Ancestry & Ethnicity in America:

A Comparative Guide to over 200 Ethnic Backgrounds

2012

Second Edition

Ancestry & Ethnicity in America:
A Comparative Guide to over 200 Ethnic Backgrounds

Where We Come From • How We Identify Ourselves • Where We Live Now

Volume II

State Population Profiles: North Carolina–Wyoming

Statistical Rankings

Master Place Name Index

A Universal Reference Book

Grey House Publishing

PUBLISHER: Leslie Mackenzie
EDITORIAL DIRECTOR: Laura Mars
SENIOR EDITOR: David Garoogian
MARKETING DIRECTOR: Jessica Moody

Grey House Publishing, Inc.
4919 Route 22
Amenia, NY 12501
518.789.8700
FAX 845.373.6390
www.greyhouse.com
e-mail: books @greyhouse.com

First edition published 2003
Printed in Canada

Publisher's Cataloging-In-Publication Data
(Prepared by The Donohue Group, Inc.)

Ancestry & ethnicity in America : a comparative guide to over 200 ethnic backgrounds / Grey House Publishing.— 2nd ed.

2 v. : ill. ; cm.

"A universal reference book."
"Where we come from, how we identify ourselves, where we live now."
1st ed.: Ancestry in America: a comparative guide to over 200 ethnic backgrounds. 2003.
ISBN: 978-1-59237-997-2

1. Ethnology—United States—Statistics. 2. Population research—United States. 3. United States—Population—Statistics. I. Grey House Publishing, Inc. II. Title: Ancestry and ethnicity in America III. Title: Ancestry in America.

E184.A1 .A53 2012
305.8/00973/021

Table of Contents

NOTE: Based on US Census categories, data in all sections of *Ancestry & Ethnicity in America* is displayed in the following sequence:

- Ancestry: 106 groups and subgroups from Afghan to Zimbabwean
- Hispanic Origin: 25 groups and subgroups by country and region
- Race: 5 major groups—African American/Black; American Indian/Alaska Native; Asian; Hawaii Native/Pacific Islander; White—and 82 subgroups by country, tribe and Hispanic identification

VOLUME I

SECTION ONE: National Population Profile

SECTION TWO: State Population Profiles

Each state chapter contains a state summary and population profiles for places with population of 7,500 or more. Each profile contains population size & percent of the total population for all 218 groups & subgroups.

VOLUME II

SECTION TWO:
State Population Profiles

Each state chapter contains a state summary and population profiles for places with population of 7,500 or more. Each profile contains population size & percent of the total population for all 218 groups & subgroups.

SECTION THREE:
Statistical Rankings

Ancestry Group Rankings

Each of 106 group and subgroup chapters contains the following:

US and 50 States Sorted by Population & Percent of Total Population
Top 150 Places Sorted by Population
Top 150 Places Sorted by Percent of Total Population
Top 150 Places Sorted by Percent of Total Population (places with population of 7,500 or more)

Introduction

The first edition of *Ancestry in America: A Comparative City-by-City Guide to over 200 Ethnic Backgrounds—with Rankings* was published in 2003. It was compiled from 2000 Census data, and included all places with populations over 10,000.

This second edition, nearly ten years in the making, is new and improved in many significant ways. Now divided between two volumes, the updated title—*Ancestry & Ethnicity in America: A Comparative Guide to over 200 Ethnic Backgrounds*—indicates not only a look back but also shows *Where We Come From • How We Identify Ourselves • Where We Live Now.* It is the most detailed look at the ethnic make-up of America in 2012 on the market today.

Praise for the first edition:

> *"...finding information in this voluminous source is easy compared with [other sources]...this work is of use to researchers in demography, marketing, sociology and political science."*
>
> —Library Journal

> *"This compilation will serve a wide range of research requests for population characteristics. Since it reports data on more than 200 different ethnic and racial categories, it offers much more detail than other sources..."*
>
> —Booklist

> *"...compilation and synthesis of disparate data files...along with the comparative rankings, make this a value-added, easy-to-use publication. Recommended for academic, public and special libraries."*
>
> —Reference & User Services Quarterly

> *"...a unique statistical compilation [whose] real value is in the ethnic breakdowns.* Ancestry in America *should also prove a statistical bonanza for those doing in-depth research on ethnic populations in the U.S."*
>
> —Against the Grain

NEW CONTENT

- This second edition includes 1,765 more places, now based on population of 7,500 instead of 10,000.
- *Ethnicity & Ancestry in America* starts off with a New Section of National Profiles, both alphabetical and ranked by group.
- The National Section also includes State-by-State charts and colorful National Maps that show population concentrations of Americans in the top 20 ancestries, those with Hispanic origin, and those in census designated racial groups.
- Each of the specific ranking sections—Ancestry, Hispanic Origin, Race—begins with an Introduction and Cross Reference Guide specific to those ethnic groups.

ARRANGEMENT

The basis for this massive two-volume work is the U.S. Census. Census 2010 collected and arranged data in specific groups, and we have maintained that arrangement throughout this work. The data in all sections of *Ancestry & Ethnicity in America* are arranged in the following groups:

- Ancestry: 106 groups and subgroups from Afghan to Zimbabwean
- Hispanic Origin: 25 groups and subgroups by country and region
- Race: 5 major groups—African American/Black, American Indian/Alaska Native, Asian, Hawaii Native/Pacific Islander, White—and 82 subgroups by country, tribe and Hispanic identification

Section One: National Population Profile

This section includes two national tables—one alphabetical by group and one ranked by size of group. Both of these tables show the population of each group, plus the percent of the U.S. population.

Following the national tables are state tables that show how many people in each state are in the top 20 ancestry groups, how many are of Hispanic origin, and how many are in each racial group. You'll be able to quickly see, for example, which state has the most Panamanians, or people of African, sub-Saharan descent.

Plus, this section includes 26 colorful maps that show where, in the country, each group is concentrated.

Section Two: State Population Profiles

This section is arranged by state. Each state chapter begins with a state overview: population numbers and percentages of U.S. population for all ancestries, for people of Hispanic origin, and for all racial groups.

The state summary is followed by profiles, in alphabetical order, of places within that state that have populations of 7,500 or more. Each place profile shows the county is resides in, the type of place it is (city, town, village, etc.) and both the number of people in each of 218 groups, as well as that group's percentage of U.S. population.

You can see at a glance, for example, how many people living in Speedway, Indiana consider themselves to be of Ethiopian descent, or what percentage of Hobbs, New Mexico's total population reported Canadian ancestry.

Section Three: Statistical Rankings

This section is comprised of three subsections: Ancestry Group Rankings; Hispanic Origin Rankings; and Racial Group Rankings. Each subsection starts with an Introduction, that gives more detail about the source and presentation of data. Following the Introduction is a Cross Reference Guide for that subsection, that makes easy work of finding those ethnicities that are part of a larger category (i.e. Pakistani, *see* Race—Asian: Pakistani or Armenian, *see* Ancestry—Armenian). Then, each group and subgroup is ranked three ways:

- Top 150 places with the largest number of persons reporting that particular group, regardless of total population
- Top 150 places with the highest percentage of persons reporting that particular group, regardless of total population
- Top 150 places, with 7,500 population or more, with the highest percentage of persons reporting that particular group

Master Place Name Index

This Master Index is an alphabetical list of every place included in this second edition of *Ancestry & Ethnicity in America.* This index includes the place name, type, county, state and the page on which their profile appears.

Ancestry & Ethnicity in America is also available as an e-book. In addition, e-states are available on CD-ROM, which include profiles of all places in that state regardless of population.

Explanation of Data

Places Covered

Section One of this book covers all 5,971 places in the U.S. with populations of 7,500 or more. It also includes profiles for the United States, all 50 states, and the District of Columbia. The ranking tables in Section Two are based on 37,950 places in the U.S. Places covered fall into one of the following categories:

Incorporated Places. Depending on the state, places are incorporated as either cities, towns, villages, boroughs, municipalities, independent cities, or corporations. A few municipalities have a form of government combined with another entity (e.g. county) and are listed as special cities or consolidated, unified, or metropolitan governments.

Census Designated Places (CDP). The U.S. Bureau of the Census defines a CDP as "a statistical entity," defined for each decennial census according to Census Bureau guidelines, comprising a densely settled concentration of population that is not within an incorporated place, but is locally identified by a name. CDPs are delineated cooperatively by state and local officials and the Census Bureau, following Census Bureau guidelines.

Minor Civil Divisions (called charter townships, districts, gores, grants, locations, plantations, purchases, reservations, towns, townships, and unorganized territories) for the states where the Census Bureau has determined that they serve as general-purpose governments. Those states are Connecticut, Maine, Massachusetts, Michigan, Minnesota, New Hampshire, New Jersey, New York, Pennsylvania, Rhode Island, Vermont, and Wisconsin. In some states incorporated municipalities are part of minor civil divisions and in some states they are independent of them.

Note: Several states have incorporated municipalities and minor civil divisions in the same county with the same name. Those communities are given separate entries (e.g. Burlington, New Jersey, in Burlington County will be listed under both the city and township of Burlington). A few states have Census Designated Places and minor civil divisions in the same county with the same name. Those communities are given separate entries (e.g. Bridgewater, Massachusetts, in Plymouth County will be listed under both the CDP and town of Bridgewater).

Source of Data

The ethnicities shown in this book were compiled from two different sources. Data for Race and Hispanic Origin was taken from Census 2010 Summary File 1 (SF1) while Ancestry data was taken from the American Community Survey (ACS) 2006-2010 Five-Year Estimate. The distinction is important because SF1 contains 100-percent data, which is the information compiled from the questions asked of all people and about every housing unit. ACS estimates are compiled from a sampling of households. The 2006-2010 Five-Year Estimate is based on data collected from January 1, 2006 to December 31, 2010.

The American Community Survey (ACS) is a relatively new survey conducted by the U.S. Census Bureau. It uses a series of monthly samples to produce annually updated data for the same small areas (census tracts and block groups) formerly surveyed via the decennial census long-form sample. While some version of this survey has been in the field since 1999, it was not fully implemented in terms of coverage until 2006. In 2005 it was expanded to cover all counties in the country and the 1-in-40 households sampling rate was first applied. The full implementation of the (household) sampling strategy for ACS entails having the survey mailed to about 250,000 households nationwide every month of every year and was begun in January 2005. In January 2006 sampling of group quarters was added to complete the sample as planned. In any given year about 2.5% (1 in 40) of U.S. households will receive the survey. Over any 5-year period about 1 in 8 households should receive the survey (as compared to about 1 in 6 that received the census long form in the 2000 census). Unfortunately, receiving the survey is not the same as responding to it, since the Bureau has adopted a strategy of sampling for non-response. This has resulted in something closer to 1 in 11 households actually participating in the survey over any 5-year period. For more information about the American Community Survey visit http://www.census.gov/acs/www.

Ancestry

Ancestry refers to a person's ethnic origin, heritage, descent, or "roots," which may reflect their place of birth or that of previous generations of their family. Some ethnic identities, such as "Egyptian" or "Polish" can be traced to geographic areas outside the United States, while other ethnicities such as "Pennsylvania German" or "Cajun" evolved in the United States.

The intent of the ancestry question was not to measure the degree of attachment the respondent had to a particular ethnicity, but simply to establish that the respondent had a connection to and self-identified with a particular ethnic group. For example, a response of "Irish" might reflect total involvement in an Irish community or only a memory of ancestors several generations removed from the individual. The question was based on self-identification; the data on ancestry represent self-classification by people according to the ancestry group(s) with which they most closely identify.

The Census Bureau coded the responses into a numeric representation of over 1,000 categories. Responses initially were processed through an automated coding system; then, those that were not automatically assigned a code were coded by individuals trained in coding ancestry responses. The code list reflects the results of the Census Bureau's own research and consultations with many ethnic experts. Many decisions were made to determine the classification of responses. These decisions affected the grouping of the tabulated data. For example, the "Indonesian" category includes the responses of "Indonesian," "Celebesian," "Moluccan," and a number of other responses.

Ancestry

Afghan	Palestinian	French, ex. Basque	Scottish
African, Sub-Saharan	Syrian	French Canadian	Serbian
African	Other Arab	German	Slavic
Cape Verdean	Armenian	German Russian	Slovak
Ethiopian	Assyrian/Chaldean/Syriac	Greek	Slovene
Ghanaian	Australian	Guyanese	Soviet Union
Kenyan	Austrian	Hungarian	Swedish
Liberian	Basque	Icelander	Swiss
Nigerian	Belgian	Iranian	Turkish
Senegalese	Brazilian	Irish	Ukrainian
Sierra Leonean	British	Israeli	Welsh
Somalian	Bulgarian	Italian	West Indian, ex. Hispanic
South African	Cajun	Latvian	Bahamian
Sudanese	Canadian	Lithuanian	Barbadian
Ugandan	Carpatho Rusyn	Luxemburger	Belizean
Zimbabwean	Celtic	Macedonian	Bermudan
Other Sub-Saharan African	Croatian	Maltese	British West Indian
Albanian	Cypriot	New Zealander	Dutch West Indian
Alsatian	Czech	Northern European	Haitian
American	Czechoslovakian	Norwegian	Jamaican
Arab	Danish	Pennsylvania German	Trinidadian/Tobagonian
Arab	Dutch	Polish	U.S. Virgin Islander
Egyptian	Eastern European	Portuguese	West Indian
Iraqi	English	Romanian	Other West Indian
Jordanian	Estonian	Russian	Yugoslavian
Lebanese	European	Scandinavian	
Moroccan	Finnish	Scotch-Irish	

The ancestry question allowed respondents to report one or more ancestry groups. Generally, only the first two responses reported were coded. If a response was in terms of a dual ancestry, for example, "Irish English," the person was assigned two codes, in this case one for Irish and another for English. However, in certain cases, multiple responses such as "French Canadian," "Scotch-Irish," "Greek Cypriot," and "Black Dutch" were assigned a single code reflecting their status as unique groups. If a person reported one of these unique groups in addition to another group, for example, "Scotch-Irish English," resulting in three terms, that person received one code for the unique group (Scotch-Irish) and another one for the remaining group (English). If a person reported "English Irish French," only English and Irish were coded. If there were more than two ancestries listed and one of the ancestries was a part of another, such as "German Bavarian Hawaiian," the responses were coded using the more detailed groups (Bavarian and Hawaiian).

The Census Bureau accepted "American" as a unique ethnicity if it was given alone or with one other ancestry. There were some groups such as "American Indian," "Mexican American," and "African American" that were coded and identified separately.

The ancestry question is asked for every person in the American Community Survey, regardless of age, place of birth, Hispanic origin, or race.

Although some people consider religious affiliation a component of ethnic identity, the ancestry question was not designed to collect any information concerning religion. Thus, if a religion was given as an answer to the ancestry question, it was listed in the "Other groups" category which is not shown in this book.

Ancestry should not be confused with a person's place of birth, although a person's place of birth and ancestry may be the same.

Hispanic Origin

The data on the Hispanic or Latino population were derived from answers to a question that was asked of all people. The terms "Spanish," "Hispanic origin," and "Latino" are used interchangeably. Some respondents identify with all three terms while others may identify with only one of these three specific terms. Hispanics or Latinos who identify with the terms "Spanish," "Hispanic," or "Latino" are those who classify themselves in one of the specific Spanish, Hispanic, or Latino categories listed on the questionnaire ("Mexican," "Puerto Rican," or "Cuban") as well as those who indicate that they are "other Spanish/Hispanic/Latino." People who do not identify with one of the specific origins listed on the questionnaire but indicate that they are "other Spanish/Hispanic/Latino" are those whose origins are from Spain, the Spanish-speaking countries of Central or South America, the Dominican Republic, or people identifying themselves generally as Spanish, Spanish-American, Hispanic, Hispano, Latino, and so on. All write-in responses to the "other Spanish/Hispanic/Latino" category were coded.

Hispanic Origin

Hispanic or Latino	South American
Central American, ex. Mexican	Argentinean
Costa Rican	Bolivian
Guatemalan	Chilean
Honduran	Colombian
Nicaraguan	Ecuadorian
Panamanian	Paraguayan
Salvadoran	Peruvian
Other Central American	Uruguayan
Cuban	Venezuelan
Dominican Republic	Other South American
Mexican	Other Hispanic or Latino
Puerto Rican	

Race

African-American/Black
- *Not Hispanic*
- *Hispanic*

American Indian/Alaska Native
- *Not Hispanic*
- *Hispanic*
- Alaska Athabascan *(Ala. Nat.)*
- Aleut *(Alaska Native)*
- Apache
- Arapaho
- Blackfeet
- Canadian/French Am. Indian
- Central American Indian
- Cherokee
- Cheyenne
- Chickasaw
- Chippewa
- Choctaw
- Colville
- Comanche
- Cree
- Creek
- Crow
- Delaware
- Hopi
- Houma
- Inupiat *(Alaska Native)*
- Iroquois
- Kiowa
- Lumbee
- Menominee
- Mexican American Indian
- Navajo
- Osage
- Ottawa
- Paiute
- Pima
- Potawatomi
- Pueblo
- Puget Sound Salish
- Seminole
- Shoshone
- Sioux
- South American Indian
- Spanish American Indian
- Tlingit-Haida *(Alaska Native)*
- Tohono O'Odham
- Tsimshian *(Alaska Native)*
- Ute
- Yakama
- Yaqui
- Yuman
- Yup'ik *(Alaska Native)*

Asian
- *Not Hispanic*
- *Hispanic*
- Bangladeshi
- Bhutanese
- Burmese
- Cambodian
- Chinese, ex. Taiwanese
- Filipino
- Hmong
- Indian
- Indonesian
- Japanese
- Korean
- Laotian
- Malaysian
- Nepalese
- Pakistani
- Sri Lankan
- Taiwanese
- Thai
- Vietnamese

Hawaii Native/Pacific Islander
- *Not Hispanic*
- *Hispanic*
- Fijian
- Guamanian/Chamorro
- Marshallese
- Native Hawaiian
- Samoan
- Tongan

White
- *Not Hispanic*
- *Hispanic*

Origin can be viewed as the heritage, nationality group, lineage, or country of birth of the person or the person's parents or ancestors before their arrival in the United States. People who identify their origin as Spanish, Hispanic, or Latino may be of any race.

Ethnicities Based on Race

The data on race were derived from answers to the question on race that was asked of individuals in the United States. The Census Bureau collects racial data in accordance with guidelines provided by the U.S. Office of Management and Budget (OMB), and these data are based on self-identification.

The racial categories included in the census questionnaire generally reflect a social definition of race recognized in this country and not an attempt to define race biologically, anthropologically, or genetically. In addition, it is recognized that the categories of the race item include racial and national origin or sociocultural groups. People may choose to report more than one race to indicate their racial mixture, such as "American Indian" and "White." People who identify their origin as Hispanic, Latino, or Spanish may be of any race.

African American or Black: A person having origins in any of the Black racial groups of Africa. It includes people who indicated their race(s) as "Black, African Am., or Negro" or reported entries such as African American, Kenyan, Nigerian, or Haitian.

American Indian or Alaska Native: A person having origins in any of the original peoples of North and South America (including Central America) and who maintains tribal affiliation or community attachment. This category includes people who indicated their race(s) as "American Indian or Alaska Native" or reported their enrolled or principal tribe, such as Navajo, Blackfeet, Inupiat, Yup'ik, or Central American Indian groups or South American Indian groups.

Asian: A person having origins in any of the original peoples of the Far East, Southeast Asia, or the Indian subcontinent, including, for example, Cambodia, China, India, Japan, Korea, Malaysia, Pakistan, the Philippine Islands, Thailand, and Vietnam. It includes people who indicated their race(s) as "Asian" or reported entries such as "Asian Indian," "Chinese," "Filipino," "Korean," "Japanese," "Vietnamese," and "Other Asian" or provided other detailed Asian responses.

Native Hawaiian or Other Pacific Islander: A person having origins in any of the original peoples of Hawaii, Guam, Samoa, or other Pacific Islands. It includes people who indicated their race(s) as "Pacific Islander" or reported entries such as "Native Hawaiian," "Guamanian or Chamorro," "Samoan," and "Other Pacific Islander" or provided other detailed Pacific Islander responses.

White: A person having origins in any of the original peoples of Europe, the Middle East, or North Africa. It includes people who indicated their race(s) as "White" or reported entries such as Irish, German, Italian, Lebanese, Arab, Moroccan, or Caucasian.

Section One: National Population Profile

The first table in this section, *National Profiles: Alphabetical by Major Category & Ethnic Group,* shows the population and percentages for all 218 ethnicities alphabetically by major category (ancestry, Hispanic origin, and race) and then by ethnic group. Column one displays the ancestry/Hispanic origin/race name, column two displays the number of people reporting each ancestry/Hispanic origin/race, and column three is the percent of the total population reporting each ancestry/Hispanic origin/race. The 2010 population (based on 100-percent data from Census 2010 Summary File 1), shown in the footnote, is used to calculate the value in the "%" column for ethnicities based on race and Hispanic origin. The 2006-2010 estimated population figure from the American Community Survey, also shown in the footnote, is used to calculate the value in the "%" column for all other ancestries.

For ethnicities in the ancestries group, the value in the "Number" column includes multiple ancestries reported. For example, if a person reported a multiple ancestry such as "French Danish," that response was counted twice in the tabulations, once in the French category and again in the Danish category. Thus, the sum of the counts is not the total population but the total of all responses. Numbers in parentheses indicate the number of people reporting a single ancestry. People reporting a single ancestry includes all people who reported only one ethnic group such as "German." Also included in this category are people with only a multiple-term response such as "Scotch-Irish" who are assigned a single code because they represent one distinct group. For example, the count for German would be interpreted as "The number of people who reported that German was their only ancestry."

For ethnicities based on Hispanic origin, the value in the "Number" column represents the number of people who reported being Mexican, Puerto Rican, Cuban or other Spanish/Hispanic/Latino (all written-in responses were coded). All ethnicities based on Hispanic origin can be of any race.

For ethnicities based on race data the value in the "Number" column represents the total number of people who reported each category alone or in combination with one or more other race categories. This number represents the maximum number of people reporting and therefore the individual race categories may add to more than the total population because people may be included in more than one category. The figures in parentheses show the number of people that reported that particular ethnicity alone, not in combination with any other race. For example, the entry for Samoan shows 109,637 in parentheses and 184,440 in the "Number" column. This means that 109,637 people reported being Samoan alone and 184,440 people reported being Samoan alone or in combination with one or more other races.

The second table, *National Profiles: By Major Category, Population Size & Percent of U.S. Population,* shows the exact same information as the first table, except the data is sorted in descending order by population size, within each major category (ancestry, Hispanic origin, and race).

The third table, *Top 20 Ancestries by State,* shows the largest 20 ancestries by population in the United States, broken down by state. The figures show the percentage of the total population reporting each ancestry. For example, 46.9% of the population of North Dakota report German as an ancestry (includes persons of mixed ancestry). The 20 national maps which follow this table, give a visual representation of the same data. Please note that Alaska and Hawaii are not shown on the maps.

The last table, *Hispanic Origin & Race by State,* shows Hispanic origin and race data, broken down by state. Column two shows the percentage of the total population reporting any Hispanic origin. Columns three through seven show the percentage of the total population reporting each of the five major racial groups: White; African-American/Black; Asian; American Indian/Alaska Native; and Hawaii Native/Other Pacific Islander. For example, 14.92% of the population of California report being Asian (includes persons reporting Asian alone or in combination with any other race). The six national maps which follow this table, give a visual representation of the same data. Please note that Alaska and Hawaii are not shown on the maps.

Section Two: State Population Profiles

Each Section Two profile shows the name of the place, the county (if a place spans more than one county, the county that holds the majority of the population is shown), and the 2010 population (based on 100-percent data from Census 2010 Summary File 1). The rest of each profile is comprised of all 218 ethnicities grouped into three sections: ancestry; Hispanic origin; and race.

Column one displays the ancestry/Hispanic origin/race name, column two displays the number of people reporting each ancestry/Hispanic origin/race, and column three is the percent of the total population reporting each ancestry/Hispanic origin/race. The population figure shown is used to calculate the value in the "%" column for ethnicities based on race and Hispanic origin. The 2006-2010 estimated population figure from the American Community Survey (not shown) is used to calculate the value in the "%" column for all other ancestries.

For ethnicities in the ancestries group, the value in the "Number" column includes multiple ancestries reported. For example, if a person reported a multiple ancestry such as "French Danish," that response was counted twice in the tabulations, once in the French category and again in the Danish category. Thus, the sum of the counts is not the total population but the total of all responses. Numbers in parentheses indicate the number of people reporting a single ancestry. People reporting a single ancestry includes all people who reported only one ethnic group such as "German." Also included in this category are people with only a multiple-term response such as "Scotch-Irish" who are assigned a single code because they represent one distinct group. For example, the count for German would be interpreted as "The number of people who reported that German was their only ancestry."

For ethnicities based on Hispanic origin, the value in the "Number" column represents the number of people who reported being Mexican, Puerto Rican, Cuban or other Spanish/Hispanic/Latino (all written-in responses were coded). All ethnicities based on Hispanic origin can be of any race.

For ethnicities based on race data the value in the "Number" column represents the total number of people who reported each category alone or in combination with one or more other race categories. This number represents the maximum number of people reporting and therefore the individual race categories may add to more than the total population because people may be included in more than one category. The figures in parentheses show the number of people that reported that particular ethnicity alone, not in combination with any other race. For example, in Alabama, the entry for Korean shows 8,320 in parentheses and 10,624 in the "Number" column. This means that 8,320 people reported being Korean alone and 10,624 people reported being Korean alone or in combination with one or more other races.

Section Three: Statistical Rankings

In Section Three, each ethnicity has four ranking tables. The first table is split into two parts. Part one ranks the U.S. and all 50 states plus the District of Columbia by ethnic population. Part two ranks the same areas by percent of the total population. The second table shows the top 150 places sorted by ethnic population (based on all places, regardless of total population), the third table shows the top 150 places sorted by percent of the total population (based on all places, regardless of total population), the fourth table shows the top 150 places sorted by percent of the total population (based on places with total population of 7,500 or more).

Within each table, column one displays the place name, the state, and the county (if a place spans more than one county, the county that holds the majority of the population is shown). Column one in the first table displays the state only. Column two displays the number of people reporting each ancestry (includes people reporting multiple ancestries), Hispanic origin, or race (alone or in combination with any other race). Column three is the percent of the total population reporting each ancestry, Hispanic origin or race. For tables representing ethnicities based on race or Hispanic origin, the 100-percent population figure from SF1 is used to calculate the value in the "%" column. For all other ancestries the 2006-2010 five-year estimated population figure from the American Community Survey is used to calculate the value in the "%" column.

Alphabetical Ethnicity Cross-Reference Guide

Afghan *see* Ancestry–Afghan
African *see* Ancestry–African, Sub-Saharan: African
African-American *see* Race–African-American/Black
African-American: Hispanic *see* Race–African-American/Black: Hispanic
African-American: Not Hispanic *see* Race–African-American/Black: Not Hispanic
Alaska Athabascan *see* Race–Alaska Native: Alaska Athabascan
Alaska Native *see* Race–American Indian/Alaska Native
Alaska Native: Hispanic *see* Race–American Indian/Alaska Native: Hispanic
Alaska Native: Not Hispanic *see* Race–American Indian/Alaska Native: Not Hispanic
Albanian *see* Ancestry–Albanian
Aleut *see* Race–Alaska Native: Aleut
Alsatian *see* Ancestry–Alsatian
American *see* Ancestry–American
American Indian *see* Race–American Indian/Alaska Native
American Indian: Hispanic *see* Race–American Indian/Alaska Native: Hispanic
American Indian: Not Hispanic *see* Race–American Indian/Alaska Native: Not Hispanic
Apache *see* Race–American Indian: Apache
Arab *see* Ancestry–Arab: Arab
Arab: Other *see* Ancestry–Arab: Other
Arapaho *see* Race–American Indian: Arapaho
Argentinean *see* Hispanic Origin–South American: Argentinean
Armenian *see* Ancestry–Armenian
Asian *see* Race–Asian
Asian Indian *see* Race–Asian: Indian
Asian: Hispanic *see* Race–Asian: Hispanic
Asian: Not Hispanic *see* Race–Asian: Not Hispanic
Assyrian *see* Ancestry–Assyrian/Chaldean/Syriac
Australian *see* Ancestry–Australian
Austrian *see* Ancestry–Austrian
Bahamian *see* Ancestry–West Indian: Bahamian, except Hispanic
Bangladeshi *see* Race–Asian: Bangladeshi
Barbadian *see* Ancestry–West Indian: Barbadian, except Hispanic
Basque *see* Ancestry–Basque
Belgian *see* Ancestry–Belgian
Belizean *see* Ancestry–West Indian: Belizean, except Hispanic
Bermudan *see* Ancestry–West Indian: Bermudan, except Hispanic
Bhutanese *see* Race–Asian: Bhutanese
Black *see* Race–African-American/Black
Black: Hispanic *see* Race–African-American/Black: Hispanic
Black: Not Hispanic *see* Race–African-American/Black: Not Hispanic
Blackfeet *see* Race–American Indian: Blackfeet
Bolivian *see* Hispanic Origin–South American: Bolivian
Brazilian *see* Ancestry–Brazilian
British *see* Ancestry–British
British West Indian *see* Ancestry–West Indian: British West Indian, except Hispanic
Bulgarian *see* Ancestry–Bulgarian
Burmese *see* Race–Asian: Burmese
Cajun *see* Ancestry–Cajun
Cambodian *see* Race–Asian: Cambodian
Canadian *see* Ancestry–Canadian
Canadian/French American Indian *see* Race–American Indian: Canadian/French American Indian
Cape Verdean *see* Ancestry–African, Sub-Saharan: Cape Verdean
Carpatho Rusyn *see* Ancestry–Carpatho Rusyn
Celtic *see* Ancestry–Celtic
Central American *see* Hispanic Origin–Central American, except Mexican
Central American Indian *see* Race–American Indian: Central American Indian
Central American: Other *see* Hispanic Origin–Central American: Other Central American
Chaldean *see* Ancestry–Assyrian/Chaldean/Syriac
Chamorro *see* Race–Hawaii Native/Pacific Islander: Guamanian or Chamorro
Cherokee *see* Race–American Indian: Cherokee
Cheyenne *see* Race–American Indian: Cheyenne
Chickasaw *see* Race–American Indian: Chickasaw
Chilean *see* Hispanic Origin–South American: Chilean
Chinese (except Taiwanese) *see* Race–Asian: Chinese, except Taiwanese
Chippewa *see* Race–American Indian: Chippewa
Choctaw *see* Race–American Indian: Choctaw
Colombian *see* Hispanic Origin–South American: Colombian
Colville *see* Race–American Indian: Colville
Comanche *see* Race–American Indian: Comanche
Costa Rican *see* Hispanic Origin–Central American: Costa Rican
Cree *see* Race–American Indian: Cree
Creek *see* Race–American Indian: Creek

Croatian *see* Ancestry–Croatian
Crow *see* Race–American Indian: Crow
Cuban *see* Hispanic Origin–Cuban
Cypriot *see* Ancestry–Cypriot
Czech *see* Ancestry–Czech
Czechoslovakian *see* Ancestry–Czechoslovakian
Danish *see* Ancestry–Danish
Delaware *see* Race–American Indian: Delaware
Dominican Republic *see* Hispanic Origin–Dominican Republic
Dutch *see* Ancestry–Dutch
Dutch West Indian *see* Ancestry–West Indian: Dutch West Indian, except Hispanic
Eastern European *see* Ancestry–Eastern European
Ecuadorian *see* Hispanic Origin–South American: Ecuadorian
Egyptian *see* Ancestry–Arab: Egyptian
English *see* Ancestry–English
Eskimo *see* Race–Alaska Native: Inupiat
Estonian *see* Ancestry–Estonian
Ethiopian *see* Ancestry–African, Sub-Saharan: Ethiopian
European *see* Ancestry–European
Fijian *see* Race–Hawaii Native/Pacific Islander: Fijian
Filipino *see* Race–Asian: Filipino
Finnish *see* Ancestry–Finnish
French (except Basque) *see* Ancestry–French, except Basque
French Canadian *see* Ancestry–French Canadian
German *see* Ancestry–German
German Russian *see* Ancestry–German Russian
Ghanaian *see* Ancestry–African, Sub-Saharan: Ghanaian
Greek *see* Ancestry–Greek
Guamanian *see* Race–Hawaii Native/Pacific Islander: Guamanian or Chamorro
Guatemalan *see* Hispanic Origin–Central American: Guatemalan
Guyanese *see* Ancestry–Guyanese
Haitian *see* Ancestry–West Indian: Haitian, except Hispanic
Hawaii Native *see* Race–Hawaii Native/Pacific Islander
Hawaii Native: Hispanic *see* Race–Hawaii Native/Pacific Islander: Hispanic
Hawaii Native: Not Hispanic *see* Race–Hawaii Native/Pacific Islander: Not Hispanic
Hispanic or Latino: *see* Hispanic Origin–Hispanic or Latino (of any race)
Hispanic or Latino: Other *see* Hispanic Origin–Other Hispanic or Latino
Hmong *see* Race–Asian: Hmong
Honduran *see* Hispanic Origin–Central American: Honduran
Hopi *see* Race–American Indian: Hopi
Houma *see* Race–American Indian: Houma
Hungarian *see* Ancestry–Hungarian
Icelander *see* Ancestry–Icelander
Indonesian *see* Race–Asian: Indonesian
Inupiat *see* Race–Alaska Native: Inupiat
Iranian *see* Ancestry–Iranian
Iraqi *see* Ancestry–Arab: Iraqi
Irish *see* Ancestry–Irish
Iroquois *see* Race–American Indian: Iroquois
Israeli *see* Ancestry–Israeli
Italian *see* Ancestry–Italian
Jamaican *see* Ancestry–West Indian: Jamaican, except Hispanic
Japanese *see* Race–Asian: Japanese
Jordanian *see* Ancestry–Arab: Jordanian
Kenyan *see* Ancestry–African, Sub-Saharan: Kenyan
Kiowa *see* Race–American Indian: Kiowa
Korean *see* Race–Asian: Korean
Laotian *see* Race–Asian: Laotian
Latvian *see* Ancestry–Latvian
Lebanese *see* Ancestry–Arab: Lebanese
Liberian *see* Ancestry–African, Sub-Saharan: Liberian
Lithuanian *see* Ancestry–Lithuanian
Lumbee *see* Race–American Indian: Lumbee
Luxemburger *see* Ancestry–Luxemburger
Macedonian *see* Ancestry–Macedonian
Malaysian *see* Race–Asian: Malaysian
Maltese *see* Ancestry–Maltese
Marshallese *see* Race–Hawaii Native/Pacific Islander: Marshallese
Menominee *see* Race–American Indian: Menominee
Mexican *see* Hispanic Origin–Mexican
Mexican American Indian *see* Race–American Indian: Mexican American Indian
Moroccan *see* Ancestry–Arab: Moroccan
Native Hawaiian *see* Race–Hawaii Native/Pacific Islander: Native Hawaiian
Navajo *see* Race–American Indian: Navajo
Nepalese *see* Race–Asian: Nepalese
New Zealander *see* Ancestry–New Zealander
Nicaraguan *see* Hispanic Origin–Central American: Nicaraguan
Nigerian *see* Ancestry–African, Sub-Saharan: Nigerian
Northern European *see* Ancestry–Northern European
Norwegian *see* Ancestry–Norwegian
Osage *see* Race–American Indian: Osage
Ottawa *see* Race–American Indian: Ottawa
Pacific Islander *see* Race–Hawaii Native/Pacific Islander
Pacific Islander: Hispanic *see* Race–Hawaii Native/Pacific Islander: Hispanic
Pacific Islander: Not Hispanic *see* Race–Hawaii Native/Pacific Islander: Not Hispanic
Paiute *see* Race–American Indian: Paiute
Pakistani *see* Race–Asian: Pakistani
Palestinian *see* Ancestry–Arab: Palestinian
Panamanian *see* Hispanic Origin–Central American: Panamanian
Paraguayan *see* Hispanic Origin–South American: Paraguayan
Pennsylvania German *see* Ancestry–Pennsylvania German
Peruvian *see* Hispanic Origin–South American: Peruvian
Pima *see* Race–American Indian: Pima
Polish *see* Ancestry–Polish
Portuguese *see* Ancestry–Portuguese
Potawatomi *see* Race–American Indian: Potawatomi
Pueblo *see* Race–American Indian: Pueblo
Puerto Rican *see* Hispanic Origin–Puerto Rican
Puget Sound Salish *see* Race–American Indian: Puget Sound Salish
Romanian *see* Ancestry–Romanian
Russian *see* Ancestry–Russian
Salvadoran *see* Hispanic Origin–Central American: Salvadoran
Samoan *see* Race–Hawaii Native/Pacific Islander: Samoan
Scandinavian *see* Ancestry–Scandinavian
Scotch-Irish *see* Ancestry–Scotch-Irish
Scottish *see* Ancestry–Scottish
Seminole *see* Race–American Indian: Seminole

Senegalese *see* Ancestry–African, Sub-Saharan: Senegalese
Serbian *see* Ancestry–Serbian
Shoshone *see* Race–American Indian: Shoshone
Sierra Leonean *see* Ancestry–African, Sub-Saharan: Sierra Leonean
Sioux *see* Race–American Indian: Sioux
Slavic *see* Ancestry–Slavic
Slovak *see* Ancestry–Slovak
Slovene *see* Ancestry–Slovene
Somalian *see* Ancestry–African, Sub-Saharan: Somalian
South African *see* Ancestry–African, Sub-Saharan: South African
South American *see* Hispanic Origin–South American
South American Indian *see* Race–American Indian: South American Indian
South American: Other *see* Hispanic Origin–South American: Other South American
Soviet Union *see* Ancestry–Soviet Union
Spanish American Indian *see* Race–American Indian: Spanish American Indian
Sri Lankan *see* Race–Asian: Sri Lankan
Sub-Saharan African *see* Ancestry–African, Sub-Saharan
Sub-Saharan African: Other *see* Ancestry–African, Sub-Saharan: Other
Sudanese *see* Ancestry–African, Sub-Saharan: Sudanese
Swedish *see* Ancestry–Swedish
Swiss *see* Ancestry–Swiss
Syriac *see* Ancestry–Assyrian/Chaldean/Syriac
Syrian *see* Ancestry–Arab: Syrian
Taiwanese *see* Race–Asian: Taiwanese
Thai *see* Race–Asian: Thai
Tlingit-Haida *see* Race–Alaska Native: Tlingit-Haida
Tohono O'Odham *see* Race–American Indian: Tohono O'Odham
Tongan *see* Race–Hawaii Native/Pacific Islander: Tongan
Trinidadian and Tobagonian *see* Ancestry–West Indian: Trinidadian and Tobagonian, except Hispanic
Tsimshian *see* Race–Alaska Native: Tsimshian
Turkish *see* Ancestry–Turkish
U.S. Virgin Islander *see* Ancestry–West Indian: U.S. Virgin Islander, except Hispanic
Ugandan *see* Ancestry–African, Sub-Saharan: Ugandan
Ukrainian *see* Ancestry–Ukrainian
Uruguayan *see* Hispanic Origin–South American: Uruguayan
Ute *see* Race–American Indian: Ute
Venezuelan *see* Hispanic Origin–South American: Venezuelan
Vietnamese *see* Race–Asian: Vietnamese
Welsh *see* Ancestry–Welsh
West Indian *see* Ancestry–West Indian: West Indian, except Hispanic
West Indian (except Hispanic) *see* Ancestry–West Indian, except Hispanic
West Indian: Other *see* Ancestry–West Indian: Other, except Hispanic
White *see* Race–White
White: Hispanic *see* Race–White: Hispanic
White: Not Hispanic *see* Race–White: Not Hispanic
Yakama *see* Race–American Indian: Yakama
Yaqui *see* Race–American Indian: Yaqui
Yugoslavian *see* Ancestry–Yugoslavian
Yuman *see* Race–American Indian: Yuman
Yup'ik *see* Race–Alaska Native: Yup'ik
Zimbabwean *see* Ancestry–African, Sub-Saharan: Zimbabwean

NORTH CAROLINA

Place Type: State
Population: 9,535,483†

Ancestry‡	Population	%
Afghan (749)	841	0.01
African, Sub-Saharan (68,388)	80,649	0.87
African (45,994)	55,748	0.60
Cape Verdean (269)	568	0.01
Ethiopian (2,732)	2,813	0.03
Ghanaian (1,729)	1,745	0.02
Kenyan (1,416)	1,597	0.02
Liberian (1,765)	1,963	0.02
Nigerian (5,732)	6,162	0.07
Senegalese (156)	156	<0.01
Sierra Leonean (565)	590	0.01
Somalian (1,173)	1,308	0.01
South African (1,159)	1,690	0.02
Sudanese (1,804)	1,880	0.02
Ugandan (38)	38	<0.01
Zimbabwean (68)	79	<0.01
Other Sub-Saharan African (3,788)	4,312	0.05
Albanian (379)	762	0.01
Alsatian (69)	255	<0.01
American (1,066,458)	1,066,458	11.50
Arab (19,860)	29,140	0.31
Arab (4,327)	5,243	0.06
Egyptian (3,017)	3,860	0.04
Iraqi (164)	241	<0.01
Jordanian (1,111)	1,457	0.02
Lebanese (5,468)	10,370	0.11
Moroccan (1,703)	1,893	0.02
Palestinian (1,136)	1,551	0.02
Syrian (779)	1,848	0.02
Other Arab (2,155)	2,677	0.03
Armenian (1,742)	3,644	0.04
Assyrian/Chaldean/Syriac (102)	138	<0.01
Australian (887)	2,088	0.02
Austrian (2,639)	11,896	0.13
Basque (149)	245	<0.01
Belgian (1,756)	5,418	0.06
Brazilian (3,131)	4,247	0.05
British (24,221)	43,114	0.47
Bulgarian (1,188)	1,544	0.02
Cajun (653)	1,416	0.02
Canadian (8,325)	15,051	0.16
Carpatho Rusyn (56)	70	<0.01
Celtic (911)	1,789	0.02
Croatian (1,437)	4,404	0.05
Cypriot (104)	135	<0.01
Czech (5,482)	18,171	0.20
Czechoslovakian (2,026)	5,381	0.06
Danish (4,096)	15,824	0.17
Dutch (24,394)	119,440	1.29
Eastern European (4,541)	5,437	0.06
English (477,665)	981,696	10.59
Estonian (254)	450	<0.01
European (84,064)	95,883	1.03
Finnish (2,297)	6,261	0.07
French, ex. Basque (37,176)	170,948	1.84
French Canadian (13,727)	32,892	0.35
German (372,466)	1,078,399	11.63
German Russian (74)	350	<0.01
Greek (13,391)	25,926	0.28
Guyanese (1,530)	2,234	0.02
Hungarian (7,549)	25,192	0.27
Icelander (539)	946	0.01
Iranian (3,300)	4,273	0.05
Irish (302,526)	879,734	9.49
Israeli (689)	1,071	0.01
Italian (102,391)	284,213	3.07
Latvian (458)	1,364	0.01
Lithuanian (3,043)	9,457	0.10
Luxemburger (64)	220	<0.01
Macedonian (187)	269	<0.01
Maltese (190)	623	0.01
New Zealander (422)	562	0.01
Northern European (3,766)	4,055	0.04
Norwegian (13,455)	43,446	0.47
Pennsylvania German (1,244)	2,855	0.03
Polish (40,165)	131,740	1.42
Portuguese (4,345)	11,957	0.13
Romanian (3,889)	7,511	0.08
Russian (15,415)	41,674	0.45
Scandinavian (2,968)	8,125	0.09
Scotch-Irish (192,818)	340,482	3.67
Scottish (102,868)	246,993	2.66
Serbian (948)	2,490	0.03
Slavic (685)	2,554	0.03
Slovak (3,362)	10,408	0.11
Slovene (678)	1,847	0.02
Soviet Union (14)	14	<0.01
Swedish (14,472)	52,952	0.57
Swiss (4,057)	15,605	0.17
Turkish (2,540)	3,355	0.04
Ukrainian (7,553)	15,628	0.17
Welsh (13,091)	54,197	0.58
West Indian, ex. Hispanic (18,847)	31,296	0.34
Bahamian (536)	974	0.01
Barbadian (598)	877	0.01
Belizean (283)	459	<0.01
Bermudan (67)	141	<0.01
British West Indian (471)	1,029	0.01
Dutch West Indian (270)	653	0.01
Haitian (3,310)	4,878	0.05
Jamaican (8,187)	12,897	0.14
Trinidadian/Tobagonian (1,662)	2,499	0.03
U.S. Virgin Islander (133)	177	<0.01
West Indian (3,297)	6,660	0.07
Other West Indian (33)	52	<0.01
Yugoslavian (2,603)	4,917	0.05

Hispanic Origin	Population	%
Hispanic or Latino (of any race)	800,120	8.39
Central American, ex. Mexican	105,066	1.10
Costa Rican	4,658	0.05
Guatemalan	20,206	0.21
Honduran	30,900	0.32
Nicaraguan	4,964	0.05
Panamanian	5,708	0.06
Salvadoran	37,778	0.40
Other Central American	852	0.01
Cuban	18,079	0.19
Dominican Republic	15,225	0.16
Mexican	486,960	5.11
Puerto Rican	71,800	0.75
South American	46,307	0.49
Argentinean	3,210	0.03
Bolivian	878	0.01
Chilean	2,525	0.03
Colombian	17,648	0.19
Ecuadorian	8,110	0.09
Paraguayan	245	<0.01
Peruvian	8,247	0.09
Uruguayan	980	0.01
Venezuelan	4,070	0.04
Other South American	394	<0.01
Other Hispanic or Latino	56,683	0.59

Race*	Population	%
African-American/Black (2,048,628)	2,151,456	22.56
Not Hispanic (2,019,854)	2,107,630	22.10
Hispanic (28,774)	43,826	0.46
American Indian/Alaska Native (122,110)	184,082	1.93
Not Hispanic (108,829)	162,311	1.70
Hispanic (13,281)	21,771	0.23
Alaska Athabascan (*Ala. Nat.*) (58)	78	<0.01
Aleut (*Alaska Native*) (83)	111	<0.01
Apache (295)	927	0.01
Arapaho (13)	50	<0.01
Blackfeet (348)	2,231	0.02
Canadian/French Am. Ind. (77)	179	<0.01
Central American Ind. (285)	523	0.01
Cherokee (13,942)	32,030	0.34
Cheyenne (66)	158	<0.01
Chickasaw (127)	298	<0.01
Chippewa (566)	1,032	0.01
Choctaw (437)	1,130	0.01
Colville (16)	24	<0.01
Comanche (78)	199	<0.01
Cree (32)	104	<0.01
Creek (278)	671	0.01
Crow (25)	145	<0.01
Delaware (85)	249	<0.01
Hopi (25)	68	<0.01
Houma (37)	61	<0.01
Inupiat (*Alaska Native*) (69)	130	<0.01
Iroquois (1,515)	2,507	0.03
Kiowa (42)	68	<0.01
Lumbee (52,905)	58,306	0.61
Menominee (31)	49	<0.01
Mexican American Ind. (2,871)	3,826	0.04
Navajo (418)	774	0.01
Osage (53)	131	<0.01
Ottawa (48)	87	<0.01
Paiute (27)	39	<0.01
Pima (27)	58	<0.01
Potawatomi (114)	210	<0.01
Pueblo (86)	210	<0.01
Puget Sound Salish (26)	40	<0.01
Seminole (96)	466	<0.01
Shoshone (36)	95	<0.01
Sioux (533)	1,283	0.01
South American Ind. (295)	783	0.01
Spanish American Ind. (337)	543	0.01
Tlingit-Haida (*Alaska Native*) (52)	73	<0.01
Tohono O'Odham (28)	47	<0.01
Tsimshian (*Alaska Native*) (4)	5	<0.01
Ute (17)	37	<0.01
Yakama (19)	29	<0.01
Yaqui (30)	76	<0.01
Yuman (14)	26	<0.01
Yup'ik (*Alaska Native*) (29)	45	<0.01
Asian (208,962)	252,585	2.65
Not Hispanic (206,579)	245,810	2.58
Hispanic (2,383)	6,775	0.07
Bangladeshi (854)	945	0.01
Bhutanese (487)	614	0.01
Burmese (3,478)	3,779	0.04
Cambodian (3,559)	4,345	0.05
Chinese, ex. Taiwanese (32,301)	38,764	0.41
Filipino (18,643)	29,314	0.31
Hmong (10,433)	10,864	0.11
Indian (57,400)	63,852	0.67
Indonesian (767)	1,121	0.01
Japanese (6,411)	12,878	0.14
Korean (19,221)	25,420	0.27
Laotian (5,566)	6,562	0.07
Malaysian (214)	363	<0.01
Nepalese (875)	1,039	0.01
Pakistani (5,757)	6,477	0.07
Sri Lankan (612)	721	0.01
Taiwanese (1,780)	2,151	0.02
Thai (2,947)	4,782	0.05
Vietnamese (27,304)	30,665	0.32
Hawaii Native/Pacific Islander (6,604)	14,774	0.15
Not Hispanic (5,259)	11,417	0.12
Hispanic (1,345)	3,357	0.04
Fijian (34)	76	<0.01
Guamanian/Chamorro (2,505)	3,682	0.04
Marshallese (152)	182	<0.01
Native Hawaiian (1,389)	4,182	0.04
Samoan (716)	1,600	0.02
Tongan (54)	123	<0.01
White (6,528,950)	6,697,465	70.24
Not Hispanic (6,223,995)	6,354,005	66.64
Hispanic (304,955)	343,460	3.60

*Notes: † The Census 2010 population figure is used to calculate the percentages in the Hispanic Origin and Race categories. Ancestry percentages are based on the 2006-2010 American Community Survey population (not shown); ‡ Numbers in parentheses indicate the number of people reporting a single ancestry; * Numbers in parentheses indicate the number of persons reporting this race alone, not in combination with any other race; Please refer to the Explanation of Data for more information.*

Albemarle

Place Type: City
County: Stanly
Population: 15,903†

Ancestry‡	Population	%
African, Sub-Saharan (222)	280	1.76
African (222)	280	1.76
Albanian (9)	9	0.06
American (1,359)	1,359	8.54
Arab (10)	10	0.06
Arab (10)	10	0.06
Armenian (0)	31	0.19
Austrian (0)	8	0.05
Belgian (45)	60	0.38
British (9)	9	0.06
Canadian (0)	55	0.35
Celtic (7)	21	0.13
Dutch (0)	140	0.88
English (1,420)	2,058	12.93
European (45)	45	0.28
French, ex. Basque (103)	177	1.11
French Canadian (0)	23	0.14
German (990)	2,121	13.33
Hungarian (9)	23	0.14
Irish (643)	1,128	7.09
Italian (15)	76	0.48
Norwegian (14)	32	0.20
Pennsylvania German (8)	8	0.05
Polish (89)	111	0.70
Portuguese (0)	8	0.05
Russian (10)	28	0.18
Scotch-Irish (223)	415	2.61
Scottish (112)	441	2.77
Serbian (0)	10	0.06
Slovak (0)	11	0.07
Swedish (0)	60	0.38
Swiss (10)	10	0.06
Welsh (49)	75	0.47
West Indian, ex. Hispanic (82)	82	0.52
Jamaican (82)	82	0.52

Hispanic Origin	Population	%
Hispanic or Latino (of any race)	719	4.52
Central American, ex. Mexican	30	0.19
Guatemalan	4	0.03
Honduran	7	0.04
Panamanian	3	0.02
Salvadoran	16	0.10
Cuban	5	0.03
Dominican Republic	8	0.05
Mexican	570	3.58
Puerto Rican	37	0.23
South American	7	0.04
Bolivian	1	0.01
Ecuadorian	5	0.03
Peruvian	1	0.01
Other Hispanic or Latino	62	0.39

Race*	Population	%
African-American/Black (3,562)	3,762	23.66
Not Hispanic (3,538)	3,725	23.42
Hispanic (24)	37	0.23
American Indian/Alaska Native (49)	102	0.64
Not Hispanic (45)	97	0.61
Hispanic (4)	5	0.03
Cherokee (11)	31	0.19
Chickasaw (1)	1	0.01
Chippewa (2)	2	0.01
Lumbee (7)	12	0.08
Sioux (1)	1	0.01
Asian (466)	515	3.24
Not Hispanic (465)	511	3.21
Hispanic (1)	4	0.03
Burmese (2)	2	0.01
Cambodian (0)	2	0.01
Chinese, ex. Taiwanese (11)	21	0.13
Filipino (17)	22	0.14
Hmong (289)	291	1.83
Indian (59)	69	0.43
Japanese (7)	14	0.09
Korean (8)	9	0.06
Laotian (27)	31	0.19
Pakistani (0)	1	0.01
Taiwanese (4)	4	0.03
Thai (8)	8	0.05
Vietnamese (10)	12	0.08
Hawaii Native/Pacific Islander (1)	8	0.05
Not Hispanic (1)	3	0.02
Hispanic (0)	5	0.03
Fijian (1)	1	0.01
Native Hawaiian (0)	2	0.01
White (11,152)	11,408	71.73
Not Hispanic (10,865)	11,102	69.81
Hispanic (287)	306	1.92

Apex

Place Type: Town
County: Wake
Population: 37,476†

Ancestry‡	Population	%
African, Sub-Saharan (169)	323	0.94
African (31)	31	0.09
Cape Verdean (38)	192	0.56
Ethiopian (43)	43	0.12
Somalian (41)	41	0.12
South African (16)	16	0.05
Albanian (0)	73	0.21
American (2,761)	2,761	8.02
Arab (74)	188	0.55
Arab (15)	15	0.04
Egyptian (45)	82	0.24
Lebanese (0)	15	0.04
Syrian (0)	62	0.18
Other Arab (14)	14	0.04
Armenian (0)	13	0.04
Australian (0)	45	0.13
Austrian (0)	114	0.33
Belgian (11)	11	0.03
Brazilian (8)	54	0.16
British (192)	443	1.29
Bulgarian (24)	24	0.07
Cajun (32)	42	0.12
Canadian (61)	205	0.60
Croatian (0)	12	0.03
Czech (0)	186	0.54
Czechoslovakian (10)	10	0.03
Danish (38)	149	0.43
Dutch (181)	723	2.10
Eastern European (73)	198	0.58
English (1,659)	4,353	12.64
European (562)	630	1.83
Finnish (21)	21	0.06
French, ex. Basque (188)	1,186	3.44
French Canadian (26)	247	0.72
German (1,310)	6,799	19.75
Greek (17)	162	0.47
Hungarian (20)	215	0.62
Icelander (0)	42	0.12
Iranian (62)	75	0.22
Irish (1,284)	5,423	15.75
Italian (1,035)	3,402	9.88
Lithuanian (14)	38	0.11
New Zealander (11)	11	0.03
Norwegian (44)	202	0.59
Pennsylvania German (0)	31	0.09
Polish (285)	1,385	4.02
Portuguese (74)	200	0.58
Russian (277)	480	1.39
Scandinavian (0)	53	0.15
Scotch-Irish (732)	1,461	4.24
Scottish (538)	1,285	3.73
Slavic (0)	17	0.05
Slovak (49)	263	0.76
Slovene (22)	60	0.17
Swedish (169)	397	1.15
Swiss (28)	205	0.60
Turkish (64)	64	0.19
Ukrainian (80)	142	0.41
Welsh (47)	322	0.94
West Indian, ex. Hispanic (28)	89	0.26
Bermudan (10)	10	0.03
Jamaican (18)	29	0.08
West Indian (0)	50	0.15

Hispanic Origin	Population	%
Hispanic or Latino (of any race)	2,655	7.08
Central American, ex. Mexican	216	0.58
Costa Rican	25	0.07
Guatemalan	39	0.10
Honduran	43	0.11
Nicaraguan	30	0.08
Panamanian	15	0.04
Salvadoran	60	0.16
Other Central American	4	0.01
Cuban	134	0.36
Dominican Republic	74	0.20
Mexican	1,243	3.32
Puerto Rican	403	1.08
South American	399	1.06
Argentinean	28	0.07
Bolivian	6	0.02
Chilean	24	0.06
Colombian	164	0.44
Ecuadorian	51	0.14
Peruvian	87	0.23
Uruguayan	4	0.01
Venezuelan	32	0.09
Other South American	3	0.01
Other Hispanic or Latino	186	0.50

Race*	Population	%
African-American/Black (2,862)	3,190	8.51
Not Hispanic (2,785)	3,075	8.21
Hispanic (77)	115	0.31
American Indian/Alaska Native (106)	321	0.86
Not Hispanic (77)	252	0.67
Hispanic (29)	69	0.18
Alaska Athabascan *(Ala. Nat.)* (1)	1	<0.01
Aleut *(Alaska Native)* (2)	3	0.01
Apache (1)	4	0.01
Blackfeet (0)	9	0.02
Central American Ind. (1)	5	0.01
Cherokee (16)	77	0.21
Chickasaw (0)	1	<0.01
Chippewa (2)	9	0.02
Choctaw (0)	11	0.03
Creek (4)	7	0.02
Delaware (2)	4	0.01
Iroquois (1)	14	0.04
Lumbee (19)	25	0.07
Mexican American Ind. (3)	5	0.01
Paiute (0)	1	<0.01
Potawatomi (0)	2	0.01
Seminole (0)	2	0.01
Sioux (0)	3	0.01
South American Ind. (1)	2	0.01
Spanish American Ind. (2)	8	0.02
Tlingit-Haida *(Alaska Native)* (1)	1	<0.01
Asian (2,652)	3,083	8.23
Not Hispanic (2,641)	3,045	8.13
Hispanic (11)	38	0.10
Bangladeshi (35)	35	0.09
Burmese (0)	3	0.01
Cambodian (2)	4	0.01
Chinese, ex. Taiwanese (561)	652	1.74
Filipino (140)	220	0.59
Hmong (6)	6	0.02
Indian (1,268)	1,339	3.57
Indonesian (13)	15	0.04
Japanese (40)	111	0.30
Korean (186)	268	0.72
Laotian (10)	17	0.05
Malaysian (2)	2	0.01
Nepalese (6)	8	0.02
Pakistani (97)	104	0.28
Sri Lankan (22)	27	0.07

*Notes: † The Census 2010 population figure is used to calculate the percentages in the Hispanic Origin and Race categories. Ancestry percentages are based on the 2006-2010 American Community Survey population (not shown); ‡ Numbers in parentheses indicate the number of people reporting a single ancestry; * Numbers in parentheses indicate the number of persons reporting this race alone, not in combination with any other race; Please refer to the Explanation of Data for more information.*

Taiwanese (46)	50	0.13
Thai (32)	49	0.13
Vietnamese (117)	142	0.38
Hawaii Native/Pacific Islander (31)	53	0.14
Not Hispanic (16)	38	0.10
Hispanic (15)	15	0.04
Guamanian/Chamorro (17)	24	0.06
Native Hawaiian (1)	10	0.03
Samoan (2)	7	0.02
White (29,796)	30,601	81.65
Not Hispanic (28,465)	29,103	77.66
Hispanic (1,331)	1,498	4.00

Archdale

Place Type: City
County: Randolph
Population: 11,415†

Ancestry‡	Population	%
African, Sub-Saharan (41)	41	0.37
African (22)	22	0.20
Liberian (19)	19	0.17
American (1,594)	1,594	14.54
Arab (24)	24	0.22
Arab (24)	24	0.22
British (0)	83	0.76
Canadian (19)	19	0.17
Dutch (8)	271	2.47
English (983)	1,693	15.44
European (55)	89	0.81
French, ex. Basque (8)	46	0.42
French Canadian (6)	6	0.05
German (654)	1,606	14.65
Hungarian (12)	12	0.11
Irish (469)	1,150	10.49
Italian (32)	147	1.34
Norwegian (34)	43	0.39
Polish (18)	79	0.72
Scandinavian (0)	16	0.15
Scotch-Irish (200)	358	3.27
Scottish (152)	424	3.87
Swedish (0)	19	0.17
Swiss (55)	55	0.50
Welsh (0)	99	0.90
West Indian, ex. Hispanic (5)	21	0.19
Barbadian (0)	8	0.07
Jamaican (5)	13	0.12

Hispanic Origin	Population	%
Hispanic or Latino (of any race)	462	4.05
Central American, ex. Mexican	38	0.33
Guatemalan	5	0.04
Honduran	16	0.14
Panamanian	1	0.01
Salvadoran	16	0.14
Cuban	23	0.20
Dominican Republic	5	0.04
Mexican	311	2.72
Puerto Rican	24	0.21
South American	28	0.25
Argentinean	1	0.01
Chilean	8	0.07
Colombian	8	0.07
Paraguayan	2	0.02
Peruvian	8	0.07
Other South American	1	0.01
Other Hispanic or Latino	33	0.29

Race*	Population	%
African-American/Black (461)	524	4.59
Not Hispanic (445)	497	4.35
Hispanic (16)	27	0.24
American Indian/Alaska Native (63)	107	0.94
Not Hispanic (60)	103	0.90
Hispanic (3)	4	0.04
Blackfeet (0)	3	0.03
Cherokee (4)	19	0.17
Iroquois (1)	1	0.01
Lumbee (31)	42	0.37
Navajo (0)	1	0.01
Puget Sound Salish (0)	1	0.01
Yaqui (1)	1	0.01
Asian (547)	582	5.10
Not Hispanic (543)	572	5.01
Hispanic (4)	10	0.09
Cambodian (26)	34	0.30
Chinese, ex. Taiwanese (16)	23	0.20
Filipino (8)	11	0.10
Indian (64)	67	0.59
Indonesian (0)	2	0.02
Japanese (7)	14	0.12
Korean (20)	20	0.18
Laotian (29)	30	0.26
Pakistani (210)	211	1.85
Thai (3)	7	0.06
Vietnamese (132)	133	1.17
Hawaii Native/Pacific Islander (0)	4	0.04
Not Hispanic (0)	1	0.01
Hispanic (0)	3	0.03
White (10,020)	10,167	89.07
Not Hispanic (9,763)	9,884	86.59
Hispanic (257)	283	2.48

Asheboro

Place Type: City
County: Randolph
Population: 25,012†

Ancestry‡	Population	%
African, Sub-Saharan (10)	10	0.04
African (10)	10	0.04
American (2,221)	2,221	9.07
Arab (102)	115	0.47
Egyptian (55)	68	0.28
Other Arab (47)	47	0.19
Australian (8)	8	0.03
Austrian (0)	13	0.05
Belgian (0)	9	0.04
Brazilian (41)	41	0.17
British (37)	45	0.18
Czech (14)	14	0.06
Dutch (25)	308	1.26
Eastern European (13)	13	0.05
English (1,268)	2,436	9.95
European (89)	169	0.69
French, ex. Basque (139)	412	1.68
French Canadian (0)	18	0.07
German (750)	2,068	8.45
Irish (594)	1,807	7.38
Italian (230)	364	1.49
Latvian (13)	13	0.05
Lithuanian (0)	25	0.10
Northern European (19)	19	0.08
Norwegian (0)	28	0.11
Polish (215)	259	1.06
Portuguese (12)	38	0.16
Romanian (13)	13	0.05
Russian (17)	17	0.07
Scandinavian (14)	27	0.11
Scotch-Irish (394)	534	2.18
Scottish (336)	579	2.37
Swedish (13)	45	0.18
Swiss (0)	64	0.26
Welsh (55)	112	0.46

Hispanic Origin	Population	%
Hispanic or Latino (of any race)	6,719	26.86
Central American, ex. Mexican	607	2.43
Costa Rican	48	0.19
Guatemalan	180	0.72
Honduran	84	0.34
Nicaraguan	98	0.39
Panamanian	9	0.04
Salvadoran	183	0.73
Other Central American	5	0.02
Cuban	47	0.19
Dominican Republic	78	0.31
Mexican	5,469	21.87
Puerto Rican	137	0.55
South American	86	0.34
Argentinean	7	0.03
Bolivian	1	<0.01
Chilean	4	0.02
Colombian	36	0.14
Ecuadorian	15	0.06
Paraguayan	2	0.01
Peruvian	14	0.06
Venezuelan	5	0.02
Other South American	2	0.01
Other Hispanic or Latino	295	1.18

Race*	Population	%
African-American/Black (3,001)	3,316	13.26
Not Hispanic (2,919)	3,175	12.69
Hispanic (82)	141	0.56
American Indian/Alaska Native (219)	352	1.41
Not Hispanic (93)	189	0.76
Hispanic (126)	163	0.65
Apache (2)	14	0.06
Blackfeet (0)	4	0.02
Cherokee (23)	63	0.25
Chickasaw (3)	3	0.01
Chippewa (1)	2	0.01
Choctaw (5)	7	0.03
Cree (2)	2	0.01
Creek (0)	1	<0.01
Lumbee (22)	30	0.12
Mexican American Ind. (27)	35	0.14
Sioux (0)	3	0.01
Spanish American Ind. (1)	1	<0.01
Ute (0)	2	0.01
Yaqui (0)	6	0.02
Asian (346)	412	1.65
Not Hispanic (332)	384	1.54
Hispanic (14)	28	0.11
Cambodian (10)	14	0.06
Chinese, ex. Taiwanese (47)	53	0.21
Filipino (24)	36	0.14
Indian (82)	94	0.38
Indonesian (5)	6	0.02
Japanese (2)	5	0.02
Korean (26)	39	0.16
Laotian (4)	8	0.03
Pakistani (45)	51	0.20
Taiwanese (4)	4	0.02
Thai (5)	6	0.02
Vietnamese (52)	55	0.22
Hawaii Native/Pacific Islander (15)	55	0.22
Not Hispanic (8)	25	0.10
Hispanic (7)	30	0.12
Guamanian/Chamorro (10)	13	0.05
Native Hawaiian (3)	12	0.05
Samoan (0)	1	<0.01
White (16,968)	17,586	70.31
Not Hispanic (14,504)	14,877	59.48
Hispanic (2,464)	2,709	10.83

Asheville

Place Type: City
County: Buncombe
Population: 83,393†

Ancestry‡	Population	%
African, Sub-Saharan (298)	355	0.43
African (286)	302	0.37
Ethiopian (12)	12	0.01
South African (0)	41	0.05
Albanian (13)	13	0.02
Alsatian (10)	10	0.01
American (9,825)	9,825	11.99
Arab (67)	361	0.44
Arab (13)	13	0.02
Jordanian (0)	12	0.01
Lebanese (39)	259	0.32
Palestinian (0)	12	0.01
Syrian (15)	25	0.03
Other Arab (0)	40	0.05

SECTION TWO

*Notes: † The Census 2010 population figure is used to calculate the percentages in the Hispanic Origin and Race categories. Ancestry percentages are based on the 2006-2010 American Community Survey population (not shown); ‡ Numbers in parentheses indicate the number of people reporting a single ancestry; * Numbers in parentheses indicate the number of persons reporting this race alone, not in combination with any other race; Please refer to the Explanation of Data for more information.*

Armenian (13)	50	0.06
Australian (0)	7	0.01
Austrian (34)	207	0.25
Belgian (0)	56	0.07
British (278)	635	0.77
Bulgarian (12)	12	0.01
Cajun (17)	17	0.02
Canadian (109)	192	0.23
Carpatho Rusyn (8)	8	0.01
Celtic (73)	84	0.10
Croatian (47)	98	0.12
Czech (113)	366	0.45
Czechoslovakian (0)	58	0.07
Danish (145)	465	0.57
Dutch (175)	1,295	1.58
Eastern European (139)	139	0.17
English (4,371)	12,259	14.96
European (1,274)	1,449	1.77
Finnish (26)	78	0.10
French, ex. Basque (389)	2,612	3.19
French Canadian (176)	357	0.44
German (3,116)	12,009	14.65
German Russian (0)	53	0.06
Greek (244)	443	0.54
Hungarian (66)	174	0.21
Icelander (0)	11	0.01
Iranian (24)	41	0.05
Irish (2,766)	9,641	11.76
Israeli (27)	27	0.03
Italian (825)	2,842	3.47
Latvian (12)	21	0.03
Lithuanian (31)	173	0.21
Luxemburger (0)	12	0.01
Northern European (132)	132	0.16
Norwegian (230)	841	1.03
Pennsylvania German (7)	21	0.03
Polish (950)	2,531	3.09
Portuguese (35)	63	0.08
Romanian (732)	759	0.93
Russian (348)	655	0.80
Scandinavian (62)	279	0.34
Scotch-Irish (2,496)	4,845	5.91
Scottish (1,092)	3,480	4.25
Serbian (0)	10	0.01
Slavic (0)	32	0.04
Slovak (25)	25	0.03
Slovene (0)	44	0.05
Swedish (125)	620	0.76
Swiss (108)	492	0.60
Turkish (20)	20	0.02
Ukrainian (540)	745	0.91
Welsh (313)	1,103	1.35
West Indian, ex. Hispanic (180)	239	0.29
Haitian (20)	20	0.02
Jamaican (68)	127	0.15
Trinidadian/Tobagonian (92)	92	0.11
Yugoslavian (8)	8	0.01

Hispanic Origin	Population	%
Hispanic or Latino (of any race)	5,455	6.54
Central American, ex. Mexican	847	1.02
Costa Rican	17	0.02
Guatemalan	87	0.10
Honduran	181	0.22
Nicaraguan	26	0.03
Panamanian	11	0.01
Salvadoran	525	0.63
Cuban	223	0.27
Dominican Republic	27	0.03
Mexican	3,059	3.67
Puerto Rican	419	0.50
South American	404	0.48
Argentinean	57	0.07
Bolivian	4	<0.01
Chilean	38	0.05
Colombian	135	0.16
Ecuadorian	61	0.07
Paraguayan	2	<0.01
Peruvian	43	0.05
Uruguayan	3	<0.01
Venezuelan	53	0.06
Other South American	8	0.01
Other Hispanic or Latino	476	0.57

Race*	Population	%
African-American/Black (11,134)	12,247	14.69
Not Hispanic (11,024)	12,038	14.44
Hispanic (110)	209	0.25
American Indian/Alaska Native (280)	932	1.12
Not Hispanic (217)	798	0.96
Hispanic (63)	134	0.16
Alaska Athabascan *(Ala. Nat.)* (1)	1	<0.01
Aleut *(Alaska Native)* (1)	1	<0.01
Apache (2)	12	0.01
Arapaho (0)	1	<0.01
Blackfeet (4)	20	0.02
Canadian/French Am. Ind. (0)	3	<0.01
Central American Ind. (0)	8	0.01
Cherokee (89)	342	0.41
Cheyenne (1)	2	<0.01
Chickasaw (0)	1	<0.01
Chippewa (2)	8	0.01
Choctaw (3)	12	0.01
Comanche (1)	2	<0.01
Cree (0)	2	<0.01
Creek (1)	2	<0.01
Delaware (0)	1	<0.01
Houma (1)	1	<0.01
Iroquois (4)	13	0.02
Lumbee (25)	37	0.04
Mexican American Ind. (11)	16	0.02
Navajo (6)	12	0.01
Paiute (0)	1	<0.01
Potawatomi (1)	1	<0.01
Seminole (0)	6	0.01
Shoshone (0)	1	<0.01
Sioux (4)	9	0.01
South American Ind. (4)	7	0.01
Spanish American Ind. (4)	4	<0.01
Ute (1)	1	<0.01
Yaqui (0)	4	<0.01
Yuman (0)	1	<0.01
Asian (1,142)	1,518	1.82
Not Hispanic (1,130)	1,491	1.79
Hispanic (12)	27	0.03
Bhutanese (1)	1	<0.01
Burmese (2)	2	<0.01
Cambodian (11)	12	0.01
Chinese, ex. Taiwanese (230)	290	0.35
Filipino (175)	250	0.30
Hmong (4)	4	<0.01
Indian (241)	292	0.35
Indonesian (30)	32	0.04
Japanese (71)	146	0.18
Korean (179)	220	0.26
Laotian (0)	5	0.01
Malaysian (1)	2	<0.01
Nepalese (6)	6	0.01
Pakistani (16)	20	0.02
Sri Lankan (3)	4	<0.01
Taiwanese (4)	8	0.01
Thai (33)	39	0.05
Vietnamese (85)	97	0.12
Hawaii Native/Pacific Islander (126)	203	0.24
Not Hispanic (123)	179	0.21
Hispanic (3)	24	0.03
Fijian (0)	1	<0.01
Guamanian/Chamorro (5)	5	0.01
Marshallese (22)	26	0.03
Native Hawaiian (8)	41	0.05
Samoan (15)	22	0.03
Tongan (0)	1	<0.01
White (66,143)	68,075	81.63
Not Hispanic (63,508)	65,118	78.09
Hispanic (2,635)	2,957	3.55

Belmont

Place Type: City
County: Gaston
Population: 10,076[†]

Ancestry[‡]	Population	%
American (526)	526	5.35
Arab (25)	25	0.25
Other Arab (25)	25	0.25
Austrian (0)	14	0.14
Belgian (0)	12	0.12
British (44)	44	0.45
Danish (10)	24	0.24
Dutch (42)	294	2.99
English (618)	1,355	13.79
European (84)	141	1.43
French, ex. Basque (27)	156	1.59
French Canadian (7)	7	0.07
German (579)	1,763	17.94
Hungarian (11)	11	0.11
Irish (218)	1,168	11.88
Italian (72)	293	2.98
Lithuanian (0)	30	0.31
Norwegian (45)	57	0.58
Polish (8)	63	0.64
Russian (25)	25	0.25
Scotch-Irish (612)	837	8.52
Scottish (199)	377	3.84
Slovak (0)	52	0.53
Slovene (0)	15	0.15
Swedish (102)	102	1.04
Ukrainian (0)	15	0.15
Welsh (0)	49	0.50
West Indian, ex. Hispanic (28)	28	0.28
Trinidadian/Tobagonian (28)	28	0.28

Hispanic Origin	Population	%
Hispanic or Latino (of any race)	355	3.52
Central American, ex. Mexican	44	0.44
Costa Rican	1	0.01
Guatemalan	10	0.10
Honduran	5	0.05
Nicaraguan	8	0.08
Panamanian	5	0.05
Salvadoran	15	0.15
Cuban	33	0.33
Dominican Republic	10	0.10
Mexican	162	1.61
Puerto Rican	49	0.49
South American	30	0.30
Argentinean	1	0.01
Bolivian	7	0.07
Chilean	1	0.01
Colombian	10	0.10
Ecuadorian	1	0.01
Peruvian	6	0.06
Venezuelan	4	0.04
Other Hispanic or Latino	27	0.27

Race*	Population	%
African-American/Black (894)	963	9.56
Not Hispanic (878)	946	9.39
Hispanic (16)	17	0.17
American Indian/Alaska Native (34)	87	0.86
Not Hispanic (32)	84	0.83
Hispanic (2)	3	0.03
Blackfeet (0)	5	0.05
Cherokee (7)	34	0.34
Chippewa (1)	1	0.01
Choctaw (1)	2	0.02
Iroquois (2)	4	0.04
Lumbee (13)	16	0.16
Asian (410)	444	4.41
Not Hispanic (409)	442	4.39
Hispanic (1)	2	0.02
Cambodian (5)	7	0.07
Chinese, ex. Taiwanese (23)	32	0.32
Filipino (17)	21	0.21
Hmong (8)	8	0.08

*Notes: † The Census 2010 population figure is used to calculate the percentages in the Hispanic Origin and Race categories. Ancestry percentages are based on the 2006-2010 American Community Survey population (not shown); ‡ Numbers in parentheses indicate the number of people reporting a single ancestry; * Numbers in parentheses indicate the number of persons reporting this race alone, not in combination with any other race; Please refer to the Explanation of Data for more information.*

Indian (91)	94	0.93
Japanese (3)	7	0.07
Korean (18)	22	0.22
Laotian (20)	21	0.21
Pakistani (26)	30	0.30
Vietnamese (181)	190	1.89
Hawaii Native/Pacific Islander (16)	25	0.25
Not Hispanic (11)	20	0.20
Hispanic (5)	5	0.05
Guamanian/Chamorro (11)	11	0.11
Native Hawaiian (2)	5	0.05
Samoan (0)	1	0.01
White (8,422)	8,560	84.95
Not Hispanic (8,242)	8,362	82.99
Hispanic (180)	198	1.97

Black Mountain

Place Type: Town
County: Buncombe
Population: 7,848†

Ancestry‡	Population	%
African, Sub-Saharan (23)	23	0.29
African (23)	23	0.29
American (789)	789	10.10
Arab (14)	44	0.56
Lebanese (14)	44	0.56
Austrian (12)	12	0.15
Celtic (16)	16	0.20
Czech (0)	12	0.15
Danish (0)	12	0.15
Dutch (5)	148	1.90
English (464)	1,209	15.48
European (40)	53	0.68
Finnish (0)	8	0.10
French, ex. Basque (71)	418	5.35
French Canadian (13)	13	0.17
German (657)	1,601	20.50
Hungarian (24)	98	1.25
Irish (241)	911	11.67
Italian (33)	253	3.24
Norwegian (0)	21	0.27
Polish (67)	256	3.28
Portuguese (37)	247	3.16
Russian (50)	66	0.85
Scotch-Irish (336)	579	7.41
Scottish (272)	622	7.97
Slovene (12)	12	0.15
Swedish (29)	41	0.53
Swiss (0)	69	0.88
Welsh (32)	46	0.59

Hispanic Origin	Population	%
Hispanic or Latino (of any race)	193	2.46
Central American, ex. Mexican	50	0.64
Guatemalan	2	0.03
Honduran	7	0.09
Nicaraguan	4	0.05
Panamanian	2	0.03
Salvadoran	35	0.45
Cuban	21	0.27
Mexican	64	0.82
Puerto Rican	27	0.34
South American	16	0.20
Argentinean	4	0.05
Colombian	5	0.06
Ecuadorian	3	0.04
Venezuelan	4	0.05
Other Hispanic or Latino	15	0.19

Race*	Population	%
African-American/Black (470)	546	6.96
Not Hispanic (466)	538	6.86
Hispanic (4)	8	0.10
American Indian/Alaska Native (20)	103	1.31
Not Hispanic (13)	89	1.13
Hispanic (7)	14	0.18
Blackfeet (0)	4	0.05
Central American Ind. (0)	4	0.05
Cherokee (3)	48	0.61
Chippewa (0)	2	0.03
Choctaw (0)	4	0.05
Creek (0)	2	0.03
Iroquois (1)	2	0.03
Lumbee (3)	4	0.05
Mexican American Ind. (8)	8	0.10
Seminole (0)	1	0.01
Sioux (1)	2	0.03
Asian (49)	68	0.87
Not Hispanic (47)	66	0.84
Hispanic (2)	2	0.03
Cambodian (16)	16	0.20
Chinese, ex. Taiwanese (7)	12	0.15
Filipino (13)	19	0.24
Indian (4)	5	0.06
Japanese (2)	6	0.08
Korean (1)	1	0.01
Pakistani (1)	3	0.04
Sri Lankan (1)	1	0.01
Vietnamese (3)	3	0.04
Hawaii Native/Pacific Islander (2)	5	0.06
Not Hispanic (0)	3	0.04
Hispanic (2)	2	0.03
Guamanian/Chamorro (2)	2	0.03
Native Hawaiian (0)	1	0.01
Samoan (0)	1	0.01
White (7,064)	7,231	92.14
Not Hispanic (6,964)	7,117	90.69
Hispanic (100)	114	1.45

Boone

Place Type: Town
County: Watauga
Population: 17,122†

Ancestry‡	Population	%
American (675)	675	4.07
Arab (10)	38	0.23
Egyptian (10)	10	0.06
Lebanese (0)	28	0.17
Austrian (13)	26	0.16
British (99)	139	0.84
Canadian (12)	12	0.07
Czech (0)	57	0.34
Czechoslovakian (0)	30	0.18
Danish (31)	101	0.61
Dutch (104)	309	1.87
English (1,022)	2,369	14.30
European (197)	197	1.19
Finnish (0)	18	0.11
French, ex. Basque (196)	557	3.36
German (1,542)	4,303	25.97
Greek (104)	148	0.89
Hungarian (89)	158	0.95
Icelander (0)	69	0.42
Iranian (0)	95	0.57
Irish (693)	2,330	14.06
Italian (333)	1,008	6.08
Lithuanian (14)	27	0.16
Norwegian (38)	242	1.46
Polish (106)	265	1.60
Portuguese (25)	38	0.23
Romanian (25)	25	0.15
Russian (13)	87	0.53
Scandinavian (33)	90	0.54
Scotch-Irish (688)	1,169	7.06
Scottish (325)	1,112	6.71
Slavic (15)	15	0.09
Slovak (0)	33	0.20
Swedish (13)	150	0.91
Swiss (48)	85	0.51
Turkish (0)	25	0.15
Ukrainian (13)	13	0.08
Welsh (35)	193	1.17
West Indian, ex. Hispanic (13)	25	0.15
Trinidadian/Tobagonian (13)	13	0.08
West Indian (0)	12	0.07
Yugoslavian (0)	21	0.13

Hispanic Origin	Population	%
Hispanic or Latino (of any race)	568	3.32
Central American, ex. Mexican	49	0.29
Costa Rican	8	0.05
Guatemalan	4	0.02
Honduran	22	0.13
Nicaraguan	5	0.03
Panamanian	2	0.01
Salvadoran	8	0.05
Cuban	47	0.27
Dominican Republic	9	0.05
Mexican	290	1.69
Puerto Rican	80	0.47
South American	58	0.34
Argentinean	2	0.01
Bolivian	2	0.01
Chilean	5	0.03
Colombian	31	0.18
Ecuadorian	6	0.04
Paraguayan	1	0.01
Peruvian	6	0.04
Uruguayan	1	0.01
Venezuelan	4	0.02
Other Hispanic or Latino	35	0.20

Race*	Population	%
African-American/Black (603)	708	4.14
Not Hispanic (584)	672	3.92
Hispanic (19)	36	0.21
American Indian/Alaska Native (39)	142	0.83
Not Hispanic (32)	122	0.71
Hispanic (7)	20	0.12
Apache (1)	5	0.03
Blackfeet (0)	1	0.01
Canadian/French Am. Ind. (1)	1	0.01
Cherokee (7)	41	0.24
Chippewa (4)	7	0.04
Choctaw (1)	1	0.01
Creek (0)	1	0.01
Crow (0)	1	0.01
Delaware (2)	3	0.02
Iroquois (0)	1	0.01
Lumbee (6)	13	0.08
South American Ind. (0)	1	0.01
Asian (268)	364	2.13
Not Hispanic (263)	354	2.07
Hispanic (5)	10	0.06
Burmese (2)	2	0.01
Cambodian (1)	1	0.01
Chinese, ex. Taiwanese (90)	102	0.60
Filipino (15)	41	0.24
Hmong (16)	16	0.09
Indian (39)	52	0.30
Indonesian (2)	3	0.02
Japanese (13)	30	0.18
Korean (36)	57	0.33
Laotian (3)	3	0.02
Nepalese (1)	1	0.01
Pakistani (2)	2	0.01
Taiwanese (1)	3	0.02
Thai (3)	8	0.05
Vietnamese (31)	38	0.22
Hawaii Native/Pacific Islander (6)	17	0.10
Not Hispanic (6)	14	0.08
Hispanic (0)	3	0.02
Guamanian/Chamorro (0)	3	0.02
Marshallese (1)	1	0.01
Native Hawaiian (1)	5	0.03
Samoan (2)	2	0.01
White (15,746)	16,014	93.53
Not Hispanic (15,396)	15,624	91.25
Hispanic (350)	390	2.28

Brevard

Place Type: City
County: Transylvania
Population: 7,609†

SECTION TWO

*Notes: † The Census 2010 population figure is used to calculate the percentages in the Hispanic Origin and Race categories. Ancestry percentages are based on the 2006-2010 American Community Survey population (not shown); ‡ Numbers in parentheses indicate the number of people reporting a single ancestry; * Numbers in parentheses indicate the number of persons reporting this race alone, not in combination with any other race; Please refer to the Explanation of Data for more information.*

Ancestry‡	Population	%
American (876)	876	11.70
Austrian (15)	15	0.20
British (68)	128	1.71
Czechoslovakian (0)	13	0.17
Danish (0)	14	0.19
Dutch (53)	139	1.86
English (889)	1,568	20.94
French, ex. Basque (15)	199	2.66
German (247)	1,100	14.69
Greek (31)	31	0.41
Hungarian (15)	15	0.20
Irish (226)	949	12.67
Italian (57)	158	2.11
Northern European (23)	23	0.31
Norwegian (0)	150	2.00
Polish (54)	83	1.11
Russian (24)	24	0.32
Scotch-Irish (307)	496	6.62
Scottish (123)	466	6.22
Swedish (22)	109	1.46
Swiss (27)	70	0.93
Welsh (0)	92	1.23

Hispanic Origin	Population	%
Hispanic or Latino (of any race)	285	3.75
Central American, ex. Mexican	17	0.22
Costa Rican	2	0.03
Guatemalan	9	0.12
Honduran	5	0.07
Salvadoran	1	0.01
Cuban	9	0.12
Dominican Republic	1	0.01
Mexican	175	2.30
Puerto Rican	46	0.60
South American	21	0.28
Chilean	1	0.01
Colombian	2	0.03
Peruvian	9	0.12
Uruguayan	1	0.01
Venezuelan	7	0.09
Other South American	1	0.01
Other Hispanic or Latino	16	0.21

Race*	Population	%
African-American/Black (840)	973	12.79
Not Hispanic (836)	965	12.68
Hispanic (4)	8	0.11
American Indian/Alaska Native (21)	85	1.12
Not Hispanic (20)	78	1.03
Hispanic (1)	7	0.09
Blackfeet (0)	3	0.04
Cherokee (0)	31	0.41
Chickasaw (1)	3	0.04
Choctaw (1)	1	0.01
Creek (0)	1	0.01
Iroquois (0)	1	0.01
Lumbee (3)	3	0.04
Ottawa (0)	1	0.01
Sioux (1)	2	0.03
Asian (74)	98	1.29
Not Hispanic (73)	96	1.26
Hispanic (1)	2	0.03
Cambodian (5)	5	0.07
Chinese, ex. Taiwanese (24)	26	0.34
Filipino (6)	13	0.17
Indian (12)	15	0.20
Indonesian (7)	8	0.11
Japanese (4)	10	0.13
Korean (7)	8	0.11
Malaysian (0)	3	0.04
Vietnamese (8)	8	0.11
Hawaii Native/Pacific Islander (0)	8	0.11
Not Hispanic (0)	8	0.11
Native Hawaiian (0)	5	0.07
White (6,339)	6,519	85.67
Not Hispanic (6,187)	6,355	83.52
Hispanic (152)	164	2.16

Burlington

Place Type: City
County: Alamance
Population: 49,963†

Ancestry‡	Population	%
African, Sub-Saharan (172)	365	0.75
African (124)	275	0.56
South African (0)	42	0.09
Sudanese (48)	48	0.10
American (3,898)	3,898	8.00
Arab (55)	146	0.30
Egyptian (19)	19	0.04
Lebanese (24)	51	0.10
Palestinian (12)	12	0.02
Syrian (0)	64	0.13
Armenian (14)	35	0.07
Austrian (34)	69	0.14
Belgian (0)	27	0.06
Brazilian (32)	32	0.07
British (9)	37	0.08
Cajun (10)	10	0.02
Canadian (0)	21	0.04
Celtic (0)	11	0.02
Danish (0)	54	0.11
Dutch (65)	310	0.64
English (2,069)	4,615	9.47
European (339)	350	0.72
Finnish (18)	18	0.04
French, ex. Basque (118)	721	1.48
French Canadian (39)	162	0.33
German (1,397)	4,654	9.55
Greek (118)	137	0.28
Hungarian (0)	58	0.12
Irish (1,263)	3,793	7.78
Italian (417)	1,194	2.45
Lithuanian (6)	6	0.01
Norwegian (38)	103	0.21
Pennsylvania German (0)	14	0.03
Polish (101)	425	0.87
Romanian (0)	7	0.01
Russian (67)	136	0.28
Scotch-Irish (1,387)	2,205	4.52
Scottish (527)	1,210	2.48
Serbian (16)	16	0.03
Slovak (25)	58	0.12
Swedish (37)	185	0.38
Swiss (0)	71	0.15
Turkish (36)	36	0.07
Ukrainian (34)	42	0.09
Welsh (57)	134	0.27
West Indian, ex. Hispanic (0)	25	0.05
West Indian (0)	25	0.05

Hispanic Origin	Population	%
Hispanic or Latino (of any race)	7,990	15.99
Central American, ex. Mexican	1,275	2.55
Costa Rican	8	0.02
Guatemalan	72	0.14
Honduran	281	0.56
Nicaraguan	35	0.07
Panamanian	18	0.04
Salvadoran	859	1.72
Other Central American	2	<0.01
Cuban	72	0.14
Dominican Republic	48	0.10
Mexican	5,402	10.81
Puerto Rican	389	0.78
South American	271	0.54
Argentinean	13	0.03
Bolivian	3	0.01
Chilean	36	0.07
Colombian	48	0.10
Ecuadorian	123	0.25
Paraguayan	4	0.01
Peruvian	26	0.05
Uruguayan	6	0.01
Venezuelan	12	0.02
Other Hispanic or Latino	533	1.07

Race*	Population	%
African-American/Black (13,998)	14,670	29.36
Not Hispanic (13,808)	14,366	28.75
Hispanic (190)	304	0.61
American Indian/Alaska Native (335)	650	1.30
Not Hispanic (162)	394	0.79
Hispanic (173)	256	0.51
Apache (1)	2	<0.01
Blackfeet (2)	8	0.02
Central American Ind. (6)	6	0.01
Cherokee (33)	104	0.21
Chippewa (3)	4	0.01
Choctaw (1)	1	<0.01
Creek (0)	4	0.01
Crow (0)	1	<0.01
Iroquois (0)	2	<0.01
Lumbee (28)	38	0.08
Mexican American Ind. (34)	38	0.08
Pueblo (1)	1	<0.01
Seminole (3)	6	0.01
Sioux (1)	2	<0.01
South American Ind. (4)	5	0.01
Spanish American Ind. (12)	25	0.05
Ute (1)	1	<0.01
Asian (1,027)	1,158	2.32
Not Hispanic (1,013)	1,127	2.26
Hispanic (14)	31	0.06
Bangladeshi (7)	7	0.01
Burmese (12)	12	0.02
Chinese, ex. Taiwanese (129)	141	0.28
Filipino (64)	87	0.17
Hmong (35)	35	0.07
Indian (265)	294	0.59
Indonesian (5)	5	0.01
Japanese (12)	19	0.04
Korean (80)	105	0.21
Laotian (155)	178	0.36
Malaysian (0)	1	<0.01
Nepalese (1)	1	<0.01
Pakistani (66)	73	0.15
Taiwanese (7)	7	0.01
Thai (10)	16	0.03
Vietnamese (143)	148	0.30
Hawaii Native/Pacific Islander (35)	81	0.16
Not Hispanic (33)	63	0.13
Hispanic (2)	18	0.04
Fijian (0)	2	<0.01
Guamanian/Chamorro (11)	13	0.03
Native Hawaiian (7)	20	0.04
Samoan (1)	13	0.03
White (28,760)	29,741	59.53
Not Hispanic (26,087)	26,709	53.46
Hispanic (2,673)	3,032	6.07

Butner

Place Type: Town
County: Granville
Population: 7,591†

Ancestry‡	Population	%
African, Sub-Saharan (48)	57	0.77
African (48)	57	0.77
American (956)	956	12.89
Arab (34)	34	0.46
Moroccan (34)	34	0.46
Dutch (0)	7	0.09
English (163)	467	6.30
French, ex. Basque (0)	47	0.63
French Canadian (0)	70	0.94
German (182)	493	6.65
Greek (8)	8	0.11
Irish (164)	491	6.62
Italian (9)	55	0.74
Latvian (0)	8	0.11
Polish (8)	32	0.43
Scotch-Irish (157)	240	3.24
Scottish (116)	214	2.89
Serbian (10)	36	0.49

*Notes: † The Census 2010 population figure is used to calculate the percentages in the Hispanic Origin and Race categories. Ancestry percentages are based on the 2006-2010 American Community Survey population (not shown); ‡ Numbers in parentheses indicate the number of people reporting a single ancestry; * Numbers in parentheses indicate the number of persons reporting this race alone, not in combination with any other race; Please refer to the Explanation of Data for more information.*

Swedish (0)	26	0.35
Swiss (0)	65	0.88
Welsh (0)	8	0.11

Hispanic Origin	Population	%
Hispanic or Latino (of any race)	1,118	14.73
Central American, ex. Mexican	68	0.90
Costa Rican	1	0.01
Honduran	25	0.33
Panamanian	1	0.01
Salvadoran	36	0.47
Other Central American	5	0.07
Cuban	3	0.04
Dominican Republic	2	0.03
Mexican	882	11.62
Puerto Rican	100	1.32
South American	16	0.21
Chilean	6	0.08
Colombian	3	0.04
Peruvian	7	0.09
Other Hispanic or Latino	47	0.62

Race*	Population	%
African-American/Black (2,286)	2,394	31.54
Not Hispanic (2,259)	2,353	31.00
Hispanic (27)	41	0.54
American Indian/Alaska Native (51)	106	1.40
Not Hispanic (17)	59	0.78
Hispanic (34)	47	0.62
Cherokee (3)	9	0.12
Comanche (0)	3	0.04
Delaware (1)	1	0.01
Iroquois (1)	1	0.01
Lumbee (3)	9	0.12
Mexican American Ind. (9)	10	0.13
Seminole (3)	3	0.04
South American Ind. (0)	4	0.05
Asian (65)	85	1.12
Not Hispanic (65)	80	1.05
Hispanic (0)	5	0.07
Bangladeshi (8)	8	0.11
Chinese, ex. Taiwanese (12)	13	0.17
Filipino (9)	17	0.22
Indian (14)	15	0.20
Japanese (0)	3	0.04
Korean (1)	5	0.07
Vietnamese (20)	20	0.26
Hawaii Native/Pacific Islander (0)	5	0.07
Not Hispanic (0)	1	0.01
Hispanic (0)	4	0.05
White (4,516)	4,667	61.48
Not Hispanic (4,007)	4,116	54.22
Hispanic (509)	551	7.26

Carrboro

Place Type: Town
County: Orange
Population: 19,582†

Ancestry‡	Population	%
African, Sub-Saharan (405)	405	2.12
African (266)	266	1.39
Liberian (5)	5	0.03
Nigerian (104)	104	0.55
South African (30)	30	0.16
American (589)	589	3.09
Arab (34)	49	0.26
Lebanese (34)	34	0.18
Syrian (0)	15	0.08
Armenian (0)	23	0.12
Australian (12)	12	0.06
Austrian (18)	39	0.20
Belgian (48)	48	0.25
British (66)	137	0.72
Bulgarian (41)	88	0.46
Canadian (39)	123	0.64
Celtic (62)	62	0.33
Croatian (23)	54	0.28
Cypriot (10)	10	0.05
Czech (10)	21	0.11
Danish (15)	127	0.67
Dutch (69)	225	1.18
Eastern European (83)	103	0.54
English (672)	2,890	15.15
Estonian (0)	20	0.10
European (450)	509	2.67
Finnish (0)	11	0.06
French, ex. Basque (25)	316	1.66
French Canadian (0)	42	0.22
German (605)	2,780	14.57
Greek (27)	155	0.81
Hungarian (13)	194	1.02
Iranian (19)	39	0.20
Irish (536)	1,741	9.13
Israeli (14)	14	0.07
Italian (238)	1,016	5.33
Lithuanian (12)	186	0.98
Northern European (84)	84	0.44
Norwegian (58)	141	0.74
Polish (250)	884	4.63
Portuguese (0)	13	0.07
Romanian (0)	7	0.04
Russian (174)	522	2.74
Scandinavian (20)	20	0.10
Scotch-Irish (232)	692	3.63
Scottish (156)	693	3.63
Serbian (21)	21	0.11
Swedish (110)	345	1.81
Swiss (15)	119	0.62
Turkish (15)	15	0.08
Ukrainian (37)	65	0.34
Welsh (13)	156	0.82
West Indian, ex. Hispanic (14)	59	0.31
Haitian (0)	15	0.08
Jamaican (14)	14	0.07
West Indian (0)	30	0.16
Yugoslavian (0)	42	0.22

Hispanic Origin	Population	%
Hispanic or Latino (of any race)	2,706	13.82
Central American, ex. Mexican	328	1.68
Costa Rican	5	0.03
Guatemalan	129	0.66
Honduran	54	0.28
Nicaraguan	5	0.03
Panamanian	5	0.03
Salvadoran	123	0.63
Other Central American	7	0.04
Cuban	58	0.30
Dominican Republic	18	0.09
Mexican	1,799	9.19
Puerto Rican	96	0.49
South American	236	1.21
Argentinean	40	0.20
Bolivian	6	0.03
Chilean	24	0.12
Colombian	89	0.45
Ecuadorian	17	0.09
Paraguayan	5	0.03
Peruvian	26	0.13
Uruguayan	2	0.01
Venezuelan	25	0.13
Other South American	2	0.01
Other Hispanic or Latino	171	0.87

Race*	Population	%
African-American/Black (1,969)	2,154	11.00
Not Hispanic (1,933)	2,084	10.64
Hispanic (36)	70	0.36
American Indian/Alaska Native (82)	213	1.09
Not Hispanic (49)	152	0.78
Hispanic (33)	61	0.31
Apache (0)	1	0.01
Blackfeet (0)	5	0.03
Canadian/French Am. Ind. (1)	2	0.01
Cherokee (1)	41	0.21
Chippewa (3)	3	0.02
Choctaw (0)	1	0.01
Cree (1)	1	0.01
Creek (1)	4	0.02
Delaware (1)	1	0.01
Iroquois (1)	7	0.04
Lumbee (13)	18	0.09
Menominee (1)	1	0.01
Mexican American Ind. (13)	18	0.09
Osage (1)	1	0.01
Pueblo (1)	1	0.01
Sioux (1)	3	0.02
South American Ind. (2)	11	0.06
Spanish American Ind. (0)	1	0.01
Tlingit-Haida *(Alaska Native)* (1)	1	0.01
Asian (1,596)	1,822	9.30
Not Hispanic (1,585)	1,802	9.20
Hispanic (11)	20	0.10
Bangladeshi (6)	6	0.03
Burmese (306)	339	1.73
Cambodian (8)	11	0.06
Chinese, ex. Taiwanese (523)	595	3.04
Filipino (70)	93	0.47
Hmong (6)	6	0.03
Indian (302)	341	1.74
Indonesian (1)	2	0.01
Japanese (51)	110	0.56
Korean (136)	182	0.93
Laotian (2)	2	0.01
Malaysian (4)	5	0.03
Pakistani (11)	19	0.10
Sri Lankan (10)	12	0.06
Taiwanese (34)	40	0.20
Thai (14)	23	0.12
Vietnamese (42)	53	0.27
Hawaii Native/Pacific Islander (8)	28	0.14
Not Hispanic (7)	26	0.13
Hispanic (1)	2	0.01
Guamanian/Chamorro (2)	4	0.02
Native Hawaiian (3)	6	0.03
Samoan (2)	2	0.01
Tongan (0)	2	0.01
White (13,891)	14,376	73.41
Not Hispanic (12,794)	13,168	67.25
Hispanic (1,097)	1,208	6.17

Cary

Place Type: Town
County: Wake
Population: 135,234†

Ancestry‡	Population	%
Afghan (369)	369	0.29
African, Sub-Saharan (627)	900	0.71
African (453)	618	0.48
Kenyan (60)	60	0.05
Nigerian (101)	101	0.08
South African (13)	121	0.09
Albanian (48)	48	0.04
Alsatian (0)	16	0.01
American (9,424)	9,424	7.39
Arab (1,035)	1,244	0.98
Arab (59)	71	0.06
Egyptian (200)	271	0.21
Iraqi (12)	12	0.01
Jordanian (75)	75	0.06
Lebanese (189)	315	0.25
Moroccan (301)	301	0.24
Palestinian (108)	108	0.08
Syrian (14)	14	0.01
Other Arab (77)	77	0.06
Armenian (54)	206	0.16
Austrian (71)	407	0.32
Basque (25)	38	0.03
Belgian (56)	343	0.27
Brazilian (19)	69	0.05
British (638)	1,185	0.93
Bulgarian (215)	215	0.17
Cajun (29)	40	0.03
Canadian (399)	525	0.41
Celtic (21)	29	0.02
Croatian (10)	86	0.07

*Notes: † The Census 2010 population figure is used to calculate the percentages in the Hispanic Origin and Race categories. Ancestry percentages are based on the 2006-2010 American Community Survey population (not shown); ‡ Numbers in parentheses indicate the number of people reporting a single ancestry; * Numbers in parentheses indicate the number of persons reporting this race alone, not in combination with any other race; Please refer to the Explanation of Data for more information.*

Czech (155)	642	0.50
Czechoslovakian (32)	139	0.11
Danish (87)	498	0.39
Dutch (379)	1,854	1.45
Eastern European (229)	320	0.25
English (7,252)	17,916	14.04
Estonian (11)	11	0.01
European (2,831)	3,166	2.48
Finnish (38)	148	0.12
French, ex. Basque (539)	3,176	2.49
French Canadian (430)	1,019	0.80
German (5,605)	19,577	15.34
German Russian (0)	13	0.01
Greek (313)	728	0.57
Guyanese (18)	18	0.01
Hungarian (388)	950	0.74
Icelander (11)	11	0.01
Iranian (116)	205	0.16
Irish (4,338)	15,501	12.15
Israeli (102)	102	0.08
Italian (3,188)	9,428	7.39
Latvian (8)	30	0.02
Lithuanian (27)	356	0.28
Macedonian (0)	13	0.01
Maltese (0)	29	0.02
Northern European (236)	236	0.18
Norwegian (379)	1,260	0.99
Pennsylvania German (0)	10	0.01
Polish (988)	4,181	3.28
Portuguese (63)	267	0.21
Romanian (46)	211	0.17
Russian (490)	1,625	1.27
Scandinavian (164)	251	0.20
Scotch-Irish (2,326)	4,549	3.57
Scottish (1,239)	3,944	3.09
Serbian (0)	36	0.03
Slavic (0)	41	0.03
Slovak (141)	448	0.35
Slovene (20)	70	0.05
Swedish (455)	1,679	1.32
Swiss (83)	345	0.27
Turkish (130)	147	0.12
Ukrainian (140)	630	0.49
Welsh (212)	1,388	1.09
West Indian, ex. Hispanic (782)	1,010	0.79
Belizean (18)	40	0.03
Haitian (126)	151	0.12
Jamaican (280)	325	0.25
Trinidadian/Tobagonian (35)	96	0.08
U.S. Virgin Islander (0)	12	0.01
West Indian (323)	386	0.30
Yugoslavian (35)	202	0.16

Hispanic Origin	Population	%
Hispanic or Latino (of any race)	10,364	7.66
Central American, ex. Mexican	1,351	1.00
Costa Rican	82	0.06
Guatemalan	391	0.29
Honduran	244	0.18
Nicaraguan	89	0.07
Panamanian	78	0.06
Salvadoran	450	0.33
Other Central American	17	0.01
Cuban	529	0.39
Dominican Republic	248	0.18
Mexican	5,012	3.71
Puerto Rican	1,169	0.86
South American	1,259	0.93
Argentinean	115	0.09
Bolivian	40	0.03
Chilean	83	0.06
Colombian	423	0.31
Ecuadorian	140	0.10
Paraguayan	9	0.01
Peruvian	258	0.19
Uruguayan	23	0.02
Venezuelan	156	0.12
Other South American	12	0.01
Other Hispanic or Latino	796	0.59

Race*	Population	%
African-American/Black (10,787)	11,966	8.85
Not Hispanic (10,485)	11,504	8.51
Hispanic (302)	462	0.34
American Indian/Alaska Native (559)	1,353	1.00
Not Hispanic (284)	949	0.70
Hispanic (275)	404	0.30
Alaska Athabascan *(Ala. Nat.)* (9)	10	0.01
Apache (2)	11	0.01
Blackfeet (14)	39	0.03
Canadian/French Am. Ind. (1)	2	<0.01
Central American Ind. (5)	6	<0.01
Cherokee (31)	214	0.16
Cheyenne (0)	1	<0.01
Chickasaw (0)	5	<0.01
Chippewa (11)	21	0.02
Choctaw (4)	20	0.01
Colville (0)	1	<0.01
Cree (1)	3	<0.01
Creek (2)	6	<0.01
Crow (0)	6	<0.01
Delaware (1)	5	<0.01
Hopi (0)	1	<0.01
Iroquois (8)	24	0.02
Kiowa (1)	1	<0.01
Lumbee (78)	124	0.09
Mexican American Ind. (50)	59	0.04
Navajo (1)	6	<0.01
Osage (0)	7	0.01
Ottawa (1)	2	<0.01
Pima (1)	1	<0.01
Potawatomi (0)	1	<0.01
Pueblo (2)	2	<0.01
Puget Sound Salish (3)	3	<0.01
Seminole (1)	8	0.01
Sioux (5)	14	0.01
South American Ind. (20)	39	0.03
Tlingit-Haida *(Alaska Native)* (1)	1	<0.01
Yaqui (1)	1	<0.01
Asian (17,668)	19,370	14.32
Not Hispanic (17,620)	19,231	14.22
Hispanic (48)	139	0.10
Bangladeshi (115)	124	0.09
Burmese (1)	5	<0.01
Cambodian (15)	31	0.02
Chinese, ex. Taiwanese (3,979)	4,330	3.20
Filipino (582)	847	0.63
Hmong (10)	10	0.01
Indian (8,769)	9,217	6.82
Indonesian (28)	70	0.05
Japanese (314)	561	0.41
Korean (1,273)	1,455	1.08
Laotian (23)	26	0.02
Malaysian (10)	14	0.01
Nepalese (184)	190	0.14
Pakistani (506)	579	0.43
Sri Lankan (137)	161	0.12
Taiwanese (305)	346	0.26
Thai (74)	114	0.08
Vietnamese (969)	1,081	0.80
Hawaii Native/Pacific Islander (46)	179	0.13
Not Hispanic (39)	160	0.12
Hispanic (7)	19	0.01
Fijian (1)	2	<0.01
Guamanian/Chamorro (15)	28	0.02
Native Hawaiian (19)	54	0.04
Samoan (1)	7	0.01
White (98,907)	101,785	75.27
Not Hispanic (93,202)	95,613	70.70
Hispanic (5,705)	6,172	4.56

Chapel Hill

Place Type: Town
County: Orange
Population: 57,233†

Ancestry‡	Population	%
African, Sub-Saharan (353)	429	0.78
African (172)	216	0.39
Ethiopian (20)	20	0.04
Ghanaian (26)	26	0.05
Kenyan (32)	32	0.06
Nigerian (44)	70	0.13
South African (5)	11	0.02
Zimbabwean (39)	39	0.07
Other Sub-Saharan African (15)	15	0.03
Albanian (7)	19	0.03
Alsatian (0)	14	0.03
American (1,650)	1,650	2.99
Arab (193)	381	0.69
Arab (63)	96	0.17
Egyptian (23)	43	0.08
Iraqi (0)	20	0.04
Jordanian (2)	2	<0.01
Lebanese (98)	148	0.27
Moroccan (7)	7	0.01
Palestinian (0)	14	0.03
Syrian (0)	14	0.03
Other Arab (0)	37	0.07
Armenian (33)	91	0.16
Australian (34)	44	0.08
Austrian (53)	243	0.44
Belgian (70)	116	0.21
British (612)	1,225	2.22
Bulgarian (46)	75	0.14
Canadian (181)	279	0.51
Celtic (0)	36	0.07
Croatian (8)	84	0.15
Czech (144)	430	0.78
Czechoslovakian (0)	33	0.06
Danish (12)	217	0.39
Dutch (284)	1,052	1.91
Eastern European (171)	196	0.36
English (3,591)	10,042	18.20
Estonian (17)	17	0.03
European (1,345)	1,435	2.60
Finnish (26)	78	0.14
French, ex. Basque (184)	1,546	2.80
French Canadian (123)	477	0.86
German (2,021)	8,076	14.64
Greek (146)	442	0.80
Guyanese (0)	15	0.03
Hungarian (77)	281	0.51
Icelander (14)	27	0.05
Iranian (47)	47	0.09
Irish (1,255)	5,429	9.84
Israeli (84)	109	0.20
Italian (636)	2,665	4.83
Latvian (28)	68	0.12
Lithuanian (85)	224	0.41
New Zealander (49)	49	0.09
Northern European (156)	156	0.28
Norwegian (180)	526	0.95
Pennsylvania German (0)	16	0.03
Polish (474)	1,646	2.98
Portuguese (0)	96	0.17
Romanian (75)	176	0.32
Russian (318)	946	1.71
Scandinavian (25)	102	0.18
Scotch-Irish (1,278)	2,806	5.09
Scottish (827)	2,770	5.02
Serbian (3)	3	0.01
Slavic (33)	122	0.22
Slovak (51)	124	0.22
Slovene (0)	32	0.06
Swedish (128)	795	1.44
Swiss (127)	422	0.76
Turkish (55)	68	0.12
Ukrainian (144)	334	0.61
Welsh (180)	805	1.46
West Indian, ex. Hispanic (317)	411	0.74
Barbadian (0)	14	0.03
British West Indian (44)	55	0.10
Haitian (19)	57	0.10
Jamaican (227)	258	0.47
West Indian (27)	27	0.05
Yugoslavian (11)	54	0.10

*Notes: † The Census 2010 population figure is used to calculate the percentages in the Hispanic Origin and Race categories. Ancestry percentages are based on the 2006-2010 American Community Survey population (not shown); ‡ Numbers in parentheses indicate the number of people reporting a single ancestry; * Numbers in parentheses indicate the number of persons reporting this race alone, not in combination with any other race; Please refer to the Explanation of Data for more information.*

Hispanic Origin	Population	%
Hispanic or Latino (of any race)	3,638	6.36
Central American, ex. Mexican	667	1.17
Costa Rican	29	0.05
Guatemalan	223	0.39
Honduran	112	0.20
Nicaraguan	29	0.05
Panamanian	43	0.08
Salvadoran	227	0.40
Other Central American	4	0.01
Cuban	197	0.34
Dominican Republic	45	0.08
Mexican	1,566	2.74
Puerto Rican	332	0.58
South American	529	0.92
Argentinean	74	0.13
Bolivian	12	0.02
Chilean	45	0.08
Colombian	204	0.36
Ecuadorian	35	0.06
Paraguayan	12	0.02
Peruvian	78	0.14
Uruguayan	7	0.01
Venezuelan	58	0.10
Other South American	4	0.01
Other Hispanic or Latino	302	0.53

Race*	Population	%
African-American/Black (5,530)	6,061	10.59
Not Hispanic (5,460)	5,915	10.33
Hispanic (70)	146	0.26
American Indian/Alaska Native (176)	471	0.82
Not Hispanic (152)	396	0.69
Hispanic (24)	75	0.13
Aleut *(Alaska Native)* (0)	1	<0.01
Apache (0)	2	<0.01
Blackfeet (0)	7	0.01
Central American Ind. (2)	3	0.01
Cherokee (30)	109	0.19
Chickasaw (1)	1	<0.01
Chippewa (5)	13	0.02
Choctaw (1)	15	0.03
Comanche (0)	4	0.01
Creek (1)	2	<0.01
Delaware (0)	7	0.01
Hopi (1)	1	<0.01
Iroquois (4)	10	0.02
Kiowa (1)	1	<0.01
Lumbee (48)	65	0.11
Mexican American Ind. (15)	24	0.04
Navajo (2)	8	0.01
Pueblo (0)	3	0.01
Sioux (1)	4	0.01
South American Ind. (1)	12	0.02
Spanish American Ind. (0)	2	<0.01
Asian (6,788)	7,548	13.19
Not Hispanic (6,775)	7,495	13.10
Hispanic (13)	53	0.09
Bangladeshi (34)	35	0.06
Burmese (380)	393	0.69
Cambodian (7)	13	0.02
Chinese, ex. Taiwanese (2,638)	2,866	5.01
Filipino (155)	269	0.47
Hmong (6)	6	0.01
Indian (1,260)	1,418	2.48
Indonesian (15)	20	0.03
Japanese (293)	387	0.68
Korean (1,285)	1,377	2.41
Laotian (4)	6	0.01
Malaysian (8)	8	0.01
Nepalese (11)	11	0.02
Pakistani (66)	89	0.16
Sri Lankan (38)	42	0.07
Taiwanese (170)	201	0.35
Thai (77)	105	0.18
Vietnamese (186)	216	0.38
Hawaii Native/Pacific Islander (14)	55	0.10
Not Hispanic (11)	47	0.08
Hispanic (3)	8	0.01
Fijian (1)	3	0.01
Guamanian/Chamorro (3)	7	0.01
Native Hawaiian (3)	9	0.02
Samoan (2)	6	0.01
White (41,641)	43,000	75.13
Not Hispanic (39,777)	40,897	71.46
Hispanic (1,864)	2,103	3.67

Charlotte

Place Type: City
County: Mecklenburg
Population: 731,424†

Ancestry‡	Population	%
Afghan (0)	13	<0.01
African, Sub-Saharan (10,123)	11,247	1.59
African (4,575)	5,460	0.77
Cape Verdean (27)	48	0.01
Ethiopian (954)	954	0.14
Ghanaian (523)	539	0.08
Kenyan (282)	282	0.04
Liberian (618)	633	0.09
Nigerian (1,182)	1,192	0.17
Senegalese (47)	47	0.01
Sierra Leonean (70)	70	0.01
Somalian (485)	485	0.07
South African (170)	194	0.03
Sudanese (42)	101	0.01
Other Sub-Saharan African (1,148)	1,242	0.18
Albanian (149)	177	0.03
Alsatian (0)	19	<0.01
American (30,441)	30,441	4.31
Arab (3,391)	4,490	0.64
Arab (754)	840	0.12
Egyptian (522)	604	0.09
Jordanian (106)	117	0.02
Lebanese (850)	1,598	0.23
Moroccan (368)	382	0.05
Palestinian (111)	122	0.02
Syrian (163)	254	0.04
Other Arab (517)	573	0.08
Armenian (397)	612	0.09
Assyrian/Chaldean/Syriac (7)	7	<0.01
Australian (32)	152	0.02
Austrian (261)	1,273	0.18
Basque (6)	6	<0.01
Belgian (294)	690	0.10
Brazilian (1,163)	1,399	0.20
British (1,891)	3,557	0.50
Bulgarian (91)	123	0.02
Cajun (115)	208	0.03
Canadian (819)	1,520	0.22
Carpatho Rusyn (15)	15	<0.01
Celtic (38)	100	0.01
Croatian (178)	618	0.09
Czech (505)	1,654	0.23
Czechoslovakian (207)	759	0.11
Danish (414)	1,486	0.21
Dutch (1,395)	7,656	1.08
Eastern European (831)	862	0.12
English (22,165)	58,078	8.23
Estonian (30)	41	0.01
European (5,975)	6,521	0.92
Finnish (166)	402	0.06
French, ex. Basque (2,435)	12,074	1.71
French Canadian (973)	2,489	0.35
German (21,410)	71,671	10.15
German Russian (0)	9	<0.01
Greek (2,642)	4,046	0.57
Guyanese (246)	298	0.04
Hungarian (528)	2,059	0.29
Icelander (11)	11	<0.01
Iranian (661)	786	0.11
Irish (15,980)	54,824	7.77
Israeli (36)	51	0.01
Italian (9,960)	28,643	4.06
Latvian (52)	105	0.01
Lithuanian (401)	856	0.12
Maltese (0)	156	0.02
New Zealander (34)	72	0.01
Northern European (328)	357	0.05
Norwegian (1,027)	3,212	0.46
Pennsylvania German (42)	203	0.03
Polish (3,483)	12,055	1.71
Portuguese (509)	1,157	0.16
Romanian (487)	1,248	0.18
Russian (2,439)	5,549	0.79
Scandinavian (316)	609	0.09
Scotch-Irish (15,704)	25,971	3.68
Scottish (6,409)	17,085	2.42
Serbian (79)	362	0.05
Slavic (112)	340	0.05
Slovak (410)	1,441	0.20
Slovene (124)	255	0.04
Swedish (1,191)	4,136	0.59
Swiss (284)	1,724	0.24
Turkish (691)	809	0.11
Ukrainian (989)	1,867	0.26
Welsh (1,158)	4,719	0.67
West Indian, ex. Hispanic (2,750)	4,254	0.60
Bahamian (76)	122	0.02
Barbadian (83)	148	0.02
Belizean (13)	20	<0.01
Bermudan (0)	16	<0.01
British West Indian (82)	82	0.01
Dutch West Indian (34)	56	0.01
Haitian (266)	403	0.06
Jamaican (1,489)	2,278	0.32
Trinidadian/Tobagonian (128)	241	0.03
U.S. Virgin Islander (0)	12	<0.01
West Indian (558)	855	0.12
Other West Indian (21)	21	<0.01
Yugoslavian (1,013)	1,220	0.17

Hispanic Origin	Population	%
Hispanic or Latino (of any race)	95,688	13.08
Central American, ex. Mexican	22,359	3.06
Costa Rican	673	0.09
Guatemalan	2,421	0.33
Honduran	7,557	1.03
Nicaraguan	1,320	0.18
Panamanian	608	0.08
Salvadoran	9,516	1.30
Other Central American	264	0.04
Cuban	2,902	0.40
Dominican Republic	3,280	0.45
Mexican	40,601	5.55
Puerto Rican	7,521	1.03
South American	10,729	1.47
Argentinean	514	0.07
Bolivian	138	0.02
Chilean	368	0.05
Colombian	3,338	0.46
Ecuadorian	3,008	0.41
Paraguayan	28	<0.01
Peruvian	2,177	0.30
Uruguayan	262	0.04
Venezuelan	818	0.11
Other South American	78	0.01
Other Hispanic or Latino	8,296	1.13

Race*	Population	%
African-American/Black (256,241)	266,822	36.48
Not Hispanic (252,007)	260,726	35.65
Hispanic (4,234)	6,096	0.83
American Indian/Alaska Native (3,483)	8,397	1.15
Not Hispanic (2,250)	6,096	0.83
Hispanic (1,233)	2,301	0.31
Alaska Athabascan *(Ala. Nat.)* (4)	5	<0.01
Aleut *(Alaska Native)* (5)	8	<0.01
Apache (9)	46	0.01
Arapaho (1)	1	<0.01
Blackfeet (29)	186	0.03
Canadian/French Am. Ind. (2)	15	<0.01
Central American Ind. (20)	67	0.01
Cherokee (270)	1,294	0.18
Cheyenne (3)	5	<0.01
Chickasaw (10)	36	<0.01
Chippewa (31)	60	0.01
Choctaw (19)	67	0.01

*Notes: † The Census 2010 population figure is used to calculate the percentages in the Hispanic Origin and Race categories. Ancestry percentages are based on the 2006-2010 American Community Survey population (not shown); ‡ Numbers in parentheses indicate the number of people reporting a single ancestry; * Numbers in parentheses indicate the number of persons reporting this race alone, not in combination with any other race; Please refer to the Explanation of Data for more information.*

Comanche (2)	5	<0.01
Cree (6)	10	<0.01
Creek (14)	38	0.01
Crow (1)	13	<0.01
Delaware (11)	26	<0.01
Hopi (0)	1	<0.01
Houma (1)	1	<0.01
Inupiat *(Alaska Native)* (6)	12	<0.01
Iroquois (56)	116	0.02
Kiowa (0)	2	<0.01
Lumbee (548)	763	0.10
Menominee (0)	4	<0.01
Mexican American Ind. (236)	331	0.05
Navajo (9)	33	<0.01
Osage (3)	5	<0.01
Ottawa (1)	2	<0.01
Pima (1)	1	<0.01
Potawatomi (1)	4	<0.01
Pueblo (1)	18	<0.01
Puget Sound Salish (2)	2	<0.01
Seminole (5)	34	<0.01
Shoshone (1)	4	<0.01
Sioux (23)	66	0.01
South American Ind. (25)	88	0.01
Spanish American Ind. (15)	101	0.01
Tlingit-Haida *(Alaska Native)* (2)	3	<0.01
Tohono O'Odham (1)	1	<0.01
Tsimshian *(Alaska Native)* (1)	1	<0.01
Ute (1)	4	<0.01
Yaqui (1)	6	<0.01
Yuman (1)	4	<0.01
Yup'ik *(Alaska Native)* (1)	2	<0.01
Asian (36,403)	40,918	5.59
Not Hispanic (36,115)	40,149	5.49
Hispanic (288)	769	0.11
Bangladeshi (62)	82	0.01
Bhutanese (224)	277	0.04
Burmese (503)	542	0.07
Cambodian (1,071)	1,236	0.17
Chinese, ex. Taiwanese (4,139)	4,883	0.67
Filipino (1,508)	2,240	0.31
Hmong (1,230)	1,304	0.18
Indian (13,329)	14,258	1.95
Indonesian (118)	163	0.02
Japanese (710)	1,149	0.16
Korean (2,575)	3,168	0.43
Laotian (1,245)	1,426	0.19
Malaysian (50)	78	0.01
Nepalese (107)	157	0.02
Pakistani (548)	625	0.09
Sri Lankan (51)	66	0.01
Taiwanese (192)	223	0.03
Thai (272)	461	0.06
Vietnamese (6,964)	7,550	1.03
Hawaii Native/Pacific Islander (581)	1,315	0.18
Not Hispanic (436)	986	0.13
Hispanic (145)	329	0.04
Fijian (3)	8	<0.01
Guamanian/Chamorro (196)	268	0.04
Marshallese (3)	5	<0.01
Native Hawaiian (95)	268	0.04
Samoan (58)	139	0.02
Tongan (11)	20	<0.01
White (365,384)	379,739	51.92
Not Hispanic (329,545)	339,512	46.42
Hispanic (35,839)	40,227	5.50

Clayton

Place Type: Town
County: Johnston
Population: 16,116†

Ancestry‡	Population	%
African, Sub-Saharan (312)	312	2.12
African (234)	234	1.59
Other Sub-Saharan African (78)	78	0.53
American (1,552)	1,552	10.55
Arab (49)	65	0.44
Egyptian (33)	33	0.22
Lebanese (16)	32	0.22
Armenian (0)	10	0.07
Austrian (0)	14	0.10
Brazilian (17)	17	0.12
British (66)	122	0.83
Czech (5)	16	0.11
Dutch (36)	141	0.96
English (835)	1,957	13.30
European (138)	153	1.04
French, ex. Basque (15)	275	1.87
French Canadian (0)	93	0.63
German (630)	1,825	12.40
Greek (49)	87	0.59
Hungarian (14)	159	1.08
Iranian (19)	19	0.13
Irish (462)	1,687	11.47
Italian (214)	886	6.02
Lithuanian (44)	191	1.30
Norwegian (0)	159	1.08
Polish (78)	594	4.04
Romanian (5)	5	0.03
Russian (15)	44	0.30
Scandinavian (0)	71	0.48
Scotch-Irish (192)	551	3.74
Scottish (62)	215	1.46
Swedish (21)	131	0.89
Ukrainian (6)	89	0.60
Welsh (0)	20	0.14
West Indian, ex. Hispanic (115)	115	0.78
Jamaican (53)	53	0.36
West Indian (62)	62	0.42

Hispanic Origin	Population	%
Hispanic or Latino (of any race)	1,725	10.70
Central American, ex. Mexican	249	1.55
Costa Rican	10	0.06
Guatemalan	27	0.17
Honduran	145	0.90
Nicaraguan	11	0.07
Panamanian	26	0.16
Salvadoran	30	0.19
Cuban	32	0.20
Dominican Republic	78	0.48
Mexican	853	5.29
Puerto Rican	264	1.64
South American	121	0.75
Argentinean	14	0.09
Bolivian	3	0.02
Chilean	2	0.01
Colombian	39	0.24
Ecuadorian	15	0.09
Peruvian	19	0.12
Uruguayan	2	0.01
Venezuelan	27	0.17
Other Hispanic or Latino	128	0.79

Race*	Population	%
African-American/Black (3,507)	3,675	22.80
Not Hispanic (3,403)	3,529	21.90
Hispanic (104)	146	0.91
American Indian/Alaska Native (65)	154	0.96
Not Hispanic (47)	123	0.76
Hispanic (18)	31	0.19
Blackfeet (1)	2	0.01
Cherokee (11)	35	0.22
Chippewa (1)	3	0.02
Choctaw (1)	1	0.01
Creek (0)	1	0.01
Inupiat *(Alaska Native)* (1)	1	0.01
Lumbee (17)	19	0.12
Mexican American Ind. (1)	1	0.01
Navajo (0)	7	0.04
Asian (224)	320	1.99
Not Hispanic (216)	305	1.89
Hispanic (8)	15	0.09
Cambodian (1)	2	0.01
Chinese, ex. Taiwanese (47)	53	0.33
Filipino (37)	68	0.42
Hmong (3)	3	0.02
Indian (64)	77	0.48
Indonesian (2)	3	0.02
Japanese (10)	22	0.14
Korean (24)	36	0.22
Laotian (1)	1	0.01
Nepalese (4)	4	0.02
Taiwanese (2)	3	0.02
Thai (2)	4	0.02
Vietnamese (25)	28	0.17
Hawaii Native/Pacific Islander (2)	14	0.09
Not Hispanic (0)	11	0.07
Hispanic (2)	3	0.02
Guamanian/Chamorro (2)	8	0.05
Native Hawaiian (0)	1	0.01
Tongan (0)	2	0.01
White (11,195)	11,473	71.19
Not Hispanic (10,430)	10,643	66.04
Hispanic (765)	830	5.15

Clemmons

Place Type: Village
County: Forsyth
Population: 18,627†

Ancestry‡	Population	%
African, Sub-Saharan (105)	127	0.70
African (22)	22	0.12
South African (83)	83	0.46
Other Sub-Saharan African (0)	22	0.12
American (2,010)	2,010	11.08
Arab (30)	39	0.21
Jordanian (16)	16	0.09
Lebanese (14)	23	0.13
Armenian (9)	9	0.05
Austrian (29)	74	0.41
British (128)	148	0.82
Canadian (0)	14	0.08
Croatian (7)	27	0.15
Czech (6)	113	0.62
Danish (0)	15	0.08
Dutch (45)	213	1.17
Eastern European (16)	16	0.09
English (1,123)	2,276	12.54
European (155)	238	1.31
French, ex. Basque (185)	527	2.90
French Canadian (68)	81	0.45
German (1,235)	3,416	18.83
Greek (222)	291	1.60
Guyanese (8)	8	0.04
Hungarian (6)	49	0.27
Irish (713)	2,339	12.89
Italian (141)	853	4.70
Lithuanian (23)	61	0.34
Luxemburger (0)	13	0.07
Northern European (126)	126	0.69
Norwegian (68)	129	0.71
Polish (30)	274	1.51
Portuguese (26)	47	0.26
Romanian (0)	50	0.28
Russian (33)	119	0.66
Scandinavian (0)	9	0.05
Scotch-Irish (395)	866	4.77
Scottish (176)	830	4.57
Slavic (4)	4	0.02
Slovak (12)	109	0.60
Slovene (12)	12	0.07
Swedish (40)	177	0.98
Swiss (0)	28	0.15
Ukrainian (8)	15	0.08
Welsh (0)	223	1.23
West Indian, ex. Hispanic (135)	135	0.74
Jamaican (135)	135	0.74

Hispanic Origin	Population	%
Hispanic or Latino (of any race)	1,571	8.43
Central American, ex. Mexican	148	0.79
Costa Rican	4	0.02
Guatemalan	56	0.30
Honduran	13	0.07
Nicaraguan	19	0.10

*Notes: † The Census 2010 population figure is used to calculate the percentages in the Hispanic Origin and Race categories. Ancestry percentages are based on the 2006-2010 American Community Survey population (not shown); ‡ Numbers in parentheses indicate the number of people reporting a single ancestry; * Numbers in parentheses indicate the number of persons reporting this race alone, not in combination with any other race; Please refer to the Explanation of Data for more information.*

	Population	%
Panamanian	6	0.03
Salvadoran	50	0.27
Cuban	44	0.24
Dominican Republic	28	0.15
Mexican	1,014	5.44
Puerto Rican	75	0.40
South American	170	0.91
Argentinean	12	0.06
Chilean	5	0.03
Colombian	64	0.34
Ecuadorian	30	0.16
Paraguayan	3	0.02
Peruvian	7	0.04
Venezuelan	49	0.26
Other Hispanic or Latino	92	0.49

Race*	Population	%
African-American/Black (1,255)	1,407	7.55
Not Hispanic (1,234)	1,369	7.35
Hispanic (21)	38	0.20
American Indian/Alaska Native (48)	104	0.56
Not Hispanic (18)	65	0.35
Hispanic (30)	39	0.21
Alaska Athabascan *(Ala. Nat.)* (1)	1	0.01
Blackfeet (0)	4	0.02
Central American Ind. (3)	3	0.02
Cherokee (6)	35	0.19
Choctaw (1)	1	0.01
Cree (1)	1	0.01
Lumbee (6)	9	0.05
Mexican American Ind. (12)	15	0.08
Pueblo (1)	1	0.01
Sioux (0)	1	0.01
South American Ind. (0)	2	0.01
Asian (690)	749	4.02
Not Hispanic (686)	741	3.98
Hispanic (4)	8	0.04
Cambodian (8)	8	0.04
Chinese, ex. Taiwanese (190)	200	1.07
Filipino (109)	129	0.69
Hmong (1)	1	0.01
Indian (198)	203	1.09
Indonesian (1)	5	0.03
Japanese (8)	22	0.12
Korean (49)	56	0.30
Pakistani (33)	33	0.18
Taiwanese (4)	4	0.02
Thai (3)	5	0.03
Vietnamese (76)	76	0.41
Hawaii Native/Pacific Islander (5)	11	0.06
Not Hispanic (2)	6	0.03
Hispanic (3)	5	0.03
Guamanian/Chamorro (3)	5	0.03
Native Hawaiian (0)	2	0.01
Samoan (1)	1	0.01
White (15,500)	15,756	84.59
Not Hispanic (14,866)	15,071	80.91
Hispanic (634)	685	3.68

Clinton

Place Type: City
County: Sampson
Population: 8,639†

Ancestry‡	Population	%
African, Sub-Saharan (34)	79	0.92
African (34)	79	0.92
American (720)	720	8.39
Arab (13)	13	0.15
Arab (2)	2	0.02
Lebanese (10)	10	0.12
Moroccan (1)	1	0.01
Austrian (4)	4	0.05
Brazilian (4)	7	0.08
British (18)	34	0.40
Croatian (5)	5	0.06
Czechoslovakian (7)	7	0.08
Danish (0)	5	0.06
Dutch (9)	88	1.03
English (435)	656	7.64
European (78)	78	0.91
French, ex. Basque (60)	133	1.55
German (155)	448	5.22
Greek (4)	7	0.08
Irish (261)	450	5.24
Italian (21)	69	0.80
Norwegian (31)	50	0.58
Polish (45)	121	1.41
Portuguese (2)	56	0.65
Russian (0)	4	0.05
Scandinavian (0)	5	0.06
Scotch-Irish (228)	293	3.41
Scottish (151)	244	2.84
Slovak (0)	5	0.06
Swedish (9)	46	0.54
Swiss (0)	4	0.05
Welsh (14)	38	0.44

Hispanic Origin	Population	%
Hispanic or Latino (of any race)	791	9.16
Central American, ex. Mexican	280	3.24
Guatemalan	45	0.52
Honduran	186	2.15
Nicaraguan	14	0.16
Panamanian	6	0.07
Salvadoran	28	0.32
Other Central American	1	0.01
Cuban	6	0.07
Dominican Republic	15	0.17
Mexican	318	3.68
Puerto Rican	91	1.05
South American	32	0.37
Argentinean	1	0.01
Chilean	4	0.05
Colombian	8	0.09
Ecuadorian	6	0.07
Peruvian	7	0.08
Venezuelan	6	0.07
Other Hispanic or Latino	49	0.57

Race*	Population	%
African-American/Black (3,500)	3,609	41.78
Not Hispanic (3,481)	3,561	41.22
Hispanic (19)	48	0.56
American Indian/Alaska Native (103)	168	1.94
Not Hispanic (100)	154	1.78
Hispanic (3)	14	0.16
Blackfeet (0)	8	0.09
Cherokee (1)	17	0.20
Creek (1)	1	0.01
Inupiat *(Alaska Native)* (0)	1	0.01
Lumbee (8)	18	0.21
Mexican American Ind. (1)	5	0.06
Navajo (0)	1	0.01
Asian (95)	122	1.41
Not Hispanic (95)	119	1.38
Hispanic (0)	3	0.03
Chinese, ex. Taiwanese (29)	35	0.41
Filipino (13)	17	0.20
Indian (8)	11	0.13
Japanese (2)	2	0.02
Korean (14)	19	0.22
Thai (2)	4	0.05
Vietnamese (12)	13	0.15
Hawaii Native/Pacific Islander (4)	10	0.12
Not Hispanic (4)	6	0.07
Hispanic (0)	4	0.05
Guamanian/Chamorro (1)	1	0.01
Native Hawaiian (0)	1	0.01
Samoan (1)	1	0.01
White (4,225)	4,343	50.27
Not Hispanic (4,021)	4,103	47.49
Hispanic (204)	240	2.78

Concord

Place Type: City
County: Cabarrus
Population: 79,066†

Ancestry‡	Population	%
African, Sub-Saharan (161)	203	0.27
African (95)	137	0.18
Liberian (52)	52	0.07
South African (14)	14	0.02
American (6,736)	6,736	8.96
Arab (61)	168	0.22
Arab (0)	21	0.03
Egyptian (31)	31	0.04
Lebanese (30)	54	0.07
Moroccan (0)	18	0.02
Syrian (0)	44	0.06
Armenian (14)	14	0.02
Austrian (0)	41	0.05
British (272)	391	0.52
Bulgarian (0)	8	0.01
Canadian (27)	45	0.06
Celtic (0)	28	0.04
Croatian (0)	18	0.02
Czech (38)	151	0.20
Czechoslovakian (129)	157	0.21
Danish (104)	340	0.45
Dutch (283)	1,450	1.93
English (3,070)	7,361	9.79
European (746)	822	1.09
Finnish (40)	52	0.07
French, ex. Basque (358)	1,485	1.98
French Canadian (134)	261	0.35
German (4,245)	11,684	15.54
Greek (84)	200	0.27
Guyanese (191)	260	0.35
Hungarian (170)	385	0.51
Icelander (31)	63	0.08
Irish (2,196)	7,316	9.73
Italian (1,860)	4,223	5.62
Lithuanian (0)	76	0.10
Northern European (81)	81	0.11
Norwegian (55)	211	0.28
Pennsylvania German (48)	48	0.06
Polish (302)	1,562	2.08
Portuguese (0)	56	0.07
Romanian (29)	104	0.14
Russian (243)	594	0.79
Scandinavian (36)	50	0.07
Scotch-Irish (1,842)	3,224	4.29
Scottish (706)	1,983	2.64
Serbian (0)	9	0.01
Slavic (2)	16	0.02
Slovak (29)	50	0.07
Swedish (81)	272	0.36
Swiss (60)	125	0.17
Ukrainian (6)	139	0.18
Welsh (68)	399	0.53
West Indian, ex. Hispanic (620)	794	1.06
Haitian (248)	248	0.33
Jamaican (200)	233	0.31
Trinidadian/Tobagonian (111)	193	0.26
West Indian (61)	120	0.16

Hispanic Origin	Population	%
Hispanic or Latino (of any race)	9,754	12.34
Central American, ex. Mexican	708	0.90
Costa Rican	43	0.05
Guatemalan	137	0.17
Honduran	180	0.23
Nicaraguan	72	0.09
Panamanian	47	0.06
Salvadoran	225	0.28
Other Central American	4	0.01
Cuban	314	0.40
Dominican Republic	188	0.24
Mexican	6,528	8.26
Puerto Rican	881	1.11
South American	591	0.75
Argentinean	41	0.05
Bolivian	4	0.01
Chilean	22	0.03
Colombian	226	0.29
Ecuadorian	151	0.19
Peruvian	92	0.12

SECTION TWO

*Notes: † The Census 2010 population figure is used to calculate the percentages in the Hispanic Origin and Race categories. Ancestry percentages are based on the 2006-2010 American Community Survey population (not shown); ‡ Numbers in parentheses indicate the number of people reporting a single ancestry; * Numbers in parentheses indicate the number of persons reporting this race alone, not in combination with any other race; Please refer to the Explanation of Data for more information.*

Uruguayan	9	0.01
Venezuelan	35	0.04
Other South American	11	0.01
Other Hispanic or Latino	544	0.69

Race*	Population	%
African-American/Black (14,110)	15,064	19.05
Not Hispanic (13,717)	14,518	18.36
Hispanic (393)	546	0.69
American Indian/Alaska Native (274)	664	0.84
Not Hispanic (189)	535	0.68
Hispanic (85)	129	0.16
Aleut *(Alaska Native)* (1)	1	<0.01
Apache (1)	4	0.01
Blackfeet (1)	21	0.03
Central American Ind. (1)	1	<0.01
Cherokee (35)	188	0.24
Cheyenne (0)	1	<0.01
Chickasaw (0)	2	<0.01
Chippewa (3)	5	0.01
Choctaw (4)	7	0.01
Colville (1)	1	<0.01
Creek (0)	8	0.01
Crow (2)	2	<0.01
Houma (1)	3	<0.01
Iroquois (8)	10	0.01
Kiowa (1)	1	<0.01
Lumbee (54)	87	0.11
Mexican American Ind. (33)	34	0.04
Navajo (1)	3	<0.01
Ottawa (2)	2	<0.01
Pueblo (1)	1	<0.01
Puget Sound Salish (2)	2	<0.01
Seminole (0)	1	<0.01
Sioux (0)	5	0.01
South American Ind. (3)	3	<0.01
Spanish American Ind. (3)	3	<0.01
Tohono O'Odham (0)	5	0.01
Yup'ik *(Alaska Native)* (1)	1	<0.01
Asian (2,046)	2,436	3.08
Not Hispanic (2,018)	2,374	3.00
Hispanic (28)	62	0.08
Burmese (5)	5	0.01
Cambodian (12)	23	0.03
Chinese, ex. Taiwanese (249)	319	0.40
Filipino (227)	331	0.42
Hmong (62)	70	0.09
Indian (954)	1,017	1.29
Indonesian (12)	12	0.02
Japanese (47)	88	0.11
Korean (136)	169	0.21
Laotian (49)	66	0.08
Nepalese (3)	3	<0.01
Pakistani (34)	38	0.05
Sri Lankan (9)	11	0.01
Taiwanese (6)	6	0.01
Thai (11)	28	0.04
Vietnamese (160)	197	0.25
Hawaii Native/Pacific Islander (50)	108	0.14
Not Hispanic (47)	90	0.11
Hispanic (3)	18	0.02
Guamanian/Chamorro (8)	16	0.02
Native Hawaiian (15)	43	0.05
Samoan (2)	18	0.02
White (55,691)	57,201	72.35
Not Hispanic (51,843)	53,001	67.03
Hispanic (3,848)	4,200	5.31

Conover

Place Type: City
County: Catawba
Population: 8,165†

Ancestry‡	Population	%
African, Sub-Saharan (13)	13	0.16
African (13)	13	0.16
American (1,038)	1,038	13.09
British (24)	34	0.43
Danish (10)	47	0.59
Dutch (0)	150	1.89
English (297)	561	7.08
European (77)	77	0.97
French, ex. Basque (17)	86	1.08
French Canadian (28)	52	0.66
German (911)	1,845	23.27
Hungarian (11)	11	0.14
Irish (331)	947	11.95
Italian (92)	122	1.54
Norwegian (0)	69	0.87
Polish (0)	29	0.37
Portuguese (14)	14	0.18
Scandinavian (0)	12	0.15
Scotch-Irish (119)	262	3.30
Scottish (0)	60	0.76
Swedish (12)	30	0.38
Swiss (39)	97	1.22
Welsh (11)	23	0.29

Hispanic Origin	Population	%
Hispanic or Latino (of any race)	993	12.16
Central American, ex. Mexican	135	1.65
Costa Rican	14	0.17
Guatemalan	17	0.21
Honduran	12	0.15
Nicaraguan	6	0.07
Panamanian	3	0.04
Salvadoran	83	1.02
Cuban	4	0.05
Dominican Republic	18	0.22
Mexican	664	8.13
Puerto Rican	67	0.82
South American	60	0.73
Chilean	1	0.01
Colombian	52	0.64
Ecuadorian	1	0.01
Peruvian	6	0.07
Other Hispanic or Latino	45	0.55

Race*	Population	%
African-American/Black (749)	848	10.39
Not Hispanic (740)	828	10.14
Hispanic (9)	20	0.24
American Indian/Alaska Native (20)	63	0.77
Not Hispanic (14)	50	0.61
Hispanic (6)	13	0.16
Cherokee (5)	16	0.20
Choctaw (0)	1	0.01
Cree (0)	1	0.01
Creek (0)	1	0.01
Lumbee (0)	4	0.05
Asian (344)	383	4.69
Not Hispanic (339)	377	4.62
Hispanic (5)	6	0.07
Cambodian (2)	3	0.04
Chinese, ex. Taiwanese (27)	27	0.33
Filipino (11)	13	0.16
Hmong (146)	160	1.96
Indian (40)	60	0.73
Japanese (3)	8	0.10
Korean (10)	17	0.21
Laotian (26)	28	0.34
Malaysian (0)	2	0.02
Nepalese (3)	5	0.06
Pakistani (3)	3	0.04
Taiwanese (1)	1	0.01
Thai (28)	34	0.42
Vietnamese (18)	21	0.26
Hawaii Native/Pacific Islander (4)	8	0.10
Not Hispanic (0)	2	0.02
Hispanic (4)	6	0.07
Guamanian/Chamorro (4)	5	0.06
White (6,375)	6,560	80.34
Not Hispanic (5,919)	6,061	74.23
Hispanic (456)	499	6.11

Cornelius

Place Type: Town
County: Mecklenburg
Population: 24,866†

Ancestry‡	Population	%
African, Sub-Saharan (10)	10	0.04
African (10)	10	0.04
American (1,516)	1,516	6.60
Arab (0)	14	0.06
Lebanese (0)	14	0.06
Austrian (0)	39	0.17
Belgian (17)	61	0.27
Brazilian (0)	23	0.10
British (109)	187	0.81
Canadian (59)	67	0.29
Croatian (17)	64	0.28
Czech (69)	110	0.48
Czechoslovakian (27)	57	0.25
Danish (45)	94	0.41
Dutch (12)	308	1.34
Eastern European (46)	46	0.20
English (1,711)	3,903	16.99
European (228)	248	1.08
Finnish (19)	65	0.28
French, ex. Basque (171)	877	3.82
French Canadian (141)	275	1.20
German (1,710)	5,180	22.55
Greek (11)	102	0.44
Hungarian (83)	282	1.23
Iranian (50)	50	0.22
Irish (1,203)	3,378	14.71
Italian (762)	2,090	9.10
Lithuanian (14)	46	0.20
Macedonian (19)	19	0.08
Norwegian (73)	199	0.87
Polish (149)	675	2.94
Portuguese (28)	48	0.21
Romanian (21)	41	0.18
Russian (10)	70	0.30
Scandinavian (22)	140	0.61
Scotch-Irish (667)	1,194	5.20
Scottish (238)	726	3.16
Slavic (13)	30	0.13
Slovak (0)	11	0.05
Slovene (10)	24	0.10
Swedish (139)	551	2.40
Swiss (14)	61	0.27
Turkish (39)	39	0.17
Ukrainian (12)	27	0.12
Welsh (66)	233	1.01
West Indian, ex. Hispanic (86)	86	0.37
Haitian (35)	35	0.15
Jamaican (51)	51	0.22
Yugoslavian (0)	63	0.27

Hispanic Origin	Population	%
Hispanic or Latino (of any race)	1,327	5.34
Central American, ex. Mexican	76	0.31
Costa Rican	2	0.01
Guatemalan	32	0.13
Honduran	17	0.07
Nicaraguan	5	0.02
Panamanian	4	0.02
Salvadoran	15	0.06
Other Central American	1	<0.01
Cuban	77	0.31
Dominican Republic	45	0.18
Mexican	659	2.65
Puerto Rican	169	0.68
South American	204	0.82
Argentinean	11	0.04
Bolivian	5	0.02
Colombian	97	0.39
Ecuadorian	40	0.16
Peruvian	37	0.15
Uruguayan	2	0.01
Venezuelan	11	0.04
Other South American	1	<0.01

*Notes: † The Census 2010 population figure is used to calculate the percentages in the Hispanic Origin and Race categories. Ancestry percentages are based on the 2006-2010 American Community Survey population (not shown); ‡ Numbers in parentheses indicate the number of people reporting a single ancestry; * Numbers in parentheses indicate the number of persons reporting this race alone, not in combination with any other race; Please refer to the Explanation of Data for more information.*

Other Hispanic or Latino	97	0.39

Race*	Population	%
African-American/Black (1,445)	1,587	6.38
Not Hispanic (1,408)	1,539	6.19
Hispanic (37)	48	0.19
American Indian/Alaska Native (72)	158	0.64
Not Hispanic (66)	144	0.58
Hispanic (6)	14	0.06
Apache (0)	1	<0.01
Blackfeet (1)	5	0.02
Cherokee (17)	46	0.18
Chippewa (1)	2	0.01
Choctaw (3)	4	0.02
Creek (0)	1	<0.01
Iroquois (0)	2	0.01
Lumbee (12)	17	0.07
Mexican American Ind. (3)	8	0.03
Ottawa (2)	2	0.01
Seminole (0)	1	<0.01
Sioux (0)	1	<0.01
Asian (560)	680	2.73
Not Hispanic (554)	664	2.67
Hispanic (6)	16	0.06
Burmese (3)	3	0.01
Chinese, ex. Taiwanese (74)	91	0.37
Filipino (45)	71	0.29
Hmong (14)	14	0.06
Indian (199)	221	0.89
Indonesian (2)	3	0.01
Japanese (33)	47	0.19
Korean (52)	66	0.27
Laotian (13)	21	0.08
Malaysian (1)	1	<0.01
Nepalese (1)	2	0.01
Pakistani (9)	11	0.04
Sri Lankan (2)	3	0.01
Taiwanese (5)	5	0.02
Thai (2)	7	0.03
Vietnamese (84)	95	0.38
Hawaii Native/Pacific Islander (8)	16	0.06
Not Hispanic (8)	14	0.06
Hispanic (0)	2	0.01
Fijian (2)	2	0.01
Native Hawaiian (1)	3	0.01
Samoan (0)	2	0.01
White (21,947)	22,299	89.68
Not Hispanic (21,178)	21,460	86.30
Hispanic (769)	839	3.37

Davidson

Place Type: Town
County: Mecklenburg
Population: 10,944†

Ancestry‡	Population	%
African, Sub-Saharan (105)	105	1.02
African (19)	19	0.18
Kenyan (72)	72	0.70
Zimbabwean (14)	14	0.14
American (306)	306	2.97
Arab (23)	23	0.22
Lebanese (23)	23	0.22
Austrian (13)	77	0.75
British (100)	135	1.31
Cajun (0)	7	0.07
Canadian (0)	9	0.09
Croatian (0)	11	0.11
Czech (17)	94	0.91
Czechoslovakian (0)	28	0.27
Dutch (54)	293	2.84
Eastern European (12)	12	0.12
English (781)	2,164	20.97
European (280)	280	2.71
Finnish (0)	18	0.17
French, ex. Basque (27)	239	2.32
French Canadian (0)	42	0.41
German (746)	2,146	20.79
Greek (89)	158	1.53
Hungarian (36)	61	0.59
Irish (543)	1,786	17.31
Italian (314)	585	5.67
Lithuanian (15)	67	0.65
Northern European (31)	31	0.30
Norwegian (0)	15	0.15
Polish (12)	61	0.59
Romanian (0)	54	0.52
Russian (53)	90	0.87
Scandinavian (0)	13	0.13
Scotch-Irish (221)	397	3.85
Scottish (104)	503	4.87
Serbian (0)	17	0.16
Slovak (45)	65	0.63
Slovene (18)	18	0.17
Swedish (39)	121	1.17
Swiss (0)	44	0.43
Ukrainian (12)	48	0.47
Welsh (105)	344	3.33
West Indian, ex. Hispanic (13)	13	0.13
Jamaican (13)	13	0.13
Yugoslavian (0)	13	0.13

Hispanic Origin	Population	%
Hispanic or Latino (of any race)	411	3.76
Central American, ex. Mexican	38	0.35
Guatemalan	13	0.12
Honduran	9	0.08
Nicaraguan	1	0.01
Panamanian	4	0.04
Salvadoran	11	0.10
Cuban	32	0.29
Dominican Republic	13	0.12
Mexican	160	1.46
Puerto Rican	51	0.47
South American	64	0.58
Argentinean	2	0.02
Bolivian	6	0.05
Chilean	1	0.01
Colombian	14	0.13
Ecuadorian	11	0.10
Peruvian	15	0.14
Uruguayan	5	0.05
Venezuelan	10	0.09
Other Hispanic or Latino	53	0.48

Race*	Population	%
African-American/Black (695)	762	6.96
Not Hispanic (679)	734	6.71
Hispanic (16)	28	0.26
American Indian/Alaska Native (21)	56	0.51
Not Hispanic (19)	51	0.47
Hispanic (2)	5	0.05
Central American Ind. (0)	1	0.01
Cherokee (3)	11	0.10
Chickasaw (1)	1	0.01
Choctaw (0)	3	0.03
Creek (1)	1	0.01
Iroquois (0)	1	0.01
Lumbee (2)	7	0.06
Navajo (0)	1	0.01
Osage (0)	1	0.01
Ottawa (1)	2	0.02
Puget Sound Salish (1)	1	0.01
South American Ind. (0)	4	0.04
Asian (305)	380	3.47
Not Hispanic (299)	372	3.40
Hispanic (6)	8	0.07
Bangladeshi (0)	1	0.01
Burmese (3)	3	0.03
Cambodian (0)	1	0.01
Chinese, ex. Taiwanese (86)	105	0.96
Filipino (23)	34	0.31
Hmong (5)	7	0.06
Indian (116)	128	1.17
Indonesian (2)	4	0.04
Japanese (11)	24	0.22
Korean (28)	43	0.39
Malaysian (0)	2	0.02
Nepalese (2)	3	0.03
Pakistani (6)	6	0.05
Sri Lankan (2)	4	0.04
Taiwanese (2)	3	0.03
Thai (2)	2	0.02
Vietnamese (4)	9	0.08
Hawaii Native/Pacific Islander (2)	9	0.08
Not Hispanic (1)	4	0.04
Hispanic (1)	5	0.05
Native Hawaiian (1)	2	0.02
White (9,609)	9,781	89.37
Not Hispanic (9,368)	9,510	86.90
Hispanic (241)	271	2.48

Dunn

Place Type: City
County: Harnett
Population: 9,263†

Ancestry‡	Population	%
African, Sub-Saharan (531)	534	5.85
African (531)	534	5.85
American (785)	785	8.60
British (9)	42	0.46
Danish (2)	2	0.02
Dutch (16)	37	0.41
English (344)	604	6.62
European (16)	16	0.18
French, ex. Basque (32)	84	0.92
French Canadian (6)	9	0.10
German (108)	337	3.69
Hungarian (0)	7	0.08
Irish (224)	484	5.31
Italian (56)	112	1.23
Lithuanian (0)	11	0.12
Norwegian (3)	3	0.03
Pennsylvania German (14)	14	0.15
Polish (13)	23	0.25
Portuguese (4)	4	0.04
Romanian (0)	1	0.01
Russian (0)	16	0.18
Scotch-Irish (189)	238	2.61
Scottish (133)	193	2.12
Slovak (0)	9	0.10
Swedish (10)	19	0.21
Ukrainian (0)	10	0.11
Welsh (0)	44	0.48

Hispanic Origin	Population	%
Hispanic or Latino (of any race)	491	5.30
Central American, ex. Mexican	74	0.80
Costa Rican	24	0.26
Guatemalan	19	0.21
Honduran	13	0.14
Panamanian	1	0.01
Salvadoran	13	0.14
Other Central American	4	0.04
Cuban	5	0.05
Dominican Republic	3	0.03
Mexican	284	3.07
Puerto Rican	57	0.62
South American	26	0.28
Argentinean	2	0.02
Chilean	1	0.01
Colombian	12	0.13
Peruvian	5	0.05
Venezuelan	6	0.06
Other Hispanic or Latino	42	0.45

Race*	Population	%
African-American/Black (3,940)	4,086	44.11
Not Hispanic (3,909)	4,043	43.65
Hispanic (31)	43	0.46
American Indian/Alaska Native (90)	157	1.69
Not Hispanic (86)	141	1.52
Hispanic (4)	16	0.17
Central American Ind. (0)	1	0.01
Cherokee (14)	30	0.32
Iroquois (2)	2	0.02
Lumbee (13)	17	0.18

SECTION TWO

*Notes: † The Census 2010 population figure is used to calculate the percentages in the Hispanic Origin and Race categories. Ancestry percentages are based on the 2006-2010 American Community Survey population (not shown); ‡ Numbers in parentheses indicate the number of people reporting a single ancestry; * Numbers in parentheses indicate the number of persons reporting this race alone, not in combination with any other race; Please refer to the Explanation of Data for more information.*

Sioux (0)	1	0.01
Asian (77)	97	1.05
Not Hispanic (76)	96	1.04
Hispanic (1)	1	0.01
Chinese, ex. Taiwanese (24)	27	0.29
Filipino (7)	11	0.12
Indian (24)	31	0.33
Japanese (0)	1	0.01
Korean (7)	9	0.10
Vietnamese (9)	11	0.12
Hawaii Native/Pacific Islander (8)	17	0.18
Not Hispanic (4)	11	0.12
Hispanic (4)	6	0.06
Guamanian/Chamorro (4)	4	0.04
Native Hawaiian (1)	4	0.04
Samoan (0)	1	0.01
White (4,653)	4,791	51.72
Not Hispanic (4,516)	4,633	50.02
Hispanic (137)	158	1.71

Durham

Place Type: City
County: Durham
Population: 228,330†

Ancestry‡	Population	%
Afghan (27)	27	0.01
African, Sub-Saharan (4,325)	5,147	2.34
African (2,755)	3,418	1.55
Ethiopian (156)	203	0.09
Ghanaian (144)	144	0.07
Kenyan (57)	64	0.03
Liberian (191)	265	0.12
Nigerian (598)	604	0.27
Senegalese (16)	16	0.01
Sierra Leonean (58)	83	0.04
Somalian (11)	11	<0.01
South African (75)	75	0.03
Sudanese (134)	134	0.06
Other Sub-Saharan African (130)	130	0.06
Albanian (27)	38	0.02
American (8,730)	8,730	3.96
Arab (436)	751	0.34
Arab (131)	279	0.13
Egyptian (94)	94	0.04
Iraqi (28)	28	0.01
Jordanian (22)	22	0.01
Lebanese (15)	120	0.05
Moroccan (61)	78	0.04
Palestinian (14)	27	0.01
Syrian (13)	45	0.02
Other Arab (58)	58	0.03
Armenian (103)	340	0.15
Assyrian/Chaldean/Syriac (13)	13	0.01
Australian (9)	127	0.06
Austrian (70)	423	0.19
Basque (0)	11	<0.01
Belgian (10)	43	0.02
Brazilian (31)	56	0.03
British (768)	1,500	0.68
Bulgarian (52)	52	0.02
Canadian (501)	821	0.37
Celtic (16)	119	0.05
Croatian (62)	165	0.07
Czech (123)	388	0.18
Czechoslovakian (0)	113	0.05
Danish (106)	348	0.16
Dutch (410)	1,816	0.82
Eastern European (350)	375	0.17
English (6,753)	18,137	8.23
Estonian (22)	43	0.02
European (2,211)	2,559	1.16
Finnish (28)	229	0.10
French, ex. Basque (601)	3,230	1.47
French Canadian (241)	649	0.29
German (5,215)	18,806	8.54
German Russian (13)	47	0.02
Greek (268)	448	0.20
Guyanese (30)	108	0.05
Hungarian (136)	571	0.26
Iranian (124)	163	0.07
Irish (4,097)	14,557	6.61
Israeli (112)	130	0.06
Italian (1,809)	6,105	2.77
Latvian (0)	42	0.02
Lithuanian (106)	270	0.12
Macedonian (0)	11	<0.01
New Zealander (0)	12	0.01
Northern European (243)	261	0.12
Norwegian (267)	1,246	0.57
Pennsylvania German (17)	53	0.02
Polish (948)	3,725	1.69
Portuguese (123)	279	0.13
Romanian (185)	421	0.19
Russian (676)	1,774	0.81
Scandinavian (124)	287	0.13
Scotch-Irish (2,989)	6,163	2.80
Scottish (1,532)	4,809	2.18
Serbian (68)	74	0.03
Slavic (28)	67	0.03
Slovak (84)	281	0.13
Slovene (46)	104	0.05
Swedish (274)	1,342	0.61
Swiss (58)	381	0.17
Turkish (262)	262	0.12
Ukrainian (226)	597	0.27
Welsh (235)	1,397	0.63
West Indian, ex. Hispanic (1,002)	2,283	1.04
Bahamian (0)	42	0.02
British West Indian (11)	60	0.03
Dutch West Indian (16)	46	0.02
Haitian (260)	452	0.21
Jamaican (370)	885	0.40
Trinidadian/Tobagonian (41)	58	0.03
U.S. Virgin Islander (8)	8	<0.01
West Indian (296)	732	0.33
Yugoslavian (0)	66	0.03

Hispanic Origin	Population	%
Hispanic or Latino (of any race)	32,459	14.22
Central American, ex. Mexican	8,052	3.53
Costa Rican	64	0.03
Guatemalan	1,323	0.58
Honduran	3,451	1.51
Nicaraguan	77	0.03
Panamanian	159	0.07
Salvadoran	2,929	1.28
Other Central American	49	0.02
Cuban	445	0.19
Dominican Republic	428	0.19
Mexican	17,626	7.72
Puerto Rican	1,641	0.72
South American	1,448	0.63
Argentinean	210	0.09
Bolivian	58	0.03
Chilean	140	0.06
Colombian	478	0.21
Ecuadorian	169	0.07
Paraguayan	6	<0.01
Peruvian	193	0.08
Uruguayan	33	0.01
Venezuelan	143	0.06
Other South American	18	0.01
Other Hispanic or Latino	2,819	1.23

Race*	Population	%
African-American/Black (93,517)	96,706	42.35
Not Hispanic (92,285)	94,986	41.60
Hispanic (1,232)	1,720	0.75
American Indian/Alaska Native (1,161)	2,744	1.20
Not Hispanic (611)	1,853	0.81
Hispanic (550)	891	0.39
Alaska Athabascan *(Ala. Nat.)* (1)	1	<0.01
Aleut *(Alaska Native)* (0)	1	<0.01
Apache (4)	11	<0.01
Blackfeet (9)	57	0.02
Canadian/French Am. Ind. (2)	4	<0.01
Central American Ind. (28)	29	0.01
Cherokee (54)	417	0.18
Cheyenne (0)	1	<0.01
Chickasaw (1)	11	<0.01
Chippewa (6)	10	<0.01
Choctaw (9)	25	0.01
Comanche (0)	3	<0.01
Cree (2)	3	<0.01
Creek (2)	14	0.01
Delaware (4)	7	<0.01
Hopi (0)	2	<0.01
Iroquois (8)	34	0.01
Kiowa (1)	1	<0.01
Lumbee (102)	155	0.07
Mexican American Ind. (111)	156	0.07
Navajo (2)	16	0.01
Osage (0)	4	<0.01
Ottawa (1)	1	<0.01
Paiute (0)	1	<0.01
Potawatomi (1)	2	<0.01
Pueblo (0)	4	<0.01
Seminole (1)	13	0.01
Shoshone (0)	1	<0.01
Sioux (10)	29	0.01
South American Ind. (10)	24	0.01
Spanish American Ind. (15)	22	0.01
Tlingit-Haida *(Alaska Native)* (3)	3	<0.01
Tohono O'Odham (1)	1	<0.01
Ute (0)	2	<0.01
Yakama (3)	5	<0.01
Yaqui (2)	3	<0.01
Asian (11,574)	13,147	5.76
Not Hispanic (11,478)	12,897	5.65
Hispanic (96)	250	0.11
Bangladeshi (90)	96	0.04
Bhutanese (13)	29	0.01
Burmese (83)	90	0.04
Cambodian (65)	80	0.04
Chinese, ex. Taiwanese (2,777)	3,150	1.38
Filipino (1,130)	1,419	0.62
Hmong (19)	20	0.01
Indian (2,982)	3,306	1.45
Indonesian (23)	44	0.02
Japanese (380)	589	0.26
Korean (947)	1,146	0.50
Laotian (18)	23	0.01
Malaysian (10)	19	0.01
Nepalese (29)	48	0.02
Pakistani (261)	294	0.13
Sri Lankan (28)	35	0.02
Taiwanese (233)	269	0.12
Thai (156)	207	0.09
Vietnamese (701)	795	0.35
Hawaii Native/Pacific Islander (166)	331	0.14
Not Hispanic (129)	256	0.11
Hispanic (37)	75	0.03
Fijian (2)	3	<0.01
Guamanian/Chamorro (33)	49	0.02
Native Hawaiian (34)	79	0.03
Samoan (14)	34	0.01
Tongan (0)	2	<0.01
White (96,932)	101,410	44.41
Not Hispanic (86,519)	89,618	39.25
Hispanic (10,413)	11,792	5.16

Eden

Place Type: City
County: Rockingham
Population: 15,527†

Ancestry‡	Population	%
African, Sub-Saharan (54)	83	0.53
African (54)	83	0.53
American (2,237)	2,237	14.34
Arab (32)	32	0.21
Moroccan (32)	32	0.21
Armenian (0)	26	0.17
British (8)	25	0.16
Czech (14)	14	0.09
Dutch (26)	177	1.13
English (807)	1,408	9.02

*Notes: † The Census 2010 population figure is used to calculate the percentages in the Hispanic Origin and Race categories. Ancestry percentages are based on the 2006-2010 American Community Survey population (not shown); ‡ Numbers in parentheses indicate the number of people reporting a single ancestry; * Numbers in parentheses indicate the number of persons reporting this race alone, not in combination with any other race; Please refer to the Explanation of Data for more information.*

European (128)	479	3.07
French, ex. Basque (33)	193	1.24
German (290)	930	5.96
Iranian (0)	49	0.31
Irish (695)	1,526	9.78
Italian (186)	295	1.89
Polish (86)	168	1.08
Romanian (0)	37	0.24
Russian (54)	61	0.39
Scotch-Irish (163)	297	1.90
Scottish (174)	293	1.88
Swedish (44)	54	0.35
Ukrainian (14)	14	0.09
Welsh (0)	195	1.25

Hispanic Origin	**Population**	**%**
Hispanic or Latino (of any race)	753	4.85
Central American, ex. Mexican	68	0.44
Guatemalan	44	0.28
Honduran	12	0.08
Panamanian	3	0.02
Salvadoran	9	0.06
Cuban	9	0.06
Dominican Republic	2	0.01
Mexican	542	3.49
Puerto Rican	50	0.32
South American	17	0.11
Argentinean	4	0.03
Colombian	1	0.01
Ecuadorian	4	0.03
Peruvian	5	0.03
Uruguayan	2	0.01
Venezuelan	1	0.01
Other Hispanic or Latino	65	0.42

Race*	**Population**	**%**
African-American/Black (3,701)	3,868	24.91
Not Hispanic (3,662)	3,819	24.60
Hispanic (39)	49	0.32
American Indian/Alaska Native (67)	146	0.94
Not Hispanic (63)	138	0.89
Hispanic (4)	8	0.05
Apache (0)	2	0.01
Blackfeet (0)	5	0.03
Cherokee (20)	56	0.36
Choctaw (1)	1	0.01
Lumbee (29)	29	0.19
Paiute (0)	1	0.01
Seminole (0)	3	0.02
Sioux (1)	1	0.01
Spanish American Ind. (1)	1	0.01
Asian (105)	143	0.92
Not Hispanic (105)	141	0.91
Hispanic (0)	2	0.01
Cambodian (2)	2	0.01
Chinese, ex. Taiwanese (16)	16	0.10
Filipino (16)	24	0.15
Indian (34)	37	0.24
Japanese (1)	9	0.06
Korean (7)	12	0.08
Pakistani (16)	18	0.12
Thai (1)	1	0.01
Vietnamese (2)	2	0.01
Hawaii Native/Pacific Islander (26)	38	0.24
Not Hispanic (21)	32	0.21
Hispanic (5)	6	0.04
Guamanian/Chamorro (21)	24	0.15
Native Hawaiian (5)	9	0.06
White (11,058)	11,336	73.01
Not Hispanic (10,661)	10,892	70.15
Hispanic (397)	444	2.86

Elizabeth City

Place Type: City
County: Pasquotank
Population: 18,683†

Ancestry‡	**Population**	**%**
African, Sub-Saharan (208)	292	1.57
African (208)	292	1.57
American (1,796)	1,796	9.63
Brazilian (0)	16	0.09
British (28)	39	0.21
Canadian (0)	25	0.13
Czechoslovakian (0)	21	0.11
Dutch (10)	31	0.17
English (569)	1,111	5.96
European (105)	156	0.84
Finnish (28)	90	0.48
French, ex. Basque (45)	185	0.99
French Canadian (21)	44	0.24
German (182)	719	3.86
Hungarian (8)	40	0.21
Irish (318)	697	3.74
Italian (168)	455	2.44
Norwegian (17)	49	0.26
Polish (27)	140	0.75
Portuguese (0)	16	0.09
Russian (0)	69	0.37
Scandinavian (0)	10	0.05
Scotch-Irish (108)	201	1.08
Scottish (103)	419	2.25
Slavic (0)	14	0.08
Swedish (0)	41	0.22
Swiss (23)	23	0.12
Welsh (31)	130	0.70

Hispanic Origin	**Population**	**%**
Hispanic or Latino (of any race)	943	5.05
Central American, ex. Mexican	56	0.30
Costa Rican	3	0.02
Guatemalan	22	0.12
Honduran	17	0.09
Nicaraguan	2	0.01
Panamanian	4	0.02
Salvadoran	8	0.04
Cuban	19	0.10
Dominican Republic	7	0.04
Mexican	605	3.24
Puerto Rican	147	0.79
South American	42	0.22
Argentinean	2	0.01
Colombian	21	0.11
Ecuadorian	3	0.02
Peruvian	9	0.05
Venezuelan	3	0.02
Other South American	4	0.02
Other Hispanic or Latino	67	0.36

Race*	**Population**	**%**
African-American/Black (10,090)	10,387	55.60
Not Hispanic (10,027)	10,289	55.07
Hispanic (63)	98	0.52
American Indian/Alaska Native (67)	166	0.89
Not Hispanic (59)	148	0.79
Hispanic (8)	18	0.10
Blackfeet (3)	7	0.04
Cherokee (8)	33	0.18
Chippewa (2)	3	0.02
Creek (1)	2	0.01
Inupiat *(Alaska Native)* (3)	3	0.02
Iroquois (4)	5	0.03
Lumbee (5)	5	0.03
Mexican American Ind. (5)	5	0.03
Navajo (0)	1	0.01
Ottawa (2)	2	0.01
Potawatomi (1)	1	0.01
Seminole (0)	1	0.01
Sioux (1)	3	0.02
South American Ind. (0)	1	0.01
Tohono O'Odham (0)	3	0.02
Yaqui (1)	1	0.01
Asian (229)	311	1.66
Not Hispanic (227)	305	1.63
Hispanic (2)	6	0.03
Bangladeshi (1)	1	0.01
Chinese, ex. Taiwanese (41)	49	0.26
Filipino (26)	56	0.30
Indian (80)	89	0.48
Indonesian (1)	2	0.01
Japanese (11)	26	0.14
Korean (4)	22	0.12
Pakistani (0)	2	0.01
Thai (1)	2	0.01
Vietnamese (62)	64	0.34
Hawaii Native/Pacific Islander (10)	29	0.16
Not Hispanic (6)	22	0.12
Hispanic (4)	7	0.04
Guamanian/Chamorro (6)	10	0.05
Native Hawaiian (1)	9	0.05
Samoan (2)	4	0.02
White (7,389)	7,694	41.18
Not Hispanic (7,026)	7,293	39.04
Hispanic (363)	401	2.15

Elon

Place Type: Town
County: Alamance
Population: 9,419†

Ancestry‡	**Population**	**%**
African, Sub-Saharan (18)	36	0.40
African (18)	36	0.40
American (415)	415	4.65
Arab (47)	47	0.53
Lebanese (47)	47	0.53
Austrian (0)	43	0.48
British (23)	23	0.26
Canadian (49)	49	0.55
Cypriot (12)	34	0.38
Czech (0)	24	0.27
Danish (0)	7	0.08
Dutch (0)	160	1.79
English (689)	1,307	14.63
European (76)	76	0.85
French, ex. Basque (0)	107	1.20
French Canadian (11)	38	0.43
German (423)	1,626	18.20
Greek (0)	28	0.31
Hungarian (0)	10	0.11
Irish (409)	1,102	12.34
Italian (318)	659	7.38
Lithuanian (27)	27	0.30
Norwegian (9)	137	1.53
Polish (0)	165	1.85
Russian (21)	69	0.77
Scotch-Irish (111)	308	3.45
Scottish (239)	293	3.28
Slavic (28)	28	0.31
Slovak (0)	13	0.15
Swedish (16)	56	0.63
Swiss (31)	49	0.55
Ukrainian (0)	52	0.58
Welsh (37)	69	0.77
West Indian, ex. Hispanic (0)	11	0.12
West Indian (0)	11	0.12

Hispanic Origin	**Population**	**%**
Hispanic or Latino (of any race)	246	2.61
Central American, ex. Mexican	41	0.44
Costa Rican	8	0.08
Guatemalan	8	0.08
Honduran	10	0.11
Nicaraguan	1	0.01
Panamanian	2	0.02
Salvadoran	12	0.13
Cuban	18	0.19
Dominican Republic	8	0.08
Mexican	83	0.88
Puerto Rican	24	0.25
South American	38	0.40
Argentinean	3	0.03
Bolivian	5	0.05
Chilean	2	0.02
Colombian	15	0.16
Ecuadorian	8	0.08
Paraguayan	1	0.01
Peruvian	3	0.03

*Notes: † The Census 2010 population figure is used to calculate the percentages in the Hispanic Origin and Race categories. Ancestry percentages are based on the 2006-2010 American Community Survey population (not shown); ‡ Numbers in parentheses indicate the number of people reporting a single ancestry; * Numbers in parentheses indicate the number of persons reporting this race alone, not in combination with any other race; Please refer to the Explanation of Data for more information.*

Uruguayan	1	0.01
Other Hispanic or Latino	34	0.36

Race*	Population	%
African-American/Black (803)	870	9.24
Not Hispanic (799)	866	9.19
Hispanic (4)	4	0.04
American Indian/Alaska Native (14)	33	0.35
Not Hispanic (12)	29	0.31
Hispanic (2)	4	0.04
Apache (0)	1	0.01
Blackfeet (0)	1	0.01
Cherokee (4)	16	0.17
Choctaw (2)	2	0.02
Asian (184)	248	2.63
Not Hispanic (182)	245	2.60
Hispanic (2)	3	0.03
Burmese (0)	1	0.01
Cambodian (1)	1	0.01
Chinese, ex. Taiwanese (35)	54	0.57
Filipino (11)	25	0.27
Indian (56)	62	0.66
Japanese (5)	11	0.12
Korean (23)	30	0.32
Laotian (5)	6	0.06
Pakistani (1)	2	0.02
Taiwanese (3)	4	0.04
Thai (2)	4	0.04
Vietnamese (19)	22	0.23
Hawaii Native/Pacific Islander (3)	8	0.08
Not Hispanic (3)	8	0.08
Guamanian/Chamorro (0)	1	0.01
Native Hawaiian (2)	4	0.04
Samoan (0)	1	0.01
White (8,166)	8,299	88.11
Not Hispanic (8,023)	8,146	86.48
Hispanic (143)	153	1.62

Fayetteville

Place Type: City
County: Cumberland
Population: 200,564†

Ancestry‡	Population	%
African, Sub-Saharan (1,702)	2,422	1.22
African (844)	1,373	0.69
Cape Verdean (13)	46	0.02
Ethiopian (56)	56	0.03
Ghanaian (106)	106	0.05
Liberian (11)	11	0.01
Nigerian (355)	412	0.21
Sierra Leonean (36)	36	0.02
Somalian (33)	134	0.07
South African (33)	33	0.02
Sudanese (107)	107	0.05
Other Sub-Saharan African (108)	108	0.05
American (8,601)	8,601	4.32
Arab (229)	327	0.16
Arab (87)	87	0.04
Iraqi (26)	26	0.01
Lebanese (97)	195	0.10
Other Arab (19)	19	0.01
Armenian (48)	48	0.02
Australian (27)	40	0.02
Austrian (200)	349	0.18
Basque (29)	29	0.01
Belgian (0)	36	0.02
British (262)	512	0.26
Bulgarian (18)	18	0.01
Cajun (0)	16	0.01
Canadian (170)	303	0.15
Croatian (11)	67	0.03
Czech (129)	353	0.18
Czechoslovakian (7)	70	0.04
Danish (75)	345	0.17
Dutch (208)	1,635	0.82
English (4,711)	12,565	6.32
Estonian (14)	64	0.03
European (1,063)	1,435	0.72
Finnish (82)	255	0.13
French, ex. Basque (787)	3,489	1.75
French Canadian (346)	899	0.45
German (7,097)	21,911	11.02
German Russian (0)	8	<0.01
Greek (363)	542	0.27
Guyanese (131)	139	0.07
Hungarian (170)	488	0.25
Icelander (0)	27	0.01
Iranian (82)	100	0.05
Irish (4,648)	16,748	8.42
Italian (1,731)	6,535	3.29
Latvian (16)	33	0.02
Lithuanian (67)	165	0.08
Maltese (15)	25	0.01
Northern European (23)	23	0.01
Norwegian (311)	1,032	0.52
Pennsylvania German (19)	45	0.02
Polish (604)	2,868	1.44
Portuguese (242)	503	0.25
Romanian (28)	51	0.03
Russian (295)	914	0.46
Scandinavian (19)	98	0.05
Scotch-Irish (3,290)	5,414	2.72
Scottish (2,220)	4,887	2.46
Serbian (2)	29	0.01
Slavic (27)	27	0.01
Slovak (89)	174	0.09
Slovene (0)	21	0.01
Swedish (318)	1,416	0.71
Swiss (30)	144	0.07
Turkish (94)	124	0.06
Ukrainian (72)	192	0.10
Welsh (62)	983	0.49
West Indian, ex. Hispanic (1,230)	2,462	1.24
Bahamian (0)	31	0.02
Barbadian (12)	31	0.02
Belizean (0)	7	<0.01
British West Indian (86)	333	0.17
Dutch West Indian (28)	28	0.01
Haitian (102)	406	0.20
Jamaican (511)	803	0.40
Trinidadian/Tobagonian (121)	147	0.07
U.S. Virgin Islander (44)	61	0.03
West Indian (326)	615	0.31
Yugoslavian (0)	33	0.02

Hispanic Origin	Population	%
Hispanic or Latino (of any race)	20,256	10.10
Central American, ex. Mexican	2,238	1.12
Costa Rican	81	0.04
Guatemalan	176	0.09
Honduran	282	0.14
Nicaraguan	157	0.08
Panamanian	1,154	0.58
Salvadoran	379	0.19
Other Central American	9	<0.01
Cuban	534	0.27
Dominican Republic	730	0.36
Mexican	6,448	3.21
Puerto Rican	7,526	3.75
South American	1,227	0.61
Argentinean	74	0.04
Bolivian	53	0.03
Chilean	55	0.03
Colombian	492	0.25
Ecuadorian	195	0.10
Paraguayan	14	0.01
Peruvian	244	0.12
Uruguayan	10	<0.01
Venezuelan	80	0.04
Other South American	10	<0.01
Other Hispanic or Latino	1,553	0.77

Race*	Population	%
African-American/Black (84,040)	89,916	44.83
Not Hispanic (81,768)	86,376	43.07
Hispanic (2,272)	3,540	1.77
American Indian/Alaska Native (2,165)	4,901	2.44
Not Hispanic (1,907)	4,180	2.08
Hispanic (258)	721	0.36
Alaska Athabascan *(Ala. Nat.)* (5)	8	<0.01
Aleut *(Alaska Native)* (3)	7	<0.01
Apache (16)	52	0.03
Arapaho (1)	3	<0.01
Blackfeet (17)	143	0.07
Canadian/French Am. Ind. (2)	4	<0.01
Central American Ind. (5)	17	0.01
Cherokee (169)	815	0.41
Cheyenne (5)	12	0.01
Chickasaw (3)	12	0.01
Chippewa (17)	55	0.03
Choctaw (26)	55	0.03
Colville (1)	1	<0.01
Comanche (6)	13	0.01
Cree (2)	11	0.01
Creek (11)	29	0.01
Crow (0)	4	<0.01
Delaware (1)	12	0.01
Hopi (2)	4	<0.01
Houma (1)	3	<0.01
Inupiat *(Alaska Native)* (0)	2	<0.01
Iroquois (40)	60	0.03
Kiowa (2)	7	<0.01
Lumbee (630)	893	0.45
Menominee (1)	2	<0.01
Mexican American Ind. (14)	27	0.01
Navajo (80)	109	0.05
Osage (3)	7	<0.01
Ottawa (1)	4	<0.01
Paiute (2)	2	<0.01
Pima (4)	8	<0.01
Potawatomi (4)	9	<0.01
Pueblo (4)	11	0.01
Puget Sound Salish (3)	5	<0.01
Seminole (4)	24	0.01
Shoshone (3)	11	0.01
Sioux (41)	87	0.04
South American Ind. (12)	94	0.05
Spanish American Ind. (14)	15	0.01
Tlingit-Haida *(Alaska Native)* (6)	6	<0.01
Tohono O'Odham (2)	4	<0.01
Ute (0)	1	<0.01
Yaqui (2)	4	<0.01
Yup'ik *(Alaska Native)* (3)	3	<0.01
Asian (5,291)	7,899	3.94
Not Hispanic (5,147)	7,423	3.70
Hispanic (144)	476	0.24
Bangladeshi (48)	51	0.03
Burmese (34)	37	0.02
Cambodian (44)	73	0.04
Chinese, ex. Taiwanese (418)	741	0.37
Filipino (956)	1,754	0.87
Hmong (9)	16	0.01
Indian (717)	908	0.45
Indonesian (5)	21	0.01
Japanese (327)	775	0.39
Korean (1,590)	2,323	1.16
Laotian (49)	67	0.03
Malaysian (1)	1	<0.01
Nepalese (12)	12	0.01
Pakistani (70)	85	0.04
Sri Lankan (15)	19	0.01
Taiwanese (27)	32	0.02
Thai (220)	364	0.18
Vietnamese (471)	611	0.30
Hawaii Native/Pacific Islander (896)	1,631	0.81
Not Hispanic (823)	1,376	0.69
Hispanic (73)	255	0.13
Fijian (3)	4	<0.01
Guamanian/Chamorro (367)	528	0.26
Marshallese (17)	22	0.01
Native Hawaiian (158)	473	0.24
Samoan (143)	226	0.11
Tongan (4)	10	<0.01
White (91,653)	99,113	49.42
Not Hispanic (82,797)	88,521	44.14
Hispanic (8,856)	10,592	5.28

*Notes: † The Census 2010 population figure is used to calculate the percentages in the Hispanic Origin and Race categories. Ancestry percentages are based on the 2006-2010 American Community Survey population (not shown); ‡ Numbers in parentheses indicate the number of people reporting a single ancestry; * Numbers in parentheses indicate the number of persons reporting this race alone, not in combination with any other race; Please refer to the Explanation of Data for more information.*

Fuquay-Varina

Place Type: Town
County: Wake
Population: 17,937†

Ancestry‡	Population	%
African, Sub-Saharan (0)	48	0.30
African (0)	48	0.30
American (1,678)	1,678	10.39
Arab (68)	96	0.59
Egyptian (68)	96	0.59
Armenian (34)	34	0.21
Austrian (17)	17	0.11
British (57)	115	0.71
Bulgarian (0)	15	0.09
Canadian (25)	35	0.22
Croatian (27)	27	0.17
Czech (0)	89	0.55
Dutch (23)	284	1.76
English (503)	2,099	13.00
European (206)	248	1.54
Finnish (9)	18	0.11
French, ex. Basque (36)	373	2.31
French Canadian (108)	166	1.03
German (390)	1,995	12.35
Greek (18)	18	0.11
Hungarian (0)	46	0.28
Irish (425)	2,283	14.13
Italian (314)	907	5.62
Lithuanian (21)	36	0.22
Norwegian (62)	178	1.10
Polish (133)	586	3.63
Portuguese (0)	12	0.07
Romanian (30)	63	0.39
Russian (28)	109	0.67
Scotch-Irish (320)	596	3.69
Scottish (247)	681	4.22
Slovak (15)	63	0.39
Swedish (0)	46	0.28
Swiss (12)	41	0.25
Turkish (168)	168	1.04
Ukrainian (8)	33	0.20
Welsh (6)	36	0.22
West Indian, ex. Hispanic (109)	129	0.80
Haitian (22)	33	0.20
Jamaican (75)	84	0.52
Trinidadian/Tobagonian (12)	12	0.07

Hispanic Origin	Population	%
Hispanic or Latino (of any race)	1,738	9.69
Central American, ex. Mexican	212	1.18
Costa Rican	10	0.06
Guatemalan	95	0.53
Honduran	17	0.09
Nicaraguan	18	0.10
Panamanian	22	0.12
Salvadoran	50	0.28
Cuban	60	0.33
Dominican Republic	64	0.36
Mexican	831	4.63
Puerto Rican	280	1.56
South American	208	1.16
Argentinean	2	0.01
Bolivian	9	0.05
Chilean	9	0.05
Colombian	87	0.49
Ecuadorian	38	0.21
Paraguayan	3	0.02
Peruvian	27	0.15
Venezuelan	33	0.18
Other Hispanic or Latino	83	0.46

Race*	Population	%
African-American/Black (3,527)	3,766	21.00
Not Hispanic (3,455)	3,670	20.46
Hispanic (72)	96	0.54
American Indian/Alaska Native (110)	240	1.34
Not Hispanic (70)	179	1.00
Hispanic (40)	61	0.34
Blackfeet (1)	1	0.01
Central American Ind. (0)	3	0.02
Cherokee (11)	50	0.28
Chippewa (1)	2	0.01
Choctaw (0)	3	0.02
Creek (1)	5	0.03
Iroquois (0)	2	0.01
Lumbee (18)	24	0.13
Mexican American Ind. (2)	6	0.03
Sioux (0)	2	0.01
South American Ind. (5)	13	0.07
Spanish American Ind. (12)	12	0.07
Yup'ik *(Alaska Native)* (1)	1	0.01
Asian (361)	504	2.81
Not Hispanic (348)	477	2.66
Hispanic (13)	27	0.15
Bangladeshi (3)	3	0.02
Chinese, ex. Taiwanese (51)	68	0.38
Filipino (107)	156	0.87
Indian (80)	102	0.57
Indonesian (3)	4	0.02
Japanese (8)	28	0.16
Korean (25)	42	0.23
Laotian (3)	3	0.02
Nepalese (13)	13	0.07
Pakistani (5)	5	0.03
Sri Lankan (0)	1	0.01
Taiwanese (6)	9	0.05
Thai (2)	3	0.02
Vietnamese (46)	51	0.28
Hawaii Native/Pacific Islander (5)	22	0.12
Not Hispanic (3)	20	0.11
Hispanic (2)	2	0.01
Guamanian/Chamorro (2)	2	0.01
Native Hawaiian (2)	10	0.06
Samoan (1)	4	0.02
White (12,967)	13,397	74.69
Not Hispanic (11,920)	12,265	68.38
Hispanic (1,047)	1,132	6.31

Garner

Place Type: Town
County: Wake
Population: 25,745†

Ancestry‡	Population	%
African, Sub-Saharan (26)	55	0.23
African (15)	44	0.18
Kenyan (11)	11	0.05
American (2,131)	2,131	8.73
Arab (71)	85	0.35
Egyptian (71)	71	0.29
Moroccan (0)	14	0.06
Australian (0)	27	0.11
Austrian (11)	11	0.05
Belgian (28)	56	0.23
British (42)	96	0.39
Canadian (57)	57	0.23
Czech (70)	70	0.29
Danish (0)	26	0.11
Dutch (113)	265	1.09
English (1,093)	2,311	9.46
Estonian (66)	66	0.27
European (208)	261	1.07
French, ex. Basque (103)	406	1.66
French Canadian (135)	269	1.10
German (973)	3,260	13.35
Greek (10)	10	0.04
Hungarian (56)	173	0.71
Iranian (0)	10	0.04
Irish (533)	2,083	8.53
Italian (259)	866	3.55
Lithuanian (25)	42	0.17
Norwegian (78)	191	0.78
Pennsylvania German (13)	13	0.05
Polish (118)	669	2.74
Portuguese (0)	9	0.04
Russian (62)	178	0.73
Scandinavian (0)	16	0.07
Scotch-Irish (498)	898	3.68
Scottish (334)	719	2.94
Slovak (0)	39	0.16
Slovene (0)	18	0.07
Swedish (24)	100	0.41
Swiss (0)	61	0.25
Ukrainian (0)	23	0.09
Welsh (10)	57	0.23
West Indian, ex. Hispanic (26)	42	0.17
Belizean (16)	16	0.07
West Indian (10)	26	0.11

Hispanic Origin	Population	%
Hispanic or Latino (of any race)	2,561	9.95
Central American, ex. Mexican	301	1.17
Costa Rican	9	0.03
Guatemalan	64	0.25
Honduran	102	0.40
Nicaraguan	4	0.02
Panamanian	31	0.12
Salvadoran	89	0.35
Other Central American	2	0.01
Cuban	52	0.20
Dominican Republic	51	0.20
Mexican	1,488	5.78
Puerto Rican	344	1.34
South American	172	0.67
Argentinean	32	0.12
Bolivian	14	0.05
Chilean	5	0.02
Colombian	54	0.21
Ecuadorian	15	0.06
Peruvian	38	0.15
Uruguayan	1	<0.01
Venezuelan	12	0.05
Other South American	1	<0.01
Other Hispanic or Latino	153	0.59

Race*	Population	%
African-American/Black (8,468)	8,827	34.29
Not Hispanic (8,339)	8,618	33.47
Hispanic (129)	209	0.81
American Indian/Alaska Native (140)	289	1.12
Not Hispanic (99)	220	0.85
Hispanic (41)	69	0.27
Apache (0)	1	<0.01
Blackfeet (0)	6	0.02
Canadian/French Am. Ind. (0)	2	0.01
Cherokee (6)	53	0.21
Chippewa (4)	4	0.02
Creek (0)	2	0.01
Crow (0)	3	0.01
Hopi (1)	1	<0.01
Iroquois (0)	4	0.02
Lumbee (23)	31	0.12
Mexican American Ind. (4)	5	0.02
Navajo (1)	1	<0.01
Osage (0)	1	<0.01
Potawatomi (4)	4	0.02
Seminole (0)	4	0.02
Sioux (5)	5	0.02
South American Ind. (3)	5	0.02
Spanish American Ind. (1)	5	0.02
Tsimshian *(Alaska Native)* (1)	1	<0.01
Asian (474)	586	2.28
Not Hispanic (468)	570	2.21
Hispanic (6)	16	0.06
Bangladeshi (11)	11	0.04
Burmese (6)	6	0.02
Cambodian (0)	2	0.01
Chinese, ex. Taiwanese (63)	84	0.33
Filipino (69)	94	0.37
Indian (89)	102	0.40
Indonesian (2)	2	0.01
Japanese (13)	27	0.10
Korean (46)	71	0.28
Laotian (7)	12	0.05
Malaysian (2)	2	0.01
Pakistani (14)	14	0.05
Sri Lankan (2)	2	0.01

*Notes: † The Census 2010 population figure is used to calculate the percentages in the Hispanic Origin and Race categories. Ancestry percentages are based on the 2006-2010 American Community Survey population (not shown); ‡ Numbers in parentheses indicate the number of people reporting a single ancestry; * Numbers in parentheses indicate the number of persons reporting this race alone, not in combination with any other race; Please refer to the Explanation of Data for more information.*

Taiwanese (11)	11	0.04
Thai (12)	19	0.07
Vietnamese (97)	114	0.44
Hawaii Native/Pacific Islander (12)	25	0.10
Not Hispanic (12)	24	0.09
Hispanic (0)	1	<0.01
Guamanian/Chamorro (9)	12	0.05
Native Hawaiian (2)	7	0.03
Samoan (0)	1	<0.01
White (14,888)	15,360	59.66
Not Hispanic (13,789)	14,154	54.98
Hispanic (1,099)	1,206	4.68

Gastonia

Place Type: City
County: Gaston
Population: 71,741†

Ancestry‡	Population	%
African, Sub-Saharan (622)	682	0.96
African (395)	455	0.64
Ethiopian (96)	96	0.14
Kenyan (13)	13	0.02
Nigerian (87)	87	0.12
Senegalese (8)	8	0.01
Somalian (23)	23	0.03
Albanian (9)	9	0.01
American (5,604)	5,604	7.93
Arab (90)	208	0.29
Arab (0)	26	0.04
Egyptian (15)	39	0.06
Lebanese (30)	30	0.04
Moroccan (13)	13	0.02
Syrian (32)	92	0.13
Other Arab (0)	8	0.01
Armenian (0)	69	0.10
Australian (13)	13	0.02
Austrian (28)	67	0.09
Belgian (0)	13	0.02
Brazilian (14)	14	0.02
British (129)	289	0.41
Bulgarian (79)	79	0.11
Canadian (19)	67	0.09
Croatian (0)	23	0.03
Czech (0)	87	0.12
Czechoslovakian (39)	47	0.07
Danish (22)	22	0.03
Dutch (215)	1,116	1.58
Eastern European (26)	30	0.04
English (2,543)	5,568	7.87
European (354)	473	0.67
Finnish (47)	47	0.07
French, ex. Basque (158)	901	1.27
French Canadian (115)	268	0.38
German (2,591)	7,258	10.26
Greek (270)	576	0.81
Hungarian (0)	15	0.02
Irish (1,788)	5,979	8.46
Italian (327)	1,119	1.58
Northern European (14)	14	0.02
Norwegian (5)	42	0.06
Pennsylvania German (11)	11	0.02
Polish (135)	514	0.73
Portuguese (34)	45	0.06
Romanian (0)	11	0.02
Russian (67)	214	0.30
Scotch-Irish (2,096)	3,416	4.83
Scottish (1,049)	1,911	2.70
Slovak (20)	65	0.09
Swedish (41)	182	0.26
Swiss (0)	61	0.09
Turkish (10)	10	0.01
Ukrainian (6)	20	0.03
Welsh (122)	327	0.46
West Indian, ex. Hispanic (135)	135	0.19
Bahamian (12)	12	0.02
Haitian (36)	36	0.05
Jamaican (9)	9	0.01
West Indian (78)	78	0.11
Yugoslavian (19)	19	0.03

Hispanic Origin	Population	%
Hispanic or Latino (of any race)	6,901	9.62
Central American, ex. Mexican	606	0.84
Costa Rican	72	0.10
Guatemalan	79	0.11
Honduran	206	0.29
Nicaraguan	73	0.10
Panamanian	18	0.03
Salvadoran	134	0.19
Other Central American	24	0.03
Cuban	136	0.19
Dominican Republic	171	0.24
Mexican	3,849	5.37
Puerto Rican	561	0.78
South American	1,042	1.45
Argentinean	10	0.01
Bolivian	3	<0.01
Chilean	63	0.09
Colombian	812	1.13
Ecuadorian	72	0.10
Peruvian	52	0.07
Uruguayan	15	0.02
Venezuelan	13	0.02
Other South American	2	<0.01
Other Hispanic or Latino	536	0.75

Race*	Population	%
African-American/Black (19,953)	20,917	29.16
Not Hispanic (19,661)	20,521	28.60
Hispanic (292)	396	0.55
American Indian/Alaska Native (289)	691	0.96
Not Hispanic (201)	576	0.80
Hispanic (88)	115	0.16
Apache (2)	5	0.01
Blackfeet (1)	14	0.02
Central American Ind. (1)	1	<0.01
Cherokee (61)	184	0.26
Cheyenne (1)	1	<0.01
Chippewa (4)	6	0.01
Choctaw (5)	9	0.01
Creek (8)	10	0.01
Crow (0)	1	<0.01
Delaware (1)	1	<0.01
Iroquois (1)	2	<0.01
Kiowa (1)	1	<0.01
Lumbee (27)	44	0.06
Mexican American Ind. (22)	23	0.03
Navajo (1)	3	<0.01
Osage (0)	1	<0.01
Potawatomi (0)	3	<0.01
Seminole (0)	9	0.01
Sioux (2)	4	0.01
South American Ind. (4)	7	0.01
Spanish American Ind. (2)	2	<0.01
Yuman (1)	1	<0.01
Asian (964)	1,175	1.64
Not Hispanic (956)	1,144	1.59
Hispanic (8)	31	0.04
Cambodian (13)	17	0.02
Chinese, ex. Taiwanese (143)	161	0.22
Filipino (69)	96	0.13
Hmong (15)	15	0.02
Indian (339)	389	0.54
Indonesian (11)	13	0.02
Japanese (23)	49	0.07
Korean (52)	75	0.10
Laotian (37)	51	0.07
Malaysian (1)	1	<0.01
Pakistani (92)	98	0.14
Sri Lankan (7)	8	0.01
Thai (12)	28	0.04
Vietnamese (112)	143	0.20
Hawaii Native/Pacific Islander (16)	53	0.07
Not Hispanic (7)	36	0.05
Hispanic (9)	17	0.02
Fijian (1)	1	<0.01
Guamanian/Chamorro (1)	5	0.01
Native Hawaiian (6)	14	0.02
Samoan (8)	10	0.01
White (45,199)	46,580	64.93
Not Hispanic (42,614)	43,719	60.94
Hispanic (2,585)	2,861	3.99

Goldsboro

Place Type: City
County: Wayne
Population: 36,437†

Ancestry‡	Population	%
African, Sub-Saharan (246)	311	0.84
African (213)	236	0.64
Nigerian (33)	75	0.20
American (2,565)	2,565	6.97
Arab (73)	94	0.26
Egyptian (18)	18	0.05
Lebanese (46)	67	0.18
Other Arab (9)	9	0.02
Australian (20)	30	0.08
Austrian (0)	5	0.01
Belgian (4)	8	0.02
Brazilian (14)	17	0.05
British (108)	151	0.41
Canadian (12)	42	0.11
Croatian (0)	13	0.04
Czech (20)	54	0.15
Danish (0)	64	0.17
Dutch (27)	185	0.50
English (1,098)	2,293	6.23
European (276)	303	0.82
Finnish (0)	4	0.01
French, ex. Basque (127)	454	1.23
French Canadian (31)	115	0.31
German (752)	2,482	6.74
Greek (8)	20	0.05
Hungarian (18)	50	0.14
Icelander (0)	11	0.03
Iranian (10)	14	0.04
Irish (688)	2,306	6.26
Italian (200)	652	1.77
Lithuanian (8)	8	0.02
Northern European (18)	18	0.05
Norwegian (94)	217	0.59
Pennsylvania German (33)	39	0.11
Polish (87)	301	0.82
Portuguese (40)	155	0.42
Romanian (0)	10	0.03
Russian (18)	29	0.08
Scandinavian (9)	12	0.03
Scotch-Irish (489)	772	2.10
Scottish (226)	492	1.34
Serbian (10)	10	0.03
Slavic (0)	3	0.01
Slovene (3)	3	0.01
Swedish (18)	52	0.14
Swiss (7)	18	0.05
Turkish (3)	3	0.01
Ukrainian (4)	16	0.04
Welsh (6)	118	0.32
West Indian, ex. Hispanic (80)	143	0.39
British West Indian (8)	8	0.02
Dutch West Indian (7)	7	0.02
Haitian (21)	30	0.08
Jamaican (11)	65	0.18
Trinidadian/Tobagonian (18)	18	0.05
U.S. Virgin Islander (3)	3	0.01
West Indian (12)	12	0.03

Hispanic Origin	Population	%
Hispanic or Latino (of any race)	1,583	4.34
Central American, ex. Mexican	194	0.53
Costa Rican	8	0.02
Guatemalan	48	0.13
Honduran	88	0.24
Nicaraguan	3	0.01
Panamanian	28	0.08
Salvadoran	16	0.04
Other Central American	3	0.01

*Notes: † The Census 2010 population figure is used to calculate the percentages in the Hispanic Origin and Race categories. Ancestry percentages are based on the 2006-2010 American Community Survey population (not shown); ‡ Numbers in parentheses indicate the number of people reporting a single ancestry; * Numbers in parentheses indicate the number of persons reporting this race alone, not in combination with any other race; Please refer to the Explanation of Data for more information.*

Cuban	34	0.09
Dominican Republic	36	0.10
Mexican	661	1.81
Puerto Rican	405	1.11
South American	72	0.20
Argentinean	4	0.01
Bolivian	1	<0.01
Chilean	3	0.01
Colombian	21	0.06
Ecuadorian	17	0.05
Peruvian	11	0.03
Uruguayan	1	<0.01
Venezuelan	10	0.03
Other South American	4	0.01
Other Hispanic or Latino	181	0.50

Race*	Population	%
African-American/Black (19,786)	20,383	55.94
Not Hispanic (19,593)	20,112	55.20
Hispanic (193)	271	0.74
American Indian/Alaska Native (133)	354	0.97
Not Hispanic (112)	302	0.83
Hispanic (21)	52	0.14
Alaska Athabascan *(Ala. Nat.)* (1)	1	<0.01
Aleut *(Alaska Native)* (1)	1	<0.01
Apache (1)	2	0.01
Blackfeet (0)	9	0.02
Central American Ind. (1)	5	0.01
Cherokee (17)	77	0.21
Chickasaw (1)	3	0.01
Chippewa (2)	3	0.01
Creek (1)	2	0.01
Houma (0)	3	0.01
Iroquois (1)	4	0.01
Lumbee (13)	24	0.07
Mexican American Ind. (5)	5	0.01
Pima (0)	1	<0.01
Potawatomi (0)	1	<0.01
Pueblo (0)	2	0.01
Sioux (1)	4	0.01
South American Ind. (5)	5	0.01
Asian (651)	963	2.64
Not Hispanic (646)	933	2.56
Hispanic (5)	30	0.08
Bangladeshi (5)	6	0.02
Cambodian (4)	4	0.01
Chinese, ex. Taiwanese (138)	174	0.48
Filipino (137)	250	0.69
Hmong (8)	8	0.02
Indian (80)	103	0.28
Japanese (48)	98	0.27
Korean (87)	128	0.35
Laotian (7)	7	0.02
Pakistani (11)	11	0.03
Taiwanese (10)	11	0.03
Thai (46)	74	0.20
Vietnamese (40)	44	0.12
Hawaii Native/Pacific Islander (23)	82	0.23
Not Hispanic (18)	60	0.16
Hispanic (5)	22	0.06
Guamanian/Chamorro (10)	22	0.06
Native Hawaiian (3)	32	0.09
Samoan (0)	6	0.02
Tongan (0)	1	<0.01
White (14,295)	14,997	41.16
Not Hispanic (13,628)	14,251	39.11
Hispanic (667)	746	2.05

Graham

Place Type: City
County: Alamance
Population: 14,153†

Ancestry‡	Population	%
African, Sub-Saharan (14)	14	0.10
South African (14)	14	0.10
American (1,084)	1,084	7.79
Arab (14)	30	0.22
Arab (14)	14	0.10
Lebanese (0)	16	0.11
Australian (0)	12	0.09
Austrian (0)	20	0.14
British (90)	106	0.76
Czech (0)	14	0.10
Danish (0)	8	0.06
Dutch (0)	87	0.62
English (728)	1,498	10.76
European (91)	124	0.89
French, ex. Basque (10)	241	1.73
French Canadian (19)	35	0.25
German (357)	1,242	8.92
Hungarian (0)	16	0.11
Irish (173)	934	6.71
Italian (99)	231	1.66
Polish (11)	166	1.19
Russian (0)	14	0.10
Scandinavian (0)	52	0.37
Scotch-Irish (459)	691	4.96
Scottish (96)	231	1.66
Slovak (0)	8	0.06
Swedish (11)	11	0.08
Swiss (14)	14	0.10
Turkish (0)	13	0.09
Ukrainian (12)	12	0.09
Welsh (9)	64	0.46

Hispanic Origin	Population	%
Hispanic or Latino (of any race)	2,229	15.75
Central American, ex. Mexican	259	1.83
Guatemalan	8	0.06
Honduran	40	0.28
Nicaraguan	12	0.08
Panamanian	5	0.04
Salvadoran	194	1.37
Cuban	15	0.11
Dominican Republic	36	0.25
Mexican	1,681	11.88
Puerto Rican	82	0.58
South American	32	0.23
Argentinean	4	0.03
Bolivian	1	0.01
Chilean	11	0.08
Colombian	12	0.08
Ecuadorian	1	0.01
Peruvian	3	0.02
Other Hispanic or Latino	124	0.88

Race*	Population	%
African-American/Black (3,229)	3,425	24.20
Not Hispanic (3,191)	3,364	23.77
Hispanic (38)	61	0.43
American Indian/Alaska Native (172)	267	1.89
Not Hispanic (74)	139	0.98
Hispanic (98)	128	0.90
Apache (0)	1	0.01
Blackfeet (0)	3	0.02
Central American Ind. (0)	2	0.01
Cherokee (12)	31	0.22
Iroquois (1)	1	0.01
Lumbee (13)	18	0.13
Mexican American Ind. (37)	48	0.34
Potawatomi (3)	3	0.02
Spanish American Ind. (12)	13	0.09
Tohono O'Odham (4)	4	0.03
Asian (179)	231	1.63
Not Hispanic (171)	217	1.53
Hispanic (8)	14	0.10
Bangladeshi (3)	3	0.02
Cambodian (1)	1	0.01
Chinese, ex. Taiwanese (25)	34	0.24
Filipino (10)	25	0.18
Indian (33)	38	0.27
Japanese (2)	12	0.08
Korean (11)	19	0.13
Laotian (54)	67	0.47
Taiwanese (2)	2	0.01
Thai (1)	7	0.05
Vietnamese (31)	34	0.24
Hawaii Native/Pacific Islander (1)	8	0.06
Not Hispanic (0)	5	0.04
Hispanic (1)	3	0.02
Guamanian/Chamorro (1)	1	0.01
Native Hawaiian (0)	5	0.04
White (8,908)	9,159	64.71
Not Hispanic (8,241)	8,410	59.42
Hispanic (667)	749	5.29

Greensboro

Place Type: City
County: Guilford
Population: 269,666†

Ancestry‡	Population	%
Afghan (16)	16	0.01
African, Sub-Saharan (5,627)	6,270	2.38
African (2,320)	2,798	1.06
Ethiopian (87)	87	0.03
Ghanaian (375)	375	0.14
Kenyan (15)	15	0.01
Liberian (175)	204	0.08
Nigerian (498)	553	0.21
Senegalese (13)	13	<0.01
Sierra Leonean (210)	210	0.08
Somalian (118)	118	0.04
South African (8)	45	0.02
Sudanese (1,127)	1,144	0.43
Ugandan (38)	38	0.01
Other Sub-Saharan African (643)	670	0.25
American (12,778)	12,778	4.85
Arab (813)	1,120	0.43
Arab (108)	151	0.06
Egyptian (137)	151	0.06
Jordanian (126)	159	0.06
Lebanese (254)	361	0.14
Moroccan (17)	26	0.01
Palestinian (65)	111	0.04
Syrian (75)	130	0.05
Other Arab (31)	31	0.01
Australian (10)	66	0.03
Austrian (119)	326	0.12
Basque (21)	21	0.01
Belgian (46)	193	0.07
Brazilian (205)	232	0.09
British (839)	1,727	0.66
Bulgarian (37)	52	0.02
Cajun (36)	66	0.03
Canadian (271)	359	0.14
Celtic (38)	51	0.02
Croatian (101)	166	0.06
Czech (94)	523	0.20
Czechoslovakian (50)	136	0.05
Danish (95)	372	0.14
Dutch (414)	2,321	0.88
Eastern European (422)	476	0.18
English (10,090)	22,926	8.71
European (2,522)	2,845	1.08
Finnish (35)	292	0.11
French, ex. Basque (750)	4,077	1.55
French Canadian (189)	633	0.24
German (7,590)	22,704	8.62
Greek (325)	526	0.20
Guyanese (182)	209	0.08
Hungarian (121)	666	0.25
Icelander (0)	14	0.01
Iranian (365)	397	0.15
Irish (6,207)	18,092	6.87
Italian (2,254)	6,358	2.41
Latvian (9)	9	<0.01
Lithuanian (37)	243	0.09
Luxemburger (0)	9	<0.01
Maltese (9)	9	<0.01
Northern European (116)	116	0.04
Norwegian (207)	1,013	0.38
Pennsylvania German (37)	143	0.05
Polish (1,041)	3,312	1.26
Portuguese (66)	273	0.10
Romanian (125)	160	0.06
Russian (561)	1,444	0.55

SECTION TWO

*Notes: † The Census 2010 population figure is used to calculate the percentages in the Hispanic Origin and Race categories. Ancestry percentages are based on the 2006-2010 American Community Survey population (not shown); ‡ Numbers in parentheses indicate the number of people reporting a single ancestry; * Numbers in parentheses indicate the number of persons reporting this race alone, not in combination with any other race; Please refer to the Explanation of Data for more information.*

Scandinavian (77)	313	0.12
Scotch-Irish (4,966)	8,719	3.31
Scottish (2,606)	6,491	2.46
Serbian (61)	93	0.04
Slavic (38)	38	0.01
Slovak (109)	331	0.13
Slovene (11)	38	0.01
Swedish (435)	1,509	0.57
Swiss (130)	367	0.14
Turkish (15)	32	0.01
Ukrainian (137)	323	0.12
Welsh (300)	1,239	0.47
West Indian, ex. Hispanic (725)	1,334	0.51
Bahamian (0)	15	0.01
Barbadian (29)	57	0.02
Bermudan (34)	34	0.01
Haitian (34)	45	0.02
Jamaican (470)	860	0.33
Trinidadian/Tobagonian (85)	123	0.05
West Indian (73)	200	0.08
Yugoslavian (202)	252	0.10

Hispanic Origin	Population	%
Hispanic or Latino (of any race)	20,336	7.54
Central American, ex. Mexican	2,246	0.83
Costa Rican	132	0.05
Guatemalan	518	0.19
Honduran	352	0.13
Nicaraguan	159	0.06
Panamanian	191	0.07
Salvadoran	887	0.33
Other Central American	7	<0.01
Cuban	520	0.19
Dominican Republic	568	0.21
Mexican	12,293	4.56
Puerto Rican	1,872	0.69
South American	1,456	0.54
Argentinean	89	0.03
Bolivian	32	0.01
Chilean	102	0.04
Colombian	562	0.21
Ecuadorian	128	0.05
Paraguayan	7	<0.01
Peruvian	285	0.11
Uruguayan	27	0.01
Venezuelan	203	0.08
Other South American	21	0.01
Other Hispanic or Latino	1,381	0.51

Race*	Population	%
African-American/Black (109,586)	114,156	42.33
Not Hispanic (108,233)	112,136	41.58
Hispanic (1,353)	2,020	0.75
American Indian/Alaska Native (1,385)	3,454	1.28
Not Hispanic (1,096)	2,892	1.07
Hispanic (289)	562	0.21
Aleut *(Alaska Native)* (1)	2	<0.01
Apache (4)	23	0.01
Arapaho (0)	1	<0.01
Blackfeet (12)	123	0.05
Canadian/French Am. Ind. (1)	4	<0.01
Central American Ind. (11)	19	0.01
Cherokee (159)	789	0.29
Cheyenne (2)	4	<0.01
Chickasaw (2)	6	<0.01
Chippewa (15)	33	0.01
Choctaw (2)	22	0.01
Comanche (1)	7	<0.01
Cree (0)	1	<0.01
Creek (1)	11	<0.01
Crow (1)	2	<0.01
Delaware (2)	5	<0.01
Hopi (0)	2	<0.01
Inupiat *(Alaska Native)* (1)	2	<0.01
Iroquois (13)	56	0.02
Kiowa (1)	1	<0.01
Lumbee (336)	488	0.18
Mexican American Ind. (44)	72	0.03
Navajo (7)	21	0.01
Ottawa (1)	3	<0.01
Potawatomi (1)	1	<0.01
Pueblo (0)	3	<0.01
Seminole (1)	5	<0.01
Sioux (10)	24	0.01
South American Ind. (5)	18	0.01
Spanish American Ind. (7)	8	<0.01
Tlingit-Haida *(Alaska Native)* (1)	1	<0.01
Tohono O'Odham (1)	1	<0.01
Yuman (0)	1	<0.01
Yup'ik *(Alaska Native)* (1)	1	<0.01
Asian (10,772)	12,291	4.56
Not Hispanic (10,711)	12,120	4.49
Hispanic (61)	171	0.06
Bangladeshi (38)	43	0.02
Bhutanese (158)	173	0.06
Burmese (266)	272	0.10
Cambodian (551)	648	0.24
Chinese, ex. Taiwanese (961)	1,197	0.44
Filipino (384)	672	0.25
Hmong (84)	85	0.03
Indian (1,810)	2,030	0.75
Indonesian (21)	35	0.01
Japanese (183)	369	0.14
Korean (778)	997	0.37
Laotian (328)	389	0.14
Malaysian (7)	14	0.01
Nepalese (74)	81	0.03
Pakistani (205)	230	0.09
Sri Lankan (31)	37	0.01
Taiwanese (46)	59	0.02
Thai (112)	177	0.07
Vietnamese (4,198)	4,474	1.66
Hawaii Native/Pacific Islander (157)	429	0.16
Not Hispanic (128)	342	0.13
Hispanic (29)	87	0.03
Fijian (1)	4	<0.01
Guamanian/Chamorro (35)	72	0.03
Marshallese (7)	7	<0.01
Native Hawaiian (50)	125	0.05
Samoan (16)	47	0.02
Tongan (0)	2	<0.01
White (130,396)	135,483	50.24
Not Hispanic (122,888)	126,944	47.07
Hispanic (7,508)	8,539	3.17

Greenville

Place Type: City
County: Pitt
Population: 84,554†

Ancestry‡	Population	%
African, Sub-Saharan (393)	462	0.57
African (169)	238	0.30
Ghanaian (129)	129	0.16
Kenyan (14)	14	0.02
Liberian (12)	12	0.01
Nigerian (69)	69	0.09
American (3,891)	3,891	4.84
Arab (642)	670	0.83
Arab (86)	86	0.11
Egyptian (368)	368	0.46
Jordanian (10)	10	0.01
Lebanese (123)	151	0.19
Moroccan (44)	44	0.05
Other Arab (11)	11	0.01
Armenian (14)	14	0.02
Australian (0)	11	0.01
Austrian (41)	110	0.14
Belgian (7)	36	0.04
Brazilian (11)	51	0.06
British (220)	359	0.45
Bulgarian (30)	30	0.04
Cajun (16)	32	0.04
Canadian (74)	136	0.17
Carpatho Rusyn (18)	18	0.02
Czech (27)	129	0.16
Czechoslovakian (20)	20	0.02
Danish (26)	97	0.12
Dutch (164)	705	0.88
Eastern European (22)	22	0.03
English (3,459)	7,419	9.22
European (880)	1,041	1.29
Finnish (13)	40	0.05
French, ex. Basque (320)	1,491	1.85
French Canadian (62)	314	0.39
German (1,999)	6,913	8.59
Greek (50)	170	0.21
Hungarian (105)	274	0.34
Icelander (0)	33	0.04
Iranian (101)	101	0.13
Irish (2,568)	7,908	9.83
Israeli (27)	27	0.03
Italian (1,157)	3,183	3.96
Latvian (0)	14	0.02
Lithuanian (54)	130	0.16
Northern European (11)	24	0.03
Norwegian (139)	536	0.67
Pennsylvania German (13)	13	0.02
Polish (362)	1,159	1.44
Portuguese (56)	183	0.23
Romanian (12)	12	0.01
Russian (77)	232	0.29
Scandinavian (0)	9	0.01
Scotch-Irish (1,266)	2,036	2.53
Scottish (819)	2,193	2.73
Slavic (0)	17	0.02
Slovak (26)	65	0.08
Slovene (11)	11	0.01
Swedish (61)	287	0.36
Swiss (87)	142	0.18
Turkish (31)	31	0.04
Ukrainian (28)	161	0.20
Welsh (206)	536	0.67
West Indian, ex. Hispanic (247)	339	0.42
Dutch West Indian (0)	8	0.01
Haitian (0)	35	0.04
Jamaican (84)	101	0.13
Trinidadian/Tobagonian (163)	195	0.24
Yugoslavian (62)	62	0.08

Hispanic Origin	Population	%
Hispanic or Latino (of any race)	3,183	3.76
Central American, ex. Mexican	350	0.41
Costa Rican	38	0.04
Guatemalan	44	0.05
Honduran	65	0.08
Nicaraguan	39	0.05
Panamanian	35	0.04
Salvadoran	125	0.15
Other Central American	4	<0.01
Cuban	111	0.13
Dominican Republic	72	0.09
Mexican	1,558	1.84
Puerto Rican	547	0.65
South American	277	0.33
Argentinean	14	0.02
Bolivian	2	<0.01
Chilean	23	0.03
Colombian	112	0.13
Ecuadorian	29	0.03
Paraguayan	7	0.01
Peruvian	48	0.06
Uruguayan	3	<0.01
Venezuelan	29	0.03
Other South American	10	0.01
Other Hispanic or Latino	268	0.32

Race*	Population	%
African-American/Black (31,272)	32,386	38.30
Not Hispanic (31,010)	31,978	37.82
Hispanic (262)	408	0.48
American Indian/Alaska Native (303)	735	0.87
Not Hispanic (265)	651	0.77
Hispanic (38)	84	0.10
Aleut *(Alaska Native)* (5)	5	0.01
Blackfeet (1)	11	0.01
Canadian/French Am. Ind. (5)	7	0.01
Central American Ind. (1)	8	0.01
Cherokee (33)	134	0.16

*Notes: † The Census 2010 population figure is used to calculate the percentages in the Hispanic Origin and Race categories. Ancestry percentages are based on the 2006-2010 American Community Survey population (not shown); ‡ Numbers in parentheses indicate the number of people reporting a single ancestry; * Numbers in parentheses indicate the number of persons reporting this race alone, not in combination with any other race; Please refer to the Explanation of Data for more information.*

Cheyenne (0)	4	<0.01
Chickasaw (0)	1	<0.01
Chippewa (5)	12	0.01
Choctaw (4)	9	0.01
Comanche (1)	7	0.01
Cree (1)	1	<0.01
Creek (1)	6	0.01
Delaware (1)	1	<0.01
Inupiat *(Alaska Native)* (0)	1	<0.01
Iroquois (9)	17	0.02
Lumbee (53)	72	0.09
Mexican American Ind. (5)	12	0.01
Navajo (2)	2	<0.01
Ottawa (1)	1	<0.01
Potawatomi (1)	1	<0.01
Pueblo (0)	2	<0.01
Seminole (1)	5	0.01
Shoshone (1)	1	<0.01
Sioux (1)	6	0.01
South American Ind. (6)	8	0.01
Tlingit-Haida *(Alaska Native)* (1)	1	<0.01
Asian (2,025)	2,560	3.03
Not Hispanic (1,996)	2,504	2.96
Hispanic (29)	56	0.07
Bangladeshi (7)	10	0.01
Burmese (14)	30	0.04
Cambodian (4)	8	0.01
Chinese, ex. Taiwanese (412)	468	0.55
Filipino (196)	308	0.36
Hmong (39)	41	0.05
Indian (665)	733	0.87
Indonesian (0)	11	0.01
Japanese (96)	173	0.20
Korean (200)	285	0.34
Laotian (8)	11	0.01
Malaysian (1)	3	<0.01
Nepalese (2)	2	<0.01
Pakistani (100)	116	0.14
Sri Lankan (1)	1	<0.01
Taiwanese (24)	28	0.03
Thai (21)	39	0.05
Vietnamese (125)	166	0.20
Hawaii Native/Pacific Islander (34)	100	0.12
Not Hispanic (31)	87	0.10
Hispanic (3)	13	0.02
Fijian (1)	1	<0.01
Guamanian/Chamorro (11)	20	0.02
Native Hawaiian (4)	19	0.02
Samoan (8)	15	0.02
Tongan (3)	3	<0.01
White (47,579)	49,010	57.96
Not Hispanic (46,368)	47,591	56.28
Hispanic (1,211)	1,419	1.68

Half Moon

Place Type: CDP
County: Onslow
Population: 8,352†

Ancestry‡	Population	%
African, Sub-Saharan (67)	67	0.82
African (67)	67	0.82
American (501)	501	6.14
Arab (0)	131	1.60
Lebanese (0)	131	1.60
Australian (0)	16	0.20
Canadian (150)	150	1.84
Czech (8)	8	0.10
Danish (34)	34	0.42
Dutch (0)	46	0.56
English (199)	604	7.40
European (31)	31	0.38
French, ex. Basque (0)	255	3.12
French Canadian (0)	23	0.28
German (474)	1,628	19.95
Hungarian (14)	71	0.87
Icelander (0)	9	0.11
Irish (444)	1,179	14.44
Italian (161)	417	5.11
Norwegian (24)	93	1.14
Pennsylvania German (0)	16	0.20
Polish (211)	328	4.02
Portuguese (31)	44	0.54
Scandinavian (0)	55	0.67
Scotch-Irish (69)	114	1.40
Scottish (77)	235	2.88
Slavic (0)	46	0.56
Swedish (15)	31	0.38
Swiss (0)	11	0.13
West Indian, ex. Hispanic (30)	30	0.37
Haitian (30)	30	0.37

Hispanic Origin	Population	%
Hispanic or Latino (of any race)	816	9.77
Central American, ex. Mexican	90	1.08
Costa Rican	2	0.02
Guatemalan	11	0.13
Honduran	18	0.22
Nicaraguan	18	0.22
Panamanian	25	0.30
Salvadoran	16	0.19
Cuban	18	0.22
Dominican Republic	26	0.31
Mexican	329	3.94
Puerto Rican	233	2.79
South American	44	0.53
Argentinean	2	0.02
Bolivian	2	0.02
Colombian	14	0.17
Ecuadorian	5	0.06
Peruvian	18	0.22
Uruguayan	1	0.01
Venezuelan	2	0.02
Other Hispanic or Latino	76	0.91

Race*	Population	%
African-American/Black (1,736)	1,960	23.47
Not Hispanic (1,675)	1,854	22.20
Hispanic (61)	106	1.27
American Indian/Alaska Native (56)	132	1.58
Not Hispanic (52)	110	1.32
Hispanic (4)	22	0.26
Blackfeet (0)	5	0.06
Canadian/French Am. Ind. (1)	1	0.01
Cherokee (6)	21	0.25
Cheyenne (0)	1	0.01
Chippewa (1)	1	0.01
Choctaw (1)	5	0.06
Colville (1)	1	0.01
Delaware (0)	4	0.05
Iroquois (2)	2	0.02
Lumbee (8)	10	0.12
Navajo (2)	2	0.02
Pueblo (1)	3	0.04
Seminole (0)	1	0.01
Shoshone (3)	3	0.04
Sioux (4)	5	0.06
Tlingit-Haida *(Alaska Native)* (3)	3	0.04
Asian (182)	330	3.95
Not Hispanic (163)	291	3.48
Hispanic (19)	39	0.47
Cambodian (11)	11	0.13
Chinese, ex. Taiwanese (4)	20	0.24
Filipino (95)	176	2.11
Indian (6)	11	0.13
Japanese (29)	77	0.92
Korean (8)	21	0.25
Laotian (1)	2	0.02
Pakistani (1)	1	0.01
Taiwanese (0)	2	0.02
Thai (7)	10	0.12
Vietnamese (5)	7	0.08
Hawaii Native/Pacific Islander (31)	72	0.86
Not Hispanic (30)	64	0.77
Hispanic (1)	8	0.10
Guamanian/Chamorro (7)	16	0.19
Native Hawaiian (11)	37	0.44
Samoan (11)	20	0.24
White (5,689)	6,069	72.67
Not Hispanic (5,270)	5,564	66.62
Hispanic (419)	505	6.05

Harrisburg

Place Type: Town
County: Cabarrus
Population: 11,526†

Ancestry‡	Population	%
African, Sub-Saharan (79)	92	0.89
African (62)	75	0.73
South African (9)	9	0.09
Sudanese (8)	8	0.08
Albanian (0)	8	0.08
American (1,103)	1,103	10.68
Arab (0)	13	0.13
Arab (0)	13	0.13
British (0)	13	0.13
Bulgarian (0)	13	0.13
Canadian (0)	10	0.10
Croatian (0)	24	0.23
Czech (9)	29	0.28
Dutch (22)	171	1.66
English (589)	1,269	12.29
European (181)	181	1.75
French, ex. Basque (28)	261	2.53
French Canadian (17)	17	0.16
German (836)	2,228	21.57
Greek (30)	81	0.78
Guyanese (24)	24	0.23
Hungarian (0)	17	0.16
Irish (258)	1,075	10.41
Italian (78)	429	4.15
Lithuanian (0)	11	0.11
Norwegian (20)	20	0.19
Polish (11)	144	1.39
Portuguese (46)	62	0.60
Russian (0)	160	1.55
Scotch-Irish (274)	574	5.56
Scottish (47)	204	1.98
Slovak (59)	106	1.03
Swedish (6)	22	0.21
Swiss (0)	6	0.06
Welsh (51)	75	0.73

Hispanic Origin	Population	%
Hispanic or Latino (of any race)	421	3.65
Central American, ex. Mexican	44	0.38
Costa Rican	2	0.02
Guatemalan	8	0.07
Honduran	8	0.07
Nicaraguan	2	0.02
Panamanian	8	0.07
Salvadoran	16	0.14
Cuban	66	0.57
Dominican Republic	27	0.23
Mexican	64	0.56
Puerto Rican	99	0.86
South American	88	0.76
Argentinean	4	0.03
Chilean	3	0.03
Colombian	47	0.41
Ecuadorian	9	0.08
Paraguayan	1	0.01
Peruvian	19	0.16
Uruguayan	1	0.01
Venezuelan	4	0.03
Other Hispanic or Latino	33	0.29

Race*	Population	%
African-American/Black (1,892)	2,014	17.47
Not Hispanic (1,870)	1,980	17.18
Hispanic (22)	34	0.29
American Indian/Alaska Native (52)	98	0.85
Not Hispanic (47)	82	0.71
Hispanic (5)	16	0.14
Cherokee (4)	25	0.22
Chickasaw (1)	1	0.01
Choctaw (3)	3	0.03

*Notes: † The Census 2010 population figure is used to calculate the percentages in the Hispanic Origin and Race categories. Ancestry percentages are based on the 2006-2010 American Community Survey population (not shown); ‡ Numbers in parentheses indicate the number of people reporting a single ancestry; * Numbers in parentheses indicate the number of persons reporting this race alone, not in combination with any other race; Please refer to the Explanation of Data for more information.*

SECTION TWO

Creek (1)	1	0.01
Lumbee (12)	15	0.13
Mexican American Ind. (4)	5	0.04
Navajo (1)	4	0.03
Spanish American Ind. (0)	2	0.02
Asian (522)	589	5.11
Not Hispanic (522)	584	5.07
Hispanic (0)	5	0.04
Chinese, ex. Taiwanese (103)	112	0.97
Filipino (32)	44	0.38
Hmong (18)	18	0.16
Indian (195)	211	1.83
Japanese (5)	10	0.09
Korean (63)	74	0.64
Laotian (12)	16	0.14
Malaysian (1)	1	0.01
Nepalese (13)	13	0.11
Pakistani (16)	18	0.16
Taiwanese (8)	10	0.09
Thai (2)	7	0.06
Vietnamese (37)	42	0.36
Hawaii Native/Pacific Islander (0)	8	0.07
Not Hispanic (0)	5	0.04
Hispanic (0)	3	0.03
Guamanian/Chamorro (0)	1	0.01
Native Hawaiian (0)	1	0.01
White (8,735)	8,915	77.35
Not Hispanic (8,455)	8,602	74.63
Hispanic (280)	313	2.72

Havelock

Place Type: City
County: Craven
Population: 20,735†

Ancestry‡	Population	%
African, Sub-Saharan (311)	470	2.28
African (228)	344	1.67
Cape Verdean (19)	55	0.27
Ethiopian (64)	64	0.31
Kenyan (0)	7	0.03
American (1,080)	1,080	5.24
Arab (0)	64	0.31
Lebanese (0)	62	0.30
Other Arab (0)	2	0.01
Australian (8)	15	0.07
Austrian (0)	8	0.04
Belgian (7)	33	0.16
Brazilian (0)	25	0.12
British (41)	163	0.79
Cajun (21)	21	0.10
Canadian (0)	25	0.12
Croatian (10)	10	0.05
Czech (0)	7	0.03
Czechoslovakian (11)	20	0.10
Danish (0)	8	0.04
Dutch (41)	450	2.18
Eastern European (17)	17	0.08
English (564)	1,823	8.84
European (224)	289	1.40
Finnish (0)	11	0.05
French, ex. Basque (91)	479	2.32
French Canadian (99)	186	0.90
German (939)	4,006	19.42
Greek (0)	23	0.11
Hungarian (17)	17	0.08
Iranian (10)	10	0.05
Irish (957)	3,269	15.85
Italian (420)	950	4.61
Lithuanian (12)	24	0.12
Macedonian (12)	12	0.06
Norwegian (74)	123	0.60
Pennsylvania German (0)	12	0.06
Polish (220)	608	2.95
Portuguese (32)	46	0.22
Russian (0)	104	0.50
Scandinavian (19)	130	0.63
Scotch-Irish (240)	568	2.75
Scottish (94)	330	1.60
Swedish (28)	165	0.80
Swiss (0)	13	0.06
Ukrainian (38)	49	0.24
Welsh (40)	115	0.56
West Indian, ex. Hispanic (317)	416	2.02
Belizean (0)	32	0.16
British West Indian (38)	38	0.18
Haitian (33)	42	0.20
Jamaican (202)	260	1.26
West Indian (44)	44	0.21
Yugoslavian (11)	11	0.05

Hispanic Origin	Population	%
Hispanic or Latino (of any race)	2,413	11.64
Central American, ex. Mexican	158	0.76
Costa Rican	2	0.01
Guatemalan	17	0.08
Honduran	35	0.17
Nicaraguan	19	0.09
Panamanian	16	0.08
Salvadoran	69	0.33
Cuban	64	0.31
Dominican Republic	102	0.49
Mexican	1,188	5.73
Puerto Rican	598	2.88
South American	130	0.63
Argentinean	10	0.05
Bolivian	11	0.05
Chilean	5	0.02
Colombian	60	0.29
Ecuadorian	25	0.12
Paraguayan	1	<0.01
Peruvian	12	0.06
Uruguayan	1	<0.01
Venezuelan	5	0.02
Other Hispanic or Latino	173	0.83

Race*	Population	%
African-American/Black (3,611)	4,092	19.73
Not Hispanic (3,475)	3,888	18.75
Hispanic (136)	204	0.98
American Indian/Alaska Native (155)	307	1.48
Not Hispanic (130)	259	1.25
Hispanic (25)	48	0.23
Apache (7)	11	0.05
Blackfeet (2)	5	0.02
Canadian/French Am. Ind. (0)	1	<0.01
Cherokee (23)	55	0.27
Chickasaw (2)	2	0.01
Chippewa (0)	2	0.01
Choctaw (1)	5	0.02
Cree (0)	1	<0.01
Creek (1)	2	0.01
Crow (0)	1	<0.01
Delaware (0)	5	0.02
Houma (1)	2	0.01
Iroquois (2)	5	0.02
Kiowa (2)	2	0.01
Lumbee (11)	13	0.06
Menominee (1)	1	<0.01
Mexican American Ind. (5)	7	0.03
Navajo (20)	23	0.11
Pima (0)	2	0.01
Potawatomi (0)	1	<0.01
Pueblo (4)	4	0.02
Seminole (1)	1	<0.01
Sioux (9)	16	0.08
Tlingit-Haida *(Alaska Native)* (0)	2	0.01
Yaqui (1)	1	<0.01
Asian (599)	925	4.46
Not Hispanic (580)	876	4.22
Hispanic (19)	49	0.24
Cambodian (5)	11	0.05
Chinese, ex. Taiwanese (26)	52	0.25
Filipino (278)	432	2.08
Hmong (7)	9	0.04
Indian (32)	40	0.19
Indonesian (4)	6	0.03
Japanese (113)	201	0.97
Korean (41)	70	0.34
Laotian (2)	3	0.01
Pakistani (2)	2	0.01
Taiwanese (2)	7	0.03
Thai (6)	21	0.10
Vietnamese (51)	67	0.32
Hawaii Native/Pacific Islander (68)	157	0.76
Not Hispanic (60)	130	0.63
Hispanic (8)	27	0.13
Guamanian/Chamorro (47)	67	0.32
Native Hawaiian (6)	35	0.17
Samoan (7)	15	0.07
White (14,513)	15,318	73.88
Not Hispanic (13,280)	13,916	67.11
Hispanic (1,233)	1,402	6.76

Henderson

Place Type: City
County: Vance
Population: 15,368†

Ancestry‡	Population	%
African, Sub-Saharan (68)	68	0.44
African (68)	68	0.44
American (1,984)	1,984	12.77
Arab (0)	31	0.20
Lebanese (0)	31	0.20
Armenian (0)	9	0.06
Austrian (10)	10	0.06
British (30)	30	0.19
Danish (9)	9	0.06
Dutch (0)	20	0.13
English (810)	1,164	7.49
European (8)	8	0.05
Finnish (12)	12	0.08
French, ex. Basque (26)	39	0.25
German (182)	387	2.49
Greek (0)	25	0.16
Hungarian (10)	10	0.06
Irish (158)	331	2.13
Italian (55)	136	0.88
Norwegian (6)	6	0.04
Portuguese (10)	10	0.06
Russian (0)	14	0.09
Scotch-Irish (63)	138	0.89
Scottish (12)	34	0.22
Welsh (14)	21	0.14
West Indian, ex. Hispanic (0)	27	0.17
Jamaican (0)	27	0.17

Hispanic Origin	Population	%
Hispanic or Latino (of any race)	982	6.39
Central American, ex. Mexican	46	0.30
Guatemalan	10	0.07
Honduran	9	0.06
Nicaraguan	1	0.01
Panamanian	8	0.05
Salvadoran	18	0.12
Cuban	2	0.01
Dominican Republic	4	0.03
Mexican	807	5.25
Puerto Rican	71	0.46
South American	8	0.05
Argentinean	1	0.01
Colombian	4	0.03
Peruvian	3	0.02
Other Hispanic or Latino	44	0.29

Race*	Population	%
African-American/Black (9,842)	9,996	65.04
Not Hispanic (9,748)	9,875	64.26
Hispanic (94)	121	0.79
American Indian/Alaska Native (48)	132	0.86
Not Hispanic (37)	107	0.70
Hispanic (11)	25	0.16
Blackfeet (0)	1	0.01
Cherokee (1)	26	0.17
Chickasaw (0)	1	0.01
Lumbee (5)	9	0.06
Mexican American Ind. (10)	12	0.08

*Notes: † The Census 2010 population figure is used to calculate the percentages in the Hispanic Origin and Race categories. Ancestry percentages are based on the 2006-2010 American Community Survey population (not shown); ‡ Numbers in parentheses indicate the number of people reporting a single ancestry; * Numbers in parentheses indicate the number of persons reporting this race alone, not in combination with any other race; Please refer to the Explanation of Data for more information.*

	Population	%
Navajo (3)	3	0.02
South American Ind. (0)	1	0.01
Asian (127)	146	0.95
Not Hispanic (127)	142	0.92
Hispanic (0)	4	0.03
Burmese (2)	2	0.01
Chinese, ex. Taiwanese (23)	24	0.16
Filipino (23)	24	0.16
Indian (40)	46	0.30
Japanese (1)	6	0.04
Korean (2)	3	0.02
Pakistani (1)	1	0.01
Thai (2)	2	0.01
Vietnamese (16)	17	0.11
Hawaii Native/Pacific Islander (0)	15	0.10
Not Hispanic (0)	13	0.08
Hispanic (0)	2	0.01
Guamanian/Chamorro (0)	2	0.01
Native Hawaiian (0)	1	0.01
White (4,611)	4,752	30.92
Not Hispanic (4,290)	4,403	28.65
Hispanic (321)	349	2.27

Hendersonville

Place Type: City
County: Henderson
Population: 13,137†

Ancestry‡	Population	%
African, Sub-Saharan (0)	9	0.07
Nigerian (0)	9	0.07
American (1,239)	1,239	9.60
Arab (12)	12	0.09
Egyptian (12)	12	0.09
Austrian (0)	9	0.07
British (43)	123	0.95
Canadian (15)	43	0.33
Celtic (0)	22	0.17
Croatian (14)	14	0.11
Czech (23)	34	0.26
Czechoslovakian (0)	11	0.09
Danish (0)	62	0.48
Dutch (50)	154	1.19
Eastern European (41)	41	0.32
English (764)	1,803	13.98
European (91)	91	0.71
Finnish (19)	25	0.19
French, ex. Basque (86)	360	2.79
French Canadian (28)	104	0.81
German (503)	1,672	12.96
Hungarian (16)	43	0.33
Irish (602)	1,717	13.31
Italian (107)	292	2.26
Lithuanian (0)	16	0.12
Norwegian (12)	113	0.88
Pennsylvania German (0)	15	0.12
Polish (73)	170	1.32
Portuguese (0)	38	0.29
Russian (34)	50	0.39
Scotch-Irish (535)	968	7.50
Scottish (139)	425	3.29
Slovak (0)	33	0.26
Slovene (0)	14	0.11
Swedish (77)	235	1.82
Turkish (0)	12	0.09
Ukrainian (8)	15	0.12
Welsh (0)	121	0.94
West Indian, ex. Hispanic (38)	52	0.40
Haitian (29)	29	0.22
Jamaican (9)	23	0.18

Hispanic Origin	Population	%
Hispanic or Latino (of any race)	1,774	13.50
Central American, ex. Mexican	89	0.68
Costa Rican	17	0.13
Guatemalan	18	0.14
Honduran	18	0.14
Nicaraguan	9	0.07
Panamanian	1	0.01
Salvadoran	25	0.19
Other Central American	1	0.01
Cuban	23	0.18
Dominican Republic	7	0.05
Mexican	1,410	10.73
Puerto Rican	74	0.56
South American	61	0.46
Argentinean	6	0.05
Bolivian	1	0.01
Chilean	3	0.02
Colombian	35	0.27
Ecuadorian	4	0.03
Peruvian	3	0.02
Uruguayan	4	0.03
Venezuelan	5	0.04
Other Hispanic or Latino	110	0.84

Race*	Population	%
African-American/Black (1,203)	1,346	10.25
Not Hispanic (1,183)	1,320	10.05
Hispanic (20)	26	0.20
American Indian/Alaska Native (59)	104	0.79
Not Hispanic (32)	67	0.51
Hispanic (27)	37	0.28
Apache (2)	4	0.03
Cherokee (10)	24	0.18
Chippewa (1)	1	0.01
Iroquois (1)	3	0.02
Lumbee (3)	7	0.05
Mexican American Ind. (11)	11	0.08
Navajo (0)	1	0.01
Potawatomi (1)	1	0.01
Seminole (0)	1	0.01
Shoshone (0)	1	0.01
Spanish American Ind. (5)	5	0.04
Asian (154)	203	1.55
Not Hispanic (150)	195	1.48
Hispanic (4)	8	0.06
Cambodian (12)	18	0.14
Chinese, ex. Taiwanese (35)	39	0.30
Filipino (15)	17	0.13
Indian (37)	48	0.37
Indonesian (0)	1	0.01
Japanese (5)	12	0.09
Korean (18)	36	0.27
Laotian (1)	1	0.01
Pakistani (7)	7	0.05
Sri Lankan (0)	1	0.01
Taiwanese (0)	1	0.01
Thai (6)	7	0.05
Vietnamese (5)	6	0.05
Hawaii Native/Pacific Islander (41)	52	0.40
Not Hispanic (35)	42	0.32
Hispanic (6)	10	0.08
Native Hawaiian (4)	4	0.03
Tongan (0)	1	0.01
White (10,475)	10,738	81.74
Not Hispanic (9,738)	9,911	75.44
Hispanic (737)	827	6.30

Hickory

Place Type: City
County: Catawba
Population: 40,010†

Ancestry‡	Population	%
African, Sub-Saharan (37)	55	0.14
African (37)	55	0.14
American (3,722)	3,722	9.32
Austrian (16)	64	0.16
Belgian (6)	11	0.03
British (56)	91	0.23
Canadian (45)	110	0.28
Celtic (0)	12	0.03
Czech (19)	25	0.06
Czechoslovakian (8)	8	0.02
Danish (0)	49	0.12
Dutch (104)	733	1.84
Eastern European (12)	12	0.03
English (2,480)	5,157	12.91
European (358)	358	0.90
French, ex. Basque (157)	690	1.73
French Canadian (0)	218	0.55
German (2,940)	7,114	17.82
Greek (32)	45	0.11
Hungarian (68)	125	0.31
Irish (1,379)	4,318	10.81
Italian (431)	1,146	2.87
Latvian (5)	19	0.05
Lithuanian (26)	52	0.13
Northern European (17)	17	0.04
Norwegian (21)	103	0.26
Pennsylvania German (5)	5	0.01
Polish (156)	346	0.87
Portuguese (0)	16	0.04
Romanian (52)	52	0.13
Russian (88)	207	0.52
Scotch-Irish (792)	1,622	4.06
Scottish (533)	1,616	4.05
Slovak (31)	113	0.28
Slovene (0)	13	0.03
Swedish (71)	134	0.34
Swiss (0)	70	0.18
Ukrainian (28)	70	0.18
Welsh (48)	117	0.29
West Indian, ex. Hispanic (7)	34	0.09
Dutch West Indian (7)	7	0.02
Jamaican (0)	11	0.03
Trinidadian/Tobagonian (0)	16	0.04

Hispanic Origin	Population	%
Hispanic or Latino (of any race)	4,544	11.36
Central American, ex. Mexican	401	1.00
Costa Rican	105	0.26
Guatemalan	108	0.27
Honduran	78	0.19
Nicaraguan	18	0.04
Panamanian	7	0.02
Salvadoran	83	0.21
Other Central American	2	<0.01
Cuban	82	0.20
Dominican Republic	37	0.09
Mexican	3,303	8.26
Puerto Rican	258	0.64
South American	250	0.62
Argentinean	13	0.03
Chilean	24	0.06
Colombian	107	0.27
Ecuadorian	16	0.04
Peruvian	61	0.15
Uruguayan	2	<0.01
Venezuelan	26	0.06
Other South American	1	<0.01
Other Hispanic or Latino	213	0.53

Race*	Population	%
African-American/Black (5,707)	6,254	15.63
Not Hispanic (5,638)	6,115	15.28
Hispanic (69)	139	0.35
American Indian/Alaska Native (131)	279	0.70
Not Hispanic (76)	202	0.50
Hispanic (55)	77	0.19
Alaska Athabascan *(Ala. Nat.)* (0)	3	0.01
Apache (0)	2	<0.01
Blackfeet (1)	9	0.02
Central American Ind. (1)	1	<0.01
Cherokee (19)	56	0.14
Chippewa (8)	9	0.02
Comanche (0)	1	<0.01
Creek (0)	4	0.01
Hopi (1)	1	<0.01
Iroquois (0)	1	<0.01
Lumbee (15)	20	0.05
Menominee (1)	1	<0.01
Navajo (0)	1	<0.01
Ottawa (1)	1	<0.01
Potawatomi (0)	5	0.01
Pueblo (1)	1	<0.01
Seminole (0)	1	<0.01

SECTION TWO

*Notes: † The Census 2010 population figure is used to calculate the percentages in the Hispanic Origin and Race categories. Ancestry percentages are based on the 2006-2010 American Community Survey population (not shown); ‡ Numbers in parentheses indicate the number of people reporting a single ancestry; * Numbers in parentheses indicate the number of persons reporting this race alone, not in combination with any other race; Please refer to the Explanation of Data for more information.*

Sioux (1)	1	<0.01
South American Ind. (1)	1	<0.01
Spanish American Ind. (0)	4	0.01
Yup'ik *(Alaska Native)* (0)	1	<0.01
Asian (1,262)	1,428	3.57
Not Hispanic (1,255)	1,405	3.51
Hispanic (7)	23	0.06
Cambodian (1)	3	0.01
Chinese, ex. Taiwanese (116)	134	0.33
Filipino (38)	56	0.14
Hmong (462)	479	1.20
Indian (129)	163	0.41
Indonesian (0)	1	<0.01
Japanese (43)	71	0.18
Korean (23)	41	0.10
Laotian (28)	34	0.08
Malaysian (0)	1	<0.01
Pakistani (32)	42	0.10
Sri Lankan (2)	2	<0.01
Taiwanese (1)	1	<0.01
Thai (25)	34	0.08
Vietnamese (297)	315	0.79
Hawaii Native/Pacific Islander (15)	30	0.07
Not Hispanic (9)	22	0.05
Hispanic (6)	8	0.02
Guamanian/Chamorro (3)	4	0.01
Native Hawaiian (6)	15	0.04
Samoan (1)	4	0.01
White (29,948)	30,721	76.78
Not Hispanic (27,750)	28,366	70.90
Hispanic (2,198)	2,355	5.89

High Point

Place Type: City
County: Guilford
Population: 104,371†

Ancestry‡	Population	%
African, Sub-Saharan (1,677)	1,717	1.70
African (496)	536	0.53
Ethiopian (266)	266	0.26
Ghanaian (27)	27	0.03
Liberian (376)	376	0.37
Nigerian (110)	110	0.11
Sudanese (327)	327	0.32
Other Sub-Saharan African (75)	75	0.07
American (5,633)	5,633	5.58
Arab (18)	134	0.13
Arab (0)	13	0.01
Lebanese (11)	114	0.11
Syrian (7)	7	0.01
Armenian (73)	73	0.07
Australian (0)	8	0.01
Austrian (19)	162	0.16
Belgian (0)	15	0.01
British (91)	155	0.15
Bulgarian (0)	10	0.01
Canadian (12)	69	0.07
Croatian (28)	98	0.10
Czech (54)	432	0.43
Czechoslovakian (0)	66	0.07
Danish (60)	102	0.10
Dutch (161)	959	0.95
Eastern European (15)	15	0.01
English (4,724)	9,115	9.03
European (771)	974	0.97
Finnish (0)	70	0.07
French, ex. Basque (301)	1,210	1.20
French Canadian (121)	335	0.33
German (3,102)	9,603	9.52
Greek (211)	468	0.46
Guyanese (0)	207	0.21
Hungarian (70)	265	0.26
Iranian (9)	9	0.01
Irish (2,379)	7,037	6.97
Italian (1,172)	2,523	2.50
Latvian (0)	17	0.02
Lithuanian (28)	78	0.08
Northern European (11)	11	0.01
Norwegian (208)	629	0.62
Pennsylvania German (12)	12	0.01
Polish (398)	983	0.97
Portuguese (0)	253	0.25
Romanian (19)	31	0.03
Russian (56)	196	0.19
Scandinavian (0)	19	0.02
Scotch-Irish (1,704)	3,160	3.13
Scottish (986)	2,043	2.02
Serbian (64)	250	0.25
Slavic (36)	109	0.11
Slovak (64)	96	0.10
Slovene (17)	34	0.03
Swedish (161)	838	0.83
Swiss (18)	73	0.07
Ukrainian (14)	239	0.24
Welsh (170)	402	0.40
West Indian, ex. Hispanic (436)	626	0.62
Bahamian (155)	155	0.15
British West Indian (0)	22	0.02
Dutch West Indian (7)	24	0.02
Haitian (115)	115	0.11
Jamaican (71)	116	0.11
Trinidadian/Tobagonian (88)	186	0.18
West Indian (0)	8	0.01
Yugoslavian (88)	269	0.27

Hispanic Origin	Population	%
Hispanic or Latino (of any race)	8,847	8.48
Central American, ex. Mexican	1,086	1.04
Costa Rican	43	0.04
Guatemalan	157	0.15
Honduran	380	0.36
Nicaraguan	21	0.02
Panamanian	72	0.07
Salvadoran	408	0.39
Other Central American	5	<0.01
Cuban	253	0.24
Dominican Republic	258	0.25
Mexican	5,092	4.88
Puerto Rican	883	0.85
South American	700	0.67
Argentinean	37	0.04
Bolivian	18	0.02
Chilean	49	0.05
Colombian	318	0.30
Ecuadorian	93	0.09
Paraguayan	1	<0.01
Peruvian	131	0.13
Uruguayan	6	0.01
Venezuelan	45	0.04
Other South American	2	<0.01
Other Hispanic or Latino	575	0.55

Race*	Population	%
African-American/Black (34,394)	35,767	34.27
Not Hispanic (33,983)	35,168	33.70
Hispanic (411)	599	0.57
American Indian/Alaska Native (579)	1,205	1.15
Not Hispanic (436)	981	0.94
Hispanic (143)	224	0.21
Apache (6)	13	0.01
Blackfeet (3)	22	0.02
Canadian/French Am. Ind. (0)	1	<0.01
Central American Ind. (6)	8	0.01
Cherokee (56)	216	0.21
Cheyenne (0)	2	<0.01
Chippewa (5)	13	0.01
Choctaw (3)	13	0.01
Comanche (3)	7	0.01
Cree (0)	2	<0.01
Creek (2)	7	0.01
Crow (0)	1	<0.01
Delaware (1)	2	<0.01
Hopi (0)	1	<0.01
Inupiat *(Alaska Native)* (0)	1	<0.01
Iroquois (7)	17	0.02
Lumbee (107)	161	0.15
Mexican American Ind. (38)	52	0.05
Navajo (2)	11	0.01
Ottawa (1)	2	<0.01
Potawatomi (0)	3	<0.01
Pueblo (2)	3	<0.01
Seminole (1)	2	<0.01
Sioux (1)	9	0.01
South American Ind. (1)	5	<0.01
Spanish American Ind. (1)	1	<0.01
Yaqui (0)	1	<0.01
Yuman (1)	1	<0.01
Asian (6,345)	6,916	6.63
Not Hispanic (6,302)	6,828	6.54
Hispanic (43)	88	0.08
Bangladeshi (9)	16	0.02
Bhutanese (44)	61	0.06
Burmese (384)	406	0.39
Cambodian (72)	111	0.11
Chinese, ex. Taiwanese (387)	468	0.45
Filipino (352)	459	0.44
Hmong (11)	13	0.01
Indian (978)	1,152	1.10
Indonesian (1)	1	<0.01
Japanese (79)	119	0.11
Korean (560)	630	0.60
Laotian (515)	579	0.55
Malaysian (12)	12	0.01
Nepalese (130)	147	0.14
Pakistani (1,293)	1,399	1.34
Sri Lankan (7)	7	0.01
Taiwanese (16)	21	0.02
Thai (56)	81	0.08
Vietnamese (1,032)	1,085	1.04
Hawaii Native/Pacific Islander (45)	135	0.13
Not Hispanic (38)	104	0.10
Hispanic (7)	31	0.03
Guamanian/Chamorro (13)	27	0.03
Native Hawaiian (5)	31	0.03
Samoan (6)	15	0.01
White (55,989)	57,866	55.44
Not Hispanic (52,612)	54,075	51.81
Hispanic (3,377)	3,791	3.63

Holly Springs

Place Type: Town
County: Wake
Population: 24,661†

Ancestry‡	Population	%
African, Sub-Saharan (109)	118	0.54
African (10)	19	0.09
Ethiopian (43)	43	0.20
Kenyan (17)	17	0.08
Sierra Leonean (30)	30	0.14
South African (9)	9	0.04
American (1,541)	1,541	7.01
Arab (39)	175	0.80
Arab (9)	9	0.04
Jordanian (10)	10	0.05
Lebanese (0)	53	0.24
Syrian (0)	24	0.11
Other Arab (20)	79	0.36
Armenian (14)	43	0.20
Austrian (10)	22	0.10
Belgian (35)	103	0.47
British (157)	168	0.76
Canadian (24)	96	0.44
Czech (0)	127	0.58
Czechoslovakian (0)	92	0.42
Danish (10)	133	0.61
Dutch (200)	412	1.88
English (913)	2,932	13.35
European (412)	553	2.52
Finnish (0)	11	0.05
French, ex. Basque (114)	702	3.20
French Canadian (101)	218	0.99
German (1,294)	4,173	19.00
Greek (11)	54	0.25
Hungarian (49)	140	0.64
Irish (762)	3,353	15.26
Italian (832)	2,339	10.65

*Notes: † The Census 2010 population figure is used to calculate the percentages in the Hispanic Origin and Race categories. Ancestry percentages are based on the 2006-2010 American Community Survey population (not shown); ‡ Numbers in parentheses indicate the number of people reporting a single ancestry; * Numbers in parentheses indicate the number of persons reporting this race alone, not in combination with any other race; Please refer to the Explanation of Data for more information.*

Ancestry	Population	%
Lithuanian (10)	42	0.19
Norwegian (47)	191	0.87
Polish (336)	1,517	6.91
Portuguese (0)	63	0.29
Romanian (12)	48	0.22
Russian (65)	198	0.90
Scandinavian (30)	48	0.22
Scotch-Irish (309)	728	3.31
Scottish (201)	730	3.32
Serbian (0)	33	0.15
Slavic (11)	47	0.21
Slovak (0)	56	0.25
Slovene (0)	25	0.11
Swedish (38)	237	1.08
Swiss (0)	60	0.27
Turkish (19)	78	0.36
Ukrainian (42)	129	0.59
Welsh (0)	47	0.21
West Indian, ex. Hispanic (32)	32	0.15
Jamaican (32)	32	0.15
Yugoslavian (12)	22	0.10

Hispanic Origin	Population	%
Hispanic or Latino (of any race)	1,544	6.26
Central American, ex. Mexican	149	0.60
Costa Rican	19	0.08
Guatemalan	37	0.15
Honduran	26	0.11
Nicaraguan	23	0.09
Panamanian	8	0.03
Salvadoran	36	0.15
Cuban	83	0.34
Dominican Republic	32	0.13
Mexican	567	2.30
Puerto Rican	304	1.23
South American	277	1.12
Argentinean	20	0.08
Bolivian	3	0.01
Chilean	19	0.08
Colombian	104	0.42
Ecuadorian	55	0.22
Peruvian	45	0.18
Uruguayan	7	0.03
Venezuelan	24	0.10
Other Hispanic or Latino	132	0.54

Race*	Population	%
African-American/Black (3,101)	3,398	13.78
Not Hispanic (3,053)	3,321	13.47
Hispanic (48)	77	0.31
American Indian/Alaska Native (103)	239	0.97
Not Hispanic (75)	193	0.78
Hispanic (28)	46	0.19
Alaska Athabascan *(Ala. Nat.)* (0)	1	<0.01
Apache (3)	3	0.01
Arapaho (0)	5	0.02
Blackfeet (0)	6	0.02
Canadian/French Am. Ind. (1)	1	<0.01
Cherokee (13)	46	0.19
Cheyenne (1)	3	0.01
Chickasaw (0)	1	<0.01
Choctaw (0)	1	<0.01
Comanche (1)	1	<0.01
Creek (0)	1	<0.01
Houma (0)	3	0.01
Iroquois (8)	9	0.04
Lumbee (19)	33	0.13
Mexican American Ind. (1)	2	0.01
Navajo (5)	5	0.02
Seminole (0)	1	<0.01
Sioux (0)	4	0.02
South American Ind. (3)	3	0.01
Asian (724)	931	3.78
Not Hispanic (717)	915	3.71
Hispanic (7)	16	0.06
Bangladeshi (8)	12	0.05
Cambodian (0)	1	<0.01
Chinese, ex. Taiwanese (92)	127	0.51
Filipino (88)	140	0.57
Indian (326)	362	1.47
Indonesian (13)	13	0.05
Japanese (18)	54	0.22
Korean (59)	89	0.36
Laotian (14)	14	0.06
Nepalese (5)	5	0.02
Pakistani (11)	14	0.06
Taiwanese (9)	19	0.08
Thai (14)	14	0.06
Vietnamese (46)	66	0.27
Hawaii Native/Pacific Islander (13)	32	0.13
Not Hispanic (13)	28	0.11
Hispanic (0)	4	0.02
Guamanian/Chamorro (6)	6	0.02
Native Hawaiian (0)	8	0.03
Samoan (0)	11	0.04
Tongan (0)	4	0.02
White (19,674)	20,224	82.01
Not Hispanic (18,703)	19,163	77.71
Hispanic (971)	1,061	4.30

Hope Mills

Place Type: Town
County: Cumberland
Population: 15,176†

Ancestry‡	Population	%
African, Sub-Saharan (65)	79	0.55
African (65)	79	0.55
American (1,297)	1,297	9.00
Arab (0)	22	0.15
Arab (0)	22	0.15
Austrian (0)	41	0.28
British (29)	37	0.26
Cajun (0)	18	0.12
Canadian (12)	12	0.08
Czech (12)	12	0.08
Danish (30)	37	0.26
Dutch (26)	119	0.83
Eastern European (18)	18	0.12
English (392)	1,181	8.19
European (183)	183	1.27
Finnish (14)	44	0.31
French, ex. Basque (21)	603	4.18
French Canadian (39)	68	0.47
German (617)	1,749	12.13
German Russian (17)	17	0.12
Greek (15)	15	0.10
Hungarian (45)	53	0.37
Irish (307)	1,271	8.82
Italian (188)	420	2.91
Lithuanian (0)	5	0.03
Norwegian (4)	62	0.43
Pennsylvania German (0)	17	0.12
Polish (54)	187	1.30
Portuguese (0)	14	0.10
Russian (0)	112	0.78
Scotch-Irish (235)	654	4.54
Scottish (46)	202	1.40
Slovak (0)	8	0.06
Swedish (15)	126	0.87
Turkish (25)	25	0.17
Ukrainian (0)	19	0.13
Welsh (0)	71	0.49
West Indian, ex. Hispanic (300)	330	2.29
Bahamian (0)	11	0.08
Jamaican (126)	126	0.87
Trinidadian/Tobagonian (0)	19	0.13
West Indian (174)	174	1.21

Hispanic Origin	Population	%
Hispanic or Latino (of any race)	1,519	10.01
Central American, ex. Mexican	179	1.18
Costa Rican	2	0.01
Guatemalan	12	0.08
Honduran	23	0.15
Nicaraguan	18	0.12
Panamanian	88	0.58
Salvadoran	28	0.18
Other Central American	8	0.05
Cuban	64	0.42
Dominican Republic	49	0.32
Mexican	390	2.57
Puerto Rican	649	4.28
South American	72	0.47
Bolivian	2	0.01
Chilean	6	0.04
Colombian	29	0.19
Ecuadorian	17	0.11
Peruvian	12	0.08
Uruguayan	1	0.01
Venezuelan	5	0.03
Other Hispanic or Latino	116	0.76

Race*	Population	%
African-American/Black (4,025)	4,387	28.91
Not Hispanic (3,885)	4,149	27.34
Hispanic (140)	238	1.57
American Indian/Alaska Native (294)	523	3.45
Not Hispanic (269)	466	3.07
Hispanic (25)	57	0.38
Alaska Athabascan *(Ala. Nat.)* (0)	1	0.01
Aleut *(Alaska Native)* (0)	1	0.01
Blackfeet (0)	3	0.02
Central American Ind. (2)	2	0.01
Cherokee (17)	60	0.40
Chickasaw (4)	4	0.03
Choctaw (4)	9	0.06
Creek (3)	3	0.02
Delaware (0)	1	0.01
Iroquois (8)	13	0.09
Kiowa (1)	1	0.01
Lumbee (140)	177	1.17
Menominee (2)	3	0.02
Mexican American Ind. (6)	10	0.07
Navajo (1)	1	0.01
Potawatomi (0)	2	0.01
Sioux (0)	9	0.06
South American Ind. (2)	7	0.05
Asian (275)	445	2.93
Not Hispanic (267)	412	2.71
Hispanic (8)	33	0.22
Cambodian (0)	1	0.01
Chinese, ex. Taiwanese (27)	47	0.31
Filipino (69)	114	0.75
Indian (22)	27	0.18
Indonesian (0)	2	0.01
Japanese (15)	58	0.38
Korean (87)	143	0.94
Laotian (1)	4	0.03
Pakistani (0)	2	0.01
Taiwanese (1)	1	0.01
Thai (12)	20	0.13
Vietnamese (27)	31	0.20
Hawaii Native/Pacific Islander (39)	74	0.49
Not Hispanic (32)	50	0.33
Hispanic (7)	24	0.16
Guamanian/Chamorro (17)	27	0.18
Native Hawaiian (3)	20	0.13
Samoan (5)	7	0.05
White (9,392)	9,980	65.76
Not Hispanic (8,633)	9,101	59.97
Hispanic (759)	879	5.79

Huntersville

Place Type: Town
County: Mecklenburg
Population: 46,773†

Ancestry‡	Population	%
African, Sub-Saharan (61)	104	0.24
African (61)	104	0.24
Albanian (0)	17	0.04
American (2,274)	2,274	5.28
Arab (191)	341	0.79
Arab (36)	46	0.11
Egyptian (99)	99	0.23
Jordanian (39)	39	0.09
Lebanese (8)	133	0.31

*Notes: † The Census 2010 population figure is used to calculate the percentages in the Hispanic Origin and Race categories. Ancestry percentages are based on the 2006-2010 American Community Survey population (not shown); ‡ Numbers in parentheses indicate the number of people reporting a single ancestry; * Numbers in parentheses indicate the number of persons reporting this race alone, not in combination with any other race; Please refer to the Explanation of Data for more information.*

Syrian (9)	24	0.06
Armenian (43)	110	0.26
Austrian (58)	96	0.22
Belgian (0)	103	0.24
Brazilian (0)	37	0.09
British (144)	443	1.03
Canadian (123)	148	0.34
Croatian (62)	180	0.42
Czech (20)	197	0.46
Czechoslovakian (15)	68	0.16
Danish (19)	266	0.62
Dutch (257)	772	1.79
Eastern European (50)	57	0.13
English (2,469)	6,305	14.63
European (547)	565	1.31
Finnish (10)	65	0.15
French, ex. Basque (196)	1,421	3.30
French Canadian (239)	463	1.07
German (2,602)	8,620	20.00
Greek (202)	309	0.72
Guyanese (0)	44	0.10
Hungarian (56)	280	0.65
Irish (1,788)	6,643	15.41
Italian (1,177)	4,606	10.69
Latvian (23)	23	0.05
Lithuanian (0)	105	0.24
Macedonian (0)	11	0.03
Northern European (29)	29	0.07
Norwegian (156)	515	1.19
Pennsylvania German (13)	78	0.18
Polish (524)	1,552	3.60
Portuguese (17)	80	0.19
Romanian (61)	188	0.44
Russian (169)	509	1.18
Scandinavian (47)	144	0.33
Scotch-Irish (1,114)	2,052	4.76
Scottish (602)	1,554	3.61
Serbian (17)	42	0.10
Slavic (11)	96	0.22
Slovak (80)	277	0.64
Slovene (11)	24	0.06
Swedish (79)	480	1.11
Swiss (33)	194	0.45
Ukrainian (59)	207	0.48
Welsh (129)	574	1.33
West Indian, ex. Hispanic (50)	96	0.22
Jamaican (50)	96	0.22
Yugoslavian (54)	68	0.16

Hispanic Origin	Population	%
Hispanic or Latino (of any race)	3,441	7.36
Central American, ex. Mexican	222	0.47
Costa Rican	23	0.05
Guatemalan	47	0.10
Honduran	54	0.12
Nicaraguan	16	0.03
Panamanian	20	0.04
Salvadoran	62	0.13
Cuban	186	0.40
Dominican Republic	81	0.17
Mexican	1,746	3.73
Puerto Rican	503	1.08
South American	475	1.02
Argentinean	25	0.05
Bolivian	6	0.01
Chilean	10	0.02
Colombian	206	0.44
Ecuadorian	79	0.17
Paraguayan	2	<0.01
Peruvian	82	0.18
Uruguayan	11	0.02
Venezuelan	52	0.11
Other South American	2	<0.01
Other Hispanic or Latino	228	0.49

Race*	Population	%
African-American/Black (4,404)	4,806	10.28
Not Hispanic (4,320)	4,672	9.99
Hispanic (84)	134	0.29
American Indian/Alaska Native (163)	387	0.83
Not Hispanic (107)	311	0.66
Hispanic (56)	76	0.16
Apache (0)	1	<0.01
Blackfeet (0)	12	0.03
Central American Ind. (1)	1	<0.01
Cherokee (11)	75	0.16
Cheyenne (0)	2	<0.01
Chickasaw (1)	1	<0.01
Chippewa (3)	5	0.01
Choctaw (9)	12	0.03
Creek (0)	5	0.01
Houma (0)	1	<0.01
Iroquois (3)	7	0.01
Lumbee (32)	42	0.09
Menominee (1)	2	<0.01
Mexican American Ind. (20)	20	0.04
Ottawa (0)	1	<0.01
Paiute (0)	3	0.01
Potawatomi (2)	2	<0.01
Seminole (0)	2	<0.01
Shoshone (1)	5	0.01
Sioux (0)	2	<0.01
South American Ind. (0)	3	0.01
Tlingit-Haida *(Alaska Native)* (0)	1	<0.01
Asian (1,250)	1,562	3.34
Not Hispanic (1,234)	1,523	3.26
Hispanic (16)	39	0.08
Burmese (2)	3	0.01
Cambodian (6)	9	0.02
Chinese, ex. Taiwanese (276)	337	0.72
Filipino (128)	219	0.47
Hmong (3)	4	0.01
Indian (490)	521	1.11
Indonesian (7)	7	0.01
Japanese (46)	103	0.22
Korean (97)	147	0.31
Laotian (22)	28	0.06
Malaysian (4)	7	0.01
Pakistani (12)	18	0.04
Taiwanese (3)	4	0.01
Thai (11)	23	0.05
Vietnamese (107)	135	0.29
Hawaii Native/Pacific Islander (19)	51	0.11
Not Hispanic (17)	45	0.10
Hispanic (2)	6	0.01
Fijian (1)	3	0.01
Guamanian/Chamorro (2)	8	0.02
Native Hawaiian (4)	12	0.03
Samoan (0)	7	0.01
White (38,730)	39,603	84.67
Not Hispanic (36,791)	37,491	80.16
Hispanic (1,939)	2,112	4.52

Indian Trail

Place Type: Town
County: Union
Population: 33,518†

Ancestry‡	Population	%
African, Sub-Saharan (198)	232	0.76
African (50)	76	0.25
Ethiopian (89)	89	0.29
Nigerian (35)	35	0.12
South African (24)	32	0.11
Albanian (0)	8	0.03
American (3,931)	3,931	12.95
Arab (81)	142	0.47
Jordanian (81)	81	0.27
Moroccan (0)	11	0.04
Syrian (0)	32	0.11
Other Arab (0)	18	0.06
Armenian (121)	121	0.40
Austrian (0)	15	0.05
Belgian (0)	4	0.01
Brazilian (150)	150	0.49
British (40)	188	0.62
Bulgarian (15)	26	0.09
Canadian (45)	90	0.30
Croatian (0)	13	0.04
Czech (0)	58	0.19
Danish (74)	122	0.40
Dutch (35)	391	1.29
English (1,139)	2,755	9.07
European (227)	236	0.78
Finnish (13)	22	0.07
French, ex. Basque (79)	744	2.45
French Canadian (121)	321	1.06
German (1,337)	4,655	15.33
Greek (0)	112	0.37
Hungarian (32)	159	0.52
Iranian (37)	37	0.12
Irish (1,321)	4,078	13.43
Israeli (0)	7	0.02
Italian (1,014)	2,581	8.50
Latvian (0)	18	0.06
Lithuanian (0)	11	0.04
Northern European (20)	20	0.07
Norwegian (61)	167	0.55
Polish (180)	766	2.52
Portuguese (22)	22	0.07
Romanian (13)	85	0.28
Russian (197)	408	1.34
Scotch-Irish (936)	1,640	5.40
Scottish (295)	703	2.32
Serbian (9)	48	0.16
Slovak (14)	35	0.12
Swedish (44)	232	0.76
Swiss (14)	78	0.26
Ukrainian (272)	418	1.38
Welsh (27)	266	0.88
West Indian, ex. Hispanic (36)	36	0.12
Jamaican (36)	36	0.12
Yugoslavian (47)	84	0.28

Hispanic Origin	Population	%
Hispanic or Latino (of any race)	3,658	10.91
Central American, ex. Mexican	317	0.95
Costa Rican	40	0.12
Guatemalan	51	0.15
Honduran	19	0.06
Nicaraguan	29	0.09
Panamanian	25	0.07
Salvadoran	145	0.43
Other Central American	8	0.02
Cuban	136	0.41
Dominican Republic	120	0.36
Mexican	1,613	4.81
Puerto Rican	524	1.56
South American	706	2.11
Argentinean	47	0.14
Bolivian	7	0.02
Chilean	18	0.05
Colombian	316	0.94
Ecuadorian	178	0.53
Paraguayan	1	<0.01
Peruvian	95	0.28
Uruguayan	3	0.01
Venezuelan	38	0.11
Other South American	3	0.01
Other Hispanic or Latino	242	0.72

Race*	Population	%
African-American/Black (3,341)	3,656	10.91
Not Hispanic (3,241)	3,512	10.48
Hispanic (100)	144	0.43
American Indian/Alaska Native (179)	359	1.07
Not Hispanic (149)	311	0.93
Hispanic (30)	48	0.14
Aleut *(Alaska Native)* (3)	3	0.01
Apache (0)	3	0.01
Blackfeet (0)	3	0.01
Cherokee (30)	90	0.27
Chippewa (0)	2	0.01
Choctaw (1)	6	0.02
Creek (0)	1	<0.01
Delaware (1)	1	<0.01
Hopi (0)	5	0.01
Houma (1)	1	<0.01
Iroquois (5)	12	0.04

*Notes: † The Census 2010 population figure is used to calculate the percentages in the Hispanic Origin and Race categories. Ancestry percentages are based on the 2006-2010 American Community Survey population (not shown); ‡ Numbers in parentheses indicate the number of people reporting a single ancestry; * Numbers in parentheses indicate the number of persons reporting this race alone, not in combination with any other race; Please refer to the Explanation of Data for more information.*

Kiowa (1)	1	<0.01
Lumbee (50)	86	0.26
Mexican American Ind. (8)	9	0.03
Ottawa (3)	3	0.01
Potawatomi (0)	1	<0.01
Sioux (1)	1	<0.01
South American Ind. (0)	3	0.01
Spanish American Ind. (1)	3	0.01
Yakama (0)	1	<0.01
Yaqui (1)	1	<0.01
Asian (589)	781	2.33
Not Hispanic (586)	747	2.23
Hispanic (3)	34	0.10
Bangladeshi (0)	2	0.01
Burmese (1)	1	<0.01
Cambodian (9)	10	0.03
Chinese, ex. Taiwanese (76)	99	0.30
Filipino (79)	143	0.43
Hmong (1)	2	0.01
Indian (125)	146	0.44
Indonesian (12)	15	0.04
Japanese (22)	36	0.11
Korean (99)	128	0.38
Laotian (3)	10	0.03
Pakistani (3)	4	0.01
Sri Lankan (1)	2	0.01
Taiwanese (0)	1	<0.01
Thai (5)	11	0.03
Vietnamese (130)	145	0.43
Hawaii Native/Pacific Islander (9)	33	0.10
Not Hispanic (8)	26	0.08
Hispanic (1)	7	0.02
Guamanian/Chamorro (5)	8	0.02
Native Hawaiian (1)	9	0.03
Samoan (2)	4	0.01
White (27,160)	27,816	82.99
Not Hispanic (25,220)	25,698	76.67
Hispanic (1,940)	2,118	6.32

Jacksonville

Place Type: City
County: Onslow
Population: 70,145†

Ancestry‡	Population	%
Afghan (5)	5	0.01
African, Sub-Saharan (512)	1,157	1.68
African (500)	1,109	1.61
Cape Verdean (0)	12	0.02
Nigerian (0)	14	0.02
Senegalese (12)	12	0.02
South African (0)	10	0.01
American (2,778)	2,778	4.03
Arab (173)	306	0.44
Arab (0)	15	0.02
Egyptian (7)	7	0.01
Iraqi (46)	46	0.07
Lebanese (86)	133	0.19
Syrian (16)	76	0.11
Other Arab (18)	29	0.04
Armenian (16)	16	0.02
Austrian (0)	30	0.04
Belgian (19)	31	0.04
Brazilian (14)	32	0.05
British (279)	525	0.76
Cajun (0)	48	0.07
Canadian (43)	168	0.24
Carpatho Rusyn (11)	11	0.02
Celtic (0)	12	0.02
Croatian (1)	1	<0.01
Cypriot (19)	19	0.03
Czech (50)	156	0.23
Czechoslovakian (13)	48	0.07
Danish (37)	194	0.28
Dutch (129)	606	0.88
Eastern European (26)	26	0.04
English (1,635)	5,174	7.50
European (818)	889	1.29
Finnish (22)	88	0.13
French, ex. Basque (448)	2,249	3.26
French Canadian (244)	505	0.73
German (3,786)	12,255	17.76
Greek (54)	161	0.23
Guyanese (59)	59	0.09
Hungarian (51)	377	0.55
Irish (3,487)	11,545	16.73
Israeli (9)	25	0.04
Italian (1,684)	4,366	6.33
Lithuanian (9)	33	0.05
Luxemburger (10)	22	0.03
New Zealander (0)	23	0.03
Norwegian (129)	487	0.71
Pennsylvania German (39)	39	0.06
Polish (540)	1,751	2.54
Portuguese (177)	317	0.46
Romanian (83)	102	0.15
Russian (155)	471	0.68
Scandinavian (30)	120	0.17
Scotch-Irish (939)	1,730	2.51
Scottish (703)	1,917	2.78
Serbian (52)	95	0.14
Slavic (12)	54	0.08
Slovak (22)	74	0.11
Slovene (14)	14	0.02
Swedish (161)	661	0.96
Swiss (19)	95	0.14
Ukrainian (38)	120	0.17
Welsh (129)	397	0.58
West Indian, ex. Hispanic (440)	773	1.12
Barbadian (6)	6	0.01
Belizean (0)	15	0.02
Dutch West Indian (0)	13	0.02
Haitian (65)	89	0.13
Jamaican (223)	450	0.65
Trinidadian/Tobagonian (35)	52	0.08
West Indian (111)	148	0.21
Yugoslavian (0)	72	0.10

Hispanic Origin	Population	%
Hispanic or Latino (of any race)	9,106	12.98
Central American, ex. Mexican	641	0.91
Costa Rican	43	0.06
Guatemalan	111	0.16
Honduran	90	0.13
Nicaraguan	80	0.11
Panamanian	115	0.16
Salvadoran	196	0.28
Other Central American	6	0.01
Cuban	367	0.52
Dominican Republic	413	0.59
Mexican	4,045	5.77
Puerto Rican	2,356	3.36
South American	577	0.82
Argentinean	23	0.03
Bolivian	27	0.04
Chilean	36	0.05
Colombian	249	0.35
Ecuadorian	95	0.14
Paraguayan	3	<0.01
Peruvian	85	0.12
Uruguayan	4	0.01
Venezuelan	44	0.06
Other South American	11	0.02
Other Hispanic or Latino	707	1.01

Race*	Population	%
African-American/Black (14,055)	15,798	22.52
Not Hispanic (13,453)	14,855	21.18
Hispanic (602)	943	1.34
American Indian/Alaska Native (502)	1,150	1.64
Not Hispanic (390)	899	1.28
Hispanic (112)	251	0.36
Alaska Athabascan *(Ala. Nat.)* (1)	1	<0.01
Apache (11)	17	0.02
Arapaho (2)	2	<0.01
Blackfeet (9)	45	0.06
Canadian/French Am. Ind. (1)	2	<0.01
Central American Ind. (0)	4	0.01
Cherokee (58)	220	0.31
Cheyenne (1)	1	<0.01
Chickasaw (3)	5	0.01
Chippewa (15)	23	0.03
Choctaw (9)	17	0.02
Cree (0)	2	<0.01
Creek (5)	8	0.01
Crow (0)	1	<0.01
Delaware (1)	2	<0.01
Hopi (1)	3	<0.01
Houma (2)	2	<0.01
Inupiat *(Alaska Native)* (0)	6	0.01
Iroquois (9)	24	0.03
Kiowa (3)	4	0.01
Lumbee (51)	77	0.11
Menominee (1)	1	<0.01
Mexican American Ind. (19)	25	0.04
Navajo (44)	52	0.07
Ottawa (1)	2	<0.01
Paiute (2)	2	<0.01
Pima (0)	4	0.01
Potawatomi (1)	7	0.01
Pueblo (2)	7	0.01
Puget Sound Salish (2)	4	0.01
Seminole (2)	7	0.01
Shoshone (1)	1	<0.01
Sioux (15)	31	0.04
South American Ind. (1)	2	<0.01
Spanish American Ind. (1)	1	<0.01
Tohono O'Odham (2)	2	<0.01
Yakama (1)	5	0.01
Yaqui (1)	3	<0.01
Asian (1,748)	2,775	3.96
Not Hispanic (1,653)	2,531	3.61
Hispanic (95)	244	0.35
Bangladeshi (1)	2	<0.01
Burmese (2)	3	<0.01
Cambodian (19)	24	0.03
Chinese, ex. Taiwanese (168)	271	0.39
Filipino (689)	1,167	1.66
Hmong (33)	33	0.05
Indian (130)	219	0.31
Indonesian (11)	16	0.02
Japanese (201)	449	0.64
Korean (129)	229	0.33
Laotian (35)	45	0.06
Malaysian (2)	3	<0.01
Pakistani (13)	17	0.02
Taiwanese (4)	5	0.01
Thai (53)	87	0.12
Vietnamese (156)	212	0.30
Hawaii Native/Pacific Islander (208)	432	0.62
Not Hispanic (184)	376	0.54
Hispanic (24)	56	0.08
Fijian (1)	2	<0.01
Guamanian/Chamorro (54)	93	0.13
Native Hawaiian (48)	144	0.21
Samoan (35)	67	0.10
Tongan (0)	1	<0.01
White (47,460)	50,136	71.47
Not Hispanic (42,797)	44,804	63.87
Hispanic (4,663)	5,332	7.60

Kannapolis

Place Type: City
County: Cabarrus
Population: 42,625†

Ancestry‡	Population	%
African, Sub-Saharan (428)	443	1.06
African (428)	443	1.06
American (4,085)	4,085	9.80
Arab (7)	43	0.10
Lebanese (7)	43	0.10
Armenian (14)	14	0.03
Austrian (0)	35	0.08
British (32)	140	0.34
Canadian (54)	54	0.13
Croatian (0)	14	0.03
Czech (0)	37	0.09

SECTION TWO

*Notes: † The Census 2010 population figure is used to calculate the percentages in the Hispanic Origin and Race categories. Ancestry percentages are based on the 2006-2010 American Community Survey population (not shown); ‡ Numbers in parentheses indicate the number of people reporting a single ancestry; * Numbers in parentheses indicate the number of persons reporting this race alone, not in combination with any other race; Please refer to the Explanation of Data for more information.*

Czechoslovakian (27)	27	0.06
Dutch (77)	667	1.60
English (1,103)	2,491	5.98
European (354)	354	0.85
French, ex. Basque (217)	606	1.45
French Canadian (114)	126	0.30
German (2,341)	5,389	12.93
Greek (67)	67	0.16
Hungarian (0)	28	0.07
Iranian (16)	78	0.19
Irish (841)	3,218	7.72
Italian (395)	793	1.90
Lithuanian (0)	18	0.04
New Zealander (37)	37	0.09
Norwegian (15)	60	0.14
Pennsylvania German (0)	9	0.02
Polish (99)	499	1.20
Portuguese (0)	64	0.15
Romanian (0)	25	0.06
Russian (0)	29	0.07
Scotch-Irish (785)	1,459	3.50
Scottish (653)	934	2.24
Slavic (0)	14	0.03
Swedish (8)	80	0.19
Turkish (49)	49	0.12
Ukrainian (6)	6	0.01
Welsh (93)	156	0.37
West Indian, ex. Hispanic (0)	84	0.20
Jamaican (0)	14	0.03
West Indian (0)	70	0.17

Hispanic Origin	**Population**	**%**
Hispanic or Latino (of any race)	5,166	12.12
Central American, ex. Mexican	348	0.82
Costa Rican	1	<0.01
Guatemalan	64	0.15
Honduran	91	0.21
Nicaraguan	23	0.05
Panamanian	16	0.04
Salvadoran	151	0.35
Other Central American	2	<0.01
Cuban	84	0.20
Dominican Republic	51	0.12
Mexican	3,997	9.38
Puerto Rican	318	0.75
South American	148	0.35
Argentinean	14	0.03
Chilean	3	0.01
Colombian	33	0.08
Ecuadorian	45	0.11
Peruvian	47	0.11
Uruguayan	1	<0.01
Venezuelan	5	0.01
Other Hispanic or Latino	220	0.52

Race*	**Population**	**%**
African-American/Black (8,659)	9,224	21.64
Not Hispanic (8,527)	8,991	21.09
Hispanic (132)	233	0.55
American Indian/Alaska Native (144)	381	0.89
Not Hispanic (113)	328	0.77
Hispanic (31)	53	0.12
Alaska Athabascan *(Ala. Nat.)* (1)	2	<0.01
Aleut *(Alaska Native)* (1)	1	<0.01
Apache (0)	1	<0.01
Blackfeet (0)	11	0.03
Canadian/French Am. Ind. (0)	1	<0.01
Cherokee (28)	88	0.21
Chickasaw (1)	1	<0.01
Chippewa (0)	5	0.01
Choctaw (2)	5	0.01
Creek (1)	5	0.01
Hopi (0)	1	<0.01
Iroquois (5)	10	0.02
Lumbee (28)	40	0.09
Mexican American Ind. (3)	5	0.01
Navajo (7)	9	0.02
Seminole (0)	2	<0.01
Sioux (1)	2	<0.01
South American Ind. (1)	1	<0.01
Spanish American Ind. (3)	3	0.01
Tlingit-Haida *(Alaska Native)* (0)	1	<0.01
Tohono O'Odham (1)	1	<0.01
Asian (487)	626	1.47
Not Hispanic (470)	577	1.35
Hispanic (17)	49	0.11
Bangladeshi (2)	2	<0.01
Cambodian (1)	4	0.01
Chinese, ex. Taiwanese (49)	63	0.15
Filipino (41)	68	0.16
Hmong (92)	93	0.22
Indian (104)	128	0.30
Indonesian (2)	7	0.02
Japanese (9)	17	0.04
Korean (15)	34	0.08
Laotian (107)	116	0.27
Sri Lankan (1)	1	<0.01
Thai (13)	17	0.04
Vietnamese (14)	24	0.06
Hawaii Native/Pacific Islander (12)	33	0.08
Not Hispanic (8)	20	0.05
Hispanic (4)	13	0.03
Guamanian/Chamorro (4)	8	0.02
Native Hawaiian (1)	5	0.01
Samoan (4)	5	0.01
White (29,214)	30,064	70.53
Not Hispanic (27,574)	28,221	66.21
Hispanic (1,640)	1,843	4.32

Kernersville

Place Type: Town
County: Forsyth
Population: 23,123†

Ancestry‡	**Population**	**%**
African, Sub-Saharan (22)	31	0.14
African (11)	20	0.09
Liberian (11)	11	0.05
American (2,081)	2,081	9.32
Arab (9)	22	0.10
Arab (9)	9	0.04
Jordanian (0)	13	0.06
Assyrian/Chaldean/Syriac (0)	15	0.07
Austrian (19)	19	0.09
Brazilian (37)	37	0.17
British (69)	106	0.47
Canadian (12)	42	0.19
Croatian (0)	12	0.05
Czech (6)	27	0.12
Czechoslovakian (0)	17	0.08
Danish (0)	20	0.09
Dutch (77)	362	1.62
English (1,570)	2,876	12.88
European (283)	307	1.37
Finnish (0)	17	0.08
French, ex. Basque (50)	472	2.11
French Canadian (32)	40	0.18
German (1,106)	3,509	15.71
Greek (127)	127	0.57
Guyanese (12)	40	0.18
Hungarian (0)	52	0.23
Irish (811)	2,358	10.56
Italian (164)	562	2.52
Lithuanian (0)	13	0.06
Norwegian (37)	227	1.02
Pennsylvania German (16)	16	0.07
Polish (114)	309	1.38
Russian (47)	79	0.35
Scotch-Irish (332)	627	2.81
Scottish (228)	668	2.99
Slovak (10)	38	0.17
Swedish (0)	109	0.49
Swiss (10)	10	0.04
Welsh (13)	67	0.30
West Indian, ex. Hispanic (25)	49	0.22
Jamaican (25)	49	0.22
Yugoslavian (81)	98	0.44

Hispanic Origin	**Population**	**%**
Hispanic or Latino (of any race)	2,246	9.71
Central American, ex. Mexican	267	1.15
Costa Rican	11	0.05
Guatemalan	25	0.11
Honduran	24	0.10
Panamanian	4	0.02
Salvadoran	203	0.88
Cuban	71	0.31
Dominican Republic	17	0.07
Mexican	1,474	6.37
Puerto Rican	167	0.72
South American	116	0.50
Argentinean	15	0.06
Bolivian	1	<0.01
Chilean	1	<0.01
Colombian	41	0.18
Ecuadorian	18	0.08
Paraguayan	1	<0.01
Peruvian	29	0.13
Venezuelan	10	0.04
Other Hispanic or Latino	134	0.58

Race*	**Population**	**%**
African-American/Black (2,905)	3,154	13.64
Not Hispanic (2,866)	3,067	13.26
Hispanic (39)	87	0.38
American Indian/Alaska Native (106)	248	1.07
Not Hispanic (67)	180	0.78
Hispanic (39)	68	0.29
Blackfeet (4)	4	0.02
Cherokee (12)	54	0.23
Chickasaw (3)	3	0.01
Chippewa (2)	4	0.02
Comanche (0)	1	<0.01
Creek (0)	1	<0.01
Iroquois (1)	1	<0.01
Lumbee (19)	35	0.15
Mexican American Ind. (24)	38	0.16
Navajo (1)	1	<0.01
Shoshone (0)	2	0.01
Sioux (0)	4	0.02
South American Ind. (0)	2	0.01
Asian (446)	542	2.34
Not Hispanic (436)	526	2.27
Hispanic (10)	16	0.07
Bangladeshi (1)	1	<0.01
Burmese (2)	2	0.01
Cambodian (30)	32	0.14
Chinese, ex. Taiwanese (93)	110	0.48
Filipino (53)	75	0.32
Indian (87)	96	0.42
Indonesian (1)	1	<0.01
Japanese (13)	35	0.15
Korean (67)	82	0.35
Laotian (9)	10	0.04
Malaysian (1)	1	<0.01
Pakistani (5)	5	0.02
Taiwanese (2)	2	0.01
Thai (6)	15	0.06
Vietnamese (49)	57	0.25
Hawaii Native/Pacific Islander (6)	25	0.11
Not Hispanic (3)	17	0.07
Hispanic (3)	8	0.03
Fijian (0)	1	<0.01
Guamanian/Chamorro (3)	8	0.03
Native Hawaiian (3)	9	0.04
White (17,979)	18,440	79.75
Not Hispanic (17,103)	17,429	75.38
Hispanic (876)	1,011	4.37

Kings Grant

Place Type: CDP
County: New Hanover
Population: 8,113†

Ancestry‡	**Population**	**%**
American (1,620)	1,620	19.41
Armenian (17)	17	0.20

*Notes: † The Census 2010 population figure is used to calculate the percentages in the Hispanic Origin and Race categories. Ancestry percentages are based on the 2006-2010 American Community Survey population (not shown); ‡ Numbers in parentheses indicate the number of people reporting a single ancestry; * Numbers in parentheses indicate the number of persons reporting this race alone, not in combination with any other race; Please refer to the Explanation of Data for more information.*

Australian (37)	37	0.44
British (0)	90	1.08
Canadian (12)	12	0.14
Dutch (0)	66	0.79
English (356)	981	11.75
European (135)	174	2.08
French, ex. Basque (0)	103	1.23
French Canadian (12)	12	0.14
German (216)	1,020	12.22
Hungarian (12)	12	0.14
Irish (500)	1,137	13.62
Italian (85)	307	3.68
Lithuanian (20)	20	0.24
New Zealander (34)	34	0.41
Norwegian (17)	35	0.42
Polish (31)	153	1.83
Romanian (19)	19	0.23
Russian (10)	40	0.48
Scandinavian (41)	60	0.72
Scotch-Irish (150)	279	3.34
Scottish (69)	352	4.22
Slovak (0)	12	0.14
Swedish (16)	101	1.21
Ukrainian (0)	88	1.05
Welsh (33)	71	0.85

Hispanic Origin	Population	%
Hispanic or Latino (of any race)	555	6.84
Central American, ex. Mexican	39	0.48
Guatemalan	13	0.16
Honduran	17	0.21
Nicaraguan	1	0.01
Panamanian	2	0.02
Salvadoran	6	0.07
Cuban	13	0.16
Dominican Republic	9	0.11
Mexican	375	4.62
Puerto Rican	49	0.60
South American	34	0.42
Argentinean	1	0.01
Chilean	2	0.02
Colombian	14	0.17
Ecuadorian	5	0.06
Peruvian	8	0.10
Venezuelan	4	0.05
Other Hispanic or Latino	36	0.44

Race*	Population	%
African-American/Black (1,163)	1,242	15.31
Not Hispanic (1,150)	1,229	15.15
Hispanic (13)	13	0.16
American Indian/Alaska Native (56)	90	1.11
Not Hispanic (43)	76	0.94
Hispanic (13)	14	0.17
Apache (1)	1	0.01
Central American Ind. (3)	3	0.04
Cherokee (4)	9	0.11
Chickasaw (1)	1	0.01
Chippewa (3)	4	0.05
Comanche (1)	1	0.01
Iroquois (3)	4	0.05
Lumbee (6)	9	0.11
Mexican American Ind. (6)	7	0.09
Osage (0)	1	0.01
Puget Sound Salish (2)	2	0.02
Seminole (1)	1	0.01
Sioux (1)	1	0.01
Asian (88)	124	1.53
Not Hispanic (88)	122	1.50
Hispanic (0)	2	0.02
Burmese (7)	7	0.09
Chinese, ex. Taiwanese (21)	32	0.39
Filipino (14)	26	0.32
Indian (0)	2	0.02
Japanese (0)	5	0.06
Korean (13)	18	0.22
Thai (4)	8	0.10
Vietnamese (19)	22	0.27
Hawaii Native/Pacific Islander (11)	37	0.46
Not Hispanic (10)	33	0.41
Hispanic (1)	4	0.05
Guamanian/Chamorro (2)	3	0.04
Native Hawaiian (0)	8	0.10
Samoan (1)	2	0.02
White (6,315)	6,437	79.34
Not Hispanic (6,113)	6,223	76.70
Hispanic (202)	214	2.64

Kings Mountain

Place Type: City
County: Cleveland
Population: 10,296†

Ancestry‡	Population	%
African, Sub-Saharan (0)	14	0.13
African (0)	14	0.13
American (1,672)	1,672	15.73
Armenian (14)	14	0.13
Austrian (0)	9	0.08
Dutch (115)	186	1.75
English (517)	1,005	9.45
European (9)	29	0.27
French, ex. Basque (18)	128	1.20
French Canadian (19)	19	0.18
German (448)	1,171	11.01
Greek (10)	50	0.47
Irish (531)	1,100	10.35
Italian (11)	227	2.14
Norwegian (32)	73	0.69
Russian (0)	13	0.12
Scotch-Irish (283)	565	5.31
Scottish (218)	243	2.29
Slovene (8)	8	0.08
Swiss (13)	13	0.12
Welsh (14)	24	0.23
West Indian, ex. Hispanic (0)	14	0.13
Bahamian (0)	14	0.13

Hispanic Origin	Population	%
Hispanic or Latino (of any race)	268	2.60
Central American, ex. Mexican	13	0.13
Honduran	2	0.02
Nicaraguan	3	0.03
Panamanian	2	0.02
Salvadoran	6	0.06
Cuban	19	0.18
Dominican Republic	2	0.02
Mexican	141	1.37
Puerto Rican	42	0.41
South American	15	0.15
Colombian	13	0.13
Peruvian	1	0.01
Other South American	1	0.01
Other Hispanic or Latino	36	0.35

Race*	Population	%
African-American/Black (2,315)	2,427	23.57
Not Hispanic (2,307)	2,410	23.41
Hispanic (8)	17	0.17
American Indian/Alaska Native (22)	58	0.56
Not Hispanic (19)	54	0.52
Hispanic (3)	4	0.04
Blackfeet (0)	3	0.03
Cherokee (7)	18	0.17
Creek (1)	1	0.01
Lumbee (2)	2	0.02
Asian (161)	190	1.85
Not Hispanic (158)	186	1.81
Hispanic (3)	4	0.04
Chinese, ex. Taiwanese (19)	20	0.19
Filipino (4)	5	0.05
Indian (21)	24	0.23
Japanese (4)	5	0.05
Korean (3)	8	0.08
Laotian (89)	111	1.08
Pakistani (2)	2	0.02
Taiwanese (1)	7	0.07
Thai (4)	10	0.10
Vietnamese (2)	9	0.09
Hawaii Native/Pacific Islander (1)	3	0.03
Not Hispanic (1)	3	0.03
Guamanian/Chamorro (1)	3	0.03
White (7,511)	7,662	74.42
Not Hispanic (7,378)	7,510	72.94
Hispanic (133)	152	1.48

Kinston

Place Type: City
County: Lenoir
Population: 21,677†

Ancestry‡	Population	%
African, Sub-Saharan (706)	837	3.80
African (640)	759	3.45
Liberian (14)	14	0.06
Nigerian (9)	9	0.04
Other Sub-Saharan African (43)	55	0.25
American (1,314)	1,314	5.97
Arab (55)	55	0.25
Arab (33)	33	0.15
Lebanese (22)	22	0.10
British (77)	86	0.39
Danish (14)	33	0.15
Dutch (23)	23	0.10
English (942)	1,557	7.08
European (93)	93	0.42
French, ex. Basque (29)	109	0.50
German (242)	613	2.79
German Russian (0)	36	0.16
Greek (9)	9	0.04
Hungarian (0)	18	0.08
Irish (404)	889	4.04
Italian (90)	167	0.76
Norwegian (46)	241	1.10
Polish (28)	61	0.28
Russian (14)	14	0.06
Scotch-Irish (198)	342	1.55
Scottish (111)	251	1.14
Swedish (21)	40	0.18
Swiss (9)	9	0.04
Welsh (0)	31	0.14
West Indian, ex. Hispanic (107)	187	0.85
Barbadian (0)	40	0.18
Jamaican (87)	110	0.50
Trinidadian/Tobagonian (20)	37	0.17

Hispanic Origin	Population	%
Hispanic or Latino (of any race)	512	2.36
Central American, ex. Mexican	41	0.19
Costa Rican	1	<0.01
Guatemalan	8	0.04
Honduran	19	0.09
Nicaraguan	1	<0.01
Panamanian	3	0.01
Salvadoran	9	0.04
Cuban	6	0.03
Dominican Republic	13	0.06
Mexican	300	1.38
Puerto Rican	78	0.36
South American	30	0.14
Argentinean	5	0.02
Chilean	7	0.03
Colombian	10	0.05
Ecuadorian	4	0.02
Peruvian	2	0.01
Venezuelan	1	<0.01
Other South American	1	<0.01
Other Hispanic or Latino	44	0.20

Race*	Population	%
African-American/Black (14,749)	14,944	68.94
Not Hispanic (14,673)	14,851	68.51
Hispanic (76)	93	0.43
American Indian/Alaska Native (50)	123	0.57
Not Hispanic (41)	113	0.52
Hispanic (9)	10	0.05
Arapaho (0)	1	<0.01
Blackfeet (0)	5	0.02

*Notes: † The Census 2010 population figure is used to calculate the percentages in the Hispanic Origin and Race categories. Ancestry percentages are based on the 2006-2010 American Community Survey population (not shown); ‡ Numbers in parentheses indicate the number of people reporting a single ancestry; * Numbers in parentheses indicate the number of persons reporting this race alone, not in combination with any other race; Please refer to the Explanation of Data for more information.*

SECTION TWO

Cherokee (5)	27	0.12
Choctaw (2)	2	0.01
Creek (0)	2	0.01
Kiowa (1)	1	<0.01
Lumbee (2)	5	0.02
Mexican American Ind. (2)	2	0.01
Navajo (0)	1	<0.01
Seminole (0)	2	0.01
Asian (152)	218	1.01
Not Hispanic (146)	209	0.96
Hispanic (6)	9	0.04
Chinese, ex. Taiwanese (31)	38	0.18
Filipino (25)	35	0.16
Indian (38)	47	0.22
Japanese (2)	5	0.02
Korean (19)	30	0.14
Laotian (7)	7	0.03
Pakistani (1)	1	<0.01
Thai (10)	16	0.07
Vietnamese (19)	28	0.13
Hawaii Native/Pacific Islander (12)	32	0.15
Not Hispanic (12)	29	0.13
Hispanic (0)	3	0.01
Guamanian/Chamorro (4)	8	0.04
Native Hawaiian (1)	1	<0.01
Samoan (3)	7	0.03
Tongan (2)	8	0.04
White (6,211)	6,401	29.53
Not Hispanic (6,022)	6,193	28.57
Hispanic (189)	208	0.96

Knightdale

Place Type: Town
County: Wake
Population: 11,401†

Ancestry‡	Population	%
African, Sub-Saharan (811)	953	9.10
African (414)	556	5.31
Nigerian (199)	199	1.90
Other Sub-Saharan African (198)	198	1.89
American (457)	457	4.36
Arab (15)	99	0.94
Egyptian (15)	88	0.84
Lebanese (0)	11	0.10
British (0)	114	1.09
Canadian (23)	23	0.22
Danish (0)	34	0.32
Dutch (0)	78	0.74
English (499)	1,008	9.62
European (34)	115	1.10
French, ex. Basque (0)	105	1.00
French Canadian (27)	27	0.26
German (286)	829	7.91
Greek (55)	67	0.64
Hungarian (10)	10	0.10
Iranian (10)	10	0.10
Irish (158)	462	4.41
Italian (229)	535	5.11
Norwegian (27)	128	1.22
Polish (38)	143	1.36
Portuguese (0)	16	0.15
Russian (0)	9	0.09
Scandinavian (28)	70	0.67
Scotch-Irish (113)	312	2.98
Scottish (34)	161	1.54
Swedish (9)	9	0.09
Welsh (25)	259	2.47
West Indian, ex. Hispanic (36)	36	0.34
Bahamian (18)	18	0.17
Jamaican (18)	18	0.17

Hispanic Origin	Population	%
Hispanic or Latino (of any race)	1,299	11.39
Central American, ex. Mexican	261	2.29
Guatemalan	29	0.25
Honduran	82	0.72
Nicaraguan	12	0.11
Panamanian	19	0.17
Salvadoran	111	0.97
Other Central American	8	0.07
Cuban	41	0.36
Dominican Republic	52	0.46
Mexican	554	4.86
Puerto Rican	177	1.55
South American	106	0.93
Argentinean	8	0.07
Chilean	1	0.01
Colombian	30	0.26
Ecuadorian	11	0.10
Peruvian	30	0.26
Uruguayan	13	0.11
Venezuelan	12	0.11
Other South American	1	0.01
Other Hispanic or Latino	108	0.95

Race*	Population	%
African-American/Black (4,368)	4,632	40.63
Not Hispanic (4,318)	4,529	39.72
Hispanic (50)	103	0.90
American Indian/Alaska Native (66)	175	1.53
Not Hispanic (44)	137	1.20
Hispanic (22)	38	0.33
Apache (0)	2	0.02
Blackfeet (0)	3	0.03
Central American Ind. (0)	4	0.04
Cherokee (8)	20	0.18
Chippewa (1)	1	0.01
Choctaw (0)	4	0.04
Comanche (0)	3	0.03
Delaware (0)	1	0.01
Houma (1)	1	0.01
Lumbee (4)	6	0.05
Menominee (1)	1	0.01
Mexican American Ind. (3)	6	0.05
Seminole (0)	2	0.02
Sioux (1)	1	0.01
South American Ind. (2)	2	0.02
Tohono O'Odham (0)	3	0.03
Asian (193)	278	2.44
Not Hispanic (187)	261	2.29
Hispanic (6)	17	0.15
Bangladeshi (4)	5	0.04
Burmese (1)	2	0.02
Cambodian (1)	3	0.03
Chinese, ex. Taiwanese (18)	34	0.30
Filipino (38)	56	0.49
Indian (32)	44	0.39
Japanese (9)	26	0.23
Korean (7)	13	0.11
Pakistani (15)	20	0.18
Sri Lankan (3)	3	0.03
Taiwanese (3)	5	0.04
Thai (3)	6	0.05
Vietnamese (33)	45	0.39
Hawaii Native/Pacific Islander (6)	17	0.15
Not Hispanic (5)	14	0.12
Hispanic (1)	3	0.03
Guamanian/Chamorro (2)	2	0.02
Native Hawaiian (2)	9	0.08
White (5,698)	5,995	52.58
Not Hispanic (5,235)	5,455	47.85
Hispanic (463)	540	4.74

Laurinburg

Place Type: City
County: Scotland
Population: 15,962†

Ancestry‡	Population	%
African, Sub-Saharan (84)	120	0.75
African (84)	120	0.75
American (632)	632	3.93
Arab (22)	22	0.14
Lebanese (11)	11	0.07
Other Arab (11)	11	0.07
Austrian (0)	11	0.07
Belgian (13)	36	0.22
Brazilian (6)	6	0.04
British (54)	54	0.34
Dutch (0)	73	0.45
English (678)	1,198	7.46
European (19)	19	0.12
French, ex. Basque (34)	79	0.49
French Canadian (0)	23	0.14
German (404)	1,137	7.08
Guyanese (47)	47	0.29
Hungarian (11)	39	0.24
Irish (237)	643	4.00
Italian (29)	197	1.23
Lithuanian (14)	14	0.09
Northern European (9)	9	0.06
Norwegian (13)	13	0.08
Polish (132)	231	1.44
Portuguese (28)	38	0.24
Scandinavian (9)	9	0.06
Scotch-Irish (394)	662	4.12
Scottish (276)	354	2.20
Swedish (8)	8	0.05
Swiss (0)	24	0.15
Ukrainian (0)	10	0.06
Welsh (0)	102	0.63

Hispanic Origin	Population	%
Hispanic or Latino (of any race)	326	2.04
Central American, ex. Mexican	18	0.11
Costa Rican	6	0.04
Guatemalan	1	0.01
Honduran	5	0.03
Nicaraguan	4	0.03
Salvadoran	2	0.01
Cuban	5	0.03
Dominican Republic	3	0.02
Mexican	178	1.12
Puerto Rican	67	0.42
South American	14	0.09
Colombian	5	0.03
Ecuadorian	7	0.04
Peruvian	1	0.01
Venezuelan	1	0.01
Other Hispanic or Latino	41	0.26

Race*	Population	%
African-American/Black (7,470)	7,623	47.76
Not Hispanic (7,447)	7,592	47.56
Hispanic (23)	31	0.19
American Indian/Alaska Native (971)	1,195	7.49
Not Hispanic (949)	1,170	7.33
Hispanic (22)	25	0.16
Blackfeet (0)	2	0.01
Cherokee (40)	85	0.53
Choctaw (1)	3	0.02
Colville (1)	1	0.01
Creek (1)	1	0.01
Crow (0)	3	0.02
Iroquois (3)	4	0.03
Lumbee (568)	662	4.15
Mexican American Ind. (2)	2	0.01
Navajo (1)	4	0.03
Potawatomi (1)	1	0.01
Sioux (1)	1	0.01
Spanish American Ind. (4)	4	0.03
Asian (155)	177	1.11
Not Hispanic (155)	177	1.11
Cambodian (0)	1	0.01
Chinese, ex. Taiwanese (28)	30	0.19
Filipino (24)	27	0.17
Indian (30)	38	0.24
Japanese (0)	5	0.03
Korean (13)	19	0.12
Pakistani (31)	31	0.19
Thai (2)	2	0.01
Vietnamese (24)	26	0.16
Hawaii Native/Pacific Islander (6)	11	0.07
Not Hispanic (5)	10	0.06
Hispanic (1)	1	0.01
Guamanian/Chamorro (2)	6	0.04
Native Hawaiian (1)	1	0.01

*Notes: † The Census 2010 population figure is used to calculate the percentages in the Hispanic Origin and Race categories. Ancestry percentages are based on the 2006-2010 American Community Survey population (not shown); ‡ Numbers in parentheses indicate the number of people reporting a single ancestry; * Numbers in parentheses indicate the number of persons reporting this race alone, not in combination with any other race; Please refer to the Explanation of Data for more information.*

Samoan (2)	3	0.02
White (6,861)	7,093	44.44
Not Hispanic (6,767)	6,985	43.76
Hispanic (94)	108	0.68

Leland

Place Type: Town
County: Brunswick
Population: 13,527†

Ancestry‡	Population	%
African, Sub-Saharan (17)	17	0.14
Ethiopian (17)	17	0.14
American (1,410)	1,410	11.82
Arab (61)	73	0.61
Lebanese (61)	61	0.51
Syrian (0)	12	0.10
Austrian (0)	54	0.45
British (26)	86	0.72
Canadian (22)	22	0.18
Croatian (0)	34	0.29
Danish (0)	34	0.29
Dutch (0)	334	2.80
English (479)	1,647	13.81
European (139)	199	1.67
French, ex. Basque (64)	319	2.68
French Canadian (36)	148	1.24
German (602)	2,330	19.54
Hungarian (0)	65	0.55
Irish (566)	1,601	13.43
Italian (413)	1,094	9.17
Lithuanian (28)	56	0.47
Norwegian (0)	37	0.31
Polish (164)	233	1.95
Russian (14)	116	0.97
Scotch-Irish (228)	725	6.08
Scottish (212)	460	3.86
Slavic (0)	30	0.25
Swedish (40)	252	2.11
Swiss (0)	30	0.25
Turkish (0)	43	0.36
Ukrainian (14)	14	0.12
Welsh (0)	86	0.72
West Indian, ex. Hispanic (40)	40	0.34
Haitian (40)	40	0.34
Yugoslavian (24)	24	0.20

Hispanic Origin	Population	%
Hispanic or Latino (of any race)	662	4.89
Central American, ex. Mexican	88	0.65
Costa Rican	11	0.08
Guatemalan	11	0.08
Honduran	20	0.15
Nicaraguan	3	0.02
Panamanian	5	0.04
Salvadoran	38	0.28
Cuban	15	0.11
Dominican Republic	16	0.12
Mexican	333	2.46
Puerto Rican	111	0.82
South American	58	0.43
Argentinean	4	0.03
Bolivian	1	0.01
Chilean	3	0.02
Colombian	15	0.11
Ecuadorian	22	0.16
Peruvian	9	0.07
Uruguayan	1	0.01
Venezuelan	3	0.02
Other Hispanic or Latino	41	0.30

Race*	Population	%
African-American/Black (1,356)	1,487	10.99
Not Hispanic (1,342)	1,464	10.82
Hispanic (14)	23	0.17
American Indian/Alaska Native (83)	159	1.18
Not Hispanic (72)	140	1.03
Hispanic (11)	19	0.14
Apache (0)	2	0.01
Blackfeet (1)	4	0.03
Cherokee (3)	31	0.23
Cheyenne (0)	1	0.01
Creek (0)	1	0.01
Hopi (0)	1	0.01
Iroquois (1)	1	0.01
Lumbee (19)	22	0.16
Mexican American Ind. (1)	1	0.01
Sioux (4)	5	0.04
South American Ind. (1)	1	0.01
Asian (201)	253	1.87
Not Hispanic (195)	241	1.78
Hispanic (6)	12	0.09
Cambodian (4)	4	0.03
Chinese, ex. Taiwanese (40)	49	0.36
Filipino (27)	42	0.31
Indian (29)	37	0.27
Indonesian (0)	1	0.01
Japanese (6)	12	0.09
Korean (20)	29	0.21
Laotian (6)	8	0.06
Malaysian (1)	1	0.01
Pakistani (6)	6	0.04
Sri Lankan (2)	2	0.01
Taiwanese (1)	1	0.01
Thai (9)	9	0.07
Vietnamese (38)	42	0.31
Hawaii Native/Pacific Islander (2)	11	0.08
Not Hispanic (0)	9	0.07
Hispanic (2)	2	0.01
Fijian (0)	3	0.02
Guamanian/Chamorro (2)	2	0.01
White (11,343)	11,588	85.67
Not Hispanic (11,020)	11,206	82.84
Hispanic (323)	382	2.82

Lenoir

Place Type: City
County: Caldwell
Population: 18,228†

Ancestry‡	Population	%
African, Sub-Saharan (37)	47	0.26
African (10)	20	0.11
Ethiopian (27)	27	0.15
American (2,273)	2,273	12.47
Belgian (0)	13	0.07
British (10)	10	0.05
Danish (152)	152	0.83
Dutch (115)	479	2.63
English (994)	1,982	10.88
European (148)	160	0.88
Finnish (10)	34	0.19
French, ex. Basque (10)	131	0.72
French Canadian (13)	13	0.07
German (827)	2,131	11.69
Irish (453)	1,725	9.47
Israeli (0)	64	0.35
Italian (87)	275	1.51
Northern European (63)	63	0.35
Norwegian (0)	41	0.22
Pennsylvania German (12)	12	0.07
Polish (19)	32	0.18
Russian (7)	38	0.21
Scotch-Irish (349)	495	2.72
Scottish (121)	482	2.64
Slavic (0)	75	0.41
Slovak (0)	20	0.11
Swedish (20)	43	0.24
Ukrainian (15)	38	0.21
Welsh (10)	19	0.10
West Indian, ex. Hispanic (40)	40	0.22
British West Indian (26)	26	0.14
West Indian (14)	14	0.08
Yugoslavian (34)	34	0.19

Hispanic Origin	Population	%
Hispanic or Latino (of any race)	1,640	9.00
Central American, ex. Mexican	590	3.24
Costa Rican	9	0.05
Guatemalan	135	0.74
Honduran	343	1.88
Nicaraguan	1	0.01
Panamanian	1	0.01
Salvadoran	101	0.55
Cuban	76	0.42
Dominican Republic	4	0.02
Mexican	655	3.59
Puerto Rican	76	0.42
South American	29	0.16
Argentinean	3	0.02
Bolivian	2	0.01
Chilean	1	0.01
Colombian	9	0.05
Ecuadorian	4	0.02
Peruvian	5	0.03
Uruguayan	3	0.02
Venezuelan	2	0.01
Other Hispanic or Latino	210	1.15

Race*	Population	%
African-American/Black (2,311)	2,570	14.10
Not Hispanic (2,277)	2,513	13.79
Hispanic (34)	57	0.31
American Indian/Alaska Native (76)	185	1.01
Not Hispanic (37)	123	0.67
Hispanic (39)	62	0.34
Aleut *(Alaska Native)* (6)	6	0.03
Blackfeet (0)	8	0.04
Central American Ind. (0)	1	0.01
Cherokee (11)	43	0.24
Choctaw (0)	1	0.01
Creek (0)	1	0.01
Iroquois (1)	1	0.01
Lumbee (5)	10	0.05
Navajo (1)	1	0.01
Sioux (2)	4	0.02
Yaqui (0)	1	0.01
Asian (155)	186	1.02
Not Hispanic (152)	176	0.97
Hispanic (3)	10	0.05
Chinese, ex. Taiwanese (36)	44	0.24
Filipino (10)	21	0.12
Hmong (17)	17	0.09
Indian (43)	47	0.26
Japanese (3)	5	0.03
Korean (12)	17	0.09
Laotian (4)	4	0.02
Thai (1)	2	0.01
Vietnamese (22)	24	0.13
Hawaii Native/Pacific Islander (12)	23	0.13
Not Hispanic (5)	8	0.04
Hispanic (7)	15	0.08
Guamanian/Chamorro (6)	9	0.05
Native Hawaiian (1)	4	0.02
Samoan (1)	1	0.01
White (14,282)	14,668	80.47
Not Hispanic (13,776)	14,070	77.19
Hispanic (506)	598	3.28

Lewisville

Place Type: Town
County: Forsyth
Population: 12,639†

Ancestry‡	Population	%
African, Sub-Saharan (0)	52	0.42
African (0)	52	0.42
Alsatian (0)	14	0.11
American (1,560)	1,560	12.46
Arab (68)	68	0.54
Lebanese (39)	39	0.31
Other Arab (29)	29	0.23
Armenian (27)	27	0.22
Australian (11)	34	0.27
Austrian (12)	44	0.35
British (55)	98	0.78
Canadian (0)	34	0.27

SECTION TWO

*Notes: † The Census 2010 population figure is used to calculate the percentages in the Hispanic Origin and Race categories. Ancestry percentages are based on the 2006-2010 American Community Survey population (not shown); ‡ Numbers in parentheses indicate the number of people reporting a single ancestry; * Numbers in parentheses indicate the number of persons reporting this race alone, not in combination with any other race; Please refer to the Explanation of Data for more information.*

Czech (64)	78	0.62
Danish (8)	38	0.30
Dutch (44)	235	1.88
English (927)	1,898	15.16
European (269)	269	2.15
French, ex. Basque (155)	372	2.97
French Canadian (40)	77	0.62
German (612)	2,313	18.48
Greek (54)	101	0.81
Hungarian (0)	60	0.48
Iranian (40)	56	0.45
Irish (509)	1,497	11.96
Italian (396)	802	6.41
Lithuanian (33)	47	0.38
Norwegian (10)	68	0.54
Polish (39)	346	2.76
Portuguese (19)	63	0.50
Romanian (0)	29	0.23
Russian (54)	85	0.68
Scandinavian (7)	7	0.06
Scotch-Irish (254)	579	4.63
Scottish (236)	459	3.67
Slovak (10)	72	0.58
Swedish (9)	67	0.54
Swiss (43)	71	0.57
Turkish (38)	38	0.30
Ukrainian (0)	15	0.12
Welsh (65)	165	1.32
West Indian, ex. Hispanic (0)	61	0.49
West Indian (0)	61	0.49

Hispanic Origin	Population	%
Hispanic or Latino (of any race)	429	3.39
Central American, ex. Mexican	71	0.56
Costa Rican	2	0.02
Guatemalan	6	0.05
Honduran	4	0.03
Nicaraguan	9	0.07
Panamanian	9	0.07
Salvadoran	41	0.32
Cuban	15	0.12
Dominican Republic	11	0.09
Mexican	162	1.28
Puerto Rican	76	0.60
South American	65	0.51
Argentinean	17	0.13
Bolivian	1	0.01
Chilean	5	0.04
Colombian	23	0.18
Ecuadorian	8	0.06
Peruvian	2	0.02
Venezuelan	9	0.07
Other Hispanic or Latino	29	0.23

Race*	Population	%
African-American/Black (635)	728	5.76
Not Hispanic (631)	713	5.64
Hispanic (4)	15	0.12
American Indian/Alaska Native (38)	79	0.63
Not Hispanic (29)	67	0.53
Hispanic (9)	12	0.09
Blackfeet (0)	1	0.01
Cherokee (7)	17	0.13
Chickasaw (3)	3	0.02
Choctaw (4)	8	0.06
Iroquois (0)	1	0.01
Lumbee (6)	12	0.09
Sioux (0)	1	0.01
Tlingit-Haida *(Alaska Native)* (1)	1	0.01
Asian (215)	268	2.12
Not Hispanic (214)	260	2.06
Hispanic (1)	8	0.06
Chinese, ex. Taiwanese (51)	57	0.45
Filipino (15)	21	0.17
Indian (70)	80	0.63
Japanese (9)	17	0.13
Korean (17)	20	0.16
Pakistani (13)	13	0.10
Taiwanese (6)	6	0.05
Thai (1)	1	0.01
Vietnamese (32)	35	0.28
Hawaii Native/Pacific Islander (5)	7	0.06
Not Hispanic (2)	4	0.03
Hispanic (3)	3	0.02
Guamanian/Chamorro (3)	3	0.02
Native Hawaiian (0)	2	0.02
White (11,408)	11,586	91.67
Not Hispanic (11,162)	11,310	89.48
Hispanic (246)	276	2.18

Lexington

Place Type: City
County: Davidson
Population: 18,931†

Ancestry‡	Population	%
African, Sub-Saharan (0)	9	0.05
Kenyan (0)	9	0.05
American (1,481)	1,481	7.73
Arab (25)	25	0.13
Lebanese (25)	25	0.13
Armenian (18)	18	0.09
British (40)	40	0.21
Canadian (16)	33	0.17
Dutch (26)	236	1.23
English (681)	1,105	5.77
European (31)	31	0.16
French, ex. Basque (47)	302	1.58
French Canadian (38)	45	0.23
German (792)	1,886	9.85
Greek (10)	26	0.14
Guyanese (33)	33	0.17
Hungarian (0)	20	0.10
Irish (369)	1,199	6.26
Italian (37)	74	0.39
Norwegian (13)	13	0.07
Polish (49)	83	0.43
Scandinavian (15)	34	0.18
Scotch-Irish (190)	363	1.90
Scottish (205)	390	2.04
Swedish (18)	53	0.28
Swiss (19)	95	0.50

Hispanic Origin	Population	%
Hispanic or Latino (of any race)	3,082	16.28
Central American, ex. Mexican	168	0.89
Costa Rican	3	0.02
Guatemalan	30	0.16
Honduran	34	0.18
Nicaraguan	3	0.02
Panamanian	13	0.07
Salvadoran	84	0.44
Other Central American	1	0.01
Cuban	15	0.08
Dominican Republic	7	0.04
Mexican	2,505	13.23
Puerto Rican	86	0.45
South American	60	0.32
Argentinean	7	0.04
Chilean	5	0.03
Colombian	24	0.13
Peruvian	5	0.03
Uruguayan	7	0.04
Venezuelan	4	0.02
Other South American	8	0.04
Other Hispanic or Latino	241	1.27

Race*	Population	%
African-American/Black (5,377)	5,682	30.01
Not Hispanic (5,331)	5,598	29.57
Hispanic (46)	84	0.44
American Indian/Alaska Native (126)	247	1.30
Not Hispanic (93)	192	1.01
Hispanic (33)	55	0.29
Apache (1)	5	0.03
Arapaho (0)	1	0.01
Blackfeet (1)	1	0.01
Cherokee (32)	87	0.46
Chippewa (2)	2	0.01
Comanche (2)	2	0.01
Creek (1)	1	0.01
Iroquois (7)	7	0.04
Lumbee (14)	18	0.10
Mexican American Ind. (15)	26	0.14
Navajo (0)	1	0.01
Seminole (0)	2	0.01
Sioux (0)	2	0.01
South American Ind. (2)	3	0.02
Spanish American Ind. (3)	3	0.02
Asian (554)	606	3.20
Not Hispanic (549)	591	3.12
Hispanic (5)	15	0.08
Cambodian (338)	365	1.93
Chinese, ex. Taiwanese (24)	32	0.17
Filipino (22)	30	0.16
Indian (76)	83	0.44
Japanese (3)	6	0.03
Korean (2)	7	0.04
Laotian (24)	30	0.16
Pakistani (3)	3	0.02
Taiwanese (2)	2	0.01
Thai (3)	5	0.03
Vietnamese (12)	14	0.07
Hawaii Native/Pacific Islander (1)	17	0.09
Not Hispanic (1)	12	0.06
Hispanic (0)	5	0.03
Guamanian/Chamorro (0)	1	0.01
Native Hawaiian (1)	7	0.04
Samoan (0)	1	0.01
White (10,358)	10,751	56.79
Not Hispanic (9,424)	9,747	51.49
Hispanic (934)	1,004	5.30

Lincolnton

Place Type: City
County: Lincoln
Population: 10,486†

Ancestry‡	Population	%
African, Sub-Saharan (0)	22	0.21
African (0)	22	0.21
American (1,164)	1,164	11.15
Austrian (0)	8	0.08
British (17)	17	0.16
Celtic (0)	16	0.15
Czech (0)	109	1.04
Czechoslovakian (0)	15	0.14
Danish (0)	17	0.16
Dutch (29)	300	2.87
English (509)	1,097	10.51
European (66)	66	0.63
Finnish (10)	10	0.10
French, ex. Basque (13)	122	1.17
French Canadian (0)	11	0.11
German (395)	1,497	14.34
Greek (0)	7	0.07
Irish (272)	1,043	9.99
Italian (95)	138	1.32
Polish (32)	137	1.31
Portuguese (9)	9	0.09
Russian (51)	51	0.49
Scotch-Irish (291)	522	5.00
Scottish (103)	271	2.60
Swedish (9)	9	0.09
Swiss (0)	60	0.57
Welsh (0)	33	0.32

Hispanic Origin	Population	%
Hispanic or Latino (of any race)	1,683	16.05
Central American, ex. Mexican	544	5.19
Costa Rican	431	4.11
Guatemalan	18	0.17
Honduran	29	0.28
Nicaraguan	30	0.29
Salvadoran	34	0.32
Other Central American	2	0.02
Cuban	36	0.34
Dominican Republic	76	0.72

*Notes: † The Census 2010 population figure is used to calculate the percentages in the Hispanic Origin and Race categories. Ancestry percentages are based on the 2006-2010 American Community Survey population (not shown); ‡ Numbers in parentheses indicate the number of people reporting a single ancestry; * Numbers in parentheses indicate the number of persons reporting this race alone, not in combination with any other race; Please refer to the Explanation of Data for more information.*

Mexican	786	7.50
Puerto Rican	66	0.63
South American	94	0.90
Argentinean	24	0.23
Bolivian	2	0.02
Chilean	7	0.07
Colombian	13	0.12
Ecuadorian	8	0.08
Peruvian	25	0.24
Uruguayan	13	0.12
Venezuelan	2	0.02
Other Hispanic or Latino	81	0.77

Race*	Population	%
African-American/Black (1,433)	1,592	15.18
Not Hispanic (1,394)	1,529	14.58
Hispanic (39)	63	0.60
American Indian/Alaska Native (32)	72	0.69
Not Hispanic (29)	64	0.61
Hispanic (3)	8	0.08
Blackfeet (0)	3	0.03
Cherokee (9)	22	0.21
Chippewa (0)	2	0.02
Choctaw (4)	4	0.04
Lumbee (5)	5	0.05
Navajo (0)	1	0.01
Seminole (0)	1	0.01
Sioux (2)	2	0.02
Tlingit-Haida *(Alaska Native)* (3)	3	0.03
Asian (58)	81	0.77
Not Hispanic (54)	69	0.66
Hispanic (4)	12	0.11
Burmese (1)	1	0.01
Chinese, ex. Taiwanese (11)	12	0.11
Filipino (8)	16	0.15
Hmong (18)	19	0.18
Indian (6)	7	0.07
Japanese (3)	8	0.08
Korean (4)	6	0.06
Vietnamese (6)	7	0.07
Hawaii Native/Pacific Islander (0)	17	0.16
Not Hispanic (0)	4	0.04
Hispanic (0)	13	0.12
Guamanian/Chamorro (0)	1	0.01
Native Hawaiian (0)	4	0.04
Samoan (0)	2	0.02
White (8,029)	8,273	78.90
Not Hispanic (7,135)	7,289	69.51
Hispanic (894)	984	9.38

Lumberton

Place Type: City
County: Robeson
Population: 21,542†

Ancestry‡	Population	%
African, Sub-Saharan (232)	232	1.08
African (232)	232	1.08
American (1,037)	1,037	4.83
Arab (101)	406	1.89
Arab (44)	44	0.21
Jordanian (31)	179	0.83
Moroccan (0)	9	0.04
Palestinian (26)	174	0.81
Belgian (0)	16	0.07
British (21)	39	0.18
Canadian (20)	20	0.09
Czech (8)	15	0.07
Dutch (0)	30	0.14
English (943)	1,369	6.38
European (34)	40	0.19
Finnish (0)	8	0.04
French, ex. Basque (113)	237	1.10
French Canadian (13)	34	0.16
German (185)	649	3.03
Greek (13)	13	0.06
Hungarian (11)	23	0.11
Irish (295)	751	3.50
Italian (86)	199	0.93
Lithuanian (14)	14	0.07
Norwegian (17)	100	0.47
Polish (26)	48	0.22
Portuguese (0)	18	0.08
Romanian (15)	15	0.07
Scandinavian (7)	7	0.03
Scotch-Irish (490)	578	2.69
Scottish (323)	480	2.24
Swedish (0)	45	0.21
Welsh (43)	43	0.20
West Indian, ex. Hispanic (9)	27	0.13
Haitian (0)	10	0.05
Jamaican (9)	9	0.04
West Indian (0)	8	0.04

Hispanic Origin	Population	%
Hispanic or Latino (of any race)	1,451	6.74
Central American, ex. Mexican	188	0.87
Costa Rican	2	0.01
Guatemalan	138	0.64
Honduran	21	0.10
Nicaraguan	5	0.02
Panamanian	7	0.03
Salvadoran	14	0.06
Other Central American	1	<0.01
Cuban	19	0.09
Dominican Republic	22	0.10
Mexican	835	3.88
Puerto Rican	113	0.52
South American	27	0.13
Argentinean	2	0.01
Chilean	2	0.01
Colombian	16	0.07
Ecuadorian	5	0.02
Venezuelan	2	0.01
Other Hispanic or Latino	247	1.15

Race*	Population	%
African-American/Black (8,005)	8,286	38.46
Not Hispanic (7,914)	8,164	37.90
Hispanic (91)	122	0.57
American Indian/Alaska Native (2,820)	3,178	14.75
Not Hispanic (2,738)	3,076	14.28
Hispanic (82)	102	0.47
Apache (1)	1	<0.01
Arapaho (0)	2	0.01
Blackfeet (0)	1	<0.01
Central American Ind. (14)	14	0.06
Cherokee (36)	54	0.25
Choctaw (1)	11	0.05
Comanche (0)	2	0.01
Iroquois (11)	16	0.07
Kiowa (0)	1	<0.01
Lumbee (1,783)	1,952	9.06
Mexican American Ind. (11)	16	0.07
Ottawa (0)	1	<0.01
Sioux (2)	3	0.01
Asian (519)	579	2.69
Not Hispanic (512)	570	2.65
Hispanic (7)	9	0.04
Burmese (119)	134	0.62
Cambodian (4)	4	0.02
Chinese, ex. Taiwanese (53)	55	0.26
Filipino (92)	93	0.43
Indian (100)	129	0.60
Japanese (4)	7	0.03
Korean (26)	29	0.13
Laotian (3)	3	0.01
Pakistani (12)	12	0.06
Thai (11)	11	0.05
Vietnamese (36)	45	0.21
Hawaii Native/Pacific Islander (42)	52	0.24
Not Hispanic (25)	34	0.16
Hispanic (17)	18	0.08
Guamanian/Chamorro (19)	21	0.10
Native Hawaiian (7)	11	0.05
Samoan (7)	8	0.04
White (8,794)	9,174	42.59
Not Hispanic (8,411)	8,713	40.45
Hispanic (383)	461	2.14

Marion

Place Type: City
County: McDowell
Population: 7,838†

Ancestry‡	Population	%
African, Sub-Saharan (10)	10	0.12
African (10)	10	0.12
American (1,521)	1,521	18.87
Arab (8)	8	0.10
Moroccan (8)	8	0.10
Australian (0)	5	0.06
Belgian (18)	18	0.22
British (5)	5	0.06
Dutch (0)	99	1.23
English (597)	883	10.95
European (131)	136	1.69
French, ex. Basque (47)	199	2.47
French Canadian (10)	10	0.12
German (424)	941	11.67
Irish (470)	991	12.29
Italian (0)	136	1.69
Latvian (0)	38	0.47
Norwegian (0)	62	0.77
Polish (0)	62	0.77
Russian (0)	59	0.73
Scotch-Irish (205)	358	4.44
Scottish (113)	286	3.55
Swedish (0)	10	0.12
Welsh (0)	40	0.50

Hispanic Origin	Population	%
Hispanic or Latino (of any race)	1,028	13.12
Central American, ex. Mexican	37	0.47
Costa Rican	3	0.04
Guatemalan	18	0.23
Honduran	6	0.08
Panamanian	2	0.03
Salvadoran	8	0.10
Cuban	7	0.09
Mexican	846	10.79
Puerto Rican	9	0.11
South American	18	0.23
Argentinean	2	0.03
Colombian	6	0.08
Ecuadorian	10	0.13
Other Hispanic or Latino	111	1.42

Race*	Population	%
African-American/Black (872)	945	12.06
Not Hispanic (846)	908	11.58
Hispanic (26)	37	0.47
American Indian/Alaska Native (40)	95	1.21
Not Hispanic (29)	83	1.06
Hispanic (11)	12	0.15
Blackfeet (0)	2	0.03
Cherokee (16)	39	0.50
Chippewa (0)	1	0.01
Comanche (0)	1	0.01
Asian (59)	77	0.98
Not Hispanic (57)	70	0.89
Hispanic (2)	7	0.09
Cambodian (1)	1	0.01
Chinese, ex. Taiwanese (7)	8	0.10
Filipino (4)	10	0.13
Hmong (5)	5	0.06
Indian (21)	27	0.34
Japanese (2)	5	0.06
Korean (3)	5	0.06
Nepalese (4)	7	0.09
Taiwanese (1)	1	0.01
Vietnamese (6)	6	0.08
Hawaii Native/Pacific Islander (0)	1	0.01
Hispanic (0)	1	0.01
White (5,999)	6,132	78.23
Not Hispanic (5,748)	5,859	74.75
Hispanic (251)	273	3.48

*Notes: † The Census 2010 population figure is used to calculate the percentages in the Hispanic Origin and Race categories. Ancestry percentages are based on the 2006-2010 American Community Survey population (not shown); ‡ Numbers in parentheses indicate the number of people reporting a single ancestry; * Numbers in parentheses indicate the number of persons reporting this race alone, not in combination with any other race; Please refer to the Explanation of Data for more information.*

Matthews

Place Type: Town
County: Mecklenburg
Population: 27,198†

Ancestry‡	Population	%
African, Sub-Saharan (267)	304	1.14
African (75)	112	0.42
Ethiopian (181)	181	0.68
South African (11)	11	0.04
American (3,210)	3,210	12.09
Arab (82)	256	0.96
Arab (16)	16	0.06
Egyptian (0)	19	0.07
Lebanese (8)	163	0.61
Palestinian (18)	18	0.07
Other Arab (40)	40	0.15
Australian (11)	11	0.04
Austrian (8)	29	0.11
Belgian (0)	51	0.19
British (150)	252	0.95
Canadian (12)	12	0.05
Croatian (0)	52	0.20
Czech (0)	13	0.05
Czechoslovakian (38)	49	0.18
Danish (33)	119	0.45
Dutch (75)	546	2.06
Eastern European (22)	22	0.08
English (1,506)	3,813	14.36
European (535)	570	2.15
Finnish (7)	7	0.03
French, ex. Basque (208)	785	2.96
French Canadian (17)	214	0.81
German (1,499)	4,722	17.78
Greek (57)	113	0.43
Hungarian (10)	100	0.38
Iranian (13)	13	0.05
Irish (867)	3,161	11.90
Israeli (8)	8	0.03
Italian (871)	1,920	7.23
Lithuanian (0)	57	0.21
Norwegian (48)	326	1.23
Polish (149)	634	2.39
Portuguese (41)	81	0.31
Romanian (37)	49	0.18
Russian (153)	431	1.62
Scandinavian (11)	36	0.14
Scotch-Irish (696)	1,544	5.81
Scottish (432)	1,433	5.40
Serbian (13)	13	0.05
Slovak (12)	62	0.23
Slovene (13)	13	0.05
Swedish (14)	160	0.60
Swiss (0)	12	0.05
Ukrainian (81)	220	0.83
Welsh (107)	343	1.29
West Indian, ex. Hispanic (83)	87	0.33
Haitian (27)	27	0.10
Jamaican (43)	43	0.16
Trinidadian/Tobagonian (13)	13	0.05
West Indian (0)	4	0.02

Hispanic Origin	Population	%
Hispanic or Latino (of any race)	1,579	5.81
Central American, ex. Mexican	259	0.95
Costa Rican	17	0.06
Guatemalan	29	0.11
Honduran	48	0.18
Nicaraguan	39	0.14
Panamanian	25	0.09
Salvadoran	100	0.37
Other Central American	1	<0.01
Cuban	82	0.30
Dominican Republic	75	0.28
Mexican	432	1.59
Puerto Rican	271	1.00
South American	306	1.13
Argentinean	20	0.07
Bolivian	2	0.01
Chilean	13	0.05
Colombian	97	0.36
Ecuadorian	87	0.32
Paraguayan	5	0.02
Peruvian	59	0.22
Venezuelan	23	0.08
Other Hispanic or Latino	154	0.57

Race*	Population	%
African-American/Black (2,609)	2,868	10.54
Not Hispanic (2,555)	2,767	10.17
Hispanic (54)	101	0.37
American Indian/Alaska Native (90)	182	0.67
Not Hispanic (79)	153	0.56
Hispanic (11)	29	0.11
Apache (1)	1	<0.01
Arapaho (1)	1	<0.01
Blackfeet (2)	3	0.01
Central American Ind. (0)	2	0.01
Cherokee (10)	33	0.12
Chickasaw (1)	1	<0.01
Chippewa (1)	1	<0.01
Choctaw (3)	4	0.01
Creek (2)	3	0.01
Iroquois (0)	2	0.01
Lumbee (32)	38	0.14
Mexican American Ind. (2)	2	0.01
Navajo (0)	1	<0.01
Potawatomi (3)	3	0.01
Seminole (1)	1	<0.01
South American Ind. (3)	5	0.02
Asian (1,155)	1,316	4.84
Not Hispanic (1,148)	1,297	4.77
Hispanic (7)	19	0.07
Burmese (5)	7	0.03
Cambodian (15)	25	0.09
Chinese, ex. Taiwanese (163)	202	0.74
Filipino (102)	146	0.54
Hmong (2)	2	0.01
Indian (283)	313	1.15
Indonesian (4)	4	0.01
Japanese (14)	39	0.14
Korean (163)	173	0.64
Laotian (15)	18	0.07
Pakistani (18)	18	0.07
Sri Lankan (9)	9	0.03
Taiwanese (6)	9	0.03
Thai (9)	16	0.06
Vietnamese (299)	335	1.23
Hawaii Native/Pacific Islander (9)	18	0.07
Not Hispanic (8)	17	0.06
Hispanic (1)	1	<0.01
Guamanian/Chamorro (2)	2	0.01
Native Hawaiian (1)	3	0.01
Samoan (2)	4	0.01
White (22,235)	22,697	83.45
Not Hispanic (21,344)	21,717	79.85
Hispanic (891)	980	3.60

Mebane

Place Type: City
County: Alamance
Population: 11,393†

Ancestry‡	Population	%
African, Sub-Saharan (25)	25	0.24
African (25)	25	0.24
American (950)	950	9.13
Arab (0)	17	0.16
Egyptian (0)	17	0.16
British (22)	22	0.21
Celtic (12)	12	0.12
Croatian (11)	11	0.11
Danish (47)	59	0.57
Dutch (45)	291	2.80
English (420)	1,189	11.43
European (173)	173	1.66
French, ex. Basque (39)	511	4.91
French Canadian (76)	86	0.83
German (362)	1,419	13.64
Greek (0)	5	0.05
Guyanese (0)	12	0.12
Irish (316)	1,154	11.10
Italian (54)	230	2.21
Lithuanian (0)	12	0.12
Norwegian (0)	67	0.64
Polish (62)	229	2.20
Portuguese (82)	82	0.79
Russian (14)	83	0.80
Scotch-Irish (188)	405	3.89
Scottish (192)	452	4.35
Slovak (11)	37	0.36
Swedish (39)	94	0.90
Yugoslavian (9)	9	0.09

Hispanic Origin	Population	%
Hispanic or Latino (of any race)	684	6.00
Central American, ex. Mexican	114	1.00
Costa Rican	4	0.04
Guatemalan	11	0.10
Honduran	39	0.34
Nicaraguan	14	0.12
Panamanian	5	0.04
Salvadoran	41	0.36
Cuban	21	0.18
Dominican Republic	31	0.27
Mexican	268	2.35
Puerto Rican	136	1.19
South American	58	0.51
Argentinean	2	0.02
Bolivian	4	0.04
Colombian	31	0.27
Ecuadorian	3	0.03
Peruvian	3	0.03
Venezuelan	15	0.13
Other Hispanic or Latino	56	0.49

Race*	Population	%
African-American/Black (2,324)	2,496	21.91
Not Hispanic (2,298)	2,428	21.31
Hispanic (26)	68	0.60
American Indian/Alaska Native (52)	120	1.05
Not Hispanic (29)	89	0.78
Hispanic (23)	31	0.27
Apache (0)	1	0.01
Blackfeet (0)	5	0.04
Central American Ind. (4)	4	0.04
Cherokee (0)	20	0.18
Chippewa (2)	4	0.04
Choctaw (1)	1	0.01
Iroquois (2)	7	0.06
Lumbee (8)	8	0.07
Mexican American Ind. (11)	12	0.11
Spanish American Ind. (1)	1	0.01
Yaqui (0)	1	0.01
Asian (142)	203	1.78
Not Hispanic (140)	193	1.69
Hispanic (2)	10	0.09
Burmese (15)	15	0.13
Chinese, ex. Taiwanese (20)	29	0.25
Filipino (24)	35	0.31
Indian (39)	43	0.38
Japanese (7)	12	0.11
Korean (21)	41	0.36
Laotian (2)	2	0.02
Malaysian (0)	5	0.04
Pakistani (3)	7	0.06
Thai (1)	2	0.02
Vietnamese (6)	9	0.08
Hawaii Native/Pacific Islander (13)	19	0.17
Not Hispanic (13)	15	0.13
Hispanic (0)	4	0.04
Guamanian/Chamorro (3)	4	0.04
Native Hawaiian (3)	8	0.07
Samoan (5)	5	0.04
White (8,378)	8,634	75.78
Not Hispanic (7,995)	8,185	71.84
Hispanic (383)	449	3.94

*Notes: † The Census 2010 population figure is used to calculate the percentages in the Hispanic Origin and Race categories. Ancestry percentages are based on the 2006-2010 American Community Survey population (not shown); ‡ Numbers in parentheses indicate the number of people reporting a single ancestry; * Numbers in parentheses indicate the number of persons reporting this race alone, not in combination with any other race; Please refer to the Explanation of Data for more information.*

Mint Hill

Place Type: Town
County: Mecklenburg
Population: 22,722†

Ancestry‡	Population	%
African, Sub-Saharan (114)	128	0.58
African (93)	107	0.49
Ghanaian (21)	21	0.10
American (2,278)	2,278	10.38
Arab (8)	16	0.07
Lebanese (8)	8	0.04
Moroccan (0)	8	0.04
Austrian (12)	48	0.22
British (84)	142	0.65
Canadian (16)	61	0.28
Croatian (0)	16	0.07
Czech (44)	55	0.25
Czechoslovakian (0)	11	0.05
Danish (0)	40	0.18
Dutch (39)	372	1.70
English (860)	2,921	13.31
European (276)	276	1.26
French, ex. Basque (127)	451	2.06
French Canadian (27)	51	0.23
German (1,088)	3,712	16.92
Greek (78)	110	0.50
Hungarian (0)	78	0.36
Icelander (0)	14	0.06
Irish (1,205)	3,060	13.95
Italian (236)	800	3.65
Lithuanian (30)	59	0.27
Norwegian (13)	138	0.63
Polish (115)	381	1.74
Portuguese (59)	73	0.33
Romanian (14)	43	0.20
Russian (64)	74	0.34
Scandinavian (32)	45	0.21
Scotch-Irish (1,010)	1,625	7.41
Scottish (298)	863	3.93
Serbian (0)	11	0.05
Slovak (9)	43	0.20
Swedish (60)	220	1.00
Swiss (8)	37	0.17
Ukrainian (179)	242	1.10
Welsh (84)	182	0.83
West Indian, ex. Hispanic (8)	24	0.11
Trinidadian/Tobagonian (0)	16	0.07
West Indian (8)	8	0.04
Yugoslavian (79)	79	0.36

Hispanic Origin	Population	%
Hispanic or Latino (of any race)	1,883	8.29
Central American, ex. Mexican	437	1.92
Costa Rican	12	0.05
Guatemalan	47	0.21
Honduran	99	0.44
Nicaraguan	40	0.18
Panamanian	4	0.02
Salvadoran	235	1.03
Cuban	97	0.43
Dominican Republic	59	0.26
Mexican	629	2.77
Puerto Rican	277	1.22
South American	250	1.10
Argentinean	27	0.12
Bolivian	4	0.02
Chilean	9	0.04
Colombian	114	0.50
Ecuadorian	39	0.17
Paraguayan	2	0.01
Peruvian	31	0.14
Uruguayan	2	0.01
Venezuelan	20	0.09
Other South American	2	0.01
Other Hispanic or Latino	134	0.59

Race*	Population	%
African-American/Black (2,804)	3,010	13.25
Not Hispanic (2,735)	2,921	12.86
Hispanic (69)	89	0.39
American Indian/Alaska Native (139)	244	1.07
Not Hispanic (113)	193	0.85
Hispanic (26)	51	0.22
Aleut *(Alaska Native)* (2)	3	0.01
Apache (0)	7	0.03
Blackfeet (2)	4	0.02
Cherokee (11)	40	0.18
Choctaw (0)	1	<0.01
Creek (0)	2	0.01
Crow (0)	1	<0.01
Delaware (0)	2	0.01
Iroquois (1)	1	<0.01
Kiowa (0)	4	0.02
Lumbee (52)	58	0.26
Mexican American Ind. (12)	12	0.05
Pueblo (1)	2	0.01
Sioux (1)	3	0.01
Asian (576)	705	3.10
Not Hispanic (559)	673	2.96
Hispanic (17)	32	0.14
Cambodian (13)	14	0.06
Chinese, ex. Taiwanese (75)	102	0.45
Filipino (33)	58	0.26
Hmong (29)	29	0.13
Indian (66)	82	0.36
Indonesian (3)	4	0.02
Japanese (15)	33	0.15
Korean (139)	156	0.69
Laotian (12)	12	0.05
Malaysian (0)	2	0.01
Pakistani (24)	24	0.11
Sri Lankan (1)	2	0.01
Thai (7)	7	0.03
Vietnamese (139)	153	0.67
Hawaii Native/Pacific Islander (6)	15	0.07
Not Hispanic (6)	14	0.06
Hispanic (0)	1	<0.01
Guamanian/Chamorro (0)	3	0.01
Native Hawaiian (2)	3	0.01
Samoan (0)	1	<0.01
White (17,818)	18,202	80.11
Not Hispanic (17,016)	17,334	76.29
Hispanic (802)	868	3.82

Monroe

Place Type: City
County: Union
Population: 32,797†

Ancestry‡	Population	%
African, Sub-Saharan (75)	75	0.23
African (53)	53	0.16
Other Sub-Saharan African (22)	22	0.07
American (3,398)	3,398	10.52
Arab (24)	48	0.15
Lebanese (24)	36	0.11
Syrian (0)	12	0.04
Austrian (0)	9	0.03
British (26)	39	0.12
Czech (10)	65	0.20
Danish (0)	102	0.32
Dutch (102)	253	0.78
English (1,102)	2,025	6.27
European (181)	198	0.61
French, ex. Basque (42)	298	0.92
French Canadian (31)	119	0.37
German (1,108)	3,316	10.27
Greek (76)	116	0.36
Hungarian (0)	22	0.07
Irish (567)	2,195	6.80
Italian (582)	1,001	3.10
Lithuanian (12)	33	0.10
Luxemburger (17)	17	0.05
Norwegian (36)	59	0.18
Pennsylvania German (0)	12	0.04
Polish (176)	482	1.49
Portuguese (0)	6	0.02
Romanian (20)	55	0.17
Russian (21)	21	0.07
Scotch-Irish (500)	752	2.33
Scottish (185)	661	2.05
Slovene (0)	27	0.08
Swedish (69)	122	0.38
Swiss (0)	8	0.02
Ukrainian (72)	78	0.24
Welsh (0)	31	0.10

Hispanic Origin	Population	%
Hispanic or Latino (of any race)	9,651	29.43
Central American, ex. Mexican	778	2.37
Costa Rican	20	0.06
Guatemalan	342	1.04
Honduran	156	0.48
Nicaraguan	33	0.10
Panamanian	14	0.04
Salvadoran	212	0.65
Other Central American	1	<0.01
Cuban	69	0.21
Dominican Republic	112	0.34
Mexican	7,773	23.70
Puerto Rican	359	1.09
South American	244	0.74
Argentinean	14	0.04
Chilean	9	0.03
Colombian	114	0.35
Ecuadorian	56	0.17
Peruvian	29	0.09
Uruguayan	4	0.01
Venezuelan	17	0.05
Other South American	1	<0.01
Other Hispanic or Latino	316	0.96

Race*	Population	%
African-American/Black (8,274)	8,696	26.51
Not Hispanic (8,142)	8,452	25.77
Hispanic (132)	244	0.74
American Indian/Alaska Native (204)	353	1.08
Not Hispanic (92)	201	0.61
Hispanic (112)	152	0.46
Apache (2)	2	0.01
Blackfeet (0)	12	0.04
Canadian/French Am. Ind. (1)	1	<0.01
Central American Ind. (2)	2	0.01
Cherokee (15)	53	0.16
Chippewa (1)	2	0.01
Cree (0)	2	0.01
Creek (2)	4	0.01
Delaware (0)	2	0.01
Iroquois (6)	7	0.02
Lumbee (38)	47	0.14
Mexican American Ind. (20)	23	0.07
Navajo (1)	1	<0.01
Osage (3)	4	0.01
Potawatomi (0)	1	<0.01
Pueblo (1)	1	<0.01
Shoshone (0)	1	<0.01
Sioux (2)	6	0.02
South American Ind. (1)	3	0.01
Spanish American Ind. (5)	5	0.02
Yaqui (0)	3	0.01
Asian (301)	385	1.17
Not Hispanic (287)	348	1.06
Hispanic (14)	37	0.11
Chinese, ex. Taiwanese (52)	58	0.18
Filipino (54)	91	0.28
Hmong (14)	14	0.04
Indian (91)	107	0.33
Indonesian (0)	1	<0.01
Japanese (1)	15	0.05
Korean (26)	47	0.14
Laotian (3)	3	0.01
Thai (2)	4	0.01
Vietnamese (40)	40	0.12
Hawaii Native/Pacific Islander (7)	24	0.07
Not Hispanic (4)	12	0.04
Hispanic (3)	12	0.04
Guamanian/Chamorro (3)	3	0.01

SECTION TWO

*Notes: † The Census 2010 population figure is used to calculate the percentages in the Hispanic Origin and Race categories. Ancestry percentages are based on the 2006-2010 American Community Survey population (not shown); ‡ Numbers in parentheses indicate the number of people reporting a single ancestry; * Numbers in parentheses indicate the number of persons reporting this race alone, not in combination with any other race; Please refer to the Explanation of Data for more information.*

Native Hawaiian (2)	11	0.03
Samoan (1)	2	0.01
White (17,063)	17,748	54.11
Not Hispanic (14,149)	14,500	44.21
Hispanic (2,914)	3,248	9.90

Mooresville

Place Type: Town
County: Iredell
Population: 32,711†

Ancestry‡	Population	%
African, Sub-Saharan (101)	148	0.48
African (26)	73	0.24
Cape Verdean (17)	17	0.06
Ghanaian (58)	58	0.19
American (2,940)	2,940	9.61
Arab (11)	147	0.48
Lebanese (11)	99	0.32
Syrian (0)	48	0.16
Austrian (0)	19	0.06
British (84)	213	0.70
Canadian (38)	38	0.12
Croatian (18)	56	0.18
Czech (23)	82	0.27
Danish (0)	12	0.04
Dutch (55)	548	1.79
Eastern European (27)	27	0.09
English (1,501)	3,183	10.41
European (148)	160	0.52
Finnish (0)	25	0.08
French, ex. Basque (108)	695	2.27
French Canadian (22)	87	0.28
German (1,413)	4,434	14.50
Greek (52)	105	0.34
Hungarian (52)	134	0.44
Irish (1,113)	4,076	13.33
Italian (844)	2,217	7.25
Lithuanian (0)	10	0.03
New Zealander (44)	44	0.14
Northern European (14)	14	0.05
Norwegian (95)	269	0.88
Pennsylvania German (0)	21	0.07
Polish (135)	849	2.78
Portuguese (0)	20	0.07
Romanian (0)	14	0.05
Russian (52)	156	0.51
Scandinavian (11)	60	0.20
Scotch-Irish (485)	848	2.77
Scottish (371)	835	2.73
Slovak (19)	52	0.17
Swedish (24)	219	0.72
Swiss (57)	125	0.41
Ukrainian (19)	19	0.06
Welsh (15)	110	0.36
West Indian, ex. Hispanic (219)	262	0.86
Haitian (219)	219	0.72
West Indian (0)	43	0.14

Hispanic Origin	Population	%
Hispanic or Latino (of any race)	2,252	6.88
Central American, ex. Mexican	204	0.62
Costa Rican	32	0.10
Guatemalan	36	0.11
Honduran	19	0.06
Nicaraguan	16	0.05
Panamanian	12	0.04
Salvadoran	88	0.27
Other Central American	1	<0.01
Cuban	110	0.34
Dominican Republic	50	0.15
Mexican	1,196	3.66
Puerto Rican	241	0.74
South American	291	0.89
Argentinean	10	0.03
Chilean	13	0.04
Colombian	143	0.44
Ecuadorian	42	0.13
Peruvian	55	0.17
Uruguayan	8	0.02
Venezuelan	20	0.06
Other Hispanic or Latino	160	0.49

Race*	Population	%
African-American/Black (3,567)	3,965	12.12
Not Hispanic (3,507)	3,863	11.81
Hispanic (60)	102	0.31
American Indian/Alaska Native (162)	359	1.10
Not Hispanic (122)	296	0.90
Hispanic (40)	63	0.19
Apache (0)	5	0.02
Blackfeet (3)	12	0.04
Cherokee (30)	91	0.28
Chickasaw (0)	1	<0.01
Chippewa (0)	2	0.01
Choctaw (3)	6	0.02
Creek (1)	3	0.01
Crow (4)	4	0.01
Delaware (1)	2	0.01
Iroquois (7)	11	0.03
Lumbee (18)	35	0.11
Mexican American Ind. (3)	6	0.02
Navajo (1)	3	0.01
Paiute (1)	1	<0.01
Pueblo (1)	1	<0.01
Seminole (0)	1	<0.01
Shoshone (0)	3	0.01
Sioux (1)	4	0.01
Spanish American Ind. (2)	3	0.01
Tlingit-Haida *(Alaska Native)* (2)	2	0.01
Asian (1,073)	1,275	3.90
Not Hispanic (1,068)	1,248	3.82
Hispanic (5)	27	0.08
Cambodian (11)	11	0.03
Chinese, ex. Taiwanese (158)	181	0.55
Filipino (110)	152	0.46
Hmong (28)	29	0.09
Indian (544)	583	1.78
Indonesian (4)	6	0.02
Japanese (42)	77	0.24
Korean (47)	66	0.20
Laotian (21)	29	0.09
Malaysian (1)	1	<0.01
Pakistani (32)	34	0.10
Thai (9)	19	0.06
Vietnamese (40)	55	0.17
Hawaii Native/Pacific Islander (12)	31	0.09
Not Hispanic (10)	22	0.07
Hispanic (2)	9	0.03
Guamanian/Chamorro (9)	13	0.04
Native Hawaiian (2)	9	0.03
Samoan (0)	1	<0.01
White (26,229)	26,921	82.30
Not Hispanic (25,074)	25,630	78.35
Hispanic (1,155)	1,291	3.95

Morehead City

Place Type: Town
County: Carteret
Population: 8,661†

Ancestry‡	Population	%
African, Sub-Saharan (21)	21	0.25
African (21)	21	0.25
American (1,267)	1,267	14.87
Armenian (10)	39	0.46
Austrian (0)	37	0.43
British (126)	162	1.90
Canadian (0)	98	1.15
Croatian (0)	20	0.23
Czech (0)	143	1.68
Czechoslovakian (51)	64	0.75
Dutch (19)	68	0.80
English (660)	1,230	14.43
European (111)	140	1.64
French, ex. Basque (76)	271	3.18
French Canadian (14)	14	0.16
German (241)	976	11.45
Greek (39)	39	0.46
Hungarian (0)	22	0.26
Irish (314)	1,225	14.37
Italian (99)	297	3.48
Maltese (18)	18	0.21
New Zealander (22)	22	0.26
Norwegian (28)	28	0.33
Polish (13)	141	1.65
Romanian (50)	50	0.59
Russian (41)	65	0.76
Scandinavian (11)	11	0.13
Scotch-Irish (203)	477	5.60
Scottish (44)	105	1.23
Welsh (0)	71	0.83

Hispanic Origin	Population	%
Hispanic or Latino (of any race)	598	6.90
Central American, ex. Mexican	62	0.72
Costa Rican	2	0.02
Guatemalan	21	0.24
Honduran	21	0.24
Nicaraguan	4	0.05
Panamanian	3	0.03
Salvadoran	11	0.13
Cuban	15	0.17
Dominican Republic	1	0.01
Mexican	440	5.08
Puerto Rican	47	0.54
South American	14	0.16
Argentinean	2	0.02
Bolivian	1	0.01
Colombian	2	0.02
Ecuadorian	2	0.02
Peruvian	4	0.05
Uruguayan	3	0.03
Other Hispanic or Latino	19	0.22

Race*	Population	%
African-American/Black (931)	1,052	12.15
Not Hispanic (920)	1,030	11.89
Hispanic (11)	22	0.25
American Indian/Alaska Native (46)	112	1.29
Not Hispanic (39)	99	1.14
Hispanic (7)	13	0.15
Blackfeet (1)	8	0.09
Cherokee (6)	32	0.37
Chippewa (3)	5	0.06
Choctaw (0)	1	0.01
Iroquois (1)	2	0.02
Lumbee (7)	15	0.17
Pima (0)	1	0.01
Sioux (0)	1	0.01
Asian (136)	194	2.24
Not Hispanic (136)	185	2.14
Hispanic (0)	9	0.10
Burmese (18)	19	0.22
Chinese, ex. Taiwanese (39)	48	0.55
Filipino (24)	47	0.54
Indian (17)	31	0.36
Japanese (12)	18	0.21
Korean (3)	4	0.05
Malaysian (2)	2	0.02
Pakistani (1)	1	0.01
Thai (7)	11	0.13
Vietnamese (10)	12	0.14
Hawaii Native/Pacific Islander (21)	33	0.38
Not Hispanic (20)	26	0.30
Hispanic (1)	7	0.08
Fijian (0)	1	0.01
Guamanian/Chamorro (6)	6	0.07
Native Hawaiian (10)	13	0.15
Samoan (1)	3	0.03
White (7,102)	7,279	84.04
Not Hispanic (6,746)	6,904	79.71
Hispanic (356)	375	4.33

*Notes: † The Census 2010 population figure is used to calculate the percentages in the Hispanic Origin and Race categories. Ancestry percentages are based on the 2006-2010 American Community Survey population (not shown); ‡ Numbers in parentheses indicate the number of people reporting a single ancestry; * Numbers in parentheses indicate the number of persons reporting this race alone, not in combination with any other race; Please refer to the Explanation of Data for more information.*

Morganton

Place Type: City
County: Burke
Population: 16,918†

Ancestry‡	Population	%
African, Sub-Saharan (77)	77	0.45
African (77)	77	0.45
American (2,950)	2,950	17.38
Arab (41)	63	0.37
Egyptian (34)	34	0.20
Lebanese (7)	29	0.17
Austrian (0)	51	0.30
British (127)	148	0.87
Czech (8)	8	0.05
Dutch (38)	187	1.10
English (753)	1,884	11.10
European (205)	217	1.28
Finnish (0)	9	0.05
French, ex. Basque (54)	323	1.90
French Canadian (45)	56	0.33
German (846)	2,364	13.93
Hungarian (25)	66	0.39
Irish (572)	1,663	9.80
Italian (70)	290	1.71
Maltese (9)	9	0.05
Norwegian (15)	45	0.27
Polish (0)	25	0.15
Portuguese (0)	8	0.05
Russian (0)	20	0.12
Scandinavian (6)	6	0.04
Scotch-Irish (481)	899	5.30
Scottish (254)	708	4.17
Swedish (0)	30	0.18
Swiss (0)	10	0.06
Welsh (12)	64	0.38

Hispanic Origin	Population	%
Hispanic or Latino (of any race)	2,777	16.41
Central American, ex. Mexican	1,633	9.65
Costa Rican	12	0.07
Guatemalan	1,507	8.91
Honduran	61	0.36
Panamanian	3	0.02
Salvadoran	44	0.26
Other Central American	6	0.04
Cuban	15	0.09
Dominican Republic	3	0.02
Mexican	580	3.43
Puerto Rican	45	0.27
South American	25	0.15
Argentinean	4	0.02
Bolivian	1	0.01
Chilean	2	0.01
Colombian	7	0.04
Ecuadorian	3	0.02
Peruvian	5	0.03
Venezuelan	3	0.02
Other Hispanic or Latino	476	2.81

Race*	Population	%
African-American/Black (2,057)	2,274	13.44
Not Hispanic (2,020)	2,227	13.16
Hispanic (37)	47	0.28
American Indian/Alaska Native (144)	243	1.44
Not Hispanic (34)	107	0.63
Hispanic (110)	136	0.80
Apache (0)	1	0.01
Blackfeet (0)	4	0.02
Central American Ind. (20)	31	0.18
Cherokee (11)	49	0.29
Chippewa (2)	2	0.01
Comanche (0)	1	0.01
Iroquois (1)	1	0.01
Lumbee (3)	3	0.02
Mexican American Ind. (77)	80	0.47
Paiute (0)	1	0.01
Sioux (1)	2	0.01
South American Ind. (2)	3	0.02
Asian (399)	483	2.85
Not Hispanic (391)	437	2.58
Hispanic (8)	46	0.27
Bangladeshi (4)	4	0.02
Chinese, ex. Taiwanese (46)	49	0.29
Filipino (19)	33	0.20
Hmong (142)	163	0.96
Indian (111)	129	0.76
Indonesian (5)	5	0.03
Japanese (8)	8	0.05
Korean (7)	14	0.08
Laotian (17)	17	0.10
Malaysian (1)	1	0.01
Nepalese (4)	4	0.02
Pakistani (7)	7	0.04
Thai (4)	4	0.02
Vietnamese (5)	8	0.05
Hawaii Native/Pacific Islander (250)	272	1.61
Not Hispanic (136)	139	0.82
Hispanic (114)	133	0.79
Guamanian/Chamorro (244)	246	1.45
Native Hawaiian (1)	3	0.02
Samoan (1)	2	0.01
White (11,854)	12,264	72.49
Not Hispanic (11,240)	11,516	68.07
Hispanic (614)	748	4.42

Morrisville

Place Type: Town
County: Wake
Population: 18,576†

Ancestry‡	Population	%
African, Sub-Saharan (106)	186	1.15
African (54)	95	0.59
Nigerian (32)	43	0.27
South African (20)	37	0.23
Zimbabwean (0)	11	0.07
Alsatian (12)	23	0.14
American (628)	628	3.89
Arab (128)	128	0.79
Jordanian (14)	14	0.09
Lebanese (51)	51	0.32
Palestinian (63)	63	0.39
Austrian (14)	42	0.26
Belgian (17)	34	0.21
Brazilian (14)	31	0.19
British (222)	268	1.66
Bulgarian (17)	17	0.11
Canadian (10)	10	0.06
Czech (13)	277	1.72
Danish (16)	43	0.27
Dutch (73)	183	1.13
English (342)	1,487	9.21
European (88)	258	1.60
Finnish (0)	44	0.27
French, ex. Basque (66)	278	1.72
French Canadian (44)	110	0.68
German (335)	1,618	10.02
Hungarian (19)	103	0.64
Iranian (76)	76	0.47
Irish (533)	1,516	9.39
Israeli (15)	15	0.09
Italian (418)	1,005	6.22
Lithuanian (0)	124	0.77
Maltese (0)	12	0.07
Northern European (13)	13	0.08
Norwegian (0)	34	0.21
Polish (108)	477	2.95
Romanian (11)	11	0.07
Russian (76)	153	0.95
Scandinavian (0)	159	0.98
Scotch-Irish (176)	534	3.31
Scottish (75)	372	2.30
Slovak (31)	39	0.24
Swedish (58)	106	0.66
Swiss (21)	28	0.17
Turkish (33)	33	0.20
Ukrainian (0)	46	0.28
Welsh (85)	267	1.65

Hispanic Origin	Population	%
Hispanic or Latino (of any race)	1,092	5.88
Central American, ex. Mexican	95	0.51
Costa Rican	9	0.05
Guatemalan	9	0.05
Honduran	16	0.09
Nicaraguan	3	0.02
Panamanian	21	0.11
Salvadoran	36	0.19
Other Central American	1	0.01
Cuban	64	0.34
Dominican Republic	78	0.42
Mexican	257	1.38
Puerto Rican	221	1.19
South American	286	1.54
Argentinean	4	0.02
Bolivian	2	0.01
Chilean	19	0.10
Colombian	119	0.64
Ecuadorian	36	0.19
Paraguayan	1	0.01
Peruvian	73	0.39
Uruguayan	2	0.01
Venezuelan	30	0.16
Other Hispanic or Latino	91	0.49

Race*	Population	%
African-American/Black (2,402)	2,669	14.37
Not Hispanic (2,352)	2,568	13.82
Hispanic (50)	101	0.54
American Indian/Alaska Native (75)	198	1.07
Not Hispanic (71)	180	0.97
Hispanic (4)	18	0.10
Central American Ind. (0)	4	0.02
Cherokee (12)	31	0.17
Chickasaw (1)	1	0.01
Chippewa (4)	4	0.02
Choctaw (0)	4	0.02
Creek (0)	2	0.01
Iroquois (2)	3	0.02
Lumbee (18)	28	0.15
Mexican American Ind. (1)	2	0.01
Ottawa (1)	1	0.01
Pueblo (0)	3	0.02
Sioux (1)	1	0.01
South American Ind. (1)	4	0.02
Asian (5,058)	5,378	28.95
Not Hispanic (5,051)	5,354	28.82
Hispanic (7)	24	0.13
Bangladeshi (40)	41	0.22
Cambodian (3)	5	0.03
Chinese, ex. Taiwanese (454)	502	2.70
Filipino (100)	162	0.87
Hmong (3)	3	0.02
Indian (3,717)	3,809	20.50
Indonesian (9)	14	0.08
Japanese (67)	111	0.60
Korean (160)	198	1.07
Laotian (2)	6	0.03
Malaysian (5)	11	0.06
Nepalese (62)	70	0.38
Pakistani (140)	144	0.78
Sri Lankan (31)	34	0.18
Taiwanese (26)	29	0.16
Thai (22)	38	0.20
Vietnamese (158)	181	0.97
Hawaii Native/Pacific Islander (12)	37	0.20
Not Hispanic (12)	37	0.20
Guamanian/Chamorro (0)	1	0.01
Native Hawaiian (9)	20	0.11
White (10,030)	10,479	56.41
Not Hispanic (9,417)	9,818	52.85
Hispanic (613)	661	3.56

*Notes: † The Census 2010 population figure is used to calculate the percentages in the Hispanic Origin and Race categories. Ancestry percentages are based on the 2006-2010 American Community Survey population (not shown); ‡ Numbers in parentheses indicate the number of people reporting a single ancestry; * Numbers in parentheses indicate the number of persons reporting this race alone, not in combination with any other race; Please refer to the Explanation of Data for more information.*

Mount Airy

Place Type: City
County: Surry
Population: 10,388†

Ancestry‡	Population	%
African, Sub-Saharan (44)	44	0.42
African (44)	44	0.42
American (1,774)	1,774	16.86
British (29)	38	0.36
Bulgarian (64)	64	0.61
Canadian (0)	22	0.21
Dutch (30)	175	1.66
English (823)	1,446	13.75
European (43)	43	0.41
French, ex. Basque (47)	163	1.55
French Canadian (107)	107	1.02
German (520)	1,086	10.32
Hungarian (0)	12	0.11
Irish (284)	771	7.33
Italian (57)	102	0.97
Polish (44)	44	0.42
Romanian (39)	52	0.49
Russian (117)	173	1.64
Scotch-Irish (309)	509	4.84
Scottish (59)	120	1.14
Slovak (14)	14	0.13
Swedish (0)	27	0.26
Swiss (0)	15	0.14
Ukrainian (36)	36	0.34
Welsh (0)	28	0.27
West Indian, ex. Hispanic (14)	14	0.13
Bahamian (14)	14	0.13

Hispanic Origin	Population	%
Hispanic or Latino (of any race)	699	6.73
Central American, ex. Mexican	15	0.14
Costa Rican	4	0.04
Guatemalan	6	0.06
Honduran	3	0.03
Salvadoran	2	0.02
Cuban	6	0.06
Dominican Republic	5	0.05
Mexican	569	5.48
Puerto Rican	35	0.34
South American	12	0.12
Argentinean	3	0.03
Chilean	2	0.02
Peruvian	1	0.01
Venezuelan	4	0.04
Other South American	2	0.02
Other Hispanic or Latino	57	0.55

Race*	Population	%
African-American/Black (856)	971	9.35
Not Hispanic (846)	946	9.11
Hispanic (10)	25	0.24
American Indian/Alaska Native (29)	104	1.00
Not Hispanic (29)	94	0.90
Hispanic (0)	10	0.10
Aleut *(Alaska Native)* (2)	2	0.02
Apache (0)	2	0.02
Canadian/French Am. Ind. (1)	1	0.01
Cherokee (6)	25	0.24
Chickasaw (1)	2	0.02
Choctaw (0)	1	0.01
Comanche (1)	2	0.02
Lumbee (8)	8	0.08
Mexican American Ind. (0)	1	0.01
Sioux (1)	1	0.01
Asian (148)	173	1.67
Not Hispanic (147)	170	1.64
Hispanic (1)	3	0.03
Chinese, ex. Taiwanese (20)	21	0.20
Filipino (26)	36	0.35
Hmong (46)	46	0.44
Indian (22)	23	0.22
Indonesian (3)	3	0.03
Japanese (1)	9	0.09
Korean (7)	7	0.07
Pakistani (6)	6	0.06
Vietnamese (14)	15	0.14
Hawaii Native/Pacific Islander (6)	11	0.11
Not Hispanic (3)	6	0.06
Hispanic (3)	5	0.05
Guamanian/Chamorro (3)	3	0.03
Native Hawaiian (1)	3	0.03
White (8,741)	8,959	86.24
Not Hispanic (8,484)	8,658	83.35
Hispanic (257)	301	2.90

Mount Holly

Place Type: City
County: Gaston
Population: 13,656†

Ancestry‡	Population	%
African, Sub-Saharan (22)	22	0.17
African (22)	22	0.17
American (1,166)	1,166	9.03
Arab (225)	262	2.03
Jordanian (175)	205	1.59
Syrian (0)	7	0.05
Other Arab (50)	50	0.39
Austrian (0)	11	0.09
Belgian (0)	17	0.13
British (38)	49	0.38
Bulgarian (30)	30	0.23
Dutch (71)	368	2.85
English (479)	1,462	11.32
European (49)	89	0.69
French, ex. Basque (248)	503	3.89
French Canadian (13)	30	0.23
German (616)	2,173	16.83
Greek (0)	11	0.09
Hungarian (8)	19	0.15
Irish (147)	1,129	8.74
Italian (84)	211	1.63
Norwegian (25)	95	0.74
Pennsylvania German (0)	20	0.15
Polish (48)	148	1.15
Romanian (11)	36	0.28
Russian (0)	12	0.09
Scandinavian (0)	20	0.15
Scotch-Irish (379)	662	5.13
Scottish (19)	518	4.01
Slavic (14)	14	0.11
Slovak (0)	16	0.12
Swedish (0)	6	0.05
Swiss (0)	119	0.92
Welsh (0)	13	0.10
West Indian, ex. Hispanic (13)	29	0.22
Haitian (13)	29	0.22

Hispanic Origin	Population	%
Hispanic or Latino (of any race)	749	5.48
Central American, ex. Mexican	92	0.67
Costa Rican	9	0.07
Guatemalan	21	0.15
Honduran	25	0.18
Nicaraguan	8	0.06
Panamanian	6	0.04
Salvadoran	23	0.17
Cuban	21	0.15
Dominican Republic	6	0.04
Mexican	354	2.59
Puerto Rican	94	0.69
South American	91	0.67
Argentinean	5	0.04
Bolivian	1	0.01
Chilean	1	0.01
Colombian	32	0.23
Ecuadorian	29	0.21
Paraguayan	1	0.01
Peruvian	8	0.06
Uruguayan	3	0.02
Venezuelan	11	0.08
Other Hispanic or Latino	91	0.67

Race*	Population	%
African-American/Black (1,735)	1,837	13.45
Not Hispanic (1,717)	1,810	13.25
Hispanic (18)	27	0.20
American Indian/Alaska Native (53)	107	0.78
Not Hispanic (39)	93	0.68
Hispanic (14)	14	0.10
Blackfeet (3)	4	0.03
Central American Ind. (6)	6	0.04
Cherokee (12)	25	0.18
Chippewa (0)	2	0.01
Choctaw (0)	1	0.01
Creek (5)	9	0.07
Delaware (0)	1	0.01
Iroquois (0)	1	0.01
Lumbee (17)	22	0.16
Mexican American Ind. (1)	1	0.01
Ottawa (0)	1	0.01
Asian (332)	395	2.89
Not Hispanic (331)	393	2.88
Hispanic (1)	2	0.01
Cambodian (13)	14	0.10
Chinese, ex. Taiwanese (12)	15	0.11
Filipino (17)	40	0.29
Hmong (6)	6	0.04
Indian (43)	47	0.34
Japanese (6)	8	0.06
Korean (18)	22	0.16
Laotian (154)	170	1.24
Pakistani (0)	2	0.01
Thai (4)	5	0.04
Vietnamese (43)	46	0.34
Hawaii Native/Pacific Islander (7)	15	0.11
Not Hispanic (7)	15	0.11
Guamanian/Chamorro (3)	3	0.02
Native Hawaiian (4)	9	0.07
Samoan (0)	2	0.01
White (10,979)	11,177	81.85
Not Hispanic (10,588)	10,767	78.84
Hispanic (391)	410	3.00

Murraysville

Place Type: CDP
County: New Hanover
Population: 14,215†

Ancestry‡	Population	%
African, Sub-Saharan (31)	57	0.43
African (31)	57	0.43
American (2,175)	2,175	16.36
Arab (0)	14	0.11
Syrian (0)	14	0.11
Belgian (0)	7	0.05
Brazilian (0)	11	0.08
British (41)	107	0.80
Canadian (41)	41	0.31
Croatian (19)	19	0.14
Czech (22)	73	0.55
Danish (0)	20	0.15
Dutch (11)	155	1.17
Eastern European (34)	34	0.26
English (689)	1,655	12.45
European (49)	60	0.45
French, ex. Basque (78)	309	2.32
French Canadian (77)	123	0.93
German (659)	1,819	13.68
Greek (18)	18	0.14
Hungarian (15)	29	0.22
Irish (561)	1,813	13.64
Italian (490)	835	6.28
Lithuanian (9)	58	0.44
Maltese (14)	14	0.11
Norwegian (18)	34	0.26
Pennsylvania German (11)	11	0.08
Polish (43)	294	2.21
Russian (16)	63	0.47
Scandinavian (0)	41	0.31
Scotch-Irish (359)	549	4.13

*Notes: † The Census 2010 population figure is used to calculate the percentages in the Hispanic Origin and Race categories. Ancestry percentages are based on the 2006-2010 American Community Survey population (not shown); ‡ Numbers in parentheses indicate the number of people reporting a single ancestry; * Numbers in parentheses indicate the number of persons reporting this race alone, not in combination with any other race; Please refer to the Explanation of Data for more information.*

Scottish (146)	373	2.81
Slavic (0)	8	0.06
Slovak (26)	144	1.08
Swedish (24)	138	1.04
Swiss (0)	32	0.24
Turkish (38)	38	0.29
Ukrainian (14)	71	0.53
Welsh (69)	99	0.74
West Indian, ex. Hispanic (18)	18	0.14
Haitian (18)	18	0.14
Yugoslavian (49)	49	0.37

Hispanic Origin	Population	%
Hispanic or Latino (of any race)	748	5.26
Central American, ex. Mexican	149	1.05
Costa Rican	1	0.01
Guatemalan	14	0.10
Honduran	15	0.11
Nicaraguan	1	0.01
Panamanian	12	0.08
Salvadoran	106	0.75
Cuban	31	0.22
Dominican Republic	15	0.11
Mexican	316	2.22
Puerto Rican	128	0.90
South American	46	0.32
Argentinean	6	0.04
Bolivian	3	0.02
Chilean	8	0.06
Colombian	9	0.06
Ecuadorian	8	0.06
Peruvian	5	0.04
Uruguayan	1	0.01
Venezuelan	6	0.04
Other Hispanic or Latino	63	0.44

Race*	Population	%
African-American/Black (1,943)	2,080	14.63
Not Hispanic (1,922)	2,046	14.39
Hispanic (21)	34	0.24
American Indian/Alaska Native (45)	104	0.73
Not Hispanic (36)	87	0.61
Hispanic (9)	17	0.12
Apache (0)	1	0.01
Central American Ind. (0)	1	0.01
Cherokee (5)	33	0.23
Chippewa (4)	4	0.03
Choctaw (1)	2	0.01
Lumbee (9)	12	0.08
Mexican American Ind. (2)	2	0.01
Navajo (0)	1	0.01
Osage (1)	1	0.01
Ottawa (1)	1	0.01
Sioux (0)	1	0.01
Asian (276)	371	2.61
Not Hispanic (274)	357	2.51
Hispanic (2)	14	0.10
Burmese (1)	1	0.01
Cambodian (2)	4	0.03
Chinese, ex. Taiwanese (49)	64	0.45
Filipino (22)	43	0.30
Indian (46)	50	0.35
Japanese (8)	34	0.24
Korean (20)	33	0.23
Laotian (5)	5	0.04
Malaysian (0)	2	0.01
Pakistani (0)	3	0.02
Taiwanese (2)	2	0.01
Thai (5)	11	0.08
Vietnamese (107)	114	0.80
Hawaii Native/Pacific Islander (8)	29	0.20
Not Hispanic (7)	24	0.17
Hispanic (1)	5	0.04
Guamanian/Chamorro (2)	2	0.01
Native Hawaiian (3)	17	0.12
Samoan (3)	3	0.02
White (11,314)	11,563	81.34
Not Hispanic (10,974)	11,173	78.60
Hispanic (340)	390	2.74

Myrtle Grove

Place Type: CDP
County: New Hanover
Population: 8,875†

Ancestry‡	Population	%
American (1,301)	1,301	15.08
Austrian (0)	14	0.16
British (112)	112	1.30
Canadian (0)	12	0.14
Czech (0)	32	0.37
Czechoslovakian (14)	14	0.16
Danish (10)	21	0.24
Dutch (23)	195	2.26
Eastern European (11)	11	0.13
English (675)	1,654	19.17
European (21)	21	0.24
French, ex. Basque (54)	217	2.52
French Canadian (27)	27	0.31
German (502)	1,440	16.69
Greek (89)	147	1.70
Hungarian (19)	29	0.34
Iranian (19)	19	0.22
Irish (298)	1,307	15.15
Israeli (14)	14	0.16
Italian (167)	607	7.04
Northern European (23)	23	0.27
Norwegian (14)	117	1.36
Polish (70)	158	1.83
Portuguese (45)	61	0.71
Romanian (19)	35	0.41
Russian (35)	35	0.41
Scandinavian (0)	40	0.46
Scotch-Irish (116)	323	3.74
Scottish (64)	250	2.90
Slovak (13)	13	0.15
Swedish (0)	107	1.24
Ukrainian (22)	117	1.36
Welsh (23)	100	1.16

Hispanic Origin	Population	%
Hispanic or Latino (of any race)	184	2.07
Central American, ex. Mexican	14	0.16
Costa Rican	3	0.03
Guatemalan	2	0.02
Honduran	2	0.02
Nicaraguan	2	0.02
Panamanian	3	0.03
Salvadoran	2	0.02
Cuban	5	0.06
Dominican Republic	9	0.10
Mexican	58	0.65
Puerto Rican	61	0.69
South American	18	0.20
Argentinean	2	0.02
Bolivian	1	0.01
Chilean	3	0.03
Colombian	4	0.05
Ecuadorian	1	0.01
Peruvian	6	0.07
Venezuelan	1	0.01
Other Hispanic or Latino	19	0.21

Race*	Population	%
African-American/Black (285)	332	3.74
Not Hispanic (279)	321	3.62
Hispanic (6)	11	0.12
American Indian/Alaska Native (29)	62	0.70
Not Hispanic (29)	60	0.68
Hispanic (0)	2	0.02
Cherokee (1)	11	0.12
Chickasaw (1)	1	0.01
Chippewa (1)	2	0.02
Choctaw (0)	1	0.01
Lumbee (9)	12	0.14
South American Ind. (0)	1	0.01
Asian (103)	136	1.53
Not Hispanic (102)	131	1.48
Hispanic (1)	5	0.06
Chinese, ex. Taiwanese (21)	22	0.25
Filipino (16)	21	0.24
Indian (22)	26	0.29
Japanese (4)	5	0.06
Korean (7)	14	0.16
Thai (7)	7	0.08
Vietnamese (23)	25	0.28
Hawaii Native/Pacific Islander (7)	20	0.23
Not Hispanic (7)	20	0.23
Guamanian/Chamorro (1)	1	0.01
Native Hawaiian (4)	7	0.08
Samoan (1)	4	0.05
White (8,254)	8,362	94.22
Not Hispanic (8,149)	8,244	92.89
Hispanic (105)	118	1.33

New Bern

Place Type: City
County: Craven
Population: 29,524†

Ancestry‡	Population	%
African, Sub-Saharan (220)	287	1.02
African (220)	249	0.89
South African (0)	38	0.14
American (1,631)	1,631	5.81
Arab (47)	122	0.43
Lebanese (47)	112	0.40
Syrian (0)	10	0.04
Armenian (16)	16	0.06
Austrian (0)	47	0.17
Belgian (0)	37	0.13
British (52)	65	0.23
Canadian (52)	52	0.19
Croatian (0)	70	0.25
Czech (0)	35	0.12
Czechoslovakian (8)	22	0.08
Danish (11)	65	0.23
Dutch (57)	224	0.80
English (1,841)	4,017	14.31
European (469)	469	1.67
Finnish (11)	35	0.12
French, ex. Basque (284)	1,178	4.20
French Canadian (44)	71	0.25
German (810)	2,764	9.85
Greek (0)	38	0.14
Guyanese (13)	13	0.05
Hungarian (63)	107	0.38
Irish (879)	3,257	11.60
Italian (383)	1,373	4.89
Lithuanian (48)	92	0.33
Macedonian (14)	14	0.05
Norwegian (55)	151	0.54
Pennsylvania German (37)	37	0.13
Polish (199)	711	2.53
Portuguese (17)	25	0.09
Romanian (0)	7	0.02
Russian (15)	105	0.37
Scandinavian (53)	53	0.19
Scotch-Irish (403)	951	3.39
Scottish (284)	745	2.65
Slovak (0)	68	0.24
Swedish (44)	222	0.79
Swiss (58)	161	0.57
Ukrainian (27)	44	0.16
Welsh (0)	232	0.83
West Indian, ex. Hispanic (70)	82	0.29
Belizean (70)	70	0.25
West Indian (0)	12	0.04
Yugoslavian (43)	43	0.15

Hispanic Origin	Population	%
Hispanic or Latino (of any race)	1,712	5.80
Central American, ex. Mexican	139	0.47
Costa Rican	5	0.02
Guatemalan	40	0.14
Honduran	55	0.19
Nicaraguan	1	<0.01
Panamanian	11	0.04

*Notes: † The Census 2010 population figure is used to calculate the percentages in the Hispanic Origin and Race categories. Ancestry percentages are based on the 2006-2010 American Community Survey population (not shown); ‡ Numbers in parentheses indicate the number of people reporting a single ancestry; * Numbers in parentheses indicate the number of persons reporting this race alone, not in combination with any other race; Please refer to the Explanation of Data for more information.*

Salvadoran	27	0.09
Cuban	41	0.14
Dominican Republic	22	0.07
Mexican	960	3.25
Puerto Rican	307	1.04
South American	104	0.35
Argentinean	5	0.02
Bolivian	3	0.01
Chilean	1	<0.01
Colombian	48	0.16
Ecuadorian	13	0.04
Paraguayan	13	0.04
Peruvian	7	0.02
Venezuelan	13	0.04
Other South American	1	<0.01
Other Hispanic or Latino	139	0.47

Race*	Population	%
African-American/Black (9,790)	10,146	34.37
Not Hispanic (9,679)	9,992	33.84
Hispanic (111)	154	0.52
American Indian/Alaska Native (108)	279	0.94
Not Hispanic (82)	231	0.78
Hispanic (26)	48	0.16
Apache (0)	1	<0.01
Arapaho (2)	2	0.01
Blackfeet (1)	6	0.02
Cherokee (14)	42	0.14
Chickasaw (0)	3	0.01
Chippewa (1)	1	<0.01
Choctaw (1)	4	0.01
Creek (1)	1	<0.01
Crow (0)	3	0.01
Inupiat *(Alaska Native)* (0)	1	<0.01
Iroquois (8)	14	0.05
Lumbee (16)	22	0.07
Mexican American Ind. (2)	4	0.01
Navajo (5)	8	0.03
Seminole (0)	2	0.01
Sioux (0)	3	0.01
South American Ind. (0)	1	<0.01
Tohono O'Odham (2)	2	0.01
Asian (1,054)	1,251	4.24
Not Hispanic (1,049)	1,226	4.15
Hispanic (5)	25	0.08
Burmese (585)	623	2.11
Cambodian (10)	10	0.03
Chinese, ex. Taiwanese (61)	71	0.24
Filipino (61)	135	0.46
Indian (56)	68	0.23
Indonesian (2)	2	0.01
Japanese (30)	64	0.22
Korean (27)	50	0.17
Laotian (3)	3	0.01
Malaysian (0)	7	0.02
Pakistani (10)	10	0.03
Sri Lankan (0)	1	<0.01
Thai (25)	43	0.15
Vietnamese (127)	136	0.46
Hawaii Native/Pacific Islander (34)	80	0.27
Not Hispanic (23)	61	0.21
Hispanic (11)	19	0.06
Guamanian/Chamorro (5)	13	0.04
Marshallese (3)	3	0.01
Native Hawaiian (7)	18	0.06
Samoan (9)	15	0.05
White (17,099)	17,672	59.86
Not Hispanic (16,400)	16,855	57.09
Hispanic (699)	817	2.77

Newton

Place Type: City
County: Catawba
Population: 12,968†

Ancestry‡	Population	%
American (1,624)	1,624	12.52
Arab (0)	21	0.16
Egyptian (0)	10	0.08
Other Arab (0)	11	0.08
British (16)	16	0.12
Celtic (0)	8	0.06
Dutch (25)	336	2.59
English (307)	948	7.31
French, ex. Basque (15)	124	0.96
French Canadian (15)	15	0.12
German (1,197)	2,525	19.47
Hungarian (0)	27	0.21
Irish (377)	1,011	7.80
Italian (53)	177	1.37
Norwegian (0)	52	0.40
Polish (19)	79	0.61
Portuguese (13)	13	0.10
Russian (0)	10	0.08
Scotch-Irish (145)	231	1.78
Scottish (66)	154	1.19
Swedish (0)	63	0.49
Swiss (16)	68	0.52
Welsh (0)	48	0.37
West Indian, ex. Hispanic (20)	37	0.29
Haitian (20)	37	0.29

Hispanic Origin	Population	%
Hispanic or Latino (of any race)	1,678	12.94
Central American, ex. Mexican	192	1.48
Costa Rican	31	0.24
Guatemalan	49	0.38
Honduran	28	0.22
Nicaraguan	25	0.19
Panamanian	1	0.01
Salvadoran	58	0.45
Cuban	17	0.13
Dominican Republic	11	0.08
Mexican	1,224	9.44
Puerto Rican	101	0.78
South American	89	0.69
Argentinean	3	0.02
Chilean	1	0.01
Colombian	66	0.51
Ecuadorian	10	0.08
Peruvian	5	0.04
Venezuelan	3	0.02
Other South American	1	0.01
Other Hispanic or Latino	44	0.34

Race*	Population	%
African-American/Black (1,804)	1,988	15.33
Not Hispanic (1,775)	1,931	14.89
Hispanic (29)	57	0.44
American Indian/Alaska Native (47)	122	0.94
Not Hispanic (30)	91	0.70
Hispanic (17)	31	0.24
Apache (0)	2	0.02
Blackfeet (3)	5	0.04
Canadian/French Am. Ind. (1)	1	0.01
Cherokee (7)	37	0.29
Creek (0)	2	0.02
Iroquois (1)	1	0.01
Lumbee (9)	10	0.08
Mexican American Ind. (6)	8	0.06
Navajo (0)	3	0.02
Sioux (3)	3	0.02
South American Ind. (0)	3	0.02
Asian (427)	455	3.51
Not Hispanic (426)	449	3.46
Hispanic (1)	6	0.05
Cambodian (3)	3	0.02
Chinese, ex. Taiwanese (17)	21	0.16
Filipino (20)	25	0.19
Hmong (257)	262	2.02
Indian (29)	30	0.23
Indonesian (1)	1	0.01
Japanese (1)	5	0.04
Korean (7)	12	0.09
Laotian (28)	32	0.25
Pakistani (0)	1	0.01
Thai (23)	24	0.19
Vietnamese (10)	13	0.10
Hawaii Native/Pacific Islander (2)	8	0.06
Not Hispanic (1)	5	0.04
Hispanic (1)	3	0.02
Guamanian/Chamorro (1)	1	0.01
Native Hawaiian (1)	6	0.05
White (9,551)	9,843	75.90
Not Hispanic (8,805)	9,017	69.53
Hispanic (746)	826	6.37

Oxford

Place Type: City
County: Granville
Population: 8,461†

Ancestry‡	Population	%
African, Sub-Saharan (35)	44	0.52
African (35)	44	0.52
American (883)	883	10.40
Arab (4)	53	0.62
Egyptian (0)	37	0.44
Palestinian (4)	16	0.19
Croatian (0)	7	0.08
Czech (6)	8	0.09
Danish (0)	21	0.25
Dutch (0)	35	0.41
English (311)	481	5.67
European (114)	163	1.92
French, ex. Basque (40)	116	1.37
German (73)	263	3.10
Greek (0)	11	0.13
Irish (172)	325	3.83
Italian (0)	80	0.94
Lithuanian (0)	8	0.09
Polish (0)	7	0.08
Russian (0)	8	0.09
Scotch-Irish (97)	157	1.85
Scottish (14)	51	0.60
Welsh (0)	19	0.22
West Indian, ex. Hispanic (30)	30	0.35
British West Indian (7)	7	0.08
Haitian (14)	14	0.16
Jamaican (9)	9	0.11

Hispanic Origin	Population	%
Hispanic or Latino (of any race)	405	4.79
Central American, ex. Mexican	17	0.20
Guatemalan	5	0.06
Panamanian	1	0.01
Salvadoran	10	0.12
Other Central American	1	0.01
Cuban	6	0.07
Dominican Republic	3	0.04
Mexican	332	3.92
Puerto Rican	17	0.20
South American	9	0.11
Argentinean	1	0.01
Chilean	1	0.01
Colombian	2	0.02
Peruvian	5	0.06
Other Hispanic or Latino	21	0.25

Race*	Population	%
African-American/Black (4,704)	4,811	56.86
Not Hispanic (4,681)	4,775	56.44
Hispanic (23)	36	0.43
American Indian/Alaska Native (36)	78	0.92
Not Hispanic (20)	58	0.69
Hispanic (16)	20	0.24
Blackfeet (0)	1	0.01
Cherokee (12)	26	0.31
Colville (0)	1	0.01
Delaware (1)	1	0.01
Lumbee (1)	1	0.01
Mexican American Ind. (10)	10	0.12
Sioux (1)	1	0.01
Asian (92)	128	1.51
Not Hispanic (92)	117	1.38
Hispanic (0)	11	0.13
Chinese, ex. Taiwanese (11)	12	0.14
Filipino (10)	11	0.13

*Notes: † The Census 2010 population figure is used to calculate the percentages in the Hispanic Origin and Race categories. Ancestry percentages are based on the 2006-2010 American Community Survey population (not shown); ‡ Numbers in parentheses indicate the number of people reporting a single ancestry; * Numbers in parentheses indicate the number of persons reporting this race alone, not in combination with any other race; Please refer to the Explanation of Data for more information.*

Hmong (1)	1	0.01
Indian (47)	56	0.66
Japanese (1)	8	0.09
Korean (1)	4	0.05
Laotian (7)	9	0.11
Pakistani (1)	1	0.01
Thai (1)	1	0.01
Vietnamese (12)	12	0.14
White (3,265)	3,380	39.95
Not Hispanic (3,137)	3,234	38.22
Hispanic (128)	146	1.73

Pinehurst

Place Type: Village
County: Moore
Population: 13,124†

Ancestry‡	Population	%
American (998)	998	7.97
Arab (12)	206	1.65
Lebanese (12)	206	1.65
Austrian (14)	60	0.48
Belgian (16)	45	0.36
British (51)	62	0.50
Canadian (15)	68	0.54
Croatian (0)	26	0.21
Czech (32)	57	0.46
Czechoslovakian (0)	63	0.50
Danish (28)	92	0.73
Dutch (174)	536	4.28
English (1,020)	2,658	21.23
European (51)	51	0.41
Finnish (13)	13	0.10
French, ex. Basque (82)	678	5.41
French Canadian (63)	82	0.65
German (992)	2,895	23.12
Greek (49)	49	0.39
Hungarian (73)	82	0.65
Irish (769)	1,774	14.17
Italian (543)	948	7.57
Lithuanian (66)	206	1.65
Maltese (0)	45	0.36
Norwegian (0)	235	1.88
Pennsylvania German (0)	15	0.12
Polish (104)	460	3.67
Portuguese (14)	48	0.38
Romanian (17)	30	0.24
Russian (22)	92	0.73
Scotch-Irish (195)	466	3.72
Scottish (409)	861	6.88
Slavic (11)	11	0.09
Slovak (0)	61	0.49
Slovene (17)	60	0.48
Swedish (14)	146	1.17
Swiss (14)	66	0.53
Ukrainian (0)	13	0.10
Welsh (29)	221	1.77

Hispanic Origin	Population	%
Hispanic or Latino (of any race)	279	2.13
Central American, ex. Mexican	19	0.14
Guatemalan	3	0.02
Honduran	3	0.02
Nicaraguan	4	0.03
Panamanian	5	0.04
Salvadoran	4	0.03
Cuban	12	0.09
Dominican Republic	6	0.05
Mexican	117	0.89
Puerto Rican	50	0.38
South American	22	0.17
Colombian	10	0.08
Ecuadorian	3	0.02
Peruvian	6	0.05
Venezuelan	3	0.02
Other Hispanic or Latino	53	0.40

Race*	Population	%
African-American/Black (494)	551	4.20
Not Hispanic (492)	539	4.11
Hispanic (2)	12	0.09
American Indian/Alaska Native (53)	108	0.82
Not Hispanic (53)	99	0.75
Hispanic (0)	9	0.07
Blackfeet (1)	1	0.01
Cherokee (6)	21	0.16
Creek (0)	2	0.02
Delaware (0)	1	0.01
Inupiat *(Alaska Native)* (2)	2	0.02
Lumbee (27)	34	0.26
Sioux (0)	3	0.02
South American Ind. (1)	4	0.03
Asian (167)	220	1.68
Not Hispanic (164)	216	1.65
Hispanic (3)	4	0.03
Cambodian (1)	1	0.01
Chinese, ex. Taiwanese (31)	40	0.30
Filipino (44)	60	0.46
Indian (13)	14	0.11
Indonesian (1)	1	0.01
Japanese (19)	34	0.26
Korean (25)	37	0.28
Taiwanese (2)	2	0.02
Thai (8)	9	0.07
Vietnamese (19)	19	0.14
Hawaii Native/Pacific Islander (1)	9	0.07
Not Hispanic (1)	8	0.06
Hispanic (0)	1	0.01
Guamanian/Chamorro (1)	1	0.01
Native Hawaiian (0)	5	0.04
White (12,182)	12,316	93.84
Not Hispanic (11,993)	12,107	92.25
Hispanic (189)	209	1.59

Piney Green

Place Type: CDP
County: Onslow
Population: 13,293†

Ancestry‡	Population	%
African, Sub-Saharan (32)	67	0.48
African (32)	67	0.48
American (797)	797	5.76
Arab (0)	26	0.19
Lebanese (0)	26	0.19
Brazilian (9)	9	0.06
British (4)	26	0.19
Canadian (23)	58	0.42
Czech (12)	37	0.27
Danish (12)	12	0.09
Dutch (122)	353	2.55
English (379)	1,239	8.95
European (24)	37	0.27
French, ex. Basque (129)	732	5.29
French Canadian (37)	106	0.77
German (590)	2,241	16.18
Greek (0)	9	0.06
Guyanese (8)	8	0.06
Hungarian (31)	41	0.30
Irish (482)	2,206	15.93
Italian (268)	814	5.88
Lithuanian (0)	24	0.17
Northern European (33)	33	0.24
Norwegian (14)	144	1.04
Polish (135)	684	4.94
Russian (69)	111	0.80
Scandinavian (0)	20	0.14
Scotch-Irish (119)	230	1.66
Scottish (124)	479	3.46
Swedish (0)	117	0.84
Swiss (0)	14	0.10
Welsh (0)	49	0.35
West Indian, ex. Hispanic (132)	278	2.01
Jamaican (60)	74	0.53
Trinidadian/Tobagonian (22)	22	0.16
West Indian (50)	182	1.31
Yugoslavian (0)	12	0.09

Hispanic Origin	Population	%
Hispanic or Latino (of any race)	1,628	12.25
Central American, ex. Mexican	145	1.09
Costa Rican	12	0.09
Guatemalan	9	0.07
Honduran	47	0.35
Nicaraguan	15	0.11
Panamanian	51	0.38
Salvadoran	11	0.08
Cuban	69	0.52
Dominican Republic	38	0.29
Mexican	652	4.90
Puerto Rican	531	3.99
South American	70	0.53
Argentinean	1	0.01
Bolivian	5	0.04
Chilean	5	0.04
Colombian	32	0.24
Ecuadorian	7	0.05
Peruvian	18	0.14
Uruguayan	2	0.02
Other Hispanic or Latino	123	0.93

Race*	Population	%
African-American/Black (2,978)	3,389	25.49
Not Hispanic (2,884)	3,214	24.18
Hispanic (94)	175	1.32
American Indian/Alaska Native (96)	229	1.72
Not Hispanic (72)	186	1.40
Hispanic (24)	43	0.32
Apache (1)	2	0.02
Arapaho (0)	1	0.01
Blackfeet (0)	1	0.01
Central American Ind. (3)	3	0.02
Cherokee (16)	53	0.40
Cheyenne (2)	3	0.02
Chippewa (1)	5	0.04
Choctaw (3)	15	0.11
Colville (0)	1	0.01
Cree (1)	1	0.01
Crow (0)	4	0.03
Iroquois (0)	1	0.01
Kiowa (2)	2	0.02
Lumbee (7)	12	0.09
Mexican American Ind. (7)	9	0.07
Navajo (0)	1	0.01
Potawatomi (1)	1	0.01
Seminole (0)	1	0.01
Sioux (2)	5	0.04
Tlingit-Haida *(Alaska Native)* (1)	1	0.01
Asian (374)	653	4.91
Not Hispanic (361)	606	4.56
Hispanic (13)	47	0.35
Cambodian (2)	5	0.04
Chinese, ex. Taiwanese (24)	46	0.35
Filipino (169)	284	2.14
Hmong (2)	2	0.02
Indian (11)	25	0.19
Japanese (102)	178	1.34
Korean (16)	31	0.23
Laotian (0)	1	0.01
Pakistani (1)	1	0.01
Taiwanese (2)	2	0.02
Thai (16)	38	0.29
Vietnamese (14)	21	0.16
Hawaii Native/Pacific Islander (57)	140	1.05
Not Hispanic (50)	96	0.72
Hispanic (7)	44	0.33
Guamanian/Chamorro (25)	30	0.23
Marshallese (1)	5	0.04
Native Hawaiian (14)	42	0.32
Samoan (5)	17	0.13
Tongan (1)	1	0.01
White (8,420)	9,076	68.28
Not Hispanic (7,674)	8,183	61.56
Hispanic (746)	893	6.72

*Notes: † The Census 2010 population figure is used to calculate the percentages in the Hispanic Origin and Race categories. Ancestry percentages are based on the 2006-2010 American Community Survey population (not shown); ‡ Numbers in parentheses indicate the number of people reporting a single ancestry; * Numbers in parentheses indicate the number of persons reporting this race alone, not in combination with any other race; Please refer to the Explanation of Data for more information.*

Raleigh

Place Type: City
County: Wake
Population: 403,892†

Ancestry‡	Population	%
Afghan (272)	318	0.08
African, Sub-Saharan (11,388)	12,222	3.19
African (7,418)	7,836	2.05
Cape Verdean (75)	95	0.02
Ethiopian (312)	323	0.08
Ghanaian (109)	109	0.03
Kenyan (753)	766	0.20
Liberian (0)	14	<0.01
Nigerian (1,281)	1,375	0.36
Senegalese (45)	45	0.01
Sierra Leonean (161)	161	0.04
Somalian (462)	496	0.13
South African (108)	163	0.04
Other Sub-Saharan African (664)	839	0.22
Albanian (66)	94	0.02
Alsatian (17)	17	<0.01
American (37,404)	37,404	9.77
Arab (2,923)	3,836	1.00
Arab (1,015)	1,105	0.29
Egyptian (530)	703	0.18
Iraqi (30)	87	0.02
Jordanian (106)	186	0.05
Lebanese (521)	837	0.22
Moroccan (258)	258	0.07
Palestinian (97)	119	0.03
Syrian (25)	85	0.02
Other Arab (341)	456	0.12
Armenian (153)	213	0.06
Assyrian/Chaldean/Syriac (18)	18	<0.01
Australian (44)	356	0.09
Austrian (103)	670	0.18
Basque (0)	25	0.01
Belgian (40)	288	0.08
Brazilian (265)	444	0.12
British (1,389)	2,874	0.75
Bulgarian (71)	85	0.02
Cajun (9)	49	0.01
Canadian (406)	740	0.19
Celtic (53)	53	0.01
Croatian (59)	221	0.06
Cypriot (27)	27	0.01
Czech (387)	959	0.25
Czechoslovakian (68)	198	0.05
Danish (161)	689	0.18
Dutch (955)	4,068	1.06
Eastern European (404)	549	0.14
English (16,908)	39,630	10.35
Estonian (45)	77	0.02
European (4,570)	5,405	1.41
Finnish (76)	310	0.08
French, ex. Basque (1,448)	7,025	1.84
French Canadian (601)	1,561	0.41
German (10,684)	38,247	9.99
Greek (717)	1,389	0.36
Guyanese (138)	202	0.05
Hungarian (210)	972	0.25
Icelander (24)	67	0.02
Iranian (411)	532	0.14
Irish (10,384)	31,339	8.19
Israeli (63)	95	0.02
Italian (4,925)	14,642	3.83
Latvian (22)	119	0.03
Lithuanian (215)	566	0.15
Luxemburger (0)	17	<0.01
Maltese (33)	94	0.02
Northern European (261)	261	0.07
Norwegian (810)	2,108	0.55
Pennsylvania German (17)	44	0.01
Polish (2,380)	7,411	1.94
Portuguese (156)	370	0.10
Romanian (208)	418	0.11
Russian (795)	2,411	0.63
Scandinavian (132)	318	0.08
Scotch-Irish (6,243)	12,189	3.18
Scottish (3,579)	10,633	2.78
Serbian (60)	72	0.02
Slavic (25)	66	0.02
Slovak (283)	651	0.17
Slovene (0)	39	0.01
Swedish (676)	2,719	0.71
Swiss (185)	846	0.22
Turkish (260)	329	0.09
Ukrainian (520)	846	0.22
Welsh (671)	3,130	0.82
West Indian, ex. Hispanic (1,182)	2,282	0.60
Bahamian (69)	184	0.05
Barbadian (0)	31	0.01
Belizean (29)	29	0.01
British West Indian (28)	83	0.02
Haitian (198)	300	0.08
Jamaican (618)	914	0.24
Trinidadian/Tobagonian (65)	107	0.03
U.S. Virgin Islander (14)	14	<0.01
West Indian (161)	620	0.16
Yugoslavian (79)	196	0.05

Hispanic Origin	Population	%
Hispanic or Latino (of any race)	45,868	11.36
Central American, ex. Mexican	7,519	1.86
Costa Rican	164	0.04
Guatemalan	978	0.24
Honduran	2,345	0.58
Nicaraguan	184	0.05
Panamanian	313	0.08
Salvadoran	3,476	0.86
Other Central American	59	0.01
Cuban	1,082	0.27
Dominican Republic	2,378	0.59
Mexican	23,867	5.91
Puerto Rican	4,340	1.07
South American	3,574	0.88
Argentinean	313	0.08
Bolivian	94	0.02
Chilean	196	0.05
Colombian	1,261	0.31
Ecuadorian	352	0.09
Paraguayan	9	<0.01
Peruvian	729	0.18
Uruguayan	146	0.04
Venezuelan	457	0.11
Other South American	17	<0.01
Other Hispanic or Latino	3,108	0.77

Race*	Population	%
African-American/Black (118,471)	124,035	30.71
Not Hispanic (115,976)	120,403	29.81
Hispanic (2,495)	3,632	0.90
American Indian/Alaska Native (1,963)	4,541	1.12
Not Hispanic (1,019)	3,015	0.75
Hispanic (944)	1,526	0.38
Alaska Athabascan *(Ala. Nat.)* (2)	3	<0.01
Aleut *(Alaska Native)* (4)	5	<0.01
Apache (4)	26	0.01
Arapaho (0)	1	<0.01
Blackfeet (12)	101	0.03
Canadian/French Am. Ind. (7)	11	<0.01
Central American Ind. (6)	23	0.01
Cherokee (149)	775	0.19
Cheyenne (3)	9	<0.01
Chickasaw (6)	9	<0.01
Chippewa (9)	36	0.01
Choctaw (11)	36	0.01
Comanche (0)	4	<0.01
Cree (1)	6	<0.01
Creek (3)	21	0.01
Crow (2)	4	<0.01
Delaware (4)	10	<0.01
Hopi (0)	2	<0.01
Houma (2)	2	<0.01
Inupiat *(Alaska Native)* (0)	3	<0.01
Iroquois (13)	52	0.01
Lumbee (268)	392	0.10
Menominee (1)	2	<0.01
Mexican American Ind. (201)	242	0.06
Navajo (6)	19	<0.01
Osage (9)	9	<0.01
Ottawa (1)	1	<0.01
Paiute (2)	2	<0.01
Pima (3)	3	<0.01
Potawatomi (1)	2	<0.01
Pueblo (6)	13	<0.01
Puget Sound Salish (1)	1	<0.01
Seminole (1)	20	<0.01
Sioux (11)	42	0.01
South American Ind. (8)	46	0.01
Spanish American Ind. (37)	44	0.01
Tlingit-Haida *(Alaska Native)* (1)	2	<0.01
Tohono O'Odham (5)	5	<0.01
Tsimshian *(Alaska Native)* (0)	1	<0.01
Ute (1)	2	<0.01
Yaqui (1)	1	<0.01
Yup'ik *(Alaska Native)* (0)	3	<0.01
Asian (17,434)	20,389	5.05
Not Hispanic (17,309)	20,006	4.95
Hispanic (125)	383	0.09
Bangladeshi (167)	177	0.04
Bhutanese (42)	68	0.02
Burmese (360)	397	0.10
Cambodian (39)	63	0.02
Chinese, ex. Taiwanese (3,135)	3,607	0.89
Filipino (1,486)	2,141	0.53
Hmong (53)	55	0.01
Indian (4,681)	5,143	1.27
Indonesian (91)	121	0.03
Japanese (443)	821	0.20
Korean (1,957)	2,357	0.58
Laotian (219)	259	0.06
Malaysian (31)	44	0.01
Nepalese (101)	140	0.03
Pakistani (497)	545	0.13
Sri Lankan (71)	75	0.02
Taiwanese (230)	269	0.07
Thai (232)	343	0.08
Vietnamese (2,954)	3,210	0.79
Hawaii Native/Pacific Islander (173)	595	0.15
Not Hispanic (139)	417	0.10
Hispanic (34)	178	0.04
Fijian (2)	3	<0.01
Guamanian/Chamorro (56)	121	0.03
Native Hawaiian (49)	156	0.04
Samoan (10)	43	0.01
Tongan (0)	1	<0.01
White (232,377)	240,430	59.53
Not Hispanic (215,204)	221,203	54.77
Hispanic (17,173)	19,227	4.76

Reidsville

Place Type: City
County: Rockingham
Population: 14,520†

Ancestry‡	Population	%
African, Sub-Saharan (54)	54	0.37
African (54)	54	0.37
American (1,401)	1,401	9.65
Austrian (0)	99	0.68
British (31)	31	0.21
Danish (0)	12	0.08
Dutch (12)	208	1.43
English (665)	1,051	7.24
European (260)	326	2.25
French, ex. Basque (41)	203	1.40
German (257)	1,006	6.93
Irish (429)	1,016	7.00
Italian (23)	189	1.30
Lithuanian (15)	15	0.10
Northern European (21)	21	0.14
Norwegian (46)	108	0.74
Polish (65)	144	0.99
Russian (0)	16	0.11
Scotch-Irish (212)	349	2.41

*Notes: † The Census 2010 population figure is used to calculate the percentages in the Hispanic Origin and Race categories. Ancestry percentages are based on the 2006-2010 American Community Survey population (not shown); ‡ Numbers in parentheses indicate the number of people reporting a single ancestry; * Numbers in parentheses indicate the number of persons reporting this race alone, not in combination with any other race; Please refer to the Explanation of Data for more information.*

Scottish (35)	148	1.02
Swedish (37)	49	0.34
Welsh (22)	40	0.28
West Indian, ex. Hispanic (36)	36	0.25
Jamaican (36)	36	0.25

Hispanic Origin	Population	%
Hispanic or Latino (of any race)	683	4.70
Central American, ex. Mexican	81	0.56
Costa Rican	2	0.01
Guatemalan	33	0.23
Honduran	20	0.14
Panamanian	2	0.01
Salvadoran	24	0.17
Cuban	6	0.04
Mexican	508	3.50
Puerto Rican	34	0.23
South American	7	0.05
Colombian	6	0.04
Venezuelan	1	0.01
Other Hispanic or Latino	47	0.32

Race*	Population	%
African-American/Black (6,082)	6,311	43.46
Not Hispanic (6,046)	6,257	43.09
Hispanic (36)	54	0.37
American Indian/Alaska Native (49)	117	0.81
Not Hispanic (38)	102	0.70
Hispanic (11)	15	0.10
Apache (0)	1	0.01
Blackfeet (0)	1	0.01
Central American Ind. (2)	2	0.01
Cherokee (16)	40	0.28
Cree (0)	2	0.01
Lumbee (9)	11	0.08
Seminole (0)	1	0.01
South American Ind. (1)	1	0.01
Asian (92)	121	0.83
Not Hispanic (88)	112	0.77
Hispanic (4)	9	0.06
Chinese, ex. Taiwanese (24)	32	0.22
Filipino (14)	20	0.14
Indian (29)	31	0.21
Japanese (3)	8	0.06
Korean (14)	14	0.10
Laotian (0)	1	0.01
Pakistani (1)	1	0.01
Thai (2)	5	0.03
Vietnamese (4)	5	0.03
Hawaii Native/Pacific Islander (3)	9	0.06
Not Hispanic (2)	5	0.03
Hispanic (1)	4	0.03
Guamanian/Chamorro (2)	3	0.02
Native Hawaiian (1)	1	0.01
Samoan (0)	1	0.01
White (7,607)	7,864	54.16
Not Hispanic (7,389)	7,617	52.46
Hispanic (218)	247	1.70

Roanoke Rapids

Place Type: City
County: Halifax
Population: 15,754†

Ancestry‡	Population	%
African, Sub-Saharan (130)	130	0.82
African (130)	130	0.82
American (2,006)	2,006	12.64
Belgian (0)	13	0.08
British (67)	80	0.50
Canadian (9)	13	0.08
Czech (0)	19	0.12
Danish (35)	35	0.22
Dutch (41)	56	0.35
English (1,005)	1,947	12.27
European (22)	22	0.14
French, ex. Basque (33)	225	1.42
French Canadian (23)	359	2.26
German (125)	927	5.84
Greek (19)	30	0.19
Hungarian (8)	46	0.29
Iranian (14)	14	0.09
Irish (660)	1,494	9.42
Italian (209)	441	2.78
Norwegian (0)	19	0.12
Polish (18)	72	0.45
Russian (0)	22	0.14
Scotch-Irish (162)	349	2.20
Scottish (221)	555	3.50
Slavic (0)	13	0.08
Slovak (0)	31	0.20
Swedish (0)	50	0.32
Swiss (18)	60	0.38
Welsh (0)	19	0.12
West Indian, ex. Hispanic (62)	419	2.64
Bahamian (0)	141	0.89
British West Indian (34)	142	0.90
Jamaican (28)	136	0.86

Hispanic Origin	Population	%
Hispanic or Latino (of any race)	502	3.19
Central American, ex. Mexican	86	0.55
Costa Rican	3	0.02
Guatemalan	15	0.10
Honduran	12	0.08
Nicaraguan	7	0.04
Panamanian	1	0.01
Salvadoran	48	0.30
Cuban	2	0.01
Dominican Republic	2	0.01
Mexican	283	1.80
Puerto Rican	60	0.38
South American	20	0.13
Chilean	1	0.01
Colombian	11	0.07
Ecuadorian	1	0.01
Paraguayan	1	0.01
Peruvian	5	0.03
Venezuelan	1	0.01
Other Hispanic or Latino	49	0.31

Race*	Population	%
African-American/Black (4,912)	5,029	31.92
Not Hispanic (4,871)	4,979	31.60
Hispanic (41)	50	0.32
American Indian/Alaska Native (91)	147	0.93
Not Hispanic (77)	126	0.80
Hispanic (14)	21	0.13
Blackfeet (8)	10	0.06
Cherokee (12)	29	0.18
Cheyenne (1)	1	0.01
Chippewa (2)	2	0.01
Choctaw (1)	2	0.01
Iroquois (2)	3	0.02
Lumbee (2)	2	0.01
Mexican American Ind. (1)	2	0.01
Navajo (1)	1	0.01
Asian (267)	301	1.91
Not Hispanic (264)	295	1.87
Hispanic (3)	6	0.04
Cambodian (1)	1	0.01
Chinese, ex. Taiwanese (56)	56	0.36
Filipino (70)	75	0.48
Indian (73)	80	0.51
Japanese (4)	8	0.05
Korean (3)	5	0.03
Pakistani (4)	4	0.03
Thai (4)	5	0.03
Vietnamese (51)	55	0.35
Hawaii Native/Pacific Islander (5)	12	0.08
Not Hispanic (2)	8	0.05
Hispanic (3)	4	0.03
Guamanian/Chamorro (3)	4	0.03
Native Hawaiian (2)	5	0.03
Samoan (0)	1	0.01
White (10,016)	10,188	64.67
Not Hispanic (9,851)	9,997	63.46
Hispanic (165)	191	1.21

Rockingham

Place Type: City
County: Richmond
Population: 9,558†

Ancestry‡	Population	%
African, Sub-Saharan (0)	7	0.07
African (0)	7	0.07
American (1,259)	1,259	13.22
British (0)	27	0.28
Canadian (5)	5	0.05
Czech (0)	18	0.19
Dutch (0)	23	0.24
English (489)	911	9.57
European (35)	35	0.37
French, ex. Basque (47)	183	1.92
German (121)	454	4.77
Guyanese (0)	22	0.23
Irish (200)	421	4.42
Italian (53)	118	1.24
Norwegian (15)	32	0.34
Pennsylvania German (17)	17	0.18
Polish (7)	7	0.07
Scotch-Irish (145)	324	3.40
Scottish (162)	273	2.87
Swedish (10)	27	0.28
Welsh (5)	54	0.57
West Indian, ex. Hispanic (0)	27	0.28
Belizean (0)	5	0.05
West Indian (0)	22	0.23

Hispanic Origin	Population	%
Hispanic or Latino (of any race)	484	5.06
Central American, ex. Mexican	34	0.36
Guatemalan	4	0.04
Honduran	13	0.14
Nicaraguan	1	0.01
Panamanian	1	0.01
Salvadoran	15	0.16
Cuban	13	0.14
Dominican Republic	16	0.17
Mexican	325	3.40
Puerto Rican	28	0.29
South American	31	0.32
Argentinean	5	0.05
Bolivian	1	0.01
Chilean	5	0.05
Colombian	12	0.13
Peruvian	3	0.03
Venezuelan	5	0.05
Other Hispanic or Latino	37	0.39

Race*	Population	%
African-American/Black (3,257)	3,358	35.13
Not Hispanic (3,229)	3,320	34.74
Hispanic (28)	38	0.40
American Indian/Alaska Native (164)	239	2.50
Not Hispanic (137)	210	2.20
Hispanic (27)	29	0.30
Blackfeet (1)	1	0.01
Cherokee (20)	42	0.44
Hopi (1)	1	0.01
Iroquois (1)	6	0.06
Lumbee (65)	89	0.93
Mexican American Ind. (3)	3	0.03
Sioux (1)	4	0.04
South American Ind. (2)	2	0.02
Spanish American Ind. (1)	1	0.01
Asian (199)	225	2.35
Not Hispanic (197)	220	2.30
Hispanic (2)	5	0.05
Bangladeshi (5)	5	0.05
Burmese (44)	44	0.46
Chinese, ex. Taiwanese (13)	13	0.14
Filipino (5)	11	0.12
Indian (66)	72	0.75
Japanese (1)	7	0.07
Korean (2)	3	0.03
Laotian (38)	42	0.44

*Notes: † The Census 2010 population figure is used to calculate the percentages in the Hispanic Origin and Race categories. Ancestry percentages are based on the 2006-2010 American Community Survey population (not shown); ‡ Numbers in parentheses indicate the number of people reporting a single ancestry; * Numbers in parentheses indicate the number of persons reporting this race alone, not in combination with any other race; Please refer to the Explanation of Data for more information.*

Pakistani (2)	2	0.02
Taiwanese (5)	5	0.05
Vietnamese (14)	19	0.20
Hawaii Native/Pacific Islander (1)	5	0.05
Not Hispanic (1)	5	0.05
Native Hawaiian (1)	3	0.03
White (5,482)	5,639	59.00
Not Hispanic (5,337)	5,473	57.26
Hispanic (145)	166	1.74

Rocky Mount

Place Type: City
County: Nash
Population: 57,477†

Ancestry‡	Population	%
African, Sub-Saharan (938)	1,253	2.17
African (925)	1,167	2.02
Ethiopian (13)	13	0.02
Other Sub-Saharan African (0)	73	0.13
American (3,523)	3,523	6.10
Arab (492)	492	0.85
Arab (74)	74	0.13
Jordanian (47)	47	0.08
Lebanese (55)	55	0.10
Palestinian (222)	222	0.38
Other Arab (94)	94	0.16
Austrian (0)	27	0.05
Belgian (12)	75	0.13
British (91)	150	0.26
Canadian (34)	34	0.06
Croatian (15)	15	0.03
Czech (0)	29	0.05
Danish (0)	7	0.01
Dutch (111)	457	0.79
Eastern European (10)	27	0.05
English (2,975)	4,711	8.15
European (140)	140	0.24
Finnish (18)	18	0.03
French, ex. Basque (123)	619	1.07
French Canadian (53)	94	0.16
German (561)	2,438	4.22
German Russian (0)	47	0.08
Greek (10)	69	0.12
Hungarian (31)	117	0.20
Irish (1,178)	3,313	5.73
Italian (293)	684	1.18
Latvian (0)	4	0.01
Lithuanian (18)	18	0.03
Northern European (0)	19	0.03
Norwegian (13)	116	0.20
Pennsylvania German (0)	16	0.03
Polish (120)	172	0.30
Portuguese (14)	33	0.06
Romanian (0)	17	0.03
Russian (46)	52	0.09
Scotch-Irish (857)	1,076	1.86
Scottish (280)	507	0.88
Slavic (0)	16	0.03
Slovak (53)	53	0.09
Swedish (13)	140	0.24
Swiss (5)	25	0.04
Ukrainian (21)	45	0.08
Welsh (50)	123	0.21
West Indian, ex. Hispanic (120)	270	0.47
Barbadian (0)	27	0.05
Haitian (0)	39	0.07
Jamaican (120)	204	0.35
Yugoslavian (0)	27	0.05

Hispanic Origin	Population	%
Hispanic or Latino (of any race)	2,106	3.66
Central American, ex. Mexican	183	0.32
Costa Rican	10	0.02
Guatemalan	30	0.05
Honduran	60	0.10
Nicaraguan	5	0.01
Panamanian	21	0.04
Salvadoran	57	0.10
Cuban	29	0.05
Dominican Republic	22	0.04
Mexican	1,376	2.39
Puerto Rican	253	0.44
South American	94	0.16
Argentinean	12	0.02
Bolivian	2	<0.01
Chilean	4	0.01
Colombian	40	0.07
Ecuadorian	12	0.02
Paraguayan	2	<0.01
Peruvian	16	0.03
Venezuelan	6	0.01
Other Hispanic or Latino	149	0.26

Race*	Population	%
African-American/Black (35,245)	35,854	62.38
Not Hispanic (35,069)	35,605	61.95
Hispanic (176)	249	0.43
American Indian/Alaska Native (350)	660	1.15
Not Hispanic (329)	615	1.07
Hispanic (21)	45	0.08
Aleut *(Alaska Native)* (3)	3	0.01
Blackfeet (3)	18	0.03
Central American Ind. (0)	3	0.01
Cherokee (10)	63	0.11
Cheyenne (0)	1	<0.01
Choctaw (1)	4	0.01
Cree (0)	3	0.01
Creek (2)	2	<0.01
Crow (0)	2	<0.01
Iroquois (0)	4	0.01
Lumbee (15)	24	0.04
Mexican American Ind. (11)	13	0.02
Potawatomi (0)	1	<0.01
Seminole (0)	1	<0.01
Sioux (0)	1	<0.01
South American Ind. (0)	1	<0.01
Spanish American Ind. (1)	2	<0.01
Asian (563)	714	1.24
Not Hispanic (540)	677	1.18
Hispanic (23)	37	0.06
Bangladeshi (15)	15	0.03
Cambodian (1)	1	<0.01
Chinese, ex. Taiwanese (73)	91	0.16
Filipino (87)	127	0.22
Hmong (9)	9	0.02
Indian (180)	198	0.34
Indonesian (1)	1	<0.01
Japanese (10)	20	0.03
Korean (43)	59	0.10
Malaysian (3)	8	0.01
Pakistani (29)	29	0.05
Sri Lankan (2)	2	<0.01
Thai (6)	7	0.01
Vietnamese (75)	81	0.14
Hawaii Native/Pacific Islander (12)	52	0.09
Not Hispanic (10)	41	0.07
Hispanic (2)	11	0.02
Guamanian/Chamorro (2)	4	0.01
Native Hawaiian (4)	23	0.04
Samoan (4)	8	0.01
White (19,228)	19,851	34.54
Not Hispanic (18,610)	19,138	33.30
Hispanic (618)	713	1.24

Roxboro

Place Type: City
County: Person
Population: 8,362†

Ancestry‡	Population	%
African, Sub-Saharan (43)	43	0.51
African (43)	43	0.51
American (860)	860	10.13
British (10)	10	0.12
Dutch (0)	10	0.12
English (709)	963	11.34
European (64)	101	1.19
French, ex. Basque (24)	131	1.54
German (57)	415	4.89
Irish (273)	477	5.62
Italian (13)	13	0.15
Norwegian (6)	6	0.07
Polish (27)	107	1.26
Russian (0)	34	0.40
Scotch-Irish (61)	112	1.32
Scottish (116)	187	2.20
Swedish (0)	21	0.25
Swiss (0)	12	0.14
Welsh (0)	42	0.49

Hispanic Origin	Population	%
Hispanic or Latino (of any race)	730	8.73
Central American, ex. Mexican	6	0.07
Costa Rican	1	0.01
Honduran	3	0.04
Nicaraguan	1	0.01
Salvadoran	1	0.01
Cuban	6	0.07
Dominican Republic	8	0.10
Mexican	574	6.86
Puerto Rican	36	0.43
South American	21	0.25
Chilean	1	0.01
Colombian	5	0.06
Ecuadorian	8	0.10
Peruvian	7	0.08
Other Hispanic or Latino	79	0.94

Race*	Population	%
African-American/Black (3,917)	4,042	48.34
Not Hispanic (3,898)	4,006	47.91
Hispanic (19)	36	0.43
American Indian/Alaska Native (54)	99	1.18
Not Hispanic (48)	90	1.08
Hispanic (6)	9	0.11
Aleut *(Alaska Native)* (0)	1	0.01
Arapaho (0)	2	0.02
Cherokee (2)	6	0.07
Lumbee (6)	8	0.10
Potawatomi (0)	1	0.01
Sioux (1)	4	0.05
Asian (31)	39	0.47
Not Hispanic (31)	36	0.43
Hispanic (0)	3	0.04
Chinese, ex. Taiwanese (1)	4	0.05
Filipino (3)	5	0.06
Indian (18)	18	0.22
Japanese (0)	3	0.04
Korean (4)	4	0.05
Taiwanese (1)	1	0.01
Vietnamese (4)	4	0.05
Hawaii Native/Pacific Islander (2)	6	0.07
Not Hispanic (2)	5	0.06
Hispanic (0)	1	0.01
Native Hawaiian (1)	1	0.01
Samoan (1)	5	0.06
White (3,753)	3,896	46.59
Not Hispanic (3,510)	3,627	43.37
Hispanic (243)	269	3.22

Salisbury

Place Type: City
County: Rowan
Population: 33,662†

Ancestry‡	Population	%
African, Sub-Saharan (1,812)	1,859	5.63
African (1,789)	1,836	5.56
Nigerian (23)	23	0.07
Albanian (31)	31	0.09
American (2,939)	2,939	8.90
Arab (75)	89	0.27
Arab (13)	13	0.04
Egyptian (21)	21	0.06
Lebanese (32)	46	0.14
Syrian (9)	9	0.03

*Notes: † The Census 2010 population figure is used to calculate the percentages in the Hispanic Origin and Race categories. Ancestry percentages are based on the 2006-2010 American Community Survey population (not shown); ‡ Numbers in parentheses indicate the number of people reporting a single ancestry; * Numbers in parentheses indicate the number of persons reporting this race alone, not in combination with any other race; Please refer to the Explanation of Data for more information.*

Austrian (10)	24	0.07
Belgian (8)	8	0.02
Brazilian (0)	22	0.07
British (116)	149	0.45
Canadian (36)	36	0.11
Czech (16)	54	0.16
Czechoslovakian (13)	24	0.07
Danish (0)	10	0.03
Dutch (122)	401	1.21
Eastern European (38)	38	0.12
English (1,061)	2,300	6.97
European (83)	83	0.25
Finnish (0)	13	0.04
French, ex. Basque (56)	396	1.20
French Canadian (72)	130	0.39
German (1,739)	4,433	13.43
Greek (24)	106	0.32
Guyanese (13)	13	0.04
Hungarian (17)	78	0.24
Irish (619)	2,253	6.82
Italian (154)	659	2.00
Lithuanian (7)	7	0.02
Maltese (11)	11	0.03
Northern European (23)	23	0.07
Norwegian (19)	69	0.21
Polish (33)	249	0.75
Portuguese (0)	8	0.02
Russian (0)	5	0.02
Scandinavian (0)	12	0.04
Scotch-Irish (711)	1,279	3.87
Scottish (373)	967	2.93
Slavic (8)	39	0.12
Slovak (0)	12	0.04
Slovene (0)	11	0.03
Swedish (22)	304	0.92
Swiss (32)	94	0.28
Ukrainian (0)	9	0.03
Welsh (32)	89	0.27
West Indian, ex. Hispanic (34)	58	0.18
Bahamian (20)	20	0.06
Haitian (0)	13	0.04
Jamaican (7)	7	0.02
West Indian (7)	18	0.05
Yugoslavian (0)	25	0.08

Hispanic Origin	Population	%
Hispanic or Latino (of any race)	3,563	10.58
Central American, ex. Mexican	788	2.34
Costa Rican	4	0.01
Guatemalan	34	0.10
Honduran	488	1.45
Nicaraguan	9	0.03
Panamanian	13	0.04
Salvadoran	226	0.67
Other Central American	14	0.04
Cuban	94	0.28
Dominican Republic	44	0.13
Mexican	2,156	6.40
Puerto Rican	167	0.50
South American	72	0.21
Argentinean	4	0.01
Bolivian	1	<0.01
Chilean	1	<0.01
Colombian	34	0.10
Ecuadorian	19	0.06
Peruvian	4	0.01
Uruguayan	1	<0.01
Venezuelan	7	0.02
Other South American	1	<0.01
Other Hispanic or Latino	242	0.72

Race*	Population	%
African-American/Black (12,694)	13,039	38.74
Not Hispanic (12,572)	12,881	38.27
Hispanic (122)	158	0.47
American Indian/Alaska Native (121)	331	0.98
Not Hispanic (88)	283	0.84
Hispanic (33)	48	0.14
Apache (0)	3	0.01
Blackfeet (1)	11	0.03
Canadian/French Am. Ind. (1)	1	<0.01
Cherokee (21)	85	0.25
Choctaw (0)	6	0.02
Comanche (1)	3	0.01
Creek (0)	2	0.01
Iroquois (2)	8	0.02
Lumbee (21)	23	0.07
Mexican American Ind. (6)	6	0.02
Osage (0)	5	0.01
Ottawa (0)	1	<0.01
Sioux (0)	1	<0.01
South American Ind. (0)	1	<0.01
Asian (523)	612	1.82
Not Hispanic (513)	596	1.77
Hispanic (10)	16	0.05
Cambodian (2)	3	0.01
Chinese, ex. Taiwanese (48)	65	0.19
Filipino (50)	69	0.20
Hmong (40)	42	0.12
Indian (155)	171	0.51
Indonesian (2)	2	0.01
Japanese (1)	10	0.03
Korean (24)	34	0.10
Laotian (24)	27	0.08
Pakistani (7)	7	0.02
Sri Lankan (1)	1	<0.01
Taiwanese (5)	7	0.02
Thai (14)	30	0.09
Vietnamese (119)	131	0.39
Hawaii Native/Pacific Islander (16)	39	0.12
Not Hispanic (16)	32	0.10
Hispanic (0)	7	0.02
Guamanian/Chamorro (5)	5	0.01
Native Hawaiian (9)	15	0.04
Samoan (0)	11	0.03
White (17,652)	18,206	54.08
Not Hispanic (16,346)	16,764	49.80
Hispanic (1,306)	1,442	4.28

Sanford

Place Type: City
County: Lee
Population: 28,094†

Ancestry‡	Population	%
African, Sub-Saharan (0)	24	0.09
African (0)	24	0.09
American (1,915)	1,915	7.12
Arab (12)	33	0.12
Arab (12)	12	0.04
Lebanese (0)	11	0.04
Syrian (0)	10	0.04
Australian (37)	37	0.14
Belgian (0)	6	0.02
British (12)	27	0.10
Canadian (8)	25	0.09
Celtic (18)	18	0.07
Croatian (44)	44	0.16
Czech (4)	22	0.08
Dutch (65)	129	0.48
English (1,268)	2,436	9.06
European (631)	650	2.42
French, ex. Basque (44)	300	1.12
French Canadian (50)	119	0.44
German (681)	1,783	6.63
Greek (0)	67	0.25
Hungarian (14)	74	0.28
Irish (382)	1,276	4.74
Italian (163)	412	1.53
Norwegian (43)	61	0.23
Polish (63)	139	0.52
Portuguese (0)	53	0.20
Russian (18)	53	0.20
Scotch-Irish (514)	803	2.99
Scottish (334)	727	2.70
Swedish (0)	122	0.45
Swiss (0)	22	0.08
Ukrainian (13)	13	0.05
Welsh (33)	133	0.49
West Indian, ex. Hispanic (59)	78	0.29
Haitian (14)	14	0.05
Jamaican (20)	20	0.07
West Indian (25)	44	0.16

Hispanic Origin	Population	%
Hispanic or Latino (of any race)	7,190	25.59
Central American, ex. Mexican	1,749	6.23
Costa Rican	10	0.04
Guatemalan	429	1.53
Honduran	351	1.25
Nicaraguan	26	0.09
Panamanian	46	0.16
Salvadoran	880	3.13
Other Central American	7	0.02
Cuban	23	0.08
Dominican Republic	64	0.23
Mexican	4,409	15.69
Puerto Rican	379	1.35
South American	161	0.57
Argentinean	3	0.01
Bolivian	2	0.01
Colombian	56	0.20
Ecuadorian	23	0.08
Peruvian	61	0.22
Uruguayan	4	0.01
Venezuelan	12	0.04
Other Hispanic or Latino	405	1.44

Race*	Population	%
African-American/Black (7,763)	8,111	28.87
Not Hispanic (7,622)	7,868	28.01
Hispanic (141)	243	0.86
American Indian/Alaska Native (232)	404	1.44
Not Hispanic (116)	234	0.83
Hispanic (116)	170	0.61
Apache (1)	1	<0.01
Blackfeet (1)	5	0.02
Central American Ind. (8)	14	0.05
Cherokee (37)	86	0.31
Chippewa (1)	1	<0.01
Choctaw (2)	2	0.01
Comanche (0)	1	<0.01
Creek (1)	1	<0.01
Inupiat *(Alaska Native)* (0)	1	<0.01
Iroquois (5)	11	0.04
Lumbee (22)	41	0.15
Mexican American Ind. (29)	47	0.17
Navajo (1)	2	0.01
Pima (1)	1	<0.01
Seminole (1)	1	<0.01
Sioux (3)	4	0.01
South American Ind. (2)	4	0.01
Spanish American Ind. (5)	5	0.02
Asian (309)	430	1.53
Not Hispanic (301)	398	1.42
Hispanic (8)	32	0.11
Cambodian (4)	4	0.01
Chinese, ex. Taiwanese (38)	40	0.14
Filipino (67)	102	0.36
Hmong (1)	1	<0.01
Indian (80)	106	0.38
Japanese (15)	22	0.08
Korean (18)	29	0.10
Laotian (1)	1	<0.01
Pakistani (2)	2	0.01
Thai (6)	12	0.04
Vietnamese (66)	81	0.29
Hawaii Native/Pacific Islander (12)	37	0.13
Not Hispanic (7)	16	0.06
Hispanic (5)	21	0.07
Fijian (0)	1	<0.01
Guamanian/Chamorro (5)	6	0.02
Native Hawaiian (1)	5	0.02
Tongan (1)	3	0.01
White (15,512)	16,115	57.36
Not Hispanic (12,416)	12,733	45.32
Hispanic (3,096)	3,382	12.04

*Notes: † The Census 2010 population figure is used to calculate the percentages in the Hispanic Origin and Race categories. Ancestry percentages are based on the 2006-2010 American Community Survey population (not shown); ‡ Numbers in parentheses indicate the number of people reporting a single ancestry; * Numbers in parentheses indicate the number of persons reporting this race alone, not in combination with any other race; Please refer to the Explanation of Data for more information.*

Shelby

Place Type: City
County: Cleveland
Population: 20,323†

Ancestry‡	Population	%
African, Sub-Saharan (255)	268	1.31
African (133)	146	0.72
Nigerian (22)	22	0.11
Other Sub-Saharan African (100)	100	0.49
Albanian (0)	20	0.10
American (2,661)	2,661	13.03
Armenian (8)	8	0.04
British (10)	22	0.11
Czech (0)	6	0.03
Danish (0)	1	<0.01
Dutch (10)	128	0.63
Eastern European (12)	12	0.06
English (1,033)	1,800	8.82
Estonian (9)	9	0.04
European (144)	191	0.94
French, ex. Basque (26)	175	0.86
French Canadian (0)	58	0.28
German (606)	1,596	7.82
Hungarian (0)	18	0.09
Irish (405)	1,032	5.05
Italian (81)	263	1.29
Norwegian (11)	62	0.30
Pennsylvania German (0)	7	0.03
Polish (7)	7	0.03
Russian (7)	7	0.03
Scotch-Irish (539)	730	3.58
Scottish (123)	274	1.34
Slovak (14)	46	0.23
Swedish (10)	61	0.30
Swiss (9)	9	0.04
Ukrainian (0)	6	0.03
Welsh (0)	17	0.08
West Indian, ex. Hispanic (113)	113	0.55
Haitian (113)	113	0.55
Yugoslavian (0)	31	0.15

Hispanic Origin	Population	%
Hispanic or Latino (of any race)	640	3.15
Central American, ex. Mexican	53	0.26
Costa Rican	13	0.06
Guatemalan	2	0.01
Honduran	2	0.01
Nicaraguan	13	0.06
Panamanian	16	0.08
Salvadoran	7	0.03
Cuban	34	0.17
Dominican Republic	25	0.12
Mexican	352	1.73
Puerto Rican	100	0.49
South American	13	0.06
Argentinean	6	0.03
Colombian	4	0.02
Peruvian	2	0.01
Venezuelan	1	<0.01
Other Hispanic or Latino	63	0.31

Race*	Population	%
African-American/Black (8,397)	8,632	42.47
Not Hispanic (8,339)	8,556	42.10
Hispanic (58)	76	0.37
American Indian/Alaska Native (73)	164	0.81
Not Hispanic (54)	144	0.71
Hispanic (19)	20	0.10
Blackfeet (0)	4	0.02
Canadian/French Am. Ind. (1)	1	<0.01
Central American Ind. (1)	1	<0.01
Cherokee (5)	30	0.15
Chickasaw (0)	4	0.02
Iroquois (6)	6	0.03
Lumbee (7)	9	0.04
Mexican American Ind. (5)	5	0.02
Navajo (0)	1	<0.01
Sioux (4)	4	0.02
Asian (167)	214	1.05
Not Hispanic (167)	211	1.04
Hispanic (0)	3	0.01
Bangladeshi (5)	5	0.02
Chinese, ex. Taiwanese (31)	45	0.22
Filipino (17)	19	0.09
Hmong (6)	9	0.04
Indian (51)	71	0.35
Japanese (4)	5	0.02
Korean (3)	8	0.04
Laotian (4)	6	0.03
Pakistani (10)	13	0.06
Taiwanese (0)	2	0.01
Thai (1)	5	0.02
Vietnamese (24)	27	0.13
Hawaii Native/Pacific Islander (6)	12	0.06
Not Hispanic (6)	12	0.06
Guamanian/Chamorro (1)	1	<0.01
Native Hawaiian (2)	2	0.01
Samoan (2)	3	0.01
Tongan (0)	3	0.01
White (11,115)	11,403	56.11
Not Hispanic (10,799)	11,055	54.40
Hispanic (316)	348	1.71

Siler City

Place Type: Town
County: Chatham
Population: 7,887†

Ancestry‡	Population	%
African, Sub-Saharan (28)	28	0.36
African (28)	28	0.36
American (440)	440	5.64
Arab (0)	54	0.69
Egyptian (0)	27	0.35
Syrian (0)	27	0.35
British (26)	26	0.33
Dutch (0)	23	0.29
English (190)	387	4.96
European (0)	13	0.17
French, ex. Basque (0)	21	0.27
German (82)	245	3.14
Irish (55)	196	2.51
Italian (33)	33	0.42
Scotch-Irish (65)	117	1.50
Scottish (14)	26	0.33
Slovak (12)	12	0.15
Swedish (0)	13	0.17

Hispanic Origin	Population	%
Hispanic or Latino (of any race)	3,925	49.77
Central American, ex. Mexican	995	12.62
Costa Rican	2	0.03
Guatemalan	502	6.36
Honduran	87	1.10
Nicaraguan	11	0.14
Panamanian	3	0.04
Salvadoran	370	4.69
Other Central American	20	0.25
Cuban	6	0.08
Dominican Republic	4	0.05
Mexican	2,638	33.45
Puerto Rican	24	0.30
South American	22	0.28
Bolivian	2	0.03
Colombian	16	0.20
Ecuadorian	1	0.01
Peruvian	3	0.04
Other Hispanic or Latino	236	2.99

Race*	Population	%
African-American/Black (1,508)	1,624	20.59
Not Hispanic (1,469)	1,552	19.68
Hispanic (39)	72	0.91
American Indian/Alaska Native (136)	196	2.49
Not Hispanic (17)	34	0.43
Hispanic (119)	162	2.05
Blackfeet (0)	1	0.01
Central American Ind. (1)	2	0.03
Cherokee (4)	8	0.10
Lumbee (8)	12	0.15
Mexican American Ind. (32)	50	0.63
South American Ind. (0)	6	0.08
Spanish American Ind. (5)	10	0.13
Asian (34)	39	0.49
Not Hispanic (33)	37	0.47
Hispanic (1)	2	0.03
Chinese, ex. Taiwanese (6)	8	0.10
Filipino (3)	3	0.04
Indian (7)	9	0.11
Korean (1)	2	0.03
Laotian (1)	1	0.01
Pakistani (9)	11	0.14
Thai (1)	2	0.03
Hawaii Native/Pacific Islander (15)	21	0.27
Not Hispanic (7)	11	0.14
Hispanic (8)	10	0.13
Guamanian/Chamorro (14)	15	0.19
Samoan (1)	5	0.06
White (3,471)	3,672	46.56
Not Hispanic (2,305)	2,384	30.23
Hispanic (1,166)	1,288	16.33

Smithfield

Place Type: Town
County: Johnston
Population: 10,966†

Ancestry‡	Population	%
African, Sub-Saharan (97)	97	0.88
African (97)	97	0.88
American (1,644)	1,644	14.98
Arab (154)	154	1.40
Arab (101)	101	0.92
Other Arab (53)	53	0.48
British (11)	11	0.10
Canadian (43)	43	0.39
Danish (0)	21	0.19
Dutch (0)	14	0.13
English (1,157)	1,579	14.39
European (47)	47	0.43
Finnish (38)	38	0.35
French, ex. Basque (49)	127	1.16
French Canadian (25)	35	0.32
German (30)	199	1.81
Irish (219)	681	6.21
Italian (62)	183	1.67
Northern European (12)	18	0.16
Norwegian (0)	26	0.24
Pennsylvania German (14)	29	0.26
Polish (0)	3	0.03
Portuguese (31)	31	0.28
Scotch-Irish (276)	399	3.64
Scottish (93)	206	1.88
Swedish (25)	58	0.53
Swiss (0)	20	0.18
Welsh (8)	101	0.92
West Indian, ex. Hispanic (4)	14	0.13
Jamaican (0)	10	0.09
West Indian (4)	4	0.04

Hispanic Origin	Population	%
Hispanic or Latino (of any race)	2,114	19.28
Central American, ex. Mexican	389	3.55
Costa Rican	2	0.02
Guatemalan	48	0.44
Honduran	274	2.50
Nicaraguan	5	0.05
Panamanian	20	0.18
Salvadoran	31	0.28
Other Central American	9	0.08
Cuban	19	0.17
Dominican Republic	27	0.25
Mexican	1,365	12.45
Puerto Rican	98	0.89
South American	48	0.44
Argentinean	4	0.04

*Notes: † The Census 2010 population figure is used to calculate the percentages in the Hispanic Origin and Race categories. Ancestry percentages are based on the 2006-2010 American Community Survey population (not shown); ‡ Numbers in parentheses indicate the number of people reporting a single ancestry; * Numbers in parentheses indicate the number of persons reporting this race alone, not in combination with any other race; Please refer to the Explanation of Data for more information.*

Chilean	5	0.05
Colombian	18	0.16
Ecuadorian	4	0.04
Peruvian	7	0.06
Uruguayan	6	0.05
Venezuelan	4	0.04
Other Hispanic or Latino	168	1.53

Race*	Population	%
African-American/Black (2,986)	3,101	28.28
Not Hispanic (2,937)	3,031	27.64
Hispanic (49)	70	0.64
American Indian/Alaska Native (53)	105	0.96
Not Hispanic (24)	68	0.62
Hispanic (29)	37	0.34
Blackfeet (0)	1	0.01
Central American Ind. (3)	4	0.04
Cherokee (5)	11	0.10
Chippewa (1)	1	0.01
Choctaw (0)	1	0.01
Lumbee (4)	5	0.05
Mexican American Ind. (10)	10	0.09
Navajo (0)	1	0.01
Yaqui (0)	1	0.01
Asian (88)	122	1.11
Not Hispanic (82)	110	1.00
Hispanic (6)	12	0.11
Cambodian (0)	1	0.01
Chinese, ex. Taiwanese (10)	15	0.14
Filipino (8)	19	0.17
Indian (32)	34	0.31
Japanese (5)	11	0.10
Korean (7)	8	0.07
Laotian (1)	1	0.01
Pakistani (5)	6	0.05
Thai (3)	7	0.06
Vietnamese (17)	17	0.16
Hawaii Native/Pacific Islander (7)	21	0.19
Not Hispanic (3)	11	0.10
Hispanic (4)	10	0.09
Guamanian/Chamorro (4)	5	0.05
Native Hawaiian (3)	7	0.06
Samoan (0)	1	0.01
White (6,243)	6,412	58.47
Not Hispanic (5,658)	5,774	52.65
Hispanic (585)	638	5.82

Southern Pines

Place Type: Town
County: Moore
Population: 12,334†

Ancestry‡	Population	%
African, Sub-Saharan (81)	81	0.67
African (81)	81	0.67
American (839)	839	6.92
Arab (12)	50	0.41
Lebanese (12)	50	0.41
Australian (22)	22	0.18
British (68)	68	0.56
Canadian (28)	37	0.31
Croatian (0)	13	0.11
Czech (11)	30	0.25
Czechoslovakian (0)	48	0.40
Danish (0)	69	0.57
Dutch (66)	161	1.33
Eastern European (7)	15	0.12
English (1,291)	2,326	19.20
European (168)	168	1.39
French, ex. Basque (86)	292	2.41
French Canadian (36)	55	0.45
German (458)	1,414	11.67
Greek (18)	18	0.15
Hungarian (12)	12	0.10
Irish (514)	1,138	9.39
Italian (94)	318	2.62
Norwegian (38)	75	0.62
Pennsylvania German (0)	23	0.19
Polish (134)	214	1.77
Portuguese (19)	19	0.16
Russian (0)	36	0.30
Scandinavian (8)	8	0.07
Scotch-Irish (420)	626	5.17
Scottish (475)	727	6.00
Slovak (0)	26	0.21
Swedish (23)	157	1.30
Swiss (0)	18	0.15
Turkish (11)	11	0.09
Ukrainian (13)	13	0.11
Welsh (25)	157	1.30
West Indian, ex. Hispanic (38)	93	0.77
Jamaican (38)	80	0.66
West Indian (0)	13	0.11
Yugoslavian (0)	12	0.10

Hispanic Origin	Population	%
Hispanic or Latino (of any race)	482	3.91
Central American, ex. Mexican	46	0.37
Costa Rican	4	0.03
Guatemalan	30	0.24
Honduran	2	0.02
Panamanian	7	0.06
Salvadoran	3	0.02
Cuban	12	0.10
Dominican Republic	4	0.03
Mexican	283	2.29
Puerto Rican	50	0.41
South American	31	0.25
Argentinean	7	0.06
Bolivian	1	0.01
Chilean	7	0.06
Colombian	15	0.12
Ecuadorian	1	0.01
Other Hispanic or Latino	56	0.45

Race*	Population	%
African-American/Black (2,959)	3,054	24.76
Not Hispanic (2,947)	3,026	24.53
Hispanic (12)	28	0.23
American Indian/Alaska Native (74)	125	1.01
Not Hispanic (67)	109	0.88
Hispanic (7)	16	0.13
Blackfeet (0)	1	0.01
Cherokee (17)	36	0.29
Choctaw (2)	3	0.02
Lumbee (28)	37	0.30
Navajo (3)	3	0.02
Yaqui (1)	1	0.01
Asian (104)	152	1.23
Not Hispanic (100)	146	1.18
Hispanic (4)	6	0.05
Cambodian (1)	1	0.01
Chinese, ex. Taiwanese (26)	31	0.25
Filipino (5)	18	0.15
Indian (29)	37	0.30
Japanese (8)	15	0.12
Korean (18)	29	0.24
Pakistani (3)	3	0.02
Thai (2)	3	0.02
Vietnamese (10)	12	0.10
Hawaii Native/Pacific Islander (8)	17	0.14
Not Hispanic (6)	15	0.12
Hispanic (2)	2	0.02
Guamanian/Chamorro (2)	5	0.04
Native Hawaiian (4)	9	0.07
White (8,848)	8,978	72.79
Not Hispanic (8,579)	8,686	70.42
Hispanic (269)	292	2.37

Spring Lake

Place Type: Town
County: Cumberland
Population: 11,964†

Ancestry‡	Population	%
African, Sub-Saharan (0)	88	0.74
African (0)	44	0.37
Other Sub-Saharan African (0)	44	0.37
American (517)	517	4.37
Arab (41)	74	0.63
Arab (0)	33	0.28
Moroccan (41)	41	0.35
British (68)	68	0.57
Croatian (0)	30	0.25
Czech (9)	25	0.21
Danish (0)	13	0.11
Dutch (0)	40	0.34
English (52)	609	5.15
European (46)	69	0.58
French, ex. Basque (67)	310	2.62
French Canadian (39)	184	1.56
German (280)	1,163	9.83
Guyanese (0)	22	0.19
Hungarian (9)	18	0.15
Irish (389)	1,119	9.46
Italian (87)	1,099	9.29
Norwegian (0)	3	0.03
Polish (74)	421	3.56
Russian (16)	49	0.41
Scotch-Irish (82)	243	2.05
Scottish (39)	175	1.48
Swedish (0)	17	0.14
Swiss (28)	28	0.24
Turkish (0)	23	0.19
Welsh (12)	79	0.67
West Indian, ex. Hispanic (180)	253	2.14
Haitian (53)	53	0.45
Jamaican (25)	62	0.52
West Indian (102)	138	1.17

Hispanic Origin	Population	%
Hispanic or Latino (of any race)	1,839	15.37
Central American, ex. Mexican	126	1.05
Costa Rican	6	0.05
Guatemalan	16	0.13
Honduran	9	0.08
Nicaraguan	1	0.01
Panamanian	80	0.67
Salvadoran	13	0.11
Other Central American	1	0.01
Cuban	24	0.20
Dominican Republic	58	0.48
Mexican	691	5.78
Puerto Rican	740	6.19
South American	76	0.64
Argentinean	1	0.01
Bolivian	5	0.04
Chilean	3	0.03
Colombian	27	0.23
Ecuadorian	19	0.16
Peruvian	18	0.15
Venezuelan	2	0.02
Other South American	1	0.01
Other Hispanic or Latino	124	1.04

Race*	Population	%
African-American/Black (4,346)	4,852	40.55
Not Hispanic (4,131)	4,517	37.75
Hispanic (215)	335	2.80
American Indian/Alaska Native (127)	290	2.42
Not Hispanic (111)	227	1.90
Hispanic (16)	63	0.53
Apache (1)	2	0.02
Blackfeet (1)	15	0.13
Cherokee (11)	44	0.37
Cheyenne (4)	4	0.03
Chickasaw (2)	3	0.03
Choctaw (1)	5	0.04
Creek (0)	2	0.02
Delaware (0)	1	0.01
Houma (2)	2	0.02
Iroquois (3)	7	0.06
Lumbee (13)	15	0.13
Mexican American Ind. (1)	6	0.05
Navajo (5)	6	0.05
Seminole (0)	1	0.01
Sioux (14)	22	0.18
South American Ind. (1)	5	0.04

*Notes: † The Census 2010 population figure is used to calculate the percentages in the Hispanic Origin and Race categories. Ancestry percentages are based on the 2006-2010 American Community Survey population (not shown); ‡ Numbers in parentheses indicate the number of people reporting a single ancestry; * Numbers in parentheses indicate the number of persons reporting this race alone, not in combination with any other race; Please refer to the Explanation of Data for more information.*

Tlingit-Haida *(Alaska Native)* (0)	2	0.02
Tohono O'Odham (0)	1	0.01
Asian (354)	629	5.26
Not Hispanic (335)	562	4.70
Hispanic (19)	67	0.56
Cambodian (4)	4	0.03
Chinese, ex. Taiwanese (38)	68	0.57
Filipino (76)	178	1.49
Hmong (3)	7	0.06
Indian (13)	15	0.13
Indonesian (4)	5	0.04
Japanese (17)	64	0.53
Korean (145)	200	1.67
Laotian (4)	12	0.10
Pakistani (1)	1	0.01
Sri Lankan (2)	2	0.02
Taiwanese (1)	1	0.01
Thai (9)	50	0.42
Vietnamese (21)	34	0.28
Hawaii Native/Pacific Islander (58)	144	1.20
Not Hispanic (47)	94	0.79
Hispanic (11)	50	0.42
Guamanian/Chamorro (24)	32	0.27
Native Hawaiian (2)	32	0.27
Samoan (16)	31	0.26
Tongan (0)	3	0.03
White (5,644)	6,229	52.06
Not Hispanic (4,889)	5,313	44.41
Hispanic (755)	916	7.66

St. Stephens

Place Type: CDP
County: Catawba
Population: 8,759†

Ancestry‡	Population	%
American (1,578)	1,578	16.89
Austrian (0)	7	0.07
British (16)	50	0.54
Dutch (134)	418	4.47
Eastern European (27)	27	0.29
English (438)	676	7.23
European (173)	183	1.96
French, ex. Basque (49)	119	1.27
German (1,003)	1,998	21.38
Greek (0)	25	0.27
Hungarian (42)	42	0.45
Irish (214)	977	10.46
Italian (11)	140	1.50
Lithuanian (0)	15	0.16
Luxemburger (22)	22	0.24
Norwegian (0)	46	0.49
Polish (12)	100	1.07
Romanian (40)	40	0.43
Russian (34)	104	1.11
Scotch-Irish (286)	393	4.21
Scottish (66)	243	2.60
Swedish (13)	57	0.61
Welsh (0)	31	0.33

Hispanic Origin	Population	%
Hispanic or Latino (of any race)	904	10.32
Central American, ex. Mexican	104	1.19
Costa Rican	30	0.34
Guatemalan	26	0.30
Honduran	11	0.13
Nicaraguan	4	0.05
Panamanian	5	0.06
Salvadoran	28	0.32
Cuban	8	0.09
Dominican Republic	3	0.03
Mexican	683	7.80
Puerto Rican	26	0.30
South American	34	0.39
Argentinean	1	0.01
Chilean	1	0.01
Colombian	10	0.11
Ecuadorian	2	0.02
Peruvian	20	0.23
Other Hispanic or Latino	46	0.53

Race*	Population	%
African-American/Black (366)	473	5.40
Not Hispanic (359)	460	5.25
Hispanic (7)	13	0.15
American Indian/Alaska Native (22)	68	0.78
Not Hispanic (17)	55	0.63
Hispanic (5)	13	0.15
Blackfeet (0)	6	0.07
Cherokee (9)	26	0.30
Creek (1)	1	0.01
Iroquois (0)	2	0.02
Lumbee (5)	9	0.10
Mexican American Ind. (4)	15	0.17
Osage (0)	1	0.01
Potawatomi (1)	1	0.01
Asian (388)	422	4.82
Not Hispanic (388)	413	4.72
Hispanic (0)	9	0.10
Burmese (1)	1	0.01
Cambodian (1)	3	0.03
Chinese, ex. Taiwanese (25)	25	0.29
Filipino (3)	10	0.11
Hmong (246)	250	2.85
Indian (16)	22	0.25
Japanese (1)	8	0.09
Korean (1)	9	0.10
Laotian (24)	28	0.32
Pakistani (4)	4	0.05
Thai (1)	2	0.02
Vietnamese (46)	50	0.57
Hawaii Native/Pacific Islander (7)	11	0.13
Not Hispanic (2)	4	0.05
Hispanic (5)	7	0.08
Guamanian/Chamorro (0)	1	0.01
Marshallese (1)	1	0.01
Native Hawaiian (5)	6	0.07
Samoan (0)	1	0.01
White (7,253)	7,422	84.74
Not Hispanic (6,922)	7,063	80.64
Hispanic (331)	359	4.10

Stallings

Place Type: Town
County: Union
Population: 13,831†

Ancestry‡	Population	%
African, Sub-Saharan (67)	85	0.67
African (16)	34	0.27
Nigerian (36)	36	0.28
Other Sub-Saharan African (15)	15	0.12
American (1,672)	1,672	13.18
Austrian (0)	9	0.07
Belgian (49)	98	0.77
British (41)	41	0.32
Canadian (39)	56	0.44
Croatian (48)	61	0.48
Czech (13)	53	0.42
Dutch (13)	197	1.55
Eastern European (16)	16	0.13
English (834)	1,564	12.33
European (197)	223	1.76
French, ex. Basque (25)	233	1.84
French Canadian (19)	70	0.55
German (1,002)	2,374	18.72
Greek (27)	39	0.31
Hungarian (55)	68	0.54
Irish (639)	1,496	11.80
Italian (209)	586	4.62
Lithuanian (0)	30	0.24
Maltese (41)	41	0.32
Norwegian (18)	52	0.41
Polish (124)	387	3.05
Portuguese (0)	13	0.10
Romanian (0)	18	0.14
Russian (280)	316	2.49
Scotch-Irish (305)	488	3.85
Scottish (137)	402	3.17
Slovak (9)	33	0.26
Slovene (0)	16	0.13
Swedish (316)	412	3.25
Swiss (0)	13	0.10
Ukrainian (101)	101	0.80
Welsh (39)	182	1.44
Yugoslavian (13)	13	0.10

Hispanic Origin	Population	%
Hispanic or Latino (of any race)	798	5.77
Central American, ex. Mexican	71	0.51
Costa Rican	4	0.03
Guatemalan	4	0.03
Honduran	11	0.08
Nicaraguan	20	0.14
Panamanian	4	0.03
Salvadoran	28	0.20
Cuban	32	0.23
Dominican Republic	14	0.10
Mexican	348	2.52
Puerto Rican	132	0.95
South American	134	0.97
Argentinean	11	0.08
Bolivian	4	0.03
Chilean	4	0.03
Colombian	48	0.35
Ecuadorian	30	0.22
Peruvian	23	0.17
Uruguayan	1	0.01
Venezuelan	6	0.04
Other South American	7	0.05
Other Hispanic or Latino	67	0.48

Race*	Population	%
African-American/Black (776)	870	6.29
Not Hispanic (758)	840	6.07
Hispanic (18)	30	0.22
American Indian/Alaska Native (68)	142	1.03
Not Hispanic (61)	129	0.93
Hispanic (7)	13	0.09
Blackfeet (4)	4	0.03
Cherokee (6)	26	0.19
Choctaw (0)	1	0.01
Creek (1)	3	0.02
Lumbee (30)	37	0.27
Seminole (0)	5	0.04
South American Ind. (0)	2	0.01
Asian (318)	390	2.82
Not Hispanic (316)	386	2.79
Hispanic (2)	4	0.03
Chinese, ex. Taiwanese (42)	55	0.40
Filipino (40)	52	0.38
Indian (75)	80	0.58
Indonesian (7)	7	0.05
Japanese (10)	26	0.19
Korean (81)	85	0.61
Laotian (8)	8	0.06
Pakistani (2)	2	0.01
Sri Lankan (2)	3	0.02
Taiwanese (5)	5	0.04
Thai (3)	3	0.02
Vietnamese (35)	42	0.30
Hawaii Native/Pacific Islander (5)	7	0.05
Not Hispanic (4)	6	0.04
Hispanic (1)	1	0.01
Native Hawaiian (4)	5	0.04
White (12,213)	12,403	89.68
Not Hispanic (11,671)	11,841	85.61
Hispanic (542)	562	4.06

Statesville

Place Type: City
County: Iredell
Population: 24,532†

Ancestry‡	Population	%
African, Sub-Saharan (97)	105	0.43
African (73)	81	0.33

*Notes: † The Census 2010 population figure is used to calculate the percentages in the Hispanic Origin and Race categories. Ancestry percentages are based on the 2006-2010 American Community Survey population (not shown); ‡ Numbers in parentheses indicate the number of people reporting a single ancestry; * Numbers in parentheses indicate the number of persons reporting this race alone, not in combination with any other race; Please refer to the Explanation of Data for more information.*

Ancestry	Population	%
Cape Verdean (24)	24	0.10
American (2,121)	2,121	8.62
Austrian (23)	23	0.09
Belgian (16)	16	0.06
British (67)	100	0.41
Croatian (21)	21	0.09
Czech (24)	24	0.10
Czechoslovakian (24)	24	0.10
Danish (0)	42	0.17
Dutch (116)	294	1.19
English (1,086)	1,979	8.04
European (291)	304	1.23
French, ex. Basque (61)	355	1.44
French Canadian (41)	51	0.21
German (1,024)	2,535	10.30
Greek (0)	31	0.13
Hungarian (8)	8	0.03
Irish (560)	1,711	6.95
Israeli (16)	16	0.06
Italian (225)	511	2.08
Lithuanian (0)	9	0.04
Norwegian (30)	41	0.17
Pennsylvania German (0)	6	0.02
Polish (33)	126	0.51
Portuguese (0)	52	0.21
Russian (24)	59	0.24
Scandinavian (68)	180	0.73
Scotch-Irish (723)	1,165	4.73
Scottish (74)	333	1.35
Slovak (11)	46	0.19
Swedish (28)	65	0.26
Swiss (0)	23	0.09
Welsh (16)	114	0.46
West Indian, ex. Hispanic (55)	169	0.69
Haitian (9)	9	0.04
Trinidadian/Tobagonian (32)	32	0.13
West Indian (14)	128	0.52

Hispanic Origin	Population	%
Hispanic or Latino (of any race)	2,665	10.86
Central American, ex. Mexican	487	1.99
Costa Rican	12	0.05
Guatemalan	38	0.15
Honduran	157	0.64
Nicaraguan	30	0.12
Panamanian	6	0.02
Salvadoran	244	0.99
Cuban	37	0.15
Dominican Republic	39	0.16
Mexican	1,244	5.07
Puerto Rican	155	0.63
South American	483	1.97
Argentinean	8	0.03
Bolivian	2	0.01
Chilean	18	0.07
Colombian	365	1.49
Ecuadorian	75	0.31
Peruvian	8	0.03
Uruguayan	2	0.01
Venezuelan	5	0.02
Other Hispanic or Latino	220	0.90

Race*	Population	%
African-American/Black (8,471)	8,850	36.08
Not Hispanic (8,356)	8,686	35.41
Hispanic (115)	164	0.67
American Indian/Alaska Native (77)	234	0.95
Not Hispanic (52)	181	0.74
Hispanic (25)	53	0.22
Apache (4)	4	0.02
Blackfeet (0)	10	0.04
Central American Ind. (3)	3	0.01
Cherokee (7)	61	0.25
Chippewa (1)	1	<0.01
Creek (0)	1	<0.01
Iroquois (1)	1	<0.01
Lumbee (11)	17	0.07
Mexican American Ind. (5)	6	0.02
Seminole (0)	1	<0.01
Shoshone (0)	6	0.02
Sioux (0)	5	0.02
South American Ind. (0)	3	0.01
Ute (1)	1	<0.01
Asian (460)	519	2.12
Not Hispanic (457)	507	2.07
Hispanic (3)	12	0.05
Chinese, ex. Taiwanese (28)	38	0.15
Filipino (17)	21	0.09
Hmong (134)	140	0.57
Indian (90)	97	0.40
Indonesian (1)	2	0.01
Japanese (41)	47	0.19
Korean (18)	28	0.11
Laotian (31)	36	0.15
Nepalese (2)	2	0.01
Taiwanese (2)	2	0.01
Thai (4)	5	0.02
Vietnamese (66)	77	0.31
Hawaii Native/Pacific Islander (5)	34	0.14
Not Hispanic (1)	16	0.07
Hispanic (4)	18	0.07
Guamanian/Chamorro (4)	4	0.02
Native Hawaiian (1)	12	0.05
White (13,436)	13,914	56.72
Not Hispanic (12,542)	12,886	52.53
Hispanic (894)	1,028	4.19

Summerfield

Place Type: Town
County: Guilford
Population: 10,232†

Ancestry‡	Population	%
Alsatian (12)	12	0.12
American (1,031)	1,031	10.72
Arab (0)	27	0.28
Lebanese (0)	27	0.28
Australian (0)	8	0.08
British (37)	45	0.47
Canadian (0)	14	0.15
Czech (38)	38	0.40
Czechoslovakian (11)	11	0.11
Danish (36)	134	1.39
Dutch (49)	186	1.93
English (620)	1,150	11.96
European (86)	86	0.89
French, ex. Basque (292)	584	6.07
French Canadian (0)	8	0.08
German (627)	1,708	17.76
Greek (0)	13	0.14
Hungarian (26)	79	0.82
Irish (431)	1,067	11.10
Italian (185)	465	4.84
Norwegian (0)	40	0.42
Polish (78)	160	1.66
Portuguese (0)	21	0.22
Romanian (10)	41	0.43
Russian (9)	104	1.08
Scotch-Irish (249)	382	3.97
Scottish (174)	407	4.23
Slovak (14)	14	0.15
Slovene (0)	13	0.14
Swiss (11)	23	0.24
Ukrainian (0)	10	0.10
Welsh (21)	237	2.46
West Indian, ex. Hispanic (0)	65	0.68
Haitian (0)	65	0.68

Hispanic Origin	Population	%
Hispanic or Latino (of any race)	440	4.30
Central American, ex. Mexican	62	0.61
Costa Rican	1	0.01
Guatemalan	16	0.16
Honduran	6	0.06
Panamanian	1	0.01
Salvadoran	38	0.37
Cuban	27	0.26
Dominican Republic	6	0.06
Mexican	211	2.06
Puerto Rican	49	0.48
South American	60	0.59
Argentinean	7	0.07
Chilean	4	0.04
Colombian	20	0.20
Ecuadorian	1	0.01
Paraguayan	2	0.02
Peruvian	16	0.16
Venezuelan	10	0.10
Other Hispanic or Latino	25	0.24

Race*	Population	%
African-American/Black (452)	505	4.94
Not Hispanic (448)	493	4.82
Hispanic (4)	12	0.12
American Indian/Alaska Native (41)	94	0.92
Not Hispanic (35)	85	0.83
Hispanic (6)	9	0.09
Blackfeet (0)	4	0.04
Central American Ind. (0)	1	0.01
Cherokee (2)	24	0.23
Chippewa (2)	2	0.02
Lumbee (7)	16	0.16
Mexican American Ind. (5)	5	0.05
Navajo (5)	5	0.05
Osage (2)	2	0.02
Potawatomi (1)	1	0.01
Seminole (0)	1	0.01
Spanish American Ind. (1)	1	0.01
Asian (229)	291	2.84
Not Hispanic (228)	287	2.80
Hispanic (1)	4	0.04
Cambodian (2)	4	0.04
Chinese, ex. Taiwanese (28)	44	0.43
Filipino (21)	34	0.33
Indian (46)	49	0.48
Indonesian (0)	1	0.01
Japanese (22)	39	0.38
Korean (72)	90	0.88
Laotian (1)	1	0.01
Malaysian (1)	1	0.01
Pakistani (4)	4	0.04
Taiwanese (10)	10	0.10
Thai (1)	1	0.01
Vietnamese (6)	11	0.11
Hawaii Native/Pacific Islander (2)	6	0.06
Not Hispanic (2)	6	0.06
Marshallese (0)	1	0.01
Native Hawaiian (2)	2	0.02
Samoan (0)	2	0.02
White (9,203)	9,338	91.26
Not Hispanic (8,940)	9,058	88.53
Hispanic (263)	280	2.74

Tarboro

Place Type: Town
County: Edgecombe
Population: 11,415†

Ancestry‡	Population	%
African, Sub-Saharan (31)	65	0.57
African (31)	65	0.57
American (1,757)	1,757	15.38
Arab (160)	160	1.40
Arab (160)	160	1.40
Assyrian/Chaldean/Syriac (16)	16	0.14
British (44)	44	0.39
Canadian (9)	9	0.08
Celtic (27)	27	0.24
Czechoslovakian (0)	21	0.18
Dutch (13)	27	0.24
English (667)	906	7.93
European (123)	170	1.49
French, ex. Basque (8)	67	0.59
German (199)	342	2.99
Greek (0)	13	0.11
Iranian (26)	26	0.23
Irish (242)	383	3.35
Italian (35)	68	0.60

*Notes: † The Census 2010 population figure is used to calculate the percentages in the Hispanic Origin and Race categories. Ancestry percentages are based on the 2006-2010 American Community Survey population (not shown); ‡ Numbers in parentheses indicate the number of people reporting a single ancestry; * Numbers in parentheses indicate the number of persons reporting this race alone, not in combination with any other race; Please refer to the Explanation of Data for more information.*

Northern European (19)	19	0.17
Pennsylvania German (11)	11	0.10
Polish (11)	11	0.10
Portuguese (0)	24	0.21
Russian (0)	48	0.42
Scotch-Irish (165)	221	1.93
Scottish (114)	125	1.09
Slovene (0)	57	0.50
Ukrainian (0)	48	0.42
West Indian, ex. Hispanic (43)	43	0.38
Jamaican (22)	22	0.19
West Indian (21)	21	0.18

Hispanic Origin	Population	%
Hispanic or Latino (of any race)	557	4.88
Central American, ex. Mexican	31	0.27
Costa Rican	4	0.04
Guatemalan	7	0.06
Honduran	8	0.07
Panamanian	2	0.02
Salvadoran	10	0.09
Cuban	1	0.01
Dominican Republic	21	0.18
Mexican	416	3.64
Puerto Rican	31	0.27
South American	28	0.25
Colombian	20	0.18
Paraguayan	1	0.01
Peruvian	3	0.03
Venezuelan	4	0.04
Other Hispanic or Latino	29	0.25

Race*	Population	%
African-American/Black (5,522)	5,572	48.81
Not Hispanic (5,497)	5,543	48.56
Hispanic (25)	29	0.25
American Indian/Alaska Native (12)	41	0.36
Not Hispanic (6)	33	0.29
Hispanic (6)	8	0.07
Apache (0)	2	0.02
Cherokee (0)	7	0.06
Comanche (2)	2	0.02
Mexican American Ind. (0)	1	0.01
Sioux (0)	1	0.01
Asian (53)	61	0.53
Not Hispanic (53)	59	0.52
Hispanic (0)	2	0.02
Chinese, ex. Taiwanese (24)	24	0.21
Filipino (3)	4	0.04
Indian (4)	6	0.05
Japanese (0)	4	0.04
Korean (2)	2	0.02
Laotian (1)	1	0.01
Taiwanese (2)	2	0.02
Thai (2)	2	0.02
Vietnamese (15)	15	0.13
Hawaii Native/Pacific Islander (7)	9	0.08
Not Hispanic (0)	2	0.02
Hispanic (7)	7	0.06
Guamanian/Chamorro (6)	6	0.05
Native Hawaiian (0)	2	0.02
White (5,390)	5,465	47.88
Not Hispanic (5,229)	5,278	46.24
Hispanic (161)	187	1.64

Thomasville

Place Type: City
County: Davidson
Population: 26,757†

Ancestry‡	Population	%
African, Sub-Saharan (21)	21	0.08
African (21)	21	0.08
American (2,729)	2,729	10.37
Arab (23)	23	0.09
Palestinian (23)	23	0.09
Austrian (0)	28	0.11
British (45)	85	0.32
Cajun (13)	105	0.40
Canadian (29)	72	0.27
Croatian (0)	11	0.04
Danish (0)	22	0.08
Dutch (99)	268	1.02
English (1,221)	1,982	7.53
European (200)	222	0.84
French, ex. Basque (39)	177	0.67
French Canadian (0)	15	0.06
German (1,453)	2,819	10.71
Hungarian (48)	73	0.28
Irish (557)	1,551	5.89
Italian (206)	422	1.60
Norwegian (91)	144	0.55
Polish (0)	63	0.24
Portuguese (17)	17	0.06
Russian (26)	26	0.10
Scotch-Irish (294)	516	1.96
Scottish (111)	309	1.17
Serbian (88)	88	0.33
Swedish (9)	47	0.18
Swiss (0)	120	0.46
Ukrainian (10)	24	0.09
Welsh (31)	120	0.46

Hispanic Origin	Population	%
Hispanic or Latino (of any race)	3,844	14.37
Central American, ex. Mexican	599	2.24
Costa Rican	9	0.03
Guatemalan	41	0.15
Honduran	162	0.61
Nicaraguan	1	<0.01
Panamanian	6	0.02
Salvadoran	379	1.42
Other Central American	1	<0.01
Cuban	17	0.06
Dominican Republic	79	0.30
Mexican	2,722	10.17
Puerto Rican	149	0.56
South American	40	0.15
Argentinean	1	<0.01
Chilean	3	0.01
Colombian	17	0.06
Ecuadorian	8	0.03
Paraguayan	1	<0.01
Peruvian	5	0.02
Venezuelan	5	0.02
Other Hispanic or Latino	238	0.89

Race*	Population	%
African-American/Black (5,243)	5,513	20.60
Not Hispanic (5,180)	5,411	20.22
Hispanic (63)	102	0.38
American Indian/Alaska Native (199)	364	1.36
Not Hispanic (133)	266	0.99
Hispanic (66)	98	0.37
Blackfeet (0)	12	0.04
Central American Ind. (2)	2	0.01
Cherokee (25)	80	0.30
Cheyenne (1)	1	<0.01
Chickasaw (2)	2	0.01
Cree (2)	2	0.01
Delaware (2)	3	0.01
Hopi (3)	3	0.01
Iroquois (3)	8	0.03
Lumbee (51)	70	0.26
Mexican American Ind. (3)	4	0.01
Seminole (1)	1	<0.01
Sioux (0)	7	0.03
South American Ind. (0)	2	0.01
Spanish American Ind. (0)	2	0.01
Asian (291)	374	1.40
Not Hispanic (280)	346	1.29
Hispanic (11)	28	0.10
Bangladeshi (3)	3	0.01
Burmese (8)	8	0.03
Cambodian (15)	21	0.08
Chinese, ex. Taiwanese (21)	27	0.10
Filipino (53)	66	0.25
Hmong (1)	1	<0.01
Indian (32)	38	0.14
Indonesian (0)	1	<0.01
Japanese (0)	5	0.02
Korean (11)	19	0.07
Laotian (32)	41	0.15
Pakistani (37)	40	0.15
Thai (6)	8	0.03
Vietnamese (53)	73	0.27
Hawaii Native/Pacific Islander (1)	8	0.03
Not Hispanic (1)	4	0.01
Hispanic (0)	4	0.01
Guamanian/Chamorro (1)	2	0.01
Native Hawaiian (0)	1	<0.01
White (18,285)	18,774	70.16
Not Hispanic (16,875)	17,232	64.40
Hispanic (1,410)	1,542	5.76

Wake Forest

Place Type: Town
County: Wake
Population: 30,117†

Ancestry‡	Population	%
African, Sub-Saharan (227)	269	1.00
African (60)	102	0.38
Ethiopian (72)	72	0.27
Ghanaian (64)	64	0.24
South African (31)	31	0.12
American (1,823)	1,823	6.80
Arab (96)	113	0.42
Egyptian (0)	5	0.02
Lebanese (67)	79	0.29
Other Arab (29)	29	0.11
Armenian (0)	29	0.11
Australian (36)	36	0.13
Austrian (0)	44	0.16
Belgian (9)	41	0.15
Brazilian (12)	34	0.13
British (55)	101	0.38
Canadian (112)	206	0.77
Czech (15)	125	0.47
Czechoslovakian (19)	19	0.07
Danish (7)	124	0.46
Dutch (148)	465	1.74
Eastern European (76)	76	0.28
English (1,423)	4,127	15.41
European (641)	934	3.49
Finnish (0)	37	0.14
French, ex. Basque (118)	1,061	3.96
French Canadian (111)	283	1.06
German (852)	3,442	12.85
Greek (110)	219	0.82
Hungarian (26)	109	0.41
Iranian (15)	15	0.06
Irish (1,122)	4,324	16.14
Italian (702)	2,341	8.74
Lithuanian (68)	94	0.35
Maltese (0)	45	0.17
Northern European (26)	26	0.10
Norwegian (119)	344	1.28
Pennsylvania German (0)	19	0.07
Polish (221)	781	2.92
Portuguese (13)	146	0.54
Romanian (71)	78	0.29
Russian (40)	97	0.36
Scandinavian (0)	9	0.03
Scotch-Irish (357)	938	3.50
Scottish (400)	983	3.67
Serbian (10)	10	0.04
Slavic (9)	43	0.16
Slovak (32)	70	0.26
Slovene (0)	42	0.16
Swedish (69)	267	1.00
Swiss (35)	79	0.29
Ukrainian (99)	169	0.63
Welsh (33)	178	0.66
West Indian, ex. Hispanic (114)	156	0.58
Belizean (0)	35	0.13
Jamaican (31)	31	0.12
West Indian (83)	90	0.34

*Notes: † The Census 2010 population figure is used to calculate the percentages in the Hispanic Origin and Race categories. Ancestry percentages are based on the 2006-2010 American Community Survey population (not shown); ‡ Numbers in parentheses indicate the number of people reporting a single ancestry; * Numbers in parentheses indicate the number of persons reporting this race alone, not in combination with any other race; Please refer to the Explanation of Data for more information.*

Hispanic Origin	Population	%
Hispanic or Latino (of any race)	1,681	5.58
Central American, ex. Mexican	132	0.44
Costa Rican	10	0.03
Guatemalan	30	0.10
Honduran	14	0.05
Nicaraguan	10	0.03
Panamanian	14	0.05
Salvadoran	52	0.17
Other Central American	2	0.01
Cuban	144	0.48
Dominican Republic	102	0.34
Mexican	544	1.81
Puerto Rican	371	1.23
South American	289	0.96
Argentinean	18	0.06
Bolivian	11	0.04
Chilean	8	0.03
Colombian	99	0.33
Ecuadorian	33	0.11
Paraguayan	1	<0.01
Peruvian	73	0.24
Uruguayan	4	0.01
Venezuelan	39	0.13
Other South American	3	0.01
Other Hispanic or Latino	99	0.33

Race*	Population	%
African-American/Black (4,594)	4,935	16.39
Not Hispanic (4,524)	4,810	15.97
Hispanic (70)	125	0.42
American Indian/Alaska Native (125)	329	1.09
Not Hispanic (97)	271	0.90
Hispanic (28)	58	0.19
Alaska Athabascan *(Ala. Nat.)* (2)	2	0.01
Aleut *(Alaska Native)* (0)	1	<0.01
Apache (0)	2	0.01
Blackfeet (1)	10	0.03
Cherokee (10)	72	0.24
Cheyenne (3)	3	0.01
Chickasaw (0)	1	<0.01
Chippewa (3)	8	0.03
Choctaw (8)	11	0.04
Comanche (2)	2	0.01
Creek (1)	3	0.01
Crow (0)	6	0.02
Delaware (0)	1	<0.01
Inupiat *(Alaska Native)* (0)	1	<0.01
Iroquois (3)	4	0.01
Lumbee (10)	16	0.05
Mexican American Ind. (4)	4	0.01
Navajo (1)	1	<0.01
Ottawa (0)	2	0.01
Potawatomi (1)	4	0.01
Seminole (0)	10	0.03
Shoshone (3)	3	0.01
Sioux (0)	2	0.01
South American Ind. (5)	7	0.02
Ute (1)	1	<0.01
Yuman (1)	1	<0.01
Yup'ik *(Alaska Native)* (0)	2	0.01
Asian (887)	1,121	3.72
Not Hispanic (881)	1,089	3.62
Hispanic (6)	32	0.11
Cambodian (2)	6	0.02
Chinese, ex. Taiwanese (150)	179	0.59
Filipino (146)	216	0.72
Indian (211)	244	0.81
Indonesian (2)	8	0.03
Japanese (10)	45	0.15
Korean (133)	165	0.55
Laotian (25)	26	0.09
Malaysian (2)	2	0.01
Pakistani (25)	26	0.09
Sri Lankan (6)	9	0.03
Taiwanese (7)	7	0.02
Thai (8)	16	0.05
Vietnamese (137)	146	0.48
Hawaii Native/Pacific Islander (12)	35	0.12
Not Hispanic (11)	32	0.11
Hispanic (1)	3	0.01
Marshallese (1)	4	0.01
Native Hawaiian (5)	19	0.06
Samoan (1)	3	0.01
White (23,291)	23,912	79.40
Not Hispanic (22,297)	22,795	75.69
Hispanic (994)	1,117	3.71

Washington

Place Type: City
County: Beaufort
Population: 9,744†

Ancestry‡	Population	%
African, Sub-Saharan (68)	68	0.70
African (68)	68	0.70
American (421)	421	4.34
Arab (64)	64	0.66
Lebanese (64)	64	0.66
Austrian (0)	9	0.09
British (38)	46	0.47
Cajun (0)	15	0.15
Czech (0)	15	0.15
Danish (13)	13	0.13
Dutch (24)	98	1.01
Eastern European (8)	28	0.29
English (967)	1,429	14.72
European (47)	47	0.48
French, ex. Basque (193)	263	2.71
French Canadian (0)	44	0.45
German (304)	665	6.85
Irish (178)	492	5.07
Italian (110)	148	1.52
Northern European (10)	10	0.10
Norwegian (0)	13	0.13
Polish (0)	12	0.12
Portuguese (34)	34	0.35
Russian (12)	21	0.22
Scotch-Irish (87)	211	2.17
Scottish (133)	272	2.80
Slovene (0)	12	0.12
Swedish (0)	13	0.13
Welsh (12)	117	1.21
West Indian, ex. Hispanic (16)	16	0.16
Barbadian (16)	16	0.16

Hispanic Origin	Population	%
Hispanic or Latino (of any race)	538	5.52
Central American, ex. Mexican	25	0.26
Guatemalan	10	0.10
Honduran	3	0.03
Panamanian	1	0.01
Salvadoran	11	0.11
Cuban	5	0.05
Dominican Republic	5	0.05
Mexican	420	4.31
Puerto Rican	43	0.44
South American	25	0.26
Chilean	1	0.01
Colombian	17	0.17
Ecuadorian	4	0.04
Peruvian	1	0.01
Venezuelan	2	0.02
Other Hispanic or Latino	15	0.15

Race*	Population	%
African-American/Black (4,433)	4,544	46.63
Not Hispanic (4,406)	4,503	46.21
Hispanic (27)	41	0.42
American Indian/Alaska Native (22)	61	0.63
Not Hispanic (20)	58	0.60
Hispanic (2)	3	0.03
Apache (4)	4	0.04
Cherokee (3)	14	0.14
Iroquois (0)	3	0.03
Navajo (2)	2	0.02
Seminole (0)	1	0.01
Sioux (1)	1	0.01
Asian (51)	62	0.64
Not Hispanic (51)	60	0.62
Hispanic (0)	2	0.02
Cambodian (0)	3	0.03
Chinese, ex. Taiwanese (15)	19	0.19
Filipino (7)	11	0.11
Hmong (2)	2	0.02
Indian (17)	18	0.18
Japanese (3)	5	0.05
Korean (3)	4	0.04
Vietnamese (2)	4	0.04
Hawaii Native/Pacific Islander (8)	17	0.17
Not Hispanic (0)	9	0.09
Hispanic (8)	8	0.08
Guamanian/Chamorro (8)	13	0.13
Native Hawaiian (0)	1	0.01
Samoan (0)	2	0.02
White (4,778)	4,897	50.26
Not Hispanic (4,599)	4,693	48.16
Hispanic (179)	204	2.09

Waxhaw

Place Type: Town
County: Union
Population: 9,859†

Ancestry‡	Population	%
Afghan (0)	15	0.17
American (652)	652	7.45
Arab (97)	120	1.37
Arab (14)	14	0.16
Lebanese (11)	34	0.39
Moroccan (72)	72	0.82
Austrian (0)	17	0.19
Brazilian (8)	8	0.09
British (23)	181	2.07
Canadian (29)	52	0.59
Croatian (30)	30	0.34
Czech (65)	65	0.74
Danish (0)	17	0.19
Dutch (47)	256	2.92
English (320)	757	8.65
European (0)	16	0.18
French, ex. Basque (0)	125	1.43
French Canadian (98)	98	1.12
German (359)	1,637	18.70
Greek (0)	42	0.48
Hungarian (15)	47	0.54
Iranian (31)	31	0.35
Irish (301)	1,093	12.49
Italian (82)	617	7.05
Lithuanian (0)	23	0.26
Norwegian (11)	32	0.37
Polish (128)	467	5.33
Portuguese (27)	106	1.21
Russian (0)	60	0.69
Scandinavian (23)	49	0.56
Scotch-Irish (148)	458	5.23
Scottish (37)	202	2.31
Slovak (0)	32	0.37
Swedish (0)	63	0.72
Swiss (20)	20	0.23
Ukrainian (11)	11	0.13
Welsh (45)	110	1.26

Hispanic Origin	Population	%
Hispanic or Latino (of any race)	628	6.37
Central American, ex. Mexican	58	0.59
Costa Rican	6	0.06
Guatemalan	10	0.10
Honduran	5	0.05
Nicaraguan	4	0.04
Panamanian	15	0.15
Salvadoran	18	0.18
Cuban	54	0.55
Dominican Republic	39	0.40
Mexican	152	1.54
Puerto Rican	139	1.41
South American	141	1.43
Argentinean	6	0.06

*Notes: † The Census 2010 population figure is used to calculate the percentages in the Hispanic Origin and Race categories. Ancestry percentages are based on the 2006-2010 American Community Survey population (not shown); ‡ Numbers in parentheses indicate the number of people reporting a single ancestry; * Numbers in parentheses indicate the number of persons reporting this race alone, not in combination with any other race; Please refer to the Explanation of Data for more information.*

Bolivian	1	0.01
Chilean	1	0.01
Colombian	47	0.48
Ecuadorian	47	0.48
Peruvian	27	0.27
Venezuelan	12	0.12
Other Hispanic or Latino	45	0.46

Race*	Population	%
African-American/Black (1,106)	1,230	12.48
Not Hispanic (1,082)	1,189	12.06
Hispanic (24)	41	0.42
American Indian/Alaska Native (14)	88	0.89
Not Hispanic (10)	71	0.72
Hispanic (4)	17	0.17
Blackfeet (0)	1	0.01
Cherokee (1)	34	0.34
Chippewa (0)	2	0.02
Choctaw (3)	3	0.03
Iroquois (0)	1	0.01
Lumbee (6)	11	0.11
Menominee (0)	3	0.03
Mexican American Ind. (0)	3	0.03
South American Ind. (0)	4	0.04
Yaqui (0)	1	0.01
Asian (201)	253	2.57
Not Hispanic (201)	253	2.57
Chinese, ex. Taiwanese (33)	48	0.49
Filipino (37)	57	0.58
Indian (69)	79	0.80
Indonesian (0)	1	0.01
Japanese (4)	6	0.06
Korean (35)	48	0.49
Laotian (2)	5	0.05
Thai (2)	5	0.05
Vietnamese (7)	8	0.08
Hawaii Native/Pacific Islander (4)	12	0.12
Not Hispanic (4)	7	0.07
Hispanic (0)	5	0.05
Guamanian/Chamorro (2)	2	0.02
Native Hawaiian (1)	2	0.02
Samoan (1)	2	0.02
White (8,090)	8,360	84.80
Not Hispanic (7,701)	7,903	80.16
Hispanic (389)	457	4.64

Waynesville

Place Type: Town
County: Haywood
Population: 9,869†

Ancestry‡	Population	%
American (2,603)	2,603	26.20
Australian (21)	21	0.21
British (8)	25	0.25
Canadian (0)	30	0.30
Czech (11)	11	0.11
Danish (0)	10	0.10
Dutch (49)	361	3.63
English (667)	1,162	11.70
European (147)	157	1.58
Finnish (10)	10	0.10
French, ex. Basque (30)	198	1.99
French Canadian (11)	31	0.31
German (505)	1,433	14.43
Hungarian (0)	15	0.15
Irish (294)	894	9.00
Italian (124)	307	3.09
Norwegian (9)	31	0.31
Polish (0)	56	0.56
Portuguese (0)	23	0.23
Romanian (9)	17	0.17
Russian (0)	8	0.08
Scandinavian (0)	7	0.07
Scotch-Irish (455)	741	7.46
Scottish (120)	253	2.55
Slovene (10)	10	0.10
Swedish (12)	50	0.50
Swiss (33)	45	0.45
Welsh (14)	46	0.46

Hispanic Origin	Population	%
Hispanic or Latino (of any race)	558	5.65
Central American, ex. Mexican	14	0.14
Costa Rican	1	0.01
Guatemalan	2	0.02
Honduran	6	0.06
Panamanian	2	0.02
Salvadoran	3	0.03
Cuban	24	0.24
Dominican Republic	2	0.02
Mexican	417	4.23
Puerto Rican	28	0.28
South American	25	0.25
Argentinean	3	0.03
Chilean	2	0.02
Colombian	2	0.02
Ecuadorian	9	0.09
Peruvian	7	0.07
Venezuelan	2	0.02
Other Hispanic or Latino	48	0.49

Race*	Population	%
African-American/Black (233)	259	2.62
Not Hispanic (232)	257	2.60
Hispanic (1)	2	0.02
American Indian/Alaska Native (60)	127	1.29
Not Hispanic (53)	117	1.19
Hispanic (7)	10	0.10
Central American Ind. (0)	1	0.01
Cherokee (23)	57	0.58
Cheyenne (0)	1	0.01
Chippewa (1)	1	0.01
Choctaw (0)	1	0.01
Creek (0)	1	0.01
Delaware (0)	1	0.01
Iroquois (1)	2	0.02
Lumbee (3)	5	0.05
Mexican American Ind. (4)	5	0.05
Asian (38)	63	0.64
Not Hispanic (37)	62	0.63
Hispanic (1)	1	0.01
Chinese, ex. Taiwanese (9)	18	0.18
Filipino (8)	15	0.15
Indian (7)	8	0.08
Japanese (1)	4	0.04
Korean (1)	2	0.02
Sri Lankan (2)	2	0.02
Vietnamese (4)	11	0.11
Hawaii Native/Pacific Islander (6)	15	0.15
Not Hispanic (3)	7	0.07
Hispanic (3)	8	0.08
Guamanian/Chamorro (2)	6	0.06
Native Hawaiian (1)	3	0.03
White (9,117)	9,241	93.64
Not Hispanic (8,873)	8,976	90.95
Hispanic (244)	265	2.69

Weddington

Place Type: Town
County: Union
Population: 9,459†

Ancestry‡	Population	%
American (797)	797	8.66
Arab (9)	51	0.55
Egyptian (9)	27	0.29
Lebanese (0)	15	0.16
Syrian (0)	9	0.10
Austrian (0)	14	0.15
Belgian (0)	38	0.41
Brazilian (45)	45	0.49
British (61)	166	1.80
Croatian (9)	29	0.31
Czech (13)	24	0.26
Danish (0)	12	0.13
Dutch (14)	56	0.61
English (445)	1,467	15.93
European (219)	219	2.38
French, ex. Basque (50)	271	2.94
French Canadian (11)	40	0.43
German (576)	1,530	16.62
Greek (73)	154	1.67
Hungarian (12)	12	0.13
Irish (682)	2,038	22.14
Italian (172)	534	5.80
Lithuanian (12)	22	0.24
Norwegian (27)	138	1.50
Polish (118)	266	2.89
Portuguese (16)	60	0.65
Romanian (0)	12	0.13
Russian (167)	244	2.65
Scandinavian (17)	17	0.18
Scotch-Irish (337)	629	6.83
Scottish (141)	431	4.68
Slovak (15)	29	0.31
Swedish (10)	86	0.93
Swiss (0)	30	0.33
Ukrainian (18)	18	0.20
Welsh (0)	86	0.93
Yugoslavian (14)	28	0.30

Hispanic Origin	Population	%
Hispanic or Latino (of any race)	281	2.97
Central American, ex. Mexican	33	0.35
Costa Rican	8	0.08
Guatemalan	5	0.05
Honduran	10	0.11
Nicaraguan	1	0.01
Panamanian	2	0.02
Salvadoran	7	0.07
Cuban	39	0.41
Dominican Republic	6	0.06
Mexican	93	0.98
Puerto Rican	39	0.41
South American	45	0.48
Argentinean	4	0.04
Bolivian	1	0.01
Chilean	1	0.01
Colombian	18	0.19
Ecuadorian	5	0.05
Paraguayan	1	0.01
Peruvian	9	0.10
Venezuelan	6	0.06
Other Hispanic or Latino	26	0.27

Race*	Population	%
African-American/Black (366)	414	4.38
Not Hispanic (359)	404	4.27
Hispanic (7)	10	0.11
American Indian/Alaska Native (17)	42	0.44
Not Hispanic (15)	40	0.42
Hispanic (2)	2	0.02
Apache (0)	1	0.01
Blackfeet (0)	3	0.03
Cherokee (4)	7	0.07
Choctaw (1)	3	0.03
Inupiat *(Alaska Native)* (4)	4	0.04
Lumbee (6)	7	0.07
Asian (243)	303	3.20
Not Hispanic (243)	298	3.15
Hispanic (0)	5	0.05
Cambodian (1)	3	0.03
Chinese, ex. Taiwanese (70)	78	0.82
Filipino (6)	17	0.18
Indian (87)	96	1.01
Indonesian (1)	1	0.01
Japanese (7)	14	0.15
Korean (42)	58	0.61
Laotian (2)	4	0.04
Nepalese (1)	1	0.01
Pakistani (1)	3	0.03
Taiwanese (2)	2	0.02
Vietnamese (20)	23	0.24
Hawaii Native/Pacific Islander (0)	5	0.05
Not Hispanic (0)	5	0.05
Native Hawaiian (0)	3	0.03
Samoan (0)	3	0.03

*Notes: † The Census 2010 population figure is used to calculate the percentages in the Hispanic Origin and Race categories. Ancestry percentages are based on the 2006-2010 American Community Survey population (not shown); ‡ Numbers in parentheses indicate the number of people reporting a single ancestry; * Numbers in parentheses indicate the number of persons reporting this race alone, not in combination with any other race; Please refer to the Explanation of Data for more information.*

White (8,628)	8,734	92.34
Not Hispanic (8,427)	8,520	90.07
Hispanic (201)	214	2.26

Wilmington

Place Type: City
County: New Hanover
Population: 106,476†

Ancestry‡	Population	%
African, Sub-Saharan (103)	316	0.30
African (83)	296	0.28
Nigerian (20)	20	0.02
American (15,339)	15,339	14.65
Arab (189)	262	0.25
Arab (31)	31	0.03
Egyptian (67)	67	0.06
Lebanese (64)	122	0.12
Other Arab (27)	42	0.04
Armenian (17)	43	0.04
Australian (66)	106	0.10
Austrian (22)	224	0.21
Belgian (9)	54	0.05
Brazilian (61)	61	0.06
British (547)	713	0.68
Bulgarian (58)	66	0.06
Canadian (68)	148	0.14
Celtic (38)	38	0.04
Croatian (15)	102	0.10
Czech (279)	393	0.38
Czechoslovakian (16)	46	0.04
Danish (75)	270	0.26
Dutch (281)	1,097	1.05
Eastern European (10)	27	0.03
English (5,762)	13,829	13.20
European (745)	808	0.77
Finnish (26)	142	0.14
French, ex. Basque (445)	2,934	2.80
French Canadian (121)	395	0.38
German (3,534)	11,884	11.35
Greek (291)	544	0.52
Hungarian (99)	476	0.45
Icelander (0)	11	0.01
Iranian (35)	35	0.03
Irish (4,386)	11,876	11.34
Italian (2,262)	5,142	4.91
Latvian (17)	51	0.05
Lithuanian (74)	272	0.26
New Zealander (0)	30	0.03
Northern European (29)	29	0.03
Norwegian (176)	634	0.61
Pennsylvania German (17)	30	0.03
Polish (602)	1,997	1.91
Portuguese (111)	242	0.23
Romanian (64)	82	0.08
Russian (300)	603	0.58
Scandinavian (7)	21	0.02
Scotch-Irish (2,648)	5,317	5.08
Scottish (1,472)	3,498	3.34
Slavic (25)	90	0.09
Slovak (39)	195	0.19
Slovene (15)	24	0.02
Swedish (206)	598	0.57
Swiss (38)	161	0.15
Turkish (92)	186	0.18
Ukrainian (156)	256	0.24
Welsh (169)	993	0.95
West Indian, ex. Hispanic (189)	306	0.29
Barbadian (38)	38	0.04
Haitian (0)	25	0.02
Jamaican (122)	122	0.12
West Indian (29)	121	0.12
Yugoslavian (54)	181	0.17

Hispanic Origin	Population	%
Hispanic or Latino (of any race)	6,487	6.09
Central American, ex. Mexican	826	0.78
Costa Rican	21	0.02
Guatemalan	212	0.20
Honduran	389	0.37
Nicaraguan	26	0.02
Panamanian	52	0.05
Salvadoran	122	0.11
Other Central American	4	<0.01
Cuban	170	0.16
Dominican Republic	93	0.09
Mexican	3,654	3.43
Puerto Rican	692	0.65
South American	423	0.40
Argentinean	62	0.06
Bolivian	16	0.02
Chilean	40	0.04
Colombian	160	0.15
Ecuadorian	50	0.05
Paraguayan	3	<0.01
Peruvian	52	0.05
Uruguayan	13	0.01
Venezuelan	26	0.02
Other South American	1	<0.01
Other Hispanic or Latino	629	0.59

Race*	Population	%
African-American/Black (21,158)	22,287	20.93
Not Hispanic (20,850)	21,808	20.48
Hispanic (308)	479	0.45
American Indian/Alaska Native (514)	1,276	1.20
Not Hispanic (379)	1,018	0.96
Hispanic (135)	258	0.24
Apache (3)	15	0.01
Arapaho (0)	2	<0.01
Blackfeet (2)	25	0.02
Canadian/French Am. Ind. (1)	2	<0.01
Central American Ind. (12)	25	0.02
Cherokee (72)	297	0.28
Chickasaw (3)	6	0.01
Chippewa (6)	8	0.01
Choctaw (3)	9	0.01
Comanche (2)	2	<0.01
Cree (2)	3	<0.01
Creek (4)	8	0.01
Crow (1)	3	<0.01
Delaware (1)	2	<0.01
Hopi (0)	1	<0.01
Iroquois (8)	25	0.02
Lumbee (78)	120	0.11
Menominee (3)	3	<0.01
Mexican American Ind. (37)	57	0.05
Navajo (1)	10	0.01
Osage (0)	1	<0.01
Ottawa (0)	2	<0.01
Paiute (1)	1	<0.01
Seminole (4)	13	0.01
Sioux (2)	19	0.02
South American Ind. (6)	10	0.01
Spanish American Ind. (2)	2	<0.01
Yaqui (0)	1	<0.01
Asian (1,263)	1,829	1.72
Not Hispanic (1,246)	1,766	1.66
Hispanic (17)	63	0.06
Bangladeshi (4)	4	<0.01
Burmese (6)	6	0.01
Cambodian (2)	2	<0.01
Chinese, ex. Taiwanese (345)	408	0.38
Filipino (135)	282	0.26
Hmong (1)	1	<0.01
Indian (223)	284	0.27
Indonesian (13)	26	0.02
Japanese (78)	162	0.15
Korean (176)	238	0.22
Laotian (11)	11	0.01
Malaysian (3)	5	<0.01
Nepalese (4)	5	<0.01
Pakistani (14)	18	0.02
Sri Lankan (3)	3	<0.01
Taiwanese (10)	11	0.01
Thai (19)	35	0.03
Vietnamese (152)	182	0.17
Hawaii Native/Pacific Islander (78)	189	0.18
Not Hispanic (61)	152	0.14
Hispanic (17)	37	0.03
Guamanian/Chamorro (24)	39	0.04
Native Hawaiian (27)	61	0.06
Samoan (15)	34	0.03
Tongan (1)	1	<0.01
White (78,286)	80,213	75.33
Not Hispanic (75,432)	76,964	72.28
Hispanic (2,854)	3,249	3.05

Wilson

Place Type: City
County: Wilson
Population: 49,167†

Ancestry‡	Population	%
African, Sub-Saharan (308)	414	0.86
African (293)	399	0.83
Kenyan (15)	15	0.03
American (5,626)	5,626	11.67
Arab (473)	574	1.19
Arab (297)	297	0.62
Lebanese (77)	133	0.28
Moroccan (39)	39	0.08
Syrian (15)	48	0.10
Other Arab (45)	57	0.12
Belgian (9)	9	0.02
Brazilian (0)	32	0.07
British (43)	68	0.14
Canadian (0)	13	0.03
Czech (13)	39	0.08
Danish (0)	28	0.06
Dutch (126)	313	0.65
English (2,618)	4,140	8.59
European (353)	360	0.75
French, ex. Basque (50)	522	1.08
French Canadian (15)	206	0.43
German (820)	2,310	4.79
Greek (93)	132	0.27
Guyanese (10)	10	0.02
Hungarian (13)	58	0.12
Irish (843)	2,303	4.78
Italian (185)	549	1.14
Northern European (18)	18	0.04
Norwegian (49)	49	0.10
Polish (40)	196	0.41
Portuguese (0)	22	0.05
Russian (12)	40	0.08
Scandinavian (0)	10	0.02
Scotch-Irish (818)	1,141	2.37
Scottish (289)	790	1.64
Slovak (0)	12	0.02
Swedish (13)	55	0.11
Swiss (10)	10	0.02
Ukrainian (0)	17	0.04
Welsh (17)	141	0.29
West Indian, ex. Hispanic (62)	197	0.41
Bahamian (18)	18	0.04
Belizean (13)	13	0.03
Jamaican (31)	60	0.12
West Indian (0)	106	0.22

Hispanic Origin	Population	%
Hispanic or Latino (of any race)	4,606	9.37
Central American, ex. Mexican	256	0.52
Costa Rican	5	0.01
Guatemalan	40	0.08
Honduran	71	0.14
Nicaraguan	23	0.05
Panamanian	11	0.02
Salvadoran	103	0.21
Other Central American	3	0.01
Cuban	38	0.08
Dominican Republic	24	0.05
Mexican	3,569	7.26
Puerto Rican	234	0.48
South American	110	0.22
Argentinean	16	0.03
Chilean	6	0.01
Colombian	24	0.05

*Notes: † The Census 2010 population figure is used to calculate the percentages in the Hispanic Origin and Race categories. Ancestry percentages are based on the 2006-2010 American Community Survey population (not shown); ‡ Numbers in parentheses indicate the number of people reporting a single ancestry; * Numbers in parentheses indicate the number of persons reporting this race alone, not in combination with any other race; Please refer to the Explanation of Data for more information.*

	Population	%
Ecuadorian	19	0.04
Peruvian	23	0.05
Uruguayan	16	0.03
Venezuelan	6	0.01
Other Hispanic or Latino	375	0.76

Race*	Population	%
African-American/Black (23,530)	24,034	48.88
Not Hispanic (23,361)	23,803	48.41
Hispanic (169)	231	0.47
American Indian/Alaska Native (138)	327	0.67
Not Hispanic (111)	270	0.55
Hispanic (27)	57	0.12
Alaska Athabascan *(Ala. Nat.)* (1)	1	<0.01
Blackfeet (0)	10	0.02
Canadian/French Am. Ind. (4)	4	0.01
Central American Ind. (0)	3	0.01
Cherokee (5)	44	0.09
Chippewa (3)	3	0.01
Choctaw (0)	2	<0.01
Comanche (3)	4	0.01
Crow (1)	1	<0.01
Iroquois (0)	11	0.02
Lumbee (17)	23	0.05
Mexican American Ind. (9)	10	0.02
Pima (0)	3	0.01
Potawatomi (1)	1	<0.01
Pueblo (1)	1	<0.01
Seminole (0)	1	<0.01
South American Ind. (1)	4	0.01
Tohono O'Odham (1)	1	<0.01
Asian (594)	724	1.47
Not Hispanic (590)	697	1.42
Hispanic (4)	27	0.05
Bangladeshi (2)	2	<0.01
Cambodian (6)	10	0.02
Chinese, ex. Taiwanese (79)	100	0.20
Filipino (82)	113	0.23
Indian (254)	269	0.55
Indonesian (0)	2	<0.01
Japanese (31)	44	0.09
Korean (33)	50	0.10
Pakistani (7)	12	0.02
Sri Lankan (1)	1	<0.01
Taiwanese (2)	2	<0.01
Thai (5)	13	0.03
Vietnamese (76)	80	0.16
Hawaii Native/Pacific Islander (19)	60	0.12
Not Hispanic (19)	53	0.11
Hispanic (0)	7	0.01
Guamanian/Chamorro (9)	14	0.03
Native Hawaiian (6)	24	0.05
Samoan (2)	6	0.01
White (21,090)	21,752	44.24
Not Hispanic (19,820)	20,301	41.29
Hispanic (1,270)	1,451	2.95

Winston-Salem

Place Type: City
County: Forsyth
Population: 229,617†

Ancestry‡	Population	%
African, Sub-Saharan (1,249)	1,923	0.86
African (857)	1,251	0.56
Ethiopian (16)	16	0.01
Ghanaian (70)	70	0.03
Kenyan (0)	145	0.06
Liberian (40)	106	0.05
Nigerian (254)	254	0.11
South African (12)	66	0.03
Other Sub-Saharan African (0)	15	0.01
American (11,710)	11,710	5.21
Arab (602)	806	0.36
Arab (111)	134	0.06
Egyptian (117)	176	0.08
Jordanian (50)	50	0.02
Lebanese (249)	320	0.14
Moroccan (43)	43	0.02
Palestinian (6)	6	<0.01
Syrian (26)	70	0.03
Other Arab (0)	7	<0.01
Armenian (17)	74	0.03
Australian (11)	34	0.02
Austrian (121)	325	0.14
Basque (9)	9	<0.01
Belgian (71)	120	0.05
Brazilian (64)	103	0.05
British (656)	1,064	0.47
Bulgarian (25)	25	0.01
Cajun (38)	38	0.02
Canadian (97)	168	0.07
Celtic (31)	64	0.03
Croatian (29)	65	0.03
Czech (113)	321	0.14
Czechoslovakian (24)	90	0.04
Danish (82)	256	0.11
Dutch (363)	2,351	1.05
Eastern European (117)	135	0.06
English (10,465)	22,468	10.00
European (2,088)	2,316	1.03
Finnish (68)	124	0.06
French, ex. Basque (925)	3,360	1.49
French Canadian (194)	520	0.23
German (7,850)	22,499	10.01
German Russian (21)	21	0.01
Greek (706)	1,114	0.50
Guyanese (47)	82	0.04
Hungarian (267)	554	0.25
Iranian (373)	431	0.19
Irish (5,460)	17,469	7.77
Italian (2,074)	5,218	2.32
Latvian (10)	102	0.05
Lithuanian (35)	252	0.11
New Zealander (12)	12	0.01
Northern European (58)	58	0.03
Norwegian (500)	1,252	0.56
Pennsylvania German (21)	34	0.02
Polish (637)	2,333	1.04
Portuguese (91)	268	0.12
Romanian (112)	194	0.09
Russian (435)	1,097	0.49
Scandinavian (57)	344	0.15
Scotch-Irish (3,388)	6,601	2.94
Scottish (2,174)	4,986	2.22
Serbian (21)	99	0.04
Slovak (78)	196	0.09
Slovene (0)	21	0.01
Swedish (247)	928	0.41
Swiss (52)	272	0.12
Turkish (25)	25	0.01
Ukrainian (105)	251	0.11
Welsh (360)	1,806	0.80
West Indian, ex. Hispanic (601)	968	0.43
Bahamian (0)	9	<0.01
Barbadian (222)	222	0.10
Belizean (0)	30	0.01
Haitian (160)	191	0.08
Jamaican (112)	398	0.18
Trinidadian/Tobagonian (64)	75	0.03
U.S. Virgin Islander (18)	18	0.01
West Indian (25)	25	0.01
Yugoslavian (26)	45	0.02

Hispanic Origin	Population	%
Hispanic or Latino (of any race)	33,753	14.70
Central American, ex. Mexican	3,757	1.64
Costa Rican	78	0.03
Guatemalan	882	0.38
Honduran	497	0.22
Nicaraguan	199	0.09
Panamanian	115	0.05
Salvadoran	1,954	0.85
Other Central American	32	0.01
Cuban	503	0.22
Dominican Republic	472	0.21
Mexican	23,427	10.20
Puerto Rican	1,965	0.86
South American	1,344	0.59
Argentinean	121	0.05
Bolivian	17	0.01
Chilean	79	0.03
Colombian	463	0.20
Ecuadorian	243	0.11
Paraguayan	10	<0.01
Peruvian	236	0.10
Uruguayan	25	0.01
Venezuelan	137	0.06
Other South American	13	0.01
Other Hispanic or Latino	2,285	1.00

Race*	Population	%
African-American/Black (79,598)	82,853	36.08
Not Hispanic (78,065)	80,608	35.11
Hispanic (1,533)	2,245	0.98
American Indian/Alaska Native (991)	2,391	1.04
Not Hispanic (567)	1,726	0.75
Hispanic (424)	665	0.29
Alaska Athabascan *(Ala. Nat.)* (0)	1	<0.01
Apache (6)	17	0.01
Blackfeet (9)	72	0.03
Canadian/French Am. Ind. (0)	4	<0.01
Central American Ind. (15)	25	0.01
Cherokee (98)	470	0.20
Cheyenne (0)	2	<0.01
Chickasaw (3)	11	<0.01
Chippewa (9)	17	0.01
Choctaw (6)	18	0.01
Comanche (0)	1	<0.01
Cree (0)	2	<0.01
Creek (1)	10	<0.01
Crow (0)	4	<0.01
Delaware (1)	3	<0.01
Inupiat *(Alaska Native)* (2)	2	<0.01
Iroquois (8)	18	0.01
Kiowa (1)	1	<0.01
Lumbee (120)	180	0.08
Mexican American Ind. (128)	151	0.07
Navajo (8)	11	<0.01
Osage (0)	2	<0.01
Potawatomi (1)	4	<0.01
Pueblo (1)	12	0.01
Puget Sound Salish (0)	2	<0.01
Seminole (0)	10	<0.01
Shoshone (0)	1	<0.01
Sioux (4)	18	0.01
South American Ind. (11)	22	0.01
Spanish American Ind. (4)	4	<0.01
Tlingit-Haida *(Alaska Native)* (3)	3	<0.01
Tohono O'Odham (0)	1	<0.01
Asian (4,581)	5,669	2.47
Not Hispanic (4,536)	5,513	2.40
Hispanic (45)	156	0.07
Bangladeshi (9)	10	<0.01
Burmese (154)	154	0.07
Cambodian (64)	84	0.04
Chinese, ex. Taiwanese (912)	1,116	0.49
Filipino (707)	922	0.40
Hmong (35)	47	0.02
Indian (1,206)	1,391	0.61
Indonesian (90)	97	0.04
Japanese (143)	298	0.13
Korean (344)	451	0.20
Laotian (51)	58	0.03
Malaysian (5)	5	<0.01
Nepalese (37)	38	0.02
Pakistani (124)	155	0.07
Sri Lankan (30)	36	0.02
Taiwanese (31)	38	0.02
Thai (49)	79	0.03
Vietnamese (376)	456	0.20
Hawaii Native/Pacific Islander (182)	374	0.16
Not Hispanic (138)	261	0.11
Hispanic (44)	113	0.05
Guamanian/Chamorro (68)	100	0.04
Marshallese (42)	44	0.02
Native Hawaiian (29)	90	0.04
Samoan (2)	11	<0.01
Tongan (1)	1	<0.01

*Notes: † The Census 2010 population figure is used to calculate the percentages in the Hispanic Origin and Race categories. Ancestry percentages are based on the 2006-2010 American Community Survey population (not shown); ‡ Numbers in parentheses indicate the number of people reporting a single ancestry; * Numbers in parentheses indicate the number of persons reporting this race alone, not in combination with any other race; Please refer to the Explanation of Data for more information.*

White (117,600)	121,879	53.08
Not Hispanic (108,222)	111,232	48.44
Hispanic (9,378)	10,647	4.64

Winterville

Place Type: Town
County: Pitt
Population: 9,269†

Ancestry‡	Population	%
African, Sub-Saharan (36)	36	0.43
Ghanaian (36)	36	0.43
American (979)	979	11.57
Arab (61)	61	0.72
Arab (12)	12	0.14
Lebanese (10)	10	0.12
Palestinian (39)	39	0.46
Brazilian (64)	64	0.76
Canadian (8)	8	0.09
Croatian (0)	12	0.14
Czech (0)	13	0.15
Dutch (63)	122	1.44
English (499)	923	10.91
European (80)	115	1.36
Finnish (0)	14	0.17
French, ex. Basque (0)	76	0.90
French Canadian (29)	29	0.34
German (239)	963	11.38
Greek (28)	39	0.46
Irish (130)	638	7.54
Italian (64)	176	2.08
Norwegian (10)	29	0.34
Pennsylvania German (14)	14	0.17
Polish (45)	115	1.36
Portuguese (16)	16	0.19
Romanian (13)	13	0.15
Scandinavian (0)	18	0.21
Scotch-Irish (85)	152	1.80
Scottish (10)	106	1.25
Slovene (0)	13	0.15
Swedish (0)	24	0.28
Welsh (0)	9	0.11
West Indian, ex. Hispanic (59)	63	0.74
Jamaican (47)	47	0.56
Trinidadian/Tobagonian (0)	4	0.05
West Indian (12)	12	0.14
Yugoslavian (12)	26	0.31

Hispanic Origin	Population	%
Hispanic or Latino (of any race)	309	3.33
Central American, ex. Mexican	28	0.30
Costa Rican	7	0.08
Guatemalan	11	0.12
Honduran	5	0.05
Nicaraguan	3	0.03
Panamanian	1	0.01
Salvadoran	1	0.01
Cuban	24	0.26
Dominican Republic	7	0.08
Mexican	142	1.53
Puerto Rican	51	0.55
South American	33	0.36
Argentinean	2	0.02
Chilean	1	0.01
Colombian	24	0.26
Peruvian	6	0.06
Other Hispanic or Latino	24	0.26

Race*	Population	%
African-American/Black (2,933)	3,037	32.77
Not Hispanic (2,906)	3,001	32.38
Hispanic (27)	36	0.39
American Indian/Alaska Native (31)	64	0.69
Not Hispanic (28)	54	0.58
Hispanic (3)	10	0.11
Alaska Athabascan *(Ala. Nat.)* (2)	2	0.02
Aleut *(Alaska Native)* (1)	1	0.01
Apache (0)	3	0.03
Blackfeet (3)	3	0.03
Cherokee (4)	10	0.11
Chippewa (0)	4	0.04
Choctaw (0)	1	0.01
Delaware (0)	1	0.01
Lumbee (2)	2	0.02
Navajo (5)	5	0.05
Osage (1)	1	0.01
Asian (199)	262	2.83
Not Hispanic (199)	262	2.83
Chinese, ex. Taiwanese (48)	53	0.57
Filipino (23)	44	0.47
Indian (22)	29	0.31
Japanese (39)	52	0.56
Korean (18)	31	0.33
Pakistani (8)	10	0.11
Thai (3)	4	0.04
Vietnamese (30)	32	0.35
Hawaii Native/Pacific Islander (3)	11	0.12
Not Hispanic (2)	10	0.11
Hispanic (1)	1	0.01
Guamanian/Chamorro (1)	1	0.01
Native Hawaiian (2)	10	0.11
White (5,825)	5,964	64.34
Not Hispanic (5,652)	5,776	62.32
Hispanic (173)	188	2.03

SECTION TWO

*Notes: † The Census 2010 population figure is used to calculate the percentages in the Hispanic Origin and Race categories. Ancestry percentages are based on the 2006-2010 American Community Survey population (not shown); ‡ Numbers in parentheses indicate the number of people reporting a single ancestry; * Numbers in parentheses indicate the number of persons reporting this race alone, not in combination with any other race; Please refer to the Explanation of Data for more information.*

NORTH DAKOTA

Place Type: State
Population: 672,591†

Ancestry‡	Population	%
African, Sub-Saharan (2,080)	2,284	0.35
African (1,262)	1,348	0.20
Ethiopian (57)	57	0.01
Ghanaian (19)	19	<0.01
Kenyan (29)	42	0.01
Liberian (107)	107	0.02
Nigerian (116)	119	0.02
Somalian (247)	256	0.04
South African (42)	51	0.01
Sudanese (43)	43	0.01
Ugandan (5)	68	0.01
Other Sub-Saharan African (153)	174	0.03
Albanian (144)	166	0.03
Alsatian (0)	15	<0.01
American (16,254)	16,254	2.46
Arab (637)	1,534	0.23
Arab (64)	100	0.02
Egyptian (58)	75	0.01
Iraqi (91)	132	0.02
Jordanian (13)	13	<0.01
Lebanese (258)	803	0.12
Syrian (98)	336	0.05
Other Arab (55)	75	0.01
Armenian (110)	460	0.07
Assyrian/Chaldean/Syriac (0)	12	<0.01
Australian (61)	105	0.02
Austrian (185)	1,222	0.19
Basque (13)	47	0.01
Belgian (195)	1,047	0.16
Brazilian (46)	93	0.01
British (674)	1,229	0.19
Bulgarian (136)	340	0.05
Cajun (0)	29	<0.01
Canadian (634)	1,242	0.19
Carpatho Rusyn (3)	3	<0.01
Celtic (19)	39	0.01
Croatian (129)	246	0.04
Czech (3,647)	12,732	1.93
Czechoslovakian (752)	1,354	0.21
Danish (1,763)	7,925	1.20
Dutch (1,753)	9,198	1.39
Eastern European (56)	67	0.01
English (5,814)	31,409	4.76
Estonian (33)	64	0.01
European (2,625)	2,946	0.45
Finnish (1,202)	3,921	0.59
French, ex. Basque (5,391)	27,396	4.15
French Canadian (8,178)	12,068	1.83
German (128,147)	309,500	46.90
German Russian (873)	986	0.15
Greek (142)	636	0.10
Guyanese (7)	7	<0.01
Hungarian (456)	2,728	0.41
Icelander (1,061)	2,840	0.43
Iranian (39)	41	0.01
Irish (8,989)	53,397	8.09
Italian (1,648)	7,159	1.08
Latvian (30)	102	0.02
Lithuanian (113)	258	0.04
Luxemburger (46)	312	0.05
Macedonian (4)	4	<0.01
New Zealander (0)	28	<0.01
Northern European (393)	417	0.06
Norwegian (77,815)	198,244	30.04
Pennsylvania German (108)	263	0.04
Polish (4,136)	17,488	2.65
Portuguese (132)	732	0.11
Romanian (183)	490	0.07
Russian (1,378)	25,211	3.82
Scandinavian (5,745)	8,787	1.33
Scotch-Irish (2,240)	7,878	1.19
Scottish (1,657)	8,803	1.33
Serbian (175)	329	0.05
Slavic (71)	260	0.04
Slovak (99)	286	0.04
Slovene (2)	55	0.01
Swedish (4,988)	31,513	4.78
Swiss (360)	2,149	0.33
Turkish (49)	118	0.02
Ukrainian (1,403)	3,813	0.58
Welsh (288)	1,876	0.28
West Indian, ex. Hispanic (116)	369	0.06
Bahamian (5)	5	<0.01
Barbadian (3)	3	<0.01
British West Indian (0)	5	<0.01
Dutch West Indian (0)	10	<0.01
Haitian (3)	55	0.01
Jamaican (49)	95	0.01
Trinidadian/Tobagonian (0)	71	0.01
U.S. Virgin Islander (0)	12	<0.01
West Indian (56)	113	0.02
Yugoslavian (761)	883	0.13

Hispanic Origin	Population	%
Hispanic or Latino (of any race)	13,467	2.00
Central American, ex. Mexican	452	0.07
Costa Rican	35	0.01
Guatemalan	134	0.02
Honduran	50	0.01
Nicaraguan	59	0.01
Panamanian	100	0.01
Salvadoran	73	0.01
Other Central American	1	<0.01
Cuban	260	0.04
Dominican Republic	90	0.01
Mexican	9,223	1.37
Puerto Rican	987	0.15
South American	539	0.08
Argentinean	41	0.01
Bolivian	17	<0.01
Chilean	47	0.01
Colombian	244	0.04
Ecuadorian	55	0.01
Paraguayan	5	<0.01
Peruvian	78	0.01
Uruguayan	4	<0.01
Venezuelan	43	0.01
Other South American	5	<0.01
Other Hispanic or Latino	1,916	0.28

Race*	Population	%
African-American/Black (7,960)	11,086	1.65
Not Hispanic (7,720)	10,542	1.57
Hispanic (240)	544	0.08
American Indian/Alaska Native (36,591)	42,996	6.39
Not Hispanic (35,562)	41,470	6.17
Hispanic (1,029)	1,526	0.23
Alaska Athabascan *(Ala. Nat.)* (10)	18	<0.01
Aleut *(Alaska Native)* (5)	9	<0.01
Apache (28)	67	0.01
Arapaho (11)	18	<0.01
Blackfeet (34)	84	0.01
Canadian/French Am. Ind. (51)	74	0.01
Central American Ind. (3)	5	<0.01
Cherokee (103)	361	0.05
Cheyenne (74)	98	0.01
Chickasaw (9)	18	<0.01
Chippewa (14,977)	16,994	2.53
Choctaw (34)	89	0.01
Colville (1)	3	<0.01
Comanche (8)	14	<0.01
Cree (17)	38	0.01
Creek (7)	20	<0.01
Crow (78)	96	0.01
Delaware (3)	3	<0.01
Hopi (6)	12	<0.01
Houma (1)	1	<0.01
Inupiat *(Alaska Native)* (22)	35	0.01
Iroquois (23)	36	0.01
Kiowa (3)	3	<0.01
Lumbee (10)	18	<0.01
Menominee (3)	16	<0.01
Mexican American Ind. (33)	56	0.01
Navajo (98)	144	0.02
Osage (2)	2	<0.01
Ottawa (5)	9	<0.01
Paiute (7)	9	<0.01
Pima (8)	10	<0.01
Potawatomi (17)	26	<0.01
Pueblo (22)	29	<0.01
Puget Sound Salish (3)	4	<0.01
Seminole (4)	19	<0.01
Shoshone (34)	38	0.01
Sioux (10,149)	11,210	1.67
South American Ind. (3)	6	<0.01
Spanish American Ind. (3)	3	<0.01
Tlingit-Haida *(Alaska Native)* (12)	16	<0.01
Tohono O'Odham (1)	1	<0.01
Tsimshian *(Alaska Native)* (3)	3	<0.01
Ute (21)	21	<0.01
Yakama (4)	4	<0.01
Yaqui (7)	13	<0.01
Yuman (8)	9	<0.01
Yup'ik *(Alaska Native)* (4)	8	<0.01
Asian (6,909)	9,193	1.37
Not Hispanic (6,839)	8,987	1.34
Hispanic (70)	206	0.03
Bangladeshi (62)	67	0.01
Bhutanese (264)	354	0.05
Burmese (28)	28	<0.01
Cambodian (52)	79	0.01
Chinese, ex. Taiwanese (1,455)	1,691	0.25
Filipino (924)	1,704	0.25
Hmong (26)	33	<0.01
Indian (1,543)	1,740	0.26
Indonesian (20)	34	0.01
Japanese (276)	628	0.09
Korean (609)	933	0.14
Laotian (31)	67	0.01
Malaysian (15)	22	<0.01
Nepalese (222)	294	0.04
Pakistani (87)	97	0.01
Sri Lankan (120)	131	0.02
Taiwanese (57)	74	0.01
Thai (135)	219	0.03
Vietnamese (640)	791	0.12
Hawaii Native/Pacific Islander (320)	782	0.12
Not Hispanic (290)	696	0.10
Hispanic (30)	86	0.01
Fijian (6)	10	<0.01
Guamanian/Chamorro (65)	126	0.02
Marshallese (43)	53	0.01
Native Hawaiian (88)	282	0.04
Samoan (49)	117	0.02
Tongan (8)	15	<0.01
White (605,449)	616,350	91.64
Not Hispanic (598,007)	607,632	90.34
Hispanic (7,442)	8,718	1.30

*Notes: † The Census 2010 population figure is used to calculate the percentages in the Hispanic Origin and Race categories. Ancestry percentages are based on the 2006-2010 American Community Survey population (not shown); ‡ Numbers in parentheses indicate the number of people reporting a single ancestry; * Numbers in parentheses indicate the number of persons reporting this race alone, not in combination with any other race; Please refer to the Explanation of Data for more information.*

Bismarck

Place Type: City
County: Burleigh
Population: 61,272†

Ancestry‡	Population	%
African, Sub-Saharan (122)	179	0.30
African (86)	143	0.24
Ethiopian (36)	36	0.06
Alsatian (0)	15	0.03
American (1,508)	1,508	2.51
Arab (14)	113	0.19
Arab (0)	9	0.02
Egyptian (0)	14	0.02
Lebanese (14)	82	0.14
Syrian (0)	8	0.01
Austrian (26)	135	0.23
Belgian (30)	30	0.05
British (31)	65	0.11
Bulgarian (55)	138	0.23
Canadian (30)	81	0.14
Croatian (0)	8	0.01
Czech (207)	816	1.36
Czechoslovakian (14)	56	0.09
Danish (225)	605	1.01
Dutch (258)	896	1.49
English (480)	2,174	3.62
European (225)	255	0.43
Finnish (86)	433	0.72
French, ex. Basque (228)	1,578	2.63
French Canadian (73)	295	0.49
German (17,990)	36,206	60.36
German Russian (156)	178	0.30
Greek (13)	98	0.16
Hungarian (81)	407	0.68
Icelander (21)	144	0.24
Irish (614)	3,857	6.43
Italian (181)	582	0.97
Luxemburger (6)	34	0.06
Northern European (12)	12	0.02
Norwegian (4,251)	12,463	20.78
Pennsylvania German (0)	33	0.06
Polish (288)	1,130	1.88
Romanian (0)	136	0.23
Russian (103)	4,970	8.28
Scandinavian (381)	902	1.50
Scotch-Irish (161)	602	1.00
Scottish (94)	509	0.85
Serbian (64)	72	0.12
Slovak (0)	29	0.05
Swedish (368)	2,264	3.77
Swiss (28)	72	0.12
Turkish (0)	13	0.02
Ukrainian (173)	524	0.87
Welsh (16)	154	0.26
West Indian, ex. Hispanic (30)	48	0.08
Jamaican (0)	18	0.03
West Indian (30)	30	0.05

Hispanic Origin	Population	%
Hispanic or Latino (of any race)	812	1.33
Central American, ex. Mexican	59	0.10
Costa Rican	6	0.01
Guatemalan	24	0.04
Honduran	7	0.01
Nicaraguan	3	<0.01
Panamanian	12	0.02
Salvadoran	7	0.01
Cuban	27	0.04
Dominican Republic	1	<0.01
Mexican	489	0.80
Puerto Rican	54	0.09
South American	51	0.08
Argentinean	9	0.01
Chilean	3	<0.01
Colombian	27	0.04
Ecuadorian	3	<0.01
Peruvian	6	0.01
Venezuelan	1	<0.01
Other South American	2	<0.01
Other Hispanic or Latino	131	0.21

Race*	Population	%
African-American/Black (400)	660	1.08
Not Hispanic (393)	629	1.03
Hispanic (7)	31	0.05
American Indian/Alaska Native (2,773)	3,329	5.43
Not Hispanic (2,678)	3,195	5.21
Hispanic (95)	134	0.22
Alaska Athabascan *(Ala. Nat.)* (1)	1	<0.01
Apache (5)	11	0.02
Arapaho (2)	2	<0.01
Blackfeet (4)	9	0.01
Canadian/French Am. Ind. (2)	3	<0.01
Central American Ind. (2)	4	0.01
Cherokee (4)	24	0.04
Cheyenne (12)	18	0.03
Chippewa (401)	523	0.85
Choctaw (6)	10	0.02
Cree (3)	3	<0.01
Crow (17)	18	0.03
Delaware (1)	1	<0.01
Hopi (0)	4	0.01
Inupiat *(Alaska Native)* (1)	4	0.01
Kiowa (2)	2	<0.01
Mexican American Ind. (4)	4	0.01
Navajo (17)	24	0.04
Paiute (0)	1	<0.01
Pima (3)	3	<0.01
Pueblo (2)	2	<0.01
Shoshone (11)	11	0.02
Sioux (1,108)	1,273	2.08
Spanish American Ind. (1)	1	<0.01
Tlingit-Haida *(Alaska Native)* (0)	1	<0.01
Ute (5)	5	0.01
Yakama (1)	1	<0.01
Yuman (1)	1	<0.01
Yup'ik *(Alaska Native)* (0)	1	<0.01
Asian (343)	484	0.79
Not Hispanic (340)	475	0.78
Hispanic (3)	9	0.01
Bangladeshi (0)	1	<0.01
Chinese, ex. Taiwanese (94)	103	0.17
Filipino (52)	107	0.17
Indian (108)	125	0.20
Indonesian (0)	2	<0.01
Japanese (14)	34	0.06
Korean (27)	38	0.06
Malaysian (1)	6	0.01
Nepalese (1)	1	<0.01
Pakistani (2)	2	<0.01
Sri Lankan (3)	3	<0.01
Thai (12)	15	0.02
Vietnamese (20)	28	0.05
Hawaii Native/Pacific Islander (17)	48	0.08
Not Hispanic (16)	46	0.08
Hispanic (1)	2	<0.01
Guamanian/Chamorro (0)	2	<0.01
Marshallese (5)	10	0.02
Native Hawaiian (4)	12	0.02
Samoan (0)	3	<0.01
White (56,616)	57,472	93.80
Not Hispanic (56,152)	56,940	92.93
Hispanic (464)	532	0.87

Dickinson

Place Type: City
County: Stark
Population: 17,787†

Ancestry‡	Population	%
American (599)	599	3.49
Austrian (0)	58	0.34
Belgian (0)	5	0.03
British (6)	16	0.09
Czech (351)	1,125	6.55
Czechoslovakian (102)	128	0.75
Danish (23)	100	0.58
Dutch (15)	166	0.97
Eastern European (31)	31	0.18
English (264)	962	5.60
Estonian (0)	8	0.05
European (26)	26	0.15
Finnish (0)	11	0.06
French, ex. Basque (94)	862	5.02
French Canadian (34)	88	0.51
German (4,815)	10,005	58.28
German Russian (20)	20	0.12
Hungarian (49)	503	2.93
Irish (175)	1,329	7.74
Italian (11)	51	0.30
Northern European (0)	11	0.06
Norwegian (740)	2,516	14.66
Pennsylvania German (0)	8	0.05
Polish (84)	412	2.40
Russian (38)	1,303	7.59
Scandinavian (104)	158	0.92
Scotch-Irish (108)	509	2.96
Scottish (72)	167	0.97
Swedish (68)	293	1.71
Swiss (9)	34	0.20
Ukrainian (110)	357	2.08
Welsh (8)	23	0.13
West Indian, ex. Hispanic (19)	31	0.18
Bahamian (5)	5	0.03
Jamaican (14)	14	0.08
U.S. Virgin Islander (0)	12	0.07

Hispanic Origin	Population	%
Hispanic or Latino (of any race)	382	2.15
Central American, ex. Mexican	20	0.11
Costa Rican	3	0.02
Guatemalan	2	0.01
Panamanian	10	0.06
Salvadoran	5	0.03
Cuban	4	0.02
Dominican Republic	1	0.01
Mexican	270	1.52
Puerto Rican	20	0.11
South American	22	0.12
Colombian	15	0.08
Peruvian	4	0.02
Venezuelan	2	0.01
Other South American	1	0.01
Other Hispanic or Latino	45	0.25

Race*	Population	%
African-American/Black (186)	268	1.51
Not Hispanic (175)	245	1.38
Hispanic (11)	23	0.13
American Indian/Alaska Native (217)	337	1.89
Not Hispanic (208)	325	1.83
Hispanic (9)	12	0.07
Apache (1)	4	0.02
Arapaho (1)	2	0.01
Blackfeet (1)	4	0.02
Canadian/French Am. Ind. (2)	2	0.01
Cherokee (2)	11	0.06
Cheyenne (1)	2	0.01
Chippewa (30)	46	0.26
Choctaw (0)	2	0.01
Colville (1)	3	0.02
Crow (4)	4	0.02
Inupiat *(Alaska Native)* (1)	1	0.01
Iroquois (0)	1	0.01
Mexican American Ind. (0)	1	0.01
Navajo (1)	3	0.02
Potawatomi (0)	1	0.01
Pueblo (1)	1	0.01
Seminole (0)	1	0.01
Shoshone (2)	2	0.01
Sioux (42)	58	0.33
Yaqui (1)	1	0.01
Asian (262)	292	1.64
Not Hispanic (258)	286	1.61
Hispanic (4)	6	0.03
Cambodian (1)	4	0.02
Chinese, ex. Taiwanese (128)	131	0.74

*Notes: † The Census 2010 population figure is used to calculate the percentages in the Hispanic Origin and Race categories. Ancestry percentages are based on the 2006-2010 American Community Survey population (not shown); ‡ Numbers in parentheses indicate the number of people reporting a single ancestry; * Numbers in parentheses indicate the number of persons reporting this race alone, not in combination with any other race; Please refer to the Explanation of Data for more information.*

Filipino (18)	23	0.13
Indian (28)	29	0.16
Indonesian (7)	7	0.04
Japanese (6)	8	0.04
Korean (10)	18	0.10
Laotian (1)	5	0.03
Nepalese (28)	30	0.17
Thai (2)	5	0.03
Vietnamese (7)	9	0.05
Hawaii Native/Pacific Islander (9)	23	0.13
Not Hispanic (7)	19	0.11
Hispanic (2)	4	0.02
Fijian (1)	1	0.01
Guamanian/Chamorro (1)	2	0.01
Native Hawaiian (2)	5	0.03
Samoan (1)	1	0.01
White (16,748)	17,003	95.59
Not Hispanic (16,542)	16,750	94.17
Hispanic (206)	253	1.42

Fargo

Place Type: City
County: Cass
Population: 105,549†

Ancestry‡	Population	%
African, Sub-Saharan (932)	965	0.94
African (543)	543	0.53
Ethiopian (21)	21	0.02
Ghanaian (9)	9	0.01
Kenyan (13)	26	0.03
Liberian (82)	82	0.08
Nigerian (92)	92	0.09
Somalian (63)	72	0.07
Sudanese (29)	29	0.03
Ugandan (5)	5	<0.01
Other Sub-Saharan African (75)	86	0.08
Albanian (141)	153	0.15
American (1,460)	1,460	1.42
Arab (274)	537	0.52
Arab (58)	58	0.06
Egyptian (58)	58	0.06
Iraqi (91)	91	0.09
Lebanese (28)	193	0.19
Syrian (39)	137	0.13
Armenian (28)	314	0.31
Assyrian/Chaldean/Syriac (0)	12	0.01
Australian (19)	35	0.03
Austrian (26)	274	0.27
Basque (5)	21	0.02
Belgian (60)	214	0.21
Brazilian (0)	12	0.01
British (338)	495	0.48
Bulgarian (48)	56	0.05
Cajun (0)	19	0.02
Canadian (114)	327	0.32
Celtic (13)	13	0.01
Croatian (22)	85	0.08
Czech (414)	1,537	1.50
Czechoslovakian (52)	115	0.11
Danish (245)	1,031	1.01
Dutch (189)	1,255	1.22
English (873)	5,165	5.04
European (576)	701	0.68
Finnish (224)	865	0.84
French, ex. Basque (588)	5,086	4.96
French Canadian (349)	1,108	1.08
German (14,504)	44,410	43.32
German Russian (68)	80	0.08
Greek (44)	93	0.09
Hungarian (21)	135	0.13
Icelander (130)	330	0.32
Irish (1,770)	9,591	9.35
Italian (239)	1,455	1.42
Latvian (13)	46	0.04
Lithuanian (0)	14	0.01
Luxemburger (0)	60	0.06
New Zealander (0)	6	0.01
Northern European (171)	171	0.17
Norwegian (12,992)	36,248	35.35
Pennsylvania German (11)	68	0.07
Polish (618)	2,897	2.83
Portuguese (27)	371	0.36
Romanian (104)	122	0.12
Russian (134)	2,475	2.41
Scandinavian (1,206)	1,826	1.78
Scotch-Irish (388)	1,363	1.33
Scottish (272)	1,441	1.41
Serbian (10)	29	0.03
Slavic (56)	187	0.18
Slovak (14)	58	0.06
Slovene (0)	25	0.02
Swedish (989)	6,328	6.17
Swiss (49)	196	0.19
Turkish (13)	26	0.03
Ukrainian (58)	340	0.33
Welsh (39)	242	0.24
West Indian, ex. Hispanic (0)	70	0.07
Haitian (0)	35	0.03
Jamaican (0)	22	0.02
West Indian (0)	13	0.01
Yugoslavian (523)	535	0.52

Hispanic Origin	Population	%
Hispanic or Latino (of any race)	2,308	2.19
Central American, ex. Mexican	92	0.09
Costa Rican	8	0.01
Guatemalan	32	0.03
Honduran	12	0.01
Nicaraguan	7	0.01
Panamanian	19	0.02
Salvadoran	13	0.01
Other Central American	1	<0.01
Cuban	52	0.05
Dominican Republic	22	0.02
Mexican	1,546	1.46
Puerto Rican	131	0.12
South American	147	0.14
Argentinean	8	0.01
Bolivian	1	<0.01
Chilean	23	0.02
Colombian	81	0.08
Ecuadorian	14	0.01
Peruvian	10	0.01
Uruguayan	3	<0.01
Venezuelan	7	0.01
Other Hispanic or Latino	318	0.30

Race*	Population	%
African-American/Black (2,852)	3,600	3.41
Not Hispanic (2,809)	3,487	3.30
Hispanic (43)	113	0.11
American Indian/Alaska Native (1,452)	2,315	2.19
Not Hispanic (1,326)	2,115	2.00
Hispanic (126)	200	0.19
Alaska Athabascan *(Ala. Nat.)* (1)	4	<0.01
Aleut *(Alaska Native)* (1)	1	<0.01
Apache (5)	7	0.01
Blackfeet (0)	12	0.01
Canadian/French Am. Ind. (5)	11	0.01
Cherokee (11)	43	0.04
Cheyenne (10)	16	0.02
Chickasaw (3)	3	<0.01
Chippewa (545)	810	0.77
Choctaw (4)	10	0.01
Cree (1)	4	<0.01
Crow (0)	1	<0.01
Hopi (2)	3	<0.01
Inupiat *(Alaska Native)* (2)	3	<0.01
Iroquois (5)	7	0.01
Menominee (0)	9	0.01
Mexican American Ind. (6)	9	0.01
Navajo (5)	10	0.01
Paiute (2)	2	<0.01
Pima (1)	1	<0.01
Potawatomi (1)	1	<0.01
Pueblo (4)	5	<0.01
Seminole (0)	1	<0.01
Shoshone (1)	2	<0.01
Sioux (236)	361	0.34
South American Ind. (0)	1	<0.01
Spanish American Ind. (1)	1	<0.01
Tlingit-Haida *(Alaska Native)* (3)	3	<0.01
Yuman (0)	1	<0.01
Asian (3,137)	3,713	3.52
Not Hispanic (3,132)	3,695	3.50
Hispanic (5)	18	0.02
Bangladeshi (46)	48	0.05
Bhutanese (128)	204	0.19
Burmese (19)	19	0.02
Cambodian (35)	54	0.05
Chinese, ex. Taiwanese (563)	633	0.60
Filipino (120)	261	0.25
Hmong (12)	13	0.01
Indian (915)	998	0.95
Indonesian (5)	6	0.01
Japanese (62)	132	0.13
Korean (260)	328	0.31
Laotian (7)	21	0.02
Malaysian (8)	8	0.01
Nepalese (154)	221	0.21
Pakistani (62)	66	0.06
Sri Lankan (89)	100	0.09
Taiwanese (33)	39	0.04
Thai (43)	61	0.06
Vietnamese (407)	448	0.42
Hawaii Native/Pacific Islander (44)	123	0.12
Not Hispanic (41)	116	0.11
Hispanic (3)	7	0.01
Fijian (3)	4	<0.01
Guamanian/Chamorro (7)	15	0.01
Marshallese (1)	1	<0.01
Native Hawaiian (17)	28	0.03
Samoan (7)	15	0.01
White (95,205)	97,175	92.07
Not Hispanic (93,889)	95,614	90.59
Hispanic (1,316)	1,561	1.48

Grand Forks

Place Type: City
County: Grand Forks
Population: 52,838†

Ancestry‡	Population	%
African, Sub-Saharan (459)	468	0.89
African (192)	192	0.37
Liberian (25)	25	0.05
Nigerian (20)	20	0.04
Somalian (144)	144	0.28
South African (0)	9	0.02
Other Sub-Saharan African (78)	78	0.15
Albanian (0)	10	0.02
American (1,362)	1,362	2.60
Arab (53)	72	0.14
Lebanese (9)	28	0.05
Other Arab (44)	44	0.08
Armenian (0)	27	0.05
Austrian (0)	35	0.07
Belgian (12)	138	0.26
Brazilian (0)	12	0.02
British (26)	65	0.12
Bulgarian (11)	11	0.02
Canadian (52)	100	0.19
Croatian (65)	94	0.18
Czech (329)	1,119	2.14
Czechoslovakian (110)	240	0.46
Danish (52)	529	1.01
Dutch (65)	412	0.79
English (495)	2,779	5.31
Estonian (12)	12	0.02
European (447)	464	0.89
Finnish (124)	263	0.50
French, ex. Basque (489)	2,715	5.19
French Canadian (271)	906	1.73
German (6,675)	17,981	34.38
German Russian (15)	15	0.03
Greek (0)	66	0.13
Hungarian (52)	109	0.21

*Notes: † The Census 2010 population figure is used to calculate the percentages in the Hispanic Origin and Race categories. Ancestry percentages are based on the 2006-2010 American Community Survey population (not shown); ‡ Numbers in parentheses indicate the number of people reporting a single ancestry; * Numbers in parentheses indicate the number of persons reporting this race alone, not in combination with any other race; Please refer to the Explanation of Data for more information.*

Icelander (209)	626	1.20
Iranian (33)	33	0.06
Irish (831)	4,775	9.13
Italian (261)	891	1.70
Latvian (9)	21	0.04
Lithuanian (23)	53	0.10
Luxemburger (0)	27	0.05
New Zealander (0)	13	0.02
Norwegian (7,881)	17,361	33.20
Pennsylvania German (18)	24	0.05
Polish (761)	3,109	5.95
Portuguese (58)	58	0.11
Romanian (10)	18	0.03
Russian (60)	853	1.63
Scandinavian (388)	449	0.86
Scotch-Irish (196)	691	1.32
Scottish (154)	865	1.65
Serbian (64)	82	0.16
Slavic (0)	10	0.02
Slovak (20)	36	0.07
Swedish (510)	2,332	4.46
Swiss (10)	103	0.20
Turkish (33)	33	0.06
Ukrainian (95)	300	0.57
Welsh (16)	162	0.31
West Indian, ex. Hispanic (0)	67	0.13
Jamaican (0)	6	0.01
Trinidadian/Tobagonian (0)	61	0.12
Yugoslavian (14)	24	0.05

Hispanic Origin	Population	%
Hispanic or Latino (of any race)	1,473	2.79
Central American, ex. Mexican	30	0.06
Costa Rican	2	<0.01
Guatemalan	6	0.01
Honduran	7	0.01
Panamanian	8	0.02
Salvadoran	7	0.01
Cuban	34	0.06
Dominican Republic	6	0.01
Mexican	995	1.88
Puerto Rican	99	0.19
South American	51	0.10
Argentinean	9	0.02
Bolivian	4	0.01
Chilean	6	0.01
Colombian	11	0.02
Ecuadorian	4	0.01
Paraguayan	2	<0.01
Peruvian	7	0.01
Uruguayan	1	<0.01
Venezuelan	7	0.01
Other Hispanic or Latino	258	0.49

Race*	Population	%
African-American/Black (1,061)	1,433	2.71
Not Hispanic (1,037)	1,372	2.60
Hispanic (24)	61	0.12
American Indian/Alaska Native (1,515)	2,136	4.04
Not Hispanic (1,458)	2,010	3.80
Hispanic (57)	126	0.24
Aleut *(Alaska Native)* (1)	1	<0.01
Apache (3)	10	0.02
Blackfeet (0)	7	0.01
Canadian/French Am. Ind. (7)	9	0.02
Cherokee (16)	32	0.06
Cheyenne (8)	8	0.02
Chickasaw (2)	4	0.01
Chippewa (751)	1,008	1.91
Choctaw (6)	9	0.02
Comanche (1)	2	<0.01
Cree (4)	4	0.01
Creek (1)	2	<0.01
Crow (1)	1	<0.01
Hopi (2)	2	<0.01
Inupiat *(Alaska Native)* (1)	1	<0.01
Iroquois (1)	4	0.01
Lumbee (4)	5	0.01
Mexican American Ind. (2)	7	0.01
Navajo (7)	11	0.02
Paiute (1)	2	<0.01
Pima (2)	2	<0.01
Potawatomi (1)	1	<0.01
Pueblo (0)	1	<0.01
Seminole (0)	2	<0.01
Shoshone (1)	1	<0.01
Sioux (201)	262	0.50
Tlingit-Haida *(Alaska Native)* (1)	2	<0.01
Ute (1)	1	<0.01
Yup'ik *(Alaska Native)* (0)	2	<0.01
Asian (1,178)	1,506	2.85
Not Hispanic (1,169)	1,483	2.81
Hispanic (9)	23	0.04
Bangladeshi (10)	10	0.02
Bhutanese (101)	115	0.22
Cambodian (3)	3	0.01
Chinese, ex. Taiwanese (382)	437	0.83
Filipino (123)	207	0.39
Hmong (10)	13	0.02
Indian (211)	231	0.44
Indonesian (3)	4	0.01
Japanese (85)	141	0.27
Korean (112)	152	0.29
Laotian (6)	8	0.02
Malaysian (2)	2	<0.01
Nepalese (19)	20	0.04
Pakistani (4)	8	0.02
Sri Lankan (16)	16	0.03
Taiwanese (9)	12	0.02
Thai (15)	26	0.05
Vietnamese (33)	47	0.09
Hawaii Native/Pacific Islander (20)	73	0.14
Not Hispanic (19)	68	0.13
Hispanic (1)	5	0.01
Fijian (0)	1	<0.01
Guamanian/Chamorro (0)	10	0.02
Marshallese (0)	2	<0.01
Native Hawaiian (7)	29	0.05
Samoan (7)	15	0.03
Tongan (2)	2	<0.01
White (47,382)	48,595	91.97
Not Hispanic (46,525)	47,592	90.07
Hispanic (857)	1,003	1.90

Jamestown

Place Type: City
County: Stutsman
Population: 15,427†

Ancestry‡	Population	%
American (373)	373	2.44
Austrian (0)	7	0.05
Belgian (0)	64	0.42
Brazilian (0)	10	0.07
British (17)	17	0.11
Canadian (14)	14	0.09
Czech (37)	133	0.87
Czechoslovakian (0)	9	0.06
Danish (53)	199	1.30
Dutch (54)	299	1.96
English (116)	691	4.52
European (256)	318	2.08
Finnish (8)	75	0.49
French, ex. Basque (78)	662	4.33
French Canadian (11)	57	0.37
German (3,356)	8,379	54.79
German Russian (6)	6	0.04
Greek (0)	19	0.12
Hungarian (0)	27	0.18
Icelander (0)	15	0.10
Irish (213)	1,133	7.41
Italian (19)	209	1.37
Norwegian (1,087)	4,306	28.16
Polish (160)	640	4.19
Portuguese (0)	9	0.06
Romanian (5)	13	0.09
Russian (23)	757	4.95
Scandinavian (43)	107	0.70
Scotch-Irish (13)	122	0.80
Scottish (40)	208	1.36
Swedish (100)	772	5.05
Swiss (16)	56	0.37
Ukrainian (19)	19	0.12
Welsh (0)	50	0.33

Hispanic Origin	Population	%
Hispanic or Latino (of any race)	323	2.09
Central American, ex. Mexican	7	0.05
Guatemalan	1	0.01
Honduran	1	0.01
Panamanian	5	0.03
Dominican Republic	1	0.01
Mexican	211	1.37
Puerto Rican	21	0.14
South American	16	0.10
Chilean	3	0.02
Colombian	8	0.05
Ecuadorian	1	0.01
Peruvian	4	0.03
Other Hispanic or Latino	67	0.43

Race*	Population	%
African-American/Black (129)	184	1.19
Not Hispanic (120)	161	1.04
Hispanic (9)	23	0.15
American Indian/Alaska Native (274)	363	2.35
Not Hispanic (271)	352	2.28
Hispanic (3)	11	0.07
Alaska Athabascan *(Ala. Nat.)* (1)	1	0.01
Apache (1)	3	0.02
Canadian/French Am. Ind. (0)	1	0.01
Cherokee (2)	6	0.04
Chickasaw (0)	1	0.01
Chippewa (71)	99	0.64
Choctaw (1)	1	0.01
Cree (0)	1	0.01
Creek (0)	1	0.01
Iroquois (0)	1	0.01
Lumbee (0)	1	0.01
Navajo (1)	2	0.01
Potawatomi (2)	2	0.01
Sioux (80)	90	0.58
Tlingit-Haida *(Alaska Native)* (2)	3	0.02
Ute (2)	2	0.01
Yup'ik *(Alaska Native)* (0)	1	0.01
Asian (91)	130	0.84
Not Hispanic (90)	123	0.80
Hispanic (1)	7	0.05
Burmese (4)	4	0.03
Cambodian (0)	2	0.01
Chinese, ex. Taiwanese (26)	30	0.19
Filipino (14)	31	0.20
Indian (17)	17	0.11
Indonesian (0)	1	0.01
Japanese (4)	8	0.05
Korean (12)	17	0.11
Laotian (0)	1	0.01
Nepalese (1)	1	0.01
Taiwanese (0)	1	0.01
Thai (2)	2	0.01
Vietnamese (8)	10	0.06
Hawaii Native/Pacific Islander (9)	33	0.21
Not Hispanic (9)	23	0.15
Hispanic (0)	10	0.06
Guamanian/Chamorro (1)	2	0.01
Marshallese (1)	1	0.01
Native Hawaiian (2)	8	0.05
Samoan (1)	4	0.03
White (14,599)	14,799	95.93
Not Hispanic (14,448)	14,604	94.67
Hispanic (151)	195	1.26

Mandan

Place Type: City
County: Morton
Population: 18,331†

*Notes: † The Census 2010 population figure is used to calculate the percentages in the Hispanic Origin and Race categories. Ancestry percentages are based on the 2006-2010 American Community Survey population (not shown); ‡ Numbers in parentheses indicate the number of people reporting a single ancestry; * Numbers in parentheses indicate the number of persons reporting this race alone, not in combination with any other race; Please refer to the Explanation of Data for more information.*

Ancestry‡	Population	%
American (559)	559	3.14
Arab (0)	18	0.10
Arab (0)	18	0.10
Australian (0)	11	0.06
Austrian (14)	40	0.22
Belgian (0)	9	0.05
British (8)	59	0.33
Canadian (59)	73	0.41
Czech (99)	474	2.66
Danish (27)	143	0.80
Dutch (112)	446	2.50
English (107)	810	4.55
European (58)	58	0.33
Finnish (0)	67	0.38
French, ex. Basque (0)	461	2.59
French Canadian (14)	139	0.78
German (5,175)	11,268	63.26
German Russian (31)	31	0.17
Hungarian (68)	292	1.64
Icelander (0)	59	0.33
Irish (120)	1,004	5.64
Italian (254)	516	2.90
Latvian (0)	12	0.07
Norwegian (614)	2,814	15.80
Polish (20)	130	0.73
Romanian (0)	25	0.14
Russian (0)	1,802	10.12
Scandinavian (11)	66	0.37
Scotch-Irish (26)	170	0.95
Scottish (97)	178	1.00
Swedish (63)	634	3.56
Swiss (10)	40	0.22
Ukrainian (76)	191	1.07
Welsh (0)	86	0.48
Yugoslavian (46)	46	0.26

Hispanic Origin	Population	%
Hispanic or Latino (of any race)	325	1.77
Central American, ex. Mexican	13	0.07
Guatemalan	6	0.03
Nicaraguan	4	0.02
Salvadoran	3	0.02
Cuban	11	0.06
Mexican	205	1.12
Puerto Rican	27	0.15
South American	13	0.07
Argentinean	2	0.01
Colombian	5	0.03
Ecuadorian	3	0.02
Paraguayan	2	0.01
Peruvian	1	0.01
Other Hispanic or Latino	56	0.31

Race*	Population	%
African-American/Black (112)	193	1.05
Not Hispanic (105)	181	0.99
Hispanic (7)	12	0.07
American Indian/Alaska Native (904)	1,123	6.13
Not Hispanic (878)	1,070	5.84
Hispanic (26)	53	0.29
Apache (1)	1	0.01
Arapaho (3)	3	0.02
Canadian/French Am. Ind. (1)	1	0.01
Cherokee (0)	19	0.10
Cheyenne (4)	6	0.03
Chippewa (197)	239	1.30
Comanche (1)	1	0.01
Cree (1)	2	0.01
Crow (2)	2	0.01
Mexican American Ind. (0)	1	0.01
Navajo (1)	3	0.02
Paiute (1)	1	0.01
Potawatomi (4)	5	0.03
Pueblo (1)	1	0.01
Shoshone (2)	2	0.01
Sioux (369)	416	2.27
Yakama (1)	1	0.01
Yaqui (1)	3	0.02
Yuman (1)	1	0.01
Asian (41)	88	0.48
Not Hispanic (40)	84	0.46
Hispanic (1)	4	0.02
Chinese, ex. Taiwanese (9)	11	0.06
Filipino (15)	31	0.17
Indian (1)	2	0.01
Japanese (2)	10	0.05
Korean (5)	14	0.08
Pakistani (1)	1	0.01
Thai (2)	2	0.01
Vietnamese (3)	11	0.06
Hawaii Native/Pacific Islander (14)	24	0.13
Not Hispanic (14)	24	0.13
Marshallese (4)	5	0.03
Native Hawaiian (1)	6	0.03
Samoan (2)	5	0.03
Tongan (1)	1	0.01
White (16,813)	17,150	93.56
Not Hispanic (16,661)	16,946	92.44
Hispanic (152)	204	1.11

Minot

Place Type: City
County: Ward
Population: 40,888†

Ancestry‡	Population	%
African, Sub-Saharan (122)	132	0.34
African (86)	86	0.22
Somalian (36)	36	0.09
Other Sub-Saharan African (0)	10	0.03
American (718)	718	1.84
Arab (78)	193	0.49
Arab (0)	9	0.02
Lebanese (78)	184	0.47
Armenian (56)	56	0.14
Australian (10)	10	0.03
Basque (8)	15	0.04
Belgian (11)	32	0.08
Brazilian (35)	35	0.09
British (47)	142	0.36
Bulgarian (0)	29	0.07
Canadian (68)	81	0.21
Croatian (5)	5	0.01
Czech (80)	408	1.04
Czechoslovakian (19)	19	0.05
Danish (167)	634	1.62
Dutch (47)	561	1.44
English (450)	2,135	5.47
Estonian (14)	14	0.04
European (66)	70	0.18
Finnish (8)	120	0.31
French, ex. Basque (94)	1,202	3.08
French Canadian (48)	474	1.21
German (5,696)	17,416	44.59
German Russian (13)	13	0.03
Greek (42)	149	0.38
Hungarian (32)	106	0.27
Icelander (19)	50	0.13
Irish (794)	4,569	11.70
Italian (144)	721	1.85
Latvian (0)	13	0.03
Lithuanian (13)	20	0.05
Luxemburger (6)	11	0.03
Norwegian (4,346)	12,251	31.37
Pennsylvania German (9)	9	0.02
Polish (170)	790	2.02
Portuguese (0)	53	0.14
Romanian (0)	15	0.04
Russian (263)	1,223	3.13
Scandinavian (538)	806	2.06
Scotch-Irish (153)	600	1.54
Scottish (117)	725	1.86
Slovak (26)	26	0.07
Swedish (283)	1,985	5.08
Swiss (41)	154	0.39
Turkish (0)	43	0.11
Ukrainian (131)	384	0.98
Welsh (23)	194	0.50
West Indian, ex. Hispanic (23)	43	0.11
West Indian (23)	43	0.11
Yugoslavian (14)	30	0.08

Hispanic Origin	Population	%
Hispanic or Latino (of any race)	1,117	2.73
Central American, ex. Mexican	39	0.10
Costa Rican	3	0.01
Guatemalan	7	0.02
Honduran	5	0.01
Nicaraguan	4	0.01
Panamanian	15	0.04
Salvadoran	5	0.01
Cuban	29	0.07
Dominican Republic	14	0.03
Mexican	708	1.73
Puerto Rican	159	0.39
South American	48	0.12
Argentinean	1	<0.01
Bolivian	3	0.01
Chilean	2	<0.01
Colombian	13	0.03
Ecuadorian	13	0.03
Paraguayan	1	<0.01
Peruvian	13	0.03
Venezuelan	1	<0.01
Other South American	1	<0.01
Other Hispanic or Latino	120	0.29

Race*	Population	%
African-American/Black (933)	1,319	3.23
Not Hispanic (880)	1,229	3.01
Hispanic (53)	90	0.22
American Indian/Alaska Native (1,328)	1,823	4.46
Not Hispanic (1,244)	1,699	4.16
Hispanic (84)	124	0.30
Alaska Athabascan *(Ala. Nat.)* (1)	1	<0.01
Aleut *(Alaska Native)* (0)	2	<0.01
Apache (1)	1	<0.01
Arapaho (1)	4	0.01
Blackfeet (7)	10	0.02
Canadian/French Am. Ind. (11)	15	0.04
Cherokee (5)	22	0.05
Cheyenne (8)	8	0.02
Chickasaw (0)	2	<0.01
Chippewa (536)	698	1.71
Choctaw (2)	10	0.02
Comanche (0)	3	0.01
Cree (1)	4	0.01
Creek (0)	4	0.01
Crow (2)	3	0.01
Hopi (0)	1	<0.01
Inupiat *(Alaska Native)* (3)	4	0.01
Iroquois (1)	1	<0.01
Lumbee (3)	4	0.01
Menominee (0)	1	<0.01
Mexican American Ind. (0)	2	<0.01
Navajo (6)	12	0.03
Potawatomi (1)	1	<0.01
Pueblo (2)	2	<0.01
Puget Sound Salish (1)	1	<0.01
Seminole (1)	2	<0.01
Sioux (118)	151	0.37
South American Ind. (1)	1	<0.01
Tlingit-Haida *(Alaska Native)* (2)	2	<0.01
Yaqui (0)	1	<0.01
Yup'ik *(Alaska Native)* (1)	1	<0.01
Asian (376)	593	1.45
Not Hispanic (358)	557	1.36
Hispanic (18)	36	0.09
Bhutanese (1)	1	<0.01
Burmese (3)	3	0.01
Cambodian (1)	1	<0.01
Chinese, ex. Taiwanese (53)	74	0.18
Filipino (110)	201	0.49
Hmong (3)	5	0.01
Indian (47)	60	0.15
Indonesian (0)	4	0.01
Japanese (19)	53	0.13
Korean (59)	102	0.25

*Notes: † The Census 2010 population figure is used to calculate the percentages in the Hispanic Origin and Race categories. Ancestry percentages are based on the 2006-2010 American Community Survey population (not shown); ‡ Numbers in parentheses indicate the number of people reporting a single ancestry; * Numbers in parentheses indicate the number of persons reporting this race alone, not in combination with any other race; Please refer to the Explanation of Data for more information.*

Laotian (1)	1	<0.01
Malaysian (1)	1	<0.01
Nepalese (10)	12	0.03
Pakistani (5)	7	0.02
Sri Lankan (6)	6	0.01
Taiwanese (5)	6	0.01
Thai (11)	21	0.05
Vietnamese (26)	36	0.09
Hawaii Native/Pacific Islander (42)	79	0.19
Not Hispanic (36)	69	0.17
Hispanic (6)	10	0.02
Guamanian/Chamorro (8)	17	0.04
Marshallese (6)	6	0.01
Native Hawaiian (14)	35	0.09
Samoan (8)	14	0.03
White (36,863)	37,849	92.57
Not Hispanic (36,294)	37,156	90.87
Hispanic (569)	693	1.69

Wahpeton

Place Type: City
County: Richland
Population: 7,766†

Ancestry‡	Population	%
American (172)	172	2.19
Armenian (8)	16	0.20
Austrian (0)	37	0.47
Belgian (8)	56	0.71
British (8)	19	0.24
Canadian (30)	38	0.48
Czech (79)	288	3.67
Czechoslovakian (8)	20	0.25
Danish (37)	148	1.88
Dutch (27)	84	1.07
English (9)	269	3.43
Finnish (25)	129	1.64
French, ex. Basque (9)	284	3.62
French Canadian (0)	9	0.11
German (1,281)	3,569	45.45
Greek (0)	8	0.10
Hungarian (13)	13	0.17
Irish (72)	569	7.25
Italian (0)	51	0.65
Norwegian (1,080)	2,545	32.41
Polish (46)	202	2.57
Romanian (5)	5	0.06
Russian (18)	155	1.97
Scandinavian (205)	216	2.75
Scotch-Irish (9)	61	0.78
Scottish (8)	45	0.57
Serbian (0)	51	0.65
Swedish (5)	357	4.55
Swiss (0)	71	0.90
Ukrainian (0)	7	0.09
Welsh (0)	25	0.32

Hispanic Origin	Population	%
Hispanic or Latino (of any race)	156	2.01
Central American, ex. Mexican	4	0.05
Guatemalan	1	0.01
Honduran	3	0.04
Mexican	123	1.58
Puerto Rican	8	0.10
South American	4	0.05
Colombian	4	0.05
Other Hispanic or Latino	17	0.22

Race*	Population	%
African-American/Black (98)	137	1.76
Not Hispanic (98)	129	1.66
Hispanic (0)	8	0.10
American Indian/Alaska Native (239)	313	4.03
Not Hispanic (217)	281	3.62
Hispanic (22)	32	0.41
Apache (0)	1	0.01
Blackfeet (1)	1	0.01
Cherokee (1)	4	0.05
Chickasaw (1)	2	0.03
Chippewa (87)	99	1.27
Choctaw (0)	3	0.04
Crow (2)	2	0.03
Navajo (6)	7	0.09
Ottawa (0)	3	0.04
Seminole (1)	5	0.06
Sioux (49)	70	0.90
Asian (61)	90	1.16
Not Hispanic (61)	88	1.13
Hispanic (0)	2	0.03
Chinese, ex. Taiwanese (16)	19	0.24
Filipino (28)	45	0.58
Indian (2)	2	0.03
Japanese (1)	1	0.01
Korean (2)	3	0.04
Taiwanese (0)	3	0.04
Vietnamese (12)	20	0.26
Hawaii Native/Pacific Islander (7)	8	0.10
Not Hispanic (5)	6	0.08
Hispanic (2)	2	0.03
Guamanian/Chamorro (2)	2	0.03
Native Hawaiian (1)	1	0.01
Samoan (4)	4	0.05
White (7,195)	7,330	94.39
Not Hispanic (7,105)	7,219	92.96
Hispanic (90)	111	1.43

West Fargo

Place Type: City
County: Cass
Population: 25,830†

Ancestry‡	Population	%
African, Sub-Saharan (365)	449	1.88
African (351)	372	1.56
Sudanese (14)	14	0.06
Ugandan (0)	63	0.26
American (350)	350	1.47
Arab (11)	89	0.37
Iraqi (0)	41	0.17
Lebanese (0)	17	0.07
Other Arab (11)	31	0.13
Austrian (11)	107	0.45
Belgian (9)	22	0.09
British (13)	23	0.10
Bulgarian (0)	38	0.16
Canadian (14)	24	0.10
Czech (82)	424	1.78
Czechoslovakian (13)	22	0.09
Danish (43)	177	0.74
Dutch (21)	258	1.08
English (144)	1,048	4.39
European (100)	100	0.42
Finnish (60)	81	0.34
French, ex. Basque (103)	890	3.73
French Canadian (25)	126	0.53
German (4,233)	11,892	49.82
German Russian (102)	115	0.48
Greek (0)	11	0.05
Hungarian (0)	45	0.19
Icelander (57)	139	0.58
Irish (369)	2,209	9.26
Italian (56)	308	1.29
Lithuanian (51)	74	0.31
Norwegian (2,806)	8,756	36.69
Polish (146)	658	2.76
Portuguese (0)	27	0.11
Romanian (13)	13	0.05
Russian (9)	530	2.22
Scandinavian (557)	703	2.95
Scotch-Irish (47)	263	1.10
Scottish (15)	352	1.47
Serbian (0)	11	0.05
Slovene (0)	9	0.04
Swedish (175)	1,530	6.41
Swiss (0)	39	0.16
Ukrainian (24)	41	0.17
Welsh (14)	70	0.29
West Indian, ex. Hispanic (0)	11	0.05
West Indian (0)	11	0.05
Yugoslavian (132)	198	0.83

Hispanic Origin	Population	%
Hispanic or Latino (of any race)	473	1.83
Central American, ex. Mexican	15	0.06
Guatemalan	5	0.02
Honduran	1	<0.01
Nicaraguan	8	0.03
Panamanian	1	<0.01
Cuban	9	0.03
Dominican Republic	7	0.03
Mexican	356	1.38
Puerto Rican	20	0.08
South American	14	0.05
Colombian	8	0.03
Ecuadorian	1	<0.01
Peruvian	5	0.02
Other Hispanic or Latino	52	0.20

Race*	Population	%
African-American/Black (515)	651	2.52
Not Hispanic (503)	627	2.43
Hispanic (12)	24	0.09
American Indian/Alaska Native (246)	438	1.70
Not Hispanic (232)	410	1.59
Hispanic (14)	28	0.11
Alaska Athabascan *(Ala. Nat.)* (0)	3	0.01
Apache (0)	1	<0.01
Blackfeet (1)	3	0.01
Canadian/French Am. Ind. (1)	2	0.01
Cherokee (1)	4	0.02
Cheyenne (1)	1	<0.01
Chippewa (93)	149	0.58
Choctaw (0)	3	0.01
Cree (0)	3	0.01
Crow (4)	4	0.02
Mexican American Ind. (5)	7	0.03
Navajo (0)	3	0.01
Seminole (0)	3	0.01
Sioux (44)	68	0.26
South American Ind. (0)	1	<0.01
Asian (362)	482	1.87
Not Hispanic (359)	474	1.84
Hispanic (3)	8	0.03
Bangladeshi (6)	8	0.03
Bhutanese (30)	30	0.12
Cambodian (3)	4	0.02
Chinese, ex. Taiwanese (49)	58	0.22
Filipino (37)	74	0.29
Indian (89)	106	0.41
Indonesian (2)	3	0.01
Japanese (2)	19	0.07
Korean (17)	37	0.14
Laotian (5)	13	0.05
Pakistani (2)	2	0.01
Sri Lankan (4)	4	0.02
Taiwanese (4)	4	0.02
Thai (5)	14	0.05
Vietnamese (93)	104	0.40
Hawaii Native/Pacific Islander (6)	13	0.05
Not Hispanic (6)	13	0.05
Native Hawaiian (0)	2	0.01
Samoan (5)	6	0.02
White (24,153)	24,566	95.11
Not Hispanic (23,840)	24,197	93.68
Hispanic (313)	369	1.43

Williston

Place Type: City
County: Williams
Population: 14,716†

Ancestry‡	Population	%
African, Sub-Saharan (10)	10	0.07
Ghanaian (10)	10	0.07
American (243)	243	1.75
Arab (32)	42	0.30
Lebanese (16)	26	0.19

*Notes: † The Census 2010 population figure is used to calculate the percentages in the Hispanic Origin and Race categories. Ancestry percentages are based on the 2006-2010 American Community Survey population (not shown); ‡ Numbers in parentheses indicate the number of people reporting a single ancestry; * Numbers in parentheses indicate the number of persons reporting this race alone, not in combination with any other race; Please refer to the Explanation of Data for more information.*

Ancestry	Population	%
Syrian (16)	16	0.12
Belgian (0)	12	0.09
Canadian (24)	45	0.32
Czech (29)	88	0.64
Czechoslovakian (0)	11	0.08
Danish (25)	141	1.02
Dutch (0)	300	2.17
English (55)	647	4.67
European (61)	89	0.64
Finnish (15)	38	0.27
French, ex. Basque (56)	630	4.55
French Canadian (55)	203	1.47
German (1,412)	4,907	35.42
Greek (11)	60	0.43
Icelander (0)	18	0.13
Irish (343)	1,507	10.88
Italian (31)	214	1.54
Norwegian (2,780)	6,065	43.78
Pennsylvania German (0)	12	0.09
Polish (25)	275	1.99
Portuguese (0)	13	0.09
Romanian (0)	12	0.09
Russian (93)	443	3.20
Scandinavian (56)	65	0.47
Scotch-Irish (8)	96	0.69
Scottish (11)	159	1.15
Slavic (9)	9	0.06
Swedish (90)	507	3.66
Swiss (10)	17	0.12
Ukrainian (16)	99	0.71
Welsh (0)	8	0.06

Hispanic Origin	Population	%
Hispanic or Latino (of any race)	328	2.23
Central American, ex. Mexican	9	0.06
Costa Rican	2	0.01
Honduran	1	0.01
Panamanian	1	0.01
Salvadoran	5	0.03
Cuban	5	0.03
Dominican Republic	6	0.04
Mexican	213	1.45
Puerto Rican	25	0.17
South American	18	0.12
Argentinean	5	0.03
Bolivian	1	0.01
Colombian	6	0.04
Ecuadorian	1	0.01
Peruvian	2	0.01
Venezuelan	3	0.02
Other Hispanic or Latino	52	0.35

Race*	Population	%
African-American/Black (51)	102	0.69
Not Hispanic (47)	92	0.63
Hispanic (4)	10	0.07
American Indian/Alaska Native (488)	817	5.55
Not Hispanic (471)	778	5.29
Hispanic (17)	39	0.27
Aleut *(Alaska Native)* (0)	1	0.01
Apache (0)	1	0.01
Blackfeet (2)	2	0.01
Canadian/French Am. Ind. (4)	4	0.03
Cherokee (2)	12	0.08
Chippewa (221)	382	2.60
Choctaw (0)	2	0.01
Comanche (1)	1	0.01
Cree (1)	4	0.03
Creek (0)	1	0.01
Crow (1)	1	0.01
Inupiat *(Alaska Native)* (1)	1	0.01
Iroquois (3)	5	0.03
Menominee (1)	1	0.01
Mexican American Ind. (0)	4	0.03
Navajo (5)	5	0.03
Osage (1)	1	0.01
Potawatomi (3)	3	0.02
Shoshone (1)	1	0.01
Sioux (45)	71	0.48
Tlingit-Haida *(Alaska Native)* (3)	3	0.02
Asian (48)	96	0.65
Not Hispanic (47)	88	0.60
Hispanic (1)	8	0.05
Chinese, ex. Taiwanese (12)	18	0.12
Filipino (15)	39	0.27
Indian (10)	16	0.11
Japanese (4)	11	0.07
Korean (1)	6	0.04
Laotian (1)	3	0.02
Malaysian (1)	1	0.01
Nepalese (1)	1	0.01
Taiwanese (0)	1	0.01
Thai (1)	1	0.01
Vietnamese (0)	2	0.01
Hawaii Native/Pacific Islander (4)	17	0.12
Not Hispanic (4)	13	0.09
Hispanic (0)	4	0.03
Guamanian/Chamorro (0)	1	0.01
Marshallese (1)	1	0.01
Native Hawaiian (0)	4	0.03
Samoan (0)	2	0.01
Tongan (1)	6	0.04
White (13,634)	14,056	95.52
Not Hispanic (13,428)	13,808	93.83
Hispanic (206)	248	1.69

SECTION TWO

*Notes: † The Census 2010 population figure is used to calculate the percentages in the Hispanic Origin and Race categories. Ancestry percentages are based on the 2006-2010 American Community Survey population (not shown); ‡ Numbers in parentheses indicate the number of people reporting a single ancestry; * Numbers in parentheses indicate the number of persons reporting this race alone, not in combination with any other race; Please refer to the Explanation of Data for more information.*

OHIO

Place Type: State
Population: 11,536,504†

Ancestry‡	Population	%
Afghan (334)	403	<0.01
African, Sub-Saharan (86,101)	98,709	0.86
African (56,965)	66,657	0.58
Cape Verdean (145)	396	<0.01
Ethiopian (4,654)	5,039	0.04
Ghanaian (2,800)	2,919	0.03
Kenyan (805)	948	0.01
Liberian (846)	939	0.01
Nigerian (4,600)	5,051	0.04
Senegalese (438)	537	<0.01
Sierra Leonean (530)	558	<0.01
Somalian (9,821)	10,078	0.09
South African (814)	1,304	0.01
Sudanese (348)	385	<0.01
Ugandan (139)	139	<0.01
Zimbabwean (381)	381	<0.01
Other Sub-Saharan African (2,815)	3,378	0.03
Albanian (3,200)	4,061	0.04
Alsatian (213)	705	0.01
American (911,201)	911,201	7.91
Arab (41,613)	65,834	0.57
Arab (7,980)	10,035	0.09
Egyptian (3,921)	4,801	0.04
Iraqi (1,205)	1,346	0.01
Jordanian (2,350)	2,833	0.02
Lebanese (14,495)	30,056	0.26
Moroccan (1,055)	1,497	0.01
Palestinian (4,116)	4,705	0.04
Syrian (2,939)	6,042	0.05
Other Arab (3,552)	4,519	0.04
Armenian (1,768)	4,333	0.04
Assyrian/Chaldean/Syriac (288)	389	<0.01
Australian (662)	2,134	0.02
Austrian (6,767)	28,071	0.24
Basque (8)	63	<0.01
Belgian (2,787)	10,037	0.09
Brazilian (1,749)	2,500	0.02
British (19,024)	42,018	0.36
Bulgarian (1,401)	2,864	0.02
Cajun (205)	558	<0.01
Canadian (6,805)	15,625	0.14
Carpatho Rusyn (539)	959	0.01
Celtic (1,001)	1,824	0.02
Croatian (15,181)	41,430	0.36
Cypriot (116)	141	<0.01
Czech (19,585)	73,775	0.64
Czechoslovakian (8,047)	18,742	0.16
Danish (4,624)	18,632	0.16
Dutch (34,625)	207,492	1.80
Eastern European (9,338)	10,672	0.09
English (362,859)	1,112,280	9.66
Estonian (461)	663	0.01
European (87,969)	98,058	0.85
Finnish (5,944)	19,872	0.17
French, ex. Basque (46,200)	284,589	2.47
French Canadian (11,090)	32,522	0.28
German (1,247,503)	3,220,180	27.97
German Russian (164)	481	<0.01
Greek (27,899)	58,649	0.51
Guyanese (907)	1,203	0.01
Hungarian (69,178)	210,625	1.83
Icelander (252)	808	0.01
Iranian (3,084)	4,038	0.04
Irish (413,997)	1,666,746	14.48
Israeli (907)	1,650	0.01
Italian (282,256)	748,397	6.50
Latvian (1,324)	2,580	0.02
Lithuanian (8,194)	24,321	0.21
Luxemburger (165)	665	0.01
Macedonian (2,762)	4,613	0.04
Maltese (204)	516	<0.01
New Zealander (154)	387	<0.01
Northern European (3,525)	3,939	0.03
Norwegian (12,651)	42,773	0.37
Pennsylvania German (24,371)	32,246	0.28
Polish (156,163)	462,815	4.02
Portuguese (3,847)	9,658	0.08
Romanian (13,078)	29,751	0.26
Russian (29,493)	80,848	0.70
Scandinavian (3,490)	8,810	0.08
Scotch-Irish (70,567)	190,369	1.65
Scottish (65,322)	229,371	1.99
Serbian (8,080)	17,530	0.15
Slavic (2,824)	8,235	0.07
Slovak (51,528)	144,300	1.25
Slovene (19,901)	55,482	0.48
Soviet Union (23)	36	<0.01
Swedish (17,992)	78,498	0.68
Swiss (19,738)	78,114	0.68
Turkish (2,941)	4,399	0.04
Ukrainian (22,564)	46,993	0.41
Welsh (28,763)	135,998	1.18
West Indian, ex. Hispanic (11,019)	17,473	0.15
Bahamian (276)	396	<0.01
Barbadian (223)	480	<0.01
Belizean (133)	214	<0.01
Bermudan (59)	128	<0.01
British West Indian (323)	457	<0.01
Dutch West Indian (156)	676	0.01
Haitian (2,297)	2,912	0.03
Jamaican (5,799)	8,744	0.08
Trinidadian/Tobagonian (541)	938	0.01
U.S. Virgin Islander (35)	56	<0.01
West Indian (1,168)	2,428	0.02
Other West Indian (9)	44	<0.01
Yugoslavian (6,948)	12,485	0.11

Hispanic Origin	Population	%
Hispanic or Latino (of any race)	354,674	3.07
Central American, ex. Mexican	22,756	0.20
Costa Rican	1,093	0.01
Guatemalan	8,680	0.08
Honduran	3,699	0.03
Nicaraguan	1,383	0.01
Panamanian	2,055	0.02
Salvadoran	5,627	0.05
Other Central American	219	<0.01
Cuban	7,523	0.07
Dominican Republic	6,453	0.06
Mexican	172,029	1.49
Puerto Rican	94,965	0.82
South American	17,571	0.15
Argentinean	1,921	0.02
Bolivian	649	0.01
Chilean	1,065	0.01
Colombian	5,247	0.05
Ecuadorian	2,090	0.02
Paraguayan	205	<0.01
Peruvian	3,741	0.03
Uruguayan	291	<0.01
Venezuelan	2,190	0.02
Other South American	172	<0.01
Other Hispanic or Latino	33,377	0.29

Race*	Population	%
African-American/Black (1,407,681)	1,541,771	13.36
Not Hispanic (1,389,115)	1,511,035	13.10
Hispanic (18,566)	30,736	0.27
American Indian/Alaska Native (25,292)	90,124	0.78
Not Hispanic (20,906)	79,872	0.69
Hispanic (4,386)	10,252	0.09
Alaska Athabascan *(Ala. Nat.)* (47)	100	<0.01
Aleut *(Alaska Native)* (43)	88	<0.01
Apache (362)	1,325	0.01
Arapaho (21)	95	<0.01
Blackfeet (642)	4,916	0.04
Canadian/French Am. Ind. (143)	338	<0.01
Central American Ind. (372)	458	<0.01
Cherokee (5,386)	26,584	0.23
Cheyenne (57)	236	<0.01
Chickasaw (111)	289	<0.01
Chippewa (807)	1,599	0.01
Choctaw (339)	1,194	0.01
Colville (5)	11	<0.01
Comanche (84)	237	<0.01
Cree (64)	194	<0.01
Creek (169)	579	0.01
Crow (38)	204	<0.01
Delaware (252)	608	0.01
Hopi (35)	105	<0.01
Houma (9)	22	<0.01
Inupiat *(Alaska Native)* (56)	115	<0.01
Iroquois (570)	1,807	0.02
Kiowa (33)	70	<0.01
Lumbee (235)	406	<0.01
Menominee (48)	66	<0.01
Mexican American Ind. (862)	1,472	0.01
Navajo (310)	809	0.01
Osage (47)	125	<0.01
Ottawa (91)	229	<0.01
Paiute (21)	39	<0.01
Pima (15)	27	<0.01
Potawatomi (125)	276	<0.01
Pueblo (75)	163	<0.01
Puget Sound Salish (24)	32	<0.01
Seminole (87)	460	<0.01
Shoshone (28)	99	<0.01
Sioux (613)	2,069	0.02
South American Ind. (287)	650	0.01
Spanish American Ind. (81)	124	<0.01
Tlingit-Haida *(Alaska Native)* (48)	77	<0.01
Tohono O'Odham (22)	41	<0.01
Tsimshian *(Alaska Native)* (12)	28	<0.01
Ute (5)	32	<0.01
Yakama (9)	19	<0.01
Yaqui (29)	73	<0.01
Yuman (13)	31	<0.01
Yup'ik *(Alaska Native)* (27)	47	<0.01
Asian (192,233)	238,292	2.07
Not Hispanic (190,765)	234,053	2.03
Hispanic (1,468)	4,239	0.04
Bangladeshi (928)	1,052	0.01
Bhutanese (703)	865	0.01
Burmese (1,258)	1,356	0.01
Cambodian (3,744)	4,570	0.04
Chinese, ex. Taiwanese (41,006)	47,861	0.41
Filipino (16,899)	27,661	0.24
Hmong (539)	589	0.01
Indian (64,187)	71,211	0.62
Indonesian (862)	1,354	0.01
Japanese (10,162)	16,995	0.15
Korean (15,281)	21,207	0.18
Laotian (3,355)	4,183	0.04
Malaysian (335)	528	<0.01
Nepalese (819)	992	0.01
Pakistani (4,644)	5,330	0.05
Sri Lankan (882)	1,029	0.01
Taiwanese (2,672)	3,172	0.03
Thai (2,535)	4,024	0.03
Vietnamese (13,121)	15,639	0.14
Hawaii Native/Pacific Islander (4,066)	10,525	0.09
Not Hispanic (3,400)	8,702	0.08
Hispanic (666)	1,823	0.02
Fijian (46)	90	<0.01
Guamanian/Chamorro (1,145)	1,977	0.02
Marshallese (99)	124	<0.01
Native Hawaiian (928)	3,037	0.03
Samoan (702)	1,278	0.01
Tongan (30)	81	<0.01
White (9,539,437)	9,751,547	84.53
Not Hispanic (9,359,263)	9,543,218	82.72
Hispanic (180,174)	208,329	1.81

*Notes: † The Census 2010 population figure is used to calculate the percentages in the Hispanic Origin and Race categories. Ancestry percentages are based on the 2006-2010 American Community Survey population (not shown); ‡ Numbers in parentheses indicate the number of people reporting a single ancestry; * Numbers in parentheses indicate the number of persons reporting this race alone, not in combination with any other race; Please refer to the Explanation of Data for more information.*

Akron

Place Type: City
County: Summit
Population: 199,110†

Ancestry‡	Population	%
African, Sub-Saharan (1,717)	2,290	1.13
African (1,579)	2,027	1.00
Cape Verdean (0)	33	0.02
Ethiopian (14)	42	0.02
Liberian (29)	29	0.01
Somalian (23)	23	0.01
South African (17)	17	0.01
Zimbabwean (12)	12	0.01
Other Sub-Saharan African (43)	107	0.05
Albanian (214)	304	0.15
Alsatian (0)	26	0.01
American (8,242)	8,242	4.06
Arab (714)	1,396	0.69
Arab (30)	159	0.08
Egyptian (124)	137	0.07
Iraqi (0)	7	<0.01
Lebanese (407)	914	0.45
Palestinian (10)	10	<0.01
Syrian (0)	26	0.01
Other Arab (143)	143	0.07
Armenian (26)	82	0.04
Australian (0)	21	0.01
Austrian (108)	450	0.22
Belgian (58)	109	0.05
Brazilian (0)	27	0.01
British (201)	508	0.25
Bulgarian (11)	32	0.02
Cajun (0)	27	0.01
Canadian (102)	196	0.10
Carpatho Rusyn (7)	25	0.01
Croatian (225)	584	0.29
Czech (236)	919	0.45
Czechoslovakian (176)	233	0.11
Danish (76)	260	0.13
Dutch (352)	2,805	1.38
Eastern European (115)	138	0.07
English (4,635)	15,829	7.80
European (1,068)	1,390	0.69
Finnish (12)	84	0.04
French, ex. Basque (524)	3,698	1.82
French Canadian (143)	320	0.16
German (11,486)	39,722	19.59
German Russian (0)	78	0.04
Greek (609)	1,127	0.56
Hungarian (1,222)	4,508	2.22
Icelander (19)	19	0.01
Iranian (36)	36	0.02
Irish (6,958)	26,458	13.05
Israeli (11)	11	0.01
Italian (5,897)	15,000	7.40
Latvian (27)	27	0.01
Lithuanian (87)	239	0.12
Macedonian (43)	56	0.03
Northern European (103)	103	0.05
Norwegian (220)	541	0.27
Pennsylvania German (177)	444	0.22
Polish (1,639)	4,998	2.46
Portuguese (210)	293	0.14
Romanian (344)	564	0.28
Russian (294)	893	0.44
Scandinavian (49)	130	0.06
Scotch-Irish (1,292)	3,342	1.65
Scottish (734)	2,974	1.47
Serbian (522)	945	0.47
Slavic (25)	106	0.05
Slovak (960)	2,164	1.07
Slovene (180)	588	0.29
Swedish (292)	1,161	0.57
Swiss (161)	690	0.34
Turkish (27)	61	0.03
Ukrainian (304)	693	0.34
Welsh (376)	2,022	1.00
West Indian, ex. Hispanic (142)	240	0.12
Barbadian (5)	5	<0.01
British West Indian (39)	39	0.02
Haitian (9)	36	0.02
Jamaican (30)	89	0.04
West Indian (59)	71	0.04
Yugoslavian (858)	1,145	0.56

Hispanic Origin	Population	%
Hispanic or Latino (of any race)	4,255	2.14
Central American, ex. Mexican	341	0.17
Costa Rican	10	0.01
Guatemalan	80	0.04
Honduran	93	0.05
Nicaraguan	38	0.02
Panamanian	47	0.02
Salvadoran	69	0.03
Other Central American	4	<0.01
Cuban	148	0.07
Dominican Republic	50	0.03
Mexican	1,784	0.90
Puerto Rican	1,091	0.55
South American	251	0.13
Argentinean	23	0.01
Bolivian	6	<0.01
Chilean	18	0.01
Colombian	101	0.05
Ecuadorian	39	0.02
Peruvian	24	0.01
Uruguayan	6	<0.01
Venezuelan	31	0.02
Other South American	3	<0.01
Other Hispanic or Latino	590	0.30

Race*	Population	%
African-American/Black (62,648)	67,240	33.77
Not Hispanic (62,095)	66,385	33.34
Hispanic (553)	855	0.43
American Indian/Alaska Native (486)	2,083	1.05
Not Hispanic (425)	1,899	0.95
Hispanic (61)	184	0.09
Aleut *(Alaska Native)* (1)	1	<0.01
Apache (3)	16	0.01
Arapaho (0)	3	<0.01
Blackfeet (11)	115	0.06
Canadian/French Am. Ind. (12)	18	0.01
Cherokee (91)	534	0.27
Cheyenne (4)	14	0.01
Chickasaw (3)	9	<0.01
Chippewa (13)	20	0.01
Choctaw (10)	42	0.02
Comanche (2)	5	<0.01
Cree (4)	8	<0.01
Creek (5)	16	0.01
Crow (0)	6	<0.01
Delaware (5)	17	0.01
Inupiat *(Alaska Native)* (2)	4	<0.01
Iroquois (6)	41	0.02
Lumbee (2)	5	<0.01
Mexican American Ind. (1)	14	0.01
Navajo (3)	15	0.01
Osage (0)	3	<0.01
Ottawa (3)	4	<0.01
Pima (4)	5	<0.01
Potawatomi (2)	2	<0.01
Pueblo (0)	1	<0.01
Seminole (1)	17	0.01
Shoshone (4)	10	0.01
Sioux (14)	55	0.03
South American Ind. (4)	7	<0.01
Spanish American Ind. (2)	4	<0.01
Tlingit-Haida *(Alaska Native)* (0)	1	<0.01
Ute (0)	1	<0.01
Yaqui (1)	9	<0.01
Asian (4,218)	5,081	2.55
Not Hispanic (4,201)	5,008	2.52
Hispanic (17)	73	0.04
Bangladeshi (15)	15	0.01
Bhutanese (267)	318	0.16
Burmese (585)	603	0.30
Cambodian (55)	69	0.03
Chinese, ex. Taiwanese (486)	607	0.30
Filipino (174)	317	0.16
Hmong (351)	362	0.18
Indian (713)	874	0.44
Indonesian (12)	20	0.01
Japanese (68)	207	0.10
Korean (174)	252	0.13
Laotian (346)	388	0.19
Malaysian (6)	9	<0.01
Nepalese (54)	85	0.04
Pakistani (19)	22	0.01
Sri Lankan (17)	18	0.01
Taiwanese (50)	54	0.03
Thai (77)	116	0.06
Vietnamese (427)	474	0.24
Hawaii Native/Pacific Islander (52)	189	0.09
Not Hispanic (49)	164	0.08
Hispanic (3)	25	0.01
Guamanian/Chamorro (12)	27	0.01
Native Hawaiian (20)	84	0.04
Samoan (5)	14	0.01
Tongan (1)	1	<0.01
White (123,879)	129,298	64.94
Not Hispanic (121,946)	126,928	63.75
Hispanic (1,933)	2,370	1.19

Alliance

Place Type: City
County: Stark
Population: 22,322†

Ancestry‡	Population	%
African, Sub-Saharan (60)	60	0.27
African (60)	60	0.27
Albanian (31)	31	0.14
American (2,275)	2,275	10.09
Australian (0)	14	0.06
Austrian (25)	65	0.29
Belgian (0)	11	0.05
Brazilian (16)	16	0.07
British (0)	62	0.28
Canadian (10)	20	0.09
Croatian (24)	77	0.34
Czech (14)	39	0.17
Czechoslovakian (0)	42	0.19
Danish (0)	12	0.05
Dutch (222)	639	2.83
English (629)	2,057	9.12
European (96)	96	0.43
French, ex. Basque (82)	685	3.04
French Canadian (10)	22	0.10
German (1,968)	6,105	27.08
Greek (0)	26	0.12
Hungarian (103)	436	1.93
Irish (824)	3,500	15.52
Italian (1,345)	2,501	11.09
Lithuanian (13)	26	0.12
Norwegian (15)	51	0.23
Pennsylvania German (71)	133	0.59
Polish (202)	522	2.32
Portuguese (0)	11	0.05
Romanian (119)	351	1.56
Russian (35)	55	0.24
Scandinavian (0)	14	0.06
Scotch-Irish (225)	592	2.63
Scottish (98)	276	1.22
Slavic (0)	12	0.05
Slovak (61)	99	0.44
Swedish (45)	80	0.35
Swiss (132)	540	2.40
Turkish (14)	14	0.06
Ukrainian (0)	39	0.17
Welsh (50)	299	1.33
West Indian, ex. Hispanic (13)	13	0.06
Jamaican (13)	13	0.06
Yugoslavian (11)	11	0.05

Hispanic Origin	Population	%
Hispanic or Latino (of any race)	418	1.87

*Notes: † The Census 2010 population figure is used to calculate the percentages in the Hispanic Origin and Race categories. Ancestry percentages are based on the 2006-2010 American Community Survey population (not shown); ‡ Numbers in parentheses indicate the number of people reporting a single ancestry; * Numbers in parentheses indicate the number of persons reporting this race alone, not in combination with any other race; Please refer to the Explanation of Data for more information.*

Central American, ex. Mexican	35	0.16
Guatemalan	16	0.07
Honduran	5	0.02
Panamanian	9	0.04
Salvadoran	5	0.02
Cuban	5	0.02
Dominican Republic	3	0.01
Mexican	184	0.82
Puerto Rican	121	0.54
South American	5	0.02
Colombian	3	0.01
Ecuadorian	1	<0.01
Uruguayan	1	<0.01
Other Hispanic or Latino	65	0.29

Race*	Population	%
African-American/Black (2,333)	2,929	13.12
Not Hispanic (2,304)	2,880	12.90
Hispanic (29)	49	0.22
American Indian/Alaska Native (38)	180	0.81
Not Hispanic (35)	159	0.71
Hispanic (3)	21	0.09
Alaska Athabascan *(Ala. Nat.)* (0)	1	<0.01
Apache (1)	2	0.01
Blackfeet (2)	18	0.08
Cherokee (3)	63	0.28
Cheyenne (0)	4	0.02
Chickasaw (0)	1	<0.01
Chippewa (0)	2	0.01
Choctaw (0)	3	0.01
Crow (1)	7	0.03
Delaware (4)	5	0.02
Iroquois (1)	1	<0.01
Lumbee (5)	5	0.02
Mexican American Ind. (1)	1	<0.01
Pima (1)	1	<0.01
Pueblo (1)	1	<0.01
Sioux (2)	6	0.03
South American Ind. (0)	1	<0.01
Asian (168)	217	0.97
Not Hispanic (165)	212	0.95
Hispanic (3)	5	0.02
Chinese, ex. Taiwanese (42)	51	0.23
Filipino (26)	42	0.19
Indian (22)	25	0.11
Japanese (26)	35	0.16
Korean (17)	21	0.09
Malaysian (1)	1	<0.01
Pakistani (5)	5	0.02
Thai (3)	3	0.01
Vietnamese (19)	20	0.09
Hawaii Native/Pacific Islander (4)	17	0.08
Not Hispanic (4)	17	0.08
Guamanian/Chamorro (3)	8	0.04
Native Hawaiian (1)	7	0.03
White (18,895)	19,635	87.96
Not Hispanic (18,651)	19,338	86.63
Hispanic (244)	297	1.33

Amherst

Place Type: City
County: Lorain
Population: 12,021†

Ancestry‡	Population	%
American (941)	941	7.82
Arab (65)	123	1.02
Lebanese (0)	39	0.32
Moroccan (27)	27	0.22
Palestinian (28)	28	0.23
Syrian (10)	29	0.24
Austrian (8)	121	1.01
British (37)	112	0.93
Bulgarian (11)	11	0.09
Canadian (16)	31	0.26
Croatian (27)	103	0.86
Czech (0)	80	0.66
Czechoslovakian (22)	44	0.37
Danish (28)	63	0.52
Dutch (14)	201	1.67
Eastern European (9)	9	0.07
English (246)	1,161	9.65
European (9)	9	0.07
French, ex. Basque (15)	304	2.53
French Canadian (14)	48	0.40
German (1,091)	4,300	35.74
Greek (48)	68	0.57
Hungarian (314)	938	7.80
Irish (334)	2,233	18.56
Italian (497)	1,252	10.41
Lithuanian (0)	36	0.30
Norwegian (0)	39	0.32
Pennsylvania German (13)	22	0.18
Polish (342)	1,058	8.79
Portuguese (0)	19	0.16
Romanian (0)	10	0.08
Russian (59)	239	1.99
Scotch-Irish (42)	218	1.81
Scottish (116)	316	2.63
Serbian (0)	13	0.11
Slovak (201)	714	5.93
Slovene (13)	126	1.05
Swedish (10)	58	0.48
Swiss (0)	36	0.30
Turkish (33)	33	0.27
Ukrainian (8)	34	0.28
Welsh (20)	86	0.71

Hispanic Origin	Population	%
Hispanic or Latino (of any race)	632	5.26
Central American, ex. Mexican	14	0.12
Guatemalan	7	0.06
Honduran	5	0.04
Salvadoran	2	0.02
Cuban	3	0.02
Dominican Republic	2	0.02
Mexican	216	1.80
Puerto Rican	351	2.92
South American	15	0.12
Argentinean	3	0.02
Chilean	3	0.02
Colombian	1	0.01
Ecuadorian	1	0.01
Peruvian	7	0.06
Other Hispanic or Latino	31	0.26

Race*	Population	%
African-American/Black (85)	166	1.38
Not Hispanic (76)	137	1.14
Hispanic (9)	29	0.24
American Indian/Alaska Native (27)	103	0.86
Not Hispanic (22)	79	0.66
Hispanic (5)	24	0.20
Aleut *(Alaska Native)* (1)	1	0.01
Blackfeet (1)	5	0.04
Canadian/French Am. Ind. (3)	5	0.04
Cherokee (5)	25	0.21
Chippewa (0)	1	0.01
Choctaw (0)	2	0.02
Iroquois (3)	4	0.03
Lumbee (1)	4	0.03
Mexican American Ind. (1)	2	0.02
Navajo (2)	5	0.04
Ottawa (0)	1	0.01
Paiute (2)	2	0.02
Pueblo (1)	1	0.01
Sioux (0)	2	0.02
Yup'ik *(Alaska Native)* (0)	1	0.01
Asian (83)	115	0.96
Not Hispanic (80)	112	0.93
Hispanic (3)	3	0.02
Chinese, ex. Taiwanese (6)	8	0.07
Filipino (25)	35	0.29
Indian (16)	16	0.13
Japanese (10)	21	0.17
Korean (17)	24	0.20
Pakistani (5)	5	0.04
Taiwanese (2)	2	0.02
Vietnamese (1)	5	0.04
Hawaii Native/Pacific Islander (2)	5	0.04
Not Hispanic (2)	4	0.03
Hispanic (0)	1	0.01
Native Hawaiian (1)	2	0.02
White (11,499)	11,697	97.30
Not Hispanic (11,058)	11,199	93.16
Hispanic (441)	498	4.14

Ashland

Place Type: City
County: Ashland
Population: 20,362†

Ancestry‡	Population	%
African, Sub-Saharan (32)	32	0.15
African (32)	32	0.15
Alsatian (16)	69	0.33
American (3,055)	3,055	14.80
Arab (159)	174	0.84
Arab (43)	43	0.21
Lebanese (0)	5	0.02
Moroccan (8)	8	0.04
Syrian (0)	10	0.05
Other Arab (108)	108	0.52
Australian (19)	19	0.09
Austrian (25)	51	0.25
British (92)	158	0.77
Bulgarian (11)	11	0.05
Canadian (0)	31	0.15
Croatian (30)	40	0.19
Czech (24)	48	0.23
Czechoslovakian (24)	72	0.35
Danish (0)	9	0.04
Dutch (16)	357	1.73
Eastern European (12)	12	0.06
English (1,013)	2,209	10.70
European (104)	114	0.55
French, ex. Basque (161)	597	2.89
French Canadian (7)	17	0.08
German (3,014)	6,624	32.08
German Russian (0)	22	0.11
Greek (17)	41	0.20
Hungarian (138)	298	1.44
Iranian (7)	7	0.03
Irish (686)	2,362	11.44
Italian (753)	1,518	7.35
Latvian (0)	9	0.04
Lithuanian (31)	31	0.15
Norwegian (20)	70	0.34
Pennsylvania German (109)	283	1.37
Polish (331)	674	3.26
Romanian (21)	29	0.14
Russian (32)	68	0.33
Scandinavian (26)	50	0.24
Scotch-Irish (248)	448	2.17
Scottish (69)	623	3.02
Slovak (12)	68	0.33
Swedish (22)	180	0.87
Swiss (35)	182	0.88
Ukrainian (80)	98	0.47
Welsh (46)	136	0.66
West Indian, ex. Hispanic (0)	17	0.08
Other West Indian (0)	17	0.08
Yugoslavian (22)	32	0.15

Hispanic Origin	Population	%
Hispanic or Latino (of any race)	244	1.20
Central American, ex. Mexican	26	0.13
Costa Rican	6	0.03
Guatemalan	8	0.04
Nicaraguan	2	0.01
Salvadoran	8	0.04
Other Central American	2	0.01
Cuban	5	0.02
Dominican Republic	5	0.02
Mexican	118	0.58
Puerto Rican	49	0.24
South American	9	0.04
Argentinean	3	0.01

*Notes: † The Census 2010 population figure is used to calculate the percentages in the Hispanic Origin and Race categories. Ancestry percentages are based on the 2006-2010 American Community Survey population (not shown); ‡ Numbers in parentheses indicate the number of people reporting a single ancestry; * Numbers in parentheses indicate the number of persons reporting this race alone, not in combination with any other race; Please refer to the Explanation of Data for more information.*

Colombian	2	0.01
Ecuadorian	2	0.01
Peruvian	1	<0.01
Venezuelan	1	<0.01
Other Hispanic or Latino	32	0.16

Race*	Population	%
African-American/Black (279)	407	2.00
Not Hispanic (279)	403	1.98
Hispanic (0)	4	0.02
American Indian/Alaska Native (29)	107	0.53
Not Hispanic (24)	95	0.47
Hispanic (5)	12	0.06
Apache (1)	3	0.01
Blackfeet (1)	10	0.05
Cherokee (8)	43	0.21
Chippewa (3)	3	0.01
Creek (0)	3	0.01
Iroquois (0)	2	0.01
Mexican American Ind. (5)	5	0.02
Osage (0)	1	<0.01
Potawatomi (2)	3	0.01
Sioux (3)	4	0.02
Asian (206)	265	1.30
Not Hispanic (206)	264	1.30
Hispanic (0)	1	<0.01
Bangladeshi (2)	2	0.01
Cambodian (11)	12	0.06
Chinese, ex. Taiwanese (65)	79	0.39
Filipino (15)	32	0.16
Indian (36)	54	0.27
Indonesian (2)	2	0.01
Japanese (5)	11	0.05
Korean (20)	24	0.12
Sri Lankan (8)	8	0.04
Taiwanese (21)	24	0.12
Thai (4)	8	0.04
Vietnamese (0)	1	<0.01
Hawaii Native/Pacific Islander (22)	41	0.20
Not Hispanic (22)	35	0.17
Hispanic (0)	6	0.03
Guamanian/Chamorro (13)	17	0.08
Native Hawaiian (3)	11	0.05
Samoan (1)	4	0.02
White (19,498)	19,754	97.01
Not Hispanic (19,335)	19,566	96.09
Hispanic (163)	188	0.92

Ashtabula

Place Type: City
County: Ashtabula
Population: 19,124†

Ancestry‡	Population	%
African, Sub-Saharan (74)	111	0.57
African (74)	111	0.57
American (2,377)	2,377	12.18
Arab (28)	47	0.24
Lebanese (28)	47	0.24
Austrian (9)	32	0.16
British (20)	20	0.10
Canadian (0)	9	0.05
Croatian (27)	44	0.23
Czech (0)	66	0.34
Czechoslovakian (0)	13	0.07
Danish (0)	8	0.04
Dutch (40)	438	2.25
English (631)	1,864	9.56
European (89)	89	0.46
Finnish (262)	914	4.69
French, ex. Basque (231)	546	2.80
French Canadian (23)	58	0.30
German (1,148)	3,986	20.43
Greek (11)	11	0.06
Hungarian (150)	446	2.29
Irish (573)	2,515	12.89
Italian (1,670)	3,237	16.59
Lithuanian (0)	32	0.16
Macedonian (0)	8	0.04
Norwegian (0)	81	0.42
Pennsylvania German (0)	22	0.11
Polish (273)	725	3.72
Portuguese (28)	90	0.46
Romanian (8)	18	0.09
Russian (17)	69	0.35
Scandinavian (63)	63	0.32
Scotch-Irish (99)	232	1.19
Scottish (75)	280	1.44
Slavic (0)	9	0.05
Slovak (68)	198	1.01
Slovene (6)	6	0.03
Swedish (121)	401	2.06
Swiss (0)	53	0.27
Ukrainian (2)	48	0.25
Welsh (0)	84	0.43
West Indian, ex. Hispanic (19)	19	0.10
Jamaican (19)	19	0.10

Hispanic Origin	Population	%
Hispanic or Latino (of any race)	1,773	9.27
Central American, ex. Mexican	27	0.14
Honduran	21	0.11
Panamanian	4	0.02
Salvadoran	2	0.01
Cuban	14	0.07
Dominican Republic	9	0.05
Mexican	476	2.49
Puerto Rican	1,156	6.04
South American	10	0.05
Chilean	1	0.01
Colombian	2	0.01
Ecuadorian	2	0.01
Peruvian	1	0.01
Other South American	4	0.02
Other Hispanic or Latino	81	0.42

Race*	Population	%
African-American/Black (1,711)	2,404	12.57
Not Hispanic (1,619)	2,260	11.82
Hispanic (92)	144	0.75
American Indian/Alaska Native (84)	283	1.48
Not Hispanic (68)	237	1.24
Hispanic (16)	46	0.24
Apache (0)	6	0.03
Blackfeet (1)	22	0.12
Cherokee (21)	95	0.50
Chickasaw (0)	2	0.01
Chippewa (5)	10	0.05
Choctaw (4)	5	0.03
Creek (0)	4	0.02
Crow (0)	3	0.02
Delaware (2)	6	0.03
Iroquois (3)	4	0.02
Mexican American Ind. (5)	5	0.03
Navajo (2)	4	0.02
Sioux (3)	7	0.04
Asian (54)	97	0.51
Not Hispanic (54)	92	0.48
Hispanic (0)	5	0.03
Bangladeshi (1)	1	0.01
Cambodian (1)	3	0.02
Chinese, ex. Taiwanese (16)	23	0.12
Filipino (8)	16	0.08
Indian (5)	6	0.03
Japanese (6)	9	0.05
Korean (11)	19	0.10
Vietnamese (3)	5	0.03
Hawaii Native/Pacific Islander (5)	26	0.14
Not Hispanic (4)	18	0.09
Hispanic (1)	8	0.04
Guamanian/Chamorro (2)	5	0.03
Native Hawaiian (2)	8	0.04
White (15,674)	16,565	86.62
Not Hispanic (14,790)	15,548	81.30
Hispanic (884)	1,017	5.32

Athens

Place Type: City
County: Athens
Population: 23,832†

Ancestry‡	Population	%
African, Sub-Saharan (205)	255	1.09
African (184)	234	1.00
Nigerian (15)	15	0.06
Ugandan (6)	6	0.03
Albanian (0)	14	0.06
Alsatian (21)	21	0.09
American (1,173)	1,173	4.99
Arab (186)	293	1.25
Arab (40)	40	0.17
Lebanese (45)	87	0.37
Syrian (0)	18	0.08
Other Arab (101)	148	0.63
Armenian (14)	14	0.06
Austrian (0)	63	0.27
Belgian (0)	35	0.15
Brazilian (23)	68	0.29
British (30)	78	0.33
Canadian (23)	43	0.18
Celtic (0)	11	0.05
Croatian (32)	84	0.36
Czech (79)	279	1.19
Czechoslovakian (8)	8	0.03
Dutch (47)	265	1.13
Eastern European (0)	11	0.05
English (533)	2,134	9.09
European (235)	268	1.14
Finnish (15)	44	0.19
French, ex. Basque (88)	584	2.49
French Canadian (15)	44	0.19
German (1,990)	6,409	27.29
Greek (28)	216	0.92
Hungarian (84)	436	1.86
Icelander (0)	12	0.05
Iranian (9)	9	0.04
Irish (887)	3,962	16.87
Israeli (0)	14	0.06
Italian (630)	2,079	8.85
Latvian (8)	8	0.03
Lithuanian (23)	59	0.25
Luxemburger (0)	13	0.06
Macedonian (0)	34	0.14
Norwegian (62)	162	0.69
Polish (145)	1,034	4.40
Romanian (32)	92	0.39
Russian (63)	262	1.12
Scandinavian (34)	63	0.27
Scotch-Irish (284)	668	2.84
Scottish (85)	501	2.13
Slavic (0)	8	0.03
Slovak (149)	380	1.62
Slovene (46)	107	0.46
Swedish (88)	227	0.97
Swiss (14)	89	0.38
Ukrainian (15)	117	0.50
Welsh (49)	353	1.50
Yugoslavian (13)	27	0.11

Hispanic Origin	Population	%
Hispanic or Latino (of any race)	576	2.42
Central American, ex. Mexican	44	0.18
Costa Rican	3	0.01
Guatemalan	10	0.04
Honduran	8	0.03
Nicaraguan	4	0.02
Panamanian	5	0.02
Salvadoran	14	0.06
Cuban	32	0.13
Dominican Republic	5	0.02
Mexican	226	0.95
Puerto Rican	94	0.39
South American	126	0.53
Argentinean	16	0.07
Bolivian	5	0.02

*Notes: † The Census 2010 population figure is used to calculate the percentages in the Hispanic Origin and Race categories. Ancestry percentages are based on the 2006-2010 American Community Survey population (not shown); ‡ Numbers in parentheses indicate the number of people reporting a single ancestry; * Numbers in parentheses indicate the number of persons reporting this race alone, not in combination with any other race; Please refer to the Explanation of Data for more information.*

Chilean	16	0.07
Colombian	40	0.17
Ecuadorian	14	0.06
Paraguayan	5	0.02
Peruvian	9	0.04
Uruguayan	4	0.02
Venezuelan	17	0.07
Other Hispanic or Latino	49	0.21

Race*	Population	%
African-American/Black (1,047)	1,270	5.33
Not Hispanic (1,027)	1,226	5.14
Hispanic (20)	44	0.18
American Indian/Alaska Native (37)	212	0.89
Not Hispanic (34)	196	0.82
Hispanic (3)	16	0.07
Apache (1)	2	0.01
Arapaho (0)	1	<0.01
Blackfeet (1)	11	0.05
Cherokee (7)	66	0.28
Chickasaw (1)	1	<0.01
Chippewa (2)	7	0.03
Choctaw (0)	2	0.01
Comanche (0)	1	<0.01
Delaware (0)	1	<0.01
Inupiat *(Alaska Native)* (0)	1	<0.01
Iroquois (1)	7	0.03
Lumbee (1)	2	0.01
Navajo (1)	3	0.01
Osage (0)	1	<0.01
Potawatomi (1)	1	<0.01
Seminole (0)	4	0.02
Shoshone (1)	1	<0.01
Sioux (2)	3	0.01
South American Ind. (0)	3	0.01
Asian (1,455)	1,674	7.02
Not Hispanic (1,451)	1,658	6.96
Hispanic (4)	16	0.07
Bangladeshi (7)	7	0.03
Burmese (2)	2	0.01
Cambodian (5)	5	0.02
Chinese, ex. Taiwanese (859)	900	3.78
Filipino (31)	74	0.31
Hmong (1)	5	0.02
Indian (165)	189	0.79
Indonesian (37)	41	0.17
Japanese (77)	116	0.49
Korean (111)	130	0.55
Laotian (1)	1	<0.01
Malaysian (10)	12	0.05
Nepalese (6)	6	0.03
Pakistani (14)	16	0.07
Sri Lankan (8)	8	0.03
Taiwanese (27)	28	0.12
Thai (15)	18	0.08
Vietnamese (32)	41	0.17
Hawaii Native/Pacific Islander (10)	24	0.10
Not Hispanic (8)	18	0.08
Hispanic (2)	6	0.03
Guamanian/Chamorro (0)	2	0.01
Marshallese (2)	2	0.01
Native Hawaiian (1)	11	0.05
Samoan (4)	4	0.02
White (20,586)	21,081	88.46
Not Hispanic (20,196)	20,652	86.66
Hispanic (390)	429	1.80

Aurora

Place Type: City
County: Portage
Population: 15,548†

Ancestry‡	Population	%
African, Sub-Saharan (0)	22	0.14
African (0)	22	0.14
American (345)	345	2.27
Arab (56)	179	1.18
Egyptian (13)	39	0.26
Moroccan (0)	63	0.41
Syrian (43)	54	0.36
Other Arab (0)	23	0.15
Austrian (58)	160	1.05
Belgian (41)	55	0.36
British (82)	153	1.01
Canadian (0)	77	0.51
Carpatho Rusyn (16)	65	0.43
Celtic (0)	14	0.09
Croatian (57)	177	1.16
Czech (101)	456	3.00
Czechoslovakian (18)	43	0.28
Danish (20)	104	0.68
Dutch (16)	157	1.03
Eastern European (10)	36	0.24
English (408)	1,656	10.90
European (234)	249	1.64
Finnish (0)	33	0.22
French, ex. Basque (10)	233	1.53
French Canadian (0)	31	0.20
German (881)	3,268	21.51
Greek (63)	241	1.59
Hungarian (218)	965	6.35
Irish (598)	2,043	13.44
Italian (1,046)	2,624	17.27
Latvian (30)	30	0.20
Lithuanian (33)	135	0.89
Luxemburger (0)	13	0.09
Norwegian (8)	53	0.35
Polish (375)	1,322	8.70
Romanian (52)	80	0.53
Russian (145)	265	1.74
Scandinavian (0)	10	0.07
Scotch-Irish (81)	173	1.14
Scottish (76)	458	3.01
Slavic (11)	11	0.07
Slovak (205)	724	4.76
Slovene (157)	384	2.53
Swedish (74)	202	1.33
Swiss (25)	69	0.45
Ukrainian (87)	131	0.86
Welsh (77)	255	1.68

Hispanic Origin	Population	%
Hispanic or Latino (of any race)	203	1.31
Central American, ex. Mexican	12	0.08
Guatemalan	8	0.05
Honduran	4	0.03
Cuban	22	0.14
Mexican	89	0.57
Puerto Rican	27	0.17
South American	28	0.18
Argentinean	8	0.05
Bolivian	2	0.01
Colombian	8	0.05
Ecuadorian	3	0.02
Peruvian	4	0.03
Venezuelan	3	0.02
Other Hispanic or Latino	25	0.16

Race*	Population	%
African-American/Black (467)	504	3.24
Not Hispanic (466)	495	3.18
Hispanic (1)	9	0.06
American Indian/Alaska Native (13)	40	0.26
Not Hispanic (12)	34	0.22
Hispanic (1)	6	0.04
Apache (1)	1	0.01
Blackfeet (0)	1	0.01
Cherokee (1)	10	0.06
Chippewa (4)	5	0.03
Iroquois (0)	1	0.01
Pima (1)	1	0.01
South American Ind. (0)	1	0.01
Asian (294)	366	2.35
Not Hispanic (290)	359	2.31
Hispanic (4)	7	0.05
Bangladeshi (3)	3	0.02
Burmese (3)	3	0.02
Chinese, ex. Taiwanese (78)	94	0.60
Filipino (13)	33	0.21
Indian (124)	138	0.89
Japanese (11)	20	0.13
Korean (16)	23	0.15
Laotian (2)	2	0.01
Nepalese (2)	2	0.01
Pakistani (3)	3	0.02
Sri Lankan (5)	7	0.05
Taiwanese (4)	7	0.05
Thai (1)	1	0.01
Vietnamese (23)	23	0.15
Hawaii Native/Pacific Islander (6)	9	0.06
Not Hispanic (6)	9	0.06
Native Hawaiian (0)	1	0.01
Samoan (1)	2	0.01
White (14,595)	14,731	94.75
Not Hispanic (14,451)	14,560	93.65
Hispanic (144)	171	1.10

Austintown

Place Type: CDP
County: Mahoning
Population: 29,677†

Ancestry‡	Population	%
African, Sub-Saharan (233)	245	0.81
African (233)	245	0.81
American (1,556)	1,556	5.15
Arab (41)	91	0.30
Arab (25)	75	0.25
Lebanese (16)	16	0.05
Austrian (14)	29	0.10
Belgian (0)	34	0.11
British (50)	68	0.22
Bulgarian (13)	13	0.04
Canadian (0)	13	0.04
Croatian (178)	596	1.97
Czech (6)	161	0.53
Czechoslovakian (17)	29	0.10
Dutch (55)	480	1.59
Eastern European (21)	35	0.12
English (784)	3,295	10.90
European (408)	418	1.38
Finnish (10)	52	0.17
French, ex. Basque (30)	715	2.36
French Canadian (0)	42	0.14
German (2,072)	7,809	25.82
Greek (26)	276	0.91
Hungarian (472)	1,136	3.76
Irish (1,052)	6,116	20.22
Italian (2,938)	6,154	20.35
Lithuanian (16)	47	0.16
Macedonian (21)	21	0.07
Norwegian (43)	107	0.35
Pennsylvania German (44)	107	0.35
Polish (363)	1,196	3.96
Portuguese (0)	32	0.11
Romanian (41)	99	0.33
Russian (33)	158	0.52
Scandinavian (0)	21	0.07
Scotch-Irish (147)	464	1.53
Scottish (95)	517	1.71
Serbian (87)	129	0.43
Slovak (1,004)	2,267	7.50
Slovene (34)	82	0.27
Swedish (106)	579	1.91
Swiss (0)	13	0.04
Ukrainian (328)	666	2.20
Welsh (119)	737	2.44
West Indian, ex. Hispanic (16)	40	0.13
Haitian (0)	24	0.08
Jamaican (16)	16	0.05
Yugoslavian (22)	33	0.11

Hispanic Origin	Population	%
Hispanic or Latino (of any race)	794	2.68
Central American, ex. Mexican	29	0.10
Costa Rican	1	<0.01
Guatemalan	5	0.02
Honduran	14	0.05

*Notes: † The Census 2010 population figure is used to calculate the percentages in the Hispanic Origin and Race categories. Ancestry percentages are based on the 2006-2010 American Community Survey population (not shown); ‡ Numbers in parentheses indicate the number of people reporting a single ancestry; * Numbers in parentheses indicate the number of persons reporting this race alone, not in combination with any other race; Please refer to the Explanation of Data for more information.*

SECTION TWO

Panamanian	6	0.02
Salvadoran	3	0.01
Cuban	9	0.03
Dominican Republic	9	0.03
Mexican	212	0.71
Puerto Rican	423	1.43
South American	19	0.06
Argentinean	1	<0.01
Chilean	8	0.03
Colombian	2	0.01
Ecuadorian	3	0.01
Peruvian	1	<0.01
Venezuelan	4	0.01
Other Hispanic or Latino	93	0.31

Race*	Population	%
African-American/Black (2,047)	2,338	7.88
Not Hispanic (1,994)	2,248	7.57
Hispanic (53)	90	0.30
American Indian/Alaska Native (57)	210	0.71
Not Hispanic (41)	175	0.59
Hispanic (16)	35	0.12
Apache (0)	2	0.01
Blackfeet (0)	15	0.05
Cherokee (12)	69	0.23
Cheyenne (0)	1	<0.01
Cree (0)	1	<0.01
Delaware (0)	2	0.01
Iroquois (3)	11	0.04
Mexican American Ind. (1)	2	0.01
Navajo (0)	1	<0.01
Potawatomi (0)	2	0.01
Sioux (4)	6	0.02
South American Ind. (3)	6	0.02
Asian (181)	247	0.83
Not Hispanic (177)	240	0.81
Hispanic (4)	7	0.02
Bangladeshi (3)	3	0.01
Chinese, ex. Taiwanese (38)	49	0.17
Filipino (36)	51	0.17
Indian (37)	44	0.15
Indonesian (0)	1	<0.01
Japanese (5)	10	0.03
Korean (22)	32	0.11
Pakistani (9)	20	0.07
Thai (7)	14	0.05
Vietnamese (13)	20	0.07
Hawaii Native/Pacific Islander (8)	21	0.07
Not Hispanic (8)	15	0.05
Hispanic (0)	6	0.02
Guamanian/Chamorro (2)	5	0.02
Native Hawaiian (2)	3	0.01
Samoan (3)	6	0.02
Tongan (0)	1	<0.01
White (26,687)	27,165	91.54
Not Hispanic (26,229)	26,621	89.70
Hispanic (458)	544	1.83

Avon Lake

Place Type: City
County: Lorain
Population: 22,581†

Ancestry‡	Population	%
American (570)	570	2.60
Arab (83)	220	1.01
Arab (13)	13	0.06
Egyptian (13)	13	0.06
Lebanese (28)	99	0.45
Palestinian (0)	10	0.05
Syrian (29)	85	0.39
Armenian (37)	60	0.27
Australian (12)	12	0.05
Austrian (0)	134	0.61
Brazilian (0)	14	0.06
British (96)	162	0.74
Bulgarian (0)	9	0.04
Cajun (7)	7	0.03
Canadian (106)	121	0.55
Croatian (53)	80	0.37
Czech (46)	244	1.12
Czechoslovakian (11)	92	0.42
Danish (12)	88	0.40
Dutch (83)	350	1.60
Eastern European (41)	41	0.19
English (579)	2,941	13.44
Estonian (0)	12	0.05
European (274)	284	1.30
Finnish (11)	87	0.40
French, ex. Basque (38)	412	1.88
French Canadian (46)	155	0.71
German (1,689)	6,869	31.39
Greek (19)	179	0.82
Hungarian (250)	1,062	4.85
Iranian (57)	57	0.26
Irish (1,730)	5,387	24.62
Italian (661)	2,495	11.40
Latvian (9)	28	0.13
Lithuanian (12)	100	0.46
Northern European (15)	15	0.07
Norwegian (60)	290	1.33
Polish (585)	1,867	8.53
Portuguese (17)	42	0.19
Romanian (26)	104	0.48
Russian (20)	103	0.47
Scotch-Irish (169)	469	2.14
Scottish (262)	775	3.54
Serbian (15)	46	0.21
Slavic (10)	79	0.36
Slovak (206)	1,021	4.67
Slovene (100)	431	1.97
Swedish (33)	231	1.06
Swiss (14)	131	0.60
Turkish (0)	15	0.07
Ukrainian (80)	224	1.02
Welsh (42)	321	1.47
Yugoslavian (0)	9	0.04

Hispanic Origin	Population	%
Hispanic or Latino (of any race)	544	2.41
Central American, ex. Mexican	24	0.11
Costa Rican	1	<0.01
Guatemalan	6	0.03
Honduran	12	0.05
Panamanian	4	0.02
Salvadoran	1	<0.01
Cuban	14	0.06
Dominican Republic	5	0.02
Mexican	231	1.02
Puerto Rican	208	0.92
South American	43	0.19
Argentinean	5	0.02
Chilean	5	0.02
Colombian	12	0.05
Ecuadorian	6	0.03
Paraguayan	2	0.01
Peruvian	7	0.03
Venezuelan	6	0.03
Other Hispanic or Latino	19	0.08

Race*	Population	%
African-American/Black (248)	327	1.45
Not Hispanic (234)	299	1.32
Hispanic (14)	28	0.12
American Indian/Alaska Native (27)	116	0.51
Not Hispanic (23)	94	0.42
Hispanic (4)	22	0.10
Apache (0)	1	<0.01
Blackfeet (1)	7	0.03
Canadian/French Am. Ind. (2)	4	0.02
Central American Ind. (1)	1	<0.01
Cherokee (5)	35	0.15
Chippewa (0)	1	<0.01
Choctaw (0)	2	0.01
Iroquois (4)	10	0.04
Lumbee (1)	1	<0.01
Mexican American Ind. (1)	1	<0.01
Osage (0)	3	0.01
Paiute (1)	1	<0.01
Sioux (1)	7	0.03
Tlingit-Haida *(Alaska Native)* (1)	1	<0.01
Asian (283)	401	1.78
Not Hispanic (283)	398	1.76
Hispanic (0)	3	0.01
Burmese (0)	5	0.02
Chinese, ex. Taiwanese (65)	79	0.35
Filipino (34)	59	0.26
Indian (110)	144	0.64
Indonesian (2)	2	0.01
Japanese (14)	26	0.12
Korean (30)	49	0.22
Malaysian (1)	1	<0.01
Pakistani (8)	9	0.04
Taiwanese (2)	3	0.01
Thai (3)	6	0.03
Vietnamese (9)	15	0.07
Hawaii Native/Pacific Islander (6)	10	0.04
Not Hispanic (6)	9	0.04
Hispanic (0)	1	<0.01
Native Hawaiian (0)	2	0.01
Samoan (2)	3	0.01
White (21,620)	21,907	97.02
Not Hispanic (21,234)	21,468	95.07
Hispanic (386)	439	1.94

Avon

Place Type: City
County: Lorain
Population: 21,193†

Ancestry‡	Population	%
African, Sub-Saharan (0)	16	0.08
Ethiopian (0)	4	0.02
South African (0)	12	0.06
American (443)	443	2.27
Arab (76)	144	0.74
Arab (29)	42	0.22
Lebanese (40)	69	0.35
Palestinian (7)	20	0.10
Syrian (0)	13	0.07
Austrian (57)	137	0.70
British (97)	97	0.50
Bulgarian (43)	84	0.43
Canadian (0)	27	0.14
Croatian (0)	82	0.42
Czech (35)	284	1.46
Czechoslovakian (44)	134	0.69
Danish (12)	42	0.22
Dutch (103)	242	1.24
Eastern European (13)	13	0.07
English (355)	1,927	9.87
European (294)	313	1.60
Finnish (49)	158	0.81
French, ex. Basque (80)	641	3.28
French Canadian (26)	66	0.34
German (1,747)	6,840	35.05
Greek (208)	360	1.84
Hungarian (262)	984	5.04
Irish (992)	4,479	22.95
Italian (742)	2,706	13.87
Lithuanian (0)	21	0.11
Macedonian (13)	13	0.07
Northern European (13)	13	0.07
Norwegian (47)	150	0.77
Pennsylvania German (13)	24	0.12
Polish (451)	2,083	10.67
Romanian (78)	97	0.50
Russian (58)	203	1.04
Scandinavian (9)	9	0.05
Scotch-Irish (109)	399	2.04
Scottish (57)	332	1.70
Serbian (133)	166	0.85
Slavic (0)	12	0.06
Slovak (306)	1,282	6.57
Slovene (68)	311	1.59
Swedish (53)	204	1.05
Swiss (0)	52	0.27
Ukrainian (0)	178	0.91

*Notes: † The Census 2010 population figure is used to calculate the percentages in the Hispanic Origin and Race categories. Ancestry percentages are based on the 2006-2010 American Community Survey population (not shown); ‡ Numbers in parentheses indicate the number of people reporting a single ancestry; * Numbers in parentheses indicate the number of persons reporting this race alone, not in combination with any other race; Please refer to the Explanation of Data for more information.*

Ancestry	Population	%
Welsh (46)	340	1.74
Yugoslavian (0)	9	0.05

Hispanic Origin	Population	%
Hispanic or Latino (of any race)	711	3.35
Central American, ex. Mexican	22	0.10
Guatemalan	6	0.03
Honduran	3	0.01
Nicaraguan	3	0.01
Panamanian	5	0.02
Salvadoran	5	0.02
Cuban	13	0.06
Dominican Republic	9	0.04
Mexican	169	0.80
Puerto Rican	403	1.90
South American	68	0.32
Argentinean	6	0.03
Chilean	8	0.04
Colombian	31	0.15
Peruvian	15	0.07
Uruguayan	1	<0.01
Venezuelan	7	0.03
Other Hispanic or Latino	27	0.13

Race*	Population	%
African-American/Black (480)	572	2.70
Not Hispanic (446)	528	2.49
Hispanic (34)	44	0.21
American Indian/Alaska Native (30)	93	0.44
Not Hispanic (22)	76	0.36
Hispanic (8)	17	0.08
Apache (1)	1	<0.01
Blackfeet (1)	5	0.02
Cherokee (2)	7	0.03
Chippewa (3)	3	0.01
Creek (0)	1	<0.01
Iroquois (0)	5	0.02
Kiowa (0)	1	<0.01
Lumbee (1)	2	0.01
Mexican American Ind. (2)	2	0.01
Pueblo (1)	3	0.01
Shoshone (3)	3	0.01
Sioux (2)	4	0.02
South American Ind. (1)	6	0.03
Asian (648)	776	3.66
Not Hispanic (646)	769	3.63
Hispanic (2)	7	0.03
Cambodian (8)	9	0.04
Chinese, ex. Taiwanese (94)	104	0.49
Filipino (69)	105	0.50
Indian (304)	326	1.54
Indonesian (6)	11	0.05
Japanese (47)	67	0.32
Korean (46)	56	0.26
Pakistani (23)	23	0.11
Sri Lankan (4)	4	0.02
Taiwanese (3)	5	0.02
Thai (1)	1	<0.01
Vietnamese (38)	42	0.20
Hawaii Native/Pacific Islander (5)	23	0.11
Not Hispanic (4)	13	0.06
Hispanic (1)	10	0.05
Guamanian/Chamorro (0)	1	<0.01
Native Hawaiian (4)	6	0.03
Tongan (0)	3	0.01
White (19,589)	19,847	93.65
Not Hispanic (19,072)	19,300	91.07
Hispanic (517)	547	2.58

Barberton

Place Type: City
County: Summit
Population: 26,550†

Ancestry‡	Population	%
African, Sub-Saharan (10)	10	0.04
African (10)	10	0.04
American (2,035)	2,035	7.58
Arab (112)	197	0.73
Egyptian (34)	34	0.13
Iraqi (14)	14	0.05
Jordanian (11)	57	0.21
Lebanese (53)	82	0.31
Syrian (0)	10	0.04
Austrian (10)	37	0.14
Belgian (0)	9	0.03
British (60)	132	0.49
Croatian (109)	364	1.36
Czech (31)	146	0.54
Czechoslovakian (65)	80	0.30
Danish (0)	12	0.04
Dutch (74)	487	1.81
Eastern European (18)	18	0.07
English (757)	2,533	9.44
European (86)	86	0.32
Finnish (0)	37	0.14
French, ex. Basque (46)	443	1.65
French Canadian (22)	105	0.39
German (2,100)	6,445	24.01
Greek (70)	107	0.40
Hungarian (572)	1,283	4.78
Irish (1,090)	4,217	15.71
Italian (726)	1,660	6.18
Lithuanian (137)	137	0.51
Macedonian (22)	43	0.16
Norwegian (20)	42	0.16
Pennsylvania German (56)	110	0.41
Polish (212)	859	3.20
Portuguese (0)	24	0.09
Romanian (32)	77	0.29
Russian (42)	98	0.37
Scotch-Irish (82)	474	1.77
Scottish (105)	689	2.57
Serbian (237)	358	1.33
Slavic (33)	50	0.19
Slovak (374)	759	2.83
Slovene (151)	332	1.24
Swedish (0)	89	0.33
Swiss (86)	336	1.25
Ukrainian (12)	61	0.23
Welsh (77)	340	1.27
Yugoslavian (117)	178	0.66

Hispanic Origin	Population	%
Hispanic or Latino (of any race)	359	1.35
Central American, ex. Mexican	15	0.06
Guatemalan	1	<0.01
Honduran	10	0.04
Nicaraguan	1	<0.01
Salvadoran	3	0.01
Cuban	6	0.02
Dominican Republic	2	0.01
Mexican	217	0.82
Puerto Rican	62	0.23
South American	18	0.07
Argentinean	1	<0.01
Chilean	2	0.01
Colombian	9	0.03
Ecuadorian	2	0.01
Peruvian	4	0.02
Other Hispanic or Latino	39	0.15

Race*	Population	%
African-American/Black (1,555)	1,931	7.27
Not Hispanic (1,542)	1,903	7.17
Hispanic (13)	28	0.11
American Indian/Alaska Native (85)	256	0.96
Not Hispanic (84)	238	0.90
Hispanic (1)	18	0.07
Apache (2)	6	0.02
Blackfeet (0)	13	0.05
Cherokee (16)	100	0.38
Cheyenne (1)	1	<0.01
Chickasaw (1)	3	0.01
Chippewa (2)	4	0.02
Choctaw (4)	5	0.02
Comanche (0)	1	<0.01
Delaware (0)	1	<0.01
Inupiat *(Alaska Native)* (0)	1	<0.01
Iroquois (6)	6	0.02
Mexican American Ind. (4)	7	0.03
Navajo (2)	2	0.01
Sioux (0)	2	0.01
Spanish American Ind. (0)	1	<0.01
Yaqui (1)	3	0.01
Asian (77)	140	0.53
Not Hispanic (77)	130	0.49
Hispanic (0)	10	0.04
Chinese, ex. Taiwanese (17)	35	0.13
Filipino (19)	28	0.11
Indian (22)	31	0.12
Indonesian (3)	3	0.01
Japanese (6)	12	0.05
Korean (4)	12	0.05
Laotian (0)	4	0.02
Pakistani (1)	1	<0.01
Thai (3)	14	0.05
Hawaii Native/Pacific Islander (13)	22	0.08
Not Hispanic (10)	18	0.07
Hispanic (3)	4	0.02
Guamanian/Chamorro (1)	5	0.02
Native Hawaiian (6)	11	0.04
White (24,113)	24,687	92.98
Not Hispanic (23,916)	24,442	92.06
Hispanic (197)	245	0.92

Bay Village

Place Type: City
County: Cuyahoga
Population: 15,651†

Ancestry‡	Population	%
Albanian (99)	99	0.63
American (413)	413	2.64
Arab (113)	225	1.44
Arab (36)	36	0.23
Egyptian (54)	54	0.35
Lebanese (23)	88	0.56
Syrian (0)	47	0.30
Armenian (0)	10	0.06
Austrian (16)	125	0.80
Brazilian (0)	9	0.06
British (71)	108	0.69
Bulgarian (19)	19	0.12
Canadian (8)	86	0.55
Croatian (38)	125	0.80
Czech (72)	209	1.34
Czechoslovakian (0)	21	0.13
Danish (20)	37	0.24
Dutch (53)	359	2.29
Eastern European (68)	68	0.43
English (348)	2,683	17.15
European (142)	142	0.91
Finnish (0)	58	0.37
French, ex. Basque (41)	463	2.96
French Canadian (24)	43	0.27
German (1,041)	4,973	31.78
Greek (21)	176	1.12
Hungarian (138)	723	4.62
Irish (1,202)	4,458	28.49
Italian (583)	1,944	12.42
Lithuanian (39)	118	0.75
Northern European (38)	38	0.24
Norwegian (20)	72	0.46
Pennsylvania German (0)	10	0.06
Polish (465)	1,304	8.33
Portuguese (0)	33	0.21
Romanian (34)	45	0.29
Russian (50)	132	0.84
Scandinavian (0)	10	0.06
Scotch-Irish (210)	525	3.36
Scottish (153)	692	4.42
Serbian (0)	49	0.31
Slavic (14)	31	0.20
Slovak (336)	706	4.51
Slovene (44)	201	1.28
Swedish (116)	455	2.91
Swiss (7)	121	0.77

*Notes: † The Census 2010 population figure is used to calculate the percentages in the Hispanic Origin and Race categories. Ancestry percentages are based on the 2006-2010 American Community Survey population (not shown); ‡ Numbers in parentheses indicate the number of people reporting a single ancestry; * Numbers in parentheses indicate the number of persons reporting this race alone, not in combination with any other race; Please refer to the Explanation of Data for more information.*

Ukrainian (46)	164	1.05
Welsh (9)	158	1.01
West Indian, ex. Hispanic (12)	12	0.08
Belizean (12)	12	0.08
Yugoslavian (0)	24	0.15

Hispanic Origin	Population	%
Hispanic or Latino (of any race)	251	1.60
Central American, ex. Mexican	24	0.15
Costa Rican	1	0.01
Guatemalan	6	0.04
Honduran	1	0.01
Panamanian	7	0.04
Salvadoran	9	0.06
Cuban	8	0.05
Dominican Republic	1	0.01
Mexican	63	0.40
Puerto Rican	83	0.53
South American	30	0.19
Argentinean	6	0.04
Bolivian	1	0.01
Chilean	5	0.03
Colombian	5	0.03
Ecuadorian	3	0.02
Paraguayan	1	0.01
Peruvian	5	0.03
Uruguayan	1	0.01
Venezuelan	3	0.02
Other Hispanic or Latino	42	0.27

Race*	Population	%
African-American/Black (85)	140	0.89
Not Hispanic (85)	138	0.88
Hispanic (0)	2	0.01
American Indian/Alaska Native (16)	53	0.34
Not Hispanic (14)	50	0.32
Hispanic (2)	3	0.02
Blackfeet (0)	4	0.03
Cherokee (5)	13	0.08
Chippewa (1)	3	0.02
Choctaw (0)	1	0.01
Comanche (0)	2	0.01
Creek (0)	1	0.01
Lumbee (3)	4	0.03
Mexican American Ind. (1)	1	0.01
Navajo (1)	5	0.03
Potawatomi (0)	1	0.01
Pueblo (0)	1	0.01
Asian (145)	218	1.39
Not Hispanic (145)	213	1.36
Hispanic (0)	5	0.03
Bangladeshi (1)	2	0.01
Chinese, ex. Taiwanese (57)	65	0.42
Filipino (18)	38	0.24
Indian (19)	27	0.17
Indonesian (1)	1	0.01
Japanese (7)	20	0.13
Korean (32)	50	0.32
Pakistani (4)	4	0.03
Taiwanese (1)	1	0.01
Thai (2)	2	0.01
Vietnamese (2)	2	0.01
Hawaii Native/Pacific Islander (4)	8	0.05
Not Hispanic (4)	7	0.04
Hispanic (0)	1	0.01
Guamanian/Chamorro (3)	3	0.02
Native Hawaiian (0)	1	0.01
White (15,177)	15,344	98.04
Not Hispanic (14,973)	15,125	96.64
Hispanic (204)	219	1.40

Beachwood

Place Type: City
County: Cuyahoga
Population: 11,953†

Ancestry‡	Population	%
African, Sub-Saharan (147)	147	1.23
African (56)	56	0.47
Kenyan (12)	12	0.10
South African (79)	79	0.66
American (726)	726	6.08
Arab (11)	36	0.30
Arab (11)	11	0.09
Lebanese (0)	18	0.15
Other Arab (0)	7	0.06
Austrian (6)	100	0.84
Belgian (36)	48	0.40
Canadian (15)	22	0.18
Croatian (9)	9	0.08
Czech (29)	177	1.48
Czechoslovakian (7)	16	0.13
Dutch (0)	61	0.51
Eastern European (546)	546	4.58
English (78)	412	3.45
European (229)	229	1.92
Finnish (0)	9	0.08
French, ex. Basque (11)	62	0.52
German (360)	1,263	10.58
Greek (27)	35	0.29
Hungarian (328)	733	6.14
Iranian (37)	37	0.31
Irish (202)	711	5.96
Israeli (31)	31	0.26
Italian (133)	327	2.74
Latvian (17)	17	0.14
Lithuanian (263)	299	2.51
Polish (607)	1,360	11.40
Portuguese (8)	8	0.07
Romanian (47)	124	1.04
Russian (1,123)	1,926	16.14
Scotch-Irish (58)	209	1.75
Scottish (7)	28	0.23
Serbian (40)	51	0.43
Slavic (9)	18	0.15
Slovak (62)	96	0.80
Slovene (12)	97	0.81
Swedish (33)	42	0.35
Swiss (8)	41	0.34
Turkish (24)	60	0.50
Ukrainian (84)	117	0.98
Welsh (0)	73	0.61
West Indian, ex. Hispanic (41)	41	0.34
Jamaican (41)	41	0.34
Yugoslavian (0)	11	0.09

Hispanic Origin	Population	%
Hispanic or Latino (of any race)	229	1.92
Central American, ex. Mexican	16	0.13
Guatemalan	3	0.03
Honduran	2	0.02
Panamanian	4	0.03
Salvadoran	7	0.06
Cuban	11	0.09
Dominican Republic	5	0.04
Mexican	63	0.53
Puerto Rican	25	0.21
South American	79	0.66
Argentinean	13	0.11
Bolivian	1	0.01
Chilean	7	0.06
Colombian	30	0.25
Peruvian	6	0.05
Venezuelan	22	0.18
Other Hispanic or Latino	30	0.25

Race*	Population	%
African-American/Black (1,635)	1,718	14.37
Not Hispanic (1,614)	1,690	14.14
Hispanic (21)	28	0.23
American Indian/Alaska Native (5)	30	0.25
Not Hispanic (5)	29	0.24
Hispanic (0)	1	0.01
Cherokee (0)	7	0.06
Cheyenne (0)	1	0.01
Choctaw (0)	2	0.02
Navajo (1)	1	0.01
Sioux (0)	2	0.02
Asian (886)	939	7.86
Not Hispanic (885)	937	7.84
Hispanic (1)	2	0.02
Bangladeshi (2)	2	0.02
Chinese, ex. Taiwanese (292)	303	2.53
Filipino (34)	39	0.33
Indian (305)	318	2.66
Indonesian (2)	6	0.05
Japanese (91)	92	0.77
Korean (105)	110	0.92
Nepalese (7)	7	0.06
Pakistani (5)	5	0.04
Sri Lankan (2)	3	0.03
Taiwanese (12)	12	0.10
Thai (10)	11	0.09
Vietnamese (5)	8	0.07
Hawaii Native/Pacific Islander (2)	9	0.08
Not Hispanic (1)	8	0.07
Hispanic (1)	1	0.01
Guamanian/Chamorro (1)	1	0.01
Marshallese (1)	1	0.01
Native Hawaiian (0)	1	0.01
White (9,237)	9,339	78.13
Not Hispanic (9,065)	9,161	76.64
Hispanic (172)	178	1.49

Beavercreek

Place Type: City
County: Greene
Population: 45,193†

Ancestry‡	Population	%
African, Sub-Saharan (12)	12	0.03
Kenyan (12)	12	0.03
American (5,517)	5,517	12.52
Arab (221)	309	0.70
Arab (10)	10	0.02
Egyptian (24)	24	0.05
Lebanese (95)	129	0.29
Palestinian (9)	9	0.02
Syrian (0)	16	0.04
Other Arab (83)	121	0.27
Armenian (11)	11	0.02
Australian (28)	36	0.08
Austrian (0)	82	0.19
Belgian (13)	24	0.05
British (217)	314	0.71
Cajun (15)	29	0.07
Canadian (77)	139	0.32
Celtic (9)	18	0.04
Croatian (11)	21	0.05
Czech (90)	315	0.71
Czechoslovakian (21)	88	0.20
Danish (60)	136	0.31
Dutch (106)	756	1.72
Eastern European (76)	90	0.20
English (1,962)	5,308	12.05
European (530)	544	1.23
Finnish (31)	42	0.10
French, ex. Basque (310)	1,789	4.06
French Canadian (78)	182	0.41
German (5,537)	14,048	31.88
Greek (167)	224	0.51
Hungarian (94)	458	1.04
Iranian (6)	28	0.06
Irish (1,548)	6,606	14.99
Israeli (10)	50	0.11
Italian (714)	2,114	4.80
Latvian (15)	15	0.03
Lithuanian (16)	99	0.22
Maltese (11)	11	0.02
Northern European (65)	79	0.18
Norwegian (126)	349	0.79
Pennsylvania German (27)	27	0.06
Polish (441)	1,417	3.22
Portuguese (84)	84	0.19
Romanian (0)	20	0.05
Russian (20)	141	0.32
Scandinavian (45)	156	0.35
Scotch-Irish (409)	1,136	2.58

*Notes: † The Census 2010 population figure is used to calculate the percentages in the Hispanic Origin and Race categories. Ancestry percentages are based on the 2006-2010 American Community Survey population (not shown); ‡ Numbers in parentheses indicate the number of people reporting a single ancestry; * Numbers in parentheses indicate the number of persons reporting this race alone, not in combination with any other race; Please refer to the Explanation of Data for more information.*

Scottish (486)	1,229	2.79
Slavic (0)	12	0.03
Slovak (42)	132	0.30
Slovene (0)	34	0.08
Swedish (91)	500	1.13
Swiss (29)	274	0.62
Ukrainian (32)	107	0.24
Welsh (112)	546	1.24
Yugoslavian (24)	37	0.08

Hispanic Origin	Population	%
Hispanic or Latino (of any race)	1,184	2.62
Central American, ex. Mexican	96	0.21
Costa Rican	1	<0.01
Guatemalan	27	0.06
Honduran	13	0.03
Nicaraguan	17	0.04
Panamanian	30	0.07
Salvadoran	2	<0.01
Other Central American	6	0.01
Cuban	59	0.13
Dominican Republic	8	0.02
Mexican	547	1.21
Puerto Rican	187	0.41
South American	132	0.29
Argentinean	24	0.05
Bolivian	13	0.03
Chilean	9	0.02
Colombian	53	0.12
Ecuadorian	13	0.03
Paraguayan	1	<0.01
Peruvian	16	0.04
Uruguayan	1	<0.01
Venezuelan	1	<0.01
Other South American	1	<0.01
Other Hispanic or Latino	155	0.34

Race*	Population	%
African-American/Black (1,124)	1,414	3.13
Not Hispanic (1,104)	1,374	3.04
Hispanic (20)	40	0.09
American Indian/Alaska Native (101)	355	0.79
Not Hispanic (87)	321	0.71
Hispanic (14)	34	0.08
Apache (3)	4	0.01
Blackfeet (0)	3	0.01
Cherokee (32)	118	0.26
Chickasaw (0)	1	<0.01
Chippewa (4)	10	0.02
Choctaw (4)	9	0.02
Comanche (0)	1	<0.01
Creek (0)	6	0.01
Crow (0)	1	<0.01
Hopi (1)	1	<0.01
Iroquois (1)	9	0.02
Lumbee (0)	1	<0.01
Mexican American Ind. (9)	10	0.02
Osage (0)	3	0.01
Paiute (0)	3	0.01
Potawatomi (1)	1	<0.01
Seminole (0)	1	<0.01
Sioux (1)	14	0.03
Yup'ik *(Alaska Native)* (1)	1	<0.01
Asian (2,671)	3,170	7.01
Not Hispanic (2,653)	3,130	6.93
Hispanic (18)	40	0.09
Bangladeshi (3)	3	0.01
Burmese (4)	4	0.01
Cambodian (13)	15	0.03
Chinese, ex. Taiwanese (472)	528	1.17
Filipino (231)	347	0.77
Indian (1,056)	1,127	2.49
Indonesian (6)	8	0.02
Japanese (128)	214	0.47
Korean (321)	410	0.91
Laotian (2)	2	<0.01
Malaysian (5)	8	0.02
Nepalese (4)	5	0.01
Pakistani (110)	113	0.25
Sri Lankan (12)	16	0.04
Taiwanese (47)	52	0.12
Thai (22)	42	0.09
Vietnamese (153)	188	0.42
Hawaii Native/Pacific Islander (21)	69	0.15
Not Hispanic (17)	62	0.14
Hispanic (4)	7	0.02
Fijian (0)	1	<0.01
Guamanian/Chamorro (3)	8	0.02
Native Hawaiian (12)	29	0.06
Samoan (3)	7	0.02
White (40,018)	40,947	90.60
Not Hispanic (39,143)	40,006	88.52
Hispanic (875)	941	2.08

Beckett Ridge

Place Type: CDP
County: Butler
Population: 9,187†

Ancestry‡	Population	%
African, Sub-Saharan (30)	30	0.34
African (30)	30	0.34
American (569)	569	6.39
Armenian (19)	19	0.21
Austrian (0)	11	0.12
British (63)	101	1.13
Bulgarian (32)	43	0.48
Czech (31)	120	1.35
Danish (0)	12	0.13
Dutch (31)	159	1.78
Eastern European (20)	20	0.22
English (283)	911	10.22
European (196)	196	2.20
Finnish (28)	28	0.31
French, ex. Basque (95)	323	3.62
German (1,003)	2,967	33.30
Greek (14)	14	0.16
Hungarian (0)	33	0.37
Irish (332)	1,553	17.43
Italian (205)	551	6.18
Norwegian (0)	165	1.85
Pennsylvania German (16)	16	0.18
Polish (91)	376	4.22
Portuguese (0)	31	0.35
Russian (57)	94	1.05
Scandinavian (0)	15	0.17
Scotch-Irish (37)	189	2.12
Scottish (17)	116	1.30
Slovak (0)	41	0.46
Slovene (0)	32	0.36
Swedish (49)	111	1.25
Welsh (12)	87	0.98
West Indian, ex. Hispanic (10)	10	0.11
Jamaican (10)	10	0.11

Hispanic Origin	Population	%
Hispanic or Latino (of any race)	274	2.98
Central American, ex. Mexican	26	0.28
Costa Rican	1	0.01
Guatemalan	19	0.21
Nicaraguan	3	0.03
Panamanian	1	0.01
Salvadoran	1	0.01
Other Central American	1	0.01
Cuban	25	0.27
Dominican Republic	8	0.09
Mexican	103	1.12
Puerto Rican	21	0.23
South American	57	0.62
Argentinean	3	0.03
Bolivian	1	0.01
Colombian	26	0.28
Ecuadorian	3	0.03
Peruvian	16	0.17
Venezuelan	8	0.09
Other Hispanic or Latino	34	0.37

Race*	Population	%
African-American/Black (802)	864	9.40
Not Hispanic (800)	859	9.35
Hispanic (2)	5	0.05
American Indian/Alaska Native (16)	45	0.49
Not Hispanic (12)	34	0.37
Hispanic (4)	11	0.12
Blackfeet (0)	2	0.02
Central American Ind. (1)	1	0.01
Cherokee (2)	12	0.13
Choctaw (1)	1	0.01
Creek (0)	2	0.02
Iroquois (1)	3	0.03
Mexican American Ind. (3)	3	0.03
Seminole (2)	2	0.02
Sioux (0)	1	0.01
Asian (609)	682	7.42
Not Hispanic (601)	672	7.31
Hispanic (8)	10	0.11
Bangladeshi (4)	4	0.04
Cambodian (5)	5	0.05
Chinese, ex. Taiwanese (67)	81	0.88
Filipino (20)	38	0.41
Indian (287)	303	3.30
Japanese (49)	60	0.65
Korean (59)	66	0.72
Malaysian (2)	2	0.02
Pakistani (9)	10	0.11
Taiwanese (7)	11	0.12
Thai (3)	5	0.05
Vietnamese (85)	92	1.00
Hawaii Native/Pacific Islander (7)	11	0.12
Not Hispanic (7)	11	0.12
Fijian (1)	1	0.01
Guamanian/Chamorro (1)	1	0.01
Native Hawaiian (1)	4	0.04
Samoan (0)	1	0.01
White (7,522)	7,661	83.39
Not Hispanic (7,342)	7,462	81.22
Hispanic (180)	199	2.17

Bedford Heights

Place Type: City
County: Cuyahoga
Population: 10,751†

Ancestry‡	Population	%
African, Sub-Saharan (222)	294	2.72
African (217)	248	2.30
Nigerian (5)	5	0.05
Senegalese (0)	22	0.20
Other Sub-Saharan African (0)	19	0.18
American (63)	63	0.58
Arab (2)	2	0.02
Lebanese (2)	2	0.02
Austrian (14)	14	0.13
Croatian (17)	17	0.16
Czech (22)	55	0.51
Dutch (0)	17	0.16
Eastern European (39)	39	0.36
English (37)	158	1.46
European (7)	7	0.06
French, ex. Basque (11)	20	0.19
German (171)	418	3.87
Greek (0)	47	0.44
Hungarian (36)	150	1.39
Irish (89)	233	2.16
Italian (367)	504	4.67
Lithuanian (11)	20	0.19
Norwegian (0)	9	0.08
Polish (107)	210	1.95
Russian (5)	23	0.21
Scotch-Irish (27)	27	0.25
Scottish (23)	25	0.23
Slavic (0)	11	0.10
Slovak (0)	31	0.29
Slovene (16)	45	0.42
Swedish (0)	9	0.08
Turkish (0)	47	0.44
Welsh (11)	23	0.21
West Indian, ex. Hispanic (135)	249	2.31

*Notes: † The Census 2010 population figure is used to calculate the percentages in the Hispanic Origin and Race categories. Ancestry percentages are based on the 2006-2010 American Community Survey population (not shown); ‡ Numbers in parentheses indicate the number of people reporting a single ancestry; * Numbers in parentheses indicate the number of persons reporting this race alone, not in combination with any other race; Please refer to the Explanation of Data for more information.*

Belizean (8)	8	0.07
British West Indian (34)	34	0.31
Jamaican (85)	155	1.44
West Indian (8)	52	0.48

Hispanic Origin	Population	%
Hispanic or Latino (of any race)	282	2.62
Central American, ex. Mexican	34	0.32
Costa Rican	3	0.03
Guatemalan	1	0.01
Honduran	6	0.06
Nicaraguan	4	0.04
Panamanian	8	0.07
Salvadoran	12	0.11
Cuban	7	0.07
Dominican Republic	9	0.08
Mexican	113	1.05
Puerto Rican	61	0.57
South American	38	0.35
Argentinean	7	0.07
Colombian	6	0.06
Peruvian	25	0.23
Other Hispanic or Latino	20	0.19

Race*	Population	%
African-American/Black (8,263)	8,458	78.67
Not Hispanic (8,207)	8,383	77.97
Hispanic (56)	75	0.70
American Indian/Alaska Native (11)	70	0.65
Not Hispanic (10)	64	0.60
Hispanic (1)	6	0.06
Blackfeet (0)	7	0.07
Cherokee (0)	17	0.16
Cheyenne (0)	1	0.01
Choctaw (0)	1	0.01
Creek (1)	1	0.01
Menominee (0)	1	0.01
Mexican American Ind. (1)	1	0.01
Ottawa (0)	4	0.04
Yuman (1)	1	0.01
Asian (124)	152	1.41
Not Hispanic (123)	148	1.38
Hispanic (1)	4	0.04
Burmese (0)	3	0.03
Chinese, ex. Taiwanese (16)	22	0.20
Filipino (36)	45	0.42
Indian (46)	57	0.53
Japanese (3)	4	0.04
Korean (5)	6	0.06
Malaysian (1)	1	0.01
Pakistani (4)	4	0.04
Thai (1)	1	0.01
Vietnamese (2)	8	0.07
Hawaii Native/Pacific Islander (0)	6	0.06
Not Hispanic (0)	6	0.06
Native Hawaiian (0)	2	0.02
Samoan (0)	1	0.01
White (2,009)	2,160	20.09
Not Hispanic (1,916)	2,050	19.07
Hispanic (93)	110	1.02

Bedford

Place Type: City
County: Cuyahoga
Population: 13,074†

Ancestry‡	Population	%
African, Sub-Saharan (0)	51	0.39
African (0)	51	0.39
American (256)	256	1.94
Arab (7)	7	0.05
Egyptian (7)	7	0.05
Armenian (0)	12	0.09
Austrian (0)	14	0.11
British (9)	19	0.14
Canadian (7)	19	0.14
Croatian (22)	111	0.84
Czech (207)	461	3.49
Czechoslovakian (29)	103	0.78
Dutch (7)	33	0.25
Eastern European (28)	28	0.21
English (177)	770	5.83
European (53)	53	0.40
French, ex. Basque (5)	190	1.44
German (364)	1,550	11.74
Greek (17)	36	0.27
Hungarian (299)	674	5.11
Irish (525)	1,443	10.93
Italian (532)	1,307	9.90
Lithuanian (0)	27	0.20
Pennsylvania German (0)	17	0.13
Polish (432)	1,034	7.83
Portuguese (36)	36	0.27
Romanian (37)	49	0.37
Russian (0)	139	1.05
Scotch-Irish (44)	179	1.36
Scottish (55)	185	1.40
Slavic (0)	30	0.23
Slovak (138)	337	2.55
Slovene (75)	127	0.96
Swedish (0)	11	0.08
Swiss (0)	9	0.07
Ukrainian (25)	25	0.19
Welsh (16)	47	0.36
West Indian, ex. Hispanic (10)	22	0.17
Jamaican (10)	22	0.17

Hispanic Origin	Population	%
Hispanic or Latino (of any race)	256	1.96
Central American, ex. Mexican	16	0.12
Costa Rican	1	0.01
Guatemalan	3	0.02
Honduran	4	0.03
Nicaraguan	1	0.01
Panamanian	6	0.05
Salvadoran	1	0.01
Cuban	24	0.18
Dominican Republic	16	0.12
Mexican	64	0.49
Puerto Rican	92	0.70
South American	16	0.12
Argentinean	2	0.02
Chilean	4	0.03
Colombian	2	0.02
Peruvian	5	0.04
Venezuelan	3	0.02
Other Hispanic or Latino	28	0.21

Race*	Population	%
African-American/Black (5,479)	5,740	43.90
Not Hispanic (5,417)	5,657	43.27
Hispanic (62)	83	0.63
American Indian/Alaska Native (24)	104	0.80
Not Hispanic (20)	92	0.70
Hispanic (4)	12	0.09
Blackfeet (2)	18	0.14
Cherokee (2)	17	0.13
Chickasaw (1)	1	0.01
Choctaw (2)	5	0.04
Cree (0)	1	0.01
Iroquois (0)	4	0.03
Mexican American Ind. (0)	2	0.02
Seminole (0)	2	0.02
Sioux (0)	3	0.02
South American Ind. (0)	1	0.01
Asian (115)	153	1.17
Not Hispanic (112)	148	1.13
Hispanic (3)	5	0.04
Bangladeshi (0)	3	0.02
Chinese, ex. Taiwanese (24)	36	0.28
Filipino (38)	50	0.38
Indian (41)	45	0.34
Japanese (2)	4	0.03
Korean (6)	9	0.07
Thai (2)	3	0.02
Vietnamese (1)	1	0.01
Hawaii Native/Pacific Islander (0)	6	0.05
Not Hispanic (0)	6	0.05
Native Hawaiian (0)	1	0.01
Samoan (0)	2	0.02
White (7,051)	7,303	55.86
Not Hispanic (6,963)	7,187	54.97
Hispanic (88)	116	0.89

Bellefontaine

Place Type: City
County: Logan
Population: 13,370†

Ancestry‡	Population	%
American (1,323)	1,323	10.08
Arab (72)	83	0.63
Jordanian (72)	83	0.63
Belgian (7)	7	0.05
British (33)	33	0.25
Canadian (0)	8	0.06
Dutch (40)	363	2.77
English (555)	1,172	8.93
European (39)	53	0.40
French, ex. Basque (53)	331	2.52
French Canadian (0)	8	0.06
German (1,996)	4,288	32.68
Hungarian (16)	33	0.25
Irish (507)	1,690	12.88
Italian (287)	736	5.61
Northern European (13)	13	0.10
Norwegian (14)	39	0.30
Polish (79)	262	2.00
Russian (41)	100	0.76
Scotch-Irish (71)	206	1.57
Scottish (41)	275	2.10
Swedish (35)	139	1.06
Swiss (13)	97	0.74
Ukrainian (24)	48	0.37
Welsh (12)	145	1.10

Hispanic Origin	Population	%
Hispanic or Latino (of any race)	248	1.85
Central American, ex. Mexican	18	0.13
Costa Rican	1	0.01
Guatemalan	1	0.01
Panamanian	1	0.01
Salvadoran	11	0.08
Other Central American	4	0.03
Cuban	3	0.02
Mexican	161	1.20
Puerto Rican	26	0.19
South American	2	0.01
Colombian	1	0.01
Ecuadorian	1	0.01
Other Hispanic or Latino	38	0.28

Race*	Population	%
African-American/Black (574)	934	6.99
Not Hispanic (565)	916	6.85
Hispanic (9)	18	0.13
American Indian/Alaska Native (33)	141	1.05
Not Hispanic (28)	131	0.98
Hispanic (5)	10	0.07
Aleut *(Alaska Native)* (1)	1	0.01
Apache (1)	3	0.02
Blackfeet (1)	3	0.02
Cherokee (5)	39	0.29
Cheyenne (1)	1	0.01
Chippewa (3)	7	0.05
Inupiat *(Alaska Native)* (1)	2	0.01
Iroquois (0)	2	0.01
Mexican American Ind. (1)	2	0.01
Navajo (1)	3	0.02
Seminole (2)	2	0.01
Sioux (2)	5	0.04
Asian (157)	207	1.55
Not Hispanic (156)	199	1.49
Hispanic (1)	8	0.06
Chinese, ex. Taiwanese (16)	21	0.16
Filipino (50)	67	0.50
Indian (18)	26	0.19
Indonesian (2)	2	0.01

*Notes: † The Census 2010 population figure is used to calculate the percentages in the Hispanic Origin and Race categories. Ancestry percentages are based on the 2006-2010 American Community Survey population (not shown); ‡ Numbers in parentheses indicate the number of people reporting a single ancestry; * Numbers in parentheses indicate the number of persons reporting this race alone, not in combination with any other race; Please refer to the Explanation of Data for more information.*

Japanese (52)	62	0.46
Korean (7)	16	0.12
Laotian (1)	2	0.01
Taiwanese (4)	4	0.03
Vietnamese (4)	5	0.04
Hawaii Native/Pacific Islander (1)	9	0.07
Not Hispanic (1)	7	0.05
Hispanic (0)	2	0.01
Guamanian/Chamorro (0)	2	0.01
Marshallese (1)	2	0.01
Native Hawaiian (0)	4	0.03
White (12,046)	12,508	93.55
Not Hispanic (11,902)	12,331	92.23
Hispanic (144)	177	1.32

Bellevue

Place Type: City
County: Sandusky
Population: 8,202†

Ancestry‡	Population	%
Alsatian (0)	7	0.08
American (706)	706	8.52
Australian (0)	29	0.35
Czech (0)	10	0.12
Czechoslovakian (0)	27	0.33
Dutch (11)	409	4.94
English (185)	809	9.77
European (7)	21	0.25
Finnish (8)	18	0.22
French, ex. Basque (31)	267	3.22
French Canadian (0)	60	0.72
German (1,465)	3,394	40.98
Greek (9)	26	0.31
Hungarian (34)	88	1.06
Irish (203)	1,601	19.33
Italian (198)	763	9.21
Lithuanian (0)	11	0.13
Norwegian (12)	105	1.27
Pennsylvania German (36)	50	0.60
Polish (55)	260	3.14
Portuguese (0)	8	0.10
Russian (0)	11	0.13
Scotch-Irish (28)	118	1.42
Scottish (102)	235	2.84
Slovak (10)	43	0.52
Swedish (32)	39	0.47
Swiss (0)	16	0.19
Welsh (21)	31	0.37

Hispanic Origin	Population	%
Hispanic or Latino (of any race)	260	3.17
Central American, ex. Mexican	7	0.09
Guatemalan	1	0.01
Nicaraguan	6	0.07
Cuban	3	0.04
Mexican	222	2.71
Puerto Rican	16	0.20
South American	2	0.02
Peruvian	2	0.02
Other Hispanic or Latino	10	0.12

Race*	Population	%
African-American/Black (47)	92	1.12
Not Hispanic (46)	89	1.09
Hispanic (1)	3	0.04
American Indian/Alaska Native (17)	79	0.96
Not Hispanic (16)	70	0.85
Hispanic (1)	9	0.11
Blackfeet (0)	12	0.15
Cherokee (5)	31	0.38
Chippewa (1)	2	0.02
Cree (0)	1	0.01
Iroquois (0)	5	0.06
Mexican American Ind. (1)	2	0.02
Ottawa (1)	1	0.01
Asian (20)	35	0.43
Not Hispanic (20)	33	0.40
Hispanic (0)	2	0.02
Chinese, ex. Taiwanese (4)	4	0.05
Filipino (8)	12	0.15
Japanese (3)	6	0.07
Korean (3)	5	0.06
Thai (1)	5	0.06
Vietnamese (1)	2	0.02
Hawaii Native/Pacific Islander (0)	9	0.11
Not Hispanic (0)	9	0.11
Native Hawaiian (0)	9	0.11
White (7,899)	8,059	98.26
Not Hispanic (7,737)	7,857	95.79
Hispanic (162)	202	2.46

Berea

Place Type: City
County: Cuyahoga
Population: 19,093†

Ancestry‡	Population	%
African, Sub-Saharan (224)	308	1.62
African (161)	245	1.29
Nigerian (63)	63	0.33
American (730)	730	3.85
Arab (45)	74	0.39
Lebanese (36)	65	0.34
Other Arab (9)	9	0.05
Armenian (0)	9	0.05
Australian (0)	8	0.04
Austrian (6)	48	0.25
Belgian (0)	11	0.06
British (36)	74	0.39
Canadian (19)	52	0.27
Croatian (12)	88	0.46
Czech (146)	613	3.23
Czechoslovakian (31)	38	0.20
Danish (16)	133	0.70
Dutch (21)	266	1.40
Eastern European (25)	25	0.13
English (317)	1,985	10.46
European (131)	171	0.90
Finnish (0)	14	0.07
French, ex. Basque (28)	274	1.44
French Canadian (26)	82	0.43
German (1,654)	6,486	34.17
Greek (11)	108	0.57
Hungarian (195)	782	4.12
Irish (942)	3,756	19.79
Italian (635)	1,876	9.88
Lithuanian (29)	110	0.58
Norwegian (24)	119	0.63
Pennsylvania German (0)	23	0.12
Polish (632)	1,904	10.03
Romanian (79)	165	0.87
Russian (87)	475	2.50
Scandinavian (15)	46	0.24
Scotch-Irish (94)	314	1.65
Scottish (143)	450	2.37
Slavic (0)	15	0.08
Slovak (286)	698	3.68
Slovene (58)	195	1.03
Swedish (13)	98	0.52
Swiss (0)	45	0.24
Turkish (10)	27	0.14
Ukrainian (54)	193	1.02
Welsh (29)	353	1.86
West Indian, ex. Hispanic (0)	29	0.15
Bermudan (0)	13	0.07
Trinidadian/Tobagonian (0)	16	0.08

Hispanic Origin	Population	%
Hispanic or Latino (of any race)	534	2.80
Central American, ex. Mexican	18	0.09
Costa Rican	1	0.01
Guatemalan	7	0.04
Honduran	1	0.01
Panamanian	5	0.03
Salvadoran	4	0.02
Cuban	14	0.07
Dominican Republic	9	0.05
Mexican	146	0.76
Puerto Rican	284	1.49
South American	23	0.12
Argentinean	4	0.02
Colombian	13	0.07
Ecuadorian	2	0.01
Peruvian	3	0.02
Venezuelan	1	0.01
Other Hispanic or Latino	40	0.21

Race*	Population	%
African-American/Black (1,260)	1,510	7.91
Not Hispanic (1,226)	1,452	7.60
Hispanic (34)	58	0.30
American Indian/Alaska Native (36)	148	0.78
Not Hispanic (32)	128	0.67
Hispanic (4)	20	0.10
Arapaho (1)	1	0.01
Blackfeet (1)	13	0.07
Cherokee (1)	41	0.21
Chippewa (1)	1	0.01
Creek (0)	1	0.01
Crow (1)	1	0.01
Inupiat *(Alaska Native)* (0)	1	0.01
Iroquois (0)	1	0.01
Navajo (1)	3	0.02
Osage (1)	1	0.01
Sioux (2)	9	0.05
South American Ind. (1)	1	0.01
Tlingit-Haida *(Alaska Native)* (3)	3	0.02
Yup'ik *(Alaska Native)* (0)	1	0.01
Asian (288)	379	1.99
Not Hispanic (288)	378	1.98
Hispanic (0)	1	0.01
Bangladeshi (8)	8	0.04
Cambodian (5)	9	0.05
Chinese, ex. Taiwanese (47)	64	0.34
Filipino (44)	54	0.28
Indian (69)	83	0.43
Indonesian (8)	9	0.05
Japanese (15)	36	0.19
Korean (15)	29	0.15
Pakistani (3)	5	0.03
Sri Lankan (0)	1	0.01
Thai (3)	4	0.02
Vietnamese (57)	67	0.35
Hawaii Native/Pacific Islander (3)	16	0.08
Not Hispanic (3)	11	0.06
Hispanic (0)	5	0.03
Guamanian/Chamorro (0)	2	0.01
Native Hawaiian (2)	4	0.02
Tongan (1)	1	0.01
White (16,953)	17,347	90.86
Not Hispanic (16,619)	16,963	88.84
Hispanic (334)	384	2.01

Bexley

Place Type: City
County: Franklin
Population: 13,057†

Ancestry‡	Population	%
African, Sub-Saharan (27)	42	0.32
African (27)	42	0.32
American (559)	559	4.29
Arab (38)	55	0.42
Lebanese (0)	8	0.06
Moroccan (38)	38	0.29
Syrian (0)	9	0.07
Austrian (29)	124	0.95
Brazilian (0)	36	0.28
British (10)	80	0.61
Canadian (12)	12	0.09
Czech (21)	62	0.48
Danish (0)	21	0.16
Dutch (61)	312	2.40
Eastern European (142)	151	1.16
English (434)	1,575	12.10
European (368)	368	2.83

*Notes: † The Census 2010 population figure is used to calculate the percentages in the Hispanic Origin and Race categories. Ancestry percentages are based on the 2006-2010 American Community Survey population (not shown); ‡ Numbers in parentheses indicate the number of people reporting a single ancestry; * Numbers in parentheses indicate the number of persons reporting this race alone, not in combination with any other race; Please refer to the Explanation of Data for more information.*

Finnish (34)	101	0.78
French, ex. Basque (103)	313	2.40
French Canadian (0)	25	0.19
German (1,219)	4,363	33.51
Greek (0)	29	0.22
Hungarian (127)	390	3.00
Irish (402)	1,892	14.53
Israeli (35)	35	0.27
Italian (352)	1,105	8.49
Lithuanian (9)	134	1.03
Norwegian (38)	216	1.66
Polish (224)	770	5.91
Romanian (78)	157	1.21
Russian (685)	1,210	9.29
Scotch-Irish (108)	528	4.06
Scottish (98)	277	2.13
Serbian (0)	9	0.07
Slavic (12)	34	0.26
Slovak (13)	69	0.53
Slovene (9)	9	0.07
Swedish (63)	253	1.94
Swiss (9)	100	0.77
Turkish (54)	54	0.41
Ukrainian (107)	162	1.24
Welsh (67)	257	1.97
Yugoslavian (10)	10	0.08

Hispanic Origin	Population	%
Hispanic or Latino (of any race)	234	1.79
Central American, ex. Mexican	16	0.12
Guatemalan	6	0.05
Honduran	1	0.01
Nicaraguan	3	0.02
Panamanian	3	0.02
Salvadoran	3	0.02
Cuban	21	0.16
Dominican Republic	2	0.02
Mexican	77	0.59
Puerto Rican	38	0.29
South American	48	0.37
Argentinean	9	0.07
Bolivian	7	0.05
Colombian	19	0.15
Ecuadorian	1	0.01
Paraguayan	2	0.02
Peruvian	2	0.02
Uruguayan	1	0.01
Venezuelan	7	0.05
Other Hispanic or Latino	32	0.25

Race*	Population	%
African-American/Black (771)	943	7.22
Not Hispanic (751)	913	6.99
Hispanic (20)	30	0.23
American Indian/Alaska Native (15)	84	0.64
Not Hispanic (15)	79	0.61
Hispanic (0)	5	0.04
Alaska Athabascan *(Ala. Nat.)* (1)	1	0.01
Blackfeet (2)	3	0.02
Cherokee (3)	19	0.15
Chippewa (1)	3	0.02
Choctaw (0)	1	0.01
Mexican American Ind. (0)	1	0.01
Seminole (0)	4	0.03
South American Ind. (0)	2	0.02
Yuman (0)	1	0.01
Asian (195)	302	2.31
Not Hispanic (193)	297	2.27
Hispanic (2)	5	0.04
Chinese, ex. Taiwanese (67)	95	0.73
Filipino (14)	26	0.20
Indian (33)	44	0.34
Indonesian (1)	1	0.01
Japanese (12)	34	0.26
Korean (24)	44	0.34
Laotian (8)	8	0.06
Malaysian (1)	4	0.03
Pakistani (14)	14	0.11
Taiwanese (0)	2	0.02
Thai (1)	2	0.02
Vietnamese (13)	17	0.13
Hawaii Native/Pacific Islander (2)	14	0.11
Not Hispanic (2)	14	0.11
Marshallese (0)	1	0.01
Native Hawaiian (1)	7	0.05
Samoan (1)	4	0.03
White (11,705)	12,000	91.90
Not Hispanic (11,547)	11,821	90.53
Hispanic (158)	179	1.37

Blacklick Estates

Place Type: CDP
County: Franklin
Population: 8,682†

Ancestry‡	Population	%
African, Sub-Saharan (44)	44	0.51
Nigerian (44)	44	0.51
American (879)	879	10.10
Arab (9)	18	0.21
Lebanese (9)	18	0.21
Belgian (0)	7	0.08
British (44)	60	0.69
Czech (7)	7	0.08
Danish (9)	16	0.18
Dutch (42)	273	3.14
English (437)	858	9.86
European (58)	58	0.67
French, ex. Basque (44)	128	1.47
German (748)	1,840	21.14
Greek (31)	108	1.24
Hungarian (0)	25	0.29
Irish (577)	1,571	18.05
Italian (225)	397	4.56
Lithuanian (9)	9	0.10
Northern European (14)	14	0.16
Pennsylvania German (0)	29	0.33
Polish (145)	300	3.45
Portuguese (7)	7	0.08
Russian (0)	9	0.10
Scotch-Irish (41)	70	0.80
Scottish (13)	47	0.54
Slovak (9)	9	0.10
Swedish (12)	27	0.31
Swiss (0)	6	0.07
Ukrainian (0)	10	0.11
Welsh (0)	71	0.82
West Indian, ex. Hispanic (25)	25	0.29
Trinidadian/Tobagonian (25)	25	0.29

Hispanic Origin	Population	%
Hispanic or Latino (of any race)	275	3.17
Central American, ex. Mexican	16	0.18
Costa Rican	2	0.02
Guatemalan	1	0.01
Honduran	5	0.06
Salvadoran	8	0.09
Cuban	5	0.06
Dominican Republic	18	0.21
Mexican	147	1.69
Puerto Rican	66	0.76
South American	16	0.18
Colombian	8	0.09
Peruvian	4	0.05
Venezuelan	4	0.05
Other Hispanic or Latino	7	0.08

Race*	Population	%
African-American/Black (1,705)	1,957	22.54
Not Hispanic (1,674)	1,914	22.05
Hispanic (31)	43	0.50
American Indian/Alaska Native (17)	97	1.12
Not Hispanic (16)	87	1.00
Hispanic (1)	10	0.12
Apache (1)	2	0.02
Blackfeet (1)	4	0.05
Cherokee (4)	26	0.30
Creek (1)	3	0.03
Iroquois (3)	6	0.07
Navajo (1)	1	0.01
Seminole (0)	3	0.03
Sioux (1)	1	0.01
Asian (116)	140	1.61
Not Hispanic (116)	138	1.59
Hispanic (0)	2	0.02
Cambodian (6)	8	0.09
Chinese, ex. Taiwanese (7)	12	0.14
Filipino (8)	18	0.21
Indian (7)	11	0.13
Indonesian (1)	2	0.02
Japanese (6)	7	0.08
Korean (10)	12	0.14
Laotian (40)	47	0.54
Taiwanese (0)	1	0.01
Thai (4)	8	0.09
Vietnamese (16)	20	0.23
Hawaii Native/Pacific Islander (13)	22	0.25
Not Hispanic (11)	20	0.23
Hispanic (2)	2	0.02
Guamanian/Chamorro (7)	12	0.14
Native Hawaiian (0)	1	0.01
Samoan (6)	9	0.10
White (6,381)	6,685	77.00
Not Hispanic (6,260)	6,546	75.40
Hispanic (121)	139	1.60

Blue Ash

Place Type: City
County: Hamilton
Population: 12,114†

Ancestry‡	Population	%
African, Sub-Saharan (183)	192	1.59
African (0)	9	0.07
Nigerian (11)	11	0.09
Zimbabwean (172)	172	1.43
Alsatian (9)	9	0.07
American (584)	584	4.84
Arab (0)	26	0.22
Lebanese (0)	26	0.22
Austrian (10)	18	0.15
Belgian (23)	57	0.47
British (70)	94	0.78
Canadian (10)	10	0.08
Czech (72)	215	1.78
Czechoslovakian (13)	13	0.11
Danish (13)	25	0.21
Dutch (16)	96	0.80
Eastern European (35)	35	0.29
English (398)	1,162	9.64
Estonian (0)	10	0.08
European (226)	226	1.87
Finnish (0)	9	0.07
French, ex. Basque (31)	252	2.09
French Canadian (27)	53	0.44
German (1,462)	3,467	28.75
Greek (46)	66	0.55
Hungarian (8)	45	0.37
Iranian (20)	20	0.17
Irish (533)	1,811	15.02
Israeli (50)	50	0.41
Italian (129)	424	3.52
Lithuanian (18)	40	0.33
Norwegian (0)	77	0.64
Polish (119)	340	2.82
Romanian (16)	24	0.20
Russian (259)	382	3.17
Scotch-Irish (88)	367	3.04
Scottish (72)	319	2.65
Slovak (13)	25	0.21
Slovene (13)	13	0.11
Swedish (0)	37	0.31
Swiss (21)	114	0.95
Ukrainian (42)	42	0.35
Welsh (18)	121	1.00

Hispanic Origin	Population	%
Hispanic or Latino (of any race)	308	2.54

*Notes: † The Census 2010 population figure is used to calculate the percentages in the Hispanic Origin and Race categories. Ancestry percentages are based on the 2006-2010 American Community Survey population (not shown); ‡ Numbers in parentheses indicate the number of people reporting a single ancestry; * Numbers in parentheses indicate the number of persons reporting this race alone, not in combination with any other race; Please refer to the Explanation of Data for more information.*

Central American, ex. Mexican	36	0.30
Costa Rican	2	0.02
Guatemalan	16	0.13
Honduran	9	0.07
Panamanian	2	0.02
Salvadoran	7	0.06
Cuban	10	0.08
Dominican Republic	1	0.01
Mexican	142	1.17
Puerto Rican	28	0.23
South American	60	0.50
Argentinean	16	0.13
Bolivian	2	0.02
Chilean	2	0.02
Colombian	11	0.09
Ecuadorian	4	0.03
Peruvian	19	0.16
Venezuelan	6	0.05
Other Hispanic or Latino	31	0.26

Race*	Population	%
African-American/Black (787)	891	7.36
Not Hispanic (784)	876	7.23
Hispanic (3)	15	0.12
American Indian/Alaska Native (20)	68	0.56
Not Hispanic (15)	58	0.48
Hispanic (5)	10	0.08
Blackfeet (2)	4	0.03
Central American Ind. (0)	1	0.01
Cherokee (2)	11	0.09
Creek (0)	1	0.01
Iroquois (1)	3	0.02
Mexican American Ind. (5)	5	0.04
Potawatomi (0)	1	0.01
South American Ind. (0)	1	0.01
Tlingit-Haida *(Alaska Native)* (1)	1	0.01
Asian (1,290)	1,406	11.61
Not Hispanic (1,286)	1,393	11.50
Hispanic (4)	13	0.11
Bangladeshi (5)	5	0.04
Burmese (26)	26	0.21
Cambodian (2)	5	0.04
Chinese, ex. Taiwanese (228)	247	2.04
Filipino (41)	60	0.50
Indian (778)	807	6.66
Indonesian (0)	1	0.01
Japanese (41)	49	0.40
Korean (69)	76	0.63
Malaysian (3)	3	0.02
Nepalese (9)	9	0.07
Pakistani (28)	29	0.24
Sri Lankan (2)	2	0.02
Taiwanese (27)	31	0.26
Thai (1)	3	0.02
Vietnamese (9)	12	0.10
Hawaii Native/Pacific Islander (6)	14	0.12
Not Hispanic (6)	14	0.12
Guamanian/Chamorro (1)	1	0.01
Native Hawaiian (5)	11	0.09
White (9,682)	9,889	81.63
Not Hispanic (9,467)	9,655	79.70
Hispanic (215)	234	1.93

Boardman

Place Type: CDP
County: Mahoning
Population: 35,376†

Ancestry‡	Population	%
African, Sub-Saharan (56)	197	0.56
African (46)	177	0.50
South African (0)	10	0.03
Other Sub-Saharan African (10)	10	0.03
American (1,335)	1,335	3.77
Arab (482)	703	1.99
Arab (186)	198	0.56
Jordanian (22)	22	0.06
Lebanese (204)	402	1.14
Syrian (14)	25	0.07
Other Arab (56)	56	0.16
Austrian (13)	128	0.36
Belgian (0)	51	0.14
British (40)	127	0.36
Carpatho Rusyn (19)	19	0.05
Croatian (232)	733	2.07
Cypriot (11)	11	0.03
Czech (50)	180	0.51
Czechoslovakian (86)	106	0.30
Dutch (49)	671	1.90
English (569)	3,175	8.97
European (65)	65	0.18
Finnish (29)	83	0.23
French, ex. Basque (74)	671	1.90
French Canadian (73)	198	0.56
German (1,821)	8,243	23.28
Greek (340)	783	2.21
Hungarian (302)	1,296	3.66
Irish (1,177)	6,922	19.55
Italian (3,857)	8,683	24.53
Lithuanian (42)	56	0.16
Luxemburger (0)	7	0.02
Macedonian (5)	24	0.07
Maltese (0)	152	0.43
Northern European (87)	109	0.31
Norwegian (38)	76	0.21
Pennsylvania German (94)	275	0.78
Polish (619)	1,807	5.10
Portuguese (0)	21	0.06
Romanian (169)	302	0.85
Russian (100)	428	1.21
Scandinavian (0)	22	0.06
Scotch-Irish (217)	677	1.91
Scottish (111)	599	1.69
Serbian (37)	94	0.27
Slavic (27)	41	0.12
Slovak (1,036)	2,764	7.81
Slovene (0)	67	0.19
Swedish (166)	508	1.43
Swiss (27)	137	0.39
Ukrainian (247)	653	1.84
Welsh (134)	1,078	3.04
Yugoslavian (23)	23	0.06

Hispanic Origin	Population	%
Hispanic or Latino (of any race)	1,151	3.25
Central American, ex. Mexican	17	0.05
Costa Rican	1	<0.01
Guatemalan	12	0.03
Honduran	2	0.01
Salvadoran	2	0.01
Cuban	23	0.07
Dominican Republic	24	0.07
Mexican	265	0.75
Puerto Rican	709	2.00
South American	34	0.10
Argentinean	6	0.02
Bolivian	1	<0.01
Chilean	1	<0.01
Colombian	7	0.02
Ecuadorian	3	0.01
Paraguayan	4	0.01
Peruvian	3	0.01
Uruguayan	1	<0.01
Venezuelan	7	0.02
Other South American	1	<0.01
Other Hispanic or Latino	79	0.22

Race*	Population	%
African-American/Black (2,269)	2,628	7.43
Not Hispanic (2,214)	2,512	7.10
Hispanic (55)	116	0.33
American Indian/Alaska Native (49)	187	0.53
Not Hispanic (42)	145	0.41
Hispanic (7)	42	0.12
Alaska Athabascan *(Ala. Nat.)* (0)	1	<0.01
Aleut *(Alaska Native)* (2)	2	0.01
Apache (0)	1	<0.01
Blackfeet (0)	9	0.03
Canadian/French Am. Ind. (1)	1	<0.01
Central American Ind. (0)	1	<0.01
Cherokee (6)	47	0.13
Chippewa (6)	6	0.02
Choctaw (0)	3	0.01
Comanche (1)	1	<0.01
Delaware (4)	4	0.01
Hopi (1)	1	<0.01
Mexican American Ind. (2)	3	0.01
Navajo (0)	3	0.01
Pima (0)	1	<0.01
Potawatomi (2)	2	0.01
Sioux (0)	5	0.01
South American Ind. (3)	9	0.03
Asian (430)	580	1.64
Not Hispanic (427)	565	1.60
Hispanic (3)	15	0.04
Bangladeshi (4)	4	0.01
Cambodian (4)	7	0.02
Chinese, ex. Taiwanese (79)	98	0.28
Filipino (39)	89	0.25
Indian (128)	144	0.41
Indonesian (3)	4	0.01
Japanese (9)	15	0.04
Korean (41)	45	0.13
Laotian (0)	2	0.01
Nepalese (3)	3	0.01
Pakistani (50)	51	0.14
Taiwanese (2)	3	0.01
Thai (11)	12	0.03
Vietnamese (38)	48	0.14
Hawaii Native/Pacific Islander (11)	22	0.06
Not Hispanic (10)	21	0.06
Hispanic (1)	1	<0.01
Guamanian/Chamorro (2)	2	0.01
Native Hawaiian (3)	4	0.01
White (31,706)	32,257	91.18
Not Hispanic (31,016)	31,455	88.92
Hispanic (690)	802	2.27

Bowling Green

Place Type: City
County: Wood
Population: 30,028†

Ancestry‡	Population	%
African, Sub-Saharan (188)	277	0.92
African (154)	227	0.75
Ghanaian (21)	21	0.07
Nigerian (13)	13	0.04
Other Sub-Saharan African (0)	16	0.05
American (834)	834	2.76
Arab (95)	224	0.74
Arab (26)	26	0.09
Lebanese (0)	129	0.43
Moroccan (24)	24	0.08
Other Arab (45)	45	0.15
Austrian (60)	190	0.63
Basque (0)	18	0.06
Belgian (41)	107	0.35
British (25)	82	0.27
Canadian (9)	43	0.14
Croatian (23)	153	0.51
Czech (31)	298	0.99
Czechoslovakian (0)	66	0.22
Danish (13)	75	0.25
Dutch (90)	536	1.77
Eastern European (17)	17	0.06
English (576)	3,041	10.07
European (268)	281	0.93
Finnish (29)	60	0.20
French, ex. Basque (147)	1,031	3.41
French Canadian (10)	75	0.25
German (4,725)	11,894	39.37
Greek (26)	196	0.65
Hungarian (198)	773	2.56
Icelander (14)	14	0.05
Iranian (53)	53	0.18
Irish (923)	4,867	16.11
Israeli (14)	14	0.05

*Notes: † The Census 2010 population figure is used to calculate the percentages in the Hispanic Origin and Race categories. Ancestry percentages are based on the 2006-2010 American Community Survey population (not shown); ‡ Numbers in parentheses indicate the number of people reporting a single ancestry; * Numbers in parentheses indicate the number of persons reporting this race alone, not in combination with any other race; Please refer to the Explanation of Data for more information.*

Ancestry	Population	%
Italian (878)	2,213	7.33
Lithuanian (17)	60	0.20
Norwegian (61)	206	0.68
Pennsylvania German (20)	30	0.10
Polish (343)	1,605	5.31
Portuguese (0)	14	0.05
Romanian (0)	26	0.09
Russian (34)	265	0.88
Scandinavian (9)	50	0.17
Scotch-Irish (195)	454	1.50
Scottish (309)	986	3.26
Serbian (15)	28	0.09
Slavic (0)	15	0.05
Slovak (24)	187	0.62
Slovene (0)	98	0.32
Swedish (57)	178	0.59
Swiss (20)	184	0.61
Turkish (10)	10	0.03
Ukrainian (17)	36	0.12
Welsh (57)	407	1.35
West Indian, ex. Hispanic (0)	14	0.05
Bahamian (0)	14	0.05

Hispanic Origin	Population	%
Hispanic or Latino (of any race)	1,436	4.78
Central American, ex. Mexican	33	0.11
Costa Rican	2	0.01
Guatemalan	11	0.04
Honduran	5	0.02
Nicaraguan	5	0.02
Panamanian	6	0.02
Salvadoran	4	0.01
Cuban	32	0.11
Dominican Republic	6	0.02
Mexican	1,040	3.46
Puerto Rican	139	0.46
South American	65	0.22
Argentinean	18	0.06
Bolivian	6	0.02
Chilean	2	0.01
Colombian	19	0.06
Ecuadorian	1	<0.01
Paraguayan	2	0.01
Peruvian	10	0.03
Venezuelan	7	0.02
Other Hispanic or Latino	121	0.40

Race*	Population	%
African-American/Black (1,926)	2,220	7.39
Not Hispanic (1,875)	2,130	7.09
Hispanic (51)	90	0.30
American Indian/Alaska Native (64)	246	0.82
Not Hispanic (54)	214	0.71
Hispanic (10)	32	0.11
Aleut *(Alaska Native)* (1)	1	<0.01
Apache (2)	6	0.02
Blackfeet (2)	15	0.05
Cherokee (17)	78	0.26
Chickasaw (0)	1	<0.01
Chippewa (2)	2	0.01
Choctaw (0)	3	0.01
Comanche (1)	4	0.01
Cree (0)	1	<0.01
Creek (0)	1	<0.01
Crow (0)	1	<0.01
Delaware (0)	1	<0.01
Hopi (0)	1	<0.01
Houma (0)	2	0.01
Iroquois (4)	7	0.02
Mexican American Ind. (1)	2	0.01
Navajo (1)	3	0.01
Osage (1)	1	<0.01
Seminole (0)	1	<0.01
Sioux (3)	10	0.03
South American Ind. (1)	1	<0.01
Yaqui (1)	1	<0.01
Asian (640)	807	2.69
Not Hispanic (636)	795	2.65
Hispanic (4)	12	0.04
Bangladeshi (5)	5	0.02
Burmese (0)	1	<0.01
Cambodian (3)	5	0.02
Chinese, ex. Taiwanese (269)	291	0.97
Filipino (43)	70	0.23
Indian (120)	138	0.46
Indonesian (0)	4	0.01
Japanese (38)	56	0.19
Korean (81)	110	0.37
Laotian (1)	1	<0.01
Malaysian (1)	1	<0.01
Nepalese (10)	10	0.03
Pakistani (8)	12	0.04
Sri Lankan (8)	8	0.03
Taiwanese (5)	7	0.02
Thai (7)	13	0.04
Vietnamese (16)	22	0.07
Hawaii Native/Pacific Islander (9)	30	0.10
Not Hispanic (3)	20	0.07
Hispanic (6)	10	0.03
Guamanian/Chamorro (4)	5	0.02
Marshallese (0)	1	<0.01
Native Hawaiian (4)	8	0.03
Samoan (1)	3	0.01
White (26,301)	26,889	89.55
Not Hispanic (25,466)	25,954	86.43
Hispanic (835)	935	3.11

Brecksville

Place Type: City
County: Cuyahoga
Population: 13,656†

Ancestry‡	Population	%
African, Sub-Saharan (38)	38	0.28
African (38)	38	0.28
American (315)	315	2.32
Arab (14)	78	0.58
Lebanese (14)	53	0.39
Palestinian (0)	6	0.04
Syrian (0)	19	0.14
Armenian (0)	53	0.39
Austrian (17)	131	0.97
Croatian (24)	129	0.95
Czech (143)	533	3.93
Czechoslovakian (44)	119	0.88
Danish (13)	13	0.10
Dutch (0)	56	0.41
Eastern European (16)	16	0.12
English (292)	1,629	12.02
Estonian (9)	9	0.07
European (83)	106	0.78
Finnish (12)	36	0.27
French, ex. Basque (18)	253	1.87
French Canadian (27)	73	0.54
German (780)	3,403	25.11
Greek (180)	338	2.49
Hungarian (199)	830	6.13
Irish (656)	2,312	17.06
Italian (660)	2,041	15.06
Latvian (15)	15	0.11
Lithuanian (0)	16	0.12
Macedonian (18)	18	0.13
Northern European (8)	8	0.06
Norwegian (42)	130	0.96
Pennsylvania German (12)	12	0.09
Polish (1,145)	2,565	18.93
Romanian (32)	41	0.30
Russian (125)	387	2.86
Scotch-Irish (46)	372	2.75
Scottish (81)	328	2.42
Serbian (29)	49	0.36
Slavic (9)	9	0.07
Slovak (276)	882	6.51
Slovene (142)	304	2.24
Swedish (9)	80	0.59
Swiss (0)	54	0.40
Ukrainian (134)	253	1.87
Welsh (22)	77	0.57
West Indian, ex. Hispanic (17)	17	0.13
Jamaican (17)	17	0.13
Yugoslavian (21)	34	0.25

Hispanic Origin	Population	%
Hispanic or Latino (of any race)	192	1.41
Central American, ex. Mexican	14	0.10
Costa Rican	1	0.01
Guatemalan	6	0.04
Honduran	4	0.03
Panamanian	2	0.01
Salvadoran	1	0.01
Cuban	14	0.10
Mexican	45	0.33
Puerto Rican	38	0.28
South American	63	0.46
Argentinean	11	0.08
Chilean	3	0.02
Colombian	36	0.26
Ecuadorian	4	0.03
Paraguayan	2	0.01
Peruvian	5	0.04
Venezuelan	2	0.01
Other Hispanic or Latino	18	0.13

Race*	Population	%
African-American/Black (238)	267	1.96
Not Hispanic (237)	262	1.92
Hispanic (1)	5	0.04
American Indian/Alaska Native (8)	39	0.29
Not Hispanic (7)	38	0.28
Hispanic (1)	1	0.01
Blackfeet (0)	3	0.02
Cherokee (3)	15	0.11
Chippewa (1)	1	0.01
Choctaw (0)	2	0.01
Seminole (1)	1	0.01
South American Ind. (1)	1	0.01
Asian (471)	567	4.15
Not Hispanic (470)	566	4.14
Hispanic (1)	1	0.01
Cambodian (1)	1	0.01
Chinese, ex. Taiwanese (80)	100	0.73
Filipino (59)	93	0.68
Indian (209)	233	1.71
Japanese (23)	30	0.22
Korean (42)	54	0.40
Malaysian (1)	3	0.02
Pakistani (17)	19	0.14
Sri Lankan (7)	7	0.05
Taiwanese (2)	2	0.01
Thai (4)	8	0.06
Vietnamese (11)	15	0.11
Hawaii Native/Pacific Islander (2)	3	0.02
Not Hispanic (1)	2	0.01
Hispanic (1)	1	0.01
Guamanian/Chamorro (1)	1	0.01
Native Hawaiian (1)	2	0.01
White (12,745)	12,884	94.35
Not Hispanic (12,594)	12,725	93.18
Hispanic (151)	159	1.16

Bridgetown

Place Type: CDP
County: Hamilton
Population: 14,407†

Ancestry‡	Population	%
American (765)	765	5.34
Arab (18)	18	0.13
Lebanese (18)	18	0.13
Austrian (12)	99	0.69
Brazilian (12)	12	0.08
British (11)	51	0.36
Danish (0)	13	0.09
Dutch (37)	303	2.11
English (414)	1,062	7.41
Estonian (8)	8	0.06
European (34)	34	0.24
French, ex. Basque (27)	659	4.60

*Notes: † The Census 2010 population figure is used to calculate the percentages in the Hispanic Origin and Race categories. Ancestry percentages are based on the 2006-2010 American Community Survey population (not shown); ‡ Numbers in parentheses indicate the number of people reporting a single ancestry; * Numbers in parentheses indicate the number of persons reporting this race alone, not in combination with any other race; Please refer to the Explanation of Data for more information.*

French Canadian (0)	30	0.21
German (4,147)	8,375	58.41
Greek (225)	259	1.81
Hungarian (12)	116	0.81
Irish (458)	3,020	21.06
Italian (231)	885	6.17
Polish (48)	317	2.21
Portuguese (33)	58	0.40
Romanian (12)	12	0.08
Russian (0)	12	0.08
Scotch-Irish (56)	232	1.62
Scottish (107)	247	1.72
Serbian (0)	11	0.08
Slovak (0)	9	0.06
Swedish (10)	91	0.63
Swiss (0)	78	0.54
Welsh (0)	93	0.65
Yugoslavian (35)	35	0.24

Hispanic Origin	Population	%
Hispanic or Latino (of any race)	110	0.76
Central American, ex. Mexican	3	0.02
Costa Rican	2	0.01
Honduran	1	0.01
Cuban	6	0.04
Mexican	64	0.44
Puerto Rican	17	0.12
South American	7	0.05
Chilean	3	0.02
Colombian	2	0.01
Ecuadorian	2	0.01
Other Hispanic or Latino	13	0.09

Race*	Population	%
African-American/Black (133)	209	1.45
Not Hispanic (133)	208	1.44
Hispanic (0)	1	0.01
American Indian/Alaska Native (11)	52	0.36
Not Hispanic (11)	47	0.33
Hispanic (0)	5	0.03
Apache (0)	3	0.02
Blackfeet (0)	8	0.06
Canadian/French Am. Ind. (0)	2	0.01
Cherokee (1)	4	0.03
Cheyenne (0)	1	0.01
Chippewa (1)	1	0.01
Choctaw (1)	1	0.01
Comanche (0)	1	0.01
Sioux (1)	2	0.01
Asian (111)	148	1.03
Not Hispanic (111)	143	0.99
Hispanic (0)	5	0.03
Bangladeshi (1)	3	0.02
Cambodian (0)	2	0.01
Chinese, ex. Taiwanese (46)	49	0.34
Filipino (12)	19	0.13
Indian (14)	19	0.13
Japanese (7)	18	0.12
Korean (6)	12	0.08
Taiwanese (2)	2	0.01
Thai (0)	2	0.01
Vietnamese (19)	20	0.14
Hawaii Native/Pacific Islander (8)	14	0.10
Not Hispanic (5)	11	0.08
Hispanic (3)	3	0.02
Native Hawaiian (2)	8	0.06
White (13,967)	14,117	97.99
Not Hispanic (13,891)	14,024	97.34
Hispanic (76)	93	0.65

Broadview Heights

Place Type: City
County: Cuyahoga
Population: 19,400†

Ancestry‡	Population	%
American (732)	732	3.92
Arab (144)	231	1.24
Egyptian (49)	70	0.37
Lebanese (95)	161	0.86
Armenian (17)	54	0.29
Austrian (16)	176	0.94
Brazilian (20)	20	0.11
British (0)	8	0.04
Carpatho Rusyn (18)	18	0.10
Croatian (75)	179	0.96
Czech (205)	578	3.10
Czechoslovakian (29)	69	0.37
Dutch (32)	153	0.82
Eastern European (10)	10	0.05
English (241)	1,341	7.18
Estonian (13)	27	0.14
European (90)	118	0.63
French, ex. Basque (36)	192	1.03
French Canadian (0)	11	0.06
German (968)	4,467	23.92
Greek (101)	273	1.46
Hungarian (468)	1,418	7.59
Irish (629)	2,695	14.43
Italian (1,206)	2,696	14.44
Latvian (9)	27	0.14
Lithuanian (27)	133	0.71
Macedonian (0)	11	0.06
Polish (1,585)	3,784	20.26
Romanian (27)	27	0.14
Russian (8)	214	1.15
Scotch-Irish (201)	349	1.87
Scottish (44)	236	1.26
Serbian (162)	230	1.23
Slavic (43)	54	0.29
Slovak (371)	997	5.34
Slovene (174)	420	2.25
Swedish (25)	176	0.94
Swiss (0)	28	0.15
Ukrainian (391)	520	2.78
Welsh (37)	164	0.88
Yugoslavian (61)	61	0.33

Hispanic Origin	Population	%
Hispanic or Latino (of any race)	353	1.82
Central American, ex. Mexican	17	0.09
Costa Rican	1	0.01
Guatemalan	9	0.05
Panamanian	5	0.03
Salvadoran	2	0.01
Cuban	11	0.06
Dominican Republic	3	0.02
Mexican	102	0.53
Puerto Rican	134	0.69
South American	50	0.26
Argentinean	13	0.07
Bolivian	1	0.01
Colombian	15	0.08
Ecuadorian	6	0.03
Peruvian	6	0.03
Uruguayan	1	0.01
Venezuelan	8	0.04
Other Hispanic or Latino	36	0.19

Race*	Population	%
African-American/Black (400)	464	2.39
Not Hispanic (391)	446	2.30
Hispanic (9)	18	0.09
American Indian/Alaska Native (28)	81	0.42
Not Hispanic (22)	65	0.34
Hispanic (6)	16	0.08
Blackfeet (2)	11	0.06
Cherokee (3)	16	0.08
Choctaw (0)	1	0.01
Iroquois (0)	6	0.03
Lumbee (1)	1	0.01
Navajo (1)	1	0.01
Sioux (0)	3	0.02
South American Ind. (1)	1	0.01
Asian (1,000)	1,116	5.75
Not Hispanic (999)	1,112	5.73
Hispanic (1)	4	0.02
Bangladeshi (9)	9	0.05
Chinese, ex. Taiwanese (176)	193	0.99
Filipino (85)	126	0.65
Indian (540)	567	2.92
Indonesian (3)	4	0.02
Japanese (7)	21	0.11
Korean (101)	113	0.58
Pakistani (21)	22	0.11
Sri Lankan (4)	4	0.02
Taiwanese (19)	21	0.11
Thai (4)	6	0.03
Vietnamese (14)	16	0.08
Hawaii Native/Pacific Islander (4)	22	0.11
Not Hispanic (4)	22	0.11
Guamanian/Chamorro (3)	5	0.03
Native Hawaiian (0)	4	0.02
Tongan (1)	1	0.01
White (17,652)	17,887	92.20
Not Hispanic (17,403)	17,614	90.79
Hispanic (249)	273	1.41

Brook Park

Place Type: City
County: Cuyahoga
Population: 19,212†

Ancestry‡	Population	%
African, Sub-Saharan (48)	48	0.25
African (48)	48	0.25
American (1,288)	1,288	6.61
Arab (238)	387	1.99
Arab (102)	109	0.56
Lebanese (136)	263	1.35
Syrian (0)	15	0.08
Armenian (0)	19	0.10
Austrian (0)	75	0.39
Belgian (27)	62	0.32
British (8)	8	0.04
Bulgarian (12)	12	0.06
Canadian (18)	39	0.20
Croatian (68)	127	0.65
Czech (112)	476	2.44
Czechoslovakian (29)	39	0.20
Danish (0)	31	0.16
Dutch (11)	230	1.18
English (363)	1,744	8.96
European (268)	279	1.43
Finnish (0)	22	0.11
French, ex. Basque (0)	341	1.75
French Canadian (27)	97	0.50
German (1,222)	4,777	24.53
Greek (98)	169	0.87
Hungarian (271)	855	4.39
Irish (682)	3,551	18.24
Italian (1,216)	2,863	14.70
Latvian (41)	55	0.28
Lithuanian (46)	169	0.87
Macedonian (23)	33	0.17
Norwegian (9)	9	0.05
Pennsylvania German (22)	33	0.17
Polish (1,121)	2,785	14.30
Romanian (43)	145	0.74
Russian (34)	176	0.90
Scandinavian (0)	14	0.07
Scotch-Irish (76)	275	1.41
Scottish (90)	255	1.31
Serbian (0)	87	0.45
Slavic (0)	8	0.04
Slovak (503)	1,255	6.45
Slovene (32)	102	0.52
Swedish (15)	105	0.54
Swiss (0)	30	0.15
Ukrainian (254)	325	1.67
Welsh (11)	128	0.66
West Indian, ex. Hispanic (0)	8	0.04
Jamaican (0)	8	0.04
Yugoslavian (25)	25	0.13

Hispanic Origin	Population	%
Hispanic or Latino (of any race)	662	3.45
Central American, ex. Mexican	22	0.11

SECTION TWO

*Notes: † The Census 2010 population figure is used to calculate the percentages in the Hispanic Origin and Race categories. Ancestry percentages are based on the 2006-2010 American Community Survey population (not shown); ‡ Numbers in parentheses indicate the number of people reporting a single ancestry; * Numbers in parentheses indicate the number of persons reporting this race alone, not in combination with any other race; Please refer to the Explanation of Data for more information.*

Costa Rican	1	0.01
Guatemalan	5	0.03
Nicaraguan	1	0.01
Panamanian	8	0.04
Salvadoran	7	0.04
Cuban	17	0.09
Dominican Republic	12	0.06
Mexican	109	0.57
Puerto Rican	443	2.31
South American	31	0.16
Argentinean	2	0.01
Chilean	3	0.02
Colombian	9	0.05
Ecuadorian	11	0.06
Paraguayan	1	0.01
Peruvian	4	0.02
Uruguayan	1	0.01
Other Hispanic or Latino	28	0.15

Race*	Population	%
African-American/Black (624)	832	4.33
Not Hispanic (600)	791	4.12
Hispanic (24)	41	0.21
American Indian/Alaska Native (31)	98	0.51
Not Hispanic (28)	90	0.47
Hispanic (3)	8	0.04
Blackfeet (6)	15	0.08
Canadian/French Am. Ind. (0)	2	0.01
Cherokee (8)	32	0.17
Cheyenne (1)	1	0.01
Chickasaw (0)	1	0.01
Chippewa (1)	1	0.01
Delaware (0)	1	0.01
Iroquois (0)	2	0.01
Mexican American Ind. (2)	2	0.01
Seminole (0)	2	0.01
Sioux (0)	2	0.01
Asian (301)	376	1.96
Not Hispanic (301)	371	1.93
Hispanic (0)	5	0.03
Cambodian (5)	5	0.03
Chinese, ex. Taiwanese (55)	69	0.36
Filipino (72)	86	0.45
Indian (113)	123	0.64
Indonesian (1)	2	0.01
Japanese (4)	9	0.05
Korean (5)	11	0.06
Pakistani (3)	3	0.02
Thai (2)	2	0.01
Vietnamese (33)	45	0.23
Hawaii Native/Pacific Islander (2)	16	0.08
Not Hispanic (2)	12	0.06
Hispanic (0)	4	0.02
Guamanian/Chamorro (0)	1	0.01
Native Hawaiian (1)	7	0.04
Tongan (1)	4	0.02
White (17,711)	18,060	94.00
Not Hispanic (17,286)	17,581	91.51
Hispanic (425)	479	2.49

Brooklyn

Place Type: City
County: Cuyahoga
Population: 11,169†

Ancestry‡	Population	%
American (339)	339	3.04
Arab (74)	108	0.97
Jordanian (9)	19	0.17
Lebanese (65)	71	0.64
Syrian (0)	18	0.16
Austrian (9)	42	0.38
British (18)	26	0.23
Bulgarian (18)	18	0.16
Canadian (0)	15	0.13
Croatian (95)	205	1.84
Czech (132)	386	3.46
Czechoslovakian (0)	5	0.04
Dutch (10)	160	1.43
English (201)	1,262	11.31
European (67)	67	0.60
Finnish (24)	53	0.48
French, ex. Basque (0)	76	0.68
French Canadian (0)	28	0.25
German (615)	2,887	25.88
Greek (0)	24	0.22
Hungarian (150)	419	3.76
Irish (317)	2,052	18.39
Italian (701)	1,567	14.05
Lithuanian (0)	20	0.18
Macedonian (18)	18	0.16
Northern European (15)	15	0.13
Pennsylvania German (0)	28	0.25
Polish (523)	1,415	12.68
Romanian (70)	80	0.72
Russian (122)	251	2.25
Scotch-Irish (32)	99	0.89
Scottish (22)	22	0.20
Serbian (8)	69	0.62
Slavic (0)	8	0.07
Slovak (340)	860	7.71
Slovene (55)	127	1.14
Swedish (0)	119	1.07
Swiss (0)	23	0.21
Turkish (27)	27	0.24
Ukrainian (63)	104	0.93
Welsh (0)	22	0.20
Yugoslavian (6)	36	0.32

Hispanic Origin	Population	%
Hispanic or Latino (of any race)	1,165	10.43
Central American, ex. Mexican	35	0.31
Costa Rican	2	0.02
Guatemalan	18	0.16
Honduran	4	0.04
Nicaraguan	1	0.01
Salvadoran	10	0.09
Cuban	11	0.10
Dominican Republic	25	0.22
Mexican	94	0.84
Puerto Rican	896	8.02
South American	46	0.41
Chilean	3	0.03
Colombian	7	0.06
Ecuadorian	8	0.07
Peruvian	23	0.21
Venezuelan	5	0.04
Other Hispanic or Latino	58	0.52

Race*	Population	%
African-American/Black (577)	707	6.33
Not Hispanic (529)	631	5.65
Hispanic (48)	76	0.68
American Indian/Alaska Native (18)	77	0.69
Not Hispanic (12)	61	0.55
Hispanic (6)	16	0.14
Blackfeet (0)	3	0.03
Cherokee (3)	19	0.17
Cheyenne (1)	1	0.01
Chippewa (1)	2	0.02
Choctaw (0)	1	0.01
Delaware (0)	1	0.01
Kiowa (0)	1	0.01
Ottawa (0)	1	0.01
Pueblo (1)	1	0.01
Sioux (0)	1	0.01
South American Ind. (1)	5	0.04
Spanish American Ind. (1)	1	0.01
Yaqui (0)	1	0.01
Asian (441)	513	4.59
Not Hispanic (441)	501	4.49
Hispanic (0)	12	0.11
Cambodian (41)	47	0.42
Chinese, ex. Taiwanese (76)	96	0.86
Filipino (30)	37	0.33
Hmong (1)	1	0.01
Indian (69)	84	0.75
Japanese (8)	12	0.11
Korean (12)	15	0.13
Laotian (1)	4	0.04
Malaysian (3)	3	0.03
Pakistani (6)	8	0.07
Thai (1)	1	0.01
Vietnamese (182)	193	1.73
Hawaii Native/Pacific Islander (0)	5	0.04
Not Hispanic (0)	5	0.04
White (9,415)	9,637	86.28
Not Hispanic (8,808)	8,979	80.39
Hispanic (607)	658	5.89

Brunswick

Place Type: City
County: Medina
Population: 34,255†

Ancestry‡	Population	%
African, Sub-Saharan (0)	14	0.04
Somalian (0)	14	0.04
American (2,043)	2,043	5.94
Arab (90)	169	0.49
Arab (29)	29	0.08
Jordanian (20)	20	0.06
Lebanese (41)	111	0.32
Syrian (0)	9	0.03
Armenian (12)	24	0.07
Austrian (65)	120	0.35
Belgian (0)	26	0.08
British (23)	85	0.25
Canadian (42)	46	0.13
Croatian (86)	258	0.75
Czech (174)	824	2.39
Czechoslovakian (17)	87	0.25
Danish (6)	138	0.40
Dutch (92)	667	1.94
Eastern European (9)	9	0.03
English (859)	3,086	8.97
European (240)	240	0.70
Finnish (0)	11	0.03
French, ex. Basque (73)	708	2.06
French Canadian (12)	62	0.18
German (2,508)	10,213	29.68
German Russian (0)	15	0.04
Greek (130)	359	1.04
Hungarian (512)	1,802	5.24
Irish (1,305)	7,187	20.89
Italian (1,395)	4,729	13.74
Lithuanian (9)	45	0.13
Macedonian (222)	222	0.65
Norwegian (8)	165	0.48
Pennsylvania German (29)	55	0.16
Polish (1,543)	5,132	14.92
Romanian (231)	307	0.89
Russian (82)	514	1.49
Scandinavian (32)	66	0.19
Scotch-Irish (101)	463	1.35
Scottish (140)	656	1.91
Serbian (215)	399	1.16
Slavic (39)	117	0.34
Slovak (633)	1,800	5.23
Slovene (93)	432	1.26
Swedish (102)	358	1.04
Swiss (28)	97	0.28
Turkish (0)	39	0.11
Ukrainian (200)	499	1.45
Welsh (64)	243	0.71
Yugoslavian (38)	38	0.11

Hispanic Origin	Population	%
Hispanic or Latino (of any race)	790	2.31
Central American, ex. Mexican	41	0.12
Costa Rican	4	0.01
Guatemalan	14	0.04
Honduran	5	0.01
Nicaraguan	1	<0.01
Panamanian	11	0.03
Salvadoran	5	0.01
Other Central American	1	<0.01
Cuban	13	0.04

*Notes: † The Census 2010 population figure is used to calculate the percentages in the Hispanic Origin and Race categories. Ancestry percentages are based on the 2006-2010 American Community Survey population (not shown); ‡ Numbers in parentheses indicate the number of people reporting a single ancestry; * Numbers in parentheses indicate the number of persons reporting this race alone, not in combination with any other race; Please refer to the Explanation of Data for more information.*

Dominican Republic	4	0.01
Mexican	249	0.73
Puerto Rican	375	1.09
South American	44	0.13
Argentinean	6	0.02
Bolivian	1	<0.01
Colombian	19	0.06
Ecuadorian	5	0.01
Peruvian	6	0.02
Venezuelan	7	0.02
Other Hispanic or Latino	64	0.19

Race*	Population	%
African-American/Black (422)	583	1.70
Not Hispanic (417)	553	1.61
Hispanic (5)	30	0.09
American Indian/Alaska Native (51)	210	0.61
Not Hispanic (41)	181	0.53
Hispanic (10)	29	0.08
Apache (6)	8	0.02
Blackfeet (0)	14	0.04
Canadian/French Am. Ind. (1)	1	<0.01
Central American Ind. (1)	1	<0.01
Cherokee (10)	65	0.19
Chickasaw (0)	3	0.01
Choctaw (0)	3	0.01
Creek (0)	3	0.01
Crow (0)	3	0.01
Delaware (0)	1	<0.01
Iroquois (1)	7	0.02
Lumbee (2)	4	0.01
Mexican American Ind. (3)	5	0.01
Navajo (0)	2	0.01
Potawatomi (1)	4	0.01
Pueblo (0)	2	0.01
Sioux (5)	9	0.03
Ute (0)	1	<0.01
Asian (420)	510	1.49
Not Hispanic (413)	500	1.46
Hispanic (7)	10	0.03
Cambodian (2)	5	0.01
Chinese, ex. Taiwanese (40)	46	0.13
Filipino (82)	106	0.31
Indian (153)	166	0.48
Indonesian (7)	7	0.02
Japanese (7)	23	0.07
Korean (42)	62	0.18
Laotian (5)	5	0.01
Malaysian (1)	1	<0.01
Pakistani (5)	11	0.03
Taiwanese (1)	1	<0.01
Thai (1)	1	<0.01
Vietnamese (54)	55	0.16
Hawaii Native/Pacific Islander (6)	19	0.06
Not Hispanic (6)	19	0.06
Guamanian/Chamorro (1)	1	<0.01
Native Hawaiian (1)	8	0.02
White (32,706)	33,134	96.73
Not Hispanic (32,194)	32,557	95.04
Hispanic (512)	577	1.68

Bryan

Place Type: City
County: Williams
Population: 8,545†

Ancestry‡	Population	%
American (508)	508	5.89
Arab (8)	10	0.12
Syrian (8)	10	0.12
British (0)	8	0.09
Canadian (0)	11	0.13
Croatian (0)	11	0.13
Czech (0)	11	0.13
Czechoslovakian (18)	48	0.56
Danish (0)	9	0.10
Dutch (38)	288	3.34
English (121)	661	7.67
European (67)	100	1.16
French, ex. Basque (38)	370	4.29
French Canadian (13)	37	0.43
German (2,321)	4,464	51.78
Greek (16)	51	0.59
Hungarian (9)	114	1.32
Irish (304)	1,314	15.24
Italian (33)	125	1.45
Lithuanian (0)	14	0.16
Northern European (15)	15	0.17
Norwegian (0)	28	0.32
Pennsylvania German (10)	10	0.12
Polish (49)	119	1.38
Russian (10)	10	0.12
Scotch-Irish (26)	62	0.72
Scottish (57)	144	1.67
Slovak (8)	8	0.09
Swedish (16)	16	0.19
Swiss (0)	32	0.37
Welsh (79)	231	2.68
West Indian, ex. Hispanic (17)	17	0.20
Jamaican (17)	17	0.20

Hispanic Origin	Population	%
Hispanic or Latino (of any race)	436	5.10
Central American, ex. Mexican	3	0.04
Honduran	1	0.01
Panamanian	1	0.01
Salvadoran	1	0.01
Cuban	3	0.04
Mexican	342	4.00
Puerto Rican	20	0.23
South American	1	0.01
Argentinean	1	0.01
Other Hispanic or Latino	67	0.78

Race*	Population	%
African-American/Black (47)	108	1.26
Not Hispanic (47)	104	1.22
Hispanic (0)	4	0.05
American Indian/Alaska Native (14)	70	0.82
Not Hispanic (9)	56	0.66
Hispanic (5)	14	0.16
Apache (2)	2	0.02
Blackfeet (0)	1	0.01
Cherokee (3)	21	0.25
Mexican American Ind. (0)	1	0.01
Navajo (2)	2	0.02
Sioux (0)	9	0.11
Spanish American Ind. (0)	4	0.05
Asian (73)	87	1.02
Not Hispanic (73)	85	0.99
Hispanic (0)	2	0.02
Chinese, ex. Taiwanese (26)	30	0.35
Filipino (7)	10	0.12
Indian (18)	20	0.23
Japanese (1)	3	0.04
Korean (6)	7	0.08
Laotian (11)	12	0.14
Pakistani (1)	1	0.01
Thai (1)	1	0.01
Vietnamese (0)	1	0.01
Hawaii Native/Pacific Islander (5)	7	0.08
Not Hispanic (5)	7	0.08
Guamanian/Chamorro (2)	2	0.02
White (8,056)	8,223	96.23
Not Hispanic (7,861)	7,970	93.27
Hispanic (195)	253	2.96

Bucyrus

Place Type: City
County: Crawford
Population: 12,362†

Ancestry‡	Population	%
American (1,989)	1,989	15.90
Arab (7)	16	0.13
Lebanese (7)	7	0.06
Syrian (0)	9	0.07
Armenian (11)	11	0.09
Austrian (0)	33	0.26
Belgian (3)	6	0.05
British (0)	12	0.10
Canadian (6)	6	0.05
Czechoslovakian (13)	51	0.41
Danish (0)	2	0.02
Dutch (35)	532	4.25
English (681)	1,563	12.50
European (0)	8	0.06
French, ex. Basque (30)	281	2.25
French Canadian (0)	10	0.08
German (2,358)	5,440	43.50
Greek (50)	92	0.74
Hungarian (4)	26	0.21
Irish (420)	2,000	15.99
Italian (64)	505	4.04
Pennsylvania German (7)	18	0.14
Polish (9)	137	1.10
Portuguese (0)	23	0.18
Romanian (0)	17	0.14
Scotch-Irish (53)	331	2.65
Scottish (18)	125	1.00
Swedish (39)	54	0.43
Swiss (8)	46	0.37
Ukrainian (0)	9	0.07
Welsh (30)	112	0.90
West Indian, ex. Hispanic (0)	24	0.19
West Indian (0)	24	0.19

Hispanic Origin	Population	%
Hispanic or Latino (of any race)	195	1.58
Central American, ex. Mexican	6	0.05
Costa Rican	1	0.01
Guatemalan	4	0.03
Honduran	1	0.01
Cuban	4	0.03
Mexican	131	1.06
Puerto Rican	14	0.11
South American	8	0.06
Bolivian	3	0.02
Colombian	4	0.03
Ecuadorian	1	0.01
Other Hispanic or Latino	32	0.26

Race*	Population	%
African-American/Black (134)	207	1.67
Not Hispanic (131)	202	1.63
Hispanic (3)	5	0.04
American Indian/Alaska Native (20)	70	0.57
Not Hispanic (10)	50	0.40
Hispanic (10)	20	0.16
Apache (0)	4	0.03
Blackfeet (0)	7	0.06
Cherokee (4)	20	0.16
Chippewa (0)	1	0.01
Comanche (0)	2	0.02
Creek (0)	1	0.01
Iroquois (1)	7	0.06
Mexican American Ind. (5)	9	0.07
Pueblo (0)	1	0.01
Sioux (3)	3	0.02
South American Ind. (5)	5	0.04
Asian (83)	108	0.87
Not Hispanic (83)	104	0.84
Hispanic (0)	4	0.03
Chinese, ex. Taiwanese (23)	31	0.25
Filipino (4)	5	0.04
Indian (7)	7	0.06
Japanese (44)	54	0.44
Korean (4)	7	0.06
Hawaii Native/Pacific Islander (2)	2	0.02
Not Hispanic (2)	2	0.02
Native Hawaiian (1)	1	0.01
White (11,905)	12,059	97.55
Not Hispanic (11,808)	11,932	96.52
Hispanic (97)	127	1.03

*Notes: † The Census 2010 population figure is used to calculate the percentages in the Hispanic Origin and Race categories. Ancestry percentages are based on the 2006-2010 American Community Survey population (not shown); ‡ Numbers in parentheses indicate the number of people reporting a single ancestry; * Numbers in parentheses indicate the number of persons reporting this race alone, not in combination with any other race; Please refer to the Explanation of Data for more information.*

Cambridge

Place Type: City
County: Guernsey
Population: 10,635†

Ancestry‡	Population	%
American (1,091)	1,091	10.07
Arab (63)	95	0.88
Egyptian (0)	6	0.06
Lebanese (63)	89	0.82
Austrian (0)	44	0.41
Belgian (0)	8	0.07
Brazilian (0)	9	0.08
British (0)	21	0.19
Czech (10)	56	0.52
Czechoslovakian (29)	29	0.27
Dutch (70)	247	2.28
English (529)	1,132	10.45
European (77)	95	0.88
French, ex. Basque (68)	242	2.23
French Canadian (0)	10	0.09
German (824)	2,159	19.93
Greek (90)	138	1.27
Hungarian (11)	49	0.45
Irish (432)	1,550	14.31
Italian (67)	239	2.21
Lithuanian (0)	28	0.26
Norwegian (12)	12	0.11
Polish (71)	145	1.34
Portuguese (12)	12	0.11
Romanian (6)	6	0.06
Scandinavian (0)	7	0.06
Scotch-Irish (220)	366	3.38
Scottish (30)	283	2.61
Slovak (49)	143	1.32
Welsh (39)	167	1.54
West Indian, ex. Hispanic (24)	24	0.22
Jamaican (24)	24	0.22

Hispanic Origin	Population	%
Hispanic or Latino (of any race)	129	1.21
Central American, ex. Mexican	2	0.02
Guatemalan	2	0.02
Cuban	2	0.02
Mexican	88	0.83
Puerto Rican	18	0.17
South American	3	0.03
Other South American	3	0.03
Other Hispanic or Latino	16	0.15

Race*	Population	%
African-American/Black (361)	596	5.60
Not Hispanic (354)	583	5.48
Hispanic (7)	13	0.12
American Indian/Alaska Native (32)	113	1.06
Not Hispanic (29)	108	1.02
Hispanic (3)	5	0.05
Blackfeet (1)	3	0.03
Cherokee (6)	27	0.25
Choctaw (3)	5	0.05
Delaware (0)	1	0.01
Iroquois (0)	3	0.03
Potawatomi (1)	1	0.01
Yaqui (1)	1	0.01
Asian (33)	56	0.53
Not Hispanic (33)	49	0.46
Hispanic (0)	7	0.07
Chinese, ex. Taiwanese (9)	9	0.08
Filipino (11)	20	0.19
Indian (6)	10	0.09
Japanese (2)	2	0.02
Korean (1)	6	0.06
Thai (1)	1	0.01
Vietnamese (1)	1	0.01
Hawaii Native/Pacific Islander (3)	9	0.08
Not Hispanic (3)	5	0.05
Hispanic (0)	4	0.04
Native Hawaiian (2)	4	0.04
White (9,857)	10,163	95.56
Not Hispanic (9,779)	10,071	94.70
Hispanic (78)	92	0.87

Campbell

Place Type: City
County: Mahoning
Population: 8,235†

Ancestry‡	Population	%
African, Sub-Saharan (40)	40	0.47
African (40)	40	0.47
American (468)	468	5.54
Arab (8)	55	0.65
Arab (8)	23	0.27
Lebanese (0)	32	0.38
Bulgarian (6)	6	0.07
Carpatho Rusyn (17)	17	0.20
Croatian (110)	202	2.39
Czech (0)	27	0.32
English (42)	226	2.68
Finnish (0)	10	0.12
French, ex. Basque (13)	48	0.57
German (124)	596	7.06
Greek (1,030)	1,393	16.50
Hungarian (54)	155	1.84
Irish (155)	935	11.07
Italian (555)	1,155	13.68
Macedonian (7)	7	0.08
Norwegian (0)	32	0.38
Polish (218)	469	5.55
Romanian (22)	22	0.26
Russian (10)	53	0.63
Scotch-Irish (10)	40	0.47
Scottish (40)	195	2.31
Serbian (32)	38	0.45
Slavic (0)	9	0.11
Slovak (420)	892	10.56
Swedish (0)	17	0.20
Ukrainian (34)	51	0.60
Welsh (14)	88	1.04

Hispanic Origin	Population	%
Hispanic or Latino (of any race)	1,302	15.81
Central American, ex. Mexican	21	0.26
Guatemalan	2	0.02
Honduran	11	0.13
Nicaraguan	1	0.01
Salvadoran	6	0.07
Other Central American	1	0.01
Cuban	9	0.11
Dominican Republic	15	0.18
Mexican	89	1.08
Puerto Rican	1,090	13.24
South American	29	0.35
Colombian	6	0.07
Ecuadorian	3	0.04
Peruvian	20	0.24
Other Hispanic or Latino	49	0.60

Race*	Population	%
African-American/Black (1,748)	1,980	24.04
Not Hispanic (1,670)	1,826	22.17
Hispanic (78)	154	1.87
American Indian/Alaska Native (23)	63	0.77
Not Hispanic (21)	47	0.57
Hispanic (2)	16	0.19
Blackfeet (0)	3	0.04
Cherokee (2)	15	0.18
Creek (1)	2	0.02
Delaware (2)	2	0.02
Iroquois (0)	1	0.01
South American Ind. (1)	2	0.02
Tohono O'Odham (0)	2	0.02
Asian (34)	64	0.78
Not Hispanic (24)	53	0.64
Hispanic (10)	11	0.13
Chinese, ex. Taiwanese (11)	11	0.13
Filipino (10)	17	0.21
Indian (7)	8	0.10
Indonesian (1)	1	0.01
Japanese (3)	19	0.23
Thai (2)	5	0.06
Vietnamese (0)	1	0.01
Hawaii Native/Pacific Islander (2)	14	0.17
Not Hispanic (2)	6	0.07
Hispanic (0)	8	0.10
Guamanian/Chamorro (2)	2	0.02
Native Hawaiian (0)	2	0.02
White (5,688)	5,950	72.25
Not Hispanic (5,016)	5,192	63.05
Hispanic (672)	758	9.20

Canfield

Place Type: City
County: Mahoning
Population: 7,515†

Ancestry‡	Population	%
Albanian (0)	35	0.47
American (109)	109	1.45
Arab (0)	17	0.23
Syrian (0)	17	0.23
Carpatho Rusyn (30)	41	0.55
Croatian (60)	188	2.51
Czech (13)	89	1.19
Czechoslovakian (9)	9	0.12
Danish (0)	15	0.20
Dutch (47)	115	1.53
English (301)	1,419	18.94
European (37)	37	0.49
Finnish (0)	18	0.24
French, ex. Basque (0)	105	1.40
German (521)	2,261	30.17
Greek (58)	70	0.93
Hungarian (30)	181	2.42
Iranian (10)	29	0.39
Irish (425)	1,774	23.68
Italian (632)	1,558	20.79
Lithuanian (0)	61	0.81
Norwegian (0)	52	0.69
Pennsylvania German (0)	15	0.20
Polish (140)	471	6.29
Romanian (12)	39	0.52
Russian (11)	114	1.52
Scandinavian (16)	16	0.21
Scotch-Irish (33)	72	0.96
Scottish (0)	144	1.92
Serbian (13)	63	0.84
Slavic (16)	16	0.21
Slovak (242)	594	7.93
Slovene (0)	25	0.33
Swedish (56)	130	1.73
Swiss (17)	105	1.40
Ukrainian (8)	132	1.76
Welsh (89)	601	8.02

Hispanic Origin	Population	%
Hispanic or Latino (of any race)	111	1.48
Central American, ex. Mexican	3	0.04
Guatemalan	3	0.04
Cuban	2	0.03
Dominican Republic	3	0.04
Mexican	24	0.32
Puerto Rican	53	0.71
South American	11	0.15
Argentinean	3	0.04
Chilean	2	0.03
Colombian	1	0.01
Ecuadorian	1	0.01
Paraguayan	1	0.01
Peruvian	3	0.04
Other Hispanic or Latino	15	0.20

Race*	Population	%
African-American/Black (32)	46	0.61
Not Hispanic (32)	46	0.61
American Indian/Alaska Native (6)	21	0.28
Not Hispanic (4)	17	0.23

*Notes: † The Census 2010 population figure is used to calculate the percentages in the Hispanic Origin and Race categories. Ancestry percentages are based on the 2006-2010 American Community Survey population (not shown); ‡ Numbers in parentheses indicate the number of people reporting a single ancestry; * Numbers in parentheses indicate the number of persons reporting this race alone, not in combination with any other race; Please refer to the Explanation of Data for more information.*

Hispanic (2)	4	0.05
Central American Ind. (1)	1	0.01
Cherokee (1)	6	0.08
Chippewa (0)	2	0.03
Iroquois (0)	1	0.01
Mexican American Ind. (1)	1	0.01
Sioux (0)	1	0.01
Asian (139)	165	2.20
Not Hispanic (139)	163	2.17
Hispanic (0)	2	0.03
Chinese, ex. Taiwanese (22)	35	0.47
Filipino (8)	11	0.15
Indian (64)	65	0.86
Japanese (2)	4	0.05
Korean (21)	26	0.35
Malaysian (1)	1	0.01
Pakistani (3)	3	0.04
Taiwanese (1)	1	0.01
Thai (3)	4	0.05
Vietnamese (2)	2	0.03
Hawaii Native/Pacific Islander (3)	3	0.04
Not Hispanic (2)	2	0.03
Hispanic (1)	1	0.01
Guamanian/Chamorro (1)	1	0.01
Samoan (1)	1	0.01
White (7,245)	7,301	97.15
Not Hispanic (7,162)	7,213	95.98
Hispanic (83)	88	1.17

Canton

Place Type: City
County: Stark
Population: 73,007†

Ancestry‡	Population	%
African, Sub-Saharan (2,636)	2,852	3.83
African (2,507)	2,713	3.64
Cape Verdean (46)	56	0.08
Liberian (38)	38	0.05
South African (45)	45	0.06
Albanian (14)	30	0.04
American (5,025)	5,025	6.75
Arab (443)	577	0.78
Arab (13)	23	0.03
Egyptian (0)	5	0.01
Iraqi (15)	15	0.02
Lebanese (278)	358	0.48
Syrian (137)	164	0.22
Other Arab (0)	12	0.02
Armenian (9)	35	0.05
Austrian (99)	143	0.19
Belgian (6)	152	0.20
British (75)	146	0.20
Bulgarian (11)	11	0.01
Canadian (17)	41	0.06
Carpatho Rusyn (0)	13	0.02
Celtic (0)	39	0.05
Croatian (66)	279	0.37
Czech (192)	342	0.46
Czechoslovakian (30)	51	0.07
Danish (25)	176	0.24
Dutch (88)	1,441	1.94
English (1,447)	5,256	7.06
European (341)	358	0.48
Finnish (0)	27	0.04
French, ex. Basque (135)	1,697	2.28
French Canadian (37)	122	0.16
German (5,392)	18,990	25.51
Greek (747)	1,154	1.55
Hungarian (330)	917	1.23
Irish (2,411)	9,815	13.18
Italian (2,380)	5,958	8.00
Lithuanian (29)	99	0.13
Northern European (80)	80	0.11
Norwegian (51)	143	0.19
Pennsylvania German (125)	212	0.28
Polish (447)	1,434	1.93
Portuguese (253)	367	0.49
Romanian (171)	682	0.92
Russian (185)	603	0.81
Scotch-Irish (392)	1,161	1.56
Scottish (250)	1,294	1.74
Serbian (10)	67	0.09
Slavic (25)	87	0.12
Slovak (197)	577	0.78
Slovene (5)	28	0.04
Swedish (57)	420	0.56
Swiss (41)	577	0.78
Turkish (0)	9	0.01
Ukrainian (128)	214	0.29
Welsh (91)	631	0.85
West Indian, ex. Hispanic (22)	32	0.04
Bahamian (16)	16	0.02
British West Indian (0)	10	0.01
Jamaican (6)	6	0.01
Yugoslavian (36)	48	0.06

Hispanic Origin	Population	%
Hispanic or Latino (of any race)	1,899	2.60
Central American, ex. Mexican	348	0.48
Costa Rican	2	<0.01
Guatemalan	138	0.19
Honduran	139	0.19
Nicaraguan	5	0.01
Panamanian	8	0.01
Salvadoran	42	0.06
Other Central American	14	0.02
Cuban	49	0.07
Dominican Republic	27	0.04
Mexican	666	0.91
Puerto Rican	356	0.49
South American	66	0.09
Argentinean	14	0.02
Bolivian	3	<0.01
Colombian	25	0.03
Ecuadorian	6	0.01
Peruvian	13	0.02
Uruguayan	1	<0.01
Venezuelan	4	0.01
Other Hispanic or Latino	387	0.53

Race*	Population	%
African-American/Black (17,666)	20,377	27.91
Not Hispanic (17,501)	20,069	27.49
Hispanic (165)	308	0.42
American Indian/Alaska Native (349)	1,243	1.70
Not Hispanic (274)	1,102	1.51
Hispanic (75)	141	0.19
Apache (3)	20	0.03
Blackfeet (4)	100	0.14
Canadian/French Am. Ind. (2)	5	0.01
Central American Ind. (45)	45	0.06
Cherokee (64)	327	0.45
Cheyenne (2)	5	0.01
Chickasaw (0)	2	<0.01
Chippewa (5)	5	0.01
Choctaw (1)	6	0.01
Comanche (1)	5	0.01
Creek (4)	5	0.01
Crow (0)	3	<0.01
Delaware (30)	57	0.08
Hopi (1)	4	0.01
Houma (1)	1	<0.01
Inupiat *(Alaska Native)* (1)	2	<0.01
Iroquois (4)	31	0.04
Lumbee (4)	5	0.01
Mexican American Ind. (19)	24	0.03
Navajo (3)	16	0.02
Ottawa (0)	1	<0.01
Potawatomi (3)	3	<0.01
Pueblo (1)	1	<0.01
Seminole (2)	13	0.02
Sioux (0)	8	0.01
South American Ind. (0)	4	0.01
Spanish American Ind. (1)	1	<0.01
Yuman (1)	5	0.01
Asian (253)	461	0.63
Not Hispanic (243)	442	0.61
Hispanic (10)	19	0.03
Bangladeshi (1)	1	<0.01
Burmese (0)	1	<0.01
Chinese, ex. Taiwanese (55)	78	0.11
Filipino (53)	112	0.15
Hmong (1)	1	<0.01
Indian (43)	58	0.08
Japanese (22)	60	0.08
Korean (38)	80	0.11
Laotian (2)	2	<0.01
Pakistani (1)	1	<0.01
Sri Lankan (1)	1	<0.01
Thai (5)	17	0.02
Vietnamese (22)	28	0.04
Hawaii Native/Pacific Islander (35)	93	0.13
Not Hispanic (21)	65	0.09
Hispanic (14)	28	0.04
Guamanian/Chamorro (17)	28	0.04
Native Hawaiian (8)	32	0.04
Samoan (2)	9	0.01
White (50,458)	53,661	73.50
Not Hispanic (49,591)	52,555	71.99
Hispanic (867)	1,106	1.51

Celina

Place Type: City
County: Mercer
Population: 10,400†

Ancestry‡	Population	%
American (1,042)	1,042	10.00
Arab (42)	42	0.40
Arab (42)	42	0.40
Armenian (2)	2	0.02
British (9)	12	0.12
Canadian (0)	21	0.20
Celtic (0)	7	0.07
Czech (0)	11	0.11
Czechoslovakian (0)	30	0.29
Danish (0)	8	0.08
Dutch (84)	210	2.01
English (258)	611	5.86
European (11)	32	0.31
French, ex. Basque (52)	515	4.94
French Canadian (11)	11	0.11
German (2,688)	4,739	45.46
Greek (17)	17	0.16
Hungarian (0)	34	0.33
Irish (193)	1,139	10.93
Italian (174)	446	4.28
Pennsylvania German (8)	8	0.08
Polish (46)	182	1.75
Russian (4)	4	0.04
Scandinavian (8)	8	0.08
Scotch-Irish (68)	86	0.83
Scottish (20)	144	1.38
Slavic (5)	5	0.05
Slovak (59)	59	0.57
Swedish (0)	14	0.13
Swiss (0)	35	0.34
Welsh (29)	107	1.03
Yugoslavian (13)	24	0.23

Hispanic Origin	Population	%
Hispanic or Latino (of any race)	293	2.82
Central American, ex. Mexican	3	0.03
Guatemalan	1	0.01
Panamanian	2	0.02
Cuban	3	0.03
Mexican	235	2.26
Puerto Rican	16	0.15
South American	1	0.01
Peruvian	1	0.01
Other Hispanic or Latino	35	0.34

Race*	Population	%
African-American/Black (50)	127	1.22
Not Hispanic (45)	119	1.14
Hispanic (5)	8	0.08
American Indian/Alaska Native (44)	93	0.89

*Notes: † The Census 2010 population figure is used to calculate the percentages in the Hispanic Origin and Race categories. Ancestry percentages are based on the 2006-2010 American Community Survey population (not shown); ‡ Numbers in parentheses indicate the number of people reporting a single ancestry; * Numbers in parentheses indicate the number of persons reporting this race alone, not in combination with any other race; Please refer to the Explanation of Data for more information.*

	Population	%
Not Hispanic (37)	77	0.74
Hispanic (7)	16	0.15
Alaska Athabascan *(Ala. Nat.)* (1)	1	0.01
Apache (1)	4	0.04
Blackfeet (0)	5	0.05
Cherokee (9)	34	0.33
Chippewa (0)	1	0.01
Comanche (1)	4	0.04
Crow (1)	1	0.01
Iroquois (5)	6	0.06
Mexican American Ind. (0)	3	0.03
Navajo (0)	1	0.01
Sioux (2)	3	0.03
Asian (117)	150	1.44
Not Hispanic (116)	146	1.40
Hispanic (1)	4	0.04
Cambodian (17)	20	0.19
Chinese, ex. Taiwanese (25)	27	0.26
Filipino (8)	14	0.13
Indian (40)	46	0.44
Japanese (8)	12	0.12
Korean (8)	16	0.15
Pakistani (5)	7	0.07
Thai (0)	4	0.04
Vietnamese (1)	3	0.03
Hawaii Native/Pacific Islander (41)	42	0.40
Not Hispanic (40)	40	0.38
Hispanic (1)	2	0.02
Guamanian/Chamorro (1)	1	0.01
Marshallese (24)	24	0.23
Native Hawaiian (7)	8	0.08
White (9,873)	10,027	96.41
Not Hispanic (9,734)	9,857	94.78
Hispanic (139)	170	1.63

Centerville

Place Type: City
County: Montgomery
Population: 23,999†

Ancestry‡	Population	%
African, Sub-Saharan (17)	17	0.07
African (17)	17	0.07
American (1,875)	1,875	7.87
Arab (379)	453	1.90
Arab (16)	16	0.07
Egyptian (16)	61	0.26
Iraqi (264)	264	1.11
Lebanese (24)	53	0.22
Other Arab (59)	59	0.25
Armenian (16)	16	0.07
Australian (0)	16	0.07
Austrian (17)	69	0.29
Belgian (0)	29	0.12
British (36)	242	1.02
Bulgarian (11)	11	0.05
Canadian (15)	35	0.15
Croatian (7)	7	0.03
Czech (17)	17	0.07
Czechoslovakian (0)	27	0.11
Danish (0)	27	0.11
Dutch (129)	427	1.79
Eastern European (55)	55	0.23
English (1,032)	3,483	14.61
European (214)	277	1.16
Finnish (0)	17	0.07
French, ex. Basque (63)	817	3.43
French Canadian (66)	80	0.34
German (3,364)	7,976	33.46
Greek (116)	248	1.04
Guyanese (123)	123	0.52
Hungarian (83)	233	0.98
Irish (1,071)	4,055	17.01
Italian (363)	841	3.53
Latvian (20)	41	0.17
Northern European (33)	33	0.14
Norwegian (89)	164	0.69
Pennsylvania German (11)	11	0.05
Polish (320)	794	3.33
Portuguese (0)	14	0.06
Romanian (46)	54	0.23
Russian (140)	183	0.77
Scandinavian (13)	27	0.11
Scotch-Irish (180)	690	2.89
Scottish (165)	571	2.40
Slavic (9)	9	0.04
Slovak (50)	63	0.26
Slovene (28)	59	0.25
Swedish (105)	320	1.34
Swiss (44)	91	0.38
Turkish (7)	22	0.09
Ukrainian (18)	66	0.28
Welsh (43)	197	0.83

Hispanic Origin	Population	%
Hispanic or Latino (of any race)	439	1.83
Central American, ex. Mexican	22	0.09
Costa Rican	6	0.03
Guatemalan	6	0.03
Honduran	1	<0.01
Nicaraguan	2	0.01
Panamanian	1	<0.01
Salvadoran	6	0.03
Cuban	24	0.10
Dominican Republic	2	0.01
Mexican	173	0.72
Puerto Rican	77	0.32
South American	79	0.33
Argentinean	8	0.03
Bolivian	8	0.03
Chilean	1	<0.01
Colombian	26	0.11
Ecuadorian	12	0.05
Peruvian	23	0.10
Venezuelan	1	<0.01
Other Hispanic or Latino	62	0.26

Race*	Population	%
African-American/Black (954)	1,176	4.90
Not Hispanic (939)	1,152	4.80
Hispanic (15)	24	0.10
American Indian/Alaska Native (52)	156	0.65
Not Hispanic (48)	146	0.61
Hispanic (4)	10	0.04
Alaska Athabascan *(Ala. Nat.)* (0)	1	<0.01
Apache (0)	4	0.02
Blackfeet (1)	8	0.03
Cherokee (11)	43	0.18
Chickasaw (2)	2	0.01
Chippewa (1)	3	0.01
Choctaw (4)	5	0.02
Creek (1)	1	<0.01
Crow (0)	5	0.02
Delaware (2)	2	0.01
Inupiat *(Alaska Native)* (0)	1	<0.01
Iroquois (1)	1	<0.01
Mexican American Ind. (0)	2	0.01
Navajo (1)	1	<0.01
Pueblo (1)	1	<0.01
Puget Sound Salish (1)	1	<0.01
Sioux (5)	5	0.02
Asian (770)	944	3.93
Not Hispanic (767)	932	3.88
Hispanic (3)	12	0.05
Bangladeshi (2)	2	0.01
Burmese (5)	5	0.02
Cambodian (3)	4	0.02
Chinese, ex. Taiwanese (200)	225	0.94
Filipino (40)	73	0.30
Indian (266)	279	1.16
Indonesian (6)	12	0.05
Japanese (40)	67	0.28
Korean (78)	100	0.42
Nepalese (2)	2	0.01
Pakistani (36)	37	0.15
Sri Lankan (7)	7	0.03
Taiwanese (28)	37	0.15
Thai (6)	9	0.04
Vietnamese (38)	43	0.18
Hawaii Native/Pacific Islander (11)	29	0.12
Not Hispanic (11)	26	0.11
Hispanic (0)	3	0.01
Guamanian/Chamorro (4)	5	0.02
Native Hawaiian (6)	12	0.05
White (21,654)	22,061	91.92
Not Hispanic (21,335)	21,708	90.45
Hispanic (319)	353	1.47

Cheviot

Place Type: City
County: Hamilton
Population: 8,375†

Ancestry‡	Population	%
African, Sub-Saharan (124)	124	1.47
African (124)	124	1.47
American (339)	339	4.03
Austrian (0)	9	0.11
Belgian (0)	10	0.12
British (0)	17	0.20
Canadian (0)	16	0.19
Dutch (0)	184	2.19
English (149)	575	6.83
European (103)	103	1.22
French, ex. Basque (43)	401	4.77
German (1,865)	4,015	47.72
Greek (8)	18	0.21
Hungarian (0)	101	1.20
Irish (323)	1,715	20.39
Italian (212)	438	5.21
Northern European (14)	14	0.17
Polish (43)	68	0.81
Portuguese (0)	9	0.11
Romanian (0)	44	0.52
Russian (13)	13	0.15
Scotch-Irish (56)	161	1.91
Scottish (68)	216	2.57
Welsh (0)	68	0.81

Hispanic Origin	Population	%
Hispanic or Latino (of any race)	170	2.03
Central American, ex. Mexican	27	0.32
Costa Rican	3	0.04
Guatemalan	4	0.05
Honduran	10	0.12
Salvadoran	5	0.06
Other Central American	5	0.06
Cuban	2	0.02
Dominican Republic	1	0.01
Mexican	73	0.87
Puerto Rican	19	0.23
South American	25	0.30
Argentinean	2	0.02
Colombian	4	0.05
Ecuadorian	2	0.02
Peruvian	12	0.14
Venezuelan	4	0.05
Other South American	1	0.01
Other Hispanic or Latino	23	0.27

Race*	Population	%
African-American/Black (609)	710	8.48
Not Hispanic (608)	706	8.43
Hispanic (1)	4	0.05
American Indian/Alaska Native (19)	65	0.78
Not Hispanic (17)	59	0.70
Hispanic (2)	6	0.07
Apache (0)	3	0.04
Blackfeet (1)	4	0.05
Cherokee (2)	13	0.16
Chippewa (0)	2	0.02
Comanche (1)	1	0.01
Delaware (1)	1	0.01
Iroquois (0)	1	0.01
Navajo (1)	3	0.04
Sioux (2)	6	0.07
Asian (45)	70	0.84
Not Hispanic (45)	68	0.81

*Notes: † The Census 2010 population figure is used to calculate the percentages in the Hispanic Origin and Race categories. Ancestry percentages are based on the 2006-2010 American Community Survey population (not shown); ‡ Numbers in parentheses indicate the number of people reporting a single ancestry; * Numbers in parentheses indicate the number of persons reporting this race alone, not in combination with any other race; Please refer to the Explanation of Data for more information.*

Hispanic (0)	2	0.02
Cambodian (1)	1	0.01
Chinese, ex. Taiwanese (4)	8	0.10
Filipino (4)	9	0.11
Indian (10)	11	0.13
Japanese (9)	15	0.18
Korean (2)	6	0.07
Nepalese (5)	6	0.07
Thai (2)	3	0.04
Vietnamese (7)	8	0.10
Hawaii Native/Pacific Islander (1)	3	0.04
Not Hispanic (1)	2	0.02
Hispanic (0)	1	0.01
White (7,453)	7,621	91.00
Not Hispanic (7,369)	7,516	89.74
Hispanic (84)	105	1.25

Chillicothe

Place Type: City
County: Ross
Population: 21,901†

Ancestry‡	Population	%
African, Sub-Saharan (36)	41	0.19
African (10)	15	0.07
Nigerian (13)	13	0.06
Other Sub-Saharan African (13)	13	0.06
Albanian (0)	10	0.05
American (2,626)	2,626	11.94
Armenian (0)	10	0.05
Austrian (0)	23	0.10
Belgian (17)	17	0.08
British (22)	75	0.34
Canadian (43)	43	0.20
Czech (20)	30	0.14
Czechoslovakian (0)	31	0.14
Danish (0)	14	0.06
Dutch (158)	531	2.41
English (981)	2,801	12.73
European (242)	257	1.17
Finnish (25)	25	0.11
French, ex. Basque (84)	599	2.72
French Canadian (16)	66	0.30
German (2,319)	6,104	27.75
Greek (14)	14	0.06
Hungarian (33)	67	0.30
Irish (954)	3,219	14.63
Italian (83)	520	2.36
Northern European (8)	8	0.04
Norwegian (0)	51	0.23
Polish (134)	193	0.88
Romanian (0)	12	0.05
Russian (63)	99	0.45
Scandinavian (0)	24	0.11
Scotch-Irish (380)	693	3.15
Scottish (108)	388	1.76
Slavic (11)	43	0.20
Slovak (0)	10	0.05
Swedish (55)	125	0.57
Swiss (16)	52	0.24
Turkish (9)	9	0.04
Welsh (83)	271	1.23
West Indian, ex. Hispanic (35)	58	0.26
Barbadian (4)	4	0.02
Haitian (31)	31	0.14
Trinidadian/Tobagonian (0)	23	0.10

Hispanic Origin	Population	%
Hispanic or Latino (of any race)	292	1.33
Central American, ex. Mexican	11	0.05
Honduran	2	0.01
Panamanian	1	<0.01
Salvadoran	8	0.04
Cuban	15	0.07
Mexican	139	0.63
Puerto Rican	61	0.28
South American	17	0.08
Argentinean	6	0.03
Chilean	1	<0.01
Colombian	4	0.02
Ecuadorian	1	<0.01
Peruvian	5	0.02
Other Hispanic or Latino	49	0.22

Race*	Population	%
African-American/Black (1,577)	2,053	9.37
Not Hispanic (1,559)	2,010	9.18
Hispanic (18)	43	0.20
American Indian/Alaska Native (71)	310	1.42
Not Hispanic (60)	276	1.26
Hispanic (11)	34	0.16
Apache (2)	4	0.02
Blackfeet (1)	17	0.08
Cherokee (28)	112	0.51
Chickasaw (0)	1	<0.01
Chippewa (1)	2	0.01
Crow (0)	1	<0.01
Iroquois (0)	2	0.01
Kiowa (1)	1	<0.01
Lumbee (1)	1	<0.01
Mexican American Ind. (2)	7	0.03
Potawatomi (1)	1	<0.01
Seminole (0)	3	0.01
Sioux (2)	8	0.04
Asian (112)	176	0.80
Not Hispanic (112)	169	0.77
Hispanic (0)	7	0.03
Bangladeshi (6)	6	0.03
Cambodian (1)	3	0.01
Chinese, ex. Taiwanese (18)	20	0.09
Filipino (21)	37	0.17
Indian (11)	24	0.11
Indonesian (0)	1	<0.01
Japanese (9)	19	0.09
Korean (5)	13	0.06
Laotian (1)	1	<0.01
Malaysian (0)	1	<0.01
Nepalese (5)	5	0.02
Taiwanese (2)	2	0.01
Thai (4)	8	0.04
Vietnamese (20)	23	0.11
Hawaii Native/Pacific Islander (2)	24	0.11
Not Hispanic (2)	19	0.09
Hispanic (0)	5	0.02
Fijian (0)	2	0.01
Guamanian/Chamorro (1)	2	0.01
Native Hawaiian (0)	2	0.01
Samoan (0)	1	<0.01
White (19,294)	19,987	91.26
Not Hispanic (19,148)	19,783	90.33
Hispanic (146)	204	0.93

Cincinnati

Place Type: City
County: Hamilton
Population: 296,943†

Ancestry‡	Population	%
African, Sub-Saharan (16,040)	17,006	5.67
African (14,780)	15,631	5.21
Ethiopian (432)	458	0.15
Ghanaian (23)	23	0.01
Kenyan (12)	12	<0.01
Liberian (26)	26	0.01
Nigerian (158)	158	0.05
Senegalese (144)	195	0.06
South African (13)	13	<0.01
Sudanese (63)	63	0.02
Zimbabwean (53)	53	0.02
Other Sub-Saharan African (336)	374	0.12
Alsatian (9)	67	0.02
American (18,156)	18,156	6.05
Arab (941)	1,405	0.47
Arab (142)	199	0.07
Egyptian (107)	133	0.04
Iraqi (14)	14	<0.01
Jordanian (112)	127	0.04
Lebanese (408)	704	0.23
Moroccan (65)	65	0.02
Palestinian (40)	55	0.02
Syrian (0)	38	0.01
Other Arab (53)	70	0.02
Armenian (30)	82	0.03
Assyrian/Chaldean/Syriac (0)	9	<0.01
Australian (45)	50	0.02
Austrian (82)	502	0.17
Belgian (48)	185	0.06
Brazilian (16)	23	0.01
British (770)	1,314	0.44
Bulgarian (13)	13	<0.01
Cajun (0)	41	0.01
Canadian (144)	275	0.09
Celtic (0)	29	0.01
Croatian (60)	146	0.05
Czech (240)	704	0.23
Czechoslovakian (64)	180	0.06
Danish (99)	439	0.15
Dutch (627)	2,867	0.96
Eastern European (147)	172	0.06
English (4,893)	16,011	5.33
Estonian (69)	86	0.03
European (2,291)	2,521	0.84
Finnish (7)	175	0.06
French, ex. Basque (685)	5,247	1.75
French Canadian (127)	503	0.17
German (23,192)	59,441	19.80
German Russian (0)	34	0.01
Greek (499)	840	0.28
Guyanese (77)	77	0.03
Hungarian (350)	1,319	0.44
Iranian (47)	69	0.02
Irish (8,007)	32,799	10.93
Israeli (75)	118	0.04
Italian (3,201)	9,502	3.17
Latvian (36)	67	0.02
Lithuanian (86)	212	0.07
Macedonian (13)	46	0.02
Maltese (0)	18	0.01
Northern European (69)	69	0.02
Norwegian (302)	1,024	0.34
Pennsylvania German (46)	63	0.02
Polish (972)	3,782	1.26
Portuguese (10)	142	0.05
Romanian (46)	356	0.12
Russian (598)	1,528	0.51
Scandinavian (168)	293	0.10
Scotch-Irish (988)	3,249	1.08
Scottish (987)	3,828	1.28
Serbian (10)	10	<0.01
Slavic (9)	63	0.02
Slovak (229)	659	0.22
Slovene (19)	90	0.03
Soviet Union (15)	15	<0.01
Swedish (193)	1,245	0.41
Swiss (128)	796	0.27
Turkish (75)	75	0.02
Ukrainian (128)	313	0.10
Welsh (405)	2,038	0.68
West Indian, ex. Hispanic (270)	478	0.16
Bahamian (33)	33	0.01
British West Indian (0)	20	0.01
Haitian (41)	41	0.01
Jamaican (153)	292	0.10
Trinidadian/Tobagonian (29)	29	0.01
West Indian (14)	53	0.02
Other West Indian (0)	10	<0.01
Yugoslavian (128)	158	0.05

Hispanic Origin	Population	%
Hispanic or Latino (of any race)	8,308	2.80
Central American, ex. Mexican	1,860	0.63
Costa Rican	39	0.01
Guatemalan	1,257	0.42
Honduran	230	0.08
Nicaraguan	90	0.03
Panamanian	78	0.03
Salvadoran	132	0.04
Other Central American	34	0.01

*Notes: † The Census 2010 population figure is used to calculate the percentages in the Hispanic Origin and Race categories. Ancestry percentages are based on the 2006-2010 American Community Survey population (not shown); ‡ Numbers in parentheses indicate the number of people reporting a single ancestry; * Numbers in parentheses indicate the number of persons reporting this race alone, not in combination with any other race; Please refer to the Explanation of Data for more information.*

Cuban	320	0.11
Dominican Republic	119	0.04
Mexican	3,244	1.09
Puerto Rican	973	0.33
South American	668	0.22
Argentinean	83	0.03
Bolivian	14	<0.01
Chilean	50	0.02
Colombian	215	0.07
Ecuadorian	45	0.02
Paraguayan	6	<0.01
Peruvian	138	0.05
Uruguayan	1	<0.01
Venezuelan	107	0.04
Other South American	9	<0.01
Other Hispanic or Latino	1,124	0.38

Race*	Population	%
African-American/Black (133,039)	138,296	46.57
Not Hispanic (132,307)	137,223	46.21
Hispanic (732)	1,073	0.36
American Indian/Alaska Native (759)	2,658	0.90
Not Hispanic (549)	2,276	0.77
Hispanic (210)	382	0.13
Alaska Athabascan *(Ala. Nat.)* (1)	3	<0.01
Aleut *(Alaska Native)* (4)	8	<0.01
Apache (10)	44	0.01
Arapaho (0)	4	<0.01
Blackfeet (16)	160	0.05
Canadian/French Am. Ind. (3)	6	<0.01
Central American Ind. (95)	98	0.03
Cherokee (85)	652	0.22
Chickasaw (5)	11	<0.01
Chippewa (13)	29	0.01
Choctaw (6)	26	0.01
Comanche (5)	7	<0.01
Cree (0)	6	<0.01
Creek (6)	23	0.01
Crow (0)	5	<0.01
Delaware (2)	5	<0.01
Inupiat *(Alaska Native)* (1)	1	<0.01
Iroquois (6)	18	0.01
Lumbee (4)	4	<0.01
Menominee (1)	1	<0.01
Mexican American Ind. (25)	38	0.01
Navajo (11)	31	0.01
Osage (2)	3	<0.01
Ottawa (0)	1	<0.01
Potawatomi (1)	10	<0.01
Pueblo (3)	4	<0.01
Seminole (3)	20	0.01
Shoshone (0)	2	<0.01
Sioux (12)	56	0.02
South American Ind. (2)	18	0.01
Spanish American Ind. (6)	6	<0.01
Tohono O'Odham (1)	7	<0.01
Tsimshian *(Alaska Native)* (0)	1	<0.01
Yakama (0)	1	<0.01
Yaqui (0)	2	<0.01
Yuman (2)	2	<0.01
Asian (5,481)	6,875	2.32
Not Hispanic (5,434)	6,728	2.27
Hispanic (47)	147	0.05
Bangladeshi (25)	25	0.01
Bhutanese (74)	74	0.02
Burmese (12)	13	<0.01
Cambodian (169)	212	0.07
Chinese, ex. Taiwanese (1,267)	1,558	0.52
Filipino (411)	718	0.24
Hmong (0)	3	<0.01
Indian (1,805)	2,036	0.69
Indonesian (10)	31	0.01
Japanese (222)	399	0.13
Korean (514)	674	0.23
Laotian (9)	14	<0.01
Malaysian (4)	5	<0.01
Nepalese (59)	77	0.03
Pakistani (98)	125	0.04
Sri Lankan (75)	82	0.03
Taiwanese (112)	122	0.04
Thai (108)	143	0.05
Vietnamese (303)	359	0.12
Hawaii Native/Pacific Islander (251)	465	0.16
Not Hispanic (168)	344	0.12
Hispanic (83)	121	0.04
Fijian (1)	1	<0.01
Guamanian/Chamorro (171)	202	0.07
Marshallese (1)	2	<0.01
Native Hawaiian (15)	70	0.02
Samoan (21)	51	0.02
White (146,435)	152,515	51.36
Not Hispanic (142,831)	148,354	49.96
Hispanic (3,604)	4,161	1.40

Circleville

Place Type: City
County: Pickaway
Population: 13,314†

Ancestry‡	Population	%
African, Sub-Saharan (52)	81	0.61
African (52)	81	0.61
American (2,430)	2,430	18.19
Arab (0)	6	0.04
Lebanese (0)	6	0.04
Assyrian/Chaldean/Syriac (13)	13	0.10
Belgian (17)	17	0.13
British (39)	94	0.70
Canadian (0)	9	0.07
Danish (0)	10	0.07
Dutch (56)	442	3.31
English (1,017)	1,492	11.17
European (57)	57	0.43
French, ex. Basque (65)	282	2.11
German (1,736)	3,545	26.54
Irish (447)	1,949	14.59
Italian (87)	663	4.96
Lithuanian (0)	12	0.09
Norwegian (9)	49	0.37
Pennsylvania German (0)	3	0.02
Polish (51)	120	0.90
Portuguese (24)	24	0.18
Scotch-Irish (38)	112	0.84
Scottish (177)	376	2.81
Serbian (0)	18	0.13
Slovak (0)	17	0.13
Slovene (0)	5	0.04
Swedish (24)	105	0.79
Swiss (0)	18	0.13
Ukrainian (0)	12	0.09
Welsh (88)	197	1.47

Hispanic Origin	Population	%
Hispanic or Latino (of any race)	142	1.07
Central American, ex. Mexican	15	0.11
Guatemalan	5	0.04
Honduran	6	0.05
Panamanian	3	0.02
Salvadoran	1	0.01
Cuban	1	0.01
Mexican	81	0.61
Puerto Rican	18	0.14
South American	2	0.02
Bolivian	1	0.01
Colombian	1	0.01
Other Hispanic or Latino	25	0.19

Race*	Population	%
African-American/Black (257)	383	2.88
Not Hispanic (255)	376	2.82
Hispanic (2)	7	0.05
American Indian/Alaska Native (22)	117	0.88
Not Hispanic (21)	111	0.83
Hispanic (1)	6	0.05
Alaska Athabascan *(Ala. Nat.)* (2)	3	0.02
Aleut *(Alaska Native)* (1)	1	0.01
Blackfeet (0)	7	0.05
Cherokee (10)	38	0.29
Chippewa (0)	2	0.02
Comanche (1)	2	0.02
Creek (0)	1	0.01
Navajo (0)	1	0.01
Shoshone (0)	1	0.01
Sioux (0)	5	0.04
Asian (54)	84	0.63
Not Hispanic (54)	83	0.62
Hispanic (0)	1	0.01
Chinese, ex. Taiwanese (12)	16	0.12
Filipino (12)	18	0.14
Indian (15)	24	0.18
Japanese (2)	8	0.06
Korean (2)	12	0.09
Pakistani (6)	6	0.05
Taiwanese (1)	1	0.01
Thai (1)	3	0.02
Hawaii Native/Pacific Islander (4)	10	0.08
Not Hispanic (4)	10	0.08
Guamanian/Chamorro (1)	1	0.01
Native Hawaiian (2)	3	0.02
Samoan (1)	4	0.03
White (12,699)	12,915	97.00
Not Hispanic (12,611)	12,815	96.25
Hispanic (88)	100	0.75

Clayton

Place Type: City
County: Montgomery
Population: 13,209†

Ancestry‡	Population	%
African, Sub-Saharan (17)	117	0.88
African (17)	117	0.88
American (892)	892	6.74
Arab (7)	41	0.31
Lebanese (7)	41	0.31
Armenian (35)	35	0.26
Australian (0)	13	0.10
Austrian (0)	27	0.20
British (18)	69	0.52
Canadian (23)	23	0.17
Celtic (6)	6	0.05
Croatian (6)	6	0.05
Czech (17)	67	0.51
Czechoslovakian (0)	16	0.12
Danish (24)	31	0.23
Dutch (57)	383	2.89
Eastern European (7)	7	0.05
English (409)	1,703	12.87
European (261)	319	2.41
French, ex. Basque (60)	527	3.98
French Canadian (23)	42	0.32
German (1,872)	4,145	31.33
Greek (12)	18	0.14
Hungarian (83)	161	1.22
Irish (411)	1,714	12.95
Italian (169)	470	3.55
Lithuanian (0)	23	0.17
Norwegian (38)	52	0.39
Pennsylvania German (24)	24	0.18
Polish (70)	176	1.33
Romanian (9)	9	0.07
Russian (68)	139	1.05
Scandinavian (28)	28	0.21
Scotch-Irish (0)	72	0.54
Scottish (82)	262	1.98
Slovak (13)	30	0.23
Slovene (0)	11	0.08
Swedish (0)	6	0.05
Swiss (18)	24	0.18
Ukrainian (8)	8	0.06
Welsh (19)	168	1.27
West Indian, ex. Hispanic (18)	18	0.14
Bermudan (18)	18	0.14

Hispanic Origin	Population	%
Hispanic or Latino (of any race)	182	1.38
Central American, ex. Mexican	13	0.10
Costa Rican	3	0.02

*Notes: † The Census 2010 population figure is used to calculate the percentages in the Hispanic Origin and Race categories. Ancestry percentages are based on the 2006-2010 American Community Survey population (not shown); ‡ Numbers in parentheses indicate the number of people reporting a single ancestry; * Numbers in parentheses indicate the number of persons reporting this race alone, not in combination with any other race; Please refer to the Explanation of Data for more information.*

Guatemalan	3	0.02
Honduran	3	0.02
Panamanian	1	0.01
Salvadoran	3	0.02
Cuban	6	0.05
Dominican Republic	10	0.08
Mexican	93	0.70
Puerto Rican	28	0.21
South American	6	0.05
Ecuadorian	2	0.02
Peruvian	2	0.02
Venezuelan	2	0.02
Other Hispanic or Latino	26	0.20

Race*	Population	%
African-American/Black (2,482)	2,703	20.46
Not Hispanic (2,472)	2,689	20.36
Hispanic (10)	14	0.11
American Indian/Alaska Native (23)	119	0.90
Not Hispanic (18)	105	0.79
Hispanic (5)	14	0.11
Apache (0)	3	0.02
Blackfeet (3)	6	0.05
Central American Ind. (0)	5	0.04
Cherokee (6)	34	0.26
Chippewa (0)	4	0.03
Choctaw (0)	2	0.02
Comanche (0)	1	0.01
Hopi (1)	1	0.01
Navajo (0)	1	0.01
Sioux (0)	6	0.05
Asian (182)	238	1.80
Not Hispanic (182)	237	1.79
Hispanic (0)	1	0.01
Cambodian (8)	8	0.06
Chinese, ex. Taiwanese (33)	45	0.34
Filipino (18)	41	0.31
Indian (59)	62	0.47
Japanese (14)	27	0.20
Korean (15)	23	0.17
Taiwanese (12)	14	0.11
Thai (0)	1	0.01
Vietnamese (16)	22	0.17
Hawaii Native/Pacific Islander (3)	12	0.09
Not Hispanic (3)	7	0.05
Hispanic (0)	5	0.04
Guamanian/Chamorro (1)	1	0.01
Native Hawaiian (2)	5	0.04
White (10,107)	10,392	78.67
Not Hispanic (10,010)	10,280	77.83
Hispanic (97)	112	0.85

Cleveland Heights

Place Type: City
County: Cuyahoga
Population: 46,121†

Ancestry‡	Population	%
African, Sub-Saharan (532)	608	1.30
African (357)	433	0.93
Liberian (28)	28	0.06
Nigerian (88)	88	0.19
South African (35)	35	0.07
Ugandan (12)	12	0.03
Other Sub-Saharan African (12)	12	0.03
American (972)	972	2.08
Arab (555)	742	1.59
Egyptian (32)	72	0.15
Lebanese (185)	297	0.63
Moroccan (75)	82	0.18
Palestinian (47)	47	0.10
Syrian (24)	44	0.09
Other Arab (192)	200	0.43
Armenian (16)	58	0.12
Austrian (28)	255	0.54
Belgian (0)	24	0.05
Brazilian (13)	37	0.08
British (102)	231	0.49
Bulgarian (0)	11	0.02
Canadian (42)	210	0.45
Celtic (10)	10	0.02
Croatian (114)	266	0.57
Czech (151)	482	1.03
Czechoslovakian (25)	84	0.18
Danish (137)	271	0.58
Dutch (113)	574	1.23
Eastern European (448)	475	1.02
English (506)	2,987	6.38
European (425)	608	1.30
Finnish (17)	116	0.25
French, ex. Basque (146)	892	1.91
French Canadian (32)	228	0.49
German (1,699)	6,476	13.84
Greek (68)	251	0.54
Hungarian (425)	1,224	2.62
Iranian (35)	67	0.14
Irish (1,326)	4,607	9.84
Israeli (20)	49	0.10
Italian (828)	2,318	4.95
Latvian (31)	31	0.07
Lithuanian (69)	165	0.35
New Zealander (10)	10	0.02
Northern European (27)	35	0.07
Norwegian (45)	188	0.40
Polish (476)	1,422	3.04
Portuguese (0)	35	0.07
Romanian (88)	115	0.25
Russian (656)	1,231	2.63
Scandinavian (30)	44	0.09
Scotch-Irish (237)	699	1.49
Scottish (149)	1,022	2.18
Serbian (13)	124	0.26
Slavic (7)	24	0.05
Slovak (133)	264	0.56
Slovene (34)	204	0.44
Swedish (46)	497	1.06
Swiss (39)	250	0.53
Turkish (0)	29	0.06
Ukrainian (103)	415	0.89
Welsh (59)	365	0.78
West Indian, ex. Hispanic (260)	351	0.75
Bermudan (11)	11	0.02
Haitian (0)	10	0.02
Jamaican (249)	315	0.67
West Indian (0)	15	0.03
Yugoslavian (21)	27	0.06

Hispanic Origin	Population	%
Hispanic or Latino (of any race)	903	1.96
Central American, ex. Mexican	100	0.22
Costa Rican	4	0.01
Guatemalan	14	0.03
Honduran	6	0.01
Nicaraguan	7	0.02
Panamanian	7	0.02
Salvadoran	61	0.13
Other Central American	1	<0.01
Cuban	51	0.11
Dominican Republic	28	0.06
Mexican	195	0.42
Puerto Rican	255	0.55
South American	124	0.27
Argentinean	19	0.04
Bolivian	3	0.01
Chilean	16	0.03
Colombian	30	0.07
Ecuadorian	10	0.02
Paraguayan	1	<0.01
Peruvian	23	0.05
Uruguayan	5	0.01
Venezuelan	15	0.03
Other South American	2	<0.01
Other Hispanic or Latino	150	0.33

Race*	Population	%
African-American/Black (19,587)	20,487	44.42
Not Hispanic (19,448)	20,266	43.94
Hispanic (139)	221	0.48
American Indian/Alaska Native (74)	434	0.94
Not Hispanic (61)	387	0.84
Hispanic (13)	47	0.10
Apache (0)	7	0.02
Blackfeet (4)	39	0.08
Canadian/French Am. Ind. (0)	4	0.01
Central American Ind. (0)	2	<0.01
Cherokee (8)	105	0.23
Chickasaw (2)	2	<0.01
Chippewa (2)	8	0.02
Choctaw (2)	9	0.02
Comanche (0)	1	<0.01
Cree (0)	1	<0.01
Creek (0)	4	0.01
Crow (0)	1	<0.01
Delaware (0)	1	<0.01
Inupiat *(Alaska Native)* (1)	1	<0.01
Iroquois (4)	15	0.03
Kiowa (1)	1	<0.01
Lumbee (1)	4	0.01
Mexican American Ind. (5)	12	0.03
Navajo (2)	6	0.01
Osage (0)	1	<0.01
Ottawa (0)	2	<0.01
Pueblo (0)	2	<0.01
Puget Sound Salish (1)	1	<0.01
Seminole (0)	10	0.02
Sioux (2)	14	0.03
South American Ind. (1)	3	0.01
Asian (1,900)	2,267	4.92
Not Hispanic (1,880)	2,236	4.85
Hispanic (20)	31	0.07
Bangladeshi (3)	3	0.01
Bhutanese (44)	48	0.10
Burmese (4)	6	0.01
Cambodian (8)	8	0.02
Chinese, ex. Taiwanese (558)	640	1.39
Filipino (109)	185	0.40
Indian (658)	726	1.57
Indonesian (3)	5	0.01
Japanese (52)	102	0.22
Korean (155)	186	0.40
Laotian (10)	10	0.02
Malaysian (1)	2	<0.01
Nepalese (34)	34	0.07
Pakistani (25)	31	0.07
Sri Lankan (14)	17	0.04
Taiwanese (68)	83	0.18
Thai (62)	68	0.15
Vietnamese (28)	44	0.10
Hawaii Native/Pacific Islander (6)	30	0.07
Not Hispanic (6)	26	0.06
Hispanic (0)	4	0.01
Fijian (1)	1	<0.01
Native Hawaiian (3)	15	0.03
Samoan (0)	3	0.01
Tongan (1)	3	0.01
White (22,984)	24,004	52.05
Not Hispanic (22,536)	23,458	50.86
Hispanic (448)	546	1.18

Cleveland

Place Type: City
County: Cuyahoga
Population: 396,815†

Ancestry‡	Population	%
African, Sub-Saharan (4,355)	5,454	1.33
African (3,344)	4,279	1.05
Cape Verdean (19)	58	0.01
Ethiopian (21)	21	0.01
Ghanaian (79)	79	0.02
Kenyan (0)	10	<0.01
Liberian (128)	128	0.03
Nigerian (352)	352	0.09
Senegalese (17)	17	<0.01
Somalian (41)	41	0.01
South African (19)	68	0.02
Sudanese (86)	86	0.02
Other Sub-Saharan African (249)	315	0.08

*Notes: † The Census 2010 population figure is used to calculate the percentages in the Hispanic Origin and Race categories. Ancestry percentages are based on the 2006-2010 American Community Survey population (not shown); ‡ Numbers in parentheses indicate the number of people reporting a single ancestry; * Numbers in parentheses indicate the number of persons reporting this race alone, not in combination with any other race; Please refer to the Explanation of Data for more information.*

Albanian (130)	139	0.03
American (9,836)	9,836	2.40
Arab (2,382)	3,346	0.82
Arab (466)	663	0.16
Egyptian (318)	326	0.08
Iraqi (85)	85	0.02
Jordanian (115)	115	0.03
Lebanese (551)	1,147	0.28
Moroccan (37)	75	0.02
Palestinian (553)	553	0.14
Syrian (77)	155	0.04
Other Arab (180)	227	0.06
Armenian (61)	91	0.02
Assyrian/Chaldean/Syriac (5)	5	<0.01
Australian (24)	39	0.01
Austrian (85)	589	0.14
Belgian (0)	96	0.02
Brazilian (80)	80	0.02
British (102)	474	0.12
Bulgarian (29)	54	0.01
Cajun (29)	29	0.01
Canadian (124)	343	0.08
Celtic (8)	18	<0.01
Croatian (509)	1,547	0.38
Czech (881)	2,835	0.69
Czechoslovakian (319)	553	0.14
Danish (54)	230	0.06
Dutch (180)	2,881	0.70
Eastern European (140)	140	0.03
English (4,019)	13,765	3.36
European (887)	1,116	0.27
Finnish (79)	376	0.09
French, ex. Basque (428)	4,063	0.99
French Canadian (146)	425	0.10
German (9,110)	40,200	9.82
German Russian (18)	18	<0.01
Greek (536)	1,435	0.35
Guyanese (304)	370	0.09
Hungarian (2,360)	6,822	1.67
Icelander (11)	25	0.01
Iranian (26)	26	0.01
Irish (9,753)	37,296	9.11
Israeli (10)	10	<0.01
Italian (7,160)	19,033	4.65
Latvian (62)	99	0.02
Lithuanian (435)	1,180	0.29
Macedonian (0)	10	<0.01
Northern European (48)	48	0.01
Norwegian (77)	435	0.11
Pennsylvania German (89)	157	0.04
Polish (6,968)	18,227	4.45
Portuguese (73)	277	0.07
Romanian (904)	1,296	0.32
Russian (692)	2,395	0.59
Scandinavian (29)	127	0.03
Scotch-Irish (927)	2,928	0.72
Scottish (682)	3,093	0.76
Serbian (241)	529	0.13
Slavic (72)	232	0.06
Slovak (2,328)	7,074	1.73
Slovene (1,381)	3,214	0.79
Swedish (186)	1,163	0.28
Swiss (55)	405	0.10
Turkish (45)	53	0.01
Ukrainian (858)	2,072	0.51
Welsh (131)	1,575	0.38
West Indian, ex. Hispanic (1,118)	1,835	0.45
Belizean (0)	16	<0.01
Bermudan (11)	11	<0.01
British West Indian (21)	31	0.01
Haitian (22)	31	0.01
Jamaican (904)	1,281	0.31
Trinidadian/Tobagonian (45)	94	0.02
U.S. Virgin Islander (7)	7	<0.01
West Indian (108)	364	0.09
Yugoslavian (168)	287	0.07

Hispanic Origin	Population	%
Hispanic or Latino (of any race)	39,534	9.96
Central American, ex. Mexican	2,085	0.53
Costa Rican	45	0.01
Guatemalan	786	0.20
Honduran	324	0.08
Nicaraguan	82	0.02
Panamanian	89	0.02
Salvadoran	738	0.19
Other Central American	21	0.01
Cuban	463	0.12
Dominican Republic	1,140	0.29
Mexican	3,593	0.91
Puerto Rican	29,286	7.38
South American	959	0.24
Argentinean	70	0.02
Bolivian	3	<0.01
Chilean	62	0.02
Colombian	320	0.08
Ecuadorian	113	0.03
Paraguayan	8	<0.01
Peruvian	276	0.07
Uruguayan	28	0.01
Venezuelan	54	0.01
Other South American	25	0.01
Other Hispanic or Latino	2,008	0.51

Race*	Population	%
African-American/Black (211,672)	219,027	55.20
Not Hispanic (208,208)	213,920	53.91
Hispanic (3,464)	5,107	1.29
American Indian/Alaska Native (1,340)	4,008	1.01
Not Hispanic (997)	3,202	0.81
Hispanic (343)	806	0.20
Alaska Athabascan *(Ala. Nat.)* (0)	2	<0.01
Apache (10)	43	0.01
Arapaho (0)	7	<0.01
Blackfeet (39)	240	0.06
Canadian/French Am. Ind. (2)	7	<0.01
Central American Ind. (24)	32	0.01
Cherokee (140)	865	0.22
Cheyenne (5)	7	<0.01
Chickasaw (14)	34	0.01
Chippewa (38)	54	0.01
Choctaw (29)	83	0.02
Colville (1)	3	<0.01
Comanche (1)	3	<0.01
Cree (1)	3	<0.01
Creek (7)	23	0.01
Crow (3)	10	<0.01
Delaware (3)	10	<0.01
Hopi (0)	4	<0.01
Inupiat *(Alaska Native)* (3)	6	<0.01
Iroquois (27)	62	0.02
Kiowa (6)	11	<0.01
Lumbee (6)	9	<0.01
Mexican American Ind. (44)	60	0.02
Navajo (16)	31	0.01
Ottawa (6)	7	<0.01
Pima (0)	1	<0.01
Potawatomi (1)	4	<0.01
Pueblo (13)	13	<0.01
Seminole (9)	30	0.01
Shoshone (3)	4	<0.01
Sioux (34)	91	0.02
South American Ind. (39)	105	0.03
Spanish American Ind. (2)	3	<0.01
Tlingit-Haida *(Alaska Native)* (2)	2	<0.01
Tohono O'Odham (7)	7	<0.01
Yup'ik *(Alaska Native)* (1)	3	<0.01
Asian (7,327)	8,705	2.19
Not Hispanic (7,213)	8,422	2.12
Hispanic (114)	283	0.07
Bangladeshi (8)	11	<0.01
Bhutanese (70)	94	0.02
Burmese (63)	69	0.02
Cambodian (275)	328	0.08
Chinese, ex. Taiwanese (2,620)	2,916	0.73
Filipino (643)	937	0.24
Hmong (2)	7	<0.01
Indian (1,412)	1,649	0.42
Indonesian (18)	25	0.01
Japanese (158)	349	0.09
Korean (418)	533	0.13
Laotian (87)	108	0.03
Malaysian (6)	12	<0.01
Nepalese (79)	108	0.03
Pakistani (55)	61	0.02
Sri Lankan (14)	18	<0.01
Taiwanese (94)	102	0.03
Thai (89)	121	0.03
Vietnamese (882)	990	0.25
Hawaii Native/Pacific Islander (120)	582	0.15
Not Hispanic (70)	347	0.09
Hispanic (50)	235	0.06
Guamanian/Chamorro (47)	73	0.02
Native Hawaiian (25)	127	0.03
Samoan (7)	24	0.01
Tongan (4)	6	<0.01
White (147,929)	156,136	39.35
Not Hispanic (132,710)	138,590	34.93
Hispanic (15,219)	17,546	4.42

Columbus

Place Type: City
County: Franklin
Population: 787,033†

Ancestry‡	Population	%
Afghan (67)	89	0.01
African, Sub-Saharan (25,127)	26,987	3.50
African (9,844)	10,986	1.43
Cape Verdean (28)	28	<0.01
Ethiopian (2,080)	2,207	0.29
Ghanaian (1,270)	1,303	0.17
Kenyan (433)	517	0.07
Liberian (376)	384	0.05
Nigerian (703)	861	0.11
Senegalese (104)	104	0.01
Sierra Leonean (433)	461	0.06
Somalian (8,938)	9,093	1.18
South African (97)	115	0.01
Sudanese (53)	90	0.01
Zimbabwean (125)	125	0.02
Other Sub-Saharan African (643)	713	0.09
Albanian (261)	292	0.04
Alsatian (0)	29	<0.01
American (31,925)	31,925	4.14
Arab (4,438)	6,451	0.84
Arab (974)	1,109	0.14
Egyptian (669)	911	0.12
Iraqi (279)	334	0.04
Jordanian (602)	617	0.08
Lebanese (518)	1,656	0.21
Moroccan (222)	308	0.04
Palestinian (576)	604	0.08
Syrian (163)	415	0.05
Other Arab (435)	497	0.06
Armenian (111)	163	0.02
Assyrian/Chaldean/Syriac (97)	97	0.01
Australian (43)	154	0.02
Austrian (325)	1,440	0.19
Belgian (320)	699	0.09
Brazilian (263)	284	0.04
British (1,471)	3,242	0.42
Bulgarian (55)	130	0.02
Cajun (0)	56	0.01
Canadian (509)	1,023	0.13
Carpatho Rusyn (12)	35	<0.01
Celtic (17)	95	0.01
Croatian (428)	1,158	0.15
Cypriot (0)	14	<0.01
Czech (836)	2,996	0.39
Czechoslovakian (251)	819	0.11
Danish (332)	1,200	0.16
Dutch (1,747)	10,822	1.40
Eastern European (701)	867	0.11
English (18,279)	58,155	7.55
Estonian (20)	20	<0.01
European (6,242)	7,099	0.92
Finnish (224)	858	0.11
French, ex. Basque (3,125)	14,605	1.90

*Notes: † The Census 2010 population figure is used to calculate the percentages in the Hispanic Origin and Race categories. Ancestry percentages are based on the 2006-2010 American Community Survey population (not shown); ‡ Numbers in parentheses indicate the number of people reporting a single ancestry; * Numbers in parentheses indicate the number of persons reporting this race alone, not in combination with any other race; Please refer to the Explanation of Data for more information.*

French Canadian (763)	1,886	0.24
German (59,347)	163,383	21.21
German Russian (33)	33	<0.01
Greek (1,110)	2,987	0.39
Guyanese (101)	135	0.02
Hungarian (1,716)	6,569	0.85
Icelander (15)	51	0.01
Iranian (408)	466	0.06
Irish (30,407)	99,000	12.85
Israeli (63)	138	0.02
Italian (14,391)	38,883	5.05
Latvian (150)	214	0.03
Lithuanian (193)	1,022	0.13
Luxemburger (14)	23	<0.01
Macedonian (235)	307	0.04
Maltese (0)	29	<0.01
New Zealander (48)	48	0.01
Northern European (188)	220	0.03
Norwegian (1,070)	3,594	0.47
Pennsylvania German (141)	359	0.05
Polish (5,407)	17,936	2.33
Portuguese (819)	1,667	0.22
Romanian (458)	1,256	0.16
Russian (2,348)	5,392	0.70
Scandinavian (453)	1,042	0.14
Scotch-Irish (4,412)	12,017	1.56
Scottish (4,099)	13,797	1.79
Serbian (189)	511	0.07
Slavic (192)	458	0.06
Slovak (1,091)	3,380	0.44
Slovene (592)	1,380	0.18
Swedish (985)	4,492	0.58
Swiss (563)	2,745	0.36
Turkish (530)	601	0.08
Ukrainian (989)	1,935	0.25
Welsh (2,202)	10,220	1.33
West Indian, ex. Hispanic (2,879)	3,944	0.51
Bahamian (82)	93	0.01
Barbadian (88)	132	0.02
Belizean (28)	42	0.01
Bermudan (0)	11	<0.01
British West Indian (149)	165	0.02
Dutch West Indian (0)	54	0.01
Haitian (1,450)	1,655	0.21
Jamaican (757)	1,305	0.17
Trinidadian/Tobagonian (68)	103	0.01
U.S. Virgin Islander (15)	27	<0.01
West Indian (242)	357	0.05
Yugoslavian (660)	883	0.11

Hispanic Origin	Population	%
Hispanic or Latino (of any race)	44,359	5.64
Central American, ex. Mexican	4,017	0.51
Costa Rican	129	0.02
Guatemalan	645	0.08
Honduran	784	0.10
Nicaraguan	157	0.02
Panamanian	294	0.04
Salvadoran	1,954	0.25
Other Central American	54	0.01
Cuban	922	0.12
Dominican Republic	1,553	0.20
Mexican	25,973	3.30
Puerto Rican	5,034	0.64
South American	2,730	0.35
Argentinean	273	0.03
Bolivian	81	0.01
Chilean	112	0.01
Colombian	797	0.10
Ecuadorian	491	0.06
Paraguayan	9	<0.01
Peruvian	543	0.07
Uruguayan	47	0.01
Venezuelan	355	0.05
Other South American	22	<0.01
Other Hispanic or Latino	4,130	0.52

Race*	Population	%
African-American/Black (220,241)	237,077	30.12
Not Hispanic (217,694)	233,108	29.62
Hispanic (2,547)	3,969	0.50
American Indian/Alaska Native (2,105)	8,353	1.06
Not Hispanic (1,643)	7,286	0.93
Hispanic (462)	1,067	0.14
Alaska Athabascan *(Ala. Nat.)* (8)	11	<0.01
Aleut *(Alaska Native)* (4)	9	<0.01
Apache (21)	109	0.01
Arapaho (0)	3	<0.01
Blackfeet (49)	539	0.07
Canadian/French Am. Ind. (3)	21	<0.01
Central American Ind. (11)	18	<0.01
Cherokee (333)	2,100	0.27
Cheyenne (3)	15	<0.01
Chickasaw (11)	23	<0.01
Chippewa (44)	112	0.01
Choctaw (17)	72	0.01
Colville (0)	1	<0.01
Comanche (3)	17	<0.01
Cree (6)	17	<0.01
Creek (8)	47	0.01
Crow (0)	12	<0.01
Delaware (5)	40	0.01
Hopi (3)	9	<0.01
Inupiat *(Alaska Native)* (2)	3	<0.01
Iroquois (50)	126	0.02
Kiowa (0)	1	<0.01
Lumbee (37)	56	0.01
Menominee (3)	3	<0.01
Mexican American Ind. (114)	203	0.03
Navajo (24)	68	0.01
Osage (5)	7	<0.01
Ottawa (6)	13	<0.01
Paiute (1)	1	<0.01
Pima (0)	3	<0.01
Potawatomi (5)	13	<0.01
Pueblo (9)	16	<0.01
Puget Sound Salish (0)	1	<0.01
Seminole (3)	42	0.01
Shoshone (3)	5	<0.01
Sioux (41)	182	0.02
South American Ind. (24)	51	0.01
Spanish American Ind. (14)	18	<0.01
Tlingit-Haida *(Alaska Native)* (9)	10	<0.01
Tohono O'Odham (2)	5	<0.01
Tsimshian *(Alaska Native)* (1)	1	<0.01
Ute (1)	4	<0.01
Yaqui (0)	1	<0.01
Yuman (0)	2	<0.01
Yup'ik *(Alaska Native)* (0)	2	<0.01
Asian (31,965)	37,743	4.80
Not Hispanic (31,734)	37,170	4.72
Hispanic (231)	573	0.07
Bangladeshi (334)	366	0.05
Bhutanese (71)	96	0.01
Burmese (198)	204	0.03
Cambodian (1,521)	1,794	0.23
Chinese, ex. Taiwanese (5,887)	6,780	0.86
Filipino (1,713)	2,827	0.36
Hmong (45)	51	0.01
Indian (10,495)	11,364	1.44
Indonesian (245)	326	0.04
Japanese (1,474)	2,331	0.30
Korean (2,612)	3,330	0.42
Laotian (1,161)	1,412	0.18
Malaysian (92)	121	0.02
Nepalese (163)	190	0.02
Pakistani (787)	927	0.12
Sri Lankan (188)	202	0.03
Taiwanese (535)	626	0.08
Thai (375)	594	0.08
Vietnamese (1,922)	2,319	0.29
Hawaii Native/Pacific Islander (512)	1,346	0.17
Not Hispanic (462)	1,149	0.15
Hispanic (50)	197	0.03
Fijian (4)	7	<0.01
Guamanian/Chamorro (77)	181	0.02
Native Hawaiian (78)	336	0.04
Samoan (298)	399	0.05
Tongan (0)	2	<0.01
White (483,677)	505,454	64.22
Not Hispanic (466,615)	485,567	61.70
Hispanic (17,062)	19,887	2.53

Conneaut

Place Type: City
County: Ashtabula
Population: 12,841†

Ancestry‡	Population	%
African, Sub-Saharan (45)	54	0.42
African (45)	45	0.35
Ethiopian (0)	9	0.07
American (1,388)	1,388	10.85
Arab (17)	26	0.20
Lebanese (17)	26	0.20
Austrian (0)	45	0.35
British (11)	11	0.09
Canadian (0)	12	0.09
Croatian (9)	9	0.07
Czech (0)	79	0.62
Czechoslovakian (9)	17	0.13
Danish (0)	10	0.08
Dutch (20)	151	1.18
English (369)	1,484	11.60
European (181)	181	1.41
Finnish (269)	688	5.38
French, ex. Basque (8)	217	1.70
French Canadian (18)	29	0.23
German (770)	3,214	25.11
Greek (7)	27	0.21
Hungarian (149)	421	3.29
Iranian (21)	21	0.16
Irish (541)	2,017	15.76
Israeli (0)	9	0.07
Italian (703)	1,545	12.07
Norwegian (6)	61	0.48
Pennsylvania German (18)	39	0.30
Polish (303)	774	6.05
Portuguese (9)	43	0.34
Russian (45)	77	0.60
Scotch-Irish (38)	131	1.02
Scottish (17)	228	1.78
Serbian (10)	48	0.38
Slovak (41)	236	1.84
Slovene (51)	92	0.72
Swedish (50)	230	1.80
Swiss (0)	8	0.06
Ukrainian (0)	10	0.08
Welsh (64)	173	1.35
Yugoslavian (8)	8	0.06

Hispanic Origin	Population	%
Hispanic or Latino (of any race)	230	1.79
Central American, ex. Mexican	14	0.11
Guatemalan	1	0.01
Honduran	11	0.09
Salvadoran	2	0.02
Cuban	3	0.02
Mexican	46	0.36
Puerto Rican	100	0.78
Other Hispanic or Latino	67	0.52

Race*	Population	%
African-American/Black (969)	1,085	8.45
Not Hispanic (963)	1,077	8.39
Hispanic (6)	8	0.06
American Indian/Alaska Native (23)	102	0.79
Not Hispanic (21)	91	0.71
Hispanic (2)	11	0.09
Apache (0)	1	0.01
Blackfeet (0)	6	0.05
Cherokee (3)	29	0.23
Chickasaw (0)	3	0.02
Chippewa (1)	2	0.02
Cree (1)	1	0.01
Crow (0)	1	0.01
Delaware (0)	5	0.04
Iroquois (0)	1	0.01
Mexican American Ind. (1)	1	0.01

*Notes: † The Census 2010 population figure is used to calculate the percentages in the Hispanic Origin and Race categories. Ancestry percentages are based on the 2006-2010 American Community Survey population (not shown); ‡ Numbers in parentheses indicate the number of people reporting a single ancestry; * Numbers in parentheses indicate the number of persons reporting this race alone, not in combination with any other race; Please refer to the Explanation of Data for more information.*

Spanish American Ind. (1)	1	0.01
Tohono O'Odham (0)	3	0.02
Asian (47)	75	0.58
Not Hispanic (45)	72	0.56
Hispanic (2)	3	0.02
Chinese, ex. Taiwanese (7)	11	0.09
Filipino (13)	24	0.19
Indian (14)	17	0.13
Japanese (1)	6	0.05
Korean (4)	7	0.05
Pakistani (2)	2	0.02
Thai (1)	1	0.01
Vietnamese (1)	1	0.01
Hawaii Native/Pacific Islander (2)	14	0.11
Not Hispanic (2)	13	0.10
Hispanic (0)	1	0.01
Guamanian/Chamorro (1)	8	0.06
Native Hawaiian (1)	5	0.04
White (11,527)	11,746	91.47
Not Hispanic (11,370)	11,569	90.09
Hispanic (157)	177	1.38

Coshocton

Place Type: City
County: Coshocton
Population: 11,216†

Ancestry‡	Population	%
American (1,024)	1,024	9.02
Arab (12)	18	0.16
Syrian (12)	18	0.16
Belgian (25)	25	0.22
British (148)	186	1.64
Carpatho Rusyn (0)	8	0.07
Czech (0)	51	0.45
Czechoslovakian (51)	51	0.45
Dutch (60)	261	2.30
English (924)	1,746	15.38
European (77)	77	0.68
French, ex. Basque (32)	219	1.93
French Canadian (0)	9	0.08
German (1,249)	3,154	27.79
Greek (8)	26	0.23
Hungarian (9)	74	0.65
Irish (476)	1,696	14.94
Italian (187)	310	2.73
Pennsylvania German (9)	9	0.08
Polish (64)	111	0.98
Russian (0)	11	0.10
Scotch-Irish (99)	314	2.77
Scottish (66)	294	2.59
Slovak (0)	11	0.10
Swedish (0)	8	0.07
Swiss (10)	49	0.43
Welsh (10)	137	1.21

Hispanic Origin	Population	%
Hispanic or Latino (of any race)	127	1.13
Central American, ex. Mexican	10	0.09
Panamanian	4	0.04
Salvadoran	6	0.05
Cuban	4	0.04
Mexican	89	0.79
Puerto Rican	18	0.16
South American	1	0.01
Bolivian	1	0.01
Other Hispanic or Latino	5	0.04

Race*	Population	%
African-American/Black (207)	328	2.92
Not Hispanic (205)	321	2.86
Hispanic (2)	7	0.06
American Indian/Alaska Native (20)	64	0.57
Not Hispanic (17)	57	0.51
Hispanic (3)	7	0.06
Blackfeet (1)	8	0.07
Cherokee (4)	21	0.19
Crow (0)	2	0.02
Delaware (1)	2	0.02
Iroquois (1)	1	0.01
Kiowa (1)	1	0.01
Seminole (2)	2	0.02
South American Ind. (1)	1	0.01
Asian (49)	62	0.55
Not Hispanic (49)	62	0.55
Chinese, ex. Taiwanese (7)	10	0.09
Filipino (2)	2	0.02
Indian (12)	13	0.12
Japanese (1)	3	0.03
Korean (11)	14	0.12
Laotian (2)	2	0.02
Malaysian (1)	1	0.01
Pakistani (4)	4	0.04
Vietnamese (6)	10	0.09
Hawaii Native/Pacific Islander (1)	2	0.02
Not Hispanic (1)	2	0.02
Native Hawaiian (1)	1	0.01
White (10,730)	10,902	97.20
Not Hispanic (10,651)	10,809	96.37
Hispanic (79)	93	0.83

Cuyahoga Falls

Place Type: City
County: Summit
Population: 49,652†

Ancestry‡	Population	%
African, Sub-Saharan (36)	71	0.14
African (36)	57	0.11
South African (0)	14	0.03
Alsatian (0)	11	0.02
American (2,075)	2,075	4.17
Arab (352)	533	1.07
Arab (80)	80	0.16
Lebanese (123)	291	0.59
Syrian (0)	13	0.03
Other Arab (149)	149	0.30
Armenian (27)	27	0.05
Austrian (0)	123	0.25
Belgian (15)	23	0.05
British (157)	219	0.44
Bulgarian (0)	8	0.02
Canadian (40)	130	0.26
Carpatho Rusyn (14)	14	0.03
Croatian (36)	117	0.24
Czech (55)	353	0.71
Czechoslovakian (107)	222	0.45
Danish (7)	137	0.28
Dutch (128)	1,076	2.16
Eastern European (76)	118	0.24
English (1,561)	6,483	13.04
European (415)	474	0.95
Finnish (25)	46	0.09
French, ex. Basque (171)	1,166	2.35
French Canadian (15)	136	0.27
German (4,418)	15,626	31.43
Greek (204)	382	0.77
Hungarian (369)	1,514	3.05
Iranian (9)	19	0.04
Irish (2,215)	9,658	19.43
Italian (2,576)	6,168	12.41
Lithuanian (138)	263	0.53
Macedonian (0)	59	0.12
New Zealander (0)	32	0.06
Northern European (17)	73	0.15
Norwegian (46)	263	0.53
Pennsylvania German (106)	117	0.24
Polish (675)	2,625	5.28
Portuguese (8)	60	0.12
Romanian (38)	201	0.40
Russian (37)	279	0.56
Scandinavian (7)	7	0.01
Scotch-Irish (557)	1,222	2.46
Scottish (181)	1,257	2.53
Serbian (123)	264	0.53
Slavic (91)	132	0.27
Slovak (202)	525	1.06
Slovene (62)	198	0.40
Swedish (194)	642	1.29
Swiss (47)	373	0.75
Turkish (18)	25	0.05
Ukrainian (26)	188	0.38
Welsh (141)	781	1.57
Yugoslavian (59)	125	0.25

Hispanic Origin	Population	%
Hispanic or Latino (of any race)	672	1.35
Central American, ex. Mexican	53	0.11
Costa Rican	1	<0.01
Guatemalan	11	0.02
Honduran	15	0.03
Nicaraguan	1	<0.01
Panamanian	3	0.01
Salvadoran	21	0.04
Other Central American	1	<0.01
Cuban	17	0.03
Dominican Republic	12	0.02
Mexican	284	0.57
Puerto Rican	157	0.32
South American	81	0.16
Argentinean	12	0.02
Bolivian	1	<0.01
Chilean	2	<0.01
Colombian	18	0.04
Ecuadorian	17	0.03
Paraguayan	1	<0.01
Peruvian	21	0.04
Venezuelan	9	0.02
Other Hispanic or Latino	68	0.14

Race*	Population	%
African-American/Black (1,642)	2,011	4.05
Not Hispanic (1,617)	1,972	3.97
Hispanic (25)	39	0.08
American Indian/Alaska Native (84)	344	0.69
Not Hispanic (75)	324	0.65
Hispanic (9)	20	0.04
Apache (0)	5	0.01
Blackfeet (3)	14	0.03
Central American Ind. (1)	1	<0.01
Cherokee (22)	94	0.19
Chickasaw (0)	1	<0.01
Chippewa (10)	12	0.02
Choctaw (0)	8	0.02
Comanche (0)	1	<0.01
Cree (0)	1	<0.01
Creek (1)	2	<0.01
Crow (1)	2	<0.01
Iroquois (4)	9	0.02
Kiowa (0)	1	<0.01
Lumbee (1)	1	<0.01
Mexican American Ind. (2)	3	0.01
Navajo (0)	3	0.01
Ottawa (1)	4	0.01
Shoshone (0)	1	<0.01
Sioux (8)	12	0.02
South American Ind. (0)	1	<0.01
Tlingit-Haida *(Alaska Native)* (0)	1	<0.01
Asian (573)	788	1.59
Not Hispanic (565)	776	1.56
Hispanic (8)	12	0.02
Bangladeshi (7)	7	0.01
Bhutanese (53)	54	0.11
Burmese (8)	8	0.02
Cambodian (5)	5	0.01
Chinese, ex. Taiwanese (82)	105	0.21
Filipino (56)	97	0.20
Hmong (1)	1	<0.01
Indian (134)	153	0.31
Indonesian (0)	3	0.01
Japanese (29)	48	0.10
Korean (82)	112	0.23
Laotian (12)	14	0.03
Malaysian (1)	2	<0.01
Nepalese (9)	9	0.02
Pakistani (3)	3	0.01
Sri Lankan (6)	6	0.01
Taiwanese (4)	4	0.01

*Notes: † The Census 2010 population figure is used to calculate the percentages in the Hispanic Origin and Race categories. Ancestry percentages are based on the 2006-2010 American Community Survey population (not shown); ‡ Numbers in parentheses indicate the number of people reporting a single ancestry; * Numbers in parentheses indicate the number of persons reporting this race alone, not in combination with any other race; Please refer to the Explanation of Data for more information.*

Thai (20)	25	0.05
Vietnamese (37)	46	0.09
Hawaii Native/Pacific Islander (6)	17	0.03
Not Hispanic (3)	13	0.03
Hispanic (3)	4	0.01
Guamanian/Chamorro (0)	3	0.01
Native Hawaiian (5)	6	0.01
Samoan (1)	2	<0.01
White (46,398)	47,141	94.94
Not Hispanic (45,939)	46,633	93.92
Hispanic (459)	508	1.02

Dayton

Place Type: City
County: Montgomery
Population: 141,527†

Ancestry‡	Population	%
African, Sub-Saharan (2,085)	2,395	1.64
African (1,718)	1,956	1.34
Ethiopian (78)	94	0.06
Kenyan (10)	10	0.01
Nigerian (104)	138	0.09
South African (9)	22	0.02
Other Sub-Saharan African (166)	175	0.12
Alsatian (13)	13	0.01
American (16,035)	16,035	11.01
Arab (256)	474	0.33
Arab (39)	39	0.03
Egyptian (28)	46	0.03
Iraqi (123)	123	0.08
Jordanian (0)	39	0.03
Lebanese (51)	184	0.13
Moroccan (0)	28	0.02
Palestinian (15)	15	0.01
Australian (9)	22	0.02
Austrian (11)	93	0.06
Belgian (35)	105	0.07
British (397)	727	0.50
Bulgarian (62)	125	0.09
Canadian (19)	116	0.08
Croatian (37)	81	0.06
Czech (69)	231	0.16
Czechoslovakian (27)	179	0.12
Danish (13)	94	0.06
Dutch (260)	1,660	1.14
Eastern European (0)	54	0.04
English (2,681)	7,108	4.88
European (968)	1,113	0.76
Finnish (53)	144	0.10
French, ex. Basque (165)	2,130	1.46
French Canadian (137)	280	0.19
German (8,595)	23,171	15.91
Greek (227)	451	0.31
Hungarian (312)	792	0.54
Irish (3,119)	14,086	9.67
Israeli (29)	29	0.02
Italian (1,474)	4,059	2.79
Latvian (9)	9	0.01
Lithuanian (47)	244	0.17
Macedonian (0)	14	0.01
Norwegian (78)	346	0.24
Pennsylvania German (21)	80	0.05
Polish (614)	2,017	1.39
Portuguese (0)	45	0.03
Romanian (11)	177	0.12
Russian (121)	358	0.25
Scandinavian (42)	93	0.06
Scotch-Irish (817)	1,768	1.21
Scottish (514)	1,758	1.21
Serbian (7)	30	0.02
Slavic (10)	31	0.02
Slovak (16)	154	0.11
Slovene (14)	132	0.09
Swedish (371)	927	0.64
Swiss (84)	346	0.24
Turkish (158)	203	0.14
Ukrainian (79)	150	0.10
Welsh (162)	856	0.59
West Indian, ex. Hispanic (175)	267	0.18
Haitian (32)	32	0.02
Jamaican (81)	173	0.12
Trinidadian/Tobagonian (62)	62	0.04
Yugoslavian (28)	28	0.02

Hispanic Origin	Population	%
Hispanic or Latino (of any race)	4,180	2.95
Central American, ex. Mexican	269	0.19
Costa Rican	87	0.06
Guatemalan	51	0.04
Honduran	59	0.04
Nicaraguan	14	0.01
Panamanian	37	0.03
Salvadoran	20	0.01
Other Central American	1	<0.01
Cuban	147	0.10
Dominican Republic	58	0.04
Mexican	2,541	1.80
Puerto Rican	515	0.36
South American	217	0.15
Argentinean	11	0.01
Bolivian	11	0.01
Chilean	8	0.01
Colombian	34	0.02
Ecuadorian	115	0.08
Paraguayan	1	<0.01
Peruvian	25	0.02
Uruguayan	7	<0.01
Venezuelan	5	<0.01
Other Hispanic or Latino	433	0.31

Race*	Population	%
African-American/Black (60,705)	63,535	44.89
Not Hispanic (60,342)	62,972	44.49
Hispanic (363)	563	0.40
American Indian/Alaska Native (417)	1,579	1.12
Not Hispanic (373)	1,460	1.03
Hispanic (44)	119	0.08
Aleut *(Alaska Native)* (4)	4	<0.01
Apache (5)	18	0.01
Arapaho (3)	10	0.01
Blackfeet (19)	100	0.07
Canadian/French Am. Ind. (0)	1	<0.01
Central American Ind. (1)	1	<0.01
Cherokee (90)	435	0.31
Cheyenne (0)	4	<0.01
Chickasaw (0)	1	<0.01
Chippewa (9)	23	0.02
Choctaw (1)	9	0.01
Comanche (1)	2	<0.01
Creek (6)	17	0.01
Delaware (0)	1	<0.01
Hopi (0)	1	<0.01
Iroquois (4)	19	0.01
Lumbee (1)	2	<0.01
Menominee (1)	6	<0.01
Mexican American Ind. (7)	12	0.01
Navajo (3)	13	0.01
Osage (0)	1	<0.01
Ottawa (2)	6	<0.01
Pima (1)	2	<0.01
Potawatomi (2)	3	<0.01
Pueblo (0)	5	<0.01
Puget Sound Salish (0)	2	<0.01
Seminole (2)	10	0.01
Shoshone (1)	1	<0.01
Sioux (10)	31	0.02
South American Ind. (1)	5	<0.01
Spanish American Ind. (2)	2	<0.01
Ute (0)	4	<0.01
Asian (1,206)	1,864	1.32
Not Hispanic (1,195)	1,813	1.28
Hispanic (11)	51	0.04
Bangladeshi (3)	8	0.01
Burmese (2)	2	<0.01
Cambodian (43)	59	0.04
Chinese, ex. Taiwanese (252)	324	0.23
Filipino (196)	334	0.24
Indian (220)	281	0.20
Indonesian (5)	16	0.01
Japanese (51)	147	0.10
Korean (96)	184	0.13
Laotian (0)	1	<0.01
Malaysian (9)	9	0.01
Nepalese (4)	4	<0.01
Pakistani (24)	30	0.02
Sri Lankan (8)	9	0.01
Taiwanese (10)	12	0.01
Thai (30)	54	0.04
Vietnamese (188)	220	0.16
Hawaii Native/Pacific Islander (52)	166	0.12
Not Hispanic (47)	148	0.10
Hispanic (5)	18	0.01
Guamanian/Chamorro (7)	31	0.02
Marshallese (0)	4	<0.01
Native Hawaiian (17)	57	0.04
Samoan (15)	34	0.02
Tongan (0)	2	<0.01
White (73,193)	76,680	54.18
Not Hispanic (71,458)	74,600	52.71
Hispanic (1,735)	2,080	1.47

Defiance

Place Type: City
County: Defiance
Population: 16,494†

Ancestry‡	Population	%
American (1,071)	1,071	6.46
Arab (39)	84	0.51
Arab (0)	15	0.09
Egyptian (14)	44	0.27
Lebanese (25)	25	0.15
Assyrian/Chaldean/Syriac (10)	10	0.06
Austrian (8)	59	0.36
British (11)	20	0.12
Bulgarian (7)	7	0.04
Canadian (0)	9	0.05
Croatian (0)	19	0.11
Czech (0)	65	0.39
Czechoslovakian (8)	33	0.20
Danish (0)	21	0.13
Dutch (70)	217	1.31
English (732)	1,756	10.59
European (31)	46	0.28
Finnish (9)	18	0.11
French, ex. Basque (37)	405	2.44
French Canadian (60)	69	0.42
German (2,788)	6,039	36.43
Greek (10)	10	0.06
Hungarian (97)	337	2.03
Irish (501)	2,095	12.64
Italian (187)	514	3.10
Macedonian (0)	8	0.05
Norwegian (48)	100	0.60
Pennsylvania German (17)	17	0.10
Polish (306)	517	3.12
Russian (0)	50	0.30
Scotch-Irish (53)	181	1.09
Scottish (77)	169	1.02
Serbian (0)	27	0.16
Slovak (0)	16	0.10
Slovene (0)	13	0.08
Swedish (25)	89	0.54
Swiss (28)	52	0.31
Welsh (37)	116	0.70
West Indian, ex. Hispanic (8)	8	0.05
Barbadian (8)	8	0.05

Hispanic Origin	Population	%
Hispanic or Latino (of any race)	2,376	14.41
Central American, ex. Mexican	15	0.09
Guatemalan	4	0.02
Nicaraguan	6	0.04
Panamanian	5	0.03
Mexican	1,874	11.36
Puerto Rican	217	1.32
South American	14	0.08

*Notes: † The Census 2010 population figure is used to calculate the percentages in the Hispanic Origin and Race categories. Ancestry percentages are based on the 2006-2010 American Community Survey population (not shown); ‡ Numbers in parentheses indicate the number of people reporting a single ancestry; * Numbers in parentheses indicate the number of persons reporting this race alone, not in combination with any other race; Please refer to the Explanation of Data for more information.*

Argentinean	9	0.05
Colombian	1	0.01
Ecuadorian	1	0.01
Peruvian	3	0.02
Other Hispanic or Latino	256	1.55

Race*	Population	%
African-American/Black (590)	779	4.72
Not Hispanic (532)	667	4.04
Hispanic (58)	112	0.68
American Indian/Alaska Native (49)	141	0.85
Not Hispanic (26)	98	0.59
Hispanic (23)	43	0.26
Apache (0)	4	0.02
Blackfeet (2)	9	0.05
Cherokee (7)	39	0.24
Chippewa (3)	3	0.02
Choctaw (1)	2	0.01
Comanche (0)	1	0.01
Iroquois (0)	1	0.01
Mexican American Ind. (5)	6	0.04
Sioux (1)	2	0.01
Spanish American Ind. (1)	4	0.02
Yup'ik *(Alaska Native)* (1)	1	0.01
Asian (62)	92	0.56
Not Hispanic (61)	84	0.51
Hispanic (1)	8	0.05
Cambodian (2)	2	0.01
Chinese, ex. Taiwanese (18)	20	0.12
Filipino (11)	20	0.12
Indian (6)	10	0.06
Japanese (4)	7	0.04
Korean (7)	11	0.07
Taiwanese (0)	1	0.01
Thai (2)	5	0.03
Vietnamese (8)	10	0.06
Hawaii Native/Pacific Islander (4)	10	0.06
Not Hispanic (4)	10	0.06
Native Hawaiian (1)	2	0.01
Samoan (0)	2	0.01
White (14,535)	14,972	90.77
Not Hispanic (13,270)	13,485	81.76
Hispanic (1,265)	1,487	9.02

Delaware

Place Type: City
County: Delaware
Population: 34,753†

Ancestry‡	Population	%
African, Sub-Saharan (54)	93	0.28
African (42)	68	0.20
Ghanaian (0)	13	0.04
Nigerian (12)	12	0.04
Alsatian (0)	9	0.03
American (1,875)	1,875	5.57
Arab (98)	241	0.72
Arab (18)	37	0.11
Iraqi (39)	58	0.17
Lebanese (41)	146	0.43
Armenian (9)	9	0.03
Austrian (21)	46	0.14
Belgian (21)	76	0.23
British (62)	289	0.86
Canadian (77)	98	0.29
Croatian (28)	84	0.25
Czech (56)	203	0.60
Czechoslovakian (8)	29	0.09
Danish (9)	45	0.13
Dutch (130)	805	2.39
Eastern European (0)	17	0.05
English (1,671)	4,469	13.27
European (394)	435	1.29
Finnish (0)	16	0.05
French, ex. Basque (117)	899	2.67
French Canadian (25)	79	0.23
German (3,589)	11,241	33.38
Greek (158)	342	1.02
Hungarian (132)	393	1.17
Icelander (0)	24	0.07
Iranian (40)	40	0.12
Irish (975)	5,071	15.06
Italian (558)	1,535	4.56
Lithuanian (0)	44	0.13
Luxemburger (6)	6	0.02
New Zealander (29)	29	0.09
Northern European (20)	20	0.06
Norwegian (26)	115	0.34
Polish (363)	1,342	3.99
Romanian (61)	70	0.21
Russian (83)	253	0.75
Scandinavian (21)	21	0.06
Scotch-Irish (192)	699	2.08
Scottish (245)	848	2.52
Serbian (0)	22	0.07
Slavic (0)	9	0.03
Slovak (81)	111	0.33
Slovene (0)	12	0.04
Swedish (67)	301	0.89
Swiss (52)	150	0.45
Turkish (0)	34	0.10
Ukrainian (33)	65	0.19
Welsh (154)	998	2.96
West Indian, ex. Hispanic (27)	37	0.11
British West Indian (9)	9	0.03
Jamaican (18)	23	0.07
Trinidadian/Tobagonian (0)	5	0.01

Hispanic Origin	Population	%
Hispanic or Latino (of any race)	881	2.54
Central American, ex. Mexican	83	0.24
Costa Rican	4	0.01
Guatemalan	35	0.10
Honduran	8	0.02
Nicaraguan	2	0.01
Panamanian	10	0.03
Salvadoran	24	0.07
Cuban	19	0.05
Dominican Republic	17	0.05
Mexican	520	1.50
Puerto Rican	75	0.22
South American	91	0.26
Argentinean	4	0.01
Bolivian	2	0.01
Colombian	43	0.12
Ecuadorian	14	0.04
Paraguayan	1	<0.01
Peruvian	16	0.05
Venezuelan	11	0.03
Other Hispanic or Latino	76	0.22

Race*	Population	%
African-American/Black (1,573)	2,059	5.92
Not Hispanic (1,545)	2,009	5.78
Hispanic (28)	50	0.14
American Indian/Alaska Native (65)	290	0.83
Not Hispanic (47)	254	0.73
Hispanic (18)	36	0.10
Apache (0)	1	<0.01
Blackfeet (1)	16	0.05
Canadian/French Am. Ind. (1)	1	<0.01
Central American Ind. (6)	6	0.02
Cherokee (11)	72	0.21
Chippewa (1)	4	0.01
Choctaw (0)	1	<0.01
Creek (1)	6	0.02
Delaware (0)	3	0.01
Iroquois (0)	12	0.03
Lumbee (1)	8	0.02
Mexican American Ind. (3)	3	0.01
Navajo (5)	5	0.01
Sioux (2)	12	0.03
South American Ind. (0)	1	<0.01
Asian (472)	617	1.78
Not Hispanic (460)	602	1.73
Hispanic (12)	15	0.04
Bangladeshi (2)	2	0.01
Burmese (0)	1	<0.01
Cambodian (4)	7	0.02
Chinese, ex. Taiwanese (116)	136	0.39
Filipino (40)	69	0.20
Indian (100)	113	0.33
Indonesian (4)	5	0.01
Japanese (29)	66	0.19
Korean (57)	73	0.21
Laotian (3)	3	0.01
Malaysian (2)	4	0.01
Nepalese (5)	5	0.01
Pakistani (21)	21	0.06
Sri Lankan (3)	4	0.01
Taiwanese (1)	6	0.02
Thai (7)	10	0.03
Vietnamese (58)	68	0.20
Hawaii Native/Pacific Islander (12)	43	0.12
Not Hispanic (10)	36	0.10
Hispanic (2)	7	0.02
Guamanian/Chamorro (6)	10	0.03
Native Hawaiian (3)	12	0.03
White (31,503)	32,314	92.98
Not Hispanic (30,966)	31,701	91.22
Hispanic (537)	613	1.76

Dent

Place Type: CDP
County: Hamilton
Population: 10,497†

Ancestry‡	Population	%
African, Sub-Saharan (48)	48	0.49
Nigerian (48)	48	0.49
Alsatian (13)	30	0.31
American (533)	533	5.44
Arab (10)	119	1.22
Arab (10)	29	0.30
Lebanese (0)	8	0.08
Syrian (0)	82	0.84
Austrian (0)	9	0.09
Basque (0)	17	0.17
British (18)	25	0.26
Canadian (13)	13	0.13
Czech (0)	14	0.14
Dutch (15)	178	1.82
Eastern European (30)	43	0.44
English (185)	589	6.01
European (40)	49	0.50
French, ex. Basque (15)	260	2.65
French Canadian (0)	37	0.38
German (2,517)	4,721	48.21
Greek (80)	80	0.82
Hungarian (27)	131	1.34
Irish (390)	1,818	18.56
Italian (440)	963	9.83
Lithuanian (15)	26	0.27
Norwegian (14)	96	0.98
Pennsylvania German (0)	13	0.13
Polish (28)	72	0.74
Romanian (0)	7	0.07
Russian (0)	128	1.31
Scotch-Irish (27)	106	1.08
Scottish (15)	131	1.34
Slovene (0)	9	0.09
Swiss (0)	53	0.54
Welsh (14)	56	0.57
West Indian, ex. Hispanic (16)	16	0.16
British West Indian (16)	16	0.16
Yugoslavian (0)	18	0.18

Hispanic Origin	Population	%
Hispanic or Latino (of any race)	117	1.11
Central American, ex. Mexican	16	0.15
Costa Rican	1	0.01
Guatemalan	12	0.11
Honduran	1	0.01
Salvadoran	2	0.02
Cuban	7	0.07
Mexican	48	0.46
Puerto Rican	17	0.16
South American	14	0.13

*Notes: † The Census 2010 population figure is used to calculate the percentages in the Hispanic Origin and Race categories. Ancestry percentages are based on the 2006-2010 American Community Survey population (not shown); ‡ Numbers in parentheses indicate the number of people reporting a single ancestry; * Numbers in parentheses indicate the number of persons reporting this race alone, not in combination with any other race; Please refer to the Explanation of Data for more information.*

Bolivian	2	0.02
Colombian	4	0.04
Ecuadorian	2	0.02
Peruvian	6	0.06
Other Hispanic or Latino	15	0.14

Race*	Population	%
African-American/Black (139)	176	1.68
Not Hispanic (137)	172	1.64
Hispanic (2)	4	0.04
American Indian/Alaska Native (6)	46	0.44
Not Hispanic (6)	43	0.41
Hispanic (0)	3	0.03
Apache (0)	4	0.04
Cherokee (2)	19	0.18
Colville (0)	3	0.03
Navajo (1)	1	0.01
Sioux (0)	1	0.01
Asian (164)	195	1.86
Not Hispanic (163)	192	1.83
Hispanic (1)	3	0.03
Chinese, ex. Taiwanese (25)	38	0.36
Filipino (11)	16	0.15
Indian (57)	65	0.62
Japanese (17)	27	0.26
Korean (9)	9	0.09
Sri Lankan (1)	1	0.01
Vietnamese (30)	35	0.33
Hawaii Native/Pacific Islander (1)	4	0.04
Not Hispanic (1)	3	0.03
Hispanic (0)	1	0.01
Native Hawaiian (1)	1	0.01
Samoan (0)	1	0.01
White (10,045)	10,150	96.69
Not Hispanic (9,959)	10,058	95.82
Hispanic (86)	92	0.88

Dover

Place Type: City
County: Tuscarawas
Population: 12,826†

Ancestry‡	Population	%
American (693)	693	5.42
Armenian (0)	20	0.16
Austrian (12)	54	0.42
Belgian (10)	30	0.23
British (0)	27	0.21
Croatian (9)	24	0.19
Czech (21)	39	0.31
Danish (0)	9	0.07
Dutch (15)	433	3.39
English (481)	1,321	10.34
European (234)	234	1.83
French, ex. Basque (42)	539	4.22
French Canadian (0)	43	0.34
German (1,901)	5,164	40.42
Greek (0)	58	0.45
Hungarian (24)	52	0.41
Irish (470)	2,144	16.78
Italian (702)	1,460	11.43
Lithuanian (10)	10	0.08
Norwegian (9)	49	0.38
Pennsylvania German (36)	59	0.46
Polish (65)	354	2.77
Romanian (0)	32	0.25
Russian (0)	81	0.63
Scandinavian (0)	15	0.12
Scotch-Irish (132)	409	3.20
Scottish (70)	323	2.53
Serbian (0)	15	0.12
Slovak (9)	96	0.75
Swedish (52)	121	0.95
Swiss (93)	541	4.23
Ukrainian (8)	8	0.06
Welsh (58)	320	2.50

Hispanic Origin	Population	%
Hispanic or Latino (of any race)	531	4.14
Central American, ex. Mexican	280	2.18
Guatemalan	273	2.13
Honduran	7	0.05
Cuban	4	0.03
Dominican Republic	3	0.02
Mexican	157	1.22
Puerto Rican	37	0.29
South American	2	0.02
Colombian	2	0.02
Other Hispanic or Latino	48	0.37

Race*	Population	%
African-American/Black (138)	208	1.62
Not Hispanic (125)	194	1.51
Hispanic (13)	14	0.11
American Indian/Alaska Native (75)	116	0.90
Not Hispanic (24)	65	0.51
Hispanic (51)	51	0.40
Apache (1)	1	0.01
Blackfeet (0)	3	0.02
Central American Ind. (32)	33	0.26
Cherokee (4)	17	0.13
Crow (1)	1	0.01
Delaware (2)	4	0.03
Iroquois (0)	2	0.02
Mexican American Ind. (0)	1	0.01
Sioux (1)	1	0.01
Yaqui (1)	1	0.01
Asian (68)	111	0.87
Not Hispanic (68)	111	0.87
Burmese (10)	10	0.08
Chinese, ex. Taiwanese (13)	16	0.12
Filipino (21)	33	0.26
Indian (16)	21	0.16
Japanese (2)	13	0.10
Korean (2)	6	0.05
Thai (2)	7	0.05
Hawaii Native/Pacific Islander (84)	100	0.78
Not Hispanic (31)	41	0.32
Hispanic (53)	59	0.46
Guamanian/Chamorro (83)	89	0.69
Native Hawaiian (0)	1	0.01
Samoan (1)	6	0.05
White (12,069)	12,236	95.40
Not Hispanic (11,891)	12,034	93.83
Hispanic (178)	202	1.57

Dublin

Place Type: City
County: Franklin
Population: 41,751†

Ancestry‡	Population	%
Afghan (38)	38	0.10
African, Sub-Saharan (176)	195	0.50
African (99)	118	0.30
Somalian (77)	77	0.20
American (1,504)	1,504	3.83
Arab (415)	610	1.55
Arab (103)	138	0.35
Egyptian (164)	164	0.42
Jordanian (48)	48	0.12
Lebanese (88)	153	0.39
Moroccan (8)	39	0.10
Syrian (4)	33	0.08
Other Arab (0)	35	0.09
Armenian (31)	31	0.08
Assyrian/Chaldean/Syriac (10)	10	0.03
Austrian (14)	28	0.07
Belgian (24)	37	0.09
Brazilian (116)	155	0.39
British (255)	287	0.73
Bulgarian (0)	13	0.03
Canadian (66)	107	0.27
Croatian (12)	50	0.13
Czech (83)	329	0.84
Czechoslovakian (49)	98	0.25
Danish (0)	35	0.09
Dutch (126)	646	1.65
Eastern European (51)	62	0.16
English (1,844)	5,519	14.06
European (782)	836	2.13
Finnish (22)	68	0.17
French, ex. Basque (82)	904	2.30
French Canadian (27)	215	0.55
German (4,512)	11,866	30.24
Greek (379)	624	1.59
Hungarian (171)	579	1.48
Iranian (98)	98	0.25
Irish (1,459)	5,865	14.94
Italian (1,174)	3,348	8.53
Latvian (12)	12	0.03
Lithuanian (27)	36	0.09
Luxemburger (8)	8	0.02
Macedonian (49)	49	0.12
Northern European (77)	77	0.20
Norwegian (54)	284	0.72
Polish (453)	1,513	3.86
Portuguese (28)	76	0.19
Romanian (0)	30	0.08
Russian (113)	253	0.64
Scandinavian (10)	121	0.31
Scotch-Irish (382)	907	2.31
Scottish (328)	1,328	3.38
Serbian (0)	60	0.15
Slavic (31)	88	0.22
Slovak (137)	475	1.21
Slovene (71)	148	0.38
Swedish (193)	978	2.49
Swiss (61)	287	0.73
Ukrainian (59)	181	0.46
Welsh (172)	748	1.91

Hispanic Origin	Population	%
Hispanic or Latino (of any race)	764	1.83
Central American, ex. Mexican	70	0.17
Costa Rican	3	0.01
Guatemalan	23	0.06
Honduran	11	0.03
Nicaraguan	6	0.01
Panamanian	9	0.02
Salvadoran	13	0.03
Other Central American	5	0.01
Cuban	27	0.06
Dominican Republic	13	0.03
Mexican	303	0.73
Puerto Rican	107	0.26
South American	149	0.36
Argentinean	6	0.01
Bolivian	14	0.03
Chilean	12	0.03
Colombian	47	0.11
Ecuadorian	6	0.01
Paraguayan	3	0.01
Peruvian	23	0.06
Uruguayan	1	<0.01
Venezuelan	37	0.09
Other Hispanic or Latino	95	0.23

Race*	Population	%
African-American/Black (752)	919	2.20
Not Hispanic (722)	878	2.10
Hispanic (30)	41	0.10
American Indian/Alaska Native (25)	153	0.37
Not Hispanic (22)	139	0.33
Hispanic (3)	14	0.03
Blackfeet (1)	8	0.02
Central American Ind. (0)	1	<0.01
Cherokee (2)	36	0.09
Cheyenne (0)	1	<0.01
Chippewa (2)	2	<0.01
Choctaw (1)	4	0.01
Cree (0)	1	<0.01
Creek (0)	1	<0.01
Iroquois (0)	9	0.02
Lumbee (1)	4	0.01
Mexican American Ind. (3)	5	0.01
Potawatomi (1)	1	<0.01
Shoshone (0)	1	<0.01

*Notes: † The Census 2010 population figure is used to calculate the percentages in the Hispanic Origin and Race categories. Ancestry percentages are based on the 2006-2010 American Community Survey population (not shown); ‡ Numbers in parentheses indicate the number of people reporting a single ancestry; * Numbers in parentheses indicate the number of persons reporting this race alone, not in combination with any other race; Please refer to the Explanation of Data for more information.*

Sioux (0)	3	0.01
Asian (6,384)	6,891	16.50
Not Hispanic (6,370)	6,866	16.45
Hispanic (14)	25	0.06
Bangladeshi (47)	53	0.13
Burmese (5)	9	0.02
Cambodian (2)	6	0.01
Chinese, ex. Taiwanese (1,250)	1,343	3.22
Filipino (98)	171	0.41
Indian (2,864)	2,986	7.15
Indonesian (22)	30	0.07
Japanese (1,071)	1,154	2.76
Korean (529)	611	1.46
Laotian (7)	9	0.02
Malaysian (1)	3	0.01
Nepalese (6)	6	0.01
Pakistani (94)	105	0.25
Sri Lankan (28)	35	0.08
Taiwanese (117)	121	0.29
Thai (12)	21	0.05
Vietnamese (100)	127	0.30
Hawaii Native/Pacific Islander (17)	32	0.08
Not Hispanic (12)	26	0.06
Hispanic (5)	6	0.01
Guamanian/Chamorro (4)	7	0.02
Native Hawaiian (2)	5	0.01
Samoan (2)	2	<0.01
White (33,608)	34,260	82.06
Not Hispanic (33,089)	33,697	80.71
Hispanic (519)	563	1.35

East Cleveland

Place Type: City
County: Cuyahoga
Population: 17,843†

Ancestry‡	Population	%
African, Sub-Saharan (322)	418	2.15
African (322)	418	2.15
Albanian (7)	7	0.04
American (237)	237	1.22
Arab (14)	14	0.07
Lebanese (14)	14	0.07
Armenian (8)	8	0.04
English (24)	122	0.63
European (12)	12	0.06
French, ex. Basque (0)	20	0.10
French Canadian (19)	19	0.10
German (66)	163	0.84
Hungarian (22)	35	0.18
Irish (98)	233	1.20
Italian (10)	60	0.31
Polish (0)	28	0.14
Russian (122)	122	0.63
Scandinavian (0)	9	0.05
Scotch-Irish (9)	34	0.18
Scottish (0)	39	0.20
Slovak (5)	18	0.09
Slovene (14)	21	0.11
Swedish (18)	56	0.29
Ukrainian (15)	15	0.08
Welsh (9)	16	0.08
West Indian, ex. Hispanic (184)	193	0.99
Jamaican (150)	159	0.82
West Indian (34)	34	0.18

Hispanic Origin	Population	%
Hispanic or Latino (of any race)	179	1.00
Central American, ex. Mexican	8	0.04
Costa Rican	1	0.01
Guatemalan	4	0.02
Panamanian	3	0.02
Cuban	16	0.09
Dominican Republic	3	0.02
Mexican	39	0.22
Puerto Rican	74	0.41
South American	7	0.04
Chilean	2	0.01
Colombian	1	0.01
Peruvian	1	0.01
Venezuelan	3	0.02
Other Hispanic or Latino	32	0.18

Race*	Population	%
African-American/Black (16,638)	16,901	94.72
Not Hispanic (16,532)	16,770	93.99
Hispanic (106)	131	0.73
American Indian/Alaska Native (40)	145	0.81
Not Hispanic (38)	131	0.73
Hispanic (2)	14	0.08
Apache (0)	2	0.01
Blackfeet (0)	15	0.08
Central American Ind. (1)	2	0.01
Cherokee (6)	23	0.13
Chippewa (0)	2	0.01
Choctaw (0)	2	0.01
Creek (1)	1	0.01
Iroquois (0)	6	0.03
Navajo (1)	1	0.01
Sioux (1)	5	0.03
Asian (40)	67	0.38
Not Hispanic (40)	65	0.36
Hispanic (0)	2	0.01
Burmese (6)	6	0.03
Chinese, ex. Taiwanese (10)	17	0.10
Filipino (3)	12	0.07
Indian (11)	16	0.09
Japanese (2)	3	0.02
Korean (3)	4	0.02
Vietnamese (0)	4	0.02
Hawaii Native/Pacific Islander (0)	11	0.06
Not Hispanic (0)	7	0.04
Hispanic (0)	4	0.02
Guamanian/Chamorro (0)	5	0.03
Native Hawaiian (0)	5	0.03
Samoan (0)	1	0.01
White (817)	977	5.48
Not Hispanic (796)	938	5.26
Hispanic (21)	39	0.22

East Liverpool

Place Type: City
County: Columbiana
Population: 11,195†

Ancestry‡	Population	%
African, Sub-Saharan (16)	16	0.14
African (16)	16	0.14
American (885)	885	7.67
Belgian (29)	57	0.49
British (0)	13	0.11
Canadian (17)	47	0.41
Czech (0)	31	0.27
Czechoslovakian (0)	23	0.20
Danish (10)	18	0.16
Dutch (60)	221	1.92
English (675)	2,071	17.95
European (8)	8	0.07
French, ex. Basque (17)	65	0.56
German (639)	2,413	20.92
Hungarian (7)	35	0.30
Irish (456)	2,059	17.85
Italian (246)	604	5.24
Norwegian (11)	26	0.23
Pennsylvania German (20)	20	0.17
Polish (28)	198	1.72
Portuguese (0)	6	0.05
Russian (0)	9	0.08
Scotch-Irish (154)	393	3.41
Scottish (130)	256	2.22
Serbian (6)	16	0.14
Slavic (17)	17	0.15
Slovak (16)	65	0.56
Swiss (0)	16	0.14
Ukrainian (12)	34	0.29
Welsh (174)	361	3.13
West Indian, ex. Hispanic (7)	7	0.06
Jamaican (7)	7	0.06

Hispanic Origin	Population	%
Hispanic or Latino (of any race)	121	1.08
Central American, ex. Mexican	5	0.04
Guatemalan	1	0.01
Panamanian	4	0.04
Cuban	2	0.02
Mexican	72	0.64
Puerto Rican	19	0.17
South American	1	0.01
Colombian	1	0.01
Other Hispanic or Latino	22	0.20

Race*	Population	%
African-American/Black (511)	749	6.69
Not Hispanic (510)	745	6.65
Hispanic (1)	4	0.04
American Indian/Alaska Native (22)	110	0.98
Not Hispanic (20)	101	0.90
Hispanic (2)	9	0.08
Alaska Athabascan *(Ala. Nat.)* (1)	1	0.01
Apache (1)	1	0.01
Blackfeet (0)	7	0.06
Cherokee (3)	42	0.38
Cheyenne (1)	1	0.01
Chickasaw (1)	1	0.01
Chippewa (1)	4	0.04
Choctaw (0)	5	0.04
Cree (0)	1	0.01
Creek (0)	1	0.01
Iroquois (0)	1	0.01
Mexican American Ind. (1)	1	0.01
Navajo (0)	2	0.02
Paiute (0)	1	0.01
Sioux (0)	1	0.01
South American Ind. (0)	4	0.04
Asian (22)	32	0.29
Not Hispanic (22)	32	0.29
Chinese, ex. Taiwanese (8)	8	0.07
Filipino (7)	8	0.07
Indian (2)	3	0.03
Japanese (0)	3	0.03
Korean (0)	5	0.04
Pakistani (4)	4	0.04
Vietnamese (1)	1	0.01
Hawaii Native/Pacific Islander (2)	6	0.05
Not Hispanic (2)	6	0.05
Guamanian/Chamorro (1)	5	0.04
Native Hawaiian (1)	1	0.01
White (10,270)	10,591	94.60
Not Hispanic (10,198)	10,505	93.84
Hispanic (72)	86	0.77

Eastlake

Place Type: City
County: Lake
Population: 18,577†

Ancestry‡	Population	%
American (592)	592	3.14
Arab (15)	40	0.21
Arab (15)	15	0.08
Lebanese (0)	25	0.13
Armenian (27)	27	0.14
Austrian (32)	166	0.88
Brazilian (0)	9	0.05
Canadian (8)	27	0.14
Croatian (431)	689	3.65
Czech (49)	249	1.32
Czechoslovakian (12)	36	0.19
Danish (41)	93	0.49
Dutch (19)	228	1.21
English (422)	2,147	11.37
European (94)	94	0.50
Finnish (24)	50	0.26
French, ex. Basque (42)	391	2.07
French Canadian (47)	126	0.67
German (1,189)	5,248	27.80
Greek (9)	59	0.31
Guyanese (0)	9	0.05

*Notes: † The Census 2010 population figure is used to calculate the percentages in the Hispanic Origin and Race categories. Ancestry percentages are based on the 2006-2010 American Community Survey population (not shown); ‡ Numbers in parentheses indicate the number of people reporting a single ancestry; * Numbers in parentheses indicate the number of persons reporting this race alone, not in combination with any other race; Please refer to the Explanation of Data for more information.*

Hungarian (281)	942	4.99
Irish (961)	3,593	19.03
Italian (1,387)	3,466	18.36
Latvian (12)	12	0.06
Lithuanian (106)	286	1.51
Macedonian (6)	6	0.03
Norwegian (0)	74	0.39
Pennsylvania German (0)	16	0.08
Polish (583)	1,616	8.56
Romanian (37)	118	0.63
Russian (16)	202	1.07
Scandinavian (0)	6	0.03
Scotch-Irish (19)	315	1.67
Scottish (31)	200	1.06
Serbian (19)	76	0.40
Slavic (0)	91	0.48
Slovak (239)	619	3.28
Slovene (675)	1,595	8.45
Swedish (45)	162	0.86
Turkish (0)	19	0.10
Ukrainian (64)	137	0.73
Welsh (48)	322	1.71
Yugoslavian (239)	265	1.40

Hispanic Origin	Population	%
Hispanic or Latino (of any race)	263	1.42
Central American, ex. Mexican	7	0.04
Honduran	2	0.01
Panamanian	3	0.02
Salvadoran	2	0.01
Cuban	11	0.06
Dominican Republic	2	0.01
Mexican	97	0.52
Puerto Rican	92	0.50
South American	9	0.05
Colombian	5	0.03
Peruvian	2	0.01
Uruguayan	2	0.01
Other Hispanic or Latino	45	0.24

Race*	Population	%
African-American/Black (266)	356	1.92
Not Hispanic (251)	334	1.80
Hispanic (15)	22	0.12
American Indian/Alaska Native (26)	88	0.47
Not Hispanic (22)	80	0.43
Hispanic (4)	8	0.04
Apache (0)	3	0.02
Blackfeet (0)	1	0.01
Cherokee (8)	32	0.17
Chippewa (0)	3	0.02
Choctaw (0)	1	0.01
Crow (0)	3	0.02
Inupiat *(Alaska Native)* (1)	1	0.01
Iroquois (2)	5	0.03
Lumbee (1)	1	0.01
Mexican American Ind. (1)	1	0.01
Navajo (0)	1	0.01
Potawatomi (2)	2	0.01
Seminole (1)	1	0.01
Shoshone (0)	1	0.01
Sioux (0)	3	0.02
South American Ind. (3)	3	0.02
Tohono O'Odham (3)	3	0.02
Asian (185)	248	1.33
Not Hispanic (184)	247	1.33
Hispanic (1)	1	0.01
Burmese (3)	3	0.02
Chinese, ex. Taiwanese (27)	33	0.18
Filipino (17)	32	0.17
Indian (87)	91	0.49
Japanese (12)	37	0.20
Korean (11)	18	0.10
Laotian (1)	1	0.01
Thai (4)	5	0.03
Vietnamese (13)	16	0.09
Hawaii Native/Pacific Islander (0)	6	0.03
Not Hispanic (0)	6	0.03
Native Hawaiian (0)	1	0.01
White (17,823)	18,040	97.11
Not Hispanic (17,644)	17,835	96.01
Hispanic (179)	205	1.10

Eaton

Place Type: City
County: Preble
Population: 8,407†

Ancestry‡	Population	%
American (894)	894	10.62
Austrian (73)	123	1.46
British (11)	66	0.78
Czech (0)	30	0.36
Czechoslovakian (0)	10	0.12
Danish (0)	8	0.10
Dutch (12)	153	1.82
English (262)	797	9.47
European (20)	62	0.74
French, ex. Basque (20)	288	3.42
French Canadian (0)	25	0.30
German (1,356)	3,197	37.98
Greek (11)	11	0.13
Irish (505)	1,675	19.90
Italian (0)	26	0.31
Polish (24)	61	0.72
Scotch-Irish (46)	276	3.28
Scottish (189)	386	4.59
Slavic (0)	13	0.15
Slovak (0)	41	0.49
Swedish (10)	10	0.12
Swiss (0)	13	0.15
Welsh (7)	17	0.20

Hispanic Origin	Population	%
Hispanic or Latino (of any race)	69	0.82
Central American, ex. Mexican	2	0.02
Guatemalan	2	0.02
Cuban	1	0.01
Mexican	50	0.59
Puerto Rican	4	0.05
South American	3	0.04
Chilean	1	0.01
Uruguayan	2	0.02
Other Hispanic or Latino	9	0.11

Race*	Population	%
African-American/Black (47)	117	1.39
Not Hispanic (47)	117	1.39
American Indian/Alaska Native (15)	63	0.75
Not Hispanic (13)	59	0.70
Hispanic (2)	4	0.05
Apache (0)	1	0.01
Blackfeet (1)	1	0.01
Cherokee (3)	28	0.33
Chippewa (1)	1	0.01
Cree (1)	3	0.04
Lumbee (2)	2	0.02
Mexican American Ind. (2)	2	0.02
Ottawa (1)	1	0.01
Asian (83)	94	1.12
Not Hispanic (83)	94	1.12
Cambodian (1)	1	0.01
Chinese, ex. Taiwanese (2)	2	0.02
Filipino (5)	7	0.08
Indian (19)	19	0.23
Japanese (50)	52	0.62
Korean (5)	5	0.06
Hawaii Native/Pacific Islander (1)	11	0.13
Not Hispanic (1)	11	0.13
Native Hawaiian (0)	1	0.01
White (8,098)	8,220	97.78
Not Hispanic (8,064)	8,172	97.20
Hispanic (34)	48	0.57

Elyria

Place Type: City
County: Lorain
Population: 54,533†

Ancestry‡	Population	%
African, Sub-Saharan (102)	138	0.25
African (29)	65	0.12
Kenyan (18)	18	0.03
Sudanese (55)	55	0.10
American (5,042)	5,042	9.17
Arab (31)	112	0.20
Arab (1)	1	<0.01
Jordanian (30)	30	0.05
Lebanese (0)	72	0.13
Syrian (0)	9	0.02
Armenian (0)	10	0.02
Austrian (30)	154	0.28
Belgian (0)	21	0.04
British (72)	137	0.25
Canadian (11)	100	0.18
Croatian (33)	123	0.22
Czech (85)	556	1.01
Czechoslovakian (26)	312	0.57
Danish (39)	183	0.33
Dutch (123)	1,082	1.97
Eastern European (31)	31	0.06
English (1,799)	6,659	12.11
European (78)	88	0.16
Finnish (6)	36	0.07
French, ex. Basque (74)	896	1.63
French Canadian (78)	376	0.68
German (3,671)	13,579	24.69
Greek (203)	317	0.58
Hungarian (968)	2,358	4.29
Irish (1,823)	8,207	14.92
Italian (1,155)	3,507	6.38
Lithuanian (64)	132	0.24
Macedonian (74)	95	0.17
Northern European (0)	28	0.05
Norwegian (52)	234	0.43
Pennsylvania German (68)	68	0.12
Polish (1,483)	4,359	7.93
Portuguese (8)	58	0.11
Romanian (89)	165	0.30
Russian (131)	599	1.09
Scandinavian (20)	20	0.04
Scotch-Irish (311)	730	1.33
Scottish (316)	1,571	2.86
Serbian (8)	57	0.10
Slavic (0)	43	0.08
Slovak (531)	1,549	2.82
Slovene (57)	165	0.30
Swedish (196)	509	0.93
Swiss (32)	318	0.58
Ukrainian (6)	229	0.42
Welsh (149)	612	1.11
West Indian, ex. Hispanic (10)	22	0.04
Jamaican (10)	22	0.04
Yugoslavian (11)	41	0.07

Hispanic Origin	Population	%
Hispanic or Latino (of any race)	2,649	4.86
Central American, ex. Mexican	34	0.06
Costa Rican	3	0.01
Guatemalan	16	0.03
Honduran	3	0.01
Nicaraguan	1	<0.01
Panamanian	3	0.01
Salvadoran	7	0.01
Other Central American	1	<0.01
Cuban	28	0.05
Dominican Republic	18	0.03
Mexican	578	1.06
Puerto Rican	1,719	3.15
South American	50	0.09
Argentinean	2	<0.01
Bolivian	1	<0.01
Chilean	3	0.01
Colombian	16	0.03
Ecuadorian	8	0.01
Peruvian	13	0.02
Venezuelan	5	0.01
Other South American	2	<0.01
Other Hispanic or Latino	222	0.41

*Notes: † The Census 2010 population figure is used to calculate the percentages in the Hispanic Origin and Race categories. Ancestry percentages are based on the 2006-2010 American Community Survey population (not shown); ‡ Numbers in parentheses indicate the number of people reporting a single ancestry; * Numbers in parentheses indicate the number of persons reporting this race alone, not in combination with any other race; Please refer to the Explanation of Data for more information.*

Race*	Population	%
African-American/Black (8,441)	10,098	18.52
Not Hispanic (8,161)	9,622	17.64
Hispanic (280)	476	0.87
American Indian/Alaska Native (162)	631	1.16
Not Hispanic (131)	531	0.97
Hispanic (31)	100	0.18
Aleut *(Alaska Native)* (1)	1	<0.01
Apache (0)	6	0.01
Arapaho (1)	1	<0.01
Blackfeet (7)	44	0.08
Cherokee (32)	197	0.36
Cheyenne (0)	4	0.01
Chickasaw (0)	3	0.01
Chippewa (7)	11	0.02
Choctaw (0)	3	0.01
Delaware (0)	1	<0.01
Inupiat *(Alaska Native)* (0)	1	<0.01
Iroquois (7)	17	0.03
Lumbee (5)	8	0.01
Mexican American Ind. (3)	4	0.01
Navajo (0)	6	0.01
Osage (0)	1	<0.01
Paiute (0)	1	<0.01
Potawatomi (1)	2	<0.01
Pueblo (1)	1	<0.01
Puget Sound Salish (0)	1	<0.01
Seminole (3)	4	0.01
Sioux (4)	11	0.02
South American Ind. (3)	3	0.01
Asian (435)	628	1.15
Not Hispanic (421)	590	1.08
Hispanic (14)	38	0.07
Cambodian (0)	1	<0.01
Chinese, ex. Taiwanese (60)	78	0.14
Filipino (185)	273	0.50
Indian (70)	88	0.16
Indonesian (1)	2	<0.01
Japanese (16)	33	0.06
Korean (39)	76	0.14
Malaysian (2)	2	<0.01
Pakistani (6)	7	0.01
Sri Lankan (2)	8	0.01
Taiwanese (3)	3	0.01
Thai (6)	13	0.02
Vietnamese (25)	31	0.06
Hawaii Native/Pacific Islander (4)	65	0.12
Not Hispanic (3)	45	0.08
Hispanic (1)	20	0.04
Guamanian/Chamorro (2)	13	0.02
Native Hawaiian (1)	16	0.03
Samoan (1)	5	0.01
White (42,601)	44,643	81.86
Not Hispanic (41,226)	42,979	78.81
Hispanic (1,375)	1,664	3.05

Englewood

Place Type: City
County: Montgomery
Population: 13,465†

Ancestry‡	Population	%
African, Sub-Saharan (38)	141	1.07
African (20)	47	0.36
Cape Verdean (18)	94	0.71
American (903)	903	6.84
Arab (39)	84	0.64
Lebanese (0)	45	0.34
Moroccan (39)	39	0.30
Assyrian/Chaldean/Syriac (10)	10	0.08
Austrian (0)	10	0.08
Belgian (0)	12	0.09
British (0)	19	0.14
Croatian (0)	14	0.11
Danish (0)	76	0.58
Dutch (22)	300	2.27
English (678)	1,401	10.61
European (147)	161	1.22
Finnish (12)	64	0.48
French, ex. Basque (113)	300	2.27
French Canadian (32)	53	0.40
German (2,358)	4,785	36.24
Greek (105)	119	0.90
Hungarian (142)	180	1.36
Irish (379)	1,726	13.07
Italian (229)	483	3.66
Lithuanian (9)	9	0.07
Norwegian (12)	12	0.09
Polish (120)	313	2.37
Portuguese (0)	14	0.11
Romanian (13)	13	0.10
Russian (121)	249	1.89
Scotch-Irish (37)	127	0.96
Scottish (41)	293	2.22
Serbian (0)	99	0.75
Slovak (12)	24	0.18
Swedish (0)	28	0.21
Swiss (39)	61	0.46
Welsh (36)	195	1.48

Hispanic Origin	Population	%
Hispanic or Latino (of any race)	151	1.12
Central American, ex. Mexican	12	0.09
Costa Rican	4	0.03
Guatemalan	4	0.03
Salvadoran	4	0.03
Cuban	14	0.10
Dominican Republic	4	0.03
Mexican	76	0.56
Puerto Rican	16	0.12
South American	5	0.04
Argentinean	1	0.01
Bolivian	1	0.01
Colombian	1	0.01
Peruvian	2	0.01
Other Hispanic or Latino	24	0.18

Race*	Population	%
African-American/Black (1,742)	1,937	14.39
Not Hispanic (1,735)	1,923	14.28
Hispanic (7)	14	0.10
American Indian/Alaska Native (22)	81	0.60
Not Hispanic (21)	80	0.59
Hispanic (1)	1	0.01
Blackfeet (2)	4	0.03
Cherokee (1)	20	0.15
Chippewa (2)	3	0.02
Choctaw (1)	1	0.01
Creek (0)	1	0.01
Iroquois (1)	1	0.01
Potawatomi (1)	1	0.01
Seminole (0)	3	0.02
Sioux (1)	3	0.02
Asian (216)	294	2.18
Not Hispanic (216)	294	2.18
Bangladeshi (3)	3	0.02
Burmese (2)	2	0.01
Chinese, ex. Taiwanese (46)	51	0.38
Filipino (46)	56	0.42
Indian (37)	41	0.30
Indonesian (0)	1	0.01
Japanese (30)	47	0.35
Korean (25)	52	0.39
Taiwanese (8)	13	0.10
Thai (2)	3	0.02
Vietnamese (15)	21	0.16
Hawaii Native/Pacific Islander (10)	18	0.13
Not Hispanic (10)	18	0.13
Guamanian/Chamorro (6)	6	0.04
Native Hawaiian (0)	1	0.01
Samoan (1)	4	0.03
White (11,086)	11,364	84.40
Not Hispanic (11,010)	11,276	83.74
Hispanic (76)	88	0.65

Euclid

Place Type: City
County: Cuyahoga
Population: 48,920†

Ancestry‡	Population	%
African, Sub-Saharan (564)	686	1.39
African (406)	485	0.98
Nigerian (53)	71	0.14
South African (0)	25	0.05
Other Sub-Saharan African (105)	105	0.21
Albanian (32)	32	0.06
American (1,085)	1,085	2.20
Arab (23)	60	0.12
Arab (12)	12	0.02
Lebanese (11)	44	0.09
Syrian (0)	4	0.01
Armenian (7)	7	0.01
Assyrian/Chaldean/Syriac (0)	5	0.01
Austrian (49)	181	0.37
Brazilian (9)	9	0.02
British (54)	102	0.21
Bulgarian (28)	28	0.06
Canadian (0)	9	0.02
Celtic (0)	11	0.02
Croatian (487)	1,084	2.20
Czech (125)	464	0.94
Czechoslovakian (26)	39	0.08
Danish (13)	38	0.08
Dutch (30)	156	0.32
English (416)	1,950	3.95
European (127)	141	0.29
Finnish (19)	44	0.09
French, ex. Basque (88)	570	1.16
French Canadian (76)	132	0.27
German (1,120)	5,611	11.37
Greek (45)	117	0.24
Hungarian (313)	1,228	2.49
Irish (1,116)	4,809	9.75
Israeli (9)	9	0.02
Italian (2,008)	4,242	8.60
Lithuanian (223)	568	1.15
Luxemburger (0)	12	0.02
Norwegian (7)	16	0.03
Polish (524)	1,637	3.32
Portuguese (9)	32	0.06
Romanian (33)	79	0.16
Russian (64)	332	0.67
Scandinavian (26)	26	0.05
Scotch-Irish (117)	333	0.67
Scottish (80)	725	1.47
Serbian (8)	24	0.05
Slavic (37)	62	0.13
Slovak (460)	1,043	2.11
Slovene (1,341)	2,895	5.87
Swedish (121)	327	0.66
Swiss (21)	45	0.09
Turkish (11)	20	0.04
Ukrainian (38)	86	0.17
Welsh (55)	283	0.57
West Indian, ex. Hispanic (120)	229	0.46
Bahamian (11)	15	0.03
Barbadian (0)	10	0.02
Belizean (10)	10	0.02
Haitian (41)	49	0.10
Jamaican (23)	23	0.05
Trinidadian/Tobagonian (14)	14	0.03
West Indian (21)	108	0.22
Yugoslavian (65)	65	0.13

Hispanic Origin	Population	%
Hispanic or Latino (of any race)	769	1.57
Central American, ex. Mexican	53	0.11
Costa Rican	4	0.01
Guatemalan	3	0.01
Honduran	8	0.02
Nicaraguan	6	0.01
Panamanian	19	0.04
Salvadoran	13	0.03

*Notes: † The Census 2010 population figure is used to calculate the percentages in the Hispanic Origin and Race categories. Ancestry percentages are based on the 2006-2010 American Community Survey population (not shown); ‡ Numbers in parentheses indicate the number of people reporting a single ancestry; * Numbers in parentheses indicate the number of persons reporting this race alone, not in combination with any other race; Please refer to the Explanation of Data for more information.*

Cuban	16	0.03
Dominican Republic	29	0.06
Mexican	158	0.32
Puerto Rican	344	0.70
South American	43	0.09
Argentinean	6	0.01
Chilean	1	<0.01
Colombian	15	0.03
Ecuadorian	3	0.01
Peruvian	9	0.02
Uruguayan	6	0.01
Venezuelan	3	0.01
Other Hispanic or Latino	126	0.26

Race*	Population	%
African-American/Black (25,751)	26,672	54.52
Not Hispanic (25,522)	26,370	53.90
Hispanic (229)	302	0.62
American Indian/Alaska Native (102)	370	0.76
Not Hispanic (94)	339	0.69
Hispanic (8)	31	0.06
Apache (1)	2	<0.01
Blackfeet (1)	19	0.04
Canadian/French Am. Ind. (5)	5	0.01
Cherokee (6)	81	0.17
Cheyenne (0)	1	<0.01
Chickasaw (0)	1	<0.01
Chippewa (4)	6	0.01
Choctaw (0)	4	0.01
Creek (0)	2	<0.01
Crow (0)	1	<0.01
Inupiat *(Alaska Native)* (1)	1	<0.01
Iroquois (2)	3	0.01
Menominee (2)	2	<0.01
Mexican American Ind. (2)	3	0.01
Navajo (2)	3	0.01
Seminole (8)	13	0.03
Sioux (0)	6	0.01
South American Ind. (1)	1	<0.01
Tlingit-Haida *(Alaska Native)* (1)	1	<0.01
Asian (359)	541	1.11
Not Hispanic (354)	522	1.07
Hispanic (5)	19	0.04
Burmese (1)	1	<0.01
Cambodian (2)	2	<0.01
Chinese, ex. Taiwanese (78)	109	0.22
Filipino (100)	145	0.30
Indian (57)	76	0.16
Indonesian (5)	8	0.02
Japanese (28)	57	0.12
Korean (12)	32	0.07
Laotian (30)	42	0.09
Nepalese (2)	2	<0.01
Pakistani (6)	6	0.01
Taiwanese (0)	3	0.01
Thai (6)	22	0.04
Vietnamese (20)	24	0.05
Hawaii Native/Pacific Islander (4)	22	0.04
Not Hispanic (3)	16	0.03
Hispanic (1)	6	0.01
Guamanian/Chamorro (2)	4	0.01
Native Hawaiian (2)	7	0.01
Samoan (0)	1	<0.01
White (21,417)	22,300	45.58
Not Hispanic (21,101)	21,909	44.79
Hispanic (316)	391	0.80

Fairborn

Place Type: City
County: Greene
Population: 32,352†

Ancestry‡	Population	%
African, Sub-Saharan (185)	212	0.66
African (173)	184	0.57
Cape Verdean (12)	28	0.09
American (6,052)	6,052	18.82
Arab (0)	17	0.05
Egyptian (0)	10	0.03
Lebanese (0)	7	0.02
Australian (11)	11	0.03
Austrian (0)	16	0.05
Belgian (0)	23	0.07
Brazilian (19)	19	0.06
British (69)	166	0.52
Canadian (0)	20	0.06
Croatian (32)	32	0.10
Czech (8)	82	0.26
Czechoslovakian (13)	43	0.13
Danish (0)	15	0.05
Dutch (211)	588	1.83
English (1,101)	3,136	9.75
European (211)	265	0.82
Finnish (0)	22	0.07
French, ex. Basque (145)	667	2.07
French Canadian (35)	54	0.17
German (2,995)	6,901	21.46
Greek (27)	62	0.19
Hungarian (115)	338	1.05
Irish (1,014)	3,452	10.74
Italian (313)	709	2.20
Lithuanian (19)	45	0.14
Northern European (54)	54	0.17
Norwegian (31)	93	0.29
Pennsylvania German (55)	55	0.17
Polish (146)	442	1.37
Portuguese (0)	13	0.04
Romanian (10)	18	0.06
Russian (61)	105	0.33
Scandinavian (19)	27	0.08
Scotch-Irish (243)	584	1.82
Scottish (257)	845	2.63
Slavic (0)	29	0.09
Slovak (10)	29	0.09
Swedish (93)	187	0.58
Swiss (22)	57	0.18
Turkish (43)	43	0.13
Ukrainian (21)	34	0.11
Welsh (70)	445	1.38
Yugoslavian (4)	4	0.01

Hispanic Origin	Population	%
Hispanic or Latino (of any race)	778	2.40
Central American, ex. Mexican	62	0.19
Costa Rican	11	0.03
Guatemalan	26	0.08
Honduran	4	0.01
Nicaraguan	4	0.01
Panamanian	14	0.04
Salvadoran	3	0.01
Cuban	14	0.04
Dominican Republic	9	0.03
Mexican	360	1.11
Puerto Rican	173	0.53
South American	66	0.20
Argentinean	3	0.01
Bolivian	8	0.02
Chilean	1	<0.01
Colombian	21	0.06
Ecuadorian	9	0.03
Peruvian	15	0.05
Uruguayan	1	<0.01
Venezuelan	8	0.02
Other Hispanic or Latino	94	0.29

Race*	Population	%
African-American/Black (2,507)	3,020	9.33
Not Hispanic (2,468)	2,954	9.13
Hispanic (39)	66	0.20
American Indian/Alaska Native (108)	368	1.14
Not Hispanic (88)	323	1.00
Hispanic (20)	45	0.14
Aleut *(Alaska Native)* (1)	1	<0.01
Apache (5)	7	0.02
Blackfeet (1)	10	0.03
Canadian/French Am. Ind. (0)	3	0.01
Central American Ind. (1)	1	<0.01
Cherokee (17)	117	0.36
Chickasaw (5)	5	0.02
Chippewa (2)	6	0.02
Choctaw (1)	8	0.02
Creek (4)	7	0.02
Delaware (0)	1	<0.01
Iroquois (0)	1	<0.01
Mexican American Ind. (5)	5	0.02
Navajo (1)	1	<0.01
Osage (2)	2	0.01
Pueblo (1)	5	0.02
Seminole (1)	5	0.02
Shoshone (1)	1	<0.01
Sioux (5)	9	0.03
South American Ind. (0)	2	0.01
Tlingit-Haida *(Alaska Native)* (1)	1	<0.01
Asian (1,015)	1,305	4.03
Not Hispanic (1,009)	1,291	3.99
Hispanic (6)	14	0.04
Bangladeshi (12)	12	0.04
Cambodian (23)	36	0.11
Chinese, ex. Taiwanese (140)	157	0.49
Filipino (126)	209	0.65
Hmong (1)	1	<0.01
Indian (286)	321	0.99
Japanese (46)	109	0.34
Korean (145)	183	0.57
Laotian (10)	12	0.04
Nepalese (2)	5	0.02
Pakistani (19)	19	0.06
Sri Lankan (11)	12	0.04
Taiwanese (8)	8	0.02
Thai (35)	63	0.19
Vietnamese (103)	112	0.35
Hawaii Native/Pacific Islander (40)	79	0.24
Not Hispanic (37)	69	0.21
Hispanic (3)	10	0.03
Fijian (0)	1	<0.01
Guamanian/Chamorro (13)	22	0.07
Native Hawaiian (13)	30	0.09
Samoan (2)	4	0.01
White (27,427)	28,327	87.56
Not Hispanic (26,978)	27,811	85.96
Hispanic (449)	516	1.59

Fairfield

Place Type: City
County: Butler
Population: 42,510†

Ancestry‡	Population	%
African, Sub-Saharan (1,010)	1,080	2.53
African (556)	626	1.47
Ethiopian (47)	47	0.11
Ghanaian (368)	368	0.86
Nigerian (25)	25	0.06
Other Sub-Saharan African (14)	14	0.03
American (4,423)	4,423	10.37
Arab (69)	102	0.24
Arab (69)	81	0.19
Lebanese (0)	9	0.02
Other Arab (0)	12	0.03
Austrian (35)	103	0.24
Belgian (0)	61	0.14
Brazilian (67)	131	0.31
British (57)	83	0.19
Cajun (12)	12	0.03
Canadian (9)	48	0.11
Celtic (13)	13	0.03
Czech (73)	248	0.58
Czechoslovakian (38)	88	0.21
Danish (24)	53	0.12
Dutch (102)	533	1.25
Eastern European (9)	9	0.02
English (1,473)	3,629	8.51
European (228)	291	0.68
Finnish (9)	14	0.03
French, ex. Basque (421)	1,202	2.82
French Canadian (9)	21	0.05
German (6,113)	13,044	30.60
Greek (87)	147	0.34

*Notes: † The Census 2010 population figure is used to calculate the percentages in the Hispanic Origin and Race categories. Ancestry percentages are based on the 2006-2010 American Community Survey population (not shown); ‡ Numbers in parentheses indicate the number of people reporting a single ancestry; * Numbers in parentheses indicate the number of persons reporting this race alone, not in combination with any other race; Please refer to the Explanation of Data for more information.*

Hungarian (76)	246	0.58
Iranian (14)	14	0.03
Irish (1,244)	6,158	14.44
Israeli (13)	13	0.03
Italian (680)	1,916	4.49
Latvian (26)	26	0.06
Lithuanian (12)	22	0.05
Norwegian (77)	98	0.23
Polish (179)	718	1.68
Portuguese (23)	29	0.07
Russian (113)	258	0.61
Scandinavian (12)	36	0.08
Scotch-Irish (335)	674	1.58
Scottish (190)	693	1.63
Slavic (0)	15	0.04
Slovak (29)	29	0.07
Slovene (12)	12	0.03
Swedish (123)	328	0.77
Swiss (30)	102	0.24
Ukrainian (10)	41	0.10
Welsh (67)	254	0.60
West Indian, ex. Hispanic (0)	6	0.01
Trinidadian/Tobagonian (0)	6	0.01
Yugoslavian (45)	120	0.28

Hispanic Origin	Population	%
Hispanic or Latino (of any race)	2,357	5.54
Central American, ex. Mexican	299	0.70
Costa Rican	2	<0.01
Guatemalan	133	0.31
Honduran	79	0.19
Nicaraguan	5	0.01
Panamanian	17	0.04
Salvadoran	62	0.15
Other Central American	1	<0.01
Cuban	48	0.11
Dominican Republic	233	0.55
Mexican	1,155	2.72
Puerto Rican	177	0.42
South American	250	0.59
Argentinean	4	0.01
Bolivian	1	<0.01
Chilean	5	0.01
Colombian	47	0.11
Ecuadorian	25	0.06
Paraguayan	3	0.01
Peruvian	145	0.34
Uruguayan	2	<0.01
Venezuelan	18	0.04
Other Hispanic or Latino	195	0.46

Race*	Population	%
African-American/Black (5,457)	6,048	14.23
Not Hispanic (5,338)	5,882	13.84
Hispanic (119)	166	0.39
American Indian/Alaska Native (112)	300	0.71
Not Hispanic (84)	257	0.60
Hispanic (28)	43	0.10
Apache (1)	1	<0.01
Blackfeet (2)	5	0.01
Canadian/French Am. Ind. (2)	3	0.01
Cherokee (24)	83	0.20
Chippewa (7)	9	0.02
Choctaw (1)	5	0.01
Comanche (1)	2	<0.01
Creek (0)	1	<0.01
Iroquois (1)	3	0.01
Mexican American Ind. (11)	13	0.03
Navajo (4)	6	0.01
Osage (1)	1	<0.01
Potawatomi (0)	1	<0.01
Puget Sound Salish (1)	1	<0.01
Seminole (0)	1	<0.01
Sioux (7)	14	0.03
Spanish American Ind. (0)	3	0.01
Asian (1,032)	1,272	2.99
Not Hispanic (1,029)	1,252	2.95
Hispanic (3)	20	0.05
Bangladeshi (3)	3	0.01
Burmese (2)	5	0.01
Cambodian (113)	133	0.31
Chinese, ex. Taiwanese (146)	189	0.44
Filipino (97)	160	0.38
Indian (274)	311	0.73
Indonesian (3)	3	0.01
Japanese (23)	65	0.15
Korean (43)	63	0.15
Laotian (0)	2	<0.01
Malaysian (0)	2	<0.01
Nepalese (2)	2	<0.01
Pakistani (13)	15	0.04
Sri Lankan (5)	5	0.01
Taiwanese (27)	30	0.07
Thai (25)	34	0.08
Vietnamese (200)	224	0.53
Hawaii Native/Pacific Islander (30)	53	0.12
Not Hispanic (30)	48	0.11
Hispanic (0)	5	0.01
Guamanian/Chamorro (1)	2	<0.01
Native Hawaiian (5)	7	0.02
Samoan (1)	2	<0.01
White (33,586)	34,500	81.16
Not Hispanic (32,739)	33,509	78.83
Hispanic (847)	991	2.33

Fairview Park

Place Type: City
County: Cuyahoga
Population: 16,826†

Ancestry‡	Population	%
African, Sub-Saharan (0)	20	0.12
Ethiopian (0)	10	0.06
Somalian (0)	10	0.06
Albanian (223)	223	1.32
American (392)	392	2.32
Arab (375)	495	2.93
Arab (0)	53	0.31
Jordanian (107)	107	0.63
Lebanese (77)	118	0.70
Palestinian (94)	94	0.56
Syrian (97)	123	0.73
Austrian (15)	88	0.52
Belgian (10)	10	0.06
British (53)	73	0.43
Bulgarian (94)	107	0.63
Canadian (12)	22	0.13
Carpatho Rusyn (30)	30	0.18
Croatian (20)	138	0.82
Czech (161)	509	3.01
Czechoslovakian (30)	67	0.40
Danish (8)	17	0.10
Dutch (0)	192	1.14
English (329)	1,472	8.71
European (97)	125	0.74
Finnish (9)	26	0.15
French, ex. Basque (25)	308	1.82
French Canadian (0)	157	0.93
German (1,240)	5,374	31.81
Greek (19)	79	0.47
Hungarian (246)	889	5.26
Irish (1,379)	4,785	28.32
Italian (536)	2,023	11.97
Latvian (9)	40	0.24
Lithuanian (12)	24	0.14
Macedonian (23)	36	0.21
Norwegian (0)	18	0.11
Polish (458)	1,905	11.28
Portuguese (0)	53	0.31
Romanian (84)	122	0.72
Russian (58)	238	1.41
Scandinavian (9)	9	0.05
Scotch-Irish (119)	316	1.87
Scottish (83)	328	1.94
Serbian (11)	94	0.56
Slavic (0)	20	0.12
Slovak (291)	891	5.27
Slovene (161)	259	1.53
Swedish (0)	46	0.27
Swiss (0)	87	0.51
Ukrainian (95)	137	0.81
Welsh (24)	115	0.68
West Indian, ex. Hispanic (0)	28	0.17
Jamaican (0)	14	0.08
West Indian (0)	14	0.08
Yugoslavian (31)	31	0.18

Hispanic Origin	Population	%
Hispanic or Latino (of any race)	557	3.31
Central American, ex. Mexican	18	0.11
Costa Rican	2	0.01
Guatemalan	4	0.02
Honduran	3	0.02
Panamanian	4	0.02
Salvadoran	5	0.03
Cuban	15	0.09
Dominican Republic	3	0.02
Mexican	140	0.83
Puerto Rican	307	1.82
South American	44	0.26
Argentinean	4	0.02
Bolivian	1	0.01
Chilean	4	0.02
Colombian	8	0.05
Paraguayan	8	0.05
Peruvian	15	0.09
Venezuelan	4	0.02
Other Hispanic or Latino	30	0.18

Race*	Population	%
African-American/Black (303)	375	2.23
Not Hispanic (292)	354	2.10
Hispanic (11)	21	0.12
American Indian/Alaska Native (19)	68	0.40
Not Hispanic (12)	56	0.33
Hispanic (7)	12	0.07
Blackfeet (1)	11	0.07
Cherokee (5)	16	0.10
Chippewa (6)	9	0.05
Choctaw (0)	1	0.01
Comanche (0)	1	0.01
Osage (0)	1	0.01
Ottawa (1)	2	0.01
Sioux (1)	1	0.01
Asian (272)	346	2.06
Not Hispanic (267)	339	2.01
Hispanic (5)	7	0.04
Cambodian (9)	12	0.07
Chinese, ex. Taiwanese (77)	94	0.56
Filipino (55)	75	0.45
Indian (50)	59	0.35
Indonesian (1)	3	0.02
Japanese (10)	24	0.14
Korean (20)	24	0.14
Malaysian (1)	1	0.01
Nepalese (2)	2	0.01
Pakistani (3)	3	0.02
Thai (5)	7	0.04
Vietnamese (30)	32	0.19
Hawaii Native/Pacific Islander (1)	8	0.05
Not Hispanic (1)	8	0.05
Guamanian/Chamorro (0)	2	0.01
Native Hawaiian (0)	2	0.01
Samoan (1)	1	0.01
White (15,889)	16,077	95.55
Not Hispanic (15,512)	15,671	93.14
Hispanic (377)	406	2.41

Findlay

Place Type: City
County: Hancock
Population: 41,202†

Ancestry‡	Population	%
African, Sub-Saharan (59)	59	0.14
African (8)	8	0.02
South African (51)	51	0.12
American (2,652)	2,652	6.44

*Notes: † The Census 2010 population figure is used to calculate the percentages in the Hispanic Origin and Race categories. Ancestry percentages are based on the 2006-2010 American Community Survey population (not shown); ‡ Numbers in parentheses indicate the number of people reporting a single ancestry; * Numbers in parentheses indicate the number of persons reporting this race alone, not in combination with any other race; Please refer to the Explanation of Data for more information.*

Arab (137)	254	0.62
Lebanese (0)	117	0.28
Other Arab (137)	137	0.33
Austrian (0)	16	0.04
Belgian (31)	116	0.28
British (222)	261	0.63
Bulgarian (22)	22	0.05
Canadian (0)	56	0.14
Croatian (14)	20	0.05
Czech (43)	121	0.29
Czechoslovakian (23)	23	0.06
Danish (25)	67	0.16
Dutch (249)	989	2.40
Eastern European (31)	31	0.08
English (1,416)	4,129	10.02
European (650)	845	2.05
Finnish (24)	24	0.06
French, ex. Basque (237)	1,383	3.36
French Canadian (27)	115	0.28
German (8,382)	16,605	40.31
Greek (10)	10	0.02
Hungarian (176)	461	1.12
Irish (1,215)	5,038	12.23
Italian (506)	1,450	3.52
Lithuanian (55)	97	0.24
Luxemburger (0)	12	0.03
Macedonian (14)	14	0.03
Norwegian (70)	124	0.30
Pennsylvania German (100)	133	0.32
Polish (198)	1,452	3.53
Portuguese (48)	65	0.16
Romanian (18)	18	0.04
Russian (0)	209	0.51
Scandinavian (0)	20	0.05
Scotch-Irish (289)	827	2.01
Scottish (281)	1,042	2.53
Serbian (47)	75	0.18
Slovak (47)	116	0.28
Slovene (84)	112	0.27
Swedish (105)	338	0.82
Swiss (74)	434	1.05
Ukrainian (23)	32	0.08
Welsh (126)	509	1.24
West Indian, ex. Hispanic (8)	8	0.02
U.S. Virgin Islander (8)	8	0.02

Hispanic Origin	Population	%
Hispanic or Latino (of any race)	2,335	5.67
Central American, ex. Mexican	52	0.13
Costa Rican	1	<0.01
Guatemalan	22	0.05
Honduran	6	0.01
Nicaraguan	3	0.01
Panamanian	5	0.01
Salvadoran	15	0.04
Cuban	26	0.06
Dominican Republic	7	0.02
Mexican	1,926	4.67
Puerto Rican	98	0.24
South American	36	0.09
Argentinean	3	0.01
Bolivian	2	<0.01
Colombian	5	0.01
Paraguayan	1	<0.01
Peruvian	13	0.03
Venezuelan	12	0.03
Other Hispanic or Latino	190	0.46

Race*	Population	%
African-American/Black (886)	1,303	3.16
Not Hispanic (820)	1,175	2.85
Hispanic (66)	128	0.31
American Indian/Alaska Native (123)	305	0.74
Not Hispanic (91)	234	0.57
Hispanic (32)	71	0.17
Alaska Athabascan *(Ala. Nat.)* (0)	1	<0.01
Apache (3)	5	0.01
Blackfeet (6)	15	0.04
Canadian/French Am. Ind. (3)	5	0.01
Central American Ind. (2)	5	0.01
Cherokee (19)	83	0.20
Chickasaw (1)	1	<0.01
Chippewa (2)	2	<0.01
Choctaw (4)	5	0.01
Comanche (0)	2	<0.01
Crow (0)	2	<0.01
Delaware (0)	2	<0.01
Iroquois (7)	9	0.02
Lumbee (1)	3	0.01
Mexican American Ind. (4)	11	0.03
Navajo (2)	2	<0.01
Ottawa (0)	1	<0.01
Potawatomi (1)	1	<0.01
Puget Sound Salish (4)	4	0.01
Seminole (1)	1	<0.01
Shoshone (0)	1	<0.01
Sioux (6)	11	0.03
South American Ind. (1)	1	<0.01
Asian (1,025)	1,182	2.87
Not Hispanic (1,020)	1,169	2.84
Hispanic (5)	13	0.03
Cambodian (1)	1	<0.01
Chinese, ex. Taiwanese (160)	175	0.42
Filipino (93)	129	0.31
Hmong (0)	1	<0.01
Indian (216)	231	0.56
Indonesian (9)	9	0.02
Japanese (247)	274	0.67
Korean (54)	77	0.19
Laotian (130)	133	0.32
Malaysian (1)	3	0.01
Nepalese (3)	3	0.01
Pakistani (10)	10	0.02
Taiwanese (25)	25	0.06
Thai (9)	17	0.04
Vietnamese (27)	30	0.07
Hawaii Native/Pacific Islander (5)	21	0.05
Not Hispanic (4)	18	0.04
Hispanic (1)	3	0.01
Fijian (0)	1	<0.01
Native Hawaiian (2)	8	0.02
Samoan (2)	3	0.01
Tongan (1)	1	<0.01
White (37,584)	38,373	93.13
Not Hispanic (36,270)	36,836	89.40
Hispanic (1,314)	1,537	3.73

Finneytown

Place Type: CDP
County: Hamilton
Population: 12,741†

Ancestry‡	Population	%
African, Sub-Saharan (195)	211	1.62
African (64)	80	0.61
Senegalese (131)	131	1.01
Alsatian (12)	12	0.09
American (564)	564	4.33
Arab (11)	58	0.45
Lebanese (11)	44	0.34
Syrian (0)	14	0.11
Armenian (0)	10	0.08
British (0)	53	0.41
Canadian (0)	13	0.10
Croatian (12)	12	0.09
Czech (24)	36	0.28
Czechoslovakian (0)	23	0.18
Danish (0)	25	0.19
Dutch (57)	94	0.72
English (202)	1,059	8.13
European (99)	99	0.76
Finnish (0)	9	0.07
French, ex. Basque (16)	248	1.90
French Canadian (44)	55	0.42
German (1,929)	3,896	29.92
Greek (37)	52	0.40
Hungarian (0)	28	0.22
Irish (248)	1,519	11.66
Israeli (9)	9	0.07
Italian (200)	680	5.22
Latvian (12)	12	0.09
Lithuanian (16)	35	0.27
Northern European (25)	25	0.19
Norwegian (26)	83	0.64
Polish (94)	207	1.59
Russian (27)	44	0.34
Scotch-Irish (52)	157	1.21
Scottish (10)	314	2.41
Slovak (13)	61	0.47
Slovene (0)	14	0.11
Swedish (13)	101	0.78
Swiss (11)	91	0.70
Welsh (11)	34	0.26
West Indian, ex. Hispanic (25)	25	0.19
Jamaican (15)	15	0.12
West Indian (10)	10	0.08

Hispanic Origin	Population	%
Hispanic or Latino (of any race)	241	1.89
Central American, ex. Mexican	43	0.34
Guatemalan	19	0.15
Honduran	4	0.03
Nicaraguan	3	0.02
Panamanian	11	0.09
Salvadoran	6	0.05
Cuban	7	0.05
Dominican Republic	3	0.02
Mexican	98	0.77
Puerto Rican	25	0.20
South American	31	0.24
Bolivian	1	0.01
Colombian	17	0.13
Ecuadorian	8	0.06
Peruvian	5	0.04
Other Hispanic or Latino	34	0.27

Race*	Population	%
African-American/Black (4,293)	4,521	35.48
Not Hispanic (4,259)	4,467	35.06
Hispanic (34)	54	0.42
American Indian/Alaska Native (13)	63	0.49
Not Hispanic (12)	61	0.48
Hispanic (1)	2	0.02
Blackfeet (0)	4	0.03
Cherokee (1)	20	0.16
Chickasaw (0)	1	0.01
Iroquois (1)	2	0.02
Lumbee (1)	1	0.01
Navajo (0)	2	0.02
Potawatomi (0)	1	0.01
Asian (181)	238	1.87
Not Hispanic (181)	233	1.83
Hispanic (0)	5	0.04
Bhutanese (13)	25	0.20
Burmese (1)	1	0.01
Cambodian (3)	4	0.03
Chinese, ex. Taiwanese (38)	46	0.36
Filipino (27)	50	0.39
Indian (27)	43	0.34
Indonesian (2)	2	0.02
Japanese (7)	10	0.08
Korean (11)	21	0.16
Laotian (1)	1	0.01
Nepalese (1)	1	0.01
Sri Lankan (5)	5	0.04
Taiwanese (4)	4	0.03
Thai (5)	8	0.06
Vietnamese (15)	15	0.12
Hawaii Native/Pacific Islander (13)	23	0.18
Not Hispanic (13)	18	0.14
Hispanic (0)	5	0.04
Guamanian/Chamorro (1)	2	0.02
Native Hawaiian (5)	9	0.07
Samoan (0)	1	0.01
White (7,856)	8,090	63.50
Not Hispanic (7,732)	7,953	62.42
Hispanic (124)	137	1.08

*Notes: † The Census 2010 population figure is used to calculate the percentages in the Hispanic Origin and Race categories. Ancestry percentages are based on the 2006-2010 American Community Survey population (not shown); ‡ Numbers in parentheses indicate the number of people reporting a single ancestry; * Numbers in parentheses indicate the number of persons reporting this race alone, not in combination with any other race; Please refer to the Explanation of Data for more information.*

Forest Park

Place Type: City
County: Hamilton
Population: 18,720†

Ancestry‡	Population	%
African, Sub-Saharan (552)	654	3.51
African (127)	148	0.79
Ethiopian (96)	96	0.51
Ghanaian (39)	39	0.21
Nigerian (5)	5	0.03
Other Sub-Saharan African (285)	366	1.96
American (421)	421	2.26
Arab (53)	53	0.28
Palestinian (53)	53	0.28
Austrian (0)	26	0.14
Brazilian (135)	135	0.72
British (0)	55	0.30
Canadian (0)	4	0.02
Czech (0)	15	0.08
Dutch (13)	59	0.32
Eastern European (0)	15	0.08
English (298)	1,125	6.03
European (52)	52	0.28
Finnish (0)	10	0.05
French, ex. Basque (26)	114	0.61
German (692)	2,081	11.16
Greek (18)	43	0.23
Hungarian (5)	43	0.23
Irish (262)	1,124	6.03
Italian (180)	400	2.15
Norwegian (0)	10	0.05
Polish (22)	75	0.40
Russian (16)	16	0.09
Scandinavian (9)	19	0.10
Scotch-Irish (49)	242	1.30
Scottish (23)	207	1.11
Slovak (33)	33	0.18
Swedish (27)	85	0.46
Turkish (14)	14	0.08
Welsh (0)	27	0.14
West Indian, ex. Hispanic (80)	99	0.53
Jamaican (47)	66	0.35
West Indian (33)	33	0.18

Hispanic Origin	Population	%
Hispanic or Latino (of any race)	1,204	6.43
Central American, ex. Mexican	270	1.44
Costa Rican	1	0.01
Guatemalan	148	0.79
Honduran	17	0.09
Nicaraguan	7	0.04
Salvadoran	93	0.50
Other Central American	4	0.02
Cuban	21	0.11
Dominican Republic	50	0.27
Mexican	623	3.33
Puerto Rican	69	0.37
South American	51	0.27
Chilean	1	0.01
Colombian	12	0.06
Ecuadorian	2	0.01
Peruvian	27	0.14
Venezuelan	9	0.05
Other Hispanic or Latino	120	0.64

Race*	Population	%
African-American/Black (12,159)	12,711	67.90
Not Hispanic (12,088)	12,617	67.40
Hispanic (71)	94	0.50
American Indian/Alaska Native (45)	166	0.89
Not Hispanic (40)	149	0.80
Hispanic (5)	17	0.09
Blackfeet (2)	7	0.04
Cherokee (11)	54	0.29
Chippewa (0)	1	0.01
Choctaw (1)	4	0.02
Creek (2)	2	0.01
Mexican American Ind. (3)	3	0.02
Navajo (1)	1	0.01
Seminole (0)	1	0.01
Sioux (1)	1	0.01
Asian (412)	513	2.74
Not Hispanic (402)	489	2.61
Hispanic (10)	24	0.13
Burmese (1)	2	0.01
Cambodian (32)	37	0.20
Chinese, ex. Taiwanese (35)	44	0.24
Filipino (69)	105	0.56
Indian (93)	113	0.60
Japanese (7)	18	0.10
Korean (13)	22	0.12
Nepalese (12)	12	0.06
Pakistani (18)	20	0.11
Taiwanese (1)	1	0.01
Thai (1)	2	0.01
Vietnamese (101)	101	0.54
Hawaii Native/Pacific Islander (39)	71	0.38
Not Hispanic (31)	61	0.33
Hispanic (8)	10	0.05
Guamanian/Chamorro (11)	18	0.10
Native Hawaiian (7)	14	0.07
White (4,657)	5,204	27.80
Not Hispanic (4,266)	4,752	25.38
Hispanic (391)	452	2.41

Forestville

Place Type: CDP
County: Hamilton
Population: 10,532†

Ancestry‡	Population	%
African, Sub-Saharan (96)	96	0.88
Ethiopian (96)	96	0.88
Alsatian (0)	10	0.09
American (1,887)	1,887	17.38
Arab (0)	26	0.24
Syrian (0)	26	0.24
Armenian (31)	31	0.29
British (33)	72	0.66
Bulgarian (51)	51	0.47
Canadian (0)	15	0.14
Croatian (35)	112	1.03
Czech (0)	65	0.60
Dutch (53)	253	2.33
Eastern European (11)	11	0.10
English (595)	1,474	13.58
European (64)	94	0.87
Finnish (0)	16	0.15
French, ex. Basque (37)	280	2.58
French Canadian (12)	12	0.11
German (1,557)	3,627	33.41
Greek (21)	99	0.91
Hungarian (50)	205	1.89
Irish (436)	1,930	17.78
Italian (405)	693	6.38
Lithuanian (14)	14	0.13
Norwegian (0)	14	0.13
Polish (21)	139	1.28
Romanian (21)	45	0.41
Russian (52)	121	1.11
Scotch-Irish (19)	136	1.25
Scottish (37)	290	2.67
Slovak (12)	27	0.25
Swedish (9)	37	0.34
Swiss (0)	130	1.20
Ukrainian (14)	14	0.13
Welsh (36)	228	2.10
Yugoslavian (16)	16	0.15

Hispanic Origin	Population	%
Hispanic or Latino (of any race)	160	1.52
Central American, ex. Mexican	17	0.16
Costa Rican	2	0.02
Guatemalan	7	0.07
Nicaraguan	2	0.02
Panamanian	5	0.05
Salvadoran	1	0.01
Cuban	12	0.11
Dominican Republic	3	0.03
Mexican	45	0.43
Puerto Rican	34	0.32
South American	28	0.27
Argentinean	1	0.01
Bolivian	2	0.02
Chilean	1	0.01
Colombian	4	0.04
Ecuadorian	3	0.03
Peruvian	13	0.12
Uruguayan	2	0.02
Venezuelan	2	0.02
Other Hispanic or Latino	21	0.20

Race*	Population	%
African-American/Black (148)	210	1.99
Not Hispanic (145)	198	1.88
Hispanic (3)	12	0.11
American Indian/Alaska Native (13)	81	0.77
Not Hispanic (7)	69	0.66
Hispanic (6)	12	0.11
Blackfeet (2)	2	0.02
Cherokee (1)	26	0.25
Chickasaw (0)	1	0.01
Iroquois (0)	5	0.05
Mexican American Ind. (1)	1	0.01
Potawatomi (1)	1	0.01
Sioux (0)	3	0.03
Spanish American Ind. (1)	1	0.01
Asian (265)	342	3.25
Not Hispanic (265)	335	3.18
Hispanic (0)	7	0.07
Burmese (3)	3	0.03
Cambodian (1)	1	0.01
Chinese, ex. Taiwanese (82)	93	0.88
Filipino (13)	32	0.30
Indian (116)	125	1.19
Indonesian (1)	3	0.03
Japanese (14)	30	0.28
Korean (13)	17	0.16
Pakistani (9)	10	0.09
Sri Lankan (1)	3	0.03
Taiwanese (4)	4	0.04
Thai (4)	4	0.04
Vietnamese (1)	3	0.03
Hawaii Native/Pacific Islander (15)	19	0.18
Not Hispanic (14)	18	0.17
Hispanic (1)	1	0.01
Guamanian/Chamorro (1)	1	0.01
Native Hawaiian (8)	8	0.08
Samoan (0)	2	0.02
White (9,841)	10,044	95.37
Not Hispanic (9,744)	9,918	94.17
Hispanic (97)	126	1.20

Fostoria

Place Type: City
County: Seneca
Population: 13,441†

Ancestry‡	Population	%
African, Sub-Saharan (0)	34	0.26
African (0)	34	0.26
American (974)	974	7.47
Belgian (10)	19	0.15
Croatian (0)	11	0.08
Czech (0)	9	0.07
Dutch (57)	261	2.00
English (431)	895	6.86
European (18)	18	0.14
French, ex. Basque (21)	382	2.93
French Canadian (38)	53	0.41
German (2,304)	4,431	33.98
Greek (36)	36	0.28
Hungarian (9)	53	0.41
Icelander (24)	24	0.18
Irish (275)	1,128	8.65
Italian (192)	502	3.85

*Notes: † The Census 2010 population figure is used to calculate the percentages in the Hispanic Origin and Race categories. Ancestry percentages are based on the 2006-2010 American Community Survey population (not shown); ‡ Numbers in parentheses indicate the number of people reporting a single ancestry; * Numbers in parentheses indicate the number of persons reporting this race alone, not in combination with any other race; Please refer to the Explanation of Data for more information.*

Norwegian (19)	39	0.30
Pennsylvania German (21)	21	0.16
Polish (88)	242	1.86
Russian (0)	18	0.14
Scotch-Irish (54)	126	0.97
Scottish (43)	251	1.92
Swedish (21)	21	0.16
Swiss (10)	31	0.24
Welsh (37)	160	1.23

Hispanic Origin	Population	%
Hispanic or Latino (of any race)	1,550	11.53
Central American, ex. Mexican	3	0.02
Honduran	1	0.01
Salvadoran	2	0.01
Mexican	1,409	10.48
Puerto Rican	19	0.14
South American	2	0.01
Bolivian	1	0.01
Colombian	1	0.01
Other Hispanic or Latino	117	0.87

Race*	Population	%
African-American/Black (854)	1,321	9.83
Not Hispanic (793)	1,175	8.74
Hispanic (61)	146	1.09
American Indian/Alaska Native (20)	131	0.97
Not Hispanic (14)	101	0.75
Hispanic (6)	30	0.22
Blackfeet (3)	10	0.07
Cherokee (8)	35	0.26
Cheyenne (0)	1	0.01
Choctaw (0)	1	0.01
Iroquois (0)	1	0.01
Mexican American Ind. (0)	1	0.01
Navajo (0)	2	0.01
Sioux (0)	9	0.07
Asian (60)	89	0.66
Not Hispanic (57)	82	0.61
Hispanic (3)	7	0.05
Cambodian (1)	1	0.01
Chinese, ex. Taiwanese (15)	22	0.16
Filipino (9)	17	0.13
Indian (6)	8	0.06
Indonesian (1)	1	0.01
Japanese (7)	8	0.06
Korean (3)	6	0.04
Laotian (14)	18	0.13
Thai (2)	3	0.02
Vietnamese (2)	8	0.06
Hawaii Native/Pacific Islander (2)	5	0.04
Not Hispanic (0)	2	0.01
Hispanic (2)	3	0.02
Native Hawaiian (2)	3	0.02
Samoan (0)	1	0.01
White (11,304)	11,881	88.39
Not Hispanic (10,526)	10,962	81.56
Hispanic (778)	919	6.84

Franklin

Place Type: City
County: Warren
Population: 11,771†

Ancestry‡	Population	%
American (2,062)	2,062	17.24
Arab (0)	36	0.30
Lebanese (0)	36	0.30
Belgian (20)	20	0.17
British (53)	53	0.44
Danish (0)	13	0.11
Dutch (0)	282	2.36
English (595)	1,114	9.31
European (163)	189	1.58
French, ex. Basque (54)	430	3.59
German (781)	2,225	18.60
Greek (7)	46	0.38
Irish (375)	1,547	12.93
Italian (119)	629	5.26
Norwegian (0)	39	0.33
Polish (0)	75	0.63
Scotch-Irish (131)	147	1.23
Scottish (101)	155	1.30
Swiss (0)	12	0.10
Welsh (0)	41	0.34
West Indian, ex. Hispanic (129)	129	1.08
West Indian (129)	129	1.08
Yugoslavian (9)	9	0.08

Hispanic Origin	Population	%
Hispanic or Latino (of any race)	183	1.55
Central American, ex. Mexican	16	0.14
Guatemalan	1	0.01
Honduran	6	0.05
Nicaraguan	4	0.03
Panamanian	1	0.01
Salvadoran	4	0.03
Cuban	4	0.03
Dominican Republic	3	0.03
Mexican	79	0.67
Puerto Rican	42	0.36
South American	12	0.10
Colombian	4	0.03
Peruvian	8	0.07
Other Hispanic or Latino	27	0.23

Race*	Population	%
African-American/Black (110)	177	1.50
Not Hispanic (110)	175	1.49
Hispanic (0)	2	0.02
American Indian/Alaska Native (25)	106	0.90
Not Hispanic (22)	94	0.80
Hispanic (3)	12	0.10
Apache (2)	2	0.02
Blackfeet (0)	5	0.04
Canadian/French Am. Ind. (3)	3	0.03
Cherokee (3)	26	0.22
Cheyenne (0)	7	0.06
Chippewa (1)	3	0.03
Crow (0)	1	0.01
Iroquois (3)	4	0.03
Lumbee (0)	1	0.01
Mexican American Ind. (1)	2	0.02
Navajo (0)	4	0.03
Ute (1)	4	0.03
Asian (62)	102	0.87
Not Hispanic (62)	102	0.87
Burmese (4)	6	0.05
Chinese, ex. Taiwanese (8)	12	0.10
Filipino (10)	22	0.19
Indian (20)	31	0.26
Japanese (3)	5	0.04
Korean (3)	15	0.13
Taiwanese (1)	1	0.01
Thai (2)	3	0.03
Hawaii Native/Pacific Islander (0)	4	0.03
Not Hispanic (0)	3	0.03
Hispanic (0)	1	0.01
Native Hawaiian (0)	1	0.01
White (11,325)	11,516	97.83
Not Hispanic (11,208)	11,381	96.69
Hispanic (117)	135	1.15

Fremont

Place Type: City
County: Sandusky
Population: 16,734†

Ancestry‡	Population	%
African, Sub-Saharan (259)	269	1.59
African (259)	269	1.59
American (958)	958	5.65
Arab (44)	110	0.65
Lebanese (44)	103	0.61
Syrian (0)	7	0.04
Armenian (0)	5	0.03
Austrian (11)	35	0.21
Belgian (9)	9	0.05
British (7)	24	0.14
Canadian (0)	18	0.11
Croatian (11)	20	0.12
Czechoslovakian (9)	18	0.11
Danish (12)	12	0.07
Dutch (14)	359	2.12
English (271)	1,172	6.91
European (8)	8	0.05
French, ex. Basque (73)	564	3.33
French Canadian (37)	47	0.28
German (2,859)	5,631	33.20
Greek (7)	7	0.04
Hungarian (14)	53	0.31
Irish (362)	1,545	9.11
Italian (131)	487	2.87
Northern European (9)	9	0.05
Norwegian (80)	133	0.78
Pennsylvania German (24)	34	0.20
Polish (286)	713	4.20
Russian (11)	27	0.16
Scandinavian (9)	9	0.05
Scotch-Irish (49)	100	0.59
Scottish (45)	118	0.70
Slovak (24)	67	0.40
Slovene (0)	24	0.14
Swedish (0)	55	0.32
Swiss (15)	74	0.44
Welsh (17)	69	0.41
West Indian, ex. Hispanic (0)	67	0.40
Jamaican (0)	67	0.40

Hispanic Origin	Population	%
Hispanic or Latino (of any race)	2,700	16.13
Central American, ex. Mexican	15	0.09
Honduran	7	0.04
Nicaraguan	7	0.04
Salvadoran	1	0.01
Cuban	8	0.05
Mexican	2,331	13.93
Puerto Rican	127	0.76
South American	13	0.08
Argentinean	4	0.02
Colombian	8	0.05
Peruvian	1	0.01
Other Hispanic or Latino	206	1.23

Race*	Population	%
African-American/Black (1,384)	1,933	11.55
Not Hispanic (1,303)	1,775	10.61
Hispanic (81)	158	0.94
American Indian/Alaska Native (40)	137	0.82
Not Hispanic (29)	110	0.66
Hispanic (11)	27	0.16
Apache (2)	9	0.05
Blackfeet (1)	19	0.11
Canadian/French Am. Ind. (0)	3	0.02
Cherokee (3)	34	0.20
Chippewa (2)	2	0.01
Choctaw (0)	1	0.01
Comanche (1)	1	0.01
Creek (1)	1	0.01
Inupiat *(Alaska Native)* (0)	6	0.04
Lumbee (0)	1	0.01
Mexican American Ind. (1)	1	0.01
Potawatomi (1)	1	0.01
Sioux (0)	2	0.01
Yakama (2)	2	0.01
Asian (54)	100	0.60
Not Hispanic (54)	92	0.55
Hispanic (0)	8	0.05
Chinese, ex. Taiwanese (25)	34	0.20
Filipino (14)	31	0.19
Indian (2)	2	0.01
Japanese (2)	17	0.10
Korean (4)	15	0.09
Laotian (0)	1	0.01
Taiwanese (2)	2	0.01
Vietnamese (5)	5	0.03
Hawaii Native/Pacific Islander (3)	15	0.09
Not Hispanic (3)	15	0.09

*Notes: † The Census 2010 population figure is used to calculate the percentages in the Hispanic Origin and Race categories. Ancestry percentages are based on the 2006-2010 American Community Survey population (not shown); ‡ Numbers in parentheses indicate the number of people reporting a single ancestry; * Numbers in parentheses indicate the number of persons reporting this race alone, not in combination with any other race; Please refer to the Explanation of Data for more information.*

Fijian (0)	6	0.04
Guamanian/Chamorro (1)	2	0.01
Native Hawaiian (1)	3	0.02
Samoan (1)	1	0.01
Tongan (0)	6	0.04
White (13,510)	14,331	85.64
Not Hispanic (12,059)	12,607	75.34
Hispanic (1,451)	1,724	10.30

Gahanna

Place Type: City
County: Franklin
Population: 33,248†

Ancestry‡	Population	%
African, Sub-Saharan (170)	170	0.52
African (117)	117	0.36
Ethiopian (45)	45	0.14
Nigerian (8)	8	0.02
American (1,896)	1,896	5.82
Arab (224)	224	0.69
Egyptian (100)	100	0.31
Lebanese (50)	50	0.15
Moroccan (24)	24	0.07
Syrian (50)	50	0.15
Australian (14)	14	0.04
Austrian (0)	90	0.28
Belgian (25)	25	0.08
British (42)	145	0.44
Canadian (13)	157	0.48
Celtic (51)	51	0.16
Croatian (23)	82	0.25
Czech (88)	204	0.63
Czechoslovakian (30)	57	0.17
Danish (0)	57	0.17
Dutch (70)	602	1.85
Eastern European (60)	60	0.18
English (1,545)	4,680	14.36
European (464)	582	1.79
Finnish (56)	122	0.37
French, ex. Basque (78)	835	2.56
French Canadian (88)	180	0.55
German (3,557)	10,153	31.15
Greek (165)	188	0.58
Hungarian (54)	248	0.76
Irish (1,703)	5,629	17.27
Israeli (27)	47	0.14
Italian (807)	2,414	7.41
Latvian (12)	48	0.15
Lithuanian (15)	36	0.11
Macedonian (103)	103	0.32
New Zealander (14)	14	0.04
Norwegian (61)	239	0.73
Pennsylvania German (36)	58	0.18
Polish (411)	1,160	3.56
Portuguese (8)	17	0.05
Romanian (14)	24	0.07
Russian (205)	427	1.31
Scandinavian (15)	57	0.17
Scotch-Irish (181)	714	2.19
Scottish (269)	916	2.81
Serbian (31)	31	0.10
Slavic (9)	9	0.03
Slovak (58)	240	0.74
Slovene (0)	57	0.17
Swedish (57)	399	1.22
Swiss (46)	238	0.73
Turkish (0)	31	0.10
Ukrainian (33)	169	0.52
Welsh (341)	927	2.84
West Indian, ex. Hispanic (54)	54	0.17
Jamaican (54)	54	0.17
Yugoslavian (0)	28	0.09

Hispanic Origin	Population	%
Hispanic or Latino (of any race)	849	2.55
Central American, ex. Mexican	76	0.23
Costa Rican	7	0.02
Guatemalan	20	0.06
Honduran	16	0.05
Nicaraguan	7	0.02
Panamanian	11	0.03
Salvadoran	15	0.05
Cuban	34	0.10
Dominican Republic	24	0.07
Mexican	376	1.13
Puerto Rican	176	0.53
South American	97	0.29
Argentinean	19	0.06
Bolivian	3	0.01
Chilean	5	0.02
Colombian	43	0.13
Ecuadorian	9	0.03
Peruvian	16	0.05
Venezuelan	2	0.01
Other Hispanic or Latino	66	0.20

Race*	Population	%
African-American/Black (3,723)	4,185	12.59
Not Hispanic (3,650)	4,070	12.24
Hispanic (73)	115	0.35
American Indian/Alaska Native (65)	295	0.89
Not Hispanic (58)	271	0.82
Hispanic (7)	24	0.07
Aleut *(Alaska Native)* (0)	1	<0.01
Apache (0)	3	0.01
Blackfeet (0)	19	0.06
Cherokee (13)	88	0.26
Cheyenne (0)	1	<0.01
Chippewa (1)	1	<0.01
Choctaw (6)	13	0.04
Cree (0)	1	<0.01
Creek (0)	1	<0.01
Crow (1)	1	<0.01
Lumbee (0)	2	0.01
Mexican American Ind. (2)	4	0.01
Navajo (2)	2	0.01
Ottawa (2)	3	0.01
Pima (0)	1	<0.01
Potawatomi (1)	1	<0.01
Sioux (2)	3	0.01
South American Ind. (0)	1	<0.01
Spanish American Ind. (1)	1	<0.01
Tlingit-Haida *(Alaska Native)* (0)	2	0.01
Tsimshian *(Alaska Native)* (0)	2	0.01
Asian (1,038)	1,262	3.80
Not Hispanic (1,034)	1,244	3.74
Hispanic (4)	18	0.05
Bangladeshi (8)	8	0.02
Cambodian (16)	26	0.08
Chinese, ex. Taiwanese (228)	271	0.82
Filipino (69)	122	0.37
Indian (347)	384	1.15
Indonesian (7)	11	0.03
Japanese (48)	74	0.22
Korean (104)	129	0.39
Laotian (22)	28	0.08
Malaysian (3)	4	0.01
Nepalese (3)	3	0.01
Pakistani (34)	39	0.12
Taiwanese (25)	27	0.08
Thai (7)	19	0.06
Vietnamese (69)	86	0.26
Hawaii Native/Pacific Islander (14)	22	0.07
Not Hispanic (14)	21	0.06
Hispanic (0)	1	<0.01
Fijian (1)	2	0.01
Guamanian/Chamorro (1)	2	0.01
Native Hawaiian (2)	3	0.01
Samoan (8)	8	0.02
White (27,291)	27,984	84.17
Not Hispanic (26,834)	27,472	82.63
Hispanic (457)	512	1.54

Galion

Place Type: City
County: Crawford
Population: 10,512†

Ancestry‡	Population	%
American (1,145)	1,145	10.72
Arab (25)	25	0.23
Other Arab (25)	25	0.23
Austrian (6)	15	0.14
Belgian (0)	9	0.08
British (8)	36	0.34
Czech (0)	29	0.27
Czechoslovakian (13)	13	0.12
Dutch (63)	225	2.11
English (591)	1,494	13.99
European (27)	27	0.25
French, ex. Basque (18)	143	1.34
French Canadian (41)	49	0.46
German (1,460)	3,745	35.07
Greek (0)	9	0.08
Hungarian (13)	38	0.36
Irish (267)	2,117	19.82
Italian (285)	711	6.66
Lithuanian (0)	17	0.16
Pennsylvania German (12)	30	0.28
Polish (72)	225	2.11
Russian (0)	45	0.42
Scotch-Irish (76)	231	2.16
Scottish (99)	203	1.90
Slovak (33)	50	0.47
Swedish (0)	14	0.13
Swiss (0)	16	0.15
Ukrainian (0)	13	0.12
Welsh (52)	91	0.85
Yugoslavian (16)	16	0.15

Hispanic Origin	Population	%
Hispanic or Latino (of any race)	140	1.33
Central American, ex. Mexican	3	0.03
Costa Rican	1	0.01
Guatemalan	2	0.02
Cuban	3	0.03
Mexican	99	0.94
Puerto Rican	14	0.13
South American	1	0.01
Peruvian	1	0.01
Other Hispanic or Latino	20	0.19

Race*	Population	%
African-American/Black (50)	102	0.97
Not Hispanic (50)	97	0.92
Hispanic (0)	5	0.05
American Indian/Alaska Native (14)	58	0.55
Not Hispanic (14)	53	0.50
Hispanic (0)	5	0.05
Alaska Athabascan *(Ala. Nat.)* (1)	1	0.01
Apache (0)	1	0.01
Blackfeet (0)	4	0.04
Cherokee (4)	18	0.17
Cheyenne (0)	1	0.01
Choctaw (1)	2	0.02
Asian (21)	35	0.33
Not Hispanic (21)	35	0.33
Chinese, ex. Taiwanese (9)	11	0.10
Filipino (3)	7	0.07
Indian (4)	4	0.04
Japanese (1)	5	0.05
Korean (0)	3	0.03
Taiwanese (0)	2	0.02
Vietnamese (2)	4	0.04
Hawaii Native/Pacific Islander (1)	5	0.05
Not Hispanic (1)	3	0.03
Hispanic (0)	2	0.02
Guamanian/Chamorro (0)	1	0.01
Native Hawaiian (0)	1	0.01
White (10,264)	10,380	98.74
Not Hispanic (10,170)	10,266	97.66
Hispanic (94)	114	1.08

Garfield Heights

Place Type: City
County: Cuyahoga
Population: 28,849†

*Notes: † The Census 2010 population figure is used to calculate the percentages in the Hispanic Origin and Race categories. Ancestry percentages are based on the 2006-2010 American Community Survey population (not shown); ‡ Numbers in parentheses indicate the number of people reporting a single ancestry; * Numbers in parentheses indicate the number of persons reporting this race alone, not in combination with any other race; Please refer to the Explanation of Data for more information.*

Ancestry‡	Population	%
African, Sub-Saharan (82)	133	0.46
African (35)	44	0.15
Kenyan (30)	51	0.18
Liberian (7)	7	0.02
Other Sub-Saharan African (10)	31	0.11
American (626)	626	2.15
Arab (48)	105	0.36
Arab (13)	13	0.04
Lebanese (22)	67	0.23
Syrian (13)	25	0.09
Armenian (0)	15	0.05
Austrian (43)	143	0.49
Belgian (0)	36	0.12
British (0)	6	0.02
Canadian (13)	24	0.08
Carpatho Rusyn (9)	9	0.03
Croatian (57)	147	0.51
Czech (201)	945	3.25
Czechoslovakian (60)	95	0.33
Danish (0)	4	0.01
Dutch (8)	122	0.42
English (177)	1,087	3.74
European (97)	97	0.33
Finnish (13)	13	0.04
French, ex. Basque (25)	488	1.68
French Canadian (7)	7	0.02
German (942)	4,753	16.36
German Russian (0)	28	0.10
Greek (58)	85	0.29
Hungarian (309)	986	3.39
Irish (586)	3,067	10.55
Italian (1,394)	3,290	11.32
Lithuanian (38)	145	0.50
Macedonian (0)	13	0.04
Norwegian (9)	30	0.10
Pennsylvania German (0)	12	0.04
Polish (3,045)	6,009	20.68
Portuguese (0)	17	0.06
Romanian (0)	48	0.17
Russian (71)	179	0.62
Scandinavian (47)	97	0.33
Scotch-Irish (43)	182	0.63
Scottish (22)	162	0.56
Serbian (0)	10	0.03
Slovak (513)	1,253	4.31
Slovene (231)	717	2.47
Swedish (0)	54	0.19
Swiss (0)	50	0.17
Ukrainian (68)	319	1.10
Welsh (17)	78	0.27
West Indian, ex. Hispanic (0)	9	0.03
Haitian (0)	9	0.03
Yugoslavian (10)	18	0.06

Hispanic Origin	Population	%
Hispanic or Latino (of any race)	656	2.27
Central American, ex. Mexican	49	0.17
Costa Rican	3	0.01
Guatemalan	24	0.08
Honduran	3	0.01
Panamanian	5	0.02
Salvadoran	14	0.05
Cuban	14	0.05
Dominican Republic	5	0.02
Mexican	190	0.66
Puerto Rican	321	1.11
South American	17	0.06
Argentinean	5	0.02
Chilean	1	<0.01
Colombian	1	<0.01
Ecuadorian	1	<0.01
Peruvian	8	0.03
Venezuelan	1	<0.01
Other Hispanic or Latino	60	0.21

Race*	Population	%
African-American/Black (10,288)	10,731	37.20
Not Hispanic (10,184)	10,584	36.69
Hispanic (104)	147	0.51
American Indian/Alaska Native (45)	180	0.62
Not Hispanic (35)	169	0.59
Hispanic (10)	11	0.04
Alaska Athabascan *(Ala. Nat.)* (1)	1	<0.01
Apache (4)	6	0.02
Blackfeet (0)	11	0.04
Canadian/French Am. Ind. (2)	3	0.01
Cherokee (5)	43	0.15
Chippewa (3)	3	0.01
Creek (0)	2	0.01
Iroquois (4)	7	0.02
Navajo (1)	1	<0.01
Ottawa (1)	1	<0.01
Pueblo (3)	3	0.01
Shoshone (0)	4	0.01
Sioux (1)	4	0.01
South American Ind. (1)	1	<0.01
Asian (388)	499	1.73
Not Hispanic (387)	496	1.72
Hispanic (1)	3	0.01
Cambodian (5)	5	0.02
Chinese, ex. Taiwanese (33)	49	0.17
Filipino (185)	222	0.77
Indian (110)	124	0.43
Indonesian (0)	1	<0.01
Japanese (8)	28	0.10
Korean (10)	22	0.08
Laotian (6)	8	0.03
Pakistani (1)	2	0.01
Vietnamese (12)	21	0.07
Hawaii Native/Pacific Islander (7)	27	0.09
Not Hispanic (6)	25	0.09
Hispanic (1)	2	0.01
Guamanian/Chamorro (1)	3	0.01
Native Hawaiian (4)	5	0.02
Samoan (1)	3	0.01
White (17,362)	17,820	61.77
Not Hispanic (17,019)	17,430	60.42
Hispanic (343)	390	1.35

Girard

Place Type: City
County: Trumbull
Population: 9,958†

Ancestry‡	Population	%
American (1,751)	1,751	17.07
Arab (53)	53	0.52
Lebanese (25)	25	0.24
Palestinian (28)	28	0.27
Belgian (0)	17	0.17
Croatian (30)	107	1.04
Czech (12)	37	0.36
Czechoslovakian (15)	55	0.54
Dutch (0)	123	1.20
English (105)	790	7.70
European (0)	10	0.10
Finnish (10)	40	0.39
French, ex. Basque (0)	184	1.79
French Canadian (26)	106	1.03
German (474)	2,235	21.79
Greek (29)	61	0.59
Hungarian (37)	199	1.94
Irish (210)	1,724	16.81
Italian (1,379)	2,806	27.35
Lithuanian (5)	10	0.10
Macedonian (0)	24	0.23
Pennsylvania German (17)	30	0.29
Polish (147)	541	5.27
Romanian (0)	11	0.11
Russian (14)	33	0.32
Scotch-Irish (70)	188	1.83
Scottish (0)	147	1.43
Serbian (0)	83	0.81
Slavic (0)	11	0.11
Slovak (65)	391	3.81
Slovene (34)	96	0.94
Swedish (32)	142	1.38
Ukrainian (88)	154	1.50
Welsh (14)	210	2.05

Hispanic Origin	Population	%
Hispanic or Latino (of any race)	208	2.09
Central American, ex. Mexican	3	0.03
Guatemalan	1	0.01
Honduran	2	0.02
Cuban	1	0.01
Dominican Republic	2	0.02
Mexican	95	0.95
Puerto Rican	91	0.91
South American	4	0.04
Argentinean	1	0.01
Chilean	3	0.03
Other Hispanic or Latino	12	0.12

Race*	Population	%
African-American/Black (399)	520	5.22
Not Hispanic (383)	491	4.93
Hispanic (16)	29	0.29
American Indian/Alaska Native (10)	71	0.71
Not Hispanic (8)	64	0.64
Hispanic (2)	7	0.07
Blackfeet (0)	2	0.02
Cherokee (5)	28	0.28
Chippewa (0)	2	0.02
Creek (0)	3	0.03
Inupiat *(Alaska Native)* (0)	1	0.01
Iroquois (0)	2	0.02
Mexican American Ind. (0)	2	0.02
Asian (28)	50	0.50
Not Hispanic (27)	49	0.49
Hispanic (1)	1	0.01
Chinese, ex. Taiwanese (13)	13	0.13
Filipino (9)	16	0.16
Indian (2)	3	0.03
Japanese (1)	3	0.03
Korean (0)	7	0.07
Thai (3)	3	0.03
Hawaii Native/Pacific Islander (1)	3	0.03
Not Hispanic (1)	3	0.03
Guamanian/Chamorro (0)	1	0.01
Native Hawaiian (1)	1	0.01
White (9,278)	9,493	95.33
Not Hispanic (9,141)	9,320	93.59
Hispanic (137)	173	1.74

Green

Place Type: City
County: Summit
Population: 25,699†

Ancestry‡	Population	%
African, Sub-Saharan (30)	62	0.25
African (0)	16	0.06
Kenyan (30)	46	0.18
American (1,714)	1,714	6.80
Arab (207)	332	1.32
Lebanese (103)	216	0.86
Palestinian (25)	25	0.10
Syrian (13)	25	0.10
Other Arab (66)	66	0.26
Armenian (21)	45	0.18
Australian (0)	38	0.15
Austrian (14)	111	0.44
Belgian (7)	28	0.11
British (11)	40	0.16
Cajun (0)	15	0.06
Croatian (41)	245	0.97
Czech (44)	273	1.08
Czechoslovakian (40)	119	0.47
Danish (20)	134	0.53
Dutch (85)	431	1.71
Eastern European (19)	19	0.08
English (814)	3,140	12.45
Estonian (13)	13	0.05
European (257)	297	1.18
Finnish (20)	20	0.08
French, ex. Basque (93)	713	2.83

SECTION TWO

*Notes: † The Census 2010 population figure is used to calculate the percentages in the Hispanic Origin and Race categories. Ancestry percentages are based on the 2006-2010 American Community Survey population (not shown); ‡ Numbers in parentheses indicate the number of people reporting a single ancestry; * Numbers in parentheses indicate the number of persons reporting this race alone, not in combination with any other race; Please refer to the Explanation of Data for more information.*

French Canadian (72)	102	0.40
German (2,229)	7,637	30.28
Greek (196)	389	1.54
Hungarian (422)	1,380	5.47
Irish (941)	4,029	15.97
Italian (1,310)	3,330	13.20
Latvian (0)	17	0.07
Lithuanian (17)	46	0.18
Luxemburger (14)	14	0.06
Macedonian (0)	11	0.04
Northern European (32)	32	0.13
Norwegian (10)	50	0.20
Pennsylvania German (85)	152	0.60
Polish (268)	1,073	4.25
Portuguese (15)	15	0.06
Romanian (53)	64	0.25
Russian (14)	70	0.28
Scandinavian (11)	37	0.15
Scotch-Irish (210)	523	2.07
Scottish (137)	678	2.69
Serbian (40)	170	0.67
Slavic (0)	17	0.07
Slovak (246)	568	2.25
Slovene (21)	52	0.21
Swedish (53)	155	0.61
Swiss (38)	164	0.65
Ukrainian (63)	127	0.50
Welsh (68)	367	1.45
Yugoslavian (0)	13	0.05

Hispanic Origin	Population	%
Hispanic or Latino (of any race)	313	1.22
Central American, ex. Mexican	13	0.05
Guatemalan	8	0.03
Honduran	4	0.02
Panamanian	1	<0.01
Cuban	7	0.03
Mexican	148	0.58
Puerto Rican	65	0.25
South American	39	0.15
Argentinean	1	<0.01
Bolivian	1	<0.01
Chilean	3	0.01
Colombian	22	0.09
Ecuadorian	1	<0.01
Peruvian	7	0.03
Uruguayan	4	0.02
Other Hispanic or Latino	41	0.16

Race*	Population	%
African-American/Black (463)	568	2.21
Not Hispanic (456)	556	2.16
Hispanic (7)	12	0.05
American Indian/Alaska Native (51)	142	0.55
Not Hispanic (47)	127	0.49
Hispanic (4)	15	0.06
Apache (1)	1	<0.01
Blackfeet (0)	2	0.01
Central American Ind. (1)	1	<0.01
Cherokee (13)	48	0.19
Chickasaw (0)	1	<0.01
Chippewa (0)	1	<0.01
Choctaw (1)	1	<0.01
Iroquois (2)	8	0.03
Mexican American Ind. (1)	1	<0.01
Navajo (1)	1	<0.01
Seminole (0)	1	<0.01
Sioux (5)	8	0.03
Tsimshian *(Alaska Native)* (1)	2	0.01
Yup'ik *(Alaska Native)* (3)	3	0.01
Asian (381)	495	1.93
Not Hispanic (380)	490	1.91
Hispanic (1)	5	0.02
Bangladeshi (4)	9	0.04
Cambodian (1)	1	<0.01
Chinese, ex. Taiwanese (58)	67	0.26
Filipino (37)	57	0.22
Hmong (27)	31	0.12
Indian (94)	105	0.41
Indonesian (2)	6	0.02
Japanese (18)	28	0.11
Korean (41)	55	0.21
Laotian (14)	14	0.05
Malaysian (1)	3	0.01
Pakistani (27)	27	0.11
Taiwanese (1)	2	0.01
Thai (2)	10	0.04
Vietnamese (40)	43	0.17
Hawaii Native/Pacific Islander (7)	11	0.04
Not Hispanic (7)	11	0.04
Native Hawaiian (1)	2	0.01
White (24,413)	24,720	96.19
Not Hispanic (24,187)	24,459	95.17
Hispanic (226)	261	1.02

Greenville

Place Type: City
County: Darke
Population: 13,227†

Ancestry‡	Population	%
African, Sub-Saharan (82)	82	0.62
African (7)	7	0.05
South African (75)	75	0.57
American (1,819)	1,819	13.71
Arab (10)	10	0.08
Egyptian (10)	10	0.08
Belgian (0)	17	0.13
British (13)	76	0.57
Dutch (12)	288	2.17
English (441)	1,287	9.70
European (92)	92	0.69
French, ex. Basque (151)	689	5.19
French Canadian (0)	10	0.08
German (2,037)	4,438	33.45
Greek (0)	77	0.58
Hungarian (0)	35	0.26
Irish (400)	1,689	12.73
Italian (141)	262	1.97
Norwegian (36)	55	0.41
Pennsylvania German (69)	69	0.52
Polish (0)	31	0.23
Romanian (0)	19	0.14
Russian (0)	29	0.22
Scotch-Irish (52)	178	1.34
Scottish (97)	354	2.67
Swedish (65)	78	0.59
Swiss (38)	136	1.03
Ukrainian (0)	16	0.12
Welsh (13)	41	0.31

Hispanic Origin	Population	%
Hispanic or Latino (of any race)	185	1.40
Central American, ex. Mexican	3	0.02
Guatemalan	1	0.01
Panamanian	2	0.02
Cuban	16	0.12
Mexican	124	0.94
Puerto Rican	11	0.08
South American	5	0.04
Ecuadorian	5	0.04
Other Hispanic or Latino	26	0.20

Race*	Population	%
African-American/Black (117)	198	1.50
Not Hispanic (113)	194	1.47
Hispanic (4)	4	0.03
American Indian/Alaska Native (31)	73	0.55
Not Hispanic (27)	66	0.50
Hispanic (4)	7	0.05
Apache (2)	3	0.02
Blackfeet (1)	6	0.05
Cherokee (7)	17	0.13
Iroquois (0)	2	0.02
Menominee (0)	1	0.01
Mexican American Ind. (2)	2	0.02
Navajo (2)	2	0.02
Shoshone (1)	1	0.01
Sioux (1)	5	0.04
South American Ind. (1)	1	0.01
Asian (92)	123	0.93
Not Hispanic (92)	120	0.91
Hispanic (0)	3	0.02
Chinese, ex. Taiwanese (15)	16	0.12
Filipino (21)	30	0.23
Indian (22)	27	0.20
Japanese (23)	28	0.21
Korean (2)	8	0.06
Pakistani (5)	5	0.04
Vietnamese (4)	6	0.05
Hawaii Native/Pacific Islander (3)	9	0.07
Not Hispanic (3)	7	0.05
Hispanic (0)	2	0.02
Guamanian/Chamorro (0)	1	0.01
Native Hawaiian (3)	5	0.04
White (12,795)	12,933	97.78
Not Hispanic (12,663)	12,790	96.70
Hispanic (132)	143	1.08

Grove City

Place Type: City
County: Franklin
Population: 35,575†

Ancestry‡	Population	%
African, Sub-Saharan (35)	56	0.16
African (7)	28	0.08
Somalian (28)	28	0.08
Alsatian (0)	30	0.09
American (3,070)	3,070	9.04
Arab (13)	40	0.12
Syrian (13)	25	0.07
Other Arab (0)	15	0.04
Austrian (0)	44	0.13
British (153)	324	0.95
Bulgarian (0)	28	0.08
Canadian (29)	52	0.15
Croatian (6)	22	0.06
Czech (13)	76	0.22
Czechoslovakian (0)	33	0.10
Danish (0)	38	0.11
Dutch (157)	886	2.61
Eastern European (10)	10	0.03
English (1,222)	4,183	12.32
European (483)	558	1.64
Finnish (36)	57	0.17
French, ex. Basque (160)	797	2.35
French Canadian (38)	69	0.20
German (4,127)	10,344	30.47
German Russian (0)	29	0.09
Greek (147)	337	0.99
Hungarian (108)	277	0.82
Irish (1,780)	6,026	17.75
Italian (955)	2,132	6.28
Lithuanian (19)	40	0.12
Northern European (80)	80	0.24
Norwegian (54)	227	0.67
Pennsylvania German (32)	53	0.16
Polish (176)	1,003	2.95
Romanian (40)	64	0.19
Russian (23)	141	0.42
Scandinavian (30)	85	0.25
Scotch-Irish (248)	712	2.10
Scottish (422)	860	2.53
Serbian (0)	13	0.04
Slavic (0)	7	0.02
Slovak (17)	43	0.13
Slovene (15)	15	0.04
Swedish (86)	342	1.01
Swiss (0)	187	0.55
Ukrainian (12)	35	0.10
Welsh (246)	784	2.31
West Indian, ex. Hispanic (0)	10	0.03
Haitian (0)	10	0.03
Yugoslavian (0)	11	0.03

Hispanic Origin	Population	%
Hispanic or Latino (of any race)	912	2.56

*Notes: † The Census 2010 population figure is used to calculate the percentages in the Hispanic Origin and Race categories. Ancestry percentages are based on the 2006-2010 American Community Survey population (not shown); ‡ Numbers in parentheses indicate the number of people reporting a single ancestry; * Numbers in parentheses indicate the number of persons reporting this race alone, not in combination with any other race; Please refer to the Explanation of Data for more information.*

Central American, ex. Mexican	114	0.32
Costa Rican	10	0.03
Guatemalan	7	0.02
Honduran	11	0.03
Nicaraguan	2	0.01
Panamanian	7	0.02
Salvadoran	77	0.22
Cuban	21	0.06
Dominican Republic	32	0.09
Mexican	464	1.30
Puerto Rican	110	0.31
South American	76	0.21
Argentinean	10	0.03
Bolivian	5	0.01
Chilean	4	0.01
Colombian	23	0.06
Ecuadorian	6	0.02
Peruvian	26	0.07
Venezuelan	2	0.01
Other Hispanic or Latino	95	0.27

Race*	Population	%
African-American/Black (997)	1,356	3.81
Not Hispanic (979)	1,322	3.72
Hispanic (18)	34	0.10
American Indian/Alaska Native (65)	291	0.82
Not Hispanic (53)	267	0.75
Hispanic (12)	24	0.07
Aleut *(Alaska Native)* (1)	2	0.01
Apache (2)	3	0.01
Blackfeet (0)	4	0.01
Cherokee (12)	116	0.33
Cheyenne (0)	1	<0.01
Chippewa (3)	8	0.02
Choctaw (3)	4	0.01
Comanche (0)	8	0.02
Crow (0)	1	<0.01
Delaware (0)	1	<0.01
Iroquois (0)	5	0.01
Lumbee (1)	1	<0.01
Mexican American Ind. (3)	5	0.01
Navajo (1)	3	0.01
Osage (0)	2	0.01
Sioux (1)	2	0.01
Tsimshian *(Alaska Native)* (1)	1	<0.01
Asian (455)	631	1.77
Not Hispanic (454)	624	1.75
Hispanic (1)	7	0.02
Cambodian (67)	87	0.24
Chinese, ex. Taiwanese (74)	95	0.27
Filipino (52)	88	0.25
Indian (134)	152	0.43
Indonesian (1)	1	<0.01
Japanese (21)	48	0.13
Korean (14)	44	0.12
Laotian (14)	24	0.07
Pakistani (2)	5	0.01
Taiwanese (7)	7	0.02
Thai (6)	9	0.03
Vietnamese (36)	54	0.15
Hawaii Native/Pacific Islander (17)	26	0.07
Not Hispanic (14)	23	0.06
Hispanic (3)	3	0.01
Guamanian/Chamorro (1)	2	0.01
Native Hawaiian (11)	11	0.03
Samoan (2)	3	0.01
White (32,954)	33,657	94.61
Not Hispanic (32,438)	33,079	92.98
Hispanic (516)	578	1.62

Hamilton

Place Type: City
County: Butler
Population: 62,477†

Ancestry‡	Population	%
African, Sub-Saharan (289)	348	0.56
African (289)	348	0.56
American (15,067)	15,067	24.12
Arab (81)	81	0.13
Iraqi (8)	8	0.01
Jordanian (58)	58	0.09
Other Arab (15)	15	0.02
Australian (0)	10	0.02
Austrian (49)	93	0.15
Belgian (0)	16	0.03
British (139)	270	0.43
Czech (10)	114	0.18
Czechoslovakian (0)	36	0.06
Danish (48)	48	0.08
Dutch (179)	873	1.40
Eastern European (24)	24	0.04
English (1,890)	4,631	7.41
European (327)	357	0.57
Finnish (0)	49	0.08
French, ex. Basque (188)	844	1.35
French Canadian (9)	19	0.03
German (6,035)	13,275	21.25
Greek (26)	71	0.11
Hungarian (64)	193	0.31
Irish (1,930)	6,846	10.96
Italian (1,003)	2,251	3.60
Lithuanian (16)	16	0.03
New Zealander (0)	8	0.01
Northern European (28)	28	0.04
Norwegian (139)	199	0.32
Pennsylvania German (24)	24	0.04
Polish (70)	477	0.76
Portuguese (0)	18	0.03
Romanian (0)	34	0.05
Russian (45)	206	0.33
Scotch-Irish (276)	655	1.05
Scottish (239)	801	1.28
Slavic (8)	8	0.01
Slovak (33)	59	0.09
Swedish (28)	142	0.23
Swiss (160)	202	0.32
Ukrainian (47)	47	0.08
Welsh (52)	242	0.39
West Indian, ex. Hispanic (29)	29	0.05
Jamaican (17)	17	0.03
Trinidadian/Tobagonian (12)	12	0.02
Yugoslavian (0)	15	0.02

Hispanic Origin	Population	%
Hispanic or Latino (of any race)	3,981	6.37
Central American, ex. Mexican	166	0.27
Costa Rican	3	<0.01
Guatemalan	41	0.07
Honduran	64	0.10
Nicaraguan	2	<0.01
Panamanian	3	<0.01
Salvadoran	50	0.08
Other Central American	3	<0.01
Cuban	48	0.08
Dominican Republic	300	0.48
Mexican	2,897	4.64
Puerto Rican	209	0.33
South American	60	0.10
Argentinean	4	0.01
Bolivian	2	<0.01
Chilean	3	<0.01
Colombian	18	0.03
Ecuadorian	5	0.01
Paraguayan	4	0.01
Peruvian	20	0.03
Venezuelan	3	<0.01
Other South American	1	<0.01
Other Hispanic or Latino	301	0.48

Race*	Population	%
African-American/Black (5,336)	6,394	10.23
Not Hispanic (5,232)	6,226	9.97
Hispanic (104)	168	0.27
American Indian/Alaska Native (150)	518	0.83
Not Hispanic (113)	451	0.72
Hispanic (37)	67	0.11
Aleut *(Alaska Native)* (1)	4	0.01
Apache (1)	6	0.01
Arapaho (0)	1	<0.01
Blackfeet (1)	16	0.03
Central American Ind. (1)	1	<0.01
Cherokee (33)	172	0.28
Cheyenne (1)	2	<0.01
Chickasaw (0)	1	<0.01
Chippewa (0)	4	0.01
Choctaw (6)	6	0.01
Comanche (1)	2	<0.01
Cree (2)	2	<0.01
Creek (0)	6	0.01
Iroquois (2)	11	0.02
Kiowa (0)	2	<0.01
Mexican American Ind. (10)	11	0.02
Navajo (2)	4	0.01
Seminole (2)	3	<0.01
Sioux (3)	14	0.02
South American Ind. (1)	5	0.01
Spanish American Ind. (3)	3	<0.01
Yakama (0)	5	0.01
Yaqui (0)	1	<0.01
Asian (384)	576	0.92
Not Hispanic (379)	552	0.88
Hispanic (5)	24	0.04
Cambodian (9)	12	0.02
Chinese, ex. Taiwanese (48)	65	0.10
Filipino (118)	164	0.26
Indian (50)	73	0.12
Indonesian (7)	11	0.02
Japanese (23)	52	0.08
Korean (20)	56	0.09
Nepalese (3)	3	<0.01
Pakistani (2)	9	0.01
Sri Lankan (0)	1	<0.01
Taiwanese (1)	1	<0.01
Thai (5)	19	0.03
Vietnamese (83)	98	0.16
Hawaii Native/Pacific Islander (46)	104	0.17
Not Hispanic (40)	82	0.13
Hispanic (6)	22	0.04
Guamanian/Chamorro (18)	30	0.05
Marshallese (0)	5	0.01
Native Hawaiian (8)	22	0.04
Samoan (2)	9	0.01
Tongan (6)	7	0.01
White (52,487)	54,183	86.72
Not Hispanic (51,198)	52,579	84.16
Hispanic (1,289)	1,604	2.57

Harrison

Place Type: City
County: Hamilton
Population: 9,897†

Ancestry‡	Population	%
American (1,024)	1,024	10.90
Belgian (0)	48	0.51
British (0)	38	0.40
Czech (9)	27	0.29
Dutch (12)	161	1.71
English (241)	980	10.43
European (14)	24	0.26
French, ex. Basque (64)	413	4.40
German (2,467)	4,837	51.49
Hungarian (0)	18	0.19
Irish (322)	2,301	24.49
Italian (171)	444	4.73
Lithuanian (0)	28	0.30
Norwegian (0)	23	0.24
Polish (14)	24	0.26
Romanian (6)	19	0.20
Scandinavian (18)	28	0.30
Scotch-Irish (0)	25	0.27
Scottish (45)	156	1.66
Swedish (38)	44	0.47
Welsh (0)	11	0.12
Yugoslavian (0)	10	0.11

*Notes: † The Census 2010 population figure is used to calculate the percentages in the Hispanic Origin and Race categories. Ancestry percentages are based on the 2006-2010 American Community Survey population (not shown); ‡ Numbers in parentheses indicate the number of people reporting a single ancestry; * Numbers in parentheses indicate the number of persons reporting this race alone, not in combination with any other race; Please refer to the Explanation of Data for more information.*

Hispanic Origin	Population	%
Hispanic or Latino (of any race)	107	1.08
Central American, ex. Mexican	5	0.05
Nicaraguan	5	0.05
Cuban	2	0.02
Dominican Republic	3	0.03
Mexican	63	0.64
Puerto Rican	15	0.15
South American	13	0.13
Argentinean	5	0.05
Colombian	4	0.04
Peruvian	4	0.04
Other Hispanic or Latino	6	0.06

Race*	Population	%
African-American/Black (29)	65	0.66
Not Hispanic (29)	65	0.66
American Indian/Alaska Native (20)	35	0.35
Not Hispanic (19)	34	0.34
Hispanic (1)	1	0.01
Cherokee (2)	10	0.10
Chippewa (1)	3	0.03
Choctaw (0)	1	0.01
Creek (2)	2	0.02
Delaware (1)	1	0.01
Osage (1)	1	0.01
Sioux (0)	2	0.02
Asian (63)	84	0.85
Not Hispanic (61)	82	0.83
Hispanic (2)	2	0.02
Chinese, ex. Taiwanese (16)	16	0.16
Filipino (7)	19	0.19
Indian (4)	5	0.05
Japanese (3)	10	0.10
Korean (6)	7	0.07
Thai (3)	3	0.03
Vietnamese (13)	13	0.13
Hawaii Native/Pacific Islander (1)	2	0.02
Not Hispanic (1)	2	0.02
Native Hawaiian (1)	1	0.01
White (9,662)	9,738	98.39
Not Hispanic (9,596)	9,666	97.67
Hispanic (66)	72	0.73

Heath

Place Type: City
County: Licking
Population: 10,310†

Ancestry‡	Population	%
African, Sub-Saharan (25)	25	0.25
African (25)	25	0.25
American (1,418)	1,418	14.08
Arab (49)	57	0.57
Syrian (0)	8	0.08
Other Arab (49)	49	0.49
Australian (0)	8	0.08
Austrian (11)	49	0.49
British (45)	61	0.61
Croatian (0)	11	0.11
Dutch (16)	125	1.24
English (430)	1,247	12.38
European (146)	158	1.57
French, ex. Basque (19)	258	2.56
German (767)	2,685	26.65
Hungarian (13)	32	0.32
Iranian (10)	10	0.10
Irish (446)	1,557	15.46
Italian (300)	397	3.94
Norwegian (0)	16	0.16
Pennsylvania German (0)	16	0.16
Polish (105)	188	1.87
Russian (0)	49	0.49
Scotch-Irish (102)	216	2.14
Scottish (28)	212	2.10
Slavic (0)	18	0.18
Swedish (0)	43	0.43
Swiss (0)	24	0.24
Welsh (45)	116	1.15
West Indian, ex. Hispanic (47)	78	0.77
British West Indian (0)	31	0.31
Jamaican (47)	47	0.47

Hispanic Origin	Population	%
Hispanic or Latino (of any race)	157	1.52
Central American, ex. Mexican	1	0.01
Panamanian	1	0.01
Cuban	4	0.04
Dominican Republic	1	0.01
Mexican	103	1.00
Puerto Rican	17	0.16
South American	10	0.10
Chilean	3	0.03
Peruvian	5	0.05
Venezuelan	2	0.02
Other Hispanic or Latino	21	0.20

Race*	Population	%
African-American/Black (271)	392	3.80
Not Hispanic (269)	389	3.77
Hispanic (2)	3	0.03
American Indian/Alaska Native (20)	83	0.81
Not Hispanic (18)	79	0.77
Hispanic (2)	4	0.04
Blackfeet (0)	7	0.07
Canadian/French Am. Ind. (2)	2	0.02
Cherokee (6)	29	0.28
Chippewa (1)	3	0.03
Comanche (4)	4	0.04
Cree (0)	3	0.03
Iroquois (0)	1	0.01
Seminole (0)	1	0.01
Sioux (0)	1	0.01
Asian (74)	109	1.06
Not Hispanic (71)	104	1.01
Hispanic (3)	5	0.05
Chinese, ex. Taiwanese (24)	31	0.30
Filipino (16)	21	0.20
Indian (14)	19	0.18
Japanese (2)	4	0.04
Korean (8)	20	0.19
Laotian (1)	1	0.01
Malaysian (0)	1	0.01
Thai (1)	13	0.13
Vietnamese (4)	8	0.08
Hawaii Native/Pacific Islander (0)	4	0.04
Not Hispanic (0)	4	0.04
Native Hawaiian (0)	3	0.03
White (9,664)	9,878	95.81
Not Hispanic (9,573)	9,771	94.77
Hispanic (91)	107	1.04

Highland Heights

Place Type: City
County: Cuyahoga
Population: 8,345†

Ancestry‡	Population	%
American (228)	228	2.77
Arab (138)	199	2.41
Egyptian (28)	28	0.34
Lebanese (110)	171	2.07
Armenian (11)	11	0.13
Assyrian/Chaldean/Syriac (10)	10	0.12
Austrian (18)	54	0.65
British (12)	12	0.15
Cajun (8)	8	0.10
Canadian (0)	13	0.16
Croatian (33)	268	3.25
Czech (41)	157	1.90
Czechoslovakian (6)	36	0.44
Danish (0)	91	1.10
Dutch (22)	64	0.78
Eastern European (0)	10	0.12
English (195)	688	8.34
European (66)	66	0.80
Finnish (0)	37	0.45
French, ex. Basque (19)	179	2.17
French Canadian (15)	15	0.18
German (307)	1,494	18.12
Greek (92)	111	1.35
Hungarian (124)	296	3.59
Irish (268)	1,409	17.09
Italian (1,251)	2,187	26.53
Latvian (0)	10	0.12
Lithuanian (39)	113	1.37
Macedonian (0)	22	0.27
Norwegian (0)	19	0.23
Pennsylvania German (0)	12	0.15
Polish (212)	669	8.11
Romanian (78)	175	2.12
Russian (216)	352	4.27
Scotch-Irish (17)	57	0.69
Scottish (12)	109	1.32
Serbian (0)	43	0.52
Slavic (10)	17	0.21
Slovak (99)	296	3.59
Slovene (134)	476	5.77
Swedish (27)	100	1.21
Swiss (0)	10	0.12
Ukrainian (58)	83	1.01
Welsh (0)	80	0.97
Yugoslavian (0)	11	0.13

Hispanic Origin	Population	%
Hispanic or Latino (of any race)	116	1.39
Central American, ex. Mexican	14	0.17
Costa Rican	2	0.02
Guatemalan	6	0.07
Nicaraguan	1	0.01
Panamanian	5	0.06
Cuban	5	0.06
Mexican	25	0.30
Puerto Rican	25	0.30
South American	32	0.38
Argentinean	6	0.07
Colombian	18	0.22
Paraguayan	3	0.04
Peruvian	1	0.01
Uruguayan	4	0.05
Other Hispanic or Latino	15	0.18

Race*	Population	%
African-American/Black (155)	178	2.13
Not Hispanic (151)	171	2.05
Hispanic (4)	7	0.08
American Indian/Alaska Native (10)	26	0.31
Not Hispanic (10)	26	0.31
Cherokee (5)	10	0.12
Chippewa (3)	3	0.04
Iroquois (1)	1	0.01
Tlingit-Haida *(Alaska Native)* (1)	1	0.01
Asian (483)	525	6.29
Not Hispanic (483)	523	6.27
Hispanic (0)	2	0.02
Bangladeshi (5)	5	0.06
Burmese (1)	1	0.01
Chinese, ex. Taiwanese (143)	160	1.92
Filipino (7)	15	0.18
Indian (217)	226	2.71
Japanese (12)	15	0.18
Korean (37)	44	0.53
Pakistani (24)	24	0.29
Taiwanese (15)	16	0.19
Thai (1)	1	0.01
Vietnamese (14)	14	0.17
Hawaii Native/Pacific Islander (0)	2	0.02
Not Hispanic (0)	2	0.02
White (7,590)	7,663	91.83
Not Hispanic (7,496)	7,567	90.68
Hispanic (94)	96	1.15

Hilliard

Place Type: City
County: Franklin
Population: 28,435†

*Notes: † The Census 2010 population figure is used to calculate the percentages in the Hispanic Origin and Race categories. Ancestry percentages are based on the 2006-2010 American Community Survey population (not shown); ‡ Numbers in parentheses indicate the number of people reporting a single ancestry; * Numbers in parentheses indicate the number of persons reporting this race alone, not in combination with any other race; Please refer to the Explanation of Data for more information.*

Ancestry‡	Population	%
African, Sub-Saharan (152)	163	0.59
African (0)	11	0.04
Somalian (130)	130	0.47
South African (22)	22	0.08
Albanian (48)	48	0.17
American (2,112)	2,112	7.68
Arab (119)	172	0.63
Arab (7)	7	0.03
Egyptian (53)	53	0.19
Lebanese (0)	44	0.16
Palestinian (59)	59	0.21
Syrian (0)	9	0.03
Austrian (178)	255	0.93
Belgian (0)	7	0.03
British (113)	290	1.05
Canadian (24)	170	0.62
Croatian (13)	56	0.20
Czech (44)	171	0.62
Czechoslovakian (12)	34	0.12
Danish (34)	87	0.32
Dutch (90)	345	1.25
Eastern European (27)	65	0.24
English (1,320)	3,702	13.46
European (294)	339	1.23
Finnish (12)	36	0.13
French, ex. Basque (107)	756	2.75
French Canadian (53)	82	0.30
German (2,957)	8,873	32.26
Greek (81)	356	1.29
Hungarian (128)	397	1.44
Iranian (14)	14	0.05
Irish (1,537)	5,020	18.25
Italian (921)	2,379	8.65
Latvian (10)	51	0.19
Lithuanian (45)	59	0.21
Luxemburger (6)	6	0.02
Northern European (11)	11	0.04
Norwegian (9)	95	0.35
Pennsylvania German (79)	79	0.29
Polish (168)	847	3.08
Portuguese (24)	98	0.36
Romanian (0)	49	0.18
Russian (86)	198	0.72
Scandinavian (24)	24	0.09
Scotch-Irish (192)	480	1.75
Scottish (384)	1,055	3.84
Serbian (0)	34	0.12
Slavic (0)	8	0.03
Slovak (34)	139	0.51
Slovene (0)	29	0.11
Swedish (63)	296	1.08
Swiss (0)	78	0.28
Turkish (53)	53	0.19
Ukrainian (0)	24	0.09
Welsh (162)	680	2.47
West Indian, ex. Hispanic (8)	29	0.11
British West Indian (8)	8	0.03
Dutch West Indian (0)	21	0.08
Yugoslavian (18)	18	0.07

Hispanic Origin	Population	%
Hispanic or Latino (of any race)	663	2.33
Central American, ex. Mexican	43	0.15
Costa Rican	2	0.01
Guatemalan	15	0.05
Honduran	7	0.02
Nicaraguan	2	0.01
Panamanian	6	0.02
Salvadoran	11	0.04
Cuban	35	0.12
Dominican Republic	16	0.06
Mexican	288	1.01
Puerto Rican	112	0.39
South American	84	0.30
Argentinean	10	0.04
Bolivian	9	0.03
Chilean	5	0.02
Colombian	22	0.08
Ecuadorian	16	0.06
Paraguayan	1	<0.01
Peruvian	10	0.04
Venezuelan	11	0.04
Other Hispanic or Latino	85	0.30

Race*	Population	%
African-American/Black (840)	1,086	3.82
Not Hispanic (823)	1,043	3.67
Hispanic (17)	43	0.15
American Indian/Alaska Native (43)	137	0.48
Not Hispanic (37)	123	0.43
Hispanic (6)	14	0.05
Apache (0)	1	<0.01
Blackfeet (1)	6	0.02
Cherokee (6)	29	0.10
Chickasaw (0)	1	<0.01
Chippewa (1)	4	0.01
Choctaw (1)	5	0.02
Cree (1)	1	<0.01
Creek (0)	7	0.02
Iroquois (0)	1	<0.01
Lumbee (0)	1	<0.01
Mexican American Ind. (3)	5	0.02
Navajo (4)	4	0.01
Ottawa (0)	1	<0.01
Potawatomi (0)	5	0.02
Seminole (0)	1	<0.01
Sioux (1)	2	0.01
Asian (1,595)	1,818	6.39
Not Hispanic (1,588)	1,800	6.33
Hispanic (7)	18	0.06
Bangladeshi (27)	28	0.10
Cambodian (40)	48	0.17
Chinese, ex. Taiwanese (237)	271	0.95
Filipino (95)	160	0.56
Indian (623)	678	2.38
Indonesian (30)	38	0.13
Japanese (104)	135	0.47
Korean (92)	111	0.39
Laotian (9)	17	0.06
Malaysian (1)	1	<0.01
Nepalese (3)	3	0.01
Pakistani (158)	177	0.62
Sri Lankan (21)	21	0.07
Taiwanese (13)	17	0.06
Thai (19)	22	0.08
Vietnamese (48)	56	0.20
Hawaii Native/Pacific Islander (8)	18	0.06
Not Hispanic (8)	18	0.06
Native Hawaiian (1)	2	0.01
Samoan (7)	7	0.02
White (25,177)	25,678	90.30
Not Hispanic (24,798)	25,250	88.80
Hispanic (379)	428	1.51

Hubbard

Place Type: City
County: Trumbull
Population: 7,874†

Ancestry‡	Population	%
African, Sub-Saharan (0)	16	0.20
African (0)	16	0.20
American (1,343)	1,343	16.96
Arab (10)	10	0.13
Lebanese (10)	10	0.13
Croatian (97)	203	2.56
Czech (0)	86	1.09
Czechoslovakian (0)	22	0.28
Dutch (0)	99	1.25
English (112)	714	9.02
European (15)	32	0.40
French, ex. Basque (25)	138	1.74
German (551)	2,030	25.63
Greek (0)	37	0.47
Hungarian (76)	446	5.63
Iranian (10)	10	0.13
Irish (198)	1,241	15.67
Italian (736)	1,723	21.76
Lithuanian (44)	44	0.56
Macedonian (0)	38	0.48
Pennsylvania German (0)	11	0.14
Polish (71)	519	6.55
Romanian (20)	20	0.25
Russian (0)	32	0.40
Scotch-Irish (39)	219	2.77
Scottish (52)	124	1.57
Serbian (0)	29	0.37
Slavic (0)	12	0.15
Slovak (146)	569	7.18
Slovene (16)	44	0.56
Swedish (0)	13	0.16
Swiss (24)	58	0.73
Ukrainian (13)	28	0.35
Welsh (52)	78	0.98
Yugoslavian (0)	12	0.15

Hispanic Origin	Population	%
Hispanic or Latino (of any race)	104	1.32
Central American, ex. Mexican	3	0.04
Guatemalan	1	0.01
Panamanian	1	0.01
Salvadoran	1	0.01
Cuban	8	0.10
Mexican	18	0.23
Puerto Rican	63	0.80
South American	4	0.05
Colombian	2	0.03
Venezuelan	2	0.03
Other Hispanic or Latino	8	0.10

Race*	Population	%
African-American/Black (118)	154	1.96
Not Hispanic (116)	145	1.84
Hispanic (2)	9	0.11
American Indian/Alaska Native (8)	33	0.42
Not Hispanic (7)	32	0.41
Hispanic (1)	1	0.01
Blackfeet (0)	1	0.01
Cherokee (2)	9	0.11
Chippewa (0)	1	0.01
Iroquois (0)	1	0.01
Navajo (1)	4	0.05
Asian (22)	51	0.65
Not Hispanic (22)	49	0.62
Hispanic (0)	2	0.03
Chinese, ex. Taiwanese (12)	14	0.18
Filipino (3)	9	0.11
Indian (1)	1	0.01
Japanese (0)	4	0.05
Korean (4)	8	0.10
Thai (1)	3	0.04
Vietnamese (0)	1	0.01
Hawaii Native/Pacific Islander (5)	9	0.11
Not Hispanic (5)	7	0.09
Hispanic (0)	2	0.03
Native Hawaiian (2)	3	0.04
Samoan (0)	2	0.03
White (7,602)	7,694	97.71
Not Hispanic (7,535)	7,615	96.71
Hispanic (67)	79	1.00

Huber Heights

Place Type: City
County: Montgomery
Population: 38,101†

Ancestry‡	Population	%
African, Sub-Saharan (181)	235	0.62
African (124)	178	0.47
Other Sub-Saharan African (57)	57	0.15
American (4,927)	4,927	13.02
Arab (159)	173	0.46
Arab (102)	102	0.27
Jordanian (57)	57	0.15
Lebanese (0)	7	0.02
Syrian (0)	7	0.02
Armenian (0)	14	0.04

*Notes: † The Census 2010 population figure is used to calculate the percentages in the Hispanic Origin and Race categories. Ancestry percentages are based on the 2006-2010 American Community Survey population (not shown); ‡ Numbers in parentheses indicate the number of people reporting a single ancestry; * Numbers in parentheses indicate the number of persons reporting this race alone, not in combination with any other race; Please refer to the Explanation of Data for more information.*

Austrian (24)	41	0.11
Belgian (0)	27	0.07
British (53)	87	0.23
Bulgarian (13)	52	0.14
Canadian (6)	55	0.15
Croatian (9)	56	0.15
Czech (7)	35	0.09
Czechoslovakian (0)	26	0.07
Danish (0)	38	0.10
Dutch (83)	590	1.56
Eastern European (27)	27	0.07
English (1,366)	3,441	9.09
European (457)	503	1.33
Finnish (11)	11	0.03
French, ex. Basque (82)	1,004	2.65
French Canadian (32)	239	0.63
German (3,787)	9,215	24.35
Greek (41)	83	0.22
Hungarian (90)	323	0.85
Irish (1,367)	4,900	12.95
Italian (412)	1,544	4.08
Latvian (0)	26	0.07
Lithuanian (26)	108	0.29
Macedonian (0)	11	0.03
Northern European (22)	22	0.06
Norwegian (165)	190	0.50
Pennsylvania German (40)	48	0.13
Polish (389)	808	2.14
Portuguese (0)	75	0.20
Romanian (8)	27	0.07
Russian (69)	90	0.24
Scandinavian (36)	128	0.34
Scotch-Irish (369)	796	2.10
Scottish (273)	695	1.84
Slavic (24)	34	0.09
Slovak (68)	102	0.27
Slovene (0)	21	0.06
Swedish (60)	193	0.51
Swiss (5)	129	0.34
Ukrainian (0)	13	0.03
Welsh (125)	333	0.88
West Indian, ex. Hispanic (40)	98	0.26
Dutch West Indian (0)	43	0.11
Haitian (0)	15	0.04
Jamaican (40)	40	0.11

Hispanic Origin	Population	%
Hispanic or Latino (of any race)	1,178	3.09
Central American, ex. Mexican	54	0.14
Costa Rican	6	0.02
Guatemalan	9	0.02
Honduran	9	0.02
Panamanian	18	0.05
Salvadoran	12	0.03
Cuban	27	0.07
Dominican Republic	10	0.03
Mexican	658	1.73
Puerto Rican	217	0.57
South American	76	0.20
Argentinean	12	0.03
Chilean	22	0.06
Colombian	7	0.02
Ecuadorian	27	0.07
Peruvian	5	0.01
Uruguayan	1	<0.01
Venezuelan	1	<0.01
Other South American	1	<0.01
Other Hispanic or Latino	136	0.36

Race*	Population	%
African-American/Black (4,947)	5,798	15.22
Not Hispanic (4,891)	5,661	14.86
Hispanic (56)	137	0.36
American Indian/Alaska Native (101)	377	0.99
Not Hispanic (92)	318	0.83
Hispanic (9)	59	0.15
Alaska Athabascan *(Ala. Nat.)* (1)	1	<0.01
Apache (1)	5	0.01
Blackfeet (0)	7	0.02
Canadian/French Am. Ind. (0)	3	0.01
Cherokee (20)	126	0.33
Cheyenne (0)	1	<0.01
Chickasaw (4)	4	0.01
Chippewa (0)	2	0.01
Choctaw (7)	10	0.03
Comanche (0)	1	<0.01
Creek (2)	6	0.02
Hopi (1)	1	<0.01
Inupiat *(Alaska Native)* (1)	1	<0.01
Iroquois (0)	1	<0.01
Lumbee (3)	3	0.01
Menominee (0)	1	<0.01
Mexican American Ind. (3)	9	0.02
Navajo (1)	1	<0.01
Ottawa (0)	1	<0.01
Pueblo (0)	2	0.01
Shoshone (0)	2	0.01
Sioux (0)	9	0.02
Yup'ik *(Alaska Native)* (5)	5	0.01
Asian (967)	1,308	3.43
Not Hispanic (951)	1,277	3.35
Hispanic (16)	31	0.08
Burmese (0)	4	0.01
Cambodian (5)	7	0.02
Chinese, ex. Taiwanese (62)	82	0.22
Filipino (248)	382	1.00
Hmong (2)	2	0.01
Indian (133)	154	0.40
Indonesian (3)	6	0.02
Japanese (66)	130	0.34
Korean (65)	117	0.31
Laotian (14)	18	0.05
Malaysian (1)	2	0.01
Pakistani (23)	30	0.08
Taiwanese (4)	4	0.01
Thai (37)	49	0.13
Vietnamese (271)	294	0.77
Hawaii Native/Pacific Islander (30)	81	0.21
Not Hispanic (29)	74	0.19
Hispanic (1)	7	0.02
Fijian (0)	5	0.01
Guamanian/Chamorro (16)	33	0.09
Native Hawaiian (11)	18	0.05
Samoan (2)	6	0.02
White (30,325)	31,509	82.70
Not Hispanic (29,681)	30,739	80.68
Hispanic (644)	770	2.02

Hudson

Place Type: City
County: Summit
Population: 22,262†

Ancestry‡	Population	%
Alsatian (0)	11	0.05
American (561)	561	2.51
Arab (85)	192	0.86
Egyptian (9)	27	0.12
Lebanese (22)	111	0.50
Other Arab (54)	54	0.24
Armenian (0)	6	0.03
Austrian (63)	143	0.64
Belgian (0)	6	0.03
British (188)	276	1.24
Canadian (126)	201	0.90
Carpatho Rusyn (10)	10	0.04
Croatian (62)	138	0.62
Czech (83)	292	1.31
Czechoslovakian (25)	51	0.23
Danish (25)	74	0.33
Dutch (33)	546	2.45
Eastern European (0)	28	0.13
English (804)	4,056	18.16
European (359)	404	1.81
Finnish (25)	54	0.24
French, ex. Basque (54)	642	2.87
French Canadian (13)	34	0.15
German (1,359)	6,741	30.19
Greek (38)	90	0.40
Hungarian (158)	1,021	4.57
Irish (931)	4,732	21.19
Italian (987)	2,831	12.68
Latvian (19)	19	0.09
Lithuanian (34)	96	0.43
Macedonian (0)	10	0.04
Norwegian (60)	175	0.78
Pennsylvania German (14)	25	0.11
Polish (383)	1,893	8.48
Portuguese (6)	26	0.12
Romanian (10)	61	0.27
Russian (169)	617	2.76
Scotch-Irish (187)	575	2.57
Scottish (94)	702	3.14
Serbian (26)	104	0.47
Slavic (0)	33	0.15
Slovak (80)	397	1.78
Slovene (89)	196	0.88
Swedish (39)	341	1.53
Swiss (62)	260	1.16
Ukrainian (47)	127	0.57
Welsh (88)	502	2.25
West Indian, ex. Hispanic (13)	13	0.06
West Indian (13)	13	0.06
Yugoslavian (30)	30	0.13

Hispanic Origin	Population	%
Hispanic or Latino (of any race)	378	1.70
Central American, ex. Mexican	48	0.22
Costa Rican	14	0.06
Guatemalan	18	0.08
Honduran	3	0.01
Nicaraguan	7	0.03
Panamanian	4	0.02
Salvadoran	2	0.01
Cuban	37	0.17
Dominican Republic	9	0.04
Mexican	124	0.56
Puerto Rican	48	0.22
South American	58	0.26
Argentinean	6	0.03
Bolivian	4	0.02
Chilean	16	0.07
Colombian	20	0.09
Ecuadorian	1	<0.01
Paraguayan	3	0.01
Peruvian	3	0.01
Venezuelan	4	0.02
Other South American	1	<0.01
Other Hispanic or Latino	54	0.24

Race*	Population	%
African-American/Black (282)	350	1.57
Not Hispanic (272)	336	1.51
Hispanic (10)	14	0.06
American Indian/Alaska Native (20)	73	0.33
Not Hispanic (18)	65	0.29
Hispanic (2)	8	0.04
Alaska Athabascan *(Ala. Nat.)* (1)	4	0.02
Blackfeet (0)	1	<0.01
Cherokee (3)	23	0.10
Chippewa (1)	3	0.01
Choctaw (0)	2	0.01
Colville (2)	2	0.01
Iroquois (1)	7	0.03
Mexican American Ind. (1)	1	<0.01
Navajo (1)	1	<0.01
Seminole (1)	1	<0.01
South American Ind. (1)	1	<0.01
Asian (966)	1,126	5.06
Not Hispanic (964)	1,124	5.05
Hispanic (2)	2	0.01
Cambodian (1)	1	<0.01
Chinese, ex. Taiwanese (371)	411	1.85
Filipino (58)	117	0.53
Indian (238)	265	1.19
Indonesian (3)	4	0.02
Japanese (62)	91	0.41
Korean (148)	161	0.72
Laotian (0)	4	0.02

*Notes: † The Census 2010 population figure is used to calculate the percentages in the Hispanic Origin and Race categories. Ancestry percentages are based on the 2006-2010 American Community Survey population (not shown); ‡ Numbers in parentheses indicate the number of people reporting a single ancestry; * Numbers in parentheses indicate the number of persons reporting this race alone, not in combination with any other race; Please refer to the Explanation of Data for more information.*

Nepalese (1)	4	0.02
Pakistani (11)	11	0.05
Taiwanese (31)	37	0.17
Thai (5)	7	0.03
Vietnamese (16)	21	0.09
Hawaii Native/Pacific Islander (4)	11	0.05
Not Hispanic (4)	11	0.05
Marshallese (1)	1	<0.01
Native Hawaiian (1)	2	0.01
Samoan (2)	5	0.02
White (20,644)	20,916	93.95
Not Hispanic (20,356)	20,600	92.53
Hispanic (288)	316	1.42

Ironton

Place Type: City
County: Lawrence
Population: 11,129†

Ancestry‡	Population	%
African, Sub-Saharan (56)	103	0.92
African (56)	103	0.92
American (1,921)	1,921	17.24
Arab (21)	32	0.29
Lebanese (21)	32	0.29
Austrian (23)	23	0.21
Czech (0)	14	0.13
Dutch (11)	145	1.30
English (510)	1,084	9.73
European (68)	68	0.61
French, ex. Basque (53)	213	1.91
French Canadian (8)	8	0.07
German (806)	2,167	19.45
Irish (527)	1,466	13.16
Italian (134)	161	1.44
Pennsylvania German (0)	26	0.23
Polish (24)	27	0.24
Russian (13)	13	0.12
Scotch-Irish (60)	195	1.75
Scottish (30)	175	1.57
Slovak (13)	13	0.12
Swedish (0)	18	0.16
Swiss (0)	53	0.48
Welsh (8)	193	1.73
Yugoslavian (15)	46	0.41

Hispanic Origin	Population	%
Hispanic or Latino (of any race)	61	0.55
Central American, ex. Mexican	3	0.03
Guatemalan	1	0.01
Honduran	1	0.01
Nicaraguan	1	0.01
Cuban	3	0.03
Mexican	23	0.21
Puerto Rican	14	0.13
South American	5	0.04
Colombian	1	0.01
Paraguayan	1	0.01
Peruvian	3	0.03
Other Hispanic or Latino	13	0.12

Race*	Population	%
African-American/Black (525)	686	6.16
Not Hispanic (521)	679	6.10
Hispanic (4)	7	0.06
American Indian/Alaska Native (20)	87	0.78
Not Hispanic (20)	86	0.77
Hispanic (0)	1	0.01
Apache (0)	1	0.01
Blackfeet (1)	2	0.02
Cherokee (9)	36	0.32
Chippewa (0)	5	0.04
Kiowa (0)	3	0.03
Sioux (0)	1	0.01
Asian (29)	46	0.41
Not Hispanic (28)	44	0.40
Hispanic (1)	2	0.02
Burmese (1)	1	0.01
Chinese, ex. Taiwanese (11)	13	0.12
Filipino (11)	12	0.11
Indian (1)	7	0.06
Japanese (1)	2	0.02
Korean (1)	2	0.02
Laotian (3)	3	0.03
Vietnamese (0)	4	0.04
Hawaii Native/Pacific Islander (0)	1	0.01
Not Hispanic (0)	1	0.01
White (10,308)	10,542	94.73
Not Hispanic (10,264)	10,488	94.24
Hispanic (44)	54	0.49

Kent

Place Type: City
County: Portage
Population: 28,904†

Ancestry‡	Population	%
African, Sub-Saharan (99)	129	0.45
African (0)	24	0.08
Ghanaian (23)	23	0.08
Nigerian (76)	76	0.26
South African (0)	6	0.02
Albanian (1)	1	<0.01
American (1,114)	1,114	3.86
Arab (165)	197	0.68
Arab (37)	37	0.13
Egyptian (46)	46	0.16
Lebanese (69)	87	0.30
Palestinian (0)	14	0.05
Syrian (13)	13	0.05
Armenian (0)	10	0.03
Austrian (15)	41	0.14
Belgian (18)	57	0.20
Brazilian (16)	16	0.06
British (57)	157	0.54
Cajun (0)	11	0.04
Canadian (0)	20	0.07
Croatian (20)	92	0.32
Czech (15)	262	0.91
Czechoslovakian (40)	110	0.38
Danish (14)	73	0.25
Dutch (66)	404	1.40
Eastern European (30)	30	0.10
English (572)	2,796	9.69
European (138)	221	0.77
Finnish (10)	31	0.11
French, ex. Basque (87)	620	2.15
French Canadian (33)	33	0.11
German (2,677)	9,921	34.39
Greek (161)	270	0.94
Guyanese (16)	16	0.06
Hungarian (145)	994	3.45
Icelander (0)	10	0.03
Iranian (10)	10	0.03
Irish (1,209)	5,439	18.86
Italian (1,496)	4,095	14.20
Latvian (0)	12	0.04
Lithuanian (0)	118	0.41
Macedonian (0)	15	0.05
Northern European (18)	18	0.06
Norwegian (58)	280	0.97
Pennsylvania German (82)	156	0.54
Polish (528)	1,865	6.47
Romanian (25)	91	0.32
Russian (82)	415	1.44
Scandinavian (23)	43	0.15
Scotch-Irish (138)	626	2.17
Scottish (32)	531	1.84
Serbian (0)	49	0.17
Slavic (23)	61	0.21
Slovak (90)	555	1.92
Slovene (10)	59	0.20
Swedish (77)	297	1.03
Swiss (39)	217	0.75
Turkish (24)	35	0.12
Ukrainian (80)	306	1.06
Welsh (64)	495	1.72
West Indian, ex. Hispanic (40)	69	0.24
Jamaican (40)	69	0.24
Yugoslavian (28)	66	0.23

Hispanic Origin	Population	%
Hispanic or Latino (of any race)	642	2.22
Central American, ex. Mexican	43	0.15
Costa Rican	9	0.03
Guatemalan	9	0.03
Honduran	10	0.03
Nicaraguan	3	0.01
Panamanian	3	0.01
Salvadoran	9	0.03
Cuban	26	0.09
Dominican Republic	7	0.02
Mexican	232	0.80
Puerto Rican	154	0.53
South American	61	0.21
Argentinean	3	0.01
Bolivian	1	<0.01
Chilean	6	0.02
Colombian	25	0.09
Ecuadorian	6	0.02
Peruvian	10	0.03
Uruguayan	2	0.01
Venezuelan	8	0.03
Other Hispanic or Latino	119	0.41

Race*	Population	%
African-American/Black (2,782)	3,300	11.42
Not Hispanic (2,744)	3,229	11.17
Hispanic (38)	71	0.25
American Indian/Alaska Native (52)	267	0.92
Not Hispanic (45)	244	0.84
Hispanic (7)	23	0.08
Apache (1)	3	0.01
Arapaho (0)	1	<0.01
Blackfeet (0)	17	0.06
Cherokee (9)	74	0.26
Cheyenne (0)	1	<0.01
Chippewa (6)	10	0.03
Choctaw (0)	1	<0.01
Comanche (0)	1	<0.01
Cree (0)	1	<0.01
Crow (0)	2	0.01
Delaware (0)	1	<0.01
Inupiat *(Alaska Native)* (1)	1	<0.01
Iroquois (0)	2	0.01
Mexican American Ind. (2)	4	0.01
Navajo (1)	3	0.01
Potawatomi (0)	2	0.01
Seminole (2)	3	0.01
Sioux (3)	5	0.02
South American Ind. (3)	3	0.01
Asian (1,065)	1,259	4.36
Not Hispanic (1,060)	1,249	4.32
Hispanic (5)	10	0.03
Bangladeshi (3)	4	0.01
Bhutanese (15)	15	0.05
Burmese (1)	1	<0.01
Cambodian (0)	1	<0.01
Chinese, ex. Taiwanese (454)	480	1.66
Filipino (38)	67	0.23
Indian (239)	266	0.92
Indonesian (7)	8	0.03
Japanese (36)	73	0.25
Korean (93)	112	0.39
Laotian (3)	3	0.01
Malaysian (9)	10	0.03
Nepalese (39)	39	0.13
Pakistani (14)	17	0.06
Sri Lankan (10)	10	0.03
Taiwanese (34)	36	0.12
Thai (4)	7	0.02
Vietnamese (36)	38	0.13
Hawaii Native/Pacific Islander (17)	47	0.16
Not Hispanic (12)	42	0.15
Hispanic (5)	5	0.02
Guamanian/Chamorro (3)	10	0.03
Native Hawaiian (3)	12	0.04
Samoan (3)	4	0.01

SECTION TWO

*Notes: † The Census 2010 population figure is used to calculate the percentages in the Hispanic Origin and Race categories. Ancestry percentages are based on the 2006-2010 American Community Survey population (not shown); ‡ Numbers in parentheses indicate the number of people reporting a single ancestry; * Numbers in parentheses indicate the number of persons reporting this race alone, not in combination with any other race; Please refer to the Explanation of Data for more information.*

White (24,019)	24,777	85.72
Not Hispanic (23,595)	24,283	84.01
Hispanic (424)	494	1.71

Kenton

Place Type: City
County: Hardin
Population: 8,262†

Ancestry‡	Population	%
American (1,289)	1,289	15.43
Arab (0)	13	0.16
Syrian (0)	13	0.16
British (6)	42	0.50
Dutch (59)	240	2.87
English (507)	765	9.16
European (32)	32	0.38
French, ex. Basque (0)	88	1.05
French Canadian (16)	50	0.60
German (815)	1,899	22.73
Irish (459)	1,270	15.20
Italian (25)	121	1.45
Norwegian (0)	10	0.12
Polish (79)	115	1.38
Scandinavian (25)	25	0.30
Scotch-Irish (97)	134	1.60
Scottish (23)	120	1.44
Swedish (0)	29	0.35
Swiss (10)	17	0.20
Welsh (36)	228	2.73

Hispanic Origin	Population	%
Hispanic or Latino (of any race)	184	2.23
Central American, ex. Mexican	12	0.15
Guatemalan	10	0.12
Salvadoran	2	0.02
Cuban	2	0.02
Dominican Republic	4	0.05
Mexican	149	1.80
Puerto Rican	2	0.02
Other Hispanic or Latino	15	0.18

Race*	Population	%
African-American/Black (72)	128	1.55
Not Hispanic (70)	123	1.49
Hispanic (2)	5	0.06
American Indian/Alaska Native (14)	56	0.68
Not Hispanic (10)	49	0.59
Hispanic (4)	7	0.08
Apache (0)	1	0.01
Blackfeet (0)	3	0.04
Cherokee (10)	26	0.31
Cheyenne (0)	1	0.01
Chippewa (0)	1	0.01
Iroquois (1)	3	0.04
Navajo (1)	1	0.01
Ottawa (0)	2	0.02
Asian (23)	43	0.52
Not Hispanic (23)	42	0.51
Hispanic (0)	1	0.01
Chinese, ex. Taiwanese (1)	4	0.05
Filipino (3)	8	0.10
Indian (6)	8	0.10
Japanese (8)	14	0.17
Korean (2)	6	0.07
Vietnamese (3)	3	0.04
Hawaii Native/Pacific Islander (11)	11	0.13
Not Hispanic (2)	2	0.02
Hispanic (9)	9	0.11
Guamanian/Chamorro (9)	9	0.11
Samoan (2)	2	0.02
White (7,949)	8,064	97.60
Not Hispanic (7,862)	7,968	96.44
Hispanic (87)	96	1.16

Kettering

Place Type: City
County: Montgomery
Population: 56,163†

Ancestry‡	Population	%
African, Sub-Saharan (11)	42	0.07
African (0)	31	0.06
Other Sub-Saharan African (11)	11	0.02
Albanian (15)	15	0.03
Alsatian (0)	13	0.02
American (4,961)	4,961	8.83
Arab (345)	458	0.82
Arab (0)	11	0.02
Egyptian (10)	10	0.02
Jordanian (78)	78	0.14
Lebanese (184)	251	0.45
Syrian (56)	81	0.14
Other Arab (17)	27	0.05
Australian (0)	4	0.01
Austrian (36)	160	0.28
Belgian (19)	63	0.11
Brazilian (59)	59	0.11
British (119)	352	0.63
Cajun (31)	66	0.12
Canadian (28)	58	0.10
Croatian (13)	58	0.10
Czech (53)	220	0.39
Czechoslovakian (36)	136	0.24
Danish (20)	174	0.31
Dutch (254)	1,420	2.53
Eastern European (95)	104	0.19
English (2,059)	6,441	11.46
Estonian (0)	39	0.07
European (633)	692	1.23
Finnish (23)	84	0.15
French, ex. Basque (480)	2,149	3.83
French Canadian (69)	237	0.42
German (8,550)	20,845	37.10
Greek (100)	224	0.40
Hungarian (298)	714	1.27
Iranian (9)	9	0.02
Irish (2,170)	9,275	16.51
Italian (1,188)	2,845	5.06
Lithuanian (46)	202	0.36
Northern European (18)	18	0.03
Norwegian (112)	264	0.47
Pennsylvania German (81)	118	0.21
Polish (395)	1,457	2.59
Portuguese (8)	22	0.04
Romanian (55)	70	0.12
Russian (91)	238	0.42
Scandinavian (42)	120	0.21
Scotch-Irish (467)	1,103	1.96
Scottish (452)	1,568	2.79
Serbian (0)	12	0.02
Slavic (0)	15	0.03
Slovak (51)	208	0.37
Slovene (11)	41	0.07
Swedish (77)	648	1.15
Swiss (63)	263	0.47
Ukrainian (55)	157	0.28
Welsh (170)	757	1.35
West Indian, ex. Hispanic (8)	74	0.13
Haitian (0)	9	0.02
Jamaican (8)	8	0.01
West Indian (0)	57	0.10
Yugoslavian (60)	81	0.14

Hispanic Origin	Population	%
Hispanic or Latino (of any race)	1,178	2.10
Central American, ex. Mexican	116	0.21
Costa Rican	29	0.05
Guatemalan	28	0.05
Honduran	11	0.02
Nicaraguan	5	0.01
Panamanian	28	0.05
Salvadoran	15	0.03
Cuban	84	0.15
Dominican Republic	7	0.01
Mexican	542	0.97
Puerto Rican	151	0.27
South American	125	0.22
Argentinean	7	0.01
Bolivian	13	0.02
Chilean	5	0.01
Colombian	44	0.08
Ecuadorian	18	0.03
Paraguayan	3	0.01
Peruvian	15	0.03
Uruguayan	3	0.01
Venezuelan	15	0.03
Other South American	2	<0.01
Other Hispanic or Latino	153	0.27

Race*	Population	%
African-American/Black (1,840)	2,386	4.25
Not Hispanic (1,806)	2,323	4.14
Hispanic (34)	63	0.11
American Indian/Alaska Native (106)	414	0.74
Not Hispanic (98)	382	0.68
Hispanic (8)	32	0.06
Aleut *(Alaska Native)* (0)	1	<0.01
Apache (1)	5	0.01
Blackfeet (4)	15	0.03
Canadian/French Am. Ind. (2)	2	<0.01
Cherokee (18)	134	0.24
Chippewa (4)	8	0.01
Choctaw (3)	5	0.01
Comanche (1)	1	<0.01
Creek (4)	8	0.01
Crow (0)	1	<0.01
Inupiat *(Alaska Native)* (1)	1	<0.01
Iroquois (1)	2	<0.01
Lumbee (1)	1	<0.01
Mexican American Ind. (0)	1	<0.01
Navajo (3)	6	0.01
Ottawa (1)	1	<0.01
Seminole (0)	1	<0.01
Sioux (4)	14	0.02
South American Ind. (0)	6	0.01
Spanish American Ind. (0)	3	0.01
Ute (1)	1	<0.01
Yuman (1)	1	<0.01
Asian (752)	1,101	1.96
Not Hispanic (745)	1,080	1.92
Hispanic (7)	21	0.04
Bangladeshi (1)	3	0.01
Burmese (7)	7	0.01
Cambodian (20)	23	0.04
Chinese, ex. Taiwanese (161)	197	0.35
Filipino (120)	213	0.38
Indian (148)	182	0.32
Indonesian (2)	13	0.02
Japanese (55)	119	0.21
Korean (58)	124	0.22
Laotian (7)	7	0.01
Malaysian (3)	3	0.01
Pakistani (14)	21	0.04
Sri Lankan (2)	2	<0.01
Taiwanese (13)	15	0.03
Thai (13)	26	0.05
Vietnamese (96)	116	0.21
Hawaii Native/Pacific Islander (12)	46	0.08
Not Hispanic (12)	45	0.08
Hispanic (0)	1	<0.01
Guamanian/Chamorro (2)	6	0.01
Native Hawaiian (5)	15	0.03
Samoan (2)	4	0.01
White (51,982)	53,090	94.53
Not Hispanic (51,191)	52,203	92.95
Hispanic (791)	887	1.58

Lakewood

Place Type: City
County: Cuyahoga
Population: 52,131†

*Notes: † The Census 2010 population figure is used to calculate the percentages in the Hispanic Origin and Race categories. Ancestry percentages are based on the 2006-2010 American Community Survey population (not shown); ‡ Numbers in parentheses indicate the number of people reporting a single ancestry; * Numbers in parentheses indicate the number of persons reporting this race alone, not in combination with any other race; Please refer to the Explanation of Data for more information.*

Ancestry‡	Population	%
African, Sub-Saharan (363)	406	0.77
African (159)	169	0.32
Ghanaian (67)	67	0.13
Kenyan (13)	13	0.02
Nigerian (19)	52	0.10
Sudanese (23)	23	0.04
Ugandan (9)	9	0.02
Other Sub-Saharan African (73)	73	0.14
Albanian (741)	766	1.45
American (1,234)	1,234	2.34
Arab (997)	1,450	2.75
Arab (151)	218	0.41
Egyptian (172)	172	0.33
Lebanese (360)	706	1.34
Palestinian (105)	116	0.22
Syrian (207)	213	0.40
Other Arab (2)	25	0.05
Armenian (13)	29	0.06
Australian (0)	10	0.02
Austrian (22)	233	0.44
Belgian (24)	53	0.10
Brazilian (0)	21	0.04
British (64)	313	0.59
Bulgarian (23)	23	0.04
Canadian (0)	16	0.03
Carpatho Rusyn (12)	25	0.05
Croatian (108)	563	1.07
Cypriot (12)	12	0.02
Czech (240)	758	1.44
Czechoslovakian (38)	126	0.24
Danish (61)	219	0.42
Dutch (59)	553	1.05
Eastern European (107)	129	0.24
English (1,284)	5,509	10.46
Estonian (9)	9	0.02
European (373)	385	0.73
Finnish (77)	386	0.73
French, ex. Basque (16)	1,255	2.38
French Canadian (55)	227	0.43
German (2,948)	14,246	27.05
Greek (343)	607	1.15
Hungarian (632)	2,499	4.74
Iranian (0)	118	0.22
Irish (3,451)	12,740	24.19
Israeli (14)	14	0.03
Italian (2,167)	6,124	11.63
Latvian (44)	60	0.11
Lithuanian (140)	291	0.55
Macedonian (11)	11	0.02
Maltese (30)	30	0.06
Northern European (9)	9	0.02
Norwegian (64)	366	0.69
Pennsylvania German (12)	12	0.02
Polish (907)	4,284	8.13
Portuguese (8)	31	0.06
Romanian (147)	293	0.56
Russian (209)	673	1.28
Scandinavian (11)	66	0.13
Scotch-Irish (447)	1,371	2.60
Scottish (236)	1,113	2.11
Serbian (85)	183	0.35
Slavic (27)	47	0.09
Slovak (795)	2,432	4.62
Slovene (199)	761	1.44
Swedish (94)	528	1.00
Swiss (29)	154	0.29
Turkish (222)	222	0.42
Ukrainian (235)	528	1.00
Welsh (121)	657	1.25
West Indian, ex. Hispanic (90)	193	0.37
Haitian (13)	27	0.05
Jamaican (69)	158	0.30
West Indian (8)	8	0.02
Yugoslavian (87)	109	0.21

Hispanic Origin	Population	%
Hispanic or Latino (of any race)	2,147	4.12
Central American, ex. Mexican	98	0.19
Costa Rican	5	0.01
Guatemalan	21	0.04
Honduran	16	0.03
Nicaraguan	17	0.03
Panamanian	13	0.02
Salvadoran	26	0.05
Cuban	80	0.15
Dominican Republic	82	0.16
Mexican	442	0.85
Puerto Rican	1,077	2.07
South American	179	0.34
Argentinean	32	0.06
Bolivian	1	<0.01
Chilean	11	0.02
Colombian	37	0.07
Ecuadorian	5	0.01
Paraguayan	1	<0.01
Peruvian	31	0.06
Uruguayan	7	0.01
Venezuelan	52	0.10
Other South American	2	<0.01
Other Hispanic or Latino	189	0.36

Race*	Population	%
African-American/Black (3,340)	4,052	7.77
Not Hispanic (3,238)	3,858	7.40
Hispanic (102)	194	0.37
American Indian/Alaska Native (149)	503	0.96
Not Hispanic (127)	428	0.82
Hispanic (22)	75	0.14
Alaska Athabascan *(Ala. Nat.)* (2)	2	<0.01
Aleut *(Alaska Native)* (1)	1	<0.01
Apache (1)	4	0.01
Blackfeet (7)	27	0.05
Canadian/French Am. Ind. (0)	1	<0.01
Central American Ind. (3)	3	0.01
Cherokee (26)	132	0.25
Cheyenne (0)	2	<0.01
Chickasaw (2)	6	0.01
Chippewa (9)	11	0.02
Choctaw (1)	9	0.02
Comanche (1)	1	<0.01
Cree (1)	1	<0.01
Creek (0)	7	0.01
Delaware (2)	4	0.01
Iroquois (1)	10	0.02
Mexican American Ind. (4)	9	0.02
Navajo (5)	13	0.02
Potawatomi (1)	1	<0.01
Pueblo (1)	1	<0.01
Seminole (1)	7	0.01
Sioux (15)	35	0.07
South American Ind. (0)	2	<0.01
Spanish American Ind. (5)	5	0.01
Tlingit-Haida *(Alaska Native)* (1)	2	<0.01
Tsimshian *(Alaska Native)* (1)	2	<0.01
Yuman (0)	1	<0.01
Asian (988)	1,344	2.58
Not Hispanic (977)	1,323	2.54
Hispanic (11)	21	0.04
Bangladeshi (5)	8	0.02
Bhutanese (29)	49	0.09
Burmese (146)	146	0.28
Cambodian (6)	7	0.01
Chinese, ex. Taiwanese (150)	189	0.36
Filipino (73)	137	0.26
Indian (217)	277	0.53
Indonesian (13)	21	0.04
Japanese (49)	95	0.18
Korean (68)	96	0.18
Laotian (3)	6	0.01
Nepalese (16)	29	0.06
Pakistani (68)	75	0.14
Sri Lankan (1)	1	<0.01
Taiwanese (8)	8	0.02
Thai (34)	47	0.09
Vietnamese (49)	62	0.12
Hawaii Native/Pacific Islander (9)	41	0.08
Not Hispanic (9)	37	0.07
Hispanic (0)	4	0.01
Guamanian/Chamorro (3)	5	0.01
Native Hawaiian (4)	8	0.02
White (45,598)	46,836	89.84
Not Hispanic (44,341)	45,393	87.07
Hispanic (1,257)	1,443	2.77

Lancaster

Place Type: City
County: Fairfield
Population: 38,780†

Ancestry‡	Population	%
African, Sub-Saharan (50)	124	0.32
African (50)	124	0.32
American (4,044)	4,044	10.46
Arab (12)	12	0.03
Egyptian (12)	12	0.03
Austrian (25)	34	0.09
Belgian (17)	26	0.07
British (180)	323	0.84
Canadian (32)	60	0.16
Czech (21)	53	0.14
Czechoslovakian (9)	21	0.05
Danish (14)	14	0.04
Dutch (280)	1,384	3.58
English (1,609)	4,120	10.66
European (305)	305	0.79
French, ex. Basque (217)	1,013	2.62
French Canadian (25)	25	0.06
German (4,710)	11,880	30.73
Greek (58)	62	0.16
Hungarian (57)	173	0.45
Iranian (12)	24	0.06
Irish (1,842)	5,851	15.14
Italian (562)	1,486	3.84
Lithuanian (9)	31	0.08
Norwegian (72)	239	0.62
Pennsylvania German (35)	54	0.14
Polish (183)	543	1.40
Romanian (27)	78	0.20
Russian (137)	179	0.46
Scotch-Irish (370)	679	1.76
Scottish (314)	1,141	2.95
Serbian (0)	28	0.07
Slovak (22)	37	0.10
Slovene (0)	9	0.02
Swedish (55)	224	0.58
Swiss (52)	199	0.51
Ukrainian (12)	54	0.14
Welsh (199)	654	1.69
Yugoslavian (0)	28	0.07

Hispanic Origin	Population	%
Hispanic or Latino (of any race)	631	1.63
Central American, ex. Mexican	44	0.11
Costa Rican	6	0.02
Guatemalan	12	0.03
Honduran	7	0.02
Nicaraguan	1	<0.01
Panamanian	9	0.02
Salvadoran	9	0.02
Cuban	8	0.02
Dominican Republic	5	0.01
Mexican	370	0.95
Puerto Rican	106	0.27
South American	21	0.05
Bolivian	1	<0.01
Chilean	2	0.01
Colombian	11	0.03
Ecuadorian	4	0.01
Other South American	3	0.01
Other Hispanic or Latino	77	0.20

Race*	Population	%
African-American/Black (394)	725	1.87
Not Hispanic (378)	690	1.78
Hispanic (16)	35	0.09
American Indian/Alaska Native (100)	347	0.89
Not Hispanic (96)	329	0.85
Hispanic (4)	18	0.05

*Notes: † The Census 2010 population figure is used to calculate the percentages in the Hispanic Origin and Race categories. Ancestry percentages are based on the 2006-2010 American Community Survey population (not shown); ‡ Numbers in parentheses indicate the number of people reporting a single ancestry; * Numbers in parentheses indicate the number of persons reporting this race alone, not in combination with any other race; Please refer to the Explanation of Data for more information.*

Alaska Athabascan *(Ala. Nat.)* (0)	1	<0.01
Aleut *(Alaska Native)* (0)	2	0.01
Apache (5)	19	0.05
Blackfeet (2)	19	0.05
Canadian/French Am. Ind. (0)	1	<0.01
Cherokee (20)	128	0.33
Chippewa (5)	6	0.02
Choctaw (3)	4	0.01
Creek (1)	12	0.03
Delaware (0)	2	0.01
Hopi (0)	1	<0.01
Iroquois (2)	10	0.03
Lumbee (0)	2	0.01
Navajo (0)	7	0.02
Seminole (1)	6	0.02
Sioux (2)	8	0.02
Asian (184)	281	0.72
Not Hispanic (182)	275	0.71
Hispanic (2)	6	0.02
Cambodian (0)	1	<0.01
Chinese, ex. Taiwanese (34)	38	0.10
Filipino (35)	62	0.16
Indian (36)	49	0.13
Indonesian (2)	4	0.01
Japanese (15)	26	0.07
Korean (13)	34	0.09
Laotian (1)	1	<0.01
Malaysian (2)	4	0.01
Pakistani (1)	1	<0.01
Taiwanese (3)	4	0.01
Thai (10)	16	0.04
Vietnamese (26)	31	0.08
Hawaii Native/Pacific Islander (14)	34	0.09
Not Hispanic (9)	25	0.06
Hispanic (5)	9	0.02
Fijian (0)	1	<0.01
Guamanian/Chamorro (2)	5	0.01
Native Hawaiian (5)	16	0.04
Samoan (0)	2	0.01
White (37,178)	37,822	97.53
Not Hispanic (36,853)	37,436	96.53
Hispanic (325)	386	1.00

Lebanon

Place Type: City
County: Warren
Population: 20,033†

Ancestry‡	Population	%
Afghan (0)	12	0.06
African, Sub-Saharan (0)	109	0.55
African (0)	109	0.55
American (1,981)	1,981	9.93
Arab (55)	141	0.71
Arab (47)	108	0.54
Jordanian (0)	8	0.04
Syrian (8)	25	0.13
Armenian (0)	37	0.19
Austrian (0)	16	0.08
Belgian (0)	54	0.27
British (63)	125	0.63
Canadian (30)	64	0.32
Croatian (16)	16	0.08
Czech (0)	103	0.52
Danish (0)	65	0.33
Dutch (68)	386	1.94
Eastern European (32)	32	0.16
English (967)	2,400	12.03
European (197)	263	1.32
Finnish (49)	166	0.83
French, ex. Basque (23)	227	1.14
French Canadian (0)	10	0.05
German (2,132)	4,931	24.73
Greek (15)	64	0.32
Hungarian (20)	80	0.40
Irish (594)	2,569	12.88
Italian (265)	789	3.96
Lithuanian (0)	12	0.06
Norwegian (10)	97	0.49
Pennsylvania German (17)	17	0.09
Polish (81)	435	2.18
Portuguese (0)	17	0.09
Russian (31)	51	0.26
Scandinavian (0)	39	0.20
Scotch-Irish (215)	353	1.77
Scottish (123)	593	2.97
Serbian (15)	44	0.22
Slovene (0)	19	0.10
Swedish (14)	129	0.65
Swiss (0)	29	0.15
Turkish (0)	9	0.05
Welsh (21)	93	0.47
West Indian, ex. Hispanic (0)	17	0.09
Haitian (0)	17	0.09

Hispanic Origin	Population	%
Hispanic or Latino (of any race)	711	3.55
Central American, ex. Mexican	35	0.17
Costa Rican	7	0.03
Guatemalan	8	0.04
Honduran	2	0.01
Nicaraguan	1	<0.01
Panamanian	3	0.01
Salvadoran	14	0.07
Cuban	13	0.06
Dominican Republic	2	0.01
Mexican	510	2.55
Puerto Rican	76	0.38
South American	35	0.17
Chilean	1	<0.01
Colombian	14	0.07
Ecuadorian	6	0.03
Peruvian	4	0.02
Venezuelan	9	0.04
Other South American	1	<0.01
Other Hispanic or Latino	40	0.20

Race*	Population	%
African-American/Black (525)	695	3.47
Not Hispanic (509)	676	3.37
Hispanic (16)	19	0.09
American Indian/Alaska Native (43)	168	0.84
Not Hispanic (37)	149	0.74
Hispanic (6)	19	0.09
Apache (0)	1	<0.01
Blackfeet (0)	8	0.04
Central American Ind. (0)	2	0.01
Cherokee (15)	75	0.37
Choctaw (2)	5	0.02
Comanche (1)	1	<0.01
Creek (0)	4	0.02
Crow (0)	1	<0.01
Hopi (0)	1	<0.01
Iroquois (2)	4	0.02
Navajo (2)	7	0.03
Potawatomi (0)	3	0.01
Pueblo (0)	1	<0.01
Shoshone (0)	2	0.01
Asian (166)	244	1.22
Not Hispanic (166)	242	1.21
Hispanic (0)	2	0.01
Burmese (1)	2	0.01
Cambodian (1)	1	<0.01
Chinese, ex. Taiwanese (37)	46	0.23
Filipino (30)	43	0.21
Indian (32)	47	0.23
Japanese (14)	30	0.15
Korean (18)	32	0.16
Malaysian (1)	1	<0.01
Pakistani (1)	1	<0.01
Taiwanese (1)	1	<0.01
Thai (3)	3	0.01
Vietnamese (17)	17	0.08
Hawaii Native/Pacific Islander (4)	15	0.07
Not Hispanic (4)	12	0.06
Hispanic (0)	3	0.01
Marshallese (2)	2	0.01
Native Hawaiian (2)	10	0.05
White (18,569)	18,944	94.56
Not Hispanic (18,247)	18,564	92.67
Hispanic (322)	380	1.90

Lima

Place Type: City
County: Allen
Population: 38,771†

Ancestry‡	Population	%
African, Sub-Saharan (992)	1,042	2.68
African (945)	995	2.56
Nigerian (13)	13	0.03
Somalian (34)	34	0.09
American (3,914)	3,914	10.06
Arab (11)	99	0.25
Arab (0)	55	0.14
Lebanese (11)	44	0.11
Austrian (9)	47	0.12
Belgian (0)	32	0.08
British (34)	134	0.34
Bulgarian (7)	7	0.02
Canadian (26)	41	0.11
Croatian (8)	28	0.07
Czech (9)	65	0.17
Czechoslovakian (0)	19	0.05
Danish (10)	18	0.05
Dutch (174)	787	2.02
English (814)	2,063	5.30
European (92)	92	0.24
Finnish (24)	91	0.23
French, ex. Basque (130)	872	2.24
French Canadian (0)	34	0.09
German (4,226)	9,651	24.81
Greek (52)	141	0.36
Hungarian (85)	155	0.40
Irish (950)	3,772	9.70
Italian (479)	1,232	3.17
Lithuanian (7)	35	0.09
Norwegian (11)	88	0.23
Pennsylvania German (16)	16	0.04
Polish (119)	428	1.10
Portuguese (0)	10	0.03
Russian (33)	197	0.51
Scotch-Irish (149)	387	0.99
Scottish (106)	458	1.18
Slovak (8)	96	0.25
Swedish (11)	99	0.25
Swiss (54)	234	0.60
Ukrainian (0)	9	0.02
Welsh (116)	403	1.04
West Indian, ex. Hispanic (116)	222	0.57
Haitian (14)	52	0.13
Jamaican (91)	159	0.41
Trinidadian/Tobagonian (11)	11	0.03

Hispanic Origin	Population	%
Hispanic or Latino (of any race)	1,420	3.66
Central American, ex. Mexican	31	0.08
Costa Rican	5	0.01
Guatemalan	2	0.01
Honduran	6	0.02
Nicaraguan	3	0.01
Panamanian	4	0.01
Salvadoran	11	0.03
Cuban	27	0.07
Dominican Republic	3	0.01
Mexican	845	2.18
Puerto Rican	120	0.31
South American	14	0.04
Argentinean	2	0.01
Bolivian	1	<0.01
Chilean	4	0.01
Colombian	4	0.01
Peruvian	1	<0.01
Venezuelan	2	0.01
Other Hispanic or Latino	380	0.98

Race*	Population	%
African-American/Black (10,253)	11,630	30.00

*Notes: † The Census 2010 population figure is used to calculate the percentages in the Hispanic Origin and Race categories. Ancestry percentages are based on the 2006-2010 American Community Survey population (not shown); ‡ Numbers in parentheses indicate the number of people reporting a single ancestry; * Numbers in parentheses indicate the number of persons reporting this race alone, not in combination with any other race; Please refer to the Explanation of Data for more information.*

Not Hispanic (10,139)	11,407	29.42
Hispanic (114)	223	0.58
American Indian/Alaska Native (113)	420	1.08
Not Hispanic (85)	340	0.88
Hispanic (28)	80	0.21
Apache (5)	10	0.03
Blackfeet (0)	17	0.04
Canadian/French Am. Ind. (1)	3	0.01
Cherokee (19)	115	0.30
Cheyenne (0)	2	0.01
Chippewa (1)	12	0.03
Choctaw (0)	3	0.01
Creek (0)	3	0.01
Delaware (3)	3	0.01
Inupiat *(Alaska Native)* (0)	1	<0.01
Iroquois (4)	9	0.02
Menominee (4)	4	0.01
Mexican American Ind. (5)	10	0.03
Navajo (0)	1	<0.01
Osage (2)	3	0.01
Potawatomi (0)	1	<0.01
Seminole (0)	3	0.01
Sioux (2)	8	0.02
South American Ind. (4)	4	0.01
Asian (189)	306	0.79
Not Hispanic (181)	279	0.72
Hispanic (8)	27	0.07
Chinese, ex. Taiwanese (11)	26	0.07
Filipino (48)	75	0.19
Hmong (1)	2	0.01
Indian (36)	56	0.14
Japanese (10)	14	0.04
Korean (12)	30	0.08
Laotian (24)	28	0.07
Nepalese (3)	3	0.01
Pakistani (0)	1	<0.01
Thai (4)	11	0.03
Vietnamese (16)	22	0.06
Hawaii Native/Pacific Islander (6)	40	0.10
Not Hispanic (6)	35	0.09
Hispanic (0)	5	0.01
Guamanian/Chamorro (0)	6	0.02
Native Hawaiian (4)	9	0.02
Samoan (1)	1	<0.01
White (26,012)	27,581	71.14
Not Hispanic (25,282)	26,665	68.78
Hispanic (730)	916	2.36

Lincoln Village

Place Type: CDP
County: Franklin
Population: 9,032†

Ancestry‡	Population	%
African, Sub-Saharan (50)	50	0.53
African (50)	50	0.53
American (671)	671	7.12
Austrian (17)	28	0.30
British (19)	56	0.59
Canadian (10)	10	0.11
Czech (0)	19	0.20
Dutch (22)	170	1.80
English (350)	874	9.27
European (108)	121	1.28
French, ex. Basque (40)	280	2.97
German (779)	2,092	22.18
Greek (0)	18	0.19
Hungarian (0)	58	0.62
Irish (519)	1,614	17.12
Italian (233)	404	4.28
Norwegian (0)	22	0.23
Polish (37)	55	0.58
Scotch-Irish (150)	267	2.83
Scottish (216)	309	3.28
Serbian (0)	10	0.11
Slovak (17)	24	0.25
Swedish (69)	102	1.08
Swiss (17)	17	0.18
Ukrainian (0)	19	0.20
Welsh (26)	159	1.69

Hispanic Origin	Population	%
Hispanic or Latino (of any race)	962	10.65
Central American, ex. Mexican	98	1.09
Guatemalan	8	0.09
Honduran	32	0.35
Nicaraguan	3	0.03
Panamanian	1	0.01
Salvadoran	54	0.60
Cuban	2	0.02
Dominican Republic	38	0.42
Mexican	709	7.85
Puerto Rican	54	0.60
South American	13	0.14
Chilean	4	0.04
Colombian	1	0.01
Ecuadorian	2	0.02
Peruvian	2	0.02
Venezuelan	4	0.04
Other Hispanic or Latino	48	0.53

Race*	Population	%
African-American/Black (570)	719	7.96
Not Hispanic (548)	687	7.61
Hispanic (22)	32	0.35
American Indian/Alaska Native (40)	121	1.34
Not Hispanic (33)	111	1.23
Hispanic (7)	10	0.11
Blackfeet (2)	12	0.13
Cherokee (8)	47	0.52
Chippewa (0)	4	0.04
Choctaw (0)	2	0.02
Comanche (1)	1	0.01
Iroquois (3)	6	0.07
Lumbee (4)	4	0.04
Mexican American Ind. (6)	6	0.07
Navajo (1)	1	0.01
Potawatomi (0)	1	0.01
Asian (81)	119	1.32
Not Hispanic (79)	115	1.27
Hispanic (2)	4	0.04
Burmese (7)	7	0.08
Cambodian (1)	1	0.01
Chinese, ex. Taiwanese (9)	12	0.13
Filipino (11)	20	0.22
Indian (16)	18	0.20
Japanese (4)	13	0.14
Korean (11)	17	0.19
Laotian (4)	9	0.10
Malaysian (0)	1	0.01
Pakistani (3)	4	0.04
Sri Lankan (3)	4	0.04
Taiwanese (2)	2	0.02
Thai (3)	7	0.08
Vietnamese (1)	5	0.06
Hawaii Native/Pacific Islander (0)	3	0.03
Not Hispanic (0)	3	0.03
Guamanian/Chamorro (0)	1	0.01
White (7,414)	7,662	84.83
Not Hispanic (7,159)	7,378	81.69
Hispanic (255)	284	3.14

London

Place Type: City
County: Madison
Population: 9,904†

Ancestry‡	Population	%
American (1,892)	1,892	19.49
Arab (35)	35	0.36
Other Arab (35)	35	0.36
Austrian (0)	9	0.09
British (8)	55	0.57
Canadian (13)	13	0.13
Dutch (69)	237	2.44
English (387)	871	8.97
European (9)	9	0.09
French, ex. Basque (55)	176	1.81
French Canadian (0)	13	0.13
German (1,661)	3,398	35.00
Greek (29)	29	0.30
Hungarian (0)	53	0.55
Irish (369)	1,305	13.44
Italian (234)	497	5.12
Norwegian (0)	9	0.09
Pennsylvania German (13)	13	0.13
Polish (50)	79	0.81
Romanian (13)	13	0.13
Russian (0)	29	0.30
Scotch-Irish (32)	77	0.79
Scottish (91)	183	1.88
Slovak (0)	117	1.21
Swedish (34)	47	0.48
Swiss (19)	124	1.28
Welsh (26)	173	1.78

Hispanic Origin	Population	%
Hispanic or Latino (of any race)	169	1.71
Central American, ex. Mexican	5	0.05
Guatemalan	3	0.03
Salvadoran	2	0.02
Cuban	2	0.02
Mexican	125	1.26
Puerto Rican	15	0.15
South American	10	0.10
Bolivian	2	0.02
Colombian	3	0.03
Ecuadorian	2	0.02
Peruvian	3	0.03
Other Hispanic or Latino	12	0.12

Race*	Population	%
African-American/Black (596)	805	8.13
Not Hispanic (594)	797	8.05
Hispanic (2)	8	0.08
American Indian/Alaska Native (30)	86	0.87
Not Hispanic (23)	75	0.76
Hispanic (7)	11	0.11
Arapaho (0)	2	0.02
Blackfeet (0)	2	0.02
Cherokee (7)	24	0.24
Cheyenne (0)	2	0.02
Choctaw (0)	4	0.04
Lumbee (1)	6	0.06
Mexican American Ind. (5)	5	0.05
Navajo (2)	2	0.02
Sioux (0)	2	0.02
Asian (100)	133	1.34
Not Hispanic (100)	131	1.32
Hispanic (0)	2	0.02
Cambodian (1)	1	0.01
Chinese, ex. Taiwanese (4)	9	0.09
Filipino (8)	13	0.13
Hmong (1)	1	0.01
Indian (20)	30	0.30
Japanese (54)	59	0.60
Laotian (1)	4	0.04
Malaysian (1)	1	0.01
Pakistani (0)	1	0.01
Thai (1)	2	0.02
Vietnamese (6)	6	0.06
White (8,830)	9,104	91.92
Not Hispanic (8,729)	8,990	90.77
Hispanic (101)	114	1.15

Lorain

Place Type: City
County: Lorain
Population: 64,097†

Ancestry‡	Population	%
African, Sub-Saharan (258)	473	0.73
African (258)	451	0.69
Ghanaian (0)	11	0.02
Nigerian (0)	11	0.02
American (2,165)	2,165	3.32
Arab (222)	383	0.59

*Notes: † The Census 2010 population figure is used to calculate the percentages in the Hispanic Origin and Race categories. Ancestry percentages are based on the 2006-2010 American Community Survey population (not shown); ‡ Numbers in parentheses indicate the number of people reporting a single ancestry; * Numbers in parentheses indicate the number of persons reporting this race alone, not in combination with any other race; Please refer to the Explanation of Data for more information.*

Arab (211)	211	0.32
Lebanese (0)	153	0.23
Syrian (11)	19	0.03
Austrian (24)	110	0.17
Belgian (0)	31	0.05
British (85)	93	0.14
Bulgarian (15)	15	0.02
Canadian (8)	26	0.04
Carpatho Rusyn (26)	26	0.04
Croatian (319)	569	0.87
Czech (32)	104	0.16
Czechoslovakian (64)	186	0.29
Danish (18)	53	0.08
Dutch (46)	824	1.26
Eastern European (156)	156	0.24
English (581)	3,807	5.84
European (77)	87	0.13
Finnish (11)	23	0.04
French, ex. Basque (190)	1,057	1.62
French Canadian (4)	42	0.06
German (2,443)	9,408	14.42
German Russian (18)	18	0.03
Greek (160)	365	0.56
Hungarian (1,136)	3,113	4.77
Irish (1,573)	7,298	11.19
Italian (1,682)	4,912	7.53
Latvian (0)	23	0.04
Lithuanian (25)	66	0.10
Macedonian (62)	97	0.15
Norwegian (25)	71	0.11
Pennsylvania German (25)	25	0.04
Polish (1,803)	4,052	6.21
Romanian (44)	135	0.21
Russian (81)	399	0.61
Scandinavian (0)	33	0.05
Scotch-Irish (232)	1,107	1.70
Scottish (77)	613	0.94
Serbian (95)	206	0.32
Slavic (7)	15	0.02
Slovak (769)	1,882	2.89
Slovene (175)	546	0.84
Swedish (27)	125	0.19
Swiss (11)	115	0.18
Ukrainian (284)	521	0.80
Welsh (50)	314	0.48
West Indian, ex. Hispanic (78)	122	0.19
Haitian (43)	43	0.07
Jamaican (22)	29	0.04
West Indian (13)	50	0.08
Yugoslavian (0)	23	0.04

Hispanic Origin	Population	%
Hispanic or Latino (of any race)	16,177	25.24
Central American, ex. Mexican	118	0.18
Costa Rican	4	0.01
Guatemalan	32	0.05
Honduran	17	0.03
Nicaraguan	8	0.01
Panamanian	28	0.04
Salvadoran	29	0.05
Cuban	79	0.12
Dominican Republic	115	0.18
Mexican	2,934	4.58
Puerto Rican	12,413	19.37
South American	60	0.09
Argentinean	9	0.01
Bolivian	4	0.01
Chilean	3	<0.01
Colombian	12	0.02
Ecuadorian	12	0.02
Peruvian	10	0.02
Venezuelan	10	0.02
Other Hispanic or Latino	458	0.71

Race*	Population	%
African-American/Black (11,262)	13,512	21.08
Not Hispanic (10,245)	11,803	18.41
Hispanic (1,017)	1,709	2.67
American Indian/Alaska Native (324)	966	1.51
Not Hispanic (177)	651	1.02
Hispanic (147)	315	0.49
Apache (2)	13	0.02
Arapaho (2)	2	<0.01
Blackfeet (8)	54	0.08
Canadian/French Am. Ind. (1)	1	<0.01
Central American Ind. (6)	9	0.01
Cherokee (41)	227	0.35
Cheyenne (0)	1	<0.01
Chickasaw (4)	5	0.01
Chippewa (6)	11	0.02
Choctaw (1)	6	0.01
Comanche (0)	1	<0.01
Cree (1)	1	<0.01
Creek (0)	4	0.01
Delaware (0)	2	<0.01
Hopi (0)	1	<0.01
Iroquois (3)	14	0.02
Kiowa (1)	2	<0.01
Lumbee (0)	2	<0.01
Mexican American Ind. (10)	16	0.02
Navajo (2)	7	0.01
Ottawa (2)	2	<0.01
Potawatomi (3)	3	<0.01
Pueblo (7)	14	0.02
Seminole (0)	1	<0.01
Sioux (8)	26	0.04
South American Ind. (31)	79	0.12
Spanish American Ind. (1)	1	<0.01
Yaqui (0)	1	<0.01
Asian (228)	428	0.67
Not Hispanic (206)	342	0.53
Hispanic (22)	86	0.13
Cambodian (0)	3	<0.01
Chinese, ex. Taiwanese (36)	70	0.11
Filipino (70)	131	0.20
Hmong (6)	6	0.01
Indian (38)	59	0.09
Indonesian (4)	5	0.01
Japanese (11)	29	0.05
Korean (25)	53	0.08
Nepalese (1)	1	<0.01
Pakistani (5)	7	0.01
Thai (11)	13	0.02
Vietnamese (13)	22	0.03
Hawaii Native/Pacific Islander (9)	88	0.14
Not Hispanic (4)	27	0.04
Hispanic (5)	61	0.10
Guamanian/Chamorro (4)	6	0.01
Native Hawaiian (1)	15	0.02
Samoan (1)	4	0.01
White (43,505)	46,446	72.46
Not Hispanic (35,269)	37,080	57.85
Hispanic (8,236)	9,366	14.61

Louisville

Place Type: City
County: Stark
Population: 9,186†

Ancestry‡	Population	%
American (515)	515	5.65
Arab (0)	19	0.21
Lebanese (0)	10	0.11
Syrian (0)	9	0.10
Austrian (20)	57	0.62
British (10)	10	0.11
Croatian (0)	8	0.09
Czech (0)	10	0.11
Danish (0)	30	0.33
Dutch (48)	258	2.83
English (419)	1,330	14.58
European (41)	41	0.45
French, ex. Basque (167)	634	6.95
German (988)	3,318	36.38
Greek (11)	31	0.34
Hungarian (57)	173	1.90
Irish (586)	1,610	17.65
Italian (426)	1,247	13.67
Lithuanian (26)	73	0.80
Macedonian (15)	15	0.16
Norwegian (9)	27	0.30
Polish (74)	252	2.76
Romanian (0)	91	1.00
Russian (0)	279	3.06
Scotch-Irish (45)	122	1.34
Scottish (64)	181	1.98
Slovak (12)	89	0.98
Swedish (0)	69	0.76
Swiss (64)	187	2.05
Ukrainian (0)	14	0.15
Welsh (19)	74	0.81

Hispanic Origin	Population	%
Hispanic or Latino (of any race)	117	1.27
Central American, ex. Mexican	2	0.02
Guatemalan	1	0.01
Honduran	1	0.01
Mexican	54	0.59
Puerto Rican	13	0.14
South American	3	0.03
Colombian	1	0.01
Peruvian	1	0.01
Venezuelan	1	0.01
Other Hispanic or Latino	45	0.49

Race*	Population	%
African-American/Black (16)	39	0.42
Not Hispanic (15)	38	0.41
Hispanic (1)	1	0.01
American Indian/Alaska Native (15)	48	0.52
Not Hispanic (14)	47	0.51
Hispanic (1)	1	0.01
Apache (0)	2	0.02
Blackfeet (1)	2	0.02
Cherokee (1)	20	0.22
Chippewa (4)	4	0.04
Delaware (0)	1	0.01
Potawatomi (0)	1	0.01
Sioux (4)	4	0.04
Asian (26)	37	0.40
Not Hispanic (26)	37	0.40
Chinese, ex. Taiwanese (8)	12	0.13
Filipino (3)	6	0.07
Indian (6)	9	0.10
Korean (3)	3	0.03
Pakistani (2)	3	0.03
Taiwanese (0)	1	0.01
Thai (1)	1	0.01
Hawaii Native/Pacific Islander (0)	1	0.01
Not Hispanic (0)	1	0.01
Native Hawaiian (0)	1	0.01
White (9,033)	9,112	99.19
Not Hispanic (8,942)	9,008	98.06
Hispanic (91)	104	1.13

Loveland

Place Type: City
County: Hamilton
Population: 12,081†

Ancestry‡	Population	%
American (1,040)	1,040	8.78
Arab (52)	94	0.79
Lebanese (52)	86	0.73
Syrian (0)	8	0.07
Australian (17)	33	0.28
Austrian (0)	115	0.97
Brazilian (14)	14	0.12
British (55)	80	0.68
Canadian (0)	10	0.08
Czech (0)	43	0.36
Danish (0)	15	0.13
Dutch (53)	193	1.63
Eastern European (66)	66	0.56
English (372)	1,273	10.75
European (99)	99	0.84
French, ex. Basque (87)	295	2.49
French Canadian (0)	68	0.57

*Notes: † The Census 2010 population figure is used to calculate the percentages in the Hispanic Origin and Race categories. Ancestry percentages are based on the 2006-2010 American Community Survey population (not shown); ‡ Numbers in parentheses indicate the number of people reporting a single ancestry; * Numbers in parentheses indicate the number of persons reporting this race alone, not in combination with any other race; Please refer to the Explanation of Data for more information.*

Ancestry	Population	%
German (1,814)	4,834	40.81
Greek (0)	7	0.06
Hungarian (63)	141	1.19
Irish (387)	2,468	20.84
Italian (162)	551	4.65
Lithuanian (11)	22	0.19
Norwegian (0)	44	0.37
Polish (45)	396	3.34
Portuguese (6)	18	0.15
Romanian (12)	23	0.19
Russian (256)	370	3.12
Scotch-Irish (95)	261	2.20
Scottish (59)	320	2.70
Slavic (48)	48	0.41
Slovak (11)	62	0.52
Swedish (0)	55	0.46
Ukrainian (33)	152	1.28
Welsh (0)	28	0.24

Hispanic Origin	Population	%
Hispanic or Latino (of any race)	295	2.44
Central American, ex. Mexican	27	0.22
Costa Rican	3	0.02
Guatemalan	5	0.04
Honduran	9	0.07
Nicaraguan	3	0.02
Panamanian	3	0.02
Salvadoran	4	0.03
Cuban	16	0.13
Mexican	156	1.29
Puerto Rican	17	0.14
South American	38	0.31
Argentinean	4	0.03
Bolivian	1	0.01
Colombian	15	0.12
Ecuadorian	8	0.07
Peruvian	5	0.04
Uruguayan	1	0.01
Venezuelan	4	0.03
Other Hispanic or Latino	41	0.34

Race*	Population	%
African-American/Black (253)	360	2.98
Not Hispanic (246)	350	2.90
Hispanic (7)	10	0.08
American Indian/Alaska Native (16)	59	0.49
Not Hispanic (9)	50	0.41
Hispanic (7)	9	0.07
Blackfeet (0)	1	0.01
Cherokee (8)	29	0.24
Chippewa (1)	2	0.02
Comanche (0)	1	0.01
Crow (4)	4	0.03
Navajo (0)	1	0.01
Sioux (0)	2	0.02
Yaqui (0)	1	0.01
Asian (203)	270	2.23
Not Hispanic (198)	263	2.18
Hispanic (5)	7	0.06
Bangladeshi (1)	1	0.01
Burmese (1)	1	0.01
Cambodian (2)	4	0.03
Chinese, ex. Taiwanese (41)	56	0.46
Filipino (20)	30	0.25
Indian (74)	78	0.65
Japanese (16)	34	0.28
Korean (14)	19	0.16
Laotian (1)	2	0.02
Pakistani (12)	12	0.10
Taiwanese (0)	2	0.02
Thai (7)	7	0.06
Vietnamese (11)	11	0.09
Hawaii Native/Pacific Islander (11)	18	0.15
Not Hispanic (11)	17	0.14
Hispanic (0)	1	0.01
Guamanian/Chamorro (0)	1	0.01
Native Hawaiian (6)	9	0.07
Samoan (4)	4	0.03
White (11,300)	11,512	95.29
Not Hispanic (11,100)	11,294	93.49
Hispanic (200)	218	1.80

Lyndhurst

Place Type: City
County: Cuyahoga
Population: 14,001†

Ancestry‡	Population	%
African, Sub-Saharan (21)	35	0.25
African (14)	28	0.20
South African (7)	7	0.05
American (529)	529	3.74
Arab (134)	146	1.03
Arab (56)	56	0.40
Egyptian (5)	5	0.04
Lebanese (73)	85	0.60
Armenian (14)	14	0.10
Australian (0)	9	0.06
Austrian (29)	216	1.53
British (23)	76	0.54
Bulgarian (4)	4	0.03
Canadian (0)	30	0.21
Croatian (44)	71	0.50
Czech (63)	275	1.94
Czechoslovakian (0)	47	0.33
Danish (38)	98	0.69
Dutch (27)	58	0.41
Eastern European (56)	56	0.40
English (348)	1,479	10.46
European (175)	175	1.24
Finnish (13)	33	0.23
French, ex. Basque (0)	120	0.85
French Canadian (21)	21	0.15
German (781)	3,083	21.80
Greek (98)	187	1.32
Hungarian (274)	904	6.39
Iranian (36)	36	0.25
Irish (611)	2,176	15.38
Israeli (62)	136	0.96
Italian (1,377)	2,468	17.45
Latvian (0)	8	0.06
Lithuanian (78)	260	1.84
Norwegian (39)	39	0.28
Polish (376)	1,111	7.85
Portuguese (8)	31	0.22
Romanian (45)	87	0.62
Russian (555)	973	6.88
Scotch-Irish (83)	262	1.85
Scottish (73)	236	1.67
Serbian (0)	65	0.46
Slavic (0)	10	0.07
Slovak (150)	295	2.09
Slovene (219)	398	2.81
Swedish (25)	53	0.37
Swiss (11)	32	0.23
Ukrainian (58)	94	0.66
Welsh (6)	97	0.69
Yugoslavian (0)	7	0.05

Hispanic Origin	Population	%
Hispanic or Latino (of any race)	185	1.32
Central American, ex. Mexican	18	0.13
Costa Rican	1	0.01
Guatemalan	9	0.06
Panamanian	1	0.01
Salvadoran	7	0.05
Cuban	7	0.05
Dominican Republic	1	0.01
Mexican	50	0.36
Puerto Rican	25	0.18
South American	60	0.43
Argentinean	2	0.01
Chilean	2	0.01
Colombian	14	0.10
Peruvian	21	0.15
Uruguayan	1	0.01
Venezuelan	17	0.12
Other South American	3	0.02
Other Hispanic or Latino	24	0.17

Race*	Population	%
African-American/Black (901)	995	7.11
Not Hispanic (894)	980	7.00
Hispanic (7)	15	0.11
American Indian/Alaska Native (5)	35	0.25
Not Hispanic (5)	33	0.24
Hispanic (0)	2	0.01
Cherokee (0)	7	0.05
Choctaw (0)	4	0.03
Iroquois (3)	3	0.02
Lumbee (1)	1	0.01
Pueblo (0)	1	0.01
Asian (223)	281	2.01
Not Hispanic (223)	280	2.00
Hispanic (0)	1	0.01
Cambodian (1)	1	0.01
Chinese, ex. Taiwanese (87)	100	0.71
Filipino (18)	34	0.24
Indian (49)	60	0.43
Indonesian (3)	3	0.02
Japanese (7)	10	0.07
Korean (21)	31	0.22
Nepalese (1)	1	0.01
Pakistani (1)	2	0.01
Taiwanese (9)	14	0.10
Thai (0)	4	0.03
Vietnamese (18)	21	0.15
Hawaii Native/Pacific Islander (1)	4	0.03
Not Hispanic (0)	3	0.02
Hispanic (1)	1	0.01
Native Hawaiian (1)	3	0.02
White (12,646)	12,793	91.37
Not Hispanic (12,531)	12,666	90.46
Hispanic (115)	127	0.91

Macedonia

Place Type: City
County: Summit
Population: 11,188†

Ancestry‡	Population	%
Albanian (0)	3	0.03
American (373)	373	3.43
Arab (255)	275	2.53
Arab (42)	42	0.39
Lebanese (0)	20	0.18
Palestinian (213)	213	1.96
Bulgarian (0)	14	0.13
Canadian (82)	100	0.92
Croatian (64)	261	2.40
Czech (163)	333	3.07
Czechoslovakian (17)	17	0.16
Danish (0)	11	0.10
Dutch (11)	95	0.87
Eastern European (12)	12	0.11
English (325)	1,074	9.89
European (72)	72	0.66
Finnish (14)	32	0.29
French, ex. Basque (25)	209	1.92
French Canadian (18)	18	0.17
German (636)	2,631	24.22
Greek (13)	23	0.21
Hungarian (98)	905	8.33
Iranian (41)	41	0.38
Irish (193)	1,448	13.33
Italian (609)	1,792	16.50
Lithuanian (28)	62	0.57
Macedonian (0)	14	0.13
Norwegian (20)	64	0.59
Pennsylvania German (0)	2	0.02
Polish (483)	1,422	13.09
Romanian (11)	11	0.10
Russian (63)	170	1.56
Scotch-Irish (36)	89	0.82
Scottish (38)	315	2.90
Serbian (10)	10	0.09
Slovak (111)	420	3.87
Slovene (40)	181	1.67

*Notes: † The Census 2010 population figure is used to calculate the percentages in the Hispanic Origin and Race categories. Ancestry percentages are based on the 2006-2010 American Community Survey population (not shown); ‡ Numbers in parentheses indicate the number of people reporting a single ancestry; * Numbers in parentheses indicate the number of persons reporting this race alone, not in combination with any other race; Please refer to the Explanation of Data for more information.*

Swedish (0)	167	1.54
Swiss (0)	13	0.12
Ukrainian (55)	102	0.94
Welsh (0)	79	0.73
West Indian, ex. Hispanic (9)	9	0.08
Bermudan (9)	9	0.08

Hispanic Origin	Population	%
Hispanic or Latino (of any race)	146	1.30
Central American, ex. Mexican	10	0.09
Guatemalan	2	0.02
Honduran	2	0.02
Panamanian	4	0.04
Salvadoran	2	0.02
Cuban	4	0.04
Dominican Republic	1	0.01
Mexican	49	0.44
Puerto Rican	51	0.46
South American	8	0.07
Argentinean	2	0.02
Colombian	3	0.03
Ecuadorian	3	0.03
Other Hispanic or Latino	23	0.21

Race*	Population	%
African-American/Black (1,168)	1,261	11.27
Not Hispanic (1,165)	1,257	11.24
Hispanic (3)	4	0.04
American Indian/Alaska Native (10)	58	0.52
Not Hispanic (9)	57	0.51
Hispanic (1)	1	0.01
Blackfeet (1)	4	0.04
Cherokee (1)	12	0.11
Chippewa (0)	2	0.02
Choctaw (0)	4	0.04
Iroquois (2)	6	0.05
Mexican American Ind. (1)	1	0.01
Navajo (0)	1	0.01
Seminole (0)	1	0.01
Sioux (2)	4	0.04
Asian (437)	484	4.33
Not Hispanic (434)	480	4.29
Hispanic (3)	4	0.04
Bangladeshi (1)	1	0.01
Cambodian (0)	10	0.09
Chinese, ex. Taiwanese (52)	57	0.51
Filipino (61)	74	0.66
Indian (269)	275	2.46
Japanese (1)	7	0.06
Korean (22)	24	0.21
Pakistani (1)	1	0.01
Taiwanese (2)	2	0.02
Thai (6)	6	0.05
Vietnamese (9)	19	0.17
Hawaii Native/Pacific Islander (0)	4	0.04
Not Hispanic (0)	3	0.03
Hispanic (0)	1	0.01
White (9,351)	9,505	84.96
Not Hispanic (9,247)	9,396	83.98
Hispanic (104)	109	0.97

Mack

Place Type: CDP
County: Hamilton
Population: 11,585†

Ancestry‡	Population	%
American (426)	426	3.72
Arab (0)	26	0.23
Lebanese (0)	10	0.09
Syrian (0)	16	0.14
Armenian (10)	32	0.28
Austrian (10)	45	0.39
Belgian (0)	15	0.13
British (0)	24	0.21
Canadian (0)	9	0.08
Czech (9)	9	0.08
Czechoslovakian (0)	9	0.08
Dutch (36)	124	1.08
English (198)	775	6.76
European (181)	181	1.58
French, ex. Basque (25)	258	2.25
French Canadian (7)	7	0.06
German (3,285)	6,720	58.65
Greek (117)	125	1.09
Hungarian (71)	290	2.53
Irish (447)	2,545	22.21
Italian (335)	1,183	10.32
Lithuanian (0)	24	0.21
Macedonian (26)	72	0.63
Norwegian (0)	12	0.10
Polish (13)	177	1.54
Romanian (0)	123	1.07
Russian (18)	78	0.68
Scotch-Irish (57)	124	1.08
Scottish (0)	198	1.73
Serbian (40)	70	0.61
Slavic (0)	21	0.18
Slovak (0)	29	0.25
Swedish (0)	15	0.13
Swiss (0)	29	0.25
Welsh (16)	96	0.84

Hispanic Origin	Population	%
Hispanic or Latino (of any race)	73	0.63
Central American, ex. Mexican	8	0.07
Costa Rican	1	0.01
Guatemalan	5	0.04
Panamanian	2	0.02
Dominican Republic	3	0.03
Mexican	28	0.24
Puerto Rican	5	0.04
South American	14	0.12
Argentinean	1	0.01
Bolivian	3	0.03
Ecuadorian	7	0.06
Peruvian	3	0.03
Other Hispanic or Latino	15	0.13

Race*	Population	%
African-American/Black (41)	60	0.52
Not Hispanic (38)	52	0.45
Hispanic (3)	8	0.07
American Indian/Alaska Native (13)	32	0.28
Not Hispanic (8)	27	0.23
Hispanic (5)	5	0.04
Blackfeet (0)	1	0.01
Cherokee (2)	11	0.09
Creek (4)	4	0.03
Mexican American Ind. (1)	1	0.01
Navajo (1)	2	0.02
Asian (45)	80	0.69
Not Hispanic (44)	78	0.67
Hispanic (1)	2	0.02
Chinese, ex. Taiwanese (9)	15	0.13
Filipino (9)	14	0.12
Indian (14)	21	0.18
Japanese (2)	12	0.10
Korean (6)	11	0.09
Laotian (1)	2	0.02
Thai (1)	1	0.01
Vietnamese (3)	3	0.03
Hawaii Native/Pacific Islander (1)	1	0.01
Hispanic (1)	1	0.01
Guamanian/Chamorro (1)	1	0.01
White (11,375)	11,450	98.83
Not Hispanic (11,332)	11,401	98.41
Hispanic (43)	49	0.42

Madeira

Place Type: City
County: Hamilton
Population: 8,726†

Ancestry‡	Population	%
African, Sub-Saharan (0)	12	0.14
African (0)	12	0.14
American (490)	490	5.65
Arab (20)	20	0.23
Lebanese (20)	20	0.23
Belgian (12)	12	0.14
British (21)	69	0.80
Canadian (13)	54	0.62
Czech (15)	44	0.51
Czechoslovakian (11)	11	0.13
Danish (11)	11	0.13
Dutch (30)	149	1.72
Eastern European (14)	42	0.48
English (365)	1,031	11.89
European (170)	170	1.96
French, ex. Basque (25)	227	2.62
French Canadian (13)	13	0.15
German (1,695)	4,193	48.34
Greek (0)	40	0.46
Hungarian (80)	137	1.58
Irish (355)	1,953	22.52
Italian (157)	478	5.51
Norwegian (14)	62	0.71
Polish (61)	340	3.92
Russian (14)	156	1.80
Scandinavian (0)	12	0.14
Scotch-Irish (145)	264	3.04
Scottish (60)	248	2.86
Serbian (0)	31	0.36
Swedish (0)	84	0.97
Ukrainian (0)	32	0.37
Welsh (0)	161	1.86

Hispanic Origin	Population	%
Hispanic or Latino (of any race)	198	2.27
Central American, ex. Mexican	27	0.31
Costa Rican	5	0.06
Guatemalan	11	0.13
Honduran	7	0.08
Nicaraguan	2	0.02
Salvadoran	2	0.02
Cuban	11	0.13
Dominican Republic	3	0.03
Mexican	94	1.08
Puerto Rican	17	0.19
South American	28	0.32
Argentinean	4	0.05
Chilean	1	0.01
Colombian	4	0.05
Ecuadorian	5	0.06
Peruvian	4	0.05
Uruguayan	1	0.01
Venezuelan	8	0.09
Other South American	1	0.01
Other Hispanic or Latino	18	0.21

Race*	Population	%
African-American/Black (222)	247	2.83
Not Hispanic (219)	243	2.78
Hispanic (3)	4	0.05
American Indian/Alaska Native (12)	26	0.30
Not Hispanic (7)	20	0.23
Hispanic (5)	6	0.07
Blackfeet (1)	1	0.01
Cherokee (0)	1	0.01
Mexican American Ind. (4)	5	0.06
Potawatomi (1)	1	0.01
Asian (244)	311	3.56
Not Hispanic (242)	308	3.53
Hispanic (2)	3	0.03
Burmese (9)	9	0.10
Cambodian (28)	40	0.46
Chinese, ex. Taiwanese (87)	99	1.13
Filipino (9)	27	0.31
Indian (29)	49	0.56
Japanese (7)	13	0.15
Korean (31)	33	0.38
Laotian (6)	6	0.07
Pakistani (3)	3	0.03
Taiwanese (1)	1	0.01
Vietnamese (17)	18	0.21
Hawaii Native/Pacific Islander (0)	1	0.01
Not Hispanic (0)	1	0.01

*Notes: † The Census 2010 population figure is used to calculate the percentages in the Hispanic Origin and Race categories. Ancestry percentages are based on the 2006-2010 American Community Survey population (not shown); ‡ Numbers in parentheses indicate the number of people reporting a single ancestry; * Numbers in parentheses indicate the number of persons reporting this race alone, not in combination with any other race; Please refer to the Explanation of Data for more information.*

White (8,115)	8,214	94.13
Not Hispanic (7,950)	8,047	92.22
Hispanic (165)	167	1.91

Mansfield

Place Type: City
County: Richland
Population: 47,821†

Ancestry‡	Population	%
African, Sub-Saharan (698)	863	1.77
African (679)	827	1.69
Ghanaian (19)	19	0.04
Senegalese (0)	8	0.02
Other Sub-Saharan African (0)	9	0.02
Albanian (23)	23	0.05
American (2,984)	2,984	6.11
Arab (44)	49	0.10
Arab (9)	9	0.02
Iraqi (4)	4	0.01
Jordanian (18)	18	0.04
Palestinian (13)	18	0.04
Armenian (11)	43	0.09
Australian (0)	39	0.08
Austrian (36)	253	0.52
Belgian (0)	21	0.04
Brazilian (8)	21	0.04
British (69)	175	0.36
Bulgarian (6)	15	0.03
Canadian (24)	24	0.05
Carpatho Rusyn (0)	43	0.09
Croatian (51)	106	0.22
Czech (69)	169	0.35
Czechoslovakian (47)	260	0.53
Danish (0)	94	0.19
Dutch (126)	796	1.63
Eastern European (18)	18	0.04
English (2,170)	4,965	10.17
European (160)	160	0.33
Finnish (13)	59	0.12
French, ex. Basque (150)	848	1.74
French Canadian (23)	29	0.06
German (4,871)	12,189	24.98
Greek (103)	216	0.44
Hungarian (215)	715	1.47
Irish (1,361)	5,835	11.96
Italian (598)	2,245	4.60
Latvian (8)	30	0.06
Lithuanian (48)	58	0.12
Macedonian (42)	58	0.12
Maltese (26)	26	0.05
Norwegian (38)	125	0.26
Pennsylvania German (36)	130	0.27
Polish (339)	1,106	2.27
Romanian (0)	67	0.14
Russian (0)	77	0.16
Scotch-Irish (251)	1,110	2.27
Scottish (221)	817	1.67
Serbian (17)	17	0.03
Slavic (22)	22	0.05
Slovak (37)	123	0.25
Slovene (0)	8	0.02
Swedish (52)	186	0.38
Swiss (75)	353	0.72
Turkish (0)	9	0.02
Ukrainian (0)	5	0.01
Welsh (39)	513	1.05
West Indian, ex. Hispanic (146)	226	0.46
Barbadian (0)	40	0.08
Haitian (9)	9	0.02
Jamaican (129)	169	0.35
West Indian (8)	8	0.02
Yugoslavian (147)	307	0.63

Hispanic Origin	Population	%
Hispanic or Latino (of any race)	921	1.93
Central American, ex. Mexican	35	0.07
Guatemalan	9	0.02
Honduran	3	0.01
Nicaraguan	4	0.01
Panamanian	13	0.03
Salvadoran	1	<0.01
Other Central American	5	0.01
Cuban	28	0.06
Dominican Republic	12	0.03
Mexican	476	1.00
Puerto Rican	199	0.42
South American	51	0.11
Argentinean	10	0.02
Chilean	2	<0.01
Colombian	22	0.05
Peruvian	14	0.03
Venezuelan	3	0.01
Other Hispanic or Latino	120	0.25

Race*	Population	%
African-American/Black (10,592)	11,594	24.24
Not Hispanic (10,505)	11,447	23.94
Hispanic (87)	147	0.31
American Indian/Alaska Native (96)	442	0.92
Not Hispanic (86)	415	0.87
Hispanic (10)	27	0.06
Aleut *(Alaska Native)* (0)	1	<0.01
Apache (1)	14	0.03
Blackfeet (4)	28	0.06
Canadian/French Am. Ind. (1)	3	0.01
Cherokee (23)	157	0.33
Cheyenne (0)	2	<0.01
Chickasaw (0)	1	<0.01
Chippewa (2)	4	0.01
Choctaw (1)	7	0.01
Comanche (0)	1	<0.01
Creek (0)	3	0.01
Crow (0)	1	<0.01
Delaware (0)	1	<0.01
Hopi (1)	1	<0.01
Iroquois (3)	7	0.01
Mexican American Ind. (1)	1	<0.01
Navajo (0)	2	<0.01
Ottawa (0)	1	<0.01
Seminole (0)	1	<0.01
Shoshone (0)	1	<0.01
Sioux (1)	10	0.02
Tohono O'Odham (1)	1	<0.01
Yakama (2)	4	0.01
Yup'ik *(Alaska Native)* (1)	1	<0.01
Asian (354)	498	1.04
Not Hispanic (346)	488	1.02
Hispanic (8)	10	0.02
Burmese (3)	3	0.01
Cambodian (1)	2	<0.01
Chinese, ex. Taiwanese (28)	45	0.09
Filipino (49)	76	0.16
Indian (139)	160	0.33
Indonesian (1)	1	<0.01
Japanese (23)	42	0.09
Korean (36)	75	0.16
Laotian (4)	4	0.01
Nepalese (2)	2	<0.01
Pakistani (12)	14	0.03
Sri Lankan (2)	3	0.01
Taiwanese (10)	14	0.03
Thai (4)	9	0.02
Vietnamese (19)	21	0.04
Hawaii Native/Pacific Islander (26)	65	0.14
Not Hispanic (21)	54	0.11
Hispanic (5)	11	0.02
Guamanian/Chamorro (11)	17	0.04
Native Hawaiian (5)	16	0.03
Samoan (5)	14	0.03
White (35,058)	36,391	76.10
Not Hispanic (34,521)	35,766	74.79
Hispanic (537)	625	1.31

Maple Heights

Place Type: City
County: Cuyahoga
Population: 23,138†

Ancestry‡	Population	%
African, Sub-Saharan (328)	386	1.64
African (316)	374	1.59
Nigerian (12)	12	0.05
American (165)	165	0.70
Arab (8)	18	0.08
Lebanese (8)	18	0.08
Austrian (15)	28	0.12
British (18)	29	0.12
Canadian (0)	39	0.17
Croatian (10)	27	0.11
Czech (283)	612	2.60
Czechoslovakian (37)	37	0.16
Danish (0)	26	0.11
Dutch (21)	37	0.16
English (195)	403	1.71
European (46)	46	0.20
French, ex. Basque (0)	48	0.20
German (629)	1,695	7.19
German Russian (54)	68	0.29
Greek (26)	60	0.25
Hungarian (273)	736	3.12
Irish (276)	916	3.89
Italian (689)	1,213	5.15
Latvian (0)	10	0.04
Lithuanian (10)	35	0.15
Pennsylvania German (0)	8	0.03
Polish (759)	1,566	6.64
Portuguese (14)	26	0.11
Russian (63)	127	0.54
Scotch-Irish (36)	97	0.41
Scottish (0)	84	0.36
Serbian (0)	4	0.02
Slavic (9)	9	0.04
Slovak (367)	647	2.74
Slovene (87)	318	1.35
Swedish (0)	147	0.62
Swiss (24)	95	0.40
Ukrainian (39)	51	0.22
Welsh (10)	113	0.48
West Indian, ex. Hispanic (144)	235	1.00
Jamaican (91)	182	0.77
West Indian (53)	53	0.22
Yugoslavian (0)	10	0.04

Hispanic Origin	Population	%
Hispanic or Latino (of any race)	357	1.54
Central American, ex. Mexican	28	0.12
Guatemalan	2	0.01
Honduran	1	<0.01
Nicaraguan	12	0.05
Panamanian	12	0.05
Salvadoran	1	<0.01
Cuban	8	0.03
Dominican Republic	10	0.04
Mexican	91	0.39
Puerto Rican	157	0.68
South American	25	0.11
Colombian	6	0.03
Ecuadorian	5	0.02
Peruvian	11	0.05
Venezuelan	3	0.01
Other Hispanic or Latino	38	0.16

Race*	Population	%
African-American/Black (15,788)	16,216	70.08
Not Hispanic (15,682)	16,072	69.46
Hispanic (106)	144	0.62
American Indian/Alaska Native (39)	169	0.73
Not Hispanic (35)	150	0.65
Hispanic (4)	19	0.08
Apache (0)	1	<0.01
Blackfeet (1)	14	0.06
Central American Ind. (2)	2	0.01
Cherokee (4)	40	0.17
Chickasaw (1)	1	<0.01
Chippewa (0)	1	<0.01
Choctaw (0)	5	0.02
Creek (0)	1	<0.01
Iroquois (0)	1	<0.01

*Notes: † The Census 2010 population figure is used to calculate the percentages in the Hispanic Origin and Race categories. Ancestry percentages are based on the 2006-2010 American Community Survey population (not shown); ‡ Numbers in parentheses indicate the number of people reporting a single ancestry; * Numbers in parentheses indicate the number of persons reporting this race alone, not in combination with any other race; Please refer to the Explanation of Data for more information.*

Sioux (1)	2	0.01
Asian (236)	292	1.26
Not Hispanic (233)	284	1.23
Hispanic (3)	8	0.03
Bangladeshi (3)	3	0.01
Chinese, ex. Taiwanese (20)	22	0.10
Filipino (51)	71	0.31
Indian (135)	157	0.68
Japanese (3)	15	0.06
Korean (8)	12	0.05
Nepalese (0)	4	0.02
Thai (1)	2	0.01
Vietnamese (10)	12	0.05
Hawaii Native/Pacific Islander (0)	7	0.03
Not Hispanic (0)	6	0.03
Hispanic (0)	1	<0.01
Guamanian/Chamorro (0)	2	0.01
Native Hawaiian (0)	1	<0.01
Samoan (0)	2	0.01
White (6,477)	6,828	29.51
Not Hispanic (6,373)	6,687	28.90
Hispanic (104)	141	0.61

Marietta

Place Type: City
County: Washington
Population: 14,085†

Ancestry‡	Population	%
African, Sub-Saharan (41)	41	0.29
African (41)	41	0.29
American (1,428)	1,428	10.05
Arab (0)	25	0.18
Lebanese (0)	25	0.18
Austrian (0)	24	0.17
Belgian (46)	54	0.38
British (47)	57	0.40
Croatian (0)	34	0.24
Czech (33)	126	0.89
Czechoslovakian (10)	21	0.15
Dutch (34)	234	1.65
Eastern European (7)	15	0.11
English (617)	1,734	12.20
European (97)	124	0.87
French, ex. Basque (77)	242	1.70
French Canadian (0)	47	0.33
German (1,661)	3,738	26.30
Hungarian (14)	19	0.13
Irish (918)	2,383	16.77
Italian (164)	564	3.97
Lithuanian (0)	12	0.08
Norwegian (7)	54	0.38
Polish (59)	505	3.55
Romanian (0)	34	0.24
Russian (0)	13	0.09
Scotch-Irish (220)	432	3.04
Scottish (82)	346	2.43
Slovak (29)	42	0.30
Slovene (16)	16	0.11
Swedish (33)	62	0.44
Swiss (0)	22	0.15
Ukrainian (14)	39	0.27
Welsh (16)	157	1.10
Yugoslavian (20)	20	0.14

Hispanic Origin	Population	%
Hispanic or Latino (of any race)	151	1.07
Central American, ex. Mexican	13	0.09
Costa Rican	1	0.01
Guatemalan	6	0.04
Honduran	4	0.03
Panamanian	1	0.01
Salvadoran	1	0.01
Cuban	7	0.05
Mexican	72	0.51
Puerto Rican	14	0.10
South American	5	0.04
Bolivian	3	0.02
Peruvian	1	0.01
Uruguayan	1	0.01
Other Hispanic or Latino	40	0.28

Race*	Population	%
African-American/Black (188)	281	2.00
Not Hispanic (186)	276	1.96
Hispanic (2)	5	0.04
American Indian/Alaska Native (38)	142	1.01
Not Hispanic (38)	136	0.97
Hispanic (0)	6	0.04
Apache (2)	2	0.01
Blackfeet (0)	3	0.02
Canadian/French Am. Ind. (1)	1	0.01
Cherokee (10)	44	0.31
Chickasaw (0)	1	0.01
Chippewa (1)	2	0.01
Choctaw (0)	3	0.02
Creek (0)	2	0.01
Iroquois (0)	1	0.01
Lumbee (0)	2	0.01
Menominee (1)	1	0.01
Navajo (0)	1	0.01
Osage (0)	1	0.01
Sioux (3)	8	0.06
Yaqui (0)	4	0.03
Yup'ik *(Alaska Native)* (1)	1	0.01
Asian (202)	239	1.70
Not Hispanic (202)	237	1.68
Hispanic (0)	2	0.01
Burmese (0)	1	0.01
Chinese, ex. Taiwanese (46)	49	0.35
Filipino (17)	23	0.16
Indian (16)	21	0.15
Japanese (4)	18	0.13
Korean (6)	9	0.06
Sri Lankan (2)	2	0.01
Taiwanese (1)	3	0.02
Thai (0)	2	0.01
Vietnamese (0)	1	0.01
Hawaii Native/Pacific Islander (4)	9	0.06
Not Hispanic (4)	9	0.06
Guamanian/Chamorro (2)	3	0.02
Native Hawaiian (1)	3	0.02
Samoan (1)	1	0.01
White (13,366)	13,569	96.34
Not Hispanic (13,271)	13,464	95.59
Hispanic (95)	105	0.75

Marion

Place Type: City
County: Marion
Population: 36,837†

Ancestry‡	Population	%
African, Sub-Saharan (147)	212	0.57
African (104)	169	0.46
Nigerian (23)	23	0.06
Other Sub-Saharan African (20)	20	0.05
American (5,427)	5,427	14.63
Arab (0)	40	0.11
Arab (0)	10	0.03
Egyptian (0)	13	0.04
Lebanese (0)	17	0.05
Australian (59)	59	0.16
Austrian (20)	48	0.13
Belgian (0)	15	0.04
British (41)	133	0.36
Canadian (32)	60	0.16
Croatian (0)	93	0.25
Czech (16)	73	0.20
Czechoslovakian (0)	30	0.08
Dutch (168)	978	2.64
Eastern European (9)	9	0.02
English (1,157)	3,399	9.16
European (145)	159	0.43
Finnish (59)	59	0.16
French, ex. Basque (119)	678	1.83
French Canadian (8)	45	0.12
German (3,487)	9,475	25.54
Greek (84)	96	0.26
Hungarian (38)	184	0.50
Irish (2,194)	5,832	15.72
Italian (442)	1,257	3.39
Latvian (0)	13	0.04
Lithuanian (0)	11	0.03
Northern European (9)	9	0.02
Norwegian (9)	22	0.06
Pennsylvania German (17)	25	0.07
Polish (303)	672	1.81
Romanian (25)	61	0.16
Russian (61)	142	0.38
Scandinavian (0)	26	0.07
Scotch-Irish (330)	831	2.24
Scottish (223)	686	1.85
Serbian (0)	10	0.03
Slovak (22)	22	0.06
Slovene (0)	78	0.21
Swedish (21)	214	0.58
Swiss (23)	82	0.22
Welsh (108)	398	1.07
West Indian, ex. Hispanic (35)	41	0.11
Dutch West Indian (0)	6	0.02
Jamaican (35)	35	0.09
Yugoslavian (24)	24	0.06

Hispanic Origin	Population	%
Hispanic or Latino (of any race)	1,098	2.98
Central American, ex. Mexican	44	0.12
Guatemalan	28	0.08
Honduran	11	0.03
Panamanian	1	<0.01
Salvadoran	4	0.01
Cuban	11	0.03
Dominican Republic	8	0.02
Mexican	768	2.08
Puerto Rican	135	0.37
South American	14	0.04
Argentinean	1	<0.01
Bolivian	1	<0.01
Colombian	4	0.01
Peruvian	3	0.01
Venezuelan	5	0.01
Other Hispanic or Latino	118	0.32

Race*	Population	%
African-American/Black (3,538)	4,011	10.89
Not Hispanic (3,499)	3,945	10.71
Hispanic (39)	66	0.18
American Indian/Alaska Native (68)	292	0.79
Not Hispanic (59)	272	0.74
Hispanic (9)	20	0.05
Apache (0)	4	0.01
Blackfeet (2)	22	0.06
Central American Ind. (2)	2	0.01
Cherokee (14)	104	0.28
Choctaw (1)	2	0.01
Creek (0)	4	0.01
Iroquois (1)	3	0.01
Mexican American Ind. (1)	1	<0.01
Navajo (2)	2	0.01
Osage (0)	2	0.01
Ottawa (1)	1	<0.01
Pueblo (1)	1	<0.01
Seminole (0)	2	0.01
Sioux (1)	10	0.03
Yup'ik *(Alaska Native)* (1)	1	<0.01
Asian (134)	194	0.53
Not Hispanic (128)	178	0.48
Hispanic (6)	16	0.04
Chinese, ex. Taiwanese (21)	28	0.08
Filipino (38)	56	0.15
Indian (37)	40	0.11
Indonesian (1)	3	0.01
Japanese (4)	10	0.03
Korean (10)	21	0.06
Laotian (2)	2	0.01
Thai (7)	12	0.03
Vietnamese (13)	14	0.04
Hawaii Native/Pacific Islander (9)	29	0.08

*Notes: † The Census 2010 population figure is used to calculate the percentages in the Hispanic Origin and Race categories. Ancestry percentages are based on the 2006-2010 American Community Survey population (not shown); ‡ Numbers in parentheses indicate the number of people reporting a single ancestry; * Numbers in parentheses indicate the number of persons reporting this race alone, not in combination with any other race; Please refer to the Explanation of Data for more information.*

Not Hispanic (8)	23	0.06
Hispanic (1)	6	0.02
Guamanian/Chamorro (1)	4	0.01
Native Hawaiian (3)	11	0.03
Samoan (2)	4	0.01
White (31,930)	32,663	88.67
Not Hispanic (31,329)	31,978	86.81
Hispanic (601)	685	1.86

Marysville

Place Type: City
County: Union
Population: 22,094†

Ancestry‡	Population	%
African, Sub-Saharan (9)	9	0.04
African (9)	9	0.04
American (2,434)	2,434	11.43
Arab (33)	45	0.21
Egyptian (22)	22	0.10
Lebanese (11)	11	0.05
Syrian (0)	12	0.06
Austrian (13)	13	0.06
British (58)	65	0.31
Canadian (8)	22	0.10
Celtic (12)	12	0.06
Czech (26)	103	0.48
Czechoslovakian (16)	16	0.08
Danish (12)	12	0.06
Dutch (129)	566	2.66
English (671)	2,527	11.87
European (387)	402	1.89
Finnish (21)	64	0.30
French, ex. Basque (35)	804	3.78
French Canadian (27)	49	0.23
German (2,517)	6,792	31.89
Greek (82)	175	0.82
Hungarian (61)	273	1.28
Irish (779)	3,615	16.98
Italian (246)	1,084	5.09
Latvian (18)	18	0.08
Norwegian (19)	75	0.35
Pennsylvania German (21)	44	0.21
Polish (331)	719	3.38
Romanian (0)	24	0.11
Scotch-Irish (239)	445	2.09
Scottish (104)	415	1.95
Slavic (22)	36	0.17
Slovak (72)	138	0.65
Slovene (0)	20	0.09
Swedish (0)	45	0.21
Swiss (0)	183	0.86
Turkish (15)	15	0.07
Welsh (143)	490	2.30
West Indian, ex. Hispanic (52)	52	0.24
Belizean (20)	20	0.09
Haitian (10)	10	0.05
Jamaican (22)	22	0.10

Hispanic Origin	Population	%
Hispanic or Latino (of any race)	392	1.77
Central American, ex. Mexican	29	0.13
Costa Rican	4	0.02
Guatemalan	10	0.05
Honduran	3	0.01
Nicaraguan	5	0.02
Panamanian	6	0.03
Salvadoran	1	<0.01
Cuban	8	0.04
Dominican Republic	11	0.05
Mexican	209	0.95
Puerto Rican	80	0.36
South American	20	0.09
Argentinean	1	<0.01
Bolivian	1	<0.01
Colombian	2	0.01
Ecuadorian	3	0.01
Peruvian	9	0.04
Venezuelan	4	0.02
Other Hispanic or Latino	35	0.16

Race*	Population	%
African-American/Black (1,004)	1,165	5.27
Not Hispanic (990)	1,140	5.16
Hispanic (14)	25	0.11
American Indian/Alaska Native (61)	176	0.80
Not Hispanic (55)	161	0.73
Hispanic (6)	15	0.07
Apache (0)	1	<0.01
Blackfeet (6)	14	0.06
Cherokee (19)	64	0.29
Cheyenne (2)	2	0.01
Chippewa (0)	1	<0.01
Comanche (0)	1	<0.01
Cree (0)	1	<0.01
Hopi (0)	1	<0.01
Iroquois (2)	2	0.01
Kiowa (2)	2	0.01
Lumbee (1)	1	<0.01
Navajo (1)	6	0.03
Sioux (2)	7	0.03
Asian (508)	638	2.89
Not Hispanic (499)	624	2.82
Hispanic (9)	14	0.06
Bangladeshi (3)	3	0.01
Cambodian (6)	7	0.03
Chinese, ex. Taiwanese (66)	82	0.37
Filipino (83)	115	0.52
Indian (210)	232	1.05
Indonesian (1)	8	0.04
Japanese (50)	78	0.35
Korean (22)	39	0.18
Laotian (0)	2	0.01
Pakistani (1)	1	<0.01
Taiwanese (7)	7	0.03
Thai (4)	14	0.06
Vietnamese (25)	28	0.13
Hawaii Native/Pacific Islander (14)	26	0.12
Not Hispanic (12)	24	0.11
Hispanic (2)	2	0.01
Guamanian/Chamorro (6)	7	0.03
Marshallese (1)	1	<0.01
Native Hawaiian (2)	5	0.02
Samoan (1)	1	<0.01
White (19,980)	20,359	92.15
Not Hispanic (19,765)	20,099	90.97
Hispanic (215)	260	1.18

Mason

Place Type: City
County: Warren
Population: 30,712†

Ancestry‡	Population	%
African, Sub-Saharan (118)	163	0.55
African (118)	163	0.55
Albanian (0)	10	0.03
American (2,427)	2,427	8.13
Arab (87)	101	0.34
Egyptian (60)	60	0.20
Jordanian (18)	18	0.06
Lebanese (9)	23	0.08
Australian (12)	12	0.04
Austrian (13)	50	0.17
Brazilian (49)	49	0.16
British (74)	104	0.35
Canadian (55)	124	0.42
Czech (24)	202	0.68
Danish (0)	79	0.26
Dutch (164)	535	1.79
Eastern European (25)	38	0.13
English (1,317)	3,755	12.57
European (448)	460	1.54
Finnish (10)	33	0.11
French, ex. Basque (84)	883	2.96
French Canadian (33)	118	0.40
German (3,701)	10,266	34.38
Greek (72)	242	0.81
Hungarian (50)	296	0.99
Iranian (13)	13	0.04
Irish (873)	4,271	14.30
Israeli (15)	15	0.05
Italian (544)	2,099	7.03
Northern European (26)	26	0.09
Norwegian (92)	338	1.13
Pennsylvania German (14)	14	0.05
Polish (411)	1,362	4.56
Romanian (12)	12	0.04
Russian (66)	233	0.78
Scandinavian (31)	49	0.16
Scotch-Irish (251)	651	2.18
Scottish (179)	976	3.27
Serbian (0)	87	0.29
Slavic (0)	8	0.03
Slovak (0)	45	0.15
Slovene (29)	82	0.27
Swedish (110)	300	1.00
Swiss (0)	106	0.35
Turkish (43)	43	0.14
Ukrainian (33)	85	0.28
Welsh (86)	323	1.08
Yugoslavian (12)	12	0.04

Hispanic Origin	Population	%
Hispanic or Latino (of any race)	988	3.22
Central American, ex. Mexican	80	0.26
Costa Rican	10	0.03
Guatemalan	38	0.12
Honduran	8	0.03
Nicaraguan	13	0.04
Panamanian	6	0.02
Salvadoran	5	0.02
Cuban	55	0.18
Dominican Republic	8	0.03
Mexican	502	1.63
Puerto Rican	113	0.37
South American	172	0.56
Argentinean	12	0.04
Bolivian	2	0.01
Chilean	3	0.01
Colombian	41	0.13
Ecuadorian	11	0.04
Peruvian	22	0.07
Uruguayan	3	0.01
Venezuelan	78	0.25
Other Hispanic or Latino	58	0.19

Race*	Population	%
African-American/Black (1,013)	1,142	3.72
Not Hispanic (990)	1,103	3.59
Hispanic (23)	39	0.13
American Indian/Alaska Native (50)	105	0.34
Not Hispanic (36)	87	0.28
Hispanic (14)	18	0.06
Alaska Athabascan *(Ala. Nat.)* (0)	1	<0.01
Apache (3)	3	0.01
Blackfeet (0)	5	0.02
Cherokee (4)	19	0.06
Chippewa (3)	3	0.01
Choctaw (2)	6	0.02
Creek (1)	3	0.01
Crow (0)	2	0.01
Iroquois (3)	3	0.01
Mexican American Ind. (10)	10	0.03
Navajo (5)	8	0.03
Sioux (1)	2	0.01
Asian (2,757)	3,049	9.93
Not Hispanic (2,754)	3,035	9.88
Hispanic (3)	14	0.05
Burmese (1)	1	<0.01
Cambodian (10)	15	0.05
Chinese, ex. Taiwanese (599)	667	2.17
Filipino (87)	145	0.47
Indian (1,331)	1,384	4.51
Indonesian (3)	4	0.01
Japanese (135)	165	0.54
Korean (152)	192	0.63
Laotian (6)	13	0.04

*Notes: † The Census 2010 population figure is used to calculate the percentages in the Hispanic Origin and Race categories. Ancestry percentages are based on the 2006-2010 American Community Survey population (not shown); ‡ Numbers in parentheses indicate the number of people reporting a single ancestry; * Numbers in parentheses indicate the number of persons reporting this race alone, not in combination with any other race; Please refer to the Explanation of Data for more information.*

Malaysian (3)	17	0.06
Nepalese (3)	3	0.01
Pakistani (174)	190	0.62
Sri Lankan (10)	15	0.05
Taiwanese (49)	56	0.18
Thai (12)	15	0.05
Vietnamese (115)	129	0.42
Hawaii Native/Pacific Islander (35)	64	0.21
Not Hispanic (35)	64	0.21
Guamanian/Chamorro (2)	7	0.02
Native Hawaiian (4)	8	0.03
Samoan (1)	1	<0.01
White (26,141)	26,545	86.43
Not Hispanic (25,434)	25,797	84.00
Hispanic (707)	748	2.44

Massillon

Place Type: City
County: Stark
Population: 32,149†

Ancestry‡	Population	%
African, Sub-Saharan (321)	368	1.15
African (321)	368	1.15
Albanian (14)	64	0.20
American (3,843)	3,843	12.00
Arab (94)	260	0.81
Arab (15)	133	0.42
Lebanese (79)	127	0.40
Austrian (17)	28	0.09
British (42)	89	0.28
Bulgarian (0)	21	0.07
Canadian (13)	34	0.11
Celtic (0)	12	0.04
Croatian (45)	127	0.40
Czech (34)	202	0.63
Czechoslovakian (23)	34	0.11
Danish (0)	10	0.03
Dutch (112)	1,134	3.54
English (667)	2,716	8.48
European (280)	310	0.97
French, ex. Basque (240)	1,378	4.30
French Canadian (31)	39	0.12
German (4,244)	11,536	36.03
Greek (169)	268	0.84
Hungarian (129)	400	1.25
Irish (955)	5,050	15.77
Italian (865)	2,771	8.65
Lithuanian (0)	94	0.29
Luxemburger (13)	13	0.04
Macedonian (16)	38	0.12
Norwegian (22)	89	0.28
Pennsylvania German (37)	52	0.16
Polish (202)	638	1.99
Portuguese (0)	12	0.04
Romanian (105)	355	1.11
Russian (12)	25	0.08
Scandinavian (0)	6	0.02
Scotch-Irish (98)	617	1.93
Scottish (104)	467	1.46
Serbian (62)	96	0.30
Slavic (9)	14	0.04
Slovak (82)	383	1.20
Slovene (23)	64	0.20
Swedish (53)	263	0.82
Swiss (102)	422	1.32
Ukrainian (48)	127	0.40
Welsh (112)	683	2.13
Yugoslavian (45)	110	0.34

Hispanic Origin	Population	%
Hispanic or Latino (of any race)	651	2.02
Central American, ex. Mexican	116	0.36
Costa Rican	2	0.01
Guatemalan	81	0.25
Honduran	4	0.01
Nicaraguan	15	0.05
Panamanian	5	0.02
Salvadoran	9	0.03
Cuban	37	0.12
Dominican Republic	2	0.01
Mexican	297	0.92
Puerto Rican	74	0.23
South American	10	0.03
Argentinean	5	0.02
Colombian	2	0.01
Ecuadorian	2	0.01
Peruvian	1	<0.01
Other Hispanic or Latino	115	0.36

Race*	Population	%
African-American/Black (2,822)	3,433	10.68
Not Hispanic (2,792)	3,388	10.54
Hispanic (30)	45	0.14
American Indian/Alaska Native (95)	285	0.89
Not Hispanic (61)	239	0.74
Hispanic (34)	46	0.14
Apache (0)	2	0.01
Blackfeet (0)	16	0.05
Central American Ind. (27)	27	0.08
Cherokee (11)	67	0.21
Cheyenne (0)	2	0.01
Chippewa (0)	4	0.01
Choctaw (0)	4	0.01
Comanche (0)	1	<0.01
Cree (0)	1	<0.01
Creek (2)	4	0.01
Delaware (2)	7	0.02
Inupiat *(Alaska Native)* (1)	1	<0.01
Iroquois (5)	13	0.04
Menominee (0)	1	<0.01
Ottawa (1)	1	<0.01
Potawatomi (3)	3	0.01
Pueblo (0)	2	0.01
Sioux (3)	10	0.03
Asian (128)	188	0.58
Not Hispanic (123)	173	0.54
Hispanic (5)	15	0.05
Cambodian (0)	1	<0.01
Chinese, ex. Taiwanese (23)	28	0.09
Filipino (32)	55	0.17
Indian (20)	26	0.08
Indonesian (1)	1	<0.01
Japanese (6)	17	0.05
Korean (22)	26	0.08
Malaysian (0)	1	<0.01
Taiwanese (2)	2	0.01
Thai (7)	10	0.03
Vietnamese (9)	15	0.05
Hawaii Native/Pacific Islander (7)	24	0.07
Not Hispanic (4)	17	0.05
Hispanic (3)	7	0.02
Guamanian/Chamorro (3)	6	0.02
Native Hawaiian (3)	11	0.03
Tongan (0)	2	0.01
White (28,094)	28,885	89.85
Not Hispanic (27,678)	28,418	88.39
Hispanic (416)	467	1.45

Maumee

Place Type: City
County: Lucas
Population: 14,286†

Ancestry‡	Population	%
African, Sub-Saharan (8)	8	0.06
Nigerian (8)	8	0.06
American (546)	546	3.79
Arab (76)	94	0.65
Arab (51)	60	0.42
Syrian (25)	34	0.24
Austrian (10)	57	0.40
Belgian (24)	56	0.39
British (22)	44	0.31
Canadian (27)	93	0.64
Croatian (0)	10	0.07
Czech (19)	60	0.42
Czechoslovakian (0)	16	0.11
Danish (12)	75	0.52
Dutch (67)	284	1.97
English (425)	1,674	11.61
European (35)	45	0.31
Finnish (0)	61	0.42
French, ex. Basque (135)	1,051	7.29
French Canadian (21)	61	0.42
German (2,185)	6,099	42.30
Greek (6)	107	0.74
Hungarian (97)	468	3.25
Irish (380)	2,336	16.20
Italian (206)	757	5.25
Latvian (0)	13	0.09
Lithuanian (0)	17	0.12
Luxemburger (0)	10	0.07
Norwegian (10)	63	0.44
Polish (889)	1,770	12.28
Romanian (0)	69	0.48
Russian (15)	87	0.60
Scandinavian (0)	12	0.08
Scotch-Irish (50)	151	1.05
Scottish (47)	356	2.47
Serbian (26)	26	0.18
Slavic (9)	34	0.24
Slovak (23)	62	0.43
Swedish (40)	172	1.19
Swiss (0)	22	0.15
Ukrainian (10)	10	0.07
Welsh (21)	115	0.80
West Indian, ex. Hispanic (17)	26	0.18
Dutch West Indian (9)	18	0.12
Jamaican (8)	8	0.06

Hispanic Origin	Population	%
Hispanic or Latino (of any race)	481	3.37
Central American, ex. Mexican	20	0.14
Guatemalan	6	0.04
Nicaraguan	7	0.05
Panamanian	7	0.05
Cuban	8	0.06
Dominican Republic	2	0.01
Mexican	388	2.72
Puerto Rican	18	0.13
South American	10	0.07
Colombian	1	0.01
Ecuadorian	1	0.01
Paraguayan	2	0.01
Venezuelan	6	0.04
Other Hispanic or Latino	35	0.24

Race*	Population	%
African-American/Black (255)	346	2.42
Not Hispanic (245)	329	2.30
Hispanic (10)	17	0.12
American Indian/Alaska Native (23)	74	0.52
Not Hispanic (22)	72	0.50
Hispanic (1)	2	0.01
Apache (0)	4	0.03
Blackfeet (2)	4	0.03
Cherokee (3)	11	0.08
Chippewa (4)	6	0.04
Mexican American Ind. (1)	1	0.01
Ottawa (0)	1	0.01
Potawatomi (1)	1	0.01
Sioux (0)	3	0.02
South American Ind. (0)	1	0.01
Asian (132)	183	1.28
Not Hispanic (129)	176	1.23
Hispanic (3)	7	0.05
Bangladeshi (2)	2	0.01
Cambodian (10)	10	0.07
Chinese, ex. Taiwanese (32)	42	0.29
Filipino (10)	20	0.14
Indian (37)	38	0.27
Japanese (9)	13	0.09
Korean (8)	23	0.16
Laotian (6)	6	0.04
Pakistani (3)	5	0.03
Thai (0)	4	0.03
Vietnamese (11)	23	0.16

*Notes: † The Census 2010 population figure is used to calculate the percentages in the Hispanic Origin and Race categories. Ancestry percentages are based on the 2006-2010 American Community Survey population (not shown); ‡ Numbers in parentheses indicate the number of people reporting a single ancestry; * Numbers in parentheses indicate the number of persons reporting this race alone, not in combination with any other race; Please refer to the Explanation of Data for more information.*

Hawaii Native/Pacific Islander (0)	1	0.01
Not Hispanic (0)	1	0.01
White (13,532)	13,767	96.37
Not Hispanic (13,223)	13,389	93.72
Hispanic (309)	378	2.65

Mayfield Heights

Place Type: City
County: Cuyahoga
Population: 19,155†

Ancestry‡	Population	%
African, Sub-Saharan (31)	47	0.25
African (23)	23	0.12
Nigerian (0)	16	0.08
Sudanese (8)	8	0.04
Albanian (17)	17	0.09
American (532)	532	2.78
Arab (514)	529	2.77
Arab (101)	101	0.53
Lebanese (393)	401	2.10
Syrian (9)	16	0.08
Other Arab (11)	11	0.06
Armenian (16)	16	0.08
Austrian (22)	161	0.84
Belgian (10)	10	0.05
British (0)	44	0.23
Bulgarian (0)	31	0.16
Canadian (0)	92	0.48
Croatian (55)	106	0.55
Czech (76)	228	1.19
Czechoslovakian (40)	98	0.51
Danish (19)	19	0.10
Dutch (32)	135	0.71
Eastern European (98)	98	0.51
English (196)	1,387	7.26
European (118)	118	0.62
French, ex. Basque (21)	329	1.72
German (660)	2,852	14.92
Greek (77)	169	0.88
Hungarian (344)	939	4.91
Iranian (0)	27	0.14
Irish (594)	2,310	12.09
Israeli (13)	13	0.07
Italian (2,543)	4,365	22.84
Latvian (21)	31	0.16
Lithuanian (16)	27	0.14
Northern European (11)	11	0.06
Norwegian (0)	27	0.14
Pennsylvania German (0)	26	0.14
Polish (423)	1,173	6.14
Portuguese (24)	70	0.37
Romanian (9)	87	0.46
Russian (866)	1,185	6.20
Scotch-Irish (28)	139	0.73
Scottish (78)	257	1.34
Serbian (12)	43	0.23
Slavic (0)	14	0.07
Slovak (228)	529	2.77
Slovene (177)	455	2.38
Swedish (23)	133	0.70
Swiss (63)	150	0.78
Turkish (31)	31	0.16
Ukrainian (609)	649	3.40
Welsh (0)	220	1.15
West Indian, ex. Hispanic (13)	13	0.07
Jamaican (13)	13	0.07
Yugoslavian (28)	28	0.15

Hispanic Origin	Population	%
Hispanic or Latino (of any race)	391	2.04
Central American, ex. Mexican	37	0.19
Guatemalan	17	0.09
Panamanian	2	0.01
Salvadoran	18	0.09
Cuban	16	0.08
Dominican Republic	5	0.03
Mexican	148	0.77
Puerto Rican	63	0.33
South American	61	0.32
Argentinean	13	0.07
Chilean	2	0.01
Colombian	9	0.05
Ecuadorian	1	0.01
Paraguayan	2	0.01
Peruvian	15	0.08
Uruguayan	15	0.08
Venezuelan	4	0.02
Other Hispanic or Latino	61	0.32

Race*	Population	%
African-American/Black (1,979)	2,133	11.14
Not Hispanic (1,958)	2,100	10.96
Hispanic (21)	33	0.17
American Indian/Alaska Native (19)	75	0.39
Not Hispanic (15)	63	0.33
Hispanic (4)	12	0.06
Blackfeet (0)	4	0.02
Cherokee (4)	15	0.08
Lumbee (1)	1	0.01
Mexican American Ind. (0)	1	0.01
Navajo (0)	2	0.01
Seminole (1)	1	0.01
Sioux (1)	1	0.01
Yaqui (0)	1	0.01
Asian (1,340)	1,469	7.67
Not Hispanic (1,331)	1,452	7.58
Hispanic (9)	17	0.09
Bangladeshi (9)	9	0.05
Chinese, ex. Taiwanese (288)	300	1.57
Filipino (59)	82	0.43
Indian (797)	836	4.36
Indonesian (6)	8	0.04
Japanese (54)	74	0.39
Korean (61)	77	0.40
Laotian (2)	4	0.02
Malaysian (2)	2	0.01
Nepalese (3)	3	0.02
Pakistani (15)	18	0.09
Sri Lankan (0)	4	0.02
Taiwanese (4)	6	0.03
Thai (0)	2	0.01
Vietnamese (12)	12	0.06
Hawaii Native/Pacific Islander (2)	20	0.10
Not Hispanic (2)	19	0.10
Hispanic (0)	1	0.01
Guamanian/Chamorro (0)	1	0.01
Native Hawaiian (1)	9	0.05
White (15,397)	15,662	81.76
Not Hispanic (15,141)	15,381	80.30
Hispanic (256)	281	1.47

Medina

Place Type: City
County: Medina
Population: 26,678†

Ancestry‡	Population	%
African, Sub-Saharan (38)	38	0.14
African (25)	25	0.09
Senegalese (13)	13	0.05
American (1,662)	1,662	6.23
Arab (30)	173	0.65
Arab (0)	18	0.07
Egyptian (10)	31	0.12
Jordanian (9)	9	0.03
Lebanese (0)	71	0.27
Syrian (11)	44	0.17
Austrian (27)	78	0.29
Belgian (0)	15	0.06
British (45)	81	0.30
Canadian (25)	25	0.09
Croatian (31)	94	0.35
Czech (74)	576	2.16
Czechoslovakian (27)	89	0.33
Danish (20)	75	0.28
Dutch (97)	475	1.78
Eastern European (7)	7	0.03
English (902)	3,526	13.23
European (218)	218	0.82
Finnish (6)	98	0.37
French, ex. Basque (119)	1,028	3.86
French Canadian (15)	184	0.69
German (2,321)	9,474	35.54
Greek (44)	177	0.66
Hungarian (378)	1,176	4.41
Iranian (12)	12	0.05
Irish (757)	4,905	18.40
Italian (625)	3,266	12.25
Lithuanian (19)	43	0.16
Macedonian (8)	27	0.10
Northern European (0)	14	0.05
Norwegian (26)	295	1.11
Pennsylvania German (23)	60	0.23
Polish (667)	2,571	9.64
Portuguese (148)	214	0.80
Romanian (10)	79	0.30
Russian (32)	162	0.61
Scandinavian (0)	25	0.09
Scotch-Irish (221)	401	1.50
Scottish (90)	591	2.22
Serbian (11)	79	0.30
Slavic (12)	12	0.05
Slovak (306)	873	3.27
Slovene (0)	163	0.61
Swedish (30)	106	0.40
Swiss (35)	158	0.59
Turkish (63)	199	0.75
Ukrainian (103)	329	1.23
Welsh (75)	315	1.18
Yugoslavian (75)	278	1.04

Hispanic Origin	Population	%
Hispanic or Latino (of any race)	480	1.80
Central American, ex. Mexican	47	0.18
Guatemalan	15	0.06
Honduran	4	0.01
Nicaraguan	6	0.02
Panamanian	12	0.04
Salvadoran	10	0.04
Cuban	16	0.06
Dominican Republic	5	0.02
Mexican	160	0.60
Puerto Rican	170	0.64
South American	36	0.13
Argentinean	5	0.02
Chilean	1	<0.01
Colombian	11	0.04
Ecuadorian	3	0.01
Paraguayan	2	0.01
Peruvian	14	0.05
Other Hispanic or Latino	46	0.17

Race*	Population	%
African-American/Black (837)	1,173	4.40
Not Hispanic (815)	1,130	4.24
Hispanic (22)	43	0.16
American Indian/Alaska Native (23)	147	0.55
Not Hispanic (18)	135	0.51
Hispanic (5)	12	0.04
Apache (1)	5	0.02
Blackfeet (0)	9	0.03
Central American Ind. (0)	3	0.01
Cherokee (8)	57	0.21
Cheyenne (0)	1	<0.01
Chippewa (1)	5	0.02
Choctaw (1)	3	0.01
Cree (0)	1	<0.01
Delaware (0)	1	<0.01
Lumbee (3)	3	0.01
Sioux (0)	4	0.01
Asian (241)	351	1.32
Not Hispanic (240)	346	1.30
Hispanic (1)	5	0.02
Chinese, ex. Taiwanese (44)	48	0.18
Filipino (34)	81	0.30
Hmong (7)	7	0.03
Indian (80)	99	0.37

*Notes: † The Census 2010 population figure is used to calculate the percentages in the Hispanic Origin and Race categories. Ancestry percentages are based on the 2006-2010 American Community Survey population (not shown); ‡ Numbers in parentheses indicate the number of people reporting a single ancestry; * Numbers in parentheses indicate the number of persons reporting this race alone, not in combination with any other race; Please refer to the Explanation of Data for more information.*

Japanese (20)	41	0.15
Korean (20)	32	0.12
Laotian (0)	1	<0.01
Pakistani (1)	2	0.01
Taiwanese (8)	8	0.03
Thai (3)	4	0.01
Vietnamese (13)	19	0.07
Hawaii Native/Pacific Islander (4)	11	0.04
Not Hispanic (4)	10	0.04
Hispanic (0)	1	<0.01
Native Hawaiian (0)	1	<0.01
Samoan (2)	2	0.01
White (24,888)	25,429	95.32
Not Hispanic (24,601)	25,092	94.06
Hispanic (287)	337	1.26

Mentor

Place Type: City
County: Lake
Population: 47,159†

Ancestry‡	Population	%
African, Sub-Saharan (15)	15	0.03
Somalian (15)	15	0.03
Albanian (0)	14	0.03
American (1,590)	1,590	3.34
Arab (137)	249	0.52
Lebanese (137)	249	0.52
Armenian (0)	13	0.03
Australian (0)	15	0.03
Austrian (49)	123	0.26
Belgian (21)	36	0.08
British (79)	102	0.21
Canadian (18)	39	0.08
Carpatho Rusyn (11)	11	0.02
Celtic (15)	15	0.03
Croatian (944)	1,797	3.77
Czech (146)	672	1.41
Czechoslovakian (33)	97	0.20
Danish (0)	39	0.08
Dutch (64)	791	1.66
Eastern European (41)	41	0.09
English (1,236)	6,049	12.70
Estonian (17)	17	0.04
European (521)	586	1.23
Finnish (85)	280	0.59
French, ex. Basque (40)	936	1.96
French Canadian (29)	326	0.68
German (3,396)	13,848	29.07
Greek (57)	112	0.24
Hungarian (1,179)	2,998	6.29
Irish (2,034)	9,297	19.52
Italian (2,813)	8,526	17.90
Lithuanian (68)	497	1.04
Luxemburger (22)	44	0.09
Norwegian (30)	110	0.23
Pennsylvania German (52)	76	0.16
Polish (1,427)	4,015	8.43
Portuguese (32)	184	0.39
Romanian (80)	158	0.33
Russian (114)	700	1.47
Scandinavian (27)	37	0.08
Scotch-Irish (329)	790	1.66
Scottish (225)	1,464	3.07
Serbian (21)	34	0.07
Slavic (74)	112	0.24
Slovak (412)	1,279	2.68
Slovene (1,066)	3,037	6.38
Swedish (92)	446	0.94
Swiss (0)	84	0.18
Ukrainian (37)	258	0.54
Welsh (132)	480	1.01
Yugoslavian (185)	241	0.51

Hispanic Origin	Population	%
Hispanic or Latino (of any race)	624	1.32
Central American, ex. Mexican	44	0.09
Costa Rican	1	<0.01
Guatemalan	13	0.03
Honduran	14	0.03
Nicaraguan	1	<0.01
Panamanian	4	0.01
Salvadoran	11	0.02
Cuban	28	0.06
Dominican Republic	9	0.02
Mexican	181	0.38
Puerto Rican	161	0.34
South American	85	0.18
Argentinean	7	0.01
Chilean	13	0.03
Colombian	14	0.03
Peruvian	33	0.07
Uruguayan	1	<0.01
Venezuelan	16	0.03
Other South American	1	<0.01
Other Hispanic or Latino	116	0.25

Race*	Population	%
African-American/Black (454)	639	1.35
Not Hispanic (443)	612	1.30
Hispanic (11)	27	0.06
American Indian/Alaska Native (37)	121	0.26
Not Hispanic (34)	108	0.23
Hispanic (3)	13	0.03
Apache (2)	6	0.01
Blackfeet (1)	5	0.01
Canadian/French Am. Ind. (1)	1	<0.01
Central American Ind. (1)	1	<0.01
Cherokee (13)	32	0.07
Chickasaw (0)	1	<0.01
Chippewa (1)	3	0.01
Choctaw (0)	1	<0.01
Creek (0)	1	<0.01
Inupiat *(Alaska Native)* (0)	2	<0.01
Mexican American Ind. (1)	5	0.01
Navajo (1)	4	0.01
Potawatomi (0)	3	0.01
Sioux (2)	3	0.01
Asian (646)	803	1.70
Not Hispanic (637)	783	1.66
Hispanic (9)	20	0.04
Chinese, ex. Taiwanese (166)	193	0.41
Filipino (59)	104	0.22
Indian (225)	248	0.53
Indonesian (1)	1	<0.01
Japanese (29)	60	0.13
Korean (63)	86	0.18
Laotian (5)	5	0.01
Nepalese (1)	2	<0.01
Pakistani (4)	4	0.01
Taiwanese (5)	6	0.01
Thai (4)	7	0.01
Vietnamese (70)	75	0.16
Hawaii Native/Pacific Islander (6)	32	0.07
Not Hispanic (4)	25	0.05
Hispanic (2)	7	0.01
Fijian (0)	1	<0.01
Guamanian/Chamorro (2)	3	0.01
Native Hawaiian (0)	10	0.02
Samoan (1)	6	0.01
White (45,404)	45,859	97.24
Not Hispanic (44,984)	45,377	96.22
Hispanic (420)	482	1.02

Miamisburg

Place Type: City
County: Montgomery
Population: 20,181†

Ancestry‡	Population	%
African, Sub-Saharan (13)	13	0.07
African (13)	13	0.07
American (2,092)	2,092	10.47
Arab (207)	317	1.59
Arab (74)	74	0.37
Iraqi (14)	14	0.07
Jordanian (15)	105	0.53
Lebanese (0)	20	0.10
Palestinian (104)	104	0.52
Australian (0)	15	0.08
Austrian (31)	99	0.50
Belgian (0)	18	0.09
British (49)	62	0.31
Canadian (0)	17	0.09
Czech (4)	32	0.16
Czechoslovakian (15)	15	0.08
Danish (0)	58	0.29
Dutch (127)	649	3.25
English (1,061)	2,380	11.91
European (104)	170	0.85
French, ex. Basque (122)	494	2.47
French Canadian (57)	70	0.35
German (2,501)	6,349	31.77
Hungarian (3)	47	0.24
Icelander (0)	43	0.22
Irish (933)	3,342	16.72
Italian (251)	677	3.39
Lithuanian (23)	23	0.12
Norwegian (33)	81	0.41
Polish (147)	396	1.98
Romanian (11)	11	0.06
Russian (0)	114	0.57
Scandinavian (0)	15	0.08
Scotch-Irish (108)	261	1.31
Scottish (303)	689	3.45
Slavic (0)	14	0.07
Slovak (0)	37	0.19
Swedish (0)	31	0.16
Swiss (0)	15	0.08
Ukrainian (9)	9	0.05
Welsh (14)	264	1.32
West Indian, ex. Hispanic (12)	12	0.06
West Indian (12)	12	0.06
Yugoslavian (24)	35	0.18

Hispanic Origin	Population	%
Hispanic or Latino (of any race)	327	1.62
Central American, ex. Mexican	44	0.22
Costa Rican	1	<0.01
Guatemalan	10	0.05
Honduran	12	0.06
Nicaraguan	8	0.04
Panamanian	4	0.02
Salvadoran	6	0.03
Other Central American	3	0.01
Cuban	6	0.03
Dominican Republic	4	0.02
Mexican	159	0.79
Puerto Rican	46	0.23
South American	27	0.13
Bolivian	5	0.02
Chilean	3	0.01
Colombian	3	0.01
Ecuadorian	13	0.06
Paraguayan	1	<0.01
Peruvian	2	0.01
Other Hispanic or Latino	41	0.20

Race*	Population	%
African-American/Black (615)	767	3.80
Not Hispanic (606)	744	3.69
Hispanic (9)	23	0.11
American Indian/Alaska Native (35)	97	0.48
Not Hispanic (33)	89	0.44
Hispanic (2)	8	0.04
Blackfeet (0)	3	0.01
Canadian/French Am. Ind. (2)	2	0.01
Cherokee (8)	27	0.13
Chickasaw (0)	1	<0.01
Choctaw (2)	2	0.01
Comanche (4)	4	0.02
Inupiat *(Alaska Native)* (0)	1	<0.01
Mexican American Ind. (0)	5	0.02
Navajo (7)	11	0.05
Sioux (3)	3	0.01
Asian (206)	309	1.53
Not Hispanic (205)	297	1.47
Hispanic (1)	12	0.06

*Notes: † The Census 2010 population figure is used to calculate the percentages in the Hispanic Origin and Race categories. Ancestry percentages are based on the 2006-2010 American Community Survey population (not shown); ‡ Numbers in parentheses indicate the number of people reporting a single ancestry; * Numbers in parentheses indicate the number of persons reporting this race alone, not in combination with any other race; Please refer to the Explanation of Data for more information.*

Chinese, ex. Taiwanese (32)	45	0.22
Filipino (26)	57	0.28
Indian (65)	68	0.34
Indonesian (4)	4	0.02
Japanese (15)	26	0.13
Korean (21)	35	0.17
Laotian (4)	12	0.06
Malaysian (2)	2	0.01
Sri Lankan (2)	4	0.02
Taiwanese (4)	4	0.02
Thai (2)	9	0.04
Vietnamese (24)	32	0.16
Hawaii Native/Pacific Islander (2)	6	0.03
Not Hispanic (0)	4	0.02
Hispanic (2)	2	0.01
Guamanian/Chamorro (2)	2	0.01
Native Hawaiian (0)	3	0.01
White (18,939)	19,231	95.29
Not Hispanic (18,705)	18,976	94.03
Hispanic (234)	255	1.26

Middleburg Heights

Place Type: City
County: Cuyahoga
Population: 15,946†

Ancestry‡	Population	%
American (443)	443	2.80
Arab (464)	596	3.77
Arab (41)	53	0.34
Lebanese (371)	479	3.03
Palestinian (52)	52	0.33
Syrian (0)	12	0.08
Armenian (9)	40	0.25
Austrian (57)	86	0.54
Belgian (0)	5	0.03
British (26)	49	0.31
Canadian (6)	9	0.06
Croatian (67)	84	0.53
Czech (103)	335	2.12
Czechoslovakian (18)	69	0.44
Danish (0)	10	0.06
Dutch (63)	198	1.25
Eastern European (43)	43	0.27
English (367)	1,285	8.13
European (66)	66	0.42
Finnish (0)	36	0.23
French, ex. Basque (20)	290	1.84
French Canadian (0)	34	0.22
German (1,183)	4,071	25.77
Greek (120)	188	1.19
Guyanese (33)	33	0.21
Hungarian (288)	730	4.62
Irish (340)	2,531	16.02
Italian (820)	2,309	14.62
Latvian (39)	94	0.60
Lithuanian (35)	61	0.39
Macedonian (0)	8	0.05
Norwegian (0)	16	0.10
Pennsylvania German (0)	42	0.27
Polish (847)	2,266	14.34
Romanian (122)	195	1.23
Russian (76)	284	1.80
Scandinavian (11)	11	0.07
Scotch-Irish (16)	278	1.76
Scottish (57)	314	1.99
Serbian (59)	138	0.87
Slovak (503)	971	6.15
Slovene (56)	296	1.87
Swedish (0)	105	0.66
Swiss (45)	64	0.41
Turkish (24)	24	0.15
Ukrainian (218)	517	3.27
Welsh (41)	143	0.91
West Indian, ex. Hispanic (0)	18	0.11
Haitian (0)	18	0.11
Yugoslavian (23)	23	0.15

Hispanic Origin	Population	%
Hispanic or Latino (of any race)	356	2.23
Central American, ex. Mexican	23	0.14
Costa Rican	1	0.01
Guatemalan	5	0.03
Honduran	7	0.04
Nicaraguan	3	0.02
Panamanian	1	0.01
Salvadoran	2	0.01
Other Central American	4	0.03
Cuban	7	0.04
Dominican Republic	1	0.01
Mexican	87	0.55
Puerto Rican	197	1.24
South American	22	0.14
Argentinean	3	0.02
Bolivian	2	0.01
Chilean	1	0.01
Colombian	5	0.03
Ecuadorian	2	0.01
Peruvian	8	0.05
Venezuelan	1	0.01
Other Hispanic or Latino	19	0.12

Race*	Population	%
African-American/Black (253)	289	1.81
Not Hispanic (249)	282	1.77
Hispanic (4)	7	0.04
American Indian/Alaska Native (27)	54	0.34
Not Hispanic (25)	51	0.32
Hispanic (2)	3	0.02
Blackfeet (0)	2	0.01
Cherokee (9)	16	0.10
Choctaw (1)	4	0.03
Hopi (0)	1	0.01
Inupiat *(Alaska Native)* (1)	1	0.01
Iroquois (0)	3	0.02
Asian (887)	958	6.01
Not Hispanic (882)	949	5.95
Hispanic (5)	9	0.06
Burmese (1)	1	0.01
Cambodian (16)	17	0.11
Chinese, ex. Taiwanese (70)	77	0.48
Filipino (61)	72	0.45
Indian (662)	676	4.24
Indonesian (0)	2	0.01
Japanese (9)	10	0.06
Korean (13)	16	0.10
Pakistani (16)	19	0.12
Thai (1)	1	0.01
Vietnamese (32)	34	0.21
Hawaii Native/Pacific Islander (4)	12	0.08
Not Hispanic (4)	12	0.08
Native Hawaiian (3)	3	0.02
Tongan (1)	3	0.02
White (14,528)	14,651	91.88
Not Hispanic (14,287)	14,398	90.29
Hispanic (241)	253	1.59

Middletown

Place Type: City
County: Butler
Population: 48,694†

Ancestry‡	Population	%
African, Sub-Saharan (24)	50	0.10
African (24)	50	0.10
American (5,061)	5,061	10.34
Arab (90)	90	0.18
Arab (66)	66	0.13
Syrian (24)	24	0.05
Austrian (0)	17	0.03
Belgian (11)	49	0.10
British (83)	152	0.31
Canadian (19)	46	0.09
Celtic (0)	27	0.06
Croatian (28)	80	0.16
Czech (64)	214	0.44
Czechoslovakian (33)	33	0.07
Danish (0)	10	0.02
Dutch (131)	1,001	2.05
English (2,060)	4,682	9.57
European (425)	499	1.02
Finnish (0)	23	0.05
French, ex. Basque (134)	768	1.57
French Canadian (121)	147	0.30
German (3,688)	9,559	19.53
Greek (133)	251	0.51
Hungarian (66)	196	0.40
Iranian (0)	28	0.06
Irish (2,151)	7,332	14.98
Italian (645)	1,622	3.31
Lithuanian (66)	142	0.29
Northern European (12)	12	0.02
Norwegian (114)	215	0.44
Pennsylvania German (11)	21	0.04
Polish (176)	539	1.10
Romanian (0)	47	0.10
Russian (92)	188	0.38
Scandinavian (14)	14	0.03
Scotch-Irish (252)	559	1.14
Scottish (223)	912	1.86
Slavic (8)	8	0.02
Slovak (34)	62	0.13
Slovene (15)	15	0.03
Swedish (81)	174	0.36
Swiss (0)	29	0.06
Turkish (22)	75	0.15
Ukrainian (11)	31	0.06
Welsh (107)	336	0.69
West Indian, ex. Hispanic (44)	68	0.14
Barbadian (22)	36	0.07
Dutch West Indian (0)	10	0.02
Trinidadian/Tobagonian (22)	22	0.04
Yugoslavian (0)	8	0.02

Hispanic Origin	Population	%
Hispanic or Latino (of any race)	1,838	3.77
Central American, ex. Mexican	176	0.36
Costa Rican	5	0.01
Guatemalan	28	0.06
Honduran	30	0.06
Nicaraguan	18	0.04
Panamanian	47	0.10
Salvadoran	48	0.10
Cuban	73	0.15
Dominican Republic	182	0.37
Mexican	892	1.83
Puerto Rican	316	0.65
South American	49	0.10
Argentinean	3	0.01
Chilean	1	<0.01
Colombian	22	0.05
Ecuadorian	9	0.02
Peruvian	9	0.02
Venezuelan	5	0.01
Other Hispanic or Latino	150	0.31

Race*	Population	%
African-American/Black (5,691)	6,655	13.67
Not Hispanic (5,556)	6,469	13.29
Hispanic (135)	186	0.38
American Indian/Alaska Native (105)	337	0.69
Not Hispanic (97)	319	0.66
Hispanic (8)	18	0.04
Apache (1)	5	0.01
Blackfeet (1)	17	0.03
Central American Ind. (1)	1	<0.01
Cherokee (31)	112	0.23
Chippewa (5)	7	0.01
Choctaw (3)	4	0.01
Comanche (1)	2	<0.01
Cree (0)	1	<0.01
Crow (1)	3	0.01
Delaware (0)	1	<0.01
Houma (0)	1	<0.01
Inupiat *(Alaska Native)* (1)	1	<0.01
Iroquois (5)	9	0.02
Kiowa (0)	1	<0.01

*Notes: † The Census 2010 population figure is used to calculate the percentages in the Hispanic Origin and Race categories. Ancestry percentages are based on the 2006-2010 American Community Survey population (not shown); ‡ Numbers in parentheses indicate the number of people reporting a single ancestry; * Numbers in parentheses indicate the number of persons reporting this race alone, not in combination with any other race; Please refer to the Explanation of Data for more information.*

Lumbee (4)	4	0.01
Mexican American Ind. (0)	2	<0.01
Navajo (0)	3	0.01
Osage (0)	1	<0.01
Pueblo (1)	1	<0.01
Seminole (1)	5	0.01
Sioux (6)	14	0.03
South American Ind. (1)	1	<0.01
Spanish American Ind. (3)	3	0.01
Asian (232)	360	0.74
Not Hispanic (228)	352	0.72
Hispanic (4)	8	0.02
Bangladeshi (7)	10	0.02
Burmese (3)	3	0.01
Cambodian (9)	9	0.02
Chinese, ex. Taiwanese (26)	34	0.07
Filipino (59)	91	0.19
Indian (38)	70	0.14
Indonesian (2)	3	0.01
Japanese (11)	21	0.04
Korean (21)	45	0.09
Laotian (2)	3	0.01
Malaysian (1)	2	<0.01
Nepalese (1)	1	<0.01
Pakistani (2)	8	0.02
Sri Lankan (6)	6	0.01
Taiwanese (1)	1	<0.01
Thai (4)	6	0.01
Vietnamese (7)	13	0.03
Hawaii Native/Pacific Islander (23)	56	0.12
Not Hispanic (20)	50	0.10
Hispanic (3)	6	0.01
Fijian (1)	3	0.01
Guamanian/Chamorro (4)	9	0.02
Native Hawaiian (11)	15	0.03
Samoan (1)	5	0.01
White (40,545)	41,760	85.76
Not Hispanic (39,678)	40,788	83.76
Hispanic (867)	972	2.00

Monfort Heights

Place Type: CDP
County: Hamilton
Population: 11,948†

Ancestry‡	Population	%
African, Sub-Saharan (160)	204	1.77
African (160)	168	1.46
South African (0)	36	0.31
Alsatian (9)	9	0.08
American (618)	618	5.35
Belgian (0)	13	0.11
British (0)	11	0.10
Canadian (33)	66	0.57
Celtic (0)	19	0.16
Czech (0)	42	0.36
Danish (0)	5	0.04
Dutch (12)	272	2.36
English (246)	1,049	9.09
European (40)	40	0.35
French, ex. Basque (79)	446	3.86
German (3,394)	6,127	53.08
Greek (10)	10	0.09
Hungarian (21)	127	1.10
Icelander (0)	35	0.30
Irish (506)	2,320	20.10
Italian (315)	881	7.63
Lithuanian (11)	24	0.21
Macedonian (21)	21	0.18
Polish (36)	99	0.86
Romanian (0)	37	0.32
Russian (0)	46	0.40
Scandinavian (13)	13	0.11
Scotch-Irish (90)	205	1.78
Scottish (10)	72	0.62
Slavic (7)	20	0.17
Slovak (11)	11	0.10
Swedish (0)	36	0.31
Swiss (0)	12	0.10
Ukrainian (9)	13	0.11
Welsh (41)	86	0.75

Hispanic Origin	Population	%
Hispanic or Latino (of any race)	106	0.89
Central American, ex. Mexican	6	0.05
Guatemalan	2	0.02
Honduran	3	0.03
Panamanian	1	0.01
Cuban	4	0.03
Dominican Republic	5	0.04
Mexican	71	0.59
Puerto Rican	14	0.12
South American	2	0.02
Argentinean	2	0.02
Other Hispanic or Latino	4	0.03

Race*	Population	%
African-American/Black (787)	870	7.28
Not Hispanic (784)	864	7.23
Hispanic (3)	6	0.05
American Indian/Alaska Native (11)	47	0.39
Not Hispanic (10)	46	0.39
Hispanic (1)	1	0.01
Blackfeet (0)	1	0.01
Cherokee (2)	21	0.18
Choctaw (0)	1	0.01
Iroquois (1)	2	0.02
Menominee (1)	1	0.01
Mexican American Ind. (1)	1	0.01
Osage (2)	2	0.02
Asian (155)	225	1.88
Not Hispanic (155)	224	1.87
Hispanic (0)	1	0.01
Bhutanese (6)	6	0.05
Cambodian (5)	5	0.04
Chinese, ex. Taiwanese (16)	28	0.23
Filipino (29)	56	0.47
Indian (41)	51	0.43
Indonesian (1)	1	0.01
Japanese (10)	26	0.22
Korean (5)	7	0.06
Nepalese (4)	4	0.03
Pakistani (6)	6	0.05
Sri Lankan (3)	3	0.03
Thai (6)	7	0.06
Vietnamese (10)	16	0.13
Hawaii Native/Pacific Islander (2)	5	0.04
Not Hispanic (1)	4	0.03
Hispanic (1)	1	0.01
Guamanian/Chamorro (0)	1	0.01
Native Hawaiian (1)	1	0.01
White (10,761)	10,933	91.50
Not Hispanic (10,694)	10,861	90.90
Hispanic (67)	72	0.60

Monroe

Place Type: City
County: Butler
Population: 12,442†

Ancestry‡	Population	%
African, Sub-Saharan (8)	8	0.07
African (8)	8	0.07
American (1,395)	1,395	11.75
Austrian (0)	10	0.08
Belgian (7)	28	0.24
British (17)	24	0.20
Canadian (12)	12	0.10
Dutch (10)	135	1.14
English (611)	1,343	11.32
European (155)	155	1.31
French, ex. Basque (0)	237	2.00
French Canadian (27)	59	0.50
German (1,822)	3,562	30.01
Greek (0)	38	0.32
Hungarian (10)	39	0.33
Irish (511)	1,685	14.20
Italian (169)	616	5.19
Norwegian (18)	45	0.38
Polish (28)	61	0.51
Russian (11)	27	0.23
Scotch-Irish (39)	150	1.26
Scottish (244)	442	3.72
Slovak (45)	148	1.25
Swedish (27)	133	1.12
Swiss (14)	59	0.50
Welsh (25)	25	0.21
Yugoslavian (21)	21	0.18

Hispanic Origin	Population	%
Hispanic or Latino (of any race)	224	1.80
Central American, ex. Mexican	23	0.18
Costa Rican	2	0.02
Guatemalan	2	0.02
Honduran	10	0.08
Panamanian	8	0.06
Salvadoran	1	0.01
Cuban	3	0.02
Dominican Republic	3	0.02
Mexican	110	0.88
Puerto Rican	44	0.35
South American	17	0.14
Bolivian	1	0.01
Colombian	6	0.05
Peruvian	8	0.06
Venezuelan	2	0.02
Other Hispanic or Latino	24	0.19

Race*	Population	%
African-American/Black (455)	537	4.32
Not Hispanic (453)	529	4.25
Hispanic (2)	8	0.06
American Indian/Alaska Native (20)	49	0.39
Not Hispanic (18)	46	0.37
Hispanic (2)	3	0.02
Blackfeet (0)	1	0.01
Cherokee (10)	18	0.14
Chippewa (1)	1	0.01
Iroquois (3)	3	0.02
Mexican American Ind. (2)	2	0.02
Sioux (0)	1	0.01
Asian (208)	252	2.03
Not Hispanic (207)	249	2.00
Hispanic (1)	3	0.02
Cambodian (4)	5	0.04
Chinese, ex. Taiwanese (33)	37	0.30
Filipino (27)	43	0.35
Indian (98)	105	0.84
Indonesian (1)	1	0.01
Japanese (2)	13	0.10
Korean (13)	22	0.18
Laotian (5)	5	0.04
Pakistani (1)	1	0.01
Vietnamese (13)	16	0.13
Hawaii Native/Pacific Islander (0)	2	0.02
Not Hispanic (0)	2	0.02
Native Hawaiian (0)	2	0.02
White (11,519)	11,668	93.78
Not Hispanic (11,392)	11,527	92.65
Hispanic (127)	141	1.13

Montgomery

Place Type: City
County: Hamilton
Population: 10,251†

Ancestry‡	Population	%
American (629)	629	6.20
Arab (17)	17	0.17
Egyptian (8)	8	0.08
Lebanese (9)	9	0.09
Australian (22)	22	0.22
Austrian (0)	35	0.34
Belgian (0)	9	0.09
British (125)	165	1.63
Canadian (34)	83	0.82
Croatian (11)	11	0.11

*Notes: † The Census 2010 population figure is used to calculate the percentages in the Hispanic Origin and Race categories. Ancestry percentages are based on the 2006-2010 American Community Survey population (not shown); ‡ Numbers in parentheses indicate the number of people reporting a single ancestry; * Numbers in parentheses indicate the number of persons reporting this race alone, not in combination with any other race; Please refer to the Explanation of Data for more information.*

Ancestry (cont.)	Population	%
Czech (11)	177	1.74
Czechoslovakian (0)	15	0.15
Danish (0)	26	0.26
Dutch (0)	206	2.03
Eastern European (53)	53	0.52
English (326)	1,184	11.67
European (249)	266	2.62
French, ex. Basque (60)	442	4.35
French Canadian (19)	19	0.19
German (1,172)	3,384	33.34
Greek (18)	69	0.68
Hungarian (73)	137	1.35
Iranian (29)	29	0.29
Irish (389)	2,095	20.64
Italian (199)	767	7.56
Latvian (0)	9	0.09
Lithuanian (6)	6	0.06
Norwegian (18)	73	0.72
Polish (122)	450	4.43
Portuguese (0)	17	0.17
Romanian (0)	7	0.07
Russian (85)	264	2.60
Scandinavian (15)	24	0.24
Scotch-Irish (36)	102	1.00
Scottish (104)	210	2.07
Serbian (10)	10	0.10
Slovak (7)	32	0.32
Slovene (11)	11	0.11
Swedish (32)	72	0.71
Swiss (28)	97	0.96
Ukrainian (34)	53	0.52
Welsh (19)	102	1.00
West Indian, ex. Hispanic (9)	9	0.09
Other West Indian (9)	9	0.09

Hispanic Origin	Population	%
Hispanic or Latino (of any race)	184	1.79
Central American, ex. Mexican	13	0.13
Costa Rican	2	0.02
Guatemalan	3	0.03
Nicaraguan	3	0.03
Panamanian	5	0.05
Cuban	21	0.20
Mexican	67	0.65
Puerto Rican	16	0.16
South American	46	0.45
Argentinean	3	0.03
Bolivian	2	0.02
Chilean	1	0.01
Colombian	26	0.25
Ecuadorian	6	0.06
Peruvian	6	0.06
Venezuelan	2	0.02
Other Hispanic or Latino	21	0.20

Race*	Population	%
African-American/Black (275)	322	3.14
Not Hispanic (275)	315	3.07
Hispanic (0)	7	0.07
American Indian/Alaska Native (7)	27	0.26
Not Hispanic (6)	23	0.22
Hispanic (1)	4	0.04
Arapaho (0)	3	0.03
Blackfeet (0)	3	0.03
Cherokee (2)	9	0.09
Creek (1)	1	0.01
Iroquois (0)	1	0.01
Potawatomi (1)	1	0.01
Asian (569)	654	6.38
Not Hispanic (569)	648	6.32
Hispanic (0)	6	0.06
Burmese (17)	17	0.17
Chinese, ex. Taiwanese (150)	182	1.78
Filipino (32)	53	0.52
Indian (176)	192	1.87
Indonesian (2)	5	0.05
Japanese (79)	92	0.90
Korean (65)	73	0.71
Malaysian (0)	4	0.04
Nepalese (8)	8	0.08
Pakistani (4)	4	0.04
Taiwanese (12)	12	0.12
Thai (2)	4	0.04
Vietnamese (5)	12	0.12
Hawaii Native/Pacific Islander (3)	7	0.07
Not Hispanic (3)	6	0.06
Hispanic (0)	1	0.01
Guamanian/Chamorro (2)	5	0.05
Native Hawaiian (1)	1	0.01
White (9,212)	9,345	91.16
Not Hispanic (9,077)	9,196	89.71
Hispanic (135)	149	1.45

Mount Vernon

Place Type: City
County: Knox
Population: 16,990†

Ancestry‡	Population	%
African, Sub-Saharan (16)	16	0.09
Nigerian (16)	16	0.09
American (1,500)	1,500	8.89
Arab (23)	23	0.14
Lebanese (11)	11	0.07
Other Arab (12)	12	0.07
Austrian (0)	36	0.21
Belgian (32)	79	0.47
British (29)	139	0.82
Canadian (8)	23	0.14
Celtic (14)	29	0.17
Croatian (12)	12	0.07
Czech (8)	20	0.12
Czechoslovakian (14)	22	0.13
Danish (0)	34	0.20
Dutch (72)	347	2.06
English (1,112)	2,411	14.30
Estonian (15)	15	0.09
European (504)	504	2.99
Finnish (0)	10	0.06
French, ex. Basque (83)	481	2.85
French Canadian (21)	81	0.48
German (1,898)	4,455	26.42
Greek (97)	106	0.63
Guyanese (39)	120	0.71
Hungarian (64)	177	1.05
Irish (746)	2,465	14.62
Italian (419)	893	5.30
Lithuanian (0)	15	0.09
Norwegian (40)	43	0.25
Pennsylvania German (0)	13	0.08
Polish (41)	236	1.40
Portuguese (0)	10	0.06
Russian (22)	55	0.33
Scandinavian (16)	16	0.09
Scotch-Irish (142)	355	2.11
Scottish (365)	747	4.43
Slovak (11)	16	0.09
Slovene (0)	11	0.07
Swedish (18)	118	0.70
Swiss (12)	89	0.53
Ukrainian (24)	33	0.20
Welsh (8)	205	1.22

Hispanic Origin	Population	%
Hispanic or Latino (of any race)	305	1.80
Central American, ex. Mexican	33	0.19
Guatemalan	7	0.04
Honduran	7	0.04
Nicaraguan	4	0.02
Panamanian	1	0.01
Salvadoran	14	0.08
Cuban	15	0.09
Dominican Republic	3	0.02
Mexican	148	0.87
Puerto Rican	33	0.19
South American	11	0.06
Argentinean	2	0.01
Colombian	7	0.04
Peruvian	1	0.01
Venezuelan	1	0.01
Other Hispanic or Latino	62	0.36

Race*	Population	%
African-American/Black (191)	331	1.95
Not Hispanic (186)	322	1.90
Hispanic (5)	9	0.05
American Indian/Alaska Native (35)	117	0.69
Not Hispanic (34)	113	0.67
Hispanic (1)	4	0.02
Apache (1)	2	0.01
Blackfeet (2)	2	0.01
Cherokee (12)	42	0.25
Chippewa (0)	3	0.02
Cree (0)	1	0.01
Iroquois (0)	5	0.03
Potawatomi (0)	1	0.01
Pueblo (1)	2	0.01
Sioux (2)	3	0.02
Asian (181)	213	1.25
Not Hispanic (180)	210	1.24
Hispanic (1)	3	0.02
Burmese (6)	6	0.04
Chinese, ex. Taiwanese (48)	57	0.34
Filipino (19)	26	0.15
Indian (64)	68	0.40
Indonesian (1)	5	0.03
Japanese (5)	5	0.03
Korean (20)	25	0.15
Pakistani (6)	6	0.04
Taiwanese (1)	1	0.01
Thai (4)	4	0.02
Vietnamese (5)	8	0.05
Hawaii Native/Pacific Islander (7)	17	0.10
Not Hispanic (7)	16	0.09
Hispanic (0)	1	0.01
Guamanian/Chamorro (0)	1	0.01
Native Hawaiian (7)	9	0.05
Samoan (0)	7	0.04
White (16,196)	16,453	96.84
Not Hispanic (16,024)	16,260	95.70
Hispanic (172)	193	1.14

Napoleon

Place Type: City
County: Henry
Population: 8,749†

Ancestry‡	Population	%
American (597)	597	7.02
Austrian (0)	48	0.56
Belgian (19)	32	0.38
British (22)	47	0.55
Canadian (0)	12	0.14
Czech (12)	22	0.26
Danish (0)	15	0.18
Dutch (57)	225	2.65
English (194)	711	8.36
European (20)	20	0.24
Finnish (0)	9	0.11
French, ex. Basque (87)	281	3.31
French Canadian (34)	61	0.72
German (2,471)	4,409	51.86
Greek (12)	43	0.51
Hungarian (35)	96	1.13
Irish (223)	796	9.36
Italian (67)	141	1.66
Lithuanian (0)	34	0.40
Norwegian (0)	62	0.73
Polish (209)	346	4.07
Russian (0)	23	0.27
Scandinavian (12)	12	0.14
Scotch-Irish (12)	89	1.05
Scottish (48)	146	1.72
Slovak (0)	49	0.58
Slovene (0)	25	0.29
Swedish (10)	66	0.78
Swiss (0)	197	2.32
Welsh (10)	70	0.82

*Notes: † The Census 2010 population figure is used to calculate the percentages in the Hispanic Origin and Race categories. Ancestry percentages are based on the 2006-2010 American Community Survey population (not shown); ‡ Numbers in parentheses indicate the number of people reporting a single ancestry; * Numbers in parentheses indicate the number of persons reporting this race alone, not in combination with any other race; Please refer to the Explanation of Data for more information.*

Hispanic Origin	Population	%
Hispanic or Latino (of any race)	698	7.98
Central American, ex. Mexican	41	0.47
Guatemalan	21	0.24
Honduran	3	0.03
Nicaraguan	14	0.16
Salvadoran	2	0.02
Other Central American	1	0.01
Mexican	527	6.02
Puerto Rican	18	0.21
South American	14	0.16
Argentinean	2	0.02
Bolivian	7	0.08
Peruvian	5	0.06
Other Hispanic or Latino	98	1.12

Race*	Population	%
African-American/Black (78)	119	1.36
Not Hispanic (68)	104	1.19
Hispanic (10)	15	0.17
American Indian/Alaska Native (35)	75	0.86
Not Hispanic (23)	50	0.57
Hispanic (12)	25	0.29
Blackfeet (0)	6	0.07
Cherokee (7)	14	0.16
Chickasaw (2)	8	0.09
Chippewa (1)	1	0.01
Choctaw (0)	6	0.07
Delaware (4)	4	0.05
Mexican American Ind. (3)	4	0.05
Navajo (1)	1	0.01
Potawatomi (0)	1	0.01
Puget Sound Salish (1)	1	0.01
Seminole (0)	1	0.01
Sioux (1)	2	0.02
Asian (34)	49	0.56
Not Hispanic (34)	46	0.53
Hispanic (0)	3	0.03
Cambodian (1)	1	0.01
Chinese, ex. Taiwanese (8)	9	0.10
Filipino (15)	21	0.24
Indian (0)	2	0.02
Japanese (2)	4	0.05
Korean (1)	5	0.06
Vietnamese (7)	7	0.08
Hawaii Native/Pacific Islander (0)	1	0.01
Not Hispanic (0)	1	0.01
Native Hawaiian (0)	1	0.01
White (8,201)	8,338	95.30
Not Hispanic (7,854)	7,922	90.55
Hispanic (347)	416	4.75

New Albany

Place Type: Village
County: Franklin
Population: 7,724†

Ancestry‡	Population	%
American (481)	481	6.77
Arab (77)	121	1.70
Egyptian (62)	62	0.87
Palestinian (15)	59	0.83
Austrian (14)	68	0.96
Belgian (0)	80	1.13
Brazilian (22)	22	0.31
British (31)	107	1.51
Croatian (11)	31	0.44
Czech (0)	13	0.18
Czechoslovakian (0)	18	0.25
Danish (0)	26	0.37
Dutch (5)	70	0.99
Eastern European (27)	27	0.38
English (287)	813	11.45
European (161)	167	2.35
French, ex. Basque (28)	293	4.13
French Canadian (0)	26	0.37
German (841)	2,262	31.85
Greek (85)	123	1.73
Hungarian (51)	125	1.76
Iranian (15)	46	0.65
Irish (317)	1,178	16.58
Italian (247)	642	9.04
Lithuanian (0)	43	0.61
Macedonian (44)	44	0.62
Norwegian (20)	83	1.17
Polish (37)	257	3.62
Romanian (0)	14	0.20
Russian (70)	205	2.89
Scandinavian (8)	64	0.90
Scotch-Irish (69)	154	2.17
Scottish (40)	145	2.04
Serbian (0)	18	0.25
Slavic (0)	12	0.17
Slovak (15)	44	0.62
Slovene (13)	132	1.86
Swedish (14)	202	2.84
Swiss (0)	68	0.96
Ukrainian (0)	29	0.41
Welsh (0)	80	1.13
Yugoslavian (0)	12	0.17

Hispanic Origin	Population	%
Hispanic or Latino (of any race)	153	1.98
Central American, ex. Mexican	15	0.19
Guatemalan	5	0.06
Nicaraguan	8	0.10
Salvadoran	2	0.03
Cuban	30	0.39
Dominican Republic	1	0.01
Mexican	57	0.74
Puerto Rican	11	0.14
South American	29	0.38
Argentinean	4	0.05
Chilean	4	0.05
Colombian	7	0.09
Ecuadorian	3	0.04
Peruvian	7	0.09
Uruguayan	2	0.03
Venezuelan	2	0.03
Other Hispanic or Latino	10	0.13

Race*	Population	%
African-American/Black (239)	285	3.69
Not Hispanic (238)	282	3.65
Hispanic (1)	3	0.04
American Indian/Alaska Native (6)	31	0.40
Not Hispanic (6)	26	0.34
Hispanic (0)	5	0.06
Cherokee (1)	7	0.09
Chippewa (1)	1	0.01
Choctaw (0)	4	0.05
Cree (0)	1	0.01
Mexican American Ind. (0)	3	0.04
Asian (500)	601	7.78
Not Hispanic (500)	595	7.70
Hispanic (0)	6	0.08
Cambodian (2)	4	0.05
Chinese, ex. Taiwanese (152)	173	2.24
Filipino (17)	38	0.49
Indian (229)	252	3.26
Indonesian (2)	2	0.03
Japanese (5)	17	0.22
Korean (45)	66	0.85
Laotian (1)	1	0.01
Pakistani (8)	9	0.12
Sri Lankan (0)	1	0.01
Taiwanese (4)	4	0.05
Thai (4)	7	0.09
Vietnamese (11)	13	0.17
Hawaii Native/Pacific Islander (8)	15	0.19
Not Hispanic (8)	15	0.19
Native Hawaiian (3)	3	0.04
Samoan (1)	8	0.10
White (6,777)	6,925	89.66
Not Hispanic (6,656)	6,791	87.92
Hispanic (121)	134	1.73

New Franklin

Place Type: City
County: Summit
Population: 14,227†

Ancestry‡	Population	%
American (1,203)	1,203	8.41
Arab (0)	59	0.41
Lebanese (0)	54	0.38
Syrian (0)	5	0.03
Australian (0)	12	0.08
Austrian (0)	9	0.06
British (35)	79	0.55
Canadian (9)	21	0.15
Croatian (58)	86	0.60
Czech (49)	211	1.47
Czechoslovakian (8)	17	0.12
Dutch (33)	172	1.20
Eastern European (8)	8	0.06
English (615)	2,067	14.45
Estonian (9)	9	0.06
European (148)	148	1.03
French, ex. Basque (102)	562	3.93
French Canadian (7)	42	0.29
German (1,256)	4,300	30.05
Greek (89)	140	0.98
Hungarian (301)	850	5.94
Irish (612)	2,563	17.91
Italian (448)	1,261	8.81
Lithuanian (26)	75	0.52
Norwegian (8)	8	0.06
Pennsylvania German (19)	68	0.48
Polish (84)	357	2.49
Romanian (47)	103	0.72
Russian (53)	198	1.38
Scotch-Irish (142)	314	2.19
Scottish (174)	424	2.96
Serbian (27)	40	0.28
Slavic (8)	8	0.06
Slovak (162)	352	2.46
Slovene (31)	108	0.75
Swedish (20)	183	1.28
Swiss (0)	53	0.37
Turkish (0)	8	0.06
Ukrainian (38)	78	0.55
Welsh (28)	271	1.89
West Indian, ex. Hispanic (0)	20	0.14
Jamaican (0)	20	0.14
Yugoslavian (48)	69	0.48

Hispanic Origin	Population	%
Hispanic or Latino (of any race)	118	0.83
Central American, ex. Mexican	5	0.04
Guatemalan	2	0.01
Panamanian	1	0.01
Salvadoran	2	0.01
Dominican Republic	1	0.01
Mexican	53	0.37
Puerto Rican	30	0.21
South American	8	0.06
Argentinean	1	0.01
Colombian	4	0.03
Uruguayan	3	0.02
Other Hispanic or Latino	21	0.15

Race*	Population	%
African-American/Black (82)	126	0.89
Not Hispanic (82)	123	0.86
Hispanic (0)	3	0.02
American Indian/Alaska Native (21)	91	0.64
Not Hispanic (21)	90	0.63
Hispanic (0)	1	0.01
Apache (0)	3	0.02
Blackfeet (3)	13	0.09
Canadian/French Am. Ind. (2)	3	0.02
Cherokee (3)	44	0.31
Cheyenne (0)	1	0.01
Chickasaw (1)	1	0.01
Choctaw (2)	3	0.02

*Notes: † The Census 2010 population figure is used to calculate the percentages in the Hispanic Origin and Race categories. Ancestry percentages are based on the 2006-2010 American Community Survey population (not shown); ‡ Numbers in parentheses indicate the number of people reporting a single ancestry; * Numbers in parentheses indicate the number of persons reporting this race alone, not in combination with any other race; Please refer to the Explanation of Data for more information.*

Cree (1)	1	0.01
Delaware (0)	1	0.01
Iroquois (0)	1	0.01
Lumbee (4)	4	0.03
Sioux (0)	2	0.01
Asian (57)	77	0.54
Not Hispanic (56)	76	0.53
Hispanic (1)	1	0.01
Chinese, ex. Taiwanese (9)	11	0.08
Filipino (6)	12	0.08
Hmong (12)	12	0.08
Indian (6)	10	0.07
Japanese (9)	14	0.10
Korean (11)	16	0.11
Vietnamese (3)	9	0.06
Hawaii Native/Pacific Islander (3)	5	0.04
Not Hispanic (1)	2	0.01
Hispanic (2)	3	0.02
Guamanian/Chamorro (0)	1	0.01
Native Hawaiian (3)	4	0.03
White (13,904)	14,036	98.66
Not Hispanic (13,812)	13,938	97.97
Hispanic (92)	98	0.69

New Philadelphia

Place Type: City
County: Tuscarawas
Population: 17,288†

Ancestry‡	Population	%
American (1,276)	1,276	7.38
Australian (0)	18	0.10
Austrian (42)	114	0.66
Belgian (16)	16	0.09
Brazilian (42)	42	0.24
British (33)	74	0.43
Czech (88)	103	0.60
Czechoslovakian (32)	48	0.28
Dutch (96)	342	1.98
English (568)	1,844	10.66
European (22)	22	0.13
French, ex. Basque (50)	348	2.01
French Canadian (29)	29	0.17
German (1,980)	5,964	34.49
Greek (64)	177	1.02
Hungarian (90)	135	0.78
Irish (686)	2,719	15.72
Italian (657)	1,656	9.58
Lithuanian (0)	10	0.06
Norwegian (0)	8	0.05
Pennsylvania German (90)	138	0.80
Polish (199)	528	3.05
Romanian (14)	58	0.34
Russian (0)	19	0.11
Scandinavian (0)	19	0.11
Scotch-Irish (80)	284	1.64
Scottish (111)	423	2.45
Slavic (11)	11	0.06
Slovak (107)	225	1.30
Swedish (17)	122	0.71
Swiss (129)	620	3.59
Welsh (16)	268	1.55

Hispanic Origin	Population	%
Hispanic or Latino (of any race)	734	4.25
Central American, ex. Mexican	365	2.11
Guatemalan	353	2.04
Honduran	3	0.02
Panamanian	7	0.04
Other Central American	2	0.01
Cuban	4	0.02
Dominican Republic	11	0.06
Mexican	198	1.15
Puerto Rican	67	0.39
South American	5	0.03
Chilean	2	0.01
Venezuelan	3	0.02
Other Hispanic or Latino	84	0.49

Race*	Population	%
African-American/Black (208)	329	1.90
Not Hispanic (206)	318	1.84
Hispanic (2)	11	0.06
American Indian/Alaska Native (69)	181	1.05
Not Hispanic (26)	121	0.70
Hispanic (43)	60	0.35
Apache (1)	1	0.01
Arapaho (2)	2	0.01
Blackfeet (1)	2	0.01
Central American Ind. (30)	35	0.20
Cherokee (4)	34	0.20
Cheyenne (1)	1	0.01
Chippewa (2)	2	0.01
Choctaw (1)	1	0.01
Crow (0)	1	0.01
Delaware (3)	8	0.05
Iroquois (0)	2	0.01
Mexican American Ind. (11)	21	0.12
Sioux (1)	8	0.05
South American Ind. (0)	3	0.02
Asian (106)	146	0.84
Not Hispanic (105)	143	0.83
Hispanic (1)	3	0.02
Chinese, ex. Taiwanese (28)	31	0.18
Filipino (28)	41	0.24
Indian (36)	48	0.28
Japanese (1)	4	0.02
Korean (3)	10	0.06
Nepalese (4)	4	0.02
Taiwanese (1)	1	0.01
Thai (1)	1	0.01
Vietnamese (3)	3	0.02
Hawaii Native/Pacific Islander (65)	77	0.45
Not Hispanic (23)	27	0.16
Hispanic (42)	50	0.29
Guamanian/Chamorro (61)	65	0.38
Native Hawaiian (2)	5	0.03
Samoan (2)	3	0.02
White (16,255)	16,547	95.71
Not Hispanic (15,937)	16,177	93.57
Hispanic (318)	370	2.14

Newark

Place Type: City
County: Licking
Population: 47,573†

Ancestry‡	Population	%
African, Sub-Saharan (61)	61	0.13
African (61)	61	0.13
American (5,240)	5,240	11.01
Arab (0)	39	0.08
Lebanese (0)	12	0.03
Syrian (0)	27	0.06
Armenian (17)	17	0.04
Australian (8)	20	0.04
Austrian (20)	68	0.14
Belgian (7)	32	0.07
British (99)	251	0.53
Canadian (0)	34	0.07
Croatian (0)	14	0.03
Czech (33)	198	0.42
Czechoslovakian (9)	87	0.18
Danish (21)	45	0.09
Dutch (114)	1,010	2.12
Eastern European (25)	25	0.05
English (2,569)	5,718	12.01
European (820)	901	1.89
Finnish (0)	67	0.14
French, ex. Basque (197)	1,071	2.25
French Canadian (51)	74	0.16
German (4,405)	12,659	26.59
Greek (9)	36	0.08
Hungarian (91)	296	0.62
Iranian (31)	31	0.07
Irish (1,947)	7,924	16.65
Italian (810)	2,238	4.70
Lithuanian (0)	13	0.03
Macedonian (50)	50	0.11
Northern European (34)	34	0.07
Norwegian (63)	109	0.23
Pennsylvania German (202)	202	0.42
Polish (209)	639	1.34
Portuguese (129)	186	0.39
Romanian (0)	38	0.08
Russian (0)	149	0.31
Scandinavian (64)	102	0.21
Scotch-Irish (479)	1,163	2.44
Scottish (300)	837	1.76
Serbian (32)	61	0.13
Slavic (13)	38	0.08
Slovak (11)	104	0.22
Slovene (0)	71	0.15
Swedish (30)	164	0.34
Swiss (45)	264	0.55
Turkish (10)	10	0.02
Ukrainian (50)	95	0.20
Welsh (213)	890	1.87
West Indian, ex. Hispanic (0)	38	0.08
Jamaican (0)	30	0.06
Other West Indian (0)	8	0.02
Yugoslavian (0)	12	0.03

Hispanic Origin	Population	%
Hispanic or Latino (of any race)	570	1.20
Central American, ex. Mexican	35	0.07
Costa Rican	5	0.01
Guatemalan	8	0.02
Honduran	5	0.01
Nicaraguan	2	<0.01
Panamanian	4	0.01
Salvadoran	11	0.02
Cuban	12	0.03
Dominican Republic	6	0.01
Mexican	281	0.59
Puerto Rican	114	0.24
South American	46	0.10
Argentinean	6	0.01
Bolivian	1	<0.01
Chilean	6	0.01
Colombian	25	0.05
Ecuadorian	2	<0.01
Peruvian	1	<0.01
Venezuelan	5	0.01
Other Hispanic or Latino	76	0.16

Race*	Population	%
African-American/Black (1,575)	2,387	5.02
Not Hispanic (1,560)	2,346	4.93
Hispanic (15)	41	0.09
American Indian/Alaska Native (162)	463	0.97
Not Hispanic (153)	438	0.92
Hispanic (9)	25	0.05
Apache (2)	5	0.01
Blackfeet (5)	35	0.07
Canadian/French Am. Ind. (4)	5	0.01
Cherokee (46)	167	0.35
Cheyenne (0)	1	<0.01
Chickasaw (1)	2	<0.01
Chippewa (7)	10	0.02
Choctaw (4)	6	0.01
Comanche (0)	1	<0.01
Creek (0)	1	<0.01
Crow (0)	1	<0.01
Delaware (4)	7	0.01
Inupiat *(Alaska Native)* (0)	1	<0.01
Iroquois (5)	7	0.01
Kiowa (0)	1	<0.01
Lumbee (1)	3	0.01
Mexican American Ind. (1)	2	<0.01
Navajo (2)	2	<0.01
Osage (0)	1	<0.01
Seminole (1)	3	0.01
Sioux (2)	13	0.03
Asian (279)	393	0.83
Not Hispanic (278)	390	0.82
Hispanic (1)	3	0.01

*Notes: † The Census 2010 population figure is used to calculate the percentages in the Hispanic Origin and Race categories. Ancestry percentages are based on the 2006-2010 American Community Survey population (not shown); ‡ Numbers in parentheses indicate the number of people reporting a single ancestry; * Numbers in parentheses indicate the number of persons reporting this race alone, not in combination with any other race; Please refer to the Explanation of Data for more information.*

Cambodian (7)	15	0.03
Chinese, ex. Taiwanese (42)	61	0.13
Filipino (37)	53	0.11
Indian (49)	62	0.13
Indonesian (3)	7	0.01
Japanese (19)	43	0.09
Korean (65)	74	0.16
Laotian (2)	2	<0.01
Malaysian (1)	1	<0.01
Pakistani (0)	2	<0.01
Sri Lankan (1)	2	<0.01
Taiwanese (3)	4	0.01
Thai (3)	9	0.02
Vietnamese (27)	40	0.08
Hawaii Native/Pacific Islander (12)	44	0.09
Not Hispanic (11)	39	0.08
Hispanic (1)	5	0.01
Guamanian/Chamorro (2)	6	0.01
Native Hawaiian (2)	9	0.02
Samoan (1)	4	0.01
Tongan (4)	8	0.02
White (44,165)	45,348	95.32
Not Hispanic (43,811)	44,924	94.43
Hispanic (354)	424	0.89

Niles

Place Type: City
County: Trumbull
Population: 19,266†

Ancestry‡	Population	%
African, Sub-Saharan (46)	92	0.47
African (46)	92	0.47
Albanian (14)	14	0.07
American (3,000)	3,000	15.41
Arab (17)	145	0.74
Arab (0)	21	0.11
Lebanese (0)	107	0.55
Moroccan (17)	17	0.09
Austrian (40)	40	0.21
Belgian (0)	13	0.07
British (8)	8	0.04
Canadian (30)	41	0.21
Celtic (23)	64	0.33
Croatian (43)	196	1.01
Czech (0)	44	0.23
Czechoslovakian (16)	16	0.08
Dutch (18)	520	2.67
English (641)	2,207	11.34
European (158)	158	0.81
Finnish (30)	72	0.37
French, ex. Basque (25)	300	1.54
French Canadian (13)	13	0.07
German (821)	3,939	20.24
Greek (20)	111	0.57
Hungarian (162)	579	2.97
Irish (795)	2,732	14.04
Italian (2,448)	4,355	22.37
Latvian (12)	12	0.06
Lithuanian (0)	7	0.04
Norwegian (0)	30	0.15
Pennsylvania German (39)	48	0.25
Polish (295)	1,063	5.46
Romanian (68)	119	0.61
Russian (36)	127	0.65
Scandinavian (10)	10	0.05
Scotch-Irish (80)	252	1.29
Scottish (63)	309	1.59
Serbian (30)	54	0.28
Slovak (213)	698	3.59
Slovene (45)	103	0.53
Swedish (0)	27	0.14
Swiss (0)	45	0.23
Ukrainian (42)	201	1.03
Welsh (200)	898	4.61
West Indian, ex. Hispanic (0)	38	0.20
Jamaican (0)	38	0.20
Yugoslavian (0)	17	0.09

Hispanic Origin	Population	%
Hispanic or Latino (of any race)	254	1.32
Central American, ex. Mexican	2	0.01
Guatemalan	1	0.01
Panamanian	1	0.01
Cuban	5	0.03
Dominican Republic	2	0.01
Mexican	112	0.58
Puerto Rican	95	0.49
South American	12	0.06
Argentinean	1	0.01
Colombian	5	0.03
Ecuadorian	4	0.02
Peruvian	1	0.01
Venezuelan	1	0.01
Other Hispanic or Latino	26	0.13

Race*	Population	%
African-American/Black (667)	945	4.91
Not Hispanic (661)	917	4.76
Hispanic (6)	28	0.15
American Indian/Alaska Native (35)	152	0.79
Not Hispanic (35)	142	0.74
Hispanic (0)	10	0.05
Apache (0)	4	0.02
Blackfeet (0)	7	0.04
Cherokee (13)	57	0.30
Chippewa (0)	4	0.02
Comanche (0)	2	0.01
Hopi (0)	1	0.01
Iroquois (0)	8	0.04
Sioux (1)	3	0.02
Tlingit-Haida *(Alaska Native)* (0)	2	0.01
Asian (139)	184	0.96
Not Hispanic (139)	171	0.89
Hispanic (0)	13	0.07
Bangladeshi (1)	1	0.01
Bhutanese (1)	1	0.01
Chinese, ex. Taiwanese (34)	43	0.22
Filipino (9)	27	0.14
Indian (46)	51	0.26
Indonesian (2)	2	0.01
Japanese (8)	13	0.07
Korean (16)	19	0.10
Malaysian (0)	1	0.01
Nepalese (0)	2	0.01
Thai (2)	9	0.05
Vietnamese (7)	7	0.04
Hawaii Native/Pacific Islander (1)	18	0.09
Not Hispanic (1)	8	0.04
Hispanic (0)	10	0.05
Native Hawaiian (1)	7	0.04
White (17,940)	18,339	95.19
Not Hispanic (17,789)	18,150	94.21
Hispanic (151)	189	0.98

North Canton

Place Type: City
County: Stark
Population: 17,488†

Ancestry‡	Population	%
African, Sub-Saharan (11)	11	0.06
African (11)	11	0.06
Albanian (19)	34	0.20
American (1,010)	1,010	5.82
Arab (30)	155	0.89
Egyptian (0)	36	0.21
Lebanese (26)	90	0.52
Syrian (4)	29	0.17
Armenian (0)	17	0.10
Austrian (17)	31	0.18
British (59)	113	0.65
Canadian (42)	42	0.24
Croatian (47)	175	1.01
Cypriot (15)	15	0.09
Czech (0)	114	0.66
Czechoslovakian (41)	55	0.32
Danish (11)	22	0.13
Dutch (93)	347	2.00
English (485)	2,373	13.68
European (209)	237	1.37
Finnish (0)	31	0.18
French, ex. Basque (89)	623	3.59
French Canadian (9)	130	0.75
German (2,085)	6,171	35.58
Greek (40)	119	0.69
Hungarian (185)	529	3.05
Irish (639)	3,344	19.28
Italian (989)	2,502	14.43
Latvian (14)	28	0.16
Lithuanian (33)	43	0.25
Norwegian (25)	98	0.57
Pennsylvania German (20)	20	0.12
Polish (229)	686	3.96
Portuguese (0)	57	0.33
Romanian (75)	114	0.66
Russian (7)	102	0.59
Scandinavian (23)	62	0.36
Scotch-Irish (101)	400	2.31
Scottish (139)	471	2.72
Serbian (16)	27	0.16
Slavic (0)	48	0.28
Slovak (83)	391	2.25
Swedish (31)	324	1.87
Swiss (52)	235	1.35
Ukrainian (0)	19	0.11
Welsh (47)	444	2.56

Hispanic Origin	Population	%
Hispanic or Latino (of any race)	259	1.48
Central American, ex. Mexican	17	0.10
Costa Rican	1	0.01
Guatemalan	2	0.01
Honduran	11	0.06
Nicaraguan	1	0.01
Panamanian	1	0.01
Salvadoran	1	0.01
Cuban	10	0.06
Mexican	115	0.66
Puerto Rican	19	0.11
South American	17	0.10
Argentinean	7	0.04
Bolivian	1	0.01
Colombian	6	0.03
Peruvian	1	0.01
Venezuelan	2	0.01
Other Hispanic or Latino	81	0.46

Race*	Population	%
African-American/Black (356)	478	2.73
Not Hispanic (347)	465	2.66
Hispanic (9)	13	0.07
American Indian/Alaska Native (28)	99	0.57
Not Hispanic (22)	90	0.51
Hispanic (6)	9	0.05
Blackfeet (0)	7	0.04
Cherokee (10)	34	0.19
Choctaw (1)	3	0.02
Creek (0)	1	0.01
Delaware (1)	2	0.01
Inupiat *(Alaska Native)* (3)	3	0.02
Navajo (1)	1	0.01
Pima (0)	1	0.01
Potawatomi (0)	3	0.02
Sioux (3)	5	0.03
South American Ind. (1)	1	0.01
Asian (200)	267	1.53
Not Hispanic (200)	265	1.52
Hispanic (0)	2	0.01
Burmese (2)	2	0.01
Chinese, ex. Taiwanese (53)	62	0.35
Filipino (19)	40	0.23
Indian (61)	66	0.38
Japanese (12)	22	0.13
Korean (20)	25	0.14
Laotian (0)	1	0.01
Malaysian (0)	1	0.01
Pakistani (9)	11	0.06

*Notes: † The Census 2010 population figure is used to calculate the percentages in the Hispanic Origin and Race categories. Ancestry percentages are based on the 2006-2010 American Community Survey population (not shown); ‡ Numbers in parentheses indicate the number of people reporting a single ancestry; * Numbers in parentheses indicate the number of persons reporting this race alone, not in combination with any other race; Please refer to the Explanation of Data for more information.*

Taiwanese (3)	3	0.02
Thai (1)	2	0.01
Vietnamese (16)	17	0.10
Hawaii Native/Pacific Islander (4)	7	0.04
Not Hispanic (4)	7	0.04
Native Hawaiian (4)	6	0.03
White (16,585)	16,827	96.22
Not Hispanic (16,408)	16,632	95.11
Hispanic (177)	195	1.12

North College Hill

Place Type: City
County: Hamilton
Population: 9,397†

Ancestry‡	Population	%
African, Sub-Saharan (137)	148	1.57
African (94)	105	1.11
Ghanaian (33)	33	0.35
Nigerian (10)	10	0.11
American (412)	412	4.37
Arab (11)	11	0.12
Arab (11)	11	0.12
Austrian (0)	26	0.28
British (10)	35	0.37
Danish (23)	23	0.24
Dutch (0)	199	2.11
English (201)	461	4.89
European (225)	225	2.38
French, ex. Basque (0)	68	0.72
French Canadian (0)	10	0.11
German (1,234)	2,381	25.23
Greek (21)	56	0.59
Hungarian (0)	3	0.03
Irish (96)	825	8.74
Israeli (0)	12	0.13
Italian (105)	197	2.09
Norwegian (0)	12	0.13
Polish (32)	36	0.38
Romanian (41)	41	0.43
Russian (0)	22	0.23
Scandinavian (19)	19	0.20
Scotch-Irish (11)	35	0.37
Scottish (37)	56	0.59
Slovak (9)	17	0.18
Swedish (0)	61	0.65
Welsh (8)	16	0.17
West Indian, ex. Hispanic (7)	7	0.07
Jamaican (7)	7	0.07
Yugoslavian (10)	10	0.11

Hispanic Origin	Population	%
Hispanic or Latino (of any race)	125	1.33
Central American, ex. Mexican	7	0.07
Costa Rican	1	0.01
Honduran	1	0.01
Panamanian	1	0.01
Salvadoran	4	0.04
Cuban	7	0.07
Dominican Republic	1	0.01
Mexican	57	0.61
Puerto Rican	27	0.29
South American	9	0.10
Argentinean	2	0.02
Chilean	1	0.01
Peruvian	4	0.04
Venezuelan	2	0.02
Other Hispanic or Latino	17	0.18

Race*	Population	%
African-American/Black (4,382)	4,621	49.18
Not Hispanic (4,365)	4,600	48.95
Hispanic (17)	21	0.22
American Indian/Alaska Native (14)	69	0.73
Not Hispanic (12)	64	0.68
Hispanic (2)	5	0.05
Apache (0)	1	0.01
Blackfeet (0)	4	0.04
Cherokee (2)	18	0.19
Chickasaw (2)	2	0.02
Chippewa (3)	5	0.05
Asian (53)	99	1.05
Not Hispanic (53)	97	1.03
Hispanic (0)	2	0.02
Cambodian (4)	5	0.05
Chinese, ex. Taiwanese (13)	22	0.23
Filipino (14)	39	0.42
Indian (10)	12	0.13
Japanese (0)	4	0.04
Korean (2)	6	0.06
Malaysian (1)	3	0.03
Pakistani (1)	1	0.01
Taiwanese (1)	4	0.04
Thai (0)	8	0.09
Vietnamese (2)	6	0.06
Hawaii Native/Pacific Islander (6)	12	0.13
Not Hispanic (6)	12	0.13
Guamanian/Chamorro (0)	1	0.01
Native Hawaiian (3)	6	0.06
Samoan (0)	1	0.01
White (4,603)	4,864	51.76
Not Hispanic (4,542)	4,785	50.92
Hispanic (61)	79	0.84

North Madison

Place Type: CDP
County: Lake
Population: 8,547†

Ancestry‡	Population	%
American (504)	504	5.60
Austrian (6)	53	0.59
British (37)	70	0.78
Canadian (13)	34	0.38
Croatian (0)	42	0.47
Czech (0)	66	0.73
Czechoslovakian (34)	34	0.38
Danish (17)	39	0.43
Dutch (22)	121	1.34
English (378)	1,204	13.38
European (95)	95	1.06
Finnish (69)	226	2.51
French, ex. Basque (37)	208	2.31
French Canadian (16)	131	1.46
German (752)	2,378	26.43
Greek (7)	98	1.09
Hungarian (196)	458	5.09
Irish (572)	2,139	23.77
Italian (493)	1,430	15.89
Lithuanian (6)	40	0.44
Norwegian (0)	20	0.22
Polish (192)	720	8.00
Portuguese (17)	17	0.19
Romanian (0)	38	0.42
Russian (8)	33	0.37
Scotch-Irish (91)	219	2.43
Scottish (38)	206	2.29
Slovak (45)	79	0.88
Slovene (28)	203	2.26
Swedish (0)	170	1.89
Ukrainian (24)	32	0.36
Welsh (24)	63	0.70
West Indian, ex. Hispanic (0)	7	0.08
Belizean (0)	7	0.08

Hispanic Origin	Population	%
Hispanic or Latino (of any race)	156	1.83
Central American, ex. Mexican	2	0.02
Costa Rican	1	0.01
Salvadoran	1	0.01
Cuban	4	0.05
Mexican	83	0.97
Puerto Rican	43	0.50
South American	3	0.04
Argentinean	2	0.02
Colombian	1	0.01
Other Hispanic or Latino	21	0.25

Race*	Population	%
African-American/Black (43)	80	0.94
Not Hispanic (43)	78	0.91
Hispanic (0)	2	0.02
American Indian/Alaska Native (21)	65	0.76
Not Hispanic (18)	61	0.71
Hispanic (3)	4	0.05
Apache (0)	1	0.01
Blackfeet (1)	5	0.06
Cherokee (1)	18	0.21
Chippewa (0)	1	0.01
Delaware (1)	1	0.01
Ottawa (2)	2	0.02
Pueblo (2)	5	0.06
Asian (34)	51	0.60
Not Hispanic (34)	51	0.60
Chinese, ex. Taiwanese (9)	13	0.15
Filipino (3)	11	0.13
Japanese (2)	4	0.05
Korean (5)	6	0.07
Laotian (15)	15	0.18
Hawaii Native/Pacific Islander (2)	5	0.06
Not Hispanic (2)	5	0.06
Guamanian/Chamorro (1)	3	0.04
Native Hawaiian (1)	2	0.02
White (8,312)	8,411	98.41
Not Hispanic (8,200)	8,291	97.00
Hispanic (112)	120	1.40

North Olmsted

Place Type: City
County: Cuyahoga
Population: 32,718†

Ancestry‡	Population	%
African, Sub-Saharan (21)	21	0.06
African (21)	21	0.06
Albanian (64)	176	0.54
American (1,020)	1,020	3.11
Arab (1,114)	1,223	3.73
Arab (431)	447	1.36
Egyptian (10)	10	0.03
Jordanian (74)	74	0.23
Lebanese (193)	286	0.87
Palestinian (331)	331	1.01
Syrian (51)	51	0.16
Other Arab (24)	24	0.07
Austrian (38)	104	0.32
Belgian (0)	11	0.03
British (60)	69	0.21
Canadian (0)	17	0.05
Croatian (297)	525	1.60
Czech (322)	982	2.99
Czechoslovakian (55)	98	0.30
Danish (10)	114	0.35
Dutch (36)	378	1.15
Eastern European (88)	88	0.27
English (751)	3,342	10.19
Estonian (0)	15	0.05
European (145)	198	0.60
Finnish (27)	78	0.24
French, ex. Basque (89)	549	1.67
French Canadian (0)	46	0.14
German (2,412)	10,479	31.96
Greek (289)	603	1.84
Hungarian (508)	1,755	5.35
Iranian (53)	53	0.16
Irish (2,055)	7,707	23.50
Israeli (68)	80	0.24
Italian (1,338)	3,577	10.91
Latvian (43)	43	0.13
Lithuanian (18)	153	0.47
Macedonian (0)	10	0.03
Norwegian (9)	164	0.50
Pennsylvania German (0)	19	0.06
Polish (683)	3,204	9.77
Portuguese (0)	9	0.03
Romanian (306)	398	1.21

*Notes: † The Census 2010 population figure is used to calculate the percentages in the Hispanic Origin and Race categories. Ancestry percentages are based on the 2006-2010 American Community Survey population (not shown); ‡ Numbers in parentheses indicate the number of people reporting a single ancestry; * Numbers in parentheses indicate the number of persons reporting this race alone, not in combination with any other race; Please refer to the Explanation of Data for more information.*

Russian (93)	543	1.66
Scandinavian (0)	17	0.05
Scotch-Irish (208)	754	2.30
Scottish (204)	632	1.93
Serbian (10)	47	0.14
Slavic (18)	44	0.13
Slovak (626)	2,024	6.17
Slovene (172)	438	1.34
Swedish (57)	215	0.66
Swiss (0)	85	0.26
Turkish (7)	7	0.02
Ukrainian (227)	338	1.03
Welsh (23)	336	1.02
West Indian, ex. Hispanic (15)	104	0.32
Barbadian (0)	74	0.23
Jamaican (15)	30	0.09
Yugoslavian (17)	76	0.23

Hispanic Origin	Population	%
Hispanic or Latino (of any race)	1,136	3.47
Central American, ex. Mexican	64	0.20
Costa Rican	1	<0.01
Guatemalan	18	0.06
Honduran	3	0.01
Nicaraguan	5	0.02
Panamanian	2	0.01
Salvadoran	35	0.11
Cuban	26	0.08
Dominican Republic	21	0.06
Mexican	302	0.92
Puerto Rican	538	1.64
South American	82	0.25
Argentinean	8	0.02
Bolivian	1	<0.01
Chilean	3	0.01
Colombian	31	0.09
Ecuadorian	2	0.01
Peruvian	27	0.08
Uruguayan	1	<0.01
Venezuelan	8	0.02
Other South American	1	<0.01
Other Hispanic or Latino	103	0.31

Race*	Population	%
African-American/Black (642)	841	2.57
Not Hispanic (617)	787	2.41
Hispanic (25)	54	0.17
American Indian/Alaska Native (34)	160	0.49
Not Hispanic (31)	134	0.41
Hispanic (3)	26	0.08
Apache (1)	6	0.02
Blackfeet (1)	7	0.02
Cherokee (3)	16	0.05
Chippewa (3)	7	0.02
Choctaw (1)	2	0.01
Creek (0)	4	0.01
Delaware (1)	1	<0.01
Iroquois (3)	5	0.02
Mexican American Ind. (1)	2	0.01
Navajo (0)	5	0.02
Sioux (1)	5	0.02
South American Ind. (1)	3	0.01
Spanish American Ind. (0)	1	<0.01
Tlingit-Haida *(Alaska Native)* (0)	6	0.02
Asian (879)	1,064	3.25
Not Hispanic (877)	1,053	3.22
Hispanic (2)	11	0.03
Bangladeshi (2)	2	0.01
Burmese (3)	3	0.01
Cambodian (34)	35	0.11
Chinese, ex. Taiwanese (172)	190	0.58
Filipino (63)	97	0.30
Indian (371)	402	1.23
Japanese (29)	41	0.13
Korean (74)	84	0.26
Laotian (1)	2	0.01
Pakistani (17)	17	0.05
Taiwanese (7)	7	0.02
Thai (5)	7	0.02
Vietnamese (77)	88	0.27
Hawaii Native/Pacific Islander (10)	27	0.08
Not Hispanic (10)	22	0.07
Hispanic (0)	5	0.02
Guamanian/Chamorro (0)	2	0.01
Native Hawaiian (0)	1	<0.01
White (30,307)	30,793	94.12
Not Hispanic (29,568)	29,956	91.56
Hispanic (739)	837	2.56

North Ridgeville

Place Type: City
County: Lorain
Population: 29,465†

Ancestry‡	Population	%
Albanian (3)	12	0.04
Alsatian (0)	13	0.05
American (2,098)	2,098	7.41
Arab (101)	129	0.46
Arab (29)	29	0.10
Lebanese (55)	71	0.25
Palestinian (17)	17	0.06
Syrian (0)	12	0.04
Armenian (0)	24	0.08
Austrian (57)	100	0.35
British (0)	69	0.24
Cajun (13)	13	0.05
Canadian (0)	32	0.11
Celtic (0)	31	0.11
Croatian (30)	105	0.37
Czech (140)	577	2.04
Czechoslovakian (50)	115	0.41
Danish (11)	123	0.43
Dutch (37)	416	1.47
Eastern European (9)	9	0.03
English (741)	3,146	11.12
European (230)	230	0.81
Finnish (51)	72	0.25
French, ex. Basque (28)	443	1.57
French Canadian (35)	133	0.47
German (2,520)	7,710	27.24
Greek (100)	206	0.73
Hungarian (712)	1,613	5.70
Irish (1,728)	5,712	20.18
Italian (1,039)	2,970	10.49
Latvian (0)	15	0.05
Lithuanian (0)	128	0.45
Norwegian (77)	191	0.67
Pennsylvania German (28)	63	0.22
Polish (961)	2,730	9.65
Portuguese (0)	32	0.11
Romanian (181)	251	0.89
Russian (136)	290	1.02
Scandinavian (0)	8	0.03
Scotch-Irish (76)	415	1.47
Scottish (151)	775	2.74
Serbian (34)	96	0.34
Slavic (16)	29	0.10
Slovak (512)	1,428	5.05
Slovene (13)	223	0.79
Swedish (38)	99	0.35
Swiss (18)	166	0.59
Ukrainian (196)	470	1.66
Welsh (17)	293	1.04
Yugoslavian (32)	41	0.14

Hispanic Origin	Population	%
Hispanic or Latino (of any race)	973	3.30
Central American, ex. Mexican	56	0.19
Costa Rican	11	0.04
Guatemalan	13	0.04
Honduran	7	0.02
Nicaraguan	18	0.06
Panamanian	1	<0.01
Salvadoran	6	0.02
Cuban	23	0.08
Dominican Republic	7	0.02
Mexican	268	0.91
Puerto Rican	504	1.71
South American	59	0.20
Argentinean	9	0.03
Bolivian	1	<0.01
Chilean	24	0.08
Colombian	10	0.03
Ecuadorian	1	<0.01
Peruvian	3	0.01
Venezuelan	9	0.03
Other South American	2	0.01
Other Hispanic or Latino	56	0.19

Race*	Population	%
African-American/Black (429)	594	2.02
Not Hispanic (405)	552	1.87
Hispanic (24)	42	0.14
American Indian/Alaska Native (65)	206	0.70
Not Hispanic (48)	174	0.59
Hispanic (17)	32	0.11
Apache (0)	1	<0.01
Blackfeet (1)	9	0.03
Canadian/French Am. Ind. (0)	1	<0.01
Cherokee (16)	70	0.24
Cheyenne (0)	1	<0.01
Chippewa (4)	8	0.03
Choctaw (3)	3	0.01
Creek (0)	1	<0.01
Crow (1)	3	0.01
Iroquois (0)	2	0.01
Mexican American Ind. (1)	1	<0.01
Navajo (1)	2	0.01
Sioux (4)	11	0.04
South American Ind. (0)	1	<0.01
Tlingit-Haida *(Alaska Native)* (0)	1	<0.01
Asian (356)	504	1.71
Not Hispanic (352)	486	1.65
Hispanic (4)	18	0.06
Bangladeshi (1)	1	<0.01
Cambodian (12)	12	0.04
Chinese, ex. Taiwanese (58)	81	0.27
Filipino (58)	106	0.36
Indian (95)	111	0.38
Indonesian (3)	4	0.01
Japanese (7)	31	0.11
Korean (39)	69	0.23
Pakistani (4)	4	0.01
Sri Lankan (3)	3	0.01
Taiwanese (0)	4	0.01
Thai (5)	11	0.04
Vietnamese (57)	62	0.21
Hawaii Native/Pacific Islander (0)	13	0.04
Not Hispanic (0)	9	0.03
Hispanic (0)	4	0.01
Guamanian/Chamorro (0)	2	0.01
Native Hawaiian (0)	3	0.01
Samoan (0)	3	0.01
White (27,982)	28,401	96.39
Not Hispanic (27,291)	27,636	93.79
Hispanic (691)	765	2.60

North Royalton

Place Type: City
County: Cuyahoga
Population: 30,444†

Ancestry‡	Population	%
African, Sub-Saharan (0)	29	0.10
African (0)	29	0.10
Albanian (8)	8	0.03
American (932)	932	3.11
Arab (221)	304	1.01
Arab (29)	29	0.10
Jordanian (50)	50	0.17
Lebanese (119)	191	0.64
Other Arab (23)	34	0.11
Austrian (46)	239	0.80
British (25)	38	0.13
Bulgarian (15)	15	0.05
Canadian (0)	15	0.05
Croatian (191)	364	1.21

*Notes: † The Census 2010 population figure is used to calculate the percentages in the Hispanic Origin and Race categories. Ancestry percentages are based on the 2006-2010 American Community Survey population (not shown); ‡ Numbers in parentheses indicate the number of people reporting a single ancestry; * Numbers in parentheses indicate the number of persons reporting this race alone, not in combination with any other race; Please refer to the Explanation of Data for more information.*

Czech (300)	1,263	4.21
Czechoslovakian (51)	85	0.28
Danish (11)	62	0.21
Dutch (12)	179	0.60
Eastern European (20)	20	0.07
English (445)	2,181	7.28
Estonian (25)	35	0.12
European (225)	257	0.86
Finnish (11)	163	0.54
French, ex. Basque (75)	395	1.32
French Canadian (0)	18	0.06
German (2,444)	8,225	27.45
Greek (276)	489	1.63
Hungarian (341)	1,230	4.10
Irish (997)	4,870	16.25
Italian (1,543)	4,359	14.55
Latvian (0)	11	0.04
Lithuanian (29)	157	0.52
Norwegian (95)	167	0.56
Pennsylvania German (0)	14	0.05
Polish (2,274)	5,749	19.19
Portuguese (0)	15	0.05
Romanian (249)	323	1.08
Russian (112)	310	1.03
Scandinavian (9)	33	0.11
Scotch-Irish (91)	282	0.94
Scottish (98)	427	1.42
Serbian (295)	433	1.45
Slavic (23)	57	0.19
Slovak (629)	1,719	5.74
Slovene (114)	666	2.22
Swedish (75)	311	1.04
Swiss (11)	182	0.61
Ukrainian (771)	1,113	3.71
Welsh (25)	316	1.05
West Indian, ex. Hispanic (0)	45	0.15
Bermudan (0)	45	0.15
Yugoslavian (35)	55	0.18

Hispanic Origin	Population	%
Hispanic or Latino (of any race)	473	1.55
Central American, ex. Mexican	37	0.12
Costa Rican	10	0.03
Guatemalan	12	0.04
Honduran	6	0.02
Nicaraguan	4	0.01
Panamanian	1	<0.01
Salvadoran	4	0.01
Cuban	7	0.02
Dominican Republic	8	0.03
Mexican	113	0.37
Puerto Rican	205	0.67
South American	48	0.16
Argentinean	1	<0.01
Bolivian	1	<0.01
Chilean	2	0.01
Colombian	14	0.05
Ecuadorian	1	<0.01
Paraguayan	5	0.02
Peruvian	10	0.03
Uruguayan	4	0.01
Venezuelan	10	0.03
Other Hispanic or Latino	55	0.18

Race*	Population	%
African-American/Black (348)	435	1.43
Not Hispanic (340)	424	1.39
Hispanic (8)	11	0.04
American Indian/Alaska Native (19)	113	0.37
Not Hispanic (16)	104	0.34
Hispanic (3)	9	0.03
Blackfeet (0)	5	0.02
Cherokee (3)	35	0.11
Chickasaw (0)	1	<0.01
Chippewa (1)	2	0.01
Choctaw (0)	1	<0.01
Creek (0)	2	0.01
Delaware (0)	2	0.01
Iroquois (1)	3	0.01
Mexican American Ind. (2)	2	0.01
Navajo (0)	1	<0.01
Sioux (0)	2	0.01
South American Ind. (0)	1	<0.01
Asian (837)	979	3.22
Not Hispanic (837)	973	3.20
Hispanic (0)	6	0.02
Cambodian (11)	14	0.05
Chinese, ex. Taiwanese (110)	129	0.42
Filipino (112)	163	0.54
Indian (440)	465	1.53
Japanese (11)	23	0.08
Korean (70)	87	0.29
Laotian (1)	2	0.01
Pakistani (21)	27	0.09
Sri Lankan (0)	5	0.02
Taiwanese (1)	1	<0.01
Thai (15)	17	0.06
Vietnamese (27)	35	0.11
Hawaii Native/Pacific Islander (6)	9	0.03
Not Hispanic (6)	9	0.03
Guamanian/Chamorro (4)	4	0.01
Native Hawaiian (0)	1	<0.01
White (28,810)	29,120	95.65
Not Hispanic (28,449)	28,727	94.36
Hispanic (361)	393	1.29

Northbrook

Place Type: CDP
County: Hamilton
Population: 10,668†

Ancestry‡	Population	%
African, Sub-Saharan (164)	164	1.62
African (150)	150	1.48
Senegalese (14)	14	0.14
American (761)	761	7.52
Austrian (0)	9	0.09
British (0)	18	0.18
Celtic (0)	7	0.07
Danish (16)	16	0.16
Dutch (20)	139	1.37
English (128)	693	6.85
European (26)	26	0.26
French, ex. Basque (39)	275	2.72
German (1,445)	3,259	32.21
Greek (0)	8	0.08
Hungarian (0)	8	0.08
Irish (204)	1,185	11.71
Italian (165)	513	5.07
Norwegian (0)	16	0.16
Pennsylvania German (0)	9	0.09
Polish (8)	58	0.57
Portuguese (9)	9	0.09
Romanian (0)	27	0.27
Russian (0)	88	0.87
Scandinavian (0)	8	0.08
Scotch-Irish (117)	273	2.70
Scottish (19)	101	1.00
Slovak (0)	16	0.16
Swedish (0)	51	0.50
Swiss (0)	12	0.12
Welsh (0)	25	0.25
Yugoslavian (7)	28	0.28

Hispanic Origin	Population	%
Hispanic or Latino (of any race)	377	3.53
Central American, ex. Mexican	82	0.77
Costa Rican	2	0.02
Guatemalan	53	0.50
Honduran	3	0.03
Panamanian	7	0.07
Salvadoran	17	0.16
Cuban	4	0.04
Dominican Republic	9	0.08
Mexican	180	1.69
Puerto Rican	54	0.51
South American	7	0.07
Colombian	2	0.02
Ecuadorian	2	0.02
Peruvian	3	0.03
Other Hispanic or Latino	41	0.38

Race*	Population	%
African-American/Black (2,974)	3,273	30.68
Not Hispanic (2,950)	3,216	30.15
Hispanic (24)	57	0.53
American Indian/Alaska Native (48)	127	1.19
Not Hispanic (22)	82	0.77
Hispanic (26)	45	0.42
Blackfeet (0)	5	0.05
Canadian/French Am. Ind. (3)	3	0.03
Central American Ind. (10)	10	0.09
Cherokee (3)	28	0.26
Cheyenne (0)	3	0.03
Choctaw (0)	3	0.03
Creek (0)	1	0.01
Mexican American Ind. (17)	30	0.28
Sioux (2)	3	0.03
South American Ind. (0)	2	0.02
Asian (125)	170	1.59
Not Hispanic (125)	159	1.49
Hispanic (0)	11	0.10
Cambodian (13)	13	0.12
Chinese, ex. Taiwanese (7)	14	0.13
Filipino (59)	79	0.74
Indian (11)	13	0.12
Indonesian (1)	2	0.02
Japanese (3)	6	0.06
Korean (5)	17	0.16
Laotian (1)	1	0.01
Pakistani (3)	3	0.03
Taiwanese (1)	1	0.01
Thai (2)	2	0.02
Vietnamese (16)	16	0.15
Hawaii Native/Pacific Islander (6)	19	0.18
Not Hispanic (6)	19	0.18
Guamanian/Chamorro (4)	4	0.04
Native Hawaiian (0)	3	0.03
Samoan (1)	3	0.03
White (6,995)	7,313	68.55
Not Hispanic (6,830)	7,107	66.62
Hispanic (165)	206	1.93

Northridge

Place Type: CDP
County: Clark
Population: 7,572†

Ancestry‡	Population	%
American (728)	728	9.39
Belgian (0)	6	0.08
British (16)	26	0.34
Croatian (24)	70	0.90
Czechoslovakian (11)	11	0.14
Dutch (38)	151	1.95
English (253)	949	12.24
French, ex. Basque (21)	180	2.32
French Canadian (14)	26	0.34
German (1,001)	2,539	32.74
Greek (0)	48	0.62
Hungarian (0)	74	0.95
Irish (726)	1,868	24.09
Italian (188)	331	4.27
Northern European (27)	27	0.35
Norwegian (0)	14	0.18
Polish (45)	150	1.93
Scotch-Irish (96)	209	2.70
Scottish (67)	203	2.62
Swedish (0)	49	0.63
Swiss (10)	10	0.13
Ukrainian (0)	12	0.15
Welsh (62)	130	1.68

Hispanic Origin	Population	%
Hispanic or Latino (of any race)	84	1.11
Central American, ex. Mexican	16	0.21
Guatemalan	2	0.03
Nicaraguan	5	0.07

*Notes: † The Census 2010 population figure is used to calculate the percentages in the Hispanic Origin and Race categories. Ancestry percentages are based on the 2006-2010 American Community Survey population (not shown); ‡ Numbers in parentheses indicate the number of people reporting a single ancestry; * Numbers in parentheses indicate the number of persons reporting this race alone, not in combination with any other race; Please refer to the Explanation of Data for more information.*

Salvadoran	9	0.12
Cuban	3	0.04
Mexican	40	0.53
Puerto Rican	9	0.12
South American	1	0.01
Venezuelan	1	0.01
Other Hispanic or Latino	15	0.20

Race*	Population	%
African-American/Black (129)	181	2.39
Not Hispanic (129)	178	2.35
Hispanic (0)	3	0.04
American Indian/Alaska Native (5)	22	0.29
Not Hispanic (5)	22	0.29
Alaska Athabascan *(Ala. Nat.)* (0)	3	0.04
Cherokee (1)	3	0.04
Choctaw (0)	2	0.03
Iroquois (0)	1	0.01
Sioux (1)	1	0.01
Asian (45)	64	0.85
Not Hispanic (45)	63	0.83
Hispanic (0)	1	0.01
Chinese, ex. Taiwanese (5)	5	0.07
Filipino (9)	20	0.26
Indian (16)	19	0.25
Japanese (1)	3	0.04
Korean (2)	3	0.04
Pakistani (5)	5	0.07
Sri Lankan (1)	1	0.01
Vietnamese (4)	6	0.08
Hawaii Native/Pacific Islander (1)	3	0.04
Not Hispanic (1)	2	0.03
Hispanic (0)	1	0.01
Fijian (1)	1	0.01
Native Hawaiian (0)	2	0.03
White (7,267)	7,355	97.13
Not Hispanic (7,218)	7,297	96.37
Hispanic (49)	58	0.77

Norton

Place Type: City
County: Summit
Population: 12,085†

Ancestry‡	Population	%
American (976)	976	8.13
Arab (11)	78	0.65
Lebanese (11)	78	0.65
Austrian (9)	50	0.42
Brazilian (0)	9	0.07
British (11)	11	0.09
Canadian (10)	30	0.25
Carpatho Rusyn (11)	11	0.09
Croatian (13)	46	0.38
Czech (32)	108	0.90
Czechoslovakian (21)	42	0.35
Danish (47)	81	0.67
Dutch (22)	191	1.59
English (530)	1,508	12.56
European (129)	151	1.26
Finnish (0)	26	0.22
French, ex. Basque (35)	277	2.31
French Canadian (47)	47	0.39
German (1,288)	3,751	31.24
Greek (72)	95	0.79
Hungarian (263)	837	6.97
Irish (388)	1,827	15.21
Italian (311)	805	6.70
Lithuanian (24)	36	0.30
Norwegian (0)	20	0.17
Pennsylvania German (10)	19	0.16
Polish (101)	344	2.86
Portuguese (11)	11	0.09
Romanian (6)	19	0.16
Russian (0)	54	0.45
Scandinavian (0)	9	0.07
Scotch-Irish (119)	261	2.17
Scottish (52)	274	2.28
Serbian (172)	205	1.71
Slovak (63)	199	1.66
Slovene (94)	190	1.58
Swedish (9)	46	0.38
Swiss (0)	42	0.35
Ukrainian (56)	127	1.06
Welsh (37)	117	0.97
Yugoslavian (11)	44	0.37

Hispanic Origin	Population	%
Hispanic or Latino (of any race)	114	0.94
Central American, ex. Mexican	5	0.04
Guatemalan	5	0.04
Cuban	1	0.01
Mexican	61	0.50
Puerto Rican	10	0.08
South American	23	0.19
Argentinean	1	0.01
Bolivian	2	0.02
Chilean	6	0.05
Colombian	7	0.06
Ecuadorian	1	0.01
Peruvian	6	0.05
Other Hispanic or Latino	14	0.12

Race*	Population	%
African-American/Black (208)	252	2.09
Not Hispanic (207)	249	2.06
Hispanic (1)	3	0.02
American Indian/Alaska Native (20)	62	0.51
Not Hispanic (18)	56	0.46
Hispanic (2)	6	0.05
Blackfeet (0)	4	0.03
Cherokee (7)	20	0.17
Cheyenne (0)	1	0.01
Iroquois (3)	4	0.03
Mexican American Ind. (1)	1	0.01
Seminole (0)	1	0.01
Shoshone (0)	1	0.01
Asian (91)	115	0.95
Not Hispanic (90)	114	0.94
Hispanic (1)	1	0.01
Bangladeshi (1)	1	0.01
Cambodian (1)	3	0.02
Chinese, ex. Taiwanese (9)	11	0.09
Filipino (9)	17	0.14
Indian (29)	31	0.26
Japanese (3)	7	0.06
Korean (2)	7	0.06
Laotian (5)	7	0.06
Taiwanese (1)	1	0.01
Thai (4)	4	0.03
Vietnamese (26)	27	0.22
Hawaii Native/Pacific Islander (8)	11	0.09
Not Hispanic (8)	11	0.09
Guamanian/Chamorro (0)	1	0.01
Native Hawaiian (2)	3	0.02
White (11,628)	11,739	97.14
Not Hispanic (11,539)	11,636	96.28
Hispanic (89)	103	0.85

Norwalk

Place Type: City
County: Huron
Population: 17,012†

Ancestry‡	Population	%
Alsatian (10)	10	0.06
American (1,598)	1,598	9.40
Austrian (21)	73	0.43
British (41)	49	0.29
Canadian (0)	54	0.32
Croatian (0)	12	0.07
Czech (6)	65	0.38
Czechoslovakian (0)	69	0.41
Danish (29)	117	0.69
Dutch (12)	338	1.99
Eastern European (0)	8	0.05
English (578)	2,000	11.76
Estonian (17)	17	0.10
European (59)	66	0.39
French, ex. Basque (100)	549	3.23
French Canadian (17)	26	0.15
German (2,879)	6,587	38.73
Hungarian (119)	332	1.95
Irish (897)	2,788	16.39
Italian (306)	797	4.69
Latvian (10)	10	0.06
Lithuanian (0)	12	0.07
Macedonian (76)	76	0.45
Maltese (11)	11	0.06
Norwegian (33)	96	0.56
Polish (171)	456	2.68
Portuguese (36)	53	0.31
Romanian (0)	22	0.13
Russian (11)	49	0.29
Scandinavian (12)	12	0.07
Scotch-Irish (10)	112	0.66
Scottish (165)	351	2.06
Slavic (0)	19	0.11
Slovak (0)	52	0.31
Swedish (0)	68	0.40
Swiss (0)	23	0.14
Ukrainian (0)	8	0.05
Welsh (30)	66	0.39
Yugoslavian (49)	122	0.72

Hispanic Origin	Population	%
Hispanic or Latino (of any race)	1,221	7.18
Central American, ex. Mexican	37	0.22
Costa Rican	3	0.02
Guatemalan	8	0.05
Honduran	14	0.08
Nicaraguan	2	0.01
Panamanian	7	0.04
Salvadoran	3	0.02
Cuban	3	0.02
Dominican Republic	3	0.02
Mexican	1,010	5.94
Puerto Rican	90	0.53
South American	13	0.08
Colombian	11	0.06
Ecuadorian	1	0.01
Peruvian	1	0.01
Other Hispanic or Latino	65	0.38

Race*	Population	%
African-American/Black (317)	513	3.02
Not Hispanic (291)	460	2.70
Hispanic (26)	53	0.31
American Indian/Alaska Native (33)	114	0.67
Not Hispanic (31)	109	0.64
Hispanic (2)	5	0.03
Blackfeet (0)	3	0.02
Canadian/French Am. Ind. (0)	1	0.01
Cherokee (20)	56	0.33
Cheyenne (0)	1	0.01
Iroquois (0)	2	0.01
Potawatomi (1)	2	0.01
Seminole (0)	2	0.01
Sioux (0)	2	0.01
Asian (80)	111	0.65
Not Hispanic (79)	109	0.64
Hispanic (1)	2	0.01
Chinese, ex. Taiwanese (25)	30	0.18
Filipino (19)	29	0.17
Indian (18)	20	0.12
Indonesian (0)	1	0.01
Japanese (2)	4	0.02
Korean (7)	9	0.05
Pakistani (0)	1	0.01
Thai (2)	7	0.04
Vietnamese (3)	4	0.02
Hawaii Native/Pacific Islander (2)	29	0.17
Not Hispanic (2)	21	0.12
Hispanic (0)	8	0.05
Guamanian/Chamorro (1)	1	0.01
Native Hawaiian (0)	12	0.07
Samoan (1)	5	0.03
White (15,689)	16,023	94.19

*Notes: † The Census 2010 population figure is used to calculate the percentages in the Hispanic Origin and Race categories. Ancestry percentages are based on the 2006-2010 American Community Survey population (not shown); ‡ Numbers in parentheses indicate the number of people reporting a single ancestry; * Numbers in parentheses indicate the number of persons reporting this race alone, not in combination with any other race; Please refer to the Explanation of Data for more information.*

	Population	%
Not Hispanic (15,107)	15,365	90.32
Hispanic (582)	658	3.87

Norwood

Place Type: City
County: Hamilton
Population: 19,207†

Ancestry‡	Population	%
African, Sub-Saharan (13)	13	0.07
South African (13)	13	0.07
American (5,029)	5,029	25.84
Arab (94)	126	0.65
Arab (30)	30	0.15
Lebanese (33)	65	0.33
Palestinian (21)	21	0.11
Other Arab (10)	10	0.05
Brazilian (0)	22	0.11
British (29)	115	0.59
Canadian (36)	36	0.18
Croatian (0)	28	0.14
Czech (0)	19	0.10
Czechoslovakian (0)	10	0.05
Danish (0)	9	0.05
Dutch (42)	340	1.75
Eastern European (11)	11	0.06
English (505)	1,432	7.36
European (171)	184	0.95
French, ex. Basque (146)	371	1.91
French Canadian (9)	9	0.05
German (1,695)	4,700	24.15
German Russian (0)	9	0.05
Greek (12)	43	0.22
Hungarian (8)	29	0.15
Irish (710)	2,919	15.00
Italian (376)	906	4.65
Norwegian (0)	59	0.30
Pennsylvania German (0)	12	0.06
Polish (41)	318	1.63
Russian (7)	108	0.55
Scotch-Irish (84)	259	1.33
Scottish (96)	226	1.16
Slovak (8)	49	0.25
Swedish (16)	50	0.26
Swiss (43)	161	0.83
Turkish (9)	9	0.05
Welsh (17)	100	0.51
Yugoslavian (0)	28	0.14

Hispanic Origin	Population	%
Hispanic or Latino (of any race)	972	5.06
Central American, ex. Mexican	168	0.87
Costa Rican	1	0.01
Guatemalan	39	0.20
Honduran	81	0.42
Nicaraguan	25	0.13
Panamanian	12	0.06
Salvadoran	10	0.05
Cuban	19	0.10
Dominican Republic	20	0.10
Mexican	611	3.18
Puerto Rican	50	0.26
South American	34	0.18
Argentinean	5	0.03
Chilean	8	0.04
Colombian	6	0.03
Ecuadorian	3	0.02
Peruvian	3	0.02
Venezuelan	9	0.05
Other Hispanic or Latino	70	0.36

Race*	Population	%
African-American/Black (1,465)	1,704	8.87
Not Hispanic (1,448)	1,668	8.68
Hispanic (17)	36	0.19
American Indian/Alaska Native (80)	211	1.10
Not Hispanic (52)	173	0.90
Hispanic (28)	38	0.20
Aleut *(Alaska Native)* (2)	2	0.01
Apache (0)	1	0.01
Blackfeet (1)	4	0.02
Central American Ind. (8)	8	0.04
Cherokee (18)	67	0.35
Cheyenne (0)	1	0.01
Chickasaw (0)	1	0.01
Choctaw (6)	8	0.04
Comanche (0)	1	0.01
Creek (2)	2	0.01
Iroquois (1)	1	0.01
Lumbee (1)	2	0.01
Mexican American Ind. (6)	6	0.03
Navajo (2)	4	0.02
Pueblo (0)	1	0.01
Sioux (2)	6	0.03
Tlingit-Haida *(Alaska Native)* (1)	1	0.01
Asian (154)	214	1.11
Not Hispanic (148)	204	1.06
Hispanic (6)	10	0.05
Cambodian (5)	10	0.05
Chinese, ex. Taiwanese (30)	44	0.23
Filipino (29)	44	0.23
Indian (16)	23	0.12
Indonesian (1)	2	0.01
Japanese (8)	14	0.07
Korean (13)	23	0.12
Laotian (3)	3	0.02
Pakistani (1)	3	0.02
Taiwanese (1)	1	0.01
Thai (6)	10	0.05
Vietnamese (32)	34	0.18
Hawaii Native/Pacific Islander (12)	21	0.11
Not Hispanic (4)	10	0.05
Hispanic (8)	11	0.06
Guamanian/Chamorro (9)	9	0.05
Native Hawaiian (0)	5	0.03
Samoan (1)	1	0.01
Tongan (1)	1	0.01
White (16,632)	17,072	88.88
Not Hispanic (16,168)	16,530	86.06
Hispanic (464)	542	2.82

Oakwood

Place Type: City
County: Montgomery
Population: 9,202†

Ancestry‡	Population	%
American (154)	154	1.68
Arab (17)	54	0.59
Lebanese (17)	26	0.28
Palestinian (0)	9	0.10
Other Arab (0)	19	0.21
Austrian (60)	60	0.65
British (29)	72	0.78
Celtic (0)	10	0.11
Croatian (13)	13	0.14
Czech (0)	10	0.11
Czechoslovakian (0)	11	0.12
Danish (20)	49	0.53
Dutch (32)	212	2.31
Eastern European (0)	19	0.21
English (290)	1,376	14.98
European (250)	250	2.72
Finnish (0)	10	0.11
French, ex. Basque (39)	274	2.98
French Canadian (12)	12	0.13
German (1,004)	3,177	34.58
Greek (91)	167	1.82
Hungarian (0)	44	0.48
Iranian (32)	77	0.84
Irish (376)	1,578	17.17
Italian (198)	742	8.08
Latvian (0)	32	0.35
Lithuanian (0)	35	0.38
New Zealander (0)	11	0.12
Northern European (11)	11	0.12
Norwegian (0)	139	1.51
Polish (172)	501	5.45
Romanian (10)	40	0.44
Russian (35)	188	2.05
Scandinavian (15)	15	0.16
Scotch-Irish (151)	425	4.63
Scottish (177)	357	3.89
Slovak (0)	87	0.95
Slovene (14)	14	0.15
Swedish (37)	121	1.32
Swiss (15)	59	0.64
Ukrainian (9)	9	0.10
Welsh (12)	117	1.27

Hispanic Origin	Population	%
Hispanic or Latino (of any race)	163	1.77
Central American, ex. Mexican	20	0.22
Costa Rican	1	0.01
Guatemalan	5	0.05
Honduran	1	0.01
Panamanian	5	0.05
Salvadoran	8	0.09
Cuban	7	0.08
Mexican	65	0.71
Puerto Rican	24	0.26
South American	24	0.26
Argentinean	1	0.01
Bolivian	3	0.03
Chilean	2	0.02
Colombian	9	0.10
Ecuadorian	1	0.01
Peruvian	6	0.07
Venezuelan	2	0.02
Other Hispanic or Latino	23	0.25

Race*	Population	%
African-American/Black (83)	124	1.35
Not Hispanic (83)	121	1.31
Hispanic (0)	3	0.03
American Indian/Alaska Native (17)	53	0.58
Not Hispanic (17)	48	0.52
Hispanic (0)	5	0.05
Blackfeet (3)	3	0.03
Cherokee (7)	24	0.26
Chippewa (1)	1	0.01
Crow (0)	3	0.03
Iroquois (0)	3	0.03
Potawatomi (1)	1	0.01
Sioux (2)	2	0.02
South American Ind. (0)	3	0.03
Asian (126)	203	2.21
Not Hispanic (124)	196	2.13
Hispanic (2)	7	0.08
Chinese, ex. Taiwanese (47)	62	0.67
Filipino (17)	31	0.34
Indian (19)	30	0.33
Indonesian (0)	1	0.01
Japanese (16)	40	0.43
Korean (15)	23	0.25
Pakistani (0)	1	0.01
Thai (4)	5	0.05
Vietnamese (4)	8	0.09
Hawaii Native/Pacific Islander (1)	3	0.03
Not Hispanic (0)	2	0.02
Hispanic (1)	1	0.01
Guamanian/Chamorro (1)	1	0.01
Native Hawaiian (0)	1	0.01
Samoan (0)	1	0.01
White (8,771)	8,915	96.88
Not Hispanic (8,655)	8,787	95.49
Hispanic (116)	128	1.39

Oberlin

Place Type: City
County: Lorain
Population: 8,286†

Ancestry‡	Population	%
African, Sub-Saharan (49)	77	0.93
African (22)	50	0.60
Ethiopian (10)	10	0.12

*Notes: † The Census 2010 population figure is used to calculate the percentages in the Hispanic Origin and Race categories. Ancestry percentages are based on the 2006-2010 American Community Survey population (not shown); ‡ Numbers in parentheses indicate the number of people reporting a single ancestry; * Numbers in parentheses indicate the number of persons reporting this race alone, not in combination with any other race; Please refer to the Explanation of Data for more information.*

SECTION TWO

Kenyan (17)	17	0.20
American (436)	436	5.25
Arab (17)	50	0.60
Lebanese (17)	36	0.43
Other Arab (0)	14	0.17
Australian (0)	14	0.17
Austrian (9)	93	1.12
Belgian (0)	5	0.06
Brazilian (0)	14	0.17
British (39)	113	1.36
Canadian (13)	39	0.47
Carpatho Rusyn (0)	14	0.17
Croatian (22)	47	0.57
Czech (0)	69	0.83
Czechoslovakian (22)	22	0.27
Danish (22)	44	0.53
Dutch (4)	50	0.60
Eastern European (0)	31	0.37
English (191)	1,305	15.73
Estonian (5)	5	0.06
European (53)	91	1.10
Finnish (20)	20	0.24
French, ex. Basque (17)	117	1.41
French Canadian (9)	9	0.11
German (509)	1,836	22.13
Greek (32)	86	1.04
Hungarian (75)	279	3.36
Irish (197)	1,301	15.68
Israeli (16)	37	0.45
Italian (129)	489	5.89
Latvian (0)	30	0.36
Lithuanian (29)	34	0.41
Macedonian (0)	8	0.10
Norwegian (0)	53	0.64
Pennsylvania German (0)	11	0.13
Polish (111)	356	4.29
Portuguese (0)	3	0.04
Romanian (0)	58	0.70
Russian (99)	336	4.05
Scotch-Irish (87)	304	3.66
Scottish (61)	294	3.54
Serbian (16)	24	0.29
Slovak (26)	74	0.89
Swedish (0)	90	1.08
Swiss (0)	45	0.54
Ukrainian (12)	55	0.66
Welsh (26)	89	1.07
West Indian, ex. Hispanic (13)	33	0.40
Jamaican (13)	33	0.40

Hispanic Origin	Population	%
Hispanic or Latino (of any race)	423	5.10
Central American, ex. Mexican	29	0.35
Costa Rican	7	0.08
Guatemalan	3	0.04
Honduran	3	0.04
Nicaraguan	5	0.06
Panamanian	7	0.08
Salvadoran	4	0.05
Cuban	20	0.24
Dominican Republic	2	0.02
Mexican	128	1.54
Puerto Rican	148	1.79
South American	45	0.54
Argentinean	9	0.11
Bolivian	2	0.02
Chilean	4	0.05
Colombian	10	0.12
Ecuadorian	3	0.04
Paraguayan	3	0.04
Peruvian	7	0.08
Uruguayan	2	0.02
Venezuelan	5	0.06
Other Hispanic or Latino	51	0.62

Race*	Population	%
African-American/Black (1,230)	1,563	18.86
Not Hispanic (1,186)	1,491	17.99
Hispanic (44)	72	0.87
American Indian/Alaska Native (19)	146	1.76
Not Hispanic (18)	132	1.59
Hispanic (1)	14	0.17
Blackfeet (0)	17	0.21
Central American Ind. (0)	1	0.01
Cherokee (3)	33	0.40
Chickasaw (0)	3	0.04
Chippewa (2)	5	0.06
Choctaw (0)	4	0.05
Hopi (1)	1	0.01
Houma (0)	1	0.01
Iroquois (0)	2	0.02
Mexican American Ind. (1)	2	0.02
Navajo (0)	6	0.07
Ottawa (1)	1	0.01
Pueblo (0)	1	0.01
Sioux (0)	4	0.05
South American Ind. (0)	2	0.02
Tohono O'Odham (0)	1	0.01
Asian (335)	473	5.71
Not Hispanic (333)	459	5.54
Hispanic (2)	14	0.17
Burmese (1)	2	0.02
Cambodian (1)	3	0.04
Chinese, ex. Taiwanese (124)	178	2.15
Filipino (7)	24	0.29
Indian (39)	59	0.71
Indonesian (1)	3	0.04
Japanese (26)	69	0.83
Korean (70)	85	1.03
Laotian (0)	4	0.05
Malaysian (1)	1	0.01
Nepalese (2)	2	0.02
Pakistani (7)	7	0.08
Taiwanese (18)	21	0.25
Thai (4)	8	0.10
Vietnamese (11)	16	0.19
Hawaii Native/Pacific Islander (1)	7	0.08
Not Hispanic (1)	3	0.04
Hispanic (0)	4	0.05
Native Hawaiian (0)	3	0.04
Samoan (1)	1	0.01
White (6,047)	6,535	78.87
Not Hispanic (5,827)	6,263	75.59
Hispanic (220)	272	3.28

Olmsted Falls

Place Type: City
County: Cuyahoga
Population: 9,024†

Ancestry‡	Population	%
African, Sub-Saharan (36)	36	0.41
Sierra Leonean (36)	36	0.41
American (396)	396	4.52
Arab (205)	343	3.92
Jordanian (16)	48	0.55
Lebanese (11)	85	0.97
Syrian (178)	210	2.40
Armenian (0)	13	0.15
Australian (0)	10	0.11
Austrian (0)	10	0.11
Brazilian (31)	31	0.35
Canadian (0)	25	0.29
Croatian (0)	33	0.38
Czech (15)	60	0.69
Czechoslovakian (0)	12	0.14
Danish (23)	23	0.26
Dutch (39)	153	1.75
English (169)	918	10.49
Finnish (0)	20	0.23
French, ex. Basque (8)	261	2.98
French Canadian (13)	23	0.26
German (928)	2,711	30.98
Greek (0)	92	1.05
Hungarian (182)	522	5.96
Irish (618)	2,147	24.53
Italian (326)	1,094	12.50
Lithuanian (0)	8	0.09
Norwegian (44)	134	1.53
Polish (138)	812	9.28
Russian (40)	136	1.55
Scotch-Irish (38)	249	2.85
Scottish (73)	219	2.50
Serbian (83)	83	0.95
Slavic (0)	11	0.13
Slovak (133)	331	3.78
Slovene (20)	133	1.52
Swedish (0)	36	0.41
Swiss (0)	9	0.10
Ukrainian (21)	76	0.87
Welsh (0)	120	1.37
West Indian, ex. Hispanic (15)	15	0.17
Jamaican (15)	15	0.17
Yugoslavian (0)	9	0.10

Hispanic Origin	Population	%
Hispanic or Latino (of any race)	231	2.56
Central American, ex. Mexican	9	0.10
Guatemalan	6	0.07
Honduran	2	0.02
Salvadoran	1	0.01
Cuban	9	0.10
Dominican Republic	2	0.02
Mexican	64	0.71
Puerto Rican	117	1.30
South American	15	0.17
Colombian	10	0.11
Peruvian	4	0.04
Venezuelan	1	0.01
Other Hispanic or Latino	15	0.17

Race*	Population	%
African-American/Black (179)	235	2.60
Not Hispanic (171)	213	2.36
Hispanic (8)	22	0.24
American Indian/Alaska Native (8)	58	0.64
Not Hispanic (3)	47	0.52
Hispanic (5)	11	0.12
Apache (1)	1	0.01
Blackfeet (0)	1	0.01
Cherokee (2)	14	0.16
Chippewa (0)	1	0.01
Iroquois (1)	2	0.02
Mexican American Ind. (2)	2	0.02
Navajo (2)	2	0.02
South American Ind. (0)	2	0.02
Asian (109)	143	1.58
Not Hispanic (109)	138	1.53
Hispanic (0)	5	0.06
Burmese (1)	1	0.01
Cambodian (0)	1	0.01
Chinese, ex. Taiwanese (16)	18	0.20
Filipino (21)	33	0.37
Indian (27)	27	0.30
Indonesian (1)	1	0.01
Japanese (3)	6	0.07
Korean (19)	25	0.28
Vietnamese (21)	22	0.24
Hawaii Native/Pacific Islander (0)	1	0.01
Hispanic (0)	1	0.01
White (8,567)	8,677	96.15
Not Hispanic (8,405)	8,496	94.15
Hispanic (162)	181	2.01

Oregon

Place Type: City
County: Lucas
Population: 20,291†

Ancestry‡	Population	%
American (1,062)	1,062	5.28
Arab (217)	268	1.33
Arab (0)	7	0.03
Lebanese (217)	261	1.30
Austrian (33)	60	0.30
British (5)	93	0.46
Bulgarian (60)	77	0.38
Canadian (56)	67	0.33

*Notes: † The Census 2010 population figure is used to calculate the percentages in the Hispanic Origin and Race categories. Ancestry percentages are based on the 2006-2010 American Community Survey population (not shown); ‡ Numbers in parentheses indicate the number of people reporting a single ancestry; * Numbers in parentheses indicate the number of persons reporting this race alone, not in combination with any other race; Please refer to the Explanation of Data for more information.*

Croatian (29)	58	0.29
Czech (105)	198	0.98
Czechoslovakian (31)	50	0.25
Danish (9)	9	0.04
Dutch (58)	531	2.64
Eastern European (0)	22	0.11
English (437)	1,448	7.20
Estonian (11)	11	0.05
European (122)	122	0.61
French, ex. Basque (218)	1,492	7.42
French Canadian (102)	417	2.07
German (2,926)	7,629	37.92
Greek (117)	201	1.00
Hungarian (656)	1,686	8.38
Irish (490)	2,342	11.64
Italian (312)	1,127	5.60
Lithuanian (11)	21	0.10
Maltese (7)	7	0.03
Norwegian (9)	32	0.16
Pennsylvania German (11)	24	0.12
Polish (932)	2,036	10.12
Romanian (0)	21	0.10
Russian (0)	27	0.13
Scotch-Irish (41)	64	0.32
Scottish (179)	363	1.80
Slavic (10)	10	0.05
Slovak (72)	133	0.66
Swedish (31)	344	1.71
Swiss (10)	256	1.27
Ukrainian (0)	7	0.03
Welsh (12)	92	0.46

Hispanic Origin	Population	%
Hispanic or Latino (of any race)	1,516	7.47
Central American, ex. Mexican	11	0.05
Guatemalan	3	0.01
Nicaraguan	3	0.01
Panamanian	2	0.01
Other Central American	3	0.01
Cuban	16	0.08
Dominican Republic	1	<0.01
Mexican	1,325	6.53
Puerto Rican	61	0.30
South American	2	0.01
Argentinean	1	<0.01
Peruvian	1	<0.01
Other Hispanic or Latino	100	0.49

Race*	Population	%
African-American/Black (291)	422	2.08
Not Hispanic (259)	369	1.82
Hispanic (32)	53	0.26
American Indian/Alaska Native (38)	131	0.65
Not Hispanic (26)	103	0.51
Hispanic (12)	28	0.14
Aleut *(Alaska Native)* (0)	1	<0.01
Apache (0)	2	0.01
Blackfeet (0)	2	0.01
Cherokee (8)	41	0.20
Chippewa (1)	11	0.05
Choctaw (3)	3	0.01
Cree (0)	1	<0.01
Iroquois (1)	2	0.01
Mexican American Ind. (2)	13	0.06
Navajo (0)	2	0.01
Ottawa (1)	2	0.01
Asian (155)	208	1.03
Not Hispanic (153)	202	1.00
Hispanic (2)	6	0.03
Chinese, ex. Taiwanese (48)	58	0.29
Filipino (28)	31	0.15
Indian (22)	23	0.11
Japanese (4)	10	0.05
Korean (8)	18	0.09
Laotian (2)	8	0.04
Pakistani (8)	8	0.04
Thai (6)	14	0.07
Vietnamese (23)	25	0.12
Hawaii Native/Pacific Islander (3)	8	0.04
Not Hispanic (1)	5	0.02
Hispanic (2)	3	0.01
Guamanian/Chamorro (1)	1	<0.01
Samoan (2)	3	0.01
White (18,978)	19,341	95.32
Not Hispanic (18,082)	18,303	90.20
Hispanic (896)	1,038	5.12

Orrville

Place Type: City
County: Wayne
Population: 8,380†

Ancestry‡	Population	%
American (945)	945	11.20
Arab (38)	49	0.58
Lebanese (27)	38	0.45
Moroccan (11)	11	0.13
Austrian (8)	8	0.09
British (22)	22	0.26
Croatian (0)	10	0.12
Czech (15)	53	0.63
Danish (0)	12	0.14
Dutch (12)	275	3.26
English (180)	756	8.96
European (38)	82	0.97
Finnish (44)	52	0.62
French, ex. Basque (27)	271	3.21
French Canadian (0)	25	0.30
German (956)	2,852	33.80
Greek (40)	124	1.47
Hungarian (63)	147	1.74
Irish (261)	1,292	15.31
Italian (191)	446	5.28
Norwegian (13)	54	0.64
Pennsylvania German (12)	28	0.33
Polish (47)	90	1.07
Russian (17)	45	0.53
Scotch-Irish (48)	170	2.01
Scottish (44)	223	2.64
Slovak (8)	16	0.19
Swedish (48)	81	0.96
Swiss (181)	622	7.37
Welsh (10)	63	0.75

Hispanic Origin	Population	%
Hispanic or Latino (of any race)	292	3.48
Central American, ex. Mexican	8	0.10
Guatemalan	3	0.04
Honduran	4	0.05
Nicaraguan	1	0.01
Cuban	3	0.04
Dominican Republic	3	0.04
Mexican	228	2.72
Puerto Rican	9	0.11
South American	8	0.10
Ecuadorian	8	0.10
Other Hispanic or Latino	33	0.39

Race*	Population	%
African-American/Black (408)	539	6.43
Not Hispanic (407)	530	6.32
Hispanic (1)	9	0.11
American Indian/Alaska Native (11)	48	0.57
Not Hispanic (11)	43	0.51
Hispanic (0)	5	0.06
Apache (0)	1	0.01
Blackfeet (0)	4	0.05
Canadian/French Am. Ind. (1)	1	0.01
Cherokee (2)	15	0.18
Crow (1)	1	0.01
Iroquois (1)	1	0.01
Mexican American Ind. (0)	1	0.01
Sioux (0)	2	0.02
Asian (107)	141	1.68
Not Hispanic (107)	138	1.65
Hispanic (0)	3	0.04
Chinese, ex. Taiwanese (2)	10	0.12
Filipino (6)	15	0.18
Indian (17)	23	0.27
Japanese (0)	3	0.04
Korean (3)	3	0.04
Laotian (63)	76	0.91
Pakistani (1)	1	0.01
Thai (3)	3	0.04
Vietnamese (3)	8	0.10
Hawaii Native/Pacific Islander (3)	10	0.12
Not Hispanic (1)	8	0.10
Hispanic (2)	2	0.02
Guamanian/Chamorro (2)	4	0.05
Native Hawaiian (1)	6	0.07
White (7,517)	7,728	92.22
Not Hispanic (7,365)	7,545	90.04
Hispanic (152)	183	2.18

Oxford

Place Type: City
County: Butler
Population: 21,371†

Ancestry‡	Population	%
African, Sub-Saharan (313)	342	1.59
African (209)	238	1.11
Nigerian (48)	48	0.22
Ugandan (8)	8	0.04
Other Sub-Saharan African (48)	48	0.22
American (3,563)	3,563	16.55
Arab (17)	30	0.14
Lebanese (0)	13	0.06
Palestinian (17)	17	0.08
Austrian (0)	85	0.39
Belgian (14)	14	0.07
Brazilian (15)	15	0.07
British (54)	96	0.45
Canadian (38)	61	0.28
Croatian (0)	14	0.07
Czech (14)	226	1.05
Czechoslovakian (12)	39	0.18
Danish (19)	54	0.25
Dutch (54)	284	1.32
Eastern European (0)	14	0.07
English (511)	1,866	8.67
Estonian (27)	27	0.13
European (476)	606	2.81
Finnish (15)	50	0.23
French, ex. Basque (80)	568	2.64
French Canadian (17)	51	0.24
German (1,371)	4,767	22.14
Greek (43)	114	0.53
Hungarian (29)	180	0.84
Icelander (14)	14	0.07
Irish (632)	2,827	13.13
Italian (544)	1,287	5.98
Lithuanian (29)	79	0.37
Norwegian (37)	182	0.85
Polish (208)	867	4.03
Portuguese (0)	42	0.20
Romanian (0)	57	0.26
Russian (66)	261	1.21
Scandinavian (8)	15	0.07
Scotch-Irish (112)	376	1.75
Scottish (115)	357	1.66
Slavic (0)	13	0.06
Slovak (51)	96	0.45
Slovene (0)	15	0.07
Swedish (13)	214	0.99
Swiss (26)	85	0.39
Turkish (13)	38	0.18
Ukrainian (15)	53	0.25
Welsh (77)	262	1.22
Yugoslavian (16)	16	0.07

Hispanic Origin	Population	%
Hispanic or Latino (of any race)	491	2.30
Central American, ex. Mexican	30	0.14
Costa Rican	6	0.03
Guatemalan	7	0.03
Honduran	7	0.03
Nicaraguan	5	0.02

*Notes: † The Census 2010 population figure is used to calculate the percentages in the Hispanic Origin and Race categories. Ancestry percentages are based on the 2006-2010 American Community Survey population (not shown); ‡ Numbers in parentheses indicate the number of people reporting a single ancestry; * Numbers in parentheses indicate the number of persons reporting this race alone, not in combination with any other race; Please refer to the Explanation of Data for more information.*

Panamanian	2	0.01
Salvadoran	3	0.01
Cuban	31	0.15
Dominican Republic	17	0.08
Mexican	200	0.94
Puerto Rican	70	0.33
South American	84	0.39
Argentinean	10	0.05
Chilean	4	0.02
Colombian	14	0.07
Ecuadorian	9	0.04
Paraguayan	2	0.01
Peruvian	18	0.08
Uruguayan	6	0.03
Venezuelan	18	0.08
Other South American	3	0.01
Other Hispanic or Latino	59	0.28

Race*	Population	%
African-American/Black (859)	1,049	4.91
Not Hispanic (844)	1,022	4.78
Hispanic (15)	27	0.13
American Indian/Alaska Native (33)	155	0.73
Not Hispanic (30)	134	0.63
Hispanic (3)	21	0.10
Blackfeet (0)	3	0.01
Cherokee (1)	29	0.14
Cheyenne (0)	1	<0.01
Chippewa (2)	4	0.02
Choctaw (0)	3	0.01
Iroquois (2)	7	0.03
Mexican American Ind. (0)	2	0.01
Navajo (0)	2	0.01
Osage (1)	2	0.01
Potawatomi (0)	2	0.01
Shoshone (0)	1	<0.01
Sioux (1)	4	0.02
South American Ind. (0)	1	<0.01
Spanish American Ind. (0)	1	<0.01
Asian (1,153)	1,363	6.38
Not Hispanic (1,149)	1,355	6.34
Hispanic (4)	8	0.04
Bangladeshi (4)	4	0.02
Burmese (3)	3	0.01
Cambodian (6)	6	0.03
Chinese, ex. Taiwanese (663)	716	3.35
Filipino (32)	76	0.36
Indian (184)	214	1.00
Indonesian (3)	6	0.03
Japanese (38)	83	0.39
Korean (110)	135	0.63
Laotian (1)	2	0.01
Malaysian (4)	7	0.03
Nepalese (21)	21	0.10
Pakistani (9)	19	0.09
Sri Lankan (4)	4	0.02
Taiwanese (10)	11	0.05
Thai (7)	11	0.05
Vietnamese (26)	34	0.16
Hawaii Native/Pacific Islander (2)	12	0.06
Not Hispanic (2)	12	0.06
Native Hawaiian (2)	6	0.03
Samoan (0)	1	<0.01
White (18,719)	19,152	89.62
Not Hispanic (18,390)	18,795	87.95
Hispanic (329)	357	1.67

Painesville

Place Type: City
County: Lake
Population: 19,563†

Ancestry‡	Population	%
African, Sub-Saharan (0)	42	0.22
African (0)	30	0.16
Kenyan (0)	12	0.06
American (651)	651	3.39
Arab (0)	54	0.28
Arab (0)	9	0.05
Lebanese (0)	45	0.23
Australian (0)	20	0.10
Austrian (0)	37	0.19
British (4)	4	0.02
Bulgarian (17)	17	0.09
Canadian (20)	48	0.25
Croatian (27)	130	0.68
Czech (45)	186	0.97
Czechoslovakian (28)	28	0.15
Danish (18)	57	0.30
Dutch (8)	201	1.05
Eastern European (31)	31	0.16
English (482)	1,662	8.66
European (78)	125	0.65
Finnish (108)	290	1.51
French, ex. Basque (11)	282	1.47
French Canadian (48)	78	0.41
German (916)	4,094	21.33
Greek (16)	28	0.15
Hungarian (249)	851	4.43
Irish (465)	3,008	15.67
Italian (691)	2,264	11.80
Lithuanian (57)	65	0.34
Norwegian (67)	174	0.91
Pennsylvania German (13)	20	0.10
Polish (135)	694	3.62
Romanian (28)	77	0.40
Russian (0)	120	0.63
Scandinavian (0)	29	0.15
Scotch-Irish (219)	443	2.31
Scottish (74)	252	1.31
Serbian (10)	10	0.05
Slavic (7)	21	0.11
Slovak (33)	252	1.31
Slovene (46)	260	1.35
Swedish (59)	396	2.06
Swiss (0)	8	0.04
Turkish (15)	15	0.08
Ukrainian (0)	73	0.38
Welsh (7)	88	0.46

Hispanic Origin	Population	%
Hispanic or Latino (of any race)	4,298	21.97
Central American, ex. Mexican	41	0.21
Costa Rican	6	0.03
Guatemalan	8	0.04
Honduran	11	0.06
Salvadoran	16	0.08
Cuban	15	0.08
Dominican Republic	7	0.04
Mexican	3,614	18.47
Puerto Rican	457	2.34
South American	33	0.17
Argentinean	5	0.03
Bolivian	1	0.01
Chilean	6	0.03
Colombian	8	0.04
Ecuadorian	4	0.02
Peruvian	5	0.03
Venezuelan	4	0.02
Other Hispanic or Latino	131	0.67

Race*	Population	%
African-American/Black (2,555)	3,184	16.28
Not Hispanic (2,491)	3,050	15.59
Hispanic (64)	134	0.68
American Indian/Alaska Native (53)	227	1.16
Not Hispanic (34)	182	0.93
Hispanic (19)	45	0.23
Blackfeet (1)	7	0.04
Cherokee (5)	70	0.36
Cheyenne (0)	1	0.01
Chickasaw (0)	1	0.01
Chippewa (1)	4	0.02
Choctaw (1)	9	0.05
Cree (1)	1	0.01
Creek (0)	1	0.01
Iroquois (3)	6	0.03
Lumbee (2)	2	0.01
Mexican American Ind. (1)	13	0.07
Navajo (5)	10	0.05
Osage (0)	1	0.01
Pueblo (1)	1	0.01
Sioux (0)	2	0.01
Asian (149)	219	1.12
Not Hispanic (146)	211	1.08
Hispanic (3)	8	0.04
Chinese, ex. Taiwanese (34)	49	0.25
Filipino (28)	45	0.23
Indian (32)	45	0.23
Indonesian (0)	1	0.01
Japanese (8)	23	0.12
Korean (16)	21	0.11
Laotian (5)	5	0.03
Pakistani (1)	2	0.01
Taiwanese (2)	4	0.02
Thai (1)	3	0.02
Vietnamese (20)	20	0.10
Hawaii Native/Pacific Islander (6)	23	0.12
Not Hispanic (4)	16	0.08
Hispanic (2)	7	0.04
Fijian (2)	2	0.01
Guamanian/Chamorro (1)	3	0.02
Native Hawaiian (1)	5	0.03
White (13,345)	14,108	72.12
Not Hispanic (11,882)	12,491	63.85
Hispanic (1,463)	1,617	8.27

Parma Heights

Place Type: City
County: Cuyahoga
Population: 20,718†

Ancestry‡	Population	%
African, Sub-Saharan (91)	91	0.44
Other Sub-Saharan African (91)	91	0.44
Albanian (164)	164	0.79
American (911)	911	4.38
Arab (443)	660	3.18
Arab (148)	148	0.71
Egyptian (110)	110	0.53
Lebanese (143)	285	1.37
Palestinian (24)	24	0.12
Syrian (18)	93	0.45
Austrian (31)	114	0.55
British (13)	24	0.12
Bulgarian (42)	112	0.54
Canadian (11)	23	0.11
Croatian (151)	272	1.31
Czech (146)	593	2.85
Czechoslovakian (57)	126	0.61
Danish (64)	112	0.54
Dutch (12)	294	1.41
Eastern European (0)	11	0.05
English (549)	1,628	7.83
European (152)	168	0.81
Finnish (12)	70	0.34
French, ex. Basque (16)	298	1.43
French Canadian (84)	91	0.44
German (1,447)	4,988	24.00
Greek (202)	275	1.32
Hungarian (420)	1,046	5.03
Irish (519)	2,816	13.55
Israeli (37)	37	0.18
Italian (1,030)	2,261	10.88
Lithuanian (37)	122	0.59
Macedonian (0)	8	0.04
Norwegian (38)	38	0.18
Pennsylvania German (10)	26	0.13
Polish (1,144)	2,908	13.99
Romanian (398)	549	2.64
Russian (112)	354	1.70
Scotch-Irish (105)	302	1.45
Scottish (47)	176	0.85
Serbian (212)	234	1.13
Slovak (444)	1,023	4.92
Slovene (113)	346	1.66
Swedish (16)	92	0.44
Swiss (18)	102	0.49

*Notes: † The Census 2010 population figure is used to calculate the percentages in the Hispanic Origin and Race categories. Ancestry percentages are based on the 2006-2010 American Community Survey population (not shown); ‡ Numbers in parentheses indicate the number of people reporting a single ancestry; * Numbers in parentheses indicate the number of persons reporting this race alone, not in combination with any other race; Please refer to the Explanation of Data for more information.*

Turkish (0)	11	0.05
Ukrainian (609)	883	4.25
Welsh (7)	85	0.41
Yugoslavian (12)	50	0.24

Hispanic Origin	Population	%
Hispanic or Latino (of any race)	793	3.83
Central American, ex. Mexican	40	0.19
Costa Rican	1	<0.01
Guatemalan	23	0.11
Honduran	1	<0.01
Nicaraguan	9	0.04
Panamanian	4	0.02
Salvadoran	2	0.01
Cuban	11	0.05
Dominican Republic	39	0.19
Mexican	148	0.71
Puerto Rican	469	2.26
South American	52	0.25
Argentinean	7	0.03
Colombian	15	0.07
Ecuadorian	5	0.02
Peruvian	21	0.10
Venezuelan	1	<0.01
Other South American	3	0.01
Other Hispanic or Latino	34	0.16

Race*	Population	%
African-American/Black (571)	721	3.48
Not Hispanic (536)	654	3.16
Hispanic (35)	67	0.32
American Indian/Alaska Native (35)	127	0.61
Not Hispanic (30)	111	0.54
Hispanic (5)	16	0.08
Apache (1)	3	0.01
Blackfeet (0)	6	0.03
Central American Ind. (1)	1	<0.01
Cherokee (3)	29	0.14
Chippewa (6)	9	0.04
Creek (1)	1	<0.01
Iroquois (0)	1	<0.01
Menominee (0)	1	<0.01
Mexican American Ind. (0)	1	<0.01
Navajo (0)	3	0.01
Potawatomi (2)	3	0.01
Shoshone (2)	2	0.01
Sioux (1)	6	0.03
South American Ind. (0)	1	<0.01
Asian (631)	750	3.62
Not Hispanic (622)	732	3.53
Hispanic (9)	18	0.09
Bangladeshi (7)	11	0.05
Cambodian (7)	11	0.05
Chinese, ex. Taiwanese (71)	82	0.40
Filipino (96)	116	0.56
Indian (322)	337	1.63
Indonesian (1)	3	0.01
Japanese (11)	21	0.10
Korean (21)	46	0.22
Malaysian (1)	2	0.01
Pakistani (34)	35	0.17
Sri Lankan (3)	3	0.01
Thai (0)	1	<0.01
Vietnamese (30)	33	0.16
Hawaii Native/Pacific Islander (9)	25	0.12
Not Hispanic (6)	21	0.10
Hispanic (3)	4	0.02
Guamanian/Chamorro (6)	10	0.05
Native Hawaiian (0)	2	0.01
Samoan (2)	3	0.01
White (18,880)	19,215	92.75
Not Hispanic (18,400)	18,669	90.11
Hispanic (480)	546	2.64

Parma

Place Type: City
County: Cuyahoga
Population: 81,601†

Ancestry‡	Population	%
African, Sub-Saharan (341)	341	0.42
African (122)	122	0.15
Kenyan (31)	31	0.04
Nigerian (180)	180	0.22
Ugandan (8)	8	0.01
Albanian (26)	41	0.05
American (3,084)	3,084	3.77
Arab (743)	1,340	1.64
Arab (55)	184	0.22
Iraqi (153)	153	0.19
Lebanese (356)	813	0.99
Moroccan (83)	83	0.10
Palestinian (34)	34	0.04
Syrian (62)	62	0.08
Other Arab (0)	11	0.01
Armenian (35)	80	0.10
Australian (0)	44	0.05
Austrian (64)	283	0.35
Belgian (0)	163	0.20
British (66)	189	0.23
Bulgarian (52)	73	0.09
Canadian (43)	85	0.10
Carpatho Rusyn (95)	116	0.14
Croatian (256)	1,112	1.36
Czech (648)	2,231	2.72
Czechoslovakian (215)	299	0.37
Danish (0)	32	0.04
Dutch (49)	589	0.72
Eastern European (91)	102	0.12
English (959)	5,050	6.17
European (367)	420	0.51
Finnish (20)	42	0.05
French, ex. Basque (83)	1,339	1.64
French Canadian (46)	178	0.22
German (5,153)	21,335	26.05
Greek (712)	1,087	1.33
Hungarian (1,279)	4,239	5.18
Iranian (24)	24	0.03
Irish (2,406)	11,502	14.04
Italian (3,782)	11,434	13.96
Latvian (24)	24	0.03
Lithuanian (183)	613	0.75
Macedonian (10)	10	0.01
Norwegian (43)	152	0.19
Pennsylvania German (12)	25	0.03
Polish (5,990)	14,703	17.95
Portuguese (50)	97	0.12
Romanian (460)	761	0.93
Russian (437)	1,152	1.41
Scotch-Irish (230)	831	1.01
Scottish (146)	883	1.08
Serbian (1,540)	1,778	2.17
Slavic (56)	145	0.18
Slovak (2,503)	6,760	8.25
Slovene (501)	1,677	2.05
Swedish (58)	382	0.47
Swiss (36)	206	0.25
Ukrainian (3,660)	4,857	5.93
Welsh (76)	411	0.50
West Indian, ex. Hispanic (139)	160	0.20
Barbadian (44)	44	0.05
Haitian (0)	21	0.03
U.S. Virgin Islander (5)	5	0.01
West Indian (90)	90	0.11
Yugoslavian (264)	332	0.41

Hispanic Origin	Population	%
Hispanic or Latino (of any race)	2,915	3.57
Central American, ex. Mexican	117	0.14
Costa Rican	6	0.01
Guatemalan	34	0.04
Honduran	19	0.02
Nicaraguan	13	0.02
Panamanian	8	0.01
Salvadoran	37	0.05
Cuban	58	0.07
Dominican Republic	64	0.08
Mexican	566	0.69
Puerto Rican	1,665	2.04
South American	252	0.31
Argentinean	19	0.02
Chilean	4	<0.01
Colombian	45	0.06
Ecuadorian	44	0.05
Paraguayan	1	<0.01
Peruvian	129	0.16
Venezuelan	7	0.01
Other South American	3	<0.01
Other Hispanic or Latino	193	0.24

Race*	Population	%
African-American/Black (1,887)	2,340	2.87
Not Hispanic (1,797)	2,211	2.71
Hispanic (90)	129	0.16
American Indian/Alaska Native (151)	435	0.53
Not Hispanic (121)	368	0.45
Hispanic (30)	67	0.08
Alaska Athabascan *(Ala. Nat.)* (1)	3	<0.01
Apache (6)	13	0.02
Blackfeet (5)	27	0.03
Central American Ind. (3)	3	<0.01
Cherokee (18)	115	0.14
Cheyenne (2)	5	0.01
Chickasaw (0)	1	<0.01
Chippewa (1)	6	0.01
Choctaw (8)	15	0.02
Comanche (0)	3	<0.01
Crow (0)	1	<0.01
Inupiat *(Alaska Native)* (1)	2	<0.01
Iroquois (3)	13	0.02
Lumbee (1)	3	<0.01
Mexican American Ind. (3)	5	0.01
Navajo (7)	13	0.02
Osage (0)	1	<0.01
Potawatomi (0)	3	<0.01
Pueblo (1)	2	<0.01
Sioux (0)	9	0.01
South American Ind. (8)	10	0.01
Spanish American Ind. (1)	1	<0.01
Tlingit-Haida *(Alaska Native)* (5)	6	0.01
Tsimshian *(Alaska Native)* (0)	2	<0.01
Asian (1,511)	1,920	2.35
Not Hispanic (1,497)	1,891	2.32
Hispanic (14)	29	0.04
Bangladeshi (0)	1	<0.01
Cambodian (52)	54	0.07
Chinese, ex. Taiwanese (174)	218	0.27
Filipino (392)	515	0.63
Indian (543)	630	0.77
Indonesian (1)	4	<0.01
Japanese (48)	86	0.11
Korean (60)	86	0.11
Laotian (16)	18	0.02
Nepalese (5)	5	0.01
Pakistani (20)	21	0.03
Sri Lankan (5)	8	0.01
Taiwanese (2)	4	<0.01
Thai (12)	16	0.02
Vietnamese (149)	176	0.22
Hawaii Native/Pacific Islander (13)	79	0.10
Not Hispanic (11)	71	0.09
Hispanic (2)	8	0.01
Guamanian/Chamorro (4)	8	0.01
Native Hawaiian (6)	16	0.02
Samoan (1)	9	0.01
White (75,921)	77,034	94.40
Not Hispanic (74,186)	75,053	91.98
Hispanic (1,735)	1,981	2.43

Pataskala

Place Type: City
County: Licking
Population: 14,962†

Ancestry‡	Population	%
African, Sub-Saharan (77)	77	0.54
African (19)	19	0.13
Liberian (58)	58	0.41

SECTION TWO

*Notes: † The Census 2010 population figure is used to calculate the percentages in the Hispanic Origin and Race categories. Ancestry percentages are based on the 2006-2010 American Community Survey population (not shown); ‡ Numbers in parentheses indicate the number of people reporting a single ancestry; * Numbers in parentheses indicate the number of persons reporting this race alone, not in combination with any other race; Please refer to the Explanation of Data for more information.*

American (1,684)	1,684	11.88
Australian (0)	32	0.23
Austrian (8)	8	0.06
Belgian (8)	8	0.06
British (0)	22	0.16
Czech (0)	8	0.06
Czechoslovakian (8)	8	0.06
Dutch (55)	404	2.85
English (565)	1,543	10.89
European (34)	56	0.40
French, ex. Basque (85)	325	2.29
French Canadian (38)	45	0.32
German (1,851)	4,748	33.51
Greek (75)	75	0.53
Hungarian (31)	46	0.32
Irish (509)	1,845	13.02
Italian (457)	1,092	7.71
Lithuanian (0)	10	0.07
Macedonian (30)	30	0.21
Norwegian (0)	62	0.44
Pennsylvania German (19)	19	0.13
Polish (241)	520	3.67
Romanian (8)	23	0.16
Russian (49)	97	0.68
Scotch-Irish (79)	201	1.42
Scottish (224)	484	3.42
Slavic (0)	7	0.05
Slovak (0)	13	0.09
Swedish (41)	239	1.69
Swiss (0)	16	0.11
Ukrainian (38)	38	0.27
Welsh (9)	204	1.44

Hispanic Origin	Population	%
Hispanic or Latino (of any race)	306	2.05
Central American, ex. Mexican	24	0.16
Guatemalan	4	0.03
Honduran	5	0.03
Panamanian	3	0.02
Salvadoran	12	0.08
Cuban	13	0.09
Dominican Republic	13	0.09
Mexican	131	0.88
Puerto Rican	70	0.47
South American	20	0.13
Argentinean	3	0.02
Bolivian	1	0.01
Chilean	1	0.01
Colombian	9	0.06
Ecuadorian	1	0.01
Paraguayan	1	0.01
Venezuelan	4	0.03
Other Hispanic or Latino	35	0.23

Race*	Population	%
African-American/Black (891)	1,071	7.16
Not Hispanic (887)	1,052	7.03
Hispanic (4)	19	0.13
American Indian/Alaska Native (41)	147	0.98
Not Hispanic (40)	143	0.96
Hispanic (1)	4	0.03
Blackfeet (0)	1	0.01
Canadian/French Am. Ind. (0)	1	0.01
Cherokee (6)	30	0.20
Chippewa (2)	5	0.03
Choctaw (0)	5	0.03
Cree (0)	1	0.01
Creek (5)	5	0.03
Delaware (1)	4	0.03
Iroquois (1)	3	0.02
Mexican American Ind. (0)	1	0.01
Navajo (1)	3	0.02
Shoshone (0)	4	0.03
Sioux (7)	9	0.06
Asian (101)	183	1.22
Not Hispanic (100)	176	1.18
Hispanic (1)	7	0.05
Cambodian (0)	6	0.04
Chinese, ex. Taiwanese (29)	44	0.29
Filipino (12)	36	0.24
Indian (11)	16	0.11
Japanese (8)	17	0.11
Korean (4)	13	0.09
Laotian (13)	20	0.13
Pakistani (11)	11	0.07
Taiwanese (0)	3	0.02
Thai (1)	5	0.03
Vietnamese (5)	9	0.06
Hawaii Native/Pacific Islander (3)	8	0.05
Not Hispanic (3)	8	0.05
Guamanian/Chamorro (0)	3	0.02
Native Hawaiian (3)	4	0.03
White (13,461)	13,801	92.24
Not Hispanic (13,296)	13,576	90.74
Hispanic (165)	225	1.50

Perry Heights

Place Type: CDP
County: Stark
Population: 8,441†

Ancestry‡	Population	%
African, Sub-Saharan (15)	15	0.17
Other Sub-Saharan African (15)	15	0.17
American (864)	864	9.99
Arab (27)	27	0.31
Lebanese (27)	27	0.31
Austrian (8)	8	0.09
Croatian (15)	15	0.17
Czechoslovakian (13)	13	0.15
Dutch (0)	87	1.01
English (365)	901	10.41
French, ex. Basque (142)	441	5.10
French Canadian (0)	33	0.38
German (1,032)	3,029	35.01
Greek (49)	61	0.71
Hungarian (17)	59	0.68
Irish (220)	1,208	13.96
Italian (270)	862	9.96
Macedonian (0)	7	0.08
Norwegian (10)	67	0.77
Pennsylvania German (50)	109	1.26
Polish (46)	301	3.48
Romanian (34)	82	0.95
Russian (0)	33	0.38
Scotch-Irish (149)	322	3.72
Scottish (45)	149	1.72
Serbian (0)	7	0.08
Slovak (40)	125	1.44
Soviet Union (0)	13	0.15
Swedish (0)	12	0.14
Swiss (18)	247	2.86
Ukrainian (0)	57	0.66
Welsh (39)	160	1.85

Hispanic Origin	Population	%
Hispanic or Latino (of any race)	184	2.18
Central American, ex. Mexican	10	0.12
Guatemalan	5	0.06
Honduran	1	0.01
Panamanian	2	0.02
Salvadoran	2	0.02
Cuban	1	0.01
Dominican Republic	1	0.01
Mexican	119	1.41
Puerto Rican	13	0.15
South American	4	0.05
Chilean	2	0.02
Ecuadorian	1	0.01
Peruvian	1	0.01
Other Hispanic or Latino	36	0.43

Race*	Population	%
African-American/Black (246)	345	4.09
Not Hispanic (246)	338	4.00
Hispanic (0)	7	0.08
American Indian/Alaska Native (12)	49	0.58
Not Hispanic (12)	46	0.54
Hispanic (0)	3	0.04
Apache (0)	1	0.01
Blackfeet (1)	5	0.06
Cherokee (2)	14	0.17
Crow (0)	2	0.02
Delaware (4)	4	0.05
Ottawa (2)	2	0.02
Asian (43)	62	0.73
Not Hispanic (43)	62	0.73
Chinese, ex. Taiwanese (9)	11	0.13
Filipino (5)	10	0.12
Indian (9)	12	0.14
Japanese (1)	2	0.02
Korean (7)	13	0.15
Taiwanese (1)	1	0.01
Vietnamese (10)	17	0.20
Hawaii Native/Pacific Islander (0)	1	0.01
Hispanic (0)	1	0.01
Native Hawaiian (0)	1	0.01
White (7,902)	8,050	95.37
Not Hispanic (7,802)	7,938	94.04
Hispanic (100)	112	1.33

Perrysburg

Place Type: City
County: Wood
Population: 20,623†

Ancestry‡	Population	%
African, Sub-Saharan (7)	7	0.03
Nigerian (7)	7	0.03
American (838)	838	4.14
Arab (92)	112	0.55
Egyptian (12)	12	0.06
Lebanese (80)	100	0.49
Armenian (14)	24	0.12
Australian (0)	18	0.09
Austrian (0)	38	0.19
Belgian (14)	78	0.38
British (46)	181	0.89
Bulgarian (16)	16	0.08
Canadian (9)	9	0.04
Croatian (13)	84	0.41
Czech (29)	220	1.09
Czechoslovakian (17)	94	0.46
Danish (16)	56	0.28
Dutch (46)	343	1.69
English (574)	2,434	12.01
European (312)	325	1.60
Finnish (59)	99	0.49
French, ex. Basque (121)	961	4.74
French Canadian (35)	123	0.61
German (3,541)	7,975	39.36
Greek (0)	85	0.42
Hungarian (259)	659	3.25
Iranian (15)	15	0.07
Irish (662)	3,237	15.97
Italian (238)	989	4.88
Lithuanian (0)	51	0.25
Macedonian (17)	17	0.08
Maltese (12)	39	0.19
Norwegian (107)	186	0.92
Pennsylvania German (0)	18	0.09
Polish (922)	1,786	8.81
Romanian (10)	72	0.36
Russian (42)	87	0.43
Scandinavian (17)	17	0.08
Scotch-Irish (33)	208	1.03
Scottish (131)	477	2.35
Serbian (0)	13	0.06
Slavic (12)	38	0.19
Slovak (84)	163	0.80
Swedish (26)	188	0.93
Swiss (123)	364	1.80
Turkish (176)	176	0.87
Ukrainian (0)	33	0.16
Welsh (54)	168	0.83
West Indian, ex. Hispanic (11)	11	0.05
West Indian (11)	11	0.05
Yugoslavian (0)	13	0.06

*Notes: † The Census 2010 population figure is used to calculate the percentages in the Hispanic Origin and Race categories. Ancestry percentages are based on the 2006-2010 American Community Survey population (not shown); ‡ Numbers in parentheses indicate the number of people reporting a single ancestry; * Numbers in parentheses indicate the number of persons reporting this race alone, not in combination with any other race; Please refer to the Explanation of Data for more information.*

Hispanic Origin	Population	%
Hispanic or Latino (of any race)	657	3.19
Central American, ex. Mexican	19	0.09
Costa Rican	1	<0.01
Guatemalan	13	0.06
Panamanian	1	<0.01
Salvadoran	4	0.02
Cuban	7	0.03
Mexican	472	2.29
Puerto Rican	51	0.25
South American	60	0.29
Argentinean	1	<0.01
Colombian	22	0.11
Ecuadorian	7	0.03
Paraguayan	6	0.03
Peruvian	10	0.05
Uruguayan	1	<0.01
Venezuelan	13	0.06
Other Hispanic or Latino	48	0.23

Race*	Population	%
African-American/Black (297)	380	1.84
Not Hispanic (291)	361	1.75
Hispanic (6)	19	0.09
American Indian/Alaska Native (29)	101	0.49
Not Hispanic (20)	78	0.38
Hispanic (9)	23	0.11
Apache (1)	1	<0.01
Blackfeet (0)	7	0.03
Cherokee (5)	35	0.17
Cheyenne (0)	1	<0.01
Chippewa (0)	2	0.01
Choctaw (1)	1	<0.01
Inupiat *(Alaska Native)* (3)	3	0.01
Iroquois (0)	5	0.02
Mexican American Ind. (5)	7	0.03
Ottawa (1)	1	<0.01
Potawatomi (1)	1	<0.01
Shoshone (0)	2	0.01
South American Ind. (0)	1	<0.01
Asian (632)	778	3.77
Not Hispanic (621)	748	3.63
Hispanic (11)	30	0.15
Bangladeshi (7)	11	0.05
Chinese, ex. Taiwanese (152)	176	0.85
Filipino (63)	89	0.43
Indian (184)	214	1.04
Indonesian (11)	11	0.05
Japanese (21)	24	0.12
Korean (55)	78	0.38
Laotian (5)	8	0.04
Malaysian (4)	4	0.02
Pakistani (55)	61	0.30
Sri Lankan (1)	3	0.01
Taiwanese (3)	3	0.01
Thai (9)	13	0.06
Vietnamese (28)	34	0.16
Hawaii Native/Pacific Islander (8)	13	0.06
Not Hispanic (8)	10	0.05
Hispanic (0)	3	0.01
Fijian (0)	1	<0.01
Native Hawaiian (1)	2	0.01
Samoan (1)	4	0.02
White (19,169)	19,465	94.38
Not Hispanic (18,770)	18,979	92.03
Hispanic (399)	486	2.36

Pickerington

Place Type: City
County: Fairfield
Population: 18,291†

Ancestry‡	Population	%
African, Sub-Saharan (9)	19	0.11
African (9)	9	0.05
South African (0)	10	0.06
American (760)	760	4.47
Arab (92)	236	1.39
Arab (37)	37	0.22
Lebanese (14)	136	0.80
Syrian (41)	63	0.37
Assyrian/Chaldean/Syriac (0)	12	0.07
Austrian (26)	94	0.55
Belgian (18)	65	0.38
Brazilian (52)	118	0.69
British (51)	102	0.60
Canadian (27)	27	0.16
Croatian (25)	166	0.98
Czech (0)	31	0.18
Danish (18)	124	0.73
Dutch (68)	318	1.87
English (504)	2,300	13.53
European (275)	285	1.68
French, ex. Basque (64)	289	1.70
French Canadian (15)	30	0.18
German (1,621)	5,045	29.67
Greek (66)	179	1.05
Hungarian (351)	426	2.51
Irish (766)	2,885	16.97
Italian (414)	1,313	7.72
Macedonian (56)	116	0.68
Northern European (27)	27	0.16
Norwegian (21)	109	0.64
Polish (104)	856	5.03
Romanian (0)	82	0.48
Russian (51)	171	1.01
Scandinavian (0)	24	0.14
Scotch-Irish (25)	339	1.99
Scottish (28)	309	1.82
Serbian (0)	14	0.08
Slavic (11)	11	0.06
Slovak (13)	120	0.71
Swedish (56)	154	0.91
Swiss (0)	29	0.17
Ukrainian (0)	78	0.46
Welsh (0)	258	1.52
West Indian, ex. Hispanic (137)	137	0.81
Bahamian (100)	100	0.59
Haitian (12)	12	0.07
Jamaican (25)	25	0.15
Yugoslavian (0)	28	0.16

Hispanic Origin	Population	%
Hispanic or Latino (of any race)	461	2.52
Central American, ex. Mexican	30	0.16
Costa Rican	6	0.03
Guatemalan	15	0.08
Panamanian	3	0.02
Salvadoran	6	0.03
Cuban	35	0.19
Dominican Republic	20	0.11
Mexican	171	0.93
Puerto Rican	89	0.49
South American	54	0.30
Argentinean	11	0.06
Bolivian	5	0.03
Colombian	16	0.09
Ecuadorian	6	0.03
Peruvian	8	0.04
Uruguayan	3	0.02
Venezuelan	2	0.01
Other South American	3	0.02
Other Hispanic or Latino	62	0.34

Race*	Population	%
African-American/Black (2,374)	2,683	14.67
Not Hispanic (2,354)	2,655	14.52
Hispanic (20)	28	0.15
American Indian/Alaska Native (34)	149	0.81
Not Hispanic (29)	131	0.72
Hispanic (5)	18	0.10
Blackfeet (0)	4	0.02
Central American Ind. (3)	3	0.02
Cherokee (5)	30	0.16
Chippewa (1)	3	0.02
Choctaw (0)	1	0.01
Comanche (0)	1	0.01
Crow (0)	1	0.01
Delaware (0)	4	0.02
Iroquois (1)	5	0.03
Paiute (0)	3	0.02
Potawatomi (1)	1	0.01
Sioux (1)	5	0.03
South American Ind. (1)	1	0.01
Asian (533)	712	3.89
Not Hispanic (527)	702	3.84
Hispanic (6)	10	0.05
Bangladeshi (1)	3	0.02
Burmese (4)	4	0.02
Cambodian (19)	23	0.13
Chinese, ex. Taiwanese (83)	113	0.62
Filipino (59)	98	0.54
Indian (133)	154	0.84
Japanese (36)	76	0.42
Korean (18)	31	0.17
Laotian (26)	26	0.14
Malaysian (2)	2	0.01
Pakistani (81)	89	0.49
Sri Lankan (5)	5	0.03
Taiwanese (1)	1	0.01
Thai (6)	17	0.09
Vietnamese (25)	33	0.18
Hawaii Native/Pacific Islander (9)	30	0.16
Not Hispanic (9)	29	0.16
Hispanic (0)	1	0.01
Guamanian/Chamorro (1)	12	0.07
Native Hawaiian (3)	12	0.07
Samoan (4)	4	0.02
White (14,648)	15,159	82.88
Not Hispanic (14,337)	14,814	80.99
Hispanic (311)	345	1.89

Piqua

Place Type: City
County: Miami
Population: 20,522†

Ancestry‡	Population	%
African, Sub-Saharan (63)	63	0.30
African (63)	63	0.30
American (2,421)	2,421	11.72
Australian (0)	14	0.07
Austrian (0)	13	0.06
Belgian (0)	12	0.06
British (18)	60	0.29
Canadian (51)	51	0.25
Croatian (6)	20	0.10
Czech (0)	42	0.20
Dutch (88)	419	2.03
English (581)	1,532	7.42
European (163)	180	0.87
French, ex. Basque (224)	748	3.62
French Canadian (33)	44	0.21
German (2,884)	6,233	30.17
Greek (46)	112	0.54
Hungarian (47)	72	0.35
Icelander (0)	9	0.04
Irish (706)	2,415	11.69
Italian (264)	669	3.24
Luxemburger (0)	12	0.06
Northern European (40)	50	0.24
Norwegian (24)	71	0.34
Pennsylvania German (46)	78	0.38
Polish (110)	229	1.11
Portuguese (23)	47	0.23
Russian (9)	29	0.14
Scandinavian (23)	23	0.11
Scotch-Irish (190)	411	1.99
Scottish (52)	227	1.10
Slovak (0)	22	0.11
Swedish (0)	40	0.19
Swiss (16)	169	0.82
Ukrainian (15)	15	0.07
Welsh (10)	141	0.68

Hispanic Origin	Population	%
Hispanic or Latino (of any race)	278	1.35
Central American, ex. Mexican	12	0.06

*Notes: † The Census 2010 population figure is used to calculate the percentages in the Hispanic Origin and Race categories. Ancestry percentages are based on the 2006-2010 American Community Survey population (not shown); ‡ Numbers in parentheses indicate the number of people reporting a single ancestry; * Numbers in parentheses indicate the number of persons reporting this race alone, not in combination with any other race; Please refer to the Explanation of Data for more information.*

Guatemalan	10	0.05
Honduran	1	<0.01
Nicaraguan	1	<0.01
Cuban	8	0.04
Dominican Republic	2	0.01
Mexican	174	0.85
Puerto Rican	30	0.15
South American	7	0.03
Chilean	1	<0.01
Colombian	4	0.02
Venezuelan	2	0.01
Other Hispanic or Latino	45	0.22

Race*	Population	%
African-American/Black (684)	1,126	5.49
Not Hispanic (679)	1,112	5.42
Hispanic (5)	14	0.07
American Indian/Alaska Native (49)	172	0.84
Not Hispanic (43)	159	0.77
Hispanic (6)	13	0.06
Blackfeet (1)	10	0.05
Cherokee (13)	37	0.18
Cheyenne (0)	2	0.01
Chippewa (1)	1	<0.01
Creek (0)	1	<0.01
Delaware (2)	2	0.01
Iroquois (0)	6	0.03
Lumbee (0)	5	0.02
Mexican American Ind. (1)	2	0.01
Navajo (0)	1	<0.01
Sioux (0)	1	<0.01
Spanish American Ind. (1)	1	<0.01
Yaqui (0)	1	<0.01
Asian (137)	202	0.98
Not Hispanic (137)	198	0.96
Hispanic (0)	4	0.02
Cambodian (1)	1	<0.01
Chinese, ex. Taiwanese (23)	25	0.12
Filipino (41)	65	0.32
Indian (42)	52	0.25
Japanese (9)	18	0.09
Korean (4)	11	0.05
Sri Lankan (1)	2	0.01
Taiwanese (2)	2	0.01
Thai (1)	1	<0.01
Vietnamese (9)	17	0.08
Hawaii Native/Pacific Islander (2)	6	0.03
Not Hispanic (2)	6	0.03
Native Hawaiian (0)	4	0.02
Samoan (1)	1	<0.01
White (18,958)	19,538	95.21
Not Hispanic (18,785)	19,338	94.23
Hispanic (173)	200	0.97

Portsmouth

Place Type: City
County: Scioto
Population: 20,226†

Ancestry‡	Population	%
African, Sub-Saharan (12)	12	0.06
African (12)	12	0.06
American (1,747)	1,747	8.63
Arab (9)	9	0.04
Arab (9)	9	0.04
Armenian (52)	126	0.62
Austrian (0)	22	0.11
British (17)	113	0.56
Czech (0)	13	0.06
Czechoslovakian (0)	16	0.08
Danish (0)	14	0.07
Dutch (15)	391	1.93
English (1,020)	2,111	10.43
European (65)	77	0.38
French, ex. Basque (99)	696	3.44
French Canadian (9)	9	0.04
German (1,774)	4,753	23.48
Greek (0)	6	0.03
Hungarian (0)	19	0.09
Irish (990)	3,483	17.21
Italian (246)	520	2.57
Lithuanian (12)	12	0.06
Norwegian (36)	45	0.22
Pennsylvania German (0)	15	0.07
Polish (95)	198	0.98
Portuguese (16)	22	0.11
Scandinavian (0)	16	0.08
Scotch-Irish (155)	346	1.71
Scottish (97)	323	1.60
Swedish (14)	137	0.68
Swiss (0)	83	0.41
Welsh (61)	346	1.71

Hispanic Origin	Population	%
Hispanic or Latino (of any race)	439	2.17
Central American, ex. Mexican	15	0.07
Costa Rican	1	<0.01
Guatemalan	1	<0.01
Honduran	3	0.01
Nicaraguan	10	0.05
Cuban	9	0.04
Dominican Republic	3	0.01
Mexican	346	1.71
Puerto Rican	16	0.08
South American	6	0.03
Argentinean	1	<0.01
Chilean	1	<0.01
Colombian	2	0.01
Peruvian	2	0.01
Other Hispanic or Latino	44	0.22

Race*	Population	%
African-American/Black (1,032)	1,406	6.95
Not Hispanic (1,018)	1,369	6.77
Hispanic (14)	37	0.18
American Indian/Alaska Native (91)	288	1.42
Not Hispanic (88)	270	1.33
Hispanic (3)	18	0.09
Apache (1)	5	0.02
Arapaho (1)	2	0.01
Blackfeet (1)	6	0.03
Canadian/French Am. Ind. (0)	1	<0.01
Cherokee (40)	107	0.53
Chippewa (3)	9	0.04
Choctaw (0)	2	0.01
Comanche (0)	2	0.01
Creek (1)	2	0.01
Crow (0)	3	0.01
Iroquois (0)	3	0.01
Kiowa (0)	1	<0.01
Mexican American Ind. (0)	2	0.01
Navajo (0)	1	<0.01
Ottawa (0)	3	0.01
Seminole (0)	5	0.02
Sioux (0)	1	<0.01
Asian (124)	165	0.82
Not Hispanic (122)	155	0.77
Hispanic (2)	10	0.05
Cambodian (3)	4	0.02
Chinese, ex. Taiwanese (36)	37	0.18
Filipino (24)	35	0.17
Indian (27)	31	0.15
Indonesian (2)	2	0.01
Japanese (2)	9	0.04
Korean (14)	25	0.12
Laotian (1)	1	<0.01
Malaysian (1)	1	<0.01
Pakistani (1)	1	<0.01
Thai (5)	6	0.03
Vietnamese (3)	4	0.02
Hawaii Native/Pacific Islander (5)	27	0.13
Not Hispanic (5)	21	0.10
Hispanic (0)	6	0.03
Guamanian/Chamorro (0)	1	<0.01
Native Hawaiian (3)	10	0.05
Samoan (0)	2	0.01
White (18,229)	18,794	92.92
Not Hispanic (17,988)	18,502	91.48
Hispanic (241)	292	1.44

Powell

Place Type: City
County: Delaware
Population: 11,500†

Ancestry‡	Population	%
African, Sub-Saharan (81)	81	0.75
African (37)	37	0.34
Ethiopian (20)	20	0.19
Nigerian (24)	24	0.22
American (361)	361	3.35
Arab (91)	144	1.34
Lebanese (79)	108	1.00
Other Arab (12)	36	0.33
Armenian (46)	66	0.61
Austrian (0)	35	0.32
Belgian (0)	8	0.07
British (0)	61	0.57
Canadian (55)	69	0.64
Croatian (0)	79	0.73
Czech (21)	82	0.76
Dutch (30)	143	1.33
Eastern European (22)	22	0.20
English (434)	1,464	13.59
European (114)	169	1.57
Finnish (12)	24	0.22
French, ex. Basque (96)	264	2.45
French Canadian (8)	61	0.57
German (1,176)	3,292	30.56
Greek (93)	250	2.32
Hungarian (59)	224	2.08
Iranian (56)	56	0.52
Irish (423)	1,884	17.49
Italian (500)	1,293	12.00
Lithuanian (13)	61	0.57
Macedonian (37)	60	0.56
Norwegian (0)	68	0.63
Polish (213)	833	7.73
Portuguese (0)	24	0.22
Romanian (0)	105	0.97
Russian (22)	77	0.71
Scotch-Irish (194)	359	3.33
Scottish (115)	375	3.48
Serbian (19)	64	0.59
Slovak (70)	174	1.62
Slovene (26)	86	0.80
Swedish (8)	99	0.92
Swiss (0)	35	0.32
Ukrainian (0)	16	0.15
Welsh (33)	166	1.54
West Indian, ex. Hispanic (12)	12	0.11
Jamaican (12)	12	0.11
Yugoslavian (0)	25	0.23

Hispanic Origin	Population	%
Hispanic or Latino (of any race)	161	1.40
Central American, ex. Mexican	15	0.13
Costa Rican	4	0.03
Guatemalan	2	0.02
Nicaraguan	3	0.03
Salvadoran	6	0.05
Cuban	6	0.05
Dominican Republic	3	0.03
Mexican	55	0.48
Puerto Rican	36	0.31
South American	19	0.17
Argentinean	2	0.02
Colombian	14	0.12
Peruvian	1	0.01
Venezuelan	2	0.02
Other Hispanic or Latino	27	0.23

Race*	Population	%
African-American/Black (221)	263	2.29
Not Hispanic (221)	259	2.25
Hispanic (0)	4	0.03
American Indian/Alaska Native (13)	49	0.43
Not Hispanic (13)	49	0.43
Blackfeet (0)	2	0.02

*Notes: † The Census 2010 population figure is used to calculate the percentages in the Hispanic Origin and Race categories. Ancestry percentages are based on the 2006-2010 American Community Survey population (not shown); ‡ Numbers in parentheses indicate the number of people reporting a single ancestry; * Numbers in parentheses indicate the number of persons reporting this race alone, not in combination with any other race; Please refer to the Explanation of Data for more information.*

Cherokee (6)	19	0.17
Chickasaw (2)	2	0.02
Iroquois (0)	1	0.01
Sioux (1)	1	0.01
Asian (859)	955	8.30
Not Hispanic (859)	951	8.27
Hispanic (0)	4	0.03
Cambodian (7)	7	0.06
Chinese, ex. Taiwanese (153)	179	1.56
Filipino (12)	19	0.17
Indian (495)	530	4.61
Indonesian (5)	5	0.04
Japanese (49)	53	0.46
Korean (61)	77	0.67
Laotian (7)	11	0.10
Pakistani (8)	10	0.09
Sri Lankan (2)	2	0.02
Taiwanese (7)	11	0.10
Thai (1)	1	0.01
Vietnamese (32)	39	0.34
Hawaii Native/Pacific Islander (4)	11	0.10
Not Hispanic (4)	8	0.07
Hispanic (0)	3	0.03
Native Hawaiian (4)	11	0.10
White (10,172)	10,354	90.03
Not Hispanic (10,059)	10,211	88.79
Hispanic (113)	143	1.24

Ravenna

Place Type: City
County: Portage
Population: 11,724†

Ancestry‡	Population	%
African, Sub-Saharan (8)	8	0.07
African (8)	8	0.07
American (688)	688	5.84
Arab (107)	107	0.91
Jordanian (94)	94	0.80
Lebanese (13)	13	0.11
Australian (0)	6	0.05
Austrian (0)	9	0.08
British (0)	6	0.05
Canadian (0)	16	0.14
Croatian (10)	25	0.21
Czech (16)	55	0.47
Czechoslovakian (13)	29	0.25
Danish (9)	40	0.34
Dutch (39)	321	2.73
English (262)	1,182	10.04
European (24)	24	0.20
Finnish (15)	15	0.13
French, ex. Basque (65)	313	2.66
French Canadian (19)	50	0.42
German (1,184)	3,459	29.38
Greek (9)	40	0.34
Hungarian (79)	288	2.45
Irish (663)	2,271	19.29
Italian (477)	1,198	10.18
Lithuanian (0)	9	0.08
Norwegian (22)	47	0.40
Pennsylvania German (8)	28	0.24
Polish (136)	460	3.91
Romanian (35)	35	0.30
Russian (26)	49	0.42
Scandinavian (0)	9	0.08
Scotch-Irish (201)	352	2.99
Scottish (63)	317	2.69
Slavic (11)	19	0.16
Slovak (52)	103	0.87
Slovene (18)	27	0.23
Swedish (17)	34	0.29
Swiss (9)	47	0.40
Ukrainian (12)	12	0.10
Welsh (44)	142	1.21
Yugoslavian (0)	49	0.42

Hispanic Origin	Population	%
Hispanic or Latino (of any race)	163	1.39
Central American, ex. Mexican	16	0.14
Guatemalan	2	0.02
Honduran	4	0.03
Panamanian	4	0.03
Salvadoran	6	0.05
Cuban	8	0.07
Mexican	73	0.62
Puerto Rican	52	0.44
South American	3	0.03
Colombian	3	0.03
Other Hispanic or Latino	11	0.09

Race*	Population	%
African-American/Black (659)	840	7.16
Not Hispanic (650)	817	6.97
Hispanic (9)	23	0.20
American Indian/Alaska Native (27)	108	0.92
Not Hispanic (26)	105	0.90
Hispanic (1)	3	0.03
Blackfeet (4)	8	0.07
Canadian/French Am. Ind. (1)	1	0.01
Cherokee (5)	44	0.38
Chippewa (4)	6	0.05
Comanche (0)	1	0.01
Cree (0)	1	0.01
Creek (0)	1	0.01
Iroquois (1)	3	0.03
Lumbee (1)	3	0.03
Menominee (1)	1	0.01
Mexican American Ind. (1)	1	0.01
Navajo (1)	1	0.01
Osage (0)	1	0.01
Sioux (1)	5	0.04
Asian (52)	70	0.60
Not Hispanic (49)	67	0.57
Hispanic (3)	3	0.03
Chinese, ex. Taiwanese (13)	14	0.12
Filipino (11)	15	0.13
Indian (6)	8	0.07
Japanese (3)	9	0.08
Korean (2)	7	0.06
Malaysian (3)	3	0.03
Pakistani (1)	1	0.01
Taiwanese (2)	2	0.02
Thai (1)	2	0.02
Vietnamese (4)	4	0.03
Hawaii Native/Pacific Islander (3)	14	0.12
Not Hispanic (3)	12	0.10
Hispanic (0)	2	0.02
Guamanian/Chamorro (1)	7	0.06
Native Hawaiian (1)	3	0.03
Samoan (0)	2	0.02
White (10,677)	10,934	93.26
Not Hispanic (10,567)	10,802	92.14
Hispanic (110)	132	1.13

Reading

Place Type: City
County: Hamilton
Population: 10,385†

Ancestry‡	Population	%
African, Sub-Saharan (18)	18	0.17
Other Sub-Saharan African (18)	18	0.17
American (816)	816	7.83
Arab (13)	49	0.47
Lebanese (13)	49	0.47
British (8)	8	0.08
Canadian (0)	14	0.13
Celtic (0)	8	0.08
Czech (8)	19	0.18
Danish (0)	16	0.15
Dutch (22)	62	0.59
English (641)	1,217	11.68
European (7)	7	0.07
French, ex. Basque (36)	301	2.89
German (1,390)	3,407	32.69
Hungarian (30)	162	1.55
Irish (559)	2,101	20.16
Italian (340)	593	5.69
Norwegian (11)	11	0.11
Polish (61)	121	1.16
Russian (39)	47	0.45
Scotch-Irish (29)	120	1.15
Scottish (22)	173	1.66
Swedish (34)	34	0.33
Swiss (18)	27	0.26
Ukrainian (80)	98	0.94
Welsh (10)	149	1.43
Yugoslavian (0)	30	0.29

Hispanic Origin	Population	%
Hispanic or Latino (of any race)	175	1.69
Central American, ex. Mexican	12	0.12
Guatemalan	5	0.05
Honduran	2	0.02
Panamanian	1	0.01
Salvadoran	4	0.04
Cuban	3	0.03
Dominican Republic	9	0.09
Mexican	112	1.08
Puerto Rican	19	0.18
South American	7	0.07
Colombian	2	0.02
Peruvian	5	0.05
Other Hispanic or Latino	13	0.13

Race*	Population	%
African-American/Black (756)	848	8.17
Not Hispanic (751)	841	8.10
Hispanic (5)	7	0.07
American Indian/Alaska Native (13)	82	0.79
Not Hispanic (10)	79	0.76
Hispanic (3)	3	0.03
Blackfeet (0)	7	0.07
Cherokee (4)	21	0.20
Cheyenne (0)	2	0.02
Chippewa (0)	4	0.04
Mexican American Ind. (3)	3	0.03
Navajo (1)	1	0.01
Asian (100)	137	1.32
Not Hispanic (100)	137	1.32
Cambodian (0)	1	0.01
Chinese, ex. Taiwanese (16)	19	0.18
Filipino (11)	24	0.23
Indian (49)	57	0.55
Japanese (1)	8	0.08
Korean (3)	8	0.08
Pakistani (1)	2	0.02
Sri Lankan (1)	1	0.01
Taiwanese (1)	1	0.01
Thai (2)	4	0.04
Vietnamese (7)	11	0.11
Hawaii Native/Pacific Islander (4)	10	0.10
Not Hispanic (4)	9	0.09
Hispanic (0)	1	0.01
Guamanian/Chamorro (0)	1	0.01
Native Hawaiian (4)	9	0.09
White (9,251)	9,441	90.91
Not Hispanic (9,152)	9,324	89.78
Hispanic (99)	117	1.13

Reynoldsburg

Place Type: City
County: Franklin
Population: 35,893†

Ancestry‡	Population	%
African, Sub-Saharan (751)	751	2.15
African (397)	397	1.14
Ethiopian (297)	297	0.85
Kenyan (57)	57	0.16
American (1,834)	1,834	5.24
Arab (181)	225	0.64
Arab (113)	113	0.32
Lebanese (40)	84	0.24
Other Arab (28)	28	0.08
Australian (0)	13	0.04

SECTION TWO

*Notes: † The Census 2010 population figure is used to calculate the percentages in the Hispanic Origin and Race categories. Ancestry percentages are based on the 2006-2010 American Community Survey population (not shown); ‡ Numbers in parentheses indicate the number of people reporting a single ancestry; * Numbers in parentheses indicate the number of persons reporting this race alone, not in combination with any other race; Please refer to the Explanation of Data for more information.*

Ancestry	Population	%
Austrian (0)	40	0.11
Belgian (0)	10	0.03
British (40)	114	0.33
Canadian (0)	129	0.37
Carpatho Rusyn (9)	9	0.03
Croatian (0)	44	0.13
Czech (140)	337	0.96
Czechoslovakian (39)	39	0.11
Danish (0)	55	0.16
Dutch (36)	548	1.57
Eastern European (53)	53	0.15
English (1,346)	3,729	10.66
Estonian (0)	14	0.04
European (239)	316	0.90
Finnish (0)	9	0.03
French, ex. Basque (147)	791	2.26
French Canadian (19)	76	0.22
German (2,783)	8,183	23.40
Greek (55)	55	0.16
Hungarian (241)	436	1.25
Iranian (8)	8	0.02
Irish (1,469)	6,059	17.32
Italian (970)	2,056	5.88
Lithuanian (13)	22	0.06
Luxemburger (12)	12	0.03
Macedonian (41)	41	0.12
Northern European (41)	41	0.12
Norwegian (47)	132	0.38
Pennsylvania German (0)	17	0.05
Polish (204)	699	2.00
Portuguese (20)	20	0.06
Romanian (42)	75	0.21
Russian (264)	389	1.11
Scandinavian (15)	15	0.04
Scotch-Irish (338)	859	2.46
Scottish (189)	586	1.68
Slavic (14)	25	0.07
Slovak (41)	333	0.95
Slovene (25)	66	0.19
Swedish (0)	303	0.87
Swiss (0)	47	0.13
Ukrainian (13)	44	0.13
Welsh (78)	567	1.62
West Indian, ex. Hispanic (144)	270	0.77
Barbadian (18)	47	0.13
Haitian (119)	145	0.41
Jamaican (0)	42	0.12
Trinidadian/Tobagonian (0)	29	0.08
West Indian (7)	7	0.02
Yugoslavian (104)	132	0.38

Hispanic Origin	Population	%
Hispanic or Latino (of any race)	1,233	3.44
Central American, ex. Mexican	113	0.31
Costa Rican	2	0.01
Guatemalan	27	0.08
Honduran	19	0.05
Nicaraguan	22	0.06
Panamanian	13	0.04
Salvadoran	30	0.08
Cuban	28	0.08
Dominican Republic	109	0.30
Mexican	583	1.62
Puerto Rican	210	0.59
South American	74	0.21
Argentinean	9	0.03
Bolivian	8	0.02
Chilean	2	0.01
Colombian	21	0.06
Ecuadorian	2	0.01
Paraguayan	1	<0.01
Peruvian	16	0.04
Uruguayan	1	<0.01
Venezuelan	14	0.04
Other Hispanic or Latino	116	0.32

Race*	Population	%
African-American/Black (8,374)	9,247	25.76
Not Hispanic (8,278)	9,098	25.35
Hispanic (96)	149	0.42
American Indian/Alaska Native (83)	406	1.13
Not Hispanic (71)	363	1.01
Hispanic (12)	43	0.12
Apache (0)	1	<0.01
Blackfeet (0)	27	0.08
Canadian/French Am. Ind. (1)	2	0.01
Cherokee (9)	96	0.27
Chickasaw (0)	1	<0.01
Chippewa (2)	6	0.02
Choctaw (0)	3	0.01
Comanche (1)	1	<0.01
Cree (0)	1	<0.01
Creek (2)	5	0.01
Delaware (0)	2	0.01
Houma (0)	3	0.01
Iroquois (7)	11	0.03
Lumbee (2)	3	0.01
Mexican American Ind. (1)	4	0.01
Navajo (0)	2	0.01
Ottawa (3)	3	0.01
Paiute (2)	2	0.01
Pueblo (1)	3	0.01
Seminole (0)	1	<0.01
Sioux (3)	21	0.06
Tsimshian *(Alaska Native)* (1)	1	<0.01
Ute (0)	1	<0.01
Asian (656)	866	2.41
Not Hispanic (646)	839	2.34
Hispanic (10)	27	0.08
Burmese (9)	9	0.03
Cambodian (15)	15	0.04
Chinese, ex. Taiwanese (109)	132	0.37
Filipino (57)	109	0.30
Indian (182)	230	0.64
Indonesian (8)	10	0.03
Japanese (24)	59	0.16
Korean (49)	68	0.19
Laotian (52)	70	0.20
Nepalese (3)	5	0.01
Pakistani (43)	49	0.14
Sri Lankan (6)	6	0.02
Taiwanese (12)	13	0.04
Thai (23)	35	0.10
Vietnamese (24)	26	0.07
Hawaii Native/Pacific Islander (22)	48	0.13
Not Hispanic (18)	40	0.11
Hispanic (4)	8	0.02
Guamanian/Chamorro (4)	6	0.02
Native Hawaiian (10)	24	0.07
Samoan (1)	1	<0.01
White (25,009)	26,112	72.75
Not Hispanic (24,457)	25,446	70.89
Hispanic (552)	666	1.86

Richmond Heights

Place Type: City
County: Cuyahoga
Population: 10,546†

Ancestry‡	Population	%
African, Sub-Saharan (127)	127	1.20
African (50)	50	0.47
Liberian (65)	65	0.61
Nigerian (12)	12	0.11
Albanian (46)	46	0.44
American (158)	158	1.49
Arab (66)	91	0.86
Egyptian (10)	10	0.09
Lebanese (56)	81	0.77
Austrian (7)	15	0.14
British (0)	30	0.28
Canadian (0)	14	0.13
Carpatho Rusyn (0)	8	0.08
Croatian (58)	79	0.75
Czech (70)	107	1.01
Czechoslovakian (15)	15	0.14
Dutch (0)	21	0.20
Eastern European (16)	16	0.15
English (131)	452	4.28
Estonian (10)	10	0.09
European (78)	78	0.74
Finnish (0)	9	0.09
French, ex. Basque (0)	24	0.23
French Canadian (5)	34	0.32
German (138)	1,069	10.11
Greek (16)	58	0.55
Hungarian (130)	208	1.97
Irish (193)	974	9.21
Italian (558)	852	8.06
Latvian (10)	17	0.16
Lithuanian (128)	128	1.21
Polish (195)	574	5.43
Romanian (54)	72	0.68
Russian (148)	355	3.36
Scotch-Irish (19)	29	0.27
Scottish (16)	25	0.24
Slovak (78)	149	1.41
Slovene (173)	271	2.56
Swedish (38)	68	0.64
Swiss (0)	71	0.67
Turkish (65)	75	0.71
Ukrainian (24)	38	0.36
Welsh (0)	114	1.08
West Indian, ex. Hispanic (38)	38	0.36
Jamaican (38)	38	0.36
Yugoslavian (0)	8	0.08

Hispanic Origin	Population	%
Hispanic or Latino (of any race)	189	1.79
Central American, ex. Mexican	8	0.08
Honduran	1	0.01
Panamanian	1	0.01
Salvadoran	6	0.06
Cuban	8	0.08
Dominican Republic	3	0.03
Mexican	64	0.61
Puerto Rican	47	0.45
South American	29	0.27
Argentinean	1	0.01
Colombian	3	0.03
Peruvian	14	0.13
Uruguayan	10	0.09
Other South American	1	0.01
Other Hispanic or Latino	30	0.28

Race*	Population	%
African-American/Black (4,731)	4,867	46.15
Not Hispanic (4,693)	4,823	45.73
Hispanic (38)	44	0.42
American Indian/Alaska Native (7)	41	0.39
Not Hispanic (4)	36	0.34
Hispanic (3)	5	0.05
Apache (0)	1	0.01
Blackfeet (0)	3	0.03
Cherokee (0)	10	0.09
Chippewa (1)	1	0.01
Choctaw (0)	2	0.02
Delaware (0)	1	0.01
Mexican American Ind. (3)	3	0.03
South American Ind. (0)	1	0.01
Asian (457)	522	4.95
Not Hispanic (449)	512	4.85
Hispanic (8)	10	0.09
Bangladeshi (0)	2	0.02
Burmese (0)	1	0.01
Chinese, ex. Taiwanese (124)	147	1.39
Filipino (64)	84	0.80
Indian (141)	150	1.42
Japanese (6)	19	0.18
Korean (13)	17	0.16
Laotian (6)	6	0.06
Malaysian (3)	3	0.03
Nepalese (3)	3	0.03
Pakistani (25)	27	0.26
Sri Lankan (1)	1	0.01
Taiwanese (11)	12	0.11
Thai (1)	6	0.06
Vietnamese (43)	45	0.43
Hawaii Native/Pacific Islander (2)	9	0.09

*Notes: † The Census 2010 population figure is used to calculate the percentages in the Hispanic Origin and Race categories. Ancestry percentages are based on the 2006-2010 American Community Survey population (not shown); ‡ Numbers in parentheses indicate the number of people reporting a single ancestry; * Numbers in parentheses indicate the number of persons reporting this race alone, not in combination with any other race; Please refer to the Explanation of Data for more information.*

Not Hispanic (2)	9	0.09
Native Hawaiian (2)	6	0.06
White (5,112)	5,243	49.72
Not Hispanic (5,012)	5,135	48.69
Hispanic (100)	108	1.02

Riverside

Place Type: City
County: Montgomery
Population: 25,201†

Ancestry‡	Population	%
African, Sub-Saharan (91)	91	0.36
African (91)	91	0.36
American (4,612)	4,612	18.08
Arab (14)	14	0.05
Lebanese (14)	14	0.05
Austrian (0)	104	0.41
British (48)	171	0.67
Canadian (10)	10	0.04
Croatian (77)	87	0.34
Czech (5)	90	0.35
Czechoslovakian (24)	33	0.13
Dutch (120)	536	2.10
English (922)	2,477	9.71
European (226)	244	0.96
French, ex. Basque (80)	394	1.54
French Canadian (0)	29	0.11
German (2,678)	6,164	24.16
Greek (51)	83	0.33
Hungarian (65)	120	0.47
Irish (931)	3,872	15.18
Italian (313)	864	3.39
Lithuanian (12)	92	0.36
Norwegian (38)	82	0.32
Polish (339)	824	3.23
Portuguese (29)	58	0.23
Romanian (9)	9	0.04
Scandinavian (6)	25	0.10
Scotch-Irish (212)	489	1.92
Scottish (210)	533	2.09
Slovak (46)	46	0.18
Swedish (35)	188	0.74
Swiss (28)	93	0.36
Welsh (76)	349	1.37
West Indian, ex. Hispanic (51)	51	0.20
Dutch West Indian (26)	26	0.10
Haitian (25)	25	0.10
Yugoslavian (11)	19	0.07

Hispanic Origin	Population	%
Hispanic or Latino (of any race)	826	3.28
Central American, ex. Mexican	34	0.13
Costa Rican	5	0.02
Guatemalan	8	0.03
Honduran	4	0.02
Nicaraguan	2	0.01
Panamanian	12	0.05
Salvadoran	3	0.01
Cuban	21	0.08
Dominican Republic	7	0.03
Mexican	477	1.89
Puerto Rican	182	0.72
South American	28	0.11
Argentinean	3	0.01
Bolivian	1	<0.01
Chilean	2	0.01
Colombian	14	0.06
Ecuadorian	3	0.01
Peruvian	5	0.02
Other Hispanic or Latino	77	0.31

Race*	Population	%
African-American/Black (1,671)	2,022	8.02
Not Hispanic (1,630)	1,948	7.73
Hispanic (41)	74	0.29
American Indian/Alaska Native (74)	239	0.95
Not Hispanic (61)	217	0.86
Hispanic (13)	22	0.09
Aleut *(Alaska Native)* (0)	1	<0.01
Apache (5)	5	0.02
Blackfeet (3)	8	0.03
Canadian/French Am. Ind. (0)	1	<0.01
Cherokee (17)	79	0.31
Chippewa (5)	9	0.04
Choctaw (0)	2	0.01
Comanche (1)	1	<0.01
Cree (1)	2	0.01
Crow (1)	1	<0.01
Iroquois (0)	4	0.02
Mexican American Ind. (1)	1	<0.01
Navajo (5)	8	0.03
Sioux (1)	5	0.02
South American Ind. (3)	3	0.01
Asian (480)	696	2.76
Not Hispanic (473)	667	2.65
Hispanic (7)	29	0.12
Cambodian (5)	7	0.03
Chinese, ex. Taiwanese (41)	57	0.23
Filipino (97)	169	0.67
Indian (64)	85	0.34
Indonesian (0)	9	0.04
Japanese (48)	98	0.39
Korean (24)	62	0.25
Pakistani (4)	6	0.02
Sri Lankan (0)	1	<0.01
Taiwanese (3)	3	0.01
Thai (17)	33	0.13
Vietnamese (149)	160	0.63
Hawaii Native/Pacific Islander (10)	38	0.15
Not Hispanic (10)	35	0.14
Hispanic (0)	3	0.01
Guamanian/Chamorro (3)	10	0.04
Native Hawaiian (7)	15	0.06
Samoan (0)	2	0.01
White (21,984)	22,606	89.70
Not Hispanic (21,540)	22,097	87.68
Hispanic (444)	509	2.02

Rocky River

Place Type: City
County: Cuyahoga
Population: 20,213†

Ancestry‡	Population	%
African, Sub-Saharan (27)	27	0.13
African (27)	27	0.13
Albanian (328)	328	1.62
American (684)	684	3.39
Arab (429)	471	2.33
Egyptian (72)	72	0.36
Jordanian (62)	62	0.31
Lebanese (171)	213	1.05
Palestinian (35)	35	0.17
Syrian (89)	89	0.44
Armenian (19)	19	0.09
Austrian (17)	158	0.78
Belgian (0)	17	0.08
British (0)	35	0.17
Canadian (28)	69	0.34
Carpatho Rusyn (14)	14	0.07
Celtic (42)	42	0.21
Croatian (84)	201	1.00
Czech (263)	687	3.40
Czechoslovakian (28)	115	0.57
Danish (34)	172	0.85
Dutch (54)	229	1.13
Eastern European (20)	20	0.10
English (301)	2,224	11.01
European (146)	191	0.95
Finnish (12)	44	0.22
French, ex. Basque (34)	386	1.91
French Canadian (14)	56	0.28
German (1,299)	6,094	30.17
Greek (102)	102	0.51
Hungarian (376)	1,041	5.15
Irish (1,765)	5,241	25.95
Italian (808)	2,212	10.95
Latvian (10)	29	0.14
Lithuanian (27)	105	0.52
Northern European (27)	27	0.13
Norwegian (72)	190	0.94
Pennsylvania German (16)	16	0.08
Polish (564)	1,306	6.47
Romanian (136)	199	0.99
Russian (109)	218	1.08
Scandinavian (0)	14	0.07
Scotch-Irish (63)	310	1.53
Scottish (116)	554	2.74
Serbian (28)	28	0.14
Slovak (310)	892	4.42
Slovene (86)	180	0.89
Swedish (42)	227	1.12
Swiss (12)	158	0.78
Turkish (42)	42	0.21
Ukrainian (119)	235	1.16
Welsh (33)	213	1.05
Yugoslavian (12)	99	0.49

Hispanic Origin	Population	%
Hispanic or Latino (of any race)	367	1.82
Central American, ex. Mexican	11	0.05
Costa Rican	2	0.01
Guatemalan	6	0.03
Honduran	1	<0.01
Nicaraguan	1	<0.01
Panamanian	1	<0.01
Cuban	15	0.07
Dominican Republic	12	0.06
Mexican	95	0.47
Puerto Rican	123	0.61
South American	68	0.34
Argentinean	10	0.05
Chilean	14	0.07
Colombian	17	0.08
Ecuadorian	4	0.02
Paraguayan	4	0.02
Peruvian	6	0.03
Venezuelan	13	0.06
Other Hispanic or Latino	43	0.21

Race*	Population	%
African-American/Black (204)	287	1.42
Not Hispanic (196)	265	1.31
Hispanic (8)	22	0.11
American Indian/Alaska Native (19)	60	0.30
Not Hispanic (14)	49	0.24
Hispanic (5)	11	0.05
Apache (0)	3	0.01
Blackfeet (3)	5	0.02
Canadian/French Am. Ind. (0)	1	<0.01
Cherokee (1)	10	0.05
Cheyenne (1)	1	<0.01
Chippewa (1)	2	0.01
Delaware (0)	1	<0.01
Iroquois (1)	2	0.01
Mexican American Ind. (1)	3	0.01
Navajo (0)	1	<0.01
Osage (1)	1	<0.01
Pueblo (0)	5	0.02
Seminole (0)	1	<0.01
Spanish American Ind. (2)	2	0.01
Asian (359)	490	2.42
Not Hispanic (357)	480	2.37
Hispanic (2)	10	0.05
Bangladeshi (4)	4	0.02
Cambodian (1)	2	0.01
Chinese, ex. Taiwanese (131)	153	0.76
Filipino (50)	97	0.48
Indian (73)	92	0.46
Indonesian (1)	1	<0.01
Japanese (8)	26	0.13
Korean (25)	37	0.18
Pakistani (15)	18	0.09
Sri Lankan (2)	2	0.01
Taiwanese (4)	6	0.03
Thai (8)	8	0.04
Vietnamese (15)	18	0.09

SECTION TWO

*Notes: † The Census 2010 population figure is used to calculate the percentages in the Hispanic Origin and Race categories. Ancestry percentages are based on the 2006-2010 American Community Survey population (not shown); ‡ Numbers in parentheses indicate the number of people reporting a single ancestry; * Numbers in parentheses indicate the number of persons reporting this race alone, not in combination with any other race; Please refer to the Explanation of Data for more information.*

Hawaii Native/Pacific Islander (5)	22	0.11
Not Hispanic (5)	19	0.09
Hispanic (0)	3	0.01
Guamanian/Chamorro (2)	3	0.01
Native Hawaiian (1)	4	0.02
Samoan (1)	2	0.01
White (19,295)	19,538	96.66
Not Hispanic (19,040)	19,254	95.26
Hispanic (255)	284	1.41

Salem

Place Type: City
County: Columbiana
Population: 12,303†

Ancestry‡	Population	%
Albanian (13)	13	0.10
American (787)	787	6.36
Arab (0)	30	0.24
Lebanese (0)	30	0.24
Austrian (0)	31	0.25
British (58)	58	0.47
Carpatho Rusyn (0)	12	0.10
Celtic (0)	18	0.15
Croatian (14)	56	0.45
Czech (12)	26	0.21
Czechoslovakian (16)	31	0.25
Dutch (40)	279	2.25
English (330)	1,142	9.22
European (12)	12	0.10
French, ex. Basque (0)	220	1.78
French Canadian (0)	3	0.02
German (887)	3,408	27.52
Greek (16)	16	0.13
Hungarian (112)	419	3.38
Irish (360)	1,815	14.66
Italian (732)	1,668	13.47
Lithuanian (51)	64	0.52
Norwegian (13)	118	0.95
Pennsylvania German (0)	5	0.04
Polish (243)	685	5.53
Romanian (15)	42	0.34
Russian (0)	12	0.10
Scotch-Irish (198)	339	2.74
Scottish (74)	271	2.19
Serbian (0)	8	0.06
Slavic (0)	36	0.29
Slovak (150)	308	2.49
Slovene (8)	26	0.21
Swedish (0)	19	0.15
Swiss (76)	245	1.98
Ukrainian (15)	35	0.28
Welsh (83)	301	2.43
Yugoslavian (0)	11	0.09

Hispanic Origin	Population	%
Hispanic or Latino (of any race)	310	2.52
Central American, ex. Mexican	138	1.12
Guatemalan	133	1.08
Honduran	5	0.04
Cuban	5	0.04
Mexican	99	0.80
Puerto Rican	31	0.25
South American	5	0.04
Argentinean	1	0.01
Colombian	1	0.01
Peruvian	3	0.02
Other Hispanic or Latino	32	0.26

Race*	Population	%
African-American/Black (84)	149	1.21
Not Hispanic (76)	137	1.11
Hispanic (8)	12	0.10
American Indian/Alaska Native (24)	75	0.61
Not Hispanic (24)	73	0.59
Hispanic (0)	2	0.02
Apache (1)	6	0.05
Blackfeet (1)	6	0.05
Canadian/French Am. Ind. (6)	6	0.05
Cherokee (4)	26	0.21
Chippewa (3)	3	0.02
Choctaw (1)	2	0.02
Inupiat *(Alaska Native)* (1)	1	0.01
Sioux (1)	4	0.03
Asian (50)	83	0.67
Not Hispanic (50)	79	0.64
Hispanic (0)	4	0.03
Chinese, ex. Taiwanese (22)	32	0.26
Filipino (10)	23	0.19
Indian (3)	4	0.03
Japanese (4)	5	0.04
Korean (1)	12	0.10
Laotian (2)	2	0.02
Taiwanese (0)	1	0.01
Thai (1)	3	0.02
Vietnamese (0)	3	0.02
Hawaii Native/Pacific Islander (3)	7	0.06
Not Hispanic (3)	7	0.06
Native Hawaiian (2)	6	0.05
White (11,795)	11,933	96.99
Not Hispanic (11,708)	11,828	96.14
Hispanic (87)	105	0.85

Sandusky

Place Type: City
County: Erie
Population: 25,793†

Ancestry‡	Population	%
African, Sub-Saharan (141)	141	0.54
African (141)	141	0.54
American (961)	961	3.68
Arab (0)	12	0.05
Lebanese (0)	12	0.05
Austrian (0)	22	0.08
Belgian (11)	11	0.04
British (34)	53	0.20
Canadian (11)	33	0.13
Czech (19)	56	0.21
Czechoslovakian (5)	5	0.02
Danish (10)	32	0.12
Dutch (158)	605	2.31
English (628)	2,194	8.39
European (75)	128	0.49
Finnish (0)	75	0.29
French, ex. Basque (44)	581	2.22
French Canadian (20)	107	0.41
German (3,316)	9,006	34.44
Greek (99)	110	0.42
Hungarian (58)	296	1.13
Irish (1,020)	4,157	15.90
Italian (617)	1,810	6.92
Lithuanian (24)	91	0.35
Northern European (18)	18	0.07
Norwegian (0)	23	0.09
Pennsylvania German (45)	73	0.28
Polish (248)	718	2.75
Portuguese (0)	5	0.02
Romanian (0)	23	0.09
Russian (26)	111	0.42
Scotch-Irish (55)	331	1.27
Scottish (42)	339	1.30
Slovak (36)	188	0.72
Swedish (52)	187	0.72
Swiss (14)	39	0.15
Ukrainian (48)	48	0.18
Welsh (28)	119	0.46
West Indian, ex. Hispanic (24)	86	0.33
Jamaican (14)	14	0.05
West Indian (10)	72	0.28
Yugoslavian (14)	14	0.05

Hispanic Origin	Population	%
Hispanic or Latino (of any race)	1,265	4.90
Central American, ex. Mexican	15	0.06
Guatemalan	1	<0.01
Honduran	13	0.05
Salvadoran	1	<0.01
Cuban	10	0.04
Dominican Republic	3	0.01
Mexican	948	3.68
Puerto Rican	170	0.66
South American	21	0.08
Chilean	6	0.02
Colombian	11	0.04
Peruvian	1	<0.01
Venezuelan	3	0.01
Other Hispanic or Latino	98	0.38

Race*	Population	%
African-American/Black (5,686)	6,845	26.54
Not Hispanic (5,607)	6,628	25.70
Hispanic (79)	217	0.84
American Indian/Alaska Native (104)	336	1.30
Not Hispanic (78)	267	1.04
Hispanic (26)	69	0.27
Apache (3)	19	0.07
Blackfeet (3)	22	0.09
Canadian/French Am. Ind. (0)	3	0.01
Cherokee (26)	90	0.35
Cheyenne (1)	1	<0.01
Chippewa (3)	4	0.02
Choctaw (1)	9	0.03
Comanche (3)	3	0.01
Crow (0)	3	0.01
Delaware (0)	1	<0.01
Hopi (1)	1	<0.01
Inupiat *(Alaska Native)* (0)	2	0.01
Iroquois (2)	8	0.03
Menominee (1)	1	<0.01
Mexican American Ind. (3)	4	0.02
Ottawa (3)	9	0.03
Potawatomi (4)	6	0.02
Seminole (1)	1	<0.01
South American Ind. (0)	2	0.01
Yaqui (1)	1	<0.01
Yup'ik *(Alaska Native)* (0)	3	0.01
Asian (150)	194	0.75
Not Hispanic (149)	187	0.73
Hispanic (1)	7	0.03
Cambodian (1)	2	0.01
Chinese, ex. Taiwanese (29)	35	0.14
Filipino (33)	48	0.19
Hmong (0)	1	<0.01
Indian (14)	16	0.06
Japanese (9)	17	0.07
Korean (18)	25	0.10
Laotian (3)	3	0.01
Taiwanese (1)	1	<0.01
Thai (33)	33	0.13
Vietnamese (5)	8	0.03
Hawaii Native/Pacific Islander (6)	19	0.07
Not Hispanic (4)	9	0.03
Hispanic (2)	10	0.04
Guamanian/Chamorro (3)	4	0.02
Native Hawaiian (2)	6	0.02
White (18,158)	19,465	75.47
Not Hispanic (17,487)	18,577	72.02
Hispanic (671)	888	3.44

Seven Hills

Place Type: City
County: Cuyahoga
Population: 11,804†

Ancestry‡	Population	%
African, Sub-Saharan (14)	21	0.18
South African (0)	7	0.06
Other Sub-Saharan African (14)	14	0.12
Albanian (37)	59	0.50
American (188)	188	1.59
Arab (176)	368	3.12
Egyptian (27)	27	0.23
Jordanian (0)	20	0.17
Lebanese (149)	259	2.20
Palestinian (0)	45	0.38
Syrian (0)	17	0.14

*Notes: † The Census 2010 population figure is used to calculate the percentages in the Hispanic Origin and Race categories. Ancestry percentages are based on the 2006-2010 American Community Survey population (not shown); ‡ Numbers in parentheses indicate the number of people reporting a single ancestry; * Numbers in parentheses indicate the number of persons reporting this race alone, not in combination with any other race; Please refer to the Explanation of Data for more information.*

Ancestry	Population	%
Armenian (0)	30	0.25
Australian (0)	8	0.07
Austrian (58)	80	0.68
Belgian (0)	11	0.09
British (0)	17	0.14
Canadian (15)	41	0.35
Carpatho Rusyn (7)	7	0.06
Croatian (102)	146	1.24
Czech (218)	756	6.41
Czechoslovakian (40)	70	0.59
Dutch (44)	128	1.09
Eastern European (13)	13	0.11
English (125)	884	7.49
Finnish (11)	28	0.24
French, ex. Basque (20)	136	1.15
French Canadian (0)	10	0.08
German (619)	2,421	20.52
Greek (66)	101	0.86
Hungarian (259)	707	5.99
Irish (279)	1,399	11.86
Italian (1,055)	2,177	18.45
Lithuanian (35)	80	0.68
Macedonian (25)	25	0.21
Norwegian (0)	11	0.09
Polish (1,285)	2,569	21.78
Romanian (162)	227	1.92
Russian (130)	325	2.75
Scotch-Irish (47)	219	1.86
Scottish (16)	124	1.05
Serbian (0)	71	0.60
Slovak (360)	845	7.16
Slovene (129)	299	2.53
Swedish (20)	56	0.47
Swiss (0)	29	0.25
Ukrainian (230)	394	3.34
Welsh (9)	9	0.08

Hispanic Origin	Population	%
Hispanic or Latino (of any race)	153	1.30
Central American, ex. Mexican	11	0.09
Guatemalan	8	0.07
Honduran	3	0.03
Cuban	11	0.09
Dominican Republic	1	0.01
Mexican	16	0.14
Puerto Rican	71	0.60
South American	24	0.20
Argentinean	7	0.06
Bolivian	1	0.01
Colombian	7	0.06
Peruvian	7	0.06
Venezuelan	2	0.02
Other Hispanic or Latino	19	0.16

Race*	Population	%
African-American/Black (96)	109	0.92
Not Hispanic (85)	96	0.81
Hispanic (11)	13	0.11
American Indian/Alaska Native (8)	34	0.29
Not Hispanic (3)	28	0.24
Hispanic (5)	6	0.05
Blackfeet (0)	1	0.01
Cherokee (0)	3	0.03
Chickasaw (0)	2	0.02
Creek (0)	2	0.02
Inupiat *(Alaska Native)* (2)	2	0.02
Iroquois (0)	1	0.01
Sioux (1)	1	0.01
Asian (294)	340	2.88
Not Hispanic (293)	338	2.86
Hispanic (1)	2	0.02
Chinese, ex. Taiwanese (90)	99	0.84
Filipino (64)	91	0.77
Indian (69)	74	0.63
Indonesian (1)	1	0.01
Japanese (2)	2	0.02
Korean (34)	36	0.30
Vietnamese (28)	31	0.26
Hawaii Native/Pacific Islander (0)	4	0.03
Not Hispanic (0)	4	0.03
White (11,289)	11,373	96.35
Not Hispanic (11,175)	11,257	95.37
Hispanic (114)	116	0.98

Shaker Heights

Place Type: City
County: Cuyahoga
Population: 28,448†

Ancestry‡	Population	%
African, Sub-Saharan (304)	377	1.32
African (266)	292	1.03
Ghanaian (0)	15	0.05
Nigerian (28)	28	0.10
South African (10)	35	0.12
Other Sub-Saharan African (0)	7	0.02
Albanian (14)	14	0.05
American (744)	744	2.61
Arab (78)	89	0.31
Lebanese (60)	71	0.25
Syrian (9)	9	0.03
Other Arab (9)	9	0.03
Armenian (33)	33	0.12
Australian (30)	30	0.11
Austrian (26)	218	0.77
Belgian (21)	55	0.19
British (73)	179	0.63
Bulgarian (8)	8	0.03
Canadian (0)	24	0.08
Croatian (16)	62	0.22
Czech (16)	221	0.78
Czechoslovakian (20)	33	0.12
Danish (0)	61	0.21
Dutch (59)	289	1.02
Eastern European (526)	545	1.92
English (491)	2,593	9.11
European (437)	472	1.66
Finnish (0)	21	0.07
French, ex. Basque (62)	441	1.55
French Canadian (11)	76	0.27
German (656)	3,421	12.02
Greek (70)	130	0.46
Hungarian (234)	798	2.80
Icelander (0)	8	0.03
Iranian (59)	96	0.34
Irish (622)	2,526	8.88
Israeli (0)	10	0.04
Italian (434)	1,408	4.95
Latvian (11)	63	0.22
Lithuanian (52)	204	0.72
Macedonian (0)	30	0.11
Northern European (38)	55	0.19
Norwegian (0)	102	0.36
Polish (329)	1,251	4.40
Romanian (0)	23	0.08
Russian (426)	1,019	3.58
Scandinavian (77)	86	0.30
Scotch-Irish (133)	405	1.42
Scottish (124)	766	2.69
Serbian (11)	51	0.18
Slavic (7)	18	0.06
Slovak (17)	158	0.56
Slovene (20)	70	0.25
Swedish (76)	164	0.58
Swiss (7)	294	1.03
Turkish (47)	47	0.17
Ukrainian (128)	262	0.92
Welsh (9)	197	0.69
West Indian, ex. Hispanic (47)	72	0.25
Bermudan (10)	10	0.04
Jamaican (25)	25	0.09
Trinidadian/Tobagonian (12)	21	0.07
West Indian (0)	16	0.06
Yugoslavian (0)	9	0.03

Hispanic Origin	Population	%
Hispanic or Latino (of any race)	626	2.20
Central American, ex. Mexican	51	0.18
Costa Rican	4	0.01
Guatemalan	21	0.07
Honduran	8	0.03
Nicaraguan	8	0.03
Panamanian	5	0.02
Salvadoran	5	0.02
Cuban	43	0.15
Dominican Republic	17	0.06
Mexican	165	0.58
Puerto Rican	147	0.52
South American	130	0.46
Argentinean	32	0.11
Bolivian	1	<0.01
Chilean	6	0.02
Colombian	29	0.10
Ecuadorian	5	0.02
Paraguayan	2	0.01
Peruvian	31	0.11
Uruguayan	12	0.04
Venezuelan	12	0.04
Other Hispanic or Latino	73	0.26

Race*	Population	%
African-American/Black (10,545)	11,013	38.71
Not Hispanic (10,446)	10,875	38.23
Hispanic (99)	138	0.49
American Indian/Alaska Native (42)	218	0.77
Not Hispanic (33)	188	0.66
Hispanic (9)	30	0.11
Alaska Athabascan *(Ala. Nat.)* (1)	3	0.01
Apache (1)	1	<0.01
Blackfeet (1)	10	0.04
Cherokee (2)	44	0.15
Cheyenne (1)	1	<0.01
Chickasaw (0)	1	<0.01
Choctaw (0)	11	0.04
Inupiat *(Alaska Native)* (1)	1	<0.01
Iroquois (3)	5	0.02
Mexican American Ind. (6)	7	0.02
Navajo (1)	5	0.02
Pueblo (2)	2	0.01
Seminole (0)	6	0.02
Sioux (0)	1	<0.01
South American Ind. (0)	4	0.01
Asian (1,306)	1,569	5.52
Not Hispanic (1,300)	1,557	5.47
Hispanic (6)	12	0.04
Bangladeshi (4)	5	0.02
Cambodian (1)	2	0.01
Chinese, ex. Taiwanese (467)	547	1.92
Filipino (120)	164	0.58
Indian (395)	461	1.62
Indonesian (1)	2	0.01
Japanese (55)	82	0.29
Korean (111)	134	0.47
Laotian (1)	2	0.01
Malaysian (2)	4	0.01
Nepalese (1)	1	<0.01
Pakistani (21)	27	0.09
Sri Lankan (7)	11	0.04
Taiwanese (45)	51	0.18
Thai (13)	15	0.05
Vietnamese (11)	18	0.06
Hawaii Native/Pacific Islander (4)	17	0.06
Not Hispanic (3)	16	0.06
Hispanic (1)	1	<0.01
Fijian (0)	1	<0.01
Native Hawaiian (0)	8	0.03
Samoan (0)	1	<0.01
White (15,635)	16,250	57.12
Not Hispanic (15,270)	15,836	55.67
Hispanic (365)	414	1.46

Sharonville

Place Type: City
County: Hamilton
Population: 13,560†

Ancestry‡	Population	%
American (678)	678	5.09

*Notes: † The Census 2010 population figure is used to calculate the percentages in the Hispanic Origin and Race categories. Ancestry percentages are based on the 2006-2010 American Community Survey population (not shown); ‡ Numbers in parentheses indicate the number of people reporting a single ancestry; * Numbers in parentheses indicate the number of persons reporting this race alone, not in combination with any other race; Please refer to the Explanation of Data for more information.*

Arab (0)	40	0.30
Lebanese (0)	40	0.30
Armenian (0)	15	0.11
Austrian (18)	57	0.43
Belgian (0)	16	0.12
British (29)	71	0.53
Czech (14)	29	0.22
Czechoslovakian (0)	26	0.20
Danish (3)	11	0.08
Dutch (30)	227	1.71
English (555)	1,393	10.47
European (136)	153	1.15
French, ex. Basque (61)	360	2.70
French Canadian (27)	83	0.62
German (1,767)	4,302	32.32
Greek (38)	38	0.29
Hungarian (14)	28	0.21
Iranian (12)	24	0.18
Irish (701)	2,507	18.83
Italian (180)	564	4.24
Lithuanian (0)	12	0.09
Norwegian (87)	112	0.84
Polish (89)	356	2.67
Romanian (38)	38	0.29
Russian (72)	160	1.20
Scotch-Irish (84)	287	2.16
Scottish (103)	370	2.78
Swedish (28)	70	0.53
Swiss (36)	36	0.27
Turkish (11)	11	0.08
Ukrainian (11)	11	0.08
Welsh (101)	200	1.50
West Indian, ex. Hispanic (18)	18	0.14
Jamaican (18)	18	0.14

Hispanic Origin	Population	%
Hispanic or Latino (of any race)	948	6.99
Central American, ex. Mexican	82	0.60
Costa Rican	3	0.02
Guatemalan	62	0.46
Honduran	3	0.02
Nicaraguan	1	0.01
Panamanian	3	0.02
Salvadoran	10	0.07
Cuban	14	0.10
Dominican Republic	17	0.13
Mexican	662	4.88
Puerto Rican	31	0.23
South American	42	0.31
Argentinean	6	0.04
Chilean	1	0.01
Colombian	11	0.08
Ecuadorian	4	0.03
Peruvian	8	0.06
Venezuelan	11	0.08
Other South American	1	0.01
Other Hispanic or Latino	100	0.74

Race*	Population	%
African-American/Black (1,181)	1,352	9.97
Not Hispanic (1,177)	1,330	9.81
Hispanic (4)	22	0.16
American Indian/Alaska Native (23)	114	0.84
Not Hispanic (18)	96	0.71
Hispanic (5)	18	0.13
Apache (1)	3	0.02
Blackfeet (0)	2	0.01
Central American Ind. (3)	6	0.04
Cherokee (5)	37	0.27
Chippewa (0)	2	0.01
Choctaw (0)	3	0.02
Iroquois (1)	2	0.01
Mexican American Ind. (1)	1	0.01
Pima (1)	1	0.01
Seminole (0)	1	0.01
Sioux (4)	4	0.03
South American Ind. (0)	1	0.01
Asian (539)	700	5.16
Not Hispanic (537)	696	5.13
Hispanic (2)	4	0.03
Burmese (2)	2	0.01
Cambodian (20)	23	0.17
Chinese, ex. Taiwanese (67)	84	0.62
Filipino (21)	32	0.24
Indian (295)	325	2.40
Japanese (14)	24	0.18
Korean (30)	42	0.31
Malaysian (1)	1	0.01
Nepalese (1)	1	0.01
Pakistani (5)	7	0.05
Taiwanese (19)	25	0.18
Thai (3)	6	0.04
Vietnamese (26)	32	0.24
Hawaii Native/Pacific Islander (45)	66	0.49
Not Hispanic (44)	59	0.44
Hispanic (1)	7	0.05
Guamanian/Chamorro (2)	3	0.02
Native Hawaiian (0)	7	0.05
White (10,814)	11,133	82.10
Not Hispanic (10,447)	10,733	79.15
Hispanic (367)	400	2.95

Sheffield Lake

Place Type: City
County: Lorain
Population: 9,137†

Ancestry‡	Population	%
American (695)	695	7.53
Austrian (15)	56	0.61
British (34)	34	0.37
Canadian (0)	56	0.61
Croatian (0)	14	0.15
Czech (22)	37	0.40
Danish (0)	9	0.10
Dutch (56)	333	3.61
English (214)	1,405	15.23
European (92)	92	1.00
Finnish (0)	55	0.60
French, ex. Basque (6)	115	1.25
French Canadian (0)	94	1.02
German (683)	2,937	31.84
Greek (0)	13	0.14
Hungarian (215)	591	6.41
Irish (277)	1,786	19.36
Italian (262)	764	8.28
Lithuanian (0)	91	0.99
Macedonian (22)	35	0.38
Norwegian (29)	72	0.78
Pennsylvania German (21)	31	0.34
Polish (292)	980	10.62
Portuguese (0)	38	0.41
Romanian (11)	11	0.12
Russian (47)	72	0.78
Scotch-Irish (115)	312	3.38
Scottish (63)	312	3.38
Serbian (40)	40	0.43
Slovak (118)	322	3.49
Slovene (9)	87	0.94
Swedish (74)	187	2.03
Ukrainian (56)	110	1.19
Welsh (0)	159	1.72
Yugoslavian (11)	11	0.12

Hispanic Origin	Population	%
Hispanic or Latino (of any race)	449	4.91
Central American, ex. Mexican	12	0.13
Guatemalan	4	0.04
Nicaraguan	1	0.01
Panamanian	7	0.08
Cuban	8	0.09
Dominican Republic	3	0.03
Mexican	142	1.55
Puerto Rican	246	2.69
South American	10	0.11
Chilean	3	0.03
Ecuadorian	2	0.02
Peruvian	1	0.01
Uruguayan	1	0.01
Other South American	3	0.03
Other Hispanic or Latino	28	0.31

Race*	Population	%
African-American/Black (153)	235	2.57
Not Hispanic (145)	214	2.34
Hispanic (8)	21	0.23
American Indian/Alaska Native (24)	91	1.00
Not Hispanic (22)	82	0.90
Hispanic (2)	9	0.10
Apache (1)	1	0.01
Blackfeet (0)	2	0.02
Cherokee (6)	34	0.37
Chippewa (1)	3	0.03
Choctaw (2)	6	0.07
Creek (0)	7	0.08
Iroquois (0)	2	0.02
Mexican American Ind. (0)	4	0.04
Navajo (1)	1	0.01
Pueblo (1)	2	0.02
Seminole (3)	7	0.08
Sioux (1)	2	0.02
Asian (46)	70	0.77
Not Hispanic (43)	61	0.67
Hispanic (3)	9	0.10
Cambodian (2)	2	0.02
Chinese, ex. Taiwanese (8)	10	0.11
Filipino (7)	16	0.18
Indian (14)	15	0.16
Indonesian (1)	1	0.01
Japanese (2)	6	0.07
Korean (2)	7	0.08
Vietnamese (6)	6	0.07
Hawaii Native/Pacific Islander (1)	3	0.03
Not Hispanic (1)	3	0.03
Marshallese (1)	1	0.01
Native Hawaiian (0)	1	0.01
White (8,632)	8,818	96.51
Not Hispanic (8,323)	8,460	92.59
Hispanic (309)	358	3.92

Shelby

Place Type: City
County: Richland
Population: 9,317†

Ancestry‡	Population	%
American (708)	708	7.71
Austrian (0)	31	0.34
Belgian (0)	40	0.44
British (22)	45	0.49
Canadian (12)	12	0.13
Croatian (0)	12	0.13
Czech (18)	18	0.20
Czechoslovakian (29)	29	0.32
Danish (16)	16	0.17
Dutch (41)	237	2.58
English (531)	1,270	13.84
European (18)	18	0.20
Finnish (0)	9	0.10
French, ex. Basque (0)	202	2.20
French Canadian (10)	19	0.21
German (1,234)	3,171	34.55
Greek (8)	25	0.27
Hungarian (20)	65	0.71
Irish (455)	1,790	19.51
Italian (103)	164	1.79
Pennsylvania German (12)	12	0.13
Polish (66)	184	2.01
Scandinavian (0)	56	0.61
Scotch-Irish (93)	276	3.01
Scottish (49)	187	2.04
Slavic (0)	20	0.22
Slovak (9)	9	0.10
Swedish (12)	61	0.66
Swiss (39)	103	1.12
Welsh (62)	138	1.50
Yugoslavian (0)	11	0.12

*Notes: † The Census 2010 population figure is used to calculate the percentages in the Hispanic Origin and Race categories. Ancestry percentages are based on the 2006-2010 American Community Survey population (not shown); ‡ Numbers in parentheses indicate the number of people reporting a single ancestry; * Numbers in parentheses indicate the number of persons reporting this race alone, not in combination with any other race; Please refer to the Explanation of Data for more information.*

Hispanic Origin	Population	%
Hispanic or Latino (of any race)	108	1.16
Central American, ex. Mexican	2	0.02
Costa Rican	1	0.01
Salvadoran	1	0.01
Cuban	6	0.06
Mexican	77	0.83
Puerto Rican	8	0.09
South American	7	0.08
Argentinean	1	0.01
Colombian	2	0.02
Ecuadorian	2	0.02
Peruvian	2	0.02
Other Hispanic or Latino	8	0.09

Race*	Population	%
African-American/Black (19)	40	0.43
Not Hispanic (17)	38	0.41
Hispanic (2)	2	0.02
American Indian/Alaska Native (16)	70	0.75
Not Hispanic (15)	68	0.73
Hispanic (1)	2	0.02
Blackfeet (1)	3	0.03
Cherokee (3)	27	0.29
Chippewa (1)	2	0.02
Ottawa (0)	1	0.01
Pueblo (1)	1	0.01
Sioux (0)	4	0.04
Asian (26)	35	0.38
Not Hispanic (26)	35	0.38
Chinese, ex. Taiwanese (1)	2	0.02
Filipino (9)	12	0.13
Indian (8)	9	0.10
Japanese (1)	1	0.01
Korean (4)	4	0.04
Vietnamese (2)	2	0.02
Hawaii Native/Pacific Islander (0)	1	0.01
Not Hispanic (0)	1	0.01
White (9,149)	9,239	99.16
Not Hispanic (9,062)	9,146	98.16
Hispanic (87)	93	1.00

Sidney

Place Type: City
County: Shelby
Population: 21,229†

Ancestry‡	Population	%
African, Sub-Saharan (172)	172	0.82
African (108)	108	0.51
Other Sub-Saharan African (64)	64	0.30
American (1,800)	1,800	8.55
Arab (0)	8	0.04
Syrian (0)	8	0.04
British (63)	81	0.38
Canadian (83)	94	0.45
Czech (15)	29	0.14
Danish (19)	19	0.09
Dutch (63)	430	2.04
English (587)	1,724	8.19
European (107)	119	0.57
Finnish (0)	11	0.05
French, ex. Basque (264)	852	4.05
French Canadian (10)	40	0.19
German (3,546)	6,451	30.65
Hungarian (0)	10	0.05
Irish (677)	2,275	10.81
Italian (148)	426	2.02
Norwegian (9)	117	0.56
Pennsylvania German (9)	85	0.40
Polish (74)	164	0.78
Russian (21)	34	0.16
Scotch-Irish (80)	192	0.91
Scottish (122)	221	1.05
Swedish (0)	7	0.03
Swiss (0)	33	0.16
Turkish (12)	30	0.14
Ukrainian (63)	63	0.30
Welsh (11)	63	0.30

Hispanic Origin	Population	%
Hispanic or Latino (of any race)	463	2.18
Central American, ex. Mexican	23	0.11
Costa Rican	2	0.01
Guatemalan	6	0.03
Honduran	13	0.06
Salvadoran	1	<0.01
Other Central American	1	<0.01
Cuban	8	0.04
Mexican	330	1.55
Puerto Rican	48	0.23
South American	7	0.03
Bolivian	1	<0.01
Chilean	3	0.01
Uruguayan	1	<0.01
Venezuelan	1	<0.01
Other South American	1	<0.01
Other Hispanic or Latino	47	0.22

Race*	Population	%
African-American/Black (778)	1,234	5.81
Not Hispanic (773)	1,214	5.72
Hispanic (5)	20	0.09
American Indian/Alaska Native (43)	158	0.74
Not Hispanic (43)	150	0.71
Hispanic (0)	8	0.04
Apache (0)	1	<0.01
Blackfeet (3)	7	0.03
Cherokee (14)	71	0.33
Cheyenne (0)	1	<0.01
Chickasaw (1)	1	<0.01
Chippewa (1)	1	<0.01
Choctaw (0)	2	0.01
Cree (1)	2	0.01
Delaware (2)	2	0.01
Iroquois (0)	1	<0.01
Lumbee (0)	1	<0.01
Seminole (1)	1	<0.01
Sioux (8)	10	0.05
Asian (350)	419	1.97
Not Hispanic (349)	414	1.95
Hispanic (1)	5	0.02
Burmese (2)	2	0.01
Chinese, ex. Taiwanese (30)	37	0.17
Filipino (27)	41	0.19
Indian (80)	101	0.48
Japanese (172)	178	0.84
Korean (2)	9	0.04
Laotian (30)	31	0.15
Malaysian (1)	1	<0.01
Nepalese (2)	2	0.01
Pakistani (0)	2	0.01
Thai (1)	10	0.05
Vietnamese (3)	4	0.02
Hawaii Native/Pacific Islander (32)	58	0.27
Not Hispanic (32)	55	0.26
Hispanic (0)	3	0.01
Fijian (1)	1	<0.01
Guamanian/Chamorro (21)	29	0.14
Native Hawaiian (7)	22	0.10
White (19,165)	19,831	93.41
Not Hispanic (18,923)	19,511	91.91
Hispanic (242)	320	1.51

Solon

Place Type: City
County: Cuyahoga
Population: 23,348†

Ancestry‡	Population	%
African, Sub-Saharan (312)	327	1.42
African (93)	93	0.40
Ghanaian (34)	34	0.15
Nigerian (168)	168	0.73
South African (17)	17	0.07
Other Sub-Saharan African (0)	15	0.07
American (829)	829	3.61
Arab (80)	223	0.97
Arab (0)	26	0.11
Lebanese (80)	171	0.74
Syrian (0)	13	0.06
Other Arab (0)	13	0.06
Armenian (55)	55	0.24
Australian (13)	26	0.11
Austrian (22)	300	1.31
British (55)	172	0.75
Canadian (0)	22	0.10
Carpatho Rusyn (11)	11	0.05
Croatian (45)	141	0.61
Czech (243)	754	3.28
Czechoslovakian (58)	103	0.45
Dutch (0)	128	0.56
Eastern European (420)	420	1.83
English (554)	2,068	9.00
European (196)	218	0.95
Finnish (20)	56	0.24
French, ex. Basque (28)	374	1.63
German (911)	3,402	14.80
Greek (46)	80	0.35
Hungarian (476)	1,333	5.80
Iranian (28)	28	0.12
Irish (460)	1,911	8.31
Israeli (30)	124	0.54
Italian (1,414)	2,793	12.15
Lithuanian (20)	207	0.90
Norwegian (58)	150	0.65
Polish (1,047)	2,535	11.03
Portuguese (0)	15	0.07
Romanian (108)	146	0.64
Russian (763)	1,498	6.52
Scandinavian (17)	64	0.28
Scotch-Irish (214)	437	1.90
Scottish (97)	358	1.56
Serbian (0)	24	0.10
Slavic (9)	51	0.22
Slovak (300)	824	3.59
Slovene (90)	394	1.71
Swedish (27)	202	0.88
Swiss (9)	43	0.19
Turkish (69)	112	0.49
Ukrainian (235)	408	1.78
Welsh (22)	220	0.96
Yugoslavian (12)	31	0.13

Hispanic Origin	Population	%
Hispanic or Latino (of any race)	357	1.53
Central American, ex. Mexican	28	0.12
Costa Rican	1	<0.01
Guatemalan	13	0.06
Honduran	3	0.01
Panamanian	9	0.04
Salvadoran	2	0.01
Cuban	11	0.05
Dominican Republic	7	0.03
Mexican	142	0.61
Puerto Rican	65	0.28
South American	75	0.32
Argentinean	18	0.08
Bolivian	4	0.02
Chilean	4	0.02
Colombian	18	0.08
Ecuadorian	6	0.03
Peruvian	10	0.04
Uruguayan	5	0.02
Venezuelan	10	0.04
Other Hispanic or Latino	29	0.12

Race*	Population	%
African-American/Black (2,476)	2,624	11.24
Not Hispanic (2,441)	2,568	11.00
Hispanic (35)	56	0.24
American Indian/Alaska Native (14)	65	0.28
Not Hispanic (8)	53	0.23
Hispanic (6)	12	0.05
Apache (0)	1	<0.01
Cherokee (0)	8	0.03
Cheyenne (0)	1	<0.01
Chippewa (0)	1	<0.01
Mexican American Ind. (1)	2	0.01

*Notes: † The Census 2010 population figure is used to calculate the percentages in the Hispanic Origin and Race categories. Ancestry percentages are based on the 2006-2010 American Community Survey population (not shown); ‡ Numbers in parentheses indicate the number of people reporting a single ancestry; * Numbers in parentheses indicate the number of persons reporting this race alone, not in combination with any other race; Please refer to the Explanation of Data for more information.*

Seminole (0)	7	0.03
Sioux (0)	1	<0.01
South American Ind. (0)	1	<0.01
Asian (2,344)	2,491	10.67
Not Hispanic (2,336)	2,482	10.63
Hispanic (8)	9	0.04
Bangladeshi (9)	10	0.04
Cambodian (1)	1	<0.01
Chinese, ex. Taiwanese (928)	965	4.13
Filipino (66)	78	0.33
Indian (1,052)	1,107	4.74
Indonesian (1)	3	0.01
Japanese (24)	36	0.15
Korean (132)	141	0.60
Malaysian (1)	3	0.01
Pakistani (20)	21	0.09
Sri Lankan (7)	11	0.05
Taiwanese (50)	52	0.22
Thai (5)	5	0.02
Vietnamese (18)	22	0.09
Hawaii Native/Pacific Islander (3)	6	0.03
Not Hispanic (3)	6	0.03
Guamanian/Chamorro (2)	2	0.01
Native Hawaiian (0)	1	<0.01
White (18,104)	18,357	78.62
Not Hispanic (17,867)	18,106	77.55
Hispanic (237)	251	1.08

South Euclid

Place Type: City
County: Cuyahoga
Population: 22,295†

Ancestry‡	Population	%
African, Sub-Saharan (119)	174	0.78
African (63)	105	0.47
Ghanaian (39)	39	0.17
Nigerian (5)	5	0.02
South African (12)	25	0.11
Albanian (0)	10	0.04
American (341)	341	1.53
Arab (129)	193	0.86
Lebanese (111)	175	0.78
Moroccan (7)	7	0.03
Other Arab (11)	11	0.05
Armenian (3)	3	0.01
Austrian (14)	166	0.74
Belgian (0)	26	0.12
British (14)	28	0.13
Canadian (12)	78	0.35
Croatian (52)	163	0.73
Czech (109)	325	1.46
Czechoslovakian (61)	75	0.34
Danish (0)	25	0.11
Dutch (31)	218	0.98
Eastern European (19)	19	0.09
English (319)	1,101	4.93
European (145)	180	0.81
Finnish (0)	51	0.23
French, ex. Basque (0)	432	1.93
French Canadian (0)	53	0.24
German (721)	3,404	15.25
Greek (7)	86	0.39
Hungarian (281)	684	3.06
Irish (542)	2,643	11.84
Israeli (17)	69	0.31
Italian (1,166)	2,624	11.75
Latvian (10)	23	0.10
Lithuanian (75)	125	0.56
Luxemburger (6)	6	0.03
Norwegian (14)	74	0.33
Polish (439)	1,415	6.34
Romanian (68)	166	0.74
Russian (399)	1,011	4.53
Scotch-Irish (125)	311	1.39
Scottish (29)	273	1.22
Serbian (0)	16	0.07
Slavic (8)	60	0.27
Slovak (100)	309	1.38
Slovene (54)	295	1.32
Swedish (95)	272	1.22
Swiss (6)	14	0.06
Ukrainian (105)	149	0.67
Welsh (85)	222	0.99
West Indian, ex. Hispanic (75)	86	0.39
Haitian (13)	13	0.06
Jamaican (62)	73	0.33

Hispanic Origin	Population	%
Hispanic or Latino (of any race)	447	2.00
Central American, ex. Mexican	42	0.19
Costa Rican	1	<0.01
Guatemalan	14	0.06
Honduran	3	0.01
Nicaraguan	1	<0.01
Panamanian	11	0.05
Salvadoran	12	0.05
Cuban	33	0.15
Dominican Republic	19	0.09
Mexican	109	0.49
Puerto Rican	129	0.58
South American	60	0.27
Argentinean	2	0.01
Bolivian	2	0.01
Chilean	3	0.01
Colombian	17	0.08
Ecuadorian	3	0.01
Peruvian	27	0.12
Uruguayan	2	0.01
Venezuelan	4	0.02
Other Hispanic or Latino	55	0.25

Race*	Population	%
African-American/Black (9,073)	9,505	42.63
Not Hispanic (8,988)	9,355	41.96
Hispanic (85)	150	0.67
American Indian/Alaska Native (16)	141	0.63
Not Hispanic (16)	128	0.57
Hispanic (0)	13	0.06
Apache (0)	3	0.01
Blackfeet (0)	5	0.02
Cherokee (2)	25	0.11
Creek (0)	2	0.01
Iroquois (0)	6	0.03
Lumbee (1)	1	<0.01
Seminole (0)	4	0.02
Sioux (0)	1	<0.01
South American Ind. (0)	5	0.02
Asian (436)	565	2.53
Not Hispanic (433)	551	2.47
Hispanic (3)	14	0.06
Bangladeshi (1)	1	<0.01
Bhutanese (32)	55	0.25
Cambodian (1)	2	0.01
Chinese, ex. Taiwanese (98)	120	0.54
Filipino (57)	81	0.36
Indian (105)	140	0.63
Indonesian (0)	2	0.01
Japanese (25)	53	0.24
Korean (20)	31	0.14
Laotian (2)	2	0.01
Malaysian (1)	1	<0.01
Nepalese (13)	22	0.10
Pakistani (2)	4	0.02
Sri Lankan (7)	7	0.03
Taiwanese (3)	4	0.02
Thai (15)	18	0.08
Vietnamese (19)	22	0.10
Hawaii Native/Pacific Islander (4)	15	0.07
Not Hispanic (2)	13	0.06
Hispanic (2)	2	0.01
Guamanian/Chamorro (2)	2	0.01
Native Hawaiian (1)	8	0.04
Samoan (0)	3	0.01
White (12,063)	12,486	56.00
Not Hispanic (11,867)	12,238	54.89
Hispanic (196)	248	1.11

Springboro

Place Type: City
County: Warren
Population: 17,409†

Ancestry‡	Population	%
African, Sub-Saharan (14)	29	0.17
African (0)	15	0.09
Nigerian (14)	14	0.08
American (1,084)	1,084	6.35
Arab (68)	68	0.40
Egyptian (26)	26	0.15
Lebanese (27)	27	0.16
Palestinian (15)	15	0.09
Austrian (68)	101	0.59
British (30)	30	0.18
Croatian (0)	20	0.12
Czech (10)	78	0.46
Danish (0)	13	0.08
Dutch (11)	299	1.75
English (1,003)	2,462	14.42
European (245)	245	1.44
Finnish (0)	29	0.17
French, ex. Basque (47)	369	2.16
French Canadian (0)	32	0.19
German (1,875)	5,675	33.24
Greek (50)	100	0.59
Hungarian (47)	174	1.02
Iranian (86)	86	0.50
Irish (901)	2,600	15.23
Italian (357)	1,500	8.79
Lithuanian (7)	24	0.14
Norwegian (97)	162	0.95
Pennsylvania German (20)	20	0.12
Polish (127)	530	3.10
Portuguese (0)	7	0.04
Romanian (0)	12	0.07
Russian (20)	98	0.57
Scotch-Irish (60)	317	1.86
Scottish (71)	261	1.53
Serbian (0)	12	0.07
Slovak (56)	172	1.01
Slovene (0)	6	0.04
Swedish (63)	221	1.29
Swiss (0)	13	0.08
Ukrainian (21)	104	0.61
Welsh (7)	231	1.35
Yugoslavian (32)	50	0.29

Hispanic Origin	Population	%
Hispanic or Latino (of any race)	308	1.77
Central American, ex. Mexican	23	0.13
Costa Rican	2	0.01
Guatemalan	5	0.03
Honduran	5	0.03
Nicaraguan	3	0.02
Panamanian	4	0.02
Salvadoran	4	0.02
Cuban	18	0.10
Mexican	116	0.67
Puerto Rican	75	0.43
South American	39	0.22
Bolivian	3	0.02
Chilean	1	0.01
Colombian	26	0.15
Ecuadorian	4	0.02
Peruvian	2	0.01
Venezuelan	3	0.02
Other Hispanic or Latino	37	0.21

Race*	Population	%
African-American/Black (398)	515	2.96
Not Hispanic (382)	487	2.80
Hispanic (16)	28	0.16
American Indian/Alaska Native (19)	67	0.38
Not Hispanic (17)	64	0.37
Hispanic (2)	3	0.02
Apache (0)	3	0.02
Cherokee (8)	25	0.14

*Notes: † The Census 2010 population figure is used to calculate the percentages in the Hispanic Origin and Race categories. Ancestry percentages are based on the 2006-2010 American Community Survey population (not shown); ‡ Numbers in parentheses indicate the number of people reporting a single ancestry; * Numbers in parentheses indicate the number of persons reporting this race alone, not in combination with any other race; Please refer to the Explanation of Data for more information.*

Choctaw (0)	1	0.01
Creek (0)	1	0.01
Hopi (0)	1	0.01
Iroquois (1)	2	0.01
Mexican American Ind. (1)	1	0.01
Navajo (0)	1	0.01
Asian (598)	732	4.20
Not Hispanic (591)	721	4.14
Hispanic (7)	11	0.06
Chinese, ex. Taiwanese (88)	111	0.64
Filipino (38)	73	0.42
Indian (301)	316	1.82
Japanese (18)	41	0.24
Korean (44)	75	0.43
Laotian (0)	3	0.02
Malaysian (1)	5	0.03
Pakistani (20)	20	0.11
Sri Lankan (5)	5	0.03
Taiwanese (2)	3	0.02
Thai (4)	9	0.05
Vietnamese (60)	63	0.36
Hawaii Native/Pacific Islander (1)	13	0.07
Not Hispanic (1)	13	0.07
Native Hawaiian (0)	6	0.03
White (16,041)	16,312	93.70
Not Hispanic (15,826)	16,075	92.34
Hispanic (215)	237	1.36

Springdale

Place Type: City
County: Hamilton
Population: 11,223†

Ancestry‡	Population	%
African, Sub-Saharan (37)	46	0.42
African (37)	46	0.42
American (435)	435	3.95
Austrian (0)	8	0.07
Celtic (14)	14	0.13
Czech (12)	23	0.21
Dutch (13)	170	1.54
English (379)	792	7.19
European (11)	11	0.10
Finnish (0)	8	0.07
French, ex. Basque (76)	178	1.62
German (856)	1,877	17.03
Greek (50)	66	0.60
Guyanese (0)	21	0.19
Hungarian (11)	19	0.17
Irish (229)	885	8.03
Italian (105)	140	1.27
Norwegian (8)	23	0.21
Pennsylvania German (11)	11	0.10
Polish (45)	147	1.33
Russian (22)	70	0.64
Scandinavian (12)	12	0.11
Scotch-Irish (96)	138	1.25
Scottish (15)	104	0.94
Swedish (7)	7	0.06
Welsh (0)	44	0.40
West Indian, ex. Hispanic (0)	98	0.89
Trinidadian/Tobagonian (0)	98	0.89

Hispanic Origin	Population	%
Hispanic or Latino (of any race)	1,965	17.51
Central American, ex. Mexican	613	5.46
Costa Rican	3	0.03
Guatemalan	562	5.01
Honduran	15	0.13
Nicaraguan	3	0.03
Panamanian	7	0.06
Salvadoran	21	0.19
Other Central American	2	0.02
Cuban	11	0.10
Dominican Republic	18	0.16
Mexican	1,114	9.93
Puerto Rican	54	0.48
South American	35	0.31
Argentinean	3	0.03
Colombian	6	0.05
Ecuadorian	4	0.04
Peruvian	22	0.20
Other Hispanic or Latino	120	1.07

Race*	Population	%
African-American/Black (3,355)	3,551	31.64
Not Hispanic (3,312)	3,489	31.09
Hispanic (43)	62	0.55
American Indian/Alaska Native (35)	101	0.90
Not Hispanic (7)	61	0.54
Hispanic (28)	40	0.36
Central American Ind. (4)	14	0.12
Cherokee (1)	19	0.17
Comanche (1)	1	0.01
Crow (0)	1	0.01
Mexican American Ind. (1)	5	0.04
Navajo (0)	2	0.02
Sioux (1)	1	0.01
Asian (312)	385	3.43
Not Hispanic (306)	370	3.30
Hispanic (6)	15	0.13
Cambodian (4)	4	0.04
Chinese, ex. Taiwanese (23)	28	0.25
Filipino (31)	41	0.37
Indian (141)	156	1.39
Indonesian (0)	1	0.01
Japanese (12)	23	0.20
Korean (7)	8	0.07
Laotian (1)	1	0.01
Malaysian (1)	1	0.01
Pakistani (3)	3	0.03
Taiwanese (12)	14	0.12
Thai (0)	3	0.03
Vietnamese (75)	92	0.82
Hawaii Native/Pacific Islander (44)	60	0.53
Not Hispanic (34)	45	0.40
Hispanic (10)	15	0.13
Guamanian/Chamorro (7)	10	0.09
Native Hawaiian (13)	21	0.19
Samoan (3)	5	0.04
White (6,169)	6,428	57.28
Not Hispanic (5,312)	5,508	49.08
Hispanic (857)	920	8.20

Springfield

Place Type: City
County: Clark
Population: 60,608†

Ancestry‡	Population	%
African, Sub-Saharan (658)	729	1.19
African (627)	691	1.12
Cape Verdean (6)	13	0.02
Nigerian (25)	25	0.04
American (8,078)	8,078	13.14
Arab (35)	35	0.06
Other Arab (35)	35	0.06
Armenian (0)	12	0.02
Austrian (0)	11	0.02
Belgian (12)	12	0.02
British (25)	83	0.13
Bulgarian (0)	22	0.04
Canadian (22)	61	0.10
Celtic (12)	12	0.02
Czech (16)	153	0.25
Czechoslovakian (15)	15	0.02
Danish (0)	35	0.06
Dutch (186)	1,199	1.95
English (1,994)	4,701	7.64
European (473)	473	0.77
Finnish (78)	106	0.17
French, ex. Basque (201)	1,220	1.98
French Canadian (19)	177	0.29
German (5,064)	13,145	21.37
Greek (123)	244	0.40
Hungarian (85)	267	0.43
Iranian (28)	28	0.05
Irish (2,254)	7,564	12.30
Italian (754)	1,570	2.55
Latvian (8)	8	0.01
Lithuanian (26)	84	0.14
Macedonian (55)	145	0.24
Northern European (11)	11	0.02
Norwegian (25)	151	0.25
Pennsylvania German (9)	9	0.01
Polish (134)	661	1.07
Portuguese (87)	116	0.19
Romanian (38)	60	0.10
Russian (81)	192	0.31
Scandinavian (59)	67	0.11
Scotch-Irish (557)	1,143	1.86
Scottish (545)	1,400	2.28
Slavic (0)	14	0.02
Slovak (20)	139	0.23
Swedish (212)	498	0.81
Swiss (12)	63	0.10
Ukrainian (0)	41	0.07
Welsh (182)	505	0.82
West Indian, ex. Hispanic (40)	103	0.17
Dutch West Indian (0)	35	0.06
Haitian (6)	6	0.01
Jamaican (34)	62	0.10
Yugoslavian (0)	11	0.02

Hispanic Origin	Population	%
Hispanic or Latino (of any race)	1,824	3.01
Central American, ex. Mexican	77	0.13
Costa Rican	3	<0.01
Guatemalan	26	0.04
Honduran	10	0.02
Nicaraguan	13	0.02
Panamanian	11	0.02
Salvadoran	14	0.02
Cuban	40	0.07
Dominican Republic	13	0.02
Mexican	1,342	2.21
Puerto Rican	115	0.19
South American	19	0.03
Colombian	12	0.02
Ecuadorian	2	<0.01
Paraguayan	1	<0.01
Peruvian	2	<0.01
Venezuelan	2	<0.01
Other Hispanic or Latino	218	0.36

Race*	Population	%
African-American/Black (10,981)	12,807	21.13
Not Hispanic (10,876)	12,597	20.78
Hispanic (105)	210	0.35
American Indian/Alaska Native (201)	748	1.23
Not Hispanic (167)	660	1.09
Hispanic (34)	88	0.15
Apache (4)	9	0.01
Blackfeet (5)	47	0.08
Canadian/French Am. Ind. (0)	3	<0.01
Central American Ind. (0)	1	<0.01
Cherokee (46)	230	0.38
Cheyenne (2)	4	0.01
Chippewa (1)	2	<0.01
Choctaw (7)	9	0.01
Comanche (4)	6	0.01
Cree (1)	2	<0.01
Creek (4)	7	0.01
Crow (1)	2	<0.01
Delaware (0)	6	0.01
Hopi (0)	5	0.01
Iroquois (2)	6	0.01
Lumbee (1)	1	<0.01
Mexican American Ind. (1)	8	0.01
Navajo (0)	2	<0.01
Osage (0)	6	0.01
Ottawa (1)	1	<0.01
Potawatomi (1)	4	0.01
Seminole (0)	7	0.01
Sioux (3)	12	0.02
Spanish American Ind. (2)	2	<0.01
Tohono O'Odham (3)	3	<0.01
Yaqui (1)	1	<0.01

*Notes: † The Census 2010 population figure is used to calculate the percentages in the Hispanic Origin and Race categories. Ancestry percentages are based on the 2006-2010 American Community Survey population (not shown); ‡ Numbers in parentheses indicate the number of people reporting a single ancestry; * Numbers in parentheses indicate the number of persons reporting this race alone, not in combination with any other race; Please refer to the Explanation of Data for more information.*

Asian (455)	667	1.10
Not Hispanic (446)	634	1.05
Hispanic (9)	33	0.05
Cambodian (3)	6	0.01
Chinese, ex. Taiwanese (76)	97	0.16
Filipino (64)	102	0.17
Indian (163)	196	0.32
Indonesian (1)	6	0.01
Japanese (36)	68	0.11
Korean (18)	48	0.08
Laotian (16)	22	0.04
Pakistani (35)	38	0.06
Sri Lankan (2)	2	<0.01
Taiwanese (1)	2	<0.01
Thai (5)	16	0.03
Vietnamese (17)	38	0.06
Hawaii Native/Pacific Islander (25)	96	0.16
Not Hispanic (21)	73	0.12
Hispanic (4)	23	0.04
Fijian (7)	11	0.02
Guamanian/Chamorro (4)	12	0.02
Marshallese (1)	1	<0.01
Native Hawaiian (4)	16	0.03
Samoan (6)	10	0.02
Tongan (0)	2	<0.01
White (45,607)	47,786	78.84
Not Hispanic (44,946)	46,921	77.42
Hispanic (661)	865	1.43

St. Marys

Place Type: City
County: Auglaize
Population: 8,332†

Ancestry‡	Population	%
African, Sub-Saharan (0)	4	0.05
African (0)	4	0.05
American (541)	541	6.50
Arab (8)	8	0.10
Syrian (8)	8	0.10
Austrian (0)	14	0.17
British (7)	22	0.26
Celtic (0)	18	0.22
Czech (0)	10	0.12
Czechoslovakian (38)	38	0.46
Dutch (162)	369	4.44
English (129)	608	7.31
European (14)	18	0.22
French, ex. Basque (121)	278	3.34
German (2,043)	3,954	47.54
Hungarian (0)	50	0.60
Iranian (16)	16	0.19
Irish (254)	1,286	15.46
Italian (86)	198	2.38
Lithuanian (9)	9	0.11
Polish (62)	265	3.19
Romanian (11)	33	0.40
Russian (16)	26	0.31
Scotch-Irish (30)	137	1.65
Scottish (7)	175	2.10
Swedish (43)	55	0.66
Swiss (9)	121	1.45
Turkish (11)	11	0.13
Welsh (0)	10	0.12

Hispanic Origin	Population	%
Hispanic or Latino (of any race)	106	1.27
Central American, ex. Mexican	6	0.07
Guatemalan	4	0.05
Panamanian	2	0.02
Cuban	6	0.07
Mexican	71	0.85
Puerto Rican	13	0.16
South American	4	0.05
Chilean	2	0.02
Venezuelan	2	0.02
Other Hispanic or Latino	6	0.07

Race*	Population	%
African-American/Black (37)	106	1.27
Not Hispanic (34)	100	1.20
Hispanic (3)	6	0.07
American Indian/Alaska Native (12)	66	0.79
Not Hispanic (11)	60	0.72
Hispanic (1)	6	0.07
Blackfeet (0)	2	0.02
Cherokee (4)	23	0.28
Choctaw (1)	2	0.02
Inupiat *(Alaska Native)* (1)	1	0.01
Iroquois (1)	1	0.01
Kiowa (1)	4	0.05
Sioux (0)	4	0.05
Ute (0)	2	0.02
Asian (57)	74	0.89
Not Hispanic (57)	72	0.86
Hispanic (0)	2	0.02
Chinese, ex. Taiwanese (6)	6	0.07
Filipino (4)	9	0.11
Indian (5)	8	0.10
Japanese (32)	32	0.38
Korean (4)	4	0.05
Laotian (1)	5	0.06
Pakistani (2)	2	0.02
Thai (0)	6	0.07
Vietnamese (3)	3	0.04
Hawaii Native/Pacific Islander (6)	13	0.16
Not Hispanic (6)	8	0.10
Hispanic (0)	5	0.06
Guamanian/Chamorro (0)	2	0.02
Marshallese (6)	6	0.07
Native Hawaiian (0)	3	0.04
White (8,061)	8,179	98.16
Not Hispanic (8,000)	8,108	97.31
Hispanic (61)	71	0.85

Steubenville

Place Type: City
County: Jefferson
Population: 18,659†

Ancestry‡	Population	%
African, Sub-Saharan (49)	53	0.29
African (49)	53	0.29
American (413)	413	2.22
Arab (47)	170	0.92
Arab (36)	56	0.30
Lebanese (11)	71	0.38
Syrian (0)	43	0.23
Austrian (9)	22	0.12
Belgian (13)	25	0.13
British (113)	158	0.85
Celtic (10)	10	0.05
Czech (27)	131	0.71
Czechoslovakian (9)	42	0.23
Danish (19)	72	0.39
Dutch (12)	132	0.71
English (368)	1,121	6.03
European (207)	225	1.21
French, ex. Basque (22)	257	1.38
French Canadian (31)	111	0.60
German (687)	3,036	16.34
Greek (206)	253	1.36
Hungarian (44)	214	1.15
Irish (799)	2,903	15.63
Italian (1,445)	2,956	15.91
Latvian (0)	9	0.05
Lithuanian (11)	127	0.68
Luxemburger (0)	54	0.29
Norwegian (0)	25	0.13
Pennsylvania German (24)	24	0.13
Polish (368)	1,345	7.24
Romanian (18)	18	0.10
Russian (44)	219	1.18
Scandinavian (14)	14	0.08
Scotch-Irish (92)	389	2.09
Scottish (131)	287	1.54
Serbian (128)	226	1.22
Slavic (0)	26	0.14
Slovak (133)	303	1.63
Slovene (0)	14	0.08
Swedish (0)	44	0.24
Swiss (0)	47	0.25
Turkish (13)	13	0.07
Ukrainian (0)	18	0.10
Welsh (31)	251	1.35

Hispanic Origin	Population	%
Hispanic or Latino (of any race)	453	2.43
Central American, ex. Mexican	32	0.17
Costa Rican	4	0.02
Guatemalan	9	0.05
Honduran	1	0.01
Nicaraguan	15	0.08
Panamanian	2	0.01
Salvadoran	1	0.01
Cuban	21	0.11
Dominican Republic	4	0.02
Mexican	202	1.08
Puerto Rican	77	0.41
South American	32	0.17
Argentinean	5	0.03
Bolivian	5	0.03
Chilean	2	0.01
Colombian	9	0.05
Ecuadorian	3	0.02
Peruvian	4	0.02
Uruguayan	3	0.02
Venezuelan	1	0.01
Other Hispanic or Latino	85	0.46

Race*	Population	%
African-American/Black (2,966)	3,462	18.55
Not Hispanic (2,949)	3,428	18.37
Hispanic (17)	34	0.18
American Indian/Alaska Native (35)	153	0.82
Not Hispanic (30)	132	0.71
Hispanic (5)	21	0.11
Apache (4)	7	0.04
Blackfeet (0)	7	0.04
Cherokee (9)	44	0.24
Chippewa (2)	3	0.02
Choctaw (1)	1	0.01
Comanche (0)	6	0.03
Creek (0)	1	0.01
Iroquois (0)	4	0.02
Mexican American Ind. (3)	6	0.03
Navajo (1)	1	0.01
Sioux (1)	5	0.03
Yaqui (1)	2	0.01
Asian (151)	229	1.23
Not Hispanic (148)	215	1.15
Hispanic (3)	14	0.08
Chinese, ex. Taiwanese (46)	59	0.32
Filipino (39)	75	0.40
Indian (23)	33	0.18
Japanese (7)	15	0.08
Korean (12)	13	0.07
Laotian (0)	1	0.01
Sri Lankan (1)	1	0.01
Thai (3)	3	0.02
Vietnamese (16)	23	0.12
Hawaii Native/Pacific Islander (3)	25	0.13
Not Hispanic (2)	20	0.11
Hispanic (1)	5	0.03
Guamanian/Chamorro (2)	4	0.02
Native Hawaiian (0)	8	0.04
Samoan (1)	2	0.01
Tongan (0)	1	0.01
White (14,742)	15,339	82.21
Not Hispanic (14,427)	14,982	80.29
Hispanic (315)	357	1.91

*Notes: † The Census 2010 population figure is used to calculate the percentages in the Hispanic Origin and Race categories. Ancestry percentages are based on the 2006-2010 American Community Survey population (not shown); ‡ Numbers in parentheses indicate the number of people reporting a single ancestry; * Numbers in parentheses indicate the number of persons reporting this race alone, not in combination with any other race; Please refer to the Explanation of Data for more information.*

Stow

Place Type: City
County: Summit
Population: 34,837†

Ancestry‡	Population	%
African, Sub-Saharan (27)	27	0.08
African (15)	15	0.04
Nigerian (12)	12	0.03
American (1,160)	1,160	3.36
Arab (253)	341	0.99
Arab (79)	79	0.23
Egyptian (15)	29	0.08
Iraqi (44)	44	0.13
Lebanese (85)	146	0.42
Moroccan (0)	13	0.04
Syrian (12)	12	0.03
Other Arab (18)	18	0.05
Armenian (23)	47	0.14
Australian (0)	22	0.06
Austrian (37)	195	0.57
Belgian (0)	12	0.03
British (69)	155	0.45
Bulgarian (18)	18	0.05
Canadian (48)	75	0.22
Croatian (60)	185	0.54
Czech (89)	540	1.57
Czechoslovakian (61)	140	0.41
Danish (9)	50	0.15
Dutch (119)	758	2.20
Eastern European (26)	26	0.08
English (935)	4,473	12.97
European (250)	261	0.76
Finnish (54)	167	0.48
French, ex. Basque (183)	1,098	3.18
French Canadian (37)	152	0.44
German (3,172)	10,787	31.29
Greek (39)	131	0.38
Hungarian (343)	1,184	3.43
Icelander (10)	32	0.09
Iranian (20)	20	0.06
Irish (1,378)	5,659	16.41
Italian (1,724)	4,137	12.00
Lithuanian (32)	187	0.54
Luxemburger (0)	10	0.03
Macedonian (0)	14	0.04
Northern European (21)	21	0.06
Norwegian (83)	287	0.83
Pennsylvania German (9)	9	0.03
Polish (609)	2,201	6.38
Portuguese (14)	71	0.21
Romanian (101)	263	0.76
Russian (195)	349	1.01
Scandinavian (8)	8	0.02
Scotch-Irish (233)	767	2.22
Scottish (249)	829	2.40
Serbian (41)	160	0.46
Slavic (13)	48	0.14
Slovak (207)	676	1.96
Slovene (108)	279	0.81
Swedish (46)	398	1.15
Swiss (112)	356	1.03
Turkish (152)	152	0.44
Ukrainian (56)	281	0.82
Welsh (86)	625	1.81
Yugoslavian (0)	45	0.13

Hispanic Origin	Population	%
Hispanic or Latino (of any race)	514	1.48
Central American, ex. Mexican	31	0.09
Costa Rican	3	0.01
Guatemalan	4	0.01
Honduran	8	0.02
Nicaraguan	2	0.01
Panamanian	3	0.01
Salvadoran	11	0.03
Cuban	25	0.07
Dominican Republic	1	<0.01
Mexican	229	0.66
Puerto Rican	120	0.34
South American	60	0.17
Argentinean	7	0.02
Chilean	2	0.01
Colombian	15	0.04
Ecuadorian	1	<0.01
Paraguayan	1	<0.01
Peruvian	18	0.05
Venezuelan	16	0.05
Other Hispanic or Latino	48	0.14

Race*	Population	%
African-American/Black (943)	1,142	3.28
Not Hispanic (918)	1,100	3.16
Hispanic (25)	42	0.12
American Indian/Alaska Native (23)	150	0.43
Not Hispanic (23)	139	0.40
Hispanic (0)	11	0.03
Apache (0)	1	<0.01
Blackfeet (1)	12	0.03
Canadian/French Am. Ind. (1)	2	0.01
Cherokee (8)	61	0.18
Chickasaw (0)	3	0.01
Chippewa (1)	1	<0.01
Choctaw (0)	4	0.01
Crow (0)	1	<0.01
Iroquois (1)	4	0.01
Osage (1)	1	<0.01
Ottawa (1)	1	<0.01
Pueblo (1)	1	<0.01
Sioux (1)	2	0.01
Asian (844)	1,012	2.90
Not Hispanic (838)	1,003	2.88
Hispanic (6)	9	0.03
Bangladeshi (1)	1	<0.01
Cambodian (7)	7	0.02
Chinese, ex. Taiwanese (228)	262	0.75
Filipino (74)	108	0.31
Indian (230)	249	0.71
Indonesian (9)	18	0.05
Japanese (29)	43	0.12
Korean (113)	146	0.42
Laotian (11)	12	0.03
Nepalese (1)	1	<0.01
Pakistani (33)	33	0.09
Taiwanese (17)	22	0.06
Thai (9)	15	0.04
Vietnamese (44)	47	0.13
Hawaii Native/Pacific Islander (9)	25	0.07
Not Hispanic (9)	25	0.07
Guamanian/Chamorro (0)	5	0.01
Native Hawaiian (7)	12	0.03
White (32,409)	32,893	94.42
Not Hispanic (32,054)	32,495	93.28
Hispanic (355)	398	1.14

Streetsboro

Place Type: City
County: Portage
Population: 16,028†

Ancestry‡	Population	%
African, Sub-Saharan (23)	105	0.68
Sierra Leonean (23)	23	0.15
Other Sub-Saharan African (0)	82	0.53
American (497)	497	3.23
Arab (93)	125	0.81
Lebanese (0)	32	0.21
Other Arab (93)	93	0.60
Austrian (0)	27	0.18
Belgian (0)	7	0.05
British (11)	11	0.07
Canadian (8)	16	0.10
Croatian (7)	84	0.55
Czech (106)	335	2.18
Czechoslovakian (25)	53	0.34
Danish (0)	15	0.10
Dutch (76)	417	2.71
English (353)	1,564	10.17
European (129)	129	0.84
Finnish (6)	36	0.23
French, ex. Basque (55)	463	3.01
French Canadian (49)	99	0.64
German (982)	4,110	26.72
Greek (10)	10	0.07
Hungarian (174)	647	4.21
Irish (489)	2,520	16.38
Italian (829)	2,000	13.00
Norwegian (0)	23	0.15
Pennsylvania German (38)	45	0.29
Polish (640)	1,684	10.95
Romanian (0)	22	0.14
Russian (21)	179	1.16
Scandinavian (0)	28	0.18
Scotch-Irish (129)	361	2.35
Scottish (48)	338	2.20
Serbian (18)	32	0.21
Slavic (32)	32	0.21
Slovak (131)	578	3.76
Slovene (35)	148	0.96
Swedish (0)	99	0.64
Swiss (13)	96	0.62
Ukrainian (22)	104	0.68
Welsh (21)	298	1.94
Yugoslavian (0)	32	0.21

Hispanic Origin	Population	%
Hispanic or Latino (of any race)	269	1.68
Central American, ex. Mexican	28	0.17
Costa Rican	5	0.03
Guatemalan	5	0.03
Honduran	8	0.05
Nicaraguan	2	0.01
Panamanian	1	0.01
Salvadoran	7	0.04
Cuban	12	0.07
Dominican Republic	6	0.04
Mexican	102	0.64
Puerto Rican	90	0.56
South American	11	0.07
Argentinean	4	0.02
Chilean	1	0.01
Colombian	4	0.02
Venezuelan	2	0.01
Other Hispanic or Latino	20	0.12

Race*	Population	%
African-American/Black (1,268)	1,392	8.68
Not Hispanic (1,258)	1,372	8.56
Hispanic (10)	20	0.12
American Indian/Alaska Native (26)	112	0.70
Not Hispanic (23)	99	0.62
Hispanic (3)	13	0.08
Apache (0)	2	0.01
Blackfeet (4)	6	0.04
Cherokee (3)	19	0.12
Cheyenne (0)	1	0.01
Choctaw (1)	5	0.03
Creek (0)	2	0.01
Delaware (0)	1	0.01
Iroquois (1)	3	0.02
Navajo (1)	3	0.02
Asian (350)	431	2.69
Not Hispanic (343)	418	2.61
Hispanic (7)	13	0.08
Cambodian (1)	1	0.01
Chinese, ex. Taiwanese (64)	70	0.44
Filipino (58)	87	0.54
Indian (155)	180	1.12
Indonesian (1)	1	0.01
Japanese (11)	21	0.13
Korean (19)	25	0.16
Laotian (5)	5	0.03
Pakistani (7)	7	0.04
Sri Lankan (2)	3	0.02
Thai (2)	4	0.02
Vietnamese (16)	22	0.14
Hawaii Native/Pacific Islander (4)	18	0.11
Not Hispanic (4)	18	0.11

*Notes: † The Census 2010 population figure is used to calculate the percentages in the Hispanic Origin and Race categories. Ancestry percentages are based on the 2006-2010 American Community Survey population (not shown); ‡ Numbers in parentheses indicate the number of people reporting a single ancestry; * Numbers in parentheses indicate the number of persons reporting this race alone, not in combination with any other race; Please refer to the Explanation of Data for more information.*

Guamanian/Chamorro (4)	11	0.07
Native Hawaiian (0)	7	0.04
White (14,057)	14,301	89.23
Not Hispanic (13,875)	14,084	87.87
Hispanic (182)	217	1.35

Strongsville

Place Type: City
County: Cuyahoga
Population: 44,750†

Ancestry‡	Population	%
African, Sub-Saharan (42)	42	0.09
African (35)	35	0.08
Nigerian (7)	7	0.02
Albanian (10)	10	0.02
American (1,760)	1,760	3.97
Arab (742)	988	2.23
Arab (37)	37	0.08
Egyptian (159)	179	0.40
Lebanese (239)	410	0.92
Moroccan (0)	13	0.03
Palestinian (186)	211	0.48
Syrian (0)	17	0.04
Other Arab (121)	121	0.27
Armenian (41)	41	0.09
Australian (0)	12	0.03
Austrian (14)	209	0.47
Belgian (0)	26	0.06
British (45)	100	0.23
Bulgarian (0)	34	0.08
Cajun (0)	9	0.02
Canadian (0)	56	0.13
Carpatho Rusyn (15)	15	0.03
Croatian (45)	237	0.53
Czech (388)	1,236	2.79
Czechoslovakian (133)	217	0.49
Danish (30)	147	0.33
Dutch (49)	611	1.38
Eastern European (65)	65	0.15
English (888)	4,157	9.37
Estonian (15)	15	0.03
European (420)	426	0.96
Finnish (54)	155	0.35
French, ex. Basque (109)	960	2.16
French Canadian (94)	213	0.48
German (3,708)	13,097	29.52
Greek (454)	748	1.69
Hungarian (452)	1,610	3.63
Icelander (29)	29	0.07
Iranian (66)	85	0.19
Irish (1,820)	7,586	17.10
Israeli (3)	16	0.04
Italian (2,016)	5,792	13.06
Latvian (9)	25	0.06
Lithuanian (56)	250	0.56
Macedonian (12)	23	0.05
Northern European (31)	31	0.07
Norwegian (40)	248	0.56
Pennsylvania German (0)	7	0.02
Polish (1,994)	5,938	13.39
Portuguese (16)	68	0.15
Romanian (251)	468	1.06
Russian (92)	344	0.78
Scandinavian (0)	18	0.04
Scotch-Irish (187)	451	1.02
Scottish (175)	917	2.07
Serbian (93)	163	0.37
Slavic (34)	49	0.11
Slovak (834)	2,962	6.68
Slovene (205)	726	1.64
Swedish (44)	394	0.89
Swiss (8)	126	0.28
Ukrainian (420)	741	1.67
Welsh (30)	383	0.86
West Indian, ex. Hispanic (250)	250	0.56
Haitian (14)	14	0.03
Jamaican (236)	236	0.53
Yugoslavian (57)	65	0.15

Hispanic Origin	Population	%
Hispanic or Latino (of any race)	912	2.04
Central American, ex. Mexican	44	0.10
Guatemalan	15	0.03
Honduran	6	0.01
Nicaraguan	8	0.02
Panamanian	10	0.02
Salvadoran	5	0.01
Cuban	18	0.04
Dominican Republic	8	0.02
Mexican	300	0.67
Puerto Rican	385	0.86
South American	106	0.24
Argentinean	1	<0.01
Chilean	6	0.01
Colombian	30	0.07
Ecuadorian	22	0.05
Paraguayan	7	0.02
Peruvian	30	0.07
Uruguayan	1	<0.01
Venezuelan	7	0.02
Other South American	2	<0.01
Other Hispanic or Latino	51	0.11

Race*	Population	%
African-American/Black (845)	998	2.23
Not Hispanic (813)	933	2.08
Hispanic (32)	65	0.15
American Indian/Alaska Native (42)	185	0.41
Not Hispanic (34)	157	0.35
Hispanic (8)	28	0.06
Apache (1)	3	0.01
Blackfeet (0)	4	0.01
Canadian/French Am. Ind. (3)	4	0.01
Central American Ind. (1)	1	<0.01
Cherokee (5)	43	0.10
Chickasaw (0)	1	<0.01
Chippewa (1)	1	<0.01
Choctaw (1)	2	<0.01
Cree (0)	1	<0.01
Creek (0)	5	0.01
Delaware (1)	4	0.01
Iroquois (3)	13	0.03
Lumbee (1)	12	0.03
Mexican American Ind. (1)	3	0.01
Seminole (0)	1	<0.01
Sioux (2)	9	0.02
South American Ind. (3)	7	0.02
Yaqui (0)	3	0.01
Asian (1,833)	2,167	4.84
Not Hispanic (1,816)	2,146	4.80
Hispanic (17)	21	0.05
Bangladeshi (5)	12	0.03
Burmese (8)	12	0.03
Cambodian (51)	56	0.13
Chinese, ex. Taiwanese (335)	373	0.83
Filipino (149)	247	0.55
Indian (911)	971	2.17
Indonesian (2)	5	0.01
Japanese (33)	65	0.15
Korean (130)	158	0.35
Laotian (1)	3	0.01
Malaysian (2)	7	0.02
Pakistani (49)	51	0.11
Sri Lankan (6)	9	0.02
Taiwanese (24)	24	0.05
Thai (13)	16	0.04
Vietnamese (65)	80	0.18
Hawaii Native/Pacific Islander (14)	39	0.09
Not Hispanic (13)	36	0.08
Hispanic (1)	3	0.01
Guamanian/Chamorro (1)	5	0.01
Native Hawaiian (12)	26	0.06
White (41,185)	41,774	93.35
Not Hispanic (40,559)	41,068	91.77
Hispanic (626)	706	1.58

Struthers

Place Type: City
County: Mahoning
Population: 10,713†

Ancestry‡	Population	%
American (512)	512	4.70
Arab (17)	17	0.16
Other Arab (17)	17	0.16
Australian (0)	42	0.39
Belgian (0)	34	0.31
British (9)	37	0.34
Celtic (38)	51	0.47
Croatian (113)	269	2.47
Czech (0)	50	0.46
Czechoslovakian (0)	58	0.53
Dutch (59)	180	1.65
English (239)	929	8.53
European (49)	57	0.52
Finnish (6)	6	0.06
French, ex. Basque (0)	222	2.04
French Canadian (0)	22	0.20
German (418)	2,724	25.01
Greek (12)	91	0.84
Hungarian (198)	497	4.56
Irish (270)	2,180	20.01
Italian (1,147)	3,090	28.37
Lithuanian (0)	11	0.10
Macedonian (0)	12	0.11
Pennsylvania German (66)	86	0.79
Polish (168)	844	7.75
Romanian (33)	180	1.65
Russian (0)	14	0.13
Scotch-Irish (52)	125	1.15
Scottish (27)	229	2.10
Slavic (0)	24	0.22
Slovak (626)	1,441	13.23
Slovene (46)	46	0.42
Swedish (18)	48	0.44
Ukrainian (62)	83	0.76
Welsh (6)	90	0.83

Hispanic Origin	Population	%
Hispanic or Latino (of any race)	327	3.05
Central American, ex. Mexican	1	0.01
Nicaraguan	1	0.01
Cuban	2	0.02
Mexican	71	0.66
Puerto Rican	218	2.03
South American	5	0.05
Colombian	1	0.01
Ecuadorian	2	0.02
Peruvian	2	0.02
Other Hispanic or Latino	30	0.28

Race*	Population	%
African-American/Black (308)	418	3.90
Not Hispanic (299)	391	3.65
Hispanic (9)	27	0.25
American Indian/Alaska Native (18)	73	0.68
Not Hispanic (17)	60	0.56
Hispanic (1)	13	0.12
Blackfeet (0)	3	0.03
Cherokee (2)	9	0.08
Chippewa (1)	2	0.02
Creek (0)	1	0.01
Iroquois (1)	5	0.05
Mexican American Ind. (0)	5	0.05
Sioux (2)	3	0.03
Asian (20)	41	0.38
Not Hispanic (19)	34	0.32
Hispanic (1)	7	0.07
Filipino (2)	10	0.09
Indian (1)	1	0.01
Japanese (5)	5	0.05
Korean (2)	9	0.08
Pakistani (5)	5	0.05
Vietnamese (5)	9	0.08
Hawaii Native/Pacific Islander (1)	9	0.08

*Notes: † The Census 2010 population figure is used to calculate the percentages in the Hispanic Origin and Race categories. Ancestry percentages are based on the 2006-2010 American Community Survey population (not shown); ‡ Numbers in parentheses indicate the number of people reporting a single ancestry; * Numbers in parentheses indicate the number of persons reporting this race alone, not in combination with any other race; Please refer to the Explanation of Data for more information.*

Not Hispanic (1)	9	0.08
Native Hawaiian (1)	5	0.05
White (10,101)	10,295	96.10
Not Hispanic (9,892)	10,046	93.77
Hispanic (209)	249	2.32

Sylvania

Place Type: City
County: Lucas
Population: 18,965†

Ancestry‡	Population	%
African, Sub-Saharan (13)	13	0.07
Other Sub-Saharan African (13)	13	0.07
American (553)	553	2.91
Arab (449)	514	2.71
Arab (93)	93	0.49
Egyptian (114)	114	0.60
Jordanian (48)	48	0.25
Lebanese (137)	202	1.06
Syrian (57)	57	0.30
Austrian (44)	79	0.42
Belgian (0)	48	0.25
British (32)	74	0.39
Canadian (24)	75	0.39
Croatian (0)	24	0.13
Czech (7)	53	0.28
Czechoslovakian (11)	116	0.61
Danish (20)	52	0.27
Dutch (56)	458	2.41
Eastern European (13)	30	0.16
English (465)	2,614	13.77
European (379)	462	2.43
Finnish (10)	35	0.18
French, ex. Basque (94)	957	5.04
French Canadian (69)	266	1.40
German (2,289)	7,180	37.81
Greek (17)	49	0.26
Hungarian (144)	515	2.71
Iranian (10)	10	0.05
Irish (678)	3,430	18.06
Italian (277)	1,121	5.90
Lithuanian (14)	35	0.18
Macedonian (12)	12	0.06
Maltese (0)	7	0.04
Northern European (29)	29	0.15
Norwegian (0)	40	0.21
Polish (970)	2,599	13.69
Romanian (18)	130	0.68
Russian (96)	268	1.41
Scotch-Irish (86)	245	1.29
Scottish (80)	507	2.67
Serbian (45)	45	0.24
Slovak (15)	30	0.16
Slovene (7)	22	0.12
Swedish (0)	88	0.46
Swiss (28)	171	0.90
Turkish (0)	18	0.09
Ukrainian (62)	188	0.99
Welsh (48)	120	0.63
Yugoslavian (0)	8	0.04

Hispanic Origin	Population	%
Hispanic or Latino (of any race)	548	2.89
Central American, ex. Mexican	19	0.10
Costa Rican	1	0.01
Guatemalan	7	0.04
Honduran	1	0.01
Nicaraguan	3	0.02
Panamanian	6	0.03
Salvadoran	1	0.01
Cuban	19	0.10
Dominican Republic	8	0.04
Mexican	397	2.09
Puerto Rican	31	0.16
South American	30	0.16
Argentinean	2	0.01
Chilean	4	0.02
Colombian	4	0.02
Ecuadorian	1	0.01
Paraguayan	6	0.03
Peruvian	2	0.01
Venezuelan	11	0.06
Other Hispanic or Latino	44	0.23

Race*	Population	%
African-American/Black (513)	632	3.33
Not Hispanic (499)	608	3.21
Hispanic (14)	24	0.13
American Indian/Alaska Native (23)	106	0.56
Not Hispanic (15)	84	0.44
Hispanic (8)	22	0.12
Apache (0)	1	0.01
Blackfeet (0)	1	0.01
Cherokee (1)	24	0.13
Chippewa (2)	9	0.05
Choctaw (0)	1	0.01
Inupiat *(Alaska Native)* (0)	4	0.02
Iroquois (0)	2	0.01
Mexican American Ind. (3)	8	0.04
Ottawa (0)	1	0.01
Potawatomi (0)	1	0.01
Seminole (4)	4	0.02
Sioux (1)	2	0.01
Asian (430)	537	2.83
Not Hispanic (423)	524	2.76
Hispanic (7)	13	0.07
Burmese (3)	5	0.03
Chinese, ex. Taiwanese (77)	95	0.50
Filipino (39)	70	0.37
Indian (129)	145	0.76
Indonesian (1)	3	0.02
Japanese (22)	32	0.17
Korean (73)	94	0.50
Pakistani (20)	27	0.14
Sri Lankan (0)	2	0.01
Taiwanese (12)	19	0.10
Thai (16)	17	0.09
Vietnamese (5)	15	0.08
Hawaii Native/Pacific Islander (12)	20	0.11
Not Hispanic (11)	17	0.09
Hispanic (1)	3	0.02
Guamanian/Chamorro (3)	3	0.02
Native Hawaiian (3)	5	0.03
Samoan (1)	4	0.02
White (17,528)	17,843	94.08
Not Hispanic (17,185)	17,443	91.97
Hispanic (343)	400	2.11

Tallmadge

Place Type: City
County: Summit
Population: 17,537†

Ancestry‡	Population	%
Afghan (13)	13	0.07
Alsatian (9)	9	0.05
American (732)	732	4.22
Arab (245)	274	1.58
Lebanese (46)	75	0.43
Palestinian (199)	199	1.15
Armenian (0)	53	0.31
Austrian (28)	50	0.29
Belgian (25)	25	0.14
British (27)	62	0.36
Bulgarian (0)	10	0.06
Canadian (22)	59	0.34
Carpatho Rusyn (14)	51	0.29
Croatian (42)	147	0.85
Czech (17)	104	0.60
Czechoslovakian (35)	46	0.27
Danish (0)	50	0.29
Dutch (67)	283	1.63
English (757)	2,512	14.48
European (221)	263	1.52
Finnish (8)	8	0.05
French, ex. Basque (28)	544	3.14
French Canadian (10)	30	0.17
German (1,589)	5,181	29.86
Greek (129)	142	0.82
Hungarian (72)	480	2.77
Irish (590)	2,832	16.32
Italian (1,021)	2,318	13.36
Latvian (0)	12	0.07
Lithuanian (0)	38	0.22
Luxemburger (7)	7	0.04
Norwegian (20)	70	0.40
Pennsylvania German (53)	75	0.43
Polish (272)	999	5.76
Romanian (0)	25	0.14
Russian (0)	32	0.18
Scotch-Irish (56)	261	1.50
Scottish (191)	492	2.84
Serbian (119)	138	0.80
Slavic (12)	12	0.07
Slovak (70)	210	1.21
Slovene (41)	41	0.24
Swedish (79)	277	1.60
Swiss (0)	90	0.52
Ukrainian (7)	29	0.17
Welsh (23)	184	1.06
Yugoslavian (38)	71	0.41

Hispanic Origin	Population	%
Hispanic or Latino (of any race)	178	1.01
Central American, ex. Mexican	13	0.07
Costa Rican	1	0.01
Guatemalan	5	0.03
Panamanian	3	0.02
Salvadoran	4	0.02
Cuban	8	0.05
Dominican Republic	1	0.01
Mexican	77	0.44
Puerto Rican	38	0.22
South American	17	0.10
Argentinean	4	0.02
Bolivian	8	0.05
Colombian	2	0.01
Uruguayan	1	0.01
Venezuelan	2	0.01
Other Hispanic or Latino	24	0.14

Race*	Population	%
African-American/Black (583)	726	4.14
Not Hispanic (577)	708	4.04
Hispanic (6)	18	0.10
American Indian/Alaska Native (45)	116	0.66
Not Hispanic (42)	110	0.63
Hispanic (3)	6	0.03
Alaska Athabascan *(Ala. Nat.)* (3)	3	0.02
Apache (0)	1	0.01
Blackfeet (1)	10	0.06
Cherokee (19)	36	0.21
Chippewa (3)	5	0.03
Choctaw (0)	2	0.01
Iroquois (0)	6	0.03
Mexican American Ind. (1)	1	0.01
Navajo (1)	2	0.01
Pueblo (1)	1	0.01
Seminole (0)	1	0.01
Sioux (0)	2	0.01
Asian (183)	236	1.35
Not Hispanic (183)	236	1.35
Cambodian (5)	7	0.04
Chinese, ex. Taiwanese (55)	59	0.34
Filipino (19)	36	0.21
Hmong (4)	5	0.03
Indian (42)	50	0.29
Indonesian (2)	2	0.01
Japanese (2)	5	0.03
Korean (12)	16	0.09
Laotian (1)	1	0.01
Nepalese (1)	1	0.01
Pakistani (5)	5	0.03
Taiwanese (2)	3	0.02
Thai (4)	8	0.05
Vietnamese (26)	28	0.16
Hawaii Native/Pacific Islander (16)	22	0.13

SECTION TWO

*Notes: † The Census 2010 population figure is used to calculate the percentages in the Hispanic Origin and Race categories. Ancestry percentages are based on the 2006-2010 American Community Survey population (not shown); ‡ Numbers in parentheses indicate the number of people reporting a single ancestry; * Numbers in parentheses indicate the number of persons reporting this race alone, not in combination with any other race; Please refer to the Explanation of Data for more information.*

Not Hispanic (15)	21	0.12
Hispanic (1)	1	0.01
Guamanian/Chamorro (5)	5	0.03
Native Hawaiian (10)	10	0.06
Samoan (0)	2	0.01
White (16,407)	16,644	94.91
Not Hispanic (16,293)	16,517	94.18
Hispanic (114)	127	0.72

Tiffin

Place Type: City
County: Seneca
Population: 17,963†

Ancestry‡	Population	%
American (1,485)	1,485	8.28
Arab (9)	9	0.05
Lebanese (9)	9	0.05
Austrian (67)	80	0.45
Belgian (0)	65	0.36
British (27)	47	0.26
Bulgarian (17)	17	0.09
Croatian (0)	21	0.12
Czech (25)	135	0.75
Czechoslovakian (13)	53	0.30
Danish (0)	24	0.13
Dutch (46)	248	1.38
English (312)	1,129	6.29
European (48)	48	0.27
French, ex. Basque (44)	496	2.77
French Canadian (13)	137	0.76
German (4,616)	9,113	50.81
Greek (25)	47	0.26
Hungarian (47)	119	0.66
Irish (515)	2,484	13.85
Italian (473)	1,144	6.38
Luxemburger (0)	56	0.31
Northern European (18)	18	0.10
Norwegian (49)	66	0.37
Pennsylvania German (17)	56	0.31
Polish (177)	613	3.42
Romanian (0)	7	0.04
Russian (0)	14	0.08
Scandinavian (0)	28	0.16
Scotch-Irish (92)	294	1.64
Scottish (32)	160	0.89
Serbian (12)	26	0.14
Slavic (0)	8	0.04
Slovak (57)	72	0.40
Swedish (0)	76	0.42
Swiss (40)	280	1.56
Welsh (10)	69	0.38
West Indian, ex. Hispanic (20)	20	0.11
Bahamian (6)	6	0.03
Haitian (14)	14	0.08

Hispanic Origin	Population	%
Hispanic or Latino (of any race)	551	3.07
Central American, ex. Mexican	6	0.03
Guatemalan	1	0.01
Honduran	1	0.01
Panamanian	2	0.01
Salvadoran	2	0.01
Cuban	2	0.01
Dominican Republic	2	0.01
Mexican	460	2.56
Puerto Rican	31	0.17
South American	6	0.03
Argentinean	2	0.01
Chilean	1	0.01
Colombian	1	0.01
Paraguayan	1	0.01
Venezuelan	1	0.01
Other Hispanic or Latino	44	0.24

Race*	Population	%
African-American/Black (467)	624	3.47
Not Hispanic (453)	600	3.34
Hispanic (14)	24	0.13
American Indian/Alaska Native (31)	87	0.48
Not Hispanic (21)	75	0.42
Hispanic (10)	12	0.07
Apache (3)	3	0.02
Arapaho (0)	1	0.01
Blackfeet (1)	2	0.01
Cherokee (3)	18	0.10
Chippewa (0)	1	0.01
Choctaw (0)	1	0.01
Hopi (2)	2	0.01
Iroquois (1)	5	0.03
Mexican American Ind. (4)	5	0.03
South American Ind. (0)	1	0.01
Tohono O'Odham (0)	1	0.01
Asian (175)	206	1.15
Not Hispanic (175)	198	1.10
Hispanic (0)	8	0.04
Chinese, ex. Taiwanese (98)	99	0.55
Filipino (22)	28	0.16
Indian (20)	24	0.13
Japanese (24)	34	0.19
Korean (5)	14	0.08
Thai (1)	1	0.01
Vietnamese (2)	2	0.01
Hawaii Native/Pacific Islander (7)	17	0.09
Not Hispanic (5)	11	0.06
Hispanic (2)	6	0.03
Guamanian/Chamorro (2)	4	0.02
Native Hawaiian (2)	5	0.03
Samoan (2)	3	0.02
Tongan (1)	1	0.01
White (16,871)	17,138	95.41
Not Hispanic (16,522)	16,725	93.11
Hispanic (349)	413	2.30

Tipp City

Place Type: City
County: Miami
Population: 9,689†

Ancestry‡	Population	%
American (476)	476	4.94
Austrian (0)	15	0.16
British (14)	28	0.29
Canadian (30)	30	0.31
Czech (0)	21	0.22
Dutch (48)	224	2.32
English (674)	1,329	13.78
European (74)	90	0.93
Finnish (13)	13	0.13
French, ex. Basque (35)	294	3.05
French Canadian (0)	15	0.16
German (1,684)	3,565	36.96
Hungarian (17)	114	1.18
Irish (499)	1,424	14.76
Italian (104)	407	4.22
Norwegian (0)	32	0.33
Polish (104)	405	4.20
Portuguese (0)	11	0.11
Romanian (0)	19	0.20
Russian (16)	39	0.40
Scotch-Irish (84)	277	2.87
Scottish (130)	318	3.30
Swedish (0)	135	1.40
Swiss (0)	85	0.88
Welsh (35)	165	1.71
Yugoslavian (21)	80	0.83

Hispanic Origin	Population	%
Hispanic or Latino (of any race)	151	1.56
Central American, ex. Mexican	5	0.05
Guatemalan	4	0.04
Honduran	1	0.01
Cuban	3	0.03
Mexican	100	1.03
Puerto Rican	12	0.12
South American	3	0.03
Argentinean	1	0.01
Ecuadorian	2	0.02
Other Hispanic or Latino	28	0.29

Race*	Population	%
African-American/Black (54)	91	0.94
Not Hispanic (52)	89	0.92
Hispanic (2)	2	0.02
American Indian/Alaska Native (15)	63	0.65
Not Hispanic (15)	63	0.65
Blackfeet (0)	4	0.04
Canadian/French Am. Ind. (0)	3	0.03
Cherokee (5)	37	0.38
Delaware (0)	2	0.02
Iroquois (3)	3	0.03
Menominee (0)	1	0.01
Navajo (0)	1	0.01
Seminole (0)	1	0.01
Sioux (0)	2	0.02
Asian (145)	174	1.80
Not Hispanic (145)	174	1.80
Chinese, ex. Taiwanese (25)	25	0.26
Filipino (20)	31	0.32
Indian (55)	56	0.58
Indonesian (0)	1	0.01
Japanese (22)	26	0.27
Korean (10)	16	0.17
Taiwanese (4)	4	0.04
Thai (1)	2	0.02
Vietnamese (2)	2	0.02
Hawaii Native/Pacific Islander (0)	3	0.03
Not Hispanic (0)	1	0.01
Hispanic (0)	2	0.02
Guamanian/Chamorro (0)	2	0.02
Native Hawaiian (0)	1	0.01
White (9,291)	9,402	97.04
Not Hispanic (9,201)	9,306	96.05
Hispanic (90)	96	0.99

Toledo

Place Type: City
County: Lucas
Population: 287,208†

Ancestry‡	Population	%
African, Sub-Saharan (2,462)	3,260	1.12
African (1,781)	2,419	0.83
Cape Verdean (0)	46	0.02
Ghanaian (69)	69	0.02
Kenyan (19)	19	0.01
Nigerian (528)	642	0.22
Senegalese (15)	15	0.01
South African (27)	27	0.01
Other Sub-Saharan African (23)	23	0.01
Alsatian (0)	6	<0.01
American (10,051)	10,051	3.44
Arab (2,777)	3,428	1.17
Arab (592)	614	0.21
Egyptian (9)	28	0.01
Iraqi (15)	28	0.01
Jordanian (201)	201	0.07
Lebanese (1,284)	1,656	0.57
Palestinian (183)	216	0.07
Syrian (209)	381	0.13
Other Arab (284)	304	0.10
Armenian (48)	234	0.08
Assyrian/Chaldean/Syriac (27)	27	0.01
Australian (9)	9	<0.01
Austrian (103)	628	0.22
Belgian (34)	215	0.07
British (325)	785	0.27
Bulgarian (66)	217	0.07
Canadian (235)	521	0.18
Carpatho Rusyn (6)	15	0.01
Celtic (57)	73	0.03
Croatian (0)	125	0.04
Cypriot (0)	11	<0.01
Czech (143)	833	0.29
Czechoslovakian (116)	304	0.10
Danish (101)	499	0.17
Dutch (454)	3,569	1.22

*Notes: † The Census 2010 population figure is used to calculate the percentages in the Hispanic Origin and Race categories. Ancestry percentages are based on the 2006-2010 American Community Survey population (not shown); ‡ Numbers in parentheses indicate the number of people reporting a single ancestry; * Numbers in parentheses indicate the number of persons reporting this race alone, not in combination with any other race; Please refer to the Explanation of Data for more information.*

Eastern European (63)	63	0.02
English (5,068)	18,826	6.45
Estonian (19)	19	0.01
European (1,540)	1,626	0.56
Finnish (95)	295	0.10
French, ex. Basque (1,553)	13,787	4.72
French Canadian (664)	2,025	0.69
German (27,798)	76,635	26.26
Greek (510)	910	0.31
Guyanese (60)	60	0.02
Hungarian (2,245)	6,352	2.18
Icelander (13)	44	0.02
Iranian (73)	73	0.03
Irish (8,029)	34,827	11.93
Israeli (28)	35	0.01
Italian (3,020)	9,356	3.21
Latvian (21)	21	0.01
Lithuanian (38)	264	0.09
Macedonian (8)	18	0.01
Maltese (9)	17	0.01
Northern European (13)	13	<0.01
Norwegian (197)	1,161	0.40
Pennsylvania German (65)	245	0.08
Polish (10,864)	25,480	8.73
Portuguese (48)	154	0.05
Romanian (114)	436	0.15
Russian (227)	959	0.33
Scandinavian (12)	101	0.03
Scotch-Irish (695)	2,388	0.82
Scottish (805)	3,645	1.25
Serbian (35)	69	0.02
Slavic (0)	58	0.02
Slovak (237)	945	0.32
Slovene (70)	149	0.05
Swedish (278)	1,344	0.46
Swiss (165)	1,134	0.39
Turkish (120)	120	0.04
Ukrainian (159)	499	0.17
Welsh (246)	1,296	0.44
West Indian, ex. Hispanic (812)	1,077	0.37
Belizean (19)	19	0.01
British West Indian (22)	22	0.01
Haitian (64)	97	0.03
Jamaican (667)	879	0.30
Trinidadian/Tobagonian (11)	11	<0.01
West Indian (29)	49	0.02
Yugoslavian (75)	115	0.04

Hispanic Origin	Population	%
Hispanic or Latino (of any race)	21,231	7.39
Central American, ex. Mexican	240	0.08
Costa Rican	15	0.01
Guatemalan	61	0.02
Honduran	26	0.01
Nicaraguan	72	0.03
Panamanian	33	0.01
Salvadoran	33	0.01
Cuban	299	0.10
Dominican Republic	69	0.02
Mexican	17,576	6.12
Puerto Rican	1,143	0.40
South American	219	0.08
Argentinean	24	0.01
Bolivian	4	<0.01
Chilean	18	0.01
Colombian	49	0.02
Ecuadorian	27	0.01
Paraguayan	6	<0.01
Peruvian	51	0.02
Venezuelan	32	0.01
Other South American	8	<0.01
Other Hispanic or Latino	1,685	0.59

Race*	Population	%
African-American/Black (78,073)	85,254	29.68
Not Hispanic (76,820)	82,886	28.86
Hispanic (1,253)	2,368	0.82
American Indian/Alaska Native (1,065)	3,359	1.17
Not Hispanic (755)	2,675	0.93
Hispanic (310)	684	0.24
Alaska Athabascan *(Ala. Nat.)* (1)	2	<0.01
Aleut *(Alaska Native)* (1)	2	<0.01
Apache (21)	66	0.02
Arapaho (0)	6	<0.01
Blackfeet (25)	158	0.06
Canadian/French Am. Ind. (7)	23	0.01
Cherokee (163)	784	0.27
Cheyenne (0)	6	<0.01
Chickasaw (3)	7	<0.01
Chippewa (77)	139	0.05
Choctaw (13)	59	0.02
Comanche (1)	3	<0.01
Cree (1)	6	<0.01
Creek (2)	23	0.01
Crow (0)	5	<0.01
Delaware (9)	11	<0.01
Hopi (3)	4	<0.01
Inupiat *(Alaska Native)* (2)	3	<0.01
Iroquois (15)	39	0.01
Kiowa (0)	1	<0.01
Lumbee (5)	14	<0.01
Menominee (9)	11	<0.01
Mexican American Ind. (38)	96	0.03
Navajo (13)	30	0.01
Osage (0)	3	<0.01
Ottawa (10)	41	0.01
Potawatomi (13)	33	0.01
Pueblo (6)	15	0.01
Seminole (1)	9	<0.01
Shoshone (0)	3	<0.01
Sioux (14)	39	0.01
South American Ind. (14)	17	0.01
Spanish American Ind. (2)	6	<0.01
Tlingit-Haida *(Alaska Native)* (1)	2	<0.01
Yaqui (3)	4	<0.01
Asian (3,264)	4,559	1.59
Not Hispanic (3,204)	4,312	1.50
Hispanic (60)	247	0.09
Bangladeshi (2)	5	<0.01
Burmese (5)	5	<0.01
Cambodian (2)	7	<0.01
Chinese, ex. Taiwanese (1,015)	1,177	0.41
Filipino (355)	610	0.21
Hmong (4)	4	<0.01
Indian (836)	995	0.35
Indonesian (14)	28	0.01
Japanese (84)	272	0.09
Korean (216)	382	0.13
Laotian (91)	129	0.04
Malaysian (11)	22	0.01
Nepalese (32)	36	0.01
Pakistani (81)	97	0.03
Sri Lankan (16)	18	0.01
Taiwanese (26)	30	0.01
Thai (72)	116	0.04
Vietnamese (236)	286	0.10
Hawaii Native/Pacific Islander (77)	275	0.10
Not Hispanic (64)	220	0.08
Hispanic (13)	55	0.02
Fijian (2)	2	<0.01
Guamanian/Chamorro (13)	28	0.01
Native Hawaiian (23)	86	0.03
Samoan (17)	34	0.01
Tongan (1)	2	<0.01
White (186,188)	195,953	68.23
Not Hispanic (176,468)	183,797	63.99
Hispanic (9,720)	12,156	4.23

Trenton

Place Type: City
County: Butler
Population: 11,869†

Ancestry‡	Population	%
American (1,556)	1,556	13.70
Austrian (27)	59	0.52
British (0)	47	0.41
Dutch (16)	336	2.96
English (413)	874	7.70
European (0)	15	0.13
Finnish (21)	104	0.92
French, ex. Basque (56)	362	3.19
German (1,739)	3,324	29.28
Greek (14)	14	0.12
Hungarian (19)	19	0.17
Irish (437)	1,729	15.23
Italian (219)	568	5.00
Norwegian (0)	33	0.29
Polish (9)	84	0.74
Russian (83)	195	1.72
Scotch-Irish (135)	309	2.72
Scottish (0)	243	2.14
Swiss (0)	59	0.52
Ukrainian (12)	26	0.23
Welsh (28)	104	0.92

Hispanic Origin	Population	%
Hispanic or Latino (of any race)	198	1.67
Central American, ex. Mexican	14	0.12
Costa Rican	3	0.03
Guatemalan	4	0.03
Honduran	2	0.02
Panamanian	4	0.03
Salvadoran	1	0.01
Cuban	4	0.03
Mexican	99	0.83
Puerto Rican	38	0.32
South American	16	0.13
Chilean	1	0.01
Colombian	7	0.06
Paraguayan	3	0.03
Peruvian	3	0.03
Venezuelan	1	0.01
Other South American	1	0.01
Other Hispanic or Latino	27	0.23

Race*	Population	%
African-American/Black (115)	209	1.76
Not Hispanic (111)	198	1.67
Hispanic (4)	11	0.09
American Indian/Alaska Native (18)	88	0.74
Not Hispanic (17)	80	0.67
Hispanic (1)	8	0.07
Blackfeet (0)	8	0.07
Cherokee (3)	24	0.20
Comanche (2)	2	0.02
Creek (0)	1	0.01
Iroquois (1)	7	0.06
Asian (57)	104	0.88
Not Hispanic (53)	98	0.83
Hispanic (4)	6	0.05
Chinese, ex. Taiwanese (15)	18	0.15
Filipino (17)	40	0.34
Indian (13)	15	0.13
Indonesian (0)	1	0.01
Japanese (2)	6	0.05
Korean (0)	2	0.02
Malaysian (2)	2	0.02
Nepalese (4)	6	0.05
Pakistani (0)	1	0.01
Taiwanese (1)	3	0.03
Thai (0)	7	0.06
Vietnamese (2)	3	0.03
Hawaii Native/Pacific Islander (2)	9	0.08
Not Hispanic (2)	9	0.08
Native Hawaiian (1)	4	0.03
White (11,418)	11,640	98.07
Not Hispanic (11,292)	11,481	96.73
Hispanic (126)	159	1.34

Trotwood

Place Type: City
County: Montgomery
Population: 24,431†

Ancestry‡	Population	%
African, Sub-Saharan (285)	476	1.91
African (132)	323	1.30

*Notes: † The Census 2010 population figure is used to calculate the percentages in the Hispanic Origin and Race categories. Ancestry percentages are based on the 2006-2010 American Community Survey population (not shown); ‡ Numbers in parentheses indicate the number of people reporting a single ancestry; * Numbers in parentheses indicate the number of persons reporting this race alone, not in combination with any other race; Please refer to the Explanation of Data for more information.*

Nigerian (153)	153	0.61
American (977)	977	3.92
Austrian (0)	12	0.05
Brazilian (0)	11	0.04
Canadian (11)	11	0.04
Croatian (13)	13	0.05
Czech (24)	36	0.14
Danish (0)	10	0.04
Dutch (79)	183	0.73
English (274)	813	3.26
European (42)	46	0.18
French, ex. Basque (50)	215	0.86
French Canadian (13)	18	0.07
German (715)	1,912	7.68
Greek (0)	36	0.14
Hungarian (24)	63	0.25
Irish (314)	1,253	5.03
Italian (23)	111	0.45
Luxemburger (0)	13	0.05
Northern European (0)	12	0.05
Norwegian (0)	11	0.04
Pennsylvania German (9)	9	0.04
Polish (21)	247	0.99
Portuguese (0)	11	0.04
Romanian (0)	7	0.03
Russian (52)	59	0.24
Scandinavian (0)	9	0.04
Scotch-Irish (155)	282	1.13
Scottish (60)	193	0.77
Slovak (0)	23	0.09
Swedish (0)	6	0.02
Ukrainian (18)	18	0.07
Welsh (18)	71	0.29
West Indian, ex. Hispanic (25)	155	0.62
Jamaican (25)	34	0.14
West Indian (0)	121	0.49
Yugoslavian (6)	22	0.09

Hispanic Origin	Population	%
Hispanic or Latino (of any race)	231	0.95
Central American, ex. Mexican	5	0.02
Guatemalan	2	0.01
Panamanian	1	<0.01
Salvadoran	1	<0.01
Other Central American	1	<0.01
Dominican Republic	7	0.03
Mexican	121	0.50
Puerto Rican	48	0.20
South American	23	0.09
Colombian	6	0.02
Ecuadorian	14	0.06
Peruvian	2	0.01
Venezuelan	1	<0.01
Other Hispanic or Latino	27	0.11

Race*	Population	%
African-American/Black (16,660)	17,195	70.38
Not Hispanic (16,604)	17,113	70.05
Hispanic (56)	82	0.34
American Indian/Alaska Native (59)	271	1.11
Not Hispanic (52)	258	1.06
Hispanic (7)	13	0.05
Apache (2)	3	0.01
Blackfeet (2)	27	0.11
Cherokee (11)	76	0.31
Chickasaw (0)	1	<0.01
Chippewa (0)	2	0.01
Choctaw (0)	2	0.01
Cree (0)	1	<0.01
Creek (1)	3	0.01
Crow (0)	2	0.01
Iroquois (0)	3	0.01
Mexican American Ind. (1)	2	0.01
Navajo (0)	1	<0.01
Osage (1)	1	<0.01
Potawatomi (1)	1	<0.01
Seminole (1)	2	0.01
Sioux (2)	11	0.05
South American Ind. (0)	1	<0.01
Asian (81)	141	0.58
Not Hispanic (81)	137	0.56
Hispanic (0)	4	0.02
Chinese, ex. Taiwanese (23)	29	0.12
Filipino (20)	43	0.18
Indian (7)	15	0.06
Japanese (8)	17	0.07
Korean (7)	11	0.05
Laotian (4)	4	0.02
Taiwanese (4)	4	0.02
Thai (3)	9	0.04
Vietnamese (3)	3	0.01
Hawaii Native/Pacific Islander (7)	28	0.11
Not Hispanic (4)	25	0.10
Hispanic (3)	3	0.01
Guamanian/Chamorro (3)	9	0.04
Native Hawaiian (3)	11	0.05
Samoan (0)	1	<0.01
White (6,864)	7,338	30.04
Not Hispanic (6,796)	7,252	29.68
Hispanic (68)	86	0.35

Troy

Place Type: City
County: Miami
Population: 25,058†

Ancestry‡	Population	%
African, Sub-Saharan (37)	47	0.19
African (37)	47	0.19
American (2,328)	2,328	9.38
Arab (42)	51	0.21
Arab (19)	19	0.08
Lebanese (9)	18	0.07
Syrian (14)	14	0.06
Austrian (53)	74	0.30
Belgian (0)	23	0.09
British (76)	112	0.45
Canadian (0)	8	0.03
Czech (40)	94	0.38
Czechoslovakian (67)	80	0.32
Danish (18)	36	0.14
Dutch (89)	566	2.28
Eastern European (38)	38	0.15
English (820)	2,457	9.90
European (369)	382	1.54
French, ex. Basque (152)	738	2.97
French Canadian (26)	104	0.42
German (3,724)	8,130	32.75
Greek (16)	16	0.06
Hungarian (34)	106	0.43
Irish (1,076)	3,763	15.16
Italian (198)	676	2.72
Lithuanian (0)	16	0.06
Macedonian (0)	8	0.03
Norwegian (0)	49	0.20
Pennsylvania German (30)	53	0.21
Polish (83)	222	0.89
Portuguese (0)	9	0.04
Romanian (30)	30	0.12
Russian (11)	19	0.08
Scotch-Irish (126)	489	1.97
Scottish (319)	583	2.35
Slavic (18)	44	0.18
Slovak (23)	40	0.16
Swedish (4)	132	0.53
Swiss (26)	45	0.18
Ukrainian (35)	35	0.14
Welsh (68)	370	1.49
West Indian, ex. Hispanic (0)	10	0.04
Bahamian (0)	10	0.04

Hispanic Origin	Population	%
Hispanic or Latino (of any race)	455	1.82
Central American, ex. Mexican	16	0.06
Costa Rican	1	<0.01
Guatemalan	9	0.04
Honduran	3	0.01
Panamanian	2	0.01
Salvadoran	1	<0.01
Cuban	8	0.03
Dominican Republic	5	0.02
Mexican	308	1.23
Puerto Rican	39	0.16
South American	22	0.09
Bolivian	1	<0.01
Colombian	8	0.03
Ecuadorian	3	0.01
Peruvian	5	0.02
Venezuelan	5	0.02
Other Hispanic or Latino	57	0.23

Race*	Population	%
African-American/Black (1,057)	1,440	5.75
Not Hispanic (1,046)	1,414	5.64
Hispanic (11)	26	0.10
American Indian/Alaska Native (51)	172	0.69
Not Hispanic (46)	162	0.65
Hispanic (5)	10	0.04
Apache (0)	2	0.01
Blackfeet (5)	10	0.04
Central American Ind. (3)	3	0.01
Cherokee (20)	61	0.24
Chippewa (2)	2	0.01
Choctaw (1)	1	<0.01
Delaware (0)	1	<0.01
Seminole (1)	1	<0.01
Sioux (1)	4	0.02
Asian (613)	714	2.85
Not Hispanic (611)	708	2.83
Hispanic (2)	6	0.02
Bangladeshi (3)	3	0.01
Cambodian (2)	2	0.01
Chinese, ex. Taiwanese (77)	88	0.35
Filipino (44)	80	0.32
Indian (180)	184	0.73
Indonesian (3)	4	0.02
Japanese (217)	251	1.00
Korean (30)	38	0.15
Laotian (2)	2	0.01
Pakistani (1)	1	<0.01
Sri Lankan (6)	6	0.02
Taiwanese (5)	5	0.02
Thai (0)	5	0.02
Vietnamese (32)	34	0.14
Hawaii Native/Pacific Islander (1)	6	0.02
Not Hispanic (1)	5	0.02
Hispanic (0)	1	<0.01
Native Hawaiian (1)	2	0.01
Samoan (0)	1	<0.01
White (22,579)	23,153	92.40
Not Hispanic (22,305)	22,843	91.16
Hispanic (274)	310	1.24

Twinsburg

Place Type: City
County: Summit
Population: 18,795†

Ancestry‡	Population	%
African, Sub-Saharan (13)	81	0.44
African (13)	81	0.44
American (575)	575	3.11
Arab (74)	74	0.40
Lebanese (63)	63	0.34
Other Arab (11)	11	0.06
Armenian (20)	58	0.31
Austrian (0)	29	0.16
British (0)	27	0.15
Canadian (49)	49	0.26
Croatian (54)	173	0.93
Czech (209)	505	2.73
Czechoslovakian (92)	122	0.66
Danish (0)	20	0.11
Dutch (26)	462	2.50
Eastern European (20)	20	0.11
English (316)	1,300	7.02
European (619)	619	3.34
Finnish (43)	94	0.51

*Notes: † The Census 2010 population figure is used to calculate the percentages in the Hispanic Origin and Race categories. Ancestry percentages are based on the 2006-2010 American Community Survey population (not shown); ‡ Numbers in parentheses indicate the number of people reporting a single ancestry; * Numbers in parentheses indicate the number of persons reporting this race alone, not in combination with any other race; Please refer to the Explanation of Data for more information.*

French, ex. Basque (31)	412	2.23
French Canadian (12)	21	0.11
German (1,122)	4,115	22.23
Greek (13)	192	1.04
Hungarian (370)	1,158	6.26
Irish (613)	2,738	14.79
Italian (1,078)	2,877	15.54
Lithuanian (7)	26	0.14
Macedonian (0)	30	0.16
Norwegian (39)	128	0.69
Polish (651)	1,742	9.41
Romanian (52)	199	1.07
Russian (183)	293	1.58
Scotch-Irish (192)	413	2.23
Scottish (94)	375	2.03
Serbian (9)	9	0.05
Slavic (0)	6	0.03
Slovak (270)	663	3.58
Slovene (102)	460	2.48
Swedish (24)	138	0.75
Swiss (0)	17	0.09
Ukrainian (35)	75	0.41
Welsh (22)	208	1.12
West Indian, ex. Hispanic (12)	21	0.11
Jamaican (12)	12	0.06
Trinidadian/Tobagonian (0)	9	0.05
Yugoslavian (22)	30	0.16

Hispanic Origin	Population	%
Hispanic or Latino (of any race)	227	1.21
Central American, ex. Mexican	17	0.09
Guatemalan	14	0.07
Honduran	1	0.01
Panamanian	1	0.01
Salvadoran	1	0.01
Cuban	8	0.04
Dominican Republic	6	0.03
Mexican	74	0.39
Puerto Rican	66	0.35
South American	29	0.15
Argentinean	5	0.03
Chilean	3	0.02
Colombian	11	0.06
Ecuadorian	3	0.02
Peruvian	5	0.03
Venezuelan	2	0.01
Other Hispanic or Latino	27	0.14

Race*	Population	%
African-American/Black (2,527)	2,727	14.51
Not Hispanic (2,496)	2,676	14.24
Hispanic (31)	51	0.27
American Indian/Alaska Native (18)	109	0.58
Not Hispanic (14)	95	0.51
Hispanic (4)	14	0.07
Apache (0)	3	0.02
Blackfeet (2)	7	0.04
Cherokee (0)	14	0.07
Chickasaw (0)	1	0.01
Chippewa (0)	2	0.01
Choctaw (0)	4	0.02
Creek (0)	2	0.01
Delaware (6)	6	0.03
Mexican American Ind. (2)	2	0.01
Navajo (0)	1	0.01
Sioux (1)	1	0.01
South American Ind. (0)	3	0.02
Asian (1,080)	1,215	6.46
Not Hispanic (1,080)	1,214	6.46
Hispanic (0)	1	0.01
Bangladeshi (12)	12	0.06
Chinese, ex. Taiwanese (179)	198	1.05
Filipino (67)	97	0.52
Indian (689)	726	3.86
Indonesian (10)	12	0.06
Japanese (15)	33	0.18
Korean (38)	50	0.27
Laotian (1)	1	0.01
Malaysian (1)	1	0.01
Pakistani (11)	11	0.06
Sri Lankan (6)	6	0.03
Taiwanese (13)	14	0.07
Thai (8)	8	0.04
Vietnamese (22)	24	0.13
Hawaii Native/Pacific Islander (0)	1	0.01
Not Hispanic (0)	1	0.01
Native Hawaiian (0)	1	0.01
White (14,749)	15,027	79.95
Not Hispanic (14,626)	14,883	79.19
Hispanic (123)	144	0.77

University Heights

Place Type: City
County: Cuyahoga
Population: 13,539†

Ancestry‡	Population	%
African, Sub-Saharan (90)	122	0.90
African (57)	57	0.42
Liberian (20)	25	0.18
Nigerian (13)	25	0.18
Other Sub-Saharan African (0)	15	0.11
American (417)	417	3.07
Arab (103)	204	1.50
Egyptian (0)	12	0.09
Lebanese (69)	158	1.16
Palestinian (17)	17	0.13
Other Arab (17)	17	0.13
Armenian (10)	10	0.07
Austrian (23)	59	0.43
Belgian (0)	10	0.07
Brazilian (9)	17	0.13
British (33)	41	0.30
Bulgarian (0)	11	0.08
Canadian (12)	115	0.85
Croatian (27)	27	0.20
Czech (80)	187	1.38
Czechoslovakian (37)	88	0.65
Danish (0)	36	0.27
Dutch (28)	114	0.84
Eastern European (411)	457	3.37
English (163)	774	5.70
Estonian (16)	30	0.22
European (124)	124	0.91
Finnish (9)	9	0.07
French, ex. Basque (40)	285	2.10
French Canadian (43)	109	0.80
German (497)	2,115	15.58
Greek (27)	98	0.72
Hungarian (269)	647	4.77
Iranian (29)	46	0.34
Irish (397)	2,146	15.81
Israeli (5)	38	0.28
Italian (540)	1,511	11.13
Latvian (0)	39	0.29
Lithuanian (45)	234	1.72
New Zealander (22)	22	0.16
Northern European (18)	18	0.13
Norwegian (8)	26	0.19
Polish (256)	898	6.62
Portuguese (91)	116	0.85
Russian (221)	435	3.20
Scandinavian (0)	8	0.06
Scotch-Irish (26)	133	0.98
Scottish (17)	158	1.16
Serbian (59)	75	0.55
Slovak (58)	247	1.82
Slovene (14)	124	0.91
Swedish (0)	74	0.55
Swiss (0)	49	0.36
Turkish (0)	8	0.06
Ukrainian (60)	109	0.80
Welsh (17)	111	0.82
West Indian, ex. Hispanic (34)	34	0.25
Jamaican (34)	34	0.25

Hispanic Origin	Population	%
Hispanic or Latino (of any race)	374	2.76
Central American, ex. Mexican	44	0.32
Guatemalan	17	0.13
Honduran	2	0.01
Nicaraguan	2	0.01
Salvadoran	22	0.16
Other Central American	1	0.01
Cuban	9	0.07
Dominican Republic	12	0.09
Mexican	133	0.98
Puerto Rican	76	0.56
South American	59	0.44
Argentinean	11	0.08
Bolivian	1	0.01
Chilean	6	0.04
Colombian	6	0.04
Ecuadorian	4	0.03
Paraguayan	1	0.01
Peruvian	16	0.12
Uruguayan	1	0.01
Venezuelan	13	0.10
Other Hispanic or Latino	41	0.30

Race*	Population	%
African-American/Black (3,133)	3,259	24.07
Not Hispanic (3,120)	3,233	23.88
Hispanic (13)	26	0.19
American Indian/Alaska Native (14)	59	0.44
Not Hispanic (13)	50	0.37
Hispanic (1)	9	0.07
Blackfeet (0)	4	0.03
Cherokee (0)	8	0.06
Cheyenne (1)	1	0.01
Creek (1)	2	0.01
Mexican American Ind. (1)	1	0.01
Seminole (0)	1	0.01
South American Ind. (0)	1	0.01
Asian (326)	395	2.92
Not Hispanic (319)	385	2.84
Hispanic (7)	10	0.07
Burmese (1)	1	0.01
Chinese, ex. Taiwanese (89)	99	0.73
Filipino (28)	54	0.40
Indian (104)	115	0.85
Japanese (20)	25	0.18
Korean (33)	42	0.31
Nepalese (4)	4	0.03
Pakistani (13)	14	0.10
Sri Lankan (1)	2	0.01
Taiwanese (6)	6	0.04
Thai (6)	9	0.07
Vietnamese (12)	14	0.10
Hawaii Native/Pacific Islander (4)	7	0.05
Not Hispanic (3)	6	0.04
Hispanic (1)	1	0.01
Fijian (1)	1	0.01
Guamanian/Chamorro (1)	2	0.01
Native Hawaiian (2)	2	0.01
White (9,726)	9,907	73.17
Not Hispanic (9,497)	9,662	71.36
Hispanic (229)	245	1.81

Upper Arlington

Place Type: City
County: Franklin
Population: 33,771†

Ancestry‡	Population	%
African, Sub-Saharan (20)	20	0.06
African (15)	15	0.04
South African (5)	5	0.01
Albanian (11)	34	0.10
American (1,409)	1,409	4.19
Arab (183)	313	0.93
Arab (49)	71	0.21
Egyptian (58)	58	0.17
Jordanian (9)	9	0.03
Lebanese (31)	139	0.41
Palestinian (28)	28	0.08
Other Arab (8)	8	0.02
Armenian (9)	49	0.15

SECTION TWO

*Notes: † The Census 2010 population figure is used to calculate the percentages in the Hispanic Origin and Race categories. Ancestry percentages are based on the 2006-2010 American Community Survey population (not shown); ‡ Numbers in parentheses indicate the number of people reporting a single ancestry; * Numbers in parentheses indicate the number of persons reporting this race alone, not in combination with any other race; Please refer to the Explanation of Data for more information.*

Assyrian/Chaldean/Syriac (51)	51	0.15
Australian (0)	25	0.07
Austrian (57)	98	0.29
Belgian (22)	33	0.10
Brazilian (23)	72	0.21
British (159)	394	1.17
Bulgarian (45)	67	0.20
Canadian (20)	39	0.12
Croatian (6)	124	0.37
Czech (25)	196	0.58
Czechoslovakian (34)	47	0.14
Danish (28)	105	0.31
Dutch (157)	499	1.48
Eastern European (77)	77	0.23
English (1,353)	5,359	15.93
European (416)	467	1.39
Finnish (32)	70	0.21
French, ex. Basque (164)	1,141	3.39
French Canadian (105)	195	0.58
German (4,066)	11,224	33.36
Greek (259)	602	1.79
Hungarian (162)	538	1.60
Iranian (138)	161	0.48
Irish (2,060)	6,898	20.50
Italian (912)	2,953	8.78
Latvian (7)	7	0.02
Lithuanian (44)	90	0.27
Luxemburger (0)	12	0.04
Macedonian (0)	33	0.10
Northern European (13)	13	0.04
Norwegian (122)	392	1.17
Polish (370)	1,246	3.70
Portuguese (11)	27	0.08
Romanian (66)	101	0.30
Russian (174)	444	1.32
Scandinavian (18)	34	0.10
Scotch-Irish (465)	1,039	3.09
Scottish (400)	1,256	3.73
Serbian (20)	20	0.06
Slavic (0)	50	0.15
Slovak (59)	203	0.60
Slovene (42)	139	0.41
Swedish (68)	335	1.00
Swiss (147)	521	1.55
Turkish (9)	9	0.03
Ukrainian (143)	168	0.50
Welsh (184)	983	2.92
West Indian, ex. Hispanic (0)	9	0.03
Dutch West Indian (0)	9	0.03
Yugoslavian (0)	25	0.07

Hispanic Origin	Population	%
Hispanic or Latino (of any race)	547	1.62
Central American, ex. Mexican	42	0.12
Costa Rican	2	0.01
Guatemalan	14	0.04
Honduran	4	0.01
Nicaraguan	8	0.02
Panamanian	9	0.03
Salvadoran	5	0.01
Cuban	29	0.09
Dominican Republic	13	0.04
Mexican	210	0.62
Puerto Rican	53	0.16
South American	142	0.42
Argentinean	35	0.10
Bolivian	11	0.03
Chilean	6	0.02
Colombian	34	0.10
Ecuadorian	8	0.02
Paraguayan	1	<0.01
Peruvian	22	0.07
Uruguayan	2	0.01
Venezuelan	21	0.06
Other South American	2	0.01
Other Hispanic or Latino	58	0.17

Race*	Population	%
African-American/Black (269)	418	1.24
Not Hispanic (262)	388	1.15
Hispanic (7)	30	0.09
American Indian/Alaska Native (36)	152	0.45
Not Hispanic (30)	130	0.38
Hispanic (6)	22	0.07
Apache (0)	2	0.01
Arapaho (3)	3	0.01
Blackfeet (0)	7	0.02
Cherokee (4)	33	0.10
Chippewa (1)	7	0.02
Cree (1)	3	0.01
Delaware (0)	3	0.01
Inupiat *(Alaska Native)* (1)	1	<0.01
Iroquois (2)	2	0.01
Mexican American Ind. (0)	4	0.01
Navajo (1)	2	0.01
Potawatomi (0)	5	0.01
Seminole (0)	1	<0.01
Sioux (0)	1	<0.01
South American Ind. (0)	7	0.02
Asian (1,665)	1,957	5.79
Not Hispanic (1,660)	1,940	5.74
Hispanic (5)	17	0.05
Bangladeshi (2)	2	0.01
Cambodian (7)	10	0.03
Chinese, ex. Taiwanese (669)	758	2.24
Filipino (69)	90	0.27
Hmong (2)	4	0.01
Indian (385)	435	1.29
Indonesian (16)	23	0.07
Japanese (88)	129	0.38
Korean (183)	214	0.63
Laotian (17)	22	0.07
Malaysian (1)	5	0.01
Nepalese (22)	23	0.07
Pakistani (10)	10	0.03
Sri Lankan (6)	6	0.02
Taiwanese (101)	109	0.32
Thai (14)	19	0.06
Vietnamese (41)	56	0.17
Hawaii Native/Pacific Islander (7)	16	0.05
Not Hispanic (6)	13	0.04
Hispanic (1)	3	0.01
Guamanian/Chamorro (1)	3	0.01
Native Hawaiian (2)	3	0.01
Samoan (1)	1	<0.01
White (31,118)	31,635	93.68
Not Hispanic (30,726)	31,181	92.33
Hispanic (392)	454	1.34

Urbana

Place Type: City
County: Champaign
Population: 11,793†

Ancestry‡	Population	%
African, Sub-Saharan (0)	19	0.16
African (0)	19	0.16
American (1,709)	1,709	14.56
British (38)	52	0.44
Canadian (7)	7	0.06
Croatian (0)	11	0.09
Czech (0)	32	0.27
Danish (0)	16	0.14
Dutch (96)	350	2.98
English (869)	1,527	13.01
European (141)	141	1.20
French, ex. Basque (104)	348	2.96
French Canadian (11)	25	0.21
German (1,021)	2,605	22.19
Greek (8)	34	0.29
Hungarian (58)	104	0.89
Irish (568)	1,779	15.15
Italian (105)	284	2.42
Lithuanian (0)	16	0.14
Norwegian (0)	33	0.28
Pennsylvania German (4)	4	0.03
Polish (42)	97	0.83
Russian (8)	17	0.14
Scotch-Irish (105)	161	1.37
Scottish (33)	201	1.71
Slovak (8)	8	0.07
Swedish (9)	9	0.08
Swiss (0)	49	0.42
Ukrainian (5)	5	0.04
Welsh (79)	160	1.36

Hispanic Origin	Population	%
Hispanic or Latino (of any race)	240	2.04
Central American, ex. Mexican	4	0.03
Guatemalan	1	0.01
Honduran	2	0.02
Panamanian	1	0.01
Cuban	4	0.03
Dominican Republic	4	0.03
Mexican	156	1.32
Puerto Rican	14	0.12
South American	1	0.01
Venezuelan	1	0.01
Other Hispanic or Latino	57	0.48

Race*	Population	%
African-American/Black (631)	881	7.47
Not Hispanic (620)	860	7.29
Hispanic (11)	21	0.18
American Indian/Alaska Native (52)	157	1.33
Not Hispanic (48)	149	1.26
Hispanic (4)	8	0.07
Apache (0)	1	0.01
Blackfeet (3)	5	0.04
Cherokee (6)	38	0.32
Cheyenne (1)	2	0.02
Chickasaw (0)	2	0.02
Chippewa (2)	2	0.02
Choctaw (0)	2	0.02
Iroquois (7)	7	0.06
Navajo (1)	4	0.03
Sioux (1)	2	0.02
Asian (80)	96	0.81
Not Hispanic (78)	93	0.79
Hispanic (2)	3	0.03
Chinese, ex. Taiwanese (64)	67	0.57
Filipino (3)	7	0.06
Indian (3)	5	0.04
Indonesian (1)	1	0.01
Japanese (1)	2	0.02
Korean (5)	10	0.08
Laotian (1)	1	0.01
Vietnamese (1)	1	0.01
Hawaii Native/Pacific Islander (1)	2	0.02
Not Hispanic (0)	1	0.01
Hispanic (1)	1	0.01
Native Hawaiian (1)	1	0.01
White (10,584)	10,921	92.61
Not Hispanic (10,473)	10,774	91.36
Hispanic (111)	147	1.25

Van Wert

Place Type: City
County: Van Wert
Population: 10,846†

Ancestry‡	Population	%
African, Sub-Saharan (5)	5	0.05
African (5)	5	0.05
American (1,191)	1,191	10.79
Belgian (9)	28	0.25
British (19)	94	0.85
Canadian (21)	61	0.55
Czech (15)	25	0.23
Danish (8)	8	0.07
Dutch (32)	200	1.81
English (761)	1,762	15.96
European (20)	31	0.28
French, ex. Basque (45)	189	1.71
French Canadian (0)	27	0.24
German (1,784)	3,921	35.52
Greek (21)	44	0.40
Hungarian (12)	131	1.19

*Notes: † The Census 2010 population figure is used to calculate the percentages in the Hispanic Origin and Race categories. Ancestry percentages are based on the 2006-2010 American Community Survey population (not shown); ‡ Numbers in parentheses indicate the number of people reporting a single ancestry; * Numbers in parentheses indicate the number of persons reporting this race alone, not in combination with any other race; Please refer to the Explanation of Data for more information.*

Iranian (26)	26	0.24
Irish (389)	1,483	13.43
Italian (68)	215	1.95
Macedonian (0)	9	0.08
Norwegian (8)	59	0.53
Pennsylvania German (26)	26	0.24
Polish (8)	196	1.78
Russian (0)	10	0.09
Scotch-Irish (68)	196	1.78
Scottish (21)	109	0.99
Swedish (0)	19	0.17
Swiss (19)	71	0.64
Welsh (32)	153	1.39

Hispanic Origin	Population	%
Hispanic or Latino (of any race)	435	4.01
Central American, ex. Mexican	1	0.01
Nicaraguan	1	0.01
Cuban	3	0.03
Dominican Republic	1	0.01
Mexican	368	3.39
Puerto Rican	19	0.18
South American	1	0.01
Peruvian	1	0.01
Other Hispanic or Latino	42	0.39

Race*	Population	%
African-American/Black (180)	293	2.70
Not Hispanic (168)	276	2.54
Hispanic (12)	17	0.16
American Indian/Alaska Native (10)	52	0.48
Not Hispanic (9)	46	0.42
Hispanic (1)	6	0.06
Apache (0)	1	0.01
Canadian/French Am. Ind. (0)	1	0.01
Cherokee (4)	21	0.19
Chickasaw (0)	1	0.01
Chippewa (0)	1	0.01
Potawatomi (3)	3	0.03
Asian (41)	72	0.66
Not Hispanic (40)	68	0.63
Hispanic (1)	4	0.04
Chinese, ex. Taiwanese (16)	22	0.20
Filipino (8)	19	0.18
Indian (4)	7	0.06
Japanese (2)	3	0.03
Korean (5)	13	0.12
Vietnamese (5)	5	0.05
Hawaii Native/Pacific Islander (1)	6	0.06
Not Hispanic (1)	6	0.06
Guamanian/Chamorro (0)	3	0.03
Native Hawaiian (0)	2	0.02
White (10,263)	10,482	96.64
Not Hispanic (10,019)	10,182	93.88
Hispanic (244)	300	2.77

Vandalia

Place Type: City
County: Montgomery
Population: 15,246†

Ancestry‡	Population	%
African, Sub-Saharan (42)	42	0.28
Nigerian (42)	42	0.28
American (1,114)	1,114	7.38
British (10)	66	0.44
Canadian (0)	9	0.06
Czech (13)	90	0.60
Czechoslovakian (12)	12	0.08
Danish (0)	15	0.10
Dutch (88)	247	1.64
English (541)	1,489	9.86
European (217)	257	1.70
French, ex. Basque (130)	432	2.86
French Canadian (32)	57	0.38
German (1,804)	4,067	26.94
Greek (59)	138	0.91
Hungarian (102)	220	1.46
Irish (576)	1,999	13.24
Italian (242)	653	4.33
Lithuanian (61)	134	0.89
Norwegian (23)	37	0.25
Pennsylvania German (13)	13	0.09
Polish (134)	473	3.13
Romanian (0)	7	0.05
Russian (0)	63	0.42
Scotch-Irish (88)	296	1.96
Scottish (195)	399	2.64
Slovak (19)	37	0.25
Slovene (0)	8	0.05
Swedish (10)	227	1.50
Swiss (13)	64	0.42
Ukrainian (18)	30	0.20
Welsh (42)	162	1.07
West Indian, ex. Hispanic (10)	61	0.40
Jamaican (10)	10	0.07
West Indian (0)	51	0.34

Hispanic Origin	Population	%
Hispanic or Latino (of any race)	246	1.61
Central American, ex. Mexican	12	0.08
Guatemalan	7	0.05
Nicaraguan	2	0.01
Panamanian	1	0.01
Salvadoran	2	0.01
Cuban	2	0.01
Dominican Republic	1	0.01
Mexican	142	0.93
Puerto Rican	41	0.27
South American	18	0.12
Argentinean	1	0.01
Colombian	8	0.05
Ecuadorian	2	0.01
Peruvian	6	0.04
Venezuelan	1	0.01
Other Hispanic or Latino	30	0.20

Race*	Population	%
African-American/Black (631)	809	5.31
Not Hispanic (624)	793	5.20
Hispanic (7)	16	0.10
American Indian/Alaska Native (20)	89	0.58
Not Hispanic (18)	83	0.54
Hispanic (2)	6	0.04
Apache (1)	1	0.01
Arapaho (0)	1	0.01
Blackfeet (2)	8	0.05
Cherokee (7)	39	0.26
Cheyenne (0)	1	0.01
Iroquois (1)	1	0.01
Lumbee (1)	1	0.01
Sioux (1)	3	0.02
Asian (219)	305	2.00
Not Hispanic (218)	303	1.99
Hispanic (1)	2	0.01
Chinese, ex. Taiwanese (44)	48	0.31
Filipino (31)	61	0.40
Indian (80)	87	0.57
Japanese (8)	19	0.12
Korean (12)	31	0.20
Laotian (4)	8	0.05
Malaysian (0)	1	0.01
Pakistani (6)	8	0.05
Sri Lankan (1)	1	0.01
Thai (4)	6	0.04
Vietnamese (14)	16	0.10
Hawaii Native/Pacific Islander (4)	11	0.07
Not Hispanic (4)	11	0.07
Native Hawaiian (4)	8	0.05
White (13,955)	14,264	93.56
Not Hispanic (13,815)	14,108	92.54
Hispanic (140)	156	1.02

Vermilion

Place Type: City
County: Lorain
Population: 10,594†

Ancestry‡	Population	%
American (603)	603	5.59
Arab (12)	12	0.11
Lebanese (12)	12	0.11
Australian (0)	15	0.14
Austrian (9)	44	0.41
British (60)	139	1.29
Bulgarian (0)	46	0.43
Croatian (43)	102	0.95
Czech (74)	152	1.41
Czechoslovakian (14)	69	0.64
Danish (17)	26	0.24
Dutch (11)	126	1.17
English (337)	1,559	14.45
European (77)	77	0.71
French, ex. Basque (38)	488	4.52
French Canadian (0)	18	0.17
German (1,112)	3,494	32.38
Greek (30)	52	0.48
Hungarian (118)	368	3.41
Irish (513)	1,684	15.61
Italian (260)	803	7.44
Luxemburger (0)	12	0.11
Northern European (33)	33	0.31
Norwegian (0)	79	0.73
Polish (345)	1,018	9.44
Romanian (0)	17	0.16
Russian (0)	73	0.68
Scotch-Irish (98)	299	2.77
Scottish (62)	237	2.20
Serbian (0)	98	0.91
Slavic (16)	16	0.15
Slovak (122)	221	2.05
Slovene (16)	84	0.78
Swedish (16)	66	0.61
Swiss (7)	24	0.22
Ukrainian (35)	48	0.44
Welsh (15)	203	1.88
Yugoslavian (0)	34	0.32

Hispanic Origin	Population	%
Hispanic or Latino (of any race)	300	2.83
Central American, ex. Mexican	5	0.05
Guatemalan	1	0.01
Nicaraguan	1	0.01
Panamanian	3	0.03
Cuban	3	0.03
Mexican	101	0.95
Puerto Rican	160	1.51
South American	3	0.03
Colombian	2	0.02
Peruvian	1	0.01
Other Hispanic or Latino	28	0.26

Race*	Population	%
African-American/Black (35)	91	0.86
Not Hispanic (25)	77	0.73
Hispanic (10)	14	0.13
American Indian/Alaska Native (17)	125	1.18
Not Hispanic (16)	123	1.16
Hispanic (1)	2	0.02
Blackfeet (0)	18	0.17
Cherokee (9)	54	0.51
Chippewa (0)	1	0.01
Crow (0)	2	0.02
Delaware (0)	4	0.04
Houma (0)	3	0.03
Iroquois (0)	2	0.02
Lumbee (1)	1	0.01
Navajo (0)	3	0.03
Sioux (0)	2	0.02
Asian (33)	53	0.50
Not Hispanic (30)	48	0.45
Hispanic (3)	5	0.05
Chinese, ex. Taiwanese (7)	10	0.09
Filipino (12)	20	0.19
Indian (3)	7	0.07
Japanese (2)	5	0.05
Korean (7)	8	0.08
Thai (1)	1	0.01

*Notes: † The Census 2010 population figure is used to calculate the percentages in the Hispanic Origin and Race categories. Ancestry percentages are based on the 2006-2010 American Community Survey population (not shown); ‡ Numbers in parentheses indicate the number of people reporting a single ancestry; * Numbers in parentheses indicate the number of persons reporting this race alone, not in combination with any other race; Please refer to the Explanation of Data for more information.*

	Population	%
Vietnamese (1)	2	0.02
Hawaii Native/Pacific Islander (0)	1	0.01
Not Hispanic (0)	1	0.01
Native Hawaiian (0)	1	0.01
White (10,259)	10,450	98.64
Not Hispanic (10,042)	10,212	96.39
Hispanic (217)	238	2.25

Wadsworth

Place Type: City
County: Medina
Population: 21,567†

Ancestry‡	Population	%
American (1,736)	1,736	8.18
Arab (9)	47	0.22
Lebanese (9)	47	0.22
Armenian (15)	62	0.29
Austrian (8)	89	0.42
Belgian (0)	14	0.07
British (80)	89	0.42
Croatian (22)	107	0.50
Czech (0)	176	0.83
Czechoslovakian (12)	113	0.53
Danish (0)	39	0.18
Dutch (72)	469	2.21
English (949)	2,857	13.47
Estonian (11)	11	0.05
European (130)	168	0.79
French, ex. Basque (229)	1,082	5.10
French Canadian (13)	42	0.20
German (2,081)	6,577	31.01
Greek (94)	199	0.94
Hungarian (261)	755	3.56
Iranian (0)	50	0.24
Irish (942)	3,507	16.53
Israeli (8)	8	0.04
Italian (775)	1,560	7.35
Latvian (13)	13	0.06
Lithuanian (0)	10	0.05
Norwegian (12)	54	0.25
Pennsylvania German (38)	99	0.47
Polish (206)	878	4.14
Portuguese (170)	170	0.80
Romanian (80)	132	0.62
Russian (12)	207	0.98
Scotch-Irish (151)	354	1.67
Scottish (161)	679	3.20
Serbian (49)	168	0.79
Slavic (25)	35	0.17
Slovak (190)	522	2.46
Slovene (38)	91	0.43
Swedish (67)	193	0.91
Swiss (83)	413	1.95
Ukrainian (63)	92	0.43
Welsh (73)	340	1.60
West Indian, ex. Hispanic (0)	10	0.05
Dutch West Indian (0)	10	0.05
Yugoslavian (0)	17	0.08

Hispanic Origin	Population	%
Hispanic or Latino (of any race)	267	1.24
Central American, ex. Mexican	19	0.09
Costa Rican	1	<0.01
Guatemalan	7	0.03
Honduran	4	0.02
Nicaraguan	5	0.02
Salvadoran	2	0.01
Cuban	8	0.04
Dominican Republic	6	0.03
Mexican	133	0.62
Puerto Rican	55	0.26
South American	14	0.06
Argentinean	7	0.03
Colombian	4	0.02
Ecuadorian	2	0.01
Venezuelan	1	<0.01
Other Hispanic or Latino	32	0.15

Race*	Population	%
African-American/Black (168)	252	1.17
Not Hispanic (166)	244	1.13
Hispanic (2)	8	0.04
American Indian/Alaska Native (51)	133	0.62
Not Hispanic (43)	117	0.54
Hispanic (8)	16	0.07
Apache (1)	2	0.01
Blackfeet (0)	3	0.01
Canadian/French Am. Ind. (1)	1	<0.01
Cherokee (14)	39	0.18
Cheyenne (0)	1	<0.01
Chippewa (4)	6	0.03
Comanche (4)	8	0.04
Delaware (0)	2	0.01
Iroquois (0)	1	<0.01
Lumbee (2)	3	0.01
Mexican American Ind. (1)	2	0.01
Navajo (1)	3	0.01
Sioux (0)	2	0.01
Yuman (2)	4	0.02
Asian (159)	220	1.02
Not Hispanic (157)	213	0.99
Hispanic (2)	7	0.03
Cambodian (0)	2	0.01
Chinese, ex. Taiwanese (55)	56	0.26
Filipino (10)	15	0.07
Indian (24)	34	0.16
Japanese (9)	31	0.14
Korean (30)	43	0.20
Laotian (12)	15	0.07
Pakistani (2)	2	0.01
Taiwanese (1)	1	<0.01
Thai (2)	2	0.01
Vietnamese (8)	8	0.04
Hawaii Native/Pacific Islander (3)	6	0.03
Not Hispanic (2)	5	0.02
Hispanic (1)	1	<0.01
Guamanian/Chamorro (1)	1	<0.01
Marshallese (1)	1	<0.01
Native Hawaiian (0)	1	<0.01
Samoan (1)	2	0.01
White (20,895)	21,138	98.01
Not Hispanic (20,717)	20,921	97.00
Hispanic (178)	217	1.01

Wapakoneta

Place Type: City
County: Auglaize
Population: 9,867†

Ancestry‡	Population	%
African, Sub-Saharan (3)	7	0.07
African (3)	7	0.07
American (841)	841	8.50
Austrian (0)	10	0.10
Dutch (41)	219	2.21
English (202)	544	5.50
European (25)	25	0.25
French, ex. Basque (20)	367	3.71
French Canadian (0)	8	0.08
German (3,041)	5,472	55.30
Greek (22)	22	0.22
Hungarian (20)	32	0.32
Irish (404)	1,502	15.18
Italian (91)	362	3.66
Norwegian (12)	12	0.12
Polish (60)	120	1.21
Russian (48)	149	1.51
Scotch-Irish (39)	106	1.07
Scottish (16)	66	0.67
Serbian (0)	11	0.11
Slovene (0)	12	0.12
Swedish (0)	34	0.34
Swiss (0)	18	0.18
Welsh (66)	222	2.24
West Indian, ex. Hispanic (3)	3	0.03
Haitian (3)	3	0.03

Hispanic Origin	Population	%
Hispanic or Latino (of any race)	160	1.62
Central American, ex. Mexican	7	0.07
Panamanian	7	0.07
Cuban	6	0.06
Dominican Republic	5	0.05
Mexican	106	1.07
Puerto Rican	13	0.13
Other Hispanic or Latino	23	0.23

Race*	Population	%
African-American/Black (43)	92	0.93
Not Hispanic (39)	87	0.88
Hispanic (4)	5	0.05
American Indian/Alaska Native (26)	54	0.55
Not Hispanic (23)	47	0.48
Hispanic (3)	7	0.07
Apache (1)	2	0.02
Canadian/French Am. Ind. (1)	4	0.04
Cherokee (3)	10	0.10
Chippewa (3)	3	0.03
Choctaw (0)	1	0.01
Creek (0)	1	0.01
Iroquois (0)	1	0.01
Mexican American Ind. (0)	1	0.01
Pueblo (0)	1	0.01
South American Ind. (1)	2	0.02
Asian (38)	74	0.75
Not Hispanic (37)	71	0.72
Hispanic (1)	3	0.03
Chinese, ex. Taiwanese (10)	11	0.11
Filipino (5)	14	0.14
Indian (7)	8	0.08
Japanese (3)	3	0.03
Korean (5)	8	0.08
Laotian (4)	16	0.16
Vietnamese (4)	16	0.16
Hawaii Native/Pacific Islander (1)	13	0.13
Not Hispanic (1)	12	0.12
Hispanic (0)	1	0.01
Guamanian/Chamorro (1)	9	0.09
Native Hawaiian (0)	4	0.04
White (9,577)	9,692	98.23
Not Hispanic (9,484)	9,588	97.17
Hispanic (93)	104	1.05

Warren

Place Type: City
County: Trumbull
Population: 41,557†

Ancestry‡	Population	%
African, Sub-Saharan (79)	134	0.31
African (79)	134	0.31
American (7,537)	7,537	17.66
Arab (109)	125	0.29
Arab (9)	25	0.06
Egyptian (49)	49	0.11
Lebanese (51)	51	0.12
Austrian (11)	64	0.15
Belgian (12)	79	0.19
British (14)	122	0.29
Cajun (13)	13	0.03
Canadian (28)	51	0.12
Carpatho Rusyn (10)	10	0.02
Croatian (124)	309	0.72
Czech (28)	136	0.32
Czechoslovakian (0)	41	0.10
Danish (11)	23	0.05
Dutch (53)	718	1.68
English (493)	2,716	6.37
European (46)	78	0.18
Finnish (52)	190	0.45
French, ex. Basque (55)	441	1.03
French Canadian (11)	140	0.33
German (1,329)	6,004	14.07
Greek (572)	876	2.05
Hungarian (329)	929	2.18
Iranian (64)	64	0.15

*Notes: † The Census 2010 population figure is used to calculate the percentages in the Hispanic Origin and Race categories. Ancestry percentages are based on the 2006-2010 American Community Survey population (not shown); ‡ Numbers in parentheses indicate the number of people reporting a single ancestry; * Numbers in parentheses indicate the number of persons reporting this race alone, not in combination with any other race; Please refer to the Explanation of Data for more information.*

Ancestry	Population	%
Irish (1,205)	4,963	11.63
Italian (1,593)	3,677	8.62
Lithuanian (0)	46	0.11
Macedonian (0)	15	0.04
Northern European (13)	13	0.03
Norwegian (7)	66	0.15
Pennsylvania German (33)	145	0.34
Polish (326)	1,180	2.77
Portuguese (0)	17	0.04
Romanian (190)	372	0.87
Russian (92)	304	0.71
Scandinavian (0)	42	0.10
Scotch-Irish (97)	421	0.99
Scottish (157)	503	1.18
Serbian (44)	127	0.30
Slavic (14)	25	0.06
Slovak (542)	1,161	2.72
Slovene (27)	95	0.22
Swedish (89)	189	0.44
Swiss (0)	73	0.17
Ukrainian (80)	182	0.43
Welsh (181)	720	1.69
West Indian, ex. Hispanic (94)	110	0.26
Barbadian (0)	8	0.02
Jamaican (37)	37	0.09
West Indian (57)	65	0.15
Yugoslavian (33)	33	0.08

Hispanic Origin	Population	%
Hispanic or Latino (of any race)	797	1.92
Central American, ex. Mexican	32	0.08
Guatemalan	5	0.01
Honduran	7	0.02
Nicaraguan	3	0.01
Panamanian	9	0.02
Salvadoran	8	0.02
Cuban	29	0.07
Dominican Republic	13	0.03
Mexican	282	0.68
Puerto Rican	268	0.64
South American	25	0.06
Argentinean	1	<0.01
Chilean	2	<0.01
Colombian	5	0.01
Peruvian	8	0.02
Venezuelan	9	0.02
Other Hispanic or Latino	148	0.36

Race*	Population	%
African-American/Black (11,522)	12,586	30.29
Not Hispanic (11,411)	12,405	29.85
Hispanic (111)	181	0.44
American Indian/Alaska Native (96)	449	1.08
Not Hispanic (82)	407	0.98
Hispanic (14)	42	0.10
Apache (1)	7	0.02
Blackfeet (7)	33	0.08
Canadian/French Am. Ind. (0)	1	<0.01
Central American Ind. (0)	1	<0.01
Cherokee (21)	152	0.37
Cheyenne (1)	6	0.01
Chickasaw (1)	1	<0.01
Chippewa (1)	3	0.01
Choctaw (0)	13	0.03
Comanche (0)	6	0.01
Cree (2)	5	0.01
Creek (1)	3	0.01
Delaware (3)	3	0.01
Iroquois (0)	4	0.01
Mexican American Ind. (1)	3	0.01
Navajo (0)	1	<0.01
Paiute (0)	5	0.01
Sioux (0)	11	0.03
Asian (166)	279	0.67
Not Hispanic (165)	269	0.65
Hispanic (1)	10	0.02
Bangladeshi (2)	2	<0.01
Chinese, ex. Taiwanese (25)	44	0.11
Filipino (35)	66	0.16
Indian (33)	56	0.13
Indonesian (1)	1	<0.01
Japanese (13)	43	0.10
Korean (20)	28	0.07
Laotian (1)	1	<0.01
Malaysian (5)	5	0.01
Pakistani (0)	10	0.02
Thai (3)	4	0.01
Vietnamese (6)	14	0.03
Hawaii Native/Pacific Islander (6)	23	0.06
Not Hispanic (5)	17	0.04
Hispanic (1)	6	0.01
Guamanian/Chamorro (1)	2	<0.01
Native Hawaiian (3)	14	0.03
Samoan (0)	3	0.01
White (28,114)	29,369	70.67
Not Hispanic (27,693)	28,889	69.52
Hispanic (421)	480	1.16

Warrensville Heights

Place Type: City
County: Cuyahoga
Population: 13,542†

Ancestry‡	Population	%
African, Sub-Saharan (296)	296	2.15
African (163)	163	1.19
Somalian (119)	119	0.87
Other Sub-Saharan African (14)	14	0.10
American (56)	56	0.41
Czech (6)	6	0.04
Dutch (4)	12	0.09
English (18)	21	0.15
European (0)	7	0.05
French, ex. Basque (0)	15	0.11
French Canadian (0)	3	0.02
German (19)	133	0.97
Hungarian (36)	46	0.33
Irish (49)	226	1.64
Italian (101)	146	1.06
Polish (41)	228	1.66
Russian (0)	19	0.14
Scottish (0)	35	0.25
Slovene (10)	10	0.07
Turkish (0)	7	0.05
Ukrainian (24)	24	0.17
West Indian, ex. Hispanic (88)	132	0.96
Bahamian (0)	11	0.08
Jamaican (78)	78	0.57
Trinidadian/Tobagonian (0)	33	0.24
West Indian (10)	10	0.07

Hispanic Origin	Population	%
Hispanic or Latino (of any race)	192	1.42
Central American, ex. Mexican	5	0.04
Panamanian	4	0.03
Salvadoran	1	0.01
Cuban	8	0.06
Dominican Republic	11	0.08
Mexican	51	0.38
Puerto Rican	88	0.65
South American	4	0.03
Colombian	3	0.02
Other South American	1	0.01
Other Hispanic or Latino	25	0.18

Race*	Population	%
African-American/Black (12,657)	12,909	95.33
Not Hispanic (12,549)	12,764	94.25
Hispanic (108)	145	1.07
American Indian/Alaska Native (24)	139	1.03
Not Hispanic (21)	129	0.95
Hispanic (3)	10	0.07
Apache (0)	1	0.01
Arapaho (0)	1	0.01
Blackfeet (0)	9	0.07
Cherokee (5)	32	0.24
Chippewa (1)	1	0.01
Choctaw (0)	1	0.01
Cree (0)	1	0.01
Iroquois (0)	6	0.04
Seminole (0)	1	0.01
Sioux (0)	2	0.01
Asian (34)	61	0.45
Not Hispanic (33)	60	0.44
Hispanic (1)	1	0.01
Chinese, ex. Taiwanese (10)	11	0.08
Filipino (5)	11	0.08
Indian (12)	14	0.10
Korean (3)	9	0.07
Pakistani (0)	2	0.01
Thai (1)	1	0.01
Vietnamese (1)	2	0.01
Hawaii Native/Pacific Islander (1)	6	0.04
Not Hispanic (1)	5	0.04
Hispanic (0)	1	0.01
Native Hawaiian (0)	2	0.01
Samoan (1)	1	0.01
White (494)	653	4.82
Not Hispanic (487)	627	4.63
Hispanic (7)	26	0.19

Washington Court House

Place Type: City
County: Fayette
Population: 14,192†

Ancestry‡	Population	%
American (2,329)	2,329	16.54
Armenian (0)	14	0.10
Brazilian (0)	9	0.06
British (23)	47	0.33
Canadian (7)	36	0.26
Czech (0)	62	0.44
Czechoslovakian (9)	65	0.46
Danish (0)	8	0.06
Dutch (69)	346	2.46
English (735)	1,382	9.82
European (126)	155	1.10
French, ex. Basque (47)	130	0.92
French Canadian (13)	54	0.38
German (1,300)	2,510	17.83
German Russian (0)	23	0.16
Greek (36)	36	0.26
Hungarian (50)	50	0.36
Irish (455)	1,169	8.30
Italian (46)	217	1.54
Norwegian (0)	18	0.13
Polish (0)	29	0.21
Russian (0)	15	0.11
Scotch-Irish (168)	219	1.56
Scottish (60)	329	2.34
Slovak (0)	12	0.09
Swedish (8)	16	0.11
Swiss (0)	60	0.43
Welsh (23)	68	0.48
West Indian, ex. Hispanic (13)	13	0.09
Dutch West Indian (13)	13	0.09

Hispanic Origin	Population	%
Hispanic or Latino (of any race)	257	1.81
Central American, ex. Mexican	28	0.20
Costa Rican	4	0.03
Guatemalan	3	0.02
Honduran	3	0.02
Nicaraguan	13	0.09
Panamanian	1	0.01
Salvadoran	4	0.03
Cuban	20	0.14
Mexican	171	1.20
Puerto Rican	8	0.06
South American	11	0.08
Colombian	3	0.02
Ecuadorian	4	0.03
Peruvian	3	0.02
Other South American	1	0.01
Other Hispanic or Latino	19	0.13

*Notes: † The Census 2010 population figure is used to calculate the percentages in the Hispanic Origin and Race categories. Ancestry percentages are based on the 2006-2010 American Community Survey population (not shown); ‡ Numbers in parentheses indicate the number of people reporting a single ancestry; * Numbers in parentheses indicate the number of persons reporting this race alone, not in combination with any other race; Please refer to the Explanation of Data for more information.*

Race*	Population	%
African-American/Black (385)	589	4.15
Not Hispanic (372)	569	4.01
Hispanic (13)	20	0.14
American Indian/Alaska Native (39)	95	0.67
Not Hispanic (33)	86	0.61
Hispanic (6)	9	0.06
Aleut *(Alaska Native)* (1)	1	0.01
Apache (2)	2	0.01
Blackfeet (1)	9	0.06
Cherokee (11)	26	0.18
Cheyenne (1)	1	0.01
Chippewa (2)	3	0.02
Creek (0)	1	0.01
Delaware (0)	1	0.01
Iroquois (0)	2	0.01
Mexican American Ind. (0)	1	0.01
Asian (107)	142	1.00
Not Hispanic (107)	142	1.00
Cambodian (2)	2	0.01
Chinese, ex. Taiwanese (13)	15	0.11
Filipino (11)	30	0.21
Hmong (1)	1	0.01
Indian (16)	20	0.14
Japanese (41)	46	0.32
Korean (6)	14	0.10
Laotian (1)	1	0.01
Pakistani (9)	9	0.06
Vietnamese (2)	2	0.01
Hawaii Native/Pacific Islander (1)	3	0.02
Not Hispanic (1)	3	0.02
Native Hawaiian (1)	2	0.01
White (13,269)	13,560	95.55
Not Hispanic (13,130)	13,397	94.40
Hispanic (139)	163	1.15

West Carrollton

Place Type: City
County: Montgomery
Population: 13,143†

Ancestry‡	Population	%
African, Sub-Saharan (40)	58	0.44
African (17)	17	0.13
Nigerian (23)	23	0.17
South African (0)	18	0.14
Albanian (129)	129	0.97
American (1,717)	1,717	12.97
Arab (0)	17	0.13
Lebanese (0)	17	0.13
Belgian (0)	26	0.20
British (21)	97	0.73
Canadian (39)	87	0.66
Croatian (0)	25	0.19
Czechoslovakian (36)	36	0.27
Dutch (38)	118	0.89
English (734)	1,587	11.99
European (131)	131	0.99
Finnish (10)	30	0.23
French, ex. Basque (26)	265	2.00
French Canadian (0)	28	0.21
German (1,569)	3,609	27.26
Greek (36)	36	0.27
Hungarian (0)	13	0.10
Icelander (9)	18	0.14
Irish (470)	2,039	15.40
Italian (124)	332	2.51
Norwegian (31)	83	0.63
Pennsylvania German (10)	10	0.08
Polish (31)	144	1.09
Romanian (11)	21	0.16
Russian (0)	23	0.17
Scotch-Irish (63)	157	1.19
Scottish (129)	264	1.99
Serbian (0)	12	0.09
Slovak (12)	12	0.09
Swedish (65)	117	0.88
Swiss (13)	104	0.79
Ukrainian (0)	31	0.23
Welsh (12)	88	0.66
West Indian, ex. Hispanic (10)	10	0.08
Barbadian (10)	10	0.08

Hispanic Origin	Population	%
Hispanic or Latino (of any race)	338	2.57
Central American, ex. Mexican	27	0.21
Costa Rican	4	0.03
Guatemalan	2	0.02
Honduran	10	0.08
Panamanian	6	0.05
Salvadoran	5	0.04
Cuban	16	0.12
Dominican Republic	12	0.09
Mexican	176	1.34
Puerto Rican	44	0.33
South American	43	0.33
Argentinean	1	0.01
Bolivian	9	0.07
Colombian	14	0.11
Ecuadorian	11	0.08
Peruvian	1	0.01
Venezuelan	7	0.05
Other Hispanic or Latino	20	0.15

Race*	Population	%
African-American/Black (1,174)	1,324	10.07
Not Hispanic (1,165)	1,305	9.93
Hispanic (9)	19	0.14
American Indian/Alaska Native (36)	104	0.79
Not Hispanic (35)	103	0.78
Hispanic (1)	1	0.01
Apache (1)	1	0.01
Blackfeet (3)	7	0.05
Cherokee (18)	42	0.32
Chippewa (0)	2	0.02
Choctaw (0)	1	0.01
Iroquois (4)	5	0.04
Shoshone (0)	1	0.01
Asian (148)	214	1.63
Not Hispanic (148)	210	1.60
Hispanic (0)	4	0.03
Chinese, ex. Taiwanese (17)	19	0.14
Filipino (42)	60	0.46
Indian (38)	38	0.29
Japanese (5)	17	0.13
Korean (8)	17	0.13
Pakistani (6)	8	0.06
Taiwanese (4)	4	0.03
Thai (6)	11	0.08
Vietnamese (17)	19	0.14
Hawaii Native/Pacific Islander (1)	14	0.11
Not Hispanic (1)	14	0.11
Native Hawaiian (1)	9	0.07
Tongan (0)	1	0.01
White (11,404)	11,640	88.56
Not Hispanic (11,200)	11,412	86.83
Hispanic (204)	228	1.73

Westerville

Place Type: City
County: Franklin
Population: 36,120†

Ancestry‡	Population	%
African, Sub-Saharan (752)	752	2.09
African (365)	365	1.01
Ethiopian (68)	68	0.19
Ghanaian (262)	262	0.73
Nigerian (11)	11	0.03
Other Sub-Saharan African (46)	46	0.13
American (1,933)	1,933	5.37
Arab (102)	133	0.37
Arab (54)	54	0.15
Jordanian (0)	4	0.01
Lebanese (20)	25	0.07
Palestinian (21)	43	0.12
Syrian (7)	7	0.02
Armenian (32)	51	0.14
Austrian (0)	60	0.17
Belgian (12)	52	0.14
Brazilian (0)	11	0.03
British (361)	538	1.50
Bulgarian (0)	16	0.04
Canadian (41)	187	0.52
Carpatho Rusyn (28)	28	0.08
Celtic (27)	27	0.08
Croatian (29)	90	0.25
Czech (82)	271	0.75
Czechoslovakian (17)	48	0.13
Danish (43)	114	0.32
Dutch (249)	833	2.32
Eastern European (25)	25	0.07
English (1,219)	5,250	14.60
Estonian (16)	16	0.04
European (705)	733	2.04
Finnish (16)	39	0.11
French, ex. Basque (182)	1,113	3.09
French Canadian (38)	109	0.30
German (4,397)	12,500	34.75
Greek (145)	281	0.78
Hungarian (96)	619	1.72
Iranian (42)	53	0.15
Irish (1,507)	7,631	21.21
Italian (1,043)	2,943	8.18
Latvian (0)	12	0.03
Lithuanian (24)	67	0.19
Macedonian (15)	15	0.04
Northern European (31)	31	0.09
Norwegian (59)	231	0.64
Pennsylvania German (12)	12	0.03
Polish (428)	1,496	4.16
Portuguese (0)	31	0.09
Romanian (46)	89	0.25
Russian (45)	133	0.37
Scandinavian (74)	80	0.22
Scotch-Irish (205)	670	1.86
Scottish (538)	1,430	3.98
Slavic (0)	29	0.08
Slovak (31)	155	0.43
Swedish (126)	411	1.14
Swiss (33)	288	0.80
Turkish (15)	15	0.04
Ukrainian (23)	196	0.54
Welsh (240)	688	1.91

Hispanic Origin	Population	%
Hispanic or Latino (of any race)	698	1.93
Central American, ex. Mexican	64	0.18
Costa Rican	4	0.01
Guatemalan	17	0.05
Honduran	11	0.03
Nicaraguan	3	0.01
Panamanian	7	0.02
Salvadoran	22	0.06
Cuban	51	0.14
Dominican Republic	28	0.08
Mexican	235	0.65
Puerto Rican	143	0.40
South American	86	0.24
Argentinean	7	0.02
Bolivian	10	0.03
Chilean	14	0.04
Colombian	14	0.04
Ecuadorian	5	0.01
Paraguayan	2	0.01
Peruvian	23	0.06
Uruguayan	1	<0.01
Venezuelan	10	0.03
Other Hispanic or Latino	91	0.25

Race*	Population	%
African-American/Black (2,300)	2,660	7.36
Not Hispanic (2,267)	2,601	7.20
Hispanic (33)	59	0.16
American Indian/Alaska Native (57)	250	0.69
Not Hispanic (51)	224	0.62
Hispanic (6)	26	0.07

*Notes: † The Census 2010 population figure is used to calculate the percentages in the Hispanic Origin and Race categories. Ancestry percentages are based on the 2006-2010 American Community Survey population (not shown); ‡ Numbers in parentheses indicate the number of people reporting a single ancestry; * Numbers in parentheses indicate the number of persons reporting this race alone, not in combination with any other race; Please refer to the Explanation of Data for more information.*

Apache (1)	2	0.01
Blackfeet (0)	8	0.02
Canadian/French Am. Ind. (0)	5	0.01
Cherokee (11)	75	0.21
Chickasaw (0)	1	<0.01
Chippewa (1)	3	0.01
Choctaw (0)	4	0.01
Creek (2)	2	0.01
Hopi (0)	2	0.01
Iroquois (3)	8	0.02
Lumbee (3)	3	0.01
Mexican American Ind. (2)	3	0.01
Navajo (2)	5	0.01
Ottawa (1)	1	<0.01
Paiute (0)	1	<0.01
Potawatomi (2)	3	0.01
Seminole (0)	1	<0.01
Shoshone (0)	4	0.01
Sioux (3)	6	0.02
South American Ind. (2)	2	0.01
Spanish American Ind. (1)	1	<0.01
Yup'ik *(Alaska Native)* (1)	1	<0.01
Asian (827)	1,060	2.93
Not Hispanic (824)	1,051	2.91
Hispanic (3)	9	0.02
Bangladeshi (3)	3	0.01
Burmese (1)	1	<0.01
Cambodian (18)	21	0.06
Chinese, ex. Taiwanese (241)	287	0.79
Filipino (91)	143	0.40
Indian (197)	219	0.61
Indonesian (5)	5	0.01
Japanese (38)	78	0.22
Korean (62)	87	0.24
Laotian (11)	14	0.04
Pakistani (7)	13	0.04
Sri Lankan (5)	5	0.01
Taiwanese (12)	18	0.05
Thai (16)	22	0.06
Vietnamese (89)	105	0.29
Hawaii Native/Pacific Islander (4)	21	0.06
Not Hispanic (2)	18	0.05
Hispanic (2)	3	0.01
Guamanian/Chamorro (1)	6	0.02
Native Hawaiian (0)	4	0.01
Samoan (2)	7	0.02
White (32,002)	32,714	90.57
Not Hispanic (31,540)	32,184	89.10
Hispanic (462)	530	1.47

Westlake

Place Type: City
County: Cuyahoga
Population: 32,729†

Ancestry‡	Population	%
African, Sub-Saharan (117)	141	0.44
African (65)	65	0.20
Somalian (52)	76	0.23
American (954)	954	2.95
Arab (852)	1,183	3.66
Arab (338)	344	1.06
Egyptian (87)	111	0.34
Lebanese (165)	431	1.33
Palestinian (145)	145	0.45
Syrian (104)	126	0.39
Other Arab (13)	26	0.08
Armenian (37)	63	0.19
Austrian (29)	114	0.35
Belgian (0)	8	0.02
British (130)	282	0.87
Bulgarian (0)	25	0.08
Canadian (20)	102	0.32
Celtic (0)	18	0.06
Croatian (366)	498	1.54
Czech (89)	543	1.68
Czechoslovakian (87)	204	0.63
Danish (0)	37	0.11
Dutch (33)	227	0.70
Eastern European (34)	34	0.11
English (612)	3,458	10.69
European (246)	298	0.92
Finnish (29)	44	0.14
French, ex. Basque (34)	686	2.12
French Canadian (22)	36	0.11
German (2,488)	9,453	29.22
Greek (374)	545	1.68
Hungarian (618)	1,410	4.36
Icelander (11)	33	0.10
Iranian (60)	60	0.19
Irish (2,086)	7,076	21.87
Israeli (2)	2	0.01
Italian (1,144)	3,097	9.57
Latvian (41)	41	0.13
Lithuanian (37)	141	0.44
Norwegian (34)	253	0.78
Pennsylvania German (0)	18	0.06
Polish (665)	1,949	6.02
Portuguese (32)	83	0.26
Romanian (90)	187	0.58
Russian (91)	281	0.87
Scotch-Irish (263)	485	1.50
Scottish (150)	634	1.96
Serbian (13)	178	0.55
Slavic (7)	30	0.09
Slovak (333)	1,268	3.92
Slovene (154)	555	1.72
Swedish (143)	503	1.55
Swiss (11)	157	0.49
Turkish (83)	83	0.26
Ukrainian (142)	201	0.62
Welsh (48)	422	1.30
Yugoslavian (10)	41	0.13

Hispanic Origin	Population	%
Hispanic or Latino (of any race)	812	2.48
Central American, ex. Mexican	35	0.11
Guatemalan	10	0.03
Nicaraguan	4	0.01
Panamanian	7	0.02
Salvadoran	14	0.04
Cuban	31	0.09
Dominican Republic	17	0.05
Mexican	228	0.70
Puerto Rican	250	0.76
South American	113	0.35
Argentinean	21	0.06
Bolivian	3	0.01
Chilean	9	0.03
Colombian	51	0.16
Paraguayan	1	<0.01
Peruvian	20	0.06
Venezuelan	8	0.02
Other Hispanic or Latino	138	0.42

Race*	Population	%
African-American/Black (518)	644	1.97
Not Hispanic (498)	618	1.89
Hispanic (20)	26	0.08
American Indian/Alaska Native (23)	81	0.25
Not Hispanic (15)	67	0.20
Hispanic (8)	14	0.04
Apache (3)	5	0.02
Blackfeet (0)	1	<0.01
Cherokee (4)	15	0.05
Chippewa (0)	4	0.01
Choctaw (2)	5	0.02
Delaware (0)	1	<0.01
Iroquois (2)	5	0.02
Lumbee (1)	1	<0.01
Mexican American Ind. (2)	2	0.01
Potawatomi (2)	4	0.01
South American Ind. (0)	1	<0.01
Asian (1,599)	1,900	5.81
Not Hispanic (1,595)	1,889	5.77
Hispanic (4)	11	0.03
Bangladeshi (9)	9	0.03
Burmese (6)	6	0.02
Cambodian (26)	30	0.09
Chinese, ex. Taiwanese (333)	367	1.12
Filipino (112)	157	0.48
Indian (703)	767	2.34
Indonesian (0)	4	0.01
Japanese (44)	62	0.19
Korean (146)	180	0.55
Laotian (2)	4	0.01
Malaysian (1)	1	<0.01
Pakistani (83)	98	0.30
Sri Lankan (7)	9	0.03
Taiwanese (18)	23	0.07
Thai (8)	10	0.03
Vietnamese (53)	69	0.21
Hawaii Native/Pacific Islander (18)	37	0.11
Not Hispanic (18)	36	0.11
Hispanic (0)	1	<0.01
Guamanian/Chamorro (4)	7	0.02
Marshallese (1)	1	<0.01
Native Hawaiian (1)	2	0.01
Samoan (0)	1	<0.01
White (29,847)	30,336	92.69
Not Hispanic (29,279)	29,716	90.79
Hispanic (568)	620	1.89

White Oak

Place Type: CDP
County: Hamilton
Population: 19,167†

Ancestry‡	Population	%
African, Sub-Saharan (59)	84	0.44
African (59)	84	0.44
Alsatian (20)	20	0.11
American (893)	893	4.69
Arab (0)	10	0.05
Lebanese (0)	10	0.05
Austrian (12)	32	0.17
British (13)	44	0.23
Canadian (0)	16	0.08
Czech (0)	16	0.08
Danish (0)	23	0.12
Dutch (26)	236	1.24
Eastern European (10)	10	0.05
English (689)	1,967	10.33
European (238)	238	1.25
Finnish (0)	10	0.05
French, ex. Basque (82)	486	2.55
French Canadian (0)	28	0.15
German (5,461)	10,268	53.93
Greek (62)	177	0.93
Guyanese (22)	22	0.12
Hungarian (142)	220	1.16
Iranian (0)	10	0.05
Irish (405)	3,856	20.25
Italian (409)	1,276	6.70
Lithuanian (17)	17	0.09
Macedonian (123)	123	0.65
Norwegian (0)	20	0.11
Pennsylvania German (0)	14	0.07
Polish (110)	204	1.07
Portuguese (9)	23	0.12
Romanian (29)	38	0.20
Russian (34)	62	0.33
Scandinavian (0)	11	0.06
Scotch-Irish (63)	157	0.82
Scottish (103)	234	1.23
Serbian (0)	20	0.11
Slavic (0)	12	0.06
Slovak (0)	11	0.06
Swedish (19)	158	0.83
Swiss (9)	20	0.11
Ukrainian (0)	7	0.04
Welsh (0)	51	0.27
Yugoslavian (0)	11	0.06

Hispanic Origin	Population	%
Hispanic or Latino (of any race)	270	1.41
Central American, ex. Mexican	43	0.22
Guatemalan	28	0.15

*Notes: † The Census 2010 population figure is used to calculate the percentages in the Hispanic Origin and Race categories. Ancestry percentages are based on the 2006-2010 American Community Survey population (not shown); ‡ Numbers in parentheses indicate the number of people reporting a single ancestry; * Numbers in parentheses indicate the number of persons reporting this race alone, not in combination with any other race; Please refer to the Explanation of Data for more information.*

SECTION TWO

Honduran	6	0.03
Panamanian	3	0.02
Salvadoran	6	0.03
Cuban	2	0.01
Dominican Republic	1	0.01
Mexican	141	0.74
Puerto Rican	45	0.23
South American	20	0.10
Argentinean	1	0.01
Colombian	3	0.02
Ecuadorian	3	0.02
Paraguayan	1	0.01
Peruvian	12	0.06
Other Hispanic or Latino	18	0.09

Race*	Population	%
African-American/Black (1,625)	1,820	9.50
Not Hispanic (1,618)	1,801	9.40
Hispanic (7)	19	0.10
American Indian/Alaska Native (41)	129	0.67
Not Hispanic (39)	117	0.61
Hispanic (2)	12	0.06
Apache (2)	2	0.01
Blackfeet (0)	1	0.01
Cherokee (6)	26	0.14
Cheyenne (0)	2	0.01
Chippewa (0)	2	0.01
Creek (1)	1	0.01
Iroquois (1)	1	0.01
Mexican American Ind. (0)	2	0.01
Navajo (3)	6	0.03
Ottawa (0)	3	0.02
Potawatomi (0)	2	0.01
Seminole (0)	1	0.01
Sioux (3)	9	0.05
Ute (0)	2	0.01
Asian (206)	294	1.53
Not Hispanic (206)	292	1.52
Hispanic (0)	2	0.01
Bhutanese (15)	16	0.08
Cambodian (14)	14	0.07
Chinese, ex. Taiwanese (28)	38	0.20
Filipino (43)	74	0.39
Indian (22)	39	0.20
Indonesian (6)	6	0.03
Japanese (3)	8	0.04
Korean (8)	20	0.10
Nepalese (6)	6	0.03
Pakistani (11)	11	0.06
Thai (7)	8	0.04
Vietnamese (34)	44	0.23
Hawaii Native/Pacific Islander (1)	6	0.03
Not Hispanic (0)	5	0.03
Hispanic (1)	1	0.01
Guamanian/Chamorro (1)	1	0.01
Native Hawaiian (0)	1	0.01
White (16,823)	17,144	89.45
Not Hispanic (16,678)	16,963	88.50
Hispanic (145)	181	0.94

Whitehall

Place Type: City
County: Franklin
Population: 18,062†

Ancestry‡	Population	%
African, Sub-Saharan (870)	932	5.13
African (128)	190	1.05
Ethiopian (565)	565	3.11
Ghanaian (9)	9	0.05
Nigerian (36)	36	0.20
Somalian (37)	37	0.20
Sudanese (50)	50	0.28
Other Sub-Saharan African (45)	45	0.25
Albanian (105)	105	0.58
American (1,408)	1,408	7.75
Arab (0)	13	0.07
Lebanese (0)	13	0.07
Australian (0)	156	0.86
Austrian (9)	31	0.17
British (10)	30	0.17
Canadian (0)	10	0.06
Czech (0)	16	0.09
Danish (0)	26	0.14
Dutch (48)	274	1.51
English (327)	956	5.26
European (155)	189	1.04
French, ex. Basque (40)	220	1.21
French Canadian (21)	44	0.24
German (1,091)	3,592	19.77
Greek (0)	29	0.16
Hungarian (36)	59	0.32
Iranian (13)	13	0.07
Irish (424)	2,548	14.02
Italian (151)	812	4.47
Lithuanian (20)	20	0.11
Macedonian (12)	12	0.07
Norwegian (26)	69	0.38
Polish (77)	221	1.22
Portuguese (0)	20	0.11
Russian (0)	6	0.03
Scotch-Irish (253)	388	2.14
Scottish (29)	226	1.24
Slovak (16)	28	0.15
Swedish (0)	31	0.17
Swiss (0)	19	0.10
Welsh (17)	380	2.09
West Indian, ex. Hispanic (29)	107	0.59
Jamaican (0)	78	0.43
West Indian (29)	29	0.16
Yugoslavian (23)	23	0.13

Hispanic Origin	Population	%
Hispanic or Latino (of any race)	1,784	9.88
Central American, ex. Mexican	338	1.87
Costa Rican	13	0.07
Guatemalan	40	0.22
Honduran	35	0.19
Nicaraguan	12	0.07
Panamanian	2	0.01
Salvadoran	236	1.31
Cuban	17	0.09
Dominican Republic	37	0.20
Mexican	931	5.15
Puerto Rican	145	0.80
South American	119	0.66
Argentinean	100	0.55
Bolivian	2	0.01
Colombian	7	0.04
Ecuadorian	2	0.01
Peruvian	5	0.03
Other South American	3	0.02
Other Hispanic or Latino	197	1.09

Race*	Population	%
African-American/Black (5,289)	5,803	32.13
Not Hispanic (5,217)	5,683	31.46
Hispanic (72)	120	0.66
American Indian/Alaska Native (87)	273	1.51
Not Hispanic (63)	217	1.20
Hispanic (24)	56	0.31
Apache (1)	5	0.03
Blackfeet (0)	12	0.07
Canadian/French Am. Ind. (0)	1	0.01
Cherokee (9)	65	0.36
Chippewa (0)	1	0.01
Choctaw (3)	3	0.02
Cree (1)	1	0.01
Delaware (5)	6	0.03
Iroquois (1)	1	0.01
Lumbee (4)	4	0.02
Mexican American Ind. (7)	13	0.07
Seminole (0)	2	0.01
Sioux (3)	9	0.05
South American Ind. (1)	3	0.02
Asian (270)	342	1.89
Not Hispanic (267)	332	1.84
Hispanic (3)	10	0.06
Bangladeshi (6)	6	0.03
Bhutanese (0)	1	0.01
Burmese (3)	3	0.02
Cambodian (10)	11	0.06
Chinese, ex. Taiwanese (90)	99	0.55
Filipino (28)	47	0.26
Indian (28)	33	0.18
Indonesian (1)	1	0.01
Japanese (3)	17	0.09
Korean (11)	15	0.08
Laotian (47)	56	0.31
Pakistani (1)	1	0.01
Thai (4)	4	0.02
Vietnamese (21)	24	0.13
Hawaii Native/Pacific Islander (7)	20	0.11
Not Hispanic (6)	18	0.10
Hispanic (1)	2	0.01
Fijian (1)	1	0.01
Guamanian/Chamorro (1)	1	0.01
Native Hawaiian (1)	3	0.02
Samoan (4)	6	0.03
White (10,614)	11,323	62.69
Not Hispanic (10,071)	10,610	58.74
Hispanic (543)	713	3.95

Wickliffe

Place Type: City
County: Lake
Population: 12,750†

Ancestry‡	Population	%
Afghan (8)	8	0.06
Albanian (0)	21	0.16
American (626)	626	4.87
Arab (10)	10	0.08
Jordanian (10)	10	0.08
Austrian (50)	61	0.47
British (19)	36	0.28
Canadian (22)	22	0.17
Croatian (228)	580	4.51
Czech (41)	198	1.54
Czechoslovakian (58)	90	0.70
Danish (12)	45	0.35
Dutch (17)	177	1.38
English (186)	1,096	8.53
European (49)	70	0.54
Finnish (0)	21	0.16
French, ex. Basque (11)	356	2.77
French Canadian (0)	71	0.55
German (726)	3,030	23.58
Greek (16)	50	0.39
Hungarian (127)	409	3.18
Irish (464)	2,332	18.15
Italian (1,158)	3,047	23.71
Lithuanian (54)	144	1.12
Norwegian (10)	89	0.69
Pennsylvania German (0)	8	0.06
Polish (393)	1,149	8.94
Portuguese (0)	13	0.10
Romanian (17)	36	0.28
Russian (43)	190	1.48
Scandinavian (11)	11	0.09
Scotch-Irish (24)	427	3.32
Scottish (101)	374	2.91
Serbian (11)	19	0.15
Slavic (10)	61	0.47
Slovak (252)	612	4.76
Slovene (575)	1,137	8.85
Swedish (20)	179	1.39
Swiss (10)	55	0.43
Turkish (0)	10	0.08
Ukrainian (37)	184	1.43
Welsh (22)	122	0.95
Yugoslavian (10)	10	0.08

Hispanic Origin	Population	%
Hispanic or Latino (of any race)	154	1.21
Central American, ex. Mexican	14	0.11
Guatemalan	3	0.02
Panamanian	6	0.05

*Notes: † The Census 2010 population figure is used to calculate the percentages in the Hispanic Origin and Race categories. Ancestry percentages are based on the 2006-2010 American Community Survey population (not shown); ‡ Numbers in parentheses indicate the number of people reporting a single ancestry; * Numbers in parentheses indicate the number of persons reporting this race alone, not in combination with any other race; Please refer to the Explanation of Data for more information.*

Salvadoran	5	0.04
Cuban	9	0.07
Mexican	45	0.35
Puerto Rican	58	0.45
South American	9	0.07
Argentinean	5	0.04
Chilean	3	0.02
Colombian	1	0.01
Other Hispanic or Latino	19	0.15

Race*	Population	%
African-American/Black (571)	687	5.39
Not Hispanic (566)	681	5.34
Hispanic (5)	6	0.05
American Indian/Alaska Native (11)	59	0.46
Not Hispanic (11)	59	0.46
Blackfeet (0)	6	0.05
Cherokee (4)	22	0.17
Chickasaw (0)	1	0.01
Chippewa (0)	1	0.01
Iroquois (0)	3	0.02
Navajo (1)	1	0.01
Asian (106)	151	1.18
Not Hispanic (105)	150	1.18
Hispanic (1)	1	0.01
Burmese (0)	1	0.01
Cambodian (2)	2	0.02
Chinese, ex. Taiwanese (15)	26	0.20
Filipino (17)	30	0.24
Indian (25)	28	0.22
Japanese (17)	31	0.24
Korean (15)	18	0.14
Thai (0)	1	0.01
Vietnamese (7)	13	0.10
Hawaii Native/Pacific Islander (1)	5	0.04
Not Hispanic (1)	5	0.04
Samoan (1)	2	0.02
White (11,830)	12,011	94.20
Not Hispanic (11,709)	11,879	93.17
Hispanic (121)	132	1.04

Willoughby Hills

Place Type: City
County: Lake
Population: 9,485†

Ancestry‡	Population	%
African, Sub-Saharan (0)	13	0.14
African (0)	13	0.14
American (205)	205	2.18
Arab (35)	56	0.60
Lebanese (10)	31	0.33
Other Arab (25)	25	0.27
Armenian (24)	24	0.26
Austrian (0)	22	0.23
British (15)	15	0.16
Croatian (325)	505	5.38
Czech (23)	69	0.73
Danish (0)	31	0.33
Dutch (12)	17	0.18
Eastern European (20)	20	0.21
English (183)	747	7.96
European (64)	64	0.68
Finnish (0)	46	0.49
French, ex. Basque (13)	83	0.88
French Canadian (0)	13	0.14
German (436)	1,581	16.84
Greek (65)	157	1.67
Hungarian (109)	216	2.30
Iranian (15)	15	0.16
Irish (319)	1,248	13.29
Italian (519)	1,190	12.67
Lithuanian (62)	116	1.24
New Zealander (8)	8	0.09
Norwegian (0)	9	0.10
Polish (298)	503	5.36
Russian (241)	348	3.71
Scotch-Irish (107)	169	1.80
Scottish (28)	189	2.01
Slavic (9)	9	0.10
Slovak (63)	74	0.79
Slovene (334)	736	7.84
Swedish (84)	145	1.54
Swiss (0)	31	0.33
Ukrainian (10)	19	0.20
Welsh (0)	69	0.73
Yugoslavian (107)	107	1.14

Hispanic Origin	Population	%
Hispanic or Latino (of any race)	121	1.28
Central American, ex. Mexican	5	0.05
Honduran	1	0.01
Nicaraguan	2	0.02
Salvadoran	2	0.02
Cuban	1	0.01
Dominican Republic	1	0.01
Mexican	45	0.47
Puerto Rican	39	0.41
South American	17	0.18
Argentinean	2	0.02
Colombian	10	0.11
Peruvian	2	0.02
Venezuelan	3	0.03
Other Hispanic or Latino	13	0.14

Race*	Population	%
African-American/Black (1,526)	1,601	16.88
Not Hispanic (1,512)	1,575	16.61
Hispanic (14)	26	0.27
American Indian/Alaska Native (3)	39	0.41
Not Hispanic (3)	38	0.40
Hispanic (0)	1	0.01
Apache (1)	1	0.01
Blackfeet (0)	1	0.01
Cherokee (1)	5	0.05
Comanche (0)	1	0.01
Hopi (0)	1	0.01
Puget Sound Salish (0)	1	0.01
Asian (409)	469	4.94
Not Hispanic (408)	466	4.91
Hispanic (1)	3	0.03
Burmese (3)	3	0.03
Cambodian (1)	1	0.01
Chinese, ex. Taiwanese (44)	49	0.52
Filipino (15)	19	0.20
Indian (282)	295	3.11
Indonesian (2)	2	0.02
Japanese (2)	2	0.02
Korean (8)	10	0.11
Laotian (2)	3	0.03
Malaysian (1)	1	0.01
Nepalese (5)	6	0.06
Pakistani (17)	17	0.18
Sri Lankan (3)	3	0.03
Thai (2)	5	0.05
Vietnamese (10)	10	0.11
Hawaii Native/Pacific Islander (1)	8	0.08
Not Hispanic (1)	8	0.08
Guamanian/Chamorro (1)	3	0.03
White (7,357)	7,482	78.88
Not Hispanic (7,282)	7,396	77.98
Hispanic (75)	86	0.91

Willoughby

Place Type: City
County: Lake
Population: 22,268†

Ancestry‡	Population	%
African, Sub-Saharan (17)	17	0.08
South African (17)	17	0.08
Alsatian (9)	9	0.04
American (845)	845	3.80
Arab (37)	72	0.32
Lebanese (37)	72	0.32
Armenian (0)	12	0.05
Austrian (0)	110	0.49
Belgian (0)	31	0.14
British (72)	152	0.68
Bulgarian (8)	8	0.04
Canadian (13)	23	0.10
Croatian (413)	769	3.46
Czech (60)	333	1.50
Czechoslovakian (41)	65	0.29
Dutch (27)	260	1.17
Eastern European (27)	52	0.23
English (487)	2,273	10.22
European (41)	96	0.43
Finnish (0)	97	0.44
French, ex. Basque (34)	548	2.46
French Canadian (20)	69	0.31
German (1,356)	5,553	24.97
Greek (80)	106	0.48
Hungarian (198)	775	3.49
Irish (936)	4,301	19.34
Italian (1,664)	3,799	17.08
Lithuanian (150)	338	1.52
Northern European (8)	17	0.08
Norwegian (119)	169	0.76
Pennsylvania German (9)	26	0.12
Polish (623)	1,615	7.26
Portuguese (0)	11	0.05
Romanian (0)	19	0.09
Russian (296)	485	2.18
Scandinavian (0)	7	0.03
Scotch-Irish (304)	631	2.84
Scottish (156)	579	2.60
Serbian (45)	165	0.74
Slavic (63)	94	0.42
Slovak (312)	789	3.55
Slovene (778)	1,861	8.37
Swedish (50)	269	1.21
Swiss (22)	144	0.65
Ukrainian (210)	338	1.52
Welsh (43)	417	1.88
Yugoslavian (18)	18	0.08

Hispanic Origin	Population	%
Hispanic or Latino (of any race)	287	1.29
Central American, ex. Mexican	6	0.03
Costa Rican	1	<0.01
Guatemalan	1	<0.01
Honduran	2	0.01
Panamanian	1	<0.01
Salvadoran	1	<0.01
Cuban	7	0.03
Dominican Republic	1	<0.01
Mexican	122	0.55
Puerto Rican	87	0.39
South American	39	0.18
Argentinean	11	0.05
Chilean	5	0.02
Colombian	5	0.02
Ecuadorian	4	0.02
Peruvian	8	0.04
Uruguayan	1	<0.01
Venezuelan	5	0.02
Other Hispanic or Latino	25	0.11

Race*	Population	%
African-American/Black (691)	883	3.97
Not Hispanic (683)	866	3.89
Hispanic (8)	17	0.08
American Indian/Alaska Native (23)	104	0.47
Not Hispanic (22)	96	0.43
Hispanic (1)	8	0.04
Apache (0)	11	0.05
Blackfeet (2)	3	0.01
Cherokee (5)	28	0.13
Chippewa (0)	4	0.02
Choctaw (1)	1	<0.01
Iroquois (1)	8	0.04
Kiowa (0)	1	<0.01
Mexican American Ind. (1)	1	<0.01
Navajo (0)	1	<0.01
Shoshone (0)	1	<0.01
Tohono O'Odham (1)	1	<0.01
Asian (325)	407	1.83

*Notes: † The Census 2010 population figure is used to calculate the percentages in the Hispanic Origin and Race categories. Ancestry percentages are based on the 2006-2010 American Community Survey population (not shown); ‡ Numbers in parentheses indicate the number of people reporting a single ancestry; * Numbers in parentheses indicate the number of persons reporting this race alone, not in combination with any other race; Please refer to the Explanation of Data for more information.*

Not Hispanic (325)	398	1.79
Hispanic (0)	9	0.04
Burmese (2)	2	0.01
Cambodian (2)	7	0.03
Chinese, ex. Taiwanese (73)	76	0.34
Filipino (46)	71	0.32
Indian (118)	134	0.60
Indonesian (1)	1	<0.01
Japanese (29)	45	0.20
Korean (23)	38	0.17
Laotian (3)	3	0.01
Pakistani (3)	3	0.01
Taiwanese (1)	1	<0.01
Thai (2)	3	0.01
Vietnamese (15)	18	0.08
Hawaii Native/Pacific Islander (3)	18	0.08
Not Hispanic (3)	15	0.07
Hispanic (0)	3	0.01
Guamanian/Chamorro (1)	1	<0.01
Native Hawaiian (0)	11	0.05
Samoan (1)	4	0.02
White (20,846)	21,136	94.92
Not Hispanic (20,632)	20,900	93.86
Hispanic (214)	236	1.06

Willowick

Place Type: City
County: Lake
Population: 14,171†

Ancestry‡	Population	%
African, Sub-Saharan (13)	13	0.09
African (13)	13	0.09
Albanian (111)	132	0.93
American (364)	364	2.56
Arab (9)	63	0.44
Arab (9)	23	0.16
Lebanese (0)	40	0.28
Austrian (11)	20	0.14
British (24)	26	0.18
Canadian (0)	10	0.07
Croatian (352)	705	4.96
Czech (24)	275	1.94
Czechoslovakian (24)	47	0.33
Danish (0)	8	0.06
Dutch (0)	119	0.84
Eastern European (25)	25	0.18
English (431)	1,477	10.39
European (153)	153	1.08
Finnish (0)	57	0.40
French, ex. Basque (66)	341	2.40
French Canadian (17)	35	0.25
German (763)	3,507	24.68
Greek (60)	96	0.68
Hungarian (206)	621	4.37
Irish (809)	2,920	20.55
Italian (985)	2,313	16.28
Lithuanian (150)	316	2.22
Norwegian (0)	44	0.31
Polish (263)	1,346	9.47
Portuguese (0)	9	0.06
Romanian (42)	116	0.82
Russian (18)	117	0.82
Scotch-Irish (188)	417	2.93
Scottish (47)	453	3.19
Serbian (16)	28	0.20
Slavic (28)	28	0.20
Slovak (214)	531	3.74
Slovene (495)	1,273	8.96
Swedish (25)	73	0.51
Swiss (0)	62	0.44
Ukrainian (0)	53	0.37
Welsh (24)	192	1.35
Yugoslavian (51)	51	0.36

Hispanic Origin	Population	%
Hispanic or Latino (of any race)	187	1.32
Central American, ex. Mexican	12	0.08
Guatemalan	9	0.06
Honduran	2	0.01
Salvadoran	1	0.01
Cuban	13	0.09
Mexican	46	0.32
Puerto Rican	60	0.42
South American	32	0.23
Argentinean	8	0.06
Chilean	1	0.01
Colombian	4	0.03
Paraguayan	1	0.01
Peruvian	11	0.08
Uruguayan	3	0.02
Venezuelan	4	0.03
Other Hispanic or Latino	24	0.17

Race*	Population	%
African-American/Black (358)	430	3.03
Not Hispanic (356)	423	2.98
Hispanic (2)	7	0.05
American Indian/Alaska Native (21)	79	0.56
Not Hispanic (21)	70	0.49
Hispanic (0)	9	0.06
Aleut *(Alaska Native)* (1)	1	0.01
Apache (0)	1	0.01
Blackfeet (0)	7	0.05
Cherokee (5)	25	0.18
Chickasaw (2)	2	0.01
Delaware (0)	3	0.02
Inupiat *(Alaska Native)* (4)	7	0.05
Mexican American Ind. (0)	2	0.01
Osage (2)	2	0.01
Sioux (0)	1	0.01
South American Ind. (0)	1	0.01
Asian (109)	159	1.12
Not Hispanic (109)	159	1.12
Chinese, ex. Taiwanese (22)	33	0.23
Filipino (8)	17	0.12
Indian (26)	38	0.27
Japanese (11)	15	0.11
Korean (12)	14	0.10
Laotian (6)	7	0.05
Malaysian (0)	2	0.01
Thai (5)	8	0.06
Vietnamese (8)	15	0.11
Hawaii Native/Pacific Islander (0)	6	0.04
Not Hispanic (0)	6	0.04
Native Hawaiian (0)	1	0.01
Samoan (0)	5	0.04
White (13,469)	13,648	96.31
Not Hispanic (13,330)	13,491	95.20
Hispanic (139)	157	1.11

Wilmington

Place Type: City
County: Clinton
Population: 12,520†

Ancestry‡	Population	%
African, Sub-Saharan (63)	63	0.50
African (54)	54	0.43
Kenyan (9)	9	0.07
American (1,179)	1,179	9.33
Austrian (0)	78	0.62
British (10)	37	0.29
Canadian (29)	29	0.23
Czech (9)	62	0.49
Danish (0)	26	0.21
Dutch (16)	242	1.91
English (841)	1,656	13.10
European (17)	27	0.21
Finnish (0)	13	0.10
French, ex. Basque (79)	241	1.91
French Canadian (16)	40	0.32
German (1,740)	3,571	28.25
Hungarian (52)	52	0.41
Irish (444)	1,582	12.52
Italian (72)	270	2.14
Lithuanian (0)	13	0.10
Norwegian (17)	17	0.13
Polish (28)	104	0.82
Scandinavian (11)	11	0.09
Scotch-Irish (110)	232	1.84
Scottish (45)	185	1.46
Serbian (19)	19	0.15
Slovak (10)	33	0.26
Swedish (0)	9	0.07
Swiss (0)	70	0.55
Welsh (12)	118	0.93
Yugoslavian (16)	16	0.13

Hispanic Origin	Population	%
Hispanic or Latino (of any race)	320	2.56
Central American, ex. Mexican	8	0.06
Costa Rican	1	0.01
Honduran	2	0.02
Nicaraguan	1	0.01
Panamanian	4	0.03
Cuban	6	0.05
Dominican Republic	3	0.02
Mexican	178	1.42
Puerto Rican	86	0.69
South American	5	0.04
Colombian	3	0.02
Peruvian	1	0.01
Venezuelan	1	0.01
Other Hispanic or Latino	34	0.27

Race*	Population	%
African-American/Black (766)	1,085	8.67
Not Hispanic (746)	1,058	8.45
Hispanic (20)	27	0.22
American Indian/Alaska Native (29)	127	1.01
Not Hispanic (25)	118	0.94
Hispanic (4)	9	0.07
Aleut *(Alaska Native)* (0)	3	0.02
Apache (1)	4	0.03
Blackfeet (0)	4	0.03
Canadian/French Am. Ind. (0)	1	0.01
Cherokee (4)	44	0.35
Chippewa (0)	1	0.01
Creek (0)	1	0.01
Hopi (0)	1	0.01
Iroquois (0)	4	0.03
Mexican American Ind. (1)	4	0.03
Navajo (1)	6	0.05
Pima (0)	1	0.01
Tohono O'Odham (0)	1	0.01
Asian (101)	137	1.09
Not Hispanic (99)	135	1.08
Hispanic (2)	2	0.02
Chinese, ex. Taiwanese (19)	19	0.15
Filipino (18)	30	0.24
Indian (11)	17	0.14
Indonesian (0)	1	0.01
Japanese (26)	28	0.22
Korean (5)	8	0.06
Thai (2)	2	0.02
Vietnamese (17)	23	0.18
Hawaii Native/Pacific Islander (9)	14	0.11
Not Hispanic (9)	14	0.11
Native Hawaiian (0)	1	0.01
Samoan (0)	2	0.02
Tongan (0)	2	0.02
White (11,059)	11,485	91.73
Not Hispanic (10,886)	11,289	90.17
Hispanic (173)	196	1.57

Wooster

Place Type: City
County: Wayne
Population: 26,119†

Ancestry‡	Population	%
African, Sub-Saharan (109)	196	0.75
African (93)	162	0.62
Ghanaian (16)	16	0.06
South African (0)	18	0.07
American (2,729)	2,729	10.46

*Notes: † The Census 2010 population figure is used to calculate the percentages in the Hispanic Origin and Race categories. Ancestry percentages are based on the 2006-2010 American Community Survey population (not shown); ‡ Numbers in parentheses indicate the number of people reporting a single ancestry; * Numbers in parentheses indicate the number of persons reporting this race alone, not in combination with any other race; Please refer to the Explanation of Data for more information.*

Arab (0)	11	0.04
Lebanese (0)	11	0.04
Armenian (0)	69	0.26
Austrian (8)	113	0.43
Belgian (0)	16	0.06
British (28)	83	0.32
Bulgarian (12)	34	0.13
Canadian (42)	94	0.36
Croatian (38)	71	0.27
Czech (10)	136	0.52
Czechoslovakian (0)	11	0.04
Danish (0)	10	0.04
Dutch (22)	656	2.51
Eastern European (18)	18	0.07
English (808)	2,536	9.72
European (202)	247	0.95
Finnish (0)	28	0.11
French, ex. Basque (181)	792	3.03
French Canadian (35)	50	0.19
German (3,864)	9,422	36.10
Greek (11)	24	0.09
Hungarian (171)	375	1.44
Iranian (0)	19	0.07
Irish (654)	3,740	14.33
Italian (579)	1,455	5.58
Lithuanian (9)	50	0.19
Norwegian (13)	74	0.28
Pennsylvania German (68)	68	0.26
Polish (148)	510	1.95
Romanian (0)	10	0.04
Russian (30)	154	0.59
Scotch-Irish (169)	571	2.19
Scottish (236)	844	3.23
Slovak (42)	99	0.38
Slovene (7)	31	0.12
Swedish (46)	288	1.10
Swiss (161)	722	2.77
Turkish (15)	15	0.06
Ukrainian (39)	76	0.29
Welsh (85)	286	1.10
West Indian, ex. Hispanic (38)	38	0.15
Jamaican (38)	38	0.15
Yugoslavian (52)	94	0.36

Hispanic Origin	Population	%
Hispanic or Latino (of any race)	570	2.18
Central American, ex. Mexican	65	0.25
Costa Rican	4	0.02
Guatemalan	12	0.05
Honduran	13	0.05
Panamanian	1	<0.01
Salvadoran	31	0.12
Other Central American	4	0.02
Cuban	41	0.16
Dominican Republic	11	0.04
Mexican	256	0.98
Puerto Rican	79	0.30
South American	49	0.19
Argentinean	6	0.02
Bolivian	5	0.02
Chilean	5	0.02
Colombian	10	0.04
Ecuadorian	10	0.04
Paraguayan	1	<0.01
Peruvian	6	0.02
Uruguayan	1	<0.01
Venezuelan	5	0.02
Other Hispanic or Latino	69	0.26

Race*	Population	%
African-American/Black (929)	1,316	5.04
Not Hispanic (914)	1,280	4.90
Hispanic (15)	36	0.14
American Indian/Alaska Native (74)	218	0.83
Not Hispanic (56)	187	0.72
Hispanic (18)	31	0.12
Alaska Athabascan *(Ala. Nat.)* (1)	1	<0.01
Apache (1)	1	<0.01
Blackfeet (0)	8	0.03
Central American Ind. (2)	5	0.02
Cherokee (25)	63	0.24
Cheyenne (0)	1	<0.01
Chippewa (2)	9	0.03
Choctaw (0)	2	0.01
Comanche (1)	1	<0.01
Cree (1)	2	0.01
Hopi (0)	1	<0.01
Houma (1)	3	0.01
Iroquois (0)	6	0.02
Mexican American Ind. (4)	9	0.03
Navajo (0)	2	0.01
Sioux (5)	8	0.03
South American Ind. (2)	2	0.01
Asian (490)	588	2.25
Not Hispanic (488)	580	2.22
Hispanic (2)	8	0.03
Bangladeshi (0)	1	<0.01
Chinese, ex. Taiwanese (140)	157	0.60
Filipino (31)	63	0.24
Indian (174)	190	0.73
Indonesian (2)	3	0.01
Japanese (11)	34	0.13
Korean (62)	72	0.28
Laotian (0)	1	<0.01
Malaysian (0)	1	<0.01
Nepalese (5)	5	0.02
Pakistani (12)	13	0.05
Taiwanese (1)	1	<0.01
Thai (2)	4	0.02
Vietnamese (38)	39	0.15
Hawaii Native/Pacific Islander (8)	20	0.08
Not Hispanic (7)	19	0.07
Hispanic (1)	1	<0.01
Guamanian/Chamorro (2)	5	0.02
Native Hawaiian (0)	7	0.03
Samoan (3)	3	0.01
White (23,818)	24,408	93.45
Not Hispanic (23,485)	24,021	91.97
Hispanic (333)	387	1.48

Worthington

Place Type: City
County: Franklin
Population: 13,575†

Ancestry‡	Population	%
African, Sub-Saharan (84)	84	0.61
African (84)	84	0.61
Alsatian (0)	8	0.06
American (537)	537	3.90
Arab (40)	70	0.51
Egyptian (11)	11	0.08
Lebanese (29)	59	0.43
Armenian (11)	22	0.16
Austrian (9)	91	0.66
Belgian (8)	8	0.06
Brazilian (45)	45	0.33
British (80)	187	1.36
Bulgarian (0)	10	0.07
Canadian (8)	8	0.06
Carpatho Rusyn (0)	10	0.07
Croatian (9)	38	0.28
Czech (25)	87	0.63
Czechoslovakian (0)	76	0.55
Danish (12)	53	0.38
Dutch (38)	381	2.77
Eastern European (39)	39	0.28
English (621)	2,598	18.85
European (308)	308	2.24
Finnish (27)	87	0.63
French, ex. Basque (118)	398	2.89
French Canadian (8)	34	0.25
German (1,688)	4,642	33.69
Greek (13)	142	1.03
Hungarian (54)	131	0.95
Iranian (10)	10	0.07
Irish (687)	2,882	20.92
Italian (348)	1,152	8.36
Lithuanian (0)	8	0.06
Northern European (9)	22	0.16
Norwegian (47)	192	1.39
Polish (100)	503	3.65
Romanian (8)	8	0.06
Russian (65)	245	1.78
Scandinavian (45)	58	0.42
Scotch-Irish (159)	384	2.79
Scottish (174)	627	4.55
Serbian (8)	8	0.06
Slavic (17)	25	0.18
Slovak (28)	75	0.54
Swedish (0)	117	0.85
Swiss (9)	102	0.74
Turkish (8)	8	0.06
Ukrainian (16)	16	0.12
Welsh (61)	506	3.67
West Indian, ex. Hispanic (0)	63	0.46
Bahamian (0)	63	0.46

Hispanic Origin	Population	%
Hispanic or Latino (of any race)	231	1.70
Central American, ex. Mexican	18	0.13
Costa Rican	3	0.02
Guatemalan	6	0.04
Honduran	4	0.03
Nicaraguan	2	0.01
Panamanian	2	0.01
Salvadoran	1	0.01
Cuban	13	0.10
Dominican Republic	4	0.03
Mexican	80	0.59
Puerto Rican	35	0.26
South American	64	0.47
Argentinean	5	0.04
Bolivian	6	0.04
Chilean	6	0.04
Colombian	15	0.11
Ecuadorian	9	0.07
Peruvian	15	0.11
Uruguayan	2	0.01
Venezuelan	6	0.04
Other Hispanic or Latino	17	0.13

Race*	Population	%
African-American/Black (300)	415	3.06
Not Hispanic (292)	397	2.92
Hispanic (8)	18	0.13
American Indian/Alaska Native (5)	59	0.43
Not Hispanic (2)	49	0.36
Hispanic (3)	10	0.07
Apache (0)	1	0.01
Blackfeet (0)	10	0.07
Cherokee (0)	10	0.07
Chippewa (0)	1	0.01
Iroquois (0)	4	0.03
Mexican American Ind. (1)	3	0.02
Navajo (0)	1	0.01
Pueblo (0)	1	0.01
Sioux (0)	2	0.01
Asian (307)	427	3.15
Not Hispanic (305)	422	3.11
Hispanic (2)	5	0.04
Bangladeshi (0)	1	0.01
Cambodian (5)	5	0.04
Chinese, ex. Taiwanese (112)	147	1.08
Filipino (17)	41	0.30
Indian (74)	87	0.64
Indonesian (1)	3	0.02
Japanese (17)	37	0.27
Korean (44)	64	0.47
Malaysian (5)	6	0.04
Taiwanese (6)	10	0.07
Thai (7)	7	0.05
Vietnamese (5)	10	0.07
Hawaii Native/Pacific Islander (4)	12	0.09
Not Hispanic (2)	10	0.07
Hispanic (2)	2	0.01
Guamanian/Chamorro (2)	2	0.01
Native Hawaiian (0)	3	0.02
White (12,622)	12,872	94.82

*Notes: † The Census 2010 population figure is used to calculate the percentages in the Hispanic Origin and Race categories. Ancestry percentages are based on the 2006-2010 American Community Survey population (not shown); ‡ Numbers in parentheses indicate the number of people reporting a single ancestry; * Numbers in parentheses indicate the number of persons reporting this race alone, not in combination with any other race; Please refer to the Explanation of Data for more information.*

Not Hispanic (12,470)	12,693	93.50
Hispanic (152)	179	1.32

Wyoming

Place Type: City
County: Hamilton
Population: 8,428†

Ancestry‡	Population	%
African, Sub-Saharan (11)	11	0.13
Ethiopian (11)	11	0.13
American (493)	493	5.93
Arab (0)	15	0.18
Syrian (0)	15	0.18
Austrian (0)	11	0.13
British (0)	18	0.22
Canadian (13)	13	0.16
Czech (0)	42	0.50
Danish (0)	80	0.96
Dutch (20)	162	1.95
Eastern European (84)	84	1.01
English (378)	1,298	15.60
European (99)	110	1.32
French, ex. Basque (78)	228	2.74
French Canadian (10)	46	0.55
German (1,308)	3,128	37.61
Greek (0)	46	0.55
Hungarian (8)	122	1.47
Irish (174)	1,447	17.40
Italian (135)	499	6.00
Latvian (0)	17	0.20
Lithuanian (19)	52	0.63
Northern European (14)	14	0.17
Norwegian (11)	71	0.85
Pennsylvania German (0)	11	0.13
Polish (77)	224	2.69
Romanian (0)	27	0.32
Russian (12)	149	1.79
Scandinavian (0)	15	0.18
Scotch-Irish (8)	188	2.26
Scottish (29)	250	3.01
Slovak (0)	54	0.65
Swedish (27)	156	1.88
Swiss (28)	88	1.06
Turkish (4)	4	0.05
Ukrainian (33)	74	0.89
Welsh (12)	66	0.79
West Indian, ex. Hispanic (11)	41	0.49
Barbadian (11)	41	0.49

Hispanic Origin	Population	%
Hispanic or Latino (of any race)	149	1.77
Central American, ex. Mexican	11	0.13
Guatemalan	2	0.02
Honduran	5	0.06
Salvadoran	4	0.05
Cuban	6	0.07
Mexican	58	0.69
Puerto Rican	29	0.34
South American	26	0.31
Argentinean	2	0.02
Bolivian	3	0.04
Chilean	4	0.05
Colombian	10	0.12
Ecuadorian	1	0.01
Peruvian	1	0.01
Uruguayan	1	0.01
Venezuelan	4	0.05
Other Hispanic or Latino	19	0.23

Race*	Population	%
African-American/Black (954)	1,066	12.65
Not Hispanic (944)	1,049	12.45
Hispanic (10)	17	0.20
American Indian/Alaska Native (11)	51	0.61
Not Hispanic (10)	40	0.47
Hispanic (1)	11	0.13
Apache (0)	3	0.04
Cherokee (2)	15	0.18
Choctaw (0)	2	0.02
Mexican American Ind. (1)	4	0.05
Navajo (0)	3	0.04
Seminole (1)	1	0.01
Asian (180)	248	2.94
Not Hispanic (180)	241	2.86
Hispanic (0)	7	0.08
Chinese, ex. Taiwanese (51)	80	0.95
Filipino (9)	23	0.27
Indian (49)	60	0.71
Japanese (8)	18	0.21
Korean (12)	16	0.19
Laotian (7)	7	0.08
Nepalese (2)	2	0.02
Pakistani (3)	5	0.06
Sri Lankan (1)	1	0.01
Taiwanese (16)	18	0.21
Thai (1)	1	0.01
Vietnamese (10)	14	0.17
Hawaii Native/Pacific Islander (2)	9	0.11
Not Hispanic (2)	9	0.11
Marshallese (2)	2	0.02
Native Hawaiian (0)	2	0.02
White (7,048)	7,205	85.49
Not Hispanic (6,941)	7,085	84.07
Hispanic (107)	120	1.42

Xenia

Place Type: City
County: Greene
Population: 25,719†

Ancestry‡	Population	%
African, Sub-Saharan (234)	254	0.99
African (137)	157	0.61
Nigerian (97)	97	0.38
American (5,196)	5,196	20.30
Arab (0)	14	0.05
Lebanese (0)	14	0.05
Austrian (0)	10	0.04
British (68)	172	0.67
Czech (20)	50	0.20
Danish (9)	27	0.11
Dutch (26)	504	1.97
English (901)	1,940	7.58
European (152)	242	0.95
Finnish (0)	8	0.03
French, ex. Basque (114)	515	2.01
French Canadian (39)	39	0.15
German (1,849)	4,695	18.35
Greek (0)	26	0.10
Hungarian (35)	88	0.34
Irish (1,118)	3,409	13.32
Italian (198)	452	1.77
Lithuanian (0)	53	0.21
Norwegian (94)	155	0.61
Polish (59)	236	0.92
Portuguese (0)	21	0.08
Romanian (0)	15	0.06
Russian (15)	97	0.38
Scotch-Irish (255)	453	1.77
Scottish (214)	423	1.65
Slavic (0)	11	0.04
Slovak (14)	39	0.15
Swedish (13)	136	0.53
Swiss (0)	40	0.16
Ukrainian (10)	10	0.04
Welsh (64)	268	1.05
West Indian, ex. Hispanic (0)	7	0.03
Jamaican (0)	7	0.03

Hispanic Origin	Population	%
Hispanic or Latino (of any race)	426	1.66
Central American, ex. Mexican	28	0.11
Costa Rican	3	0.01
Guatemalan	12	0.05
Honduran	5	0.02
Nicaraguan	1	<0.01
Panamanian	6	0.02
Salvadoran	1	<0.01
Cuban	20	0.08
Dominican Republic	3	0.01
Mexican	200	0.78
Puerto Rican	72	0.28
South American	14	0.05
Argentinean	1	<0.01
Colombian	10	0.04
Venezuelan	3	0.01
Other Hispanic or Latino	89	0.35

Race*	Population	%
African-American/Black (3,446)	4,020	15.63
Not Hispanic (3,412)	3,952	15.37
Hispanic (34)	68	0.26
American Indian/Alaska Native (95)	302	1.17
Not Hispanic (87)	273	1.06
Hispanic (8)	29	0.11
Apache (1)	1	<0.01
Blackfeet (1)	18	0.07
Canadian/French Am. Ind. (1)	1	<0.01
Cherokee (18)	75	0.29
Chippewa (7)	10	0.04
Choctaw (0)	2	0.01
Comanche (0)	2	0.01
Cree (0)	2	0.01
Creek (0)	3	0.01
Delaware (0)	1	<0.01
Iroquois (1)	8	0.03
Kiowa (0)	2	0.01
Mexican American Ind. (1)	2	0.01
Navajo (0)	1	<0.01
Potawatomi (2)	5	0.02
Seminole (0)	1	<0.01
Sioux (2)	4	0.02
South American Ind. (1)	1	<0.01
Asian (120)	218	0.85
Not Hispanic (115)	204	0.79
Hispanic (5)	14	0.05
Chinese, ex. Taiwanese (27)	35	0.14
Filipino (35)	60	0.23
Indian (14)	22	0.09
Japanese (8)	32	0.12
Korean (13)	31	0.12
Taiwanese (2)	2	0.01
Thai (1)	3	0.01
Vietnamese (14)	20	0.08
Hawaii Native/Pacific Islander (11)	40	0.16
Not Hispanic (10)	39	0.15
Hispanic (1)	1	<0.01
Fijian (1)	1	<0.01
Guamanian/Chamorro (6)	13	0.05
Native Hawaiian (1)	13	0.05
Samoan (1)	5	0.02
White (21,095)	21,858	84.99
Not Hispanic (20,866)	21,565	83.85
Hispanic (229)	293	1.14

Youngstown

Place Type: City
County: Mahoning
Population: 66,982†

Ancestry‡	Population	%
African, Sub-Saharan (2,618)	2,765	3.97
African (2,559)	2,655	3.82
Ethiopian (14)	65	0.09
Other Sub-Saharan African (45)	45	0.06
Albanian (10)	22	0.03
American (2,278)	2,278	3.27
Arab (104)	274	0.39
Arab (84)	110	0.16
Lebanese (20)	139	0.20
Syrian (0)	25	0.04
Armenian (0)	11	0.02
Australian (0)	18	0.03
British (82)	115	0.17
Bulgarian (10)	33	0.05
Canadian (11)	46	0.07

*Notes: † The Census 2010 population figure is used to calculate the percentages in the Hispanic Origin and Race categories. Ancestry percentages are based on the 2006-2010 American Community Survey population (not shown); ‡ Numbers in parentheses indicate the number of people reporting a single ancestry; * Numbers in parentheses indicate the number of persons reporting this race alone, not in combination with any other race; Please refer to the Explanation of Data for more information.*

Carpatho Rusyn (0)	20	0.03
Croatian (314)	688	0.99
Czech (28)	160	0.23
Czechoslovakian (24)	32	0.05
Danish (0)	141	0.20
Dutch (72)	662	0.95
Eastern European (11)	11	0.02
English (656)	3,017	4.34
European (103)	119	0.17
Finnish (0)	29	0.04
French, ex. Basque (130)	542	0.78
French Canadian (58)	106	0.15
German (1,840)	7,654	11.00
German Russian (0)	1	<0.01
Greek (110)	312	0.45
Hungarian (389)	1,409	2.02
Irish (1,479)	6,661	9.57
Italian (3,495)	7,337	10.54
Lithuanian (33)	79	0.11
Northern European (7)	7	0.01
Norwegian (7)	22	0.03
Pennsylvania German (19)	113	0.16
Polish (807)	2,036	2.93
Portuguese (10)	25	0.04
Romanian (146)	267	0.38
Russian (152)	351	0.50
Scotch-Irish (218)	730	1.05
Scottish (79)	466	0.67
Serbian (16)	43	0.06
Slavic (9)	16	0.02
Slovak (1,477)	3,113	4.47
Slovene (20)	44	0.06
Swedish (128)	228	0.33
Swiss (12)	96	0.14
Turkish (12)	12	0.02
Ukrainian (218)	533	0.77
Welsh (70)	877	1.26
West Indian, ex. Hispanic (86)	152	0.22
Barbadian (0)	8	0.01
Haitian (9)	19	0.03
Jamaican (77)	125	0.18
Yugoslavian (7)	34	0.05

Hispanic Origin	Population	%
Hispanic or Latino (of any race)	6,207	9.27
Central American, ex. Mexican	152	0.23
Costa Rican	5	0.01
Guatemalan	26	0.04
Honduran	46	0.07
Nicaraguan	7	0.01
Panamanian	19	0.03
Salvadoran	49	0.07
Cuban	98	0.15
Dominican Republic	239	0.36
Mexican	1,270	1.90
Puerto Rican	3,836	5.73
South American	155	0.23
Argentinean	9	0.01
Bolivian	2	<0.01
Chilean	3	<0.01
Colombian	104	0.16
Ecuadorian	7	0.01
Peruvian	18	0.03
Uruguayan	1	<0.01
Venezuelan	9	0.01
Other South American	2	<0.01
Other Hispanic or Latino	457	0.68

Race*	Population	%
African-American/Black (30,257)	32,093	47.91
Not Hispanic (29,448)	30,939	46.19
Hispanic (809)	1,154	1.72
American Indian/Alaska Native (237)	870	1.30
Not Hispanic (183)	715	1.07
Hispanic (54)	155	0.23
Alaska Athabascan *(Ala. Nat.)* (0)	3	<0.01
Apache (1)	19	0.03
Arapaho (0)	4	0.01
Blackfeet (9)	60	0.09
Cherokee (55)	234	0.35
Chickasaw (1)	1	<0.01
Chippewa (0)	7	0.01
Choctaw (3)	14	0.02
Comanche (2)	6	0.01
Creek (0)	1	<0.01
Crow (0)	2	<0.01
Delaware (0)	1	<0.01
Hopi (2)	2	<0.01
Inupiat *(Alaska Native)* (1)	2	<0.01
Iroquois (6)	11	0.02
Lumbee (2)	2	<0.01
Menominee (0)	1	<0.01
Mexican American Ind. (8)	19	0.03
Navajo (2)	3	<0.01
Seminole (2)	6	0.01
Shoshone (1)	1	<0.01
Sioux (2)	11	0.02
South American Ind. (8)	15	0.02
Spanish American Ind. (3)	3	<0.01
Tlingit-Haida *(Alaska Native)* (0)	1	<0.01
Ute (1)	1	<0.01
Yaqui (2)	2	<0.01
Asian (297)	499	0.74
Not Hispanic (283)	449	0.67
Hispanic (14)	50	0.07
Bangladeshi (0)	1	<0.01
Cambodian (7)	9	0.01
Chinese, ex. Taiwanese (31)	43	0.06
Filipino (34)	74	0.11
Hmong (3)	3	<0.01
Indian (100)	128	0.19
Indonesian (1)	1	<0.01
Japanese (8)	27	0.04
Korean (19)	59	0.09
Laotian (7)	10	0.01
Nepalese (6)	7	0.01
Pakistani (11)	12	0.02
Sri Lankan (0)	1	<0.01
Taiwanese (3)	3	<0.01
Thai (1)	3	<0.01
Vietnamese (50)	67	0.10
Hawaii Native/Pacific Islander (17)	87	0.13
Not Hispanic (7)	54	0.08
Hispanic (10)	33	0.05
Guamanian/Chamorro (3)	10	0.01
Native Hawaiian (5)	25	0.04
Samoan (2)	6	0.01
White (31,508)	33,448	49.94
Not Hispanic (28,918)	30,411	45.40
Hispanic (2,590)	3,037	4.53

Zanesville

Place Type: City
County: Muskingum
Population: 25,487†

Ancestry‡	Population	%
African, Sub-Saharan (0)	13	0.05
Liberian (0)	13	0.05
American (2,775)	2,775	10.85
Arab (157)	237	0.93
Lebanese (134)	171	0.67
Moroccan (12)	12	0.05
Syrian (11)	54	0.21
Austrian (105)	105	0.41
Belgian (23)	50	0.20
British (10)	17	0.07
Croatian (0)	13	0.05
Czech (19)	120	0.47
Czechoslovakian (13)	24	0.09
Danish (17)	28	0.11
Dutch (93)	683	2.67
Eastern European (55)	55	0.22
English (884)	2,347	9.18
European (43)	64	0.25
French, ex. Basque (135)	359	1.40
French Canadian (0)	24	0.09
German (1,499)	5,196	20.32
Greek (40)	103	0.40
Hungarian (54)	178	0.70
Iranian (10)	10	0.04
Irish (827)	3,584	14.02
Italian (271)	619	2.42
Lithuanian (6)	6	0.02
Pennsylvania German (51)	73	0.29
Polish (76)	132	0.52
Russian (78)	89	0.35
Scotch-Irish (144)	465	1.82
Scottish (114)	363	1.42
Slavic (108)	108	0.42
Slovak (32)	79	0.31
Swedish (0)	138	0.54
Swiss (62)	94	0.37
Welsh (58)	311	1.22
West Indian, ex. Hispanic (0)	16	0.06
Jamaican (0)	16	0.06

Hispanic Origin	Population	%
Hispanic or Latino (of any race)	316	1.24
Central American, ex. Mexican	11	0.04
Guatemalan	3	0.01
Honduran	4	0.02
Nicaraguan	1	<0.01
Salvadoran	3	0.01
Cuban	11	0.04
Dominican Republic	1	<0.01
Mexican	118	0.46
Puerto Rican	95	0.37
South American	17	0.07
Argentinean	1	<0.01
Colombian	5	0.02
Peruvian	8	0.03
Uruguayan	3	0.01
Other Hispanic or Latino	63	0.25

Race*	Population	%
African-American/Black (2,472)	3,450	13.54
Not Hispanic (2,441)	3,385	13.28
Hispanic (31)	65	0.26
American Indian/Alaska Native (101)	414	1.62
Not Hispanic (93)	397	1.56
Hispanic (8)	17	0.07
Arapaho (1)	3	0.01
Blackfeet (7)	20	0.08
Canadian/French Am. Ind. (0)	1	<0.01
Cherokee (27)	125	0.49
Cheyenne (0)	6	0.02
Chippewa (0)	2	0.01
Cree (0)	6	0.02
Delaware (9)	12	0.05
Iroquois (2)	6	0.02
Lumbee (1)	1	<0.01
Mexican American Ind. (2)	2	0.01
Navajo (0)	2	0.01
Osage (3)	5	0.02
Shoshone (0)	1	<0.01
Sioux (4)	5	0.02
Asian (100)	156	0.61
Not Hispanic (99)	152	0.60
Hispanic (1)	4	0.02
Chinese, ex. Taiwanese (32)	39	0.15
Filipino (12)	22	0.09
Indian (31)	41	0.16
Japanese (2)	10	0.04
Korean (1)	8	0.03
Laotian (2)	4	0.02
Nepalese (1)	3	0.01
Pakistani (5)	7	0.03
Thai (1)	8	0.03
Vietnamese (8)	12	0.05
Hawaii Native/Pacific Islander (3)	17	0.07
Not Hispanic (2)	13	0.05
Hispanic (1)	4	0.02
Guamanian/Chamorro (1)	2	0.01
Native Hawaiian (1)	6	0.02
Samoan (0)	3	0.01
White (21,508)	22,631	88.79
Not Hispanic (21,330)	22,410	87.93
Hispanic (178)	221	0.87

*Notes: † The Census 2010 population figure is used to calculate the percentages in the Hispanic Origin and Race categories. Ancestry percentages are based on the 2006-2010 American Community Survey population (not shown); ‡ Numbers in parentheses indicate the number of people reporting a single ancestry; * Numbers in parentheses indicate the number of persons reporting this race alone, not in combination with any other race; Please refer to the Explanation of Data for more information.*

OKLAHOMA

Place Type: State
Population: 3,751,351†

Ancestry‡	Population	%
African, Sub-Saharan (11,783)	15,106	0.41
African (7,005)	9,374	0.26
Cape Verdean (70)	187	0.01
Ethiopian (249)	418	0.01
Ghanaian (388)	411	0.01
Kenyan (627)	769	0.02
Liberian (314)	314	0.01
Nigerian (1,998)	2,222	0.06
Senegalese (24)	24	<0.01
Somalian (6)	6	<0.01
South African (104)	191	0.01
Sudanese (428)	428	0.01
Ugandan (63)	73	<0.01
Zimbabwean (18)	18	<0.01
Other Sub-Saharan African (489)	671	0.02
Albanian (318)	363	0.01
Alsatian (14)	14	<0.01
American (351,499)	351,499	9.56
Arab (6,549)	10,688	0.29
Arab (1,152)	1,596	0.04
Egyptian (292)	477	0.01
Iraqi (129)	129	<0.01
Jordanian (581)	649	0.02
Lebanese (2,319)	4,427	0.12
Moroccan (418)	548	0.01
Palestinian (301)	485	0.01
Syrian (507)	1,065	0.03
Other Arab (850)	1,312	0.04
Armenian (553)	967	0.03
Assyrian/Chaldean/Syriac (49)	56	<0.01
Australian (484)	980	0.03
Austrian (972)	3,679	0.10
Basque (104)	251	0.01
Belgian (497)	1,559	0.04
Brazilian (519)	731	0.02
British (6,200)	12,462	0.34
Bulgarian (433)	750	0.02
Cajun (578)	1,293	0.04
Canadian (2,097)	3,818	0.10
Carpatho Rusyn (12)	50	<0.01
Celtic (125)	420	0.01
Croatian (256)	843	0.02
Czech (6,207)	16,698	0.45
Czechoslovakian (1,786)	3,045	0.08
Danish (2,335)	8,389	0.23
Dutch (16,056)	80,729	2.20
Eastern European (469)	697	0.02
English (124,057)	324,282	8.82
Estonian (47)	65	<0.01
European (47,699)	57,453	1.56
Finnish (770)	2,060	0.06
French, ex. Basque (18,515)	89,301	2.43
French Canadian (4,083)	9,274	0.25
German (202,589)	567,850	15.45
German Russian (145)	371	0.01
Greek (2,593)	5,871	0.16
Guyanese (43)	74	<0.01
Hungarian (1,783)	5,046	0.14
Icelander (113)	310	0.01
Iranian (3,009)	3,720	0.10
Irish (141,537)	478,190	13.01
Israeli (184)	254	0.01
Italian (21,893)	62,365	1.70
Latvian (101)	304	0.01
Lithuanian (732)	1,755	0.05
Luxemburger (52)	117	<0.01
Macedonian (84)	93	<0.01
Maltese (84)	134	<0.01
New Zealander (76)	127	<0.01
Northern European (1,040)	1,267	0.03
Norwegian (8,701)	23,782	0.65
Pennsylvania German (867)	1,635	0.04
Polish (9,954)	32,979	0.90
Portuguese (1,537)	3,923	0.11
Romanian (432)	1,033	0.03
Russian (3,581)	10,943	0.30
Scandinavian (1,497)	3,624	0.10
Scotch-Irish (27,640)	68,107	1.85
Scottish (25,164)	71,037	1.93
Serbian (247)	385	0.01
Slavic (276)	655	0.02
Slovak (462)	1,425	0.04
Slovene (92)	336	0.01
Swedish (7,781)	28,013	0.76
Swiss (1,630)	7,635	0.21
Turkish (514)	977	0.03
Ukrainian (1,281)	2,676	0.07
Welsh (5,111)	19,204	0.52
West Indian, ex. Hispanic (6,006)	23,128	0.63
Bahamian (137)	288	0.01
Barbadian (54)	54	<0.01
Belizean (183)	200	0.01
Bermudan (0)	41	<0.01
British West Indian (154)	189	0.01
Dutch West Indian (4,079)	20,181	0.55
Haitian (219)	306	0.01
Jamaican (658)	1,188	0.03
Trinidadian/Tobagonian (96)	150	<0.01
U.S. Virgin Islander (48)	59	<0.01
West Indian (372)	466	0.01
Other West Indian (6)	6	<0.01
Yugoslavian (578)	956	0.03

Hispanic Origin	Population	%
Hispanic or Latino (of any race)	332,007	8.85
Central American, ex. Mexican	15,641	0.42
Costa Rican	413	0.01
Guatemalan	7,960	0.21
Honduran	2,711	0.07
Nicaraguan	470	0.01
Panamanian	1,122	0.03
Salvadoran	2,788	0.07
Other Central American	177	<0.01
Cuban	2,755	0.07
Dominican Republic	727	0.02
Mexican	267,016	7.12
Puerto Rican	12,223	0.33
South American	7,134	0.19
Argentinean	590	0.02
Bolivian	300	0.01
Chilean	289	0.01
Colombian	2,122	0.06
Ecuadorian	474	0.01
Paraguayan	44	<0.01
Peruvian	1,805	0.05
Uruguayan	78	<0.01
Venezuelan	1,352	0.04
Other South American	80	<0.01
Other Hispanic or Latino	26,511	0.71

Race*	Population	%
African-American/Black (277,644)	327,621	8.73
Not Hispanic (272,071)	316,902	8.45
Hispanic (5,573)	10,719	0.29
American Indian/Alaska Native (321,687)	482,760	12.87
Not Hispanic (308,733)	459,178	12.24
Hispanic (12,954)	23,582	0.63
Alaska Athabascan *(Ala. Nat.)* (72)	103	<0.01
Aleut *(Alaska Native)* (102)	168	<0.01
Apache (2,125)	3,576	0.10
Arapaho (669)	961	0.03
Blackfeet (225)	1,325	0.04
Canadian/French Am. Ind. (29)	99	<0.01
Central American Ind. (69)	116	<0.01
Cherokee (114,533)	185,850	4.95
Cheyenne (2,152)	3,157	0.08
Chickasaw (16,826)	27,538	0.73
Chippewa (541)	984	0.03
Choctaw (51,431)	79,006	2.11
Colville (48)	89	<0.01
Comanche (6,413)	8,741	0.23
Cree (51)	132	<0.01
Creek (28,364)	44,170	1.18
Crow (118)	210	0.01
Delaware (1,938)	3,100	0.08
Hopi (64)	137	<0.01
Houma (25)	44	<0.01
Inupiat *(Alaska Native)* (90)	196	0.01
Iroquois (2,398)	3,548	0.09
Kiowa (5,724)	7,711	0.21
Lumbee (79)	137	<0.01
Menominee (30)	51	<0.01
Mexican American Ind. (913)	1,470	0.04
Navajo (1,310)	1,954	0.05
Osage (4,746)	7,586	0.20
Ottawa (411)	637	0.02
Paiute (35)	94	<0.01
Pima (85)	122	<0.01
Potawatomi (5,428)	8,078	0.22
Pueblo (300)	436	0.01
Puget Sound Salish (35)	52	<0.01
Seminole (7,429)	11,493	0.31
Shoshone (109)	198	0.01
Sioux (1,280)	2,352	0.06
South American Ind. (69)	167	<0.01
Spanish American Ind. (72)	109	<0.01
Tlingit-Haida *(Alaska Native)* (70)	122	<0.01
Tohono O'Odham (55)	86	<0.01
Tsimshian *(Alaska Native)* (13)	20	<0.01
Ute (30)	66	<0.01
Yakama (36)	46	<0.01
Yaqui (47)	108	<0.01
Yuman (94)	112	<0.01
Yup'ik *(Alaska Native)* (32)	63	<0.01
Asian (65,076)	84,170	2.24
Not Hispanic (64,154)	81,353	2.17
Hispanic (922)	2,817	0.08
Bangladeshi (562)	630	0.02
Burmese (1,074)	1,146	0.03
Cambodian (373)	504	0.01
Chinese, ex. Taiwanese (8,616)	11,104	0.30
Filipino (5,901)	10,850	0.29
Hmong (3,180)	3,369	0.09
Indian (11,906)	14,078	0.38
Indonesian (371)	527	0.01
Japanese (2,113)	5,580	0.15
Korean (5,949)	9,072	0.24
Laotian (1,183)	1,469	0.04
Malaysian (209)	299	0.01
Nepalese (441)	464	0.01
Pakistani (1,931)	2,236	0.06
Sri Lankan (140)	164	<0.01
Taiwanese (475)	591	0.02
Thai (1,159)	1,943	0.05
Vietnamese (16,258)	18,098	0.48
Hawaii Native/Pacific Islander (4,369)	8,206	0.22
Not Hispanic (3,977)	7,062	0.19
Hispanic (392)	1,144	0.03
Fijian (27)	40	<0.01
Guamanian/Chamorro (924)	1,470	0.04
Marshallese (978)	1,028	0.03
Native Hawaiian (942)	2,766	0.07
Samoan (411)	855	0.02
Tongan (27)	58	<0.01
White (2,706,845)	2,906,285	77.47
Not Hispanic (2,575,381)	2,750,713	73.33
Hispanic (131,464)	155,572	4.15

*Notes: † The Census 2010 population figure is used to calculate the percentages in the Hispanic Origin and Race categories. Ancestry percentages are based on the 2006-2010 American Community Survey population (not shown); ‡ Numbers in parentheses indicate the number of people reporting a single ancestry; * Numbers in parentheses indicate the number of persons reporting this race alone, not in combination with any other race; Please refer to the Explanation of Data for more information.*

Ada

Place Type: City
County: Pontotoc
Population: 16,810†

Ancestry‡	Population	%
African, Sub-Saharan (21)	21	0.13
African (21)	21	0.13
American (1,362)	1,362	8.23
Arab (33)	33	0.20
Lebanese (33)	33	0.20
Belgian (10)	10	0.06
Brazilian (54)	54	0.33
British (24)	48	0.29
Czech (49)	73	0.44
Czechoslovakian (15)	24	0.15
Danish (12)	58	0.35
Dutch (124)	489	2.96
English (488)	1,167	7.05
European (136)	152	0.92
French, ex. Basque (34)	269	1.63
French Canadian (28)	28	0.17
German (679)	2,524	15.26
Hungarian (11)	30	0.18
Irish (876)	2,929	17.71
Italian (78)	148	0.89
Norwegian (35)	147	0.89
Polish (147)	210	1.27
Portuguese (7)	7	0.04
Russian (9)	34	0.21
Scandinavian (0)	10	0.06
Scotch-Irish (177)	322	1.95
Scottish (131)	275	1.66
Slovak (0)	17	0.10
Swedish (0)	101	0.61
Swiss (0)	19	0.11
Welsh (0)	131	0.79
West Indian, ex. Hispanic (58)	436	2.64
Dutch West Indian (58)	436	2.64

Hispanic Origin	Population	%
Hispanic or Latino (of any race)	946	5.63
Central American, ex. Mexican	20	0.12
Honduran	6	0.04
Nicaraguan	2	0.01
Panamanian	8	0.05
Salvadoran	1	0.01
Other Central American	3	0.02
Cuban	8	0.05
Dominican Republic	1	0.01
Mexican	801	4.77
Puerto Rican	30	0.18
South American	22	0.13
Bolivian	1	0.01
Chilean	1	0.01
Colombian	9	0.05
Ecuadorian	4	0.02
Peruvian	4	0.02
Venezuelan	3	0.02
Other Hispanic or Latino	64	0.38

Race*	Population	%
African-American/Black (714)	1,045	6.22
Not Hispanic (691)	1,006	5.98
Hispanic (23)	39	0.23
American Indian/Alaska Native (2,850)	3,925	23.35
Not Hispanic (2,753)	3,771	22.43
Hispanic (97)	154	0.92
Alaska Athabascan *(Ala. Nat.)* (2)	3	0.02
Apache (3)	12	0.07
Arapaho (2)	2	0.01
Blackfeet (0)	6	0.04
Cherokee (187)	372	2.21
Cheyenne (4)	9	0.05
Chickasaw (1,131)	1,568	9.33
Chippewa (5)	6	0.04
Choctaw (681)	1,053	6.26
Comanche (15)	23	0.14
Cree (1)	1	0.01
Creek (150)	227	1.35
Crow (5)	5	0.03
Delaware (1)	2	0.01
Inupiat *(Alaska Native)* (2)	3	0.02
Iroquois (2)	2	0.01
Kiowa (26)	31	0.18
Mexican American Ind. (6)	8	0.05
Navajo (20)	23	0.14
Osage (5)	7	0.04
Ottawa (0)	1	0.01
Potawatomi (28)	38	0.23
Pueblo (1)	1	0.01
Seminole (118)	210	1.25
Shoshone (2)	6	0.04
Sioux (5)	15	0.09
Asian (197)	249	1.48
Not Hispanic (197)	248	1.48
Hispanic (0)	1	0.01
Bangladeshi (4)	4	0.02
Cambodian (9)	9	0.05
Chinese, ex. Taiwanese (34)	37	0.22
Filipino (25)	41	0.24
Hmong (12)	12	0.07
Indian (74)	82	0.49
Japanese (2)	8	0.05
Korean (9)	15	0.09
Malaysian (0)	4	0.02
Nepalese (1)	1	0.01
Pakistani (4)	4	0.02
Sri Lankan (0)	1	0.01
Thai (1)	1	0.01
Vietnamese (9)	11	0.07
Hawaii Native/Pacific Islander (11)	31	0.18
Not Hispanic (11)	31	0.18
Fijian (0)	2	0.01
Guamanian/Chamorro (1)	2	0.01
Native Hawaiian (7)	15	0.09
Samoan (0)	2	0.01
White (11,469)	12,574	74.80
Not Hispanic (11,036)	12,054	71.71
Hispanic (433)	520	3.09

Altus

Place Type: City
County: Jackson
Population: 19,813†

Ancestry‡	Population	%
African, Sub-Saharan (65)	150	0.76
African (65)	150	0.76
Albanian (97)	97	0.49
American (1,189)	1,189	6.01
Arab (34)	69	0.35
Lebanese (34)	69	0.35
Austrian (8)	32	0.16
British (27)	116	0.59
Cajun (6)	30	0.15
Canadian (9)	9	0.05
Czech (56)	80	0.40
Danish (0)	21	0.11
Dutch (150)	286	1.45
English (767)	1,819	9.19
European (96)	114	0.58
French, ex. Basque (109)	470	2.38
French Canadian (25)	50	0.25
German (987)	2,396	12.11
Greek (9)	49	0.25
Hungarian (10)	10	0.05
Iranian (0)	19	0.10
Irish (679)	2,448	12.37
Italian (113)	447	2.26
Lithuanian (19)	56	0.28
Norwegian (91)	136	0.69
Pennsylvania German (11)	11	0.06
Polish (33)	368	1.86
Portuguese (0)	26	0.13
Russian (7)	58	0.29
Scandinavian (0)	11	0.06
Scotch-Irish (339)	654	3.31
Scottish (72)	142	0.72
Slavic (9)	9	0.05
Slovak (11)	11	0.06
Swedish (27)	107	0.54
Swiss (9)	47	0.24
Turkish (12)	12	0.06
Welsh (47)	52	0.26
West Indian, ex. Hispanic (13)	56	0.28
Barbadian (13)	13	0.07
Dutch West Indian (0)	15	0.08
West Indian (0)	28	0.14

Hispanic Origin	Population	%
Hispanic or Latino (of any race)	4,699	23.72
Central American, ex. Mexican	71	0.36
Costa Rican	1	0.01
Guatemalan	11	0.06
Honduran	8	0.04
Nicaraguan	2	0.01
Panamanian	35	0.18
Salvadoran	14	0.07
Cuban	35	0.18
Dominican Republic	8	0.04
Mexican	4,089	20.64
Puerto Rican	107	0.54
South American	21	0.11
Argentinean	3	0.02
Colombian	10	0.05
Ecuadorian	4	0.02
Paraguayan	3	0.02
Venezuelan	1	0.01
Other Hispanic or Latino	368	1.86

Race*	Population	%
African-American/Black (1,895)	2,241	11.31
Not Hispanic (1,833)	2,087	10.53
Hispanic (62)	154	0.78
American Indian/Alaska Native (334)	644	3.25
Not Hispanic (280)	531	2.68
Hispanic (54)	113	0.57
Apache (6)	9	0.05
Blackfeet (1)	13	0.07
Canadian/French Am. Ind. (0)	1	0.01
Cherokee (72)	158	0.80
Cheyenne (2)	7	0.04
Chickasaw (31)	51	0.26
Chippewa (0)	1	0.01
Choctaw (50)	89	0.45
Comanche (7)	8	0.04
Creek (21)	35	0.18
Crow (0)	1	0.01
Houma (0)	1	0.01
Inupiat *(Alaska Native)* (4)	4	0.02
Kiowa (17)	27	0.14
Mexican American Ind. (3)	6	0.03
Navajo (2)	4	0.02
Osage (2)	4	0.02
Pima (1)	1	0.01
Potawatomi (1)	3	0.02
Pueblo (1)	1	0.01
Seminole (3)	6	0.03
Sioux (3)	13	0.07
South American Ind. (0)	5	0.03
Spanish American Ind. (1)	1	0.01
Yaqui (4)	4	0.02
Asian (278)	464	2.34
Not Hispanic (269)	428	2.16
Hispanic (9)	36	0.18
Cambodian (12)	12	0.06
Chinese, ex. Taiwanese (18)	32	0.16
Filipino (94)	177	0.89
Hmong (1)	1	0.01
Indian (10)	15	0.08
Japanese (23)	53	0.27
Korean (32)	55	0.28
Laotian (8)	11	0.06
Pakistani (9)	10	0.05
Thai (19)	38	0.19
Vietnamese (45)	59	0.30
Hawaii Native/Pacific Islander (56)	103	0.52

*Notes: † The Census 2010 population figure is used to calculate the percentages in the Hispanic Origin and Race categories. Ancestry percentages are based on the 2006-2010 American Community Survey population (not shown); ‡ Numbers in parentheses indicate the number of people reporting a single ancestry; * Numbers in parentheses indicate the number of persons reporting this race alone, not in combination with any other race; Please refer to the Explanation of Data for more information.*

Not Hispanic (52)	95	0.48
Hispanic (4)	8	0.04
Guamanian/Chamorro (34)	40	0.20
Marshallese (0)	3	0.02
Native Hawaiian (0)	22	0.11
Samoan (1)	4	0.02
Tongan (1)	1	0.01
White (13,592)	14,410	72.73
Not Hispanic (12,037)	12,572	63.45
Hispanic (1,555)	1,838	9.28

Ardmore

Place Type: City
County: Carter
Population: 24,283†

Ancestry‡	Population	%
African, Sub-Saharan (109)	178	0.74
African (109)	178	0.74
American (6,658)	6,658	27.58
Arab (67)	67	0.28
Palestinian (67)	67	0.28
Austrian (12)	12	0.05
British (32)	75	0.31
Cajun (0)	27	0.11
Canadian (10)	20	0.08
Czech (61)	61	0.25
Czechoslovakian (12)	50	0.21
Danish (0)	10	0.04
Dutch (17)	353	1.46
English (857)	1,792	7.42
European (216)	247	1.02
Finnish (0)	8	0.03
French, ex. Basque (75)	358	1.48
French Canadian (13)	13	0.05
German (504)	1,723	7.14
Hungarian (0)	30	0.12
Iranian (0)	6	0.02
Irish (778)	2,017	8.35
Italian (112)	314	1.30
Luxemburger (7)	7	0.03
New Zealander (24)	24	0.10
Northern European (21)	21	0.09
Norwegian (25)	71	0.29
Polish (41)	179	0.74
Russian (0)	14	0.06
Scandinavian (10)	29	0.12
Scotch-Irish (130)	350	1.45
Scottish (53)	280	1.16
Swedish (9)	50	0.21
Swiss (0)	22	0.09
Welsh (0)	48	0.20
West Indian, ex. Hispanic (120)	200	0.83
Bermudan (0)	41	0.17
Dutch West Indian (21)	60	0.25
Haitian (99)	99	0.41

Hispanic Origin	Population	%
Hispanic or Latino (of any race)	1,800	7.41
Central American, ex. Mexican	84	0.35
Costa Rican	1	<0.01
Guatemalan	2	0.01
Honduran	36	0.15
Nicaraguan	7	0.03
Panamanian	2	0.01
Salvadoran	32	0.13
Other Central American	4	0.02
Cuban	11	0.05
Dominican Republic	6	0.02
Mexican	1,495	6.16
Puerto Rican	27	0.11
South American	20	0.08
Argentinean	2	0.01
Bolivian	1	<0.01
Colombian	10	0.04
Peruvian	5	0.02
Venezuelan	2	0.01
Other Hispanic or Latino	157	0.65

Race*	Population	%
African-American/Black (2,485)	3,121	12.85
Not Hispanic (2,429)	3,022	12.44
Hispanic (56)	99	0.41
American Indian/Alaska Native (2,219)	3,508	14.45
Not Hispanic (2,116)	3,323	13.68
Hispanic (103)	185	0.76
Aleut *(Alaska Native)* (0)	2	0.01
Apache (8)	11	0.05
Blackfeet (5)	11	0.05
Canadian/French Am. Ind. (0)	1	<0.01
Cherokee (117)	263	1.08
Cheyenne (0)	1	<0.01
Chickasaw (746)	1,324	5.45
Chippewa (1)	5	0.02
Choctaw (842)	1,330	5.48
Comanche (3)	11	0.05
Creek (33)	64	0.26
Delaware (2)	3	0.01
Houma (0)	1	<0.01
Inupiat *(Alaska Native)* (3)	3	0.01
Iroquois (1)	6	0.02
Kiowa (14)	24	0.10
Menominee (0)	3	0.01
Mexican American Ind. (8)	9	0.04
Navajo (14)	25	0.10
Osage (19)	21	0.09
Pima (0)	2	0.01
Potawatomi (8)	12	0.05
Seminole (29)	54	0.22
Sioux (1)	14	0.06
Yakama (0)	1	<0.01
Asian (448)	537	2.21
Not Hispanic (448)	520	2.14
Hispanic (0)	17	0.07
Bangladeshi (4)	4	0.02
Cambodian (5)	5	0.02
Chinese, ex. Taiwanese (135)	145	0.60
Filipino (28)	52	0.21
Indian (134)	143	0.59
Japanese (13)	18	0.07
Korean (19)	30	0.12
Laotian (1)	1	<0.01
Malaysian (1)	1	<0.01
Nepalese (14)	14	0.06
Pakistani (14)	14	0.06
Sri Lankan (4)	5	0.02
Taiwanese (1)	1	<0.01
Thai (6)	16	0.07
Vietnamese (66)	73	0.30
Hawaii Native/Pacific Islander (6)	35	0.14
Not Hispanic (5)	24	0.10
Hispanic (1)	11	0.05
Guamanian/Chamorro (1)	1	<0.01
Native Hawaiian (3)	14	0.06
Samoan (1)	2	0.01
White (16,508)	17,925	73.82
Not Hispanic (15,941)	17,183	70.76
Hispanic (567)	742	3.06

Bartlesville

Place Type: City
County: Washington
Population: 35,750†

Ancestry‡	Population	%
African, Sub-Saharan (13)	13	0.04
African (13)	13	0.04
Albanian (0)	13	0.04
American (2,575)	2,575	7.28
Arab (42)	42	0.12
Egyptian (42)	42	0.12
Armenian (9)	9	0.03
Austrian (15)	104	0.29
Belgian (12)	31	0.09
British (78)	219	0.62
Canadian (23)	23	0.06
Croatian (10)	10	0.03
Czech (64)	64	0.18
Czechoslovakian (8)	8	0.02
Danish (13)	35	0.10
Dutch (130)	896	2.53
Eastern European (0)	11	0.03
English (1,557)	4,187	11.83
European (483)	580	1.64
Finnish (0)	16	0.05
French, ex. Basque (156)	1,025	2.90
French Canadian (11)	155	0.44
German (2,239)	6,658	18.81
Greek (40)	40	0.11
Hungarian (61)	127	0.36
Irish (1,641)	5,830	16.47
Italian (127)	542	1.53
Lithuanian (12)	12	0.03
Northern European (55)	55	0.16
Norwegian (131)	270	0.76
Pennsylvania German (40)	51	0.14
Polish (306)	699	1.98
Portuguese (12)	50	0.14
Romanian (7)	7	0.02
Russian (67)	128	0.36
Scandinavian (17)	36	0.10
Scotch-Irish (367)	776	2.19
Scottish (376)	1,207	3.41
Slovak (20)	33	0.09
Swedish (94)	404	1.14
Swiss (11)	45	0.13
Ukrainian (32)	32	0.09
Welsh (42)	221	0.62
West Indian, ex. Hispanic (68)	125	0.35
Dutch West Indian (32)	89	0.25
Jamaican (26)	26	0.07
Trinidadian/Tobagonian (10)	10	0.03

Hispanic Origin	Population	%
Hispanic or Latino (of any race)	2,112	5.91
Central American, ex. Mexican	115	0.32
Costa Rican	12	0.03
Guatemalan	13	0.04
Honduran	39	0.11
Nicaraguan	3	0.01
Panamanian	12	0.03
Salvadoran	36	0.10
Cuban	19	0.05
Dominican Republic	3	0.01
Mexican	1,611	4.51
Puerto Rican	58	0.16
South American	89	0.25
Argentinean	17	0.05
Chilean	1	<0.01
Colombian	22	0.06
Ecuadorian	6	0.02
Peruvian	16	0.04
Venezuelan	27	0.08
Other Hispanic or Latino	217	0.61

Race*	Population	%
African-American/Black (1,123)	1,577	4.41
Not Hispanic (1,092)	1,518	4.25
Hispanic (31)	59	0.17
American Indian/Alaska Native (3,118)	4,649	13.00
Not Hispanic (3,019)	4,422	12.37
Hispanic (99)	227	0.63
Alaska Athabascan *(Ala. Nat.)* (1)	1	<0.01
Aleut *(Alaska Native)* (4)	8	0.02
Apache (12)	25	0.07
Arapaho (0)	2	0.01
Blackfeet (2)	19	0.05
Canadian/French Am. Ind. (3)	3	0.01
Cherokee (1,626)	2,549	7.13
Cheyenne (7)	17	0.05
Chickasaw (36)	58	0.16
Chippewa (7)	10	0.03
Choctaw (112)	190	0.53
Comanche (5)	9	0.03
Cree (0)	2	0.01
Creek (101)	149	0.42
Delaware (171)	255	0.71

*Notes: † The Census 2010 population figure is used to calculate the percentages in the Hispanic Origin and Race categories. Ancestry percentages are based on the 2006-2010 American Community Survey population (not shown); ‡ Numbers in parentheses indicate the number of people reporting a single ancestry; * Numbers in parentheses indicate the number of persons reporting this race alone, not in combination with any other race; Please refer to the Explanation of Data for more information.*

Iroquois (32)	52	0.15
Kiowa (22)	35	0.10
Mexican American Ind. (5)	23	0.06
Navajo (9)	24	0.07
Osage (248)	358	1.00
Ottawa (1)	3	0.01
Potawatomi (41)	53	0.15
Pueblo (2)	2	0.01
Seminole (20)	30	0.08
Sioux (20)	25	0.07
South American Ind. (0)	3	0.01
Spanish American Ind. (4)	5	0.01
Tlingit-Haida *(Alaska Native)* (1)	1	<0.01
Ute (1)	1	<0.01
Asian (497)	642	1.80
Not Hispanic (495)	626	1.75
Hispanic (2)	16	0.04
Burmese (3)	3	0.01
Chinese, ex. Taiwanese (108)	114	0.32
Filipino (52)	88	0.25
Hmong (2)	2	0.01
Indian (159)	178	0.50
Indonesian (6)	9	0.03
Japanese (18)	49	0.14
Korean (44)	52	0.15
Malaysian (3)	6	0.02
Nepalese (1)	2	0.01
Pakistani (20)	20	0.06
Sri Lankan (3)	3	0.01
Taiwanese (1)	1	<0.01
Thai (6)	8	0.02
Vietnamese (63)	67	0.19
Hawaii Native/Pacific Islander (13)	46	0.13
Not Hispanic (13)	40	0.11
Hispanic (0)	6	0.02
Native Hawaiian (11)	35	0.10
Samoan (0)	1	<0.01
Tongan (1)	1	<0.01
White (28,226)	30,076	84.13
Not Hispanic (27,204)	28,851	80.70
Hispanic (1,022)	1,225	3.43

Bethany

Place Type: City
County: Oklahoma
Population: 19,051†

Ancestry‡	Population	%
African, Sub-Saharan (21)	84	0.44
African (0)	40	0.21
Nigerian (9)	9	0.05
Senegalese (12)	12	0.06
South African (0)	23	0.12
American (1,369)	1,369	7.13
Arab (48)	68	0.35
Iraqi (48)	48	0.25
Lebanese (0)	8	0.04
Other Arab (0)	12	0.06
Belgian (0)	6	0.03
British (124)	124	0.65
Canadian (9)	19	0.10
Czech (0)	26	0.14
Danish (0)	13	0.07
Dutch (97)	495	2.58
English (990)	2,202	11.47
European (250)	259	1.35
French, ex. Basque (47)	290	1.51
French Canadian (17)	87	0.45
German (1,344)	3,723	19.39
German Russian (0)	29	0.15
Greek (9)	9	0.05
Hungarian (0)	20	0.10
Iranian (0)	8	0.04
Irish (489)	2,214	11.53
Italian (76)	302	1.57
Lithuanian (29)	29	0.15
Macedonian (60)	60	0.31
Norwegian (188)	327	1.70
Polish (46)	195	1.02
Portuguese (0)	11	0.06
Russian (0)	22	0.11
Scandinavian (0)	9	0.05
Scotch-Irish (246)	572	2.98
Scottish (167)	508	2.65
Swedish (133)	306	1.59
Swiss (17)	138	0.72
Welsh (60)	90	0.47
West Indian, ex. Hispanic (0)	75	0.39
British West Indian (0)	29	0.15
Dutch West Indian (0)	23	0.12
Trinidadian/Tobagonian (0)	23	0.12

Hispanic Origin	Population	%
Hispanic or Latino (of any race)	2,546	13.36
Central American, ex. Mexican	173	0.91
Costa Rican	3	0.02
Guatemalan	90	0.47
Honduran	30	0.16
Nicaraguan	6	0.03
Panamanian	3	0.02
Salvadoran	40	0.21
Other Central American	1	0.01
Cuban	16	0.08
Dominican Republic	2	0.01
Mexican	2,081	10.92
Puerto Rican	64	0.34
South American	36	0.19
Argentinean	5	0.03
Colombian	8	0.04
Ecuadorian	3	0.02
Peruvian	17	0.09
Venezuelan	3	0.02
Other Hispanic or Latino	174	0.91

Race*	Population	%
African-American/Black (1,071)	1,375	7.22
Not Hispanic (1,042)	1,319	6.92
Hispanic (29)	56	0.29
American Indian/Alaska Native (578)	1,079	5.66
Not Hispanic (539)	997	5.23
Hispanic (39)	82	0.43
Aleut *(Alaska Native)* (3)	3	0.02
Apache (6)	15	0.08
Arapaho (3)	6	0.03
Blackfeet (1)	4	0.02
Canadian/French Am. Ind. (0)	2	0.01
Cherokee (72)	210	1.10
Cheyenne (7)	20	0.10
Chickasaw (42)	73	0.38
Chippewa (4)	14	0.07
Choctaw (85)	200	1.05
Comanche (18)	27	0.14
Creek (32)	62	0.33
Crow (0)	2	0.01
Delaware (9)	14	0.07
Iroquois (7)	13	0.07
Kiowa (21)	26	0.14
Mexican American Ind. (2)	3	0.02
Navajo (8)	8	0.04
Osage (12)	16	0.08
Ottawa (2)	4	0.02
Potawatomi (24)	28	0.15
Pueblo (1)	5	0.03
Seminole (25)	40	0.21
Sioux (6)	11	0.06
South American Ind. (0)	1	0.01
Tohono O'Odham (0)	1	0.01
Asian (245)	348	1.83
Not Hispanic (242)	331	1.74
Hispanic (3)	17	0.09
Cambodian (0)	2	0.01
Chinese, ex. Taiwanese (15)	26	0.14
Filipino (39)	76	0.40
Indian (56)	70	0.37
Indonesian (1)	6	0.03
Japanese (8)	18	0.09
Korean (3)	11	0.06
Laotian (7)	8	0.04
Malaysian (2)	3	0.02
Nepalese (1)	1	0.01
Pakistani (5)	5	0.03
Taiwanese (1)	1	0.01
Thai (3)	4	0.02
Vietnamese (95)	105	0.55
Hawaii Native/Pacific Islander (26)	70	0.37
Not Hispanic (19)	56	0.29
Hispanic (7)	14	0.07
Guamanian/Chamorro (12)	17	0.09
Native Hawaiian (6)	34	0.18
Samoan (5)	5	0.03
White (14,792)	15,642	82.11
Not Hispanic (13,883)	14,572	76.49
Hispanic (909)	1,070	5.62

Bixby

Place Type: City
County: Tulsa
Population: 20,884†

Ancestry‡	Population	%
African, Sub-Saharan (7)	14	0.07
South African (7)	14	0.07
American (2,175)	2,175	11.20
Arab (42)	107	0.55
Lebanese (16)	68	0.35
Syrian (26)	39	0.20
Austrian (11)	21	0.11
Belgian (20)	69	0.36
Brazilian (5)	5	0.03
British (0)	83	0.43
Canadian (15)	15	0.08
Croatian (12)	12	0.06
Czech (40)	129	0.66
Czechoslovakian (9)	9	0.05
Danish (13)	65	0.33
Dutch (249)	666	3.43
Eastern European (9)	9	0.05
English (899)	2,264	11.66
European (187)	214	1.10
Finnish (10)	75	0.39
French, ex. Basque (165)	501	2.58
French Canadian (0)	19	0.10
German (1,197)	3,468	17.86
Greek (28)	71	0.37
Hungarian (0)	8	0.04
Iranian (104)	104	0.54
Irish (921)	2,946	15.17
Italian (215)	476	2.45
Lithuanian (0)	19	0.10
Norwegian (74)	149	0.77
Polish (80)	196	1.01
Portuguese (0)	58	0.30
Romanian (14)	14	0.07
Russian (80)	127	0.65
Scandinavian (10)	10	0.05
Scotch-Irish (149)	301	1.55
Scottish (164)	357	1.84
Slavic (25)	25	0.13
Swedish (50)	203	1.05
Swiss (0)	39	0.20
Welsh (20)	127	0.65
West Indian, ex. Hispanic (11)	90	0.46
Dutch West Indian (11)	90	0.46

Hispanic Origin	Population	%
Hispanic or Latino (of any race)	1,033	4.95
Central American, ex. Mexican	41	0.20
Costa Rican	5	0.02
Guatemalan	13	0.06
Honduran	8	0.04
Nicaraguan	3	0.01
Salvadoran	12	0.06
Cuban	22	0.11
Dominican Republic	2	0.01
Mexican	812	3.89
Puerto Rican	36	0.17
South American	29	0.14
Chilean	1	<0.01

*Notes: † The Census 2010 population figure is used to calculate the percentages in the Hispanic Origin and Race categories. Ancestry percentages are based on the 2006-2010 American Community Survey population (not shown); ‡ Numbers in parentheses indicate the number of people reporting a single ancestry; * Numbers in parentheses indicate the number of persons reporting this race alone, not in combination with any other race; Please refer to the Explanation of Data for more information.*

Colombian	8	0.04
Ecuadorian	3	0.01
Peruvian	7	0.03
Venezuelan	10	0.05
Other Hispanic or Latino	91	0.44

Race*	Population	%
African-American/Black (329)	444	2.13
Not Hispanic (326)	436	2.09
Hispanic (3)	8	0.04
American Indian/Alaska Native (1,242)	1,988	9.52
Not Hispanic (1,204)	1,924	9.21
Hispanic (38)	64	0.31
Blackfeet (4)	6	0.03
Canadian/French Am. Ind. (1)	1	<0.01
Cherokee (550)	965	4.62
Cheyenne (2)	3	0.01
Chickasaw (24)	39	0.19
Chippewa (1)	8	0.04
Choctaw (119)	206	0.99
Comanche (10)	10	0.05
Creek (288)	386	1.85
Delaware (5)	8	0.04
Iroquois (22)	27	0.13
Kiowa (6)	10	0.05
Mexican American Ind. (0)	1	<0.01
Navajo (9)	11	0.05
Osage (19)	41	0.20
Potawatomi (17)	27	0.13
Pueblo (1)	1	<0.01
Seminole (10)	21	0.10
Sioux (6)	12	0.06
Spanish American Ind. (2)	2	0.01
Tohono O'Odham (0)	1	<0.01
Asian (341)	488	2.34
Not Hispanic (337)	480	2.30
Hispanic (4)	8	0.04
Bangladeshi (4)	4	0.02
Cambodian (1)	1	<0.01
Chinese, ex. Taiwanese (54)	79	0.38
Filipino (44)	66	0.32
Indian (77)	100	0.48
Indonesian (0)	3	0.01
Japanese (17)	45	0.22
Korean (42)	67	0.32
Laotian (2)	2	0.01
Malaysian (4)	4	0.02
Pakistani (17)	20	0.10
Taiwanese (1)	1	<0.01
Thai (5)	17	0.08
Vietnamese (63)	69	0.33
Hawaii Native/Pacific Islander (1)	10	0.05
Not Hispanic (1)	10	0.05
Native Hawaiian (1)	8	0.04
Samoan (0)	2	0.01
White (17,574)	18,548	88.81
Not Hispanic (17,048)	17,952	85.96
Hispanic (526)	596	2.85

Blanchard

Place Type: City
County: McClain
Population: 7,670†

Ancestry‡	Population	%
American (908)	908	12.57
Australian (0)	59	0.82
Austrian (24)	24	0.33
British (12)	12	0.17
Canadian (0)	13	0.18
Danish (128)	195	2.70
Dutch (37)	189	2.62
English (217)	811	11.23
European (22)	71	0.98
French, ex. Basque (16)	192	2.66
French Canadian (11)	11	0.15
German (452)	1,396	19.33
Hungarian (41)	50	0.69
Irish (628)	1,885	26.10
Italian (26)	26	0.36
Norwegian (0)	26	0.36
Pennsylvania German (0)	35	0.48
Polish (26)	174	2.41
Portuguese (0)	24	0.33
Scotch-Irish (72)	156	2.16
Scottish (74)	140	1.94
Slavic (17)	17	0.24
Swedish (29)	56	0.78
Swiss (0)	11	0.15
Welsh (0)	11	0.15
West Indian, ex. Hispanic (0)	148	2.05
Dutch West Indian (0)	148	2.05

Hispanic Origin	Population	%
Hispanic or Latino (of any race)	298	3.89
Central American, ex. Mexican	9	0.12
Costa Rican	1	0.01
Guatemalan	4	0.05
Honduran	3	0.04
Salvadoran	1	0.01
Cuban	2	0.03
Dominican Republic	4	0.05
Mexican	239	3.12
Puerto Rican	14	0.18
South American	5	0.07
Ecuadorian	1	0.01
Peruvian	1	0.01
Venezuelan	3	0.04
Other Hispanic or Latino	25	0.33

Race*	Population	%
African-American/Black (35)	72	0.94
Not Hispanic (30)	67	0.87
Hispanic (5)	5	0.07
American Indian/Alaska Native (385)	664	8.66
Not Hispanic (371)	637	8.31
Hispanic (14)	27	0.35
Blackfeet (0)	2	0.03
Cherokee (72)	175	2.28
Cheyenne (0)	1	0.01
Chickasaw (59)	90	1.17
Chippewa (1)	1	0.01
Choctaw (118)	188	2.45
Comanche (15)	15	0.20
Creek (26)	55	0.72
Delaware (2)	3	0.04
Kiowa (2)	4	0.05
Mexican American Ind. (1)	3	0.04
Navajo (1)	5	0.07
Osage (1)	1	0.01
Potawatomi (12)	14	0.18
Pueblo (3)	5	0.07
Seminole (3)	8	0.10
South American Ind. (0)	1	0.01
Asian (24)	40	0.52
Not Hispanic (24)	39	0.51
Hispanic (0)	1	0.01
Cambodian (1)	4	0.05
Chinese, ex. Taiwanese (5)	5	0.07
Filipino (3)	4	0.05
Indian (4)	8	0.10
Japanese (1)	11	0.14
Korean (5)	7	0.09
Laotian (1)	2	0.03
Vietnamese (1)	2	0.03
Hawaii Native/Pacific Islander (0)	2	0.03
Not Hispanic (0)	2	0.03
Samoan (0)	1	0.01
White (6,823)	7,171	93.49
Not Hispanic (6,637)	6,946	90.56
Hispanic (186)	225	2.93

Broken Arrow

Place Type: City
County: Tulsa
Population: 98,850†

Ancestry‡	Population	%
African, Sub-Saharan (233)	286	0.30
African (84)	117	0.12
Cape Verdean (0)	20	0.02
Ethiopian (19)	19	0.02
Ghanaian (9)	9	0.01
Nigerian (97)	97	0.10
Other Sub-Saharan African (24)	24	0.03
American (8,737)	8,737	9.22
Arab (78)	191	0.20
Arab (0)	12	0.01
Lebanese (50)	113	0.12
Syrian (28)	57	0.06
Other Arab (0)	9	0.01
Armenian (10)	17	0.02
Australian (7)	7	0.01
Austrian (51)	101	0.11
Basque (0)	6	0.01
Belgian (12)	12	0.01
Brazilian (20)	50	0.05
British (95)	395	0.42
Bulgarian (34)	43	0.05
Cajun (17)	34	0.04
Canadian (191)	335	0.35
Croatian (10)	33	0.03
Czech (94)	381	0.40
Czechoslovakian (10)	39	0.04
Danish (42)	293	0.31
Dutch (521)	2,309	2.44
English (3,894)	10,684	11.28
European (776)	905	0.96
Finnish (35)	67	0.07
French, ex. Basque (512)	2,768	2.92
French Canadian (68)	188	0.20
German (5,724)	15,684	16.55
Greek (81)	250	0.26
Hungarian (104)	305	0.32
Iranian (126)	177	0.19
Irish (3,074)	11,642	12.29
Israeli (0)	14	0.01
Italian (870)	2,481	2.62
Lithuanian (21)	46	0.05
Maltese (5)	16	0.02
Northern European (56)	56	0.06
Norwegian (262)	1,005	1.06
Pennsylvania German (11)	48	0.05
Polish (373)	1,425	1.50
Portuguese (46)	83	0.09
Romanian (17)	96	0.10
Russian (196)	431	0.45
Scandinavian (56)	139	0.15
Scotch-Irish (862)	2,036	2.15
Scottish (801)	2,069	2.18
Serbian (9)	9	0.01
Slavic (0)	19	0.02
Slovak (36)	86	0.09
Slovene (0)	18	0.02
Swedish (257)	1,056	1.11
Swiss (120)	429	0.45
Turkish (74)	85	0.09
Ukrainian (224)	392	0.41
Welsh (160)	599	0.63
West Indian, ex. Hispanic (180)	342	0.36
Belizean (52)	52	0.05
Dutch West Indian (68)	221	0.23
Haitian (19)	19	0.02
Jamaican (41)	50	0.05
Yugoslavian (19)	19	0.02

Hispanic Origin	Population	%
Hispanic or Latino (of any race)	6,378	6.45
Central American, ex. Mexican	293	0.30
Costa Rican	19	0.02
Guatemalan	86	0.09
Honduran	36	0.04
Nicaraguan	35	0.04
Panamanian	25	0.03
Salvadoran	90	0.09
Other Central American	2	<0.01
Cuban	139	0.14

SECTION TWO

*Notes: † The Census 2010 population figure is used to calculate the percentages in the Hispanic Origin and Race categories. Ancestry percentages are based on the 2006-2010 American Community Survey population (not shown); ‡ Numbers in parentheses indicate the number of people reporting a single ancestry; * Numbers in parentheses indicate the number of persons reporting this race alone, not in combination with any other race; Please refer to the Explanation of Data for more information.*

Dominican Republic	29	0.03
Mexican	4,361	4.41
Puerto Rican	417	0.42
South American	514	0.52
Argentinean	21	0.02
Bolivian	12	0.01
Chilean	36	0.04
Colombian	135	0.14
Ecuadorian	30	0.03
Paraguayan	3	<0.01
Peruvian	108	0.11
Uruguayan	21	0.02
Venezuelan	142	0.14
Other South American	6	0.01
Other Hispanic or Latino	625	0.63

Race*	Population	%
African-American/Black (4,282)	5,389	5.45
Not Hispanic (4,169)	5,178	5.24
Hispanic (113)	211	0.21
American Indian/Alaska Native (5,097)	8,786	8.89
Not Hispanic (4,882)	8,336	8.43
Hispanic (215)	450	0.46
Alaska Athabascan *(Ala. Nat.)* (1)	1	<0.01
Aleut *(Alaska Native)* (2)	4	<0.01
Apache (12)	47	0.05
Arapaho (5)	5	0.01
Blackfeet (10)	41	0.04
Canadian/French Am. Ind. (0)	1	<0.01
Central American Ind. (0)	3	<0.01
Cherokee (2,443)	4,505	4.56
Cheyenne (16)	19	0.02
Chickasaw (120)	212	0.21
Chippewa (9)	23	0.02
Choctaw (459)	804	0.81
Colville (1)	1	<0.01
Comanche (23)	44	0.04
Creek (767)	1,259	1.27
Crow (3)	8	0.01
Delaware (31)	51	0.05
Hopi (0)	1	<0.01
Houma (1)	1	<0.01
Inupiat *(Alaska Native)* (1)	4	<0.01
Iroquois (61)	85	0.09
Kiowa (11)	20	0.02
Lumbee (1)	1	<0.01
Mexican American Ind. (22)	28	0.03
Navajo (26)	38	0.04
Osage (106)	205	0.21
Ottawa (13)	31	0.03
Paiute (0)	4	<0.01
Pima (1)	1	<0.01
Potawatomi (42)	89	0.09
Pueblo (10)	12	0.01
Puget Sound Salish (0)	3	<0.01
Seminole (53)	72	0.07
Shoshone (1)	5	0.01
Sioux (23)	60	0.06
South American Ind. (1)	4	<0.01
Tlingit-Haida *(Alaska Native)* (2)	2	<0.01
Tsimshian *(Alaska Native)* (4)	4	<0.01
Yaqui (4)	4	<0.01
Asian (3,585)	4,332	4.38
Not Hispanic (3,568)	4,278	4.33
Hispanic (17)	54	0.05
Bangladeshi (44)	45	0.05
Burmese (4)	5	0.01
Cambodian (25)	47	0.05
Chinese, ex. Taiwanese (374)	476	0.48
Filipino (233)	437	0.44
Hmong (313)	322	0.33
Indian (705)	788	0.80
Indonesian (17)	34	0.03
Japanese (54)	162	0.16
Korean (305)	432	0.44
Laotian (30)	42	0.04
Malaysian (6)	18	0.02
Nepalese (2)	2	<0.01
Pakistani (243)	266	0.27
Sri Lankan (10)	12	0.01
Taiwanese (7)	8	0.01
Thai (23)	48	0.05
Vietnamese (1,021)	1,111	1.12
Hawaii Native/Pacific Islander (48)	143	0.14
Not Hispanic (42)	129	0.13
Hispanic (6)	14	0.01
Guamanian/Chamorro (5)	16	0.02
Native Hawaiian (20)	68	0.07
Samoan (10)	13	0.01
Tongan (1)	1	<0.01
White (78,345)	83,250	84.22
Not Hispanic (75,008)	79,384	80.31
Hispanic (3,337)	3,866	3.91

Chickasha

Place Type: City
County: Grady
Population: 16,036†

Ancestry‡	Population	%
American (1,905)	1,905	11.76
Austrian (0)	12	0.07
Belgian (0)	11	0.07
British (11)	11	0.07
Czech (10)	37	0.23
Czechoslovakian (0)	13	0.08
Danish (8)	28	0.17
Dutch (137)	652	4.03
English (533)	1,074	6.63
European (100)	100	0.62
French, ex. Basque (144)	417	2.57
French Canadian (32)	41	0.25
German (977)	2,812	17.36
Irish (1,184)	2,771	17.11
Italian (128)	276	1.70
Lithuanian (9)	21	0.13
Norwegian (101)	229	1.41
Polish (7)	69	0.43
Portuguese (52)	52	0.32
Russian (12)	50	0.31
Scotch-Irish (73)	210	1.30
Scottish (47)	242	1.49
Slovak (9)	9	0.06
Swedish (29)	134	0.83
Swiss (0)	24	0.15
Ukrainian (0)	31	0.19
Welsh (77)	108	0.67
West Indian, ex. Hispanic (8)	303	1.87
Dutch West Indian (8)	303	1.87

Hispanic Origin	Population	%
Hispanic or Latino (of any race)	1,037	6.47
Central American, ex. Mexican	9	0.06
Guatemalan	1	0.01
Honduran	1	0.01
Salvadoran	7	0.04
Cuban	2	0.01
Mexican	903	5.63
Puerto Rican	30	0.19
South American	6	0.04
Argentinean	1	0.01
Peruvian	2	0.01
Venezuelan	3	0.02
Other Hispanic or Latino	87	0.54

Race*	Population	%
African-American/Black (1,141)	1,359	8.47
Not Hispanic (1,126)	1,329	8.29
Hispanic (15)	30	0.19
American Indian/Alaska Native (774)	1,382	8.62
Not Hispanic (680)	1,242	7.75
Hispanic (94)	140	0.87
Aleut *(Alaska Native)* (2)	2	0.01
Apache (33)	41	0.26
Arapaho (2)	2	0.01
Blackfeet (2)	10	0.06
Cherokee (113)	235	1.47
Cheyenne (2)	2	0.01
Chickasaw (61)	123	0.77
Chippewa (2)	7	0.04
Choctaw (177)	332	2.07
Comanche (53)	88	0.55
Creek (20)	39	0.24
Crow (1)	1	0.01
Delaware (22)	34	0.21
Inupiat *(Alaska Native)* (1)	1	0.01
Iroquois (1)	2	0.01
Kiowa (64)	100	0.62
Mexican American Ind. (6)	6	0.04
Navajo (1)	2	0.01
Osage (0)	5	0.03
Ottawa (0)	2	0.01
Pima (2)	2	0.01
Potawatomi (16)	28	0.17
Seminole (9)	15	0.09
Shoshone (3)	3	0.02
Sioux (3)	8	0.05
Tlingit-Haida *(Alaska Native)* (0)	2	0.01
Yuman (4)	4	0.02
Yup'ik *(Alaska Native)* (1)	3	0.02
Asian (85)	138	0.86
Not Hispanic (81)	128	0.80
Hispanic (4)	10	0.06
Chinese, ex. Taiwanese (31)	37	0.23
Filipino (5)	17	0.11
Indian (19)	25	0.16
Japanese (6)	11	0.07
Korean (12)	29	0.18
Laotian (6)	6	0.04
Pakistani (1)	1	0.01
Taiwanese (2)	2	0.01
Thai (1)	3	0.02
Vietnamese (2)	6	0.04
Hawaii Native/Pacific Islander (11)	26	0.16
Not Hispanic (8)	15	0.09
Hispanic (3)	11	0.07
Guamanian/Chamorro (1)	5	0.03
Native Hawaiian (10)	16	0.10
Samoan (0)	3	0.02
White (12,832)	13,638	85.05
Not Hispanic (12,363)	13,040	81.32
Hispanic (469)	598	3.73

Choctaw

Place Type: City
County: Oklahoma
Population: 11,146†

Ancestry‡	Population	%
American (1,719)	1,719	15.94
Armenian (18)	18	0.17
Austrian (25)	25	0.23
British (11)	33	0.31
Canadian (0)	32	0.30
Czech (14)	113	1.05
Czechoslovakian (0)	23	0.21
Dutch (18)	292	2.71
English (377)	879	8.15
European (67)	97	0.90
French, ex. Basque (41)	276	2.56
French Canadian (13)	13	0.12
German (886)	2,361	21.90
Greek (49)	49	0.45
Irish (507)	1,272	11.80
Italian (148)	248	2.30
Norwegian (43)	52	0.48
Polish (70)	236	2.19
Portuguese (40)	40	0.37
Russian (19)	39	0.36
Scotch-Irish (110)	255	2.37
Scottish (120)	279	2.59
Slovene (14)	59	0.55
Swedish (9)	9	0.08
Swiss (0)	11	0.10
Ukrainian (24)	109	1.01
Welsh (13)	115	1.07
West Indian, ex. Hispanic (0)	9	0.08
Dutch West Indian (0)	9	0.08

*Notes: † The Census 2010 population figure is used to calculate the percentages in the Hispanic Origin and Race categories. Ancestry percentages are based on the 2006-2010 American Community Survey population (not shown); ‡ Numbers in parentheses indicate the number of people reporting a single ancestry; * Numbers in parentheses indicate the number of persons reporting this race alone, not in combination with any other race; Please refer to the Explanation of Data for more information.*

Hispanic Origin	Population	%
Hispanic or Latino (of any race)	412	3.70
Central American, ex. Mexican	12	0.11
Costa Rican	3	0.03
Guatemalan	1	0.01
Panamanian	4	0.04
Salvadoran	4	0.04
Dominican Republic	1	0.01
Mexican	292	2.62
Puerto Rican	35	0.31
South American	5	0.04
Bolivian	1	0.01
Chilean	1	0.01
Colombian	1	0.01
Peruvian	2	0.02
Other Hispanic or Latino	67	0.60

Race*	Population	%
African-American/Black (267)	389	3.49
Not Hispanic (257)	372	3.34
Hispanic (10)	17	0.15
American Indian/Alaska Native (534)	994	8.92
Not Hispanic (514)	959	8.60
Hispanic (20)	35	0.31
Apache (5)	9	0.08
Blackfeet (2)	5	0.04
Cherokee (113)	303	2.72
Cheyenne (3)	3	0.03
Chickasaw (61)	96	0.86
Chippewa (1)	1	0.01
Choctaw (140)	228	2.05
Comanche (1)	1	0.01
Creek (43)	73	0.65
Crow (0)	1	0.01
Delaware (8)	9	0.08
Inupiat *(Alaska Native)* (2)	2	0.02
Iroquois (0)	2	0.02
Kiowa (0)	2	0.02
Lumbee (3)	5	0.04
Navajo (1)	6	0.05
Osage (5)	6	0.05
Potawatomi (31)	72	0.65
Seminole (29)	39	0.35
Asian (77)	185	1.66
Not Hispanic (76)	174	1.56
Hispanic (1)	11	0.10
Chinese, ex. Taiwanese (9)	26	0.23
Filipino (15)	64	0.57
Indian (4)	7	0.06
Japanese (7)	22	0.20
Korean (17)	36	0.32
Pakistani (8)	10	0.09
Sri Lankan (1)	3	0.03
Taiwanese (3)	6	0.05
Thai (5)	9	0.08
Vietnamese (8)	10	0.09
Hawaii Native/Pacific Islander (11)	26	0.23
Not Hispanic (11)	26	0.23
Guamanian/Chamorro (3)	5	0.04
Native Hawaiian (7)	15	0.13
White (9,485)	10,137	90.95
Not Hispanic (9,238)	9,841	88.29
Hispanic (247)	296	2.66

Claremore

Place Type: City
County: Rogers
Population: 18,581†

Ancestry‡	Population	%
American (1,963)	1,963	10.66
Arab (0)	12	0.07
Lebanese (0)	12	0.07
Austrian (16)	25	0.14
Belgian (0)	22	0.12
British (61)	91	0.49
Croatian (0)	9	0.05
Czech (0)	50	0.27
Danish (13)	35	0.19
Dutch (159)	513	2.79
English (390)	1,376	7.47
European (127)	192	1.04
Finnish (36)	36	0.20
French, ex. Basque (41)	349	1.90
German (1,197)	2,807	15.24
Greek (38)	68	0.37
Irish (839)	2,505	13.60
Italian (124)	349	1.90
Norwegian (28)	172	0.93
Polish (40)	105	0.57
Portuguese (0)	11	0.06
Scandinavian (0)	13	0.07
Scotch-Irish (61)	173	0.94
Scottish (103)	284	1.54
Swedish (43)	180	0.98
Welsh (0)	50	0.27
West Indian, ex. Hispanic (0)	31	0.17
Dutch West Indian (0)	31	0.17

Hispanic Origin	Population	%
Hispanic or Latino (of any race)	926	4.98
Central American, ex. Mexican	35	0.19
Costa Rican	2	0.01
Guatemalan	12	0.06
Honduran	8	0.04
Nicaraguan	3	0.02
Panamanian	3	0.02
Salvadoran	7	0.04
Cuban	4	0.02
Dominican Republic	19	0.10
Mexican	654	3.52
Puerto Rican	96	0.52
South American	36	0.19
Argentinean	3	0.02
Bolivian	1	0.01
Chilean	1	0.01
Colombian	8	0.04
Ecuadorian	4	0.02
Paraguayan	3	0.02
Peruvian	16	0.09
Other Hispanic or Latino	82	0.44

Race*	Population	%
African-American/Black (393)	577	3.11
Not Hispanic (374)	536	2.88
Hispanic (19)	41	0.22
American Indian/Alaska Native (2,953)	4,334	23.32
Not Hispanic (2,913)	4,241	22.82
Hispanic (40)	93	0.50
Aleut *(Alaska Native)* (0)	3	0.02
Apache (7)	13	0.07
Arapaho (6)	7	0.04
Blackfeet (2)	7	0.04
Cherokee (1,977)	3,042	16.37
Cheyenne (0)	3	0.02
Chickasaw (33)	48	0.26
Chippewa (2)	3	0.02
Choctaw (138)	222	1.19
Comanche (17)	20	0.11
Creek (196)	262	1.41
Delaware (35)	52	0.28
Hopi (1)	1	0.01
Iroquois (23)	37	0.20
Kiowa (27)	37	0.20
Lumbee (0)	2	0.01
Mexican American Ind. (0)	3	0.02
Navajo (3)	6	0.03
Osage (45)	61	0.33
Ottawa (8)	8	0.04
Paiute (1)	1	0.01
Potawatomi (22)	26	0.14
Pueblo (1)	1	0.01
Seminole (25)	41	0.22
Shoshone (1)	2	0.01
Sioux (10)	27	0.15
South American Ind. (0)	3	0.02
Yakama (2)	2	0.01
Asian (114)	175	0.94
Not Hispanic (111)	168	0.90
Hispanic (3)	7	0.04
Bangladeshi (9)	9	0.05
Chinese, ex. Taiwanese (27)	31	0.17
Filipino (20)	48	0.26
Hmong (1)	1	0.01
Indian (18)	22	0.12
Indonesian (1)	1	0.01
Japanese (8)	21	0.11
Korean (9)	17	0.09
Thai (1)	3	0.02
Vietnamese (16)	18	0.10
Hawaii Native/Pacific Islander (12)	38	0.20
Not Hispanic (12)	34	0.18
Hispanic (0)	4	0.02
Guamanian/Chamorro (2)	10	0.05
Native Hawaiian (4)	13	0.07
Samoan (4)	9	0.05
White (13,203)	14,718	79.21
Not Hispanic (12,760)	14,170	76.26
Hispanic (443)	548	2.95

Clinton

Place Type: City
County: Custer
Population: 9,033†

Ancestry‡	Population	%
American (568)	568	6.40
Arab (15)	15	0.17
Egyptian (15)	15	0.17
Canadian (0)	12	0.14
Czech (22)	30	0.34
Dutch (12)	79	0.89
English (228)	645	7.27
European (92)	92	1.04
French, ex. Basque (15)	101	1.14
French Canadian (0)	38	0.43
German (412)	1,008	11.36
Irish (245)	582	6.56
Italian (22)	218	2.46
Norwegian (27)	109	1.23
Polish (26)	48	0.54
Russian (0)	22	0.25
Scotch-Irish (77)	151	1.70
Scottish (15)	78	0.88
Swedish (10)	22	0.25
West Indian, ex. Hispanic (0)	147	1.66
Dutch West Indian (0)	147	1.66

Hispanic Origin	Population	%
Hispanic or Latino (of any race)	2,512	27.81
Central American, ex. Mexican	51	0.56
Guatemalan	42	0.46
Salvadoran	9	0.10
Cuban	1	0.01
Mexican	2,278	25.22
Puerto Rican	23	0.25
South American	5	0.06
Argentinean	4	0.04
Colombian	1	0.01
Other Hispanic or Latino	154	1.70

Race*	Population	%
African-American/Black (464)	567	6.28
Not Hispanic (439)	532	5.89
Hispanic (25)	35	0.39
American Indian/Alaska Native (639)	857	9.49
Not Hispanic (594)	761	8.42
Hispanic (45)	96	1.06
Apache (1)	10	0.11
Arapaho (25)	27	0.30
Central American Ind. (0)	3	0.03
Cherokee (49)	81	0.90
Cheyenne (160)	202	2.24
Chickasaw (8)	13	0.14
Chippewa (1)	1	0.01
Choctaw (34)	52	0.58
Comanche (8)	13	0.14
Creek (23)	67	0.74

*Notes: † The Census 2010 population figure is used to calculate the percentages in the Hispanic Origin and Race categories. Ancestry percentages are based on the 2006-2010 American Community Survey population (not shown); ‡ Numbers in parentheses indicate the number of people reporting a single ancestry; * Numbers in parentheses indicate the number of persons reporting this race alone, not in combination with any other race; Please refer to the Explanation of Data for more information.*

Delaware (5)	5	0.06
Iroquois (3)	6	0.07
Kiowa (15)	24	0.27
Mexican American Ind. (5)	10	0.11
Navajo (14)	21	0.23
Osage (3)	5	0.06
Paiute (1)	1	0.01
Potawatomi (3)	10	0.11
Pueblo (2)	10	0.11
Seminole (7)	11	0.12
Sioux (5)	6	0.07
Spanish American Ind. (3)	3	0.03
Asian (71)	87	0.96
Not Hispanic (70)	86	0.95
Hispanic (1)	1	0.01
Chinese, ex. Taiwanese (16)	18	0.20
Filipino (5)	11	0.12
Indian (11)	13	0.14
Korean (6)	11	0.12
Thai (3)	3	0.03
Vietnamese (28)	31	0.34
Hawaii Native/Pacific Islander (5)	13	0.14
Not Hispanic (1)	5	0.06
Hispanic (4)	8	0.09
Guamanian/Chamorro (1)	1	0.01
Native Hawaiian (3)	8	0.09
Samoan (0)	1	0.01
White (5,932)	6,255	69.25
Not Hispanic (5,189)	5,353	59.26
Hispanic (743)	902	9.99

Coweta

Place Type: City
County: Wagoner
Population: 9,943†

Ancestry‡	Population	%
American (749)	749	7.86
Armenian (0)	24	0.25
Australian (0)	13	0.14
British (14)	14	0.15
Cajun (14)	14	0.15
Celtic (0)	10	0.10
Czech (0)	9	0.09
Danish (9)	9	0.09
Dutch (69)	223	2.34
English (520)	837	8.79
European (29)	29	0.30
French, ex. Basque (40)	193	2.03
German (388)	1,064	11.17
Greek (0)	36	0.38
Irish (263)	1,236	12.98
Italian (13)	79	0.83
Norwegian (27)	71	0.75
Polish (17)	68	0.71
Portuguese (0)	14	0.15
Russian (15)	20	0.21
Scandinavian (6)	21	0.22
Scotch-Irish (11)	119	1.25
Scottish (23)	149	1.56
Slovak (0)	13	0.14
Swedish (0)	113	1.19
Turkish (0)	25	0.26
West Indian, ex. Hispanic (0)	32	0.34
Dutch West Indian (0)	32	0.34

Hispanic Origin	Population	%
Hispanic or Latino (of any race)	407	4.09
Central American, ex. Mexican	18	0.18
Guatemalan	1	0.01
Honduran	12	0.12
Nicaraguan	2	0.02
Panamanian	1	0.01
Salvadoran	2	0.02
Cuban	4	0.04
Mexican	331	3.33
Puerto Rican	13	0.13
South American	6	0.06
Argentinean	3	0.03
Colombian	3	0.03
Other Hispanic or Latino	35	0.35

Race*	Population	%
African-American/Black (346)	478	4.81
Not Hispanic (345)	472	4.75
Hispanic (1)	6	0.06
American Indian/Alaska Native (1,102)	1,788	17.98
Not Hispanic (1,088)	1,744	17.54
Hispanic (14)	44	0.44
Aleut *(Alaska Native)* (0)	6	0.06
Apache (2)	12	0.12
Blackfeet (0)	2	0.02
Canadian/French Am. Ind. (0)	1	0.01
Cherokee (478)	873	8.78
Cheyenne (1)	1	0.01
Chickasaw (6)	14	0.14
Chippewa (1)	3	0.03
Choctaw (88)	140	1.41
Comanche (1)	2	0.02
Cree (3)	3	0.03
Creek (314)	490	4.93
Delaware (3)	4	0.04
Houma (3)	3	0.03
Iroquois (6)	8	0.08
Kiowa (6)	13	0.13
Lumbee (0)	1	0.01
Navajo (6)	6	0.06
Osage (19)	25	0.25
Paiute (3)	3	0.03
Potawatomi (16)	18	0.18
Pueblo (1)	4	0.04
Seminole (14)	18	0.18
Shoshone (4)	8	0.08
Sioux (1)	2	0.02
Yuman (1)	1	0.01
Asian (82)	117	1.18
Not Hispanic (81)	114	1.15
Hispanic (1)	3	0.03
Cambodian (0)	3	0.03
Chinese, ex. Taiwanese (8)	10	0.10
Filipino (22)	32	0.32
Hmong (24)	24	0.24
Indian (7)	13	0.13
Japanese (2)	13	0.13
Korean (4)	5	0.05
Laotian (2)	2	0.02
Nepalese (2)	2	0.02
Sri Lankan (2)	2	0.02
Taiwanese (1)	1	0.01
Thai (1)	1	0.01
Hawaii Native/Pacific Islander (9)	14	0.14
Not Hispanic (9)	13	0.13
Hispanic (0)	1	0.01
Guamanian/Chamorro (1)	3	0.03
Native Hawaiian (8)	10	0.10
Samoan (0)	2	0.02
White (7,469)	8,208	82.55
Not Hispanic (7,261)	7,963	80.09
Hispanic (208)	245	2.46

Cushing

Place Type: City
County: Payne
Population: 7,826†

Ancestry‡	Population	%
American (747)	747	9.62
Arab (0)	31	0.40
Lebanese (0)	31	0.40
Belgian (13)	13	0.17
Czech (0)	17	0.22
Czechoslovakian (0)	48	0.62
Dutch (15)	38	0.49
English (253)	625	8.05
French, ex. Basque (0)	359	4.62
French Canadian (50)	50	0.64
German (530)	1,879	24.19
Irish (398)	1,290	16.61
Italian (36)	69	0.89
Norwegian (0)	42	0.54
Polish (13)	79	1.02
Portuguese (10)	10	0.13
Russian (17)	79	1.02
Scotch-Irish (51)	193	2.48
Scottish (10)	127	1.64
Swedish (0)	17	0.22
Welsh (0)	57	0.73
West Indian, ex. Hispanic (15)	29	0.37
Dutch West Indian (15)	29	0.37

Hispanic Origin	Population	%
Hispanic or Latino (of any race)	388	4.96
Central American, ex. Mexican	8	0.10
Honduran	1	0.01
Panamanian	6	0.08
Salvadoran	1	0.01
Cuban	1	0.01
Mexican	318	4.06
Puerto Rican	9	0.12
South American	12	0.15
Colombian	2	0.03
Ecuadorian	3	0.04
Peruvian	7	0.09
Other Hispanic or Latino	40	0.51

Race*	Population	%
African-American/Black (416)	480	6.13
Not Hispanic (413)	473	6.04
Hispanic (3)	7	0.09
American Indian/Alaska Native (566)	968	12.37
Not Hispanic (531)	895	11.44
Hispanic (35)	73	0.93
Alaska Athabascan *(Ala. Nat.)* (1)	1	0.01
Apache (3)	17	0.22
Arapaho (3)	5	0.06
Blackfeet (0)	4	0.05
Cherokee (142)	291	3.72
Cheyenne (0)	2	0.03
Chickasaw (18)	45	0.58
Chippewa (0)	1	0.01
Choctaw (33)	91	1.16
Comanche (10)	11	0.14
Cree (0)	2	0.03
Creek (59)	84	1.07
Crow (0)	1	0.01
Delaware (3)	4	0.05
Houma (0)	2	0.03
Inupiat *(Alaska Native)* (1)	4	0.05
Iroquois (1)	4	0.05
Kiowa (7)	18	0.23
Mexican American Ind. (6)	7	0.09
Navajo (7)	8	0.10
Osage (15)	16	0.20
Ottawa (0)	2	0.03
Potawatomi (6)	7	0.09
Pueblo (1)	1	0.01
Seminole (2)	3	0.04
Sioux (12)	19	0.24
Tohono O'Odham (0)	1	0.01
Asian (32)	68	0.87
Not Hispanic (30)	58	0.74
Hispanic (2)	10	0.13
Chinese, ex. Taiwanese (10)	15	0.19
Filipino (8)	17	0.22
Indian (3)	6	0.08
Japanese (1)	7	0.09
Korean (1)	13	0.17
Thai (0)	3	0.04
Vietnamese (5)	5	0.06
Hawaii Native/Pacific Islander (4)	9	0.12
Not Hispanic (3)	7	0.09
Hispanic (1)	2	0.03
Fijian (1)	3	0.04
Guamanian/Chamorro (2)	3	0.04
Native Hawaiian (1)	2	0.03
Samoan (0)	1	0.01
White (6,193)	6,699	85.60
Not Hispanic (6,007)	6,450	82.42

*Notes: † The Census 2010 population figure is used to calculate the percentages in the Hispanic Origin and Race categories. Ancestry percentages are based on the 2006-2010 American Community Survey population (not shown); ‡ Numbers in parentheses indicate the number of people reporting a single ancestry; * Numbers in parentheses indicate the number of persons reporting this race alone, not in combination with any other race; Please refer to the Explanation of Data for more information.*

Hispanic (186)	249	3.18

Del City

Place Type: City
County: Oklahoma
Population: 21,332†

Ancestry‡	Population	%
African, Sub-Saharan (11)	23	0.11
African (11)	23	0.11
American (1,549)	1,549	7.25
Arab (20)	36	0.17
Arab (0)	10	0.05
Lebanese (20)	26	0.12
Armenian (11)	11	0.05
Australian (37)	37	0.17
Austrian (0)	9	0.04
British (0)	11	0.05
Cajun (10)	33	0.15
Canadian (26)	49	0.23
Czech (52)	99	0.46
Czechoslovakian (27)	27	0.13
Danish (10)	30	0.14
Dutch (72)	223	1.04
English (492)	1,688	7.90
European (400)	425	1.99
French, ex. Basque (44)	410	1.92
French Canadian (0)	29	0.14
German (886)	2,481	11.60
Hungarian (0)	23	0.11
Iranian (0)	18	0.08
Irish (594)	1,979	9.26
Italian (120)	283	1.32
Lithuanian (0)	10	0.05
Norwegian (0)	31	0.14
Pennsylvania German (0)	7	0.03
Polish (72)	273	1.28
Portuguese (0)	16	0.07
Russian (10)	46	0.22
Scotch-Irish (131)	348	1.63
Scottish (45)	261	1.22
Swedish (0)	34	0.16
Swiss (0)	31	0.14
Welsh (0)	30	0.14
West Indian, ex. Hispanic (29)	111	0.52
Dutch West Indian (29)	106	0.50
Jamaican (0)	5	0.02

Hispanic Origin	Population	%
Hispanic or Latino (of any race)	1,544	7.24
Central American, ex. Mexican	45	0.21
Costa Rican	1	<0.01
Guatemalan	7	0.03
Honduran	12	0.06
Nicaraguan	5	0.02
Panamanian	10	0.05
Salvadoran	8	0.04
Other Central American	2	0.01
Cuban	24	0.11
Dominican Republic	4	0.02
Mexican	1,214	5.69
Puerto Rican	123	0.58
South American	32	0.15
Argentinean	7	0.03
Bolivian	2	0.01
Colombian	10	0.05
Ecuadorian	1	<0.01
Paraguayan	3	0.01
Peruvian	6	0.03
Venezuelan	3	0.01
Other Hispanic or Latino	102	0.48

Race*	Population	%
African-American/Black (3,773)	4,485	21.02
Not Hispanic (3,708)	4,332	20.31
Hispanic (65)	153	0.72
American Indian/Alaska Native (909)	1,824	8.55
Not Hispanic (868)	1,692	7.93
Hispanic (41)	132	0.62
Apache (7)	20	0.09
Arapaho (0)	5	0.02
Blackfeet (1)	14	0.07
Canadian/French Am. Ind. (1)	1	<0.01
Cherokee (109)	339	1.59
Cheyenne (18)	30	0.14
Chickasaw (65)	114	0.53
Chippewa (8)	13	0.06
Choctaw (176)	313	1.47
Colville (0)	2	0.01
Comanche (10)	16	0.08
Cree (0)	1	<0.01
Creek (137)	247	1.16
Delaware (5)	11	0.05
Hopi (1)	1	<0.01
Inupiat *(Alaska Native)* (4)	11	0.05
Iroquois (0)	11	0.05
Kiowa (24)	42	0.20
Mexican American Ind. (1)	8	0.04
Navajo (7)	10	0.05
Osage (3)	11	0.05
Ottawa (0)	6	0.03
Potawatomi (27)	33	0.15
Pueblo (1)	4	0.02
Seminole (46)	110	0.52
Sioux (2)	3	0.01
South American Ind. (0)	2	0.01
Tlingit-Haida *(Alaska Native)* (1)	1	<0.01
Yaqui (1)	2	0.01
Asian (339)	602	2.82
Not Hispanic (331)	571	2.68
Hispanic (8)	31	0.15
Cambodian (2)	2	0.01
Chinese, ex. Taiwanese (29)	60	0.28
Filipino (76)	151	0.71
Hmong (0)	1	<0.01
Indian (9)	20	0.09
Japanese (28)	100	0.47
Korean (48)	89	0.42
Laotian (1)	1	<0.01
Malaysian (1)	1	<0.01
Pakistani (4)	5	0.02
Thai (27)	41	0.19
Vietnamese (106)	110	0.52
Hawaii Native/Pacific Islander (42)	82	0.38
Not Hispanic (40)	77	0.36
Hispanic (2)	5	0.02
Guamanian/Chamorro (29)	32	0.15
Marshallese (2)	2	0.01
Native Hawaiian (5)	21	0.10
Samoan (0)	5	0.02
Tongan (1)	2	0.01
White (14,156)	15,500	72.66
Not Hispanic (13,419)	14,595	68.42
Hispanic (737)	905	4.24

Duncan

Place Type: City
County: Stephens
Population: 23,431†

Ancestry‡	Population	%
American (4,167)	4,167	17.99
British (73)	73	0.32
Canadian (0)	22	0.10
Czech (24)	124	0.54
Czechoslovakian (13)	33	0.14
Danish (0)	52	0.22
Dutch (179)	541	2.34
Eastern European (30)	30	0.13
English (801)	2,096	9.05
European (61)	78	0.34
French, ex. Basque (52)	315	1.36
French Canadian (36)	36	0.16
German (1,190)	3,209	13.86
German Russian (29)	29	0.13
Greek (9)	9	0.04
Hungarian (20)	20	0.09
Irish (1,415)	3,963	17.11
Italian (132)	271	1.17
Norwegian (57)	110	0.48
Polish (82)	139	0.60
Portuguese (32)	42	0.18
Russian (43)	63	0.27
Scandinavian (36)	40	0.17
Scotch-Irish (165)	309	1.33
Scottish (264)	559	2.41
Swedish (97)	182	0.79
Swiss (0)	9	0.04
Welsh (0)	12	0.05
West Indian, ex. Hispanic (20)	117	0.51
Dutch West Indian (20)	111	0.48
West Indian (0)	6	0.03

Hispanic Origin	Population	%
Hispanic or Latino (of any race)	2,085	8.90
Central American, ex. Mexican	49	0.21
Guatemalan	10	0.04
Honduran	28	0.12
Panamanian	4	0.02
Salvadoran	7	0.03
Cuban	14	0.06
Dominican Republic	4	0.02
Mexican	1,687	7.20
Puerto Rican	62	0.26
South American	44	0.19
Argentinean	1	<0.01
Bolivian	1	<0.01
Colombian	4	0.02
Ecuadorian	5	0.02
Peruvian	13	0.06
Venezuelan	15	0.06
Other South American	5	0.02
Other Hispanic or Latino	225	0.96

Race*	Population	%
African-American/Black (780)	1,077	4.60
Not Hispanic (757)	1,010	4.31
Hispanic (23)	67	0.29
American Indian/Alaska Native (1,090)	1,873	7.99
Not Hispanic (1,026)	1,728	7.37
Hispanic (64)	145	0.62
Aleut *(Alaska Native)* (2)	2	0.01
Apache (20)	39	0.17
Arapaho (1)	5	0.02
Blackfeet (1)	16	0.07
Canadian/French Am. Ind. (0)	1	<0.01
Central American Ind. (0)	1	<0.01
Cherokee (139)	359	1.53
Cheyenne (0)	2	0.01
Chickasaw (167)	276	1.18
Chippewa (2)	4	0.02
Choctaw (365)	615	2.62
Comanche (78)	107	0.46
Creek (25)	46	0.20
Delaware (2)	3	0.01
Iroquois (4)	17	0.07
Kiowa (22)	35	0.15
Menominee (2)	2	0.01
Mexican American Ind. (4)	8	0.03
Navajo (11)	22	0.09
Osage (8)	13	0.06
Potawatomi (18)	23	0.10
Pueblo (5)	6	0.03
Seminole (8)	14	0.06
Shoshone (8)	8	0.03
Sioux (3)	13	0.06
South American Ind. (1)	4	0.02
Spanish American Ind. (1)	6	0.03
Yup'ik *(Alaska Native)* (1)	1	<0.01
Asian (183)	271	1.16
Not Hispanic (172)	256	1.09
Hispanic (11)	15	0.06
Chinese, ex. Taiwanese (32)	46	0.20
Filipino (34)	60	0.26
Indian (41)	54	0.23
Indonesian (11)	13	0.06
Japanese (8)	29	0.12
Korean (7)	16	0.07

SECTION TWO

*Notes: † The Census 2010 population figure is used to calculate the percentages in the Hispanic Origin and Race categories. Ancestry percentages are based on the 2006-2010 American Community Survey population (not shown); ‡ Numbers in parentheses indicate the number of people reporting a single ancestry; * Numbers in parentheses indicate the number of persons reporting this race alone, not in combination with any other race; Please refer to the Explanation of Data for more information.*

Pakistani (4)	4	0.02
Taiwanese (2)	3	0.01
Thai (5)	8	0.03
Vietnamese (35)	41	0.17
Hawaii Native/Pacific Islander (5)	16	0.07
Not Hispanic (4)	10	0.04
Hispanic (1)	6	0.03
Native Hawaiian (1)	6	0.03
Samoan (2)	6	0.03
White (19,278)	20,368	86.93
Not Hispanic (18,434)	19,336	82.52
Hispanic (844)	1,032	4.40

Durant

Place Type: City
County: Bryan
Population: 15,856†

Ancestry‡	Population	%
African, Sub-Saharan (12)	12	0.08
Nigerian (12)	12	0.08
American (3,210)	3,210	20.56
Arab (66)	66	0.42
Iraqi (31)	31	0.20
Lebanese (35)	35	0.22
Australian (34)	34	0.22
Austrian (0)	20	0.13
Brazilian (11)	11	0.07
British (31)	59	0.38
Celtic (0)	9	0.06
Czech (9)	9	0.06
Czechoslovakian (0)	15	0.10
Danish (0)	34	0.22
Dutch (65)	343	2.20
English (385)	1,030	6.60
European (30)	49	0.31
French, ex. Basque (51)	193	1.24
French Canadian (35)	99	0.63
German (708)	1,731	11.09
Iranian (16)	16	0.10
Irish (691)	1,794	11.49
Italian (25)	155	0.99
Norwegian (32)	57	0.37
Polish (0)	67	0.43
Portuguese (53)	61	0.39
Romanian (11)	11	0.07
Russian (14)	23	0.15
Scotch-Irish (78)	214	1.37
Scottish (37)	148	0.95
Swedish (16)	55	0.35
Swiss (0)	17	0.11
Welsh (19)	62	0.40
West Indian, ex. Hispanic (0)	82	0.53
Dutch West Indian (0)	82	0.53

Hispanic Origin	Population	%
Hispanic or Latino (of any race)	1,131	7.13
Central American, ex. Mexican	20	0.13
Costa Rican	1	0.01
Guatemalan	1	0.01
Honduran	4	0.03
Nicaraguan	1	0.01
Panamanian	2	0.01
Salvadoran	11	0.07
Cuban	8	0.05
Dominican Republic	3	0.02
Mexican	989	6.24
Puerto Rican	13	0.08
South American	28	0.18
Argentinean	8	0.05
Colombian	11	0.07
Ecuadorian	2	0.01
Peruvian	6	0.04
Venezuelan	1	0.01
Other Hispanic or Latino	70	0.44

Race*	Population	%
African-American/Black (356)	518	3.27
Not Hispanic (347)	489	3.08
Hispanic (9)	29	0.18
American Indian/Alaska Native (2,112)	2,975	18.76
Not Hispanic (2,050)	2,860	18.04
Hispanic (62)	115	0.73
Apache (5)	5	0.03
Arapaho (1)	2	0.01
Cherokee (122)	263	1.66
Cheyenne (1)	3	0.02
Chickasaw (174)	326	2.06
Chippewa (7)	8	0.05
Choctaw (1,416)	1,961	12.37
Comanche (1)	5	0.03
Creek (21)	50	0.32
Delaware (1)	2	0.01
Inupiat *(Alaska Native)* (1)	1	0.01
Iroquois (0)	1	0.01
Kiowa (1)	2	0.01
Mexican American Ind. (2)	3	0.02
Navajo (1)	3	0.02
Osage (5)	8	0.05
Paiute (1)	5	0.03
Potawatomi (11)	18	0.11
Seminole (6)	12	0.08
Shoshone (2)	2	0.01
Sioux (8)	14	0.09
South American Ind. (1)	1	0.01
Tlingit-Haida *(Alaska Native)* (0)	1	0.01
Ute (1)	1	0.01
Asian (112)	149	0.94
Not Hispanic (110)	147	0.93
Hispanic (2)	2	0.01
Bangladeshi (4)	4	0.03
Chinese, ex. Taiwanese (15)	17	0.11
Filipino (23)	33	0.21
Indian (30)	34	0.21
Japanese (11)	29	0.18
Korean (4)	6	0.04
Pakistani (7)	7	0.04
Thai (0)	2	0.01
Vietnamese (16)	19	0.12
Hawaii Native/Pacific Islander (2)	10	0.06
Not Hispanic (2)	10	0.06
Guamanian/Chamorro (1)	3	0.02
Native Hawaiian (1)	3	0.02
Samoan (0)	3	0.02
White (11,848)	12,803	80.75
Not Hispanic (11,286)	12,160	76.69
Hispanic (562)	643	4.06

Edmond

Place Type: City
County: Oklahoma
Population: 81,405†

Ancestry‡	Population	%
African, Sub-Saharan (287)	316	0.40
African (216)	245	0.31
Nigerian (59)	59	0.08
Senegalese (12)	12	0.02
Albanian (64)	64	0.08
American (6,065)	6,065	7.72
Arab (217)	465	0.59
Arab (0)	12	0.02
Lebanese (69)	203	0.26
Moroccan (28)	28	0.04
Syrian (64)	117	0.15
Other Arab (56)	105	0.13
Armenian (43)	43	0.05
Australian (22)	40	0.05
Austrian (13)	179	0.23
Belgian (17)	45	0.06
Brazilian (96)	96	0.12
British (231)	604	0.77
Bulgarian (21)	21	0.03
Cajun (0)	20	0.03
Canadian (109)	226	0.29
Celtic (0)	62	0.08
Croatian (45)	127	0.16
Czech (205)	534	0.68
Czechoslovakian (91)	108	0.14
Danish (100)	374	0.48
Dutch (319)	1,568	1.99
Eastern European (35)	35	0.04
English (3,781)	10,195	12.97
European (5,089)	5,462	6.95
Finnish (6)	20	0.03
French, ex. Basque (527)	2,291	2.91
French Canadian (146)	376	0.48
German (5,764)	15,420	19.62
German Russian (31)	46	0.06
Greek (165)	458	0.58
Guyanese (13)	21	0.03
Hungarian (38)	107	0.14
Iranian (414)	448	0.57
Irish (3,000)	10,259	13.05
Italian (597)	1,987	2.53
Latvian (8)	33	0.04
Lithuanian (45)	53	0.07
Northern European (51)	84	0.11
Norwegian (289)	926	1.18
Polish (330)	1,176	1.50
Portuguese (28)	49	0.06
Romanian (6)	62	0.08
Russian (195)	573	0.73
Scandinavian (68)	158	0.20
Scotch-Irish (866)	1,998	2.54
Scottish (715)	2,246	2.86
Slavic (0)	12	0.02
Slovak (13)	75	0.10
Slovene (0)	11	0.01
Swedish (167)	889	1.13
Swiss (20)	329	0.42
Turkish (12)	24	0.03
Ukrainian (33)	87	0.11
Welsh (125)	549	0.70
West Indian, ex. Hispanic (101)	317	0.40
Bahamian (8)	92	0.12
British West Indian (47)	47	0.06
Dutch West Indian (21)	139	0.18
Jamaican (25)	39	0.05
Yugoslavian (30)	55	0.07

Hispanic Origin	Population	%
Hispanic or Latino (of any race)	4,144	5.09
Central American, ex. Mexican	159	0.20
Costa Rican	7	0.01
Guatemalan	51	0.06
Honduran	37	0.05
Nicaraguan	7	0.01
Panamanian	38	0.05
Salvadoran	19	0.02
Cuban	81	0.10
Dominican Republic	10	0.01
Mexican	2,925	3.59
Puerto Rican	204	0.25
South American	222	0.27
Argentinean	12	0.01
Bolivian	13	0.02
Chilean	6	0.01
Colombian	66	0.08
Ecuadorian	22	0.03
Paraguayan	2	<0.01
Peruvian	59	0.07
Uruguayan	3	<0.01
Venezuelan	35	0.04
Other South American	4	<0.01
Other Hispanic or Latino	543	0.67

Race*	Population	%
African-American/Black (4,500)	5,331	6.55
Not Hispanic (4,412)	5,165	6.34
Hispanic (88)	166	0.20
American Indian/Alaska Native (2,132)	4,095	5.03
Not Hispanic (2,040)	3,879	4.77
Hispanic (92)	216	0.27
Aleut *(Alaska Native)* (0)	2	<0.01
Apache (7)	18	0.02
Arapaho (3)	5	0.01
Blackfeet (2)	26	0.03

*Notes: † The Census 2010 population figure is used to calculate the percentages in the Hispanic Origin and Race categories. Ancestry percentages are based on the 2006-2010 American Community Survey population (not shown); ‡ Numbers in parentheses indicate the number of people reporting a single ancestry; * Numbers in parentheses indicate the number of persons reporting this race alone, not in combination with any other race; Please refer to the Explanation of Data for more information.*

Canadian/French Am. Ind. (1)	2	<0.01
Central American Ind. (1)	1	<0.01
Cherokee (471)	1,098	1.35
Cheyenne (15)	17	0.02
Chickasaw (195)	395	0.49
Chippewa (11)	20	0.02
Choctaw (406)	723	0.89
Comanche (28)	46	0.06
Cree (0)	1	<0.01
Creek (184)	341	0.42
Crow (1)	1	<0.01
Delaware (21)	46	0.06
Hopi (1)	2	<0.01
Inupiat *(Alaska Native)* (1)	1	<0.01
Iroquois (4)	4	<0.01
Kiowa (33)	48	0.06
Lumbee (5)	5	0.01
Menominee (1)	1	<0.01
Mexican American Ind. (10)	23	0.03
Navajo (9)	24	0.03
Osage (27)	58	0.07
Ottawa (4)	4	<0.01
Paiute (0)	3	<0.01
Pima (0)	3	<0.01
Potawatomi (80)	126	0.15
Pueblo (10)	15	0.02
Puget Sound Salish (1)	3	<0.01
Seminole (55)	108	0.13
Sioux (3)	15	0.02
Spanish American Ind. (0)	1	<0.01
Tlingit-Haida *(Alaska Native)* (1)	1	<0.01
Tohono O'Odham (2)	2	<0.01
Yaqui (0)	2	<0.01
Yup'ik *(Alaska Native)* (4)	4	<0.01
Asian (2,619)	3,271	4.02
Not Hispanic (2,599)	3,211	3.94
Hispanic (20)	60	0.07
Bangladeshi (45)	47	0.06
Burmese (1)	2	<0.01
Cambodian (6)	12	0.01
Chinese, ex. Taiwanese (612)	710	0.87
Filipino (120)	260	0.32
Indian (543)	615	0.76
Indonesian (26)	33	0.04
Japanese (124)	259	0.32
Korean (403)	483	0.59
Laotian (15)	18	0.02
Malaysian (20)	28	0.03
Nepalese (83)	89	0.11
Pakistani (106)	119	0.15
Sri Lankan (17)	17	0.02
Taiwanese (48)	54	0.07
Thai (24)	45	0.06
Vietnamese (218)	258	0.32
Hawaii Native/Pacific Islander (102)	171	0.21
Not Hispanic (100)	163	0.20
Hispanic (2)	8	0.01
Guamanian/Chamorro (8)	24	0.03
Native Hawaiian (32)	54	0.07
Samoan (5)	12	0.01
White (67,237)	70,323	86.39
Not Hispanic (65,076)	67,771	83.25
Hispanic (2,161)	2,552	3.13

El Reno

Place Type: City
County: Canadian
Population: 16,749†

Ancestry‡	Population	%
African, Sub-Saharan (194)	220	1.33
African (180)	180	1.09
Nigerian (14)	14	0.08
Other Sub-Saharan African (0)	26	0.16
American (1,201)	1,201	7.26
Arab (19)	19	0.11
Moroccan (19)	19	0.11
British (9)	9	0.05
Canadian (5)	9	0.05
Czech (30)	209	1.26
Danish (28)	36	0.22
Dutch (71)	357	2.16
English (496)	1,129	6.83
European (68)	80	0.48
Finnish (0)	10	0.06
French, ex. Basque (78)	433	2.62
French Canadian (7)	26	0.16
German (1,287)	2,676	16.18
Irish (696)	2,400	14.51
Italian (57)	110	0.66
Northern European (0)	3	0.02
Norwegian (34)	55	0.33
Pennsylvania German (0)	31	0.19
Polish (19)	67	0.41
Russian (13)	13	0.08
Scotch-Irish (73)	192	1.16
Scottish (41)	170	1.03
Swedish (20)	74	0.45
Swiss (12)	97	0.59
Welsh (23)	41	0.25
West Indian, ex. Hispanic (2)	12	0.07
Dutch West Indian (2)	12	0.07

Hispanic Origin	Population	%
Hispanic or Latino (of any race)	2,156	12.87
Central American, ex. Mexican	30	0.18
Costa Rican	1	0.01
Guatemalan	14	0.08
Honduran	5	0.03
Salvadoran	9	0.05
Other Central American	1	0.01
Cuban	14	0.08
Dominican Republic	1	0.01
Mexican	1,797	10.73
Puerto Rican	51	0.30
South American	16	0.10
Bolivian	6	0.04
Chilean	2	0.01
Colombian	3	0.02
Peruvian	5	0.03
Other Hispanic or Latino	247	1.47

Race*	Population	%
African-American/Black (1,209)	1,439	8.59
Not Hispanic (1,171)	1,371	8.19
Hispanic (38)	68	0.41
American Indian/Alaska Native (1,860)	2,385	14.24
Not Hispanic (1,713)	2,162	12.91
Hispanic (147)	223	1.33
Apache (11)	15	0.09
Arapaho (67)	93	0.56
Blackfeet (5)	9	0.05
Cherokee (99)	203	1.21
Cheyenne (198)	244	1.46
Chickasaw (31)	54	0.32
Chippewa (4)	5	0.03
Choctaw (91)	144	0.86
Comanche (13)	23	0.14
Creek (36)	63	0.38
Crow (1)	1	0.01
Delaware (2)	12	0.07
Inupiat *(Alaska Native)* (1)	2	0.01
Iroquois (4)	9	0.05
Kiowa (50)	76	0.45
Mexican American Ind. (11)	12	0.07
Navajo (16)	22	0.13
Osage (8)	8	0.05
Potawatomi (14)	29	0.17
Pueblo (2)	3	0.02
Seminole (19)	38	0.23
Sioux (16)	30	0.18
South American Ind. (0)	1	0.01
Tohono O'Odham (1)	1	0.01
Ute (4)	4	0.02
Yakama (2)	2	0.01
Yuman (1)	1	0.01
Asian (87)	134	0.80
Not Hispanic (84)	123	0.73
Hispanic (3)	11	0.07
Chinese, ex. Taiwanese (14)	18	0.11
Filipino (16)	25	0.15
Indian (22)	30	0.18
Japanese (4)	9	0.05
Korean (6)	16	0.10
Laotian (3)	3	0.02
Pakistani (0)	3	0.02
Thai (3)	8	0.05
Vietnamese (10)	15	0.09
Hawaii Native/Pacific Islander (9)	17	0.10
Not Hispanic (9)	16	0.10
Hispanic (0)	1	0.01
Native Hawaiian (5)	11	0.07
Samoan (1)	8	0.05
White (12,025)	12,711	75.89
Not Hispanic (11,006)	11,552	68.97
Hispanic (1,019)	1,159	6.92

Elk City

Place Type: City
County: Beckham
Population: 11,693†

Ancestry‡	Population	%
African, Sub-Saharan (0)	27	0.23
African (0)	27	0.23
American (692)	692	5.98
Arab (31)	37	0.32
Lebanese (31)	37	0.32
British (0)	14	0.12
Canadian (13)	13	0.11
Celtic (0)	16	0.14
Czech (14)	55	0.48
Czechoslovakian (11)	11	0.10
Danish (0)	9	0.08
Dutch (129)	324	2.80
English (372)	1,010	8.73
European (9)	36	0.31
French, ex. Basque (40)	209	1.81
French Canadian (11)	11	0.10
German (815)	2,451	21.19
Greek (0)	12	0.10
Irish (642)	2,339	20.22
Italian (0)	217	1.88
Northern European (5)	5	0.04
Norwegian (6)	15	0.13
Scotch-Irish (41)	291	2.52
Scottish (145)	344	2.97
Slavic (0)	18	0.16
Swedish (0)	43	0.37
Welsh (0)	8	0.07
West Indian, ex. Hispanic (12)	72	0.62
Dutch West Indian (12)	72	0.62

Hispanic Origin	Population	%
Hispanic or Latino (of any race)	1,204	10.30
Central American, ex. Mexican	23	0.20
Honduran	2	0.02
Nicaraguan	1	0.01
Panamanian	2	0.02
Salvadoran	18	0.15
Cuban	6	0.05
Mexican	978	8.36
Puerto Rican	13	0.11
South American	18	0.15
Argentinean	3	0.03
Chilean	2	0.02
Colombian	3	0.03
Ecuadorian	1	0.01
Peruvian	8	0.07
Venezuelan	1	0.01
Other Hispanic or Latino	166	1.42

Race*	Population	%
African-American/Black (345)	445	3.81
Not Hispanic (337)	429	3.67
Hispanic (8)	16	0.14
American Indian/Alaska Native (439)	658	5.63
Not Hispanic (406)	612	5.23

*Notes: † The Census 2010 population figure is used to calculate the percentages in the Hispanic Origin and Race categories. Ancestry percentages are based on the 2006-2010 American Community Survey population (not shown); ‡ Numbers in parentheses indicate the number of people reporting a single ancestry; * Numbers in parentheses indicate the number of persons reporting this race alone, not in combination with any other race; Please refer to the Explanation of Data for more information.*

Hispanic (33)	46	0.39
Apache (4)	6	0.05
Arapaho (3)	4	0.03
Blackfeet (0)	3	0.03
Cherokee (55)	117	1.00
Cheyenne (76)	85	0.73
Chickasaw (12)	16	0.14
Choctaw (63)	117	1.00
Colville (3)	6	0.05
Comanche (1)	3	0.03
Creek (23)	53	0.45
Delaware (3)	3	0.03
Iroquois (1)	4	0.03
Kiowa (8)	9	0.08
Navajo (12)	13	0.11
Osage (5)	11	0.09
Ottawa (1)	1	0.01
Potawatomi (6)	7	0.06
Pueblo (1)	1	0.01
Seminole (2)	2	0.02
Sioux (1)	6	0.05
Tlingit-Haida *(Alaska Native)* (2)	2	0.02
Ute (0)	1	0.01
Asian (104)	125	1.07
Not Hispanic (99)	116	0.99
Hispanic (5)	9	0.08
Chinese, ex. Taiwanese (16)	21	0.18
Filipino (17)	21	0.18
Indian (49)	56	0.48
Japanese (0)	3	0.03
Korean (1)	3	0.03
Laotian (3)	3	0.03
Vietnamese (9)	9	0.08
Hawaii Native/Pacific Islander (0)	3	0.03
Hispanic (0)	3	0.03
Guamanian/Chamorro (0)	3	0.03
White (9,846)	10,174	87.01
Not Hispanic (9,350)	9,609	82.18
Hispanic (496)	565	4.83

Enid

Place Type: City
County: Garfield
Population: 49,379†

Ancestry‡	Population	%
African, Sub-Saharan (61)	90	0.19
African (61)	90	0.19
Albanian (22)	22	0.05
American (4,199)	4,199	8.73
Arab (78)	78	0.16
Arab (30)	30	0.06
Lebanese (13)	13	0.03
Syrian (35)	35	0.07
Austrian (7)	54	0.11
Belgian (0)	25	0.05
British (11)	79	0.16
Canadian (19)	43	0.09
Croatian (0)	2	<0.01
Czech (278)	694	1.44
Czechoslovakian (50)	88	0.18
Danish (63)	211	0.44
Dutch (283)	1,650	3.43
English (2,283)	5,489	11.41
European (301)	323	0.67
Finnish (0)	28	0.06
French, ex. Basque (372)	1,563	3.25
French Canadian (72)	240	0.50
German (4,190)	10,564	21.95
Greek (78)	87	0.18
Hungarian (24)	128	0.27
Iranian (13)	13	0.03
Irish (1,682)	6,275	13.04
Italian (350)	847	1.76
Latvian (0)	13	0.03
Lithuanian (14)	14	0.03
Norwegian (103)	320	0.66
Pennsylvania German (33)	61	0.13
Polish (84)	302	0.63
Romanian (13)	27	0.06
Russian (57)	147	0.31
Scandinavian (124)	182	0.38
Scotch-Irish (337)	732	1.52
Scottish (312)	762	1.58
Slovak (0)	59	0.12
Swedish (121)	345	0.72
Swiss (9)	59	0.12
Welsh (97)	326	0.68
West Indian, ex. Hispanic (39)	61	0.13
Dutch West Indian (39)	61	0.13
Yugoslavian (63)	131	0.27

Hispanic Origin	Population	%
Hispanic or Latino (of any race)	5,066	10.26
Central American, ex. Mexican	78	0.16
Costa Rican	1	<0.01
Guatemalan	45	0.09
Honduran	8	0.02
Nicaraguan	4	0.01
Panamanian	6	0.01
Salvadoran	14	0.03
Cuban	25	0.05
Dominican Republic	6	0.01
Mexican	4,327	8.76
Puerto Rican	207	0.42
South American	74	0.15
Argentinean	6	0.01
Chilean	3	0.01
Colombian	23	0.05
Ecuadorian	9	0.02
Peruvian	21	0.04
Uruguayan	1	<0.01
Venezuelan	8	0.02
Other South American	3	0.01
Other Hispanic or Latino	349	0.71

Race*	Population	%
African-American/Black (1,768)	2,372	4.80
Not Hispanic (1,722)	2,243	4.54
Hispanic (46)	129	0.26
American Indian/Alaska Native (1,144)	2,096	4.24
Not Hispanic (1,054)	1,910	3.87
Hispanic (90)	186	0.38
Aleut *(Alaska Native)* (6)	6	0.01
Apache (43)	73	0.15
Arapaho (10)	15	0.03
Blackfeet (9)	31	0.06
Cherokee (269)	621	1.26
Cheyenne (31)	49	0.10
Chickasaw (64)	104	0.21
Chippewa (5)	7	0.01
Choctaw (120)	222	0.45
Comanche (9)	23	0.05
Cree (0)	2	<0.01
Creek (36)	82	0.17
Crow (1)	5	0.01
Delaware (13)	26	0.05
Hopi (2)	2	<0.01
Iroquois (10)	13	0.03
Kiowa (3)	5	0.01
Lumbee (1)	1	<0.01
Mexican American Ind. (5)	12	0.02
Navajo (16)	25	0.05
Osage (27)	43	0.09
Potawatomi (23)	33	0.07
Pueblo (0)	2	<0.01
Seminole (10)	19	0.04
Sioux (13)	27	0.05
Spanish American Ind. (2)	4	0.01
Tlingit-Haida *(Alaska Native)* (1)	2	<0.01
Tohono O'Odham (1)	4	0.01
Ute (1)	1	<0.01
Yup'ik *(Alaska Native)* (1)	7	0.01
Asian (531)	784	1.59
Not Hispanic (520)	741	1.50
Hispanic (11)	43	0.09
Cambodian (3)	3	0.01
Chinese, ex. Taiwanese (47)	77	0.16
Filipino (121)	191	0.39
Indian (79)	97	0.20
Indonesian (11)	14	0.03
Japanese (25)	91	0.18
Korean (126)	167	0.34
Laotian (4)	4	0.01
Malaysian (1)	1	<0.01
Nepalese (1)	1	<0.01
Pakistani (6)	8	0.02
Taiwanese (0)	1	<0.01
Thai (21)	31	0.06
Vietnamese (55)	69	0.14
Hawaii Native/Pacific Islander (1,082)	1,156	2.34
Not Hispanic (1,075)	1,139	2.31
Hispanic (7)	17	0.03
Fijian (4)	4	0.01
Guamanian/Chamorro (5)	10	0.02
Marshallese (899)	934	1.89
Native Hawaiian (46)	90	0.18
Samoan (0)	2	<0.01
Tongan (1)	2	<0.01
White (40,300)	42,040	85.14
Not Hispanic (38,390)	39,782	80.56
Hispanic (1,910)	2,258	4.57

Glenpool

Place Type: City
County: Tulsa
Population: 10,808†

Ancestry‡	Population	%
African, Sub-Saharan (14)	14	0.14
African (14)	14	0.14
American (1,145)	1,145	11.10
Austrian (10)	45	0.44
British (0)	120	1.16
Canadian (0)	17	0.16
Croatian (22)	22	0.21
Czech (23)	32	0.31
Czechoslovakian (9)	9	0.09
Danish (0)	28	0.27
Dutch (51)	509	4.93
English (196)	889	8.62
French, ex. Basque (82)	272	2.64
German (598)	1,803	17.47
Greek (0)	15	0.15
Irish (299)	1,343	13.01
Italian (57)	181	1.75
Lithuanian (9)	17	0.16
Polish (14)	121	1.17
Portuguese (16)	31	0.30
Russian (37)	48	0.47
Scandinavian (0)	16	0.16
Scotch-Irish (72)	333	3.23
Scottish (119)	311	3.01
Swedish (15)	139	1.35
Swiss (0)	12	0.12
Welsh (5)	188	1.82
West Indian, ex. Hispanic (69)	69	0.67
Dutch West Indian (69)	69	0.67

Hispanic Origin	Population	%
Hispanic or Latino (of any race)	636	5.88
Central American, ex. Mexican	29	0.27
Costa Rican	2	0.02
Guatemalan	9	0.08
Honduran	9	0.08
Panamanian	3	0.03
Salvadoran	6	0.06
Cuban	2	0.02
Mexican	491	4.54
Puerto Rican	24	0.22
South American	29	0.27
Argentinean	1	0.01
Chilean	1	0.01
Colombian	20	0.19
Peruvian	7	0.06
Other Hispanic or Latino	61	0.56

*Notes: † The Census 2010 population figure is used to calculate the percentages in the Hispanic Origin and Race categories. Ancestry percentages are based on the 2006-2010 American Community Survey population (not shown); ‡ Numbers in parentheses indicate the number of people reporting a single ancestry; * Numbers in parentheses indicate the number of persons reporting this race alone, not in combination with any other race; Please refer to the Explanation of Data for more information.*

Race*	Population	%
African-American/Black (264)	402	3.72
Not Hispanic (260)	387	3.58
Hispanic (4)	15	0.14
American Indian/Alaska Native (1,428)	2,210	20.45
Not Hispanic (1,399)	2,137	19.77
Hispanic (29)	73	0.68
Aleut *(Alaska Native)* (1)	1	0.01
Apache (0)	7	0.06
Blackfeet (2)	3	0.03
Cherokee (372)	758	7.01
Cheyenne (3)	5	0.05
Chickasaw (21)	38	0.35
Chippewa (5)	9	0.08
Choctaw (95)	182	1.68
Comanche (1)	5	0.05
Creek (615)	893	8.26
Delaware (4)	7	0.06
Iroquois (8)	11	0.10
Kiowa (7)	8	0.07
Mexican American Ind. (1)	6	0.06
Navajo (3)	3	0.03
Osage (18)	24	0.22
Ottawa (4)	10	0.09
Paiute (0)	2	0.02
Pima (1)	2	0.02
Potawatomi (10)	15	0.14
Seminole (38)	58	0.54
Sioux (6)	13	0.12
Tlingit-Haida *(Alaska Native)* (2)	3	0.03
Yup'ik *(Alaska Native)* (1)	1	0.01
Asian (102)	167	1.55
Not Hispanic (100)	154	1.42
Hispanic (2)	13	0.12
Bangladeshi (5)	5	0.05
Burmese (4)	6	0.06
Chinese, ex. Taiwanese (5)	10	0.09
Filipino (46)	74	0.68
Indian (12)	19	0.18
Indonesian (1)	5	0.05
Japanese (5)	14	0.13
Korean (9)	13	0.12
Laotian (4)	4	0.04
Pakistani (4)	9	0.08
Thai (1)	2	0.02
Vietnamese (5)	8	0.07
Hawaii Native/Pacific Islander (9)	21	0.19
Not Hispanic (7)	14	0.13
Hispanic (2)	7	0.06
Guamanian/Chamorro (2)	3	0.03
Native Hawaiian (7)	13	0.12
White (7,846)	8,711	80.60
Not Hispanic (7,556)	8,348	77.24
Hispanic (290)	363	3.36

Guthrie

Place Type: City
County: Logan
Population: 10,191†

Ancestry‡	Population	%
African, Sub-Saharan (48)	48	0.48
African (48)	48	0.48
American (1,095)	1,095	10.96
Arab (5)	5	0.05
Lebanese (5)	5	0.05
Austrian (12)	39	0.39
British (0)	61	0.61
Canadian (7)	7	0.07
Czech (17)	17	0.17
Czechoslovakian (0)	20	0.20
Danish (9)	9	0.09
Dutch (34)	272	2.72
English (464)	1,104	11.05
European (229)	252	2.52
French, ex. Basque (44)	305	3.05
German (587)	1,816	18.18
German Russian (0)	19	0.19
Irish (319)	1,249	12.51
Italian (76)	195	1.95
Norwegian (0)	30	0.30
Polish (20)	107	1.07
Russian (0)	26	0.26
Scandinavian (7)	7	0.07
Scotch-Irish (46)	135	1.35
Scottish (37)	187	1.87
Serbian (0)	13	0.13
Slavic (0)	13	0.13
Swedish (47)	78	0.78
Swiss (18)	70	0.70
West Indian, ex. Hispanic (0)	30	0.30
Dutch West Indian (0)	30	0.30

Hispanic Origin	Population	%
Hispanic or Latino (of any race)	465	4.56
Central American, ex. Mexican	6	0.06
Guatemalan	1	0.01
Honduran	3	0.03
Salvadoran	2	0.02
Cuban	3	0.03
Mexican	372	3.65
Puerto Rican	30	0.29
South American	8	0.08
Colombian	3	0.03
Peruvian	4	0.04
Venezuelan	1	0.01
Other Hispanic or Latino	46	0.45

Race*	Population	%
African-American/Black (1,365)	1,572	15.43
Not Hispanic (1,348)	1,531	15.02
Hispanic (17)	41	0.40
American Indian/Alaska Native (318)	670	6.57
Not Hispanic (302)	640	6.28
Hispanic (16)	30	0.29
Apache (0)	1	0.01
Blackfeet (0)	11	0.11
Canadian/French Am. Ind. (1)	1	0.01
Cherokee (74)	230	2.26
Chickasaw (30)	60	0.59
Chippewa (1)	5	0.05
Choctaw (56)	97	0.95
Colville (0)	2	0.02
Comanche (4)	16	0.16
Creek (26)	43	0.42
Delaware (0)	4	0.04
Iroquois (9)	11	0.11
Kiowa (4)	5	0.05
Osage (3)	9	0.09
Paiute (1)	6	0.06
Potawatomi (21)	23	0.23
Seminole (3)	10	0.10
Sioux (1)	3	0.03
Asian (45)	72	0.71
Not Hispanic (45)	72	0.71
Cambodian (1)	1	0.01
Chinese, ex. Taiwanese (12)	19	0.19
Filipino (8)	22	0.22
Indian (9)	14	0.14
Japanese (4)	7	0.07
Korean (3)	4	0.04
Pakistani (2)	3	0.03
Thai (0)	1	0.01
Vietnamese (0)	1	0.01
Hawaii Native/Pacific Islander (7)	16	0.16
Not Hispanic (7)	14	0.14
Hispanic (0)	2	0.02
Guamanian/Chamorro (2)	2	0.02
Native Hawaiian (4)	10	0.10
White (7,751)	8,222	80.68
Not Hispanic (7,542)	7,961	78.12
Hispanic (209)	261	2.56

Guymon

Place Type: City
County: Texas
Population: 11,442†

Ancestry‡	Population	%
American (511)	511	4.69
Arab (0)	36	0.33
Lebanese (0)	15	0.14
Other Arab (0)	21	0.19
Dutch (66)	212	1.94
English (281)	812	7.45
European (50)	50	0.46
French, ex. Basque (12)	113	1.04
German (609)	1,407	12.90
Hungarian (52)	66	0.61
Irish (308)	920	8.44
Italian (79)	146	1.34
Northern European (34)	34	0.31
Norwegian (42)	42	0.39
Polish (0)	19	0.17
Scotch-Irish (58)	138	1.27
Scottish (0)	53	0.49
Swedish (0)	8	0.07
West Indian, ex. Hispanic (0)	38	0.35
Dutch West Indian (0)	38	0.35

Hispanic Origin	Population	%
Hispanic or Latino (of any race)	5,896	51.53
Central American, ex. Mexican	803	7.02
Costa Rican	1	0.01
Guatemalan	704	6.15
Honduran	24	0.21
Salvadoran	6	0.05
Other Central American	68	0.59
Cuban	122	1.07
Dominican Republic	9	0.08
Mexican	4,578	40.01
Puerto Rican	12	0.10
South American	7	0.06
Argentinean	5	0.04
Colombian	1	0.01
Peruvian	1	0.01
Other Hispanic or Latino	365	3.19

Race*	Population	%
African-American/Black (178)	242	2.12
Not Hispanic (147)	183	1.60
Hispanic (31)	59	0.52
American Indian/Alaska Native (168)	261	2.28
Not Hispanic (94)	146	1.28
Hispanic (74)	115	1.01
Apache (2)	7	0.06
Central American Ind. (13)	20	0.17
Cherokee (33)	57	0.50
Cheyenne (6)	11	0.10
Chickasaw (6)	7	0.06
Choctaw (8)	11	0.10
Comanche (0)	1	0.01
Creek (5)	9	0.08
Iroquois (0)	4	0.03
Mexican American Ind. (26)	27	0.24
Navajo (1)	1	0.01
Osage (0)	8	0.07
Ottawa (1)	1	0.01
Potawatomi (1)	4	0.03
Pueblo (3)	6	0.05
Seminole (2)	6	0.05
Sioux (2)	4	0.03
South American Ind. (3)	4	0.03
Spanish American Ind. (5)	5	0.04
Ute (0)	1	0.01
Yaqui (1)	1	0.01
Asian (311)	364	3.18
Not Hispanic (304)	333	2.91
Hispanic (7)	31	0.27
Bangladeshi (3)	3	0.03
Burmese (145)	153	1.34
Cambodian (2)	2	0.02
Chinese, ex. Taiwanese (17)	28	0.24
Filipino (35)	43	0.38
Indian (18)	23	0.20
Japanese (4)	16	0.14
Korean (6)	18	0.16
Laotian (15)	21	0.18

*Notes: † The Census 2010 population figure is used to calculate the percentages in the Hispanic Origin and Race categories. Ancestry percentages are based on the 2006-2010 American Community Survey population (not shown); ‡ Numbers in parentheses indicate the number of people reporting a single ancestry; * Numbers in parentheses indicate the number of persons reporting this race alone, not in combination with any other race; Please refer to the Explanation of Data for more information.*

Thai (18)	28	0.24
Vietnamese (32)	35	0.31
Hawaii Native/Pacific Islander (30)	43	0.38
Not Hispanic (5)	9	0.08
Hispanic (25)	34	0.30
Guamanian/Chamorro (25)	32	0.28
Native Hawaiian (3)	7	0.06
Samoan (2)	5	0.04
White (8,312)	8,588	75.06
Not Hispanic (4,858)	4,964	43.38
Hispanic (3,454)	3,624	31.67

Jenks

Place Type: City
County: Tulsa
Population: 16,924†

Ancestry‡	Population	%
African, Sub-Saharan (91)	91	0.59
African (86)	86	0.56
Nigerian (5)	5	0.03
Albanian (0)	23	0.15
American (1,264)	1,264	8.18
Arab (66)	106	0.69
Lebanese (21)	61	0.39
Other Arab (45)	45	0.29
Austrian (10)	43	0.28
British (23)	92	0.60
Bulgarian (0)	8	0.05
Canadian (11)	33	0.21
Czech (47)	95	0.62
Danish (39)	39	0.25
Dutch (106)	505	3.27
Eastern European (12)	12	0.08
English (1,044)	2,376	15.38
European (221)	354	2.29
French, ex. Basque (128)	463	3.00
French Canadian (11)	83	0.54
German (1,171)	3,483	22.55
Greek (34)	34	0.22
Hungarian (9)	9	0.06
Irish (725)	2,364	15.30
Italian (102)	311	2.01
Norwegian (15)	113	0.73
Polish (110)	559	3.62
Portuguese (13)	13	0.08
Russian (14)	124	0.80
Scandinavian (9)	27	0.17
Scotch-Irish (35)	210	1.36
Scottish (60)	357	2.31
Slovak (0)	6	0.04
Swedish (78)	288	1.86
Swiss (0)	22	0.14
Welsh (8)	136	0.88
West Indian, ex. Hispanic (14)	40	0.26
Dutch West Indian (14)	40	0.26

Hispanic Origin	Population	%
Hispanic or Latino (of any race)	815	4.82
Central American, ex. Mexican	23	0.14
Guatemalan	3	0.02
Honduran	1	0.01
Nicaraguan	3	0.02
Panamanian	6	0.04
Salvadoran	10	0.06
Cuban	7	0.04
Dominican Republic	1	0.01
Mexican	515	3.04
Puerto Rican	75	0.44
South American	106	0.63
Argentinean	1	0.01
Chilean	4	0.02
Colombian	49	0.29
Ecuadorian	13	0.08
Peruvian	9	0.05
Uruguayan	2	0.01
Venezuelan	27	0.16
Other South American	1	0.01
Other Hispanic or Latino	88	0.52

Race*	Population	%
African-American/Black (474)	583	3.44
Not Hispanic (461)	563	3.33
Hispanic (13)	20	0.12
American Indian/Alaska Native (935)	1,522	8.99
Not Hispanic (917)	1,483	8.76
Hispanic (18)	39	0.23
Aleut *(Alaska Native)* (1)	1	0.01
Apache (5)	13	0.08
Blackfeet (0)	6	0.04
Cherokee (368)	670	3.96
Cheyenne (1)	1	0.01
Chickasaw (36)	58	0.34
Choctaw (79)	162	0.96
Comanche (2)	4	0.02
Cree (0)	1	0.01
Creek (236)	356	2.10
Delaware (3)	5	0.03
Iroquois (4)	9	0.05
Kiowa (7)	8	0.05
Menominee (1)	1	0.01
Mexican American Ind. (1)	4	0.02
Navajo (2)	2	0.01
Osage (24)	43	0.25
Ottawa (5)	5	0.03
Potawatomi (27)	33	0.19
Pueblo (4)	4	0.02
Seminole (3)	10	0.06
Sioux (1)	1	0.01
Yakama (1)	1	0.01
Asian (386)	492	2.91
Not Hispanic (385)	483	2.85
Hispanic (1)	9	0.05
Bangladeshi (10)	10	0.06
Burmese (39)	40	0.24
Cambodian (1)	1	0.01
Chinese, ex. Taiwanese (37)	59	0.35
Filipino (33)	53	0.31
Hmong (6)	6	0.04
Indian (110)	120	0.71
Japanese (16)	34	0.20
Korean (44)	55	0.32
Laotian (14)	15	0.09
Malaysian (1)	4	0.02
Pakistani (11)	13	0.08
Sri Lankan (3)	3	0.02
Taiwanese (5)	5	0.03
Thai (4)	6	0.04
Vietnamese (34)	42	0.25
Hawaii Native/Pacific Islander (4)	32	0.19
Not Hispanic (4)	29	0.17
Hispanic (0)	3	0.02
Fijian (0)	1	0.01
Guamanian/Chamorro (0)	2	0.01
Native Hawaiian (1)	13	0.08
White (14,008)	14,771	87.28
Not Hispanic (13,584)	14,285	84.41
Hispanic (424)	486	2.87

Lawton

Place Type: City
County: Comanche
Population: 96,867†

Ancestry‡	Population	%
African, Sub-Saharan (739)	942	1.00
African (567)	724	0.77
Ethiopian (12)	12	0.01
Nigerian (120)	144	0.15
South African (24)	24	0.03
Other Sub-Saharan African (16)	38	0.04
American (8,455)	8,455	8.97
Arab (253)	416	0.44
Arab (63)	137	0.15
Egyptian (43)	65	0.07
Jordanian (17)	17	0.02
Lebanese (80)	140	0.15
Moroccan (50)	57	0.06
Assyrian/Chaldean/Syriac (0)	7	0.01
Austrian (52)	97	0.10
Belgian (18)	54	0.06
Brazilian (72)	117	0.12
British (134)	216	0.23
Cajun (0)	9	0.01
Canadian (40)	97	0.10
Carpatho Rusyn (12)	50	0.05
Celtic (0)	9	0.01
Croatian (0)	6	0.01
Czech (40)	162	0.17
Czechoslovakian (137)	227	0.24
Danish (115)	230	0.24
Dutch (169)	1,164	1.24
Eastern European (0)	17	0.02
English (1,798)	6,012	6.38
European (1,995)	2,956	3.14
Finnish (60)	304	0.32
French, ex. Basque (644)	2,539	2.69
French Canadian (122)	395	0.42
German (5,314)	14,688	15.59
German Russian (0)	14	0.01
Greek (25)	124	0.13
Guyanese (0)	23	0.02
Hungarian (13)	249	0.26
Iranian (35)	53	0.06
Irish (2,490)	9,338	9.91
Italian (981)	2,967	3.15
Lithuanian (0)	15	0.02
New Zealander (0)	41	0.04
Norwegian (244)	598	0.63
Pennsylvania German (0)	10	0.01
Polish (215)	1,236	1.31
Portuguese (48)	140	0.15
Romanian (9)	16	0.02
Russian (77)	236	0.25
Scandinavian (0)	28	0.03
Scotch-Irish (853)	1,964	2.08
Scottish (509)	1,695	1.80
Slavic (0)	37	0.04
Slovak (0)	17	0.02
Slovene (0)	22	0.02
Swedish (218)	766	0.81
Swiss (104)	252	0.27
Turkish (5)	33	0.04
Ukrainian (16)	16	0.02
Welsh (60)	391	0.41
West Indian, ex. Hispanic (438)	737	0.78
British West Indian (88)	88	0.09
Dutch West Indian (11)	192	0.20
Haitian (44)	74	0.08
Jamaican (46)	98	0.10
Trinidadian/Tobagonian (19)	19	0.02
U.S. Virgin Islander (31)	31	0.03
West Indian (199)	235	0.25
Yugoslavian (65)	73	0.08

Hispanic Origin	Population	%
Hispanic or Latino (of any race)	12,160	12.55
Central American, ex. Mexican	483	0.50
Costa Rican	12	0.01
Guatemalan	46	0.05
Honduran	75	0.08
Nicaraguan	32	0.03
Panamanian	243	0.25
Salvadoran	74	0.08
Other Central American	1	<0.01
Cuban	150	0.15
Dominican Republic	157	0.16
Mexican	7,547	7.79
Puerto Rican	2,727	2.82
South American	209	0.22
Argentinean	21	0.02
Bolivian	9	0.01
Chilean	12	0.01
Colombian	81	0.08
Ecuadorian	20	0.02
Paraguayan	1	<0.01
Peruvian	33	0.03
Uruguayan	4	<0.01

*Notes: † The Census 2010 population figure is used to calculate the percentages in the Hispanic Origin and Race categories. Ancestry percentages are based on the 2006-2010 American Community Survey population (not shown); ‡ Numbers in parentheses indicate the number of people reporting a single ancestry; * Numbers in parentheses indicate the number of persons reporting this race alone, not in combination with any other race; Please refer to the Explanation of Data for more information.*

Venezuelan	26	0.03
Other South American	2	<0.01
Other Hispanic or Latino	887	0.92

Race*	Population	%
African-American/Black (20,684)	24,002	24.78
Not Hispanic (19,848)	22,600	23.33
Hispanic (836)	1,402	1.45
American Indian/Alaska Native (4,544)	7,008	7.23
Not Hispanic (4,031)	6,037	6.23
Hispanic (513)	971	1.00
Alaska Athabascan *(Ala. Nat.)* (3)	5	0.01
Aleut *(Alaska Native)* (4)	8	0.01
Apache (133)	218	0.23
Arapaho (33)	39	0.04
Blackfeet (8)	55	0.06
Canadian/French Am. Ind. (3)	5	0.01
Central American Ind. (0)	3	<0.01
Cherokee (303)	679	0.70
Cheyenne (58)	79	0.08
Chickasaw (145)	255	0.26
Chippewa (15)	30	0.03
Choctaw (287)	544	0.56
Colville (3)	4	<0.01
Comanche (1,407)	1,874	1.93
Cree (0)	5	0.01
Creek (83)	148	0.15
Crow (7)	13	0.01
Delaware (18)	29	0.03
Hopi (3)	7	0.01
Houma (1)	1	<0.01
Inupiat *(Alaska Native)* (1)	5	0.01
Iroquois (18)	41	0.04
Kiowa (532)	757	0.78
Lumbee (5)	10	0.01
Menominee (1)	1	<0.01
Mexican American Ind. (21)	47	0.05
Navajo (74)	106	0.11
Osage (8)	22	0.02
Ottawa (7)	7	0.01
Paiute (1)	2	<0.01
Pima (9)	12	0.01
Potawatomi (33)	56	0.06
Pueblo (10)	11	0.01
Puget Sound Salish (1)	2	<0.01
Seminole (64)	112	0.12
Shoshone (11)	13	0.01
Sioux (60)	94	0.10
South American Ind. (9)	15	0.02
Spanish American Ind. (3)	8	0.01
Tlingit-Haida *(Alaska Native)* (1)	4	<0.01
Tohono O'Odham (1)	3	<0.01
Ute (1)	3	<0.01
Yakama (0)	1	<0.01
Yaqui (1)	2	<0.01
Yuman (6)	6	0.01
Yup'ik *(Alaska Native)* (2)	2	<0.01
Asian (2,532)	4,122	4.26
Not Hispanic (2,423)	3,806	3.93
Hispanic (109)	316	0.33
Bangladeshi (4)	4	<0.01
Burmese (6)	7	0.01
Cambodian (51)	66	0.07
Chinese, ex. Taiwanese (161)	316	0.33
Filipino (560)	955	0.99
Hmong (11)	12	0.01
Indian (231)	310	0.32
Indonesian (1)	7	0.01
Japanese (184)	522	0.54
Korean (887)	1,499	1.55
Laotian (6)	10	0.01
Malaysian (1)	1	<0.01
Nepalese (26)	30	0.03
Pakistani (27)	29	0.03
Sri Lankan (3)	3	<0.01
Taiwanese (13)	15	0.02
Thai (61)	115	0.12
Vietnamese (163)	242	0.25
Hawaii Native/Pacific Islander (612)	1,027	1.06
Not Hispanic (564)	911	0.94
Hispanic (48)	116	0.12
Fijian (13)	15	0.02
Guamanian/Chamorro (218)	297	0.31
Marshallese (5)	5	0.01
Native Hawaiian (109)	298	0.31
Samoan (150)	248	0.26
Tongan (2)	4	<0.01
White (58,450)	63,852	65.92
Not Hispanic (52,540)	56,791	58.63
Hispanic (5,910)	7,061	7.29

McAlester

Place Type: City
County: Pittsburg
Population: 18,383†

Ancestry‡	Population	%
African, Sub-Saharan (143)	171	0.93
African (143)	171	0.93
American (1,423)	1,423	7.75
Arab (95)	100	0.54
Arab (90)	90	0.49
Lebanese (3)	8	0.04
Other Arab (2)	2	0.01
Austrian (14)	26	0.14
British (11)	30	0.16
Czech (11)	67	0.36
Czechoslovakian (15)	15	0.08
Danish (0)	27	0.15
Dutch (176)	597	3.25
English (750)	2,109	11.48
European (116)	116	0.63
French, ex. Basque (29)	406	2.21
French Canadian (0)	20	0.11
German (787)	2,301	12.53
Greek (13)	13	0.07
Hungarian (40)	40	0.22
Irish (953)	2,759	15.02
Italian (480)	767	4.18
Norwegian (13)	52	0.28
Polish (0)	215	1.17
Portuguese (0)	21	0.11
Russian (9)	19	0.10
Scandinavian (0)	9	0.05
Scotch-Irish (266)	599	3.26
Scottish (73)	175	0.95
Swedish (38)	94	0.51
Swiss (0)	10	0.05
Ukrainian (0)	8	0.04
Welsh (12)	61	0.33
West Indian, ex. Hispanic (40)	187	1.02
Dutch West Indian (13)	160	0.87
Jamaican (8)	8	0.04
West Indian (19)	19	0.10

Hispanic Origin	Population	%
Hispanic or Latino (of any race)	1,198	6.52
Central American, ex. Mexican	15	0.08
Costa Rican	3	0.02
Guatemalan	1	0.01
Honduran	3	0.02
Nicaraguan	2	0.01
Panamanian	2	0.01
Salvadoran	4	0.02
Cuban	13	0.07
Dominican Republic	2	0.01
Mexican	1,020	5.55
Puerto Rican	27	0.15
South American	10	0.05
Bolivian	1	0.01
Chilean	1	0.01
Colombian	2	0.01
Ecuadorian	2	0.01
Venezuelan	4	0.02
Other Hispanic or Latino	111	0.60

Race*	Population	%
African-American/Black (1,306)	1,617	8.80
Not Hispanic (1,279)	1,571	8.55
Hispanic (27)	46	0.25
American Indian/Alaska Native (2,338)	3,355	18.25
Not Hispanic (2,227)	3,159	17.18
Hispanic (111)	196	1.07
Aleut *(Alaska Native)* (1)	1	0.01
Apache (4)	6	0.03
Blackfeet (3)	5	0.03
Canadian/French Am. Ind. (1)	1	0.01
Central American Ind. (2)	2	0.01
Cherokee (288)	567	3.08
Cheyenne (5)	8	0.04
Chickasaw (77)	136	0.74
Chippewa (1)	5	0.03
Choctaw (1,327)	1,853	10.08
Comanche (16)	22	0.12
Creek (89)	139	0.76
Delaware (2)	3	0.02
Iroquois (0)	3	0.02
Kiowa (11)	14	0.08
Mexican American Ind. (6)	9	0.05
Osage (15)	20	0.11
Ottawa (2)	2	0.01
Paiute (0)	1	0.01
Potawatomi (16)	19	0.10
Pueblo (3)	5	0.03
Seminole (16)	24	0.13
Shoshone (3)	3	0.02
Sioux (7)	15	0.08
Asian (122)	175	0.95
Not Hispanic (119)	168	0.91
Hispanic (3)	7	0.04
Chinese, ex. Taiwanese (46)	51	0.28
Filipino (18)	29	0.16
Indian (24)	33	0.18
Japanese (3)	12	0.07
Korean (11)	15	0.08
Pakistani (1)	1	0.01
Thai (5)	10	0.05
Vietnamese (10)	14	0.08
Hawaii Native/Pacific Islander (11)	25	0.14
Not Hispanic (10)	21	0.11
Hispanic (1)	4	0.02
Guamanian/Chamorro (7)	7	0.04
Native Hawaiian (2)	9	0.05
Samoan (0)	3	0.02
White (12,942)	14,044	76.40
Not Hispanic (12,425)	13,415	72.98
Hispanic (517)	629	3.42

Miami

Place Type: City
County: Ottawa
Population: 13,570†

Ancestry‡	Population	%
African, Sub-Saharan (9)	20	0.15
African (0)	10	0.07
Kenyan (9)	10	0.07
American (993)	993	7.27
Austrian (0)	35	0.26
Belgian (0)	8	0.06
British (31)	34	0.25
Canadian (0)	3	0.02
Celtic (6)	12	0.09
Czech (13)	15	0.11
Czechoslovakian (0)	7	0.05
Danish (3)	19	0.14
Dutch (99)	456	3.34
English (386)	1,306	9.56
European (41)	63	0.46
French, ex. Basque (89)	510	3.73
French Canadian (7)	28	0.20
German (693)	2,147	15.71
Greek (5)	5	0.04
Hungarian (0)	18	0.13
Irish (470)	1,763	12.90
Italian (68)	258	1.89
Lithuanian (0)	3	0.02
Norwegian (24)	41	0.30

*Notes: † The Census 2010 population figure is used to calculate the percentages in the Hispanic Origin and Race categories. Ancestry percentages are based on the 2006-2010 American Community Survey population (not shown); ‡ Numbers in parentheses indicate the number of people reporting a single ancestry; * Numbers in parentheses indicate the number of persons reporting this race alone, not in combination with any other race; Please refer to the Explanation of Data for more information.*

Pennsylvania German (0)	8	0.06
Polish (25)	78	0.57
Portuguese (5)	18	0.13
Romanian (3)	3	0.02
Russian (7)	7	0.05
Scotch-Irish (74)	248	1.82
Scottish (72)	236	1.73
Serbian (3)	3	0.02
Slavic (7)	18	0.13
Slovak (0)	12	0.09
Swedish (49)	117	0.86
Swiss (7)	33	0.24
Turkish (3)	3	0.02
Ukrainian (0)	2	0.01
Welsh (6)	18	0.13
West Indian, ex. Hispanic (16)	92	0.67
Dutch West Indian (16)	92	0.67

Hispanic Origin	Population	%
Hispanic or Latino (of any race)	657	4.84
Central American, ex. Mexican	42	0.31
Guatemalan	31	0.23
Honduran	3	0.02
Nicaraguan	1	0.01
Panamanian	7	0.05
Cuban	3	0.02
Dominican Republic	1	0.01
Mexican	508	3.74
Puerto Rican	25	0.18
South American	5	0.04
Ecuadorian	1	0.01
Peruvian	2	0.01
Venezuelan	2	0.01
Other Hispanic or Latino	73	0.54

Race*	Population	%
African-American/Black (182)	272	2.00
Not Hispanic (175)	256	1.89
Hispanic (7)	16	0.12
American Indian/Alaska Native (2,317)	3,246	23.92
Not Hispanic (2,274)	3,163	23.31
Hispanic (43)	83	0.61
Apache (3)	3	0.02
Arapaho (7)	13	0.10
Cherokee (893)	1,399	10.31
Cheyenne (12)	19	0.14
Chickasaw (7)	20	0.15
Chippewa (3)	6	0.04
Choctaw (38)	74	0.55
Comanche (3)	3	0.02
Creek (43)	62	0.46
Delaware (25)	36	0.27
Iroquois (242)	334	2.46
Kiowa (2)	5	0.04
Menominee (1)	1	0.01
Mexican American Ind. (2)	2	0.01
Navajo (5)	10	0.07
Osage (11)	20	0.15
Ottawa (58)	73	0.54
Potawatomi (10)	11	0.08
Puget Sound Salish (1)	1	0.01
Seminole (7)	7	0.05
Sioux (7)	12	0.09
South American Ind. (1)	1	0.01
Ute (0)	1	0.01
Yaqui (0)	2	0.01
Asian (71)	135	0.99
Not Hispanic (71)	130	0.96
Hispanic (0)	5	0.04
Cambodian (4)	4	0.03
Chinese, ex. Taiwanese (24)	29	0.21
Filipino (8)	14	0.10
Indian (13)	22	0.16
Japanese (3)	30	0.22
Korean (3)	14	0.10
Taiwanese (0)	1	0.01
Vietnamese (10)	12	0.09
Hawaii Native/Pacific Islander (271)	306	2.25
Not Hispanic (270)	297	2.19
Hispanic (1)	9	0.07
Guamanian/Chamorro (8)	10	0.07
Native Hawaiian (28)	52	0.38
Tongan (0)	1	0.01
White (9,355)	10,406	76.68
Not Hispanic (9,100)	10,080	74.28
Hispanic (255)	326	2.40

Midwest City

Place Type: City
County: Oklahoma
Population: 54,371†

Ancestry‡	Population	%
African, Sub-Saharan (252)	262	0.49
African (172)	182	0.34
Ghanaian (68)	68	0.13
Liberian (12)	12	0.02
American (4,982)	4,982	9.24
Arab (8)	74	0.14
Lebanese (8)	59	0.11
Syrian (0)	15	0.03
Armenian (0)	16	0.03
Austrian (10)	26	0.05
Belgian (16)	27	0.05
British (137)	224	0.42
Bulgarian (0)	18	0.03
Cajun (9)	9	0.02
Canadian (34)	69	0.13
Czech (27)	166	0.31
Czechoslovakian (32)	32	0.06
Danish (119)	188	0.35
Dutch (152)	902	1.67
Eastern European (11)	11	0.02
English (1,536)	4,341	8.05
European (348)	426	0.79
Finnish (19)	31	0.06
French, ex. Basque (252)	1,453	2.69
French Canadian (29)	57	0.11
German (2,592)	7,555	14.01
Greek (27)	34	0.06
Hungarian (24)	35	0.06
Iranian (59)	59	0.11
Irish (1,546)	5,958	11.05
Italian (194)	812	1.51
Lithuanian (10)	37	0.07
Luxemburger (10)	24	0.04
Maltese (0)	12	0.02
Northern European (50)	50	0.09
Norwegian (185)	313	0.58
Pennsylvania German (56)	85	0.16
Polish (159)	471	0.87
Portuguese (33)	55	0.10
Romanian (0)	13	0.02
Russian (33)	216	0.40
Scotch-Irish (380)	856	1.59
Scottish (316)	906	1.68
Swedish (16)	175	0.32
Swiss (10)	65	0.12
Turkish (86)	86	0.16
Ukrainian (27)	49	0.09
Welsh (27)	262	0.49
West Indian, ex. Hispanic (71)	258	0.48
Bahamian (32)	32	0.06
British West Indian (10)	10	0.02
Dutch West Indian (23)	210	0.39
Other West Indian (6)	6	0.01

Hispanic Origin	Population	%
Hispanic or Latino (of any race)	3,019	5.55
Central American, ex. Mexican	92	0.17
Guatemalan	17	0.03
Honduran	22	0.04
Nicaraguan	9	0.02
Panamanian	33	0.06
Salvadoran	11	0.02
Cuban	36	0.07
Dominican Republic	18	0.03
Mexican	2,169	3.99
Puerto Rican	280	0.51
South American	81	0.15
Argentinean	1	<0.01
Bolivian	5	0.01
Chilean	7	0.01
Colombian	32	0.06
Ecuadorian	5	0.01
Peruvian	27	0.05
Venezuelan	4	0.01
Other Hispanic or Latino	343	0.63

Race*	Population	%
African-American/Black (11,888)	13,394	24.63
Not Hispanic (11,723)	13,069	24.04
Hispanic (165)	325	0.60
American Indian/Alaska Native (2,029)	4,057	7.46
Not Hispanic (1,884)	3,767	6.93
Hispanic (145)	290	0.53
Alaska Athabascan *(Ala. Nat.)* (3)	3	0.01
Apache (8)	44	0.08
Arapaho (10)	13	0.02
Blackfeet (1)	26	0.05
Canadian/French Am. Ind. (0)	2	<0.01
Cherokee (361)	905	1.66
Cheyenne (8)	28	0.05
Chickasaw (196)	379	0.70
Chippewa (17)	28	0.05
Choctaw (353)	695	1.28
Comanche (31)	54	0.10
Creek (178)	347	0.64
Crow (2)	7	0.01
Delaware (19)	25	0.05
Hopi (3)	7	0.01
Inupiat *(Alaska Native)* (1)	3	0.01
Iroquois (13)	19	0.03
Kiowa (56)	84	0.15
Lumbee (4)	4	0.01
Mexican American Ind. (6)	15	0.03
Navajo (18)	25	0.05
Osage (11)	30	0.06
Ottawa (0)	1	<0.01
Potawatomi (75)	111	0.20
Pueblo (7)	9	0.02
Seminole (87)	203	0.37
Shoshone (0)	2	<0.01
Sioux (15)	29	0.05
South American Ind. (0)	3	0.01
Tohono O'Odham (0)	6	0.01
Ute (0)	3	0.01
Yakama (0)	1	<0.01
Yaqui (1)	2	<0.01
Asian (913)	1,445	2.66
Not Hispanic (890)	1,353	2.49
Hispanic (23)	92	0.17
Burmese (3)	3	0.01
Cambodian (3)	3	0.01
Chinese, ex. Taiwanese (51)	100	0.18
Filipino (289)	488	0.90
Hmong (3)	3	0.01
Indian (85)	103	0.19
Indonesian (4)	10	0.02
Japanese (87)	207	0.38
Korean (98)	180	0.33
Laotian (3)	5	0.01
Nepalese (1)	1	<0.01
Pakistani (5)	11	0.02
Taiwanese (8)	13	0.02
Thai (54)	91	0.17
Vietnamese (177)	203	0.37
Hawaii Native/Pacific Islander (62)	173	0.32
Not Hispanic (50)	141	0.26
Hispanic (12)	32	0.06
Guamanian/Chamorro (24)	43	0.08
Native Hawaiian (19)	73	0.13
Samoan (13)	21	0.04
Tongan (0)	2	<0.01
White (35,113)	38,040	69.96
Not Hispanic (33,697)	36,233	66.64
Hispanic (1,416)	1,807	3.32

*Notes: † The Census 2010 population figure is used to calculate the percentages in the Hispanic Origin and Race categories. Ancestry percentages are based on the 2006-2010 American Community Survey population (not shown); ‡ Numbers in parentheses indicate the number of people reporting a single ancestry; * Numbers in parentheses indicate the number of persons reporting this race alone, not in combination with any other race; Please refer to the Explanation of Data for more information.*

Moore

Place Type: City
County: Cleveland
Population: 55,081†

Ancestry‡	Population	%
African, Sub-Saharan (67)	67	0.13
African (55)	55	0.10
Other Sub-Saharan African (12)	12	0.02
Albanian (11)	11	0.02
American (4,884)	4,884	9.30
Arab (10)	33	0.06
Arab (10)	10	0.02
Lebanese (0)	23	0.04
Australian (0)	22	0.04
Austrian (46)	55	0.10
Belgian (12)	24	0.05
British (141)	261	0.50
Bulgarian (7)	7	0.01
Canadian (27)	58	0.11
Croatian (0)	9	0.02
Czech (57)	186	0.35
Czechoslovakian (0)	13	0.02
Danish (0)	88	0.17
Dutch (104)	1,278	2.43
English (1,576)	4,615	8.79
Estonian (12)	12	0.02
European (529)	680	1.30
Finnish (0)	34	0.06
French, ex. Basque (391)	1,505	2.87
French Canadian (61)	117	0.22
German (2,687)	8,923	16.99
Greek (16)	88	0.17
Hungarian (29)	83	0.16
Icelander (8)	8	0.02
Iranian (22)	35	0.07
Irish (1,809)	8,109	15.44
Italian (269)	1,139	2.17
Lithuanian (0)	40	0.08
New Zealander (11)	21	0.04
Northern European (0)	29	0.06
Norwegian (175)	572	1.09
Polish (113)	591	1.13
Portuguese (21)	21	0.04
Russian (0)	273	0.52
Scandinavian (8)	102	0.19
Scotch-Irish (435)	871	1.66
Scottish (482)	957	1.82
Slavic (0)	7	0.01
Slovak (8)	8	0.02
Slovene (0)	13	0.02
Swedish (50)	344	0.66
Swiss (0)	69	0.13
Turkish (39)	117	0.22
Ukrainian (22)	60	0.11
Welsh (52)	351	0.67
West Indian, ex. Hispanic (186)	548	1.04
British West Indian (9)	9	0.02
Dutch West Indian (85)	409	0.78
Jamaican (86)	124	0.24
Trinidadian/Tobagonian (6)	6	0.01
Yugoslavian (0)	7	0.01

Hispanic Origin	Population	%
Hispanic or Latino (of any race)	4,900	8.90
Central American, ex. Mexican	359	0.65
Costa Rican	4	0.01
Guatemalan	195	0.35
Honduran	36	0.07
Nicaraguan	8	0.01
Panamanian	35	0.06
Salvadoran	70	0.13
Other Central American	11	0.02
Cuban	58	0.11
Dominican Republic	14	0.03
Mexican	3,448	6.26
Puerto Rican	304	0.55
South American	183	0.33
Argentinean	22	0.04
Bolivian	3	0.01
Colombian	86	0.16
Ecuadorian	10	0.02
Paraguayan	4	0.01
Peruvian	32	0.06
Uruguayan	1	<0.01
Venezuelan	23	0.04
Other South American	2	<0.01
Other Hispanic or Latino	534	0.97

Race*	Population	%
African-American/Black (2,511)	3,451	6.27
Not Hispanic (2,430)	3,274	5.94
Hispanic (81)	177	0.32
American Indian/Alaska Native (2,463)	4,642	8.43
Not Hispanic (2,284)	4,265	7.74
Hispanic (179)	377	0.68
Alaska Athabascan *(Ala. Nat.)* (1)	3	0.01
Apache (11)	30	0.05
Arapaho (7)	15	0.03
Blackfeet (6)	32	0.06
Canadian/French Am. Ind. (1)	4	0.01
Cherokee (502)	1,235	2.24
Cheyenne (12)	22	0.04
Chickasaw (281)	500	0.91
Chippewa (11)	17	0.03
Choctaw (552)	1,057	1.92
Colville (0)	1	<0.01
Comanche (41)	82	0.15
Cree (1)	1	<0.01
Creek (170)	330	0.60
Crow (2)	2	<0.01
Delaware (16)	41	0.07
Hopi (4)	8	0.01
Houma (2)	2	<0.01
Inupiat *(Alaska Native)* (6)	7	0.01
Iroquois (4)	13	0.02
Kiowa (59)	100	0.18
Lumbee (1)	1	<0.01
Menominee (0)	2	<0.01
Mexican American Ind. (15)	18	0.03
Navajo (25)	40	0.07
Osage (19)	33	0.06
Paiute (1)	1	<0.01
Pima (3)	3	0.01
Potawatomi (114)	182	0.33
Pueblo (14)	17	0.03
Puget Sound Salish (3)	4	0.01
Seminole (101)	175	0.32
Shoshone (1)	1	<0.01
Sioux (15)	26	0.05
Spanish American Ind. (0)	1	<0.01
Tlingit-Haida *(Alaska Native)* (5)	10	0.02
Ute (0)	1	<0.01
Yakama (1)	2	<0.01
Yaqui (1)	2	<0.01
Yup'ik *(Alaska Native)* (1)	1	<0.01
Asian (1,256)	1,817	3.30
Not Hispanic (1,234)	1,733	3.15
Hispanic (22)	84	0.15
Bangladeshi (6)	7	0.01
Cambodian (13)	19	0.03
Chinese, ex. Taiwanese (95)	154	0.28
Filipino (161)	343	0.62
Indian (121)	158	0.29
Indonesian (0)	1	<0.01
Japanese (55)	142	0.26
Korean (230)	357	0.65
Laotian (7)	16	0.03
Malaysian (1)	3	0.01
Nepalese (12)	12	0.02
Pakistani (13)	16	0.03
Sri Lankan (3)	3	0.01
Taiwanese (5)	8	0.01
Thai (23)	51	0.09
Vietnamese (441)	515	0.93
Hawaii Native/Pacific Islander (40)	112	0.20
Not Hispanic (35)	92	0.17
Hispanic (5)	20	0.04
Guamanian/Chamorro (17)	34	0.06
Marshallese (2)	2	<0.01
Native Hawaiian (12)	44	0.08
Samoan (0)	10	0.02
Tongan (1)	1	<0.01
White (43,459)	46,897	85.14
Not Hispanic (41,077)	43,970	79.83
Hispanic (2,382)	2,927	5.31

Muskogee

Place Type: City
County: Muskogee
Population: 39,223†

Ancestry‡	Population	%
African, Sub-Saharan (117)	152	0.39
African (43)	47	0.12
Cape Verdean (0)	31	0.08
Ethiopian (50)	50	0.13
Nigerian (24)	24	0.06
Albanian (77)	77	0.20
American (5,190)	5,190	13.29
Arab (54)	78	0.20
Arab (0)	12	0.03
Jordanian (13)	13	0.03
Lebanese (15)	15	0.04
Palestinian (0)	12	0.03
Syrian (26)	26	0.07
Australian (0)	8	0.02
Austrian (19)	19	0.05
Belgian (20)	51	0.13
British (24)	155	0.40
Canadian (14)	14	0.04
Celtic (11)	11	0.03
Czech (17)	45	0.12
Czechoslovakian (0)	33	0.08
Danish (14)	23	0.06
Dutch (27)	511	1.31
English (816)	2,158	5.53
European (147)	169	0.43
Finnish (44)	57	0.15
French, ex. Basque (151)	724	1.85
French Canadian (0)	32	0.08
German (1,308)	4,320	11.06
German Russian (22)	22	0.06
Greek (12)	23	0.06
Hungarian (55)	55	0.14
Iranian (0)	9	0.02
Irish (1,051)	4,544	11.64
Italian (95)	626	1.60
Norwegian (56)	230	0.59
Pennsylvania German (0)	13	0.03
Polish (69)	111	0.28
Russian (68)	68	0.17
Scandinavian (11)	11	0.03
Scotch-Irish (218)	609	1.56
Scottish (269)	558	1.43
Swedish (35)	140	0.36
Welsh (23)	93	0.24
West Indian, ex. Hispanic (56)	142	0.36
Dutch West Indian (39)	125	0.32
West Indian (17)	17	0.04

Hispanic Origin	Population	%
Hispanic or Latino (of any race)	2,781	7.09
Central American, ex. Mexican	107	0.27
Guatemalan	58	0.15
Honduran	27	0.07
Nicaraguan	6	0.02
Panamanian	6	0.02
Salvadoran	10	0.03
Cuban	15	0.04
Dominican Republic	2	0.01
Mexican	2,252	5.74
Puerto Rican	84	0.21
South American	26	0.07
Argentinean	9	0.02
Chilean	1	<0.01
Colombian	8	0.02
Ecuadorian	1	<0.01

*Notes: † The Census 2010 population figure is used to calculate the percentages in the Hispanic Origin and Race categories. Ancestry percentages are based on the 2006-2010 American Community Survey population (not shown); ‡ Numbers in parentheses indicate the number of people reporting a single ancestry; * Numbers in parentheses indicate the number of persons reporting this race alone, not in combination with any other race; Please refer to the Explanation of Data for more information.*

Peruvian	2	0.01
Venezuelan	5	0.01
Other Hispanic or Latino	295	0.75

Race*	Population	%
African-American/Black (6,311)	7,320	18.66
Not Hispanic (6,254)	7,202	18.36
Hispanic (57)	118	0.30
American Indian/Alaska Native (6,017)	8,610	21.95
Not Hispanic (5,846)	8,314	21.20
Hispanic (171)	296	0.75
Apache (21)	33	0.08
Arapaho (6)	7	0.02
Blackfeet (1)	12	0.03
Cherokee (3,449)	5,163	13.16
Cheyenne (8)	10	0.03
Chickasaw (67)	131	0.33
Chippewa (12)	17	0.04
Choctaw (471)	714	1.82
Colville (0)	2	0.01
Comanche (16)	21	0.05
Creek (839)	1,317	3.36
Delaware (2)	5	0.01
Hopi (2)	2	0.01
Houma (1)	1	<0.01
Iroquois (12)	14	0.04
Kiowa (26)	29	0.07
Lumbee (4)	5	0.01
Mexican American Ind. (10)	12	0.03
Navajo (22)	27	0.07
Osage (35)	46	0.12
Ottawa (5)	5	0.01
Paiute (1)	5	0.01
Pima (1)	1	<0.01
Potawatomi (20)	39	0.10
Pueblo (2)	3	0.01
Puget Sound Salish (1)	2	0.01
Seminole (47)	78	0.20
Shoshone (4)	7	0.02
Sioux (14)	22	0.06
Tlingit-Haida *(Alaska Native)* (0)	4	0.01
Yakama (3)	3	0.01
Yaqui (2)	3	0.01
Asian (335)	418	1.07
Not Hispanic (324)	397	1.01
Hispanic (11)	21	0.05
Burmese (7)	7	0.02
Cambodian (1)	1	<0.01
Chinese, ex. Taiwanese (46)	54	0.14
Filipino (45)	70	0.18
Hmong (9)	9	0.02
Indian (55)	62	0.16
Japanese (12)	28	0.07
Korean (22)	38	0.10
Laotian (1)	1	<0.01
Nepalese (1)	1	<0.01
Pakistani (2)	2	0.01
Taiwanese (0)	1	<0.01
Thai (1)	5	0.01
Vietnamese (120)	126	0.32
Hawaii Native/Pacific Islander (15)	42	0.11
Not Hispanic (13)	32	0.08
Hispanic (2)	10	0.03
Guamanian/Chamorro (8)	10	0.03
Native Hawaiian (7)	18	0.05
White (21,926)	24,536	62.56
Not Hispanic (21,119)	23,511	59.94
Hispanic (807)	1,025	2.61

Mustang

Place Type: City
County: Canadian
Population: 17,395†

Ancestry‡	Population	%
African, Sub-Saharan (0)	186	1.13
Kenyan (0)	93	0.56
Other Sub-Saharan African (0)	93	0.56
American (1,452)	1,452	8.78
Arab (0)	14	0.08
Lebanese (0)	10	0.06
Moroccan (0)	4	0.02
Austrian (0)	8	0.05
British (122)	135	0.82
Cajun (10)	34	0.21
Croatian (9)	9	0.05
Czech (141)	208	1.26
Czechoslovakian (35)	47	0.28
Dutch (66)	386	2.34
Eastern European (0)	37	0.22
English (759)	1,905	11.53
European (215)	249	1.51
Finnish (0)	13	0.08
French, ex. Basque (133)	485	2.93
French Canadian (48)	73	0.44
German (1,398)	3,585	21.69
Greek (0)	47	0.28
Hungarian (22)	22	0.13
Irish (630)	1,946	11.77
Italian (145)	340	2.06
Norwegian (51)	124	0.75
Polish (58)	276	1.67
Russian (33)	43	0.26
Scandinavian (0)	36	0.22
Scotch-Irish (110)	280	1.69
Scottish (129)	420	2.54
Slovak (8)	8	0.05
Swedish (124)	234	1.42
Swiss (21)	60	0.36
Ukrainian (12)	12	0.07
Welsh (44)	145	0.88
West Indian, ex. Hispanic (25)	82	0.50
Dutch West Indian (25)	82	0.50

Hispanic Origin	Population	%
Hispanic or Latino (of any race)	1,054	6.06
Central American, ex. Mexican	48	0.28
Costa Rican	2	0.01
Guatemalan	25	0.14
Honduran	9	0.05
Nicaraguan	1	0.01
Panamanian	2	0.01
Salvadoran	9	0.05
Cuban	16	0.09
Dominican Republic	2	0.01
Mexican	783	4.50
Puerto Rican	54	0.31
South American	30	0.17
Argentinean	1	0.01
Bolivian	1	0.01
Colombian	12	0.07
Ecuadorian	2	0.01
Peruvian	12	0.07
Venezuelan	1	0.01
Other South American	1	0.01
Other Hispanic or Latino	121	0.70

Race*	Population	%
African-American/Black (166)	283	1.63
Not Hispanic (153)	259	1.49
Hispanic (13)	24	0.14
American Indian/Alaska Native (674)	1,145	6.58
Not Hispanic (649)	1,096	6.30
Hispanic (25)	49	0.28
Aleut *(Alaska Native)* (0)	1	0.01
Apache (1)	1	0.01
Arapaho (1)	2	0.01
Blackfeet (0)	1	0.01
Canadian/French Am. Ind. (0)	1	0.01
Central American Ind. (0)	1	0.01
Cherokee (134)	286	1.64
Cheyenne (10)	11	0.06
Chickasaw (72)	117	0.67
Chippewa (5)	5	0.03
Choctaw (193)	310	1.78
Comanche (9)	9	0.05
Creek (49)	78	0.45
Delaware (4)	10	0.06
Inupiat *(Alaska Native)* (0)	2	0.01
Iroquois (3)	4	0.02
Kiowa (7)	13	0.07
Lumbee (1)	1	0.01
Mexican American Ind. (0)	2	0.01
Navajo (1)	1	0.01
Osage (9)	23	0.13
Pima (1)	1	0.01
Potawatomi (25)	62	0.36
Pueblo (1)	4	0.02
Seminole (17)	21	0.12
Shoshone (0)	1	0.01
Sioux (1)	7	0.04
South American Ind. (0)	2	0.01
Yaqui (0)	2	0.01
Asian (160)	231	1.33
Not Hispanic (156)	222	1.28
Hispanic (4)	9	0.05
Bangladeshi (7)	7	0.04
Chinese, ex. Taiwanese (12)	31	0.18
Filipino (23)	52	0.30
Hmong (1)	2	0.01
Indian (26)	31	0.18
Japanese (8)	26	0.15
Korean (9)	15	0.09
Laotian (0)	1	0.01
Pakistani (1)	1	0.01
Thai (2)	2	0.01
Vietnamese (65)	73	0.42
Hawaii Native/Pacific Islander (8)	27	0.16
Not Hispanic (7)	22	0.13
Hispanic (1)	5	0.03
Guamanian/Chamorro (4)	6	0.03
Native Hawaiian (2)	14	0.08
Samoan (0)	3	0.02
White (15,371)	16,058	92.31
Not Hispanic (14,768)	15,352	88.26
Hispanic (603)	706	4.06

Newcastle

Place Type: City
County: McClain
Population: 7,685†

Ancestry‡	Population	%
American (893)	893	12.31
British (204)	204	2.81
Croatian (0)	7	0.10
Czech (0)	8	0.11
Czechoslovakian (0)	15	0.21
Danish (42)	70	0.96
Dutch (22)	96	1.32
English (267)	679	9.36
European (11)	119	1.64
French, ex. Basque (84)	155	2.14
German (696)	1,580	21.78
Irish (298)	1,268	17.48
Italian (70)	70	0.96
Norwegian (0)	23	0.32
Pennsylvania German (30)	30	0.41
Polish (47)	86	1.19
Scotch-Irish (53)	188	2.59
Scottish (43)	127	1.75
Slovak (0)	10	0.14
Swedish (13)	21	0.29
Ukrainian (0)	9	0.12
Welsh (0)	13	0.18
West Indian, ex. Hispanic (0)	24	0.33
Dutch West Indian (0)	24	0.33

Hispanic Origin	Population	%
Hispanic or Latino (of any race)	301	3.92
Central American, ex. Mexican	13	0.17
Honduran	2	0.03
Nicaraguan	2	0.03
Salvadoran	8	0.10
Other Central American	1	0.01
Cuban	1	0.01
Mexican	250	3.25
Puerto Rican	7	0.09

*Notes: † The Census 2010 population figure is used to calculate the percentages in the Hispanic Origin and Race categories. Ancestry percentages are based on the 2006-2010 American Community Survey population (not shown); ‡ Numbers in parentheses indicate the number of people reporting a single ancestry; * Numbers in parentheses indicate the number of persons reporting this race alone, not in combination with any other race; Please refer to the Explanation of Data for more information.*

South American	4	0.05
Chilean	3	0.04
Colombian	1	0.01
Other Hispanic or Latino	26	0.34

Race*	Population	%
African-American/Black (49)	77	1.00
Not Hispanic (45)	72	0.94
Hispanic (4)	5	0.07
American Indian/Alaska Native (490)	833	10.84
Not Hispanic (481)	811	10.55
Hispanic (9)	22	0.29
Apache (1)	3	0.04
Arapaho (1)	1	0.01
Cherokee (74)	188	2.45
Cheyenne (1)	1	0.01
Chickasaw (119)	182	2.37
Choctaw (115)	202	2.63
Comanche (8)	9	0.12
Creek (31)	49	0.64
Delaware (1)	2	0.03
Inupiat *(Alaska Native)* (1)	1	0.01
Iroquois (4)	4	0.05
Kiowa (5)	7	0.09
Osage (5)	10	0.13
Ottawa (1)	2	0.03
Potawatomi (26)	44	0.57
Pueblo (1)	1	0.01
Seminole (9)	16	0.21
Sioux (1)	1	0.01
Asian (51)	80	1.04
Not Hispanic (51)	80	1.04
Chinese, ex. Taiwanese (7)	8	0.10
Filipino (13)	21	0.27
Indian (10)	12	0.16
Japanese (4)	7	0.09
Korean (7)	18	0.23
Malaysian (1)	1	0.01
Pakistani (5)	5	0.07
Taiwanese (1)	1	0.01
Thai (1)	3	0.04
Vietnamese (1)	3	0.04
Hawaii Native/Pacific Islander (2)	8	0.10
Not Hispanic (2)	8	0.10
Native Hawaiian (2)	7	0.09
Samoan (0)	1	0.01
White (6,596)	6,997	91.05
Not Hispanic (6,426)	6,799	88.47
Hispanic (170)	198	2.58

Norman

Place Type: City
County: Cleveland
Population: 110,925†

Ancestry‡	Population	%
African, Sub-Saharan (1,384)	1,650	1.52
African (396)	525	0.48
Cape Verdean (0)	11	0.01
Ethiopian (10)	10	0.01
Ghanaian (13)	13	0.01
Kenyan (236)	236	0.22
Liberian (19)	19	0.02
Nigerian (700)	815	0.75
South African (0)	11	0.01
Zimbabwean (10)	10	0.01
American (7,435)	7,435	6.87
Arab (579)	876	0.81
Arab (138)	212	0.20
Egyptian (7)	59	0.05
Iraqi (22)	22	0.02
Lebanese (252)	412	0.38
Palestinian (28)	28	0.03
Syrian (48)	59	0.05
Other Arab (84)	84	0.08
Armenian (32)	43	0.04
Australian (89)	139	0.13
Austrian (31)	260	0.24
Basque (0)	10	0.01
Belgian (40)	133	0.12
British (366)	599	0.55
Bulgarian (127)	127	0.12
Cajun (23)	23	0.02
Canadian (71)	176	0.16
Celtic (0)	37	0.03
Czech (249)	827	0.76
Czechoslovakian (117)	223	0.21
Danish (115)	560	0.52
Dutch (265)	1,646	1.52
Eastern European (72)	176	0.16
English (4,521)	13,827	12.77
European (2,549)	3,162	2.92
Finnish (40)	89	0.08
French, ex. Basque (536)	2,729	2.52
French Canadian (126)	388	0.36
German (6,265)	19,576	18.08
Greek (261)	410	0.38
Hungarian (77)	199	0.18
Icelander (25)	34	0.03
Iranian (387)	466	0.43
Irish (4,940)	16,093	14.86
Israeli (19)	30	0.03
Italian (952)	2,919	2.70
Latvian (23)	47	0.04
Lithuanian (87)	155	0.14
Luxemburger (0)	10	0.01
New Zealander (7)	7	0.01
Northern European (44)	93	0.09
Norwegian (304)	1,053	0.97
Pennsylvania German (50)	60	0.06
Polish (457)	1,690	1.56
Portuguese (82)	163	0.15
Romanian (8)	42	0.04
Russian (44)	349	0.32
Scandinavian (85)	234	0.22
Scotch-Irish (1,008)	2,960	2.73
Scottish (1,274)	4,134	3.82
Serbian (149)	149	0.14
Slavic (0)	32	0.03
Slovak (40)	96	0.09
Slovene (10)	31	0.03
Swedish (427)	1,167	1.08
Swiss (33)	169	0.16
Turkish (53)	73	0.07
Ukrainian (107)	388	0.36
Welsh (485)	1,207	1.11
West Indian, ex. Hispanic (176)	411	0.38
Bahamian (11)	11	0.01
Dutch West Indian (37)	251	0.23
Haitian (35)	35	0.03
Jamaican (82)	103	0.10
Trinidadian/Tobagonian (11)	11	0.01
Yugoslavian (0)	17	0.02

Hispanic Origin	Population	%
Hispanic or Latino (of any race)	7,082	6.38
Central American, ex. Mexican	530	0.48
Costa Rican	48	0.04
Guatemalan	170	0.15
Honduran	41	0.04
Nicaraguan	21	0.02
Panamanian	66	0.06
Salvadoran	183	0.16
Other Central American	1	<0.01
Cuban	123	0.11
Dominican Republic	29	0.03
Mexican	4,635	4.18
Puerto Rican	406	0.37
South American	501	0.45
Argentinean	59	0.05
Bolivian	44	0.04
Chilean	21	0.02
Colombian	157	0.14
Ecuadorian	15	0.01
Paraguayan	3	<0.01
Peruvian	71	0.06
Uruguayan	2	<0.01
Venezuelan	124	0.11
Other South American	5	<0.01
Other Hispanic or Latino	858	0.77

Race*	Population	%
African-American/Black (4,794)	6,302	5.68
Not Hispanic (4,674)	6,048	5.45
Hispanic (120)	254	0.23
American Indian/Alaska Native (5,260)	8,972	8.09
Not Hispanic (5,027)	8,455	7.62
Hispanic (233)	517	0.47
Alaska Athabascan *(Ala. Nat.)* (4)	4	<0.01
Aleut *(Alaska Native)* (10)	12	0.01
Apache (42)	74	0.07
Arapaho (7)	16	0.01
Blackfeet (6)	26	0.02
Canadian/French Am. Ind. (0)	1	<0.01
Central American Ind. (0)	4	<0.01
Cherokee (862)	1,952	1.76
Cheyenne (37)	61	0.05
Chickasaw (554)	911	0.82
Chippewa (6)	23	0.02
Choctaw (999)	1,807	1.63
Colville (1)	5	<0.01
Comanche (189)	280	0.25
Cree (1)	4	<0.01
Creek (327)	580	0.52
Crow (3)	3	<0.01
Delaware (51)	95	0.09
Hopi (4)	9	0.01
Inupiat *(Alaska Native)* (3)	7	0.01
Iroquois (42)	66	0.06
Kiowa (162)	212	0.19
Lumbee (2)	6	0.01
Mexican American Ind. (19)	32	0.03
Navajo (53)	72	0.06
Osage (72)	135	0.12
Ottawa (5)	17	0.02
Pima (3)	4	<0.01
Potawatomi (269)	439	0.40
Pueblo (18)	24	0.02
Seminole (161)	255	0.23
Shoshone (2)	6	0.01
Sioux (35)	63	0.06
South American Ind. (2)	10	0.01
Spanish American Ind. (2)	2	<0.01
Tlingit-Haida *(Alaska Native)* (4)	8	0.01
Tsimshian *(Alaska Native)* (1)	2	<0.01
Ute (1)	1	<0.01
Yakama (1)	2	<0.01
Yaqui (0)	1	<0.01
Yup'ik *(Alaska Native)* (2)	2	<0.01
Asian (4,245)	5,258	4.74
Not Hispanic (4,211)	5,170	4.66
Hispanic (34)	88	0.08
Bangladeshi (52)	55	0.05
Burmese (19)	23	0.02
Cambodian (8)	8	0.01
Chinese, ex. Taiwanese (1,174)	1,361	1.23
Filipino (303)	538	0.49
Hmong (26)	28	0.03
Indian (942)	1,069	0.96
Indonesian (24)	34	0.03
Japanese (138)	312	0.28
Korean (448)	596	0.54
Laotian (36)	52	0.05
Malaysian (12)	20	0.02
Nepalese (43)	43	0.04
Pakistani (154)	178	0.16
Sri Lankan (33)	35	0.03
Taiwanese (89)	105	0.09
Thai (87)	143	0.13
Vietnamese (450)	536	0.48
Hawaii Native/Pacific Islander (90)	229	0.21
Not Hispanic (74)	186	0.17
Hispanic (16)	43	0.04
Fijian (2)	3	<0.01
Guamanian/Chamorro (28)	52	0.05
Marshallese (0)	1	<0.01
Native Hawaiian (29)	75	0.07
Samoan (14)	36	0.03
Tongan (1)	3	<0.01

*Notes: † The Census 2010 population figure is used to calculate the percentages in the Hispanic Origin and Race categories. Ancestry percentages are based on the 2006-2010 American Community Survey population (not shown); ‡ Numbers in parentheses indicate the number of people reporting a single ancestry; * Numbers in parentheses indicate the number of persons reporting this race alone, not in combination with any other race; Please refer to the Explanation of Data for more information.*

White (88,382)	94,008	84.75
Not Hispanic (84,384)	89,381	80.58
Hispanic (3,998)	4,627	4.17

Oklahoma City

Place Type: City
County: Oklahoma
Population: 579,999†

Ancestry‡	Population	%
African, Sub-Saharan (3,824)	4,569	0.81
African (2,152)	2,648	0.47
Cape Verdean (50)	50	0.01
Ethiopian (66)	235	0.04
Ghanaian (182)	205	0.04
Kenyan (262)	262	0.05
Liberian (107)	107	0.02
Nigerian (533)	559	0.10
South African (55)	64	0.01
Sudanese (385)	385	0.07
Ugandan (22)	22	<0.01
Other Sub-Saharan African (10)	32	0.01
Albanian (47)	47	0.01
American (36,023)	36,023	6.39
Arab (1,809)	2,661	0.47
Arab (416)	499	0.09
Egyptian (12)	25	<0.01
Jordanian (303)	303	0.05
Lebanese (612)	928	0.16
Moroccan (168)	244	0.04
Palestinian (55)	75	0.01
Syrian (32)	150	0.03
Other Arab (211)	437	0.08
Armenian (153)	226	0.04
Assyrian/Chaldean/Syriac (13)	13	<0.01
Australian (93)	160	0.03
Austrian (128)	577	0.10
Basque (17)	80	0.01
Belgian (91)	229	0.04
Brazilian (59)	150	0.03
British (1,335)	2,582	0.46
Bulgarian (150)	234	0.04
Cajun (164)	168	0.03
Canadian (155)	374	0.07
Celtic (0)	8	<0.01
Croatian (34)	192	0.03
Czech (971)	2,994	0.53
Czechoslovakian (226)	459	0.08
Danish (284)	1,333	0.24
Dutch (1,665)	10,020	1.78
Eastern European (85)	117	0.02
English (16,894)	47,135	8.36
Estonian (0)	8	<0.01
European (5,865)	6,973	1.24
Finnish (113)	257	0.05
French, ex. Basque (2,466)	12,990	2.30
French Canadian (660)	1,333	0.24
German (28,050)	78,776	13.98
German Russian (11)	75	0.01
Greek (667)	1,392	0.25
Guyanese (30)	30	0.01
Hungarian (398)	1,061	0.19
Icelander (18)	69	0.01
Iranian (1,068)	1,297	0.23
Irish (17,825)	62,334	11.06
Israeli (130)	139	0.02
Italian (3,535)	10,410	1.85
Latvian (12)	66	0.01
Lithuanian (107)	281	0.05
Luxemburger (0)	8	<0.01
Macedonian (19)	28	<0.01
Northern European (288)	330	0.06
Norwegian (1,244)	3,656	0.65
Pennsylvania German (137)	257	0.05
Polish (1,378)	5,061	0.90
Portuguese (277)	693	0.12
Romanian (119)	198	0.04
Russian (486)	1,534	0.27
Scandinavian (212)	524	0.09
Scotch-Irish (3,601)	9,958	1.77
Scottish (4,034)	10,551	1.87
Serbian (19)	19	<0.01
Slavic (144)	223	0.04
Slovak (59)	241	0.04
Slovene (18)	59	0.01
Swedish (1,098)	4,355	0.77
Swiss (438)	1,461	0.26
Turkish (12)	135	0.02
Ukrainian (138)	270	0.05
Welsh (838)	2,967	0.53
West Indian, ex. Hispanic (505)	2,596	0.46
Bahamian (43)	63	0.01
Barbadian (27)	27	<0.01
Belizean (28)	28	<0.01
Dutch West Indian (276)	2,248	0.40
Haitian (9)	16	<0.01
Jamaican (87)	159	0.03
Trinidadian/Tobagonian (35)	55	0.01
Yugoslavian (162)	208	0.04

Hispanic Origin	Population	%
Hispanic or Latino (of any race)	100,038	17.25
Central American, ex. Mexican	6,506	1.12
Costa Rican	93	0.02
Guatemalan	4,256	0.73
Honduran	944	0.16
Nicaraguan	140	0.02
Panamanian	228	0.04
Salvadoran	799	0.14
Other Central American	46	0.01
Cuban	594	0.10
Dominican Republic	106	0.02
Mexican	82,318	14.19
Puerto Rican	2,211	0.38
South American	1,762	0.30
Argentinean	125	0.02
Bolivian	54	0.01
Chilean	68	0.01
Colombian	552	0.10
Ecuadorian	137	0.02
Paraguayan	9	<0.01
Peruvian	540	0.09
Uruguayan	13	<0.01
Venezuelan	257	0.04
Other South American	7	<0.01
Other Hispanic or Latino	6,541	1.13

Race*	Population	%
African-American/Black (87,354)	98,344	16.96
Not Hispanic (85,744)	95,377	16.44
Hispanic (1,610)	2,967	0.51
American Indian/Alaska Native (20,533)	36,572	6.31
Not Hispanic (18,208)	32,292	5.57
Hispanic (2,325)	4,280	0.74
Alaska Athabascan *(Ala. Nat.)* (8)	11	<0.01
Aleut *(Alaska Native)* (10)	17	<0.01
Apache (238)	412	0.07
Arapaho (82)	132	0.02
Blackfeet (19)	200	0.03
Canadian/French Am. Ind. (1)	10	<0.01
Central American Ind. (13)	26	<0.01
Cherokee (2,900)	7,210	1.24
Cheyenne (279)	444	0.08
Chickasaw (1,427)	2,766	0.48
Chippewa (63)	142	0.02
Choctaw (3,746)	6,527	1.13
Colville (4)	10	<0.01
Comanche (435)	672	0.12
Cree (8)	22	<0.01
Creek (1,513)	2,905	0.50
Crow (8)	22	<0.01
Delaware (148)	280	0.05
Hopi (7)	27	<0.01
Houma (2)	4	<0.01
Inupiat *(Alaska Native)* (5)	21	<0.01
Iroquois (98)	195	0.03
Kiowa (645)	950	0.16
Lumbee (19)	26	<0.01
Mexican American Ind. (252)	402	0.07
Navajo (171)	244	0.04
Osage (157)	308	0.05
Ottawa (13)	27	<0.01
Paiute (4)	14	<0.01
Pima (17)	30	0.01
Potawatomi (597)	982	0.17
Pueblo (44)	66	0.01
Puget Sound Salish (11)	12	<0.01
Seminole (988)	1,745	0.30
Shoshone (10)	25	<0.01
Sioux (130)	271	0.05
South American Ind. (13)	33	0.01
Spanish American Ind. (24)	30	0.01
Tlingit-Haida *(Alaska Native)* (12)	17	<0.01
Tohono O'Odham (11)	18	<0.01
Tsimshian *(Alaska Native)* (1)	4	<0.01
Ute (1)	4	<0.01
Yakama (7)	9	<0.01
Yaqui (5)	17	<0.01
Yuman (12)	16	<0.01
Yup'ik *(Alaska Native)* (1)	4	<0.01
Asian (23,310)	27,716	4.78
Not Hispanic (23,051)	26,942	4.65
Hispanic (259)	774	0.13
Bangladeshi (222)	247	0.04
Burmese (191)	222	0.04
Cambodian (120)	160	0.03
Chinese, ex. Taiwanese (2,239)	2,952	0.51
Filipino (1,318)	2,379	0.41
Hmong (23)	32	0.01
Indian (4,252)	4,765	0.82
Indonesian (102)	136	0.02
Japanese (426)	1,073	0.19
Korean (1,320)	1,998	0.34
Laotian (653)	805	0.14
Malaysian (76)	89	0.02
Nepalese (146)	153	0.03
Pakistani (707)	782	0.13
Sri Lankan (16)	20	<0.01
Taiwanese (118)	145	0.03
Thai (332)	529	0.09
Vietnamese (10,095)	10,848	1.87
Hawaii Native/Pacific Islander (586)	1,322	0.23
Not Hispanic (464)	975	0.17
Hispanic (122)	347	0.06
Fijian (1)	1	<0.01
Guamanian/Chamorro (255)	384	0.07
Marshallese (9)	12	<0.01
Native Hawaiian (138)	435	0.08
Samoan (70)	138	0.02
Tongan (7)	13	<0.01
White (363,646)	388,546	66.99
Not Hispanic (328,582)	348,078	60.01
Hispanic (35,064)	40,468	6.98

Okmulgee

Place Type: City
County: Okmulgee
Population: 12,321†

Ancestry‡	Population	%
African, Sub-Saharan (4)	71	0.58
African (4)	49	0.40
Nigerian (0)	22	0.18
American (1,196)	1,196	9.72
Belgian (9)	9	0.07
British (29)	29	0.24
Canadian (10)	10	0.08
Dutch (6)	465	3.78
English (319)	697	5.67
French, ex. Basque (89)	265	2.15
French Canadian (21)	21	0.17
German (461)	2,093	17.01
Greek (0)	48	0.39
Irish (269)	2,096	17.04
Italian (18)	46	0.37
Lithuanian (0)	37	0.30
Norwegian (0)	31	0.25
Russian (0)	7	0.06

*Notes: † The Census 2010 population figure is used to calculate the percentages in the Hispanic Origin and Race categories. Ancestry percentages are based on the 2006-2010 American Community Survey population (not shown); ‡ Numbers in parentheses indicate the number of people reporting a single ancestry; * Numbers in parentheses indicate the number of persons reporting this race alone, not in combination with any other race; Please refer to the Explanation of Data for more information.*

Ancestry	Population	%
Scotch-Irish (62)	264	2.15
Scottish (97)	291	2.37
Swedish (0)	10	0.08
Welsh (0)	19	0.15
West Indian, ex. Hispanic (16)	31	0.25
Belizean (16)	16	0.13
Dutch West Indian (0)	15	0.12
Yugoslavian (27)	27	0.22

Hispanic Origin	Population	%
Hispanic or Latino (of any race)	393	3.19
Central American, ex. Mexican	13	0.11
Nicaraguan	7	0.06
Panamanian	3	0.02
Salvadoran	3	0.02
Cuban	2	0.02
Dominican Republic	2	0.02
Mexican	294	2.39
Puerto Rican	22	0.18
South American	7	0.06
Argentinean	1	0.01
Colombian	1	0.01
Peruvian	3	0.02
Venezuelan	2	0.02
Other Hispanic or Latino	53	0.43

Race*	Population	%
African-American/Black (2,320)	2,722	22.09
Not Hispanic (2,299)	2,685	21.79
Hispanic (21)	37	0.30
American Indian/Alaska Native (2,259)	3,142	25.50
Not Hispanic (2,192)	3,027	24.57
Hispanic (67)	115	0.93
Apache (2)	17	0.14
Arapaho (4)	5	0.04
Blackfeet (0)	7	0.06
Cherokee (250)	481	3.90
Chickasaw (47)	66	0.54
Chippewa (6)	6	0.05
Choctaw (131)	196	1.59
Comanche (7)	8	0.06
Creek (1,415)	1,882	15.27
Delaware (0)	2	0.02
Hopi (1)	1	0.01
Inupiat *(Alaska Native)* (2)	2	0.02
Iroquois (0)	1	0.01
Kiowa (17)	18	0.15
Lumbee (1)	1	0.01
Mexican American Ind. (0)	1	0.01
Navajo (3)	7	0.06
Osage (0)	2	0.02
Potawatomi (5)	5	0.04
Seminole (53)	81	0.66
Sioux (10)	12	0.10
Tohono O'Odham (1)	1	0.01
Yuman (5)	5	0.04
Asian (83)	127	1.03
Not Hispanic (80)	121	0.98
Hispanic (3)	6	0.05
Chinese, ex. Taiwanese (16)	22	0.18
Filipino (17)	27	0.22
Indian (19)	27	0.22
Japanese (5)	18	0.15
Korean (6)	10	0.08
Pakistani (5)	5	0.04
Thai (2)	2	0.02
Vietnamese (11)	13	0.11
Hawaii Native/Pacific Islander (0)	12	0.10
Not Hispanic (0)	9	0.07
Hispanic (0)	3	0.02
Guamanian/Chamorro (0)	3	0.02
Native Hawaiian (0)	5	0.04
White (6,536)	7,354	59.69
Not Hispanic (6,353)	7,116	57.76
Hispanic (183)	238	1.93

Owasso

Place Type: City
County: Tulsa
Population: 28,915†

Ancestry‡	Population	%
African, Sub-Saharan (48)	100	0.37
African (48)	63	0.23
South African (0)	37	0.14
American (2,530)	2,530	9.40
Arab (0)	27	0.10
Lebanese (0)	13	0.05
Other Arab (0)	14	0.05
Austrian (0)	38	0.14
Belgian (5)	5	0.02
British (20)	93	0.35
Bulgarian (6)	6	0.02
Canadian (13)	43	0.16
Croatian (0)	7	0.03
Czech (21)	113	0.42
Danish (17)	106	0.39
Dutch (86)	933	3.47
English (1,049)	3,100	11.52
European (95)	213	0.79
French, ex. Basque (123)	758	2.82
French Canadian (49)	131	0.49
German (1,289)	4,912	18.26
Greek (95)	121	0.45
Hungarian (0)	13	0.05
Irish (965)	3,513	13.06
Italian (167)	658	2.45
Luxemburger (0)	7	0.03
Northern European (11)	11	0.04
Norwegian (142)	423	1.57
Pennsylvania German (0)	4	0.01
Polish (115)	291	1.08
Portuguese (18)	62	0.23
Russian (10)	86	0.32
Scandinavian (19)	19	0.07
Scotch-Irish (172)	359	1.33
Scottish (315)	921	3.42
Swedish (169)	270	1.00
Swiss (12)	12	0.04
Ukrainian (14)	60	0.22
Welsh (5)	173	0.64
West Indian, ex. Hispanic (44)	182	0.68
Dutch West Indian (38)	163	0.61
Jamaican (6)	19	0.07
Yugoslavian (22)	30	0.11

Hispanic Origin	Population	%
Hispanic or Latino (of any race)	1,942	6.72
Central American, ex. Mexican	141	0.49
Costa Rican	5	0.02
Guatemalan	71	0.25
Honduran	28	0.10
Nicaraguan	4	0.01
Panamanian	5	0.02
Salvadoran	28	0.10
Cuban	21	0.07
Dominican Republic	2	0.01
Mexican	1,452	5.02
Puerto Rican	83	0.29
South American	77	0.27
Argentinean	4	0.01
Chilean	3	0.01
Colombian	25	0.09
Ecuadorian	1	<0.01
Peruvian	14	0.05
Venezuelan	23	0.08
Other South American	7	0.02
Other Hispanic or Latino	166	0.57

Race*	Population	%
African-American/Black (801)	1,038	3.59
Not Hispanic (785)	993	3.43
Hispanic (16)	45	0.16
American Indian/Alaska Native (1,959)	3,291	11.38
Not Hispanic (1,893)	3,164	10.94
Hispanic (66)	127	0.44
Aleut *(Alaska Native)* (1)	1	<0.01
Apache (4)	11	0.04
Blackfeet (0)	10	0.03
Cherokee (1,153)	2,030	7.02
Cheyenne (1)	1	<0.01
Chickasaw (28)	54	0.19
Chippewa (3)	7	0.02
Choctaw (140)	254	0.88
Comanche (11)	13	0.04
Creek (154)	232	0.80
Crow (3)	4	0.01
Delaware (14)	28	0.10
Iroquois (26)	38	0.13
Kiowa (8)	14	0.05
Mexican American Ind. (3)	8	0.03
Navajo (10)	11	0.04
Osage (54)	86	0.30
Ottawa (2)	11	0.04
Potawatomi (14)	28	0.10
Pueblo (1)	1	<0.01
Seminole (25)	34	0.12
Shoshone (0)	1	<0.01
Sioux (4)	9	0.03
Tsimshian *(Alaska Native)* (0)	1	<0.01
Yaqui (0)	1	<0.01
Asian (529)	707	2.45
Not Hispanic (525)	695	2.40
Hispanic (4)	12	0.04
Bangladeshi (1)	1	<0.01
Chinese, ex. Taiwanese (80)	91	0.31
Filipino (51)	94	0.33
Hmong (186)	204	0.71
Indian (73)	111	0.38
Indonesian (1)	2	0.01
Japanese (14)	46	0.16
Korean (42)	73	0.25
Laotian (0)	7	0.02
Malaysian (1)	1	<0.01
Pakistani (4)	8	0.03
Sri Lankan (1)	1	<0.01
Thai (7)	21	0.07
Vietnamese (41)	50	0.17
Hawaii Native/Pacific Islander (57)	100	0.35
Not Hispanic (56)	91	0.31
Hispanic (1)	9	0.03
Fijian (1)	1	<0.01
Guamanian/Chamorro (12)	21	0.07
Native Hawaiian (7)	28	0.10
Samoan (3)	3	0.01
Tongan (2)	4	0.01
White (22,956)	24,616	85.13
Not Hispanic (22,106)	23,629	81.72
Hispanic (850)	987	3.41

Ponca City

Place Type: City
County: Kay
Population: 25,387†

Ancestry‡	Population	%
African, Sub-Saharan (20)	25	0.10
African (20)	25	0.10
American (2,002)	2,002	7.90
Arab (33)	33	0.13
Lebanese (20)	20	0.08
Other Arab (13)	13	0.05
Austrian (10)	22	0.09
Belgian (7)	51	0.20
British (45)	64	0.25
Cajun (7)	13	0.05
Canadian (23)	23	0.09
Czech (69)	209	0.83
Czechoslovakian (19)	19	0.08
Danish (0)	78	0.31
Dutch (146)	888	3.51
Eastern European (7)	7	0.03
English (1,359)	2,857	11.28
European (298)	313	1.24

*Notes: † The Census 2010 population figure is used to calculate the percentages in the Hispanic Origin and Race categories. Ancestry percentages are based on the 2006-2010 American Community Survey population (not shown); ‡ Numbers in parentheses indicate the number of people reporting a single ancestry; * Numbers in parentheses indicate the number of persons reporting this race alone, not in combination with any other race; Please refer to the Explanation of Data for more information.*

French, ex. Basque (268)	923	3.64
French Canadian (14)	48	0.19
German (1,813)	4,706	18.58
Greek (6)	20	0.08
Hungarian (21)	21	0.08
Irish (1,302)	3,533	13.95
Italian (133)	467	1.84
Lithuanian (0)	25	0.10
Norwegian (56)	124	0.49
Pennsylvania German (6)	6	0.02
Polish (97)	218	0.86
Portuguese (0)	17	0.07
Romanian (16)	16	0.06
Russian (33)	122	0.48
Scandinavian (21)	33	0.13
Scotch-Irish (334)	741	2.93
Scottish (118)	514	2.03
Slovak (3)	3	0.01
Swedish (56)	260	1.03
Swiss (11)	46	0.18
Turkish (14)	14	0.06
Ukrainian (23)	23	0.09
Welsh (61)	109	0.43
West Indian, ex. Hispanic (25)	37	0.15
Dutch West Indian (25)	25	0.10
Jamaican (0)	12	0.05

Hispanic Origin	Population	%
Hispanic or Latino (of any race)	1,819	7.17
Central American, ex. Mexican	36	0.14
Guatemalan	25	0.10
Honduran	6	0.02
Nicaraguan	1	<0.01
Panamanian	1	<0.01
Salvadoran	1	<0.01
Other Central American	2	0.01
Cuban	21	0.08
Dominican Republic	3	0.01
Mexican	1,564	6.16
Puerto Rican	31	0.12
South American	18	0.07
Colombian	7	0.03
Ecuadorian	4	0.02
Peruvian	6	0.02
Venezuelan	1	<0.01
Other Hispanic or Latino	146	0.58

Race*	Population	%
African-American/Black (825)	1,077	4.24
Not Hispanic (776)	1,004	3.95
Hispanic (49)	73	0.29
American Indian/Alaska Native (2,257)	3,271	12.88
Not Hispanic (2,113)	3,037	11.96
Hispanic (144)	234	0.92
Aleut *(Alaska Native)* (4)	5	0.02
Apache (8)	18	0.07
Arapaho (12)	13	0.05
Blackfeet (3)	5	0.02
Canadian/French Am. Ind. (1)	6	0.02
Cherokee (336)	644	2.54
Cheyenne (11)	26	0.10
Chickasaw (40)	57	0.22
Chippewa (5)	10	0.04
Choctaw (105)	174	0.69
Comanche (16)	41	0.16
Creek (49)	81	0.32
Delaware (6)	7	0.03
Houma (3)	6	0.02
Inupiat *(Alaska Native)* (1)	10	0.04
Iroquois (24)	47	0.19
Kiowa (19)	28	0.11
Mexican American Ind. (8)	10	0.04
Navajo (11)	16	0.06
Osage (92)	179	0.71
Ottawa (0)	3	0.01
Potawatomi (29)	39	0.15
Pueblo (8)	10	0.04
Puget Sound Salish (5)	5	0.02
Seminole (17)	25	0.10
Shoshone (1)	1	<0.01
Sioux (25)	38	0.15
South American Ind. (1)	2	0.01
Tlingit-Haida *(Alaska Native)* (0)	2	0.01
Tohono O'Odham (1)	1	<0.01
Tsimshian *(Alaska Native)* (0)	2	0.01
Ute (0)	1	<0.01
Yuman (0)	1	<0.01
Yup'ik *(Alaska Native)* (0)	4	0.02
Asian (170)	262	1.03
Not Hispanic (169)	255	1.00
Hispanic (1)	7	0.03
Bangladeshi (3)	3	0.01
Chinese, ex. Taiwanese (38)	45	0.18
Filipino (34)	64	0.25
Indian (39)	42	0.17
Indonesian (2)	2	0.01
Japanese (5)	32	0.13
Korean (14)	24	0.09
Pakistani (1)	1	<0.01
Taiwanese (7)	7	0.03
Thai (2)	3	0.01
Vietnamese (23)	32	0.13
Hawaii Native/Pacific Islander (12)	34	0.13
Not Hispanic (6)	26	0.10
Hispanic (6)	8	0.03
Guamanian/Chamorro (0)	7	0.03
Native Hawaiian (5)	14	0.06
Samoan (6)	11	0.04
White (20,072)	21,323	83.99
Not Hispanic (19,340)	20,446	80.54
Hispanic (732)	877	3.45

Poteau

Place Type: City
County: Le Flore
Population: 8,520†

Ancestry‡	Population	%
American (861)	861	10.23
British (0)	22	0.26
Cajun (13)	105	1.25
Czech (0)	14	0.17
Czechoslovakian (22)	60	0.71
Dutch (0)	82	0.97
English (130)	434	5.16
European (39)	39	0.46
French, ex. Basque (114)	197	2.34
French Canadian (0)	89	1.06
German (163)	720	8.55
Hungarian (0)	25	0.30
Irish (290)	1,159	13.77
Italian (20)	82	0.97
Norwegian (0)	22	0.26
Portuguese (22)	22	0.26
Scotch-Irish (57)	88	1.05
Scottish (71)	81	0.96
Swedish (0)	11	0.13
Swiss (0)	13	0.15
West Indian, ex. Hispanic (0)	102	1.21
Dutch West Indian (0)	102	1.21

Hispanic Origin	Population	%
Hispanic or Latino (of any race)	854	10.02
Central American, ex. Mexican	8	0.09
Costa Rican	1	0.01
Panamanian	1	0.01
Salvadoran	6	0.07
Cuban	5	0.06
Mexican	774	9.08
Puerto Rican	6	0.07
South American	5	0.06
Venezuelan	5	0.06
Other Hispanic or Latino	56	0.66

Race*	Population	%
African-American/Black (123)	195	2.29
Not Hispanic (121)	182	2.14
Hispanic (2)	13	0.15
American Indian/Alaska Native (963)	1,401	16.44
Not Hispanic (941)	1,354	15.89
Hispanic (22)	47	0.55
Aleut *(Alaska Native)* (4)	4	0.05
Apache (1)	2	0.02
Blackfeet (0)	1	0.01
Cherokee (144)	281	3.30
Cheyenne (2)	4	0.05
Chickasaw (16)	21	0.25
Chippewa (3)	3	0.04
Choctaw (594)	811	9.52
Colville (0)	1	0.01
Comanche (2)	2	0.02
Creek (9)	15	0.18
Kiowa (5)	7	0.08
Navajo (7)	7	0.08
Osage (1)	1	0.01
Potawatomi (13)	14	0.16
Seminole (10)	11	0.13
Shoshone (0)	3	0.04
Sioux (1)	8	0.09
Spanish American Ind. (0)	1	0.01
Yaqui (1)	1	0.01
Asian (52)	66	0.77
Not Hispanic (49)	62	0.73
Hispanic (3)	4	0.05
Cambodian (3)	3	0.04
Chinese, ex. Taiwanese (0)	1	0.01
Filipino (12)	14	0.16
Indian (11)	11	0.13
Japanese (3)	10	0.12
Korean (2)	3	0.04
Laotian (5)	5	0.06
Thai (1)	1	0.01
Vietnamese (12)	15	0.18
Hawaii Native/Pacific Islander (5)	12	0.14
Not Hispanic (5)	11	0.13
Hispanic (0)	1	0.01
Guamanian/Chamorro (2)	2	0.02
Marshallese (0)	1	0.01
Native Hawaiian (1)	7	0.08
White (6,340)	6,848	80.38
Not Hispanic (6,080)	6,522	76.55
Hispanic (260)	326	3.83

Pryor Creek

Place Type: City
County: Mayes
Population: 9,539†

Ancestry‡	Population	%
American (881)	881	9.34
Czech (8)	153	1.62
Danish (40)	175	1.86
Dutch (27)	164	1.74
English (196)	655	6.94
European (27)	27	0.29
French, ex. Basque (123)	298	3.16
French Canadian (8)	88	0.93
German (433)	1,408	14.93
Greek (12)	12	0.13
Irish (299)	1,643	17.42
Italian (28)	100	1.06
Norwegian (60)	157	1.66
Polish (31)	66	0.70
Portuguese (0)	39	0.41
Russian (0)	11	0.12
Scotch-Irish (44)	151	1.60
Scottish (0)	70	0.74
Slovene (16)	16	0.17
Swedish (29)	139	1.47
Swiss (38)	180	1.91
Welsh (0)	32	0.34
West Indian, ex. Hispanic (21)	76	0.81
Dutch West Indian (21)	76	0.81

Hispanic Origin	Population	%
Hispanic or Latino (of any race)	465	4.87
Central American, ex. Mexican	8	0.08
Guatemalan	2	0.02

*Notes: † The Census 2010 population figure is used to calculate the percentages in the Hispanic Origin and Race categories. Ancestry percentages are based on the 2006-2010 American Community Survey population (not shown); ‡ Numbers in parentheses indicate the number of people reporting a single ancestry; * Numbers in parentheses indicate the number of persons reporting this race alone, not in combination with any other race; Please refer to the Explanation of Data for more information.*

Honduran	2	0.02
Salvadoran	4	0.04
Cuban	5	0.05
Mexican	381	3.99
Puerto Rican	13	0.14
South American	7	0.07
Argentinean	4	0.04
Peruvian	1	0.01
Venezuelan	2	0.02
Other Hispanic or Latino	51	0.53

Race*	Population	%
African-American/Black (63)	93	0.97
Not Hispanic (57)	84	0.88
Hispanic (6)	9	0.09
American Indian/Alaska Native (1,609)	2,275	23.85
Not Hispanic (1,559)	2,207	23.14
Hispanic (50)	68	0.71
Blackfeet (1)	1	0.01
Cherokee (1,051)	1,525	15.99
Cheyenne (7)	11	0.12
Chickasaw (18)	39	0.41
Chippewa (5)	5	0.05
Choctaw (59)	81	0.85
Comanche (6)	8	0.08
Creek (49)	80	0.84
Delaware (2)	5	0.05
Iroquois (11)	18	0.19
Kiowa (8)	10	0.10
Mexican American Ind. (8)	9	0.09
Navajo (4)	6	0.06
Osage (7)	17	0.18
Ottawa (3)	3	0.03
Potawatomi (9)	15	0.16
Seminole (4)	10	0.10
Shoshone (0)	3	0.03
Sioux (3)	5	0.05
Asian (56)	80	0.84
Not Hispanic (54)	78	0.82
Hispanic (2)	2	0.02
Bangladeshi (2)	2	0.02
Chinese, ex. Taiwanese (10)	13	0.14
Filipino (9)	18	0.19
Indian (6)	6	0.06
Indonesian (2)	3	0.03
Japanese (3)	11	0.12
Korean (1)	2	0.02
Pakistani (1)	2	0.02
Taiwanese (1)	1	0.01
Vietnamese (18)	19	0.20
Hawaii Native/Pacific Islander (3)	8	0.08
Not Hispanic (3)	6	0.06
Hispanic (0)	2	0.02
Native Hawaiian (1)	5	0.05
Samoan (1)	2	0.02
White (6,894)	7,617	79.85
Not Hispanic (6,707)	7,385	77.42
Hispanic (187)	232	2.43

Sallisaw

Place Type: City
County: Sequoyah
Population: 8,880†

Ancestry‡	Population	%
American (502)	502	5.73
Czech (0)	68	0.78
Danish (0)	5	0.06
Dutch (22)	75	0.86
English (175)	470	5.37
European (11)	85	0.97
French, ex. Basque (23)	85	0.97
French Canadian (9)	46	0.53
German (159)	387	4.42
Hungarian (0)	8	0.09
Irish (336)	869	9.92
Italian (19)	79	0.90
Norwegian (8)	16	0.18
Polish (8)	37	0.42
Scotch-Irish (12)	45	0.51
Scottish (50)	53	0.61
Slavic (9)	17	0.19
Slovak (0)	9	0.10
Welsh (9)	38	0.43
West Indian, ex. Hispanic (0)	23	0.26
Dutch West Indian (0)	23	0.26

Hispanic Origin	Population	%
Hispanic or Latino (of any race)	499	5.62
Central American, ex. Mexican	8	0.09
Honduran	2	0.02
Salvadoran	6	0.07
Mexican	445	5.01
Puerto Rican	7	0.08
South American	4	0.05
Argentinean	2	0.02
Peruvian	2	0.02
Other Hispanic or Latino	35	0.39

Race*	Population	%
African-American/Black (144)	209	2.35
Not Hispanic (129)	187	2.11
Hispanic (15)	22	0.25
American Indian/Alaska Native (1,916)	2,804	31.58
Not Hispanic (1,869)	2,705	30.46
Hispanic (47)	99	1.11
Apache (0)	1	0.01
Arapaho (0)	1	0.01
Blackfeet (0)	3	0.03
Canadian/French Am. Ind. (0)	1	0.01
Cherokee (1,561)	2,267	25.53
Cheyenne (1)	1	0.01
Chickasaw (12)	20	0.23
Chippewa (2)	4	0.05
Choctaw (73)	148	1.67
Creek (21)	41	0.46
Iroquois (6)	7	0.08
Kiowa (0)	1	0.01
Lumbee (1)	4	0.05
Mexican American Ind. (1)	2	0.02
Navajo (0)	6	0.07
Osage (3)	4	0.05
Pima (0)	4	0.05
Potawatomi (4)	9	0.10
Pueblo (1)	1	0.01
Seminole (1)	3	0.03
Sioux (7)	8	0.09
Tlingit-Haida *(Alaska Native)* (4)	4	0.05
Yup'ik *(Alaska Native)* (3)	3	0.03
Asian (46)	85	0.96
Not Hispanic (44)	74	0.83
Hispanic (2)	11	0.12
Chinese, ex. Taiwanese (1)	3	0.03
Filipino (4)	27	0.30
Indian (30)	34	0.38
Japanese (4)	14	0.16
Korean (4)	4	0.05
Thai (0)	1	0.01
Vietnamese (2)	3	0.03
Hawaii Native/Pacific Islander (3)	15	0.17
Not Hispanic (3)	13	0.15
Hispanic (0)	2	0.02
Native Hawaiian (2)	13	0.15
White (5,599)	6,548	73.74
Not Hispanic (5,433)	6,311	71.07
Hispanic (166)	237	2.67

Sand Springs

Place Type: City
County: Tulsa
Population: 18,906†

Ancestry‡	Population	%
African, Sub-Saharan (0)	55	0.30
Cape Verdean (0)	55	0.30
American (1,900)	1,900	10.30
Arab (28)	28	0.15
Syrian (28)	28	0.15
Armenian (8)	8	0.04
Austrian (8)	22	0.12
British (48)	124	0.67
Canadian (36)	45	0.24
Czech (74)	97	0.53
Danish (0)	27	0.15
Dutch (64)	422	2.29
English (785)	1,743	9.44
European (130)	185	1.00
French, ex. Basque (52)	406	2.20
French Canadian (44)	44	0.24
German (1,187)	3,410	18.48
Greek (14)	25	0.14
Irish (959)	2,846	15.42
Italian (242)	401	2.17
Luxemburger (0)	13	0.07
Norwegian (47)	122	0.66
Polish (43)	109	0.59
Portuguese (0)	11	0.06
Russian (0)	29	0.16
Scotch-Irish (121)	400	2.17
Scottish (204)	445	2.41
Slavic (17)	17	0.09
Swedish (37)	129	0.70
Swiss (13)	35	0.19
Ukrainian (11)	11	0.06
Welsh (70)	99	0.54
West Indian, ex. Hispanic (21)	107	0.58
Dutch West Indian (21)	107	0.58
Yugoslavian (14)	69	0.37

Hispanic Origin	Population	%
Hispanic or Latino (of any race)	643	3.40
Central American, ex. Mexican	24	0.13
Guatemalan	8	0.04
Honduran	2	0.01
Nicaraguan	1	0.01
Salvadoran	12	0.06
Other Central American	1	0.01
Cuban	9	0.05
Mexican	485	2.57
Puerto Rican	41	0.22
South American	16	0.08
Argentinean	4	0.02
Bolivian	1	0.01
Colombian	7	0.04
Paraguayan	1	0.01
Peruvian	1	0.01
Venezuelan	2	0.01
Other Hispanic or Latino	68	0.36

Race*	Population	%
African-American/Black (458)	564	2.98
Not Hispanic (452)	553	2.92
Hispanic (6)	11	0.06
American Indian/Alaska Native (1,667)	2,512	13.29
Not Hispanic (1,631)	2,420	12.80
Hispanic (36)	92	0.49
Apache (4)	7	0.04
Arapaho (0)	4	0.02
Blackfeet (1)	3	0.02
Central American Ind. (1)	1	0.01
Cherokee (831)	1,268	6.71
Cheyenne (0)	3	0.02
Chickasaw (35)	49	0.26
Chippewa (7)	11	0.06
Choctaw (177)	277	1.47
Colville (2)	2	0.01
Comanche (3)	4	0.02
Creek (251)	390	2.06
Crow (0)	1	0.01
Delaware (12)	24	0.13
Inupiat *(Alaska Native)* (0)	1	0.01
Iroquois (6)	10	0.05
Kiowa (9)	12	0.06
Lumbee (1)	2	0.01
Menominee (0)	3	0.02
Mexican American Ind. (6)	6	0.03
Navajo (1)	3	0.02
Osage (53)	76	0.40

SECTION TWO

*Notes: † The Census 2010 population figure is used to calculate the percentages in the Hispanic Origin and Race categories. Ancestry percentages are based on the 2006-2010 American Community Survey population (not shown); ‡ Numbers in parentheses indicate the number of people reporting a single ancestry; * Numbers in parentheses indicate the number of persons reporting this race alone, not in combination with any other race; Please refer to the Explanation of Data for more information.*

Ottawa (2)	3	0.02
Paiute (0)	1	0.01
Pima (1)	5	0.03
Potawatomi (9)	26	0.14
Pueblo (0)	1	0.01
Puget Sound Salish (0)	2	0.01
Seminole (8)	9	0.05
Sioux (4)	6	0.03
South American Ind. (0)	2	0.01
Spanish American Ind. (3)	3	0.02
Tlingit-Haida *(Alaska Native)* (1)	1	0.01
Asian (112)	207	1.09
Not Hispanic (112)	203	1.07
Hispanic (0)	4	0.02
Bangladeshi (7)	7	0.04
Cambodian (1)	1	0.01
Chinese, ex. Taiwanese (28)	38	0.20
Filipino (15)	42	0.22
Indian (3)	8	0.04
Indonesian (0)	2	0.01
Japanese (10)	39	0.21
Korean (12)	25	0.13
Laotian (1)	1	0.01
Nepalese (1)	3	0.02
Pakistani (9)	9	0.05
Sri Lankan (1)	2	0.01
Taiwanese (1)	1	0.01
Thai (1)	1	0.01
Vietnamese (13)	21	0.11
Hawaii Native/Pacific Islander (2)	15	0.08
Not Hispanic (2)	15	0.08
Native Hawaiian (1)	11	0.06
Samoan (1)	1	0.01
White (15,463)	16,457	87.05
Not Hispanic (15,115)	16,021	84.74
Hispanic (348)	436	2.31

Sapulpa

Place Type: City
County: Creek
Population: 20,544†

Ancestry‡	Population	%
African, Sub-Saharan (15)	15	0.07
African (15)	15	0.07
American (2,445)	2,445	11.97
Arab (20)	74	0.36
Lebanese (20)	74	0.36
Armenian (3)	9	0.04
Austrian (11)	11	0.05
Belgian (26)	26	0.13
British (34)	59	0.29
Cajun (0)	23	0.11
Canadian (21)	21	0.10
Czech (12)	18	0.09
Czechoslovakian (21)	43	0.21
Danish (7)	39	0.19
Dutch (60)	474	2.32
English (859)	1,837	8.99
European (210)	267	1.31
Finnish (13)	13	0.06
French, ex. Basque (112)	597	2.92
French Canadian (8)	10	0.05
German (1,090)	3,185	15.59
Greek (58)	58	0.28
Hungarian (24)	63	0.31
Irish (980)	3,050	14.93
Italian (101)	363	1.78
Lithuanian (0)	9	0.04
Norwegian (67)	100	0.49
Pennsylvania German (0)	8	0.04
Polish (24)	140	0.69
Portuguese (7)	16	0.08
Russian (0)	23	0.11
Scandinavian (7)	7	0.03
Scotch-Irish (136)	332	1.62
Scottish (175)	350	1.71
Slovak (0)	9	0.04
Slovene (0)	3	0.01
Swedish (30)	148	0.72
Swiss (0)	126	0.62
Ukrainian (24)	24	0.12
Welsh (13)	41	0.20
West Indian, ex. Hispanic (13)	118	0.58
Dutch West Indian (13)	118	0.58
Yugoslavian (9)	16	0.08

Hispanic Origin	Population	%
Hispanic or Latino (of any race)	845	4.11
Central American, ex. Mexican	30	0.15
Costa Rican	1	<0.01
Guatemalan	3	0.01
Honduran	7	0.03
Nicaraguan	6	0.03
Panamanian	8	0.04
Salvadoran	4	0.02
Other Central American	1	<0.01
Cuban	15	0.07
Mexican	648	3.15
Puerto Rican	33	0.16
South American	28	0.14
Argentinean	4	0.02
Bolivian	3	0.01
Chilean	1	<0.01
Colombian	8	0.04
Peruvian	10	0.05
Venezuelan	2	0.01
Other Hispanic or Latino	91	0.44

Race*	Population	%
African-American/Black (623)	819	3.99
Not Hispanic (621)	809	3.94
Hispanic (2)	10	0.05
American Indian/Alaska Native (2,233)	3,318	16.15
Not Hispanic (2,168)	3,210	15.63
Hispanic (65)	108	0.53
Alaska Athabascan *(Ala. Nat.)* (1)	1	<0.01
Aleut *(Alaska Native)* (6)	7	0.03
Apache (9)	18	0.09
Arapaho (2)	3	0.01
Blackfeet (0)	2	0.01
Canadian/French Am. Ind. (0)	1	<0.01
Cherokee (665)	1,202	5.85
Cheyenne (4)	10	0.05
Chickasaw (31)	51	0.25
Chippewa (1)	2	0.01
Choctaw (123)	212	1.03
Comanche (10)	13	0.06
Cree (0)	3	0.01
Creek (793)	1,143	5.56
Delaware (4)	8	0.04
Inupiat *(Alaska Native)* (0)	1	<0.01
Iroquois (8)	11	0.05
Kiowa (11)	11	0.05
Menominee (4)	4	0.02
Mexican American Ind. (0)	4	0.02
Navajo (2)	2	0.01
Osage (19)	31	0.15
Potawatomi (9)	10	0.05
Pueblo (1)	1	<0.01
Seminole (44)	63	0.31
Shoshone (2)	2	0.01
Sioux (13)	22	0.11
Tlingit-Haida *(Alaska Native)* (1)	1	<0.01
Yuman (1)	1	<0.01
Asian (117)	177	0.86
Not Hispanic (117)	168	0.82
Hispanic (0)	9	0.04
Bangladeshi (5)	8	0.04
Cambodian (2)	6	0.03
Chinese, ex. Taiwanese (20)	29	0.14
Filipino (15)	31	0.15
Indian (19)	39	0.19
Japanese (6)	19	0.09
Korean (7)	13	0.06
Pakistani (0)	1	<0.01
Thai (1)	2	0.01
Vietnamese (25)	37	0.18
Hawaii Native/Pacific Islander (31)	42	0.20
Not Hispanic (29)	34	0.17
Hispanic (2)	8	0.04
Guamanian/Chamorro (1)	1	<0.01
Native Hawaiian (8)	13	0.06
White (15,928)	17,143	83.45
Not Hispanic (15,571)	16,675	81.17
Hispanic (357)	468	2.28

Shawnee

Place Type: City
County: Pottawatomie
Population: 29,857†

Ancestry‡	Population	%
African, Sub-Saharan (31)	38	0.13
African (22)	29	0.10
Other Sub-Saharan African (9)	9	0.03
American (2,329)	2,329	7.83
Arab (8)	11	0.04
Arab (0)	3	0.01
Lebanese (8)	8	0.03
Armenian (0)	3	0.01
Australian (0)	9	0.03
Austrian (0)	6	0.02
Brazilian (7)	15	0.05
British (63)	111	0.37
Cajun (5)	13	0.04
Canadian (6)	6	0.02
Czech (27)	160	0.54
Czechoslovakian (9)	15	0.05
Danish (15)	27	0.09
Dutch (69)	292	0.98
English (1,089)	2,184	7.34
European (195)	251	0.84
Finnish (18)	18	0.06
French, ex. Basque (85)	540	1.81
French Canadian (14)	60	0.20
German (1,146)	3,397	11.42
Hungarian (5)	5	0.02
Iranian (0)	13	0.04
Irish (1,114)	3,277	11.01
Italian (177)	318	1.07
Norwegian (45)	92	0.31
Pennsylvania German (6)	6	0.02
Polish (177)	340	1.14
Portuguese (22)	35	0.12
Romanian (0)	4	0.01
Russian (17)	60	0.20
Scandinavian (6)	62	0.21
Scotch-Irish (251)	584	1.96
Scottish (165)	423	1.42
Serbian (4)	4	0.01
Slavic (5)	5	0.02
Slovak (7)	15	0.05
Swedish (41)	116	0.39
Swiss (0)	60	0.20
Welsh (38)	95	0.32
West Indian, ex. Hispanic (23)	98	0.33
Dutch West Indian (23)	80	0.27
Jamaican (0)	7	0.02
U.S. Virgin Islander (0)	11	0.04

Hispanic Origin	Population	%
Hispanic or Latino (of any race)	1,522	5.10
Central American, ex. Mexican	34	0.11
Costa Rican	4	0.01
Guatemalan	7	0.02
Honduran	5	0.02
Panamanian	3	0.01
Salvadoran	15	0.05
Cuban	15	0.05
Dominican Republic	2	0.01
Mexican	1,248	4.18
Puerto Rican	66	0.22
South American	35	0.12
Bolivian	4	0.01
Colombian	21	0.07
Ecuadorian	2	0.01
Peruvian	5	0.02

*Notes: † The Census 2010 population figure is used to calculate the percentages in the Hispanic Origin and Race categories. Ancestry percentages are based on the 2006-2010 American Community Survey population (not shown); ‡ Numbers in parentheses indicate the number of people reporting a single ancestry; * Numbers in parentheses indicate the number of persons reporting this race alone, not in combination with any other race; Please refer to the Explanation of Data for more information.*

Venezuelan	2	0.01
Other South American	1	<0.01
Other Hispanic or Latino	122	0.41

Race*	Population	%
African-American/Black (1,261)	1,724	5.77
Not Hispanic (1,229)	1,647	5.52
Hispanic (32)	77	0.26
American Indian/Alaska Native (4,225)	5,732	19.20
Not Hispanic (3,991)	5,373	18.00
Hispanic (234)	359	1.20
Alaska Athabascan *(Ala. Nat.)* (1)	1	<0.01
Aleut *(Alaska Native)* (0)	2	0.01
Apache (9)	19	0.06
Arapaho (3)	5	0.02
Blackfeet (4)	7	0.02
Cherokee (350)	682	2.28
Cheyenne (22)	39	0.13
Chickasaw (179)	278	0.93
Chippewa (14)	17	0.06
Choctaw (337)	537	1.80
Comanche (45)	61	0.20
Cree (1)	1	<0.01
Creek (337)	586	1.96
Crow (1)	3	0.01
Delaware (19)	28	0.09
Hopi (2)	3	0.01
Houma (0)	1	<0.01
Inupiat *(Alaska Native)* (5)	5	0.02
Iroquois (15)	16	0.05
Kiowa (60)	72	0.24
Mexican American Ind. (6)	7	0.02
Navajo (14)	24	0.08
Osage (6)	16	0.05
Potawatomi (397)	559	1.87
Pueblo (3)	3	0.01
Puget Sound Salish (3)	4	0.01
Seminole (528)	738	2.47
Sioux (26)	38	0.13
South American Ind. (1)	1	<0.01
Tlingit-Haida *(Alaska Native)* (1)	4	0.01
Yuman (1)	1	<0.01
Asian (238)	394	1.32
Not Hispanic (229)	363	1.22
Hispanic (9)	31	0.10
Cambodian (2)	2	0.01
Chinese, ex. Taiwanese (66)	84	0.28
Filipino (25)	55	0.18
Indian (35)	46	0.15
Japanese (19)	48	0.16
Korean (18)	52	0.17
Laotian (3)	3	0.01
Pakistani (6)	17	0.06
Taiwanese (6)	10	0.03
Thai (7)	12	0.04
Vietnamese (45)	56	0.19
Hawaii Native/Pacific Islander (13)	47	0.16
Not Hispanic (13)	39	0.13
Hispanic (0)	8	0.03
Guamanian/Chamorro (5)	8	0.03
Native Hawaiian (8)	30	0.10
Samoan (0)	1	<0.01
White (21,824)	23,513	78.75
Not Hispanic (21,135)	22,670	75.93
Hispanic (689)	843	2.82

Stillwater

Place Type: City
County: Payne
Population: 45,688†

Ancestry‡	Population	%
African, Sub-Saharan (257)	264	0.59
African (64)	71	0.16
Ethiopian (92)	92	0.21
Sudanese (29)	29	0.06
Other Sub-Saharan African (72)	72	0.16
American (2,674)	2,674	5.98
Arab (305)	403	0.90
Arab (42)	42	0.09
Egyptian (64)	64	0.14
Lebanese (144)	242	0.54
Other Arab (55)	55	0.12
Austrian (14)	163	0.36
Belgian (0)	82	0.18
British (199)	340	0.76
Cajun (0)	135	0.30
Canadian (131)	131	0.29
Czech (133)	683	1.53
Czechoslovakian (76)	117	0.26
Danish (88)	259	0.58
Dutch (202)	943	2.11
English (1,552)	4,596	10.29
European (652)	765	1.71
Finnish (17)	17	0.04
French, ex. Basque (163)	1,371	3.07
French Canadian (96)	124	0.28
German (3,521)	8,727	19.53
Greek (0)	40	0.09
Hungarian (0)	56	0.13
Iranian (30)	44	0.10
Irish (1,905)	5,955	13.33
Israeli (0)	13	0.03
Italian (291)	920	2.06
Luxemburger (14)	14	0.03
Maltese (0)	27	0.06
Northern European (26)	40	0.09
Norwegian (219)	443	0.99
Pennsylvania German (38)	52	0.12
Polish (223)	545	1.22
Portuguese (6)	89	0.20
Romanian (32)	61	0.14
Russian (84)	257	0.58
Scandinavian (24)	51	0.11
Scotch-Irish (462)	1,265	2.83
Scottish (318)	1,235	2.76
Serbian (14)	43	0.10
Slovak (30)	63	0.14
Swedish (140)	363	0.81
Swiss (0)	96	0.21
Turkish (0)	24	0.05
Ukrainian (29)	40	0.09
Welsh (136)	422	0.94
West Indian, ex. Hispanic (0)	80	0.18
Dutch West Indian (0)	80	0.18

Hispanic Origin	Population	%
Hispanic or Latino (of any race)	1,947	4.26
Central American, ex. Mexican	80	0.18
Costa Rican	5	0.01
Guatemalan	14	0.03
Honduran	21	0.05
Nicaraguan	6	0.01
Panamanian	10	0.02
Salvadoran	20	0.04
Other Central American	4	0.01
Cuban	43	0.09
Dominican Republic	6	0.01
Mexican	1,343	2.94
Puerto Rican	121	0.26
South American	144	0.32
Argentinean	17	0.04
Bolivian	8	0.02
Chilean	4	0.01
Colombian	28	0.06
Ecuadorian	7	0.02
Paraguayan	2	<0.01
Peruvian	21	0.05
Uruguayan	2	<0.01
Venezuelan	53	0.12
Other South American	2	<0.01
Other Hispanic or Latino	210	0.46

Race*	Population	%
African-American/Black (2,152)	2,748	6.01
Not Hispanic (2,104)	2,671	5.85
Hispanic (48)	77	0.17
American Indian/Alaska Native (1,797)	3,213	7.03
Not Hispanic (1,744)	3,068	6.72
Hispanic (53)	145	0.32
Apache (8)	27	0.06
Arapaho (4)	7	0.02
Blackfeet (3)	12	0.03
Canadian/French Am. Ind. (0)	5	0.01
Cherokee (502)	1,033	2.26
Cheyenne (6)	21	0.05
Chickasaw (88)	154	0.34
Chippewa (5)	9	0.02
Choctaw (233)	413	0.90
Colville (0)	3	0.01
Comanche (9)	23	0.05
Cree (1)	1	<0.01
Creek (144)	254	0.56
Crow (2)	3	0.01
Delaware (6)	11	0.02
Hopi (0)	1	<0.01
Iroquois (8)	20	0.04
Kiowa (15)	23	0.05
Lumbee (2)	4	0.01
Mexican American Ind. (2)	9	0.02
Navajo (20)	25	0.05
Osage (79)	133	0.29
Ottawa (1)	2	<0.01
Potawatomi (31)	55	0.12
Pueblo (3)	3	0.01
Seminole (27)	61	0.13
Shoshone (0)	1	<0.01
Sioux (20)	24	0.05
South American Ind. (3)	5	0.01
Tohono O'Odham (1)	1	<0.01
Yaqui (0)	1	<0.01
Yuman (2)	2	<0.01
Asian (2,539)	2,925	6.40
Not Hispanic (2,533)	2,899	6.35
Hispanic (6)	26	0.06
Bangladeshi (36)	38	0.08
Burmese (4)	5	0.01
Cambodian (3)	6	0.01
Chinese, ex. Taiwanese (645)	689	1.51
Filipino (56)	115	0.25
Hmong (18)	19	0.04
Indian (779)	827	1.81
Indonesian (58)	61	0.13
Japanese (70)	131	0.29
Korean (289)	333	0.73
Laotian (6)	7	0.02
Malaysian (31)	45	0.10
Nepalese (69)	70	0.15
Pakistani (14)	24	0.05
Sri Lankan (29)	31	0.07
Taiwanese (47)	52	0.11
Thai (79)	89	0.19
Vietnamese (222)	240	0.53
Hawaii Native/Pacific Islander (28)	69	0.15
Not Hispanic (27)	67	0.15
Hispanic (1)	2	<0.01
Guamanian/Chamorro (5)	8	0.02
Marshallese (2)	2	<0.01
Native Hawaiian (3)	21	0.05
Samoan (4)	7	0.02
Tongan (2)	3	0.01
White (36,323)	38,480	84.22
Not Hispanic (35,170)	37,146	81.30
Hispanic (1,153)	1,334	2.92

Tahlequah

Place Type: City
County: Cherokee
Population: 15,753†

Ancestry‡	Population	%
African, Sub-Saharan (13)	13	0.08
African (13)	13	0.08
American (1,103)	1,103	7.06
Austrian (0)	32	0.20
Belgian (0)	24	0.15
British (0)	109	0.70
Czech (0)	27	0.17

*Notes: † The Census 2010 population figure is used to calculate the percentages in the Hispanic Origin and Race categories. Ancestry percentages are based on the 2006-2010 American Community Survey population (not shown); ‡ Numbers in parentheses indicate the number of people reporting a single ancestry; * Numbers in parentheses indicate the number of persons reporting this race alone, not in combination with any other race; Please refer to the Explanation of Data for more information.*

Ancestry (continued)	Population	%
Czechoslovakian (0)	5	0.03
Dutch (37)	156	1.00
English (469)	1,102	7.05
European (55)	64	0.41
French, ex. Basque (81)	271	1.73
German (504)	1,627	10.42
Greek (0)	16	0.10
Icelander (0)	12	0.08
Iranian (15)	15	0.10
Irish (296)	1,416	9.06
Italian (122)	271	1.73
Northern European (32)	32	0.20
Norwegian (0)	36	0.23
Polish (28)	90	0.58
Scandinavian (0)	109	0.70
Scotch-Irish (160)	313	2.00
Scottish (42)	161	1.03
Slovak (0)	13	0.08
Swedish (55)	98	0.63
Turkish (61)	61	0.39
Welsh (0)	33	0.21
West Indian, ex. Hispanic (44)	67	0.43
Dutch West Indian (0)	23	0.15
Jamaican (29)	29	0.19
Trinidadian/Tobagonian (15)	15	0.10

Hispanic Origin	Population	%
Hispanic or Latino (of any race)	1,542	9.79
Central American, ex. Mexican	18	0.11
Costa Rican	4	0.03
Guatemalan	5	0.03
Honduran	2	0.01
Panamanian	1	0.01
Salvadoran	6	0.04
Cuban	6	0.04
Dominican Republic	5	0.03
Mexican	1,331	8.45
Puerto Rican	34	0.22
South American	24	0.15
Argentinean	1	0.01
Bolivian	1	0.01
Colombian	11	0.07
Ecuadorian	2	0.01
Paraguayan	2	0.01
Peruvian	6	0.04
Venezuelan	1	0.01
Other Hispanic or Latino	124	0.79

Race*	Population	%
African-American/Black (384)	579	3.68
Not Hispanic (377)	554	3.52
Hispanic (7)	25	0.16
American Indian/Alaska Native (4,731)	5,971	37.90
Not Hispanic (4,538)	5,707	36.23
Hispanic (193)	264	1.68
Alaska Athabascan *(Ala. Nat.)* (1)	1	0.01
Apache (3)	5	0.03
Arapaho (1)	2	0.01
Blackfeet (1)	2	0.01
Canadian/French Am. Ind. (1)	1	0.01
Cherokee (3,520)	4,490	28.50
Cheyenne (11)	21	0.13
Chickasaw (19)	36	0.23
Chippewa (2)	4	0.03
Choctaw (178)	261	1.66
Comanche (13)	20	0.13
Cree (0)	5	0.03
Creek (164)	232	1.47
Crow (5)	5	0.03
Delaware (8)	10	0.06
Iroquois (9)	21	0.13
Kiowa (25)	34	0.22
Lumbee (0)	1	0.01
Mexican American Ind. (14)	17	0.11
Navajo (14)	17	0.11
Osage (25)	42	0.27
Ottawa (0)	1	0.01
Paiute (1)	1	0.01
Potawatomi (9)	11	0.07
Pueblo (8)	8	0.05
Seminole (23)	35	0.22
Sioux (9)	15	0.10
Tlingit-Haida *(Alaska Native)* (0)	1	0.01
Tohono O'Odham (1)	1	0.01
Asian (205)	256	1.63
Not Hispanic (184)	225	1.43
Hispanic (21)	31	0.20
Chinese, ex. Taiwanese (22)	23	0.15
Filipino (14)	27	0.17
Hmong (22)	22	0.14
Indian (12)	22	0.14
Indonesian (1)	1	0.01
Japanese (87)	98	0.62
Korean (15)	21	0.13
Laotian (5)	6	0.04
Pakistani (11)	12	0.08
Taiwanese (1)	1	0.01
Thai (0)	2	0.01
Vietnamese (12)	13	0.08
Hawaii Native/Pacific Islander (5)	20	0.13
Not Hispanic (3)	17	0.11
Hispanic (2)	3	0.02
Fijian (0)	1	0.01
Guamanian/Chamorro (0)	1	0.01
Native Hawaiian (3)	13	0.08
Samoan (2)	3	0.02
White (8,472)	9,724	61.73
Not Hispanic (7,842)	9,008	57.18
Hispanic (630)	716	4.55

The Village

Place Type: City
County: Oklahoma
Population: 8,929†

Ancestry‡	Population	%
African, Sub-Saharan (8)	8	0.09
African (8)	8	0.09
American (780)	780	8.57
Arab (19)	98	1.08
Lebanese (19)	98	1.08
British (18)	54	0.59
Bulgarian (36)	36	0.40
Canadian (0)	2	0.02
Czech (28)	47	0.52
Danish (16)	26	0.29
Dutch (49)	130	1.43
English (439)	950	10.43
European (33)	52	0.57
French, ex. Basque (71)	279	3.06
German (568)	1,686	18.52
Greek (10)	26	0.29
Iranian (31)	31	0.34
Irish (365)	1,271	13.96
Italian (188)	246	2.70
Norwegian (27)	89	0.98
Polish (20)	106	1.16
Portuguese (0)	17	0.19
Russian (0)	29	0.32
Scandinavian (12)	64	0.70
Scotch-Irish (93)	214	2.35
Scottish (71)	296	3.25
Slavic (14)	42	0.46
Swedish (17)	40	0.44
Swiss (11)	21	0.23
Welsh (0)	106	1.16
West Indian, ex. Hispanic (0)	22	0.24
Dutch West Indian (0)	22	0.24
Yugoslavian (0)	12	0.13

Hispanic Origin	Population	%
Hispanic or Latino (of any race)	547	6.13
Central American, ex. Mexican	38	0.43
Guatemalan	16	0.18
Honduran	11	0.12
Nicaraguan	2	0.02
Salvadoran	9	0.10
Cuban	11	0.12
Mexican	383	4.29
Puerto Rican	31	0.35
South American	24	0.27
Argentinean	1	0.01
Colombian	7	0.08
Peruvian	15	0.17
Venezuelan	1	0.01
Other Hispanic or Latino	60	0.67

Race*	Population	%
African-American/Black (749)	878	9.83
Not Hispanic (744)	866	9.70
Hispanic (5)	12	0.13
American Indian/Alaska Native (276)	557	6.24
Not Hispanic (258)	522	5.85
Hispanic (18)	35	0.39
Apache (1)	5	0.06
Arapaho (0)	1	0.01
Blackfeet (1)	2	0.02
Cherokee (53)	136	1.52
Cheyenne (1)	8	0.09
Chickasaw (24)	39	0.44
Choctaw (43)	89	1.00
Comanche (2)	6	0.07
Creek (22)	40	0.45
Crow (1)	1	0.01
Delaware (5)	6	0.07
Hopi (0)	3	0.03
Iroquois (3)	4	0.04
Kiowa (5)	11	0.12
Mexican American Ind. (1)	1	0.01
Navajo (1)	2	0.02
Osage (3)	6	0.07
Ottawa (2)	2	0.02
Potawatomi (10)	18	0.20
Pueblo (1)	1	0.01
Seminole (11)	17	0.19
Sioux (1)	2	0.02
Asian (163)	214	2.40
Not Hispanic (163)	209	2.34
Hispanic (0)	5	0.06
Cambodian (1)	1	0.01
Chinese, ex. Taiwanese (31)	40	0.45
Filipino (6)	19	0.21
Indian (14)	22	0.25
Indonesian (2)	7	0.08
Japanese (8)	14	0.16
Korean (4)	12	0.13
Laotian (10)	12	0.13
Malaysian (2)	2	0.02
Nepalese (2)	2	0.02
Pakistani (1)	2	0.02
Taiwanese (2)	3	0.03
Thai (0)	1	0.01
Vietnamese (71)	77	0.86
Hawaii Native/Pacific Islander (7)	15	0.17
Not Hispanic (7)	15	0.17
Native Hawaiian (6)	10	0.11
White (7,100)	7,486	83.84
Not Hispanic (6,819)	7,158	80.17
Hispanic (281)	328	3.67

Tulsa

Place Type: City
County: Tulsa
Population: 391,906†

Ancestry‡	Population	%
African, Sub-Saharan (1,953)	2,611	0.67
African (1,121)	1,671	0.43
Cape Verdean (12)	12	<0.01
Ghanaian (105)	105	0.03
Kenyan (98)	144	0.04
Liberian (153)	153	0.04
Nigerian (245)	282	0.07
South African (18)	18	<0.01
Ugandan (41)	51	0.01
Other Sub-Saharan African (160)	175	0.05
Albanian (0)	9	<0.01
Alsatian (14)	14	<0.01

*Notes: † The Census 2010 population figure is used to calculate the percentages in the Hispanic Origin and Race categories. Ancestry percentages are based on the 2006-2010 American Community Survey population (not shown); ‡ Numbers in parentheses indicate the number of people reporting a single ancestry; * Numbers in parentheses indicate the number of persons reporting this race alone, not in combination with any other race; Please refer to the Explanation of Data for more information.*

American (27,566)	27,566	7.10
Arab (1,662)	2,615	0.67
Arab (331)	470	0.12
Egyptian (77)	77	0.02
Jordanian (121)	189	0.05
Lebanese (412)	874	0.23
Moroccan (100)	100	0.03
Palestinian (135)	230	0.06
Syrian (169)	259	0.07
Other Arab (317)	416	0.11
Armenian (83)	244	0.06
Assyrian/Chaldean/Syriac (36)	36	0.01
Australian (80)	142	0.04
Austrian (179)	490	0.13
Basque (36)	68	0.02
Belgian (48)	156	0.04
Brazilian (133)	133	0.03
British (602)	1,200	0.31
Bulgarian (24)	139	0.04
Cajun (45)	237	0.06
Canadian (429)	761	0.20
Celtic (50)	68	0.02
Croatian (92)	174	0.04
Czech (336)	976	0.25
Czechoslovakian (169)	298	0.08
Danish (220)	957	0.25
Dutch (1,576)	7,047	1.82
Eastern European (105)	115	0.03
English (13,579)	38,383	9.89
Estonian (0)	10	<0.01
European (12,805)	15,267	3.93
Finnish (119)	301	0.08
French, ex. Basque (2,413)	10,197	2.63
French Canadian (492)	1,075	0.28
German (17,962)	54,997	14.17
German Russian (15)	15	<0.01
Greek (406)	893	0.23
Hungarian (215)	704	0.18
Icelander (31)	72	0.02
Iranian (444)	516	0.13
Irish (13,948)	45,390	11.69
Israeli (25)	25	0.01
Italian (2,596)	7,456	1.92
Latvian (32)	67	0.02
Lithuanian (120)	402	0.10
Maltese (14)	14	<0.01
New Zealander (25)	25	0.01
Northern European (204)	212	0.05
Norwegian (1,650)	3,507	0.90
Pennsylvania German (21)	69	0.02
Polish (933)	3,972	1.02
Portuguese (71)	214	0.06
Romanian (36)	111	0.03
Russian (1,019)	2,019	0.52
Scandinavian (226)	424	0.11
Scotch-Irish (3,103)	7,681	1.98
Scottish (3,306)	9,394	2.42
Serbian (13)	98	0.03
Slavic (25)	84	0.02
Slovak (48)	169	0.04
Slovene (26)	31	0.01
Swedish (940)	3,856	0.99
Swiss (233)	851	0.22
Turkish (99)	150	0.04
Ukrainian (131)	357	0.09
Welsh (573)	2,688	0.69
West Indian, ex. Hispanic (597)	1,441	0.37
Bahamian (19)	66	0.02
Belizean (31)	42	0.01
Dutch West Indian (268)	944	0.24
Haitian (9)	54	0.01
Jamaican (203)	239	0.06
Trinidadian/Tobagonian (0)	11	<0.01
U.S. Virgin Islander (8)	8	<0.01
West Indian (59)	77	0.02
Yugoslavian (28)	45	0.01

Hispanic Origin	Population	%
Hispanic or Latino (of any race)	55,266	14.10
Central American, ex. Mexican	3,059	0.78
Costa Rican	101	0.03
Guatemalan	1,352	0.34
Honduran	803	0.20
Nicaraguan	76	0.02
Panamanian	122	0.03
Salvadoran	594	0.15
Other Central American	11	<0.01
Cuban	458	0.12
Dominican Republic	168	0.04
Mexican	45,013	11.49
Puerto Rican	1,574	0.40
South American	1,615	0.41
Argentinean	119	0.03
Bolivian	82	0.02
Chilean	57	0.01
Colombian	382	0.10
Ecuadorian	90	0.02
Paraguayan	7	<0.01
Peruvian	457	0.12
Uruguayan	13	<0.01
Venezuelan	388	0.10
Other South American	20	0.01
Other Hispanic or Latino	3,379	0.86

Race*	Population	%
African-American/Black (62,164)	70,084	17.88
Not Hispanic (61,230)	68,332	17.44
Hispanic (934)	1,752	0.45
American Indian/Alaska Native (20,817)	35,990	9.18
Not Hispanic (19,473)	33,420	8.53
Hispanic (1,344)	2,570	0.66
Alaska Athabascan *(Ala. Nat.)* (4)	10	<0.01
Aleut *(Alaska Native)* (4)	6	<0.01
Apache (75)	182	0.05
Arapaho (14)	22	0.01
Blackfeet (18)	189	0.05
Canadian/French Am. Ind. (2)	7	<0.01
Central American Ind. (31)	39	0.01
Cherokee (8,810)	16,720	4.27
Cheyenne (76)	125	0.03
Chickasaw (345)	705	0.18
Chippewa (46)	108	0.03
Choctaw (1,678)	3,043	0.78
Colville (5)	5	<0.01
Comanche (105)	186	0.05
Cree (9)	15	<0.01
Creek (3,303)	5,849	1.49
Crow (17)	34	0.01
Delaware (123)	232	0.06
Hopi (5)	11	<0.01
Houma (4)	6	<0.01
Inupiat *(Alaska Native)* (11)	17	<0.01
Iroquois (163)	272	0.07
Kiowa (193)	276	0.07
Lumbee (13)	24	0.01
Menominee (2)	5	<0.01
Mexican American Ind. (178)	279	0.07
Navajo (147)	196	0.05
Osage (501)	855	0.22
Ottawa (39)	73	0.02
Paiute (5)	7	<0.01
Pima (3)	4	<0.01
Potawatomi (193)	306	0.08
Pueblo (25)	39	0.01
Puget Sound Salish (2)	2	<0.01
Seminole (351)	554	0.14
Shoshone (3)	6	<0.01
Sioux (149)	266	0.07
South American Ind. (23)	39	0.01
Spanish American Ind. (8)	9	<0.01
Tlingit-Haida *(Alaska Native)* (3)	7	<0.01
Tohono O'Odham (1)	2	<0.01
Tsimshian *(Alaska Native)* (3)	3	<0.01
Ute (3)	10	<0.01
Yakama (0)	1	<0.01
Yaqui (3)	18	<0.01
Yuman (1)	5	<0.01
Yup'ik *(Alaska Native)* (6)	7	<0.01
Asian (9,077)	11,207	2.86
Not Hispanic (8,926)	10,851	2.77
Hispanic (151)	356	0.09
Bangladeshi (71)	96	0.02
Burmese (638)	659	0.17
Cambodian (34)	45	0.01
Chinese, ex. Taiwanese (1,277)	1,632	0.42
Filipino (558)	993	0.25
Hmong (925)	972	0.25
Indian (1,799)	2,090	0.53
Indonesian (65)	82	0.02
Japanese (217)	542	0.14
Korean (727)	970	0.25
Laotian (73)	92	0.02
Malaysian (40)	46	0.01
Nepalese (14)	16	<0.01
Pakistani (380)	450	0.11
Sri Lankan (11)	16	<0.01
Taiwanese (60)	75	0.02
Thai (106)	164	0.04
Vietnamese (1,596)	1,806	0.46
Hawaii Native/Pacific Islander (316)	704	0.18
Not Hispanic (278)	570	0.15
Hispanic (38)	134	0.03
Fijian (4)	5	<0.01
Guamanian/Chamorro (51)	72	0.02
Marshallese (7)	10	<0.01
Native Hawaiian (96)	284	0.07
Samoan (29)	76	0.02
Tongan (1)	1	<0.01
White (245,309)	264,373	67.46
Not Hispanic (227,021)	243,101	62.03
Hispanic (18,288)	21,272	5.43

Wagoner

Place Type: City
County: Wagoner
Population: 8,323†

Ancestry‡	Population	%
American (1,069)	1,069	12.93
Belgian (11)	11	0.13
Czech (38)	38	0.46
Dutch (8)	125	1.51
English (189)	448	5.42
French, ex. Basque (20)	188	2.27
French Canadian (42)	42	0.51
German (347)	1,103	13.34
Greek (11)	11	0.13
Irish (419)	1,315	15.91
Italian (84)	135	1.63
Lithuanian (0)	12	0.15
Norwegian (37)	50	0.60
Polish (0)	11	0.13
Russian (0)	14	0.17
Scandinavian (0)	12	0.15
Scotch-Irish (147)	187	2.26
Scottish (48)	77	0.93
Slavic (0)	12	0.15
Swedish (0)	36	0.44
Swiss (0)	44	0.53
Ukrainian (0)	11	0.13
Welsh (0)	13	0.16
West Indian, ex. Hispanic (0)	8	0.10
Dutch West Indian (0)	8	0.10

Hispanic Origin	Population	%
Hispanic or Latino (of any race)	243	2.92
Central American, ex. Mexican	6	0.07
Guatemalan	2	0.02
Nicaraguan	1	0.01
Panamanian	2	0.02
Salvadoran	1	0.01
Cuban	1	0.01
Mexican	194	2.33
Puerto Rican	14	0.17
South American	2	0.02
Argentinean	1	0.01
Colombian	1	0.01
Other Hispanic or Latino	26	0.31

*Notes: † The Census 2010 population figure is used to calculate the percentages in the Hispanic Origin and Race categories. Ancestry percentages are based on the 2006-2010 American Community Survey population (not shown); ‡ Numbers in parentheses indicate the number of people reporting a single ancestry; * Numbers in parentheses indicate the number of persons reporting this race alone, not in combination with any other race; Please refer to the Explanation of Data for more information.*

Race*	Population	%
African-American/Black (708)	907	10.90
Not Hispanic (703)	896	10.77
Hispanic (5)	11	0.13
American Indian/Alaska Native (1,195)	1,955	23.49
Not Hispanic (1,173)	1,919	23.06
Hispanic (22)	36	0.43
Apache (2)	4	0.05
Blackfeet (0)	2	0.02
Cherokee (815)	1,357	16.30
Cheyenne (1)	2	0.02
Chickasaw (13)	31	0.37
Chippewa (0)	5	0.06
Choctaw (77)	114	1.37
Comanche (0)	1	0.01
Cree (0)	3	0.04
Creek (121)	222	2.67
Delaware (5)	5	0.06
Iroquois (0)	4	0.05
Kiowa (0)	2	0.02
Mexican American Ind. (0)	2	0.02
Navajo (2)	2	0.02
Osage (3)	15	0.18
Potawatomi (11)	18	0.22
Seminole (1)	2	0.02
Sioux (1)	1	0.01
Asian (31)	67	0.80
Not Hispanic (31)	63	0.76
Hispanic (0)	4	0.05
Chinese, ex. Taiwanese (9)	10	0.12
Filipino (8)	20	0.24
Indian (6)	13	0.16
Japanese (0)	5	0.06
Korean (2)	9	0.11
Pakistani (1)	2	0.02
Thai (0)	3	0.04
Vietnamese (4)	7	0.08
Hawaii Native/Pacific Islander (1)	18	0.22
Not Hispanic (1)	17	0.20
Hispanic (0)	1	0.01
Guamanian/Chamorro (0)	1	0.01
Native Hawaiian (0)	9	0.11
Samoan (1)	2	0.02
White (5,447)	6,240	74.97
Not Hispanic (5,310)	6,076	73.00
Hispanic (137)	164	1.97

Warr Acres

Place Type: City
County: Oklahoma
Population: 10,043†

Ancestry‡	Population	%
African, Sub-Saharan (231)	346	3.47
African (68)	183	1.83
Nigerian (163)	163	1.63
American (551)	551	5.52
Arab (109)	109	1.09
Jordanian (99)	99	0.99
Lebanese (10)	10	0.10
British (58)	94	0.94
Cajun (7)	7	0.07
Canadian (9)	9	0.09
Czech (16)	40	0.40
Danish (0)	8	0.08
Dutch (0)	216	2.16
English (366)	894	8.95
Estonian (7)	7	0.07
European (106)	118	1.18
French, ex. Basque (49)	303	3.03
French Canadian (51)	90	0.90
German (639)	1,645	16.48
Greek (18)	74	0.74
Hungarian (0)	41	0.41
Iranian (54)	54	0.54
Irish (203)	1,124	11.26
Italian (95)	180	1.80
Lithuanian (0)	23	0.23
Norwegian (12)	62	0.62
Polish (19)	38	0.38
Portuguese (27)	27	0.27
Scandinavian (12)	72	0.72
Scotch-Irish (122)	239	2.39
Scottish (70)	236	2.36
Swedish (0)	126	1.26
Swiss (9)	9	0.09
Turkish (0)	16	0.16
Ukrainian (9)	19	0.19
Welsh (39)	97	0.97

Hispanic Origin	Population	%
Hispanic or Latino (of any race)	2,030	20.21
Central American, ex. Mexican	166	1.65
Costa Rican	5	0.05
Guatemalan	61	0.61
Honduran	75	0.75
Nicaraguan	5	0.05
Panamanian	4	0.04
Salvadoran	16	0.16
Cuban	11	0.11
Dominican Republic	6	0.06
Mexican	1,622	16.15
Puerto Rican	38	0.38
South American	56	0.56
Argentinean	8	0.08
Bolivian	3	0.03
Colombian	12	0.12
Ecuadorian	2	0.02
Peruvian	26	0.26
Uruguayan	1	0.01
Venezuelan	4	0.04
Other Hispanic or Latino	131	1.30

Race*	Population	%
African-American/Black (988)	1,239	12.34
Not Hispanic (961)	1,181	11.76
Hispanic (27)	58	0.58
American Indian/Alaska Native (300)	577	5.75
Not Hispanic (251)	492	4.90
Hispanic (49)	85	0.85
Apache (5)	14	0.14
Blackfeet (1)	1	0.01
Central American Ind. (2)	2	0.02
Cherokee (37)	133	1.32
Cheyenne (6)	12	0.12
Chickasaw (19)	46	0.46
Choctaw (50)	89	0.89
Colville (2)	2	0.02
Comanche (9)	11	0.11
Creek (14)	30	0.30
Delaware (6)	7	0.07
Iroquois (1)	12	0.12
Kiowa (11)	15	0.15
Lumbee (0)	1	0.01
Mexican American Ind. (11)	21	0.21
Navajo (4)	13	0.13
Osage (1)	10	0.10
Potawatomi (10)	11	0.11
Seminole (20)	21	0.21
Shoshone (1)	3	0.03
Sioux (3)	5	0.05
South American Ind. (1)	1	0.01
Asian (220)	268	2.67
Not Hispanic (214)	257	2.56
Hispanic (6)	11	0.11
Bangladeshi (5)	8	0.08
Cambodian (4)	4	0.04
Chinese, ex. Taiwanese (33)	48	0.48
Filipino (12)	27	0.27
Indian (30)	33	0.33
Indonesian (9)	9	0.09
Japanese (6)	11	0.11
Korean (14)	20	0.20
Laotian (2)	2	0.02
Taiwanese (3)	3	0.03
Thai (1)	2	0.02
Vietnamese (92)	103	1.03
Hawaii Native/Pacific Islander (7)	17	0.17
Not Hispanic (3)	10	0.10
Hispanic (4)	7	0.07
Guamanian/Chamorro (6)	7	0.07
Native Hawaiian (0)	5	0.05
White (6,751)	7,301	72.70
Not Hispanic (6,118)	6,535	65.07
Hispanic (633)	766	7.63

Weatherford

Place Type: City
County: Custer
Population: 10,833†

Ancestry‡	Population	%
African, Sub-Saharan (133)	141	1.34
African (88)	96	0.91
Ghanaian (11)	11	0.10
Nigerian (13)	13	0.12
Other Sub-Saharan African (21)	21	0.20
American (686)	686	6.52
Arab (5)	5	0.05
Other Arab (5)	5	0.05
Austrian (0)	13	0.12
Belgian (0)	13	0.12
British (20)	20	0.19
Cajun (12)	12	0.11
Czech (11)	49	0.47
Czechoslovakian (14)	14	0.13
Danish (14)	51	0.49
Dutch (64)	301	2.86
English (656)	1,281	12.18
European (246)	246	2.34
French, ex. Basque (32)	282	2.68
French Canadian (23)	122	1.16
German (1,114)	2,526	24.02
Hungarian (16)	27	0.26
Irish (270)	1,398	13.30
Italian (19)	157	1.49
Norwegian (38)	58	0.55
Polish (87)	142	1.35
Romanian (12)	12	0.11
Russian (11)	58	0.55
Scotch-Irish (55)	124	1.18
Scottish (80)	231	2.20
Swedish (0)	197	1.87
Swiss (0)	20	0.19
Welsh (9)	37	0.35
West Indian, ex. Hispanic (38)	81	0.77
Dutch West Indian (38)	81	0.77
Yugoslavian (63)	63	0.60

Hispanic Origin	Population	%
Hispanic or Latino (of any race)	811	7.49
Central American, ex. Mexican	8	0.07
Guatemalan	1	0.01
Honduran	1	0.01
Nicaraguan	1	0.01
Salvadoran	5	0.05
Cuban	3	0.03
Dominican Republic	3	0.03
Mexican	688	6.35
Puerto Rican	33	0.30
South American	10	0.09
Argentinean	3	0.03
Colombian	7	0.06
Other Hispanic or Latino	66	0.61

Race*	Population	%
African-American/Black (327)	415	3.83
Not Hispanic (315)	397	3.66
Hispanic (12)	18	0.17
American Indian/Alaska Native (613)	891	8.22
Not Hispanic (582)	823	7.60
Hispanic (31)	68	0.63
Aleut *(Alaska Native)* (0)	2	0.02
Apache (2)	4	0.04
Arapaho (15)	32	0.30
Blackfeet (0)	1	0.01
Cherokee (60)	140	1.29

*Notes: † The Census 2010 population figure is used to calculate the percentages in the Hispanic Origin and Race categories. Ancestry percentages are based on the 2006-2010 American Community Survey population (not shown); ‡ Numbers in parentheses indicate the number of people reporting a single ancestry; * Numbers in parentheses indicate the number of persons reporting this race alone, not in combination with any other race; Please refer to the Explanation of Data for more information.*

Cheyenne (89)	113	1.04
Chickasaw (28)	40	0.37
Chippewa (2)	4	0.04
Choctaw (50)	90	0.83
Comanche (13)	20	0.18
Creek (20)	33	0.30
Crow (0)	1	0.01
Delaware (0)	7	0.06
Iroquois (0)	2	0.02
Kiowa (31)	44	0.41
Mexican American Ind. (1)	4	0.04
Navajo (3)	5	0.05
Osage (5)	8	0.07
Ottawa (0)	1	0.01
Potawatomi (10)	19	0.18
Pueblo (1)	2	0.02
Seminole (12)	22	0.20
Shoshone (1)	5	0.05
Sioux (1)	4	0.04
Ute (1)	1	0.01
Asian (177)	228	2.10
Not Hispanic (177)	219	2.02
Hispanic (0)	9	0.08
Chinese, ex. Taiwanese (20)	26	0.24
Filipino (4)	13	0.12
Indian (52)	61	0.56
Japanese (4)	7	0.06
Korean (7)	17	0.16
Laotian (1)	2	0.02
Nepalese (14)	14	0.13
Taiwanese (8)	8	0.07
Vietnamese (39)	44	0.41
Hawaii Native/Pacific Islander (7)	18	0.17
Not Hispanic (6)	17	0.16
Hispanic (1)	1	0.01
Guamanian/Chamorro (1)	3	0.03
Native Hawaiian (3)	8	0.07
Samoan (0)	1	0.01
Tongan (1)	3	0.03
White (8,930)	9,325	86.08
Not Hispanic (8,590)	8,908	82.23
Hispanic (340)	417	3.85

Woodward

Place Type: City
County: Woodward
Population: 12,051†

Ancestry‡	Population	%
American (2,631)	2,631	21.79
Czech (60)	60	0.50
Danish (0)	8	0.07
Dutch (40)	244	2.02
English (341)	878	7.27
European (38)	50	0.41
French, ex. Basque (9)	173	1.43
French Canadian (94)	94	0.78
German (1,097)	2,227	18.44
Irish (449)	1,474	12.21
Italian (38)	118	0.98
Lithuanian (24)	24	0.20
Norwegian (0)	9	0.07
Pennsylvania German (0)	7	0.06
Polish (34)	52	0.43
Portuguese (0)	10	0.08
Russian (17)	54	0.45
Scotch-Irish (70)	147	1.22
Scottish (64)	84	0.70
Slovak (16)	16	0.13
Swedish (10)	79	0.65
Welsh (0)	39	0.32
West Indian, ex. Hispanic (0)	10	0.08
Dutch West Indian (0)	10	0.08
Yugoslavian (0)	19	0.16

Hispanic Origin	Population	%
Hispanic or Latino (of any race)	1,571	13.04
Central American, ex. Mexican	47	0.39
Costa Rican	3	0.02
Guatemalan	10	0.08
Honduran	32	0.27
Nicaraguan	1	0.01
Panamanian	1	0.01
Cuban	9	0.07
Mexican	1,378	11.43
Puerto Rican	12	0.10
South American	5	0.04
Colombian	1	0.01
Venezuelan	4	0.03
Other Hispanic or Latino	120	1.00

Race*	Population	%
African-American/Black (41)	75	0.62
Not Hispanic (37)	62	0.51
Hispanic (4)	13	0.11
American Indian/Alaska Native (318)	524	4.35
Not Hispanic (293)	450	3.73
Hispanic (25)	74	0.61
Apache (5)	6	0.05
Arapaho (5)	7	0.06
Blackfeet (2)	12	0.10
Cherokee (53)	147	1.22
Cheyenne (48)	69	0.57
Chickasaw (14)	22	0.18
Chippewa (4)	4	0.03
Choctaw (35)	58	0.48
Comanche (0)	7	0.06
Creek (13)	15	0.12
Delaware (2)	2	0.02
Iroquois (1)	2	0.02
Kiowa (2)	2	0.02
Mexican American Ind. (1)	4	0.03
Navajo (4)	9	0.07
Osage (1)	2	0.02
Ottawa (0)	4	0.03
Potawatomi (10)	13	0.11
Seminole (2)	5	0.04
Sioux (1)	1	0.01
Tlingit-Haida *(Alaska Native)* (1)	1	0.01
Yakama (1)	1	0.01
Asian (102)	130	1.08
Not Hispanic (102)	130	1.08
Cambodian (4)	5	0.04
Chinese, ex. Taiwanese (23)	27	0.22
Filipino (22)	33	0.27
Indian (16)	23	0.19
Japanese (2)	6	0.05
Korean (9)	13	0.11
Pakistani (1)	1	0.01
Taiwanese (2)	2	0.02
Thai (1)	3	0.02
Vietnamese (16)	23	0.19
Hawaii Native/Pacific Islander (6)	12	0.10
Not Hispanic (6)	8	0.07
Hispanic (0)	4	0.03
Guamanian/Chamorro (1)	1	0.01
Native Hawaiian (2)	3	0.02
Samoan (2)	3	0.02
White (10,340)	10,670	88.54
Not Hispanic (9,815)	10,012	83.08
Hispanic (525)	658	5.46

Yukon

Place Type: City
County: Canadian
Population: 22,709†

Ancestry‡	Population	%
African, Sub-Saharan (50)	55	0.25
African (32)	37	0.17
Somalian (6)	6	0.03
Other Sub-Saharan African (12)	12	0.05
American (2,486)	2,486	11.17
Arab (0)	18	0.08
Lebanese (0)	12	0.05
Syrian (0)	6	0.03
Australian (29)	115	0.52
Austrian (0)	12	0.05
Belgian (0)	22	0.10
Brazilian (31)	31	0.14
British (109)	119	0.53
Canadian (8)	8	0.04
Czech (181)	307	1.38
Czechoslovakian (17)	31	0.14
Danish (0)	21	0.09
Dutch (236)	625	2.81
English (985)	2,540	11.41
European (305)	331	1.49
Finnish (0)	13	0.06
French, ex. Basque (110)	560	2.52
French Canadian (36)	51	0.23
German (1,278)	4,234	19.02
Greek (0)	36	0.16
Hungarian (16)	28	0.13
Iranian (12)	12	0.05
Irish (1,256)	3,455	15.52
Italian (198)	461	2.07
Lithuanian (73)	73	0.33
Norwegian (137)	248	1.11
Polish (79)	260	1.17
Russian (4)	7	0.03
Scotch-Irish (187)	580	2.60
Scottish (336)	671	3.01
Slovak (7)	21	0.09
Slovene (0)	11	0.05
Swedish (63)	212	0.95
Swiss (14)	88	0.40
Welsh (60)	171	0.77
West Indian, ex. Hispanic (33)	175	0.79
Dutch West Indian (33)	175	0.79

Hispanic Origin	Population	%
Hispanic or Latino (of any race)	1,114	4.91
Central American, ex. Mexican	43	0.19
Costa Rican	3	0.01
Guatemalan	13	0.06
Honduran	1	<0.01
Nicaraguan	5	0.02
Panamanian	3	0.01
Salvadoran	18	0.08
Cuban	22	0.10
Dominican Republic	3	0.01
Mexican	831	3.66
Puerto Rican	57	0.25
South American	36	0.16
Argentinean	1	<0.01
Chilean	4	0.02
Colombian	24	0.11
Ecuadorian	2	0.01
Peruvian	1	<0.01
Uruguayan	1	<0.01
Venezuelan	3	0.01
Other Hispanic or Latino	122	0.54

Race*	Population	%
African-American/Black (279)	452	1.99
Not Hispanic (269)	433	1.91
Hispanic (10)	19	0.08
American Indian/Alaska Native (838)	1,362	6.00
Not Hispanic (804)	1,279	5.63
Hispanic (34)	83	0.37
Apache (16)	23	0.10
Arapaho (3)	5	0.02
Blackfeet (1)	8	0.04
Cherokee (151)	325	1.43
Cheyenne (11)	16	0.07
Chickasaw (74)	100	0.44
Chippewa (4)	6	0.03
Choctaw (179)	279	1.23
Comanche (33)	40	0.18
Creek (62)	96	0.42
Delaware (9)	11	0.05
Iroquois (5)	6	0.03
Kiowa (20)	34	0.15
Mexican American Ind. (5)	6	0.03
Navajo (8)	8	0.04
Osage (15)	15	0.07
Potawatomi (42)	65	0.29

*Notes: † The Census 2010 population figure is used to calculate the percentages in the Hispanic Origin and Race categories. Ancestry percentages are based on the 2006-2010 American Community Survey population (not shown); ‡ Numbers in parentheses indicate the number of people reporting a single ancestry; * Numbers in parentheses indicate the number of persons reporting this race alone, not in combination with any other race; Please refer to the Explanation of Data for more information.*

Pueblo (1)	1	<0.01
Seminole (12)	32	0.14
Sioux (2)	5	0.02
Tlingit-Haida *(Alaska Native)* (1)	1	<0.01
Yaqui (1)	1	<0.01
Asian (455)	556	2.45
Not Hispanic (453)	551	2.43
Hispanic (2)	5	0.02
Burmese (5)	5	0.02
Cambodian (1)	1	<0.01
Chinese, ex. Taiwanese (29)	36	0.16
Filipino (18)	57	0.25
Indian (261)	283	1.25
Japanese (8)	16	0.07
Korean (9)	16	0.07
Laotian (16)	23	0.10
Sri Lankan (1)	2	0.01
Taiwanese (2)	3	0.01
Thai (5)	10	0.04
Vietnamese (92)	103	0.45
Hawaii Native/Pacific Islander (19)	32	0.14
Not Hispanic (16)	28	0.12
Hispanic (3)	4	0.02
Guamanian/Chamorro (3)	3	0.01
Marshallese (1)	1	<0.01
Native Hawaiian (12)	18	0.08
Samoan (1)	1	<0.01
White (19,940)	20,734	91.30
Not Hispanic (19,326)	19,997	88.06
Hispanic (614)	737	3.25

*Notes: † The Census 2010 population figure is used to calculate the percentages in the Hispanic Origin and Race categories. Ancestry percentages are based on the 2006-2010 American Community Survey population (not shown); ‡ Numbers in parentheses indicate the number of people reporting a single ancestry; * Numbers in parentheses indicate the number of persons reporting this race alone, not in combination with any other race; Please refer to the Explanation of Data for more information.*

OREGON

Place Type: State
Population: 3,831,074†

Ancestry‡	Population	%
Afghan (163)	237	0.01
African, Sub-Saharan (11,001)	15,318	0.41
African (5,385)	8,398	0.22
Cape Verdean (98)	98	<0.01
Ethiopian (1,686)	1,812	0.05
Ghanaian (299)	341	0.01
Kenyan (239)	254	0.01
Liberian (224)	262	0.01
Nigerian (352)	541	0.01
Senegalese (25)	25	<0.01
Sierra Leonean (88)	98	<0.01
Somalian (1,749)	2,061	0.05
South African (298)	715	0.02
Sudanese (81)	97	<0.01
Zimbabwean (0)	64	<0.01
Other Sub-Saharan African (477)	552	0.01
Albanian (254)	369	0.01
Alsatian (75)	195	0.01
American (183,475)	183,475	4.88
Arab (8,817)	14,161	0.38
Arab (2,571)	3,593	0.10
Egyptian (1,115)	1,582	0.04
Iraqi (228)	320	0.01
Jordanian (559)	624	0.02
Lebanese (1,696)	3,731	0.10
Moroccan (169)	388	0.01
Palestinian (639)	702	0.02
Syrian (564)	1,366	0.04
Other Arab (1,276)	1,855	0.05
Armenian (1,245)	2,488	0.07
Assyrian/Chaldean/Syriac (58)	117	<0.01
Australian (1,051)	2,291	0.06
Austrian (2,957)	11,540	0.31
Basque (1,253)	3,233	0.09
Belgian (1,649)	5,731	0.15
Brazilian (784)	1,235	0.03
British (11,313)	24,488	0.65
Bulgarian (966)	1,633	0.04
Cajun (260)	614	0.02
Canadian (6,196)	14,475	0.38
Carpatho Rusyn (30)	40	<0.01
Celtic (620)	1,382	0.04
Croatian (2,024)	5,124	0.14
Cypriot (0)	13	<0.01
Czech (6,878)	21,728	0.58
Czechoslovakian (2,106)	4,612	0.12
Danish (12,507)	43,160	1.15
Dutch (20,513)	95,959	2.55
Eastern European (3,688)	4,436	0.12
English (148,384)	508,156	13.51
Estonian (223)	683	0.02
European (73,903)	85,676	2.28
Finnish (7,980)	23,213	0.62
French, ex. Basque (19,832)	138,537	3.68
French Canadian (10,375)	27,843	0.74
German (247,014)	824,204	21.91
German Russian (104)	302	0.01
Greek (4,636)	13,213	0.35
Guyanese (55)	119	<0.01
Hungarian (4,344)	14,213	0.38
Icelander (336)	1,456	0.04
Iranian (3,643)	4,567	0.12
Irish (119,704)	487,695	12.96
Israeli (483)	755	0.02
Italian (47,073)	142,467	3.79
Latvian (626)	1,701	0.05
Lithuanian (1,716)	5,342	0.14
Luxemburger (120)	450	0.01
Macedonian (44)	311	0.01
Maltese (39)	230	0.01
New Zealander (258)	546	0.01
Northern European (8,851)	9,578	0.25
Norwegian (51,311)	151,447	4.03
Pennsylvania German (1,229)	2,702	0.07
Polish (17,732)	67,107	1.78
Portuguese (7,385)	20,812	0.55
Romanian (7,404)	10,676	0.28
Russian (22,591)	51,468	1.37
Scandinavian (11,200)	23,693	0.63
Scotch-Irish (32,291)	96,630	2.57
Scottish (35,333)	129,950	3.45
Serbian (591)	1,313	0.03
Slavic (642)	1,847	0.05
Slovak (1,341)	3,684	0.10
Slovene (287)	1,079	0.03
Soviet Union (30)	33	<0.01
Swedish (28,634)	117,209	3.12
Swiss (7,303)	30,820	0.82
Turkish (807)	1,472	0.04
Ukrainian (14,235)	21,179	0.56
Welsh (7,780)	42,581	1.13
West Indian, ex. Hispanic (1,674)	3,580	0.10
Bahamian (66)	180	<0.01
Barbadian (24)	102	<0.01
Belizean (37)	71	<0.01
Bermudan (13)	13	<0.01
British West Indian (15)	52	<0.01
Dutch West Indian (180)	628	0.02
Haitian (407)	601	0.02
Jamaican (582)	1,234	0.03
Trinidadian/Tobagonian (40)	41	<0.01
U.S. Virgin Islander (0)	18	<0.01
West Indian (286)	568	0.02
Other West Indian (24)	72	<0.01
Yugoslavian (1,875)	4,596	0.12

Hispanic Origin	Population	%
Hispanic or Latino (of any race)	450,062	11.75
Central American, ex. Mexican	18,190	0.47
Costa Rican	911	0.02
Guatemalan	7,703	0.20
Honduran	1,644	0.04
Nicaraguan	1,104	0.03
Panamanian	725	0.02
Salvadoran	5,906	0.15
Other Central American	197	0.01
Cuban	4,923	0.13
Dominican Republic	574	0.01
Mexican	369,817	9.65
Puerto Rican	8,845	0.23
South American	9,648	0.25
Argentinean	1,381	0.04
Bolivian	345	0.01
Chilean	1,274	0.03
Colombian	2,067	0.05
Ecuadorian	851	0.02
Paraguayan	112	<0.01
Peruvian	2,650	0.07
Uruguayan	132	<0.01
Venezuelan	712	0.02
Other South American	124	<0.01
Other Hispanic or Latino	38,065	0.99

Race*	Population	%
African-American/Black (69,206)	98,479	2.57
Not Hispanic (64,984)	89,808	2.34
Hispanic (4,222)	8,671	0.23
American Indian/Alaska Native (53,203)	109,223	2.85
Not Hispanic (42,706)	89,776	2.34
Hispanic (10,497)	19,447	0.51
Alaska Athabascan *(Ala. Nat.)* (274)	445	0.01
Aleut *(Alaska Native)* (329)	631	0.02
Apache (659)	1,811	0.05
Arapaho (57)	106	<0.01
Blackfeet (737)	2,943	0.08
Canadian/French Am. Ind. (135)	376	0.01
Central American Ind. (142)	210	0.01
Cherokee (4,027)	16,203	0.42
Cheyenne (190)	453	0.01
Chickasaw (336)	774	0.02
Chippewa (1,388)	3,023	0.08
Choctaw (1,416)	3,637	0.09
Colville (194)	328	0.01
Comanche (78)	301	0.01
Cree (42)	274	0.01
Creek (312)	837	0.02
Crow (87)	238	0.01
Delaware (100)	290	0.01
Hopi (62)	160	<0.01
Houma (15)	34	<0.01
Inupiat *(Alaska Native)* (248)	487	0.01
Iroquois (340)	1,039	0.03
Kiowa (62)	116	<0.01
Lumbee (64)	139	<0.01
Menominee (44)	106	<0.01
Mexican American Ind. (3,090)	4,397	0.11
Navajo (824)	1,533	0.04
Osage (235)	580	0.02
Ottawa (91)	179	<0.01
Paiute (466)	732	0.02
Pima (117)	202	0.01
Potawatomi (307)	546	0.01
Pueblo (152)	365	0.01
Puget Sound Salish (311)	507	0.01
Seminole (93)	354	0.01
Shoshone (113)	294	0.01
Sioux (1,513)	3,823	0.10
South American Ind. (121)	310	0.01
Spanish American Ind. (104)	195	0.01
Tlingit-Haida *(Alaska Native)* (647)	1,225	0.03
Tohono O'Odham (51)	103	<0.01
Tsimshian *(Alaska Native)* (90)	153	<0.01
Ute (73)	155	<0.01
Yakama (644)	1,025	0.03
Yaqui (141)	351	0.01
Yuman (41)	76	<0.01
Yup'ik *(Alaska Native)* (140)	300	0.01
Asian (141,263)	186,281	4.86
Not Hispanic (139,436)	180,139	4.70
Hispanic (1,827)	6,142	0.16
Bangladeshi (327)	378	0.01
Bhutanese (257)	281	0.01
Burmese (855)	977	0.03
Cambodian (3,093)	3,934	0.10
Chinese, ex. Taiwanese (29,313)	39,589	1.03
Filipino (15,861)	29,101	0.76
Hmong (2,722)	2,920	0.08
Indian (16,740)	20,200	0.53
Indonesian (875)	1,830	0.05
Japanese (12,085)	24,535	0.64
Korean (15,212)	20,395	0.53
Laotian (4,692)	5,792	0.15
Malaysian (159)	296	0.01
Nepalese (467)	543	0.01
Pakistani (851)	1,074	0.03
Sri Lankan (389)	491	0.01
Taiwanese (1,528)	1,888	0.05
Thai (2,519)	3,692	0.10
Vietnamese (26,195)	29,485	0.77
Hawaii Native/Pacific Islander (13,404)	25,785	0.67
Not Hispanic (12,697)	23,486	0.61
Hispanic (707)	2,299	0.06
Fijian (646)	888	0.02
Guamanian/Chamorro (1,755)	3,014	0.08
Marshallese (858)	970	0.03
Native Hawaiian (3,060)	9,719	0.25
Samoan (1,559)	2,892	0.08
Tongan (759)	1,006	0.03
White (3,204,614)	3,337,309	87.11
Not Hispanic (3,005,848)	3,107,886	81.12
Hispanic (198,766)	229,423	5.99

*Notes: † The Census 2010 population figure is used to calculate the percentages in the Hispanic Origin and Race categories. Ancestry percentages are based on the 2006-2010 American Community Survey population (not shown); ‡ Numbers in parentheses indicate the number of people reporting a single ancestry; * Numbers in parentheses indicate the number of persons reporting this race alone, not in combination with any other race; Please refer to the Explanation of Data for more information.*

Albany

Place Type: City
County: Linn
Population: 50,158†

Ancestry‡	Population	%
African, Sub-Saharan (39)	126	0.26
African (0)	54	0.11
Nigerian (39)	72	0.15
American (2,590)	2,590	5.33
Arab (0)	28	0.06
Lebanese (0)	15	0.03
Palestinian (0)	13	0.03
Australian (52)	74	0.15
Austrian (0)	27	0.06
Belgian (16)	59	0.12
British (80)	188	0.39
Cajun (13)	13	0.03
Canadian (56)	133	0.27
Celtic (0)	23	0.05
Czech (55)	155	0.32
Czechoslovakian (48)	48	0.10
Danish (97)	404	0.83
Dutch (279)	1,149	2.37
English (2,564)	7,643	15.74
Estonian (0)	13	0.03
European (457)	598	1.23
Finnish (139)	205	0.42
French, ex. Basque (292)	1,365	2.81
French Canadian (43)	215	0.44
German (3,062)	10,616	21.86
Greek (118)	190	0.39
Hungarian (28)	88	0.18
Icelander (0)	8	0.02
Irish (1,416)	5,678	11.69
Italian (240)	1,259	2.59
Latvian (0)	33	0.07
Lithuanian (0)	32	0.07
Northern European (165)	165	0.34
Norwegian (772)	1,970	4.06
Pennsylvania German (80)	80	0.16
Polish (260)	821	1.69
Portuguese (27)	54	0.11
Romanian (7)	25	0.05
Russian (154)	545	1.12
Scandinavian (166)	345	0.71
Scotch-Irish (397)	1,216	2.50
Scottish (399)	1,433	2.95
Swedish (372)	1,793	3.69
Swiss (83)	538	1.11
Ukrainian (43)	57	0.12
Welsh (124)	475	0.98
Yugoslavian (0)	9	0.02

Hispanic Origin	Population	%
Hispanic or Latino (of any race)	5,700	11.36
Central American, ex. Mexican	149	0.30
Costa Rican	6	0.01
Guatemalan	49	0.10
Honduran	11	0.02
Nicaraguan	11	0.02
Panamanian	11	0.02
Salvadoran	61	0.12
Cuban	27	0.05
Dominican Republic	9	0.02
Mexican	4,872	9.71
Puerto Rican	124	0.25
South American	69	0.14
Argentinean	17	0.03
Chilean	2	<0.01
Colombian	23	0.05
Ecuadorian	7	0.01
Paraguayan	6	0.01
Peruvian	9	0.02
Uruguayan	1	<0.01
Venezuelan	1	<0.01
Other South American	3	0.01
Other Hispanic or Latino	450	0.90

Race*	Population	%
African-American/Black (333)	613	1.22
Not Hispanic (275)	518	1.03
Hispanic (58)	95	0.19
American Indian/Alaska Native (592)	1,335	2.66
Not Hispanic (473)	1,109	2.21
Hispanic (119)	226	0.45
Alaska Athabascan *(Ala. Nat.)* (6)	6	0.01
Aleut *(Alaska Native)* (2)	3	0.01
Apache (13)	25	0.05
Arapaho (3)	7	0.01
Blackfeet (9)	40	0.08
Canadian/French Am. Ind. (0)	5	0.01
Central American Ind. (1)	2	<0.01
Cherokee (72)	245	0.49
Cheyenne (0)	1	<0.01
Chickasaw (5)	9	0.02
Chippewa (19)	42	0.08
Choctaw (16)	53	0.11
Colville (4)	4	0.01
Cree (1)	5	0.01
Creek (6)	11	0.02
Crow (0)	3	0.01
Delaware (10)	15	0.03
Hopi (0)	1	<0.01
Inupiat *(Alaska Native)* (6)	14	0.03
Iroquois (2)	7	0.01
Kiowa (0)	3	0.01
Mexican American Ind. (14)	29	0.06
Navajo (3)	12	0.02
Osage (3)	10	0.02
Ottawa (0)	1	<0.01
Paiute (2)	6	0.01
Potawatomi (13)	17	0.03
Pueblo (2)	6	0.01
Puget Sound Salish (2)	3	0.01
Seminole (0)	1	<0.01
Shoshone (2)	6	0.01
Sioux (12)	62	0.12
South American Ind. (0)	2	<0.01
Spanish American Ind. (5)	6	0.01
Tlingit-Haida *(Alaska Native)* (9)	12	0.02
Yakama (2)	8	0.02
Yaqui (2)	4	0.01
Yup'ik *(Alaska Native)* (9)	9	0.02
Asian (682)	1,161	2.31
Not Hispanic (657)	1,094	2.18
Hispanic (25)	67	0.13
Bangladeshi (5)	5	0.01
Cambodian (28)	38	0.08
Chinese, ex. Taiwanese (152)	220	0.44
Filipino (124)	293	0.58
Hmong (2)	4	0.01
Indian (80)	102	0.20
Indonesian (6)	28	0.06
Japanese (51)	171	0.34
Korean (84)	136	0.27
Laotian (13)	18	0.04
Nepalese (1)	1	<0.01
Pakistani (1)	5	0.01
Taiwanese (10)	20	0.04
Thai (20)	34	0.07
Vietnamese (76)	94	0.19
Hawaii Native/Pacific Islander (93)	223	0.44
Not Hispanic (88)	201	0.40
Hispanic (5)	22	0.04
Fijian (1)	3	0.01
Guamanian/Chamorro (32)	50	0.10
Marshallese (6)	7	0.01
Native Hawaiian (38)	112	0.22
Samoan (6)	11	0.02
Tongan (0)	2	<0.01
White (44,057)	45,743	91.20
Not Hispanic (41,591)	42,830	85.39
Hispanic (2,466)	2,913	5.81

Aloha

Place Type: CDP
County: Washington
Population: 49,425†

Ancestry‡	Population	%
Afghan (7)	7	0.01
African, Sub-Saharan (236)	520	1.09
African (84)	226	0.48
Ethiopian (103)	103	0.22
Liberian (9)	9	0.02
Nigerian (17)	17	0.04
Somalian (0)	142	0.30
South African (23)	23	0.05
American (1,409)	1,409	2.96
Arab (273)	331	0.70
Arab (206)	233	0.49
Egyptian (10)	10	0.02
Lebanese (18)	33	0.07
Palestinian (9)	9	0.02
Syrian (0)	16	0.03
Other Arab (30)	30	0.06
Armenian (24)	24	0.05
Austrian (0)	91	0.19
Belgian (26)	42	0.09
Brazilian (13)	13	0.03
British (105)	257	0.54
Bulgarian (39)	39	0.08
Canadian (99)	171	0.36
Celtic (0)	17	0.04
Croatian (0)	70	0.15
Czech (112)	245	0.51
Czechoslovakian (0)	19	0.04
Danish (63)	240	0.50
Dutch (126)	911	1.91
Eastern European (0)	8	0.02
English (1,183)	4,776	10.04
Estonian (11)	16	0.03
European (672)	1,100	2.31
Finnish (95)	252	0.53
French, ex. Basque (249)	1,495	3.14
French Canadian (258)	395	0.83
German (2,448)	8,885	18.68
Greek (39)	104	0.22
Hungarian (122)	254	0.53
Icelander (11)	11	0.02
Iranian (368)	445	0.94
Irish (1,581)	5,337	11.22
Italian (499)	1,651	3.47
Lithuanian (24)	41	0.09
New Zealander (20)	20	0.04
Northern European (84)	102	0.21
Norwegian (728)	1,479	3.11
Polish (223)	833	1.75
Portuguese (67)	278	0.58
Romanian (135)	180	0.38
Russian (119)	471	0.99
Scandinavian (74)	172	0.36
Scotch-Irish (514)	1,381	2.90
Scottish (379)	1,375	2.89
Swedish (237)	1,190	2.50
Swiss (136)	499	1.05
Ukrainian (94)	154	0.32
Welsh (27)	213	0.45
West Indian, ex. Hispanic (89)	159	0.33
Jamaican (8)	31	0.07
West Indian (81)	128	0.27
Yugoslavian (43)	97	0.20

Hispanic Origin	Population	%
Hispanic or Latino (of any race)	10,443	21.13
Central American, ex. Mexican	751	1.52
Costa Rican	19	0.04
Guatemalan	430	0.87
Honduran	48	0.10
Nicaraguan	25	0.05
Panamanian	26	0.05
Salvadoran	184	0.37
Other Central American	19	0.04

*Notes: † The Census 2010 population figure is used to calculate the percentages in the Hispanic Origin and Race categories. Ancestry percentages are based on the 2006-2010 American Community Survey population (not shown); ‡ Numbers in parentheses indicate the number of people reporting a single ancestry; * Numbers in parentheses indicate the number of persons reporting this race alone, not in combination with any other race; Please refer to the Explanation of Data for more information.*

Cuban	48	0.10
Dominican Republic	16	0.03
Mexican	8,417	17.03
Puerto Rican	186	0.38
South American	237	0.48
Argentinean	34	0.07
Bolivian	7	0.01
Chilean	20	0.04
Colombian	44	0.09
Ecuadorian	16	0.03
Paraguayan	3	0.01
Peruvian	72	0.15
Uruguayan	1	<0.01
Venezuelan	40	0.08
Other Hispanic or Latino	788	1.59

Race*	Population	%
African-American/Black (1,270)	1,874	3.79
Not Hispanic (1,168)	1,679	3.40
Hispanic (102)	195	0.39
American Indian/Alaska Native (489)	1,044	2.11
Not Hispanic (304)	726	1.47
Hispanic (185)	318	0.64
Alaska Athabascan *(Ala. Nat.)* (1)	2	<0.01
Aleut *(Alaska Native)* (1)	3	0.01
Apache (13)	32	0.06
Arapaho (0)	1	<0.01
Blackfeet (6)	38	0.08
Central American Ind. (9)	11	0.02
Cherokee (22)	138	0.28
Cheyenne (2)	3	0.01
Chickasaw (5)	12	0.02
Chippewa (20)	33	0.07
Choctaw (13)	32	0.06
Colville (1)	2	<0.01
Comanche (1)	5	0.01
Cree (0)	1	<0.01
Creek (2)	10	0.02
Crow (0)	1	<0.01
Hopi (1)	2	<0.01
Houma (0)	3	0.01
Inupiat *(Alaska Native)* (1)	2	<0.01
Iroquois (6)	10	0.02
Mexican American Ind. (30)	46	0.09
Navajo (19)	29	0.06
Osage (1)	6	0.01
Ottawa (5)	5	0.01
Paiute (6)	6	0.01
Pima (5)	5	0.01
Potawatomi (8)	11	0.02
Pueblo (1)	1	<0.01
Puget Sound Salish (10)	17	0.03
Seminole (2)	3	0.01
Shoshone (0)	5	0.01
Sioux (16)	42	0.08
South American Ind. (1)	2	<0.01
Spanish American Ind. (1)	1	<0.01
Tlingit-Haida *(Alaska Native)* (5)	13	0.03
Tohono O'Odham (1)	2	<0.01
Tsimshian *(Alaska Native)* (0)	1	<0.01
Yakama (2)	5	0.01
Yaqui (11)	16	0.03
Yup'ik *(Alaska Native)* (0)	3	0.01
Asian (4,407)	5,511	11.15
Not Hispanic (4,345)	5,335	10.79
Hispanic (62)	176	0.36
Bangladeshi (7)	7	0.01
Bhutanese (7)	7	0.01
Burmese (14)	19	0.04
Cambodian (342)	400	0.81
Chinese, ex. Taiwanese (413)	623	1.26
Filipino (729)	1,093	2.21
Hmong (122)	134	0.27
Indian (273)	357	0.72
Indonesian (19)	41	0.08
Japanese (222)	478	0.97
Korean (383)	533	1.08
Laotian (254)	307	0.62
Malaysian (1)	6	0.01
Nepalese (26)	29	0.06
Pakistani (28)	30	0.06
Sri Lankan (29)	37	0.07
Taiwanese (14)	17	0.03
Thai (104)	141	0.29
Vietnamese (1,199)	1,337	2.71
Hawaii Native/Pacific Islander (232)	541	1.09
Not Hispanic (220)	471	0.95
Hispanic (12)	70	0.14
Fijian (19)	27	0.05
Guamanian/Chamorro (56)	95	0.19
Marshallese (1)	4	0.01
Native Hawaiian (69)	260	0.53
Samoan (21)	54	0.11
Tongan (21)	28	0.06
White (35,051)	37,293	75.45
Not Hispanic (31,007)	32,665	66.09
Hispanic (4,044)	4,628	9.36

Altamont

Place Type: CDP
County: Klamath
Population: 19,257†

Ancestry‡	Population	%
American (1,195)	1,195	5.86
Arab (10)	10	0.05
Lebanese (10)	10	0.05
Austrian (0)	96	0.47
Basque (9)	20	0.10
Belgian (13)	44	0.22
British (57)	105	0.51
Canadian (15)	37	0.18
Croatian (0)	11	0.05
Czech (72)	166	0.81
Danish (46)	165	0.81
Dutch (91)	621	3.05
Eastern European (43)	119	0.58
English (857)	2,478	12.15
European (176)	311	1.53
Finnish (0)	18	0.09
French, ex. Basque (152)	857	4.20
French Canadian (110)	189	0.93
German (1,503)	4,730	23.20
Greek (116)	174	0.85
Hungarian (0)	26	0.13
Icelander (19)	48	0.24
Irish (439)	2,824	13.85
Italian (336)	895	4.39
Northern European (16)	16	0.08
Norwegian (253)	605	2.97
Polish (97)	372	1.82
Portuguese (85)	138	0.68
Russian (59)	123	0.60
Scandinavian (78)	120	0.59
Scotch-Irish (176)	774	3.80
Scottish (193)	791	3.88
Swedish (174)	453	2.22
Swiss (20)	116	0.57
Welsh (54)	154	0.76
Yugoslavian (0)	8	0.04

Hispanic Origin	Population	%
Hispanic or Latino (of any race)	2,029	10.54
Central American, ex. Mexican	47	0.24
Guatemalan	3	0.02
Honduran	1	0.01
Nicaraguan	3	0.02
Panamanian	2	0.01
Salvadoran	37	0.19
Other Central American	1	0.01
Cuban	11	0.06
Dominican Republic	3	0.02
Mexican	1,738	9.03
Puerto Rican	52	0.27
South American	17	0.09
Argentinean	2	0.01
Bolivian	2	0.01
Colombian	8	0.04
Paraguayan	1	0.01
Peruvian	3	0.02
Uruguayan	1	0.01
Other Hispanic or Latino	161	0.84

Race*	Population	%
African-American/Black (132)	236	1.23
Not Hispanic (118)	209	1.09
Hispanic (14)	27	0.14
American Indian/Alaska Native (732)	1,170	6.08
Not Hispanic (646)	1,021	5.30
Hispanic (86)	149	0.77
Alaska Athabascan *(Ala. Nat.)* (1)	1	0.01
Aleut *(Alaska Native)* (1)	2	0.01
Apache (4)	7	0.04
Arapaho (1)	3	0.02
Blackfeet (5)	17	0.09
Canadian/French Am. Ind. (0)	1	0.01
Cherokee (48)	116	0.60
Cheyenne (4)	8	0.04
Chickasaw (0)	1	0.01
Chippewa (5)	9	0.05
Choctaw (12)	29	0.15
Cree (0)	2	0.01
Creek (1)	6	0.03
Crow (1)	1	0.01
Inupiat *(Alaska Native)* (0)	1	0.01
Iroquois (5)	8	0.04
Kiowa (0)	2	0.01
Lumbee (0)	3	0.02
Mexican American Ind. (15)	21	0.11
Navajo (3)	6	0.03
Osage (1)	5	0.03
Paiute (10)	13	0.07
Pima (1)	1	0.01
Potawatomi (3)	3	0.02
Pueblo (3)	3	0.02
Puget Sound Salish (1)	1	0.01
Seminole (0)	3	0.02
Shoshone (1)	2	0.01
Sioux (3)	12	0.06
South American Ind. (1)	4	0.02
Tlingit-Haida *(Alaska Native)* (2)	2	0.01
Tohono O'Odham (3)	3	0.02
Ute (0)	1	0.01
Yaqui (2)	2	0.01
Yup'ik *(Alaska Native)* (3)	3	0.02
Asian (145)	233	1.21
Not Hispanic (144)	215	1.12
Hispanic (1)	18	0.09
Cambodian (0)	2	0.01
Chinese, ex. Taiwanese (14)	22	0.11
Filipino (35)	72	0.37
Hmong (1)	1	0.01
Indian (7)	15	0.08
Indonesian (4)	11	0.06
Japanese (15)	27	0.14
Korean (15)	22	0.11
Laotian (1)	9	0.05
Nepalese (4)	4	0.02
Thai (1)	7	0.04
Vietnamese (30)	38	0.20
Hawaii Native/Pacific Islander (21)	55	0.29
Not Hispanic (18)	50	0.26
Hispanic (3)	5	0.03
Fijian (1)	2	0.01
Guamanian/Chamorro (1)	4	0.02
Marshallese (3)	3	0.02
Native Hawaiian (9)	25	0.13
Samoan (6)	10	0.05
White (16,638)	17,350	90.10
Not Hispanic (15,740)	16,271	84.49
Hispanic (898)	1,079	5.60

Ashland

Place Type: City
County: Jackson
Population: 20,078†

*Notes: † The Census 2010 population figure is used to calculate the percentages in the Hispanic Origin and Race categories. Ancestry percentages are based on the 2006-2010 American Community Survey population (not shown); ‡ Numbers in parentheses indicate the number of people reporting a single ancestry; * Numbers in parentheses indicate the number of persons reporting this race alone, not in combination with any other race; Please refer to the Explanation of Data for more information.*

SECTION TWO

Ancestry‡	Population	%
African, Sub-Saharan (39)	39	0.19
African (16)	16	0.08
Ethiopian (23)	23	0.11
American (471)	471	2.34
Arab (24)	92	0.46
Lebanese (12)	61	0.30
Syrian (0)	19	0.09
Other Arab (12)	12	0.06
Assyrian/Chaldean/Syriac (15)	31	0.15
Austrian (23)	148	0.74
Belgian (11)	59	0.29
British (147)	296	1.47
Bulgarian (0)	81	0.40
Canadian (41)	41	0.20
Carpatho Rusyn (0)	10	0.05
Celtic (31)	31	0.15
Croatian (9)	76	0.38
Czech (48)	113	0.56
Czechoslovakian (0)	75	0.37
Danish (61)	385	1.92
Dutch (65)	713	3.55
Eastern European (54)	54	0.27
English (834)	3,331	16.57
European (622)	622	3.09
Finnish (11)	335	1.67
French, ex. Basque (126)	1,148	5.71
French Canadian (49)	138	0.69
German (1,087)	4,535	22.56
Greek (22)	82	0.41
Hungarian (10)	86	0.43
Icelander (41)	41	0.20
Iranian (0)	17	0.08
Irish (638)	3,054	15.19
Italian (159)	704	3.50
Latvian (0)	15	0.07
Lithuanian (42)	97	0.48
Maltese (0)	35	0.17
Northern European (74)	74	0.37
Norwegian (251)	977	4.86
Polish (95)	494	2.46
Portuguese (48)	177	0.88
Romanian (0)	11	0.05
Russian (89)	630	3.13
Scandinavian (9)	118	0.59
Scotch-Irish (199)	879	4.37
Scottish (212)	933	4.64
Slavic (0)	16	0.08
Slovak (0)	49	0.24
Swedish (88)	609	3.03
Swiss (0)	143	0.71
Ukrainian (30)	124	0.62
Welsh (191)	452	2.25
West Indian, ex. Hispanic (51)	51	0.25
Jamaican (51)	51	0.25
Yugoslavian (0)	21	0.10

Hispanic Origin	Population	%
Hispanic or Latino (of any race)	1,028	5.12
Central American, ex. Mexican	62	0.31
Costa Rican	4	0.02
Guatemalan	30	0.15
Honduran	4	0.02
Nicaraguan	15	0.07
Panamanian	3	0.01
Salvadoran	6	0.03
Cuban	11	0.05
Dominican Republic	6	0.03
Mexican	662	3.30
Puerto Rican	49	0.24
South American	81	0.40
Argentinean	17	0.08
Bolivian	1	<0.01
Chilean	18	0.09
Colombian	16	0.08
Ecuadorian	5	0.02
Paraguayan	2	0.01
Peruvian	10	0.05
Uruguayan	3	0.01
Venezuelan	7	0.03
Other South American	2	0.01
Other Hispanic or Latino	157	0.78

Race*	Population	%
African-American/Black (225)	382	1.90
Not Hispanic (211)	347	1.73
Hispanic (14)	35	0.17
American Indian/Alaska Native (174)	521	2.59
Not Hispanic (147)	423	2.11
Hispanic (27)	98	0.49
Alaska Athabascan *(Ala. Nat.)* (2)	2	0.01
Aleut *(Alaska Native)* (2)	2	0.01
Apache (3)	10	0.05
Blackfeet (3)	13	0.06
Canadian/French Am. Ind. (1)	3	0.01
Cherokee (8)	90	0.45
Cheyenne (1)	3	0.01
Chippewa (6)	21	0.10
Choctaw (3)	18	0.09
Comanche (0)	4	0.02
Cree (0)	1	<0.01
Creek (1)	6	0.03
Hopi (0)	1	<0.01
Inupiat *(Alaska Native)* (2)	3	0.01
Iroquois (2)	5	0.02
Lumbee (1)	1	<0.01
Mexican American Ind. (5)	13	0.06
Navajo (3)	4	0.02
Osage (0)	5	0.02
Ottawa (1)	1	<0.01
Paiute (1)	2	0.01
Potawatomi (4)	5	0.02
Pueblo (0)	1	<0.01
Puget Sound Salish (2)	2	0.01
Seminole (0)	3	0.01
Sioux (10)	22	0.11
Tlingit-Haida *(Alaska Native)* (3)	5	0.02
Ute (0)	1	<0.01
Yaqui (1)	4	0.02
Yuman (0)	1	<0.01
Yup'ik *(Alaska Native)* (1)	1	<0.01
Asian (423)	702	3.50
Not Hispanic (413)	678	3.38
Hispanic (10)	24	0.12
Bangladeshi (1)	1	<0.01
Burmese (2)	2	0.01
Cambodian (9)	11	0.05
Chinese, ex. Taiwanese (100)	158	0.79
Filipino (53)	134	0.67
Hmong (3)	3	0.01
Indian (33)	58	0.29
Indonesian (3)	6	0.03
Japanese (76)	177	0.88
Korean (55)	89	0.44
Laotian (1)	1	<0.01
Malaysian (2)	4	0.02
Nepalese (2)	2	0.01
Pakistani (2)	3	0.01
Sri Lankan (1)	1	<0.01
Taiwanese (3)	6	0.03
Thai (17)	21	0.10
Vietnamese (22)	28	0.14
Hawaii Native/Pacific Islander (55)	137	0.68
Not Hispanic (52)	128	0.64
Hispanic (3)	9	0.04
Fijian (1)	1	<0.01
Guamanian/Chamorro (2)	4	0.02
Marshallese (1)	1	<0.01
Native Hawaiian (27)	89	0.44
Samoan (7)	15	0.07
Tongan (3)	3	0.01
White (18,126)	18,869	93.98
Not Hispanic (17,540)	18,150	90.40
Hispanic (586)	719	3.58

Astoria

Place Type: City
County: Clatsop
Population: 9,477†

Ancestry‡	Population	%
African, Sub-Saharan (39)	39	0.41
Ethiopian (3)	3	0.03
Nigerian (36)	36	0.38
Alsatian (12)	12	0.13
American (826)	826	8.64
Austrian (0)	39	0.41
British (42)	90	0.94
Canadian (15)	38	0.40
Celtic (0)	10	0.10
Croatian (25)	41	0.43
Czech (0)	67	0.70
Czechoslovakian (0)	20	0.21
Danish (49)	128	1.34
Dutch (19)	137	1.43
Eastern European (51)	51	0.53
English (379)	1,378	14.41
European (148)	148	1.55
Finnish (179)	429	4.49
French, ex. Basque (0)	446	4.67
French Canadian (31)	51	0.53
German (523)	1,662	17.38
Greek (0)	38	0.40
Hungarian (0)	13	0.14
Irish (291)	1,088	11.38
Italian (72)	404	4.23
New Zealander (0)	17	0.18
Northern European (23)	23	0.24
Norwegian (252)	832	8.70
Pennsylvania German (0)	8	0.08
Polish (79)	239	2.50
Russian (12)	31	0.32
Scandinavian (98)	210	2.20
Scotch-Irish (100)	396	4.14
Scottish (96)	381	3.99
Swedish (78)	370	3.87
Swiss (0)	37	0.39
Turkish (0)	8	0.08
Ukrainian (20)	20	0.21
Welsh (64)	206	2.15
Yugoslavian (0)	17	0.18

Hispanic Origin	Population	%
Hispanic or Latino (of any race)	932	9.83
Central American, ex. Mexican	18	0.19
Costa Rican	2	0.02
Guatemalan	5	0.05
Honduran	3	0.03
Nicaraguan	4	0.04
Panamanian	1	0.01
Salvadoran	3	0.03
Cuban	8	0.08
Dominican Republic	1	0.01
Mexican	766	8.08
Puerto Rican	24	0.25
South American	18	0.19
Chilean	3	0.03
Colombian	5	0.05
Ecuadorian	2	0.02
Peruvian	5	0.05
Venezuelan	3	0.03
Other Hispanic or Latino	97	1.02

Race*	Population	%
African-American/Black (57)	94	0.99
Not Hispanic (44)	77	0.81
Hispanic (13)	17	0.18
American Indian/Alaska Native (104)	259	2.73
Not Hispanic (78)	214	2.26
Hispanic (26)	45	0.47
Alaska Athabascan *(Ala. Nat.)* (3)	3	0.03
Aleut *(Alaska Native)* (0)	4	0.04
Blackfeet (0)	5	0.05
Cherokee (5)	41	0.43
Chippewa (7)	16	0.17
Choctaw (1)	1	0.01
Colville (1)	4	0.04
Creek (2)	2	0.02
Iroquois (2)	2	0.02
Mexican American Ind. (3)	5	0.05

*Notes: † The Census 2010 population figure is used to calculate the percentages in the Hispanic Origin and Race categories. Ancestry percentages are based on the 2006-2010 American Community Survey population (not shown); ‡ Numbers in parentheses indicate the number of people reporting a single ancestry; * Numbers in parentheses indicate the number of persons reporting this race alone, not in combination with any other race; Please refer to the Explanation of Data for more information.*

Ottawa (1)	1	0.01
Pueblo (0)	1	0.01
Puget Sound Salish (1)	2	0.02
Shoshone (0)	1	0.01
Sioux (3)	11	0.12
South American Ind. (1)	2	0.02
Tlingit-Haida *(Alaska Native)* (6)	9	0.09
Yakama (0)	1	0.01
Yaqui (0)	1	0.01
Yup'ik *(Alaska Native)* (2)	3	0.03
Asian (166)	268	2.83
Not Hispanic (160)	255	2.69
Hispanic (6)	13	0.14
Burmese (5)	5	0.05
Chinese, ex. Taiwanese (64)	81	0.85
Filipino (31)	75	0.79
Indian (12)	17	0.18
Indonesian (1)	6	0.06
Japanese (17)	37	0.39
Korean (10)	17	0.18
Laotian (1)	3	0.03
Sri Lankan (5)	5	0.05
Taiwanese (1)	2	0.02
Thai (7)	10	0.11
Vietnamese (3)	5	0.05
Hawaii Native/Pacific Islander (10)	44	0.46
Not Hispanic (10)	42	0.44
Hispanic (0)	2	0.02
Native Hawaiian (1)	27	0.28
Samoan (2)	3	0.03
Tongan (2)	2	0.02
White (8,458)	8,758	92.41
Not Hispanic (7,979)	8,232	86.86
Hispanic (479)	526	5.55

Baker City

Place Type: City
County: Baker
Population: 9,828†

Ancestry‡	Population	%
American (846)	846	8.64
Basque (0)	16	0.16
Belgian (8)	8	0.08
British (48)	58	0.59
Canadian (0)	28	0.29
Czech (0)	9	0.09
Danish (26)	61	0.62
Dutch (60)	331	3.38
Eastern European (8)	8	0.08
English (356)	1,201	12.27
European (210)	210	2.15
Finnish (12)	12	0.12
French, ex. Basque (22)	349	3.57
French Canadian (15)	52	0.53
German (748)	2,202	22.50
Hungarian (5)	72	0.74
Irish (300)	1,346	13.75
Italian (49)	324	3.31
Lithuanian (0)	72	0.74
Northern European (63)	63	0.64
Norwegian (116)	451	4.61
Polish (41)	101	1.03
Portuguese (10)	41	0.42
Romanian (0)	59	0.60
Russian (7)	86	0.88
Scotch-Irish (150)	341	3.48
Scottish (25)	213	2.18
Slovene (13)	13	0.13
Swedish (161)	308	3.15
Swiss (0)	15	0.15
Welsh (12)	75	0.77
West Indian, ex. Hispanic (0)	12	0.12
Dutch West Indian (0)	12	0.12

Hispanic Origin	Population	%
Hispanic or Latino (of any race)	346	3.52
Central American, ex. Mexican	4	0.04
Guatemalan	1	0.01
Nicaraguan	1	0.01
Panamanian	1	0.01
Salvadoran	1	0.01
Cuban	2	0.02
Mexican	287	2.92
Puerto Rican	4	0.04
South American	3	0.03
Chilean	1	0.01
Ecuadorian	1	0.01
Peruvian	1	0.01
Other Hispanic or Latino	46	0.47

Race*	Population	%
African-American/Black (45)	74	0.75
Not Hispanic (40)	63	0.64
Hispanic (5)	11	0.11
American Indian/Alaska Native (110)	278	2.83
Not Hispanic (101)	255	2.59
Hispanic (9)	23	0.23
Alaska Athabascan *(Ala. Nat.)* (1)	1	0.01
Aleut *(Alaska Native)* (3)	3	0.03
Apache (1)	3	0.03
Arapaho (2)	2	0.02
Blackfeet (1)	2	0.02
Canadian/French Am. Ind. (1)	2	0.02
Cherokee (26)	91	0.93
Cheyenne (0)	1	0.01
Chickasaw (2)	4	0.04
Chippewa (4)	9	0.09
Choctaw (1)	9	0.09
Cree (0)	3	0.03
Creek (1)	3	0.03
Kiowa (0)	1	0.01
Navajo (0)	1	0.01
Osage (3)	3	0.03
Ottawa (1)	1	0.01
Paiute (0)	1	0.01
Sioux (7)	9	0.09
South American Ind. (0)	2	0.02
Tlingit-Haida *(Alaska Native)* (1)	1	0.01
Asian (52)	81	0.82
Not Hispanic (52)	79	0.80
Hispanic (0)	2	0.02
Chinese, ex. Taiwanese (17)	22	0.22
Filipino (10)	20	0.20
Indian (1)	3	0.03
Japanese (2)	5	0.05
Korean (7)	15	0.15
Thai (3)	3	0.03
Vietnamese (2)	3	0.03
Hawaii Native/Pacific Islander (1)	12	0.12
Not Hispanic (1)	9	0.09
Hispanic (0)	3	0.03
Native Hawaiian (1)	6	0.06
Samoan (0)	6	0.06
White (9,294)	9,516	96.83
Not Hispanic (9,080)	9,278	94.40
Hispanic (214)	238	2.42

Beaverton

Place Type: City
County: Washington
Population: 89,803†

Ancestry‡	Population	%
African, Sub-Saharan (451)	599	0.68
African (200)	308	0.35
Ethiopian (15)	15	0.02
Ghanaian (0)	11	0.01
Somalian (112)	112	0.13
South African (81)	81	0.09
Other Sub-Saharan African (43)	72	0.08
Alsatian (8)	8	0.01
American (2,672)	2,672	3.04
Arab (1,196)	1,419	1.61
Arab (286)	311	0.35
Egyptian (47)	47	0.05
Iraqi (145)	145	0.16
Jordanian (347)	347	0.39
Lebanese (147)	273	0.31
Palestinian (86)	86	0.10
Syrian (0)	30	0.03
Other Arab (138)	180	0.20
Armenian (183)	183	0.21
Australian (0)	61	0.07
Austrian (121)	384	0.44
Basque (16)	26	0.03
Belgian (14)	69	0.08
Brazilian (26)	26	0.03
British (339)	816	0.93
Bulgarian (131)	131	0.15
Canadian (197)	343	0.39
Celtic (9)	39	0.04
Croatian (77)	273	0.31
Czech (131)	355	0.40
Czechoslovakian (23)	62	0.07
Danish (254)	750	0.85
Dutch (604)	2,090	2.37
Eastern European (73)	79	0.09
English (2,473)	9,542	10.84
Estonian (10)	10	0.01
European (2,108)	2,357	2.68
Finnish (150)	707	0.80
French, ex. Basque (297)	2,566	2.91
French Canadian (178)	431	0.49
German (4,645)	17,444	19.81
German Russian (45)	45	0.05
Greek (210)	336	0.38
Guyanese (0)	11	0.01
Hungarian (106)	224	0.25
Iranian (328)	393	0.45
Irish (2,918)	11,391	12.94
Israeli (61)	61	0.07
Italian (1,209)	3,771	4.28
Latvian (27)	51	0.06
Lithuanian (45)	151	0.17
Luxemburger (0)	12	0.01
New Zealander (25)	25	0.03
Northern European (181)	268	0.30
Norwegian (900)	3,201	3.64
Polish (408)	1,751	1.99
Portuguese (125)	416	0.47
Romanian (152)	221	0.25
Russian (639)	1,504	1.71
Scandinavian (270)	533	0.61
Scotch-Irish (793)	2,038	2.31
Scottish (712)	2,808	3.19
Slavic (75)	144	0.16
Slovak (12)	78	0.09
Slovene (34)	72	0.08
Swedish (1,025)	2,976	3.38
Swiss (234)	837	0.95
Turkish (0)	13	0.01
Ukrainian (389)	559	0.63
Welsh (95)	813	0.92
West Indian, ex. Hispanic (75)	98	0.11
Jamaican (28)	51	0.06
Trinidadian/Tobagonian (24)	24	0.03
West Indian (23)	23	0.03
Yugoslavian (46)	179	0.20

Hispanic Origin	Population	%
Hispanic or Latino (of any race)	14,628	16.29
Central American, ex. Mexican	1,210	1.35
Costa Rican	44	0.05
Guatemalan	703	0.78
Honduran	104	0.12
Nicaraguan	42	0.05
Panamanian	32	0.04
Salvadoran	268	0.30
Other Central American	17	0.02
Cuban	168	0.19
Dominican Republic	12	0.01
Mexican	11,114	12.38
Puerto Rican	275	0.31
South American	600	0.67
Argentinean	54	0.06
Bolivian	19	0.02
Chilean	55	0.06

*Notes: † The Census 2010 population figure is used to calculate the percentages in the Hispanic Origin and Race categories. Ancestry percentages are based on the 2006-2010 American Community Survey population (not shown); ‡ Numbers in parentheses indicate the number of people reporting a single ancestry; * Numbers in parentheses indicate the number of persons reporting this race alone, not in combination with any other race; Please refer to the Explanation of Data for more information.*

Colombian	124	0.14
Ecuadorian	46	0.05
Paraguayan	6	0.01
Peruvian	206	0.23
Uruguayan	16	0.02
Venezuelan	67	0.07
Other South American	7	0.01
Other Hispanic or Latino	1,249	1.39

Race*	Population	%
African-American/Black (2,370)	3,340	3.72
Not Hispanic (2,219)	3,031	3.38
Hispanic (151)	309	0.34
American Indian/Alaska Native (576)	1,515	1.69
Not Hispanic (387)	1,127	1.25
Hispanic (189)	388	0.43
Alaska Athabascan *(Ala. Nat.)* (4)	7	0.01
Aleut *(Alaska Native)* (8)	12	0.01
Apache (13)	37	0.04
Arapaho (1)	2	<0.01
Blackfeet (16)	59	0.07
Canadian/French Am. Ind. (2)	6	0.01
Central American Ind. (11)	16	0.02
Cherokee (48)	222	0.25
Cheyenne (5)	8	0.01
Chickasaw (0)	8	0.01
Chippewa (19)	50	0.06
Choctaw (9)	51	0.06
Colville (1)	1	<0.01
Comanche (0)	1	<0.01
Cree (1)	2	<0.01
Creek (10)	21	0.02
Crow (2)	2	<0.01
Delaware (4)	14	0.02
Hopi (2)	8	0.01
Inupiat *(Alaska Native)* (10)	18	0.02
Iroquois (2)	22	0.02
Lumbee (0)	1	<0.01
Menominee (0)	1	<0.01
Mexican American Ind. (51)	88	0.10
Navajo (11)	35	0.04
Osage (3)	4	<0.01
Ottawa (3)	6	0.01
Paiute (3)	6	0.01
Pima (0)	1	<0.01
Potawatomi (4)	9	0.01
Pueblo (3)	9	0.01
Puget Sound Salish (2)	9	0.01
Seminole (0)	5	0.01
Shoshone (0)	2	<0.01
Sioux (7)	35	0.04
South American Ind. (4)	9	0.01
Spanish American Ind. (1)	2	<0.01
Tlingit-Haida *(Alaska Native)* (9)	13	0.01
Tohono O'Odham (1)	1	<0.01
Tsimshian *(Alaska Native)* (1)	1	<0.01
Yakama (3)	9	0.01
Yaqui (1)	6	0.01
Yuman (2)	3	<0.01
Asian (9,438)	11,270	12.55
Not Hispanic (9,368)	11,044	12.30
Hispanic (70)	226	0.25
Bangladeshi (25)	27	0.03
Bhutanese (56)	60	0.07
Burmese (14)	17	0.02
Cambodian (252)	290	0.32
Chinese, ex. Taiwanese (1,426)	1,881	2.09
Filipino (855)	1,309	1.46
Hmong (48)	60	0.07
Indian (2,257)	2,432	2.71
Indonesian (53)	79	0.09
Japanese (795)	1,364	1.52
Korean (1,495)	1,689	1.88
Laotian (121)	155	0.17
Malaysian (10)	18	0.02
Nepalese (38)	38	0.04
Pakistani (78)	100	0.11
Sri Lankan (36)	56	0.06
Taiwanese (115)	133	0.15
Thai (163)	205	0.23
Vietnamese (1,221)	1,367	1.52
Hawaii Native/Pacific Islander (415)	820	0.91
Not Hispanic (395)	739	0.82
Hispanic (20)	81	0.09
Fijian (38)	49	0.05
Guamanian/Chamorro (122)	177	0.20
Marshallese (1)	4	<0.01
Native Hawaiian (101)	320	0.36
Samoan (17)	56	0.06
Tongan (45)	51	0.06
White (65,566)	69,141	76.99
Not Hispanic (59,559)	62,289	69.36
Hispanic (6,007)	6,852	7.63

Bend

Place Type: City
County: Deschutes
Population: 76,639†

Ancestry‡	Population	%
African, Sub-Saharan (57)	140	0.19
African (32)	115	0.15
South African (25)	25	0.03
American (3,038)	3,038	4.09
Arab (69)	213	0.29
Egyptian (0)	51	0.07
Lebanese (21)	43	0.06
Moroccan (0)	45	0.06
Palestinian (12)	12	0.02
Syrian (36)	62	0.08
Assyrian/Chaldean/Syriac (0)	11	0.01
Australian (0)	45	0.06
Austrian (198)	557	0.75
Basque (65)	253	0.34
Belgian (20)	142	0.19
Brazilian (16)	16	0.02
British (282)	470	0.63
Canadian (94)	151	0.20
Celtic (17)	60	0.08
Croatian (19)	48	0.06
Czech (128)	398	0.54
Czechoslovakian (40)	114	0.15
Danish (143)	760	1.02
Dutch (495)	1,756	2.36
Eastern European (156)	171	0.23
English (3,219)	11,087	14.92
European (2,001)	2,148	2.89
Finnish (152)	339	0.46
French, ex. Basque (466)	2,972	4.00
French Canadian (121)	543	0.73
German (5,241)	17,784	23.93
Greek (38)	148	0.20
Hungarian (200)	511	0.69
Icelander (12)	60	0.08
Irish (3,463)	11,806	15.88
Italian (1,844)	4,057	5.46
Latvian (10)	10	0.01
Lithuanian (22)	85	0.11
New Zealander (15)	15	0.02
Northern European (305)	332	0.45
Norwegian (1,101)	3,444	4.63
Pennsylvania German (21)	21	0.03
Polish (835)	1,988	2.67
Portuguese (228)	390	0.52
Romanian (30)	60	0.08
Russian (191)	766	1.03
Scandinavian (235)	646	0.87
Scotch-Irish (664)	2,131	2.87
Scottish (1,056)	3,198	4.30
Serbian (21)	21	0.03
Slavic (67)	76	0.10
Slovak (87)	171	0.23
Slovene (21)	21	0.03
Swedish (751)	3,094	4.16
Swiss (15)	455	0.61
Ukrainian (46)	92	0.12
Welsh (113)	985	1.33
Yugoslavian (56)	81	0.11

Hispanic Origin	Population	%
Hispanic or Latino (of any race)	6,256	8.16
Central American, ex. Mexican	326	0.43
Costa Rican	20	0.03
Guatemalan	73	0.10
Honduran	34	0.04
Nicaraguan	14	0.02
Panamanian	16	0.02
Salvadoran	166	0.22
Other Central American	3	<0.01
Cuban	70	0.09
Dominican Republic	11	0.01
Mexican	4,902	6.40
Puerto Rican	140	0.18
South American	170	0.22
Argentinean	22	0.03
Bolivian	5	0.01
Chilean	17	0.02
Colombian	36	0.05
Ecuadorian	25	0.03
Paraguayan	10	0.01
Peruvian	46	0.06
Uruguayan	1	<0.01
Venezuelan	4	0.01
Other South American	4	0.01
Other Hispanic or Latino	637	0.83

Race*	Population	%
African-American/Black (357)	698	0.91
Not Hispanic (333)	635	0.83
Hispanic (24)	63	0.08
American Indian/Alaska Native (642)	1,367	1.78
Not Hispanic (486)	1,085	1.42
Hispanic (156)	282	0.37
Alaska Athabascan *(Ala. Nat.)* (2)	2	<0.01
Aleut *(Alaska Native)* (7)	21	0.03
Apache (15)	29	0.04
Blackfeet (15)	38	0.05
Canadian/French Am. Ind. (0)	5	0.01
Central American Ind. (1)	2	<0.01
Cherokee (55)	184	0.24
Cheyenne (1)	4	0.01
Chickasaw (14)	26	0.03
Chippewa (24)	47	0.06
Choctaw (11)	45	0.06
Colville (5)	6	0.01
Comanche (5)	7	0.01
Cree (1)	1	<0.01
Creek (1)	12	0.02
Crow (1)	1	<0.01
Delaware (0)	2	<0.01
Hopi (0)	2	<0.01
Houma (1)	1	<0.01
Inupiat *(Alaska Native)* (8)	12	0.02
Iroquois (11)	19	0.02
Kiowa (2)	2	<0.01
Lumbee (3)	3	<0.01
Mexican American Ind. (49)	59	0.08
Navajo (16)	33	0.04
Osage (4)	10	0.01
Paiute (9)	12	0.02
Pima (4)	4	0.01
Potawatomi (6)	12	0.02
Pueblo (4)	11	0.01
Puget Sound Salish (2)	4	0.01
Seminole (0)	4	0.01
Shoshone (3)	9	0.01
Sioux (27)	56	0.07
South American Ind. (0)	2	<0.01
Spanish American Ind. (1)	1	<0.01
Tlingit-Haida *(Alaska Native)* (7)	13	0.02
Tsimshian *(Alaska Native)* (1)	2	<0.01
Ute (0)	3	<0.01
Yakama (3)	10	0.01
Yaqui (1)	4	0.01
Yup'ik *(Alaska Native)* (4)	7	0.01
Asian (956)	1,637	2.14
Not Hispanic (918)	1,548	2.02
Hispanic (38)	89	0.12
Bangladeshi (0)	1	<0.01

*Notes: † The Census 2010 population figure is used to calculate the percentages in the Hispanic Origin and Race categories. Ancestry percentages are based on the 2006-2010 American Community Survey population (not shown); ‡ Numbers in parentheses indicate the number of people reporting a single ancestry; * Numbers in parentheses indicate the number of persons reporting this race alone, not in combination with any other race; Please refer to the Explanation of Data for more information.*

Burmese (6)	7	0.01
Cambodian (4)	5	0.01
Chinese, ex. Taiwanese (242)	396	0.52
Filipino (151)	344	0.45
Indian (97)	142	0.19
Indonesian (5)	17	0.02
Japanese (139)	358	0.47
Korean (123)	208	0.27
Laotian (1)	4	0.01
Malaysian (3)	10	0.01
Nepalese (5)	9	0.01
Pakistani (0)	7	0.01
Sri Lankan (1)	1	<0.01
Taiwanese (10)	14	0.02
Thai (27)	42	0.05
Vietnamese (84)	113	0.15
Hawaii Native/Pacific Islander (108)	288	0.38
Not Hispanic (89)	254	0.33
Hispanic (19)	34	0.04
Guamanian/Chamorro (13)	22	0.03
Native Hawaiian (67)	184	0.24
Samoan (9)	30	0.04
Tongan (0)	4	0.01
White (69,977)	71,880	93.79
Not Hispanic (66,911)	68,419	89.27
Hispanic (3,066)	3,461	4.52

Bethany

Place Type: CDP
County: Washington
Population: 20,646†

Ancestry‡	Population	%
Afghan (31)	31	0.16
American (473)	473	2.43
Arab (61)	138	0.71
Egyptian (8)	8	0.04
Iraqi (10)	10	0.05
Syrian (7)	14	0.07
Other Arab (36)	106	0.54
Armenian (10)	10	0.05
Australian (0)	40	0.21
Austrian (24)	98	0.50
Basque (36)	44	0.23
Belgian (56)	69	0.35
British (94)	156	0.80
Canadian (82)	112	0.58
Croatian (0)	27	0.14
Czech (15)	27	0.14
Danish (115)	319	1.64
Dutch (171)	350	1.80
Eastern European (70)	70	0.36
English (651)	1,986	10.20
Estonian (23)	23	0.12
European (203)	313	1.61
Finnish (8)	180	0.92
French, ex. Basque (227)	658	3.38
French Canadian (30)	92	0.47
German (1,050)	3,154	16.20
Greek (44)	147	0.75
Hungarian (42)	96	0.49
Iranian (109)	134	0.69
Irish (290)	1,434	7.36
Italian (111)	846	4.34
Latvian (29)	85	0.44
Lithuanian (14)	14	0.07
Northern European (50)	50	0.26
Norwegian (210)	671	3.45
Polish (94)	384	1.97
Portuguese (42)	281	1.44
Romanian (36)	36	0.18
Russian (258)	533	2.74
Scandinavian (34)	82	0.42
Scotch-Irish (160)	523	2.69
Scottish (83)	675	3.47
Slovak (0)	110	0.56
Swedish (359)	897	4.61
Swiss (55)	88	0.45
Turkish (0)	15	0.08
Ukrainian (0)	21	0.11
Welsh (47)	251	1.29
Yugoslavian (0)	103	0.53

Hispanic Origin	Population	%
Hispanic or Latino (of any race)	1,048	5.08
Central American, ex. Mexican	48	0.23
Costa Rican	2	0.01
Guatemalan	26	0.13
Honduran	3	0.01
Nicaraguan	4	0.02
Panamanian	4	0.02
Salvadoran	8	0.04
Other Central American	1	<0.01
Cuban	12	0.06
Mexican	685	3.32
Puerto Rican	90	0.44
South American	114	0.55
Argentinean	6	0.03
Bolivian	3	0.01
Chilean	18	0.09
Colombian	22	0.11
Ecuadorian	20	0.10
Paraguayan	1	<0.01
Peruvian	36	0.17
Uruguayan	1	<0.01
Venezuelan	6	0.03
Other South American	1	<0.01
Other Hispanic or Latino	99	0.48

Race*	Population	%
African-American/Black (358)	538	2.61
Not Hispanic (352)	507	2.46
Hispanic (6)	31	0.15
American Indian/Alaska Native (61)	185	0.90
Not Hispanic (49)	142	0.69
Hispanic (12)	43	0.21
Aleut *(Alaska Native)* (2)	2	0.01
Apache (1)	4	0.02
Blackfeet (1)	1	<0.01
Cherokee (3)	21	0.10
Chickasaw (1)	1	<0.01
Chippewa (0)	3	0.01
Choctaw (4)	10	0.05
Creek (1)	4	0.02
Crow (0)	2	0.01
Menominee (1)	1	<0.01
Mexican American Ind. (4)	9	0.04
Navajo (0)	1	<0.01
Paiute (0)	1	<0.01
Pima (0)	1	<0.01
Puget Sound Salish (0)	1	<0.01
Seminole (2)	5	0.02
Sioux (1)	1	<0.01
South American Ind. (0)	1	<0.01
Spanish American Ind. (0)	1	<0.01
Tlingit-Haida *(Alaska Native)* (7)	21	0.10
Tsimshian *(Alaska Native)* (0)	1	<0.01
Yakama (4)	4	0.02
Yaqui (1)	4	0.02
Asian (6,551)	7,061	34.20
Not Hispanic (6,535)	7,019	34.00
Hispanic (16)	42	0.20
Bangladeshi (126)	132	0.64
Burmese (1)	4	0.02
Cambodian (47)	53	0.26
Chinese, ex. Taiwanese (1,627)	1,818	8.81
Filipino (218)	316	1.53
Hmong (12)	12	0.06
Indian (2,302)	2,380	11.53
Indonesian (50)	74	0.36
Japanese (294)	420	2.03
Korean (835)	913	4.42
Laotian (31)	45	0.22
Malaysian (2)	3	0.01
Nepalese (8)	8	0.04
Pakistani (44)	49	0.24
Sri Lankan (15)	15	0.07
Taiwanese (194)	211	1.02
Thai (37)	53	0.26
Vietnamese (514)	562	2.72
Hawaii Native/Pacific Islander (43)	140	0.68
Not Hispanic (34)	122	0.59
Hispanic (9)	18	0.09
Fijian (2)	4	0.02
Guamanian/Chamorro (6)	12	0.06
Marshallese (2)	2	0.01
Native Hawaiian (11)	62	0.30
Samoan (11)	23	0.11
White (12,474)	13,224	64.05
Not Hispanic (11,872)	12,519	60.64
Hispanic (602)	705	3.41

Bull Mountain

Place Type: CDP
County: Washington
Population: 9,133†

Ancestry‡	Population	%
Afghan (13)	13	0.14
African, Sub-Saharan (0)	29	0.32
Ethiopian (0)	29	0.32
American (297)	297	3.24
Arab (231)	300	3.27
Arab (7)	7	0.08
Egyptian (10)	10	0.11
Iraqi (0)	14	0.15
Jordanian (57)	98	1.07
Lebanese (107)	107	1.17
Palestinian (50)	50	0.55
Other Arab (0)	14	0.15
Austrian (12)	57	0.62
British (37)	65	0.71
Croatian (26)	39	0.43
Czech (26)	45	0.49
Czechoslovakian (0)	13	0.14
Danish (26)	78	0.85
Dutch (8)	117	1.28
English (278)	1,620	17.67
European (100)	209	2.28
Finnish (22)	55	0.60
French, ex. Basque (23)	376	4.10
French Canadian (0)	27	0.29
German (675)	2,259	24.65
Greek (50)	91	0.99
Hungarian (0)	14	0.15
Iranian (152)	152	1.66
Irish (253)	1,532	16.71
Italian (54)	131	1.43
Latvian (0)	13	0.14
Norwegian (99)	331	3.61
Polish (59)	132	1.44
Portuguese (12)	29	0.32
Romanian (16)	16	0.17
Russian (9)	101	1.10
Scandinavian (26)	43	0.47
Scotch-Irish (76)	133	1.45
Scottish (190)	404	4.41
Serbian (60)	60	0.65
Slavic (16)	16	0.17
Swedish (49)	319	3.48
Swiss (11)	102	1.11
Turkish (10)	10	0.11
Welsh (8)	140	1.53
Yugoslavian (11)	21	0.23

Hispanic Origin	Population	%
Hispanic or Latino (of any race)	492	5.39
Central American, ex. Mexican	39	0.43
Costa Rican	4	0.04
Guatemalan	8	0.09
Honduran	2	0.02
Nicaraguan	4	0.04
Panamanian	7	0.08
Salvadoran	14	0.15
Cuban	8	0.09
Dominican Republic	1	0.01
Mexican	322	3.53
Puerto Rican	20	0.22

*Notes: † The Census 2010 population figure is used to calculate the percentages in the Hispanic Origin and Race categories. Ancestry percentages are based on the 2006-2010 American Community Survey population (not shown); ‡ Numbers in parentheses indicate the number of people reporting a single ancestry; * Numbers in parentheses indicate the number of persons reporting this race alone, not in combination with any other race; Please refer to the Explanation of Data for more information.*

South American	57	0.62
Argentinean	15	0.16
Chilean	2	0.02
Colombian	13	0.14
Ecuadorian	6	0.07
Peruvian	13	0.14
Uruguayan	2	0.02
Venezuelan	6	0.07
Other Hispanic or Latino	45	0.49

Race*	Population	%
African-American/Black (137)	227	2.49
Not Hispanic (131)	207	2.27
Hispanic (6)	20	0.22
American Indian/Alaska Native (46)	110	1.20
Not Hispanic (34)	85	0.93
Hispanic (12)	25	0.27
Apache (0)	4	0.04
Blackfeet (0)	4	0.04
Cherokee (3)	23	0.25
Chippewa (0)	1	0.01
Choctaw (4)	4	0.04
Mexican American Ind. (5)	5	0.05
Navajo (4)	4	0.04
Osage (3)	3	0.03
Shoshone (0)	1	0.01
Sioux (1)	1	0.01
South American Ind. (0)	3	0.03
Ute (2)	2	0.02
Asian (988)	1,247	13.65
Not Hispanic (985)	1,227	13.43
Hispanic (3)	20	0.22
Burmese (12)	12	0.13
Cambodian (22)	27	0.30
Chinese, ex. Taiwanese (190)	255	2.79
Filipino (95)	162	1.77
Hmong (3)	3	0.03
Indian (124)	146	1.60
Indonesian (8)	13	0.14
Japanese (75)	148	1.62
Korean (131)	181	1.98
Laotian (9)	17	0.19
Nepalese (9)	13	0.14
Pakistani (10)	11	0.12
Taiwanese (11)	18	0.20
Thai (24)	27	0.30
Vietnamese (184)	207	2.27
Hawaii Native/Pacific Islander (23)	73	0.80
Not Hispanic (20)	58	0.64
Hispanic (3)	15	0.16
Fijian (0)	1	0.01
Guamanian/Chamorro (5)	13	0.14
Native Hawaiian (2)	31	0.34
Samoan (1)	11	0.12
Tongan (5)	5	0.05
White (7,428)	7,812	85.54
Not Hispanic (7,098)	7,424	81.29
Hispanic (330)	388	4.25

Canby

Place Type: City
County: Clackamas
Population: 15,829†

Ancestry‡	Population	%
American (399)	399	2.59
Arab (16)	16	0.10
Other Arab (16)	16	0.10
Austrian (23)	71	0.46
British (76)	126	0.82
Canadian (32)	80	0.52
Celtic (0)	19	0.12
Croatian (46)	122	0.79
Czech (7)	19	0.12
Danish (17)	146	0.95
Dutch (120)	455	2.96
Eastern European (11)	11	0.07
English (472)	1,940	12.61
European (122)	154	1.00
Finnish (41)	134	0.87
French, ex. Basque (90)	520	3.38
French Canadian (8)	131	0.85
German (1,238)	3,228	20.98
Greek (0)	40	0.26
Hungarian (0)	12	0.08
Iranian (11)	24	0.16
Irish (343)	1,764	11.46
Italian (138)	393	2.55
Maltese (0)	14	0.09
Northern European (11)	11	0.07
Norwegian (249)	656	4.26
Polish (54)	220	1.43
Portuguese (0)	13	0.08
Russian (26)	125	0.81
Scandinavian (39)	53	0.34
Scotch-Irish (141)	379	2.46
Scottish (49)	327	2.13
Slovak (0)	21	0.14
Swedish (79)	341	2.22
Swiss (0)	33	0.21
Ukrainian (77)	90	0.58
Welsh (56)	247	1.61

Hispanic Origin	Population	%
Hispanic or Latino (of any race)	3,368	21.28
Central American, ex. Mexican	37	0.23
Guatemalan	13	0.08
Honduran	4	0.03
Nicaraguan	2	0.01
Panamanian	2	0.01
Salvadoran	13	0.08
Other Central American	3	0.02
Cuban	7	0.04
Mexican	3,099	19.58
Puerto Rican	20	0.13
South American	18	0.11
Argentinean	2	0.01
Bolivian	1	0.01
Chilean	1	0.01
Colombian	5	0.03
Ecuadorian	2	0.01
Peruvian	3	0.02
Venezuelan	3	0.02
Other South American	1	0.01
Other Hispanic or Latino	187	1.18

Race*	Population	%
African-American/Black (93)	157	0.99
Not Hispanic (35)	91	0.57
Hispanic (58)	66	0.42
American Indian/Alaska Native (192)	334	2.11
Not Hispanic (124)	246	1.55
Hispanic (68)	88	0.56
Aleut *(Alaska Native)* (0)	1	0.01
Arapaho (0)	1	0.01
Blackfeet (3)	6	0.04
Canadian/French Am. Ind. (1)	2	0.01
Cherokee (21)	55	0.35
Chickasaw (0)	1	0.01
Chippewa (11)	17	0.11
Choctaw (3)	7	0.04
Comanche (1)	2	0.01
Cree (0)	2	0.01
Inupiat *(Alaska Native)* (2)	2	0.01
Iroquois (0)	1	0.01
Mexican American Ind. (27)	29	0.18
Navajo (1)	1	0.01
Ottawa (1)	1	0.01
Paiute (0)	3	0.02
Potawatomi (3)	5	0.03
Pueblo (1)	1	0.01
Sioux (6)	14	0.09
South American Ind. (1)	4	0.03
Spanish American Ind. (2)	5	0.03
Tlingit-Haida *(Alaska Native)* (6)	13	0.08
Ute (0)	2	0.01
Yakama (1)	2	0.01
Yaqui (3)	4	0.03
Yup'ik *(Alaska Native)* (3)	4	0.03
Asian (169)	270	1.71
Not Hispanic (168)	260	1.64
Hispanic (1)	10	0.06
Cambodian (8)	9	0.06
Chinese, ex. Taiwanese (29)	55	0.35
Filipino (11)	37	0.23
Indian (14)	21	0.13
Indonesian (3)	6	0.04
Japanese (12)	48	0.30
Korean (21)	33	0.21
Laotian (4)	4	0.03
Pakistani (1)	1	0.01
Thai (9)	14	0.09
Vietnamese (40)	47	0.30
Hawaii Native/Pacific Islander (29)	54	0.34
Not Hispanic (19)	41	0.26
Hispanic (10)	13	0.08
Guamanian/Chamorro (3)	5	0.03
Native Hawaiian (14)	27	0.17
Samoan (0)	2	0.01
Tongan (1)	1	0.01
White (12,816)	13,244	83.67
Not Hispanic (11,825)	12,084	76.34
Hispanic (991)	1,160	7.33

Cedar Hills

Place Type: CDP
County: Washington
Population: 8,300†

Ancestry‡	Population	%
African, Sub-Saharan (19)	19	0.23
African (19)	19	0.23
American (127)	127	1.53
Arab (35)	35	0.42
Lebanese (35)	35	0.42
Australian (16)	26	0.31
Austrian (0)	11	0.13
Belgian (0)	12	0.14
Brazilian (45)	45	0.54
British (36)	131	1.57
Canadian (39)	68	0.82
Czech (0)	33	0.40
Danish (0)	105	1.26
Dutch (63)	130	1.56
Eastern European (24)	62	0.74
English (376)	1,683	20.22
European (83)	113	1.36
Finnish (27)	42	0.50
French, ex. Basque (86)	410	4.93
German (657)	2,184	26.24
Greek (27)	27	0.32
Hungarian (14)	53	0.64
Irish (374)	1,552	18.65
Italian (137)	429	5.15
Latvian (0)	16	0.19
Lithuanian (12)	12	0.14
Northern European (27)	27	0.32
Norwegian (233)	434	5.21
Pennsylvania German (14)	14	0.17
Polish (40)	137	1.65
Portuguese (16)	32	0.38
Romanian (0)	24	0.29
Russian (11)	11	0.13
Scandinavian (0)	17	0.20
Scotch-Irish (9)	197	2.37
Scottish (39)	276	3.32
Slovak (16)	31	0.37
Swedish (21)	323	3.88
Swiss (0)	66	0.79
Ukrainian (0)	33	0.40
Welsh (20)	295	3.54
Yugoslavian (10)	10	0.12

Hispanic Origin	Population	%
Hispanic or Latino (of any race)	1,149	13.84
Central American, ex. Mexican	73	0.88
Costa Rican	4	0.05
Guatemalan	33	0.40

*Notes: † The Census 2010 population figure is used to calculate the percentages in the Hispanic Origin and Race categories. Ancestry percentages are based on the 2006-2010 American Community Survey population (not shown); ‡ Numbers in parentheses indicate the number of people reporting a single ancestry; * Numbers in parentheses indicate the number of persons reporting this race alone, not in combination with any other race; Please refer to the Explanation of Data for more information.*

Honduran	4	0.05
Nicaraguan	1	0.01
Panamanian	2	0.02
Salvadoran	28	0.34
Other Central American	1	0.01
Cuban	7	0.08
Dominican Republic	5	0.06
Mexican	853	10.28
Puerto Rican	29	0.35
South American	33	0.40
Argentinean	4	0.05
Bolivian	1	0.01
Chilean	10	0.12
Colombian	7	0.08
Ecuadorian	5	0.06
Peruvian	6	0.07
Other Hispanic or Latino	149	1.80

Race*	Population	%
African-American/Black (103)	180	2.17
Not Hispanic (92)	157	1.89
Hispanic (11)	23	0.28
American Indian/Alaska Native (51)	143	1.72
Not Hispanic (30)	97	1.17
Hispanic (21)	46	0.55
Aleut *(Alaska Native)* (1)	1	0.01
Apache (0)	4	0.05
Blackfeet (1)	4	0.05
Central American Ind. (3)	3	0.04
Cherokee (9)	25	0.30
Chickasaw (0)	1	0.01
Chippewa (0)	6	0.07
Choctaw (0)	1	0.01
Delaware (0)	1	0.01
Inupiat *(Alaska Native)* (0)	4	0.05
Lumbee (0)	1	0.01
Mexican American Ind. (4)	4	0.05
Navajo (3)	3	0.04
Potawatomi (0)	3	0.04
Sioux (4)	9	0.11
Tlingit-Haida *(Alaska Native)* (0)	2	0.02
Yakama (3)	3	0.04
Asian (399)	553	6.66
Not Hispanic (396)	532	6.41
Hispanic (3)	21	0.25
Cambodian (2)	3	0.04
Chinese, ex. Taiwanese (75)	105	1.27
Filipino (67)	120	1.45
Indian (44)	56	0.67
Indonesian (3)	8	0.10
Japanese (61)	99	1.19
Korean (41)	53	0.64
Laotian (8)	8	0.10
Malaysian (1)	2	0.02
Pakistani (7)	7	0.08
Taiwanese (10)	12	0.14
Thai (13)	25	0.30
Vietnamese (45)	50	0.60
Hawaii Native/Pacific Islander (26)	77	0.93
Not Hispanic (23)	58	0.70
Hispanic (3)	19	0.23
Fijian (4)	4	0.05
Guamanian/Chamorro (14)	27	0.33
Native Hawaiian (5)	31	0.37
Samoan (0)	12	0.14
White (6,727)	7,064	85.11
Not Hispanic (6,335)	6,575	79.22
Hispanic (392)	489	5.89

Cedar Mill

Place Type: CDP
County: Washington
Population: 14,546†

Ancestry‡	Population	%
African, Sub-Saharan (26)	26	0.18
African (11)	11	0.08
Other Sub-Saharan African (15)	15	0.10
American (516)	516	3.55
Armenian (0)	12	0.08
Austrian (28)	68	0.47
Belgian (11)	45	0.31
Brazilian (0)	14	0.10
British (183)	327	2.25
Canadian (12)	110	0.76
Celtic (15)	15	0.10
Croatian (0)	37	0.25
Czech (17)	42	0.29
Czechoslovakian (24)	125	0.86
Danish (54)	208	1.43
Dutch (52)	226	1.55
English (607)	1,941	13.35
Estonian (0)	61	0.42
European (618)	637	4.38
Finnish (12)	23	0.16
French, ex. Basque (65)	519	3.57
French Canadian (0)	13	0.09
German (791)	3,192	21.96
Greek (0)	122	0.84
Hungarian (58)	148	1.02
Icelander (0)	7	0.05
Iranian (38)	50	0.34
Irish (609)	1,910	13.14
Italian (174)	576	3.96
Latvian (0)	14	0.10
Lithuanian (19)	44	0.30
New Zealander (0)	14	0.10
Northern European (120)	120	0.83
Norwegian (200)	751	5.17
Pennsylvania German (18)	18	0.12
Polish (69)	203	1.40
Portuguese (11)	55	0.38
Romanian (12)	12	0.08
Russian (57)	256	1.76
Scandinavian (67)	92	0.63
Scotch-Irish (107)	298	2.05
Scottish (151)	569	3.91
Serbian (29)	29	0.20
Slavic (0)	39	0.27
Slovak (14)	43	0.30
Swedish (78)	468	3.22
Swiss (38)	206	1.42
Ukrainian (134)	195	1.34
Welsh (43)	166	1.14
Yugoslavian (0)	17	0.12

Hispanic Origin	Population	%
Hispanic or Latino (of any race)	911	6.26
Central American, ex. Mexican	77	0.53
Costa Rican	5	0.03
Guatemalan	50	0.34
Honduran	5	0.03
Nicaraguan	2	0.01
Panamanian	6	0.04
Salvadoran	9	0.06
Cuban	26	0.18
Mexican	580	3.99
Puerto Rican	40	0.27
South American	89	0.61
Argentinean	21	0.14
Bolivian	2	0.01
Chilean	7	0.05
Colombian	18	0.12
Ecuadorian	15	0.10
Peruvian	17	0.12
Uruguayan	3	0.02
Venezuelan	6	0.04
Other Hispanic or Latino	99	0.68

Race*	Population	%
African-American/Black (143)	213	1.46
Not Hispanic (139)	204	1.40
Hispanic (4)	9	0.06
American Indian/Alaska Native (32)	131	0.90
Not Hispanic (15)	108	0.74
Hispanic (17)	23	0.16
Apache (1)	1	0.01
Blackfeet (0)	12	0.08
Cherokee (2)	19	0.13
Chickasaw (0)	4	0.03
Choctaw (0)	1	0.01
Comanche (0)	2	0.01
Delaware (0)	2	0.01
Inupiat *(Alaska Native)* (0)	3	0.02
Iroquois (1)	3	0.02
Kiowa (0)	2	0.01
Lumbee (0)	1	0.01
Mexican American Ind. (0)	1	0.01
Navajo (3)	3	0.02
Osage (0)	4	0.03
Potawatomi (0)	3	0.02
Sioux (0)	1	0.01
South American Ind. (2)	2	0.01
Spanish American Ind. (1)	1	0.01
Tlingit-Haida *(Alaska Native)* (1)	2	0.01
Yakama (0)	1	0.01
Asian (1,913)	2,305	15.85
Not Hispanic (1,908)	2,291	15.75
Hispanic (5)	14	0.10
Bangladeshi (24)	25	0.17
Burmese (1)	2	0.01
Cambodian (10)	15	0.10
Chinese, ex. Taiwanese (482)	583	4.01
Filipino (92)	160	1.10
Hmong (14)	16	0.11
Indian (574)	623	4.28
Indonesian (12)	27	0.19
Japanese (106)	212	1.46
Korean (319)	388	2.67
Laotian (5)	18	0.12
Malaysian (1)	2	0.01
Nepalese (1)	1	0.01
Pakistani (18)	20	0.14
Sri Lankan (2)	4	0.03
Taiwanese (49)	64	0.44
Thai (13)	20	0.14
Vietnamese (123)	144	0.99
Hawaii Native/Pacific Islander (32)	83	0.57
Not Hispanic (27)	75	0.52
Hispanic (5)	8	0.05
Guamanian/Chamorro (11)	14	0.10
Native Hawaiian (4)	20	0.14
Samoan (5)	6	0.04
Tongan (1)	1	0.01
White (11,500)	12,057	82.89
Not Hispanic (10,973)	11,471	78.86
Hispanic (527)	586	4.03

Central Point

Place Type: City
County: Jackson
Population: 17,169†

Ancestry‡	Population	%
American (918)	918	5.58
Arab (0)	11	0.07
Syrian (0)	11	0.07
Austrian (0)	30	0.18
Belgian (12)	12	0.07
British (12)	72	0.44
Czech (36)	61	0.37
Czechoslovakian (7)	7	0.04
Danish (0)	111	0.67
Dutch (85)	352	2.14
English (612)	2,502	15.20
European (155)	163	0.99
Finnish (29)	29	0.18
French, ex. Basque (28)	333	2.02
French Canadian (55)	105	0.64
German (1,111)	3,564	21.66
German Russian (16)	16	0.10
Greek (0)	54	0.33
Hungarian (37)	37	0.22
Icelander (0)	21	0.13
Irish (568)	2,579	15.67
Italian (194)	715	4.34
Norwegian (347)	635	3.86
Polish (108)	457	2.78

*Notes: † The Census 2010 population figure is used to calculate the percentages in the Hispanic Origin and Race categories. Ancestry percentages are based on the 2006-2010 American Community Survey population (not shown); ‡ Numbers in parentheses indicate the number of people reporting a single ancestry; * Numbers in parentheses indicate the number of persons reporting this race alone, not in combination with any other race; Please refer to the Explanation of Data for more information.*

SECTION TWO

Portuguese (91)	166	1.01
Romanian (0)	9	0.05
Russian (44)	152	0.92
Scandinavian (21)	83	0.50
Scotch-Irish (82)	242	1.47
Scottish (81)	476	2.89
Swedish (28)	331	2.01
Swiss (20)	71	0.43
Ukrainian (8)	24	0.15
Welsh (0)	55	0.33
Yugoslavian (19)	34	0.21

Hispanic Origin	Population	%
Hispanic or Latino (of any race)	1,553	9.05
Central American, ex. Mexican	49	0.29
Costa Rican	7	0.04
Guatemalan	22	0.13
Honduran	5	0.03
Salvadoran	15	0.09
Cuban	3	0.02
Dominican Republic	4	0.02
Mexican	1,297	7.55
Puerto Rican	52	0.30
South American	27	0.16
Argentinean	5	0.03
Bolivian	1	0.01
Chilean	3	0.02
Colombian	4	0.02
Ecuadorian	4	0.02
Peruvian	8	0.05
Venezuelan	2	0.01
Other Hispanic or Latino	121	0.70

Race*	Population	%
African-American/Black (64)	172	1.00
Not Hispanic (56)	142	0.83
Hispanic (8)	30	0.17
American Indian/Alaska Native (180)	432	2.52
Not Hispanic (149)	368	2.14
Hispanic (31)	64	0.37
Aleut *(Alaska Native)* (1)	1	0.01
Apache (1)	4	0.02
Blackfeet (4)	13	0.08
Cherokee (25)	75	0.44
Cheyenne (0)	3	0.02
Chickasaw (0)	2	0.01
Chippewa (2)	5	0.03
Choctaw (9)	19	0.11
Comanche (0)	1	0.01
Creek (4)	5	0.03
Crow (0)	3	0.02
Delaware (1)	1	0.01
Hopi (0)	1	0.01
Iroquois (4)	4	0.02
Mexican American Ind. (10)	15	0.09
Navajo (3)	6	0.03
Osage (0)	2	0.01
Paiute (0)	3	0.02
Puget Sound Salish (1)	2	0.01
Seminole (0)	1	0.01
Sioux (2)	16	0.09
Tlingit-Haida *(Alaska Native)* (4)	4	0.02
Yaqui (2)	4	0.02
Yuman (0)	3	0.02
Asian (180)	304	1.77
Not Hispanic (168)	278	1.62
Hispanic (12)	26	0.15
Chinese, ex. Taiwanese (30)	47	0.27
Filipino (58)	111	0.65
Hmong (4)	4	0.02
Indian (9)	17	0.10
Indonesian (3)	3	0.02
Japanese (21)	53	0.31
Korean (22)	41	0.24
Taiwanese (2)	2	0.01
Thai (11)	16	0.09
Vietnamese (12)	13	0.08
Hawaii Native/Pacific Islander (67)	120	0.70
Not Hispanic (63)	115	0.67
Hispanic (4)	5	0.03
Guamanian/Chamorro (10)	24	0.14
Native Hawaiian (11)	36	0.21
Samoan (37)	46	0.27
Tongan (0)	2	0.01
White (15,598)	16,125	93.92
Not Hispanic (14,757)	15,158	88.29
Hispanic (841)	967	5.63

Coos Bay

Place Type: City
County: Coos
Population: 15,967†

Ancestry‡	Population	%
American (975)	975	6.12
Arab (20)	31	0.19
Lebanese (20)	31	0.19
Australian (0)	41	0.26
Austrian (30)	73	0.46
Belgian (31)	74	0.46
British (16)	58	0.36
Canadian (21)	21	0.13
Czech (10)	25	0.16
Danish (69)	252	1.58
Dutch (89)	474	2.97
Eastern European (17)	17	0.11
English (728)	2,426	15.22
European (204)	237	1.49
Finnish (21)	71	0.45
French, ex. Basque (45)	661	4.15
French Canadian (67)	151	0.95
German (1,347)	3,620	22.70
Greek (28)	190	1.19
Hungarian (10)	67	0.42
Icelander (0)	14	0.09
Iranian (6)	6	0.04
Irish (517)	1,841	11.55
Italian (202)	710	4.45
Northern European (9)	41	0.26
Norwegian (175)	608	3.81
Polish (0)	275	1.72
Portuguese (0)	36	0.23
Romanian (0)	28	0.18
Russian (102)	117	0.73
Scandinavian (32)	91	0.57
Scotch-Irish (152)	446	2.80
Scottish (395)	1,093	6.86
Slovak (13)	21	0.13
Swedish (61)	444	2.78
Swiss (28)	112	0.70
Ukrainian (0)	15	0.09
Welsh (81)	310	1.94
Yugoslavian (0)	102	0.64

Hispanic Origin	Population	%
Hispanic or Latino (of any race)	1,220	7.64
Central American, ex. Mexican	28	0.18
Costa Rican	6	0.04
Guatemalan	7	0.04
Honduran	1	0.01
Nicaraguan	9	0.06
Panamanian	3	0.02
Salvadoran	2	0.01
Cuban	13	0.08
Dominican Republic	2	0.01
Mexican	993	6.22
Puerto Rican	27	0.17
South American	36	0.23
Chilean	13	0.08
Colombian	9	0.06
Paraguayan	1	0.01
Peruvian	11	0.07
Venezuelan	2	0.01
Other Hispanic or Latino	121	0.76

Race*	Population	%
African-American/Black (91)	184	1.15
Not Hispanic (84)	163	1.02
Hispanic (7)	21	0.13
American Indian/Alaska Native (415)	899	5.63
Not Hispanic (375)	817	5.12
Hispanic (40)	82	0.51
Alaska Athabascan *(Ala. Nat.)* (1)	2	0.01
Aleut *(Alaska Native)* (4)	8	0.05
Apache (5)	10	0.06
Blackfeet (0)	17	0.11
Canadian/French Am. Ind. (2)	2	0.01
Cherokee (35)	174	1.09
Chickasaw (3)	4	0.03
Chippewa (5)	16	0.10
Choctaw (12)	20	0.13
Colville (1)	6	0.04
Comanche (1)	5	0.03
Creek (2)	5	0.03
Crow (5)	6	0.04
Delaware (0)	1	0.01
Inupiat *(Alaska Native)* (0)	1	0.01
Iroquois (5)	12	0.08
Lumbee (0)	1	0.01
Menominee (5)	6	0.04
Mexican American Ind. (8)	13	0.08
Navajo (3)	6	0.04
Potawatomi (2)	4	0.03
Pueblo (1)	5	0.03
Puget Sound Salish (0)	9	0.06
Shoshone (0)	2	0.01
Sioux (8)	17	0.11
South American Ind. (0)	2	0.01
Tlingit-Haida *(Alaska Native)* (10)	18	0.11
Ute (0)	2	0.01
Yakama (0)	1	0.01
Yaqui (0)	3	0.02
Asian (217)	385	2.41
Not Hispanic (212)	369	2.31
Hispanic (5)	16	0.10
Chinese, ex. Taiwanese (26)	58	0.36
Filipino (79)	136	0.85
Indian (16)	34	0.21
Indonesian (1)	2	0.01
Japanese (34)	72	0.45
Korean (14)	33	0.21
Laotian (1)	3	0.02
Pakistani (0)	2	0.01
Thai (4)	11	0.07
Vietnamese (32)	36	0.23
Hawaii Native/Pacific Islander (54)	132	0.83
Not Hispanic (52)	126	0.79
Hispanic (2)	6	0.04
Fijian (16)	24	0.15
Guamanian/Chamorro (5)	8	0.05
Native Hawaiian (15)	64	0.40
Samoan (9)	11	0.07
White (13,908)	14,682	91.95
Not Hispanic (13,319)	13,969	87.49
Hispanic (589)	713	4.47

Cornelius

Place Type: City
County: Washington
Population: 11,869†

Ancestry‡	Population	%
African, Sub-Saharan (19)	19	0.17
African (19)	19	0.17
American (259)	259	2.25
Arab (10)	10	0.09
Arab (10)	10	0.09
Basque (0)	26	0.23
British (0)	50	0.43
Cajun (55)	55	0.48
Czech (24)	24	0.21
Danish (90)	186	1.62
Dutch (22)	139	1.21
English (301)	977	8.49
European (93)	143	1.24
Finnish (10)	21	0.18
French, ex. Basque (24)	188	1.63
French Canadian (9)	37	0.32

*Notes: † The Census 2010 population figure is used to calculate the percentages in the Hispanic Origin and Race categories. Ancestry percentages are based on the 2006-2010 American Community Survey population (not shown); ‡ Numbers in parentheses indicate the number of people reporting a single ancestry; * Numbers in parentheses indicate the number of persons reporting this race alone, not in combination with any other race; Please refer to the Explanation of Data for more information.*

German (647)	1,814	15.76
Irish (288)	1,236	10.74
Italian (38)	198	1.72
Norwegian (184)	400	3.47
Polish (63)	103	0.89
Portuguese (0)	10	0.09
Russian (16)	46	0.40
Scandinavian (15)	32	0.28
Scotch-Irish (26)	155	1.35
Scottish (88)	256	2.22
Swedish (0)	178	1.55
Swiss (18)	38	0.33
Ukrainian (30)	30	0.26
Welsh (0)	105	0.91
Yugoslavian (0)	34	0.30

Hispanic Origin	Population	%
Hispanic or Latino (of any race)	5,948	50.11
Central American, ex. Mexican	283	2.38
Costa Rican	6	0.05
Guatemalan	228	1.92
Honduran	12	0.10
Panamanian	8	0.07
Salvadoran	28	0.24
Other Central American	1	0.01
Cuban	2	0.02
Dominican Republic	1	0.01
Mexican	5,356	45.13
Puerto Rican	32	0.27
South American	34	0.29
Argentinean	1	0.01
Chilean	9	0.08
Colombian	2	0.02
Ecuadorian	3	0.03
Paraguayan	8	0.07
Peruvian	2	0.02
Venezuelan	9	0.08
Other Hispanic or Latino	240	2.02

Race*	Population	%
African-American/Black (145)	206	1.74
Not Hispanic (80)	119	1.00
Hispanic (65)	87	0.73
American Indian/Alaska Native (155)	278	2.34
Not Hispanic (71)	151	1.27
Hispanic (84)	127	1.07
Aleut *(Alaska Native)* (1)	3	0.03
Apache (5)	7	0.06
Blackfeet (1)	10	0.08
Canadian/French Am. Ind. (0)	2	0.02
Central American Ind. (8)	10	0.08
Cherokee (10)	31	0.26
Chippewa (1)	2	0.02
Choctaw (2)	5	0.04
Comanche (0)	5	0.04
Creek (0)	6	0.05
Mexican American Ind. (32)	36	0.30
Ottawa (1)	3	0.03
Paiute (2)	3	0.03
Pima (0)	1	0.01
Puget Sound Salish (1)	1	0.01
Shoshone (0)	3	0.03
Sioux (1)	4	0.03
Spanish American Ind. (1)	2	0.02
Tlingit-Haida *(Alaska Native)* (0)	4	0.03
Yakama (7)	13	0.11
Asian (263)	407	3.43
Not Hispanic (256)	365	3.08
Hispanic (7)	42	0.35
Cambodian (28)	30	0.25
Chinese, ex. Taiwanese (26)	73	0.62
Filipino (81)	130	1.10
Indian (29)	40	0.34
Indonesian (2)	3	0.03
Japanese (11)	45	0.38
Korean (21)	31	0.26
Laotian (15)	24	0.20
Malaysian (1)	1	0.01
Pakistani (5)	5	0.04
Taiwanese (1)	2	0.02
Vietnamese (23)	37	0.31
Hawaii Native/Pacific Islander (11)	57	0.48
Not Hispanic (9)	47	0.40
Hispanic (2)	10	0.08
Fijian (0)	3	0.03
Guamanian/Chamorro (2)	12	0.10
Native Hawaiian (4)	34	0.29
Samoan (2)	3	0.03
White (7,600)	7,998	67.39
Not Hispanic (5,267)	5,470	46.09
Hispanic (2,333)	2,528	21.30

Corvallis

Place Type: City
County: Benton
Population: 54,462†

Ancestry‡	Population	%
African, Sub-Saharan (262)	319	0.60
African (0)	12	0.02
Ethiopian (84)	84	0.16
Ghanaian (36)	36	0.07
Nigerian (9)	9	0.02
Somalian (122)	135	0.25
South African (3)	35	0.07
Sudanese (8)	8	0.01
Albanian (0)	7	0.01
American (1,360)	1,360	2.55
Arab (248)	307	0.57
Arab (43)	43	0.08
Egyptian (87)	120	0.22
Lebanese (11)	17	0.03
Moroccan (0)	12	0.02
Other Arab (107)	115	0.22
Armenian (11)	73	0.14
Australian (22)	34	0.06
Austrian (32)	197	0.37
Basque (23)	56	0.10
Belgian (0)	38	0.07
Brazilian (36)	45	0.08
British (314)	654	1.22
Canadian (160)	300	0.56
Celtic (0)	21	0.04
Croatian (38)	75	0.14
Czech (120)	551	1.03
Czechoslovakian (10)	44	0.08
Danish (132)	808	1.51
Dutch (333)	1,165	2.18
Eastern European (69)	69	0.13
English (2,360)	8,003	14.98
Estonian (0)	17	0.03
European (2,662)	3,268	6.12
Finnish (82)	336	0.63
French, ex. Basque (252)	1,913	3.58
French Canadian (194)	442	0.83
German (2,687)	11,820	22.12
Greek (65)	201	0.38
Hungarian (49)	239	0.45
Iranian (91)	110	0.21
Irish (1,637)	7,567	14.16
Israeli (13)	13	0.02
Italian (597)	2,052	3.84
Latvian (0)	10	0.02
Lithuanian (32)	169	0.32
Luxemburger (11)	11	0.02
New Zealander (0)	19	0.04
Northern European (177)	239	0.45
Norwegian (717)	2,574	4.82
Pennsylvania German (0)	45	0.08
Polish (364)	1,266	2.37
Portuguese (198)	446	0.83
Romanian (0)	68	0.13
Russian (200)	634	1.19
Scandinavian (223)	481	0.90
Scotch-Irish (419)	1,385	2.59
Scottish (441)	2,130	3.99
Serbian (50)	72	0.13
Slavic (147)	172	0.32
Slovak (78)	139	0.26
Soviet Union (0)	3	0.01
Swedish (317)	1,852	3.47
Swiss (67)	551	1.03
Turkish (22)	33	0.06
Ukrainian (81)	145	0.27
Welsh (64)	582	1.09
West Indian, ex. Hispanic (19)	19	0.04
West Indian (19)	19	0.04
Yugoslavian (54)	66	0.12

Hispanic Origin	Population	%
Hispanic or Latino (of any race)	4,049	7.43
Central American, ex. Mexican	168	0.31
Costa Rican	20	0.04
Guatemalan	44	0.08
Honduran	20	0.04
Nicaraguan	11	0.02
Panamanian	7	0.01
Salvadoran	66	0.12
Cuban	44	0.08
Dominican Republic	11	0.02
Mexican	3,096	5.68
Puerto Rican	116	0.21
South American	236	0.43
Argentinean	37	0.07
Bolivian	8	0.01
Chilean	41	0.08
Colombian	51	0.09
Ecuadorian	32	0.06
Paraguayan	1	<0.01
Peruvian	43	0.08
Uruguayan	9	0.02
Venezuelan	12	0.02
Other South American	2	<0.01
Other Hispanic or Latino	378	0.69

Race*	Population	%
African-American/Black (615)	997	1.83
Not Hispanic (579)	920	1.69
Hispanic (36)	77	0.14
American Indian/Alaska Native (376)	977	1.79
Not Hispanic (284)	796	1.46
Hispanic (92)	181	0.33
Alaska Athabascan *(Ala. Nat.)* (3)	11	0.02
Aleut *(Alaska Native)* (3)	6	0.01
Apache (9)	15	0.03
Arapaho (1)	3	0.01
Blackfeet (7)	33	0.06
Canadian/French Am. Ind. (4)	5	0.01
Central American Ind. (1)	2	<0.01
Cherokee (42)	156	0.29
Cheyenne (2)	7	0.01
Chickasaw (1)	4	0.01
Chippewa (14)	38	0.07
Choctaw (12)	38	0.07
Colville (3)	9	0.02
Comanche (0)	1	<0.01
Cree (0)	6	0.01
Creek (0)	2	<0.01
Crow (0)	3	0.01
Delaware (0)	3	0.01
Hopi (2)	3	0.01
Inupiat *(Alaska Native)* (6)	9	0.02
Iroquois (0)	10	0.02
Kiowa (1)	1	<0.01
Lumbee (0)	2	<0.01
Menominee (0)	4	0.01
Mexican American Ind. (18)	29	0.05
Navajo (6)	17	0.03
Osage (2)	5	0.01
Paiute (4)	6	0.01
Potawatomi (5)	7	0.01
Pueblo (1)	1	<0.01
Puget Sound Salish (3)	6	0.01
Seminole (1)	5	0.01
Shoshone (0)	1	<0.01
Sioux (10)	27	0.05
South American Ind. (2)	5	0.01
Tlingit-Haida *(Alaska Native)* (14)	22	0.04
Tsimshian *(Alaska Native)* (1)	3	0.01

*Notes: † The Census 2010 population figure is used to calculate the percentages in the Hispanic Origin and Race categories. Ancestry percentages are based on the 2006-2010 American Community Survey population (not shown); ‡ Numbers in parentheses indicate the number of people reporting a single ancestry; * Numbers in parentheses indicate the number of persons reporting this race alone, not in combination with any other race; Please refer to the Explanation of Data for more information.*

Ute (3)	5	0.01
Yaqui (2)	3	0.01
Yup'ik *(Alaska Native)* (4)	5	0.01
Asian (3,977)	5,043	9.26
Not Hispanic (3,956)	4,971	9.13
Hispanic (21)	72	0.13
Bangladeshi (11)	12	0.02
Burmese (3)	5	0.01
Cambodian (44)	52	0.10
Chinese, ex. Taiwanese (1,162)	1,499	2.75
Filipino (215)	471	0.86
Hmong (31)	31	0.06
Indian (542)	614	1.13
Indonesian (36)	54	0.10
Japanese (371)	758	1.39
Korean (642)	754	1.38
Laotian (24)	30	0.06
Malaysian (16)	21	0.04
Nepalese (7)	11	0.02
Pakistani (30)	40	0.07
Sri Lankan (18)	19	0.03
Taiwanese (109)	122	0.22
Thai (111)	138	0.25
Vietnamese (405)	453	0.83
Hawaii Native/Pacific Islander (182)	434	0.80
Not Hispanic (169)	402	0.74
Hispanic (13)	32	0.06
Fijian (3)	6	0.01
Guamanian/Chamorro (19)	35	0.06
Marshallese (16)	18	0.03
Native Hawaiian (84)	249	0.46
Samoan (23)	49	0.09
Tongan (22)	25	0.05
White (45,613)	47,633	87.46
Not Hispanic (43,472)	45,193	82.98
Hispanic (2,141)	2,440	4.48

Cottage Grove

Place Type: City
County: Lane
Population: 9,686†

Ancestry‡	Population	%
American (602)	602	6.34
Austrian (14)	14	0.15
Basque (13)	13	0.14
Belgian (49)	49	0.52
British (41)	41	0.43
Canadian (13)	24	0.25
Celtic (9)	9	0.09
Croatian (30)	30	0.32
Czech (7)	23	0.24
Danish (0)	36	0.38
Dutch (93)	439	4.62
English (482)	1,149	12.10
Estonian (41)	41	0.43
European (98)	110	1.16
Finnish (28)	39	0.41
French, ex. Basque (117)	465	4.90
French Canadian (35)	67	0.71
German (588)	1,918	20.20
Hungarian (0)	34	0.36
Irish (354)	1,332	14.03
Italian (71)	209	2.20
Northern European (35)	35	0.37
Norwegian (89)	214	2.25
Pennsylvania German (8)	8	0.08
Polish (46)	178	1.88
Portuguese (12)	99	1.04
Romanian (11)	25	0.26
Russian (55)	128	1.35
Scandinavian (0)	33	0.35
Scotch-Irish (144)	308	3.24
Scottish (33)	124	1.31
Slavic (0)	29	0.31
Swedish (95)	450	4.74
Swiss (0)	40	0.42
Ukrainian (13)	23	0.24
Welsh (32)	136	1.43
West Indian, ex. Hispanic (20)	20	0.21
Haitian (20)	20	0.21

Hispanic Origin	Population	%
Hispanic or Latino (of any race)	774	7.99
Central American, ex. Mexican	50	0.52
Costa Rican	1	0.01
Guatemalan	13	0.13
Honduran	11	0.11
Panamanian	3	0.03
Salvadoran	22	0.23
Cuban	5	0.05
Mexican	573	5.92
Puerto Rican	20	0.21
South American	10	0.10
Argentinean	2	0.02
Colombian	5	0.05
Peruvian	3	0.03
Other Hispanic or Latino	116	1.20

Race*	Population	%
African-American/Black (27)	91	0.94
Not Hispanic (24)	84	0.87
Hispanic (3)	7	0.07
American Indian/Alaska Native (125)	334	3.45
Not Hispanic (102)	287	2.96
Hispanic (23)	47	0.49
Alaska Athabascan *(Ala. Nat.)* (0)	2	0.02
Aleut *(Alaska Native)* (1)	5	0.05
Apache (2)	4	0.04
Blackfeet (4)	16	0.17
Canadian/French Am. Ind. (0)	1	0.01
Cherokee (15)	81	0.84
Cheyenne (0)	1	0.01
Chippewa (4)	10	0.10
Choctaw (3)	9	0.09
Cree (0)	2	0.02
Creek (3)	3	0.03
Hopi (1)	1	0.01
Inupiat *(Alaska Native)* (3)	4	0.04
Iroquois (0)	1	0.01
Mexican American Ind. (9)	14	0.14
Navajo (1)	6	0.06
Osage (0)	1	0.01
Ottawa (7)	8	0.08
Paiute (0)	1	0.01
Potawatomi (2)	2	0.02
Pueblo (0)	1	0.01
Seminole (0)	1	0.01
Shoshone (0)	1	0.01
Sioux (5)	14	0.14
South American Ind. (0)	6	0.06
Tlingit-Haida *(Alaska Native)* (1)	1	0.01
Asian (107)	167	1.72
Not Hispanic (106)	164	1.69
Hispanic (1)	3	0.03
Bangladeshi (0)	1	0.01
Burmese (1)	1	0.01
Chinese, ex. Taiwanese (27)	36	0.37
Filipino (14)	27	0.28
Indian (19)	28	0.29
Indonesian (1)	1	0.01
Japanese (16)	29	0.30
Korean (12)	21	0.22
Laotian (6)	7	0.07
Pakistani (1)	3	0.03
Thai (2)	5	0.05
Vietnamese (5)	7	0.07
Hawaii Native/Pacific Islander (7)	25	0.26
Not Hispanic (7)	20	0.21
Hispanic (0)	5	0.05
Guamanian/Chamorro (1)	4	0.04
Native Hawaiian (5)	9	0.09
Samoan (0)	3	0.03
Tongan (1)	1	0.01
White (8,758)	9,105	94.00
Not Hispanic (8,365)	8,649	89.29
Hispanic (393)	456	4.71

Dallas

Place Type: City
County: Polk
Population: 14,583†

Ancestry‡	Population	%
American (892)	892	6.22
Arab (18)	35	0.24
Arab (18)	35	0.24
Armenian (35)	35	0.24
Australian (16)	16	0.11
Austrian (0)	27	0.19
Brazilian (11)	22	0.15
British (56)	160	1.12
Canadian (116)	116	0.81
Czech (32)	117	0.82
Czechoslovakian (25)	57	0.40
Danish (0)	51	0.36
Dutch (40)	236	1.64
English (501)	2,573	17.93
European (189)	241	1.68
Finnish (14)	106	0.74
French, ex. Basque (124)	459	3.20
French Canadian (81)	107	0.75
German (1,206)	3,576	24.92
German Russian (0)	74	0.52
Greek (13)	166	1.16
Irish (264)	1,383	9.64
Italian (77)	334	2.33
Latvian (0)	10	0.07
Lithuanian (0)	8	0.06
New Zealander (0)	8	0.06
Northern European (10)	21	0.15
Norwegian (282)	869	6.06
Pennsylvania German (6)	14	0.10
Polish (31)	148	1.03
Portuguese (26)	70	0.49
Romanian (0)	38	0.26
Russian (27)	170	1.18
Scandinavian (0)	59	0.41
Scotch-Irish (192)	585	4.08
Scottish (86)	542	3.78
Slovene (0)	11	0.08
Swedish (107)	615	4.29
Swiss (17)	117	0.82
Ukrainian (7)	20	0.14
Welsh (0)	93	0.65
Yugoslavian (0)	11	0.08

Hispanic Origin	Population	%
Hispanic or Latino (of any race)	867	5.95
Central American, ex. Mexican	14	0.10
Costa Rican	5	0.03
Guatemalan	1	0.01
Honduran	4	0.03
Nicaraguan	1	0.01
Panamanian	2	0.01
Salvadoran	1	0.01
Cuban	5	0.03
Mexican	715	4.90
Puerto Rican	41	0.28
South American	17	0.12
Bolivian	2	0.01
Chilean	3	0.02
Colombian	6	0.04
Peruvian	6	0.04
Other Hispanic or Latino	75	0.51

Race*	Population	%
African-American/Black (33)	87	0.60
Not Hispanic (33)	84	0.58
Hispanic (0)	3	0.02
American Indian/Alaska Native (297)	501	3.44
Not Hispanic (287)	469	3.22
Hispanic (10)	32	0.22
Apache (3)	7	0.05
Arapaho (0)	1	0.01
Blackfeet (5)	12	0.08
Canadian/French Am. Ind. (0)	1	0.01

*Notes: † The Census 2010 population figure is used to calculate the percentages in the Hispanic Origin and Race categories. Ancestry percentages are based on the 2006-2010 American Community Survey population (not shown); ‡ Numbers in parentheses indicate the number of people reporting a single ancestry; * Numbers in parentheses indicate the number of persons reporting this race alone, not in combination with any other race; Please refer to the Explanation of Data for more information.*

Cherokee (23)	79	0.54
Cheyenne (2)	3	0.02
Chickasaw (3)	6	0.04
Chippewa (7)	13	0.09
Choctaw (6)	22	0.15
Comanche (0)	1	0.01
Cree (0)	3	0.02
Creek (5)	11	0.08
Hopi (0)	3	0.02
Inupiat *(Alaska Native)* (3)	3	0.02
Iroquois (3)	11	0.08
Kiowa (0)	1	0.01
Menominee (1)	2	0.01
Mexican American Ind. (1)	1	0.01
Navajo (0)	4	0.03
Osage (11)	13	0.09
Potawatomi (1)	1	0.01
Pueblo (1)	5	0.03
Puget Sound Salish (8)	8	0.05
Sioux (18)	23	0.16
Tlingit-Haida *(Alaska Native)* (9)	12	0.08
Tohono O'Odham (1)	3	0.02
Tsimshian *(Alaska Native)* (2)	2	0.01
Yakama (4)	4	0.03
Yuman (1)	1	0.01
Asian (111)	176	1.21
Not Hispanic (110)	165	1.13
Hispanic (1)	11	0.08
Burmese (0)	1	0.01
Cambodian (0)	1	0.01
Chinese, ex. Taiwanese (16)	19	0.13
Filipino (17)	44	0.30
Indian (11)	19	0.13
Indonesian (2)	3	0.02
Japanese (18)	42	0.29
Korean (12)	15	0.10
Laotian (1)	4	0.03
Malaysian (2)	2	0.01
Pakistani (1)	1	0.01
Taiwanese (1)	1	0.01
Thai (10)	11	0.08
Vietnamese (14)	16	0.11
Hawaii Native/Pacific Islander (19)	47	0.32
Not Hispanic (17)	38	0.26
Hispanic (2)	9	0.06
Guamanian/Chamorro (2)	2	0.01
Marshallese (5)	5	0.03
Native Hawaiian (5)	17	0.12
Samoan (1)	8	0.05
White (13,497)	13,872	95.12
Not Hispanic (12,967)	13,250	90.86
Hispanic (530)	622	4.27

Damascus

Place Type: City
County: Clackamas
Population: 10,539†

Ancestry‡	Population	%
Albanian (19)	54	0.53
American (933)	933	9.08
Arab (12)	25	0.24
Arab (12)	12	0.12
Lebanese (0)	13	0.13
Belgian (0)	12	0.12
British (17)	42	0.41
Canadian (0)	52	0.51
Croatian (76)	76	0.74
Czech (8)	46	0.45
Danish (0)	73	0.71
Dutch (25)	236	2.30
English (642)	1,686	16.40
European (327)	349	3.39
Finnish (53)	109	1.06
French, ex. Basque (58)	587	5.71
French Canadian (14)	39	0.38
German (896)	2,454	23.87
Greek (14)	14	0.14
Hungarian (46)	126	1.23
Irish (269)	1,336	13.00
Italian (113)	439	4.27
Lithuanian (0)	11	0.11
Northern European (21)	21	0.20
Norwegian (160)	534	5.19
Pennsylvania German (0)	9	0.09
Polish (27)	66	0.64
Portuguese (0)	22	0.21
Romanian (22)	22	0.21
Russian (46)	96	0.93
Scandinavian (124)	230	2.24
Scotch-Irish (0)	54	0.53
Scottish (86)	267	2.60
Serbian (0)	35	0.34
Slavic (0)	35	0.34
Swedish (81)	370	3.60
Swiss (37)	121	1.18
Welsh (14)	119	1.16
Yugoslavian (10)	96	0.93

Hispanic Origin	Population	%
Hispanic or Latino (of any race)	467	4.43
Central American, ex. Mexican	30	0.28
Guatemalan	6	0.06
Nicaraguan	4	0.04
Panamanian	7	0.07
Salvadoran	13	0.12
Cuban	15	0.14
Mexican	323	3.06
Puerto Rican	16	0.15
South American	22	0.21
Argentinean	6	0.06
Chilean	2	0.02
Colombian	9	0.09
Ecuadorian	3	0.03
Peruvian	2	0.02
Other Hispanic or Latino	61	0.58

Race*	Population	%
African-American/Black (66)	107	1.02
Not Hispanic (66)	96	0.91
Hispanic (0)	11	0.10
American Indian/Alaska Native (65)	171	1.62
Not Hispanic (54)	141	1.34
Hispanic (11)	30	0.28
Alaska Athabascan *(Ala. Nat.)* (0)	1	0.01
Apache (0)	1	0.01
Arapaho (0)	3	0.03
Blackfeet (1)	2	0.02
Canadian/French Am. Ind. (1)	2	0.02
Cherokee (3)	17	0.16
Cheyenne (0)	3	0.03
Chickasaw (1)	3	0.03
Chippewa (4)	7	0.07
Choctaw (1)	8	0.08
Colville (3)	3	0.03
Crow (1)	1	0.01
Iroquois (2)	8	0.08
Mexican American Ind. (1)	1	0.01
Navajo (2)	8	0.08
Pima (1)	1	0.01
Potawatomi (0)	1	0.01
Puget Sound Salish (1)	1	0.01
Sioux (1)	2	0.02
Spanish American Ind. (0)	2	0.02
Ute (1)	1	0.01
Yakama (2)	2	0.02
Asian (358)	476	4.52
Not Hispanic (356)	460	4.36
Hispanic (2)	16	0.15
Cambodian (18)	20	0.19
Chinese, ex. Taiwanese (51)	86	0.82
Filipino (56)	92	0.87
Hmong (12)	12	0.11
Indian (25)	39	0.37
Indonesian (0)	1	0.01
Japanese (27)	55	0.52
Korean (37)	48	0.46
Laotian (61)	67	0.64
Malaysian (0)	5	0.05
Taiwanese (6)	6	0.06
Thai (2)	6	0.06
Vietnamese (44)	56	0.53
Hawaii Native/Pacific Islander (20)	49	0.46
Not Hispanic (20)	49	0.46
Fijian (2)	2	0.02
Marshallese (1)	1	0.01
Native Hawaiian (8)	28	0.27
Samoan (2)	5	0.05
Tongan (2)	3	0.03
White (9,623)	9,870	93.65
Not Hispanic (9,343)	9,549	90.61
Hispanic (280)	321	3.05

Eagle Point

Place Type: City
County: Jackson
Population: 8,469†

Ancestry‡	Population	%
American (290)	290	3.69
Armenian (0)	9	0.11
Austrian (7)	20	0.25
British (0)	13	0.17
Croatian (0)	7	0.09
Czech (52)	148	1.88
Czechoslovakian (0)	70	0.89
Danish (10)	42	0.53
Dutch (35)	150	1.91
Eastern European (5)	5	0.06
English (199)	812	10.32
European (98)	98	1.25
Finnish (16)	41	0.52
French, ex. Basque (124)	333	4.23
French Canadian (0)	88	1.12
German (410)	1,702	21.63
Greek (69)	69	0.88
Hungarian (16)	29	0.37
Irish (272)	1,628	20.69
Italian (101)	335	4.26
Lithuanian (58)	58	0.74
Norwegian (116)	303	3.85
Polish (21)	142	1.80
Portuguese (42)	78	0.99
Scotch-Irish (124)	313	3.98
Scottish (57)	278	3.53
Swedish (68)	204	2.59
Swiss (0)	33	0.42
Ukrainian (0)	22	0.28
Welsh (0)	34	0.43

Hispanic Origin	Population	%
Hispanic or Latino (of any race)	579	6.84
Central American, ex. Mexican	22	0.26
Costa Rican	1	0.01
Guatemalan	13	0.15
Honduran	4	0.05
Salvadoran	4	0.05
Cuban	11	0.13
Dominican Republic	1	0.01
Mexican	476	5.62
Puerto Rican	15	0.18
South American	7	0.08
Argentinean	3	0.04
Bolivian	1	0.01
Chilean	1	0.01
Colombian	1	0.01
Ecuadorian	1	0.01
Other Hispanic or Latino	47	0.55

Race*	Population	%
African-American/Black (19)	51	0.60
Not Hispanic (19)	48	0.57
Hispanic (0)	3	0.04
American Indian/Alaska Native (109)	272	3.21
Not Hispanic (90)	223	2.63
Hispanic (19)	49	0.58
Aleut *(Alaska Native)* (2)	2	0.02
Apache (3)	17	0.20

*Notes: † The Census 2010 population figure is used to calculate the percentages in the Hispanic Origin and Race categories. Ancestry percentages are based on the 2006-2010 American Community Survey population (not shown); ‡ Numbers in parentheses indicate the number of people reporting a single ancestry; * Numbers in parentheses indicate the number of persons reporting this race alone, not in combination with any other race; Please refer to the Explanation of Data for more information.*

Blackfeet (2)	9	0.11
Canadian/French Am. Ind. (3)	4	0.05
Cherokee (8)	42	0.50
Chickasaw (1)	1	0.01
Chippewa (2)	8	0.09
Choctaw (4)	12	0.14
Creek (1)	1	0.01
Iroquois (3)	3	0.04
Mexican American Ind. (1)	6	0.07
Navajo (1)	5	0.06
Potawatomi (2)	2	0.02
Shoshone (4)	4	0.05
Sioux (3)	6	0.07
Asian (83)	149	1.76
Not Hispanic (81)	131	1.55
Hispanic (2)	18	0.21
Chinese, ex. Taiwanese (5)	9	0.11
Filipino (23)	57	0.67
Indian (4)	6	0.07
Indonesian (1)	1	0.01
Japanese (19)	32	0.38
Korean (9)	14	0.17
Laotian (1)	1	0.01
Taiwanese (0)	1	0.01
Vietnamese (20)	21	0.25
Hawaii Native/Pacific Islander (9)	37	0.44
Not Hispanic (8)	25	0.30
Hispanic (1)	12	0.14
Guamanian/Chamorro (0)	2	0.02
Native Hawaiian (9)	26	0.31
Samoan (0)	2	0.02
White (7,800)	8,086	95.48
Not Hispanic (7,476)	7,680	90.68
Hispanic (324)	406	4.79

Eugene

Place Type: City
County: Lane
Population: 156,185†

Ancestry‡	Population	%
African, Sub-Saharan (549)	784	0.51
African (146)	318	0.21
Cape Verdean (45)	45	0.03
Ethiopian (186)	186	0.12
Liberian (30)	30	0.02
Nigerian (15)	15	0.01
Somalian (0)	63	0.04
South African (21)	21	0.01
Other Sub-Saharan African (106)	106	0.07
Albanian (51)	51	0.03
Alsatian (0)	9	0.01
American (5,982)	5,982	3.90
Arab (613)	826	0.54
Arab (278)	317	0.21
Egyptian (32)	74	0.05
Jordanian (12)	12	0.01
Lebanese (52)	127	0.08
Palestinian (10)	10	0.01
Syrian (23)	74	0.05
Other Arab (206)	212	0.14
Armenian (62)	105	0.07
Assyrian/Chaldean/Syriac (12)	12	0.01
Australian (0)	80	0.05
Austrian (69)	495	0.32
Basque (34)	146	0.10
Belgian (45)	409	0.27
Brazilian (103)	128	0.08
British (625)	1,376	0.90
Bulgarian (37)	45	0.03
Cajun (12)	36	0.02
Canadian (333)	591	0.39
Carpatho Rusyn (10)	10	0.01
Celtic (35)	43	0.03
Croatian (189)	322	0.21
Czech (190)	976	0.64
Czechoslovakian (40)	181	0.12
Danish (877)	2,211	1.44
Dutch (808)	3,771	2.46
Eastern European (168)	230	0.15
English (6,640)	22,769	14.85
Estonian (0)	25	0.02
European (4,712)	5,529	3.61
Finnish (449)	1,044	0.68
French, ex. Basque (731)	5,920	3.86
French Canadian (377)	1,035	0.68
German (9,001)	32,438	21.16
Greek (134)	512	0.33
Hungarian (220)	892	0.58
Icelander (0)	34	0.02
Iranian (136)	206	0.13
Irish (5,502)	21,708	14.16
Israeli (9)	23	0.02
Italian (2,059)	6,586	4.30
Latvian (42)	93	0.06
Lithuanian (182)	456	0.30
Luxemburger (12)	24	0.02
Macedonian (0)	27	0.02
New Zealander (56)	86	0.06
Northern European (640)	734	0.48
Norwegian (2,210)	6,754	4.41
Pennsylvania German (39)	67	0.04
Polish (1,121)	3,747	2.44
Portuguese (261)	765	0.50
Romanian (103)	234	0.15
Russian (609)	2,079	1.36
Scandinavian (522)	1,005	0.66
Scotch-Irish (1,285)	4,061	2.65
Scottish (1,382)	5,572	3.63
Serbian (28)	28	0.02
Slavic (10)	75	0.05
Slovak (36)	122	0.08
Slovene (0)	21	0.01
Swedish (790)	4,137	2.70
Swiss (190)	930	0.61
Turkish (74)	82	0.05
Ukrainian (315)	693	0.45
Welsh (473)	2,309	1.51
West Indian, ex. Hispanic (59)	253	0.17
Bahamian (0)	15	0.01
Barbadian (0)	10	0.01
Belizean (0)	7	<0.01
Dutch West Indian (0)	3	<0.01
Haitian (0)	15	0.01
Jamaican (48)	164	0.11
West Indian (11)	39	0.03
Yugoslavian (83)	160	0.10

Hispanic Origin	Population	%
Hispanic or Latino (of any race)	12,200	7.81
Central American, ex. Mexican	789	0.51
Costa Rican	63	0.04
Guatemalan	229	0.15
Honduran	76	0.05
Nicaraguan	64	0.04
Panamanian	51	0.03
Salvadoran	302	0.19
Other Central American	4	<0.01
Cuban	155	0.10
Dominican Republic	32	0.02
Mexican	8,830	5.65
Puerto Rican	374	0.24
South American	625	0.40
Argentinean	69	0.04
Bolivian	44	0.03
Chilean	79	0.05
Colombian	117	0.07
Ecuadorian	67	0.04
Paraguayan	2	<0.01
Peruvian	217	0.14
Venezuelan	29	0.02
Other South American	1	<0.01
Other Hispanic or Latino	1,395	0.89

Race*	Population	%
African-American/Black (2,126)	3,815	2.44
Not Hispanic (1,955)	3,391	2.17
Hispanic (171)	424	0.27
American Indian/Alaska Native (1,606)	4,346	2.78
Not Hispanic (1,267)	3,517	2.25
Hispanic (339)	829	0.53
Alaska Athabascan *(Ala. Nat.)* (8)	17	0.01
Aleut *(Alaska Native)* (13)	26	0.02
Apache (22)	69	0.04
Arapaho (4)	6	<0.01
Blackfeet (24)	107	0.07
Canadian/French Am. Ind. (1)	12	0.01
Central American Ind. (3)	4	<0.01
Cherokee (134)	732	0.47
Cheyenne (4)	21	0.01
Chickasaw (9)	29	0.02
Chippewa (34)	112	0.07
Choctaw (56)	187	0.12
Colville (8)	9	0.01
Comanche (6)	20	0.01
Cree (0)	13	0.01
Creek (9)	38	0.02
Crow (4)	13	0.01
Delaware (2)	12	0.01
Hopi (6)	18	0.01
Houma (3)	3	<0.01
Inupiat *(Alaska Native)* (18)	31	0.02
Iroquois (9)	38	0.02
Kiowa (8)	13	0.01
Lumbee (3)	10	0.01
Menominee (0)	1	<0.01
Mexican American Ind. (69)	122	0.08
Navajo (23)	58	0.04
Osage (14)	31	0.02
Ottawa (0)	2	<0.01
Paiute (16)	25	0.02
Pima (11)	14	0.01
Potawatomi (24)	38	0.02
Pueblo (7)	29	0.02
Puget Sound Salish (9)	12	0.01
Seminole (0)	31	0.02
Shoshone (11)	19	0.01
Sioux (45)	173	0.11
South American Ind. (18)	24	0.02
Spanish American Ind. (5)	18	0.01
Tlingit-Haida *(Alaska Native)* (16)	51	0.03
Tsimshian *(Alaska Native)* (6)	19	0.01
Ute (1)	2	<0.01
Yakama (8)	11	0.01
Yaqui (4)	18	0.01
Yuman (2)	2	<0.01
Yup'ik *(Alaska Native)* (7)	17	0.01
Asian (6,283)	8,947	5.73
Not Hispanic (6,205)	8,660	5.54
Hispanic (78)	287	0.18
Bangladeshi (3)	4	<0.01
Bhutanese (2)	2	<0.01
Burmese (8)	12	0.01
Cambodian (48)	63	0.04
Chinese, ex. Taiwanese (2,001)	2,633	1.69
Filipino (460)	1,118	0.72
Hmong (7)	7	<0.01
Indian (553)	756	0.48
Indonesian (46)	101	0.06
Japanese (807)	1,622	1.04
Korean (1,298)	1,610	1.03
Laotian (55)	88	0.06
Malaysian (11)	16	0.01
Nepalese (15)	17	0.01
Pakistani (25)	44	0.03
Sri Lankan (18)	21	0.01
Taiwanese (150)	176	0.11
Thai (117)	187	0.12
Vietnamese (374)	515	0.33
Hawaii Native/Pacific Islander (364)	963	0.62
Not Hispanic (341)	864	0.55
Hispanic (23)	99	0.06
Fijian (19)	35	0.02
Guamanian/Chamorro (53)	125	0.08
Marshallese (24)	30	0.02
Native Hawaiian (145)	467	0.30
Samoan (42)	119	0.08
Tongan (9)	17	0.01
White (134,018)	140,868	90.19

*Notes: † The Census 2010 population figure is used to calculate the percentages in the Hispanic Origin and Race categories. Ancestry percentages are based on the 2006-2010 American Community Survey population (not shown); ‡ Numbers in parentheses indicate the number of people reporting a single ancestry; * Numbers in parentheses indicate the number of persons reporting this race alone, not in combination with any other race; Please refer to the Explanation of Data for more information.*

Not Hispanic (128,031)	133,599	85.54
Hispanic (5,987)	7,269	4.65

Fairview

Place Type: City
County: Multnomah
Population: 8,920†

Ancestry‡	Population	%
African, Sub-Saharan (0)	43	0.51
African (0)	28	0.33
Kenyan (0)	15	0.18
American (436)	436	5.13
Austrian (0)	10	0.12
Belgian (80)	80	0.94
British (0)	12	0.14
Czech (0)	63	0.74
Czechoslovakian (8)	8	0.09
Danish (0)	86	1.01
Dutch (9)	114	1.34
English (240)	885	10.41
European (106)	106	1.25
Finnish (12)	51	0.60
French, ex. Basque (36)	290	3.41
French Canadian (0)	19	0.22
German (440)	1,576	18.53
Hungarian (30)	43	0.51
Iranian (14)	14	0.16
Irish (184)	723	8.50
Italian (137)	366	4.30
Luxemburger (9)	15	0.18
Northern European (9)	9	0.11
Norwegian (55)	214	2.52
Polish (70)	222	2.61
Portuguese (20)	37	0.44
Romanian (30)	46	0.54
Russian (0)	38	0.45
Scandinavian (64)	64	0.75
Scotch-Irish (18)	112	1.32
Scottish (104)	270	3.17
Swedish (94)	423	4.97
Swiss (0)	30	0.35
Welsh (0)	54	0.63
Yugoslavian (0)	17	0.20

Hispanic Origin	Population	%
Hispanic or Latino (of any race)	1,463	16.40
Central American, ex. Mexican	56	0.63
Costa Rican	1	0.01
Guatemalan	13	0.15
Honduran	21	0.24
Nicaraguan	2	0.02
Panamanian	2	0.02
Salvadoran	16	0.18
Other Central American	1	0.01
Cuban	18	0.20
Mexican	1,218	13.65
Puerto Rican	20	0.22
South American	28	0.31
Argentinean	2	0.02
Chilean	4	0.04
Colombian	11	0.12
Ecuadorian	1	0.01
Peruvian	8	0.09
Venezuelan	2	0.02
Other Hispanic or Latino	123	1.38

Race*	Population	%
African-American/Black (408)	544	6.10
Not Hispanic (391)	508	5.70
Hispanic (17)	36	0.40
American Indian/Alaska Native (101)	233	2.61
Not Hispanic (71)	181	2.03
Hispanic (30)	52	0.58
Aleut *(Alaska Native)* (3)	3	0.03
Blackfeet (0)	8	0.09
Canadian/French Am. Ind. (5)	5	0.06
Cherokee (10)	38	0.43
Cheyenne (0)	1	0.01
Chickasaw (0)	1	0.01
Chippewa (2)	7	0.08
Choctaw (2)	11	0.12
Cree (0)	1	0.01
Creek (1)	4	0.04
Delaware (1)	1	0.01
Inupiat *(Alaska Native)* (1)	1	0.01
Iroquois (0)	1	0.01
Lumbee (0)	3	0.03
Menominee (0)	3	0.03
Mexican American Ind. (8)	9	0.10
Navajo (5)	5	0.06
Osage (1)	2	0.02
Ottawa (0)	1	0.01
Puget Sound Salish (2)	3	0.03
Seminole (0)	2	0.02
Shoshone (0)	1	0.01
Sioux (3)	5	0.06
Tsimshian *(Alaska Native)* (3)	3	0.03
Yakama (1)	2	0.02
Asian (491)	620	6.95
Not Hispanic (478)	594	6.66
Hispanic (13)	26	0.29
Bangladeshi (4)	4	0.04
Cambodian (3)	7	0.08
Chinese, ex. Taiwanese (39)	59	0.66
Filipino (72)	129	1.45
Hmong (21)	21	0.24
Indian (23)	34	0.38
Indonesian (5)	8	0.09
Japanese (30)	64	0.72
Korean (26)	36	0.40
Laotian (52)	60	0.67
Pakistani (0)	2	0.02
Sri Lankan (0)	3	0.03
Taiwanese (1)	2	0.02
Thai (2)	2	0.02
Vietnamese (186)	209	2.34
Hawaii Native/Pacific Islander (88)	145	1.63
Not Hispanic (87)	137	1.54
Hispanic (1)	8	0.09
Fijian (7)	11	0.12
Guamanian/Chamorro (9)	15	0.17
Native Hawaiian (6)	27	0.30
Samoan (8)	13	0.15
Tongan (3)	3	0.03
White (6,521)	6,899	77.34
Not Hispanic (6,075)	6,378	71.50
Hispanic (446)	521	5.84

Florence

Place Type: City
County: Lane
Population: 8,466†

Ancestry‡	Population	%
American (460)	460	5.57
Arab (17)	17	0.21
Lebanese (17)	17	0.21
Austrian (16)	31	0.38
Belgian (15)	15	0.18
British (17)	33	0.40
Canadian (0)	49	0.59
Czech (40)	56	0.68
Czechoslovakian (0)	12	0.15
Danish (77)	132	1.60
Dutch (10)	203	2.46
English (494)	1,796	21.73
European (60)	60	0.73
Finnish (15)	33	0.40
French, ex. Basque (38)	456	5.52
French Canadian (11)	47	0.57
German (604)	2,069	25.04
Greek (0)	40	0.48
Irish (295)	1,188	14.38
Italian (176)	343	4.15
Lithuanian (0)	16	0.19
Norwegian (89)	268	3.24
Polish (0)	76	0.92
Portuguese (0)	173	2.09
Romanian (0)	22	0.27
Russian (41)	55	0.67
Scandinavian (8)	77	0.93
Scotch-Irish (86)	298	3.61
Scottish (75)	261	3.16
Slovak (50)	68	0.82
Swedish (132)	239	2.89
Swiss (27)	27	0.33
Ukrainian (0)	17	0.21
Welsh (12)	101	1.22

Hispanic Origin	Population	%
Hispanic or Latino (of any race)	454	5.36
Central American, ex. Mexican	9	0.11
Guatemalan	2	0.02
Nicaraguan	1	0.01
Panamanian	4	0.05
Salvadoran	2	0.02
Cuban	15	0.18
Mexican	370	4.37
Puerto Rican	8	0.09
South American	9	0.11
Argentinean	2	0.02
Chilean	5	0.06
Colombian	1	0.01
Peruvian	1	0.01
Other Hispanic or Latino	43	0.51

Race*	Population	%
African-American/Black (25)	48	0.57
Not Hispanic (24)	45	0.53
Hispanic (1)	3	0.04
American Indian/Alaska Native (111)	295	3.48
Not Hispanic (100)	272	3.21
Hispanic (11)	23	0.27
Alaska Athabascan *(Ala. Nat.)* (1)	3	0.04
Aleut *(Alaska Native)* (1)	2	0.02
Apache (3)	5	0.06
Blackfeet (3)	13	0.15
Cherokee (14)	40	0.47
Chickasaw (1)	1	0.01
Chippewa (2)	5	0.06
Choctaw (3)	11	0.13
Comanche (0)	1	0.01
Cree (0)	1	0.01
Creek (0)	2	0.02
Delaware (2)	11	0.13
Inupiat *(Alaska Native)* (1)	1	0.01
Iroquois (0)	2	0.02
Lumbee (0)	2	0.02
Menominee (0)	1	0.01
Osage (1)	3	0.04
Pima (1)	1	0.01
Potawatomi (5)	6	0.07
Pueblo (1)	1	0.01
Puget Sound Salish (2)	2	0.02
Shoshone (0)	1	0.01
Sioux (7)	16	0.19
Tlingit-Haida *(Alaska Native)* (1)	2	0.02
Yakama (0)	1	0.01
Yaqui (0)	2	0.02
Asian (83)	131	1.55
Not Hispanic (79)	126	1.49
Hispanic (4)	5	0.06
Burmese (3)	3	0.04
Cambodian (1)	1	0.01
Chinese, ex. Taiwanese (25)	31	0.37
Filipino (19)	32	0.38
Indian (4)	10	0.12
Indonesian (1)	3	0.04
Japanese (9)	23	0.27
Korean (4)	13	0.15
Pakistani (0)	3	0.04
Thai (8)	10	0.12
Vietnamese (2)	5	0.06
Hawaii Native/Pacific Islander (28)	38	0.45
Not Hispanic (28)	36	0.43
Hispanic (0)	2	0.02
Guamanian/Chamorro (0)	2	0.02

*Notes: † The Census 2010 population figure is used to calculate the percentages in the Hispanic Origin and Race categories. Ancestry percentages are based on the 2006-2010 American Community Survey population (not shown); ‡ Numbers in parentheses indicate the number of people reporting a single ancestry; * Numbers in parentheses indicate the number of persons reporting this race alone, not in combination with any other race; Please refer to the Explanation of Data for more information.*

Native Hawaiian (11)	17	0.20
Samoan (15)	16	0.19
Tongan (0)	1	0.01
White (7,835)	8,091	95.57
Not Hispanic (7,544)	7,772	91.80
Hispanic (291)	319	3.77

Forest Grove

Place Type: City
County: Washington
Population: 21,083†

Ancestry‡	Population	%
African, Sub-Saharan (0)	13	0.06
African (0)	13	0.06
American (951)	951	4.61
Arab (13)	29	0.14
Lebanese (13)	29	0.14
Armenian (0)	26	0.13
Austrian (1)	58	0.28
Belgian (0)	63	0.31
British (79)	92	0.45
Canadian (69)	104	0.50
Celtic (0)	30	0.15
Croatian (14)	23	0.11
Czech (24)	76	0.37
Czechoslovakian (11)	16	0.08
Danish (43)	213	1.03
Dutch (180)	695	3.37
English (668)	2,638	12.78
European (372)	459	2.22
Finnish (55)	98	0.47
French, ex. Basque (12)	423	2.05
French Canadian (18)	59	0.29
German (1,081)	4,147	20.10
Greek (0)	25	0.12
Hungarian (0)	9	0.04
Iranian (38)	38	0.18
Irish (600)	2,230	10.81
Italian (150)	480	2.33
Lithuanian (12)	59	0.29
Norwegian (422)	1,231	5.97
Pennsylvania German (0)	14	0.07
Polish (67)	401	1.94
Portuguese (38)	38	0.18
Russian (15)	54	0.26
Scandinavian (16)	105	0.51
Scotch-Irish (180)	498	2.41
Scottish (199)	569	2.76
Slavic (8)	20	0.10
Slovene (0)	13	0.06
Swedish (91)	493	2.39
Swiss (52)	207	1.00
Ukrainian (16)	41	0.20
Welsh (70)	241	1.17
Yugoslavian (0)	12	0.06

Hispanic Origin	Population	%
Hispanic or Latino (of any race)	4,874	23.12
Central American, ex. Mexican	192	0.91
Costa Rican	1	<0.01
Guatemalan	131	0.62
Honduran	13	0.06
Nicaraguan	7	0.03
Panamanian	2	0.01
Salvadoran	32	0.15
Other Central American	6	0.03
Cuban	18	0.09
Dominican Republic	1	<0.01
Mexican	4,138	19.63
Puerto Rican	49	0.23
South American	52	0.25
Argentinean	4	0.02
Chilean	2	0.01
Colombian	6	0.03
Ecuadorian	4	0.02
Paraguayan	6	0.03
Peruvian	24	0.11
Venezuelan	6	0.03
Other Hispanic or Latino	424	2.01

Race*	Population	%
African-American/Black (164)	272	1.29
Not Hispanic (119)	203	0.96
Hispanic (45)	69	0.33
American Indian/Alaska Native (231)	438	2.08
Not Hispanic (126)	296	1.40
Hispanic (105)	142	0.67
Alaska Athabascan *(Ala. Nat.)* (1)	1	<0.01
Aleut *(Alaska Native)* (4)	7	0.03
Apache (2)	11	0.05
Blackfeet (2)	11	0.05
Canadian/French Am. Ind. (0)	1	<0.01
Central American Ind. (2)	2	0.01
Cherokee (21)	64	0.30
Chickasaw (2)	2	0.01
Chippewa (7)	13	0.06
Choctaw (5)	19	0.09
Colville (2)	2	0.01
Comanche (0)	1	<0.01
Creek (1)	8	0.04
Crow (1)	3	0.01
Iroquois (2)	8	0.04
Mexican American Ind. (53)	67	0.32
Navajo (4)	4	0.02
Osage (3)	3	0.01
Ottawa (1)	1	<0.01
Potawatomi (1)	4	0.02
Pueblo (3)	3	0.01
Puget Sound Salish (1)	1	<0.01
Seminole (1)	1	<0.01
Shoshone (0)	1	<0.01
Sioux (12)	18	0.09
South American Ind. (1)	1	<0.01
Tlingit-Haida *(Alaska Native)* (2)	3	0.01
Yup'ik *(Alaska Native)* (0)	1	<0.01
Asian (556)	866	4.11
Not Hispanic (533)	800	3.79
Hispanic (23)	66	0.31
Bangladeshi (2)	2	0.01
Burmese (0)	1	<0.01
Cambodian (2)	2	0.01
Chinese, ex. Taiwanese (95)	215	1.02
Filipino (111)	234	1.11
Indian (29)	41	0.19
Indonesian (4)	9	0.04
Japanese (136)	282	1.34
Korean (61)	111	0.53
Laotian (3)	9	0.04
Malaysian (0)	1	<0.01
Pakistani (6)	8	0.04
Sri Lankan (2)	2	0.01
Taiwanese (1)	1	<0.01
Thai (5)	7	0.03
Vietnamese (35)	51	0.24
Hawaii Native/Pacific Islander (62)	201	0.95
Not Hispanic (58)	180	0.85
Hispanic (4)	21	0.10
Fijian (2)	2	0.01
Guamanian/Chamorro (4)	13	0.06
Marshallese (4)	4	0.02
Native Hawaiian (48)	149	0.71
Samoan (1)	14	0.07
Tongan (0)	4	0.02
White (16,615)	17,348	82.28
Not Hispanic (14,796)	15,300	72.57
Hispanic (1,819)	2,048	9.71

Four Corners

Place Type: CDP
County: Marion
Population: 15,947†

Ancestry‡	Population	%
African, Sub-Saharan (0)	7	0.04
African (0)	7	0.04
American (671)	671	4.25
Australian (0)	15	0.09
British (42)	59	0.37
Canadian (12)	12	0.08
Celtic (0)	77	0.49
Czech (20)	53	0.34
Danish (49)	91	0.58
Dutch (31)	261	1.65
English (471)	1,472	9.32
Estonian (5)	18	0.11
European (119)	234	1.48
Finnish (61)	97	0.61
French, ex. Basque (87)	462	2.92
French Canadian (50)	125	0.79
German (1,054)	3,105	19.65
Greek (13)	136	0.86
Hungarian (11)	34	0.22
Irish (284)	1,866	11.81
Italian (71)	456	2.89
Norwegian (253)	706	4.47
Polish (56)	153	0.97
Portuguese (20)	32	0.20
Romanian (0)	11	0.07
Scandinavian (47)	64	0.41
Scotch-Irish (35)	331	2.10
Scottish (51)	316	2.00
Slovak (0)	14	0.09
Swedish (58)	224	1.42
Swiss (10)	90	0.57
Turkish (0)	20	0.13
Ukrainian (23)	23	0.15
Welsh (24)	127	0.80
Yugoslavian (13)	13	0.08

Hispanic Origin	Population	%
Hispanic or Latino (of any race)	5,381	33.74
Central American, ex. Mexican	104	0.65
Costa Rican	3	0.02
Guatemalan	15	0.09
Honduran	5	0.03
Nicaraguan	16	0.10
Panamanian	4	0.03
Salvadoran	61	0.38
Cuban	6	0.04
Mexican	4,917	30.83
Puerto Rican	35	0.22
South American	29	0.18
Argentinean	3	0.02
Bolivian	2	0.01
Chilean	9	0.06
Colombian	6	0.04
Ecuadorian	2	0.01
Peruvian	7	0.04
Other Hispanic or Latino	290	1.82

Race*	Population	%
African-American/Black (230)	379	2.38
Not Hispanic (170)	276	1.73
Hispanic (60)	103	0.65
American Indian/Alaska Native (316)	588	3.69
Not Hispanic (214)	415	2.60
Hispanic (102)	173	1.08
Alaska Athabascan *(Ala. Nat.)* (0)	1	0.01
Apache (2)	6	0.04
Blackfeet (1)	13	0.08
Canadian/French Am. Ind. (1)	7	0.04
Cherokee (15)	62	0.39
Cheyenne (0)	5	0.03
Chickasaw (0)	2	0.01
Chippewa (5)	18	0.11
Choctaw (7)	18	0.11
Comanche (3)	5	0.03
Creek (4)	4	0.03
Crow (1)	1	0.01
Iroquois (0)	2	0.01
Kiowa (0)	1	0.01
Mexican American Ind. (25)	39	0.24
Navajo (7)	10	0.06
Osage (1)	6	0.04
Paiute (0)	5	0.03
Potawatomi (1)	1	0.01
Seminole (0)	3	0.02

*Notes: † The Census 2010 population figure is used to calculate the percentages in the Hispanic Origin and Race categories. Ancestry percentages are based on the 2006-2010 American Community Survey population (not shown); ‡ Numbers in parentheses indicate the number of people reporting a single ancestry; * Numbers in parentheses indicate the number of persons reporting this race alone, not in combination with any other race; Please refer to the Explanation of Data for more information.*

Shoshone (2)	2	0.01
Sioux (8)	16	0.10
South American Ind. (1)	2	0.01
Spanish American Ind. (1)	4	0.03
Tlingit-Haida *(Alaska Native)* (3)	5	0.03
Tohono O'Odham (5)	5	0.03
Tsimshian *(Alaska Native)* (1)	1	0.01
Yakama (1)	2	0.01
Yaqui (0)	2	0.01
Yuman (1)	1	0.01
Yup'ik *(Alaska Native)* (2)	8	0.05
Asian (313)	443	2.78
Not Hispanic (296)	407	2.55
Hispanic (17)	36	0.23
Cambodian (27)	33	0.21
Chinese, ex. Taiwanese (54)	67	0.42
Filipino (63)	109	0.68
Hmong (55)	57	0.36
Indian (27)	44	0.28
Indonesian (5)	7	0.04
Japanese (17)	39	0.24
Korean (14)	21	0.13
Laotian (15)	23	0.14
Malaysian (1)	1	0.01
Taiwanese (1)	1	0.01
Thai (5)	10	0.06
Vietnamese (11)	16	0.10
Hawaii Native/Pacific Islander (281)	336	2.11
Not Hispanic (278)	330	2.07
Hispanic (3)	6	0.04
Fijian (3)	3	0.02
Guamanian/Chamorro (30)	36	0.23
Marshallese (66)	80	0.50
Native Hawaiian (18)	32	0.20
Samoan (6)	11	0.07
Tongan (1)	5	0.03
White (10,953)	11,614	72.83
Not Hispanic (9,172)	9,556	59.92
Hispanic (1,781)	2,058	12.91

Gladstone

Place Type: City
County: Clackamas
Population: 11,497†

Ancestry‡	Population	%
American (714)	714	6.19
Austrian (0)	10	0.09
Belgian (5)	5	0.04
British (53)	100	0.87
Canadian (21)	154	1.34
Croatian (0)	24	0.21
Czech (31)	60	0.52
Dutch (87)	298	2.58
English (696)	1,837	15.93
European (297)	347	3.01
Finnish (93)	209	1.81
French, ex. Basque (90)	606	5.26
French Canadian (168)	233	2.02
German (868)	2,601	22.56
Greek (0)	59	0.51
Hungarian (20)	144	1.25
Iranian (16)	16	0.14
Irish (275)	1,300	11.27
Italian (242)	510	4.42
Lithuanian (15)	73	0.63
Northern European (15)	15	0.13
Norwegian (116)	434	3.76
Polish (14)	111	0.96
Russian (33)	124	1.08
Scandinavian (34)	34	0.29
Scotch-Irish (88)	316	2.74
Scottish (29)	245	2.12
Swedish (42)	306	2.65
Swiss (14)	67	0.58
Ukrainian (80)	107	0.93
Welsh (0)	84	0.73

Hispanic Origin	Population	%
Hispanic or Latino (of any race)	1,001	8.71
Central American, ex. Mexican	51	0.44
Costa Rican	7	0.06
Guatemalan	14	0.12
Honduran	2	0.02
Nicaraguan	4	0.03
Panamanian	2	0.02
Salvadoran	22	0.19
Cuban	8	0.07
Mexican	775	6.74
Puerto Rican	37	0.32
South American	18	0.16
Argentinean	5	0.04
Bolivian	1	0.01
Chilean	1	0.01
Colombian	4	0.03
Ecuadorian	2	0.02
Peruvian	4	0.03
Venezuelan	1	0.01
Other Hispanic or Latino	112	0.97

Race*	Population	%
African-American/Black (99)	232	2.02
Not Hispanic (90)	203	1.77
Hispanic (9)	29	0.25
American Indian/Alaska Native (111)	276	2.40
Not Hispanic (82)	232	2.02
Hispanic (29)	44	0.38
Aleut *(Alaska Native)* (2)	4	0.03
Apache (1)	3	0.03
Blackfeet (1)	10	0.09
Central American Ind. (1)	1	0.01
Cherokee (14)	50	0.43
Cheyenne (2)	2	0.02
Chickasaw (1)	1	0.01
Chippewa (1)	5	0.04
Choctaw (1)	13	0.11
Colville (0)	1	0.01
Cree (0)	1	0.01
Creek (3)	8	0.07
Iroquois (2)	3	0.03
Mexican American Ind. (3)	10	0.09
Navajo (2)	3	0.03
Osage (0)	3	0.03
Puget Sound Salish (2)	2	0.02
Shoshone (0)	1	0.01
Sioux (2)	8	0.07
Tlingit-Haida *(Alaska Native)* (2)	6	0.05
Ute (0)	2	0.02
Yakama (4)	4	0.03
Yaqui (1)	1	0.01
Asian (180)	286	2.49
Not Hispanic (176)	269	2.34
Hispanic (4)	17	0.15
Cambodian (12)	14	0.12
Chinese, ex. Taiwanese (30)	52	0.45
Filipino (43)	79	0.69
Hmong (3)	3	0.03
Indian (22)	33	0.29
Indonesian (1)	5	0.04
Japanese (14)	46	0.40
Korean (27)	39	0.34
Laotian (3)	5	0.04
Thai (5)	7	0.06
Vietnamese (8)	13	0.11
Hawaii Native/Pacific Islander (44)	73	0.63
Not Hispanic (34)	61	0.53
Hispanic (10)	12	0.10
Fijian (3)	3	0.03
Guamanian/Chamorro (3)	7	0.06
Native Hawaiian (12)	34	0.30
Samoan (1)	8	0.07
White (10,260)	10,654	92.67
Not Hispanic (9,760)	10,086	87.73
Hispanic (500)	568	4.94

Grants Pass

Place Type: City
County: Josephine
Population: 34,533†

Ancestry‡	Population	%
African, Sub-Saharan (0)	94	0.28
African (0)	94	0.28
Albanian (11)	11	0.03
American (1,807)	1,807	5.33
Arab (37)	193	0.57
Arab (0)	156	0.46
Lebanese (37)	37	0.11
Armenian (8)	8	0.02
Austrian (0)	67	0.20
Belgian (0)	85	0.25
British (85)	185	0.55
Canadian (88)	162	0.48
Croatian (24)	59	0.17
Czech (68)	142	0.42
Czechoslovakian (8)	8	0.02
Danish (81)	281	0.83
Dutch (202)	1,045	3.08
Eastern European (38)	38	0.11
English (1,238)	4,663	13.76
European (274)	274	0.81
Finnish (13)	76	0.22
French, ex. Basque (255)	2,003	5.91
French Canadian (219)	278	0.82
German (2,623)	9,055	26.72
Greek (15)	37	0.11
Hungarian (59)	192	0.57
Irish (1,643)	5,284	15.59
Italian (788)	1,973	5.82
Lithuanian (0)	9	0.03
Northern European (41)	41	0.12
Norwegian (297)	1,134	3.35
Pennsylvania German (0)	30	0.09
Polish (144)	694	2.05
Portuguese (43)	290	0.86
Russian (20)	133	0.39
Scandinavian (115)	190	0.56
Scotch-Irish (162)	845	2.49
Scottish (217)	889	2.62
Slovak (14)	22	0.06
Swedish (330)	1,143	3.37
Swiss (96)	297	0.88
Ukrainian (111)	172	0.51
Welsh (82)	294	0.87
West Indian, ex. Hispanic (0)	45	0.13
Jamaican (0)	24	0.07
Other West Indian (0)	21	0.06
Yugoslavian (11)	30	0.09

Hispanic Origin	Population	%
Hispanic or Latino (of any race)	2,940	8.51
Central American, ex. Mexican	93	0.27
Costa Rican	15	0.04
Guatemalan	15	0.04
Honduran	6	0.02
Nicaraguan	1	<0.01
Panamanian	2	0.01
Salvadoran	54	0.16
Cuban	21	0.06
Dominican Republic	3	0.01
Mexican	2,302	6.67
Puerto Rican	95	0.28
South American	46	0.13
Argentinean	11	0.03
Bolivian	2	0.01
Chilean	7	0.02
Colombian	9	0.03
Ecuadorian	5	0.01
Peruvian	9	0.03
Venezuelan	3	0.01
Other Hispanic or Latino	380	1.10

Race*	Population	%
African-American/Black (187)	355	1.03

*Notes: † The Census 2010 population figure is used to calculate the percentages in the Hispanic Origin and Race categories. Ancestry percentages are based on the 2006-2010 American Community Survey population (not shown); ‡ Numbers in parentheses indicate the number of people reporting a single ancestry; * Numbers in parentheses indicate the number of persons reporting this race alone, not in combination with any other race; Please refer to the Explanation of Data for more information.*

Not Hispanic (158)	293	0.85
Hispanic (29)	62	0.18
American Indian/Alaska Native (427)	1,105	3.20
Not Hispanic (342)	889	2.57
Hispanic (85)	216	0.63
Alaska Athabascan *(Ala. Nat.)* (4)	6	0.02
Aleut *(Alaska Native)* (1)	4	0.01
Apache (14)	40	0.12
Blackfeet (4)	43	0.12
Canadian/French Am. Ind. (4)	11	0.03
Cherokee (63)	245	0.71
Cheyenne (0)	4	0.01
Chickasaw (4)	10	0.03
Chippewa (4)	10	0.03
Choctaw (23)	52	0.15
Comanche (1)	1	<0.01
Cree (0)	1	<0.01
Creek (7)	9	0.03
Crow (1)	8	0.02
Delaware (0)	3	0.01
Hopi (0)	1	<0.01
Inupiat *(Alaska Native)* (0)	2	0.01
Iroquois (2)	6	0.02
Kiowa (0)	1	<0.01
Lumbee (0)	2	0.01
Menominee (2)	2	0.01
Mexican American Ind. (2)	16	0.05
Navajo (6)	29	0.08
Osage (7)	11	0.03
Paiute (4)	6	0.02
Potawatomi (2)	8	0.02
Pueblo (2)	11	0.03
Puget Sound Salish (6)	7	0.02
Shoshone (2)	5	0.01
Sioux (7)	31	0.09
South American Ind. (1)	1	<0.01
Tlingit-Haida *(Alaska Native)* (6)	7	0.02
Tsimshian *(Alaska Native)* (1)	1	<0.01
Yakama (1)	2	0.01
Yaqui (1)	9	0.03
Yup'ik *(Alaska Native)* (1)	1	<0.01
Asian (368)	646	1.87
Not Hispanic (359)	587	1.70
Hispanic (9)	59	0.17
Cambodian (3)	3	0.01
Chinese, ex. Taiwanese (68)	114	0.33
Filipino (96)	187	0.54
Indian (37)	57	0.17
Indonesian (7)	22	0.06
Japanese (53)	128	0.37
Korean (28)	58	0.17
Laotian (3)	10	0.03
Pakistani (1)	2	0.01
Taiwanese (2)	3	0.01
Thai (28)	33	0.10
Vietnamese (23)	36	0.10
Hawaii Native/Pacific Islander (89)	201	0.58
Not Hispanic (65)	163	0.47
Hispanic (24)	38	0.11
Fijian (1)	2	0.01
Guamanian/Chamorro (19)	26	0.08
Native Hawaiian (30)	94	0.27
Samoan (21)	38	0.11
White (31,388)	32,628	94.48
Not Hispanic (29,700)	30,618	88.66
Hispanic (1,688)	2,010	5.82

Green

Place Type: CDP
County: Douglas
Population: 7,515†

Ancestry‡	Population	%
American (401)	401	5.13
British (0)	26	0.33
Canadian (8)	21	0.27
Czech (55)	55	0.70
Czechoslovakian (0)	10	0.13
Danish (0)	10	0.13
Dutch (56)	322	4.12
English (320)	874	11.18
Finnish (16)	35	0.45
French, ex. Basque (123)	391	5.00
French Canadian (31)	132	1.69
German (559)	2,251	28.80
Greek (0)	23	0.29
Hungarian (21)	69	0.88
Irish (78)	992	12.69
Italian (16)	358	4.58
Norwegian (0)	166	2.12
Polish (0)	31	0.40
Portuguese (55)	88	1.13
Scandinavian (25)	25	0.32
Scotch-Irish (77)	154	1.97
Scottish (75)	198	2.53
Slavic (0)	13	0.17
Slovak (16)	16	0.20
Slovene (29)	29	0.37
Swedish (17)	98	1.25
Swiss (0)	31	0.40
Ukrainian (0)	32	0.41
Welsh (10)	108	1.38

Hispanic Origin	Population	%
Hispanic or Latino (of any race)	438	5.83
Central American, ex. Mexican	17	0.23
Costa Rican	6	0.08
Honduran	8	0.11
Salvadoran	3	0.04
Mexican	345	4.59
Puerto Rican	9	0.12
South American	11	0.15
Argentinean	1	0.01
Bolivian	1	0.01
Chilean	6	0.08
Colombian	2	0.03
Peruvian	1	0.01
Other Hispanic or Latino	56	0.75

Race*	Population	%
African-American/Black (18)	53	0.71
Not Hispanic (18)	49	0.65
Hispanic (0)	4	0.05
American Indian/Alaska Native (136)	252	3.35
Not Hispanic (105)	208	2.77
Hispanic (31)	44	0.59
Aleut *(Alaska Native)* (0)	1	0.01
Apache (0)	1	0.01
Blackfeet (1)	2	0.03
Cherokee (28)	57	0.76
Chickasaw (6)	7	0.09
Chippewa (3)	5	0.07
Choctaw (12)	22	0.29
Creek (8)	8	0.11
Delaware (0)	2	0.03
Hopi (0)	1	0.01
Inupiat *(Alaska Native)* (0)	2	0.03
Iroquois (1)	1	0.01
Mexican American Ind. (1)	3	0.04
Navajo (2)	5	0.07
Potawatomi (1)	2	0.03
Shoshone (0)	1	0.01
Sioux (1)	8	0.11
Yakama (2)	2	0.03
Yaqui (0)	1	0.01
Asian (63)	100	1.33
Not Hispanic (59)	93	1.24
Hispanic (4)	7	0.09
Chinese, ex. Taiwanese (13)	21	0.28
Filipino (16)	23	0.31
Indian (11)	15	0.20
Japanese (8)	16	0.21
Korean (8)	13	0.17
Laotian (0)	1	0.01
Thai (5)	9	0.12
Vietnamese (2)	5	0.07
Hawaii Native/Pacific Islander (3)	19	0.25
Not Hispanic (3)	17	0.23
Hispanic (0)	2	0.03
Guamanian/Chamorro (1)	3	0.04
Native Hawaiian (1)	6	0.08
Samoan (1)	5	0.07
White (7,010)	7,206	95.89
Not Hispanic (6,720)	6,877	91.51
Hispanic (290)	329	4.38

Gresham

Place Type: City
County: Multnomah
Population: 105,594†

Ancestry‡	Population	%
African, Sub-Saharan (482)	690	0.68
African (392)	600	0.59
Ethiopian (12)	12	0.01
Sierra Leonean (78)	78	0.08
American (4,249)	4,249	4.19
Arab (698)	759	0.75
Arab (46)	72	0.07
Egyptian (110)	110	0.11
Jordanian (27)	27	0.03
Lebanese (462)	476	0.47
Syrian (53)	74	0.07
Armenian (61)	80	0.08
Austrian (11)	103	0.10
Basque (0)	39	0.04
Belgian (14)	42	0.04
Brazilian (29)	29	0.03
British (238)	578	0.57
Bulgarian (0)	12	0.01
Cajun (0)	43	0.04
Canadian (199)	363	0.36
Celtic (37)	37	0.04
Croatian (55)	120	0.12
Czech (137)	452	0.45
Czechoslovakian (235)	349	0.34
Danish (331)	1,109	1.09
Dutch (421)	1,615	1.59
Eastern European (9)	9	0.01
English (3,223)	10,237	10.09
European (1,343)	1,733	1.71
Finnish (145)	490	0.48
French, ex. Basque (263)	3,372	3.32
French Canadian (266)	783	0.77
German (5,939)	19,393	19.12
German Russian (0)	12	0.01
Greek (74)	215	0.21
Guyanese (36)	36	0.04
Hungarian (67)	279	0.28
Icelander (15)	15	0.01
Iranian (21)	21	0.02
Irish (2,978)	10,233	10.09
Israeli (39)	39	0.04
Italian (1,078)	3,331	3.28
Lithuanian (27)	76	0.07
Luxemburger (18)	18	0.02
Macedonian (7)	118	0.12
New Zealander (0)	10	0.01
Northern European (89)	109	0.11
Norwegian (1,412)	4,152	4.09
Pennsylvania German (10)	40	0.04
Polish (449)	1,509	1.49
Portuguese (151)	294	0.29
Romanian (1,285)	1,399	1.38
Russian (875)	1,672	1.65
Scandinavian (221)	414	0.41
Scotch-Irish (625)	1,738	1.71
Scottish (547)	2,348	2.31
Serbian (0)	12	0.01
Slavic (22)	40	0.04
Slovak (41)	67	0.07
Slovene (0)	16	0.02
Swedish (655)	2,642	2.60
Swiss (230)	592	0.58
Ukrainian (986)	1,136	1.12
Welsh (134)	798	0.79
West Indian, ex. Hispanic (8)	8	0.01
British West Indian (8)	8	0.01

*Notes: † The Census 2010 population figure is used to calculate the percentages in the Hispanic Origin and Race categories. Ancestry percentages are based on the 2006-2010 American Community Survey population (not shown); ‡ Numbers in parentheses indicate the number of people reporting a single ancestry; * Numbers in parentheses indicate the number of persons reporting this race alone, not in combination with any other race; Please refer to the Explanation of Data for more information.*

Yugoslavian (16)	67	0.07

Hispanic Origin	Population	%
Hispanic or Latino (of any race)	19,984	18.93
Central American, ex. Mexican	719	0.68
Costa Rican	32	0.03
Guatemalan	259	0.25
Honduran	69	0.07
Nicaraguan	49	0.05
Panamanian	22	0.02
Salvadoran	269	0.25
Other Central American	19	0.02
Cuban	326	0.31
Dominican Republic	24	0.02
Mexican	16,995	16.09
Puerto Rican	236	0.22
South American	302	0.29
Argentinean	26	0.02
Bolivian	3	<0.01
Chilean	49	0.05
Colombian	89	0.08
Ecuadorian	17	0.02
Paraguayan	1	<0.01
Peruvian	87	0.08
Uruguayan	10	0.01
Venezuelan	10	0.01
Other South American	10	0.01
Other Hispanic or Latino	1,382	1.31

Race*	Population	%
African-American/Black (3,732)	5,132	4.86
Not Hispanic (3,530)	4,718	4.47
Hispanic (202)	414	0.39
American Indian/Alaska Native (1,343)	2,723	2.58
Not Hispanic (808)	1,894	1.79
Hispanic (535)	829	0.79
Alaska Athabascan *(Ala. Nat.)* (6)	12	0.01
Aleut *(Alaska Native)* (3)	10	0.01
Apache (8)	28	0.03
Arapaho (1)	1	<0.01
Blackfeet (25)	101	0.10
Canadian/French Am. Ind. (2)	7	0.01
Central American Ind. (2)	2	<0.01
Cherokee (81)	370	0.35
Cheyenne (10)	29	0.03
Chickasaw (14)	30	0.03
Chippewa (44)	95	0.09
Choctaw (16)	60	0.06
Colville (5)	6	0.01
Comanche (2)	5	<0.01
Cree (2)	9	0.01
Creek (7)	20	0.02
Crow (3)	13	0.01
Delaware (1)	7	0.01
Inupiat *(Alaska Native)* (7)	12	0.01
Iroquois (5)	18	0.02
Kiowa (2)	2	<0.01
Lumbee (0)	4	<0.01
Menominee (1)	2	<0.01
Mexican American Ind. (249)	319	0.30
Navajo (26)	50	0.05
Osage (2)	8	0.01
Ottawa (1)	7	0.01
Paiute (4)	8	0.01
Pima (16)	18	0.02
Potawatomi (1)	9	0.01
Pueblo (5)	9	0.01
Puget Sound Salish (5)	8	0.01
Seminole (2)	7	0.01
Shoshone (1)	6	0.01
Sioux (47)	106	0.10
South American Ind. (6)	7	0.01
Spanish American Ind. (8)	12	0.01
Tlingit-Haida *(Alaska Native)* (24)	38	0.04
Tohono O'Odham (4)	4	<0.01
Tsimshian *(Alaska Native)* (4)	4	<0.01
Ute (1)	5	<0.01
Yakama (11)	23	0.02
Yaqui (4)	9	0.01
Asian (4,507)	5,936	5.62
Not Hispanic (4,446)	5,739	5.43
Hispanic (61)	197	0.19
Bhutanese (22)	22	0.02
Burmese (18)	34	0.03
Cambodian (139)	169	0.16
Chinese, ex. Taiwanese (546)	819	0.78
Filipino (784)	1,274	1.21
Hmong (436)	450	0.43
Indian (176)	280	0.27
Indonesian (36)	71	0.07
Japanese (346)	717	0.68
Korean (286)	438	0.41
Laotian (461)	569	0.54
Malaysian (10)	11	0.01
Nepalese (9)	13	0.01
Pakistani (15)	25	0.02
Sri Lankan (3)	5	<0.01
Taiwanese (15)	16	0.02
Thai (63)	120	0.11
Vietnamese (842)	975	0.92
Hawaii Native/Pacific Islander (717)	1,173	1.11
Not Hispanic (698)	1,083	1.03
Hispanic (19)	90	0.09
Fijian (27)	42	0.04
Guamanian/Chamorro (91)	130	0.12
Marshallese (1)	3	<0.01
Native Hawaiian (121)	346	0.33
Samoan (104)	144	0.14
Tongan (36)	39	0.04
White (80,260)	84,477	80.00
Not Hispanic (72,549)	75,636	71.63
Hispanic (7,711)	8,841	8.37

Happy Valley

Place Type: City
County: Clackamas
Population: 13,903†

Ancestry‡	Population	%
American (495)	495	3.93
Arab (230)	239	1.90
Arab (102)	102	0.81
Lebanese (14)	23	0.18
Syrian (114)	114	0.91
Armenian (0)	15	0.12
Austrian (0)	22	0.17
Belgian (0)	18	0.14
British (59)	113	0.90
Bulgarian (114)	135	1.07
Canadian (13)	26	0.21
Croatian (11)	20	0.16
Czech (0)	61	0.48
Czechoslovakian (0)	17	0.14
Danish (20)	111	0.88
Dutch (4)	126	1.00
English (603)	1,619	12.87
European (233)	233	1.85
Finnish (0)	53	0.42
French, ex. Basque (21)	281	2.23
German (816)	2,182	17.34
Greek (0)	32	0.25
Guyanese (12)	26	0.21
Hungarian (9)	26	0.21
Icelander (0)	5	0.04
Irish (321)	1,290	10.25
Italian (123)	558	4.43
Lithuanian (11)	22	0.17
Northern European (25)	25	0.20
Norwegian (202)	684	5.44
Polish (63)	275	2.19
Romanian (89)	89	0.71
Russian (224)	346	2.75
Scandinavian (63)	78	0.62
Scotch-Irish (0)	159	1.26
Scottish (195)	368	2.92
Swedish (152)	332	2.64
Swiss (0)	7	0.06
Ukrainian (651)	753	5.98
Welsh (70)	169	1.34

Hispanic Origin	Population	%
Hispanic or Latino (of any race)	563	4.05
Central American, ex. Mexican	24	0.17
Costa Rican	1	0.01
Guatemalan	4	0.03
Honduran	3	0.02
Nicaraguan	1	0.01
Panamanian	7	0.05
Salvadoran	8	0.06
Cuban	24	0.17
Dominican Republic	1	0.01
Mexican	370	2.66
Puerto Rican	22	0.16
South American	49	0.35
Argentinean	7	0.05
Bolivian	3	0.02
Chilean	5	0.04
Colombian	21	0.15
Ecuadorian	1	0.01
Peruvian	11	0.08
Other South American	1	0.01
Other Hispanic or Latino	73	0.53

Race*	Population	%
African-American/Black (150)	236	1.70
Not Hispanic (138)	216	1.55
Hispanic (12)	20	0.14
American Indian/Alaska Native (68)	154	1.11
Not Hispanic (60)	137	0.99
Hispanic (8)	17	0.12
Alaska Athabascan *(Ala. Nat.)* (1)	3	0.02
Aleut *(Alaska Native)* (0)	5	0.04
Apache (2)	2	0.01
Arapaho (0)	3	0.02
Blackfeet (2)	2	0.01
Cherokee (3)	14	0.10
Chickasaw (1)	1	0.01
Chippewa (2)	5	0.04
Colville (0)	1	0.01
Creek (0)	4	0.03
Kiowa (0)	3	0.02
Mexican American Ind. (1)	1	0.01
Navajo (0)	4	0.03
Osage (0)	3	0.02
Paiute (2)	3	0.02
Potawatomi (0)	1	0.01
Pueblo (1)	1	0.01
Sioux (8)	9	0.06
Asian (2,417)	2,728	19.62
Not Hispanic (2,406)	2,696	19.39
Hispanic (11)	32	0.23
Burmese (13)	13	0.09
Cambodian (49)	62	0.45
Chinese, ex. Taiwanese (530)	673	4.84
Filipino (136)	208	1.50
Hmong (26)	31	0.22
Indian (164)	200	1.44
Indonesian (7)	17	0.12
Japanese (77)	184	1.32
Korean (422)	475	3.42
Laotian (68)	81	0.58
Malaysian (0)	2	0.01
Pakistani (24)	24	0.17
Sri Lankan (5)	5	0.04
Taiwanese (23)	24	0.17
Thai (8)	12	0.09
Vietnamese (742)	819	5.89
Hawaii Native/Pacific Islander (21)	57	0.41
Not Hispanic (19)	50	0.36
Hispanic (2)	7	0.05
Guamanian/Chamorro (3)	10	0.07
Marshallese (1)	1	0.01
Native Hawaiian (4)	24	0.17
Samoan (0)	3	0.02
Tongan (3)	5	0.04
White (10,590)	11,089	79.76
Not Hispanic (10,267)	10,676	76.79
Hispanic (323)	413	2.97

SECTION TWO

*Notes: † The Census 2010 population figure is used to calculate the percentages in the Hispanic Origin and Race categories. Ancestry percentages are based on the 2006-2010 American Community Survey population (not shown); ‡ Numbers in parentheses indicate the number of people reporting a single ancestry; * Numbers in parentheses indicate the number of persons reporting this race alone, not in combination with any other race; Please refer to the Explanation of Data for more information.*

Hayesville

Place Type: CDP
County: Marion
Population: 19,936†

Ancestry‡	Population	%
African, Sub-Saharan (0)	9	0.05
African (0)	9	0.05
American (640)	640	3.25
Austrian (0)	8	0.04
Basque (43)	86	0.44
Belgian (15)	15	0.08
British (14)	28	0.14
Canadian (67)	99	0.50
Czech (97)	116	0.59
Czechoslovakian (12)	12	0.06
Danish (48)	221	1.12
Dutch (72)	406	2.06
Eastern European (15)	15	0.08
English (252)	1,464	7.43
European (330)	363	1.84
Finnish (8)	51	0.26
French, ex. Basque (37)	513	2.60
French Canadian (41)	141	0.72
German (1,181)	3,398	17.24
Greek (8)	107	0.54
Hungarian (0)	38	0.19
Irish (289)	1,787	9.07
Italian (150)	361	1.83
Lithuanian (15)	25	0.13
Norwegian (151)	577	2.93
Pennsylvania German (0)	17	0.09
Polish (82)	223	1.13
Romanian (13)	13	0.07
Russian (52)	113	0.57
Scandinavian (24)	115	0.58
Scotch-Irish (34)	294	1.49
Scottish (54)	298	1.51
Slovak (0)	8	0.04
Swedish (52)	403	2.04
Swiss (21)	79	0.40
Ukrainian (203)	246	1.25
Welsh (7)	159	0.81
West Indian, ex. Hispanic (48)	75	0.38
Haitian (48)	75	0.38
Yugoslavian (18)	18	0.09

Hispanic Origin	Population	%
Hispanic or Latino (of any race)	7,932	39.79
Central American, ex. Mexican	189	0.95
Costa Rican	1	0.01
Guatemalan	65	0.33
Honduran	26	0.13
Nicaraguan	5	0.03
Panamanian	1	0.01
Salvadoran	91	0.46
Cuban	13	0.07
Dominican Republic	5	0.03
Mexican	7,150	35.86
Puerto Rican	38	0.19
South American	42	0.21
Argentinean	2	0.01
Bolivian	3	0.02
Chilean	4	0.02
Colombian	7	0.04
Ecuadorian	4	0.02
Peruvian	16	0.08
Uruguayan	1	0.01
Venezuelan	5	0.03
Other Hispanic or Latino	495	2.48

Race*	Population	%
African-American/Black (232)	391	1.96
Not Hispanic (188)	304	1.52
Hispanic (44)	87	0.44
American Indian/Alaska Native (352)	662	3.32
Not Hispanic (236)	480	2.41
Hispanic (116)	182	0.91
Alaska Athabascan *(Ala. Nat.)* (3)	3	0.02
Apache (1)	11	0.06
Blackfeet (17)	26	0.13
Cherokee (15)	75	0.38
Cheyenne (3)	5	0.03
Chickasaw (3)	3	0.02
Chippewa (5)	16	0.08
Choctaw (9)	20	0.10
Colville (2)	2	0.01
Creek (0)	2	0.01
Inupiat *(Alaska Native)* (2)	2	0.01
Iroquois (0)	5	0.03
Kiowa (0)	1	0.01
Lumbee (1)	1	0.01
Mexican American Ind. (39)	52	0.26
Navajo (9)	15	0.08
Osage (3)	8	0.04
Ottawa (2)	3	0.02
Paiute (6)	8	0.04
Pima (1)	1	0.01
Potawatomi (1)	1	0.01
Pueblo (1)	1	0.01
Puget Sound Salish (0)	1	0.01
Shoshone (0)	1	0.01
Sioux (10)	30	0.15
South American Ind. (0)	5	0.03
Spanish American Ind. (1)	1	0.01
Tlingit-Haida *(Alaska Native)* (1)	1	0.01
Tohono O'Odham (1)	1	0.01
Yakama (4)	6	0.03
Yup'ik *(Alaska Native)* (0)	14	0.07
Asian (578)	719	3.61
Not Hispanic (557)	679	3.41
Hispanic (21)	40	0.20
Bangladeshi (0)	4	0.02
Cambodian (36)	49	0.25
Chinese, ex. Taiwanese (89)	121	0.61
Filipino (104)	167	0.84
Hmong (49)	52	0.26
Indian (28)	31	0.16
Indonesian (1)	1	0.01
Japanese (23)	53	0.27
Korean (26)	36	0.18
Laotian (32)	35	0.18
Pakistani (0)	3	0.02
Sri Lankan (0)	3	0.02
Thai (7)	10	0.05
Vietnamese (150)	171	0.86
Hawaii Native/Pacific Islander (288)	381	1.91
Not Hispanic (278)	352	1.77
Hispanic (10)	29	0.15
Guamanian/Chamorro (58)	66	0.33
Marshallese (25)	27	0.14
Native Hawaiian (18)	51	0.26
Samoan (1)	8	0.04
Tongan (5)	5	0.03
White (13,138)	13,942	69.93
Not Hispanic (10,241)	10,667	53.51
Hispanic (2,897)	3,275	16.43

Hermiston

Place Type: City
County: Umatilla
Population: 16,745†

Ancestry‡	Population	%
African, Sub-Saharan (7)	7	0.04
African (7)	7	0.04
American (786)	786	4.91
Australian (0)	7	0.04
British (16)	41	0.26
Canadian (19)	74	0.46
Czech (14)	39	0.24
Czechoslovakian (14)	27	0.17
Danish (0)	93	0.58
Dutch (54)	299	1.87
English (484)	1,680	10.49
European (163)	239	1.49
Finnish (7)	20	0.12
French, ex. Basque (33)	179	1.12
French Canadian (99)	195	1.22
German (922)	2,680	16.73
Icelander (0)	31	0.19
Irish (226)	1,675	10.46
Italian (274)	540	3.37
Norwegian (120)	481	3.00
Polish (8)	138	0.86
Portuguese (0)	11	0.07
Russian (34)	103	0.64
Scandinavian (13)	82	0.51
Scotch-Irish (187)	362	2.26
Scottish (98)	378	2.36
Slovak (10)	31	0.19
Swedish (56)	309	1.93
Swiss (0)	26	0.16
Welsh (21)	152	0.95

Hispanic Origin	Population	%
Hispanic or Latino (of any race)	5,852	34.95
Central American, ex. Mexican	136	0.81
Costa Rican	1	0.01
Guatemalan	37	0.22
Honduran	24	0.14
Nicaraguan	4	0.02
Salvadoran	69	0.41
Other Central American	1	0.01
Cuban	7	0.04
Mexican	5,334	31.85
Puerto Rican	22	0.13
South American	36	0.21
Argentinean	7	0.04
Colombian	2	0.01
Ecuadorian	5	0.03
Paraguayan	1	0.01
Peruvian	21	0.13
Other Hispanic or Latino	317	1.89

Race*	Population	%
African-American/Black (136)	193	1.15
Not Hispanic (94)	140	0.84
Hispanic (42)	53	0.32
American Indian/Alaska Native (221)	397	2.37
Not Hispanic (135)	263	1.57
Hispanic (86)	134	0.80
Alaska Athabascan *(Ala. Nat.)* (2)	3	0.02
Aleut *(Alaska Native)* (0)	1	0.01
Apache (1)	2	0.01
Blackfeet (1)	7	0.04
Central American Ind. (2)	2	0.01
Cherokee (18)	50	0.30
Chickasaw (0)	1	0.01
Chippewa (6)	14	0.08
Choctaw (2)	13	0.08
Comanche (0)	2	0.01
Crow (2)	2	0.01
Inupiat *(Alaska Native)* (1)	4	0.02
Iroquois (1)	1	0.01
Lumbee (0)	1	0.01
Mexican American Ind. (31)	46	0.27
Navajo (5)	5	0.03
Osage (1)	1	0.01
Potawatomi (1)	1	0.01
Puget Sound Salish (1)	1	0.01
Seminole (1)	1	0.01
Shoshone (0)	3	0.02
Sioux (7)	23	0.14
South American Ind. (1)	1	0.01
Spanish American Ind. (0)	1	0.01
Tlingit-Haida *(Alaska Native)* (4)	6	0.04
Tsimshian *(Alaska Native)* (4)	4	0.02
Yakama (3)	4	0.02
Asian (252)	350	2.09
Not Hispanic (238)	306	1.83
Hispanic (14)	44	0.26
Cambodian (25)	25	0.15
Chinese, ex. Taiwanese (41)	60	0.36
Filipino (49)	68	0.41
Indian (11)	19	0.11
Indonesian (2)	8	0.05
Japanese (14)	29	0.17

*Notes: † The Census 2010 population figure is used to calculate the percentages in the Hispanic Origin and Race categories. Ancestry percentages are based on the 2006-2010 American Community Survey population (not shown); ‡ Numbers in parentheses indicate the number of people reporting a single ancestry; * Numbers in parentheses indicate the number of persons reporting this race alone, not in combination with any other race; Please refer to the Explanation of Data for more information.*

Korean (15)	30	0.18
Laotian (15)	20	0.12
Nepalese (1)	1	0.01
Sri Lankan (6)	6	0.04
Taiwanese (2)	2	0.01
Thai (8)	19	0.11
Vietnamese (45)	50	0.30
Hawaii Native/Pacific Islander (39)	58	0.35
Not Hispanic (36)	43	0.26
Hispanic (3)	15	0.09
Fijian (0)	4	0.02
Guamanian/Chamorro (1)	2	0.01
Native Hawaiian (12)	16	0.10
Samoan (12)	16	0.10
Tongan (0)	4	0.02
White (12,420)	12,866	76.83
Not Hispanic (10,138)	10,373	61.95
Hispanic (2,282)	2,493	14.89

Hillsboro

Place Type: City
County: Washington
Population: 91,611†

Ancestry‡	Population	%
Afghan (35)	35	0.04
African, Sub-Saharan (474)	523	0.59
African (199)	236	0.27
Ethiopian (17)	17	0.02
Nigerian (49)	49	0.06
Somalian (199)	199	0.23
Other Sub-Saharan African (10)	22	0.02
Albanian (0)	13	0.01
American (2,538)	2,538	2.88
Arab (175)	268	0.30
Arab (7)	7	0.01
Egyptian (94)	94	0.11
Lebanese (0)	14	0.02
Moroccan (22)	68	0.08
Palestinian (9)	9	0.01
Other Arab (43)	76	0.09
Australian (60)	93	0.11
Austrian (62)	219	0.25
Basque (26)	26	0.03
Belgian (149)	383	0.43
Brazilian (41)	67	0.08
British (166)	486	0.55
Canadian (123)	273	0.31
Croatian (12)	125	0.14
Cypriot (0)	13	0.01
Czech (144)	523	0.59
Czechoslovakian (101)	173	0.20
Danish (208)	953	1.08
Dutch (541)	1,922	2.18
Eastern European (22)	75	0.09
English (2,648)	8,139	9.24
European (1,711)	2,031	2.30
Finnish (160)	334	0.38
French, ex. Basque (433)	2,413	2.74
French Canadian (214)	676	0.77
German (5,829)	16,251	18.44
Greek (91)	269	0.31
Hungarian (163)	245	0.28
Icelander (12)	38	0.04
Iranian (48)	81	0.09
Irish (2,295)	8,760	9.94
Italian (1,114)	2,789	3.16
Lithuanian (14)	14	0.02
Luxemburger (16)	16	0.02
New Zealander (21)	65	0.07
Northern European (254)	254	0.29
Norwegian (1,234)	3,221	3.66
Pennsylvania German (25)	50	0.06
Polish (449)	1,264	1.43
Portuguese (131)	287	0.33
Romanian (34)	51	0.06
Russian (247)	798	0.91
Scandinavian (439)	909	1.03
Scotch-Irish (684)	1,639	1.86
Scottish (722)	2,704	3.07
Serbian (17)	67	0.08
Slavic (19)	19	0.02
Slovak (32)	78	0.09
Slovene (40)	40	0.05
Swedish (547)	2,585	2.93
Swiss (98)	562	0.64
Turkish (23)	23	0.03
Ukrainian (92)	217	0.25
Welsh (257)	1,096	1.24
West Indian, ex. Hispanic (91)	122	0.14
Jamaican (0)	31	0.04
West Indian (91)	91	0.10
Yugoslavian (38)	38	0.04

Hispanic Origin	Population	%
Hispanic or Latino (of any race)	20,726	22.62
Central American, ex. Mexican	1,005	1.10
Costa Rican	47	0.05
Guatemalan	604	0.66
Honduran	70	0.08
Nicaraguan	63	0.07
Panamanian	27	0.03
Salvadoran	188	0.21
Other Central American	6	0.01
Cuban	123	0.13
Dominican Republic	28	0.03
Mexican	17,490	19.09
Puerto Rican	400	0.44
South American	376	0.41
Argentinean	33	0.04
Bolivian	19	0.02
Chilean	45	0.05
Colombian	65	0.07
Ecuadorian	28	0.03
Paraguayan	4	<0.01
Peruvian	109	0.12
Uruguayan	7	0.01
Venezuelan	64	0.07
Other South American	2	<0.01
Other Hispanic or Latino	1,304	1.42

Race*	Population	%
African-American/Black (1,812)	2,598	2.84
Not Hispanic (1,635)	2,293	2.50
Hispanic (177)	305	0.33
American Indian/Alaska Native (943)	1,960	2.14
Not Hispanic (515)	1,287	1.40
Hispanic (428)	673	0.73
Alaska Athabascan *(Ala. Nat.)* (3)	9	0.01
Aleut *(Alaska Native)* (4)	16	0.02
Apache (7)	26	0.03
Blackfeet (9)	46	0.05
Canadian/French Am. Ind. (6)	11	0.01
Central American Ind. (12)	16	0.02
Cherokee (56)	251	0.27
Cheyenne (4)	9	0.01
Chickasaw (2)	2	<0.01
Chippewa (14)	54	0.06
Choctaw (24)	56	0.06
Colville (2)	3	<0.01
Comanche (4)	7	0.01
Cree (0)	6	0.01
Creek (1)	12	0.01
Crow (5)	12	0.01
Delaware (1)	3	<0.01
Hopi (0)	1	<0.01
Inupiat *(Alaska Native)* (7)	10	0.01
Iroquois (11)	20	0.02
Kiowa (1)	1	<0.01
Lumbee (4)	4	<0.01
Mexican American Ind. (121)	164	0.18
Navajo (22)	41	0.04
Osage (3)	5	0.01
Ottawa (2)	3	<0.01
Paiute (12)	15	0.02
Potawatomi (9)	17	0.02
Pueblo (6)	9	0.01
Puget Sound Salish (6)	14	0.02
Seminole (1)	8	0.01
Shoshone (3)	5	0.01
Sioux (30)	69	0.08
South American Ind. (7)	20	0.02
Spanish American Ind. (1)	2	<0.01
Tlingit-Haida *(Alaska Native)* (8)	19	0.02
Tohono O'Odham (0)	1	<0.01
Tsimshian *(Alaska Native)* (1)	1	<0.01
Ute (1)	1	<0.01
Yakama (7)	7	0.01
Yaqui (5)	8	0.01
Yup'ik *(Alaska Native)* (2)	5	0.01
Asian (7,872)	9,694	10.58
Not Hispanic (7,782)	9,410	10.27
Hispanic (90)	284	0.31
Bangladeshi (28)	34	0.04
Burmese (12)	12	0.01
Cambodian (308)	361	0.39
Chinese, ex. Taiwanese (948)	1,412	1.54
Filipino (1,194)	1,915	2.09
Hmong (171)	188	0.21
Indian (1,994)	2,144	2.34
Indonesian (70)	92	0.10
Japanese (457)	911	0.99
Korean (520)	742	0.81
Laotian (226)	284	0.31
Malaysian (13)	18	0.02
Nepalese (47)	48	0.05
Pakistani (51)	58	0.06
Sri Lankan (37)	46	0.05
Taiwanese (80)	90	0.10
Thai (89)	135	0.15
Vietnamese (1,303)	1,449	1.58
Hawaii Native/Pacific Islander (412)	955	1.04
Not Hispanic (366)	825	0.90
Hispanic (46)	130	0.14
Fijian (36)	46	0.05
Guamanian/Chamorro (132)	202	0.22
Marshallese (1)	4	<0.01
Native Hawaiian (124)	477	0.52
Samoan (36)	84	0.09
Tongan (16)	23	0.03
White (67,145)	70,861	77.35
Not Hispanic (57,442)	60,089	65.59
Hispanic (9,703)	10,772	11.76

Independence

Place Type: City
County: Polk
Population: 8,590†

Ancestry‡	Population	%
American (402)	402	4.89
Austrian (0)	17	0.21
Brazilian (11)	11	0.13
British (11)	11	0.13
Croatian (25)	36	0.44
Czech (46)	72	0.88
Danish (72)	157	1.91
Dutch (0)	103	1.25
English (175)	722	8.79
European (43)	58	0.71
Finnish (0)	13	0.16
French, ex. Basque (84)	180	2.19
French Canadian (247)	260	3.16
German (246)	1,166	14.19
Hungarian (0)	72	0.88
Icelander (0)	18	0.22
Irish (113)	336	4.09
Italian (51)	134	1.63
Norwegian (58)	210	2.56
Polish (12)	12	0.15
Romanian (75)	75	0.91
Russian (9)	19	0.23
Scandinavian (0)	24	0.29
Scotch-Irish (121)	240	2.92
Scottish (0)	170	2.07
Swedish (56)	99	1.21
Swiss (13)	27	0.33
Ukrainian (0)	17	0.21

*Notes: † The Census 2010 population figure is used to calculate the percentages in the Hispanic Origin and Race categories. Ancestry percentages are based on the 2006-2010 American Community Survey population (not shown); ‡ Numbers in parentheses indicate the number of people reporting a single ancestry; * Numbers in parentheses indicate the number of persons reporting this race alone, not in combination with any other race; Please refer to the Explanation of Data for more information.*

Welsh (12)	61	0.74

Hispanic Origin	Population	%
Hispanic or Latino (of any race)	3,031	35.29
Central American, ex. Mexican	27	0.31
Guatemalan	5	0.06
Honduran	2	0.02
Nicaraguan	1	0.01
Panamanian	3	0.03
Salvadoran	16	0.19
Cuban	9	0.10
Dominican Republic	6	0.07
Mexican	2,830	32.95
Puerto Rican	24	0.28
South American	7	0.08
Argentinean	1	0.01
Chilean	1	0.01
Colombian	4	0.05
Venezuelan	1	0.01
Other Hispanic or Latino	128	1.49

Race*	Population	%
African-American/Black (33)	89	1.04
Not Hispanic (28)	71	0.83
Hispanic (5)	18	0.21
American Indian/Alaska Native (157)	301	3.50
Not Hispanic (95)	215	2.50
Hispanic (62)	86	1.00
Alaska Athabascan *(Ala. Nat.)* (1)	1	0.01
Aleut *(Alaska Native)* (2)	2	0.02
Apache (1)	9	0.10
Blackfeet (1)	7	0.08
Cherokee (14)	47	0.55
Chickasaw (2)	3	0.03
Chippewa (2)	7	0.08
Choctaw (4)	6	0.07
Comanche (0)	2	0.02
Creek (0)	3	0.03
Lumbee (4)	4	0.05
Mexican American Ind. (28)	30	0.35
Navajo (7)	8	0.09
Pueblo (0)	5	0.06
Seminole (0)	2	0.02
Sioux (3)	4	0.05
Spanish American Ind. (1)	1	0.01
Tlingit-Haida *(Alaska Native)* (2)	3	0.03
Tsimshian *(Alaska Native)* (6)	6	0.07
Yaqui (0)	3	0.03
Yup'ik *(Alaska Native)* (0)	1	0.01
Asian (102)	157	1.83
Not Hispanic (94)	146	1.70
Hispanic (8)	11	0.13
Chinese, ex. Taiwanese (29)	33	0.38
Filipino (21)	41	0.48
Hmong (2)	2	0.02
Indian (19)	27	0.31
Indonesian (1)	1	0.01
Japanese (12)	31	0.36
Korean (10)	11	0.13
Laotian (1)	4	0.05
Pakistani (0)	1	0.01
Taiwanese (1)	1	0.01
Vietnamese (3)	4	0.05
Hawaii Native/Pacific Islander (14)	50	0.58
Not Hispanic (11)	40	0.47
Hispanic (3)	10	0.12
Marshallese (2)	3	0.03
Native Hawaiian (4)	25	0.29
Samoan (0)	7	0.08
Tongan (2)	5	0.06
White (6,296)	6,618	77.04
Not Hispanic (5,104)	5,311	61.83
Hispanic (1,192)	1,307	15.22

Keizer

Place Type: City
County: Marion
Population: 36,478†

Ancestry‡	Population	%
African, Sub-Saharan (76)	95	0.27
African (50)	69	0.19
Somalian (26)	26	0.07
Alsatian (0)	12	0.03
American (2,100)	2,100	5.88
Arab (0)	11	0.03
Jordanian (0)	11	0.03
Armenian (72)	72	0.20
Australian (12)	12	0.03
Austrian (18)	55	0.15
Basque (0)	6	0.02
Belgian (15)	71	0.20
British (70)	136	0.38
Canadian (49)	117	0.33
Czech (54)	180	0.50
Czechoslovakian (13)	13	0.04
Danish (41)	195	0.55
Dutch (425)	1,373	3.84
English (1,280)	4,183	11.71
Estonian (8)	8	0.02
European (1,340)	1,449	4.06
Finnish (50)	105	0.29
French, ex. Basque (221)	1,573	4.40
French Canadian (76)	185	0.52
German (2,849)	8,996	25.18
Greek (68)	95	0.27
Hungarian (13)	61	0.17
Iranian (50)	50	0.14
Irish (967)	4,461	12.49
Italian (399)	1,282	3.59
Lithuanian (21)	80	0.22
New Zealander (0)	26	0.07
Northern European (0)	22	0.06
Norwegian (500)	1,161	3.25
Pennsylvania German (20)	58	0.16
Polish (176)	713	2.00
Portuguese (34)	190	0.53
Russian (61)	233	0.65
Scandinavian (117)	287	0.80
Scotch-Irish (177)	698	1.95
Scottish (115)	990	2.77
Serbian (0)	17	0.05
Slovak (10)	21	0.06
Swedish (229)	1,003	2.81
Swiss (151)	410	1.15
Ukrainian (134)	161	0.45
Welsh (132)	473	1.32
West Indian, ex. Hispanic (0)	49	0.14
Dutch West Indian (0)	38	0.11
Haitian (0)	11	0.03
Yugoslavian (0)	14	0.04

Hispanic Origin	Population	%
Hispanic or Latino (of any race)	6,693	18.35
Central American, ex. Mexican	180	0.49
Costa Rican	15	0.04
Guatemalan	48	0.13
Honduran	5	0.01
Nicaraguan	4	0.01
Panamanian	14	0.04
Salvadoran	94	0.26
Cuban	20	0.05
Dominican Republic	3	0.01
Mexican	5,796	15.89
Puerto Rican	80	0.22
South American	64	0.18
Argentinean	2	0.01
Bolivian	4	0.01
Chilean	9	0.02
Colombian	15	0.04
Ecuadorian	5	0.01
Paraguayan	2	0.01
Peruvian	13	0.04
Venezuelan	14	0.04
Other Hispanic or Latino	550	1.51

Race*	Population	%
African-American/Black (289)	532	1.46
Not Hispanic (248)	435	1.19
Hispanic (41)	97	0.27
American Indian/Alaska Native (480)	988	2.71
Not Hispanic (373)	756	2.07
Hispanic (107)	232	0.64
Alaska Athabascan *(Ala. Nat.)* (4)	10	0.03
Aleut *(Alaska Native)* (7)	9	0.02
Apache (4)	29	0.08
Blackfeet (10)	19	0.05
Canadian/French Am. Ind. (4)	5	0.01
Cherokee (40)	112	0.31
Cheyenne (11)	13	0.04
Chickasaw (1)	4	0.01
Chippewa (9)	21	0.06
Choctaw (14)	35	0.10
Colville (0)	2	0.01
Comanche (2)	5	0.01
Creek (4)	7	0.02
Delaware (0)	4	0.01
Hopi (4)	4	0.01
Inupiat *(Alaska Native)* (1)	12	0.03
Iroquois (5)	18	0.05
Kiowa (5)	5	0.01
Mexican American Ind. (11)	26	0.07
Navajo (9)	14	0.04
Osage (0)	4	0.01
Ottawa (0)	3	0.01
Paiute (4)	4	0.01
Pima (0)	1	<0.01
Potawatomi (1)	3	0.01
Pueblo (2)	7	0.02
Puget Sound Salish (4)	5	0.01
Shoshone (0)	1	<0.01
Sioux (27)	57	0.16
Spanish American Ind. (1)	1	<0.01
Tlingit-Haida *(Alaska Native)* (14)	32	0.09
Tsimshian *(Alaska Native)* (1)	1	<0.01
Ute (2)	2	0.01
Yakama (3)	4	0.01
Yaqui (1)	2	0.01
Yup'ik *(Alaska Native)* (1)	11	0.03
Asian (599)	1,014	2.78
Not Hispanic (569)	910	2.49
Hispanic (30)	104	0.29
Bangladeshi (3)	3	0.01
Cambodian (37)	47	0.13
Chinese, ex. Taiwanese (88)	148	0.41
Filipino (149)	326	0.89
Hmong (5)	6	0.02
Indian (83)	107	0.29
Indonesian (0)	4	0.01
Japanese (75)	187	0.51
Korean (66)	101	0.28
Laotian (10)	14	0.04
Nepalese (4)	4	0.01
Pakistani (1)	2	0.01
Taiwanese (1)	3	0.01
Thai (11)	18	0.05
Vietnamese (36)	58	0.16
Hawaii Native/Pacific Islander (230)	370	1.01
Not Hispanic (224)	351	0.96
Hispanic (6)	19	0.05
Fijian (1)	1	<0.01
Guamanian/Chamorro (21)	35	0.10
Marshallese (78)	78	0.21
Native Hawaiian (49)	121	0.33
Samoan (14)	37	0.10
Tongan (0)	1	<0.01
White (30,110)	31,468	86.27
Not Hispanic (27,390)	28,253	77.45
Hispanic (2,720)	3,215	8.81

Klamath Falls

Place Type: City
County: Klamath
Population: 20,840†

Ancestry‡	Population	%
African, Sub-Saharan (0)	15	0.07
African (0)	15	0.07

*Notes: † The Census 2010 population figure is used to calculate the percentages in the Hispanic Origin and Race categories. Ancestry percentages are based on the 2006-2010 American Community Survey population (not shown); ‡ Numbers in parentheses indicate the number of people reporting a single ancestry; * Numbers in parentheses indicate the number of persons reporting this race alone, not in combination with any other race; Please refer to the Explanation of Data for more information.*

American (1,058)	1,058	5.07
Arab (63)	63	0.30
Other Arab (63)	63	0.30
Armenian (24)	24	0.12
Belgian (9)	29	0.14
British (20)	44	0.21
Canadian (71)	81	0.39
Celtic (0)	10	0.05
Croatian (0)	17	0.08
Czech (26)	128	0.61
Czechoslovakian (0)	43	0.21
Danish (71)	237	1.14
Dutch (45)	399	1.91
Eastern European (19)	19	0.09
English (573)	1,996	9.56
European (166)	166	0.80
Finnish (29)	123	0.59
French, ex. Basque (103)	553	2.65
French Canadian (34)	187	0.90
German (1,379)	3,647	17.48
Greek (34)	34	0.16
Hungarian (30)	83	0.40
Icelander (0)	9	0.04
Irish (680)	2,997	14.36
Israeli (0)	57	0.27
Italian (356)	987	4.73
Latvian (26)	26	0.12
Lithuanian (21)	69	0.33
Luxemburger (0)	11	0.05
Northern European (48)	48	0.23
Norwegian (299)	1,324	6.34
Polish (244)	387	1.85
Portuguese (93)	218	1.04
Romanian (58)	94	0.45
Russian (18)	69	0.33
Scandinavian (83)	83	0.40
Scotch-Irish (210)	405	1.94
Scottish (289)	803	3.85
Slovak (22)	56	0.27
Swedish (186)	591	2.83
Swiss (56)	81	0.39
Ukrainian (22)	38	0.18
Welsh (8)	105	0.50
West Indian, ex. Hispanic (19)	19	0.09
Dutch West Indian (19)	19	0.09

Hispanic Origin	Population	%
Hispanic or Latino (of any race)	2,468	11.84
Central American, ex. Mexican	65	0.31
Costa Rican	7	0.03
Guatemalan	16	0.08
Honduran	7	0.03
Nicaraguan	10	0.05
Panamanian	4	0.02
Salvadoran	21	0.10
Cuban	25	0.12
Dominican Republic	3	0.01
Mexican	2,086	10.01
Puerto Rican	76	0.36
South American	31	0.15
Argentinean	8	0.04
Colombian	7	0.03
Peruvian	11	0.05
Venezuelan	5	0.02
Other Hispanic or Latino	182	0.87

Race*	Population	%
African-American/Black (215)	424	2.03
Not Hispanic (199)	378	1.81
Hispanic (16)	46	0.22
American Indian/Alaska Native (897)	1,486	7.13
Not Hispanic (756)	1,233	5.92
Hispanic (141)	253	1.21
Aleut *(Alaska Native)* (2)	3	0.01
Apache (9)	19	0.09
Arapaho (1)	1	<0.01
Blackfeet (1)	13	0.06
Cherokee (43)	154	0.74
Cheyenne (2)	7	0.03
Chickasaw (4)	8	0.04
Chippewa (10)	18	0.09
Choctaw (10)	25	0.12
Colville (1)	1	<0.01
Cree (1)	1	<0.01
Creek (2)	9	0.04
Crow (1)	1	<0.01
Hopi (2)	5	0.02
Inupiat *(Alaska Native)* (2)	6	0.03
Iroquois (8)	9	0.04
Kiowa (1)	1	<0.01
Lumbee (0)	1	<0.01
Menominee (1)	1	<0.01
Mexican American Ind. (20)	29	0.14
Navajo (10)	14	0.07
Osage (3)	7	0.03
Paiute (26)	55	0.26
Pima (3)	3	0.01
Potawatomi (0)	4	0.02
Pueblo (1)	7	0.03
Puget Sound Salish (15)	22	0.11
Seminole (1)	1	<0.01
Shoshone (0)	3	0.01
Sioux (5)	23	0.11
South American Ind. (0)	1	<0.01
Tlingit-Haida *(Alaska Native)* (4)	5	0.02
Tsimshian *(Alaska Native)* (3)	3	0.01
Ute (4)	4	0.02
Yakama (6)	8	0.04
Yaqui (2)	11	0.05
Asian (340)	512	2.46
Not Hispanic (339)	491	2.36
Hispanic (1)	21	0.10
Bangladeshi (1)	1	<0.01
Chinese, ex. Taiwanese (104)	137	0.66
Filipino (73)	130	0.62
Indian (34)	40	0.19
Indonesian (7)	22	0.11
Japanese (31)	74	0.36
Korean (29)	47	0.23
Laotian (8)	10	0.05
Malaysian (0)	1	<0.01
Sri Lankan (1)	1	<0.01
Taiwanese (9)	9	0.04
Thai (4)	4	0.02
Vietnamese (26)	35	0.17
Hawaii Native/Pacific Islander (24)	85	0.41
Not Hispanic (22)	70	0.34
Hispanic (2)	15	0.07
Guamanian/Chamorro (5)	13	0.06
Native Hawaiian (11)	37	0.18
Samoan (2)	4	0.02
White (17,380)	18,354	88.07
Not Hispanic (16,257)	16,990	81.53
Hispanic (1,123)	1,364	6.55

La Grande

Place Type: City
County: Union
Population: 13,082†

Ancestry‡	Population	%
African, Sub-Saharan (0)	27	0.21
Nigerian (0)	27	0.21
American (832)	832	6.46
Arab (11)	11	0.09
Arab (11)	11	0.09
Austrian (13)	44	0.34
Basque (18)	18	0.14
British (96)	120	0.93
Canadian (0)	41	0.32
Croatian (14)	28	0.22
Czech (136)	215	1.67
Czechoslovakian (14)	14	0.11
Danish (93)	166	1.29
Dutch (46)	284	2.20
Eastern European (0)	14	0.11
English (613)	1,985	15.41
European (134)	160	1.24
Finnish (0)	54	0.42
French, ex. Basque (90)	736	5.71
French Canadian (35)	116	0.90
German (999)	3,171	24.62
Greek (34)	47	0.36
Hungarian (0)	11	0.09
Icelander (0)	27	0.21
Irish (779)	2,209	17.15
Italian (52)	315	2.45
Northern European (75)	75	0.58
Norwegian (147)	458	3.56
Pennsylvania German (0)	8	0.06
Polish (57)	106	0.82
Portuguese (23)	50	0.39
Romanian (0)	13	0.10
Russian (24)	80	0.62
Scandinavian (31)	62	0.48
Scotch-Irish (117)	358	2.78
Scottish (122)	491	3.81
Serbian (0)	18	0.14
Slovene (0)	11	0.09
Swedish (66)	268	2.08
Swiss (45)	181	1.41
Ukrainian (0)	9	0.07
Welsh (29)	38	0.29
Yugoslavian (0)	12	0.09

Hispanic Origin	Population	%
Hispanic or Latino (of any race)	601	4.59
Central American, ex. Mexican	13	0.10
Costa Rican	1	0.01
Guatemalan	5	0.04
Honduran	2	0.02
Nicaraguan	2	0.02
Salvadoran	3	0.02
Cuban	8	0.06
Dominican Republic	7	0.05
Mexican	463	3.54
Puerto Rican	20	0.15
South American	12	0.09
Chilean	5	0.04
Colombian	4	0.03
Peruvian	1	0.01
Venezuelan	2	0.02
Other Hispanic or Latino	78	0.60

Race*	Population	%
African-American/Black (111)	183	1.40
Not Hispanic (105)	167	1.28
Hispanic (6)	16	0.12
American Indian/Alaska Native (178)	316	2.42
Not Hispanic (150)	272	2.08
Hispanic (28)	44	0.34
Apache (0)	1	0.01
Arapaho (1)	1	0.01
Blackfeet (1)	3	0.02
Canadian/French Am. Ind. (3)	4	0.03
Cherokee (19)	50	0.38
Chickasaw (0)	3	0.02
Chippewa (3)	4	0.03
Choctaw (8)	23	0.18
Colville (0)	1	0.01
Inupiat *(Alaska Native)* (1)	1	0.01
Iroquois (0)	3	0.02
Menominee (0)	3	0.02
Mexican American Ind. (3)	3	0.02
Navajo (2)	4	0.03
Osage (0)	2	0.02
Paiute (2)	2	0.02
Potawatomi (1)	1	0.01
Pueblo (0)	1	0.01
Puget Sound Salish (2)	4	0.03
Shoshone (2)	3	0.02
Sioux (2)	4	0.03
Tohono O'Odham (1)	3	0.02
Yakama (1)	2	0.02
Yup'ik *(Alaska Native)* (1)	4	0.03
Asian (149)	237	1.81
Not Hispanic (144)	225	1.72
Hispanic (5)	12	0.09
Cambodian (4)	4	0.03

*Notes: † The Census 2010 population figure is used to calculate the percentages in the Hispanic Origin and Race categories. Ancestry percentages are based on the 2006-2010 American Community Survey population (not shown); ‡ Numbers in parentheses indicate the number of people reporting a single ancestry; * Numbers in parentheses indicate the number of persons reporting this race alone, not in combination with any other race; Please refer to the Explanation of Data for more information.*

Chinese, ex. Taiwanese (38)	51	0.39
Filipino (24)	51	0.39
Indian (18)	22	0.17
Indonesian (0)	4	0.03
Japanese (15)	42	0.32
Korean (16)	30	0.23
Nepalese (3)	3	0.02
Pakistani (1)	1	0.01
Taiwanese (0)	1	0.01
Thai (3)	8	0.06
Vietnamese (15)	15	0.11
Hawaii Native/Pacific Islander (193)	237	1.81
Not Hispanic (191)	233	1.78
Hispanic (2)	4	0.03
Guamanian/Chamorro (8)	19	0.15
Marshallese (51)	51	0.39
Native Hawaiian (13)	22	0.17
Samoan (14)	16	0.12
White (11,944)	12,255	93.68
Not Hispanic (11,606)	11,861	90.67
Hispanic (338)	394	3.01

Lake Oswego

Place Type: City
County: Clackamas
Population: 36,619†

Ancestry‡	Population	%
Afghan (61)	61	0.17
African, Sub-Saharan (220)	232	0.63
African (19)	19	0.05
Ethiopian (62)	62	0.17
Nigerian (17)	17	0.05
South African (53)	65	0.18
Other Sub-Saharan African (69)	69	0.19
American (1,116)	1,116	3.05
Arab (325)	451	1.23
Arab (148)	184	0.50
Egyptian (0)	36	0.10
Iraqi (61)	61	0.17
Lebanese (49)	73	0.20
Syrian (0)	30	0.08
Other Arab (67)	67	0.18
Armenian (45)	45	0.12
Australian (39)	39	0.11
Austrian (56)	220	0.60
Basque (45)	76	0.21
Belgian (0)	9	0.02
Brazilian (54)	54	0.15
British (341)	450	1.23
Canadian (115)	224	0.61
Celtic (24)	24	0.07
Croatian (33)	98	0.27
Czech (90)	225	0.61
Czechoslovakian (13)	13	0.04
Danish (195)	688	1.88
Dutch (202)	639	1.75
Eastern European (48)	53	0.14
English (1,793)	5,802	15.86
European (1,343)	1,541	4.21
Finnish (106)	235	0.64
French, ex. Basque (257)	1,242	3.39
French Canadian (31)	141	0.39
German (2,190)	7,721	21.10
Greek (76)	171	0.47
Hungarian (44)	266	0.73
Icelander (0)	65	0.18
Iranian (313)	408	1.12
Irish (1,587)	5,618	15.36
Israeli (25)	38	0.10
Italian (681)	1,881	5.14
Latvian (38)	95	0.26
Lithuanian (19)	127	0.35
Luxemburger (0)	12	0.03
Northern European (165)	165	0.45
Norwegian (752)	2,063	5.64
Polish (281)	1,213	3.32
Portuguese (0)	135	0.37
Romanian (29)	59	0.16
Russian (201)	808	2.21
Scandinavian (162)	263	0.72
Scotch-Irish (903)	1,534	4.19
Scottish (448)	1,847	5.05
Serbian (0)	17	0.05
Slovak (32)	75	0.20
Slovene (0)	13	0.04
Swedish (534)	1,599	4.37
Swiss (124)	342	0.93
Turkish (15)	36	0.10
Ukrainian (155)	271	0.74
Welsh (63)	542	1.48
West Indian, ex. Hispanic (0)	12	0.03
Jamaican (0)	12	0.03
Yugoslavian (72)	161	0.44

Hispanic Origin	Population	%
Hispanic or Latino (of any race)	1,356	3.70
Central American, ex. Mexican	77	0.21
Costa Rican	17	0.05
Guatemalan	16	0.04
Honduran	5	0.01
Nicaraguan	12	0.03
Panamanian	5	0.01
Salvadoran	20	0.05
Other Central American	2	0.01
Cuban	45	0.12
Dominican Republic	4	0.01
Mexican	745	2.03
Puerto Rican	87	0.24
South American	180	0.49
Argentinean	26	0.07
Bolivian	2	0.01
Chilean	30	0.08
Colombian	50	0.14
Ecuadorian	6	0.02
Paraguayan	1	<0.01
Peruvian	57	0.16
Venezuelan	6	0.02
Other South American	2	0.01
Other Hispanic or Latino	218	0.60

Race*	Population	%
African-American/Black (264)	434	1.19
Not Hispanic (252)	404	1.10
Hispanic (12)	30	0.08
American Indian/Alaska Native (149)	383	1.05
Not Hispanic (127)	324	0.88
Hispanic (22)	59	0.16
Alaska Athabascan *(Ala. Nat.)* (1)	1	<0.01
Aleut *(Alaska Native)* (4)	5	0.01
Apache (3)	6	0.02
Blackfeet (1)	9	0.02
Central American Ind. (1)	2	0.01
Cherokee (15)	84	0.23
Cheyenne (0)	2	0.01
Chickasaw (1)	5	0.01
Chippewa (2)	7	0.02
Choctaw (6)	15	0.04
Colville (1)	4	0.01
Comanche (2)	2	0.01
Cree (0)	3	0.01
Creek (2)	3	0.01
Delaware (0)	1	<0.01
Iroquois (7)	13	0.04
Mexican American Ind. (1)	1	<0.01
Navajo (8)	13	0.04
Ottawa (1)	1	<0.01
Pima (1)	1	<0.01
Pueblo (0)	4	0.01
Puget Sound Salish (4)	4	0.01
Seminole (0)	4	0.01
Shoshone (2)	2	0.01
Sioux (3)	5	0.01
South American Ind. (1)	1	<0.01
Tlingit-Haida *(Alaska Native)* (2)	2	0.01
Yakama (0)	1	<0.01
Yuman (0)	2	0.01
Asian (2,056)	2,662	7.27
Not Hispanic (2,039)	2,622	7.16
Hispanic (17)	40	0.11
Burmese (1)	2	0.01
Cambodian (3)	13	0.04
Chinese, ex. Taiwanese (708)	911	2.49
Filipino (88)	187	0.51
Indian (266)	302	0.82
Indonesian (2)	15	0.04
Japanese (278)	465	1.27
Korean (437)	531	1.45
Laotian (0)	1	<0.01
Malaysian (3)	3	0.01
Nepalese (5)	9	0.02
Pakistani (15)	22	0.06
Sri Lankan (5)	7	0.02
Taiwanese (71)	81	0.22
Thai (25)	44	0.12
Vietnamese (53)	76	0.21
Hawaii Native/Pacific Islander (66)	148	0.40
Not Hispanic (64)	139	0.38
Hispanic (2)	9	0.02
Guamanian/Chamorro (26)	33	0.09
Marshallese (1)	1	<0.01
Native Hawaiian (14)	67	0.18
Samoan (6)	13	0.04
Tongan (11)	12	0.03
White (32,694)	33,726	92.10
Not Hispanic (31,815)	32,702	89.30
Hispanic (879)	1,024	2.80

Lebanon

Place Type: City
County: Linn
Population: 15,518†

Ancestry‡	Population	%
American (1,345)	1,345	8.92
Austrian (0)	45	0.30
Canadian (0)	14	0.09
Czech (61)	106	0.70
Danish (52)	139	0.92
Dutch (88)	645	4.28
Eastern European (17)	17	0.11
English (815)	1,940	12.87
European (66)	79	0.52
French, ex. Basque (159)	492	3.26
French Canadian (20)	54	0.36
German (1,067)	3,543	23.51
German Russian (0)	11	0.07
Greek (0)	28	0.19
Hungarian (0)	137	0.91
Irish (478)	2,181	14.47
Italian (91)	494	3.28
Lithuanian (11)	11	0.07
Northern European (41)	41	0.27
Norwegian (223)	627	4.16
Pennsylvania German (30)	30	0.20
Polish (14)	218	1.45
Portuguese (0)	11	0.07
Russian (21)	105	0.70
Scandinavian (0)	53	0.35
Scotch-Irish (153)	447	2.97
Scottish (181)	461	3.06
Swedish (79)	222	1.47
Swiss (32)	158	1.05
Ukrainian (84)	113	0.75
Welsh (69)	173	1.15

Hispanic Origin	Population	%
Hispanic or Latino (of any race)	901	5.81
Central American, ex. Mexican	14	0.09
Costa Rican	1	0.01
Guatemalan	12	0.08
Salvadoran	1	0.01
Cuban	7	0.05
Mexican	685	4.41
Puerto Rican	39	0.25
South American	17	0.11
Chilean	7	0.05
Ecuadorian	1	0.01

*Notes: † The Census 2010 population figure is used to calculate the percentages in the Hispanic Origin and Race categories. Ancestry percentages are based on the 2006-2010 American Community Survey population (not shown); ‡ Numbers in parentheses indicate the number of people reporting a single ancestry; * Numbers in parentheses indicate the number of persons reporting this race alone, not in combination with any other race; Please refer to the Explanation of Data for more information.*

Peruvian	6	0.04
Venezuelan	3	0.02
Other Hispanic or Latino	139	0.90

Race*	Population	%
African-American/Black (71)	154	0.99
Not Hispanic (58)	134	0.86
Hispanic (13)	20	0.13
American Indian/Alaska Native (223)	538	3.47
Not Hispanic (200)	472	3.04
Hispanic (23)	66	0.43
Alaska Athabascan *(Ala. Nat.)* (0)	2	0.01
Aleut *(Alaska Native)* (1)	1	0.01
Apache (5)	10	0.06
Arapaho (1)	1	0.01
Blackfeet (5)	25	0.16
Central American Ind. (1)	1	0.01
Cherokee (28)	92	0.59
Cheyenne (1)	3	0.02
Chickasaw (0)	3	0.02
Chippewa (5)	13	0.08
Choctaw (17)	41	0.26
Colville (2)	2	0.01
Comanche (4)	5	0.03
Cree (0)	2	0.01
Creek (1)	6	0.04
Hopi (1)	1	0.01
Inupiat *(Alaska Native)* (1)	1	0.01
Iroquois (0)	5	0.03
Lumbee (0)	1	0.01
Mexican American Ind. (1)	5	0.03
Navajo (0)	1	0.01
Osage (3)	6	0.04
Ottawa (1)	1	0.01
Potawatomi (4)	10	0.06
Pueblo (0)	2	0.01
Puget Sound Salish (1)	1	0.01
Shoshone (2)	5	0.03
Sioux (6)	17	0.11
Spanish American Ind. (0)	1	0.01
Tlingit-Haida *(Alaska Native)* (2)	10	0.06
Tohono O'Odham (1)	4	0.03
Yaqui (1)	2	0.01
Yup'ik *(Alaska Native)* (1)	5	0.03
Asian (170)	281	1.81
Not Hispanic (168)	266	1.71
Hispanic (2)	15	0.10
Cambodian (2)	2	0.01
Chinese, ex. Taiwanese (49)	73	0.47
Filipino (22)	49	0.32
Indian (48)	55	0.35
Japanese (6)	33	0.21
Korean (19)	48	0.31
Laotian (1)	3	0.02
Sri Lankan (1)	1	0.01
Taiwanese (1)	1	0.01
Thai (4)	5	0.03
Vietnamese (12)	12	0.08
Hawaii Native/Pacific Islander (16)	62	0.40
Not Hispanic (15)	58	0.37
Hispanic (1)	4	0.03
Fijian (1)	1	0.01
Guamanian/Chamorro (3)	8	0.05
Native Hawaiian (7)	34	0.22
Samoan (2)	3	0.02
Tongan (2)	5	0.03
White (14,150)	14,682	94.61
Not Hispanic (13,715)	14,137	91.10
Hispanic (435)	545	3.51

Lincoln City

Place Type: City
County: Lincoln
Population: 7,930†

Ancestry‡	Population	%
American (285)	285	3.61
Arab (0)	5	0.06
Egyptian (0)	5	0.06
Australian (0)	3	0.04
Austrian (11)	21	0.27
British (39)	39	0.49
Canadian (0)	6	0.08
Czech (7)	7	0.09
Danish (29)	47	0.60
Dutch (20)	121	1.53
English (406)	1,392	17.64
European (356)	356	4.51
Finnish (36)	36	0.46
French, ex. Basque (65)	217	2.75
French Canadian (52)	90	1.14
German (739)	1,754	22.23
Greek (55)	60	0.76
Hungarian (0)	138	1.75
Irish (307)	1,060	13.44
Italian (252)	625	7.92
Lithuanian (13)	13	0.16
Norwegian (102)	228	2.89
Polish (0)	51	0.65
Portuguese (19)	47	0.60
Romanian (29)	45	0.57
Scandinavian (0)	29	0.37
Scotch-Irish (36)	141	1.79
Scottish (85)	172	2.18
Swedish (11)	147	1.86
Swiss (0)	23	0.29
Turkish (16)	16	0.20
Ukrainian (9)	9	0.11
Welsh (0)	61	0.77
Yugoslavian (41)	41	0.52

Hispanic Origin	Population	%
Hispanic or Latino (of any race)	1,048	13.22
Central American, ex. Mexican	2	0.03
Salvadoran	2	0.03
Cuban	11	0.14
Mexican	919	11.59
Puerto Rican	18	0.23
South American	17	0.21
Bolivian	1	0.01
Chilean	1	0.01
Colombian	1	0.01
Ecuadorian	1	0.01
Peruvian	13	0.16
Other Hispanic or Latino	81	1.02

Race*	Population	%
African-American/Black (32)	75	0.95
Not Hispanic (27)	53	0.67
Hispanic (5)	22	0.28
American Indian/Alaska Native (279)	448	5.65
Not Hispanic (243)	387	4.88
Hispanic (36)	61	0.77
Alaska Athabascan *(Ala. Nat.)* (6)	9	0.11
Aleut *(Alaska Native)* (1)	1	0.01
Apache (6)	9	0.11
Blackfeet (8)	14	0.18
Canadian/French Am. Ind. (1)	2	0.03
Cherokee (5)	24	0.30
Chickasaw (0)	2	0.03
Chippewa (7)	12	0.15
Choctaw (0)	3	0.04
Cree (0)	1	0.01
Hopi (0)	2	0.03
Iroquois (0)	1	0.01
Mexican American Ind. (7)	11	0.14
Osage (0)	3	0.04
Shoshone (0)	1	0.01
Sioux (3)	11	0.14
South American Ind. (0)	1	0.01
Tlingit-Haida *(Alaska Native)* (3)	8	0.10
Ute (1)	1	0.01
Yakama (4)	4	0.05
Yaqui (0)	2	0.03
Yup'ik *(Alaska Native)* (1)	4	0.05
Asian (122)	162	2.04
Not Hispanic (119)	143	1.80
Hispanic (3)	19	0.24
Cambodian (1)	1	0.01
Chinese, ex. Taiwanese (32)	49	0.62
Filipino (29)	40	0.50
Indian (17)	23	0.29
Japanese (9)	16	0.20
Korean (15)	18	0.23
Laotian (0)	2	0.03
Nepalese (1)	1	0.01
Taiwanese (0)	1	0.01
Thai (4)	8	0.10
Vietnamese (9)	12	0.15
Hawaii Native/Pacific Islander (11)	30	0.38
Not Hispanic (10)	24	0.30
Hispanic (1)	6	0.08
Native Hawaiian (9)	20	0.25
Samoan (2)	6	0.08
Tongan (0)	1	0.01
White (6,635)	6,902	87.04
Not Hispanic (6,286)	6,471	81.60
Hispanic (349)	431	5.44

McMinnville

Place Type: City
County: Yamhill
Population: 32,187†

Ancestry‡	Population	%
American (1,709)	1,709	5.47
Arab (0)	15	0.05
Moroccan (0)	15	0.05
Australian (0)	16	0.05
Austrian (34)	100	0.32
Basque (0)	11	0.04
Belgian (23)	37	0.12
British (11)	97	0.31
Bulgarian (0)	25	0.08
Canadian (0)	42	0.13
Croatian (0)	18	0.06
Czech (121)	360	1.15
Czechoslovakian (13)	13	0.04
Danish (291)	530	1.70
Dutch (231)	1,279	4.09
English (1,154)	4,181	13.37
Estonian (0)	32	0.10
European (472)	508	1.63
Finnish (62)	115	0.37
French, ex. Basque (164)	1,057	3.38
French Canadian (127)	468	1.50
German (1,443)	6,300	20.15
Greek (13)	13	0.04
Hungarian (44)	64	0.20
Irish (756)	3,439	11.00
Italian (205)	850	2.72
Norwegian (407)	1,079	3.45
Pennsylvania German (39)	39	0.12
Polish (148)	554	1.77
Portuguese (68)	150	0.48
Russian (270)	403	1.29
Scandinavian (169)	235	0.75
Scotch-Irish (178)	548	1.75
Scottish (277)	1,333	4.26
Slovak (0)	15	0.05
Swedish (217)	588	1.88
Swiss (12)	128	0.41
Ukrainian (0)	12	0.04
Welsh (0)	257	0.82
West Indian, ex. Hispanic (73)	86	0.28
Haitian (73)	73	0.23
Jamaican (0)	13	0.04
Yugoslavian (13)	35	0.11

Hispanic Origin	Population	%
Hispanic or Latino (of any race)	6,630	20.60
Central American, ex. Mexican	151	0.47
Costa Rican	4	0.01
Guatemalan	55	0.17
Honduran	10	0.03
Nicaraguan	6	0.02
Panamanian	4	0.01
Salvadoran	69	0.21

*Notes: † The Census 2010 population figure is used to calculate the percentages in the Hispanic Origin and Race categories. Ancestry percentages are based on the 2006-2010 American Community Survey population (not shown); ‡ Numbers in parentheses indicate the number of people reporting a single ancestry; * Numbers in parentheses indicate the number of persons reporting this race alone, not in combination with any other race; Please refer to the Explanation of Data for more information.*

Other Central American	3	0.01
Cuban	18	0.06
Dominican Republic	6	0.02
Mexican	5,890	18.30
Puerto Rican	52	0.16
South American	74	0.23
Argentinean	7	0.02
Bolivian	1	<0.01
Chilean	7	0.02
Colombian	30	0.09
Ecuadorian	4	0.01
Peruvian	12	0.04
Venezuelan	2	0.01
Other South American	11	0.03
Other Hispanic or Latino	439	1.36

Race*	Population	%
African-American/Black (233)	364	1.13
Not Hispanic (186)	298	0.93
Hispanic (47)	66	0.21
American Indian/Alaska Native (402)	816	2.54
Not Hispanic (347)	699	2.17
Hispanic (55)	117	0.36
Alaska Athabascan *(Ala. Nat.)* (3)	3	0.01
Aleut *(Alaska Native)* (10)	12	0.04
Apache (6)	19	0.06
Blackfeet (8)	20	0.06
Canadian/French Am. Ind. (2)	4	0.01
Cherokee (39)	89	0.28
Cheyenne (0)	1	<0.01
Chickasaw (0)	11	0.03
Chippewa (10)	18	0.06
Choctaw (11)	28	0.09
Comanche (0)	4	0.01
Creek (4)	6	0.02
Crow (1)	3	0.01
Hopi (1)	1	<0.01
Inupiat *(Alaska Native)* (4)	6	0.02
Iroquois (5)	15	0.05
Menominee (0)	1	<0.01
Mexican American Ind. (12)	18	0.06
Navajo (9)	11	0.03
Osage (4)	12	0.04
Ottawa (0)	2	0.01
Paiute (1)	1	<0.01
Pima (1)	1	<0.01
Potawatomi (0)	3	0.01
Puget Sound Salish (3)	6	0.02
Seminole (0)	6	0.02
Sioux (10)	27	0.08
Tlingit-Haida *(Alaska Native)* (15)	28	0.09
Tohono O'Odham (1)	1	<0.01
Tsimshian *(Alaska Native)* (0)	1	<0.01
Yakama (4)	4	0.01
Yaqui (2)	2	0.01
Yup'ik *(Alaska Native)* (6)	8	0.02
Asian (494)	796	2.47
Not Hispanic (481)	741	2.30
Hispanic (13)	55	0.17
Cambodian (1)	1	<0.01
Chinese, ex. Taiwanese (133)	199	0.62
Filipino (72)	189	0.59
Indian (36)	50	0.16
Indonesian (1)	7	0.02
Japanese (62)	183	0.57
Korean (64)	92	0.29
Laotian (21)	26	0.08
Malaysian (2)	2	0.01
Nepalese (3)	4	0.01
Pakistani (9)	9	0.03
Sri Lankan (2)	2	0.01
Taiwanese (1)	1	<0.01
Thai (15)	23	0.07
Vietnamese (42)	52	0.16
Hawaii Native/Pacific Islander (61)	160	0.50
Not Hispanic (59)	144	0.45
Hispanic (2)	16	0.05
Fijian (2)	3	0.01
Guamanian/Chamorro (12)	22	0.07
Native Hawaiian (31)	86	0.27
Samoan (6)	19	0.06
Tongan (2)	2	0.01
White (26,455)	27,494	85.42
Not Hispanic (23,693)	24,392	75.78
Hispanic (2,762)	3,102	9.64

Medford

Place Type: City
County: Jackson
Population: 74,907†

Ancestry‡	Population	%
African, Sub-Saharan (64)	205	0.28
African (47)	72	0.10
Ethiopian (17)	17	0.02
Ghanaian (0)	13	0.02
South African (0)	103	0.14
American (3,922)	3,922	5.31
Arab (9)	44	0.06
Arab (0)	16	0.02
Lebanese (0)	19	0.03
Syrian (9)	9	0.01
Australian (0)	29	0.04
Austrian (53)	122	0.17
Basque (43)	165	0.22
Belgian (10)	27	0.04
Brazilian (31)	31	0.04
British (221)	351	0.48
Bulgarian (16)	16	0.02
Cajun (33)	33	0.04
Canadian (53)	374	0.51
Croatian (67)	81	0.11
Czech (64)	295	0.40
Czechoslovakian (71)	204	0.28
Danish (322)	776	1.05
Dutch (278)	1,914	2.59
Eastern European (9)	18	0.02
English (2,838)	10,068	13.64
European (1,007)	1,183	1.60
Finnish (34)	162	0.22
French, ex. Basque (453)	3,262	4.42
French Canadian (233)	558	0.76
German (3,838)	14,390	19.49
Greek (40)	261	0.35
Hungarian (72)	232	0.31
Icelander (0)	19	0.03
Iranian (0)	23	0.03
Irish (2,442)	10,077	13.65
Italian (844)	2,906	3.94
Latvian (0)	36	0.05
Lithuanian (14)	132	0.18
Maltese (0)	19	0.03
Northern European (81)	97	0.13
Norwegian (578)	1,736	2.35
Pennsylvania German (27)	83	0.11
Polish (559)	1,190	1.61
Portuguese (470)	956	1.30
Romanian (37)	121	0.16
Russian (98)	375	0.51
Scandinavian (98)	207	0.28
Scotch-Irish (486)	1,897	2.57
Scottish (807)	2,624	3.55
Serbian (27)	69	0.09
Slovak (41)	79	0.11
Swedish (468)	2,265	3.07
Swiss (136)	248	0.34
Turkish (131)	175	0.24
Ukrainian (18)	26	0.04
Welsh (170)	736	1.00
West Indian, ex. Hispanic (0)	13	0.02
West Indian (0)	13	0.02
Yugoslavian (13)	152	0.21

Hispanic Origin	Population	%
Hispanic or Latino (of any race)	10,319	13.78
Central American, ex. Mexican	320	0.43
Costa Rican	13	0.02
Guatemalan	148	0.20
Honduran	36	0.05
Nicaraguan	9	0.01
Panamanian	11	0.01
Salvadoran	100	0.13
Other Central American	3	<0.01
Cuban	58	0.08
Dominican Republic	17	0.02
Mexican	8,652	11.55
Puerto Rican	176	0.23
South American	124	0.17
Argentinean	12	0.02
Bolivian	9	0.01
Chilean	5	0.01
Colombian	39	0.05
Ecuadorian	18	0.02
Paraguayan	1	<0.01
Peruvian	33	0.04
Venezuelan	5	0.01
Other South American	2	<0.01
Other Hispanic or Latino	972	1.30

Race*	Population	%
African-American/Black (666)	1,234	1.65
Not Hispanic (598)	1,079	1.44
Hispanic (68)	155	0.21
American Indian/Alaska Native (935)	2,184	2.92
Not Hispanic (691)	1,741	2.32
Hispanic (244)	443	0.59
Alaska Athabascan *(Ala. Nat.)* (3)	4	0.01
Aleut *(Alaska Native)* (5)	6	0.01
Apache (18)	51	0.07
Arapaho (0)	1	<0.01
Blackfeet (13)	48	0.06
Canadian/French Am. Ind. (4)	5	0.01
Central American Ind. (0)	1	<0.01
Cherokee (108)	436	0.58
Cheyenne (3)	6	0.01
Chickasaw (9)	15	0.02
Chippewa (10)	32	0.04
Choctaw (40)	106	0.14
Colville (0)	1	<0.01
Comanche (3)	6	0.01
Cree (0)	2	<0.01
Creek (5)	14	0.02
Crow (4)	5	0.01
Delaware (3)	7	0.01
Hopi (1)	3	<0.01
Houma (6)	6	0.01
Inupiat *(Alaska Native)* (4)	6	0.01
Iroquois (10)	26	0.03
Kiowa (1)	2	<0.01
Lumbee (1)	7	0.01
Mexican American Ind. (54)	88	0.12
Navajo (20)	41	0.05
Osage (3)	8	0.01
Ottawa (0)	1	<0.01
Paiute (9)	9	0.01
Pima (3)	9	0.01
Potawatomi (6)	16	0.02
Pueblo (4)	5	0.01
Puget Sound Salish (2)	6	0.01
Seminole (0)	4	0.01
Shoshone (5)	15	0.02
Sioux (14)	51	0.07
South American Ind. (0)	1	<0.01
Spanish American Ind. (4)	10	0.01
Tlingit-Haida *(Alaska Native)* (7)	16	0.02
Tohono O'Odham (1)	1	<0.01
Tsimshian *(Alaska Native)* (1)	3	<0.01
Ute (5)	6	0.01
Yakama (4)	6	0.01
Yaqui (7)	10	0.01
Yuman (3)	4	0.01
Asian (1,113)	1,749	2.33
Not Hispanic (1,084)	1,620	2.16
Hispanic (29)	129	0.17
Burmese (3)	5	0.01
Cambodian (4)	7	0.01
Chinese, ex. Taiwanese (239)	337	0.45
Filipino (285)	530	0.71
Hmong (1)	1	<0.01

*Notes: † The Census 2010 population figure is used to calculate the percentages in the Hispanic Origin and Race categories. Ancestry percentages are based on the 2006-2010 American Community Survey population (not shown); ‡ Numbers in parentheses indicate the number of people reporting a single ancestry; * Numbers in parentheses indicate the number of persons reporting this race alone, not in combination with any other race; Please refer to the Explanation of Data for more information.*

Indian (120)	171	0.23
Indonesian (9)	18	0.02
Japanese (105)	256	0.34
Korean (138)	203	0.27
Laotian (4)	8	0.01
Nepalese (4)	4	0.01
Pakistani (15)	19	0.03
Sri Lankan (6)	6	0.01
Taiwanese (7)	16	0.02
Thai (48)	68	0.09
Vietnamese (82)	107	0.14
Hawaii Native/Pacific Islander (345)	620	0.83
Not Hispanic (328)	554	0.74
Hispanic (17)	66	0.09
Fijian (1)	2	<0.01
Guamanian/Chamorro (41)	79	0.11
Marshallese (3)	3	<0.01
Native Hawaiian (68)	206	0.28
Samoan (178)	214	0.29
Tongan (4)	13	0.02
White (64,452)	67,183	89.69
Not Hispanic (59,756)	61,716	82.39
Hispanic (4,696)	5,467	7.30

Milwaukie

Place Type: City
County: Clackamas
Population: 20,291[†]

Ancestry[‡]	Population	%
American (999)	999	4.90
Arab (194)	204	1.00
Lebanese (11)	21	0.10
Palestinian (107)	107	0.52
Other Arab (76)	76	0.37
Armenian (0)	26	0.13
Australian (0)	7	0.03
Austrian (0)	155	0.76
Basque (0)	16	0.08
Belgian (0)	20	0.10
British (17)	83	0.41
Bulgarian (14)	14	0.07
Canadian (109)	175	0.86
Celtic (44)	44	0.22
Croatian (24)	24	0.12
Czech (32)	131	0.64
Czechoslovakian (0)	8	0.04
Danish (9)	295	1.45
Dutch (58)	344	1.69
Eastern European (26)	26	0.13
English (813)	2,327	11.41
European (407)	412	2.02
Finnish (12)	150	0.74
French, ex. Basque (184)	718	3.52
French Canadian (39)	186	0.91
German (1,656)	5,765	28.27
Greek (29)	66	0.32
Hungarian (32)	32	0.16
Iranian (0)	26	0.13
Irish (772)	2,619	12.84
Italian (416)	1,144	5.61
Lithuanian (0)	18	0.09
Macedonian (0)	13	0.06
Northern European (34)	34	0.17
Norwegian (297)	862	4.23
Polish (143)	511	2.51
Portuguese (0)	91	0.45
Romanian (6)	6	0.03
Russian (113)	416	2.04
Scandinavian (27)	33	0.16
Scotch-Irish (253)	528	2.59
Scottish (350)	932	4.57
Serbian (0)	8	0.04
Slovak (5)	32	0.16
Swedish (175)	748	3.67
Swiss (72)	302	1.48
Ukrainian (37)	56	0.27
Welsh (11)	278	1.36
West Indian, ex. Hispanic (15)	15	0.07
Haitian (15)	15	0.07
Yugoslavian (9)	16	0.08

Hispanic Origin	Population	%
Hispanic or Latino (of any race)	1,426	7.03
Central American, ex. Mexican	76	0.37
Costa Rican	4	0.02
Guatemalan	19	0.09
Honduran	7	0.03
Nicaraguan	6	0.03
Panamanian	7	0.03
Salvadoran	33	0.16
Cuban	27	0.13
Dominican Republic	3	0.01
Mexican	1,110	5.47
Puerto Rican	48	0.24
South American	29	0.14
Argentinean	8	0.04
Chilean	5	0.02
Colombian	2	0.01
Ecuadorian	1	<0.01
Peruvian	12	0.06
Venezuelan	1	<0.01
Other Hispanic or Latino	133	0.66

Race*	Population	%
African-American/Black (271)	423	2.08
Not Hispanic (262)	402	1.98
Hispanic (9)	21	0.10
American Indian/Alaska Native (273)	557	2.75
Not Hispanic (164)	395	1.95
Hispanic (109)	162	0.80
Alaska Athabascan *(Ala. Nat.)* (0)	2	0.01
Aleut *(Alaska Native)* (2)	3	0.01
Apache (4)	8	0.04
Blackfeet (2)	13	0.06
Cherokee (22)	79	0.39
Cheyenne (1)	3	0.01
Chickasaw (0)	4	0.02
Chippewa (21)	30	0.15
Choctaw (7)	17	0.08
Comanche (1)	2	0.01
Creek (1)	3	0.01
Delaware (0)	4	0.02
Inupiat *(Alaska Native)* (4)	4	0.02
Iroquois (2)	3	0.01
Kiowa (1)	1	<0.01
Mexican American Ind. (10)	25	0.12
Navajo (3)	12	0.06
Osage (4)	4	0.02
Ottawa (1)	3	0.01
Paiute (0)	5	0.02
Pima (0)	1	<0.01
Potawatomi (1)	3	0.01
Pueblo (1)	4	0.02
Puget Sound Salish (0)	5	0.02
Seminole (0)	1	<0.01
Shoshone (1)	2	0.01
Sioux (8)	22	0.11
Tlingit-Haida *(Alaska Native)* (4)	8	0.04
Tohono O'Odham (1)	1	<0.01
Yakama (0)	3	0.01
Yaqui (1)	5	0.02
Asian (503)	729	3.59
Not Hispanic (494)	704	3.47
Hispanic (9)	25	0.12
Cambodian (27)	31	0.15
Chinese, ex. Taiwanese (74)	115	0.57
Filipino (92)	162	0.80
Hmong (1)	1	<0.01
Indian (33)	55	0.27
Indonesian (2)	5	0.02
Japanese (69)	129	0.64
Korean (62)	83	0.41
Laotian (27)	39	0.19
Pakistani (6)	8	0.04
Sri Lankan (2)	2	0.01
Taiwanese (3)	3	0.01
Thai (13)	18	0.09
Vietnamese (66)	86	0.42
Hawaii Native/Pacific Islander (60)	127	0.63
Not Hispanic (57)	118	0.58
Hispanic (3)	9	0.04
Guamanian/Chamorro (3)	9	0.04
Marshallese (2)	2	0.01
Native Hawaiian (21)	55	0.27
Samoan (25)	36	0.18
Tongan (0)	4	0.02
White (17,960)	18,643	91.88
Not Hispanic (17,276)	17,827	87.86
Hispanic (684)	816	4.02

Molalla

Place Type: City
County: Clackamas
Population: 8,108[†]

Ancestry[‡]	Population	%
American (449)	449	5.83
Arab (42)	104	1.35
Arab (21)	21	0.27
Lebanese (21)	83	1.08
Basque (12)	12	0.16
British (0)	30	0.39
Canadian (0)	16	0.21
Czech (0)	86	1.12
Czechoslovakian (63)	96	1.25
Danish (37)	60	0.78
Dutch (15)	91	1.18
English (372)	1,004	13.05
European (173)	173	2.25
Finnish (0)	16	0.21
French, ex. Basque (27)	224	2.91
French Canadian (11)	11	0.14
German (563)	1,971	25.61
Irish (195)	998	12.97
Italian (23)	143	1.86
Latvian (0)	75	0.97
Norwegian (185)	871	11.32
Polish (0)	9	0.12
Portuguese (0)	53	0.69
Scandinavian (0)	33	0.43
Scotch-Irish (78)	207	2.69
Scottish (7)	101	1.31
Slavic (0)	30	0.39
Swedish (45)	275	3.57
Swiss (0)	70	0.91
Welsh (36)	126	1.64
Yugoslavian (0)	42	0.55

Hispanic Origin	Population	%
Hispanic or Latino (of any race)	1,173	14.47
Central American, ex. Mexican	23	0.28
Costa Rican	4	0.05
Guatemalan	10	0.12
Honduran	3	0.04
Nicaraguan	1	0.01
Salvadoran	5	0.06
Cuban	4	0.05
Mexican	1,046	12.90
Puerto Rican	12	0.15
South American	13	0.16
Chilean	7	0.09
Colombian	5	0.06
Other South American	1	0.01
Other Hispanic or Latino	75	0.93

Race*	Population	%
African-American/Black (49)	78	0.96
Not Hispanic (30)	47	0.58
Hispanic (19)	31	0.38
American Indian/Alaska Native (85)	184	2.27
Not Hispanic (55)	128	1.58
Hispanic (30)	56	0.69
Apache (1)	6	0.07
Blackfeet (0)	6	0.07
Central American Ind. (1)	1	0.01
Cherokee (8)	24	0.30
Chippewa (0)	3	0.04

*Notes: † The Census 2010 population figure is used to calculate the percentages in the Hispanic Origin and Race categories. Ancestry percentages are based on the 2006-2010 American Community Survey population (not shown); ‡ Numbers in parentheses indicate the number of people reporting a single ancestry; * Numbers in parentheses indicate the number of persons reporting this race alone, not in combination with any other race; Please refer to the Explanation of Data for more information.*

Race*	Population	%
Choctaw (5)	5	0.06
Creek (2)	5	0.06
Delaware (1)	1	0.01
Inupiat *(Alaska Native)* (0)	4	0.05
Iroquois (0)	1	0.01
Menominee (1)	1	0.01
Mexican American Ind. (8)	11	0.14
Navajo (3)	3	0.04
Paiute (3)	3	0.04
Puget Sound Salish (1)	4	0.05
Seminole (1)	3	0.04
Sioux (0)	3	0.04
Tlingit-Haida *(Alaska Native)* (0)	5	0.06
Asian (66)	129	1.59
Not Hispanic (50)	99	1.22
Hispanic (16)	30	0.37
Chinese, ex. Taiwanese (6)	14	0.17
Filipino (8)	23	0.28
Indian (14)	19	0.23
Indonesian (0)	6	0.07
Japanese (5)	17	0.21
Korean (8)	12	0.15
Laotian (6)	6	0.07
Taiwanese (0)	4	0.05
Vietnamese (10)	13	0.16
Hawaii Native/Pacific Islander (21)	44	0.54
Not Hispanic (20)	34	0.42
Hispanic (1)	10	0.12
Fijian (4)	4	0.05
Guamanian/Chamorro (1)	1	0.01
Native Hawaiian (2)	11	0.14
Samoan (3)	13	0.16
Tongan (1)	1	0.01
White (7,045)	7,264	89.59
Not Hispanic (6,619)	6,767	83.46
Hispanic (426)	497	6.13

Monmouth

Place Type: City
County: Polk
Population: 9,534†

Ancestry‡	Population	%
African, Sub-Saharan (0)	60	0.65
African (0)	60	0.65
American (315)	315	3.39
Arab (41)	41	0.44
Arab (41)	41	0.44
Austrian (0)	22	0.24
Basque (0)	27	0.29
British (14)	64	0.69
Canadian (0)	32	0.34
Danish (52)	88	0.95
Dutch (173)	490	5.28
English (435)	1,517	16.34
European (247)	260	2.80
French, ex. Basque (47)	316	3.40
French Canadian (0)	20	0.22
German (668)	2,082	22.43
Greek (41)	41	0.44
Hungarian (0)	11	0.12
Irish (186)	1,098	11.83
Italian (69)	219	2.36
Latvian (0)	37	0.40
Norwegian (250)	430	4.63
Pennsylvania German (0)	12	0.13
Polish (25)	153	1.65
Scandinavian (30)	64	0.69
Scotch-Irish (37)	162	1.75
Scottish (67)	285	3.07
Swedish (40)	339	3.65
Swiss (0)	14	0.15
Welsh (0)	182	1.96

Hispanic Origin	Population	%
Hispanic or Latino (of any race)	1,280	13.43
Central American, ex. Mexican	13	0.14
Costa Rican	1	0.01
Guatemalan	3	0.03
Honduran	1	0.01
Nicaraguan	2	0.02
Panamanian	1	0.01
Salvadoran	5	0.05
Cuban	9	0.09
Dominican Republic	1	0.01
Mexican	1,159	12.16
Puerto Rican	25	0.26
South American	13	0.14
Colombian	5	0.05
Peruvian	4	0.04
Venezuelan	4	0.04
Other Hispanic or Latino	60	0.63

Race*	Population	%
African-American/Black (109)	187	1.96
Not Hispanic (101)	162	1.70
Hispanic (8)	25	0.26
American Indian/Alaska Native (141)	273	2.86
Not Hispanic (95)	194	2.03
Hispanic (46)	79	0.83
Alaska Athabascan *(Ala. Nat.)* (0)	1	0.01
Aleut *(Alaska Native)* (1)	2	0.02
Blackfeet (3)	6	0.06
Cherokee (13)	42	0.44
Chickasaw (0)	2	0.02
Chippewa (6)	12	0.13
Choctaw (4)	6	0.06
Cree (0)	1	0.01
Creek (1)	1	0.01
Delaware (0)	1	0.01
Inupiat *(Alaska Native)* (0)	1	0.01
Iroquois (0)	2	0.02
Mexican American Ind. (8)	25	0.26
Navajo (5)	7	0.07
Osage (1)	1	0.01
Ottawa (1)	1	0.01
Paiute (1)	1	0.01
Potawatomi (1)	1	0.01
Puget Sound Salish (0)	1	0.01
Sioux (5)	7	0.07
Tlingit-Haida *(Alaska Native)* (0)	2	0.02
Tsimshian *(Alaska Native)* (1)	1	0.01
Yakama (0)	1	0.01
Yup'ik *(Alaska Native)* (1)	2	0.02
Asian (313)	457	4.79
Not Hispanic (305)	433	4.54
Hispanic (8)	24	0.25
Cambodian (2)	4	0.04
Chinese, ex. Taiwanese (169)	207	2.17
Filipino (25)	83	0.87
Hmong (1)	1	0.01
Indian (23)	29	0.30
Japanese (39)	82	0.86
Korean (23)	30	0.31
Laotian (1)	1	0.01
Pakistani (0)	5	0.05
Sri Lankan (0)	1	0.01
Thai (1)	2	0.02
Vietnamese (8)	10	0.10
Hawaii Native/Pacific Islander (55)	116	1.22
Not Hispanic (52)	109	1.14
Hispanic (3)	7	0.07
Fijian (1)	1	0.01
Guamanian/Chamorro (2)	8	0.08
Marshallese (8)	8	0.08
Native Hawaiian (23)	57	0.60
Samoan (2)	5	0.05
Tongan (1)	3	0.03
White (7,890)	8,231	86.33
Not Hispanic (7,390)	7,657	80.31
Hispanic (500)	574	6.02

Newberg

Place Type: City
County: Yamhill
Population: 22,068†

Ancestry‡	Population	%
African, Sub-Saharan (12)	12	0.06
Ethiopian (12)	12	0.06
American (843)	843	3.94
Arab (22)	35	0.16
Arab (9)	9	0.04
Lebanese (13)	26	0.12
Armenian (0)	48	0.22
Austrian (0)	21	0.10
Basque (0)	13	0.06
Belgian (0)	26	0.12
Brazilian (0)	2	0.01
British (133)	176	0.82
Canadian (32)	72	0.34
Croatian (57)	91	0.42
Czech (63)	233	1.09
Danish (39)	335	1.56
Dutch (174)	1,322	6.17
Eastern European (43)	43	0.20
English (711)	2,628	12.27
European (539)	608	2.84
Finnish (14)	54	0.25
French, ex. Basque (82)	734	3.43
French Canadian (87)	172	0.80
German (1,764)	5,807	27.11
Greek (0)	70	0.33
Hungarian (0)	79	0.37
Irish (621)	2,717	12.68
Italian (170)	726	3.39
Macedonian (0)	11	0.05
Northern European (13)	13	0.06
Norwegian (301)	1,021	4.77
Pennsylvania German (0)	10	0.05
Polish (72)	282	1.32
Portuguese (53)	53	0.25
Romanian (21)	21	0.10
Russian (100)	218	1.02
Scandinavian (60)	162	0.76
Scotch-Irish (166)	673	3.14
Scottish (423)	1,102	5.14
Slovak (0)	36	0.17
Slovene (9)	9	0.04
Swedish (139)	687	3.21
Swiss (35)	177	0.83
Ukrainian (23)	74	0.35
Welsh (49)	458	2.14
West Indian, ex. Hispanic (25)	25	0.12
Bahamian (25)	25	0.12

Hispanic Origin	Population	%
Hispanic or Latino (of any race)	2,985	13.53
Central American, ex. Mexican	82	0.37
Costa Rican	6	0.03
Guatemalan	37	0.17
Honduran	1	<0.01
Nicaraguan	2	0.01
Panamanian	1	<0.01
Salvadoran	34	0.15
Other Central American	1	<0.01
Cuban	17	0.08
Dominican Republic	9	0.04
Mexican	2,634	11.94
Puerto Rican	61	0.28
South American	20	0.09
Argentinean	2	0.01
Chilean	4	0.02
Colombian	5	0.02
Ecuadorian	1	<0.01
Peruvian	8	0.04
Other Hispanic or Latino	162	0.73

Race*	Population	%
African-American/Black (168)	290	1.31
Not Hispanic (146)	243	1.10
Hispanic (22)	47	0.21
American Indian/Alaska Native (172)	408	1.85
Not Hispanic (101)	285	1.29
Hispanic (71)	123	0.56
Alaska Athabascan *(Ala. Nat.)* (6)	6	0.03
Aleut *(Alaska Native)* (4)	8	0.04

*Notes: † The Census 2010 population figure is used to calculate the percentages in the Hispanic Origin and Race categories. Ancestry percentages are based on the 2006-2010 American Community Survey population (not shown); ‡ Numbers in parentheses indicate the number of people reporting a single ancestry; * Numbers in parentheses indicate the number of persons reporting this race alone, not in combination with any other race; Please refer to the Explanation of Data for more information.*

Apache (0)	1	<0.01
Arapaho (2)	2	0.01
Blackfeet (4)	16	0.07
Canadian/French Am. Ind. (0)	6	0.03
Central American Ind. (2)	4	0.02
Cherokee (5)	68	0.31
Cheyenne (0)	1	<0.01
Chickasaw (0)	1	<0.01
Chippewa (4)	10	0.05
Choctaw (1)	17	0.08
Creek (2)	5	0.02
Crow (1)	3	0.01
Delaware (0)	6	0.03
Inupiat *(Alaska Native)* (1)	3	0.01
Iroquois (1)	6	0.03
Mexican American Ind. (14)	18	0.08
Navajo (2)	9	0.04
Osage (1)	2	0.01
Potawatomi (2)	2	0.01
Pueblo (0)	1	<0.01
Puget Sound Salish (2)	3	0.01
Seminole (0)	1	<0.01
Shoshone (1)	2	0.01
Sioux (11)	15	0.07
South American Ind. (1)	5	0.02
Tlingit-Haida *(Alaska Native)* (4)	5	0.02
Yakama (1)	1	<0.01
Yup'ik *(Alaska Native)* (3)	4	0.02
Asian (486)	716	3.24
Not Hispanic (476)	681	3.09
Hispanic (10)	35	0.16
Burmese (2)	3	0.01
Cambodian (3)	8	0.04
Chinese, ex. Taiwanese (141)	206	0.93
Filipino (78)	149	0.68
Hmong (2)	2	0.01
Indian (36)	50	0.23
Indonesian (9)	13	0.06
Japanese (50)	123	0.56
Korean (74)	100	0.45
Laotian (5)	7	0.03
Malaysian (0)	1	<0.01
Pakistani (9)	11	0.05
Sri Lankan (0)	1	<0.01
Taiwanese (2)	4	0.02
Thai (2)	3	0.01
Vietnamese (45)	56	0.25
Hawaii Native/Pacific Islander (38)	91	0.41
Not Hispanic (35)	78	0.35
Hispanic (3)	13	0.06
Fijian (1)	1	<0.01
Guamanian/Chamorro (4)	11	0.05
Native Hawaiian (15)	48	0.22
Samoan (12)	19	0.09
Tongan (1)	1	<0.01
White (18,966)	19,609	88.86
Not Hispanic (17,803)	18,285	82.86
Hispanic (1,163)	1,324	6.00

Newport

Place Type: City
County: Lincoln
Population: 9,989†

Ancestry‡	Population	%
African, Sub-Saharan (44)	44	0.44
African (44)	44	0.44
American (373)	373	3.75
Arab (9)	18	0.18
Other Arab (9)	18	0.18
Armenian (7)	7	0.07
Austrian (10)	38	0.38
British (12)	99	1.00
Canadian (43)	94	0.95
Czech (28)	131	1.32
Czechoslovakian (37)	37	0.37
Danish (37)	123	1.24
Dutch (47)	162	1.63
Eastern European (6)	6	0.06
English (737)	2,156	21.69
European (108)	131	1.32
Finnish (0)	12	0.12
French, ex. Basque (27)	312	3.14
French Canadian (25)	33	0.33
German (786)	2,053	20.65
Hungarian (0)	27	0.27
Irish (569)	1,702	17.12
Italian (215)	388	3.90
Lithuanian (11)	42	0.42
Northern European (36)	36	0.36
Norwegian (143)	490	4.93
Polish (54)	148	1.49
Portuguese (38)	77	0.77
Romanian (0)	13	0.13
Russian (11)	30	0.30
Scandinavian (73)	92	0.93
Scotch-Irish (39)	259	2.61
Scottish (141)	363	3.65
Swedish (96)	400	4.02
Swiss (42)	145	1.46
Ukrainian (0)	60	0.60
Welsh (9)	107	1.08

Hispanic Origin	Population	%
Hispanic or Latino (of any race)	1,525	15.27
Central American, ex. Mexican	67	0.67
Costa Rican	1	0.01
Guatemalan	57	0.57
Salvadoran	9	0.09
Cuban	7	0.07
Dominican Republic	1	0.01
Mexican	1,318	13.19
Puerto Rican	20	0.20
South American	16	0.16
Argentinean	1	0.01
Chilean	3	0.03
Colombian	6	0.06
Ecuadorian	3	0.03
Peruvian	3	0.03
Other Hispanic or Latino	96	0.96

Race*	Population	%
African-American/Black (63)	112	1.12
Not Hispanic (44)	87	0.87
Hispanic (19)	25	0.25
American Indian/Alaska Native (205)	398	3.98
Not Hispanic (162)	329	3.29
Hispanic (43)	69	0.69
Aleut *(Alaska Native)* (4)	9	0.09
Apache (15)	15	0.15
Arapaho (0)	1	0.01
Blackfeet (7)	11	0.11
Canadian/French Am. Ind. (2)	3	0.03
Central American Ind. (2)	4	0.04
Cherokee (6)	39	0.39
Cheyenne (0)	3	0.03
Chickasaw (2)	9	0.09
Chippewa (5)	6	0.06
Choctaw (3)	7	0.07
Colville (2)	6	0.06
Comanche (0)	1	0.01
Cree (0)	1	0.01
Creek (1)	1	0.01
Delaware (1)	1	0.01
Inupiat *(Alaska Native)* (1)	1	0.01
Iroquois (0)	2	0.02
Kiowa (0)	1	0.01
Mexican American Ind. (8)	10	0.10
Navajo (3)	3	0.03
Osage (7)	9	0.09
Pima (1)	1	0.01
Potawatomi (2)	2	0.02
Puget Sound Salish (0)	1	0.01
Shoshone (1)	1	0.01
Sioux (3)	7	0.07
South American Ind. (0)	1	0.01
Tlingit-Haida *(Alaska Native)* (7)	12	0.12
Tsimshian *(Alaska Native)* (0)	2	0.02
Yakama (1)	1	0.01
Yaqui (0)	1	0.01
Asian (164)	258	2.58
Not Hispanic (163)	240	2.40
Hispanic (1)	18	0.18
Bangladeshi (3)	3	0.03
Cambodian (5)	5	0.05
Chinese, ex. Taiwanese (38)	63	0.63
Filipino (25)	56	0.56
Indian (16)	24	0.24
Indonesian (1)	1	0.01
Japanese (26)	46	0.46
Korean (15)	25	0.25
Sri Lankan (1)	2	0.02
Taiwanese (4)	4	0.04
Thai (6)	6	0.06
Vietnamese (21)	29	0.29
Hawaii Native/Pacific Islander (15)	37	0.37
Not Hispanic (15)	31	0.31
Hispanic (0)	6	0.06
Fijian (2)	2	0.02
Guamanian/Chamorro (0)	1	0.01
Native Hawaiian (8)	22	0.22
Samoan (4)	6	0.06
White (8,398)	8,776	87.86
Not Hispanic (7,794)	8,069	80.78
Hispanic (604)	707	7.08

North Bend

Place Type: City
County: Coos
Population: 9,695†

Ancestry‡	Population	%
American (772)	772	7.95
Austrian (0)	19	0.20
British (21)	54	0.56
Canadian (39)	48	0.49
Celtic (26)	26	0.27
Czech (22)	65	0.67
Danish (25)	44	0.45
Dutch (38)	243	2.50
English (408)	1,317	13.56
European (260)	287	2.96
Finnish (12)	53	0.55
French, ex. Basque (87)	255	2.63
French Canadian (18)	57	0.59
German (615)	2,221	22.87
Greek (0)	9	0.09
Irish (185)	1,063	10.95
Italian (225)	506	5.21
Northern European (51)	51	0.53
Norwegian (328)	559	5.76
Polish (67)	99	1.02
Portuguese (24)	31	0.32
Romanian (27)	27	0.28
Russian (41)	54	0.56
Scandinavian (30)	42	0.43
Scotch-Irish (48)	174	1.79
Scottish (231)	444	4.57
Swedish (51)	226	2.33
Swiss (0)	18	0.19
Ukrainian (9)	9	0.09
Welsh (10)	41	0.42
West Indian, ex. Hispanic (10)	10	0.10
Dutch West Indian (10)	10	0.10
Yugoslavian (10)	10	0.10

Hispanic Origin	Population	%
Hispanic or Latino (of any race)	564	5.82
Central American, ex. Mexican	14	0.14
Costa Rican	2	0.02
Guatemalan	4	0.04
Honduran	1	0.01
Nicaraguan	1	0.01
Panamanian	4	0.04
Salvadoran	1	0.01
Other Central American	1	0.01
Cuban	13	0.13
Mexican	398	4.11

SECTION TWO

*Notes: † The Census 2010 population figure is used to calculate the percentages in the Hispanic Origin and Race categories. Ancestry percentages are based on the 2006-2010 American Community Survey population (not shown); ‡ Numbers in parentheses indicate the number of people reporting a single ancestry; * Numbers in parentheses indicate the number of persons reporting this race alone, not in combination with any other race; Please refer to the Explanation of Data for more information.*

Puerto Rican	26	0.27
South American	31	0.32
Bolivian	1	0.01
Chilean	2	0.02
Colombian	7	0.07
Ecuadorian	1	0.01
Peruvian	17	0.18
Venezuelan	2	0.02
Other South American	1	0.01
Other Hispanic or Latino	82	0.85

Race*	Population	%
African-American/Black (31)	104	1.07
Not Hispanic (30)	87	0.90
Hispanic (1)	17	0.18
American Indian/Alaska Native (223)	516	5.32
Not Hispanic (199)	458	4.72
Hispanic (24)	58	0.60
Alaska Athabascan *(Ala. Nat.)* (5)	8	0.08
Aleut *(Alaska Native)* (1)	3	0.03
Apache (0)	5	0.05
Blackfeet (2)	11	0.11
Cherokee (25)	84	0.87
Cheyenne (0)	2	0.02
Chickasaw (1)	2	0.02
Chippewa (13)	17	0.18
Choctaw (10)	18	0.19
Creek (1)	3	0.03
Crow (1)	1	0.01
Delaware (0)	3	0.03
Iroquois (1)	3	0.03
Lumbee (4)	4	0.04
Menominee (0)	10	0.10
Mexican American Ind. (4)	6	0.06
Navajo (0)	1	0.01
Osage (0)	1	0.01
Paiute (1)	1	0.01
Pima (0)	1	0.01
Pueblo (0)	4	0.04
Puget Sound Salish (2)	4	0.04
Sioux (3)	13	0.13
Tlingit-Haida *(Alaska Native)* (1)	1	0.01
Yup'ik *(Alaska Native)* (1)	2	0.02
Asian (162)	260	2.68
Not Hispanic (160)	252	2.60
Hispanic (2)	8	0.08
Burmese (2)	2	0.02
Cambodian (1)	1	0.01
Chinese, ex. Taiwanese (51)	66	0.68
Filipino (43)	77	0.79
Indian (13)	23	0.24
Japanese (13)	36	0.37
Korean (22)	31	0.32
Laotian (1)	2	0.02
Malaysian (0)	2	0.02
Pakistani (1)	1	0.01
Thai (2)	2	0.02
Vietnamese (11)	14	0.14
Hawaii Native/Pacific Islander (22)	61	0.63
Not Hispanic (22)	57	0.59
Hispanic (0)	4	0.04
Fijian (3)	8	0.08
Native Hawaiian (6)	33	0.34
Samoan (3)	6	0.06
White (8,658)	9,103	93.89
Not Hispanic (8,322)	8,686	89.59
Hispanic (336)	417	4.30

Oak Grove

Place Type: CDP
County: Clackamas
Population: 16,629†

Ancestry‡	Population	%
African, Sub-Saharan (14)	14	0.08
African (14)	14	0.08
American (914)	914	5.40
Arab (0)	206	1.22
Lebanese (0)	206	1.22
Austrian (29)	175	1.03
Basque (15)	30	0.18
Belgian (0)	12	0.07
British (35)	72	0.43
Bulgarian (14)	14	0.08
Cajun (0)	10	0.06
Canadian (16)	64	0.38
Croatian (42)	147	0.87
Czech (137)	183	1.08
Czechoslovakian (0)	35	0.21
Danish (32)	163	0.96
Dutch (52)	347	2.05
English (535)	2,273	13.43
European (454)	588	3.47
Finnish (42)	85	0.50
French, ex. Basque (133)	688	4.06
French Canadian (90)	177	1.05
German (1,349)	4,518	26.68
Greek (8)	83	0.49
Hungarian (37)	37	0.22
Iranian (48)	48	0.28
Irish (697)	2,570	15.18
Italian (144)	835	4.93
Lithuanian (15)	15	0.09
Northern European (44)	44	0.26
Norwegian (218)	934	5.52
Polish (17)	105	0.62
Portuguese (0)	4	0.02
Romanian (24)	35	0.21
Russian (18)	326	1.93
Scandinavian (68)	127	0.75
Scotch-Irish (270)	684	4.04
Scottish (155)	670	3.96
Slovak (0)	50	0.30
Slovene (13)	27	0.16
Swedish (155)	491	2.90
Swiss (23)	156	0.92
Ukrainian (89)	104	0.61
Welsh (112)	194	1.15
Yugoslavian (0)	35	0.21

Hispanic Origin	Population	%
Hispanic or Latino (of any race)	1,403	8.44
Central American, ex. Mexican	70	0.42
Guatemalan	13	0.08
Honduran	6	0.04
Nicaraguan	4	0.02
Panamanian	1	0.01
Salvadoran	46	0.28
Cuban	18	0.11
Dominican Republic	2	0.01
Mexican	1,086	6.53
Puerto Rican	50	0.30
South American	50	0.30
Argentinean	7	0.04
Chilean	15	0.09
Colombian	3	0.02
Peruvian	22	0.13
Venezuelan	3	0.02
Other Hispanic or Latino	127	0.76

Race*	Population	%
African-American/Black (158)	299	1.80
Not Hispanic (144)	260	1.56
Hispanic (14)	39	0.23
American Indian/Alaska Native (135)	336	2.02
Not Hispanic (104)	256	1.54
Hispanic (31)	80	0.48
Aleut *(Alaska Native)* (2)	6	0.04
Apache (1)	8	0.05
Blackfeet (1)	8	0.05
Canadian/French Am. Ind. (1)	4	0.02
Central American Ind. (1)	1	0.01
Cherokee (18)	54	0.32
Cheyenne (0)	1	0.01
Chippewa (7)	11	0.07
Choctaw (3)	7	0.04
Colville (2)	4	0.02
Creek (2)	2	0.01
Inupiat *(Alaska Native)* (1)	1	0.01
Iroquois (1)	1	0.01
Lumbee (1)	4	0.02
Menominee (0)	1	0.01
Mexican American Ind. (10)	13	0.08
Navajo (1)	1	0.01
Potawatomi (3)	3	0.02
Pueblo (1)	1	0.01
Shoshone (1)	1	0.01
Sioux (3)	7	0.04
Tlingit-Haida *(Alaska Native)* (2)	6	0.04
Yakama (1)	4	0.02
Yaqui (0)	1	0.01
Asian (289)	479	2.88
Not Hispanic (285)	443	2.66
Hispanic (4)	36	0.22
Cambodian (8)	14	0.08
Chinese, ex. Taiwanese (52)	91	0.55
Filipino (70)	127	0.76
Hmong (1)	2	0.01
Indian (12)	19	0.11
Indonesian (1)	6	0.04
Japanese (31)	81	0.49
Korean (26)	37	0.22
Laotian (7)	20	0.12
Nepalese (1)	1	0.01
Pakistani (1)	1	0.01
Taiwanese (1)	1	0.01
Thai (25)	33	0.20
Vietnamese (36)	49	0.29
Hawaii Native/Pacific Islander (41)	89	0.54
Not Hispanic (38)	83	0.50
Hispanic (3)	6	0.04
Fijian (0)	2	0.01
Guamanian/Chamorro (1)	6	0.04
Native Hawaiian (17)	48	0.29
Samoan (5)	13	0.08
White (14,917)	15,445	92.88
Not Hispanic (14,220)	14,619	87.91
Hispanic (697)	826	4.97

Oak Hills

Place Type: CDP
County: Washington
Population: 11,333†

Ancestry‡	Population	%
Alsatian (0)	13	0.12
American (322)	322	2.96
Arab (41)	41	0.38
Arab (32)	32	0.29
Egyptian (9)	9	0.08
Armenian (9)	23	0.21
Australian (14)	14	0.13
Austrian (29)	29	0.27
Basque (11)	24	0.22
Belgian (0)	16	0.15
British (45)	110	1.01
Canadian (16)	16	0.15
Croatian (14)	33	0.30
Czech (0)	9	0.08
Danish (32)	92	0.85
Dutch (48)	377	3.46
Eastern European (40)	44	0.40
English (186)	1,212	11.14
European (316)	343	3.15
Finnish (12)	53	0.49
French, ex. Basque (64)	482	4.43
French Canadian (10)	62	0.57
German (588)	2,308	21.21
Greek (59)	203	1.87
Hungarian (0)	56	0.51
Iranian (15)	15	0.14
Irish (313)	1,305	11.99
Italian (111)	669	6.15
Lithuanian (0)	29	0.27
Northern European (13)	13	0.12
Norwegian (69)	350	3.22
Polish (126)	221	2.03
Portuguese (13)	27	0.25

*Notes: † The Census 2010 population figure is used to calculate the percentages in the Hispanic Origin and Race categories. Ancestry percentages are based on the 2006-2010 American Community Survey population (not shown); ‡ Numbers in parentheses indicate the number of people reporting a single ancestry; * Numbers in parentheses indicate the number of persons reporting this race alone, not in combination with any other race; Please refer to the Explanation of Data for more information.*

Romanian (30)	41	0.38
Russian (17)	67	0.62
Scandinavian (34)	34	0.31
Scotch-Irish (108)	303	2.78
Scottish (66)	341	3.13
Swedish (37)	295	2.71
Swiss (9)	49	0.45
Ukrainian (136)	136	1.25
Welsh (0)	269	2.47

Hispanic Origin	Population	%
Hispanic or Latino (of any race)	784	6.92
Central American, ex. Mexican	61	0.54
Guatemalan	31	0.27
Honduran	9	0.08
Nicaraguan	2	0.02
Panamanian	2	0.02
Salvadoran	17	0.15
Cuban	21	0.19
Dominican Republic	2	0.02
Mexican	503	4.44
Puerto Rican	37	0.33
South American	61	0.54
Argentinean	10	0.09
Bolivian	1	0.01
Chilean	1	0.01
Colombian	11	0.10
Ecuadorian	14	0.12
Peruvian	17	0.15
Venezuelan	6	0.05
Other South American	1	0.01
Other Hispanic or Latino	99	0.87

Race*	Population	%
African-American/Black (173)	263	2.32
Not Hispanic (163)	246	2.17
Hispanic (10)	17	0.15
American Indian/Alaska Native (35)	115	1.01
Not Hispanic (29)	98	0.86
Hispanic (6)	17	0.15
Alaska Athabascan *(Ala. Nat.)* (0)	1	0.01
Apache (2)	5	0.04
Blackfeet (2)	9	0.08
Cherokee (3)	13	0.11
Chippewa (4)	9	0.08
Choctaw (0)	1	0.01
Creek (1)	7	0.06
Iroquois (0)	1	0.01
Navajo (0)	5	0.04
Osage (0)	2	0.02
Pueblo (0)	1	0.01
Seminole (1)	1	0.01
Sioux (0)	3	0.03
South American Ind. (0)	1	0.01
Tlingit-Haida *(Alaska Native)* (0)	1	0.01
Tsimshian *(Alaska Native)* (0)	1	0.01
Ute (0)	1	0.01
Yakama (5)	5	0.04
Asian (2,189)	2,469	21.79
Not Hispanic (2,180)	2,445	21.57
Hispanic (9)	24	0.21
Bangladeshi (16)	20	0.18
Burmese (2)	2	0.02
Cambodian (28)	37	0.33
Chinese, ex. Taiwanese (416)	505	4.46
Filipino (91)	165	1.46
Hmong (11)	11	0.10
Indian (751)	780	6.88
Indonesian (14)	17	0.15
Japanese (133)	219	1.93
Korean (326)	367	3.24
Laotian (22)	23	0.20
Malaysian (6)	8	0.07
Nepalese (1)	1	0.01
Pakistani (19)	21	0.19
Sri Lankan (3)	4	0.04
Taiwanese (76)	85	0.75
Thai (8)	13	0.11
Vietnamese (189)	216	1.91
Hawaii Native/Pacific Islander (49)	109	0.96
Not Hispanic (45)	102	0.90
Hispanic (4)	7	0.06
Fijian (4)	5	0.04
Guamanian/Chamorro (14)	15	0.13
Marshallese (2)	2	0.02
Native Hawaiian (18)	71	0.63
Samoan (3)	8	0.07
Tongan (3)	8	0.07
White (8,089)	8,517	75.15
Not Hispanic (7,705)	8,067	71.18
Hispanic (384)	450	3.97

Oatfield

Place Type: CDP
County: Clackamas
Population: 13,415†

Ancestry‡	Population	%
American (693)	693	5.09
Arab (82)	82	0.60
Lebanese (74)	74	0.54
Syrian (8)	8	0.06
Australian (0)	22	0.16
Austrian (12)	34	0.25
Belgian (13)	13	0.10
British (34)	45	0.33
Canadian (71)	175	1.28
Croatian (0)	9	0.07
Czech (60)	191	1.40
Danish (41)	275	2.02
Dutch (36)	336	2.47
Eastern European (16)	31	0.23
English (519)	2,089	15.34
European (502)	588	4.32
Finnish (6)	17	0.12
French, ex. Basque (88)	629	4.62
French Canadian (0)	75	0.55
German (1,391)	3,436	25.23
Greek (10)	59	0.43
Hungarian (18)	38	0.28
Irish (527)	1,817	13.34
Italian (214)	458	3.36
Lithuanian (0)	27	0.20
Northern European (24)	24	0.18
Norwegian (237)	792	5.82
Pennsylvania German (0)	8	0.06
Polish (32)	353	2.59
Portuguese (0)	51	0.37
Romanian (53)	53	0.39
Russian (62)	128	0.94
Scandinavian (31)	31	0.23
Scotch-Irish (102)	261	1.92
Scottish (115)	317	2.33
Serbian (19)	19	0.14
Slavic (0)	34	0.25
Slovak (34)	46	0.34
Swedish (47)	534	3.92
Swiss (60)	219	1.61
Ukrainian (132)	232	1.70
Welsh (61)	184	1.35
Yugoslavian (0)	10	0.07

Hispanic Origin	Population	%
Hispanic or Latino (of any race)	871	6.49
Central American, ex. Mexican	49	0.37
Costa Rican	3	0.02
Guatemalan	27	0.20
Honduran	3	0.02
Panamanian	9	0.07
Salvadoran	7	0.05
Cuban	31	0.23
Dominican Republic	4	0.03
Mexican	660	4.92
Puerto Rican	21	0.16
South American	37	0.28
Argentinean	3	0.02
Bolivian	9	0.07
Chilean	5	0.04
Colombian	10	0.07
Ecuadorian	2	0.01
Peruvian	8	0.06
Other Hispanic or Latino	69	0.51

Race*	Population	%
African-American/Black (112)	217	1.62
Not Hispanic (107)	193	1.44
Hispanic (5)	24	0.18
American Indian/Alaska Native (124)	287	2.14
Not Hispanic (94)	236	1.76
Hispanic (30)	51	0.38
Alaska Athabascan *(Ala. Nat.)* (1)	2	0.01
Aleut *(Alaska Native)* (6)	6	0.04
Apache (1)	6	0.04
Blackfeet (1)	12	0.09
Central American Ind. (5)	5	0.04
Cherokee (20)	60	0.45
Chippewa (7)	18	0.13
Choctaw (5)	16	0.12
Colville (2)	2	0.01
Cree (0)	1	0.01
Creek (1)	5	0.04
Crow (0)	1	0.01
Inupiat *(Alaska Native)* (1)	4	0.03
Iroquois (6)	7	0.05
Mexican American Ind. (3)	4	0.03
Navajo (3)	4	0.03
Paiute (5)	6	0.04
Puget Sound Salish (0)	1	0.01
Seminole (0)	2	0.01
Shoshone (0)	3	0.02
Sioux (3)	7	0.05
South American Ind. (1)	1	0.01
Tlingit-Haida *(Alaska Native)* (1)	1	0.01
Tsimshian *(Alaska Native)* (0)	1	0.01
Yaqui (0)	1	0.01
Asian (432)	598	4.46
Not Hispanic (430)	577	4.30
Hispanic (2)	21	0.16
Burmese (1)	1	0.01
Cambodian (23)	28	0.21
Chinese, ex. Taiwanese (61)	95	0.71
Filipino (80)	127	0.95
Hmong (18)	18	0.13
Indian (34)	42	0.31
Indonesian (4)	8	0.06
Japanese (43)	89	0.66
Korean (54)	73	0.54
Laotian (20)	26	0.19
Sri Lankan (5)	5	0.04
Thai (3)	3	0.02
Vietnamese (70)	83	0.62
Hawaii Native/Pacific Islander (15)	53	0.40
Not Hispanic (15)	48	0.36
Hispanic (0)	5	0.04
Guamanian/Chamorro (0)	4	0.03
Native Hawaiian (14)	32	0.24
Samoan (0)	1	0.01
Tongan (1)	1	0.01
White (12,001)	12,422	92.60
Not Hispanic (11,509)	11,838	88.24
Hispanic (492)	584	4.35

Ontario

Place Type: City
County: Malheur
Population: 11,366†

Ancestry‡	Population	%
African, Sub-Saharan (8)	60	0.53
African (7)	59	0.52
Kenyan (1)	1	0.01
American (765)	765	6.77
Austrian (0)	9	0.08
Basque (69)	133	1.18
Canadian (12)	37	0.33
Czech (0)	25	0.22
Czechoslovakian (15)	15	0.13
Danish (9)	48	0.42

*Notes: † The Census 2010 population figure is used to calculate the percentages in the Hispanic Origin and Race categories. Ancestry percentages are based on the 2006-2010 American Community Survey population (not shown); ‡ Numbers in parentheses indicate the number of people reporting a single ancestry; * Numbers in parentheses indicate the number of persons reporting this race alone, not in combination with any other race; Please refer to the Explanation of Data for more information.*

Ancestry (continued)	Population	%
Dutch (45)	240	2.12
Eastern European (7)	7	0.06
English (749)	1,303	11.52
European (132)	171	1.51
Finnish (22)	22	0.19
French, ex. Basque (36)	157	1.39
French Canadian (12)	30	0.27
German (445)	1,481	13.10
Greek (0)	40	0.35
Irish (216)	955	8.45
Italian (205)	364	3.22
Norwegian (72)	304	2.69
Portuguese (0)	9	0.08
Russian (0)	240	2.12
Scandinavian (0)	11	0.10
Scotch-Irish (105)	240	2.12
Scottish (89)	264	2.33
Swedish (43)	243	2.15
Welsh (9)	77	0.68
West Indian, ex. Hispanic (7)	7	0.06
British West Indian (7)	7	0.06

Hispanic Origin	Population	%
Hispanic or Latino (of any race)	4,691	41.27
Central American, ex. Mexican	17	0.15
Guatemalan	3	0.03
Honduran	1	0.01
Nicaraguan	3	0.03
Panamanian	4	0.04
Salvadoran	6	0.05
Cuban	7	0.06
Mexican	4,137	36.40
Puerto Rican	15	0.13
South American	8	0.07
Argentinean	1	0.01
Colombian	4	0.04
Ecuadorian	1	0.01
Peruvian	2	0.02
Other Hispanic or Latino	507	4.46

Race*	Population	%
African-American/Black (74)	129	1.13
Not Hispanic (50)	88	0.77
Hispanic (24)	41	0.36
American Indian/Alaska Native (153)	300	2.64
Not Hispanic (89)	192	1.69
Hispanic (64)	108	0.95
Alaska Athabascan *(Ala. Nat.)* (1)	1	0.01
Aleut *(Alaska Native)* (0)	1	0.01
Apache (1)	1	0.01
Blackfeet (9)	13	0.11
Canadian/French Am. Ind. (0)	1	0.01
Cherokee (15)	36	0.32
Cheyenne (4)	4	0.04
Chickasaw (0)	1	0.01
Chippewa (6)	13	0.11
Choctaw (1)	3	0.03
Cree (0)	1	0.01
Creek (2)	2	0.02
Crow (0)	3	0.03
Delaware (1)	3	0.03
Iroquois (0)	2	0.02
Mexican American Ind. (27)	35	0.31
Navajo (1)	4	0.04
Osage (1)	1	0.01
Paiute (6)	17	0.15
Seminole (0)	1	0.01
Shoshone (1)	1	0.01
Sioux (4)	16	0.14
Spanish American Ind. (0)	5	0.04
Ute (0)	1	0.01
Yakama (1)	1	0.01
Yaqui (2)	3	0.03
Asian (251)	330	2.90
Not Hispanic (239)	301	2.65
Hispanic (12)	29	0.26
Chinese, ex. Taiwanese (18)	28	0.25
Filipino (28)	41	0.36
Indian (8)	14	0.12
Japanese (177)	220	1.94
Korean (9)	16	0.14
Pakistani (4)	4	0.04
Vietnamese (5)	7	0.06
Hawaii Native/Pacific Islander (14)	20	0.18
Not Hispanic (2)	6	0.05
Hispanic (12)	14	0.12
Guamanian/Chamorro (11)	12	0.11
Native Hawaiian (0)	1	0.01
Samoan (0)	2	0.02
Tongan (1)	1	0.01
White (7,902)	8,280	72.85
Not Hispanic (6,083)	6,277	55.23
Hispanic (1,819)	2,003	17.62

Oregon City

Place Type: City
County: Clackamas
Population: 31,859†

Ancestry‡	Population	%
African, Sub-Saharan (22)	22	0.07
African (22)	22	0.07
American (1,787)	1,787	5.77
Arab (0)	50	0.16
Arab (0)	18	0.06
Syrian (0)	32	0.10
Armenian (0)	32	0.10
Austrian (0)	88	0.28
Belgian (0)	65	0.21
British (38)	100	0.32
Canadian (30)	71	0.23
Celtic (0)	10	0.03
Croatian (27)	27	0.09
Czech (18)	138	0.45
Czechoslovakian (33)	44	0.14
Danish (272)	531	1.71
Dutch (248)	1,030	3.32
Eastern European (15)	15	0.05
English (1,136)	4,386	14.16
European (418)	556	1.79
Finnish (95)	365	1.18
French, ex. Basque (212)	1,041	3.36
French Canadian (113)	265	0.86
German (2,901)	8,586	27.71
Greek (14)	125	0.40
Hungarian (54)	214	0.69
Iranian (21)	28	0.09
Irish (785)	4,004	12.92
Italian (303)	947	3.06
Lithuanian (22)	22	0.07
Luxemburger (5)	5	0.02
Maltese (31)	31	0.10
New Zealander (0)	32	0.10
Northern European (75)	75	0.24
Norwegian (678)	1,664	5.37
Polish (124)	511	1.65
Portuguese (0)	111	0.36
Romanian (146)	146	0.47
Russian (405)	755	2.44
Scandinavian (174)	379	1.22
Scotch-Irish (223)	860	2.78
Scottish (227)	953	3.08
Slovak (16)	32	0.10
Swedish (318)	1,243	4.01
Swiss (104)	191	0.62
Ukrainian (342)	483	1.56
Welsh (86)	288	0.93

Hispanic Origin	Population	%
Hispanic or Latino (of any race)	2,339	7.34
Central American, ex. Mexican	105	0.33
Costa Rican	3	0.01
Guatemalan	20	0.06
Honduran	14	0.04
Nicaraguan	5	0.02
Panamanian	4	0.01
Salvadoran	57	0.18
Other Central American	2	0.01
Cuban	28	0.09
Dominican Republic	6	0.02
Mexican	1,829	5.74
Puerto Rican	75	0.24
South American	82	0.26
Argentinean	11	0.03
Bolivian	4	0.01
Chilean	8	0.03
Colombian	28	0.09
Ecuadorian	3	0.01
Paraguayan	1	<0.01
Peruvian	21	0.07
Uruguayan	3	0.01
Venezuelan	1	<0.01
Other South American	2	0.01
Other Hispanic or Latino	214	0.67

Race*	Population	%
African-American/Black (191)	423	1.33
Not Hispanic (167)	365	1.15
Hispanic (24)	58	0.18
American Indian/Alaska Native (271)	665	2.09
Not Hispanic (206)	531	1.67
Hispanic (65)	134	0.42
Aleut *(Alaska Native)* (2)	5	0.02
Apache (9)	21	0.07
Arapaho (3)	4	0.01
Blackfeet (1)	22	0.07
Canadian/French Am. Ind. (3)	4	0.01
Central American Ind. (1)	1	<0.01
Cherokee (19)	71	0.22
Cheyenne (1)	3	0.01
Chickasaw (4)	6	0.02
Chippewa (9)	19	0.06
Choctaw (18)	28	0.09
Colville (1)	1	<0.01
Cree (0)	3	0.01
Creek (1)	11	0.03
Delaware (2)	3	0.01
Hopi (1)	5	0.02
Inupiat *(Alaska Native)* (1)	2	0.01
Iroquois (4)	6	0.02
Lumbee (1)	1	<0.01
Menominee (0)	2	0.01
Mexican American Ind. (14)	21	0.07
Navajo (2)	6	0.02
Osage (0)	7	0.02
Ottawa (1)	1	<0.01
Paiute (1)	1	<0.01
Pima (0)	4	0.01
Potawatomi (1)	3	0.01
Puget Sound Salish (0)	3	0.01
Seminole (0)	1	<0.01
Shoshone (1)	2	0.01
Sioux (9)	24	0.08
South American Ind. (1)	2	0.01
Spanish American Ind. (1)	1	<0.01
Tlingit-Haida *(Alaska Native)* (4)	5	0.02
Ute (0)	2	0.01
Yakama (2)	8	0.03
Yaqui (0)	3	0.01
Yup'ik *(Alaska Native)* (1)	4	0.01
Asian (548)	867	2.72
Not Hispanic (542)	838	2.63
Hispanic (6)	29	0.09
Cambodian (8)	17	0.05
Chinese, ex. Taiwanese (86)	137	0.43
Filipino (98)	182	0.57
Hmong (31)	34	0.11
Indian (21)	45	0.14
Indonesian (11)	33	0.10
Japanese (51)	141	0.44
Korean (67)	103	0.32
Laotian (24)	27	0.08
Nepalese (4)	5	0.02
Pakistani (7)	8	0.03
Sri Lankan (1)	1	<0.01
Taiwanese (3)	3	0.01
Thai (12)	24	0.08
Vietnamese (79)	91	0.29
Hawaii Native/Pacific Islander (71)	159	0.50

*Notes: † The Census 2010 population figure is used to calculate the percentages in the Hispanic Origin and Race categories. Ancestry percentages are based on the 2006-2010 American Community Survey population (not shown); ‡ Numbers in parentheses indicate the number of people reporting a single ancestry; * Numbers in parentheses indicate the number of persons reporting this race alone, not in combination with any other race; Please refer to the Explanation of Data for more information.*

Not Hispanic (68)	152	0.48
Hispanic (3)	7	0.02
Fijian (6)	7	0.02
Guamanian/Chamorro (4)	11	0.03
Marshallese (2)	2	0.01
Native Hawaiian (21)	58	0.18
Samoan (12)	17	0.05
Tongan (6)	7	0.02
White (29,033)	29,960	94.04
Not Hispanic (27,722)	28,461	89.33
Hispanic (1,311)	1,499	4.71

Pendleton

Place Type: City
County: Umatilla
Population: 16,612†

Ancestry‡	Population	%
African, Sub-Saharan (19)	36	0.22
African (19)	36	0.22
American (1,082)	1,082	6.50
Arab (0)	33	0.20
Other Arab (0)	33	0.20
Basque (0)	44	0.26
Belgian (0)	89	0.53
British (0)	13	0.08
Cajun (0)	11	0.07
Canadian (0)	54	0.32
Czech (0)	42	0.25
Czechoslovakian (9)	24	0.14
Danish (76)	261	1.57
Dutch (33)	355	2.13
English (618)	2,431	14.60
European (193)	240	1.44
Finnish (28)	58	0.35
French, ex. Basque (52)	361	2.17
French Canadian (64)	164	0.98
German (1,355)	4,302	25.84
Greek (27)	38	0.23
Hungarian (0)	59	0.35
Irish (614)	2,663	15.99
Italian (93)	305	1.83
Norwegian (144)	619	3.72
Pennsylvania German (0)	27	0.16
Polish (34)	152	0.91
Portuguese (49)	93	0.56
Russian (46)	103	0.62
Scandinavian (20)	119	0.71
Scotch-Irish (123)	457	2.74
Scottish (98)	597	3.59
Slovak (0)	10	0.06
Swedish (72)	463	2.78
Swiss (8)	150	0.90
Welsh (108)	186	1.12
Yugoslavian (9)	9	0.05

Hispanic Origin	Population	%
Hispanic or Latino (of any race)	1,605	9.66
Central American, ex. Mexican	23	0.14
Costa Rican	1	0.01
Honduran	13	0.08
Salvadoran	9	0.05
Cuban	5	0.03
Dominican Republic	8	0.05
Mexican	1,427	8.59
Puerto Rican	29	0.17
South American	19	0.11
Chilean	1	0.01
Colombian	2	0.01
Peruvian	14	0.08
Venezuelan	2	0.01
Other Hispanic or Latino	94	0.57

Race*	Population	%
African-American/Black (231)	306	1.84
Not Hispanic (223)	289	1.74
Hispanic (8)	17	0.10
American Indian/Alaska Native (528)	833	5.01
Not Hispanic (479)	749	4.51
Hispanic (49)	84	0.51
Aleut *(Alaska Native)* (1)	1	0.01
Apache (1)	5	0.03
Arapaho (1)	1	0.01
Blackfeet (3)	12	0.07
Canadian/French Am. Ind. (1)	1	0.01
Central American Ind. (1)	2	0.01
Cherokee (16)	59	0.36
Cheyenne (0)	5	0.03
Chickasaw (5)	5	0.03
Chippewa (17)	25	0.15
Choctaw (6)	10	0.06
Colville (6)	8	0.05
Cree (1)	5	0.03
Creek (0)	1	0.01
Crow (0)	2	0.01
Delaware (3)	5	0.03
Inupiat *(Alaska Native)* (1)	1	0.01
Iroquois (3)	7	0.04
Lumbee (2)	2	0.01
Mexican American Ind. (1)	1	0.01
Navajo (6)	10	0.06
Osage (1)	2	0.01
Paiute (3)	3	0.02
Potawatomi (3)	5	0.03
Puget Sound Salish (1)	2	0.01
Shoshone (2)	2	0.01
Sioux (14)	30	0.18
Tlingit-Haida *(Alaska Native)* (8)	12	0.07
Tsimshian *(Alaska Native)* (0)	1	0.01
Yakama (28)	37	0.22
Yaqui (1)	1	0.01
Yuman (3)	3	0.02
Asian (187)	267	1.61
Not Hispanic (183)	253	1.52
Hispanic (4)	14	0.08
Cambodian (23)	24	0.14
Chinese, ex. Taiwanese (36)	41	0.25
Filipino (38)	66	0.40
Indian (9)	14	0.08
Japanese (11)	21	0.13
Korean (16)	27	0.16
Laotian (3)	6	0.04
Pakistani (0)	2	0.01
Taiwanese (4)	4	0.02
Thai (7)	13	0.08
Vietnamese (12)	16	0.10
Hawaii Native/Pacific Islander (26)	50	0.30
Not Hispanic (26)	48	0.29
Hispanic (0)	2	0.01
Guamanian/Chamorro (1)	1	0.01
Native Hawaiian (6)	22	0.13
Samoan (7)	10	0.06
White (14,507)	15,021	90.42
Not Hispanic (13,690)	14,074	84.72
Hispanic (817)	947	5.70

Portland

Place Type: City
County: Multnomah
Population: 583,776†

Ancestry‡	Population	%
Afghan (16)	35	0.01
African, Sub-Saharan (5,387)	6,834	1.21
African (2,796)	3,921	0.69
Ethiopian (863)	940	0.17
Ghanaian (199)	217	0.04
Kenyan (153)	153	0.03
Liberian (119)	157	0.03
Nigerian (84)	138	0.02
Senegalese (25)	25	<0.01
Sierra Leonean (10)	20	<0.01
Somalian (910)	1,004	0.18
South African (0)	15	<0.01
Sudanese (73)	73	0.01
Zimbabwean (0)	16	<0.01
Other Sub-Saharan African (155)	155	0.03
Albanian (117)	160	0.03
Alsatian (47)	122	0.02
American (23,846)	23,846	4.21
Arab (1,765)	3,494	0.62
Arab (703)	1,017	0.18
Egyptian (139)	253	0.04
Iraqi (12)	56	0.01
Jordanian (0)	13	<0.01
Lebanese (284)	1,079	0.19
Moroccan (44)	75	0.01
Palestinian (180)	196	0.03
Syrian (81)	235	0.04
Other Arab (322)	570	0.10
Armenian (152)	347	0.06
Assyrian/Chaldean/Syriac (0)	32	0.01
Australian (187)	455	0.08
Austrian (398)	1,912	0.34
Basque (130)	409	0.07
Belgian (232)	995	0.18
Brazilian (177)	233	0.04
British (2,172)	5,218	0.92
Bulgarian (310)	665	0.12
Cajun (88)	132	0.02
Canadian (964)	2,161	0.38
Carpatho Rusyn (8)	8	<0.01
Celtic (124)	226	0.04
Croatian (603)	1,270	0.22
Czech (1,034)	3,510	0.62
Czechoslovakian (222)	720	0.13
Danish (1,144)	6,203	1.09
Dutch (2,017)	11,114	1.96
Eastern European (1,430)	1,654	0.29
English (17,127)	65,820	11.61
Estonian (27)	58	0.01
European (12,250)	14,432	2.55
Finnish (1,279)	3,748	0.66
French, ex. Basque (2,785)	20,676	3.65
French Canadian (1,150)	3,683	0.65
German (28,476)	108,939	19.22
German Russian (15)	50	0.01
Greek (1,005)	2,676	0.47
Guyanese (7)	22	<0.01
Hungarian (694)	2,509	0.44
Icelander (35)	380	0.07
Iranian (451)	648	0.11
Irish (19,036)	72,114	12.73
Israeli (199)	277	0.05
Italian (8,478)	24,417	4.31
Latvian (230)	500	0.09
Lithuanian (364)	1,309	0.23
Luxemburger (16)	153	0.03
Macedonian (11)	58	0.01
Maltese (0)	71	0.01
New Zealander (15)	27	<0.01
Northern European (2,035)	2,177	0.38
Norwegian (7,947)	23,053	4.07
Pennsylvania German (238)	450	0.08
Polish (2,741)	12,757	2.25
Portuguese (756)	2,108	0.37
Romanian (2,735)	3,976	0.70
Russian (6,667)	13,188	2.33
Scandinavian (1,622)	3,477	0.61
Scotch-Irish (4,694)	14,767	2.61
Scottish (4,378)	19,960	3.52
Serbian (137)	405	0.07
Slavic (153)	412	0.07
Slovak (179)	689	0.12
Slovene (24)	275	0.05
Soviet Union (21)	21	<0.01
Swedish (3,980)	17,319	3.06
Swiss (913)	4,649	0.82
Turkish (245)	499	0.09
Ukrainian (5,321)	7,584	1.34
Welsh (1,268)	7,213	1.27
West Indian, ex. Hispanic (559)	1,275	0.22
Bahamian (35)	110	0.02
Barbadian (0)	68	0.01
Bermudan (13)	13	<0.01
British West Indian (0)	27	<0.01
Dutch West Indian (22)	113	0.02
Haitian (168)	259	0.05

*Notes: † The Census 2010 population figure is used to calculate the percentages in the Hispanic Origin and Race categories. Ancestry percentages are based on the 2006-2010 American Community Survey population (not shown); ‡ Numbers in parentheses indicate the number of people reporting a single ancestry; * Numbers in parentheses indicate the number of persons reporting this race alone, not in combination with any other race; Please refer to the Explanation of Data for more information.*

SECTION TWO

Jamaican (283)	452	0.08
U.S. Virgin Islander (0)	18	<0.01
West Indian (38)	215	0.04
Yugoslavian (735)	1,111	0.20

Hispanic Origin	Population	%
Hispanic or Latino (of any race)	54,840	9.39
Central American, ex. Mexican	3,941	0.68
Costa Rican	144	0.02
Guatemalan	1,894	0.32
Honduran	423	0.07
Nicaraguan	284	0.05
Panamanian	137	0.02
Salvadoran	1,027	0.18
Other Central American	32	0.01
Cuban	2,172	0.37
Dominican Republic	138	0.02
Mexican	39,181	6.71
Puerto Rican	1,729	0.30
South American	2,215	0.38
Argentinean	381	0.07
Bolivian	83	0.01
Chilean	307	0.05
Colombian	446	0.08
Ecuadorian	215	0.04
Paraguayan	20	<0.01
Peruvian	537	0.09
Uruguayan	33	0.01
Venezuelan	161	0.03
Other South American	32	0.01
Other Hispanic or Latino	5,464	0.94

Race*	Population	%
African-American/Black (36,695)	45,545	7.80
Not Hispanic (35,462)	43,057	7.38
Hispanic (1,233)	2,488	0.43
American Indian/Alaska Native (5,991)	14,262	2.44
Not Hispanic (4,381)	11,163	1.91
Hispanic (1,610)	3,099	0.53
Alaska Athabascan *(Ala. Nat.)* (34)	57	0.01
Aleut *(Alaska Native)* (40)	74	0.01
Apache (100)	299	0.05
Arapaho (8)	11	<0.01
Blackfeet (156)	515	0.09
Canadian/French Am. Ind. (21)	67	0.01
Central American Ind. (49)	59	0.01
Cherokee (355)	1,874	0.32
Cheyenne (34)	66	0.01
Chickasaw (26)	74	0.01
Chippewa (260)	588	0.10
Choctaw (82)	401	0.07
Colville (35)	61	0.01
Comanche (11)	36	0.01
Cree (9)	48	0.01
Creek (47)	152	0.03
Crow (10)	35	0.01
Delaware (6)	40	0.01
Hopi (7)	28	<0.01
Houma (2)	13	<0.01
Inupiat *(Alaska Native)* (32)	64	0.01
Iroquois (45)	152	0.03
Kiowa (14)	27	<0.01
Lumbee (5)	15	<0.01
Menominee (7)	13	<0.01
Mexican American Ind. (565)	786	0.13
Navajo (125)	245	0.04
Osage (15)	58	0.01
Ottawa (8)	21	<0.01
Paiute (37)	69	0.01
Pima (14)	34	0.01
Potawatomi (14)	45	0.01
Pueblo (28)	65	0.01
Puget Sound Salish (35)	68	0.01
Seminole (19)	68	0.01
Shoshone (18)	44	0.01
Sioux (349)	786	0.13
South American Ind. (25)	72	0.01
Spanish American Ind. (15)	30	0.01
Tlingit-Haida *(Alaska Native)* (107)	188	0.03
Tohono O'Odham (1)	18	<0.01
Tsimshian *(Alaska Native)* (18)	32	0.01
Ute (11)	21	<0.01
Yakama (66)	166	0.03
Yaqui (15)	43	0.01
Yuman (7)	15	<0.01
Yup'ik *(Alaska Native)* (23)	45	0.01
Asian (41,692)	51,854	8.88
Not Hispanic (41,335)	50,635	8.67
Hispanic (357)	1,219	0.21
Bangladeshi (33)	43	0.01
Bhutanese (156)	168	0.03
Burmese (681)	747	0.13
Cambodian (767)	1,018	0.17
Chinese, ex. Taiwanese (9,765)	12,434	2.13
Filipino (3,225)	5,688	0.97
Hmong (1,038)	1,115	0.19
Indian (2,155)	3,053	0.52
Indonesian (160)	370	0.06
Japanese (2,826)	5,543	0.95
Korean (2,403)	3,438	0.59
Laotian (2,223)	2,603	0.45
Malaysian (40)	83	0.01
Nepalese (157)	180	0.03
Pakistani (195)	249	0.04
Sri Lankan (69)	89	0.02
Taiwanese (239)	337	0.06
Thai (654)	960	0.16
Vietnamese (12,796)	13,921	2.38
Hawaii Native/Pacific Islander (3,109)	5,229	0.90
Not Hispanic (2,978)	4,848	0.83
Hispanic (131)	381	0.07
Fijian (277)	366	0.06
Guamanian/Chamorro (265)	470	0.08
Marshallese (14)	19	<0.01
Native Hawaiian (403)	1,314	0.23
Samoan (270)	497	0.09
Tongan (411)	497	0.09
White (444,216)	468,194	80.20
Not Hispanic (421,773)	441,039	75.55
Hispanic (22,443)	27,155	4.65

Prineville

Place Type: City
County: Crook
Population: 9,253†

Ancestry‡	Population	%
American (575)	575	6.08
Armenian (23)	23	0.24
Austrian (0)	29	0.31
Basque (11)	23	0.24
British (11)	28	0.30
Canadian (11)	39	0.41
Celtic (0)	23	0.24
Czech (0)	43	0.46
Czechoslovakian (0)	10	0.11
Danish (63)	109	1.15
Dutch (101)	329	3.48
English (344)	1,180	12.49
European (78)	78	0.83
Finnish (48)	67	0.71
French, ex. Basque (59)	293	3.10
French Canadian (0)	73	0.77
German (328)	1,500	15.87
Greek (0)	33	0.35
Irish (259)	966	10.22
Italian (0)	250	2.65
Norwegian (52)	211	2.23
Polish (0)	61	0.65
Russian (34)	162	1.71
Scandinavian (11)	25	0.26
Scotch-Irish (139)	368	3.89
Scottish (167)	324	3.43
Slavic (0)	21	0.22
Swedish (68)	174	1.84
Swiss (0)	46	0.49
Welsh (0)	85	0.90
Yugoslavian (0)	10	0.11

Hispanic Origin	Population	%
Hispanic or Latino (of any race)	934	10.09
Central American, ex. Mexican	5	0.05
Costa Rican	1	0.01
Honduran	2	0.02
Nicaraguan	2	0.02
Cuban	1	0.01
Mexican	828	8.95
Puerto Rican	16	0.17
South American	2	0.02
Chilean	1	0.01
Peruvian	1	0.01
Other Hispanic or Latino	82	0.89

Race*	Population	%
African-American/Black (15)	39	0.42
Not Hispanic (12)	36	0.39
Hispanic (3)	3	0.03
American Indian/Alaska Native (137)	270	2.92
Not Hispanic (115)	227	2.45
Hispanic (22)	43	0.46
Alaska Athabascan *(Ala. Nat.)* (1)	4	0.04
Aleut *(Alaska Native)* (3)	5	0.05
Apache (0)	1	0.01
Blackfeet (5)	11	0.12
Canadian/French Am. Ind. (1)	2	0.02
Cherokee (11)	25	0.27
Cheyenne (0)	1	0.01
Chickasaw (1)	6	0.06
Chippewa (0)	1	0.01
Choctaw (9)	16	0.17
Cree (0)	1	0.01
Creek (0)	1	0.01
Hopi (1)	1	0.01
Inupiat *(Alaska Native)* (1)	1	0.01
Iroquois (4)	4	0.04
Mexican American Ind. (11)	11	0.12
Paiute (4)	4	0.04
Potawatomi (2)	2	0.02
Shoshone (1)	1	0.01
Sioux (8)	17	0.18
Tlingit-Haida *(Alaska Native)* (1)	1	0.01
Yakama (1)	1	0.01
Yaqui (0)	1	0.01
Asian (62)	99	1.07
Not Hispanic (62)	88	0.95
Hispanic (0)	11	0.12
Cambodian (0)	1	0.01
Chinese, ex. Taiwanese (30)	33	0.36
Filipino (18)	34	0.37
Indian (1)	1	0.01
Japanese (2)	7	0.08
Korean (2)	6	0.06
Pakistani (1)	3	0.03
Vietnamese (6)	7	0.08
Hawaii Native/Pacific Islander (9)	19	0.21
Not Hispanic (9)	14	0.15
Hispanic (0)	5	0.05
Guamanian/Chamorro (0)	1	0.01
Native Hawaiian (4)	14	0.15
Tongan (2)	2	0.02
White (8,366)	8,556	92.47
Not Hispanic (7,953)	8,112	87.67
Hispanic (413)	444	4.80

Redmond

Place Type: City
County: Deschutes
Population: 26,215†

Ancestry‡	Population	%
African, Sub-Saharan (8)	8	0.03
African (8)	8	0.03
American (1,211)	1,211	4.85
Arab (0)	148	0.59
Egyptian (0)	74	0.30
Lebanese (0)	74	0.30
Armenian (0)	29	0.12
Australian (0)	34	0.14

*Notes: † The Census 2010 population figure is used to calculate the percentages in the Hispanic Origin and Race categories. Ancestry percentages are based on the 2006-2010 American Community Survey population (not shown); ‡ Numbers in parentheses indicate the number of people reporting a single ancestry; * Numbers in parentheses indicate the number of persons reporting this race alone, not in combination with any other race; Please refer to the Explanation of Data for more information.*

Austrian (34)	84	0.34
Basque (52)	60	0.24
Belgian (0)	11	0.04
British (26)	59	0.24
Canadian (43)	91	0.36
Croatian (10)	10	0.04
Danish (168)	384	1.54
Dutch (82)	949	3.80
English (1,053)	2,913	11.67
European (408)	544	2.18
Finnish (26)	144	0.58
French, ex. Basque (172)	850	3.41
French Canadian (79)	215	0.86
German (1,834)	5,477	21.95
Greek (24)	122	0.49
Hungarian (15)	80	0.32
Icelander (0)	12	0.05
Irish (758)	3,798	15.22
Italian (525)	1,207	4.84
Macedonian (10)	18	0.07
Norwegian (444)	1,111	4.45
Pennsylvania German (13)	13	0.05
Polish (266)	501	2.01
Portuguese (45)	91	0.36
Romanian (18)	127	0.51
Russian (14)	158	0.63
Scandinavian (22)	95	0.38
Scotch-Irish (340)	501	2.01
Scottish (175)	747	2.99
Serbian (0)	8	0.03
Slovak (0)	9	0.04
Swedish (132)	562	2.25
Swiss (47)	199	0.80
Welsh (57)	182	0.73
Yugoslavian (0)	9	0.04

Hispanic Origin	Population	%
Hispanic or Latino (of any race)	3,275	12.49
Central American, ex. Mexican	164	0.63
Costa Rican	2	0.01
Guatemalan	41	0.16
Honduran	7	0.03
Nicaraguan	16	0.06
Panamanian	2	0.01
Salvadoran	96	0.37
Cuban	10	0.04
Dominican Republic	3	0.01
Mexican	2,761	10.53
Puerto Rican	38	0.14
South American	38	0.14
Argentinean	7	0.03
Chilean	5	0.02
Colombian	5	0.02
Ecuadorian	5	0.02
Paraguayan	3	0.01
Peruvian	7	0.03
Uruguayan	1	<0.01
Venezuelan	5	0.02
Other Hispanic or Latino	261	1.00

Race*	Population	%
African-American/Black (104)	239	0.91
Not Hispanic (88)	200	0.76
Hispanic (16)	39	0.15
American Indian/Alaska Native (333)	680	2.59
Not Hispanic (290)	584	2.23
Hispanic (43)	96	0.37
Alaska Athabascan *(Ala. Nat.)* (2)	4	0.02
Aleut *(Alaska Native)* (6)	7	0.03
Apache (2)	11	0.04
Arapaho (0)	1	<0.01
Blackfeet (6)	17	0.06
Canadian/French Am. Ind. (1)	2	0.01
Cherokee (16)	106	0.40
Cheyenne (0)	1	<0.01
Chickasaw (1)	4	0.02
Chippewa (6)	12	0.05
Choctaw (13)	18	0.07
Colville (7)	7	0.03
Comanche (0)	3	0.01
Cree (0)	2	0.01
Creek (1)	1	<0.01
Crow (2)	2	0.01
Hopi (0)	3	0.01
Inupiat *(Alaska Native)* (0)	3	0.01
Iroquois (0)	3	0.01
Lumbee (0)	1	<0.01
Mexican American Ind. (6)	14	0.05
Navajo (16)	19	0.07
Osage (1)	1	<0.01
Paiute (0)	4	0.02
Pima (2)	2	0.01
Potawatomi (0)	1	<0.01
Puget Sound Salish (4)	7	0.03
Seminole (0)	3	0.01
Shoshone (1)	5	0.02
Sioux (7)	23	0.09
Tlingit-Haida *(Alaska Native)* (12)	15	0.06
Ute (1)	2	0.01
Yakama (3)	5	0.02
Yaqui (3)	5	0.02
Yuman (1)	5	0.02
Yup'ik *(Alaska Native)* (3)	3	0.01
Asian (203)	356	1.36
Not Hispanic (190)	319	1.22
Hispanic (13)	37	0.14
Cambodian (0)	4	0.02
Chinese, ex. Taiwanese (27)	51	0.19
Filipino (40)	105	0.40
Indian (12)	15	0.06
Indonesian (1)	6	0.02
Japanese (18)	47	0.18
Korean (51)	72	0.27
Laotian (1)	2	0.01
Sri Lankan (4)	4	0.02
Taiwanese (1)	2	0.01
Thai (8)	12	0.05
Vietnamese (26)	31	0.12
Hawaii Native/Pacific Islander (53)	143	0.55
Not Hispanic (50)	133	0.51
Hispanic (3)	10	0.04
Guamanian/Chamorro (5)	12	0.05
Native Hawaiian (36)	90	0.34
Samoan (7)	16	0.06
White (23,341)	24,072	91.83
Not Hispanic (21,749)	22,275	84.97
Hispanic (1,592)	1,797	6.85

Rockcreek

Place Type: CDP
County: Washington
Population: 9,316†

Ancestry‡	Population	%
American (289)	289	2.96
Arab (36)	42	0.43
Lebanese (36)	36	0.37
Syrian (0)	6	0.06
Armenian (0)	28	0.29
Austrian (0)	36	0.37
Belgian (0)	11	0.11
British (0)	52	0.53
Bulgarian (0)	9	0.09
Canadian (19)	25	0.26
Celtic (0)	6	0.06
Croatian (9)	54	0.55
Czech (17)	77	0.79
Czechoslovakian (13)	13	0.13
Danish (6)	152	1.55
Dutch (23)	168	1.72
Eastern European (9)	9	0.09
English (371)	1,517	15.51
Estonian (0)	44	0.45
European (388)	474	4.85
Finnish (88)	125	1.28
French, ex. Basque (27)	453	4.63
French Canadian (24)	171	1.75
German (935)	2,758	28.21
Greek (0)	57	0.58
Hungarian (22)	35	0.36
Iranian (34)	34	0.35
Irish (192)	1,125	11.51
Italian (287)	564	5.77
Latvian (39)	39	0.40
Northern European (7)	7	0.07
Norwegian (102)	478	4.89
Polish (17)	45	0.46
Russian (38)	141	1.44
Scandinavian (0)	119	1.22
Scotch-Irish (71)	203	2.08
Scottish (92)	316	3.23
Slovene (8)	33	0.34
Swedish (157)	240	2.45
Swiss (0)	81	0.83
Ukrainian (0)	48	0.49
Welsh (37)	170	1.74
West Indian, ex. Hispanic (54)	73	0.75
Jamaican (54)	73	0.75
Yugoslavian (0)	16	0.16

Hispanic Origin	Population	%
Hispanic or Latino (of any race)	681	7.31
Central American, ex. Mexican	43	0.46
Costa Rican	3	0.03
Guatemalan	22	0.24
Honduran	1	0.01
Nicaraguan	1	0.01
Panamanian	2	0.02
Salvadoran	14	0.15
Cuban	7	0.08
Dominican Republic	2	0.02
Mexican	484	5.20
Puerto Rican	21	0.23
South American	42	0.45
Argentinean	3	0.03
Chilean	7	0.08
Colombian	12	0.13
Ecuadorian	9	0.10
Peruvian	10	0.11
Venezuelan	1	0.01
Other Hispanic or Latino	82	0.88

Race*	Population	%
African-American/Black (126)	224	2.40
Not Hispanic (123)	208	2.23
Hispanic (3)	16	0.17
American Indian/Alaska Native (60)	157	1.69
Not Hispanic (55)	132	1.42
Hispanic (5)	25	0.27
Alaska Athabascan *(Ala. Nat.)* (1)	2	0.02
Apache (1)	5	0.05
Blackfeet (0)	3	0.03
Cherokee (11)	20	0.21
Chickasaw (2)	2	0.02
Chippewa (1)	4	0.04
Choctaw (2)	8	0.09
Comanche (0)	1	0.01
Creek (0)	1	0.01
Inupiat *(Alaska Native)* (0)	2	0.02
Iroquois (1)	1	0.01
Lumbee (1)	1	0.01
Mexican American Ind. (3)	3	0.03
Navajo (4)	7	0.08
Potawatomi (2)	2	0.02
Pueblo (0)	1	0.01
Puget Sound Salish (4)	4	0.04
Sioux (2)	10	0.11
Spanish American Ind. (0)	1	0.01
Tlingit-Haida *(Alaska Native)* (2)	3	0.03
Asian (782)	990	10.63
Not Hispanic (778)	964	10.35
Hispanic (4)	26	0.28
Bangladeshi (6)	9	0.10
Cambodian (12)	13	0.14
Chinese, ex. Taiwanese (167)	227	2.44
Filipino (67)	118	1.27
Hmong (15)	17	0.18
Indian (154)	168	1.80
Indonesian (3)	6	0.06

*Notes: † The Census 2010 population figure is used to calculate the percentages in the Hispanic Origin and Race categories. Ancestry percentages are based on the 2006-2010 American Community Survey population (not shown); ‡ Numbers in parentheses indicate the number of people reporting a single ancestry; * Numbers in parentheses indicate the number of persons reporting this race alone, not in combination with any other race; Please refer to the Explanation of Data for more information.*

Japanese (73)	131	1.41
Korean (124)	165	1.77
Laotian (3)	4	0.04
Malaysian (1)	5	0.05
Pakistani (4)	4	0.04
Sri Lankan (8)	8	0.09
Taiwanese (11)	11	0.12
Thai (4)	6	0.06
Vietnamese (107)	125	1.34
Hawaii Native/Pacific Islander (33)	83	0.89
Not Hispanic (29)	78	0.84
Hispanic (4)	5	0.05
Guamanian/Chamorro (2)	5	0.05
Native Hawaiian (9)	53	0.57
Samoan (1)	3	0.03
White (7,597)	7,994	85.81
Not Hispanic (7,293)	7,615	81.74
Hispanic (304)	379	4.07

Roseburg

Place Type: City
County: Douglas
Population: 21,181†

Ancestry‡	Population	%
African, Sub-Saharan (17)	17	0.08
African (17)	17	0.08
American (879)	879	4.17
Austrian (27)	76	0.36
Basque (0)	24	0.11
Belgian (16)	16	0.08
British (31)	63	0.30
Canadian (49)	49	0.23
Croatian (0)	124	0.59
Czech (28)	37	0.18
Czechoslovakian (24)	24	0.11
Danish (76)	182	0.86
Dutch (44)	522	2.47
English (708)	3,149	14.93
Estonian (0)	59	0.28
European (271)	353	1.67
Finnish (32)	161	0.76
French, ex. Basque (144)	1,031	4.89
French Canadian (44)	174	0.82
German (1,666)	5,144	24.39
Greek (0)	65	0.31
Hungarian (27)	138	0.65
Irish (790)	3,948	18.72
Italian (266)	592	2.81
Lithuanian (0)	40	0.19
Northern European (108)	108	0.51
Norwegian (215)	659	3.12
Polish (54)	268	1.27
Portuguese (63)	158	0.75
Russian (17)	42	0.20
Scandinavian (152)	260	1.23
Scotch-Irish (226)	648	3.07
Scottish (230)	768	3.64
Slavic (0)	24	0.11
Slovak (0)	35	0.17
Slovene (0)	9	0.04
Swedish (132)	613	2.91
Swiss (0)	11	0.05
Ukrainian (158)	192	0.91
Welsh (41)	305	1.45
West Indian, ex. Hispanic (69)	69	0.33
Haitian (47)	47	0.22
Jamaican (22)	22	0.10
Yugoslavian (0)	11	0.05

Hispanic Origin	Population	%
Hispanic or Latino (of any race)	1,155	5.45
Central American, ex. Mexican	46	0.22
Guatemalan	8	0.04
Honduran	9	0.04
Nicaraguan	5	0.02
Panamanian	3	0.01
Salvadoran	17	0.08
Other Central American	4	0.02
Cuban	6	0.03
Mexican	872	4.12
Puerto Rican	52	0.25
South American	18	0.08
Bolivian	5	0.02
Chilean	4	0.02
Colombian	6	0.03
Peruvian	2	0.01
Venezuelan	1	<0.01
Other Hispanic or Latino	161	0.76

Race*	Population	%
African-American/Black (97)	195	0.92
Not Hispanic (86)	171	0.81
Hispanic (11)	24	0.11
American Indian/Alaska Native (370)	781	3.69
Not Hispanic (341)	700	3.30
Hispanic (29)	81	0.38
Alaska Athabascan *(Ala. Nat.)* (3)	5	0.02
Apache (7)	16	0.08
Blackfeet (2)	19	0.09
Canadian/French Am. Ind. (2)	2	0.01
Central American Ind. (0)	1	<0.01
Cherokee (43)	143	0.68
Cheyenne (2)	2	0.01
Chickasaw (4)	5	0.02
Chippewa (6)	28	0.13
Choctaw (12)	22	0.10
Comanche (0)	3	0.01
Cree (0)	1	<0.01
Creek (2)	2	0.01
Crow (0)	1	<0.01
Delaware (1)	5	0.02
Inupiat *(Alaska Native)* (2)	3	0.01
Iroquois (0)	5	0.02
Lumbee (1)	1	<0.01
Menominee (1)	1	<0.01
Mexican American Ind. (3)	8	0.04
Navajo (7)	10	0.05
Osage (1)	7	0.03
Ottawa (1)	4	0.02
Paiute (1)	5	0.02
Potawatomi (2)	7	0.03
Pueblo (4)	5	0.02
Puget Sound Salish (0)	3	0.01
Seminole (1)	4	0.02
Shoshone (0)	1	<0.01
Sioux (17)	32	0.15
Tlingit-Haida *(Alaska Native)* (1)	6	0.03
Yakama (2)	2	0.01
Asian (341)	513	2.42
Not Hispanic (334)	488	2.30
Hispanic (7)	25	0.12
Cambodian (11)	16	0.08
Chinese, ex. Taiwanese (66)	92	0.43
Filipino (76)	134	0.63
Indian (59)	67	0.32
Indonesian (1)	2	0.01
Japanese (25)	73	0.34
Korean (35)	60	0.28
Laotian (4)	4	0.02
Pakistani (1)	1	<0.01
Sri Lankan (2)	2	0.01
Thai (9)	14	0.07
Vietnamese (35)	41	0.19
Hawaii Native/Pacific Islander (53)	140	0.66
Not Hispanic (46)	121	0.57
Hispanic (7)	19	0.09
Fijian (1)	3	0.01
Guamanian/Chamorro (3)	9	0.04
Marshallese (2)	2	0.01
Native Hawaiian (28)	84	0.40
Samoan (12)	24	0.11
Tongan (2)	2	0.01
White (19,279)	19,984	94.35
Not Hispanic (18,578)	19,169	90.50
Hispanic (701)	815	3.85

Salem

Place Type: City
County: Marion
Population: 154,637†

Ancestry‡	Population	%
African, Sub-Saharan (211)	327	0.22
African (59)	140	0.09
Ethiopian (110)	110	0.07
Ghanaian (24)	24	0.02
Nigerian (0)	9	0.01
South African (18)	44	0.03
American (7,330)	7,330	4.83
Arab (70)	148	0.10
Arab (15)	15	0.01
Egyptian (11)	11	0.01
Lebanese (11)	63	0.04
Moroccan (33)	33	0.02
Syrian (0)	26	0.02
Armenian (44)	93	0.06
Australian (81)	176	0.12
Austrian (46)	323	0.21
Basque (11)	35	0.02
Belgian (84)	310	0.20
Brazilian (17)	63	0.04
British (148)	691	0.46
Bulgarian (38)	66	0.04
Canadian (166)	554	0.36
Celtic (40)	60	0.04
Croatian (13)	42	0.03
Czech (143)	641	0.42
Czechoslovakian (82)	121	0.08
Danish (360)	1,560	1.03
Dutch (695)	3,203	2.11
Eastern European (73)	159	0.10
English (5,416)	20,013	13.18
European (2,457)	2,750	1.81
Finnish (200)	515	0.34
French, ex. Basque (587)	5,620	3.70
French Canadian (198)	947	0.62
German (9,318)	33,574	22.12
Greek (163)	550	0.36
Hungarian (92)	348	0.23
Icelander (0)	28	0.02
Iranian (158)	180	0.12
Irish (4,018)	18,415	12.13
Israeli (9)	19	0.01
Italian (1,384)	5,048	3.33
Latvian (0)	44	0.03
Lithuanian (16)	67	0.04
New Zealander (35)	35	0.02
Northern European (405)	443	0.29
Norwegian (2,208)	6,482	4.27
Pennsylvania German (17)	29	0.02
Polish (496)	2,083	1.37
Portuguese (378)	1,021	0.67
Romanian (258)	313	0.21
Russian (997)	1,780	1.17
Scandinavian (391)	874	0.58
Scotch-Irish (1,026)	3,213	2.12
Scottish (1,620)	5,618	3.70
Serbian (30)	54	0.04
Slavic (16)	51	0.03
Slovak (14)	66	0.04
Slovene (0)	36	0.02
Swedish (1,036)	4,012	2.64
Swiss (189)	1,425	0.94
Turkish (17)	69	0.05
Ukrainian (485)	759	0.50
Welsh (245)	1,418	0.93
West Indian, ex. Hispanic (47)	168	0.11
Bahamian (0)	15	0.01
Belizean (37)	64	0.04
Dutch West Indian (0)	33	0.02
Haitian (0)	9	0.01
Jamaican (10)	24	0.02
Other West Indian (0)	23	0.02
Yugoslavian (87)	171	0.11

*Notes: † The Census 2010 population figure is used to calculate the percentages in the Hispanic Origin and Race categories. Ancestry percentages are based on the 2006-2010 American Community Survey population (not shown); ‡ Numbers in parentheses indicate the number of people reporting a single ancestry; * Numbers in parentheses indicate the number of persons reporting this race alone, not in combination with any other race; Please refer to the Explanation of Data for more information.*

Hispanic Origin	Population	%
Hispanic or Latino (of any race)	31,359	20.28
Central American, ex. Mexican	759	0.49
Costa Rican	46	0.03
Guatemalan	271	0.18
Honduran	56	0.04
Nicaraguan	46	0.03
Panamanian	18	0.01
Salvadoran	320	0.21
Other Central American	2	<0.01
Cuban	121	0.08
Dominican Republic	22	0.01
Mexican	27,534	17.81
Puerto Rican	357	0.23
South American	343	0.22
Argentinean	55	0.04
Bolivian	10	0.01
Chilean	27	0.02
Colombian	60	0.04
Ecuadorian	33	0.02
Paraguayan	1	<0.01
Peruvian	108	0.07
Uruguayan	9	0.01
Venezuelan	33	0.02
Other South American	7	<0.01
Other Hispanic or Latino	2,223	1.44

Race*	Population	%
African-American/Black (2,283)	3,647	2.36
Not Hispanic (2,081)	3,168	2.05
Hispanic (202)	479	0.31
American Indian/Alaska Native (2,284)	4,503	2.91
Not Hispanic (1,750)	3,487	2.25
Hispanic (534)	1,016	0.66
Alaska Athabascan *(Ala. Nat.)* (22)	37	0.02
Aleut *(Alaska Native)* (3)	17	0.01
Apache (39)	102	0.07
Arapaho (6)	10	0.01
Blackfeet (66)	158	0.10
Canadian/French Am. Ind. (4)	10	0.01
Central American Ind. (1)	4	<0.01
Cherokee (128)	542	0.35
Cheyenne (8)	16	0.01
Chickasaw (19)	44	0.03
Chippewa (108)	169	0.11
Choctaw (71)	135	0.09
Colville (2)	5	<0.01
Comanche (5)	18	0.01
Cree (5)	20	0.01
Creek (10)	28	0.02
Crow (4)	8	0.01
Delaware (1)	4	<0.01
Hopi (2)	5	<0.01
Inupiat *(Alaska Native)* (17)	33	0.02
Iroquois (18)	46	0.03
Kiowa (6)	8	0.01
Lumbee (4)	4	<0.01
Menominee (0)	1	<0.01
Mexican American Ind. (119)	182	0.12
Navajo (35)	60	0.04
Osage (16)	32	0.02
Ottawa (1)	1	<0.01
Paiute (10)	20	0.01
Pima (8)	11	0.01
Potawatomi (8)	24	0.02
Pueblo (3)	18	0.01
Puget Sound Salish (6)	13	0.01
Seminole (7)	12	0.01
Shoshone (5)	9	0.01
Sioux (118)	219	0.14
South American Ind. (5)	15	0.01
Spanish American Ind. (4)	10	0.01
Tlingit-Haida *(Alaska Native)* (30)	60	0.04
Tohono O'Odham (3)	3	<0.01
Tsimshian *(Alaska Native)* (9)	9	0.01
Ute (5)	11	0.01
Yakama (8)	16	0.01
Yaqui (3)	8	0.01
Yuman (2)	6	<0.01
Yup'ik *(Alaska Native)* (7)	22	0.01
Asian (4,215)	6,029	3.90
Not Hispanic (4,134)	5,695	3.68
Hispanic (81)	334	0.22
Bangladeshi (9)	9	0.01
Cambodian (175)	265	0.17
Chinese, ex. Taiwanese (764)	1,096	0.71
Filipino (590)	1,175	0.76
Hmong (63)	67	0.04
Indian (531)	629	0.41
Indonesian (24)	40	0.03
Japanese (384)	875	0.57
Korean (335)	550	0.36
Laotian (114)	178	0.12
Malaysian (3)	10	0.01
Nepalese (14)	15	0.01
Pakistani (15)	17	0.01
Sri Lankan (7)	8	0.01
Taiwanese (29)	39	0.03
Thai (57)	103	0.07
Vietnamese (832)	955	0.62
Hawaii Native/Pacific Islander (1,460)	2,018	1.30
Not Hispanic (1,429)	1,934	1.25
Hispanic (31)	84	0.05
Fijian (0)	1	<0.01
Guamanian/Chamorro (162)	238	0.15
Marshallese (314)	334	0.22
Native Hawaiian (167)	383	0.25
Samoan (64)	125	0.08
Tongan (10)	18	0.01
White (122,213)	128,226	82.92
Not Hispanic (109,352)	113,323	73.28
Hispanic (12,861)	14,903	9.64

Sandy

Place Type: City
County: Clackamas
Population: 9,570†

Ancestry‡	Population	%
American (408)	408	4.60
Austrian (10)	34	0.38
Belgian (36)	36	0.41
British (23)	109	1.23
Canadian (43)	161	1.82
Croatian (0)	13	0.15
Czech (0)	66	0.74
Czechoslovakian (13)	13	0.15
Danish (39)	167	1.88
Dutch (50)	217	2.45
English (275)	1,487	16.78
European (37)	37	0.42
Finnish (13)	34	0.38
French, ex. Basque (26)	541	6.11
French Canadian (0)	36	0.41
German (868)	2,709	30.58
Greek (34)	34	0.38
Hungarian (14)	43	0.49
Irish (488)	1,625	18.34
Italian (6)	104	1.17
Lithuanian (9)	9	0.10
Northern European (13)	49	0.55
Norwegian (11)	654	7.38
Pennsylvania German (14)	14	0.16
Polish (35)	81	0.91
Portuguese (38)	104	1.17
Romanian (0)	20	0.23
Russian (0)	21	0.24
Scandinavian (23)	108	1.22
Scotch-Irish (73)	274	3.09
Scottish (142)	498	5.62
Swedish (119)	586	6.61
Swiss (0)	41	0.46
Ukrainian (7)	7	0.08
Welsh (0)	79	0.89

Hispanic Origin	Population	%
Hispanic or Latino (of any race)	884	9.24
Central American, ex. Mexican	48	0.50
Costa Rican	15	0.16
Guatemalan	12	0.13
Honduran	5	0.05
Panamanian	1	0.01
Salvadoran	15	0.16
Cuban	19	0.20
Dominican Republic	3	0.03
Mexican	696	7.27
Puerto Rican	18	0.19
South American	14	0.15
Chilean	1	0.01
Colombian	2	0.02
Ecuadorian	3	0.03
Paraguayan	1	0.01
Peruvian	7	0.07
Other Hispanic or Latino	86	0.90

Race*	Population	%
African-American/Black (40)	94	0.98
Not Hispanic (35)	87	0.91
Hispanic (5)	7	0.07
American Indian/Alaska Native (124)	248	2.59
Not Hispanic (107)	222	2.32
Hispanic (17)	26	0.27
Alaska Athabascan *(Ala. Nat.)* (0)	4	0.04
Aleut *(Alaska Native)* (0)	1	0.01
Apache (0)	1	0.01
Blackfeet (2)	8	0.08
Canadian/French Am. Ind. (3)	4	0.04
Cherokee (10)	28	0.29
Cheyenne (0)	4	0.04
Chickasaw (1)	1	0.01
Chippewa (8)	12	0.13
Choctaw (5)	14	0.15
Colville (1)	3	0.03
Creek (0)	3	0.03
Crow (1)	1	0.01
Inupiat *(Alaska Native)* (0)	2	0.02
Iroquois (0)	1	0.01
Kiowa (0)	1	0.01
Mexican American Ind. (15)	17	0.18
Navajo (1)	1	0.01
Paiute (1)	3	0.03
Potawatomi (3)	3	0.03
Sioux (3)	7	0.07
Tlingit-Haida *(Alaska Native)* (2)	4	0.04
Asian (118)	225	2.35
Not Hispanic (114)	210	2.19
Hispanic (4)	15	0.16
Burmese (0)	2	0.02
Cambodian (1)	2	0.02
Chinese, ex. Taiwanese (15)	34	0.36
Filipino (15)	48	0.50
Hmong (10)	10	0.10
Indian (11)	17	0.18
Indonesian (1)	7	0.07
Japanese (15)	54	0.56
Korean (15)	22	0.23
Laotian (0)	1	0.01
Nepalese (1)	1	0.01
Pakistani (5)	6	0.06
Taiwanese (1)	1	0.01
Thai (12)	14	0.15
Vietnamese (10)	14	0.15
Hawaii Native/Pacific Islander (19)	57	0.60
Not Hispanic (19)	55	0.57
Hispanic (0)	2	0.02
Guamanian/Chamorro (1)	3	0.03
Marshallese (2)	5	0.05
Native Hawaiian (2)	23	0.24
Samoan (6)	12	0.13
White (8,616)	8,923	93.24
Not Hispanic (8,139)	8,389	87.66
Hispanic (477)	534	5.58

Sherwood

Place Type: City
County: Washington
Population: 18,194†

*Notes: † The Census 2010 population figure is used to calculate the percentages in the Hispanic Origin and Race categories. Ancestry percentages are based on the 2006-2010 American Community Survey population (not shown); ‡ Numbers in parentheses indicate the number of people reporting a single ancestry; * Numbers in parentheses indicate the number of persons reporting this race alone, not in combination with any other race; Please refer to the Explanation of Data for more information.*

Ancestry‡	Population	%
American (705)	705	4.12
Arab (55)	66	0.39
Arab (0)	11	0.06
Other Arab (55)	55	0.32
Austrian (19)	28	0.16
Basque (19)	28	0.16
Belgian (24)	56	0.33
British (32)	127	0.74
Canadian (36)	58	0.34
Celtic (42)	84	0.49
Croatian (38)	49	0.29
Czech (0)	35	0.20
Danish (0)	67	0.39
Dutch (80)	355	2.07
Eastern European (17)	17	0.10
English (655)	2,603	15.21
European (131)	198	1.16
Finnish (7)	37	0.22
French, ex. Basque (90)	737	4.31
French Canadian (47)	105	0.61
German (1,414)	4,780	27.93
Greek (12)	81	0.47
Hungarian (8)	32	0.19
Iranian (26)	26	0.15
Irish (487)	2,520	14.72
Italian (302)	840	4.91
Lithuanian (0)	31	0.18
New Zealander (0)	9	0.05
Northern European (60)	60	0.35
Norwegian (157)	782	4.57
Polish (56)	401	2.34
Portuguese (133)	195	1.14
Romanian (77)	77	0.45
Russian (137)	179	1.05
Scandinavian (66)	82	0.48
Scotch-Irish (103)	439	2.56
Scottish (248)	711	4.15
Swedish (100)	644	3.76
Swiss (42)	124	0.72
Ukrainian (22)	22	0.13
Welsh (16)	145	0.85
West Indian, ex. Hispanic (0)	9	0.05
West Indian (0)	9	0.05
Yugoslavian (0)	25	0.15

Hispanic Origin	Population	%
Hispanic or Latino (of any race)	1,279	7.03
Central American, ex. Mexican	50	0.27
Guatemalan	17	0.09
Honduran	5	0.03
Nicaraguan	13	0.07
Salvadoran	15	0.08
Cuban	45	0.25
Dominican Republic	5	0.03
Mexican	983	5.40
Puerto Rican	46	0.25
South American	63	0.35
Argentinean	13	0.07
Bolivian	3	0.02
Chilean	12	0.07
Colombian	8	0.04
Ecuadorian	9	0.05
Peruvian	8	0.04
Uruguayan	1	0.01
Venezuelan	9	0.05
Other Hispanic or Latino	87	0.48

Race*	Population	%
African-American/Black (144)	252	1.39
Not Hispanic (125)	224	1.23
Hispanic (19)	28	0.15
American Indian/Alaska Native (87)	235	1.29
Not Hispanic (68)	200	1.10
Hispanic (19)	35	0.19
Alaska Athabascan *(Ala. Nat.)* (0)	1	0.01
Aleut *(Alaska Native)* (2)	2	0.01
Apache (3)	9	0.05
Cherokee (6)	51	0.28
Cheyenne (2)	3	0.02
Chippewa (1)	5	0.03
Choctaw (7)	10	0.05
Comanche (0)	3	0.02
Cree (1)	1	0.01
Creek (1)	4	0.02
Hopi (1)	1	0.01
Inupiat *(Alaska Native)* (0)	3	0.02
Iroquois (0)	5	0.03
Kiowa (1)	1	0.01
Mexican American Ind. (8)	12	0.07
Navajo (4)	5	0.03
Paiute (0)	1	0.01
Potawatomi (0)	2	0.01
Shoshone (2)	2	0.01
Sioux (4)	6	0.03
South American Ind. (1)	1	0.01
Tlingit-Haida *(Alaska Native)* (3)	5	0.03
Asian (630)	989	5.44
Not Hispanic (619)	958	5.27
Hispanic (11)	31	0.17
Burmese (1)	3	0.02
Cambodian (13)	13	0.07
Chinese, ex. Taiwanese (139)	230	1.26
Filipino (112)	241	1.32
Hmong (3)	3	0.02
Indian (47)	67	0.37
Indonesian (10)	12	0.07
Japanese (48)	126	0.69
Korean (81)	132	0.73
Laotian (17)	27	0.15
Malaysian (0)	1	0.01
Pakistani (9)	9	0.05
Taiwanese (7)	9	0.05
Thai (8)	13	0.07
Vietnamese (94)	115	0.63
Hawaii Native/Pacific Islander (61)	149	0.82
Not Hispanic (55)	142	0.78
Hispanic (6)	7	0.04
Guamanian/Chamorro (10)	21	0.12
Marshallese (2)	2	0.01
Native Hawaiian (15)	66	0.36
Samoan (6)	19	0.10
Tongan (15)	17	0.09
White (16,097)	16,732	91.96
Not Hispanic (15,413)	15,971	87.78
Hispanic (684)	761	4.18

Silverton

Place Type: City
County: Marion
Population: 9,222†

Ancestry‡	Population	%
American (352)	352	3.94
Arab (30)	30	0.34
Moroccan (30)	30	0.34
British (25)	76	0.85
Canadian (63)	96	1.07
Czech (0)	26	0.29
Danish (25)	87	0.97
Dutch (56)	210	2.35
English (285)	1,043	11.67
European (195)	230	2.57
Finnish (36)	51	0.57
French, ex. Basque (0)	207	2.32
French Canadian (63)	63	0.70
German (947)	2,355	26.34
Hungarian (0)	74	0.83
Irish (486)	1,529	17.10
Israeli (17)	17	0.19
Italian (65)	318	3.56
Northern European (12)	21	0.23
Norwegian (113)	446	4.99
Polish (29)	138	1.54
Romanian (9)	9	0.10
Russian (197)	418	4.68
Scandinavian (59)	102	1.14
Scotch-Irish (191)	266	2.98
Scottish (146)	251	2.81
Slovak (0)	30	0.34
Swedish (112)	467	5.22
Swiss (26)	78	0.87
Ukrainian (9)	9	0.10
Welsh (63)	102	1.14

Hispanic Origin	Population	%
Hispanic or Latino (of any race)	1,131	12.26
Central American, ex. Mexican	10	0.11
Costa Rican	2	0.02
Guatemalan	4	0.04
Honduran	2	0.02
Salvadoran	2	0.02
Cuban	6	0.07
Dominican Republic	1	0.01
Mexican	974	10.56
Puerto Rican	20	0.22
South American	11	0.12
Argentinean	5	0.05
Bolivian	1	0.01
Colombian	2	0.02
Peruvian	3	0.03
Other Hispanic or Latino	109	1.18

Race*	Population	%
African-American/Black (32)	53	0.57
Not Hispanic (21)	39	0.42
Hispanic (11)	14	0.15
American Indian/Alaska Native (74)	172	1.87
Not Hispanic (61)	142	1.54
Hispanic (13)	30	0.33
Aleut *(Alaska Native)* (2)	2	0.02
Apache (0)	2	0.02
Blackfeet (2)	4	0.04
Canadian/French Am. Ind. (0)	2	0.02
Cherokee (3)	21	0.23
Chippewa (1)	4	0.04
Choctaw (4)	5	0.05
Colville (0)	4	0.04
Comanche (0)	1	0.01
Creek (2)	2	0.02
Iroquois (1)	1	0.01
Kiowa (3)	3	0.03
Mexican American Ind. (1)	2	0.02
Navajo (6)	6	0.07
Ottawa (1)	1	0.01
Paiute (4)	4	0.04
Puget Sound Salish (4)	8	0.09
Sioux (1)	6	0.07
South American Ind. (1)	3	0.03
Tlingit-Haida *(Alaska Native)* (0)	4	0.04
Tohono O'Odham (3)	3	0.03
Ute (1)	2	0.02
Asian (95)	143	1.55
Not Hispanic (95)	132	1.43
Hispanic (0)	11	0.12
Chinese, ex. Taiwanese (12)	22	0.24
Filipino (18)	39	0.42
Indian (12)	16	0.17
Indonesian (1)	7	0.08
Japanese (8)	18	0.20
Korean (26)	30	0.33
Laotian (4)	4	0.04
Thai (9)	9	0.10
Vietnamese (2)	3	0.03
Hawaii Native/Pacific Islander (7)	27	0.29
Not Hispanic (5)	20	0.22
Hispanic (2)	7	0.08
Guamanian/Chamorro (2)	2	0.02
Native Hawaiian (3)	15	0.16
Samoan (2)	2	0.02
White (8,211)	8,452	91.65
Not Hispanic (7,756)	7,886	85.51
Hispanic (455)	566	6.14

Springfield

Place Type: City
County: Lane
Population: 59,403†

*Notes: † The Census 2010 population figure is used to calculate the percentages in the Hispanic Origin and Race categories. Ancestry percentages are based on the 2006-2010 American Community Survey population (not shown); ‡ Numbers in parentheses indicate the number of people reporting a single ancestry; * Numbers in parentheses indicate the number of persons reporting this race alone, not in combination with any other race; Please refer to the Explanation of Data for more information.*

Ancestry‡	Population	%
African, Sub-Saharan (31)	64	0.11
African (0)	5	0.01
Kenyan (20)	20	0.03
Nigerian (11)	32	0.05
Other Sub-Saharan African (0)	7	0.01
American (3,904)	3,904	6.68
Arab (68)	91	0.16
Arab (0)	23	0.04
Egyptian (35)	35	0.06
Moroccan (23)	23	0.04
Syrian (10)	10	0.02
Australian (12)	12	0.02
Austrian (20)	157	0.27
Basque (37)	37	0.06
Belgian (15)	78	0.13
British (147)	209	0.36
Canadian (68)	197	0.34
Celtic (0)	17	0.03
Croatian (0)	12	0.02
Czech (47)	194	0.33
Czechoslovakian (79)	97	0.17
Danish (174)	681	1.17
Dutch (299)	1,542	2.64
Eastern European (24)	24	0.04
English (2,732)	7,906	13.54
European (1,163)	1,259	2.16
Finnish (87)	292	0.50
French, ex. Basque (248)	2,028	3.47
French Canadian (208)	305	0.52
German (3,667)	12,072	20.67
Greek (19)	64	0.11
Hungarian (36)	161	0.28
Icelander (9)	28	0.05
Iranian (0)	16	0.03
Irish (1,861)	7,878	13.49
Israeli (20)	20	0.03
Italian (559)	2,050	3.51
Latvian (11)	17	0.03
Lithuanian (20)	34	0.06
Luxemburger (0)	6	0.01
Macedonian (13)	13	0.02
Northern European (53)	53	0.09
Norwegian (816)	2,197	3.76
Pennsylvania German (0)	57	0.10
Polish (117)	650	1.11
Portuguese (187)	479	0.82
Russian (115)	441	0.76
Scandinavian (95)	357	0.61
Scotch-Irish (290)	1,252	2.14
Scottish (377)	1,814	3.11
Serbian (23)	23	0.04
Slavic (10)	23	0.04
Slovene (0)	36	0.06
Swedish (384)	1,649	2.82
Swiss (17)	231	0.40
Turkish (29)	83	0.14
Ukrainian (86)	187	0.32
Welsh (57)	527	0.90
West Indian, ex. Hispanic (0)	20	0.03
Dutch West Indian (0)	20	0.03
Yugoslavian (0)	9	0.02

Hispanic Origin	Population	%
Hispanic or Latino (of any race)	7,194	12.11
Central American, ex. Mexican	403	0.68
Costa Rican	11	0.02
Guatemalan	151	0.25
Honduran	45	0.08
Nicaraguan	23	0.04
Panamanian	17	0.03
Salvadoran	141	0.24
Other Central American	15	0.03
Cuban	39	0.07
Dominican Republic	7	0.01
Mexican	5,828	9.81
Puerto Rican	204	0.34
South American	113	0.19
Argentinean	8	0.01
Bolivian	2	<0.01
Chilean	8	0.01
Colombian	33	0.06
Ecuadorian	7	0.01
Paraguayan	5	0.01
Peruvian	33	0.06
Uruguayan	4	0.01
Venezuelan	11	0.02
Other South American	2	<0.01
Other Hispanic or Latino	600	1.01

Race*	Population	%
African-American/Black (649)	1,227	2.07
Not Hispanic (585)	1,099	1.85
Hispanic (64)	128	0.22
American Indian/Alaska Native (851)	2,185	3.68
Not Hispanic (720)	1,841	3.10
Hispanic (131)	344	0.58
Alaska Athabascan *(Ala. Nat.)* (7)	10	0.02
Aleut *(Alaska Native)* (8)	12	0.02
Apache (19)	40	0.07
Arapaho (2)	3	0.01
Blackfeet (13)	55	0.09
Canadian/French Am. Ind. (0)	7	0.01
Cherokee (72)	386	0.65
Cheyenne (5)	9	0.02
Chickasaw (17)	32	0.05
Chippewa (20)	58	0.10
Choctaw (20)	79	0.13
Comanche (0)	13	0.02
Cree (0)	6	0.01
Creek (0)	18	0.03
Crow (3)	4	0.01
Delaware (0)	2	<0.01
Hopi (0)	3	0.01
Houma (1)	1	<0.01
Inupiat *(Alaska Native)* (6)	10	0.02
Iroquois (2)	9	0.02
Kiowa (0)	1	<0.01
Lumbee (2)	4	0.01
Mexican American Ind. (33)	52	0.09
Navajo (7)	15	0.03
Osage (15)	27	0.05
Ottawa (0)	1	<0.01
Paiute (4)	8	0.01
Pima (1)	5	0.01
Potawatomi (9)	18	0.03
Pueblo (4)	4	0.01
Puget Sound Salish (3)	3	0.01
Seminole (4)	11	0.02
Shoshone (0)	7	0.01
Sioux (17)	73	0.12
South American Ind. (1)	4	0.01
Tlingit-Haida *(Alaska Native)* (14)	35	0.06
Tsimshian *(Alaska Native)* (0)	2	<0.01
Ute (0)	2	<0.01
Yakama (7)	18	0.03
Yaqui (2)	7	0.01
Yuman (0)	1	<0.01
Yup'ik *(Alaska Native)* (5)	9	0.02
Asian (758)	1,336	2.25
Not Hispanic (730)	1,252	2.11
Hispanic (28)	84	0.14
Cambodian (0)	1	<0.01
Chinese, ex. Taiwanese (97)	171	0.29
Filipino (196)	383	0.64
Hmong (1)	1	<0.01
Indian (99)	153	0.26
Indonesian (9)	27	0.05
Japanese (65)	206	0.35
Korean (65)	117	0.20
Laotian (84)	97	0.16
Malaysian (3)	3	0.01
Nepalese (2)	3	0.01
Pakistani (5)	6	0.01
Taiwanese (0)	2	<0.01
Thai (24)	38	0.06
Vietnamese (77)	105	0.18
Hawaii Native/Pacific Islander (189)	349	0.59
Not Hispanic (184)	326	0.55
Hispanic (5)	23	0.04
Fijian (35)	42	0.07
Guamanian/Chamorro (23)	39	0.07
Marshallese (38)	39	0.07
Native Hawaiian (27)	98	0.16
Samoan (22)	44	0.07
Tongan (2)	3	0.01
White (51,005)	53,682	90.37
Not Hispanic (47,827)	49,822	83.87
Hispanic (3,178)	3,860	6.50

St. Helens

Place Type: City
County: Columbia
Population: 12,883†

Ancestry‡	Population	%
African, Sub-Saharan (8)	8	0.06
Other Sub-Saharan African (8)	8	0.06
American (643)	643	5.13
Austrian (81)	81	0.65
Basque (0)	12	0.10
Belgian (0)	14	0.11
British (11)	50	0.40
Canadian (26)	46	0.37
Celtic (9)	9	0.07
Croatian (4)	4	0.03
Czech (28)	137	1.09
Danish (40)	93	0.74
Dutch (19)	344	2.74
English (460)	1,674	13.35
European (214)	250	1.99
Finnish (45)	79	0.63
French, ex. Basque (34)	459	3.66
French Canadian (77)	146	1.16
German (708)	3,188	25.41
Greek (14)	22	0.18
Hungarian (0)	56	0.45
Irish (557)	2,223	17.72
Italian (125)	414	3.30
Norwegian (173)	695	5.54
Polish (19)	247	1.97
Portuguese (6)	44	0.35
Russian (17)	56	0.45
Scandinavian (17)	166	1.32
Scotch-Irish (31)	183	1.46
Scottish (138)	347	2.77
Slavic (16)	16	0.13
Slovene (0)	22	0.18
Swedish (207)	546	4.35
Swiss (0)	62	0.49
Ukrainian (0)	22	0.18
Welsh (12)	49	0.39
West Indian, ex. Hispanic (12)	42	0.33
Haitian (12)	42	0.33
Yugoslavian (0)	12	0.10

Hispanic Origin	Population	%
Hispanic or Latino (of any race)	785	6.09
Central American, ex. Mexican	49	0.38
Guatemalan	26	0.20
Honduran	2	0.02
Nicaraguan	2	0.02
Salvadoran	19	0.15
Cuban	19	0.15
Dominican Republic	1	0.01
Mexican	584	4.53
Puerto Rican	30	0.23
South American	14	0.11
Argentinean	1	0.01
Chilean	1	0.01
Colombian	12	0.09
Other Hispanic or Latino	88	0.68

Race*	Population	%
African-American/Black (79)	172	1.34
Not Hispanic (73)	156	1.21
Hispanic (6)	16	0.12
American Indian/Alaska Native (208)	509	3.95
Not Hispanic (173)	440	3.42

*Notes: † The Census 2010 population figure is used to calculate the percentages in the Hispanic Origin and Race categories. Ancestry percentages are based on the 2006-2010 American Community Survey population (not shown); ‡ Numbers in parentheses indicate the number of people reporting a single ancestry; * Numbers in parentheses indicate the number of persons reporting this race alone, not in combination with any other race; Please refer to the Explanation of Data for more information.*

SECTION TWO

Hispanic (35)	69	0.54
Alaska Athabascan *(Ala. Nat.)* (2)	2	0.02
Aleut *(Alaska Native)* (3)	4	0.03
Apache (0)	5	0.04
Arapaho (5)	5	0.04
Blackfeet (1)	15	0.12
Cherokee (27)	93	0.72
Cheyenne (7)	7	0.05
Chippewa (13)	25	0.19
Choctaw (0)	1	0.01
Colville (0)	1	0.01
Cree (0)	2	0.02
Creek (1)	13	0.10
Crow (0)	1	0.01
Delaware (0)	2	0.02
Inupiat *(Alaska Native)* (2)	3	0.02
Iroquois (1)	7	0.05
Mexican American Ind. (1)	6	0.05
Navajo (3)	9	0.07
Osage (1)	4	0.03
Ottawa (1)	5	0.04
Paiute (1)	1	0.01
Potawatomi (6)	8	0.06
Pueblo (0)	4	0.03
Puget Sound Salish (1)	2	0.02
Seminole (0)	3	0.02
Shoshone (0)	1	0.01
Sioux (13)	26	0.20
Tlingit-Haida *(Alaska Native)* (4)	10	0.08
Tsimshian *(Alaska Native)* (0)	2	0.02
Yakama (8)	8	0.06
Yup'ik *(Alaska Native)* (1)	1	0.01
Asian (168)	311	2.41
Not Hispanic (163)	294	2.28
Hispanic (5)	17	0.13
Cambodian (10)	10	0.08
Chinese, ex. Taiwanese (28)	47	0.36
Filipino (42)	98	0.76
Hmong (6)	9	0.07
Indian (12)	20	0.16
Indonesian (1)	4	0.03
Japanese (17)	51	0.40
Korean (14)	30	0.23
Laotian (6)	8	0.06
Malaysian (0)	1	0.01
Taiwanese (1)	1	0.01
Thai (10)	30	0.23
Vietnamese (10)	14	0.11
Hawaii Native/Pacific Islander (42)	102	0.79
Not Hispanic (42)	96	0.75
Hispanic (0)	6	0.05
Fijian (5)	5	0.04
Guamanian/Chamorro (10)	16	0.12
Native Hawaiian (22)	55	0.43
Samoan (0)	5	0.04
Tongan (2)	6	0.05
White (11,636)	12,178	94.53
Not Hispanic (11,170)	11,624	90.23
Hispanic (466)	554	4.30

Stayton

Place Type: City
County: Marion
Population: 7,644†

Ancestry‡	Population	%
American (329)	329	4.39
Arab (0)	14	0.19
Lebanese (0)	14	0.19
Belgian (13)	13	0.17
British (20)	40	0.53
Canadian (35)	67	0.89
Czech (27)	91	1.21
Danish (12)	40	0.53
Dutch (15)	245	3.27
English (122)	871	11.62
European (152)	227	3.03
Finnish (0)	100	1.33
French, ex. Basque (156)	609	8.13
French Canadian (27)	49	0.65
German (629)	1,921	25.63
Greek (0)	22	0.29
Irish (297)	1,008	13.45
Italian (0)	107	1.43
Norwegian (132)	253	3.38
Polish (64)	134	1.79
Portuguese (0)	46	0.61
Scandinavian (33)	71	0.95
Scotch-Irish (38)	61	0.81
Scottish (19)	160	2.13
Swedish (19)	171	2.28
Swiss (0)	46	0.61
Welsh (0)	29	0.39
West Indian, ex. Hispanic (0)	19	0.25
Dutch West Indian (0)	19	0.25

Hispanic Origin	Population	%
Hispanic or Latino (of any race)	1,096	14.34
Central American, ex. Mexican	20	0.26
Costa Rican	3	0.04
Guatemalan	9	0.12
Panamanian	3	0.04
Salvadoran	5	0.07
Dominican Republic	6	0.08
Mexican	938	12.27
Puerto Rican	12	0.16
South American	1	0.01
Argentinean	1	0.01
Other Hispanic or Latino	119	1.56

Race*	Population	%
African-American/Black (36)	79	1.03
Not Hispanic (33)	70	0.92
Hispanic (3)	9	0.12
American Indian/Alaska Native (105)	207	2.71
Not Hispanic (93)	187	2.45
Hispanic (12)	20	0.26
Alaska Athabascan *(Ala. Nat.)* (7)	8	0.10
Apache (4)	5	0.07
Blackfeet (2)	8	0.10
Canadian/French Am. Ind. (0)	1	0.01
Cherokee (17)	40	0.52
Chippewa (0)	7	0.09
Choctaw (7)	12	0.16
Cree (0)	4	0.05
Creek (7)	12	0.16
Delaware (0)	1	0.01
Inupiat *(Alaska Native)* (1)	1	0.01
Iroquois (1)	1	0.01
Kiowa (0)	1	0.01
Mexican American Ind. (0)	1	0.01
Navajo (1)	3	0.04
Seminole (1)	1	0.01
Sioux (3)	5	0.07
Tlingit-Haida *(Alaska Native)* (1)	6	0.08
Asian (57)	112	1.47
Not Hispanic (56)	105	1.37
Hispanic (1)	7	0.09
Chinese, ex. Taiwanese (25)	39	0.51
Filipino (15)	42	0.55
Indian (6)	6	0.08
Indonesian (2)	2	0.03
Japanese (2)	14	0.18
Korean (5)	8	0.10
Pakistani (0)	1	0.01
Thai (1)	5	0.07
Vietnamese (1)	2	0.03
Hawaii Native/Pacific Islander (13)	52	0.68
Not Hispanic (13)	45	0.59
Hispanic (0)	7	0.09
Guamanian/Chamorro (4)	9	0.12
Marshallese (1)	1	0.01
Native Hawaiian (7)	28	0.37
Samoan (0)	3	0.04
White (6,707)	6,965	91.12
Not Hispanic (6,157)	6,338	82.91
Hispanic (550)	627	8.20

Sutherlin

Place Type: City
County: Douglas
Population: 7,810†

Ancestry‡	Population	%
American (544)	544	7.09
Arab (0)	7	0.09
Syrian (0)	7	0.09
Australian (14)	14	0.18
Austrian (0)	35	0.46
Czech (0)	17	0.22
Danish (21)	74	0.97
Dutch (49)	304	3.96
English (300)	936	12.21
European (16)	16	0.21
French, ex. Basque (12)	360	4.69
French Canadian (9)	172	2.24
German (489)	1,672	21.80
Greek (0)	16	0.21
Hungarian (0)	84	1.10
Irish (198)	1,071	13.97
Italian (75)	299	3.90
Northern European (12)	12	0.16
Norwegian (44)	124	1.62
Polish (12)	77	1.00
Portuguese (9)	106	1.38
Russian (10)	26	0.34
Scandinavian (19)	19	0.25
Scotch-Irish (90)	199	2.60
Scottish (142)	331	4.32
Swedish (64)	143	1.86
Ukrainian (0)	9	0.12
Welsh (47)	78	1.02

Hispanic Origin	Population	%
Hispanic or Latino (of any race)	476	6.09
Central American, ex. Mexican	12	0.15
Costa Rican	1	0.01
Guatemalan	3	0.04
Honduran	4	0.05
Panamanian	2	0.03
Salvadoran	2	0.03
Cuban	6	0.08
Mexican	363	4.65
Puerto Rican	22	0.28
South American	6	0.08
Chilean	1	0.01
Colombian	2	0.03
Venezuelan	3	0.04
Other Hispanic or Latino	67	0.86

Race*	Population	%
African-American/Black (19)	47	0.60
Not Hispanic (17)	43	0.55
Hispanic (2)	4	0.05
American Indian/Alaska Native (150)	302	3.87
Not Hispanic (137)	273	3.50
Hispanic (13)	29	0.37
Aleut *(Alaska Native)* (4)	4	0.05
Apache (0)	4	0.05
Arapaho (1)	2	0.03
Blackfeet (1)	6	0.08
Central American Ind. (0)	1	0.01
Cherokee (19)	69	0.88
Cheyenne (2)	2	0.03
Chickasaw (2)	2	0.03
Chippewa (4)	9	0.12
Choctaw (10)	13	0.17
Colville (2)	9	0.12
Cree (0)	2	0.03
Crow (0)	1	0.01
Inupiat *(Alaska Native)* (1)	1	0.01
Navajo (4)	5	0.06
Osage (1)	1	0.01
Potawatomi (1)	1	0.01
Puget Sound Salish (0)	1	0.01
Shoshone (0)	1	0.01
Sioux (3)	7	0.09

*Notes: † The Census 2010 population figure is used to calculate the percentages in the Hispanic Origin and Race categories. Ancestry percentages are based on the 2006-2010 American Community Survey population (not shown); ‡ Numbers in parentheses indicate the number of people reporting a single ancestry; * Numbers in parentheses indicate the number of persons reporting this race alone, not in combination with any other race; Please refer to the Explanation of Data for more information.*

Tlingit-Haida *(Alaska Native)* (2)	6	0.08
Ute (1)	1	0.01
Yaqui (0)	1	0.01
Asian (44)	68	0.87
Not Hispanic (43)	65	0.83
Hispanic (1)	3	0.04
Chinese, ex. Taiwanese (6)	11	0.14
Filipino (18)	29	0.37
Indian (5)	9	0.12
Japanese (3)	12	0.15
Korean (6)	6	0.08
Thai (1)	1	0.01
Vietnamese (5)	9	0.12
Hawaii Native/Pacific Islander (7)	27	0.35
Not Hispanic (7)	25	0.32
Hispanic (0)	2	0.03
Guamanian/Chamorro (2)	7	0.09
Native Hawaiian (4)	10	0.13
Samoan (0)	1	0.01
White (7,219)	7,443	95.30
Not Hispanic (6,923)	7,115	91.10
Hispanic (296)	328	4.20

Sweet Home

Place Type: City
County: Linn
Population: 8,925†

Ancestry‡	Population	%
American (763)	763	8.70
Czech (0)	20	0.23
Danish (107)	126	1.44
Dutch (82)	469	5.35
English (343)	928	10.58
European (98)	114	1.30
Finnish (14)	42	0.48
French, ex. Basque (37)	398	4.54
French Canadian (16)	36	0.41
German (770)	1,808	20.62
Hungarian (133)	169	1.93
Irish (262)	1,118	12.75
Italian (45)	248	2.83
Norwegian (186)	288	3.28
Pennsylvania German (0)	21	0.24
Polish (155)	519	5.92
Russian (46)	46	0.52
Scandinavian (16)	16	0.18
Scotch-Irish (131)	255	2.91
Scottish (110)	313	3.57
Slavic (0)	56	0.64
Swedish (57)	158	1.80
Swiss (14)	116	1.32
West Indian, ex. Hispanic (12)	12	0.14
Dutch West Indian (12)	12	0.14

Hispanic Origin	Population	%
Hispanic or Latino (of any race)	418	4.68
Central American, ex. Mexican	7	0.08
Costa Rican	3	0.03
Guatemalan	2	0.02
Nicaraguan	1	0.01
Panamanian	1	0.01
Cuban	7	0.08
Mexican	348	3.90
Puerto Rican	19	0.21
South American	1	0.01
Venezuelan	1	0.01
Other Hispanic or Latino	36	0.40

Race*	Population	%
African-American/Black (23)	53	0.59
Not Hispanic (22)	49	0.55
Hispanic (1)	4	0.04
American Indian/Alaska Native (120)	278	3.11
Not Hispanic (99)	239	2.68
Hispanic (21)	39	0.44
Alaska Athabascan *(Ala. Nat.)* (4)	5	0.06
Aleut *(Alaska Native)* (5)	5	0.06
Apache (2)	5	0.06
Blackfeet (1)	8	0.09
Cherokee (13)	38	0.43
Cheyenne (0)	3	0.03
Chickasaw (1)	1	0.01
Chippewa (3)	6	0.07
Choctaw (14)	26	0.29
Comanche (0)	1	0.01
Creek (1)	2	0.02
Inupiat *(Alaska Native)* (0)	1	0.01
Iroquois (1)	2	0.02
Kiowa (1)	1	0.01
Navajo (2)	2	0.02
Osage (1)	3	0.03
Ottawa (0)	3	0.03
Pima (0)	5	0.06
Potawatomi (1)	2	0.02
Pueblo (0)	1	0.01
Puget Sound Salish (2)	2	0.02
Shoshone (1)	3	0.03
Sioux (1)	12	0.13
Tlingit-Haida *(Alaska Native)* (3)	4	0.04
Asian (72)	118	1.32
Not Hispanic (71)	115	1.29
Hispanic (1)	3	0.03
Chinese, ex. Taiwanese (13)	19	0.21
Filipino (23)	47	0.53
Indian (8)	13	0.15
Indonesian (3)	5	0.06
Japanese (3)	9	0.10
Korean (17)	22	0.25
Laotian (0)	1	0.01
Malaysian (1)	1	0.01
Taiwanese (1)	3	0.03
Thai (1)	1	0.01
Hawaii Native/Pacific Islander (12)	44	0.49
Not Hispanic (12)	37	0.41
Hispanic (0)	7	0.08
Guamanian/Chamorro (2)	12	0.13
Native Hawaiian (9)	30	0.34
Samoan (1)	1	0.01
White (8,330)	8,585	96.19
Not Hispanic (8,083)	8,293	92.92
Hispanic (247)	292	3.27

The Dalles

Place Type: City
County: Wasco
Population: 13,620†

Ancestry‡	Population	%
American (817)	817	6.15
Australian (9)	9	0.07
Austrian (35)	35	0.26
Belgian (0)	32	0.24
British (11)	20	0.15
Cajun (13)	13	0.10
Canadian (12)	19	0.14
Croatian (8)	8	0.06
Czech (39)	87	0.66
Czechoslovakian (28)	28	0.21
Danish (73)	173	1.30
Dutch (52)	297	2.24
English (829)	1,941	14.62
European (81)	120	0.90
Finnish (37)	91	0.69
French, ex. Basque (140)	481	3.62
French Canadian (37)	103	0.78
German (1,046)	2,836	21.36
German Russian (0)	7	0.05
Greek (24)	108	0.81
Hungarian (0)	17	0.13
Irish (606)	1,488	11.21
Italian (117)	422	3.18
Luxemburger (0)	24	0.18
Northern European (65)	65	0.49
Norwegian (156)	429	3.23
Pennsylvania German (0)	9	0.07
Polish (0)	75	0.56
Portuguese (0)	15	0.11
Romanian (4)	4	0.03
Russian (11)	81	0.61
Scandinavian (45)	105	0.79
Scotch-Irish (119)	290	2.18
Scottish (102)	339	2.55
Slavic (11)	22	0.17
Slovak (0)	33	0.25
Swedish (146)	735	5.54
Swiss (15)	54	0.41
Ukrainian (0)	19	0.14
Welsh (22)	75	0.56

Hispanic Origin	Population	%
Hispanic or Latino (of any race)	2,318	17.02
Central American, ex. Mexican	29	0.21
Guatemalan	8	0.06
Honduran	6	0.04
Nicaraguan	2	0.01
Panamanian	4	0.03
Salvadoran	9	0.07
Cuban	9	0.07
Mexican	2,157	15.84
Puerto Rican	12	0.09
South American	16	0.12
Chilean	7	0.05
Colombian	2	0.01
Peruvian	4	0.03
Venezuelan	1	0.01
Other South American	2	0.01
Other Hispanic or Latino	95	0.70

Race*	Population	%
African-American/Black (64)	108	0.79
Not Hispanic (54)	85	0.62
Hispanic (10)	23	0.17
American Indian/Alaska Native (205)	379	2.78
Not Hispanic (177)	314	2.31
Hispanic (28)	65	0.48
Aleut *(Alaska Native)* (0)	1	0.01
Apache (1)	1	0.01
Blackfeet (5)	16	0.12
Canadian/French Am. Ind. (1)	2	0.01
Cherokee (26)	49	0.36
Chickasaw (7)	9	0.07
Chippewa (3)	10	0.07
Choctaw (6)	15	0.11
Colville (0)	1	0.01
Creek (1)	1	0.01
Iroquois (5)	7	0.05
Mexican American Ind. (6)	9	0.07
Navajo (6)	7	0.05
Osage (1)	1	0.01
Paiute (0)	4	0.03
Pueblo (0)	1	0.01
Puget Sound Salish (0)	3	0.02
Seminole (4)	5	0.04
Sioux (2)	7	0.05
Spanish American Ind. (1)	1	0.01
Ute (2)	2	0.01
Yakama (23)	31	0.23
Asian (132)	200	1.47
Not Hispanic (131)	193	1.42
Hispanic (1)	7	0.05
Chinese, ex. Taiwanese (28)	36	0.26
Filipino (21)	31	0.23
Indian (17)	20	0.15
Japanese (29)	57	0.42
Korean (18)	31	0.23
Laotian (4)	6	0.04
Pakistani (1)	1	0.01
Sri Lankan (1)	1	0.01
Taiwanese (1)	1	0.01
Thai (6)	7	0.05
Vietnamese (3)	6	0.04
Hawaii Native/Pacific Islander (103)	137	1.01
Not Hispanic (103)	130	0.95
Hispanic (0)	7	0.05
Native Hawaiian (3)	15	0.11
Samoan (89)	107	0.79
White (11,966)	12,306	90.35

*Notes: † The Census 2010 population figure is used to calculate the percentages in the Hispanic Origin and Race categories. Ancestry percentages are based on the 2006-2010 American Community Survey population (not shown); ‡ Numbers in parentheses indicate the number of people reporting a single ancestry; * Numbers in parentheses indicate the number of persons reporting this race alone, not in combination with any other race; Please refer to the Explanation of Data for more information.*

Not Hispanic (10,578)	10,821	79.45
Hispanic (1,388)	1,485	10.90

Tigard

Place Type: City
County: Washington
Population: 48,035†

Ancestry‡	Population	%
African, Sub-Saharan (233)	321	0.68
African (52)	140	0.30
Kenyan (29)	29	0.06
Nigerian (13)	13	0.03
Somalian (139)	139	0.29
American (2,077)	2,077	4.40
Arab (580)	662	1.40
Arab (150)	198	0.42
Egyptian (161)	161	0.34
Jordanian (106)	106	0.22
Lebanese (0)	17	0.04
Moroccan (17)	17	0.04
Palestinian (67)	67	0.14
Syrian (34)	51	0.11
Other Arab (45)	45	0.10
Armenian (8)	19	0.04
Australian (0)	26	0.06
Austrian (29)	146	0.31
Basque (5)	5	0.01
Belgian (0)	93	0.20
Brazilian (0)	13	0.03
British (82)	238	0.50
Bulgarian (44)	44	0.09
Cajun (22)	22	0.05
Canadian (91)	214	0.45
Celtic (58)	83	0.18
Croatian (14)	77	0.16
Czech (172)	393	0.83
Czechoslovakian (17)	30	0.06
Danish (123)	677	1.43
Dutch (237)	1,040	2.20
English (1,974)	7,067	14.96
European (916)	1,119	2.37
Finnish (171)	395	0.84
French, ex. Basque (141)	1,689	3.58
French Canadian (97)	320	0.68
German (2,933)	9,835	20.82
Greek (123)	212	0.45
Guyanese (0)	24	0.05
Hungarian (72)	121	0.26
Iranian (149)	193	0.41
Irish (1,274)	5,443	11.52
Israeli (17)	26	0.06
Italian (599)	2,074	4.39
Latvian (45)	45	0.10
Lithuanian (16)	80	0.17
Luxemburger (8)	8	0.02
Northern European (157)	157	0.33
Norwegian (664)	2,314	4.90
Pennsylvania German (10)	26	0.06
Polish (167)	949	2.01
Portuguese (136)	311	0.66
Romanian (176)	209	0.44
Russian (426)	779	1.65
Scandinavian (47)	182	0.39
Scotch-Irish (374)	1,144	2.42
Scottish (449)	1,337	2.83
Slovak (136)	152	0.32
Slovene (0)	17	0.04
Swedish (378)	1,776	3.76
Swiss (88)	417	0.88
Turkish (62)	119	0.25
Ukrainian (96)	199	0.42
Welsh (34)	490	1.04
West Indian, ex. Hispanic (0)	11	0.02
Haitian (0)	11	0.02
Yugoslavian (104)	127	0.27

Hispanic Origin	Population	%
Hispanic or Latino (of any race)	6,106	12.71
Central American, ex. Mexican	442	0.92
Costa Rican	25	0.05
Guatemalan	195	0.41
Honduran	40	0.08
Nicaraguan	16	0.03
Panamanian	12	0.02
Salvadoran	153	0.32
Other Central American	1	<0.01
Cuban	54	0.11
Dominican Republic	7	0.01
Mexican	4,820	10.03
Puerto Rican	138	0.29
South American	177	0.37
Argentinean	26	0.05
Bolivian	5	0.01
Chilean	24	0.05
Colombian	34	0.07
Ecuadorian	11	0.02
Peruvian	65	0.14
Venezuelan	12	0.02
Other Hispanic or Latino	468	0.97

Race*	Population	%
African-American/Black (845)	1,258	2.62
Not Hispanic (772)	1,122	2.34
Hispanic (73)	136	0.28
American Indian/Alaska Native (327)	786	1.64
Not Hispanic (251)	653	1.36
Hispanic (76)	133	0.28
Alaska Athabascan *(Ala. Nat.)* (5)	12	0.02
Aleut *(Alaska Native)* (0)	1	<0.01
Apache (4)	9	0.02
Arapaho (0)	3	0.01
Blackfeet (3)	26	0.05
Canadian/French Am. Ind. (1)	4	0.01
Central American Ind. (3)	4	0.01
Cherokee (26)	128	0.27
Cheyenne (2)	3	0.01
Chickasaw (1)	6	0.01
Chippewa (9)	37	0.08
Choctaw (5)	31	0.06
Colville (0)	1	<0.01
Comanche (0)	1	<0.01
Cree (0)	1	<0.01
Creek (2)	5	0.01
Crow (1)	4	0.01
Delaware (2)	2	<0.01
Hopi (2)	2	<0.01
Houma (1)	1	<0.01
Inupiat *(Alaska Native)* (4)	5	0.01
Iroquois (5)	14	0.03
Kiowa (1)	3	0.01
Mexican American Ind. (23)	35	0.07
Navajo (3)	15	0.03
Ottawa (3)	4	0.01
Pueblo (1)	2	<0.01
Puget Sound Salish (16)	21	0.04
Seminole (0)	12	0.02
Shoshone (0)	1	<0.01
Sioux (3)	17	0.04
South American Ind. (0)	1	<0.01
Spanish American Ind. (1)	3	0.01
Tlingit-Haida *(Alaska Native)* (13)	17	0.04
Tohono O'Odham (0)	3	0.01
Tsimshian *(Alaska Native)* (1)	2	<0.01
Ute (3)	3	0.01
Yakama (0)	1	<0.01
Yaqui (1)	5	0.01
Yuman (1)	1	<0.01
Yup'ik *(Alaska Native)* (3)	8	0.02
Asian (3,456)	4,304	8.96
Not Hispanic (3,416)	4,209	8.76
Hispanic (40)	95	0.20
Bangladeshi (3)	10	0.02
Burmese (3)	3	0.01
Cambodian (65)	95	0.20
Chinese, ex. Taiwanese (671)	900	1.87
Filipino (347)	590	1.23
Hmong (19)	24	0.05
Indian (292)	358	0.75
Indonesian (32)	52	0.11
Japanese (267)	513	1.07
Korean (476)	576	1.20
Laotian (37)	56	0.12
Malaysian (3)	3	0.01
Nepalese (31)	35	0.07
Pakistani (34)	37	0.08
Sri Lankan (12)	12	0.02
Taiwanese (46)	59	0.12
Thai (66)	84	0.17
Vietnamese (861)	967	2.01
Hawaii Native/Pacific Islander (414)	627	1.31
Not Hispanic (411)	606	1.26
Hispanic (3)	21	0.04
Fijian (12)	21	0.04
Guamanian/Chamorro (65)	87	0.18
Marshallese (89)	98	0.20
Native Hawaiian (55)	167	0.35
Samoan (44)	60	0.12
Tongan (9)	9	0.02
White (38,253)	39,951	83.17
Not Hispanic (35,460)	36,853	76.72
Hispanic (2,793)	3,098	6.45

Troutdale

Place Type: City
County: Multnomah
Population: 15,962†

Ancestry‡	Population	%
African, Sub-Saharan (111)	111	0.72
African (45)	45	0.29
Nigerian (48)	48	0.31
Other Sub-Saharan African (18)	18	0.12
American (498)	498	3.24
Arab (0)	102	0.66
Arab (0)	47	0.31
Syrian (0)	55	0.36
Austrian (11)	11	0.07
Basque (0)	11	0.07
Belgian (5)	15	0.10
British (21)	50	0.33
Canadian (4)	49	0.32
Czech (23)	116	0.76
Czechoslovakian (7)	7	0.05
Danish (25)	96	0.63
Dutch (82)	315	2.05
English (566)	1,536	10.01
Estonian (0)	7	0.05
European (593)	630	4.11
Finnish (0)	46	0.30
French, ex. Basque (87)	442	2.88
French Canadian (34)	140	0.91
German (1,068)	3,370	21.96
Greek (0)	8	0.05
Hungarian (0)	7	0.05
Icelander (7)	7	0.05
Iranian (23)	23	0.15
Irish (410)	1,758	11.46
Italian (162)	524	3.41
Latvian (45)	53	0.35
Northern European (30)	30	0.20
Norwegian (197)	685	4.46
Polish (21)	159	1.04
Portuguese (11)	18	0.12
Romanian (195)	204	1.33
Russian (42)	168	1.09
Scandinavian (43)	149	0.97
Scotch-Irish (204)	425	2.77
Scottish (126)	495	3.23
Slavic (0)	10	0.07
Slovene (0)	11	0.07
Swedish (112)	517	3.37
Swiss (25)	93	0.61
Ukrainian (395)	395	2.57
Welsh (46)	190	1.24
West Indian, ex. Hispanic (38)	102	0.66
Dutch West Indian (0)	12	0.08
Jamaican (38)	90	0.59

*Notes: † The Census 2010 population figure is used to calculate the percentages in the Hispanic Origin and Race categories. Ancestry percentages are based on the 2006-2010 American Community Survey population (not shown); ‡ Numbers in parentheses indicate the number of people reporting a single ancestry; * Numbers in parentheses indicate the number of persons reporting this race alone, not in combination with any other race; Please refer to the Explanation of Data for more information.*

Yugoslavian (0)	11	0.07

Hispanic Origin	Population	%
Hispanic or Latino (of any race)	1,692	10.60
Central American, ex. Mexican	91	0.57
Guatemalan	52	0.33
Honduran	1	0.01
Nicaraguan	1	0.01
Panamanian	3	0.02
Salvadoran	32	0.20
Other Central American	2	0.01
Cuban	12	0.08
Dominican Republic	5	0.03
Mexican	1,326	8.31
Puerto Rican	59	0.37
South American	64	0.40
Argentinean	17	0.11
Bolivian	5	0.03
Chilean	1	0.01
Colombian	19	0.12
Ecuadorian	6	0.04
Peruvian	9	0.06
Uruguayan	3	0.02
Venezuelan	4	0.03
Other Hispanic or Latino	135	0.85

Race*	Population	%
African-American/Black (335)	497	3.11
Not Hispanic (321)	458	2.87
Hispanic (14)	39	0.24
American Indian/Alaska Native (165)	340	2.13
Not Hispanic (124)	265	1.66
Hispanic (41)	75	0.47
Aleut *(Alaska Native)* (7)	9	0.06
Apache (2)	4	0.03
Blackfeet (3)	7	0.04
Canadian/French Am. Ind. (2)	3	0.02
Cherokee (5)	45	0.28
Cheyenne (4)	4	0.03
Chickasaw (0)	1	0.01
Chippewa (11)	21	0.13
Choctaw (1)	6	0.04
Comanche (0)	1	0.01
Creek (1)	2	0.01
Delaware (1)	1	0.01
Inupiat *(Alaska Native)* (1)	1	0.01
Iroquois (6)	6	0.04
Mexican American Ind. (9)	10	0.06
Navajo (7)	13	0.08
Osage (0)	1	0.01
Ottawa (2)	2	0.01
Pima (1)	1	0.01
Puget Sound Salish (1)	1	0.01
Sioux (4)	14	0.09
Tlingit-Haida *(Alaska Native)* (2)	3	0.02
Tsimshian *(Alaska Native)* (1)	2	0.01
Yakama (1)	1	0.01
Asian (729)	947	5.93
Not Hispanic (725)	921	5.77
Hispanic (4)	26	0.16
Burmese (8)	10	0.06
Cambodian (21)	33	0.21
Chinese, ex. Taiwanese (62)	122	0.76
Filipino (105)	183	1.15
Hmong (55)	63	0.39
Indian (37)	51	0.32
Indonesian (11)	13	0.08
Japanese (56)	122	0.76
Korean (51)	72	0.45
Laotian (114)	124	0.78
Malaysian (0)	1	0.01
Pakistani (1)	3	0.02
Thai (12)	16	0.10
Vietnamese (144)	158	0.99
Hawaii Native/Pacific Islander (69)	140	0.88
Not Hispanic (62)	113	0.71
Hispanic (7)	27	0.17
Fijian (0)	1	0.01
Guamanian/Chamorro (15)	31	0.19
Marshallese (8)	8	0.05
Native Hawaiian (25)	61	0.38
Samoan (4)	20	0.13
Tongan (4)	4	0.03
White (13,345)	13,926	87.24
Not Hispanic (12,542)	12,979	81.31
Hispanic (803)	947	5.93

Tualatin

Place Type: City
County: Washington
Population: 26,054†

Ancestry‡	Population	%
African, Sub-Saharan (108)	108	0.42
Cape Verdean (53)	53	0.21
Ghanaian (40)	40	0.16
Somalian (15)	15	0.06
American (651)	651	2.54
Arab (0)	62	0.24
Palestinian (0)	24	0.09
Syrian (0)	38	0.15
Armenian (6)	24	0.09
Australian (7)	30	0.12
Austrian (36)	67	0.26
Basque (40)	156	0.61
Brazilian (37)	71	0.28
British (131)	351	1.37
Canadian (28)	142	0.55
Croatian (6)	13	0.05
Czech (7)	101	0.39
Czechoslovakian (0)	12	0.05
Danish (44)	299	1.17
Dutch (162)	491	1.92
Eastern European (30)	30	0.12
English (1,084)	3,812	14.90
European (513)	543	2.12
Finnish (0)	129	0.50
French, ex. Basque (102)	798	3.12
French Canadian (76)	160	0.63
German (1,531)	5,725	22.37
Greek (110)	207	0.81
Hungarian (55)	163	0.64
Icelander (0)	11	0.04
Iranian (59)	69	0.27
Irish (853)	3,565	13.93
Italian (520)	1,196	4.67
Latvian (0)	6	0.02
Northern European (217)	217	0.85
Norwegian (375)	1,051	4.11
Polish (51)	311	1.22
Portuguese (94)	179	0.70
Romanian (0)	48	0.19
Russian (55)	227	0.89
Scandinavian (78)	137	0.54
Scotch-Irish (448)	944	3.69
Scottish (213)	699	2.73
Slavic (0)	12	0.05
Slovak (20)	62	0.24
Slovene (0)	10	0.04
Swedish (167)	559	2.18
Swiss (44)	148	0.58
Ukrainian (14)	53	0.21
Welsh (82)	266	1.04
Yugoslavian (35)	74	0.29

Hispanic Origin	Population	%
Hispanic or Latino (of any race)	4,498	17.26
Central American, ex. Mexican	147	0.56
Costa Rican	12	0.05
Guatemalan	43	0.17
Honduran	18	0.07
Nicaraguan	2	0.01
Panamanian	11	0.04
Salvadoran	61	0.23
Cuban	33	0.13
Dominican Republic	1	<0.01
Mexican	3,847	14.77
Puerto Rican	61	0.23
South American	95	0.36
Argentinean	25	0.10
Bolivian	2	0.01
Chilean	12	0.05
Colombian	18	0.07
Ecuadorian	4	0.02
Peruvian	18	0.07
Venezuelan	16	0.06
Other Hispanic or Latino	314	1.21

Race*	Population	%
African-American/Black (325)	527	2.02
Not Hispanic (297)	453	1.74
Hispanic (28)	74	0.28
American Indian/Alaska Native (188)	442	1.70
Not Hispanic (135)	322	1.24
Hispanic (53)	120	0.46
Alaska Athabascan *(Ala. Nat.)* (2)	3	0.01
Aleut *(Alaska Native)* (0)	1	<0.01
Apache (0)	5	0.02
Blackfeet (2)	10	0.04
Canadian/French Am. Ind. (0)	1	<0.01
Cherokee (8)	43	0.17
Chickasaw (6)	6	0.02
Chippewa (4)	17	0.07
Choctaw (3)	8	0.03
Comanche (0)	1	<0.01
Creek (0)	3	0.01
Crow (3)	6	0.02
Inupiat *(Alaska Native)* (0)	1	<0.01
Iroquois (0)	5	0.02
Kiowa (1)	1	<0.01
Mexican American Ind. (13)	25	0.10
Navajo (9)	18	0.07
Osage (0)	1	<0.01
Paiute (6)	6	0.02
Potawatomi (2)	2	0.01
Pueblo (0)	1	<0.01
Puget Sound Salish (1)	2	0.01
Sioux (0)	15	0.06
Spanish American Ind. (2)	4	0.02
Tlingit-Haida *(Alaska Native)* (2)	7	0.03
Tohono O'Odham (4)	5	0.02
Tsimshian *(Alaska Native)* (1)	1	<0.01
Yaqui (3)	4	0.02
Yup'ik *(Alaska Native)* (1)	8	0.03
Asian (915)	1,405	5.39
Not Hispanic (909)	1,349	5.18
Hispanic (6)	56	0.21
Burmese (7)	7	0.03
Cambodian (12)	13	0.05
Chinese, ex. Taiwanese (174)	271	1.04
Filipino (135)	281	1.08
Hmong (9)	10	0.04
Indian (137)	166	0.64
Indonesian (7)	17	0.07
Japanese (107)	259	0.99
Korean (127)	199	0.76
Laotian (15)	21	0.08
Malaysian (5)	6	0.02
Pakistani (2)	3	0.01
Sri Lankan (7)	8	0.03
Taiwanese (14)	15	0.06
Thai (25)	40	0.15
Vietnamese (99)	116	0.45
Hawaii Native/Pacific Islander (249)	370	1.42
Not Hispanic (230)	327	1.26
Hispanic (19)	43	0.17
Fijian (8)	8	0.03
Guamanian/Chamorro (29)	44	0.17
Marshallese (36)	36	0.14
Native Hawaiian (28)	99	0.38
Samoan (26)	49	0.19
White (20,950)	21,939	84.21
Not Hispanic (19,187)	19,901	76.38
Hispanic (1,763)	2,038	7.82

*Notes: † The Census 2010 population figure is used to calculate the percentages in the Hispanic Origin and Race categories. Ancestry percentages are based on the 2006-2010 American Community Survey population (not shown); ‡ Numbers in parentheses indicate the number of people reporting a single ancestry; * Numbers in parentheses indicate the number of persons reporting this race alone, not in combination with any other race; Please refer to the Explanation of Data for more information.*

West Haven-Sylvan

Place Type: CDP
County: Washington
Population: 8,001†

Ancestry‡	Population	%
African, Sub-Saharan (0)	33	0.47
African (0)	33	0.47
American (69)	69	0.98
Arab (35)	54	0.77
Egyptian (35)	35	0.50
Lebanese (0)	19	0.27
Austrian (32)	32	0.46
British (17)	72	1.03
Croatian (0)	45	0.64
Czech (50)	80	1.14
Czechoslovakian (0)	10	0.14
Danish (0)	43	0.61
Dutch (73)	314	4.48
Eastern European (111)	111	1.58
English (269)	1,203	17.15
European (176)	231	3.29
Finnish (41)	68	0.97
French, ex. Basque (39)	390	5.56
French Canadian (32)	32	0.46
German (444)	1,739	24.79
Greek (35)	59	0.84
Hungarian (0)	100	1.43
Iranian (154)	154	2.19
Irish (244)	927	13.21
Italian (93)	298	4.25
Lithuanian (0)	43	0.61
New Zealander (0)	30	0.43
Northern European (63)	63	0.90
Norwegian (31)	244	3.48
Pennsylvania German (17)	17	0.24
Polish (99)	272	3.88
Romanian (6)	62	0.88
Russian (6)	35	0.50
Scandinavian (9)	71	1.01
Scotch-Irish (47)	199	2.84
Scottish (25)	289	4.12
Slovak (16)	16	0.23
Swedish (11)	240	3.42
Swiss (14)	48	0.68
Ukrainian (0)	9	0.13
Welsh (20)	53	0.76
Yugoslavian (16)	65	0.93

Hispanic Origin	Population	%
Hispanic or Latino (of any race)	327	4.09
Central American, ex. Mexican	29	0.36
Costa Rican	6	0.07
Guatemalan	5	0.06
Honduran	5	0.06
Nicaraguan	4	0.05
Panamanian	4	0.05
Salvadoran	5	0.06
Cuban	11	0.14
Dominican Republic	3	0.04
Mexican	173	2.16
Puerto Rican	13	0.16
South American	55	0.69
Argentinean	6	0.07
Chilean	10	0.12
Colombian	6	0.07
Ecuadorian	2	0.02
Peruvian	23	0.29
Venezuelan	5	0.06
Other South American	3	0.04
Other Hispanic or Latino	43	0.54

Race*	Population	%
African-American/Black (82)	127	1.59
Not Hispanic (79)	120	1.50
Hispanic (3)	7	0.09
American Indian/Alaska Native (28)	85	1.06
Not Hispanic (25)	74	0.92
Hispanic (3)	11	0.14
Apache (0)	1	0.01
Blackfeet (0)	2	0.02
Cherokee (5)	13	0.16
Chickasaw (3)	3	0.04
Chippewa (3)	6	0.07
Choctaw (1)	2	0.02
Creek (0)	3	0.04
Delaware (0)	1	0.01
Iroquois (1)	2	0.02
Mexican American Ind. (2)	2	0.02
Navajo (2)	2	0.02
Osage (0)	1	0.01
Pueblo (2)	3	0.04
Puget Sound Salish (0)	1	0.01
Sioux (0)	2	0.02
Spanish American Ind. (0)	1	0.01
Tlingit-Haida *(Alaska Native)* (0)	1	0.01
Asian (506)	656	8.20
Not Hispanic (504)	648	8.10
Hispanic (2)	8	0.10
Bangladeshi (1)	1	0.01
Cambodian (4)	5	0.06
Chinese, ex. Taiwanese (130)	189	2.36
Filipino (46)	81	1.01
Indian (64)	77	0.96
Indonesian (5)	8	0.10
Japanese (85)	134	1.67
Korean (76)	93	1.16
Malaysian (1)	2	0.02
Nepalese (4)	4	0.05
Pakistani (3)	4	0.05
Taiwanese (20)	21	0.26
Thai (7)	10	0.12
Vietnamese (31)	41	0.51
Hawaii Native/Pacific Islander (15)	50	0.62
Not Hispanic (14)	48	0.60
Hispanic (1)	2	0.02
Guamanian/Chamorro (2)	5	0.06
Native Hawaiian (8)	30	0.37
Samoan (1)	2	0.02
Tongan (1)	3	0.04
White (6,990)	7,233	90.40
Not Hispanic (6,798)	7,020	87.74
Hispanic (192)	213	2.66

West Linn

Place Type: City
County: Clackamas
Population: 25,109†

Ancestry‡	Population	%
African, Sub-Saharan (0)	201	0.82
South African (0)	201	0.82
American (714)	714	2.90
Arab (211)	306	1.24
Arab (190)	285	1.16
Lebanese (21)	21	0.09
Armenian (0)	187	0.76
Australian (44)	132	0.54
Austrian (58)	58	0.24
Basque (35)	78	0.32
Belgian (14)	30	0.12
British (143)	273	1.11
Canadian (126)	230	0.93
Croatian (0)	27	0.11
Czech (58)	133	0.54
Czechoslovakian (24)	56	0.23
Danish (134)	264	1.07
Dutch (115)	793	3.22
Eastern European (90)	90	0.37
English (1,241)	4,824	19.56
Estonian (0)	14	0.06
European (622)	664	2.69
Finnish (16)	53	0.21
French, ex. Basque (182)	1,024	4.15
French Canadian (44)	94	0.38
German (1,886)	6,325	25.65
Greek (46)	107	0.43
Hungarian (85)	213	0.86
Iranian (107)	107	0.43
Irish (974)	4,025	16.32
Italian (251)	1,331	5.40
Latvian (0)	31	0.13
Northern European (81)	81	0.33
Norwegian (346)	1,033	4.19
Polish (72)	582	2.36
Portuguese (22)	48	0.19
Romanian (142)	157	0.64
Russian (184)	483	1.96
Scandinavian (184)	360	1.46
Scotch-Irish (217)	590	2.39
Scottish (178)	886	3.59
Serbian (0)	14	0.06
Slovene (0)	6	0.02
Swedish (243)	1,304	5.29
Swiss (0)	181	0.73
Ukrainian (36)	86	0.35
Welsh (41)	434	1.76
Yugoslavian (0)	52	0.21

Hispanic Origin	Population	%
Hispanic or Latino (of any race)	998	3.97
Central American, ex. Mexican	71	0.28
Costa Rican	16	0.06
Guatemalan	23	0.09
Honduran	5	0.02
Nicaraguan	6	0.02
Panamanian	3	0.01
Salvadoran	18	0.07
Cuban	28	0.11
Dominican Republic	4	0.02
Mexican	627	2.50
Puerto Rican	64	0.25
South American	55	0.22
Argentinean	5	0.02
Bolivian	5	0.02
Chilean	8	0.03
Colombian	13	0.05
Ecuadorian	4	0.02
Peruvian	15	0.06
Venezuelan	3	0.01
Other South American	2	0.01
Other Hispanic or Latino	149	0.59

Race*	Population	%
African-American/Black (168)	299	1.19
Not Hispanic (164)	274	1.09
Hispanic (4)	25	0.10
American Indian/Alaska Native (87)	276	1.10
Not Hispanic (80)	240	0.96
Hispanic (7)	36	0.14
Alaska Athabascan *(Ala. Nat.)* (1)	1	<0.01
Aleut *(Alaska Native)* (0)	2	0.01
Apache (3)	9	0.04
Blackfeet (0)	7	0.03
Canadian/French Am. Ind. (0)	1	<0.01
Cherokee (6)	54	0.22
Cheyenne (1)	1	<0.01
Chickasaw (2)	7	0.03
Chippewa (7)	12	0.05
Choctaw (1)	10	0.04
Comanche (0)	5	0.02
Cree (1)	1	<0.01
Creek (1)	4	0.02
Crow (1)	1	<0.01
Delaware (0)	1	<0.01
Hopi (0)	1	<0.01
Inupiat *(Alaska Native)* (0)	1	<0.01
Iroquois (0)	1	<0.01
Mexican American Ind. (1)	2	0.01
Navajo (2)	2	0.01
Osage (0)	1	<0.01
Ottawa (1)	1	<0.01
Paiute (3)	3	0.01
Potawatomi (1)	1	<0.01
Puget Sound Salish (1)	2	0.01
Sioux (1)	3	0.01
South American Ind. (0)	1	<0.01
Tlingit-Haida *(Alaska Native)* (4)	4	0.02

*Notes: † The Census 2010 population figure is used to calculate the percentages in the Hispanic Origin and Race categories. Ancestry percentages are based on the 2006-2010 American Community Survey population (not shown); ‡ Numbers in parentheses indicate the number of people reporting a single ancestry; * Numbers in parentheses indicate the number of persons reporting this race alone, not in combination with any other race; Please refer to the Explanation of Data for more information.*

Tsimshian *(Alaska Native)* (0)	1	<0.01
Yakama (0)	1	<0.01
Yaqui (0)	5	0.02
Asian (1,012)	1,432	5.70
Not Hispanic (992)	1,392	5.54
Hispanic (20)	40	0.16
Bangladeshi (4)	4	0.02
Cambodian (21)	21	0.08
Chinese, ex. Taiwanese (308)	414	1.65
Filipino (74)	174	0.69
Indian (129)	158	0.63
Indonesian (3)	12	0.05
Japanese (130)	257	1.02
Korean (152)	222	0.88
Laotian (2)	6	0.02
Malaysian (2)	8	0.03
Nepalese (7)	10	0.04
Pakistani (11)	13	0.05
Sri Lankan (1)	1	<0.01
Taiwanese (30)	35	0.14
Thai (24)	36	0.14
Vietnamese (51)	76	0.30
Hawaii Native/Pacific Islander (37)	104	0.41
Not Hispanic (35)	102	0.41
Hispanic (2)	2	0.01
Fijian (0)	1	<0.01
Guamanian/Chamorro (7)	13	0.05
Native Hawaiian (18)	56	0.22
Samoan (0)	3	0.01
Tongan (3)	3	0.01
White (22,778)	23,512	93.64
Not Hispanic (22,122)	22,754	90.62
Hispanic (656)	758	3.02

White City

Place Type: CDP
County: Jackson
Population: 7,975†

Ancestry‡	Population	%
African, Sub-Saharan (19)	28	0.36
African (19)	28	0.36
American (222)	222	2.83
Armenian (0)	45	0.57
Austrian (0)	9	0.11
British (0)	14	0.18
Canadian (0)	57	0.73
Croatian (0)	9	0.11
Czech (19)	19	0.24
Danish (0)	3	0.04
Dutch (0)	133	1.70
English (230)	428	5.46
European (42)	66	0.84
French, ex. Basque (22)	132	1.69
French Canadian (0)	8	0.10
German (425)	1,142	14.58
Hungarian (9)	9	0.11
Irish (325)	804	10.26
Italian (179)	271	3.46
Norwegian (76)	291	3.72
Pennsylvania German (0)	8	0.10
Polish (17)	35	0.45
Portuguese (25)	100	1.28
Russian (6)	6	0.08
Scotch-Irish (73)	205	2.62
Scottish (20)	100	1.28
Swedish (48)	148	1.89
Swiss (0)	28	0.36
Welsh (15)	46	0.59
West Indian, ex. Hispanic (21)	40	0.51
Dutch West Indian (0)	19	0.24
West Indian (21)	21	0.27

Hispanic Origin	Population	%
Hispanic or Latino (of any race)	2,300	28.84
Central American, ex. Mexican	36	0.45
Costa Rican	2	0.03
Guatemalan	18	0.23
Honduran	6	0.08
Salvadoran	10	0.13
Cuban	3	0.04
Dominican Republic	1	0.01
Mexican	2,074	26.01
Puerto Rican	12	0.15
South American	7	0.09
Argentinean	1	0.01
Colombian	5	0.06
Other South American	1	0.01
Other Hispanic or Latino	167	2.09

Race*	Population	%
African-American/Black (103)	130	1.63
Not Hispanic (91)	113	1.42
Hispanic (12)	17	0.21
American Indian/Alaska Native (107)	238	2.98
Not Hispanic (77)	180	2.26
Hispanic (30)	58	0.73
Apache (4)	7	0.09
Blackfeet (0)	6	0.08
Cherokee (12)	46	0.58
Cheyenne (0)	3	0.04
Chippewa (1)	5	0.06
Choctaw (5)	14	0.18
Comanche (0)	1	0.01
Cree (0)	1	0.01
Creek (1)	2	0.03
Inupiat *(Alaska Native)* (1)	1	0.01
Iroquois (0)	1	0.01
Lumbee (0)	3	0.04
Mexican American Ind. (4)	10	0.13
Navajo (0)	4	0.05
Ottawa (0)	2	0.03
Paiute (1)	1	0.01
Pueblo (1)	1	0.01
Sioux (1)	4	0.05
Tlingit-Haida *(Alaska Native)* (3)	6	0.08
Tohono O'Odham (0)	3	0.04
Ute (0)	3	0.04
Yakama (0)	1	0.01
Yup'ik *(Alaska Native)* (1)	1	0.01
Asian (67)	114	1.43
Not Hispanic (64)	102	1.28
Hispanic (3)	12	0.15
Burmese (5)	5	0.06
Chinese, ex. Taiwanese (14)	25	0.31
Filipino (31)	56	0.70
Indian (3)	5	0.06
Japanese (4)	20	0.25
Korean (5)	9	0.11
Thai (0)	1	0.01
Hawaii Native/Pacific Islander (5)	15	0.19
Not Hispanic (5)	12	0.15
Hispanic (0)	3	0.04
Guamanian/Chamorro (1)	3	0.04
Native Hawaiian (3)	6	0.08
Samoan (0)	1	0.01
White (5,955)	6,246	78.32
Not Hispanic (5,282)	5,433	68.13
Hispanic (673)	813	10.19

Wilsonville

Place Type: City
County: Clackamas
Population: 19,509†

Ancestry‡	Population	%
African, Sub-Saharan (115)	130	0.69
African (26)	26	0.14
Ethiopian (89)	89	0.47
South African (0)	15	0.08
American (899)	899	4.76
Arab (0)	31	0.16
Syrian (0)	31	0.16
Armenian (34)	34	0.18
Austrian (11)	112	0.59
Belgian (0)	26	0.14
British (205)	289	1.53
Canadian (19)	84	0.44
Croatian (0)	12	0.06
Czech (13)	89	0.47
Czechoslovakian (13)	60	0.32
Danish (57)	176	0.93
Dutch (121)	405	2.14
Eastern European (7)	7	0.04
English (576)	2,521	13.34
European (363)	363	1.92
Finnish (53)	134	0.71
French, ex. Basque (65)	584	3.09
French Canadian (58)	142	0.75
German (1,135)	4,731	25.03
Greek (21)	31	0.16
Hungarian (31)	104	0.55
Icelander (0)	11	0.06
Iranian (63)	63	0.33
Irish (582)	2,536	13.42
Italian (288)	1,273	6.74
Latvian (0)	11	0.06
Lithuanian (15)	15	0.08
Northern European (29)	29	0.15
Norwegian (135)	606	3.21
Pennsylvania German (0)	10	0.05
Polish (83)	297	1.57
Portuguese (27)	195	1.03
Romanian (70)	70	0.37
Russian (141)	277	1.47
Scandinavian (92)	147	0.78
Scotch-Irish (138)	425	2.25
Scottish (121)	578	3.06
Slovak (19)	19	0.10
Swedish (196)	482	2.55
Swiss (38)	230	1.22
Ukrainian (28)	44	0.23
Welsh (76)	284	1.50
Yugoslavian (12)	12	0.06

Hispanic Origin	Population	%
Hispanic or Latino (of any race)	2,360	12.10
Central American, ex. Mexican	75	0.38
Costa Rican	3	0.02
Guatemalan	35	0.18
Honduran	4	0.02
Nicaraguan	6	0.03
Panamanian	8	0.04
Salvadoran	19	0.10
Cuban	18	0.09
Mexican	1,942	9.95
Puerto Rican	67	0.34
South American	54	0.28
Argentinean	6	0.03
Bolivian	1	0.01
Chilean	8	0.04
Colombian	11	0.06
Ecuadorian	7	0.04
Peruvian	14	0.07
Uruguayan	3	0.02
Venezuelan	3	0.02
Other South American	1	0.01
Other Hispanic or Latino	204	1.05

Race*	Population	%
African-American/Black (296)	414	2.12
Not Hispanic (271)	362	1.86
Hispanic (25)	52	0.27
American Indian/Alaska Native (190)	348	1.78
Not Hispanic (147)	277	1.42
Hispanic (43)	71	0.36
Apache (4)	10	0.05
Blackfeet (6)	10	0.05
Cherokee (11)	42	0.22
Chippewa (4)	12	0.06
Choctaw (4)	6	0.03
Comanche (0)	5	0.03
Cree (1)	3	0.02
Crow (0)	1	0.01
Iroquois (1)	3	0.02
Mexican American Ind. (6)	9	0.05
Navajo (3)	5	0.03
Ottawa (3)	3	0.02

*Notes: † The Census 2010 population figure is used to calculate the percentages in the Hispanic Origin and Race categories. Ancestry percentages are based on the 2006-2010 American Community Survey population (not shown); ‡ Numbers in parentheses indicate the number of people reporting a single ancestry; * Numbers in parentheses indicate the number of persons reporting this race alone, not in combination with any other race; Please refer to the Explanation of Data for more information.*

Paiute (0)	1	0.01
Pima (1)	2	0.01
Potawatomi (1)	1	0.01
Pueblo (1)	1	0.01
Puget Sound Salish (0)	1	0.01
Seminole (2)	2	0.01
Shoshone (0)	2	0.01
Sioux (1)	5	0.03
South American Ind. (1)	1	0.01
Spanish American Ind. (0)	1	0.01
Tlingit-Haida *(Alaska Native)* (5)	5	0.03
Yakama (0)	2	0.01
Asian (746)	948	4.86
Not Hispanic (732)	920	4.72
Hispanic (14)	28	0.14
Cambodian (6)	11	0.06
Chinese, ex. Taiwanese (143)	202	1.04
Filipino (54)	120	0.62
Hmong (9)	9	0.05
Indian (221)	237	1.21
Indonesian (6)	10	0.05
Japanese (63)	103	0.53
Korean (118)	150	0.77
Laotian (2)	5	0.03
Malaysian (5)	6	0.03
Pakistani (2)	2	0.01
Sri Lankan (1)	2	0.01
Taiwanese (4)	6	0.03
Thai (23)	23	0.12
Vietnamese (44)	50	0.26
Hawaii Native/Pacific Islander (85)	133	0.68
Not Hispanic (78)	121	0.62
Hispanic (7)	12	0.06
Guamanian/Chamorro (26)	27	0.14
Marshallese (1)	4	0.02
Native Hawaiian (18)	40	0.21
Samoan (12)	15	0.08
White (16,644)	17,220	88.27
Not Hispanic (15,487)	15,879	81.39
Hispanic (1,157)	1,341	6.87

Woodburn

Place Type: City
County: Marion
Population: 24,080†

Ancestry‡	Population	%
American (849)	849	3.65
Austrian (0)	12	0.05
Basque (0)	15	0.06
Belgian (14)	14	0.06
British (34)	51	0.22
Canadian (10)	10	0.04
Croatian (0)	18	0.08
Czech (45)	51	0.22
Danish (92)	229	0.99
Dutch (0)	261	1.12
English (546)	1,661	7.15
European (58)	64	0.28
Finnish (0)	31	0.13
French, ex. Basque (57)	343	1.48
French Canadian (41)	86	0.37
German (545)	2,680	11.53
Greek (10)	66	0.28
Iranian (0)	11	0.05
Irish (314)	1,519	6.53
Israeli (0)	16	0.07
Italian (10)	118	0.51
Lithuanian (17)	17	0.07
Northern European (29)	29	0.12
Norwegian (204)	520	2.24
Pennsylvania German (0)	13	0.06
Polish (34)	93	0.40
Romanian (0)	12	0.05
Russian (1,032)	1,251	5.38
Scotch-Irish (134)	354	1.52
Scottish (94)	364	1.57
Swedish (85)	268	1.15
Swiss (10)	87	0.37
Ukrainian (481)	549	2.36
Welsh (0)	264	1.14

Hispanic Origin	Population	%
Hispanic or Latino (of any race)	14,183	58.90
Central American, ex. Mexican	211	0.88
Costa Rican	5	0.02
Guatemalan	47	0.20
Honduran	11	0.05
Nicaraguan	12	0.05
Panamanian	2	0.01
Salvadoran	133	0.55
Other Central American	1	<0.01
Cuban	21	0.09
Dominican Republic	6	0.02
Mexican	13,275	55.13
Puerto Rican	35	0.15
South American	45	0.19
Argentinean	23	0.10
Chilean	1	<0.01
Colombian	11	0.05
Peruvian	6	0.02
Venezuelan	3	0.01
Other South American	1	<0.01
Other Hispanic or Latino	590	2.45

Race*	Population	%
African-American/Black (129)	249	1.03
Not Hispanic (60)	117	0.49
Hispanic (69)	132	0.55
American Indian/Alaska Native (675)	937	3.89
Not Hispanic (99)	197	0.82
Hispanic (576)	740	3.07
Aleut *(Alaska Native)* (4)	4	0.02
Apache (2)	8	0.03
Blackfeet (1)	5	0.02
Canadian/French Am. Ind. (1)	1	<0.01
Central American Ind. (1)	8	0.03
Cherokee (19)	63	0.26
Chippewa (3)	7	0.03
Choctaw (1)	5	0.02
Comanche (0)	7	0.03
Hopi (0)	1	<0.01
Inupiat *(Alaska Native)* (1)	1	<0.01
Iroquois (3)	5	0.02
Menominee (4)	12	0.05
Mexican American Ind. (451)	532	2.21
Navajo (1)	4	0.02
Osage (2)	4	0.02
Paiute (2)	2	0.01
Potawatomi (2)	2	0.01
Pueblo (1)	1	<0.01
Seminole (0)	2	0.01
Sioux (6)	9	0.04
South American Ind. (0)	6	0.02
Spanish American Ind. (20)	30	0.12
Tlingit-Haida *(Alaska Native)* (2)	3	0.01
Tohono O'Odham (3)	4	0.02
Yakama (3)	3	0.01
Yaqui (2)	2	0.01
Yup'ik *(Alaska Native)* (1)	4	0.02
Asian (191)	352	1.46
Not Hispanic (158)	262	1.09
Hispanic (33)	90	0.37
Burmese (1)	1	<0.01
Cambodian (1)	1	<0.01
Chinese, ex. Taiwanese (37)	81	0.34
Filipino (41)	90	0.37
Hmong (9)	10	0.04
Indian (9)	30	0.12
Indonesian (4)	5	0.02
Japanese (13)	43	0.18
Korean (34)	41	0.17
Laotian (9)	10	0.04
Nepalese (2)	2	0.01
Taiwanese (1)	1	<0.01
Thai (2)	3	0.01
Vietnamese (22)	29	0.12
Hawaii Native/Pacific Islander (26)	87	0.36
Not Hispanic (17)	57	0.24
Hispanic (9)	30	0.12
Guamanian/Chamorro (4)	8	0.03
Native Hawaiian (13)	56	0.23
Samoan (2)	6	0.02
Tongan (3)	3	0.01
White (14,551)	15,329	63.66
Not Hispanic (9,265)	9,508	39.49
Hispanic (5,286)	5,821	24.17

*Notes: † The Census 2010 population figure is used to calculate the percentages in the Hispanic Origin and Race categories. Ancestry percentages are based on the 2006-2010 American Community Survey population (not shown); ‡ Numbers in parentheses indicate the number of people reporting a single ancestry; * Numbers in parentheses indicate the number of persons reporting this race alone, not in combination with any other race; Please refer to the Explanation of Data for more information.*

PENNSYLVANIA

Place Type: State
Population: 12,702,379†

Ancestry‡	Population	%
Afghan (704)	876	0.01
African, Sub-Saharan (69,793)	83,254	0.66
African (44,115)	53,706	0.43
Cape Verdean (199)	355	<0.01
Ethiopian (3,174)	3,372	0.03
Ghanaian (1,632)	1,774	0.01
Kenyan (1,115)	1,277	0.01
Liberian (6,971)	7,515	0.06
Nigerian (5,398)	6,451	0.05
Senegalese (396)	477	<0.01
Sierra Leonean (952)	1,036	0.01
Somalian (239)	250	<0.01
South African (850)	1,323	0.01
Sudanese (1,003)	1,027	0.01
Ugandan (192)	215	<0.01
Zimbabwean (201)	201	<0.01
Other Sub-Saharan African (3,356)	4,275	0.03
Albanian (6,778)	8,869	0.07
Alsatian (150)	599	<0.01
American (550,441)	550,441	4.36
Arab (35,720)	61,004	0.48
Arab (5,177)	6,995	0.06
Egyptian (5,649)	6,728	0.05
Iraqi (838)	955	0.01
Jordanian (1,528)	1,616	0.01
Lebanese (7,381)	19,891	0.16
Moroccan (2,390)	2,980	0.02
Palestinian (1,360)	1,727	0.01
Syrian (7,413)	14,843	0.12
Other Arab (3,984)	5,269	0.04
Armenian (5,101)	9,325	0.07
Assyrian/Chaldean/Syriac (267)	386	<0.01
Australian (1,239)	2,907	0.02
Austrian (14,151)	59,263	0.47
Basque (192)	521	<0.01
Belgian (2,483)	9,754	0.08
Brazilian (5,805)	7,831	0.06
British (18,564)	39,949	0.32
Bulgarian (1,970)	2,544	0.02
Cajun (153)	425	<0.01
Canadian (6,707)	14,976	0.12
Carpatho Rusyn (1,228)	2,480	0.02
Celtic (792)	1,798	0.01
Croatian (17,378)	50,995	0.40
Cypriot (343)	375	<0.01
Czech (12,702)	57,652	0.46
Czechoslovakian (10,228)	23,548	0.19
Danish (4,295)	19,001	0.15
Dutch (52,955)	268,376	2.13
Eastern European (20,336)	22,509	0.18
English (274,054)	1,052,986	8.35
Estonian (444)	1,136	0.01
European (73,687)	79,980	0.63
Finnish (2,224)	8,401	0.07
French, ex. Basque (34,470)	234,946	1.86
French Canadian (10,441)	30,828	0.24
German (1,302,473)	3,533,978	28.02
German Russian (178)	320	<0.01
Greek (30,129)	66,404	0.53
Guyanese (1,783)	2,750	0.02
Hungarian (39,070)	144,444	1.15
Icelander (248)	638	0.01
Iranian (3,731)	4,863	0.04
Irish (591,624)	2,251,268	17.85
Israeli (2,306)	3,461	0.03
Italian (608,889)	1,577,604	12.51
Latvian (1,817)	3,754	0.03
Lithuanian (24,057)	82,290	0.65
Luxemburger (110)	415	<0.01
Macedonian (463)	1,117	0.01
Maltese (203)	703	0.01
New Zealander (203)	346	<0.01
Northern European (4,286)	4,622	0.04
Norwegian (11,722)	43,252	0.34
Pennsylvania German (116,138)	173,129	1.37
Polish (291,984)	880,890	6.98
Portuguese (8,178)	19,008	0.15
Romanian (8,849)	19,304	0.15
Russian (77,198)	202,430	1.60
Scandinavian (3,016)	7,796	0.06
Scotch-Irish (86,484)	251,093	1.99
Scottish (50,503)	210,517	1.67
Serbian (7,086)	19,549	0.15
Slavic (6,153)	17,175	0.14
Slovak (88,698)	244,706	1.94
Slovene (6,310)	16,861	0.13
Soviet Union (59)	59	<0.01
Swedish (26,095)	114,312	0.91
Swiss (17,438)	71,887	0.57
Turkish (4,739)	6,319	0.05
Ukrainian (49,800)	117,955	0.94
Welsh (31,875)	187,607	1.49
West Indian, ex. Hispanic (49,541)	63,964	0.51
Bahamian (383)	516	<0.01
Barbadian (1,533)	2,183	0.02
Belizean (566)	624	<0.01
Bermudan (292)	423	<0.01
British West Indian (1,114)	1,596	0.01
Dutch West Indian (156)	267	<0.01
Haitian (17,394)	19,433	0.15
Jamaican (19,465)	25,515	0.20
Trinidadian/Tobagonian (3,782)	5,362	0.04
U.S. Virgin Islander (784)	835	0.01
West Indian (4,023)	7,115	0.06
Other West Indian (49)	95	<0.01
Yugoslavian (6,768)	12,582	0.10

Hispanic Origin	Population	%
Hispanic or Latino (of any race)	719,660	5.67
Central American, ex. Mexican	35,453	0.28
Costa Rican	3,048	0.02
Guatemalan	11,462	0.09
Honduran	7,055	0.06
Nicaraguan	2,400	0.02
Panamanian	3,234	0.03
Salvadoran	7,952	0.06
Other Central American	302	<0.01
Cuban	17,930	0.14
Dominican Republic	62,348	0.49
Mexican	129,568	1.02
Puerto Rican	366,082	2.88
South American	48,126	0.38
Argentinean	4,269	0.03
Bolivian	895	0.01
Chilean	2,521	0.02
Colombian	16,525	0.13
Ecuadorian	10,680	0.08
Paraguayan	500	<0.01
Peruvian	7,783	0.06
Uruguayan	1,181	0.01
Venezuelan	3,243	0.03
Other South American	529	<0.01
Other Hispanic or Latino	60,153	0.47

Race*	Population	%
African-American/Black (1,377,689)	1,507,965	11.87
Not Hispanic (1,327,091)	1,432,537	11.28
Hispanic (50,598)	75,428	0.59
American Indian/Alaska Native (26,843)	81,092	0.64
Not Hispanic (16,909)	62,066	0.49
Hispanic (9,934)	19,026	0.15
Alaska Athabascan *(Ala. Nat.)* (58)	92	<0.01
Aleut *(Alaska Native)* (63)	108	<0.01
Apache (215)	911	0.01
Arapaho (7)	41	<0.01
Blackfeet (447)	3,347	0.03
Canadian/French Am. Ind. (118)	288	<0.01
Central American Ind. (280)	443	<0.01
Cherokee (2,612)	14,552	0.11
Cheyenne (50)	185	<0.01
Chickasaw (50)	186	<0.01
Chippewa (348)	770	0.01
Choctaw (227)	787	0.01
Colville (4)	15	<0.01
Comanche (49)	133	<0.01
Cree (53)	217	<0.01
Creek (130)	393	<0.01
Crow (23)	150	<0.01
Delaware (407)	1,680	0.01
Hopi (30)	82	<0.01
Houma (18)	28	<0.01
Inupiat *(Alaska Native)* (43)	91	<0.01
Iroquois (942)	2,816	0.02
Kiowa (40)	98	<0.01
Lumbee (250)	505	<0.01
Menominee (9)	27	<0.01
Mexican American Ind. (1,048)	1,520	0.01
Navajo (252)	619	<0.01
Osage (18)	80	<0.01
Ottawa (11)	36	<0.01
Paiute (9)	36	<0.01
Pima (19)	36	<0.01
Potawatomi (85)	157	<0.01
Pueblo (92)	204	<0.01
Puget Sound Salish (29)	41	<0.01
Seminole (105)	660	0.01
Shoshone (36)	98	<0.01
Sioux (491)	1,695	0.01
South American Ind. (970)	2,122	0.02
Spanish American Ind. (253)	383	<0.01
Tlingit-Haida *(Alaska Native)* (48)	95	<0.01
Tohono O'Odham (34)	63	<0.01
Tsimshian *(Alaska Native)* (7)	13	<0.01
Ute (13)	33	<0.01
Yakama (5)	10	<0.01
Yaqui (29)	61	<0.01
Yuman (7)	18	<0.01
Yup'ik *(Alaska Native)* (13)	25	<0.01
Asian (349,088)	402,587	3.17
Not Hispanic (346,288)	394,941	3.11
Hispanic (2,800)	7,646	0.06
Bangladeshi (3,812)	4,262	0.03
Bhutanese (946)	1,198	0.01
Burmese (1,665)	1,822	0.01
Cambodian (12,042)	14,118	0.11
Chinese, ex. Taiwanese (81,419)	92,970	0.73
Filipino (21,948)	33,021	0.26
Hmong (945)	1,021	0.01
Indian (103,026)	113,389	0.89
Indonesian (3,165)	3,926	0.03
Japanese (6,492)	12,699	0.10
Korean (40,505)	47,429	0.37
Laotian (2,589)	3,280	0.03
Malaysian (543)	768	0.01
Nepalese (1,078)	1,429	0.01
Pakistani (9,252)	10,330	0.08
Sri Lankan (954)	1,100	0.01
Taiwanese (3,220)	3,830	0.03
Thai (2,721)	4,103	0.03
Vietnamese (39,008)	44,605	0.35
Hawaii Native/Pacific Islander (3,653)	12,424	0.10
Not Hispanic (2,715)	8,756	0.07
Hispanic (938)	3,668	0.03
Fijian (39)	92	<0.01
Guamanian/Chamorro (968)	1,605	0.01
Marshallese (19)	22	<0.01
Native Hawaiian (940)	3,043	0.02
Samoan (453)	1,118	0.01
Tongan (85)	137	<0.01
White (10,406,288)	10,604,187	83.48
Not Hispanic (10,094,652)	10,248,965	80.69
Hispanic (311,636)	355,222	2.80

*Notes: † The Census 2010 population figure is used to calculate the percentages in the Hispanic Origin and Race categories. Ancestry percentages are based on the 2006-2010 American Community Survey population (not shown); ‡ Numbers in parentheses indicate the number of people reporting a single ancestry; * Numbers in parentheses indicate the number of persons reporting this race alone, not in combination with any other race; Please refer to the Explanation of Data for more information.*

Abington

Place Type: Township
County: Montgomery
Population: 55,310†

Ancestry‡	Population	%
African, Sub-Saharan (183)	240	0.43
African (150)	164	0.30
Nigerian (14)	14	0.03
Sierra Leonean (0)	10	0.02
Other Sub-Saharan African (19)	52	0.09
Albanian (82)	121	0.22
American (2,004)	2,004	3.62
Arab (38)	159	0.29
Egyptian (23)	23	0.04
Lebanese (0)	94	0.17
Palestinian (0)	11	0.02
Syrian (0)	16	0.03
Other Arab (15)	15	0.03
Armenian (10)	10	0.02
Australian (27)	37	0.07
Austrian (94)	410	0.74
Belgian (23)	75	0.14
Brazilian (10)	32	0.06
British (81)	298	0.54
Bulgarian (26)	26	0.05
Canadian (11)	56	0.10
Croatian (33)	33	0.06
Czech (92)	173	0.31
Czechoslovakian (40)	73	0.13
Danish (9)	41	0.07
Dutch (60)	322	0.58
Eastern European (282)	337	0.61
English (792)	4,855	8.76
Estonian (11)	11	0.02
European (516)	590	1.06
Finnish (0)	20	0.04
French, ex. Basque (100)	1,102	1.99
French Canadian (49)	101	0.18
German (3,011)	12,435	22.44
Greek (132)	337	0.61
Guyanese (74)	74	0.13
Hungarian (104)	458	0.83
Iranian (56)	65	0.12
Irish (4,660)	14,146	25.53
Israeli (20)	79	0.14
Italian (2,864)	7,624	13.76
Latvian (57)	70	0.13
Lithuanian (92)	330	0.60
Maltese (0)	14	0.03
Northern European (63)	63	0.11
Norwegian (31)	115	0.21
Pennsylvania German (121)	336	0.61
Polish (975)	4,038	7.29
Portuguese (141)	240	0.43
Romanian (95)	279	0.50
Russian (1,139)	2,330	4.20
Scandinavian (0)	5	0.01
Scotch-Irish (375)	1,152	2.08
Scottish (270)	1,043	1.88
Slavic (0)	22	0.04
Slovak (102)	282	0.51
Slovene (28)	28	0.05
Swedish (34)	470	0.85
Swiss (6)	162	0.29
Turkish (0)	17	0.03
Ukrainian (471)	885	1.60
Welsh (29)	562	1.01
West Indian, ex. Hispanic (529)	672	1.21
Barbadian (50)	60	0.11
British West Indian (11)	11	0.02
Haitian (87)	119	0.21
Jamaican (222)	264	0.48
Trinidadian/Tobagonian (15)	74	0.13
West Indian (144)	144	0.26
Yugoslavian (22)	32	0.06

Hispanic Origin	Population	%
Hispanic or Latino (of any race)	1,771	3.20
Central American, ex. Mexican	187	0.34
Costa Rican	21	0.04
Guatemalan	62	0.11
Honduran	15	0.03
Nicaraguan	17	0.03
Panamanian	18	0.03
Salvadoran	43	0.08
Other Central American	11	0.02
Cuban	111	0.20
Dominican Republic	27	0.05
Mexican	261	0.47
Puerto Rican	683	1.23
South American	294	0.53
Argentinean	42	0.08
Bolivian	4	0.01
Chilean	11	0.02
Colombian	100	0.18
Ecuadorian	28	0.05
Paraguayan	1	<0.01
Peruvian	69	0.12
Uruguayan	10	0.02
Venezuelan	29	0.05
Other Hispanic or Latino	208	0.38

Race*	Population	%
African-American/Black (6,850)	7,513	13.58
Not Hispanic (6,711)	7,266	13.14
Hispanic (139)	247	0.45
American Indian/Alaska Native (57)	296	0.54
Not Hispanic (40)	231	0.42
Hispanic (17)	65	0.12
Alaska Athabascan *(Ala. Nat.)* (1)	1	<0.01
Apache (0)	6	0.01
Blackfeet (1)	9	0.02
Canadian/French Am. Ind. (0)	1	<0.01
Cherokee (15)	91	0.16
Choctaw (0)	1	<0.01
Cree (1)	3	0.01
Delaware (1)	5	0.01
Inupiat *(Alaska Native)* (0)	3	0.01
Iroquois (0)	2	<0.01
Lumbee (3)	10	0.02
Mexican American Ind. (3)	3	0.01
Navajo (0)	4	0.01
Sioux (1)	3	0.01
South American Ind. (4)	8	0.01
Asian (2,686)	3,030	5.48
Not Hispanic (2,673)	2,985	5.40
Hispanic (13)	45	0.08
Bangladeshi (19)	19	0.03
Burmese (10)	10	0.02
Cambodian (37)	46	0.08
Chinese, ex. Taiwanese (346)	424	0.77
Filipino (130)	212	0.38
Hmong (2)	2	<0.01
Indian (401)	455	0.82
Indonesian (8)	10	0.02
Japanese (45)	92	0.17
Korean (1,337)	1,396	2.52
Laotian (28)	37	0.07
Malaysian (1)	1	<0.01
Nepalese (7)	7	0.01
Pakistani (51)	55	0.10
Sri Lankan (4)	4	0.01
Taiwanese (21)	31	0.06
Thai (21)	29	0.05
Vietnamese (155)	186	0.34
Hawaii Native/Pacific Islander (8)	53	0.10
Not Hispanic (7)	48	0.09
Hispanic (1)	5	0.01
Guamanian/Chamorro (0)	3	0.01
Native Hawaiian (1)	6	0.01
Samoan (2)	3	0.01
White (44,083)	45,025	81.40
Not Hispanic (43,122)	43,861	79.30
Hispanic (961)	1,164	2.10

Adams

Place Type: Township
County: Butler
Population: 11,652†

Ancestry‡	Population	%
African, Sub-Saharan (9)	16	0.15
Nigerian (9)	9	0.08
South African (0)	7	0.06
American (375)	375	3.47
Arab (0)	34	0.32
Syrian (0)	34	0.32
Austrian (0)	38	0.35
Belgian (15)	15	0.14
British (8)	22	0.20
Croatian (27)	111	1.03
Czech (16)	168	1.56
Czechoslovakian (7)	20	0.19
Danish (0)	11	0.10
Dutch (0)	98	0.91
Eastern European (13)	26	0.24
English (312)	1,128	10.45
European (39)	55	0.51
Finnish (0)	52	0.48
French, ex. Basque (128)	570	5.28
French Canadian (76)	125	1.16
German (1,362)	4,528	41.95
Greek (18)	62	0.57
Hungarian (36)	151	1.40
Irish (259)	2,438	22.59
Italian (416)	2,186	20.25
Lithuanian (0)	72	0.67
Northern European (0)	15	0.14
Norwegian (13)	43	0.40
Pennsylvania German (0)	27	0.25
Polish (112)	559	5.18
Russian (34)	107	0.99
Scotch-Irish (166)	461	4.27
Scottish (74)	247	2.29
Serbian (25)	133	1.23
Slavic (0)	11	0.10
Slovak (40)	243	2.25
Slovene (15)	28	0.26
Swedish (11)	11	0.10
Swiss (19)	163	1.51
Ukrainian (39)	137	1.27
Welsh (35)	126	1.17
Yugoslavian (0)	7	0.06

Hispanic Origin	Population	%
Hispanic or Latino (of any race)	161	1.38
Central American, ex. Mexican	12	0.10
Costa Rican	1	0.01
Guatemalan	5	0.04
Honduran	1	0.01
Salvadoran	5	0.04
Cuban	11	0.09
Dominican Republic	2	0.02
Mexican	34	0.29
Puerto Rican	32	0.27
South American	43	0.37
Argentinean	13	0.11
Colombian	10	0.09
Ecuadorian	9	0.08
Venezuelan	9	0.08
Other South American	2	0.02
Other Hispanic or Latino	27	0.23

Race*	Population	%
African-American/Black (118)	135	1.16
Not Hispanic (117)	128	1.10
Hispanic (1)	7	0.06
American Indian/Alaska Native (4)	17	0.15
Not Hispanic (3)	14	0.12
Hispanic (1)	3	0.03
Blackfeet (0)	1	0.01
Cherokee (0)	3	0.03
Choctaw (0)	1	0.01
Mexican American Ind. (1)	1	0.01

*Notes: † The Census 2010 population figure is used to calculate the percentages in the Hispanic Origin and Race categories. Ancestry percentages are based on the 2006-2010 American Community Survey population (not shown); ‡ Numbers in parentheses indicate the number of people reporting a single ancestry; * Numbers in parentheses indicate the number of persons reporting this race alone, not in combination with any other race; Please refer to the Explanation of Data for more information.*

Asian (273)	341	2.93
Not Hispanic (272)	340	2.92
Hispanic (1)	1	0.01
Chinese, ex. Taiwanese (46)	59	0.51
Filipino (10)	20	0.17
Indian (93)	107	0.92
Indonesian (5)	5	0.04
Japanese (49)	54	0.46
Korean (47)	64	0.55
Pakistani (1)	1	0.01
Sri Lankan (10)	10	0.09
Thai (3)	3	0.03
Vietnamese (5)	10	0.09
Hawaii Native/Pacific Islander (1)	9	0.08
Not Hispanic (1)	9	0.08
Native Hawaiian (1)	1	0.01
White (11,116)	11,207	96.18
Not Hispanic (10,994)	11,079	95.08
Hispanic (122)	128	1.10

Aliquippa

Place Type: City
County: Beaver
Population: 9,438†

Ancestry‡	Population	%
African, Sub-Saharan (80)	80	0.82
African (80)	80	0.82
American (173)	173	1.77
Arab (104)	185	1.89
Arab (17)	17	0.17
Lebanese (87)	143	1.46
Syrian (0)	25	0.26
Austrian (0)	24	0.25
British (0)	8	0.08
Croatian (102)	223	2.28
Czech (0)	22	0.22
Czechoslovakian (10)	19	0.19
Dutch (36)	147	1.50
English (19)	230	2.35
Estonian (0)	46	0.47
European (9)	9	0.09
French, ex. Basque (47)	146	1.49
French Canadian (0)	7	0.07
German (193)	1,203	12.30
Greek (147)	236	2.41
Hungarian (9)	44	0.45
Irish (242)	1,163	11.89
Italian (1,014)	1,867	19.09
Pennsylvania German (11)	23	0.24
Polish (133)	449	4.59
Romanian (0)	33	0.34
Russian (10)	27	0.28
Scotch-Irish (85)	167	1.71
Scottish (33)	189	1.93
Serbian (117)	158	1.62
Slavic (20)	42	0.43
Slovak (159)	265	2.71
Slovene (9)	9	0.09
Swiss (0)	10	0.10
Ukrainian (26)	63	0.64
Welsh (0)	14	0.14
West Indian, ex. Hispanic (30)	30	0.31
Haitian (13)	13	0.13
Jamaican (17)	17	0.17
Yugoslavian (9)	18	0.18

Hispanic Origin	Population	%
Hispanic or Latino (of any race)	125	1.32
Central American, ex. Mexican	4	0.04
Guatemalan	1	0.01
Salvadoran	3	0.03
Cuban	5	0.05
Mexican	55	0.58
Puerto Rican	24	0.25
South American	5	0.05
Chilean	1	0.01
Peruvian	3	0.03
Venezuelan	1	0.01
Other Hispanic or Latino	32	0.34

Race*	Population	%
African-American/Black (3,645)	3,870	41.00
Not Hispanic (3,627)	3,838	40.67
Hispanic (18)	32	0.34
American Indian/Alaska Native (10)	70	0.74
Not Hispanic (9)	64	0.68
Hispanic (1)	6	0.06
Blackfeet (2)	4	0.04
Cherokee (0)	10	0.11
Choctaw (0)	1	0.01
Iroquois (1)	1	0.01
Osage (0)	2	0.02
Shoshone (0)	1	0.01
Sioux (0)	5	0.05
Asian (42)	62	0.66
Not Hispanic (41)	61	0.65
Hispanic (1)	1	0.01
Chinese, ex. Taiwanese (7)	7	0.07
Filipino (7)	13	0.14
Hmong (1)	1	0.01
Indian (8)	9	0.10
Japanese (1)	6	0.06
Korean (2)	6	0.06
Pakistani (4)	4	0.04
Thai (2)	2	0.02
Vietnamese (7)	7	0.07
Hawaii Native/Pacific Islander (2)	6	0.06
Not Hispanic (2)	6	0.06
Native Hawaiian (1)	5	0.05
Samoan (1)	1	0.01
White (5,435)	5,647	59.83
Not Hispanic (5,374)	5,574	59.06
Hispanic (61)	73	0.77

Allegheny

Place Type: Township
County: Westmoreland
Population: 8,164†

Ancestry‡	Population	%
American (347)	347	4.27
Arab (36)	60	0.74
Lebanese (0)	12	0.15
Syrian (36)	48	0.59
Austrian (0)	23	0.28
Belgian (8)	8	0.10
Croatian (13)	35	0.43
Czech (22)	128	1.57
Czechoslovakian (37)	37	0.46
Dutch (24)	127	1.56
Eastern European (0)	13	0.16
English (187)	871	10.71
European (33)	46	0.57
French, ex. Basque (0)	125	1.54
German (986)	2,885	35.49
Greek (21)	21	0.26
Hungarian (11)	133	1.64
Irish (197)	1,041	12.80
Italian (667)	1,972	24.26
Latvian (32)	32	0.39
Lithuanian (66)	101	1.24
Norwegian (15)	29	0.36
Pennsylvania German (70)	70	0.86
Polish (348)	975	11.99
Russian (33)	163	2.00
Scotch-Irish (54)	246	3.03
Scottish (30)	212	2.61
Serbian (0)	8	0.10
Slovak (327)	666	8.19
Slovene (14)	19	0.23
Swedish (29)	95	1.17
Swiss (0)	74	0.91
Ukrainian (0)	13	0.16
Welsh (17)	63	0.77

Hispanic Origin	Population	%
Hispanic or Latino (of any race)	30	0.37
Central American, ex. Mexican	3	0.04
Costa Rican	1	0.01
Guatemalan	1	0.01
Salvadoran	1	0.01
Mexican	17	0.21
Puerto Rican	1	0.01
South American	1	0.01
Argentinean	1	0.01
Other Hispanic or Latino	8	0.10

Race*	Population	%
African-American/Black (77)	124	1.52
Not Hispanic (77)	124	1.52
American Indian/Alaska Native (11)	33	0.40
Not Hispanic (10)	31	0.38
Hispanic (1)	2	0.02
Blackfeet (0)	2	0.02
Canadian/French Am. Ind. (1)	1	0.01
Central American Ind. (1)	1	0.01
Cherokee (2)	12	0.15
Cree (0)	1	0.01
Creek (0)	3	0.04
Iroquois (1)	1	0.01
Pueblo (1)	1	0.01
Sioux (0)	2	0.02
Asian (6)	22	0.27
Not Hispanic (6)	22	0.27
Chinese, ex. Taiwanese (2)	5	0.06
Filipino (0)	6	0.07
Indian (1)	1	0.01
Japanese (0)	4	0.05
Korean (3)	6	0.07
Hawaii Native/Pacific Islander (3)	3	0.04
Not Hispanic (3)	3	0.04
Samoan (3)	3	0.04
White (7,976)	8,059	98.71
Not Hispanic (7,952)	8,032	98.38
Hispanic (24)	27	0.33

Allentown

Place Type: City
County: Lehigh
Population: 118,032†

Ancestry‡	Population	%
African, Sub-Saharan (526)	562	0.48
African (423)	459	0.39
Cape Verdean (16)	16	0.01
Ethiopian (24)	24	0.02
Kenyan (31)	31	0.03
Nigerian (32)	32	0.03
Albanian (111)	126	0.11
Alsatian (0)	9	0.01
American (3,325)	3,325	2.86
Arab (2,632)	3,112	2.67
Arab (335)	360	0.31
Egyptian (166)	166	0.14
Lebanese (66)	113	0.10
Moroccan (13)	13	0.01
Palestinian (46)	46	0.04
Syrian (1,751)	2,119	1.82
Other Arab (255)	295	0.25
Armenian (15)	15	0.01
Assyrian/Chaldean/Syriac (9)	20	0.02
Australian (10)	120	0.10
Austrian (610)	1,440	1.24
Belgian (20)	20	0.02
Brazilian (29)	43	0.04
British (84)	217	0.19
Bulgarian (47)	47	0.04
Canadian (51)	64	0.05
Croatian (24)	24	0.02
Czech (62)	163	0.14
Czechoslovakian (180)	338	0.29
Danish (0)	57	0.05
Dutch (665)	2,721	2.34
Eastern European (110)	110	0.09
English (982)	4,215	3.62
European (213)	264	0.23

SECTION TWO

*Notes: † The Census 2010 population figure is used to calculate the percentages in the Hispanic Origin and Race categories. Ancestry percentages are based on the 2006-2010 American Community Survey population (not shown); ‡ Numbers in parentheses indicate the number of people reporting a single ancestry; * Numbers in parentheses indicate the number of persons reporting this race alone, not in combination with any other race; Please refer to the Explanation of Data for more information.*

Ancestry	Population	%
Finnish (0)	15	0.01
French, ex. Basque (288)	1,293	1.11
French Canadian (45)	185	0.16
German (8,060)	20,043	17.22
Greek (214)	573	0.49
Guyanese (79)	79	0.07
Hungarian (468)	1,829	1.57
Iranian (43)	56	0.05
Irish (2,162)	8,860	7.61
Italian (2,866)	7,606	6.53
Lithuanian (76)	232	0.20
Luxemburger (0)	11	0.01
Macedonian (0)	19	0.02
Northern European (38)	38	0.03
Norwegian (37)	141	0.12
Pennsylvania German (2,851)	4,292	3.69
Polish (1,174)	3,566	3.06
Portuguese (51)	136	0.12
Romanian (103)	147	0.13
Russian (248)	919	0.79
Scandinavian (0)	1	<0.01
Scotch-Irish (200)	913	0.78
Scottish (257)	970	0.83
Serbian (13)	24	0.02
Slavic (0)	13	0.01
Slovak (648)	1,543	1.33
Slovene (73)	73	0.06
Soviet Union (10)	10	0.01
Swedish (125)	502	0.43
Swiss (42)	242	0.21
Turkish (41)	53	0.05
Ukrainian (418)	1,122	0.96
Welsh (208)	1,050	0.90
West Indian, ex. Hispanic (1,069)	1,351	1.16
Bahamian (32)	32	0.03
Barbadian (23)	23	0.02
British West Indian (47)	63	0.05
Haitian (265)	265	0.23
Jamaican (590)	724	0.62
Trinidadian/Tobagonian (51)	67	0.06
West Indian (61)	177	0.15
Yugoslavian (25)	25	0.02

Hispanic Origin	Population	%
Hispanic or Latino (of any race)	50,461	42.75
Central American, ex. Mexican	1,911	1.62
Costa Rican	65	0.06
Guatemalan	420	0.36
Honduran	749	0.63
Nicaraguan	89	0.08
Panamanian	143	0.12
Salvadoran	440	0.37
Other Central American	5	<0.01
Cuban	458	0.39
Dominican Republic	9,340	7.91
Mexican	2,448	2.07
Puerto Rican	29,640	25.11
South American	3,048	2.58
Argentinean	49	0.04
Bolivian	20	0.02
Chilean	259	0.22
Colombian	755	0.64
Ecuadorian	1,241	1.05
Paraguayan	3	<0.01
Peruvian	565	0.48
Uruguayan	61	0.05
Venezuelan	75	0.06
Other South American	20	0.02
Other Hispanic or Latino	3,616	3.06

Race*	Population	%
African-American/Black (14,812)	17,916	15.18
Not Hispanic (11,336)	12,976	10.99
Hispanic (3,476)	4,940	4.19
American Indian/Alaska Native (893)	1,792	1.52
Not Hispanic (200)	645	0.55
Hispanic (693)	1,147	0.97
Aleut *(Alaska Native)* (2)	2	<0.01
Apache (0)	8	0.01
Blackfeet (4)	33	0.03
Canadian/French Am. Ind. (1)	1	<0.01
Central American Ind. (27)	40	0.03
Cherokee (41)	170	0.14
Cheyenne (1)	1	<0.01
Chickasaw (1)	1	<0.01
Chippewa (6)	12	0.01
Choctaw (1)	13	0.01
Comanche (3)	4	<0.01
Cree (5)	5	<0.01
Creek (0)	2	<0.01
Crow (0)	5	<0.01
Delaware (7)	21	0.02
Hopi (0)	3	<0.01
Iroquois (13)	19	0.02
Lumbee (0)	4	<0.01
Mexican American Ind. (43)	51	0.04
Navajo (3)	4	<0.01
Pueblo (0)	1	<0.01
Puget Sound Salish (0)	1	<0.01
Seminole (1)	5	<0.01
Shoshone (2)	5	<0.01
Sioux (7)	18	0.02
South American Ind. (69)	135	0.11
Spanish American Ind. (23)	27	0.02
Tohono O'Odham (3)	3	<0.01
Yaqui (1)	1	<0.01
Yup'ik *(Alaska Native)* (0)	1	<0.01
Asian (2,542)	3,274	2.77
Not Hispanic (2,452)	2,981	2.53
Hispanic (90)	293	0.25
Bangladeshi (15)	18	0.02
Burmese (108)	121	0.10
Cambodian (64)	80	0.07
Chinese, ex. Taiwanese (390)	502	0.43
Filipino (220)	324	0.27
Indian (542)	688	0.58
Indonesian (5)	7	0.01
Japanese (40)	93	0.08
Korean (168)	192	0.16
Laotian (10)	20	0.02
Malaysian (2)	7	0.01
Nepalese (5)	5	<0.01
Pakistani (68)	76	0.06
Sri Lankan (11)	12	0.01
Taiwanese (13)	15	0.01
Thai (25)	35	0.03
Vietnamese (736)	853	0.72
Hawaii Native/Pacific Islander (55)	307	0.26
Not Hispanic (11)	83	0.07
Hispanic (44)	224	0.19
Guamanian/Chamorro (8)	11	0.01
Native Hawaiian (10)	43	0.04
Samoan (10)	23	0.02
Tongan (0)	1	<0.01
White (69,061)	73,671	62.42
Not Hispanic (50,964)	53,079	44.97
Hispanic (18,097)	20,592	17.45

Allison Park

Place Type: CDP
County: Allegheny
Population: 21,552†

Ancestry‡	Population	%
African, Sub-Saharan (83)	83	0.37
African (55)	55	0.25
Ghanaian (16)	16	0.07
Other Sub-Saharan African (12)	12	0.05
Alsatian (0)	9	0.04
American (635)	635	2.85
Arab (91)	145	0.65
Lebanese (65)	119	0.53
Syrian (26)	26	0.12
Australian (28)	28	0.13
Austrian (10)	90	0.40
British (12)	21	0.09
Bulgarian (35)	35	0.16
Canadian (15)	15	0.07
Croatian (314)	668	3.00
Czech (62)	335	1.50
Czechoslovakian (36)	98	0.44
Danish (0)	42	0.19
Dutch (0)	83	0.37
Eastern European (28)	28	0.13
English (330)	1,727	7.75
European (72)	72	0.32
French, ex. Basque (38)	474	2.13
French Canadian (21)	181	0.81
German (3,151)	9,184	41.20
Greek (64)	113	0.51
Hungarian (18)	170	0.76
Irish (1,268)	4,862	21.81
Italian (1,320)	3,787	16.99
Latvian (0)	20	0.09
Lithuanian (16)	114	0.51
Macedonian (14)	54	0.24
Norwegian (17)	82	0.37
Pennsylvania German (17)	17	0.08
Polish (724)	2,437	10.93
Portuguese (15)	15	0.07
Romanian (0)	42	0.19
Russian (176)	406	1.82
Scandinavian (0)	19	0.09
Scotch-Irish (282)	722	3.24
Scottish (107)	484	2.17
Serbian (12)	23	0.10
Slavic (0)	24	0.11
Slovak (151)	573	2.57
Slovene (13)	46	0.21
Swedish (42)	351	1.57
Swiss (77)	186	0.83
Ukrainian (89)	210	0.94
Welsh (193)	551	2.47
Yugoslavian (19)	37	0.17

Hispanic Origin	Population	%
Hispanic or Latino (of any race)	187	0.87
Central American, ex. Mexican	14	0.06
Costa Rican	1	<0.01
Guatemalan	8	0.04
Nicaraguan	1	<0.01
Panamanian	3	0.01
Salvadoran	1	<0.01
Cuban	11	0.05
Dominican Republic	5	0.02
Mexican	71	0.33
Puerto Rican	32	0.15
South American	31	0.14
Argentinean	5	0.02
Bolivian	7	0.03
Chilean	7	0.03
Colombian	5	0.02
Paraguayan	1	<0.01
Peruvian	4	0.02
Venezuelan	2	0.01
Other Hispanic or Latino	23	0.11

Race*	Population	%
African-American/Black (323)	386	1.79
Not Hispanic (321)	379	1.76
Hispanic (2)	7	0.03
American Indian/Alaska Native (15)	51	0.24
Not Hispanic (14)	47	0.22
Hispanic (1)	4	0.02
Aleut *(Alaska Native)* (1)	3	0.01
Blackfeet (1)	2	0.01
Cherokee (1)	12	0.06
Chippewa (1)	1	<0.01
Cree (1)	1	<0.01
Creek (0)	1	<0.01
Iroquois (1)	1	<0.01
Mexican American Ind. (1)	1	<0.01
Seminole (0)	1	<0.01
South American Ind. (0)	1	<0.01
Asian (665)	743	3.45
Not Hispanic (661)	736	3.41
Hispanic (4)	7	0.03
Bangladeshi (2)	2	0.01
Cambodian (1)	1	<0.01

*Notes: † The Census 2010 population figure is used to calculate the percentages in the Hispanic Origin and Race categories. Ancestry percentages are based on the 2006-2010 American Community Survey population (not shown); ‡ Numbers in parentheses indicate the number of people reporting a single ancestry; * Numbers in parentheses indicate the number of persons reporting this race alone, not in combination with any other race; Please refer to the Explanation of Data for more information.*

Chinese, ex. Taiwanese (178)	196	0.91
Filipino (30)	39	0.18
Indian (232)	240	1.11
Indonesian (5)	5	0.02
Japanese (30)	43	0.20
Korean (135)	138	0.64
Laotian (3)	5	0.02
Nepalese (5)	5	0.02
Pakistani (4)	4	0.02
Sri Lankan (3)	4	0.02
Taiwanese (1)	2	0.01
Thai (2)	5	0.02
Vietnamese (15)	25	0.12
Hawaii Native/Pacific Islander (5)	11	0.05
Not Hispanic (5)	8	0.04
Hispanic (0)	3	0.01
Guamanian/Chamorro (1)	1	<0.01
Native Hawaiian (0)	3	0.01
Tongan (3)	4	0.02
White (20,335)	20,493	95.09
Not Hispanic (20,194)	20,337	94.36
Hispanic (141)	156	0.72

Altoona

Place Type: City
County: Blair
Population: 46,320†

Ancestry‡	Population	%
African, Sub-Saharan (100)	100	0.21
African (59)	59	0.13
Ethiopian (13)	13	0.03
Ghanaian (28)	28	0.06
Albanian (14)	14	0.03
American (2,185)	2,185	4.66
Arab (35)	91	0.19
Lebanese (26)	71	0.15
Syrian (9)	20	0.04
Armenian (0)	66	0.14
Austrian (12)	40	0.09
Belgian (0)	15	0.03
Brazilian (0)	39	0.08
British (30)	79	0.17
Cajun (0)	17	0.04
Canadian (13)	37	0.08
Croatian (34)	85	0.18
Czech (8)	70	0.15
Czechoslovakian (0)	71	0.15
Danish (0)	21	0.04
Dutch (52)	846	1.80
Eastern European (17)	17	0.04
English (1,189)	3,510	7.49
European (206)	206	0.44
Finnish (6)	53	0.11
French, ex. Basque (137)	1,070	2.28
French Canadian (8)	84	0.18
German (7,236)	19,843	42.32
Greek (110)	187	0.40
Hungarian (49)	323	0.69
Irish (2,268)	10,230	21.82
Italian (2,771)	7,090	15.12
Lithuanian (14)	48	0.10
Macedonian (0)	8	0.02
Northern European (8)	8	0.02
Norwegian (23)	61	0.13
Pennsylvania German (296)	509	1.09
Polish (586)	2,457	5.24
Portuguese (0)	14	0.03
Russian (68)	169	0.36
Scotch-Irish (323)	1,085	2.31
Scottish (214)	798	1.70
Serbian (0)	16	0.03
Slavic (0)	34	0.07
Slovak (112)	325	0.69
Slovene (0)	19	0.04
Swedish (97)	422	0.90
Swiss (45)	218	0.46
Ukrainian (33)	154	0.33
Welsh (67)	497	1.06
West Indian, ex. Hispanic (61)	138	0.29
Haitian (47)	124	0.26
Trinidadian/Tobagonian (14)	14	0.03
Yugoslavian (0)	26	0.06

Hispanic Origin	Population	%
Hispanic or Latino (of any race)	609	1.31
Central American, ex. Mexican	22	0.05
Costa Rican	8	0.02
Guatemalan	1	<0.01
Honduran	1	<0.01
Nicaraguan	6	0.01
Panamanian	5	0.01
Salvadoran	1	<0.01
Cuban	30	0.06
Dominican Republic	16	0.03
Mexican	195	0.42
Puerto Rican	213	0.46
South American	45	0.10
Argentinean	4	0.01
Bolivian	1	<0.01
Chilean	4	0.01
Colombian	5	0.01
Ecuadorian	2	<0.01
Peruvian	23	0.05
Venezuelan	6	0.01
Other Hispanic or Latino	88	0.19

Race*	Population	%
African-American/Black (1,540)	2,178	4.70
Not Hispanic (1,484)	2,088	4.51
Hispanic (56)	90	0.19
American Indian/Alaska Native (63)	239	0.52
Not Hispanic (49)	207	0.45
Hispanic (14)	32	0.07
Apache (0)	7	0.02
Blackfeet (1)	8	0.02
Cherokee (9)	45	0.10
Chippewa (2)	3	0.01
Comanche (0)	1	<0.01
Cree (0)	1	<0.01
Delaware (3)	12	0.03
Iroquois (4)	17	0.04
Lumbee (1)	2	<0.01
Mexican American Ind. (1)	3	0.01
Navajo (1)	1	<0.01
Potawatomi (1)	1	<0.01
Seminole (1)	2	<0.01
Shoshone (0)	1	<0.01
Sioux (0)	2	<0.01
South American Ind. (1)	2	<0.01
Yaqui (2)	2	<0.01
Asian (195)	309	0.67
Not Hispanic (189)	288	0.62
Hispanic (6)	21	0.05
Bangladeshi (1)	2	<0.01
Chinese, ex. Taiwanese (75)	83	0.18
Filipino (27)	49	0.11
Indian (34)	54	0.12
Japanese (7)	14	0.03
Korean (24)	51	0.11
Laotian (0)	3	0.01
Malaysian (3)	3	0.01
Taiwanese (3)	3	0.01
Thai (9)	14	0.03
Vietnamese (6)	24	0.05
Hawaii Native/Pacific Islander (16)	44	0.09
Not Hispanic (15)	41	0.09
Hispanic (1)	3	0.01
Guamanian/Chamorro (2)	6	0.01
Native Hawaiian (1)	6	0.01
Samoan (1)	3	0.01
White (43,435)	44,294	95.63
Not Hispanic (43,094)	43,892	94.76
Hispanic (341)	402	0.87

Amity

Place Type: Township
County: Berks
Population: 12,583†

Ancestry‡	Population	%
African, Sub-Saharan (0)	19	0.16
African (0)	19	0.16
American (1,102)	1,102	9.21
Arab (13)	29	0.24
Arab (13)	13	0.11
Other Arab (0)	16	0.13
Austrian (9)	9	0.08
Belgian (38)	38	0.32
British (34)	56	0.47
Czech (9)	58	0.48
Czechoslovakian (0)	50	0.42
Danish (35)	70	0.58
Dutch (78)	570	4.76
Eastern European (19)	19	0.16
English (303)	1,438	12.01
European (14)	14	0.12
French, ex. Basque (16)	259	2.16
French Canadian (47)	106	0.89
German (1,556)	4,217	35.23
Greek (0)	11	0.09
Hungarian (24)	414	3.46
Irish (341)	2,398	20.03
Italian (595)	2,007	16.77
Lithuanian (11)	35	0.29
Pennsylvania German (182)	306	2.56
Polish (153)	685	5.72
Russian (206)	326	2.72
Scandinavian (10)	10	0.08
Scotch-Irish (9)	129	1.08
Scottish (37)	164	1.37
Slavic (0)	19	0.16
Slovak (75)	120	1.00
Swedish (0)	27	0.23
Swiss (40)	52	0.43
Ukrainian (73)	114	0.95
Welsh (12)	211	1.76
West Indian, ex. Hispanic (36)	36	0.30
West Indian (36)	36	0.30

Hispanic Origin	Population	%
Hispanic or Latino (of any race)	304	2.42
Central American, ex. Mexican	18	0.14
Costa Rican	2	0.02
Guatemalan	5	0.04
Honduran	1	0.01
Nicaraguan	1	0.01
Panamanian	6	0.05
Salvadoran	2	0.02
Other Central American	1	0.01
Cuban	22	0.17
Dominican Republic	18	0.14
Mexican	45	0.36
Puerto Rican	134	1.06
South American	43	0.34
Argentinean	4	0.03
Colombian	11	0.09
Ecuadorian	4	0.03
Peruvian	18	0.14
Uruguayan	3	0.02
Venezuelan	3	0.02
Other Hispanic or Latino	24	0.19

Race*	Population	%
African-American/Black (465)	549	4.36
Not Hispanic (459)	536	4.26
Hispanic (6)	13	0.10
American Indian/Alaska Native (17)	64	0.51
Not Hispanic (17)	59	0.47
Hispanic (0)	5	0.04
Arapaho (0)	1	0.01
Blackfeet (0)	1	0.01
Cherokee (1)	4	0.03
Chippewa (1)	7	0.06

*Notes: † The Census 2010 population figure is used to calculate the percentages in the Hispanic Origin and Race categories. Ancestry percentages are based on the 2006-2010 American Community Survey population (not shown); ‡ Numbers in parentheses indicate the number of people reporting a single ancestry; * Numbers in parentheses indicate the number of persons reporting this race alone, not in combination with any other race; Please refer to the Explanation of Data for more information.*

Iroquois (4)	4	0.03
Navajo (0)	3	0.02
Sioux (1)	6	0.05
Asian (248)	334	2.65
Not Hispanic (248)	325	2.58
Hispanic (0)	9	0.07
Bangladeshi (6)	6	0.05
Cambodian (1)	1	0.01
Chinese, ex. Taiwanese (34)	40	0.32
Filipino (45)	68	0.54
Indian (40)	49	0.39
Japanese (5)	24	0.19
Korean (25)	42	0.33
Laotian (7)	7	0.06
Pakistani (0)	1	0.01
Thai (2)	2	0.02
Vietnamese (69)	73	0.58
Hawaii Native/Pacific Islander (0)	1	0.01
Hispanic (0)	1	0.01
White (11,562)	11,743	93.32
Not Hispanic (11,370)	11,525	91.59
Hispanic (192)	218	1.73

Antrim

Place Type: Township
County: Franklin
Population: 14,893†

Ancestry‡	Population	%
African, Sub-Saharan (15)	30	0.21
Nigerian (15)	30	0.21
American (1,873)	1,873	12.90
Arab (29)	29	0.20
Other Arab (29)	29	0.20
Austrian (0)	43	0.30
Belgian (12)	49	0.34
British (14)	78	0.54
Czech (0)	53	0.36
Czechoslovakian (42)	42	0.29
Danish (0)	12	0.08
Dutch (25)	329	2.27
English (272)	1,071	7.37
European (211)	211	1.45
Finnish (14)	14	0.10
French, ex. Basque (171)	459	3.16
French Canadian (0)	52	0.36
German (3,685)	6,150	42.35
Greek (12)	24	0.17
Hungarian (0)	52	0.36
Irish (256)	1,432	9.86
Israeli (18)	18	0.12
Italian (245)	670	4.61
Lithuanian (23)	23	0.16
Northern European (27)	27	0.19
Norwegian (25)	31	0.21
Polish (125)	262	1.80
Russian (0)	16	0.11
Scotch-Irish (82)	203	1.40
Scottish (110)	345	2.38
Slovak (46)	46	0.32
Swedish (0)	17	0.12
Swiss (91)	328	2.26
Welsh (0)	36	0.25

Hispanic Origin	Population	%
Hispanic or Latino (of any race)	260	1.75
Central American, ex. Mexican	51	0.34
Costa Rican	1	0.01
Guatemalan	19	0.13
Honduran	7	0.05
Nicaraguan	3	0.02
Panamanian	11	0.07
Salvadoran	10	0.07
Cuban	9	0.06
Dominican Republic	4	0.03
Mexican	91	0.61
Puerto Rican	49	0.33
South American	28	0.19
Argentinean	1	0.01
Chilean	1	0.01
Colombian	9	0.06
Ecuadorian	3	0.02
Peruvian	10	0.07
Venezuelan	4	0.03
Other Hispanic or Latino	28	0.19

Race*	Population	%
African-American/Black (221)	319	2.14
Not Hispanic (200)	283	1.90
Hispanic (21)	36	0.24
American Indian/Alaska Native (24)	84	0.56
Not Hispanic (20)	73	0.49
Hispanic (4)	11	0.07
Blackfeet (0)	3	0.02
Cherokee (5)	17	0.11
Cree (0)	2	0.01
Iroquois (1)	1	0.01
Lumbee (0)	3	0.02
Navajo (6)	6	0.04
Seminole (2)	2	0.01
South American Ind. (0)	5	0.03
Asian (118)	162	1.09
Not Hispanic (118)	158	1.06
Hispanic (0)	4	0.03
Burmese (1)	1	0.01
Cambodian (4)	4	0.03
Chinese, ex. Taiwanese (14)	19	0.13
Filipino (17)	26	0.17
Indian (19)	24	0.16
Indonesian (2)	2	0.01
Japanese (4)	10	0.07
Korean (15)	19	0.13
Pakistani (7)	7	0.05
Taiwanese (2)	2	0.01
Thai (4)	9	0.06
Vietnamese (14)	19	0.13
Hawaii Native/Pacific Islander (2)	9	0.06
Not Hispanic (1)	8	0.05
Hispanic (1)	1	0.01
Guamanian/Chamorro (1)	1	0.01
Tongan (1)	2	0.01
White (14,245)	14,423	96.84
Not Hispanic (14,122)	14,268	95.80
Hispanic (123)	155	1.04

Ardmore

Place Type: CDP
County: Montgomery
Population: 12,455†

Ancestry‡	Population	%
African, Sub-Saharan (90)	90	0.72
African (63)	63	0.50
South African (27)	27	0.22
American (263)	263	2.10
Austrian (0)	62	0.50
Brazilian (26)	39	0.31
British (77)	193	1.54
Canadian (64)	103	0.82
Celtic (10)	10	0.08
Czech (0)	25	0.20
Dutch (32)	81	0.65
Eastern European (104)	104	0.83
English (252)	1,314	10.50
Estonian (13)	13	0.10
European (160)	160	1.28
Finnish (22)	38	0.30
French, ex. Basque (79)	259	2.07
French Canadian (30)	45	0.36
German (501)	2,554	20.41
Greek (66)	89	0.71
Hungarian (27)	180	1.44
Icelander (0)	32	0.26
Iranian (25)	59	0.47
Irish (1,171)	2,595	20.74
Israeli (0)	35	0.28
Italian (1,051)	1,948	15.57
Latvian (11)	30	0.24
Lithuanian (0)	61	0.49
Northern European (18)	18	0.14
Norwegian (0)	83	0.66
Pennsylvania German (0)	10	0.08
Polish (117)	415	3.32
Romanian (112)	143	1.14
Russian (253)	468	3.74
Scotch-Irish (70)	257	2.05
Scottish (73)	313	2.50
Slovak (0)	22	0.18
Swedish (34)	137	1.09
Swiss (24)	55	0.44
Turkish (0)	34	0.27
Ukrainian (44)	80	0.64
Welsh (0)	177	1.41
West Indian, ex. Hispanic (211)	261	2.09
Barbadian (21)	21	0.17
Haitian (125)	125	1.00
Jamaican (65)	76	0.61
Trinidadian/Tobagonian (0)	39	0.31
Yugoslavian (27)	67	0.54

Hispanic Origin	Population	%
Hispanic or Latino (of any race)	502	4.03
Central American, ex. Mexican	99	0.79
Costa Rican	6	0.05
Guatemalan	27	0.22
Honduran	23	0.18
Nicaraguan	14	0.11
Panamanian	12	0.10
Salvadoran	17	0.14
Cuban	20	0.16
Dominican Republic	15	0.12
Mexican	136	1.09
Puerto Rican	77	0.62
South American	117	0.94
Argentinean	24	0.19
Bolivian	2	0.02
Chilean	9	0.07
Colombian	32	0.26
Ecuadorian	12	0.10
Paraguayan	3	0.02
Peruvian	27	0.22
Venezuelan	5	0.04
Other South American	3	0.02
Other Hispanic or Latino	38	0.31

Race*	Population	%
African-American/Black (1,607)	1,751	14.06
Not Hispanic (1,579)	1,711	13.74
Hispanic (28)	40	0.32
American Indian/Alaska Native (16)	89	0.71
Not Hispanic (11)	69	0.55
Hispanic (5)	20	0.16
Apache (0)	1	0.01
Blackfeet (0)	1	0.01
Cherokee (2)	14	0.11
Cheyenne (0)	1	0.01
Choctaw (0)	3	0.02
Creek (0)	2	0.02
Mexican American Ind. (1)	4	0.03
Seminole (0)	5	0.04
Sioux (0)	1	0.01
South American Ind. (1)	4	0.03
Asian (510)	629	5.05
Not Hispanic (509)	622	4.99
Hispanic (1)	7	0.06
Cambodian (7)	7	0.06
Chinese, ex. Taiwanese (179)	218	1.75
Filipino (34)	44	0.35
Indian (102)	120	0.96
Japanese (31)	57	0.46
Korean (91)	100	0.80
Malaysian (6)	6	0.05
Nepalese (2)	2	0.02
Pakistani (12)	12	0.10
Sri Lankan (4)	5	0.04
Taiwanese (6)	8	0.06
Thai (9)	14	0.11
Vietnamese (16)	21	0.17

*Notes: † The Census 2010 population figure is used to calculate the percentages in the Hispanic Origin and Race categories. Ancestry percentages are based on the 2006-2010 American Community Survey population (not shown); ‡ Numbers in parentheses indicate the number of people reporting a single ancestry; * Numbers in parentheses indicate the number of persons reporting this race alone, not in combination with any other race; Please refer to the Explanation of Data for more information.*

Hawaii Native/Pacific Islander (9)	24	0.19
Not Hispanic (9)	22	0.18
Hispanic (0)	2	0.02
Fijian (1)	1	0.01
Native Hawaiian (2)	6	0.05
Samoan (0)	1	0.01
Tongan (6)	13	0.10
White (9,877)	10,119	81.24
Not Hispanic (9,569)	9,783	78.55
Hispanic (308)	336	2.70

Aston

Place Type: Township
County: Delaware
Population: 16,592†

Ancestry‡	Population	%
African, Sub-Saharan (1)	1	0.01
African (1)	1	0.01
Albanian (0)	22	0.13
American (636)	636	3.86
Arab (10)	20	0.12
Lebanese (10)	20	0.12
Armenian (29)	76	0.46
Belgian (0)	57	0.35
British (60)	113	0.69
Croatian (0)	9	0.05
Czech (10)	61	0.37
Danish (0)	26	0.16
Dutch (36)	306	1.86
English (518)	1,931	11.73
European (36)	36	0.22
Finnish (35)	74	0.45
French, ex. Basque (0)	336	2.04
French Canadian (21)	44	0.27
German (656)	3,687	22.39
Greek (12)	41	0.25
Hungarian (0)	170	1.03
Irish (1,970)	5,606	34.05
Italian (1,603)	4,523	27.47
Lithuanian (12)	120	0.73
Norwegian (50)	83	0.50
Pennsylvania German (39)	104	0.63
Polish (444)	1,693	10.28
Russian (114)	224	1.36
Scotch-Irish (224)	473	2.87
Scottish (40)	324	1.97
Slavic (0)	17	0.10
Slovak (36)	166	1.01
Swedish (66)	218	1.32
Swiss (8)	8	0.05
Ukrainian (61)	294	1.79
Welsh (47)	253	1.54
West Indian, ex. Hispanic (8)	19	0.12
Jamaican (8)	8	0.05
West Indian (0)	11	0.07

Hispanic Origin	Population	%
Hispanic or Latino (of any race)	266	1.60
Central American, ex. Mexican	8	0.05
Guatemalan	2	0.01
Honduran	1	0.01
Nicaraguan	4	0.02
Salvadoran	1	0.01
Cuban	17	0.10
Dominican Republic	3	0.02
Mexican	59	0.36
Puerto Rican	111	0.67
South American	35	0.21
Argentinean	6	0.04
Colombian	18	0.11
Ecuadorian	4	0.02
Peruvian	6	0.04
Venezuelan	1	0.01
Other Hispanic or Latino	33	0.20

Race*	Population	%
African-American/Black (470)	529	3.19
Not Hispanic (463)	515	3.10
Hispanic (7)	14	0.08
American Indian/Alaska Native (18)	64	0.39
Not Hispanic (16)	55	0.33
Hispanic (2)	9	0.05
Blackfeet (2)	2	0.01
Cherokee (2)	20	0.12
Delaware (0)	3	0.02
Iroquois (3)	7	0.04
Lumbee (0)	5	0.03
Navajo (1)	1	0.01
South American Ind. (0)	1	0.01
Asian (263)	311	1.87
Not Hispanic (258)	301	1.81
Hispanic (5)	10	0.06
Bangladeshi (1)	1	0.01
Cambodian (1)	4	0.02
Chinese, ex. Taiwanese (64)	78	0.47
Filipino (35)	47	0.28
Indian (80)	87	0.52
Indonesian (1)	1	0.01
Japanese (6)	10	0.06
Korean (38)	46	0.28
Laotian (1)	1	0.01
Sri Lankan (3)	3	0.02
Taiwanese (1)	1	0.01
Vietnamese (13)	18	0.11
Hawaii Native/Pacific Islander (1)	6	0.04
Not Hispanic (1)	6	0.04
Fijian (1)	4	0.02
Native Hawaiian (0)	2	0.01
Samoan (0)	3	0.02
White (15,652)	15,790	95.17
Not Hispanic (15,461)	15,578	93.89
Hispanic (191)	212	1.28

Audubon

Place Type: CDP
County: Montgomery
Population: 8,433†

Ancestry‡	Population	%
African, Sub-Saharan (8)	8	0.10
African (8)	8	0.10
American (607)	607	7.44
Arab (0)	11	0.13
Lebanese (0)	11	0.13
Australian (0)	10	0.12
Austrian (11)	68	0.83
British (32)	38	0.47
Canadian (11)	11	0.13
Croatian (0)	79	0.97
Czech (39)	39	0.48
Czechoslovakian (10)	40	0.49
Danish (0)	29	0.36
Dutch (81)	100	1.23
English (181)	666	8.16
European (46)	46	0.56
French, ex. Basque (29)	83	1.02
French Canadian (34)	143	1.75
German (419)	1,708	20.94
Greek (10)	22	0.27
Guyanese (12)	12	0.15
Hungarian (64)	200	2.45
Iranian (37)	37	0.45
Irish (606)	1,850	22.68
Italian (583)	1,589	19.48
Lithuanian (11)	21	0.26
Norwegian (34)	34	0.42
Pennsylvania German (65)	131	1.61
Polish (84)	499	6.12
Romanian (66)	66	0.81
Russian (107)	160	1.96
Scotch-Irish (91)	331	4.06
Scottish (6)	51	0.63
Slovak (84)	149	1.83
Swedish (40)	163	2.00
Ukrainian (29)	42	0.51
Welsh (0)	30	0.37
West Indian, ex. Hispanic (9)	9	0.11
Jamaican (9)	9	0.11

Hispanic Origin	Population	%
Hispanic or Latino (of any race)	195	2.31
Central American, ex. Mexican	5	0.06
Guatemalan	3	0.04
Honduran	2	0.02
Cuban	7	0.08
Dominican Republic	4	0.05
Mexican	73	0.87
Puerto Rican	69	0.82
South American	17	0.20
Argentinean	2	0.02
Chilean	1	0.01
Colombian	3	0.04
Ecuadorian	1	0.01
Peruvian	6	0.07
Uruguayan	2	0.02
Venezuelan	2	0.02
Other Hispanic or Latino	20	0.24

Race*	Population	%
African-American/Black (436)	472	5.60
Not Hispanic (423)	458	5.43
Hispanic (13)	14	0.17
American Indian/Alaska Native (3)	15	0.18
Not Hispanic (2)	14	0.17
Hispanic (1)	1	0.01
Cherokee (0)	3	0.04
Iroquois (0)	1	0.01
Lumbee (0)	1	0.01
Asian (1,127)	1,183	14.03
Not Hispanic (1,120)	1,174	13.92
Hispanic (7)	9	0.11
Burmese (1)	1	0.01
Cambodian (4)	8	0.09
Chinese, ex. Taiwanese (308)	328	3.89
Filipino (39)	51	0.60
Indian (645)	663	7.86
Indonesian (1)	2	0.02
Japanese (12)	16	0.19
Korean (16)	21	0.25
Laotian (4)	4	0.05
Nepalese (1)	1	0.01
Pakistani (31)	32	0.38
Sri Lankan (4)	4	0.05
Taiwanese (9)	9	0.11
Thai (3)	3	0.04
Vietnamese (41)	47	0.56
Hawaii Native/Pacific Islander (2)	3	0.04
Not Hispanic (2)	3	0.04
Samoan (1)	1	0.01
White (6,705)	6,794	80.56
Not Hispanic (6,590)	6,671	79.11
Hispanic (115)	123	1.46

Baldwin

Place Type: Borough
County: Allegheny
Population: 19,767†

Ancestry‡	Population	%
African, Sub-Saharan (87)	87	0.44
African (87)	87	0.44
American (432)	432	2.20
Arab (12)	105	0.54
Lebanese (12)	95	0.48
Syrian (0)	10	0.05
Armenian (17)	47	0.24
Austrian (48)	145	0.74
Belgian (0)	25	0.13
British (8)	43	0.22
Bulgarian (25)	25	0.13
Carpatho Rusyn (12)	24	0.12
Croatian (56)	424	2.16
Czech (51)	127	0.65
Czechoslovakian (20)	56	0.29
Danish (0)	24	0.12
Dutch (0)	115	0.59

*Notes: † The Census 2010 population figure is used to calculate the percentages in the Hispanic Origin and Race categories. Ancestry percentages are based on the 2006-2010 American Community Survey population (not shown); ‡ Numbers in parentheses indicate the number of people reporting a single ancestry; * Numbers in parentheses indicate the number of persons reporting this race alone, not in combination with any other race; Please refer to the Explanation of Data for more information.*

Eastern European (10)	10	0.05
English (174)	1,399	7.13
European (20)	20	0.10
Finnish (0)	9	0.05
French, ex. Basque (27)	482	2.46
French Canadian (11)	11	0.06
German (1,983)	7,865	40.08
Greek (38)	113	0.58
Hungarian (24)	434	2.21
Irish (822)	5,019	25.58
Italian (999)	3,834	19.54
Lithuanian (152)	284	1.45
Northern European (21)	21	0.11
Norwegian (0)	125	0.64
Pennsylvania German (10)	21	0.11
Polish (1,013)	2,920	14.88
Russian (52)	231	1.18
Scotch-Irish (85)	499	2.54
Scottish (108)	338	1.72
Serbian (38)	271	1.38
Slavic (17)	58	0.30
Slovak (435)	1,136	5.79
Slovene (11)	85	0.43
Swedish (0)	118	0.60
Swiss (0)	67	0.34
Ukrainian (68)	197	1.00
Welsh (3)	331	1.69

Hispanic Origin	Population	%
Hispanic or Latino (of any race)	214	1.08
Central American, ex. Mexican	15	0.08
Costa Rican	2	0.01
Guatemalan	6	0.03
Honduran	3	0.02
Panamanian	3	0.02
Salvadoran	1	0.01
Cuban	5	0.03
Dominican Republic	4	0.02
Mexican	63	0.32
Puerto Rican	72	0.36
South American	15	0.08
Argentinean	5	0.03
Chilean	4	0.02
Colombian	4	0.02
Ecuadorian	1	0.01
Paraguayan	1	0.01
Other Hispanic or Latino	40	0.20

Race*	Population	%
African-American/Black (1,056)	1,247	6.31
Not Hispanic (1,044)	1,222	6.18
Hispanic (12)	25	0.13
American Indian/Alaska Native (21)	96	0.49
Not Hispanic (17)	86	0.44
Hispanic (4)	10	0.05
Arapaho (0)	1	0.01
Blackfeet (0)	9	0.05
Cherokee (3)	29	0.15
Creek (0)	1	0.01
Delaware (0)	1	0.01
Iroquois (4)	6	0.03
Mexican American Ind. (0)	1	0.01
Sioux (1)	5	0.03
South American Ind. (0)	1	0.01
Asian (246)	283	1.43
Not Hispanic (244)	276	1.40
Hispanic (2)	7	0.04
Bangladeshi (3)	3	0.02
Bhutanese (5)	5	0.03
Burmese (17)	17	0.09
Cambodian (1)	1	0.01
Chinese, ex. Taiwanese (56)	67	0.34
Filipino (15)	26	0.13
Indian (56)	63	0.32
Indonesian (0)	3	0.02
Japanese (4)	5	0.03
Korean (8)	9	0.05
Nepalese (3)	6	0.03
Pakistani (13)	14	0.07
Thai (10)	10	0.05
Vietnamese (38)	50	0.25
Hawaii Native/Pacific Islander (4)	11	0.06
Not Hispanic (4)	11	0.06
Guamanian/Chamorro (0)	1	0.01
Native Hawaiian (3)	4	0.02
White (18,110)	18,366	92.91
Not Hispanic (17,986)	18,218	92.16
Hispanic (124)	148	0.75

Beaver Falls

Place Type: City
County: Beaver
Population: 8,987†

Ancestry‡	Population	%
African, Sub-Saharan (3)	9	0.10
Liberian (3)	9	0.10
American (172)	172	1.89
Arab (10)	64	0.70
Arab (0)	13	0.14
Lebanese (10)	41	0.45
Syrian (0)	10	0.11
British (0)	20	0.22
Canadian (0)	53	0.58
Croatian (10)	67	0.74
Czech (0)	71	0.78
Czechoslovakian (9)	36	0.40
Danish (0)	8	0.09
Dutch (0)	106	1.17
English (140)	845	9.29
European (39)	39	0.43
French, ex. Basque (29)	138	1.52
French Canadian (17)	17	0.19
German (668)	2,587	28.45
Greek (103)	132	1.45
Hungarian (37)	170	1.87
Irish (273)	1,587	17.45
Italian (368)	1,044	11.48
Lithuanian (9)	19	0.21
Norwegian (0)	34	0.37
Pennsylvania German (8)	8	0.09
Polish (167)	533	5.86
Portuguese (0)	29	0.32
Romanian (0)	130	1.43
Russian (0)	26	0.29
Scotch-Irish (101)	541	5.95
Scottish (10)	225	2.47
Serbian (0)	102	1.12
Slavic (0)	8	0.09
Slovak (9)	91	1.00
Swedish (0)	25	0.27
Swiss (0)	8	0.09
Ukrainian (9)	49	0.54
Welsh (0)	54	0.59

Hispanic Origin	Population	%
Hispanic or Latino (of any race)	105	1.17
Central American, ex. Mexican	6	0.07
Panamanian	6	0.07
Cuban	10	0.11
Dominican Republic	11	0.12
Mexican	29	0.32
Puerto Rican	23	0.26
South American	11	0.12
Argentinean	4	0.04
Colombian	4	0.04
Ecuadorian	1	0.01
Peruvian	1	0.01
Venezuelan	1	0.01
Other Hispanic or Latino	15	0.17

Race*	Population	%
African-American/Black (1,736)	2,075	23.09
Not Hispanic (1,725)	2,050	22.81
Hispanic (11)	25	0.28
American Indian/Alaska Native (15)	93	1.03
Not Hispanic (11)	82	0.91
Hispanic (4)	11	0.12
Cherokee (2)	16	0.18
Choctaw (0)	1	0.01
Cree (0)	1	0.01
Creek (0)	1	0.01
Delaware (1)	1	0.01
Iroquois (1)	5	0.06
South American Ind. (1)	1	0.01
Asian (38)	61	0.68
Not Hispanic (37)	59	0.66
Hispanic (1)	2	0.02
Chinese, ex. Taiwanese (12)	13	0.14
Filipino (6)	14	0.16
Indian (7)	8	0.09
Japanese (0)	1	0.01
Korean (9)	17	0.19
Pakistani (1)	1	0.01
Sri Lankan (0)	1	0.01
Thai (1)	1	0.01
Vietnamese (2)	2	0.02
Hawaii Native/Pacific Islander (2)	6	0.07
Not Hispanic (1)	4	0.04
Hispanic (1)	2	0.02
Guamanian/Chamorro (0)	1	0.01
Native Hawaiian (1)	4	0.04
White (6,768)	7,129	79.33
Not Hispanic (6,712)	7,058	78.54
Hispanic (56)	71	0.79

Bellevue

Place Type: Borough
County: Allegheny
Population: 8,370†

Ancestry‡	Population	%
African, Sub-Saharan (29)	29	0.35
African (29)	29	0.35
American (311)	311	3.71
Armenian (12)	12	0.14
Austrian (29)	118	1.41
Belgian (0)	10	0.12
British (0)	19	0.23
Croatian (31)	153	1.83
Czech (11)	192	2.29
Czechoslovakian (7)	47	0.56
Dutch (41)	128	1.53
English (175)	632	7.55
European (14)	14	0.17
Finnish (0)	10	0.12
French, ex. Basque (0)	76	0.91
French Canadian (0)	9	0.11
German (605)	3,057	36.50
Greek (40)	67	0.80
Hungarian (33)	132	1.58
Irish (411)	1,988	23.74
Italian (368)	1,257	15.01
Lithuanian (0)	19	0.23
Norwegian (14)	14	0.17
Pennsylvania German (12)	40	0.48
Polish (211)	906	10.82
Russian (83)	169	2.02
Scotch-Irish (19)	222	2.65
Scottish (30)	219	2.61
Serbian (0)	22	0.26
Slavic (8)	19	0.23
Slovak (123)	258	3.08
Slovene (34)	42	0.50
Swedish (12)	70	0.84
Swiss (0)	49	0.59
Ukrainian (60)	195	2.33
Welsh (0)	129	1.54
Yugoslavian (7)	18	0.21

Hispanic Origin	Population	%
Hispanic or Latino (of any race)	162	1.94
Central American, ex. Mexican	24	0.29
Costa Rican	5	0.06
Guatemalan	3	0.04
Honduran	5	0.06
Nicaraguan	1	0.01
Panamanian	8	0.10

*Notes: † The Census 2010 population figure is used to calculate the percentages in the Hispanic Origin and Race categories. Ancestry percentages are based on the 2006-2010 American Community Survey population (not shown); ‡ Numbers in parentheses indicate the number of people reporting a single ancestry; * Numbers in parentheses indicate the number of persons reporting this race alone, not in combination with any other race; Please refer to the Explanation of Data for more information.*

Salvadoran	2	0.02
Cuban	8	0.10
Mexican	53	0.63
Puerto Rican	40	0.48
South American	18	0.22
Bolivian	3	0.04
Chilean	3	0.04
Colombian	1	0.01
Ecuadorian	4	0.05
Peruvian	6	0.07
Venezuelan	1	0.01
Other Hispanic or Latino	19	0.23

Race*	Population	%
African-American/Black (748)	886	10.59
Not Hispanic (737)	872	10.42
Hispanic (11)	14	0.17
American Indian/Alaska Native (5)	54	0.65
Not Hispanic (4)	46	0.55
Hispanic (1)	8	0.10
Cherokee (0)	13	0.16
Chippewa (0)	2	0.02
Cree (0)	1	0.01
Crow (0)	1	0.01
Iroquois (1)	1	0.01
Mexican American Ind. (0)	1	0.01
Osage (0)	1	0.01
Sioux (0)	1	0.01
Spanish American Ind. (1)	1	0.01
Ute (1)	1	0.01
Yuman (0)	1	0.01
Asian (90)	136	1.62
Not Hispanic (90)	134	1.60
Hispanic (0)	2	0.02
Bhutanese (0)	9	0.11
Burmese (3)	4	0.05
Cambodian (0)	1	0.01
Chinese, ex. Taiwanese (16)	33	0.39
Filipino (9)	17	0.20
Indian (15)	23	0.27
Japanese (3)	11	0.13
Korean (6)	12	0.14
Nepalese (2)	11	0.13
Pakistani (2)	2	0.02
Taiwanese (1)	1	0.01
Thai (4)	5	0.06
Vietnamese (9)	19	0.23
Hawaii Native/Pacific Islander (3)	6	0.07
Not Hispanic (3)	6	0.07
Native Hawaiian (3)	6	0.07
White (7,266)	7,462	89.15
Not Hispanic (7,162)	7,334	87.62
Hispanic (104)	128	1.53

Bensalem

Place Type: Township
County: Bucks
Population: 60,427†

Ancestry‡	Population	%
African, Sub-Saharan (283)	356	0.59
African (262)	319	0.53
Liberian (11)	27	0.04
Nigerian (10)	10	0.02
Albanian (16)	51	0.08
American (1,276)	1,276	2.12
Arab (51)	103	0.17
Egyptian (13)	13	0.02
Lebanese (8)	26	0.04
Syrian (0)	16	0.03
Other Arab (30)	48	0.08
Armenian (40)	40	0.07
Austrian (27)	236	0.39
Belgian (0)	14	0.02
Brazilian (79)	100	0.17
British (34)	57	0.09
Canadian (20)	26	0.04
Celtic (26)	26	0.04
Croatian (0)	24	0.04
Czech (16)	112	0.19
Czechoslovakian (8)	8	0.01
Danish (8)	58	0.10
Dutch (44)	301	0.50
Eastern European (94)	94	0.16
English (1,113)	4,695	7.79
European (282)	306	0.51
Finnish (15)	22	0.04
French, ex. Basque (355)	1,378	2.29
French Canadian (7)	96	0.16
German (3,900)	13,336	22.13
Greek (147)	270	0.45
Guyanese (0)	81	0.13
Hungarian (161)	453	0.75
Irish (5,404)	15,954	26.47
Israeli (23)	23	0.04
Italian (3,471)	8,721	14.47
Latvian (0)	16	0.03
Lithuanian (125)	370	0.61
Macedonian (17)	52	0.09
Northern European (24)	24	0.04
Norwegian (21)	183	0.30
Pennsylvania German (71)	219	0.36
Polish (1,888)	5,563	9.23
Portuguese (38)	67	0.11
Romanian (30)	106	0.18
Russian (758)	1,323	2.19
Scotch-Irish (383)	962	1.60
Scottish (165)	579	0.96
Slovak (132)	265	0.44
Slovene (0)	11	0.02
Soviet Union (10)	10	0.02
Swedish (36)	276	0.46
Swiss (16)	57	0.09
Turkish (107)	107	0.18
Ukrainian (950)	1,352	2.24
Welsh (49)	420	0.70
West Indian, ex. Hispanic (167)	179	0.30
Bahamian (11)	11	0.02
Barbadian (99)	99	0.16
Jamaican (26)	38	0.06
Trinidadian/Tobagonian (14)	14	0.02
U.S. Virgin Islander (17)	17	0.03
Yugoslavian (38)	71	0.12

Hispanic Origin	Population	%
Hispanic or Latino (of any race)	5,091	8.43
Central American, ex. Mexican	539	0.89
Costa Rican	74	0.12
Guatemalan	272	0.45
Honduran	77	0.13
Nicaraguan	22	0.04
Panamanian	15	0.02
Salvadoran	79	0.13
Cuban	92	0.15
Dominican Republic	75	0.12
Mexican	1,879	3.11
Puerto Rican	1,452	2.40
South American	689	1.14
Argentinean	26	0.04
Bolivian	2	<0.01
Chilean	11	0.02
Colombian	121	0.20
Ecuadorian	416	0.69
Peruvian	80	0.13
Uruguayan	7	0.01
Venezuelan	20	0.03
Other South American	6	0.01
Other Hispanic or Latino	365	0.60

Race*	Population	%
African-American/Black (4,419)	5,040	8.34
Not Hispanic (4,240)	4,750	7.86
Hispanic (179)	290	0.48
American Indian/Alaska Native (296)	638	1.06
Not Hispanic (108)	409	0.68
Hispanic (188)	229	0.38
Alaska Athabascan *(Ala. Nat.)* (0)	1	<0.01
Apache (4)	13	0.02
Blackfeet (2)	24	0.04
Canadian/French Am. Ind. (0)	2	<0.01
Central American Ind. (2)	2	<0.01
Cherokee (10)	74	0.12
Chippewa (1)	2	<0.01
Choctaw (0)	1	<0.01
Comanche (0)	1	<0.01
Creek (3)	5	0.01
Delaware (4)	13	0.02
Iroquois (5)	21	0.03
Lumbee (0)	5	0.01
Menominee (1)	1	<0.01
Mexican American Ind. (112)	113	0.19
Navajo (1)	6	0.01
Pima (2)	3	<0.01
Potawatomi (0)	1	<0.01
Pueblo (2)	2	<0.01
Seminole (0)	4	0.01
Sioux (3)	11	0.02
South American Ind. (6)	14	0.02
Spanish American Ind. (4)	5	0.01
Asian (6,163)	6,706	11.10
Not Hispanic (6,150)	6,653	11.01
Hispanic (13)	53	0.09
Bangladeshi (57)	67	0.11
Cambodian (23)	32	0.05
Chinese, ex. Taiwanese (467)	537	0.89
Filipino (338)	423	0.70
Indian (4,272)	4,480	7.41
Indonesian (8)	8	0.01
Japanese (40)	81	0.13
Korean (268)	312	0.52
Laotian (7)	12	0.02
Malaysian (3)	5	0.01
Nepalese (13)	16	0.03
Pakistani (260)	284	0.47
Sri Lankan (6)	6	0.01
Taiwanese (12)	19	0.03
Thai (15)	23	0.04
Vietnamese (219)	251	0.42
Hawaii Native/Pacific Islander (23)	81	0.13
Not Hispanic (8)	53	0.09
Hispanic (15)	28	0.05
Guamanian/Chamorro (17)	19	0.03
Native Hawaiian (4)	16	0.03
White (45,712)	46,896	77.61
Not Hispanic (43,561)	44,411	73.50
Hispanic (2,151)	2,485	4.11

Berwick

Place Type: Borough
County: Columbia
Population: 10,477†

Ancestry‡	Population	%
American (612)	612	5.78
Armenian (0)	38	0.36
Austrian (0)	46	0.43
British (15)	35	0.33
Carpatho Rusyn (11)	11	0.10
Czech (35)	35	0.33
Czechoslovakian (0)	13	0.12
Dutch (311)	821	7.76
English (401)	864	8.17
European (59)	59	0.56
French, ex. Basque (8)	96	0.91
French Canadian (0)	19	0.18
German (1,500)	3,166	29.92
Greek (57)	88	0.83
Hungarian (48)	148	1.40
Irish (413)	1,324	12.51
Italian (627)	1,323	12.50
Lithuanian (0)	51	0.48
Norwegian (13)	32	0.30
Pennsylvania German (372)	721	6.81
Polish (145)	545	5.15
Russian (65)	80	0.76
Scotch-Irish (92)	127	1.20
Scottish (31)	107	1.01
Slovak (16)	58	0.55

SECTION TWO

*Notes: † The Census 2010 population figure is used to calculate the percentages in the Hispanic Origin and Race categories. Ancestry percentages are based on the 2006-2010 American Community Survey population (not shown); ‡ Numbers in parentheses indicate the number of people reporting a single ancestry; * Numbers in parentheses indicate the number of persons reporting this race alone, not in combination with any other race; Please refer to the Explanation of Data for more information.*

Swedish (25)	25	0.24
Swiss (0)	16	0.15
Ukrainian (231)	310	2.93
Welsh (47)	174	1.64

Hispanic Origin	Population	%
Hispanic or Latino (of any race)	386	3.68
Central American, ex. Mexican	121	1.15
Costa Rican	2	0.02
Guatemalan	2	0.02
Honduran	4	0.04
Nicaraguan	6	0.06
Salvadoran	102	0.97
Other Central American	5	0.05
Cuban	2	0.02
Dominican Republic	18	0.17
Mexican	58	0.55
Puerto Rican	106	1.01
South American	28	0.27
Argentinean	2	0.02
Colombian	4	0.04
Ecuadorian	6	0.06
Peruvian	15	0.14
Uruguayan	1	0.01
Other Hispanic or Latino	53	0.51

Race*	Population	%
African-American/Black (156)	224	2.14
Not Hispanic (144)	206	1.97
Hispanic (12)	18	0.17
American Indian/Alaska Native (21)	97	0.93
Not Hispanic (8)	75	0.72
Hispanic (13)	22	0.21
Apache (0)	8	0.08
Blackfeet (0)	10	0.10
Cherokee (2)	13	0.12
Cheyenne (0)	1	0.01
Choctaw (0)	1	0.01
Comanche (0)	1	0.01
Crow (1)	1	0.01
Delaware (0)	2	0.02
Iroquois (3)	8	0.08
Lumbee (2)	2	0.02
Sioux (0)	2	0.02
South American Ind. (0)	1	0.01
Asian (86)	110	1.05
Not Hispanic (81)	101	0.96
Hispanic (5)	9	0.09
Bangladeshi (0)	5	0.05
Chinese, ex. Taiwanese (18)	21	0.20
Filipino (9)	13	0.12
Indian (33)	38	0.36
Indonesian (9)	9	0.09
Japanese (1)	10	0.10
Korean (4)	6	0.06
Laotian (0)	1	0.01
Thai (1)	1	0.01
Vietnamese (6)	6	0.06
Hawaii Native/Pacific Islander (0)	1	0.01
Hispanic (0)	1	0.01
White (9,887)	10,055	95.97
Not Hispanic (9,702)	9,847	93.99
Hispanic (185)	208	1.99

Bethel Park

Place Type: Municipality
County: Allegheny
Population: 32,313†

Ancestry‡	Population	%
African, Sub-Saharan (0)	11	0.03
Nigerian (0)	11	0.03
American (745)	745	2.31
Arab (117)	253	0.78
Iraqi (11)	11	0.03
Lebanese (47)	74	0.23
Palestinian (45)	45	0.14
Syrian (0)	89	0.28
Other Arab (14)	34	0.11
Austrian (22)	252	0.78
Belgian (0)	8	0.02
Brazilian (0)	25	0.08
British (56)	102	0.32
Bulgarian (10)	20	0.06
Canadian (13)	20	0.06
Carpatho Rusyn (15)	26	0.08
Croatian (49)	407	1.26
Czech (39)	206	0.64
Czechoslovakian (13)	75	0.23
Danish (0)	69	0.21
Dutch (107)	466	1.45
Eastern European (62)	62	0.19
English (704)	3,569	11.07
European (217)	237	0.73
Finnish (23)	23	0.07
French, ex. Basque (55)	748	2.32
French Canadian (27)	111	0.34
German (2,956)	12,147	37.67
Greek (177)	280	0.87
Hungarian (132)	784	2.43
Irish (1,748)	7,953	24.66
Israeli (27)	27	0.08
Italian (2,295)	6,938	21.51
Lithuanian (98)	247	0.77
Macedonian (20)	20	0.06
Norwegian (21)	131	0.41
Pennsylvania German (25)	39	0.12
Polish (813)	3,552	11.01
Romanian (0)	17	0.05
Russian (135)	484	1.50
Scandinavian (0)	53	0.16
Scotch-Irish (326)	838	2.60
Scottish (121)	485	1.50
Serbian (45)	150	0.47
Slavic (69)	105	0.33
Slovak (441)	1,579	4.90
Slovene (99)	186	0.58
Swedish (37)	266	0.82
Swiss (13)	124	0.38
Turkish (22)	62	0.19
Ukrainian (99)	562	1.74
Welsh (73)	432	1.34
Yugoslavian (16)	16	0.05

Hispanic Origin	Population	%
Hispanic or Latino (of any race)	313	0.97
Central American, ex. Mexican	25	0.08
Guatemalan	10	0.03
Honduran	4	0.01
Panamanian	6	0.02
Salvadoran	5	0.02
Cuban	4	0.01
Dominican Republic	1	<0.01
Mexican	154	0.48
Puerto Rican	33	0.10
South American	53	0.16
Argentinean	1	<0.01
Bolivian	7	0.02
Chilean	4	0.01
Colombian	15	0.05
Ecuadorian	2	0.01
Peruvian	15	0.05
Uruguayan	1	<0.01
Venezuelan	8	0.02
Other Hispanic or Latino	43	0.13

Race*	Population	%
African-American/Black (411)	534	1.65
Not Hispanic (403)	523	1.62
Hispanic (8)	11	0.03
American Indian/Alaska Native (19)	83	0.26
Not Hispanic (11)	74	0.23
Hispanic (8)	9	0.03
Blackfeet (0)	7	0.02
Cherokee (1)	13	0.04
Choctaw (1)	1	<0.01
Creek (0)	1	<0.01
Delaware (0)	1	<0.01
Iroquois (1)	7	0.02
Menominee (0)	1	<0.01
Mexican American Ind. (5)	6	0.02
Navajo (1)	3	0.01
South American Ind. (2)	2	0.01
Tlingit-Haida *(Alaska Native)* (0)	2	0.01
Asian (462)	578	1.79
Not Hispanic (462)	573	1.77
Hispanic (0)	5	0.02
Bangladeshi (6)	6	0.02
Burmese (0)	3	0.01
Chinese, ex. Taiwanese (106)	130	0.40
Filipino (30)	73	0.23
Indian (195)	210	0.65
Indonesian (0)	2	0.01
Japanese (21)	39	0.12
Korean (29)	48	0.15
Pakistani (2)	3	0.01
Sri Lankan (1)	2	0.01
Thai (6)	8	0.02
Vietnamese (32)	39	0.12
Hawaii Native/Pacific Islander (4)	21	0.06
Not Hispanic (4)	18	0.06
Hispanic (0)	3	0.01
Native Hawaiian (2)	11	0.03
Samoan (1)	2	0.01
White (31,049)	31,315	96.91
Not Hispanic (30,846)	31,087	96.21
Hispanic (203)	228	0.71

Bethel

Place Type: Township
County: Delaware
Population: 8,791†

Ancestry‡	Population	%
African, Sub-Saharan (0)	29	0.35
African (0)	29	0.35
Albanian (22)	22	0.26
American (180)	180	2.15
Austrian (0)	7	0.08
British (41)	125	1.50
Canadian (14)	14	0.17
Croatian (0)	62	0.74
Czech (0)	13	0.16
Czechoslovakian (0)	13	0.16
Dutch (0)	128	1.53
Eastern European (23)	23	0.28
English (326)	1,388	16.60
European (38)	38	0.45
French, ex. Basque (11)	133	1.59
French Canadian (0)	20	0.24
German (269)	1,622	19.40
Greek (44)	78	0.93
Hungarian (13)	52	0.62
Irish (660)	2,693	32.21
Italian (1,006)	2,855	34.15
Lithuanian (29)	53	0.63
Norwegian (6)	69	0.83
Polish (149)	548	6.56
Romanian (14)	14	0.17
Russian (69)	114	1.36
Scotch-Irish (45)	94	1.12
Scottish (59)	125	1.50
Slovak (8)	16	0.19
Slovene (0)	36	0.43
Swedish (0)	47	0.56
Ukrainian (12)	51	0.61
Welsh (20)	47	0.56
West Indian, ex. Hispanic (29)	29	0.35
Jamaican (20)	20	0.24
Trinidadian/Tobagonian (9)	9	0.11

Hispanic Origin	Population	%
Hispanic or Latino (of any race)	190	2.16
Central American, ex. Mexican	5	0.06
Guatemalan	1	0.01
Nicaraguan	1	0.01
Panamanian	1	0.01
Salvadoran	2	0.02

*Notes: † The Census 2010 population figure is used to calculate the percentages in the Hispanic Origin and Race categories. Ancestry percentages are based on the 2006-2010 American Community Survey population (not shown); ‡ Numbers in parentheses indicate the number of people reporting a single ancestry; * Numbers in parentheses indicate the number of persons reporting this race alone, not in combination with any other race; Please refer to the Explanation of Data for more information.*

Cuban	22	0.25
Dominican Republic	3	0.03
Mexican	83	0.94
Puerto Rican	38	0.43
South American	24	0.27
Argentinean	2	0.02
Bolivian	1	0.01
Chilean	1	0.01
Colombian	9	0.10
Ecuadorian	2	0.02
Paraguayan	1	0.01
Peruvian	4	0.05
Venezuelan	4	0.05
Other Hispanic or Latino	15	0.17

Race*	Population	%
African-American/Black (158)	193	2.20
Not Hispanic (157)	189	2.15
Hispanic (1)	4	0.05
American Indian/Alaska Native (16)	36	0.41
Not Hispanic (12)	28	0.32
Hispanic (4)	8	0.09
Blackfeet (0)	5	0.06
Cherokee (1)	5	0.06
Delaware (0)	2	0.02
Iroquois (1)	1	0.01
Lumbee (0)	1	0.01
Mexican American Ind. (1)	1	0.01
Seminole (0)	2	0.02
Asian (539)	581	6.61
Not Hispanic (539)	580	6.60
Hispanic (0)	1	0.01
Bangladeshi (4)	4	0.05
Cambodian (2)	2	0.02
Chinese, ex. Taiwanese (201)	216	2.46
Filipino (24)	41	0.47
Indian (204)	216	2.46
Indonesian (4)	4	0.05
Japanese (0)	1	0.01
Korean (35)	42	0.48
Laotian (1)	1	0.01
Pakistani (9)	9	0.10
Sri Lankan (4)	4	0.05
Taiwanese (5)	5	0.06
Thai (1)	1	0.01
Vietnamese (33)	37	0.42
Hawaii Native/Pacific Islander (3)	5	0.06
Not Hispanic (3)	4	0.05
Hispanic (0)	1	0.01
Guamanian/Chamorro (1)	1	0.01
Native Hawaiian (0)	2	0.02
Samoan (1)	1	0.01
White (7,936)	8,032	91.37
Not Hispanic (7,791)	7,873	89.56
Hispanic (145)	159	1.81

Bethlehem

Place Type: City
County: Lehigh
Population: 19,343†

Ancestry‡	Population	%
Afghan (0)	63	0.33
African, Sub-Saharan (94)	164	0.85
African (94)	164	0.85
American (487)	487	2.52
Arab (107)	180	0.93
Jordanian (5)	5	0.03
Lebanese (13)	13	0.07
Syrian (89)	140	0.72
Other Arab (0)	22	0.11
Australian (0)	9	0.05
Austrian (31)	239	1.24
Brazilian (17)	17	0.09
British (30)	104	0.54
Canadian (0)	30	0.16
Celtic (0)	11	0.06
Croatian (10)	21	0.11
Czech (0)	71	0.37
Czechoslovakian (17)	75	0.39
Danish (8)	33	0.17
Dutch (160)	807	4.18
Eastern European (0)	10	0.05
English (334)	1,319	6.83
European (158)	158	0.82
French, ex. Basque (25)	431	2.23
French Canadian (19)	19	0.10
German (1,547)	4,918	25.47
Greek (39)	104	0.54
Guyanese (0)	40	0.21
Hungarian (189)	935	4.84
Irish (801)	3,356	17.38
Italian (531)	1,942	10.06
Latvian (0)	8	0.04
Lithuanian (26)	122	0.63
Norwegian (13)	54	0.28
Pennsylvania German (642)	911	4.72
Polish (273)	1,202	6.22
Portuguese (20)	38	0.20
Romanian (22)	22	0.11
Russian (81)	325	1.68
Scotch-Irish (87)	305	1.58
Scottish (51)	215	1.11
Serbian (24)	32	0.17
Slavic (0)	17	0.09
Slovak (292)	915	4.74
Slovene (30)	85	0.44
Swedish (8)	180	0.93
Swiss (23)	57	0.30
Turkish (15)	15	0.08
Ukrainian (40)	140	0.72
Welsh (186)	502	2.60
West Indian, ex. Hispanic (22)	62	0.32
Jamaican (12)	12	0.06
Trinidadian/Tobagonian (10)	10	0.05
West Indian (0)	40	0.21
Yugoslavian (8)	8	0.04

Hispanic Origin	Population	%
Hispanic or Latino (of any race)	2,972	15.36
Central American, ex. Mexican	109	0.56
Costa Rican	9	0.05
Guatemalan	35	0.18
Honduran	15	0.08
Nicaraguan	14	0.07
Panamanian	4	0.02
Salvadoran	32	0.17
Cuban	33	0.17
Dominican Republic	227	1.17
Mexican	222	1.15
Puerto Rican	2,007	10.38
South American	176	0.91
Argentinean	5	0.03
Bolivian	1	0.01
Chilean	11	0.06
Colombian	42	0.22
Ecuadorian	56	0.29
Paraguayan	1	0.01
Peruvian	42	0.22
Uruguayan	10	0.05
Venezuelan	8	0.04
Other Hispanic or Latino	198	1.02

Race*	Population	%
African-American/Black (994)	1,298	6.71
Not Hispanic (843)	1,043	5.39
Hispanic (151)	255	1.32
American Indian/Alaska Native (55)	143	0.74
Not Hispanic (25)	76	0.39
Hispanic (30)	67	0.35
Apache (0)	1	0.01
Blackfeet (0)	5	0.03
Central American Ind. (2)	3	0.02
Cherokee (4)	24	0.12
Choctaw (0)	1	0.01
Delaware (1)	7	0.04
Navajo (2)	2	0.01
Ottawa (1)	2	0.01
Pueblo (0)	1	0.01
Puget Sound Salish (1)	1	0.01
Seminole (0)	1	0.01
Sioux (2)	3	0.02
South American Ind. (8)	19	0.10
Asian (439)	518	2.68
Not Hispanic (437)	503	2.60
Hispanic (2)	15	0.08
Burmese (9)	9	0.05
Cambodian (5)	7	0.04
Chinese, ex. Taiwanese (77)	92	0.48
Filipino (55)	77	0.40
Indian (152)	155	0.80
Indonesian (3)	5	0.03
Japanese (4)	15	0.08
Korean (57)	62	0.32
Malaysian (2)	2	0.01
Pakistani (8)	13	0.07
Sri Lankan (3)	3	0.02
Thai (4)	5	0.03
Vietnamese (56)	58	0.30
Hawaii Native/Pacific Islander (7)	29	0.15
Not Hispanic (6)	24	0.12
Hispanic (1)	5	0.03
Guamanian/Chamorro (1)	3	0.02
Native Hawaiian (3)	12	0.06
Samoan (1)	1	0.01
White (16,012)	16,479	85.19
Not Hispanic (14,703)	14,981	77.45
Hispanic (1,309)	1,498	7.74

Bethlehem

Place Type: City
County: Northampton
Population: 55,639†

Ancestry‡	Population	%
Afghan (40)	40	0.07
African, Sub-Saharan (231)	249	0.45
African (103)	121	0.22
Ethiopian (20)	20	0.04
Kenyan (35)	35	0.06
Nigerian (30)	30	0.05
Senegalese (43)	43	0.08
American (1,272)	1,272	2.29
Arab (306)	384	0.69
Arab (225)	225	0.41
Egyptian (16)	16	0.03
Lebanese (14)	47	0.08
Syrian (39)	84	0.15
Other Arab (12)	12	0.02
Armenian (0)	21	0.04
Assyrian/Chaldean/Syriac (8)	8	0.01
Austrian (135)	544	0.98
Basque (0)	12	0.02
Belgian (0)	14	0.03
Brazilian (22)	22	0.04
British (97)	342	0.62
Bulgarian (10)	10	0.02
Canadian (53)	117	0.21
Carpatho Rusyn (13)	13	0.02
Croatian (11)	54	0.10
Czech (27)	344	0.62
Czechoslovakian (23)	91	0.16
Danish (26)	64	0.12
Dutch (220)	1,021	1.84
Eastern European (73)	93	0.17
English (696)	3,258	5.88
European (314)	329	0.59
Finnish (29)	29	0.05
French, ex. Basque (142)	1,049	1.89
French Canadian (37)	67	0.12
German (3,712)	12,068	21.77
Greek (241)	553	1.00
Guyanese (12)	133	0.24
Hungarian (830)	2,523	4.55
Iranian (64)	64	0.12
Irish (1,337)	7,207	13.00
Italian (2,062)	6,357	11.47
Lithuanian (154)	308	0.56

SECTION TWO

*Notes: † The Census 2010 population figure is used to calculate the percentages in the Hispanic Origin and Race categories. Ancestry percentages are based on the 2006-2010 American Community Survey population (not shown); ‡ Numbers in parentheses indicate the number of people reporting a single ancestry; * Numbers in parentheses indicate the number of persons reporting this race alone, not in combination with any other race; Please refer to the Explanation of Data for more information.*

Macedonian (16)	16	0.03
New Zealander (14)	14	0.03
Norwegian (58)	178	0.32
Pennsylvania German (952)	1,688	3.04
Polish (768)	2,523	4.55
Portuguese (413)	587	1.06
Romanian (26)	54	0.10
Russian (205)	717	1.29
Scandinavian (12)	22	0.04
Scotch-Irish (169)	630	1.14
Scottish (229)	864	1.56
Serbian (0)	11	0.02
Slavic (12)	63	0.11
Slovak (681)	1,659	2.99
Slovene (173)	231	0.42
Swedish (35)	376	0.68
Swiss (19)	228	0.41
Turkish (142)	169	0.30
Ukrainian (295)	724	1.31
Welsh (78)	931	1.68
West Indian, ex. Hispanic (239)	366	0.66
Barbadian (0)	12	0.02
Dutch West Indian (0)	12	0.02
Haitian (134)	134	0.24
Jamaican (78)	142	0.26
Trinidadian/Tobagonian (9)	19	0.03
U.S. Virgin Islander (3)	3	0.01
West Indian (15)	44	0.08
Yugoslavian (45)	55	0.10

Hispanic Origin	Population	%
Hispanic or Latino (of any race)	15,296	27.49
Central American, ex. Mexican	534	0.96
Costa Rican	18	0.03
Guatemalan	240	0.43
Honduran	75	0.13
Nicaraguan	72	0.13
Panamanian	42	0.08
Salvadoran	84	0.15
Other Central American	3	0.01
Cuban	163	0.29
Dominican Republic	783	1.41
Mexican	863	1.55
Puerto Rican	11,715	21.06
South American	628	1.13
Argentinean	32	0.06
Bolivian	16	0.03
Chilean	68	0.12
Colombian	198	0.36
Ecuadorian	144	0.26
Paraguayan	2	<0.01
Peruvian	113	0.20
Uruguayan	12	0.02
Venezuelan	42	0.08
Other South American	1	<0.01
Other Hispanic or Latino	610	1.10

Race*	Population	%
African-American/Black (4,205)	5,221	9.38
Not Hispanic (3,244)	3,772	6.78
Hispanic (961)	1,449	2.60
American Indian/Alaska Native (204)	465	0.84
Not Hispanic (58)	231	0.42
Hispanic (146)	234	0.42
Apache (0)	1	<0.01
Blackfeet (3)	17	0.03
Central American Ind. (4)	7	0.01
Cherokee (6)	55	0.10
Choctaw (1)	2	<0.01
Comanche (0)	1	<0.01
Delaware (2)	15	0.03
Iroquois (4)	13	0.02
Lumbee (1)	2	<0.01
Mexican American Ind. (1)	5	0.01
Navajo (2)	5	0.01
Ottawa (3)	3	0.01
Paiute (0)	1	<0.01
Pueblo (5)	5	0.01
Seminole (1)	6	0.01
Sioux (0)	5	0.01
South American Ind. (39)	54	0.10
Spanish American Ind. (1)	1	<0.01
Asian (1,704)	2,012	3.62
Not Hispanic (1,666)	1,915	3.44
Hispanic (38)	97	0.17
Bangladeshi (2)	3	0.01
Burmese (13)	14	0.03
Cambodian (4)	5	0.01
Chinese, ex. Taiwanese (537)	601	1.08
Filipino (95)	144	0.26
Indian (436)	478	0.86
Indonesian (9)	13	0.02
Japanese (44)	80	0.14
Korean (183)	221	0.40
Laotian (1)	2	<0.01
Malaysian (9)	12	0.02
Nepalese (3)	6	0.01
Pakistani (69)	70	0.13
Sri Lankan (12)	12	0.02
Taiwanese (32)	35	0.06
Thai (51)	57	0.10
Vietnamese (134)	159	0.29
Hawaii Native/Pacific Islander (24)	92	0.17
Not Hispanic (16)	45	0.08
Hispanic (8)	47	0.08
Guamanian/Chamorro (4)	7	0.01
Native Hawaiian (7)	24	0.04
Tongan (5)	5	0.01
White (41,293)	42,972	77.23
Not Hispanic (34,329)	35,169	63.21
Hispanic (6,964)	7,803	14.02

Bethlehem

Place Type: City
County: Northampton
Population: 74,982†

Ancestry‡	Population	%
Afghan (40)	103	0.14
African, Sub-Saharan (325)	413	0.55
African (197)	285	0.38
Ethiopian (20)	20	0.03
Kenyan (35)	35	0.05
Nigerian (30)	30	0.04
Senegalese (43)	43	0.06
American (1,759)	1,759	2.35
Arab (413)	564	0.75
Arab (225)	225	0.30
Egyptian (16)	16	0.02
Jordanian (5)	5	0.01
Lebanese (27)	60	0.08
Syrian (128)	224	0.30
Other Arab (12)	34	0.05
Armenian (0)	21	0.03
Assyrian/Chaldean/Syriac (8)	8	0.01
Australian (0)	9	0.01
Austrian (166)	783	1.05
Basque (0)	12	0.02
Belgian (0)	14	0.02
Brazilian (39)	39	0.05
British (127)	446	0.60
Bulgarian (10)	10	0.01
Canadian (53)	147	0.20
Carpatho Rusyn (13)	13	0.02
Celtic (0)	11	0.01
Croatian (21)	75	0.10
Czech (27)	415	0.56
Czechoslovakian (40)	166	0.22
Danish (34)	97	0.13
Dutch (380)	1,828	2.45
Eastern European (73)	103	0.14
English (1,030)	4,577	6.12
European (472)	487	0.65
Finnish (29)	29	0.04
French, ex. Basque (167)	1,480	1.98
French Canadian (56)	86	0.12
German (5,259)	16,986	22.72
Greek (280)	657	0.88
Guyanese (12)	173	0.23
Hungarian (1,019)	3,458	4.63
Iranian (64)	64	0.09
Irish (2,138)	10,563	14.13
Italian (2,593)	8,299	11.10
Latvian (0)	8	0.01
Lithuanian (180)	430	0.58
Macedonian (16)	16	0.02
New Zealander (14)	14	0.02
Norwegian (71)	232	0.31
Pennsylvania German (1,594)	2,599	3.48
Polish (1,041)	3,725	4.98
Portuguese (433)	625	0.84
Romanian (48)	76	0.10
Russian (286)	1,042	1.39
Scandinavian (12)	22	0.03
Scotch-Irish (256)	935	1.25
Scottish (280)	1,079	1.44
Serbian (24)	43	0.06
Slavic (12)	80	0.11
Slovak (973)	2,574	3.44
Slovene (203)	316	0.42
Swedish (43)	556	0.74
Swiss (42)	285	0.38
Turkish (157)	184	0.25
Ukrainian (335)	864	1.16
Welsh (264)	1,433	1.92
West Indian, ex. Hispanic (261)	428	0.57
Barbadian (0)	12	0.02
Dutch West Indian (0)	12	0.02
Haitian (134)	134	0.18
Jamaican (90)	154	0.21
Trinidadian/Tobagonian (19)	29	0.04
U.S. Virgin Islander (3)	3	<0.01
West Indian (15)	84	0.11
Yugoslavian (53)	63	0.08

Hispanic Origin	Population	%
Hispanic or Latino (of any race)	18,268	24.36
Central American, ex. Mexican	643	0.86
Costa Rican	27	0.04
Guatemalan	275	0.37
Honduran	90	0.12
Nicaraguan	86	0.11
Panamanian	46	0.06
Salvadoran	116	0.15
Other Central American	3	<0.01
Cuban	196	0.26
Dominican Republic	1,010	1.35
Mexican	1,085	1.45
Puerto Rican	13,722	18.30
South American	804	1.07
Argentinean	37	0.05
Bolivian	17	0.02
Chilean	79	0.11
Colombian	240	0.32
Ecuadorian	200	0.27
Paraguayan	3	<0.01
Peruvian	155	0.21
Uruguayan	22	0.03
Venezuelan	50	0.07
Other South American	1	<0.01
Other Hispanic or Latino	808	1.08

Race*	Population	%
African-American/Black (5,199)	6,519	8.69
Not Hispanic (4,087)	4,815	6.42
Hispanic (1,112)	1,704	2.27
American Indian/Alaska Native (259)	608	0.81
Not Hispanic (83)	307	0.41
Hispanic (176)	301	0.40
Apache (0)	2	<0.01
Blackfeet (3)	22	0.03
Central American Ind. (6)	10	0.01
Cherokee (10)	79	0.11
Choctaw (1)	3	<0.01
Comanche (0)	1	<0.01
Delaware (3)	22	0.03
Iroquois (4)	13	0.02
Lumbee (1)	2	<0.01
Mexican American Ind. (1)	5	0.01

*Notes: † The Census 2010 population figure is used to calculate the percentages in the Hispanic Origin and Race categories. Ancestry percentages are based on the 2006-2010 American Community Survey population (not shown); ‡ Numbers in parentheses indicate the number of people reporting a single ancestry; * Numbers in parentheses indicate the number of persons reporting this race alone, not in combination with any other race; Please refer to the Explanation of Data for more information.*

Navajo (4)	7	0.01
Ottawa (4)	5	0.01
Paiute (0)	1	<0.01
Pueblo (5)	6	0.01
Puget Sound Salish (1)	1	<0.01
Seminole (1)	7	0.01
Sioux (2)	8	0.01
South American Ind. (47)	73	0.10
Spanish American Ind. (1)	1	<0.01
Asian (2,143)	2,530	3.37
Not Hispanic (2,103)	2,418	3.22
Hispanic (40)	112	0.15
Bangladeshi (2)	3	<0.01
Burmese (22)	23	0.03
Cambodian (9)	12	0.02
Chinese, ex. Taiwanese (614)	693	0.92
Filipino (150)	221	0.29
Indian (588)	633	0.84
Indonesian (12)	18	0.02
Japanese (48)	95	0.13
Korean (240)	283	0.38
Laotian (1)	2	<0.01
Malaysian (11)	14	0.02
Nepalese (3)	6	0.01
Pakistani (77)	83	0.11
Sri Lankan (15)	15	0.02
Taiwanese (32)	35	0.05
Thai (55)	62	0.08
Vietnamese (190)	217	0.29
Hawaii Native/Pacific Islander (31)	121	0.16
Not Hispanic (22)	69	0.09
Hispanic (9)	52	0.07
Guamanian/Chamorro (5)	10	0.01
Native Hawaiian (10)	36	0.05
Samoan (1)	1	<0.01
Tongan (5)	5	0.01
White (57,305)	59,451	79.29
Not Hispanic (49,032)	50,150	66.88
Hispanic (8,273)	9,301	12.40

Bethlehem

Place Type: Township
County: Northampton
Population: 23,730†

Ancestry‡	Population	%
African, Sub-Saharan (52)	52	0.22
African (32)	32	0.14
Nigerian (16)	16	0.07
South African (2)	2	0.01
Other Sub-Saharan African (2)	2	0.01
American (1,230)	1,230	5.25
Arab (227)	419	1.79
Egyptian (122)	230	0.98
Lebanese (49)	133	0.57
Syrian (56)	56	0.24
Armenian (46)	60	0.26
Assyrian/Chaldean/Syriac (23)	23	0.10
Austrian (64)	166	0.71
Basque (0)	38	0.16
Belgian (17)	17	0.07
Brazilian (266)	266	1.13
British (11)	21	0.09
Canadian (56)	96	0.41
Croatian (41)	93	0.40
Czech (0)	58	0.25
Czechoslovakian (24)	45	0.19
Danish (10)	69	0.29
Dutch (192)	516	2.20
Eastern European (105)	105	0.45
English (362)	1,391	5.93
European (226)	226	0.96
French, ex. Basque (141)	615	2.62
French Canadian (0)	40	0.17
German (1,962)	5,944	25.35
Greek (51)	141	0.60
Hungarian (551)	1,213	5.17
Irish (864)	3,547	15.13
Israeli (9)	48	0.20
Italian (2,110)	4,577	19.52
Lithuanian (17)	129	0.55
Norwegian (8)	47	0.20
Pennsylvania German (269)	486	2.07
Polish (579)	1,476	6.29
Portuguese (267)	318	1.36
Romanian (41)	75	0.32
Russian (133)	212	0.90
Scotch-Irish (154)	317	1.35
Scottish (87)	327	1.39
Serbian (17)	56	0.24
Slavic (0)	43	0.18
Slovak (130)	651	2.78
Slovene (8)	23	0.10
Swedish (19)	72	0.31
Swiss (0)	121	0.52
Turkish (3)	3	0.01
Ukrainian (129)	318	1.36
Welsh (67)	192	0.82
West Indian, ex. Hispanic (208)	208	0.89
Belizean (12)	12	0.05
Haitian (140)	140	0.60
Jamaican (20)	20	0.09
West Indian (36)	36	0.15

Hispanic Origin	Population	%
Hispanic or Latino (of any race)	1,865	7.86
Central American, ex. Mexican	151	0.64
Costa Rican	19	0.08
Guatemalan	56	0.24
Honduran	22	0.09
Nicaraguan	8	0.03
Panamanian	6	0.03
Salvadoran	34	0.14
Other Central American	6	0.03
Cuban	70	0.29
Dominican Republic	102	0.43
Mexican	130	0.55
Puerto Rican	1,070	4.51
South American	220	0.93
Argentinean	15	0.06
Bolivian	1	<0.01
Chilean	7	0.03
Colombian	94	0.40
Ecuadorian	59	0.25
Paraguayan	3	0.01
Peruvian	23	0.10
Uruguayan	4	0.02
Venezuelan	11	0.05
Other South American	3	0.01
Other Hispanic or Latino	122	0.51

Race*	Population	%
African-American/Black (1,117)	1,295	5.46
Not Hispanic (1,041)	1,164	4.91
Hispanic (76)	131	0.55
American Indian/Alaska Native (38)	113	0.48
Not Hispanic (28)	83	0.35
Hispanic (10)	30	0.13
Apache (1)	5	0.02
Cherokee (6)	22	0.09
Chickasaw (1)	1	<0.01
Delaware (1)	8	0.03
Mexican American Ind. (1)	1	<0.01
Navajo (1)	2	0.01
Sioux (4)	7	0.03
South American Ind. (3)	13	0.05
Asian (1,034)	1,154	4.86
Not Hispanic (1,030)	1,136	4.79
Hispanic (4)	18	0.08
Bangladeshi (6)	6	0.03
Chinese, ex. Taiwanese (163)	179	0.75
Filipino (106)	134	0.56
Indian (508)	527	2.22
Indonesian (1)	1	<0.01
Japanese (6)	20	0.08
Korean (48)	65	0.27
Nepalese (3)	3	0.01
Pakistani (50)	53	0.22
Sri Lankan (6)	6	0.03
Taiwanese (12)	14	0.06
Thai (4)	5	0.02
Vietnamese (105)	110	0.46
Hawaii Native/Pacific Islander (23)	44	0.19
Not Hispanic (23)	42	0.18
Hispanic (0)	2	0.01
Guamanian/Chamorro (15)	22	0.09
Native Hawaiian (8)	8	0.03
White (20,569)	20,929	88.20
Not Hispanic (19,435)	19,671	82.90
Hispanic (1,134)	1,258	5.30

Bloomsburg

Place Type: Town
County: Columbia
Population: 14,855†

Ancestry‡	Population	%
African, Sub-Saharan (28)	28	0.20
African (14)	14	0.10
Ethiopian (13)	13	0.09
Ghanaian (1)	1	0.01
Albanian (0)	13	0.09
American (321)	321	2.24
Arab (28)	28	0.20
Lebanese (13)	13	0.09
Other Arab (15)	15	0.10
Austrian (16)	36	0.25
Basque (0)	17	0.12
Belgian (16)	16	0.11
British (33)	97	0.68
Canadian (16)	16	0.11
Carpatho Rusyn (0)	14	0.10
Croatian (15)	27	0.19
Czech (85)	139	0.97
Czechoslovakian (0)	43	0.30
Danish (36)	61	0.43
Dutch (34)	470	3.29
English (695)	1,492	10.43
European (11)	11	0.08
French, ex. Basque (284)	663	4.64
French Canadian (0)	8	0.06
German (2,123)	4,810	33.64
Greek (73)	105	0.73
Hungarian (61)	326	2.28
Irish (765)	2,357	16.48
Italian (576)	1,368	9.57
Lithuanian (0)	54	0.38
Norwegian (44)	92	0.64
Pennsylvania German (163)	324	2.27
Polish (337)	1,130	7.90
Portuguese (66)	66	0.46
Romanian (14)	14	0.10
Russian (69)	192	1.34
Scotch-Irish (46)	103	0.72
Scottish (112)	319	2.23
Serbian (0)	12	0.08
Slovak (75)	284	1.99
Swedish (0)	99	0.69
Swiss (0)	49	0.34
Ukrainian (31)	103	0.72
Welsh (233)	566	3.96
West Indian, ex. Hispanic (25)	26	0.18
Jamaican (25)	26	0.18

Hispanic Origin	Population	%
Hispanic or Latino (of any race)	508	3.42
Central American, ex. Mexican	58	0.39
Costa Rican	6	0.04
Guatemalan	26	0.18
Honduran	5	0.03
Nicaraguan	5	0.03
Panamanian	4	0.03
Salvadoran	12	0.08
Cuban	30	0.20
Dominican Republic	29	0.20
Mexican	88	0.59
Puerto Rican	243	1.64
South American	33	0.22

*Notes: † The Census 2010 population figure is used to calculate the percentages in the Hispanic Origin and Race categories. Ancestry percentages are based on the 2006-2010 American Community Survey population (not shown); ‡ Numbers in parentheses indicate the number of people reporting a single ancestry; * Numbers in parentheses indicate the number of persons reporting this race alone, not in combination with any other race; Please refer to the Explanation of Data for more information.*

Argentinean	1	0.01
Bolivian	2	0.01
Chilean	8	0.05
Colombian	11	0.07
Ecuadorian	6	0.04
Peruvian	5	0.03
Other Hispanic or Latino	27	0.18

Race*	Population	%
African-American/Black (914)	1,009	6.79
Not Hispanic (880)	963	6.48
Hispanic (34)	46	0.31
American Indian/Alaska Native (16)	72	0.48
Not Hispanic (12)	63	0.42
Hispanic (4)	9	0.06
Aleut *(Alaska Native)* (1)	1	0.01
Apache (0)	2	0.01
Blackfeet (0)	4	0.03
Cherokee (1)	8	0.05
Choctaw (0)	2	0.01
Creek (0)	2	0.01
Delaware (0)	3	0.02
Iroquois (0)	8	0.05
Lumbee (1)	1	0.01
Mexican American Ind. (1)	3	0.02
Seminole (0)	1	0.01
Sioux (0)	1	0.01
South American Ind. (0)	1	0.01
Asian (232)	285	1.92
Not Hispanic (225)	274	1.84
Hispanic (7)	11	0.07
Bangladeshi (2)	6	0.04
Burmese (0)	3	0.02
Cambodian (2)	3	0.02
Chinese, ex. Taiwanese (63)	75	0.50
Filipino (15)	34	0.23
Indian (66)	73	0.49
Indonesian (1)	1	0.01
Japanese (6)	9	0.06
Korean (24)	31	0.21
Malaysian (1)	1	0.01
Nepalese (9)	11	0.07
Pakistani (7)	8	0.05
Taiwanese (2)	2	0.01
Thai (2)	3	0.02
Vietnamese (24)	26	0.18
Hawaii Native/Pacific Islander (3)	9	0.06
Not Hispanic (2)	7	0.05
Hispanic (1)	2	0.01
Guamanian/Chamorro (1)	2	0.01
Native Hawaiian (1)	2	0.01
Samoan (0)	1	0.01
White (13,305)	13,481	90.75
Not Hispanic (13,050)	13,197	88.84
Hispanic (255)	284	1.91

Bradford

Place Type: City
County: McKean
Population: 8,770†

Ancestry‡	Population	%
African, Sub-Saharan (6)	6	0.07
African (6)	6	0.07
American (567)	567	6.41
Arab (32)	32	0.36
Arab (13)	13	0.15
Moroccan (19)	19	0.21
Armenian (24)	24	0.27
Austrian (40)	52	0.59
Belgian (0)	31	0.35
Brazilian (9)	9	0.10
British (0)	35	0.40
Canadian (22)	22	0.25
Czech (0)	14	0.16
Danish (9)	9	0.10
Dutch (0)	77	0.87
English (260)	900	10.17
European (94)	94	1.06
French, ex. Basque (51)	268	3.03
French Canadian (23)	116	1.31
German (713)	2,507	28.34
Greek (24)	24	0.27
Hungarian (0)	25	0.28
Irish (458)	1,387	15.68
Italian (794)	1,801	20.36
Pennsylvania German (14)	58	0.66
Polish (209)	633	7.15
Scotch-Irish (68)	170	1.92
Scottish (36)	288	3.26
Serbian (0)	8	0.09
Slovak (19)	29	0.33
Slovene (0)	14	0.16
Swedish (152)	509	5.75
Swiss (10)	18	0.20
Ukrainian (0)	7	0.08
Welsh (11)	59	0.67
West Indian, ex. Hispanic (0)	5	0.06
West Indian (0)	5	0.06

Hispanic Origin	Population	%
Hispanic or Latino (of any race)	119	1.36
Central American, ex. Mexican	7	0.08
Guatemalan	2	0.02
Panamanian	3	0.03
Salvadoran	2	0.02
Cuban	7	0.08
Dominican Republic	2	0.02
Mexican	34	0.39
Puerto Rican	44	0.50
South American	4	0.05
Argentinean	2	0.02
Colombian	2	0.02
Other Hispanic or Latino	21	0.24

Race*	Population	%
African-American/Black (86)	142	1.62
Not Hispanic (86)	139	1.58
Hispanic (0)	3	0.03
American Indian/Alaska Native (33)	87	0.99
Not Hispanic (29)	77	0.88
Hispanic (4)	10	0.11
Aleut *(Alaska Native)* (1)	1	0.01
Apache (0)	3	0.03
Blackfeet (0)	8	0.09
Cherokee (7)	17	0.19
Chippewa (1)	1	0.01
Comanche (0)	3	0.03
Iroquois (8)	18	0.21
Sioux (1)	2	0.02
Asian (64)	81	0.92
Not Hispanic (64)	79	0.90
Hispanic (0)	2	0.02
Bangladeshi (5)	5	0.06
Chinese, ex. Taiwanese (24)	27	0.31
Filipino (12)	14	0.16
Indian (10)	13	0.15
Japanese (2)	8	0.09
Korean (4)	6	0.07
Pakistani (2)	2	0.02
Taiwanese (1)	1	0.01
Vietnamese (4)	4	0.05
Hawaii Native/Pacific Islander (2)	4	0.05
Not Hispanic (2)	4	0.05
Samoan (0)	1	0.01
White (8,444)	8,557	97.57
Not Hispanic (8,360)	8,459	96.45
Hispanic (84)	98	1.12

Brentwood

Place Type: Borough
County: Allegheny
Population: 9,643†

Ancestry‡	Population	%
African, Sub-Saharan (90)	90	0.93
Other Sub-Saharan African (90)	90	0.93
American (245)	245	2.52
Austrian (16)	82	0.84
Belgian (0)	12	0.12
Croatian (48)	103	1.06
Czech (0)	78	0.80
Czechoslovakian (11)	36	0.37
Dutch (0)	22	0.23
English (123)	627	6.46
European (60)	60	0.62
Finnish (0)	14	0.14
French, ex. Basque (0)	120	1.24
German (1,201)	3,853	39.68
Hungarian (16)	286	2.95
Irish (518)	2,553	26.29
Italian (697)	1,870	19.26
Lithuanian (47)	205	2.11
Norwegian (31)	52	0.54
Polish (383)	1,242	12.79
Russian (0)	164	1.69
Scotch-Irish (102)	304	3.13
Scottish (0)	101	1.04
Serbian (0)	26	0.27
Slavic (0)	35	0.36
Slovak (80)	337	3.47
Slovene (0)	11	0.11
Swedish (7)	110	1.13
Swiss (0)	11	0.11
Ukrainian (53)	128	1.32
Welsh (72)	403	4.15

Hispanic Origin	Population	%
Hispanic or Latino (of any race)	169	1.75
Central American, ex. Mexican	24	0.25
Guatemalan	18	0.19
Honduran	5	0.05
Panamanian	1	0.01
Cuban	6	0.06
Dominican Republic	1	0.01
Mexican	62	0.64
Puerto Rican	22	0.23
South American	19	0.20
Argentinean	1	0.01
Chilean	1	0.01
Colombian	3	0.03
Ecuadorian	7	0.07
Peruvian	3	0.03
Venezuelan	4	0.04
Other Hispanic or Latino	35	0.36

Race*	Population	%
African-American/Black (197)	275	2.85
Not Hispanic (190)	263	2.73
Hispanic (7)	12	0.12
American Indian/Alaska Native (17)	51	0.53
Not Hispanic (13)	45	0.47
Hispanic (4)	6	0.06
Blackfeet (0)	2	0.02
Cherokee (1)	11	0.11
Cheyenne (0)	1	0.01
Delaware (1)	1	0.01
Houma (3)	3	0.03
Inupiat *(Alaska Native)* (1)	1	0.01
Iroquois (0)	3	0.03
Mexican American Ind. (2)	4	0.04
Pima (0)	1	0.01
Potawatomi (3)	3	0.03
South American Ind. (1)	2	0.02
Asian (76)	97	1.01
Not Hispanic (76)	95	0.99
Hispanic (0)	2	0.02
Chinese, ex. Taiwanese (30)	35	0.36
Filipino (5)	10	0.10
Indian (12)	14	0.15
Indonesian (3)	3	0.03
Japanese (1)	3	0.03
Korean (12)	16	0.17
Vietnamese (5)	13	0.13
Hawaii Native/Pacific Islander (4)	4	0.04
Not Hispanic (4)	4	0.04
White (9,177)	9,299	96.43
Not Hispanic (9,064)	9,173	95.13

*Notes: † The Census 2010 population figure is used to calculate the percentages in the Hispanic Origin and Race categories. Ancestry percentages are based on the 2006-2010 American Community Survey population (not shown); ‡ Numbers in parentheses indicate the number of people reporting a single ancestry; * Numbers in parentheses indicate the number of persons reporting this race alone, not in combination with any other race; Please refer to the Explanation of Data for more information.*

Hispanic (113)	126	1.31

Brighton

Place Type: Township
County: Beaver
Population: 8,227†

Ancestry‡	Population	%
American (270)	270	3.32
Arab (11)	11	0.14
Syrian (11)	11	0.14
Austrian (0)	42	0.52
British (0)	30	0.37
Canadian (88)	101	1.24
Carpatho Rusyn (0)	10	0.12
Croatian (54)	151	1.85
Czech (20)	77	0.95
Czechoslovakian (13)	36	0.44
Danish (6)	16	0.20
Dutch (24)	254	3.12
English (237)	947	11.63
European (78)	78	0.96
Finnish (11)	23	0.28
French, ex. Basque (42)	129	1.58
French Canadian (13)	23	0.28
German (803)	2,779	34.14
Greek (139)	211	2.59
Hungarian (11)	159	1.95
Irish (343)	1,531	18.81
Italian (442)	1,296	15.92
Lithuanian (33)	54	0.66
Pennsylvania German (0)	15	0.18
Polish (127)	464	5.70
Romanian (10)	21	0.26
Russian (30)	107	1.31
Scotch-Irish (103)	285	3.50
Scottish (40)	140	1.72
Serbian (59)	136	1.67
Slovak (73)	252	3.10
Slovene (0)	21	0.26
Swedish (10)	32	0.39
Swiss (17)	17	0.21
Ukrainian (33)	115	1.41
Welsh (0)	166	2.04
Yugoslavian (14)	14	0.17

Hispanic Origin	Population	%
Hispanic or Latino (of any race)	89	1.08
Central American, ex. Mexican	19	0.23
Costa Rican	7	0.09
Guatemalan	6	0.07
Nicaraguan	1	0.01
Panamanian	1	0.01
Salvadoran	4	0.05
Cuban	2	0.02
Dominican Republic	3	0.04
Mexican	38	0.46
Puerto Rican	9	0.11
South American	3	0.04
Colombian	2	0.02
Ecuadorian	1	0.01
Other Hispanic or Latino	15	0.18

Race*	Population	%
African-American/Black (94)	127	1.54
Not Hispanic (94)	125	1.52
Hispanic (0)	2	0.02
American Indian/Alaska Native (6)	28	0.34
Not Hispanic (3)	23	0.28
Hispanic (3)	5	0.06
Cherokee (0)	3	0.04
Iroquois (0)	2	0.02
Sioux (0)	5	0.06
South American Ind. (1)	1	0.01
Asian (54)	64	0.78
Not Hispanic (53)	60	0.73
Hispanic (1)	4	0.05
Chinese, ex. Taiwanese (15)	18	0.22
Filipino (6)	10	0.12
Indian (8)	8	0.10
Japanese (3)	6	0.07
Korean (4)	8	0.10
Pakistani (5)	5	0.06
Vietnamese (12)	12	0.15
Hawaii Native/Pacific Islander (8)	8	0.10
Not Hispanic (7)	7	0.09
Hispanic (1)	1	0.01
Guamanian/Chamorro (2)	2	0.02
White (7,985)	8,043	97.76
Not Hispanic (7,928)	7,976	96.95
Hispanic (57)	67	0.81

Bristol

Place Type: Borough
County: Bucks
Population: 9,726†

Ancestry‡	Population	%
African, Sub-Saharan (37)	37	0.38
African (37)	37	0.38
American (283)	283	2.88
Arab (10)	10	0.10
Other Arab (10)	10	0.10
Australian (0)	16	0.16
Austrian (0)	4	0.04
Belgian (0)	4	0.04
British (20)	54	0.55
Celtic (0)	67	0.68
Czech (8)	40	0.41
Dutch (16)	252	2.56
English (195)	928	9.44
European (46)	46	0.47
French, ex. Basque (25)	117	1.19
French Canadian (0)	13	0.13
German (319)	1,768	17.98
Greek (0)	15	0.15
Hungarian (12)	48	0.49
Irish (1,171)	3,537	35.98
Italian (1,164)	2,719	27.66
Lithuanian (0)	41	0.42
Pennsylvania German (0)	62	0.63
Polish (93)	499	5.08
Russian (0)	18	0.18
Scotch-Irish (25)	111	1.13
Scottish (8)	37	0.38
Slovak (25)	38	0.39
Swedish (15)	51	0.52
Swiss (0)	3	0.03
Ukrainian (8)	93	0.95
Welsh (13)	38	0.39

Hispanic Origin	Population	%
Hispanic or Latino (of any race)	1,378	14.17
Central American, ex. Mexican	46	0.47
Costa Rican	12	0.12
Guatemalan	24	0.25
Honduran	2	0.02
Salvadoran	8	0.08
Cuban	13	0.13
Dominican Republic	7	0.07
Mexican	89	0.92
Puerto Rican	1,098	11.29
South American	47	0.48
Argentinean	1	0.01
Colombian	22	0.23
Ecuadorian	20	0.21
Peruvian	3	0.03
Venezuelan	1	0.01
Other Hispanic or Latino	78	0.80

Race*	Population	%
African-American/Black (926)	1,130	11.62
Not Hispanic (865)	1,028	10.57
Hispanic (61)	102	1.05
American Indian/Alaska Native (22)	75	0.77
Not Hispanic (16)	60	0.62
Hispanic (6)	15	0.15
Blackfeet (0)	2	0.02
Cherokee (3)	16	0.16
Cheyenne (0)	1	0.01
Choctaw (0)	1	0.01
Delaware (1)	4	0.04
Iroquois (1)	1	0.01
Lumbee (0)	4	0.04
Mexican American Ind. (3)	3	0.03
Seminole (0)	2	0.02
Sioux (1)	4	0.04
South American Ind. (2)	2	0.02
Asian (56)	81	0.83
Not Hispanic (55)	74	0.76
Hispanic (1)	7	0.07
Chinese, ex. Taiwanese (6)	8	0.08
Filipino (14)	25	0.26
Indian (17)	20	0.21
Japanese (2)	6	0.06
Korean (4)	8	0.08
Pakistani (3)	3	0.03
Thai (1)	1	0.01
Vietnamese (7)	7	0.07
Hawaii Native/Pacific Islander (1)	6	0.06
Not Hispanic (0)	2	0.02
Hispanic (1)	4	0.04
Guamanian/Chamorro (1)	1	0.01
Native Hawaiian (0)	2	0.02
White (7,890)	8,201	84.32
Not Hispanic (7,180)	7,383	75.91
Hispanic (710)	818	8.41

Bristol

Place Type: Township
County: Bucks
Population: 54,582†

Ancestry‡	Population	%
African, Sub-Saharan (1,318)	1,378	2.51
African (1,011)	1,057	1.92
Ghanaian (55)	62	0.11
Liberian (243)	243	0.44
Nigerian (9)	16	0.03
Albanian (27)	27	0.05
Alsatian (12)	12	0.02
American (1,396)	1,396	2.54
Arab (182)	245	0.45
Egyptian (97)	97	0.18
Lebanese (18)	42	0.08
Syrian (35)	74	0.13
Other Arab (32)	32	0.06
Armenian (0)	13	0.02
Austrian (26)	85	0.15
Belgian (19)	118	0.21
British (77)	120	0.22
Bulgarian (0)	13	0.02
Canadian (0)	18	0.03
Carpatho Rusyn (19)	19	0.03
Czech (12)	72	0.13
Czechoslovakian (25)	88	0.16
Danish (30)	75	0.14
Dutch (142)	942	1.71
Eastern European (17)	24	0.04
English (1,398)	5,476	9.96
European (84)	101	0.18
Finnish (0)	60	0.11
French, ex. Basque (88)	927	1.69
French Canadian (85)	233	0.42
German (4,960)	13,990	25.43
Greek (131)	307	0.56
Guyanese (53)	53	0.10
Hungarian (156)	648	1.18
Iranian (0)	10	0.02
Irish (5,896)	16,287	29.61
Italian (2,898)	7,904	14.37
Lithuanian (118)	379	0.69
Macedonian (14)	14	0.03
Northern European (40)	40	0.07
Norwegian (31)	88	0.16
Pennsylvania German (68)	196	0.36
Polish (1,630)	5,282	9.60

*Notes: † The Census 2010 population figure is used to calculate the percentages in the Hispanic Origin and Race categories. Ancestry percentages are based on the 2006-2010 American Community Survey population (not shown); ‡ Numbers in parentheses indicate the number of people reporting a single ancestry; * Numbers in parentheses indicate the number of persons reporting this race alone, not in combination with any other race; Please refer to the Explanation of Data for more information.*

Portuguese (14)	73	0.13
Romanian (12)	37	0.07
Russian (194)	478	0.87
Scandinavian (10)	65	0.12
Scotch-Irish (412)	1,261	2.29
Scottish (252)	809	1.47
Serbian (0)	15	0.03
Slavic (29)	96	0.17
Slovak (317)	558	1.01
Slovene (0)	13	0.02
Swedish (46)	295	0.54
Swiss (0)	72	0.13
Turkish (167)	201	0.37
Ukrainian (433)	704	1.28
Welsh (120)	715	1.30
West Indian, ex. Hispanic (239)	264	0.48
Haitian (199)	206	0.37
Jamaican (40)	58	0.11
Yugoslavian (0)	14	0.03

Hispanic Origin	Population	%
Hispanic or Latino (of any race)	4,040	7.40
Central American, ex. Mexican	335	0.61
Costa Rican	113	0.21
Guatemalan	108	0.20
Honduran	20	0.04
Nicaraguan	20	0.04
Panamanian	10	0.02
Salvadoran	59	0.11
Other Central American	5	0.01
Cuban	65	0.12
Dominican Republic	121	0.22
Mexican	1,100	2.02
Puerto Rican	1,873	3.43
South American	260	0.48
Argentinean	19	0.03
Chilean	13	0.02
Colombian	93	0.17
Ecuadorian	69	0.13
Paraguayan	1	<0.01
Peruvian	32	0.06
Uruguayan	6	0.01
Venezuelan	20	0.04
Other South American	7	0.01
Other Hispanic or Latino	286	0.52

Race*	Population	%
African-American/Black (5,576)	6,353	11.64
Not Hispanic (5,425)	6,069	11.12
Hispanic (151)	284	0.52
American Indian/Alaska Native (136)	473	0.87
Not Hispanic (92)	381	0.70
Hispanic (44)	92	0.17
Alaska Athabascan *(Ala. Nat.)* (0)	3	0.01
Apache (0)	8	0.01
Arapaho (0)	1	<0.01
Blackfeet (1)	27	0.05
Central American Ind. (4)	9	0.02
Cherokee (8)	73	0.13
Chippewa (0)	3	0.01
Choctaw (3)	3	0.01
Cree (0)	3	0.01
Delaware (3)	13	0.02
Iroquois (7)	22	0.04
Kiowa (0)	1	<0.01
Lumbee (2)	4	0.01
Mexican American Ind. (12)	17	0.03
Navajo (0)	2	<0.01
Seminole (0)	6	0.01
Sioux (3)	16	0.03
South American Ind. (7)	11	0.02
Asian (1,546)	1,896	3.47
Not Hispanic (1,527)	1,840	3.37
Hispanic (19)	56	0.10
Bangladeshi (10)	11	0.02
Burmese (2)	2	<0.01
Cambodian (62)	72	0.13
Chinese, ex. Taiwanese (123)	162	0.30
Filipino (231)	319	0.58
Indian (810)	899	1.65
Indonesian (3)	4	0.01
Japanese (15)	44	0.08
Korean (95)	135	0.25
Laotian (1)	1	<0.01
Nepalese (4)	4	0.01
Pakistani (35)	59	0.11
Sri Lankan (5)	9	0.02
Taiwanese (1)	1	<0.01
Thai (12)	18	0.03
Vietnamese (95)	110	0.20
Hawaii Native/Pacific Islander (18)	73	0.13
Not Hispanic (18)	65	0.12
Hispanic (0)	8	0.01
Guamanian/Chamorro (14)	19	0.03
Native Hawaiian (0)	9	0.02
Samoan (0)	2	<0.01
White (44,190)	45,446	83.26
Not Hispanic (42,197)	43,161	79.08
Hispanic (1,993)	2,285	4.19

Brookhaven

Place Type: Borough
County: Delaware
Population: 8,006†

Ancestry‡	Population	%
African, Sub-Saharan (40)	40	0.50
African (40)	40	0.50
American (166)	166	2.08
Austrian (0)	23	0.29
Brazilian (0)	14	0.18
British (74)	118	1.48
Canadian (24)	34	0.43
Croatian (14)	14	0.18
Danish (0)	10	0.13
Dutch (0)	85	1.07
English (167)	864	10.83
European (12)	12	0.15
French, ex. Basque (0)	38	0.48
French Canadian (8)	21	0.26
German (244)	1,289	16.15
Greek (72)	98	1.23
Hungarian (23)	23	0.29
Irish (674)	2,313	28.98
Italian (977)	2,304	28.87
Lithuanian (18)	45	0.56
Norwegian (0)	17	0.21
Pennsylvania German (22)	22	0.28
Polish (239)	617	7.73
Portuguese (17)	17	0.21
Russian (17)	71	0.89
Scotch-Irish (66)	142	1.78
Scottish (0)	66	0.83
Serbian (11)	11	0.14
Slovene (0)	16	0.20
Swedish (0)	80	1.00
Swiss (0)	43	0.54
Turkish (54)	54	0.68
Ukrainian (85)	229	2.87
Welsh (0)	84	1.05

Hispanic Origin	Population	%
Hispanic or Latino (of any race)	161	2.01
Central American, ex. Mexican	16	0.20
Costa Rican	1	0.01
Panamanian	3	0.04
Salvadoran	12	0.15
Cuban	4	0.05
Dominican Republic	5	0.06
Mexican	32	0.40
Puerto Rican	71	0.89
South American	22	0.27
Colombian	11	0.14
Ecuadorian	2	0.02
Peruvian	5	0.06
Venezuelan	4	0.05
Other Hispanic or Latino	11	0.14

Race*	Population	%
African-American/Black (299)	355	4.43
Not Hispanic (291)	338	4.22
Hispanic (8)	17	0.21
American Indian/Alaska Native (6)	40	0.50
Not Hispanic (6)	33	0.41
Hispanic (0)	7	0.09
Blackfeet (0)	3	0.04
Cherokee (0)	11	0.14
Choctaw (0)	1	0.01
Lumbee (1)	1	0.01
Asian (152)	193	2.41
Not Hispanic (151)	192	2.40
Hispanic (1)	1	0.01
Cambodian (3)	5	0.06
Chinese, ex. Taiwanese (21)	28	0.35
Filipino (12)	24	0.30
Indian (56)	62	0.77
Indonesian (1)	3	0.04
Japanese (4)	6	0.07
Korean (10)	10	0.12
Laotian (7)	7	0.09
Malaysian (1)	1	0.01
Pakistani (8)	8	0.10
Sri Lankan (0)	1	0.01
Taiwanese (7)	7	0.09
Thai (1)	1	0.01
Vietnamese (15)	17	0.21
Hawaii Native/Pacific Islander (0)	2	0.02
Not Hispanic (0)	2	0.02
Guamanian/Chamorro (0)	2	0.02
White (7,394)	7,511	93.82
Not Hispanic (7,281)	7,380	92.18
Hispanic (113)	131	1.64

Broomall

Place Type: CDP
County: Delaware
Population: 10,789†

Ancestry‡	Population	%
American (279)	279	2.48
Arab (59)	78	0.69
Arab (53)	53	0.47
Lebanese (6)	25	0.22
Armenian (106)	125	1.11
Australian (0)	12	0.11
Austrian (0)	22	0.20
Canadian (5)	5	0.04
Croatian (36)	36	0.32
Czech (0)	9	0.08
Dutch (29)	216	1.92
Eastern European (38)	38	0.34
English (153)	929	8.25
European (64)	64	0.57
Finnish (5)	10	0.09
French, ex. Basque (21)	171	1.52
French Canadian (9)	38	0.34
German (234)	1,511	13.42
Greek (313)	373	3.31
Hungarian (7)	53	0.47
Iranian (216)	216	1.92
Irish (1,107)	2,859	25.40
Italian (1,949)	3,369	29.93
Latvian (9)	9	0.08
Lithuanian (0)	29	0.26
Norwegian (0)	35	0.31
Pennsylvania German (0)	12	0.11
Polish (220)	450	4.00
Romanian (16)	16	0.14
Russian (157)	219	1.95
Scotch-Irish (204)	329	2.92
Scottish (17)	220	1.95
Slavic (7)	7	0.06
Slovak (11)	43	0.38
Swedish (17)	36	0.32
Swiss (0)	30	0.27
Ukrainian (18)	37	0.33

*Notes: † The Census 2010 population figure is used to calculate the percentages in the Hispanic Origin and Race categories. Ancestry percentages are based on the 2006-2010 American Community Survey population (not shown); ‡ Numbers in parentheses indicate the number of people reporting a single ancestry; * Numbers in parentheses indicate the number of persons reporting this race alone, not in combination with any other race; Please refer to the Explanation of Data for more information.*

Welsh (22)	117	1.04

Hispanic Origin	Population	%
Hispanic or Latino (of any race)	146	1.35
Central American, ex. Mexican	8	0.07
Costa Rican	1	0.01
Guatemalan	2	0.02
Honduran	5	0.05
Cuban	6	0.06
Dominican Republic	4	0.04
Mexican	23	0.21
Puerto Rican	20	0.19
South American	56	0.52
Argentinean	10	0.09
Bolivian	4	0.04
Chilean	3	0.03
Colombian	4	0.04
Ecuadorian	15	0.14
Paraguayan	6	0.06
Peruvian	7	0.06
Uruguayan	1	0.01
Venezuelan	3	0.03
Other South American	3	0.03
Other Hispanic or Latino	29	0.27

Race*	Population	%
African-American/Black (199)	225	2.09
Not Hispanic (196)	222	2.06
Hispanic (3)	3	0.03
American Indian/Alaska Native (2)	21	0.19
Not Hispanic (2)	16	0.15
Hispanic (0)	5	0.05
Cherokee (0)	3	0.03
Asian (832)	899	8.33
Not Hispanic (829)	895	8.30
Hispanic (3)	4	0.04
Bangladeshi (7)	7	0.06
Chinese, ex. Taiwanese (154)	166	1.54
Filipino (10)	21	0.19
Indian (186)	204	1.89
Japanese (13)	21	0.19
Korean (280)	291	2.70
Laotian (12)	13	0.12
Pakistani (9)	9	0.08
Taiwanese (14)	14	0.13
Thai (10)	12	0.11
Vietnamese (118)	120	1.11
Hawaii Native/Pacific Islander (0)	2	0.02
Not Hispanic (0)	2	0.02
White (9,613)	9,694	89.85
Not Hispanic (9,515)	9,587	88.86
Hispanic (98)	107	0.99

Buckingham

Place Type: Township
County: Bucks
Population: 20,075†

Ancestry‡	Population	%
African, Sub-Saharan (8)	8	0.04
African (8)	8	0.04
Albanian (0)	12	0.06
American (1,020)	1,020	5.23
Arab (70)	97	0.50
Egyptian (0)	11	0.06
Lebanese (70)	86	0.44
Armenian (22)	53	0.27
Austrian (31)	154	0.79
Brazilian (52)	52	0.27
British (54)	81	0.42
Canadian (10)	25	0.13
Croatian (0)	14	0.07
Czech (16)	38	0.19
Czechoslovakian (120)	147	0.75
Danish (11)	61	0.31
Dutch (10)	262	1.34
Eastern European (57)	85	0.44
English (554)	2,504	12.84
European (329)	385	1.97
French, ex. Basque (26)	358	1.84
French Canadian (44)	108	0.55
German (1,210)	4,042	20.72
Greek (22)	78	0.40
Hungarian (173)	402	2.06
Irish (1,342)	5,562	28.52
Israeli (0)	32	0.16
Italian (1,597)	4,448	22.81
Lithuanian (38)	145	0.74
Northern European (16)	16	0.08
Norwegian (86)	201	1.03
Pennsylvania German (134)	178	0.91
Polish (477)	1,567	8.03
Portuguese (13)	50	0.26
Romanian (23)	52	0.27
Russian (421)	854	4.38
Scotch-Irish (87)	389	1.99
Scottish (147)	392	2.01
Slavic (27)	42	0.22
Slovak (40)	149	0.76
Swedish (58)	191	0.98
Swiss (0)	97	0.50
Turkish (0)	45	0.23
Ukrainian (159)	260	1.33
Welsh (88)	368	1.89
West Indian, ex. Hispanic (168)	214	1.10
Jamaican (46)	92	0.47
West Indian (122)	122	0.63
Yugoslavian (0)	10	0.05

Hispanic Origin	Population	%
Hispanic or Latino (of any race)	490	2.44
Central American, ex. Mexican	42	0.21
Costa Rican	2	0.01
Guatemalan	12	0.06
Honduran	7	0.03
Panamanian	8	0.04
Salvadoran	13	0.06
Cuban	84	0.42
Dominican Republic	8	0.04
Mexican	85	0.42
Puerto Rican	128	0.64
South American	67	0.33
Argentinean	9	0.04
Chilean	5	0.02
Colombian	28	0.14
Ecuadorian	4	0.02
Peruvian	11	0.05
Uruguayan	3	0.01
Venezuelan	7	0.03
Other Hispanic or Latino	76	0.38

Race*	Population	%
African-American/Black (215)	287	1.43
Not Hispanic (210)	268	1.33
Hispanic (5)	19	0.09
American Indian/Alaska Native (27)	82	0.41
Not Hispanic (22)	64	0.32
Hispanic (5)	18	0.09
Alaska Athabascan *(Ala. Nat.)* (1)	1	<0.01
Apache (3)	3	0.01
Blackfeet (2)	9	0.04
Central American Ind. (1)	1	<0.01
Cherokee (2)	8	0.04
Delaware (0)	12	0.06
Hopi (5)	5	0.02
Iroquois (4)	5	0.02
Mexican American Ind. (1)	1	<0.01
South American Ind. (1)	6	0.03
Asian (689)	819	4.08
Not Hispanic (687)	811	4.04
Hispanic (2)	8	0.04
Bangladeshi (4)	4	0.02
Cambodian (0)	2	0.01
Chinese, ex. Taiwanese (218)	247	1.23
Filipino (46)	67	0.33
Indian (231)	269	1.34
Japanese (7)	14	0.07
Korean (123)	153	0.76
Pakistani (7)	8	0.04
Taiwanese (22)	22	0.11
Thai (5)	8	0.04
Vietnamese (13)	16	0.08
Hawaii Native/Pacific Islander (1)	6	0.03
Not Hispanic (1)	5	0.02
Hispanic (0)	1	<0.01
Guamanian/Chamorro (0)	1	<0.01
Native Hawaiian (1)	1	<0.01
White (18,821)	19,046	94.87
Not Hispanic (18,431)	18,623	92.77
Hispanic (390)	423	2.11

Bushkill

Place Type: Township
County: Northampton
Population: 8,178†

Ancestry‡	Population	%
American (409)	409	5.09
Armenian (30)	30	0.37
Austrian (116)	223	2.77
Belgian (0)	19	0.24
Brazilian (0)	16	0.20
Croatian (0)	21	0.26
Czech (0)	46	0.57
Czechoslovakian (0)	39	0.49
Dutch (84)	413	5.14
English (141)	710	8.83
European (37)	37	0.46
French, ex. Basque (50)	157	1.95
German (1,420)	2,983	37.11
Hungarian (104)	298	3.71
Irish (204)	1,089	13.55
Italian (392)	1,014	12.62
Latvian (0)	28	0.35
Lithuanian (8)	26	0.32
Pennsylvania German (365)	465	5.79
Polish (256)	875	10.89
Portuguese (0)	16	0.20
Russian (32)	75	0.93
Scotch-Irish (21)	110	1.37
Scottish (22)	122	1.52
Slavic (0)	11	0.14
Slovak (48)	190	2.36
Swedish (0)	43	0.53
Swiss (0)	8	0.10
Ukrainian (24)	55	0.68
Welsh (13)	118	1.47
Yugoslavian (10)	10	0.12

Hispanic Origin	Population	%
Hispanic or Latino (of any race)	167	2.04
Central American, ex. Mexican	15	0.18
Guatemalan	5	0.06
Honduran	1	0.01
Nicaraguan	4	0.05
Panamanian	5	0.06
Cuban	11	0.13
Dominican Republic	6	0.07
Mexican	18	0.22
Puerto Rican	69	0.84
South American	25	0.31
Argentinean	2	0.02
Chilean	1	0.01
Colombian	20	0.24
Peruvian	1	0.01
Venezuelan	1	0.01
Other Hispanic or Latino	23	0.28

Race*	Population	%
African-American/Black (59)	79	0.97
Not Hispanic (55)	73	0.89
Hispanic (4)	6	0.07
American Indian/Alaska Native (7)	29	0.35
Not Hispanic (7)	28	0.34
Hispanic (0)	1	0.01
Blackfeet (0)	2	0.02
Cherokee (0)	5	0.06
Cree (1)	1	0.01

SECTION TWO

*Notes: † The Census 2010 population figure is used to calculate the percentages in the Hispanic Origin and Race categories. Ancestry percentages are based on the 2006-2010 American Community Survey population (not shown); ‡ Numbers in parentheses indicate the number of people reporting a single ancestry; * Numbers in parentheses indicate the number of persons reporting this race alone, not in combination with any other race; Please refer to the Explanation of Data for more information.*

Delaware (0)	7	0.09
Iroquois (3)	4	0.05
Asian (76)	110	1.35
Not Hispanic (74)	108	1.32
Hispanic (2)	2	0.02
Chinese, ex. Taiwanese (11)	16	0.20
Filipino (8)	18	0.22
Indian (35)	42	0.51
Indonesian (0)	3	0.04
Japanese (2)	7	0.09
Korean (9)	10	0.12
Pakistani (3)	3	0.04
Vietnamese (2)	9	0.11
Hawaii Native/Pacific Islander (0)	6	0.07
Not Hispanic (0)	6	0.07
Native Hawaiian (0)	4	0.05
White (7,918)	8,002	97.85
Not Hispanic (7,791)	7,864	96.16
Hispanic (127)	138	1.69

Butler

Place Type: City
County: Butler
Population: 13,757†

Ancestry‡	Population	%
American (687)	687	4.89
Arab (10)	18	0.13
Syrian (10)	18	0.13
Austrian (0)	13	0.09
British (0)	38	0.27
Canadian (25)	91	0.65
Croatian (7)	65	0.46
Czech (9)	9	0.06
Czechoslovakian (58)	69	0.49
Danish (11)	25	0.18
Dutch (9)	313	2.23
Eastern European (17)	17	0.12
English (286)	1,471	10.48
European (46)	46	0.33
Finnish (0)	37	0.26
French, ex. Basque (10)	372	2.65
French Canadian (63)	95	0.68
German (1,702)	5,957	42.44
Greek (87)	109	0.78
Hungarian (21)	150	1.07
Irish (365)	3,178	22.64
Israeli (28)	28	0.20
Italian (446)	1,727	12.30
Lithuanian (16)	142	1.01
Norwegian (43)	43	0.31
Pennsylvania German (62)	132	0.94
Polish (259)	808	5.76
Portuguese (8)	8	0.06
Romanian (15)	15	0.11
Russian (10)	98	0.70
Scandinavian (0)	32	0.23
Scotch-Irish (238)	601	4.28
Scottish (51)	172	1.23
Slavic (0)	8	0.06
Slovak (0)	175	1.25
Slovene (13)	13	0.09
Swedish (1)	161	1.15
Swiss (0)	22	0.16
Ukrainian (63)	156	1.11
Welsh (16)	110	0.78
Yugoslavian (23)	23	0.16

Hispanic Origin	Population	%
Hispanic or Latino (of any race)	331	2.41
Central American, ex. Mexican	9	0.07
Guatemalan	1	0.01
Panamanian	3	0.02
Salvadoran	5	0.04
Cuban	6	0.04
Dominican Republic	4	0.03
Mexican	118	0.86
Puerto Rican	147	1.07
South American	5	0.04
Argentinean	1	0.01
Bolivian	1	0.01
Colombian	2	0.01
Peruvian	1	0.01
Other Hispanic or Latino	42	0.31

Race*	Population	%
African-American/Black (372)	549	3.99
Not Hispanic (357)	530	3.85
Hispanic (15)	19	0.14
American Indian/Alaska Native (34)	125	0.91
Not Hispanic (27)	116	0.84
Hispanic (7)	9	0.07
Apache (0)	1	0.01
Blackfeet (0)	11	0.08
Cherokee (6)	28	0.20
Cheyenne (0)	1	0.01
Chippewa (0)	1	0.01
Choctaw (0)	1	0.01
Creek (0)	2	0.01
Crow (0)	2	0.01
Iroquois (2)	7	0.05
Mexican American Ind. (2)	2	0.01
Sioux (2)	6	0.04
Tlingit-Haida *(Alaska Native)* (0)	1	0.01
Tohono O'Odham (0)	1	0.01
Asian (66)	102	0.74
Not Hispanic (65)	99	0.72
Hispanic (1)	3	0.02
Chinese, ex. Taiwanese (26)	33	0.24
Filipino (16)	25	0.18
Indian (6)	9	0.07
Japanese (2)	9	0.07
Korean (8)	12	0.09
Thai (3)	5	0.04
Vietnamese (3)	3	0.02
Hawaii Native/Pacific Islander (5)	22	0.16
Not Hispanic (5)	21	0.15
Hispanic (0)	1	0.01
Guamanian/Chamorro (1)	2	0.01
Native Hawaiian (3)	7	0.05
Samoan (1)	7	0.05
Tongan (0)	1	0.01
White (12,874)	13,163	95.68
Not Hispanic (12,671)	12,945	94.10
Hispanic (203)	218	1.58

Butler

Place Type: Township
County: Butler
Population: 17,248†

Ancestry‡	Population	%
African, Sub-Saharan (30)	45	0.26
African (30)	45	0.26
American (595)	595	3.43
Arab (24)	52	0.30
Egyptian (8)	8	0.05
Syrian (16)	44	0.25
Austrian (39)	145	0.84
Belgian (12)	116	0.67
British (9)	47	0.27
Carpatho Rusyn (7)	14	0.08
Croatian (30)	151	0.87
Czech (38)	231	1.33
Czechoslovakian (0)	16	0.09
Danish (0)	9	0.05
Dutch (30)	282	1.63
Eastern European (11)	11	0.06
English (447)	2,005	11.56
European (62)	62	0.36
French, ex. Basque (17)	497	2.86
French Canadian (0)	32	0.18
German (2,108)	7,354	42.39
Greek (23)	101	0.58
Hungarian (79)	361	2.08
Irish (524)	3,186	18.37
Italian (711)	2,374	13.68
Lithuanian (29)	77	0.44
Norwegian (9)	50	0.29
Pennsylvania German (29)	60	0.35
Polish (458)	1,560	8.99
Romanian (7)	25	0.14
Russian (80)	577	3.33
Scandinavian (20)	30	0.17
Scotch-Irish (163)	927	5.34
Scottish (162)	680	3.92
Serbian (12)	21	0.12
Slavic (9)	38	0.22
Slovak (314)	791	4.56
Slovene (33)	40	0.23
Swedish (7)	31	0.18
Swiss (21)	103	0.59
Turkish (0)	26	0.15
Ukrainian (328)	543	3.13
Welsh (11)	331	1.91
Yugoslavian (11)	21	0.12

Hispanic Origin	Population	%
Hispanic or Latino (of any race)	174	1.01
Central American, ex. Mexican	8	0.05
Guatemalan	6	0.03
Honduran	1	0.01
Salvadoran	1	0.01
Cuban	3	0.02
Dominican Republic	2	0.01
Mexican	82	0.48
Puerto Rican	45	0.26
South American	7	0.04
Colombian	1	0.01
Ecuadorian	4	0.02
Paraguayan	1	0.01
Peruvian	1	0.01
Other Hispanic or Latino	27	0.16

Race*	Population	%
African-American/Black (145)	218	1.26
Not Hispanic (141)	213	1.23
Hispanic (4)	5	0.03
American Indian/Alaska Native (13)	70	0.41
Not Hispanic (12)	67	0.39
Hispanic (1)	3	0.02
Apache (1)	5	0.03
Blackfeet (0)	3	0.02
Cherokee (1)	17	0.10
Chippewa (2)	3	0.02
Comanche (2)	2	0.01
Delaware (2)	2	0.01
Iroquois (0)	3	0.02
Ottawa (0)	1	0.01
Seminole (0)	2	0.01
Sioux (0)	1	0.01
Asian (85)	125	0.72
Not Hispanic (85)	120	0.70
Hispanic (0)	5	0.03
Chinese, ex. Taiwanese (11)	17	0.10
Filipino (13)	24	0.14
Indian (22)	29	0.17
Indonesian (1)	3	0.02
Japanese (3)	11	0.06
Korean (7)	11	0.06
Pakistani (2)	2	0.01
Taiwanese (1)	1	0.01
Thai (0)	1	0.01
Vietnamese (25)	29	0.17
Hawaii Native/Pacific Islander (3)	7	0.04
Not Hispanic (3)	5	0.03
Hispanic (0)	2	0.01
Guamanian/Chamorro (2)	3	0.02
Native Hawaiian (0)	1	0.01
White (16,792)	16,940	98.21
Not Hispanic (16,662)	16,801	97.41
Hispanic (130)	139	0.81

Butler

Place Type: Township
County: Luzerne
Population: 9,221†

*Notes: † The Census 2010 population figure is used to calculate the percentages in the Hispanic Origin and Race categories. Ancestry percentages are based on the 2006-2010 American Community Survey population (not shown); ‡ Numbers in parentheses indicate the number of people reporting a single ancestry; * Numbers in parentheses indicate the number of persons reporting this race alone, not in combination with any other race; Please refer to the Explanation of Data for more information.*

Ancestry‡	Population	%
African, Sub-Saharan (13)	13	0.15
African (6)	6	0.07
Other Sub-Saharan African (7)	7	0.08
American (175)	175	1.99
Arab (0)	62	0.70
Lebanese (0)	52	0.59
Syrian (0)	10	0.11
Austrian (85)	230	2.61
Brazilian (33)	33	0.37
British (0)	32	0.36
Czech (17)	93	1.06
Czechoslovakian (34)	46	0.52
Danish (15)	15	0.17
Dutch (62)	583	6.62
Eastern European (31)	31	0.35
English (73)	499	5.67
European (18)	18	0.20
Finnish (0)	9	0.10
French, ex. Basque (0)	37	0.42
German (615)	2,080	23.62
Greek (0)	49	0.56
Hungarian (0)	25	0.28
Irish (250)	1,877	21.32
Italian (1,040)	2,619	29.74
Lithuanian (81)	175	1.99
Norwegian (41)	127	1.44
Pennsylvania German (60)	95	1.08
Polish (677)	1,597	18.14
Portuguese (17)	17	0.19
Romanian (78)	78	0.89
Russian (0)	58	0.66
Scotch-Irish (0)	151	1.71
Scottish (49)	68	0.77
Slavic (0)	76	0.86
Slovak (297)	682	7.74
Swedish (0)	47	0.53
Swiss (0)	56	0.64
Ukrainian (32)	65	0.74
Welsh (0)	102	1.16
West Indian, ex. Hispanic (0)	6	0.07
Jamaican (0)	6	0.07
Yugoslavian (17)	17	0.19

Hispanic Origin	Population	%
Hispanic or Latino (of any race)	269	2.92
Central American, ex. Mexican	6	0.07
Guatemalan	1	0.01
Honduran	2	0.02
Salvadoran	3	0.03
Cuban	7	0.08
Dominican Republic	49	0.53
Mexican	39	0.42
Puerto Rican	110	1.19
South American	29	0.31
Bolivian	2	0.02
Colombian	6	0.07
Ecuadorian	4	0.04
Peruvian	6	0.07
Venezuelan	8	0.09
Other South American	3	0.03
Other Hispanic or Latino	29	0.31

Race*	Population	%
African-American/Black (419)	462	5.01
Not Hispanic (393)	426	4.62
Hispanic (26)	36	0.39
American Indian/Alaska Native (17)	48	0.52
Not Hispanic (10)	30	0.33
Hispanic (7)	18	0.20
Apache (0)	3	0.03
Cherokee (1)	4	0.04
Chippewa (1)	1	0.01
Choctaw (1)	2	0.02
Creek (0)	1	0.01
Delaware (0)	2	0.02
Iroquois (0)	1	0.01
Asian (97)	121	1.31
Not Hispanic (97)	121	1.31
Bhutanese (1)	1	0.01
Cambodian (1)	1	0.01
Chinese, ex. Taiwanese (7)	12	0.13
Filipino (10)	17	0.18
Indian (46)	49	0.53
Indonesian (0)	1	0.01
Japanese (3)	4	0.04
Korean (9)	19	0.21
Pakistani (9)	9	0.10
Thai (1)	1	0.01
Vietnamese (2)	3	0.03
Hawaii Native/Pacific Islander (1)	6	0.07
Not Hispanic (0)	3	0.03
Hispanic (1)	3	0.03
Guamanian/Chamorro (1)	1	0.01
Native Hawaiian (0)	3	0.03
Samoan (0)	1	0.01
White (8,490)	8,567	92.91
Not Hispanic (8,369)	8,431	91.43
Hispanic (121)	136	1.47

Caln

Place Type: Township
County: Chester
Population: 13,817†

Ancestry‡	Population	%
African, Sub-Saharan (132)	171	1.26
African (61)	100	0.74
Other Sub-Saharan African (71)	71	0.52
American (360)	360	2.65
Arab (13)	13	0.10
Lebanese (13)	13	0.10
Armenian (11)	33	0.24
Austrian (0)	16	0.12
British (42)	54	0.40
Canadian (44)	58	0.43
Celtic (0)	36	0.26
Croatian (0)	30	0.22
Czech (9)	23	0.17
Danish (12)	12	0.09
Dutch (32)	196	1.44
Eastern European (13)	13	0.10
English (121)	1,260	9.27
European (41)	54	0.40
French, ex. Basque (49)	241	1.77
French Canadian (8)	48	0.35
German (543)	2,622	19.30
Greek (16)	46	0.34
Hungarian (15)	55	0.40
Irish (894)	3,519	25.90
Israeli (15)	31	0.23
Italian (869)	2,278	16.76
Lithuanian (64)	114	0.84
Norwegian (12)	74	0.54
Pennsylvania German (57)	70	0.52
Polish (313)	790	5.81
Russian (68)	185	1.36
Scandinavian (14)	53	0.39
Scotch-Irish (30)	125	0.92
Scottish (35)	110	0.81
Serbian (0)	16	0.12
Slavic (15)	51	0.38
Slovak (16)	76	0.56
Swedish (30)	131	0.96
Swiss (26)	65	0.48
Turkish (32)	32	0.24
Ukrainian (105)	133	0.98
Welsh (0)	104	0.77
West Indian, ex. Hispanic (0)	35	0.26
Jamaican (0)	35	0.26

Hispanic Origin	Population	%
Hispanic or Latino (of any race)	761	5.51
Central American, ex. Mexican	35	0.25
Costa Rican	5	0.04
Guatemalan	11	0.08
Honduran	8	0.06
Nicaraguan	3	0.02
Panamanian	1	0.01
Salvadoran	7	0.05
Cuban	15	0.11
Dominican Republic	11	0.08
Mexican	215	1.56
Puerto Rican	284	2.06
South American	130	0.94
Argentinean	17	0.12
Bolivian	9	0.07
Chilean	3	0.02
Colombian	52	0.38
Ecuadorian	32	0.23
Peruvian	4	0.03
Uruguayan	2	0.01
Venezuelan	11	0.08
Other Hispanic or Latino	71	0.51

Race*	Population	%
African-American/Black (2,239)	2,452	17.75
Not Hispanic (2,185)	2,362	17.09
Hispanic (54)	90	0.65
American Indian/Alaska Native (17)	76	0.55
Not Hispanic (16)	71	0.51
Hispanic (1)	5	0.04
Blackfeet (1)	1	0.01
Cherokee (5)	18	0.13
Chippewa (0)	1	0.01
Choctaw (1)	1	0.01
Delaware (0)	2	0.01
Iroquois (1)	1	0.01
Lumbee (1)	4	0.03
Asian (544)	589	4.26
Not Hispanic (540)	583	4.22
Hispanic (4)	6	0.04
Cambodian (9)	10	0.07
Chinese, ex. Taiwanese (80)	88	0.64
Filipino (101)	111	0.80
Indian (189)	197	1.43
Japanese (5)	9	0.07
Korean (31)	39	0.28
Laotian (13)	13	0.09
Pakistani (29)	31	0.22
Sri Lankan (5)	5	0.04
Taiwanese (1)	1	0.01
Thai (2)	3	0.02
Vietnamese (63)	67	0.48
Hawaii Native/Pacific Islander (8)	16	0.12
Not Hispanic (6)	8	0.06
Hispanic (2)	8	0.06
Fijian (1)	5	0.04
Guamanian/Chamorro (4)	4	0.03
Native Hawaiian (1)	3	0.02
White (10,460)	10,728	77.64
Not Hispanic (10,052)	10,268	74.31
Hispanic (408)	460	3.33

Camp Hill

Place Type: Borough
County: Cumberland
Population: 7,888†

Ancestry‡	Population	%
American (366)	366	4.67
Arab (13)	30	0.38
Arab (7)	7	0.09
Lebanese (6)	17	0.22
Syrian (0)	6	0.08
Austrian (111)	188	2.40
Belgian (0)	17	0.22
British (35)	105	1.34
Canadian (8)	8	0.10
Carpatho Rusyn (13)	13	0.17
Croatian (0)	20	0.26
Czech (0)	9	0.11
Czechoslovakian (0)	13	0.17
Dutch (52)	150	1.92
English (226)	1,011	12.91
European (173)	173	2.21
Finnish (0)	14	0.18
French, ex. Basque (104)	268	3.42

SECTION TWO

*Notes: † The Census 2010 population figure is used to calculate the percentages in the Hispanic Origin and Race categories. Ancestry percentages are based on the 2006-2010 American Community Survey population (not shown); ‡ Numbers in parentheses indicate the number of people reporting a single ancestry; * Numbers in parentheses indicate the number of persons reporting this race alone, not in combination with any other race; Please refer to the Explanation of Data for more information.*

Ancestry	Population	%
French Canadian (9)	22	0.28
German (915)	2,922	37.32
Greek (27)	68	0.87
Guyanese (28)	35	0.45
Hungarian (9)	66	0.84
Irish (275)	1,641	20.96
Italian (150)	510	6.51
Lithuanian (6)	77	0.98
Macedonian (26)	26	0.33
New Zealander (8)	8	0.10
Northern European (20)	20	0.26
Norwegian (0)	12	0.15
Pennsylvania German (28)	39	0.50
Polish (81)	364	4.65
Portuguese (0)	9	0.11
Romanian (0)	7	0.09
Russian (21)	167	2.13
Scotch-Irish (41)	220	2.81
Scottish (23)	248	3.17
Serbian (13)	13	0.17
Slavic (0)	38	0.49
Slovak (60)	137	1.75
Slovene (13)	32	0.41
Swedish (0)	48	0.61
Swiss (0)	21	0.27
Ukrainian (0)	25	0.32
Welsh (21)	262	3.35
Yugoslavian (111)	140	1.79

Hispanic Origin	Population	%
Hispanic or Latino (of any race)	211	2.67
Central American, ex. Mexican	29	0.37
Costa Rican	3	0.04
Guatemalan	12	0.15
Honduran	1	0.01
Panamanian	4	0.05
Salvadoran	8	0.10
Other Central American	1	0.01
Cuban	5	0.06
Dominican Republic	10	0.13
Mexican	64	0.81
Puerto Rican	59	0.75
South American	24	0.30
Argentinean	1	0.01
Chilean	1	0.01
Colombian	3	0.04
Ecuadorian	10	0.13
Peruvian	8	0.10
Uruguayan	1	0.01
Other Hispanic or Latino	20	0.25

Race*	Population	%
African-American/Black (141)	193	2.45
Not Hispanic (130)	175	2.22
Hispanic (11)	18	0.23
American Indian/Alaska Native (8)	27	0.34
Not Hispanic (6)	23	0.29
Hispanic (2)	4	0.05
Blackfeet (0)	3	0.04
Canadian/French Am. Ind. (0)	2	0.03
Cherokee (0)	3	0.04
Choctaw (0)	2	0.03
Delaware (1)	1	0.01
Osage (0)	3	0.04
Puget Sound Salish (1)	2	0.03
South American Ind. (2)	3	0.04
Asian (530)	593	7.52
Not Hispanic (528)	586	7.43
Hispanic (2)	7	0.09
Bangladeshi (0)	1	0.01
Burmese (4)	4	0.05
Cambodian (7)	7	0.09
Chinese, ex. Taiwanese (22)	32	0.41
Filipino (19)	29	0.37
Indian (346)	363	4.60
Indonesian (2)	3	0.04
Japanese (7)	12	0.15
Korean (25)	32	0.41
Laotian (4)	5	0.06
Pakistani (7)	8	0.10
Sri Lankan (5)	12	0.15
Taiwanese (1)	1	0.01
Thai (7)	15	0.19
Vietnamese (56)	68	0.86
Hawaii Native/Pacific Islander (0)	1	0.01
Not Hispanic (0)	1	0.01
Samoan (0)	1	0.01
White (7,007)	7,143	90.56
Not Hispanic (6,891)	7,001	88.76
Hispanic (116)	142	1.80

Canonsburg

Place Type: Borough
County: Washington
Population: 8,992†

Ancestry‡	Population	%
African, Sub-Saharan (42)	48	0.54
African (42)	48	0.54
American (144)	144	1.61
Arab (0)	6	0.07
Syrian (0)	6	0.07
Austrian (69)	83	0.93
Belgian (0)	10	0.11
British (0)	9	0.10
Canadian (14)	22	0.25
Croatian (8)	33	0.37
Czech (32)	52	0.58
Czechoslovakian (0)	8	0.09
Dutch (0)	50	0.56
English (134)	790	8.86
French, ex. Basque (10)	203	2.28
French Canadian (0)	12	0.13
German (321)	2,294	25.73
Greek (156)	258	2.89
Hungarian (9)	208	2.33
Irish (287)	1,362	15.27
Italian (763)	1,794	20.12
Lithuanian (15)	58	0.65
Pennsylvania German (14)	24	0.27
Polish (426)	1,275	14.30
Portuguese (0)	30	0.34
Russian (97)	304	3.41
Scotch-Irish (110)	695	7.79
Scottish (24)	214	2.40
Slovak (234)	364	4.08
Slovene (47)	134	1.50
Swiss (9)	81	0.91
Ukrainian (16)	37	0.41
Welsh (14)	127	1.42
Yugoslavian (0)	25	0.28

Hispanic Origin	Population	%
Hispanic or Latino (of any race)	162	1.80
Central American, ex. Mexican	11	0.12
Honduran	9	0.10
Panamanian	2	0.02
Cuban	2	0.02
Dominican Republic	3	0.03
Mexican	70	0.78
Puerto Rican	33	0.37
South American	12	0.13
Chilean	7	0.08
Colombian	2	0.02
Peruvian	2	0.02
Venezuelan	1	0.01
Other Hispanic or Latino	31	0.34

Race*	Population	%
African-American/Black (686)	907	10.09
Not Hispanic (674)	888	9.88
Hispanic (12)	19	0.21
American Indian/Alaska Native (13)	51	0.57
Not Hispanic (13)	51	0.57
Alaska Athabascan *(Ala. Nat.)* (0)	1	0.01
Apache (0)	3	0.03
Blackfeet (0)	1	0.01
Cherokee (2)	9	0.10
Creek (0)	1	0.01
Iroquois (1)	1	0.01
Navajo (1)	1	0.01
Sioux (3)	4	0.04
Asian (94)	131	1.46
Not Hispanic (94)	131	1.46
Bangladeshi (2)	2	0.02
Chinese, ex. Taiwanese (15)	17	0.19
Filipino (10)	25	0.28
Indian (38)	43	0.48
Indonesian (2)	6	0.07
Japanese (1)	6	0.07
Korean (15)	17	0.19
Thai (1)	4	0.04
Vietnamese (5)	7	0.08
Hawaii Native/Pacific Islander (1)	11	0.12
Not Hispanic (1)	11	0.12
Native Hawaiian (1)	1	0.01
Samoan (0)	7	0.08
White (7,857)	8,115	90.25
Not Hispanic (7,764)	8,011	89.09
Hispanic (93)	104	1.16

Canton

Place Type: Township
County: Washington
Population: 8,375†

Ancestry‡	Population	%
American (481)	481	5.68
Arab (14)	76	0.90
Lebanese (0)	62	0.73
Syrian (14)	14	0.17
Australian (15)	43	0.51
Belgian (0)	55	0.65
Croatian (0)	52	0.61
Czech (8)	38	0.45
Czechoslovakian (18)	18	0.21
Dutch (0)	269	3.17
English (268)	1,014	11.97
European (0)	3	0.04
Finnish (0)	69	0.81
French, ex. Basque (0)	187	2.21
French Canadian (13)	49	0.58
German (429)	2,430	28.68
Greek (0)	85	1.00
Hungarian (32)	59	0.70
Irish (292)	1,934	22.82
Italian (522)	1,323	15.61
Lithuanian (18)	31	0.37
Norwegian (0)	48	0.57
Pennsylvania German (0)	10	0.12
Polish (404)	1,107	13.06
Russian (0)	26	0.31
Scotch-Irish (254)	675	7.97
Scottish (0)	25	0.30
Serbian (9)	9	0.11
Slavic (0)	12	0.14
Slovak (38)	250	2.95
Slovene (14)	14	0.17
Swedish (17)	44	0.52
Swiss (0)	12	0.14
Ukrainian (35)	47	0.55
Welsh (38)	122	1.44

Hispanic Origin	Population	%
Hispanic or Latino (of any race)	88	1.05
Central American, ex. Mexican	10	0.12
Guatemalan	5	0.06
Honduran	3	0.04
Salvadoran	2	0.02
Cuban	1	0.01
Mexican	42	0.50
Puerto Rican	15	0.18
South American	2	0.02
Ecuadorian	2	0.02
Other Hispanic or Latino	18	0.21

Race*	Population	%
African-American/Black (254)	322	3.84

*Notes: † The Census 2010 population figure is used to calculate the percentages in the Hispanic Origin and Race categories. Ancestry percentages are based on the 2006-2010 American Community Survey population (not shown); ‡ Numbers in parentheses indicate the number of people reporting a single ancestry; * Numbers in parentheses indicate the number of persons reporting this race alone, not in combination with any other race; Please refer to the Explanation of Data for more information.*

Not Hispanic (248)	316	3.77
Hispanic (6)	6	0.07
American Indian/Alaska Native (7)	33	0.39
Not Hispanic (5)	31	0.37
Hispanic (2)	2	0.02
Blackfeet (0)	3	0.04
Cherokee (1)	11	0.13
Iroquois (0)	3	0.04
Sioux (0)	1	0.01
Asian (10)	23	0.27
Not Hispanic (10)	23	0.27
Filipino (3)	3	0.04
Japanese (2)	4	0.05
Korean (2)	7	0.08
Laotian (1)	1	0.01
Taiwanese (1)	1	0.01
Thai (0)	5	0.06
Vietnamese (1)	2	0.02
Hawaii Native/Pacific Islander (0)	4	0.05
Not Hispanic (0)	4	0.05
Native Hawaiian (0)	3	0.04
White (7,970)	8,080	96.48
Not Hispanic (7,908)	8,016	95.71
Hispanic (62)	64	0.76

Carbondale

Place Type: City
County: Lackawanna
Population: 8,891†

Ancestry‡	Population	%
American (273)	273	3.03
Australian (0)	8	0.09
Austrian (0)	19	0.21
British (0)	12	0.13
Carpatho Rusyn (29)	29	0.32
Croatian (5)	10	0.11
Czech (23)	34	0.38
Czechoslovakian (10)	10	0.11
Danish (6)	6	0.07
Dutch (15)	158	1.76
English (120)	892	9.91
European (32)	42	0.47
French, ex. Basque (0)	62	0.69
French Canadian (1)	2	0.02
German (341)	2,117	23.52
Greek (0)	23	0.26
Hungarian (0)	292	3.24
Irish (1,253)	3,237	35.96
Israeli (10)	10	0.11
Italian (874)	2,019	22.43
Lithuanian (9)	121	1.34
Norwegian (0)	43	0.48
Pennsylvania German (12)	19	0.21
Polish (301)	1,258	13.97
Portuguese (108)	108	1.20
Romanian (0)	25	0.28
Russian (59)	344	3.82
Scotch-Irish (0)	131	1.46
Scottish (36)	228	2.53
Slovak (59)	196	2.18
Swedish (0)	38	0.42
Swiss (0)	7	0.08
Ukrainian (0)	48	0.53
Welsh (50)	267	2.97

Hispanic Origin	Population	%
Hispanic or Latino (of any race)	274	3.08
Central American, ex. Mexican	18	0.20
Costa Rican	2	0.02
Guatemalan	2	0.02
Honduran	10	0.11
Nicaraguan	2	0.02
Salvadoran	2	0.02
Cuban	10	0.11
Dominican Republic	15	0.17
Mexican	36	0.40
Puerto Rican	147	1.65
South American	19	0.21
Argentinean	3	0.03
Bolivian	1	0.01
Colombian	3	0.03
Ecuadorian	1	0.01
Paraguayan	3	0.03
Peruvian	8	0.09
Other Hispanic or Latino	29	0.33

Race*	Population	%
African-American/Black (90)	158	1.78
Not Hispanic (89)	144	1.62
Hispanic (1)	14	0.16
American Indian/Alaska Native (14)	43	0.48
Not Hispanic (9)	33	0.37
Hispanic (5)	10	0.11
Blackfeet (0)	1	0.01
Canadian/French Am. Ind. (0)	1	0.01
Cherokee (0)	2	0.02
Choctaw (0)	1	0.01
Crow (0)	1	0.01
Delaware (0)	1	0.01
Iroquois (0)	4	0.04
Pueblo (5)	5	0.06
Seminole (2)	2	0.02
Sioux (0)	1	0.01
Tohono O'Odham (2)	2	0.02
Asian (33)	55	0.62
Not Hispanic (30)	52	0.58
Hispanic (3)	3	0.03
Chinese, ex. Taiwanese (12)	13	0.15
Filipino (4)	8	0.09
Indian (3)	6	0.07
Japanese (1)	5	0.06
Korean (3)	3	0.03
Pakistani (3)	7	0.08
Vietnamese (2)	8	0.09
Hawaii Native/Pacific Islander (2)	3	0.03
Not Hispanic (2)	2	0.02
Hispanic (0)	1	0.01
Native Hawaiian (1)	1	0.01
Samoan (0)	1	0.01
White (8,563)	8,690	97.74
Not Hispanic (8,376)	8,478	95.35
Hispanic (187)	212	2.38

Carlisle

Place Type: Borough
County: Cumberland
Population: 18,682†

Ancestry‡	Population	%
African, Sub-Saharan (74)	191	1.03
African (42)	130	0.70
South African (0)	15	0.08
Other Sub-Saharan African (32)	46	0.25
American (798)	798	4.31
Arab (52)	84	0.45
Moroccan (32)	32	0.17
Syrian (20)	52	0.28
Australian (18)	18	0.10
Austrian (0)	140	0.76
Belgian (11)	24	0.13
British (0)	63	0.34
Bulgarian (22)	22	0.12
Canadian (14)	85	0.46
Croatian (18)	118	0.64
Czech (36)	131	0.71
Czechoslovakian (0)	29	0.16
Danish (44)	73	0.39
Dutch (130)	536	2.89
Eastern European (30)	30	0.16
English (391)	1,634	8.82
Estonian (33)	33	0.18
European (357)	365	1.97
Finnish (0)	24	0.13
French, ex. Basque (12)	466	2.52
French Canadian (26)	82	0.44
German (2,218)	5,680	30.68
Greek (64)	150	0.81
Hungarian (56)	263	1.42
Irish (829)	2,945	15.91
Italian (408)	1,280	6.91
Lithuanian (25)	143	0.77
Maltese (35)	35	0.19
Norwegian (98)	174	0.94
Pennsylvania German (146)	211	1.14
Polish (161)	795	4.29
Portuguese (0)	15	0.08
Romanian (0)	26	0.14
Russian (49)	170	0.92
Scotch-Irish (275)	827	4.47
Scottish (194)	513	2.77
Slavic (0)	12	0.06
Slovak (17)	115	0.62
Slovene (12)	63	0.34
Swedish (29)	239	1.29
Swiss (39)	167	0.90
Ukrainian (26)	59	0.32
Welsh (150)	302	1.63
West Indian, ex. Hispanic (43)	58	0.31
Barbadian (13)	13	0.07
British West Indian (14)	14	0.08
Jamaican (12)	12	0.06
West Indian (4)	19	0.10
Yugoslavian (162)	162	0.87

Hispanic Origin	Population	%
Hispanic or Latino (of any race)	846	4.53
Central American, ex. Mexican	99	0.53
Costa Rican	1	0.01
Guatemalan	26	0.14
Honduran	17	0.09
Nicaraguan	2	0.01
Panamanian	24	0.13
Salvadoran	29	0.16
Cuban	19	0.10
Dominican Republic	36	0.19
Mexican	235	1.26
Puerto Rican	310	1.66
South American	89	0.48
Argentinean	15	0.08
Bolivian	6	0.03
Chilean	6	0.03
Colombian	23	0.12
Ecuadorian	6	0.03
Peruvian	16	0.09
Uruguayan	13	0.07
Venezuelan	4	0.02
Other Hispanic or Latino	58	0.31

Race*	Population	%
African-American/Black (1,547)	2,015	10.79
Not Hispanic (1,479)	1,894	10.14
Hispanic (68)	121	0.65
American Indian/Alaska Native (36)	128	0.69
Not Hispanic (20)	94	0.50
Hispanic (16)	34	0.18
Alaska Athabascan *(Ala. Nat.)* (1)	1	0.01
Aleut *(Alaska Native)* (0)	1	0.01
Apache (0)	1	0.01
Arapaho (0)	1	0.01
Blackfeet (1)	3	0.02
Cherokee (2)	23	0.12
Chippewa (0)	1	0.01
Choctaw (1)	1	0.01
Comanche (1)	1	0.01
Inupiat *(Alaska Native)* (0)	2	0.01
Iroquois (1)	1	0.01
Mexican American Ind. (8)	12	0.06
Navajo (2)	4	0.02
Seminole (1)	2	0.01
Sioux (1)	2	0.01
South American Ind. (5)	7	0.04
Asian (434)	574	3.07
Not Hispanic (431)	553	2.96
Hispanic (3)	21	0.11
Bangladeshi (4)	4	0.02
Cambodian (4)	9	0.05
Chinese, ex. Taiwanese (107)	128	0.69

*Notes: † The Census 2010 population figure is used to calculate the percentages in the Hispanic Origin and Race categories. Ancestry percentages are based on the 2006-2010 American Community Survey population (not shown); ‡ Numbers in parentheses indicate the number of people reporting a single ancestry; * Numbers in parentheses indicate the number of persons reporting this race alone, not in combination with any other race; Please refer to the Explanation of Data for more information.*

Filipino (44)	71	0.38
Indian (71)	92	0.49
Indonesian (1)	2	0.01
Japanese (9)	37	0.20
Korean (77)	94	0.50
Malaysian (3)	3	0.02
Nepalese (0)	1	0.01
Pakistani (3)	7	0.04
Sri Lankan (1)	1	0.01
Taiwanese (5)	6	0.03
Thai (2)	6	0.03
Vietnamese (82)	91	0.49
Hawaii Native/Pacific Islander (5)	23	0.12
Not Hispanic (5)	13	0.07
Hispanic (0)	10	0.05
Guamanian/Chamorro (0)	2	0.01
Native Hawaiian (1)	7	0.04
Samoan (3)	3	0.02
White (15,754)	16,336	87.44
Not Hispanic (15,333)	15,838	84.78
Hispanic (421)	498	2.67

Carnegie

Place Type: Borough
County: Allegheny
Population: 7,972†

Ancestry‡	Population	%
American (232)	232	2.91
Arab (32)	70	0.88
Lebanese (0)	12	0.15
Syrian (32)	58	0.73
Austrian (0)	15	0.19
Belgian (0)	22	0.28
Bulgarian (15)	15	0.19
Canadian (0)	11	0.14
Croatian (40)	77	0.97
Czech (33)	55	0.69
Czechoslovakian (9)	9	0.11
Dutch (0)	45	0.56
Eastern European (11)	11	0.14
English (120)	558	7.00
European (47)	47	0.59
French, ex. Basque (22)	192	2.41
German (634)	2,508	31.46
Greek (29)	102	1.28
Hungarian (6)	60	0.75
Irish (327)	1,679	21.06
Italian (570)	1,853	23.24
Lithuanian (26)	75	0.94
Norwegian (12)	35	0.44
Polish (343)	1,169	14.66
Russian (44)	116	1.45
Scotch-Irish (82)	394	4.94
Scottish (21)	85	1.07
Serbian (0)	11	0.14
Slavic (0)	5	0.06
Slovak (88)	130	1.63
Slovene (14)	55	0.69
Swedish (0)	28	0.35
Swiss (12)	40	0.50
Ukrainian (138)	429	5.38
Welsh (12)	89	1.12
Yugoslavian (12)	22	0.28

Hispanic Origin	Population	%
Hispanic or Latino (of any race)	130	1.63
Central American, ex. Mexican	8	0.10
Honduran	6	0.08
Nicaraguan	1	0.01
Salvadoran	1	0.01
Mexican	60	0.75
Puerto Rican	27	0.34
South American	12	0.15
Argentinean	2	0.03
Chilean	6	0.08
Colombian	1	0.01
Paraguayan	2	0.03
Peruvian	1	0.01
Other Hispanic or Latino	23	0.29

Race*	Population	%
African-American/Black (589)	735	9.22
Not Hispanic (584)	718	9.01
Hispanic (5)	17	0.21
American Indian/Alaska Native (13)	44	0.55
Not Hispanic (13)	39	0.49
Hispanic (0)	5	0.06
Blackfeet (0)	1	0.01
Cherokee (4)	13	0.16
Delaware (1)	1	0.01
South American Ind. (1)	1	0.01
Tohono O'Odham (0)	1	0.01
Asian (129)	169	2.12
Not Hispanic (129)	165	2.07
Hispanic (0)	4	0.05
Bhutanese (10)	10	0.13
Burmese (7)	7	0.09
Chinese, ex. Taiwanese (12)	17	0.21
Filipino (9)	20	0.25
Indian (71)	81	1.02
Indonesian (2)	2	0.03
Japanese (0)	2	0.03
Korean (2)	8	0.10
Nepalese (5)	5	0.06
Pakistani (3)	3	0.04
Sri Lankan (1)	1	0.01
Taiwanese (2)	2	0.03
Thai (3)	5	0.06
Vietnamese (1)	1	0.01
Hawaii Native/Pacific Islander (6)	13	0.16
Not Hispanic (6)	13	0.16
Guamanian/Chamorro (0)	1	0.01
Native Hawaiian (1)	3	0.04
White (6,988)	7,193	90.23
Not Hispanic (6,909)	7,090	88.94
Hispanic (79)	103	1.29

Carnot-Moon

Place Type: CDP
County: Allegheny
Population: 11,372†

Ancestry‡	Population	%
American (405)	405	3.59
Arab (67)	191	1.69
Arab (15)	15	0.13
Lebanese (52)	176	1.56
Australian (19)	25	0.22
Austrian (0)	57	0.51
Belgian (0)	37	0.33
Brazilian (41)	41	0.36
Canadian (16)	16	0.14
Croatian (0)	122	1.08
Czech (85)	151	1.34
Dutch (31)	129	1.14
English (117)	886	7.86
European (89)	102	0.90
Finnish (13)	28	0.25
French, ex. Basque (23)	249	2.21
German (1,065)	3,804	33.73
Greek (49)	130	1.15
Hungarian (69)	126	1.12
Iranian (9)	22	0.20
Irish (658)	2,713	24.05
Italian (450)	1,946	17.25
Lithuanian (6)	28	0.25
Norwegian (16)	24	0.21
Polish (335)	1,122	9.95
Portuguese (15)	15	0.13
Russian (50)	229	2.03
Scandinavian (13)	13	0.12
Scotch-Irish (103)	293	2.60
Scottish (107)	173	1.53
Serbian (33)	83	0.74
Slavic (11)	11	0.10
Slovak (60)	316	2.80
Swedish (16)	76	0.67
Swiss (0)	57	0.51
Turkish (10)	20	0.18
Ukrainian (73)	188	1.67
Welsh (4)	213	1.89
West Indian, ex. Hispanic (13)	13	0.12
Jamaican (13)	13	0.12

Hispanic Origin	Population	%
Hispanic or Latino (of any race)	285	2.51
Central American, ex. Mexican	27	0.24
Guatemalan	6	0.05
Honduran	5	0.04
Panamanian	4	0.04
Salvadoran	12	0.11
Cuban	10	0.09
Dominican Republic	1	0.01
Mexican	120	1.06
Puerto Rican	36	0.32
South American	41	0.36
Argentinean	7	0.06
Bolivian	3	0.03
Chilean	2	0.02
Colombian	3	0.03
Ecuadorian	6	0.05
Paraguayan	5	0.04
Peruvian	8	0.07
Uruguayan	1	0.01
Venezuelan	6	0.05
Other Hispanic or Latino	50	0.44

Race*	Population	%
African-American/Black (731)	870	7.65
Not Hispanic (708)	844	7.42
Hispanic (23)	26	0.23
American Indian/Alaska Native (13)	57	0.50
Not Hispanic (13)	53	0.47
Hispanic (0)	4	0.04
Apache (0)	1	0.01
Blackfeet (0)	1	0.01
Cherokee (2)	12	0.11
Chippewa (1)	1	0.01
Choctaw (0)	1	0.01
Delaware (0)	3	0.03
Iroquois (4)	4	0.04
Navajo (0)	1	0.01
Seminole (0)	1	0.01
South American Ind. (0)	2	0.02
Asian (400)	459	4.04
Not Hispanic (398)	457	4.02
Hispanic (2)	2	0.02
Cambodian (1)	4	0.04
Chinese, ex. Taiwanese (88)	90	0.79
Filipino (33)	52	0.46
Indian (169)	183	1.61
Indonesian (0)	1	0.01
Japanese (7)	22	0.19
Korean (18)	24	0.21
Malaysian (3)	3	0.03
Nepalese (1)	1	0.01
Pakistani (53)	55	0.48
Sri Lankan (1)	1	0.01
Taiwanese (4)	4	0.04
Thai (2)	5	0.04
Vietnamese (16)	16	0.14
Hawaii Native/Pacific Islander (0)	9	0.08
Not Hispanic (0)	7	0.06
Hispanic (0)	2	0.02
Native Hawaiian (0)	3	0.03
White (9,867)	10,070	88.55
Not Hispanic (9,715)	9,902	87.07
Hispanic (152)	168	1.48

Castle Shannon

Place Type: Borough
County: Allegheny
Population: 8,316†

Ancestry‡	Population	%
African, Sub-Saharan (10)	10	0.12

*Notes: † The Census 2010 population figure is used to calculate the percentages in the Hispanic Origin and Race categories. Ancestry percentages are based on the 2006-2010 American Community Survey population (not shown); ‡ Numbers in parentheses indicate the number of people reporting a single ancestry; * Numbers in parentheses indicate the number of persons reporting this race alone, not in combination with any other race; Please refer to the Explanation of Data for more information.*

Ancestry	Population	%
Ghanaian (10)	10	0.12
American (530)	530	6.38
Arab (81)	92	1.11
Arab (51)	51	0.61
Lebanese (15)	26	0.31
Syrian (15)	15	0.18
Austrian (0)	59	0.71
Belgian (0)	13	0.16
British (0)	12	0.14
Croatian (9)	64	0.77
Czech (0)	21	0.25
Czechoslovakian (15)	39	0.47
Dutch (0)	74	0.89
English (67)	757	9.12
European (38)	38	0.46
Finnish (0)	13	0.16
French, ex. Basque (0)	164	1.98
German (619)	3,312	39.90
Greek (28)	149	1.79
Hungarian (24)	103	1.24
Irish (446)	2,117	25.50
Israeli (0)	26	0.31
Italian (341)	1,336	16.09
Lithuanian (42)	80	0.96
Norwegian (0)	28	0.34
Polish (357)	1,076	12.96
Portuguese (0)	10	0.12
Romanian (10)	54	0.65
Russian (181)	205	2.47
Scotch-Irish (48)	235	2.83
Scottish (15)	305	3.67
Serbian (0)	13	0.16
Slavic (0)	10	0.12
Slovak (41)	438	5.28
Slovene (10)	26	0.31
Swedish (12)	58	0.70
Swiss (0)	14	0.17
Turkish (67)	67	0.81
Ukrainian (43)	135	1.63
Welsh (12)	122	1.47

Hispanic Origin	Population	%
Hispanic or Latino (of any race)	94	1.13
Central American, ex. Mexican	12	0.14
Costa Rican	3	0.04
Guatemalan	6	0.07
Honduran	3	0.04
Cuban	7	0.08
Mexican	25	0.30
Puerto Rican	19	0.23
South American	21	0.25
Argentinean	4	0.05
Chilean	5	0.06
Colombian	4	0.05
Ecuadorian	1	0.01
Peruvian	6	0.07
Venezuelan	1	0.01
Other Hispanic or Latino	10	0.12

Race*	Population	%
African-American/Black (169)	220	2.65
Not Hispanic (167)	217	2.61
Hispanic (2)	3	0.04
American Indian/Alaska Native (3)	21	0.25
Not Hispanic (1)	19	0.23
Hispanic (2)	2	0.02
Cherokee (0)	2	0.02
Mexican American Ind. (2)	2	0.02
Osage (1)	1	0.01
Sioux (0)	1	0.01
Asian (199)	241	2.90
Not Hispanic (199)	241	2.90
Bhutanese (41)	51	0.61
Burmese (21)	25	0.30
Cambodian (2)	4	0.05
Chinese, ex. Taiwanese (10)	14	0.17
Filipino (8)	15	0.18
Indian (37)	43	0.52
Indonesian (1)	1	0.01
Japanese (0)	5	0.06
Korean (5)	10	0.12
Nepalese (25)	36	0.43
Pakistani (9)	9	0.11
Thai (2)	2	0.02
Vietnamese (21)	29	0.35
Hawaii Native/Pacific Islander (0)	5	0.06
Not Hispanic (0)	5	0.06
Native Hawaiian (0)	2	0.02
White (7,806)	7,897	94.96
Not Hispanic (7,751)	7,837	94.24
Hispanic (55)	60	0.72

Cecil

Place Type: Township
County: Washington
Population: 11,271†

Ancestry‡	Population	%
Alsatian (0)	12	0.11
American (293)	293	2.66
Arab (20)	58	0.53
Lebanese (20)	47	0.43
Syrian (0)	11	0.10
Austrian (0)	107	0.97
Belgian (9)	118	1.07
British (11)	11	0.10
Canadian (0)	13	0.12
Carpatho Rusyn (0)	19	0.17
Croatian (32)	277	2.52
Czech (31)	132	1.20
Czechoslovakian (11)	20	0.18
Dutch (23)	116	1.06
English (154)	1,002	9.11
European (59)	59	0.54
Finnish (0)	9	0.08
French, ex. Basque (93)	402	3.66
French Canadian (0)	10	0.09
German (806)	3,391	30.84
Greek (74)	166	1.51
Hungarian (55)	243	2.21
Irish (428)	2,277	20.71
Italian (989)	2,654	24.14
Lithuanian (0)	40	0.36
Norwegian (0)	26	0.24
Pennsylvania German (0)	10	0.09
Polish (618)	1,859	16.91
Portuguese (0)	48	0.44
Russian (100)	383	3.48
Scotch-Irish (84)	337	3.07
Scottish (49)	210	1.91
Serbian (18)	70	0.64
Slavic (43)	71	0.65
Slovak (180)	567	5.16
Slovene (108)	225	2.05
Swedish (6)	91	0.83
Swiss (0)	20	0.18
Turkish (0)	10	0.09
Ukrainian (34)	77	0.70
Welsh (10)	121	1.10
West Indian, ex. Hispanic (0)	29	0.26
Barbadian (0)	20	0.18
Jamaican (0)	9	0.08
Yugoslavian (0)	20	0.18

Hispanic Origin	Population	%
Hispanic or Latino (of any race)	82	0.73
Central American, ex. Mexican	3	0.03
Costa Rican	1	0.01
Panamanian	2	0.02
Cuban	5	0.04
Mexican	38	0.34
Puerto Rican	9	0.08
South American	8	0.07
Argentinean	1	0.01
Bolivian	1	0.01
Colombian	2	0.02
Venezuelan	4	0.04
Other Hispanic or Latino	19	0.17

Race*	Population	%
African-American/Black (197)	253	2.24
Not Hispanic (195)	251	2.23
Hispanic (2)	2	0.02
American Indian/Alaska Native (13)	34	0.30
Not Hispanic (13)	33	0.29
Hispanic (0)	1	0.01
Cherokee (4)	7	0.06
Choctaw (0)	1	0.01
Iroquois (1)	1	0.01
Mexican American Ind. (1)	1	0.01
Asian (84)	108	0.96
Not Hispanic (84)	108	0.96
Chinese, ex. Taiwanese (25)	29	0.26
Filipino (8)	11	0.10
Indian (26)	34	0.30
Indonesian (0)	1	0.01
Japanese (2)	5	0.04
Korean (6)	12	0.11
Pakistani (4)	6	0.05
Thai (2)	3	0.03
Vietnamese (9)	9	0.08
Hawaii Native/Pacific Islander (2)	5	0.04
Not Hispanic (2)	5	0.04
Native Hawaiian (1)	4	0.04
White (10,848)	10,941	97.07
Not Hispanic (10,793)	10,882	96.55
Hispanic (55)	59	0.52

Center

Place Type: Township
County: Beaver
Population: 11,795†

Ancestry‡	Population	%
African, Sub-Saharan (21)	21	0.18
African (21)	21	0.18
American (309)	309	2.65
Arab (66)	109	0.93
Lebanese (53)	96	0.82
Syrian (13)	13	0.11
Austrian (0)	38	0.33
British (17)	36	0.31
Bulgarian (0)	14	0.12
Croatian (147)	434	3.72
Czech (32)	172	1.47
Czechoslovakian (0)	25	0.21
Dutch (11)	90	0.77
Eastern European (25)	25	0.21
English (178)	1,146	9.81
European (53)	53	0.45
French, ex. Basque (11)	159	1.36
German (854)	3,410	29.20
Greek (152)	163	1.40
Hungarian (0)	152	1.30
Irish (370)	2,259	19.35
Italian (1,402)	3,310	28.35
Lithuanian (9)	25	0.21
Norwegian (11)	11	0.09
Polish (269)	648	5.55
Romanian (0)	11	0.09
Russian (32)	189	1.62
Scotch-Irish (208)	467	4.00
Scottish (99)	261	2.24
Serbian (108)	296	2.53
Slovak (195)	698	5.98
Slovene (16)	41	0.35
Swedish (0)	36	0.31
Ukrainian (93)	192	1.64
Welsh (44)	137	1.17
Yugoslavian (23)	34	0.29

Hispanic Origin	Population	%
Hispanic or Latino (of any race)	155	1.31
Cuban	8	0.07
Dominican Republic	8	0.07
Mexican	82	0.70
Puerto Rican	28	0.24
South American	4	0.03

*Notes: † The Census 2010 population figure is used to calculate the percentages in the Hispanic Origin and Race categories. Ancestry percentages are based on the 2006-2010 American Community Survey population (not shown); ‡ Numbers in parentheses indicate the number of people reporting a single ancestry; * Numbers in parentheses indicate the number of persons reporting this race alone, not in combination with any other race; Please refer to the Explanation of Data for more information.*

Colombian	2	0.02
Venezuelan	2	0.02
Other Hispanic or Latino	25	0.21

Race*	Population	%
African-American/Black (408)	465	3.94
Not Hispanic (406)	462	3.92
Hispanic (2)	3	0.03
American Indian/Alaska Native (5)	44	0.37
Not Hispanic (5)	43	0.36
Hispanic (0)	1	0.01
Blackfeet (0)	2	0.02
Cherokee (0)	11	0.09
Delaware (0)	1	0.01
Iroquois (1)	4	0.03
Sioux (2)	5	0.04
Spanish American Ind. (0)	1	0.01
Asian (109)	135	1.14
Not Hispanic (109)	134	1.14
Hispanic (0)	1	0.01
Chinese, ex. Taiwanese (44)	51	0.43
Filipino (9)	15	0.13
Indian (12)	14	0.12
Indonesian (2)	2	0.02
Japanese (2)	8	0.07
Korean (11)	13	0.11
Pakistani (2)	2	0.02
Taiwanese (3)	3	0.03
Thai (1)	2	0.02
Vietnamese (18)	19	0.16
Hawaii Native/Pacific Islander (1)	6	0.05
Not Hispanic (1)	5	0.04
Hispanic (0)	1	0.01
Guamanian/Chamorro (0)	1	0.01
Native Hawaiian (1)	4	0.03
White (11,105)	11,225	95.17
Not Hispanic (10,995)	11,104	94.14
Hispanic (110)	121	1.03

Center

Place Type: Township
County: Butler
Population: 7,898†

Ancestry‡	Population	%
American (494)	494	6.24
Arab (24)	44	0.56
Syrian (24)	44	0.56
Austrian (25)	49	0.62
British (11)	28	0.35
Croatian (15)	39	0.49
Czech (10)	115	1.45
Czechoslovakian (14)	14	0.18
Danish (0)	27	0.34
Dutch (15)	181	2.29
Eastern European (23)	23	0.29
English (270)	962	12.15
European (52)	52	0.66
Finnish (0)	8	0.10
French, ex. Basque (25)	224	2.83
German (945)	3,403	42.98
Hungarian (16)	90	1.14
Irish (209)	1,560	19.70
Italian (333)	1,291	16.31
Lithuanian (0)	4	0.05
Norwegian (0)	8	0.10
Pennsylvania German (16)	28	0.35
Polish (34)	352	4.45
Russian (0)	103	1.30
Scandinavian (0)	14	0.18
Scotch-Irish (140)	336	4.24
Scottish (15)	166	2.10
Serbian (10)	28	0.35
Slavic (0)	18	0.23
Slovak (68)	289	3.65
Swedish (26)	90	1.14
Swiss (38)	66	0.83
Ukrainian (85)	253	3.20
Welsh (7)	104	1.31

Hispanic Origin	Population	%
Hispanic or Latino (of any race)	64	0.81
Central American, ex. Mexican	5	0.06
Guatemalan	1	0.01
Panamanian	3	0.04
Salvadoran	1	0.01
Cuban	4	0.05
Dominican Republic	6	0.08
Mexican	28	0.35
Puerto Rican	8	0.10
South American	4	0.05
Peruvian	4	0.05
Other Hispanic or Latino	9	0.11

Race*	Population	%
African-American/Black (36)	62	0.79
Not Hispanic (36)	61	0.77
Hispanic (0)	1	0.01
American Indian/Alaska Native (9)	32	0.41
Not Hispanic (6)	28	0.35
Hispanic (3)	4	0.05
Blackfeet (0)	10	0.13
Cherokee (1)	12	0.15
Iroquois (1)	1	0.01
Tohono O'Odham (2)	2	0.03
Asian (78)	93	1.18
Not Hispanic (77)	92	1.16
Hispanic (1)	1	0.01
Chinese, ex. Taiwanese (16)	16	0.20
Filipino (20)	23	0.29
Indian (10)	16	0.20
Japanese (1)	4	0.05
Korean (2)	3	0.04
Thai (1)	2	0.03
Vietnamese (28)	28	0.35
Hawaii Native/Pacific Islander (0)	1	0.01
Not Hispanic (0)	1	0.01
Native Hawaiian (0)	1	0.01
White (7,697)	7,757	98.21
Not Hispanic (7,650)	7,706	97.57
Hispanic (47)	51	0.65

Chambersburg

Place Type: Borough
County: Franklin
Population: 20,268†

Ancestry‡	Population	%
African, Sub-Saharan (8)	37	0.19
African (5)	34	0.17
Liberian (3)	3	0.02
American (1,221)	1,221	6.13
Arab (11)	11	0.06
Lebanese (11)	11	0.06
Austrian (10)	55	0.28
Belgian (0)	15	0.08
British (41)	78	0.39
Croatian (0)	11	0.06
Czech (0)	23	0.12
Danish (0)	96	0.48
Dutch (45)	286	1.44
English (451)	1,355	6.80
European (153)	160	0.80
Finnish (0)	57	0.29
French, ex. Basque (87)	504	2.53
French Canadian (14)	102	0.51
German (2,946)	6,163	30.93
Greek (112)	153	0.77
Hungarian (13)	34	0.17
Irish (753)	2,591	13.00
Italian (154)	641	3.22
Lithuanian (10)	76	0.38
New Zealander (13)	13	0.07
Norwegian (22)	52	0.26
Pennsylvania German (252)	313	1.57
Polish (130)	486	2.44
Portuguese (0)	31	0.16
Romanian (16)	16	0.08
Russian (4)	21	0.11
Scandinavian (11)	39	0.20
Scotch-Irish (196)	526	2.64
Scottish (19)	353	1.77
Serbian (0)	18	0.09
Slavic (0)	10	0.05
Slovak (28)	78	0.39
Slovene (14)	14	0.07
Swedish (52)	139	0.70
Swiss (0)	144	0.72
Ukrainian (0)	25	0.13
Welsh (24)	185	0.93
West Indian, ex. Hispanic (100)	125	0.63
Haitian (11)	11	0.06
Jamaican (89)	114	0.57

Hispanic Origin	Population	%
Hispanic or Latino (of any race)	3,175	15.67
Central American, ex. Mexican	821	4.05
Costa Rican	8	0.04
Guatemalan	621	3.06
Honduran	55	0.27
Nicaraguan	2	0.01
Panamanian	7	0.03
Salvadoran	126	0.62
Other Central American	2	0.01
Cuban	22	0.11
Dominican Republic	168	0.83
Mexican	1,298	6.40
Puerto Rican	536	2.64
South American	57	0.28
Argentinean	1	<0.01
Bolivian	17	0.08
Chilean	5	0.02
Colombian	6	0.03
Ecuadorian	4	0.02
Peruvian	16	0.08
Uruguayan	1	<0.01
Venezuelan	7	0.03
Other Hispanic or Latino	273	1.35

Race*	Population	%
African-American/Black (1,857)	2,361	11.65
Not Hispanic (1,681)	2,101	10.37
Hispanic (176)	260	1.28
American Indian/Alaska Native (70)	193	0.95
Not Hispanic (45)	160	0.79
Hispanic (25)	33	0.16
Apache (0)	3	0.01
Blackfeet (0)	7	0.03
Cherokee (5)	37	0.18
Chippewa (1)	1	<0.01
Choctaw (1)	7	0.03
Creek (1)	2	0.01
Inupiat *(Alaska Native)* (0)	1	<0.01
Iroquois (2)	3	0.01
Lumbee (2)	3	0.01
Mexican American Ind. (2)	3	0.01
Navajo (1)	2	0.01
Potawatomi (1)	1	<0.01
Shoshone (0)	1	<0.01
Sioux (3)	3	0.01
Tlingit-Haida *(Alaska Native)* (0)	1	<0.01
Tohono O'Odham (0)	2	0.01
Asian (281)	396	1.95
Not Hispanic (281)	376	1.86
Hispanic (0)	20	0.10
Burmese (2)	2	0.01
Cambodian (1)	1	<0.01
Chinese, ex. Taiwanese (40)	54	0.27
Filipino (23)	42	0.21
Indian (57)	76	0.37
Indonesian (45)	46	0.23
Japanese (6)	25	0.12
Korean (28)	52	0.26
Malaysian (1)	5	0.02
Pakistani (22)	24	0.12
Taiwanese (3)	3	0.01
Thai (1)	7	0.03
Vietnamese (35)	50	0.25
Hawaii Native/Pacific Islander (11)	30	0.15

*Notes: † The Census 2010 population figure is used to calculate the percentages in the Hispanic Origin and Race categories. Ancestry percentages are based on the 2006-2010 American Community Survey population (not shown); ‡ Numbers in parentheses indicate the number of people reporting a single ancestry; * Numbers in parentheses indicate the number of persons reporting this race alone, not in combination with any other race; Please refer to the Explanation of Data for more information.*

	Population	%
Not Hispanic (2)	15	0.07
Hispanic (9)	15	0.07
Guamanian/Chamorro (11)	15	0.07
Native Hawaiian (0)	6	0.03
White (15,616)	16,316	80.50
Not Hispanic (14,457)	14,984	73.93
Hispanic (1,159)	1,332	6.57

Chartiers

Place Type: Township
County: Washington
Population: 7,818†

Ancestry‡	Population	%
American (255)	255	3.31
Austrian (10)	58	0.75
Belgian (13)	29	0.38
British (0)	27	0.35
Croatian (0)	27	0.35
Czech (0)	63	0.82
Czechoslovakian (10)	24	0.31
Dutch (0)	74	0.96
English (273)	875	11.34
French, ex. Basque (49)	357	4.63
German (516)	1,945	25.22
Hungarian (82)	249	3.23
Irish (213)	1,133	14.69
Italian (467)	1,599	20.73
Lithuanian (3)	12	0.16
Pennsylvania German (0)	26	0.34
Polish (483)	1,250	16.21
Russian (51)	175	2.27
Scotch-Irish (148)	376	4.87
Scottish (44)	108	1.40
Serbian (0)	62	0.80
Slavic (8)	8	0.10
Slovak (169)	429	5.56
Slovene (49)	171	2.22
Swedish (0)	37	0.48
Swiss (9)	19	0.25
Ukrainian (15)	25	0.32
Welsh (11)	31	0.40

Hispanic Origin	Population	%
Hispanic or Latino (of any race)	102	1.30
Central American, ex. Mexican	1	0.01
Honduran	1	0.01
Cuban	1	0.01
Mexican	50	0.64
Puerto Rican	7	0.09
South American	6	0.08
Colombian	3	0.04
Uruguayan	2	0.03
Venezuelan	1	0.01
Other Hispanic or Latino	37	0.47

Race*	Population	%
African-American/Black (221)	274	3.50
Not Hispanic (221)	272	3.48
Hispanic (0)	2	0.03
American Indian/Alaska Native (11)	28	0.36
Not Hispanic (11)	27	0.35
Hispanic (0)	1	0.01
Cherokee (1)	6	0.08
Choctaw (0)	1	0.01
Asian (19)	38	0.49
Not Hispanic (19)	37	0.47
Hispanic (0)	1	0.01
Chinese, ex. Taiwanese (4)	12	0.15
Filipino (6)	8	0.10
Indian (2)	3	0.04
Indonesian (0)	1	0.01
Japanese (3)	4	0.05
Korean (1)	4	0.05
Vietnamese (1)	4	0.05
Hawaii Native/Pacific Islander (1)	6	0.08
Not Hispanic (1)	4	0.05
Hispanic (0)	2	0.03
Guamanian/Chamorro (0)	2	0.03
Native Hawaiian (1)	4	0.05
White (7,431)	7,515	96.12
Not Hispanic (7,380)	7,445	95.23
Hispanic (51)	70	0.90

Cheltenham

Place Type: Township
County: Montgomery
Population: 36,793†

Ancestry‡	Population	%
African, Sub-Saharan (461)	568	1.54
African (276)	346	0.94
Cape Verdean (69)	96	0.26
Ethiopian (24)	24	0.07
Ghanaian (53)	53	0.14
Nigerian (29)	29	0.08
Senegalese (10)	20	0.05
Albanian (0)	10	0.03
Alsatian (0)	12	0.03
American (1,390)	1,390	3.78
Arab (121)	171	0.46
Egyptian (91)	125	0.34
Syrian (0)	16	0.04
Other Arab (30)	30	0.08
Armenian (53)	89	0.24
Austrian (72)	137	0.37
British (95)	128	0.35
Canadian (8)	27	0.07
Croatian (14)	14	0.04
Czech (22)	97	0.26
Danish (0)	104	0.28
Dutch (68)	236	0.64
Eastern European (506)	566	1.54
English (485)	2,358	6.41
Estonian (0)	44	0.12
European (157)	174	0.47
French, ex. Basque (58)	423	1.15
French Canadian (0)	16	0.04
German (964)	4,409	11.98
German Russian (0)	11	0.03
Greek (56)	127	0.35
Guyanese (9)	9	0.02
Hungarian (254)	465	1.26
Icelander (13)	25	0.07
Iranian (8)	8	0.02
Irish (1,486)	5,481	14.90
Israeli (32)	37	0.10
Italian (962)	2,938	7.98
Latvian (23)	33	0.09
Lithuanian (94)	188	0.51
New Zealander (8)	8	0.02
Northern European (31)	31	0.08
Norwegian (12)	63	0.17
Pennsylvania German (108)	292	0.79
Polish (601)	1,761	4.79
Portuguese (0)	19	0.05
Romanian (68)	94	0.26
Russian (1,380)	2,477	6.73
Scandinavian (0)	13	0.04
Scotch-Irish (110)	422	1.15
Scottish (30)	361	0.98
Serbian (11)	95	0.26
Slovak (10)	82	0.22
Swedish (9)	150	0.41
Swiss (22)	35	0.10
Ukrainian (274)	571	1.55
Welsh (41)	365	0.99
West Indian, ex. Hispanic (1,088)	1,325	3.60
Barbadian (26)	59	0.16
Belizean (117)	117	0.32
British West Indian (0)	20	0.05
Haitian (266)	280	0.76
Jamaican (543)	713	1.94
Trinidadian/Tobagonian (30)	30	0.08
West Indian (80)	80	0.22
Other West Indian (26)	26	0.07
Yugoslavian (5)	5	0.01

Hispanic Origin	Population	%
Hispanic or Latino (of any race)	1,428	3.88
Central American, ex. Mexican	107	0.29
Costa Rican	16	0.04
Guatemalan	42	0.11
Honduran	18	0.05
Nicaraguan	6	0.02
Panamanian	8	0.02
Salvadoran	17	0.05
Cuban	90	0.24
Dominican Republic	96	0.26
Mexican	172	0.47
Puerto Rican	631	1.72
South American	200	0.54
Argentinean	39	0.11
Bolivian	5	0.01
Chilean	7	0.02
Colombian	65	0.18
Ecuadorian	39	0.11
Paraguayan	2	0.01
Peruvian	22	0.06
Uruguayan	5	0.01
Venezuelan	13	0.04
Other South American	3	0.01
Other Hispanic or Latino	132	0.36

Race*	Population	%
African-American/Black (11,426)	12,042	32.73
Not Hispanic (11,203)	11,712	31.83
Hispanic (223)	330	0.90
American Indian/Alaska Native (89)	313	0.85
Not Hispanic (68)	254	0.69
Hispanic (21)	59	0.16
Apache (0)	2	0.01
Blackfeet (0)	6	0.02
Central American Ind. (0)	2	0.01
Cherokee (6)	71	0.19
Choctaw (0)	4	0.01
Delaware (2)	9	0.02
Inupiat *(Alaska Native)* (0)	1	<0.01
Iroquois (1)	3	0.01
Lumbee (5)	7	0.02
Mexican American Ind. (5)	6	0.02
Navajo (0)	1	<0.01
Potawatomi (1)	1	<0.01
Pueblo (1)	1	<0.01
Seminole (2)	4	0.01
Sioux (0)	6	0.02
South American Ind. (6)	7	0.02
Spanish American Ind. (0)	3	0.01
Tlingit-Haida *(Alaska Native)* (0)	2	0.01
Asian (2,825)	3,128	8.50
Not Hispanic (2,814)	3,092	8.40
Hispanic (11)	36	0.10
Bangladeshi (6)	6	0.02
Burmese (32)	32	0.09
Cambodian (110)	133	0.36
Chinese, ex. Taiwanese (550)	623	1.69
Filipino (171)	228	0.62
Hmong (1)	1	<0.01
Indian (417)	475	1.29
Indonesian (8)	10	0.03
Japanese (32)	77	0.21
Korean (1,002)	1,066	2.90
Laotian (18)	28	0.08
Malaysian (2)	2	0.01
Nepalese (6)	6	0.02
Pakistani (16)	17	0.05
Sri Lankan (8)	14	0.04
Taiwanese (17)	23	0.06
Thai (7)	19	0.05
Vietnamese (332)	366	0.99
Hawaii Native/Pacific Islander (15)	44	0.12
Not Hispanic (11)	37	0.10
Hispanic (4)	7	0.02
Guamanian/Chamorro (5)	6	0.02
Native Hawaiian (1)	9	0.02
White (21,116)	21,793	59.23
Not Hispanic (20,439)	21,019	57.13
Hispanic (677)	774	2.10

*Notes: † The Census 2010 population figure is used to calculate the percentages in the Hispanic Origin and Race categories. Ancestry percentages are based on the 2006-2010 American Community Survey population (not shown); ‡ Numbers in parentheses indicate the number of people reporting a single ancestry; * Numbers in parentheses indicate the number of persons reporting this race alone, not in combination with any other race; Please refer to the Explanation of Data for more information.*

Chester

Place Type: City
County: Delaware
Population: 33,972†

Ancestry‡	Population	%
African, Sub-Saharan (264)	292	0.85
African (189)	217	0.63
Liberian (57)	57	0.17
Sudanese (18)	18	0.05
American (107)	107	0.31
Arab (12)	12	0.03
Other Arab (12)	12	0.03
Armenian (18)	18	0.05
Assyrian/Chaldean/Syriac (8)	8	0.02
Austrian (0)	22	0.06
Brazilian (0)	14	0.04
British (12)	12	0.03
Croatian (0)	13	0.04
Dutch (0)	75	0.22
English (153)	479	1.39
Estonian (0)	11	0.03
French, ex. Basque (0)	52	0.15
German (272)	806	2.34
Greek (33)	52	0.15
Hungarian (12)	12	0.03
Icelander (10)	10	0.03
Irish (284)	1,014	2.94
Italian (264)	670	1.94
Lithuanian (15)	34	0.10
Norwegian (9)	50	0.15
Pennsylvania German (0)	28	0.08
Polish (150)	386	1.12
Portuguese (9)	9	0.03
Russian (0)	55	0.16
Scotch-Irish (53)	202	0.59
Scottish (7)	121	0.35
Slavic (14)	27	0.08
Slovak (0)	37	0.11
Swedish (0)	81	0.24
Swiss (0)	43	0.12
Ukrainian (32)	89	0.26
Welsh (0)	75	0.22
West Indian, ex. Hispanic (276)	380	1.10
Haitian (121)	180	0.52
Jamaican (104)	122	0.35
West Indian (51)	78	0.23

Hispanic Origin	Population	%
Hispanic or Latino (of any race)	3,054	8.99
Central American, ex. Mexican	111	0.33
Costa Rican	4	0.01
Guatemalan	62	0.18
Honduran	3	0.01
Nicaraguan	3	0.01
Panamanian	10	0.03
Salvadoran	29	0.09
Cuban	47	0.14
Dominican Republic	59	0.17
Mexican	296	0.87
Puerto Rican	2,107	6.20
South American	26	0.08
Argentinean	6	0.02
Colombian	10	0.03
Paraguayan	1	<0.01
Peruvian	7	0.02
Venezuelan	2	0.01
Other Hispanic or Latino	408	1.20

Race*	Population	%
African-American/Black (25,393)	26,257	77.29
Not Hispanic (24,803)	25,408	74.79
Hispanic (590)	849	2.50
American Indian/Alaska Native (121)	460	1.35
Not Hispanic (69)	335	0.99
Hispanic (52)	125	0.37
Apache (0)	2	0.01
Blackfeet (2)	16	0.05
Canadian/French Am. Ind. (0)	1	<0.01
Cherokee (14)	82	0.24
Cheyenne (0)	1	<0.01
Creek (0)	6	0.02
Delaware (2)	9	0.03
Iroquois (0)	3	0.01
Lumbee (0)	1	<0.01
Mexican American Ind. (2)	6	0.02
Navajo (4)	6	0.02
Shoshone (0)	3	0.01
Sioux (0)	10	0.03
South American Ind. (6)	25	0.07
Spanish American Ind. (7)	7	0.02
Tohono O'Odham (3)	3	0.01
Asian (217)	326	0.96
Not Hispanic (213)	291	0.86
Hispanic (4)	35	0.10
Bangladeshi (2)	2	0.01
Burmese (1)	1	<0.01
Cambodian (6)	8	0.02
Chinese, ex. Taiwanese (45)	65	0.19
Filipino (22)	51	0.15
Indian (47)	68	0.20
Japanese (1)	7	0.02
Korean (26)	31	0.09
Laotian (2)	3	0.01
Pakistani (12)	14	0.04
Sri Lankan (0)	1	<0.01
Taiwanese (3)	3	0.01
Thai (3)	10	0.03
Vietnamese (26)	32	0.09
Hawaii Native/Pacific Islander (20)	46	0.14
Not Hispanic (9)	21	0.06
Hispanic (11)	25	0.07
Fijian (1)	1	<0.01
Guamanian/Chamorro (11)	15	0.04
Native Hawaiian (4)	17	0.05
Samoan (1)	5	0.01
White (5,860)	6,507	19.15
Not Hispanic (5,117)	5,560	16.37
Hispanic (743)	947	2.79

Chestnuthill

Place Type: Township
County: Monroe
Population: 17,156†

Ancestry‡	Population	%
Albanian (58)	58	0.34
American (714)	714	4.18
Arab (220)	243	1.42
Jordanian (175)	175	1.03
Lebanese (0)	23	0.13
Moroccan (45)	45	0.26
Armenian (0)	32	0.19
Austrian (103)	151	0.88
British (20)	40	0.23
Bulgarian (0)	32	0.19
Canadian (8)	8	0.05
Czech (15)	97	0.57
Czechoslovakian (0)	42	0.25
Danish (0)	69	0.40
Dutch (164)	610	3.57
Eastern European (14)	14	0.08
English (247)	1,391	8.15
European (76)	107	0.63
French, ex. Basque (0)	185	1.08
French Canadian (0)	136	0.80
German (1,404)	4,528	26.52
Greek (110)	190	1.11
Guyanese (9)	9	0.05
Hungarian (70)	219	1.28
Irish (757)	2,970	17.40
Italian (1,049)	3,447	20.19
Latvian (0)	9	0.05
Lithuanian (12)	154	0.90
Norwegian (20)	20	0.12
Pennsylvania German (178)	358	2.10
Polish (270)	1,533	8.98
Portuguese (31)	31	0.18
Romanian (16)	49	0.29
Russian (62)	210	1.23
Scotch-Irish (99)	307	1.80
Scottish (76)	218	1.28
Slovak (14)	101	0.59
Slovene (18)	51	0.30
Swedish (0)	173	1.01
Swiss (71)	97	0.57
Ukrainian (42)	164	0.96
Welsh (24)	323	1.89
West Indian, ex. Hispanic (307)	328	1.92
Barbadian (50)	50	0.29
Belizean (175)	175	1.03
British West Indian (17)	38	0.22
Jamaican (65)	65	0.38
Yugoslavian (8)	8	0.05

Hispanic Origin	Population	%
Hispanic or Latino (of any race)	1,834	10.69
Central American, ex. Mexican	87	0.51
Costa Rican	6	0.03
Guatemalan	18	0.10
Honduran	11	0.06
Nicaraguan	9	0.05
Panamanian	13	0.08
Salvadoran	30	0.17
Cuban	70	0.41
Dominican Republic	137	0.80
Mexican	100	0.58
Puerto Rican	1,068	6.23
South American	230	1.34
Argentinean	12	0.07
Bolivian	5	0.03
Chilean	11	0.06
Colombian	68	0.40
Ecuadorian	69	0.40
Peruvian	39	0.23
Uruguayan	10	0.06
Venezuelan	7	0.04
Other South American	9	0.05
Other Hispanic or Latino	142	0.83

Race*	Population	%
African-American/Black (1,514)	1,695	9.88
Not Hispanic (1,388)	1,528	8.91
Hispanic (126)	167	0.97
American Indian/Alaska Native (46)	142	0.83
Not Hispanic (34)	115	0.67
Hispanic (12)	27	0.16
Aleut *(Alaska Native)* (1)	1	0.01
Blackfeet (0)	3	0.02
Cherokee (10)	24	0.14
Chippewa (0)	3	0.02
Choctaw (0)	2	0.01
Delaware (1)	16	0.09
Iroquois (5)	5	0.03
Mexican American Ind. (1)	1	0.01
Potawatomi (1)	1	0.01
Sioux (0)	1	0.01
South American Ind. (6)	11	0.06
Spanish American Ind. (1)	1	0.01
Asian (217)	314	1.83
Not Hispanic (207)	294	1.71
Hispanic (10)	20	0.12
Chinese, ex. Taiwanese (38)	60	0.35
Filipino (46)	79	0.46
Hmong (2)	2	0.01
Indian (60)	75	0.44
Japanese (6)	16	0.09
Korean (17)	27	0.16
Pakistani (29)	31	0.18
Taiwanese (3)	3	0.02
Thai (8)	9	0.05
Vietnamese (4)	6	0.03
Hawaii Native/Pacific Islander (7)	23	0.13
Not Hispanic (3)	17	0.10
Hispanic (4)	6	0.03
Guamanian/Chamorro (4)	4	0.02
Native Hawaiian (1)	4	0.02
Samoan (2)	3	0.02

*Notes: † The Census 2010 population figure is used to calculate the percentages in the Hispanic Origin and Race categories. Ancestry percentages are based on the 2006-2010 American Community Survey population (not shown); ‡ Numbers in parentheses indicate the number of people reporting a single ancestry; * Numbers in parentheses indicate the number of persons reporting this race alone, not in combination with any other race; Please refer to the Explanation of Data for more information.*

White (14,435)	14,766	86.07
Not Hispanic (13,368)	13,583	79.17
Hispanic (1,067)	1,183	6.90

Chippewa

Place Type: Township
County: Beaver
Population: 7,620†

Ancestry‡	Population	%
African, Sub-Saharan (0)	17	0.23
South African (0)	17	0.23
American (454)	454	6.09
Arab (0)	55	0.74
Lebanese (0)	36	0.48
Syrian (0)	19	0.25
Armenian (0)	25	0.34
Austrian (0)	10	0.13
Belgian (0)	12	0.16
British (9)	27	0.36
Croatian (64)	192	2.58
Czech (0)	12	0.16
Czechoslovakian (8)	8	0.11
Dutch (18)	231	3.10
English (209)	1,042	13.98
European (17)	17	0.23
Finnish (24)	50	0.67
French, ex. Basque (27)	97	1.30
German (857)	3,244	43.53
Hungarian (53)	206	2.76
Irish (134)	1,635	21.94
Italian (494)	1,313	17.62
Lithuanian (11)	11	0.15
Norwegian (14)	33	0.44
Pennsylvania German (11)	11	0.15
Polish (383)	795	10.67
Romanian (0)	12	0.16
Russian (16)	72	0.97
Scotch-Irish (33)	81	1.09
Scottish (11)	84	1.13
Serbian (0)	21	0.28
Slavic (0)	8	0.11
Slovak (40)	206	2.76
Slovene (8)	20	0.27
Swedish (15)	116	1.56
Swiss (0)	71	0.95
Ukrainian (0)	11	0.15
Welsh (0)	43	0.58

Hispanic Origin	Population	%
Hispanic or Latino (of any race)	47	0.62
Central American, ex. Mexican	1	0.01
Costa Rican	1	0.01
Dominican Republic	1	0.01
Mexican	16	0.21
Puerto Rican	12	0.16
South American	8	0.10
Argentinean	5	0.07
Colombian	2	0.03
Venezuelan	1	0.01
Other Hispanic or Latino	9	0.12

Race*	Population	%
African-American/Black (64)	101	1.33
Not Hispanic (63)	100	1.31
Hispanic (1)	1	0.01
American Indian/Alaska Native (3)	25	0.33
Not Hispanic (2)	24	0.31
Hispanic (1)	1	0.01
Blackfeet (1)	4	0.05
Cherokee (0)	7	0.09
Choctaw (0)	3	0.04
Iroquois (0)	1	0.01
Asian (58)	80	1.05
Not Hispanic (56)	78	1.02
Hispanic (2)	2	0.03
Chinese, ex. Taiwanese (19)	21	0.28
Filipino (7)	11	0.14
Indian (22)	25	0.33
Japanese (3)	9	0.12
Korean (4)	6	0.08
Thai (3)	4	0.05
Hawaii Native/Pacific Islander (5)	5	0.07
Not Hispanic (5)	5	0.07
White (7,396)	7,476	98.11
Not Hispanic (7,360)	7,437	97.60
Hispanic (36)	39	0.51

Coal

Place Type: Township
County: Northumberland
Population: 10,383†

Ancestry‡	Population	%
African, Sub-Saharan (0)	9	0.09
African (0)	9	0.09
American (410)	410	3.97
Arab (15)	15	0.15
Syrian (15)	15	0.15
Austrian (11)	75	0.73
Czechoslovakian (11)	26	0.25
Dutch (240)	895	8.66
English (85)	429	4.15
French, ex. Basque (0)	142	1.37
French Canadian (0)	8	0.08
German (653)	1,824	17.65
Greek (0)	16	0.15
Hungarian (25)	37	0.36
Irish (180)	1,061	10.27
Italian (384)	1,152	11.15
Lithuanian (24)	110	1.06
Norwegian (0)	8	0.08
Pennsylvania German (143)	222	2.15
Polish (1,090)	2,422	23.43
Russian (14)	93	0.90
Scotch-Irish (18)	57	0.55
Scottish (9)	38	0.37
Slovak (32)	95	0.92
Swiss (0)	20	0.19
Ukrainian (172)	365	3.53
Welsh (28)	203	1.96
West Indian, ex. Hispanic (9)	26	0.25
Jamaican (9)	26	0.25

Hispanic Origin	Population	%
Hispanic or Latino (of any race)	262	2.52
Central American, ex. Mexican	4	0.04
Guatemalan	3	0.03
Honduran	1	0.01
Cuban	5	0.05
Mexican	37	0.36
Puerto Rican	85	0.82
South American	3	0.03
Colombian	2	0.02
Peruvian	1	0.01
Other Hispanic or Latino	128	1.23

Race*	Population	%
African-American/Black (1,055)	1,081	10.41
Not Hispanic (1,041)	1,063	10.24
Hispanic (14)	18	0.17
American Indian/Alaska Native (18)	33	0.32
Not Hispanic (15)	29	0.28
Hispanic (3)	4	0.04
Apache (0)	1	0.01
Blackfeet (0)	1	0.01
Cherokee (2)	3	0.03
Cree (0)	1	0.01
Navajo (1)	1	0.01
Sioux (1)	2	0.02
South American Ind. (0)	1	0.01
Asian (24)	37	0.36
Not Hispanic (22)	35	0.34
Hispanic (2)	2	0.02
Chinese, ex. Taiwanese (2)	2	0.02
Filipino (7)	12	0.12
Indian (3)	4	0.04
Indonesian (2)	2	0.02
Japanese (3)	4	0.04
Korean (1)	7	0.07
Vietnamese (1)	1	0.01
Hawaii Native/Pacific Islander (1)	2	0.02
Not Hispanic (1)	2	0.02
Native Hawaiian (1)	2	0.02
White (9,049)	9,099	87.63
Not Hispanic (8,966)	9,012	86.80
Hispanic (83)	87	0.84

Coatesville

Place Type: City
County: Chester
Population: 13,100†

Ancestry‡	Population	%
African, Sub-Saharan (121)	137	1.07
African (107)	123	0.96
Sierra Leonean (14)	14	0.11
American (418)	418	3.27
Arab (135)	150	1.17
Egyptian (21)	21	0.16
Jordanian (38)	38	0.30
Lebanese (76)	91	0.71
Armenian (20)	20	0.16
British (0)	13	0.10
Canadian (0)	7	0.05
Croatian (15)	15	0.12
Czech (18)	33	0.26
Czechoslovakian (20)	20	0.16
Danish (0)	8	0.06
Dutch (28)	179	1.40
English (52)	433	3.39
European (22)	22	0.17
Finnish (0)	25	0.20
French, ex. Basque (0)	74	0.58
French Canadian (9)	19	0.15
German (174)	754	5.90
Greek (30)	40	0.31
Hungarian (109)	117	0.92
Irish (289)	830	6.50
Italian (229)	619	4.85
Latvian (0)	8	0.06
Lithuanian (0)	16	0.13
Macedonian (0)	10	0.08
Pennsylvania German (0)	4	0.03
Polish (79)	217	1.70
Russian (0)	56	0.44
Scotch-Irish (39)	83	0.65
Scottish (0)	14	0.11
Slovak (9)	125	0.98
Swedish (8)	15	0.12
Swiss (0)	30	0.23
Ukrainian (15)	40	0.31
Welsh (6)	64	0.50
West Indian, ex. Hispanic (34)	34	0.27
Belizean (12)	12	0.09
Haitian (11)	11	0.09
Jamaican (11)	11	0.09

Hispanic Origin	Population	%
Hispanic or Latino (of any race)	3,008	22.96
Central American, ex. Mexican	88	0.67
Guatemalan	8	0.06
Honduran	38	0.29
Nicaraguan	4	0.03
Panamanian	10	0.08
Salvadoran	21	0.16
Other Central American	7	0.05
Cuban	18	0.14
Dominican Republic	21	0.16
Mexican	1,772	13.53
Puerto Rican	846	6.46
South American	108	0.82
Argentinean	3	0.02
Bolivian	3	0.02
Colombian	19	0.15
Ecuadorian	81	0.62
Venezuelan	2	0.02

*Notes: † The Census 2010 population figure is used to calculate the percentages in the Hispanic Origin and Race categories. Ancestry percentages are based on the 2006-2010 American Community Survey population (not shown); ‡ Numbers in parentheses indicate the number of people reporting a single ancestry; * Numbers in parentheses indicate the number of persons reporting this race alone, not in combination with any other race; Please refer to the Explanation of Data for more information.*

Other Hispanic or Latino	155	1.18

Race*	Population	%
African-American/Black (6,079)	6,645	50.73
Not Hispanic (5,841)	6,285	47.98
Hispanic (238)	360	2.75
American Indian/Alaska Native (61)	199	1.52
Not Hispanic (37)	146	1.11
Hispanic (24)	53	0.40
Blackfeet (0)	13	0.10
Cherokee (3)	47	0.36
Choctaw (0)	1	0.01
Creek (0)	1	0.01
Delaware (1)	2	0.02
Inupiat *(Alaska Native)* (0)	1	0.01
Iroquois (4)	4	0.03
Seminole (0)	2	0.02
South American Ind. (0)	1	0.01
Asian (109)	168	1.28
Not Hispanic (109)	153	1.17
Hispanic (0)	15	0.11
Chinese, ex. Taiwanese (25)	45	0.34
Filipino (19)	30	0.23
Indian (33)	43	0.33
Japanese (3)	8	0.06
Korean (8)	10	0.08
Laotian (6)	6	0.05
Pakistani (2)	3	0.02
Sri Lankan (0)	1	0.01
Thai (4)	4	0.03
Vietnamese (2)	3	0.02
Hawaii Native/Pacific Islander (13)	42	0.32
Not Hispanic (9)	25	0.19
Hispanic (4)	17	0.13
Fijian (1)	5	0.04
Native Hawaiian (5)	8	0.06
Tongan (2)	7	0.05
White (4,982)	5,527	42.19
Not Hispanic (3,565)	3,978	30.37
Hispanic (1,417)	1,549	11.82

College

Place Type: Township
County: Centre
Population: 9,521†

Ancestry‡	Population	%
African, Sub-Saharan (47)	54	0.59
African (0)	7	0.08
Nigerian (47)	47	0.51
American (796)	796	8.65
Arab (0)	14	0.15
Egyptian (0)	14	0.15
Armenian (13)	13	0.14
Austrian (30)	86	0.93
Brazilian (0)	21	0.23
British (29)	94	1.02
Canadian (13)	27	0.29
Carpatho Rusyn (0)	13	0.14
Croatian (10)	19	0.21
Czech (10)	42	0.46
Czechoslovakian (17)	17	0.18
Danish (17)	91	0.99
Dutch (40)	252	2.74
Eastern European (29)	29	0.32
English (455)	1,327	14.43
European (196)	196	2.13
Finnish (0)	56	0.61
French, ex. Basque (73)	286	3.11
French Canadian (10)	19	0.21
German (1,099)	2,852	31.00
Greek (0)	97	1.05
Hungarian (23)	56	0.61
Irish (167)	887	9.64
Italian (283)	692	7.52
Lithuanian (10)	10	0.11
Pennsylvania German (61)	79	0.86
Polish (99)	411	4.47
Portuguese (9)	12	0.13
Russian (138)	166	1.80
Scotch-Irish (110)	227	2.47
Scottish (54)	311	3.38
Slavic (13)	13	0.14
Slovak (11)	163	1.77
Slovene (16)	16	0.17
Swedish (50)	131	1.42
Swiss (30)	58	0.63
Turkish (13)	13	0.14
Ukrainian (35)	45	0.49
Welsh (64)	116	1.26

Hispanic Origin	Population	%
Hispanic or Latino (of any race)	232	2.44
Central American, ex. Mexican	24	0.25
Costa Rican	1	0.01
Guatemalan	7	0.07
Honduran	4	0.04
Nicaraguan	3	0.03
Panamanian	2	0.02
Salvadoran	7	0.07
Cuban	16	0.17
Dominican Republic	11	0.12
Mexican	33	0.35
Puerto Rican	76	0.80
South American	43	0.45
Argentinean	6	0.06
Chilean	3	0.03
Colombian	9	0.09
Ecuadorian	4	0.04
Peruvian	12	0.13
Venezuelan	8	0.08
Other South American	1	0.01
Other Hispanic or Latino	29	0.30

Race*	Population	%
African-American/Black (224)	287	3.01
Not Hispanic (213)	273	2.87
Hispanic (11)	14	0.15
American Indian/Alaska Native (18)	49	0.51
Not Hispanic (16)	44	0.46
Hispanic (2)	5	0.05
Blackfeet (0)	1	0.01
Cherokee (3)	8	0.08
Comanche (1)	1	0.01
Creek (0)	1	0.01
Crow (1)	1	0.01
Iroquois (1)	3	0.03
Mexican American Ind. (1)	1	0.01
Navajo (3)	3	0.03
Potawatomi (0)	1	0.01
Sioux (1)	4	0.04
Spanish American Ind. (0)	1	0.01
Tohono O'Odham (0)	4	0.04
Asian (321)	393	4.13
Not Hispanic (315)	379	3.98
Hispanic (6)	14	0.15
Bangladeshi (3)	3	0.03
Chinese, ex. Taiwanese (127)	142	1.49
Filipino (16)	29	0.30
Indian (66)	76	0.80
Indonesian (0)	5	0.05
Japanese (14)	33	0.35
Korean (41)	45	0.47
Malaysian (3)	4	0.04
Pakistani (13)	13	0.14
Sri Lankan (1)	1	0.01
Taiwanese (15)	15	0.16
Thai (0)	1	0.01
Vietnamese (16)	20	0.21
Hawaii Native/Pacific Islander (5)	13	0.14
Not Hispanic (5)	13	0.14
Guamanian/Chamorro (2)	4	0.04
Native Hawaiian (1)	2	0.02
Samoan (2)	2	0.02
White (8,724)	8,877	93.24
Not Hispanic (8,581)	8,718	91.57
Hispanic (143)	159	1.67

Collingdale

Place Type: Borough
County: Delaware
Population: 8,786†

Ancestry‡	Population	%
African, Sub-Saharan (367)	426	4.86
African (164)	223	2.55
Liberian (203)	203	2.32
Albanian (0)	16	0.18
American (256)	256	2.92
Arab (28)	28	0.32
Other Arab (28)	28	0.32
Armenian (8)	24	0.27
Austrian (0)	24	0.27
Czech (0)	16	0.18
Czechoslovakian (5)	5	0.06
Dutch (0)	43	0.49
English (89)	750	8.56
European (39)	39	0.45
French, ex. Basque (0)	231	2.64
French Canadian (0)	5	0.06
German (341)	1,278	14.59
Greek (23)	32	0.37
Hungarian (9)	9	0.10
Irish (835)	2,284	26.08
Israeli (143)	143	1.63
Italian (382)	1,207	13.78
Lithuanian (9)	44	0.50
Norwegian (8)	13	0.15
Pennsylvania German (40)	58	0.66
Polish (43)	260	2.97
Russian (0)	9	0.10
Scotch-Irish (4)	88	1.00
Scottish (38)	163	1.86
Swedish (8)	88	1.00
Swiss (0)	10	0.11
Ukrainian (22)	29	0.33
Welsh (28)	125	1.43
West Indian, ex. Hispanic (119)	162	1.85
Haitian (51)	51	0.58
Jamaican (68)	111	1.27

Hispanic Origin	Population	%
Hispanic or Latino (of any race)	274	3.12
Central American, ex. Mexican	21	0.24
Costa Rican	4	0.05
Panamanian	2	0.02
Salvadoran	15	0.17
Cuban	3	0.03
Dominican Republic	16	0.18
Mexican	23	0.26
Puerto Rican	162	1.84
South American	13	0.15
Argentinean	1	0.01
Colombian	6	0.07
Ecuadorian	5	0.06
Peruvian	1	0.01
Other Hispanic or Latino	36	0.41

Race*	Population	%
African-American/Black (3,192)	3,467	39.46
Not Hispanic (3,115)	3,354	38.17
Hispanic (77)	113	1.29
American Indian/Alaska Native (26)	113	1.29
Not Hispanic (22)	99	1.13
Hispanic (4)	14	0.16
Blackfeet (0)	7	0.08
Cherokee (0)	21	0.24
Chippewa (2)	2	0.02
Cree (0)	1	0.01
Crow (0)	2	0.02
Delaware (0)	2	0.02
Iroquois (3)	4	0.05
Potawatomi (3)	3	0.03
Shoshone (0)	1	0.01
South American Ind. (2)	6	0.07
Asian (252)	285	3.24
Not Hispanic (248)	277	3.15

*Notes: † The Census 2010 population figure is used to calculate the percentages in the Hispanic Origin and Race categories. Ancestry percentages are based on the 2006-2010 American Community Survey population (not shown); ‡ Numbers in parentheses indicate the number of people reporting a single ancestry; * Numbers in parentheses indicate the number of persons reporting this race alone, not in combination with any other race; Please refer to the Explanation of Data for more information.*

Hispanic (4)	8	0.09
Bangladeshi (4)	4	0.05
Cambodian (14)	20	0.23
Chinese, ex. Taiwanese (45)	58	0.66
Filipino (32)	44	0.50
Indian (33)	40	0.46
Japanese (0)	1	0.01
Korean (4)	6	0.07
Laotian (38)	48	0.55
Pakistani (7)	8	0.09
Thai (4)	8	0.09
Vietnamese (44)	51	0.58
Hawaii Native/Pacific Islander (1)	9	0.10
Not Hispanic (1)	8	0.09
Hispanic (0)	1	0.01
Guamanian/Chamorro (0)	3	0.03
Native Hawaiian (1)	3	0.03
White (4,911)	5,158	58.71
Not Hispanic (4,823)	5,045	57.42
Hispanic (88)	113	1.29

Colonial Park

Place Type: CDP
County: Dauphin
Population: 13,229†

Ancestry‡	Population	%
African, Sub-Saharan (162)	162	1.24
African (82)	82	0.63
Cape Verdean (15)	15	0.11
Ethiopian (23)	23	0.18
Sudanese (42)	42	0.32
American (464)	464	3.54
Arab (141)	141	1.08
Egyptian (131)	131	1.00
Other Arab (10)	10	0.08
Armenian (62)	62	0.47
Austrian (8)	23	0.18
British (0)	62	0.47
Canadian (0)	16	0.12
Croatian (42)	146	1.11
Czech (17)	135	1.03
Dutch (103)	458	3.49
English (197)	943	7.19
Estonian (0)	13	0.10
European (75)	85	0.65
French, ex. Basque (11)	308	2.35
French Canadian (0)	48	0.37
German (1,650)	4,248	32.39
Greek (30)	61	0.47
Hungarian (60)	97	0.74
Irish (330)	1,709	13.03
Italian (392)	1,134	8.65
Lithuanian (55)	114	0.87
Macedonian (0)	12	0.09
Norwegian (0)	47	0.36
Pennsylvania German (59)	90	0.69
Polish (189)	514	3.92
Portuguese (16)	16	0.12
Russian (11)	81	0.62
Scandinavian (14)	14	0.11
Scotch-Irish (70)	224	1.71
Scottish (62)	179	1.36
Serbian (11)	50	0.38
Slavic (0)	14	0.11
Slovak (59)	111	0.85
Swedish (13)	174	1.33
Swiss (0)	37	0.28
Turkish (0)	24	0.18
Ukrainian (16)	43	0.33
Welsh (55)	260	1.98
West Indian, ex. Hispanic (41)	41	0.31
Haitian (6)	6	0.05
Jamaican (35)	35	0.27
Yugoslavian (44)	86	0.66

Hispanic Origin	Population	%
Hispanic or Latino (of any race)	1,026	7.76
Central American, ex. Mexican	27	0.20
Costa Rican	3	0.02
Guatemalan	8	0.06
Honduran	6	0.05
Nicaraguan	3	0.02
Panamanian	5	0.04
Salvadoran	2	0.02
Cuban	55	0.42
Dominican Republic	91	0.69
Mexican	190	1.44
Puerto Rican	509	3.85
South American	98	0.74
Argentinean	2	0.02
Bolivian	2	0.02
Colombian	15	0.11
Ecuadorian	33	0.25
Peruvian	43	0.33
Venezuelan	3	0.02
Other Hispanic or Latino	56	0.42

Race*	Population	%
African-American/Black (2,107)	2,431	18.38
Not Hispanic (1,971)	2,243	16.96
Hispanic (136)	188	1.42
American Indian/Alaska Native (25)	112	0.85
Not Hispanic (14)	83	0.63
Hispanic (11)	29	0.22
Apache (0)	3	0.02
Blackfeet (0)	10	0.08
Canadian/French Am. Ind. (1)	1	0.01
Central American Ind. (1)	1	0.01
Cherokee (2)	17	0.13
Cree (0)	1	0.01
Delaware (0)	1	0.01
Iroquois (3)	4	0.03
Mexican American Ind. (1)	1	0.01
Navajo (1)	1	0.01
Seminole (0)	1	0.01
Sioux (1)	2	0.02
South American Ind. (1)	9	0.07
Yakama (0)	2	0.02
Asian (604)	707	5.34
Not Hispanic (596)	686	5.19
Hispanic (8)	21	0.16
Bhutanese (14)	14	0.11
Cambodian (2)	2	0.02
Chinese, ex. Taiwanese (57)	69	0.52
Filipino (26)	45	0.34
Indian (330)	346	2.62
Indonesian (5)	5	0.04
Japanese (5)	22	0.17
Korean (12)	24	0.18
Laotian (0)	1	0.01
Nepalese (16)	16	0.12
Pakistani (59)	62	0.47
Taiwanese (3)	5	0.04
Thai (1)	1	0.01
Vietnamese (59)	76	0.57
Hawaii Native/Pacific Islander (9)	19	0.14
Not Hispanic (9)	17	0.13
Hispanic (0)	2	0.02
Guamanian/Chamorro (3)	4	0.03
Native Hawaiian (4)	5	0.04
Samoan (1)	1	0.01
White (9,650)	10,043	75.92
Not Hispanic (9,225)	9,554	72.22
Hispanic (425)	489	3.70

Columbia

Place Type: Borough
County: Lancaster
Population: 10,400†

Ancestry‡	Population	%
African, Sub-Saharan (185)	185	1.78
African (185)	185	1.78
American (964)	964	9.28
Arab (97)	97	0.93
Egyptian (97)	97	0.93
Austrian (0)	10	0.10
British (8)	8	0.08
Danish (0)	22	0.21
Dutch (9)	104	1.00
English (202)	611	5.88
European (48)	48	0.46
French, ex. Basque (196)	331	3.19
French Canadian (11)	22	0.21
German (2,153)	3,815	36.71
Greek (9)	17	0.16
Guyanese (3)	3	0.03
Hungarian (0)	29	0.28
Irish (193)	950	9.14
Italian (279)	576	5.54
Norwegian (0)	13	0.13
Pennsylvania German (24)	33	0.32
Polish (78)	302	2.91
Romanian (19)	34	0.33
Russian (9)	117	1.13
Scotch-Irish (49)	117	1.13
Scottish (20)	107	1.03
Serbian (0)	11	0.11
Slovak (0)	10	0.10
Swedish (0)	31	0.30
Swiss (0)	27	0.26
Ukrainian (0)	12	0.12
Welsh (22)	141	1.36

Hispanic Origin	Population	%
Hispanic or Latino (of any race)	938	9.02
Central American, ex. Mexican	12	0.12
Guatemalan	1	0.01
Honduran	1	0.01
Nicaraguan	2	0.02
Salvadoran	8	0.08
Cuban	25	0.24
Dominican Republic	26	0.25
Mexican	60	0.58
Puerto Rican	736	7.08
South American	12	0.12
Colombian	3	0.03
Ecuadorian	4	0.04
Peruvian	1	0.01
Venezuelan	4	0.04
Other Hispanic or Latino	67	0.64

Race*	Population	%
African-American/Black (528)	768	7.38
Not Hispanic (471)	662	6.37
Hispanic (57)	106	1.02
American Indian/Alaska Native (23)	68	0.65
Not Hispanic (19)	56	0.54
Hispanic (4)	12	0.12
Blackfeet (0)	2	0.02
Canadian/French Am. Ind. (0)	1	0.01
Cherokee (1)	13	0.13
Chickasaw (0)	1	0.01
Chippewa (0)	1	0.01
Choctaw (0)	1	0.01
Cree (1)	1	0.01
Iroquois (2)	3	0.03
Shoshone (5)	5	0.05
South American Ind. (0)	6	0.06
Asian (64)	92	0.88
Not Hispanic (60)	80	0.77
Hispanic (4)	12	0.12
Cambodian (1)	1	0.01
Chinese, ex. Taiwanese (11)	12	0.12
Filipino (7)	12	0.12
Indian (17)	19	0.18
Japanese (1)	6	0.06
Korean (3)	8	0.08
Taiwanese (7)	7	0.07
Thai (1)	1	0.01
Vietnamese (15)	16	0.15
Hawaii Native/Pacific Islander (3)	10	0.10
Not Hispanic (0)	6	0.06
Hispanic (3)	4	0.04
Guamanian/Chamorro (1)	3	0.03
White (9,055)	9,392	90.31
Not Hispanic (8,662)	8,899	85.57

SECTION TWO

*Notes: † The Census 2010 population figure is used to calculate the percentages in the Hispanic Origin and Race categories. Ancestry percentages are based on the 2006-2010 American Community Survey population (not shown); ‡ Numbers in parentheses indicate the number of people reporting a single ancestry; * Numbers in parentheses indicate the number of persons reporting this race alone, not in combination with any other race; Please refer to the Explanation of Data for more information.*

Hispanic (393)	493	4.74

Concord

Place Type: Township
County: Delaware
Population: 17,231†

Ancestry‡	Population	%
African, Sub-Saharan (0)	35	0.22
African (0)	35	0.22
Albanian (12)	12	0.07
American (540)	540	3.35
Arab (9)	25	0.16
Lebanese (9)	18	0.11
Palestinian (0)	7	0.04
Armenian (48)	160	0.99
Austrian (0)	8	0.05
Brazilian (14)	55	0.34
British (63)	85	0.53
Cajun (23)	23	0.14
Croatian (64)	64	0.40
Czech (0)	26	0.16
Czechoslovakian (40)	49	0.30
Danish (0)	9	0.06
Dutch (53)	175	1.09
English (448)	2,181	13.52
European (183)	194	1.20
Finnish (0)	8	0.05
French, ex. Basque (86)	504	3.13
French Canadian (0)	110	0.68
German (523)	2,717	16.85
Greek (50)	123	0.76
Hungarian (96)	173	1.07
Irish (1,387)	3,933	24.39
Italian (1,239)	2,877	17.84
Lithuanian (58)	127	0.79
Maltese (0)	9	0.06
Northern European (36)	36	0.22
Norwegian (27)	144	0.89
Pennsylvania German (11)	28	0.17
Polish (327)	847	5.25
Portuguese (0)	37	0.23
Romanian (0)	150	0.93
Russian (83)	374	2.32
Scandinavian (16)	25	0.16
Scotch-Irish (74)	240	1.49
Scottish (52)	264	1.64
Slovak (0)	133	0.82
Swedish (53)	186	1.15
Swiss (0)	59	0.37
Turkish (0)	12	0.07
Ukrainian (76)	237	1.47
Welsh (56)	352	2.18
West Indian, ex. Hispanic (24)	59	0.37
Bahamian (0)	35	0.22
Haitian (12)	12	0.07
Trinidadian/Tobagonian (12)	12	0.07

Hispanic Origin	Population	%
Hispanic or Latino (of any race)	345	2.00
Central American, ex. Mexican	17	0.10
Guatemalan	10	0.06
Honduran	5	0.03
Nicaraguan	1	0.01
Salvadoran	1	0.01
Cuban	26	0.15
Dominican Republic	9	0.05
Mexican	92	0.53
Puerto Rican	61	0.35
South American	58	0.34
Argentinean	9	0.05
Bolivian	3	0.02
Chilean	3	0.02
Colombian	22	0.13
Ecuadorian	5	0.03
Peruvian	8	0.05
Uruguayan	2	0.01
Venezuelan	5	0.03
Other South American	1	0.01
Other Hispanic or Latino	82	0.48

Race*	Population	%
African-American/Black (1,190)	1,253	7.27
Not Hispanic (1,179)	1,232	7.15
Hispanic (11)	21	0.12
American Indian/Alaska Native (12)	42	0.24
Not Hispanic (8)	34	0.20
Hispanic (4)	8	0.05
Blackfeet (0)	3	0.02
Central American Ind. (2)	2	0.01
Cherokee (0)	6	0.03
Choctaw (0)	1	0.01
Iroquois (2)	2	0.01
Lumbee (1)	3	0.02
Mexican American Ind. (2)	2	0.01
Osage (0)	1	0.01
Seminole (0)	1	0.01
South American Ind. (2)	2	0.01
Asian (883)	1,002	5.82
Not Hispanic (878)	988	5.73
Hispanic (5)	14	0.08
Bangladeshi (2)	2	0.01
Burmese (2)	4	0.02
Cambodian (19)	22	0.13
Chinese, ex. Taiwanese (256)	281	1.63
Filipino (26)	54	0.31
Hmong (2)	2	0.01
Indian (376)	396	2.30
Japanese (13)	28	0.16
Korean (89)	111	0.64
Nepalese (1)	1	0.01
Pakistani (23)	26	0.15
Sri Lankan (3)	3	0.02
Taiwanese (5)	7	0.04
Thai (2)	2	0.01
Vietnamese (43)	54	0.31
Hawaii Native/Pacific Islander (2)	6	0.03
Not Hispanic (1)	4	0.02
Hispanic (1)	2	0.01
Guamanian/Chamorro (1)	1	0.01
Native Hawaiian (0)	1	0.01
White (14,832)	14,997	87.03
Not Hispanic (14,629)	14,767	85.70
Hispanic (203)	230	1.33

Conewago

Place Type: Township
County: York
Population: 7,510†

Ancestry‡	Population	%
African, Sub-Saharan (60)	198	2.77
African (46)	46	0.64
Nigerian (0)	100	1.40
Other Sub-Saharan African (14)	52	0.73
American (573)	573	8.01
Austrian (0)	27	0.38
British (7)	7	0.10
Canadian (0)	11	0.15
Czechoslovakian (0)	22	0.31
Dutch (116)	216	3.02
English (188)	581	8.12
European (38)	38	0.53
Finnish (7)	7	0.10
French, ex. Basque (9)	212	2.96
French Canadian (23)	66	0.92
German (1,267)	2,909	40.67
Hungarian (0)	35	0.49
Irish (137)	890	12.44
Italian (98)	314	4.39
Lithuanian (0)	37	0.52
Norwegian (16)	25	0.35
Pennsylvania German (115)	115	1.61
Polish (33)	178	2.49
Russian (61)	79	1.10
Scotch-Irish (73)	261	3.65
Scottish (28)	110	1.54
Serbian (9)	19	0.27
Slavic (0)	18	0.25
Swedish (36)	129	1.80
Swiss (9)	9	0.13
Ukrainian (0)	10	0.14
Welsh (0)	48	0.67
West Indian, ex. Hispanic (13)	13	0.18
Trinidadian/Tobagonian (13)	13	0.18

Hispanic Origin	Population	%
Hispanic or Latino (of any race)	292	3.89
Central American, ex. Mexican	19	0.25
Honduran	3	0.04
Panamanian	3	0.04
Salvadoran	13	0.17
Cuban	2	0.03
Dominican Republic	11	0.15
Mexican	82	1.09
Puerto Rican	128	1.70
South American	25	0.33
Bolivian	1	0.01
Chilean	1	0.01
Colombian	4	0.05
Ecuadorian	15	0.20
Other South American	4	0.05
Other Hispanic or Latino	25	0.33

Race*	Population	%
African-American/Black (632)	693	9.23
Not Hispanic (607)	661	8.80
Hispanic (25)	32	0.43
American Indian/Alaska Native (12)	50	0.67
Not Hispanic (11)	43	0.57
Hispanic (1)	7	0.09
Apache (0)	3	0.04
Blackfeet (0)	1	0.01
Cherokee (1)	13	0.17
Cree (1)	1	0.01
Delaware (1)	1	0.01
Iroquois (0)	4	0.05
Sioux (0)	1	0.01
Asian (76)	120	1.60
Not Hispanic (75)	118	1.57
Hispanic (1)	2	0.03
Cambodian (11)	14	0.19
Chinese, ex. Taiwanese (3)	5	0.07
Filipino (10)	18	0.24
Indian (20)	31	0.41
Indonesian (0)	1	0.01
Japanese (1)	4	0.05
Korean (8)	16	0.21
Pakistani (13)	19	0.25
Vietnamese (8)	9	0.12
Hawaii Native/Pacific Islander (0)	7	0.09
Not Hispanic (0)	7	0.09
Native Hawaiian (0)	3	0.04
Samoan (0)	1	0.01
White (6,563)	6,696	89.16
Not Hispanic (6,390)	6,506	86.63
Hispanic (173)	190	2.53

Connellsville

Place Type: City
County: Fayette
Population: 7,637†

Ancestry‡	Population	%
American (460)	460	5.84
Arab (0)	2	0.03
Syrian (0)	2	0.03
Belgian (0)	58	0.74
Croatian (11)	31	0.39
Dutch (46)	507	6.43
English (204)	899	11.41
European (12)	12	0.15
French, ex. Basque (0)	109	1.38
German (949)	2,562	32.50
Greek (0)	23	0.29
Hungarian (66)	200	2.54
Irish (331)	1,386	17.58

*Notes: † The Census 2010 population figure is used to calculate the percentages in the Hispanic Origin and Race categories. Ancestry percentages are based on the 2006-2010 American Community Survey population (not shown); ‡ Numbers in parentheses indicate the number of people reporting a single ancestry; * Numbers in parentheses indicate the number of persons reporting this race alone, not in combination with any other race; Please refer to the Explanation of Data for more information.*

Ancestry	Population	%
Italian (386)	999	12.67
Pennsylvania German (63)	122	1.55
Polish (453)	925	11.74
Russian (0)	21	0.27
Scotch-Irish (43)	124	1.57
Scottish (0)	40	0.51
Slavic (0)	7	0.09
Slovak (196)	471	5.98
Slovene (0)	11	0.14
Swedish (16)	29	0.37
Ukrainian (0)	37	0.47
Welsh (17)	58	0.74

Hispanic Origin	Population	%
Hispanic or Latino (of any race)	55	0.72
Central American, ex. Mexican	1	0.01
Salvadoran	1	0.01
Cuban	2	0.03
Dominican Republic	1	0.01
Mexican	23	0.30
Puerto Rican	20	0.26
South American	1	0.01
Colombian	1	0.01
Other Hispanic or Latino	7	0.09

Race*	Population	%
African-American/Black (343)	419	5.49
Not Hispanic (338)	413	5.41
Hispanic (5)	6	0.08
American Indian/Alaska Native (6)	29	0.38
Not Hispanic (5)	28	0.37
Hispanic (1)	1	0.01
Blackfeet (0)	4	0.05
Cherokee (1)	3	0.04
Choctaw (1)	1	0.01
Mexican American Ind. (1)	1	0.01
Sioux (0)	2	0.03
Asian (29)	37	0.48
Not Hispanic (29)	36	0.47
Hispanic (0)	1	0.01
Chinese, ex. Taiwanese (9)	10	0.13
Filipino (3)	7	0.09
Indian (2)	4	0.05
Indonesian (1)	1	0.01
Japanese (9)	11	0.14
Korean (4)	4	0.05
Thai (1)	1	0.01
Vietnamese (0)	1	0.01
Hawaii Native/Pacific Islander (10)	12	0.16
Not Hispanic (10)	11	0.14
Hispanic (0)	1	0.01
Guamanian/Chamorro (0)	1	0.01
Native Hawaiian (0)	1	0.01
Samoan (10)	10	0.13
White (7,117)	7,228	94.64
Not Hispanic (7,083)	7,190	94.15
Hispanic (34)	38	0.50

Conshohocken

Place Type: Borough
County: Montgomery
Population: 7,833†

Ancestry‡	Population	%
African, Sub-Saharan (65)	65	0.83
African (65)	65	0.83
American (177)	177	2.27
Australian (0)	11	0.14
Austrian (0)	55	0.71
British (0)	36	0.46
Czech (0)	52	0.67
Czechoslovakian (0)	52	0.67
Danish (0)	32	0.41
Dutch (0)	323	4.15
English (99)	595	7.64
European (79)	79	1.01
French, ex. Basque (52)	107	1.37
French Canadian (52)	58	0.74
German (317)	1,498	19.23
Greek (40)	56	0.72
Hungarian (0)	62	0.80
Irish (913)	2,400	30.81
Italian (1,081)	2,045	26.25
Lithuanian (0)	13	0.17
Norwegian (14)	143	1.84
Pennsylvania German (26)	125	1.60
Polish (416)	988	12.68
Romanian (0)	18	0.23
Russian (26)	81	1.04
Scotch-Irish (41)	141	1.81
Scottish (42)	114	1.46
Slavic (0)	24	0.31
Slovak (18)	174	2.23
Swedish (0)	37	0.48
Swiss (0)	19	0.24
Ukrainian (33)	71	0.91
Welsh (9)	159	2.04
West Indian, ex. Hispanic (21)	21	0.27
Jamaican (21)	21	0.27

Hispanic Origin	Population	%
Hispanic or Latino (of any race)	274	3.50
Central American, ex. Mexican	20	0.26
Costa Rican	4	0.05
Guatemalan	5	0.06
Honduran	4	0.05
Nicaraguan	5	0.06
Salvadoran	2	0.03
Cuban	12	0.15
Dominican Republic	4	0.05
Mexican	130	1.66
Puerto Rican	53	0.68
South American	29	0.37
Argentinean	3	0.04
Bolivian	2	0.03
Chilean	3	0.04
Colombian	9	0.11
Ecuadorian	4	0.05
Peruvian	5	0.06
Uruguayan	1	0.01
Venezuelan	2	0.03
Other Hispanic or Latino	26	0.33

Race*	Population	%
African-American/Black (508)	583	7.44
Not Hispanic (494)	564	7.20
Hispanic (14)	19	0.24
American Indian/Alaska Native (10)	38	0.49
Not Hispanic (5)	32	0.41
Hispanic (5)	6	0.08
Cherokee (0)	16	0.20
Chippewa (1)	1	0.01
Mexican American Ind. (5)	5	0.06
Puget Sound Salish (1)	1	0.01
Asian (142)	174	2.22
Not Hispanic (140)	168	2.14
Hispanic (2)	6	0.08
Cambodian (2)	2	0.03
Chinese, ex. Taiwanese (26)	33	0.42
Filipino (25)	33	0.42
Indian (30)	35	0.45
Indonesian (1)	1	0.01
Japanese (3)	5	0.06
Korean (20)	27	0.34
Nepalese (1)	1	0.01
Pakistani (2)	3	0.04
Sri Lankan (6)	6	0.08
Taiwanese (4)	5	0.06
Thai (5)	5	0.06
Vietnamese (14)	16	0.20
Hawaii Native/Pacific Islander (0)	2	0.03
Not Hispanic (0)	1	0.01
Hispanic (0)	1	0.01
White (6,944)	7,062	90.16
Not Hispanic (6,790)	6,892	87.99
Hispanic (154)	170	2.17

Coolbaugh

Place Type: Township
County: Monroe
Population: 20,564†

Ancestry‡	Population	%
African, Sub-Saharan (310)	326	1.63
African (196)	212	1.06
Kenyan (53)	53	0.26
Nigerian (37)	37	0.18
Other Sub-Saharan African (24)	24	0.12
American (330)	330	1.65
Austrian (0)	44	0.22
Belgian (12)	50	0.25
Brazilian (13)	13	0.06
British (65)	102	0.51
Croatian (61)	123	0.61
Czech (40)	188	0.94
Danish (0)	30	0.15
Dutch (56)	320	1.60
English (123)	805	4.01
European (12)	12	0.06
French, ex. Basque (16)	339	1.69
German (748)	2,304	11.49
Greek (225)	241	1.20
Guyanese (14)	36	0.18
Hungarian (0)	34	0.17
Irish (803)	2,394	11.93
Israeli (0)	46	0.23
Italian (1,194)	2,314	11.54
Lithuanian (26)	70	0.35
Norwegian (31)	193	0.96
Pennsylvania German (43)	43	0.21
Polish (625)	1,254	6.25
Portuguese (9)	137	0.68
Russian (112)	211	1.05
Scandinavian (0)	46	0.23
Scotch-Irish (150)	170	0.85
Scottish (39)	169	0.84
Slovak (154)	203	1.01
Swedish (31)	65	0.32
Ukrainian (37)	94	0.47
Welsh (9)	81	0.40
West Indian, ex. Hispanic (293)	563	2.81
Barbadian (25)	25	0.12
Haitian (18)	54	0.27
Jamaican (101)	279	1.39
Trinidadian/Tobagonian (32)	32	0.16
West Indian (117)	173	0.86

Hispanic Origin	Population	%
Hispanic or Latino (of any race)	4,789	23.29
Central American, ex. Mexican	384	1.87
Costa Rican	15	0.07
Guatemalan	108	0.53
Honduran	71	0.35
Nicaraguan	28	0.14
Panamanian	75	0.36
Salvadoran	79	0.38
Other Central American	8	0.04
Cuban	137	0.67
Dominican Republic	455	2.21
Mexican	169	0.82
Puerto Rican	2,757	13.41
South American	502	2.44
Argentinean	19	0.09
Bolivian	10	0.05
Chilean	8	0.04
Colombian	151	0.73
Ecuadorian	131	0.64
Peruvian	139	0.68
Uruguayan	3	0.01
Venezuelan	30	0.15
Other South American	11	0.05
Other Hispanic or Latino	385	1.87

Race*	Population	%
African-American/Black (5,727)	6,318	30.72
Not Hispanic (5,235)	5,590	27.18

SECTION TWO

*Notes: † The Census 2010 population figure is used to calculate the percentages in the Hispanic Origin and Race categories. Ancestry percentages are based on the 2006-2010 American Community Survey population (not shown); ‡ Numbers in parentheses indicate the number of people reporting a single ancestry; * Numbers in parentheses indicate the number of persons reporting this race alone, not in combination with any other race; Please refer to the Explanation of Data for more information.*

Hispanic (492)	728	3.54
American Indian/Alaska Native (138)	355	1.73
Not Hispanic (72)	225	1.09
Hispanic (66)	130	0.63
Apache (0)	1	<0.01
Blackfeet (2)	18	0.09
Central American Ind. (4)	4	0.02
Cherokee (22)	84	0.41
Chippewa (0)	4	0.02
Creek (1)	1	<0.01
Delaware (6)	14	0.07
Iroquois (0)	13	0.06
Lumbee (1)	1	<0.01
Mexican American Ind. (2)	2	0.01
Pima (0)	2	0.01
Potawatomi (2)	2	0.01
Seminole (0)	2	0.01
Sioux (2)	3	0.01
South American Ind. (22)	28	0.14
Asian (376)	471	2.29
Not Hispanic (360)	432	2.10
Hispanic (16)	39	0.19
Bangladeshi (6)	6	0.03
Cambodian (2)	2	0.01
Chinese, ex. Taiwanese (47)	73	0.35
Filipino (124)	152	0.74
Indian (126)	151	0.73
Indonesian (4)	4	0.02
Japanese (8)	13	0.06
Korean (26)	33	0.16
Laotian (1)	8	0.04
Pakistani (8)	8	0.04
Taiwanese (4)	4	0.02
Thai (5)	5	0.02
Vietnamese (4)	7	0.03
Hawaii Native/Pacific Islander (15)	75	0.36
Not Hispanic (13)	48	0.23
Hispanic (2)	27	0.13
Fijian (2)	2	0.01
Native Hawaiian (4)	8	0.04
Samoan (1)	5	0.02
White (11,603)	12,239	59.52
Not Hispanic (9,510)	9,849	47.89
Hispanic (2,093)	2,390	11.62

Cranberry

Place Type: Township
County: Butler
Population: 28,098†

Ancestry‡	Population	%
American (982)	982	3.59
Arab (85)	263	0.96
Jordanian (33)	33	0.12
Lebanese (23)	175	0.64
Palestinian (29)	29	0.11
Syrian (0)	26	0.10
Armenian (18)	18	0.07
Austrian (26)	99	0.36
Belgian (0)	23	0.08
Brazilian (35)	70	0.26
British (33)	138	0.50
Bulgarian (15)	15	0.05
Canadian (9)	9	0.03
Croatian (106)	375	1.37
Czech (42)	169	0.62
Czechoslovakian (54)	107	0.39
Dutch (64)	322	1.18
Eastern European (57)	57	0.21
English (572)	2,465	9.01
European (463)	463	1.69
Finnish (24)	62	0.23
French, ex. Basque (50)	527	1.93
French Canadian (0)	91	0.33
German (2,599)	9,754	35.65
Greek (79)	115	0.42
Hungarian (124)	549	2.01
Iranian (0)	9	0.03
Irish (1,342)	6,124	22.38
Italian (1,519)	5,589	20.42
Latvian (0)	11	0.04
Lithuanian (23)	267	0.98
Maltese (0)	15	0.05
Norwegian (31)	49	0.18
Pennsylvania German (8)	8	0.03
Polish (479)	2,289	8.37
Romanian (0)	36	0.13
Russian (115)	301	1.10
Scandinavian (8)	39	0.14
Scotch-Irish (181)	922	3.37
Scottish (192)	740	2.70
Serbian (55)	283	1.03
Slavic (0)	9	0.03
Slovak (278)	1,119	4.09
Slovene (12)	84	0.31
Swedish (106)	363	1.33
Swiss (0)	65	0.24
Ukrainian (82)	344	1.26
Welsh (97)	414	1.51
West Indian, ex. Hispanic (43)	43	0.16
Jamaican (43)	43	0.16
Yugoslavian (27)	43	0.16

Hispanic Origin	Population	%
Hispanic or Latino (of any race)	446	1.59
Central American, ex. Mexican	61	0.22
Guatemalan	37	0.13
Honduran	11	0.04
Nicaraguan	6	0.02
Panamanian	1	<0.01
Salvadoran	6	0.02
Cuban	17	0.06
Dominican Republic	23	0.08
Mexican	165	0.59
Puerto Rican	78	0.28
South American	53	0.19
Argentinean	11	0.04
Colombian	18	0.06
Ecuadorian	6	0.02
Peruvian	5	0.02
Uruguayan	1	<0.01
Venezuelan	12	0.04
Other Hispanic or Latino	49	0.17

Race*	Population	%
African-American/Black (351)	488	1.74
Not Hispanic (336)	468	1.67
Hispanic (15)	20	0.07
American Indian/Alaska Native (26)	76	0.27
Not Hispanic (20)	64	0.23
Hispanic (6)	12	0.04
Blackfeet (0)	3	0.01
Cherokee (12)	26	0.09
Iroquois (1)	2	0.01
Lumbee (1)	1	<0.01
Mexican American Ind. (1)	2	0.01
Seminole (0)	5	0.02
Sioux (2)	4	0.01
South American Ind. (1)	1	<0.01
Spanish American Ind. (1)	1	<0.01
Tohono O'Odham (1)	1	<0.01
Yaqui (0)	1	<0.01
Asian (777)	892	3.17
Not Hispanic (776)	886	3.15
Hispanic (1)	6	0.02
Burmese (9)	9	0.03
Cambodian (6)	6	0.02
Chinese, ex. Taiwanese (169)	198	0.70
Filipino (48)	74	0.26
Indian (307)	321	1.14
Indonesian (6)	6	0.02
Japanese (14)	23	0.08
Korean (87)	104	0.37
Laotian (2)	2	0.01
Malaysian (0)	3	0.01
Nepalese (1)	1	<0.01
Pakistani (32)	32	0.11
Sri Lankan (10)	10	0.04
Taiwanese (7)	10	0.04
Thai (8)	9	0.03
Vietnamese (53)	57	0.20
Hawaii Native/Pacific Islander (6)	15	0.05
Not Hispanic (5)	14	0.05
Hispanic (1)	1	<0.01
Guamanian/Chamorro (1)	1	<0.01
Native Hawaiian (3)	10	0.04
Tongan (1)	1	<0.01
White (26,535)	26,814	95.43
Not Hispanic (26,225)	26,478	94.23
Hispanic (310)	336	1.20

Croydon

Place Type: CDP
County: Bucks
Population: 9,950†

Ancestry‡	Population	%
African, Sub-Saharan (276)	276	2.73
African (242)	242	2.40
Ghanaian (34)	34	0.34
American (235)	235	2.33
Arab (0)	24	0.24
Lebanese (0)	24	0.24
Austrian (0)	33	0.33
British (16)	16	0.16
Danish (24)	48	0.48
Dutch (0)	204	2.02
English (286)	1,215	12.03
Finnish (0)	12	0.12
French, ex. Basque (23)	230	2.28
French Canadian (0)	46	0.46
German (1,262)	3,253	32.20
Greek (24)	65	0.64
Hungarian (52)	147	1.46
Irish (1,251)	3,306	32.73
Italian (315)	1,051	10.40
Lithuanian (16)	51	0.50
Norwegian (0)	10	0.10
Pennsylvania German (23)	37	0.37
Polish (169)	776	7.68
Russian (29)	103	1.02
Scandinavian (10)	10	0.10
Scotch-Irish (57)	171	1.69
Scottish (14)	119	1.18
Serbian (0)	15	0.15
Slovak (21)	66	0.65
Swedish (0)	41	0.41
Swiss (0)	12	0.12
Turkish (8)	8	0.08
Ukrainian (9)	65	0.64
Welsh (12)	165	1.63

Hispanic Origin	Population	%
Hispanic or Latino (of any race)	737	7.41
Central American, ex. Mexican	57	0.57
Costa Rican	14	0.14
Guatemalan	28	0.28
Salvadoran	10	0.10
Other Central American	5	0.05
Cuban	10	0.10
Dominican Republic	23	0.23
Mexican	234	2.35
Puerto Rican	261	2.62
South American	75	0.75
Argentinean	2	0.02
Chilean	1	0.01
Colombian	21	0.21
Ecuadorian	41	0.41
Paraguayan	1	0.01
Peruvian	7	0.07
Uruguayan	2	0.02
Other Hispanic or Latino	77	0.77

Race*	Population	%
African-American/Black (491)	605	6.08
Not Hispanic (478)	565	5.68
Hispanic (13)	40	0.40
American Indian/Alaska Native (25)	92	0.92

*Notes: † The Census 2010 population figure is used to calculate the percentages in the Hispanic Origin and Race categories. Ancestry percentages are based on the 2006-2010 American Community Survey population (not shown); ‡ Numbers in parentheses indicate the number of people reporting a single ancestry; * Numbers in parentheses indicate the number of persons reporting this race alone, not in combination with any other race; Please refer to the Explanation of Data for more information.*

Not Hispanic (18)	77	0.77
Hispanic (7)	15	0.15
Apache (0)	1	0.01
Blackfeet (0)	3	0.03
Cherokee (1)	10	0.10
Delaware (0)	3	0.03
Iroquois (2)	3	0.03
Mexican American Ind. (7)	7	0.07
Seminole (0)	1	0.01
Sioux (1)	5	0.05
Asian (293)	331	3.33
Not Hispanic (293)	327	3.29
Hispanic (0)	4	0.04
Bangladeshi (6)	6	0.06
Cambodian (11)	11	0.11
Chinese, ex. Taiwanese (20)	24	0.24
Filipino (52)	66	0.66
Indian (135)	152	1.53
Japanese (3)	13	0.13
Korean (12)	14	0.14
Pakistani (20)	27	0.27
Thai (1)	1	0.01
Vietnamese (17)	19	0.19
Hawaii Native/Pacific Islander (0)	7	0.07
Not Hispanic (0)	7	0.07
White (8,612)	8,823	88.67
Not Hispanic (8,253)	8,397	84.39
Hispanic (359)	426	4.28

Cumru

Place Type: Township
County: Berks
Population: 15,147†

Ancestry‡	Population	%
African, Sub-Saharan (82)	108	0.72
African (65)	91	0.61
South African (8)	8	0.05
Other Sub-Saharan African (9)	9	0.06
American (462)	462	3.07
Arab (0)	9	0.06
Lebanese (0)	9	0.06
Armenian (0)	7	0.05
Austrian (35)	98	0.65
British (42)	70	0.47
Canadian (11)	11	0.07
Czech (0)	30	0.20
Czechoslovakian (14)	37	0.25
Dutch (56)	439	2.92
Eastern European (12)	12	0.08
English (219)	1,137	7.57
European (53)	68	0.45
Finnish (0)	11	0.07
French, ex. Basque (71)	287	1.91
French Canadian (0)	19	0.13
German (2,843)	6,556	43.63
Greek (45)	81	0.54
Guyanese (25)	25	0.17
Hungarian (63)	133	0.89
Irish (258)	2,016	13.42
Italian (407)	1,863	12.40
Lithuanian (91)	236	1.57
Norwegian (9)	28	0.19
Pennsylvania German (342)	682	4.54
Polish (375)	1,652	10.99
Portuguese (8)	8	0.05
Russian (78)	368	2.45
Scandinavian (8)	42	0.28
Scotch-Irish (71)	223	1.48
Scottish (9)	118	0.79
Serbian (0)	18	0.12
Slavic (0)	11	0.07
Slovak (148)	372	2.48
Swedish (24)	81	0.54
Swiss (11)	66	0.44
Ukrainian (47)	114	0.76
Welsh (28)	402	2.68
West Indian, ex. Hispanic (107)	107	0.71
Bermudan (17)	17	0.11
Haitian (69)	69	0.46
West Indian (21)	21	0.14
Yugoslavian (0)	13	0.09

Hispanic Origin	Population	%
Hispanic or Latino (of any race)	979	6.46
Central American, ex. Mexican	34	0.22
Guatemalan	14	0.09
Honduran	4	0.03
Nicaraguan	3	0.02
Panamanian	9	0.06
Salvadoran	4	0.03
Cuban	29	0.19
Dominican Republic	102	0.67
Mexican	86	0.57
Puerto Rican	599	3.95
South American	55	0.36
Argentinean	2	0.01
Chilean	1	0.01
Colombian	36	0.24
Ecuadorian	6	0.04
Peruvian	4	0.03
Uruguayan	5	0.03
Venezuelan	1	0.01
Other Hispanic or Latino	74	0.49

Race*	Population	%
African-American/Black (510)	625	4.13
Not Hispanic (453)	537	3.55
Hispanic (57)	88	0.58
American Indian/Alaska Native (19)	74	0.49
Not Hispanic (14)	53	0.35
Hispanic (5)	21	0.14
Apache (0)	3	0.02
Blackfeet (0)	5	0.03
Cherokee (2)	13	0.09
Chippewa (3)	3	0.02
Crow (0)	1	0.01
Delaware (1)	4	0.03
Iroquois (0)	2	0.01
Lumbee (0)	3	0.02
Potawatomi (4)	4	0.03
South American Ind. (1)	1	0.01
Asian (276)	354	2.34
Not Hispanic (274)	342	2.26
Hispanic (2)	12	0.08
Bangladeshi (4)	4	0.03
Chinese, ex. Taiwanese (41)	52	0.34
Filipino (21)	42	0.28
Hmong (6)	6	0.04
Indian (120)	135	0.89
Indonesian (3)	3	0.02
Japanese (9)	17	0.11
Korean (23)	35	0.23
Laotian (7)	8	0.05
Pakistani (13)	15	0.10
Thai (1)	1	0.01
Vietnamese (22)	23	0.15
Hawaii Native/Pacific Islander (0)	8	0.05
Not Hispanic (0)	4	0.03
Hispanic (0)	4	0.03
Native Hawaiian (0)	1	0.01
Samoan (0)	1	0.01
White (13,752)	13,975	92.26
Not Hispanic (13,234)	13,401	88.47
Hispanic (518)	574	3.79

Dallas

Place Type: Township
County: Luzerne
Population: 8,994†

Ancestry‡	Population	%
American (267)	267	3.03
Arab (56)	74	0.84
Egyptian (45)	45	0.51
Lebanese (11)	11	0.12
Syrian (0)	18	0.20
Assyrian/Chaldean/Syriac (17)	17	0.19
Austrian (0)	64	0.73
Belgian (0)	19	0.22
British (90)	90	1.02
Croatian (0)	8	0.09
Czech (0)	36	0.41
Czechoslovakian (51)	51	0.58
Danish (16)	16	0.18
Dutch (0)	216	2.45
English (176)	865	9.82
European (75)	75	0.85
Finnish (18)	18	0.20
French, ex. Basque (42)	318	3.61
German (559)	1,981	22.49
Greek (0)	19	0.22
Hungarian (30)	49	0.56
Irish (383)	1,608	18.26
Italian (448)	1,213	13.77
Lithuanian (87)	235	2.67
Norwegian (18)	18	0.20
Pennsylvania German (171)	242	2.75
Polish (639)	1,625	18.45
Russian (13)	357	4.05
Scotch-Irish (102)	355	4.03
Scottish (30)	61	0.69
Slovak (237)	457	5.19
Slovene (0)	11	0.12
Swedish (11)	45	0.51
Ukrainian (110)	190	2.16
Welsh (318)	820	9.31
Yugoslavian (0)	8	0.09

Hispanic Origin	Population	%
Hispanic or Latino (of any race)	87	0.97
Central American, ex. Mexican	5	0.06
Costa Rican	3	0.03
Guatemalan	2	0.02
Cuban	18	0.20
Dominican Republic	2	0.02
Mexican	19	0.21
Puerto Rican	28	0.31
South American	8	0.09
Argentinean	2	0.02
Colombian	4	0.04
Ecuadorian	1	0.01
Peruvian	1	0.01
Other Hispanic or Latino	7	0.08

Race*	Population	%
African-American/Black (30)	46	0.51
Not Hispanic (27)	41	0.46
Hispanic (3)	5	0.06
American Indian/Alaska Native (6)	19	0.21
Not Hispanic (6)	19	0.21
Central American Ind. (1)	1	0.01
Cherokee (1)	4	0.04
Iroquois (3)	4	0.04
Sioux (0)	2	0.02
Asian (78)	105	1.17
Not Hispanic (78)	104	1.16
Hispanic (0)	1	0.01
Burmese (1)	1	0.01
Chinese, ex. Taiwanese (10)	14	0.16
Filipino (12)	21	0.23
Indian (32)	44	0.49
Japanese (3)	9	0.10
Korean (13)	13	0.14
Taiwanese (1)	1	0.01
Thai (0)	1	0.01
Hawaii Native/Pacific Islander (0)	3	0.03
Not Hispanic (0)	1	0.01
Hispanic (0)	2	0.02
Guamanian/Chamorro (0)	1	0.01
Samoan (0)	1	0.01
White (8,803)	8,863	98.54
Not Hispanic (8,742)	8,792	97.75
Hispanic (61)	71	0.79

*Notes: † The Census 2010 population figure is used to calculate the percentages in the Hispanic Origin and Race categories. Ancestry percentages are based on the 2006-2010 American Community Survey population (not shown); ‡ Numbers in parentheses indicate the number of people reporting a single ancestry; * Numbers in parentheses indicate the number of persons reporting this race alone, not in combination with any other race; Please refer to the Explanation of Data for more information.*

Darby

Place Type: Borough
County: Delaware
Population: 10,687†

Ancestry‡	Population	%
African, Sub-Saharan (1,531)	1,568	14.79
African (770)	777	7.33
Ghanaian (22)	22	0.21
Liberian (566)	566	5.34
Nigerian (37)	37	0.35
Sierra Leonean (126)	156	1.47
Other Sub-Saharan African (10)	10	0.09
American (80)	80	0.75
Arab (13)	13	0.12
Other Arab (13)	13	0.12
Armenian (7)	7	0.07
British (17)	30	0.28
Canadian (8)	8	0.08
Czech (0)	25	0.24
Dutch (14)	79	0.75
English (0)	89	0.84
French, ex. Basque (0)	22	0.21
German (67)	434	4.09
Hungarian (15)	15	0.14
Irish (173)	643	6.07
Italian (390)	758	7.15
Lithuanian (8)	8	0.08
Pennsylvania German (11)	11	0.10
Polish (43)	144	1.36
Russian (0)	16	0.15
Scotch-Irish (6)	26	0.25
Scottish (0)	10	0.09
Ukrainian (8)	49	0.46
Welsh (0)	21	0.20
West Indian, ex. Hispanic (172)	190	1.79
Haitian (16)	34	0.32
Jamaican (156)	156	1.47

Hispanic Origin	Population	%
Hispanic or Latino (of any race)	228	2.13
Central American, ex. Mexican	21	0.20
Guatemalan	5	0.05
Nicaraguan	7	0.07
Panamanian	7	0.07
Other Central American	2	0.02
Cuban	18	0.17
Dominican Republic	14	0.13
Mexican	21	0.20
Puerto Rican	116	1.09
South American	11	0.10
Bolivian	5	0.05
Chilean	1	0.01
Ecuadorian	3	0.03
Peruvian	1	0.01
Venezuelan	1	0.01
Other Hispanic or Latino	27	0.25

Race*	Population	%
African-American/Black (8,428)	8,751	81.88
Not Hispanic (8,330)	8,616	80.62
Hispanic (98)	135	1.26
American Indian/Alaska Native (26)	141	1.32
Not Hispanic (26)	127	1.19
Hispanic (0)	14	0.13
Apache (0)	1	0.01
Blackfeet (1)	3	0.03
Cherokee (5)	36	0.34
Choctaw (0)	1	0.01
Iroquois (0)	1	0.01
Lumbee (0)	1	0.01
Pueblo (1)	2	0.02
Asian (74)	110	1.03
Not Hispanic (74)	101	0.95
Hispanic (0)	9	0.08
Bangladeshi (0)	1	0.01
Cambodian (0)	1	0.01
Chinese, ex. Taiwanese (10)	21	0.20
Filipino (7)	13	0.12
Indian (20)	25	0.23
Indonesian (1)	2	0.02
Japanese (1)	3	0.03
Korean (2)	7	0.07
Laotian (10)	13	0.12
Malaysian (0)	1	0.01
Thai (1)	3	0.03
Vietnamese (18)	21	0.20
Hawaii Native/Pacific Islander (3)	24	0.22
Not Hispanic (3)	23	0.22
Hispanic (0)	1	0.01
Guamanian/Chamorro (0)	2	0.02
Native Hawaiian (3)	5	0.05
White (1,735)	1,972	18.45
Not Hispanic (1,706)	1,917	17.94
Hispanic (29)	55	0.51

Darby

Place Type: Township
County: Delaware
Population: 9,264†

Ancestry‡	Population	%
American (250)	250	2.69
Dutch (0)	12	0.13
English (79)	457	4.91
European (19)	19	0.20
French, ex. Basque (14)	182	1.96
French Canadian (19)	19	0.20
German (140)	1,013	10.89
Hungarian (0)	51	0.55
Irish (1,111)	2,916	31.34
Italian (928)	2,116	22.75
Lithuanian (30)	75	0.81
Norwegian (0)	10	0.11
Pennsylvania German (19)	28	0.30
Polish (74)	500	5.37
Russian (8)	16	0.17
Scotch-Irish (68)	182	1.96
Scottish (11)	27	0.29
Slovak (19)	19	0.20
Swedish (0)	11	0.12
Swiss (0)	26	0.28
Ukrainian (0)	44	0.47
Welsh (0)	36	0.39
West Indian, ex. Hispanic (28)	54	0.58
Jamaican (28)	54	0.58

Hispanic Origin	Population	%
Hispanic or Latino (of any race)	189	2.04
Central American, ex. Mexican	11	0.12
Costa Rican	8	0.09
Guatemalan	1	0.01
Nicaraguan	1	0.01
Panamanian	1	0.01
Cuban	16	0.17
Dominican Republic	2	0.02
Mexican	17	0.18
Puerto Rican	94	1.01
South American	17	0.18
Argentinean	7	0.08
Colombian	1	0.01
Ecuadorian	7	0.08
Peruvian	2	0.02
Other Hispanic or Latino	32	0.35

Race*	Population	%
African-American/Black (3,608)	3,763	40.62
Not Hispanic (3,546)	3,678	39.70
Hispanic (62)	85	0.92
American Indian/Alaska Native (10)	84	0.91
Not Hispanic (9)	65	0.70
Hispanic (1)	19	0.21
Blackfeet (0)	1	0.01
Central American Ind. (0)	1	0.01
Cherokee (0)	10	0.11
Iroquois (1)	1	0.01
Navajo (1)	4	0.04
Sioux (1)	3	0.03
Asian (55)	81	0.87
Not Hispanic (55)	81	0.87
Cambodian (6)	6	0.06
Chinese, ex. Taiwanese (17)	27	0.29
Filipino (10)	22	0.24
Indian (5)	14	0.15
Japanese (1)	4	0.04
Korean (3)	3	0.03
Pakistani (2)	4	0.04
Thai (1)	2	0.02
Vietnamese (1)	7	0.08
Hawaii Native/Pacific Islander (2)	7	0.08
Not Hispanic (2)	7	0.08
Guamanian/Chamorro (0)	1	0.01
Native Hawaiian (2)	6	0.06
Samoan (0)	2	0.02
White (5,343)	5,491	59.27
Not Hispanic (5,283)	5,407	58.37
Hispanic (60)	84	0.91

Derry

Place Type: Township
County: Dauphin
Population: 24,679†

Ancestry‡	Population	%
African, Sub-Saharan (192)	301	1.25
African (131)	183	0.76
Nigerian (18)	18	0.07
South African (29)	86	0.36
Sudanese (14)	14	0.06
American (607)	607	2.53
Arab (160)	225	0.94
Egyptian (125)	125	0.52
Iraqi (0)	26	0.11
Lebanese (0)	39	0.16
Syrian (12)	12	0.05
Other Arab (23)	23	0.10
Australian (12)	36	0.15
Austrian (23)	144	0.60
Belgian (12)	57	0.24
British (40)	114	0.47
Canadian (54)	107	0.45
Carpatho Rusyn (0)	11	0.05
Celtic (0)	70	0.29
Croatian (0)	9	0.04
Czech (67)	280	1.17
Czechoslovakian (0)	45	0.19
Danish (10)	10	0.04
Dutch (108)	491	2.04
Eastern European (65)	73	0.30
English (505)	2,891	12.03
European (271)	281	1.17
Finnish (12)	25	0.10
French, ex. Basque (36)	747	3.11
French Canadian (38)	114	0.47
German (3,247)	8,558	35.61
Greek (19)	72	0.30
Hungarian (44)	395	1.64
Iranian (14)	40	0.17
Irish (753)	4,264	17.74
Italian (1,265)	3,493	14.54
Lithuanian (17)	134	0.56
Norwegian (88)	328	1.36
Pennsylvania German (252)	337	1.40
Polish (127)	899	3.74
Portuguese (13)	78	0.32
Romanian (0)	27	0.11
Russian (113)	460	1.91
Scandinavian (0)	63	0.26
Scotch-Irish (119)	666	2.77
Scottish (84)	616	2.56
Serbian (13)	78	0.32
Slavic (27)	198	0.82
Slovak (52)	278	1.16
Slovene (16)	28	0.12
Swedish (66)	285	1.19
Swiss (24)	216	0.90
Turkish (86)	96	0.40

*Notes: † The Census 2010 population figure is used to calculate the percentages in the Hispanic Origin and Race categories. Ancestry percentages are based on the 2006-2010 American Community Survey population (not shown); ‡ Numbers in parentheses indicate the number of people reporting a single ancestry; * Numbers in parentheses indicate the number of persons reporting this race alone, not in combination with any other race; Please refer to the Explanation of Data for more information.*

Ukrainian (33)	167	0.69
Welsh (159)	625	2.60

Hispanic Origin	Population	%
Hispanic or Latino (of any race)	733	2.97
Central American, ex. Mexican	29	0.12
Costa Rican	2	0.01
Guatemalan	11	0.04
Honduran	2	0.01
Nicaraguan	1	<0.01
Panamanian	9	0.04
Salvadoran	4	0.02
Cuban	33	0.13
Dominican Republic	35	0.14
Mexican	142	0.58
Puerto Rican	292	1.18
South American	115	0.47
Argentinean	20	0.08
Chilean	4	0.02
Colombian	36	0.15
Ecuadorian	25	0.10
Peruvian	20	0.08
Uruguayan	1	<0.01
Venezuelan	8	0.03
Other South American	1	<0.01
Other Hispanic or Latino	87	0.35

Race*	Population	%
African-American/Black (1,122)	1,321	5.35
Not Hispanic (1,103)	1,284	5.20
Hispanic (19)	37	0.15
American Indian/Alaska Native (42)	122	0.49
Not Hispanic (30)	104	0.42
Hispanic (12)	18	0.07
Aleut *(Alaska Native)* (0)	3	0.01
Apache (0)	1	<0.01
Arapaho (0)	4	0.02
Blackfeet (0)	2	0.01
Canadian/French Am. Ind. (1)	2	0.01
Central American Ind. (1)	3	0.01
Cherokee (4)	20	0.08
Chippewa (4)	5	0.02
Creek (1)	1	<0.01
Iroquois (0)	4	0.02
Lumbee (3)	3	0.01
Navajo (1)	1	<0.01
Seminole (0)	1	<0.01
Yaqui (0)	2	0.01
Asian (1,861)	2,067	8.38
Not Hispanic (1,856)	2,052	8.31
Hispanic (5)	15	0.06
Bangladeshi (12)	16	0.06
Burmese (4)	4	0.02
Cambodian (38)	46	0.19
Chinese, ex. Taiwanese (619)	664	2.69
Filipino (70)	99	0.40
Indian (606)	651	2.64
Indonesian (2)	2	0.01
Japanese (37)	52	0.21
Korean (116)	144	0.58
Laotian (2)	2	0.01
Nepalese (4)	4	0.02
Pakistani (85)	86	0.35
Sri Lankan (6)	7	0.03
Taiwanese (34)	40	0.16
Thai (83)	89	0.36
Vietnamese (110)	123	0.50
Hawaii Native/Pacific Islander (11)	30	0.12
Not Hispanic (11)	29	0.12
Hispanic (0)	1	<0.01
Guamanian/Chamorro (0)	1	<0.01
Native Hawaiian (1)	5	0.02
Samoan (1)	1	<0.01
White (20,898)	21,297	86.30
Not Hispanic (20,430)	20,797	84.27
Hispanic (468)	500	2.03

Derry

Place Type: Township
County: Westmoreland
Population: 14,502†

Ancestry‡	Population	%
American (995)	995	6.87
Arab (0)	41	0.28
Syrian (0)	41	0.28
Austrian (22)	44	0.30
British (0)	13	0.09
Canadian (0)	8	0.06
Croatian (37)	46	0.32
Czech (141)	260	1.80
Czechoslovakian (32)	57	0.39
Dutch (70)	369	2.55
Eastern European (18)	18	0.12
English (395)	1,104	7.62
French, ex. Basque (25)	88	0.61
German (876)	4,833	33.37
Greek (22)	53	0.37
Hungarian (164)	355	2.45
Irish (497)	2,526	17.44
Italian (969)	2,615	18.06
Lithuanian (0)	28	0.19
Pennsylvania German (75)	147	1.02
Polish (480)	1,267	8.75
Russian (130)	186	1.28
Scotch-Irish (155)	761	5.26
Scottish (71)	155	1.07
Serbian (0)	10	0.07
Slavic (0)	11	0.08
Slovak (356)	1,164	8.04
Slovene (0)	14	0.10
Swedish (20)	92	0.64
Ukrainian (85)	128	0.88
Welsh (35)	140	0.97
Yugoslavian (0)	9	0.06

Hispanic Origin	Population	%
Hispanic or Latino (of any race)	83	0.57
Central American, ex. Mexican	5	0.03
Guatemalan	4	0.03
Panamanian	1	0.01
Cuban	1	0.01
Mexican	37	0.26
Puerto Rican	15	0.10
South American	3	0.02
Argentinean	1	0.01
Peruvian	2	0.01
Other Hispanic or Latino	22	0.15

Race*	Population	%
African-American/Black (188)	233	1.61
Not Hispanic (186)	231	1.59
Hispanic (2)	2	0.01
American Indian/Alaska Native (16)	41	0.28
Not Hispanic (15)	40	0.28
Hispanic (1)	1	0.01
Blackfeet (1)	1	0.01
Cherokee (3)	5	0.03
Chippewa (1)	1	0.01
Choctaw (0)	1	0.01
Iroquois (1)	3	0.02
Asian (32)	45	0.31
Not Hispanic (32)	45	0.31
Chinese, ex. Taiwanese (0)	1	0.01
Filipino (8)	10	0.07
Indian (8)	11	0.08
Indonesian (1)	1	0.01
Japanese (2)	8	0.06
Korean (7)	10	0.07
Thai (2)	2	0.01
Hawaii Native/Pacific Islander (2)	4	0.03
Not Hispanic (2)	4	0.03
Native Hawaiian (1)	1	0.01
White (14,149)	14,234	98.15
Not Hispanic (14,093)	14,175	97.75
Hispanic (56)	59	0.41

Dingman

Place Type: Township
County: Pike
Population: 11,926†

Ancestry‡	Population	%
African, Sub-Saharan (28)	28	0.24
African (28)	28	0.24
American (334)	334	2.86
Arab (0)	11	0.09
Lebanese (0)	11	0.09
Assyrian/Chaldean/Syriac (10)	10	0.09
Austrian (16)	37	0.32
Belgian (0)	35	0.30
British (14)	14	0.12
Canadian (0)	25	0.21
Croatian (0)	28	0.24
Czech (0)	116	0.99
Danish (55)	167	1.43
Dutch (28)	438	3.75
English (454)	1,422	12.17
European (44)	67	0.57
Finnish (8)	63	0.54
French, ex. Basque (98)	374	3.20
French Canadian (23)	68	0.58
German (711)	2,760	23.62
Greek (22)	33	0.28
Hungarian (58)	132	1.13
Irish (690)	2,676	22.90
Italian (1,311)	2,920	24.99
Lithuanian (0)	40	0.34
Norwegian (12)	62	0.53
Pennsylvania German (19)	134	1.15
Polish (366)	1,200	10.27
Portuguese (0)	47	0.40
Romanian (29)	38	0.33
Russian (101)	349	2.99
Scandinavian (9)	9	0.08
Scotch-Irish (10)	83	0.71
Scottish (22)	390	3.34
Slovak (158)	158	1.35
Swedish (25)	116	0.99
Swiss (0)	120	1.03
Ukrainian (61)	138	1.18
Welsh (11)	247	2.11
West Indian, ex. Hispanic (50)	71	0.61
Barbadian (0)	21	0.18
Jamaican (50)	50	0.43
Yugoslavian (25)	25	0.21

Hispanic Origin	Population	%
Hispanic or Latino (of any race)	1,055	8.85
Central American, ex. Mexican	50	0.42
Costa Rican	4	0.03
Guatemalan	6	0.05
Honduran	3	0.03
Nicaraguan	9	0.08
Panamanian	7	0.06
Salvadoran	21	0.18
Cuban	66	0.55
Dominican Republic	79	0.66
Mexican	62	0.52
Puerto Rican	583	4.89
South American	121	1.01
Argentinean	9	0.08
Chilean	2	0.02
Colombian	39	0.33
Ecuadorian	35	0.29
Peruvian	31	0.26
Venezuelan	1	0.01
Other South American	4	0.03
Other Hispanic or Latino	94	0.79

Race*	Population	%
African-American/Black (408)	515	4.32
Not Hispanic (385)	463	3.88
Hispanic (23)	52	0.44
American Indian/Alaska Native (36)	119	1.00
Not Hispanic (22)	90	0.75

*Notes: † The Census 2010 population figure is used to calculate the percentages in the Hispanic Origin and Race categories. Ancestry percentages are based on the 2006-2010 American Community Survey population (not shown); ‡ Numbers in parentheses indicate the number of people reporting a single ancestry; * Numbers in parentheses indicate the number of persons reporting this race alone, not in combination with any other race; Please refer to the Explanation of Data for more information.*

Hispanic (14)	29	0.24
Apache (0)	1	0.01
Blackfeet (0)	1	0.01
Cherokee (2)	12	0.10
Chippewa (2)	2	0.02
Delaware (1)	22	0.18
Iroquois (2)	5	0.04
Mexican American Ind. (0)	1	0.01
Navajo (1)	2	0.02
Sioux (2)	3	0.03
South American Ind. (5)	5	0.04
Asian (98)	144	1.21
Not Hispanic (98)	137	1.15
Hispanic (0)	7	0.06
Cambodian (4)	4	0.03
Chinese, ex. Taiwanese (27)	34	0.29
Filipino (11)	27	0.23
Indian (27)	39	0.33
Japanese (3)	8	0.07
Korean (14)	20	0.17
Taiwanese (0)	1	0.01
Vietnamese (7)	9	0.08
Hawaii Native/Pacific Islander (8)	11	0.09
Not Hispanic (7)	9	0.08
Hispanic (1)	2	0.02
Guamanian/Chamorro (1)	1	0.01
Native Hawaiian (2)	4	0.03
White (10,942)	11,161	93.59
Not Hispanic (10,178)	10,330	86.62
Hispanic (764)	831	6.97

Dormont

Place Type: Borough
County: Allegheny
Population: 8,593†

Ancestry‡	Population	%
American (182)	182	2.10
Arab (67)	91	1.05
Arab (21)	45	0.52
Jordanian (9)	9	0.10
Lebanese (5)	5	0.06
Syrian (32)	32	0.37
Austrian (0)	18	0.21
British (28)	46	0.53
Bulgarian (0)	12	0.14
Canadian (0)	11	0.13
Croatian (17)	72	0.83
Czech (0)	8	0.09
Danish (0)	21	0.24
Dutch (0)	49	0.57
Eastern European (19)	19	0.22
English (69)	689	7.96
European (174)	174	2.01
Finnish (14)	26	0.30
French, ex. Basque (20)	239	2.76
German (603)	2,932	33.89
Greek (212)	293	3.39
Guyanese (8)	67	0.77
Hungarian (24)	167	1.93
Icelander (0)	13	0.15
Irish (701)	2,321	26.83
Italian (766)	1,891	21.86
Lithuanian (0)	21	0.24
Pennsylvania German (14)	14	0.16
Polish (271)	877	10.14
Portuguese (0)	37	0.43
Russian (0)	113	1.31
Scandinavian (0)	9	0.10
Scotch-Irish (118)	283	3.27
Scottish (10)	89	1.03
Serbian (30)	48	0.55
Slavic (12)	50	0.58
Slovak (85)	241	2.79
Slovene (0)	13	0.15
Swedish (0)	64	0.74
Swiss (0)	100	1.16
Turkish (13)	13	0.15
Ukrainian (20)	107	1.24
Welsh (0)	94	1.09
West Indian, ex. Hispanic (39)	39	0.45
Jamaican (39)	39	0.45

Hispanic Origin	Population	%
Hispanic or Latino (of any race)	214	2.49
Central American, ex. Mexican	10	0.12
Costa Rican	3	0.03
Guatemalan	4	0.05
Panamanian	3	0.03
Cuban	4	0.05
Dominican Republic	1	0.01
Mexican	118	1.37
Puerto Rican	21	0.24
South American	39	0.45
Argentinean	5	0.06
Chilean	2	0.02
Colombian	4	0.05
Ecuadorian	11	0.13
Peruvian	10	0.12
Venezuelan	7	0.08
Other Hispanic or Latino	21	0.24

Race*	Population	%
African-American/Black (181)	233	2.71
Not Hispanic (180)	231	2.69
Hispanic (1)	2	0.02
American Indian/Alaska Native (7)	32	0.37
Not Hispanic (6)	31	0.36
Hispanic (1)	1	0.01
Blackfeet (0)	2	0.02
Cherokee (1)	4	0.05
Choctaw (0)	3	0.03
Mexican American Ind. (1)	1	0.01
Seminole (0)	1	0.01
Sioux (2)	2	0.02
Asian (132)	158	1.84
Not Hispanic (131)	156	1.82
Hispanic (1)	2	0.02
Burmese (3)	3	0.03
Chinese, ex. Taiwanese (27)	37	0.43
Filipino (12)	18	0.21
Indian (9)	11	0.13
Japanese (6)	9	0.10
Korean (8)	11	0.13
Nepalese (1)	1	0.01
Thai (1)	1	0.01
Vietnamese (59)	68	0.79
Hawaii Native/Pacific Islander (0)	6	0.07
Not Hispanic (0)	6	0.07
Native Hawaiian (0)	2	0.02
White (8,092)	8,196	95.38
Not Hispanic (7,946)	8,035	93.51
Hispanic (146)	161	1.87

Douglass

Place Type: Township
County: Montgomery
Population: 10,195†

Ancestry‡	Population	%
American (559)	559	5.60
Arab (9)	51	0.51
Arab (9)	18	0.18
Lebanese (0)	33	0.33
Austrian (9)	39	0.39
British (34)	48	0.48
Bulgarian (14)	28	0.28
Canadian (18)	25	0.25
Croatian (14)	14	0.14
Czech (6)	39	0.39
Czechoslovakian (0)	11	0.11
Dutch (195)	839	8.40
English (252)	867	8.68
European (39)	39	0.39
French, ex. Basque (24)	194	1.94
French Canadian (0)	8	0.08
German (1,647)	3,750	37.56
Greek (0)	29	0.29
Hungarian (65)	209	2.09
Irish (442)	2,175	21.78
Italian (417)	1,335	13.37
Lithuanian (0)	29	0.29
Norwegian (7)	7	0.07
Pennsylvania German (252)	344	3.45
Polish (311)	897	8.98
Portuguese (45)	73	0.73
Romanian (0)	11	0.11
Russian (8)	70	0.70
Scandinavian (0)	9	0.09
Scotch-Irish (39)	218	2.18
Scottish (89)	329	3.30
Slavic (0)	12	0.12
Slovak (71)	198	1.98
Swedish (0)	32	0.32
Swiss (0)	41	0.41
Turkish (0)	10	0.10
Ukrainian (54)	94	0.94
Welsh (9)	217	2.17
West Indian, ex. Hispanic (13)	13	0.13
British West Indian (7)	7	0.07
Haitian (6)	6	0.06
Yugoslavian (16)	16	0.16

Hispanic Origin	Population	%
Hispanic or Latino (of any race)	187	1.83
Central American, ex. Mexican	13	0.13
Costa Rican	1	0.01
Guatemalan	1	0.01
Honduran	7	0.07
Panamanian	4	0.04
Cuban	16	0.16
Mexican	34	0.33
Puerto Rican	89	0.87
South American	16	0.16
Argentinean	3	0.03
Colombian	7	0.07
Peruvian	6	0.06
Other Hispanic or Latino	19	0.19

Race*	Population	%
African-American/Black (106)	159	1.56
Not Hispanic (104)	155	1.52
Hispanic (2)	4	0.04
American Indian/Alaska Native (28)	50	0.49
Not Hispanic (19)	36	0.35
Hispanic (9)	14	0.14
Cherokee (5)	12	0.12
Choctaw (7)	7	0.07
Delaware (0)	2	0.02
Lumbee (1)	1	0.01
Navajo (1)	1	0.01
Asian (117)	164	1.61
Not Hispanic (116)	160	1.57
Hispanic (1)	4	0.04
Burmese (1)	1	0.01
Chinese, ex. Taiwanese (24)	27	0.26
Filipino (14)	29	0.28
Indian (31)	33	0.32
Japanese (1)	9	0.09
Korean (6)	14	0.14
Laotian (12)	12	0.12
Pakistani (1)	1	0.01
Taiwanese (2)	2	0.02
Thai (2)	6	0.06
Vietnamese (22)	25	0.25
Hawaii Native/Pacific Islander (2)	4	0.04
Not Hispanic (2)	4	0.04
Native Hawaiian (1)	1	0.01
White (9,783)	9,897	97.08
Not Hispanic (9,644)	9,752	95.65
Hispanic (139)	145	1.42

Dover

Place Type: Township
County: York
Population: 21,078†

*Notes: † The Census 2010 population figure is used to calculate the percentages in the Hispanic Origin and Race categories. Ancestry percentages are based on the 2006-2010 American Community Survey population (not shown); ‡ Numbers in parentheses indicate the number of people reporting a single ancestry; * Numbers in parentheses indicate the number of persons reporting this race alone, not in combination with any other race; Please refer to the Explanation of Data for more information.*

Ancestry‡	Population	%
African, Sub-Saharan (0)	27	0.13
African (0)	27	0.13
American (1,756)	1,756	8.49
Austrian (0)	32	0.15
British (40)	56	0.27
Canadian (35)	35	0.17
Czech (0)	33	0.16
Dutch (97)	658	3.18
English (424)	1,568	7.58
European (148)	148	0.72
French, ex. Basque (48)	369	1.78
French Canadian (11)	35	0.17
German (5,963)	9,883	47.81
Greek (22)	39	0.19
Irish (490)	2,414	11.68
Italian (352)	760	3.68
Lithuanian (0)	29	0.14
Norwegian (34)	118	0.57
Pennsylvania German (229)	242	1.17
Polish (103)	548	2.65
Romanian (0)	12	0.06
Russian (19)	78	0.38
Scotch-Irish (106)	241	1.17
Scottish (115)	286	1.38
Serbian (14)	14	0.07
Slavic (0)	21	0.10
Slovak (30)	120	0.58
Slovene (0)	14	0.07
Swedish (46)	135	0.65
Swiss (0)	12	0.06
Ukrainian (15)	15	0.07
Welsh (74)	239	1.16

Hispanic Origin	Population	%
Hispanic or Latino (of any race)	672	3.19
Central American, ex. Mexican	36	0.17
Guatemalan	2	0.01
Honduran	1	<0.01
Nicaraguan	6	0.03
Panamanian	4	0.02
Salvadoran	23	0.11
Cuban	24	0.11
Dominican Republic	16	0.08
Mexican	151	0.72
Puerto Rican	362	1.72
South American	39	0.19
Argentinean	3	0.01
Bolivian	1	<0.01
Chilean	4	0.02
Colombian	13	0.06
Ecuadorian	11	0.05
Paraguayan	1	<0.01
Peruvian	6	0.03
Other Hispanic or Latino	44	0.21

Race*	Population	%
African-American/Black (693)	861	4.08
Not Hispanic (659)	799	3.79
Hispanic (34)	62	0.29
American Indian/Alaska Native (67)	143	0.68
Not Hispanic (42)	113	0.54
Hispanic (25)	30	0.14
Apache (1)	1	<0.01
Blackfeet (0)	1	<0.01
Central American Ind. (7)	7	0.03
Cherokee (8)	34	0.16
Choctaw (1)	1	<0.01
Creek (3)	3	0.01
Delaware (0)	3	0.01
Hopi (0)	3	0.01
Iroquois (3)	12	0.06
Lumbee (3)	3	0.01
Mexican American Ind. (10)	10	0.05
Paiute (0)	1	<0.01
Sioux (4)	7	0.03
Asian (151)	204	0.97
Not Hispanic (148)	201	0.95
Hispanic (3)	3	0.01
Chinese, ex. Taiwanese (23)	27	0.13
Filipino (38)	51	0.24
Indian (35)	39	0.19
Indonesian (1)	1	<0.01
Japanese (4)	20	0.09
Korean (15)	26	0.12
Laotian (0)	3	0.01
Nepalese (8)	8	0.04
Pakistani (1)	1	<0.01
Sri Lankan (4)	4	0.02
Thai (1)	4	0.02
Vietnamese (18)	21	0.10
Hawaii Native/Pacific Islander (6)	18	0.09
Not Hispanic (6)	12	0.06
Hispanic (0)	6	0.03
Guamanian/Chamorro (1)	1	<0.01
Native Hawaiian (4)	8	0.04
Samoan (1)	1	<0.01
White (19,623)	19,919	94.50
Not Hispanic (19,281)	19,523	92.62
Hispanic (342)	396	1.88

Downingtown

Place Type: Borough
County: Chester
Population: 7,891†

Ancestry‡	Population	%
African, Sub-Saharan (92)	92	1.16
African (73)	73	0.92
Liberian (19)	19	0.24
American (292)	292	3.69
Arab (37)	37	0.47
Egyptian (27)	27	0.34
Lebanese (10)	10	0.13
Assyrian/Chaldean/Syriac (57)	57	0.72
Austrian (0)	62	0.78
Belgian (0)	14	0.18
British (68)	81	1.02
Bulgarian (33)	33	0.42
Czech (10)	10	0.13
Czechoslovakian (0)	10	0.13
Danish (0)	11	0.14
Dutch (14)	90	1.14
Eastern European (4)	4	0.05
English (206)	955	12.08
European (31)	60	0.76
French, ex. Basque (6)	271	3.43
German (378)	1,720	21.75
Greek (35)	73	0.92
Hungarian (6)	79	1.00
Irish (607)	2,022	25.57
Israeli (0)	8	0.10
Italian (693)	1,589	20.10
Lithuanian (11)	110	1.39
Norwegian (8)	8	0.10
Pennsylvania German (41)	41	0.52
Polish (50)	215	2.72
Portuguese (10)	10	0.13
Russian (9)	169	2.14
Scotch-Irish (185)	424	5.36
Scottish (17)	209	2.64
Serbian (39)	39	0.49
Slovak (36)	46	0.58
Swedish (8)	53	0.67
Swiss (5)	11	0.14
Ukrainian (0)	20	0.25
Welsh (44)	122	1.54
West Indian, ex. Hispanic (48)	69	0.87
British West Indian (31)	52	0.66
Jamaican (17)	17	0.21

Hispanic Origin	Population	%
Hispanic or Latino (of any race)	567	7.19
Central American, ex. Mexican	13	0.16
Costa Rican	2	0.03
Guatemalan	3	0.04
Honduran	2	0.03
Panamanian	6	0.08
Cuban	1	0.01
Dominican Republic	5	0.06
Mexican	214	2.71
Puerto Rican	229	2.90
South American	50	0.63
Argentinean	5	0.06
Bolivian	1	0.01
Chilean	2	0.03
Colombian	17	0.22
Ecuadorian	16	0.20
Peruvian	4	0.05
Uruguayan	1	0.01
Venezuelan	4	0.05
Other Hispanic or Latino	55	0.70

Race*	Population	%
African-American/Black (948)	1,119	14.18
Not Hispanic (898)	1,045	13.24
Hispanic (50)	74	0.94
American Indian/Alaska Native (6)	59	0.75
Not Hispanic (5)	45	0.57
Hispanic (1)	14	0.18
Apache (0)	1	0.01
Canadian/French Am. Ind. (0)	1	0.01
Cherokee (0)	9	0.11
Chippewa (0)	1	0.01
Delaware (1)	4	0.05
Iroquois (0)	1	0.01
Sioux (0)	1	0.01
South American Ind. (1)	2	0.03
Asian (216)	270	3.42
Not Hispanic (209)	254	3.22
Hispanic (7)	16	0.20
Burmese (2)	2	0.03
Cambodian (4)	4	0.05
Chinese, ex. Taiwanese (43)	53	0.67
Filipino (28)	43	0.54
Indian (66)	75	0.95
Japanese (4)	15	0.19
Korean (7)	8	0.10
Laotian (3)	3	0.04
Pakistani (6)	8	0.10
Taiwanese (1)	1	0.01
Vietnamese (39)	43	0.54
Hawaii Native/Pacific Islander (9)	14	0.18
Not Hispanic (9)	14	0.18
Guamanian/Chamorro (1)	1	0.01
Native Hawaiian (1)	2	0.03
Samoan (4)	5	0.06
Tongan (1)	2	0.03
White (6,255)	6,466	81.94
Not Hispanic (5,999)	6,166	78.14
Hispanic (256)	300	3.80

Doylestown

Place Type: Borough
County: Bucks
Population: 8,380†

Ancestry‡	Population	%
American (362)	362	4.32
Arab (63)	88	1.05
Arab (0)	10	0.12
Lebanese (55)	55	0.66
Other Arab (8)	23	0.27
Armenian (10)	10	0.12
Austrian (24)	76	0.91
Belgian (15)	25	0.30
Brazilian (12)	12	0.14
British (53)	76	0.91
Canadian (14)	43	0.51
Czech (0)	49	0.58
Czechoslovakian (0)	13	0.15
Danish (7)	68	0.81
Dutch (20)	216	2.58
Eastern European (68)	68	0.81
English (342)	1,293	15.41
European (34)	34	0.41
French, ex. Basque (10)	238	2.84
French Canadian (26)	47	0.56

*Notes: † The Census 2010 population figure is used to calculate the percentages in the Hispanic Origin and Race categories. Ancestry percentages are based on the 2006-2010 American Community Survey population (not shown); ‡ Numbers in parentheses indicate the number of people reporting a single ancestry; * Numbers in parentheses indicate the number of persons reporting this race alone, not in combination with any other race; Please refer to the Explanation of Data for more information.*

Ancestry (continued)	Population	%
German (679)	2,405	28.67
Greek (0)	28	0.33
Hungarian (11)	125	1.49
Irish (589)	2,202	26.25
Italian (251)	1,087	12.96
Lithuanian (25)	113	1.35
Norwegian (34)	48	0.57
Pennsylvania German (16)	49	0.58
Polish (185)	497	5.93
Portuguese (7)	47	0.56
Romanian (10)	34	0.41
Russian (141)	331	3.95
Scotch-Irish (52)	166	1.98
Scottish (60)	283	3.37
Slavic (25)	40	0.48
Slovak (21)	80	0.95
Slovene (12)	12	0.14
Swedish (13)	94	1.12
Swiss (11)	148	1.76
Ukrainian (111)	140	1.67
Welsh (24)	241	2.87
West Indian, ex. Hispanic (11)	11	0.13
Jamaican (11)	11	0.13

Hispanic Origin	Population	%
Hispanic or Latino (of any race)	171	2.04
Central American, ex. Mexican	12	0.14
Guatemalan	10	0.12
Honduran	1	0.01
Salvadoran	1	0.01
Cuban	15	0.18
Dominican Republic	2	0.02
Mexican	43	0.51
Puerto Rican	59	0.70
South American	25	0.30
Argentinean	3	0.04
Chilean	1	0.01
Colombian	5	0.06
Ecuadorian	6	0.07
Peruvian	4	0.05
Uruguayan	2	0.02
Venezuelan	4	0.05
Other Hispanic or Latino	15	0.18

Race*	Population	%
African-American/Black (106)	162	1.93
Not Hispanic (103)	153	1.83
Hispanic (3)	9	0.11
American Indian/Alaska Native (11)	28	0.33
Not Hispanic (10)	26	0.31
Hispanic (1)	2	0.02
Blackfeet (0)	1	0.01
Cherokee (1)	3	0.04
Creek (1)	1	0.01
Delaware (0)	5	0.06
Hopi (5)	5	0.06
Iroquois (1)	1	0.01
Seminole (0)	1	0.01
Asian (158)	221	2.64
Not Hispanic (157)	220	2.63
Hispanic (1)	1	0.01
Burmese (1)	1	0.01
Chinese, ex. Taiwanese (35)	45	0.54
Filipino (21)	41	0.49
Indian (39)	47	0.56
Indonesian (2)	2	0.02
Japanese (2)	7	0.08
Korean (13)	27	0.32
Taiwanese (8)	8	0.10
Thai (6)	8	0.10
Vietnamese (28)	33	0.39
Hawaii Native/Pacific Islander (5)	6	0.07
Not Hispanic (5)	6	0.07
Fijian (1)	2	0.02
Guamanian/Chamorro (4)	4	0.05
White (7,946)	8,059	96.17
Not Hispanic (7,814)	7,918	94.49
Hispanic (132)	141	1.68

Doylestown

Place Type: Township
County: Bucks
Population: 17,565†

Ancestry‡	Population	%
African, Sub-Saharan (56)	56	0.32
African (53)	53	0.30
South African (3)	3	0.02
Albanian (0)	30	0.17
American (703)	703	3.98
Arab (30)	69	0.39
Egyptian (15)	15	0.08
Lebanese (0)	12	0.07
Moroccan (15)	15	0.08
Syrian (0)	27	0.15
Armenian (0)	11	0.06
Australian (5)	5	0.03
Austrian (8)	33	0.19
British (110)	142	0.80
Canadian (23)	47	0.27
Czech (5)	24	0.14
Czechoslovakian (11)	28	0.16
Danish (7)	46	0.26
Dutch (28)	112	0.63
Eastern European (30)	30	0.17
English (694)	2,804	15.87
European (178)	178	1.01
Finnish (0)	13	0.07
French, ex. Basque (46)	412	2.33
French Canadian (25)	39	0.22
German (1,447)	5,259	29.76
Greek (43)	140	0.79
Hungarian (68)	216	1.22
Icelander (0)	7	0.04
Irish (1,275)	4,361	24.68
Italian (1,382)	3,061	17.32
Lithuanian (27)	122	0.69
Luxemburger (0)	8	0.05
Norwegian (19)	115	0.65
Pennsylvania German (9)	37	0.21
Polish (554)	1,607	9.09
Romanian (59)	65	0.37
Russian (90)	321	1.82
Scotch-Irish (83)	290	1.64
Scottish (110)	491	2.78
Serbian (23)	23	0.13
Slovak (33)	127	0.72
Slovene (10)	21	0.12
Swedish (153)	447	2.53
Swiss (0)	55	0.31
Ukrainian (87)	230	1.30
Welsh (30)	337	1.91
Yugoslavian (9)	64	0.36

Hispanic Origin	Population	%
Hispanic or Latino (of any race)	485	2.76
Central American, ex. Mexican	23	0.13
Costa Rican	1	0.01
Guatemalan	5	0.03
Honduran	10	0.06
Panamanian	1	0.01
Salvadoran	6	0.03
Cuban	30	0.17
Dominican Republic	10	0.06
Mexican	144	0.82
Puerto Rican	145	0.83
South American	70	0.40
Argentinean	5	0.03
Chilean	3	0.02
Colombian	27	0.15
Ecuadorian	12	0.07
Paraguayan	1	0.01
Peruvian	13	0.07
Uruguayan	3	0.02
Venezuelan	5	0.03
Other South American	1	0.01
Other Hispanic or Latino	63	0.36

Race*	Population	%
African-American/Black (411)	459	2.61
Not Hispanic (388)	432	2.46
Hispanic (23)	27	0.15
American Indian/Alaska Native (30)	73	0.42
Not Hispanic (19)	51	0.29
Hispanic (11)	22	0.13
Apache (1)	7	0.04
Blackfeet (1)	1	0.01
Cherokee (2)	12	0.07
Chickasaw (0)	1	0.01
Chippewa (0)	1	0.01
Choctaw (0)	1	0.01
Cree (0)	1	0.01
Delaware (1)	3	0.02
Iroquois (1)	1	0.01
Mexican American Ind. (6)	6	0.03
Navajo (0)	4	0.02
Puget Sound Salish (1)	1	0.01
South American Ind. (0)	4	0.02
Asian (243)	347	1.98
Not Hispanic (239)	336	1.91
Hispanic (4)	11	0.06
Cambodian (1)	1	0.01
Chinese, ex. Taiwanese (60)	76	0.43
Filipino (14)	49	0.28
Indian (52)	60	0.34
Japanese (11)	28	0.16
Korean (56)	73	0.42
Sri Lankan (2)	2	0.01
Taiwanese (8)	13	0.07
Thai (4)	7	0.04
Vietnamese (24)	26	0.15
Hawaii Native/Pacific Islander (10)	27	0.15
Not Hispanic (10)	23	0.13
Hispanic (0)	4	0.02
Native Hawaiian (5)	11	0.06
Samoan (3)	4	0.02
White (16,538)	16,745	95.33
Not Hispanic (16,235)	16,399	93.36
Hispanic (303)	346	1.97

Drexel Hill

Place Type: CDP
County: Delaware
Population: 28,043†

Ancestry‡	Population	%
African, Sub-Saharan (263)	280	0.98
African (143)	160	0.56
Ghanaian (49)	49	0.17
Nigerian (71)	71	0.25
Albanian (108)	158	0.55
American (533)	533	1.86
Arab (110)	147	0.51
Egyptian (99)	128	0.45
Lebanese (11)	19	0.07
Armenian (115)	265	0.92
Austrian (0)	40	0.14
Basque (0)	33	0.12
Belgian (19)	19	0.07
British (21)	69	0.24
Canadian (0)	11	0.04
Czech (0)	81	0.28
Czechoslovakian (11)	24	0.08
Danish (0)	51	0.18
Dutch (49)	317	1.11
English (355)	1,851	6.46
European (150)	160	0.56
Finnish (0)	23	0.08
French, ex. Basque (62)	603	2.10
French Canadian (20)	66	0.23
German (755)	5,139	17.93
Greek (136)	223	0.78
Hungarian (12)	74	0.26
Icelander (0)	41	0.14
Irish (4,699)	11,374	39.69
Italian (3,345)	7,166	25.00

*Notes: † The Census 2010 population figure is used to calculate the percentages in the Hispanic Origin and Race categories. Ancestry percentages are based on the 2006-2010 American Community Survey population (not shown); ‡ Numbers in parentheses indicate the number of people reporting a single ancestry; * Numbers in parentheses indicate the number of persons reporting this race alone, not in combination with any other race; Please refer to the Explanation of Data for more information.*

Latvian (0)	17	0.06
Lithuanian (38)	137	0.48
Northern European (30)	30	0.10
Norwegian (5)	70	0.24
Pennsylvania German (22)	76	0.27
Polish (310)	1,297	4.53
Romanian (14)	117	0.41
Russian (156)	344	1.20
Scotch-Irish (243)	450	1.57
Scottish (147)	458	1.60
Slovak (32)	171	0.60
Swedish (27)	206	0.72
Swiss (16)	63	0.22
Turkish (53)	53	0.18
Ukrainian (29)	212	0.74
Welsh (55)	334	1.17
West Indian, ex. Hispanic (158)	182	0.64
Haitian (150)	150	0.52
Jamaican (8)	32	0.11
Yugoslavian (14)	45	0.16

Hispanic Origin	Population	%
Hispanic or Latino (of any race)	728	2.60
Central American, ex. Mexican	77	0.27
Costa Rican	6	0.02
Guatemalan	14	0.05
Honduran	22	0.08
Nicaraguan	7	0.02
Panamanian	7	0.02
Salvadoran	18	0.06
Other Central American	3	0.01
Cuban	50	0.18
Dominican Republic	32	0.11
Mexican	122	0.44
Puerto Rican	209	0.75
South American	179	0.64
Argentinean	13	0.05
Bolivian	2	0.01
Chilean	6	0.02
Colombian	45	0.16
Ecuadorian	64	0.23
Paraguayan	5	0.02
Peruvian	28	0.10
Uruguayan	5	0.02
Venezuelan	10	0.04
Other South American	1	<0.01
Other Hispanic or Latino	59	0.21

Race*	Population	%
African-American/Black (2,161)	2,399	8.55
Not Hispanic (2,121)	2,336	8.33
Hispanic (40)	63	0.22
American Indian/Alaska Native (34)	133	0.47
Not Hispanic (24)	106	0.38
Hispanic (10)	27	0.10
Blackfeet (0)	4	0.01
Canadian/French Am. Ind. (2)	2	0.01
Cherokee (3)	21	0.07
Chippewa (0)	1	<0.01
Choctaw (1)	4	0.01
Creek (0)	1	<0.01
Iroquois (2)	3	0.01
Mexican American Ind. (3)	4	0.01
Seminole (0)	1	<0.01
Sioux (1)	6	0.02
South American Ind. (1)	2	0.01
Tlingit-Haida *(Alaska Native)* (1)	1	<0.01
Asian (1,207)	1,346	4.80
Not Hispanic (1,197)	1,328	4.74
Hispanic (10)	18	0.06
Bangladeshi (9)	10	0.04
Cambodian (23)	30	0.11
Chinese, ex. Taiwanese (396)	455	1.62
Filipino (98)	136	0.48
Hmong (2)	3	0.01
Indian (242)	262	0.93
Indonesian (2)	2	0.01
Japanese (41)	58	0.21
Korean (131)	147	0.52
Laotian (4)	6	0.02
Nepalese (0)	2	0.01
Pakistani (59)	66	0.24
Sri Lankan (3)	3	0.01
Taiwanese (4)	9	0.03
Thai (8)	12	0.04
Vietnamese (135)	158	0.56
Hawaii Native/Pacific Islander (7)	11	0.04
Not Hispanic (6)	9	0.03
Hispanic (1)	2	0.01
Native Hawaiian (5)	6	0.02
Samoan (2)	3	0.01
White (23,988)	24,402	87.02
Not Hispanic (23,539)	23,888	85.18
Hispanic (449)	514	1.83

DuBois

Place Type: City
County: Clearfield
Population: 7,794†

Ancestry‡	Population	%
African, Sub-Saharan (4)	4	0.05
Sierra Leonean (4)	4	0.05
American (1,514)	1,514	19.30
Arab (11)	60	0.76
Lebanese (0)	49	0.62
Syrian (11)	11	0.14
Austrian (8)	37	0.47
Carpatho Rusyn (0)	18	0.23
Croatian (0)	12	0.15
Czech (0)	25	0.32
Dutch (0)	179	2.28
English (318)	812	10.35
European (22)	22	0.28
French, ex. Basque (20)	128	1.63
French Canadian (0)	12	0.15
German (536)	1,803	22.98
Greek (19)	92	1.17
Hungarian (0)	16	0.20
Iranian (0)	11	0.14
Irish (365)	1,289	16.43
Italian (333)	911	11.61
Lithuanian (74)	185	2.36
Norwegian (0)	26	0.33
Pennsylvania German (27)	52	0.66
Polish (324)	712	9.07
Portuguese (0)	16	0.20
Russian (0)	29	0.37
Scotch-Irish (90)	182	2.32
Scottish (84)	226	2.88
Serbian (0)	12	0.15
Slavic (9)	53	0.68
Slovak (66)	149	1.90
Slovene (10)	10	0.13
Swedish (94)	382	4.87
Swiss (8)	17	0.22
Ukrainian (9)	61	0.78
Welsh (13)	111	1.41
West Indian, ex. Hispanic (10)	10	0.13
Dutch West Indian (10)	10	0.13

Hispanic Origin	Population	%
Hispanic or Latino (of any race)	95	1.22
Central American, ex. Mexican	1	0.01
Salvadoran	1	0.01
Dominican Republic	2	0.03
Mexican	29	0.37
Puerto Rican	47	0.60
South American	5	0.06
Colombian	2	0.03
Ecuadorian	3	0.04
Other Hispanic or Latino	11	0.14

Race*	Population	%
African-American/Black (49)	87	1.12
Not Hispanic (43)	76	0.98
Hispanic (6)	11	0.14
American Indian/Alaska Native (4)	20	0.26
Not Hispanic (4)	18	0.23
Hispanic (0)	2	0.03
Blackfeet (0)	2	0.03
Cherokee (0)	2	0.03
Choctaw (1)	1	0.01
Iroquois (0)	1	0.01
Sioux (0)	1	0.01
Asian (67)	100	1.28
Not Hispanic (66)	98	1.26
Hispanic (1)	2	0.03
Bangladeshi (2)	2	0.03
Chinese, ex. Taiwanese (21)	22	0.28
Filipino (6)	10	0.13
Indian (15)	19	0.24
Japanese (2)	12	0.15
Korean (11)	18	0.23
Vietnamese (9)	10	0.13
Hawaii Native/Pacific Islander (1)	2	0.03
Not Hispanic (1)	2	0.03
Guamanian/Chamorro (0)	1	0.01
Native Hawaiian (1)	1	0.01
White (7,557)	7,637	97.99
Not Hispanic (7,503)	7,574	97.18
Hispanic (54)	63	0.81

Dunmore

Place Type: Borough
County: Lackawanna
Population: 14,057†

Ancestry‡	Population	%
American (182)	182	1.29
Arab (33)	209	1.48
Lebanese (0)	176	1.25
Other Arab (33)	33	0.23
Armenian (0)	24	0.17
Austrian (17)	246	1.75
British (0)	18	0.13
Bulgarian (18)	18	0.13
Carpatho Rusyn (49)	69	0.49
Croatian (9)	9	0.06
Czech (31)	82	0.58
Czechoslovakian (32)	32	0.23
Dutch (28)	161	1.14
Eastern European (8)	16	0.11
English (148)	767	5.44
European (26)	26	0.18
French, ex. Basque (10)	28	0.20
French Canadian (0)	23	0.16
German (351)	1,915	13.59
Greek (32)	51	0.36
Hungarian (0)	164	1.16
Irish (1,794)	4,541	32.22
Italian (2,230)	5,026	35.67
Lithuanian (96)	362	2.57
Norwegian (0)	8	0.06
Pennsylvania German (29)	39	0.28
Polish (387)	1,429	10.14
Romanian (0)	8	0.06
Russian (70)	450	3.19
Scotch-Irish (62)	194	1.38
Scottish (62)	178	1.26
Slovak (223)	617	4.38
Slovene (0)	30	0.21
Swedish (6)	33	0.23
Swiss (0)	42	0.30
Ukrainian (88)	130	0.92
Welsh (60)	600	4.26

Hispanic Origin	Population	%
Hispanic or Latino (of any race)	319	2.27
Central American, ex. Mexican	22	0.16
Guatemalan	5	0.04
Honduran	5	0.04
Panamanian	3	0.02
Salvadoran	9	0.06
Cuban	15	0.11
Dominican Republic	21	0.15
Mexican	64	0.46
Puerto Rican	124	0.88

*Notes: † The Census 2010 population figure is used to calculate the percentages in the Hispanic Origin and Race categories. Ancestry percentages are based on the 2006-2010 American Community Survey population (not shown); ‡ Numbers in parentheses indicate the number of people reporting a single ancestry; * Numbers in parentheses indicate the number of persons reporting this race alone, not in combination with any other race; Please refer to the Explanation of Data for more information.*

	Population	%
South American	39	0.28
Argentinean	4	0.03
Chilean	3	0.02
Colombian	18	0.13
Ecuadorian	8	0.06
Paraguayan	1	0.01
Peruvian	5	0.04
Other Hispanic or Latino	34	0.24

Race*	Population	%
African-American/Black (160)	224	1.59
Not Hispanic (142)	193	1.37
Hispanic (18)	31	0.22
American Indian/Alaska Native (10)	35	0.25
Not Hispanic (8)	32	0.23
Hispanic (2)	3	0.02
Blackfeet (1)	6	0.04
Cherokee (0)	8	0.06
Cheyenne (1)	1	0.01
Chippewa (0)	1	0.01
Crow (0)	1	0.01
Delaware (0)	1	0.01
Sioux (0)	2	0.01
Asian (247)	290	2.06
Not Hispanic (246)	287	2.04
Hispanic (1)	3	0.02
Bangladeshi (4)	4	0.03
Cambodian (0)	1	0.01
Chinese, ex. Taiwanese (34)	43	0.31
Filipino (36)	47	0.33
Indian (138)	144	1.02
Indonesian (6)	6	0.04
Japanese (2)	6	0.04
Korean (4)	7	0.05
Laotian (0)	2	0.01
Nepalese (4)	4	0.03
Pakistani (7)	8	0.06
Thai (7)	9	0.06
Vietnamese (1)	1	0.01
Hawaii Native/Pacific Islander (3)	8	0.06
Not Hispanic (2)	7	0.05
Hispanic (1)	1	0.01
Guamanian/Chamorro (1)	1	0.01
Native Hawaiian (2)	2	0.01
Samoan (0)	4	0.03
White (13,386)	13,514	96.14
Not Hispanic (13,215)	13,322	94.77
Hispanic (171)	192	1.37

East Bradford

Place Type: Township
County: Chester
Population: 9,942†

Ancestry‡	Population	%
African, Sub-Saharan (47)	47	0.47
African (32)	32	0.32
Nigerian (15)	15	0.15
American (462)	462	4.66
Arab (9)	38	0.38
Syrian (9)	38	0.38
Armenian (0)	15	0.15
Austrian (40)	134	1.35
British (32)	79	0.80
Canadian (11)	11	0.11
Celtic (26)	36	0.36
Croatian (0)	19	0.19
Czech (30)	67	0.68
Czechoslovakian (0)	58	0.58
Danish (0)	29	0.29
Dutch (20)	196	1.98
Eastern European (22)	22	0.22
English (465)	2,197	22.14
European (101)	101	1.02
French, ex. Basque (30)	370	3.73
French Canadian (14)	53	0.53
German (341)	2,231	22.48
Greek (33)	86	0.87
Hungarian (25)	170	1.71
Iranian (10)	22	0.22
Irish (544)	2,540	25.59
Italian (494)	1,772	17.86
Latvian (13)	35	0.35
Lithuanian (15)	53	0.53
Norwegian (25)	35	0.35
Polish (183)	601	6.06
Romanian (13)	24	0.24
Russian (37)	130	1.31
Scotch-Irish (112)	282	2.84
Scottish (40)	553	5.57
Slovak (0)	68	0.69
Slovene (13)	74	0.75
Swedish (44)	161	1.62
Swiss (0)	37	0.37
Ukrainian (47)	153	1.54
Welsh (38)	318	3.20
West Indian, ex. Hispanic (19)	57	0.57
Jamaican (19)	57	0.57

Hispanic Origin	Population	%
Hispanic or Latino (of any race)	197	1.98
Central American, ex. Mexican	13	0.13
Costa Rican	4	0.04
Guatemalan	4	0.04
Honduran	2	0.02
Nicaraguan	1	0.01
Panamanian	1	0.01
Salvadoran	1	0.01
Cuban	14	0.14
Dominican Republic	6	0.06
Mexican	67	0.67
Puerto Rican	50	0.50
South American	31	0.31
Bolivian	3	0.03
Chilean	5	0.05
Colombian	14	0.14
Ecuadorian	4	0.04
Peruvian	5	0.05
Other Hispanic or Latino	16	0.16

Race*	Population	%
African-American/Black (325)	392	3.94
Not Hispanic (318)	379	3.81
Hispanic (7)	13	0.13
American Indian/Alaska Native (10)	42	0.42
Not Hispanic (8)	36	0.36
Hispanic (2)	6	0.06
Cherokee (0)	12	0.12
Iroquois (1)	1	0.01
Seminole (0)	1	0.01
South American Ind. (2)	4	0.04
Asian (200)	258	2.60
Not Hispanic (198)	248	2.49
Hispanic (2)	10	0.10
Cambodian (1)	1	0.01
Chinese, ex. Taiwanese (53)	69	0.69
Filipino (3)	9	0.09
Indian (74)	95	0.96
Indonesian (0)	1	0.01
Japanese (3)	13	0.13
Korean (22)	29	0.29
Laotian (2)	2	0.02
Nepalese (1)	1	0.01
Pakistani (1)	1	0.01
Sri Lankan (1)	1	0.01
Thai (5)	7	0.07
Vietnamese (25)	31	0.31
Hawaii Native/Pacific Islander (1)	4	0.04
Not Hispanic (0)	2	0.02
Hispanic (1)	2	0.02
Guamanian/Chamorro (1)	1	0.01
White (9,223)	9,343	93.98
Not Hispanic (9,099)	9,202	92.56
Hispanic (124)	141	1.42

East Cocalico

Place Type: Township
County: Lancaster
Population: 10,310†

Ancestry‡	Population	%
American (976)	976	9.52
British (16)	28	0.27
Czechoslovakian (0)	10	0.10
Danish (10)	10	0.10
Dutch (91)	302	2.95
Eastern European (11)	11	0.11
English (213)	889	8.67
European (193)	216	2.11
French, ex. Basque (0)	159	1.55
French Canadian (50)	50	0.49
German (2,837)	4,703	45.89
Greek (12)	35	0.34
Irish (190)	885	8.63
Italian (160)	482	4.70
Norwegian (0)	45	0.44
Pennsylvania German (245)	266	2.60
Polish (140)	301	2.94
Portuguese (39)	60	0.59
Romanian (12)	12	0.12
Russian (103)	180	1.76
Scotch-Irish (26)	61	0.60
Scottish (94)	261	2.55
Slavic (0)	31	0.30
Slovak (0)	53	0.52
Swedish (12)	69	0.67
Swiss (254)	578	5.64
Ukrainian (42)	81	0.79
Welsh (0)	79	0.77

Hispanic Origin	Population	%
Hispanic or Latino (of any race)	189	1.83
Central American, ex. Mexican	8	0.08
Costa Rican	2	0.02
Guatemalan	3	0.03
Honduran	1	0.01
Nicaraguan	1	0.01
Salvadoran	1	0.01
Cuban	1	0.01
Dominican Republic	1	0.01
Mexican	41	0.40
Puerto Rican	103	1.00
South American	23	0.22
Colombian	18	0.17
Uruguayan	5	0.05
Other Hispanic or Latino	12	0.12

Race*	Population	%
African-American/Black (89)	134	1.30
Not Hispanic (83)	117	1.13
Hispanic (6)	17	0.16
American Indian/Alaska Native (12)	30	0.29
Not Hispanic (10)	26	0.25
Hispanic (2)	4	0.04
Apache (0)	3	0.03
Canadian/French Am. Ind. (0)	1	0.01
Cherokee (3)	8	0.08
Chippewa (1)	1	0.01
Delaware (1)	2	0.02
Mexican American Ind. (1)	1	0.01
Asian (212)	222	2.15
Not Hispanic (212)	221	2.14
Hispanic (0)	1	0.01
Cambodian (1)	1	0.01
Chinese, ex. Taiwanese (16)	18	0.17
Filipino (8)	8	0.08
Hmong (110)	120	1.16
Indian (19)	23	0.22
Japanese (0)	1	0.01
Korean (9)	10	0.10
Laotian (14)	21	0.20
Malaysian (3)	3	0.03
Taiwanese (4)	4	0.04
Thai (2)	2	0.02

*Notes: † The Census 2010 population figure is used to calculate the percentages in the Hispanic Origin and Race categories. Ancestry percentages are based on the 2006-2010 American Community Survey population (not shown); ‡ Numbers in parentheses indicate the number of people reporting a single ancestry; * Numbers in parentheses indicate the number of persons reporting this race alone, not in combination with any other race; Please refer to the Explanation of Data for more information.*

Vietnamese (12)	13	0.13
Hawaii Native/Pacific Islander (5)	7	0.07
Not Hispanic (2)	4	0.04
Hispanic (3)	3	0.03
Guamanian/Chamorro (5)	7	0.07
White (9,867)	9,939	96.40
Not Hispanic (9,753)	9,810	95.15
Hispanic (114)	129	1.25

East Donegal

Place Type: Township
County: Lancaster
Population: 7,755†

Ancestry‡	Population	%
American (837)	837	11.40
Armenian (12)	12	0.16
Austrian (18)	48	0.65
Czech (0)	51	0.69
Dutch (26)	204	2.78
English (150)	439	5.98
European (23)	38	0.52
French, ex. Basque (48)	134	1.82
French Canadian (41)	178	2.42
German (1,555)	3,100	42.21
Hungarian (14)	31	0.42
Irish (259)	1,094	14.90
Italian (310)	736	10.02
Lithuanian (0)	28	0.38
Norwegian (8)	60	0.82
Polish (83)	318	4.33
Russian (25)	25	0.34
Scotch-Irish (25)	206	2.81
Scottish (64)	126	1.72
Slavic (0)	13	0.18
Slovak (9)	24	0.33
Swedish (11)	69	0.94
Swiss (25)	93	1.27
Welsh (0)	85	1.16

Hispanic Origin	Population	%
Hispanic or Latino (of any race)	251	3.24
Central American, ex. Mexican	32	0.41
Costa Rican	2	0.03
Guatemalan	18	0.23
Nicaraguan	3	0.04
Panamanian	1	0.01
Salvadoran	8	0.10
Cuban	7	0.09
Dominican Republic	6	0.08
Mexican	45	0.58
Puerto Rican	135	1.74
South American	11	0.14
Bolivian	1	0.01
Chilean	2	0.03
Colombian	5	0.06
Venezuelan	3	0.04
Other Hispanic or Latino	15	0.19

Race*	Population	%
African-American/Black (143)	203	2.62
Not Hispanic (132)	182	2.35
Hispanic (11)	21	0.27
American Indian/Alaska Native (6)	28	0.36
Not Hispanic (6)	19	0.25
Hispanic (0)	9	0.12
Cherokee (1)	4	0.05
Choctaw (0)	1	0.01
Iroquois (0)	1	0.01
Sioux (0)	3	0.04
Asian (63)	111	1.43
Not Hispanic (61)	102	1.32
Hispanic (2)	9	0.12
Cambodian (1)	5	0.06
Chinese, ex. Taiwanese (10)	18	0.23
Filipino (8)	13	0.17
Indian (22)	22	0.28
Indonesian (2)	4	0.05
Japanese (2)	15	0.19
Korean (8)	12	0.15
Pakistani (1)	4	0.05
Vietnamese (5)	12	0.15
Hawaii Native/Pacific Islander (4)	12	0.15
Not Hispanic (4)	12	0.15
Native Hawaiian (0)	3	0.04
Samoan (1)	4	0.05
White (7,352)	7,467	96.29
Not Hispanic (7,196)	7,293	94.04
Hispanic (156)	174	2.24

East Goshen

Place Type: Township
County: Chester
Population: 18,026†

Ancestry‡	Population	%
African, Sub-Saharan (49)	61	0.34
African (35)	35	0.19
Nigerian (14)	26	0.14
Albanian (0)	9	0.05
American (664)	664	3.69
Arab (60)	102	0.57
Egyptian (13)	13	0.07
Lebanese (25)	67	0.37
Moroccan (13)	13	0.07
Palestinian (9)	9	0.05
Armenian (69)	148	0.82
Austrian (0)	82	0.46
Belgian (0)	9	0.05
British (51)	66	0.37
Canadian (20)	40	0.22
Croatian (0)	40	0.22
Czech (13)	73	0.41
Danish (0)	30	0.17
Dutch (20)	189	1.05
Eastern European (11)	11	0.06
English (619)	3,113	17.32
European (84)	97	0.54
Finnish (0)	11	0.06
French, ex. Basque (115)	521	2.90
French Canadian (10)	10	0.06
German (1,085)	4,431	24.65
Greek (88)	202	1.12
Hungarian (10)	125	0.70
Iranian (91)	91	0.51
Irish (1,735)	5,772	32.11
Italian (1,284)	3,735	20.78
Latvian (19)	50	0.28
Lithuanian (0)	91	0.51
Norwegian (24)	73	0.41
Pennsylvania German (34)	45	0.25
Polish (297)	1,135	6.31
Romanian (0)	30	0.17
Russian (75)	373	2.07
Scotch-Irish (173)	699	3.89
Scottish (128)	578	3.22
Slavic (16)	55	0.31
Slovak (47)	212	1.18
Slovene (9)	9	0.05
Swedish (51)	92	0.51
Swiss (0)	26	0.14
Ukrainian (35)	200	1.11
Welsh (62)	375	2.09
West Indian, ex. Hispanic (10)	10	0.06
Jamaican (10)	10	0.06
Yugoslavian (0)	41	0.23

Hispanic Origin	Population	%
Hispanic or Latino (of any race)	405	2.25
Central American, ex. Mexican	32	0.18
Costa Rican	1	0.01
Guatemalan	13	0.07
Honduran	3	0.02
Panamanian	8	0.04
Salvadoran	7	0.04
Cuban	28	0.16
Dominican Republic	6	0.03
Mexican	123	0.68
Puerto Rican	96	0.53
South American	70	0.39
Argentinean	11	0.06
Bolivian	5	0.03
Chilean	11	0.06
Colombian	13	0.07
Ecuadorian	11	0.06
Peruvian	7	0.04
Uruguayan	1	0.01
Venezuelan	11	0.06
Other Hispanic or Latino	50	0.28

Race*	Population	%
African-American/Black (484)	572	3.17
Not Hispanic (461)	536	2.97
Hispanic (23)	36	0.20
American Indian/Alaska Native (13)	59	0.33
Not Hispanic (8)	36	0.20
Hispanic (5)	23	0.13
Apache (0)	4	0.02
Cherokee (3)	12	0.07
Chippewa (1)	4	0.02
Creek (0)	1	0.01
Delaware (0)	6	0.03
Iroquois (0)	1	0.01
Mexican American Ind. (4)	9	0.05
Navajo (1)	4	0.02
Sioux (0)	2	0.01
South American Ind. (0)	4	0.02
Asian (517)	593	3.29
Not Hispanic (510)	583	3.23
Hispanic (7)	10	0.06
Bangladeshi (4)	4	0.02
Chinese, ex. Taiwanese (121)	139	0.77
Filipino (27)	34	0.19
Indian (228)	238	1.32
Indonesian (6)	10	0.06
Japanese (12)	22	0.12
Korean (66)	72	0.40
Laotian (1)	6	0.03
Pakistani (17)	18	0.10
Sri Lankan (2)	2	0.01
Taiwanese (5)	5	0.03
Thai (7)	9	0.05
Vietnamese (15)	16	0.09
Hawaii Native/Pacific Islander (3)	4	0.02
Not Hispanic (3)	4	0.02
Native Hawaiian (1)	1	0.01
White (16,699)	16,880	93.64
Not Hispanic (16,453)	16,607	92.13
Hispanic (246)	273	1.51

East Hempfield

Place Type: Township
County: Lancaster
Population: 23,522†

Ancestry‡	Population	%
African, Sub-Saharan (14)	73	0.32
African (0)	32	0.14
Liberian (14)	14	0.06
South African (0)	13	0.06
Other Sub-Saharan African (0)	14	0.06
American (1,059)	1,059	4.57
Arab (14)	54	0.23
Lebanese (14)	54	0.23
Austrian (0)	22	0.10
British (20)	38	0.16
Canadian (0)	18	0.08
Croatian (0)	47	0.20
Czech (42)	199	0.86
Czechoslovakian (20)	95	0.41
Danish (37)	132	0.57
Dutch (54)	439	1.90
Eastern European (79)	123	0.53
English (729)	2,836	12.25
European (236)	236	1.02
French, ex. Basque (78)	488	2.11
French Canadian (10)	44	0.19

SECTION TWO

*Notes: † The Census 2010 population figure is used to calculate the percentages in the Hispanic Origin and Race categories. Ancestry percentages are based on the 2006-2010 American Community Survey population (not shown); ‡ Numbers in parentheses indicate the number of people reporting a single ancestry; * Numbers in parentheses indicate the number of persons reporting this race alone, not in combination with any other race; Please refer to the Explanation of Data for more information.*

German (4,255)	9,395	40.57
Greek (110)	172	0.74
Hungarian (71)	117	0.51
Irish (814)	3,931	16.98
Italian (669)	1,902	8.21
Lithuanian (0)	15	0.06
Macedonian (10)	10	0.04
Northern European (139)	139	0.60
Norwegian (26)	162	0.70
Pennsylvania German (57)	57	0.25
Polish (230)	901	3.89
Portuguese (16)	63	0.27
Romanian (8)	8	0.03
Russian (84)	342	1.48
Scandinavian (0)	18	0.08
Scotch-Irish (147)	549	2.37
Scottish (196)	480	2.07
Serbian (10)	10	0.04
Slavic (0)	9	0.04
Slovak (65)	200	0.86
Slovene (0)	82	0.35
Swedish (76)	198	0.86
Swiss (62)	519	2.24
Ukrainian (90)	130	0.56
Welsh (94)	393	1.70
Yugoslavian (18)	35	0.15

Hispanic Origin	Population	%
Hispanic or Latino (of any race)	1,625	6.91
Central American, ex. Mexican	44	0.19
Costa Rican	5	0.02
Guatemalan	9	0.04
Honduran	14	0.06
Nicaraguan	1	<0.01
Panamanian	6	0.03
Salvadoran	9	0.04
Cuban	45	0.19
Dominican Republic	98	0.42
Mexican	184	0.78
Puerto Rican	1,070	4.55
South American	102	0.43
Argentinean	7	0.03
Bolivian	4	0.02
Chilean	3	0.01
Colombian	63	0.27
Ecuadorian	5	0.02
Peruvian	16	0.07
Venezuelan	4	0.02
Other Hispanic or Latino	82	0.35

Race*	Population	%
African-American/Black (662)	858	3.65
Not Hispanic (588)	735	3.12
Hispanic (74)	123	0.52
American Indian/Alaska Native (34)	98	0.42
Not Hispanic (15)	67	0.28
Hispanic (19)	31	0.13
Apache (0)	2	0.01
Blackfeet (0)	3	0.01
Canadian/French Am. Ind. (1)	1	<0.01
Cherokee (4)	13	0.06
Choctaw (0)	1	<0.01
Delaware (1)	2	0.01
Iroquois (1)	5	0.02
Navajo (1)	3	0.01
Pima (0)	1	<0.01
Sioux (0)	2	0.01
South American Ind. (7)	9	0.04
Asian (829)	958	4.07
Not Hispanic (824)	947	4.03
Hispanic (5)	11	0.05
Bangladeshi (10)	10	0.04
Cambodian (40)	49	0.21
Chinese, ex. Taiwanese (171)	206	0.88
Filipino (44)	69	0.29
Hmong (0)	1	<0.01
Indian (111)	135	0.57
Indonesian (3)	5	0.02
Japanese (18)	43	0.18
Korean (76)	93	0.40
Laotian (14)	16	0.07
Malaysian (1)	4	0.02
Nepalese (4)	6	0.03
Pakistani (10)	14	0.06
Thai (1)	1	<0.01
Vietnamese (275)	299	1.27
Hawaii Native/Pacific Islander (8)	18	0.08
Not Hispanic (6)	12	0.05
Hispanic (2)	6	0.03
Native Hawaiian (0)	8	0.03
White (20,881)	21,267	90.41
Not Hispanic (20,134)	20,417	86.80
Hispanic (747)	850	3.61

East Huntingdon

Place Type: Township
County: Westmoreland
Population: 7,963†

Ancestry‡	Population	%
American (353)	353	4.44
Arab (42)	42	0.53
Egyptian (14)	14	0.18
Lebanese (28)	28	0.35
Australian (0)	11	0.14
Austrian (0)	41	0.52
Croatian (14)	43	0.54
Czech (9)	70	0.88
Czechoslovakian (16)	16	0.20
Dutch (23)	253	3.19
English (317)	952	11.99
European (21)	21	0.26
French, ex. Basque (10)	189	2.38
German (998)	2,823	35.54
Hungarian (11)	74	0.93
Irish (242)	1,442	18.15
Italian (491)	1,087	13.69
Lithuanian (8)	20	0.25
Pennsylvania German (65)	122	1.54
Polish (297)	871	10.97
Scotch-Irish (34)	106	1.33
Scottish (85)	188	2.37
Slavic (0)	20	0.25
Slovak (171)	476	5.99
Slovene (0)	18	0.23
Swedish (0)	57	0.72
Swiss (14)	14	0.18
Ukrainian (0)	32	0.40
Welsh (0)	41	0.52
West Indian, ex. Hispanic (0)	12	0.15
Jamaican (0)	12	0.15
Yugoslavian (9)	9	0.11

Hispanic Origin	Population	%
Hispanic or Latino (of any race)	66	0.83
Central American, ex. Mexican	2	0.03
Guatemalan	1	0.01
Salvadoran	1	0.01
Cuban	2	0.03
Mexican	36	0.45
Puerto Rican	11	0.14
South American	4	0.05
Argentinean	3	0.04
Peruvian	1	0.01
Other Hispanic or Latino	11	0.14

Race*	Population	%
African-American/Black (59)	97	1.22
Not Hispanic (59)	93	1.17
Hispanic (0)	4	0.05
American Indian/Alaska Native (8)	40	0.50
Not Hispanic (6)	34	0.43
Hispanic (2)	6	0.08
Apache (1)	1	0.01
Cherokee (0)	10	0.13
Iroquois (0)	2	0.03
Lumbee (2)	2	0.03
Mexican American Ind. (1)	1	0.01
Ottawa (0)	1	0.01
Seminole (0)	1	0.01
Sioux (0)	3	0.04
Asian (41)	47	0.59
Not Hispanic (41)	46	0.58
Hispanic (0)	1	0.01
Chinese, ex. Taiwanese (20)	21	0.26
Filipino (5)	8	0.10
Indian (2)	2	0.03
Japanese (2)	3	0.04
Korean (2)	3	0.04
Thai (1)	1	0.01
Vietnamese (9)	9	0.11
Hawaii Native/Pacific Islander (2)	8	0.10
Not Hispanic (2)	8	0.10
Guamanian/Chamorro (2)	8	0.10
White (7,756)	7,832	98.35
Not Hispanic (7,715)	7,785	97.76
Hispanic (41)	47	0.59

East Lampeter

Place Type: Township
County: Lancaster
Population: 16,424†

Ancestry‡	Population	%
African, Sub-Saharan (98)	121	0.76
African (0)	23	0.14
Ethiopian (70)	70	0.44
Kenyan (28)	28	0.18
Albanian (25)	25	0.16
American (1,057)	1,057	6.64
Arab (5)	5	0.03
Lebanese (5)	5	0.03
Austrian (0)	26	0.16
Belgian (16)	16	0.10
Brazilian (27)	27	0.17
British (21)	42	0.26
Canadian (0)	44	0.28
Czech (0)	10	0.06
Dutch (155)	213	1.34
Eastern European (12)	12	0.08
English (305)	1,286	8.07
European (175)	175	1.10
Finnish (24)	24	0.15
French, ex. Basque (96)	381	2.39
French Canadian (0)	29	0.18
German (3,078)	5,983	37.57
Greek (40)	60	0.38
Hungarian (0)	78	0.49
Irish (509)	2,177	13.67
Italian (396)	1,008	6.33
Latvian (22)	43	0.27
Lithuanian (12)	52	0.33
Northern European (10)	10	0.06
Norwegian (25)	55	0.35
Pennsylvania German (447)	495	3.11
Polish (89)	305	1.91
Romanian (63)	63	0.40
Russian (15)	67	0.42
Scotch-Irish (85)	381	2.39
Scottish (44)	139	0.87
Slovak (24)	95	0.60
Swedish (24)	133	0.84
Swiss (126)	756	4.75
Ukrainian (9)	9	0.06
Welsh (34)	256	1.61
West Indian, ex. Hispanic (0)	52	0.33
Jamaican (0)	52	0.33

Hispanic Origin	Population	%
Hispanic or Latino (of any race)	1,500	9.13
Central American, ex. Mexican	59	0.36
Costa Rican	18	0.11
Guatemalan	17	0.10
Honduran	9	0.05
Nicaraguan	3	0.02
Salvadoran	12	0.07
Cuban	55	0.33
Dominican Republic	126	0.77

*Notes: † The Census 2010 population figure is used to calculate the percentages in the Hispanic Origin and Race categories. Ancestry percentages are based on the 2006-2010 American Community Survey population (not shown); ‡ Numbers in parentheses indicate the number of people reporting a single ancestry; * Numbers in parentheses indicate the number of persons reporting this race alone, not in combination with any other race; Please refer to the Explanation of Data for more information.*

Mexican	124	0.75
Puerto Rican	961	5.85
South American	116	0.71
Argentinean	11	0.07
Chilean	4	0.02
Colombian	58	0.35
Ecuadorian	24	0.15
Peruvian	14	0.09
Venezuelan	3	0.02
Other South American	2	0.01
Other Hispanic or Latino	59	0.36

Race*	Population	%
African-American/Black (775)	970	5.91
Not Hispanic (654)	795	4.84
Hispanic (121)	175	1.07
American Indian/Alaska Native (31)	93	0.57
Not Hispanic (14)	67	0.41
Hispanic (17)	26	0.16
Apache (0)	1	0.01
Blackfeet (0)	5	0.03
Cherokee (2)	25	0.15
Comanche (0)	6	0.04
Cree (1)	3	0.02
Delaware (0)	3	0.02
Iroquois (1)	1	0.01
Navajo (1)	2	0.01
Sioux (0)	1	0.01
South American Ind. (5)	7	0.04
Asian (672)	731	4.45
Not Hispanic (668)	721	4.39
Hispanic (4)	10	0.06
Burmese (10)	10	0.06
Cambodian (21)	24	0.15
Chinese, ex. Taiwanese (118)	133	0.81
Filipino (23)	31	0.19
Hmong (10)	10	0.06
Indian (186)	200	1.22
Japanese (16)	26	0.16
Korean (32)	41	0.25
Laotian (8)	10	0.06
Malaysian (1)	1	0.01
Nepalese (4)	4	0.02
Pakistani (34)	36	0.22
Sri Lankan (1)	1	0.01
Taiwanese (1)	4	0.02
Thai (3)	4	0.02
Vietnamese (173)	183	1.11
Hawaii Native/Pacific Islander (6)	16	0.10
Not Hispanic (5)	9	0.05
Hispanic (1)	7	0.04
Guamanian/Chamorro (2)	2	0.01
Native Hawaiian (1)	1	0.01
Samoan (2)	4	0.02
White (14,055)	14,324	87.21
Not Hispanic (13,328)	13,524	82.34
Hispanic (727)	800	4.87

East Norriton

Place Type: Township
County: Montgomery
Population: 13,590†

Ancestry‡	Population	%
American (483)	483	3.57
Arab (30)	30	0.22
Arab (30)	30	0.22
Armenian (0)	11	0.08
Australian (0)	14	0.10
Austrian (10)	23	0.17
Brazilian (30)	30	0.22
British (113)	124	0.92
Canadian (42)	42	0.31
Croatian (12)	25	0.18
Czech (0)	72	0.53
Czechoslovakian (0)	7	0.05
Danish (0)	7	0.05
Dutch (36)	143	1.06
English (290)	1,309	9.68
European (22)	85	0.63
French, ex. Basque (26)	255	1.89
French Canadian (9)	103	0.76
German (875)	3,109	22.99
Greek (10)	10	0.07
Hungarian (27)	75	0.55
Irish (907)	3,514	25.99
Italian (1,646)	3,391	25.08
Latvian (14)	14	0.10
Lithuanian (34)	162	1.20
Norwegian (21)	59	0.44
Pennsylvania German (35)	70	0.52
Polish (399)	965	7.14
Romanian (0)	32	0.24
Russian (66)	254	1.88
Scandinavian (10)	10	0.07
Scotch-Irish (165)	366	2.71
Scottish (8)	183	1.35
Slovak (24)	121	0.89
Swedish (12)	111	0.82
Swiss (0)	61	0.45
Ukrainian (54)	145	1.07
Welsh (34)	164	1.21
West Indian, ex. Hispanic (9)	9	0.07
Jamaican (9)	9	0.07
Yugoslavian (0)	10	0.07

Hispanic Origin	Population	%
Hispanic or Latino (of any race)	430	3.16
Central American, ex. Mexican	10	0.07
Costa Rican	1	0.01
Guatemalan	4	0.03
Honduran	1	0.01
Panamanian	4	0.03
Cuban	19	0.14
Dominican Republic	14	0.10
Mexican	167	1.23
Puerto Rican	137	1.01
South American	41	0.30
Argentinean	13	0.10
Chilean	5	0.04
Colombian	3	0.02
Ecuadorian	3	0.02
Peruvian	6	0.04
Venezuelan	11	0.08
Other Hispanic or Latino	42	0.31

Race*	Population	%
African-American/Black (1,217)	1,326	9.76
Not Hispanic (1,198)	1,296	9.54
Hispanic (19)	30	0.22
American Indian/Alaska Native (18)	68	0.50
Not Hispanic (12)	56	0.41
Hispanic (6)	12	0.09
Blackfeet (0)	1	0.01
Cherokee (0)	17	0.13
Creek (1)	1	0.01
Delaware (0)	1	0.01
Iroquois (0)	1	0.01
Lumbee (0)	1	0.01
Ottawa (0)	1	0.01
Seminole (0)	1	0.01
Sioux (0)	2	0.01
Yuman (1)	1	0.01
Asian (855)	920	6.77
Not Hispanic (851)	909	6.69
Hispanic (4)	11	0.08
Bangladeshi (1)	1	0.01
Burmese (1)	1	0.01
Cambodian (16)	18	0.13
Chinese, ex. Taiwanese (89)	118	0.87
Filipino (56)	66	0.49
Indian (339)	355	2.61
Indonesian (2)	3	0.02
Japanese (13)	18	0.13
Korean (217)	229	1.69
Laotian (3)	6	0.04
Malaysian (2)	2	0.01
Nepalese (6)	7	0.05
Pakistani (11)	12	0.09
Sri Lankan (4)	4	0.03
Taiwanese (2)	6	0.04
Thai (10)	13	0.10
Vietnamese (56)	65	0.48
Hawaii Native/Pacific Islander (3)	7	0.05
Not Hispanic (3)	6	0.04
Hispanic (0)	1	0.01
Guamanian/Chamorro (1)	1	0.01
Native Hawaiian (2)	2	0.01
White (11,147)	11,316	83.27
Not Hispanic (10,893)	11,038	81.22
Hispanic (254)	278	2.05

East Nottingham

Place Type: Township
County: Chester
Population: 8,650†

Ancestry‡	Population	%
African, Sub-Saharan (25)	25	0.31
African (25)	25	0.31
American (479)	479	5.86
Austrian (58)	58	0.71
British (3)	43	0.53
Canadian (55)	55	0.67
Czech (0)	39	0.48
Czechoslovakian (19)	47	0.57
Dutch (74)	194	2.37
Eastern European (69)	69	0.84
English (273)	1,276	15.61
European (74)	74	0.91
Finnish (10)	10	0.12
French, ex. Basque (28)	184	2.25
French Canadian (0)	91	1.11
German (600)	2,127	26.02
German Russian (0)	33	0.40
Greek (0)	18	0.22
Hungarian (0)	31	0.38
Irish (488)	1,918	23.46
Italian (382)	1,424	17.42
Lithuanian (0)	3	0.04
Norwegian (0)	45	0.55
Pennsylvania German (300)	331	4.05
Polish (28)	425	5.20
Russian (0)	16	0.20
Scotch-Irish (128)	397	4.86
Scottish (37)	303	3.71
Slovak (11)	96	1.17
Slovene (0)	4	0.05
Swedish (0)	52	0.64
Swiss (0)	114	1.39
Ukrainian (0)	65	0.80
Welsh (0)	64	0.78

Hispanic Origin	Population	%
Hispanic or Latino (of any race)	800	9.25
Central American, ex. Mexican	22	0.25
Costa Rican	1	0.01
Guatemalan	12	0.14
Honduran	2	0.02
Panamanian	3	0.03
Salvadoran	4	0.05
Cuban	7	0.08
Mexican	549	6.35
Puerto Rican	185	2.14
South American	23	0.27
Argentinean	1	0.01
Chilean	4	0.05
Colombian	4	0.05
Ecuadorian	9	0.10
Venezuelan	4	0.05
Other South American	1	0.01
Other Hispanic or Latino	14	0.16

Race*	Population	%
African-American/Black (271)	341	3.94
Not Hispanic (255)	310	3.58
Hispanic (16)	31	0.36
American Indian/Alaska Native (0)	35	0.40

*Notes: † The Census 2010 population figure is used to calculate the percentages in the Hispanic Origin and Race categories. Ancestry percentages are based on the 2006-2010 American Community Survey population (not shown); ‡ Numbers in parentheses indicate the number of people reporting a single ancestry; * Numbers in parentheses indicate the number of persons reporting this race alone, not in combination with any other race; Please refer to the Explanation of Data for more information.*

Not Hispanic (0)	31	0.36
Hispanic (0)	4	0.05
Blackfeet (0)	4	0.05
Cherokee (0)	18	0.21
Delaware (0)	1	0.01
Hopi (0)	1	0.01
Seminole (0)	1	0.01
Sioux (0)	2	0.02
South American Ind. (0)	1	0.01
Asian (37)	84	0.97
Not Hispanic (36)	77	0.89
Hispanic (1)	7	0.08
Chinese, ex. Taiwanese (10)	20	0.23
Filipino (4)	8	0.09
Indian (8)	14	0.16
Japanese (1)	2	0.02
Korean (8)	20	0.23
Malaysian (1)	3	0.03
Taiwanese (3)	4	0.05
Thai (0)	5	0.06
Vietnamese (1)	5	0.06
Hawaii Native/Pacific Islander (4)	6	0.07
Not Hispanic (4)	4	0.05
Hispanic (0)	2	0.02
White (7,785)	7,933	91.71
Not Hispanic (7,437)	7,537	87.13
Hispanic (348)	396	4.58

East Pennsboro

Place Type: Township
County: Cumberland
Population: 20,228†

Ancestry‡	Population	%
African, Sub-Saharan (90)	152	0.77
African (16)	78	0.39
Ghanaian (12)	12	0.06
Liberian (62)	62	0.31
American (1,081)	1,081	5.46
Arab (145)	189	0.95
Arab (0)	11	0.06
Egyptian (122)	122	0.62
Lebanese (13)	35	0.18
Moroccan (10)	21	0.11
Armenian (55)	63	0.32
Austrian (0)	53	0.27
Belgian (14)	14	0.07
Brazilian (0)	62	0.31
British (18)	37	0.19
Canadian (0)	27	0.14
Celtic (0)	13	0.07
Croatian (23)	102	0.51
Czech (8)	75	0.38
Czechoslovakian (17)	17	0.09
Danish (9)	21	0.11
Dutch (96)	369	1.86
English (208)	1,531	7.73
European (149)	149	0.75
French, ex. Basque (182)	536	2.71
French Canadian (28)	39	0.20
German (3,353)	7,880	39.77
Greek (118)	131	0.66
Hungarian (9)	174	0.88
Irish (828)	3,556	17.95
Israeli (15)	15	0.08
Italian (653)	1,924	9.71
Lithuanian (27)	58	0.29
Norwegian (18)	34	0.17
Pennsylvania German (302)	450	2.27
Polish (219)	795	4.01
Romanian (0)	28	0.14
Russian (49)	58	0.29
Scotch-Irish (86)	335	1.69
Scottish (95)	242	1.22
Slovak (30)	207	1.04
Swedish (8)	145	0.73
Swiss (67)	106	0.54
Turkish (9)	9	0.05
Ukrainian (57)	104	0.52
Welsh (20)	336	1.70
West Indian, ex. Hispanic (19)	74	0.37
Jamaican (0)	55	0.28
West Indian (19)	19	0.10
Yugoslavian (140)	201	1.01

Hispanic Origin	Population	%
Hispanic or Latino (of any race)	566	2.80
Central American, ex. Mexican	39	0.19
Guatemalan	4	0.02
Honduran	10	0.05
Panamanian	5	0.02
Salvadoran	19	0.09
Other Central American	1	<0.01
Cuban	19	0.09
Dominican Republic	14	0.07
Mexican	95	0.47
Puerto Rican	297	1.47
South American	54	0.27
Chilean	4	0.02
Colombian	8	0.04
Ecuadorian	16	0.08
Paraguayan	4	0.02
Peruvian	21	0.10
Venezuelan	1	<0.01
Other Hispanic or Latino	48	0.24

Race*	Population	%
African-American/Black (554)	791	3.91
Not Hispanic (528)	742	3.67
Hispanic (26)	49	0.24
American Indian/Alaska Native (29)	103	0.51
Not Hispanic (19)	86	0.43
Hispanic (10)	17	0.08
Aleut *(Alaska Native)* (1)	1	<0.01
Apache (1)	2	0.01
Blackfeet (1)	5	0.02
Cherokee (8)	34	0.17
Chippewa (3)	3	0.01
Creek (0)	1	<0.01
Iroquois (1)	1	<0.01
Mexican American Ind. (3)	4	0.02
Pueblo (2)	2	0.01
Seminole (0)	3	0.01
Sioux (0)	4	0.02
South American Ind. (1)	2	0.01
Yup'ik *(Alaska Native)* (1)	1	<0.01
Asian (1,033)	1,144	5.66
Not Hispanic (1,025)	1,128	5.58
Hispanic (8)	16	0.08
Bangladeshi (4)	4	0.02
Burmese (25)	25	0.12
Cambodian (3)	3	0.01
Chinese, ex. Taiwanese (98)	116	0.57
Filipino (93)	113	0.56
Indian (551)	573	2.83
Indonesian (0)	1	<0.01
Japanese (9)	16	0.08
Korean (60)	86	0.43
Laotian (1)	1	<0.01
Nepalese (6)	7	0.03
Pakistani (5)	5	0.02
Sri Lankan (12)	12	0.06
Taiwanese (4)	4	0.02
Thai (5)	8	0.04
Vietnamese (139)	150	0.74
Hawaii Native/Pacific Islander (2)	20	0.10
Not Hispanic (2)	19	0.09
Hispanic (0)	1	<0.01
Guamanian/Chamorro (0)	6	0.03
Native Hawaiian (0)	4	0.02
Samoan (1)	3	0.01
White (17,995)	18,341	90.67
Not Hispanic (17,709)	18,010	89.04
Hispanic (286)	331	1.64

East Stroudsburg

Place Type: Borough
County: Monroe
Population: 9,840†

Ancestry‡	Population	%
American (160)	160	1.60
Arab (0)	44	0.44
Syrian (0)	44	0.44
Armenian (0)	28	0.28
Austrian (11)	30	0.30
Brazilian (7)	20	0.20
British (6)	33	0.33
Bulgarian (104)	104	1.04
Cajun (0)	10	0.10
Canadian (19)	24	0.24
Czech (8)	31	0.31
Czechoslovakian (0)	15	0.15
Danish (25)	62	0.62
Dutch (28)	298	2.98
English (91)	609	6.09
European (5)	5	0.05
Finnish (0)	15	0.15
French, ex. Basque (43)	233	2.33
French Canadian (13)	13	0.13
German (606)	2,431	24.31
Greek (32)	102	1.02
Hungarian (44)	164	1.64
Irish (879)	2,694	26.94
Italian (620)	2,097	20.97
Lithuanian (0)	34	0.34
Norwegian (0)	34	0.34
Pennsylvania German (41)	110	1.10
Polish (214)	880	8.80
Portuguese (0)	92	0.92
Romanian (17)	25	0.25
Russian (41)	153	1.53
Scandinavian (0)	7	0.07
Scotch-Irish (10)	183	1.83
Scottish (7)	121	1.21
Slovak (33)	76	0.76
Swedish (15)	107	1.07
Swiss (0)	13	0.13
Turkish (14)	14	0.14
Ukrainian (10)	70	0.70
Welsh (12)	106	1.06
West Indian, ex. Hispanic (71)	79	0.79
Bahamian (20)	20	0.20
Jamaican (0)	8	0.08
Trinidadian/Tobagonian (51)	51	0.51

Hispanic Origin	Population	%
Hispanic or Latino (of any race)	1,166	11.85
Central American, ex. Mexican	56	0.57
Costa Rican	4	0.04
Guatemalan	11	0.11
Honduran	15	0.15
Nicaraguan	10	0.10
Panamanian	7	0.07
Salvadoran	9	0.09
Cuban	48	0.49
Dominican Republic	111	1.13
Mexican	60	0.61
Puerto Rican	617	6.27
South American	177	1.80
Argentinean	7	0.07
Chilean	8	0.08
Colombian	49	0.50
Ecuadorian	71	0.72
Peruvian	37	0.38
Uruguayan	1	0.01
Venezuelan	2	0.02
Other South American	2	0.02
Other Hispanic or Latino	97	0.99

Race*	Population	%
African-American/Black (1,092)	1,266	12.87
Not Hispanic (982)	1,109	11.27
Hispanic (110)	157	1.60

*Notes: † The Census 2010 population figure is used to calculate the percentages in the Hispanic Origin and Race categories. Ancestry percentages are based on the 2006-2010 American Community Survey population (not shown); ‡ Numbers in parentheses indicate the number of people reporting a single ancestry; * Numbers in parentheses indicate the number of persons reporting this race alone, not in combination with any other race; Please refer to the Explanation of Data for more information.*

American Indian/Alaska Native (24)	88	0.89
Not Hispanic (13)	50	0.51
Hispanic (11)	38	0.39
Aleut *(Alaska Native)* (1)	1	0.01
Blackfeet (1)	4	0.04
Central American Ind. (3)	3	0.03
Cherokee (2)	15	0.15
Chippewa (1)	2	0.02
Delaware (1)	2	0.02
Iroquois (0)	5	0.05
Mexican American Ind. (0)	1	0.01
Shoshone (0)	2	0.02
Sioux (1)	2	0.02
South American Ind. (5)	10	0.10
Asian (246)	313	3.18
Not Hispanic (240)	291	2.96
Hispanic (6)	22	0.22
Cambodian (6)	7	0.07
Chinese, ex. Taiwanese (47)	57	0.58
Filipino (55)	76	0.77
Indian (72)	79	0.80
Indonesian (2)	3	0.03
Japanese (3)	8	0.08
Korean (21)	22	0.22
Nepalese (5)	5	0.05
Pakistani (19)	25	0.25
Thai (3)	3	0.03
Vietnamese (7)	12	0.12
Hawaii Native/Pacific Islander (3)	10	0.10
Not Hispanic (0)	1	0.01
Hispanic (3)	9	0.09
Native Hawaiian (0)	1	0.01
White (7,793)	8,079	82.10
Not Hispanic (7,205)	7,390	75.10
Hispanic (588)	689	7.00

East Whiteland

Place Type: Township
County: Chester
Population: 10,650†

Ancestry‡	Population	%
African, Sub-Saharan (47)	47	0.45
Ugandan (23)	23	0.22
Other Sub-Saharan African (24)	24	0.23
American (106)	106	1.01
Arab (72)	72	0.69
Egyptian (72)	72	0.69
Armenian (44)	44	0.42
Austrian (13)	161	1.54
Basque (0)	36	0.34
British (18)	110	1.05
Carpatho Rusyn (0)	14	0.13
Croatian (19)	19	0.18
Czech (0)	32	0.31
Czechoslovakian (8)	8	0.08
Danish (27)	37	0.35
Dutch (42)	162	1.55
English (385)	1,247	11.90
European (52)	52	0.50
French, ex. Basque (34)	276	2.63
French Canadian (18)	142	1.35
German (507)	2,290	21.85
Greek (0)	43	0.41
Hungarian (12)	43	0.41
Irish (706)	2,558	24.41
Italian (758)	2,077	19.82
Lithuanian (16)	40	0.38
Norwegian (9)	95	0.91
Pennsylvania German (0)	9	0.09
Polish (54)	367	3.50
Russian (78)	196	1.87
Scotch-Irish (65)	174	1.66
Scottish (61)	356	3.40
Serbian (14)	41	0.39
Slovak (10)	38	0.36
Swedish (0)	42	0.40
Ukrainian (9)	9	0.09
Welsh (28)	120	1.14
West Indian, ex. Hispanic (8)	8	0.08
Jamaican (8)	8	0.08
Yugoslavian (12)	12	0.11

Hispanic Origin	Population	%
Hispanic or Latino (of any race)	732	6.87
Central American, ex. Mexican	105	0.99
Costa Rican	1	0.01
Guatemalan	4	0.04
Honduran	70	0.66
Panamanian	7	0.07
Salvadoran	23	0.22
Cuban	22	0.21
Dominican Republic	13	0.12
Mexican	238	2.23
Puerto Rican	66	0.62
South American	229	2.15
Argentinean	22	0.21
Colombian	28	0.26
Ecuadorian	152	1.43
Paraguayan	5	0.05
Peruvian	14	0.13
Venezuelan	8	0.08
Other Hispanic or Latino	59	0.55

Race*	Population	%
African-American/Black (352)	412	3.87
Not Hispanic (325)	372	3.49
Hispanic (27)	40	0.38
American Indian/Alaska Native (20)	79	0.74
Not Hispanic (16)	61	0.57
Hispanic (4)	18	0.17
Apache (0)	1	0.01
Blackfeet (0)	2	0.02
Cherokee (1)	6	0.06
Creek (0)	4	0.04
Delaware (0)	1	0.01
Iroquois (0)	5	0.05
Mexican American Ind. (0)	7	0.07
Potawatomi (0)	5	0.05
Sioux (0)	1	0.01
Asian (1,233)	1,288	12.09
Not Hispanic (1,230)	1,284	12.06
Hispanic (3)	4	0.04
Bangladeshi (5)	5	0.05
Chinese, ex. Taiwanese (278)	295	2.77
Filipino (40)	46	0.43
Indian (657)	672	6.31
Japanese (13)	18	0.17
Korean (81)	88	0.83
Laotian (2)	2	0.02
Nepalese (1)	1	0.01
Pakistani (26)	26	0.24
Sri Lankan (4)	4	0.04
Taiwanese (18)	18	0.17
Thai (4)	6	0.06
Vietnamese (97)	101	0.95
Hawaii Native/Pacific Islander (3)	6	0.06
Not Hispanic (3)	6	0.06
Marshallese (1)	1	0.01
Native Hawaiian (2)	4	0.04
Samoan (0)	1	0.01
White (8,613)	8,760	82.25
Not Hispanic (8,206)	8,318	78.10
Hispanic (407)	442	4.15

East York

Place Type: CDP
County: York
Population: 8,777†

Ancestry‡	Population	%
African, Sub-Saharan (0)	89	0.97
African (0)	89	0.97
American (616)	616	6.69
Armenian (0)	17	0.18
Austrian (0)	26	0.28
Brazilian (0)	205	2.23
British (30)	40	0.43
Bulgarian (17)	17	0.18
Canadian (18)	34	0.37
Croatian (13)	27	0.29
Czech (15)	42	0.46
Danish (0)	15	0.16
Dutch (40)	188	2.04
English (332)	1,019	11.06
European (15)	15	0.16
French, ex. Basque (0)	167	1.81
French Canadian (8)	23	0.25
German (1,873)	4,038	43.83
Greek (33)	33	0.36
Hungarian (60)	72	0.78
Irish (265)	1,302	14.13
Italian (221)	559	6.07
Lithuanian (0)	7	0.08
Norwegian (9)	40	0.43
Pennsylvania German (73)	103	1.12
Polish (98)	262	2.84
Russian (14)	75	0.81
Scotch-Irish (133)	375	4.07
Scottish (43)	269	2.92
Slovak (25)	60	0.65
Swedish (15)	85	0.92
Swiss (0)	36	0.39
Welsh (0)	145	1.57

Hispanic Origin	Population	%
Hispanic or Latino (of any race)	334	3.81
Central American, ex. Mexican	31	0.35
Costa Rican	1	0.01
Guatemalan	6	0.07
Honduran	5	0.06
Panamanian	4	0.05
Salvadoran	15	0.17
Cuban	14	0.16
Dominican Republic	12	0.14
Mexican	60	0.68
Puerto Rican	150	1.71
South American	43	0.49
Argentinean	5	0.06
Chilean	4	0.05
Colombian	4	0.05
Ecuadorian	13	0.15
Peruvian	13	0.15
Uruguayan	4	0.05
Other Hispanic or Latino	24	0.27

Race*	Population	%
African-American/Black (362)	430	4.90
Not Hispanic (344)	405	4.61
Hispanic (18)	25	0.28
American Indian/Alaska Native (14)	40	0.46
Not Hispanic (13)	35	0.40
Hispanic (1)	5	0.06
Apache (1)	1	0.01
Blackfeet (0)	2	0.02
Cherokee (2)	9	0.10
Chippewa (1)	1	0.01
Houma (4)	4	0.05
Lumbee (1)	1	0.01
Navajo (1)	1	0.01
Potawatomi (2)	2	0.02
Sioux (0)	4	0.05
Asian (372)	400	4.56
Not Hispanic (371)	399	4.55
Hispanic (1)	1	0.01
Bangladeshi (8)	8	0.09
Cambodian (14)	15	0.17
Chinese, ex. Taiwanese (50)	53	0.60
Filipino (9)	23	0.26
Indian (53)	56	0.64
Japanese (6)	12	0.14
Korean (23)	28	0.32
Laotian (8)	8	0.09
Malaysian (3)	3	0.03
Nepalese (3)	3	0.03
Pakistani (14)	14	0.16
Sri Lankan (4)	4	0.05
Thai (3)	6	0.07

*Notes: † The Census 2010 population figure is used to calculate the percentages in the Hispanic Origin and Race categories. Ancestry percentages are based on the 2006-2010 American Community Survey population (not shown); ‡ Numbers in parentheses indicate the number of people reporting a single ancestry; * Numbers in parentheses indicate the number of persons reporting this race alone, not in combination with any other race; Please refer to the Explanation of Data for more information.*

Vietnamese (164)	168	1.91
Hawaii Native/Pacific Islander (2)	3	0.03
Not Hispanic (2)	2	0.02
Hispanic (0)	1	0.01
Native Hawaiian (2)	2	0.02
White (7,785)	7,902	90.03
Not Hispanic (7,596)	7,698	87.71
Hispanic (189)	204	2.32

Easton

Place Type: City
County: Northampton
Population: 26,800†

Ancestry‡	Population	%
African, Sub-Saharan (213)	243	0.90
African (57)	87	0.32
Kenyan (46)	46	0.17
Liberian (24)	24	0.09
Nigerian (70)	70	0.26
South African (10)	10	0.04
Other Sub-Saharan African (6)	6	0.02
American (1,439)	1,439	5.35
Arab (120)	165	0.61
Lebanese (104)	139	0.52
Syrian (0)	10	0.04
Other Arab (16)	16	0.06
Armenian (0)	8	0.03
Austrian (37)	100	0.37
Basque (0)	9	0.03
British (26)	49	0.18
Canadian (15)	41	0.15
Croatian (17)	17	0.06
Czech (26)	228	0.85
Czechoslovakian (12)	22	0.08
Danish (0)	13	0.05
Dutch (93)	783	2.91
Eastern European (28)	57	0.21
English (249)	1,496	5.56
European (101)	149	0.55
Finnish (15)	24	0.09
French, ex. Basque (37)	369	1.37
French Canadian (20)	61	0.23
German (1,366)	5,845	21.73
Greek (50)	92	0.34
Guyanese (24)	32	0.12
Hungarian (192)	507	1.88
Irish (473)	3,456	12.85
Italian (1,147)	3,669	13.64
Lithuanian (10)	100	0.37
Norwegian (11)	73	0.27
Pennsylvania German (512)	711	2.64
Polish (247)	1,144	4.25
Portuguese (13)	46	0.17
Romanian (52)	52	0.19
Russian (80)	434	1.61
Scotch-Irish (9)	216	0.80
Scottish (25)	325	1.21
Slavic (8)	8	0.03
Slovak (9)	111	0.41
Swedish (35)	299	1.11
Swiss (15)	64	0.24
Ukrainian (19)	115	0.43
Welsh (87)	272	1.01
West Indian, ex. Hispanic (472)	574	2.13
Belizean (14)	14	0.05
British West Indian (32)	32	0.12
Dutch West Indian (8)	8	0.03
Haitian (14)	14	0.05
Jamaican (120)	174	0.65
Trinidadian/Tobagonian (237)	237	0.88
West Indian (47)	95	0.35

Hispanic Origin	Population	%
Hispanic or Latino (of any race)	5,331	19.89
Central American, ex. Mexican	562	2.10
Costa Rican	40	0.15
Guatemalan	183	0.68
Honduran	104	0.39
Nicaraguan	38	0.14
Panamanian	19	0.07
Salvadoran	177	0.66
Other Central American	1	<0.01
Cuban	96	0.36
Dominican Republic	403	1.50
Mexican	1,203	4.49
Puerto Rican	1,956	7.30
South American	575	2.15
Argentinean	32	0.12
Bolivian	1	<0.01
Chilean	7	0.03
Colombian	248	0.93
Ecuadorian	95	0.35
Paraguayan	4	0.01
Peruvian	149	0.56
Uruguayan	21	0.08
Venezuelan	13	0.05
Other South American	5	0.02
Other Hispanic or Latino	536	2.00

Race*	Population	%
African-American/Black (4,506)	5,355	19.98
Not Hispanic (4,123)	4,778	17.83
Hispanic (383)	577	2.15
American Indian/Alaska Native (106)	307	1.15
Not Hispanic (64)	229	0.85
Hispanic (42)	78	0.29
Apache (0)	3	0.01
Blackfeet (0)	13	0.05
Canadian/French Am. Ind. (0)	2	0.01
Central American Ind. (1)	2	0.01
Cherokee (11)	73	0.27
Chippewa (2)	10	0.04
Choctaw (1)	2	0.01
Delaware (4)	13	0.05
Iroquois (2)	3	0.01
Mexican American Ind. (3)	6	0.02
Navajo (3)	9	0.03
Ottawa (0)	1	<0.01
Seminole (0)	1	<0.01
Sioux (1)	2	0.01
South American Ind. (7)	14	0.05
Spanish American Ind. (1)	1	<0.01
Yakama (0)	1	<0.01
Asian (639)	778	2.90
Not Hispanic (629)	747	2.79
Hispanic (10)	31	0.12
Bangladeshi (15)	15	0.06
Burmese (4)	4	0.01
Cambodian (3)	3	0.01
Chinese, ex. Taiwanese (132)	157	0.59
Filipino (44)	71	0.26
Indian (149)	183	0.68
Indonesian (3)	5	0.02
Japanese (20)	38	0.14
Korean (35)	49	0.18
Malaysian (0)	1	<0.01
Nepalese (10)	11	0.04
Pakistani (20)	23	0.09
Sri Lankan (1)	1	<0.01
Taiwanese (5)	8	0.03
Thai (5)	6	0.02
Vietnamese (159)	164	0.61
Hawaii Native/Pacific Islander (28)	62	0.23
Not Hispanic (15)	32	0.12
Hispanic (13)	30	0.11
Guamanian/Chamorro (16)	17	0.06
Native Hawaiian (1)	1	<0.01
Samoan (1)	1	<0.01
White (17,997)	19,129	71.38
Not Hispanic (15,714)	16,502	61.57
Hispanic (2,283)	2,627	9.80

Easttown

Place Type: Township
County: Chester
Population: 10,477†

Ancestry‡	Population	%
Albanian (10)	31	0.29
American (391)	391	3.71
Arab (23)	63	0.60
Lebanese (15)	29	0.28
Moroccan (8)	34	0.32
Armenian (16)	16	0.15
Austrian (26)	46	0.44
Basque (12)	12	0.11
Brazilian (39)	39	0.37
British (35)	126	1.20
Bulgarian (14)	14	0.13
Croatian (10)	35	0.33
Czech (0)	49	0.46
Danish (0)	28	0.27
Dutch (23)	253	2.40
Eastern European (100)	119	1.13
English (404)	1,638	15.54
European (221)	237	2.25
Finnish (0)	45	0.43
French, ex. Basque (22)	230	2.18
French Canadian (0)	69	0.65
German (314)	2,228	21.14
Greek (122)	177	1.68
Hungarian (0)	56	0.53
Irish (1,127)	2,988	28.35
Italian (770)	1,925	18.27
Lithuanian (10)	85	0.81
Macedonian (35)	35	0.33
Norwegian (45)	132	1.25
Polish (110)	349	3.31
Portuguese (0)	30	0.28
Romanian (10)	20	0.19
Russian (67)	217	2.06
Scotch-Irish (64)	292	2.77
Scottish (114)	271	2.57
Serbian (35)	142	1.35
Slovak (54)	230	2.18
Swedish (24)	200	1.90
Swiss (11)	105	1.00
Ukrainian (23)	90	0.85
Welsh (31)	164	1.56
West Indian, ex. Hispanic (9)	9	0.09
Haitian (9)	9	0.09
Yugoslavian (9)	15	0.14

Hispanic Origin	Population	%
Hispanic or Latino (of any race)	210	2.00
Central American, ex. Mexican	18	0.17
Costa Rican	4	0.04
Guatemalan	4	0.04
Honduran	2	0.02
Nicaraguan	2	0.02
Panamanian	1	0.01
Salvadoran	5	0.05
Cuban	35	0.33
Dominican Republic	6	0.06
Mexican	42	0.40
Puerto Rican	29	0.28
South American	55	0.52
Argentinean	4	0.04
Chilean	2	0.02
Colombian	19	0.18
Ecuadorian	6	0.06
Peruvian	13	0.12
Uruguayan	1	0.01
Venezuelan	10	0.10
Other Hispanic or Latino	25	0.24

Race*	Population	%
African-American/Black (205)	243	2.32
Not Hispanic (205)	240	2.29
Hispanic (0)	3	0.03
American Indian/Alaska Native (9)	34	0.32
Not Hispanic (9)	33	0.31
Hispanic (0)	1	0.01
Blackfeet (0)	1	0.01
Cherokee (1)	9	0.09
Choctaw (0)	6	0.06
Delaware (1)	1	0.01

*Notes: † The Census 2010 population figure is used to calculate the percentages in the Hispanic Origin and Race categories. Ancestry percentages are based on the 2006-2010 American Community Survey population (not shown); ‡ Numbers in parentheses indicate the number of people reporting a single ancestry; * Numbers in parentheses indicate the number of persons reporting this race alone, not in combination with any other race; Please refer to the Explanation of Data for more information.*

Shoshone (1)	1	0.01
Tlingit-Haida *(Alaska Native)* (2)	2	0.02
Asian (558)	625	5.97
Not Hispanic (558)	625	5.97
Burmese (2)	2	0.02
Cambodian (9)	9	0.09
Chinese, ex. Taiwanese (266)	280	2.67
Filipino (26)	32	0.31
Hmong (1)	1	0.01
Indian (92)	102	0.97
Japanese (7)	12	0.11
Korean (73)	95	0.91
Pakistani (12)	12	0.11
Taiwanese (26)	27	0.26
Thai (3)	3	0.03
Vietnamese (34)	37	0.35
Hawaii Native/Pacific Islander (0)	1	0.01
Not Hispanic (0)	1	0.01
White (9,557)	9,653	92.14
Not Hispanic (9,375)	9,461	90.30
Hispanic (182)	192	1.83

Economy

Place Type: Borough
County: Beaver
Population: 8,970†

Ancestry‡	Population	%
American (300)	300	3.33
Austrian (0)	41	0.46
British (42)	42	0.47
Canadian (26)	26	0.29
Carpatho Rusyn (12)	12	0.13
Croatian (139)	328	3.64
Czech (48)	117	1.30
Czechoslovakian (0)	30	0.33
Dutch (26)	128	1.42
Eastern European (7)	17	0.19
English (151)	574	6.37
European (83)	93	1.03
French, ex. Basque (7)	197	2.19
French Canadian (39)	75	0.83
German (902)	2,966	32.94
Greek (73)	158	1.75
Hungarian (70)	250	2.78
Irish (243)	1,815	20.16
Italian (397)	1,281	14.23
Lithuanian (0)	18	0.20
Pennsylvania German (83)	83	0.92
Polish (451)	1,383	15.36
Portuguese (0)	17	0.19
Romanian (10)	10	0.11
Russian (53)	146	1.62
Scotch-Irish (75)	311	3.45
Scottish (31)	163	1.81
Serbian (0)	39	0.43
Slavic (14)	71	0.79
Slovak (140)	522	5.80
Slovene (0)	18	0.20
Swedish (8)	49	0.54
Swiss (20)	20	0.22
Ukrainian (149)	447	4.96
Welsh (18)	103	1.14
Yugoslavian (0)	13	0.14

Hispanic Origin	Population	%
Hispanic or Latino (of any race)	68	0.76
Central American, ex. Mexican	11	0.12
Costa Rican	3	0.03
Guatemalan	3	0.03
Nicaraguan	1	0.01
Salvadoran	4	0.04
Cuban	3	0.03
Dominican Republic	1	0.01
Mexican	32	0.36
Puerto Rican	5	0.06
South American	7	0.08
Colombian	3	0.03
Peruvian	3	0.03
Venezuelan	1	0.01
Other Hispanic or Latino	9	0.10

Race*	Population	%
African-American/Black (58)	89	0.99
Not Hispanic (57)	86	0.96
Hispanic (1)	3	0.03
American Indian/Alaska Native (9)	26	0.29
Not Hispanic (9)	25	0.28
Hispanic (0)	1	0.01
Cherokee (0)	6	0.07
Sioux (0)	4	0.04
Asian (34)	48	0.54
Not Hispanic (34)	48	0.54
Chinese, ex. Taiwanese (7)	9	0.10
Filipino (3)	5	0.06
Indian (2)	5	0.06
Indonesian (3)	4	0.04
Japanese (6)	6	0.07
Korean (5)	6	0.07
Sri Lankan (2)	2	0.02
Taiwanese (2)	2	0.02
Thai (1)	2	0.02
Vietnamese (1)	6	0.07
Hawaii Native/Pacific Islander (1)	1	0.01
Hispanic (1)	1	0.01
Guamanian/Chamorro (1)	1	0.01
White (8,806)	8,858	98.75
Not Hispanic (8,748)	8,798	98.08
Hispanic (58)	60	0.67

Elizabeth

Place Type: Township
County: Allegheny
Population: 13,271†

Ancestry‡	Population	%
American (401)	401	3.02
Arab (0)	30	0.23
Lebanese (0)	30	0.23
Austrian (0)	91	0.69
Carpatho Rusyn (52)	52	0.39
Croatian (178)	319	2.40
Czech (48)	189	1.42
Czechoslovakian (0)	14	0.11
Dutch (0)	212	1.60
English (613)	1,820	13.70
European (34)	34	0.26
French, ex. Basque (33)	197	1.48
French Canadian (0)	13	0.10
German (1,059)	3,921	29.52
Greek (48)	83	0.62
Hungarian (253)	742	5.59
Irish (976)	3,014	22.69
Italian (995)	2,193	16.51
Lithuanian (22)	74	0.56
Norwegian (0)	38	0.29
Pennsylvania German (0)	13	0.10
Polish (617)	1,381	10.40
Romanian (13)	21	0.16
Russian (76)	213	1.60
Scotch-Irish (87)	398	3.00
Scottish (57)	308	2.32
Serbian (18)	18	0.14
Slavic (66)	121	0.91
Slovak (400)	1,052	7.92
Swedish (45)	303	2.28
Swiss (0)	9	0.07
Turkish (0)	12	0.09
Ukrainian (67)	124	0.93
Welsh (17)	257	1.93
Yugoslavian (13)	30	0.23

Hispanic Origin	Population	%
Hispanic or Latino (of any race)	83	0.63
Central American, ex. Mexican	15	0.11
Guatemalan	4	0.03
Nicaraguan	6	0.05
Panamanian	4	0.03
Salvadoran	1	0.01
Cuban	2	0.02
Dominican Republic	3	0.02
Mexican	21	0.16
Puerto Rican	18	0.14
South American	2	0.02
Argentinean	1	0.01
Ecuadorian	1	0.01
Other Hispanic or Latino	22	0.17

Race*	Population	%
African-American/Black (203)	256	1.93
Not Hispanic (203)	254	1.91
Hispanic (0)	2	0.02
American Indian/Alaska Native (12)	39	0.29
Not Hispanic (10)	35	0.26
Hispanic (2)	4	0.03
Cherokee (5)	15	0.11
Choctaw (3)	3	0.02
Delaware (1)	1	0.01
Sioux (1)	1	0.01
Asian (37)	69	0.52
Not Hispanic (37)	68	0.51
Hispanic (0)	1	0.01
Chinese, ex. Taiwanese (8)	9	0.07
Filipino (10)	17	0.13
Indian (9)	16	0.12
Japanese (1)	6	0.05
Korean (6)	15	0.11
Taiwanese (1)	1	0.01
Vietnamese (1)	1	0.01
Hawaii Native/Pacific Islander (2)	3	0.02
Not Hispanic (1)	2	0.02
Hispanic (1)	1	0.01
Guamanian/Chamorro (1)	1	0.01
Native Hawaiian (0)	1	0.01
White (12,887)	12,985	97.84
Not Hispanic (12,823)	12,915	97.32
Hispanic (64)	70	0.53

Elizabethtown

Place Type: Borough
County: Lancaster
Population: 11,545†

Ancestry‡	Population	%
Alsatian (0)	11	0.09
American (871)	871	7.51
Austrian (8)	73	0.63
British (11)	29	0.25
Bulgarian (11)	11	0.09
Canadian (11)	25	0.22
Croatian (0)	21	0.18
Czech (24)	50	0.43
Czechoslovakian (0)	66	0.57
Dutch (19)	146	1.26
Eastern European (24)	24	0.21
English (392)	968	8.35
European (53)	79	0.68
French, ex. Basque (56)	212	1.83
French Canadian (19)	34	0.29
German (3,034)	5,320	45.90
Greek (0)	40	0.35
Hungarian (28)	57	0.49
Iranian (0)	13	0.11
Irish (422)	1,368	11.80
Italian (182)	659	5.69
Lithuanian (10)	62	0.53
Norwegian (0)	10	0.09
Pennsylvania German (28)	137	1.18
Polish (201)	438	3.78
Portuguese (12)	12	0.10
Romanian (7)	13	0.11
Russian (21)	93	0.80
Scotch-Irish (113)	280	2.42
Scottish (14)	197	1.70
Slovak (0)	59	0.51
Swedish (37)	174	1.50
Swiss (94)	388	3.35

*Notes: † The Census 2010 population figure is used to calculate the percentages in the Hispanic Origin and Race categories. Ancestry percentages are based on the 2006-2010 American Community Survey population (not shown); ‡ Numbers in parentheses indicate the number of people reporting a single ancestry; * Numbers in parentheses indicate the number of persons reporting this race alone, not in combination with any other race; Please refer to the Explanation of Data for more information.*

SECTION TWO

Ancestry	Population	%
Ukrainian (35)	77	0.66
Welsh (17)	104	0.90

Hispanic Origin	Population	%
Hispanic or Latino (of any race)	381	3.30
Central American, ex. Mexican	36	0.31
Costa Rican	1	0.01
Guatemalan	15	0.13
Honduran	7	0.06
Nicaraguan	1	0.01
Panamanian	1	0.01
Salvadoran	11	0.10
Cuban	10	0.09
Dominican Republic	6	0.05
Mexican	132	1.14
Puerto Rican	136	1.18
South American	30	0.26
Argentinean	3	0.03
Bolivian	2	0.02
Colombian	3	0.03
Ecuadorian	5	0.04
Peruvian	4	0.03
Venezuelan	12	0.10
Other South American	1	0.01
Other Hispanic or Latino	31	0.27

Race*	Population	%
African-American/Black (141)	203	1.76
Not Hispanic (133)	188	1.63
Hispanic (8)	15	0.13
American Indian/Alaska Native (26)	74	0.64
Not Hispanic (17)	61	0.53
Hispanic (9)	13	0.11
Blackfeet (0)	4	0.03
Central American Ind. (0)	1	0.01
Cherokee (1)	9	0.08
Chippewa (0)	5	0.04
Choctaw (6)	6	0.05
Cree (1)	1	0.01
Inupiat *(Alaska Native)* (0)	1	0.01
Iroquois (1)	2	0.02
Navajo (1)	2	0.02
Pueblo (0)	1	0.01
Sioux (2)	2	0.02
South American Ind. (2)	2	0.02
Asian (132)	179	1.55
Not Hispanic (132)	179	1.55
Bangladeshi (6)	6	0.05
Burmese (6)	7	0.06
Cambodian (7)	12	0.10
Chinese, ex. Taiwanese (31)	35	0.30
Filipino (11)	21	0.18
Indian (20)	20	0.17
Japanese (5)	16	0.14
Korean (13)	25	0.22
Laotian (0)	1	0.01
Nepalese (1)	1	0.01
Pakistani (4)	4	0.03
Thai (7)	9	0.08
Vietnamese (16)	16	0.14
Hawaii Native/Pacific Islander (7)	10	0.09
Not Hispanic (7)	10	0.09
Native Hawaiian (2)	3	0.03
Samoan (3)	4	0.03
White (10,949)	11,104	96.18
Not Hispanic (10,734)	10,860	94.07
Hispanic (215)	244	2.11

Ellwood City

Place Type: Borough
County: Lawrence
Population: 7,921†

Ancestry‡	Population	%
American (206)	206	2.51
Arab (8)	17	0.21
Arab (0)	9	0.11
Syrian (8)	8	0.10
Austrian (40)	73	0.89
British (11)	60	0.73
Croatian (44)	137	1.67
Czech (0)	35	0.43
Czechoslovakian (0)	9	0.11
Danish (0)	8	0.10
Dutch (21)	85	1.04
English (186)	710	8.65
European (37)	37	0.45
French, ex. Basque (19)	164	2.00
German (754)	2,656	32.37
Greek (28)	126	1.54
Hungarian (70)	169	2.06
Irish (294)	1,307	15.93
Italian (1,493)	2,912	35.49
Lithuanian (9)	18	0.22
Macedonian (0)	46	0.56
Norwegian (0)	15	0.18
Pennsylvania German (0)	9	0.11
Polish (227)	883	10.76
Romanian (42)	77	0.94
Russian (0)	24	0.29
Scandinavian (0)	8	0.10
Scotch-Irish (94)	438	5.34
Scottish (0)	136	1.66
Serbian (13)	33	0.40
Slovak (31)	80	0.97
Slovene (0)	32	0.39
Swedish (0)	18	0.22
Swiss (13)	60	0.73
Welsh (27)	139	1.69

Hispanic Origin	Population	%
Hispanic or Latino (of any race)	101	1.28
Central American, ex. Mexican	7	0.09
Guatemalan	1	0.01
Honduran	3	0.04
Nicaraguan	3	0.04
Cuban	1	0.01
Dominican Republic	4	0.05
Mexican	55	0.69
Puerto Rican	20	0.25
South American	8	0.10
Chilean	1	0.01
Colombian	4	0.05
Peruvian	3	0.04
Other Hispanic or Latino	6	0.08

Race*	Population	%
African-American/Black (91)	155	1.96
Not Hispanic (91)	147	1.86
Hispanic (0)	8	0.10
American Indian/Alaska Native (11)	27	0.34
Not Hispanic (5)	21	0.27
Hispanic (6)	6	0.08
Blackfeet (0)	2	0.03
Central American Ind. (0)	1	0.01
Choctaw (3)	3	0.04
Delaware (0)	2	0.03
South American Ind. (0)	1	0.01
Asian (26)	40	0.50
Not Hispanic (26)	38	0.48
Hispanic (0)	2	0.03
Chinese, ex. Taiwanese (6)	10	0.13
Filipino (4)	11	0.14
Indian (5)	5	0.06
Korean (2)	4	0.05
Pakistani (8)	11	0.14
Thai (1)	1	0.01
Hawaii Native/Pacific Islander (1)	1	0.01
Not Hispanic (1)	1	0.01
Guamanian/Chamorro (1)	1	0.01
White (7,680)	7,775	98.16
Not Hispanic (7,610)	7,694	97.13
Hispanic (70)	81	1.02

Emmaus

Place Type: Borough
County: Lehigh
Population: 11,211†

Ancestry‡	Population	%
African, Sub-Saharan (89)	89	0.79
Other Sub-Saharan African (89)	89	0.79
Albanian (0)	223	1.98
American (463)	463	4.11
Arab (19)	31	0.28
Arab (19)	19	0.17
Syrian (0)	12	0.11
Austrian (77)	325	2.88
British (13)	32	0.28
Canadian (0)	19	0.17
Celtic (0)	39	0.35
Czech (0)	34	0.30
Czechoslovakian (34)	34	0.30
Dutch (115)	451	4.00
English (265)	742	6.58
European (55)	88	0.78
French, ex. Basque (25)	160	1.42
French Canadian (19)	89	0.79
German (1,834)	4,184	37.13
Greek (16)	23	0.20
Hungarian (37)	264	2.34
Irish (667)	2,187	19.41
Italian (360)	1,134	10.06
Lithuanian (17)	30	0.27
Macedonian (0)	16	0.14
Norwegian (12)	38	0.34
Pennsylvania German (687)	939	8.33
Polish (51)	491	4.36
Romanian (15)	15	0.13
Russian (20)	163	1.45
Scandinavian (14)	14	0.12
Scotch-Irish (75)	246	2.18
Scottish (53)	211	1.87
Slavic (0)	13	0.12
Slovak (179)	417	3.70
Swedish (15)	62	0.55
Swiss (0)	23	0.20
Ukrainian (132)	264	2.34
Welsh (118)	371	3.29
Yugoslavian (161)	384	3.41

Hispanic Origin	Population	%
Hispanic or Latino (of any race)	529	4.72
Central American, ex. Mexican	33	0.29
Guatemalan	22	0.20
Honduran	1	0.01
Panamanian	2	0.02
Salvadoran	8	0.07
Cuban	12	0.11
Dominican Republic	58	0.52
Mexican	75	0.67
Puerto Rican	264	2.35
South American	50	0.45
Argentinean	3	0.03
Chilean	2	0.02
Colombian	15	0.13
Ecuadorian	13	0.12
Peruvian	9	0.08
Venezuelan	8	0.07
Other Hispanic or Latino	37	0.33

Race*	Population	%
African-American/Black (175)	247	2.20
Not Hispanic (147)	208	1.86
Hispanic (28)	39	0.35
American Indian/Alaska Native (20)	59	0.53
Not Hispanic (11)	40	0.36
Hispanic (9)	19	0.17
Apache (0)	1	0.01
Blackfeet (3)	3	0.03
Cherokee (0)	9	0.08
Comanche (0)	1	0.01
Delaware (0)	3	0.03
Iroquois (0)	1	0.01
Mexican American Ind. (0)	1	0.01
Seminole (0)	1	0.01
Sioux (1)	1	0.01
Asian (164)	211	1.88
Not Hispanic (163)	209	1.86

*Notes: † The Census 2010 population figure is used to calculate the percentages in the Hispanic Origin and Race categories. Ancestry percentages are based on the 2006-2010 American Community Survey population (not shown); ‡ Numbers in parentheses indicate the number of people reporting a single ancestry; * Numbers in parentheses indicate the number of persons reporting this race alone, not in combination with any other race; Please refer to the Explanation of Data for more information.*

Hispanic (1)	2	0.02
Burmese (6)	6	0.05
Cambodian (2)	2	0.02
Chinese, ex. Taiwanese (36)	39	0.35
Filipino (8)	24	0.21
Indian (56)	58	0.52
Indonesian (6)	6	0.05
Japanese (10)	21	0.19
Korean (13)	25	0.22
Pakistani (6)	6	0.05
Thai (0)	3	0.03
Vietnamese (17)	18	0.16
Hawaii Native/Pacific Islander (2)	11	0.10
Not Hispanic (0)	9	0.08
Hispanic (2)	2	0.02
Guamanian/Chamorro (2)	3	0.03
Native Hawaiian (0)	3	0.03
White (10,472)	10,646	94.96
Not Hispanic (10,220)	10,347	92.29
Hispanic (252)	299	2.67

Ephrata

Place Type: Borough
County: Lancaster
Population: 13,394†

Ancestry‡	Population	%
American (1,151)	1,151	8.60
Arab (0)	9	0.07
Lebanese (0)	9	0.07
Austrian (0)	26	0.19
Belgian (0)	9	0.07
Canadian (29)	29	0.22
Czech (0)	51	0.38
Czechoslovakian (13)	13	0.10
Dutch (29)	104	0.78
Eastern European (8)	8	0.06
English (231)	691	5.16
Estonian (9)	9	0.07
European (88)	88	0.66
Finnish (15)	15	0.11
French, ex. Basque (43)	267	1.99
French Canadian (57)	66	0.49
German (2,857)	5,733	42.83
Greek (30)	96	0.72
Hungarian (0)	29	0.22
Icelander (0)	16	0.12
Irish (227)	1,374	10.27
Italian (181)	719	5.37
Lithuanian (16)	32	0.24
Northern European (15)	15	0.11
Norwegian (98)	114	0.85
Pennsylvania German (97)	149	1.11
Polish (217)	463	3.46
Romanian (0)	36	0.27
Russian (129)	171	1.28
Scotch-Irish (95)	347	2.59
Scottish (25)	236	1.76
Serbian (0)	9	0.07
Slovak (23)	147	1.10
Swedish (47)	198	1.48
Swiss (33)	673	5.03
Ukrainian (262)	262	1.96
Welsh (9)	103	0.77
West Indian, ex. Hispanic (74)	74	0.55
West Indian (74)	74	0.55

Hispanic Origin	Population	%
Hispanic or Latino (of any race)	693	5.17
Central American, ex. Mexican	22	0.16
Guatemalan	7	0.05
Honduran	3	0.02
Panamanian	1	0.01
Salvadoran	11	0.08
Cuban	20	0.15
Dominican Republic	29	0.22
Mexican	141	1.05
Puerto Rican	312	2.33
South American	118	0.88
Argentinean	5	0.04
Bolivian	3	0.02
Chilean	1	0.01
Colombian	81	0.60
Ecuadorian	11	0.08
Peruvian	11	0.08
Uruguayan	3	0.02
Venezuelan	3	0.02
Other Hispanic or Latino	51	0.38

Race*	Population	%
African-American/Black (128)	238	1.78
Not Hispanic (109)	203	1.52
Hispanic (19)	35	0.26
American Indian/Alaska Native (23)	78	0.58
Not Hispanic (19)	64	0.48
Hispanic (4)	14	0.10
Blackfeet (1)	2	0.01
Cherokee (7)	18	0.13
Chickasaw (4)	4	0.03
Chippewa (0)	1	0.01
Delaware (1)	4	0.03
Iroquois (2)	4	0.03
Kiowa (0)	1	0.01
Sioux (1)	4	0.03
Tohono O'Odham (1)	1	0.01
Asian (171)	215	1.61
Not Hispanic (170)	210	1.57
Hispanic (1)	5	0.04
Cambodian (12)	14	0.10
Chinese, ex. Taiwanese (25)	27	0.20
Filipino (4)	11	0.08
Hmong (37)	39	0.29
Indian (27)	33	0.25
Japanese (4)	9	0.07
Korean (17)	21	0.16
Laotian (10)	11	0.08
Pakistani (2)	2	0.01
Vietnamese (24)	35	0.26
Hawaii Native/Pacific Islander (0)	10	0.07
Not Hispanic (0)	9	0.07
Hispanic (0)	1	0.01
Native Hawaiian (0)	4	0.03
White (12,590)	12,810	95.64
Not Hispanic (12,218)	12,388	92.49
Hispanic (372)	422	3.15

Ephrata

Place Type: Township
County: Lancaster
Population: 9,400†

Ancestry‡	Population	%
American (772)	772	8.40
Arab (20)	82	0.89
Lebanese (20)	59	0.64
Other Arab (0)	23	0.25
Australian (0)	7	0.08
Austrian (11)	39	0.42
Canadian (33)	33	0.36
Dutch (7)	105	1.14
English (113)	640	6.96
Estonian (0)	7	0.08
European (37)	37	0.40
French, ex. Basque (0)	88	0.96
French Canadian (22)	82	0.89
German (2,204)	3,851	41.91
Hungarian (9)	37	0.40
Irish (276)	784	8.53
Italian (300)	550	5.99
Lithuanian (10)	10	0.11
Northern European (8)	8	0.09
Pennsylvania German (255)	303	3.30
Polish (99)	164	1.78
Russian (165)	178	1.94
Scotch-Irish (29)	98	1.07
Scottish (34)	234	2.55
Slovak (0)	52	0.57
Swedish (188)	280	3.05
Swiss (233)	785	8.54
Ukrainian (28)	28	0.30
Welsh (28)	193	2.10

Hispanic Origin	Population	%
Hispanic or Latino (of any race)	291	3.10
Central American, ex. Mexican	19	0.20
Guatemalan	8	0.09
Honduran	2	0.02
Nicaraguan	3	0.03
Salvadoran	6	0.06
Cuban	15	0.16
Dominican Republic	6	0.06
Mexican	35	0.37
Puerto Rican	136	1.45
South American	63	0.67
Argentinean	2	0.02
Chilean	2	0.02
Colombian	42	0.45
Ecuadorian	10	0.11
Peruvian	3	0.03
Uruguayan	2	0.02
Venezuelan	2	0.02
Other Hispanic or Latino	17	0.18

Race*	Population	%
African-American/Black (90)	136	1.45
Not Hispanic (83)	124	1.32
Hispanic (7)	12	0.13
American Indian/Alaska Native (12)	34	0.36
Not Hispanic (9)	24	0.26
Hispanic (3)	10	0.11
Apache (1)	1	0.01
Cherokee (1)	5	0.05
Cheyenne (1)	1	0.01
Chippewa (0)	1	0.01
Iroquois (2)	3	0.03
Mexican American Ind. (2)	2	0.02
Ottawa (0)	1	0.01
Sioux (0)	1	0.01
South American Ind. (1)	1	0.01
Asian (176)	206	2.19
Not Hispanic (173)	203	2.16
Hispanic (3)	3	0.03
Bangladeshi (2)	2	0.02
Cambodian (12)	16	0.17
Chinese, ex. Taiwanese (23)	26	0.28
Filipino (2)	5	0.05
Hmong (65)	65	0.69
Indian (18)	23	0.24
Indonesian (1)	1	0.01
Japanese (1)	3	0.03
Korean (13)	15	0.16
Laotian (27)	29	0.31
Pakistani (1)	1	0.01
Thai (0)	5	0.05
Vietnamese (10)	12	0.13
Hawaii Native/Pacific Islander (1)	4	0.04
Not Hispanic (1)	3	0.03
Hispanic (0)	1	0.01
Guamanian/Chamorro (1)	1	0.01
Native Hawaiian (0)	2	0.02
White (8,909)	9,014	95.89
Not Hispanic (8,756)	8,836	94.00
Hispanic (153)	178	1.89

Erie

Place Type: City
County: Erie
Population: 101,786†

Ancestry‡	Population	%
Afghan (85)	85	0.08
African, Sub-Saharan (3,074)	4,228	4.16
African (2,494)	3,634	3.58
Kenyan (17)	17	0.02
Nigerian (7)	7	0.01
Somalian (96)	96	0.09
South African (27)	27	0.03

SECTION TWO

*Notes: † The Census 2010 population figure is used to calculate the percentages in the Hispanic Origin and Race categories. Ancestry percentages are based on the 2006-2010 American Community Survey population (not shown); ‡ Numbers in parentheses indicate the number of people reporting a single ancestry; * Numbers in parentheses indicate the number of persons reporting this race alone, not in combination with any other race; Please refer to the Explanation of Data for more information.*

Ancestry	Population	%
Sudanese (221)	221	0.22
Other Sub-Saharan African (212)	226	0.22
Albanian (136)	136	0.13
Alsatian (0)	7	0.01
American (2,350)	2,350	2.31
Arab (262)	532	0.52
Arab (46)	152	0.15
Egyptian (8)	8	0.01
Iraqi (166)	208	0.20
Lebanese (36)	98	0.10
Moroccan (6)	6	0.01
Syrian (0)	37	0.04
Other Arab (0)	23	0.02
Armenian (153)	183	0.18
Australian (0)	22	0.02
Austrian (45)	350	0.34
Belgian (14)	89	0.09
Brazilian (53)	107	0.11
British (98)	151	0.15
Bulgarian (12)	12	0.01
Canadian (79)	88	0.09
Carpatho Rusyn (17)	37	0.04
Celtic (0)	15	0.01
Croatian (123)	352	0.35
Czech (134)	626	0.62
Czechoslovakian (114)	187	0.18
Danish (40)	310	0.31
Dutch (169)	1,425	1.40
Eastern European (19)	19	0.02
English (1,236)	5,870	5.78
Estonian (0)	12	0.01
European (424)	436	0.43
Finnish (0)	182	0.18
French, ex. Basque (80)	1,680	1.65
French Canadian (105)	199	0.20
German (6,379)	27,772	27.33
German Russian (2)	2	<0.01
Greek (173)	350	0.34
Guyanese (0)	7	0.01
Hungarian (225)	1,120	1.10
Iranian (11)	20	0.02
Irish (3,859)	17,685	17.40
Israeli (6)	6	0.01
Italian (5,781)	15,798	15.54
Latvian (0)	20	0.02
Lithuanian (92)	349	0.34
Luxemburger (0)	10	0.01
Macedonian (10)	10	0.01
Norwegian (51)	188	0.18
Pennsylvania German (101)	329	0.32
Polish (5,072)	12,920	12.71
Portuguese (80)	415	0.41
Romanian (52)	174	0.17
Russian (554)	1,342	1.32
Scotch-Irish (667)	2,432	2.39
Scottish (278)	984	0.97
Serbian (32)	69	0.07
Slavic (22)	127	0.12
Slovak (383)	1,499	1.47
Slovene (22)	61	0.06
Swedish (214)	1,830	1.80
Swiss (20)	167	0.16
Turkish (11)	69	0.07
Ukrainian (637)	864	0.85
Welsh (39)	743	0.73
West Indian, ex. Hispanic (345)	353	0.35
British West Indian (20)	20	0.02
Haitian (211)	211	0.21
Jamaican (79)	87	0.09
West Indian (35)	35	0.03
Yugoslavian (684)	697	0.69

Hispanic Origin	Population	%
Hispanic or Latino (of any race)	7,005	6.88
Central American, ex. Mexican	188	0.18
Costa Rican	29	0.03
Guatemalan	22	0.02
Honduran	23	0.02
Nicaraguan	18	0.02
Panamanian	14	0.01
Salvadoran	82	0.08
Cuban	98	0.10
Dominican Republic	110	0.11
Mexican	1,271	1.25
Puerto Rican	4,752	4.67
South American	132	0.13
Argentinean	7	0.01
Chilean	6	0.01
Colombian	74	0.07
Ecuadorian	8	0.01
Peruvian	19	0.02
Uruguayan	1	<0.01
Venezuelan	17	0.02
Other Hispanic or Latino	454	0.45

Race*	Population	%
African-American/Black (17,141)	20,022	19.67
Not Hispanic (16,535)	19,010	18.68
Hispanic (606)	1,012	0.99
American Indian/Alaska Native (291)	909	0.89
Not Hispanic (210)	743	0.73
Hispanic (81)	166	0.16
Aleut *(Alaska Native)* (1)	1	<0.01
Apache (2)	9	0.01
Blackfeet (6)	48	0.05
Canadian/French Am. Ind. (1)	4	<0.01
Central American Ind. (1)	4	<0.01
Cherokee (22)	135	0.13
Chickasaw (0)	4	<0.01
Chippewa (3)	7	0.01
Choctaw (2)	10	0.01
Comanche (1)	1	<0.01
Cree (0)	2	<0.01
Creek (4)	7	0.01
Crow (0)	3	<0.01
Delaware (1)	1	<0.01
Hopi (1)	1	<0.01
Iroquois (50)	105	0.10
Mexican American Ind. (7)	17	0.02
Navajo (3)	7	0.01
Pueblo (1)	1	<0.01
Seminole (0)	5	<0.01
Shoshone (1)	2	<0.01
Sioux (6)	33	0.03
South American Ind. (0)	7	0.01
Tlingit-Haida *(Alaska Native)* (2)	5	<0.01
Ute (0)	1	<0.01
Yuman (2)	2	<0.01
Asian (1,515)	1,997	1.96
Not Hispanic (1,498)	1,951	1.92
Hispanic (17)	46	0.05
Bangladeshi (2)	2	<0.01
Bhutanese (332)	395	0.39
Burmese (110)	121	0.12
Cambodian (1)	2	<0.01
Chinese, ex. Taiwanese (145)	182	0.18
Filipino (102)	185	0.18
Indian (230)	294	0.29
Indonesian (4)	4	<0.01
Japanese (21)	72	0.07
Korean (47)	100	0.10
Laotian (7)	7	0.01
Malaysian (2)	3	<0.01
Nepalese (68)	138	0.14
Pakistani (9)	9	0.01
Taiwanese (2)	2	<0.01
Thai (18)	32	0.03
Vietnamese (288)	326	0.32
Hawaii Native/Pacific Islander (53)	154	0.15
Not Hispanic (43)	135	0.13
Hispanic (10)	19	0.02
Fijian (0)	1	<0.01
Guamanian/Chamorro (12)	31	0.03
Native Hawaiian (8)	29	0.03
Samoan (3)	6	0.01
White (76,327)	79,875	78.47
Not Hispanic (73,073)	76,023	74.69
Hispanic (3,254)	3,852	3.78

Exeter

Place Type: Township
County: Berks
Population: 25,550†

Ancestry‡	Population	%
African, Sub-Saharan (43)	57	0.23
African (22)	36	0.14
Kenyan (21)	21	0.08
Alsatian (0)	3	0.01
American (1,334)	1,334	5.35
Arab (77)	77	0.31
Egyptian (57)	57	0.23
Lebanese (10)	10	0.04
Other Arab (10)	10	0.04
Austrian (47)	227	0.91
Belgian (0)	9	0.04
British (90)	220	0.88
Cajun (16)	16	0.06
Canadian (6)	6	0.02
Czech (0)	102	0.41
Czechoslovakian (14)	25	0.10
Danish (12)	26	0.10
Dutch (231)	858	3.44
English (480)	2,325	9.32
European (48)	48	0.19
Finnish (0)	18	0.07
French, ex. Basque (43)	570	2.28
French Canadian (45)	222	0.89
German (4,353)	10,117	40.55
Greek (74)	224	0.90
Hungarian (83)	313	1.25
Irish (826)	4,374	17.53
Italian (1,040)	3,779	15.15
Lithuanian (21)	111	0.44
Norwegian (34)	134	0.54
Pennsylvania German (551)	748	3.00
Polish (840)	2,486	9.96
Russian (96)	233	0.93
Scandinavian (21)	62	0.25
Scotch-Irish (99)	387	1.55
Scottish (72)	310	1.24
Slavic (7)	78	0.31
Slovak (192)	354	1.42
Slovene (16)	28	0.11
Swedish (42)	172	0.69
Swiss (24)	59	0.24
Ukrainian (75)	292	1.17
Welsh (62)	373	1.49
West Indian, ex. Hispanic (211)	211	0.85
Haitian (211)	211	0.85
Yugoslavian (15)	27	0.11

Hispanic Origin	Population	%
Hispanic or Latino (of any race)	923	3.61
Central American, ex. Mexican	36	0.14
Guatemalan	9	0.04
Honduran	3	0.01
Nicaraguan	5	0.02
Panamanian	10	0.04
Salvadoran	9	0.04
Cuban	42	0.16
Dominican Republic	64	0.25
Mexican	116	0.45
Puerto Rican	529	2.07
South American	66	0.26
Argentinean	5	0.02
Chilean	7	0.03
Colombian	31	0.12
Ecuadorian	8	0.03
Peruvian	9	0.04
Venezuelan	6	0.02
Other Hispanic or Latino	70	0.27

Race*	Population	%
African-American/Black (838)	1,041	4.07
Not Hispanic (796)	955	3.74
Hispanic (42)	86	0.34
American Indian/Alaska Native (37)	135	0.53

*Notes: † The Census 2010 population figure is used to calculate the percentages in the Hispanic Origin and Race categories. Ancestry percentages are based on the 2006-2010 American Community Survey population (not shown); ‡ Numbers in parentheses indicate the number of people reporting a single ancestry; * Numbers in parentheses indicate the number of persons reporting this race alone, not in combination with any other race; Please refer to the Explanation of Data for more information.*

Not Hispanic (34)	126	0.49
Hispanic (3)	9	0.04
Apache (0)	6	0.02
Blackfeet (0)	3	0.01
Cherokee (8)	24	0.09
Cheyenne (0)	1	<0.01
Chippewa (3)	4	0.02
Choctaw (0)	1	<0.01
Comanche (1)	3	0.01
Iroquois (0)	1	<0.01
Mexican American Ind. (2)	2	0.01
Navajo (1)	1	<0.01
Potawatomi (1)	1	<0.01
Seminole (0)	5	0.02
Sioux (0)	6	0.02
South American Ind. (1)	2	0.01
Asian (497)	605	2.37
Not Hispanic (485)	584	2.29
Hispanic (12)	21	0.08
Bangladeshi (3)	5	0.02
Cambodian (1)	1	<0.01
Chinese, ex. Taiwanese (112)	143	0.56
Filipino (57)	96	0.38
Indian (153)	167	0.65
Japanese (6)	24	0.09
Korean (28)	43	0.17
Laotian (9)	10	0.04
Malaysian (0)	2	0.01
Pakistani (16)	18	0.07
Sri Lankan (1)	3	0.01
Taiwanese (5)	6	0.02
Thai (3)	3	0.01
Vietnamese (82)	85	0.33
Hawaii Native/Pacific Islander (0)	10	0.04
Not Hispanic (0)	7	0.03
Hispanic (0)	3	0.01
Fijian (0)	4	0.02
White (23,481)	23,846	93.33
Not Hispanic (22,972)	23,257	91.03
Hispanic (509)	589	2.31

Fairless Hills

Place Type: CDP
County: Bucks
Population: 8,466†

Ancestry‡	Population	%
African, Sub-Saharan (124)	124	1.42
African (45)	45	0.52
Liberian (79)	79	0.90
Albanian (45)	45	0.52
American (353)	353	4.04
Arab (0)	14	0.16
Lebanese (0)	14	0.16
Austrian (0)	10	0.11
Belgian (6)	6	0.07
Brazilian (7)	13	0.15
Canadian (0)	14	0.16
Croatian (65)	79	0.90
Czech (0)	25	0.29
Danish (0)	9	0.10
Dutch (25)	177	2.03
Eastern European (10)	10	0.11
English (298)	1,288	14.75
European (46)	59	0.68
French, ex. Basque (9)	42	0.48
French Canadian (17)	17	0.19
German (705)	2,310	26.45
Hungarian (28)	153	1.75
Irish (974)	2,650	30.34
Italian (434)	1,208	13.83
Lithuanian (6)	66	0.76
Northern European (11)	11	0.13
Pennsylvania German (39)	54	0.62
Polish (115)	524	6.00
Russian (85)	234	2.68
Scandinavian (16)	16	0.18
Scotch-Irish (32)	96	1.10
Scottish (11)	78	0.89
Slovak (60)	115	1.32
Swedish (17)	63	0.72
Ukrainian (187)	187	2.14
Welsh (15)	215	2.46
West Indian, ex. Hispanic (0)	6	0.07
Dutch West Indian (0)	6	0.07
Yugoslavian (28)	37	0.42

Hispanic Origin	Population	%
Hispanic or Latino (of any race)	308	3.64
Central American, ex. Mexican	30	0.35
Costa Rican	9	0.11
Guatemalan	16	0.19
Panamanian	1	0.01
Salvadoran	4	0.05
Cuban	20	0.24
Dominican Republic	10	0.12
Mexican	30	0.35
Puerto Rican	170	2.01
South American	19	0.22
Argentinean	5	0.06
Colombian	7	0.08
Ecuadorian	4	0.05
Peruvian	1	0.01
Uruguayan	2	0.02
Other Hispanic or Latino	29	0.34

Race*	Population	%
African-American/Black (322)	398	4.70
Not Hispanic (316)	379	4.48
Hispanic (6)	19	0.22
American Indian/Alaska Native (7)	41	0.48
Not Hispanic (6)	38	0.45
Hispanic (1)	3	0.04
Blackfeet (0)	1	0.01
Cherokee (1)	7	0.08
Delaware (1)	2	0.02
Iroquois (2)	3	0.04
Mexican American Ind. (1)	1	0.01
Asian (470)	512	6.05
Not Hispanic (470)	508	6.00
Hispanic (0)	4	0.05
Chinese, ex. Taiwanese (41)	43	0.51
Filipino (46)	58	0.69
Indian (249)	259	3.06
Indonesian (1)	2	0.02
Japanese (3)	6	0.07
Korean (61)	66	0.78
Malaysian (0)	1	0.01
Pakistani (16)	18	0.21
Thai (4)	5	0.06
Vietnamese (46)	47	0.56
Hawaii Native/Pacific Islander (1)	2	0.02
Not Hispanic (1)	2	0.02
Guamanian/Chamorro (1)	1	0.01
White (7,394)	7,550	89.18
Not Hispanic (7,216)	7,339	86.69
Hispanic (178)	211	2.49

Fairview

Place Type: Township
County: Erie
Population: 10,102†

Ancestry‡	Population	%
African, Sub-Saharan (14)	14	0.14
African (14)	14	0.14
American (514)	514	5.11
Arab (0)	17	0.17
Syrian (0)	17	0.17
Austrian (0)	18	0.18
Brazilian (40)	40	0.40
British (25)	25	0.25
Canadian (5)	11	0.11
Celtic (0)	19	0.19
Croatian (0)	10	0.10
Czech (14)	38	0.38
Czechoslovakian (25)	37	0.37
Danish (0)	32	0.32
Dutch (30)	221	2.20
Eastern European (11)	11	0.11
English (406)	1,416	14.07
Estonian (13)	26	0.26
European (93)	101	1.00
Finnish (0)	19	0.19
French, ex. Basque (8)	156	1.55
French Canadian (0)	29	0.29
German (987)	3,561	35.39
Greek (48)	75	0.75
Hungarian (70)	92	0.91
Irish (496)	1,930	19.18
Italian (545)	1,585	15.75
Latvian (9)	9	0.09
Lithuanian (18)	144	1.43
Maltese (12)	12	0.12
Norwegian (8)	33	0.33
Polish (421)	1,066	10.59
Portuguese (0)	9	0.09
Romanian (0)	19	0.19
Russian (70)	166	1.65
Scotch-Irish (55)	138	1.37
Scottish (44)	187	1.86
Slavic (10)	21	0.21
Slovak (84)	233	2.32
Slovene (10)	10	0.10
Swedish (57)	234	2.33
Swiss (7)	70	0.70
Ukrainian (0)	20	0.20
Welsh (13)	93	0.92
Yugoslavian (0)	13	0.13

Hispanic Origin	Population	%
Hispanic or Latino (of any race)	138	1.37
Central American, ex. Mexican	5	0.05
Guatemalan	2	0.02
Honduran	2	0.02
Nicaraguan	1	0.01
Cuban	3	0.03
Dominican Republic	3	0.03
Mexican	42	0.42
Puerto Rican	55	0.54
South American	15	0.15
Argentinean	1	0.01
Bolivian	2	0.02
Chilean	3	0.03
Colombian	2	0.02
Ecuadorian	2	0.02
Peruvian	2	0.02
Venezuelan	3	0.03
Other Hispanic or Latino	15	0.15

Race*	Population	%
African-American/Black (63)	89	0.88
Not Hispanic (59)	85	0.84
Hispanic (4)	4	0.04
American Indian/Alaska Native (19)	28	0.28
Not Hispanic (7)	14	0.14
Hispanic (12)	14	0.14
Central American Ind. (1)	2	0.02
Cherokee (3)	5	0.05
Iroquois (1)	3	0.03
Mexican American Ind. (1)	2	0.02
Asian (66)	85	0.84
Not Hispanic (65)	84	0.83
Hispanic (1)	1	0.01
Chinese, ex. Taiwanese (12)	12	0.12
Filipino (7)	11	0.11
Hmong (4)	4	0.04
Indian (24)	28	0.28
Japanese (2)	4	0.04
Korean (11)	16	0.16
Laotian (1)	1	0.01
Malaysian (1)	1	0.01
Vietnamese (3)	7	0.07
Hawaii Native/Pacific Islander (1)	7	0.07
Hispanic (1)	7	0.07
Guamanian/Chamorro (1)	1	0.01
White (9,861)	9,919	98.19
Not Hispanic (9,779)	9,827	97.28

SECTION TWO

*Notes: † The Census 2010 population figure is used to calculate the percentages in the Hispanic Origin and Race categories. Ancestry percentages are based on the 2006-2010 American Community Survey population (not shown); ‡ Numbers in parentheses indicate the number of people reporting a single ancestry; * Numbers in parentheses indicate the number of persons reporting this race alone, not in combination with any other race; Please refer to the Explanation of Data for more information.*

Hispanic (82)	92	0.91

Fairview

Place Type: Township
County: York
Population: 16,668†

Ancestry‡	Population	%
African, Sub-Saharan (0)	38	0.23
African (0)	38	0.23
American (811)	811	4.96
Arab (18)	18	0.11
Egyptian (10)	10	0.06
Lebanese (8)	8	0.05
Armenian (10)	10	0.06
Australian (11)	11	0.07
Austrian (0)	51	0.31
British (50)	94	0.58
Canadian (0)	13	0.08
Croatian (58)	132	0.81
Czech (37)	52	0.32
Czechoslovakian (17)	26	0.16
Danish (18)	38	0.23
Dutch (128)	461	2.82
English (614)	1,607	9.84
European (215)	308	1.89
Finnish (10)	10	0.06
French, ex. Basque (69)	306	1.87
French Canadian (99)	111	0.68
German (3,215)	6,769	41.43
Greek (33)	33	0.20
Hungarian (0)	139	0.85
Irish (596)	2,232	13.66
Italian (590)	1,721	10.53
Lithuanian (23)	68	0.42
Norwegian (49)	122	0.75
Pennsylvania German (120)	131	0.80
Polish (261)	728	4.46
Portuguese (15)	15	0.09
Romanian (10)	10	0.06
Russian (87)	148	0.91
Scotch-Irish (107)	365	2.23
Scottish (73)	318	1.95
Slavic (10)	26	0.16
Slovak (88)	255	1.56
Slovene (0)	45	0.28
Swedish (26)	165	1.01
Swiss (53)	137	0.84
Ukrainian (65)	84	0.51
Welsh (25)	278	1.70
Yugoslavian (88)	88	0.54

Hispanic Origin	Population	%
Hispanic or Latino (of any race)	544	3.26
Central American, ex. Mexican	25	0.15
Guatemalan	4	0.02
Honduran	5	0.03
Nicaraguan	4	0.02
Panamanian	8	0.05
Salvadoran	4	0.02
Cuban	17	0.10
Dominican Republic	19	0.11
Mexican	164	0.98
Puerto Rican	255	1.53
South American	15	0.09
Argentinean	1	0.01
Bolivian	1	0.01
Colombian	4	0.02
Ecuadorian	6	0.04
Peruvian	3	0.02
Other Hispanic or Latino	49	0.29

Race*	Population	%
African-American/Black (263)	384	2.30
Not Hispanic (248)	329	1.97
Hispanic (15)	55	0.33
American Indian/Alaska Native (36)	86	0.52
Not Hispanic (35)	83	0.50
Hispanic (1)	3	0.02
Apache (1)	2	0.01
Cherokee (5)	12	0.07
Chippewa (0)	2	0.01
Choctaw (1)	2	0.01
Comanche (0)	1	0.01
Creek (3)	3	0.02
Iroquois (2)	10	0.06
Kiowa (0)	1	0.01
Lumbee (1)	1	0.01
Navajo (0)	1	0.01
Seminole (0)	1	0.01
Sioux (3)	6	0.04
South American Ind. (0)	1	0.01
Asian (229)	285	1.71
Not Hispanic (229)	275	1.65
Hispanic (0)	10	0.06
Bangladeshi (4)	4	0.02
Cambodian (2)	2	0.01
Chinese, ex. Taiwanese (41)	45	0.27
Filipino (21)	37	0.22
Indian (35)	36	0.22
Indonesian (2)	2	0.01
Japanese (13)	27	0.16
Korean (36)	48	0.29
Laotian (2)	3	0.02
Pakistani (5)	5	0.03
Taiwanese (1)	2	0.01
Thai (2)	5	0.03
Vietnamese (56)	59	0.35
Hawaii Native/Pacific Islander (7)	11	0.07
Not Hispanic (6)	6	0.04
Hispanic (1)	5	0.03
Guamanian/Chamorro (1)	1	0.01
Native Hawaiian (6)	8	0.05
White (15,756)	15,967	95.79
Not Hispanic (15,439)	15,589	93.53
Hispanic (317)	378	2.27

Falls

Place Type: Township
County: Bucks
Population: 34,300†

Ancestry‡	Population	%
African, Sub-Saharan (203)	203	0.59
African (45)	45	0.13
Liberian (158)	158	0.46
Albanian (45)	45	0.13
American (1,288)	1,288	3.73
Arab (19)	57	0.17
Egyptian (12)	12	0.03
Lebanese (7)	45	0.13
Austrian (9)	167	0.48
Belgian (6)	6	0.02
Brazilian (17)	35	0.10
British (0)	14	0.04
Canadian (0)	14	0.04
Croatian (65)	79	0.23
Czech (22)	183	0.53
Czechoslovakian (45)	45	0.13
Danish (0)	35	0.10
Dutch (141)	593	1.72
Eastern European (52)	52	0.15
English (1,049)	4,383	12.69
European (194)	225	0.65
French, ex. Basque (30)	530	1.53
French Canadian (78)	244	0.71
German (3,051)	9,606	27.81
Greek (145)	256	0.74
Guyanese (70)	70	0.20
Hungarian (74)	443	1.28
Irish (3,369)	9,744	28.21
Italian (2,016)	5,176	14.99
Lithuanian (72)	229	0.66
Northern European (11)	11	0.03
Norwegian (0)	48	0.14
Pennsylvania German (62)	154	0.45
Polish (1,297)	2,961	8.57
Portuguese (14)	42	0.12
Romanian (37)	105	0.30
Russian (241)	568	1.64
Scandinavian (16)	16	0.05
Scotch-Irish (146)	564	1.63
Scottish (150)	566	1.64
Slavic (12)	37	0.11
Slovak (239)	396	1.15
Swedish (45)	201	0.58
Swiss (0)	33	0.10
Turkish (99)	99	0.29
Ukrainian (262)	365	1.06
Welsh (43)	483	1.40
West Indian, ex. Hispanic (32)	38	0.11
Dutch West Indian (0)	6	0.02
Jamaican (24)	24	0.07
Trinidadian/Tobagonian (8)	8	0.02
Yugoslavian (28)	51	0.15

Hispanic Origin	Population	%
Hispanic or Latino (of any race)	1,501	4.38
Central American, ex. Mexican	145	0.42
Costa Rican	52	0.15
Guatemalan	66	0.19
Honduran	2	0.01
Panamanian	10	0.03
Salvadoran	15	0.04
Cuban	57	0.17
Dominican Republic	63	0.18
Mexican	171	0.50
Puerto Rican	810	2.36
South American	120	0.35
Argentinean	16	0.05
Chilean	6	0.02
Colombian	44	0.13
Ecuadorian	31	0.09
Peruvian	14	0.04
Uruguayan	5	0.01
Venezuelan	4	0.01
Other Hispanic or Latino	135	0.39

Race*	Population	%
African-American/Black (1,974)	2,331	6.80
Not Hispanic (1,899)	2,189	6.38
Hispanic (75)	142	0.41
American Indian/Alaska Native (64)	201	0.59
Not Hispanic (46)	166	0.48
Hispanic (18)	35	0.10
Apache (1)	7	0.02
Blackfeet (0)	14	0.04
Canadian/French Am. Ind. (1)	1	<0.01
Cherokee (11)	53	0.15
Chickasaw (1)	1	<0.01
Chippewa (0)	1	<0.01
Choctaw (0)	4	0.01
Delaware (8)	12	0.03
Iroquois (3)	5	0.01
Lumbee (1)	1	<0.01
Mexican American Ind. (4)	5	0.01
Navajo (0)	2	0.01
Seminole (1)	3	0.01
Sioux (2)	2	0.01
South American Ind. (4)	6	0.02
Asian (1,426)	1,611	4.70
Not Hispanic (1,422)	1,584	4.62
Hispanic (4)	27	0.08
Bangladeshi (13)	13	0.04
Cambodian (12)	14	0.04
Chinese, ex. Taiwanese (141)	166	0.48
Filipino (109)	160	0.47
Indian (786)	812	2.37
Indonesian (3)	4	0.01
Japanese (18)	47	0.14
Korean (143)	180	0.52
Laotian (1)	3	0.01
Malaysian (2)	5	0.01
Pakistani (66)	71	0.21
Taiwanese (6)	7	0.02
Thai (7)	11	0.03
Vietnamese (82)	101	0.29
Hawaii Native/Pacific Islander (8)	30	0.09

*Notes: † The Census 2010 population figure is used to calculate the percentages in the Hispanic Origin and Race categories. Ancestry percentages are based on the 2006-2010 American Community Survey population (not shown); ‡ Numbers in parentheses indicate the number of people reporting a single ancestry; * Numbers in parentheses indicate the number of persons reporting this race alone, not in combination with any other race; Please refer to the Explanation of Data for more information.*

Not Hispanic (7)	24	0.07
Hispanic (1)	6	0.02
Guamanian/Chamorro (4)	5	0.01
Native Hawaiian (1)	5	0.01
Samoan (3)	4	0.01
White (29,673)	30,283	88.29
Not Hispanic (28,830)	29,317	85.47
Hispanic (843)	966	2.82

Ferguson

Place Type: Township
County: Centre
Population: 17,690†

Ancestry‡	Population	%
African, Sub-Saharan (52)	73	0.43
African (0)	21	0.12
Nigerian (52)	52	0.30
American (688)	688	4.03
Arab (60)	130	0.76
Lebanese (17)	87	0.51
Moroccan (43)	43	0.25
Armenian (17)	54	0.32
Austrian (8)	60	0.35
Belgian (0)	18	0.11
British (68)	147	0.86
Bulgarian (12)	12	0.07
Canadian (0)	39	0.23
Croatian (16)	16	0.09
Czech (40)	134	0.78
Czechoslovakian (36)	79	0.46
Danish (0)	86	0.50
Dutch (65)	386	2.26
Eastern European (24)	24	0.14
English (252)	1,694	9.91
European (319)	331	1.94
Finnish (0)	20	0.12
French, ex. Basque (40)	432	2.53
French Canadian (0)	46	0.27
German (1,691)	5,158	30.18
Greek (18)	77	0.45
Hungarian (15)	208	1.22
Irish (492)	2,396	14.02
Italian (481)	1,623	9.50
Lithuanian (36)	36	0.21
Northern European (6)	6	0.04
Norwegian (26)	258	1.51
Pennsylvania German (0)	111	0.65
Polish (211)	898	5.25
Portuguese (11)	11	0.06
Romanian (27)	55	0.32
Russian (135)	293	1.71
Scandinavian (0)	15	0.09
Scotch-Irish (164)	510	2.98
Scottish (60)	637	3.73
Serbian (16)	16	0.09
Slavic (12)	51	0.30
Slovak (59)	218	1.28
Slovene (20)	20	0.12
Swedish (59)	337	1.97
Swiss (11)	123	0.72
Turkish (16)	16	0.09
Ukrainian (95)	148	0.87
Welsh (68)	272	1.59
West Indian, ex. Hispanic (16)	16	0.09
Trinidadian/Tobagonian (16)	16	0.09

Hispanic Origin	Population	%
Hispanic or Latino (of any race)	534	3.02
Central American, ex. Mexican	52	0.29
Costa Rican	7	0.04
Guatemalan	17	0.10
Honduran	4	0.02
Nicaraguan	3	0.02
Panamanian	9	0.05
Salvadoran	12	0.07
Cuban	20	0.11
Dominican Republic	21	0.12
Mexican	141	0.80
Puerto Rican	134	0.76
South American	112	0.63
Argentinean	9	0.05
Bolivian	6	0.03
Chilean	11	0.06
Colombian	41	0.23
Ecuadorian	5	0.03
Peruvian	18	0.10
Uruguayan	4	0.02
Venezuelan	18	0.10
Other Hispanic or Latino	54	0.31

Race*	Population	%
African-American/Black (574)	717	4.05
Not Hispanic (545)	671	3.79
Hispanic (29)	46	0.26
American Indian/Alaska Native (13)	94	0.53
Not Hispanic (10)	59	0.33
Hispanic (3)	35	0.20
Apache (0)	1	0.01
Blackfeet (1)	2	0.01
Cherokee (3)	12	0.07
Chickasaw (2)	2	0.01
Delaware (0)	1	0.01
Inupiat *(Alaska Native)* (0)	1	0.01
Iroquois (0)	2	0.01
Pueblo (0)	2	0.01
Sioux (0)	6	0.03
South American Ind. (1)	3	0.02
Yaqui (0)	1	0.01
Asian (2,017)	2,204	12.46
Not Hispanic (2,016)	2,197	12.42
Hispanic (1)	7	0.04
Bangladeshi (16)	20	0.11
Burmese (8)	8	0.05
Chinese, ex. Taiwanese (991)	1,030	5.82
Filipino (32)	67	0.38
Indian (295)	321	1.81
Indonesian (7)	11	0.06
Japanese (43)	65	0.37
Korean (419)	449	2.54
Malaysian (1)	4	0.02
Nepalese (5)	5	0.03
Pakistani (10)	12	0.07
Sri Lankan (10)	10	0.06
Taiwanese (89)	92	0.52
Thai (8)	13	0.07
Vietnamese (25)	31	0.18
Hawaii Native/Pacific Islander (1)	6	0.03
Not Hispanic (1)	3	0.02
Hispanic (0)	3	0.02
Guamanian/Chamorro (1)	1	0.01
Native Hawaiian (0)	2	0.01
White (14,514)	14,888	84.16
Not Hispanic (14,189)	14,505	82.00
Hispanic (325)	383	2.17

Fernway

Place Type: CDP
County: Butler
Population: 12,414†

Ancestry‡	Population	%
American (253)	253	2.06
Arab (23)	121	0.99
Lebanese (23)	111	0.90
Syrian (0)	10	0.08
Austrian (9)	34	0.28
Belgian (0)	10	0.08
British (20)	63	0.51
Bulgarian (15)	15	0.12
Canadian (9)	9	0.07
Croatian (59)	184	1.50
Czech (14)	78	0.64
Czechoslovakian (28)	81	0.66
Dutch (0)	65	0.53
Eastern European (57)	57	0.46
English (191)	1,173	9.55
European (215)	215	1.75
Finnish (10)	10	0.08
French, ex. Basque (9)	172	1.40
French Canadian (0)	14	0.11
German (1,086)	4,598	37.44
Greek (44)	44	0.36
Hungarian (73)	387	3.15
Iranian (0)	9	0.07
Irish (650)	2,712	22.08
Italian (619)	2,566	20.90
Latvian (0)	11	0.09
Lithuanian (23)	109	0.89
Norwegian (31)	43	0.35
Polish (231)	1,160	9.45
Romanian (0)	19	0.15
Russian (6)	96	0.78
Scandinavian (8)	39	0.32
Scotch-Irish (55)	321	2.61
Scottish (97)	385	3.14
Serbian (36)	193	1.57
Slavic (0)	9	0.07
Slovak (187)	539	4.39
Slovene (0)	25	0.20
Swedish (22)	134	1.09
Swiss (0)	53	0.43
Ukrainian (46)	205	1.67
Welsh (35)	213	1.73

Hispanic Origin	Population	%
Hispanic or Latino (of any race)	236	1.90
Central American, ex. Mexican	29	0.23
Guatemalan	16	0.13
Honduran	6	0.05
Nicaraguan	1	0.01
Salvadoran	6	0.05
Cuban	6	0.05
Dominican Republic	2	0.02
Mexican	99	0.80
Puerto Rican	48	0.39
South American	34	0.27
Argentinean	9	0.07
Colombian	12	0.10
Ecuadorian	3	0.02
Peruvian	5	0.04
Venezuelan	5	0.04
Other Hispanic or Latino	18	0.14

Race*	Population	%
African-American/Black (153)	222	1.79
Not Hispanic (148)	213	1.72
Hispanic (5)	9	0.07
American Indian/Alaska Native (10)	41	0.33
Not Hispanic (8)	35	0.28
Hispanic (2)	6	0.05
Blackfeet (0)	2	0.02
Cherokee (3)	9	0.07
Iroquois (0)	1	0.01
Mexican American Ind. (1)	1	0.01
Seminole (0)	5	0.04
Sioux (2)	2	0.02
Yaqui (0)	1	0.01
Asian (316)	371	2.99
Not Hispanic (315)	368	2.96
Hispanic (1)	3	0.02
Burmese (6)	6	0.05
Chinese, ex. Taiwanese (81)	99	0.80
Filipino (17)	29	0.23
Indian (121)	127	1.02
Japanese (2)	7	0.06
Korean (28)	40	0.32
Laotian (1)	1	0.01
Malaysian (0)	3	0.02
Pakistani (11)	11	0.09
Sri Lankan (6)	6	0.05
Taiwanese (5)	5	0.04
Thai (2)	2	0.02
Vietnamese (24)	27	0.22
Hawaii Native/Pacific Islander (1)	7	0.06
Not Hispanic (1)	7	0.06
Native Hawaiian (0)	4	0.03
Tongan (1)	1	0.01

*Notes: † The Census 2010 population figure is used to calculate the percentages in the Hispanic Origin and Race categories. Ancestry percentages are based on the 2006-2010 American Community Survey population (not shown); ‡ Numbers in parentheses indicate the number of people reporting a single ancestry; * Numbers in parentheses indicate the number of persons reporting this race alone, not in combination with any other race; Please refer to the Explanation of Data for more information.*

White (11,735)	11,877	95.67
Not Hispanic (11,564)	11,691	94.18
Hispanic (171)	186	1.50

Folsom

Place Type: CDP
County: Delaware
Population: 8,323†

Ancestry‡	Population	%
American (156)	156	1.85
Arab (0)	14	0.17
Syrian (0)	14	0.17
Armenian (18)	35	0.41
Austrian (0)	18	0.21
British (0)	14	0.17
Canadian (0)	14	0.17
Danish (16)	16	0.19
Dutch (47)	154	1.83
English (36)	984	11.67
French, ex. Basque (54)	191	2.26
French Canadian (0)	15	0.18
German (157)	1,718	20.37
Greek (0)	15	0.18
Hungarian (14)	212	2.51
Irish (1,418)	3,937	46.67
Italian (961)	2,662	31.56
Norwegian (29)	60	0.71
Pennsylvania German (27)	60	0.71
Polish (141)	526	6.24
Russian (0)	16	0.19
Scotch-Irish (14)	156	1.85
Scottish (15)	88	1.04
Slavic (14)	14	0.17
Slovak (278)	278	3.30
Swedish (0)	103	1.22
Ukrainian (0)	29	0.34
Welsh (0)	291	3.45
West Indian, ex. Hispanic (0)	10	0.12
West Indian (0)	10	0.12

Hispanic Origin	Population	%
Hispanic or Latino (of any race)	153	1.84
Central American, ex. Mexican	18	0.22
Costa Rican	7	0.08
Guatemalan	1	0.01
Nicaraguan	1	0.01
Panamanian	3	0.04
Salvadoran	6	0.07
Cuban	13	0.16
Dominican Republic	5	0.06
Mexican	18	0.22
Puerto Rican	43	0.52
South American	47	0.56
Argentinean	18	0.22
Colombian	15	0.18
Ecuadorian	10	0.12
Peruvian	2	0.02
Venezuelan	2	0.02
Other Hispanic or Latino	9	0.11

Race*	Population	%
African-American/Black (280)	315	3.78
Not Hispanic (276)	311	3.74
Hispanic (4)	4	0.05
American Indian/Alaska Native (6)	28	0.34
Not Hispanic (6)	27	0.32
Hispanic (0)	1	0.01
Apache (0)	1	0.01
Blackfeet (0)	3	0.04
Cherokee (1)	9	0.11
Creek (1)	1	0.01
Crow (1)	1	0.01
Delaware (0)	1	0.01
Seminole (0)	1	0.01
Asian (146)	189	2.27
Not Hispanic (145)	188	2.26
Hispanic (1)	1	0.01
Bangladeshi (5)	5	0.06
Cambodian (5)	5	0.06
Chinese, ex. Taiwanese (19)	26	0.31
Filipino (18)	34	0.41
Indian (33)	44	0.53
Japanese (1)	3	0.04
Korean (13)	14	0.17
Laotian (10)	10	0.12
Pakistani (3)	4	0.05
Taiwanese (1)	1	0.01
Thai (6)	6	0.07
Vietnamese (28)	30	0.36
Hawaii Native/Pacific Islander (1)	1	0.01
Hispanic (1)	1	0.01
Guamanian/Chamorro (1)	1	0.01
White (7,746)	7,832	94.10
Not Hispanic (7,644)	7,723	92.79
Hispanic (102)	109	1.31

Forks

Place Type: Township
County: Northampton
Population: 14,721†

Ancestry‡	Population	%
African, Sub-Saharan (33)	33	0.24
African (11)	11	0.08
Nigerian (22)	22	0.16
American (455)	455	3.32
Arab (47)	278	2.03
Egyptian (0)	10	0.07
Lebanese (29)	116	0.85
Syrian (18)	81	0.59
Other Arab (0)	71	0.52
Austrian (12)	84	0.61
Belgian (0)	61	0.45
British (161)	220	1.61
Canadian (58)	80	0.58
Croatian (23)	36	0.26
Czech (24)	77	0.56
Czechoslovakian (0)	13	0.09
Danish (8)	29	0.21
Dutch (116)	263	1.92
Eastern European (12)	12	0.09
English (253)	1,109	8.10
European (82)	114	0.83
French, ex. Basque (10)	198	1.45
French Canadian (8)	8	0.06
German (875)	3,237	23.65
Greek (21)	84	0.61
Guyanese (39)	39	0.28
Hungarian (179)	409	2.99
Iranian (47)	47	0.34
Irish (616)	2,760	20.17
Italian (972)	2,927	21.39
Lithuanian (0)	30	0.22
Northern European (0)	13	0.09
Norwegian (36)	55	0.40
Pennsylvania German (254)	416	3.04
Polish (285)	1,029	7.52
Portuguese (115)	150	1.10
Russian (34)	88	0.64
Scotch-Irish (65)	223	1.63
Scottish (58)	250	1.83
Serbian (0)	17	0.12
Slavic (0)	26	0.19
Slovak (35)	122	0.89
Slovene (0)	28	0.20
Swedish (0)	80	0.58
Swiss (36)	191	1.40
Ukrainian (66)	218	1.59
Welsh (34)	432	3.16
West Indian, ex. Hispanic (66)	66	0.48
Jamaican (58)	58	0.42
Trinidadian/Tobagonian (8)	8	0.06
Yugoslavian (0)	16	0.12

Hispanic Origin	Population	%
Hispanic or Latino (of any race)	1,055	7.17
Central American, ex. Mexican	138	0.94
Costa Rican	11	0.07
Guatemalan	14	0.10
Honduran	30	0.20
Nicaraguan	2	0.01
Panamanian	7	0.05
Salvadoran	74	0.50
Cuban	35	0.24
Dominican Republic	70	0.48
Mexican	109	0.74
Puerto Rican	377	2.56
South American	235	1.60
Argentinean	14	0.10
Bolivian	1	0.01
Chilean	11	0.07
Colombian	97	0.66
Ecuadorian	32	0.22
Paraguayan	3	0.02
Peruvian	51	0.35
Uruguayan	14	0.10
Venezuelan	12	0.08
Other Hispanic or Latino	91	0.62

Race*	Population	%
African-American/Black (1,031)	1,160	7.88
Not Hispanic (984)	1,094	7.43
Hispanic (47)	66	0.45
American Indian/Alaska Native (15)	74	0.50
Not Hispanic (9)	60	0.41
Hispanic (6)	14	0.10
Alaska Athabascan *(Ala. Nat.)* (0)	1	0.01
Blackfeet (0)	1	0.01
Cherokee (1)	16	0.11
Chippewa (1)	1	0.01
Creek (0)	3	0.02
Delaware (1)	2	0.01
Iroquois (0)	2	0.01
Seminole (0)	1	0.01
Sioux (1)	2	0.01
South American Ind. (1)	3	0.02
Asian (632)	739	5.02
Not Hispanic (630)	734	4.99
Hispanic (2)	5	0.03
Bangladeshi (6)	6	0.04
Cambodian (5)	5	0.03
Chinese, ex. Taiwanese (86)	100	0.68
Filipino (110)	122	0.83
Indian (278)	311	2.11
Indonesian (2)	2	0.01
Japanese (7)	16	0.11
Korean (19)	39	0.26
Pakistani (54)	64	0.43
Sri Lankan (5)	5	0.03
Thai (4)	4	0.03
Vietnamese (44)	52	0.35
Hawaii Native/Pacific Islander (6)	16	0.11
Not Hispanic (6)	11	0.07
Hispanic (0)	5	0.03
Guamanian/Chamorro (4)	5	0.03
Native Hawaiian (1)	4	0.03
Samoan (1)	4	0.03
White (12,460)	12,694	86.23
Not Hispanic (11,777)	11,967	81.29
Hispanic (683)	727	4.94

Franconia

Place Type: Township
County: Montgomery
Population: 13,064†

Ancestry‡	Population	%
American (651)	651	5.12
Arab (7)	7	0.06
Lebanese (7)	7	0.06
Armenian (29)	60	0.47
Australian (0)	14	0.11
Austrian (17)	45	0.35
Belgian (9)	27	0.21
British (5)	17	0.13
Canadian (30)	30	0.24

*Notes: † The Census 2010 population figure is used to calculate the percentages in the Hispanic Origin and Race categories. Ancestry percentages are based on the 2006-2010 American Community Survey population (not shown); ‡ Numbers in parentheses indicate the number of people reporting a single ancestry; * Numbers in parentheses indicate the number of persons reporting this race alone, not in combination with any other race; Please refer to the Explanation of Data for more information.*

Ancestry	Population	%
Croatian (9)	36	0.28
Czech (0)	64	0.50
Czechoslovakian (0)	17	0.13
Dutch (116)	250	1.97
English (298)	1,320	10.39
European (228)	228	1.79
French, ex. Basque (67)	295	2.32
French Canadian (14)	48	0.38
German (2,585)	5,347	42.08
Greek (19)	67	0.53
Hungarian (36)	106	0.83
Irish (537)	2,044	16.08
Israeli (9)	9	0.07
Italian (438)	1,014	7.98
Lithuanian (9)	50	0.39
Norwegian (10)	79	0.62
Pennsylvania German (349)	413	3.25
Polish (241)	865	6.81
Russian (102)	184	1.45
Scandinavian (0)	30	0.24
Scotch-Irish (65)	238	1.87
Scottish (74)	336	2.64
Slovak (28)	124	0.98
Swedish (8)	37	0.29
Swiss (199)	510	4.01
Turkish (0)	34	0.27
Ukrainian (105)	239	1.88
Welsh (37)	119	0.94
West Indian, ex. Hispanic (16)	16	0.13
Trinidadian/Tobagonian (16)	16	0.13
Yugoslavian (9)	18	0.14

Hispanic Origin	Population	%
Hispanic or Latino (of any race)	229	1.75
Central American, ex. Mexican	44	0.34
Costa Rican	1	0.01
Guatemalan	15	0.11
Honduran	17	0.13
Nicaraguan	6	0.05
Salvadoran	5	0.04
Cuban	21	0.16
Dominican Republic	4	0.03
Mexican	41	0.31
Puerto Rican	75	0.57
South American	27	0.21
Argentinean	1	0.01
Bolivian	1	0.01
Chilean	4	0.03
Colombian	9	0.07
Ecuadorian	7	0.05
Paraguayan	2	0.02
Peruvian	3	0.02
Other Hispanic or Latino	17	0.13

Race*	Population	%
African-American/Black (213)	275	2.11
Not Hispanic (199)	258	1.97
Hispanic (14)	17	0.13
American Indian/Alaska Native (22)	59	0.45
Not Hispanic (22)	59	0.45
Blackfeet (0)	1	0.01
Cherokee (5)	7	0.05
Choctaw (1)	1	0.01
Delaware (0)	3	0.02
Iroquois (1)	6	0.05
Lumbee (2)	4	0.03
Seminole (0)	4	0.03
Sioux (1)	3	0.02
Tlingit-Haida *(Alaska Native)* (1)	4	0.03
Asian (435)	489	3.74
Not Hispanic (434)	483	3.70
Hispanic (1)	6	0.05
Bangladeshi (14)	14	0.11
Burmese (2)	2	0.02
Cambodian (3)	3	0.02
Chinese, ex. Taiwanese (44)	49	0.38
Filipino (14)	32	0.24
Indian (112)	119	0.91
Japanese (5)	8	0.06
Korean (52)	67	0.51
Laotian (6)	8	0.06
Nepalese (4)	4	0.03
Pakistani (10)	11	0.08
Vietnamese (159)	166	1.27
Hawaii Native/Pacific Islander (6)	12	0.09
Not Hispanic (6)	12	0.09
Guamanian/Chamorro (2)	2	0.02
Native Hawaiian (1)	7	0.05
White (12,181)	12,321	94.31
Not Hispanic (12,032)	12,151	93.01
Hispanic (149)	170	1.30

Franklin Park

Place Type: Borough
County: Allegheny
Population: 13,470†

Ancestry‡	Population	%
American (459)	459	3.53
Arab (58)	127	0.98
Lebanese (58)	112	0.86
Other Arab (0)	15	0.12
Australian (39)	50	0.39
Austrian (0)	35	0.27
Belgian (0)	12	0.09
Brazilian (13)	28	0.22
British (52)	52	0.40
Canadian (20)	20	0.15
Croatian (121)	348	2.68
Czech (21)	181	1.39
Czechoslovakian (0)	30	0.23
Danish (0)	70	0.54
Dutch (13)	72	0.55
Eastern European (12)	12	0.09
English (268)	1,907	14.69
European (289)	317	2.44
French, ex. Basque (63)	477	3.67
French Canadian (0)	22	0.17
German (989)	4,280	32.96
Greek (35)	61	0.47
Hungarian (10)	188	1.45
Icelander (14)	14	0.11
Iranian (16)	16	0.12
Irish (585)	3,194	24.60
Italian (589)	1,840	14.17
Latvian (10)	10	0.08
Lithuanian (19)	77	0.59
Norwegian (72)	187	1.44
Pennsylvania German (0)	11	0.08
Polish (279)	805	6.20
Romanian (0)	18	0.14
Russian (79)	253	1.95
Scandinavian (11)	36	0.28
Scotch-Irish (46)	176	1.36
Scottish (110)	486	3.74
Serbian (35)	57	0.44
Slavic (27)	35	0.27
Slovak (121)	354	2.73
Slovene (13)	152	1.17
Swedish (15)	104	0.80
Swiss (34)	151	1.16
Ukrainian (40)	143	1.10
Welsh (35)	127	0.98
Yugoslavian (10)	10	0.08

Hispanic Origin	Population	%
Hispanic or Latino (of any race)	202	1.50
Central American, ex. Mexican	8	0.06
Costa Rican	1	0.01
Guatemalan	2	0.01
Nicaraguan	2	0.01
Salvadoran	3	0.02
Cuban	19	0.14
Mexican	66	0.49
Puerto Rican	49	0.36
South American	39	0.29
Argentinean	6	0.04
Chilean	7	0.05
Colombian	7	0.05
Ecuadorian	4	0.03
Peruvian	5	0.04
Venezuelan	10	0.07
Other Hispanic or Latino	21	0.16

Race*	Population	%
African-American/Black (163)	188	1.40
Not Hispanic (147)	171	1.27
Hispanic (16)	17	0.13
American Indian/Alaska Native (16)	40	0.30
Not Hispanic (15)	38	0.28
Hispanic (1)	2	0.01
Central American Ind. (1)	3	0.02
Cherokee (6)	15	0.11
Chippewa (0)	2	0.01
Iroquois (1)	7	0.05
Pueblo (2)	2	0.01
Sioux (0)	3	0.02
Asian (1,397)	1,501	11.14
Not Hispanic (1,393)	1,497	11.11
Hispanic (4)	4	0.03
Chinese, ex. Taiwanese (554)	569	4.22
Filipino (36)	55	0.41
Indian (615)	656	4.87
Indonesian (1)	4	0.03
Japanese (21)	22	0.16
Korean (85)	91	0.68
Nepalese (4)	4	0.03
Pakistani (31)	32	0.24
Sri Lankan (1)	1	0.01
Taiwanese (12)	12	0.09
Thai (3)	3	0.02
Vietnamese (9)	13	0.10
Hawaii Native/Pacific Islander (7)	15	0.11
Not Hispanic (7)	15	0.11
Native Hawaiian (4)	5	0.04
Tongan (2)	5	0.04
White (11,698)	11,829	87.82
Not Hispanic (11,530)	11,660	86.56
Hispanic (168)	169	1.25

Fullerton

Place Type: CDP
County: Lehigh
Population: 14,925†

Ancestry‡	Population	%
African, Sub-Saharan (195)	212	1.41
African (111)	111	0.74
Other Sub-Saharan African (84)	101	0.67
American (381)	381	2.53
Arab (639)	854	5.67
Arab (97)	113	0.75
Jordanian (8)	8	0.05
Lebanese (216)	283	1.88
Moroccan (14)	14	0.09
Syrian (239)	371	2.46
Other Arab (65)	65	0.43
Armenian (14)	23	0.15
Austrian (156)	338	2.25
Brazilian (16)	24	0.16
Canadian (0)	14	0.09
Celtic (0)	46	0.31
Croatian (0)	21	0.14
Czech (11)	11	0.07
Czechoslovakian (16)	23	0.15
Danish (17)	32	0.21
Dutch (106)	411	2.73
Eastern European (8)	20	0.13
English (107)	674	4.48
European (24)	37	0.25
Finnish (0)	10	0.07
French, ex. Basque (10)	221	1.47
French Canadian (49)	72	0.48
German (1,705)	3,779	25.11
Greek (114)	149	0.99
Guyanese (23)	23	0.15
Hungarian (98)	443	2.94
Iranian (17)	32	0.21

*Notes: † The Census 2010 population figure is used to calculate the percentages in the Hispanic Origin and Race categories. Ancestry percentages are based on the 2006-2010 American Community Survey population (not shown); ‡ Numbers in parentheses indicate the number of people reporting a single ancestry; * Numbers in parentheses indicate the number of persons reporting this race alone, not in combination with any other race; Please refer to the Explanation of Data for more information.*

Irish (436)	1,573	10.45
Italian (471)	1,081	7.18
Lithuanian (29)	62	0.41
Northern European (70)	70	0.47
Norwegian (14)	39	0.26
Pennsylvania German (360)	522	3.47
Polish (239)	576	3.83
Portuguese (0)	206	1.37
Romanian (35)	49	0.33
Russian (18)	147	0.98
Scotch-Irish (80)	160	1.06
Scottish (0)	181	1.20
Slovak (101)	402	2.67
Swedish (0)	45	0.30
Swiss (0)	13	0.09
Ukrainian (119)	284	1.89
Welsh (58)	220	1.46
West Indian, ex. Hispanic (29)	46	0.31
Haitian (12)	12	0.08
Jamaican (17)	17	0.11
West Indian (0)	17	0.11
Yugoslavian (29)	29	0.19

Hispanic Origin	Population	%
Hispanic or Latino (of any race)	2,178	14.59
Central American, ex. Mexican	105	0.70
Costa Rican	5	0.03
Guatemalan	12	0.08
Honduran	26	0.17
Nicaraguan	13	0.09
Panamanian	12	0.08
Salvadoran	25	0.17
Other Central American	12	0.08
Cuban	39	0.26
Dominican Republic	441	2.95
Mexican	104	0.70
Puerto Rican	1,066	7.14
South American	291	1.95
Argentinean	8	0.05
Bolivian	4	0.03
Chilean	20	0.13
Colombian	135	0.90
Ecuadorian	70	0.47
Paraguayan	1	0.01
Peruvian	41	0.27
Uruguayan	3	0.02
Venezuelan	5	0.03
Other South American	4	0.03
Other Hispanic or Latino	132	0.88

Race*	Population	%
African-American/Black (1,279)	1,501	10.06
Not Hispanic (1,150)	1,294	8.67
Hispanic (129)	207	1.39
American Indian/Alaska Native (66)	114	0.76
Not Hispanic (23)	57	0.38
Hispanic (43)	57	0.38
Apache (1)	2	0.01
Blackfeet (1)	1	0.01
Central American Ind. (2)	2	0.01
Cherokee (4)	20	0.13
Delaware (0)	6	0.04
Lumbee (1)	2	0.01
Seminole (1)	1	0.01
South American Ind. (9)	10	0.07
Asian (860)	1,007	6.75
Not Hispanic (855)	987	6.61
Hispanic (5)	20	0.13
Bangladeshi (4)	5	0.03
Cambodian (1)	1	0.01
Chinese, ex. Taiwanese (113)	135	0.90
Filipino (40)	55	0.37
Indian (404)	441	2.95
Indonesian (2)	7	0.05
Japanese (8)	15	0.10
Korean (34)	41	0.27
Laotian (0)	1	0.01
Nepalese (4)	5	0.03
Pakistani (28)	30	0.20
Taiwanese (1)	1	0.01
Thai (1)	1	0.01
Vietnamese (192)	220	1.47
Hawaii Native/Pacific Islander (4)	20	0.13
Not Hispanic (3)	14	0.09
Hispanic (1)	6	0.04
Guamanian/Chamorro (1)	1	0.01
Native Hawaiian (1)	2	0.01
Samoan (0)	4	0.03
White (11,313)	11,685	78.29
Not Hispanic (10,366)	10,616	71.13
Hispanic (947)	1,069	7.16

Gettysburg

Place Type: Borough
County: Adams
Population: 7,620†

Ancestry‡	Population	%
African, Sub-Saharan (35)	35	0.45
African (35)	35	0.45
American (215)	215	2.79
Arab (21)	51	0.66
Palestinian (0)	16	0.21
Other Arab (21)	35	0.45
Austrian (0)	40	0.52
Belgian (0)	11	0.14
British (44)	44	0.57
Croatian (14)	14	0.18
Czech (13)	41	0.53
Czechoslovakian (0)	16	0.21
Danish (0)	28	0.36
Dutch (19)	101	1.31
English (277)	1,055	13.71
European (31)	31	0.40
Finnish (0)	26	0.34
French, ex. Basque (99)	307	3.99
French Canadian (0)	14	0.18
German (846)	2,318	30.13
Greek (30)	169	2.20
Guyanese (0)	17	0.22
Hungarian (0)	18	0.23
Irish (552)	1,532	19.91
Italian (207)	653	8.49
Lithuanian (13)	28	0.36
Northern European (19)	19	0.25
Norwegian (28)	167	2.17
Pennsylvania German (104)	104	1.35
Polish (52)	296	3.85
Portuguese (0)	17	0.22
Romanian (0)	40	0.52
Russian (0)	151	1.96
Scandinavian (0)	20	0.26
Scotch-Irish (50)	196	2.55
Scottish (17)	251	3.26
Slavic (0)	17	0.22
Slovak (30)	94	1.22
Swedish (33)	83	1.08
Swiss (0)	17	0.22
Turkish (9)	9	0.12
Ukrainian (18)	63	0.82
Welsh (45)	153	1.99
West Indian, ex. Hispanic (70)	121	1.57
Barbadian (14)	14	0.18
Jamaican (28)	53	0.69
Trinidadian/Tobagonian (14)	31	0.40
West Indian (14)	23	0.30

Hispanic Origin	Population	%
Hispanic or Latino (of any race)	834	10.94
Central American, ex. Mexican	28	0.37
Costa Rican	3	0.04
Guatemalan	5	0.07
Honduran	7	0.09
Nicaraguan	2	0.03
Panamanian	2	0.03
Salvadoran	9	0.12
Cuban	23	0.30
Dominican Republic	22	0.29
Mexican	607	7.97
Puerto Rican	109	1.43
South American	20	0.26
Chilean	4	0.05
Colombian	10	0.13
Ecuadorian	2	0.03
Peruvian	3	0.04
Uruguayan	1	0.01
Other Hispanic or Latino	25	0.33

Race*	Population	%
African-American/Black (441)	564	7.40
Not Hispanic (411)	512	6.72
Hispanic (30)	52	0.68
American Indian/Alaska Native (25)	58	0.76
Not Hispanic (13)	36	0.47
Hispanic (12)	22	0.29
Blackfeet (1)	2	0.03
Cherokee (3)	5	0.07
Choctaw (0)	2	0.03
Hopi (3)	3	0.04
Iroquois (0)	1	0.01
Lumbee (0)	1	0.01
Mexican American Ind. (6)	8	0.10
Spanish American Ind. (0)	1	0.01
Tlingit-Haida *(Alaska Native)* (0)	1	0.01
Yaqui (0)	1	0.01
Asian (142)	179	2.35
Not Hispanic (142)	178	2.34
Hispanic (0)	1	0.01
Burmese (14)	14	0.18
Cambodian (1)	1	0.01
Chinese, ex. Taiwanese (40)	50	0.66
Filipino (13)	16	0.21
Indian (24)	32	0.42
Japanese (10)	20	0.26
Korean (9)	14	0.18
Nepalese (5)	5	0.07
Pakistani (3)	3	0.04
Taiwanese (1)	1	0.01
Thai (0)	1	0.01
Vietnamese (16)	19	0.25
Hawaii Native/Pacific Islander (0)	6	0.08
Not Hispanic (0)	5	0.07
Hispanic (0)	1	0.01
Native Hawaiian (0)	1	0.01
White (6,441)	6,602	86.64
Not Hispanic (6,066)	6,190	81.23
Hispanic (375)	412	5.41

Glenshaw

Place Type: CDP
County: Allegheny
Population: 8,981†

Ancestry‡	Population	%
American (351)	351	3.82
Arab (24)	24	0.26
Lebanese (24)	24	0.26
Austrian (0)	13	0.14
British (0)	41	0.45
Carpatho Rusyn (16)	29	0.32
Croatian (48)	103	1.12
Czech (12)	139	1.51
Dutch (0)	13	0.14
English (196)	859	9.34
European (111)	111	1.21
French, ex. Basque (0)	264	2.87
German (1,131)	3,967	43.14
Greek (45)	45	0.49
Hungarian (9)	72	0.78
Irish (238)	2,175	23.65
Italian (689)	1,699	18.48
Lithuanian (11)	36	0.39
Pennsylvania German (38)	90	0.98
Polish (387)	1,100	11.96
Russian (35)	47	0.51
Scotch-Irish (163)	440	4.78
Scottish (12)	192	2.09
Serbian (10)	20	0.22

*Notes: † The Census 2010 population figure is used to calculate the percentages in the Hispanic Origin and Race categories. Ancestry percentages are based on the 2006-2010 American Community Survey population (not shown); ‡ Numbers in parentheses indicate the number of people reporting a single ancestry; * Numbers in parentheses indicate the number of persons reporting this race alone, not in combination with any other race; Please refer to the Explanation of Data for more information.*

Slavic (43)	114	1.24
Slovak (67)	303	3.29
Slovene (26)	59	0.64
Swedish (13)	13	0.14
Swiss (0)	19	0.21
Ukrainian (15)	54	0.59
Welsh (0)	197	2.14
Yugoslavian (48)	58	0.63

Hispanic Origin	Population	%
Hispanic or Latino (of any race)	60	0.67
Central American, ex. Mexican	10	0.11
Costa Rican	1	0.01
Guatemalan	4	0.04
Panamanian	5	0.06
Cuban	8	0.09
Dominican Republic	1	0.01
Mexican	25	0.28
Puerto Rican	2	0.02
South American	7	0.08
Colombian	2	0.02
Ecuadorian	3	0.03
Peruvian	1	0.01
Venezuelan	1	0.01
Other Hispanic or Latino	7	0.08

Race*	Population	%
African-American/Black (61)	73	0.81
Not Hispanic (59)	69	0.77
Hispanic (2)	4	0.04
American Indian/Alaska Native (3)	25	0.28
Not Hispanic (3)	25	0.28
Blackfeet (0)	1	0.01
Cherokee (0)	5	0.06
Iroquois (0)	4	0.04
Navajo (1)	1	0.01
Asian (62)	89	0.99
Not Hispanic (62)	89	0.99
Chinese, ex. Taiwanese (18)	26	0.29
Filipino (12)	17	0.19
Indian (14)	15	0.17
Japanese (1)	1	0.01
Korean (8)	8	0.09
Pakistani (3)	3	0.03
Taiwanese (2)	5	0.06
Thai (3)	5	0.06
Vietnamese (0)	4	0.04
Hawaii Native/Pacific Islander (2)	2	0.02
Not Hispanic (2)	2	0.02
Samoan (2)	2	0.02
White (8,773)	8,834	98.36
Not Hispanic (8,730)	8,790	97.87
Hispanic (43)	44	0.49

Glenside

Place Type: CDP
County: Montgomery
Population: 8,384†

Ancestry‡	Population	%
African, Sub-Saharan (58)	58	0.79
African (20)	20	0.27
Ethiopian (24)	24	0.33
Nigerian (14)	14	0.19
American (298)	298	4.05
Arab (0)	41	0.56
Lebanese (0)	41	0.56
Austrian (19)	19	0.26
British (12)	12	0.16
Czech (27)	63	0.86
Dutch (23)	67	0.91
English (109)	885	12.02
European (97)	97	1.32
French, ex. Basque (13)	147	2.00
French Canadian (0)	9	0.12
German (344)	1,828	24.83
Greek (0)	28	0.38
Hungarian (8)	52	0.71
Irish (844)	2,732	37.11
Italian (327)	1,060	14.40
Lithuanian (0)	107	1.45
Northern European (11)	11	0.15
Norwegian (0)	30	0.41
Pennsylvania German (45)	90	1.22
Polish (72)	332	4.51
Portuguese (0)	10	0.14
Romanian (0)	13	0.18
Russian (77)	277	3.76
Scotch-Irish (41)	128	1.74
Scottish (13)	113	1.54
Serbian (0)	74	1.01
Swedish (0)	41	0.56
Ukrainian (11)	55	0.75
Welsh (0)	84	1.14
West Indian, ex. Hispanic (94)	94	1.28
West Indian (94)	94	1.28

Hispanic Origin	Population	%
Hispanic or Latino (of any race)	242	2.89
Central American, ex. Mexican	39	0.47
Costa Rican	2	0.02
Guatemalan	28	0.33
Honduran	4	0.05
Panamanian	3	0.04
Salvadoran	2	0.02
Cuban	17	0.20
Dominican Republic	8	0.10
Mexican	14	0.17
Puerto Rican	77	0.92
South American	41	0.49
Argentinean	2	0.02
Bolivian	3	0.04
Chilean	2	0.02
Colombian	14	0.17
Ecuadorian	7	0.08
Peruvian	11	0.13
Venezuelan	2	0.02
Other Hispanic or Latino	46	0.55

Race*	Population	%
African-American/Black (606)	670	7.99
Not Hispanic (597)	657	7.84
Hispanic (9)	13	0.16
American Indian/Alaska Native (17)	54	0.64
Not Hispanic (16)	45	0.54
Hispanic (1)	9	0.11
Cherokee (4)	20	0.24
Cree (1)	3	0.04
Delaware (2)	2	0.02
Iroquois (0)	3	0.04
Asian (231)	278	3.32
Not Hispanic (231)	273	3.26
Hispanic (0)	5	0.06
Burmese (17)	17	0.20
Cambodian (0)	1	0.01
Chinese, ex. Taiwanese (44)	55	0.66
Filipino (12)	22	0.26
Indian (51)	58	0.69
Indonesian (3)	5	0.06
Japanese (7)	12	0.14
Korean (67)	75	0.89
Laotian (2)	4	0.05
Malaysian (1)	1	0.01
Pakistani (1)	1	0.01
Sri Lankan (1)	3	0.04
Taiwanese (3)	3	0.04
Thai (0)	4	0.05
Vietnamese (16)	19	0.23
Hawaii Native/Pacific Islander (1)	6	0.07
Not Hispanic (1)	6	0.07
Native Hawaiian (0)	2	0.02
White (7,299)	7,424	88.55
Not Hispanic (7,163)	7,271	86.72
Hispanic (136)	153	1.82

Greene

Place Type: Township
County: Franklin
Population: 16,700†

Ancestry‡	Population	%
American (1,309)	1,309	8.20
Arab (217)	217	1.36
Moroccan (217)	217	1.36
Austrian (16)	62	0.39
Belgian (11)	23	0.14
Brazilian (56)	56	0.35
British (10)	75	0.47
Croatian (0)	52	0.33
Czech (0)	9	0.06
Czechoslovakian (17)	17	0.11
Danish (11)	11	0.07
Dutch (52)	279	1.75
Eastern European (15)	15	0.09
English (431)	1,278	8.01
European (125)	146	0.91
French, ex. Basque (96)	399	2.50
French Canadian (22)	22	0.14
German (3,479)	6,836	42.82
Greek (29)	39	0.24
Hungarian (67)	179	1.12
Irish (444)	2,086	13.07
Italian (170)	670	4.20
Luxemburger (0)	13	0.08
Northern European (0)	10	0.06
Norwegian (0)	20	0.13
Pennsylvania German (101)	101	0.63
Polish (213)	618	3.87
Portuguese (0)	8	0.05
Romanian (0)	21	0.13
Russian (16)	16	0.10
Scotch-Irish (249)	523	3.28
Scottish (76)	335	2.10
Slovak (75)	156	0.98
Swedish (20)	81	0.51
Swiss (149)	301	1.89
Ukrainian (0)	17	0.11
Welsh (31)	106	0.66

Hispanic Origin	Population	%
Hispanic or Latino (of any race)	518	3.10
Central American, ex. Mexican	75	0.45
Costa Rican	5	0.03
Guatemalan	34	0.20
Honduran	13	0.08
Panamanian	6	0.04
Salvadoran	17	0.10
Cuban	10	0.06
Dominican Republic	14	0.08
Mexican	199	1.19
Puerto Rican	143	0.86
South American	33	0.20
Bolivian	8	0.05
Chilean	9	0.05
Colombian	3	0.02
Ecuadorian	1	0.01
Peruvian	9	0.05
Venezuelan	3	0.02
Other Hispanic or Latino	44	0.26

Race*	Population	%
African-American/Black (456)	631	3.78
Not Hispanic (416)	570	3.41
Hispanic (40)	61	0.37
American Indian/Alaska Native (13)	76	0.46
Not Hispanic (12)	71	0.43
Hispanic (1)	5	0.03
Arapaho (0)	1	0.01
Blackfeet (0)	5	0.03
Cherokee (4)	11	0.07
Chippewa (0)	4	0.02
Choctaw (1)	1	0.01
Delaware (0)	2	0.01
Iroquois (0)	4	0.02

*Notes: † The Census 2010 population figure is used to calculate the percentages in the Hispanic Origin and Race categories. Ancestry percentages are based on the 2006-2010 American Community Survey population (not shown); ‡ Numbers in parentheses indicate the number of people reporting a single ancestry; * Numbers in parentheses indicate the number of persons reporting this race alone, not in combination with any other race; Please refer to the Explanation of Data for more information.*

Mexican American Ind. (0)	3	0.02
Navajo (1)	2	0.01
Potawatomi (3)	5	0.03
Sioux (1)	4	0.02
Asian (197)	268	1.60
Not Hispanic (193)	259	1.55
Hispanic (4)	9	0.05
Bangladeshi (7)	7	0.04
Chinese, ex. Taiwanese (36)	46	0.28
Filipino (32)	56	0.34
Indian (44)	50	0.30
Indonesian (4)	4	0.02
Japanese (10)	14	0.08
Korean (18)	31	0.19
Laotian (0)	2	0.01
Nepalese (2)	2	0.01
Pakistani (21)	25	0.15
Taiwanese (2)	2	0.01
Thai (8)	9	0.05
Vietnamese (10)	16	0.10
Hawaii Native/Pacific Islander (6)	8	0.05
Not Hispanic (6)	8	0.05
Fijian (2)	2	0.01
Guamanian/Chamorro (1)	1	0.01
Native Hawaiian (1)	2	0.01
White (15,492)	15,798	94.60
Not Hispanic (15,282)	15,527	92.98
Hispanic (210)	271	1.62

Greensburg

Place Type: City
County: Westmoreland
Population: 14,892†

Ancestry‡	Population	%
African, Sub-Saharan (223)	223	1.48
African (180)	180	1.20
Nigerian (43)	43	0.29
Alsatian (10)	10	0.07
American (554)	554	3.68
Arab (31)	68	0.45
Syrian (31)	68	0.45
Armenian (0)	11	0.07
Austrian (18)	81	0.54
Belgian (0)	10	0.07
British (38)	143	0.95
Canadian (0)	104	0.69
Carpatho Rusyn (12)	12	0.08
Croatian (49)	210	1.40
Czech (13)	58	0.39
Czechoslovakian (8)	54	0.36
Danish (0)	34	0.23
Dutch (10)	204	1.36
Eastern European (13)	13	0.09
English (456)	1,317	8.76
European (101)	101	0.67
French, ex. Basque (16)	151	1.00
French Canadian (11)	34	0.23
German (1,368)	5,189	34.51
Greek (42)	69	0.46
Hungarian (0)	181	1.20
Irish (596)	3,292	21.89
Italian (1,181)	3,053	20.30
Lithuanian (0)	77	0.51
Macedonian (0)	11	0.07
Northern European (26)	26	0.17
Norwegian (13)	36	0.24
Pennsylvania German (39)	74	0.49
Polish (185)	1,019	6.78
Romanian (0)	15	0.10
Russian (84)	207	1.38
Scotch-Irish (337)	611	4.06
Scottish (55)	414	2.75
Serbian (0)	86	0.57
Slavic (19)	59	0.39
Slovak (256)	784	5.21
Slovene (0)	20	0.13
Swedish (38)	119	0.79
Swiss (0)	16	0.11
Ukrainian (8)	78	0.52
Welsh (35)	221	1.47
Yugoslavian (11)	11	0.07

Hispanic Origin	Population	%
Hispanic or Latino (of any race)	217	1.46
Central American, ex. Mexican	11	0.07
Costa Rican	1	0.01
Guatemalan	3	0.02
Panamanian	5	0.03
Salvadoran	2	0.01
Cuban	17	0.11
Dominican Republic	6	0.04
Mexican	67	0.45
Puerto Rican	62	0.42
South American	15	0.10
Argentinean	2	0.01
Bolivian	2	0.01
Chilean	4	0.03
Colombian	2	0.01
Peruvian	2	0.01
Venezuelan	3	0.02
Other Hispanic or Latino	39	0.26

Race*	Population	%
African-American/Black (721)	1,015	6.82
Not Hispanic (711)	993	6.67
Hispanic (10)	22	0.15
American Indian/Alaska Native (28)	85	0.57
Not Hispanic (25)	79	0.53
Hispanic (3)	6	0.04
Arapaho (0)	1	0.01
Blackfeet (3)	5	0.03
Cherokee (6)	31	0.21
Cheyenne (0)	1	0.01
Chippewa (0)	1	0.01
Comanche (1)	1	0.01
Creek (1)	1	0.01
Iroquois (0)	6	0.04
Navajo (2)	5	0.03
Seminole (0)	1	0.01
Asian (119)	160	1.07
Not Hispanic (119)	160	1.07
Chinese, ex. Taiwanese (55)	57	0.38
Filipino (5)	23	0.15
Indian (10)	22	0.15
Japanese (13)	18	0.12
Korean (12)	15	0.10
Laotian (0)	1	0.01
Pakistani (0)	1	0.01
Taiwanese (1)	4	0.03
Thai (2)	5	0.03
Vietnamese (13)	15	0.10
Hawaii Native/Pacific Islander (3)	7	0.05
Not Hispanic (3)	7	0.05
Guamanian/Chamorro (0)	1	0.01
Native Hawaiian (1)	1	0.01
Samoan (2)	4	0.03
White (13,599)	13,960	93.74
Not Hispanic (13,451)	13,791	92.61
Hispanic (148)	169	1.13

Grove City

Place Type: Borough
County: Mercer
Population: 8,322†

Ancestry‡	Population	%
American (285)	285	3.44
Arab (0)	10	0.12
Syrian (0)	10	0.12
Australian (8)	8	0.10
Austrian (29)	50	0.60
British (15)	57	0.69
Canadian (15)	15	0.18
Carpatho Rusyn (0)	10	0.12
Croatian (8)	64	0.77
Czech (7)	35	0.42
Czechoslovakian (8)	8	0.10
Danish (15)	15	0.18
Dutch (74)	174	2.10
Eastern European (15)	15	0.18
English (215)	1,012	12.20
French, ex. Basque (128)	295	3.56
French Canadian (17)	55	0.66
German (709)	2,838	34.21
Greek (29)	58	0.70
Hungarian (28)	100	1.21
Irish (374)	1,475	17.78
Italian (212)	982	11.84
Latvian (0)	14	0.17
Lithuanian (10)	32	0.39
Macedonian (7)	7	0.08
Norwegian (20)	145	1.75
Pennsylvania German (0)	23	0.28
Polish (83)	436	5.26
Russian (22)	99	1.19
Scandinavian (0)	44	0.53
Scotch-Irish (235)	574	6.92
Scottish (158)	370	4.46
Slavic (30)	82	0.99
Slovak (19)	61	0.74
Slovene (0)	23	0.28
Swedish (30)	284	3.42
Swiss (0)	87	1.05
Ukrainian (23)	23	0.28
Welsh (6)	90	1.08
West Indian, ex. Hispanic (15)	15	0.18
Haitian (15)	15	0.18
Yugoslavian (0)	6	0.07

Hispanic Origin	Population	%
Hispanic or Latino (of any race)	95	1.14
Central American, ex. Mexican	3	0.04
Costa Rican	1	0.01
Panamanian	1	0.01
Salvadoran	1	0.01
Cuban	5	0.06
Mexican	27	0.32
Puerto Rican	15	0.18
South American	7	0.08
Colombian	5	0.06
Ecuadorian	1	0.01
Peruvian	1	0.01
Other Hispanic or Latino	38	0.46

Race*	Population	%
African-American/Black (106)	145	1.74
Not Hispanic (104)	141	1.69
Hispanic (2)	4	0.05
American Indian/Alaska Native (15)	35	0.42
Not Hispanic (15)	34	0.41
Hispanic (0)	1	0.01
Alaska Athabascan *(Ala. Nat.)* (1)	1	0.01
Cherokee (3)	8	0.10
Chippewa (5)	5	0.06
Delaware (3)	3	0.04
Iroquois (0)	2	0.02
Navajo (1)	1	0.01
Sioux (0)	1	0.01
Asian (113)	140	1.68
Not Hispanic (113)	140	1.68
Chinese, ex. Taiwanese (35)	38	0.46
Filipino (1)	3	0.04
Indian (13)	15	0.18
Japanese (4)	7	0.08
Korean (16)	33	0.40
Taiwanese (7)	7	0.08
Vietnamese (4)	5	0.06
Hawaii Native/Pacific Islander (0)	1	0.01
Not Hispanic (0)	1	0.01
Tongan (0)	1	0.01
White (7,987)	8,072	97.00
Not Hispanic (7,909)	7,991	96.02
Hispanic (78)	81	0.97

*Notes: † The Census 2010 population figure is used to calculate the percentages in the Hispanic Origin and Race categories. Ancestry percentages are based on the 2006-2010 American Community Survey population (not shown); ‡ Numbers in parentheses indicate the number of people reporting a single ancestry; * Numbers in parentheses indicate the number of persons reporting this race alone, not in combination with any other race; Please refer to the Explanation of Data for more information.*

Guilford

Place Type: Township
County: Franklin
Population: 14,531†

Ancestry‡	Population	%
African, Sub-Saharan (20)	20	0.14
African (20)	20	0.14
American (1,804)	1,804	12.58
Austrian (0)	98	0.68
Belgian (21)	21	0.15
British (78)	206	1.44
Cajun (0)	6	0.04
Canadian (56)	56	0.39
Czech (16)	16	0.11
Danish (16)	31	0.22
Dutch (84)	406	2.83
English (713)	1,653	11.53
European (259)	259	1.81
French, ex. Basque (29)	286	1.99
French Canadian (25)	25	0.17
German (2,752)	5,593	39.01
Greek (16)	54	0.38
Hungarian (30)	60	0.42
Irish (305)	1,641	11.45
Italian (478)	1,013	7.07
Lithuanian (23)	23	0.16
Northern European (15)	15	0.10
Norwegian (27)	27	0.19
Pennsylvania German (62)	96	0.67
Polish (58)	199	1.39
Portuguese (15)	42	0.29
Russian (35)	81	0.56
Scotch-Irish (399)	731	5.10
Scottish (117)	385	2.69
Slovak (24)	78	0.54
Slovene (15)	48	0.33
Swedish (48)	151	1.05
Swiss (49)	212	1.48
Ukrainian (39)	44	0.31
Welsh (87)	311	2.17

Hispanic Origin	Population	%
Hispanic or Latino (of any race)	537	3.70
Central American, ex. Mexican	99	0.68
Costa Rican	2	0.01
Guatemalan	62	0.43
Honduran	19	0.13
Panamanian	1	0.01
Salvadoran	15	0.10
Cuban	9	0.06
Dominican Republic	8	0.06
Mexican	228	1.57
Puerto Rican	115	0.79
South American	18	0.12
Bolivian	1	0.01
Chilean	7	0.05
Colombian	7	0.05
Peruvian	3	0.02
Other Hispanic or Latino	60	0.41

Race*	Population	%
African-American/Black (390)	499	3.43
Not Hispanic (361)	459	3.16
Hispanic (29)	40	0.28
American Indian/Alaska Native (31)	66	0.45
Not Hispanic (25)	54	0.37
Hispanic (6)	12	0.08
Apache (0)	3	0.02
Blackfeet (4)	4	0.03
Canadian/French Am. Ind. (0)	1	0.01
Cherokee (3)	9	0.06
Cree (0)	3	0.02
Crow (1)	1	0.01
Iroquois (4)	4	0.03
Lumbee (3)	3	0.02
Navajo (1)	1	0.01
Potawatomi (1)	1	0.01
Seminole (1)	1	0.01
South American Ind. (2)	2	0.01
Asian (135)	173	1.19
Not Hispanic (133)	169	1.16
Hispanic (2)	4	0.03
Burmese (1)	1	0.01
Chinese, ex. Taiwanese (35)	36	0.25
Filipino (19)	30	0.21
Indian (28)	30	0.21
Japanese (2)	6	0.04
Korean (17)	25	0.17
Laotian (2)	5	0.03
Malaysian (2)	2	0.01
Nepalese (4)	5	0.03
Pakistani (5)	5	0.03
Sri Lankan (1)	1	0.01
Taiwanese (0)	1	0.01
Thai (1)	8	0.06
Vietnamese (12)	13	0.09
Hawaii Native/Pacific Islander (1)	8	0.06
Not Hispanic (1)	6	0.04
Hispanic (0)	2	0.01
Guamanian/Chamorro (0)	1	0.01
Native Hawaiian (1)	2	0.01
White (13,548)	13,729	94.48
Not Hispanic (13,309)	13,453	92.58
Hispanic (239)	276	1.90

Hamilton

Place Type: Township
County: Franklin
Population: 10,788†

Ancestry‡	Population	%
American (1,076)	1,076	10.27
Arab (41)	87	0.83
Palestinian (21)	44	0.42
Syrian (20)	43	0.41
Austrian (13)	13	0.12
British (0)	14	0.13
Czech (0)	14	0.13
Czechoslovakian (19)	19	0.18
Dutch (33)	125	1.19
English (343)	786	7.50
European (94)	94	0.90
French, ex. Basque (33)	173	1.65
French Canadian (0)	53	0.51
German (1,797)	4,017	38.33
Greek (32)	32	0.31
Hungarian (58)	74	0.71
Irish (393)	1,658	15.82
Italian (69)	285	2.72
Lithuanian (21)	60	0.57
Luxemburger (16)	31	0.30
Pennsylvania German (72)	82	0.78
Polish (51)	166	1.58
Russian (0)	7	0.07
Scotch-Irish (90)	222	2.12
Scottish (29)	91	0.87
Serbian (60)	93	0.89
Slovak (1)	21	0.20
Swedish (33)	64	0.61
Swiss (29)	111	1.06
Ukrainian (0)	18	0.17
Welsh (0)	86	0.82
West Indian, ex. Hispanic (11)	30	0.29
Jamaican (11)	30	0.29
Yugoslavian (0)	31	0.30

Hispanic Origin	Population	%
Hispanic or Latino (of any race)	455	4.22
Central American, ex. Mexican	65	0.60
Costa Rican	1	0.01
Guatemalan	49	0.45
Honduran	1	0.01
Panamanian	2	0.02
Salvadoran	6	0.06
Other Central American	6	0.06
Cuban	10	0.09
Dominican Republic	30	0.28
Mexican	198	1.84
Puerto Rican	96	0.89
South American	20	0.19
Argentinean	1	0.01
Bolivian	4	0.04
Chilean	2	0.02
Colombian	3	0.03
Paraguayan	7	0.06
Peruvian	2	0.02
Venezuelan	1	0.01
Other Hispanic or Latino	36	0.33

Race*	Population	%
African-American/Black (351)	504	4.67
Not Hispanic (339)	471	4.37
Hispanic (12)	33	0.31
American Indian/Alaska Native (12)	88	0.82
Not Hispanic (11)	83	0.77
Hispanic (1)	5	0.05
Alaska Athabascan *(Ala. Nat.)* (0)	2	0.02
Blackfeet (0)	8	0.07
Cherokee (5)	17	0.16
Cheyenne (0)	1	0.01
Comanche (0)	2	0.02
Delaware (0)	2	0.02
Iroquois (0)	9	0.08
Sioux (2)	7	0.06
Asian (73)	102	0.95
Not Hispanic (72)	98	0.91
Hispanic (1)	4	0.04
Chinese, ex. Taiwanese (9)	15	0.14
Filipino (15)	23	0.21
Hmong (1)	1	0.01
Indian (14)	16	0.15
Japanese (5)	11	0.10
Korean (18)	22	0.20
Thai (3)	4	0.04
Vietnamese (8)	9	0.08
Hawaii Native/Pacific Islander (1)	8	0.07
Not Hispanic (1)	5	0.05
Hispanic (0)	3	0.03
Guamanian/Chamorro (1)	2	0.02
Native Hawaiian (0)	2	0.02
White (9,912)	10,135	93.95
Not Hispanic (9,703)	9,889	91.67
Hispanic (209)	246	2.28

Hamilton

Place Type: Township
County: Monroe
Population: 9,083†

Ancestry‡	Population	%
American (195)	195	2.13
Arab (186)	186	2.04
Egyptian (86)	86	0.94
Moroccan (43)	43	0.47
Palestinian (57)	57	0.62
Austrian (0)	17	0.19
Belgian (0)	17	0.19
Czech (0)	24	0.26
Danish (0)	17	0.19
Dutch (113)	330	3.61
English (207)	755	8.27
Estonian (0)	17	0.19
European (67)	67	0.73
Finnish (40)	111	1.22
French, ex. Basque (10)	243	2.66
French Canadian (0)	26	0.28
German (987)	2,760	30.22
Greek (25)	73	0.80
Hungarian (32)	57	0.62
Irish (462)	1,723	18.86
Italian (494)	1,726	18.90
Latvian (0)	21	0.23
Lithuanian (25)	43	0.47
Norwegian (0)	36	0.39
Pennsylvania German (168)	281	3.08
Polish (410)	1,058	11.58

SECTION TWO

*Notes: † The Census 2010 population figure is used to calculate the percentages in the Hispanic Origin and Race categories. Ancestry percentages are based on the 2006-2010 American Community Survey population (not shown); ‡ Numbers in parentheses indicate the number of people reporting a single ancestry; * Numbers in parentheses indicate the number of persons reporting this race alone, not in combination with any other race; Please refer to the Explanation of Data for more information.*

Portuguese (60)	159	1.74
Russian (36)	196	2.15
Scandinavian (0)	13	0.14
Scotch-Irish (5)	5	0.05
Scottish (36)	185	2.03
Slavic (51)	51	0.56
Slovak (32)	32	0.35
Swedish (73)	220	2.41
Swiss (0)	7	0.08
Ukrainian (143)	210	2.30
Welsh (49)	175	1.92
West Indian, ex. Hispanic (16)	174	1.90
Barbadian (0)	48	0.53
Jamaican (16)	16	0.18
Trinidadian/Tobagonian (0)	110	1.20

Hispanic Origin	Population	%
Hispanic or Latino (of any race)	501	5.52
Central American, ex. Mexican	14	0.15
Honduran	4	0.04
Nicaraguan	1	0.01
Panamanian	1	0.01
Salvadoran	8	0.09
Cuban	37	0.41
Dominican Republic	48	0.53
Mexican	47	0.52
Puerto Rican	257	2.83
South American	45	0.50
Argentinean	3	0.03
Colombian	17	0.19
Ecuadorian	14	0.15
Paraguayan	1	0.01
Peruvian	10	0.11
Other Hispanic or Latino	53	0.58

Race*	Population	%
African-American/Black (415)	471	5.19
Not Hispanic (387)	433	4.77
Hispanic (28)	38	0.42
American Indian/Alaska Native (22)	57	0.63
Not Hispanic (16)	47	0.52
Hispanic (6)	10	0.11
Blackfeet (3)	5	0.06
Central American Ind. (5)	5	0.06
Cherokee (1)	9	0.10
Delaware (3)	4	0.04
Iroquois (0)	4	0.04
Lumbee (1)	1	0.01
Mexican American Ind. (1)	2	0.02
Shoshone (0)	2	0.02
South American Ind. (2)	3	0.03
Spanish American Ind. (3)	3	0.03
Asian (154)	191	2.10
Not Hispanic (151)	187	2.06
Hispanic (3)	4	0.04
Chinese, ex. Taiwanese (6)	8	0.09
Filipino (16)	21	0.23
Indian (91)	105	1.16
Japanese (1)	6	0.07
Korean (16)	20	0.22
Laotian (3)	3	0.03
Pakistani (2)	2	0.02
Thai (1)	4	0.04
Vietnamese (11)	11	0.12
Hawaii Native/Pacific Islander (1)	2	0.02
Not Hispanic (1)	2	0.02
White (8,238)	8,347	91.90
Not Hispanic (7,898)	7,992	87.99
Hispanic (340)	355	3.91

Hampden

Place Type: Township
County: Cumberland
Population: 28,044†

Ancestry‡	Population	%
African, Sub-Saharan (20)	28	0.10
Kenyan (20)	20	0.07
Other Sub-Saharan African (0)	8	0.03
American (1,003)	1,003	3.66
Arab (705)	946	3.45
Egyptian (573)	600	2.19
Lebanese (61)	197	0.72
Moroccan (19)	19	0.07
Palestinian (41)	106	0.39
Syrian (11)	24	0.09
Armenian (11)	67	0.24
Australian (0)	19	0.07
Austrian (66)	113	0.41
Belgian (0)	9	0.03
Brazilian (0)	12	0.04
British (61)	157	0.57
Canadian (0)	48	0.18
Celtic (0)	11	0.04
Croatian (66)	185	0.68
Czech (28)	134	0.49
Czechoslovakian (20)	99	0.36
Danish (0)	91	0.33
Dutch (143)	590	2.15
Eastern European (49)	49	0.18
English (680)	2,899	10.58
European (461)	487	1.78
Finnish (0)	16	0.06
French, ex. Basque (76)	775	2.83
French Canadian (53)	97	0.35
German (3,629)	9,320	34.02
Greek (209)	235	0.86
Hungarian (137)	284	1.04
Iranian (0)	11	0.04
Irish (1,322)	5,341	19.49
Italian (817)	2,847	10.39
Latvian (18)	18	0.07
Lithuanian (49)	160	0.58
Macedonian (0)	15	0.05
Norwegian (118)	300	1.10
Pennsylvania German (137)	266	0.97
Polish (639)	1,608	5.87
Portuguese (25)	40	0.15
Russian (125)	241	0.88
Scotch-Irish (299)	652	2.38
Scottish (182)	862	3.15
Serbian (0)	15	0.05
Slavic (15)	42	0.15
Slovak (153)	458	1.67
Slovene (20)	35	0.13
Swedish (54)	369	1.35
Swiss (10)	165	0.60
Ukrainian (137)	333	1.22
Welsh (206)	769	2.81
West Indian, ex. Hispanic (31)	83	0.30
West Indian (31)	83	0.30
Yugoslavian (134)	145	0.53

Hispanic Origin	Population	%
Hispanic or Latino (of any race)	567	2.02
Central American, ex. Mexican	65	0.23
Costa Rican	1	<0.01
Guatemalan	22	0.08
Honduran	14	0.05
Nicaraguan	3	0.01
Panamanian	17	0.06
Salvadoran	8	0.03
Cuban	17	0.06
Dominican Republic	4	0.01
Mexican	180	0.64
Puerto Rican	175	0.62
South American	60	0.21
Argentinean	6	0.02
Bolivian	2	0.01
Chilean	2	0.01
Colombian	14	0.05
Ecuadorian	8	0.03
Paraguayan	5	0.02
Peruvian	17	0.06
Venezuelan	4	0.01
Other South American	2	0.01
Other Hispanic or Latino	66	0.24

Race*	Population	%
African-American/Black (473)	629	2.24
Not Hispanic (443)	587	2.09
Hispanic (30)	42	0.15
American Indian/Alaska Native (34)	105	0.37
Not Hispanic (30)	97	0.35
Hispanic (4)	8	0.03
Blackfeet (1)	5	0.02
Cherokee (2)	18	0.06
Chickasaw (0)	6	0.02
Chippewa (2)	2	0.01
Choctaw (1)	4	0.01
Comanche (1)	1	<0.01
Cree (2)	2	0.01
Creek (1)	2	0.01
Delaware (0)	3	0.01
Mexican American Ind. (2)	2	0.01
Osage (1)	1	<0.01
Sioux (1)	1	<0.01
Spanish American Ind. (0)	1	<0.01
Asian (1,981)	2,177	7.76
Not Hispanic (1,979)	2,171	7.74
Hispanic (2)	6	0.02
Bangladeshi (4)	4	0.01
Burmese (21)	21	0.07
Cambodian (17)	27	0.10
Chinese, ex. Taiwanese (191)	218	0.78
Filipino (63)	103	0.37
Hmong (2)	10	0.04
Indian (1,013)	1,043	3.72
Indonesian (2)	5	0.02
Japanese (28)	44	0.16
Korean (240)	279	0.99
Laotian (9)	12	0.04
Nepalese (1)	1	<0.01
Pakistani (42)	47	0.17
Sri Lankan (12)	13	0.05
Taiwanese (23)	30	0.11
Thai (9)	15	0.05
Vietnamese (245)	272	0.97
Hawaii Native/Pacific Islander (5)	39	0.14
Not Hispanic (4)	38	0.14
Hispanic (1)	1	<0.01
Guamanian/Chamorro (3)	8	0.03
Marshallese (1)	1	<0.01
Native Hawaiian (1)	13	0.05
White (24,933)	25,342	90.37
Not Hispanic (24,579)	24,950	88.97
Hispanic (354)	392	1.40

Hampton

Place Type: Township
County: Allegheny
Population: 18,363†

Ancestry‡	Population	%
African, Sub-Saharan (38)	38	0.21
African (38)	38	0.21
American (703)	703	3.89
Arab (117)	129	0.71
Egyptian (53)	53	0.29
Lebanese (38)	50	0.28
Syrian (26)	26	0.14
Australian (28)	28	0.16
Austrian (22)	108	0.60
Belgian (77)	93	0.52
British (22)	22	0.12
Bulgarian (35)	35	0.19
Canadian (15)	15	0.08
Croatian (80)	503	2.79
Czech (20)	137	0.76
Czechoslovakian (36)	95	0.53
Danish (0)	31	0.17
Dutch (11)	105	0.58
Eastern European (0)	14	0.08
English (367)	1,620	8.97
European (64)	64	0.35
French, ex. Basque (55)	297	1.64

*Notes: † The Census 2010 population figure is used to calculate the percentages in the Hispanic Origin and Race categories. Ancestry percentages are based on the 2006-2010 American Community Survey population (not shown); ‡ Numbers in parentheses indicate the number of people reporting a single ancestry; * Numbers in parentheses indicate the number of persons reporting this race alone, not in combination with any other race; Please refer to the Explanation of Data for more information.*

Ancestry	Population	%
French Canadian (22)	92	0.51
German (1,848)	6,882	38.12
Greek (39)	145	0.80
Hungarian (37)	187	1.04
Irish (965)	4,132	22.89
Italian (1,279)	3,486	19.31
Latvian (0)	49	0.27
Lithuanian (16)	109	0.60
Macedonian (14)	54	0.30
Norwegian (14)	149	0.83
Pennsylvania German (13)	13	0.07
Polish (325)	1,838	10.18
Russian (88)	182	1.01
Scandinavian (0)	19	0.11
Scotch-Irish (167)	581	3.22
Scottish (122)	430	2.38
Serbian (26)	54	0.30
Slavic (0)	15	0.08
Slovak (183)	518	2.87
Slovene (0)	97	0.54
Swedish (42)	299	1.66
Swiss (46)	91	0.50
Ukrainian (46)	170	0.94
Welsh (205)	399	2.21
Yugoslavian (13)	31	0.17

Hispanic Origin	Population	%
Hispanic or Latino (of any race)	148	0.81
Central American, ex. Mexican	12	0.07
Guatemalan	4	0.02
Honduran	1	0.01
Panamanian	1	0.01
Salvadoran	6	0.03
Cuban	11	0.06
Mexican	62	0.34
Puerto Rican	23	0.13
South American	20	0.11
Argentinean	3	0.02
Bolivian	3	0.02
Chilean	1	0.01
Colombian	9	0.05
Peruvian	2	0.01
Uruguayan	1	0.01
Venezuelan	1	0.01
Other Hispanic or Latino	20	0.11

Race*	Population	%
African-American/Black (166)	217	1.18
Not Hispanic (164)	212	1.15
Hispanic (2)	5	0.03
American Indian/Alaska Native (9)	45	0.25
Not Hispanic (9)	40	0.22
Hispanic (0)	5	0.03
Aleut *(Alaska Native)* (1)	1	0.01
Cherokee (1)	12	0.07
Iroquois (1)	1	0.01
Mexican American Ind. (0)	3	0.02
Asian (385)	441	2.40
Not Hispanic (384)	440	2.40
Hispanic (1)	1	0.01
Chinese, ex. Taiwanese (84)	96	0.52
Filipino (16)	25	0.14
Indian (173)	185	1.01
Indonesian (1)	1	0.01
Japanese (18)	24	0.13
Korean (52)	53	0.29
Laotian (3)	5	0.03
Nepalese (3)	3	0.02
Pakistani (5)	5	0.03
Sri Lankan (0)	1	0.01
Taiwanese (1)	5	0.03
Thai (1)	1	0.01
Vietnamese (16)	24	0.13
Hawaii Native/Pacific Islander (1)	10	0.05
Not Hispanic (1)	8	0.04
Hispanic (0)	2	0.01
Native Hawaiian (0)	4	0.02
Tongan (0)	1	0.01
White (17,630)	17,759	96.71
Not Hispanic (17,504)	17,624	95.98
Hispanic (126)	135	0.74

Hanover

Place Type: Borough
County: York
Population: 15,289†

Ancestry‡	Population	%
African, Sub-Saharan (34)	34	0.22
Ethiopian (34)	34	0.22
American (1,598)	1,598	10.47
Arab (0)	7	0.05
Lebanese (0)	7	0.05
British (26)	119	0.78
Croatian (45)	45	0.29
Czech (0)	28	0.18
Czechoslovakian (0)	15	0.10
Dutch (69)	377	2.47
Eastern European (38)	38	0.25
English (611)	1,315	8.62
European (45)	45	0.29
Finnish (0)	32	0.21
French, ex. Basque (70)	216	1.42
French Canadian (9)	16	0.10
German (3,501)	6,647	43.57
Greek (0)	68	0.45
Hungarian (0)	14	0.09
Irish (386)	2,210	14.49
Italian (155)	628	4.12
Latvian (7)	7	0.05
Lithuanian (0)	38	0.25
Norwegian (33)	54	0.35
Pennsylvania German (157)	203	1.33
Polish (132)	475	3.11
Russian (0)	55	0.36
Scandinavian (0)	8	0.05
Scotch-Irish (132)	494	3.24
Scottish (36)	241	1.58
Serbian (10)	10	0.07
Slovak (0)	20	0.13
Swedish (27)	58	0.38
Swiss (7)	60	0.39
Ukrainian (16)	88	0.58
Welsh (11)	92	0.60

Hispanic Origin	Population	%
Hispanic or Latino (of any race)	1,121	7.33
Central American, ex. Mexican	46	0.30
Costa Rican	5	0.03
Guatemalan	24	0.16
Honduran	5	0.03
Panamanian	2	0.01
Salvadoran	10	0.07
Cuban	2	0.01
Mexican	756	4.94
Puerto Rican	217	1.42
South American	40	0.26
Argentinean	7	0.05
Bolivian	1	0.01
Chilean	2	0.01
Colombian	4	0.03
Ecuadorian	1	0.01
Peruvian	22	0.14
Venezuelan	3	0.02
Other Hispanic or Latino	60	0.39

Race*	Population	%
African-American/Black (180)	297	1.94
Not Hispanic (155)	264	1.73
Hispanic (25)	33	0.22
American Indian/Alaska Native (25)	99	0.65
Not Hispanic (21)	85	0.56
Hispanic (4)	14	0.09
Blackfeet (0)	9	0.06
Canadian/French Am. Ind. (0)	2	0.01
Cherokee (4)	14	0.09
Cheyenne (0)	1	0.01
Chippewa (1)	1	0.01
Inupiat *(Alaska Native)* (0)	3	0.02
Iroquois (1)	3	0.02
Seminole (1)	1	0.01
Sioux (1)	2	0.01
Spanish American Ind. (1)	1	0.01
Asian (156)	186	1.22
Not Hispanic (149)	174	1.14
Hispanic (7)	12	0.08
Chinese, ex. Taiwanese (31)	32	0.21
Filipino (11)	16	0.10
Hmong (10)	10	0.07
Indian (58)	60	0.39
Japanese (5)	10	0.07
Korean (18)	26	0.17
Laotian (0)	1	0.01
Pakistani (4)	5	0.03
Thai (1)	5	0.03
Vietnamese (16)	18	0.12
Hawaii Native/Pacific Islander (7)	15	0.10
Not Hispanic (5)	10	0.07
Hispanic (2)	5	0.03
Guamanian/Chamorro (1)	3	0.02
Native Hawaiian (4)	8	0.05
Samoan (2)	2	0.01
White (14,045)	14,277	93.38
Not Hispanic (13,631)	13,821	90.40
Hispanic (414)	456	2.98

Hanover

Place Type: Township
County: Luzerne
Population: 11,076†

Ancestry‡	Population	%
American (371)	371	3.34
Arab (10)	170	1.53
Egyptian (0)	9	0.08
Lebanese (10)	126	1.13
Syrian (0)	35	0.32
Armenian (3)	3	0.03
Austrian (0)	31	0.28
Czech (0)	22	0.20
Dutch (47)	289	2.60
Eastern European (41)	41	0.37
English (113)	591	5.32
Finnish (11)	11	0.10
French, ex. Basque (24)	217	1.95
German (433)	1,753	15.79
Greek (0)	11	0.10
Hungarian (0)	25	0.23
Irish (585)	2,583	23.26
Italian (492)	1,588	14.30
Lithuanian (242)	693	6.24
Norwegian (0)	14	0.13
Pennsylvania German (72)	128	1.15
Polish (1,444)	3,378	30.42
Russian (161)	463	4.17
Scotch-Irish (9)	47	0.42
Scottish (17)	134	1.21
Serbian (0)	8	0.07
Slovak (102)	531	4.78
Slovene (0)	11	0.10
Swedish (0)	40	0.36
Ukrainian (213)	408	3.67
Welsh (159)	890	8.01
West Indian, ex. Hispanic (23)	46	0.41
Haitian (23)	46	0.41

Hispanic Origin	Population	%
Hispanic or Latino (of any race)	326	2.94
Central American, ex. Mexican	22	0.20
Costa Rican	1	0.01
Guatemalan	3	0.03
Honduran	6	0.05
Panamanian	2	0.02
Salvadoran	10	0.09
Cuban	4	0.04
Dominican Republic	31	0.28
Mexican	52	0.47
Puerto Rican	175	1.58

*Notes: † The Census 2010 population figure is used to calculate the percentages in the Hispanic Origin and Race categories. Ancestry percentages are based on the 2006-2010 American Community Survey population (not shown); ‡ Numbers in parentheses indicate the number of people reporting a single ancestry; * Numbers in parentheses indicate the number of persons reporting this race alone, not in combination with any other race; Please refer to the Explanation of Data for more information.*

South American	13	0.12
Bolivian	1	0.01
Colombian	8	0.07
Ecuadorian	2	0.02
Venezuelan	2	0.02
Other Hispanic or Latino	29	0.26

Race*	Population	%
African-American/Black (351)	500	4.51
Not Hispanic (315)	437	3.95
Hispanic (36)	63	0.57
American Indian/Alaska Native (11)	44	0.40
Not Hispanic (11)	31	0.28
Hispanic (0)	13	0.12
Apache (1)	3	0.03
Blackfeet (2)	2	0.02
Cherokee (0)	12	0.11
Navajo (0)	1	0.01
Sioux (0)	2	0.02
Asian (62)	87	0.79
Not Hispanic (62)	87	0.79
Chinese, ex. Taiwanese (17)	17	0.15
Filipino (7)	18	0.16
Indian (16)	20	0.18
Japanese (2)	6	0.05
Korean (1)	7	0.06
Vietnamese (17)	17	0.15
Hawaii Native/Pacific Islander (2)	11	0.10
Not Hispanic (1)	9	0.08
Hispanic (1)	2	0.02
Native Hawaiian (1)	4	0.04
Samoan (1)	1	0.01
White (10,355)	10,552	95.27
Not Hispanic (10,189)	10,343	93.38
Hispanic (166)	209	1.89

Hanover

Place Type: Township
County: Northampton
Population: 10,866†

Ancestry‡	Population	%
African, Sub-Saharan (80)	115	1.07
Ghanaian (28)	28	0.26
Nigerian (52)	87	0.81
American (383)	383	3.57
Arab (127)	226	2.11
Egyptian (59)	59	0.55
Jordanian (37)	59	0.55
Lebanese (0)	4	0.04
Syrian (14)	65	0.61
Other Arab (17)	39	0.36
Austrian (53)	93	0.87
British (72)	86	0.80
Carpatho Rusyn (17)	17	0.16
Croatian (18)	29	0.27
Cypriot (11)	11	0.10
Czech (17)	104	0.97
Czechoslovakian (0)	15	0.14
Danish (33)	49	0.46
Dutch (14)	210	1.96
Eastern European (10)	19	0.18
English (287)	982	9.16
European (42)	42	0.39
French, ex. Basque (23)	192	1.79
French Canadian (0)	14	0.13
German (960)	2,800	26.10
Greek (287)	302	2.82
Hungarian (131)	487	4.54
Irish (516)	2,002	18.66
Italian (520)	1,466	13.67
Lithuanian (0)	108	1.01
Norwegian (108)	199	1.86
Pennsylvania German (210)	270	2.52
Polish (191)	432	4.03
Portuguese (0)	45	0.42
Romanian (11)	11	0.10
Russian (110)	175	1.63
Scotch-Irish (71)	159	1.48
Scottish (44)	122	1.14
Slovak (90)	260	2.42
Slovene (36)	36	0.34
Swedish (0)	21	0.20
Swiss (10)	63	0.59
Turkish (115)	115	1.07
Ukrainian (28)	73	0.68
Welsh (21)	215	2.00
Yugoslavian (14)	14	0.13

Hispanic Origin	Population	%
Hispanic or Latino (of any race)	525	4.83
Central American, ex. Mexican	30	0.28
Guatemalan	11	0.10
Nicaraguan	7	0.06
Panamanian	3	0.03
Salvadoran	9	0.08
Cuban	18	0.17
Dominican Republic	46	0.42
Mexican	52	0.48
Puerto Rican	262	2.41
South American	81	0.75
Argentinean	8	0.07
Chilean	5	0.05
Colombian	27	0.25
Ecuadorian	11	0.10
Peruvian	19	0.17
Uruguayan	4	0.04
Venezuelan	7	0.06
Other Hispanic or Latino	36	0.33

Race*	Population	%
African-American/Black (298)	358	3.29
Not Hispanic (280)	328	3.02
Hispanic (18)	30	0.28
American Indian/Alaska Native (5)	28	0.26
Not Hispanic (4)	22	0.20
Hispanic (1)	6	0.06
Blackfeet (0)	2	0.02
Cherokee (1)	1	0.01
Choctaw (0)	1	0.01
Delaware (0)	1	0.01
Iroquois (1)	1	0.01
South American Ind. (0)	4	0.04
Spanish American Ind. (1)	1	0.01
Asian (710)	844	7.77
Not Hispanic (709)	829	7.63
Hispanic (1)	15	0.14
Bangladeshi (3)	3	0.03
Burmese (2)	2	0.02
Chinese, ex. Taiwanese (93)	109	1.00
Filipino (102)	128	1.18
Indian (316)	357	3.29
Indonesian (4)	4	0.04
Japanese (7)	14	0.13
Korean (76)	90	0.83
Laotian (1)	1	0.01
Pakistani (9)	11	0.10
Sri Lankan (3)	3	0.03
Taiwanese (15)	15	0.14
Thai (4)	8	0.07
Vietnamese (68)	69	0.64
Hawaii Native/Pacific Islander (0)	8	0.07
Not Hispanic (0)	6	0.06
Hispanic (0)	2	0.02
Native Hawaiian (0)	2	0.02
Samoan (0)	1	0.01
White (9,466)	9,653	88.84
Not Hispanic (9,137)	9,283	85.43
Hispanic (329)	370	3.41

Harborcreek

Place Type: Township
County: Erie
Population: 17,234†

Ancestry‡	Population	%
African, Sub-Saharan (0)	15	0.09
African (0)	15	0.09
American (929)	929	5.47
Arab (0)	46	0.27
Lebanese (0)	23	0.14
Syrian (0)	23	0.14
Armenian (0)	8	0.05
Australian (0)	15	0.09
Austrian (7)	25	0.15
British (27)	52	0.31
Canadian (0)	15	0.09
Celtic (0)	25	0.15
Croatian (44)	44	0.26
Czech (0)	91	0.54
Czechoslovakian (0)	51	0.30
Danish (11)	24	0.14
Dutch (112)	289	1.70
English (583)	1,754	10.32
Estonian (25)	25	0.15
European (51)	64	0.38
Finnish (12)	34	0.20
French, ex. Basque (33)	552	3.25
French Canadian (17)	72	0.42
German (1,604)	6,197	36.47
Greek (36)	60	0.35
Hungarian (103)	151	0.89
Icelander (0)	8	0.05
Iranian (0)	24	0.14
Irish (461)	2,683	15.79
Italian (749)	2,434	14.32
Lithuanian (7)	26	0.15
Norwegian (12)	33	0.19
Pennsylvania German (11)	60	0.35
Polish (1,303)	3,341	19.66
Portuguese (18)	18	0.11
Romanian (8)	8	0.05
Russian (76)	268	1.58
Scandinavian (6)	6	0.04
Scotch-Irish (117)	348	2.05
Scottish (30)	415	2.44
Serbian (0)	6	0.04
Slavic (17)	61	0.36
Slovak (132)	407	2.40
Slovene (31)	31	0.18
Swedish (73)	520	3.06
Swiss (0)	67	0.39
Ukrainian (10)	121	0.71
Welsh (34)	213	1.25
Yugoslavian (0)	18	0.11

Hispanic Origin	Population	%
Hispanic or Latino (of any race)	177	1.03
Central American, ex. Mexican	22	0.13
Costa Rican	2	0.01
Guatemalan	2	0.01
Honduran	2	0.01
Panamanian	8	0.05
Salvadoran	8	0.05
Cuban	3	0.02
Dominican Republic	9	0.05
Mexican	46	0.27
Puerto Rican	73	0.42
South American	10	0.06
Argentinean	1	0.01
Chilean	3	0.02
Ecuadorian	2	0.01
Venezuelan	4	0.02
Other Hispanic or Latino	14	0.08

Race*	Population	%
African-American/Black (247)	296	1.72
Not Hispanic (241)	286	1.66
Hispanic (6)	10	0.06
American Indian/Alaska Native (16)	49	0.28
Not Hispanic (13)	46	0.27
Hispanic (3)	3	0.02
Blackfeet (0)	1	0.01
Canadian/French Am. Ind. (3)	3	0.02
Cherokee (2)	5	0.03
Cree (1)	1	0.01
Iroquois (1)	3	0.02
Mexican American Ind. (1)	2	0.01

*Notes: † The Census 2010 population figure is used to calculate the percentages in the Hispanic Origin and Race categories. Ancestry percentages are based on the 2006-2010 American Community Survey population (not shown); ‡ Numbers in parentheses indicate the number of people reporting a single ancestry; * Numbers in parentheses indicate the number of persons reporting this race alone, not in combination with any other race; Please refer to the Explanation of Data for more information.*

Pueblo (0)	1	0.01
Sioux (0)	2	0.01
Tlingit-Haida *(Alaska Native)* (1)	1	0.01
Asian (140)	188	1.09
Not Hispanic (139)	187	1.09
Hispanic (1)	1	0.01
Cambodian (2)	2	0.01
Chinese, ex. Taiwanese (44)	47	0.27
Filipino (13)	24	0.14
Indian (27)	30	0.17
Japanese (4)	14	0.08
Korean (19)	24	0.14
Laotian (5)	5	0.03
Pakistani (2)	5	0.03
Taiwanese (1)	3	0.02
Thai (1)	2	0.01
Vietnamese (18)	27	0.16
Hawaii Native/Pacific Islander (0)	7	0.04
Not Hispanic (0)	7	0.04
Native Hawaiian (0)	2	0.01
Samoan (0)	1	0.01
White (16,661)	16,788	97.41
Not Hispanic (16,534)	16,649	96.61
Hispanic (127)	139	0.81

Harleysville

Place Type: CDP
County: Montgomery
Population: 9,286†

Ancestry‡	Population	%
African, Sub-Saharan (26)	26	0.27
African (26)	26	0.27
American (261)	261	2.76
Arab (8)	36	0.38
Other Arab (8)	36	0.38
Armenian (0)	7	0.07
Australian (12)	37	0.39
Austrian (20)	62	0.66
British (5)	25	0.26
Canadian (9)	9	0.10
Croatian (0)	43	0.45
Czech (11)	77	0.81
Czechoslovakian (11)	20	0.21
Danish (0)	17	0.18
Dutch (36)	95	1.00
English (171)	888	9.38
European (97)	116	1.23
French, ex. Basque (14)	192	2.03
French Canadian (0)	16	0.17
German (1,224)	3,828	40.45
Greek (27)	56	0.59
Hungarian (30)	181	1.91
Irish (597)	2,591	27.38
Italian (552)	1,547	16.35
Latvian (42)	42	0.44
Lithuanian (9)	25	0.26
Norwegian (9)	99	1.05
Pennsylvania German (186)	214	2.26
Polish (126)	659	6.96
Portuguese (0)	30	0.32
Russian (36)	59	0.62
Scotch-Irish (76)	182	1.92
Scottish (11)	208	2.20
Slavic (0)	14	0.15
Slovak (15)	119	1.26
Swedish (0)	89	0.94
Swiss (32)	117	1.24
Turkish (5)	20	0.21
Ukrainian (28)	52	0.55
Welsh (14)	89	0.94
West Indian, ex. Hispanic (0)	11	0.12
Belizean (0)	11	0.12
Yugoslavian (0)	27	0.29

Hispanic Origin	Population	%
Hispanic or Latino (of any race)	219	2.36
Central American, ex. Mexican	31	0.33
Costa Rican	1	0.01
Guatemalan	14	0.15
Honduran	10	0.11
Nicaraguan	3	0.03
Panamanian	1	0.01
Salvadoran	2	0.02
Cuban	13	0.14
Dominican Republic	5	0.05
Mexican	33	0.36
Puerto Rican	86	0.93
South American	37	0.40
Argentinean	3	0.03
Colombian	20	0.22
Ecuadorian	4	0.04
Peruvian	10	0.11
Other Hispanic or Latino	14	0.15

Race*	Population	%
African-American/Black (243)	289	3.11
Not Hispanic (232)	269	2.90
Hispanic (11)	20	0.22
American Indian/Alaska Native (5)	31	0.33
Not Hispanic (2)	23	0.25
Hispanic (3)	8	0.09
Apache (0)	1	0.01
Cherokee (0)	5	0.05
Cheyenne (0)	3	0.03
Mexican American Ind. (3)	3	0.03
Asian (328)	376	4.05
Not Hispanic (326)	374	4.03
Hispanic (2)	2	0.02
Bangladeshi (2)	2	0.02
Burmese (1)	3	0.03
Chinese, ex. Taiwanese (62)	79	0.85
Filipino (13)	19	0.20
Indian (114)	127	1.37
Indonesian (1)	3	0.03
Japanese (11)	15	0.16
Korean (40)	45	0.48
Laotian (7)	7	0.08
Pakistani (10)	10	0.11
Sri Lankan (1)	1	0.01
Thai (3)	7	0.08
Vietnamese (57)	61	0.66
Hawaii Native/Pacific Islander (0)	6	0.06
Not Hispanic (0)	3	0.03
Hispanic (0)	3	0.03
Fijian (0)	2	0.02
Native Hawaiian (0)	1	0.01
White (8,542)	8,645	93.10
Not Hispanic (8,399)	8,488	91.41
Hispanic (143)	157	1.69

Harrisburg

Place Type: City
County: Dauphin
Population: 49,528†

Ancestry‡	Population	%
African, Sub-Saharan (741)	848	1.72
African (636)	743	1.51
Ethiopian (24)	24	0.05
Nigerian (7)	7	0.01
Other Sub-Saharan African (74)	74	0.15
American (666)	666	1.35
Arab (38)	38	0.08
Moroccan (38)	38	0.08
Armenian (20)	20	0.04
Austrian (30)	73	0.15
Belgian (0)	12	0.02
Brazilian (10)	10	0.02
British (9)	60	0.12
Cajun (0)	24	0.05
Canadian (16)	16	0.03
Croatian (70)	172	0.35
Czech (21)	49	0.10
Danish (0)	10	0.02
Dutch (73)	582	1.18
Eastern European (25)	25	0.05
English (172)	1,244	2.52
European (23)	23	0.05
Finnish (0)	12	0.02
French, ex. Basque (45)	455	0.92
French Canadian (18)	25	0.05
German (2,140)	5,633	11.42
German Russian (11)	11	0.02
Greek (40)	46	0.09
Hungarian (30)	190	0.39
Iranian (23)	23	0.05
Irish (757)	2,927	5.93
Israeli (104)	104	0.21
Italian (643)	1,866	3.78
Lithuanian (17)	160	0.32
Macedonian (8)	8	0.02
Norwegian (19)	19	0.04
Pennsylvania German (72)	138	0.28
Polish (295)	779	1.58
Romanian (0)	10	0.02
Russian (81)	217	0.44
Scotch-Irish (131)	394	0.80
Scottish (59)	207	0.42
Serbian (0)	6	0.01
Slovak (61)	82	0.17
Slovene (18)	97	0.20
Swedish (64)	120	0.24
Swiss (26)	150	0.30
Turkish (28)	28	0.06
Ukrainian (13)	56	0.11
Welsh (9)	175	0.35
West Indian, ex. Hispanic (453)	752	1.52
Bahamian (0)	8	0.02
Barbadian (0)	18	0.04
British West Indian (36)	36	0.07
Haitian (132)	163	0.33
Jamaican (112)	321	0.65
Trinidadian/Tobagonian (64)	84	0.17
West Indian (109)	122	0.25
Yugoslavian (20)	38	0.08

Hispanic Origin	Population	%
Hispanic or Latino (of any race)	8,939	18.05
Central American, ex. Mexican	219	0.44
Costa Rican	4	0.01
Guatemalan	83	0.17
Honduran	73	0.15
Nicaraguan	2	<0.01
Panamanian	30	0.06
Salvadoran	25	0.05
Other Central American	2	<0.01
Cuban	219	0.44
Dominican Republic	624	1.26
Mexican	1,366	2.76
Puerto Rican	5,685	11.48
South American	309	0.62
Argentinean	7	0.01
Bolivian	5	0.01
Chilean	6	0.01
Colombian	30	0.06
Ecuadorian	144	0.29
Paraguayan	5	0.01
Peruvian	90	0.18
Uruguayan	2	<0.01
Venezuelan	15	0.03
Other South American	5	0.01
Other Hispanic or Latino	517	1.04

Race*	Population	%
African-American/Black (25,957)	27,947	56.43
Not Hispanic (24,727)	26,151	52.80
Hispanic (1,230)	1,796	3.63
American Indian/Alaska Native (251)	726	1.47
Not Hispanic (146)	511	1.03
Hispanic (105)	215	0.43
Apache (2)	9	0.02
Blackfeet (7)	24	0.05
Canadian/French Am. Ind. (5)	5	0.01
Cherokee (22)	143	0.29
Chickasaw (1)	2	<0.01
Chippewa (3)	5	0.01
Choctaw (7)	11	0.02

*Notes: † The Census 2010 population figure is used to calculate the percentages in the Hispanic Origin and Race categories. Ancestry percentages are based on the 2006-2010 American Community Survey population (not shown); ‡ Numbers in parentheses indicate the number of people reporting a single ancestry; * Numbers in parentheses indicate the number of persons reporting this race alone, not in combination with any other race; Please refer to the Explanation of Data for more information.*

Cree (0)	1	<0.01
Creek (2)	2	<0.01
Delaware (1)	8	0.02
Inupiat *(Alaska Native)* (1)	1	<0.01
Iroquois (5)	12	0.02
Kiowa (0)	1	<0.01
Lumbee (3)	4	0.01
Mexican American Ind. (4)	8	0.02
Paiute (1)	1	<0.01
Potawatomi (1)	2	<0.01
Pueblo (0)	3	0.01
Seminole (1)	13	0.03
Sioux (2)	10	0.02
South American Ind. (11)	22	0.04
Spanish American Ind. (7)	7	0.01
Tlingit-Haida *(Alaska Native)* (1)	1	<0.01
Asian (1,709)	1,964	3.97
Not Hispanic (1,692)	1,894	3.82
Hispanic (17)	70	0.14
Bangladeshi (2)	2	<0.01
Bhutanese (68)	101	0.20
Burmese (53)	61	0.12
Cambodian (74)	89	0.18
Chinese, ex. Taiwanese (158)	185	0.37
Filipino (29)	64	0.13
Indian (202)	291	0.59
Indonesian (49)	49	0.10
Japanese (17)	48	0.10
Korean (60)	87	0.18
Laotian (18)	23	0.05
Malaysian (1)	1	<0.01
Nepalese (9)	27	0.05
Pakistani (44)	70	0.14
Sri Lankan (8)	8	0.02
Taiwanese (2)	3	0.01
Thai (57)	66	0.13
Vietnamese (738)	786	1.59
Hawaii Native/Pacific Islander (29)	127	0.26
Not Hispanic (4)	49	0.10
Hispanic (25)	78	0.16
Guamanian/Chamorro (8)	12	0.02
Native Hawaiian (3)	21	0.04
Samoan (0)	7	0.01
White (15,181)	17,093	34.51
Not Hispanic (12,290)	13,615	27.49
Hispanic (2,891)	3,478	7.02

Harrison

Place Type: Township
County: Allegheny
Population: 10,461†

Ancestry‡	Population	%
American (228)	228	2.18
Arab (0)	13	0.12
Syrian (0)	13	0.12
Belgian (28)	174	1.66
British (0)	37	0.35
Croatian (0)	8	0.08
Czech (0)	50	0.48
Czechoslovakian (17)	17	0.16
Dutch (10)	84	0.80
English (204)	576	5.50
Finnish (0)	11	0.10
French, ex. Basque (35)	168	1.60
French Canadian (7)	7	0.07
German (849)	3,349	31.97
Hungarian (9)	76	0.73
Irish (190)	1,744	16.65
Italian (681)	1,550	14.79
Lithuanian (0)	7	0.07
Norwegian (0)	13	0.12
Pennsylvania German (0)	51	0.49
Polish (1,072)	1,986	18.96
Romanian (0)	15	0.14
Russian (29)	170	1.62
Scotch-Irish (219)	469	4.48
Scottish (33)	169	1.61
Serbian (13)	57	0.54
Slovak (627)	1,475	14.08
Slovene (7)	7	0.07
Swedish (33)	103	0.98
Welsh (18)	173	1.65
West Indian, ex. Hispanic (44)	44	0.42
West Indian (44)	44	0.42

Hispanic Origin	Population	%
Hispanic or Latino (of any race)	97	0.93
Central American, ex. Mexican	6	0.06
Guatemalan	3	0.03
Honduran	2	0.02
Panamanian	1	0.01
Cuban	4	0.04
Mexican	40	0.38
Puerto Rican	23	0.22
South American	4	0.04
Argentinean	1	0.01
Ecuadorian	2	0.02
Peruvian	1	0.01
Other Hispanic or Latino	20	0.19

Race*	Population	%
African-American/Black (366)	516	4.93
Not Hispanic (360)	505	4.83
Hispanic (6)	11	0.11
American Indian/Alaska Native (14)	49	0.47
Not Hispanic (13)	47	0.45
Hispanic (1)	2	0.02
Blackfeet (0)	3	0.03
Cherokee (4)	17	0.16
Comanche (1)	1	0.01
Creek (0)	1	0.01
Iroquois (0)	5	0.05
Mexican American Ind. (1)	1	0.01
Seminole (0)	2	0.02
Sioux (3)	3	0.03
Asian (61)	83	0.79
Not Hispanic (61)	80	0.76
Hispanic (0)	3	0.03
Chinese, ex. Taiwanese (17)	23	0.22
Filipino (2)	5	0.05
Indian (3)	4	0.04
Japanese (5)	11	0.11
Korean (2)	6	0.06
Malaysian (0)	2	0.02
Pakistani (4)	4	0.04
Thai (2)	2	0.02
Vietnamese (22)	23	0.22
Hawaii Native/Pacific Islander (0)	4	0.04
Not Hispanic (0)	4	0.04
Guamanian/Chamorro (0)	1	0.01
Native Hawaiian (0)	3	0.03
Samoan (0)	2	0.02
White (9,808)	9,988	95.48
Not Hispanic (9,737)	9,909	94.72
Hispanic (71)	79	0.76

Hatfield

Place Type: Township
County: Montgomery
Population: 17,249†

Ancestry‡	Population	%
African, Sub-Saharan (0)	10	0.06
African (0)	10	0.06
American (473)	473	2.76
Arab (24)	24	0.14
Egyptian (24)	24	0.14
Armenian (0)	52	0.30
Austrian (28)	39	0.23
British (0)	12	0.07
Canadian (71)	78	0.45
Croatian (0)	11	0.06
Czech (19)	61	0.36
Czechoslovakian (19)	50	0.29
Danish (0)	178	1.04
Dutch (32)	133	0.78
Eastern European (38)	47	0.27
English (354)	1,531	8.93
Estonian (6)	6	0.03
European (83)	83	0.48
Finnish (0)	42	0.24
French, ex. Basque (112)	369	2.15
French Canadian (0)	13	0.08
German (1,176)	4,314	25.15
Greek (41)	57	0.33
Hungarian (28)	161	0.94
Irish (951)	3,395	19.79
Italian (672)	2,353	13.72
Lithuanian (47)	147	0.86
Norwegian (70)	137	0.80
Pennsylvania German (103)	170	0.99
Polish (403)	1,304	7.60
Portuguese (46)	79	0.46
Russian (83)	224	1.31
Scotch-Irish (215)	420	2.45
Scottish (49)	240	1.40
Slovak (35)	126	0.73
Swedish (12)	63	0.37
Swiss (12)	49	0.29
Ukrainian (14)	184	1.07
Welsh (47)	199	1.16
West Indian, ex. Hispanic (26)	90	0.52
Barbadian (11)	45	0.26
Jamaican (8)	23	0.13
Trinidadian/Tobagonian (7)	22	0.13
Yugoslavian (0)	9	0.05

Hispanic Origin	Population	%
Hispanic or Latino (of any race)	648	3.76
Central American, ex. Mexican	112	0.65
Costa Rican	9	0.05
Guatemalan	23	0.13
Honduran	54	0.31
Nicaraguan	2	0.01
Panamanian	4	0.02
Salvadoran	20	0.12
Cuban	19	0.11
Dominican Republic	16	0.09
Mexican	137	0.79
Puerto Rican	220	1.28
South American	90	0.52
Bolivian	1	0.01
Chilean	9	0.05
Colombian	46	0.27
Ecuadorian	9	0.05
Peruvian	16	0.09
Uruguayan	1	0.01
Venezuelan	8	0.05
Other Hispanic or Latino	54	0.31

Race*	Population	%
African-American/Black (779)	942	5.46
Not Hispanic (733)	862	5.00
Hispanic (46)	80	0.46
American Indian/Alaska Native (42)	120	0.70
Not Hispanic (32)	101	0.59
Hispanic (10)	19	0.11
Blackfeet (0)	7	0.04
Cherokee (5)	30	0.17
Delaware (0)	2	0.01
Iroquois (3)	4	0.02
Lumbee (1)	2	0.01
Navajo (2)	5	0.03
Seminole (0)	1	0.01
Sioux (0)	4	0.02
South American Ind. (1)	2	0.01
Spanish American Ind. (1)	1	0.01
Ute (1)	1	0.01
Asian (2,809)	2,964	17.18
Not Hispanic (2,804)	2,949	17.10
Hispanic (5)	15	0.09
Bangladeshi (174)	192	1.11
Burmese (3)	3	0.02
Cambodian (29)	44	0.26
Chinese, ex. Taiwanese (163)	185	1.07
Filipino (50)	78	0.45
Hmong (1)	3	0.02

*Notes: † The Census 2010 population figure is used to calculate the percentages in the Hispanic Origin and Race categories. Ancestry percentages are based on the 2006-2010 American Community Survey population (not shown); ‡ Numbers in parentheses indicate the number of people reporting a single ancestry; * Numbers in parentheses indicate the number of persons reporting this race alone, not in combination with any other race; Please refer to the Explanation of Data for more information.*

Indian (1,570)	1,619	9.39
Indonesian (6)	6	0.03
Japanese (14)	29	0.17
Korean (349)	373	2.16
Laotian (6)	8	0.05
Malaysian (2)	2	0.01
Pakistani (22)	26	0.15
Sri Lankan (4)	4	0.02
Taiwanese (4)	6	0.03
Thai (6)	10	0.06
Vietnamese (341)	364	2.11
Hawaii Native/Pacific Islander (14)	31	0.18
Not Hispanic (14)	30	0.17
Hispanic (0)	1	0.01
Native Hawaiian (4)	10	0.06
Samoan (10)	17	0.10
White (13,032)	13,297	77.09
Not Hispanic (12,698)	12,910	74.84
Hispanic (334)	387	2.24

Haverford

Place Type: Township
County: Delaware
Population: 48,491†

Ancestry‡	Population	%
Afghan (48)	48	0.10
African, Sub-Saharan (59)	76	0.16
African (0)	17	0.04
Ethiopian (8)	8	0.02
Kenyan (6)	6	0.01
Nigerian (18)	18	0.04
South African (27)	27	0.06
Albanian (49)	49	0.10
American (1,240)	1,240	2.55
Arab (321)	408	0.84
Arab (0)	16	0.03
Egyptian (73)	73	0.15
Iraqi (25)	25	0.05
Lebanese (37)	92	0.19
Palestinian (0)	16	0.03
Syrian (10)	10	0.02
Other Arab (176)	176	0.36
Armenian (181)	246	0.51
Assyrian/Chaldean/Syriac (75)	75	0.15
Australian (16)	85	0.18
Austrian (69)	383	0.79
Belgian (0)	54	0.11
Brazilian (23)	36	0.07
British (134)	388	0.80
Bulgarian (31)	31	0.06
Canadian (11)	146	0.30
Celtic (10)	10	0.02
Croatian (0)	74	0.15
Czech (6)	90	0.19
Czechoslovakian (0)	51	0.11
Danish (0)	181	0.37
Dutch (42)	367	0.76
Eastern European (277)	289	0.60
English (907)	4,959	10.22
Estonian (25)	25	0.05
European (510)	530	1.09
Finnish (13)	54	0.11
French, ex. Basque (94)	747	1.54
French Canadian (151)	200	0.41
German (1,911)	9,746	20.08
Greek (195)	314	0.65
Hungarian (71)	382	0.79
Irish (8,396)	18,506	38.12
Israeli (28)	79	0.16
Italian (4,758)	9,724	20.03
Latvian (0)	21	0.04
Lithuanian (77)	443	0.91
Maltese (0)	7	0.01
Northern European (18)	18	0.04
Norwegian (29)	354	0.73
Pennsylvania German (91)	129	0.27
Polish (595)	2,215	4.56
Portuguese (12)	49	0.10
Romanian (0)	102	0.21
Russian (911)	2,125	4.38
Scandinavian (12)	20	0.04
Scotch-Irish (490)	987	2.03
Scottish (318)	1,239	2.55
Serbian (0)	11	0.02
Slavic (12)	30	0.06
Slovak (31)	248	0.51
Swedish (59)	542	1.12
Swiss (8)	30	0.06
Turkish (0)	8	0.02
Ukrainian (76)	220	0.45
Welsh (87)	613	1.26
West Indian, ex. Hispanic (61)	73	0.15
British West Indian (16)	16	0.03
Haitian (0)	12	0.02
Jamaican (33)	33	0.07
West Indian (12)	12	0.02
Yugoslavian (11)	34	0.07

Hispanic Origin	Population	%
Hispanic or Latino (of any race)	937	1.93
Central American, ex. Mexican	79	0.16
Costa Rican	19	0.04
Guatemalan	25	0.05
Honduran	7	0.01
Nicaraguan	9	0.02
Panamanian	13	0.03
Salvadoran	6	0.01
Cuban	92	0.19
Dominican Republic	23	0.05
Mexican	147	0.30
Puerto Rican	207	0.43
South American	276	0.57
Argentinean	46	0.09
Bolivian	11	0.02
Chilean	19	0.04
Colombian	56	0.12
Ecuadorian	47	0.10
Paraguayan	24	0.05
Peruvian	48	0.10
Uruguayan	4	0.01
Venezuelan	20	0.04
Other South American	1	<0.01
Other Hispanic or Latino	113	0.23

Race*	Population	%
African-American/Black (1,293)	1,581	3.26
Not Hispanic (1,265)	1,520	3.13
Hispanic (28)	61	0.13
American Indian/Alaska Native (43)	176	0.36
Not Hispanic (34)	140	0.29
Hispanic (9)	36	0.07
Blackfeet (1)	2	<0.01
Cherokee (5)	36	0.07
Chippewa (6)	6	0.01
Crow (0)	1	<0.01
Delaware (1)	3	0.01
Iroquois (4)	7	0.01
Lumbee (1)	2	<0.01
Mexican American Ind. (4)	6	0.01
Ottawa (0)	2	<0.01
Potawatomi (1)	1	<0.01
Pueblo (1)	1	<0.01
Seminole (1)	5	0.01
Sioux (0)	1	<0.01
South American Ind. (1)	10	0.02
Asian (2,048)	2,331	4.81
Not Hispanic (2,046)	2,314	4.77
Hispanic (2)	17	0.04
Bangladeshi (4)	4	0.01
Burmese (4)	6	0.01
Cambodian (47)	54	0.11
Chinese, ex. Taiwanese (636)	724	1.49
Filipino (136)	204	0.42
Indian (233)	269	0.55
Indonesian (1)	9	0.02
Japanese (61)	111	0.23
Korean (530)	559	1.15
Laotian (10)	19	0.04
Malaysian (5)	5	0.01
Nepalese (5)	5	0.01
Pakistani (46)	48	0.10
Sri Lankan (21)	23	0.05
Taiwanese (10)	19	0.04
Thai (32)	38	0.08
Vietnamese (195)	230	0.47
Hawaii Native/Pacific Islander (2)	26	0.05
Not Hispanic (2)	23	0.05
Hispanic (0)	3	0.01
Fijian (1)	5	0.01
Native Hawaiian (1)	13	0.03
Samoan (0)	4	0.01
White (44,245)	44,830	92.45
Not Hispanic (43,575)	44,100	90.94
Hispanic (670)	730	1.51

Hazle

Place Type: Township
County: Luzerne
Population: 9,549†

Ancestry‡	Population	%
Albanian (13)	13	0.14
American (142)	142	1.51
Arab (0)	9	0.10
Lebanese (0)	9	0.10
Austrian (85)	306	3.26
British (10)	48	0.51
Czech (46)	132	1.41
Czechoslovakian (24)	31	0.33
Dutch (75)	415	4.42
Eastern European (51)	51	0.54
English (84)	455	4.85
European (21)	21	0.22
French, ex. Basque (15)	100	1.07
French Canadian (0)	11	0.12
German (577)	1,874	19.98
Greek (34)	199	2.12
Hungarian (64)	94	1.00
Irish (445)	1,871	19.95
Italian (1,336)	2,305	24.57
Lithuanian (45)	151	1.61
Norwegian (0)	13	0.14
Pennsylvania German (7)	55	0.59
Polish (981)	1,882	20.06
Romanian (31)	31	0.33
Russian (0)	10	0.11
Scandinavian (30)	49	0.52
Scotch-Irish (8)	36	0.38
Scottish (9)	25	0.27
Slavic (59)	71	0.76
Slovak (554)	1,049	11.18
Swedish (0)	37	0.39
Swiss (74)	87	0.93
Ukrainian (76)	129	1.38
Welsh (19)	166	1.77
Yugoslavian (6)	19	0.20

Hispanic Origin	Population	%
Hispanic or Latino (of any race)	853	8.93
Central American, ex. Mexican	14	0.15
Guatemalan	1	0.01
Honduran	2	0.02
Panamanian	3	0.03
Salvadoran	8	0.08
Cuban	3	0.03
Dominican Republic	430	4.50
Mexican	65	0.68
Puerto Rican	209	2.19
South American	51	0.53
Colombian	10	0.10
Ecuadorian	24	0.25
Peruvian	16	0.17
Venezuelan	1	0.01
Other Hispanic or Latino	81	0.85

Race*	Population	%
African-American/Black (98)	155	1.62

*Notes: † The Census 2010 population figure is used to calculate the percentages in the Hispanic Origin and Race categories. Ancestry percentages are based on the 2006-2010 American Community Survey population (not shown); ‡ Numbers in parentheses indicate the number of people reporting a single ancestry; * Numbers in parentheses indicate the number of persons reporting this race alone, not in combination with any other race; Please refer to the Explanation of Data for more information.*

Not Hispanic (47)	63	0.66
Hispanic (51)	92	0.96
American Indian/Alaska Native (24)	43	0.45
Not Hispanic (10)	29	0.30
Hispanic (14)	14	0.15
Central American Ind. (4)	4	0.04
Cherokee (1)	2	0.02
Chippewa (2)	2	0.02
Delaware (0)	1	0.01
Iroquois (0)	1	0.01
Asian (79)	102	1.07
Not Hispanic (77)	98	1.03
Hispanic (2)	4	0.04
Cambodian (1)	3	0.03
Chinese, ex. Taiwanese (20)	26	0.27
Filipino (12)	20	0.21
Indian (22)	22	0.23
Japanese (2)	2	0.02
Korean (8)	8	0.08
Taiwanese (2)	4	0.04
Vietnamese (10)	11	0.12
Hawaii Native/Pacific Islander (0)	13	0.14
Hispanic (0)	13	0.14
White (8,803)	8,916	93.37
Not Hispanic (8,504)	8,559	89.63
Hispanic (299)	357	3.74

Hazleton

Place Type: City
County: Luzerne
Population: 25,340†

Ancestry‡	Population	%
American (618)	618	2.48
Arab (0)	41	0.16
Lebanese (0)	29	0.12
Syrian (0)	12	0.05
Austrian (141)	364	1.46
Belgian (0)	11	0.04
British (21)	21	0.08
Bulgarian (39)	39	0.16
Croatian (0)	8	0.03
Czech (13)	94	0.38
Czechoslovakian (53)	68	0.27
Dutch (85)	531	2.13
Eastern European (18)	18	0.07
English (113)	797	3.20
European (52)	52	0.21
Finnish (0)	11	0.04
French, ex. Basque (57)	334	1.34
German (876)	3,131	12.59
Greek (210)	616	2.48
Hungarian (17)	138	0.55
Iranian (0)	11	0.04
Irish (660)	2,551	10.25
Italian (2,258)	5,019	20.18
Lithuanian (85)	218	0.88
Macedonian (0)	24	0.10
Pennsylvania German (58)	133	0.53
Polish (1,278)	3,234	13.00
Portuguese (13)	23	0.09
Romanian (163)	163	0.66
Russian (39)	127	0.51
Scotch-Irish (37)	97	0.39
Scottish (24)	89	0.36
Serbian (56)	56	0.23
Slavic (40)	40	0.16
Slovak (949)	2,045	8.22
Swedish (16)	54	0.22
Swiss (0)	54	0.22
Ukrainian (90)	231	0.93
Welsh (50)	292	1.17
West Indian, ex. Hispanic (45)	45	0.18
British West Indian (45)	45	0.18
Yugoslavian (120)	138	0.55

Hispanic Origin	Population	%
Hispanic or Latino (of any race)	9,454	37.31
Central American, ex. Mexican	225	0.89
Costa Rican	17	0.07
Guatemalan	48	0.19
Honduran	60	0.24
Nicaraguan	16	0.06
Panamanian	8	0.03
Salvadoran	76	0.30
Cuban	48	0.19
Dominican Republic	5,327	21.02
Mexican	886	3.50
Puerto Rican	1,699	6.70
South American	338	1.33
Argentinean	16	0.06
Chilean	5	0.02
Colombian	42	0.17
Ecuadorian	141	0.56
Peruvian	89	0.35
Uruguayan	24	0.09
Venezuelan	14	0.06
Other South American	7	0.03
Other Hispanic or Latino	931	3.67

Race*	Population	%
African-American/Black (1,003)	1,380	5.45
Not Hispanic (497)	589	2.32
Hispanic (506)	791	3.12
American Indian/Alaska Native (112)	232	0.92
Not Hispanic (24)	72	0.28
Hispanic (88)	160	0.63
Blackfeet (3)	3	0.01
Canadian/French Am. Ind. (1)	1	<0.01
Central American Ind. (0)	4	0.02
Cherokee (7)	16	0.06
Choctaw (0)	1	<0.01
Creek (1)	1	<0.01
Delaware (0)	3	0.01
Iroquois (0)	1	<0.01
Lumbee (0)	1	<0.01
Mexican American Ind. (7)	11	0.04
Pueblo (6)	6	0.02
Seminole (0)	4	0.02
Sioux (0)	1	<0.01
South American Ind. (7)	22	0.09
Spanish American Ind. (1)	8	0.03
Asian (200)	263	1.04
Not Hispanic (184)	218	0.86
Hispanic (16)	45	0.18
Cambodian (1)	1	<0.01
Chinese, ex. Taiwanese (28)	29	0.11
Filipino (36)	49	0.19
Indian (77)	91	0.36
Indonesian (3)	3	0.01
Japanese (5)	13	0.05
Korean (8)	14	0.06
Pakistani (0)	4	0.02
Thai (2)	3	0.01
Vietnamese (32)	32	0.13
Hawaii Native/Pacific Islander (8)	68	0.27
Not Hispanic (5)	9	0.04
Hispanic (3)	59	0.23
Guamanian/Chamorro (2)	2	0.01
Native Hawaiian (0)	2	0.01
Samoan (0)	3	0.01
White (17,592)	18,210	71.86
Not Hispanic (14,955)	15,121	59.67
Hispanic (2,637)	3,089	12.19

Hempfield

Place Type: Township
County: Westmoreland
Population: 43,241†

Ancestry‡	Population	%
African, Sub-Saharan (122)	151	0.35
African (114)	130	0.30
Kenyan (8)	8	0.02
Nigerian (0)	13	0.03
Albanian (7)	7	0.02
American (1,192)	1,192	2.77
Arab (100)	239	0.56
Lebanese (24)	26	0.06
Moroccan (12)	24	0.06
Palestinian (0)	16	0.04
Syrian (64)	173	0.40
Austrian (22)	243	0.57
Belgian (10)	71	0.17
British (8)	41	0.10
Canadian (26)	140	0.33
Carpatho Rusyn (11)	28	0.07
Croatian (99)	496	1.15
Czech (101)	353	0.82
Czechoslovakian (58)	207	0.48
Danish (0)	46	0.11
Dutch (114)	774	1.80
Eastern European (67)	67	0.16
English (1,054)	4,743	11.04
European (389)	396	0.92
Finnish (0)	87	0.20
French, ex. Basque (39)	500	1.16
French Canadian (32)	128	0.30
German (4,320)	16,121	37.52
Greek (95)	231	0.54
Hungarian (301)	833	1.94
Irish (1,461)	7,113	16.56
Italian (3,286)	9,075	21.12
Lithuanian (66)	199	0.46
Norwegian (7)	121	0.28
Pennsylvania German (185)	229	0.53
Polish (1,339)	4,584	10.67
Romanian (17)	17	0.04
Russian (24)	344	0.80
Scandinavian (0)	8	0.02
Scotch-Irish (361)	1,444	3.36
Scottish (274)	1,021	2.38
Serbian (83)	360	0.84
Slavic (42)	183	0.43
Slovak (841)	2,694	6.27
Slovene (107)	328	0.76
Swedish (147)	725	1.69
Swiss (0)	84	0.20
Ukrainian (92)	447	1.04
Welsh (65)	559	1.30
West Indian, ex. Hispanic (7)	7	0.02
Jamaican (7)	7	0.02
Yugoslavian (19)	48	0.11

Hispanic Origin	Population	%
Hispanic or Latino (of any race)	395	0.91
Central American, ex. Mexican	37	0.09
Guatemalan	12	0.03
Honduran	10	0.02
Nicaraguan	3	0.01
Panamanian	4	0.01
Salvadoran	8	0.02
Cuban	20	0.05
Dominican Republic	9	0.02
Mexican	99	0.23
Puerto Rican	61	0.14
South American	25	0.06
Argentinean	1	<0.01
Chilean	1	<0.01
Colombian	16	0.04
Ecuadorian	1	<0.01
Peruvian	2	<0.01
Uruguayan	1	<0.01
Venezuelan	3	0.01
Other Hispanic or Latino	144	0.33

Race*	Population	%
African-American/Black (1,047)	1,194	2.76
Not Hispanic (1,034)	1,169	2.70
Hispanic (13)	25	0.06
American Indian/Alaska Native (47)	136	0.31
Not Hispanic (40)	126	0.29
Hispanic (7)	10	0.02
Blackfeet (0)	1	<0.01
Canadian/French Am. Ind. (0)	1	<0.01
Cherokee (11)	34	0.08
Cree (0)	1	<0.01
Creek (1)	3	0.01

*Notes: † The Census 2010 population figure is used to calculate the percentages in the Hispanic Origin and Race categories. Ancestry percentages are based on the 2006-2010 American Community Survey population (not shown); ‡ Numbers in parentheses indicate the number of people reporting a single ancestry; * Numbers in parentheses indicate the number of persons reporting this race alone, not in combination with any other race; Please refer to the Explanation of Data for more information.*

Delaware (1)	3	0.01
Iroquois (2)	6	0.01
Mexican American Ind. (2)	2	<0.01
Navajo (1)	2	<0.01
Osage (0)	1	<0.01
Puget Sound Salish (1)	1	<0.01
Shoshone (0)	1	<0.01
Sioux (4)	8	0.02
South American Ind. (1)	1	<0.01
Asian (372)	458	1.06
Not Hispanic (370)	455	1.05
Hispanic (2)	3	0.01
Bangladeshi (4)	4	0.01
Cambodian (1)	1	<0.01
Chinese, ex. Taiwanese (100)	121	0.28
Filipino (43)	54	0.12
Hmong (0)	1	<0.01
Indian (87)	97	0.22
Japanese (16)	24	0.06
Korean (34)	44	0.10
Laotian (5)	7	0.02
Pakistani (8)	9	0.02
Sri Lankan (1)	1	<0.01
Taiwanese (4)	6	0.01
Thai (2)	7	0.02
Vietnamese (47)	63	0.15
Hawaii Native/Pacific Islander (10)	20	0.05
Not Hispanic (10)	20	0.05
Guamanian/Chamorro (2)	4	0.01
Native Hawaiian (1)	5	0.01
White (41,285)	41,590	96.18
Not Hispanic (41,068)	41,347	95.62
Hispanic (217)	243	0.56

Hermitage

Place Type: City
County: Mercer
Population: 16,220†

Ancestry‡	Population	%
African, Sub-Saharan (17)	17	0.11
African (17)	17	0.11
American (472)	472	2.92
Arab (21)	62	0.38
Egyptian (21)	31	0.19
Syrian (0)	31	0.19
Austrian (26)	70	0.43
British (50)	59	0.37
Canadian (12)	12	0.07
Carpatho Rusyn (16)	64	0.40
Croatian (216)	416	2.58
Czech (20)	270	1.67
Czechoslovakian (30)	38	0.24
Danish (13)	13	0.08
Dutch (52)	346	2.14
English (383)	1,642	10.16
European (209)	228	1.41
Finnish (0)	14	0.09
French, ex. Basque (10)	255	1.58
French Canadian (0)	50	0.31
German (1,125)	5,333	33.01
Greek (150)	307	1.90
Hungarian (292)	642	3.97
Irish (565)	2,552	15.80
Italian (1,327)	3,199	19.80
Latvian (24)	24	0.15
Lithuanian (13)	32	0.20
Northern European (49)	49	0.30
Norwegian (26)	78	0.48
Pennsylvania German (43)	85	0.53
Polish (360)	1,017	6.30
Romanian (91)	133	0.82
Russian (50)	318	1.97
Scotch-Irish (167)	685	4.24
Scottish (106)	419	2.59
Serbian (62)	317	1.96
Slavic (0)	17	0.11
Slovak (455)	1,409	8.72
Slovene (0)	61	0.38
Swedish (24)	271	1.68
Ukrainian (22)	33	0.20
Welsh (33)	200	1.24
West Indian, ex. Hispanic (71)	71	0.44
Jamaican (71)	71	0.44
Yugoslavian (32)	81	0.50

Hispanic Origin	Population	%
Hispanic or Latino (of any race)	156	0.96
Central American, ex. Mexican	9	0.06
Guatemalan	2	0.01
Honduran	3	0.02
Nicaraguan	3	0.02
Salvadoran	1	0.01
Cuban	7	0.04
Dominican Republic	10	0.06
Mexican	53	0.33
Puerto Rican	44	0.27
South American	8	0.05
Colombian	2	0.01
Peruvian	1	0.01
Venezuelan	5	0.03
Other Hispanic or Latino	25	0.15

Race*	Population	%
African-American/Black (613)	733	4.52
Not Hispanic (607)	718	4.43
Hispanic (6)	15	0.09
American Indian/Alaska Native (15)	62	0.38
Not Hispanic (15)	59	0.36
Hispanic (0)	3	0.02
Apache (0)	1	0.01
Blackfeet (0)	2	0.01
Cherokee (1)	10	0.06
Cree (0)	2	0.01
Delaware (1)	3	0.02
Iroquois (4)	9	0.06
Sioux (3)	3	0.02
Asian (202)	232	1.43
Not Hispanic (202)	232	1.43
Chinese, ex. Taiwanese (35)	41	0.25
Filipino (29)	33	0.20
Indian (59)	64	0.39
Japanese (3)	4	0.02
Korean (20)	26	0.16
Pakistani (17)	17	0.10
Taiwanese (1)	1	0.01
Vietnamese (34)	37	0.23
Hawaii Native/Pacific Islander (2)	19	0.12
Not Hispanic (2)	19	0.12
Native Hawaiian (0)	16	0.10
White (15,135)	15,334	94.54
Not Hispanic (15,034)	15,216	93.81
Hispanic (101)	118	0.73

Hershey

Place Type: CDP
County: Dauphin
Population: 14,257†

Ancestry‡	Population	%
African, Sub-Saharan (96)	108	0.83
African (64)	76	0.58
Nigerian (18)	18	0.14
Sudanese (14)	14	0.11
American (297)	297	2.27
Arab (160)	172	1.31
Egyptian (125)	125	0.96
Lebanese (0)	12	0.09
Syrian (12)	12	0.09
Other Arab (23)	23	0.18
Austrian (23)	111	0.85
Belgian (0)	31	0.24
British (40)	73	0.56
Celtic (0)	70	0.54
Croatian (0)	9	0.07
Czech (27)	111	0.85
Czechoslovakian (0)	45	0.34
Danish (10)	10	0.08
Dutch (88)	388	2.97
Eastern European (36)	44	0.34
English (255)	1,221	9.33
European (92)	102	0.78
Finnish (12)	25	0.19
French, ex. Basque (25)	345	2.64
French Canadian (22)	43	0.33
German (1,877)	4,578	34.99
Greek (0)	42	0.32
Hungarian (32)	197	1.51
Iranian (14)	14	0.11
Irish (502)	2,584	19.75
Italian (933)	2,074	15.85
Lithuanian (6)	36	0.28
Norwegian (34)	148	1.13
Pennsylvania German (141)	206	1.57
Polish (68)	589	4.50
Portuguese (13)	13	0.10
Romanian (0)	13	0.10
Russian (90)	239	1.83
Scandinavian (0)	45	0.34
Scotch-Irish (89)	442	3.38
Scottish (52)	263	2.01
Serbian (13)	25	0.19
Slavic (27)	91	0.70
Slovak (19)	195	1.49
Slovene (0)	12	0.09
Swedish (46)	82	0.63
Swiss (8)	144	1.10
Turkish (41)	51	0.39
Ukrainian (17)	50	0.38
Welsh (68)	274	2.09

Hispanic Origin	Population	%
Hispanic or Latino (of any race)	485	3.40
Central American, ex. Mexican	19	0.13
Costa Rican	2	0.01
Guatemalan	6	0.04
Honduran	2	0.01
Nicaraguan	1	0.01
Panamanian	4	0.03
Salvadoran	4	0.03
Cuban	20	0.14
Dominican Republic	28	0.20
Mexican	78	0.55
Puerto Rican	206	1.44
South American	72	0.51
Argentinean	12	0.08
Chilean	1	0.01
Colombian	25	0.18
Ecuadorian	14	0.10
Peruvian	13	0.09
Uruguayan	1	0.01
Venezuelan	5	0.04
Other South American	1	0.01
Other Hispanic or Latino	62	0.43

Race*	Population	%
African-American/Black (891)	1,026	7.20
Not Hispanic (874)	1,000	7.01
Hispanic (17)	26	0.18
American Indian/Alaska Native (23)	72	0.51
Not Hispanic (17)	61	0.43
Hispanic (6)	11	0.08
Apache (0)	1	0.01
Blackfeet (0)	2	0.01
Central American Ind. (0)	2	0.01
Cherokee (2)	9	0.06
Creek (1)	1	0.01
Iroquois (0)	4	0.03
Seminole (0)	1	0.01
Yaqui (0)	1	0.01
Asian (947)	1,056	7.41
Not Hispanic (943)	1,044	7.32
Hispanic (4)	12	0.08
Bangladeshi (7)	7	0.05
Burmese (1)	1	0.01
Cambodian (29)	34	0.24
Chinese, ex. Taiwanese (260)	284	1.99
Filipino (40)	55	0.39

*Notes: † The Census 2010 population figure is used to calculate the percentages in the Hispanic Origin and Race categories. Ancestry percentages are based on the 2006-2010 American Community Survey population (not shown); ‡ Numbers in parentheses indicate the number of people reporting a single ancestry; * Numbers in parentheses indicate the number of persons reporting this race alone, not in combination with any other race; Please refer to the Explanation of Data for more information.*

Indian (315)	335	2.35
Indonesian (2)	2	0.01
Japanese (9)	16	0.11
Korean (60)	70	0.49
Laotian (2)	2	0.01
Nepalese (4)	4	0.03
Pakistani (36)	36	0.25
Sri Lankan (3)	4	0.03
Taiwanese (19)	23	0.16
Thai (75)	78	0.55
Vietnamese (66)	74	0.52
Hawaii Native/Pacific Islander (9)	23	0.16
Not Hispanic (9)	22	0.15
Hispanic (0)	1	0.01
Native Hawaiian (0)	3	0.02
Samoan (1)	1	0.01
White (11,909)	12,138	85.14
Not Hispanic (11,615)	11,824	82.93
Hispanic (294)	314	2.20

Hilltown

Place Type: Township
County: Bucks
Population: 15,029†

Ancestry‡	Population	%
American (686)	686	4.71
Arab (0)	35	0.24
Syrian (0)	35	0.24
Armenian (0)	10	0.07
Australian (0)	12	0.08
Austrian (0)	40	0.27
British (27)	85	0.58
Canadian (9)	19	0.13
Croatian (20)	43	0.30
Czech (31)	31	0.21
Czechoslovakian (0)	8	0.05
Danish (25)	25	0.17
Dutch (60)	276	1.89
Eastern European (7)	7	0.05
English (335)	1,521	10.44
European (285)	293	2.01
French, ex. Basque (60)	421	2.89
French Canadian (66)	153	1.05
German (2,373)	5,836	40.06
Greek (37)	81	0.56
Hungarian (46)	153	1.05
Irish (799)	3,520	24.16
Italian (715)	2,055	14.11
Lithuanian (36)	171	1.17
Norwegian (12)	97	0.67
Pennsylvania German (195)	325	2.23
Polish (211)	755	5.18
Portuguese (9)	45	0.31
Romanian (0)	41	0.28
Russian (0)	178	1.22
Scotch-Irish (59)	192	1.32
Scottish (56)	348	2.39
Slovak (49)	172	1.18
Swedish (67)	230	1.58
Swiss (23)	147	1.01
Ukrainian (93)	209	1.43
Welsh (10)	232	1.59
West Indian, ex. Hispanic (19)	19	0.13
Jamaican (19)	19	0.13
Yugoslavian (0)	28	0.19

Hispanic Origin	Population	%
Hispanic or Latino (of any race)	428	2.85
Central American, ex. Mexican	40	0.27
Costa Rican	9	0.06
Guatemalan	5	0.03
Honduran	11	0.07
Nicaraguan	5	0.03
Panamanian	2	0.01
Salvadoran	8	0.05
Cuban	18	0.12
Dominican Republic	17	0.11
Mexican	78	0.52
Puerto Rican	180	1.20
South American	39	0.26
Argentinean	5	0.03
Chilean	3	0.02
Colombian	14	0.09
Ecuadorian	11	0.07
Peruvian	2	0.01
Uruguayan	2	0.01
Venezuelan	2	0.01
Other Hispanic or Latino	56	0.37

Race*	Population	%
African-American/Black (303)	374	2.49
Not Hispanic (289)	354	2.36
Hispanic (14)	20	0.13
American Indian/Alaska Native (19)	75	0.50
Not Hispanic (17)	71	0.47
Hispanic (2)	4	0.03
Blackfeet (0)	7	0.05
Cherokee (2)	21	0.14
Chickasaw (1)	1	0.01
Choctaw (0)	2	0.01
Creek (0)	4	0.03
Iroquois (0)	1	0.01
Lumbee (1)	1	0.01
Navajo (2)	2	0.01
Seminole (1)	2	0.01
Sioux (0)	2	0.01
Yaqui (1)	1	0.01
Asian (466)	520	3.46
Not Hispanic (463)	516	3.43
Hispanic (3)	4	0.03
Bangladeshi (7)	7	0.05
Cambodian (7)	9	0.06
Chinese, ex. Taiwanese (60)	73	0.49
Filipino (26)	40	0.27
Indian (151)	154	1.02
Indonesian (1)	2	0.01
Japanese (6)	12	0.08
Korean (113)	124	0.83
Laotian (10)	12	0.08
Pakistani (3)	3	0.02
Taiwanese (0)	1	0.01
Vietnamese (78)	80	0.53
Hawaii Native/Pacific Islander (8)	12	0.08
Not Hispanic (6)	7	0.05
Hispanic (2)	5	0.03
Guamanian/Chamorro (1)	1	0.01
Native Hawaiian (1)	1	0.01
Tongan (1)	1	0.01
White (13,939)	14,120	93.95
Not Hispanic (13,651)	13,807	91.87
Hispanic (288)	313	2.08

Honey Brook

Place Type: Township
County: Chester
Population: 7,647†

Ancestry‡	Population	%
African, Sub-Saharan (28)	28	0.38
Other Sub-Saharan African (28)	28	0.38
American (234)	234	3.15
Austrian (0)	18	0.24
Belgian (0)	15	0.20
British (66)	115	1.55
Canadian (0)	14	0.19
Croatian (55)	71	0.96
Czech (0)	17	0.23
Dutch (0)	122	1.64
Eastern European (0)	19	0.26
English (298)	791	10.64
European (72)	72	0.97
French, ex. Basque (54)	216	2.91
French Canadian (14)	25	0.34
German (995)	2,523	33.95
Greek (15)	15	0.20
Hungarian (0)	36	0.48
Irish (394)	1,127	15.17
Italian (189)	803	10.81
Lithuanian (24)	24	0.32
Pennsylvania German (349)	428	5.76
Polish (80)	448	6.03
Romanian (146)	165	2.22
Russian (8)	61	0.82
Scandinavian (8)	8	0.11
Scotch-Irish (143)	255	3.43
Scottish (43)	231	3.11
Slovak (18)	49	0.66
Swedish (38)	83	1.12
Swiss (37)	177	2.38
Ukrainian (16)	33	0.44
Welsh (118)	232	3.12

Hispanic Origin	Population	%
Hispanic or Latino (of any race)	130	1.70
Central American, ex. Mexican	6	0.08
Costa Rican	2	0.03
Guatemalan	1	0.01
Nicaraguan	2	0.03
Panamanian	1	0.01
Cuban	2	0.03
Dominican Republic	1	0.01
Mexican	18	0.24
Puerto Rican	73	0.95
South American	7	0.09
Chilean	1	0.01
Colombian	3	0.04
Ecuadorian	3	0.04
Other Hispanic or Latino	23	0.30

Race*	Population	%
African-American/Black (73)	103	1.35
Not Hispanic (71)	96	1.26
Hispanic (2)	7	0.09
American Indian/Alaska Native (28)	77	1.01
Not Hispanic (28)	68	0.89
Hispanic (0)	9	0.12
Apache (0)	5	0.07
Blackfeet (0)	5	0.07
Cherokee (4)	19	0.25
Chippewa (0)	1	0.01
Delaware (1)	4	0.05
Iroquois (1)	2	0.03
Kiowa (0)	2	0.03
Mexican American Ind. (0)	1	0.01
Navajo (0)	2	0.03
Seminole (1)	1	0.01
Sioux (0)	8	0.10
Asian (41)	54	0.71
Not Hispanic (41)	54	0.71
Cambodian (2)	2	0.03
Chinese, ex. Taiwanese (7)	9	0.12
Filipino (5)	12	0.16
Indian (13)	14	0.18
Indonesian (1)	1	0.01
Japanese (1)	1	0.01
Korean (7)	10	0.13
Vietnamese (5)	5	0.07
Hawaii Native/Pacific Islander (0)	1	0.01
Not Hispanic (0)	1	0.01
Native Hawaiian (0)	1	0.01
White (7,378)	7,466	97.63
Not Hispanic (7,296)	7,370	96.38
Hispanic (82)	96	1.26

Hopewell

Place Type: Township
County: Beaver
Population: 12,593†

Ancestry‡	Population	%
American (468)	468	3.70
Arab (75)	243	1.92
Arab (0)	9	0.07
Lebanese (75)	234	1.85
Austrian (11)	145	1.15
Brazilian (0)	39	0.31

*Notes: † The Census 2010 population figure is used to calculate the percentages in the Hispanic Origin and Race categories. Ancestry percentages are based on the 2006-2010 American Community Survey population (not shown); ‡ Numbers in parentheses indicate the number of people reporting a single ancestry; * Numbers in parentheses indicate the number of persons reporting this race alone, not in combination with any other race; Please refer to the Explanation of Data for more information.*

Canadian (32)	32	0.25
Croatian (156)	477	3.77
Czech (64)	79	0.62
Czechoslovakian (11)	22	0.17
Danish (13)	13	0.10
Dutch (41)	279	2.21
English (142)	1,043	8.25
European (54)	54	0.43
Finnish (0)	48	0.38
French, ex. Basque (32)	235	1.86
French Canadian (12)	26	0.21
German (790)	3,232	25.56
Greek (32)	90	0.71
Hungarian (20)	209	1.65
Irish (540)	2,524	19.96
Italian (1,056)	2,782	22.00
Lithuanian (14)	65	0.51
Norwegian (19)	70	0.55
Pennsylvania German (15)	15	0.12
Polish (382)	980	7.75
Portuguese (0)	26	0.21
Romanian (0)	27	0.21
Russian (159)	259	2.05
Scotch-Irish (157)	403	3.19
Scottish (87)	284	2.25
Serbian (228)	423	3.34
Slavic (41)	135	1.07
Slovak (451)	1,103	8.72
Slovene (10)	10	0.08
Swedish (33)	155	1.23
Ukrainian (90)	201	1.59
Welsh (13)	138	1.09
Yugoslavian (14)	14	0.11

Hispanic Origin	Population	%
Hispanic or Latino (of any race)	145	1.15
Central American, ex. Mexican	9	0.07
Honduran	3	0.02
Nicaraguan	1	0.01
Panamanian	3	0.02
Salvadoran	2	0.02
Cuban	2	0.02
Mexican	68	0.54
Puerto Rican	33	0.26
South American	11	0.09
Colombian	7	0.06
Ecuadorian	1	0.01
Venezuelan	3	0.02
Other Hispanic or Latino	22	0.17

Race*	Population	%
African-American/Black (466)	537	4.26
Not Hispanic (463)	529	4.20
Hispanic (3)	8	0.06
American Indian/Alaska Native (11)	39	0.31
Not Hispanic (11)	38	0.30
Hispanic (0)	1	0.01
Apache (0)	1	0.01
Cherokee (1)	10	0.08
Delaware (0)	2	0.02
Iroquois (0)	2	0.02
Sioux (1)	2	0.02
South American Ind. (0)	1	0.01
Ute (0)	2	0.02
Asian (45)	75	0.60
Not Hispanic (45)	72	0.57
Hispanic (0)	3	0.02
Chinese, ex. Taiwanese (12)	16	0.13
Filipino (8)	16	0.13
Indian (11)	14	0.11
Indonesian (1)	1	0.01
Japanese (1)	7	0.06
Korean (1)	1	0.01
Malaysian (1)	2	0.02
Thai (1)	1	0.01
Vietnamese (7)	14	0.11
Hawaii Native/Pacific Islander (0)	2	0.02
Not Hispanic (0)	2	0.02
Native Hawaiian (0)	1	0.01
Samoan (0)	1	0.01
White (11,918)	12,043	95.63
Not Hispanic (11,805)	11,917	94.63
Hispanic (113)	126	1.00

Horsham

Place Type: CDP
County: Montgomery
Population: 14,842†

Ancestry‡	Population	%
African, Sub-Saharan (83)	83	0.58
African (83)	83	0.58
American (496)	496	3.44
Arab (53)	77	0.53
Arab (40)	40	0.28
Lebanese (13)	37	0.26
Armenian (138)	261	1.81
Austrian (48)	94	0.65
Belgian (10)	10	0.07
British (28)	72	0.50
Canadian (0)	46	0.32
Czech (0)	48	0.33
Czechoslovakian (0)	48	0.33
Danish (0)	39	0.27
Dutch (0)	274	1.90
Eastern European (12)	12	0.08
English (380)	1,915	13.29
European (95)	95	0.66
French, ex. Basque (51)	398	2.76
German (1,058)	4,506	31.26
Greek (18)	53	0.37
Hungarian (12)	137	0.95
Irish (1,114)	4,227	29.33
Italian (898)	1,942	13.47
Lithuanian (0)	42	0.29
Norwegian (0)	25	0.17
Pennsylvania German (15)	34	0.24
Polish (402)	1,264	8.77
Portuguese (12)	12	0.08
Romanian (19)	44	0.31
Russian (122)	335	2.32
Scotch-Irish (189)	371	2.57
Scottish (109)	413	2.87
Serbian (0)	19	0.13
Slavic (0)	20	0.14
Slovak (6)	30	0.21
Slovene (13)	13	0.09
Swedish (0)	122	0.85
Swiss (0)	28	0.19
Ukrainian (14)	28	0.19
Welsh (29)	188	1.30
West Indian, ex. Hispanic (97)	115	0.80
Haitian (97)	97	0.67
U.S. Virgin Islander (0)	18	0.12
Yugoslavian (0)	7	0.05

Hispanic Origin	Population	%
Hispanic or Latino (of any race)	520	3.50
Central American, ex. Mexican	91	0.61
Costa Rican	3	0.02
Guatemalan	61	0.41
Honduran	1	0.01
Nicaraguan	3	0.02
Panamanian	1	0.01
Salvadoran	18	0.12
Other Central American	4	0.03
Cuban	18	0.12
Dominican Republic	8	0.05
Mexican	117	0.79
Puerto Rican	166	1.12
South American	65	0.44
Argentinean	5	0.03
Chilean	1	0.01
Colombian	18	0.12
Ecuadorian	28	0.19
Peruvian	8	0.05
Venezuelan	4	0.03
Other South American	1	0.01
Other Hispanic or Latino	55	0.37

Race*	Population	%
African-American/Black (694)	799	5.38
Not Hispanic (678)	767	5.17
Hispanic (16)	32	0.22
American Indian/Alaska Native (25)	71	0.48
Not Hispanic (21)	61	0.41
Hispanic (4)	10	0.07
Alaska Athabascan *(Ala. Nat.)* (1)	1	0.01
Apache (1)	1	0.01
Blackfeet (1)	2	0.01
Cherokee (3)	5	0.03
Choctaw (0)	1	0.01
Delaware (0)	1	0.01
Lumbee (1)	2	0.01
Mexican American Ind. (1)	1	0.01
Sioux (1)	1	0.01
Asian (867)	958	6.45
Not Hispanic (864)	953	6.42
Hispanic (3)	5	0.03
Bangladeshi (2)	2	0.01
Cambodian (4)	4	0.03
Chinese, ex. Taiwanese (87)	105	0.71
Filipino (68)	81	0.55
Indian (267)	295	1.99
Indonesian (1)	4	0.03
Japanese (1)	8	0.05
Korean (355)	370	2.49
Laotian (11)	11	0.07
Malaysian (0)	2	0.01
Pakistani (18)	23	0.15
Taiwanese (3)	3	0.02
Thai (3)	7	0.05
Vietnamese (35)	38	0.26
Hawaii Native/Pacific Islander (8)	14	0.09
Not Hispanic (2)	7	0.05
Hispanic (6)	7	0.05
Guamanian/Chamorro (6)	7	0.05
Native Hawaiian (0)	3	0.02
White (12,837)	13,030	87.79
Not Hispanic (12,525)	12,692	85.51
Hispanic (312)	338	2.28

Horsham

Place Type: Township
County: Montgomery
Population: 26,147†

Ancestry‡	Population	%
African, Sub-Saharan (147)	167	0.65
African (83)	83	0.32
Liberian (0)	20	0.08
Nigerian (13)	13	0.05
Ugandan (51)	51	0.20
American (843)	843	3.27
Arab (86)	174	0.67
Arab (40)	40	0.16
Egyptian (33)	33	0.13
Lebanese (13)	101	0.39
Armenian (138)	261	1.01
Austrian (48)	132	0.51
Belgian (31)	31	0.12
Brazilian (0)	54	0.21
British (66)	119	0.46
Canadian (0)	46	0.18
Czech (32)	138	0.53
Czechoslovakian (16)	64	0.25
Danish (15)	93	0.36
Dutch (0)	366	1.42
Eastern European (36)	72	0.28
English (627)	3,147	12.20
Estonian (39)	39	0.15
European (201)	215	0.83
French, ex. Basque (135)	640	2.48
French Canadian (40)	71	0.28
German (1,581)	7,350	28.49
Greek (18)	53	0.21
Hungarian (60)	301	1.17
Irish (1,989)	7,371	28.57

*Notes: † The Census 2010 population figure is used to calculate the percentages in the Hispanic Origin and Race categories. Ancestry percentages are based on the 2006-2010 American Community Survey population (not shown); ‡ Numbers in parentheses indicate the number of people reporting a single ancestry; * Numbers in parentheses indicate the number of persons reporting this race alone, not in combination with any other race; Please refer to the Explanation of Data for more information.*

Italian (1,688)	4,264	16.53
Lithuanian (0)	81	0.31
Norwegian (11)	68	0.26
Pennsylvania German (61)	89	0.35
Polish (626)	2,075	8.04
Portuguese (43)	43	0.17
Romanian (19)	95	0.37
Russian (257)	878	3.40
Scotch-Irish (275)	572	2.22
Scottish (150)	660	2.56
Serbian (0)	19	0.07
Slavic (0)	20	0.08
Slovak (6)	75	0.29
Slovene (13)	13	0.05
Swedish (12)	187	0.72
Swiss (0)	28	0.11
Ukrainian (38)	81	0.31
Welsh (45)	367	1.42
West Indian, ex. Hispanic (97)	115	0.45
Haitian (97)	97	0.38
U.S. Virgin Islander (0)	18	0.07
Yugoslavian (0)	21	0.08

Hispanic Origin	Population	%
Hispanic or Latino (of any race)	753	2.88
Central American, ex. Mexican	114	0.44
Costa Rican	6	0.02
Guatemalan	72	0.28
Honduran	1	<0.01
Nicaraguan	9	0.03
Panamanian	4	0.02
Salvadoran	18	0.07
Other Central American	4	0.02
Cuban	27	0.10
Dominican Republic	13	0.05
Mexican	161	0.62
Puerto Rican	226	0.86
South American	116	0.44
Argentinean	5	0.02
Chilean	2	0.01
Colombian	40	0.15
Ecuadorian	30	0.11
Paraguayan	1	<0.01
Peruvian	21	0.08
Uruguayan	1	<0.01
Venezuelan	15	0.06
Other South American	1	<0.01
Other Hispanic or Latino	96	0.37

Race*	Population	%
African-American/Black (1,128)	1,276	4.88
Not Hispanic (1,106)	1,235	4.72
Hispanic (22)	41	0.16
American Indian/Alaska Native (34)	107	0.41
Not Hispanic (27)	92	0.35
Hispanic (7)	15	0.06
Alaska Athabascan *(Ala. Nat.)* (1)	1	<0.01
Apache (1)	1	<0.01
Blackfeet (1)	3	0.01
Cherokee (4)	11	0.04
Choctaw (0)	1	<0.01
Creek (0)	1	<0.01
Delaware (0)	1	<0.01
Iroquois (3)	5	0.02
Lumbee (1)	2	0.01
Mexican American Ind. (1)	1	<0.01
Potawatomi (0)	1	<0.01
Sioux (2)	2	0.01
South American Ind. (1)	1	<0.01
Asian (1,894)	2,030	7.76
Not Hispanic (1,889)	2,021	7.73
Hispanic (5)	9	0.03
Bangladeshi (4)	4	0.02
Cambodian (7)	12	0.05
Chinese, ex. Taiwanese (230)	266	1.02
Filipino (99)	127	0.49
Indian (644)	682	2.61
Indonesian (1)	4	0.02
Japanese (8)	17	0.07
Korean (740)	760	2.91
Laotian (11)	11	0.04
Malaysian (0)	3	0.01
Pakistani (33)	38	0.15
Sri Lankan (2)	5	0.02
Taiwanese (10)	10	0.04
Thai (6)	12	0.05
Vietnamese (63)	70	0.27
Hawaii Native/Pacific Islander (9)	22	0.08
Not Hispanic (3)	15	0.06
Hispanic (6)	7	0.03
Guamanian/Chamorro (6)	7	0.03
Native Hawaiian (0)	10	0.04
White (22,498)	22,793	87.17
Not Hispanic (22,016)	22,279	85.21
Hispanic (482)	514	1.97

Indiana

Place Type: Borough
County: Indiana
Population: 13,975†

Ancestry‡	Population	%
African, Sub-Saharan (90)	106	0.75
African (65)	81	0.58
Nigerian (25)	25	0.18
American (172)	172	1.22
Arab (110)	170	1.21
Arab (61)	61	0.43
Lebanese (23)	23	0.16
Syrian (0)	60	0.43
Other Arab (26)	26	0.18
Austrian (0)	8	0.06
Canadian (0)	24	0.17
Croatian (8)	47	0.33
Czech (29)	53	0.38
Czechoslovakian (43)	64	0.46
Dutch (46)	177	1.26
Eastern European (10)	10	0.07
English (139)	959	6.82
European (74)	74	0.53
Finnish (7)	7	0.05
French, ex. Basque (18)	192	1.37
German (1,340)	4,556	32.39
Greek (89)	136	0.97
Hungarian (39)	224	1.59
Irish (937)	3,484	24.77
Italian (866)	2,501	17.78
Lithuanian (0)	28	0.20
Norwegian (28)	105	0.75
Pennsylvania German (13)	59	0.42
Polish (436)	928	6.60
Portuguese (15)	15	0.11
Russian (30)	186	1.32
Scotch-Irish (282)	713	5.07
Scottish (176)	464	3.30
Serbian (16)	78	0.55
Slovak (123)	333	2.37
Swedish (12)	120	0.85
Swiss (0)	24	0.17
Ukrainian (47)	223	1.59
Welsh (25)	282	2.01
West Indian, ex. Hispanic (44)	75	0.53
Haitian (30)	30	0.21
Jamaican (0)	31	0.22
Trinidadian/Tobagonian (14)	14	0.10

Hispanic Origin	Population	%
Hispanic or Latino (of any race)	281	2.01
Central American, ex. Mexican	22	0.16
Costa Rican	1	0.01
Guatemalan	8	0.06
Honduran	4	0.03
Nicaraguan	3	0.02
Panamanian	3	0.02
Salvadoran	3	0.02
Cuban	19	0.14
Dominican Republic	18	0.13
Mexican	78	0.56
Puerto Rican	74	0.53
South American	31	0.22
Argentinean	4	0.03
Colombian	15	0.11
Ecuadorian	4	0.03
Peruvian	6	0.04
Venezuelan	2	0.01
Other Hispanic or Latino	39	0.28

Race*	Population	%
African-American/Black (925)	1,047	7.49
Not Hispanic (888)	990	7.08
Hispanic (37)	57	0.41
American Indian/Alaska Native (12)	61	0.44
Not Hispanic (12)	56	0.40
Hispanic (0)	5	0.04
Apache (1)	1	0.01
Blackfeet (0)	3	0.02
Cherokee (4)	15	0.11
Chippewa (0)	1	0.01
Comanche (0)	2	0.01
Delaware (0)	2	0.01
Iroquois (1)	3	0.02
Lumbee (0)	1	0.01
Potawatomi (0)	1	0.01
Sioux (0)	1	0.01
South American Ind. (0)	1	0.01
Asian (315)	374	2.68
Not Hispanic (312)	364	2.60
Hispanic (3)	10	0.07
Cambodian (0)	9	0.06
Chinese, ex. Taiwanese (109)	137	0.98
Filipino (13)	23	0.16
Indian (29)	40	0.29
Japanese (12)	22	0.16
Korean (58)	65	0.47
Malaysian (9)	9	0.06
Nepalese (2)	2	0.01
Pakistani (2)	4	0.03
Taiwanese (40)	41	0.29
Thai (5)	7	0.05
Vietnamese (18)	33	0.24
Hawaii Native/Pacific Islander (3)	12	0.09
Not Hispanic (3)	10	0.07
Hispanic (0)	2	0.01
Guamanian/Chamorro (0)	1	0.01
Native Hawaiian (1)	5	0.04
Samoan (0)	3	0.02
White (12,420)	12,584	90.05
Not Hispanic (12,294)	12,435	88.98
Hispanic (126)	149	1.07

Jackson

Place Type: Township
County: Lebanon
Population: 8,163†

Ancestry‡	Population	%
American (676)	676	8.65
Arab (0)	37	0.47
Lebanese (0)	37	0.47
Austrian (24)	24	0.31
Canadian (18)	28	0.36
Croatian (0)	16	0.20
Danish (0)	18	0.23
Dutch (183)	299	3.83
English (116)	460	5.89
European (168)	168	2.15
Finnish (15)	15	0.19
French, ex. Basque (15)	142	1.82
German (2,189)	3,590	45.94
Greek (0)	17	0.22
Hungarian (0)	47	0.60
Irish (121)	565	7.23
Italian (260)	576	7.37
Lithuanian (11)	11	0.14
Norwegian (0)	10	0.13
Pennsylvania German (174)	219	2.80
Polish (91)	170	2.18
Romanian (18)	18	0.23

*Notes: † The Census 2010 population figure is used to calculate the percentages in the Hispanic Origin and Race categories. Ancestry percentages are based on the 2006-2010 American Community Survey population (not shown); ‡ Numbers in parentheses indicate the number of people reporting a single ancestry; * Numbers in parentheses indicate the number of persons reporting this race alone, not in combination with any other race; Please refer to the Explanation of Data for more information.*

Russian (33)	65	0.83
Scotch-Irish (14)	66	0.84
Scottish (20)	74	0.95
Slavic (11)	11	0.14
Slovak (25)	82	1.05
Swedish (48)	63	0.81
Swiss (54)	249	3.19
Ukrainian (17)	17	0.22
Welsh (29)	82	1.05

Hispanic Origin	Population	%
Hispanic or Latino (of any race)	130	1.59
Central American, ex. Mexican	9	0.11
Guatemalan	5	0.06
Honduran	2	0.02
Nicaraguan	1	0.01
Salvadoran	1	0.01
Cuban	4	0.05
Dominican Republic	8	0.10
Mexican	20	0.25
Puerto Rican	73	0.89
South American	5	0.06
Chilean	1	0.01
Colombian	4	0.05
Other Hispanic or Latino	11	0.13

Race*	Population	%
African-American/Black (46)	69	0.85
Not Hispanic (37)	58	0.71
Hispanic (9)	11	0.13
American Indian/Alaska Native (6)	18	0.22
Not Hispanic (4)	13	0.16
Hispanic (2)	5	0.06
Cherokee (2)	5	0.06
Iroquois (1)	1	0.01
Mexican American Ind. (1)	1	0.01
Asian (51)	71	0.87
Not Hispanic (50)	70	0.86
Hispanic (1)	1	0.01
Cambodian (7)	10	0.12
Chinese, ex. Taiwanese (4)	4	0.05
Filipino (4)	4	0.05
Indian (8)	8	0.10
Indonesian (1)	1	0.01
Japanese (1)	4	0.05
Korean (10)	21	0.26
Pakistani (3)	3	0.04
Thai (1)	1	0.01
Vietnamese (4)	6	0.07
Hawaii Native/Pacific Islander (2)	5	0.06
Not Hispanic (2)	5	0.06
Native Hawaiian (2)	3	0.04
White (7,974)	8,032	98.40
Not Hispanic (7,889)	7,938	97.24
Hispanic (85)	94	1.15

Jeannette

Place Type: City
County: Westmoreland
Population: 9,654†

Ancestry‡	Population	%
African, Sub-Saharan (344)	344	3.50
African (344)	344	3.50
American (402)	402	4.09
Arab (0)	58	0.59
Lebanese (0)	12	0.12
Moroccan (0)	21	0.21
Syrian (0)	25	0.25
Austrian (14)	51	0.52
Belgian (0)	51	0.52
British (10)	10	0.10
Croatian (43)	98	1.00
Czech (32)	88	0.89
Czechoslovakian (12)	81	0.82
Dutch (14)	198	2.01
Eastern European (10)	10	0.10
English (170)	949	9.64
Finnish (12)	12	0.12
French, ex. Basque (0)	196	1.99
French Canadian (0)	23	0.23
German (772)	2,759	28.04
Greek (6)	16	0.16
Hungarian (18)	82	0.83
Irish (219)	1,397	14.20
Italian (1,261)	2,265	23.02
Lithuanian (13)	63	0.64
Norwegian (18)	30	0.30
Pennsylvania German (21)	32	0.33
Polish (257)	1,028	10.45
Russian (88)	133	1.35
Scotch-Irish (64)	230	2.34
Scottish (0)	101	1.03
Serbian (27)	89	0.90
Slavic (0)	12	0.12
Slovak (49)	165	1.68
Slovene (0)	22	0.22
Swedish (38)	107	1.09
Ukrainian (25)	78	0.79
Welsh (0)	72	0.73
West Indian, ex. Hispanic (9)	9	0.09
West Indian (9)	9	0.09
Yugoslavian (0)	11	0.11

Hispanic Origin	Population	%
Hispanic or Latino (of any race)	84	0.87
Central American, ex. Mexican	7	0.07
Costa Rican	3	0.03
Guatemalan	1	0.01
Nicaraguan	1	0.01
Salvadoran	2	0.02
Cuban	2	0.02
Mexican	34	0.35
Puerto Rican	21	0.22
South American	7	0.07
Argentinean	1	0.01
Bolivian	5	0.05
Other South American	1	0.01
Other Hispanic or Latino	13	0.13

Race*	Population	%
African-American/Black (665)	960	9.94
Not Hispanic (662)	955	9.89
Hispanic (3)	5	0.05
American Indian/Alaska Native (15)	70	0.73
Not Hispanic (12)	67	0.69
Hispanic (3)	3	0.03
Blackfeet (0)	6	0.06
Cherokee (1)	6	0.06
Chickasaw (0)	4	0.04
Crow (1)	1	0.01
Delaware (0)	1	0.01
Iroquois (1)	1	0.01
Seminole (0)	2	0.02
Sioux (0)	1	0.01
South American Ind. (2)	2	0.02
Asian (16)	37	0.38
Not Hispanic (16)	32	0.33
Hispanic (0)	5	0.05
Chinese, ex. Taiwanese (1)	1	0.01
Filipino (8)	15	0.16
Indian (0)	1	0.01
Indonesian (0)	2	0.02
Japanese (1)	6	0.06
Korean (4)	6	0.06
Thai (1)	1	0.01
Vietnamese (1)	5	0.05
Hawaii Native/Pacific Islander (4)	7	0.07
Not Hispanic (4)	7	0.07
Samoan (0)	1	0.01
White (8,548)	8,912	92.31
Not Hispanic (8,510)	8,858	91.75
Hispanic (38)	54	0.56

Jefferson Hills

Place Type: Borough
County: Allegheny
Population: 10,619†

Ancestry‡	Population	%
American (199)	199	1.92
Arab (50)	57	0.55
Arab (38)	38	0.37
Lebanese (0)	7	0.07
Syrian (12)	12	0.12
Austrian (15)	27	0.26
Belgian (0)	33	0.32
British (34)	55	0.53
Croatian (183)	293	2.82
Czech (7)	76	0.73
Czechoslovakian (14)	31	0.30
Dutch (0)	45	0.43
English (326)	1,038	10.00
European (94)	94	0.91
Finnish (0)	13	0.13
French, ex. Basque (7)	177	1.71
French Canadian (0)	15	0.14
German (1,032)	3,341	32.20
Greek (7)	21	0.20
Hungarian (105)	467	4.50
Irish (401)	2,143	20.66
Italian (824)	1,902	18.33
Lithuanian (54)	123	1.19
Norwegian (16)	16	0.15
Pennsylvania German (0)	40	0.39
Polish (205)	892	8.60
Russian (60)	188	1.81
Scotch-Irish (107)	314	3.03
Scottish (45)	176	1.70
Serbian (31)	46	0.44
Slovak (352)	795	7.66
Slovene (0)	26	0.25
Swedish (14)	65	0.63
Swiss (0)	49	0.47
Turkish (21)	21	0.20
Ukrainian (25)	60	0.58
Welsh (0)	93	0.90
Yugoslavian (0)	14	0.13

Hispanic Origin	Population	%
Hispanic or Latino (of any race)	96	0.90
Central American, ex. Mexican	1	0.01
Guatemalan	1	0.01
Cuban	3	0.03
Dominican Republic	3	0.03
Mexican	27	0.25
Puerto Rican	28	0.26
South American	16	0.15
Argentinean	5	0.05
Bolivian	5	0.05
Colombian	1	0.01
Uruguayan	1	0.01
Venezuelan	4	0.04
Other Hispanic or Latino	18	0.17

Race*	Population	%
African-American/Black (191)	222	2.09
Not Hispanic (191)	219	2.06
Hispanic (0)	3	0.03
American Indian/Alaska Native (11)	33	0.31
Not Hispanic (9)	27	0.25
Hispanic (2)	6	0.06
Blackfeet (0)	2	0.02
Cherokee (1)	7	0.07
Cheyenne (0)	1	0.01
Creek (0)	1	0.01
Hopi (1)	1	0.01
Navajo (4)	4	0.04
Sioux (2)	2	0.02
South American Ind. (1)	2	0.02
Asian (143)	165	1.55
Not Hispanic (143)	165	1.55
Burmese (3)	3	0.03
Chinese, ex. Taiwanese (27)	30	0.28
Filipino (19)	27	0.25
Indian (50)	53	0.50
Korean (17)	24	0.23
Laotian (1)	1	0.01
Pakistani (9)	12	0.11

*Notes: † The Census 2010 population figure is used to calculate the percentages in the Hispanic Origin and Race categories. Ancestry percentages are based on the 2006-2010 American Community Survey population (not shown); ‡ Numbers in parentheses indicate the number of people reporting a single ancestry; * Numbers in parentheses indicate the number of persons reporting this race alone, not in combination with any other race; Please refer to the Explanation of Data for more information.*

Sri Lankan (1)	1	0.01
Thai (2)	2	0.02
Vietnamese (12)	14	0.13
Hawaii Native/Pacific Islander (2)	3	0.03
Hispanic (2)	3	0.03
Samoan (2)	2	0.02
White (10,184)	10,243	96.46
Not Hispanic (10,118)	10,174	95.81
Hispanic (66)	69	0.65

Johnstown

Place Type: City
County: Cambria
Population: 20,978†

Ancestry‡	Population	%
African, Sub-Saharan (12)	36	0.17
African (12)	36	0.17
American (1,059)	1,059	4.94
Arab (112)	168	0.78
Lebanese (94)	150	0.70
Syrian (18)	18	0.08
Austrian (24)	42	0.20
Belgian (0)	10	0.05
British (13)	47	0.22
Cajun (0)	27	0.13
Canadian (11)	38	0.18
Carpatho Rusyn (17)	26	0.12
Croatian (101)	291	1.36
Czech (0)	193	0.90
Czechoslovakian (49)	49	0.23
Danish (10)	13	0.06
Dutch (8)	449	2.09
Eastern European (8)	8	0.04
English (276)	1,570	7.32
French, ex. Basque (3)	271	1.26
French Canadian (53)	75	0.35
German (1,394)	5,186	24.18
Greek (0)	69	0.32
Hungarian (99)	468	2.18
Irish (838)	3,368	15.70
Italian (858)	2,722	12.69
Lithuanian (0)	25	0.12
Macedonian (12)	12	0.06
Norwegian (0)	44	0.21
Pennsylvania German (153)	330	1.54
Polish (537)	1,418	6.61
Romanian (0)	8	0.04
Russian (106)	281	1.31
Scotch-Irish (96)	250	1.17
Scottish (0)	165	0.77
Serbian (116)	164	0.76
Slavic (62)	79	0.37
Slovak (777)	1,712	7.98
Slovene (57)	89	0.41
Swedish (0)	38	0.18
Swiss (0)	28	0.13
Ukrainian (125)	237	1.10
Welsh (59)	288	1.34
West Indian, ex. Hispanic (49)	79	0.37
Jamaican (49)	49	0.23
West Indian (0)	30	0.14
Yugoslavian (29)	40	0.19

Hispanic Origin	Population	%
Hispanic or Latino (of any race)	644	3.07
Central American, ex. Mexican	24	0.11
Guatemalan	8	0.04
Honduran	4	0.02
Panamanian	8	0.04
Salvadoran	4	0.02
Cuban	49	0.23
Dominican Republic	7	0.03
Mexican	241	1.15
Puerto Rican	219	1.04
South American	18	0.09
Argentinean	1	<0.01
Chilean	1	<0.01
Colombian	7	0.03
Ecuadorian	4	0.02
Peruvian	5	0.02
Other Hispanic or Latino	86	0.41

Race*	Population	%
African-American/Black (3,068)	3,843	18.32
Not Hispanic (2,974)	3,673	17.51
Hispanic (94)	170	0.81
American Indian/Alaska Native (35)	160	0.76
Not Hispanic (25)	138	0.66
Hispanic (10)	22	0.10
Apache (1)	1	<0.01
Blackfeet (0)	6	0.03
Cherokee (5)	36	0.17
Chickasaw (1)	1	<0.01
Creek (0)	2	0.01
Crow (0)	1	<0.01
Iroquois (3)	7	0.03
Seminole (0)	1	<0.01
South American Ind. (1)	1	<0.01
Asian (51)	106	0.51
Not Hispanic (51)	93	0.44
Hispanic (0)	13	0.06
Chinese, ex. Taiwanese (9)	14	0.07
Filipino (14)	26	0.12
Indian (6)	11	0.05
Japanese (2)	21	0.10
Korean (5)	20	0.10
Laotian (0)	3	0.01
Nepalese (1)	1	<0.01
Thai (1)	1	<0.01
Vietnamese (13)	13	0.06
Hawaii Native/Pacific Islander (5)	26	0.12
Not Hispanic (5)	20	0.10
Hispanic (0)	6	0.03
Guamanian/Chamorro (0)	2	0.01
Marshallese (2)	2	0.01
Native Hawaiian (2)	5	0.02
Samoan (1)	9	0.04
White (16,776)	17,602	83.91
Not Hispanic (16,446)	17,177	81.88
Hispanic (330)	425	2.03

Kennedy

Place Type: Township
County: Allegheny
Population: 7,672†

Ancestry‡	Population	%
African, Sub-Saharan (10)	10	0.13
African (10)	10	0.13
American (196)	196	2.58
Austrian (19)	71	0.93
Belgian (0)	10	0.13
British (0)	9	0.12
Canadian (7)	7	0.09
Croatian (73)	340	4.47
Czech (9)	39	0.51
Czechoslovakian (7)	16	0.21
Dutch (0)	48	0.63
Eastern European (8)	8	0.11
English (51)	300	3.95
European (20)	44	0.58
French, ex. Basque (11)	123	1.62
French Canadian (10)	10	0.13
German (785)	2,565	33.75
Greek (32)	53	0.70
Hungarian (36)	151	1.99
Iranian (10)	10	0.13
Irish (352)	1,522	20.03
Italian (983)	1,959	25.78
Lithuanian (9)	36	0.47
Pennsylvania German (0)	8	0.11
Polish (265)	907	11.93
Russian (71)	400	5.26
Scotch-Irish (60)	176	2.32
Scottish (34)	126	1.66
Serbian (37)	54	0.71
Slavic (0)	18	0.24
Slovak (175)	514	6.76
Slovene (0)	27	0.36
Swedish (6)	64	0.84
Swiss (14)	25	0.33
Ukrainian (62)	265	3.49
Welsh (0)	70	0.92

Hispanic Origin	Population	%
Hispanic or Latino (of any race)	45	0.59
Central American, ex. Mexican	4	0.05
Guatemalan	2	0.03
Honduran	2	0.03
Cuban	2	0.03
Dominican Republic	2	0.03
Mexican	22	0.29
Puerto Rican	4	0.05
South American	4	0.05
Colombian	2	0.03
Venezuelan	2	0.03
Other Hispanic or Latino	7	0.09

Race*	Population	%
African-American/Black (97)	119	1.55
Not Hispanic (97)	118	1.54
Hispanic (0)	1	0.01
American Indian/Alaska Native (5)	19	0.25
Not Hispanic (4)	18	0.23
Hispanic (1)	1	0.01
Chippewa (3)	3	0.04
Iroquois (0)	1	0.01
Mexican American Ind. (1)	1	0.01
Paiute (0)	4	0.05
Asian (62)	93	1.21
Not Hispanic (62)	93	1.21
Chinese, ex. Taiwanese (14)	16	0.21
Filipino (1)	7	0.09
Indian (26)	34	0.44
Japanese (1)	9	0.12
Korean (7)	11	0.14
Pakistani (9)	9	0.12
Vietnamese (3)	4	0.05
Hawaii Native/Pacific Islander (1)	1	0.01
Not Hispanic (1)	1	0.01
Native Hawaiian (1)	1	0.01
White (7,435)	7,499	97.75
Not Hispanic (7,399)	7,459	97.22
Hispanic (36)	40	0.52

Kennett

Place Type: Township
County: Chester
Population: 7,565†

Ancestry‡	Population	%
Albanian (63)	86	1.16
American (488)	488	6.58
Austrian (15)	44	0.59
Basque (15)	15	0.20
Belgian (0)	13	0.18
Brazilian (12)	12	0.16
British (87)	114	1.54
Canadian (0)	13	0.18
Croatian (16)	38	0.51
Danish (0)	13	0.18
Dutch (15)	149	2.01
English (458)	1,347	18.16
European (22)	72	0.97
Finnish (56)	56	0.75
French, ex. Basque (18)	133	1.79
French Canadian (13)	13	0.18
German (259)	1,170	15.77
Greek (74)	205	2.76
Hungarian (34)	77	1.04
Iranian (13)	13	0.18
Irish (308)	1,447	19.51
Italian (573)	1,425	19.21
Latvian (47)	47	0.63
Maltese (8)	24	0.32
Norwegian (15)	60	0.81

*Notes: † The Census 2010 population figure is used to calculate the percentages in the Hispanic Origin and Race categories. Ancestry percentages are based on the 2006-2010 American Community Survey population (not shown); ‡ Numbers in parentheses indicate the number of people reporting a single ancestry; * Numbers in parentheses indicate the number of persons reporting this race alone, not in combination with any other race; Please refer to the Explanation of Data for more information.*

Ancestry (cont.)	Population	%
Pennsylvania German (0)	10	0.13
Polish (40)	347	4.68
Russian (105)	243	3.28
Scandinavian (17)	17	0.23
Scotch-Irish (58)	96	1.29
Scottish (40)	342	4.61
Slavic (14)	14	0.19
Slovak (0)	26	0.35
Swedish (30)	73	0.98
Swiss (0)	13	0.18
Turkish (0)	13	0.18
Ukrainian (27)	27	0.36
Welsh (85)	256	3.45
Yugoslavian (14)	40	0.54

Hispanic Origin	Population	%
Hispanic or Latino (of any race)	792	10.47
Central American, ex. Mexican	6	0.08
Guatemalan	5	0.07
Salvadoran	1	0.01
Cuban	15	0.20
Mexican	615	8.13
Puerto Rican	88	1.16
South American	33	0.44
Argentinean	13	0.17
Bolivian	1	0.01
Chilean	2	0.03
Colombian	6	0.08
Ecuadorian	2	0.03
Paraguayan	2	0.03
Peruvian	4	0.05
Uruguayan	2	0.03
Venezuelan	1	0.01
Other Hispanic or Latino	35	0.46

Race*	Population	%
African-American/Black (137)	167	2.21
Not Hispanic (129)	152	2.01
Hispanic (8)	15	0.20
American Indian/Alaska Native (28)	47	0.62
Not Hispanic (0)	19	0.25
Hispanic (28)	28	0.37
Apache (0)	1	0.01
Cherokee (0)	3	0.04
Mexican American Ind. (18)	18	0.24
Sioux (0)	2	0.03
Asian (179)	236	3.12
Not Hispanic (179)	234	3.09
Hispanic (0)	2	0.03
Chinese, ex. Taiwanese (44)	53	0.70
Filipino (6)	18	0.24
Indian (80)	98	1.30
Indonesian (0)	4	0.05
Japanese (11)	17	0.22
Korean (8)	15	0.20
Laotian (12)	12	0.16
Taiwanese (1)	1	0.01
Thai (1)	1	0.01
Vietnamese (7)	11	0.15
Hawaii Native/Pacific Islander (5)	8	0.11
Not Hispanic (5)	8	0.11
Native Hawaiian (5)	8	0.11
White (6,725)	6,810	90.02
Not Hispanic (6,366)	6,437	85.09
Hispanic (359)	373	4.93

King of Prussia

Place Type: CDP
County: Montgomery
Population: 19,936†

Ancestry‡	Population	%
African, Sub-Saharan (56)	56	0.28
African (29)	29	0.15
Kenyan (11)	11	0.06
Other Sub-Saharan African (16)	16	0.08
American (445)	445	2.25
Arab (205)	307	1.56
Arab (45)	69	0.35
Egyptian (15)	15	0.08
Lebanese (0)	54	0.27
Moroccan (11)	35	0.18
Other Arab (134)	134	0.68
Armenian (15)	15	0.08
Austrian (25)	116	0.59
Belgian (0)	9	0.05
Brazilian (0)	11	0.06
British (34)	83	0.42
Canadian (8)	8	0.04
Croatian (0)	28	0.14
Czech (13)	125	0.63
Czechoslovakian (14)	41	0.21
Dutch (37)	179	0.91
Eastern European (0)	18	0.09
English (330)	1,215	6.16
European (138)	138	0.70
Finnish (0)	10	0.05
French, ex. Basque (40)	443	2.24
French Canadian (23)	69	0.35
German (1,005)	3,560	18.04
Greek (90)	146	0.74
Hungarian (18)	198	1.00
Iranian (82)	82	0.42
Irish (1,463)	4,077	20.66
Italian (1,584)	3,435	17.41
Latvian (0)	12	0.06
Lithuanian (23)	56	0.28
Norwegian (0)	40	0.20
Pennsylvania German (35)	69	0.35
Polish (508)	1,504	7.62
Portuguese (0)	29	0.15
Romanian (53)	74	0.37
Russian (299)	572	2.90
Scotch-Irish (169)	282	1.43
Scottish (11)	209	1.06
Serbian (8)	34	0.17
Slovak (161)	267	1.35
Slovene (0)	12	0.06
Swedish (56)	165	0.84
Swiss (21)	31	0.16
Turkish (30)	30	0.15
Ukrainian (131)	322	1.63
Welsh (8)	242	1.23
West Indian, ex. Hispanic (120)	183	0.93
Bermudan (0)	13	0.07
Jamaican (120)	170	0.86
Yugoslavian (0)	10	0.05

Hispanic Origin	Population	%
Hispanic or Latino (of any race)	842	4.22
Central American, ex. Mexican	41	0.21
Costa Rican	8	0.04
Guatemalan	7	0.04
Honduran	4	0.02
Nicaraguan	2	0.01
Panamanian	4	0.02
Salvadoran	16	0.08
Cuban	27	0.14
Dominican Republic	20	0.10
Mexican	388	1.95
Puerto Rican	192	0.96
South American	107	0.54
Argentinean	10	0.05
Chilean	5	0.03
Colombian	30	0.15
Ecuadorian	9	0.05
Peruvian	38	0.19
Uruguayan	7	0.04
Venezuelan	8	0.04
Other Hispanic or Latino	67	0.34

Race*	Population	%
African-American/Black (1,129)	1,288	6.46
Not Hispanic (1,094)	1,240	6.22
Hispanic (35)	48	0.24
American Indian/Alaska Native (53)	128	0.64
Not Hispanic (38)	106	0.53
Hispanic (15)	22	0.11
Apache (1)	1	0.01
Blackfeet (2)	4	0.02
Cherokee (9)	16	0.08
Choctaw (0)	3	0.02
Delaware (0)	2	0.01
Hopi (0)	1	0.01
Iroquois (1)	5	0.03
Mexican American Ind. (6)	6	0.03
Pueblo (0)	1	0.01
Sioux (0)	1	0.01
South American Ind. (1)	2	0.01
Asian (3,718)	3,952	19.82
Not Hispanic (3,694)	3,919	19.66
Hispanic (24)	33	0.17
Bangladeshi (17)	18	0.09
Burmese (6)	8	0.04
Cambodian (75)	92	0.46
Chinese, ex. Taiwanese (523)	582	2.92
Filipino (191)	222	1.11
Indian (2,136)	2,198	11.03
Indonesian (10)	11	0.06
Japanese (46)	63	0.32
Korean (206)	225	1.13
Laotian (34)	36	0.18
Malaysian (4)	12	0.06
Nepalese (10)	19	0.10
Pakistani (103)	111	0.56
Sri Lankan (4)	4	0.02
Taiwanese (34)	35	0.18
Thai (18)	18	0.09
Vietnamese (223)	248	1.24
Hawaii Native/Pacific Islander (3)	16	0.08
Not Hispanic (3)	16	0.08
Native Hawaiian (0)	2	0.01
Samoan (3)	6	0.03
White (14,320)	14,641	73.44
Not Hispanic (13,843)	14,129	70.87
Hispanic (477)	512	2.57

Kingston

Place Type: Borough
County: Luzerne
Population: 13,182†

Ancestry‡	Population	%
African, Sub-Saharan (0)	16	0.12
African (0)	16	0.12
American (626)	626	4.73
Arab (48)	208	1.57
Arab (0)	21	0.16
Jordanian (39)	39	0.29
Lebanese (9)	9	0.07
Syrian (0)	139	1.05
Australian (0)	8	0.06
Austrian (39)	91	0.69
Brazilian (8)	8	0.06
British (0)	24	0.18
Canadian (0)	52	0.39
Croatian (11)	18	0.14
Czech (0)	44	0.33
Czechoslovakian (11)	24	0.18
Danish (9)	9	0.07
Dutch (9)	327	2.47
Eastern European (31)	41	0.31
English (330)	1,106	8.35
European (118)	134	1.01
French, ex. Basque (31)	183	1.38
French Canadian (18)	18	0.14
German (474)	1,907	14.40
Greek (0)	24	0.18
Guyanese (0)	14	0.11
Hungarian (51)	69	0.52
Irish (901)	3,080	23.26
Israeli (12)	12	0.09
Italian (394)	1,396	10.54
Lithuanian (256)	625	4.72
Norwegian (13)	52	0.39
Pennsylvania German (66)	92	0.69
Polish (1,212)	2,610	19.71
Russian (128)	579	4.37

*Notes: † The Census 2010 population figure is used to calculate the percentages in the Hispanic Origin and Race categories. Ancestry percentages are based on the 2006-2010 American Community Survey population (not shown); ‡ Numbers in parentheses indicate the number of people reporting a single ancestry; * Numbers in parentheses indicate the number of persons reporting this race alone, not in combination with any other race; Please refer to the Explanation of Data for more information.*

Ancestry	Population	%
Scandinavian (0)	54	0.41
Scotch-Irish (40)	79	0.60
Scottish (120)	272	2.05
Slavic (0)	30	0.23
Slovak (211)	723	5.46
Swedish (30)	224	1.69
Swiss (0)	32	0.24
Turkish (0)	54	0.41
Ukrainian (68)	198	1.50
Welsh (234)	841	6.35
West Indian, ex. Hispanic (0)	18	0.14
Jamaican (0)	18	0.14

Hispanic Origin	Population	%
Hispanic or Latino (of any race)	422	3.20
Central American, ex. Mexican	30	0.23
Costa Rican	7	0.05
Guatemalan	6	0.05
Honduran	3	0.02
Nicaraguan	5	0.04
Panamanian	5	0.04
Salvadoran	4	0.03
Cuban	20	0.15
Dominican Republic	28	0.21
Mexican	81	0.61
Puerto Rican	198	1.50
South American	24	0.18
Argentinean	1	0.01
Colombian	12	0.09
Ecuadorian	1	0.01
Peruvian	2	0.02
Venezuelan	4	0.03
Other South American	4	0.03
Other Hispanic or Latino	41	0.31

Race*	Population	%
African-American/Black (424)	550	4.17
Not Hispanic (393)	506	3.84
Hispanic (31)	44	0.33
American Indian/Alaska Native (13)	75	0.57
Not Hispanic (7)	57	0.43
Hispanic (6)	18	0.14
Canadian/French Am. Ind. (0)	1	0.01
Cherokee (1)	18	0.14
Chippewa (1)	1	0.01
Delaware (0)	1	0.01
Iroquois (0)	3	0.02
Kiowa (0)	3	0.02
Mexican American Ind. (1)	2	0.02
Seminole (0)	4	0.03
South American Ind. (0)	3	0.02
Spanish American Ind. (1)	1	0.01
Yaqui (1)	1	0.01
Asian (311)	370	2.81
Not Hispanic (305)	363	2.75
Hispanic (6)	7	0.05
Cambodian (1)	3	0.02
Chinese, ex. Taiwanese (104)	115	0.87
Filipino (13)	30	0.23
Indian (110)	114	0.86
Indonesian (4)	4	0.03
Japanese (9)	21	0.16
Korean (28)	34	0.26
Pakistani (8)	10	0.08
Taiwanese (11)	11	0.08
Thai (5)	7	0.05
Vietnamese (14)	17	0.13
Hawaii Native/Pacific Islander (2)	8	0.06
Not Hispanic (2)	5	0.04
Hispanic (0)	3	0.02
Native Hawaiian (2)	6	0.05
White (12,104)	12,311	93.39
Not Hispanic (11,856)	12,035	91.30
Hispanic (248)	276	2.09

Kulpsville

Place Type: CDP
County: Montgomery
Population: 8,194†

Ancestry‡	Population	%
African, Sub-Saharan (56)	56	0.72
African (17)	17	0.22
Ethiopian (39)	39	0.50
American (477)	477	6.13
Austrian (0)	14	0.18
British (55)	80	1.03
Czech (9)	61	0.78
Czechoslovakian (0)	15	0.19
Dutch (0)	178	2.29
English (253)	924	11.88
European (30)	30	0.39
Finnish (10)	10	0.13
French, ex. Basque (6)	21	0.27
French Canadian (9)	40	0.51
German (638)	1,906	24.50
Greek (0)	15	0.19
Hungarian (86)	168	2.16
Irish (637)	1,988	25.55
Israeli (10)	10	0.13
Italian (542)	1,474	18.95
Lithuanian (12)	36	0.46
Norwegian (24)	72	0.93
Pennsylvania German (76)	76	0.98
Polish (173)	450	5.78
Romanian (49)	49	0.63
Russian (33)	84	1.08
Scotch-Irish (36)	177	2.28
Scottish (72)	189	2.43
Slavic (12)	88	1.13
Slovak (0)	73	0.94
Swedish (14)	14	0.18
Swiss (27)	27	0.35
Ukrainian (13)	44	0.57
Welsh (15)	82	1.05
West Indian, ex. Hispanic (0)	44	0.57
Haitian (0)	26	0.33
Jamaican (0)	18	0.23
Yugoslavian (13)	13	0.17

Hispanic Origin	Population	%
Hispanic or Latino (of any race)	192	2.34
Central American, ex. Mexican	7	0.09
Costa Rican	2	0.02
Panamanian	4	0.05
Other Central American	1	0.01
Cuban	9	0.11
Dominican Republic	6	0.07
Mexican	35	0.43
Puerto Rican	78	0.95
South American	45	0.55
Argentinean	4	0.05
Colombian	26	0.32
Ecuadorian	5	0.06
Paraguayan	1	0.01
Peruvian	6	0.07
Venezuelan	3	0.04
Other Hispanic or Latino	12	0.15

Race*	Population	%
African-American/Black (381)	458	5.59
Not Hispanic (376)	440	5.37
Hispanic (5)	18	0.22
American Indian/Alaska Native (9)	50	0.61
Not Hispanic (7)	42	0.51
Hispanic (2)	8	0.10
Blackfeet (0)	3	0.04
Cherokee (0)	6	0.07
Choctaw (0)	2	0.02
Iroquois (0)	1	0.01
Lumbee (1)	1	0.01
Mexican American Ind. (2)	2	0.02
Navajo (0)	1	0.01
Sioux (0)	1	0.01
Asian (658)	719	8.77
Not Hispanic (657)	718	8.76
Hispanic (1)	1	0.01
Bangladeshi (17)	23	0.28
Cambodian (1)	5	0.06
Chinese, ex. Taiwanese (125)	141	1.72
Filipino (17)	23	0.28
Indian (217)	237	2.89
Indonesian (1)	1	0.01
Japanese (24)	37	0.45
Korean (161)	162	1.98
Nepalese (4)	4	0.05
Pakistani (10)	10	0.12
Thai (1)	2	0.02
Vietnamese (52)	56	0.68
Hawaii Native/Pacific Islander (0)	3	0.04
Not Hispanic (0)	3	0.04
Guamanian/Chamorro (0)	3	0.04
White (6,960)	7,073	86.32
Not Hispanic (6,821)	6,924	84.50
Hispanic (139)	149	1.82

Lancaster

Place Type: City
County: Lancaster
Population: 59,322†

Ancestry‡	Population	%
African, Sub-Saharan (764)	820	1.39
African (618)	659	1.12
Cape Verdean (14)	14	0.02
Ethiopian (82)	87	0.15
Kenyan (0)	10	0.02
South African (27)	27	0.05
Sudanese (23)	23	0.04
Alsatian (4)	4	0.01
American (1,406)	1,406	2.39
Arab (0)	30	0.05
Lebanese (0)	15	0.03
Syrian (0)	15	0.03
Armenian (52)	52	0.09
Austrian (0)	93	0.16
Belgian (0)	16	0.03
Brazilian (5)	17	0.03
British (34)	188	0.32
Canadian (0)	34	0.06
Celtic (18)	18	0.03
Croatian (0)	8	0.01
Czech (30)	72	0.12
Danish (8)	73	0.12
Dutch (55)	396	0.67
Eastern European (41)	41	0.07
English (1,035)	3,009	5.12
European (197)	197	0.33
Finnish (0)	56	0.10
French, ex. Basque (111)	704	1.20
French Canadian (18)	63	0.11
German (5,665)	11,795	20.05
Greek (81)	178	0.30
Hungarian (61)	221	0.38
Irish (1,084)	4,900	8.33
Israeli (0)	13	0.02
Italian (935)	2,451	4.17
Latvian (8)	8	0.01
Lithuanian (0)	68	0.12
Norwegian (76)	166	0.28
Pennsylvania German (75)	143	0.24
Polish (381)	1,142	1.94
Portuguese (0)	20	0.03
Romanian (33)	50	0.09
Russian (109)	381	0.65
Scandinavian (16)	38	0.06
Scotch-Irish (282)	842	1.43
Scottish (35)	452	0.77
Slavic (10)	10	0.02
Slovak (21)	54	0.09
Swedish (29)	237	0.40
Swiss (115)	714	1.21
Turkish (174)	174	0.30
Ukrainian (4)	76	0.13
Welsh (16)	328	0.56
West Indian, ex. Hispanic (289)	367	0.62
Barbadian (36)	36	0.06
Belizean (32)	32	0.05
British West Indian (10)	10	0.02

*Notes: † The Census 2010 population figure is used to calculate the percentages in the Hispanic Origin and Race categories. Ancestry percentages are based on the 2006-2010 American Community Survey population (not shown); ‡ Numbers in parentheses indicate the number of people reporting a single ancestry; * Numbers in parentheses indicate the number of persons reporting this race alone, not in combination with any other race; Please refer to the Explanation of Data for more information.*

Haitian (143)	187	0.32
Jamaican (55)	78	0.13
West Indian (13)	24	0.04
Yugoslavian (44)	70	0.12

Hispanic Origin	Population	%
Hispanic or Latino (of any race)	23,329	39.33
Central American, ex. Mexican	405	0.68
Costa Rican	20	0.03
Guatemalan	103	0.17
Honduran	94	0.16
Nicaraguan	15	0.03
Panamanian	25	0.04
Salvadoran	143	0.24
Other Central American	5	0.01
Cuban	994	1.68
Dominican Republic	1,905	3.21
Mexican	1,046	1.76
Puerto Rican	17,341	29.23
South American	571	0.96
Argentinean	34	0.06
Bolivian	1	<0.01
Chilean	14	0.02
Colombian	208	0.35
Ecuadorian	157	0.26
Paraguayan	5	0.01
Peruvian	108	0.18
Uruguayan	15	0.03
Venezuelan	26	0.04
Other South American	3	0.01
Other Hispanic or Latino	1,067	1.80

Race*	Population	%
African-American/Black (9,683)	11,899	20.06
Not Hispanic (7,869)	9,178	15.47
Hispanic (1,814)	2,721	4.59
American Indian/Alaska Native (433)	900	1.52
Not Hispanic (172)	445	0.75
Hispanic (261)	455	0.77
Alaska Athabascan *(Ala. Nat.)* (2)	2	<0.01
Aleut *(Alaska Native)* (1)	1	<0.01
Apache (1)	7	0.01
Blackfeet (5)	28	0.05
Canadian/French Am. Ind. (3)	4	0.01
Central American Ind. (18)	19	0.03
Cherokee (27)	112	0.19
Chippewa (3)	6	0.01
Choctaw (0)	3	0.01
Comanche (0)	3	0.01
Cree (2)	4	0.01
Creek (0)	4	0.01
Delaware (1)	5	0.01
Hopi (0)	2	<0.01
Inupiat *(Alaska Native)* (0)	2	<0.01
Iroquois (9)	25	0.04
Mexican American Ind. (6)	10	0.02
Navajo (1)	2	<0.01
Paiute (1)	1	<0.01
Pima (1)	1	<0.01
Potawatomi (1)	1	<0.01
Pueblo (0)	1	<0.01
Puget Sound Salish (1)	1	<0.01
Seminole (0)	4	0.01
Sioux (6)	22	0.04
South American Ind. (41)	77	0.13
Spanish American Ind. (8)	11	0.02
Yakama (1)	1	<0.01
Yaqui (2)	3	0.01
Asian (1,773)	2,087	3.52
Not Hispanic (1,729)	1,965	3.31
Hispanic (44)	122	0.21
Bangladeshi (3)	8	0.01
Bhutanese (177)	209	0.35
Burmese (128)	135	0.23
Cambodian (200)	230	0.39
Chinese, ex. Taiwanese (158)	208	0.35
Filipino (80)	129	0.22
Hmong (19)	19	0.03
Indian (172)	230	0.39
Indonesian (4)	8	0.01
Japanese (28)	50	0.08
Korean (68)	94	0.16
Laotian (10)	14	0.02
Malaysian (6)	8	0.01
Nepalese (40)	87	0.15
Pakistani (10)	12	0.02
Sri Lankan (5)	6	0.01
Taiwanese (1)	1	<0.01
Thai (10)	14	0.02
Vietnamese (531)	594	1.00
Hawaii Native/Pacific Islander (43)	191	0.32
Not Hispanic (17)	56	0.09
Hispanic (26)	135	0.23
Guamanian/Chamorro (12)	27	0.05
Native Hawaiian (10)	30	0.05
Samoan (5)	8	0.01
White (32,729)	35,384	59.65
Not Hispanic (24,501)	25,936	43.72
Hispanic (8,228)	9,448	15.93

Lancaster

Place Type: Township
County: Lancaster
Population: 16,149†

Ancestry‡	Population	%
African, Sub-Saharan (52)	52	0.33
African (44)	44	0.28
Ethiopian (8)	8	0.05
Albanian (35)	35	0.22
American (636)	636	4.03
Arab (11)	28	0.18
Lebanese (0)	17	0.11
Other Arab (11)	11	0.07
Austrian (19)	44	0.28
Belgian (23)	23	0.15
British (80)	141	0.89
Canadian (11)	44	0.28
Croatian (0)	19	0.12
Cypriot (13)	13	0.08
Czech (0)	29	0.18
Czechoslovakian (13)	31	0.20
Dutch (36)	212	1.34
English (470)	1,423	9.02
European (204)	218	1.38
French, ex. Basque (119)	404	2.56
French Canadian (34)	34	0.22
German (2,534)	4,850	30.74
Greek (185)	217	1.38
Hungarian (0)	19	0.12
Irish (534)	1,805	11.44
Italian (476)	1,440	9.13
Lithuanian (49)	61	0.39
Northern European (30)	30	0.19
Norwegian (12)	12	0.08
Pennsylvania German (47)	95	0.60
Polish (54)	301	1.91
Russian (71)	159	1.01
Scotch-Irish (169)	430	2.73
Scottish (27)	194	1.23
Slovak (30)	50	0.32
Slovene (0)	19	0.12
Swedish (26)	106	0.67
Swiss (61)	245	1.55
Turkish (24)	35	0.22
Ukrainian (37)	51	0.32
Welsh (28)	175	1.11
West Indian, ex. Hispanic (27)	41	0.26
British West Indian (27)	27	0.17
Haitian (0)	14	0.09

Hispanic Origin	Population	%
Hispanic or Latino (of any race)	3,117	19.30
Central American, ex. Mexican	63	0.39
Costa Rican	7	0.04
Guatemalan	11	0.07
Honduran	20	0.12
Nicaraguan	3	0.02
Panamanian	7	0.04
Salvadoran	15	0.09
Cuban	127	0.79
Dominican Republic	224	1.39
Mexican	155	0.96
Puerto Rican	2,279	14.11
South American	105	0.65
Argentinean	5	0.03
Bolivian	2	0.01
Chilean	3	0.02
Colombian	50	0.31
Ecuadorian	16	0.10
Peruvian	15	0.09
Uruguayan	3	0.02
Venezuelan	7	0.04
Other South American	4	0.02
Other Hispanic or Latino	164	1.02

Race*	Population	%
African-American/Black (1,564)	1,924	11.91
Not Hispanic (1,304)	1,547	9.58
Hispanic (260)	377	2.33
American Indian/Alaska Native (80)	151	0.94
Not Hispanic (25)	72	0.45
Hispanic (55)	79	0.49
Blackfeet (0)	2	0.01
Central American Ind. (0)	1	0.01
Cherokee (9)	21	0.13
Comanche (1)	1	0.01
Delaware (0)	1	0.01
Mexican American Ind. (1)	1	0.01
Navajo (1)	3	0.02
Sioux (1)	4	0.02
South American Ind. (12)	13	0.08
Asian (419)	488	3.02
Not Hispanic (405)	460	2.85
Hispanic (14)	28	0.17
Burmese (4)	4	0.02
Cambodian (47)	49	0.30
Chinese, ex. Taiwanese (58)	82	0.51
Filipino (39)	51	0.32
Indian (70)	83	0.51
Indonesian (1)	4	0.02
Japanese (6)	16	0.10
Korean (22)	24	0.15
Laotian (4)	8	0.05
Malaysian (0)	1	0.01
Nepalese (18)	18	0.11
Pakistani (3)	3	0.02
Sri Lankan (1)	1	0.01
Thai (3)	10	0.06
Vietnamese (116)	138	0.85
Hawaii Native/Pacific Islander (3)	10	0.06
Not Hispanic (3)	9	0.06
Hispanic (0)	1	0.01
Marshallese (1)	1	0.01
Native Hawaiian (0)	1	0.01
White (12,171)	12,585	77.93
Not Hispanic (10,964)	11,243	69.62
Hispanic (1,207)	1,342	8.31

Lansdale

Place Type: Borough
County: Montgomery
Population: 16,269†

Ancestry‡	Population	%
African, Sub-Saharan (79)	99	0.61
African (0)	20	0.12
Sudanese (79)	79	0.49
American (436)	436	2.69
Arab (324)	344	2.12
Egyptian (324)	324	2.00
Other Arab (0)	20	0.12
Austrian (0)	103	0.64
British (11)	11	0.07
Canadian (24)	30	0.19
Celtic (12)	12	0.07
Croatian (0)	12	0.07
Czech (2)	43	0.27

*Notes: † The Census 2010 population figure is used to calculate the percentages in the Hispanic Origin and Race categories. Ancestry percentages are based on the 2006-2010 American Community Survey population (not shown); ‡ Numbers in parentheses indicate the number of people reporting a single ancestry; * Numbers in parentheses indicate the number of persons reporting this race alone, not in combination with any other race; Please refer to the Explanation of Data for more information.*

Czechoslovakian (0)	16	0.10
Danish (0)	19	0.12
Dutch (89)	411	2.54
English (347)	1,519	9.37
European (110)	110	0.68
French, ex. Basque (17)	270	1.67
French Canadian (37)	51	0.31
German (1,125)	4,184	25.81
Greek (18)	45	0.28
Hungarian (75)	156	0.96
Irish (1,022)	3,431	21.16
Italian (770)	1,907	11.76
Latvian (12)	23	0.14
Lithuanian (9)	136	0.84
Norwegian (19)	65	0.40
Pennsylvania German (175)	224	1.38
Polish (533)	1,403	8.65
Portuguese (9)	63	0.39
Russian (67)	142	0.88
Scotch-Irish (118)	316	1.95
Scottish (56)	265	1.63
Slavic (11)	11	0.07
Slovak (14)	81	0.50
Swedish (23)	103	0.64
Swiss (2)	118	0.73
Turkish (0)	24	0.15
Ukrainian (44)	94	0.58
Welsh (9)	177	1.09
West Indian, ex. Hispanic (73)	103	0.64
Bahamian (11)	11	0.07
Barbadian (0)	8	0.05
British West Indian (0)	14	0.09
Haitian (0)	8	0.05
Jamaican (29)	29	0.18
West Indian (33)	33	0.20

Hispanic Origin	Population	%
Hispanic or Latino (of any race)	806	4.95
Central American, ex. Mexican	131	0.81
Costa Rican	5	0.03
Guatemalan	65	0.40
Honduran	26	0.16
Nicaraguan	7	0.04
Panamanian	1	0.01
Salvadoran	25	0.15
Other Central American	2	0.01
Cuban	26	0.16
Dominican Republic	19	0.12
Mexican	196	1.20
Puerto Rican	253	1.56
South American	111	0.68
Argentinean	4	0.02
Bolivian	1	0.01
Chilean	8	0.05
Colombian	27	0.17
Ecuadorian	49	0.30
Peruvian	12	0.07
Uruguayan	2	0.01
Venezuelan	8	0.05
Other Hispanic or Latino	70	0.43

Race*	Population	%
African-American/Black (953)	1,178	7.24
Not Hispanic (930)	1,121	6.89
Hispanic (23)	57	0.35
American Indian/Alaska Native (39)	147	0.90
Not Hispanic (31)	115	0.71
Hispanic (8)	32	0.20
Alaska Athabascan *(Ala. Nat.)* (2)	2	0.01
Apache (1)	2	0.01
Blackfeet (0)	4	0.02
Cherokee (2)	21	0.13
Comanche (0)	3	0.02
Delaware (0)	1	0.01
Iroquois (0)	1	0.01
Lumbee (2)	2	0.01
Mexican American Ind. (0)	2	0.01
Pueblo (0)	2	0.01
Seminole (1)	3	0.02
Sioux (0)	3	0.02
South American Ind. (0)	5	0.03
Spanish American Ind. (0)	1	0.01
Asian (2,158)	2,309	14.19
Not Hispanic (2,144)	2,276	13.99
Hispanic (14)	33	0.20
Bangladeshi (524)	564	3.47
Burmese (16)	16	0.10
Cambodian (100)	125	0.77
Chinese, ex. Taiwanese (127)	145	0.89
Filipino (46)	75	0.46
Indian (757)	833	5.12
Indonesian (4)	5	0.03
Japanese (9)	18	0.11
Korean (260)	270	1.66
Laotian (7)	7	0.04
Malaysian (1)	2	0.01
Pakistani (30)	30	0.18
Taiwanese (8)	11	0.07
Thai (11)	28	0.17
Vietnamese (165)	182	1.12
Hawaii Native/Pacific Islander (22)	28	0.17
Not Hispanic (18)	22	0.14
Hispanic (4)	6	0.04
Native Hawaiian (0)	1	0.01
Samoan (17)	19	0.12
White (12,348)	12,681	77.95
Not Hispanic (11,974)	12,236	75.21
Hispanic (374)	445	2.74

Lansdowne

Place Type: Borough
County: Delaware
Population: 10,620†

Ancestry‡	Population	%
African, Sub-Saharan (170)	217	2.04
African (106)	153	1.44
Ethiopian (13)	13	0.12
South African (51)	51	0.48
American (72)	72	0.68
Arab (30)	30	0.28
Egyptian (30)	30	0.28
Armenian (12)	19	0.18
Austrian (0)	31	0.29
Belgian (14)	14	0.13
British (79)	96	0.90
Czech (0)	36	0.34
Czechoslovakian (0)	15	0.14
Danish (0)	14	0.13
Dutch (77)	153	1.44
Eastern European (20)	20	0.19
English (149)	657	6.16
European (19)	19	0.18
French, ex. Basque (12)	112	1.05
French Canadian (0)	4	0.04
German (344)	1,408	13.21
Greek (32)	42	0.39
Hungarian (0)	29	0.27
Irish (1,001)	2,445	22.94
Italian (402)	1,007	9.45
Lithuanian (22)	48	0.45
Northern European (49)	49	0.46
Norwegian (0)	31	0.29
Pennsylvania German (24)	37	0.35
Polish (188)	648	6.08
Portuguese (0)	58	0.54
Russian (89)	166	1.56
Scotch-Irish (17)	65	0.61
Scottish (78)	477	4.48
Slovak (13)	13	0.12
Swedish (0)	33	0.31
Swiss (0)	39	0.37
Ukrainian (20)	39	0.37
Welsh (0)	77	0.72
West Indian, ex. Hispanic (556)	571	5.36
Bahamian (7)	7	0.07
Barbadian (35)	35	0.33
Haitian (387)	402	3.77
Jamaican (111)	111	1.04
West Indian (16)	16	0.15
Yugoslavian (0)	31	0.29

Hispanic Origin	Population	%
Hispanic or Latino (of any race)	353	3.32
Central American, ex. Mexican	21	0.20
Costa Rican	1	0.01
Guatemalan	4	0.04
Honduran	6	0.06
Nicaraguan	1	0.01
Panamanian	6	0.06
Salvadoran	3	0.03
Cuban	28	0.26
Dominican Republic	15	0.14
Mexican	56	0.53
Puerto Rican	128	1.21
South American	55	0.52
Argentinean	3	0.03
Colombian	6	0.06
Ecuadorian	28	0.26
Peruvian	9	0.08
Uruguayan	5	0.05
Venezuelan	4	0.04
Other Hispanic or Latino	50	0.47

Race*	Population	%
African-American/Black (4,733)	5,049	47.54
Not Hispanic (4,670)	4,939	46.51
Hispanic (63)	110	1.04
American Indian/Alaska Native (20)	138	1.30
Not Hispanic (19)	118	1.11
Hispanic (1)	20	0.19
Aleut *(Alaska Native)* (1)	1	0.01
Blackfeet (0)	8	0.08
Cherokee (2)	44	0.41
Crow (0)	1	0.01
Delaware (0)	6	0.06
Houma (0)	2	0.02
Iroquois (0)	5	0.05
Kiowa (0)	6	0.06
Mexican American Ind. (2)	4	0.04
Seminole (0)	2	0.02
Sioux (2)	2	0.02
South American Ind. (0)	4	0.04
Asian (378)	465	4.38
Not Hispanic (375)	454	4.27
Hispanic (3)	11	0.10
Bangladeshi (17)	17	0.16
Cambodian (35)	43	0.40
Chinese, ex. Taiwanese (49)	66	0.62
Filipino (40)	60	0.56
Hmong (1)	3	0.03
Indian (68)	91	0.86
Indonesian (2)	2	0.02
Japanese (6)	10	0.09
Korean (42)	57	0.54
Laotian (3)	5	0.05
Malaysian (0)	1	0.01
Pakistani (48)	55	0.52
Sri Lankan (2)	2	0.02
Thai (4)	5	0.05
Vietnamese (35)	41	0.39
Hawaii Native/Pacific Islander (1)	8	0.08
Not Hispanic (1)	8	0.08
Guamanian/Chamorro (1)	4	0.04
Native Hawaiian (0)	2	0.02
White (5,005)	5,279	49.71
Not Hispanic (4,848)	5,078	47.82
Hispanic (157)	201	1.89

Latrobe

Place Type: City
County: Westmoreland
Population: 8,338†

Ancestry‡	Population	%
American (445)	445	5.25
Arab (16)	16	0.19
Egyptian (16)	16	0.19

*Notes: † The Census 2010 population figure is used to calculate the percentages in the Hispanic Origin and Race categories. Ancestry percentages are based on the 2006-2010 American Community Survey population (not shown); ‡ Numbers in parentheses indicate the number of people reporting a single ancestry; * Numbers in parentheses indicate the number of persons reporting this race alone, not in combination with any other race; Please refer to the Explanation of Data for more information.*

Austrian (0)	31	0.37
British (55)	55	0.65
Croatian (8)	62	0.73
Czech (2)	84	0.99
Czechoslovakian (11)	39	0.46
Dutch (0)	339	4.00
Eastern European (32)	32	0.38
English (148)	797	9.41
European (19)	19	0.22
French, ex. Basque (20)	201	2.37
French Canadian (0)	7	0.08
German (742)	2,538	29.95
Greek (0)	10	0.12
Hungarian (26)	166	1.96
Irish (354)	1,537	18.14
Italian (809)	1,902	22.45
Lithuanian (13)	13	0.15
Norwegian (5)	20	0.24
Pennsylvania German (0)	7	0.08
Polish (307)	967	11.41
Romanian (0)	8	0.09
Russian (9)	72	0.85
Scandinavian (23)	23	0.27
Scotch-Irish (44)	313	3.69
Scottish (33)	226	2.67
Serbian (11)	20	0.24
Slavic (21)	79	0.93
Slovak (255)	687	8.11
Slovene (8)	26	0.31
Swedish (7)	98	1.16
Swiss (0)	12	0.14
Ukrainian (52)	113	1.33
Welsh (48)	164	1.94
Yugoslavian (23)	55	0.65

Hispanic Origin	Population	%
Hispanic or Latino (of any race)	59	0.71
Central American, ex. Mexican	1	0.01
Salvadoran	1	0.01
Cuban	3	0.04
Dominican Republic	3	0.04
Mexican	20	0.24
Puerto Rican	25	0.30
South American	4	0.05
Colombian	2	0.02
Peruvian	2	0.02
Other Hispanic or Latino	3	0.04

Race*	Population	%
African-American/Black (63)	107	1.28
Not Hispanic (60)	99	1.19
Hispanic (3)	8	0.10
American Indian/Alaska Native (11)	26	0.31
Not Hispanic (11)	25	0.30
Hispanic (0)	1	0.01
Cherokee (1)	3	0.04
Delaware (1)	1	0.01
Iroquois (0)	4	0.05
Osage (0)	2	0.02
Asian (50)	63	0.76
Not Hispanic (50)	62	0.74
Hispanic (0)	1	0.01
Bangladeshi (4)	4	0.05
Chinese, ex. Taiwanese (8)	11	0.13
Filipino (7)	17	0.20
Indian (7)	7	0.08
Japanese (1)	1	0.01
Korean (7)	10	0.12
Pakistani (2)	2	0.02
Thai (1)	1	0.01
Vietnamese (11)	11	0.13
Hawaii Native/Pacific Islander (0)	5	0.06
Not Hispanic (0)	5	0.06
Native Hawaiian (0)	4	0.05
White (8,126)	8,196	98.30
Not Hispanic (8,081)	8,148	97.72
Hispanic (45)	48	0.58

Lawrence

Place Type: Township
County: Clearfield
Population: 7,681†

Ancestry‡	Population	%
American (999)	999	12.94
Austrian (9)	62	0.80
British (9)	21	0.27
Canadian (0)	21	0.27
Czech (29)	29	0.38
Czechoslovakian (0)	13	0.17
Danish (0)	10	0.13
Dutch (34)	350	4.53
English (275)	911	11.80
European (41)	52	0.67
French, ex. Basque (120)	425	5.51
French Canadian (0)	5	0.06
German (723)	2,512	32.55
Greek (10)	10	0.13
Hungarian (12)	38	0.49
Irish (291)	1,056	13.68
Italian (300)	646	8.37
Norwegian (10)	10	0.13
Pennsylvania German (25)	37	0.48
Polish (108)	275	3.56
Russian (0)	9	0.12
Scotch-Irish (104)	189	2.45
Scottish (37)	203	2.63
Serbian (11)	11	0.14
Slovak (93)	178	2.31
Slovene (9)	28	0.36
Swedish (37)	181	2.35
Swiss (0)	106	1.37
Ukrainian (19)	35	0.45
Welsh (29)	197	2.55

Hispanic Origin	Population	%
Hispanic or Latino (of any race)	35	0.46
Central American, ex. Mexican	2	0.03
Guatemalan	2	0.03
Mexican	9	0.12
Puerto Rican	14	0.18
South American	1	0.01
Peruvian	1	0.01
Other Hispanic or Latino	9	0.12

Race*	Population	%
African-American/Black (45)	58	0.76
Not Hispanic (45)	57	0.74
Hispanic (0)	1	0.01
American Indian/Alaska Native (6)	18	0.23
Not Hispanic (5)	17	0.22
Hispanic (1)	1	0.01
Blackfeet (1)	1	0.01
Cherokee (1)	6	0.08
Choctaw (0)	1	0.01
Iroquois (0)	3	0.04
Asian (35)	51	0.66
Not Hispanic (35)	51	0.66
Chinese, ex. Taiwanese (7)	7	0.09
Filipino (5)	8	0.10
Indian (19)	19	0.25
Korean (3)	11	0.14
Thai (0)	3	0.04
Vietnamese (1)	1	0.01
Hawaii Native/Pacific Islander (4)	4	0.05
Not Hispanic (4)	4	0.05
White (7,534)	7,578	98.66
Not Hispanic (7,512)	7,551	98.31
Hispanic (22)	27	0.35

Lebanon

Place Type: City
County: Lebanon
Population: 25,477†

Ancestry‡	Population	%
African, Sub-Saharan (103)	188	0.74
African (17)	102	0.40
Kenyan (86)	86	0.34
American (955)	955	3.76
Arab (11)	37	0.15
Egyptian (11)	24	0.09
Syrian (0)	13	0.05
Australian (13)	13	0.05
Austrian (14)	55	0.22
British (18)	30	0.12
Bulgarian (13)	38	0.15
Canadian (0)	32	0.13
Czech (0)	17	0.07
Czechoslovakian (10)	23	0.09
Dutch (110)	399	1.57
Eastern European (14)	14	0.06
English (221)	933	3.67
European (87)	87	0.34
French, ex. Basque (34)	330	1.30
German (4,033)	8,250	32.46
German Russian (21)	21	0.08
Greek (0)	84	0.33
Hungarian (29)	316	1.24
Irish (610)	2,983	11.74
Italian (390)	1,473	5.80
Lithuanian (12)	32	0.13
Norwegian (26)	73	0.29
Pennsylvania German (634)	1,014	3.99
Polish (88)	496	1.95
Portuguese (0)	47	0.18
Russian (0)	42	0.17
Scotch-Irish (117)	221	0.87
Scottish (15)	156	0.61
Serbian (11)	11	0.04
Slavic (13)	13	0.05
Slovak (82)	448	1.76
Swedish (0)	51	0.20
Swiss (24)	115	0.45
Ukrainian (0)	7	0.03
Welsh (52)	210	0.83
West Indian, ex. Hispanic (0)	65	0.26
Jamaican (0)	6	0.02
Trinidadian/Tobagonian (0)	59	0.23
Yugoslavian (37)	60	0.24

Hispanic Origin	Population	%
Hispanic or Latino (of any race)	8,177	32.10
Central American, ex. Mexican	161	0.63
Costa Rican	1	<0.01
Guatemalan	16	0.06
Honduran	37	0.15
Nicaraguan	25	0.10
Panamanian	14	0.05
Salvadoran	65	0.26
Other Central American	3	0.01
Cuban	152	0.60
Dominican Republic	778	3.05
Mexican	563	2.21
Puerto Rican	6,081	23.87
South American	142	0.56
Argentinean	7	0.03
Chilean	19	0.07
Colombian	48	0.19
Ecuadorian	20	0.08
Peruvian	38	0.15
Uruguayan	2	0.01
Venezuelan	8	0.03
Other Hispanic or Latino	300	1.18

Race*	Population	%
African-American/Black (1,506)	1,926	7.56
Not Hispanic (956)	1,172	4.60
Hispanic (550)	754	2.96
American Indian/Alaska Native (123)	267	1.05
Not Hispanic (43)	125	0.49
Hispanic (80)	142	0.56
Alaska Athabascan *(Ala. Nat.)* (1)	1	<0.01
Apache (0)	1	<0.01
Blackfeet (4)	6	0.02

*Notes: † The Census 2010 population figure is used to calculate the percentages in the Hispanic Origin and Race categories. Ancestry percentages are based on the 2006-2010 American Community Survey population (not shown); ‡ Numbers in parentheses indicate the number of people reporting a single ancestry; * Numbers in parentheses indicate the number of persons reporting this race alone, not in combination with any other race; Please refer to the Explanation of Data for more information.*

Central American Ind. (0)	1	<0.01
Cherokee (3)	24	0.09
Cheyenne (3)	3	0.01
Chippewa (4)	4	0.02
Choctaw (0)	1	<0.01
Cree (1)	3	0.01
Creek (5)	5	0.02
Delaware (3)	8	0.03
Iroquois (2)	2	0.01
Kiowa (2)	2	0.01
Mexican American Ind. (2)	5	0.02
Navajo (1)	2	0.01
Pueblo (0)	1	<0.01
Sioux (2)	2	0.01
South American Ind. (14)	25	0.10
Yaqui (1)	1	<0.01
Asian (286)	345	1.35
Not Hispanic (268)	304	1.19
Hispanic (18)	41	0.16
Bangladeshi (4)	4	0.02
Cambodian (56)	65	0.26
Chinese, ex. Taiwanese (59)	63	0.25
Filipino (32)	42	0.16
Indian (39)	50	0.20
Indonesian (1)	1	<0.01
Japanese (5)	11	0.04
Korean (10)	16	0.06
Laotian (3)	3	0.01
Pakistani (4)	4	0.02
Taiwanese (2)	2	0.01
Thai (2)	4	0.02
Vietnamese (50)	55	0.22
Hawaii Native/Pacific Islander (12)	47	0.18
Not Hispanic (7)	29	0.11
Hispanic (5)	18	0.07
Guamanian/Chamorro (0)	5	0.02
Native Hawaiian (5)	14	0.05
White (18,877)	19,544	76.71
Not Hispanic (15,669)	15,965	62.66
Hispanic (3,208)	3,579	14.05

Lehigh

Place Type: Township
County: Northampton
Population: 10,526†

Ancestry‡	Population	%
African, Sub-Saharan (40)	40	0.38
African (7)	7	0.07
South African (33)	33	0.32
Albanian (13)	13	0.12
American (815)	815	7.78
Arab (9)	36	0.34
Arab (9)	9	0.09
Syrian (0)	27	0.26
Austrian (54)	286	2.73
Belgian (12)	12	0.11
British (0)	10	0.10
Canadian (12)	12	0.11
Czech (17)	40	0.38
Czechoslovakian (42)	98	0.94
Dutch (280)	719	6.87
Eastern European (14)	14	0.13
English (25)	622	5.94
European (21)	21	0.20
French, ex. Basque (0)	11	0.11
French Canadian (0)	20	0.19
German (2,017)	4,035	38.53
Greek (0)	11	0.11
Hungarian (155)	475	4.54
Irish (154)	1,103	10.53
Italian (390)	917	8.76
Lithuanian (23)	57	0.54
Pennsylvania German (1,132)	1,634	15.60
Polish (167)	634	6.05
Portuguese (29)	43	0.41
Romanian (0)	7	0.07
Russian (23)	111	1.06
Scotch-Irish (8)	54	0.52
Scottish (11)	100	0.95
Slavic (0)	20	0.19
Slovak (78)	224	2.14
Swedish (0)	13	0.12
Swiss (0)	72	0.69
Ukrainian (63)	304	2.90
Welsh (57)	258	2.46

Hispanic Origin	Population	%
Hispanic or Latino (of any race)	166	1.58
Central American, ex. Mexican	1	0.01
Guatemalan	1	0.01
Cuban	7	0.07
Dominican Republic	14	0.13
Mexican	36	0.34
Puerto Rican	80	0.76
South American	10	0.10
Argentinean	2	0.02
Colombian	5	0.05
Peruvian	2	0.02
Venezuelan	1	0.01
Other Hispanic or Latino	18	0.17

Race*	Population	%
African-American/Black (54)	83	0.79
Not Hispanic (48)	74	0.70
Hispanic (6)	9	0.09
American Indian/Alaska Native (11)	34	0.32
Not Hispanic (6)	27	0.26
Hispanic (5)	7	0.07
Aleut *(Alaska Native)* (0)	2	0.02
Cherokee (1)	2	0.02
Delaware (2)	7	0.07
Iroquois (0)	1	0.01
Mexican American Ind. (1)	1	0.01
Tlingit-Haida *(Alaska Native)* (0)	2	0.02
Asian (50)	60	0.57
Not Hispanic (49)	58	0.55
Hispanic (1)	2	0.02
Cambodian (1)	6	0.06
Chinese, ex. Taiwanese (7)	11	0.10
Filipino (2)	5	0.05
Indian (13)	13	0.12
Japanese (1)	1	0.01
Korean (6)	6	0.06
Pakistani (8)	8	0.08
Thai (0)	2	0.02
Vietnamese (9)	9	0.09
Hawaii Native/Pacific Islander (0)	2	0.02
Not Hispanic (0)	2	0.02
Native Hawaiian (0)	2	0.02
White (10,313)	10,381	98.62
Not Hispanic (10,201)	10,254	97.42
Hispanic (112)	127	1.21

Lehman

Place Type: Township
County: Pike
Population: 10,663†

Ancestry‡	Population	%
African, Sub-Saharan (263)	263	2.53
African (263)	263	2.53
American (388)	388	3.73
Austrian (0)	19	0.18
Brazilian (183)	183	1.76
British (7)	28	0.27
Czech (0)	12	0.12
Czechoslovakian (15)	15	0.14
Danish (0)	20	0.19
Dutch (106)	308	2.96
English (129)	454	4.36
European (47)	47	0.45
French, ex. Basque (41)	250	2.40
German (418)	1,486	14.29
Greek (72)	179	1.72
Guyanese (26)	26	0.25
Hungarian (98)	176	1.69
Irish (363)	1,419	13.64
Italian (1,019)	1,940	18.65
Lithuanian (50)	84	0.81
Norwegian (9)	44	0.42
Polish (87)	358	3.44
Portuguese (44)	93	0.89
Romanian (79)	79	0.76
Russian (18)	93	0.89
Scotch-Irish (19)	111	1.07
Scottish (0)	60	0.58
Slovak (11)	11	0.11
Swedish (20)	49	0.47
Swiss (18)	18	0.17
Ukrainian (33)	78	0.75
Welsh (22)	41	0.39
West Indian, ex. Hispanic (157)	252	2.42
Barbadian (0)	12	0.12
British West Indian (9)	9	0.09
Haitian (26)	75	0.72
Jamaican (110)	116	1.12
Trinidadian/Tobagonian (12)	22	0.21
West Indian (0)	18	0.17

Hispanic Origin	Population	%
Hispanic or Latino (of any race)	2,343	21.97
Central American, ex. Mexican	121	1.13
Costa Rican	5	0.05
Guatemalan	25	0.23
Honduran	28	0.26
Nicaraguan	8	0.08
Panamanian	37	0.35
Salvadoran	14	0.13
Other Central American	4	0.04
Cuban	110	1.03
Dominican Republic	185	1.73
Mexican	49	0.46
Puerto Rican	1,329	12.46
South American	296	2.78
Argentinean	19	0.18
Bolivian	5	0.05
Chilean	13	0.12
Colombian	92	0.86
Ecuadorian	101	0.95
Peruvian	38	0.36
Uruguayan	10	0.09
Venezuelan	12	0.11
Other South American	6	0.06
Other Hispanic or Latino	253	2.37

Race*	Population	%
African-American/Black (2,209)	2,458	23.05
Not Hispanic (2,010)	2,150	20.16
Hispanic (199)	308	2.89
American Indian/Alaska Native (54)	157	1.47
Not Hispanic (34)	94	0.88
Hispanic (20)	63	0.59
Apache (0)	1	0.01
Blackfeet (0)	6	0.06
Cherokee (12)	39	0.37
Chippewa (2)	2	0.02
Creek (0)	1	0.01
Delaware (0)	1	0.01
Iroquois (1)	8	0.08
Mexican American Ind. (1)	1	0.01
Seminole (0)	1	0.01
Sioux (0)	2	0.02
South American Ind. (6)	34	0.32
Asian (219)	283	2.65
Not Hispanic (213)	263	2.47
Hispanic (6)	20	0.19
Burmese (6)	6	0.06
Cambodian (22)	22	0.21
Chinese, ex. Taiwanese (23)	36	0.34
Filipino (79)	96	0.90
Indian (40)	61	0.57
Japanese (5)	9	0.08
Korean (20)	29	0.27
Sri Lankan (5)	5	0.05
Thai (4)	6	0.06
Vietnamese (2)	2	0.02
Hawaii Native/Pacific Islander (2)	2	0.02

*Notes: † The Census 2010 population figure is used to calculate the percentages in the Hispanic Origin and Race categories. Ancestry percentages are based on the 2006-2010 American Community Survey population (not shown); ‡ Numbers in parentheses indicate the number of people reporting a single ancestry; * Numbers in parentheses indicate the number of persons reporting this race alone, not in combination with any other race; Please refer to the Explanation of Data for more information.*

Hispanic (2)	2	0.02
White (7,056)	7,381	69.22
Not Hispanic (5,812)	5,995	56.22
Hispanic (1,244)	1,386	13.00

Levittown

Place Type: CDP
County: Bucks
Population: 52,983†

Ancestry‡	Population	%
African, Sub-Saharan (254)	292	0.56
African (213)	244	0.47
Ghanaian (6)	13	0.03
Liberian (35)	35	0.07
Alsatian (12)	12	0.02
American (1,650)	1,650	3.17
Arab (46)	68	0.13
Egyptian (21)	21	0.04
Lebanese (25)	25	0.05
Syrian (0)	22	0.04
Armenian (30)	43	0.08
Austrian (34)	92	0.18
Basque (10)	10	0.02
Belgian (0)	99	0.19
Brazilian (0)	4	0.01
British (70)	87	0.17
Bulgarian (0)	13	0.03
Canadian (39)	86	0.17
Czech (25)	152	0.29
Czechoslovakian (55)	105	0.20
Danish (17)	60	0.12
Dutch (157)	828	1.59
Eastern European (39)	46	0.09
English (1,401)	5,585	10.74
European (190)	225	0.43
Finnish (0)	48	0.09
French, ex. Basque (76)	1,085	2.09
French Canadian (52)	344	0.66
German (5,088)	15,853	30.49
Greek (100)	302	0.58
Guyanese (70)	70	0.13
Hungarian (154)	498	0.96
Irish (6,062)	17,768	34.18
Italian (2,596)	7,926	15.25
Latvian (12)	12	0.02
Lithuanian (136)	469	0.90
Macedonian (0)	13	0.03
Maltese (0)	9	0.02
Northern European (30)	30	0.06
Norwegian (31)	137	0.26
Pennsylvania German (68)	182	0.35
Polish (1,692)	5,707	10.98
Portuguese (0)	32	0.06
Romanian (37)	129	0.25
Russian (208)	600	1.15
Scandinavian (0)	55	0.11
Scotch-Irish (408)	1,218	2.34
Scottish (321)	822	1.58
Serbian (0)	26	0.05
Slavic (28)	103	0.20
Slovak (283)	621	1.19
Swedish (37)	334	0.64
Swiss (0)	43	0.08
Turkish (175)	209	0.40
Ukrainian (361)	752	1.45
Welsh (138)	825	1.59
West Indian, ex. Hispanic (123)	130	0.25
Haitian (96)	103	0.20
Jamaican (19)	19	0.04
Trinidadian/Tobagonian (8)	8	0.02
Yugoslavian (0)	40	0.08

Hispanic Origin	Population	%
Hispanic or Latino (of any race)	2,685	5.07
Central American, ex. Mexican	220	0.42
Costa Rican	70	0.13
Guatemalan	82	0.15
Honduran	24	0.05
Nicaraguan	1	<0.01
Panamanian	7	0.01
Salvadoran	36	0.07
Cuban	84	0.16
Dominican Republic	88	0.17
Mexican	589	1.11
Puerto Rican	1,293	2.44
South American	198	0.37
Argentinean	18	0.03
Bolivian	2	<0.01
Chilean	12	0.02
Colombian	86	0.16
Ecuadorian	30	0.06
Peruvian	22	0.04
Uruguayan	5	0.01
Venezuelan	18	0.03
Other South American	5	0.01
Other Hispanic or Latino	213	0.40

Race*	Population	%
African-American/Black (2,000)	2,461	4.64
Not Hispanic (1,904)	2,274	4.29
Hispanic (96)	187	0.35
American Indian/Alaska Native (154)	392	0.74
Not Hispanic (81)	282	0.53
Hispanic (73)	110	0.21
Alaska Athabascan *(Ala. Nat.)* (0)	3	0.01
Apache (0)	8	0.02
Arapaho (0)	1	<0.01
Blackfeet (1)	26	0.05
Central American Ind. (4)	8	0.02
Cherokee (13)	61	0.12
Cheyenne (3)	3	0.01
Chippewa (0)	2	<0.01
Cree (0)	4	0.01
Creek (0)	3	0.01
Delaware (8)	15	0.03
Iroquois (6)	22	0.04
Lumbee (2)	4	0.01
Mexican American Ind. (8)	11	0.02
Navajo (0)	1	<0.01
Seminole (1)	2	<0.01
Sioux (6)	15	0.03
South American Ind. (13)	20	0.04
Asian (926)	1,231	2.32
Not Hispanic (917)	1,196	2.26
Hispanic (9)	35	0.07
Burmese (2)	2	<0.01
Cambodian (40)	49	0.09
Chinese, ex. Taiwanese (129)	166	0.31
Filipino (165)	242	0.46
Hmong (0)	1	<0.01
Indian (272)	304	0.57
Indonesian (1)	8	0.02
Japanese (20)	52	0.10
Korean (160)	215	0.41
Laotian (1)	1	<0.01
Pakistani (20)	34	0.06
Sri Lankan (6)	10	0.02
Taiwanese (11)	11	0.02
Thai (13)	20	0.04
Vietnamese (71)	97	0.18
Hawaii Native/Pacific Islander (16)	64	0.12
Not Hispanic (16)	48	0.09
Hispanic (0)	16	0.03
Fijian (0)	1	<0.01
Guamanian/Chamorro (9)	11	0.02
Native Hawaiian (0)	11	0.02
Samoan (4)	6	0.01
White (47,900)	48,870	92.24
Not Hispanic (46,421)	47,173	89.03
Hispanic (1,479)	1,697	3.20

Lewistown

Place Type: Borough
County: Mifflin
Population: 8,338†

Ancestry‡	Population	%
American (737)	737	8.75
Arab (8)	8	0.09
Lebanese (8)	8	0.09
British (10)	10	0.12
Dutch (90)	369	4.38
English (184)	565	6.71
European (47)	47	0.56
French, ex. Basque (18)	97	1.15
French Canadian (0)	10	0.12
German (1,382)	3,147	37.37
Irish (633)	1,434	17.03
Italian (198)	523	6.21
Lithuanian (0)	25	0.30
Norwegian (9)	211	2.51
Pennsylvania German (18)	44	0.52
Polish (60)	229	2.72
Portuguese (8)	8	0.09
Romanian (19)	19	0.23
Russian (0)	52	0.62
Scotch-Irish (81)	295	3.50
Scottish (29)	134	1.59
Serbian (0)	31	0.37
Slovak (6)	6	0.07
Swedish (0)	73	0.87
Swiss (0)	8	0.09
Ukrainian (0)	56	0.66
Welsh (81)	118	1.40

Hispanic Origin	Population	%
Hispanic or Latino (of any race)	256	3.07
Central American, ex. Mexican	13	0.16
Guatemalan	1	0.01
Honduran	8	0.10
Panamanian	3	0.04
Salvadoran	1	0.01
Dominican Republic	10	0.12
Mexican	52	0.62
Puerto Rican	164	1.97
South American	3	0.04
Chilean	1	0.01
Colombian	2	0.02
Other Hispanic or Latino	14	0.17

Race*	Population	%
African-American/Black (127)	218	2.61
Not Hispanic (116)	200	2.40
Hispanic (11)	18	0.22
American Indian/Alaska Native (21)	50	0.60
Not Hispanic (21)	50	0.60
Aleut *(Alaska Native)* (1)	5	0.06
Apache (0)	1	0.01
Cherokee (2)	8	0.10
Chippewa (1)	1	0.01
Cree (1)	1	0.01
Delaware (0)	4	0.05
Iroquois (0)	3	0.04
Sioux (0)	5	0.06
Asian (27)	50	0.60
Not Hispanic (27)	50	0.60
Chinese, ex. Taiwanese (11)	11	0.13
Filipino (1)	4	0.05
Indian (5)	9	0.11
Japanese (3)	12	0.14
Korean (3)	4	0.05
Laotian (3)	8	0.10
Thai (1)	3	0.04
Hawaii Native/Pacific Islander (1)	3	0.04
Not Hispanic (1)	2	0.02
Hispanic (0)	1	0.01
Native Hawaiian (1)	1	0.01
Samoan (0)	1	0.01
White (7,936)	8,087	96.99
Not Hispanic (7,779)	7,912	94.89
Hispanic (157)	175	2.10

SECTION TWO

*Notes: † The Census 2010 population figure is used to calculate the percentages in the Hispanic Origin and Race categories. Ancestry percentages are based on the 2006-2010 American Community Survey population (not shown); ‡ Numbers in parentheses indicate the number of people reporting a single ancestry; * Numbers in parentheses indicate the number of persons reporting this race alone, not in combination with any other race; Please refer to the Explanation of Data for more information.*

Limerick

Place Type: Township
County: Montgomery
Population: 18,074†

Ancestry‡	Population	%
African, Sub-Saharan (86)	118	0.68
African (20)	41	0.24
South African (11)	22	0.13
Zimbabwean (55)	55	0.32
Albanian (0)	9	0.05
American (459)	459	2.66
Arab (108)	108	0.63
Lebanese (80)	80	0.46
Palestinian (28)	28	0.16
Armenian (15)	15	0.09
Austrian (12)	41	0.24
British (26)	45	0.26
Canadian (10)	10	0.06
Czech (0)	9	0.05
Czechoslovakian (11)	26	0.15
Danish (0)	9	0.05
Dutch (46)	307	1.78
Eastern European (33)	33	0.19
English (342)	1,880	10.89
European (196)	196	1.14
French, ex. Basque (0)	363	2.10
French Canadian (10)	10	0.06
German (1,482)	4,981	28.85
Greek (62)	261	1.51
Hungarian (73)	199	1.15
Irish (1,174)	4,445	25.74
Italian (1,317)	3,955	22.90
Latvian (23)	23	0.13
Lithuanian (64)	147	0.85
Norwegian (10)	21	0.12
Pennsylvania German (115)	281	1.63
Polish (432)	1,994	11.55
Portuguese (16)	28	0.16
Romanian (0)	22	0.13
Russian (24)	137	0.79
Scotch-Irish (140)	244	1.41
Scottish (74)	259	1.50
Serbian (0)	25	0.14
Slavic (19)	28	0.16
Slovak (30)	146	0.85
Swedish (51)	121	0.70
Swiss (33)	70	0.41
Turkish (34)	34	0.20
Ukrainian (95)	257	1.49
Welsh (0)	235	1.36
West Indian, ex. Hispanic (16)	16	0.09
Jamaican (16)	16	0.09

Hispanic Origin	Population	%
Hispanic or Latino (of any race)	318	1.76
Central American, ex. Mexican	22	0.12
Costa Rican	3	0.02
Guatemalan	7	0.04
Honduran	1	0.01
Nicaraguan	3	0.02
Panamanian	3	0.02
Salvadoran	4	0.02
Other Central American	1	0.01
Cuban	22	0.12
Dominican Republic	6	0.03
Mexican	67	0.37
Puerto Rican	108	0.60
South American	52	0.29
Argentinean	3	0.02
Bolivian	6	0.03
Colombian	8	0.04
Ecuadorian	2	0.01
Paraguayan	1	0.01
Peruvian	15	0.08
Venezuelan	15	0.08
Other South American	2	0.01
Other Hispanic or Latino	41	0.23

Race*	Population	%
African-American/Black (611)	728	4.03
Not Hispanic (592)	701	3.88
Hispanic (19)	27	0.15
American Indian/Alaska Native (22)	57	0.32
Not Hispanic (18)	47	0.26
Hispanic (4)	10	0.06
Blackfeet (0)	4	0.02
Cherokee (5)	18	0.10
Chickasaw (0)	1	0.01
Creek (0)	1	0.01
Delaware (0)	1	0.01
Iroquois (0)	1	0.01
Mexican American Ind. (3)	3	0.02
Seminole (3)	3	0.02
South American Ind. (0)	3	0.02
Asian (575)	667	3.69
Not Hispanic (575)	666	3.68
Hispanic (0)	1	0.01
Cambodian (10)	13	0.07
Chinese, ex. Taiwanese (99)	128	0.71
Filipino (35)	45	0.25
Indian (233)	240	1.33
Indonesian (5)	5	0.03
Japanese (15)	23	0.13
Korean (77)	93	0.51
Laotian (4)	4	0.02
Pakistani (7)	11	0.06
Sri Lankan (1)	1	0.01
Taiwanese (6)	8	0.04
Thai (1)	5	0.03
Vietnamese (69)	79	0.44
Hawaii Native/Pacific Islander (5)	14	0.08
Not Hispanic (4)	12	0.07
Hispanic (1)	2	0.01
Guamanian/Chamorro (2)	5	0.03
Native Hawaiian (1)	1	0.01
White (16,543)	16,754	92.70
Not Hispanic (16,319)	16,509	91.34
Hispanic (224)	245	1.36

Lititz

Place Type: Borough
County: Lancaster
Population: 9,369†

Ancestry‡	Population	%
American (534)	534	5.74
Arab (20)	52	0.56
Syrian (10)	42	0.45
Other Arab (10)	10	0.11
Austrian (11)	97	1.04
Basque (0)	10	0.11
British (55)	55	0.59
Canadian (0)	24	0.26
Croatian (0)	36	0.39
Czech (0)	8	0.09
Czechoslovakian (0)	15	0.16
Danish (9)	18	0.19
Dutch (23)	127	1.37
English (154)	680	7.31
European (98)	98	1.05
Finnish (0)	77	0.83
French, ex. Basque (19)	158	1.70
French Canadian (0)	27	0.29
German (2,737)	4,290	46.14
Greek (18)	45	0.48
Hungarian (0)	52	0.56
Irish (203)	789	8.49
Italian (159)	542	5.83
Lithuanian (14)	58	0.62
Norwegian (16)	26	0.28
Pennsylvania German (23)	23	0.25
Polish (89)	379	4.08
Portuguese (10)	10	0.11
Russian (23)	23	0.25
Scandinavian (10)	10	0.11
Scotch-Irish (8)	180	1.94
Scottish (72)	122	1.31
Slovak (18)	49	0.53
Swedish (47)	96	1.03
Swiss (30)	279	3.00
Turkish (42)	42	0.45
Ukrainian (0)	104	1.12
Welsh (0)	118	1.27
West Indian, ex. Hispanic (10)	10	0.11
Haitian (10)	10	0.11

Hispanic Origin	Population	%
Hispanic or Latino (of any race)	345	3.68
Central American, ex. Mexican	7	0.07
Guatemalan	2	0.02
Honduran	2	0.02
Salvadoran	3	0.03
Cuban	5	0.05
Dominican Republic	9	0.10
Mexican	60	0.64
Puerto Rican	210	2.24
South American	25	0.27
Argentinean	1	0.01
Bolivian	2	0.02
Chilean	1	0.01
Colombian	11	0.12
Ecuadorian	5	0.05
Peruvian	2	0.02
Uruguayan	3	0.03
Other Hispanic or Latino	29	0.31

Race*	Population	%
African-American/Black (119)	190	2.03
Not Hispanic (105)	165	1.76
Hispanic (14)	25	0.27
American Indian/Alaska Native (17)	48	0.51
Not Hispanic (15)	43	0.46
Hispanic (2)	5	0.05
Alaska Athabascan *(Ala. Nat.)* (1)	1	0.01
Blackfeet (0)	1	0.01
Cherokee (2)	7	0.07
Cheyenne (0)	3	0.03
Chippewa (0)	2	0.02
Cree (1)	1	0.01
Lumbee (1)	1	0.01
Mexican American Ind. (1)	1	0.01
Seminole (0)	5	0.05
Sioux (2)	3	0.03
Asian (111)	138	1.47
Not Hispanic (111)	138	1.47
Burmese (29)	30	0.32
Cambodian (3)	4	0.04
Chinese, ex. Taiwanese (28)	30	0.32
Filipino (2)	6	0.06
Hmong (5)	5	0.05
Indian (11)	17	0.18
Indonesian (1)	1	0.01
Japanese (4)	7	0.07
Korean (9)	11	0.12
Laotian (1)	2	0.02
Malaysian (1)	1	0.01
Vietnamese (13)	14	0.15
Hawaii Native/Pacific Islander (2)	5	0.05
Not Hispanic (2)	5	0.05
Fijian (0)	1	0.01
Native Hawaiian (2)	4	0.04
White (8,852)	9,003	96.09
Not Hispanic (8,659)	8,773	93.64
Hispanic (193)	230	2.45

Lock Haven

Place Type: City
County: Clinton
Population: 9,772†

Ancestry‡	Population	%
African, Sub-Saharan (18)	18	0.19
African (3)	3	0.03
Other Sub-Saharan African (15)	15	0.16
American (396)	396	4.11

*Notes: † The Census 2010 population figure is used to calculate the percentages in the Hispanic Origin and Race categories. Ancestry percentages are based on the 2006-2010 American Community Survey population (not shown); ‡ Numbers in parentheses indicate the number of people reporting a single ancestry; * Numbers in parentheses indicate the number of persons reporting this race alone, not in combination with any other race; Please refer to the Explanation of Data for more information.*

Arab (5)	5	0.05
Egyptian (5)	5	0.05
Austrian (0)	43	0.45
British (0)	15	0.16
Cajun (0)	15	0.16
Canadian (0)	14	0.15
Croatian (0)	10	0.10
Czech (0)	32	0.33
Dutch (0)	161	1.67
English (118)	413	4.28
European (64)	81	0.84
French, ex. Basque (69)	213	2.21
French Canadian (11)	52	0.54
German (1,313)	2,939	30.47
Greek (15)	40	0.41
Hungarian (0)	30	0.31
Irish (460)	1,712	17.75
Italian (486)	1,229	12.74
Lithuanian (33)	134	1.39
Northern European (28)	44	0.46
Norwegian (14)	34	0.35
Pennsylvania German (114)	140	1.45
Polish (191)	558	5.79
Portuguese (0)	14	0.15
Russian (10)	53	0.55
Scandinavian (6)	6	0.06
Scotch-Irish (102)	167	1.73
Scottish (36)	135	1.40
Slovak (0)	68	0.71
Slovene (0)	13	0.13
Swedish (56)	139	1.44
Swiss (12)	21	0.22
Ukrainian (9)	35	0.36
Welsh (13)	125	1.30
West Indian, ex. Hispanic (23)	23	0.24
Jamaican (17)	17	0.18
Trinidadian/Tobagonian (6)	6	0.06

Hispanic Origin	Population	%
Hispanic or Latino (of any race)	183	1.87
Central American, ex. Mexican	5	0.05
Costa Rican	1	0.01
Guatemalan	2	0.02
Honduran	1	0.01
Panamanian	1	0.01
Cuban	3	0.03
Dominican Republic	10	0.10
Mexican	36	0.37
Puerto Rican	77	0.79
South American	9	0.09
Argentinean	2	0.02
Colombian	3	0.03
Peruvian	2	0.02
Uruguayan	1	0.01
Venezuelan	1	0.01
Other Hispanic or Latino	43	0.44

Race*	Population	%
African-American/Black (406)	481	4.92
Not Hispanic (399)	467	4.78
Hispanic (7)	14	0.14
American Indian/Alaska Native (8)	37	0.38
Not Hispanic (8)	37	0.38
Blackfeet (0)	1	0.01
Cherokee (2)	12	0.12
Chippewa (1)	1	0.01
Cree (0)	1	0.01
Creek (0)	1	0.01
Crow (2)	2	0.02
Iroquois (0)	2	0.02
Sioux (0)	1	0.01
Asian (93)	106	1.08
Not Hispanic (92)	105	1.07
Hispanic (1)	1	0.01
Bangladeshi (1)	1	0.01
Chinese, ex. Taiwanese (18)	18	0.18
Filipino (5)	7	0.07
Indian (39)	41	0.42
Indonesian (1)	2	0.02
Japanese (2)	4	0.04
Korean (16)	17	0.17
Pakistani (3)	3	0.03
Taiwanese (2)	2	0.02
Thai (2)	6	0.06
Vietnamese (3)	3	0.03
Hawaii Native/Pacific Islander (5)	10	0.10
Not Hispanic (5)	9	0.09
Hispanic (0)	1	0.01
Native Hawaiian (4)	4	0.04
White (9,070)	9,196	94.11
Not Hispanic (8,966)	9,075	92.87
Hispanic (104)	121	1.24

Logan

Place Type: Township
County: Blair
Population: 12,289†

Ancestry‡	Population	%
African, Sub-Saharan (4)	4	0.03
African (4)	4	0.03
American (709)	709	5.88
Arab (21)	46	0.38
Arab (12)	12	0.10
Lebanese (9)	34	0.28
Austrian (9)	9	0.07
British (15)	25	0.21
Croatian (0)	21	0.17
Czech (11)	11	0.09
Czechoslovakian (0)	9	0.07
Danish (0)	8	0.07
Dutch (19)	366	3.03
English (394)	1,118	9.26
European (11)	11	0.09
French, ex. Basque (86)	368	3.05
French Canadian (24)	104	0.86
German (1,835)	5,297	43.90
Greek (36)	102	0.85
Hungarian (13)	82	0.68
Irish (376)	2,420	20.05
Italian (796)	1,680	13.92
Pennsylvania German (278)	327	2.71
Polish (131)	417	3.46
Portuguese (0)	60	0.50
Russian (12)	118	0.98
Scotch-Irish (58)	193	1.60
Scottish (67)	230	1.91
Slavic (10)	10	0.08
Slovak (61)	142	1.18
Swedish (30)	49	0.41
Ukrainian (0)	24	0.20
Welsh (14)	175	1.45
Yugoslavian (0)	12	0.10

Hispanic Origin	Population	%
Hispanic or Latino (of any race)	112	0.91
Central American, ex. Mexican	8	0.07
Honduran	2	0.02
Nicaraguan	2	0.02
Panamanian	1	0.01
Salvadoran	3	0.02
Cuban	12	0.10
Dominican Republic	4	0.03
Mexican	33	0.27
Puerto Rican	21	0.17
South American	21	0.17
Argentinean	5	0.04
Chilean	3	0.02
Colombian	7	0.06
Ecuadorian	2	0.02
Peruvian	2	0.02
Venezuelan	2	0.02
Other Hispanic or Latino	13	0.11

Race*	Population	%
African-American/Black (153)	192	1.56
Not Hispanic (149)	185	1.51
Hispanic (4)	7	0.06
American Indian/Alaska Native (28)	56	0.46
Not Hispanic (26)	51	0.42
Hispanic (2)	5	0.04
Blackfeet (0)	3	0.02
Cherokee (0)	7	0.06
Cree (0)	1	0.01
Delaware (5)	6	0.05
Iroquois (1)	6	0.05
Asian (115)	145	1.18
Not Hispanic (114)	142	1.16
Hispanic (1)	3	0.02
Chinese, ex. Taiwanese (39)	44	0.36
Filipino (10)	17	0.14
Indian (33)	37	0.30
Indonesian (0)	1	0.01
Japanese (6)	8	0.07
Korean (12)	19	0.15
Malaysian (0)	1	0.01
Pakistani (4)	5	0.04
Sri Lankan (2)	3	0.02
Taiwanese (1)	1	0.01
Vietnamese (6)	8	0.07
Hawaii Native/Pacific Islander (2)	9	0.07
Not Hispanic (2)	8	0.07
Hispanic (0)	1	0.01
Guamanian/Chamorro (0)	1	0.01
Native Hawaiian (1)	3	0.02
Samoan (1)	2	0.02
White (11,874)	11,959	97.31
Not Hispanic (11,800)	11,877	96.65
Hispanic (74)	82	0.67

Lower Allen

Place Type: Township
County: Cumberland
Population: 17,980†

Ancestry‡	Population	%
African, Sub-Saharan (63)	122	0.68
African (9)	18	0.10
Somalian (54)	54	0.30
Other Sub-Saharan African (0)	50	0.28
American (960)	960	5.38
Arab (109)	109	0.61
Egyptian (8)	8	0.04
Iraqi (33)	33	0.18
Palestinian (32)	32	0.18
Other Arab (36)	36	0.20
Armenian (0)	17	0.10
Austrian (13)	99	0.55
Belgian (22)	33	0.18
British (27)	81	0.45
Canadian (0)	24	0.13
Celtic (0)	8	0.04
Croatian (32)	50	0.28
Czech (0)	10	0.06
Danish (11)	33	0.18
Dutch (70)	353	1.98
Eastern European (34)	34	0.19
English (429)	1,434	8.03
European (140)	166	0.93
Finnish (9)	21	0.12
French, ex. Basque (46)	466	2.61
French Canadian (28)	71	0.40
German (2,385)	5,692	31.88
Greek (0)	30	0.17
Hungarian (13)	50	0.28
Irish (448)	1,733	9.71
Italian (571)	1,435	8.04
Lithuanian (26)	112	0.63
Northern European (48)	48	0.27
Norwegian (0)	18	0.10
Pennsylvania German (161)	265	1.48
Polish (267)	806	4.51
Portuguese (35)	43	0.24
Russian (26)	157	0.88
Scandinavian (43)	43	0.24
Scotch-Irish (89)	402	2.25
Scottish (63)	427	2.39
Slovak (57)	125	0.70

*Notes: † The Census 2010 population figure is used to calculate the percentages in the Hispanic Origin and Race categories. Ancestry percentages are based on the 2006-2010 American Community Survey population (not shown); ‡ Numbers in parentheses indicate the number of people reporting a single ancestry; * Numbers in parentheses indicate the number of persons reporting this race alone, not in combination with any other race; Please refer to the Explanation of Data for more information.*

Slovene (27)	27	0.15
Swedish (17)	152	0.85
Swiss (33)	130	0.73
Ukrainian (0)	32	0.18
Welsh (105)	347	1.94
West Indian, ex. Hispanic (217)	217	1.22
British West Indian (9)	9	0.05
Jamaican (208)	208	1.16
Yugoslavian (51)	174	0.97

Hispanic Origin	Population	%
Hispanic or Latino (of any race)	955	5.31
Central American, ex. Mexican	35	0.19
Costa Rican	3	0.02
Guatemalan	5	0.03
Honduran	12	0.07
Nicaraguan	1	0.01
Panamanian	5	0.03
Salvadoran	8	0.04
Other Central American	1	0.01
Cuban	17	0.09
Dominican Republic	34	0.19
Mexican	102	0.57
Puerto Rican	230	1.28
South American	28	0.16
Argentinean	3	0.02
Bolivian	2	0.01
Chilean	2	0.01
Colombian	1	0.01
Ecuadorian	10	0.06
Peruvian	5	0.03
Venezuelan	5	0.03
Other Hispanic or Latino	509	2.83

Race*	Population	%
African-American/Black (1,846)	1,964	10.92
Not Hispanic (1,810)	1,914	10.65
Hispanic (36)	50	0.28
American Indian/Alaska Native (24)	79	0.44
Not Hispanic (23)	64	0.36
Hispanic (1)	15	0.08
Blackfeet (0)	1	0.01
Central American Ind. (0)	5	0.03
Cherokee (4)	21	0.12
Cheyenne (0)	1	0.01
Choctaw (0)	1	0.01
Cree (3)	3	0.02
Creek (0)	1	0.01
Delaware (2)	3	0.02
Iroquois (1)	2	0.01
Mexican American Ind. (0)	1	0.01
Pueblo (0)	1	0.01
Sioux (1)	1	0.01
Asian (416)	483	2.69
Not Hispanic (412)	467	2.60
Hispanic (4)	16	0.09
Bangladeshi (3)	5	0.03
Cambodian (4)	6	0.03
Chinese, ex. Taiwanese (62)	73	0.41
Filipino (30)	47	0.26
Indian (113)	116	0.65
Indonesian (1)	3	0.02
Japanese (9)	13	0.07
Korean (75)	89	0.49
Laotian (1)	6	0.03
Nepalese (2)	2	0.01
Pakistani (8)	8	0.04
Taiwanese (2)	2	0.01
Thai (0)	4	0.02
Vietnamese (79)	92	0.51
Hawaii Native/Pacific Islander (11)	16	0.09
Not Hispanic (11)	16	0.09
Guamanian/Chamorro (3)	3	0.02
Native Hawaiian (1)	1	0.01
Samoan (1)	3	0.02
White (14,841)	15,051	83.71
Not Hispanic (14,562)	14,730	81.92
Hispanic (279)	321	1.79

Lower Burrell

Place Type: City
County: Westmoreland
Population: 11,761†

Ancestry‡	Population	%
African, Sub-Saharan (192)	192	1.61
African (192)	192	1.61
American (341)	341	2.86
Arab (79)	203	1.71
Lebanese (28)	28	0.24
Syrian (33)	157	1.32
Other Arab (18)	18	0.15
Austrian (0)	48	0.40
Belgian (8)	74	0.62
British (8)	8	0.07
Croatian (9)	61	0.51
Czech (42)	146	1.23
Czechoslovakian (39)	61	0.51
Dutch (22)	160	1.34
English (159)	1,248	10.48
Finnish (10)	110	0.92
French, ex. Basque (13)	235	1.97
French Canadian (0)	57	0.48
German (874)	3,777	31.72
Greek (9)	18	0.15
Hungarian (42)	123	1.03
Iranian (10)	10	0.08
Irish (178)	2,103	17.66
Italian (1,107)	2,741	23.02
Lithuanian (74)	126	1.06
Norwegian (0)	8	0.07
Pennsylvania German (45)	73	0.61
Polish (764)	2,256	18.95
Portuguese (0)	9	0.08
Russian (19)	216	1.81
Scotch-Irish (134)	447	3.75
Scottish (9)	133	1.12
Serbian (0)	9	0.08
Slavic (0)	70	0.59
Slovak (378)	898	7.54
Slovene (10)	10	0.08
Swedish (0)	172	1.44
Swiss (6)	68	0.57
Ukrainian (26)	183	1.54
Welsh (18)	103	0.87

Hispanic Origin	Population	%
Hispanic or Latino (of any race)	64	0.54
Central American, ex. Mexican	2	0.02
Guatemalan	1	0.01
Honduran	1	0.01
Cuban	3	0.03
Dominican Republic	1	0.01
Mexican	24	0.20
Puerto Rican	22	0.19
South American	4	0.03
Argentinean	1	0.01
Peruvian	1	0.01
Venezuelan	2	0.02
Other Hispanic or Latino	8	0.07

Race*	Population	%
African-American/Black (129)	200	1.70
Not Hispanic (128)	196	1.67
Hispanic (1)	4	0.03
American Indian/Alaska Native (6)	40	0.34
Not Hispanic (6)	39	0.33
Hispanic (0)	1	0.01
Cherokee (4)	18	0.15
Spanish American Ind. (0)	1	0.01
Asian (48)	59	0.50
Not Hispanic (48)	59	0.50
Chinese, ex. Taiwanese (18)	21	0.18
Filipino (9)	11	0.09
Indian (4)	5	0.04
Japanese (1)	2	0.02
Korean (4)	6	0.05
Thai (1)	1	0.01
Vietnamese (10)	10	0.09
Hawaii Native/Pacific Islander (0)	6	0.05
Not Hispanic (0)	6	0.05
Native Hawaiian (0)	5	0.04
White (11,447)	11,559	98.28
Not Hispanic (11,402)	11,507	97.84
Hispanic (45)	52	0.44

Lower Gwynedd

Place Type: Township
County: Montgomery
Population: 11,405†

Ancestry‡	Population	%
African, Sub-Saharan (38)	38	0.34
African (38)	38	0.34
American (558)	558	4.98
Arab (18)	18	0.16
Egyptian (18)	18	0.16
Armenian (19)	56	0.50
Australian (11)	32	0.29
Austrian (22)	71	0.63
Belgian (0)	10	0.09
British (68)	143	1.28
Canadian (35)	42	0.37
Celtic (0)	12	0.11
Czech (9)	38	0.34
Czechoslovakian (76)	76	0.68
Danish (32)	52	0.46
Dutch (25)	141	1.26
Eastern European (149)	149	1.33
English (477)	1,804	16.09
European (108)	108	0.96
French, ex. Basque (38)	215	1.92
French Canadian (11)	11	0.10
German (597)	2,572	22.94
Greek (68)	102	0.91
Hungarian (9)	60	0.54
Iranian (41)	79	0.70
Irish (589)	2,156	19.23
Israeli (21)	21	0.19
Italian (777)	1,200	10.70
Lithuanian (0)	29	0.26
Northern European (30)	30	0.27
Norwegian (0)	29	0.26
Pennsylvania German (75)	83	0.74
Polish (175)	557	4.97
Romanian (22)	147	1.31
Russian (263)	601	5.36
Scandinavian (0)	9	0.08
Scotch-Irish (64)	232	2.07
Scottish (72)	244	2.18
Serbian (11)	11	0.10
Slovak (6)	72	0.64
Swedish (10)	52	0.46
Swiss (0)	20	0.18
Ukrainian (8)	56	0.50
Welsh (9)	152	1.36
West Indian, ex. Hispanic (42)	61	0.54
Bermudan (0)	9	0.08
Jamaican (42)	52	0.46

Hispanic Origin	Population	%
Hispanic or Latino (of any race)	220	1.93
Central American, ex. Mexican	21	0.18
Guatemalan	8	0.07
Honduran	4	0.04
Nicaraguan	1	0.01
Panamanian	5	0.04
Salvadoran	3	0.03
Cuban	10	0.09
Dominican Republic	13	0.11
Mexican	65	0.57
Puerto Rican	63	0.55
South American	33	0.29
Argentinean	5	0.04
Colombian	7	0.06
Ecuadorian	5	0.04
Paraguayan	2	0.02

*Notes: † The Census 2010 population figure is used to calculate the percentages in the Hispanic Origin and Race categories. Ancestry percentages are based on the 2006-2010 American Community Survey population (not shown); ‡ Numbers in parentheses indicate the number of people reporting a single ancestry; * Numbers in parentheses indicate the number of persons reporting this race alone, not in combination with any other race; Please refer to the Explanation of Data for more information.*

Peruvian	10	0.09
Venezuelan	3	0.03
Other South American	1	0.01
Other Hispanic or Latino	15	0.13

Race*	Population	%
African-American/Black (785)	851	7.46
Not Hispanic (774)	836	7.33
Hispanic (11)	15	0.13
American Indian/Alaska Native (6)	44	0.39
Not Hispanic (4)	41	0.36
Hispanic (2)	3	0.03
Central American Ind. (1)	1	0.01
Cherokee (0)	8	0.07
Iroquois (0)	1	0.01
Asian (811)	897	7.86
Not Hispanic (808)	891	7.81
Hispanic (3)	6	0.05
Bangladeshi (1)	1	0.01
Cambodian (3)	3	0.03
Chinese, ex. Taiwanese (161)	185	1.62
Filipino (23)	45	0.39
Indian (157)	176	1.54
Indonesian (1)	1	0.01
Japanese (20)	33	0.29
Korean (377)	396	3.47
Laotian (2)	3	0.03
Malaysian (1)	2	0.02
Pakistani (12)	14	0.12
Taiwanese (14)	16	0.14
Thai (1)	1	0.01
Vietnamese (16)	16	0.14
Hawaii Native/Pacific Islander (2)	3	0.03
Not Hispanic (1)	2	0.02
Hispanic (1)	1	0.01
Native Hawaiian (1)	1	0.01
White (9,583)	9,719	85.22
Not Hispanic (9,434)	9,549	83.73
Hispanic (149)	170	1.49

Lower Macungie

Place Type: Township
County: Lehigh
Population: 30,633†

Ancestry‡	Population	%
African, Sub-Saharan (48)	48	0.17
African (12)	12	0.04
Nigerian (36)	36	0.13
American (950)	950	3.32
Arab (125)	243	0.85
Lebanese (50)	136	0.47
Syrian (75)	107	0.37
Armenian (0)	20	0.07
Austrian (122)	559	1.95
Belgian (13)	32	0.11
Brazilian (14)	14	0.05
British (49)	97	0.34
Bulgarian (45)	45	0.16
Canadian (26)	37	0.13
Celtic (0)	15	0.05
Croatian (0)	21	0.07
Czech (29)	150	0.52
Czechoslovakian (9)	9	0.03
Danish (27)	83	0.29
Dutch (182)	610	2.13
Eastern European (57)	83	0.29
English (603)	2,304	8.04
European (137)	145	0.51
Finnish (11)	24	0.08
French, ex. Basque (97)	613	2.14
French Canadian (82)	249	0.87
German (3,634)	9,341	32.60
German Russian (9)	42	0.15
Greek (136)	211	0.74
Hungarian (163)	749	2.61
Irish (1,124)	5,000	17.45
Italian (1,544)	4,251	14.83
Latvian (11)	29	0.10
Lithuanian (38)	106	0.37
Maltese (0)	11	0.04
Norwegian (53)	177	0.62
Pennsylvania German (782)	1,065	3.72
Polish (524)	1,533	5.35
Portuguese (9)	94	0.33
Romanian (17)	71	0.25
Russian (172)	424	1.48
Scotch-Irish (136)	307	1.07
Scottish (219)	733	2.56
Slavic (0)	27	0.09
Slovak (274)	856	2.99
Slovene (0)	22	0.08
Swedish (61)	352	1.23
Swiss (11)	145	0.51
Turkish (8)	8	0.03
Ukrainian (113)	449	1.57
Welsh (198)	593	2.07
West Indian, ex. Hispanic (207)	281	0.98
Barbadian (0)	5	0.02
Haitian (36)	36	0.13
Jamaican (139)	183	0.64
Trinidadian/Tobagonian (0)	6	0.02
West Indian (32)	51	0.18
Yugoslavian (0)	7	0.02

Hispanic Origin	Population	%
Hispanic or Latino (of any race)	1,545	5.04
Central American, ex. Mexican	63	0.21
Costa Rican	11	0.04
Guatemalan	6	0.02
Honduran	26	0.08
Nicaraguan	2	0.01
Panamanian	9	0.03
Salvadoran	8	0.03
Other Central American	1	<0.01
Cuban	68	0.22
Dominican Republic	193	0.63
Mexican	161	0.53
Puerto Rican	637	2.08
South American	294	0.96
Argentinean	26	0.08
Bolivian	6	0.02
Chilean	18	0.06
Colombian	96	0.31
Ecuadorian	57	0.19
Peruvian	60	0.20
Uruguayan	1	<0.01
Venezuelan	27	0.09
Other South American	3	0.01
Other Hispanic or Latino	129	0.42

Race*	Population	%
African-American/Black (1,002)	1,185	3.87
Not Hispanic (919)	1,057	3.45
Hispanic (83)	128	0.42
American Indian/Alaska Native (40)	107	0.35
Not Hispanic (24)	77	0.25
Hispanic (16)	30	0.10
Alaska Athabascan *(Ala. Nat.)* (3)	3	0.01
Apache (0)	1	<0.01
Blackfeet (0)	3	0.01
Central American Ind. (3)	3	0.01
Cherokee (4)	28	0.09
Chippewa (3)	3	0.01
Crow (0)	1	<0.01
Delaware (0)	8	0.03
Iroquois (3)	4	0.01
Lumbee (1)	2	0.01
Sioux (3)	3	0.01
South American Ind. (0)	1	<0.01
Asian (1,830)	2,023	6.60
Not Hispanic (1,815)	1,994	6.51
Hispanic (15)	29	0.09
Bangladeshi (11)	17	0.06
Burmese (7)	7	0.02
Chinese, ex. Taiwanese (464)	504	1.65
Filipino (98)	134	0.44
Indian (748)	783	2.56
Indonesian (3)	5	0.02
Japanese (46)	66	0.22
Korean (143)	172	0.56
Malaysian (0)	4	0.01
Pakistani (82)	90	0.29
Sri Lankan (18)	18	0.06
Taiwanese (48)	56	0.18
Thai (3)	3	0.01
Vietnamese (117)	133	0.43
Hawaii Native/Pacific Islander (2)	9	0.03
Not Hispanic (2)	5	0.02
Hispanic (0)	4	0.01
Native Hawaiian (2)	6	0.02
White (26,773)	27,170	88.70
Not Hispanic (25,904)	26,191	85.50
Hispanic (869)	979	3.20

Lower Makefield

Place Type: Township
County: Bucks
Population: 32,559†

Ancestry‡	Population	%
African, Sub-Saharan (0)	16	0.05
African (0)	16	0.05
Alsatian (0)	7	0.02
American (1,225)	1,225	3.74
Arab (26)	76	0.23
Egyptian (6)	6	0.02
Lebanese (20)	20	0.06
Syrian (0)	12	0.04
Other Arab (0)	38	0.12
Australian (6)	18	0.06
Austrian (47)	293	0.90
Belgian (0)	34	0.10
British (51)	197	0.60
Cajun (0)	7	0.02
Canadian (83)	96	0.29
Croatian (20)	44	0.13
Czech (13)	41	0.13
Czechoslovakian (0)	43	0.13
Danish (22)	74	0.23
Dutch (44)	221	0.68
Eastern European (275)	275	0.84
English (1,049)	4,060	12.41
European (494)	528	1.61
Finnish (14)	100	0.31
French, ex. Basque (103)	836	2.55
French Canadian (70)	188	0.57
German (1,859)	7,194	21.99
Greek (149)	422	1.29
Hungarian (88)	507	1.55
Iranian (77)	77	0.24
Irish (2,143)	8,108	24.78
Israeli (7)	16	0.05
Italian (2,306)	5,346	16.34
Lithuanian (96)	321	0.98
Northern European (42)	42	0.13
Norwegian (47)	159	0.49
Pennsylvania German (47)	131	0.40
Polish (900)	2,644	8.08
Portuguese (46)	109	0.33
Romanian (66)	165	0.50
Russian (580)	1,661	5.08
Scandinavian (0)	11	0.03
Scotch-Irish (280)	792	2.42
Scottish (220)	1,032	3.15
Serbian (0)	24	0.07
Slavic (19)	43	0.13
Slovak (71)	221	0.68
Slovene (17)	17	0.05
Swedish (67)	469	1.43
Swiss (0)	130	0.40
Turkish (13)	13	0.04
Ukrainian (232)	413	1.26
Welsh (76)	395	1.21
West Indian, ex. Hispanic (22)	22	0.07
British West Indian (11)	11	0.03
Trinidadian/Tobagonian (11)	11	0.03
Yugoslavian (115)	115	0.35

SECTION TWO

*Notes: † The Census 2010 population figure is used to calculate the percentages in the Hispanic Origin and Race categories. Ancestry percentages are based on the 2006-2010 American Community Survey population (not shown); ‡ Numbers in parentheses indicate the number of people reporting a single ancestry; * Numbers in parentheses indicate the number of persons reporting this race alone, not in combination with any other race; Please refer to the Explanation of Data for more information.*

Hispanic Origin	Population	%
Hispanic or Latino (of any race)	787	2.42
Central American, ex. Mexican	61	0.19
Costa Rican	16	0.05
Guatemalan	24	0.07
Honduran	6	0.02
Nicaraguan	1	<0.01
Panamanian	11	0.03
Salvadoran	3	0.01
Cuban	53	0.16
Dominican Republic	27	0.08
Mexican	140	0.43
Puerto Rican	252	0.77
South American	158	0.49
Argentinean	34	0.10
Bolivian	4	0.01
Chilean	6	0.02
Colombian	41	0.13
Ecuadorian	11	0.03
Peruvian	32	0.10
Uruguayan	4	0.01
Venezuelan	22	0.07
Other South American	4	0.01
Other Hispanic or Latino	96	0.29

Race*	Population	%
African-American/Black (753)	854	2.62
Not Hispanic (723)	820	2.52
Hispanic (30)	34	0.10
American Indian/Alaska Native (33)	90	0.28
Not Hispanic (29)	70	0.21
Hispanic (4)	20	0.06
Blackfeet (0)	2	0.01
Cherokee (1)	8	0.02
Chippewa (4)	5	0.02
Choctaw (0)	1	<0.01
Delaware (4)	7	0.02
Iroquois (0)	3	0.01
Mexican American Ind. (1)	1	<0.01
Sioux (2)	4	0.01
South American Ind. (3)	8	0.02
Asian (2,059)	2,310	7.09
Not Hispanic (2,057)	2,298	7.06
Hispanic (2)	12	0.04
Bangladeshi (3)	4	0.01
Burmese (1)	1	<0.01
Cambodian (6)	6	0.02
Chinese, ex. Taiwanese (474)	530	1.63
Filipino (113)	168	0.52
Indian (946)	999	3.07
Indonesian (2)	4	0.01
Japanese (22)	54	0.17
Korean (256)	298	0.92
Pakistani (94)	95	0.29
Sri Lankan (13)	13	0.04
Taiwanese (20)	21	0.06
Thai (9)	9	0.03
Vietnamese (43)	62	0.19
Hawaii Native/Pacific Islander (8)	31	0.10
Not Hispanic (5)	28	0.09
Hispanic (3)	3	0.01
Guamanian/Chamorro (3)	3	0.01
Native Hawaiian (4)	15	0.05
Samoan (0)	1	<0.01
White (29,161)	29,505	90.62
Not Hispanic (28,545)	28,851	88.61
Hispanic (616)	654	2.01

Lower Merion

Place Type: Township
County: Montgomery
Population: 57,825†

Ancestry‡	Population	%
African, Sub-Saharan (375)	416	0.72
African (140)	152	0.26
Ethiopian (0)	14	0.02
Kenyan (70)	70	0.12
Nigerian (20)	35	0.06
South African (137)	137	0.24
Other Sub-Saharan African (8)	8	0.01
Albanian (18)	70	0.12
Alsatian (0)	4	0.01
American (2,084)	2,084	3.59
Arab (83)	195	0.34
Arab (0)	15	0.03
Iraqi (21)	21	0.04
Lebanese (62)	105	0.18
Moroccan (0)	28	0.05
Palestinian (0)	26	0.04
Armenian (11)	110	0.19
Australian (8)	8	0.01
Austrian (126)	648	1.12
Belgian (69)	120	0.21
Brazilian (37)	37	0.06
British (336)	509	0.88
Bulgarian (0)	6	0.01
Canadian (134)	241	0.42
Celtic (10)	10	0.02
Croatian (15)	96	0.17
Cypriot (66)	66	0.11
Czech (40)	154	0.27
Czechoslovakian (12)	44	0.08
Danish (0)	66	0.11
Dutch (70)	480	0.83
Eastern European (1,966)	1,986	3.42
English (1,445)	5,531	9.53
Estonian (0)	28	0.05
European (1,083)	1,134	1.95
Finnish (9)	22	0.04
French, ex. Basque (260)	1,058	1.82
French Canadian (76)	142	0.24
German (1,920)	8,094	13.95
Greek (285)	649	1.12
Hungarian (188)	635	1.09
Icelander (0)	32	0.06
Iranian (197)	362	0.62
Irish (3,344)	8,965	15.45
Israeli (243)	377	0.65
Italian (2,512)	5,480	9.44
Latvian (49)	151	0.26
Lithuanian (107)	514	0.89
Macedonian (18)	54	0.09
Northern European (98)	98	0.17
Norwegian (89)	260	0.45
Pennsylvania German (48)	99	0.17
Polish (1,199)	3,877	6.68
Portuguese (14)	86	0.15
Romanian (150)	478	0.82
Russian (3,632)	6,253	10.77
Scandinavian (0)	54	0.09
Scotch-Irish (419)	1,085	1.87
Scottish (403)	1,205	2.08
Serbian (33)	95	0.16
Slavic (41)	76	0.13
Slovak (25)	125	0.22
Slovene (0)	10	0.02
Soviet Union (22)	22	0.04
Swedish (195)	520	0.90
Swiss (28)	192	0.33
Turkish (5)	59	0.10
Ukrainian (394)	703	1.21
Welsh (42)	406	0.70
West Indian, ex. Hispanic (257)	378	0.65
Barbadian (21)	21	0.04
Haitian (125)	146	0.25
Jamaican (103)	154	0.27
Trinidadian/Tobagonian (0)	39	0.07
West Indian (8)	18	0.03
Yugoslavian (27)	67	0.12

Hispanic Origin	Population	%
Hispanic or Latino (of any race)	1,718	2.97
Central American, ex. Mexican	193	0.33
Costa Rican	10	0.02
Guatemalan	62	0.11
Honduran	30	0.05
Nicaraguan	26	0.04
Panamanian	34	0.06
Salvadoran	29	0.05
Other Central American	2	<0.01
Cuban	156	0.27
Dominican Republic	55	0.10
Mexican	343	0.59
Puerto Rican	319	0.55
South American	446	0.77
Argentinean	79	0.14
Bolivian	10	0.02
Chilean	37	0.06
Colombian	116	0.20
Ecuadorian	34	0.06
Paraguayan	12	0.02
Peruvian	76	0.13
Uruguayan	16	0.03
Venezuelan	60	0.10
Other South American	6	0.01
Other Hispanic or Latino	206	0.36

Race*	Population	%
African-American/Black (3,246)	3,608	6.24
Not Hispanic (3,165)	3,484	6.03
Hispanic (81)	124	0.21
American Indian/Alaska Native (39)	218	0.38
Not Hispanic (27)	168	0.29
Hispanic (12)	50	0.09
Apache (0)	1	<0.01
Arapaho (0)	1	<0.01
Blackfeet (0)	2	<0.01
Canadian/French Am. Ind. (0)	1	<0.01
Cherokee (6)	33	0.06
Cheyenne (0)	1	<0.01
Choctaw (0)	6	0.01
Creek (0)	2	<0.01
Hopi (0)	2	<0.01
Iroquois (1)	4	0.01
Kiowa (0)	2	<0.01
Lumbee (0)	3	0.01
Mexican American Ind. (4)	7	0.01
Navajo (1)	3	0.01
Ottawa (0)	2	<0.01
Seminole (0)	4	0.01
Sioux (0)	1	<0.01
South American Ind. (3)	7	0.01
Tlingit-Haida *(Alaska Native)* (0)	4	0.01
Tohono O'Odham (0)	1	<0.01
Tsimshian *(Alaska Native)* (0)	3	0.01
Asian (3,488)	4,085	7.06
Not Hispanic (3,469)	4,024	6.96
Hispanic (19)	61	0.11
Bangladeshi (8)	9	0.02
Burmese (7)	8	0.01
Cambodian (11)	11	0.02
Chinese, ex. Taiwanese (1,301)	1,477	2.55
Filipino (197)	291	0.50
Indian (783)	906	1.57
Indonesian (5)	6	0.01
Japanese (134)	221	0.38
Korean (556)	651	1.13
Laotian (5)	10	0.02
Malaysian (9)	18	0.03
Nepalese (12)	12	0.02
Pakistani (77)	95	0.16
Sri Lankan (20)	28	0.05
Taiwanese (57)	70	0.12
Thai (33)	44	0.08
Vietnamese (155)	185	0.32
Hawaii Native/Pacific Islander (19)	61	0.11
Not Hispanic (17)	56	0.10
Hispanic (2)	5	0.01
Fijian (2)	5	0.01
Guamanian/Chamorro (3)	4	0.01
Native Hawaiian (4)	12	0.02
Samoan (1)	5	0.01
Tongan (7)	18	0.03
White (49,563)	50,501	87.33
Not Hispanic (48,375)	49,193	85.07
Hispanic (1,188)	1,308	2.26

*Notes: † The Census 2010 population figure is used to calculate the percentages in the Hispanic Origin and Race categories. Ancestry percentages are based on the 2006-2010 American Community Survey population (not shown); ‡ Numbers in parentheses indicate the number of people reporting a single ancestry; * Numbers in parentheses indicate the number of persons reporting this race alone, not in combination with any other race; Please refer to the Explanation of Data for more information.*

Lower Moreland

Place Type: Township
County: Montgomery
Population: 12,982†

Ancestry‡	Population	%
American (803)	803	6.34
Arab (193)	206	1.63
Arab (16)	16	0.13
Iraqi (177)	177	1.40
Lebanese (0)	13	0.10
Armenian (18)	20	0.16
Australian (3)	3	0.02
Austrian (0)	68	0.54
British (9)	22	0.17
Bulgarian (0)	8	0.06
Canadian (20)	46	0.36
Croatian (0)	25	0.20
Czech (0)	17	0.13
Czechoslovakian (9)	17	0.13
Danish (0)	8	0.06
Dutch (11)	88	0.69
Eastern European (147)	147	1.16
English (283)	1,183	9.34
European (111)	111	0.88
Finnish (11)	53	0.42
French, ex. Basque (14)	76	0.60
French Canadian (28)	56	0.44
German (656)	1,989	15.71
Greek (139)	166	1.31
Hungarian (89)	264	2.08
Iranian (10)	30	0.24
Irish (748)	2,239	17.68
Israeli (9)	32	0.25
Italian (884)	1,992	15.73
Latvian (27)	27	0.21
Lithuanian (57)	164	1.30
Norwegian (28)	28	0.22
Pennsylvania German (23)	23	0.18
Polish (153)	956	7.55
Portuguese (47)	89	0.70
Romanian (0)	33	0.26
Russian (952)	1,614	12.75
Scandinavian (9)	29	0.23
Scotch-Irish (33)	130	1.03
Scottish (55)	92	0.73
Slovak (0)	11	0.09
Swedish (0)	234	1.85
Swiss (0)	8	0.06
Ukrainian (213)	311	2.46
Welsh (0)	53	0.42
West Indian, ex. Hispanic (10)	10	0.08
Jamaican (10)	10	0.08
Yugoslavian (0)	18	0.14

Hispanic Origin	Population	%
Hispanic or Latino (of any race)	234	1.80
Central American, ex. Mexican	10	0.08
Costa Rican	2	0.02
Guatemalan	5	0.04
Nicaraguan	2	0.02
Salvadoran	1	0.01
Cuban	25	0.19
Dominican Republic	7	0.05
Mexican	29	0.22
Puerto Rican	90	0.69
South American	47	0.36
Argentinean	11	0.08
Colombian	14	0.11
Ecuadorian	5	0.04
Peruvian	15	0.12
Venezuelan	2	0.02
Other Hispanic or Latino	26	0.20

Race*	Population	%
African-American/Black (128)	158	1.22
Not Hispanic (124)	152	1.17
Hispanic (4)	6	0.05
American Indian/Alaska Native (18)	38	0.29
Not Hispanic (13)	32	0.25
Hispanic (5)	6	0.05
Central American Ind. (1)	1	0.01
Cherokee (1)	9	0.07
Delaware (0)	1	0.01
Iroquois (1)	3	0.02
Mexican American Ind. (1)	1	0.01
Asian (1,156)	1,259	9.70
Not Hispanic (1,152)	1,248	9.61
Hispanic (4)	11	0.08
Cambodian (12)	18	0.14
Chinese, ex. Taiwanese (145)	169	1.30
Filipino (26)	34	0.26
Indian (394)	436	3.36
Japanese (7)	17	0.13
Korean (441)	462	3.56
Pakistani (16)	19	0.15
Sri Lankan (1)	1	0.01
Taiwanese (13)	15	0.12
Thai (5)	5	0.04
Vietnamese (57)	60	0.46
Hawaii Native/Pacific Islander (7)	8	0.06
Not Hispanic (7)	7	0.05
Hispanic (0)	1	0.01
Native Hawaiian (3)	4	0.03
Samoan (0)	1	0.01
White (11,456)	11,571	89.13
Not Hispanic (11,308)	11,408	87.88
Hispanic (148)	163	1.26

Lower Paxton

Place Type: Township
County: Dauphin
Population: 47,360†

Ancestry‡	Population	%
African, Sub-Saharan (474)	483	1.03
African (365)	374	0.80
Cape Verdean (15)	15	0.03
Ethiopian (23)	23	0.05
Nigerian (8)	8	0.02
Sudanese (42)	42	0.09
Ugandan (21)	21	0.04
American (2,524)	2,524	5.39
Arab (275)	520	1.11
Arab (41)	245	0.52
Egyptian (224)	224	0.48
Lebanese (0)	11	0.02
Moroccan (0)	9	0.02
Syrian (0)	21	0.04
Other Arab (10)	10	0.02
Armenian (62)	62	0.13
Assyrian/Chaldean/Syriac (0)	17	0.04
Australian (0)	22	0.05
Austrian (8)	169	0.36
Basque (0)	14	0.03
Belgian (14)	14	0.03
British (42)	157	0.34
Bulgarian (0)	12	0.03
Canadian (11)	27	0.06
Carpatho Rusyn (0)	19	0.04
Croatian (202)	668	1.43
Czech (87)	453	0.97
Czechoslovakian (13)	53	0.11
Danish (9)	9	0.02
Dutch (301)	1,222	2.61
Eastern European (83)	83	0.18
English (848)	3,771	8.06
Estonian (0)	13	0.03
European (452)	495	1.06
Finnish (0)	9	0.02
French, ex. Basque (64)	930	1.99
French Canadian (84)	243	0.52
German (6,326)	15,978	34.14
German Russian (22)	22	0.05
Greek (55)	111	0.24
Hungarian (217)	575	1.23
Iranian (31)	31	0.07
Irish (1,391)	6,575	14.05
Italian (1,518)	4,563	9.75
Lithuanian (132)	302	0.65
Macedonian (0)	31	0.07
Northern European (0)	10	0.02
Norwegian (8)	108	0.23
Pennsylvania German (432)	528	1.13
Polish (555)	2,102	4.49
Portuguese (16)	61	0.13
Romanian (34)	59	0.13
Russian (247)	613	1.31
Scandinavian (14)	14	0.03
Scotch-Irish (226)	853	1.82
Scottish (119)	651	1.39
Serbian (40)	91	0.19
Slavic (39)	232	0.50
Slovak (207)	546	1.17
Slovene (23)	48	0.10
Swedish (98)	505	1.08
Swiss (9)	151	0.32
Turkish (11)	35	0.07
Ukrainian (296)	358	0.76
Welsh (180)	895	1.91
West Indian, ex. Hispanic (289)	342	0.73
Barbadian (18)	71	0.15
Haitian (6)	6	0.01
Jamaican (49)	49	0.10
Trinidadian/Tobagonian (91)	91	0.19
West Indian (125)	125	0.27
Yugoslavian (288)	371	0.79

Hispanic Origin	Population	%
Hispanic or Latino (of any race)	2,194	4.63
Central American, ex. Mexican	72	0.15
Costa Rican	4	0.01
Guatemalan	18	0.04
Honduran	11	0.02
Nicaraguan	3	0.01
Panamanian	15	0.03
Salvadoran	21	0.04
Cuban	110	0.23
Dominican Republic	142	0.30
Mexican	392	0.83
Puerto Rican	1,085	2.29
South American	223	0.47
Argentinean	6	0.01
Bolivian	2	<0.01
Chilean	9	0.02
Colombian	52	0.11
Ecuadorian	57	0.12
Paraguayan	2	<0.01
Peruvian	80	0.17
Uruguayan	4	0.01
Venezuelan	11	0.02
Other Hispanic or Latino	170	0.36

Race*	Population	%
African-American/Black (5,780)	6,691	14.13
Not Hispanic (5,534)	6,312	13.33
Hispanic (246)	379	0.80
American Indian/Alaska Native (65)	292	0.62
Not Hispanic (50)	230	0.49
Hispanic (15)	62	0.13
Apache (1)	4	0.01
Blackfeet (1)	19	0.04
Canadian/French Am. Ind. (1)	2	<0.01
Central American Ind. (1)	1	<0.01
Cherokee (5)	58	0.12
Chickasaw (3)	5	0.01
Chippewa (5)	5	0.01
Choctaw (0)	2	<0.01
Cree (0)	1	<0.01
Delaware (0)	1	<0.01
Iroquois (3)	6	0.01
Mexican American Ind. (2)	3	0.01
Navajo (1)	3	0.01
Osage (0)	2	<0.01
Paiute (0)	1	<0.01
Pueblo (0)	2	<0.01
Seminole (0)	4	0.01
Shoshone (1)	1	<0.01

*Notes: † The Census 2010 population figure is used to calculate the percentages in the Hispanic Origin and Race categories. Ancestry percentages are based on the 2006-2010 American Community Survey population (not shown); ‡ Numbers in parentheses indicate the number of people reporting a single ancestry; * Numbers in parentheses indicate the number of persons reporting this race alone, not in combination with any other race; Please refer to the Explanation of Data for more information.*

Sioux (3)	5	0.01
South American Ind. (1)	9	0.02
Spanish American Ind. (1)	1	<0.01
Yakama (0)	2	<0.01
Asian (2,163)	2,472	5.22
Not Hispanic (2,137)	2,418	5.11
Hispanic (26)	54	0.11
Bhutanese (28)	34	0.07
Cambodian (43)	45	0.10
Chinese, ex. Taiwanese (229)	271	0.57
Filipino (110)	149	0.31
Indian (977)	1,044	2.20
Indonesian (35)	35	0.07
Japanese (15)	52	0.11
Korean (88)	131	0.28
Laotian (2)	3	0.01
Nepalese (25)	26	0.05
Pakistani (111)	121	0.26
Sri Lankan (3)	3	0.01
Taiwanese (3)	9	0.02
Thai (12)	13	0.03
Vietnamese (419)	464	0.98
Hawaii Native/Pacific Islander (11)	39	0.08
Not Hispanic (11)	35	0.07
Hispanic (0)	4	0.01
Guamanian/Chamorro (4)	7	0.01
Native Hawaiian (4)	11	0.02
Samoan (1)	2	<0.01
White (37,314)	38,492	81.28
Not Hispanic (36,276)	37,275	78.71
Hispanic (1,038)	1,217	2.57

Lower Pottsgrove

Place Type: Township
County: Montgomery
Population: 12,059†

Ancestry‡	Population	%
African, Sub-Saharan (124)	133	1.12
African (0)	9	0.08
Ghanaian (124)	124	1.04
American (459)	459	3.86
Arab (20)	30	0.25
Lebanese (20)	30	0.25
Armenian (0)	10	0.08
Austrian (25)	136	1.14
British (35)	94	0.79
Canadian (9)	9	0.08
Celtic (0)	9	0.08
Czech (25)	33	0.28
Czechoslovakian (19)	53	0.45
Danish (0)	62	0.52
Dutch (31)	277	2.33
Eastern European (42)	42	0.35
English (333)	1,230	10.34
European (29)	29	0.24
French, ex. Basque (74)	294	2.47
French Canadian (8)	35	0.29
German (1,231)	3,773	31.71
Greek (0)	29	0.24
Hungarian (27)	104	0.87
Irish (541)	2,503	21.03
Italian (552)	2,161	18.16
Lithuanian (12)	25	0.21
Norwegian (45)	45	0.38
Pennsylvania German (238)	315	2.65
Polish (217)	785	6.60
Portuguese (0)	9	0.08
Romanian (26)	49	0.41
Russian (46)	126	1.06
Scandinavian (0)	15	0.13
Scotch-Irish (124)	315	2.65
Scottish (41)	204	1.71
Slavic (0)	10	0.08
Slovak (25)	179	1.50
Swedish (30)	89	0.75
Swiss (12)	21	0.18
Ukrainian (84)	457	3.84
Welsh (8)	87	0.73
West Indian, ex. Hispanic (13)	13	0.11
Jamaican (13)	13	0.11
Yugoslavian (7)	37	0.31

Hispanic Origin	Population	%
Hispanic or Latino (of any race)	326	2.70
Central American, ex. Mexican	7	0.06
Guatemalan	2	0.02
Nicaraguan	4	0.03
Salvadoran	1	0.01
Cuban	14	0.12
Dominican Republic	4	0.03
Mexican	79	0.66
Puerto Rican	158	1.31
South American	27	0.22
Argentinean	2	0.02
Bolivian	2	0.02
Colombian	9	0.07
Ecuadorian	5	0.04
Peruvian	9	0.07
Other Hispanic or Latino	37	0.31

Race*	Population	%
African-American/Black (1,220)	1,417	11.75
Not Hispanic (1,171)	1,356	11.24
Hispanic (49)	61	0.51
American Indian/Alaska Native (11)	55	0.46
Not Hispanic (8)	50	0.41
Hispanic (3)	5	0.04
Blackfeet (0)	12	0.10
Cherokee (1)	14	0.12
Choctaw (0)	1	0.01
Crow (0)	1	0.01
Delaware (0)	2	0.02
Iroquois (0)	1	0.01
Mexican American Ind. (2)	2	0.02
Sioux (0)	3	0.02
Asian (191)	241	2.00
Not Hispanic (188)	237	1.97
Hispanic (3)	4	0.03
Burmese (1)	3	0.02
Cambodian (2)	3	0.02
Chinese, ex. Taiwanese (41)	43	0.36
Filipino (21)	33	0.27
Indian (45)	55	0.46
Japanese (6)	14	0.12
Korean (25)	31	0.26
Laotian (1)	2	0.02
Nepalese (5)	5	0.04
Pakistani (11)	11	0.09
Sri Lankan (0)	2	0.02
Taiwanese (0)	1	0.01
Thai (2)	2	0.02
Vietnamese (26)	30	0.25
Hawaii Native/Pacific Islander (7)	14	0.12
Not Hispanic (7)	13	0.11
Hispanic (0)	1	0.01
Guamanian/Chamorro (0)	1	0.01
Marshallese (1)	1	0.01
Native Hawaiian (3)	6	0.05
Samoan (1)	7	0.06
White (10,290)	10,555	87.53
Not Hispanic (10,075)	10,312	85.51
Hispanic (215)	243	2.02

Lower Providence

Place Type: Township
County: Montgomery
Population: 25,436†

Ancestry‡	Population	%
African, Sub-Saharan (15)	22	0.09
African (15)	15	0.06
Liberian (0)	7	0.03
Albanian (37)	65	0.26
American (1,407)	1,407	5.65
Arab (9)	20	0.08
Lebanese (0)	11	0.04
Syrian (9)	9	0.04
Armenian (21)	51	0.20
Australian (0)	10	0.04
Austrian (22)	108	0.43
British (43)	101	0.41
Canadian (11)	11	0.04
Croatian (10)	129	0.52
Czech (48)	79	0.32
Czechoslovakian (10)	40	0.16
Danish (0)	50	0.20
Dutch (210)	613	2.46
Eastern European (33)	33	0.13
English (422)	1,963	7.89
European (312)	326	1.31
French, ex. Basque (61)	453	1.82
French Canadian (95)	279	1.12
German (1,274)	5,557	22.33
Greek (80)	133	0.53
Guyanese (12)	12	0.05
Hungarian (187)	389	1.56
Iranian (37)	37	0.15
Irish (1,552)	5,861	23.55
Italian (2,239)	6,137	24.66
Latvian (0)	15	0.06
Lithuanian (40)	72	0.29
Norwegian (34)	93	0.37
Pennsylvania German (171)	355	1.43
Polish (364)	1,653	6.64
Portuguese (11)	62	0.25
Romanian (93)	93	0.37
Russian (247)	332	1.33
Scotch-Irish (143)	636	2.56
Scottish (16)	313	1.26
Serbian (17)	17	0.07
Slovak (113)	322	1.29
Swedish (64)	226	0.91
Swiss (0)	36	0.14
Turkish (8)	8	0.03
Ukrainian (142)	313	1.26
Welsh (11)	128	0.51
West Indian, ex. Hispanic (54)	70	0.28
Jamaican (34)	50	0.20
Trinidadian/Tobagonian (20)	20	0.08

Hispanic Origin	Population	%
Hispanic or Latino (of any race)	730	2.87
Central American, ex. Mexican	43	0.17
Costa Rican	6	0.02
Guatemalan	9	0.04
Honduran	17	0.07
Panamanian	5	0.02
Salvadoran	6	0.02
Cuban	21	0.08
Dominican Republic	19	0.07
Mexican	270	1.06
Puerto Rican	215	0.85
South American	64	0.25
Argentinean	13	0.05
Bolivian	2	0.01
Chilean	2	0.01
Colombian	12	0.05
Ecuadorian	6	0.02
Peruvian	15	0.06
Uruguayan	3	0.01
Venezuelan	11	0.04
Other Hispanic or Latino	98	0.39

Race*	Population	%
African-American/Black (1,800)	1,947	7.65
Not Hispanic (1,770)	1,903	7.48
Hispanic (30)	44	0.17
American Indian/Alaska Native (22)	95	0.37
Not Hispanic (16)	76	0.30
Hispanic (6)	19	0.07
Apache (0)	1	<0.01
Blackfeet (0)	7	0.03
Central American Ind. (2)	8	0.03
Cherokee (3)	16	0.06
Creek (1)	1	<0.01
Delaware (1)	3	0.01
Iroquois (0)	2	0.01

*Notes: † The Census 2010 population figure is used to calculate the percentages in the Hispanic Origin and Race categories. Ancestry percentages are based on the 2006-2010 American Community Survey population (not shown); ‡ Numbers in parentheses indicate the number of people reporting a single ancestry; * Numbers in parentheses indicate the number of persons reporting this race alone, not in combination with any other race; Please refer to the Explanation of Data for more information.*

Lumbee (0)	1	<0.01
Menominee (1)	1	<0.01
Sioux (3)	6	0.02
South American Ind. (2)	5	0.02
Asian (2,479)	2,602	10.23
Not Hispanic (2,465)	2,583	10.15
Hispanic (14)	19	0.07
Bangladeshi (3)	3	0.01
Burmese (4)	4	0.02
Cambodian (21)	30	0.12
Chinese, ex. Taiwanese (728)	766	3.01
Filipino (78)	97	0.38
Indian (1,230)	1,268	4.99
Indonesian (6)	7	0.03
Japanese (24)	31	0.12
Korean (158)	174	0.68
Laotian (5)	6	0.02
Nepalese (1)	1	<0.01
Pakistani (51)	53	0.21
Sri Lankan (4)	4	0.02
Taiwanese (23)	27	0.11
Thai (15)	15	0.06
Vietnamese (96)	114	0.45
Hawaii Native/Pacific Islander (2)	8	0.03
Not Hispanic (2)	8	0.03
Samoan (1)	1	<0.01
White (20,605)	20,874	82.06
Not Hispanic (20,151)	20,391	80.17
Hispanic (454)	483	1.90

Lower Salford

Place Type: Township
County: Montgomery
Population: 14,959†

Ancestry‡	Population	%
African, Sub-Saharan (26)	26	0.18
African (26)	26	0.18
American (368)	368	2.52
Arab (8)	36	0.25
Other Arab (8)	36	0.25
Armenian (0)	7	0.05
Australian (12)	37	0.25
Austrian (13)	55	0.38
British (16)	36	0.25
Croatian (0)	43	0.29
Czech (11)	48	0.33
Czechoslovakian (11)	20	0.14
Danish (6)	55	0.38
Dutch (45)	175	1.20
Eastern European (14)	54	0.37
English (282)	1,376	9.43
European (69)	88	0.60
French, ex. Basque (14)	283	1.94
French Canadian (0)	56	0.38
German (1,754)	5,451	37.36
Greek (53)	117	0.80
Hungarian (54)	234	1.60
Iranian (10)	30	0.21
Irish (859)	3,783	25.93
Italian (736)	2,467	16.91
Latvian (42)	42	0.29
Lithuanian (9)	25	0.17
Norwegian (9)	71	0.49
Pennsylvania German (262)	324	2.22
Polish (215)	930	6.37
Portuguese (0)	30	0.21
Russian (95)	158	1.08
Scotch-Irish (101)	247	1.69
Scottish (69)	316	2.17
Slavic (0)	14	0.10
Slovak (8)	114	0.78
Swedish (0)	121	0.83
Swiss (69)	188	1.29
Turkish (5)	46	0.32
Ukrainian (20)	94	0.64
Welsh (170)	367	2.52
West Indian, ex. Hispanic (44)	55	0.38
Belizean (0)	11	0.08
Trinidadian/Tobagonian (44)	44	0.30
Yugoslavian (0)	27	0.19

Hispanic Origin	Population	%
Hispanic or Latino (of any race)	384	2.57
Central American, ex. Mexican	41	0.27
Costa Rican	5	0.03
Guatemalan	14	0.09
Honduran	15	0.10
Nicaraguan	3	0.02
Panamanian	2	0.01
Salvadoran	2	0.01
Cuban	21	0.14
Dominican Republic	6	0.04
Mexican	75	0.50
Puerto Rican	154	1.03
South American	54	0.36
Argentinean	4	0.03
Bolivian	1	0.01
Colombian	27	0.18
Ecuadorian	5	0.03
Peruvian	16	0.11
Venezuelan	1	0.01
Other Hispanic or Latino	33	0.22

Race*	Population	%
African-American/Black (436)	523	3.50
Not Hispanic (422)	491	3.28
Hispanic (14)	32	0.21
American Indian/Alaska Native (9)	39	0.26
Not Hispanic (3)	25	0.17
Hispanic (6)	14	0.09
Apache (0)	1	0.01
Blackfeet (0)	1	0.01
Cherokee (1)	7	0.05
Cheyenne (0)	3	0.02
Chippewa (1)	1	0.01
Mexican American Ind. (3)	3	0.02
Asian (664)	744	4.97
Not Hispanic (662)	738	4.93
Hispanic (2)	6	0.04
Bangladeshi (6)	6	0.04
Burmese (2)	4	0.03
Cambodian (0)	5	0.03
Chinese, ex. Taiwanese (119)	147	0.98
Filipino (28)	41	0.27
Indian (249)	268	1.79
Indonesian (2)	4	0.03
Japanese (14)	23	0.15
Korean (100)	110	0.74
Laotian (8)	10	0.07
Pakistani (25)	25	0.17
Sri Lankan (1)	1	0.01
Taiwanese (3)	3	0.02
Thai (4)	8	0.05
Vietnamese (86)	96	0.64
Hawaii Native/Pacific Islander (2)	9	0.06
Not Hispanic (1)	5	0.03
Hispanic (1)	4	0.03
Fijian (0)	2	0.01
Native Hawaiian (1)	2	0.01
White (13,550)	13,725	91.75
Not Hispanic (13,299)	13,447	89.89
Hispanic (251)	278	1.86

Lower Saucon

Place Type: Township
County: Northampton
Population: 10,772†

Ancestry‡	Population	%
American (399)	399	3.72
Austrian (0)	103	0.96
Belgian (14)	25	0.23
Croatian (11)	11	0.10
Czech (0)	43	0.40
Czechoslovakian (12)	43	0.40
Danish (0)	8	0.07
Dutch (51)	385	3.59
Eastern European (71)	71	0.66
English (420)	1,300	12.11
Estonian (0)	82	0.76
European (146)	162	1.51
Finnish (0)	15	0.14
French, ex. Basque (17)	151	1.41
French Canadian (10)	10	0.09
German (1,204)	3,127	29.13
Greek (96)	170	1.58
Hungarian (221)	535	4.98
Irish (673)	1,987	18.51
Italian (653)	1,373	12.79
Latvian (10)	10	0.09
Lithuanian (9)	27	0.25
New Zealander (0)	16	0.15
Norwegian (11)	11	0.10
Pennsylvania German (484)	749	6.98
Polish (81)	656	6.11
Portuguese (66)	156	1.45
Russian (32)	102	0.95
Scotch-Irish (25)	140	1.30
Scottish (24)	150	1.40
Serbian (18)	26	0.24
Slovak (168)	537	5.00
Slovene (10)	10	0.09
Swedish (0)	40	0.37
Swiss (0)	26	0.24
Ukrainian (97)	248	2.31
Welsh (21)	203	1.89
Yugoslavian (8)	30	0.28

Hispanic Origin	Population	%
Hispanic or Latino (of any race)	408	3.79
Central American, ex. Mexican	16	0.15
Costa Rican	1	0.01
Guatemalan	2	0.02
Honduran	2	0.02
Nicaraguan	4	0.04
Panamanian	1	0.01
Salvadoran	6	0.06
Cuban	17	0.16
Dominican Republic	2	0.02
Mexican	76	0.71
Puerto Rican	180	1.67
South American	79	0.73
Argentinean	3	0.03
Bolivian	3	0.03
Chilean	12	0.11
Colombian	27	0.25
Ecuadorian	22	0.20
Peruvian	2	0.02
Uruguayan	1	0.01
Venezuelan	9	0.08
Other Hispanic or Latino	38	0.35

Race*	Population	%
African-American/Black (123)	160	1.49
Not Hispanic (109)	135	1.25
Hispanic (14)	25	0.23
American Indian/Alaska Native (21)	52	0.48
Not Hispanic (9)	36	0.33
Hispanic (12)	16	0.15
Cherokee (7)	12	0.11
Choctaw (0)	2	0.02
Delaware (0)	2	0.02
Mexican American Ind. (1)	1	0.01
Navajo (0)	1	0.01
South American Ind. (1)	2	0.02
Asian (203)	243	2.26
Not Hispanic (200)	234	2.17
Hispanic (3)	9	0.08
Chinese, ex. Taiwanese (42)	46	0.43
Filipino (13)	22	0.20
Indian (61)	61	0.57
Japanese (7)	16	0.15
Korean (32)	39	0.36
Laotian (1)	3	0.03
Pakistani (21)	24	0.22
Thai (3)	5	0.05
Vietnamese (23)	23	0.21

*Notes: † The Census 2010 population figure is used to calculate the percentages in the Hispanic Origin and Race categories. Ancestry percentages are based on the 2006-2010 American Community Survey population (not shown); ‡ Numbers in parentheses indicate the number of people reporting a single ancestry; * Numbers in parentheses indicate the number of persons reporting this race alone, not in combination with any other race; Please refer to the Explanation of Data for more information.*

Hawaii Native/Pacific Islander (0)	3	0.03
Not Hispanic (0)	3	0.03
Native Hawaiian (0)	3	0.03
White (10,230)	10,331	95.91
Not Hispanic (9,948)	10,025	93.07
Hispanic (282)	306	2.84

Lower Southampton

Place Type: Township
County: Bucks
Population: 18,909†

Ancestry‡	Population	%
Albanian (27)	85	0.45
American (819)	819	4.29
Arab (176)	176	0.92
Moroccan (176)	176	0.92
Austrian (41)	133	0.70
British (35)	54	0.28
Celtic (0)	57	0.30
Croatian (16)	16	0.08
Czech (13)	27	0.14
Czechoslovakian (0)	41	0.21
Dutch (13)	111	0.58
Eastern European (34)	34	0.18
English (419)	1,835	9.62
Estonian (0)	5	0.03
European (101)	101	0.53
Finnish (0)	5	0.03
French, ex. Basque (12)	346	1.81
French Canadian (16)	16	0.08
German (1,352)	4,970	26.06
Greek (16)	74	0.39
Hungarian (48)	238	1.25
Irish (1,778)	5,747	30.14
Italian (795)	2,491	13.06
Lithuanian (93)	182	0.95
Norwegian (22)	41	0.21
Pennsylvania German (115)	189	0.99
Polish (528)	1,841	9.65
Portuguese (26)	81	0.42
Romanian (0)	187	0.98
Russian (861)	1,580	8.29
Scandinavian (18)	26	0.14
Scotch-Irish (125)	312	1.64
Scottish (46)	340	1.78
Serbian (0)	7	0.04
Slavic (0)	44	0.23
Slovak (21)	44	0.23
Slovene (10)	10	0.05
Swedish (11)	65	0.34
Swiss (0)	23	0.12
Turkish (18)	18	0.09
Ukrainian (626)	827	4.34
Welsh (47)	249	1.31
West Indian, ex. Hispanic (17)	26	0.14
Trinidadian/Tobagonian (0)	9	0.05
West Indian (17)	17	0.09

Hispanic Origin	Population	%
Hispanic or Latino (of any race)	521	2.76
Central American, ex. Mexican	37	0.20
Costa Rican	4	0.02
Guatemalan	13	0.07
Honduran	4	0.02
Nicaraguan	6	0.03
Panamanian	1	0.01
Salvadoran	9	0.05
Cuban	17	0.09
Dominican Republic	18	0.10
Mexican	84	0.44
Puerto Rican	276	1.46
South American	59	0.31
Argentinean	6	0.03
Bolivian	3	0.02
Colombian	15	0.08
Ecuadorian	3	0.02
Paraguayan	2	0.01
Peruvian	23	0.12
Venezuelan	5	0.03
Other South American	2	0.01
Other Hispanic or Latino	30	0.16

Race*	Population	%
African-American/Black (338)	420	2.22
Not Hispanic (327)	404	2.14
Hispanic (11)	16	0.08
American Indian/Alaska Native (29)	80	0.42
Not Hispanic (22)	68	0.36
Hispanic (7)	12	0.06
Blackfeet (0)	3	0.02
Cherokee (1)	15	0.08
Chippewa (0)	3	0.02
Creek (0)	2	0.01
Delaware (1)	7	0.04
Iroquois (0)	2	0.01
Kiowa (1)	1	0.01
Potawatomi (1)	1	0.01
Sioux (2)	6	0.03
South American Ind. (6)	6	0.03
Asian (481)	555	2.94
Not Hispanic (479)	547	2.89
Hispanic (2)	8	0.04
Cambodian (1)	6	0.03
Chinese, ex. Taiwanese (54)	67	0.35
Filipino (20)	40	0.21
Indian (277)	289	1.53
Indonesian (5)	5	0.03
Japanese (7)	17	0.09
Korean (61)	76	0.40
Malaysian (1)	1	0.01
Pakistani (10)	10	0.05
Taiwanese (2)	2	0.01
Thai (6)	7	0.04
Vietnamese (18)	28	0.15
Hawaii Native/Pacific Islander (4)	8	0.04
Not Hispanic (4)	8	0.04
Native Hawaiian (4)	6	0.03
White (17,718)	17,905	94.69
Not Hispanic (17,368)	17,533	92.72
Hispanic (350)	372	1.97

Lower Swatara

Place Type: Township
County: Dauphin
Population: 8,268†

Ancestry‡	Population	%
American (625)	625	7.61
Arab (0)	40	0.49
Other Arab (0)	40	0.49
Austrian (0)	92	1.12
British (0)	12	0.15
Croatian (10)	127	1.55
Czech (0)	20	0.24
Dutch (21)	118	1.44
English (159)	446	5.43
European (83)	133	1.62
French, ex. Basque (26)	148	1.80
German (1,575)	3,076	37.46
Hungarian (0)	144	1.75
Irish (235)	1,131	13.77
Italian (217)	554	6.75
Lithuanian (37)	52	0.63
Northern European (56)	56	0.68
Pennsylvania German (117)	150	1.83
Polish (160)	540	6.58
Russian (23)	96	1.17
Scotch-Irish (37)	208	2.53
Scottish (26)	111	1.35
Serbian (31)	69	0.84
Slavic (31)	44	0.54
Slovak (68)	263	3.20
Slovene (8)	27	0.33
Swedish (20)	42	0.51
Ukrainian (17)	34	0.41
Welsh (0)	38	0.46

Hispanic Origin	Population	%
Hispanic or Latino (of any race)	330	3.99
Central American, ex. Mexican	26	0.31
Costa Rican	2	0.02
Guatemalan	5	0.06
Honduran	8	0.10
Nicaraguan	1	0.01
Panamanian	4	0.05
Salvadoran	6	0.07
Cuban	4	0.05
Dominican Republic	9	0.11
Mexican	102	1.23
Puerto Rican	121	1.46
South American	35	0.42
Argentinean	1	0.01
Bolivian	3	0.04
Chilean	1	0.01
Colombian	4	0.05
Ecuadorian	7	0.08
Peruvian	16	0.19
Venezuelan	3	0.04
Other Hispanic or Latino	33	0.40

Race*	Population	%
African-American/Black (400)	552	6.68
Not Hispanic (373)	515	6.23
Hispanic (27)	37	0.45
American Indian/Alaska Native (16)	66	0.80
Not Hispanic (13)	59	0.71
Hispanic (3)	7	0.08
Cherokee (1)	11	0.13
Chippewa (2)	3	0.04
Lumbee (1)	1	0.01
Sioux (2)	6	0.07
Asian (114)	167	2.02
Not Hispanic (114)	163	1.97
Hispanic (0)	4	0.05
Cambodian (1)	2	0.02
Chinese, ex. Taiwanese (25)	29	0.35
Filipino (10)	22	0.27
Indian (30)	33	0.40
Japanese (5)	19	0.23
Korean (17)	25	0.30
Laotian (3)	6	0.07
Pakistani (6)	10	0.12
Taiwanese (2)	2	0.02
Vietnamese (8)	17	0.21
Hawaii Native/Pacific Islander (0)	7	0.08
Not Hispanic (0)	7	0.08
Guamanian/Chamorro (0)	1	0.01
Native Hawaiian (0)	4	0.05
White (7,399)	7,625	92.22
Not Hispanic (7,220)	7,425	89.80
Hispanic (179)	200	2.42

Loyalsock

Place Type: Township
County: Lycoming
Population: 11,026†

Ancestry‡	Population	%
American (678)	678	6.19
Arab (0)	13	0.12
Lebanese (0)	13	0.12
Armenian (0)	17	0.16
Austrian (0)	41	0.37
Belgian (0)	18	0.16
British (30)	45	0.41
Cajun (0)	31	0.28
Canadian (51)	89	0.81
Czech (10)	50	0.46
Czechoslovakian (14)	14	0.13
Danish (0)	29	0.26
Dutch (86)	466	4.25
English (391)	1,175	10.72
European (16)	16	0.15
French, ex. Basque (58)	187	1.71
French Canadian (23)	61	0.56
German (1,633)	4,059	37.04

*Notes: † The Census 2010 population figure is used to calculate the percentages in the Hispanic Origin and Race categories. Ancestry percentages are based on the 2006-2010 American Community Survey population (not shown); ‡ Numbers in parentheses indicate the number of people reporting a single ancestry; * Numbers in parentheses indicate the number of persons reporting this race alone, not in combination with any other race; Please refer to the Explanation of Data for more information.*

Greek (15)	15	0.14
Hungarian (35)	35	0.32
Irish (402)	2,002	18.27
Italian (694)	1,342	12.25
Latvian (9)	9	0.08
Lithuanian (14)	26	0.24
Pennsylvania German (109)	109	0.99
Polish (153)	337	3.08
Russian (0)	79	0.72
Scotch-Irish (44)	140	1.28
Scottish (128)	418	3.81
Slavic (19)	19	0.17
Slovak (31)	31	0.28
Swedish (0)	110	1.00
Swiss (0)	15	0.14
Ukrainian (14)	107	0.98
Welsh (52)	219	2.00
West Indian, ex. Hispanic (24)	24	0.22
West Indian (24)	24	0.22

Hispanic Origin	Population	%
Hispanic or Latino (of any race)	127	1.15
Central American, ex. Mexican	1	0.01
Guatemalan	1	0.01
Cuban	5	0.05
Dominican Republic	2	0.02
Mexican	42	0.38
Puerto Rican	39	0.35
South American	12	0.11
Ecuadorian	7	0.06
Peruvian	2	0.02
Uruguayan	2	0.02
Venezuelan	1	0.01
Other Hispanic or Latino	26	0.24

Race*	Population	%
African-American/Black (313)	397	3.60
Not Hispanic (303)	384	3.48
Hispanic (10)	13	0.12
American Indian/Alaska Native (13)	48	0.44
Not Hispanic (12)	45	0.41
Hispanic (1)	3	0.03
Apache (0)	4	0.04
Blackfeet (0)	3	0.03
Cherokee (1)	8	0.07
Cheyenne (1)	1	0.01
Chippewa (2)	2	0.02
Iroquois (1)	3	0.03
Navajo (2)	3	0.03
Asian (151)	185	1.68
Not Hispanic (151)	183	1.66
Hispanic (0)	2	0.02
Chinese, ex. Taiwanese (38)	42	0.38
Filipino (20)	30	0.27
Indian (49)	60	0.54
Japanese (4)	5	0.05
Korean (15)	20	0.18
Pakistani (14)	16	0.15
Sri Lankan (4)	4	0.04
Vietnamese (4)	5	0.05
Hawaii Native/Pacific Islander (4)	18	0.16
Not Hispanic (4)	12	0.11
Hispanic (0)	6	0.05
Guamanian/Chamorro (0)	1	0.01
Native Hawaiian (1)	4	0.04
Samoan (2)	10	0.09
White (10,345)	10,482	95.07
Not Hispanic (10,269)	10,398	94.30
Hispanic (76)	84	0.76

Maidencreek

Place Type: Township
County: Berks
Population: 9,126†

Ancestry‡	Population	%
African, Sub-Saharan (48)	113	1.30
African (48)	113	1.30
American (406)	406	4.66
Austrian (0)	28	0.32
Belgian (0)	13	0.15
British (14)	70	0.80
Danish (12)	44	0.50
Dutch (68)	269	3.09
English (53)	612	7.02
French, ex. Basque (12)	168	1.93
French Canadian (83)	128	1.47
German (1,368)	3,400	39.01
Greek (14)	24	0.28
Hungarian (87)	99	1.14
Irish (291)	1,578	18.11
Italian (258)	1,284	14.73
Lithuanian (25)	67	0.77
Norwegian (48)	75	0.86
Pennsylvania German (411)	584	6.70
Polish (205)	694	7.96
Portuguese (0)	71	0.81
Romanian (0)	12	0.14
Russian (25)	133	1.53
Scotch-Irish (22)	92	1.06
Scottish (40)	217	2.49
Slavic (13)	13	0.15
Slovak (35)	142	1.63
Swedish (0)	41	0.47
Swiss (0)	26	0.30
Ukrainian (15)	58	0.67
Welsh (17)	135	1.55
West Indian, ex. Hispanic (94)	94	1.08
Jamaican (94)	94	1.08

Hispanic Origin	Population	%
Hispanic or Latino (of any race)	516	5.65
Central American, ex. Mexican	40	0.44
Costa Rican	4	0.04
Guatemalan	29	0.32
Honduran	1	0.01
Nicaraguan	3	0.03
Panamanian	3	0.03
Cuban	15	0.16
Dominican Republic	44	0.48
Mexican	77	0.84
Puerto Rican	242	2.65
South American	57	0.62
Argentinean	3	0.03
Colombian	23	0.25
Ecuadorian	26	0.28
Peruvian	5	0.05
Other Hispanic or Latino	41	0.45

Race*	Population	%
African-American/Black (281)	360	3.94
Not Hispanic (253)	306	3.35
Hispanic (28)	54	0.59
American Indian/Alaska Native (11)	44	0.48
Not Hispanic (7)	37	0.41
Hispanic (4)	7	0.08
Blackfeet (0)	4	0.04
Central American Ind. (1)	1	0.01
Cherokee (1)	8	0.09
Chippewa (3)	4	0.04
Iroquois (1)	1	0.01
South American Ind. (0)	1	0.01
Asian (144)	192	2.10
Not Hispanic (140)	178	1.95
Hispanic (4)	14	0.15
Cambodian (3)	7	0.08
Chinese, ex. Taiwanese (46)	48	0.53
Filipino (24)	34	0.37
Indian (32)	47	0.52
Japanese (0)	1	0.01
Korean (3)	6	0.07
Pakistani (15)	16	0.18
Sri Lankan (1)	3	0.03
Taiwanese (1)	1	0.01
Vietnamese (11)	20	0.22
Hawaii Native/Pacific Islander (2)	10	0.11
Not Hispanic (2)	7	0.08
Hispanic (0)	3	0.03
Samoan (2)	5	0.05
White (8,378)	8,522	93.38
Not Hispanic (8,085)	8,180	89.63
Hispanic (293)	342	3.75

Manchester

Place Type: Township
County: York
Population: 18,161†

Ancestry‡	Population	%
African, Sub-Saharan (0)	108	0.62
Nigerian (0)	108	0.62
American (1,132)	1,132	6.55
Arab (13)	13	0.08
Lebanese (8)	8	0.05
Syrian (5)	5	0.03
Austrian (0)	57	0.33
Belgian (0)	15	0.09
Brazilian (0)	19	0.11
British (12)	19	0.11
Croatian (7)	47	0.27
Czech (0)	30	0.17
Czechoslovakian (9)	9	0.05
Danish (9)	44	0.25
Dutch (71)	175	1.01
Eastern European (0)	26	0.15
English (329)	1,648	9.53
European (129)	129	0.75
Finnish (0)	24	0.14
French, ex. Basque (22)	365	2.11
French Canadian (35)	73	0.42
German (3,844)	7,667	44.34
Greek (40)	174	1.01
Hungarian (9)	90	0.52
Iranian (14)	14	0.08
Irish (419)	2,261	13.08
Italian (319)	1,146	6.63
Lithuanian (0)	47	0.27
Norwegian (0)	136	0.79
Pennsylvania German (117)	117	0.68
Polish (171)	915	5.29
Portuguese (10)	10	0.06
Romanian (0)	41	0.24
Russian (114)	203	1.17
Scandinavian (0)	11	0.06
Scotch-Irish (224)	483	2.79
Scottish (39)	199	1.15
Slavic (8)	26	0.15
Slovak (8)	98	0.57
Swedish (26)	101	0.58
Swiss (0)	64	0.37
Ukrainian (50)	92	0.53
Welsh (0)	226	1.31
West Indian, ex. Hispanic (8)	21	0.12
Haitian (8)	8	0.05
Jamaican (0)	13	0.08
Yugoslavian (10)	37	0.21

Hispanic Origin	Population	%
Hispanic or Latino (of any race)	651	3.58
Central American, ex. Mexican	61	0.34
Costa Rican	4	0.02
Guatemalan	12	0.07
Honduran	1	0.01
Nicaraguan	17	0.09
Panamanian	6	0.03
Salvadoran	21	0.12
Cuban	13	0.07
Dominican Republic	53	0.29
Mexican	99	0.55
Puerto Rican	304	1.67
South American	71	0.39
Argentinean	6	0.03
Chilean	2	0.01
Colombian	19	0.10
Ecuadorian	34	0.19
Peruvian	6	0.03
Venezuelan	4	0.02
Other Hispanic or Latino	50	0.28

*Notes: † The Census 2010 population figure is used to calculate the percentages in the Hispanic Origin and Race categories. Ancestry percentages are based on the 2006-2010 American Community Survey population (not shown); ‡ Numbers in parentheses indicate the number of people reporting a single ancestry; * Numbers in parentheses indicate the number of persons reporting this race alone, not in combination with any other race; Please refer to the Explanation of Data for more information.*

Race*	Population	%
African-American/Black (1,065)	1,239	6.82
Not Hispanic (1,033)	1,185	6.52
Hispanic (32)	54	0.30
American Indian/Alaska Native (32)	83	0.46
Not Hispanic (29)	72	0.40
Hispanic (3)	11	0.06
Apache (2)	7	0.04
Blackfeet (0)	1	0.01
Central American Ind. (0)	1	0.01
Cherokee (3)	13	0.07
Choctaw (0)	1	0.01
Creek (0)	1	0.01
Kiowa (0)	2	0.01
Mexican American Ind. (1)	3	0.02
Sioux (0)	1	0.01
Asian (633)	755	4.16
Not Hispanic (632)	748	4.12
Hispanic (1)	7	0.04
Cambodian (41)	44	0.24
Chinese, ex. Taiwanese (146)	169	0.93
Filipino (39)	62	0.34
Indian (179)	199	1.10
Indonesian (6)	6	0.03
Japanese (6)	23	0.13
Korean (47)	62	0.34
Laotian (8)	10	0.06
Nepalese (3)	3	0.02
Pakistani (12)	14	0.08
Taiwanese (1)	1	0.01
Thai (1)	1	0.01
Vietnamese (119)	144	0.79
Hawaii Native/Pacific Islander (13)	29	0.16
Not Hispanic (13)	26	0.14
Hispanic (0)	3	0.02
Guamanian/Chamorro (4)	4	0.02
Native Hawaiian (0)	9	0.05
Samoan (7)	10	0.06
Tongan (0)	3	0.02
White (15,819)	16,114	88.73
Not Hispanic (15,481)	15,736	86.65
Hispanic (338)	378	2.08

Manheim

Place Type: Township
County: Lancaster
Population: 38,133†

Ancestry‡	Population	%
African, Sub-Saharan (78)	111	0.30
African (53)	86	0.23
South African (13)	13	0.03
Zimbabwean (12)	12	0.03
Albanian (0)	10	0.03
American (1,826)	1,826	4.89
Arab (170)	251	0.67
Arab (78)	78	0.21
Egyptian (17)	17	0.05
Iraqi (16)	16	0.04
Jordanian (15)	15	0.04
Lebanese (0)	81	0.22
Other Arab (44)	44	0.12
Armenian (0)	9	0.02
Austrian (75)	214	0.57
Belgian (30)	47	0.13
British (154)	283	0.76
Canadian (53)	77	0.21
Carpatho Rusyn (8)	8	0.02
Czech (109)	211	0.56
Czechoslovakian (29)	64	0.17
Danish (13)	99	0.26
Dutch (95)	464	1.24
Eastern European (57)	57	0.15
English (1,582)	4,677	12.52
European (526)	586	1.57
Finnish (0)	12	0.03
French, ex. Basque (260)	1,188	3.18
French Canadian (70)	250	0.67
German (6,485)	13,729	36.75
Greek (350)	569	1.52
Hungarian (40)	137	0.37
Iranian (11)	11	0.03
Irish (1,067)	5,085	13.61
Italian (983)	2,422	6.48
Latvian (0)	12	0.03
Lithuanian (61)	256	0.69
Northern European (14)	14	0.04
Norwegian (65)	107	0.29
Pennsylvania German (82)	143	0.38
Polish (515)	1,728	4.63
Portuguese (12)	28	0.07
Romanian (15)	36	0.10
Russian (184)	394	1.05
Scandinavian (0)	29	0.08
Scotch-Irish (361)	979	2.62
Scottish (293)	970	2.60
Serbian (0)	12	0.03
Slavic (25)	97	0.26
Slovak (190)	341	0.91
Slovene (46)	58	0.16
Swedish (122)	450	1.20
Swiss (93)	625	1.67
Turkish (15)	15	0.04
Ukrainian (91)	203	0.54
Welsh (77)	497	1.33
West Indian, ex. Hispanic (33)	33	0.09
Haitian (33)	33	0.09
Yugoslavian (101)	128	0.34

Hispanic Origin	Population	%
Hispanic or Latino (of any race)	2,498	6.55
Central American, ex. Mexican	104	0.27
Costa Rican	3	0.01
Guatemalan	47	0.12
Honduran	17	0.04
Nicaraguan	5	0.01
Panamanian	3	0.01
Salvadoran	29	0.08
Cuban	129	0.34
Dominican Republic	142	0.37
Mexican	231	0.61
Puerto Rican	1,503	3.94
South American	219	0.57
Argentinean	22	0.06
Bolivian	4	0.01
Chilean	20	0.05
Colombian	76	0.20
Ecuadorian	25	0.07
Paraguayan	4	0.01
Peruvian	50	0.13
Uruguayan	4	0.01
Venezuelan	14	0.04
Other Hispanic or Latino	170	0.45

Race*	Population	%
African-American/Black (1,153)	1,485	3.89
Not Hispanic (1,031)	1,270	3.33
Hispanic (122)	215	0.56
American Indian/Alaska Native (42)	144	0.38
Not Hispanic (16)	82	0.22
Hispanic (26)	62	0.16
Apache (1)	1	<0.01
Canadian/French Am. Ind. (0)	4	0.01
Central American Ind. (2)	2	0.01
Cherokee (3)	22	0.06
Chickasaw (1)	1	<0.01
Chippewa (0)	1	<0.01
Choctaw (1)	1	<0.01
Cree (1)	1	<0.01
Crow (0)	2	0.01
Delaware (0)	2	0.01
Iroquois (2)	6	0.02
Mexican American Ind. (3)	4	0.01
Navajo (2)	2	0.01
South American Ind. (3)	6	0.02
Asian (1,894)	2,122	5.56
Not Hispanic (1,883)	2,083	5.46
Hispanic (11)	39	0.10
Bangladeshi (5)	5	0.01
Cambodian (135)	140	0.37
Chinese, ex. Taiwanese (323)	384	1.01
Filipino (99)	124	0.33
Hmong (4)	4	0.01
Indian (357)	385	1.01
Indonesian (4)	4	0.01
Japanese (35)	59	0.15
Korean (127)	158	0.41
Laotian (19)	24	0.06
Nepalese (9)	9	0.02
Pakistani (9)	12	0.03
Sri Lankan (5)	5	0.01
Taiwanese (3)	7	0.02
Thai (2)	9	0.02
Vietnamese (704)	760	1.99
Hawaii Native/Pacific Islander (3)	23	0.06
Not Hispanic (3)	21	0.06
Hispanic (0)	2	0.01
Guamanian/Chamorro (0)	1	<0.01
Native Hawaiian (3)	14	0.04
Samoan (0)	1	<0.01
White (33,405)	34,043	89.27
Not Hispanic (32,160)	32,629	85.57
Hispanic (1,245)	1,414	3.71

Manor

Place Type: Township
County: Lancaster
Population: 19,612†

Ancestry‡	Population	%
African, Sub-Saharan (10)	10	0.05
African (10)	10	0.05
American (1,462)	1,462	7.66
Arab (12)	34	0.18
Lebanese (0)	22	0.12
Other Arab (12)	12	0.06
Austrian (0)	38	0.20
Belgian (0)	8	0.04
British (97)	147	0.77
Canadian (0)	45	0.24
Croatian (0)	6	0.03
Czech (24)	39	0.20
Czechoslovakian (0)	9	0.05
Danish (32)	71	0.37
Dutch (84)	343	1.80
Eastern European (10)	10	0.05
English (668)	2,008	10.52
European (274)	338	1.77
French, ex. Basque (124)	550	2.88
French Canadian (15)	59	0.31
German (4,086)	8,766	45.93
Greek (51)	75	0.39
Hungarian (18)	51	0.27
Irish (294)	2,454	12.86
Italian (483)	1,584	8.30
Lithuanian (0)	104	0.54
Norwegian (35)	255	1.34
Pennsylvania German (21)	32	0.17
Polish (221)	548	2.87
Portuguese (7)	63	0.33
Russian (12)	272	1.43
Scandinavian (10)	10	0.05
Scotch-Irish (117)	210	1.10
Scottish (97)	230	1.21
Serbian (0)	13	0.07
Slavic (12)	12	0.06
Slovak (74)	106	0.56
Swedish (8)	119	0.62
Swiss (75)	564	2.96
Ukrainian (7)	87	0.46
Welsh (8)	89	0.47
West Indian, ex. Hispanic (79)	161	0.84
Jamaican (79)	161	0.84
Yugoslavian (18)	18	0.09

Hispanic Origin	Population	%
Hispanic or Latino (of any race)	1,230	6.27

*Notes: † The Census 2010 population figure is used to calculate the percentages in the Hispanic Origin and Race categories. Ancestry percentages are based on the 2006-2010 American Community Survey population (not shown); ‡ Numbers in parentheses indicate the number of people reporting a single ancestry; * Numbers in parentheses indicate the number of persons reporting this race alone, not in combination with any other race; Please refer to the Explanation of Data for more information.*

Central American, ex. Mexican	24	0.12
Costa Rican	5	0.03
Guatemalan	2	0.01
Honduran	6	0.03
Nicaraguan	1	0.01
Panamanian	4	0.02
Salvadoran	6	0.03
Cuban	43	0.22
Dominican Republic	80	0.41
Mexican	87	0.44
Puerto Rican	809	4.13
South American	78	0.40
Argentinean	5	0.03
Bolivian	1	0.01
Chilean	1	0.01
Colombian	31	0.16
Ecuadorian	11	0.06
Peruvian	14	0.07
Uruguayan	5	0.03
Venezuelan	10	0.05
Other Hispanic or Latino	109	0.56

Race*	Population	%
African-American/Black (506)	709	3.62
Not Hispanic (414)	563	2.87
Hispanic (92)	146	0.74
American Indian/Alaska Native (47)	113	0.58
Not Hispanic (33)	78	0.40
Hispanic (14)	35	0.18
Blackfeet (1)	7	0.04
Cherokee (3)	12	0.06
Chippewa (1)	2	0.01
Choctaw (1)	3	0.02
Comanche (0)	1	0.01
Delaware (1)	1	0.01
Iroquois (1)	1	0.01
Mexican American Ind. (1)	1	0.01
Navajo (1)	5	0.03
Potawatomi (5)	5	0.03
Sioux (0)	1	0.01
South American Ind. (4)	14	0.07
Asian (325)	380	1.94
Not Hispanic (324)	371	1.89
Hispanic (1)	9	0.05
Bangladeshi (3)	3	0.02
Burmese (1)	1	0.01
Cambodian (11)	18	0.09
Chinese, ex. Taiwanese (81)	98	0.50
Filipino (24)	43	0.22
Indian (47)	50	0.25
Indonesian (1)	1	0.01
Japanese (5)	6	0.03
Korean (24)	27	0.14
Pakistani (18)	19	0.10
Sri Lankan (4)	4	0.02
Thai (3)	6	0.03
Vietnamese (91)	110	0.56
Hawaii Native/Pacific Islander (6)	7	0.04
Not Hispanic (6)	7	0.04
Native Hawaiian (1)	1	0.01
White (17,998)	18,293	93.27
Not Hispanic (17,352)	17,567	89.57
Hispanic (646)	726	3.70

Marple

Place Type: Township
County: Delaware
Population: 23,428†

Ancestry‡	Population	%
African, Sub-Saharan (29)	40	0.17
African (0)	11	0.05
Other Sub-Saharan African (29)	29	0.12
Albanian (22)	22	0.09
Alsatian (0)	21	0.09
American (875)	875	3.74
Arab (76)	162	0.69
Arab (70)	70	0.30
Lebanese (6)	92	0.39
Armenian (394)	421	1.80
Australian (0)	22	0.09
Austrian (0)	64	0.27
British (10)	51	0.22
Canadian (5)	18	0.08
Croatian (46)	56	0.24
Czech (0)	9	0.04
Danish (0)	22	0.09
Dutch (31)	323	1.38
Eastern European (109)	109	0.47
English (339)	2,194	9.37
European (107)	107	0.46
Finnish (5)	10	0.04
French, ex. Basque (40)	342	1.46
French Canadian (9)	38	0.16
German (746)	3,787	16.17
Greek (540)	632	2.70
Hungarian (38)	182	0.78
Iranian (245)	245	1.05
Irish (2,424)	6,361	27.16
Italian (3,406)	6,101	26.05
Latvian (9)	9	0.04
Lithuanian (31)	189	0.81
Norwegian (35)	90	0.38
Pennsylvania German (8)	39	0.17
Polish (416)	984	4.20
Romanian (42)	54	0.23
Russian (469)	732	3.13
Scandinavian (10)	10	0.04
Scotch-Irish (353)	556	2.37
Scottish (43)	468	2.00
Serbian (12)	12	0.05
Slavic (7)	7	0.03
Slovak (23)	64	0.27
Swedish (47)	154	0.66
Swiss (10)	75	0.32
Turkish (0)	15	0.06
Ukrainian (33)	119	0.51
Welsh (34)	200	0.85

Hispanic Origin	Population	%
Hispanic or Latino (of any race)	303	1.29
Central American, ex. Mexican	23	0.10
Costa Rican	2	0.01
Guatemalan	12	0.05
Honduran	5	0.02
Nicaraguan	3	0.01
Salvadoran	1	<0.01
Cuban	25	0.11
Dominican Republic	6	0.03
Mexican	68	0.29
Puerto Rican	52	0.22
South American	81	0.35
Argentinean	12	0.05
Bolivian	4	0.02
Chilean	3	0.01
Colombian	7	0.03
Ecuadorian	28	0.12
Paraguayan	9	0.04
Peruvian	9	0.04
Uruguayan	1	<0.01
Venezuelan	5	0.02
Other South American	3	0.01
Other Hispanic or Latino	48	0.20

Race*	Population	%
African-American/Black (497)	560	2.39
Not Hispanic (489)	548	2.34
Hispanic (8)	12	0.05
American Indian/Alaska Native (15)	62	0.26
Not Hispanic (11)	44	0.19
Hispanic (4)	18	0.08
Aleut *(Alaska Native)* (0)	1	<0.01
Apache (0)	1	<0.01
Central American Ind. (0)	1	<0.01
Cherokee (0)	7	0.03
Chippewa (0)	1	<0.01
Delaware (1)	2	0.01
Mexican American Ind. (0)	2	0.01
Sioux (2)	2	0.01
Asian (1,650)	1,760	7.51
Not Hispanic (1,647)	1,756	7.50
Hispanic (3)	4	0.02
Bangladeshi (18)	18	0.08
Burmese (2)	2	0.01
Cambodian (11)	11	0.05
Chinese, ex. Taiwanese (280)	305	1.30
Filipino (16)	31	0.13
Indian (414)	437	1.87
Indonesian (0)	1	<0.01
Japanese (20)	34	0.15
Korean (587)	606	2.59
Laotian (14)	15	0.06
Pakistani (12)	12	0.05
Taiwanese (21)	26	0.11
Thai (11)	14	0.06
Vietnamese (207)	216	0.92
Hawaii Native/Pacific Islander (1)	7	0.03
Not Hispanic (1)	7	0.03
Guamanian/Chamorro (0)	2	0.01
White (20,989)	21,166	90.34
Not Hispanic (20,776)	20,930	89.34
Hispanic (213)	236	1.01

Maxatawny

Place Type: Township
County: Berks
Population: 7,906†

Ancestry‡	Population	%
African, Sub-Saharan (14)	14	0.18
Sierra Leonean (14)	14	0.18
Albanian (0)	4	0.05
American (311)	311	4.03
Arab (0)	9	0.12
Lebanese (0)	9	0.12
Australian (0)	13	0.17
Austrian (14)	94	1.22
British (0)	21	0.27
Canadian (0)	14	0.18
Carpatho Rusyn (0)	14	0.18
Croatian (0)	109	1.41
Czech (16)	48	0.62
Czechoslovakian (17)	30	0.39
Dutch (156)	270	3.50
Eastern European (0)	11	0.14
English (132)	433	5.61
European (33)	33	0.43
Finnish (0)	15	0.19
French, ex. Basque (38)	273	3.53
German (1,720)	3,167	41.01
Greek (0)	92	1.19
Hungarian (26)	98	1.27
Irish (190)	1,323	17.13
Italian (416)	1,258	16.29
Latvian (0)	4	0.05
Lithuanian (0)	16	0.21
Norwegian (18)	75	0.97
Pennsylvania German (467)	574	7.43
Polish (191)	518	6.71
Portuguese (0)	16	0.21
Romanian (0)	14	0.18
Russian (14)	92	1.19
Scandinavian (0)	16	0.21
Scotch-Irish (28)	48	0.62
Scottish (25)	134	1.74
Slavic (0)	14	0.18
Slovak (0)	33	0.43
Swedish (36)	66	0.85
Swiss (86)	167	2.16
Ukrainian (0)	13	0.17
Welsh (0)	79	1.02
West Indian, ex. Hispanic (16)	30	0.39
Bermudan (0)	14	0.18
Jamaican (16)	16	0.21
Yugoslavian (0)	14	0.18

Hispanic Origin	Population	%
Hispanic or Latino (of any race)	220	2.78

*Notes: † The Census 2010 population figure is used to calculate the percentages in the Hispanic Origin and Race categories. Ancestry percentages are based on the 2006-2010 American Community Survey population (not shown); ‡ Numbers in parentheses indicate the number of people reporting a single ancestry; * Numbers in parentheses indicate the number of persons reporting this race alone, not in combination with any other race; Please refer to the Explanation of Data for more information.*

Central American, ex. Mexican	10	0.13
Costa Rican	2	0.03
Guatemalan	1	0.01
Honduran	3	0.04
Nicaraguan	1	0.01
Panamanian	1	0.01
Salvadoran	2	0.03
Cuban	9	0.11
Dominican Republic	16	0.20
Mexican	7	0.09
Puerto Rican	77	0.97
South American	20	0.25
Colombian	7	0.09
Ecuadorian	6	0.08
Paraguayan	3	0.04
Peruvian	4	0.05
Other Hispanic or Latino	81	1.02

Race*	Population	%
African-American/Black (379)	409	5.17
Not Hispanic (373)	394	4.98
Hispanic (6)	15	0.19
American Indian/Alaska Native (24)	37	0.47
Not Hispanic (21)	31	0.39
Hispanic (3)	6	0.08
Blackfeet (1)	2	0.03
Cherokee (1)	1	0.01
Chippewa (0)	2	0.03
Iroquois (0)	1	0.01
Mexican American Ind. (1)	1	0.01
South American Ind. (1)	2	0.03
Asian (52)	87	1.10
Not Hispanic (52)	85	1.08
Hispanic (0)	2	0.03
Burmese (1)	1	0.01
Cambodian (2)	2	0.03
Chinese, ex. Taiwanese (9)	13	0.16
Filipino (7)	9	0.11
Hmong (0)	1	0.01
Indian (7)	8	0.10
Japanese (1)	5	0.06
Korean (9)	10	0.13
Pakistani (5)	5	0.06
Taiwanese (0)	1	0.01
Thai (5)	7	0.09
Vietnamese (2)	2	0.03
Hawaii Native/Pacific Islander (7)	29	0.37
Not Hispanic (6)	27	0.34
Hispanic (1)	2	0.03
Guamanian/Chamorro (1)	2	0.03
White (7,278)	7,332	92.74
Not Hispanic (7,167)	7,208	91.17
Hispanic (111)	124	1.57

McCandless

Place Type: Township
County: Allegheny
Population: 28,457†

Ancestry‡	Population	%
African, Sub-Saharan (45)	45	0.16
African (17)	17	0.06
Ghanaian (16)	16	0.06
Other Sub-Saharan African (12)	12	0.04
Alsatian (0)	9	0.03
American (931)	931	3.29
Arab (125)	254	0.90
Arab (20)	20	0.07
Egyptian (12)	12	0.04
Lebanese (27)	108	0.38
Palestinian (0)	24	0.08
Syrian (0)	24	0.08
Other Arab (66)	66	0.23
Australian (0)	16	0.06
Austrian (66)	201	0.71
Belgian (0)	12	0.04
British (9)	84	0.30
Canadian (0)	35	0.12
Carpatho Rusyn (9)	9	0.03
Croatian (346)	725	2.56
Czech (39)	330	1.17
Czechoslovakian (0)	44	0.16
Danish (36)	62	0.22
Dutch (0)	131	0.46
Eastern European (71)	71	0.25
English (421)	2,242	7.92
Estonian (9)	9	0.03
European (145)	145	0.51
Finnish (0)	10	0.04
French, ex. Basque (53)	750	2.65
French Canadian (36)	138	0.49
German (3,591)	11,024	38.95
Greek (88)	154	0.54
Hungarian (31)	340	1.20
Iranian (20)	20	0.07
Irish (1,736)	6,460	22.83
Italian (1,673)	4,547	16.07
Lithuanian (54)	135	0.48
Norwegian (48)	114	0.40
Pennsylvania German (17)	55	0.19
Polish (889)	2,844	10.05
Portuguese (15)	24	0.08
Romanian (0)	72	0.25
Russian (141)	612	2.16
Scandinavian (13)	39	0.14
Scotch-Irish (247)	885	3.13
Scottish (67)	561	1.98
Serbian (0)	39	0.14
Slavic (0)	135	0.48
Slovak (336)	1,094	3.87
Slovene (27)	98	0.35
Swedish (73)	369	1.30
Swiss (31)	338	1.19
Turkish (15)	15	0.05
Ukrainian (89)	319	1.13
Welsh (65)	539	1.90
Yugoslavian (6)	6	0.02

Hispanic Origin	Population	%
Hispanic or Latino (of any race)	311	1.09
Central American, ex. Mexican	25	0.09
Costa Rican	2	0.01
Guatemalan	11	0.04
Honduran	1	<0.01
Nicaraguan	2	0.01
Panamanian	2	0.01
Salvadoran	7	0.02
Cuban	11	0.04
Dominican Republic	2	0.01
Mexican	108	0.38
Puerto Rican	45	0.16
South American	77	0.27
Argentinean	11	0.04
Bolivian	4	0.01
Chilean	9	0.03
Colombian	11	0.04
Ecuadorian	7	0.02
Peruvian	10	0.04
Uruguayan	1	<0.01
Venezuelan	24	0.08
Other Hispanic or Latino	43	0.15

Race*	Population	%
African-American/Black (473)	566	1.99
Not Hispanic (463)	551	1.94
Hispanic (10)	15	0.05
American Indian/Alaska Native (25)	82	0.29
Not Hispanic (25)	78	0.27
Hispanic (0)	4	0.01
Aleut *(Alaska Native)* (0)	2	0.01
Apache (0)	1	<0.01
Blackfeet (1)	2	0.01
Cherokee (1)	14	0.05
Chippewa (1)	2	0.01
Cree (1)	1	<0.01
Creek (0)	7	0.02
Kiowa (5)	5	0.02
Seminole (0)	1	<0.01
Sioux (1)	7	0.02
South American Ind. (0)	1	<0.01
Asian (1,436)	1,584	5.57
Not Hispanic (1,435)	1,579	5.55
Hispanic (1)	5	0.02
Bangladeshi (2)	2	0.01
Cambodian (3)	5	0.02
Chinese, ex. Taiwanese (494)	524	1.84
Filipino (38)	55	0.19
Indian (409)	435	1.53
Indonesian (9)	17	0.06
Japanese (28)	40	0.14
Korean (257)	283	0.99
Nepalese (6)	6	0.02
Pakistani (43)	46	0.16
Sri Lankan (18)	18	0.06
Taiwanese (27)	36	0.13
Thai (7)	10	0.04
Vietnamese (70)	82	0.29
Hawaii Native/Pacific Islander (11)	25	0.09
Not Hispanic (9)	22	0.08
Hispanic (2)	3	0.01
Fijian (2)	2	0.01
Guamanian/Chamorro (8)	8	0.03
Native Hawaiian (0)	1	<0.01
Samoan (1)	3	0.01
White (26,139)	26,397	92.76
Not Hispanic (25,922)	26,157	91.92
Hispanic (217)	240	0.84

McKeesport

Place Type: City
County: Allegheny
Population: 19,731†

Ancestry‡	Population	%
African, Sub-Saharan (186)	298	1.47
African (186)	298	1.47
American (891)	891	4.38
Austrian (7)	25	0.12
British (9)	9	0.04
Carpatho Rusyn (0)	15	0.07
Croatian (225)	538	2.64
Czech (14)	39	0.19
Czechoslovakian (71)	165	0.81
Dutch (0)	53	0.26
Eastern European (25)	25	0.12
English (479)	1,455	7.15
French, ex. Basque (21)	136	0.67
French Canadian (12)	12	0.06
German (998)	3,413	16.78
Greek (28)	72	0.35
Hungarian (206)	703	3.46
Irish (799)	2,679	13.17
Italian (1,401)	2,411	11.85
Lithuanian (24)	188	0.92
Pennsylvania German (0)	7	0.03
Polish (691)	1,829	8.99
Romanian (6)	24	0.12
Russian (93)	263	1.29
Scotch-Irish (161)	410	2.02
Scottish (79)	288	1.42
Serbian (24)	122	0.60
Slavic (73)	73	0.36
Slovak (469)	1,158	5.69
Slovene (0)	49	0.24
Swedish (72)	164	0.81
Ukrainian (38)	65	0.32
Welsh (50)	148	0.73
West Indian, ex. Hispanic (6)	27	0.13
Barbadian (0)	8	0.04
Haitian (6)	6	0.03
Jamaican (0)	13	0.06

Hispanic Origin	Population	%
Hispanic or Latino (of any race)	451	2.29
Central American, ex. Mexican	20	0.10
Costa Rican	9	0.05
Guatemalan	2	0.01
Panamanian	2	0.01

*Notes: † The Census 2010 population figure is used to calculate the percentages in the Hispanic Origin and Race categories. Ancestry percentages are based on the 2006-2010 American Community Survey population (not shown); ‡ Numbers in parentheses indicate the number of people reporting a single ancestry; * Numbers in parentheses indicate the number of persons reporting this race alone, not in combination with any other race; Please refer to the Explanation of Data for more information.*

Salvadoran	7	0.04
Cuban	11	0.06
Dominican Republic	6	0.03
Mexican	162	0.82
Puerto Rican	175	0.89
South American	6	0.03
Argentinean	1	0.01
Colombian	4	0.02
Paraguayan	1	0.01
Other Hispanic or Latino	71	0.36

Race*	Population	%
African-American/Black (6,301)	7,062	35.79
Not Hispanic (6,199)	6,900	34.97
Hispanic (102)	162	0.82
American Indian/Alaska Native (60)	259	1.31
Not Hispanic (52)	228	1.16
Hispanic (8)	31	0.16
Apache (1)	11	0.06
Blackfeet (2)	8	0.04
Canadian/French Am. Ind. (0)	2	0.01
Cherokee (3)	61	0.31
Cheyenne (0)	1	0.01
Chickasaw (1)	2	0.01
Chippewa (6)	8	0.04
Choctaw (0)	2	0.01
Delaware (0)	3	0.02
Hopi (1)	2	0.01
Inupiat *(Alaska Native)* (0)	1	0.01
Iroquois (0)	5	0.03
Mexican American Ind. (1)	2	0.01
Navajo (1)	1	0.01
Potawatomi (0)	1	0.01
Seminole (2)	13	0.07
Sioux (1)	4	0.02
Yakama (0)	1	0.01
Asian (52)	101	0.51
Not Hispanic (52)	87	0.44
Hispanic (0)	14	0.07
Chinese, ex. Taiwanese (2)	15	0.08
Filipino (22)	37	0.19
Indian (8)	22	0.11
Japanese (3)	13	0.07
Korean (4)	10	0.05
Thai (0)	3	0.02
Vietnamese (5)	11	0.06
Hawaii Native/Pacific Islander (8)	28	0.14
Not Hispanic (8)	22	0.11
Hispanic (0)	6	0.03
Guamanian/Chamorro (0)	4	0.02
Native Hawaiian (3)	10	0.05
Samoan (0)	3	0.02
White (12,296)	13,077	66.28
Not Hispanic (12,132)	12,840	65.08
Hispanic (164)	237	1.20

Meadville

Place Type: City
County: Crawford
Population: 13,388†

Ancestry‡	Population	%
African, Sub-Saharan (9)	31	0.23
South African (9)	31	0.23
American (272)	272	2.02
Arab (35)	126	0.93
Lebanese (35)	126	0.93
Austrian (9)	55	0.41
Belgian (0)	17	0.13
British (17)	54	0.40
Canadian (20)	20	0.15
Celtic (17)	17	0.13
Croatian (10)	54	0.40
Czech (0)	121	0.90
Czechoslovakian (0)	15	0.11
Danish (0)	22	0.16
Dutch (41)	212	1.57
English (214)	1,525	11.31
European (114)	114	0.85
Finnish (19)	39	0.29
French, ex. Basque (54)	551	4.09
German (1,155)	4,371	32.41
Hungarian (0)	123	0.91
Irish (616)	2,676	19.84
Italian (738)	1,873	13.89
Northern European (35)	35	0.26
Norwegian (22)	211	1.56
Pennsylvania German (72)	120	0.89
Polish (241)	1,125	8.34
Portuguese (13)	13	0.10
Russian (21)	198	1.47
Scandinavian (0)	19	0.14
Scotch-Irish (286)	572	4.24
Scottish (26)	267	1.98
Serbian (0)	54	0.40
Slavic (72)	72	0.53
Slovak (33)	156	1.16
Slovene (0)	17	0.13
Swedish (66)	290	2.15
Swiss (15)	36	0.27
Turkish (40)	40	0.30
Ukrainian (42)	90	0.67
Welsh (34)	279	2.07
West Indian, ex. Hispanic (29)	29	0.22
Haitian (29)	29	0.22

Hispanic Origin	Population	%
Hispanic or Latino (of any race)	222	1.66
Central American, ex. Mexican	5	0.04
Costa Rican	3	0.02
Honduran	2	0.01
Cuban	12	0.09
Dominican Republic	2	0.01
Mexican	103	0.77
Puerto Rican	65	0.49
South American	17	0.13
Bolivian	1	0.01
Colombian	7	0.05
Ecuadorian	1	0.01
Peruvian	7	0.05
Venezuelan	1	0.01
Other Hispanic or Latino	18	0.13

Race*	Population	%
African-American/Black (675)	905	6.76
Not Hispanic (658)	873	6.52
Hispanic (17)	32	0.24
American Indian/Alaska Native (31)	113	0.84
Not Hispanic (28)	108	0.81
Hispanic (3)	5	0.04
Apache (0)	6	0.04
Blackfeet (0)	6	0.04
Cherokee (3)	23	0.17
Choctaw (0)	4	0.03
Iroquois (0)	4	0.03
Kiowa (0)	1	0.01
Mexican American Ind. (2)	2	0.01
Seminole (3)	3	0.02
Sioux (0)	10	0.07
Yaqui (0)	1	0.01
Asian (148)	190	1.42
Not Hispanic (147)	189	1.41
Hispanic (1)	1	0.01
Cambodian (0)	3	0.02
Chinese, ex. Taiwanese (59)	68	0.51
Filipino (19)	28	0.21
Indian (39)	41	0.31
Japanese (13)	24	0.18
Korean (8)	16	0.12
Taiwanese (2)	2	0.01
Thai (2)	2	0.01
Vietnamese (2)	4	0.03
Hawaii Native/Pacific Islander (3)	6	0.04
Not Hispanic (2)	5	0.04
Hispanic (1)	1	0.01
Native Hawaiian (3)	4	0.03
Samoan (0)	2	0.01
White (12,132)	12,476	93.19
Not Hispanic (12,003)	12,312	91.96
Hispanic (129)	164	1.22

Mechanicsburg

Place Type: Borough
County: Cumberland
Population: 8,981†

Ancestry‡	Population	%
African, Sub-Saharan (0)	64	0.71
African (0)	64	0.71
American (491)	491	5.47
Arab (34)	143	1.59
Arab (0)	43	0.48
Syrian (34)	100	1.11
Austrian (0)	18	0.20
Canadian (48)	61	0.68
Croatian (0)	10	0.11
Czech (13)	39	0.43
Czechoslovakian (0)	49	0.55
Danish (0)	36	0.40
Dutch (0)	183	2.04
English (273)	886	9.87
European (31)	31	0.35
Finnish (46)	46	0.51
French, ex. Basque (28)	299	3.33
French Canadian (21)	70	0.78
German (1,631)	4,060	45.21
Hungarian (17)	46	0.51
Irish (290)	1,506	16.77
Italian (330)	1,198	13.34
Lithuanian (28)	76	0.85
Norwegian (0)	11	0.12
Pennsylvania German (45)	87	0.97
Polish (96)	467	5.20
Portuguese (0)	13	0.14
Romanian (0)	17	0.19
Russian (0)	46	0.51
Scandinavian (0)	14	0.16
Scotch-Irish (122)	358	3.99
Scottish (65)	217	2.42
Serbian (14)	14	0.16
Slavic (0)	8	0.09
Slovak (34)	106	1.18
Slovene (0)	10	0.11
Swedish (66)	66	0.73
Swiss (31)	91	1.01
Ukrainian (9)	19	0.21
Welsh (5)	120	1.34
West Indian, ex. Hispanic (0)	9	0.10
West Indian (0)	9	0.10

Hispanic Origin	Population	%
Hispanic or Latino (of any race)	315	3.51
Central American, ex. Mexican	35	0.39
Costa Rican	1	0.01
Guatemalan	14	0.16
Honduran	12	0.13
Nicaraguan	1	0.01
Salvadoran	7	0.08
Cuban	11	0.12
Dominican Republic	9	0.10
Mexican	47	0.52
Puerto Rican	143	1.59
South American	50	0.56
Argentinean	1	0.01
Bolivian	3	0.03
Chilean	5	0.06
Colombian	6	0.07
Ecuadorian	28	0.31
Paraguayan	1	0.01
Peruvian	6	0.07
Other Hispanic or Latino	20	0.22

Race*	Population	%
African-American/Black (197)	293	3.26
Not Hispanic (191)	276	3.07
Hispanic (6)	17	0.19
American Indian/Alaska Native (30)	81	0.90
Not Hispanic (25)	70	0.78

*Notes: † The Census 2010 population figure is used to calculate the percentages in the Hispanic Origin and Race categories. Ancestry percentages are based on the 2006-2010 American Community Survey population (not shown); ‡ Numbers in parentheses indicate the number of people reporting a single ancestry; * Numbers in parentheses indicate the number of persons reporting this race alone, not in combination with any other race; Please refer to the Explanation of Data for more information.*

Hispanic (5)	11	0.12
Aleut *(Alaska Native)* (0)	1	0.01
Apache (1)	3	0.03
Blackfeet (0)	2	0.02
Central American Ind. (0)	1	0.01
Cherokee (4)	18	0.20
Choctaw (1)	1	0.01
Delaware (1)	1	0.01
Iroquois (4)	4	0.04
Mexican American Ind. (1)	1	0.01
Sioux (3)	5	0.06
South American Ind. (2)	2	0.02
Yup'ik *(Alaska Native)* (1)	1	0.01
Asian (159)	203	2.26
Not Hispanic (158)	200	2.23
Hispanic (1)	3	0.03
Bangladeshi (4)	4	0.04
Chinese, ex. Taiwanese (19)	30	0.33
Filipino (9)	16	0.18
Indian (33)	39	0.43
Japanese (6)	9	0.10
Korean (27)	35	0.39
Laotian (4)	4	0.04
Pakistani (5)	5	0.06
Sri Lankan (1)	1	0.01
Taiwanese (1)	1	0.01
Thai (2)	5	0.06
Vietnamese (38)	44	0.49
Hawaii Native/Pacific Islander (3)	14	0.16
Not Hispanic (3)	12	0.13
Hispanic (0)	2	0.02
Fijian (0)	2	0.02
Native Hawaiian (0)	2	0.02
Samoan (2)	2	0.02
Tongan (1)	1	0.01
White (8,292)	8,482	94.44
Not Hispanic (8,113)	8,272	92.11
Hispanic (179)	210	2.34

Middle Smithfield

Place Type: Township
County: Monroe
Population: 15,997†

Ancestry‡	Population	%
African, Sub-Saharan (426)	471	3.03
African (317)	362	2.33
Ghanaian (109)	109	0.70
American (697)	697	4.48
Arab (91)	179	1.15
Arab (43)	73	0.47
Egyptian (20)	20	0.13
Syrian (28)	86	0.55
Australian (109)	109	0.70
Austrian (0)	61	0.39
Belgian (0)	20	0.13
British (0)	58	0.37
Croatian (14)	45	0.29
Cypriot (15)	15	0.10
Czech (69)	93	0.60
Czechoslovakian (0)	41	0.26
Danish (0)	8	0.05
Dutch (29)	112	0.72
English (385)	1,079	6.94
European (27)	56	0.36
French, ex. Basque (27)	192	1.23
German (1,019)	2,988	19.21
Greek (28)	100	0.64
Guyanese (60)	60	0.39
Hungarian (78)	153	0.98
Iranian (94)	94	0.60
Irish (631)	2,187	14.06
Italian (1,010)	2,085	13.40
Lithuanian (17)	40	0.26
Norwegian (39)	179	1.15
Pennsylvania German (14)	60	0.39
Polish (397)	681	4.38
Russian (22)	225	1.45
Scandinavian (0)	59	0.38
Scotch-Irish (74)	106	0.68
Scottish (36)	343	2.20
Slovak (14)	36	0.23
Swedish (44)	115	0.74
Swiss (0)	61	0.39
Ukrainian (21)	125	0.80
Welsh (132)	240	1.54
West Indian, ex. Hispanic (437)	581	3.73
Haitian (335)	335	2.15
Jamaican (102)	246	1.58
Yugoslavian (0)	19	0.12

Hispanic Origin	Population	%
Hispanic or Latino (of any race)	2,762	17.27
Central American, ex. Mexican	108	0.68
Costa Rican	14	0.09
Guatemalan	5	0.03
Honduran	21	0.13
Nicaraguan	1	0.01
Panamanian	18	0.11
Salvadoran	49	0.31
Cuban	101	0.63
Dominican Republic	249	1.56
Mexican	114	0.71
Puerto Rican	1,606	10.04
South American	386	2.41
Argentinean	25	0.16
Bolivian	3	0.02
Chilean	14	0.09
Colombian	119	0.74
Ecuadorian	132	0.83
Paraguayan	3	0.02
Peruvian	73	0.46
Uruguayan	13	0.08
Venezuelan	4	0.03
Other Hispanic or Latino	198	1.24

Race*	Population	%
African-American/Black (2,777)	3,028	18.93
Not Hispanic (2,506)	2,677	16.73
Hispanic (271)	351	2.19
American Indian/Alaska Native (55)	150	0.94
Not Hispanic (31)	104	0.65
Hispanic (24)	46	0.29
Apache (1)	1	0.01
Blackfeet (6)	8	0.05
Central American Ind. (0)	1	0.01
Cherokee (2)	18	0.11
Chippewa (1)	2	0.01
Choctaw (0)	5	0.03
Comanche (2)	2	0.01
Delaware (0)	3	0.02
Lumbee (0)	3	0.02
Mexican American Ind. (8)	9	0.06
Sioux (1)	3	0.02
South American Ind. (6)	8	0.05
Spanish American Ind. (0)	2	0.01
Asian (501)	606	3.79
Not Hispanic (491)	577	3.61
Hispanic (10)	29	0.18
Cambodian (10)	15	0.09
Chinese, ex. Taiwanese (81)	109	0.68
Filipino (156)	181	1.13
Indian (144)	179	1.12
Indonesian (4)	6	0.04
Japanese (12)	19	0.12
Korean (40)	46	0.29
Laotian (2)	2	0.01
Malaysian (8)	8	0.05
Pakistani (13)	15	0.09
Taiwanese (4)	4	0.03
Thai (1)	4	0.03
Vietnamese (7)	12	0.08
Hawaii Native/Pacific Islander (2)	18	0.11
Not Hispanic (2)	14	0.09
Hispanic (0)	4	0.03
Native Hawaiian (1)	3	0.02
White (11,415)	11,776	73.61
Not Hispanic (9,875)	10,108	63.19
Hispanic (1,540)	1,668	10.43

Middletown

Place Type: Borough
County: Dauphin
Population: 8,901†

Ancestry‡	Population	%
African, Sub-Saharan (0)	39	0.43
African (0)	11	0.12
Cape Verdean (0)	8	0.09
Nigerian (0)	20	0.22
American (573)	573	6.39
Arab (0)	8	0.09
Syrian (0)	8	0.09
Austrian (16)	16	0.18
Belgian (0)	11	0.12
British (23)	23	0.26
Canadian (7)	15	0.17
Croatian (0)	21	0.23
Czech (0)	74	0.82
Czechoslovakian (0)	13	0.14
Dutch (59)	202	2.25
English (259)	648	7.22
European (90)	90	1.00
Finnish (7)	14	0.16
French, ex. Basque (7)	191	2.13
French Canadian (0)	23	0.26
German (1,420)	3,164	35.27
Greek (0)	15	0.17
Hungarian (38)	60	0.67
Irish (220)	1,354	15.09
Italian (297)	1,016	11.33
Lithuanian (40)	65	0.72
Macedonian (9)	9	0.10
Norwegian (0)	17	0.19
Pennsylvania German (55)	309	3.44
Polish (176)	395	4.40
Portuguese (0)	29	0.32
Russian (22)	159	1.77
Scotch-Irish (16)	145	1.62
Scottish (16)	99	1.10
Serbian (11)	26	0.29
Slovak (11)	96	1.07
Swedish (0)	30	0.33
Swiss (8)	50	0.56
Ukrainian (9)	28	0.31
Welsh (11)	65	0.72
West Indian, ex. Hispanic (17)	31	0.35
British West Indian (8)	8	0.09
Jamaican (0)	14	0.16
West Indian (9)	9	0.10
Yugoslavian (9)	9	0.10

Hispanic Origin	Population	%
Hispanic or Latino (of any race)	510	5.73
Central American, ex. Mexican	5	0.06
Costa Rican	2	0.02
Honduran	1	0.01
Nicaraguan	1	0.01
Salvadoran	1	0.01
Cuban	16	0.18
Dominican Republic	19	0.21
Mexican	79	0.89
Puerto Rican	342	3.84
South American	22	0.25
Argentinean	1	0.01
Chilean	1	0.01
Colombian	6	0.07
Ecuadorian	4	0.04
Paraguayan	1	0.01
Peruvian	8	0.09
Venezuelan	1	0.01
Other Hispanic or Latino	27	0.30

Race*	Population	%
African-American/Black (737)	984	11.05
Not Hispanic (706)	895	10.06
Hispanic (31)	89	1.00
American Indian/Alaska Native (9)	103	1.16
Not Hispanic (9)	80	0.90

*Notes: † The Census 2010 population figure is used to calculate the percentages in the Hispanic Origin and Race categories. Ancestry percentages are based on the 2006-2010 American Community Survey population (not shown); ‡ Numbers in parentheses indicate the number of people reporting a single ancestry; * Numbers in parentheses indicate the number of persons reporting this race alone, not in combination with any other race; Please refer to the Explanation of Data for more information.*

Hispanic (0)	23	0.26
Apache (0)	1	0.01
Blackfeet (0)	2	0.02
Canadian/French Am. Ind. (0)	1	0.01
Cherokee (3)	13	0.15
Chippewa (1)	3	0.03
Delaware (0)	1	0.01
Iroquois (0)	4	0.04
Mexican American Ind. (0)	1	0.01
Navajo (1)	5	0.06
Sioux (0)	1	0.01
Asian (160)	189	2.12
Not Hispanic (160)	180	2.02
Hispanic (0)	9	0.10
Burmese (7)	7	0.08
Cambodian (16)	17	0.19
Chinese, ex. Taiwanese (42)	45	0.51
Filipino (13)	27	0.30
Indian (42)	51	0.57
Indonesian (2)	2	0.02
Japanese (3)	4	0.04
Korean (16)	16	0.18
Taiwanese (3)	3	0.03
Thai (1)	2	0.02
Vietnamese (4)	6	0.07
Hawaii Native/Pacific Islander (0)	22	0.25
Not Hispanic (0)	13	0.15
Hispanic (0)	9	0.10
Guamanian/Chamorro (0)	1	0.01
Native Hawaiian (0)	13	0.15
Samoan (0)	1	0.01
White (7,444)	7,787	87.48
Not Hispanic (7,235)	7,493	84.18
Hispanic (209)	294	3.30

Middletown

Place Type: Township
County: Bucks
Population: 45,436†

Ancestry‡	Population	%
African, Sub-Saharan (237)	237	0.52
African (188)	188	0.41
South African (49)	49	0.11
American (1,277)	1,277	2.81
Arab (69)	89	0.20
Lebanese (0)	11	0.02
Moroccan (69)	69	0.15
Syrian (0)	9	0.02
Armenian (30)	76	0.17
Austrian (47)	124	0.27
Basque (10)	10	0.02
Brazilian (0)	4	0.01
British (26)	109	0.24
Cajun (9)	18	0.04
Canadian (58)	140	0.31
Czech (8)	159	0.35
Czechoslovakian (52)	63	0.14
Danish (70)	271	0.60
Dutch (85)	607	1.34
Eastern European (130)	143	0.32
English (1,222)	4,831	10.64
European (238)	238	0.52
Finnish (24)	32	0.07
French, ex. Basque (55)	873	1.92
French Canadian (21)	198	0.44
German (3,350)	12,866	28.34
Greek (52)	197	0.43
Guyanese (8)	8	0.02
Hungarian (161)	661	1.46
Iranian (10)	21	0.05
Irish (4,395)	13,269	29.23
Italian (2,677)	7,448	16.41
Latvian (72)	149	0.33
Lithuanian (61)	250	0.55
Macedonian (0)	13	0.03
Maltese (0)	9	0.02
Norwegian (6)	118	0.26
Pennsylvania German (102)	194	0.43
Polish (1,310)	4,248	9.36
Portuguese (8)	58	0.13
Romanian (39)	58	0.13
Russian (472)	921	2.03
Scandinavian (0)	8	0.02
Scotch-Irish (424)	898	1.98
Scottish (413)	944	2.08
Serbian (0)	26	0.06
Slavic (0)	8	0.02
Slovak (153)	500	1.10
Slovene (10)	10	0.02
Swedish (91)	401	0.88
Swiss (0)	58	0.13
Turkish (58)	78	0.17
Ukrainian (326)	716	1.58
Welsh (95)	614	1.35
West Indian, ex. Hispanic (89)	170	0.37
Haitian (61)	61	0.13
Jamaican (28)	109	0.24
Yugoslavian (10)	57	0.13

Hispanic Origin	Population	%
Hispanic or Latino (of any race)	1,411	3.11
Central American, ex. Mexican	117	0.26
Costa Rican	21	0.05
Guatemalan	35	0.08
Honduran	25	0.06
Nicaraguan	5	0.01
Panamanian	9	0.02
Salvadoran	20	0.04
Other Central American	2	<0.01
Cuban	76	0.17
Dominican Republic	37	0.08
Mexican	169	0.37
Puerto Rican	657	1.45
South American	173	0.38
Argentinean	16	0.04
Bolivian	5	0.01
Chilean	3	0.01
Colombian	66	0.15
Ecuadorian	34	0.07
Paraguayan	2	<0.01
Peruvian	28	0.06
Venezuelan	19	0.04
Other Hispanic or Latino	182	0.40

Race*	Population	%
African-American/Black (1,475)	1,753	3.86
Not Hispanic (1,393)	1,609	3.54
Hispanic (82)	144	0.32
American Indian/Alaska Native (109)	262	0.58
Not Hispanic (66)	192	0.42
Hispanic (43)	70	0.15
Blackfeet (3)	13	0.03
Cherokee (6)	46	0.10
Cheyenne (3)	4	0.01
Chickasaw (0)	2	<0.01
Chippewa (1)	3	0.01
Choctaw (0)	1	<0.01
Comanche (0)	1	<0.01
Cree (0)	4	0.01
Creek (0)	3	0.01
Delaware (7)	9	0.02
Iroquois (11)	16	0.04
Lumbee (6)	11	0.02
Mexican American Ind. (3)	6	0.01
Seminole (1)	1	<0.01
Sioux (4)	7	0.02
South American Ind. (5)	7	0.02
Asian (1,782)	2,070	4.56
Not Hispanic (1,777)	2,047	4.51
Hispanic (5)	23	0.05
Bangladeshi (14)	15	0.03
Burmese (5)	5	0.01
Cambodian (15)	15	0.03
Chinese, ex. Taiwanese (198)	240	0.53
Filipino (142)	213	0.47
Hmong (0)	1	<0.01
Indian (877)	929	2.04
Indonesian (3)	11	0.02
Japanese (25)	48	0.11
Korean (292)	320	0.70
Nepalese (13)	13	0.03
Pakistani (60)	60	0.13
Sri Lankan (7)	7	0.02
Taiwanese (13)	13	0.03
Thai (14)	23	0.05
Vietnamese (67)	82	0.18
Hawaii Native/Pacific Islander (8)	31	0.07
Not Hispanic (7)	24	0.05
Hispanic (1)	7	0.02
Fijian (0)	1	<0.01
Guamanian/Chamorro (3)	7	0.02
Native Hawaiian (1)	6	0.01
Samoan (2)	3	0.01
White (40,926)	41,545	91.44
Not Hispanic (40,125)	40,627	89.42
Hispanic (801)	918	2.02

Middletown

Place Type: Township
County: Delaware
Population: 15,807†

Ancestry‡	Population	%
African, Sub-Saharan (9)	19	0.12
African (9)	9	0.06
Senegalese (0)	10	0.06
Albanian (64)	74	0.47
Alsatian (10)	21	0.13
American (418)	418	2.64
Arab (5)	18	0.11
Lebanese (0)	13	0.08
Other Arab (5)	5	0.03
Armenian (46)	46	0.29
Austrian (24)	45	0.28
Belgian (0)	66	0.42
Brazilian (10)	10	0.06
British (35)	130	0.82
Cajun (0)	9	0.06
Canadian (0)	26	0.16
Celtic (5)	15	0.09
Croatian (0)	20	0.13
Czech (16)	117	0.74
Czechoslovakian (20)	20	0.13
Danish (0)	51	0.32
Dutch (18)	200	1.26
Eastern European (21)	21	0.13
English (686)	2,288	14.46
European (85)	85	0.54
Finnish (16)	25	0.16
French, ex. Basque (10)	220	1.39
French Canadian (0)	29	0.18
German (861)	3,738	23.63
Greek (143)	394	2.49
Hungarian (5)	43	0.27
Iranian (9)	9	0.06
Irish (1,755)	5,100	32.24
Italian (1,017)	2,732	17.27
Latvian (27)	27	0.17
Lithuanian (64)	192	1.21
Norwegian (41)	100	0.63
Pennsylvania German (95)	105	0.66
Polish (207)	589	3.72
Portuguese (0)	10	0.06
Romanian (11)	11	0.07
Russian (78)	136	0.86
Scandinavian (0)	27	0.17
Scotch-Irish (137)	434	2.74
Scottish (81)	431	2.72
Slavic (0)	33	0.21
Slovak (21)	92	0.58
Swedish (40)	181	1.14
Swiss (20)	157	0.99
Ukrainian (44)	77	0.49
Welsh (51)	266	1.68
West Indian, ex. Hispanic (0)	32	0.20
Barbadian (0)	32	0.20

SECTION TWO

*Notes: † The Census 2010 population figure is used to calculate the percentages in the Hispanic Origin and Race categories. Ancestry percentages are based on the 2006-2010 American Community Survey population (not shown); ‡ Numbers in parentheses indicate the number of people reporting a single ancestry; * Numbers in parentheses indicate the number of persons reporting this race alone, not in combination with any other race; Please refer to the Explanation of Data for more information.*

Hispanic Origin	Population	%
Hispanic or Latino (of any race)	251	1.59
Central American, ex. Mexican	46	0.29
Costa Rican	8	0.05
Guatemalan	9	0.06
Honduran	3	0.02
Nicaraguan	16	0.10
Panamanian	3	0.02
Salvadoran	7	0.04
Cuban	17	0.11
Mexican	80	0.51
Puerto Rican	57	0.36
South American	35	0.22
Argentinean	1	0.01
Bolivian	1	0.01
Chilean	6	0.04
Colombian	18	0.11
Ecuadorian	3	0.02
Venezuelan	6	0.04
Other Hispanic or Latino	16	0.10

Race*	Population	%
African-American/Black (532)	574	3.63
Not Hispanic (524)	561	3.55
Hispanic (8)	13	0.08
American Indian/Alaska Native (17)	53	0.34
Not Hispanic (9)	42	0.27
Hispanic (8)	11	0.07
Canadian/French Am. Ind. (0)	1	0.01
Central American Ind. (1)	1	0.01
Cherokee (0)	8	0.05
Chickasaw (0)	5	0.03
Cree (0)	1	0.01
Delaware (0)	1	0.01
Hopi (1)	1	0.01
Iroquois (0)	1	0.01
Lumbee (1)	2	0.01
Mexican American Ind. (2)	2	0.01
Shoshone (1)	1	0.01
Sioux (0)	1	0.01
Asian (437)	506	3.20
Not Hispanic (437)	506	3.20
Burmese (8)	8	0.05
Cambodian (3)	3	0.02
Chinese, ex. Taiwanese (120)	144	0.91
Filipino (19)	26	0.16
Indian (144)	149	0.94
Japanese (7)	19	0.12
Korean (78)	85	0.54
Malaysian (1)	3	0.02
Pakistani (15)	21	0.13
Sri Lankan (8)	10	0.06
Taiwanese (1)	2	0.01
Thai (4)	6	0.04
Vietnamese (13)	26	0.16
Hawaii Native/Pacific Islander (5)	7	0.04
Not Hispanic (5)	6	0.04
Hispanic (0)	1	0.01
Native Hawaiian (1)	2	0.01
White (14,590)	14,718	93.11
Not Hispanic (14,425)	14,544	92.01
Hispanic (165)	174	1.10

Milford

Place Type: Township
County: Bucks
Population: 9,902†

Ancestry‡	Population	%
African, Sub-Saharan (53)	53	0.54
African (17)	17	0.17
Ghanaian (36)	36	0.37
American (361)	361	3.69
Australian (34)	43	0.44
Austrian (0)	38	0.39
Belgian (0)	4	0.04
British (17)	87	0.89
Canadian (0)	29	0.30
Czech (0)	136	1.39
Czechoslovakian (0)	52	0.53
Dutch (40)	219	2.24
English (150)	834	8.53
European (139)	184	1.88
French, ex. Basque (69)	245	2.51
French Canadian (8)	8	0.08
German (1,739)	4,071	41.64
Greek (0)	38	0.39
Hungarian (0)	77	0.79
Irish (443)	1,687	17.26
Italian (286)	1,360	13.91
Lithuanian (0)	56	0.57
Norwegian (16)	32	0.33
Pennsylvania German (295)	359	3.67
Polish (200)	792	8.10
Russian (12)	199	2.04
Scotch-Irish (14)	76	0.78
Scottish (117)	389	3.98
Slavic (11)	45	0.46
Slovak (16)	39	0.40
Slovene (4)	4	0.04
Swedish (14)	119	1.22
Swiss (27)	42	0.43
Ukrainian (0)	129	1.32
Welsh (36)	279	2.85
West Indian, ex. Hispanic (0)	13	0.13
Jamaican (0)	13	0,13

Hispanic Origin	Population	%
Hispanic or Latino (of any race)	174	1.76
Central American, ex. Mexican	15	0.15
Costa Rican	2	0.02
Guatemalan	6	0.06
Honduran	2	0.02
Panamanian	5	0.05
Cuban	7	0.07
Dominican Republic	7	0.07
Mexican	31	0.31
Puerto Rican	69	0.70
South American	16	0.16
Argentinean	2	0.02
Chilean	3	0.03
Colombian	5	0.05
Ecuadorian	4	0.04
Peruvian	2	0.02
Other Hispanic or Latino	29	0.29

Race*	Population	%
African-American/Black (151)	205	2.07
Not Hispanic (140)	191	1.93
Hispanic (11)	14	0.14
American Indian/Alaska Native (11)	35	0.35
Not Hispanic (11)	34	0.34
Hispanic (0)	1	0.01
Cherokee (0)	2	0.02
Chippewa (0)	1	0.01
Choctaw (0)	1	0.01
Comanche (4)	4	0.04
Iroquois (1)	5	0.05
Pima (1)	1	0.01
Sioux (1)	1	0.01
Asian (138)	181	1.83
Not Hispanic (138)	176	1.78
Hispanic (0)	5	0.05
Cambodian (1)	2	0.02
Chinese, ex. Taiwanese (32)	40	0.40
Filipino (5)	13	0.13
Indian (42)	47	0.47
Japanese (4)	10	0.10
Korean (28)	38	0.38
Pakistani (1)	1	0.01
Taiwanese (1)	1	0.01
Thai (1)	1	0.01
Vietnamese (11)	16	0.16
Hawaii Native/Pacific Islander (3)	8	0.08
Not Hispanic (3)	8	0.08
Native Hawaiian (2)	7	0.07
White (9,430)	9,559	96.54
Not Hispanic (9,318)	9,428	95.21
Hispanic (112)	131	1.32

Millcreek

Place Type: Township
County: Erie
Population: 53,515†

Ancestry‡	Population	%
African, Sub-Saharan (15)	15	0.03
African (15)	15	0.03
American (1,872)	1,872	3.53
Arab (193)	276	0.52
Arab (136)	151	0.29
Egyptian (5)	5	0.01
Lebanese (0)	8	0.02
Palestinian (15)	31	0.06
Syrian (13)	44	0.08
Other Arab (24)	37	0.07
Armenian (0)	24	0.05
Austrian (113)	273	0.52
Basque (0)	9	0.02
Belgian (0)	33	0.06
Brazilian (13)	13	0.02
British (54)	209	0.39
Bulgarian (0)	16	0.03
Canadian (84)	145	0.27
Carpatho Rusyn (0)	36	0.07
Croatian (87)	201	0.38
Czech (50)	218	0.41
Czechoslovakian (143)	250	0.47
Danish (68)	179	0.34
Dutch (75)	681	1.29
Eastern European (32)	43	0.08
English (885)	5,292	9.99
Estonian (11)	19	0.04
European (89)	121	0.23
Finnish (30)	82	0.15
French, ex. Basque (136)	1,061	2.00
French Canadian (125)	199	0.38
German (5,615)	18,920	35.73
Greek (79)	226	0.43
Hungarian (208)	861	1.63
Iranian (27)	35	0.07
Irish (2,029)	10,633	20.08
Italian (3,442)	9,038	17.07
Latvian (14)	14	0.03
Lithuanian (123)	265	0.50
Luxemburger (0)	10	0.02
Northern European (39)	49	0.09
Norwegian (72)	231	0.44
Pennsylvania German (121)	191	0.36
Polish (2,232)	6,656	12.57
Portuguese (47)	247	0.47
Romanian (165)	203	0.38
Russian (508)	1,163	2.20
Scandinavian (17)	82	0.15
Scotch-Irish (349)	1,130	2.13
Scottish (299)	929	1.75
Serbian (9)	39	0.07
Slavic (21)	145	0.27
Slovak (213)	886	1.67
Slovene (14)	37	0.07
Swedish (465)	1,705	3.22
Swiss (45)	203	0.38
Turkish (54)	80	0.15
Ukrainian (316)	658	1.24
Welsh (43)	450	0.85
West Indian, ex. Hispanic (64)	80	0.15
Haitian (15)	15	0.03
Jamaican (26)	26	0.05
Trinidadian/Tobagonian (23)	39	0.07
Yugoslavian (98)	140	0.26

Hispanic Origin	Population	%
Hispanic or Latino (of any race)	983	1.84
Central American, ex. Mexican	75	0.14
Costa Rican	14	0.03
Guatemalan	17	0.03
Honduran	14	0.03
Nicaraguan	4	0.01
Panamanian	11	0.02

*Notes: † The Census 2010 population figure is used to calculate the percentages in the Hispanic Origin and Race categories. Ancestry percentages are based on the 2006-2010 American Community Survey population (not shown); ‡ Numbers in parentheses indicate the number of people reporting a single ancestry; * Numbers in parentheses indicate the number of persons reporting this race alone, not in combination with any other race; Please refer to the Explanation of Data for more information.*

Salvadoran	15	0.03
Cuban	32	0.06
Dominican Republic	18	0.03
Mexican	305	0.57
Puerto Rican	340	0.64
South American	101	0.19
Argentinean	2	<0.01
Bolivian	1	<0.01
Chilean	4	0.01
Colombian	51	0.10
Ecuadorian	10	0.02
Peruvian	18	0.03
Venezuelan	15	0.03
Other Hispanic or Latino	112	0.21

Race*	Population	%
African-American/Black (793)	1,160	2.17
Not Hispanic (758)	1,100	2.06
Hispanic (35)	60	0.11
American Indian/Alaska Native (67)	229	0.43
Not Hispanic (61)	207	0.39
Hispanic (6)	22	0.04
Aleut *(Alaska Native)* (0)	1	<0.01
Apache (1)	1	<0.01
Blackfeet (1)	11	0.02
Cherokee (6)	32	0.06
Chippewa (1)	9	0.02
Choctaw (4)	6	0.01
Cree (0)	2	<0.01
Creek (0)	1	<0.01
Crow (0)	1	<0.01
Iroquois (6)	28	0.05
Lumbee (1)	1	<0.01
Mexican American Ind. (2)	3	0.01
Navajo (0)	1	<0.01
Seminole (0)	1	<0.01
Shoshone (3)	3	0.01
Sioux (4)	6	0.01
South American Ind. (2)	5	0.01
Tlingit-Haida *(Alaska Native)* (2)	2	<0.01
Tohono O'Odham (0)	4	0.01
Ute (1)	1	<0.01
Asian (977)	1,180	2.20
Not Hispanic (962)	1,154	2.16
Hispanic (15)	26	0.05
Bangladeshi (13)	13	0.02
Burmese (8)	9	0.02
Cambodian (1)	2	<0.01
Chinese, ex. Taiwanese (235)	271	0.51
Filipino (69)	122	0.23
Hmong (1)	1	<0.01
Indian (356)	377	0.70
Indonesian (5)	7	0.01
Japanese (20)	54	0.10
Korean (91)	116	0.22
Laotian (2)	2	<0.01
Malaysian (1)	1	<0.01
Pakistani (43)	45	0.08
Sri Lankan (10)	10	0.02
Taiwanese (12)	13	0.02
Thai (9)	18	0.03
Vietnamese (75)	89	0.17
Hawaii Native/Pacific Islander (9)	26	0.05
Not Hispanic (9)	24	0.04
Hispanic (0)	2	<0.01
Guamanian/Chamorro (2)	4	0.01
Native Hawaiian (3)	8	0.01
Samoan (1)	4	0.01
White (50,677)	51,334	95.92
Not Hispanic (50,073)	50,664	94.67
Hispanic (604)	670	1.25

Millersville

Place Type: Borough
County: Lancaster
Population: 8,168†

Ancestry‡	Population	%
African, Sub-Saharan (125)	125	1.55
African (74)	74	0.92
Ethiopian (12)	12	0.15
Kenyan (39)	39	0.48
American (273)	273	3.38
Arab (0)	14	0.17
Lebanese (0)	14	0.17
Belgian (0)	34	0.42
British (28)	43	0.53
Canadian (0)	14	0.17
Carpatho Rusyn (7)	7	0.09
Croatian (0)	10	0.12
Czech (25)	64	0.79
Czechoslovakian (7)	7	0.09
Dutch (9)	67	0.83
Eastern European (26)	26	0.32
English (234)	658	8.15
European (85)	85	1.05
French, ex. Basque (50)	184	2.28
French Canadian (0)	13	0.16
German (1,759)	3,563	44.11
Greek (29)	49	0.61
Hungarian (28)	85	1.05
Irish (311)	1,268	15.70
Italian (205)	679	8.41
Lithuanian (40)	68	0.84
Norwegian (0)	8	0.10
Pennsylvania German (28)	79	0.98
Polish (53)	464	5.74
Romanian (9)	9	0.11
Russian (11)	33	0.41
Scandinavian (0)	11	0.14
Scotch-Irish (36)	212	2.62
Scottish (60)	221	2.74
Serbian (12)	23	0.28
Slovak (54)	80	0.99
Swedish (26)	113	1.40
Swiss (9)	88	1.09
Ukrainian (22)	97	1.20
Welsh (35)	167	2.07
West Indian, ex. Hispanic (12)	26	0.32
Jamaican (0)	14	0.17
Trinidadian/Tobagonian (12)	12	0.15

Hispanic Origin	Population	%
Hispanic or Latino (of any race)	351	4.30
Central American, ex. Mexican	18	0.22
Costa Rican	2	0.02
Guatemalan	3	0.04
Honduran	4	0.05
Nicaraguan	4	0.05
Panamanian	3	0.04
Salvadoran	2	0.02
Cuban	9	0.11
Dominican Republic	22	0.27
Mexican	54	0.66
Puerto Rican	190	2.33
South American	27	0.33
Argentinean	7	0.09
Chilean	4	0.05
Colombian	3	0.04
Ecuadorian	4	0.05
Peruvian	6	0.07
Uruguayan	1	0.01
Other South American	2	0.02
Other Hispanic or Latino	31	0.38

Race*	Population	%
African-American/Black (411)	483	5.91
Not Hispanic (385)	443	5.42
Hispanic (26)	40	0.49
American Indian/Alaska Native (17)	41	0.50
Not Hispanic (13)	33	0.40
Hispanic (4)	8	0.10
Cherokee (0)	5	0.06
Chippewa (2)	2	0.02
Delaware (0)	1	0.01
Iroquois (1)	2	0.02
Mexican American Ind. (1)	2	0.02
Potawatomi (0)	1	0.01
Sioux (0)	1	0.01
Asian (99)	117	1.43
Not Hispanic (98)	112	1.37
Hispanic (1)	5	0.06
Burmese (7)	7	0.09
Cambodian (11)	11	0.13
Chinese, ex. Taiwanese (20)	24	0.29
Filipino (5)	8	0.10
Indian (21)	22	0.27
Japanese (4)	7	0.09
Korean (13)	13	0.16
Pakistani (2)	2	0.02
Taiwanese (4)	4	0.05
Thai (0)	1	0.01
Vietnamese (11)	12	0.15
Hawaii Native/Pacific Islander (5)	9	0.11
Not Hispanic (3)	6	0.07
Hispanic (2)	3	0.04
Guamanian/Chamorro (4)	4	0.05
Native Hawaiian (1)	2	0.02
White (7,427)	7,523	92.10
Not Hispanic (7,227)	7,309	89.48
Hispanic (200)	214	2.62

Monessen

Place Type: City
County: Westmoreland
Population: 7,720†

Ancestry‡	Population	%
African, Sub-Saharan (164)	164	2.09
African (164)	164	2.09
American (123)	123	1.56
Arab (18)	48	0.61
Lebanese (0)	10	0.13
Syrian (18)	38	0.48
Austrian (9)	19	0.24
Belgian (0)	9	0.11
Celtic (0)	14	0.18
Croatian (91)	151	1.92
Czech (0)	28	0.36
Czechoslovakian (40)	88	1.12
Danish (10)	10	0.13
Dutch (38)	76	0.97
English (108)	560	7.12
Finnish (21)	41	0.52
French, ex. Basque (0)	87	1.11
French Canadian (0)	7	0.09
German (273)	972	12.36
Greek (131)	221	2.81
Hungarian (50)	272	3.46
Irish (64)	659	8.38
Italian (1,261)	2,118	26.94
Lithuanian (29)	56	0.71
Polish (187)	545	6.93
Russian (177)	333	4.24
Scotch-Irish (22)	155	1.97
Scottish (0)	62	0.79
Slavic (0)	30	0.38
Slovak (321)	621	7.90
Swedish (9)	45	0.57
Ukrainian (114)	204	2.59
Welsh (9)	101	1.28
West Indian, ex. Hispanic (38)	62	0.79
Haitian (38)	38	0.48
Jamaican (0)	9	0.11
West Indian (0)	15	0.19

Hispanic Origin	Population	%
Hispanic or Latino (of any race)	138	1.79
Central American, ex. Mexican	5	0.06
Guatemalan	1	0.01
Honduran	3	0.04
Panamanian	1	0.01
Cuban	9	0.12
Dominican Republic	13	0.17
Mexican	51	0.66
Puerto Rican	35	0.45
South American	1	0.01
Argentinean	1	0.01

SECTION TWO

*Notes: † The Census 2010 population figure is used to calculate the percentages in the Hispanic Origin and Race categories. Ancestry percentages are based on the 2006-2010 American Community Survey population (not shown); ‡ Numbers in parentheses indicate the number of people reporting a single ancestry; * Numbers in parentheses indicate the number of persons reporting this race alone, not in combination with any other race; Please refer to the Explanation of Data for more information.*

Other Hispanic or Latino	24	0.31

Race*	Population	%
African-American/Black (1,152)	1,403	18.17
Not Hispanic (1,136)	1,377	17.84
Hispanic (16)	26	0.34
American Indian/Alaska Native (5)	38	0.49
Not Hispanic (3)	36	0.47
Hispanic (2)	2	0.03
Apache (1)	1	0.01
Blackfeet (0)	6	0.08
Central American Ind. (1)	1	0.01
Cherokee (0)	6	0.08
Delaware (0)	1	0.01
Iroquois (0)	2	0.03
Mexican American Ind. (0)	1	0.01
Asian (23)	34	0.44
Not Hispanic (22)	31	0.40
Hispanic (1)	3	0.04
Chinese, ex. Taiwanese (4)	7	0.09
Filipino (7)	10	0.13
Indonesian (1)	1	0.01
Korean (4)	8	0.10
Thai (1)	1	0.01
Vietnamese (4)	4	0.05
Hawaii Native/Pacific Islander (1)	3	0.04
Not Hispanic (1)	3	0.04
Native Hawaiian (1)	1	0.01
White (6,219)	6,472	83.83
Not Hispanic (6,148)	6,384	82.69
Hispanic (71)	88	1.14

Monroeville

Place Type: Municipality
County: Allegheny
Population: 28,386[†]

Ancestry[‡]	Population	%
African, Sub-Saharan (124)	162	0.57
African (90)	128	0.45
Liberian (13)	13	0.05
Sierra Leonean (21)	21	0.07
Albanian (8)	18	0.06
Alsatian (0)	27	0.10
American (1,380)	1,380	4.87
Arab (41)	135	0.48
Lebanese (11)	79	0.28
Syrian (30)	56	0.20
Austrian (77)	160	0.57
Belgian (22)	31	0.11
Brazilian (12)	12	0.04
British (32)	78	0.28
Canadian (11)	44	0.16
Carpatho Rusyn (18)	24	0.08
Croatian (150)	578	2.04
Czech (100)	317	1.12
Czechoslovakian (32)	50	0.18
Danish (0)	13	0.05
Dutch (20)	368	1.30
Eastern European (62)	115	0.41
English (449)	2,010	7.10
European (144)	171	0.60
Finnish (0)	33	0.12
French, ex. Basque (45)	468	1.65
French Canadian (22)	81	0.29
German (1,450)	6,840	24.16
Greek (47)	81	0.29
Hungarian (212)	645	2.28
Icelander (9)	9	0.03
Iranian (0)	15	0.05
Irish (1,533)	5,602	19.79
Italian (1,788)	4,235	14.96
Lithuanian (87)	165	0.58
Macedonian (0)	19	0.07
Northern European (28)	28	0.10
Norwegian (0)	52	0.18
Pennsylvania German (59)	81	0.29
Polish (779)	2,059	7.27
Portuguese (6)	33	0.12
Romanian (31)	77	0.27
Russian (185)	539	1.90
Scandinavian (32)	32	0.11
Scotch-Irish (133)	435	1.54
Scottish (133)	616	2.18
Serbian (111)	255	0.90
Slavic (10)	90	0.32
Slovak (490)	1,285	4.54
Slovene (92)	111	0.39
Swedish (49)	273	0.96
Swiss (14)	112	0.40
Turkish (37)	37	0.13
Ukrainian (81)	196	0.69
Welsh (128)	532	1.88
West Indian, ex. Hispanic (271)	271	0.96
Barbadian (18)	18	0.06
Haitian (148)	148	0.52
Jamaican (105)	105	0.37
Yugoslavian (11)	25	0.09

Hispanic Origin	Population	%
Hispanic or Latino (of any race)	425	1.50
Central American, ex. Mexican	30	0.11
Costa Rican	3	0.01
Guatemalan	16	0.06
Honduran	1	<0.01
Nicaraguan	1	<0.01
Panamanian	4	0.01
Salvadoran	5	0.02
Cuban	15	0.05
Dominican Republic	7	0.02
Mexican	130	0.46
Puerto Rican	101	0.36
South American	82	0.29
Argentinean	3	0.01
Bolivian	1	<0.01
Chilean	3	0.01
Colombian	30	0.11
Ecuadorian	1	<0.01
Peruvian	22	0.08
Uruguayan	4	0.01
Venezuelan	10	0.04
Other South American	8	0.03
Other Hispanic or Latino	60	0.21

Race*	Population	%
African-American/Black (3,325)	3,736	13.16
Not Hispanic (3,294)	3,661	12.90
Hispanic (31)	75	0.26
American Indian/Alaska Native (44)	196	0.69
Not Hispanic (38)	156	0.55
Hispanic (6)	40	0.14
Alaska Athabascan *(Ala. Nat.)* (1)	1	<0.01
Aleut *(Alaska Native)* (3)	3	0.01
Blackfeet (0)	12	0.04
Cherokee (4)	35	0.12
Chickasaw (0)	4	0.01
Chippewa (1)	1	<0.01
Creek (3)	4	0.01
Iroquois (1)	3	0.01
Lumbee (1)	1	<0.01
Mexican American Ind. (2)	12	0.04
Navajo (0)	1	<0.01
Osage (0)	2	0.01
Pueblo (1)	7	0.02
Seminole (4)	10	0.04
Sioux (0)	3	0.01
South American Ind. (0)	1	<0.01
Asian (1,669)	1,847	6.51
Not Hispanic (1,660)	1,836	6.47
Hispanic (9)	11	0.04
Bangladeshi (18)	19	0.07
Burmese (3)	3	0.01
Chinese, ex. Taiwanese (267)	278	0.98
Filipino (73)	100	0.35
Indian (868)	903	3.18
Indonesian (28)	29	0.10
Japanese (29)	45	0.16
Korean (115)	140	0.49
Malaysian (1)	1	<0.01
Nepalese (3)	3	0.01
Pakistani (165)	169	0.60
Sri Lankan (2)	2	0.01
Taiwanese (21)	24	0.08
Thai (3)	6	0.02
Vietnamese (40)	44	0.16
Hawaii Native/Pacific Islander (11)	42	0.15
Not Hispanic (11)	36	0.13
Hispanic (0)	6	0.02
Guamanian/Chamorro (3)	9	0.03
Native Hawaiian (2)	13	0.05
Samoan (3)	6	0.02
White (22,570)	23,112	81.42
Not Hispanic (22,340)	22,824	80.41
Hispanic (230)	288	1.01

Montgomery

Place Type: Township
County: Montgomery
Population: 24,790[†]

Ancestry[‡]	Population	%
African, Sub-Saharan (44)	44	0.18
African (13)	13	0.05
Liberian (31)	31	0.13
Albanian (8)	8	0.03
American (451)	451	1.86
Arab (206)	283	1.17
Arab (0)	44	0.18
Egyptian (145)	145	0.60
Jordanian (10)	20	0.08
Lebanese (0)	23	0.09
Syrian (41)	41	0.17
Other Arab (10)	10	0.04
Armenian (24)	50	0.21
Austrian (8)	36	0.15
Belgian (26)	69	0.28
British (46)	81	0.33
Canadian (0)	53	0.22
Croatian (0)	45	0.19
Czech (9)	197	0.81
Czechoslovakian (7)	7	0.03
Danish (0)	42	0.17
Dutch (50)	256	1.05
Eastern European (96)	96	0.40
English (441)	2,047	8.43
European (319)	333	1.37
Finnish (10)	45	0.19
French, ex. Basque (66)	397	1.63
French Canadian (0)	74	0.30
German (1,130)	5,151	21.21
Greek (54)	198	0.82
Hungarian (27)	285	1.17
Icelander (0)	10	0.04
Irish (1,747)	6,459	26.59
Israeli (0)	14	0.06
Italian (1,560)	4,217	17.36
Latvian (14)	14	0.06
Lithuanian (100)	263	1.08
Maltese (0)	78	0.32
Norwegian (41)	68	0.28
Pennsylvania German (46)	108	0.44
Polish (389)	1,309	5.39
Portuguese (17)	17	0.07
Romanian (0)	29	0.12
Russian (555)	853	3.51
Scandinavian (0)	18	0.07
Scotch-Irish (78)	172	0.71
Scottish (108)	558	2.30
Slavic (11)	20	0.08
Slovak (53)	165	0.68
Swedish (43)	111	0.46
Swiss (27)	92	0.38
Ukrainian (29)	86	0.35
Welsh (23)	336	1.38
West Indian, ex. Hispanic (106)	120	0.49
Jamaican (106)	120	0.49
Yugoslavian (0)	10	0.04

*Notes: † The Census 2010 population figure is used to calculate the percentages in the Hispanic Origin and Race categories. Ancestry percentages are based on the 2006-2010 American Community Survey population (not shown); ‡ Numbers in parentheses indicate the number of people reporting a single ancestry; * Numbers in parentheses indicate the number of persons reporting this race alone, not in combination with any other race; Please refer to the Explanation of Data for more information.*

Hispanic Origin	Population	%
Hispanic or Latino (of any race)	551	2.22
Central American, ex. Mexican	46	0.19
Costa Rican	4	0.02
Guatemalan	27	0.11
Honduran	2	0.01
Nicaraguan	2	0.01
Panamanian	5	0.02
Salvadoran	6	0.02
Cuban	47	0.19
Dominican Republic	6	0.02
Mexican	96	0.39
Puerto Rican	167	0.67
South American	130	0.52
Argentinean	9	0.04
Bolivian	9	0.04
Chilean	12	0.05
Colombian	51	0.21
Ecuadorian	17	0.07
Paraguayan	2	0.01
Peruvian	11	0.04
Uruguayan	1	<0.01
Venezuelan	18	0.07
Other Hispanic or Latino	59	0.24

Race*	Population	%
African-American/Black (1,144)	1,259	5.08
Not Hispanic (1,133)	1,229	4.96
Hispanic (11)	30	0.12
American Indian/Alaska Native (18)	85	0.34
Not Hispanic (14)	72	0.29
Hispanic (4)	13	0.05
Blackfeet (0)	1	<0.01
Cherokee (1)	14	0.06
Chippewa (0)	1	<0.01
Delaware (0)	3	0.01
Iroquois (3)	4	0.02
Mexican American Ind. (2)	4	0.02
Puget Sound Salish (0)	1	<0.01
Seminole (0)	1	<0.01
Sioux (0)	4	0.02
Asian (4,107)	4,351	17.55
Not Hispanic (4,097)	4,336	17.49
Hispanic (10)	15	0.06
Bangladeshi (22)	25	0.10
Cambodian (11)	32	0.13
Chinese, ex. Taiwanese (578)	644	2.60
Filipino (170)	222	0.90
Indian (1,188)	1,261	5.09
Japanese (17)	49	0.20
Korean (1,721)	1,765	7.12
Malaysian (1)	1	<0.01
Pakistani (45)	53	0.21
Sri Lankan (12)	13	0.05
Taiwanese (42)	55	0.22
Thai (6)	6	0.02
Vietnamese (197)	207	0.84
Hawaii Native/Pacific Islander (0)	10	0.04
Not Hispanic (0)	10	0.04
Native Hawaiian (0)	2	0.01
White (19,022)	19,319	77.93
Not Hispanic (18,632)	18,891	76.20
Hispanic (390)	428	1.73

Montgomeryville

Place Type: CDP
County: Montgomery
Population: 12,624†

Ancestry‡	Population	%
African, Sub-Saharan (13)	13	0.10
African (13)	13	0.10
Albanian (8)	8	0.06
American (299)	299	2.29
Arab (166)	235	1.80
Arab (0)	44	0.34
Egyptian (105)	105	0.80
Jordanian (10)	20	0.15
Lebanese (0)	15	0.11
Syrian (41)	41	0.31
Other Arab (10)	10	0.08
Armenian (12)	38	0.29
Austrian (8)	17	0.13
Belgian (7)	23	0.18
British (26)	40	0.31
Czech (0)	93	0.71
Czechoslovakian (7)	7	0.05
Danish (0)	20	0.15
Dutch (17)	170	1.30
Eastern European (96)	96	0.73
English (162)	893	6.83
European (175)	189	1.45
Finnish (10)	33	0.25
French, ex. Basque (44)	288	2.20
German (637)	2,830	21.65
Greek (45)	71	0.54
Hungarian (15)	158	1.21
Icelander (0)	10	0.08
Irish (1,154)	3,622	27.71
Israeli (0)	14	0.11
Italian (899)	2,364	18.09
Lithuanian (51)	117	0.90
Maltese (0)	16	0.12
Norwegian (17)	44	0.34
Pennsylvania German (35)	64	0.49
Polish (146)	597	4.57
Portuguese (17)	17	0.13
Romanian (0)	9	0.07
Russian (299)	349	2.67
Scotch-Irish (30)	72	0.55
Scottish (43)	149	1.14
Slavic (0)	9	0.07
Slovak (24)	79	0.60
Swedish (43)	85	0.65
Swiss (27)	76	0.58
Ukrainian (20)	67	0.51
Welsh (14)	90	0.69
West Indian, ex. Hispanic (106)	120	0.92
Jamaican (106)	120	0.92

Hispanic Origin	Population	%
Hispanic or Latino (of any race)	287	2.27
Central American, ex. Mexican	12	0.10
Guatemalan	4	0.03
Honduran	1	0.01
Panamanian	1	0.01
Salvadoran	6	0.05
Cuban	25	0.20
Dominican Republic	3	0.02
Mexican	60	0.48
Puerto Rican	105	0.83
South American	60	0.48
Argentinean	4	0.03
Bolivian	6	0.05
Colombian	16	0.13
Ecuadorian	16	0.13
Paraguayan	1	0.01
Peruvian	8	0.06
Venezuelan	9	0.07
Other Hispanic or Latino	22	0.17

Race*	Population	%
African-American/Black (563)	622	4.93
Not Hispanic (557)	603	4.78
Hispanic (6)	19	0.15
American Indian/Alaska Native (8)	39	0.31
Not Hispanic (7)	36	0.29
Hispanic (1)	3	0.02
Blackfeet (0)	1	0.01
Cherokee (1)	7	0.06
Delaware (0)	1	0.01
Iroquois (2)	2	0.02
Puget Sound Salish (0)	1	0.01
Sioux (0)	1	0.01
Asian (1,845)	1,942	15.38
Not Hispanic (1,837)	1,930	15.29
Hispanic (8)	12	0.10
Bangladeshi (21)	21	0.17
Cambodian (7)	18	0.14
Chinese, ex. Taiwanese (231)	268	2.12
Filipino (76)	95	0.75
Indian (539)	575	4.55
Japanese (4)	20	0.16
Korean (777)	792	6.27
Pakistani (31)	34	0.27
Sri Lankan (3)	3	0.02
Taiwanese (12)	19	0.15
Thai (6)	6	0.05
Vietnamese (90)	95	0.75
Hawaii Native/Pacific Islander (0)	8	0.06
Not Hispanic (0)	8	0.06
Native Hawaiian (0)	1	0.01
White (9,976)	10,114	80.12
Not Hispanic (9,782)	9,896	78.39
Hispanic (194)	218	1.73

Moon

Place Type: Township
County: Allegheny
Population: 24,185†

Ancestry‡	Population	%
African, Sub-Saharan (20)	20	0.08
Ugandan (20)	20	0.08
American (713)	713	3.02
Arab (75)	254	1.07
Arab (15)	15	0.06
Egyptian (8)	8	0.03
Lebanese (52)	231	0.98
Australian (19)	25	0.11
Austrian (25)	152	0.64
Belgian (9)	46	0.19
Brazilian (41)	41	0.17
British (7)	56	0.24
Bulgarian (16)	16	0.07
Canadian (16)	16	0.07
Croatian (83)	297	1.26
Czech (115)	370	1.57
Czechoslovakian (36)	47	0.20
Dutch (49)	287	1.21
Eastern European (8)	35	0.15
English (510)	2,454	10.38
European (165)	196	0.83
Finnish (13)	28	0.12
French, ex. Basque (23)	522	2.21
French Canadian (9)	19	0.08
German (1,945)	7,647	32.35
Greek (131)	242	1.02
Hungarian (138)	376	1.59
Iranian (9)	22	0.09
Irish (995)	5,358	22.67
Italian (1,962)	5,005	21.17
Lithuanian (34)	67	0.28
Norwegian (28)	74	0.31
Pennsylvania German (0)	18	0.08
Polish (984)	2,817	11.92
Portuguese (15)	15	0.06
Romanian (11)	42	0.18
Russian (81)	325	1.37
Scandinavian (13)	13	0.05
Scotch-Irish (167)	687	2.91
Scottish (194)	658	2.78
Serbian (42)	92	0.39
Slavic (40)	40	0.17
Slovak (128)	653	2.76
Slovene (33)	33	0.14
Swedish (57)	327	1.38
Swiss (0)	79	0.33
Turkish (10)	20	0.08
Ukrainian (127)	363	1.54
Welsh (12)	244	1.03
West Indian, ex. Hispanic (21)	21	0.09
British West Indian (8)	8	0.03
Jamaican (13)	13	0.05
Yugoslavian (0)	11	0.05

Hispanic Origin	Population	%
Hispanic or Latino (of any race)	488	2.02

*Notes: † The Census 2010 population figure is used to calculate the percentages in the Hispanic Origin and Race categories. Ancestry percentages are based on the 2006-2010 American Community Survey population (not shown); ‡ Numbers in parentheses indicate the number of people reporting a single ancestry; * Numbers in parentheses indicate the number of persons reporting this race alone, not in combination with any other race; Please refer to the Explanation of Data for more information.*

Central American, ex. Mexican	32	0.13
Guatemalan	9	0.04
Honduran	6	0.02
Panamanian	4	0.02
Salvadoran	13	0.05
Cuban	20	0.08
Dominican Republic	6	0.02
Mexican	166	0.69
Puerto Rican	95	0.39
South American	93	0.38
Argentinean	14	0.06
Bolivian	3	0.01
Chilean	21	0.09
Colombian	15	0.06
Ecuadorian	9	0.04
Paraguayan	5	0.02
Peruvian	13	0.05
Uruguayan	1	<0.01
Venezuelan	12	0.05
Other Hispanic or Latino	76	0.31

Race*	Population	%
African-American/Black (1,086)	1,299	5.37
Not Hispanic (1,059)	1,263	5.22
Hispanic (27)	36	0.15
American Indian/Alaska Native (24)	90	0.37
Not Hispanic (20)	74	0.31
Hispanic (4)	16	0.07
Apache (0)	5	0.02
Blackfeet (0)	1	<0.01
Cherokee (3)	22	0.09
Chippewa (1)	1	<0.01
Choctaw (0)	5	0.02
Delaware (1)	4	0.02
Iroquois (4)	4	0.02
Mexican American Ind. (0)	4	0.02
Navajo (0)	1	<0.01
Seminole (0)	1	<0.01
South American Ind. (2)	5	0.02
Asian (759)	889	3.68
Not Hispanic (753)	882	3.65
Hispanic (6)	7	0.03
Bangladeshi (1)	1	<0.01
Cambodian (3)	11	0.05
Chinese, ex. Taiwanese (137)	149	0.62
Filipino (50)	86	0.36
Indian (392)	422	1.74
Indonesian (0)	1	<0.01
Japanese (10)	30	0.12
Korean (39)	51	0.21
Malaysian (3)	3	0.01
Nepalese (1)	1	<0.01
Pakistani (68)	73	0.30
Sri Lankan (4)	4	0.02
Taiwanese (4)	4	0.02
Thai (4)	10	0.04
Vietnamese (25)	29	0.12
Hawaii Native/Pacific Islander (6)	19	0.08
Not Hispanic (6)	17	0.07
Hispanic (0)	2	0.01
Guamanian/Chamorro (6)	7	0.03
Native Hawaiian (0)	6	0.02
White (21,712)	22,079	91.29
Not Hispanic (21,422)	21,756	89.96
Hispanic (290)	323	1.34

Moore

Place Type: Township
County: Northampton
Population: 9,198†

Ancestry‡	Population	%
African, Sub-Saharan (0)	11	0.12
African (0)	11	0.12
American (375)	375	4.09
Arab (36)	130	1.42
Lebanese (26)	104	1.14
Syrian (10)	26	0.28
Austrian (20)	55	0.60
Belgian (11)	11	0.12
British (13)	95	1.04
Croatian (0)	12	0.13
Czech (23)	119	1.30
Czechoslovakian (32)	42	0.46
Danish (0)	8	0.09
Dutch (126)	550	6.00
Eastern European (10)	10	0.11
English (263)	591	6.45
European (11)	22	0.24
French, ex. Basque (0)	150	1.64
French Canadian (38)	98	1.07
German (1,611)	3,509	38.30
Greek (12)	12	0.13
Guyanese (41)	41	0.45
Hungarian (93)	273	2.98
Irish (120)	1,013	11.06
Italian (461)	810	8.84
Latvian (0)	30	0.33
Norwegian (0)	154	1.68
Pennsylvania German (786)	920	10.04
Polish (146)	457	4.99
Russian (26)	112	1.22
Scotch-Irish (16)	85	0.93
Scottish (31)	52	0.57
Slavic (9)	63	0.69
Slovak (150)	371	4.05
Swiss (0)	21	0.23
Ukrainian (61)	223	2.43
Welsh (29)	205	2.24

Hispanic Origin	Population	%
Hispanic or Latino (of any race)	187	2.03
Central American, ex. Mexican	8	0.09
Costa Rican	2	0.02
Guatemalan	4	0.04
Honduran	2	0.02
Cuban	8	0.09
Dominican Republic	4	0.04
Mexican	20	0.22
Puerto Rican	103	1.12
South American	23	0.25
Colombian	10	0.11
Ecuadorian	9	0.10
Peruvian	3	0.03
Venezuelan	1	0.01
Other Hispanic or Latino	21	0.23

Race*	Population	%
African-American/Black (75)	98	1.07
Not Hispanic (69)	86	0.93
Hispanic (6)	12	0.13
American Indian/Alaska Native (9)	39	0.42
Not Hispanic (7)	34	0.37
Hispanic (2)	5	0.05
Cherokee (2)	13	0.14
Choctaw (0)	1	0.01
Delaware (0)	3	0.03
Iroquois (1)	1	0.01
Sioux (0)	2	0.02
Spanish American Ind. (1)	1	0.01
Asian (45)	62	0.67
Not Hispanic (45)	62	0.67
Chinese, ex. Taiwanese (4)	8	0.09
Filipino (8)	10	0.11
Indian (1)	5	0.05
Japanese (4)	5	0.05
Korean (7)	7	0.08
Malaysian (0)	3	0.03
Pakistani (9)	11	0.12
Taiwanese (0)	2	0.02
Vietnamese (10)	10	0.11
White (8,943)	9,022	98.09
Not Hispanic (8,827)	8,885	96.60
Hispanic (116)	137	1.49

Morrisville

Place Type: Borough
County: Bucks
Population: 8,728†

Ancestry‡	Population	%
African, Sub-Saharan (250)	268	2.97
African (219)	237	2.63
Liberian (31)	31	0.34
American (240)	240	2.66
Armenian (0)	27	0.30
Austrian (0)	62	0.69
British (19)	28	0.31
Croatian (0)	23	0.25
Czech (11)	36	0.40
Czechoslovakian (13)	13	0.14
Dutch (44)	51	0.57
Eastern European (9)	9	0.10
English (311)	959	10.63
European (153)	153	1.70
French, ex. Basque (0)	228	2.53
French Canadian (0)	53	0.59
German (393)	1,748	19.38
Greek (0)	52	0.58
Hungarian (74)	147	1.63
Irish (351)	1,758	19.49
Italian (364)	1,122	12.44
Lithuanian (21)	50	0.55
Norwegian (31)	49	0.54
Polish (267)	833	9.24
Portuguese (0)	28	0.31
Romanian (0)	11	0.12
Russian (29)	177	1.96
Scotch-Irish (37)	87	0.96
Scottish (84)	324	3.59
Slavic (31)	31	0.34
Slovak (88)	125	1.39
Swedish (10)	35	0.39
Swiss (0)	10	0.11
Ukrainian (50)	72	0.80
Welsh (5)	83	0.92
West Indian, ex. Hispanic (75)	93	1.03
Haitian (75)	82	0.91
West Indian (0)	11	0.12

Hispanic Origin	Population	%
Hispanic or Latino (of any race)	888	10.17
Central American, ex. Mexican	197	2.26
Costa Rican	92	1.05
Guatemalan	69	0.79
Honduran	1	0.01
Nicaraguan	3	0.03
Panamanian	7	0.08
Salvadoran	23	0.26
Other Central American	2	0.02
Cuban	14	0.16
Dominican Republic	56	0.64
Mexican	88	1.01
Puerto Rican	395	4.53
South American	68	0.78
Argentinean	5	0.06
Chilean	6	0.07
Colombian	18	0.21
Ecuadorian	10	0.11
Peruvian	23	0.26
Uruguayan	5	0.06
Venezuelan	1	0.01
Other Hispanic or Latino	70	0.80

Race*	Population	%
African-American/Black (1,345)	1,496	17.14
Not Hispanic (1,297)	1,425	16.33
Hispanic (48)	71	0.81
American Indian/Alaska Native (22)	65	0.74
Not Hispanic (11)	52	0.60
Hispanic (11)	13	0.15
Central American Ind. (1)	1	0.01
Cherokee (0)	12	0.14
Chippewa (1)	1	0.01

*Notes: † The Census 2010 population figure is used to calculate the percentages in the Hispanic Origin and Race categories. Ancestry percentages are based on the 2006-2010 American Community Survey population (not shown); ‡ Numbers in parentheses indicate the number of people reporting a single ancestry; * Numbers in parentheses indicate the number of persons reporting this race alone, not in combination with any other race; Please refer to the Explanation of Data for more information.*

Choctaw (0)	1	0.01
Creek (1)	1	0.01
Delaware (0)	3	0.03
Iroquois (0)	1	0.01
Mexican American Ind. (5)	5	0.06
Sioux (1)	2	0.02
South American Ind. (1)	4	0.05
Asian (177)	212	2.43
Not Hispanic (172)	206	2.36
Hispanic (5)	6	0.07
Bangladeshi (5)	5	0.06
Burmese (1)	1	0.01
Chinese, ex. Taiwanese (50)	60	0.69
Filipino (29)	43	0.49
Indian (53)	55	0.63
Indonesian (3)	4	0.05
Japanese (2)	6	0.07
Korean (17)	25	0.29
Pakistani (1)	1	0.01
Thai (3)	3	0.03
Vietnamese (7)	10	0.11
Hawaii Native/Pacific Islander (3)	4	0.05
Not Hispanic (3)	4	0.05
Samoan (2)	2	0.02
White (6,609)	6,824	78.19
Not Hispanic (6,164)	6,323	72.45
Hispanic (445)	501	5.74

Mount Joy

Place Type: Township
County: Lancaster
Population: 9,873†

Ancestry‡	Population	%
American (900)	900	9.43
Arab (11)	11	0.12
Lebanese (11)	11	0.12
Armenian (14)	14	0.15
Australian (0)	40	0.42
Austrian (37)	103	1.08
British (0)	20	0.21
Czech (0)	8	0.08
Czechoslovakian (15)	28	0.29
Dutch (56)	213	2.23
English (186)	572	6.00
Estonian (12)	35	0.37
European (122)	167	1.75
Finnish (11)	24	0.25
French, ex. Basque (33)	229	2.40
French Canadian (12)	12	0.13
German (2,521)	4,517	47.35
Greek (9)	9	0.09
Hungarian (26)	26	0.27
Irish (252)	1,262	13.23
Italian (166)	641	6.72
Latvian (0)	12	0.13
Lithuanian (21)	48	0.50
Northern European (31)	31	0.32
Norwegian (16)	78	0.82
Pennsylvania German (23)	41	0.43
Polish (95)	401	4.20
Russian (40)	68	0.71
Scotch-Irish (109)	202	2.12
Scottish (25)	103	1.08
Slavic (8)	8	0.08
Slovene (17)	17	0.18
Swedish (0)	39	0.41
Swiss (0)	233	2.44
Turkish (31)	31	0.32
Ukrainian (13)	50	0.52
Welsh (0)	118	1.24

Hispanic Origin	Population	%
Hispanic or Latino (of any race)	288	2.92
Central American, ex. Mexican	13	0.13
Costa Rican	1	0.01
Guatemalan	6	0.06
Honduran	3	0.03
Panamanian	3	0.03
Cuban	7	0.07
Dominican Republic	2	0.02
Mexican	83	0.84
Puerto Rican	140	1.42
South American	23	0.23
Argentinean	1	0.01
Colombian	13	0.13
Ecuadorian	3	0.03
Peruvian	3	0.03
Venezuelan	1	0.01
Other South American	2	0.02
Other Hispanic or Latino	20	0.20

Race*	Population	%
African-American/Black (107)	163	1.65
Not Hispanic (92)	145	1.47
Hispanic (15)	18	0.18
American Indian/Alaska Native (14)	48	0.49
Not Hispanic (12)	40	0.41
Hispanic (2)	8	0.08
Blackfeet (0)	6	0.06
Cherokee (3)	18	0.18
Creek (4)	4	0.04
Delaware (0)	1	0.01
Iroquois (0)	1	0.01
Mexican American Ind. (0)	1	0.01
Tohono O'Odham (0)	1	0.01
Asian (95)	128	1.30
Not Hispanic (95)	124	1.26
Hispanic (0)	4	0.04
Burmese (1)	1	0.01
Cambodian (5)	6	0.06
Chinese, ex. Taiwanese (14)	21	0.21
Filipino (21)	31	0.31
Indian (25)	26	0.26
Japanese (4)	8	0.08
Korean (15)	23	0.23
Laotian (2)	2	0.02
Sri Lankan (1)	1	0.01
Vietnamese (6)	12	0.12
Hawaii Native/Pacific Islander (0)	8	0.08
Not Hispanic (0)	7	0.07
Hispanic (0)	1	0.01
Guamanian/Chamorro (0)	1	0.01
Native Hawaiian (0)	1	0.01
Samoan (0)	1	0.01
White (9,410)	9,552	96.75
Not Hispanic (9,255)	9,364	94.84
Hispanic (155)	188	1.90

Mount Lebanon

Place Type: Township
County: Allegheny
Population: 33,137†

Ancestry‡	Population	%
African, Sub-Saharan (84)	84	0.26
African (62)	62	0.19
South African (22)	22	0.07
American (897)	897	2.73
Arab (245)	528	1.61
Arab (16)	16	0.05
Egyptian (39)	39	0.12
Lebanese (96)	248	0.76
Syrian (73)	179	0.55
Other Arab (21)	46	0.14
Austrian (17)	345	1.05
Belgian (11)	77	0.23
British (133)	306	0.93
Canadian (24)	38	0.12
Croatian (146)	267	0.81
Czech (24)	172	0.52
Czechoslovakian (58)	66	0.20
Danish (21)	70	0.21
Dutch (14)	313	0.95
Eastern European (179)	193	0.59
English (706)	4,077	12.42
European (333)	351	1.07
Finnish (12)	80	0.24
French, ex. Basque (164)	915	2.79
French Canadian (12)	50	0.15
German (1,848)	9,920	30.21
Greek (189)	373	1.14
Hungarian (126)	931	2.84
Irish (1,740)	8,148	24.81
Italian (2,153)	6,511	19.83
Latvian (0)	44	0.13
Lithuanian (169)	583	1.78
Norwegian (38)	328	1.00
Pennsylvania German (31)	79	0.24
Polish (764)	2,792	8.50
Portuguese (67)	67	0.20
Romanian (10)	65	0.20
Russian (462)	1,259	3.83
Scandinavian (68)	68	0.21
Scotch-Irish (381)	928	2.83
Scottish (107)	1,079	3.29
Serbian (17)	123	0.37
Slavic (36)	61	0.19
Slovak (202)	879	2.68
Slovene (47)	117	0.36
Swedish (34)	357	1.09
Swiss (33)	165	0.50
Turkish (147)	147	0.45
Ukrainian (114)	484	1.47
Welsh (102)	373	1.14
West Indian, ex. Hispanic (0)	11	0.03
West Indian (0)	11	0.03
Yugoslavian (42)	119	0.36

Hispanic Origin	Population	%
Hispanic or Latino (of any race)	580	1.75
Central American, ex. Mexican	48	0.14
Costa Rican	3	0.01
Guatemalan	23	0.07
Honduran	6	0.02
Nicaraguan	3	0.01
Panamanian	7	0.02
Salvadoran	5	0.02
Other Central American	1	<0.01
Cuban	64	0.19
Dominican Republic	10	0.03
Mexican	187	0.56
Puerto Rican	67	0.20
South American	128	0.39
Argentinean	21	0.06
Bolivian	4	0.01
Chilean	10	0.03
Colombian	31	0.09
Ecuadorian	8	0.02
Peruvian	28	0.08
Venezuelan	26	0.08
Other Hispanic or Latino	76	0.23

Race*	Population	%
African-American/Black (352)	482	1.45
Not Hispanic (345)	469	1.42
Hispanic (7)	13	0.04
American Indian/Alaska Native (13)	107	0.32
Not Hispanic (11)	97	0.29
Hispanic (2)	10	0.03
Blackfeet (0)	8	0.02
Central American Ind. (0)	1	<0.01
Cherokee (2)	25	0.08
Chippewa (0)	2	0.01
Choctaw (0)	1	<0.01
Iroquois (1)	1	<0.01
Mexican American Ind. (2)	4	0.01
Osage (0)	3	0.01
Seminole (0)	2	0.01
Sioux (0)	5	0.02
South American Ind. (0)	3	0.01
Asian (1,221)	1,427	4.31
Not Hispanic (1,215)	1,415	4.27
Hispanic (6)	12	0.04
Bangladeshi (2)	3	0.01
Bhutanese (3)	3	0.01
Cambodian (3)	7	0.02
Chinese, ex. Taiwanese (573)	619	1.87

*Notes: † The Census 2010 population figure is used to calculate the percentages in the Hispanic Origin and Race categories. Ancestry percentages are based on the 2006-2010 American Community Survey population (not shown); ‡ Numbers in parentheses indicate the number of people reporting a single ancestry; * Numbers in parentheses indicate the number of persons reporting this race alone, not in combination with any other race; Please refer to the Explanation of Data for more information.*

Filipino (60)	92	0.28
Indian (273)	318	0.96
Indonesian (6)	6	0.02
Japanese (37)	55	0.17
Korean (67)	93	0.28
Malaysian (3)	6	0.02
Nepalese (17)	17	0.05
Pakistani (35)	41	0.12
Sri Lankan (2)	2	0.01
Taiwanese (14)	18	0.05
Thai (15)	16	0.05
Vietnamese (71)	90	0.27
Hawaii Native/Pacific Islander (8)	21	0.06
Not Hispanic (7)	13	0.04
Hispanic (1)	8	0.02
Guamanian/Chamorro (3)	4	0.01
Native Hawaiian (1)	3	0.01
Tongan (4)	4	0.01
White (31,014)	31,421	94.82
Not Hispanic (30,567)	30,936	93.36
Hispanic (447)	485	1.46

Mount Pleasant

Place Type: Township
County: Westmoreland
Population: 10,911†

Ancestry‡	Population	%
American (593)	593	5.42
Arab (13)	88	0.80
Lebanese (13)	70	0.64
Moroccan (0)	10	0.09
Syrian (0)	8	0.07
Austrian (9)	33	0.30
Croatian (28)	81	0.74
Czech (52)	118	1.08
Czechoslovakian (11)	20	0.18
Danish (88)	88	0.80
Dutch (30)	486	4.44
English (232)	983	8.99
European (9)	9	0.08
French, ex. Basque (7)	133	1.22
German (1,211)	3,566	32.60
Greek (18)	18	0.16
Hungarian (66)	332	3.04
Irish (324)	1,751	16.01
Italian (559)	1,384	12.65
Norwegian (8)	41	0.37
Pennsylvania German (19)	86	0.79
Polish (928)	1,779	16.27
Russian (50)	112	1.02
Scotch-Irish (81)	344	3.15
Scottish (70)	172	1.57
Slavic (14)	105	0.96
Slovak (638)	1,256	11.48
Slovene (12)	58	0.53
Swedish (20)	194	1.77
Ukrainian (23)	23	0.21
Welsh (11)	86	0.79

Hispanic Origin	Population	%
Hispanic or Latino (of any race)	56	0.51
Central American, ex. Mexican	5	0.05
Guatemalan	4	0.04
Panamanian	1	0.01
Cuban	7	0.06
Mexican	24	0.22
Puerto Rican	4	0.04
South American	6	0.05
Argentinean	1	0.01
Bolivian	3	0.03
Peruvian	2	0.02
Other Hispanic or Latino	10	0.09

Race*	Population	%
African-American/Black (34)	65	0.60
Not Hispanic (33)	60	0.55
Hispanic (1)	5	0.05
American Indian/Alaska Native (10)	46	0.42
Not Hispanic (9)	44	0.40
Hispanic (1)	2	0.02
Cherokee (2)	10	0.09
Chickasaw (0)	2	0.02
Chippewa (0)	1	0.01
Iroquois (1)	3	0.03
Puget Sound Salish (1)	1	0.01
Sioux (0)	1	0.01
Asian (21)	40	0.37
Not Hispanic (21)	40	0.37
Chinese, ex. Taiwanese (3)	5	0.05
Filipino (3)	8	0.07
Indian (5)	8	0.07
Japanese (1)	1	0.01
Korean (4)	4	0.04
Pakistani (0)	1	0.01
Thai (4)	4	0.04
Vietnamese (0)	6	0.05
Hawaii Native/Pacific Islander (2)	4	0.04
Not Hispanic (2)	4	0.04
Native Hawaiian (2)	2	0.02
White (10,745)	10,827	99.23
Not Hispanic (10,705)	10,781	98.81
Hispanic (40)	46	0.42

Mountain Top

Place Type: CDP
County: Luzerne
Population: 10,982†

Ancestry‡	Population	%
American (355)	355	3.36
Arab (25)	64	0.61
Lebanese (25)	64	0.61
Austrian (7)	118	1.12
British (20)	20	0.19
Czech (48)	120	1.14
Czechoslovakian (0)	26	0.25
Dutch (24)	290	2.75
Eastern European (0)	12	0.11
English (152)	997	9.44
European (14)	19	0.18
French, ex. Basque (62)	268	2.54
French Canadian (0)	25	0.24
German (545)	2,475	23.44
Greek (0)	17	0.16
Hungarian (10)	126	1.19
Irish (536)	2,295	21.73
Italian (513)	1,510	14.30
Latvian (15)	15	0.14
Lithuanian (92)	260	2.46
Norwegian (0)	40	0.38
Pennsylvania German (71)	115	1.09
Polish (1,095)	2,321	21.98
Portuguese (24)	24	0.23
Romanian (0)	7	0.07
Russian (146)	420	3.98
Scandinavian (0)	12	0.11
Scotch-Irish (0)	71	0.67
Scottish (13)	122	1.16
Slavic (0)	41	0.39
Slovak (218)	683	6.47
Swedish (0)	37	0.35
Ukrainian (29)	169	1.60
Welsh (104)	531	5.03
West Indian, ex. Hispanic (0)	5	0.05
West Indian (0)	5	0.05

Hispanic Origin	Population	%
Hispanic or Latino (of any race)	245	2.23
Central American, ex. Mexican	17	0.15
Guatemalan	7	0.06
Nicaraguan	2	0.02
Panamanian	7	0.06
Salvadoran	1	0.01
Cuban	21	0.19
Dominican Republic	22	0.20
Mexican	39	0.36
Puerto Rican	98	0.89
South American	30	0.27
Argentinean	4	0.04
Bolivian	4	0.04
Colombian	5	0.05
Peruvian	8	0.07
Venezuelan	9	0.08
Other Hispanic or Latino	18	0.16

Race*	Population	%
African-American/Black (92)	119	1.08
Not Hispanic (83)	109	0.99
Hispanic (9)	10	0.09
American Indian/Alaska Native (6)	36	0.33
Not Hispanic (5)	30	0.27
Hispanic (1)	6	0.05
Blackfeet (0)	1	0.01
Cherokee (1)	5	0.05
Chippewa (2)	2	0.02
Kiowa (1)	3	0.03
Mexican American Ind. (1)	1	0.01
Asian (390)	439	4.00
Not Hispanic (383)	432	3.93
Hispanic (7)	7	0.06
Chinese, ex. Taiwanese (48)	56	0.51
Filipino (30)	41	0.37
Indian (228)	244	2.22
Indonesian (0)	1	0.01
Japanese (5)	6	0.05
Korean (22)	27	0.25
Pakistani (33)	35	0.32
Taiwanese (12)	12	0.11
Vietnamese (5)	5	0.05
Hawaii Native/Pacific Islander (0)	4	0.04
Not Hispanic (0)	4	0.04
Native Hawaiian (0)	2	0.02
White (10,286)	10,386	94.57
Not Hispanic (10,160)	10,245	93.29
Hispanic (126)	141	1.28

Muhlenberg

Place Type: Township
County: Berks
Population: 19,628†

Ancestry‡	Population	%
Afghan (169)	169	0.88
African, Sub-Saharan (10)	10	0.05
Ethiopian (10)	10	0.05
Alsatian (0)	14	0.07
American (798)	798	4.15
Arab (14)	69	0.36
Egyptian (14)	14	0.07
Syrian (0)	55	0.29
Austrian (12)	33	0.17
British (0)	20	0.10
Canadian (105)	105	0.55
Croatian (22)	22	0.11
Czech (12)	45	0.23
Danish (0)	14	0.07
Dutch (207)	881	4.58
English (320)	1,303	6.78
Finnish (0)	15	0.08
French, ex. Basque (25)	316	1.64
French Canadian (0)	11	0.06
German (4,065)	7,682	39.97
Greek (73)	252	1.31
Guyanese (0)	19	0.10
Hungarian (8)	82	0.43
Irish (487)	2,471	12.86
Italian (955)	2,725	14.18
Lithuanian (39)	107	0.56
Norwegian (7)	7	0.04
Pennsylvania German (762)	1,161	6.04
Polish (426)	1,089	5.67
Portuguese (0)	26	0.14
Romanian (9)	9	0.05
Russian (0)	8	0.04
Scandinavian (8)	8	0.04
Scotch-Irish (0)	137	0.71

*Notes: † The Census 2010 population figure is used to calculate the percentages in the Hispanic Origin and Race categories. Ancestry percentages are based on the 2006-2010 American Community Survey population (not shown); ‡ Numbers in parentheses indicate the number of people reporting a single ancestry; * Numbers in parentheses indicate the number of persons reporting this race alone, not in combination with any other race; Please refer to the Explanation of Data for more information.*

Scottish (111)	264	1.37
Slavic (12)	12	0.06
Slovak (118)	239	1.24
Slovene (14)	28	0.15
Swedish (0)	34	0.18
Swiss (26)	94	0.49
Ukrainian (52)	175	0.91
Welsh (69)	261	1.36
West Indian, ex. Hispanic (87)	87	0.45
Haitian (75)	75	0.39
Trinidadian/Tobagonian (12)	12	0.06
Yugoslavian (8)	22	0.11

Hispanic Origin	Population	%
Hispanic or Latino (of any race)	2,701	13.76
Central American, ex. Mexican	129	0.66
Guatemalan	26	0.13
Honduran	30	0.15
Nicaraguan	11	0.06
Panamanian	9	0.05
Salvadoran	52	0.26
Other Central American	1	0.01
Cuban	21	0.11
Dominican Republic	407	2.07
Mexican	523	2.66
Puerto Rican	1,300	6.62
South American	137	0.70
Bolivian	2	0.01
Chilean	2	0.01
Colombian	62	0.32
Ecuadorian	43	0.22
Peruvian	15	0.08
Uruguayan	5	0.03
Venezuelan	8	0.04
Other Hispanic or Latino	184	0.94

Race*	Population	%
African-American/Black (843)	1,060	5.40
Not Hispanic (708)	852	4.34
Hispanic (135)	208	1.06
American Indian/Alaska Native (53)	107	0.55
Not Hispanic (28)	66	0.34
Hispanic (25)	41	0.21
Apache (1)	4	0.02
Blackfeet (0)	4	0.02
Cherokee (3)	10	0.05
Choctaw (1)	3	0.02
Delaware (0)	2	0.01
Iroquois (1)	2	0.01
Mexican American Ind. (1)	1	0.01
Navajo (1)	1	0.01
Pueblo (3)	3	0.02
Seminole (0)	1	0.01
Sioux (1)	2	0.01
South American Ind. (3)	7	0.04
Tlingit-Haida *(Alaska Native)* (0)	1	0.01
Asian (296)	375	1.91
Not Hispanic (293)	362	1.84
Hispanic (3)	13	0.07
Chinese, ex. Taiwanese (31)	42	0.21
Filipino (11)	19	0.10
Indian (78)	88	0.45
Indonesian (0)	2	0.01
Japanese (2)	11	0.06
Korean (23)	36	0.18
Pakistani (4)	5	0.03
Taiwanese (1)	6	0.03
Thai (2)	3	0.02
Vietnamese (138)	150	0.76
Hawaii Native/Pacific Islander (6)	42	0.21
Not Hispanic (4)	25	0.13
Hispanic (2)	17	0.09
Guamanian/Chamorro (2)	15	0.08
Native Hawaiian (3)	10	0.05
Samoan (1)	1	0.01
White (16,860)	17,293	88.10
Not Hispanic (15,619)	15,870	80.85
Hispanic (1,241)	1,423	7.25

Munhall

Place Type: Borough
County: Allegheny
Population: 11,406†

Ancestry‡	Population	%
American (231)	231	2.02
Arab (25)	25	0.22
Syrian (25)	25	0.22
Austrian (12)	43	0.38
British (0)	14	0.12
Carpatho Rusyn (0)	25	0.22
Croatian (23)	231	2.02
Czech (49)	101	0.88
Czechoslovakian (42)	94	0.82
Dutch (9)	104	0.91
Eastern European (36)	36	0.31
English (157)	1,027	8.96
French, ex. Basque (0)	85	0.74
French Canadian (0)	11	0.10
German (634)	2,758	24.07
Greek (104)	149	1.30
Hungarian (278)	1,051	9.17
Irish (595)	2,694	23.52
Italian (422)	1,818	15.87
Lithuanian (37)	190	1.66
Norwegian (18)	35	0.31
Pennsylvania German (12)	12	0.10
Polish (327)	989	8.63
Portuguese (0)	22	0.19
Romanian (16)	16	0.14
Russian (47)	172	1.50
Scotch-Irish (87)	473	4.13
Scottish (64)	443	3.87
Serbian (4)	25	0.22
Slavic (0)	31	0.27
Slovak (638)	1,676	14.63
Slovene (0)	10	0.09
Swedish (0)	85	0.74
Swiss (0)	24	0.21
Ukrainian (42)	190	1.66
Welsh (31)	355	3.10

Hispanic Origin	Population	%
Hispanic or Latino (of any race)	166	1.46
Central American, ex. Mexican	7	0.06
Costa Rican	1	0.01
Guatemalan	2	0.02
Honduran	2	0.02
Salvadoran	2	0.02
Cuban	5	0.04
Dominican Republic	8	0.07
Mexican	62	0.54
Puerto Rican	38	0.33
South American	7	0.06
Chilean	5	0.04
Colombian	2	0.02
Other Hispanic or Latino	39	0.34

Race*	Population	%
African-American/Black (1,079)	1,222	10.71
Not Hispanic (1,047)	1,182	10.36
Hispanic (32)	40	0.35
American Indian/Alaska Native (14)	52	0.46
Not Hispanic (11)	49	0.43
Hispanic (3)	3	0.03
Blackfeet (1)	4	0.04
Cherokee (3)	13	0.11
Cheyenne (0)	1	0.01
Crow (1)	1	0.01
Iroquois (4)	5	0.04
Mexican American Ind. (1)	1	0.01
Ottawa (1)	1	0.01
Asian (109)	131	1.15
Not Hispanic (109)	131	1.15
Cambodian (4)	4	0.04
Chinese, ex. Taiwanese (10)	10	0.09
Filipino (8)	8	0.07
Indian (37)	39	0.34
Indonesian (1)	1	0.01
Japanese (6)	10	0.09
Korean (8)	17	0.15
Laotian (1)	4	0.04
Pakistani (2)	4	0.04
Vietnamese (32)	32	0.28
Hawaii Native/Pacific Islander (3)	11	0.10
Not Hispanic (3)	11	0.10
Guamanian/Chamorro (0)	1	0.01
Native Hawaiian (2)	3	0.03
Samoan (1)	1	0.01
White (9,979)	10,141	88.91
Not Hispanic (9,888)	10,036	87.99
Hispanic (91)	105	0.92

Murrysville

Place Type: Municipality
County: Westmoreland
Population: 20,079†

Ancestry‡	Population	%
African, Sub-Saharan (0)	11	0.06
South African (0)	11	0.06
Albanian (8)	21	0.11
American (1,038)	1,038	5.23
Arab (12)	116	0.58
Lebanese (12)	53	0.27
Syrian (0)	63	0.32
Austrian (46)	58	0.29
Belgian (13)	22	0.11
Brazilian (0)	13	0.07
British (132)	139	0.70
Canadian (147)	147	0.74
Carpatho Rusyn (12)	12	0.06
Croatian (126)	264	1.33
Czech (40)	146	0.74
Czechoslovakian (37)	73	0.37
Danish (12)	36	0.18
Dutch (89)	418	2.11
Eastern European (72)	124	0.62
English (415)	2,927	14.75
European (162)	175	0.88
French, ex. Basque (45)	341	1.72
German (1,841)	6,905	34.79
Greek (91)	326	1.64
Hungarian (58)	239	1.20
Iranian (16)	16	0.08
Irish (718)	3,680	18.54
Italian (1,486)	4,371	22.02
Lithuanian (52)	106	0.53
Maltese (0)	13	0.07
Norwegian (44)	119	0.60
Pennsylvania German (13)	53	0.27
Polish (320)	1,560	7.86
Portuguese (0)	17	0.09
Romanian (33)	78	0.39
Russian (134)	293	1.48
Scandinavian (32)	32	0.16
Scotch-Irish (226)	701	3.53
Scottish (127)	562	2.83
Serbian (12)	128	0.64
Slavic (40)	40	0.20
Slovak (385)	931	4.69
Slovene (45)	118	0.59
Swedish (50)	322	1.62
Swiss (0)	55	0.28
Ukrainian (68)	172	0.87
Welsh (68)	289	1.46
West Indian, ex. Hispanic (0)	11	0.06
Jamaican (0)	11	0.06
Yugoslavian (10)	48	0.24

Hispanic Origin	Population	%
Hispanic or Latino (of any race)	202	1.01
Central American, ex. Mexican	12	0.06
Guatemalan	6	0.03
Nicaraguan	2	0.01
Panamanian	1	<0.01
Salvadoran	3	0.01

SECTION TWO

*Notes: † The Census 2010 population figure is used to calculate the percentages in the Hispanic Origin and Race categories. Ancestry percentages are based on the 2006-2010 American Community Survey population (not shown); ‡ Numbers in parentheses indicate the number of people reporting a single ancestry; * Numbers in parentheses indicate the number of persons reporting this race alone, not in combination with any other race; Please refer to the Explanation of Data for more information.*

Cuban	11	0.05
Dominican Republic	6	0.03
Mexican	78	0.39
Puerto Rican	31	0.15
South American	36	0.18
Argentinean	4	0.02
Colombian	11	0.05
Ecuadorian	11	0.05
Paraguayan	4	0.02
Peruvian	5	0.02
Venezuelan	1	<0.01
Other Hispanic or Latino	28	0.14

Race*	Population	%
African-American/Black (167)	224	1.12
Not Hispanic (164)	219	1.09
Hispanic (3)	5	0.02
American Indian/Alaska Native (23)	56	0.28
Not Hispanic (19)	50	0.25
Hispanic (4)	6	0.03
Cherokee (5)	5	0.02
Choctaw (1)	1	<0.01
Comanche (0)	3	0.01
Creek (4)	7	0.03
Crow (2)	2	0.01
Iroquois (0)	4	0.02
Mexican American Ind. (1)	1	<0.01
Navajo (3)	3	0.01
Asian (884)	970	4.83
Not Hispanic (882)	966	4.81
Hispanic (2)	4	0.02
Chinese, ex. Taiwanese (300)	319	1.59
Filipino (14)	26	0.13
Indian (366)	388	1.93
Indonesian (1)	1	<0.01
Japanese (21)	35	0.17
Korean (53)	62	0.31
Laotian (1)	4	0.02
Pakistani (67)	69	0.34
Sri Lankan (6)	6	0.03
Taiwanese (22)	25	0.12
Thai (2)	4	0.02
Vietnamese (16)	16	0.08
Hawaii Native/Pacific Islander (2)	13	0.06
Not Hispanic (1)	12	0.06
Hispanic (1)	1	<0.01
Guamanian/Chamorro (1)	3	0.01
Native Hawaiian (1)	6	0.03
Samoan (0)	2	0.01
White (18,805)	18,944	94.35
Not Hispanic (18,650)	18,783	93.55
Hispanic (155)	161	0.80

Nanticoke

Place Type: City
County: Luzerne
Population: 10,465†

Ancestry‡	Population	%
African, Sub-Saharan (0)	31	0.30
African (0)	31	0.30
American (433)	433	4.13
Arab (19)	41	0.39
Arab (0)	12	0.11
Lebanese (19)	29	0.28
Austrian (29)	82	0.78
British (25)	25	0.24
Czech (7)	124	1.18
Czechoslovakian (9)	9	0.09
Dutch (54)	178	1.70
Eastern European (9)	9	0.09
English (112)	654	6.23
French, ex. Basque (41)	245	2.34
German (361)	1,997	19.03
Greek (0)	24	0.23
Hungarian (31)	43	0.41
Irish (299)	1,295	12.34
Italian (259)	817	7.79
Lithuanian (60)	331	3.15
Norwegian (0)	17	0.16
Pennsylvania German (116)	156	1.49
Polish (2,363)	4,390	41.84
Portuguese (21)	21	0.20
Russian (88)	330	3.15
Scotch-Irish (34)	65	0.62
Scottish (43)	105	1.00
Slavic (11)	22	0.21
Slovak (185)	518	4.94
Slovene (9)	9	0.09
Swedish (0)	93	0.89
Ukrainian (90)	164	1.56
Welsh (79)	541	5.16
West Indian, ex. Hispanic (116)	116	1.11
Dutch West Indian (84)	84	0.80
Haitian (7)	7	0.07
Jamaican (25)	25	0.24

Hispanic Origin	Population	%
Hispanic or Latino (of any race)	270	2.58
Central American, ex. Mexican	16	0.15
Guatemalan	1	0.01
Honduran	10	0.10
Panamanian	2	0.02
Salvadoran	3	0.03
Cuban	9	0.09
Dominican Republic	15	0.14
Mexican	43	0.41
Puerto Rican	136	1.30
South American	26	0.25
Argentinean	6	0.06
Bolivian	7	0.07
Colombian	5	0.05
Ecuadorian	5	0.05
Peruvian	2	0.02
Uruguayan	1	0.01
Other Hispanic or Latino	25	0.24

Race*	Population	%
African-American/Black (167)	231	2.21
Not Hispanic (145)	206	1.97
Hispanic (22)	25	0.24
American Indian/Alaska Native (13)	38	0.36
Not Hispanic (7)	30	0.29
Hispanic (6)	8	0.08
Apache (0)	2	0.02
Cherokee (0)	5	0.05
Chippewa (1)	5	0.05
Choctaw (0)	1	0.01
Iroquois (1)	3	0.03
Sioux (1)	8	0.08
Spanish American Ind. (1)	1	0.01
Asian (45)	76	0.73
Not Hispanic (43)	71	0.68
Hispanic (2)	5	0.05
Chinese, ex. Taiwanese (6)	7	0.07
Filipino (16)	28	0.27
Indian (11)	12	0.11
Japanese (1)	6	0.06
Korean (6)	9	0.09
Pakistani (2)	2	0.02
Vietnamese (3)	5	0.05
Hawaii Native/Pacific Islander (1)	8	0.08
Not Hispanic (1)	2	0.02
Hispanic (0)	6	0.06
Guamanian/Chamorro (1)	1	0.01
Native Hawaiian (0)	6	0.06
White (10,040)	10,168	97.16
Not Hispanic (9,884)	9,994	95.50
Hispanic (156)	174	1.66

Neshannock

Place Type: Township
County: Lawrence
Population: 9,609†

Ancestry‡	Population	%
Albanian (0)	14	0.15
American (497)	497	5.22
Arab (32)	211	2.21
Lebanese (0)	102	1.07
Syrian (32)	109	1.14
Austrian (0)	26	0.27
British (0)	35	0.37
Croatian (21)	132	1.39
Czech (13)	25	0.26
Czechoslovakian (0)	13	0.14
Dutch (16)	52	0.55
English (420)	936	9.82
European (23)	23	0.24
Finnish (14)	26	0.27
French, ex. Basque (54)	277	2.91
French Canadian (0)	10	0.10
German (380)	1,974	20.72
Greek (41)	80	0.84
Hungarian (13)	109	1.14
Irish (340)	1,808	18.98
Italian (1,830)	3,369	35.36
Norwegian (0)	22	0.23
Pennsylvania German (8)	8	0.08
Polish (339)	981	10.30
Romanian (31)	43	0.45
Russian (49)	128	1.34
Scotch-Irish (250)	504	5.29
Scottish (174)	277	2.91
Serbian (0)	9	0.09
Slavic (0)	16	0.17
Slovak (50)	223	2.34
Slovene (0)	11	0.12
Swedish (32)	75	0.79
Swiss (0)	27	0.28
Ukrainian (27)	35	0.37
Welsh (91)	235	2.47

Hispanic Origin	Population	%
Hispanic or Latino (of any race)	109	1.13
Central American, ex. Mexican	5	0.05
Guatemalan	2	0.02
Nicaraguan	3	0.03
Cuban	4	0.04
Dominican Republic	3	0.03
Mexican	57	0.59
Puerto Rican	20	0.21
South American	13	0.14
Argentinean	2	0.02
Colombian	1	0.01
Ecuadorian	4	0.04
Peruvian	6	0.06
Other Hispanic or Latino	7	0.07

Race*	Population	%
African-American/Black (98)	134	1.39
Not Hispanic (95)	128	1.33
Hispanic (3)	6	0.06
American Indian/Alaska Native (6)	21	0.22
Not Hispanic (3)	17	0.18
Hispanic (3)	4	0.04
Apache (0)	2	0.02
Cherokee (0)	5	0.05
Choctaw (1)	1	0.01
Delaware (0)	3	0.03
Mexican American Ind. (0)	1	0.01
Sioux (0)	1	0.01
Asian (110)	142	1.48
Not Hispanic (110)	139	1.45
Hispanic (0)	3	0.03
Cambodian (4)	4	0.04
Chinese, ex. Taiwanese (11)	13	0.14
Filipino (35)	51	0.53
Indian (25)	27	0.28
Japanese (1)	1	0.01
Korean (14)	19	0.20
Pakistani (1)	1	0.01
Sri Lankan (3)	3	0.03
Taiwanese (1)	1	0.01
Thai (2)	2	0.02
Vietnamese (10)	10	0.10
Hawaii Native/Pacific Islander (0)	7	0.07
Not Hispanic (0)	7	0.07

*Notes: † The Census 2010 population figure is used to calculate the percentages in the Hispanic Origin and Race categories. Ancestry percentages are based on the 2006-2010 American Community Survey population (not shown); ‡ Numbers in parentheses indicate the number of people reporting a single ancestry; * Numbers in parentheses indicate the number of persons reporting this race alone, not in combination with any other race; Please refer to the Explanation of Data for more information.*

Native Hawaiian (0)	3	0.03
Samoan (0)	2	0.02
White (9,287)	9,377	97.59
Not Hispanic (9,211)	9,288	96.66
Hispanic (76)	89	0.93

Nether Providence

Place Type: Township
County: Delaware
Population: 13,706†

Ancestry‡	Population	%
African, Sub-Saharan (69)	81	0.59
African (19)	31	0.23
Kenyan (50)	50	0.37
Albanian (13)	13	0.10
American (156)	156	1.15
Arab (61)	122	0.90
Egyptian (35)	35	0.26
Lebanese (16)	77	0.57
Other Arab (10)	10	0.07
Armenian (10)	10	0.07
Australian (9)	9	0.07
Austrian (0)	43	0.32
British (10)	39	0.29
Canadian (10)	41	0.30
Czech (15)	105	0.77
Czechoslovakian (10)	22	0.16
Danish (14)	64	0.47
Dutch (20)	173	1.27
Eastern European (52)	52	0.38
English (382)	1,975	14.50
European (56)	66	0.48
Finnish (18)	54	0.40
French, ex. Basque (0)	145	1.06
French Canadian (0)	30	0.22
German (443)	2,552	18.74
Greek (158)	309	2.27
Hungarian (52)	82	0.60
Iranian (16)	16	0.12
Irish (1,507)	3,841	28.20
Italian (455)	1,872	13.74
Latvian (0)	21	0.15
Lithuanian (53)	149	1.09
Luxemburger (0)	24	0.18
New Zealander (4)	4	0.03
Northern European (9)	9	0.07
Norwegian (3)	92	0.68
Pennsylvania German (0)	12	0.09
Polish (271)	1,074	7.88
Portuguese (12)	12	0.09
Romanian (52)	99	0.73
Russian (105)	293	2.15
Scandinavian (48)	59	0.43
Scotch-Irish (130)	377	2.77
Scottish (155)	566	4.16
Slavic (10)	22	0.16
Slovak (27)	54	0.40
Swedish (53)	232	1.70
Swiss (0)	55	0.40
Ukrainian (31)	186	1.37
Welsh (53)	271	1.99
West Indian, ex. Hispanic (11)	11	0.08
Jamaican (11)	11	0.08

Hispanic Origin	Population	%
Hispanic or Latino (of any race)	271	1.98
Central American, ex. Mexican	35	0.26
Costa Rican	11	0.08
Guatemalan	5	0.04
Honduran	8	0.06
Nicaraguan	7	0.05
Panamanian	2	0.01
Salvadoran	2	0.01
Cuban	25	0.18
Dominican Republic	10	0.07
Mexican	48	0.35
Puerto Rican	68	0.50
South American	52	0.38
Argentinean	16	0.12
Bolivian	1	0.01
Chilean	3	0.02
Colombian	14	0.10
Ecuadorian	8	0.06
Peruvian	5	0.04
Uruguayan	1	0.01
Venezuelan	3	0.02
Other South American	1	0.01
Other Hispanic or Latino	33	0.24

Race*	Population	%
African-American/Black (957)	1,063	7.76
Not Hispanic (941)	1,030	7.51
Hispanic (16)	33	0.24
American Indian/Alaska Native (13)	78	0.57
Not Hispanic (11)	60	0.44
Hispanic (2)	18	0.13
Blackfeet (0)	3	0.02
Cherokee (3)	11	0.08
Choctaw (0)	1	0.01
Delaware (1)	2	0.01
Iroquois (0)	1	0.01
Mexican American Ind. (2)	2	0.01
Navajo (0)	2	0.01
Osage (1)	1	0.01
Seminole (0)	2	0.01
Sioux (0)	2	0.01
South American Ind. (0)	5	0.04
Asian (706)	830	6.06
Not Hispanic (706)	828	6.04
Hispanic (0)	2	0.01
Bangladeshi (21)	22	0.16
Burmese (2)	2	0.01
Chinese, ex. Taiwanese (352)	383	2.79
Filipino (22)	38	0.28
Indian (153)	172	1.25
Indonesian (13)	14	0.10
Japanese (25)	31	0.23
Korean (81)	101	0.74
Laotian (0)	1	0.01
Pakistani (5)	6	0.04
Taiwanese (8)	9	0.07
Thai (4)	10	0.07
Vietnamese (8)	24	0.18
Hawaii Native/Pacific Islander (6)	13	0.09
Not Hispanic (6)	13	0.09
Guamanian/Chamorro (4)	4	0.03
Marshallese (0)	2	0.01
Samoan (0)	2	0.01
Tongan (2)	2	0.01
White (11,735)	11,960	87.26
Not Hispanic (11,543)	11,737	85.63
Hispanic (192)	223	1.63

New Britain

Place Type: Township
County: Bucks
Population: 11,070†

Ancestry‡	Population	%
American (227)	227	2.05
Arab (132)	166	1.50
Lebanese (120)	154	1.39
Other Arab (12)	12	0.11
Armenian (57)	57	0.52
Austrian (10)	80	0.72
Belgian (0)	9	0.08
British (47)	70	0.63
Canadian (0)	23	0.21
Carpatho Rusyn (10)	10	0.09
Croatian (21)	31	0.28
Czech (11)	49	0.44
Czechoslovakian (8)	26	0.24
Dutch (22)	185	1.67
Eastern European (58)	68	0.62
English (249)	1,131	10.24
European (85)	93	0.84
Finnish (0)	13	0.12
French, ex. Basque (60)	391	3.54
French Canadian (0)	66	0.60
German (939)	3,732	33.78
Greek (9)	41	0.37
Hungarian (40)	129	1.17
Irish (978)	3,383	30.62
Italian (605)	2,002	18.12
Latvian (0)	8	0.07
Lithuanian (25)	105	0.95
Norwegian (10)	215	1.95
Pennsylvania German (60)	104	0.94
Polish (200)	977	8.84
Romanian (0)	9	0.08
Russian (103)	198	1.79
Scandinavian (13)	13	0.12
Scotch-Irish (97)	216	1.96
Scottish (21)	184	1.67
Serbian (0)	8	0.07
Slovak (21)	30	0.27
Swedish (18)	203	1.84
Swiss (62)	91	0.82
Turkish (18)	18	0.16
Ukrainian (27)	46	0.42
Welsh (25)	266	2.41
West Indian, ex. Hispanic (13)	13	0.12
Jamaican (13)	13	0.12
Yugoslavian (9)	18	0.16

Hispanic Origin	Population	%
Hispanic or Latino (of any race)	267	2.41
Central American, ex. Mexican	22	0.20
Costa Rican	8	0.07
Guatemalan	9	0.08
Honduran	1	0.01
Salvadoran	4	0.04
Cuban	15	0.14
Dominican Republic	8	0.07
Mexican	59	0.53
Puerto Rican	85	0.77
South American	50	0.45
Argentinean	6	0.05
Colombian	17	0.15
Ecuadorian	3	0.03
Peruvian	6	0.05
Uruguayan	1	0.01
Venezuelan	17	0.15
Other Hispanic or Latino	28	0.25

Race*	Population	%
African-American/Black (177)	209	1.89
Not Hispanic (171)	198	1.79
Hispanic (6)	11	0.10
American Indian/Alaska Native (2)	17	0.15
Not Hispanic (2)	17	0.15
Blackfeet (0)	1	0.01
Cherokee (0)	6	0.05
Sioux (1)	5	0.05
Asian (362)	402	3.63
Not Hispanic (362)	399	3.60
Hispanic (0)	3	0.03
Cambodian (2)	3	0.03
Chinese, ex. Taiwanese (67)	76	0.69
Filipino (15)	24	0.22
Indian (90)	95	0.86
Indonesian (1)	1	0.01
Japanese (3)	9	0.08
Korean (130)	137	1.24
Pakistani (3)	4	0.04
Sri Lankan (1)	1	0.01
Taiwanese (7)	7	0.06
Thai (1)	1	0.01
Vietnamese (37)	37	0.33
Hawaii Native/Pacific Islander (3)	11	0.10
Not Hispanic (2)	5	0.05
Hispanic (1)	6	0.05
Native Hawaiian (3)	11	0.10
White (10,399)	10,490	94.76
Not Hispanic (10,182)	10,249	92.58
Hispanic (217)	241	2.18

*Notes: † The Census 2010 population figure is used to calculate the percentages in the Hispanic Origin and Race categories. Ancestry percentages are based on the 2006-2010 American Community Survey population (not shown); ‡ Numbers in parentheses indicate the number of people reporting a single ancestry; * Numbers in parentheses indicate the number of persons reporting this race alone, not in combination with any other race; Please refer to the Explanation of Data for more information.*

New Castle

Place Type: City
County: Lawrence
Population: 23,273†

Ancestry‡	Population	%
African, Sub-Saharan (74)	84	0.35
African (56)	66	0.28
Liberian (18)	18	0.08
American (858)	858	3.60
Arab (180)	434	1.82
Arab (26)	83	0.35
Egyptian (0)	59	0.25
Lebanese (98)	151	0.63
Syrian (56)	141	0.59
Austrian (0)	33	0.14
Belgian (0)	9	0.04
Croatian (21)	205	0.86
Czech (9)	45	0.19
Czechoslovakian (0)	31	0.13
Danish (44)	58	0.24
Dutch (22)	406	1.70
Eastern European (36)	36	0.15
English (524)	1,692	7.10
European (62)	86	0.36
Finnish (60)	97	0.41
French, ex. Basque (45)	302	1.27
French Canadian (0)	9	0.04
German (1,318)	4,945	20.75
Greek (54)	147	0.62
Hungarian (10)	96	0.40
Irish (679)	3,760	15.77
Israeli (0)	30	0.13
Italian (4,370)	7,442	31.22
Lithuanian (8)	8	0.03
Northern European (19)	29	0.12
Norwegian (5)	19	0.08
Pennsylvania German (0)	9	0.04
Polish (545)	1,958	8.21
Portuguese (11)	11	0.05
Romanian (25)	58	0.24
Russian (61)	177	0.74
Scotch-Irish (394)	997	4.18
Scottish (90)	480	2.01
Serbian (0)	20	0.08
Slavic (17)	135	0.57
Slovak (137)	444	1.86
Slovene (0)	12	0.05
Swedish (20)	160	0.67
Swiss (0)	18	0.08
Ukrainian (27)	47	0.20
Welsh (64)	501	2.10
West Indian, ex. Hispanic (13)	13	0.05
Bermudan (13)	13	0.05

Hispanic Origin	Population	%
Hispanic or Latino (of any race)	381	1.64
Central American, ex. Mexican	9	0.04
Guatemalan	3	0.01
Panamanian	3	0.01
Salvadoran	3	0.01
Cuban	11	0.05
Dominican Republic	21	0.09
Mexican	123	0.53
Puerto Rican	156	0.67
South American	11	0.05
Argentinean	3	0.01
Chilean	1	<0.01
Colombian	2	0.01
Ecuadorian	3	0.01
Paraguayan	2	0.01
Other Hispanic or Latino	50	0.21

Race*	Population	%
African-American/Black (2,836)	3,546	15.24
Not Hispanic (2,802)	3,489	14.99
Hispanic (34)	57	0.24
American Indian/Alaska Native (31)	187	0.80
Not Hispanic (24)	167	0.72
Hispanic (7)	20	0.09
Aleut *(Alaska Native)* (0)	1	<0.01
Blackfeet (2)	11	0.05
Cherokee (11)	49	0.21
Chippewa (0)	3	0.01
Choctaw (0)	1	<0.01
Crow (0)	1	<0.01
Inupiat *(Alaska Native)* (0)	1	<0.01
Iroquois (2)	2	0.01
Navajo (0)	2	0.01
Seminole (0)	2	0.01
Sioux (0)	2	0.01
Asian (87)	129	0.55
Not Hispanic (82)	119	0.51
Hispanic (5)	10	0.04
Cambodian (6)	6	0.03
Chinese, ex. Taiwanese (26)	36	0.15
Filipino (14)	17	0.07
Indian (7)	10	0.04
Indonesian (1)	1	<0.01
Japanese (4)	10	0.04
Korean (10)	20	0.09
Nepalese (3)	3	0.01
Pakistani (1)	1	<0.01
Thai (1)	4	0.02
Vietnamese (9)	11	0.05
Hawaii Native/Pacific Islander (1)	11	0.05
Not Hispanic (1)	11	0.05
Native Hawaiian (1)	3	0.01
Samoan (0)	1	<0.01
White (19,365)	20,150	86.58
Not Hispanic (19,133)	19,875	85.40
Hispanic (232)	275	1.18

New Garden

Place Type: Township
County: Chester
Population: 11,984†

Ancestry‡	Population	%
African, Sub-Saharan (0)	11	0.10
African (0)	11	0.10
American (574)	574	4.96
Arab (0)	14	0.12
Palestinian (0)	14	0.12
Austrian (0)	58	0.50
Brazilian (57)	109	0.94
British (61)	122	1.05
Canadian (13)	13	0.11
Czech (0)	27	0.23
Danish (0)	29	0.25
Dutch (49)	156	1.35
Eastern European (8)	8	0.07
English (330)	1,218	10.52
European (118)	136	1.18
Finnish (0)	16	0.14
French, ex. Basque (35)	197	1.70
German (418)	1,848	15.97
Hungarian (15)	32	0.28
Irish (251)	1,543	13.33
Italian (794)	1,951	16.86
Lithuanian (11)	11	0.10
Norwegian (25)	164	1.42
Pennsylvania German (129)	157	1.36
Polish (139)	614	5.31
Portuguese (30)	121	1.05
Russian (178)	314	2.71
Scandinavian (0)	11	0.10
Scotch-Irish (10)	112	0.97
Scottish (59)	271	2.34
Serbian (0)	19	0.16
Slovak (0)	25	0.22
Slovene (0)	19	0.16
Swedish (76)	209	1.81
Swiss (0)	79	0.68
Ukrainian (0)	62	0.54
Welsh (59)	199	1.72
West Indian, ex. Hispanic (0)	5	0.04
Trinidadian/Tobagonian (0)	5	0.04

Hispanic Origin	Population	%
Hispanic or Latino (of any race)	3,165	26.41
Central American, ex. Mexican	23	0.19
Costa Rican	4	0.03
Guatemalan	15	0.13
Honduran	2	0.02
Salvadoran	2	0.02
Cuban	22	0.18
Dominican Republic	1	0.01
Mexican	2,791	23.29
Puerto Rican	227	1.89
South American	51	0.43
Argentinean	3	0.03
Bolivian	1	0.01
Chilean	4	0.03
Colombian	26	0.22
Ecuadorian	6	0.05
Paraguayan	1	0.01
Peruvian	8	0.07
Venezuelan	2	0.02
Other Hispanic or Latino	50	0.42

Race*	Population	%
African-American/Black (354)	414	3.45
Not Hispanic (324)	365	3.05
Hispanic (30)	49	0.41
American Indian/Alaska Native (58)	101	0.84
Not Hispanic (6)	39	0.33
Hispanic (52)	62	0.52
Blackfeet (0)	2	0.02
Cherokee (4)	10	0.08
Chippewa (0)	1	0.01
Mexican American Ind. (37)	44	0.37
South American Ind. (1)	2	0.02
Asian (359)	427	3.56
Not Hispanic (357)	413	3.45
Hispanic (2)	14	0.12
Burmese (1)	1	0.01
Chinese, ex. Taiwanese (91)	123	1.03
Filipino (33)	47	0.39
Indian (135)	158	1.32
Japanese (14)	17	0.14
Korean (31)	32	0.27
Laotian (3)	4	0.03
Malaysian (1)	1	0.01
Pakistani (11)	12	0.10
Taiwanese (2)	7	0.06
Thai (6)	10	0.08
Vietnamese (16)	18	0.15
Hawaii Native/Pacific Islander (2)	4	0.03
Not Hispanic (1)	1	0.01
Hispanic (1)	3	0.03
Guamanian/Chamorro (2)	2	0.02
Native Hawaiian (0)	1	0.01
White (9,377)	9,623	80.30
Not Hispanic (8,007)	8,105	67.63
Hispanic (1,370)	1,518	12.67

New Hanover

Place Type: Township
County: Montgomery
Population: 10,939†

Ancestry‡	Population	%
American (438)	438	4.26
Arab (0)	34	0.33
Syrian (0)	34	0.33
Austrian (25)	30	0.29
British (0)	10	0.10
Croatian (0)	8	0.08
Czech (26)	219	2.13
Czechoslovakian (0)	13	0.13
Danish (0)	12	0.12
Dutch (60)	262	2.55
English (152)	1,127	10.95
European (39)	39	0.38
Finnish (13)	27	0.26
French, ex. Basque (27)	247	2.40
French Canadian (30)	45	0.44

*Notes: † The Census 2010 population figure is used to calculate the percentages in the Hispanic Origin and Race categories. Ancestry percentages are based on the 2006-2010 American Community Survey population (not shown); ‡ Numbers in parentheses indicate the number of people reporting a single ancestry; * Numbers in parentheses indicate the number of persons reporting this race alone, not in combination with any other race; Please refer to the Explanation of Data for more information.*

German (1,447)	4,014	39.00
Greek (33)	109	1.06
Hungarian (0)	75	0.73
Iranian (10)	10	0.10
Irish (475)	2,685	26.09
Italian (619)	1,762	17.12
Lithuanian (11)	144	1.40
Norwegian (33)	124	1.20
Pennsylvania German (144)	310	3.01
Polish (145)	687	6.67
Portuguese (0)	65	0.63
Russian (51)	169	1.64
Scotch-Irish (51)	79	0.77
Scottish (72)	183	1.78
Slavic (12)	12	0.12
Slovak (37)	135	1.31
Slovene (13)	13	0.13
Swedish (0)	58	0.56
Swiss (12)	23	0.22
Ukrainian (93)	134	1.30
Welsh (10)	97	0.94

Hispanic Origin	Population	%
Hispanic or Latino (of any race)	172	1.57
Central American, ex. Mexican	19	0.17
Costa Rican	7	0.06
Guatemalan	7	0.06
Honduran	1	0.01
Panamanian	2	0.02
Salvadoran	1	0.01
Other Central American	1	0.01
Cuban	18	0.16
Dominican Republic	3	0.03
Mexican	32	0.29
Puerto Rican	73	0.67
South American	12	0.11
Argentinean	1	0.01
Chilean	6	0.05
Colombian	4	0.04
Peruvian	1	0.01
Other Hispanic or Latino	15	0.14

Race*	Population	%
African-American/Black (130)	186	1.70
Not Hispanic (116)	165	1.51
Hispanic (14)	21	0.19
American Indian/Alaska Native (9)	46	0.42
Not Hispanic (8)	42	0.38
Hispanic (1)	4	0.04
Blackfeet (0)	5	0.05
Central American Ind. (1)	2	0.02
Cherokee (2)	12	0.11
Delaware (0)	4	0.04
Potawatomi (1)	1	0.01
Asian (218)	257	2.35
Not Hispanic (215)	251	2.29
Hispanic (3)	6	0.05
Cambodian (6)	6	0.05
Chinese, ex. Taiwanese (23)	36	0.33
Filipino (22)	29	0.27
Indian (84)	93	0.85
Indonesian (2)	2	0.02
Japanese (9)	10	0.09
Korean (47)	56	0.51
Malaysian (0)	3	0.03
Pakistani (6)	6	0.05
Thai (1)	2	0.02
Vietnamese (10)	11	0.10
Hawaii Native/Pacific Islander (2)	8	0.07
Not Hispanic (1)	6	0.05
Hispanic (1)	2	0.02
Guamanian/Chamorro (1)	1	0.01
Native Hawaiian (1)	5	0.05
White (10,427)	10,534	96.30
Not Hispanic (10,315)	10,405	95.12
Hispanic (112)	129	1.18

New Kensington

Place Type: City
County: Westmoreland
Population: 13,116†

Ancestry‡	Population	%
African, Sub-Saharan (70)	70	0.52
African (70)	70	0.52
American (377)	377	2.82
Arab (133)	221	1.65
Lebanese (18)	60	0.45
Palestinian (9)	9	0.07
Syrian (37)	83	0.62
Other Arab (69)	69	0.52
Armenian (0)	8	0.06
Austrian (8)	102	0.76
Belgian (0)	59	0.44
Croatian (28)	91	0.68
Czech (28)	37	0.28
Czechoslovakian (0)	8	0.06
Danish (11)	11	0.08
Dutch (0)	155	1.16
English (198)	972	7.27
French, ex. Basque (51)	277	2.07
French Canadian (8)	17	0.13
German (973)	3,768	28.18
Greek (50)	169	1.26
Hungarian (27)	124	0.93
Irish (464)	2,486	18.59
Italian (1,193)	2,436	18.22
Lithuanian (127)	207	1.55
Norwegian (16)	24	0.18
Pennsylvania German (12)	19	0.14
Polish (827)	2,166	16.20
Russian (18)	139	1.04
Scotch-Irish (102)	360	2.69
Scottish (72)	354	2.65
Serbian (9)	9	0.07
Slovak (406)	770	5.76
Slovene (0)	8	0.06
Swedish (10)	87	0.65
Swiss (0)	17	0.13
Ukrainian (42)	163	1.22
Welsh (0)	114	0.85
Yugoslavian (8)	8	0.06

Hispanic Origin	Population	%
Hispanic or Latino (of any race)	201	1.53
Central American, ex. Mexican	7	0.05
Honduran	4	0.03
Panamanian	2	0.02
Salvadoran	1	0.01
Cuban	9	0.07
Dominican Republic	7	0.05
Mexican	67	0.51
Puerto Rican	80	0.61
South American	5	0.04
Bolivian	1	0.01
Colombian	2	0.02
Ecuadorian	1	0.01
Peruvian	1	0.01
Other Hispanic or Latino	26	0.20

Race*	Population	%
African-American/Black (1,393)	1,880	14.33
Not Hispanic (1,358)	1,814	13.83
Hispanic (35)	66	0.50
American Indian/Alaska Native (26)	110	0.84
Not Hispanic (21)	93	0.71
Hispanic (5)	17	0.13
Blackfeet (0)	5	0.04
Canadian/French Am. Ind. (1)	1	0.01
Central American Ind. (3)	3	0.02
Cherokee (4)	22	0.17
Chickasaw (0)	3	0.02
Comanche (1)	1	0.01
Creek (0)	2	0.02
Iroquois (0)	5	0.04
Kiowa (1)	1	0.01
Navajo (1)	1	0.01
Pima (1)	1	0.01
Potawatomi (1)	1	0.01
Sioux (0)	5	0.04
South American Ind. (0)	1	0.01
Asian (63)	121	0.92
Not Hispanic (63)	117	0.89
Hispanic (0)	4	0.03
Chinese, ex. Taiwanese (23)	25	0.19
Filipino (12)	22	0.17
Indian (4)	11	0.08
Indonesian (1)	3	0.02
Japanese (1)	19	0.14
Korean (9)	23	0.18
Pakistani (2)	2	0.02
Sri Lankan (3)	4	0.03
Vietnamese (7)	12	0.09
Hawaii Native/Pacific Islander (2)	11	0.08
Not Hispanic (2)	11	0.08
Guamanian/Chamorro (0)	1	0.01
Native Hawaiian (0)	2	0.02
Samoan (2)	4	0.03
White (11,030)	11,545	88.02
Not Hispanic (10,932)	11,418	87.05
Hispanic (98)	127	0.97

Newberry

Place Type: Township
County: York
Population: 15,285†

Ancestry‡	Population	%
American (1,219)	1,219	8.01
Austrian (16)	16	0.11
Belgian (0)	8	0.05
British (20)	20	0.13
Canadian (21)	21	0.14
Carpatho Rusyn (15)	31	0.20
Croatian (62)	109	0.72
Czech (0)	54	0.35
Czechoslovakian (55)	66	0.43
Danish (30)	71	0.47
Dutch (18)	214	1.41
Eastern European (16)	16	0.11
English (331)	1,026	6.74
European (54)	63	0.41
French, ex. Basque (57)	264	1.74
French Canadian (9)	9	0.06
German (4,125)	7,462	49.04
Greek (31)	60	0.39
Hungarian (55)	105	0.69
Irish (404)	2,096	13.78
Italian (319)	1,037	6.82
Lithuanian (0)	57	0.37
Norwegian (32)	49	0.32
Pennsylvania German (150)	239	1.57
Polish (97)	381	2.50
Portuguese (0)	18	0.12
Romanian (0)	32	0.21
Russian (34)	119	0.78
Scandinavian (15)	58	0.38
Scotch-Irish (93)	248	1.63
Scottish (50)	364	2.39
Serbian (22)	32	0.21
Slovak (21)	36	0.24
Slovene (33)	97	0.64
Swedish (0)	181	1.19
Swiss (26)	89	0.58
Ukrainian (10)	41	0.27
Welsh (22)	259	1.70
Yugoslavian (8)	8	0.05

Hispanic Origin	Population	%
Hispanic or Latino (of any race)	329	2.15
Central American, ex. Mexican	15	0.10
Guatemalan	5	0.03
Panamanian	10	0.07
Cuban	7	0.05
Dominican Republic	11	0.07

*Notes: † The Census 2010 population figure is used to calculate the percentages in the Hispanic Origin and Race categories. Ancestry percentages are based on the 2006-2010 American Community Survey population (not shown); ‡ Numbers in parentheses indicate the number of people reporting a single ancestry; * Numbers in parentheses indicate the number of persons reporting this race alone, not in combination with any other race; Please refer to the Explanation of Data for more information.*

Mexican	66	0.43
Puerto Rican	190	1.24
South American	20	0.13
Bolivian	1	0.01
Colombian	8	0.05
Ecuadorian	5	0.03
Peruvian	5	0.03
Venezuelan	1	0.01
Other Hispanic or Latino	20	0.13

Race*	Population	%
African-American/Black (156)	237	1.55
Not Hispanic (144)	217	1.42
Hispanic (12)	20	0.13
American Indian/Alaska Native (25)	102	0.67
Not Hispanic (14)	80	0.52
Hispanic (11)	22	0.14
Apache (0)	5	0.03
Blackfeet (1)	5	0.03
Canadian/French Am. Ind. (0)	2	0.01
Central American Ind. (1)	3	0.02
Cherokee (2)	21	0.14
Choctaw (0)	1	0.01
Inupiat *(Alaska Native)* (0)	2	0.01
Iroquois (3)	4	0.03
Lumbee (1)	3	0.02
Mexican American Ind. (4)	4	0.03
Pueblo (0)	4	0.03
Sioux (1)	6	0.04
Asian (90)	134	0.88
Not Hispanic (89)	132	0.86
Hispanic (1)	2	0.01
Burmese (1)	1	0.01
Cambodian (1)	1	0.01
Chinese, ex. Taiwanese (15)	22	0.14
Filipino (10)	16	0.10
Indian (14)	15	0.10
Indonesian (5)	11	0.07
Japanese (4)	8	0.05
Korean (23)	32	0.21
Laotian (1)	2	0.01
Pakistani (0)	1	0.01
Thai (3)	3	0.02
Vietnamese (8)	15	0.10
Hawaii Native/Pacific Islander (1)	9	0.06
Not Hispanic (1)	9	0.06
Guamanian/Chamorro (0)	1	0.01
Native Hawaiian (1)	4	0.03
White (14,688)	14,891	97.42
Not Hispanic (14,520)	14,688	96.09
Hispanic (168)	203	1.33

Newtown

Place Type: Township
County: Bucks
Population: 19,299†

Ancestry‡	Population	%
African, Sub-Saharan (25)	37	0.19
African (25)	37	0.19
American (616)	616	3.21
Arab (61)	185	0.96
Lebanese (34)	110	0.57
Moroccan (27)	56	0.29
Syrian (0)	19	0.10
Armenian (24)	71	0.37
Assyrian/Chaldean/Syriac (0)	16	0.08
Australian (40)	40	0.21
Austrian (38)	176	0.92
Belgian (17)	17	0.09
British (7)	74	0.39
Bulgarian (15)	15	0.08
Canadian (0)	82	0.43
Croatian (0)	15	0.08
Cypriot (13)	13	0.07
Czech (28)	97	0.51
Czechoslovakian (25)	67	0.35
Danish (30)	94	0.49
Dutch (106)	419	2.18
Eastern European (109)	123	0.64
English (596)	2,388	12.44
Estonian (0)	17	0.09
European (262)	272	1.42
French, ex. Basque (0)	376	1.96
French Canadian (58)	117	0.61
German (947)	4,000	20.84
Greek (197)	266	1.39
Hungarian (61)	248	1.29
Iranian (43)	43	0.22
Irish (1,307)	4,981	25.95
Israeli (6)	41	0.21
Italian (1,283)	3,627	18.90
Lithuanian (44)	134	0.70
Northern European (69)	69	0.36
Norwegian (36)	102	0.53
Pennsylvania German (0)	11	0.06
Polish (496)	1,699	8.85
Portuguese (35)	83	0.43
Romanian (6)	16	0.08
Russian (581)	933	4.86
Scandinavian (0)	24	0.13
Scotch-Irish (97)	327	1.70
Scottish (61)	383	2.00
Slovak (48)	102	0.53
Swedish (13)	320	1.67
Swiss (20)	95	0.49
Ukrainian (176)	292	1.52
Welsh (50)	299	1.56
West Indian, ex. Hispanic (15)	15	0.08
Haitian (15)	15	0.08

Hispanic Origin	Population	%
Hispanic or Latino (of any race)	375	1.94
Central American, ex. Mexican	27	0.14
Costa Rican	3	0.02
Guatemalan	9	0.05
Honduran	1	0.01
Panamanian	4	0.02
Salvadoran	10	0.05
Cuban	41	0.21
Dominican Republic	2	0.01
Mexican	65	0.34
Puerto Rican	121	0.63
South American	79	0.41
Argentinean	10	0.05
Chilean	13	0.07
Colombian	37	0.19
Ecuadorian	6	0.03
Paraguayan	2	0.01
Peruvian	10	0.05
Venezuelan	1	0.01
Other Hispanic or Latino	40	0.21

Race*	Population	%
African-American/Black (229)	286	1.48
Not Hispanic (224)	278	1.44
Hispanic (5)	8	0.04
American Indian/Alaska Native (17)	74	0.38
Not Hispanic (7)	61	0.32
Hispanic (10)	13	0.07
Apache (0)	2	0.01
Canadian/French Am. Ind. (1)	1	0.01
Cherokee (0)	19	0.10
Chippewa (0)	1	0.01
Choctaw (0)	2	0.01
Delaware (0)	3	0.02
Iroquois (0)	5	0.03
Osage (2)	2	0.01
South American Ind. (1)	1	0.01
Yaqui (0)	1	0.01
Asian (1,532)	1,663	8.62
Not Hispanic (1,532)	1,661	8.61
Hispanic (0)	2	0.01
Bangladeshi (13)	13	0.07
Cambodian (3)	3	0.02
Chinese, ex. Taiwanese (484)	523	2.71
Filipino (53)	70	0.36
Indian (579)	606	3.14
Indonesian (4)	8	0.04
Japanese (14)	25	0.13
Korean (234)	254	1.32
Pakistani (44)	48	0.25
Sri Lankan (1)	1	0.01
Taiwanese (31)	35	0.18
Thai (5)	8	0.04
Vietnamese (39)	43	0.22
Hawaii Native/Pacific Islander (2)	7	0.04
Not Hispanic (2)	7	0.04
Native Hawaiian (2)	3	0.02
White (17,236)	17,424	90.28
Not Hispanic (16,939)	17,111	88.66
Hispanic (297)	313	1.62

Newtown

Place Type: Township
County: Delaware
Population: 12,216†

Ancestry‡	Population	%
Albanian (41)	41	0.34
American (477)	477	3.94
Arab (45)	176	1.45
Arab (0)	32	0.26
Lebanese (0)	57	0.47
Syrian (45)	87	0.72
Armenian (69)	108	0.89
Austrian (6)	55	0.45
Belgian (10)	18	0.15
Brazilian (10)	10	0.08
British (9)	28	0.23
Bulgarian (38)	38	0.31
Canadian (13)	19	0.16
Czech (0)	32	0.26
Czechoslovakian (17)	17	0.14
Danish (0)	36	0.30
Dutch (15)	128	1.06
Eastern European (7)	7	0.06
English (418)	1,783	14.73
European (154)	154	1.27
Finnish (0)	70	0.58
French, ex. Basque (86)	375	3.10
French Canadian (10)	10	0.08
German (437)	2,634	21.76
Greek (213)	312	2.58
Hungarian (11)	165	1.36
Iranian (17)	17	0.14
Irish (1,544)	3,875	32.01
Italian (1,084)	2,880	23.79
Latvian (23)	23	0.19
Lithuanian (24)	98	0.81
Northern European (18)	18	0.15
Norwegian (26)	158	1.31
Pennsylvania German (22)	22	0.18
Polish (14)	419	3.46
Portuguese (0)	20	0.17
Romanian (15)	15	0.12
Russian (117)	242	2.00
Scandinavian (10)	16	0.13
Scotch-Irish (189)	391	3.23
Scottish (74)	248	2.05
Slovak (0)	65	0.54
Slovene (0)	11	0.09
Swedish (19)	115	0.95
Swiss (8)	64	0.53
Ukrainian (38)	136	1.12
Welsh (7)	144	1.19

Hispanic Origin	Population	%
Hispanic or Latino (of any race)	144	1.18
Central American, ex. Mexican	17	0.14
Guatemalan	9	0.07
Honduran	3	0.02
Nicaraguan	3	0.02
Salvadoran	1	0.01
Other Central American	1	0.01
Cuban	24	0.20
Dominican Republic	1	0.01
Mexican	44	0.36

*Notes: † The Census 2010 population figure is used to calculate the percentages in the Hispanic Origin and Race categories. Ancestry percentages are based on the 2006-2010 American Community Survey population (not shown); ‡ Numbers in parentheses indicate the number of people reporting a single ancestry; * Numbers in parentheses indicate the number of persons reporting this race alone, not in combination with any other race; Please refer to the Explanation of Data for more information.*

Puerto Rican	13	0.11
South American	31	0.25
Argentinean	3	0.02
Chilean	2	0.02
Colombian	7	0.06
Ecuadorian	5	0.04
Peruvian	10	0.08
Venezuelan	3	0.02
Other South American	1	0.01
Other Hispanic or Latino	14	0.11

Race*	Population	%
African-American/Black (111)	139	1.14
Not Hispanic (110)	138	1.13
Hispanic (1)	1	0.01
American Indian/Alaska Native (16)	31	0.25
Not Hispanic (14)	29	0.24
Hispanic (2)	2	0.02
Blackfeet (0)	2	0.02
Cherokee (6)	13	0.11
Chippewa (1)	1	0.01
Crow (0)	1	0.01
Iroquois (1)	1	0.01
Potawatomi (3)	3	0.02
South American Ind. (2)	2	0.02
Asian (406)	460	3.77
Not Hispanic (402)	454	3.72
Hispanic (4)	6	0.05
Bangladeshi (8)	9	0.07
Burmese (0)	2	0.02
Cambodian (6)	8	0.07
Chinese, ex. Taiwanese (79)	95	0.78
Filipino (12)	20	0.16
Indian (94)	103	0.84
Japanese (9)	16	0.13
Korean (131)	139	1.14
Laotian (1)	2	0.02
Pakistani (13)	15	0.12
Taiwanese (4)	4	0.03
Thai (6)	7	0.06
Vietnamese (38)	39	0.32
Hawaii Native/Pacific Islander (1)	4	0.03
Not Hispanic (1)	3	0.02
Hispanic (0)	1	0.01
Guamanian/Chamorro (0)	1	0.01
Native Hawaiian (0)	1	0.01
Samoan (0)	1	0.01
White (11,557)	11,648	95.35
Not Hispanic (11,447)	11,527	94.36
Hispanic (110)	121	0.99

Norristown

Place Type: Borough
County: Montgomery
Population: 34,324†

Ancestry‡	Population	%
African, Sub-Saharan (651)	807	2.39
African (364)	491	1.45
Kenyan (45)	45	0.13
Nigerian (216)	216	0.64
Senegalese (0)	12	0.04
South African (0)	17	0.05
Sudanese (26)	26	0.08
American (1,428)	1,428	4.23
Arab (40)	59	0.17
Egyptian (2)	2	0.01
Jordanian (28)	28	0.08
Lebanese (0)	10	0.03
Other Arab (10)	19	0.06
Armenian (19)	19	0.06
Australian (0)	79	0.23
Austrian (11)	76	0.22
Brazilian (88)	235	0.70
British (15)	58	0.17
Czech (0)	109	0.32
Czechoslovakian (0)	14	0.04
Dutch (13)	280	0.83
Eastern European (9)	18	0.05
English (254)	974	2.88
European (147)	217	0.64
Finnish (0)	11	0.03
French, ex. Basque (6)	215	0.64
French Canadian (9)	45	0.13
German (707)	3,066	9.08
Greek (31)	40	0.12
Hungarian (12)	70	0.21
Irish (926)	3,940	11.66
Israeli (9)	9	0.03
Italian (2,170)	4,558	13.49
Lithuanian (58)	149	0.44
Norwegian (0)	29	0.09
Pennsylvania German (45)	90	0.27
Polish (480)	1,206	3.57
Portuguese (46)	74	0.22
Romanian (12)	12	0.04
Russian (93)	196	0.58
Scotch-Irish (167)	245	0.73
Scottish (32)	95	0.28
Slovak (33)	80	0.24
Swedish (10)	81	0.24
Swiss (0)	134	0.40
Turkish (55)	55	0.16
Ukrainian (42)	153	0.45
Welsh (9)	176	0.52
West Indian, ex. Hispanic (343)	517	1.53
British West Indian (7)	7	0.02
Haitian (53)	53	0.16
Jamaican (283)	442	1.31
West Indian (0)	15	0.04

Hispanic Origin	Population	%
Hispanic or Latino (of any race)	9,714	28.30
Central American, ex. Mexican	349	1.02
Costa Rican	23	0.07
Guatemalan	85	0.25
Honduran	126	0.37
Nicaraguan	11	0.03
Panamanian	17	0.05
Salvadoran	82	0.24
Other Central American	5	0.01
Cuban	71	0.21
Dominican Republic	136	0.40
Mexican	7,578	22.08
Puerto Rican	1,176	3.43
South American	119	0.35
Argentinean	20	0.06
Bolivian	6	0.02
Chilean	6	0.02
Colombian	35	0.10
Ecuadorian	19	0.06
Peruvian	21	0.06
Uruguayan	2	0.01
Venezuelan	10	0.03
Other Hispanic or Latino	285	0.83

Race*	Population	%
African-American/Black (12,310)	13,366	38.94
Not Hispanic (11,909)	12,756	37.16
Hispanic (401)	610	1.78
American Indian/Alaska Native (150)	427	1.24
Not Hispanic (73)	291	0.85
Hispanic (77)	136	0.40
Apache (0)	2	0.01
Blackfeet (0)	5	0.01
Central American Ind. (0)	2	0.01
Cherokee (6)	69	0.20
Cheyenne (1)	2	0.01
Creek (0)	7	0.02
Delaware (1)	7	0.02
Iroquois (0)	2	0.01
Lumbee (1)	1	<0.01
Mexican American Ind. (9)	13	0.04
Seminole (0)	4	0.01
Sioux (2)	5	0.01
South American Ind. (3)	8	0.02
Spanish American Ind. (17)	17	0.05
Tlingit-Haida *(Alaska Native)* (0)	1	<0.01
Asian (718)	833	2.43
Not Hispanic (710)	809	2.36
Hispanic (8)	24	0.07
Bangladeshi (9)	11	0.03
Burmese (10)	10	0.03
Cambodian (18)	24	0.07
Chinese, ex. Taiwanese (116)	155	0.45
Filipino (50)	72	0.21
Indian (159)	184	0.54
Indonesian (1)	1	<0.01
Japanese (3)	13	0.04
Korean (163)	183	0.53
Laotian (8)	8	0.02
Pakistani (15)	17	0.05
Sri Lankan (3)	3	0.01
Taiwanese (2)	3	0.01
Thai (6)	12	0.03
Vietnamese (133)	150	0.44
Hawaii Native/Pacific Islander (34)	91	0.27
Not Hispanic (11)	43	0.13
Hispanic (23)	48	0.14
Fijian (0)	1	<0.01
Guamanian/Chamorro (26)	29	0.08
Native Hawaiian (3)	17	0.05
Samoan (5)	16	0.05
White (14,048)	15,352	44.73
Not Hispanic (10,844)	11,683	34.04
Hispanic (3,204)	3,669	10.69

North Codorus

Place Type: Township
County: York
Population: 8,905†

Ancestry‡	Population	%
American (952)	952	10.84
Austrian (8)	91	1.04
Brazilian (16)	16	0.18
British (12)	41	0.47
Canadian (22)	22	0.25
Dutch (67)	232	2.64
English (450)	882	10.05
French, ex. Basque (9)	59	0.67
German (3,206)	4,960	56.49
Greek (0)	42	0.48
Hungarian (9)	9	0.10
Irish (182)	756	8.61
Italian (121)	396	4.51
Lithuanian (0)	9	0.10
Norwegian (40)	50	0.57
Pennsylvania German (118)	136	1.55
Polish (40)	241	2.74
Russian (0)	45	0.51
Scotch-Irish (41)	132	1.50
Scottish (12)	63	0.72
Slovak (8)	8	0.09
Swedish (0)	29	0.33
Swiss (0)	142	1.62
Ukrainian (28)	28	0.32
Welsh (0)	90	1.03

Hispanic Origin	Population	%
Hispanic or Latino (of any race)	150	1.68
Central American, ex. Mexican	16	0.18
Costa Rican	1	0.01
Guatemalan	7	0.08
Honduran	2	0.02
Panamanian	2	0.02
Salvadoran	4	0.04
Cuban	3	0.03
Dominican Republic	5	0.06
Mexican	49	0.55
Puerto Rican	49	0.55
South American	16	0.18
Ecuadorian	5	0.06
Peruvian	7	0.08
Venezuelan	4	0.04
Other Hispanic or Latino	12	0.13

*Notes: † The Census 2010 population figure is used to calculate the percentages in the Hispanic Origin and Race categories. Ancestry percentages are based on the 2006-2010 American Community Survey population (not shown); ‡ Numbers in parentheses indicate the number of people reporting a single ancestry; * Numbers in parentheses indicate the number of persons reporting this race alone, not in combination with any other race; Please refer to the Explanation of Data for more information.*

Race*	Population	%
African-American/Black (251)	293	3.29
Not Hispanic (244)	280	3.14
Hispanic (7)	13	0.15
American Indian/Alaska Native (10)	59	0.66
Not Hispanic (9)	47	0.53
Hispanic (1)	12	0.13
Apache (1)	1	0.01
Blackfeet (0)	2	0.02
Cherokee (1)	12	0.13
Crow (0)	1	0.01
Menominee (0)	2	0.02
Sioux (0)	2	0.02
South American Ind. (1)	4	0.04
Asian (47)	69	0.77
Not Hispanic (47)	69	0.77
Chinese, ex. Taiwanese (4)	4	0.04
Filipino (13)	21	0.24
Indian (8)	10	0.11
Indonesian (1)	1	0.01
Japanese (2)	10	0.11
Korean (5)	7	0.08
Laotian (4)	4	0.04
Vietnamese (4)	5	0.06
Hawaii Native/Pacific Islander (2)	16	0.18
Not Hispanic (2)	16	0.18
Native Hawaiian (2)	15	0.17
White (8,438)	8,547	95.98
Not Hispanic (8,363)	8,442	94.80
Hispanic (75)	105	1.18

North Cornwall

Place Type: Township
County: Lebanon
Population: 7,553†

Ancestry‡	Population	%
American (528)	528	7.19
Arab (25)	25	0.34
Arab (25)	25	0.34
Armenian (8)	18	0.25
Czech (27)	122	1.66
Danish (0)	36	0.49
Dutch (74)	150	2.04
English (94)	427	5.82
European (46)	46	0.63
Finnish (6)	6	0.08
French, ex. Basque (34)	231	3.15
French Canadian (12)	25	0.34
German (1,770)	3,171	43.20
Hungarian (0)	145	1.98
Irish (108)	599	8.16
Italian (216)	503	6.85
Lithuanian (0)	16	0.22
Pennsylvania German (193)	237	3.23
Polish (166)	370	5.04
Romanian (9)	33	0.45
Russian (28)	64	0.87
Scandinavian (0)	10	0.14
Scotch-Irish (0)	80	1.09
Scottish (26)	82	1.12
Serbian (0)	9	0.12
Slovak (68)	256	3.49
Swedish (0)	52	0.71
Swiss (28)	128	1.74
Ukrainian (16)	16	0.22
Welsh (0)	32	0.44
West Indian, ex. Hispanic (45)	45	0.61
Haitian (45)	45	0.61

Hispanic Origin	Population	%
Hispanic or Latino (of any race)	820	10.86
Central American, ex. Mexican	18	0.24
Costa Rican	3	0.04
Nicaraguan	3	0.04
Panamanian	2	0.03
Salvadoran	10	0.13
Cuban	11	0.15
Dominican Republic	51	0.68
Mexican	86	1.14
Puerto Rican	567	7.51
South American	48	0.64
Argentinean	2	0.03
Bolivian	1	0.01
Colombian	15	0.20
Ecuadorian	5	0.07
Peruvian	22	0.29
Venezuelan	3	0.04
Other Hispanic or Latino	39	0.52

Race*	Population	%
African-American/Black (308)	413	5.47
Not Hispanic (236)	280	3.71
Hispanic (72)	133	1.76
American Indian/Alaska Native (17)	28	0.37
Not Hispanic (11)	20	0.26
Hispanic (6)	8	0.11
Apache (1)	1	0.01
Blackfeet (0)	1	0.01
Cherokee (0)	4	0.05
Chickasaw (0)	1	0.01
Inupiat *(Alaska Native)* (1)	1	0.01
Asian (208)	239	3.16
Not Hispanic (208)	234	3.10
Hispanic (0)	5	0.07
Bangladeshi (5)	5	0.07
Cambodian (10)	12	0.16
Chinese, ex. Taiwanese (30)	32	0.42
Filipino (30)	35	0.46
Hmong (1)	3	0.04
Indian (50)	62	0.82
Japanese (1)	1	0.01
Korean (10)	14	0.19
Nepalese (5)	5	0.07
Pakistani (17)	22	0.29
Taiwanese (1)	1	0.01
Vietnamese (37)	41	0.54
Hawaii Native/Pacific Islander (0)	4	0.05
Hispanic (0)	4	0.05
White (6,591)	6,748	89.34
Not Hispanic (6,189)	6,260	82.88
Hispanic (402)	488	6.46

North Coventry

Place Type: Township
County: Chester
Population: 7,866†

Ancestry‡	Population	%
American (343)	343	4.37
Austrian (0)	37	0.47
British (26)	26	0.33
Croatian (20)	34	0.43
Czechoslovakian (0)	8	0.10
Dutch (81)	243	3.10
Eastern European (0)	32	0.41
English (172)	868	11.07
European (70)	70	0.89
French, ex. Basque (0)	212	2.70
French Canadian (25)	32	0.41
German (822)	2,397	30.57
Greek (0)	9	0.11
Hungarian (14)	105	1.34
Irish (597)	1,986	25.33
Italian (604)	1,639	20.90
Lithuanian (0)	13	0.17
Pennsylvania German (171)	274	3.49
Polish (183)	498	6.35
Portuguese (15)	15	0.19
Romanian (11)	11	0.14
Russian (60)	75	0.96
Scotch-Irish (38)	133	1.70
Scottish (25)	210	2.68
Slavic (11)	21	0.27
Slovak (53)	164	2.09
Swedish (0)	30	0.38
Swiss (0)	30	0.38
Ukrainian (28)	89	1.14
Welsh (13)	115	1.47
West Indian, ex. Hispanic (9)	26	0.33
Haitian (9)	9	0.11
Jamaican (0)	17	0.22

Hispanic Origin	Population	%
Hispanic or Latino (of any race)	180	2.29
Central American, ex. Mexican	22	0.28
Guatemalan	3	0.04
Honduran	8	0.10
Nicaraguan	3	0.04
Salvadoran	8	0.10
Cuban	2	0.03
Dominican Republic	7	0.09
Mexican	42	0.53
Puerto Rican	63	0.80
South American	21	0.27
Argentinean	5	0.06
Colombian	2	0.03
Ecuadorian	8	0.10
Peruvian	5	0.06
Venezuelan	1	0.01
Other Hispanic or Latino	23	0.29

Race*	Population	%
African-American/Black (216)	256	3.25
Not Hispanic (212)	250	3.18
Hispanic (4)	6	0.08
American Indian/Alaska Native (17)	51	0.65
Not Hispanic (13)	39	0.50
Hispanic (4)	12	0.15
Blackfeet (0)	5	0.06
Cherokee (1)	5	0.06
Chickasaw (0)	1	0.01
Creek (1)	1	0.01
Delaware (1)	1	0.01
Iroquois (1)	1	0.01
Navajo (1)	2	0.03
Potawatomi (1)	1	0.01
Tlingit-Haida *(Alaska Native)* (0)	1	0.01
Asian (98)	138	1.75
Not Hispanic (97)	134	1.70
Hispanic (1)	4	0.05
Cambodian (1)	1	0.01
Chinese, ex. Taiwanese (19)	24	0.31
Filipino (13)	32	0.41
Indian (25)	28	0.36
Japanese (3)	4	0.05
Korean (13)	18	0.23
Laotian (1)	1	0.01
Malaysian (3)	3	0.04
Nepalese (1)	1	0.01
Sri Lankan (1)	1	0.01
Taiwanese (1)	2	0.03
Thai (4)	6	0.08
Vietnamese (10)	12	0.15
Hawaii Native/Pacific Islander (0)	4	0.05
Not Hispanic (0)	1	0.01
Hispanic (0)	3	0.04
Native Hawaiian (0)	4	0.05
White (7,346)	7,465	94.90
Not Hispanic (7,260)	7,352	93.47
Hispanic (86)	113	1.44

North Fayette

Place Type: Township
County: Allegheny
Population: 13,934†

Ancestry‡	Population	%
African, Sub-Saharan (19)	19	0.14
Ethiopian (19)	19	0.14
American (320)	320	2.37
Arab (42)	63	0.47
Lebanese (21)	42	0.31
Palestinian (12)	12	0.09
Syrian (9)	9	0.07
Austrian (57)	203	1.50
Belgian (11)	76	0.56

*Notes: † The Census 2010 population figure is used to calculate the percentages in the Hispanic Origin and Race categories. Ancestry percentages are based on the 2006-2010 American Community Survey population (not shown); ‡ Numbers in parentheses indicate the number of people reporting a single ancestry; * Numbers in parentheses indicate the number of persons reporting this race alone, not in combination with any other race; Please refer to the Explanation of Data for more information.*

British (13)	38	0.28
Canadian (12)	12	0.09
Carpatho Rusyn (0)	10	0.07
Croatian (42)	97	0.72
Czech (17)	136	1.01
Czechoslovakian (30)	91	0.67
Danish (0)	97	0.72
Dutch (18)	147	1.09
Eastern European (42)	42	0.31
English (118)	1,382	10.23
European (13)	13	0.10
French, ex. Basque (44)	274	2.03
German (1,247)	4,923	36.46
Greek (11)	62	0.46
Guyanese (13)	13	0.10
Hungarian (15)	183	1.36
Irish (747)	3,085	22.85
Italian (818)	3,015	22.33
Lithuanian (30)	71	0.53
Norwegian (11)	11	0.08
Pennsylvania German (0)	10	0.07
Polish (389)	1,351	10.01
Russian (43)	286	2.12
Scotch-Irish (92)	399	2.95
Scottish (33)	338	2.50
Serbian (0)	11	0.08
Slavic (0)	11	0.08
Slovak (102)	383	2.84
Slovene (58)	246	1.82
Swedish (10)	57	0.42
Swiss (15)	39	0.29
Ukrainian (49)	129	0.96
Welsh (64)	307	2.27
Yugoslavian (10)	10	0.07

Hispanic Origin	Population	%
Hispanic or Latino (of any race)	197	1.41
Central American, ex. Mexican	11	0.08
Costa Rican	2	0.01
Guatemalan	4	0.03
Honduran	3	0.02
Nicaraguan	1	0.01
Panamanian	1	0.01
Cuban	6	0.04
Dominican Republic	1	0.01
Mexican	81	0.58
Puerto Rican	54	0.39
South American	16	0.11
Argentinean	1	0.01
Chilean	1	0.01
Colombian	8	0.06
Peruvian	2	0.01
Venezuelan	4	0.03
Other Hispanic or Latino	28	0.20

Race*	Population	%
African-American/Black (397)	490	3.52
Not Hispanic (392)	480	3.44
Hispanic (5)	10	0.07
American Indian/Alaska Native (18)	51	0.37
Not Hispanic (15)	43	0.31
Hispanic (3)	8	0.06
Blackfeet (1)	2	0.01
Cherokee (4)	9	0.06
Chippewa (3)	3	0.02
Iroquois (0)	2	0.01
Asian (347)	397	2.85
Not Hispanic (345)	395	2.83
Hispanic (2)	2	0.01
Bangladeshi (2)	2	0.01
Cambodian (3)	3	0.02
Chinese, ex. Taiwanese (65)	71	0.51
Filipino (33)	41	0.29
Indian (176)	183	1.31
Indonesian (1)	1	0.01
Japanese (17)	28	0.20
Korean (9)	12	0.09
Malaysian (0)	1	0.01
Pakistani (7)	17	0.12
Sri Lankan (1)	1	0.01
Taiwanese (1)	1	0.01
Thai (3)	4	0.03
Vietnamese (16)	16	0.11
Hawaii Native/Pacific Islander (6)	10	0.07
Not Hispanic (6)	10	0.07
Guamanian/Chamorro (1)	1	0.01
Native Hawaiian (2)	2	0.01
Samoan (3)	3	0.02
Tongan (0)	3	0.02
White (12,941)	13,104	94.04
Not Hispanic (12,802)	12,944	92.90
Hispanic (139)	160	1.15

North Huntingdon

Place Type: Township
County: Westmoreland
Population: 30,609†

Ancestry‡	Population	%
African, Sub-Saharan (9)	44	0.15
African (0)	11	0.04
South African (9)	33	0.11
American (1,207)	1,207	3.98
Arab (32)	197	0.65
Lebanese (9)	60	0.20
Syrian (14)	128	0.42
Other Arab (9)	9	0.03
Australian (0)	9	0.03
Austrian (39)	134	0.44
Belgian (0)	28	0.09
British (11)	45	0.15
Canadian (24)	79	0.26
Carpatho Rusyn (0)	20	0.07
Croatian (324)	911	3.01
Czech (85)	430	1.42
Czechoslovakian (79)	197	0.65
Danish (0)	13	0.04
Dutch (11)	485	1.60
Eastern European (12)	12	0.04
English (680)	3,383	11.16
European (68)	68	0.22
French, ex. Basque (44)	309	1.02
French Canadian (7)	7	0.02
German (2,559)	10,217	33.71
Greek (133)	317	1.05
Hungarian (376)	1,284	4.24
Irish (1,320)	6,612	21.81
Italian (1,620)	5,346	17.64
Latvian (0)	10	0.03
Lithuanian (8)	165	0.54
Norwegian (0)	62	0.20
Pennsylvania German (149)	217	0.72
Polish (1,097)	3,294	10.87
Portuguese (0)	23	0.08
Romanian (10)	29	0.10
Russian (143)	547	1.80
Scotch-Irish (229)	954	3.15
Scottish (180)	714	2.36
Serbian (143)	453	1.49
Slavic (21)	111	0.37
Slovak (1,007)	3,038	10.02
Slovene (43)	151	0.50
Swedish (97)	369	1.22
Swiss (18)	115	0.38
Ukrainian (89)	186	0.61
Welsh (92)	428	1.41
Yugoslavian (8)	22	0.07

Hispanic Origin	Population	%
Hispanic or Latino (of any race)	183	0.60
Central American, ex. Mexican	12	0.04
Guatemalan	11	0.04
Salvadoran	1	<0.01
Cuban	11	0.04
Dominican Republic	2	0.01
Mexican	94	0.31
Puerto Rican	31	0.10
South American	14	0.05
Argentinean	1	<0.01
Chilean	1	<0.01
Colombian	6	0.02
Ecuadorian	4	0.01
Peruvian	1	<0.01
Venezuelan	1	<0.01
Other Hispanic or Latino	19	0.06

Race*	Population	%
African-American/Black (205)	297	0.97
Not Hispanic (202)	286	0.93
Hispanic (3)	11	0.04
American Indian/Alaska Native (18)	93	0.30
Not Hispanic (15)	71	0.23
Hispanic (3)	22	0.07
Apache (0)	7	0.02
Blackfeet (0)	1	<0.01
Cherokee (2)	13	0.04
Choctaw (2)	7	0.02
Delaware (2)	2	0.01
Inupiat *(Alaska Native)* (3)	3	0.01
Iroquois (0)	1	<0.01
Lumbee (0)	1	<0.01
Mexican American Ind. (1)	5	0.02
Asian (189)	260	0.85
Not Hispanic (189)	256	0.84
Hispanic (0)	4	0.01
Cambodian (3)	7	0.02
Chinese, ex. Taiwanese (52)	60	0.20
Filipino (19)	36	0.12
Indian (35)	41	0.13
Japanese (4)	19	0.06
Korean (16)	24	0.08
Laotian (1)	3	0.01
Malaysian (3)	3	0.01
Taiwanese (2)	2	0.01
Thai (1)	2	0.01
Vietnamese (46)	48	0.16
Hawaii Native/Pacific Islander (0)	11	0.04
Not Hispanic (0)	7	0.02
Hispanic (0)	4	0.01
Samoan (0)	1	<0.01
White (29,933)	30,138	98.46
Not Hispanic (29,803)	29,984	97.96
Hispanic (130)	154	0.50

North Lebanon

Place Type: Township
County: Lebanon
Population: 11,429†

Ancestry‡	Population	%
African, Sub-Saharan (12)	12	0.11
Nigerian (12)	12	0.11
American (899)	899	8.02
Arab (0)	15	0.13
Lebanese (0)	15	0.13
Austrian (0)	28	0.25
Brazilian (0)	22	0.20
British (0)	44	0.39
Croatian (0)	16	0.14
Czech (41)	108	0.96
Czechoslovakian (52)	81	0.72
Danish (15)	15	0.13
Dutch (82)	195	1.74
English (157)	436	3.89
European (50)	50	0.45
French, ex. Basque (25)	59	0.53
German (2,696)	4,810	42.90
Greek (17)	24	0.21
Hungarian (50)	142	1.27
Irish (319)	1,127	10.05
Italian (231)	836	7.46
Lithuanian (28)	44	0.39
Pennsylvania German (325)	373	3.33
Polish (106)	385	3.43
Romanian (14)	14	0.12
Russian (8)	37	0.33
Scotch-Irish (136)	247	2.20
Scottish (22)	158	1.41

*Notes: † The Census 2010 population figure is used to calculate the percentages in the Hispanic Origin and Race categories. Ancestry percentages are based on the 2006-2010 American Community Survey population (not shown); ‡ Numbers in parentheses indicate the number of people reporting a single ancestry; * Numbers in parentheses indicate the number of persons reporting this race alone, not in combination with any other race; Please refer to the Explanation of Data for more information.*

Slovak (41)	174	1.55
Swedish (0)	69	0.62
Swiss (27)	145	1.29
Ukrainian (34)	72	0.64
Welsh (12)	43	0.38
Yugoslavian (12)	12	0.11

Hispanic Origin	Population	%
Hispanic or Latino (of any race)	914	8.00
Central American, ex. Mexican	18	0.16
Honduran	11	0.10
Nicaraguan	4	0.03
Salvadoran	3	0.03
Cuban	14	0.12
Dominican Republic	53	0.46
Mexican	31	0.27
Puerto Rican	722	6.32
South American	47	0.41
Argentinean	5	0.04
Chilean	3	0.03
Colombian	22	0.19
Ecuadorian	3	0.03
Paraguayan	1	0.01
Peruvian	9	0.08
Venezuelan	1	0.01
Other South American	3	0.03
Other Hispanic or Latino	29	0.25

Race*	Population	%
African-American/Black (197)	261	2.28
Not Hispanic (165)	212	1.85
Hispanic (32)	49	0.43
American Indian/Alaska Native (12)	45	0.39
Not Hispanic (2)	28	0.24
Hispanic (10)	17	0.15
Blackfeet (0)	2	0.02
Canadian/French Am. Ind. (1)	2	0.02
Cherokee (0)	4	0.03
Delaware (0)	2	0.02
Iroquois (0)	5	0.04
South American Ind. (0)	5	0.04
Asian (159)	187	1.64
Not Hispanic (157)	184	1.61
Hispanic (2)	3	0.03
Cambodian (26)	40	0.35
Chinese, ex. Taiwanese (13)	19	0.17
Filipino (13)	22	0.19
Indian (23)	31	0.27
Japanese (5)	7	0.06
Korean (6)	8	0.07
Pakistani (14)	14	0.12
Thai (2)	11	0.10
Vietnamese (40)	44	0.38
Hawaii Native/Pacific Islander (2)	4	0.03
Not Hispanic (2)	3	0.03
Hispanic (0)	1	0.01
Guamanian/Chamorro (2)	4	0.03
White (10,550)	10,700	93.62
Not Hispanic (10,075)	10,176	89.04
Hispanic (475)	524	4.58

North Londonderry

Place Type: Township
County: Lebanon
Population: 8,068†

Ancestry‡	Population	%
American (425)	425	5.41
Armenian (24)	24	0.31
Austrian (15)	28	0.36
British (0)	9	0.11
Canadian (0)	117	1.49
Croatian (0)	13	0.17
Czech (15)	27	0.34
Czechoslovakian (15)	15	0.19
Danish (9)	9	0.11
Dutch (53)	264	3.36
English (112)	684	8.71
European (89)	89	1.13
French, ex. Basque (46)	138	1.76
French Canadian (45)	53	0.67
German (2,118)	3,842	48.92
Greek (16)	68	0.87
Hungarian (13)	40	0.51
Iranian (0)	8	0.10
Irish (171)	1,138	14.49
Italian (251)	595	7.58
Latvian (0)	13	0.17
Macedonian (8)	8	0.10
Norwegian (0)	12	0.15
Pennsylvania German (67)	67	0.85
Polish (188)	431	5.49
Russian (0)	44	0.56
Scotch-Irish (75)	102	1.30
Scottish (34)	83	1.06
Slavic (0)	22	0.28
Slovak (15)	54	0.69
Swedish (0)	82	1.04
Swiss (0)	133	1.69
Ukrainian (14)	27	0.34
Welsh (0)	83	1.06

Hispanic Origin	Population	%
Hispanic or Latino (of any race)	119	1.47
Central American, ex. Mexican	18	0.22
Guatemalan	4	0.05
Honduran	4	0.05
Panamanian	2	0.02
Salvadoran	8	0.10
Cuban	1	0.01
Dominican Republic	5	0.06
Mexican	30	0.37
Puerto Rican	51	0.63
South American	10	0.12
Argentinean	2	0.02
Bolivian	1	0.01
Colombian	6	0.07
Ecuadorian	1	0.01
Other Hispanic or Latino	4	0.05

Race*	Population	%
African-American/Black (60)	91	1.13
Not Hispanic (60)	89	1.10
Hispanic (0)	2	0.02
American Indian/Alaska Native (7)	22	0.27
Not Hispanic (7)	22	0.27
Aleut *(Alaska Native)* (0)	2	0.02
Cherokee (2)	3	0.04
Iroquois (1)	1	0.01
Sioux (1)	1	0.01
Asian (131)	156	1.93
Not Hispanic (131)	156	1.93
Cambodian (31)	33	0.41
Chinese, ex. Taiwanese (24)	25	0.31
Filipino (6)	11	0.14
Indian (26)	27	0.33
Indonesian (0)	1	0.01
Japanese (1)	3	0.04
Korean (14)	18	0.22
Laotian (0)	3	0.04
Pakistani (2)	2	0.02
Taiwanese (1)	1	0.01
Vietnamese (16)	21	0.26
Hawaii Native/Pacific Islander (0)	3	0.04
Not Hispanic (0)	2	0.02
Hispanic (0)	1	0.01
Guamanian/Chamorro (0)	1	0.01
White (7,782)	7,850	97.30
Not Hispanic (7,679)	7,745	96.00
Hispanic (103)	105	1.30

North Middleton

Place Type: Township
County: Cumberland
Population: 11,143†

Ancestry‡	Population	%
African, Sub-Saharan (8)	36	0.33
Nigerian (8)	36	0.33
American (1,025)	1,025	9.39
Arab (45)	63	0.58
Moroccan (45)	45	0.41
Syrian (0)	18	0.16
Austrian (0)	11	0.10
Brazilian (9)	9	0.08
British (53)	74	0.68
Canadian (30)	30	0.27
Croatian (61)	61	0.56
Czechoslovakian (0)	14	0.13
Dutch (22)	165	1.51
English (574)	1,082	9.91
European (51)	51	0.47
French, ex. Basque (41)	169	1.55
French Canadian (7)	7	0.06
German (1,614)	3,292	30.17
Greek (37)	141	1.29
Hungarian (27)	32	0.29
Irish (330)	1,797	16.47
Italian (270)	905	8.29
Lithuanian (21)	52	0.48
Norwegian (88)	128	1.17
Pennsylvania German (38)	58	0.53
Polish (72)	357	3.27
Romanian (10)	10	0.09
Russian (12)	38	0.35
Scotch-Irish (107)	326	2.99
Scottish (23)	152	1.39
Slavic (0)	10	0.09
Slovak (0)	5	0.05
Swedish (13)	39	0.36
Swiss (0)	30	0.27
Welsh (19)	95	0.87
Yugoslavian (216)	237	2.17

Hispanic Origin	Population	%
Hispanic or Latino (of any race)	300	2.69
Central American, ex. Mexican	26	0.23
Guatemalan	7	0.06
Honduran	1	0.01
Nicaraguan	3	0.03
Panamanian	6	0.05
Salvadoran	9	0.08
Cuban	9	0.08
Dominican Republic	5	0.04
Mexican	86	0.77
Puerto Rican	133	1.19
South American	11	0.10
Colombian	4	0.04
Ecuadorian	2	0.02
Peruvian	2	0.02
Uruguayan	1	0.01
Venezuelan	2	0.02
Other Hispanic or Latino	30	0.27

Race*	Population	%
African-American/Black (433)	548	4.92
Not Hispanic (416)	519	4.66
Hispanic (17)	29	0.26
American Indian/Alaska Native (20)	57	0.51
Not Hispanic (19)	52	0.47
Hispanic (1)	5	0.04
Apache (1)	3	0.03
Arapaho (1)	1	0.01
Blackfeet (1)	4	0.04
Cherokee (1)	13	0.12
Cree (1)	2	0.02
Iroquois (2)	3	0.03
Lumbee (3)	3	0.03
Menominee (0)	1	0.01
Mexican American Ind. (1)	1	0.01
Potawatomi (0)	1	0.01
Sioux (0)	1	0.01
Asian (158)	246	2.21
Not Hispanic (158)	239	2.14
Hispanic (0)	7	0.06
Cambodian (2)	3	0.03
Chinese, ex. Taiwanese (25)	33	0.30
Filipino (31)	54	0.48

*Notes: † The Census 2010 population figure is used to calculate the percentages in the Hispanic Origin and Race categories. Ancestry percentages are based on the 2006-2010 American Community Survey population (not shown); ‡ Numbers in parentheses indicate the number of people reporting a single ancestry; * Numbers in parentheses indicate the number of persons reporting this race alone, not in combination with any other race; Please refer to the Explanation of Data for more information.*

Indian (19)	27	0.24
Indonesian (0)	1	0.01
Japanese (7)	16	0.14
Korean (29)	47	0.42
Laotian (0)	2	0.02
Malaysian (1)	2	0.02
Pakistani (6)	7	0.06
Thai (8)	8	0.07
Vietnamese (17)	26	0.23
Hawaii Native/Pacific Islander (4)	11	0.10
Not Hispanic (4)	6	0.05
Hispanic (0)	5	0.04
Native Hawaiian (2)	7	0.06
White (10,210)	10,433	93.63
Not Hispanic (10,035)	10,221	91.73
Hispanic (175)	212	1.90

North Strabane

Place Type: Township
County: Washington
Population: 13,408†

Ancestry‡	Population	%
American (278)	278	2.17
Arab (45)	58	0.45
Lebanese (36)	36	0.28
Syrian (9)	22	0.17
Australian (0)	7	0.05
Austrian (21)	144	1.13
Croatian (36)	195	1.52
Czech (12)	216	1.69
Czechoslovakian (61)	114	0.89
Danish (52)	92	0.72
Dutch (9)	101	0.79
Eastern European (15)	15	0.12
English (174)	1,474	11.52
European (367)	381	2.98
French, ex. Basque (75)	483	3.77
German (899)	3,287	25.69
Greek (101)	205	1.60
Hungarian (135)	307	2.40
Irish (511)	2,647	20.69
Italian (681)	2,564	20.04
Lithuanian (0)	80	0.63
Macedonian (0)	45	0.35
Norwegian (0)	10	0.08
Polish (477)	1,557	12.17
Russian (46)	293	2.29
Scotch-Irish (262)	686	5.36
Scottish (65)	334	2.61
Serbian (8)	78	0.61
Slavic (24)	54	0.42
Slovak (109)	501	3.92
Slovene (84)	265	2.07
Swedish (46)	124	0.97
Swiss (10)	20	0.16
Ukrainian (81)	320	2.50
Welsh (11)	173	1.35
Yugoslavian (11)	11	0.09

Hispanic Origin	Population	%
Hispanic or Latino (of any race)	146	1.09
Central American, ex. Mexican	6	0.04
Guatemalan	4	0.03
Honduran	1	0.01
Panamanian	1	0.01
Cuban	5	0.04
Mexican	66	0.49
Puerto Rican	18	0.13
South American	13	0.10
Argentinean	1	0.01
Bolivian	1	0.01
Colombian	3	0.02
Peruvian	6	0.04
Venezuelan	2	0.01
Other Hispanic or Latino	38	0.28

Race*	Population	%
African-American/Black (217)	288	2.15
Not Hispanic (217)	286	2.13
Hispanic (0)	2	0.01
American Indian/Alaska Native (8)	23	0.17
Not Hispanic (6)	19	0.14
Hispanic (2)	4	0.03
Apache (0)	1	0.01
Cherokee (2)	7	0.05
Chickasaw (1)	1	0.01
Chippewa (0)	1	0.01
Inupiat *(Alaska Native)* (2)	2	0.01
Iroquois (0)	1	0.01
Mexican American Ind. (2)	3	0.02
Asian (157)	174	1.30
Not Hispanic (153)	167	1.25
Hispanic (4)	7	0.05
Bangladeshi (1)	1	0.01
Chinese, ex. Taiwanese (27)	29	0.22
Filipino (17)	22	0.16
Indian (77)	82	0.61
Japanese (8)	11	0.08
Korean (9)	10	0.07
Taiwanese (0)	1	0.01
Thai (2)	2	0.01
Vietnamese (14)	15	0.11
Hawaii Native/Pacific Islander (2)	3	0.02
Not Hispanic (0)	1	0.01
Hispanic (2)	2	0.01
Guamanian/Chamorro (2)	2	0.01
White (12,866)	12,974	96.76
Not Hispanic (12,775)	12,874	96.02
Hispanic (91)	100	0.75

North Union

Place Type: Township
County: Fayette
Population: 12,728†

Ancestry‡	Population	%
African, Sub-Saharan (59)	66	0.51
African (50)	57	0.44
Ugandan (9)	9	0.07
American (467)	467	3.58
Arab (161)	383	2.94
Lebanese (161)	332	2.55
Syrian (0)	51	0.39
British (83)	94	0.72
Canadian (0)	11	0.08
Croatian (40)	82	0.63
Czech (28)	109	0.84
Czechoslovakian (8)	24	0.18
Dutch (31)	355	2.72
Eastern European (9)	9	0.07
English (330)	1,333	10.23
European (0)	20	0.15
French, ex. Basque (62)	267	2.05
German (859)	3,022	23.20
Greek (8)	8	0.06
Hungarian (107)	220	1.69
Irish (622)	2,136	16.40
Italian (913)	1,979	15.19
Lithuanian (13)	13	0.10
Norwegian (60)	86	0.66
Pennsylvania German (40)	50	0.38
Polish (626)	1,589	12.20
Portuguese (0)	9	0.07
Romanian (9)	20	0.15
Russian (46)	137	1.05
Scotch-Irish (32)	141	1.08
Scottish (136)	306	2.35
Serbian (0)	43	0.33
Slovak (656)	1,323	10.16
Slovene (50)	138	1.06
Swedish (10)	104	0.80
Swiss (0)	11	0.08
Ukrainian (98)	98	0.75
Welsh (26)	96	0.74
Yugoslavian (0)	7	0.05

Hispanic Origin	Population	%
Hispanic or Latino (of any race)	100	0.79
Central American, ex. Mexican	2	0.02
Nicaraguan	2	0.02
Cuban	2	0.02
Mexican	32	0.25
Puerto Rican	20	0.16
South American	10	0.08
Argentinean	7	0.05
Colombian	3	0.02
Other Hispanic or Latino	34	0.27

Race*	Population	%
African-American/Black (360)	484	3.80
Not Hispanic (353)	471	3.70
Hispanic (7)	13	0.10
American Indian/Alaska Native (15)	59	0.46
Not Hispanic (15)	55	0.43
Hispanic (0)	4	0.03
Blackfeet (0)	7	0.05
Canadian/French Am. Ind. (0)	1	0.01
Cherokee (3)	20	0.16
Comanche (2)	2	0.02
Iroquois (1)	4	0.03
Asian (44)	78	0.61
Not Hispanic (39)	62	0.49
Hispanic (5)	16	0.13
Cambodian (0)	2	0.02
Chinese, ex. Taiwanese (4)	5	0.04
Filipino (5)	12	0.09
Hmong (3)	3	0.02
Indian (23)	30	0.24
Japanese (3)	7	0.05
Korean (2)	3	0.02
Taiwanese (1)	2	0.02
Vietnamese (2)	6	0.05
Hawaii Native/Pacific Islander (1)	8	0.06
Not Hispanic (1)	1	0.01
Hispanic (0)	7	0.05
Native Hawaiian (1)	2	0.02
White (12,102)	12,280	96.48
Not Hispanic (12,041)	12,209	95.92
Hispanic (61)	71	0.56

North Versailles

Place Type: Township
County: Allegheny
Population: 10,229†

Ancestry‡	Population	%
African, Sub-Saharan (94)	94	0.91
African (94)	94	0.91
American (385)	385	3.74
Austrian (31)	40	0.39
Belgian (9)	9	0.09
Croatian (36)	65	0.63
Czech (43)	98	0.95
Czechoslovakian (31)	31	0.30
Danish (41)	41	0.40
Dutch (0)	12	0.12
English (292)	1,137	11.05
Finnish (7)	16	0.16
French, ex. Basque (0)	147	1.43
French Canadian (21)	21	0.20
German (493)	2,341	22.75
Greek (25)	59	0.57
Hungarian (98)	259	2.52
Irish (446)	2,064	20.06
Italian (830)	1,944	18.89
Lithuanian (0)	38	0.37
Pennsylvania German (25)	47	0.46
Polish (384)	1,209	11.75
Russian (0)	46	0.45
Scotch-Irish (66)	222	2.16
Scottish (37)	291	2.83
Serbian (93)	167	1.62
Slavic (12)	37	0.36
Slovak (432)	1,098	10.67
Slovene (0)	13	0.13

SECTION TWO

*Notes: † The Census 2010 population figure is used to calculate the percentages in the Hispanic Origin and Race categories. Ancestry percentages are based on the 2006-2010 American Community Survey population (not shown); ‡ Numbers in parentheses indicate the number of people reporting a single ancestry; * Numbers in parentheses indicate the number of persons reporting this race alone, not in combination with any other race; Please refer to the Explanation of Data for more information.*

Swedish (46)	146	1.42
Swiss (0)	14	0.14
Ukrainian (30)	77	0.75
Welsh (31)	79	0.77
Yugoslavian (0)	14	0.14

Hispanic Origin	Population	%
Hispanic or Latino (of any race)	92	0.90
Central American, ex. Mexican	4	0.04
Guatemalan	4	0.04
Cuban	2	0.02
Mexican	41	0.40
Puerto Rican	19	0.19
South American	2	0.02
Chilean	1	0.01
Ecuadorian	1	0.01
Other Hispanic or Latino	24	0.23

Race*	Population	%
African-American/Black (1,408)	1,579	15.44
Not Hispanic (1,395)	1,559	15.24
Hispanic (13)	20	0.20
American Indian/Alaska Native (13)	64	0.63
Not Hispanic (12)	56	0.55
Hispanic (1)	8	0.08
Blackfeet (1)	5	0.05
Canadian/French Am. Ind. (0)	1	0.01
Cherokee (2)	10	0.10
Chickasaw (0)	2	0.02
Chippewa (1)	1	0.01
Choctaw (0)	2	0.02
Creek (0)	1	0.01
Iroquois (0)	3	0.03
Mexican American Ind. (1)	1	0.01
Ute (1)	1	0.01
Yup'ik *(Alaska Native)* (0)	1	0.01
Asian (76)	108	1.06
Not Hispanic (72)	102	1.00
Hispanic (4)	6	0.06
Chinese, ex. Taiwanese (12)	26	0.25
Filipino (18)	32	0.31
Indian (9)	13	0.13
Japanese (2)	6	0.06
Korean (5)	11	0.11
Thai (2)	2	0.02
Vietnamese (21)	23	0.22
Hawaii Native/Pacific Islander (2)	7	0.07
Not Hispanic (2)	7	0.07
Guamanian/Chamorro (0)	4	0.04
Native Hawaiian (1)	2	0.02
Samoan (0)	1	0.01
White (8,483)	8,686	84.92
Not Hispanic (8,433)	8,622	84.29
Hispanic (50)	64	0.63

North Whitehall

Place Type: Township
County: Lehigh
Population: 15,703†

Ancestry‡	Population	%
American (582)	582	3.73
Arab (135)	216	1.38
Arab (47)	53	0.34
Egyptian (0)	10	0.06
Syrian (88)	153	0.98
Austrian (76)	481	3.08
Belgian (0)	43	0.28
British (0)	41	0.26
Czech (0)	131	0.84
Czechoslovakian (35)	35	0.22
Dutch (200)	449	2.88
Eastern European (59)	59	0.38
English (159)	904	5.79
European (68)	68	0.44
French, ex. Basque (16)	253	1.62
French Canadian (57)	72	0.46
German (2,759)	6,057	38.82
Greek (32)	91	0.58
Hungarian (178)	577	3.70
Icelander (0)	19	0.12
Irish (283)	2,044	13.10
Israeli (118)	118	0.76
Italian (568)	2,022	12.96
Lithuanian (28)	50	0.32
Norwegian (13)	27	0.17
Pennsylvania German (1,190)	1,556	9.97
Polish (407)	1,290	8.27
Portuguese (0)	7	0.04
Russian (45)	352	2.26
Scotch-Irish (46)	269	1.72
Scottish (71)	228	1.46
Slavic (0)	45	0.29
Slovak (104)	396	2.54
Slovene (0)	27	0.17
Swedish (24)	72	0.46
Swiss (0)	22	0.14
Turkish (0)	20	0.13
Ukrainian (79)	284	1.82
Welsh (94)	394	2.53
West Indian, ex. Hispanic (102)	102	0.65
Jamaican (102)	102	0.65

Hispanic Origin	Population	%
Hispanic or Latino (of any race)	580	3.69
Central American, ex. Mexican	27	0.17
Costa Rican	6	0.04
Guatemalan	8	0.05
Honduran	3	0.02
Nicaraguan	3	0.02
Panamanian	2	0.01
Salvadoran	5	0.03
Cuban	13	0.08
Dominican Republic	30	0.19
Mexican	73	0.46
Puerto Rican	327	2.08
South American	52	0.33
Argentinean	3	0.02
Chilean	5	0.03
Colombian	13	0.08
Ecuadorian	10	0.06
Paraguayan	1	0.01
Peruvian	12	0.08
Uruguayan	1	0.01
Venezuelan	2	0.01
Other South American	5	0.03
Other Hispanic or Latino	58	0.37

Race*	Population	%
African-American/Black (240)	311	1.98
Not Hispanic (223)	280	1.78
Hispanic (17)	31	0.20
American Indian/Alaska Native (19)	80	0.51
Not Hispanic (13)	68	0.43
Hispanic (6)	12	0.08
Aleut *(Alaska Native)* (2)	2	0.01
Blackfeet (0)	1	0.01
Cherokee (5)	23	0.15
Choctaw (1)	1	0.01
Delaware (0)	9	0.06
Iroquois (0)	2	0.01
Sioux (1)	1	0.01
South American Ind. (0)	1	0.01
Asian (211)	265	1.69
Not Hispanic (211)	260	1.66
Hispanic (0)	5	0.03
Burmese (1)	1	0.01
Cambodian (1)	1	0.01
Chinese, ex. Taiwanese (42)	57	0.36
Filipino (14)	29	0.18
Indian (72)	77	0.49
Japanese (2)	6	0.04
Korean (30)	36	0.23
Pakistani (11)	11	0.07
Sri Lankan (2)	2	0.01
Thai (3)	6	0.04
Vietnamese (29)	33	0.21
Hawaii Native/Pacific Islander (2)	6	0.04
Not Hispanic (1)	4	0.03
Hispanic (1)	2	0.01
Guamanian/Chamorro (2)	3	0.02
Native Hawaiian (0)	1	0.01
Samoan (0)	1	0.01
White (14,873)	15,054	95.87
Not Hispanic (14,501)	14,647	93.28
Hispanic (372)	407	2.59

Northampton

Place Type: Borough
County: Northampton
Population: 9,926†

Ancestry‡	Population	%
African, Sub-Saharan (0)	5	0.05
Cape Verdean (0)	5	0.05
American (356)	356	3.59
Arab (198)	228	2.30
Arab (0)	30	0.30
Syrian (198)	198	2.00
Australian (49)	65	0.66
Austrian (240)	428	4.32
British (0)	12	0.12
Croatian (0)	22	0.22
Czech (10)	71	0.72
Czechoslovakian (11)	11	0.11
Danish (17)	17	0.17
Dutch (57)	337	3.40
Eastern European (18)	18	0.18
English (167)	536	5.40
French, ex. Basque (7)	116	1.17
German (1,587)	3,989	40.22
Greek (13)	34	0.34
Hungarian (130)	562	5.67
Irish (205)	1,598	16.11
Italian (249)	1,222	12.32
Lithuanian (0)	52	0.52
Norwegian (8)	25	0.25
Pennsylvania German (442)	624	6.29
Polish (266)	1,007	10.15
Portuguese (0)	33	0.33
Romanian (14)	14	0.14
Russian (48)	143	1.44
Scandinavian (0)	26	0.26
Scotch-Irish (21)	69	0.70
Scottish (0)	55	0.55
Slavic (23)	77	0.78
Slovak (148)	673	6.79
Swedish (0)	12	0.12
Swiss (15)	26	0.26
Ukrainian (243)	435	4.39
Welsh (0)	192	1.94

Hispanic Origin	Population	%
Hispanic or Latino (of any race)	345	3.48
Central American, ex. Mexican	10	0.10
Costa Rican	1	0.01
Guatemalan	3	0.03
Panamanian	1	0.01
Salvadoran	5	0.05
Cuban	17	0.17
Dominican Republic	10	0.10
Mexican	43	0.43
Puerto Rican	186	1.87
South American	49	0.49
Argentinean	1	0.01
Chilean	3	0.03
Colombian	23	0.23
Ecuadorian	6	0.06
Peruvian	13	0.13
Venezuelan	3	0.03
Other Hispanic or Latino	30	0.30

Race*	Population	%
African-American/Black (166)	232	2.34
Not Hispanic (154)	209	2.11
Hispanic (12)	23	0.23
American Indian/Alaska Native (16)	35	0.35
Not Hispanic (10)	24	0.24

*Notes: † The Census 2010 population figure is used to calculate the percentages in the Hispanic Origin and Race categories. Ancestry percentages are based on the 2006-2010 American Community Survey population (not shown); ‡ Numbers in parentheses indicate the number of people reporting a single ancestry; * Numbers in parentheses indicate the number of persons reporting this race alone, not in combination with any other race; Please refer to the Explanation of Data for more information.*

Hispanic (6)	11	0.11
Blackfeet (0)	1	0.01
Cherokee (0)	4	0.04
Cheyenne (0)	1	0.01
Choctaw (0)	2	0.02
Delaware (3)	3	0.03
Lumbee (0)	1	0.01
Asian (73)	94	0.95
Not Hispanic (73)	90	0.91
Hispanic (0)	4	0.04
Chinese, ex. Taiwanese (12)	14	0.14
Filipino (1)	1	0.01
Indian (13)	20	0.20
Japanese (1)	9	0.09
Korean (6)	6	0.06
Pakistani (12)	12	0.12
Vietnamese (28)	30	0.30
Hawaii Native/Pacific Islander (2)	9	0.09
Not Hispanic (1)	7	0.07
Hispanic (1)	2	0.02
Native Hawaiian (1)	5	0.05
Tongan (0)	1	0.01
White (9,447)	9,574	96.45
Not Hispanic (9,248)	9,336	94.06
Hispanic (199)	238	2.40

Northampton

Place Type: Township
County: Bucks
Population: 39,726†

Ancestry‡	Population	%
African, Sub-Saharan (64)	71	0.18
Cape Verdean (0)	7	0.02
Nigerian (64)	64	0.16
Albanian (13)	28	0.07
American (2,076)	2,076	5.21
Arab (0)	50	0.13
Lebanese (0)	50	0.13
Armenian (60)	125	0.31
Austrian (44)	328	0.82
Brazilian (11)	11	0.03
British (115)	272	0.68
Canadian (103)	256	0.64
Celtic (8)	8	0.02
Croatian (0)	38	0.10
Czech (13)	177	0.44
Danish (0)	272	0.68
Dutch (115)	429	1.08
Eastern European (552)	591	1.48
English (671)	3,757	9.43
Estonian (18)	18	0.05
European (465)	494	1.24
Finnish (10)	41	0.10
French, ex. Basque (69)	613	1.54
French Canadian (25)	70	0.18
German (2,513)	9,635	24.20
Greek (130)	278	0.70
Hungarian (87)	512	1.29
Icelander (19)	19	0.05
Iranian (186)	186	0.47
Irish (3,774)	11,531	28.96
Israeli (9)	9	0.02
Italian (2,789)	7,018	17.62
Latvian (10)	61	0.15
Lithuanian (145)	282	0.71
Northern European (82)	92	0.23
Norwegian (30)	149	0.37
Pennsylvania German (20)	48	0.12
Polish (1,094)	3,419	8.59
Portuguese (71)	99	0.25
Romanian (157)	297	0.75
Russian (1,678)	2,533	6.36
Scotch-Irish (203)	699	1.76
Scottish (118)	572	1.44
Serbian (27)	27	0.07
Slavic (3)	31	0.08
Slovak (60)	222	0.56
Soviet Union (17)	17	0.04
Swedish (53)	278	0.70
Swiss (0)	7	0.02
Turkish (36)	48	0.12
Ukrainian (1,045)	1,274	3.20
Welsh (50)	298	0.75
West Indian, ex. Hispanic (9)	58	0.15
Barbadian (0)	8	0.02
Jamaican (9)	42	0.11
Trinidadian/Tobagonian (0)	8	0.02
Yugoslavian (28)	41	0.10

Hispanic Origin	Population	%
Hispanic or Latino (of any race)	580	1.46
Central American, ex. Mexican	31	0.08
Costa Rican	5	0.01
Guatemalan	9	0.02
Honduran	3	0.01
Nicaraguan	8	0.02
Panamanian	1	<0.01
Salvadoran	5	0.01
Cuban	54	0.14
Dominican Republic	8	0.02
Mexican	97	0.24
Puerto Rican	194	0.49
South American	108	0.27
Argentinean	32	0.08
Bolivian	3	0.01
Chilean	1	<0.01
Colombian	16	0.04
Ecuadorian	14	0.04
Paraguayan	5	0.01
Peruvian	25	0.06
Uruguayan	4	0.01
Venezuelan	7	0.02
Other South American	1	<0.01
Other Hispanic or Latino	88	0.22

Race*	Population	%
African-American/Black (248)	331	0.83
Not Hispanic (243)	319	0.80
Hispanic (5)	12	0.03
American Indian/Alaska Native (24)	92	0.23
Not Hispanic (21)	85	0.21
Hispanic (3)	7	0.02
Aleut *(Alaska Native)* (1)	1	<0.01
Apache (2)	2	0.01
Blackfeet (0)	2	0.01
Cherokee (1)	21	0.05
Cheyenne (0)	1	<0.01
Chippewa (1)	1	<0.01
Creek (4)	4	0.01
Delaware (0)	8	0.02
Iroquois (0)	3	0.01
Lumbee (3)	3	0.01
Mexican American Ind. (3)	4	0.01
Shoshone (0)	1	<0.01
Sioux (0)	1	<0.01
Asian (1,374)	1,540	3.88
Not Hispanic (1,368)	1,526	3.84
Hispanic (6)	14	0.04
Bangladeshi (8)	9	0.02
Burmese (6)	6	0.02
Cambodian (7)	8	0.02
Chinese, ex. Taiwanese (322)	364	0.92
Filipino (56)	83	0.21
Indian (643)	663	1.67
Indonesian (1)	5	0.01
Japanese (25)	62	0.16
Korean (163)	175	0.44
Malaysian (0)	2	0.01
Pakistani (27)	35	0.09
Sri Lankan (8)	8	0.02
Taiwanese (28)	28	0.07
Thai (3)	5	0.01
Vietnamese (57)	66	0.17
Hawaii Native/Pacific Islander (1)	13	0.03
Not Hispanic (1)	13	0.03
Native Hawaiian (0)	5	0.01
Samoan (0)	1	<0.01
White (37,685)	37,967	95.57
Not Hispanic (37,204)	37,463	94.30
Hispanic (481)	504	1.27

Northwest Harborcreek

Place Type: CDP
County: Erie
Population: 8,949†

Ancestry‡	Population	%
American (342)	342	3.78
Arab (0)	46	0.51
Lebanese (0)	23	0.25
Syrian (0)	23	0.25
Armenian (0)	8	0.09
Austrian (7)	16	0.18
British (13)	21	0.23
Celtic (0)	25	0.28
Czech (0)	64	0.71
Czechoslovakian (0)	24	0.27
Danish (11)	11	0.12
Dutch (62)	177	1.95
English (340)	962	10.62
Estonian (25)	25	0.28
European (7)	7	0.08
Finnish (0)	10	0.11
French, ex. Basque (33)	217	2.40
French Canadian (17)	17	0.19
German (1,005)	3,141	34.69
Greek (36)	36	0.40
Hungarian (93)	113	1.25
Iranian (0)	10	0.11
Irish (270)	1,391	15.36
Italian (393)	1,176	12.99
Lithuanian (7)	26	0.29
Pennsylvania German (0)	29	0.32
Polish (811)	2,185	24.13
Portuguese (18)	18	0.20
Romanian (8)	8	0.09
Russian (54)	204	2.25
Scandinavian (6)	6	0.07
Scotch-Irish (53)	127	1.40
Scottish (30)	236	2.61
Serbian (0)	6	0.07
Slavic (17)	44	0.49
Slovak (62)	223	2.46
Swedish (73)	232	2.56
Swiss (0)	67	0.74
Ukrainian (10)	67	0.74
Welsh (19)	147	1.62
Yugoslavian (0)	18	0.20

Hispanic Origin	Population	%
Hispanic or Latino (of any race)	113	1.26
Central American, ex. Mexican	15	0.17
Costa Rican	1	0.01
Guatemalan	1	0.01
Panamanian	6	0.07
Salvadoran	7	0.08
Cuban	3	0.03
Dominican Republic	3	0.03
Mexican	36	0.40
Puerto Rican	40	0.45
South American	6	0.07
Argentinean	1	0.01
Ecuadorian	1	0.01
Venezuelan	4	0.04
Other Hispanic or Latino	10	0.11

Race*	Population	%
African-American/Black (154)	171	1.91
Not Hispanic (149)	166	1.85
Hispanic (5)	5	0.06
American Indian/Alaska Native (10)	31	0.35
Not Hispanic (8)	29	0.32
Hispanic (2)	2	0.02
Blackfeet (0)	1	0.01
Canadian/French Am. Ind. (3)	3	0.03
Cherokee (0)	2	0.02
Iroquois (1)	1	0.01

*Notes: † The Census 2010 population figure is used to calculate the percentages in the Hispanic Origin and Race categories. Ancestry percentages are based on the 2006-2010 American Community Survey population (not shown); ‡ Numbers in parentheses indicate the number of people reporting a single ancestry; * Numbers in parentheses indicate the number of persons reporting this race alone, not in combination with any other race; Please refer to the Explanation of Data for more information.*

Mexican American Ind. (1)	1	0.01
Tlingit-Haida *(Alaska Native)* (1)	1	0.01
Asian (67)	81	0.91
Not Hispanic (67)	81	0.91
Cambodian (1)	1	0.01
Chinese, ex. Taiwanese (24)	25	0.28
Filipino (6)	8	0.09
Indian (11)	13	0.15
Japanese (1)	3	0.03
Korean (3)	3	0.03
Laotian (5)	5	0.06
Pakistani (0)	2	0.02
Taiwanese (1)	3	0.03
Vietnamese (14)	15	0.17
Hawaii Native/Pacific Islander (0)	2	0.02
Not Hispanic (0)	2	0.02
White (8,649)	8,699	97.21
Not Hispanic (8,559)	8,602	96.12
Hispanic (90)	97	1.08

O'Hara

Place Type: Township
County: Allegheny
Population: 8,407†

Ancestry‡	Population	%
African, Sub-Saharan (15)	15	0.18
African (15)	15	0.18
American (320)	320	3.82
Arab (61)	89	1.06
Egyptian (41)	41	0.49
Lebanese (0)	14	0.17
Syrian (20)	34	0.41
Austrian (11)	82	0.98
British (0)	25	0.30
Carpatho Rusyn (0)	12	0.14
Croatian (38)	203	2.42
Czech (74)	138	1.65
Danish (0)	13	0.16
Dutch (10)	144	1.72
Eastern European (84)	102	1.22
English (231)	857	10.23
Estonian (0)	11	0.13
European (257)	257	3.07
French, ex. Basque (20)	135	1.61
French Canadian (15)	15	0.18
German (345)	2,067	24.68
Greek (77)	137	1.64
Hungarian (23)	103	1.23
Irish (417)	1,630	19.46
Italian (699)	1,670	19.94
Latvian (0)	11	0.13
Lithuanian (10)	54	0.64
Northern European (13)	13	0.16
Norwegian (25)	73	0.87
Pennsylvania German (25)	25	0.30
Polish (191)	659	7.87
Romanian (9)	22	0.26
Russian (180)	467	5.58
Scotch-Irish (29)	125	1.49
Scottish (91)	315	3.76
Serbian (15)	15	0.18
Slavic (12)	12	0.14
Slovak (22)	194	2.32
Slovene (12)	46	0.55
Swedish (0)	77	0.92
Swiss (27)	74	0.88
Turkish (32)	58	0.69
Ukrainian (24)	58	0.69
Welsh (9)	133	1.59
Yugoslavian (0)	10	0.12

Hispanic Origin	Population	%
Hispanic or Latino (of any race)	125	1.49
Central American, ex. Mexican	7	0.08
Costa Rican	2	0.02
Guatemalan	2	0.02
Panamanian	3	0.04
Cuban	5	0.06
Mexican	28	0.33
Puerto Rican	14	0.17
South American	57	0.68
Argentinean	20	0.24
Chilean	1	0.01
Colombian	21	0.25
Ecuadorian	1	0.01
Peruvian	9	0.11
Venezuelan	4	0.05
Other South American	1	0.01
Other Hispanic or Latino	14	0.17

Race*	Population	%
African-American/Black (53)	70	0.83
Not Hispanic (50)	65	0.77
Hispanic (3)	5	0.06
American Indian/Alaska Native (6)	17	0.20
Not Hispanic (4)	11	0.13
Hispanic (2)	6	0.07
Apache (0)	1	0.01
Cherokee (0)	3	0.04
Iroquois (1)	1	0.01
Mexican American Ind. (1)	1	0.01
Sioux (0)	1	0.01
Asian (418)	470	5.59
Not Hispanic (417)	469	5.58
Hispanic (1)	1	0.01
Bangladeshi (6)	6	0.07
Chinese, ex. Taiwanese (94)	109	1.30
Filipino (11)	15	0.18
Indian (155)	176	2.09
Indonesian (1)	2	0.02
Japanese (29)	42	0.50
Korean (58)	61	0.73
Malaysian (6)	8	0.10
Nepalese (1)	1	0.01
Pakistani (2)	2	0.02
Sri Lankan (3)	5	0.06
Taiwanese (10)	13	0.15
Thai (8)	8	0.10
Vietnamese (19)	23	0.27
Hawaii Native/Pacific Islander (0)	2	0.02
Not Hispanic (0)	2	0.02
Native Hawaiian (0)	1	0.01
White (7,830)	7,903	94.00
Not Hispanic (7,724)	7,789	92.65
Hispanic (106)	114	1.36

Oil City

Place Type: City
County: Venango
Population: 10,557†

Ancestry‡	Population	%
American (595)	595	5.56
Australian (0)	11	0.10
Austrian (0)	13	0.12
Belgian (0)	10	0.09
Canadian (9)	9	0.08
Croatian (16)	47	0.44
Czech (0)	15	0.14
Czechoslovakian (0)	61	0.57
Danish (0)	11	0.10
Dutch (56)	312	2.91
English (361)	1,062	9.92
European (107)	107	1.00
French, ex. Basque (0)	259	2.42
French Canadian (10)	10	0.09
German (1,173)	3,814	35.62
Greek (10)	46	0.43
Hungarian (0)	71	0.66
Irish (291)	2,240	20.92
Italian (292)	795	7.43
Latvian (0)	6	0.06
Lithuanian (8)	11	0.10
Pennsylvania German (11)	100	0.93
Polish (407)	810	7.57
Romanian (0)	24	0.22
Russian (28)	53	0.50
Scotch-Irish (91)	363	3.39
Scottish (74)	356	3.32
Slavic (18)	52	0.49
Slovak (22)	38	0.35
Slovene (0)	4	0.04
Swedish (70)	181	1.69
Swiss (0)	13	0.12
Ukrainian (0)	72	0.67
Welsh (19)	210	1.96

Hispanic Origin	Population	%
Hispanic or Latino (of any race)	129	1.22
Central American, ex. Mexican	4	0.04
Guatemalan	3	0.03
Honduran	1	0.01
Cuban	1	0.01
Dominican Republic	4	0.04
Mexican	69	0.65
Puerto Rican	28	0.27
South American	7	0.07
Colombian	1	0.01
Ecuadorian	2	0.02
Peruvian	4	0.04
Other Hispanic or Latino	16	0.15

Race*	Population	%
African-American/Black (156)	248	2.35
Not Hispanic (154)	242	2.29
Hispanic (2)	6	0.06
American Indian/Alaska Native (20)	83	0.79
Not Hispanic (18)	77	0.73
Hispanic (2)	6	0.06
Apache (0)	4	0.04
Blackfeet (2)	6	0.06
Cherokee (1)	10	0.09
Chippewa (3)	7	0.07
Comanche (0)	1	0.01
Delaware (1)	1	0.01
Iroquois (3)	16	0.15
Pueblo (2)	2	0.02
Sioux (0)	2	0.02
South American Ind. (1)	3	0.03
Asian (34)	52	0.49
Not Hispanic (34)	52	0.49
Chinese, ex. Taiwanese (14)	15	0.14
Filipino (5)	6	0.06
Indian (6)	8	0.08
Japanese (3)	5	0.05
Korean (2)	13	0.12
Thai (1)	1	0.01
Hawaii Native/Pacific Islander (2)	10	0.09
Not Hispanic (2)	9	0.09
Hispanic (0)	1	0.01
Guamanian/Chamorro (1)	4	0.04
Native Hawaiian (0)	2	0.02
White (10,157)	10,304	97.60
Not Hispanic (10,062)	10,203	96.65
Hispanic (95)	101	0.96

Old Forge

Place Type: Borough
County: Lackawanna
Population: 8,313†

Ancestry‡	Population	%
African, Sub-Saharan (0)	12	0.14
African (0)	12	0.14
American (120)	120	1.43
Arab (25)	101	1.21
Egyptian (0)	10	0.12
Lebanese (25)	76	0.91
Syrian (0)	15	0.18
Austrian (13)	66	0.79
Belgian (18)	18	0.21
British (10)	21	0.25
Carpatho Rusyn (9)	9	0.11
Dutch (0)	49	0.59
English (157)	380	4.54
French, ex. Basque (0)	47	0.56

*Notes: † The Census 2010 population figure is used to calculate the percentages in the Hispanic Origin and Race categories. Ancestry percentages are based on the 2006-2010 American Community Survey population (not shown); ‡ Numbers in parentheses indicate the number of people reporting a single ancestry; * Numbers in parentheses indicate the number of persons reporting this race alone, not in combination with any other race; Please refer to the Explanation of Data for more information.*

German (258)	1,109	13.24
Greek (16)	23	0.27
Irish (566)	1,829	21.84
Italian (1,656)	3,455	41.26
Lithuanian (45)	145	1.73
Norwegian (0)	12	0.14
Pennsylvania German (69)	69	0.82
Polish (759)	1,890	22.57
Russian (188)	720	8.60
Scotch-Irish (48)	121	1.44
Scottish (28)	54	0.64
Slovak (80)	255	3.05
Swedish (0)	12	0.14
Swiss (0)	22	0.26
Ukrainian (38)	110	1.31
Welsh (113)	664	7.93

Hispanic Origin	Population	%
Hispanic or Latino (of any race)	234	2.81
Central American, ex. Mexican	4	0.05
Guatemalan	2	0.02
Honduran	1	0.01
Salvadoran	1	0.01
Cuban	3	0.04
Mexican	40	0.48
Puerto Rican	111	1.34
South American	52	0.63
Argentinean	1	0.01
Chilean	1	0.01
Colombian	2	0.02
Ecuadorian	1	0.01
Peruvian	2	0.02
Uruguayan	43	0.52
Other South American	2	0.02
Other Hispanic or Latino	24	0.29

Race*	Population	%
African-American/Black (85)	123	1.48
Not Hispanic (67)	103	1.24
Hispanic (18)	20	0.24
American Indian/Alaska Native (5)	17	0.20
Not Hispanic (2)	14	0.17
Hispanic (3)	3	0.04
Cherokee (1)	3	0.04
Delaware (0)	2	0.02
Asian (60)	73	0.88
Not Hispanic (56)	69	0.83
Hispanic (4)	4	0.05
Chinese, ex. Taiwanese (10)	12	0.14
Filipino (3)	5	0.06
Indian (0)	7	0.08
Indonesian (1)	2	0.02
Japanese (4)	5	0.06
Korean (4)	10	0.12
Laotian (16)	18	0.22
Pakistani (4)	4	0.05
Vietnamese (10)	10	0.12
Hawaii Native/Pacific Islander (4)	6	0.07
Not Hispanic (4)	6	0.07
Guamanian/Chamorro (4)	4	0.05
Native Hawaiian (0)	2	0.02
White (8,053)	8,112	97.58
Not Hispanic (7,896)	7,944	95.56
Hispanic (157)	168	2.02

Palmer

Place Type: Township
County: Northampton
Population: 20,691†

Ancestry‡	Population	%
African, Sub-Saharan (171)	212	1.05
Ethiopian (0)	41	0.20
Nigerian (159)	159	0.79
Sierra Leonean (12)	12	0.06
American (677)	677	3.36
Arab (158)	198	0.98
Egyptian (11)	11	0.05
Lebanese (139)	167	0.83
Syrian (8)	20	0.10
Austrian (29)	99	0.49
British (6)	44	0.22
Canadian (22)	38	0.19
Croatian (10)	10	0.05
Czech (0)	12	0.06
Danish (29)	80	0.40
Dutch (218)	698	3.46
Eastern European (0)	14	0.07
English (508)	1,891	9.39
European (48)	48	0.24
Finnish (0)	16	0.08
French, ex. Basque (104)	435	2.16
French Canadian (12)	91	0.45
German (1,767)	5,338	26.50
Greek (94)	155	0.77
Guyanese (0)	15	0.07
Hungarian (170)	522	2.59
Iranian (16)	16	0.08
Irish (840)	3,218	15.97
Italian (2,041)	4,356	21.62
Lithuanian (24)	81	0.40
Northern European (46)	59	0.29
Norwegian (85)	153	0.76
Pennsylvania German (347)	580	2.88
Polish (452)	1,314	6.52
Portuguese (122)	139	0.69
Romanian (0)	11	0.05
Russian (80)	287	1.42
Scandinavian (37)	37	0.18
Scotch-Irish (127)	360	1.79
Scottish (122)	362	1.80
Slavic (17)	17	0.08
Slovak (43)	264	1.31
Slovene (0)	9	0.04
Swedish (46)	204	1.01
Swiss (0)	176	0.87
Turkish (38)	49	0.24
Ukrainian (85)	213	1.06
Welsh (37)	290	1.44
West Indian, ex. Hispanic (49)	151	0.75
British West Indian (0)	8	0.04
Haitian (0)	41	0.20
Jamaican (38)	54	0.27
Trinidadian/Tobagonian (11)	48	0.24

Hispanic Origin	Population	%
Hispanic or Latino (of any race)	1,258	6.08
Central American, ex. Mexican	112	0.54
Costa Rican	15	0.07
Guatemalan	42	0.20
Honduran	15	0.07
Nicaraguan	7	0.03
Panamanian	8	0.04
Salvadoran	24	0.12
Other Central American	1	<0.01
Cuban	51	0.25
Dominican Republic	87	0.42
Mexican	118	0.57
Puerto Rican	500	2.42
South American	271	1.31
Argentinean	18	0.09
Bolivian	8	0.04
Chilean	11	0.05
Colombian	135	0.65
Ecuadorian	17	0.08
Peruvian	56	0.27
Uruguayan	13	0.06
Venezuelan	9	0.04
Other South American	4	0.02
Other Hispanic or Latino	119	0.58

Race*	Population	%
African-American/Black (1,105)	1,270	6.14
Not Hispanic (1,065)	1,195	5.78
Hispanic (40)	75	0.36
American Indian/Alaska Native (34)	97	0.47
Not Hispanic (22)	78	0.38
Hispanic (12)	19	0.09
Blackfeet (0)	3	0.01
Central American Ind. (0)	1	<0.01
Cherokee (0)	11	0.05
Chippewa (1)	4	0.02
Delaware (0)	13	0.06
Iroquois (1)	2	0.01
Menominee (0)	1	<0.01
Ottawa (0)	2	0.01
Shoshone (0)	2	0.01
Sioux (1)	2	0.01
South American Ind. (5)	5	0.02
Spanish American Ind. (1)	1	<0.01
Asian (845)	1,005	4.86
Not Hispanic (838)	975	4.71
Hispanic (7)	30	0.14
Cambodian (6)	9	0.04
Chinese, ex. Taiwanese (97)	118	0.57
Filipino (115)	161	0.78
Indian (388)	413	2.00
Indonesian (1)	3	0.01
Japanese (7)	34	0.16
Korean (36)	51	0.25
Malaysian (2)	2	0.01
Nepalese (1)	5	0.02
Pakistani (49)	52	0.25
Taiwanese (6)	10	0.05
Thai (4)	11	0.05
Vietnamese (104)	133	0.64
Hawaii Native/Pacific Islander (1)	14	0.07
Not Hispanic (0)	7	0.03
Hispanic (1)	7	0.03
Guamanian/Chamorro (1)	1	<0.01
Native Hawaiian (0)	5	0.02
White (17,904)	18,264	88.27
Not Hispanic (17,168)	17,432	84.25
Hispanic (736)	832	4.02

Park Forest Village

Place Type: CDP
County: Centre
Population: 9,660†

Ancestry‡	Population	%
American (382)	382	3.79
Arab (153)	223	2.21
Lebanese (22)	76	0.75
Moroccan (43)	43	0.43
Other Arab (88)	104	1.03
Armenian (0)	17	0.17
British (36)	114	1.13
Canadian (19)	19	0.19
Celtic (31)	31	0.31
Croatian (0)	12	0.12
Czech (0)	74	0.73
Czechoslovakian (0)	33	0.33
Danish (0)	61	0.61
Dutch (33)	166	1.65
Eastern European (60)	60	0.60
English (86)	798	7.92
European (194)	218	2.16
Finnish (0)	14	0.14
French, ex. Basque (12)	292	2.90
French Canadian (13)	59	0.59
German (689)	2,357	23.40
Greek (47)	47	0.47
Guyanese (18)	18	0.18
Hungarian (0)	65	0.65
Iranian (32)	32	0.32
Irish (281)	1,450	14.40
Italian (259)	1,056	10.48
Lithuanian (60)	111	1.10
Norwegian (26)	26	0.26
Pennsylvania German (0)	30	0.30
Polish (125)	475	4.72
Romanian (27)	55	0.55
Russian (108)	287	2.85
Scandinavian (0)	18	0.18
Scotch-Irish (82)	193	1.92
Scottish (0)	321	3.19
Slavic (12)	12	0.12

*Notes: † The Census 2010 population figure is used to calculate the percentages in the Hispanic Origin and Race categories. Ancestry percentages are based on the 2006-2010 American Community Survey population (not shown); ‡ Numbers in parentheses indicate the number of people reporting a single ancestry; * Numbers in parentheses indicate the number of persons reporting this race alone, not in combination with any other race; Please refer to the Explanation of Data for more information.*

Ancestry	Population	%
Slovak (10)	131	1.30
Swedish (26)	161	1.60
Swiss (24)	63	0.63
Turkish (16)	16	0.16
Ukrainian (13)	66	0.66
Welsh (29)	187	1.86
West Indian, ex. Hispanic (16)	16	0.16
Trinidadian/Tobagonian (16)	16	0.16

Hispanic Origin	Population	%
Hispanic or Latino (of any race)	313	3.24
Central American, ex. Mexican	22	0.23
Costa Rican	1	0.01
Guatemalan	2	0.02
Honduran	5	0.05
Nicaraguan	4	0.04
Panamanian	3	0.03
Salvadoran	7	0.07
Cuban	10	0.10
Dominican Republic	18	0.19
Mexican	84	0.87
Puerto Rican	85	0.88
South American	65	0.67
Argentinean	1	0.01
Bolivian	4	0.04
Chilean	11	0.11
Colombian	25	0.26
Ecuadorian	1	0.01
Peruvian	8	0.08
Uruguayan	1	0.01
Venezuelan	14	0.14
Other Hispanic or Latino	29	0.30

Race*	Population	%
African-American/Black (370)	455	4.71
Not Hispanic (349)	421	4.36
Hispanic (21)	34	0.35
American Indian/Alaska Native (7)	53	0.55
Not Hispanic (4)	42	0.43
Hispanic (3)	11	0.11
Apache (0)	1	0.01
Central American Ind. (1)	1	0.01
Cherokee (0)	6	0.06
Chickasaw (2)	2	0.02
Chippewa (0)	1	0.01
Choctaw (0)	1	0.01
Iroquois (0)	3	0.03
Mexican American Ind. (0)	1	0.01
Pueblo (0)	2	0.02
Sioux (0)	6	0.06
South American Ind. (1)	4	0.04
Yaqui (0)	1	0.01
Asian (1,044)	1,157	11.98
Not Hispanic (1,043)	1,150	11.90
Hispanic (1)	7	0.07
Bangladeshi (7)	11	0.11
Burmese (8)	8	0.08
Chinese, ex. Taiwanese (522)	547	5.66
Filipino (18)	36	0.37
Hmong (1)	1	0.01
Indian (95)	113	1.17
Indonesian (6)	6	0.06
Japanese (19)	28	0.29
Korean (243)	257	2.66
Malaysian (1)	4	0.04
Nepalese (1)	1	0.01
Pakistani (14)	15	0.16
Sri Lankan (3)	4	0.04
Taiwanese (53)	59	0.61
Thai (7)	8	0.08
Vietnamese (11)	12	0.12
Hawaii Native/Pacific Islander (3)	13	0.13
Not Hispanic (3)	10	0.10
Hispanic (0)	3	0.03
Native Hawaiian (0)	2	0.02
White (7,888)	8,117	84.03
Not Hispanic (7,696)	7,897	81.75
Hispanic (192)	220	2.28

Patton

Place Type: Township
County: Centre
Population: 15,311†

Ancestry‡	Population	%
African, Sub-Saharan (130)	130	0.89
African (48)	48	0.33
Liberian (42)	42	0.29
Nigerian (40)	40	0.27
American (472)	472	3.22
Arab (185)	260	1.78
Lebanese (22)	64	0.44
Syrian (0)	17	0.12
Other Arab (163)	179	1.22
Austrian (0)	47	0.32
British (67)	162	1.11
Canadian (19)	19	0.13
Carpatho Rusyn (0)	15	0.10
Celtic (31)	31	0.21
Croatian (0)	33	0.23
Czech (9)	38	0.26
Czechoslovakian (0)	29	0.20
Danish (0)	44	0.30
Dutch (42)	243	1.66
Eastern European (89)	89	0.61
English (185)	1,343	9.17
European (223)	249	1.70
Finnish (9)	9	0.06
French, ex. Basque (22)	385	2.63
French Canadian (13)	41	0.28
German (1,442)	3,992	27.26
Greek (47)	47	0.32
Guyanese (61)	61	0.42
Hungarian (25)	60	0.41
Iranian (32)	32	0.22
Irish (346)	1,907	13.02
Italian (426)	1,288	8.79
Lithuanian (37)	103	0.70
Northern European (19)	19	0.13
Norwegian (27)	73	0.50
Pennsylvania German (11)	42	0.29
Polish (306)	1,000	6.83
Portuguese (13)	13	0.09
Romanian (0)	9	0.06
Russian (123)	272	1.86
Scandinavian (0)	18	0.12
Scotch-Irish (221)	381	2.60
Scottish (23)	416	2.84
Slavic (12)	12	0.08
Slovak (74)	330	2.25
Slovene (0)	11	0.08
Swedish (45)	280	1.91
Swiss (37)	64	0.44
Ukrainian (40)	182	1.24
Welsh (18)	223	1.52
West Indian, ex. Hispanic (79)	79	0.54
Jamaican (79)	79	0.54

Hispanic Origin	Population	%
Hispanic or Latino (of any race)	491	3.21
Central American, ex. Mexican	47	0.31
Costa Rican	5	0.03
Guatemalan	7	0.05
Honduran	6	0.04
Nicaraguan	6	0.04
Panamanian	9	0.06
Salvadoran	14	0.09
Cuban	26	0.17
Dominican Republic	28	0.18
Mexican	103	0.67
Puerto Rican	157	1.03
South American	76	0.50
Argentinean	7	0.05
Bolivian	4	0.03
Chilean	4	0.03
Colombian	27	0.18
Ecuadorian	6	0.04
Peruvian	7	0.05
Uruguayan	3	0.02
Venezuelan	18	0.12
Other Hispanic or Latino	54	0.35

Race*	Population	%
African-American/Black (872)	989	6.46
Not Hispanic (830)	931	6.08
Hispanic (42)	58	0.38
American Indian/Alaska Native (9)	72	0.47
Not Hispanic (5)	60	0.39
Hispanic (4)	12	0.08
Central American Ind. (1)	1	0.01
Cherokee (0)	13	0.08
Chickasaw (0)	1	0.01
Chippewa (0)	1	0.01
Choctaw (0)	2	0.01
Comanche (1)	1	0.01
Delaware (0)	1	0.01
Iroquois (1)	5	0.03
Mexican American Ind. (0)	1	0.01
Navajo (0)	1	0.01
South American Ind. (3)	4	0.03
Asian (1,211)	1,361	8.89
Not Hispanic (1,199)	1,341	8.76
Hispanic (12)	20	0.13
Bangladeshi (4)	4	0.03
Burmese (4)	4	0.03
Cambodian (3)	3	0.02
Chinese, ex. Taiwanese (444)	474	3.10
Filipino (38)	53	0.35
Hmong (1)	1	0.01
Indian (351)	380	2.48
Indonesian (8)	10	0.07
Japanese (33)	58	0.38
Korean (162)	183	1.20
Laotian (2)	2	0.01
Malaysian (7)	10	0.07
Nepalese (2)	2	0.01
Pakistani (35)	38	0.25
Sri Lankan (6)	8	0.05
Taiwanese (29)	32	0.21
Thai (29)	30	0.20
Vietnamese (31)	37	0.24
Hawaii Native/Pacific Islander (10)	26	0.17
Not Hispanic (8)	22	0.14
Hispanic (2)	4	0.03
Guamanian/Chamorro (3)	3	0.02
Native Hawaiian (2)	9	0.06
Samoan (0)	1	0.01
White (12,761)	13,035	85.13
Not Hispanic (12,479)	12,714	83.04
Hispanic (282)	321	2.10

Penn Forest

Place Type: Township
County: Carbon
Population: 9,581†

Ancestry‡	Population	%
African, Sub-Saharan (0)	120	1.35
African (0)	18	0.20
South African (0)	102	1.15
American (747)	747	8.40
Austrian (9)	9	0.10
British (9)	16	0.18
Croatian (15)	15	0.17
Czech (8)	51	0.57
Danish (17)	27	0.30
Dutch (40)	156	1.75
Eastern European (33)	33	0.37
English (61)	637	7.16
European (44)	171	1.92
Finnish (0)	41	0.46
French, ex. Basque (18)	147	1.65
German (969)	2,315	26.02
Greek (20)	38	0.43
Hungarian (19)	38	0.43
Irish (775)	2,085	23.43
Italian (500)	1,460	16.41

*Notes: † The Census 2010 population figure is used to calculate the percentages in the Hispanic Origin and Race categories. Ancestry percentages are based on the 2006-2010 American Community Survey population (not shown); ‡ Numbers in parentheses indicate the number of people reporting a single ancestry; * Numbers in parentheses indicate the number of persons reporting this race alone, not in combination with any other race; Please refer to the Explanation of Data for more information.*

Ancestry	Population	%
Lithuanian (0)	43	0.48
Macedonian (10)	10	0.11
Northern European (21)	21	0.24
Norwegian (33)	33	0.37
Pennsylvania German (82)	197	2.21
Polish (141)	414	4.65
Portuguese (0)	4	0.04
Russian (0)	59	0.66
Scandinavian (0)	84	0.94
Scotch-Irish (33)	128	1.44
Scottish (0)	80	0.90
Slovak (53)	68	0.76
Swedish (23)	126	1.42
Ukrainian (0)	58	0.65
Welsh (0)	62	0.70
West Indian, ex. Hispanic (78)	116	1.30
Jamaican (39)	39	0.44
West Indian (39)	77	0.87
Yugoslavian (16)	16	0.18

Hispanic Origin	Population	%
Hispanic or Latino (of any race)	736	7.68
Central American, ex. Mexican	44	0.46
Costa Rican	2	0.02
Guatemalan	10	0.10
Honduran	18	0.19
Nicaraguan	1	0.01
Panamanian	4	0.04
Salvadoran	9	0.09
Cuban	50	0.52
Dominican Republic	31	0.32
Mexican	42	0.44
Puerto Rican	457	4.77
South American	60	0.63
Argentinean	6	0.06
Chilean	8	0.08
Colombian	15	0.16
Ecuadorian	9	0.09
Paraguayan	1	0.01
Peruvian	19	0.20
Uruguayan	1	0.01
Venezuelan	1	0.01
Other Hispanic or Latino	52	0.54

Race*	Population	%
African-American/Black (645)	728	7.60
Not Hispanic (591)	658	6.87
Hispanic (54)	70	0.73
American Indian/Alaska Native (39)	110	1.15
Not Hispanic (28)	69	0.72
Hispanic (11)	41	0.43
Blackfeet (0)	1	0.01
Cherokee (3)	10	0.10
Chippewa (1)	1	0.01
Choctaw (5)	6	0.06
Delaware (3)	3	0.03
Houma (0)	2	0.02
Iroquois (2)	2	0.02
Lumbee (2)	3	0.03
Mexican American Ind. (0)	1	0.01
Navajo (1)	1	0.01
South American Ind. (2)	12	0.13
Asian (95)	141	1.47
Not Hispanic (92)	130	1.36
Hispanic (3)	11	0.11
Chinese, ex. Taiwanese (13)	22	0.23
Filipino (24)	43	0.45
Indian (19)	36	0.38
Indonesian (0)	1	0.01
Japanese (4)	8	0.08
Korean (15)	17	0.18
Pakistani (1)	4	0.04
Sri Lankan (1)	6	0.06
Thai (1)	1	0.01
Vietnamese (2)	3	0.03
Hawaii Native/Pacific Islander (3)	7	0.07
Not Hispanic (1)	5	0.05
Hispanic (2)	2	0.02
Guamanian/Chamorro (1)	1	0.01
Native Hawaiian (0)	4	0.04
White (8,412)	8,571	89.46
Not Hispanic (7,985)	8,085	84.39
Hispanic (427)	486	5.07

Penn Hills

Place Type: Township
County: Allegheny
Population: 42,329†

Ancestry‡	Population	%
African, Sub-Saharan (310)	323	0.75
African (104)	104	0.24
Ghanaian (19)	19	0.04
Nigerian (106)	106	0.25
South African (0)	13	0.03
Other Sub-Saharan African (81)	81	0.19
Albanian (8)	8	0.02
American (1,298)	1,298	3.03
Arab (71)	99	0.23
Arab (54)	54	0.13
Lebanese (0)	17	0.04
Syrian (17)	28	0.07
Armenian (13)	13	0.03
Australian (10)	10	0.02
Austrian (15)	189	0.44
Belgian (11)	84	0.20
Brazilian (0)	13	0.03
British (69)	124	0.29
Canadian (0)	8	0.02
Carpatho Rusyn (43)	43	0.10
Croatian (125)	518	1.21
Czech (21)	124	0.29
Czechoslovakian (109)	157	0.37
Danish (0)	37	0.09
Dutch (168)	466	1.09
Eastern European (60)	60	0.14
English (637)	2,803	6.55
European (61)	145	0.34
Finnish (0)	5	0.01
French, ex. Basque (91)	611	1.43
French Canadian (0)	45	0.11
German (2,023)	8,554	19.99
Greek (187)	255	0.60
Hungarian (89)	377	0.88
Irish (1,298)	6,463	15.11
Italian (3,414)	7,186	16.80
Lithuanian (36)	130	0.30
Northern European (2)	2	<0.01
Norwegian (34)	64	0.15
Pennsylvania German (15)	67	0.16
Polish (722)	2,509	5.86
Romanian (65)	82	0.19
Russian (58)	507	1.19
Scandinavian (56)	56	0.13
Scotch-Irish (217)	834	1.95
Scottish (64)	481	1.12
Serbian (12)	155	0.36
Slavic (51)	100	0.23
Slovak (386)	1,005	2.35
Slovene (63)	180	0.42
Swedish (23)	235	0.55
Swiss (14)	242	0.57
Ukrainian (58)	132	0.31
Welsh (43)	475	1.11
West Indian, ex. Hispanic (132)	164	0.38
British West Indian (35)	35	0.08
Jamaican (66)	98	0.23
West Indian (31)	31	0.07
Yugoslavian (0)	46	0.11

Hispanic Origin	Population	%
Hispanic or Latino (of any race)	598	1.41
Central American, ex. Mexican	24	0.06
Guatemalan	10	0.02
Nicaraguan	5	0.01
Panamanian	6	0.01
Salvadoran	3	0.01
Cuban	31	0.07
Dominican Republic	13	0.03
Mexican	212	0.50
Puerto Rican	185	0.44
South American	48	0.11
Argentinean	12	0.03
Bolivian	2	<0.01
Colombian	14	0.03
Ecuadorian	3	0.01
Peruvian	12	0.03
Uruguayan	3	0.01
Venezuelan	2	<0.01
Other Hispanic or Latino	85	0.20

Race*	Population	%
African-American/Black (14,631)	15,514	36.65
Not Hispanic (14,518)	15,331	36.22
Hispanic (113)	183	0.43
American Indian/Alaska Native (89)	373	0.88
Not Hispanic (63)	312	0.74
Hispanic (26)	61	0.14
Alaska Athabascan *(Ala. Nat.)* (1)	1	<0.01
Apache (0)	3	0.01
Blackfeet (1)	34	0.08
Central American Ind. (1)	1	<0.01
Cherokee (13)	98	0.23
Cheyenne (0)	5	0.01
Chickasaw (0)	1	<0.01
Comanche (0)	2	<0.01
Cree (1)	1	<0.01
Creek (0)	3	0.01
Delaware (2)	3	0.01
Iroquois (2)	7	0.02
Lumbee (1)	3	0.01
Mexican American Ind. (4)	7	0.02
Navajo (1)	1	<0.01
Osage (0)	1	<0.01
Potawatomi (1)	3	0.01
Puget Sound Salish (0)	1	<0.01
Seminole (0)	4	0.01
Sioux (5)	12	0.03
South American Ind. (4)	5	0.01
Asian (321)	454	1.07
Not Hispanic (320)	446	1.05
Hispanic (1)	8	0.02
Bhutanese (15)	20	0.05
Chinese, ex. Taiwanese (44)	60	0.14
Filipino (24)	59	0.14
Indian (108)	131	0.31
Indonesian (1)	1	<0.01
Japanese (7)	16	0.04
Korean (17)	27	0.06
Laotian (9)	10	0.02
Malaysian (1)	1	<0.01
Nepalese (8)	23	0.05
Pakistani (2)	2	<0.01
Taiwanese (2)	2	<0.01
Thai (6)	8	0.02
Vietnamese (66)	81	0.19
Hawaii Native/Pacific Islander (3)	22	0.05
Not Hispanic (3)	22	0.05
Guamanian/Chamorro (0)	8	0.02
Native Hawaiian (1)	7	0.02
Samoan (2)	2	<0.01
White (25,996)	26,839	63.41
Not Hispanic (25,751)	26,511	62.63
Hispanic (245)	328	0.77

Penn

Place Type: Township
County: Lancaster
Population: 8,789†

Ancestry‡	Population	%
African, Sub-Saharan (21)	21	0.25
Ghanaian (21)	21	0.25
American (697)	697	8.17
Armenian (0)	18	0.21
Austrian (13)	50	0.59
British (31)	45	0.53
Czech (0)	12	0.14

SECTION TWO

*Notes: † The Census 2010 population figure is used to calculate the percentages in the Hispanic Origin and Race categories. Ancestry percentages are based on the 2006-2010 American Community Survey population (not shown); ‡ Numbers in parentheses indicate the number of people reporting a single ancestry; * Numbers in parentheses indicate the number of persons reporting this race alone, not in combination with any other race; Please refer to the Explanation of Data for more information.*

Dutch (12)	147	1.72
English (224)	565	6.63
European (115)	150	1.76
French, ex. Basque (69)	258	3.03
French Canadian (0)	7	0.08
German (2,593)	4,181	49.03
Greek (17)	67	0.79
Hungarian (23)	34	0.40
Irish (122)	638	7.48
Italian (200)	301	3.53
Latvian (0)	15	0.18
Norwegian (0)	30	0.35
Pennsylvania German (13)	13	0.15
Polish (61)	108	1.27
Russian (27)	59	0.69
Scandinavian (15)	15	0.18
Scotch-Irish (25)	103	1.21
Scottish (27)	27	0.32
Slavic (0)	24	0.28
Slovak (45)	55	0.64
Swedish (13)	67	0.79
Swiss (113)	602	7.06
Ukrainian (17)	27	0.32
Yugoslavian (0)	11	0.13

Hispanic Origin	Population	%
Hispanic or Latino (of any race)	206	2.34
Central American, ex. Mexican	8	0.09
Guatemalan	8	0.09
Cuban	2	0.02
Dominican Republic	4	0.05
Mexican	71	0.81
Puerto Rican	99	1.13
South American	6	0.07
Colombian	4	0.05
Peruvian	2	0.02
Other Hispanic or Latino	16	0.18

Race*	Population	%
African-American/Black (88)	127	1.44
Not Hispanic (85)	118	1.34
Hispanic (3)	9	0.10
American Indian/Alaska Native (9)	13	0.15
Not Hispanic (9)	13	0.15
Blackfeet (1)	1	0.01
Cherokee (2)	2	0.02
Delaware (0)	1	0.01
Iroquois (0)	1	0.01
Tlingit-Haida *(Alaska Native)* (1)	1	0.01
Asian (113)	132	1.50
Not Hispanic (113)	131	1.49
Hispanic (0)	1	0.01
Cambodian (2)	2	0.02
Chinese, ex. Taiwanese (13)	18	0.20
Filipino (8)	11	0.13
Hmong (1)	1	0.01
Indian (24)	26	0.30
Japanese (0)	1	0.01
Korean (6)	11	0.13
Laotian (15)	16	0.18
Thai (2)	2	0.02
Vietnamese (23)	25	0.28
Hawaii Native/Pacific Islander (1)	5	0.06
Not Hispanic (1)	3	0.03
Hispanic (0)	2	0.02
Guamanian/Chamorro (0)	1	0.01
Samoan (0)	1	0.01
White (8,430)	8,497	96.68
Not Hispanic (8,303)	8,356	95.07
Hispanic (127)	141	1.60

Penn

Place Type: Township
County: Westmoreland
Population: 20,005†

Ancestry‡	Population	%
American (507)	507	2.54
Arab (32)	66	0.33
Lebanese (0)	14	0.07
Syrian (32)	52	0.26
Austrian (29)	92	0.46
Belgian (22)	48	0.24
British (0)	23	0.12
Carpatho Rusyn (0)	11	0.06
Croatian (141)	410	2.06
Czech (29)	177	0.89
Czechoslovakian (0)	26	0.13
Dutch (13)	311	1.56
English (509)	2,569	12.90
European (184)	184	0.92
French, ex. Basque (87)	447	2.24
French Canadian (0)	14	0.07
German (1,881)	6,911	34.69
Greek (0)	9	0.05
Hungarian (91)	441	2.21
Irish (964)	3,917	19.66
Italian (1,673)	4,536	22.77
Lithuanian (99)	297	1.49
Pennsylvania German (109)	283	1.42
Polish (463)	1,781	8.94
Romanian (80)	80	0.40
Russian (123)	321	1.61
Scandinavian (13)	13	0.07
Scotch-Irish (185)	407	2.04
Scottish (102)	431	2.16
Serbian (109)	302	1.52
Slavic (17)	119	0.60
Slovak (418)	1,225	6.15
Slovene (11)	224	1.12
Swedish (46)	338	1.70
Swiss (0)	34	0.17
Ukrainian (49)	107	0.54
Welsh (92)	477	2.39
Yugoslavian (37)	87	0.44

Hispanic Origin	Population	%
Hispanic or Latino (of any race)	140	0.70
Central American, ex. Mexican	6	0.03
Guatemalan	5	0.02
Salvadoran	1	<0.01
Cuban	10	0.05
Dominican Republic	1	<0.01
Mexican	67	0.33
Puerto Rican	24	0.12
South American	5	0.02
Chilean	1	<0.01
Ecuadorian	3	0.01
Venezuelan	1	<0.01
Other Hispanic or Latino	27	0.13

Race*	Population	%
African-American/Black (98)	146	0.73
Not Hispanic (95)	136	0.68
Hispanic (3)	10	0.05
American Indian/Alaska Native (12)	38	0.19
Not Hispanic (12)	38	0.19
Blackfeet (0)	1	<0.01
Cherokee (6)	12	0.06
Choctaw (0)	3	0.01
Iroquois (1)	5	0.02
Navajo (1)	4	0.02
Sioux (2)	5	0.02
Tlingit-Haida *(Alaska Native)* (1)	1	<0.01
Asian (104)	155	0.77
Not Hispanic (103)	148	0.74
Hispanic (1)	7	0.03
Chinese, ex. Taiwanese (18)	26	0.13
Filipino (10)	24	0.12
Indian (40)	44	0.22
Indonesian (0)	6	0.03
Japanese (3)	9	0.04
Korean (17)	24	0.12
Pakistani (4)	4	0.02
Taiwanese (3)	3	0.01
Thai (1)	4	0.02
Vietnamese (5)	11	0.05
Hawaii Native/Pacific Islander (1)	6	0.03
Not Hispanic (1)	2	0.01
Hispanic (0)	4	0.02
Native Hawaiian (1)	1	<0.01
White (19,635)	19,751	98.73
Not Hispanic (19,538)	19,638	98.17
Hispanic (97)	113	0.56

Penn

Place Type: Township
County: York
Population: 15,612†

Ancestry‡	Population	%
American (1,834)	1,834	11.80
Australian (0)	14	0.09
Austrian (0)	32	0.21
British (12)	12	0.08
Celtic (7)	7	0.05
Czech (21)	155	1.00
Czechoslovakian (15)	52	0.33
Danish (0)	28	0.18
Dutch (0)	304	1.96
English (643)	1,490	9.59
European (32)	47	0.30
French, ex. Basque (25)	229	1.47
German (3,833)	6,968	44.83
Greek (0)	17	0.11
Hungarian (15)	48	0.31
Irish (453)	2,132	13.72
Italian (312)	902	5.80
Lithuanian (12)	26	0.17
Pennsylvania German (76)	95	0.61
Polish (220)	870	5.60
Romanian (0)	17	0.11
Russian (15)	44	0.28
Scotch-Irish (113)	295	1.90
Scottish (70)	250	1.61
Slovak (18)	32	0.21
Slovene (0)	15	0.10
Swedish (88)	161	1.04
Swiss (12)	106	0.68
Ukrainian (27)	115	0.74
Welsh (45)	208	1.34
Yugoslavian (0)	13	0.08

Hispanic Origin	Population	%
Hispanic or Latino (of any race)	355	2.27
Central American, ex. Mexican	32	0.20
Costa Rican	6	0.04
Guatemalan	11	0.07
Panamanian	3	0.02
Salvadoran	12	0.08
Cuban	11	0.07
Dominican Republic	3	0.02
Mexican	178	1.14
Puerto Rican	70	0.45
South American	34	0.22
Argentinean	2	0.01
Chilean	1	0.01
Colombian	12	0.08
Ecuadorian	2	0.01
Peruvian	13	0.08
Venezuelan	1	0.01
Other South American	3	0.02
Other Hispanic or Latino	27	0.17

Race*	Population	%
African-American/Black (189)	270	1.73
Not Hispanic (184)	258	1.65
Hispanic (5)	12	0.08
American Indian/Alaska Native (18)	82	0.53
Not Hispanic (14)	74	0.47
Hispanic (4)	8	0.05
Apache (0)	3	0.02
Central American Ind. (1)	1	0.01
Cherokee (4)	17	0.11
Choctaw (0)	3	0.02
Iroquois (2)	3	0.02
Kiowa (0)	1	0.01
Lumbee (4)	8	0.05

*Notes: † The Census 2010 population figure is used to calculate the percentages in the Hispanic Origin and Race categories. Ancestry percentages are based on the 2006-2010 American Community Survey population (not shown); ‡ Numbers in parentheses indicate the number of people reporting a single ancestry; * Numbers in parentheses indicate the number of persons reporting this race alone, not in combination with any other race; Please refer to the Explanation of Data for more information.*

Mexican American Ind. (0)	3	0.02
Asian (167)	230	1.47
Not Hispanic (166)	220	1.41
Hispanic (1)	10	0.06
Chinese, ex. Taiwanese (32)	37	0.24
Filipino (41)	58	0.37
Indian (16)	23	0.15
Japanese (8)	24	0.15
Korean (29)	52	0.33
Pakistani (16)	17	0.11
Thai (1)	1	0.01
Vietnamese (16)	17	0.11
Hawaii Native/Pacific Islander (1)	6	0.04
Not Hispanic (1)	6	0.04
Native Hawaiian (0)	4	0.03
White (14,911)	15,108	96.77
Not Hispanic (14,693)	14,864	95.21
Hispanic (218)	244	1.56

Perkasie

Place Type: Borough
County: Bucks
Population: 8,511†

Ancestry‡	Population	%
Albanian (0)	38	0.44
American (348)	348	4.04
Arab (0)	127	1.48
Arab (0)	62	0.72
Lebanese (0)	65	0.76
Austrian (0)	67	0.78
Belgian (6)	13	0.15
British (0)	7	0.08
Croatian (12)	26	0.30
Czech (15)	43	0.50
Czechoslovakian (0)	14	0.16
Danish (0)	17	0.20
Dutch (87)	389	4.52
English (154)	1,041	12.10
European (16)	16	0.19
French, ex. Basque (21)	473	5.50
German (1,335)	3,861	44.87
Greek (0)	47	0.55
Hungarian (74)	283	3.29
Irish (339)	2,108	24.50
Italian (312)	1,116	12.97
Lithuanian (16)	87	1.01
Norwegian (0)	17	0.20
Pennsylvania German (282)	519	6.03
Polish (89)	512	5.95
Portuguese (0)	83	0.96
Russian (19)	37	0.43
Scandinavian (0)	17	0.20
Scotch-Irish (25)	116	1.35
Scottish (50)	165	1.92
Slovak (29)	74	0.86
Swedish (28)	99	1.15
Swiss (14)	14	0.16
Ukrainian (29)	126	1.46
Welsh (23)	80	0.93
Yugoslavian (18)	18	0.21

Hispanic Origin	Population	%
Hispanic or Latino (of any race)	212	2.49
Central American, ex. Mexican	22	0.26
Costa Rican	1	0.01
Guatemalan	7	0.08
Honduran	12	0.14
Panamanian	1	0.01
Salvadoran	1	0.01
Cuban	15	0.18
Dominican Republic	3	0.04
Mexican	40	0.47
Puerto Rican	99	1.16
South American	20	0.23
Bolivian	1	0.01
Colombian	5	0.06
Ecuadorian	8	0.09
Paraguayan	2	0.02
Peruvian	1	0.01
Venezuelan	3	0.04
Other Hispanic or Latino	13	0.15

Race*	Population	%
African-American/Black (88)	132	1.55
Not Hispanic (85)	126	1.48
Hispanic (3)	6	0.07
American Indian/Alaska Native (18)	60	0.70
Not Hispanic (17)	58	0.68
Hispanic (1)	2	0.02
Blackfeet (0)	5	0.06
Cherokee (7)	22	0.26
Chippewa (0)	1	0.01
Choctaw (3)	7	0.08
Delaware (0)	2	0.02
Navajo (0)	2	0.02
Sioux (1)	1	0.01
Asian (86)	114	1.34
Not Hispanic (86)	114	1.34
Chinese, ex. Taiwanese (25)	31	0.36
Filipino (6)	17	0.20
Indian (11)	12	0.14
Japanese (9)	13	0.15
Korean (8)	11	0.13
Pakistani (7)	7	0.08
Thai (7)	7	0.08
Vietnamese (13)	15	0.18
Hawaii Native/Pacific Islander (4)	8	0.09
Not Hispanic (3)	4	0.05
Hispanic (1)	4	0.05
Native Hawaiian (2)	2	0.02
Samoan (2)	6	0.07
White (8,156)	8,274	97.22
Not Hispanic (7,990)	8,097	95.14
Hispanic (166)	177	2.08

Perkiomen

Place Type: Township
County: Montgomery
Population: 9,139†

Ancestry‡	Population	%
American (136)	136	1.55
Arab (0)	13	0.15
Other Arab (0)	13	0.15
Australian (0)	13	0.15
Austrian (15)	15	0.17
Belgian (0)	16	0.18
British (99)	190	2.17
Croatian (33)	33	0.38
Czech (3)	63	0.72
Dutch (0)	120	1.37
English (179)	1,195	13.63
European (60)	148	1.69
Finnish (0)	10	0.11
French, ex. Basque (15)	252	2.87
French Canadian (42)	89	1.01
German (659)	2,641	30.12
Greek (30)	53	0.60
Hungarian (33)	92	1.05
Irish (791)	2,714	30.95
Italian (341)	1,572	17.93
Lithuanian (0)	12	0.14
Norwegian (15)	42	0.48
Pennsylvania German (182)	182	2.08
Polish (179)	638	7.28
Portuguese (0)	16	0.18
Romanian (11)	26	0.30
Russian (10)	134	1.53
Scandinavian (0)	8	0.09
Scotch-Irish (42)	178	2.03
Scottish (11)	68	0.78
Slavic (18)	34	0.39
Slovak (15)	57	0.65
Swedish (0)	34	0.39
Swiss (0)	38	0.43
Ukrainian (30)	42	0.48
Welsh (0)	97	1.11
West Indian, ex. Hispanic (91)	91	1.04
Belizean (17)	17	0.19
British West Indian (46)	46	0.52
Jamaican (28)	28	0.32
Yugoslavian (0)	32	0.36

Hispanic Origin	Population	%
Hispanic or Latino (of any race)	266	2.91
Central American, ex. Mexican	13	0.14
Guatemalan	4	0.04
Panamanian	3	0.03
Salvadoran	6	0.07
Cuban	28	0.31
Dominican Republic	9	0.10
Mexican	64	0.70
Puerto Rican	87	0.95
South American	45	0.49
Argentinean	7	0.08
Colombian	13	0.14
Ecuadorian	10	0.11
Paraguayan	11	0.12
Peruvian	1	0.01
Venezuelan	2	0.02
Other South American	1	0.01
Other Hispanic or Latino	20	0.22

Race*	Population	%
African-American/Black (372)	446	4.88
Not Hispanic (363)	427	4.67
Hispanic (9)	19	0.21
American Indian/Alaska Native (3)	41	0.45
Not Hispanic (3)	38	0.42
Hispanic (0)	3	0.03
Canadian/French Am. Ind. (1)	2	0.02
Cherokee (1)	3	0.03
Creek (0)	2	0.02
Delaware (0)	1	0.01
Hopi (0)	2	0.02
Sioux (0)	3	0.03
Asian (473)	553	6.05
Not Hispanic (473)	546	5.97
Hispanic (0)	7	0.08
Cambodian (9)	9	0.10
Chinese, ex. Taiwanese (67)	80	0.88
Filipino (79)	100	1.09
Indian (140)	146	1.60
Japanese (3)	8	0.09
Korean (75)	93	1.02
Laotian (2)	4	0.04
Pakistani (20)	24	0.26
Taiwanese (2)	2	0.02
Thai (1)	8	0.09
Vietnamese (53)	61	0.67
Hawaii Native/Pacific Islander (0)	5	0.05
Not Hispanic (0)	5	0.05
Native Hawaiian (0)	3	0.03
Samoan (0)	3	0.03
White (8,047)	8,219	89.93
Not Hispanic (7,856)	7,996	87.49
Hispanic (191)	223	2.44

Peters

Place Type: Township
County: Washington
Population: 21,213†

Ancestry‡	Population	%
African, Sub-Saharan (9)	9	0.04
African (9)	9	0.04
American (379)	379	1.85
Arab (20)	130	0.63
Lebanese (0)	26	0.13
Syrian (20)	104	0.51
Austrian (16)	94	0.46
Belgian (0)	69	0.34
Brazilian (15)	31	0.15
British (13)	13	0.06
Canadian (7)	7	0.03
Carpatho Rusyn (27)	27	0.13

*Notes: † The Census 2010 population figure is used to calculate the percentages in the Hispanic Origin and Race categories. Ancestry percentages are based on the 2006-2010 American Community Survey population (not shown); ‡ Numbers in parentheses indicate the number of people reporting a single ancestry; * Numbers in parentheses indicate the number of persons reporting this race alone, not in combination with any other race; Please refer to the Explanation of Data for more information.*

Ancestry (cont.)	Population	%
Croatian (102)	283	1.38
Czech (30)	200	0.97
Czechoslovakian (17)	129	0.63
Danish (10)	20	0.10
Dutch (36)	140	0.68
Eastern European (65)	77	0.38
English (1,026)	2,850	13.88
European (367)	367	1.79
Finnish (0)	9	0.04
French, ex. Basque (71)	615	3.00
French Canadian (50)	61	0.30
German (1,444)	6,205	30.23
Greek (150)	345	1.68
Hungarian (106)	451	2.20
Irish (897)	4,478	21.81
Italian (1,188)	4,319	21.04
Lithuanian (21)	136	0.66
Norwegian (36)	53	0.26
Pennsylvania German (15)	35	0.17
Polish (605)	2,491	12.13
Portuguese (0)	12	0.06
Romanian (34)	49	0.24
Russian (132)	503	2.45
Scandinavian (9)	9	0.04
Scotch-Irish (169)	641	3.12
Scottish (96)	440	2.14
Serbian (36)	119	0.58
Slavic (9)	49	0.24
Slovak (218)	885	4.31
Slovene (54)	264	1.29
Swedish (8)	113	0.55
Swiss (10)	39	0.19
Ukrainian (114)	286	1.39
Welsh (55)	307	1.50

Hispanic Origin	Population	%
Hispanic or Latino (of any race)	316	1.49
Central American, ex. Mexican	7	0.03
Guatemalan	4	0.02
Honduran	2	0.01
Nicaraguan	1	<0.01
Cuban	16	0.08
Dominican Republic	15	0.07
Mexican	129	0.61
Puerto Rican	68	0.32
South American	26	0.12
Argentinean	14	0.07
Chilean	1	<0.01
Colombian	4	0.02
Ecuadorian	4	0.02
Peruvian	2	0.01
Venezuelan	1	<0.01
Other Hispanic or Latino	55	0.26

Race*	Population	%
African-American/Black (110)	162	0.76
Not Hispanic (106)	145	0.68
Hispanic (4)	17	0.08
American Indian/Alaska Native (17)	63	0.30
Not Hispanic (13)	50	0.24
Hispanic (4)	13	0.06
Blackfeet (0)	6	0.03
Cherokee (2)	15	0.07
Chippewa (0)	1	<0.01
Choctaw (0)	2	0.01
Iroquois (0)	12	0.06
Mexican American Ind. (1)	1	<0.01
Sioux (3)	3	0.01
South American Ind. (4)	4	0.02
Yaqui (0)	4	0.02
Asian (417)	501	2.36
Not Hispanic (414)	489	2.31
Hispanic (3)	12	0.06
Bangladeshi (1)	4	0.02
Burmese (4)	4	0.02
Chinese, ex. Taiwanese (125)	136	0.64
Filipino (23)	46	0.22
Indian (180)	195	0.92
Japanese (19)	36	0.17
Korean (31)	36	0.17
Pakistani (9)	9	0.04
Sri Lankan (2)	2	0.01
Taiwanese (4)	4	0.02
Thai (0)	4	0.02
Vietnamese (12)	18	0.08
Hawaii Native/Pacific Islander (0)	6	0.03
Not Hispanic (0)	6	0.03
Samoan (0)	1	<0.01
White (20,413)	20,588	97.05
Not Hispanic (20,209)	20,348	95.92
Hispanic (204)	240	1.13

Philadelphia

Place Type: City
County: Philadelphia
Population: 1,526,006†

Ancestry‡	Population	%
Afghan (52)	52	<0.01
African, Sub-Saharan (24,827)	29,046	1.93
African (15,876)	18,871	1.25
Cape Verdean (69)	129	0.01
Ethiopian (1,542)	1,572	0.10
Ghanaian (584)	584	0.04
Kenyan (94)	147	0.01
Liberian (2,867)	3,198	0.21
Nigerian (1,648)	1,877	0.12
Senegalese (91)	139	0.01
Sierra Leonean (136)	144	0.01
Somalian (11)	22	<0.01
South African (164)	235	0.02
Sudanese (160)	167	0.01
Ugandan (0)	8	<0.01
Zimbabwean (51)	51	<0.01
Other Sub-Saharan African (1,534)	1,902	0.13
Albanian (3,540)	3,892	0.26
Alsatian (13)	54	<0.01
American (20,637)	20,637	1.37
Arab (6,122)	7,763	0.52
Arab (1,709)	2,081	0.14
Egyptian (491)	580	0.04
Iraqi (211)	218	0.01
Jordanian (928)	939	0.06
Lebanese (507)	991	0.07
Moroccan (516)	684	0.05
Palestinian (607)	621	0.04
Syrian (294)	637	0.04
Other Arab (859)	1,012	0.07
Armenian (949)	1,315	0.09
Assyrian/Chaldean/Syriac (8)	8	<0.01
Australian (194)	243	0.02
Austrian (476)	2,580	0.17
Basque (0)	59	<0.01
Belgian (63)	214	0.01
Brazilian (2,390)	2,622	0.17
British (1,248)	2,578	0.17
Bulgarian (103)	150	0.01
Cajun (17)	38	<0.01
Canadian (534)	1,094	0.07
Carpatho Rusyn (33)	46	<0.01
Celtic (41)	41	<0.01
Croatian (382)	916	0.06
Cypriot (75)	75	<0.01
Czech (545)	2,209	0.15
Czechoslovakian (389)	721	0.05
Danish (181)	830	0.06
Dutch (1,200)	5,855	0.39
Eastern European (3,053)	3,363	0.22
English (10,881)	47,303	3.14
Estonian (55)	147	0.01
European (4,424)	4,939	0.33
Finnish (108)	326	0.02
French, ex. Basque (2,120)	12,027	0.80
French Canadian (497)	1,636	0.11
German (28,175)	122,783	8.16
Greek (2,136)	4,288	0.28
Guyanese (545)	638	0.04
Hungarian (1,262)	5,463	0.36
Icelander (58)	86	0.01
Iranian (550)	665	0.04
Irish (68,684)	195,849	13.01
Israeli (567)	861	0.06
Italian (60,356)	125,080	8.31
Latvian (250)	570	0.04
Lithuanian (1,629)	5,334	0.35
Luxemburger (15)	29	<0.01
Macedonian (10)	10	<0.01
New Zealander (38)	52	<0.01
Northern European (315)	361	0.02
Norwegian (599)	2,417	0.16
Pennsylvania German (853)	1,967	0.13
Polish (21,876)	58,395	3.88
Portuguese (2,044)	3,158	0.21
Romanian (980)	2,101	0.14
Russian (13,897)	25,520	1.70
Scandinavian (251)	504	0.03
Scotch-Irish (3,872)	9,813	0.65
Scottish (1,963)	8,768	0.58
Serbian (286)	493	0.03
Slavic (153)	498	0.03
Slovak (750)	2,480	0.16
Slovene (186)	273	0.02
Swedish (852)	3,719	0.25
Swiss (267)	1,886	0.13
Turkish (609)	786	0.05
Ukrainian (7,300)	13,262	0.88
Welsh (629)	4,345	0.29
West Indian, ex. Hispanic (21,124)	25,436	1.69
Bahamian (59)	104	0.01
Barbadian (607)	635	0.04
Belizean (0)	31	<0.01
Bermudan (29)	29	<0.01
British West Indian (458)	541	0.04
Haitian (8,400)	9,026	0.60
Jamaican (8,311)	10,082	0.67
Trinidadian/Tobagonian (1,700)	2,407	0.16
U.S. Virgin Islander (100)	100	0.01
West Indian (1,446)	2,445	0.16
Other West Indian (14)	36	<0.01
Yugoslavian (239)	406	0.03

Hispanic Origin	Population	%
Hispanic or Latino (of any race)	187,611	12.29
Central American, ex. Mexican	7,511	0.49
Costa Rican	903	0.06
Guatemalan	2,262	0.15
Honduran	1,642	0.11
Nicaraguan	874	0.06
Panamanian	737	0.05
Salvadoran	1,049	0.07
Other Central American	44	<0.01
Cuban	3,930	0.26
Dominican Republic	15,963	1.05
Mexican	15,531	1.02
Puerto Rican	121,643	7.97
South American	9,969	0.65
Argentinean	1,006	0.07
Bolivian	112	0.01
Chilean	357	0.02
Colombian	4,675	0.31
Ecuadorian	1,542	0.10
Paraguayan	74	<0.01
Peruvian	1,085	0.07
Uruguayan	234	0.02
Venezuelan	773	0.05
Other South American	111	0.01
Other Hispanic or Latino	13,064	0.86

Race*	Population	%
African-American/Black (661,839)	686,870	45.01
Not Hispanic (644,287)	662,568	43.42
Hispanic (17,552)	24,302	1.59
American Indian/Alaska Native (6,996)	17,495	1.15
Not Hispanic (3,498)	11,409	0.75
Hispanic (3,498)	6,086	0.40
Alaska Athabascan *(Ala. Nat.)* (5)	6	<0.01
Aleut *(Alaska Native)* (4)	8	<0.01
Apache (31)	118	0.01
Arapaho (4)	7	<0.01

*Notes: † The Census 2010 population figure is used to calculate the percentages in the Hispanic Origin and Race categories. Ancestry percentages are based on the 2006-2010 American Community Survey population (not shown); ‡ Numbers in parentheses indicate the number of people reporting a single ancestry; * Numbers in parentheses indicate the number of persons reporting this race alone, not in combination with any other race; Please refer to the Explanation of Data for more information.*

Blackfeet (105)	679	0.04
Canadian/French Am. Ind. (8)	34	<0.01
Central American Ind. (65)	111	0.01
Cherokee (463)	2,484	0.16
Cheyenne (0)	12	<0.01
Chickasaw (5)	28	<0.01
Chippewa (17)	63	<0.01
Choctaw (25)	92	0.01
Comanche (3)	9	<0.01
Cree (3)	25	<0.01
Creek (16)	59	<0.01
Crow (2)	15	<0.01
Delaware (71)	239	0.02
Hopi (5)	7	<0.01
Houma (1)	2	<0.01
Inupiat *(Alaska Native)* (1)	3	<0.01
Iroquois (72)	216	0.01
Kiowa (0)	9	<0.01
Lumbee (51)	121	0.01
Menominee (1)	6	<0.01
Mexican American Ind. (126)	185	0.01
Navajo (35)	99	0.01
Osage (1)	5	<0.01
Ottawa (1)	2	<0.01
Paiute (2)	4	<0.01
Pima (1)	2	<0.01
Potawatomi (4)	14	<0.01
Pueblo (13)	42	<0.01
Puget Sound Salish (3)	5	<0.01
Seminole (21)	189	0.01
Shoshone (4)	11	<0.01
Sioux (55)	199	0.01
South American Ind. (273)	657	0.04
Spanish American Ind. (98)	156	0.01
Tlingit-Haida *(Alaska Native)* (3)	18	<0.01
Tohono O'Odham (2)	3	<0.01
Tsimshian *(Alaska Native)* (0)	1	<0.01
Yakama (2)	2	<0.01
Yaqui (5)	10	<0.01
Yuman (2)	8	<0.01
Yup'ik *(Alaska Native)* (2)	5	<0.01
Asian (96,405)	106,720	6.99
Not Hispanic (95,521)	104,551	6.85
Hispanic (884)	2,169	0.14
Bangladeshi (883)	978	0.06
Bhutanese (43)	51	<0.01
Burmese (341)	388	0.03
Cambodian (8,707)	9,912	0.65
Chinese, ex. Taiwanese (29,396)	32,773	2.15
Filipino (4,978)	6,849	0.45
Hmong (77)	83	0.01
Indian (18,520)	20,809	1.36
Indonesian (1,921)	2,222	0.15
Japanese (1,034)	1,956	0.13
Korean (6,217)	7,074	0.46
Laotian (1,084)	1,350	0.09
Malaysian (88)	130	0.01
Nepalese (181)	220	0.01
Pakistani (2,423)	2,683	0.18
Sri Lankan (148)	172	0.01
Taiwanese (639)	736	0.05
Thai (386)	627	0.04
Vietnamese (14,431)	16,268	1.07
Hawaii Native/Pacific Islander (744)	3,125	0.20
Not Hispanic (457)	1,938	0.13
Hispanic (287)	1,187	0.08
Fijian (7)	14	<0.01
Guamanian/Chamorro (186)	272	0.02
Native Hawaiian (203)	538	0.04
Samoan (84)	198	0.01
Tongan (7)	9	<0.01
White (626,221)	655,021	42.92
Not Hispanic (562,585)	581,693	38.12
Hispanic (63,636)	73,328	4.81

Phoenixville

Place Type: Borough
County: Chester
Population: 16,440†

Ancestry‡	Population	%
African, Sub-Saharan (115)	115	0.71
Kenyan (15)	15	0.09
Nigerian (100)	100	0.62
Albanian (8)	36	0.22
American (295)	295	1.82
Arab (29)	59	0.36
Egyptian (0)	30	0.18
Moroccan (23)	23	0.14
Other Arab (6)	6	0.04
Australian (0)	8	0.05
Austrian (0)	103	0.63
Belgian (23)	23	0.14
Brazilian (95)	95	0.58
British (31)	65	0.40
Croatian (12)	22	0.14
Czech (37)	116	0.71
Czechoslovakian (0)	30	0.18
Dutch (74)	234	1.44
Eastern European (16)	16	0.10
English (198)	1,658	10.20
European (215)	215	1.32
Finnish (0)	25	0.15
French, ex. Basque (31)	481	2.96
French Canadian (0)	89	0.55
German (880)	3,955	24.34
Greek (65)	84	0.52
Hungarian (77)	252	1.55
Iranian (30)	45	0.28
Irish (1,315)	4,354	26.80
Italian (778)	2,737	16.84
Lithuanian (0)	76	0.47
Macedonian (30)	30	0.18
Norwegian (18)	67	0.41
Pennsylvania German (55)	216	1.33
Polish (292)	1,146	7.05
Portuguese (0)	15	0.09
Romanian (0)	24	0.15
Russian (44)	170	1.05
Scotch-Irish (70)	329	2.02
Scottish (89)	421	2.59
Slavic (0)	32	0.20
Slovak (171)	569	3.50
Swedish (15)	63	0.39
Swiss (10)	52	0.32
Ukrainian (153)	454	2.79
Welsh (67)	575	3.54
West Indian, ex. Hispanic (112)	127	0.78
British West Indian (12)	27	0.17
Jamaican (76)	76	0.47
Trinidadian/Tobagonian (15)	15	0.09
Other West Indian (9)	9	0.06

Hispanic Origin	Population	%
Hispanic or Latino (of any race)	1,220	7.42
Central American, ex. Mexican	425	2.59
Costa Rican	3	0.02
Guatemalan	355	2.16
Honduran	6	0.04
Nicaraguan	2	0.01
Panamanian	5	0.03
Salvadoran	54	0.33
Cuban	22	0.13
Dominican Republic	20	0.12
Mexican	275	1.67
Puerto Rican	291	1.77
South American	71	0.43
Argentinean	10	0.06
Bolivian	3	0.02
Colombian	25	0.15
Ecuadorian	7	0.04
Peruvian	16	0.10
Uruguayan	1	0.01
Venezuelan	9	0.05
Other Hispanic or Latino	116	0.71

Race*	Population	%
African-American/Black (1,415)	1,666	10.13
Not Hispanic (1,348)	1,576	9.59
Hispanic (67)	90	0.55
American Indian/Alaska Native (39)	107	0.65
Not Hispanic (24)	88	0.54
Hispanic (15)	19	0.12
Aleut *(Alaska Native)* (1)	1	0.01
Blackfeet (2)	6	0.04
Central American Ind. (1)	1	0.01
Cherokee (2)	25	0.15
Chippewa (0)	1	0.01
Choctaw (0)	2	0.01
Comanche (1)	1	0.01
Inupiat *(Alaska Native)* (1)	2	0.01
Lumbee (1)	1	0.01
Mexican American Ind. (7)	8	0.05
Navajo (0)	1	0.01
Shoshone (0)	1	0.01
Sioux (5)	6	0.04
Yup'ik *(Alaska Native)* (0)	1	0.01
Asian (576)	664	4.04
Not Hispanic (571)	654	3.98
Hispanic (5)	10	0.06
Burmese (1)	2	0.01
Cambodian (3)	6	0.04
Chinese, ex. Taiwanese (88)	114	0.69
Filipino (58)	78	0.47
Indian (235)	250	1.52
Indonesian (5)	5	0.03
Japanese (5)	24	0.15
Korean (42)	53	0.32
Laotian (1)	3	0.02
Pakistani (10)	10	0.06
Sri Lankan (12)	12	0.07
Taiwanese (0)	1	0.01
Thai (5)	7	0.04
Vietnamese (83)	99	0.60
Hawaii Native/Pacific Islander (25)	38	0.23
Not Hispanic (21)	31	0.19
Hispanic (4)	7	0.04
Guamanian/Chamorro (23)	26	0.16
Native Hawaiian (2)	8	0.05
White (13,464)	13,857	84.29
Not Hispanic (12,825)	13,149	79.98
Hispanic (639)	708	4.31

Pine

Place Type: Township
County: Allegheny
Population: 11,497†

Ancestry‡	Population	%
African, Sub-Saharan (8)	8	0.07
South African (8)	8	0.07
American (443)	443	4.12
Arab (62)	161	1.50
Lebanese (54)	139	1.29
Syrian (8)	22	0.20
Austrian (0)	11	0.10
Belgian (48)	48	0.45
British (25)	36	0.34
Bulgarian (88)	88	0.82
Croatian (39)	229	2.13
Czech (11)	89	0.83
Danish (15)	15	0.14
Dutch (39)	181	1.69
Eastern European (0)	12	0.11
English (66)	927	8.63
European (265)	265	2.47
French, ex. Basque (39)	223	2.08
French Canadian (0)	11	0.10
German (883)	3,698	34.43
Greek (45)	166	1.55
Hungarian (74)	312	2.90
Iranian (8)	8	0.07
Irish (560)	2,582	24.04

SECTION TWO

*Notes: † The Census 2010 population figure is used to calculate the percentages in the Hispanic Origin and Race categories. Ancestry percentages are based on the 2006-2010 American Community Survey population (not shown); ‡ Numbers in parentheses indicate the number of people reporting a single ancestry; * Numbers in parentheses indicate the number of persons reporting this race alone, not in combination with any other race; Please refer to the Explanation of Data for more information.*

Ancestry	Population	%
Italian (460)	1,918	17.86
Lithuanian (0)	25	0.23
Northern European (10)	10	0.09
Norwegian (0)	91	0.85
Polish (125)	903	8.41
Russian (12)	177	1.65
Scotch-Irish (127)	330	3.07
Scottish (99)	294	2.74
Serbian (0)	12	0.11
Slovak (77)	343	3.19
Slovene (7)	68	0.63
Swedish (42)	108	1.01
Swiss (14)	90	0.84
Ukrainian (0)	70	0.65
Welsh (25)	120	1.12
Yugoslavian (0)	30	0.28

Hispanic Origin	Population	%
Hispanic or Latino (of any race)	220	1.91
Central American, ex. Mexican	23	0.20
Costa Rican	2	0.02
Guatemalan	16	0.14
Panamanian	2	0.02
Salvadoran	3	0.03
Cuban	16	0.14
Mexican	75	0.65
Puerto Rican	39	0.34
South American	47	0.41
Argentinean	4	0.03
Chilean	3	0.03
Colombian	24	0.21
Ecuadorian	1	0.01
Paraguayan	7	0.06
Peruvian	5	0.04
Venezuelan	3	0.03
Other Hispanic or Latino	20	0.17

Race*	Population	%
African-American/Black (143)	168	1.46
Not Hispanic (139)	164	1.43
Hispanic (4)	4	0.03
American Indian/Alaska Native (13)	49	0.43
Not Hispanic (8)	34	0.30
Hispanic (5)	15	0.13
Apache (1)	1	0.01
Central American Ind. (1)	2	0.02
Cherokee (2)	9	0.08
Iroquois (2)	2	0.02
Mexican American Ind. (3)	7	0.06
Potawatomi (1)	1	0.01
South American Ind. (0)	1	0.01
Asian (460)	523	4.55
Not Hispanic (460)	523	4.55
Chinese, ex. Taiwanese (74)	91	0.79
Filipino (17)	28	0.24
Indian (213)	227	1.97
Japanese (7)	18	0.16
Korean (90)	101	0.88
Nepalese (2)	2	0.02
Pakistani (29)	34	0.30
Sri Lankan (3)	3	0.03
Taiwanese (5)	5	0.04
Thai (6)	6	0.05
Vietnamese (7)	9	0.08
Hawaii Native/Pacific Islander (1)	1	0.01
Not Hispanic (1)	1	0.01
Samoan (1)	1	0.01
White (10,701)	10,823	94.14
Not Hispanic (10,532)	10,635	92.50
Hispanic (169)	188	1.64

Pittsburgh

Place Type: City
County: Allegheny
Population: 305,704†

Ancestry‡	Population	%
African, Sub-Saharan (4,056)	4,577	1.49
African (3,209)	3,558	1.16
Cape Verdean (6)	6	<0.01
Ethiopian (112)	112	0.04
Ghanaian (45)	45	0.01
Kenyan (14)	21	0.01
Liberian (71)	71	0.02
Nigerian (267)	391	0.13
Senegalese (35)	36	0.01
Sierra Leonean (55)	55	0.02
Somalian (57)	57	0.02
South African (0)	15	<0.01
Sudanese (38)	38	0.01
Zimbabwean (36)	36	0.01
Other Sub-Saharan African (111)	136	0.04
Albanian (11)	85	0.03
Alsatian (17)	91	0.03
American (7,699)	7,699	2.50
Arab (1,839)	2,859	0.93
Arab (388)	388	0.13
Egyptian (108)	152	0.05
Iraqi (91)	104	0.03
Lebanese (395)	934	0.30
Moroccan (197)	312	0.10
Palestinian (25)	25	0.01
Syrian (275)	499	0.16
Other Arab (360)	445	0.14
Armenian (31)	77	0.02
Australian (38)	38	0.01
Austrian (218)	1,622	0.53
Belgian (19)	171	0.06
Brazilian (69)	106	0.03
British (546)	1,143	0.37
Bulgarian (113)	127	0.04
Cajun (24)	77	0.02
Canadian (201)	308	0.10
Carpatho Rusyn (20)	116	0.04
Celtic (14)	38	0.01
Croatian (771)	2,304	0.75
Cypriot (102)	102	0.03
Czech (297)	1,676	0.54
Czechoslovakian (325)	773	0.25
Danish (26)	299	0.10
Dutch (519)	2,016	0.65
Eastern European (1,035)	1,195	0.39
English (3,539)	16,692	5.42
Estonian (0)	13	<0.01
European (2,043)	2,300	0.75
Finnish (32)	181	0.06
French, ex. Basque (452)	4,106	1.33
French Canadian (278)	499	0.16
German (16,287)	66,031	21.44
Greek (979)	2,108	0.68
Guyanese (8)	57	0.02
Hungarian (1,381)	4,477	1.45
Iranian (116)	187	0.06
Irish (12,283)	51,563	16.74
Israeli (109)	210	0.07
Italian (16,620)	41,352	13.43
Latvian (68)	138	0.04
Lithuanian (729)	2,260	0.73
Luxemburger (0)	22	0.01
Macedonian (30)	44	0.01
Maltese (11)	11	<0.01
New Zealander (21)	21	0.01
Northern European (192)	192	0.06
Norwegian (150)	682	0.22
Pennsylvania German (133)	385	0.12
Polish (7,981)	24,743	8.03
Portuguese (93)	276	0.09
Romanian (155)	559	0.18
Russian (2,580)	6,191	2.01
Scandinavian (213)	337	0.11
Scotch-Irish (1,600)	5,558	1.80
Scottish (936)	4,798	1.56
Serbian (361)	993	0.32
Slavic (180)	428	0.14
Slovak (2,134)	5,935	1.93
Slovene (144)	739	0.24
Swedish (316)	2,007	0.65
Swiss (156)	838	0.27
Turkish (422)	485	0.16
Ukrainian (1,046)	2,972	0.96
Welsh (290)	2,729	0.89
West Indian, ex. Hispanic (925)	1,313	0.43
Bahamian (29)	44	0.01
Barbadian (22)	77	0.02
Belizean (10)	10	<0.01
Bermudan (14)	37	0.01
British West Indian (9)	9	<0.01
Haitian (252)	285	0.09
Jamaican (336)	480	0.16
Trinidadian/Tobagonian (123)	123	0.04
West Indian (130)	248	0.08
Yugoslavian (86)	141	0.05

Hispanic Origin	Population	%
Hispanic or Latino (of any race)	6,964	2.28
Central American, ex. Mexican	500	0.16
Costa Rican	47	0.02
Guatemalan	186	0.06
Honduran	56	0.02
Nicaraguan	36	0.01
Panamanian	81	0.03
Salvadoran	93	0.03
Other Central American	1	<0.01
Cuban	397	0.13
Dominican Republic	157	0.05
Mexican	2,292	0.75
Puerto Rican	1,336	0.44
South American	1,162	0.38
Argentinean	244	0.08
Bolivian	29	0.01
Chilean	139	0.05
Colombian	263	0.09
Ecuadorian	75	0.02
Paraguayan	20	0.01
Peruvian	211	0.07
Uruguayan	23	0.01
Venezuelan	142	0.05
Other South American	16	0.01
Other Hispanic or Latino	1,120	0.37

Race*	Population	%
African-American/Black (79,710)	84,819	27.75
Not Hispanic (78,847)	83,539	27.33
Hispanic (863)	1,280	0.42
American Indian/Alaska Native (584)	2,540	0.83
Not Hispanic (505)	2,253	0.74
Hispanic (79)	287	0.09
Alaska Athabascan *(Ala. Nat.)* (2)	5	<0.01
Aleut *(Alaska Native)* (1)	1	<0.01
Apache (8)	36	0.01
Blackfeet (6)	199	0.07
Canadian/French Am. Ind. (5)	15	<0.01
Central American Ind. (3)	10	<0.01
Cherokee (72)	533	0.17
Cheyenne (5)	11	<0.01
Chickasaw (2)	13	<0.01
Chippewa (12)	30	0.01
Choctaw (3)	22	0.01
Comanche (0)	2	<0.01
Cree (1)	6	<0.01
Creek (7)	20	0.01
Crow (0)	8	<0.01
Delaware (3)	13	<0.01
Hopi (0)	4	<0.01
Inupiat *(Alaska Native)* (1)	2	<0.01
Iroquois (10)	50	0.02
Kiowa (3)	4	<0.01
Lumbee (5)	12	<0.01
Mexican American Ind. (19)	36	0.01
Navajo (1)	16	0.01
Osage (0)	3	<0.01
Potawatomi (0)	2	<0.01
Pueblo (0)	8	<0.01
Seminole (8)	31	0.01
Shoshone (0)	1	<0.01
Sioux (18)	70	0.02
South American Ind. (9)	26	0.01
Spanish American Ind. (6)	7	<0.01
Tlingit-Haida *(Alaska Native)* (1)	3	<0.01

*Notes: † The Census 2010 population figure is used to calculate the percentages in the Hispanic Origin and Race categories. Ancestry percentages are based on the 2006-2010 American Community Survey population (not shown); ‡ Numbers in parentheses indicate the number of people reporting a single ancestry; * Numbers in parentheses indicate the number of persons reporting this race alone, not in combination with any other race; Please refer to the Explanation of Data for more information.*

Tsimshian *(Alaska Native)* (1)	1	<0.01
Ute (1)	1	<0.01
Yaqui (0)	1	<0.01
Asian (13,465)	15,412	5.04
Not Hispanic (13,393)	15,233	4.98
Hispanic (72)	179	0.06
Bangladeshi (47)	57	0.02
Bhutanese (53)	56	0.02
Burmese (141)	145	0.05
Cambodian (36)	48	0.02
Chinese, ex. Taiwanese (4,405)	4,872	1.59
Filipino (505)	807	0.26
Hmong (3)	3	<0.01
Indian (3,657)	4,025	1.32
Indonesian (54)	72	0.02
Japanese (641)	938	0.31
Korean (1,768)	2,002	0.65
Laotian (9)	17	0.01
Malaysian (49)	69	0.02
Nepalese (95)	111	0.04
Pakistani (187)	217	0.07
Sri Lankan (37)	46	0.02
Taiwanese (416)	461	0.15
Thai (207)	245	0.08
Vietnamese (693)	826	0.27
Hawaii Native/Pacific Islander (86)	286	0.09
Not Hispanic (76)	236	0.08
Hispanic (10)	50	0.02
Fijian (0)	4	<0.01
Guamanian/Chamorro (14)	29	0.01
Native Hawaiian (31)	74	0.02
Samoan (26)	72	0.02
Tongan (6)	7	<0.01
White (201,766)	208,065	68.06
Not Hispanic (198,186)	203,879	66.69
Hispanic (3,580)	4,186	1.37

Pittston

Place Type: City
County: Luzerne
Population: 7,739†

Ancestry‡	Population	%
African, Sub-Saharan (0)	10	0.13
African (0)	10	0.13
American (211)	211	2.71
Arab (0)	71	0.91
Lebanese (0)	71	0.91
Austrian (0)	41	0.53
Carpatho Rusyn (4)	4	0.05
Croatian (7)	15	0.19
Czech (1)	9	0.12
Czechoslovakian (9)	9	0.12
Dutch (0)	77	0.99
English (108)	452	5.81
European (42)	42	0.54
French, ex. Basque (0)	79	1.02
French Canadian (0)	31	0.40
German (281)	1,163	14.96
Hungarian (0)	22	0.28
Irish (837)	2,324	29.89
Italian (1,303)	2,595	33.38
Lithuanian (110)	277	3.56
Norwegian (0)	73	0.94
Pennsylvania German (22)	32	0.41
Polish (456)	1,629	20.95
Russian (24)	231	2.97
Scandinavian (6)	6	0.08
Scotch-Irish (27)	72	0.93
Scottish (74)	83	1.07
Slovak (89)	232	2.98
Swiss (0)	22	0.28
Ukrainian (22)	58	0.75
Welsh (41)	282	3.63

Hispanic Origin	Population	%
Hispanic or Latino (of any race)	209	2.70
Central American, ex. Mexican	21	0.27
Costa Rican	1	0.01
Guatemalan	1	0.01
Honduran	6	0.08
Nicaraguan	3	0.04
Salvadoran	10	0.13
Dominican Republic	20	0.26
Mexican	24	0.31
Puerto Rican	104	1.34
South American	16	0.21
Colombian	8	0.10
Ecuadorian	1	0.01
Peruvian	7	0.09
Other Hispanic or Latino	24	0.31

Race*	Population	%
African-American/Black (147)	225	2.91
Not Hispanic (115)	179	2.31
Hispanic (32)	46	0.59
American Indian/Alaska Native (14)	35	0.45
Not Hispanic (4)	23	0.30
Hispanic (10)	12	0.16
Central American Ind. (2)	2	0.03
Cherokee (0)	3	0.04
Mexican American Ind. (3)	4	0.05
Seminole (0)	1	0.01
Sioux (1)	1	0.01
South American Ind. (4)	5	0.06
Asian (42)	71	0.92
Not Hispanic (42)	70	0.90
Hispanic (0)	1	0.01
Cambodian (1)	1	0.01
Chinese, ex. Taiwanese (6)	10	0.13
Filipino (3)	8	0.10
Indian (16)	22	0.28
Japanese (0)	1	0.01
Korean (7)	9	0.12
Laotian (3)	6	0.08
Taiwanese (1)	1	0.01
Thai (0)	2	0.03
Vietnamese (1)	1	0.01
Hawaii Native/Pacific Islander (1)	12	0.16
Not Hispanic (1)	11	0.14
Hispanic (0)	1	0.01
Guamanian/Chamorro (0)	1	0.01
Native Hawaiian (0)	4	0.05
White (7,349)	7,463	96.43
Not Hispanic (7,252)	7,349	94.96
Hispanic (97)	114	1.47

Plains

Place Type: Township
County: Luzerne
Population: 9,961†

Ancestry‡	Population	%
American (102)	102	1.01
Arab (85)	160	1.59
Jordanian (37)	37	0.37
Lebanese (33)	82	0.81
Syrian (15)	41	0.41
Austrian (23)	53	0.53
Carpatho Rusyn (49)	49	0.49
Czech (10)	40	0.40
Czechoslovakian (12)	15	0.15
Dutch (11)	117	1.16
Eastern European (25)	25	0.25
English (319)	1,000	9.93
European (9)	9	0.09
French, ex. Basque (0)	144	1.43
French Canadian (0)	15	0.15
German (202)	1,590	15.80
German Russian (0)	26	0.26
Hungarian (23)	121	1.20
Irish (563)	1,975	19.62
Italian (1,003)	1,957	19.44
Lithuanian (104)	271	2.69
Pennsylvania German (0)	69	0.69
Polish (1,513)	3,066	30.46
Romanian (0)	10	0.10
Russian (195)	623	6.19
Scotch-Irish (0)	32	0.32
Scottish (19)	67	0.67
Slavic (0)	14	0.14
Slovak (193)	772	7.67
Slovene (0)	18	0.18
Swedish (0)	33	0.33
Swiss (0)	17	0.17
Turkish (45)	45	0.45
Ukrainian (39)	134	1.33
Welsh (97)	466	4.63
West Indian, ex. Hispanic (9)	9	0.09
Jamaican (9)	9	0.09
Yugoslavian (7)	29	0.29

Hispanic Origin	Population	%
Hispanic or Latino (of any race)	144	1.45
Central American, ex. Mexican	7	0.07
Costa Rican	2	0.02
Honduran	2	0.02
Nicaraguan	1	0.01
Salvadoran	2	0.02
Cuban	2	0.02
Mexican	56	0.56
Puerto Rican	53	0.53
South American	19	0.19
Bolivian	1	0.01
Colombian	6	0.06
Ecuadorian	5	0.05
Peruvian	5	0.05
Venezuelan	2	0.02
Other Hispanic or Latino	7	0.07

Race*	Population	%
African-American/Black (127)	161	1.62
Not Hispanic (124)	156	1.57
Hispanic (3)	5	0.05
American Indian/Alaska Native (10)	27	0.27
Not Hispanic (10)	25	0.25
Hispanic (0)	2	0.02
Alaska Athabascan *(Ala. Nat.)* (0)	1	0.01
Blackfeet (0)	4	0.04
Cherokee (1)	2	0.02
Navajo (1)	2	0.02
South American Ind. (0)	1	0.01
Asian (137)	167	1.68
Not Hispanic (135)	162	1.63
Hispanic (2)	5	0.05
Bangladeshi (9)	10	0.10
Cambodian (1)	1	0.01
Chinese, ex. Taiwanese (15)	17	0.17
Filipino (27)	30	0.30
Indian (51)	55	0.55
Indonesian (1)	4	0.04
Japanese (4)	7	0.07
Korean (10)	13	0.13
Pakistani (1)	3	0.03
Thai (0)	9	0.09
Vietnamese (6)	7	0.07
Hawaii Native/Pacific Islander (0)	1	0.01
Not Hispanic (0)	1	0.01
White (9,548)	9,622	96.60
Not Hispanic (9,467)	9,528	95.65
Hispanic (81)	94	0.94

Pleasant Hills

Place Type: Borough
County: Allegheny
Population: 8,268†

Ancestry‡	Population	%
African, Sub-Saharan (22)	22	0.27
African (5)	5	0.06
Kenyan (17)	17	0.21
American (243)	243	2.94
Australian (0)	20	0.24
Austrian (28)	68	0.82
British (20)	30	0.36
Canadian (28)	38	0.46
Carpatho Rusyn (10)	10	0.12

*Notes: † The Census 2010 population figure is used to calculate the percentages in the Hispanic Origin and Race categories. Ancestry percentages are based on the 2006-2010 American Community Survey population (not shown); ‡ Numbers in parentheses indicate the number of people reporting a single ancestry; * Numbers in parentheses indicate the number of persons reporting this race alone, not in combination with any other race; Please refer to the Explanation of Data for more information.*

Croatian (42)	185	2.24
Czech (46)	127	1.54
Czechoslovakian (53)	76	0.92
Danish (9)	9	0.11
Dutch (18)	92	1.11
English (262)	1,084	13.13
European (29)	29	0.35
Finnish (0)	12	0.15
French, ex. Basque (15)	176	2.13
French Canadian (0)	50	0.61
German (729)	2,680	32.45
Greek (0)	13	0.16
Hungarian (58)	289	3.50
Icelander (0)	12	0.15
Irish (423)	1,935	23.43
Italian (559)	1,237	14.98
Lithuanian (26)	81	0.98
Polish (337)	884	10.70
Romanian (18)	46	0.56
Russian (30)	107	1.30
Scotch-Irish (113)	319	3.86
Scottish (38)	222	2.69
Serbian (81)	109	1.32
Slavic (0)	42	0.51
Slovak (142)	643	7.79
Slovene (13)	41	0.50
Swedish (0)	29	0.35
Swiss (9)	55	0.67
Ukrainian (35)	120	1.45
Welsh (20)	69	0.84
Yugoslavian (32)	50	0.61

Hispanic Origin	Population	%
Hispanic or Latino (of any race)	86	1.04
Central American, ex. Mexican	9	0.11
Guatemalan	3	0.04
Honduran	2	0.02
Panamanian	4	0.05
Cuban	2	0.02
Dominican Republic	2	0.02
Mexican	38	0.46
Puerto Rican	12	0.15
South American	14	0.17
Argentinean	1	0.01
Colombian	5	0.06
Ecuadorian	1	0.01
Peruvian	2	0.02
Venezuelan	5	0.06
Other Hispanic or Latino	9	0.11

Race*	Population	%
African-American/Black (226)	269	3.25
Not Hispanic (221)	261	3.16
Hispanic (5)	8	0.10
American Indian/Alaska Native (3)	20	0.24
Not Hispanic (2)	18	0.22
Hispanic (1)	2	0.02
Cherokee (0)	2	0.02
Choctaw (2)	2	0.02
Iroquois (0)	4	0.05
Sioux (0)	2	0.02
Asian (108)	123	1.49
Not Hispanic (108)	123	1.49
Chinese, ex. Taiwanese (14)	14	0.17
Filipino (8)	13	0.16
Indian (38)	39	0.47
Japanese (5)	5	0.06
Korean (4)	7	0.08
Malaysian (0)	4	0.05
Pakistani (6)	7	0.08
Vietnamese (24)	24	0.29
Hawaii Native/Pacific Islander (2)	5	0.06
Not Hispanic (1)	4	0.05
Hispanic (1)	1	0.01
White (7,837)	7,902	95.57
Not Hispanic (7,781)	7,840	94.82
Hispanic (56)	62	0.75

Plum

Place Type: Borough
County: Allegheny
Population: 27,126†

Ancestry‡	Population	%
African, Sub-Saharan (34)	53	0.20
African (34)	53	0.20
American (931)	931	3.47
Arab (73)	149	0.55
Lebanese (19)	52	0.19
Syrian (54)	97	0.36
Austrian (110)	202	0.75
British (68)	92	0.34
Croatian (67)	259	0.96
Czech (38)	252	0.94
Czechoslovakian (54)	87	0.32
Dutch (65)	355	1.32
Eastern European (55)	55	0.20
English (594)	2,679	9.98
European (101)	136	0.51
Finnish (16)	16	0.06
French, ex. Basque (34)	647	2.41
French Canadian (17)	98	0.37
German (1,668)	8,625	32.12
Greek (123)	270	1.01
Hungarian (91)	558	2.08
Irish (968)	5,868	21.86
Italian (2,508)	6,645	24.75
Lithuanian (26)	119	0.44
Northern European (18)	18	0.07
Norwegian (0)	15	0.06
Pennsylvania German (0)	30	0.11
Polish (567)	2,419	9.01
Portuguese (0)	11	0.04
Romanian (21)	21	0.08
Russian (137)	556	2.07
Scandinavian (13)	13	0.05
Scotch-Irish (169)	662	2.47
Scottish (105)	822	3.06
Serbian (0)	132	0.49
Slavic (16)	71	0.26
Slovak (303)	1,214	4.52
Slovene (51)	104	0.39
Swedish (83)	394	1.47
Swiss (27)	152	0.57
Ukrainian (102)	247	0.92
Welsh (15)	381	1.42
West Indian, ex. Hispanic (10)	22	0.08
Jamaican (0)	12	0.04
Trinidadian/Tobagonian (10)	10	0.04
Yugoslavian (0)	37	0.14

Hispanic Origin	Population	%
Hispanic or Latino (of any race)	244	0.90
Central American, ex. Mexican	17	0.06
Guatemalan	9	0.03
Honduran	3	0.01
Nicaraguan	5	0.02
Cuban	17	0.06
Dominican Republic	10	0.04
Mexican	96	0.35
Puerto Rican	35	0.13
South American	43	0.16
Argentinean	6	0.02
Bolivian	6	0.02
Chilean	3	0.01
Colombian	7	0.03
Peruvian	2	0.01
Uruguayan	8	0.03
Venezuelan	11	0.04
Other Hispanic or Latino	26	0.10

Race*	Population	%
African-American/Black (966)	1,128	4.16
Not Hispanic (957)	1,107	4.08
Hispanic (9)	21	0.08
American Indian/Alaska Native (22)	88	0.32
Not Hispanic (19)	85	0.31
Hispanic (3)	3	0.01
Apache (0)	1	<0.01
Blackfeet (0)	7	0.03
Cherokee (4)	24	0.09
Cheyenne (0)	2	0.01
Chickasaw (0)	1	<0.01
Creek (0)	1	<0.01
Houma (1)	1	<0.01
Iroquois (0)	1	<0.01
Lumbee (0)	1	<0.01
Mexican American Ind. (1)	2	0.01
Potawatomi (0)	2	0.01
Seminole (0)	1	<0.01
Sioux (0)	1	<0.01
South American Ind. (2)	2	0.01
Ute (1)	1	<0.01
Asian (309)	387	1.43
Not Hispanic (307)	378	1.39
Hispanic (2)	9	0.03
Bangladeshi (1)	3	0.01
Chinese, ex. Taiwanese (42)	52	0.19
Filipino (23)	33	0.12
Indian (171)	182	0.67
Indonesian (0)	2	0.01
Japanese (2)	20	0.07
Korean (9)	19	0.07
Pakistani (36)	40	0.15
Taiwanese (1)	6	0.02
Thai (3)	7	0.03
Vietnamese (13)	17	0.06
Hawaii Native/Pacific Islander (2)	14	0.05
Not Hispanic (2)	14	0.05
Guamanian/Chamorro (0)	1	<0.01
Native Hawaiian (2)	4	0.01
White (25,480)	25,724	94.83
Not Hispanic (25,304)	25,527	94.11
Hispanic (176)	197	0.73

Plumstead

Place Type: Township
County: Bucks
Population: 12,442†

Ancestry‡	Population	%
African, Sub-Saharan (16)	33	0.27
Kenyan (16)	33	0.27
American (786)	786	6.41
Arab (0)	25	0.20
Syrian (0)	25	0.20
Australian (28)	42	0.34
Austrian (0)	26	0.21
Belgian (16)	33	0.27
Brazilian (12)	12	0.10
British (43)	86	0.70
Canadian (39)	48	0.39
Croatian (0)	9	0.07
Czech (0)	97	0.79
Czechoslovakian (39)	39	0.32
Danish (17)	17	0.14
Dutch (43)	133	1.08
English (236)	1,183	9.65
European (123)	123	1.00
French, ex. Basque (18)	252	2.05
French Canadian (22)	74	0.60
German (1,162)	4,209	34.32
Greek (71)	150	1.22
Hungarian (49)	92	0.75
Irish (549)	3,009	24.53
Italian (805)	2,130	17.37
Latvian (0)	49	0.40
Lithuanian (101)	288	2.35
Norwegian (0)	46	0.38
Pennsylvania German (35)	35	0.29
Polish (124)	833	6.79
Portuguese (0)	18	0.15
Romanian (0)	6	0.05
Russian (38)	220	1.79
Scotch-Irish (75)	295	2.41
Scottish (26)	169	1.38

*Notes: † The Census 2010 population figure is used to calculate the percentages in the Hispanic Origin and Race categories. Ancestry percentages are based on the 2006-2010 American Community Survey population (not shown); ‡ Numbers in parentheses indicate the number of people reporting a single ancestry; * Numbers in parentheses indicate the number of persons reporting this race alone, not in combination with any other race; Please refer to the Explanation of Data for more information.*

Slavic (10)	10	0.08
Slovak (81)	167	1.36
Swedish (40)	136	1.11
Swiss (0)	71	0.58
Ukrainian (76)	153	1.25
Welsh (10)	171	1.39

Hispanic Origin	Population	%
Hispanic or Latino (of any race)	584	4.69
Central American, ex. Mexican	94	0.76
Costa Rican	5	0.04
Guatemalan	56	0.45
Honduran	14	0.11
Nicaraguan	7	0.06
Salvadoran	12	0.10
Cuban	19	0.15
Dominican Republic	11	0.09
Mexican	225	1.81
Puerto Rican	94	0.76
South American	54	0.43
Argentinean	5	0.04
Bolivian	2	0.02
Chilean	4	0.03
Colombian	14	0.11
Ecuadorian	9	0.07
Peruvian	19	0.15
Other South American	1	0.01
Other Hispanic or Latino	87	0.70

Race*	Population	%
African-American/Black (84)	142	1.14
Not Hispanic (82)	135	1.09
Hispanic (2)	7	0.06
American Indian/Alaska Native (16)	57	0.46
Not Hispanic (10)	44	0.35
Hispanic (6)	13	0.10
Blackfeet (0)	4	0.03
Canadian/French Am. Ind. (0)	2	0.02
Cherokee (3)	8	0.06
Delaware (1)	1	0.01
Iroquois (0)	5	0.04
Kiowa (3)	3	0.02
Sioux (0)	3	0.02
Yaqui (0)	2	0.02
Asian (213)	269	2.16
Not Hispanic (212)	264	2.12
Hispanic (1)	5	0.04
Chinese, ex. Taiwanese (67)	68	0.55
Filipino (13)	39	0.31
Indian (61)	65	0.52
Indonesian (1)	1	0.01
Japanese (3)	7	0.06
Korean (34)	44	0.35
Sri Lankan (0)	1	0.01
Vietnamese (25)	32	0.26
Hawaii Native/Pacific Islander (2)	7	0.06
Not Hispanic (2)	7	0.06
Guamanian/Chamorro (1)	1	0.01
Native Hawaiian (0)	3	0.02
White (11,703)	11,869	95.39
Not Hispanic (11,407)	11,535	92.71
Hispanic (296)	334	2.68

Plymouth

Place Type: Township
County: Montgomery
Population: 16,525†

Ancestry‡	Population	%
African, Sub-Saharan (44)	59	0.36
African (44)	59	0.36
American (234)	234	1.42
Arab (50)	63	0.38
Arab (19)	19	0.12
Egyptian (18)	18	0.11
Lebanese (13)	26	0.16
Armenian (35)	35	0.21
Assyrian/Chaldean/Syriac (0)	8	0.05
Austrian (11)	72	0.44
Brazilian (31)	31	0.19
British (16)	16	0.10
Canadian (0)	8	0.05
Croatian (13)	13	0.08
Czech (22)	204	1.24
Czechoslovakian (8)	48	0.29
Danish (10)	64	0.39
Dutch (27)	244	1.49
Eastern European (77)	77	0.47
English (323)	1,330	8.10
European (82)	97	0.59
French, ex. Basque (54)	418	2.55
French Canadian (24)	39	0.24
German (877)	3,754	22.86
Greek (51)	95	0.58
Hungarian (27)	127	0.77
Iranian (7)	7	0.04
Irish (1,407)	4,410	26.85
Italian (2,204)	4,028	24.53
Latvian (8)	8	0.05
Lithuanian (40)	133	0.81
Luxemburger (16)	32	0.19
Norwegian (0)	13	0.08
Pennsylvania German (37)	103	0.63
Polish (467)	1,433	8.73
Portuguese (12)	32	0.19
Romanian (6)	55	0.33
Russian (236)	525	3.20
Scandinavian (14)	14	0.09
Scotch-Irish (22)	121	0.74
Scottish (54)	214	1.30
Slovak (71)	180	1.10
Slovene (8)	8	0.05
Swedish (70)	247	1.50
Swiss (15)	44	0.27
Ukrainian (22)	71	0.43
Welsh (7)	205	1.25
West Indian, ex. Hispanic (29)	29	0.18
Barbadian (11)	11	0.07
Haitian (18)	18	0.11

Hispanic Origin	Population	%
Hispanic or Latino (of any race)	429	2.60
Central American, ex. Mexican	25	0.15
Costa Rican	6	0.04
Guatemalan	6	0.04
Honduran	6	0.04
Panamanian	3	0.02
Salvadoran	4	0.02
Cuban	23	0.14
Dominican Republic	12	0.07
Mexican	151	0.91
Puerto Rican	146	0.88
South American	41	0.25
Argentinean	3	0.02
Colombian	17	0.10
Ecuadorian	5	0.03
Peruvian	6	0.04
Uruguayan	2	0.01
Venezuelan	7	0.04
Other South American	1	0.01
Other Hispanic or Latino	31	0.19

Race*	Population	%
African-American/Black (1,158)	1,284	7.77
Not Hispanic (1,143)	1,247	7.55
Hispanic (15)	37	0.22
American Indian/Alaska Native (23)	91	0.55
Not Hispanic (16)	74	0.45
Hispanic (7)	17	0.10
Blackfeet (0)	3	0.02
Canadian/French Am. Ind. (0)	2	0.01
Cherokee (0)	17	0.10
Choctaw (0)	3	0.02
Comanche (0)	1	0.01
Delaware (0)	6	0.04
Osage (0)	1	0.01
South American Ind. (0)	3	0.02
Asian (1,188)	1,297	7.85
Not Hispanic (1,180)	1,279	7.74
Hispanic (8)	18	0.11
Cambodian (0)	2	0.01
Chinese, ex. Taiwanese (174)	206	1.25
Filipino (70)	90	0.54
Indian (417)	455	2.75
Indonesian (4)	4	0.02
Japanese (21)	29	0.18
Korean (363)	384	2.32
Laotian (8)	10	0.06
Malaysian (1)	1	0.01
Nepalese (4)	8	0.05
Pakistani (26)	28	0.17
Sri Lankan (2)	2	0.01
Taiwanese (6)	11	0.07
Thai (9)	14	0.08
Vietnamese (46)	56	0.34
Hawaii Native/Pacific Islander (2)	12	0.07
Not Hispanic (2)	12	0.07
Guamanian/Chamorro (0)	1	0.01
Tongan (2)	3	0.02
White (13,734)	13,961	84.48
Not Hispanic (13,497)	13,693	82.86
Hispanic (237)	268	1.62

Pocono

Place Type: Township
County: Monroe
Population: 11,065†

Ancestry‡	Population	%
African, Sub-Saharan (61)	61	0.55
African (61)	61	0.55
Albanian (0)	12	0.11
American (185)	185	1.67
Arab (18)	18	0.16
Egyptian (18)	18	0.16
Austrian (0)	45	0.41
British (0)	12	0.11
Canadian (18)	18	0.16
Czech (0)	16	0.14
Danish (19)	19	0.17
Dutch (172)	364	3.29
English (362)	933	8.43
European (20)	20	0.18
Finnish (36)	36	0.33
French, ex. Basque (38)	195	1.76
French Canadian (21)	21	0.19
German (1,091)	2,667	24.10
Greek (42)	60	0.54
Guyanese (21)	21	0.19
Hungarian (24)	91	0.82
Irish (730)	2,152	19.44
Italian (1,407)	2,347	21.21
Lithuanian (16)	71	0.64
Maltese (15)	31	0.28
Norwegian (0)	64	0.58
Pennsylvania German (35)	79	0.71
Polish (485)	941	8.50
Romanian (90)	148	1.34
Russian (0)	216	1.95
Scotch-Irish (70)	124	1.12
Scottish (69)	93	0.84
Slavic (30)	30	0.27
Slovak (35)	83	0.75
Swedish (126)	186	1.68
Swiss (13)	13	0.12
Ukrainian (0)	14	0.13
Welsh (37)	125	1.13
West Indian, ex. Hispanic (179)	179	1.62
Jamaican (38)	38	0.34
West Indian (141)	141	1.27

Hispanic Origin	Population	%
Hispanic or Latino (of any race)	1,264	11.42
Central American, ex. Mexican	51	0.46
Guatemalan	7	0.06
Honduran	8	0.07
Nicaraguan	1	0.01
Panamanian	24	0.22

*Notes: † The Census 2010 population figure is used to calculate the percentages in the Hispanic Origin and Race categories. Ancestry percentages are based on the 2006-2010 American Community Survey population (not shown); ‡ Numbers in parentheses indicate the number of people reporting a single ancestry; * Numbers in parentheses indicate the number of persons reporting this race alone, not in combination with any other race; Please refer to the Explanation of Data for more information.*

Salvadoran	11	0.10
Cuban	44	0.40
Dominican Republic	171	1.55
Mexican	60	0.54
Puerto Rican	668	6.04
South American	161	1.46
Argentinean	10	0.09
Bolivian	3	0.03
Chilean	4	0.04
Colombian	58	0.52
Ecuadorian	52	0.47
Paraguayan	2	0.02
Peruvian	26	0.23
Uruguayan	2	0.02
Venezuelan	4	0.04
Other Hispanic or Latino	109	0.99

Race*	Population	%
African-American/Black (1,243)	1,402	12.67
Not Hispanic (1,143)	1,252	11.31
Hispanic (100)	150	1.36
American Indian/Alaska Native (16)	104	0.94
Not Hispanic (14)	96	0.87
Hispanic (2)	8	0.07
Apache (0)	1	0.01
Blackfeet (2)	4	0.04
Central American Ind. (0)	1	0.01
Cherokee (2)	24	0.22
Chickasaw (0)	1	0.01
Choctaw (0)	3	0.03
Delaware (0)	2	0.02
Iroquois (0)	8	0.07
Lumbee (0)	1	0.01
Mexican American Ind. (1)	2	0.02
Seminole (0)	1	0.01
Sioux (0)	1	0.01
South American Ind. (1)	1	0.01
Asian (268)	357	3.23
Not Hispanic (266)	344	3.11
Hispanic (2)	13	0.12
Cambodian (2)	2	0.02
Chinese, ex. Taiwanese (59)	89	0.80
Filipino (37)	52	0.47
Indian (88)	117	1.06
Japanese (5)	16	0.14
Korean (30)	39	0.35
Malaysian (1)	1	0.01
Pakistani (1)	1	0.01
Sri Lankan (4)	4	0.04
Taiwanese (1)	1	0.01
Thai (6)	8	0.07
Vietnamese (17)	17	0.15
Hawaii Native/Pacific Islander (14)	19	0.17
Not Hispanic (10)	14	0.13
Hispanic (4)	5	0.05
Native Hawaiian (3)	5	0.05
Samoan (11)	11	0.10
White (8,727)	8,975	81.11
Not Hispanic (8,115)	8,301	75.02
Hispanic (612)	674	6.09

Polk

Place Type: Township
County: Monroe
Population: 7,874†

Ancestry‡	Population	%
American (471)	471	6.03
Austrian (23)	64	0.82
Bulgarian (13)	13	0.17
Czechoslovakian (0)	15	0.19
Danish (18)	18	0.23
Dutch (66)	177	2.27
Eastern European (223)	223	2.86
English (113)	484	6.20
European (43)	43	0.55
Finnish (0)	18	0.23
French, ex. Basque (0)	122	1.56
German (638)	1,835	23.50
Hungarian (41)	250	3.20
Irish (570)	1,604	20.54
Italian (597)	1,285	16.45
Lithuanian (0)	13	0.17
Norwegian (0)	111	1.42
Pennsylvania German (347)	376	4.81
Polish (96)	324	4.15
Russian (34)	165	2.11
Scotch-Irish (123)	218	2.79
Scottish (12)	128	1.64
Slovak (78)	160	2.05
Swedish (11)	90	1.15
Ukrainian (97)	115	1.47
Welsh (94)	190	2.43
West Indian, ex. Hispanic (294)	294	3.76
U.S. Virgin Islander (225)	225	2.88
West Indian (69)	69	0.88
Yugoslavian (0)	39	0.50

Hispanic Origin	Population	%
Hispanic or Latino (of any race)	561	7.12
Central American, ex. Mexican	26	0.33
Costa Rican	1	0.01
Guatemalan	10	0.13
Honduran	6	0.08
Nicaraguan	1	0.01
Panamanian	6	0.08
Salvadoran	2	0.03
Cuban	37	0.47
Dominican Republic	25	0.32
Mexican	34	0.43
Puerto Rican	365	4.64
South American	47	0.60
Argentinean	3	0.04
Colombian	13	0.17
Ecuadorian	11	0.14
Paraguayan	1	0.01
Peruvian	6	0.08
Uruguayan	9	0.11
Other South American	4	0.05
Other Hispanic or Latino	27	0.34

Race*	Population	%
African-American/Black (326)	377	4.79
Not Hispanic (312)	351	4.46
Hispanic (14)	26	0.33
American Indian/Alaska Native (13)	58	0.74
Not Hispanic (13)	56	0.71
Hispanic (0)	2	0.03
Apache (0)	7	0.09
Blackfeet (0)	1	0.01
Central American Ind. (2)	2	0.03
Cherokee (2)	8	0.10
Choctaw (0)	3	0.04
Delaware (1)	3	0.04
Iroquois (0)	5	0.06
Mexican American Ind. (0)	1	0.01
Seminole (1)	1	0.01
Asian (55)	84	1.07
Not Hispanic (54)	80	1.02
Hispanic (1)	4	0.05
Chinese, ex. Taiwanese (13)	24	0.30
Filipino (6)	8	0.10
Indian (15)	26	0.33
Japanese (1)	3	0.04
Korean (7)	9	0.11
Malaysian (0)	1	0.01
Pakistani (2)	6	0.08
Vietnamese (7)	7	0.09
Hawaii Native/Pacific Islander (5)	10	0.13
Not Hispanic (4)	9	0.11
Hispanic (1)	1	0.01
Guamanian/Chamorro (4)	8	0.10
White (7,190)	7,314	92.89
Not Hispanic (6,815)	6,912	87.78
Hispanic (375)	402	5.11

Pottstown

Place Type: Borough
County: Montgomery
Population: 22,377†

Ancestry‡	Population	%
African, Sub-Saharan (97)	97	0.43
African (97)	97	0.43
Albanian (0)	9	0.04
American (905)	905	4.06
Arab (9)	9	0.04
Egyptian (9)	9	0.04
Austrian (0)	57	0.26
Belgian (0)	5	0.02
British (0)	7	0.03
Canadian (9)	18	0.08
Czech (13)	79	0.35
Czechoslovakian (33)	64	0.29
Danish (0)	10	0.04
Dutch (121)	890	3.99
English (543)	1,913	8.58
Estonian (0)	16	0.07
European (51)	115	0.52
Finnish (0)	11	0.05
French, ex. Basque (49)	376	1.69
French Canadian (0)	37	0.17
German (2,180)	5,584	25.04
Greek (0)	10	0.04
Hungarian (64)	280	1.26
Irish (786)	3,854	17.28
Italian (786)	2,648	11.87
Lithuanian (76)	116	0.52
New Zealander (13)	13	0.06
Norwegian (0)	23	0.10
Pennsylvania German (623)	986	4.42
Polish (685)	1,629	7.30
Portuguese (10)	10	0.04
Romanian (0)	6	0.03
Russian (78)	179	0.80
Scandinavian (0)	31	0.14
Scotch-Irish (133)	438	1.96
Scottish (50)	319	1.43
Slavic (5)	5	0.02
Slovak (126)	431	1.93
Swedish (21)	177	0.79
Swiss (61)	121	0.54
Ukrainian (74)	224	1.00
Welsh (5)	224	1.00
West Indian, ex. Hispanic (70)	120	0.54
Barbadian (33)	33	0.15
British West Indian (13)	33	0.15
Jamaican (24)	24	0.11
West Indian (0)	30	0.13
Yugoslavian (0)	39	0.17

Hispanic Origin	Population	%
Hispanic or Latino (of any race)	1,785	7.98
Central American, ex. Mexican	146	0.65
Costa Rican	11	0.05
Guatemalan	38	0.17
Honduran	22	0.10
Nicaraguan	3	0.01
Panamanian	10	0.04
Salvadoran	62	0.28
Cuban	35	0.16
Dominican Republic	47	0.21
Mexican	274	1.22
Puerto Rican	1,032	4.61
South American	107	0.48
Argentinean	9	0.04
Bolivian	1	<0.01
Chilean	4	0.02
Colombian	12	0.05
Ecuadorian	61	0.27
Peruvian	13	0.06
Uruguayan	2	0.01
Venezuelan	1	<0.01
Other South American	4	0.02
Other Hispanic or Latino	144	0.64

*Notes: † The Census 2010 population figure is used to calculate the percentages in the Hispanic Origin and Race categories. Ancestry percentages are based on the 2006-2010 American Community Survey population (not shown); ‡ Numbers in parentheses indicate the number of people reporting a single ancestry; * Numbers in parentheses indicate the number of persons reporting this race alone, not in combination with any other race; Please refer to the Explanation of Data for more information.*

Race*	Population	%
African-American/Black (4,366)	5,136	22.95
Not Hispanic (4,147)	4,814	21.51
Hispanic (219)	322	1.44
American Indian/Alaska Native (71)	207	0.93
Not Hispanic (39)	155	0.69
Hispanic (32)	52	0.23
Blackfeet (4)	12	0.05
Canadian/French Am. Ind. (0)	1	<0.01
Cherokee (9)	52	0.23
Cheyenne (1)	1	<0.01
Chippewa (1)	1	<0.01
Choctaw (0)	1	<0.01
Comanche (1)	1	<0.01
Creek (0)	1	<0.01
Crow (0)	6	0.03
Delaware (1)	3	0.01
Hopi (2)	5	0.02
Iroquois (0)	3	0.01
Kiowa (0)	1	<0.01
Lumbee (1)	1	<0.01
Mexican American Ind. (7)	7	0.03
Navajo (2)	4	0.02
Sioux (0)	4	0.02
Spanish American Ind. (2)	2	0.01
Asian (197)	302	1.35
Not Hispanic (196)	284	1.27
Hispanic (1)	18	0.08
Cambodian (14)	18	0.08
Chinese, ex. Taiwanese (50)	68	0.30
Filipino (39)	65	0.29
Indian (30)	45	0.20
Indonesian (1)	4	0.02
Japanese (3)	17	0.08
Korean (18)	30	0.13
Laotian (2)	2	0.01
Malaysian (1)	1	<0.01
Nepalese (1)	1	<0.01
Sri Lankan (1)	1	<0.01
Taiwanese (4)	9	0.04
Thai (0)	1	<0.01
Vietnamese (21)	38	0.17
Hawaii Native/Pacific Islander (15)	37	0.17
Not Hispanic (15)	31	0.14
Hispanic (0)	6	0.03
Guamanian/Chamorro (1)	1	<0.01
Native Hawaiian (2)	9	0.04
Samoan (6)	8	0.04
White (16,143)	17,016	76.04
Not Hispanic (15,377)	16,101	71.95
Hispanic (766)	915	4.09

Pottsville

Place Type: City
County: Schuylkill
Population: 14,324†

Ancestry‡	Population	%
African, Sub-Saharan (13)	13	0.09
South African (13)	13	0.09
American (354)	354	2.44
Arab (66)	128	0.88
Lebanese (9)	71	0.49
Other Arab (57)	57	0.39
Austrian (24)	125	0.86
Basque (7)	15	0.10
British (0)	11	0.08
Canadian (39)	111	0.76
Croatian (0)	10	0.07
Czech (0)	37	0.25
Czechoslovakian (41)	166	1.14
Dutch (172)	1,491	10.27
Eastern European (144)	144	0.99
English (177)	823	5.67
European (0)	14	0.10
French, ex. Basque (0)	226	1.56
French Canadian (0)	44	0.30
German (1,184)	4,365	30.07
Greek (49)	129	0.89
Hungarian (0)	22	0.15
Irish (1,089)	3,554	24.48
Italian (615)	1,988	13.69
Latvian (12)	12	0.08
Lithuanian (140)	715	4.92
Macedonian (7)	7	0.05
Northern European (56)	56	0.39
Norwegian (13)	43	0.30
Pennsylvania German (247)	745	5.13
Polish (201)	983	6.77
Portuguese (26)	67	0.46
Russian (32)	139	0.96
Scotch-Irish (6)	44	0.30
Scottish (24)	110	0.76
Slavic (31)	42	0.29
Slovak (103)	463	3.19
Slovene (32)	32	0.22
Swedish (57)	93	0.64
Swiss (0)	21	0.14
Ukrainian (187)	427	2.94
Welsh (49)	365	2.51
West Indian, ex. Hispanic (7)	7	0.05
Jamaican (7)	7	0.05

Hispanic Origin	Population	%
Hispanic or Latino (of any race)	362	2.53
Central American, ex. Mexican	12	0.08
Costa Rican	2	0.01
Guatemalan	1	0.01
Honduran	4	0.03
Panamanian	1	0.01
Salvadoran	4	0.03
Cuban	3	0.02
Dominican Republic	11	0.08
Mexican	64	0.45
Puerto Rican	216	1.51
South American	17	0.12
Chilean	2	0.01
Colombian	2	0.01
Peruvian	6	0.04
Uruguayan	1	0.01
Venezuelan	6	0.04
Other Hispanic or Latino	39	0.27

Race*	Population	%
African-American/Black (444)	640	4.47
Not Hispanic (416)	601	4.20
Hispanic (28)	39	0.27
American Indian/Alaska Native (22)	103	0.72
Not Hispanic (20)	95	0.66
Hispanic (2)	8	0.06
Blackfeet (0)	1	0.01
Cherokee (3)	29	0.20
Chippewa (1)	2	0.01
Choctaw (0)	3	0.02
Comanche (0)	1	0.01
Delaware (2)	5	0.03
Iroquois (0)	3	0.02
Seminole (0)	2	0.01
Sioux (2)	4	0.03
South American Ind. (0)	1	0.01
Asian (97)	119	0.83
Not Hispanic (96)	116	0.81
Hispanic (1)	3	0.02
Chinese, ex. Taiwanese (16)	18	0.13
Filipino (14)	19	0.13
Indian (22)	26	0.18
Japanese (0)	3	0.02
Korean (17)	25	0.17
Pakistani (19)	20	0.14
Thai (0)	1	0.01
Vietnamese (6)	6	0.04
Hawaii Native/Pacific Islander (0)	5	0.03
Not Hispanic (0)	5	0.03
Native Hawaiian (0)	3	0.02
White (13,342)	13,624	95.11
Not Hispanic (13,151)	13,398	93.54
Hispanic (191)	226	1.58

Progress

Place Type: CDP
County: Dauphin
Population: 9,765†

Ancestry‡	Population	%
African, Sub-Saharan (282)	297	3.10
African (242)	257	2.69
Nigerian (28)	28	0.29
Other Sub-Saharan African (12)	12	0.13
Alsatian (0)	9	0.09
American (279)	279	2.92
Austrian (32)	45	0.47
British (29)	29	0.30
Canadian (0)	12	0.13
Croatian (13)	21	0.22
Czech (12)	119	1.24
Czechoslovakian (23)	36	0.38
Dutch (9)	211	2.21
Eastern European (30)	30	0.31
English (128)	685	7.16
European (52)	52	0.54
Finnish (0)	18	0.19
French, ex. Basque (16)	113	1.18
German (1,303)	2,874	30.04
Greek (12)	31	0.32
Hungarian (10)	27	0.28
Irish (269)	1,210	12.65
Italian (138)	424	4.43
Lithuanian (18)	104	1.09
Macedonian (9)	9	0.09
Norwegian (35)	130	1.36
Pennsylvania German (128)	154	1.61
Polish (94)	328	3.43
Portuguese (0)	32	0.33
Romanian (156)	156	1.63
Russian (37)	103	1.08
Scotch-Irish (71)	117	1.22
Scottish (73)	228	2.38
Serbian (18)	18	0.19
Slavic (16)	16	0.17
Slovak (15)	93	0.97
Swedish (29)	38	0.40
Swiss (7)	18	0.19
Turkish (11)	11	0.11
Ukrainian (7)	7	0.07
Welsh (9)	131	1.37
West Indian, ex. Hispanic (165)	190	1.99
Bermudan (165)	165	1.72
West Indian (0)	25	0.26

Hispanic Origin	Population	%
Hispanic or Latino (of any race)	722	7.39
Central American, ex. Mexican	26	0.27
Costa Rican	1	0.01
Guatemalan	2	0.02
Honduran	10	0.10
Panamanian	11	0.11
Salvadoran	2	0.02
Cuban	33	0.34
Dominican Republic	38	0.39
Mexican	88	0.90
Puerto Rican	461	4.72
South American	43	0.44
Argentinean	1	0.01
Bolivian	2	0.02
Chilean	1	0.01
Colombian	7	0.07
Ecuadorian	20	0.20
Peruvian	11	0.11
Uruguayan	1	0.01
Other Hispanic or Latino	33	0.34

Race*	Population	%
African-American/Black (2,574)	2,883	29.52
Not Hispanic (2,476)	2,725	27.91
Hispanic (98)	158	1.62
American Indian/Alaska Native (19)	71	0.73
Not Hispanic (9)	51	0.52

*Notes: † The Census 2010 population figure is used to calculate the percentages in the Hispanic Origin and Race categories. Ancestry percentages are based on the 2006-2010 American Community Survey population (not shown); ‡ Numbers in parentheses indicate the number of people reporting a single ancestry; * Numbers in parentheses indicate the number of persons reporting this race alone, not in combination with any other race; Please refer to the Explanation of Data for more information.*

Hispanic (10)	20	0.20
Blackfeet (1)	9	0.09
Cherokee (0)	16	0.16
Chickasaw (0)	1	0.01
Choctaw (0)	1	0.01
Comanche (0)	1	0.01
Inupiat *(Alaska Native)* (0)	1	0.01
Seminole (0)	3	0.03
Sioux (1)	3	0.03
South American Ind. (0)	5	0.05
Spanish American Ind. (0)	1	0.01
Asian (364)	422	4.32
Not Hispanic (360)	412	4.22
Hispanic (4)	10	0.10
Cambodian (6)	6	0.06
Chinese, ex. Taiwanese (39)	43	0.44
Filipino (11)	15	0.15
Indian (54)	67	0.69
Indonesian (21)	21	0.22
Japanese (6)	17	0.17
Korean (8)	16	0.16
Laotian (1)	1	0.01
Nepalese (1)	1	0.01
Pakistani (12)	12	0.12
Sri Lankan (1)	1	0.01
Thai (1)	5	0.05
Vietnamese (196)	213	2.18
Hawaii Native/Pacific Islander (1)	13	0.13
Not Hispanic (1)	7	0.07
Hispanic (0)	6	0.06
Guamanian/Chamorro (1)	1	0.01
Native Hawaiian (0)	1	0.01
Samoan (0)	1	0.01
White (6,116)	6,471	66.27
Not Hispanic (5,876)	6,149	62.97
Hispanic (240)	322	3.30

Quakertown

Place Type: Borough
County: Bucks
Population: 8,979†

Ancestry‡	Population	%
African, Sub-Saharan (45)	45	0.50
African (45)	45	0.50
Albanian (36)	36	0.40
American (589)	589	6.50
Armenian (0)	18	0.20
Austrian (44)	79	0.87
British (18)	28	0.31
Canadian (7)	18	0.20
Celtic (0)	10	0.11
Czech (0)	19	0.21
Czechoslovakian (0)	22	0.24
Dutch (89)	360	3.98
Eastern European (9)	9	0.10
English (116)	862	9.52
European (49)	49	0.54
Finnish (10)	30	0.33
French, ex. Basque (57)	142	1.57
French Canadian (19)	39	0.43
German (1,493)	3,587	39.61
Greek (44)	79	0.87
Hungarian (0)	41	0.45
Irish (648)	1,959	21.63
Italian (239)	666	7.36
Lithuanian (20)	124	1.37
Norwegian (0)	13	0.14
Pennsylvania German (189)	242	2.67
Polish (192)	587	6.48
Romanian (11)	11	0.12
Russian (54)	64	0.71
Scotch-Irish (57)	179	1.98
Scottish (0)	39	0.43
Slavic (10)	10	0.11
Slovak (17)	53	0.59
Swedish (0)	9	0.10
Swiss (0)	43	0.47
Turkish (10)	10	0.11
Ukrainian (35)	74	0.82
Welsh (0)	177	1.95

Hispanic Origin	Population	%
Hispanic or Latino (of any race)	537	5.98
Central American, ex. Mexican	100	1.11
Costa Rican	3	0.03
Guatemalan	17	0.19
Honduran	6	0.07
Panamanian	7	0.08
Salvadoran	67	0.75
Cuban	5	0.06
Dominican Republic	12	0.13
Mexican	198	2.21
Puerto Rican	137	1.53
South American	31	0.35
Argentinean	2	0.02
Colombian	15	0.17
Ecuadorian	11	0.12
Peruvian	3	0.03
Other Hispanic or Latino	54	0.60

Race*	Population	%
African-American/Black (217)	291	3.24
Not Hispanic (205)	276	3.07
Hispanic (12)	15	0.17
American Indian/Alaska Native (29)	75	0.84
Not Hispanic (8)	46	0.51
Hispanic (21)	29	0.32
Apache (1)	1	0.01
Blackfeet (2)	2	0.02
Central American Ind. (2)	2	0.02
Cherokee (3)	11	0.12
Choctaw (0)	2	0.02
Iroquois (0)	3	0.03
Navajo (0)	2	0.02
Osage (0)	1	0.01
Shoshone (1)	1	0.01
Asian (179)	212	2.36
Not Hispanic (179)	211	2.35
Hispanic (0)	1	0.01
Bangladeshi (0)	1	0.01
Cambodian (1)	1	0.01
Chinese, ex. Taiwanese (26)	32	0.36
Filipino (12)	19	0.21
Indian (48)	58	0.65
Japanese (7)	12	0.13
Korean (32)	35	0.39
Thai (3)	5	0.06
Vietnamese (34)	35	0.39
Hawaii Native/Pacific Islander (2)	6	0.07
Not Hispanic (2)	6	0.07
Guamanian/Chamorro (1)	2	0.02
Native Hawaiian (0)	3	0.03
White (8,135)	8,290	92.33
Not Hispanic (7,906)	8,025	89.38
Hispanic (229)	265	2.95

Radnor

Place Type: Township
County: Delaware
Population: 31,531†

Ancestry‡	Population	%
African, Sub-Saharan (67)	83	0.26
African (0)	16	0.05
Liberian (38)	38	0.12
Nigerian (15)	15	0.05
South African (14)	14	0.04
Albanian (0)	18	0.06
American (728)	728	2.32
Arab (268)	385	1.23
Arab (23)	23	0.07
Egyptian (19)	31	0.10
Iraqi (0)	9	0.03
Lebanese (109)	196	0.62
Moroccan (79)	79	0.25
Syrian (38)	38	0.12
Other Arab (0)	9	0.03
Armenian (28)	55	0.18
Australian (0)	16	0.05
Austrian (19)	200	0.64
Basque (0)	15	0.05
Brazilian (25)	25	0.08
British (278)	351	1.12
Bulgarian (12)	23	0.07
Canadian (90)	253	0.81
Celtic (27)	27	0.09
Croatian (11)	83	0.26
Czech (0)	143	0.46
Czechoslovakian (25)	40	0.13
Danish (82)	212	0.68
Dutch (40)	223	0.71
Eastern European (258)	282	0.90
English (1,144)	4,241	13.51
European (513)	527	1.68
Finnish (10)	49	0.16
French, ex. Basque (124)	562	1.79
French Canadian (147)	213	0.68
German (1,159)	4,832	15.40
Greek (112)	268	0.85
Hungarian (28)	257	0.82
Iranian (209)	209	0.67
Irish (2,820)	8,032	25.60
Italian (1,551)	4,434	14.13
Lithuanian (40)	243	0.77
Norwegian (52)	185	0.59
Pennsylvania German (27)	36	0.11
Polish (385)	1,555	4.96
Portuguese (17)	88	0.28
Romanian (0)	65	0.21
Russian (359)	899	2.86
Scandinavian (30)	152	0.48
Scotch-Irish (289)	587	1.87
Scottish (275)	755	2.41
Serbian (68)	94	0.30
Slovak (58)	99	0.32
Slovene (10)	25	0.08
Swedish (117)	337	1.07
Swiss (73)	219	0.70
Ukrainian (178)	263	0.84
Welsh (108)	434	1.38
West Indian, ex. Hispanic (0)	87	0.28
British West Indian (0)	15	0.05
Haitian (0)	16	0.05
Jamaican (0)	25	0.08
Trinidadian/Tobagonian (0)	15	0.05
West Indian (0)	16	0.05
Yugoslavian (0)	13	0.04

Hispanic Origin	Population	%
Hispanic or Latino (of any race)	937	2.97
Central American, ex. Mexican	95	0.30
Costa Rican	8	0.03
Guatemalan	20	0.06
Honduran	19	0.06
Nicaraguan	8	0.03
Panamanian	6	0.02
Salvadoran	34	0.11
Cuban	103	0.33
Dominican Republic	12	0.04
Mexican	204	0.65
Puerto Rican	209	0.66
South American	212	0.67
Argentinean	28	0.09
Bolivian	5	0.02
Chilean	23	0.07
Colombian	67	0.21
Ecuadorian	18	0.06
Paraguayan	3	0.01
Peruvian	41	0.13
Uruguayan	7	0.02
Venezuelan	20	0.06
Other Hispanic or Latino	102	0.32

Race*	Population	%
African-American/Black (1,240)	1,414	4.48
Not Hispanic (1,209)	1,368	4.34
Hispanic (31)	46	0.15

*Notes: † The Census 2010 population figure is used to calculate the percentages in the Hispanic Origin and Race categories. Ancestry percentages are based on the 2006-2010 American Community Survey population (not shown); ‡ Numbers in parentheses indicate the number of people reporting a single ancestry; * Numbers in parentheses indicate the number of persons reporting this race alone, not in combination with any other race; Please refer to the Explanation of Data for more information.*

American Indian/Alaska Native (20)	108	0.34
Not Hispanic (17)	100	0.32
Hispanic (3)	8	0.03
Apache (0)	1	<0.01
Cherokee (2)	18	0.06
Chickasaw (1)	1	<0.01
Chippewa (0)	1	<0.01
Cree (0)	2	0.01
Creek (0)	1	<0.01
Crow (0)	1	<0.01
Delaware (0)	7	0.02
Iroquois (0)	1	<0.01
Lumbee (1)	1	<0.01
Mexican American Ind. (2)	2	0.01
Navajo (1)	7	0.02
Osage (0)	1	<0.01
Potawatomi (0)	1	<0.01
Pueblo (0)	2	0.01
Seminole (2)	4	0.01
Sioux (1)	2	0.01
South American Ind. (1)	1	<0.01
Asian (2,493)	2,761	8.76
Not Hispanic (2,484)	2,739	8.69
Hispanic (9)	22	0.07
Bangladeshi (12)	12	0.04
Burmese (2)	2	0.01
Cambodian (10)	13	0.04
Chinese, ex. Taiwanese (699)	800	2.54
Filipino (96)	158	0.50
Indian (562)	604	1.92
Indonesian (6)	6	0.02
Japanese (137)	189	0.60
Korean (708)	756	2.40
Nepalese (1)	1	<0.01
Pakistani (79)	79	0.25
Sri Lankan (6)	9	0.03
Taiwanese (28)	36	0.11
Thai (21)	23	0.07
Vietnamese (49)	63	0.20
Hawaii Native/Pacific Islander (7)	17	0.05
Not Hispanic (7)	15	0.05
Hispanic (0)	2	0.01
Guamanian/Chamorro (1)	2	0.01
Marshallese (0)	1	<0.01
Native Hawaiian (3)	10	0.03
Samoan (0)	2	0.01
White (27,050)	27,511	87.25
Not Hispanic (26,374)	26,793	84.97
Hispanic (676)	718	2.28

Rapho

Place Type: Township
County: Lancaster
Population: 10,442†

Ancestry‡	Population	%
American (1,266)	1,266	12.52
Arab (31)	39	0.39
Egyptian (31)	31	0.31
Syrian (0)	8	0.08
Austrian (7)	7	0.07
British (42)	69	0.68
Czech (0)	21	0.21
Danish (19)	19	0.19
Dutch (31)	122	1.21
English (337)	661	6.54
European (131)	150	1.48
Finnish (0)	9	0.09
French, ex. Basque (60)	253	2.50
French Canadian (0)	23	0.23
German (2,773)	4,331	42.83
Greek (13)	13	0.13
Hungarian (7)	7	0.07
Irish (147)	834	8.25
Italian (185)	407	4.02
Lithuanian (6)	20	0.20
Northern European (14)	14	0.14
Norwegian (16)	16	0.16
Pennsylvania German (602)	643	6.36
Polish (64)	269	2.66
Russian (0)	9	0.09
Scotch-Irish (65)	175	1.73
Scottish (46)	151	1.49
Slovak (10)	78	0.77
Swedish (26)	88	0.87
Swiss (67)	364	3.60
Turkish (14)	14	0.14
Ukrainian (19)	19	0.19
Welsh (0)	87	0.86
Yugoslavian (12)	12	0.12

Hispanic Origin	Population	%
Hispanic or Latino (of any race)	242	2.32
Central American, ex. Mexican	16	0.15
Costa Rican	1	0.01
Guatemalan	7	0.07
Honduran	3	0.03
Panamanian	1	0.01
Salvadoran	4	0.04
Cuban	8	0.08
Dominican Republic	2	0.02
Mexican	61	0.58
Puerto Rican	117	1.12
South American	22	0.21
Argentinean	3	0.03
Colombian	11	0.11
Ecuadorian	1	0.01
Paraguayan	1	0.01
Peruvian	6	0.06
Other Hispanic or Latino	16	0.15

Race*	Population	%
African-American/Black (85)	118	1.13
Not Hispanic (76)	105	1.01
Hispanic (9)	13	0.12
American Indian/Alaska Native (15)	40	0.38
Not Hispanic (7)	31	0.30
Hispanic (8)	9	0.09
Cherokee (1)	6	0.06
Delaware (0)	1	0.01
Iroquois (3)	5	0.05
Mexican American Ind. (0)	1	0.01
Sioux (1)	3	0.03
Asian (119)	140	1.34
Not Hispanic (115)	135	1.29
Hispanic (4)	5	0.05
Cambodian (3)	3	0.03
Chinese, ex. Taiwanese (10)	12	0.11
Filipino (7)	16	0.15
Indian (17)	18	0.17
Japanese (3)	5	0.05
Korean (11)	15	0.14
Laotian (41)	42	0.40
Pakistani (12)	12	0.11
Taiwanese (1)	1	0.01
Thai (2)	3	0.03
Vietnamese (9)	13	0.12
Hawaii Native/Pacific Islander (1)	7	0.07
Not Hispanic (1)	5	0.05
Hispanic (0)	2	0.02
Guamanian/Chamorro (1)	1	0.01
Samoan (0)	4	0.04
White (10,071)	10,158	97.28
Not Hispanic (9,932)	9,993	95.70
Hispanic (139)	165	1.58

Reading

Place Type: City
County: Berks
Population: 88,082†

Ancestry‡	Population	%
African, Sub-Saharan (150)	306	0.35
African (88)	212	0.24
Ethiopian (18)	18	0.02
Ghanaian (0)	14	0.02
Kenyan (13)	13	0.01
Liberian (31)	31	0.04
Other Sub-Saharan African (0)	18	0.02
Albanian (96)	96	0.11
American (1,395)	1,395	1.60
Arab (49)	83	0.09
Arab (26)	48	0.05
Lebanese (12)	12	0.01
Syrian (11)	23	0.03
Austrian (10)	132	0.15
Belgian (0)	31	0.04
Brazilian (0)	16	0.02
British (20)	103	0.12
Canadian (38)	215	0.25
Croatian (0)	76	0.09
Czech (18)	173	0.20
Czechoslovakian (17)	29	0.03
Danish (0)	14	0.02
Dutch (363)	1,551	1.77
Eastern European (13)	26	0.03
English (519)	1,859	2.13
European (148)	148	0.17
Finnish (0)	18	0.02
French, ex. Basque (94)	630	0.72
French Canadian (24)	62	0.07
German (4,070)	10,470	11.98
Greek (127)	197	0.23
Hungarian (79)	221	0.25
Irish (1,096)	5,261	6.02
Israeli (9)	9	0.01
Italian (1,314)	4,489	5.14
Latvian (21)	73	0.08
Lithuanian (103)	267	0.31
Northern European (13)	13	0.01
Norwegian (80)	183	0.21
Pennsylvania German (1,369)	2,056	2.35
Polish (1,623)	3,558	4.07
Portuguese (34)	38	0.04
Romanian (331)	436	0.50
Russian (47)	178	0.20
Scandinavian (11)	11	0.01
Scotch-Irish (56)	357	0.41
Scottish (43)	345	0.39
Serbian (8)	8	0.01
Slavic (19)	68	0.08
Slovak (109)	353	0.40
Slovene (20)	20	0.02
Swedish (10)	88	0.10
Swiss (24)	164	0.19
Turkish (46)	46	0.05
Ukrainian (61)	340	0.39
Welsh (99)	531	0.61
West Indian, ex. Hispanic (1,259)	1,590	1.82
Barbadian (57)	68	0.08
Haitian (365)	451	0.52
Jamaican (443)	575	0.66
Trinidadian/Tobagonian (121)	129	0.15
U.S. Virgin Islander (256)	289	0.33
West Indian (17)	78	0.09
Yugoslavian (60)	68	0.08

Hispanic Origin	Population	%
Hispanic or Latino (of any race)	51,230	58.16
Central American, ex. Mexican	1,436	1.63
Costa Rican	17	0.02
Guatemalan	402	0.46
Honduran	270	0.31
Nicaraguan	62	0.07
Panamanian	40	0.05
Salvadoran	637	0.72
Other Central American	8	0.01
Cuban	360	0.41
Dominican Republic	8,716	9.90
Mexican	8,602	9.77
Puerto Rican	28,160	31.97
South American	1,240	1.41
Argentinean	33	0.04
Bolivian	7	0.01
Chilean	19	0.02
Colombian	612	0.69
Ecuadorian	409	0.46
Paraguayan	6	0.01

*Notes: † The Census 2010 population figure is used to calculate the percentages in the Hispanic Origin and Race categories. Ancestry percentages are based on the 2006-2010 American Community Survey population (not shown); ‡ Numbers in parentheses indicate the number of people reporting a single ancestry; * Numbers in parentheses indicate the number of persons reporting this race alone, not in combination with any other race; Please refer to the Explanation of Data for more information.*

Peruvian	93	0.11
Uruguayan	19	0.02
Venezuelan	31	0.04
Other South American	11	0.01
Other Hispanic or Latino	2,716	3.08

Race*	Population	%
African-American/Black (11,624)	14,345	16.29
Not Hispanic (8,774)	10,042	11.40
Hispanic (2,850)	4,303	4.89
American Indian/Alaska Native (794)	1,430	1.62
Not Hispanic (183)	434	0.49
Hispanic (611)	996	1.13
Apache (2)	4	<0.01
Blackfeet (17)	49	0.06
Canadian/French Am. Ind. (1)	1	<0.01
Central American Ind. (7)	14	0.02
Cherokee (29)	120	0.14
Chippewa (9)	19	0.02
Choctaw (1)	7	0.01
Comanche (0)	1	<0.01
Cree (0)	5	0.01
Creek (0)	1	<0.01
Delaware (3)	15	0.02
Inupiat *(Alaska Native)* (3)	3	<0.01
Iroquois (8)	14	0.02
Lumbee (3)	5	0.01
Menominee (1)	1	<0.01
Mexican American Ind. (35)	59	0.07
Navajo (1)	1	<0.01
Paiute (0)	1	<0.01
Potawatomi (3)	3	<0.01
Pueblo (17)	26	0.03
Seminole (3)	4	<0.01
Sioux (4)	12	0.01
South American Ind. (32)	74	0.08
Spanish American Ind. (12)	17	0.02
Tlingit-Haida *(Alaska Native)* (1)	1	<0.01
Tohono O'Odham (2)	2	<0.01
Asian (1,039)	1,323	1.50
Not Hispanic (958)	1,097	1.25
Hispanic (81)	226	0.26
Bangladeshi (1)	1	<0.01
Burmese (4)	4	<0.01
Cambodian (3)	5	0.01
Chinese, ex. Taiwanese (169)	192	0.22
Filipino (49)	79	0.09
Hmong (1)	3	<0.01
Indian (125)	176	0.20
Indonesian (10)	13	0.01
Japanese (33)	63	0.07
Korean (47)	83	0.09
Laotian (36)	39	0.04
Pakistani (13)	18	0.02
Thai (8)	14	0.02
Vietnamese (493)	538	0.61
Hawaii Native/Pacific Islander (72)	351	0.40
Not Hispanic (20)	59	0.07
Hispanic (52)	292	0.33
Guamanian/Chamorro (24)	38	0.04
Native Hawaiian (13)	49	0.06
Samoan (6)	15	0.02
Tongan (1)	1	<0.01
White (42,617)	46,727	53.05
Not Hispanic (25,258)	26,621	30.22
Hispanic (17,359)	20,106	22.83

Richland

Place Type: Township
County: Allegheny
Population: 11,100†

Ancestry‡	Population	%
Afghan (0)	27	0.25
American (358)	358	3.35
Arab (0)	15	0.14
Syrian (0)	15	0.14
Australian (10)	10	0.09
Austrian (5)	37	0.35
British (0)	9	0.08
Canadian (16)	37	0.35
Carpatho Rusyn (10)	23	0.22
Croatian (70)	159	1.49
Czech (25)	116	1.09
Czechoslovakian (11)	33	0.31
Danish (0)	14	0.13
Dutch (22)	333	3.12
Eastern European (9)	9	0.08
English (207)	1,026	9.60
European (96)	96	0.90
French, ex. Basque (64)	234	2.19
French Canadian (0)	19	0.18
German (1,358)	4,307	40.32
Greek (10)	40	0.37
Hungarian (50)	312	2.92
Irish (384)	2,482	23.24
Italian (621)	1,745	16.34
Lithuanian (11)	34	0.32
Northern European (20)	20	0.19
Norwegian (38)	127	1.19
Pennsylvania German (0)	8	0.07
Polish (190)	1,159	10.85
Romanian (0)	7	0.07
Russian (55)	112	1.05
Scotch-Irish (80)	401	3.75
Scottish (53)	310	2.90
Slovak (149)	367	3.44
Slovene (0)	45	0.42
Swedish (47)	270	2.53
Swiss (0)	58	0.54
Ukrainian (9)	93	0.87
Welsh (7)	128	1.20
Yugoslavian (0)	9	0.08

Hispanic Origin	Population	%
Hispanic or Latino (of any race)	127	1.14
Central American, ex. Mexican	11	0.10
Costa Rican	2	0.02
Guatemalan	3	0.03
Honduran	5	0.05
Salvadoran	1	0.01
Cuban	7	0.06
Dominican Republic	11	0.10
Mexican	35	0.32
Puerto Rican	25	0.23
South American	20	0.18
Argentinean	5	0.05
Chilean	1	0.01
Colombian	3	0.03
Ecuadorian	7	0.06
Peruvian	3	0.03
Venezuelan	1	0.01
Other Hispanic or Latino	18	0.16

Race*	Population	%
African-American/Black (56)	91	0.82
Not Hispanic (56)	86	0.77
Hispanic (0)	5	0.05
American Indian/Alaska Native (14)	60	0.54
Not Hispanic (14)	55	0.50
Hispanic (0)	5	0.05
Blackfeet (0)	1	0.01
Cherokee (0)	8	0.07
Chippewa (1)	1	0.01
Choctaw (0)	1	0.01
Crow (0)	3	0.03
Delaware (0)	1	0.01
Iroquois (0)	6	0.05
Lumbee (1)	1	0.01
Potawatomi (3)	3	0.03
Sioux (1)	1	0.01
South American Ind. (0)	5	0.05
Asian (188)	207	1.86
Not Hispanic (188)	207	1.86
Cambodian (1)	3	0.03
Chinese, ex. Taiwanese (39)	44	0.40
Filipino (10)	14	0.13
Indian (75)	75	0.68
Japanese (10)	18	0.16
Korean (32)	33	0.30
Nepalese (3)	3	0.03
Pakistani (3)	4	0.04
Taiwanese (3)	5	0.05
Vietnamese (9)	10	0.09
Hawaii Native/Pacific Islander (1)	2	0.02
Not Hispanic (0)	1	0.01
Hispanic (1)	1	0.01
Guamanian/Chamorro (1)	1	0.01
White (10,730)	10,830	97.57
Not Hispanic (10,622)	10,711	96.50
Hispanic (108)	119	1.07

Richland

Place Type: Township
County: Bucks
Population: 13,052†

Ancestry‡	Population	%
Albanian (0)	6	0.05
American (588)	588	4.71
Australian (12)	35	0.28
Austrian (0)	10	0.08
Belgian (0)	7	0.06
Brazilian (232)	267	2.14
Canadian (12)	57	0.46
Czech (0)	34	0.27
Czechoslovakian (8)	8	0.06
Danish (21)	21	0.17
Dutch (110)	272	2.18
Eastern European (8)	8	0.06
English (192)	1,394	11.17
European (23)	23	0.18
Finnish (10)	10	0.08
French, ex. Basque (17)	178	1.43
French Canadian (22)	91	0.73
German (1,800)	4,700	37.67
Greek (0)	7	0.06
Hungarian (19)	131	1.05
Irish (405)	2,304	18.46
Israeli (11)	22	0.18
Italian (419)	1,682	13.48
Latvian (9)	9	0.07
Lithuanian (10)	49	0.39
Norwegian (30)	30	0.24
Pennsylvania German (283)	576	4.62
Polish (235)	942	7.55
Portuguese (0)	10	0.08
Romanian (81)	115	0.92
Russian (59)	158	1.27
Scandinavian (0)	10	0.08
Scotch-Irish (6)	173	1.39
Scottish (30)	262	2.10
Slovak (8)	74	0.59
Swedish (32)	134	1.07
Swiss (0)	48	0.38
Ukrainian (8)	64	0.51
Welsh (22)	274	2.20

Hispanic Origin	Population	%
Hispanic or Latino (of any race)	490	3.75
Central American, ex. Mexican	37	0.28
Costa Rican	6	0.05
Guatemalan	5	0.04
Honduran	9	0.07
Nicaraguan	3	0.02
Panamanian	2	0.02
Salvadoran	12	0.09
Cuban	13	0.10
Dominican Republic	11	0.08
Mexican	138	1.06
Puerto Rican	202	1.55
South American	54	0.41
Argentinean	2	0.02
Colombian	10	0.08
Ecuadorian	26	0.20
Peruvian	9	0.07
Uruguayan	1	0.01
Venezuelan	6	0.05

*Notes: † The Census 2010 population figure is used to calculate the percentages in the Hispanic Origin and Race categories. Ancestry percentages are based on the 2006-2010 American Community Survey population (not shown); ‡ Numbers in parentheses indicate the number of people reporting a single ancestry; * Numbers in parentheses indicate the number of persons reporting this race alone, not in combination with any other race; Please refer to the Explanation of Data for more information.*

Other Hispanic or Latino	35	0.27

Race*	Population	%
African-American/Black (179)	254	1.95
Not Hispanic (166)	229	1.75
Hispanic (13)	25	0.19
American Indian/Alaska Native (35)	103	0.79
Not Hispanic (19)	77	0.59
Hispanic (16)	26	0.20
Blackfeet (0)	1	0.01
Cherokee (1)	13	0.10
Chippewa (4)	4	0.03
Comanche (1)	1	0.01
Cree (0)	2	0.02
Creek (0)	2	0.02
Delaware (1)	13	0.10
Iroquois (0)	2	0.02
Lumbee (0)	1	0.01
Navajo (0)	1	0.01
Sioux (1)	4	0.03
South American Ind. (8)	12	0.09
Asian (372)	455	3.49
Not Hispanic (368)	448	3.43
Hispanic (4)	7	0.05
Burmese (1)	3	0.02
Cambodian (17)	18	0.14
Chinese, ex. Taiwanese (60)	66	0.51
Filipino (53)	80	0.61
Indian (67)	78	0.60
Indonesian (1)	1	0.01
Japanese (1)	4	0.03
Korean (50)	72	0.55
Laotian (5)	5	0.04
Malaysian (1)	3	0.02
Pakistani (2)	6	0.05
Taiwanese (3)	3	0.02
Thai (1)	4	0.03
Vietnamese (98)	105	0.80
Hawaii Native/Pacific Islander (1)	6	0.05
Not Hispanic (1)	5	0.04
Hispanic (0)	1	0.01
Native Hawaiian (0)	5	0.04
Samoan (0)	3	0.02
White (12,031)	12,242	93.79
Not Hispanic (11,802)	11,980	91.79
Hispanic (229)	262	2.01

Richland

Place Type: Township
County: Cambria
Population: 12,814†

Ancestry‡	Population	%
American (727)	727	5.71
Arab (75)	121	0.95
Lebanese (75)	121	0.95
Austrian (0)	16	0.13
Belgian (14)	14	0.11
British (0)	12	0.09
Carpatho Rusyn (12)	12	0.09
Croatian (64)	123	0.97
Czech (0)	96	0.75
Czechoslovakian (30)	118	0.93
Dutch (75)	291	2.29
English (251)	1,077	8.46
European (45)	45	0.35
French, ex. Basque (18)	173	1.36
French Canadian (0)	28	0.22
German (1,809)	4,730	37.16
Greek (47)	75	0.59
Hungarian (63)	397	3.12
Irish (400)	2,324	18.26
Italian (610)	1,596	12.54
Lithuanian (0)	42	0.33
Norwegian (0)	22	0.17
Pennsylvania German (77)	128	1.01
Polish (393)	1,269	9.97
Romanian (23)	126	0.99
Russian (83)	126	0.99
Scandinavian (0)	12	0.09
Scotch-Irish (156)	229	1.80
Scottish (25)	274	2.15
Serbian (37)	133	1.04
Slavic (0)	7	0.05
Slovak (440)	1,049	8.24
Slovene (42)	79	0.62
Swedish (0)	22	0.17
Swiss (9)	38	0.30
Ukrainian (16)	49	0.38
Welsh (77)	299	2.35
West Indian, ex. Hispanic (17)	17	0.13
Trinidadian/Tobagonian (17)	17	0.13

Hispanic Origin	Population	%
Hispanic or Latino (of any race)	134	1.05
Central American, ex. Mexican	3	0.02
Costa Rican	1	0.01
Guatemalan	2	0.02
Cuban	10	0.08
Dominican Republic	2	0.02
Mexican	60	0.47
Puerto Rican	37	0.29
South American	6	0.05
Colombian	5	0.04
Peruvian	1	0.01
Other Hispanic or Latino	16	0.12

Race*	Population	%
African-American/Black (130)	157	1.23
Not Hispanic (127)	153	1.19
Hispanic (3)	4	0.03
American Indian/Alaska Native (6)	31	0.24
Not Hispanic (5)	28	0.22
Hispanic (1)	3	0.02
Blackfeet (1)	2	0.02
Cherokee (1)	9	0.07
Comanche (0)	1	0.01
Creek (1)	1	0.01
Iroquois (1)	3	0.02
Lumbee (0)	1	0.01
Ottawa (0)	1	0.01
South American Ind. (1)	2	0.02
Asian (241)	272	2.12
Not Hispanic (241)	271	2.11
Hispanic (0)	1	0.01
Bangladeshi (8)	8	0.06
Burmese (2)	2	0.02
Chinese, ex. Taiwanese (62)	70	0.55
Filipino (24)	28	0.22
Indian (87)	91	0.71
Japanese (3)	6	0.05
Korean (18)	26	0.20
Malaysian (1)	1	0.01
Pakistani (4)	4	0.03
Thai (1)	1	0.01
Vietnamese (17)	18	0.14
Hawaii Native/Pacific Islander (1)	9	0.07
Not Hispanic (1)	9	0.07
Native Hawaiian (0)	1	0.01
Samoan (1)	1	0.01
White (12,311)	12,388	96.68
Not Hispanic (12,217)	12,290	95.91
Hispanic (94)	98	0.76

Ridley

Place Type: Township
County: Delaware
Population: 30,768†

Ancestry‡	Population	%
African, Sub-Saharan (130)	130	0.42
African (12)	12	0.04
Liberian (118)	118	0.38
Albanian (0)	70	0.23
American (810)	810	2.64
Arab (63)	100	0.33
Lebanese (6)	20	0.07
Moroccan (57)	57	0.19
Syrian (0)	23	0.07
Armenian (31)	53	0.17
Austrian (0)	105	0.34
Belgian (0)	10	0.03
British (0)	14	0.05
Canadian (0)	51	0.17
Celtic (22)	22	0.07
Czech (0)	58	0.19
Czechoslovakian (12)	58	0.19
Danish (16)	27	0.09
Dutch (95)	615	2.00
English (267)	3,490	11.35
European (74)	74	0.24
Finnish (0)	142	0.46
French, ex. Basque (80)	480	1.56
French Canadian (9)	24	0.08
German (1,231)	6,125	19.93
Greek (80)	254	0.83
Hungarian (142)	444	1.44
Irish (4,362)	13,171	42.85
Italian (3,102)	8,258	26.87
Lithuanian (156)	318	1.03
Norwegian (29)	157	0.51
Pennsylvania German (94)	200	0.65
Polish (412)	1,524	4.96
Portuguese (13)	13	0.04
Russian (41)	160	0.52
Scotch-Irish (149)	641	2.09
Scottish (99)	435	1.42
Slavic (26)	26	0.08
Slovak (292)	304	0.99
Swedish (31)	271	0.88
Swiss (0)	51	0.17
Ukrainian (153)	305	0.99
Welsh (0)	524	1.70
West Indian, ex. Hispanic (19)	42	0.14
Bermudan (7)	7	0.02
Haitian (12)	25	0.08
West Indian (0)	10	0.03
Yugoslavian (15)	15	0.05

Hispanic Origin	Population	%
Hispanic or Latino (of any race)	583	1.89
Central American, ex. Mexican	72	0.23
Costa Rican	22	0.07
Guatemalan	15	0.05
Honduran	3	0.01
Nicaraguan	3	0.01
Panamanian	4	0.01
Salvadoran	25	0.08
Cuban	21	0.07
Dominican Republic	20	0.07
Mexican	100	0.33
Puerto Rican	242	0.79
South American	91	0.30
Argentinean	31	0.10
Colombian	32	0.10
Ecuadorian	12	0.04
Paraguayan	2	0.01
Peruvian	9	0.03
Uruguayan	1	<0.01
Venezuelan	4	0.01
Other Hispanic or Latino	37	0.12

Race*	Population	%
African-American/Black (1,767)	1,974	6.42
Not Hispanic (1,735)	1,925	6.26
Hispanic (32)	49	0.16
American Indian/Alaska Native (30)	131	0.43
Not Hispanic (22)	110	0.36
Hispanic (8)	21	0.07
Apache (1)	2	0.01
Blackfeet (0)	10	0.03
Cherokee (8)	34	0.11
Chippewa (0)	2	0.01
Choctaw (0)	5	0.02
Creek (1)	1	<0.01
Crow (1)	1	<0.01
Delaware (0)	2	0.01
Iroquois (0)	4	0.01

*Notes: † The Census 2010 population figure is used to calculate the percentages in the Hispanic Origin and Race categories. Ancestry percentages are based on the 2006-2010 American Community Survey population (not shown); ‡ Numbers in parentheses indicate the number of people reporting a single ancestry; * Numbers in parentheses indicate the number of persons reporting this race alone, not in combination with any other race; Please refer to the Explanation of Data for more information.*

Lumbee (0)	2	0.01
Mexican American Ind. (2)	4	0.01
Navajo (1)	3	0.01
Paiute (1)	1	<0.01
Seminole (0)	1	<0.01
South American Ind. (0)	2	0.01
Spanish American Ind. (4)	4	0.01
Asian (677)	811	2.64
Not Hispanic (675)	808	2.63
Hispanic (2)	3	0.01
Bangladeshi (18)	18	0.06
Cambodian (27)	34	0.11
Chinese, ex. Taiwanese (113)	147	0.48
Filipino (87)	130	0.42
Hmong (1)	1	<0.01
Indian (210)	231	0.75
Indonesian (0)	1	<0.01
Japanese (11)	21	0.07
Korean (42)	46	0.15
Laotian (12)	19	0.06
Malaysian (5)	5	0.02
Nepalese (3)	3	0.01
Pakistani (18)	20	0.07
Taiwanese (13)	13	0.04
Thai (8)	15	0.05
Vietnamese (79)	107	0.35
Hawaii Native/Pacific Islander (3)	13	0.04
Not Hispanic (2)	11	0.04
Hispanic (1)	2	0.01
Guamanian/Chamorro (1)	1	<0.01
Native Hawaiian (2)	4	0.01
White (27,705)	28,071	91.23
Not Hispanic (27,341)	27,664	89.91
Hispanic (364)	407	1.32

Robinson

Place Type: Township
County: Allegheny
Population: 13,354†

Ancestry‡	Population	%
African, Sub-Saharan (14)	14	0.11
African (14)	14	0.11
American (189)	189	1.45
Arab (10)	65	0.50
Arab (0)	12	0.09
Lebanese (10)	42	0.32
Syrian (0)	11	0.08
Australian (0)	11	0.08
Austrian (58)	136	1.04
British (28)	28	0.21
Croatian (38)	142	1.09
Czech (13)	129	0.99
Czechoslovakian (27)	69	0.53
Danish (0)	28	0.21
Dutch (0)	129	0.99
Eastern European (20)	20	0.15
English (336)	1,520	11.62
European (9)	9	0.07
French, ex. Basque (0)	266	2.03
German (750)	3,840	29.36
Greek (11)	85	0.65
Hungarian (48)	207	1.58
Irish (486)	2,780	21.26
Italian (1,230)	2,897	22.15
Lithuanian (97)	247	1.89
Northern European (17)	17	0.13
Norwegian (0)	9	0.07
Polish (494)	1,652	12.63
Portuguese (0)	15	0.11
Russian (43)	221	1.69
Scandinavian (0)	23	0.18
Scotch-Irish (98)	505	3.86
Scottish (36)	228	1.74
Serbian (9)	97	0.74
Slavic (12)	55	0.42
Slovak (194)	723	5.53
Slovene (87)	215	1.64
Swedish (0)	56	0.43
Swiss (10)	41	0.31
Ukrainian (100)	245	1.87
Welsh (0)	178	1.36

Hispanic Origin	Population	%
Hispanic or Latino (of any race)	195	1.46
Central American, ex. Mexican	7	0.05
Costa Rican	1	0.01
Guatemalan	4	0.03
Salvadoran	2	0.01
Cuban	15	0.11
Dominican Republic	2	0.01
Mexican	73	0.55
Puerto Rican	43	0.32
South American	23	0.17
Argentinean	1	0.01
Chilean	1	0.01
Paraguayan	5	0.04
Peruvian	11	0.08
Venezuelan	3	0.02
Other South American	2	0.01
Other Hispanic or Latino	32	0.24

Race*	Population	%
African-American/Black (446)	519	3.89
Not Hispanic (443)	507	3.80
Hispanic (3)	12	0.09
American Indian/Alaska Native (7)	33	0.25
Not Hispanic (5)	27	0.20
Hispanic (2)	6	0.04
Cherokee (3)	8	0.06
Chickasaw (0)	1	0.01
Chippewa (1)	1	0.01
Iroquois (0)	1	0.01
Sioux (0)	3	0.02
Yaqui (1)	1	0.01
Asian (485)	535	4.01
Not Hispanic (483)	530	3.97
Hispanic (2)	5	0.04
Bangladeshi (5)	5	0.04
Cambodian (2)	2	0.01
Chinese, ex. Taiwanese (83)	96	0.72
Filipino (10)	24	0.18
Indian (287)	297	2.22
Indonesian (3)	3	0.02
Japanese (4)	8	0.06
Korean (25)	37	0.28
Pakistani (13)	13	0.10
Sri Lankan (6)	6	0.04
Taiwanese (3)	3	0.02
Thai (4)	4	0.03
Vietnamese (32)	34	0.25
Hawaii Native/Pacific Islander (1)	3	0.02
Not Hispanic (1)	2	0.01
Hispanic (0)	1	0.01
Guamanian/Chamorro (0)	1	0.01
Native Hawaiian (1)	1	0.01
White (12,205)	12,351	92.49
Not Hispanic (12,083)	12,209	91.43
Hispanic (122)	142	1.06

Ross

Place Type: Township
County: Allegheny
Population: 31,105†

Ancestry‡	Population	%
African, Sub-Saharan (16)	16	0.05
African (16)	16	0.05
Albanian (0)	15	0.05
American (1,324)	1,324	4.26
Arab (103)	242	0.78
Arab (49)	49	0.16
Egyptian (12)	12	0.04
Lebanese (15)	98	0.31
Syrian (27)	83	0.27
Australian (0)	26	0.08
Austrian (110)	273	0.88
Belgian (0)	13	0.04
Brazilian (16)	16	0.05
British (35)	73	0.23
Canadian (15)	15	0.05
Carpatho Rusyn (17)	17	0.05
Celtic (11)	21	0.07
Croatian (255)	678	2.18
Czech (89)	230	0.74
Czechoslovakian (64)	151	0.49
Danish (0)	24	0.08
Dutch (33)	174	0.56
Eastern European (8)	8	0.03
English (419)	2,734	8.79
European (324)	349	1.12
Finnish (11)	11	0.04
French, ex. Basque (84)	676	2.17
French Canadian (0)	65	0.21
German (3,527)	12,468	40.07
Greek (175)	347	1.12
Hungarian (78)	468	1.50
Irish (1,719)	7,723	24.82
Israeli (13)	13	0.04
Italian (1,629)	5,146	16.54
Lithuanian (12)	121	0.39
Macedonian (9)	24	0.08
Northern European (13)	13	0.04
Norwegian (20)	30	0.10
Pennsylvania German (11)	48	0.15
Polish (1,032)	3,153	10.13
Romanian (93)	199	0.64
Russian (131)	327	1.05
Scandinavian (36)	64	0.21
Scotch-Irish (282)	767	2.47
Scottish (75)	645	2.07
Serbian (22)	82	0.26
Slavic (6)	68	0.22
Slovak (400)	1,359	4.37
Slovene (24)	46	0.15
Swedish (51)	312	1.00
Swiss (7)	113	0.36
Ukrainian (107)	250	0.80
Welsh (37)	441	1.42
West Indian, ex. Hispanic (23)	23	0.07
Haitian (12)	12	0.04
Jamaican (11)	11	0.04
Yugoslavian (9)	41	0.13

Hispanic Origin	Population	%
Hispanic or Latino (of any race)	350	1.13
Central American, ex. Mexican	30	0.10
Costa Rican	5	0.02
Guatemalan	12	0.04
Honduran	1	<0.01
Nicaraguan	2	0.01
Panamanian	5	0.02
Salvadoran	5	0.02
Cuban	15	0.05
Dominican Republic	2	0.01
Mexican	155	0.50
Puerto Rican	50	0.16
South American	58	0.19
Argentinean	14	0.05
Bolivian	1	<0.01
Chilean	4	0.01
Colombian	6	0.02
Ecuadorian	19	0.06
Peruvian	6	0.02
Venezuelan	8	0.03
Other Hispanic or Latino	40	0.13

Race*	Population	%
African-American/Black (647)	761	2.45
Not Hispanic (641)	745	2.40
Hispanic (6)	16	0.05
American Indian/Alaska Native (30)	102	0.33
Not Hispanic (23)	86	0.28
Hispanic (7)	16	0.05
Alaska Athabascan *(Ala. Nat.)* (1)	2	0.01
Aleut *(Alaska Native)* (0)	1	<0.01
Blackfeet (1)	3	0.01
Cherokee (3)	13	0.04

*Notes: † The Census 2010 population figure is used to calculate the percentages in the Hispanic Origin and Race categories. Ancestry percentages are based on the 2006-2010 American Community Survey population (not shown); ‡ Numbers in parentheses indicate the number of people reporting a single ancestry; * Numbers in parentheses indicate the number of persons reporting this race alone, not in combination with any other race; Please refer to the Explanation of Data for more information.*

Choctaw (1)	3	0.01
Cree (0)	1	<0.01
Creek (0)	2	0.01
Iroquois (3)	9	0.03
Mexican American Ind. (0)	1	<0.01
Osage (2)	2	0.01
Seminole (0)	3	0.01
Shoshone (0)	1	<0.01
Sioux (1)	2	0.01
Asian (765)	908	2.92
Not Hispanic (763)	904	2.91
Hispanic (2)	4	0.01
Bangladeshi (5)	7	0.02
Burmese (3)	3	0.01
Cambodian (1)	2	0.01
Chinese, ex. Taiwanese (275)	312	1.00
Filipino (45)	66	0.21
Indian (246)	269	0.86
Indonesian (2)	2	0.01
Japanese (12)	24	0.08
Korean (56)	79	0.25
Laotian (2)	2	0.01
Nepalese (3)	3	0.01
Pakistani (23)	23	0.07
Sri Lankan (2)	2	0.01
Taiwanese (8)	13	0.04
Thai (3)	3	0.01
Vietnamese (64)	72	0.23
Hawaii Native/Pacific Islander (10)	15	0.05
Not Hispanic (6)	11	0.04
Hispanic (4)	4	0.01
Guamanian/Chamorro (2)	2	0.01
Native Hawaiian (1)	3	0.01
Samoan (4)	4	0.01
Tongan (1)	1	<0.01
White (29,250)	29,523	94.91
Not Hispanic (29,009)	29,259	94.07
Hispanic (241)	264	0.85

Rostraver

Place Type: Township
County: Westmoreland
Population: 11,363†

Ancestry‡	Population	%
African, Sub-Saharan (12)	12	0.11
African (12)	12	0.11
American (285)	285	2.49
Arab (56)	74	0.65
Syrian (56)	74	0.65
Austrian (9)	92	0.81
Belgian (21)	133	1.16
British (0)	27	0.24
Carpatho Rusyn (26)	26	0.23
Croatian (59)	155	1.36
Czech (21)	126	1.10
Czechoslovakian (25)	66	0.58
Danish (14)	32	0.28
Dutch (0)	82	0.72
English (336)	1,556	13.62
European (28)	42	0.37
Finnish (13)	27	0.24
French, ex. Basque (15)	146	1.28
German (525)	2,413	21.12
Greek (53)	166	1.45
Hungarian (211)	482	4.22
Irish (319)	1,563	13.68
Italian (1,059)	2,475	21.66
Lithuanian (0)	8	0.07
Pennsylvania German (38)	47	0.41
Polish (332)	1,547	13.54
Romanian (13)	41	0.36
Russian (56)	337	2.95
Scotch-Irish (64)	258	2.26
Scottish (102)	379	3.32
Serbian (4)	39	0.34
Slavic (14)	79	0.69
Slovak (590)	1,315	11.51
Slovene (38)	108	0.95
Swedish (0)	44	0.39
Ukrainian (26)	139	1.22
Welsh (122)	300	2.63
Yugoslavian (0)	27	0.24

Hispanic Origin	Population	%
Hispanic or Latino (of any race)	121	1.06
Central American, ex. Mexican	8	0.07
Guatemalan	5	0.04
Panamanian	3	0.03
Cuban	5	0.04
Mexican	44	0.39
Puerto Rican	28	0.25
South American	4	0.04
Argentinean	1	0.01
Chilean	1	0.01
Colombian	1	0.01
Venezuelan	1	0.01
Other Hispanic or Latino	32	0.28

Race*	Population	%
African-American/Black (188)	263	2.31
Not Hispanic (184)	249	2.19
Hispanic (4)	14	0.12
American Indian/Alaska Native (7)	47	0.41
Not Hispanic (7)	40	0.35
Hispanic (0)	7	0.06
Alaska Athabascan *(Ala. Nat.)* (1)	1	0.01
Apache (0)	1	0.01
Blackfeet (0)	2	0.02
Cherokee (2)	13	0.11
Houma (1)	1	0.01
Iroquois (0)	1	0.01
Asian (99)	126	1.11
Not Hispanic (99)	124	1.09
Hispanic (0)	2	0.02
Bangladeshi (1)	1	0.01
Chinese, ex. Taiwanese (26)	35	0.31
Filipino (5)	14	0.12
Indian (23)	26	0.23
Indonesian (0)	2	0.02
Japanese (2)	3	0.03
Korean (4)	7	0.06
Pakistani (5)	5	0.04
Thai (2)	2	0.02
Vietnamese (30)	31	0.27
Hawaii Native/Pacific Islander (1)	10	0.09
Not Hispanic (1)	7	0.06
Hispanic (0)	3	0.03
Native Hawaiian (1)	6	0.05
White (10,914)	11,035	97.11
Not Hispanic (10,833)	10,943	96.30
Hispanic (81)	92	0.81

Salisbury

Place Type: Township
County: Lancaster
Population: 11,062†

Ancestry‡	Population	%
African, Sub-Saharan (6)	6	0.06
African (6)	6	0.06
American (1,182)	1,182	10.85
Arab (0)	9	0.08
Syrian (0)	9	0.08
British (0)	8	0.07
Dutch (86)	208	1.91
English (444)	797	7.32
European (45)	45	0.41
French, ex. Basque (0)	163	1.50
French Canadian (0)	43	0.39
German (2,707)	3,993	36.66
Greek (10)	13	0.12
Hungarian (20)	97	0.89
Irish (267)	898	8.25
Italian (67)	269	2.47
Lithuanian (0)	3	0.03
Pennsylvania German (1,526)	1,526	14.01
Polish (65)	222	2.04
Russian (0)	8	0.07
Scotch-Irish (75)	161	1.48
Scottish (0)	65	0.60
Slovak (9)	25	0.23
Swedish (6)	40	0.37
Swiss (194)	338	3.10
Ukrainian (13)	72	0.66
Welsh (0)	59	0.54

Hispanic Origin	Population	%
Hispanic or Latino (of any race)	208	1.88
Central American, ex. Mexican	18	0.16
Costa Rican	11	0.10
Guatemalan	5	0.05
Honduran	1	0.01
Nicaraguan	1	0.01
Cuban	4	0.04
Dominican Republic	2	0.02
Mexican	29	0.26
Puerto Rican	107	0.97
South American	18	0.16
Bolivian	1	0.01
Colombian	5	0.05
Ecuadorian	7	0.06
Peruvian	5	0.05
Other Hispanic or Latino	30	0.27

Race*	Population	%
African-American/Black (118)	160	1.45
Not Hispanic (100)	139	1.26
Hispanic (18)	21	0.19
American Indian/Alaska Native (11)	49	0.44
Not Hispanic (9)	45	0.41
Hispanic (2)	4	0.04
Canadian/French Am. Ind. (0)	2	0.02
Cherokee (2)	9	0.08
Chippewa (2)	3	0.03
Delaware (0)	1	0.01
Osage (0)	1	0.01
South American Ind. (1)	1	0.01
Asian (47)	69	0.62
Not Hispanic (46)	65	0.59
Hispanic (1)	4	0.04
Chinese, ex. Taiwanese (11)	19	0.17
Filipino (8)	10	0.09
Hmong (7)	7	0.06
Indian (4)	9	0.08
Japanese (2)	3	0.03
Korean (3)	3	0.03
Laotian (7)	9	0.08
Thai (1)	2	0.02
Vietnamese (1)	1	0.01
Hawaii Native/Pacific Islander (0)	7	0.06
Not Hispanic (0)	7	0.06
Guamanian/Chamorro (0)	1	0.01
Native Hawaiian (0)	6	0.05
White (10,708)	10,817	97.79
Not Hispanic (10,603)	10,693	96.66
Hispanic (105)	124	1.12

Salisbury

Place Type: Township
County: Lehigh
Population: 13,505†

Ancestry‡	Population	%
African, Sub-Saharan (30)	30	0.22
African (30)	30	0.22
American (487)	487	3.60
Arab (167)	197	1.45
Syrian (167)	197	1.45
Austrian (122)	433	3.20
British (15)	64	0.47
Celtic (0)	12	0.09
Croatian (0)	76	0.56
Czech (14)	91	0.67
Czechoslovakian (45)	53	0.39
Danish (16)	24	0.18
Dutch (114)	570	4.21

*Notes: † The Census 2010 population figure is used to calculate the percentages in the Hispanic Origin and Race categories. Ancestry percentages are based on the 2006-2010 American Community Survey population (not shown); ‡ Numbers in parentheses indicate the number of people reporting a single ancestry; * Numbers in parentheses indicate the number of persons reporting this race alone, not in combination with any other race; Please refer to the Explanation of Data for more information.*

Ancestry	Population	%
English (134)	822	6.07
European (74)	74	0.55
Finnish (0)	18	0.13
French, ex. Basque (26)	163	1.20
French Canadian (9)	74	0.55
German (2,068)	4,632	34.20
Greek (0)	77	0.57
Hungarian (104)	551	4.07
Irish (559)	2,131	15.73
Italian (346)	1,296	9.57
Lithuanian (0)	21	0.16
Norwegian (0)	51	0.38
Pennsylvania German (364)	696	5.14
Polish (445)	880	6.50
Portuguese (10)	18	0.13
Russian (123)	196	1.45
Scotch-Irish (26)	183	1.35
Scottish (44)	146	1.08
Serbian (0)	26	0.19
Slovak (253)	534	3.94
Slovene (10)	10	0.07
Swedish (0)	104	0.77
Swiss (19)	86	0.63
Ukrainian (186)	400	2.95
Welsh (118)	436	3.22
West Indian, ex. Hispanic (15)	15	0.11
Trinidadian/Tobagonian (15)	15	0.11
Yugoslavian (32)	71	0.52

Hispanic Origin	Population	%
Hispanic or Latino (of any race)	903	6.69
Central American, ex. Mexican	65	0.48
Costa Rican	2	0.01
Guatemalan	10	0.07
Honduran	12	0.09
Nicaraguan	4	0.03
Panamanian	1	0.01
Salvadoran	36	0.27
Cuban	10	0.07
Dominican Republic	93	0.69
Mexican	79	0.58
Puerto Rican	508	3.76
South American	64	0.47
Argentinean	5	0.04
Bolivian	1	0.01
Chilean	7	0.05
Colombian	21	0.16
Ecuadorian	9	0.07
Peruvian	17	0.13
Venezuelan	3	0.02
Other South American	1	0.01
Other Hispanic or Latino	84	0.62

Race*	Population	%
African-American/Black (396)	480	3.55
Not Hispanic (362)	427	3.16
Hispanic (34)	53	0.39
American Indian/Alaska Native (4)	47	0.35
Not Hispanic (4)	42	0.31
Hispanic (0)	5	0.04
Apache (0)	3	0.02
Cherokee (0)	12	0.09
Chippewa (0)	1	0.01
Delaware (0)	4	0.03
Seminole (0)	5	0.04
Asian (216)	284	2.10
Not Hispanic (213)	277	2.05
Hispanic (3)	7	0.05
Chinese, ex. Taiwanese (44)	52	0.39
Filipino (36)	47	0.35
Indian (42)	61	0.45
Japanese (4)	10	0.07
Korean (24)	37	0.27
Taiwanese (1)	1	0.01
Thai (0)	2	0.01
Vietnamese (56)	66	0.49
Hawaii Native/Pacific Islander (3)	8	0.06
Not Hispanic (3)	8	0.06
Native Hawaiian (0)	4	0.03
Samoan (1)	2	0.01
White (12,342)	12,542	92.87
Not Hispanic (11,842)	11,987	88.76
Hispanic (500)	555	4.11

Sanatoga

Place Type: CDP
County: Montgomery
Population: 8,378†

Ancestry‡	Population	%
African, Sub-Saharan (124)	133	1.61
African (0)	9	0.11
Ghanaian (124)	124	1.50
American (262)	262	3.17
Arab (20)	30	0.36
Lebanese (20)	30	0.36
Austrian (25)	65	0.79
British (9)	60	0.73
Canadian (9)	9	0.11
Celtic (0)	9	0.11
Czech (9)	9	0.11
Czechoslovakian (11)	36	0.44
Danish (0)	62	0.75
Dutch (31)	232	2.81
Eastern European (42)	42	0.51
English (220)	817	9.89
European (20)	20	0.24
French, ex. Basque (40)	229	2.77
French Canadian (8)	19	0.23
German (856)	2,283	27.65
Greek (0)	29	0.35
Hungarian (7)	30	0.36
Irish (406)	1,625	19.68
Italian (392)	1,463	17.72
Lithuanian (12)	25	0.30
Norwegian (36)	36	0.44
Pennsylvania German (119)	176	2.13
Polish (131)	467	5.66
Romanian (8)	16	0.19
Russian (27)	60	0.73
Scotch-Irish (74)	168	2.03
Scottish (41)	186	2.25
Slovak (15)	153	1.85
Swedish (11)	34	0.41
Swiss (12)	21	0.25
Ukrainian (51)	281	3.40
Welsh (0)	18	0.22
West Indian, ex. Hispanic (13)	13	0.16
Jamaican (13)	13	0.16
Yugoslavian (0)	30	0.36

Hispanic Origin	Population	%
Hispanic or Latino (of any race)	258	3.08
Central American, ex. Mexican	7	0.08
Guatemalan	2	0.02
Nicaraguan	4	0.05
Salvadoran	1	0.01
Cuban	11	0.13
Dominican Republic	2	0.02
Mexican	58	0.69
Puerto Rican	130	1.55
South American	20	0.24
Argentinean	1	0.01
Colombian	8	0.10
Ecuadorian	3	0.04
Peruvian	8	0.10
Other Hispanic or Latino	30	0.36

Race*	Population	%
African-American/Black (1,112)	1,276	15.23
Not Hispanic (1,069)	1,221	14.57
Hispanic (43)	55	0.66
American Indian/Alaska Native (11)	51	0.61
Not Hispanic (8)	46	0.55
Hispanic (3)	5	0.06
Blackfeet (0)	10	0.12
Cherokee (1)	14	0.17
Crow (0)	1	0.01
Delaware (0)	2	0.02
Iroquois (0)	1	0.01
Mexican American Ind. (2)	2	0.02
Sioux (0)	3	0.04
Asian (160)	200	2.39
Not Hispanic (160)	199	2.38
Hispanic (0)	1	0.01
Cambodian (2)	3	0.04
Chinese, ex. Taiwanese (35)	37	0.44
Filipino (16)	24	0.29
Indian (40)	46	0.55
Japanese (5)	13	0.16
Korean (20)	26	0.31
Laotian (1)	2	0.02
Nepalese (5)	5	0.06
Pakistani (11)	11	0.13
Sri Lankan (0)	2	0.02
Taiwanese (0)	1	0.01
Thai (1)	1	0.01
Vietnamese (21)	25	0.30
Hawaii Native/Pacific Islander (6)	13	0.16
Not Hispanic (6)	12	0.14
Hispanic (0)	1	0.01
Guamanian/Chamorro (0)	1	0.01
Marshallese (1)	1	0.01
Native Hawaiian (2)	5	0.06
Samoan (1)	7	0.08
White (6,805)	7,019	83.78
Not Hispanic (6,641)	6,834	81.57
Hispanic (164)	185	2.21

Sandy

Place Type: Township
County: Clearfield
Population: 10,625†

Ancestry‡	Population	%
American (3,282)	3,282	30.33
Arab (64)	64	0.59
Lebanese (40)	40	0.37
Syrian (24)	24	0.22
Australian (15)	15	0.14
Austrian (35)	72	0.67
Belgian (15)	15	0.14
British (28)	28	0.26
Canadian (62)	62	0.57
Croatian (0)	11	0.10
Czech (0)	14	0.13
Czechoslovakian (16)	36	0.33
Danish (9)	19	0.18
Dutch (12)	168	1.55
English (322)	860	7.95
French, ex. Basque (76)	343	3.17
French Canadian (11)	69	0.64
German (778)	2,055	18.99
Greek (0)	28	0.26
Hungarian (33)	57	0.53
Irish (317)	935	8.64
Italian (531)	1,098	10.15
Lithuanian (68)	208	1.92
Norwegian (76)	76	0.70
Pennsylvania German (32)	96	0.89
Polish (116)	591	5.46
Russian (31)	31	0.29
Scotch-Irish (50)	167	1.54
Scottish (112)	207	1.91
Slavic (20)	20	0.18
Slovak (277)	390	3.60
Swedish (168)	477	4.41
Ukrainian (8)	37	0.34
Welsh (16)	105	0.97
West Indian, ex. Hispanic (4)	4	0.04
Jamaican (4)	4	0.04

Hispanic Origin	Population	%
Hispanic or Latino (of any race)	83	0.78
Central American, ex. Mexican	1	0.01
Guatemalan	1	0.01
Cuban	7	0.07
Mexican	35	0.33

*Notes: † The Census 2010 population figure is used to calculate the percentages in the Hispanic Origin and Race categories. Ancestry percentages are based on the 2006-2010 American Community Survey population (not shown); ‡ Numbers in parentheses indicate the number of people reporting a single ancestry; * Numbers in parentheses indicate the number of persons reporting this race alone, not in combination with any other race; Please refer to the Explanation of Data for more information.*

Puerto Rican	16	0.15
South American	6	0.06
Colombian	1	0.01
Paraguayan	1	0.01
Uruguayan	2	0.02
Venezuelan	2	0.02
Other Hispanic or Latino	18	0.17

Race*	Population	%
African-American/Black (37)	72	0.68
Not Hispanic (36)	70	0.66
Hispanic (1)	2	0.02
American Indian/Alaska Native (4)	39	0.37
Not Hispanic (3)	38	0.36
Hispanic (1)	1	0.01
Blackfeet (0)	2	0.02
Cherokee (0)	6	0.06
Cree (0)	1	0.01
Hopi (0)	1	0.01
Iroquois (1)	6	0.06
Mexican American Ind. (1)	1	0.01
Seminole (0)	4	0.04
Sioux (0)	1	0.01
Asian (109)	132	1.24
Not Hispanic (109)	131	1.23
Hispanic (0)	1	0.01
Chinese, ex. Taiwanese (19)	21	0.20
Filipino (10)	17	0.16
Indian (46)	48	0.45
Japanese (3)	9	0.08
Korean (14)	16	0.15
Pakistani (9)	9	0.08
Taiwanese (2)	3	0.03
Thai (1)	1	0.01
Vietnamese (4)	8	0.08
Hawaii Native/Pacific Islander (3)	3	0.03
Not Hispanic (3)	3	0.03
Guamanian/Chamorro (3)	3	0.03
White (10,366)	10,458	98.43
Not Hispanic (10,302)	10,391	97.80
Hispanic (64)	67	0.63

Schuylkill

Place Type: Township
County: Chester
Population: 8,516†

Ancestry‡	Population	%
American (239)	239	2.88
Arab (27)	63	0.76
Arab (0)	8	0.10
Egyptian (27)	43	0.52
Lebanese (0)	12	0.14
Armenian (0)	39	0.47
Austrian (0)	51	0.61
British (63)	63	0.76
Canadian (0)	10	0.12
Czechoslovakian (0)	17	0.20
Dutch (28)	74	0.89
Eastern European (60)	60	0.72
English (240)	1,090	13.12
European (157)	167	2.01
Finnish (22)	22	0.26
French, ex. Basque (28)	226	2.72
German (514)	2,152	25.91
Greek (18)	78	0.94
Hungarian (55)	163	1.96
Irish (675)	2,602	31.33
Italian (390)	1,314	15.82
Lithuanian (10)	46	0.55
Northern European (33)	33	0.40
Norwegian (16)	106	1.28
Pennsylvania German (45)	61	0.73
Polish (160)	474	5.71
Russian (27)	230	2.77
Scotch-Irish (98)	297	3.58
Scottish (100)	191	2.30
Serbian (0)	16	0.19
Slovak (49)	199	2.40
Swedish (32)	44	0.53
Swiss (0)	40	0.48
Ukrainian (16)	50	0.60
Welsh (12)	177	2.13

Hispanic Origin	Population	%
Hispanic or Latino (of any race)	225	2.64
Central American, ex. Mexican	15	0.18
Costa Rican	1	0.01
Guatemalan	8	0.09
Nicaraguan	1	0.01
Panamanian	4	0.05
Salvadoran	1	0.01
Cuban	16	0.19
Dominican Republic	3	0.04
Mexican	41	0.48
Puerto Rican	72	0.85
South American	37	0.43
Argentinean	6	0.07
Chilean	1	0.01
Colombian	16	0.19
Ecuadorian	7	0.08
Paraguayan	2	0.02
Peruvian	3	0.04
Uruguayan	1	0.01
Venezuelan	1	0.01
Other Hispanic or Latino	41	0.48

Race*	Population	%
African-American/Black (180)	227	2.67
Not Hispanic (177)	222	2.61
Hispanic (3)	5	0.06
American Indian/Alaska Native (9)	26	0.31
Not Hispanic (5)	22	0.26
Hispanic (4)	4	0.05
Blackfeet (0)	1	0.01
Cherokee (1)	5	0.06
Cheyenne (0)	1	0.01
Comanche (1)	2	0.02
Mexican American Ind. (4)	4	0.05
Shoshone (0)	1	0.01
Sioux (0)	1	0.01
Asian (343)	406	4.77
Not Hispanic (343)	406	4.77
Bangladeshi (2)	2	0.02
Cambodian (1)	1	0.01
Chinese, ex. Taiwanese (90)	110	1.29
Filipino (46)	61	0.72
Indian (110)	127	1.49
Indonesian (0)	1	0.01
Japanese (1)	8	0.09
Korean (22)	28	0.33
Pakistani (9)	11	0.13
Taiwanese (6)	7	0.08
Thai (1)	1	0.01
Vietnamese (44)	57	0.67
Hawaii Native/Pacific Islander (0)	8	0.09
Not Hispanic (0)	7	0.08
Hispanic (0)	1	0.01
Native Hawaiian (0)	4	0.05
White (7,810)	7,921	93.01
Not Hispanic (7,638)	7,746	90.96
Hispanic (172)	175	2.05

Scott

Place Type: Township
County: Allegheny
Population: 17,024†

Ancestry‡	Population	%
American (457)	457	2.70
Arab (85)	227	1.34
Arab (6)	6	0.04
Lebanese (61)	187	1.10
Syrian (18)	34	0.20
Austrian (96)	239	1.41
Belgian (0)	17	0.10
Brazilian (14)	14	0.08
Bulgarian (18)	18	0.11
Canadian (7)	7	0.04
Carpatho Rusyn (15)	15	0.09
Croatian (23)	130	0.77
Czech (24)	97	0.57
Dutch (14)	106	0.63
Eastern European (11)	11	0.06
English (221)	1,195	7.05
European (80)	80	0.47
French, ex. Basque (26)	406	2.40
French Canadian (25)	25	0.15
German (1,476)	5,047	29.78
Greek (57)	63	0.37
Hungarian (88)	293	1.73
Irish (692)	3,419	20.18
Italian (1,394)	3,294	19.44
Lithuanian (56)	280	1.65
Norwegian (18)	48	0.28
Polish (663)	2,466	14.55
Romanian (8)	17	0.10
Russian (94)	288	1.70
Scandinavian (0)	7	0.04
Scotch-Irish (163)	528	3.12
Scottish (60)	221	1.30
Serbian (54)	60	0.35
Slavic (5)	13	0.08
Slovak (146)	534	3.15
Slovene (51)	89	0.53
Swedish (27)	76	0.45
Swiss (0)	141	0.83
Turkish (23)	23	0.14
Ukrainian (114)	271	1.60
Welsh (19)	200	1.18
West Indian, ex. Hispanic (27)	27	0.16
Jamaican (27)	27	0.16
Yugoslavian (20)	20	0.12

Hispanic Origin	Population	%
Hispanic or Latino (of any race)	156	0.92
Central American, ex. Mexican	18	0.11
Guatemalan	6	0.04
Honduran	1	0.01
Panamanian	4	0.02
Salvadoran	7	0.04
Cuban	4	0.02
Dominican Republic	4	0.02
Mexican	56	0.33
Puerto Rican	32	0.19
South American	18	0.11
Argentinean	1	0.01
Bolivian	3	0.02
Colombian	2	0.01
Peruvian	3	0.02
Venezuelan	9	0.05
Other Hispanic or Latino	24	0.14

Race*	Population	%
African-American/Black (321)	408	2.40
Not Hispanic (318)	398	2.34
Hispanic (3)	10	0.06
American Indian/Alaska Native (20)	56	0.33
Not Hispanic (19)	50	0.29
Hispanic (1)	6	0.04
Blackfeet (0)	4	0.02
Cherokee (2)	14	0.08
Chickasaw (1)	1	0.01
Chippewa (1)	1	0.01
Iroquois (1)	1	0.01
Mexican American Ind. (1)	2	0.01
Navajo (0)	1	0.01
Sioux (1)	1	0.01
Asian (1,827)	1,913	11.24
Not Hispanic (1,822)	1,906	11.20
Hispanic (5)	7	0.04
Bangladeshi (7)	7	0.04
Cambodian (1)	1	0.01
Chinese, ex. Taiwanese (76)	82	0.48
Filipino (20)	30	0.18
Indian (1,594)	1,620	9.52
Indonesian (1)	2	0.01
Japanese (14)	23	0.14

*Notes: † The Census 2010 population figure is used to calculate the percentages in the Hispanic Origin and Race categories. Ancestry percentages are based on the 2006-2010 American Community Survey population (not shown); ‡ Numbers in parentheses indicate the number of people reporting a single ancestry; * Numbers in parentheses indicate the number of persons reporting this race alone, not in combination with any other race; Please refer to the Explanation of Data for more information.*

Korean (14)	18	0.11
Nepalese (5)	5	0.03
Pakistani (26)	27	0.16
Sri Lankan (1)	4	0.02
Taiwanese (8)	8	0.05
Thai (5)	6	0.04
Vietnamese (29)	34	0.20
Hawaii Native/Pacific Islander (4)	9	0.05
Not Hispanic (3)	8	0.05
Hispanic (1)	1	0.01
Guamanian/Chamorro (2)	4	0.02
Native Hawaiian (0)	2	0.01
Samoan (2)	2	0.01
White (14,568)	14,727	86.51
Not Hispanic (14,475)	14,625	85.91
Hispanic (93)	102	0.60

Scranton

Place Type: City
County: Lackawanna
Population: 76,089†

Ancestry‡	Population	%
African, Sub-Saharan (55)	93	0.12
African (47)	85	0.11
Nigerian (8)	8	0.01
American (1,834)	1,834	2.41
Arab (225)	541	0.71
Arab (36)	86	0.11
Egyptian (45)	45	0.06
Lebanese (117)	383	0.50
Moroccan (5)	5	0.01
Other Arab (22)	22	0.03
Armenian (0)	41	0.05
Australian (0)	10	0.01
Austrian (68)	301	0.40
Belgian (20)	20	0.03
Brazilian (283)	305	0.40
British (56)	88	0.12
Bulgarian (55)	55	0.07
Canadian (20)	71	0.09
Carpatho Rusyn (26)	35	0.05
Celtic (0)	3	<0.01
Croatian (0)	29	0.04
Czech (11)	209	0.27
Czechoslovakian (16)	78	0.10
Danish (48)	103	0.14
Dutch (55)	707	0.93
Eastern European (7)	7	0.01
English (936)	4,507	5.93
European (441)	457	0.60
Finnish (26)	51	0.07
French, ex. Basque (115)	787	1.03
French Canadian (63)	190	0.25
German (3,405)	14,561	19.14
Greek (59)	203	0.27
Hungarian (112)	512	0.67
Icelander (0)	8	0.01
Iranian (56)	56	0.07
Irish (8,546)	23,274	30.60
Israeli (22)	22	0.03
Italian (6,015)	16,031	21.08
Latvian (14)	26	0.03
Lithuanian (486)	1,584	2.08
New Zealander (0)	10	0.01
Norwegian (15)	53	0.07
Pennsylvania German (111)	330	0.43
Polish (3,557)	10,984	14.44
Portuguese (153)	165	0.22
Romanian (28)	83	0.11
Russian (583)	2,676	3.52
Scotch-Irish (292)	608	0.80
Scottish (153)	479	0.63
Serbian (0)	33	0.04
Slavic (40)	64	0.08
Slovak (361)	1,344	1.77
Slovene (41)	49	0.06
Swedish (78)	327	0.43
Swiss (17)	169	0.22
Turkish (172)	172	0.23
Ukrainian (535)	1,060	1.39
Welsh (829)	4,539	5.97
West Indian, ex. Hispanic (87)	161	0.21
Haitian (14)	47	0.06
Jamaican (27)	44	0.06
Trinidadian/Tobagonian (26)	26	0.03
West Indian (20)	44	0.06

Hispanic Origin	Population	%
Hispanic or Latino (of any race)	7,531	9.90
Central American, ex. Mexican	448	0.59
Costa Rican	11	0.01
Guatemalan	34	0.04
Honduran	268	0.35
Nicaraguan	18	0.02
Panamanian	12	0.02
Salvadoran	100	0.13
Other Central American	5	0.01
Cuban	125	0.16
Dominican Republic	605	0.80
Mexican	1,945	2.56
Puerto Rican	3,172	4.17
South American	466	0.61
Argentinean	39	0.05
Bolivian	8	0.01
Chilean	11	0.01
Colombian	96	0.13
Ecuadorian	125	0.16
Paraguayan	4	0.01
Peruvian	98	0.13
Uruguayan	69	0.09
Venezuelan	16	0.02
Other Hispanic or Latino	770	1.01

Race*	Population	%
African-American/Black (4,150)	5,226	6.87
Not Hispanic (3,657)	4,513	5.93
Hispanic (493)	713	0.94
American Indian/Alaska Native (178)	462	0.61
Not Hispanic (100)	353	0.46
Hispanic (78)	109	0.14
Apache (3)	5	0.01
Blackfeet (2)	14	0.02
Central American Ind. (0)	2	<0.01
Cherokee (20)	61	0.08
Chippewa (1)	4	0.01
Choctaw (0)	1	<0.01
Comanche (0)	1	<0.01
Creek (5)	6	0.01
Delaware (0)	4	0.01
Iroquois (14)	14	0.02
Mexican American Ind. (7)	7	0.01
Navajo (2)	2	<0.01
Pueblo (3)	3	<0.01
Seminole (1)	1	<0.01
Sioux (0)	16	0.02
South American Ind. (2)	6	0.01
Spanish American Ind. (0)	2	<0.01
Asian (2,269)	2,642	3.47
Not Hispanic (2,240)	2,577	3.39
Hispanic (29)	65	0.09
Bangladeshi (3)	3	<0.01
Bhutanese (54)	101	0.13
Burmese (0)	4	0.01
Cambodian (4)	7	0.01
Chinese, ex. Taiwanese (142)	186	0.24
Filipino (126)	173	0.23
Indian (1,147)	1,247	1.64
Indonesian (238)	260	0.34
Japanese (15)	42	0.06
Korean (56)	82	0.11
Laotian (112)	133	0.17
Malaysian (7)	7	0.01
Nepalese (33)	80	0.11
Pakistani (50)	54	0.07
Sri Lankan (1)	1	<0.01
Taiwanese (1)	1	<0.01
Thai (18)	33	0.04
Vietnamese (142)	159	0.21
Hawaii Native/Pacific Islander (32)	83	0.11
Not Hispanic (21)	55	0.07
Hispanic (11)	28	0.04
Guamanian/Chamorro (7)	11	0.01
Native Hawaiian (4)	12	0.02
Samoan (0)	5	0.01
White (64,001)	65,659	86.29
Not Hispanic (60,954)	62,216	81.77
Hispanic (3,047)	3,443	4.52

Shaler

Place Type: Township
County: Allegheny
Population: 28,757†

Ancestry‡	Population	%
American (715)	715	2.49
Arab (43)	88	0.31
Arab (0)	20	0.07
Lebanese (43)	68	0.24
Armenian (0)	13	0.05
Austrian (0)	102	0.36
British (0)	53	0.18
Carpatho Rusyn (16)	29	0.10
Croatian (326)	834	2.91
Czech (97)	364	1.27
Czechoslovakian (12)	39	0.14
Danish (6)	6	0.02
Dutch (0)	223	0.78
English (339)	2,226	7.76
European (332)	332	1.16
French, ex. Basque (22)	708	2.47
French Canadian (28)	120	0.42
German (3,636)	12,858	44.80
Greek (214)	263	0.92
Hungarian (52)	242	0.84
Irish (835)	6,518	22.71
Italian (2,067)	5,891	20.52
Lithuanian (60)	200	0.70
Macedonian (12)	12	0.04
Maltese (0)	37	0.13
Norwegian (25)	114	0.40
Pennsylvania German (46)	109	0.38
Polish (1,687)	4,867	16.96
Romanian (11)	11	0.04
Russian (172)	451	1.57
Scotch-Irish (344)	758	2.64
Scottish (79)	545	1.90
Serbian (12)	12	0.04
Slavic (70)	141	0.49
Slovak (254)	756	2.63
Slovene (60)	114	0.40
Swedish (13)	153	0.53
Swiss (18)	97	0.34
Ukrainian (116)	260	0.91
Welsh (7)	489	1.70
West Indian, ex. Hispanic (11)	11	0.04
U.S. Virgin Islander (11)	11	0.04
Yugoslavian (48)	58	0.20

Hispanic Origin	Population	%
Hispanic or Latino (of any race)	234	0.81
Central American, ex. Mexican	20	0.07
Costa Rican	1	<0.01
Guatemalan	10	0.03
Nicaraguan	2	0.01
Panamanian	6	0.02
Other Central American	1	<0.01
Cuban	13	0.05
Dominican Republic	7	0.02
Mexican	88	0.31
Puerto Rican	33	0.11
South American	41	0.14
Argentinean	6	0.02
Bolivian	2	0.01
Chilean	5	0.02
Colombian	13	0.05
Ecuadorian	3	0.01
Paraguayan	1	<0.01

*Notes: † The Census 2010 population figure is used to calculate the percentages in the Hispanic Origin and Race categories. Ancestry percentages are based on the 2006-2010 American Community Survey population (not shown); ‡ Numbers in parentheses indicate the number of people reporting a single ancestry; * Numbers in parentheses indicate the number of persons reporting this race alone, not in combination with any other race; Please refer to the Explanation of Data for more information.*

Peruvian	10	0.03
Venezuelan	1	<0.01
Other Hispanic or Latino	32	0.11

Race*	Population	%
African-American/Black (206)	284	0.99
Not Hispanic (203)	276	0.96
Hispanic (3)	8	0.03
American Indian/Alaska Native (18)	92	0.32
Not Hispanic (16)	77	0.27
Hispanic (2)	15	0.05
Blackfeet (0)	5	0.02
Cherokee (1)	18	0.06
Chickasaw (0)	4	0.01
Choctaw (0)	12	0.04
Delaware (0)	1	<0.01
Iroquois (2)	7	0.02
Mexican American Ind. (1)	2	0.01
Navajo (2)	2	0.01
Seminole (0)	4	0.01
Sioux (0)	3	0.01
South American Ind. (0)	1	<0.01
Asian (267)	349	1.21
Not Hispanic (264)	341	1.19
Hispanic (3)	8	0.03
Burmese (0)	1	<0.01
Cambodian (2)	6	0.02
Chinese, ex. Taiwanese (66)	91	0.32
Filipino (29)	38	0.13
Indian (69)	70	0.24
Indonesian (1)	7	0.02
Japanese (9)	21	0.07
Korean (15)	18	0.06
Nepalese (4)	4	0.01
Pakistani (10)	10	0.03
Sri Lankan (3)	3	0.01
Taiwanese (4)	5	0.02
Thai (11)	15	0.05
Vietnamese (41)	55	0.19
Hawaii Native/Pacific Islander (5)	14	0.05
Not Hispanic (5)	12	0.04
Hispanic (0)	2	0.01
Native Hawaiian (0)	2	0.01
Samoan (2)	3	0.01
Tongan (3)	3	0.01
White (27,995)	28,219	98.13
Not Hispanic (27,819)	28,024	97.45
Hispanic (176)	195	0.68

Sharon

Place Type: City
County: Mercer
Population: 14,038†

Ancestry‡	Population	%
African, Sub-Saharan (58)	58	0.40
African (58)	58	0.40
American (636)	636	4.40
Arab (12)	12	0.08
Lebanese (12)	12	0.08
Austrian (11)	52	0.36
Belgian (18)	34	0.24
British (53)	70	0.48
Croatian (57)	235	1.63
Czech (9)	188	1.30
Czechoslovakian (11)	24	0.17
Dutch (15)	494	3.42
English (245)	987	6.83
European (48)	48	0.33
Finnish (17)	17	0.12
French, ex. Basque (11)	335	2.32
French Canadian (0)	45	0.31
German (1,382)	4,430	30.64
Greek (0)	62	0.43
Hungarian (97)	352	2.43
Irish (527)	2,342	16.20
Italian (890)	2,298	15.90
Lithuanian (10)	19	0.13
Norwegian (9)	32	0.22
Pennsylvania German (45)	133	0.92
Polish (260)	864	5.98
Portuguese (0)	41	0.28
Romanian (24)	90	0.62
Russian (0)	67	0.46
Scotch-Irish (103)	424	2.93
Scottish (19)	151	1.04
Serbian (12)	12	0.08
Slavic (9)	9	0.06
Slovak (365)	848	5.87
Slovene (13)	66	0.46
Swedish (14)	83	0.57
Swiss (0)	9	0.06
Ukrainian (28)	99	0.68
Welsh (28)	138	0.95

Hispanic Origin	Population	%
Hispanic or Latino (of any race)	252	1.80
Central American, ex. Mexican	5	0.04
Guatemalan	3	0.02
Nicaraguan	1	0.01
Panamanian	1	0.01
Cuban	16	0.11
Dominican Republic	1	0.01
Mexican	89	0.63
Puerto Rican	95	0.68
South American	12	0.09
Argentinean	3	0.02
Chilean	4	0.03
Colombian	4	0.03
Peruvian	1	0.01
Other Hispanic or Latino	34	0.24

Race*	Population	%
African-American/Black (2,045)	2,441	17.39
Not Hispanic (1,988)	2,369	16.88
Hispanic (57)	72	0.51
American Indian/Alaska Native (35)	118	0.84
Not Hispanic (29)	105	0.75
Hispanic (6)	13	0.09
Blackfeet (0)	4	0.03
Canadian/French Am. Ind. (1)	3	0.02
Cherokee (3)	29	0.21
Cheyenne (0)	5	0.04
Choctaw (0)	1	0.01
Delaware (3)	4	0.03
Houma (0)	1	0.01
Inupiat *(Alaska Native)* (0)	3	0.02
Iroquois (0)	2	0.01
Mexican American Ind. (3)	3	0.02
Navajo (0)	3	0.02
Shoshone (0)	2	0.01
Sioux (2)	4	0.03
Spanish American Ind. (0)	1	0.01
Asian (76)	120	0.85
Not Hispanic (74)	114	0.81
Hispanic (2)	6	0.04
Cambodian (1)	1	0.01
Chinese, ex. Taiwanese (26)	28	0.20
Filipino (11)	19	0.14
Indian (8)	12	0.09
Japanese (4)	5	0.04
Korean (7)	23	0.16
Laotian (3)	3	0.02
Pakistani (2)	2	0.01
Taiwanese (1)	1	0.01
Thai (2)	2	0.01
Vietnamese (7)	7	0.05
Hawaii Native/Pacific Islander (3)	3	0.02
Not Hispanic (3)	3	0.02
Guamanian/Chamorro (1)	1	0.01
Native Hawaiian (2)	2	0.01
White (11,285)	11,793	84.01
Not Hispanic (11,180)	11,639	82.91
Hispanic (105)	154	1.10

Shiloh

Place Type: CDP
County: York
Population: 11,218†

Ancestry‡	Population	%
African, Sub-Saharan (186)	186	1.64
African (75)	75	0.66
Kenyan (14)	14	0.12
Other Sub-Saharan African (97)	97	0.85
American (1,229)	1,229	10.80
Austrian (0)	9	0.08
British (36)	78	0.69
Canadian (9)	9	0.08
Croatian (8)	23	0.20
Czech (0)	47	0.41
Dutch (136)	186	1.64
English (393)	1,022	8.98
European (91)	91	0.80
French, ex. Basque (23)	188	1.65
French Canadian (23)	125	1.10
German (3,069)	4,926	43.31
Greek (151)	181	1.59
Hungarian (42)	124	1.09
Irish (519)	1,439	12.65
Italian (314)	717	6.30
Lithuanian (0)	11	0.10
Northern European (15)	15	0.13
Norwegian (23)	47	0.41
Pennsylvania German (113)	140	1.23
Polish (132)	258	2.27
Russian (32)	97	0.85
Scandinavian (0)	10	0.09
Scotch-Irish (68)	226	1.99
Scottish (21)	119	1.05
Serbian (7)	7	0.06
Slovak (60)	114	1.00
Swedish (16)	86	0.76
Swiss (14)	52	0.46
Ukrainian (15)	72	0.63
Welsh (0)	81	0.71
West Indian, ex. Hispanic (0)	16	0.14
Belizean (0)	16	0.14
Yugoslavian (17)	17	0.15

Hispanic Origin	Population	%
Hispanic or Latino (of any race)	348	3.10
Central American, ex. Mexican	31	0.28
Costa Rican	3	0.03
Guatemalan	3	0.03
Panamanian	8	0.07
Salvadoran	17	0.15
Cuban	2	0.02
Dominican Republic	21	0.19
Mexican	63	0.56
Puerto Rican	189	1.68
South American	17	0.15
Argentinean	2	0.02
Bolivian	6	0.05
Chilean	1	0.01
Colombian	2	0.02
Ecuadorian	1	0.01
Peruvian	5	0.04
Other Hispanic or Latino	25	0.22

Race*	Population	%
African-American/Black (503)	627	5.59
Not Hispanic (482)	590	5.26
Hispanic (21)	37	0.33
American Indian/Alaska Native (10)	49	0.44
Not Hispanic (8)	40	0.36
Hispanic (2)	9	0.08
Blackfeet (0)	6	0.05
Cherokee (1)	14	0.12
Iroquois (3)	3	0.03
Pueblo (0)	3	0.03
Sioux (0)	3	0.03
South American Ind. (1)	1	0.01
Asian (153)	193	1.72

*Notes: † The Census 2010 population figure is used to calculate the percentages in the Hispanic Origin and Race categories. Ancestry percentages are based on the 2006-2010 American Community Survey population (not shown); ‡ Numbers in parentheses indicate the number of people reporting a single ancestry; * Numbers in parentheses indicate the number of persons reporting this race alone, not in combination with any other race; Please refer to the Explanation of Data for more information.*

Not Hispanic (153)	189	1.68
Hispanic (0)	4	0.04
Cambodian (8)	9	0.08
Chinese, ex. Taiwanese (24)	35	0.31
Filipino (25)	34	0.30
Indian (40)	46	0.41
Indonesian (0)	2	0.02
Japanese (5)	13	0.12
Korean (9)	13	0.12
Laotian (2)	2	0.02
Pakistani (0)	1	0.01
Sri Lankan (1)	1	0.01
Thai (1)	4	0.04
Vietnamese (32)	36	0.32
Hawaii Native/Pacific Islander (4)	17	0.15
Not Hispanic (4)	15	0.13
Hispanic (0)	2	0.02
Guamanian/Chamorro (1)	1	0.01
Native Hawaiian (0)	5	0.04
Samoan (3)	8	0.07
White (10,256)	10,442	93.08
Not Hispanic (10,056)	10,206	90.98
Hispanic (200)	236	2.10

Silver Spring

Place Type: Township
County: Cumberland
Population: 13,657†

Ancestry‡	Population	%
American (853)	853	6.51
Arab (40)	51	0.39
Lebanese (27)	27	0.21
Syrian (13)	24	0.18
Armenian (0)	16	0.12
Austrian (0)	90	0.69
Belgian (0)	42	0.32
British (0)	43	0.33
Croatian (12)	64	0.49
Czech (13)	24	0.18
Czechoslovakian (35)	43	0.33
Danish (0)	13	0.10
Dutch (16)	202	1.54
English (425)	1,674	12.78
European (114)	123	0.94
French, ex. Basque (145)	406	3.10
French Canadian (15)	15	0.11
German (2,191)	5,082	38.81
Greek (40)	57	0.44
Hungarian (15)	61	0.47
Irish (522)	1,944	14.84
Italian (381)	1,034	7.90
Lithuanian (32)	147	1.12
Norwegian (18)	169	1.29
Pennsylvania German (64)	74	0.57
Polish (138)	494	3.77
Portuguese (18)	51	0.39
Romanian (14)	44	0.34
Russian (30)	96	0.73
Scandinavian (0)	12	0.09
Scotch-Irish (258)	502	3.83
Scottish (100)	318	2.43
Serbian (17)	17	0.13
Slovak (0)	67	0.51
Slovene (11)	23	0.18
Swedish (0)	127	0.97
Swiss (29)	98	0.75
Ukrainian (0)	86	0.66
Welsh (27)	342	2.61
Yugoslavian (73)	73	0.56

Hispanic Origin	Population	%
Hispanic or Latino (of any race)	276	2.02
Central American, ex. Mexican	13	0.10
Costa Rican	3	0.02
Guatemalan	3	0.02
Honduran	2	0.01
Panamanian	4	0.03
Salvadoran	1	0.01
Cuban	16	0.12
Dominican Republic	9	0.07
Mexican	59	0.43
Puerto Rican	120	0.88
South American	38	0.28
Argentinean	5	0.04
Chilean	8	0.06
Colombian	14	0.10
Ecuadorian	3	0.02
Paraguayan	3	0.02
Peruvian	3	0.02
Venezuelan	1	0.01
Other South American	1	0.01
Other Hispanic or Latino	21	0.15

Race*	Population	%
African-American/Black (194)	277	2.03
Not Hispanic (184)	254	1.86
Hispanic (10)	23	0.17
American Indian/Alaska Native (16)	47	0.34
Not Hispanic (13)	42	0.31
Hispanic (3)	5	0.04
Blackfeet (0)	2	0.01
Cherokee (1)	10	0.07
Chippewa (3)	3	0.02
Crow (1)	1	0.01
Delaware (0)	3	0.02
Hopi (0)	1	0.01
Iroquois (1)	1	0.01
Mexican American Ind. (1)	1	0.01
Osage (0)	1	0.01
Sioux (1)	2	0.01
South American Ind. (1)	1	0.01
Tlingit-Haida *(Alaska Native)* (0)	1	0.01
Yakama (0)	1	0.01
Asian (738)	840	6.15
Not Hispanic (737)	832	6.09
Hispanic (1)	8	0.06
Cambodian (8)	8	0.06
Chinese, ex. Taiwanese (50)	55	0.40
Filipino (30)	51	0.37
Indian (361)	379	2.78
Japanese (8)	22	0.16
Korean (119)	150	1.10
Laotian (5)	7	0.05
Nepalese (1)	1	0.01
Pakistani (58)	61	0.45
Taiwanese (2)	3	0.02
Thai (3)	3	0.02
Vietnamese (83)	91	0.67
Hawaii Native/Pacific Islander (4)	14	0.10
Not Hispanic (3)	12	0.09
Hispanic (1)	2	0.01
Guamanian/Chamorro (3)	7	0.05
Samoan (1)	1	0.01
White (12,399)	12,596	92.23
Not Hispanic (12,243)	12,402	90.81
Hispanic (156)	194	1.42

Skippack

Place Type: Township
County: Montgomery
Population: 13,715†

Ancestry‡	Population	%
African, Sub-Saharan (26)	26	0.20
African (26)	26	0.20
American (348)	348	2.69
Arab (36)	85	0.66
Egyptian (18)	53	0.41
Lebanese (0)	14	0.11
Other Arab (18)	18	0.14
Armenian (31)	31	0.24
Australian (0)	31	0.24
Austrian (0)	20	0.15
Belgian (17)	17	0.13
British (36)	108	0.83
Canadian (28)	28	0.22
Czech (30)	89	0.69
Czechoslovakian (18)	18	0.14
Danish (30)	85	0.66
Dutch (49)	193	1.49
English (347)	1,148	8.87
European (63)	63	0.49
French, ex. Basque (16)	143	1.11
French Canadian (11)	26	0.20
German (789)	2,758	21.31
Greek (83)	148	1.14
Hungarian (0)	49	0.38
Irish (999)	2,927	22.62
Israeli (10)	10	0.08
Italian (750)	1,681	12.99
Latvian (0)	8	0.06
Lithuanian (17)	61	0.47
Norwegian (33)	146	1.13
Pennsylvania German (45)	145	1.12
Polish (236)	783	6.05
Portuguese (6)	78	0.60
Russian (27)	209	1.62
Scandinavian (21)	61	0.47
Scotch-Irish (75)	183	1.41
Scottish (0)	69	0.53
Slavic (10)	17	0.13
Slovak (54)	118	0.91
Swedish (22)	88	0.68
Swiss (0)	53	0.41
Ukrainian (0)	7	0.05
Welsh (23)	290	2.24
West Indian, ex. Hispanic (96)	105	0.81
Trinidadian/Tobagonian (96)	96	0.74
West Indian (0)	9	0.07

Hispanic Origin	Population	%
Hispanic or Latino (of any race)	651	4.75
Central American, ex. Mexican	17	0.12
Costa Rican	2	0.01
Guatemalan	10	0.07
Nicaraguan	2	0.01
Panamanian	1	0.01
Salvadoran	2	0.01
Cuban	16	0.12
Dominican Republic	5	0.04
Mexican	83	0.61
Puerto Rican	78	0.57
South American	42	0.31
Argentinean	6	0.04
Chilean	1	0.01
Colombian	12	0.09
Ecuadorian	6	0.04
Paraguayan	1	0.01
Peruvian	10	0.07
Venezuelan	2	0.01
Other South American	4	0.03
Other Hispanic or Latino	410	2.99

Race*	Population	%
African-American/Black (2,271)	2,346	17.11
Not Hispanic (2,256)	2,321	16.92
Hispanic (15)	25	0.18
American Indian/Alaska Native (7)	29	0.21
Not Hispanic (7)	29	0.21
Cherokee (1)	6	0.04
Chippewa (0)	1	0.01
Delaware (0)	2	0.01
Hopi (0)	2	0.01
Lumbee (3)	3	0.02
Tohono O'Odham (1)	1	0.01
Asian (497)	560	4.08
Not Hispanic (493)	556	4.05
Hispanic (4)	4	0.03
Bangladeshi (9)	9	0.07
Cambodian (7)	8	0.06
Chinese, ex. Taiwanese (107)	116	0.85
Filipino (30)	46	0.34
Indian (157)	166	1.21
Japanese (7)	16	0.12
Korean (123)	143	1.04
Pakistani (1)	3	0.02
Thai (2)	3	0.02

*Notes: † The Census 2010 population figure is used to calculate the percentages in the Hispanic Origin and Race categories. Ancestry percentages are based on the 2006-2010 American Community Survey population (not shown); ‡ Numbers in parentheses indicate the number of people reporting a single ancestry; * Numbers in parentheses indicate the number of persons reporting this race alone, not in combination with any other race; Please refer to the Explanation of Data for more information.*

Vietnamese (36)	39	0.28
Hawaii Native/Pacific Islander (2)	6	0.04
Not Hispanic (2)	2	0.01
Hispanic (0)	4	0.03
Marshallese (1)	1	0.01
White (10,287)	10,439	76.11
Not Hispanic (10,148)	10,283	74.98
Hispanic (139)	156	1.14

Solebury

Place Type: Township
County: Bucks
Population: 8,692†

Ancestry‡	Population	%
Albanian (129)	129	1.51
American (281)	281	3.30
Arab (30)	30	0.35
Jordanian (17)	17	0.20
Syrian (13)	13	0.15
Austrian (0)	89	1.04
Belgian (14)	14	0.16
British (79)	119	1.40
Croatian (0)	19	0.22
Czech (0)	64	0.75
Danish (12)	102	1.20
Dutch (0)	201	2.36
Eastern European (41)	41	0.48
English (748)	1,789	20.99
Estonian (24)	45	0.53
European (177)	177	2.08
French, ex. Basque (119)	363	4.26
French Canadian (21)	21	0.25
German (475)	1,608	18.86
Greek (34)	52	0.61
Hungarian (80)	148	1.74
Irish (423)	1,621	19.02
Italian (499)	1,665	19.53
Lithuanian (0)	45	0.53
Maltese (0)	29	0.34
Norwegian (80)	126	1.48
Pennsylvania German (14)	75	0.88
Polish (189)	583	6.84
Portuguese (0)	86	1.01
Romanian (0)	13	0.15
Russian (79)	382	4.48
Scotch-Irish (152)	265	3.11
Scottish (38)	235	2.76
Serbian (0)	15	0.18
Slovak (24)	164	1.92
Swedish (37)	232	2.72
Swiss (0)	34	0.40
Ukrainian (35)	178	2.09
Welsh (56)	95	1.11
West Indian, ex. Hispanic (0)	44	0.52
Jamaican (0)	44	0.52

Hispanic Origin	Population	%
Hispanic or Latino (of any race)	231	2.66
Central American, ex. Mexican	10	0.12
Guatemalan	7	0.08
Honduran	2	0.02
Salvadoran	1	0.01
Cuban	30	0.35
Dominican Republic	5	0.06
Mexican	69	0.79
Puerto Rican	49	0.56
South American	29	0.33
Argentinean	5	0.06
Colombian	17	0.20
Ecuadorian	3	0.03
Peruvian	1	0.01
Uruguayan	2	0.02
Other South American	1	0.01
Other Hispanic or Latino	39	0.45

Race*	Population	%
African-American/Black (82)	119	1.37
Not Hispanic (75)	110	1.27
Hispanic (7)	9	0.10
American Indian/Alaska Native (4)	19	0.22
Not Hispanic (3)	17	0.20
Hispanic (1)	2	0.02
Central American Ind. (0)	1	0.01
Cherokee (0)	3	0.03
Chippewa (2)	2	0.02
Choctaw (0)	2	0.02
Delaware (0)	1	0.01
Iroquois (0)	2	0.02
Asian (254)	302	3.47
Not Hispanic (254)	302	3.47
Chinese, ex. Taiwanese (98)	109	1.25
Filipino (12)	25	0.29
Indian (74)	81	0.93
Japanese (11)	18	0.21
Korean (38)	43	0.49
Sri Lankan (0)	1	0.01
Taiwanese (6)	10	0.12
Thai (2)	2	0.02
Vietnamese (7)	9	0.10
Hawaii Native/Pacific Islander (5)	11	0.13
Not Hispanic (4)	10	0.12
Hispanic (1)	1	0.01
Guamanian/Chamorro (3)	4	0.05
Native Hawaiian (2)	2	0.02
White (8,193)	8,276	95.21
Not Hispanic (8,021)	8,097	93.15
Hispanic (172)	179	2.06

Somerset

Place Type: Township
County: Somerset
Population: 12,122†

Ancestry‡	Population	%
African, Sub-Saharan (16)	24	0.20
African (16)	24	0.20
American (750)	750	6.26
Belgian (0)	14	0.12
British (0)	53	0.44
Canadian (41)	41	0.34
Croatian (11)	32	0.27
Czech (37)	45	0.38
Czechoslovakian (0)	8	0.07
Dutch (69)	417	3.48
English (174)	726	6.06
European (124)	124	1.04
French, ex. Basque (18)	94	0.78
German (2,428)	4,399	36.73
Hungarian (26)	229	1.91
Irish (220)	1,032	8.62
Italian (239)	510	4.26
Norwegian (0)	8	0.07
Pennsylvania German (119)	144	1.20
Polish (71)	400	3.34
Romanian (0)	15	0.13
Russian (18)	55	0.46
Scotch-Irish (30)	48	0.40
Scottish (38)	119	0.99
Serbian (0)	10	0.08
Slovak (94)	304	2.54
Swedish (39)	46	0.38
Swiss (0)	3	0.03
Ukrainian (0)	8	0.07
Welsh (18)	168	1.40
West Indian, ex. Hispanic (0)	7	0.06
West Indian (0)	7	0.06

Hispanic Origin	Population	%
Hispanic or Latino (of any race)	447	3.69
Central American, ex. Mexican	3	0.02
Guatemalan	1	0.01
Honduran	1	0.01
Salvadoran	1	0.01
Cuban	5	0.04
Mexican	111	0.92
Puerto Rican	12	0.10
South American	2	0.02
Argentinean	1	0.01
Paraguayan	1	0.01
Other Hispanic or Latino	314	2.59

Race*	Population	%
African-American/Black (1,708)	1,716	14.16
Not Hispanic (1,708)	1,716	14.16
American Indian/Alaska Native (12)	30	0.25
Not Hispanic (9)	26	0.21
Hispanic (3)	4	0.03
Cherokee (1)	5	0.04
Iroquois (1)	1	0.01
Mexican American Ind. (1)	1	0.01
Navajo (2)	2	0.02
Sioux (1)	4	0.03
Asian (67)	85	0.70
Not Hispanic (67)	85	0.70
Cambodian (1)	2	0.02
Chinese, ex. Taiwanese (12)	12	0.10
Filipino (2)	5	0.04
Indian (18)	19	0.16
Japanese (1)	3	0.02
Korean (8)	14	0.12
Thai (0)	1	0.01
Vietnamese (6)	6	0.05
Hawaii Native/Pacific Islander (3)	6	0.05
Not Hispanic (3)	6	0.05
Guamanian/Chamorro (1)	4	0.03
White (9,882)	9,932	81.93
Not Hispanic (9,838)	9,885	81.55
Hispanic (44)	47	0.39

South Abington

Place Type: Township
County: Lackawanna
Population: 9,073†

Ancestry‡	Population	%
Afghan (0)	12	0.13
African, Sub-Saharan (0)	14	0.16
Nigerian (0)	14	0.16
American (104)	104	1.16
Arab (202)	218	2.43
Arab (81)	81	0.90
Egyptian (121)	121	1.35
Lebanese (0)	16	0.18
Austrian (18)	36	0.40
Brazilian (15)	15	0.17
British (32)	47	0.52
Canadian (0)	22	0.25
Carpatho Rusyn (0)	12	0.13
Croatian (6)	17	0.19
Czech (0)	24	0.27
Dutch (10)	270	3.01
Eastern European (14)	14	0.16
English (290)	968	10.79
European (32)	32	0.36
Finnish (5)	5	0.06
French, ex. Basque (0)	79	0.88
French Canadian (22)	37	0.41
German (502)	1,840	20.52
Greek (67)	67	0.75
Hungarian (39)	49	0.55
Irish (650)	2,126	23.71
Israeli (0)	11	0.12
Italian (473)	1,468	16.37
Lithuanian (9)	89	0.99
Norwegian (14)	53	0.59
Pennsylvania German (0)	6	0.07
Polish (651)	1,200	13.38
Portuguese (10)	10	0.11
Romanian (4)	4	0.04
Russian (173)	445	4.96
Scotch-Irish (47)	107	1.19
Scottish (65)	181	2.02
Slovak (182)	367	4.09
Swedish (0)	58	0.65
Swiss (0)	22	0.25
Ukrainian (26)	122	1.36

*Notes: † The Census 2010 population figure is used to calculate the percentages in the Hispanic Origin and Race categories. Ancestry percentages are based on the 2006-2010 American Community Survey population (not shown); ‡ Numbers in parentheses indicate the number of people reporting a single ancestry; * Numbers in parentheses indicate the number of persons reporting this race alone, not in combination with any other race; Please refer to the Explanation of Data for more information.*

Welsh (64)	544	6.07
West Indian, ex. Hispanic (0)	14	0.16
Barbadian (0)	14	0.16

Hispanic Origin	Population	%
Hispanic or Latino (of any race)	176	1.94
Central American, ex. Mexican	8	0.09
Guatemalan	2	0.02
Honduran	1	0.01
Nicaraguan	3	0.03
Salvadoran	1	0.01
Other Central American	1	0.01
Cuban	5	0.06
Dominican Republic	9	0.10
Mexican	27	0.30
Puerto Rican	71	0.78
South American	42	0.46
Argentinean	10	0.11
Bolivian	4	0.04
Chilean	3	0.03
Colombian	9	0.10
Ecuadorian	3	0.03
Peruvian	11	0.12
Uruguayan	1	0.01
Venezuelan	1	0.01
Other Hispanic or Latino	14	0.15

Race*	Population	%
African-American/Black (117)	158	1.74
Not Hispanic (106)	139	1.53
Hispanic (11)	19	0.21
American Indian/Alaska Native (5)	24	0.26
Not Hispanic (3)	20	0.22
Hispanic (2)	4	0.04
Apache (2)	2	0.02
Canadian/French Am. Ind. (0)	1	0.01
Cherokee (1)	8	0.09
Asian (307)	352	3.88
Not Hispanic (307)	348	3.84
Hispanic (0)	4	0.04
Bangladeshi (14)	14	0.15
Burmese (3)	3	0.03
Chinese, ex. Taiwanese (43)	48	0.53
Filipino (11)	19	0.21
Indian (181)	190	2.09
Indonesian (2)	2	0.02
Japanese (2)	3	0.03
Korean (16)	20	0.22
Laotian (0)	1	0.01
Malaysian (0)	1	0.01
Pakistani (10)	13	0.14
Taiwanese (4)	4	0.04
Thai (2)	8	0.09
Vietnamese (16)	16	0.18
Hawaii Native/Pacific Islander (2)	4	0.04
Not Hispanic (2)	4	0.04
Guamanian/Chamorro (1)	3	0.03
White (8,491)	8,592	94.70
Not Hispanic (8,374)	8,454	93.18
Hispanic (117)	138	1.52

South Fayette

Place Type: Township
County: Allegheny
Population: 14,416†

Ancestry‡	Population	%
African, Sub-Saharan (2)	2	0.01
Ethiopian (2)	2	0.01
American (512)	512	3.68
Arab (4)	53	0.38
Lebanese (4)	35	0.25
Syrian (0)	18	0.13
Austrian (0)	12	0.09
Belgian (55)	132	0.95
British (25)	51	0.37
Canadian (7)	25	0.18
Croatian (72)	219	1.57
Czech (0)	97	0.70
Czechoslovakian (9)	23	0.17
Dutch (84)	219	1.57
English (232)	1,506	10.82
European (68)	93	0.67
French, ex. Basque (35)	452	3.25
French Canadian (44)	66	0.47
German (885)	3,817	27.43
Greek (46)	119	0.86
Hungarian (77)	630	4.53
Iranian (0)	10	0.07
Irish (410)	2,839	20.40
Italian (1,150)	3,495	25.12
Lithuanian (60)	185	1.33
Luxemburger (0)	30	0.22
Norwegian (14)	60	0.43
Polish (452)	1,674	12.03
Russian (31)	238	1.71
Scotch-Irish (39)	405	2.91
Scottish (58)	299	2.15
Serbian (11)	27	0.19
Slavic (0)	55	0.40
Slovak (144)	591	4.25
Slovene (108)	169	1.21
Swedish (0)	39	0.28
Swiss (0)	9	0.06
Ukrainian (199)	267	1.92
Welsh (0)	141	1.01

Hispanic Origin	Population	%
Hispanic or Latino (of any race)	141	0.98
Central American, ex. Mexican	12	0.08
Costa Rican	1	0.01
Guatemalan	2	0.01
Honduran	2	0.01
Nicaraguan	3	0.02
Panamanian	3	0.02
Salvadoran	1	0.01
Cuban	2	0.01
Dominican Republic	2	0.01
Mexican	58	0.40
Puerto Rican	30	0.21
South American	15	0.10
Argentinean	6	0.04
Bolivian	1	0.01
Chilean	1	0.01
Colombian	2	0.01
Peruvian	3	0.02
Venezuelan	2	0.01
Other Hispanic or Latino	22	0.15

Race*	Population	%
African-American/Black (324)	403	2.80
Not Hispanic (320)	395	2.74
Hispanic (4)	8	0.06
American Indian/Alaska Native (8)	44	0.31
Not Hispanic (7)	42	0.29
Hispanic (1)	2	0.01
Blackfeet (0)	1	0.01
Cherokee (2)	10	0.07
Comanche (1)	1	0.01
Iroquois (0)	1	0.01
Pueblo (1)	1	0.01
Sioux (1)	1	0.01
Asian (661)	720	4.99
Not Hispanic (658)	717	4.97
Hispanic (3)	3	0.02
Chinese, ex. Taiwanese (58)	68	0.47
Filipino (13)	21	0.15
Indian (541)	559	3.88
Japanese (7)	11	0.08
Korean (11)	19	0.13
Pakistani (8)	8	0.06
Thai (8)	10	0.07
Vietnamese (11)	13	0.09
Hawaii Native/Pacific Islander (2)	3	0.02
Not Hispanic (2)	3	0.02
Samoan (2)	2	0.01
White (13,218)	13,362	92.69
Not Hispanic (13,109)	13,249	91.90
Hispanic (109)	113	0.78

South Lebanon

Place Type: Township
County: Lebanon
Population: 9,463†

Ancestry‡	Population	%
African, Sub-Saharan (20)	20	0.22
African (20)	20	0.22
Albanian (0)	37	0.40
American (644)	644	6.95
Austrian (8)	8	0.09
British (0)	7	0.08
Croatian (48)	61	0.66
Czech (0)	31	0.33
Czechoslovakian (11)	20	0.22
Danish (0)	11	0.12
Dutch (85)	246	2.65
Eastern European (14)	14	0.15
English (252)	726	7.83
European (189)	189	2.04
French, ex. Basque (80)	166	1.79
French Canadian (21)	21	0.23
German (1,965)	3,458	37.30
Greek (29)	46	0.50
Hungarian (0)	33	0.36
Irish (202)	962	10.38
Italian (159)	561	6.05
Lithuanian (6)	27	0.29
Northern European (18)	18	0.19
Norwegian (36)	36	0.39
Pennsylvania German (92)	131	1.41
Polish (57)	367	3.96
Portuguese (0)	34	0.37
Romanian (8)	8	0.09
Russian (0)	30	0.32
Scotch-Irish (13)	121	1.31
Scottish (16)	81	0.87
Serbian (36)	60	0.65
Slavic (12)	34	0.37
Slovak (77)	170	1.83
Slovene (14)	28	0.30
Swedish (14)	144	1.55
Swiss (11)	221	2.38
Turkish (0)	7	0.08
Ukrainian (27)	38	0.41
Welsh (27)	94	1.01
Yugoslavian (0)	23	0.25

Hispanic Origin	Population	%
Hispanic or Latino (of any race)	574	6.07
Central American, ex. Mexican	5	0.05
Guatemalan	2	0.02
Honduran	3	0.03
Cuban	10	0.11
Dominican Republic	26	0.27
Mexican	20	0.21
Puerto Rican	461	4.87
South American	25	0.26
Colombian	9	0.10
Ecuadorian	5	0.05
Peruvian	11	0.12
Other Hispanic or Latino	27	0.29

Race*	Population	%
African-American/Black (215)	288	3.04
Not Hispanic (191)	242	2.56
Hispanic (24)	46	0.49
American Indian/Alaska Native (21)	49	0.52
Not Hispanic (11)	35	0.37
Hispanic (10)	14	0.15
Central American Ind. (1)	1	0.01
Cherokee (1)	4	0.04
Chippewa (0)	1	0.01
Iroquois (0)	3	0.03
Potawatomi (1)	1	0.01
South American Ind. (1)	3	0.03
Spanish American Ind. (3)	3	0.03
Asian (89)	117	1.24
Not Hispanic (88)	114	1.20

*Notes: † The Census 2010 population figure is used to calculate the percentages in the Hispanic Origin and Race categories. Ancestry percentages are based on the 2006-2010 American Community Survey population (not shown); ‡ Numbers in parentheses indicate the number of people reporting a single ancestry; * Numbers in parentheses indicate the number of persons reporting this race alone, not in combination with any other race; Please refer to the Explanation of Data for more information.*

Hispanic (1)	3	0.03
Cambodian (10)	17	0.18
Chinese, ex. Taiwanese (11)	11	0.12
Filipino (8)	15	0.16
Indian (11)	17	0.18
Indonesian (1)	3	0.03
Japanese (2)	2	0.02
Korean (14)	17	0.18
Pakistani (0)	2	0.02
Thai (2)	2	0.02
Vietnamese (27)	30	0.32
Hawaii Native/Pacific Islander (3)	9	0.10
Not Hispanic (2)	7	0.07
Hispanic (1)	2	0.02
Guamanian/Chamorro (1)	5	0.05
Native Hawaiian (0)	1	0.01
Samoan (1)	1	0.01
White (8,764)	8,902	94.07
Not Hispanic (8,488)	8,583	90.70
Hispanic (276)	319	3.37

South Middleton

Place Type: Township
County: Cumberland
Population: 14,663†

Ancestry‡	Population	%
American (1,049)	1,049	7.29
Arab (27)	27	0.19
Arab (27)	27	0.19
Austrian (13)	13	0.09
British (23)	126	0.88
Canadian (25)	38	0.26
Croatian (0)	31	0.22
Czech (14)	30	0.21
Danish (15)	101	0.70
Dutch (77)	318	2.21
Eastern European (13)	13	0.09
English (536)	1,433	9.96
European (84)	84	0.58
French, ex. Basque (48)	400	2.78
French Canadian (52)	80	0.56
German (2,910)	6,215	43.18
Greek (14)	62	0.43
Hungarian (31)	150	1.04
Irish (656)	2,344	16.28
Italian (253)	807	5.61
Lithuanian (64)	187	1.30
Norwegian (0)	89	0.62
Pennsylvania German (57)	117	0.81
Polish (211)	651	4.52
Portuguese (14)	29	0.20
Russian (41)	79	0.55
Scotch-Irish (109)	398	2.77
Scottish (99)	332	2.31
Slovak (12)	78	0.54
Slovene (0)	39	0.27
Swedish (59)	185	1.29
Swiss (83)	228	1.58
Ukrainian (14)	45	0.31
Welsh (16)	85	0.59
Yugoslavian (0)	13	0.09

Hispanic Origin	Population	%
Hispanic or Latino (of any race)	246	1.68
Central American, ex. Mexican	28	0.19
Guatemalan	21	0.14
Honduran	2	0.01
Panamanian	4	0.03
Salvadoran	1	0.01
Cuban	14	0.10
Mexican	93	0.63
Puerto Rican	76	0.52
South American	10	0.07
Argentinean	3	0.02
Colombian	4	0.03
Ecuadorian	1	0.01
Peruvian	2	0.01
Other Hispanic or Latino	25	0.17

Race*	Population	%
African-American/Black (131)	177	1.21
Not Hispanic (126)	170	1.16
Hispanic (5)	7	0.05
American Indian/Alaska Native (28)	68	0.46
Not Hispanic (24)	63	0.43
Hispanic (4)	5	0.03
Alaska Athabascan *(Ala. Nat.)* (2)	2	0.01
Blackfeet (0)	1	0.01
Canadian/French Am. Ind. (2)	2	0.01
Cherokee (2)	17	0.12
Chippewa (1)	1	0.01
Comanche (0)	1	0.01
Iroquois (12)	13	0.09
Kiowa (0)	1	0.01
Paiute (1)	1	0.01
Pueblo (0)	1	0.01
Sioux (1)	1	0.01
Asian (176)	234	1.60
Not Hispanic (173)	229	1.56
Hispanic (3)	5	0.03
Chinese, ex. Taiwanese (38)	51	0.35
Filipino (18)	35	0.24
Indian (25)	34	0.23
Japanese (8)	15	0.10
Korean (28)	37	0.25
Laotian (1)	2	0.01
Pakistani (7)	7	0.05
Taiwanese (1)	1	0.01
Thai (4)	7	0.05
Vietnamese (37)	39	0.27
Hawaii Native/Pacific Islander (2)	4	0.03
Not Hispanic (1)	3	0.02
Hispanic (1)	1	0.01
White (14,107)	14,253	97.20
Not Hispanic (13,943)	14,071	95.96
Hispanic (164)	182	1.24

South Park Township

Place Type: CDP
County: Allegheny
Population: 13,416†

Ancestry‡	Population	%
Albanian (0)	55	0.41
American (411)	411	3.06
Arab (16)	91	0.68
Lebanese (0)	27	0.20
Syrian (0)	15	0.11
Other Arab (16)	49	0.36
Austrian (9)	40	0.30
Belgian (0)	15	0.11
British (17)	33	0.25
Canadian (25)	43	0.32
Croatian (47)	141	1.05
Czech (9)	103	0.77
Czechoslovakian (18)	45	0.33
Danish (8)	20	0.15
Dutch (11)	11	0.08
English (69)	1,043	7.76
European (68)	68	0.51
Finnish (0)	13	0.10
French, ex. Basque (25)	188	1.40
German (1,126)	5,144	38.25
Greek (25)	111	0.83
Hungarian (93)	339	2.52
Iranian (8)	8	0.06
Irish (540)	3,180	23.65
Italian (1,018)	3,018	22.44
Latvian (0)	18	0.13
Lithuanian (21)	100	0.74
Polish (424)	1,683	12.51
Russian (16)	202	1.50
Scotch-Irish (78)	289	2.15
Scottish (55)	203	1.51
Serbian (0)	18	0.13
Slavic (26)	35	0.26
Slovak (180)	654	4.86
Slovene (65)	183	1.36
Swedish (58)	98	0.73
Swiss (0)	69	0.51
Ukrainian (70)	344	2.56
Welsh (15)	167	1.24
West Indian, ex. Hispanic (94)	94	0.70
West Indian (94)	94	0.70
Yugoslavian (63)	63	0.47

Hispanic Origin	Population	%
Hispanic or Latino (of any race)	112	0.83
Central American, ex. Mexican	12	0.09
Costa Rican	1	0.01
Guatemalan	6	0.04
Honduran	3	0.02
Panamanian	2	0.01
Cuban	2	0.01
Dominican Republic	9	0.07
Mexican	37	0.28
Puerto Rican	31	0.23
South American	5	0.04
Bolivian	4	0.03
Colombian	1	0.01
Other Hispanic or Latino	16	0.12

Race*	Population	%
African-American/Black (379)	467	3.48
Not Hispanic (374)	452	3.37
Hispanic (5)	15	0.11
American Indian/Alaska Native (7)	58	0.43
Not Hispanic (7)	55	0.41
Hispanic (0)	3	0.02
Apache (0)	1	0.01
Cherokee (0)	13	0.10
Chippewa (0)	5	0.04
Choctaw (1)	1	0.01
Iroquois (1)	4	0.03
Sioux (0)	1	0.01
South American Ind. (0)	1	0.01
Asian (106)	136	1.01
Not Hispanic (105)	135	1.01
Hispanic (1)	1	0.01
Chinese, ex. Taiwanese (55)	61	0.45
Filipino (5)	15	0.11
Indian (18)	19	0.14
Indonesian (0)	1	0.01
Japanese (2)	7	0.05
Korean (11)	15	0.11
Malaysian (0)	1	0.01
Taiwanese (2)	2	0.01
Thai (1)	4	0.03
Vietnamese (9)	12	0.09
Hawaii Native/Pacific Islander (6)	7	0.05
Not Hispanic (4)	5	0.04
Hispanic (2)	2	0.01
Fijian (1)	1	0.01
Guamanian/Chamorro (2)	2	0.01
White (12,738)	12,878	95.99
Not Hispanic (12,672)	12,802	95.42
Hispanic (66)	76	0.57

South Park

Place Type: Township
County: Allegheny
Population: 13,416†

Ancestry‡	Population	%
Albanian (0)	55	0.41
American (411)	411	3.06
Arab (16)	91	0.68
Lebanese (0)	27	0.20
Syrian (0)	15	0.11
Other Arab (16)	49	0.36
Austrian (9)	40	0.30
Belgian (0)	15	0.11
British (17)	33	0.25
Canadian (25)	43	0.32
Croatian (47)	141	1.05
Czech (9)	103	0.77

*Notes: † The Census 2010 population figure is used to calculate the percentages in the Hispanic Origin and Race categories. Ancestry percentages are based on the 2006-2010 American Community Survey population (not shown); ‡ Numbers in parentheses indicate the number of people reporting a single ancestry; * Numbers in parentheses indicate the number of persons reporting this race alone, not in combination with any other race; Please refer to the Explanation of Data for more information.*

Ancestry	Population	%
Czechoslovakian (18)	45	0.33
Danish (8)	20	0.15
Dutch (11)	11	0.08
English (69)	1,043	7.76
European (68)	68	0.51
Finnish (0)	13	0.10
French, ex. Basque (25)	188	1.40
German (1,126)	5,144	38.25
Greek (25)	111	0.83
Hungarian (93)	339	2.52
Iranian (8)	8	0.06
Irish (540)	3,180	23.65
Italian (1,018)	3,018	22.44
Latvian (0)	18	0.13
Lithuanian (21)	100	0.74
Polish (424)	1,683	12.51
Russian (16)	202	1.50
Scotch-Irish (78)	289	2.15
Scottish (55)	203	1.51
Serbian (0)	18	0.13
Slavic (26)	35	0.26
Slovak (180)	654	4.86
Slovene (65)	183	1.36
Swedish (58)	98	0.73
Swiss (0)	69	0.51
Ukrainian (70)	344	2.56
Welsh (15)	167	1.24
West Indian, ex. Hispanic (94)	94	0.70
West Indian (94)	94	0.70
Yugoslavian (63)	63	0.47

Hispanic Origin	Population	%
Hispanic or Latino (of any race)	112	0.83
Central American, ex. Mexican	12	0.09
Costa Rican	1	0.01
Guatemalan	6	0.04
Honduran	3	0.02
Panamanian	2	0.01
Cuban	2	0.01
Dominican Republic	9	0.07
Mexican	37	0.28
Puerto Rican	31	0.23
South American	5	0.04
Bolivian	4	0.03
Colombian	1	0.01
Other Hispanic or Latino	16	0.12

Race*	Population	%
African-American/Black (379)	467	3.48
Not Hispanic (374)	452	3.37
Hispanic (5)	15	0.11
American Indian/Alaska Native (7)	58	0.43
Not Hispanic (7)	55	0.41
Hispanic (0)	3	0.02
Apache (0)	1	0.01
Cherokee (0)	13	0.10
Chippewa (0)	5	0.04
Choctaw (1)	1	0.01
Iroquois (1)	4	0.03
Sioux (0)	1	0.01
South American Ind. (0)	1	0.01
Asian (106)	136	1.01
Not Hispanic (105)	135	1.01
Hispanic (1)	1	0.01
Chinese, ex. Taiwanese (55)	61	0.45
Filipino (5)	15	0.11
Indian (18)	19	0.14
Indonesian (0)	1	0.01
Japanese (2)	7	0.05
Korean (11)	15	0.11
Malaysian (0)	1	0.01
Taiwanese (2)	2	0.01
Thai (1)	4	0.03
Vietnamese (9)	12	0.09
Hawaii Native/Pacific Islander (6)	7	0.05
Not Hispanic (4)	5	0.04
Hispanic (2)	2	0.01
Fijian (1)	1	0.01
Guamanian/Chamorro (2)	2	0.01
White (12,738)	12,878	95.99
Not Hispanic (12,672)	12,802	95.42
Hispanic (66)	76	0.57

South Strabane

Place Type: Township
County: Washington
Population: 9,346†

Ancestry‡	Population	%
African, Sub-Saharan (0)	7	0.08
African (0)	7	0.08
American (344)	344	3.78
Arab (22)	76	0.83
Egyptian (22)	22	0.24
Lebanese (0)	19	0.21
Syrian (0)	35	0.38
Austrian (0)	43	0.47
Belgian (0)	10	0.11
British (9)	54	0.59
Carpatho Rusyn (0)	14	0.15
Croatian (14)	91	1.00
Czech (58)	90	0.99
Czechoslovakian (11)	31	0.34
Dutch (10)	232	2.55
Eastern European (9)	9	0.10
English (457)	1,481	16.26
European (33)	43	0.47
French, ex. Basque (12)	139	1.53
French Canadian (9)	22	0.24
German (522)	2,221	24.38
Greek (9)	73	0.80
Hungarian (20)	257	2.82
Irish (608)	1,632	17.91
Italian (751)	1,841	20.21
Latvian (13)	39	0.43
Lithuanian (32)	95	1.04
Norwegian (20)	20	0.22
Pennsylvania German (12)	22	0.24
Polish (301)	949	10.42
Russian (30)	163	1.79
Scotch-Irish (205)	471	5.17
Scottish (45)	204	2.24
Serbian (12)	34	0.37
Slavic (10)	30	0.33
Slovak (110)	471	5.17
Slovene (18)	49	0.54
Swedish (11)	30	0.33
Swiss (0)	19	0.21
Ukrainian (10)	129	1.42
Welsh (53)	157	1.72
Yugoslavian (18)	18	0.20

Hispanic Origin	Population	%
Hispanic or Latino (of any race)	78	0.83
Central American, ex. Mexican	7	0.07
Guatemalan	6	0.06
Panamanian	1	0.01
Cuban	3	0.03
Dominican Republic	1	0.01
Mexican	42	0.45
Puerto Rican	6	0.06
South American	8	0.09
Argentinean	1	0.01
Chilean	2	0.02
Colombian	4	0.04
Ecuadorian	1	0.01
Other Hispanic or Latino	11	0.12

Race*	Population	%
African-American/Black (165)	214	2.29
Not Hispanic (159)	204	2.18
Hispanic (6)	10	0.11
American Indian/Alaska Native (6)	38	0.41
Not Hispanic (6)	37	0.40
Hispanic (0)	1	0.01
Blackfeet (0)	1	0.01
Cherokee (0)	7	0.07
Chippewa (0)	4	0.04
Choctaw (0)	1	0.01
Creek (4)	4	0.04
Iroquois (0)	1	0.01
Mexican American Ind. (0)	1	0.01
Sioux (0)	1	0.01
Asian (96)	132	1.41
Not Hispanic (94)	119	1.27
Hispanic (2)	13	0.14
Chinese, ex. Taiwanese (20)	27	0.29
Filipino (5)	21	0.22
Indian (37)	44	0.47
Japanese (9)	14	0.15
Korean (9)	10	0.11
Laotian (0)	1	0.01
Malaysian (1)	1	0.01
Pakistani (0)	1	0.01
Vietnamese (14)	14	0.15
Hawaii Native/Pacific Islander (2)	2	0.02
Not Hispanic (2)	2	0.02
Native Hawaiian (2)	2	0.02
White (8,947)	9,051	96.84
Not Hispanic (8,910)	9,002	96.32
Hispanic (37)	49	0.52

South Union

Place Type: Township
County: Fayette
Population: 10,681†

Ancestry‡	Population	%
African, Sub-Saharan (91)	91	0.84
African (91)	91	0.84
American (396)	396	3.67
Arab (96)	125	1.16
Lebanese (96)	125	1.16
Austrian (23)	165	1.53
Croatian (87)	216	2.00
Czech (57)	164	1.52
Czechoslovakian (42)	42	0.39
Dutch (38)	411	3.81
English (354)	1,300	12.05
European (29)	29	0.27
French, ex. Basque (97)	175	1.62
German (499)	2,339	21.67
Greek (21)	36	0.33
Hungarian (36)	154	1.43
Irish (344)	2,189	20.28
Italian (770)	2,060	19.09
Lithuanian (0)	31	0.29
Norwegian (13)	50	0.46
Pennsylvania German (42)	102	0.95
Polish (561)	1,342	12.44
Russian (117)	169	1.57
Scotch-Irish (83)	264	2.45
Scottish (0)	110	1.02
Serbian (29)	97	0.90
Slavic (46)	55	0.51
Slovak (445)	1,286	11.92
Swedish (15)	25	0.23
Swiss (12)	12	0.11
Ukrainian (0)	10	0.09
Welsh (22)	140	1.30
Yugoslavian (15)	15	0.14

Hispanic Origin	Population	%
Hispanic or Latino (of any race)	65	0.61
Central American, ex. Mexican	12	0.11
Guatemalan	10	0.09
Salvadoran	2	0.02
Cuban	1	0.01
Mexican	27	0.25
Puerto Rican	5	0.05
South American	5	0.05
Colombian	4	0.04
Paraguayan	1	0.01
Other Hispanic or Latino	15	0.14

Race*	Population	%
African-American/Black (407)	511	4.78
Not Hispanic (406)	505	4.73

*Notes: † The Census 2010 population figure is used to calculate the percentages in the Hispanic Origin and Race categories. Ancestry percentages are based on the 2006-2010 American Community Survey population (not shown); ‡ Numbers in parentheses indicate the number of people reporting a single ancestry; * Numbers in parentheses indicate the number of persons reporting this race alone, not in combination with any other race; Please refer to the Explanation of Data for more information.*

Hispanic (1)	6	0.06
American Indian/Alaska Native (13)	46	0.43
Not Hispanic (8)	37	0.35
Hispanic (5)	9	0.08
Central American Ind. (1)	1	0.01
Cherokee (1)	8	0.07
Chickasaw (1)	1	0.01
Delaware (0)	1	0.01
Seminole (0)	1	0.01
South American Ind. (1)	1	0.01
Asian (124)	149	1.40
Not Hispanic (124)	146	1.37
Hispanic (0)	3	0.03
Chinese, ex. Taiwanese (21)	25	0.23
Filipino (10)	20	0.19
Indian (47)	52	0.49
Indonesian (1)	1	0.01
Japanese (0)	4	0.04
Korean (15)	20	0.19
Pakistani (5)	5	0.05
Thai (6)	7	0.07
Vietnamese (19)	21	0.20
Hawaii Native/Pacific Islander (0)	2	0.02
Not Hispanic (0)	2	0.02
Native Hawaiian (0)	2	0.02
White (9,979)	10,112	94.67
Not Hispanic (9,937)	10,061	94.20
Hispanic (42)	51	0.48

South Whitehall

Place Type: Township
County: Lehigh
Population: 19,180†

Ancestry‡	Population	%
African, Sub-Saharan (73)	73	0.38
African (61)	61	0.32
South African (12)	12	0.06
Albanian (254)	267	1.40
American (789)	789	4.14
Arab (362)	423	2.22
Arab (10)	24	0.13
Egyptian (33)	33	0.17
Lebanese (32)	32	0.17
Palestinian (0)	10	0.05
Syrian (272)	309	1.62
Other Arab (15)	15	0.08
Austrian (134)	368	1.93
Basque (12)	12	0.06
Belgian (11)	31	0.16
British (31)	66	0.35
Carpatho Rusyn (0)	11	0.06
Croatian (16)	22	0.12
Czech (19)	85	0.45
Czechoslovakian (32)	39	0.20
Danish (22)	47	0.25
Dutch (143)	581	3.05
Eastern European (236)	236	1.24
English (175)	1,129	5.93
European (109)	109	0.57
Finnish (0)	9	0.05
French, ex. Basque (95)	421	2.21
French Canadian (0)	14	0.07
German (2,433)	5,507	28.91
Greek (97)	149	0.78
Hungarian (110)	404	2.12
Iranian (9)	9	0.05
Irish (579)	2,936	15.41
Italian (707)	2,426	12.74
Lithuanian (55)	181	0.95
Northern European (10)	10	0.05
Norwegian (7)	52	0.27
Pennsylvania German (713)	1,117	5.86
Polish (283)	912	4.79
Portuguese (22)	22	0.12
Romanian (0)	57	0.30
Russian (158)	505	2.65
Scotch-Irish (17)	101	0.53
Scottish (48)	282	1.48
Slavic (7)	7	0.04
Slovak (328)	847	4.45
Slovene (11)	22	0.12
Swedish (33)	209	1.10
Swiss (35)	69	0.36
Ukrainian (111)	314	1.65
Welsh (83)	460	2.42
West Indian, ex. Hispanic (34)	34	0.18
Barbadian (5)	5	0.03
Haitian (23)	23	0.12
Jamaican (6)	6	0.03
Yugoslavian (20)	20	0.11

Hispanic Origin	Population	%
Hispanic or Latino (of any race)	896	4.67
Central American, ex. Mexican	50	0.26
Costa Rican	2	0.01
Guatemalan	9	0.05
Honduran	14	0.07
Nicaraguan	6	0.03
Panamanian	6	0.03
Salvadoran	11	0.06
Other Central American	2	0.01
Cuban	41	0.21
Dominican Republic	107	0.56
Mexican	105	0.55
Puerto Rican	415	2.16
South American	122	0.64
Argentinean	5	0.03
Bolivian	3	0.02
Chilean	5	0.03
Colombian	40	0.21
Ecuadorian	30	0.16
Peruvian	23	0.12
Venezuelan	15	0.08
Other South American	1	0.01
Other Hispanic or Latino	56	0.29

Race*	Population	%
African-American/Black (539)	634	3.31
Not Hispanic (488)	565	2.95
Hispanic (51)	69	0.36
American Indian/Alaska Native (17)	43	0.22
Not Hispanic (11)	36	0.19
Hispanic (6)	7	0.04
Blackfeet (0)	2	0.01
Cherokee (5)	12	0.06
Cheyenne (1)	1	0.01
Chippewa (1)	3	0.02
Delaware (0)	4	0.02
Mexican American Ind. (1)	4	0.02
Navajo (0)	1	0.01
Pueblo (2)	2	0.01
Puget Sound Salish (1)	1	0.01
Asian (895)	999	5.21
Not Hispanic (894)	991	5.17
Hispanic (1)	8	0.04
Bangladeshi (2)	2	0.01
Burmese (3)	4	0.02
Chinese, ex. Taiwanese (152)	177	0.92
Filipino (37)	60	0.31
Indian (399)	427	2.23
Indonesian (2)	2	0.01
Japanese (38)	53	0.28
Korean (74)	82	0.43
Malaysian (2)	2	0.01
Pakistani (43)	48	0.25
Sri Lankan (1)	1	0.01
Taiwanese (12)	16	0.08
Thai (5)	6	0.03
Vietnamese (84)	91	0.47
Hawaii Native/Pacific Islander (9)	23	0.12
Not Hispanic (9)	19	0.10
Hispanic (0)	4	0.02
Samoan (2)	2	0.01
White (17,221)	17,429	90.87
Not Hispanic (16,666)	16,836	87.78
Hispanic (555)	593	3.09

Southampton

Place Type: Township
County: Franklin
Population: 7,987†

Ancestry‡	Population	%
African, Sub-Saharan (29)	29	0.38
African (29)	29	0.38
American (817)	817	10.60
Arab (15)	15	0.19
Syrian (15)	15	0.19
Belgian (15)	27	0.35
British (0)	15	0.19
Dutch (36)	133	1.73
English (208)	592	7.68
European (79)	103	1.34
Finnish (0)	9	0.12
French, ex. Basque (0)	24	0.31
French Canadian (14)	53	0.69
German (1,881)	3,575	46.40
Hungarian (10)	29	0.38
Irish (280)	1,135	14.73
Italian (249)	550	7.14
Lithuanian (0)	23	0.30
Northern European (22)	22	0.29
Polish (102)	295	3.83
Russian (27)	67	0.87
Scandinavian (26)	70	0.91
Scotch-Irish (35)	224	2.91
Scottish (48)	289	3.75
Slovak (0)	70	0.91
Swiss (41)	194	2.52
Welsh (0)	112	1.45

Hispanic Origin	Population	%
Hispanic or Latino (of any race)	184	2.30
Central American, ex. Mexican	15	0.19
Guatemalan	6	0.08
Honduran	6	0.08
Panamanian	1	0.01
Salvadoran	2	0.03
Dominican Republic	13	0.16
Mexican	45	0.56
Puerto Rican	84	1.05
South American	5	0.06
Colombian	1	0.01
Peruvian	4	0.05
Other Hispanic or Latino	22	0.28

Race*	Population	%
African-American/Black (170)	211	2.64
Not Hispanic (161)	199	2.49
Hispanic (9)	12	0.15
American Indian/Alaska Native (12)	39	0.49
Not Hispanic (11)	29	0.36
Hispanic (1)	10	0.13
Blackfeet (0)	2	0.03
Cherokee (5)	8	0.10
Cheyenne (0)	3	0.04
Chickasaw (1)	1	0.01
Delaware (1)	1	0.01
Iroquois (0)	1	0.01
Potawatomi (1)	2	0.03
Pueblo (0)	1	0.01
Sioux (0)	1	0.01
Asian (71)	93	1.16
Not Hispanic (71)	92	1.15
Hispanic (0)	1	0.01
Cambodian (1)	1	0.01
Chinese, ex. Taiwanese (19)	22	0.28
Filipino (5)	15	0.19
Indian (14)	19	0.24
Indonesian (2)	2	0.03
Japanese (1)	1	0.01
Korean (19)	23	0.29
Nepalese (1)	1	0.01
Pakistani (5)	5	0.06
Thai (2)	2	0.03
Vietnamese (2)	2	0.03

SECTION TWO

*Notes: † The Census 2010 population figure is used to calculate the percentages in the Hispanic Origin and Race categories. Ancestry percentages are based on the 2006-2010 American Community Survey population (not shown); ‡ Numbers in parentheses indicate the number of people reporting a single ancestry; * Numbers in parentheses indicate the number of persons reporting this race alone, not in combination with any other race; Please refer to the Explanation of Data for more information.*

Hawaii Native/Pacific Islander (2)	2	0.03
Hispanic (2)	2	0.03
Guamanian/Chamorro (1)	1	0.01
Native Hawaiian (1)	1	0.01
White (7,568)	7,660	95.91
Not Hispanic (7,475)	7,548	94.50
Hispanic (93)	112	1.40

Spring Garden

Place Type: Township
County: York
Population: 12,578†

Ancestry‡	Population	%
African, Sub-Saharan (15)	29	0.23
African (15)	29	0.23
Albanian (15)	44	0.36
American (870)	870	7.02
Arab (0)	10	0.08
Syrian (0)	10	0.08
Armenian (0)	4	0.03
Austrian (0)	125	1.01
Belgian (9)	9	0.07
British (30)	34	0.27
Croatian (11)	36	0.29
Czech (15)	34	0.27
Danish (0)	15	0.12
Dutch (12)	154	1.24
Eastern European (33)	33	0.27
English (215)	939	7.58
European (252)	265	2.14
Finnish (13)	38	0.31
French, ex. Basque (78)	236	1.90
French Canadian (10)	66	0.53
German (3,019)	5,478	44.20
Greek (41)	139	1.12
Hungarian (48)	63	0.51
Irish (415)	2,067	16.68
Italian (287)	957	7.72
Lithuanian (37)	60	0.48
Norwegian (14)	67	0.54
Pennsylvania German (91)	102	0.82
Polish (136)	495	3.99
Portuguese (0)	8	0.06
Russian (21)	139	1.12
Scandinavian (11)	33	0.27
Scotch-Irish (115)	306	2.47
Scottish (46)	289	2.33
Serbian (0)	37	0.30
Slavic (0)	85	0.69
Slovak (23)	62	0.50
Swedish (12)	12	0.10
Swiss (62)	112	0.90
Turkish (15)	15	0.12
Ukrainian (41)	83	0.67
Welsh (0)	173	1.40
West Indian, ex. Hispanic (14)	29	0.23
Jamaican (0)	15	0.12
Trinidadian/Tobagonian (14)	14	0.11

Hispanic Origin	Population	%
Hispanic or Latino (of any race)	439	3.49
Central American, ex. Mexican	19	0.15
Guatemalan	4	0.03
Honduran	2	0.02
Panamanian	6	0.05
Salvadoran	7	0.06
Cuban	29	0.23
Dominican Republic	22	0.17
Mexican	72	0.57
Puerto Rican	200	1.59
South American	44	0.35
Argentinean	6	0.05
Chilean	8	0.06
Colombian	12	0.10
Paraguayan	3	0.02
Peruvian	12	0.10
Uruguayan	2	0.02
Other South American	1	0.01
Other Hispanic or Latino	53	0.42

Race*	Population	%
African-American/Black (476)	595	4.73
Not Hispanic (448)	550	4.37
Hispanic (28)	45	0.36
American Indian/Alaska Native (29)	50	0.40
Not Hispanic (25)	43	0.34
Hispanic (4)	7	0.06
Blackfeet (0)	1	0.01
Cherokee (8)	17	0.14
Cree (0)	1	0.01
Crow (0)	1	0.01
Iroquois (2)	4	0.03
Mexican American Ind. (0)	2	0.02
Navajo (5)	5	0.04
Sioux (0)	1	0.01
South American Ind. (1)	1	0.01
Asian (219)	269	2.14
Not Hispanic (216)	263	2.09
Hispanic (3)	6	0.05
Bangladeshi (6)	6	0.05
Cambodian (21)	27	0.21
Chinese, ex. Taiwanese (38)	48	0.38
Filipino (12)	24	0.19
Indian (30)	34	0.27
Japanese (6)	10	0.08
Korean (21)	27	0.21
Laotian (5)	5	0.04
Pakistani (13)	14	0.11
Sri Lankan (2)	2	0.02
Taiwanese (2)	2	0.02
Thai (0)	3	0.02
Vietnamese (58)	60	0.48
Hawaii Native/Pacific Islander (3)	5	0.04
Not Hispanic (3)	5	0.04
Native Hawaiian (0)	1	0.01
White (11,542)	11,702	93.04
Not Hispanic (11,282)	11,427	90.85
Hispanic (260)	275	2.19

Spring

Place Type: Township
County: Berks
Population: 27,119†

Ancestry‡	Population	%
African, Sub-Saharan (283)	283	1.06
African (205)	205	0.77
Ethiopian (48)	48	0.18
Kenyan (30)	30	0.11
American (1,377)	1,377	5.14
Arab (0)	46	0.17
Syrian (0)	46	0.17
Austrian (0)	59	0.22
British (43)	229	0.86
Cajun (16)	16	0.06
Canadian (13)	39	0.15
Celtic (0)	10	0.04
Croatian (60)	70	0.26
Czech (0)	66	0.25
Czechoslovakian (28)	69	0.26
Danish (8)	32	0.12
Dutch (130)	806	3.01
Eastern European (0)	10	0.04
English (394)	2,099	7.84
European (205)	205	0.77
French, ex. Basque (72)	452	1.69
French Canadian (63)	117	0.44
German (4,647)	10,729	40.09
Greek (109)	232	0.87
Guyanese (14)	36	0.13
Hungarian (23)	120	0.45
Iranian (35)	35	0.13
Irish (752)	3,934	14.70
Italian (1,364)	4,051	15.14
Latvian (29)	29	0.11
Lithuanian (39)	162	0.61
Northern European (16)	16	0.06
Pennsylvania German (483)	668	2.50
Polish (741)	2,335	8.72
Romanian (200)	243	0.91
Russian (14)	250	0.93
Scandinavian (0)	9	0.03
Scotch-Irish (77)	371	1.39
Scottish (58)	445	1.66
Slavic (10)	10	0.04
Slovak (111)	525	1.96
Slovene (10)	19	0.07
Swedish (47)	158	0.59
Swiss (28)	227	0.85
Ukrainian (66)	176	0.66
Welsh (92)	601	2.25
West Indian, ex. Hispanic (356)	356	1.33
Haitian (356)	356	1.33
Yugoslavian (0)	9	0.03

Hispanic Origin	Population	%
Hispanic or Latino (of any race)	1,650	6.08
Central American, ex. Mexican	100	0.37
Costa Rican	17	0.06
Guatemalan	14	0.05
Honduran	12	0.04
Nicaraguan	3	0.01
Panamanian	13	0.05
Salvadoran	32	0.12
Other Central American	9	0.03
Cuban	48	0.18
Dominican Republic	267	0.98
Mexican	100	0.37
Puerto Rican	821	3.03
South American	179	0.66
Argentinean	2	0.01
Chilean	6	0.02
Colombian	86	0.32
Ecuadorian	50	0.18
Peruvian	12	0.04
Uruguayan	1	<0.01
Venezuelan	12	0.04
Other South American	10	0.04
Other Hispanic or Latino	135	0.50

Race*	Population	%
African-American/Black (1,292)	1,516	5.59
Not Hispanic (1,194)	1,377	5.08
Hispanic (98)	139	0.51
American Indian/Alaska Native (47)	129	0.48
Not Hispanic (29)	105	0.39
Hispanic (18)	24	0.09
Blackfeet (0)	8	0.03
Central American Ind. (1)	1	<0.01
Cherokee (2)	23	0.08
Choctaw (2)	2	0.01
Delaware (2)	9	0.03
Iroquois (4)	4	0.01
South American Ind. (1)	1	<0.01
Asian (869)	1,010	3.72
Not Hispanic (866)	993	3.66
Hispanic (3)	17	0.06
Bangladeshi (4)	4	0.01
Cambodian (1)	1	<0.01
Chinese, ex. Taiwanese (191)	219	0.81
Filipino (65)	90	0.33
Indian (346)	389	1.43
Indonesian (2)	2	0.01
Japanese (16)	24	0.09
Korean (56)	71	0.26
Laotian (5)	13	0.05
Nepalese (0)	2	0.01
Pakistani (14)	14	0.05
Sri Lankan (3)	3	0.01
Taiwanese (6)	7	0.03
Thai (4)	12	0.04
Vietnamese (129)	149	0.55
Hawaii Native/Pacific Islander (2)	22	0.08
Not Hispanic (2)	15	0.06
Hispanic (0)	7	0.03
Guamanian/Chamorro (0)	1	<0.01
Native Hawaiian (0)	8	0.03

*Notes: † The Census 2010 population figure is used to calculate the percentages in the Hispanic Origin and Race categories. Ancestry percentages are based on the 2006-2010 American Community Survey population (not shown); ‡ Numbers in parentheses indicate the number of people reporting a single ancestry; * Numbers in parentheses indicate the number of persons reporting this race alone, not in combination with any other race; Please refer to the Explanation of Data for more information.*

Tongan (1)	1	<0.01
White (23,849)	24,255	89.44
Not Hispanic (22,980)	23,296	85.90
Hispanic (869)	959	3.54

Springettsbury

Place Type: Township
County: York
Population: 26,668†

Ancestry‡	Population	%
African, Sub-Saharan (98)	213	0.81
African (71)	177	0.67
Ghanaian (0)	9	0.03
Nigerian (8)	8	0.03
South African (12)	12	0.05
Other Sub-Saharan African (7)	7	0.03
American (1,625)	1,625	6.18
Arab (70)	85	0.32
Egyptian (28)	28	0.11
Moroccan (28)	28	0.11
Syrian (14)	29	0.11
Armenian (0)	68	0.26
Austrian (13)	49	0.19
Brazilian (45)	250	0.95
British (55)	83	0.32
Bulgarian (17)	17	0.06
Canadian (74)	101	0.38
Croatian (13)	27	0.10
Czech (36)	132	0.50
Czechoslovakian (0)	10	0.04
Danish (0)	38	0.14
Dutch (98)	603	2.29
Eastern European (11)	11	0.04
English (952)	2,699	10.26
European (91)	91	0.35
Finnish (12)	63	0.24
French, ex. Basque (134)	489	1.86
French Canadian (22)	37	0.14
German (5,743)	11,185	42.52
Greek (33)	60	0.23
Hungarian (60)	112	0.43
Irish (766)	3,226	12.26
Italian (648)	1,618	6.15
Latvian (13)	13	0.05
Lithuanian (10)	62	0.24
Maltese (0)	47	0.18
Norwegian (29)	69	0.26
Pennsylvania German (144)	205	0.78
Polish (325)	809	3.08
Portuguese (0)	9	0.03
Romanian (17)	17	0.06
Russian (65)	184	0.70
Scotch-Irish (258)	769	2.92
Scottish (77)	463	1.76
Slavic (0)	9	0.03
Slovak (47)	132	0.50
Swedish (36)	199	0.76
Swiss (35)	214	0.81
Ukrainian (0)	34	0.13
Welsh (0)	233	0.89
West Indian, ex. Hispanic (85)	94	0.36
Barbadian (8)	8	0.03
Haitian (8)	8	0.03
Jamaican (69)	69	0.26
Other West Indian (0)	9	0.03

Hispanic Origin	Population	%
Hispanic or Latino (of any race)	1,890	7.09
Central American, ex. Mexican	175	0.66
Costa Rican	2	0.01
Guatemalan	55	0.21
Honduran	30	0.11
Nicaraguan	19	0.07
Panamanian	7	0.03
Salvadoran	61	0.23
Other Central American	1	<0.01
Cuban	27	0.10
Dominican Republic	144	0.54
Mexican	513	1.92
Puerto Rican	746	2.80
South American	130	0.49
Argentinean	6	0.02
Bolivian	10	0.04
Chilean	8	0.03
Colombian	55	0.21
Ecuadorian	21	0.08
Peruvian	20	0.07
Uruguayan	5	0.02
Venezuelan	5	0.02
Other Hispanic or Latino	155	0.58

Race*	Population	%
African-American/Black (1,823)	2,120	7.95
Not Hispanic (1,744)	2,003	7.51
Hispanic (79)	117	0.44
American Indian/Alaska Native (41)	128	0.48
Not Hispanic (34)	110	0.41
Hispanic (7)	18	0.07
Apache (2)	2	0.01
Blackfeet (0)	4	0.01
Central American Ind. (1)	4	0.01
Cherokee (2)	17	0.06
Chippewa (2)	4	0.01
Comanche (1)	1	<0.01
Cree (0)	1	<0.01
Delaware (0)	1	<0.01
Houma (4)	4	0.01
Inupiat *(Alaska Native)* (0)	1	<0.01
Lumbee (1)	2	0.01
Mexican American Ind. (3)	3	0.01
Navajo (1)	2	0.01
Potawatomi (2)	2	0.01
Sioux (1)	5	0.02
Tlingit-Haida *(Alaska Native)* (0)	1	<0.01
Asian (795)	880	3.30
Not Hispanic (793)	874	3.28
Hispanic (2)	6	0.02
Bangladeshi (17)	17	0.06
Cambodian (24)	26	0.10
Chinese, ex. Taiwanese (124)	141	0.53
Filipino (31)	58	0.22
Indian (144)	158	0.59
Indonesian (0)	3	0.01
Japanese (9)	19	0.07
Korean (56)	66	0.25
Laotian (9)	9	0.03
Malaysian (3)	4	0.01
Nepalese (3)	3	0.01
Pakistani (25)	29	0.11
Sri Lankan (9)	9	0.03
Taiwanese (4)	4	0.01
Thai (4)	7	0.03
Vietnamese (308)	321	1.20
Hawaii Native/Pacific Islander (6)	26	0.10
Not Hispanic (5)	22	0.08
Hispanic (1)	4	0.01
Fijian (0)	2	0.01
Guamanian/Chamorro (0)	1	<0.01
Native Hawaiian (4)	6	0.02
Samoan (1)	2	0.01
White (22,110)	22,528	84.48
Not Hispanic (21,595)	21,959	82.34
Hispanic (515)	569	2.13

Springfield

Place Type: Township
County: Delaware
Population: 24,211†

Ancestry‡	Population	%
Afghan (34)	34	0.14
Albanian (38)	38	0.16
American (393)	393	1.63
Armenian (63)	63	0.26
Austrian (21)	106	0.44
British (39)	94	0.39
Bulgarian (0)	9	0.04
Canadian (24)	24	0.10
Carpatho Rusyn (0)	12	0.05
Celtic (61)	83	0.35
Croatian (7)	7	0.03
Czech (31)	119	0.49
Czechoslovakian (13)	39	0.16
Danish (11)	35	0.15
Dutch (49)	206	0.86
Eastern European (39)	39	0.16
English (541)	2,577	10.71
European (88)	111	0.46
Finnish (9)	9	0.04
French, ex. Basque (58)	419	1.74
French Canadian (41)	146	0.61
German (689)	4,589	19.08
Greek (35)	121	0.50
Hungarian (0)	81	0.34
Irish (3,988)	10,435	43.38
Italian (3,519)	7,492	31.15
Latvian (0)	22	0.09
Lithuanian (43)	170	0.71
Luxemburger (9)	9	0.04
Maltese (0)	6	0.02
Northern European (8)	8	0.03
Norwegian (13)	76	0.32
Pennsylvania German (68)	96	0.40
Polish (240)	959	3.99
Portuguese (70)	110	0.46
Romanian (38)	48	0.20
Russian (47)	183	0.76
Scandinavian (27)	42	0.17
Scotch-Irish (257)	611	2.54
Scottish (94)	341	1.42
Slavic (33)	38	0.16
Slovak (0)	129	0.54
Swedish (17)	164	0.68
Swiss (0)	58	0.24
Turkish (12)	24	0.10
Ukrainian (33)	157	0.65
Welsh (11)	263	1.09

Hispanic Origin	Population	%
Hispanic or Latino (of any race)	256	1.06
Central American, ex. Mexican	19	0.08
Guatemalan	6	0.02
Honduran	2	0.01
Nicaraguan	2	0.01
Panamanian	6	0.02
Salvadoran	3	0.01
Cuban	21	0.09
Dominican Republic	7	0.03
Mexican	62	0.26
Puerto Rican	59	0.24
South American	35	0.14
Argentinean	3	0.01
Chilean	6	0.02
Colombian	8	0.03
Ecuadorian	7	0.03
Peruvian	8	0.03
Venezuelan	2	0.01
Other South American	1	<0.01
Other Hispanic or Latino	53	0.22

Race*	Population	%
African-American/Black (414)	482	1.99
Not Hispanic (398)	461	1.90
Hispanic (16)	21	0.09
American Indian/Alaska Native (19)	60	0.25
Not Hispanic (16)	51	0.21
Hispanic (3)	9	0.04
Central American Ind. (1)	2	0.01
Cherokee (1)	4	0.02
Choctaw (1)	2	0.01
Delaware (0)	4	0.02
Iroquois (1)	4	0.02
Seminole (0)	2	0.01
Asian (913)	1,007	4.16
Not Hispanic (904)	997	4.12
Hispanic (9)	10	0.04
Bangladeshi (7)	7	0.03

*Notes: † The Census 2010 population figure is used to calculate the percentages in the Hispanic Origin and Race categories. Ancestry percentages are based on the 2006-2010 American Community Survey population (not shown); ‡ Numbers in parentheses indicate the number of people reporting a single ancestry; * Numbers in parentheses indicate the number of persons reporting this race alone, not in combination with any other race; Please refer to the Explanation of Data for more information.*

Burmese (3)	3	0.01
Cambodian (9)	14	0.06
Chinese, ex. Taiwanese (177)	200	0.83
Filipino (72)	104	0.43
Indian (275)	294	1.21
Indonesian (1)	2	0.01
Japanese (5)	9	0.04
Korean (150)	163	0.67
Laotian (3)	3	0.01
Malaysian (1)	1	<0.01
Pakistani (20)	23	0.09
Taiwanese (14)	14	0.06
Thai (6)	10	0.04
Vietnamese (145)	153	0.63
Hawaii Native/Pacific Islander (2)	10	0.04
Not Hispanic (2)	10	0.04
Native Hawaiian (1)	2	0.01
White (22,622)	22,799	94.17
Not Hispanic (22,427)	22,592	93.31
Hispanic (195)	207	0.85

Springfield

Place Type: Township
County: Montgomery
Population: 19,418†

Ancestry‡	Population	%
African, Sub-Saharan (20)	74	0.38
African (20)	42	0.22
Other Sub-Saharan African (0)	32	0.16
Alsatian (11)	22	0.11
American (785)	785	4.03
Arab (32)	114	0.59
Arab (32)	32	0.16
Lebanese (0)	82	0.42
Armenian (0)	30	0.15
Austrian (18)	134	0.69
British (91)	179	0.92
Canadian (11)	11	0.06
Celtic (13)	13	0.07
Czech (9)	73	0.38
Czechoslovakian (8)	42	0.22
Danish (0)	32	0.16
Dutch (18)	160	0.82
Eastern European (149)	168	0.86
English (399)	2,319	11.92
European (190)	190	0.98
French, ex. Basque (87)	618	3.18
French Canadian (11)	45	0.23
German (909)	4,130	21.23
Greek (29)	54	0.28
Hungarian (29)	261	1.34
Iranian (68)	157	0.81
Irish (2,258)	6,071	31.20
Italian (1,103)	3,231	16.60
Latvian (11)	20	0.10
Lithuanian (24)	180	0.93
Northern European (38)	38	0.20
Norwegian (20)	77	0.40
Pennsylvania German (62)	114	0.59
Polish (202)	984	5.06
Portuguese (22)	42	0.22
Romanian (10)	25	0.13
Russian (355)	595	3.06
Scotch-Irish (219)	516	2.65
Scottish (75)	448	2.30
Serbian (12)	23	0.12
Slavic (8)	26	0.13
Slovak (30)	185	0.95
Slovene (0)	38	0.20
Swedish (24)	205	1.05
Swiss (12)	92	0.47
Turkish (0)	30	0.15
Ukrainian (141)	248	1.27
Welsh (10)	290	1.49
West Indian, ex. Hispanic (148)	200	1.03
Bahamian (18)	39	0.20
Barbadian (33)	33	0.17
Haitian (58)	58	0.30
Jamaican (29)	60	0.31
Trinidadian/Tobagonian (10)	10	0.05

Hispanic Origin	Population	%
Hispanic or Latino (of any race)	462	2.38
Central American, ex. Mexican	62	0.32
Costa Rican	5	0.03
Guatemalan	35	0.18
Honduran	8	0.04
Nicaraguan	1	0.01
Panamanian	5	0.03
Salvadoran	8	0.04
Cuban	31	0.16
Dominican Republic	6	0.03
Mexican	82	0.42
Puerto Rican	135	0.70
South American	100	0.51
Argentinean	14	0.07
Bolivian	5	0.03
Chilean	6	0.03
Colombian	21	0.11
Ecuadorian	18	0.09
Paraguayan	2	0.01
Peruvian	22	0.11
Uruguayan	3	0.02
Venezuelan	5	0.03
Other South American	4	0.02
Other Hispanic or Latino	46	0.24

Race*	Population	%
African-American/Black (2,157)	2,334	12.02
Not Hispanic (2,131)	2,294	11.81
Hispanic (26)	40	0.21
American Indian/Alaska Native (25)	111	0.57
Not Hispanic (13)	87	0.45
Hispanic (12)	24	0.12
Aleut *(Alaska Native)* (1)	2	0.01
Apache (0)	2	0.01
Blackfeet (0)	3	0.02
Cherokee (0)	13	0.07
Cheyenne (0)	1	0.01
Choctaw (1)	2	0.01
Creek (0)	2	0.01
Iroquois (1)	1	0.01
Lumbee (1)	2	0.01
Mexican American Ind. (1)	1	0.01
Seminole (0)	3	0.02
Spanish American Ind. (0)	1	0.01
Asian (543)	646	3.33
Not Hispanic (542)	639	3.29
Hispanic (1)	7	0.04
Burmese (1)	1	0.01
Cambodian (8)	8	0.04
Chinese, ex. Taiwanese (145)	173	0.89
Filipino (24)	43	0.22
Indian (79)	96	0.49
Japanese (16)	32	0.16
Korean (180)	196	1.01
Malaysian (1)	1	0.01
Nepalese (1)	1	0.01
Pakistani (5)	8	0.04
Sri Lankan (4)	4	0.02
Thai (3)	6	0.03
Vietnamese (68)	75	0.39
Hawaii Native/Pacific Islander (2)	12	0.06
Not Hispanic (2)	7	0.04
Hispanic (0)	5	0.03
Guamanian/Chamorro (2)	8	0.04
Native Hawaiian (0)	7	0.04
Samoan (0)	5	0.03
White (16,235)	16,490	84.92
Not Hispanic (15,951)	16,180	83.32
Hispanic (284)	310	1.60

St. Marys

Place Type: City
County: Elk
Population: 13,070†

Ancestry‡	Population	%
American (725)	725	5.44
Arab (6)	6	0.05
Arab (6)	6	0.05
Austrian (50)	87	0.65
Belgian (0)	13	0.10
British (12)	12	0.09
Croatian (48)	140	1.05
Czech (0)	41	0.31
Dutch (0)	108	0.81
English (163)	833	6.25
French, ex. Basque (62)	345	2.59
French Canadian (53)	152	1.14
German (3,916)	7,779	58.41
Greek (0)	29	0.22
Hungarian (12)	12	0.09
Irish (232)	1,714	12.87
Italian (811)	2,352	17.66
Norwegian (0)	34	0.26
Pennsylvania German (0)	15	0.11
Polish (271)	1,082	8.12
Russian (8)	16	0.12
Scandinavian (0)	16	0.12
Scotch-Irish (64)	140	1.05
Scottish (0)	21	0.16
Slavic (34)	69	0.52
Slovak (24)	63	0.47
Slovene (12)	19	0.14
Swedish (29)	457	3.43
Swiss (0)	171	1.28
Welsh (0)	53	0.40
Yugoslavian (17)	59	0.44

Hispanic Origin	Population	%
Hispanic or Latino (of any race)	52	0.40
Central American, ex. Mexican	5	0.04
Guatemalan	4	0.03
Salvadoran	1	0.01
Cuban	1	0.01
Mexican	17	0.13
Puerto Rican	13	0.10
South American	10	0.08
Peruvian	9	0.07
Uruguayan	1	0.01
Other Hispanic or Latino	6	0.05

Race*	Population	%
African-American/Black (44)	74	0.57
Not Hispanic (41)	69	0.53
Hispanic (3)	5	0.04
American Indian/Alaska Native (8)	29	0.22
Not Hispanic (8)	29	0.22
Blackfeet (0)	3	0.02
Cherokee (1)	9	0.07
Delaware (1)	1	0.01
Iroquois (1)	2	0.02
Asian (52)	71	0.54
Not Hispanic (51)	69	0.53
Hispanic (1)	2	0.02
Cambodian (0)	2	0.02
Chinese, ex. Taiwanese (11)	14	0.11
Filipino (17)	23	0.18
Indian (11)	13	0.10
Japanese (2)	4	0.03
Korean (3)	5	0.04
Taiwanese (0)	2	0.02
Thai (0)	3	0.02
Vietnamese (6)	6	0.05
Hawaii Native/Pacific Islander (5)	14	0.11
Not Hispanic (5)	14	0.11
Guamanian/Chamorro (0)	1	0.01
Native Hawaiian (2)	6	0.05
Samoan (1)	1	0.01
Tongan (2)	4	0.03
White (12,870)	12,940	99.01
Not Hispanic (12,842)	12,903	98.72
Hispanic (28)	37	0.28

*Notes: † The Census 2010 population figure is used to calculate the percentages in the Hispanic Origin and Race categories. Ancestry percentages are based on the 2006-2010 American Community Survey population (not shown); ‡ Numbers in parentheses indicate the number of people reporting a single ancestry; * Numbers in parentheses indicate the number of persons reporting this race alone, not in combination with any other race; Please refer to the Explanation of Data for more information.*

State College

Place Type: Borough
County: Centre
Population: 42,034†

Ancestry‡	Population	%
African, Sub-Saharan (170)	225	0.54
African (54)	91	0.22
Ethiopian (56)	56	0.13
Nigerian (17)	17	0.04
Sierra Leonean (15)	33	0.08
South African (10)	10	0.02
Sudanese (18)	18	0.04
Albanian (9)	9	0.02
American (440)	440	1.05
Arab (136)	264	0.63
Arab (7)	7	0.02
Egyptian (17)	34	0.08
Jordanian (0)	16	0.04
Lebanese (2)	70	0.17
Moroccan (37)	37	0.09
Palestinian (16)	16	0.04
Syrian (27)	54	0.13
Other Arab (30)	30	0.07
Armenian (27)	37	0.09
Australian (12)	12	0.03
Austrian (37)	241	0.58
Brazilian (140)	158	0.38
British (127)	229	0.55
Bulgarian (22)	22	0.05
Canadian (16)	42	0.10
Celtic (7)	20	0.05
Croatian (59)	216	0.52
Czech (74)	357	0.85
Czechoslovakian (35)	108	0.26
Danish (79)	149	0.36
Dutch (179)	731	1.75
Eastern European (83)	83	0.20
English (371)	2,314	5.53
Estonian (0)	18	0.04
European (472)	523	1.25
Finnish (0)	41	0.10
French, ex. Basque (94)	602	1.44
French Canadian (51)	125	0.30
German (2,507)	8,904	21.26
Greek (53)	206	0.49
Guyanese (0)	18	0.04
Hungarian (162)	418	1.00
Icelander (34)	47	0.11
Iranian (4)	4	0.01
Irish (1,382)	6,171	14.74
Israeli (30)	50	0.12
Italian (1,226)	4,192	10.01
Latvian (16)	34	0.08
Lithuanian (58)	275	0.66
Luxemburger (0)	18	0.04
Macedonian (26)	43	0.10
Northern European (17)	17	0.04
Norwegian (109)	309	0.74
Pennsylvania German (35)	97	0.23
Polish (576)	2,644	6.31
Portuguese (17)	119	0.28
Romanian (64)	114	0.27
Russian (437)	1,239	2.96
Scandinavian (59)	105	0.25
Scotch-Irish (188)	632	1.51
Scottish (231)	680	1.62
Serbian (36)	75	0.18
Slavic (0)	47	0.11
Slovak (76)	542	1.29
Slovene (53)	67	0.16
Swedish (188)	524	1.25
Swiss (0)	263	0.63
Turkish (144)	171	0.41
Ukrainian (175)	487	1.16
Welsh (143)	463	1.11
West Indian, ex. Hispanic (117)	135	0.32
Belizean (11)	11	0.03
Haitian (78)	78	0.19
Jamaican (28)	46	0.11
Yugoslavian (0)	32	0.08

Hispanic Origin	Population	%
Hispanic or Latino (of any race)	1,629	3.88
Central American, ex. Mexican	122	0.29
Costa Rican	17	0.04
Guatemalan	21	0.05
Honduran	14	0.03
Nicaraguan	24	0.06
Panamanian	24	0.06
Salvadoran	22	0.05
Cuban	136	0.32
Dominican Republic	81	0.19
Mexican	296	0.70
Puerto Rican	397	0.94
South American	389	0.93
Argentinean	47	0.11
Bolivian	10	0.02
Chilean	35	0.08
Colombian	113	0.27
Ecuadorian	53	0.13
Paraguayan	2	<0.01
Peruvian	79	0.19
Uruguayan	6	0.01
Venezuelan	40	0.10
Other South American	4	0.01
Other Hispanic or Latino	208	0.49

Race*	Population	%
African-American/Black (1,602)	1,890	4.50
Not Hispanic (1,521)	1,773	4.22
Hispanic (81)	117	0.28
American Indian/Alaska Native (64)	219	0.52
Not Hispanic (45)	171	0.41
Hispanic (19)	48	0.11
Apache (0)	3	0.01
Blackfeet (0)	6	0.01
Canadian/French Am. Ind. (2)	2	<0.01
Central American Ind. (0)	1	<0.01
Cherokee (2)	33	0.08
Chickasaw (1)	2	<0.01
Chippewa (4)	5	0.01
Choctaw (1)	3	0.01
Creek (0)	2	<0.01
Crow (0)	1	<0.01
Delaware (0)	2	<0.01
Inupiat *(Alaska Native)* (1)	2	<0.01
Iroquois (2)	7	0.02
Kiowa (6)	6	0.01
Lumbee (0)	2	<0.01
Mexican American Ind. (7)	7	0.02
Navajo (5)	6	0.01
Potawatomi (0)	1	<0.01
Pueblo (2)	3	0.01
Shoshone (0)	1	<0.01
Sioux (3)	5	0.01
South American Ind. (3)	8	0.02
Tohono O'Odham (0)	1	<0.01
Asian (4,121)	4,583	10.90
Not Hispanic (4,091)	4,534	10.79
Hispanic (30)	49	0.12
Bangladeshi (22)	23	0.05
Burmese (3)	8	0.02
Cambodian (21)	29	0.07
Chinese, ex. Taiwanese (1,476)	1,618	3.85
Filipino (82)	154	0.37
Hmong (2)	2	<0.01
Indian (957)	1,027	2.44
Indonesian (17)	23	0.05
Japanese (102)	163	0.39
Korean (800)	841	2.00
Laotian (0)	2	<0.01
Malaysian (137)	145	0.34
Nepalese (10)	10	0.02
Pakistani (53)	62	0.15
Sri Lankan (20)	22	0.05
Taiwanese (155)	169	0.40
Thai (42)	55	0.13
Vietnamese (73)	104	0.25
Hawaii Native/Pacific Islander (17)	61	0.15
Not Hispanic (14)	51	0.12
Hispanic (3)	10	0.02
Guamanian/Chamorro (3)	5	0.01
Native Hawaiian (5)	17	0.04
Samoan (4)	7	0.02
Tongan (1)	1	<0.01
White (34,959)	35,705	84.94
Not Hispanic (33,901)	34,574	82.25
Hispanic (1,058)	1,131	2.69

Stroud

Place Type: Township
County: Monroe
Population: 19,213†

Ancestry‡	Population	%
African, Sub-Saharan (0)	30	0.16
African (0)	15	0.08
Liberian (0)	15	0.08
American (508)	508	2.71
Arab (98)	98	0.52
Arab (22)	22	0.12
Palestinian (76)	76	0.41
Austrian (63)	114	0.61
Belgian (20)	20	0.11
Brazilian (104)	104	0.56
British (0)	47	0.25
Bulgarian (37)	37	0.20
Croatian (12)	12	0.06
Cypriot (24)	24	0.13
Czech (0)	34	0.18
Czechoslovakian (58)	125	0.67
Danish (0)	34	0.18
Dutch (29)	214	1.14
Eastern European (32)	32	0.17
English (528)	1,398	7.47
European (165)	165	0.88
Finnish (0)	17	0.09
French, ex. Basque (60)	319	1.70
French Canadian (0)	35	0.19
German (1,458)	3,697	19.75
Greek (122)	284	1.52
Guyanese (79)	186	0.99
Hungarian (17)	54	0.29
Irish (726)	2,794	14.93
Italian (1,598)	3,167	16.92
Lithuanian (15)	106	0.57
Norwegian (25)	97	0.52
Pennsylvania German (69)	105	0.56
Polish (230)	612	3.27
Portuguese (151)	212	1.13
Romanian (134)	151	0.81
Russian (45)	114	0.61
Scandinavian (26)	26	0.14
Scotch-Irish (56)	270	1.44
Scottish (109)	249	1.33
Slavic (11)	31	0.17
Slovak (55)	101	0.54
Swedish (36)	103	0.55
Swiss (0)	125	0.67
Turkish (0)	15	0.08
Ukrainian (41)	70	0.37
Welsh (65)	294	1.57
West Indian, ex. Hispanic (543)	644	3.44
Haitian (184)	226	1.21
Jamaican (359)	418	2.23

Hispanic Origin	Population	%
Hispanic or Latino (of any race)	2,920	15.20
Central American, ex. Mexican	159	0.83
Costa Rican	10	0.05
Guatemalan	13	0.07
Honduran	39	0.20
Nicaraguan	7	0.04
Panamanian	48	0.25
Salvadoran	40	0.21
Other Central American	2	0.01

SECTION TWO

*Notes: † The Census 2010 population figure is used to calculate the percentages in the Hispanic Origin and Race categories. Ancestry percentages are based on the 2006-2010 American Community Survey population (not shown); ‡ Numbers in parentheses indicate the number of people reporting a single ancestry; * Numbers in parentheses indicate the number of persons reporting this race alone, not in combination with any other race; Please refer to the Explanation of Data for more information.*

Cuban	61	0.32
Dominican Republic	340	1.77
Mexican	139	0.72
Puerto Rican	1,580	8.22
South American	428	2.23
Argentinean	17	0.09
Bolivian	2	0.01
Chilean	14	0.07
Colombian	132	0.69
Ecuadorian	145	0.75
Paraguayan	1	0.01
Peruvian	75	0.39
Uruguayan	20	0.10
Venezuelan	13	0.07
Other South American	9	0.05
Other Hispanic or Latino	213	1.11

Race*	Population	%
African-American/Black (3,150)	3,529	18.37
Not Hispanic (2,897)	3,145	16.37
Hispanic (253)	384	2.00
American Indian/Alaska Native (57)	197	1.03
Not Hispanic (29)	140	0.73
Hispanic (28)	57	0.30
Apache (0)	2	0.01
Blackfeet (0)	9	0.05
Central American Ind. (4)	4	0.02
Cherokee (4)	44	0.23
Cheyenne (1)	2	0.01
Choctaw (0)	2	0.01
Crow (0)	2	0.01
Delaware (0)	1	0.01
Iroquois (1)	5	0.03
Mexican American Ind. (0)	1	0.01
Navajo (0)	2	0.01
Potawatomi (0)	3	0.02
Pueblo (0)	1	0.01
Seminole (0)	2	0.01
Sioux (0)	4	0.02
South American Ind. (2)	5	0.03
Spanish American Ind. (1)	1	0.01
Tohono O'Odham (3)	3	0.02
Asian (686)	821	4.27
Not Hispanic (675)	798	4.15
Hispanic (11)	23	0.12
Bangladeshi (6)	6	0.03
Cambodian (1)	1	0.01
Chinese, ex. Taiwanese (125)	155	0.81
Filipino (123)	148	0.77
Indian (196)	234	1.22
Indonesian (6)	7	0.04
Japanese (14)	29	0.15
Korean (59)	71	0.37
Pakistani (38)	50	0.26
Taiwanese (9)	10	0.05
Thai (22)	22	0.11
Vietnamese (50)	51	0.27
Hawaii Native/Pacific Islander (8)	37	0.19
Not Hispanic (8)	26	0.14
Hispanic (0)	11	0.06
Native Hawaiian (0)	3	0.02
Tongan (1)	1	0.01
White (13,595)	14,068	73.22
Not Hispanic (12,202)	12,528	65.21
Hispanic (1,393)	1,540	8.02

Sunbury

Place Type: City
County: Northumberland
Population: 9,905†

Ancestry‡	Population	%
American (1,021)	1,021	10.17
Austrian (0)	20	0.20
British (0)	17	0.17
Canadian (38)	66	0.66
Czech (0)	45	0.45
Danish (0)	23	0.23
Dutch (123)	514	5.12
English (237)	640	6.37
European (15)	15	0.15
Finnish (12)	12	0.12
French, ex. Basque (90)	242	2.41
German (1,747)	3,381	33.67
Hungarian (52)	52	0.52
Irish (296)	1,057	10.53
Italian (350)	855	8.51
Lithuanian (37)	70	0.70
Pennsylvania German (199)	272	2.71
Polish (218)	348	3.47
Russian (0)	14	0.14
Scotch-Irish (74)	85	0.85
Scottish (65)	153	1.52
Slavic (0)	4	0.04
Slovak (32)	83	0.83
Swedish (0)	42	0.42
Swiss (0)	75	0.75
Ukrainian (20)	39	0.39
Welsh (8)	52	0.52
Yugoslavian (0)	9	0.09

Hispanic Origin	Population	%
Hispanic or Latino (of any race)	660	6.66
Central American, ex. Mexican	29	0.29
Guatemalan	8	0.08
Honduran	19	0.19
Panamanian	1	0.01
Salvadoran	1	0.01
Cuban	7	0.07
Dominican Republic	11	0.11
Mexican	119	1.20
Puerto Rican	431	4.35
South American	15	0.15
Bolivian	2	0.02
Chilean	1	0.01
Colombian	3	0.03
Ecuadorian	6	0.06
Peruvian	3	0.03
Other Hispanic or Latino	48	0.48

Race*	Population	%
African-American/Black (278)	395	3.99
Not Hispanic (240)	339	3.42
Hispanic (38)	56	0.57
American Indian/Alaska Native (30)	109	1.10
Not Hispanic (20)	91	0.92
Hispanic (10)	18	0.18
Apache (0)	1	0.01
Blackfeet (1)	6	0.06
Canadian/French Am. Ind. (3)	3	0.03
Cherokee (3)	31	0.31
Cree (1)	1	0.01
Creek (0)	3	0.03
Crow (0)	1	0.01
Delaware (3)	5	0.05
Iroquois (0)	1	0.01
Lumbee (1)	1	0.01
Shoshone (0)	1	0.01
Sioux (0)	1	0.01
South American Ind. (5)	7	0.07
Asian (27)	38	0.38
Not Hispanic (25)	36	0.36
Hispanic (2)	2	0.02
Chinese, ex. Taiwanese (3)	5	0.05
Filipino (3)	8	0.08
Indian (4)	6	0.06
Indonesian (9)	9	0.09
Korean (5)	8	0.08
Laotian (1)	1	0.01
Vietnamese (1)	2	0.02
Hawaii Native/Pacific Islander (4)	7	0.07
Not Hispanic (3)	5	0.05
Hispanic (1)	2	0.02
Guamanian/Chamorro (1)	1	0.01
Native Hawaiian (2)	4	0.04
Samoan (1)	1	0.01
White (9,016)	9,233	93.22
Not Hispanic (8,771)	8,942	90.28
Hispanic (245)	291	2.94

Susquehanna

Place Type: Township
County: Dauphin
Population: 24,036†

Ancestry‡	Population	%
African, Sub-Saharan (142)	216	0.91
African (102)	176	0.75
Nigerian (28)	28	0.12
Other Sub-Saharan African (12)	12	0.05
Alsatian (0)	9	0.04
American (729)	729	3.09
Arab (95)	95	0.40
Palestinian (95)	95	0.40
Austrian (35)	69	0.29
British (29)	90	0.38
Canadian (0)	22	0.09
Croatian (24)	58	0.25
Czech (0)	170	0.72
Czechoslovakian (23)	44	0.19
Danish (47)	74	0.31
Dutch (129)	498	2.11
Eastern European (162)	162	0.69
English (331)	1,643	6.96
European (292)	300	1.27
Finnish (0)	18	0.08
French, ex. Basque (41)	328	1.39
French Canadian (0)	30	0.13
German (3,197)	7,401	31.34
German Russian (11)	11	0.05
Greek (73)	111	0.47
Hungarian (47)	143	0.61
Irish (808)	3,353	14.20
Israeli (43)	43	0.18
Italian (607)	1,627	6.89
Lithuanian (42)	156	0.66
Macedonian (9)	9	0.04
Northern European (11)	11	0.05
Norwegian (52)	143	0.61
Pennsylvania German (150)	213	0.90
Polish (205)	891	3.77
Portuguese (0)	55	0.23
Romanian (156)	156	0.66
Russian (261)	710	3.01
Scotch-Irish (236)	558	2.36
Scottish (99)	479	2.03
Serbian (0)	22	0.09
Slavic (16)	25	0.11
Slovak (22)	310	1.31
Slovene (0)	12	0.05
Swedish (54)	251	1.06
Swiss (15)	150	0.64
Turkish (9)	21	0.09
Ukrainian (33)	210	0.89
Welsh (58)	329	1.39
West Indian, ex. Hispanic (222)	297	1.26
Bermudan (165)	165	0.70
Jamaican (35)	35	0.15
West Indian (22)	97	0.41
Yugoslavian (44)	52	0.22

Hispanic Origin	Population	%
Hispanic or Latino (of any race)	1,177	4.90
Central American, ex. Mexican	57	0.24
Costa Rican	6	0.02
Guatemalan	10	0.04
Honduran	10	0.04
Nicaraguan	2	0.01
Panamanian	22	0.09
Salvadoran	7	0.03
Cuban	55	0.23
Dominican Republic	54	0.22
Mexican	155	0.64
Puerto Rican	717	2.98
South American	70	0.29
Argentinean	2	0.01
Bolivian	2	0.01
Chilean	5	0.02
Colombian	11	0.05

*Notes: † The Census 2010 population figure is used to calculate the percentages in the Hispanic Origin and Race categories. Ancestry percentages are based on the 2006-2010 American Community Survey population (not shown); ‡ Numbers in parentheses indicate the number of people reporting a single ancestry; * Numbers in parentheses indicate the number of persons reporting this race alone, not in combination with any other race; Please refer to the Explanation of Data for more information.*

Ecuadorian	27	0.11
Peruvian	21	0.09
Uruguayan	1	<0.01
Venezuelan	1	<0.01
Other Hispanic or Latino	69	0.29

Race*	Population	%
African-American/Black (5,661)	6,285	26.15
Not Hispanic (5,516)	6,041	25.13
Hispanic (145)	244	1.02
American Indian/Alaska Native (31)	147	0.61
Not Hispanic (17)	121	0.50
Hispanic (14)	26	0.11
Blackfeet (1)	14	0.06
Cherokee (2)	30	0.12
Chickasaw (0)	2	0.01
Choctaw (0)	2	0.01
Comanche (0)	1	<0.01
Cree (0)	1	<0.01
Delaware (0)	1	<0.01
Hopi (0)	1	<0.01
Inupiat *(Alaska Native)* (0)	1	<0.01
Iroquois (1)	6	0.02
Lumbee (0)	3	0.01
Navajo (1)	1	<0.01
Seminole (0)	3	0.01
Sioux (0)	3	0.01
South American Ind. (0)	5	0.02
Spanish American Ind. (0)	1	<0.01
Tohono O'Odham (1)	2	0.01
Asian (868)	1,014	4.22
Not Hispanic (863)	995	4.14
Hispanic (5)	19	0.08
Cambodian (23)	23	0.10
Chinese, ex. Taiwanese (129)	153	0.64
Filipino (46)	73	0.30
Indian (208)	237	0.99
Indonesian (20)	22	0.09
Japanese (11)	23	0.10
Korean (25)	45	0.19
Laotian (1)	1	<0.01
Malaysian (1)	1	<0.01
Nepalese (5)	5	0.02
Pakistani (29)	30	0.12
Sri Lankan (1)	2	0.01
Taiwanese (2)	2	0.01
Thai (4)	13	0.05
Vietnamese (354)	375	1.56
Hawaii Native/Pacific Islander (7)	26	0.11
Not Hispanic (7)	20	0.08
Hispanic (0)	6	0.02
Guamanian/Chamorro (1)	2	0.01
Native Hawaiian (2)	6	0.02
Samoan (0)	1	<0.01
White (16,178)	16,905	70.33
Not Hispanic (15,722)	16,339	67.98
Hispanic (456)	566	2.35

Swatara

Place Type: Township
County: Dauphin
Population: 23,362†

Ancestry‡	Population	%
African, Sub-Saharan (390)	390	1.68
African (95)	95	0.41
Ghanaian (12)	12	0.05
Senegalese (18)	18	0.08
South African (18)	18	0.08
Sudanese (217)	217	0.94
Other Sub-Saharan African (30)	30	0.13
American (1,202)	1,202	5.19
Arab (77)	77	0.33
Moroccan (77)	77	0.33
Austrian (0)	75	0.32
Belgian (0)	11	0.05
British (55)	143	0.62
Bulgarian (13)	13	0.06
Croatian (350)	692	2.99
Czech (31)	98	0.42
Czechoslovakian (0)	11	0.05
Danish (0)	26	0.11
Dutch (42)	457	1.97
Eastern European (18)	18	0.08
English (220)	1,306	5.64
European (126)	126	0.54
French, ex. Basque (22)	362	1.56
French Canadian (27)	27	0.12
German (2,560)	6,102	26.35
Greek (34)	34	0.15
Hungarian (34)	174	0.75
Irish (603)	2,834	12.24
Italian (661)	1,649	7.12
Latvian (10)	10	0.04
Lithuanian (27)	85	0.37
Macedonian (0)	33	0.14
Northern European (0)	12	0.05
Pennsylvania German (140)	205	0.89
Polish (179)	716	3.09
Russian (0)	52	0.22
Scotch-Irish (127)	423	1.83
Scottish (23)	187	0.81
Serbian (145)	244	1.05
Slavic (0)	14	0.06
Slovak (42)	110	0.48
Slovene (12)	17	0.07
Swedish (0)	197	0.85
Swiss (24)	68	0.29
Ukrainian (42)	155	0.67
Welsh (25)	459	1.98
West Indian, ex. Hispanic (10)	10	0.04
Jamaican (10)	10	0.04
Yugoslavian (26)	81	0.35

Hispanic Origin	Population	%
Hispanic or Latino (of any race)	1,932	8.27
Central American, ex. Mexican	59	0.25
Costa Rican	1	<0.01
Guatemalan	16	0.07
Honduran	16	0.07
Nicaraguan	1	<0.01
Panamanian	9	0.04
Salvadoran	13	0.06
Other Central American	3	0.01
Cuban	41	0.18
Dominican Republic	172	0.74
Mexican	460	1.97
Puerto Rican	999	4.28
South American	102	0.44
Argentinean	4	0.02
Bolivian	2	0.01
Chilean	2	0.01
Colombian	19	0.08
Ecuadorian	48	0.21
Paraguayan	1	<0.01
Peruvian	24	0.10
Venezuelan	2	0.01
Other Hispanic or Latino	99	0.42

Race*	Population	%
African-American/Black (4,288)	4,923	21.07
Not Hispanic (4,128)	4,631	19.82
Hispanic (160)	292	1.25
American Indian/Alaska Native (33)	122	0.52
Not Hispanic (22)	91	0.39
Hispanic (11)	31	0.13
Apache (0)	1	<0.01
Arapaho (0)	1	<0.01
Blackfeet (1)	8	0.03
Cherokee (10)	30	0.13
Chippewa (1)	2	0.01
Delaware (0)	3	0.01
Houma (1)	1	<0.01
Iroquois (1)	3	0.01
Menominee (1)	1	<0.01
Navajo (1)	1	<0.01
Osage (0)	1	<0.01
Seminole (0)	2	0.01
Sioux (0)	1	<0.01
South American Ind. (3)	4	0.02
Spanish American Ind. (2)	2	0.01
Asian (803)	913	3.91
Not Hispanic (802)	911	3.90
Hispanic (1)	2	0.01
Bhutanese (3)	3	0.01
Cambodian (37)	40	0.17
Chinese, ex. Taiwanese (75)	96	0.41
Filipino (69)	81	0.35
Indian (160)	181	0.77
Indonesian (43)	47	0.20
Japanese (5)	17	0.07
Korean (25)	36	0.15
Laotian (6)	7	0.03
Nepalese (1)	1	<0.01
Pakistani (42)	47	0.20
Sri Lankan (4)	4	0.02
Taiwanese (7)	9	0.04
Thai (5)	10	0.04
Vietnamese (288)	327	1.40
Hawaii Native/Pacific Islander (12)	27	0.12
Not Hispanic (7)	18	0.08
Hispanic (5)	9	0.04
Guamanian/Chamorro (1)	1	<0.01
Native Hawaiian (7)	15	0.06
Samoan (2)	4	0.02
White (16,594)	17,283	73.98
Not Hispanic (15,828)	16,371	70.08
Hispanic (766)	912	3.90

Swissvale

Place Type: Borough
County: Allegheny
Population: 8,983†

Ancestry‡	Population	%
African, Sub-Saharan (82)	139	1.54
African (12)	12	0.13
Nigerian (70)	127	1.40
Alsatian (0)	17	0.19
American (236)	236	2.61
Arab (8)	8	0.09
Syrian (8)	8	0.09
Armenian (8)	8	0.09
Austrian (0)	16	0.18
Belgian (0)	9	0.10
British (0)	21	0.23
Croatian (41)	199	2.20
Czech (0)	40	0.44
Czechoslovakian (14)	14	0.15
Dutch (0)	17	0.19
Eastern European (35)	35	0.39
English (167)	709	7.84
European (96)	96	1.06
Finnish (0)	11	0.12
French, ex. Basque (14)	88	0.97
French Canadian (9)	9	0.10
German (296)	1,372	15.18
Greek (0)	8	0.09
Hungarian (31)	133	1.47
Iranian (47)	47	0.52
Irish (402)	1,280	14.16
Italian (749)	1,260	13.94
Lithuanian (0)	28	0.31
Pennsylvania German (0)	22	0.24
Polish (66)	288	3.19
Russian (81)	168	1.86
Scandinavian (6)	18	0.20
Scotch-Irish (114)	309	3.42
Scottish (67)	261	2.89
Serbian (0)	21	0.23
Slavic (5)	12	0.13
Slovak (223)	408	4.51
Swedish (0)	23	0.25
Ukrainian (36)	55	0.61
Welsh (24)	133	1.47

Hispanic Origin	Population	%
Hispanic or Latino (of any race)	200	2.23

SECTION TWO

*Notes: † The Census 2010 population figure is used to calculate the percentages in the Hispanic Origin and Race categories. Ancestry percentages are based on the 2006-2010 American Community Survey population (not shown); ‡ Numbers in parentheses indicate the number of people reporting a single ancestry; * Numbers in parentheses indicate the number of persons reporting this race alone, not in combination with any other race; Please refer to the Explanation of Data for more information.*

Central American, ex. Mexican	4	0.04
Guatemalan	2	0.02
Panamanian	1	0.01
Salvadoran	1	0.01
Cuban	15	0.17
Dominican Republic	4	0.04
Mexican	62	0.69
Puerto Rican	65	0.72
South American	28	0.31
Argentinean	2	0.02
Chilean	4	0.04
Colombian	10	0.11
Ecuadorian	9	0.10
Peruvian	2	0.02
Venezuelan	1	0.01
Other Hispanic or Latino	22	0.24

Race*	Population	%
African-American/Black (3,148)	3,390	37.74
Not Hispanic (3,112)	3,336	37.14
Hispanic (36)	54	0.60
American Indian/Alaska Native (18)	103	1.15
Not Hispanic (12)	85	0.95
Hispanic (6)	18	0.20
Apache (0)	1	0.01
Blackfeet (0)	9	0.10
Central American Ind. (0)	1	0.01
Cherokee (3)	12	0.13
Choctaw (0)	3	0.03
Creek (0)	1	0.01
Crow (0)	2	0.02
Sioux (0)	1	0.01
Ute (0)	2	0.02
Asian (149)	194	2.16
Not Hispanic (148)	191	2.13
Hispanic (1)	3	0.03
Burmese (1)	1	0.01
Chinese, ex. Taiwanese (56)	68	0.76
Filipino (6)	13	0.14
Hmong (2)	2	0.02
Indian (26)	37	0.41
Indonesian (10)	10	0.11
Japanese (7)	15	0.17
Korean (11)	13	0.14
Pakistani (1)	1	0.01
Taiwanese (5)	5	0.06
Thai (4)	6	0.07
Vietnamese (8)	13	0.14
Hawaii Native/Pacific Islander (0)	4	0.04
Not Hispanic (0)	4	0.04
Native Hawaiian (0)	2	0.02
Samoan (0)	1	0.01
White (5,308)	5,534	61.61
Not Hispanic (5,220)	5,432	60.47
Hispanic (88)	102	1.14

Thornbury

Place Type: Township
County: Delaware
Population: 8,028†

Ancestry‡	Population	%
African, Sub-Saharan (0)	8	0.11
African (0)	4	0.05
Sudanese (0)	4	0.05
American (126)	126	1.65
Armenian (20)	20	0.26
Austrian (0)	19	0.25
Belgian (11)	21	0.28
British (24)	24	0.32
Canadian (0)	11	0.14
Czech (20)	72	0.95
Dutch (0)	104	1.37
English (247)	793	10.41
European (236)	236	3.10
French, ex. Basque (0)	71	0.93
German (277)	1,412	18.54
Greek (50)	63	0.83
Hungarian (0)	11	0.14
Irish (734)	2,150	28.23
Italian (658)	1,674	21.98
Lithuanian (11)	20	0.26
Polish (65)	420	5.52
Portuguese (0)	13	0.17
Romanian (7)	37	0.49
Russian (53)	120	1.58
Scotch-Irish (24)	91	1.20
Scottish (12)	144	1.89
Serbian (9)	9	0.12
Slavic (0)	13	0.17
Slovak (14)	71	0.93
Slovene (15)	15	0.20
Swedish (20)	69	0.91
Swiss (0)	12	0.16
Ukrainian (25)	66	0.87
Welsh (16)	88	1.16
Yugoslavian (20)	39	0.51

Hispanic Origin	Population	%
Hispanic or Latino (of any race)	190	2.37
Central American, ex. Mexican	8	0.10
Costa Rican	3	0.04
Guatemalan	2	0.02
Honduran	1	0.01
Panamanian	1	0.01
Salvadoran	1	0.01
Cuban	18	0.22
Dominican Republic	8	0.10
Mexican	26	0.32
Puerto Rican	29	0.36
South American	13	0.16
Argentinean	1	0.01
Chilean	1	0.01
Colombian	4	0.05
Paraguayan	1	0.01
Peruvian	3	0.04
Venezuelan	3	0.04
Other Hispanic or Latino	88	1.10

Race*	Population	%
African-American/Black (1,651)	1,735	21.61
Not Hispanic (1,624)	1,701	21.19
Hispanic (27)	34	0.42
American Indian/Alaska Native (19)	38	0.47
Not Hispanic (17)	33	0.41
Hispanic (2)	5	0.06
Central American Ind. (1)	2	0.02
Cherokee (5)	12	0.15
Choctaw (2)	2	0.02
Iroquois (1)	1	0.01
Yuman (1)	2	0.02
Asian (327)	360	4.48
Not Hispanic (327)	360	4.48
Cambodian (5)	5	0.06
Chinese, ex. Taiwanese (70)	96	1.20
Filipino (12)	15	0.19
Hmong (1)	1	0.01
Indian (102)	109	1.36
Indonesian (0)	4	0.05
Japanese (6)	10	0.12
Korean (68)	69	0.86
Pakistani (9)	9	0.11
Sri Lankan (2)	2	0.02
Taiwanese (5)	5	0.06
Thai (5)	8	0.10
Vietnamese (22)	34	0.42
Hawaii Native/Pacific Islander (1)	7	0.09
Not Hispanic (1)	6	0.07
Hispanic (0)	1	0.01
Native Hawaiian (0)	1	0.01
Samoan (0)	1	0.01
Tongan (0)	1	0.01
White (5,812)	5,920	73.74
Not Hispanic (5,747)	5,844	72.80
Hispanic (65)	76	0.95

Tobyhanna

Place Type: Township
County: Monroe
Population: 8,554†

Ancestry‡	Population	%
American (115)	115	1.38
Arab (34)	183	2.20
Egyptian (0)	12	0.14
Lebanese (34)	159	1.91
Other Arab (0)	12	0.14
Carpatho Rusyn (11)	11	0.13
Czech (0)	48	0.58
Danish (122)	122	1.47
Dutch (121)	144	1.73
English (106)	631	7.58
French, ex. Basque (13)	116	1.39
German (815)	2,216	26.62
Guyanese (16)	16	0.19
Hungarian (0)	107	1.29
Irish (173)	1,159	13.92
Italian (908)	2,162	25.97
Lithuanian (24)	61	0.73
Norwegian (50)	82	0.98
Pennsylvania German (171)	195	2.34
Polish (285)	642	7.71
Russian (23)	120	1.44
Scotch-Irish (50)	67	0.80
Scottish (18)	138	1.66
Swedish (51)	65	0.78
Welsh (59)	143	1.72
West Indian, ex. Hispanic (7)	7	0.08
West Indian (7)	7	0.08

Hispanic Origin	Population	%
Hispanic or Latino (of any race)	1,010	11.81
Central American, ex. Mexican	47	0.55
Costa Rican	9	0.11
Guatemalan	11	0.13
Honduran	14	0.16
Nicaraguan	6	0.07
Panamanian	3	0.04
Salvadoran	4	0.05
Cuban	41	0.48
Dominican Republic	121	1.41
Mexican	53	0.62
Puerto Rican	552	6.45
South American	107	1.25
Argentinean	13	0.15
Bolivian	5	0.06
Colombian	35	0.41
Ecuadorian	18	0.21
Paraguayan	1	0.01
Peruvian	26	0.30
Uruguayan	8	0.09
Venezuelan	1	0.01
Other Hispanic or Latino	89	1.04

Race*	Population	%
African-American/Black (854)	953	11.14
Not Hispanic (795)	848	9.91
Hispanic (59)	105	1.23
American Indian/Alaska Native (41)	88	1.03
Not Hispanic (29)	63	0.74
Hispanic (12)	25	0.29
Apache (0)	4	0.05
Blackfeet (2)	2	0.02
Central American Ind. (0)	1	0.01
Cherokee (4)	10	0.12
Choctaw (0)	2	0.02
Comanche (0)	1	0.01
Cree (0)	1	0.01
Delaware (0)	2	0.02
Iroquois (5)	11	0.13
Mexican American Ind. (0)	3	0.04
Puget Sound Salish (4)	4	0.05
Sioux (1)	4	0.05
South American Ind. (7)	12	0.14
Asian (117)	152	1.78

*Notes: † The Census 2010 population figure is used to calculate the percentages in the Hispanic Origin and Race categories. Ancestry percentages are based on the 2006-2010 American Community Survey population (not shown); ‡ Numbers in parentheses indicate the number of people reporting a single ancestry; * Numbers in parentheses indicate the number of persons reporting this race alone, not in combination with any other race; Please refer to the Explanation of Data for more information.*

Not Hispanic (115)	143	1.67
Hispanic (2)	9	0.11
Bangladeshi (4)	4	0.05
Burmese (1)	1	0.01
Chinese, ex. Taiwanese (28)	45	0.53
Filipino (27)	31	0.36
Indian (27)	33	0.39
Indonesian (1)	4	0.05
Japanese (7)	10	0.12
Korean (8)	8	0.09
Malaysian (0)	1	0.01
Pakistani (5)	5	0.06
Thai (2)	2	0.02
Vietnamese (1)	1	0.01
Hawaii Native/Pacific Islander (1)	7	0.08
Not Hispanic (0)	2	0.02
Hispanic (1)	5	0.06
Native Hawaiian (1)	5	0.06
White (6,999)	7,143	83.50
Not Hispanic (6,488)	6,570	76.81
Hispanic (511)	573	6.70

Towamencin

Place Type: Township
County: Montgomery
Population: 17,578†

Ancestry‡	Population	%
African, Sub-Saharan (117)	117	0.67
African (78)	78	0.44
Ethiopian (39)	39	0.22
American (672)	672	3.82
Arab (0)	23	0.13
Jordanian (0)	9	0.05
Lebanese (0)	14	0.08
Armenian (11)	11	0.06
Austrian (13)	76	0.43
Belgian (0)	9	0.05
British (55)	94	0.53
Cypriot (0)	9	0.05
Czech (18)	170	0.97
Czechoslovakian (36)	51	0.29
Danish (26)	35	0.20
Dutch (40)	317	1.80
English (485)	2,135	12.14
European (55)	65	0.37
Finnish (10)	10	0.06
French, ex. Basque (13)	151	0.86
French Canadian (18)	49	0.28
German (1,503)	4,878	27.74
Greek (9)	24	0.14
Hungarian (95)	265	1.51
Irish (1,233)	4,472	25.43
Israeli (10)	10	0.06
Italian (1,024)	2,981	16.95
Lithuanian (12)	138	0.78
Northern European (39)	39	0.22
Norwegian (86)	163	0.93
Pennsylvania German (241)	321	1.83
Polish (388)	924	5.25
Portuguese (8)	8	0.05
Romanian (49)	49	0.28
Russian (89)	207	1.18
Scandinavian (0)	9	0.05
Scotch-Irish (89)	310	1.76
Scottish (121)	363	2.06
Slavic (12)	88	0.50
Slovak (75)	258	1.47
Swedish (70)	136	0.77
Swiss (79)	87	0.49
Ukrainian (13)	63	0.36
Welsh (39)	461	2.62
West Indian, ex. Hispanic (0)	54	0.31
Haitian (0)	26	0.15
Jamaican (0)	18	0.10
West Indian (0)	10	0.06
Yugoslavian (13)	13	0.07

Hispanic Origin	Population	%
Hispanic or Latino (of any race)	433	2.46
Central American, ex. Mexican	18	0.10
Costa Rican	5	0.03
Guatemalan	1	0.01
Panamanian	9	0.05
Salvadoran	2	0.01
Other Central American	1	0.01
Cuban	26	0.15
Dominican Republic	15	0.09
Mexican	80	0.46
Puerto Rican	157	0.89
South American	105	0.60
Argentinean	13	0.07
Bolivian	2	0.01
Colombian	39	0.22
Ecuadorian	22	0.13
Paraguayan	2	0.01
Peruvian	21	0.12
Venezuelan	5	0.03
Other South American	1	0.01
Other Hispanic or Latino	32	0.18

Race*	Population	%
African-American/Black (727)	878	4.99
Not Hispanic (708)	831	4.73
Hispanic (19)	47	0.27
American Indian/Alaska Native (19)	88	0.50
Not Hispanic (16)	76	0.43
Hispanic (3)	12	0.07
Blackfeet (0)	4	0.02
Canadian/French Am. Ind. (7)	7	0.04
Cherokee (0)	9	0.05
Choctaw (0)	2	0.01
Iroquois (0)	1	0.01
Lumbee (1)	1	0.01
Mexican American Ind. (2)	2	0.01
Navajo (0)	2	0.01
Sioux (0)	3	0.02
Asian (1,478)	1,601	9.11
Not Hispanic (1,477)	1,599	9.10
Hispanic (1)	2	0.01
Bangladeshi (30)	36	0.20
Cambodian (16)	20	0.11
Chinese, ex. Taiwanese (228)	267	1.52
Filipino (44)	62	0.35
Hmong (2)	2	0.01
Indian (450)	482	2.74
Indonesian (5)	5	0.03
Japanese (28)	48	0.27
Korean (480)	499	2.84
Laotian (4)	5	0.03
Malaysian (0)	1	0.01
Nepalese (7)	7	0.04
Pakistani (13)	14	0.08
Sri Lankan (4)	4	0.02
Taiwanese (6)	11	0.06
Thai (6)	7	0.04
Vietnamese (103)	114	0.65
Hawaii Native/Pacific Islander (3)	8	0.05
Not Hispanic (3)	7	0.04
Hispanic (0)	1	0.01
Guamanian/Chamorro (1)	4	0.02
Native Hawaiian (0)	2	0.01
Samoan (1)	1	0.01
White (14,958)	15,181	86.36
Not Hispanic (14,658)	14,857	84.52
Hispanic (300)	324	1.84

Tredyffrin

Place Type: Township
County: Chester
Population: 29,332†

Ancestry‡	Population	%
African, Sub-Saharan (91)	91	0.31
Kenyan (12)	12	0.04
South African (32)	32	0.11
Sudanese (47)	47	0.16
Albanian (80)	100	0.34
American (998)	998	3.39
Arab (339)	415	1.41
Egyptian (58)	58	0.20
Lebanese (12)	31	0.11
Syrian (0)	57	0.19
Other Arab (269)	269	0.91
Armenian (16)	98	0.33
Austrian (48)	215	0.73
Belgian (13)	56	0.19
Brazilian (24)	37	0.13
British (122)	202	0.69
Bulgarian (27)	27	0.09
Canadian (43)	93	0.32
Celtic (10)	20	0.07
Croatian (0)	31	0.11
Czech (31)	318	1.08
Czechoslovakian (10)	10	0.03
Danish (13)	83	0.28
Dutch (19)	448	1.52
Eastern European (111)	141	0.48
English (1,084)	4,846	16.44
European (223)	253	0.86
French, ex. Basque (57)	644	2.18
French Canadian (43)	100	0.34
German (1,630)	7,033	23.86
Greek (127)	312	1.06
Hungarian (45)	204	0.69
Iranian (38)	38	0.13
Irish (2,086)	7,353	24.94
Italian (1,935)	4,375	14.84
Latvian (40)	108	0.37
Lithuanian (81)	272	0.92
Luxemburger (0)	14	0.05
Northern European (26)	35	0.12
Norwegian (37)	528	1.79
Pennsylvania German (21)	31	0.11
Polish (325)	1,358	4.61
Portuguese (22)	55	0.19
Romanian (39)	39	0.13
Russian (261)	806	2.73
Scandinavian (16)	65	0.22
Scotch-Irish (153)	614	2.08
Scottish (300)	986	3.34
Slavic (13)	23	0.08
Slovak (107)	268	0.91
Slovene (17)	58	0.20
Swedish (144)	424	1.44
Swiss (19)	128	0.43
Turkish (12)	12	0.04
Ukrainian (21)	223	0.76
Welsh (82)	629	2.13
West Indian, ex. Hispanic (53)	69	0.23
Barbadian (0)	16	0.05
Haitian (14)	14	0.05
Jamaican (39)	39	0.13

Hispanic Origin	Population	%
Hispanic or Latino (of any race)	647	2.21
Central American, ex. Mexican	50	0.17
Costa Rican	5	0.02
Guatemalan	22	0.08
Honduran	4	0.01
Nicaraguan	1	<0.01
Panamanian	8	0.03
Salvadoran	10	0.03
Cuban	53	0.18
Dominican Republic	16	0.05
Mexican	130	0.44
Puerto Rican	121	0.41
South American	189	0.64
Argentinean	19	0.06
Bolivian	6	0.02
Chilean	25	0.09
Colombian	51	0.17
Ecuadorian	21	0.07
Peruvian	42	0.14
Uruguayan	5	0.02
Venezuelan	20	0.07
Other Hispanic or Latino	88	0.30

*Notes: † The Census 2010 population figure is used to calculate the percentages in the Hispanic Origin and Race categories. Ancestry percentages are based on the 2006-2010 American Community Survey population (not shown); ‡ Numbers in parentheses indicate the number of people reporting a single ancestry; * Numbers in parentheses indicate the number of persons reporting this race alone, not in combination with any other race; Please refer to the Explanation of Data for more information.*

Race*	Population	%
African-American/Black (968)	1,092	3.72
Not Hispanic (957)	1,069	3.64
Hispanic (11)	23	0.08
American Indian/Alaska Native (21)	111	0.38
Not Hispanic (16)	95	0.32
Hispanic (5)	16	0.05
Apache (0)	1	<0.01
Blackfeet (0)	1	<0.01
Cherokee (2)	25	0.09
Chickasaw (0)	1	<0.01
Delaware (0)	2	0.01
Hopi (0)	2	0.01
Iroquois (0)	3	0.01
Mexican American Ind. (2)	3	0.01
Seminole (0)	2	0.01
Shoshone (3)	4	0.01
Sioux (0)	6	0.02
South American Ind. (1)	5	0.02
Ute (1)	1	<0.01
Asian (2,873)	3,106	10.59
Not Hispanic (2,865)	3,084	10.51
Hispanic (8)	22	0.08
Bangladeshi (12)	15	0.05
Burmese (2)	2	0.01
Cambodian (3)	3	0.01
Chinese, ex. Taiwanese (1,073)	1,130	3.85
Filipino (59)	90	0.31
Hmong (0)	1	<0.01
Indian (1,055)	1,093	3.73
Indonesian (1)	2	0.01
Japanese (58)	94	0.32
Korean (309)	364	1.24
Laotian (5)	10	0.03
Nepalese (2)	2	0.01
Pakistani (43)	47	0.16
Sri Lankan (7)	8	0.03
Taiwanese (61)	69	0.24
Thai (12)	21	0.07
Vietnamese (131)	145	0.49
Hawaii Native/Pacific Islander (1)	5	0.02
Not Hispanic (1)	5	0.02
Native Hawaiian (0)	2	0.01
Samoan (1)	2	0.01
White (24,963)	25,329	86.35
Not Hispanic (24,433)	24,763	84.42
Hispanic (530)	566	1.93

Uniontown

Place Type: City
County: Fayette
Population: 10,372†

Ancestry‡	Population	%
African, Sub-Saharan (20)	40	0.37
African (20)	40	0.37
American (220)	220	2.05
Arab (81)	374	3.49
Lebanese (81)	374	3.49
Armenian (16)	46	0.43
Austrian (26)	221	2.06
British (8)	20	0.19
Carpatho Rusyn (18)	18	0.17
Croatian (12)	175	1.63
Czech (18)	123	1.15
Dutch (32)	701	6.53
English (265)	695	6.48
European (95)	95	0.89
Finnish (0)	6	0.06
French, ex. Basque (51)	90	0.84
French Canadian (6)	18	0.17
German (376)	1,994	18.59
Greek (12)	12	0.11
Hungarian (46)	184	1.72
Irish (421)	1,785	16.64
Israeli (0)	9	0.08
Italian (611)	1,455	13.56
Lithuanian (0)	59	0.55
Pennsylvania German (102)	102	0.95
Polish (210)	949	8.85
Russian (103)	264	2.46
Scotch-Irish (52)	134	1.25
Scottish (28)	91	0.85
Slavic (0)	14	0.13
Slovak (222)	680	6.34
Swedish (0)	51	0.48
Welsh (60)	142	1.32
West Indian, ex. Hispanic (31)	37	0.34
Bahamian (31)	31	0.29
Jamaican (0)	6	0.06

Hispanic Origin	Population	%
Hispanic or Latino (of any race)	143	1.38
Central American, ex. Mexican	3	0.03
Guatemalan	1	0.01
Nicaraguan	1	0.01
Salvadoran	1	0.01
Cuban	2	0.02
Dominican Republic	1	0.01
Mexican	65	0.63
Puerto Rican	40	0.39
South American	7	0.07
Ecuadorian	2	0.02
Peruvian	1	0.01
Uruguayan	1	0.01
Venezuelan	3	0.03
Other Hispanic or Latino	25	0.24

Race*	Population	%
African-American/Black (1,874)	2,163	20.85
Not Hispanic (1,853)	2,122	20.46
Hispanic (21)	41	0.40
American Indian/Alaska Native (29)	102	0.98
Not Hispanic (22)	92	0.89
Hispanic (7)	10	0.10
Apache (0)	4	0.04
Blackfeet (0)	2	0.02
Cherokee (8)	29	0.28
Cheyenne (4)	4	0.04
Cree (0)	2	0.02
Delaware (0)	2	0.02
Iroquois (0)	3	0.03
Pima (1)	1	0.01
Potawatomi (1)	1	0.01
Sioux (0)	3	0.03
Tlingit-Haida *(Alaska Native)* (1)	1	0.01
Asian (48)	78	0.75
Not Hispanic (48)	77	0.74
Hispanic (0)	1	0.01
Cambodian (0)	1	0.01
Chinese, ex. Taiwanese (6)	12	0.12
Filipino (7)	11	0.11
Indian (17)	20	0.19
Japanese (5)	6	0.06
Korean (8)	12	0.12
Pakistani (0)	4	0.04
Thai (0)	1	0.01
Vietnamese (3)	4	0.04
Hawaii Native/Pacific Islander (1)	2	0.02
Not Hispanic (0)	1	0.01
Hispanic (1)	1	0.01
Guamanian/Chamorro (0)	1	0.01
White (8,032)	8,359	80.59
Not Hispanic (7,957)	8,265	79.69
Hispanic (75)	94	0.91

Unity

Place Type: Township
County: Westmoreland
Population: 22,607†

Ancestry‡	Population	%
African, Sub-Saharan (0)	10	0.04
African (0)	10	0.04
American (806)	806	3.60
Arab (12)	78	0.35
Lebanese (0)	16	0.07
Syrian (12)	62	0.28
Armenian (0)	81	0.36
Austrian (44)	161	0.72
Belgian (0)	13	0.06
Brazilian (0)	94	0.42
Croatian (91)	384	1.72
Czech (121)	287	1.28
Czechoslovakian (23)	61	0.27
Danish (0)	11	0.05
Dutch (106)	411	1.84
Eastern European (11)	11	0.05
English (529)	2,539	11.35
European (126)	175	0.78
French, ex. Basque (58)	513	2.29
German (1,975)	6,936	31.01
Greek (10)	10	0.04
Hungarian (206)	566	2.53
Irish (526)	4,002	17.89
Italian (2,070)	5,325	23.81
Latvian (24)	24	0.11
Lithuanian (62)	116	0.52
Norwegian (13)	49	0.22
Pennsylvania German (79)	216	0.97
Polish (630)	2,413	10.79
Portuguese (0)	37	0.17
Russian (147)	380	1.70
Scandinavian (10)	20	0.09
Scotch-Irish (383)	695	3.11
Scottish (95)	503	2.25
Serbian (9)	87	0.39
Slavic (48)	78	0.35
Slovak (636)	1,706	7.63
Slovene (25)	60	0.27
Swedish (33)	207	0.93
Swiss (13)	121	0.54
Ukrainian (64)	104	0.46
Welsh (58)	240	1.07
West Indian, ex. Hispanic (9)	14	0.06
Haitian (0)	5	0.02
Jamaican (5)	5	0.02
Trinidadian/Tobagonian (4)	4	0.02
Yugoslavian (28)	51	0.23

Hispanic Origin	Population	%
Hispanic or Latino (of any race)	199	0.88
Central American, ex. Mexican	15	0.07
Costa Rican	2	0.01
Guatemalan	7	0.03
Honduran	3	0.01
Panamanian	1	<0.01
Salvadoran	2	0.01
Cuban	11	0.05
Dominican Republic	1	<0.01
Mexican	57	0.25
Puerto Rican	60	0.27
South American	38	0.17
Argentinean	7	0.03
Bolivian	3	0.01
Chilean	7	0.03
Colombian	9	0.04
Ecuadorian	6	0.03
Peruvian	1	<0.01
Venezuelan	5	0.02
Other Hispanic or Latino	17	0.08

Race*	Population	%
African-American/Black (161)	248	1.10
Not Hispanic (155)	232	1.03
Hispanic (6)	16	0.07
American Indian/Alaska Native (14)	75	0.33
Not Hispanic (13)	71	0.31
Hispanic (1)	4	0.02
Blackfeet (0)	4	0.02
Cherokee (0)	23	0.10
Cheyenne (0)	3	0.01
Choctaw (0)	1	<0.01
Delaware (1)	1	<0.01
Iroquois (4)	9	0.04
Mexican American Ind. (1)	1	<0.01
Navajo (0)	1	<0.01

*Notes: † The Census 2010 population figure is used to calculate the percentages in the Hispanic Origin and Race categories. Ancestry percentages are based on the 2006-2010 American Community Survey population (not shown); ‡ Numbers in parentheses indicate the number of people reporting a single ancestry; * Numbers in parentheses indicate the number of persons reporting this race alone, not in combination with any other race; Please refer to the Explanation of Data for more information.*

Sioux (0)	3	0.01
South American Ind. (0)	2	0.01
Asian (222)	258	1.14
Not Hispanic (221)	254	1.12
Hispanic (1)	4	0.02
Bangladeshi (2)	2	0.01
Cambodian (0)	1	<0.01
Chinese, ex. Taiwanese (70)	75	0.33
Filipino (19)	32	0.14
Indian (74)	76	0.34
Japanese (2)	7	0.03
Korean (17)	23	0.10
Laotian (1)	3	0.01
Pakistani (4)	4	0.02
Sri Lankan (4)	4	0.02
Taiwanese (2)	3	0.01
Thai (6)	12	0.05
Vietnamese (14)	14	0.06
Hawaii Native/Pacific Islander (7)	14	0.06
Not Hispanic (7)	14	0.06
Guamanian/Chamorro (0)	1	<0.01
Marshallese (1)	1	<0.01
Native Hawaiian (1)	5	0.02
White (21,985)	22,157	98.01
Not Hispanic (21,835)	21,990	97.27
Hispanic (150)	167	0.74

Upper Allen

Place Type: Township
County: Cumberland
Population: 18,059†

Ancestry‡	Population	%
Afghan (50)	50	0.29
African, Sub-Saharan (14)	42	0.24
African (0)	28	0.16
Kenyan (14)	14	0.08
American (630)	630	3.59
Arab (32)	45	0.26
Lebanese (16)	16	0.09
Syrian (16)	29	0.17
Armenian (0)	16	0.09
Assyrian/Chaldean/Syriac (0)	15	0.09
Austrian (13)	113	0.64
Brazilian (0)	15	0.09
British (41)	181	1.03
Bulgarian (15)	28	0.16
Canadian (18)	90	0.51
Celtic (0)	16	0.09
Croatian (0)	73	0.42
Czech (40)	123	0.70
Czechoslovakian (9)	9	0.05
Danish (0)	22	0.13
Dutch (81)	673	3.84
English (470)	1,832	10.45
European (174)	239	1.36
Finnish (37)	44	0.25
French, ex. Basque (135)	588	3.35
French Canadian (27)	85	0.48
German (2,685)	6,479	36.94
Greek (82)	115	0.66
Hungarian (42)	151	0.86
Irish (745)	2,785	15.88
Italian (616)	1,907	10.87
Lithuanian (0)	48	0.27
Maltese (11)	22	0.13
Norwegian (0)	179	1.02
Pennsylvania German (115)	228	1.30
Polish (325)	1,054	6.01
Portuguese (0)	32	0.18
Russian (47)	158	0.90
Scandinavian (0)	23	0.13
Scotch-Irish (112)	495	2.82
Scottish (175)	502	2.86
Serbian (0)	9	0.05
Slavic (26)	52	0.30
Slovak (91)	196	1.12
Slovene (0)	7	0.04
Swedish (50)	215	1.23
Swiss (22)	160	0.91
Ukrainian (51)	119	0.68
Welsh (72)	499	2.85
West Indian, ex. Hispanic (56)	70	0.40
Haitian (52)	52	0.30
Jamaican (4)	18	0.10
Yugoslavian (25)	50	0.29

Hispanic Origin	Population	%
Hispanic or Latino (of any race)	475	2.63
Central American, ex. Mexican	56	0.31
Costa Rican	1	0.01
Guatemalan	15	0.08
Honduran	24	0.13
Nicaraguan	4	0.02
Panamanian	6	0.03
Salvadoran	6	0.03
Cuban	24	0.13
Dominican Republic	12	0.07
Mexican	112	0.62
Puerto Rican	161	0.89
South American	71	0.39
Argentinean	2	0.01
Bolivian	3	0.02
Chilean	1	0.01
Colombian	20	0.11
Ecuadorian	18	0.10
Paraguayan	1	0.01
Peruvian	24	0.13
Uruguayan	1	0.01
Venezuelan	1	0.01
Other Hispanic or Latino	39	0.22

Race*	Population	%
African-American/Black (589)	758	4.20
Not Hispanic (568)	705	3.90
Hispanic (21)	53	0.29
American Indian/Alaska Native (19)	71	0.39
Not Hispanic (17)	66	0.37
Hispanic (2)	5	0.03
Apache (0)	1	0.01
Blackfeet (0)	5	0.03
Central American Ind. (1)	1	0.01
Cherokee (3)	18	0.10
Chickasaw (0)	1	0.01
Chippewa (2)	2	0.01
Choctaw (3)	3	0.02
Cree (0)	1	0.01
Delaware (0)	1	0.01
Hopi (0)	2	0.01
Iroquois (0)	2	0.01
Navajo (0)	3	0.02
Osage (1)	1	0.01
Sioux (1)	1	0.01
South American Ind. (1)	1	0.01
Asian (411)	562	3.11
Not Hispanic (409)	551	3.05
Hispanic (2)	11	0.06
Bangladeshi (10)	11	0.06
Cambodian (7)	12	0.07
Chinese, ex. Taiwanese (49)	76	0.42
Filipino (36)	66	0.37
Indian (119)	129	0.71
Indonesian (0)	8	0.04
Japanese (13)	31	0.17
Korean (74)	104	0.58
Laotian (13)	16	0.09
Pakistani (18)	18	0.10
Taiwanese (2)	5	0.03
Thai (3)	5	0.03
Vietnamese (51)	70	0.39
Hawaii Native/Pacific Islander (3)	12	0.07
Not Hispanic (3)	10	0.06
Hispanic (0)	2	0.01
Guamanian/Chamorro (0)	1	0.01
Native Hawaiian (0)	2	0.01
White (16,550)	16,882	93.48
Not Hispanic (16,277)	16,564	91.72
Hispanic (273)	318	1.76

Upper Chichester

Place Type: Township
County: Delaware
Population: 16,738†

Ancestry‡	Population	%
African, Sub-Saharan (97)	108	0.65
African (97)	97	0.58
Cape Verdean (0)	11	0.07
Albanian (14)	14	0.08
American (601)	601	3.60
Arab (22)	48	0.29
Lebanese (0)	13	0.08
Syrian (0)	13	0.08
Other Arab (22)	22	0.13
Armenian (0)	65	0.39
Australian (12)	12	0.07
Austrian (0)	84	0.50
British (0)	14	0.08
Bulgarian (51)	51	0.31
Canadian (0)	61	0.37
Croatian (0)	12	0.07
Czech (25)	86	0.51
Czechoslovakian (0)	7	0.04
Dutch (26)	354	2.12
Eastern European (28)	51	0.31
English (265)	1,602	9.59
European (53)	53	0.32
Finnish (0)	11	0.07
French, ex. Basque (30)	301	1.80
French Canadian (0)	59	0.35
German (582)	3,171	18.98
Greek (24)	48	0.29
Hungarian (37)	57	0.34
Irish (1,587)	4,830	28.92
Italian (1,430)	3,366	20.15
Lithuanian (58)	174	1.04
Norwegian (0)	82	0.49
Pennsylvania German (17)	52	0.31
Polish (386)	1,443	8.64
Portuguese (0)	36	0.22
Russian (86)	174	1.04
Scotch-Irish (285)	578	3.46
Scottish (51)	331	1.98
Slovak (45)	124	0.74
Swedish (0)	101	0.60
Swiss (13)	25	0.15
Turkish (15)	15	0.09
Ukrainian (216)	474	2.84
Welsh (59)	229	1.37
West Indian, ex. Hispanic (10)	21	0.13
Jamaican (0)	11	0.07
West Indian (10)	10	0.06
Yugoslavian (0)	8	0.05

Hispanic Origin	Population	%
Hispanic or Latino (of any race)	407	2.43
Central American, ex. Mexican	10	0.06
Guatemalan	1	0.01
Honduran	2	0.01
Nicaraguan	1	0.01
Panamanian	2	0.01
Salvadoran	4	0.02
Cuban	22	0.13
Dominican Republic	12	0.07
Mexican	95	0.57
Puerto Rican	179	1.07
South American	47	0.28
Argentinean	14	0.08
Chilean	8	0.05
Colombian	15	0.09
Ecuadorian	3	0.02
Paraguayan	1	0.01
Peruvian	4	0.02
Venezuelan	2	0.01
Other Hispanic or Latino	42	0.25

Race*	Population	%
African-American/Black (1,788)	1,950	11.65

*Notes: † The Census 2010 population figure is used to calculate the percentages in the Hispanic Origin and Race categories. Ancestry percentages are based on the 2006-2010 American Community Survey population (not shown); ‡ Numbers in parentheses indicate the number of people reporting a single ancestry; * Numbers in parentheses indicate the number of persons reporting this race alone, not in combination with any other race; Please refer to the Explanation of Data for more information.*

Not Hispanic (1,764)	1,911	11.42
Hispanic (24)	39	0.23
American Indian/Alaska Native (44)	105	0.63
Not Hispanic (42)	100	0.60
Hispanic (2)	5	0.03
Blackfeet (0)	3	0.02
Cherokee (2)	10	0.06
Chippewa (2)	2	0.01
Cree (0)	1	0.01
Delaware (0)	1	0.01
Inupiat *(Alaska Native)* (1)	1	0.01
Iroquois (1)	4	0.02
Lumbee (2)	3	0.02
Mexican American Ind. (1)	2	0.01
Potawatomi (0)	1	0.01
Sioux (4)	7	0.04
South American Ind. (1)	1	0.01
Spanish American Ind. (0)	2	0.01
Asian (454)	542	3.24
Not Hispanic (446)	531	3.17
Hispanic (8)	11	0.07
Bangladeshi (2)	2	0.01
Cambodian (11)	14	0.08
Chinese, ex. Taiwanese (120)	142	0.85
Filipino (80)	111	0.66
Indian (107)	124	0.74
Japanese (5)	5	0.03
Korean (53)	66	0.39
Laotian (1)	5	0.03
Pakistani (1)	4	0.02
Taiwanese (2)	3	0.02
Thai (9)	16	0.10
Vietnamese (43)	54	0.32
Hawaii Native/Pacific Islander (1)	2	0.01
Not Hispanic (1)	2	0.01
Fijian (1)	1	0.01
White (14,063)	14,333	85.63
Not Hispanic (13,796)	14,035	83.85
Hispanic (267)	298	1.78

Upper Darby

Place Type: Township
County: Delaware
Population: 82,795†

Ancestry‡	Population	%
Afghan (115)	115	0.14
African, Sub-Saharan (3,941)	4,163	5.05
African (1,129)	1,251	1.52
Ethiopian (442)	442	0.54
Ghanaian (126)	134	0.16
Liberian (1,465)	1,530	1.86
Nigerian (284)	300	0.36
Senegalese (191)	191	0.23
Sierra Leonean (116)	116	0.14
Sudanese (7)	7	0.01
Other Sub-Saharan African (181)	192	0.23
Albanian (228)	278	0.34
American (1,141)	1,141	1.39
Arab (552)	719	0.87
Arab (79)	104	0.13
Egyptian (178)	207	0.25
Lebanese (56)	144	0.17
Moroccan (9)	9	0.01
Syrian (213)	213	0.26
Other Arab (17)	42	0.05
Armenian (188)	423	0.51
Australian (21)	21	0.03
Austrian (0)	93	0.11
Basque (0)	33	0.04
Belgian (19)	39	0.05
British (65)	196	0.24
Canadian (0)	41	0.05
Celtic (33)	33	0.04
Croatian (25)	25	0.03
Czech (0)	116	0.14
Czechoslovakian (42)	63	0.08
Danish (0)	211	0.26
Dutch (179)	748	0.91
English (837)	4,439	5.39
European (373)	383	0.46
Finnish (24)	64	0.08
French, ex. Basque (118)	1,276	1.55
French Canadian (31)	133	0.16
German (1,472)	9,780	11.87
Greek (1,046)	1,276	1.55
Guyanese (10)	10	0.01
Hungarian (78)	208	0.25
Icelander (0)	51	0.06
Iranian (8)	8	0.01
Irish (9,453)	22,488	27.30
Italian (5,974)	12,902	15.66
Latvian (0)	17	0.02
Lithuanian (38)	308	0.37
Macedonian (0)	9	0.01
Northern European (37)	37	0.04
Norwegian (19)	157	0.19
Pennsylvania German (120)	269	0.33
Polish (725)	2,753	3.34
Portuguese (28)	52	0.06
Romanian (40)	143	0.17
Russian (212)	482	0.59
Scotch-Irish (365)	808	0.98
Scottish (303)	1,018	1.24
Serbian (63)	63	0.08
Slovak (32)	214	0.26
Swedish (82)	505	0.61
Swiss (23)	70	0.08
Turkish (53)	53	0.06
Ukrainian (43)	364	0.44
Welsh (125)	619	0.75
West Indian, ex. Hispanic (2,017)	2,118	2.57
Bahamian (9)	9	0.01
Barbadian (85)	85	0.10
British West Indian (44)	75	0.09
Haitian (698)	698	0.85
Jamaican (692)	762	0.93
Trinidadian/Tobagonian (411)	411	0.50
U.S. Virgin Islander (59)	59	0.07
West Indian (19)	19	0.02
Yugoslavian (24)	55	0.07

Hispanic Origin	Population	%
Hispanic or Latino (of any race)	3,755	4.54
Central American, ex. Mexican	502	0.61
Costa Rican	33	0.04
Guatemalan	220	0.27
Honduran	143	0.17
Nicaraguan	11	0.01
Panamanian	20	0.02
Salvadoran	53	0.06
Other Central American	22	0.03
Cuban	110	0.13
Dominican Republic	133	0.16
Mexican	715	0.86
Puerto Rican	821	0.99
South American	1,080	1.30
Argentinean	32	0.04
Bolivian	7	0.01
Chilean	6	0.01
Colombian	99	0.12
Ecuadorian	783	0.95
Paraguayan	20	0.02
Peruvian	76	0.09
Uruguayan	9	0.01
Venezuelan	46	0.06
Other South American	2	<0.01
Other Hispanic or Latino	394	0.48

Race*	Population	%
African-American/Black (22,731)	24,093	29.10
Not Hispanic (22,341)	23,509	28.39
Hispanic (390)	584	0.71
American Indian/Alaska Native (165)	669	0.81
Not Hispanic (119)	555	0.67
Hispanic (46)	114	0.14
Aleut *(Alaska Native)* (0)	1	<0.01
Apache (4)	10	0.01
Blackfeet (1)	33	0.04
Canadian/French Am. Ind. (2)	2	<0.01
Cherokee (15)	92	0.11
Cheyenne (0)	2	<0.01
Chickasaw (3)	3	<0.01
Chippewa (1)	5	0.01
Choctaw (3)	20	0.02
Cree (0)	2	<0.01
Creek (0)	3	<0.01
Delaware (6)	22	0.03
Inupiat *(Alaska Native)* (0)	1	<0.01
Iroquois (3)	10	0.01
Lumbee (2)	3	<0.01
Mexican American Ind. (6)	12	0.01
Navajo (0)	3	<0.01
Ottawa (2)	2	<0.01
Seminole (0)	2	<0.01
Sioux (2)	7	0.01
South American Ind. (2)	8	0.01
Spanish American Ind. (0)	3	<0.01
Tlingit-Haida *(Alaska Native)* (1)	1	<0.01
Ute (0)	3	<0.01
Asian (9,218)	9,903	11.96
Not Hispanic (9,182)	9,825	11.87
Hispanic (36)	78	0.09
Bangladeshi (542)	605	0.73
Burmese (15)	15	0.02
Cambodian (211)	294	0.36
Chinese, ex. Taiwanese (1,398)	1,655	2.00
Filipino (433)	565	0.68
Hmong (57)	58	0.07
Indian (2,906)	3,208	3.87
Indonesian (29)	40	0.05
Japanese (69)	111	0.13
Korean (465)	526	0.64
Laotian (152)	172	0.21
Malaysian (11)	11	0.01
Nepalese (32)	34	0.04
Pakistani (626)	693	0.84
Sri Lankan (8)	9	0.01
Taiwanese (9)	14	0.02
Thai (86)	103	0.12
Vietnamese (1,702)	1,849	2.23
Hawaii Native/Pacific Islander (36)	151	0.18
Not Hispanic (29)	129	0.16
Hispanic (7)	22	0.03
Guamanian/Chamorro (7)	19	0.02
Native Hawaiian (11)	31	0.04
Samoan (2)	5	0.01
Tongan (1)	1	<0.01
White (46,835)	48,402	58.46
Not Hispanic (45,341)	46,606	56.29
Hispanic (1,494)	1,796	2.17

Upper Dublin

Place Type: Township
County: Montgomery
Population: 25,569†

Ancestry‡	Population	%
African, Sub-Saharan (74)	131	0.51
African (74)	131	0.51
Albanian (37)	37	0.14
American (973)	973	3.80
Arab (157)	232	0.91
Arab (19)	37	0.14
Egyptian (0)	57	0.22
Jordanian (40)	40	0.16
Lebanese (76)	76	0.30
Palestinian (12)	12	0.05
Syrian (10)	10	0.04
Armenian (97)	97	0.38
Austrian (24)	123	0.48
Belgian (0)	9	0.04
Brazilian (10)	10	0.04
British (59)	197	0.77
Canadian (0)	28	0.11
Croatian (8)	15	0.06
Czech (21)	95	0.37
Czechoslovakian (10)	59	0.23

*Notes: † The Census 2010 population figure is used to calculate the percentages in the Hispanic Origin and Race categories. Ancestry percentages are based on the 2006-2010 American Community Survey population (not shown); ‡ Numbers in parentheses indicate the number of people reporting a single ancestry; * Numbers in parentheses indicate the number of persons reporting this race alone, not in combination with any other race; Please refer to the Explanation of Data for more information.*

Danish (0)	26	0.10
Dutch (55)	186	0.73
Eastern European (484)	546	2.13
English (555)	2,726	10.65
Estonian (0)	12	0.05
European (199)	209	0.82
Finnish (51)	77	0.30
French, ex. Basque (99)	489	1.91
French Canadian (37)	96	0.37
German (1,204)	5,373	20.98
German Russian (4)	4	0.02
Greek (15)	160	0.62
Hungarian (30)	238	0.93
Iranian (68)	68	0.27
Irish (1,684)	5,313	20.75
Israeli (13)	13	0.05
Italian (1,541)	3,685	14.39
Latvian (6)	6	0.02
Lithuanian (48)	153	0.60
Norwegian (38)	103	0.40
Pennsylvania German (124)	193	0.75
Polish (460)	1,958	7.65
Portuguese (5)	18	0.07
Romanian (44)	124	0.48
Russian (1,089)	2,127	8.31
Scotch-Irish (119)	364	1.42
Scottish (112)	430	1.68
Serbian (0)	12	0.05
Slavic (0)	22	0.09
Slovak (28)	102	0.40
Swedish (41)	202	0.79
Swiss (11)	121	0.47
Turkish (0)	12	0.05
Ukrainian (161)	536	2.09
Welsh (23)	411	1.61
West Indian, ex. Hispanic (122)	150	0.59
Haitian (11)	11	0.04
Jamaican (101)	101	0.39
West Indian (10)	38	0.15
Yugoslavian (14)	68	0.27

Hispanic Origin	Population	%
Hispanic or Latino (of any race)	463	1.81
Central American, ex. Mexican	43	0.17
Costa Rican	11	0.04
Guatemalan	9	0.04
Honduran	4	0.02
Panamanian	13	0.05
Salvadoran	6	0.02
Cuban	41	0.16
Dominican Republic	19	0.07
Mexican	95	0.37
Puerto Rican	130	0.51
South American	91	0.36
Argentinean	24	0.09
Bolivian	1	<0.01
Chilean	10	0.04
Colombian	24	0.09
Ecuadorian	14	0.05
Paraguayan	2	0.01
Peruvian	11	0.04
Uruguayan	3	0.01
Venezuelan	1	<0.01
Other South American	1	<0.01
Other Hispanic or Latino	44	0.17

Race*	Population	%
African-American/Black (1,695)	1,851	7.24
Not Hispanic (1,656)	1,784	6.98
Hispanic (39)	67	0.26
American Indian/Alaska Native (22)	88	0.34
Not Hispanic (19)	77	0.30
Hispanic (3)	11	0.04
Alaska Athabascan *(Ala. Nat.)* (1)	3	0.01
Blackfeet (0)	3	0.01
Cherokee (0)	8	0.03
Chickasaw (0)	1	<0.01
Chippewa (3)	3	0.01
Choctaw (1)	3	0.01
Cree (0)	1	<0.01
Delaware (0)	5	0.02
Mexican American Ind. (2)	2	0.01
Navajo (0)	2	0.01
Seminole (0)	2	0.01
Sioux (0)	8	0.03
Asian (2,171)	2,342	9.16
Not Hispanic (2,163)	2,326	9.10
Hispanic (8)	16	0.06
Burmese (2)	4	0.02
Cambodian (7)	13	0.05
Chinese, ex. Taiwanese (665)	727	2.84
Filipino (46)	75	0.29
Indian (270)	296	1.16
Indonesian (2)	5	0.02
Japanese (16)	20	0.08
Korean (1,005)	1,047	4.09
Malaysian (1)	1	<0.01
Pakistani (13)	14	0.05
Sri Lankan (1)	1	<0.01
Taiwanese (37)	43	0.17
Thai (9)	16	0.06
Vietnamese (56)	74	0.29
Hawaii Native/Pacific Islander (3)	19	0.07
Not Hispanic (2)	18	0.07
Hispanic (1)	1	<0.01
Guamanian/Chamorro (2)	4	0.02
Native Hawaiian (0)	6	0.02
White (21,218)	21,493	84.06
Not Hispanic (20,937)	21,183	82.85
Hispanic (281)	310	1.21

Upper Gwynedd

Place Type: Township
County: Montgomery
Population: 15,552[†]

Ancestry[‡]	Population	%
African, Sub-Saharan (30)	30	0.20
Ethiopian (30)	30	0.20
American (289)	289	1.89
Arab (112)	192	1.25
Arab (89)	158	1.03
Lebanese (0)	11	0.07
Syrian (9)	9	0.06
Other Arab (14)	14	0.09
Armenian (22)	42	0.27
Austrian (24)	102	0.67
Belgian (11)	11	0.07
British (33)	44	0.29
Canadian (54)	54	0.35
Croatian (71)	71	0.46
Czech (10)	20	0.13
Czechoslovakian (0)	8	0.05
Danish (11)	36	0.23
Dutch (9)	172	1.12
Eastern European (51)	51	0.33
English (248)	1,448	9.45
European (196)	232	1.51
French, ex. Basque (30)	250	1.63
French Canadian (0)	29	0.19
German (1,351)	4,596	30.00
Greek (24)	49	0.32
Hungarian (36)	144	0.94
Irish (1,040)	4,073	26.58
Israeli (40)	40	0.26
Italian (959)	2,361	15.41
Lithuanian (32)	105	0.69
Macedonian (0)	10	0.07
Northern European (0)	16	0.10
Norwegian (11)	21	0.14
Pennsylvania German (66)	180	1.17
Polish (342)	1,224	7.99
Portuguese (128)	143	0.93
Russian (176)	395	2.58
Scandinavian (18)	27	0.18
Scotch-Irish (63)	202	1.32
Scottish (77)	164	1.07
Slovak (22)	64	0.42
Swedish (31)	102	0.67
Swiss (12)	87	0.57
Turkish (29)	29	0.19
Ukrainian (196)	268	1.75
Welsh (32)	167	1.09
West Indian, ex. Hispanic (44)	44	0.29
Haitian (26)	26	0.17
Jamaican (18)	18	0.12

Hispanic Origin	Population	%
Hispanic or Latino (of any race)	344	2.21
Central American, ex. Mexican	30	0.19
Costa Rican	4	0.03
Guatemalan	12	0.08
Honduran	2	0.01
Nicaraguan	7	0.05
Panamanian	2	0.01
Salvadoran	3	0.02
Cuban	17	0.11
Dominican Republic	23	0.15
Mexican	44	0.28
Puerto Rican	124	0.80
South American	61	0.39
Argentinean	4	0.03
Bolivian	2	0.01
Chilean	5	0.03
Colombian	18	0.12
Ecuadorian	4	0.03
Paraguayan	2	0.01
Peruvian	13	0.08
Uruguayan	3	0.02
Venezuelan	9	0.06
Other South American	1	0.01
Other Hispanic or Latino	45	0.29

Race*	Population	%
African-American/Black (659)	752	4.84
Not Hispanic (644)	732	4.71
Hispanic (15)	20	0.13
American Indian/Alaska Native (6)	47	0.30
Not Hispanic (5)	42	0.27
Hispanic (1)	5	0.03
Blackfeet (0)	3	0.02
Cherokee (0)	11	0.07
Choctaw (0)	3	0.02
Delaware (0)	3	0.02
Hopi (1)	1	0.01
Iroquois (0)	1	0.01
Lumbee (0)	1	0.01
Mexican American Ind. (0)	2	0.01
Osage (0)	1	0.01
South American Ind. (0)	2	0.01
Spanish American Ind. (1)	1	0.01
Asian (1,913)	2,037	13.10
Not Hispanic (1,910)	2,029	13.05
Hispanic (3)	8	0.05
Bangladeshi (30)	30	0.19
Cambodian (3)	6	0.04
Chinese, ex. Taiwanese (295)	315	2.03
Filipino (59)	78	0.50
Indian (855)	882	5.67
Indonesian (3)	3	0.02
Japanese (16)	31	0.20
Korean (496)	528	3.40
Laotian (7)	8	0.05
Nepalese (5)	5	0.03
Pakistani (26)	29	0.19
Sri Lankan (3)	3	0.02
Taiwanese (7)	14	0.09
Thai (5)	7	0.05
Vietnamese (87)	91	0.59
Hawaii Native/Pacific Islander (6)	23	0.15
Not Hispanic (6)	17	0.11
Hispanic (0)	6	0.04
Fijian (2)	2	0.01
Guamanian/Chamorro (0)	1	0.01
Native Hawaiian (0)	3	0.02
Samoan (1)	4	0.03
White (12,615)	12,802	82.32
Not Hispanic (12,401)	12,571	80.83
Hispanic (214)	231	1.49

*Notes: † The Census 2010 population figure is used to calculate the percentages in the Hispanic Origin and Race categories. Ancestry percentages are based on the 2006-2010 American Community Survey population (not shown); ‡ Numbers in parentheses indicate the number of people reporting a single ancestry; * Numbers in parentheses indicate the number of persons reporting this race alone, not in combination with any other race; Please refer to the Explanation of Data for more information.*

Upper Leacock

Place Type: Township
County: Lancaster
Population: 8,708†

Ancestry‡	Population	%
African, Sub-Saharan (33)	33	0.38
Liberian (33)	33	0.38
American (823)	823	9.52
Arab (9)	9	0.10
Lebanese (9)	9	0.10
Austrian (9)	9	0.10
British (9)	9	0.10
Czech (9)	9	0.10
Czechoslovakian (9)	9	0.10
Danish (0)	18	0.21
Dutch (94)	154	1.78
English (170)	468	5.41
European (88)	88	1.02
French, ex. Basque (97)	175	2.02
German (1,813)	3,130	36.19
Greek (5)	5	0.06
Hungarian (0)	40	0.46
Irish (168)	728	8.42
Italian (241)	425	4.91
Lithuanian (10)	42	0.49
Pennsylvania German (507)	544	6.29
Polish (44)	158	1.83
Russian (13)	13	0.15
Scotch-Irish (117)	191	2.21
Scottish (8)	38	0.44
Slovak (0)	15	0.17
Swedish (22)	30	0.35
Swiss (173)	446	5.16
Welsh (17)	69	0.80
Yugoslavian (29)	29	0.34

Hispanic Origin	Population	%
Hispanic or Latino (of any race)	538	6.18
Central American, ex. Mexican	34	0.39
Costa Rican	1	0.01
Guatemalan	16	0.18
Honduran	10	0.11
Nicaraguan	1	0.01
Salvadoran	6	0.07
Cuban	15	0.17
Dominican Republic	20	0.23
Mexican	51	0.59
Puerto Rican	324	3.72
South American	59	0.68
Argentinean	1	0.01
Colombian	52	0.60
Ecuadorian	5	0.06
Paraguayan	1	0.01
Other Hispanic or Latino	35	0.40

Race*	Population	%
African-American/Black (129)	193	2.22
Not Hispanic (97)	144	1.65
Hispanic (32)	49	0.56
American Indian/Alaska Native (12)	34	0.39
Not Hispanic (6)	26	0.30
Hispanic (6)	8	0.09
Blackfeet (1)	1	0.01
Cherokee (1)	3	0.03
Lumbee (1)	3	0.03
Potawatomi (0)	1	0.01
Asian (328)	353	4.05
Not Hispanic (320)	339	3.89
Hispanic (8)	14	0.16
Cambodian (29)	32	0.37
Chinese, ex. Taiwanese (35)	49	0.56
Filipino (18)	23	0.26
Hmong (56)	59	0.68
Indian (28)	31	0.36
Indonesian (5)	5	0.06
Japanese (2)	2	0.02
Korean (17)	21	0.24
Laotian (3)	3	0.03
Nepalese (2)	2	0.02
Sri Lankan (1)	1	0.01
Thai (5)	6	0.07
Vietnamese (103)	118	1.36
Hawaii Native/Pacific Islander (1)	1	0.01
Not Hispanic (1)	1	0.01
Native Hawaiian (1)	1	0.01
White (7,973)	8,090	92.90
Not Hispanic (7,655)	7,734	88.81
Hispanic (318)	356	4.09

Upper Macungie

Place Type: Township
County: Lehigh
Population: 20,063†

Ancestry‡	Population	%
Afghan (13)	38	0.20
African, Sub-Saharan (9)	9	0.05
Nigerian (9)	9	0.05
American (615)	615	3.23
Arab (140)	251	1.32
Arab (0)	15	0.08
Egyptian (114)	141	0.74
Lebanese (13)	51	0.27
Moroccan (0)	13	0.07
Syrian (0)	18	0.09
Other Arab (13)	13	0.07
Austrian (119)	392	2.06
British (37)	47	0.25
Canadian (20)	45	0.24
Czech (32)	76	0.40
Czechoslovakian (13)	13	0.07
Danish (0)	10	0.05
Dutch (59)	331	1.74
English (324)	1,443	7.58
European (149)	149	0.78
Finnish (0)	43	0.23
French, ex. Basque (109)	524	2.75
French Canadian (0)	22	0.12
German (2,894)	6,221	32.69
Greek (38)	173	0.91
Hungarian (61)	239	1.26
Irish (584)	3,035	15.95
Israeli (51)	68	0.36
Italian (756)	2,754	14.47
Lithuanian (6)	67	0.35
Maltese (15)	15	0.08
Northern European (14)	26	0.14
Norwegian (0)	116	0.61
Pennsylvania German (663)	703	3.69
Polish (365)	1,207	6.34
Portuguese (0)	138	0.73
Romanian (0)	19	0.10
Russian (146)	449	2.36
Scandinavian (21)	134	0.70
Scotch-Irish (110)	259	1.36
Scottish (66)	347	1.82
Slovak (147)	324	1.70
Slovene (0)	6	0.03
Swedish (56)	398	2.09
Swiss (0)	370	1.94
Ukrainian (114)	242	1.27
Welsh (155)	571	3.00

Hispanic Origin	Population	%
Hispanic or Latino (of any race)	988	4.92
Central American, ex. Mexican	53	0.26
Costa Rican	4	0.02
Guatemalan	16	0.08
Honduran	21	0.10
Panamanian	6	0.03
Salvadoran	6	0.03
Cuban	30	0.15
Dominican Republic	83	0.41
Mexican	96	0.48
Puerto Rican	452	2.25
South American	177	0.88
Argentinean	12	0.06
Bolivian	6	0.03
Chilean	7	0.03
Colombian	49	0.24
Ecuadorian	62	0.31
Peruvian	20	0.10
Uruguayan	1	<0.01
Venezuelan	15	0.07
Other South American	5	0.02
Other Hispanic or Latino	97	0.48

Race*	Population	%
African-American/Black (539)	665	3.31
Not Hispanic (498)	596	2.97
Hispanic (41)	69	0.34
American Indian/Alaska Native (29)	83	0.41
Not Hispanic (22)	72	0.36
Hispanic (7)	11	0.05
Blackfeet (0)	1	<0.01
Cherokee (3)	8	0.04
Cheyenne (1)	1	<0.01
Chippewa (1)	6	0.03
Comanche (0)	1	<0.01
Mexican American Ind. (1)	1	<0.01
Ottawa (0)	2	0.01
Sioux (1)	1	<0.01
Asian (1,799)	1,992	9.93
Not Hispanic (1,786)	1,969	9.81
Hispanic (13)	23	0.11
Bangladeshi (40)	47	0.23
Burmese (1)	2	0.01
Cambodian (2)	5	0.02
Chinese, ex. Taiwanese (260)	298	1.49
Filipino (105)	155	0.77
Hmong (10)	10	0.05
Indian (1,029)	1,092	5.44
Indonesian (1)	3	0.01
Japanese (19)	31	0.15
Korean (85)	96	0.48
Laotian (6)	6	0.03
Malaysian (5)	10	0.05
Nepalese (1)	1	<0.01
Pakistani (77)	93	0.46
Sri Lankan (4)	4	0.02
Taiwanese (6)	12	0.06
Thai (10)	12	0.06
Vietnamese (68)	86	0.43
Hawaii Native/Pacific Islander (5)	25	0.12
Not Hispanic (2)	19	0.09
Hispanic (3)	6	0.03
Guamanian/Chamorro (1)	6	0.03
Native Hawaiian (0)	1	<0.01
Samoan (1)	3	0.01
White (17,051)	17,336	86.41
Not Hispanic (16,448)	16,682	83.15
Hispanic (603)	654	3.26

Upper Makefield

Place Type: Township
County: Bucks
Population: 8,190†

Ancestry‡	Population	%
American (483)	483	6.01
Arab (44)	129	1.60
Lebanese (44)	129	1.60
Austrian (0)	14	0.17
Canadian (56)	56	0.70
Czech (14)	14	0.17
Czechoslovakian (38)	38	0.47
Dutch (13)	83	1.03
Eastern European (94)	94	1.17
English (285)	1,261	15.69
European (39)	39	0.49
French, ex. Basque (0)	212	2.64
German (643)	1,940	24.14
Greek (103)	126	1.57
Hungarian (0)	136	1.69
Irish (439)	1,684	20.95
Israeli (13)	13	0.16

*Notes: † The Census 2010 population figure is used to calculate the percentages in the Hispanic Origin and Race categories. Ancestry percentages are based on the 2006-2010 American Community Survey population (not shown); ‡ Numbers in parentheses indicate the number of people reporting a single ancestry; * Numbers in parentheses indicate the number of persons reporting this race alone, not in combination with any other race; Please refer to the Explanation of Data for more information.*

Italian (628)	1,385	17.23
Lithuanian (13)	106	1.32
Norwegian (0)	14	0.17
Polish (227)	837	10.41
Portuguese (0)	31	0.39
Romanian (15)	29	0.36
Russian (335)	629	7.83
Scotch-Irish (105)	234	2.91
Scottish (79)	378	4.70
Slovak (0)	28	0.35
Swedish (62)	62	0.77
Swiss (17)	60	0.75
Ukrainian (101)	220	2.74
Welsh (23)	49	0.61
Yugoslavian (6)	24	0.30

Hispanic Origin	Population	%
Hispanic or Latino (of any race)	186	2.27
Central American, ex. Mexican	17	0.21
Costa Rican	5	0.06
Guatemalan	6	0.07
Nicaraguan	4	0.05
Panamanian	1	0.01
Other Central American	1	0.01
Cuban	6	0.07
Mexican	44	0.54
Puerto Rican	37	0.45
South American	29	0.35
Argentinean	4	0.05
Colombian	9	0.11
Ecuadorian	4	0.05
Peruvian	8	0.10
Venezuelan	3	0.04
Other South American	1	0.01
Other Hispanic or Latino	53	0.65

Race*	Population	%
African-American/Black (94)	111	1.36
Not Hispanic (94)	103	1.26
Hispanic (0)	8	0.10
American Indian/Alaska Native (13)	30	0.37
Not Hispanic (9)	22	0.27
Hispanic (4)	8	0.10
Cherokee (3)	7	0.09
Chickasaw (0)	1	0.01
Creek (0)	1	0.01
Iroquois (0)	1	0.01
Sioux (0)	1	0.01
Asian (207)	253	3.09
Not Hispanic (207)	251	3.06
Hispanic (0)	2	0.02
Chinese, ex. Taiwanese (71)	87	1.06
Filipino (9)	19	0.23
Indian (56)	62	0.76
Japanese (7)	14	0.17
Korean (45)	55	0.67
Nepalese (1)	1	0.01
Pakistani (5)	7	0.09
Taiwanese (5)	5	0.06
Vietnamese (4)	7	0.09
Hawaii Native/Pacific Islander (0)	1	0.01
Not Hispanic (0)	1	0.01
Native Hawaiian (0)	1	0.01
White (7,758)	7,837	95.69
Not Hispanic (7,616)	7,683	93.81
Hispanic (142)	154	1.88

Upper Merion

Place Type: Township
County: Montgomery
Population: 28,395†

Ancestry‡	Population	%
Afghan (9)	9	0.03
African, Sub-Saharan (99)	115	0.41
African (72)	88	0.31
Kenyan (11)	11	0.04
Other Sub-Saharan African (16)	16	0.06
Albanian (0)	9	0.03
American (579)	579	2.06
Arab (215)	325	1.16
Arab (55)	79	0.28
Egyptian (15)	15	0.05
Lebanese (0)	62	0.22
Moroccan (11)	35	0.12
Other Arab (134)	134	0.48
Armenian (51)	71	0.25
Austrian (33)	155	0.55
Belgian (0)	9	0.03
Brazilian (14)	33	0.12
British (90)	148	0.53
Canadian (8)	8	0.03
Croatian (0)	28	0.10
Czech (13)	143	0.51
Czechoslovakian (27)	54	0.19
Dutch (66)	310	1.10
Eastern European (30)	48	0.17
English (571)	2,214	7.88
European (267)	267	0.95
Finnish (0)	10	0.04
French, ex. Basque (62)	652	2.32
French Canadian (35)	107	0.38
German (1,460)	5,205	18.52
Greek (160)	216	0.77
Hungarian (55)	320	1.14
Icelander (15)	15	0.05
Iranian (158)	158	0.56
Irish (2,012)	6,029	21.45
Israeli (0)	7	0.02
Italian (2,278)	5,080	18.08
Latvian (13)	49	0.17
Lithuanian (46)	87	0.31
Norwegian (20)	97	0.35
Pennsylvania German (35)	69	0.25
Polish (737)	2,335	8.31
Portuguese (0)	37	0.13
Romanian (53)	83	0.30
Russian (407)	883	3.14
Scandinavian (0)	8	0.03
Scotch-Irish (192)	412	1.47
Scottish (70)	409	1.46
Serbian (8)	34	0.12
Slovak (183)	371	1.32
Slovene (0)	12	0.04
Swedish (72)	215	0.77
Swiss (28)	77	0.27
Turkish (30)	30	0.11
Ukrainian (215)	428	1.52
Welsh (23)	322	1.15
West Indian, ex. Hispanic (153)	231	0.82
Bermudan (0)	13	0.05
Jamaican (127)	177	0.63
West Indian (26)	26	0.09
Other West Indian (0)	15	0.05
Yugoslavian (0)	10	0.04

Hispanic Origin	Population	%
Hispanic or Latino (of any race)	1,109	3.91
Central American, ex. Mexican	61	0.21
Costa Rican	12	0.04
Guatemalan	8	0.03
Honduran	10	0.04
Nicaraguan	4	0.01
Panamanian	4	0.01
Salvadoran	23	0.08
Cuban	37	0.13
Dominican Republic	21	0.07
Mexican	514	1.81
Puerto Rican	237	0.83
South American	153	0.54
Argentinean	15	0.05
Chilean	7	0.02
Colombian	39	0.14
Ecuadorian	14	0.05
Paraguayan	7	0.02
Peruvian	44	0.15
Uruguayan	7	0.02
Venezuelan	19	0.07
Other South American	1	<0.01
Other Hispanic or Latino	86	0.30

Race*	Population	%
African-American/Black (1,551)	1,765	6.22
Not Hispanic (1,510)	1,707	6.01
Hispanic (41)	58	0.20
American Indian/Alaska Native (63)	171	0.60
Not Hispanic (43)	140	0.49
Hispanic (20)	31	0.11
Apache (1)	1	<0.01
Arapaho (0)	1	<0.01
Blackfeet (2)	4	0.01
Cherokee (10)	26	0.09
Choctaw (0)	3	0.01
Delaware (0)	2	0.01
Hopi (0)	1	<0.01
Iroquois (1)	5	0.02
Mexican American Ind. (6)	6	0.02
Navajo (0)	1	<0.01
Pueblo (2)	3	0.01
Seminole (0)	3	0.01
Sioux (0)	2	0.01
South American Ind. (1)	2	0.01
Asian (4,184)	4,511	15.89
Not Hispanic (4,159)	4,473	15.75
Hispanic (25)	38	0.13
Bangladeshi (17)	18	0.06
Burmese (6)	8	0.03
Cambodian (75)	93	0.33
Chinese, ex. Taiwanese (677)	759	2.67
Filipino (214)	264	0.93
Indian (2,279)	2,352	8.28
Indonesian (11)	14	0.05
Japanese (52)	77	0.27
Korean (266)	296	1.04
Laotian (34)	36	0.13
Malaysian (4)	12	0.04
Nepalese (10)	19	0.07
Pakistani (125)	139	0.49
Sri Lankan (5)	5	0.02
Taiwanese (35)	38	0.13
Thai (19)	26	0.09
Vietnamese (264)	297	1.05
Hawaii Native/Pacific Islander (7)	23	0.08
Not Hispanic (7)	23	0.08
Guamanian/Chamorro (1)	1	<0.01
Native Hawaiian (3)	5	0.02
Samoan (3)	6	0.02
White (21,594)	22,078	77.75
Not Hispanic (20,960)	21,394	75.34
Hispanic (634)	684	2.41

Upper Moreland

Place Type: Township
County: Montgomery
Population: 24,015†

Ancestry‡	Population	%
African, Sub-Saharan (56)	56	0.23
African (15)	15	0.06
Kenyan (41)	41	0.17
Albanian (14)	28	0.12
Alsatian (25)	25	0.10
American (789)	789	3.25
Arab (45)	76	0.31
Arab (10)	27	0.11
Palestinian (7)	21	0.09
Other Arab (28)	28	0.12
Armenian (64)	90	0.37
Australian (0)	4	0.02
Austrian (35)	200	0.82
Belgian (0)	13	0.05
Brazilian (15)	15	0.06
British (33)	93	0.38
Canadian (0)	27	0.11
Croatian (10)	10	0.04
Czech (16)	66	0.27
Czechoslovakian (0)	9	0.04
Danish (0)	41	0.17

*Notes: † The Census 2010 population figure is used to calculate the percentages in the Hispanic Origin and Race categories. Ancestry percentages are based on the 2006-2010 American Community Survey population (not shown); ‡ Numbers in parentheses indicate the number of people reporting a single ancestry; * Numbers in parentheses indicate the number of persons reporting this race alone, not in combination with any other race; Please refer to the Explanation of Data for more information.*

SECTION TWO

Dutch (44)	486	2.00
Eastern European (60)	83	0.34
English (764)	3,023	12.47
European (151)	160	0.66
French, ex. Basque (36)	347	1.43
French Canadian (0)	88	0.36
German (1,785)	6,824	28.15
Greek (99)	127	0.52
Hungarian (59)	306	1.26
Irish (2,423)	7,493	30.91
Italian (1,363)	3,834	15.81
Lithuanian (29)	164	0.68
Maltese (10)	10	0.04
Northern European (9)	9	0.04
Norwegian (0)	133	0.55
Pennsylvania German (30)	163	0.67
Polish (421)	1,333	5.50
Portuguese (17)	17	0.07
Romanian (46)	93	0.38
Russian (327)	550	2.27
Scandinavian (41)	54	0.22
Scotch-Irish (109)	478	1.97
Scottish (110)	603	2.49
Slavic (26)	68	0.28
Slovak (68)	148	0.61
Swedish (34)	251	1.04
Swiss (0)	48	0.20
Ukrainian (53)	214	0.88
Welsh (68)	432	1.78
West Indian, ex. Hispanic (138)	186	0.77
Haitian (0)	48	0.20
Jamaican (138)	138	0.57
Yugoslavian (31)	31	0.13

Hispanic Origin	Population	%
Hispanic or Latino (of any race)	865	3.60
Central American, ex. Mexican	117	0.49
Costa Rican	22	0.09
Guatemalan	59	0.25
Honduran	19	0.08
Nicaraguan	1	<0.01
Panamanian	9	0.04
Salvadoran	7	0.03
Cuban	27	0.11
Dominican Republic	23	0.10
Mexican	210	0.87
Puerto Rican	331	1.38
South American	90	0.37
Argentinean	10	0.04
Chilean	2	0.01
Colombian	35	0.15
Ecuadorian	29	0.12
Peruvian	9	0.04
Uruguayan	2	0.01
Venezuelan	3	0.01
Other Hispanic or Latino	67	0.28

Race*	Population	%
African-American/Black (1,231)	1,478	6.15
Not Hispanic (1,200)	1,398	5.82
Hispanic (31)	80	0.33
American Indian/Alaska Native (50)	151	0.63
Not Hispanic (32)	106	0.44
Hispanic (18)	45	0.19
Apache (3)	6	0.02
Blackfeet (0)	10	0.04
Cherokee (11)	28	0.12
Creek (0)	4	0.02
Delaware (1)	2	0.01
Iroquois (1)	9	0.04
Lumbee (1)	1	<0.01
Mexican American Ind. (2)	2	0.01
Pueblo (0)	1	<0.01
Seminole (0)	1	<0.01
Sioux (1)	2	0.01
South American Ind. (2)	3	0.01
Asian (1,051)	1,181	4.92
Not Hispanic (1,050)	1,170	4.87
Hispanic (1)	11	0.05
Bangladeshi (0)	1	<0.01
Cambodian (23)	24	0.10
Chinese, ex. Taiwanese (108)	126	0.52
Filipino (72)	89	0.37
Indian (364)	392	1.63
Indonesian (1)	2	0.01
Japanese (20)	41	0.17
Korean (319)	336	1.40
Laotian (10)	10	0.04
Malaysian (2)	2	0.01
Pakistani (21)	22	0.09
Sri Lankan (5)	5	0.02
Taiwanese (9)	13	0.05
Thai (7)	8	0.03
Vietnamese (58)	63	0.26
Hawaii Native/Pacific Islander (14)	34	0.14
Not Hispanic (11)	31	0.13
Hispanic (3)	3	0.01
Fijian (0)	1	<0.01
Guamanian/Chamorro (5)	5	0.02
Native Hawaiian (3)	5	0.02
Samoan (5)	9	0.04
White (20,901)	21,275	88.59
Not Hispanic (20,465)	20,770	86.49
Hispanic (436)	505	2.10

Upper Providence

Place Type: Township
County: Delaware
Population: 10,142†

Ancestry‡	Population	%
African, Sub-Saharan (38)	45	0.44
African (0)	7	0.07
South African (38)	38	0.37
Albanian (0)	32	0.31
American (310)	310	3.04
Arab (31)	114	1.12
Lebanese (22)	69	0.68
Syrian (0)	36	0.35
Other Arab (9)	9	0.09
Armenian (68)	80	0.79
Austrian (0)	14	0.14
Belgian (8)	8	0.08
British (10)	19	0.19
Canadian (0)	22	0.22
Celtic (7)	7	0.07
Croatian (19)	19	0.19
Czech (0)	21	0.21
Czechoslovakian (0)	17	0.17
Dutch (0)	49	0.48
Eastern European (87)	87	0.85
English (183)	998	9.79
European (216)	216	2.12
Finnish (9)	36	0.35
French, ex. Basque (22)	275	2.70
French Canadian (0)	9	0.09
German (541)	2,025	19.87
Greek (83)	131	1.29
Hungarian (0)	78	0.77
Iranian (13)	30	0.29
Irish (965)	3,402	33.39
Israeli (0)	30	0.29
Italian (902)	2,123	20.83
Latvian (0)	8	0.08
Lithuanian (42)	96	0.94
Norwegian (21)	72	0.71
Pennsylvania German (0)	19	0.19
Polish (223)	596	5.85
Romanian (11)	11	0.11
Russian (60)	246	2.41
Scandinavian (0)	36	0.35
Scotch-Irish (120)	269	2.64
Scottish (41)	103	1.01
Slavic (0)	10	0.10
Slovak (10)	124	1.22
Swedish (17)	93	0.91
Swiss (12)	73	0.72
Ukrainian (19)	99	0.97
Welsh (10)	95	0.93

Hispanic Origin	Population	%
Hispanic or Latino (of any race)	156	1.54
Central American, ex. Mexican	16	0.16
Costa Rican	2	0.02
Guatemalan	5	0.05
Nicaraguan	1	0.01
Salvadoran	8	0.08
Cuban	9	0.09
Dominican Republic	4	0.04
Mexican	33	0.33
Puerto Rican	44	0.43
South American	16	0.16
Argentinean	3	0.03
Bolivian	1	0.01
Chilean	1	0.01
Colombian	5	0.05
Ecuadorian	1	0.01
Peruvian	3	0.03
Venezuelan	2	0.02
Other Hispanic or Latino	34	0.34

Race*	Population	%
African-American/Black (397)	463	4.57
Not Hispanic (386)	444	4.38
Hispanic (11)	19	0.19
American Indian/Alaska Native (5)	34	0.34
Not Hispanic (5)	34	0.34
Aleut *(Alaska Native)* (0)	2	0.02
Arapaho (0)	1	0.01
Cherokee (2)	9	0.09
Delaware (0)	2	0.02
Lumbee (1)	2	0.02
Ottawa (0)	1	0.01
Seminole (0)	3	0.03
Asian (436)	507	5.00
Not Hispanic (436)	507	5.00
Cambodian (6)	7	0.07
Chinese, ex. Taiwanese (128)	160	1.58
Filipino (26)	38	0.37
Hmong (1)	1	0.01
Indian (113)	135	1.33
Japanese (12)	17	0.17
Korean (89)	95	0.94
Pakistani (3)	3	0.03
Sri Lankan (6)	7	0.07
Taiwanese (12)	17	0.17
Thai (0)	1	0.01
Vietnamese (21)	28	0.28
Hawaii Native/Pacific Islander (4)	10	0.10
Not Hispanic (3)	9	0.09
Hispanic (1)	1	0.01
Guamanian/Chamorro (1)	1	0.01
Native Hawaiian (0)	1	0.01
Samoan (0)	1	0.01
White (9,105)	9,248	91.19
Not Hispanic (8,997)	9,130	90.02
Hispanic (108)	118	1.16

Upper Providence

Place Type: Township
County: Montgomery
Population: 21,219†

Ancestry‡	Population	%
African, Sub-Saharan (9)	9	0.04
South African (9)	9	0.04
American (522)	522	2.59
Arab (110)	121	0.60
Lebanese (110)	110	0.55
Syrian (0)	11	0.05
Austrian (0)	60	0.30
Belgian (0)	9	0.04
Brazilian (58)	58	0.29
British (38)	66	0.33
Croatian (0)	10	0.05
Czech (0)	66	0.33
Czechoslovakian (8)	59	0.29
Danish (0)	8	0.04
Dutch (67)	281	1.39

*Notes: † The Census 2010 population figure is used to calculate the percentages in the Hispanic Origin and Race categories. Ancestry percentages are based on the 2006-2010 American Community Survey population (not shown); ‡ Numbers in parentheses indicate the number of people reporting a single ancestry; * Numbers in parentheses indicate the number of persons reporting this race alone, not in combination with any other race; Please refer to the Explanation of Data for more information.*

Eastern European (10)	10	0.05
English (449)	2,111	10.48
European (70)	70	0.35
French, ex. Basque (8)	329	1.63
French Canadian (0)	41	0.20
German (1,463)	5,685	28.22
Greek (30)	101	0.50
Hungarian (10)	134	0.67
Irish (1,398)	5,118	25.40
Italian (1,725)	4,286	21.27
Latvian (61)	70	0.35
Lithuanian (8)	94	0.47
Maltese (0)	16	0.08
Norwegian (29)	128	0.64
Pennsylvania German (199)	314	1.56
Polish (454)	1,790	8.89
Romanian (0)	35	0.17
Russian (90)	211	1.05
Scandinavian (42)	42	0.21
Scotch-Irish (141)	379	1.88
Scottish (92)	516	2.56
Serbian (0)	10	0.05
Slavic (0)	87	0.43
Slovak (22)	171	0.85
Slovene (0)	30	0.15
Swedish (11)	159	0.79
Swiss (9)	64	0.32
Turkish (24)	71	0.35
Ukrainian (54)	217	1.08
Welsh (9)	267	1.33
West Indian, ex. Hispanic (26)	51	0.25
Jamaican (26)	43	0.21
West Indian (0)	8	0.04

Hispanic Origin	Population	%
Hispanic or Latino (of any race)	468	2.21
Central American, ex. Mexican	59	0.28
Costa Rican	4	0.02
Guatemalan	18	0.08
Honduran	8	0.04
Nicaraguan	1	<0.01
Panamanian	11	0.05
Salvadoran	17	0.08
Cuban	48	0.23
Dominican Republic	5	0.02
Mexican	104	0.49
Puerto Rican	115	0.54
South American	96	0.45
Argentinean	18	0.08
Bolivian	5	0.02
Chilean	17	0.08
Colombian	22	0.10
Ecuadorian	13	0.06
Paraguayan	1	<0.01
Peruvian	15	0.07
Venezuelan	5	0.02
Other Hispanic or Latino	41	0.19

Race*	Population	%
African-American/Black (736)	837	3.94
Not Hispanic (725)	815	3.84
Hispanic (11)	22	0.10
American Indian/Alaska Native (28)	108	0.51
Not Hispanic (10)	71	0.33
Hispanic (18)	37	0.17
Alaska Athabascan *(Ala. Nat.)* (3)	3	0.01
Blackfeet (0)	1	<0.01
Cherokee (0)	18	0.08
Cree (0)	1	<0.01
Creek (0)	1	<0.01
Delaware (0)	4	0.02
Iroquois (0)	1	<0.01
Lumbee (0)	2	0.01
Mexican American Ind. (9)	9	0.04
Puget Sound Salish (0)	1	<0.01
Sioux (1)	1	<0.01
South American Ind. (1)	4	0.02
Asian (1,666)	1,844	8.69
Not Hispanic (1,664)	1,832	8.63
Hispanic (2)	12	0.06
Bangladeshi (11)	16	0.08
Burmese (4)	4	0.02
Cambodian (19)	32	0.15
Chinese, ex. Taiwanese (342)	406	1.91
Filipino (95)	131	0.62
Indian (789)	827	3.90
Indonesian (6)	6	0.03
Japanese (20)	38	0.18
Korean (148)	169	0.80
Laotian (2)	2	0.01
Malaysian (1)	1	<0.01
Nepalese (6)	6	0.03
Pakistani (62)	66	0.31
Sri Lankan (2)	6	0.03
Taiwanese (3)	3	0.01
Thai (7)	10	0.05
Vietnamese (108)	119	0.56
Hawaii Native/Pacific Islander (4)	11	0.05
Not Hispanic (4)	10	0.05
Hispanic (0)	1	<0.01
Guamanian/Chamorro (1)	1	<0.01
Native Hawaiian (3)	5	0.02
White (18,380)	18,661	87.94
Not Hispanic (18,037)	18,289	86.19
Hispanic (343)	372	1.75

Upper Saucon

Place Type: Township
County: Lehigh
Population: 14,808†

Ancestry‡	Population	%
American (361)	361	2.51
Arab (83)	274	1.91
Arab (15)	15	0.10
Lebanese (30)	101	0.70
Syrian (38)	148	1.03
Other Arab (0)	10	0.07
Armenian (32)	32	0.22
Austrian (24)	123	0.86
British (82)	125	0.87
Bulgarian (20)	35	0.24
Canadian (24)	24	0.17
Carpatho Rusyn (8)	8	0.06
Croatian (0)	8	0.06
Czech (14)	294	2.05
Czechoslovakian (27)	117	0.82
Dutch (83)	316	2.20
Eastern European (15)	15	0.10
English (261)	1,327	9.24
European (80)	101	0.70
Finnish (0)	20	0.14
French, ex. Basque (63)	436	3.04
French Canadian (12)	50	0.35
German (2,142)	5,902	41.12
Greek (32)	169	1.18
Hungarian (151)	454	3.16
Irish (730)	3,100	21.60
Italian (519)	2,142	14.92
Latvian (12)	36	0.25
Lithuanian (30)	64	0.45
Maltese (13)	52	0.36
Northern European (18)	18	0.13
Norwegian (26)	165	1.15
Pennsylvania German (338)	535	3.73
Polish (377)	869	6.05
Portuguese (8)	36	0.25
Romanian (0)	78	0.54
Russian (62)	238	1.66
Scandinavian (0)	44	0.31
Scotch-Irish (32)	98	0.68
Scottish (81)	300	2.09
Slavic (13)	13	0.09
Slovak (234)	460	3.20
Slovene (0)	8	0.06
Swedish (25)	134	0.93
Swiss (0)	7	0.05
Ukrainian (56)	206	1.44
Welsh (64)	383	2.67

Hispanic Origin	Population	%
Hispanic or Latino (of any race)	466	3.15
Central American, ex. Mexican	29	0.20
Costa Rican	6	0.04
Guatemalan	9	0.06
Honduran	8	0.05
Nicaraguan	1	0.01
Panamanian	3	0.02
Salvadoran	2	0.01
Cuban	43	0.29
Dominican Republic	25	0.17
Mexican	88	0.59
Puerto Rican	195	1.32
South American	59	0.40
Argentinean	5	0.03
Bolivian	2	0.01
Chilean	8	0.05
Colombian	22	0.15
Ecuadorian	10	0.07
Peruvian	5	0.03
Uruguayan	6	0.04
Venezuelan	1	0.01
Other Hispanic or Latino	27	0.18

Race*	Population	%
African-American/Black (182)	224	1.51
Not Hispanic (176)	208	1.40
Hispanic (6)	16	0.11
American Indian/Alaska Native (15)	48	0.32
Not Hispanic (10)	39	0.26
Hispanic (5)	9	0.06
Apache (0)	1	0.01
Blackfeet (0)	4	0.03
Cherokee (3)	11	0.07
Delaware (0)	1	0.01
Iroquois (0)	3	0.02
Mexican American Ind. (2)	3	0.02
Puget Sound Salish (3)	3	0.02
Asian (494)	589	3.98
Not Hispanic (492)	583	3.94
Hispanic (2)	6	0.04
Bangladeshi (5)	6	0.04
Burmese (5)	5	0.03
Cambodian (1)	2	0.01
Chinese, ex. Taiwanese (117)	138	0.93
Filipino (26)	49	0.33
Hmong (4)	4	0.03
Indian (133)	151	1.02
Indonesian (1)	1	0.01
Japanese (34)	45	0.30
Korean (85)	93	0.63
Laotian (0)	2	0.01
Pakistani (29)	32	0.22
Taiwanese (4)	4	0.03
Thai (1)	3	0.02
Vietnamese (38)	49	0.33
Hawaii Native/Pacific Islander (8)	8	0.05
Not Hispanic (8)	8	0.05
Tongan (8)	8	0.05
White (13,853)	14,031	94.75
Not Hispanic (13,502)	13,636	92.09
Hispanic (351)	395	2.67

Upper Southampton

Place Type: Township
County: Bucks
Population: 15,152†

Ancestry‡	Population	%
African, Sub-Saharan (16)	23	0.15
African (16)	23	0.15
Albanian (86)	86	0.56
American (1,059)	1,059	6.91
Arab (81)	86	0.56
Moroccan (39)	39	0.25
Palestinian (0)	5	0.03
Other Arab (42)	42	0.27
Armenian (13)	13	0.08
Austrian (23)	141	0.92

*Notes: † The Census 2010 population figure is used to calculate the percentages in the Hispanic Origin and Race categories. Ancestry percentages are based on the 2006-2010 American Community Survey population (not shown); ‡ Numbers in parentheses indicate the number of people reporting a single ancestry; * Numbers in parentheses indicate the number of persons reporting this race alone, not in combination with any other race; Please refer to the Explanation of Data for more information.*

Belgian (15)	15	0.10
British (10)	29	0.19
Canadian (0)	64	0.42
Croatian (10)	10	0.07
Czech (15)	15	0.10
Czechoslovakian (10)	10	0.07
Danish (14)	28	0.18
Dutch (24)	63	0.41
Eastern European (71)	71	0.46
English (261)	1,652	10.77
European (65)	98	0.64
Finnish (0)	18	0.12
French, ex. Basque (99)	373	2.43
French Canadian (0)	27	0.18
German (993)	3,928	25.61
Greek (181)	276	1.80
Hungarian (51)	238	1.55
Irish (1,678)	4,893	31.91
Italian (1,008)	2,108	13.75
Lithuanian (9)	111	0.72
Northern European (20)	30	0.20
Norwegian (0)	49	0.32
Pennsylvania German (53)	110	0.72
Polish (382)	1,206	7.86
Portuguese (28)	28	0.18
Romanian (0)	36	0.23
Russian (450)	844	5.50
Scandinavian (16)	48	0.31
Scotch-Irish (91)	285	1.86
Scottish (42)	192	1.25
Slavic (0)	14	0.09
Slovak (42)	73	0.48
Swedish (14)	50	0.33
Swiss (13)	59	0.38
Ukrainian (535)	662	4.32
Welsh (37)	266	1.73
Yugoslavian (44)	44	0.29

Hispanic Origin	Population	%
Hispanic or Latino (of any race)	246	1.62
Central American, ex. Mexican	9	0.06
Guatemalan	5	0.03
Honduran	1	0.01
Nicaraguan	1	0.01
Panamanian	1	0.01
Salvadoran	1	0.01
Cuban	7	0.05
Mexican	64	0.42
Puerto Rican	90	0.59
South American	39	0.26
Argentinean	8	0.05
Chilean	1	0.01
Colombian	14	0.09
Ecuadorian	2	0.01
Peruvian	13	0.09
Other South American	1	0.01
Other Hispanic or Latino	37	0.24

Race*	Population	%
African-American/Black (115)	165	1.09
Not Hispanic (114)	158	1.04
Hispanic (1)	7	0.05
American Indian/Alaska Native (12)	56	0.37
Not Hispanic (10)	50	0.33
Hispanic (2)	6	0.04
Blackfeet (1)	3	0.02
Canadian/French Am. Ind. (0)	2	0.01
Cherokee (3)	21	0.14
Creek (0)	1	0.01
Delaware (1)	4	0.03
Lumbee (0)	3	0.02
Mexican American Ind. (2)	2	0.01
Asian (280)	352	2.32
Not Hispanic (276)	333	2.20
Hispanic (4)	19	0.13
Cambodian (3)	3	0.02
Chinese, ex. Taiwanese (46)	62	0.41
Filipino (28)	45	0.30
Indian (106)	107	0.71
Indonesian (1)	4	0.03
Japanese (5)	15	0.10
Korean (44)	55	0.36
Pakistani (10)	10	0.07
Taiwanese (3)	3	0.02
Thai (1)	1	0.01
Vietnamese (15)	24	0.16
Hawaii Native/Pacific Islander (11)	19	0.13
Not Hispanic (10)	16	0.11
Hispanic (1)	3	0.02
Guamanian/Chamorro (5)	6	0.04
Native Hawaiian (1)	5	0.03
White (14,509)	14,658	96.74
Not Hispanic (14,354)	14,469	95.49
Hispanic (155)	189	1.25

Upper St. Clair

Place Type: CDP/Township
County: Allegheny
Population: 19,229†

Ancestry‡	Population	%
African, Sub-Saharan (0)	5	0.03
African (0)	5	0.03
American (624)	624	3.25
Arab (56)	150	0.78
Lebanese (38)	101	0.53
Syrian (18)	49	0.26
Armenian (0)	30	0.16
Austrian (142)	263	1.37
Basque (54)	67	0.35
Belgian (0)	18	0.09
British (94)	157	0.82
Canadian (15)	15	0.08
Croatian (57)	120	0.63
Czech (23)	95	0.50
Czechoslovakian (0)	50	0.26
Danish (11)	79	0.41
Dutch (0)	50	0.26
Eastern European (105)	127	0.66
English (344)	2,068	10.78
European (308)	316	1.65
Finnish (9)	9	0.05
French, ex. Basque (61)	499	2.60
German (1,298)	5,970	31.11
Greek (209)	389	2.03
Hungarian (152)	495	2.58
Iranian (28)	28	0.15
Irish (986)	4,868	25.37
Italian (1,265)	3,518	18.33
Latvian (10)	10	0.05
Lithuanian (30)	103	0.54
Northern European (9)	9	0.05
Norwegian (9)	103	0.54
Pennsylvania German (8)	31	0.16
Polish (332)	1,514	7.89
Portuguese (9)	40	0.21
Romanian (11)	21	0.11
Russian (281)	544	2.84
Scandinavian (9)	30	0.16
Scotch-Irish (168)	560	2.92
Scottish (185)	699	3.64
Serbian (121)	194	1.01
Slavic (9)	18	0.09
Slovak (144)	541	2.82
Slovene (27)	100	0.52
Swedish (68)	438	2.28
Swiss (43)	68	0.35
Turkish (93)	93	0.48
Ukrainian (32)	205	1.07
Welsh (44)	421	2.19
West Indian, ex. Hispanic (12)	12	0.06
West Indian (12)	12	0.06
Yugoslavian (0)	70	0.36

Hispanic Origin	Population	%
Hispanic or Latino (of any race)	254	1.32
Central American, ex. Mexican	23	0.12
Guatemalan	16	0.08
Honduran	2	0.01
Panamanian	1	0.01
Salvadoran	4	0.02
Cuban	23	0.12
Dominican Republic	2	0.01
Mexican	59	0.31
Puerto Rican	43	0.22
South American	68	0.35
Argentinean	9	0.05
Bolivian	5	0.03
Chilean	4	0.02
Colombian	22	0.11
Ecuadorian	6	0.03
Paraguayan	2	0.01
Peruvian	2	0.01
Venezuelan	15	0.08
Other South American	3	0.02
Other Hispanic or Latino	36	0.19

Race*	Population	%
African-American/Black (152)	193	1.00
Not Hispanic (144)	178	0.93
Hispanic (8)	15	0.08
American Indian/Alaska Native (7)	26	0.14
Not Hispanic (4)	19	0.10
Hispanic (3)	7	0.04
Alaska Athabascan *(Ala. Nat.)* (1)	1	0.01
Central American Ind. (1)	1	0.01
Cherokee (0)	7	0.04
Chippewa (0)	2	0.01
Asian (1,097)	1,215	6.32
Not Hispanic (1,096)	1,207	6.28
Hispanic (1)	8	0.04
Bangladeshi (17)	17	0.09
Burmese (9)	9	0.05
Chinese, ex. Taiwanese (258)	289	1.50
Filipino (32)	63	0.33
Indian (586)	607	3.16
Japanese (25)	42	0.22
Korean (58)	79	0.41
Nepalese (4)	4	0.02
Pakistani (29)	29	0.15
Sri Lankan (10)	10	0.05
Taiwanese (18)	22	0.11
Thai (15)	16	0.08
Vietnamese (19)	24	0.12
Hawaii Native/Pacific Islander (2)	5	0.03
Not Hispanic (2)	5	0.03
Native Hawaiian (1)	1	0.01
White (17,717)	17,891	93.04
Not Hispanic (17,523)	17,678	91.93
Hispanic (194)	213	1.11

Upper Uwchlan

Place Type: Township
County: Chester
Population: 11,227†

Ancestry‡	Population	%
American (515)	515	4.91
Arab (26)	34	0.32
Lebanese (12)	20	0.19
Palestinian (14)	14	0.13
Armenian (50)	50	0.48
Australian (64)	64	0.61
Belgian (15)	44	0.42
British (167)	237	2.26
Canadian (13)	22	0.21
Czech (0)	61	0.58
Czechoslovakian (0)	12	0.11
Danish (0)	45	0.43
Dutch (39)	127	1.21
Eastern European (14)	14	0.13
English (374)	1,353	12.89
European (74)	74	0.70
Finnish (0)	36	0.34
French, ex. Basque (62)	271	2.58
French Canadian (0)	10	0.10
German (347)	2,531	24.11
Greek (19)	110	1.05

*Notes: † The Census 2010 population figure is used to calculate the percentages in the Hispanic Origin and Race categories. Ancestry percentages are based on the 2006-2010 American Community Survey population (not shown); ‡ Numbers in parentheses indicate the number of people reporting a single ancestry; * Numbers in parentheses indicate the number of persons reporting this race alone, not in combination with any other race; Please refer to the Explanation of Data for more information.*

Hungarian (20)	60	0.57
Irish (508)	2,578	24.56
Italian (373)	1,659	15.80
Lithuanian (24)	151	1.44
Norwegian (15)	49	0.47
Pennsylvania German (40)	122	1.16
Polish (176)	709	6.75
Portuguese (43)	59	0.56
Romanian (10)	45	0.43
Russian (93)	183	1.74
Scandinavian (0)	37	0.35
Scotch-Irish (78)	236	2.25
Scottish (48)	214	2.04
Slavic (0)	20	0.19
Slovak (37)	153	1.46
Swedish (17)	92	0.88
Swiss (29)	50	0.48
Ukrainian (20)	105	1.00
Welsh (16)	134	1.28

Hispanic Origin	Population	%
Hispanic or Latino (of any race)	264	2.35
Central American, ex. Mexican	7	0.06
Guatemalan	5	0.04
Panamanian	2	0.02
Cuban	12	0.11
Dominican Republic	8	0.07
Mexican	78	0.69
Puerto Rican	79	0.70
South American	55	0.49
Argentinean	3	0.03
Chilean	3	0.03
Colombian	22	0.20
Ecuadorian	5	0.04
Peruvian	11	0.10
Uruguayan	1	0.01
Venezuelan	10	0.09
Other Hispanic or Latino	25	0.22

Race*	Population	%
African-American/Black (161)	205	1.83
Not Hispanic (156)	193	1.72
Hispanic (5)	12	0.11
American Indian/Alaska Native (3)	20	0.18
Not Hispanic (1)	13	0.12
Hispanic (2)	7	0.06
Cherokee (0)	5	0.04
Chippewa (0)	2	0.02
Navajo (0)	4	0.04
Seminole (0)	1	0.01
Ute (2)	2	0.02
Asian (1,587)	1,678	14.95
Not Hispanic (1,587)	1,672	14.89
Hispanic (0)	6	0.05
Bangladeshi (6)	6	0.05
Burmese (5)	5	0.04
Cambodian (0)	3	0.03
Chinese, ex. Taiwanese (322)	355	3.16
Filipino (47)	64	0.57
Indian (993)	1,020	9.09
Indonesian (3)	3	0.03
Japanese (8)	23	0.20
Korean (68)	83	0.74
Laotian (4)	4	0.04
Pakistani (32)	33	0.29
Taiwanese (11)	15	0.13
Thai (6)	10	0.09
Vietnamese (46)	54	0.48
Hawaii Native/Pacific Islander (4)	7	0.06
Not Hispanic (3)	6	0.05
Hispanic (1)	1	0.01
Guamanian/Chamorro (1)	1	0.01
White (9,290)	9,411	83.82
Not Hispanic (9,073)	9,178	81.75
Hispanic (217)	233	2.08

Uwchlan

Place Type: Township
County: Chester
Population: 18,088†

Ancestry‡	Population	%
American (642)	642	3.58
Arab (27)	38	0.21
Egyptian (27)	27	0.15
Other Arab (0)	11	0.06
Armenian (0)	59	0.33
Australian (12)	12	0.07
Austrian (51)	141	0.79
British (135)	170	0.95
Canadian (12)	22	0.12
Celtic (0)	12	0.07
Czech (0)	88	0.49
Czechoslovakian (42)	67	0.37
Danish (30)	101	0.56
Dutch (41)	290	1.62
Eastern European (72)	72	0.40
English (431)	2,221	12.38
European (379)	412	2.30
Finnish (12)	12	0.07
French, ex. Basque (198)	608	3.39
French Canadian (35)	76	0.42
German (1,111)	4,739	26.42
Greek (103)	173	0.96
Hungarian (55)	141	0.79
Iranian (40)	40	0.22
Irish (1,866)	4,898	27.31
Israeli (53)	53	0.30
Italian (839)	2,539	14.16
Latvian (18)	35	0.20
Lithuanian (81)	141	0.79
Northern European (0)	21	0.12
Norwegian (13)	104	0.58
Pennsylvania German (33)	58	0.32
Polish (286)	911	5.08
Romanian (0)	83	0.46
Russian (162)	412	2.30
Scandinavian (2)	10	0.06
Scotch-Irish (339)	851	4.74
Scottish (116)	557	3.11
Serbian (45)	69	0.38
Slavic (12)	12	0.07
Slovak (50)	105	0.59
Slovene (15)	15	0.08
Swedish (37)	221	1.23
Swiss (33)	78	0.43
Ukrainian (65)	221	1.23
Welsh (36)	266	1.48
Yugoslavian (55)	55	0.31

Hispanic Origin	Population	%
Hispanic or Latino (of any race)	411	2.27
Central American, ex. Mexican	34	0.19
Costa Rican	2	0.01
Guatemalan	8	0.04
Honduran	8	0.04
Nicaraguan	2	0.01
Panamanian	12	0.07
Salvadoran	2	0.01
Cuban	27	0.15
Dominican Republic	18	0.10
Mexican	114	0.63
Puerto Rican	100	0.55
South American	78	0.43
Argentinean	15	0.08
Bolivian	3	0.02
Chilean	8	0.04
Colombian	17	0.09
Ecuadorian	10	0.06
Peruvian	4	0.02
Uruguayan	2	0.01
Venezuelan	19	0.11
Other Hispanic or Latino	40	0.22

Race*	Population	%
African-American/Black (445)	546	3.02
Not Hispanic (432)	523	2.89
Hispanic (13)	23	0.13
American Indian/Alaska Native (11)	56	0.31
Not Hispanic (5)	49	0.27
Hispanic (6)	7	0.04
Blackfeet (1)	1	0.01
Central American Ind. (3)	3	0.02
Cherokee (1)	10	0.06
Delaware (0)	2	0.01
Inupiat *(Alaska Native)* (0)	1	0.01
Lumbee (2)	2	0.01
Mexican American Ind. (3)	4	0.02
Pima (0)	1	0.01
Potawatomi (0)	1	0.01
Asian (943)	1,058	5.85
Not Hispanic (940)	1,051	5.81
Hispanic (3)	7	0.04
Bangladeshi (6)	10	0.06
Cambodian (2)	2	0.01
Chinese, ex. Taiwanese (174)	202	1.12
Filipino (32)	54	0.30
Hmong (2)	2	0.01
Indian (558)	582	3.22
Indonesian (2)	5	0.03
Japanese (14)	28	0.15
Korean (51)	68	0.38
Malaysian (1)	1	0.01
Pakistani (10)	10	0.06
Sri Lankan (5)	5	0.03
Taiwanese (6)	6	0.03
Thai (0)	1	0.01
Vietnamese (62)	79	0.44
Hawaii Native/Pacific Islander (1)	8	0.04
Not Hispanic (1)	8	0.04
Native Hawaiian (1)	2	0.01
White (16,348)	16,552	91.51
Not Hispanic (16,054)	16,236	89.76
Hispanic (294)	316	1.75

Village Green-Green Ridge

Place Type: CDP
County: Delaware
Population: 7,822†

Ancestry‡	Population	%
American (342)	342	4.44
Armenian (15)	43	0.56
Belgian (0)	46	0.60
British (37)	47	0.61
Croatian (0)	9	0.12
Czech (0)	11	0.14
Dutch (23)	138	1.79
English (302)	1,195	15.52
Finnish (35)	52	0.68
French, ex. Basque (0)	156	2.03
French Canadian (0)	13	0.17
German (215)	1,655	21.50
Greek (12)	41	0.53
Hungarian (0)	58	0.75
Irish (680)	2,705	35.14
Italian (710)	2,285	29.68
Lithuanian (12)	76	0.99
Norwegian (39)	39	0.51
Pennsylvania German (20)	66	0.86
Polish (241)	765	9.94
Russian (14)	37	0.48
Scotch-Irish (87)	224	2.91
Scottish (31)	90	1.17
Slovak (0)	16	0.21
Swedish (27)	85	1.10
Ukrainian (52)	195	2.53
Welsh (47)	137	1.78

Hispanic Origin	Population	%
Hispanic or Latino (of any race)	143	1.83
Central American, ex. Mexican	4	0.05
Guatemalan	2	0.03

SECTION TWO

*Notes: † The Census 2010 population figure is used to calculate the percentages in the Hispanic Origin and Race categories. Ancestry percentages are based on the 2006-2010 American Community Survey population (not shown); ‡ Numbers in parentheses indicate the number of people reporting a single ancestry; * Numbers in parentheses indicate the number of persons reporting this race alone, not in combination with any other race; Please refer to the Explanation of Data for more information.*

Honduran	1	0.01
Nicaraguan	1	0.01
Cuban	8	0.10
Dominican Republic	3	0.04
Mexican	31	0.40
Puerto Rican	75	0.96
South American	19	0.24
Argentinean	5	0.06
Colombian	8	0.10
Ecuadorian	2	0.03
Peruvian	3	0.04
Venezuelan	1	0.01
Other Hispanic or Latino	3	0.04

Race*	Population	%
African-American/Black (109)	134	1.71
Not Hispanic (109)	130	1.66
Hispanic (0)	4	0.05
American Indian/Alaska Native (8)	24	0.31
Not Hispanic (8)	17	0.22
Hispanic (0)	7	0.09
Cherokee (2)	10	0.13
Delaware (0)	2	0.03
Iroquois (2)	3	0.04
Lumbee (0)	2	0.03
South American Ind. (0)	1	0.01
Asian (56)	81	1.04
Not Hispanic (52)	73	0.93
Hispanic (4)	8	0.10
Cambodian (0)	1	0.01
Chinese, ex. Taiwanese (21)	25	0.32
Filipino (15)	26	0.33
Indian (4)	7	0.09
Japanese (3)	5	0.06
Korean (11)	14	0.18
Vietnamese (2)	3	0.04
Hawaii Native/Pacific Islander (1)	3	0.04
Not Hispanic (1)	3	0.04
Fijian (1)	1	0.01
Native Hawaiian (0)	2	0.03
White (7,556)	7,620	97.42
Not Hispanic (7,458)	7,506	95.96
Hispanic (98)	114	1.46

Warminster

Place Type: Township
County: Bucks
Population: 32,682†

Ancestry‡	Population	%
Albanian (8)	8	0.02
American (1,150)	1,150	3.53
Arab (126)	172	0.53
Arab (25)	71	0.22
Egyptian (27)	27	0.08
Other Arab (74)	74	0.23
Armenian (7)	22	0.07
Australian (0)	4	0.01
Austrian (32)	115	0.35
Belgian (38)	63	0.19
Brazilian (0)	16	0.05
British (35)	84	0.26
Cajun (0)	24	0.07
Canadian (23)	43	0.13
Croatian (18)	51	0.16
Czech (0)	104	0.32
Czechoslovakian (48)	117	0.36
Danish (0)	31	0.10
Dutch (156)	610	1.87
Eastern European (59)	59	0.18
English (734)	3,451	10.59
Estonian (4)	4	0.01
European (175)	175	0.54
French, ex. Basque (46)	497	1.53
French Canadian (19)	117	0.36
German (2,398)	8,845	27.15
Greek (42)	164	0.50
Hungarian (29)	241	0.74
Irish (2,928)	9,038	27.74
Italian (2,186)	5,403	16.58
Latvian (19)	19	0.06
Lithuanian (133)	233	0.72
Northern European (9)	9	0.03
Norwegian (33)	193	0.59
Pennsylvania German (99)	189	0.58
Polish (912)	2,651	8.14
Portuguese (27)	41	0.13
Romanian (18)	34	0.10
Russian (774)	1,078	3.31
Scandinavian (67)	117	0.36
Scotch-Irish (156)	550	1.69
Scottish (98)	477	1.46
Slavic (0)	12	0.04
Slovak (16)	46	0.14
Swedish (50)	99	0.30
Swiss (13)	40	0.12
Ukrainian (310)	615	1.89
Welsh (76)	361	1.11
West Indian, ex. Hispanic (111)	120	0.37
Bermudan (0)	9	0.03
Haitian (40)	40	0.12
Jamaican (12)	12	0.04
West Indian (59)	59	0.18
Yugoslavian (7)	24	0.07

Hispanic Origin	Population	%
Hispanic or Latino (of any race)	2,518	7.70
Central American, ex. Mexican	399	1.22
Costa Rican	11	0.03
Guatemalan	116	0.35
Honduran	37	0.11
Nicaraguan	10	0.03
Panamanian	3	0.01
Salvadoran	218	0.67
Other Central American	4	0.01
Cuban	32	0.10
Dominican Republic	62	0.19
Mexican	869	2.66
Puerto Rican	907	2.78
South American	121	0.37
Argentinean	6	0.02
Chilean	6	0.02
Colombian	29	0.09
Ecuadorian	31	0.09
Peruvian	42	0.13
Uruguayan	1	<0.01
Venezuelan	6	0.02
Other Hispanic or Latino	128	0.39

Race*	Population	%
African-American/Black (1,016)	1,296	3.97
Not Hispanic (935)	1,163	3.56
Hispanic (81)	133	0.41
American Indian/Alaska Native (63)	167	0.51
Not Hispanic (32)	129	0.39
Hispanic (31)	38	0.12
Apache (0)	2	0.01
Blackfeet (0)	5	0.02
Cherokee (1)	26	0.08
Chickasaw (0)	6	0.02
Choctaw (0)	1	<0.01
Creek (0)	1	<0.01
Delaware (0)	3	0.01
Iroquois (2)	6	0.02
Menominee (1)	1	<0.01
Mexican American Ind. (3)	3	0.01
Osage (1)	1	<0.01
Sioux (2)	3	0.01
Spanish American Ind. (1)	1	<0.01
Asian (626)	776	2.37
Not Hispanic (610)	740	2.26
Hispanic (16)	36	0.11
Bangladeshi (3)	3	0.01
Cambodian (8)	9	0.03
Chinese, ex. Taiwanese (90)	101	0.31
Filipino (103)	146	0.45
Hmong (0)	3	0.01
Indian (239)	285	0.87
Indonesian (7)	7	0.02
Japanese (16)	38	0.12
Korean (68)	89	0.27
Laotian (7)	10	0.03
Pakistani (11)	18	0.06
Taiwanese (2)	2	0.01
Thai (1)	7	0.02
Vietnamese (36)	44	0.13
Hawaii Native/Pacific Islander (20)	54	0.17
Not Hispanic (15)	40	0.12
Hispanic (5)	14	0.04
Fijian (2)	2	0.01
Guamanian/Chamorro (5)	7	0.02
Native Hawaiian (6)	10	0.03
Samoan (0)	1	<0.01
Tongan (5)	5	0.02
White (29,180)	29,645	90.71
Not Hispanic (28,113)	28,432	87.00
Hispanic (1,067)	1,213	3.71

Warren

Place Type: City
County: Warren
Population: 9,710†

Ancestry‡	Population	%
Albanian (0)	22	0.23
American (423)	423	4.33
Arab (38)	48	0.49
Egyptian (6)	6	0.06
Lebanese (26)	26	0.27
Syrian (0)	10	0.10
Other Arab (6)	6	0.06
Austrian (15)	36	0.37
Belgian (0)	11	0.11
British (0)	18	0.18
Canadian (25)	36	0.37
Croatian (0)	10	0.10
Czech (20)	46	0.47
Czechoslovakian (10)	32	0.33
Danish (39)	87	0.89
Dutch (7)	229	2.34
Eastern European (15)	15	0.15
English (461)	1,484	15.19
European (95)	99	1.01
French, ex. Basque (10)	237	2.43
French Canadian (0)	12	0.12
German (1,065)	2,932	30.00
Greek (22)	38	0.39
Hungarian (13)	89	0.91
Irish (334)	1,491	15.26
Israeli (0)	15	0.15
Italian (490)	1,265	12.95
Lithuanian (0)	38	0.39
Northern European (29)	29	0.30
Norwegian (37)	45	0.46
Pennsylvania German (10)	96	0.98
Polish (228)	700	7.16
Russian (7)	69	0.71
Scandinavian (10)	19	0.19
Scotch-Irish (90)	407	4.16
Scottish (73)	192	1.96
Slovak (37)	67	0.69
Slovene (0)	20	0.20
Swedish (372)	1,264	12.93
Swiss (0)	72	0.74
Ukrainian (0)	62	0.63
Welsh (11)	166	1.70
Yugoslavian (10)	52	0.53

Hispanic Origin	Population	%
Hispanic or Latino (of any race)	90	0.93
Central American, ex. Mexican	3	0.03
Panamanian	2	0.02
Other Central American	1	0.01
Cuban	6	0.06
Dominican Republic	1	0.01
Mexican	29	0.30
Puerto Rican	25	0.26
South American	10	0.10

*Notes: † The Census 2010 population figure is used to calculate the percentages in the Hispanic Origin and Race categories. Ancestry percentages are based on the 2006-2010 American Community Survey population (not shown); ‡ Numbers in parentheses indicate the number of people reporting a single ancestry; * Numbers in parentheses indicate the number of persons reporting this race alone, not in combination with any other race; Please refer to the Explanation of Data for more information.*

Argentinean	4	0.04
Chilean	4	0.04
Colombian	1	0.01
Peruvian	1	0.01
Other Hispanic or Latino	16	0.16

Race*	Population	%
African-American/Black (45)	91	0.94
Not Hispanic (44)	87	0.90
Hispanic (1)	4	0.04
American Indian/Alaska Native (29)	60	0.62
Not Hispanic (28)	56	0.58
Hispanic (1)	4	0.04
Apache (1)	2	0.02
Blackfeet (0)	2	0.02
Cherokee (4)	8	0.08
Choctaw (1)	1	0.01
Iroquois (8)	12	0.12
Pima (1)	1	0.01
Asian (57)	78	0.80
Not Hispanic (56)	77	0.79
Hispanic (1)	1	0.01
Chinese, ex. Taiwanese (16)	17	0.18
Filipino (3)	6	0.06
Indian (17)	24	0.25
Japanese (4)	5	0.05
Korean (6)	12	0.12
Malaysian (1)	1	0.01
Pakistani (5)	6	0.06
Vietnamese (0)	4	0.04
Hawaii Native/Pacific Islander (1)	5	0.05
Not Hispanic (1)	5	0.05
White (9,463)	9,560	98.46
Not Hispanic (9,401)	9,484	97.67
Hispanic (62)	76	0.78

Warrington

Place Type: Township
County: Bucks
Population: 23,418†

Ancestry‡	Population	%
African, Sub-Saharan (66)	66	0.29
African (66)	66	0.29
American (743)	743	3.31
Arab (116)	132	0.59
Egyptian (71)	71	0.32
Lebanese (8)	24	0.11
Other Arab (37)	37	0.16
Armenian (25)	122	0.54
Austrian (0)	68	0.30
Brazilian (11)	11	0.05
British (26)	43	0.19
Canadian (0)	27	0.12
Croatian (12)	73	0.32
Czech (9)	65	0.29
Danish (16)	42	0.19
Dutch (48)	320	1.42
Eastern European (40)	40	0.18
English (556)	2,383	10.60
European (185)	185	0.82
French, ex. Basque (28)	413	1.84
French Canadian (9)	76	0.34
German (1,212)	6,323	28.14
Greek (61)	114	0.51
Guyanese (55)	55	0.24
Hungarian (19)	251	1.12
Irish (1,861)	6,740	29.99
Italian (1,405)	4,017	17.88
Latvian (13)	13	0.06
Lithuanian (40)	162	0.72
Norwegian (34)	135	0.60
Pennsylvania German (20)	68	0.30
Polish (411)	1,838	8.18
Portuguese (63)	177	0.79
Romanian (27)	66	0.29
Russian (575)	1,097	4.88
Scandinavian (0)	13	0.06
Scotch-Irish (116)	514	2.29
Scottish (151)	468	2.08
Serbian (0)	13	0.06
Slovak (22)	65	0.29
Slovene (0)	23	0.10
Swedish (63)	237	1.05
Swiss (0)	105	0.47
Ukrainian (284)	574	2.55
Welsh (15)	278	1.24
West Indian, ex. Hispanic (24)	24	0.11
Jamaican (24)	24	0.11

Hispanic Origin	Population	%
Hispanic or Latino (of any race)	978	4.18
Central American, ex. Mexican	155	0.66
Costa Rican	4	0.02
Guatemalan	82	0.35
Honduran	7	0.03
Nicaraguan	6	0.03
Panamanian	1	<0.01
Salvadoran	51	0.22
Other Central American	4	0.02
Cuban	42	0.18
Dominican Republic	15	0.06
Mexican	316	1.35
Puerto Rican	259	1.11
South American	110	0.47
Argentinean	8	0.03
Bolivian	1	<0.01
Colombian	36	0.15
Ecuadorian	28	0.12
Peruvian	25	0.11
Venezuelan	9	0.04
Other South American	3	0.01
Other Hispanic or Latino	81	0.35

Race*	Population	%
African-American/Black (498)	612	2.61
Not Hispanic (469)	571	2.44
Hispanic (29)	41	0.18
American Indian/Alaska Native (37)	98	0.42
Not Hispanic (27)	74	0.32
Hispanic (10)	24	0.10
Apache (0)	1	<0.01
Blackfeet (0)	5	0.02
Cherokee (9)	22	0.09
Chippewa (0)	1	<0.01
Comanche (3)	3	0.01
Delaware (0)	1	<0.01
Iroquois (1)	4	0.02
Lumbee (0)	3	0.01
Mexican American Ind. (4)	11	0.05
Sioux (0)	1	<0.01
South American Ind. (2)	4	0.02
Asian (1,427)	1,564	6.68
Not Hispanic (1,426)	1,554	6.64
Hispanic (1)	10	0.04
Bangladeshi (3)	3	0.01
Cambodian (19)	21	0.09
Chinese, ex. Taiwanese (322)	362	1.55
Filipino (94)	131	0.56
Indian (477)	509	2.17
Indonesian (1)	1	<0.01
Japanese (5)	21	0.09
Korean (369)	385	1.64
Laotian (11)	16	0.07
Malaysian (2)	2	0.01
Pakistani (10)	12	0.05
Sri Lankan (3)	3	0.01
Taiwanese (9)	14	0.06
Thai (2)	3	0.01
Vietnamese (71)	86	0.37
Hawaii Native/Pacific Islander (5)	22	0.09
Not Hispanic (4)	20	0.09
Hispanic (1)	2	0.01
Guamanian/Chamorro (1)	4	0.02
Native Hawaiian (0)	12	0.05
Tongan (1)	2	0.01
White (20,720)	21,005	89.70
Not Hispanic (20,214)	20,458	87.36
Hispanic (506)	547	2.34

Warwick

Place Type: Township
County: Bucks
Population: 14,437†

Ancestry‡	Population	%
Albanian (14)	72	0.51
American (400)	400	2.85
Arab (28)	113	0.80
Palestinian (12)	24	0.17
Other Arab (16)	89	0.63
Armenian (68)	93	0.66
Austrian (18)	46	0.33
British (0)	53	0.38
Czech (18)	60	0.43
Danish (0)	38	0.27
Dutch (29)	215	1.53
Eastern European (72)	89	0.63
English (222)	1,227	8.73
European (159)	159	1.13
French, ex. Basque (0)	381	2.71
French Canadian (42)	55	0.39
German (860)	3,990	28.39
Greek (63)	167	1.19
Hungarian (45)	212	1.51
Irish (1,035)	4,090	29.11
Italian (1,172)	3,029	21.56
Latvian (20)	20	0.14
Lithuanian (37)	145	1.03
Northern European (85)	85	0.60
Norwegian (16)	26	0.19
Pennsylvania German (66)	169	1.20
Polish (390)	1,529	10.88
Portuguese (16)	60	0.43
Romanian (0)	40	0.28
Russian (580)	845	6.01
Scotch-Irish (27)	237	1.69
Scottish (66)	324	2.31
Slovak (7)	23	0.16
Swedish (22)	103	0.73
Ukrainian (366)	423	3.01
Welsh (30)	151	1.07
Yugoslavian (0)	14	0.10

Hispanic Origin	Population	%
Hispanic or Latino (of any race)	300	2.08
Central American, ex. Mexican	22	0.15
Costa Rican	4	0.03
Guatemalan	14	0.10
Honduran	3	0.02
Panamanian	1	0.01
Cuban	20	0.14
Mexican	55	0.38
Puerto Rican	143	0.99
South American	31	0.21
Argentinean	8	0.06
Bolivian	1	0.01
Chilean	7	0.05
Colombian	7	0.05
Paraguayan	2	0.01
Peruvian	4	0.03
Uruguayan	1	0.01
Venezuelan	1	0.01
Other Hispanic or Latino	29	0.20

Race*	Population	%
African-American/Black (186)	232	1.61
Not Hispanic (176)	218	1.51
Hispanic (10)	14	0.10
American Indian/Alaska Native (31)	56	0.39
Not Hispanic (19)	41	0.28
Hispanic (12)	15	0.10
Chickasaw (1)	1	0.01
Chippewa (0)	3	0.02
Choctaw (1)	1	0.01
Iroquois (1)	1	0.01
Lumbee (1)	1	0.01
Mexican American Ind. (0)	1	0.01
South American Ind. (5)	5	0.03

SECTION TWO

*Notes: † The Census 2010 population figure is used to calculate the percentages in the Hispanic Origin and Race categories. Ancestry percentages are based on the 2006-2010 American Community Survey population (not shown); ‡ Numbers in parentheses indicate the number of people reporting a single ancestry; * Numbers in parentheses indicate the number of persons reporting this race alone, not in combination with any other race; Please refer to the Explanation of Data for more information.*

Asian (538)	611	4.23
Not Hispanic (526)	596	4.13
Hispanic (12)	15	0.10
Bangladeshi (2)	2	0.01
Cambodian (1)	1	0.01
Chinese, ex. Taiwanese (145)	158	1.09
Filipino (51)	67	0.46
Indian (212)	220	1.52
Indonesian (1)	1	0.01
Japanese (1)	6	0.04
Korean (80)	96	0.66
Laotian (2)	3	0.02
Pakistani (4)	4	0.03
Taiwanese (1)	1	0.01
Thai (3)	4	0.03
Vietnamese (25)	28	0.19
Hawaii Native/Pacific Islander (4)	6	0.04
Not Hispanic (4)	6	0.04
Guamanian/Chamorro (1)	1	0.01
White (13,489)	13,623	94.36
Not Hispanic (13,276)	13,392	92.76
Hispanic (213)	231	1.60

Warwick

Place Type: Township
County: Lancaster
Population: 17,783†

Ancestry‡	Population	%
African, Sub-Saharan (54)	72	0.41
African (0)	18	0.10
Other Sub-Saharan African (54)	54	0.31
American (1,599)	1,599	9.18
Australian (15)	15	0.09
Austrian (0)	33	0.19
British (79)	86	0.49
Canadian (0)	23	0.13
Czech (14)	67	0.38
Danish (28)	37	0.21
Dutch (63)	306	1.76
Eastern European (29)	29	0.17
English (357)	1,178	6.76
European (99)	107	0.61
Finnish (35)	52	0.30
French, ex. Basque (87)	518	2.97
French Canadian (11)	105	0.60
German (4,293)	7,803	44.79
Greek (35)	179	1.03
Irish (557)	2,152	12.35
Italian (622)	1,302	7.47
Lithuanian (14)	62	0.36
Macedonian (0)	13	0.07
Maltese (0)	22	0.13
Norwegian (27)	40	0.23
Pennsylvania German (51)	81	0.46
Polish (201)	672	3.86
Romanian (14)	27	0.15
Russian (0)	10	0.06
Scotch-Irish (121)	439	2.52
Scottish (121)	255	1.46
Serbian (39)	52	0.30
Slovak (0)	49	0.28
Swedish (59)	197	1.13
Swiss (209)	628	3.60
Turkish (0)	10	0.06
Ukrainian (28)	81	0.46
Welsh (33)	455	2.61

Hispanic Origin	Population	%
Hispanic or Latino (of any race)	514	2.89
Central American, ex. Mexican	19	0.11
Guatemalan	8	0.04
Honduran	3	0.02
Nicaraguan	3	0.02
Salvadoran	4	0.02
Other Central American	1	0.01
Cuban	25	0.14
Dominican Republic	14	0.08
Mexican	101	0.57
Puerto Rican	276	1.55
South American	32	0.18
Argentinean	2	0.01
Bolivian	1	0.01
Colombian	14	0.08
Ecuadorian	4	0.02
Paraguayan	3	0.02
Peruvian	6	0.03
Venezuelan	1	0.01
Other South American	1	0.01
Other Hispanic or Latino	47	0.26

Race*	Population	%
African-American/Black (214)	289	1.63
Not Hispanic (189)	250	1.41
Hispanic (25)	39	0.22
American Indian/Alaska Native (28)	79	0.44
Not Hispanic (11)	57	0.32
Hispanic (17)	22	0.12
Apache (0)	2	0.01
Blackfeet (0)	2	0.01
Canadian/French Am. Ind. (0)	1	0.01
Cherokee (3)	18	0.10
Creek (1)	1	0.01
Delaware (3)	4	0.02
Mexican American Ind. (3)	4	0.02
Seminole (0)	1	0.01
South American Ind. (2)	3	0.02
Asian (173)	227	1.28
Not Hispanic (168)	217	1.22
Hispanic (5)	10	0.06
Chinese, ex. Taiwanese (30)	39	0.22
Filipino (17)	25	0.14
Hmong (8)	10	0.06
Indian (40)	48	0.27
Indonesian (4)	4	0.02
Japanese (8)	19	0.11
Korean (26)	32	0.18
Laotian (3)	5	0.03
Taiwanese (1)	3	0.02
Thai (8)	8	0.04
Vietnamese (22)	29	0.16
Hawaii Native/Pacific Islander (3)	5	0.03
Not Hispanic (3)	4	0.02
Hispanic (0)	1	0.01
Native Hawaiian (3)	4	0.02
White (17,026)	17,206	96.76
Not Hispanic (16,731)	16,875	94.89
Hispanic (295)	331	1.86

Washington

Place Type: City
County: Washington
Population: 13,663†

Ancestry‡	Population	%
African, Sub-Saharan (92)	92	0.66
African (92)	92	0.66
American (474)	474	3.41
Arab (91)	103	0.74
Lebanese (25)	25	0.18
Syrian (66)	78	0.56
Austrian (20)	71	0.51
Belgian (0)	29	0.21
British (15)	15	0.11
Canadian (7)	14	0.10
Croatian (0)	53	0.38
Czech (12)	12	0.09
Czechoslovakian (0)	27	0.19
Dutch (21)	178	1.28
English (186)	1,133	8.14
European (35)	55	0.40
French, ex. Basque (115)	453	3.26
French Canadian (0)	40	0.29
German (473)	2,539	18.25
Greek (28)	49	0.35
Hungarian (20)	105	0.75
Irish (605)	2,247	16.15
Italian (988)	2,029	14.58
Lithuanian (0)	67	0.48
Northern European (20)	20	0.14
Norwegian (0)	69	0.50
Pennsylvania German (0)	48	0.34
Polish (155)	771	5.54
Russian (15)	78	0.56
Scandinavian (14)	14	0.10
Scotch-Irish (343)	983	7.06
Scottish (57)	209	1.50
Serbian (0)	10	0.07
Slavic (14)	34	0.24
Slovak (76)	165	1.19
Slovene (16)	24	0.17
Swedish (0)	85	0.61
Swiss (0)	31	0.22
Ukrainian (12)	21	0.15
Welsh (49)	83	0.60

Hispanic Origin	Population	%
Hispanic or Latino (of any race)	249	1.82
Central American, ex. Mexican	21	0.15
Guatemalan	5	0.04
Honduran	1	0.01
Nicaraguan	9	0.07
Panamanian	6	0.04
Cuban	2	0.01
Dominican Republic	1	0.01
Mexican	92	0.67
Puerto Rican	61	0.45
South American	7	0.05
Argentinean	1	0.01
Chilean	2	0.01
Colombian	1	0.01
Ecuadorian	1	0.01
Peruvian	1	0.01
Venezuelan	1	0.01
Other Hispanic or Latino	65	0.48

Race*	Population	%
African-American/Black (2,172)	2,671	19.55
Not Hispanic (2,145)	2,611	19.11
Hispanic (27)	60	0.44
American Indian/Alaska Native (25)	135	0.99
Not Hispanic (24)	128	0.94
Hispanic (1)	7	0.05
Alaska Athabascan *(Ala. Nat.)* (0)	1	0.01
Blackfeet (1)	13	0.10
Cherokee (7)	36	0.26
Choctaw (1)	1	0.01
Iroquois (0)	1	0.01
Mexican American Ind. (1)	1	0.01
Navajo (1)	1	0.01
Sioux (2)	5	0.04
Asian (98)	148	1.08
Not Hispanic (96)	141	1.03
Hispanic (2)	7	0.05
Chinese, ex. Taiwanese (19)	28	0.20
Filipino (20)	42	0.31
Indian (36)	41	0.30
Indonesian (1)	5	0.04
Japanese (2)	10	0.07
Korean (5)	5	0.04
Pakistani (6)	6	0.04
Taiwanese (1)	1	0.01
Thai (2)	2	0.01
Vietnamese (4)	6	0.04
Hawaii Native/Pacific Islander (8)	19	0.14
Not Hispanic (8)	19	0.14
Guamanian/Chamorro (2)	2	0.01
Native Hawaiian (1)	3	0.02
Samoan (0)	1	0.01
Tongan (0)	1	0.01
White (10,622)	11,204	82.00
Not Hispanic (10,522)	11,074	81.05
Hispanic (100)	130	0.95

*Notes: † The Census 2010 population figure is used to calculate the percentages in the Hispanic Origin and Race categories. Ancestry percentages are based on the 2006-2010 American Community Survey population (not shown); ‡ Numbers in parentheses indicate the number of people reporting a single ancestry; * Numbers in parentheses indicate the number of persons reporting this race alone, not in combination with any other race; Please refer to the Explanation of Data for more information.*

Washington

Place Type: Township
County: Franklin
Population: 14,009†

Ancestry‡	Population	%
African, Sub-Saharan (16)	23	0.17
African (16)	23	0.17
American (1,118)	1,118	8.20
Arab (61)	88	0.65
Egyptian (35)	35	0.26
Lebanese (0)	18	0.13
Syrian (26)	35	0.26
Austrian (21)	64	0.47
British (11)	69	0.51
Canadian (10)	10	0.07
Croatian (0)	8	0.06
Czech (20)	20	0.15
Danish (11)	32	0.23
Dutch (21)	356	2.61
English (424)	1,160	8.51
Estonian (11)	22	0.16
European (246)	246	1.80
Finnish (0)	11	0.08
French, ex. Basque (52)	295	2.16
French Canadian (34)	77	0.56
German (3,214)	5,811	42.63
Greek (9)	94	0.69
Hungarian (33)	78	0.57
Irish (424)	1,981	14.53
Israeli (20)	20	0.15
Italian (167)	433	3.18
Latvian (0)	10	0.07
Lithuanian (0)	10	0.07
Norwegian (29)	37	0.27
Pennsylvania German (110)	138	1.01
Polish (175)	438	3.21
Romanian (9)	9	0.07
Russian (17)	113	0.83
Scandinavian (11)	29	0.21
Scotch-Irish (46)	258	1.89
Scottish (61)	225	1.65
Slovene (10)	10	0.07
Swedish (124)	179	1.31
Swiss (11)	22	0.16
Ukrainian (0)	9	0.07
Welsh (19)	84	0.62
West Indian, ex. Hispanic (0)	10	0.07
Jamaican (0)	10	0.07

Hispanic Origin	Population	%
Hispanic or Latino (of any race)	323	2.31
Central American, ex. Mexican	39	0.28
Costa Rican	4	0.03
Guatemalan	8	0.06
Honduran	2	0.01
Panamanian	10	0.07
Salvadoran	15	0.11
Cuban	8	0.06
Dominican Republic	8	0.06
Mexican	128	0.91
Puerto Rican	74	0.53
South American	15	0.11
Argentinean	1	0.01
Bolivian	3	0.02
Chilean	4	0.03
Colombian	5	0.04
Venezuelan	2	0.01
Other Hispanic or Latino	51	0.36

Race*	Population	%
African-American/Black (233)	333	2.38
Not Hispanic (218)	299	2.13
Hispanic (15)	34	0.24
American Indian/Alaska Native (30)	67	0.48
Not Hispanic (26)	59	0.42
Hispanic (4)	8	0.06
Apache (1)	2	0.01
Blackfeet (0)	2	0.01
Cherokee (3)	15	0.11
Chippewa (1)	1	0.01
Choctaw (1)	2	0.01
Delaware (3)	3	0.02
Shoshone (5)	5	0.04
Sioux (0)	2	0.01
Tlingit-Haida *(Alaska Native)* (1)	1	0.01
Asian (158)	187	1.33
Not Hispanic (158)	183	1.31
Hispanic (0)	4	0.03
Chinese, ex. Taiwanese (15)	16	0.11
Filipino (35)	50	0.36
Indian (26)	32	0.23
Indonesian (0)	1	0.01
Japanese (6)	7	0.05
Korean (31)	37	0.26
Nepalese (5)	5	0.04
Pakistani (6)	6	0.04
Taiwanese (2)	2	0.01
Thai (5)	8	0.06
Vietnamese (18)	21	0.15
Hawaii Native/Pacific Islander (1)	8	0.06
Not Hispanic (1)	5	0.04
Hispanic (0)	3	0.02
Native Hawaiian (1)	6	0.04
White (13,326)	13,485	96.26
Not Hispanic (13,138)	13,265	94.69
Hispanic (188)	220	1.57

Waynesboro

Place Type: Borough
County: Franklin
Population: 10,568†

Ancestry‡	Population	%
American (890)	890	8.53
Armenian (13)	13	0.12
Austrian (9)	27	0.26
Belgian (7)	15	0.14
British (18)	48	0.46
Canadian (0)	35	0.34
Croatian (0)	24	0.23
Czech (10)	32	0.31
Czechoslovakian (8)	8	0.08
Dutch (0)	177	1.70
Eastern European (7)	7	0.07
English (313)	1,010	9.68
European (9)	23	0.22
French, ex. Basque (20)	243	2.33
French Canadian (11)	19	0.18
German (1,932)	4,224	40.47
Greek (10)	20	0.19
Irish (349)	1,782	17.07
Italian (117)	511	4.90
Norwegian (0)	12	0.11
Pennsylvania German (51)	51	0.49
Polish (42)	224	2.15
Portuguese (25)	25	0.24
Russian (9)	9	0.09
Scotch-Irish (152)	332	3.18
Scottish (91)	215	2.06
Serbian (0)	12	0.11
Slovak (11)	22	0.21
Swedish (0)	99	0.95
Swiss (26)	117	1.12
Ukrainian (11)	23	0.22
Welsh (11)	91	0.87

Hispanic Origin	Population	%
Hispanic or Latino (of any race)	386	3.65
Central American, ex. Mexican	32	0.30
Costa Rican	3	0.03
Guatemalan	12	0.11
Honduran	2	0.02
Panamanian	4	0.04
Salvadoran	11	0.10
Cuban	24	0.23
Mexican	200	1.89
Puerto Rican	91	0.86
South American	11	0.10
Colombian	5	0.05
Paraguayan	1	0.01
Peruvian	5	0.05
Other Hispanic or Latino	28	0.26

Race*	Population	%
African-American/Black (319)	446	4.22
Not Hispanic (307)	416	3.94
Hispanic (12)	30	0.28
American Indian/Alaska Native (39)	120	1.14
Not Hispanic (27)	94	0.89
Hispanic (12)	26	0.25
Alaska Athabascan *(Ala. Nat.)* (1)	2	0.02
Apache (6)	10	0.09
Blackfeet (1)	7	0.07
Central American Ind. (0)	1	0.01
Cherokee (2)	30	0.28
Chippewa (1)	1	0.01
Choctaw (0)	1	0.01
Cree (0)	2	0.02
Iroquois (2)	3	0.03
Lumbee (2)	3	0.03
Mexican American Ind. (5)	6	0.06
Navajo (1)	2	0.02
Potawatomi (0)	4	0.04
Sioux (2)	4	0.04
Spanish American Ind. (0)	1	0.01
Asian (65)	113	1.07
Not Hispanic (62)	99	0.94
Hispanic (3)	14	0.13
Chinese, ex. Taiwanese (9)	18	0.17
Filipino (20)	29	0.27
Indian (6)	11	0.10
Indonesian (0)	1	0.01
Japanese (2)	9	0.09
Korean (16)	29	0.27
Taiwanese (1)	1	0.01
Thai (5)	8	0.08
Hawaii Native/Pacific Islander (1)	6	0.06
Not Hispanic (1)	4	0.04
Hispanic (0)	2	0.02
Native Hawaiian (1)	3	0.03
White (9,769)	9,998	94.61
Not Hispanic (9,578)	9,771	92.46
Hispanic (191)	227	2.15

Weigelstown

Place Type: CDP
County: York
Population: 12,875†

Ancestry‡	Population	%
African, Sub-Saharan (0)	27	0.21
African (0)	27	0.21
American (962)	962	7.45
Austrian (0)	32	0.25
British (14)	14	0.11
Canadian (14)	14	0.11
Czech (0)	33	0.26
Dutch (63)	404	3.13
English (257)	840	6.50
European (89)	89	0.69
French, ex. Basque (48)	212	1.64
German (3,547)	5,936	45.95
Greek (22)	39	0.30
Irish (390)	1,573	12.18
Italian (272)	506	3.92
Norwegian (17)	85	0.66
Pennsylvania German (106)	119	0.92
Polish (35)	313	2.42
Romanian (0)	12	0.09
Russian (19)	41	0.32
Scotch-Irish (39)	101	0.78
Scottish (21)	152	1.18
Slovak (14)	50	0.39
Slovene (0)	14	0.11
Swedish (46)	81	0.63
Swiss (0)	12	0.09

*Notes: † The Census 2010 population figure is used to calculate the percentages in the Hispanic Origin and Race categories. Ancestry percentages are based on the 2006-2010 American Community Survey population (not shown); ‡ Numbers in parentheses indicate the number of people reporting a single ancestry; * Numbers in parentheses indicate the number of persons reporting this race alone, not in combination with any other race; Please refer to the Explanation of Data for more information.*

SECTION TWO

Ukrainian (15)	15	0.12
Welsh (59)	193	1.49

Hispanic Origin	Population	%
Hispanic or Latino (of any race)	515	4.00
Central American, ex. Mexican	31	0.24
Guatemalan	1	0.01
Honduran	1	0.01
Nicaraguan	5	0.04
Panamanian	3	0.02
Salvadoran	21	0.16
Cuban	16	0.12
Dominican Republic	15	0.12
Mexican	115	0.89
Puerto Rican	288	2.24
South American	28	0.22
Argentinean	2	0.02
Bolivian	1	0.01
Chilean	4	0.03
Colombian	12	0.09
Ecuadorian	2	0.02
Paraguayan	1	0.01
Peruvian	6	0.05
Other Hispanic or Latino	22	0.17

Race*	Population	%
African-American/Black (603)	740	5.75
Not Hispanic (574)	689	5.35
Hispanic (29)	51	0.40
American Indian/Alaska Native (31)	86	0.67
Not Hispanic (24)	75	0.58
Hispanic (7)	11	0.09
Apache (1)	1	0.01
Cherokee (2)	19	0.15
Creek (3)	3	0.02
Delaware (0)	3	0.02
Hopi (0)	3	0.02
Iroquois (0)	9	0.07
Lumbee (3)	3	0.02
Mexican American Ind. (1)	1	0.01
Paiute (0)	1	0.01
Sioux (4)	7	0.05
Asian (117)	157	1.22
Not Hispanic (116)	156	1.21
Hispanic (1)	1	0.01
Chinese, ex. Taiwanese (19)	23	0.18
Filipino (27)	37	0.29
Indian (31)	34	0.26
Indonesian (1)	1	0.01
Japanese (3)	17	0.13
Korean (10)	18	0.14
Nepalese (8)	8	0.06
Pakistani (1)	1	0.01
Vietnamese (15)	16	0.12
Hawaii Native/Pacific Islander (6)	18	0.14
Not Hispanic (6)	12	0.09
Hispanic (0)	6	0.05
Guamanian/Chamorro (1)	1	0.01
Native Hawaiian (4)	8	0.06
Samoan (1)	1	0.01
White (11,707)	11,934	92.69
Not Hispanic (11,428)	11,619	90.24
Hispanic (279)	315	2.45

West Bradford

Place Type: Township
County: Chester
Population: 12,223†

Ancestry‡	Population	%
African, Sub-Saharan (9)	9	0.07
African (9)	9	0.07
American (962)	962	8.01
Arab (23)	23	0.19
Arab (12)	12	0.10
Palestinian (11)	11	0.09
Armenian (9)	44	0.37
Austrian (11)	80	0.67
Belgian (12)	12	0.10
British (33)	137	1.14
Canadian (28)	58	0.48
Czech (19)	60	0.50
Danish (0)	56	0.47
Dutch (43)	171	1.42
Eastern European (8)	8	0.07
English (322)	1,732	14.42
Estonian (0)	6	0.05
European (77)	77	0.64
Finnish (0)	8	0.07
French, ex. Basque (22)	311	2.59
French Canadian (40)	114	0.95
German (564)	3,441	28.65
Greek (39)	117	0.97
Hungarian (25)	114	0.95
Irish (1,204)	3,618	30.12
Italian (478)	1,981	16.49
Latvian (0)	13	0.11
Lithuanian (9)	142	1.18
Northern European (41)	41	0.34
Norwegian (27)	103	0.86
Pennsylvania German (11)	34	0.28
Polish (288)	1,157	9.63
Russian (25)	207	1.72
Scotch-Irish (79)	327	2.72
Scottish (64)	269	2.24
Slovak (0)	82	0.68
Swedish (0)	133	1.11
Swiss (0)	23	0.19
Ukrainian (25)	114	0.95
Welsh (35)	117	0.97

Hispanic Origin	Population	%
Hispanic or Latino (of any race)	249	2.04
Central American, ex. Mexican	6	0.05
Guatemalan	4	0.03
Honduran	1	0.01
Nicaraguan	1	0.01
Cuban	10	0.08
Dominican Republic	2	0.02
Mexican	92	0.75
Puerto Rican	59	0.48
South American	37	0.30
Argentinean	10	0.08
Bolivian	1	0.01
Chilean	2	0.02
Colombian	9	0.07
Ecuadorian	1	0.01
Peruvian	6	0.05
Uruguayan	1	0.01
Venezuelan	7	0.06
Other Hispanic or Latino	43	0.35

Race*	Population	%
African-American/Black (356)	438	3.58
Not Hispanic (356)	422	3.45
Hispanic (0)	16	0.13
American Indian/Alaska Native (20)	59	0.48
Not Hispanic (18)	46	0.38
Hispanic (2)	13	0.11
Cherokee (2)	8	0.07
Choctaw (0)	1	0.01
Delaware (0)	1	0.01
Iroquois (2)	4	0.03
Mexican American Ind. (2)	4	0.03
South American Ind. (0)	1	0.01
Asian (318)	389	3.18
Not Hispanic (313)	381	3.12
Hispanic (5)	8	0.07
Bangladeshi (5)	7	0.06
Cambodian (5)	5	0.04
Chinese, ex. Taiwanese (80)	101	0.83
Filipino (31)	41	0.34
Indian (137)	152	1.24
Indonesian (1)	2	0.02
Japanese (1)	2	0.02
Korean (16)	25	0.20
Laotian (4)	4	0.03
Malaysian (0)	1	0.01
Pakistani (9)	9	0.07
Thai (1)	4	0.03
Vietnamese (13)	27	0.22
Hawaii Native/Pacific Islander (5)	13	0.11
Not Hispanic (5)	13	0.11
Native Hawaiian (0)	2	0.02
Samoan (0)	4	0.03
White (11,293)	11,434	93.54
Not Hispanic (11,130)	11,250	92.04
Hispanic (163)	184	1.51

West Caln

Place Type: Township
County: Chester
Population: 9,014†

Ancestry‡	Population	%
American (815)	815	9.32
Arab (58)	88	1.01
Jordanian (58)	58	0.66
Lebanese (0)	30	0.34
Austrian (0)	36	0.41
British (65)	78	0.89
Czech (0)	87	0.99
Dutch (33)	235	2.69
English (408)	1,467	16.78
European (131)	142	1.62
French, ex. Basque (11)	129	1.48
German (659)	2,246	25.69
Hungarian (26)	33	0.38
Irish (659)	1,936	22.14
Italian (496)	1,215	13.90
Norwegian (15)	44	0.50
Pennsylvania German (130)	194	2.22
Polish (61)	432	4.94
Romanian (29)	44	0.50
Russian (7)	44	0.50
Scotch-Irish (53)	119	1.36
Scottish (81)	284	3.25
Slovak (45)	220	2.52
Swedish (24)	51	0.58
Swiss (14)	24	0.27
Ukrainian (26)	124	1.42
Welsh (14)	102	1.17

Hispanic Origin	Population	%
Hispanic or Latino (of any race)	204	2.26
Central American, ex. Mexican	6	0.07
Panamanian	3	0.03
Salvadoran	3	0.03
Cuban	4	0.04
Dominican Republic	3	0.03
Mexican	76	0.84
Puerto Rican	98	1.09
South American	7	0.08
Argentinean	2	0.02
Chilean	1	0.01
Colombian	2	0.02
Peruvian	2	0.02
Other Hispanic or Latino	10	0.11

Race*	Population	%
African-American/Black (350)	448	4.97
Not Hispanic (335)	422	4.68
Hispanic (15)	26	0.29
American Indian/Alaska Native (14)	56	0.62
Not Hispanic (10)	48	0.53
Hispanic (4)	8	0.09
Blackfeet (3)	5	0.06
Cherokee (1)	12	0.13
Choctaw (4)	4	0.04
Delaware (0)	7	0.08
Iroquois (1)	3	0.03
Mexican American Ind. (1)	1	0.01
Seminole (0)	2	0.02
Sioux (1)	1	0.01
Asian (66)	85	0.94
Not Hispanic (66)	83	0.92
Hispanic (0)	2	0.02
Cambodian (3)	5	0.06

*Notes: † The Census 2010 population figure is used to calculate the percentages in the Hispanic Origin and Race categories. Ancestry percentages are based on the 2006-2010 American Community Survey population (not shown); ‡ Numbers in parentheses indicate the number of people reporting a single ancestry; * Numbers in parentheses indicate the number of persons reporting this race alone, not in combination with any other race; Please refer to the Explanation of Data for more information.*

Chinese, ex. Taiwanese (17)	18	0.20
Filipino (16)	20	0.22
Indian (15)	19	0.21
Indonesian (0)	1	0.01
Japanese (3)	4	0.04
Korean (10)	14	0.16
Pakistani (1)	1	0.01
Vietnamese (1)	1	0.01
Hawaii Native/Pacific Islander (1)	3	0.03
Not Hispanic (1)	3	0.03
Guamanian/Chamorro (0)	1	0.01
Native Hawaiian (1)	1	0.01
White (8,378)	8,526	94.59
Not Hispanic (8,269)	8,385	93.02
Hispanic (109)	141	1.56

West Chester

Place Type: Borough
County: Chester
Population: 18,461†

Ancestry‡	Population	%
African, Sub-Saharan (38)	61	0.33
African (27)	27	0.15
Ethiopian (0)	23	0.12
Liberian (11)	11	0.06
Albanian (0)	15	0.08
American (986)	986	5.32
Arab (26)	66	0.36
Egyptian (0)	16	0.09
Lebanese (26)	36	0.19
Moroccan (0)	14	0.08
Australian (9)	9	0.05
Austrian (28)	75	0.40
Belgian (0)	7	0.04
British (27)	61	0.33
Canadian (0)	23	0.12
Croatian (0)	28	0.15
Czech (0)	64	0.35
Czechoslovakian (53)	67	0.36
Danish (11)	11	0.06
Dutch (48)	310	1.67
Eastern European (12)	26	0.14
English (342)	1,803	9.73
European (62)	67	0.36
Finnish (8)	8	0.04
French, ex. Basque (14)	448	2.42
French Canadian (27)	35	0.19
German (1,221)	3,861	20.84
Greek (17)	51	0.28
Guyanese (0)	15	0.08
Hungarian (10)	106	0.57
Irish (1,206)	4,248	22.92
Italian (1,088)	2,998	16.18
Latvian (31)	31	0.17
Lithuanian (18)	39	0.21
New Zealander (14)	14	0.08
Northern European (10)	10	0.05
Norwegian (24)	76	0.41
Pennsylvania German (23)	46	0.25
Polish (240)	992	5.35
Portuguese (9)	60	0.32
Romanian (0)	23	0.12
Russian (119)	364	1.96
Scotch-Irish (136)	433	2.34
Scottish (130)	402	2.17
Slovak (38)	75	0.40
Swedish (18)	133	0.72
Swiss (0)	60	0.32
Turkish (0)	14	0.08
Ukrainian (55)	100	0.54
Welsh (27)	298	1.61
West Indian, ex. Hispanic (100)	165	0.89
British West Indian (0)	14	0.08
Haitian (51)	51	0.28
Jamaican (35)	60	0.32
Trinidadian/Tobagonian (14)	14	0.08
West Indian (0)	26	0.14

Hispanic Origin	Population	%
Hispanic or Latino (of any race)	2,481	13.44
Central American, ex. Mexican	110	0.60
Costa Rican	4	0.02
Guatemalan	58	0.31
Honduran	22	0.12
Nicaraguan	8	0.04
Panamanian	10	0.05
Salvadoran	8	0.04
Cuban	42	0.23
Dominican Republic	38	0.21
Mexican	1,248	6.76
Puerto Rican	816	4.42
South American	141	0.76
Argentinean	25	0.14
Bolivian	6	0.03
Chilean	11	0.06
Colombian	51	0.28
Ecuadorian	24	0.13
Paraguayan	1	0.01
Peruvian	14	0.08
Uruguayan	1	0.01
Venezuelan	8	0.04
Other Hispanic or Latino	86	0.47

Race*	Population	%
African-American/Black (2,225)	2,451	13.28
Not Hispanic (2,082)	2,258	12.23
Hispanic (143)	193	1.05
American Indian/Alaska Native (39)	135	0.73
Not Hispanic (17)	91	0.49
Hispanic (22)	44	0.24
Apache (1)	2	0.01
Arapaho (0)	1	0.01
Blackfeet (0)	6	0.03
Cherokee (3)	23	0.12
Choctaw (0)	2	0.01
Delaware (0)	1	0.01
Inupiat *(Alaska Native)* (0)	2	0.01
Iroquois (0)	1	0.01
Kiowa (1)	1	0.01
Lumbee (2)	2	0.01
Mexican American Ind. (6)	8	0.04
Navajo (0)	1	0.01
Seminole (0)	1	0.01
Sioux (1)	5	0.03
Spanish American Ind. (0)	1	0.01
Asian (259)	341	1.85
Not Hispanic (258)	335	1.81
Hispanic (1)	6	0.03
Bangladeshi (1)	1	0.01
Cambodian (5)	10	0.05
Chinese, ex. Taiwanese (64)	81	0.44
Filipino (23)	37	0.20
Indian (55)	67	0.36
Indonesian (0)	1	0.01
Japanese (7)	19	0.10
Korean (45)	54	0.29
Laotian (4)	5	0.03
Malaysian (1)	1	0.01
Nepalese (3)	4	0.02
Pakistani (5)	8	0.04
Taiwanese (4)	4	0.02
Thai (6)	8	0.04
Vietnamese (29)	41	0.22
Hawaii Native/Pacific Islander (5)	22	0.12
Not Hispanic (2)	16	0.09
Hispanic (3)	6	0.03
Native Hawaiian (0)	4	0.02
Samoan (0)	2	0.01
Tongan (1)	1	0.01
White (14,530)	14,923	80.84
Not Hispanic (13,303)	13,567	73.49
Hispanic (1,227)	1,356	7.35

West Deer

Place Type: Township
County: Allegheny
Population: 11,771†

Ancestry‡	Population	%
American (316)	316	2.72
Arab (6)	86	0.74
Egyptian (6)	18	0.15
Lebanese (0)	32	0.28
Syrian (0)	36	0.31
Armenian (0)	18	0.15
Austrian (12)	53	0.46
Belgian (0)	7	0.06
British (19)	19	0.16
Bulgarian (17)	17	0.15
Croatian (73)	382	3.29
Czech (32)	85	0.73
Czechoslovakian (8)	35	0.30
Dutch (13)	412	3.55
English (238)	895	7.70
European (13)	13	0.11
French, ex. Basque (14)	270	2.32
French Canadian (0)	25	0.22
German (1,081)	4,075	35.08
Greek (24)	43	0.37
Hungarian (79)	229	1.97
Irish (482)	2,495	21.48
Italian (815)	2,166	18.65
Lithuanian (25)	88	0.76
Northern European (29)	29	0.25
Norwegian (0)	56	0.48
Pennsylvania German (7)	7	0.06
Polish (410)	1,563	13.46
Romanian (0)	44	0.38
Russian (63)	328	2.82
Scotch-Irish (108)	459	3.95
Scottish (48)	195	1.68
Serbian (14)	14	0.12
Slavic (20)	86	0.74
Slovak (357)	803	6.91
Slovene (38)	134	1.15
Swedish (12)	71	0.61
Swiss (9)	23	0.20
Ukrainian (28)	66	0.57
Welsh (44)	118	1.02
Yugoslavian (0)	6	0.05

Hispanic Origin	Population	%
Hispanic or Latino (of any race)	95	0.81
Central American, ex. Mexican	2	0.02
Guatemalan	2	0.02
Cuban	9	0.08
Mexican	45	0.38
Puerto Rican	21	0.18
South American	1	0.01
Colombian	1	0.01
Other Hispanic or Latino	17	0.14

Race*	Population	%
African-American/Black (60)	81	0.69
Not Hispanic (60)	81	0.69
American Indian/Alaska Native (16)	37	0.31
Not Hispanic (15)	31	0.26
Hispanic (1)	6	0.05
Blackfeet (0)	1	0.01
Cherokee (2)	7	0.06
Cheyenne (0)	1	0.01
Choctaw (0)	1	0.01
Iroquois (5)	5	0.04
Tlingit-Haida *(Alaska Native)* (1)	1	0.01
Yaqui (1)	3	0.03
Asian (52)	72	0.61
Not Hispanic (52)	70	0.59
Hispanic (0)	2	0.02
Chinese, ex. Taiwanese (12)	14	0.12
Filipino (3)	10	0.08
Indian (23)	27	0.23
Japanese (3)	5	0.04

SECTION TWO

*Notes: † The Census 2010 population figure is used to calculate the percentages in the Hispanic Origin and Race categories. Ancestry percentages are based on the 2006-2010 American Community Survey population (not shown); ‡ Numbers in parentheses indicate the number of people reporting a single ancestry; * Numbers in parentheses indicate the number of persons reporting this race alone, not in combination with any other race; Please refer to the Explanation of Data for more information.*

Korean (4)	7	0.06
Laotian (1)	1	0.01
Taiwanese (0)	1	0.01
Vietnamese (5)	5	0.04
Hawaii Native/Pacific Islander (2)	5	0.04
Not Hispanic (2)	5	0.04
Native Hawaiian (0)	1	0.01
Samoan (1)	1	0.01
White (11,570)	11,626	98.77
Not Hispanic (11,491)	11,541	98.05
Hispanic (79)	85	0.72

West Donegal

Place Type: Township
County: Lancaster
Population: 8,260†

Ancestry‡	Population	%
American (744)	744	9.33
Austrian (13)	55	0.69
British (11)	57	0.72
Dutch (62)	122	1.53
English (359)	913	11.45
European (35)	35	0.44
French, ex. Basque (62)	226	2.84
German (1,759)	3,296	41.35
Hungarian (23)	32	0.40
Irish (108)	730	9.16
Italian (264)	644	8.08
Lithuanian (0)	28	0.35
Norwegian (45)	95	1.19
Pennsylvania German (75)	89	1.12
Polish (79)	209	2.62
Russian (56)	83	1.04
Scotch-Irish (86)	157	1.97
Scottish (75)	174	2.18
Slovak (42)	56	0.70
Slovene (9)	9	0.11
Swedish (30)	43	0.54
Swiss (93)	438	5.49
Ukrainian (14)	14	0.18
Welsh (15)	70	0.88
West Indian, ex. Hispanic (29)	29	0.36
Haitian (29)	29	0.36

Hispanic Origin	Population	%
Hispanic or Latino (of any race)	122	1.48
Central American, ex. Mexican	3	0.04
Guatemalan	3	0.04
Cuban	12	0.15
Dominican Republic	3	0.04
Mexican	28	0.34
Puerto Rican	56	0.68
South American	8	0.10
Colombian	2	0.02
Ecuadorian	4	0.05
Uruguayan	2	0.02
Other Hispanic or Latino	12	0.15

Race*	Population	%
African-American/Black (57)	81	0.98
Not Hispanic (55)	74	0.90
Hispanic (2)	7	0.08
American Indian/Alaska Native (3)	19	0.23
Not Hispanic (3)	19	0.23
Cherokee (1)	3	0.04
Iroquois (1)	1	0.01
Sioux (1)	1	0.01
Asian (57)	75	0.91
Not Hispanic (57)	75	0.91
Bangladeshi (4)	5	0.06
Chinese, ex. Taiwanese (7)	10	0.12
Filipino (7)	13	0.16
Indian (11)	15	0.18
Japanese (2)	3	0.04
Korean (16)	19	0.23
Vietnamese (9)	9	0.11
Hawaii Native/Pacific Islander (0)	2	0.02
Not Hispanic (0)	2	0.02
White (8,052)	8,115	98.24
Not Hispanic (7,966)	8,015	97.03
Hispanic (86)	100	1.21

West Earl

Place Type: Township
County: Lancaster
Population: 7,868†

Ancestry‡	Population	%
American (683)	683	8.93
Arab (0)	58	0.76
Lebanese (0)	42	0.55
Syrian (0)	16	0.21
Austrian (0)	13	0.17
Czech (44)	121	1.58
Dutch (51)	119	1.56
English (140)	392	5.12
Estonian (12)	12	0.16
European (167)	167	2.18
French, ex. Basque (26)	38	0.50
French Canadian (0)	12	0.16
German (1,977)	3,208	41.92
Greek (0)	10	0.13
Hungarian (0)	10	0.13
Irish (177)	834	10.90
Italian (138)	347	4.53
Pennsylvania German (616)	628	8.21
Polish (15)	134	1.75
Russian (16)	16	0.21
Scotch-Irish (47)	83	1.08
Scottish (28)	40	0.52
Slovak (14)	14	0.18
Swedish (174)	207	2.71
Swiss (185)	535	6.99
Welsh (10)	75	0.98

Hispanic Origin	Population	%
Hispanic or Latino (of any race)	232	2.95
Central American, ex. Mexican	14	0.18
Guatemalan	9	0.11
Honduran	3	0.04
Salvadoran	2	0.03
Cuban	12	0.15
Dominican Republic	6	0.08
Mexican	33	0.42
Puerto Rican	110	1.40
South American	37	0.47
Argentinean	2	0.03
Bolivian	3	0.04
Colombian	24	0.31
Ecuadorian	3	0.04
Peruvian	5	0.06
Other Hispanic or Latino	20	0.25

Race*	Population	%
African-American/Black (61)	98	1.25
Not Hispanic (56)	89	1.13
Hispanic (5)	9	0.11
American Indian/Alaska Native (8)	28	0.36
Not Hispanic (4)	22	0.28
Hispanic (4)	6	0.08
Central American Ind. (2)	2	0.03
Cherokee (1)	1	0.01
Cree (0)	2	0.03
Iroquois (0)	1	0.01
Navajo (1)	1	0.01
Sioux (1)	1	0.01
South American Ind. (0)	2	0.03
Asian (176)	191	2.43
Not Hispanic (175)	188	2.39
Hispanic (1)	3	0.04
Cambodian (8)	8	0.10
Chinese, ex. Taiwanese (18)	26	0.33
Filipino (3)	4	0.05
Hmong (55)	55	0.70
Indian (13)	15	0.19
Japanese (1)	2	0.03
Korean (4)	5	0.06
Laotian (25)	26	0.33
Malaysian (0)	5	0.06
Pakistani (0)	1	0.01
Vietnamese (41)	46	0.58
Hawaii Native/Pacific Islander (3)	5	0.06
Not Hispanic (3)	4	0.05
Hispanic (0)	1	0.01
Guamanian/Chamorro (3)	4	0.05
Native Hawaiian (0)	1	0.01
White (7,487)	7,550	95.96
Not Hispanic (7,334)	7,381	93.81
Hispanic (153)	169	2.15

West Goshen

Place Type: Township
County: Chester
Population: 21,866†

Ancestry‡	Population	%
African, Sub-Saharan (102)	102	0.47
African (8)	8	0.04
Nigerian (94)	94	0.43
Albanian (12)	35	0.16
American (974)	974	4.47
Arab (15)	35	0.16
Egyptian (15)	15	0.07
Lebanese (0)	20	0.09
Armenian (0)	23	0.11
Austrian (11)	68	0.31
British (37)	152	0.70
Canadian (50)	124	0.57
Croatian (14)	28	0.13
Czech (11)	83	0.38
Czechoslovakian (0)	10	0.05
Danish (0)	23	0.11
Dutch (107)	301	1.38
Eastern European (40)	40	0.18
English (680)	3,549	16.30
European (241)	241	1.11
French, ex. Basque (23)	351	1.61
French Canadian (39)	39	0.18
German (1,023)	5,239	24.06
Greek (142)	277	1.27
Hungarian (17)	118	0.54
Icelander (0)	37	0.17
Irish (2,228)	6,394	29.37
Italian (1,790)	4,155	19.08
Latvian (0)	12	0.06
Lithuanian (27)	166	0.76
Northern European (43)	43	0.20
Norwegian (47)	182	0.84
Pennsylvania German (45)	97	0.45
Polish (157)	979	4.50
Romanian (0)	11	0.05
Russian (43)	316	1.45
Scandinavian (12)	24	0.11
Scotch-Irish (139)	487	2.24
Scottish (74)	514	2.36
Slavic (6)	22	0.10
Slovak (24)	97	0.45
Slovene (0)	8	0.04
Swedish (24)	186	0.85
Swiss (55)	104	0.48
Ukrainian (93)	250	1.15
Welsh (19)	296	1.36
West Indian, ex. Hispanic (17)	82	0.38
Jamaican (17)	82	0.38
Yugoslavian (58)	76	0.35

Hispanic Origin	Population	%
Hispanic or Latino (of any race)	814	3.72
Central American, ex. Mexican	35	0.16
Costa Rican	2	0.01
Guatemalan	18	0.08
Honduran	3	0.01
Panamanian	4	0.02
Salvadoran	8	0.04
Cuban	35	0.16
Dominican Republic	8	0.04

*Notes: † The Census 2010 population figure is used to calculate the percentages in the Hispanic Origin and Race categories. Ancestry percentages are based on the 2006-2010 American Community Survey population (not shown); ‡ Numbers in parentheses indicate the number of people reporting a single ancestry; * Numbers in parentheses indicate the number of persons reporting this race alone, not in combination with any other race; Please refer to the Explanation of Data for more information.*

Mexican	327	1.50
Puerto Rican	223	1.02
South American	122	0.56
Argentinean	9	0.04
Bolivian	5	0.02
Chilean	5	0.02
Colombian	45	0.21
Ecuadorian	19	0.09
Paraguayan	1	<0.01
Peruvian	21	0.10
Uruguayan	1	<0.01
Venezuelan	16	0.07
Other Hispanic or Latino	64	0.29

Race*	Population	%
African-American/Black (818)	945	4.32
Not Hispanic (800)	914	4.18
Hispanic (18)	31	0.14
American Indian/Alaska Native (43)	105	0.48
Not Hispanic (26)	85	0.39
Hispanic (17)	20	0.09
Blackfeet (1)	2	0.01
Cherokee (4)	22	0.10
Chippewa (0)	1	<0.01
Choctaw (0)	1	<0.01
Cree (0)	1	<0.01
Delaware (0)	6	0.03
Iroquois (2)	4	0.02
Mexican American Ind. (1)	1	<0.01
Navajo (1)	1	<0.01
Pima (1)	1	<0.01
Seminole (0)	2	0.01
South American Ind. (0)	2	0.01
Spanish American Ind. (7)	7	0.03
Asian (1,031)	1,154	5.28
Not Hispanic (1,022)	1,142	5.22
Hispanic (9)	12	0.05
Bangladeshi (0)	2	0.01
Burmese (6)	6	0.03
Cambodian (11)	19	0.09
Chinese, ex. Taiwanese (205)	219	1.00
Filipino (38)	63	0.29
Indian (502)	523	2.39
Japanese (18)	42	0.19
Korean (66)	82	0.38
Laotian (3)	5	0.02
Malaysian (4)	8	0.04
Pakistani (25)	25	0.11
Taiwanese (18)	21	0.10
Thai (13)	18	0.08
Vietnamese (94)	100	0.46
Hawaii Native/Pacific Islander (6)	17	0.08
Not Hispanic (4)	15	0.07
Hispanic (2)	2	0.01
Guamanian/Chamorro (1)	1	<0.01
Native Hawaiian (0)	5	0.02
Samoan (2)	5	0.02
White (19,419)	19,686	90.03
Not Hispanic (18,899)	19,147	87.57
Hispanic (520)	539	2.47

West Hanover

Place Type: Township
County: Dauphin
Population: 9,343†

Ancestry‡	Population	%
American (624)	624	7.07
Arab (16)	16	0.18
Lebanese (16)	16	0.18
Austrian (41)	41	0.46
British (27)	64	0.73
Canadian (8)	30	0.34
Croatian (98)	139	1.58
Czechoslovakian (11)	24	0.27
Danish (0)	8	0.09
Dutch (40)	209	2.37
English (114)	819	9.28
European (55)	71	0.80
French, ex. Basque (48)	207	2.35
German (1,472)	3,306	37.47
Greek (70)	113	1.28
Hungarian (64)	123	1.39
Irish (345)	1,100	12.47
Italian (183)	1,070	12.13
Lithuanian (68)	121	1.37
Norwegian (11)	32	0.36
Pennsylvania German (123)	167	1.89
Polish (154)	397	4.50
Portuguese (28)	28	0.32
Romanian (0)	12	0.14
Russian (12)	115	1.30
Scotch-Irish (118)	371	4.20
Scottish (42)	62	0.70
Serbian (14)	64	0.73
Slavic (12)	12	0.14
Slovak (30)	102	1.16
Slovene (24)	40	0.45
Swedish (0)	53	0.60
Swiss (0)	34	0.39
Ukrainian (17)	29	0.33
Welsh (31)	122	1.38

Hispanic Origin	Population	%
Hispanic or Latino (of any race)	218	2.33
Central American, ex. Mexican	11	0.12
Guatemalan	3	0.03
Panamanian	1	0.01
Salvadoran	7	0.07
Cuban	6	0.06
Dominican Republic	8	0.09
Mexican	49	0.52
Puerto Rican	106	1.13
South American	30	0.32
Chilean	1	0.01
Colombian	13	0.14
Ecuadorian	7	0.07
Paraguayan	1	0.01
Peruvian	6	0.06
Venezuelan	2	0.02
Other Hispanic or Latino	8	0.09

Race*	Population	%
African-American/Black (305)	376	4.02
Not Hispanic (290)	358	3.83
Hispanic (15)	18	0.19
American Indian/Alaska Native (17)	37	0.40
Not Hispanic (12)	32	0.34
Hispanic (5)	5	0.05
Canadian/French Am. Ind. (2)	2	0.02
Cherokee (1)	4	0.04
Iroquois (1)	1	0.01
Kiowa (4)	4	0.04
Puget Sound Salish (0)	1	0.01
Sioux (0)	2	0.02
Asian (186)	212	2.27
Not Hispanic (186)	210	2.25
Hispanic (0)	2	0.02
Cambodian (3)	4	0.04
Chinese, ex. Taiwanese (20)	21	0.22
Filipino (10)	14	0.15
Indian (115)	117	1.25
Indonesian (1)	3	0.03
Japanese (4)	9	0.10
Korean (5)	6	0.06
Laotian (1)	1	0.01
Pakistani (1)	1	0.01
Sri Lankan (0)	1	0.01
Thai (1)	2	0.02
Vietnamese (19)	23	0.25
Hawaii Native/Pacific Islander (1)	3	0.03
Not Hispanic (1)	3	0.03
Guamanian/Chamorro (1)	1	0.01
Samoan (0)	2	0.02
White (8,646)	8,775	93.92
Not Hispanic (8,519)	8,631	92.38
Hispanic (127)	144	1.54

West Hempfield

Place Type: Township
County: Lancaster
Population: 16,153†

Ancestry‡	Population	%
African, Sub-Saharan (53)	119	0.74
African (0)	66	0.41
Ethiopian (53)	53	0.33
Albanian (0)	14	0.09
American (1,030)	1,030	6.43
Arab (14)	23	0.14
Lebanese (14)	23	0.14
Armenian (27)	27	0.17
Australian (12)	65	0.41
Austrian (44)	59	0.37
Belgian (0)	13	0.08
British (19)	60	0.37
Celtic (22)	22	0.14
Croatian (10)	36	0.22
Czech (0)	14	0.09
Czechoslovakian (7)	22	0.14
Dutch (26)	258	1.61
English (390)	1,512	9.44
European (113)	113	0.71
Finnish (0)	13	0.08
French, ex. Basque (61)	260	1.62
French Canadian (7)	31	0.19
German (4,010)	6,973	43.54
Greek (27)	106	0.66
Icelander (0)	11	0.07
Irish (414)	2,291	14.30
Italian (227)	966	6.03
Lithuanian (0)	25	0.16
Norwegian (39)	81	0.51
Pennsylvania German (0)	36	0.22
Polish (121)	327	2.04
Russian (22)	68	0.42
Scotch-Irish (100)	212	1.32
Scottish (13)	220	1.37
Slovak (12)	51	0.32
Swedish (0)	101	0.63
Swiss (141)	492	3.07
Ukrainian (51)	51	0.32
Welsh (24)	161	1.01
West Indian, ex. Hispanic (45)	135	0.84
Haitian (12)	57	0.36
Jamaican (33)	78	0.49

Hispanic Origin	Population	%
Hispanic or Latino (of any race)	1,100	6.81
Central American, ex. Mexican	20	0.12
Costa Rican	2	0.01
Guatemalan	8	0.05
Honduran	2	0.01
Panamanian	2	0.01
Salvadoran	6	0.04
Cuban	23	0.14
Dominican Republic	157	0.97
Mexican	72	0.45
Puerto Rican	702	4.35
South American	53	0.33
Chilean	2	0.01
Colombian	26	0.16
Ecuadorian	10	0.06
Paraguayan	1	0.01
Peruvian	10	0.06
Other South American	4	0.02
Other Hispanic or Latino	73	0.45

Race*	Population	%
African-American/Black (445)	581	3.60
Not Hispanic (395)	505	3.13
Hispanic (50)	76	0.47
American Indian/Alaska Native (32)	72	0.45
Not Hispanic (25)	58	0.36
Hispanic (7)	14	0.09
Apache (1)	1	0.01
Blackfeet (0)	4	0.02

*Notes: † The Census 2010 population figure is used to calculate the percentages in the Hispanic Origin and Race categories. Ancestry percentages are based on the 2006-2010 American Community Survey population (not shown); ‡ Numbers in parentheses indicate the number of people reporting a single ancestry; * Numbers in parentheses indicate the number of persons reporting this race alone, not in combination with any other race; Please refer to the Explanation of Data for more information.*

Cherokee (8)	18	0.11
Chickasaw (0)	1	0.01
Chippewa (1)	1	0.01
Choctaw (0)	2	0.01
Iroquois (7)	7	0.04
Lumbee (2)	2	0.01
Mexican American Ind. (1)	1	0.01
Navajo (0)	4	0.02
Osage (1)	1	0.01
Sioux (1)	1	0.01
South American Ind. (0)	1	0.01
Asian (333)	405	2.51
Not Hispanic (328)	393	2.43
Hispanic (5)	12	0.07
Burmese (0)	1	0.01
Cambodian (33)	40	0.25
Chinese, ex. Taiwanese (71)	84	0.52
Filipino (21)	39	0.24
Hmong (1)	3	0.02
Indian (44)	50	0.31
Indonesian (1)	1	0.01
Japanese (5)	14	0.09
Korean (33)	43	0.27
Laotian (4)	5	0.03
Sri Lankan (1)	2	0.01
Taiwanese (2)	2	0.01
Thai (4)	5	0.03
Vietnamese (101)	109	0.67
Hawaii Native/Pacific Islander (2)	11	0.07
Not Hispanic (2)	7	0.04
Hispanic (0)	4	0.02
Native Hawaiian (1)	4	0.02
White (14,716)	14,963	92.63
Not Hispanic (14,087)	14,267	88.32
Hispanic (629)	696	4.31

West Lampeter

Place Type: Township
County: Lancaster
Population: 15,209†

Ancestry‡	Population	%
American (1,406)	1,406	9.48
Arab (0)	18	0.12
Lebanese (0)	18	0.12
Armenian (38)	38	0.26
Austrian (0)	35	0.24
British (105)	135	0.91
Canadian (8)	23	0.15
Croatian (0)	37	0.25
Czech (38)	55	0.37
Czechoslovakian (0)	19	0.13
Danish (23)	23	0.15
Dutch (30)	191	1.29
Eastern European (17)	17	0.11
English (662)	1,910	12.87
European (325)	366	2.47
Finnish (0)	10	0.07
French, ex. Basque (24)	200	1.35
French Canadian (13)	13	0.09
German (2,943)	6,415	43.23
Greek (14)	14	0.09
Hungarian (13)	60	0.40
Irish (502)	2,101	14.16
Italian (427)	1,422	9.58
Latvian (0)	19	0.13
Lithuanian (0)	34	0.23
Norwegian (22)	110	0.74
Pennsylvania German (91)	103	0.69
Polish (126)	669	4.51
Portuguese (0)	19	0.13
Russian (0)	32	0.22
Scotch-Irish (195)	450	3.03
Scottish (46)	393	2.65
Slavic (0)	10	0.07
Slovak (15)	29	0.20
Swedish (63)	272	1.83
Swiss (165)	647	4.36
Ukrainian (33)	53	0.36
Welsh (15)	82	0.55

Hispanic Origin	Population	%
Hispanic or Latino (of any race)	473	3.11
Central American, ex. Mexican	25	0.16
Guatemalan	6	0.04
Honduran	7	0.05
Nicaraguan	1	0.01
Panamanian	2	0.01
Salvadoran	9	0.06
Cuban	15	0.10
Dominican Republic	6	0.04
Mexican	19	0.12
Puerto Rican	346	2.27
South American	40	0.26
Argentinean	1	0.01
Chilean	1	0.01
Colombian	21	0.14
Ecuadorian	10	0.07
Peruvian	6	0.04
Other South American	1	0.01
Other Hispanic or Latino	22	0.14

Race*	Population	%
African-American/Black (144)	225	1.48
Not Hispanic (126)	190	1.25
Hispanic (18)	35	0.23
American Indian/Alaska Native (12)	52	0.34
Not Hispanic (10)	45	0.30
Hispanic (2)	7	0.05
Blackfeet (0)	1	0.01
Canadian/French Am. Ind. (0)	4	0.03
Cherokee (0)	13	0.09
Choctaw (1)	1	0.01
Iroquois (0)	3	0.02
Mexican American Ind. (1)	1	0.01
Navajo (1)	1	0.01
Sioux (0)	2	0.01
Asian (220)	263	1.73
Not Hispanic (217)	255	1.68
Hispanic (3)	8	0.05
Cambodian (9)	10	0.07
Chinese, ex. Taiwanese (57)	65	0.43
Filipino (35)	42	0.28
Hmong (8)	10	0.07
Indian (43)	52	0.34
Japanese (13)	19	0.12
Korean (21)	26	0.17
Laotian (2)	2	0.01
Nepalese (3)	3	0.02
Pakistani (2)	2	0.01
Taiwanese (1)	3	0.02
Thai (1)	1	0.01
Vietnamese (17)	21	0.14
Hawaii Native/Pacific Islander (4)	7	0.05
Not Hispanic (4)	7	0.05
Native Hawaiian (1)	3	0.02
Samoan (3)	3	0.02
White (14,502)	14,670	96.46
Not Hispanic (14,248)	14,368	94.47
Hispanic (254)	302	1.99

West Manchester

Place Type: Township
County: York
Population: 18,894†

Ancestry‡	Population	%
African, Sub-Saharan (345)	345	1.85
African (84)	84	0.45
Kenyan (14)	14	0.07
Nigerian (150)	150	0.80
Other Sub-Saharan African (97)	97	0.52
American (2,136)	2,136	11.44
Austrian (0)	20	0.11
British (36)	78	0.42
Canadian (9)	9	0.05
Croatian (8)	36	0.19
Czech (0)	47	0.25
Dutch (170)	343	1.84
English (506)	1,343	7.19
European (91)	91	0.49
Finnish (12)	12	0.06
French, ex. Basque (73)	353	1.89
French Canadian (23)	137	0.73
German (5,035)	8,052	43.13
Greek (162)	201	1.08
Hungarian (42)	124	0.66
Iranian (0)	9	0.05
Irish (703)	2,363	12.66
Italian (422)	1,002	5.37
Lithuanian (24)	44	0.24
Northern European (31)	31	0.17
Norwegian (45)	69	0.37
Pennsylvania German (159)	194	1.04
Polish (170)	365	1.96
Romanian (16)	16	0.09
Russian (43)	120	0.64
Scandinavian (0)	10	0.05
Scotch-Irish (140)	341	1.83
Scottish (41)	208	1.11
Serbian (7)	7	0.04
Slavic (0)	13	0.07
Slovak (60)	125	0.67
Swedish (16)	86	0.46
Swiss (14)	69	0.37
Ukrainian (15)	72	0.39
Welsh (18)	134	0.72
West Indian, ex. Hispanic (0)	16	0.09
Belizean (0)	16	0.09
Yugoslavian (17)	17	0.09

Hispanic Origin	Population	%
Hispanic or Latino (of any race)	559	2.96
Central American, ex. Mexican	40	0.21
Costa Rican	3	0.02
Guatemalan	4	0.02
Honduran	2	0.01
Nicaraguan	1	0.01
Panamanian	10	0.05
Salvadoran	20	0.11
Cuban	16	0.08
Dominican Republic	32	0.17
Mexican	93	0.49
Puerto Rican	300	1.59
South American	26	0.14
Argentinean	2	0.01
Bolivian	6	0.03
Chilean	1	0.01
Colombian	3	0.02
Ecuadorian	3	0.02
Peruvian	11	0.06
Other Hispanic or Latino	52	0.28

Race*	Population	%
African-American/Black (920)	1,153	6.10
Not Hispanic (888)	1,090	5.77
Hispanic (32)	63	0.33
American Indian/Alaska Native (20)	73	0.39
Not Hispanic (18)	64	0.34
Hispanic (2)	9	0.05
Apache (0)	1	0.01
Blackfeet (1)	7	0.04
Canadian/French Am. Ind. (2)	2	0.01
Cherokee (2)	22	0.12
Iroquois (3)	3	0.02
Pueblo (0)	3	0.02
Sioux (0)	3	0.02
South American Ind. (1)	1	0.01
Tohono O'Odham (0)	1	0.01
Yaqui (1)	1	0.01
Asian (232)	301	1.59
Not Hispanic (232)	290	1.53
Hispanic (0)	11	0.06
Cambodian (16)	18	0.10
Chinese, ex. Taiwanese (41)	59	0.31
Filipino (37)	51	0.27
Indian (63)	73	0.39
Indonesian (0)	2	0.01

*Notes: † The Census 2010 population figure is used to calculate the percentages in the Hispanic Origin and Race categories. Ancestry percentages are based on the 2006-2010 American Community Survey population (not shown); ‡ Numbers in parentheses indicate the number of people reporting a single ancestry; * Numbers in parentheses indicate the number of persons reporting this race alone, not in combination with any other race; Please refer to the Explanation of Data for more information.*

	Population	%
Japanese (7)	21	0.11
Korean (16)	25	0.13
Laotian (2)	2	0.01
Pakistani (0)	1	0.01
Sri Lankan (3)	3	0.02
Thai (1)	4	0.02
Vietnamese (40)	45	0.24
Hawaii Native/Pacific Islander (10)	31	0.16
Not Hispanic (10)	27	0.14
Hispanic (0)	4	0.02
Fijian (1)	1	0.01
Guamanian/Chamorro (1)	1	0.01
Native Hawaiian (1)	7	0.04
Samoan (3)	8	0.04
White (17,193)	17,522	92.74
Not Hispanic (16,896)	17,162	90.83
Hispanic (297)	360	1.91

West Manheim

Place Type: Township
County: York
Population: 7,744†

Ancestry‡	Population	%
American (966)	966	13.28
Arab (12)	46	0.63
Lebanese (12)	36	0.49
Other Arab (0)	10	0.14
Austrian (0)	64	0.88
British (33)	43	0.59
Canadian (7)	7	0.10
Czechoslovakian (7)	7	0.10
Dutch (26)	78	1.07
English (333)	751	10.32
European (120)	130	1.79
French, ex. Basque (81)	326	4.48
German (1,439)	2,972	40.85
Greek (0)	12	0.16
Hungarian (0)	22	0.30
Irish (198)	1,133	15.57
Italian (62)	379	5.21
Lithuanian (34)	34	0.47
Pennsylvania German (60)	60	0.82
Polish (116)	363	4.99
Russian (19)	49	0.67
Scandinavian (14)	14	0.19
Scotch-Irish (0)	55	0.76
Scottish (0)	53	0.73
Ukrainian (71)	71	0.98
Welsh (11)	110	1.51

Hispanic Origin	Population	%
Hispanic or Latino (of any race)	125	1.61
Central American, ex. Mexican	14	0.18
Guatemalan	3	0.04
Honduran	1	0.01
Salvadoran	9	0.12
Other Central American	1	0.01
Dominican Republic	11	0.14
Mexican	35	0.45
Puerto Rican	40	0.52
South American	15	0.19
Argentinean	7	0.09
Colombian	2	0.03
Ecuadorian	2	0.03
Peruvian	4	0.05
Other Hispanic or Latino	10	0.13

Race*	Population	%
African-American/Black (302)	357	4.61
Not Hispanic (297)	348	4.49
Hispanic (5)	9	0.12
American Indian/Alaska Native (10)	24	0.31
Not Hispanic (9)	17	0.22
Hispanic (1)	7	0.09
Apache (0)	1	0.01
Cherokee (3)	9	0.12
Lumbee (1)	1	0.01
Mexican American Ind. (1)	2	0.03
Asian (93)	124	1.60
Not Hispanic (92)	120	1.55
Hispanic (1)	4	0.05
Chinese, ex. Taiwanese (12)	15	0.19
Filipino (21)	31	0.40
Indian (15)	19	0.25
Japanese (5)	9	0.12
Korean (15)	19	0.25
Pakistani (14)	14	0.18
Taiwanese (2)	5	0.06
Vietnamese (9)	9	0.12
Hawaii Native/Pacific Islander (1)	5	0.06
Not Hispanic (1)	5	0.06
Native Hawaiian (1)	1	0.01
White (7,193)	7,282	94.03
Not Hispanic (7,126)	7,204	93.03
Hispanic (67)	78	1.01

West Mifflin

Place Type: Borough
County: Allegheny
Population: 20,313†

Ancestry‡	Population	%
African, Sub-Saharan (204)	240	1.17
African (204)	240	1.17
American (1,386)	1,386	6.76
Arab (10)	168	0.82
Arab (0)	17	0.08
Lebanese (10)	10	0.05
Syrian (0)	141	0.69
Australian (4)	4	0.02
Austrian (33)	49	0.24
Belgian (9)	21	0.10
Bulgarian (0)	9	0.04
Carpatho Rusyn (0)	19	0.09
Croatian (183)	482	2.35
Czech (76)	301	1.47
Czechoslovakian (40)	66	0.32
Dutch (0)	73	0.36
Eastern European (63)	63	0.31
English (313)	1,712	8.35
French, ex. Basque (16)	262	1.28
German (1,245)	5,404	26.36
Greek (47)	117	0.57
Guyanese (0)	12	0.06
Hungarian (302)	952	4.64
Irish (1,099)	4,384	21.39
Italian (780)	2,733	13.33
Lithuanian (35)	143	0.70
Pennsylvania German (0)	35	0.17
Polish (640)	2,178	10.63
Russian (75)	373	1.82
Scotch-Irish (53)	233	1.14
Scottish (18)	240	1.17
Serbian (91)	174	0.85
Slavic (61)	104	0.51
Slovak (1,102)	2,921	14.25
Slovene (14)	45	0.22
Swedish (8)	268	1.31
Swiss (0)	51	0.25
Ukrainian (21)	64	0.31
Welsh (12)	451	2.20
Yugoslavian (0)	14	0.07

Hispanic Origin	Population	%
Hispanic or Latino (of any race)	251	1.24
Central American, ex. Mexican	8	0.04
Guatemalan	7	0.03
Honduran	1	<0.01
Cuban	3	0.01
Dominican Republic	6	0.03
Mexican	140	0.69
Puerto Rican	44	0.22
South American	8	0.04
Bolivian	1	<0.01
Colombian	3	0.01
Peruvian	4	0.02
Other Hispanic or Latino	42	0.21

Race*	Population	%
African-American/Black (2,230)	2,502	12.32
Not Hispanic (2,198)	2,453	12.08
Hispanic (32)	49	0.24
American Indian/Alaska Native (14)	110	0.54
Not Hispanic (14)	102	0.50
Hispanic (0)	8	0.04
Apache (0)	2	0.01
Blackfeet (0)	8	0.04
Cherokee (3)	32	0.16
Chippewa (0)	3	0.01
Creek (0)	2	0.01
Iroquois (1)	4	0.02
Kiowa (0)	2	0.01
Mexican American Ind. (0)	2	0.01
Navajo (0)	1	<0.01
Sioux (2)	5	0.02
Asian (78)	118	0.58
Not Hispanic (77)	116	0.57
Hispanic (1)	2	0.01
Chinese, ex. Taiwanese (13)	15	0.07
Filipino (6)	15	0.07
Indian (12)	20	0.10
Indonesian (7)	8	0.04
Japanese (2)	7	0.03
Korean (4)	12	0.06
Sri Lankan (3)	3	0.01
Vietnamese (26)	35	0.17
Hawaii Native/Pacific Islander (0)	1	<0.01
Not Hispanic (0)	1	<0.01
White (17,580)	17,893	88.09
Not Hispanic (17,410)	17,706	87.17
Hispanic (170)	187	0.92

West Norriton

Place Type: Township
County: Montgomery
Population: 15,663†

Ancestry‡	Population	%
African, Sub-Saharan (80)	80	0.52
African (80)	80	0.52
Albanian (0)	12	0.08
American (461)	461	2.97
Arab (19)	19	0.12
Iraqi (10)	10	0.06
Lebanese (9)	9	0.06
Armenian (25)	43	0.28
Australian (13)	13	0.08
Austrian (26)	103	0.66
Belgian (0)	18	0.12
British (41)	117	0.75
Canadian (30)	40	0.26
Celtic (18)	18	0.12
Croatian (17)	29	0.19
Czech (0)	84	0.54
Czechoslovakian (20)	31	0.20
Dutch (17)	131	0.84
Eastern European (32)	42	0.27
English (235)	1,268	8.18
European (21)	21	0.14
Finnish (0)	10	0.06
French, ex. Basque (28)	211	1.36
French Canadian (20)	20	0.13
German (752)	3,573	23.05
Greek (0)	20	0.13
Hungarian (34)	214	1.38
Irish (1,302)	4,184	26.99
Italian (2,416)	4,264	27.50
Lithuanian (11)	24	0.15
Northern European (18)	18	0.12
Norwegian (11)	48	0.31
Pennsylvania German (35)	122	0.79
Polish (582)	1,303	8.40
Portuguese (11)	66	0.43
Russian (121)	351	2.26
Scotch-Irish (124)	193	1.24
Scottish (54)	258	1.66

SECTION TWO

*Notes: † The Census 2010 population figure is used to calculate the percentages in the Hispanic Origin and Race categories. Ancestry percentages are based on the 2006-2010 American Community Survey population (not shown); ‡ Numbers in parentheses indicate the number of people reporting a single ancestry; * Numbers in parentheses indicate the number of persons reporting this race alone, not in combination with any other race; Please refer to the Explanation of Data for more information.*

Slovak (39)	141	0.91
Slovene (16)	46	0.30
Swedish (41)	102	0.66
Swiss (0)	47	0.30
Ukrainian (48)	105	0.68
Welsh (11)	135	0.87
West Indian, ex. Hispanic (31)	48	0.31
Jamaican (14)	31	0.20
Trinidadian/Tobagonian (17)	17	0.11

Hispanic Origin	Population	%
Hispanic or Latino (of any race)	492	3.14
Central American, ex. Mexican	44	0.28
Costa Rican	8	0.05
Guatemalan	13	0.08
Honduran	6	0.04
Nicaraguan	3	0.02
Panamanian	2	0.01
Salvadoran	12	0.08
Cuban	23	0.15
Dominican Republic	11	0.07
Mexican	183	1.17
Puerto Rican	132	0.84
South American	61	0.39
Argentinean	12	0.08
Bolivian	1	0.01
Chilean	1	0.01
Colombian	23	0.15
Ecuadorian	7	0.04
Peruvian	11	0.07
Uruguayan	1	0.01
Venezuelan	5	0.03
Other Hispanic or Latino	38	0.24

Race*	Population	%
African-American/Black (1,409)	1,560	9.96
Not Hispanic (1,385)	1,521	9.71
Hispanic (24)	39	0.25
American Indian/Alaska Native (11)	57	0.36
Not Hispanic (10)	48	0.31
Hispanic (1)	9	0.06
Blackfeet (1)	9	0.06
Cherokee (1)	3	0.02
Chippewa (1)	2	0.01
Delaware (0)	1	0.01
Lumbee (2)	2	0.01
Mexican American Ind. (1)	1	0.01
Asian (817)	896	5.72
Not Hispanic (811)	885	5.65
Hispanic (6)	11	0.07
Bangladeshi (2)	2	0.01
Burmese (1)	1	0.01
Cambodian (8)	10	0.06
Chinese, ex. Taiwanese (114)	129	0.82
Filipino (46)	64	0.41
Indian (431)	444	2.83
Indonesian (2)	2	0.01
Japanese (3)	7	0.04
Korean (98)	109	0.70
Laotian (7)	7	0.04
Nepalese (1)	1	0.01
Pakistani (22)	22	0.14
Sri Lankan (5)	5	0.03
Taiwanese (5)	8	0.05
Thai (3)	4	0.03
Vietnamese (56)	59	0.38
Hawaii Native/Pacific Islander (11)	19	0.12
Not Hispanic (10)	15	0.10
Hispanic (1)	4	0.03
Guamanian/Chamorro (1)	1	0.01
Native Hawaiian (1)	1	0.01
Tongan (8)	9	0.06
White (13,001)	13,242	84.54
Not Hispanic (12,697)	12,902	82.37
Hispanic (304)	340	2.17

West Whiteland

Place Type: Township
County: Chester
Population: 18,274†

Ancestry‡	Population	%
African, Sub-Saharan (25)	25	0.14
Cape Verdean (10)	10	0.06
South African (15)	15	0.08
Albanian (58)	58	0.32
American (257)	257	1.42
Arab (0)	52	0.29
Lebanese (0)	52	0.29
Austrian (14)	206	1.14
Brazilian (23)	35	0.19
British (105)	185	1.02
Canadian (29)	37	0.20
Croatian (0)	7	0.04
Czech (0)	69	0.38
Danish (6)	18	0.10
Dutch (59)	424	2.35
Eastern European (24)	24	0.13
English (705)	2,364	13.08
European (140)	140	0.77
Finnish (0)	10	0.06
French, ex. Basque (52)	394	2.18
German (1,139)	4,613	25.52
Greek (68)	157	0.87
Hungarian (68)	138	0.76
Iranian (67)	67	0.37
Irish (1,283)	4,386	24.27
Italian (1,244)	3,345	18.51
Lithuanian (56)	183	1.01
Maltese (12)	12	0.07
Northern European (24)	24	0.13
Norwegian (9)	100	0.55
Pennsylvania German (39)	86	0.48
Polish (288)	934	5.17
Portuguese (44)	55	0.30
Romanian (39)	131	0.72
Russian (101)	306	1.69
Scandinavian (33)	33	0.18
Scotch-Irish (23)	154	0.85
Scottish (108)	403	2.23
Slovak (29)	173	0.96
Swedish (8)	413	2.29
Swiss (15)	98	0.54
Ukrainian (82)	156	0.86
Welsh (57)	267	1.48
West Indian, ex. Hispanic (51)	51	0.28
Bermudan (42)	42	0.23
Jamaican (9)	9	0.05
Yugoslavian (0)	12	0.07

Hispanic Origin	Population	%
Hispanic or Latino (of any race)	541	2.96
Central American, ex. Mexican	24	0.13
Costa Rican	7	0.04
Guatemalan	10	0.05
Panamanian	6	0.03
Salvadoran	1	0.01
Cuban	25	0.14
Dominican Republic	12	0.07
Mexican	151	0.83
Puerto Rican	196	1.07
South American	103	0.56
Argentinean	11	0.06
Bolivian	6	0.03
Chilean	12	0.07
Colombian	36	0.20
Ecuadorian	6	0.03
Paraguayan	2	0.01
Peruvian	7	0.04
Venezuelan	23	0.13
Other Hispanic or Latino	30	0.16

Race*	Population	%
African-American/Black (924)	1,098	6.01
Not Hispanic (896)	1,049	5.74
Hispanic (28)	49	0.27
American Indian/Alaska Native (32)	102	0.56
Not Hispanic (26)	91	0.50
Hispanic (6)	11	0.06
Apache (0)	1	0.01
Blackfeet (1)	3	0.02
Cherokee (4)	32	0.18
Chippewa (1)	2	0.01
Delaware (1)	3	0.02
Iroquois (0)	1	0.01
Lumbee (0)	3	0.02
Mexican American Ind. (1)	1	0.01
Seminole (0)	1	0.01
Sioux (0)	1	0.01
South American Ind. (3)	3	0.02
Yaqui (1)	1	0.01
Asian (2,081)	2,222	12.16
Not Hispanic (2,075)	2,209	12.09
Hispanic (6)	13	0.07
Bangladeshi (14)	14	0.08
Burmese (1)	1	0.01
Cambodian (7)	7	0.04
Chinese, ex. Taiwanese (406)	444	2.43
Filipino (98)	138	0.76
Indian (1,225)	1,250	6.84
Indonesian (4)	9	0.05
Japanese (9)	23	0.13
Korean (103)	122	0.67
Laotian (4)	6	0.03
Malaysian (4)	5	0.03
Nepalese (8)	8	0.04
Pakistani (36)	36	0.20
Sri Lankan (23)	25	0.14
Taiwanese (13)	14	0.08
Thai (9)	19	0.10
Vietnamese (64)	83	0.45
Hawaii Native/Pacific Islander (4)	26	0.14
Not Hispanic (3)	24	0.13
Hispanic (1)	2	0.01
Guamanian/Chamorro (0)	1	0.01
Native Hawaiian (1)	8	0.04
Tongan (3)	4	0.02
White (14,710)	15,026	82.23
Not Hispanic (14,393)	14,669	80.27
Hispanic (317)	357	1.95

Westtown

Place Type: Township
County: Chester
Population: 10,827†

Ancestry‡	Population	%
African, Sub-Saharan (7)	7	0.06
African (7)	7	0.06
Albanian (43)	75	0.69
American (602)	602	5.57
Arab (16)	16	0.15
Lebanese (16)	16	0.15
Armenian (44)	63	0.58
Austrian (15)	79	0.73
British (9)	9	0.08
Canadian (19)	37	0.34
Czechoslovakian (19)	19	0.18
Danish (13)	84	0.78
Dutch (21)	77	0.71
Eastern European (66)	66	0.61
English (304)	1,643	15.20
Estonian (0)	11	0.10
European (151)	166	1.54
Finnish (9)	34	0.31
French, ex. Basque (4)	216	2.00
French Canadian (12)	144	1.33
German (523)	2,380	22.01
Greek (101)	156	1.44
Hungarian (96)	120	1.11
Irish (1,237)	3,812	35.26
Italian (841)	2,347	21.71
Lithuanian (11)	21	0.19
Norwegian (6)	25	0.23

*Notes: † The Census 2010 population figure is used to calculate the percentages in the Hispanic Origin and Race categories. Ancestry percentages are based on the 2006-2010 American Community Survey population (not shown); ‡ Numbers in parentheses indicate the number of people reporting a single ancestry; * Numbers in parentheses indicate the number of persons reporting this race alone, not in combination with any other race; Please refer to the Explanation of Data for more information.*

Pennsylvania German (16)	118	1.09
Polish (179)	574	5.31
Portuguese (0)	32	0.30
Russian (105)	218	2.02
Scandinavian (10)	25	0.23
Scotch-Irish (106)	375	3.47
Scottish (84)	246	2.28
Serbian (0)	13	0.12
Slovak (27)	63	0.58
Slovene (0)	15	0.14
Swedish (47)	185	1.71
Swiss (0)	29	0.27
Ukrainian (117)	140	1.29
Welsh (0)	55	0.51
West Indian, ex. Hispanic (0)	24	0.22
Haitian (0)	24	0.22

Hispanic Origin	Population	%
Hispanic or Latino (of any race)	258	2.38
Central American, ex. Mexican	22	0.20
Costa Rican	1	0.01
Guatemalan	9	0.08
Honduran	5	0.05
Nicaraguan	2	0.02
Panamanian	1	0.01
Salvadoran	4	0.04
Cuban	15	0.14
Dominican Republic	11	0.10
Mexican	43	0.40
Puerto Rican	91	0.84
South American	47	0.43
Argentinean	9	0.08
Bolivian	4	0.04
Colombian	10	0.09
Ecuadorian	5	0.05
Paraguayan	2	0.02
Peruvian	10	0.09
Uruguayan	1	0.01
Venezuelan	5	0.05
Other South American	1	0.01
Other Hispanic or Latino	29	0.27

Race*	Population	%
African-American/Black (408)	467	4.31
Not Hispanic (389)	435	4.02
Hispanic (19)	32	0.30
American Indian/Alaska Native (10)	33	0.30
Not Hispanic (8)	29	0.27
Hispanic (2)	4	0.04
Cherokee (5)	13	0.12
Chippewa (3)	4	0.04
Delaware (0)	2	0.02
Iroquois (0)	2	0.02
Mexican American Ind. (1)	1	0.01
Seminole (0)	1	0.01
South American Ind. (1)	1	0.01
Asian (351)	415	3.83
Not Hispanic (351)	413	3.81
Hispanic (0)	2	0.02
Bangladeshi (6)	7	0.06
Cambodian (1)	1	0.01
Chinese, ex. Taiwanese (106)	117	1.08
Filipino (7)	22	0.20
Indian (130)	145	1.34
Japanese (7)	20	0.18
Korean (59)	65	0.60
Nepalese (3)	3	0.03
Pakistani (4)	8	0.07
Taiwanese (4)	5	0.05
Thai (6)	8	0.07
Vietnamese (14)	14	0.13
Hawaii Native/Pacific Islander (6)	20	0.18
Not Hispanic (4)	16	0.15
Hispanic (2)	4	0.04
Guamanian/Chamorro (4)	4	0.04
Native Hawaiian (0)	6	0.06
Samoan (0)	1	0.01
White (9,848)	9,972	92.10
Not Hispanic (9,684)	9,787	90.39
Hispanic (164)	185	1.71

White Oak

Place Type: Borough
County: Allegheny
Population: 7,862†

Ancestry‡	Population	%
American (590)	590	7.47
Arab (14)	14	0.18
Egyptian (14)	14	0.18
Armenian (15)	15	0.19
Austrian (8)	13	0.16
British (0)	10	0.13
Canadian (12)	26	0.33
Croatian (105)	199	2.52
Czech (11)	38	0.48
Czechoslovakian (10)	24	0.30
Danish (0)	26	0.33
Dutch (0)	29	0.37
Eastern European (14)	14	0.18
English (262)	1,040	13.16
European (40)	40	0.51
French, ex. Basque (10)	23	0.29
German (537)	2,183	27.62
Greek (153)	303	3.83
Hungarian (167)	357	4.52
Iranian (0)	15	0.19
Irish (263)	1,240	15.69
Italian (361)	919	11.63
Lithuanian (0)	31	0.39
Norwegian (10)	10	0.13
Pennsylvania German (0)	18	0.23
Polish (391)	922	11.67
Romanian (14)	14	0.18
Russian (26)	154	1.95
Scotch-Irish (95)	334	4.23
Scottish (36)	292	3.69
Serbian (38)	142	1.80
Slavic (0)	30	0.38
Slovak (416)	878	11.11
Slovene (0)	9	0.11
Swedish (33)	83	1.05
Swiss (0)	9	0.11
Ukrainian (14)	61	0.77
Welsh (43)	207	2.62

Hispanic Origin	Population	%
Hispanic or Latino (of any race)	73	0.93
Central American, ex. Mexican	2	0.03
Guatemalan	2	0.03
Cuban	7	0.09
Dominican Republic	3	0.04
Mexican	37	0.47
Puerto Rican	14	0.18
South American	4	0.05
Chilean	1	0.01
Ecuadorian	2	0.03
Uruguayan	1	0.01
Other Hispanic or Latino	6	0.08

Race*	Population	%
African-American/Black (280)	359	4.57
Not Hispanic (277)	350	4.45
Hispanic (3)	9	0.11
American Indian/Alaska Native (9)	29	0.37
Not Hispanic (7)	24	0.31
Hispanic (2)	5	0.06
Apache (0)	2	0.03
Blackfeet (2)	5	0.06
Cherokee (1)	4	0.05
Delaware (1)	5	0.06
Iroquois (2)	3	0.04
Yaqui (1)	1	0.01
Asian (71)	90	1.14
Not Hispanic (70)	88	1.12
Hispanic (1)	2	0.03
Chinese, ex. Taiwanese (18)	22	0.28
Filipino (16)	20	0.25
Indian (12)	13	0.17
Japanese (0)	4	0.05
Korean (14)	17	0.22
Pakistani (2)	3	0.04
Taiwanese (1)	1	0.01
Thai (1)	1	0.01
Vietnamese (6)	9	0.11
Hawaii Native/Pacific Islander (6)	10	0.13
Not Hispanic (6)	10	0.13
Native Hawaiian (1)	2	0.03
White (7,367)	7,469	95.00
Not Hispanic (7,320)	7,414	94.30
Hispanic (47)	55	0.70

White

Place Type: Township
County: Indiana
Population: 15,821†

Ancestry‡	Population	%
American (646)	646	4.18
Arab (6)	35	0.23
Lebanese (0)	20	0.13
Syrian (0)	9	0.06
Other Arab (6)	6	0.04
Austrian (11)	91	0.59
Belgian (8)	40	0.26
Bulgarian (0)	11	0.07
Carpatho Rusyn (10)	20	0.13
Croatian (9)	57	0.37
Czech (40)	213	1.38
Czechoslovakian (20)	46	0.30
Dutch (50)	466	3.01
Eastern European (9)	9	0.06
English (421)	1,619	10.47
European (29)	29	0.19
French, ex. Basque (75)	320	2.07
French Canadian (19)	19	0.12
German (1,330)	4,122	26.67
Greek (63)	63	0.41
Hungarian (40)	346	2.24
Irish (839)	2,705	17.50
Italian (639)	1,549	10.02
Lithuanian (0)	24	0.16
Northern European (10)	10	0.06
Norwegian (37)	90	0.58
Pennsylvania German (54)	132	0.85
Polish (397)	1,074	6.95
Portuguese (11)	33	0.21
Romanian (0)	21	0.14
Russian (63)	249	1.61
Scandinavian (0)	5	0.03
Scotch-Irish (280)	618	4.00
Scottish (104)	429	2.78
Serbian (26)	35	0.23
Slavic (11)	16	0.10
Slovak (365)	753	4.87
Slovene (0)	52	0.34
Swedish (91)	239	1.55
Swiss (7)	144	0.93
Ukrainian (22)	165	1.07
Welsh (11)	163	1.05
Yugoslavian (6)	56	0.36

Hispanic Origin	Population	%
Hispanic or Latino (of any race)	297	1.88
Central American, ex. Mexican	18	0.11
Costa Rican	1	0.01
Guatemalan	7	0.04
Honduran	4	0.03
Panamanian	2	0.01
Salvadoran	4	0.03
Cuban	12	0.08
Dominican Republic	13	0.08
Mexican	67	0.42
Puerto Rican	45	0.28
South American	24	0.15
Argentinean	5	0.03
Colombian	2	0.01
Ecuadorian	1	0.01
Peruvian	4	0.03

*Notes: † The Census 2010 population figure is used to calculate the percentages in the Hispanic Origin and Race categories. Ancestry percentages are based on the 2006-2010 American Community Survey population (not shown); ‡ Numbers in parentheses indicate the number of people reporting a single ancestry; * Numbers in parentheses indicate the number of persons reporting this race alone, not in combination with any other race; Please refer to the Explanation of Data for more information.*

Uruguayan	5	0.03
Venezuelan	7	0.04
Other Hispanic or Latino	118	0.75

Race*	Population	%
African-American/Black (1,181)	1,289	8.15
Not Hispanic (1,173)	1,273	8.05
Hispanic (8)	16	0.10
American Indian/Alaska Native (34)	76	0.48
Not Hispanic (30)	69	0.44
Hispanic (4)	7	0.04
Blackfeet (1)	6	0.04
Cherokee (5)	11	0.07
Chippewa (2)	3	0.02
Choctaw (1)	1	0.01
Delaware (2)	3	0.02
Iroquois (5)	14	0.09
Mexican American Ind. (0)	1	0.01
Navajo (1)	1	0.01
Sioux (0)	2	0.01
Asian (353)	418	2.64
Not Hispanic (351)	412	2.60
Hispanic (2)	6	0.04
Bangladeshi (6)	10	0.06
Chinese, ex. Taiwanese (83)	87	0.55
Filipino (13)	26	0.16
Indian (99)	112	0.71
Indonesian (8)	8	0.05
Japanese (7)	13	0.08
Korean (54)	60	0.38
Malaysian (2)	2	0.01
Nepalese (0)	1	0.01
Pakistani (33)	34	0.21
Sri Lankan (4)	4	0.03
Taiwanese (15)	15	0.09
Thai (3)	3	0.02
Vietnamese (10)	11	0.07
Hawaii Native/Pacific Islander (3)	12	0.08
Not Hispanic (2)	9	0.06
Hispanic (1)	3	0.02
Native Hawaiian (0)	8	0.05
Samoan (1)	1	0.01
White (13,900)	14,090	89.06
Not Hispanic (13,757)	13,938	88.10
Hispanic (143)	152	0.96

Whitehall

Place Type: Borough
County: Allegheny
Population: 13,944†

Ancestry‡	Population	%
African, Sub-Saharan (178)	255	1.83
African (148)	194	1.39
Nigerian (30)	61	0.44
American (343)	343	2.46
Arab (54)	126	0.91
Egyptian (39)	39	0.28
Lebanese (15)	87	0.62
Austrian (28)	81	0.58
Belgian (10)	10	0.07
British (0)	8	0.06
Carpatho Rusyn (14)	14	0.10
Croatian (24)	172	1.24
Czech (0)	43	0.31
Czechoslovakian (41)	90	0.65
Danish (0)	10	0.07
Dutch (8)	62	0.45
English (128)	916	6.58
European (51)	51	0.37
French, ex. Basque (14)	176	1.26
French Canadian (0)	11	0.08
German (1,239)	4,867	34.96
Greek (34)	54	0.39
Hungarian (116)	306	2.20
Irish (848)	3,500	25.14
Italian (1,018)	3,055	21.95
Lithuanian (29)	177	1.27
Macedonian (19)	19	0.14
Norwegian (0)	26	0.19
Pennsylvania German (0)	14	0.10
Polish (430)	1,579	11.34
Romanian (0)	9	0.06
Russian (63)	187	1.34
Scandinavian (0)	11	0.08
Scotch-Irish (94)	377	2.71
Scottish (24)	117	0.84
Serbian (55)	125	0.90
Slavic (21)	41	0.29
Slovak (138)	880	6.32
Slovene (0)	50	0.36
Swedish (14)	55	0.40
Swiss (0)	110	0.79
Turkish (223)	223	1.60
Ukrainian (45)	167	1.20
Welsh (23)	195	1.40
Yugoslavian (261)	272	1.95

Hispanic Origin	Population	%
Hispanic or Latino (of any race)	132	0.95
Central American, ex. Mexican	12	0.09
Guatemalan	5	0.04
Honduran	3	0.02
Nicaraguan	1	0.01
Panamanian	3	0.02
Cuban	2	0.01
Dominican Republic	2	0.01
Mexican	63	0.45
Puerto Rican	23	0.16
South American	8	0.06
Colombian	5	0.04
Ecuadorian	1	0.01
Peruvian	1	0.01
Uruguayan	1	0.01
Other Hispanic or Latino	22	0.16

Race*	Population	%
African-American/Black (521)	587	4.21
Not Hispanic (513)	572	4.10
Hispanic (8)	15	0.11
American Indian/Alaska Native (11)	43	0.31
Not Hispanic (10)	41	0.29
Hispanic (1)	2	0.01
Blackfeet (0)	1	0.01
Cherokee (3)	7	0.05
Chippewa (0)	1	0.01
Choctaw (0)	3	0.02
Iroquois (0)	1	0.01
Puget Sound Salish (2)	2	0.01
Sioux (0)	3	0.02
Asian (532)	590	4.23
Not Hispanic (531)	586	4.20
Hispanic (1)	4	0.03
Bhutanese (77)	105	0.75
Burmese (145)	151	1.08
Cambodian (0)	4	0.03
Chinese, ex. Taiwanese (39)	43	0.31
Filipino (7)	18	0.13
Indian (56)	70	0.50
Indonesian (0)	1	0.01
Japanese (1)	4	0.03
Korean (7)	9	0.06
Nepalese (49)	55	0.39
Taiwanese (1)	1	0.01
Thai (12)	18	0.13
Vietnamese (56)	73	0.52
Hawaii Native/Pacific Islander (3)	10	0.07
Not Hispanic (3)	10	0.07
White (12,701)	12,830	92.01
Not Hispanic (12,611)	12,725	91.26
Hispanic (90)	105	0.75

Whitehall

Place Type: Township
County: Lehigh
Population: 26,738†

Ancestry‡	Population	%
African, Sub-Saharan (195)	212	0.80
African (111)	111	0.42
Other Sub-Saharan African (84)	101	0.38
American (867)	867	3.27
Arab (1,033)	1,261	4.76
Arab (111)	127	0.48
Egyptian (21)	21	0.08
Jordanian (8)	8	0.03
Lebanese (229)	309	1.17
Moroccan (14)	14	0.05
Syrian (585)	717	2.71
Other Arab (65)	65	0.25
Armenian (33)	42	0.16
Austrian (361)	902	3.40
Belgian (0)	11	0.04
Brazilian (16)	24	0.09
Canadian (0)	14	0.05
Celtic (36)	91	0.34
Croatian (31)	83	0.31
Czech (11)	47	0.18
Czechoslovakian (58)	130	0.49
Danish (30)	45	0.17
Dutch (229)	727	2.74
Eastern European (8)	20	0.08
English (206)	1,121	4.23
European (129)	142	0.54
Finnish (23)	56	0.21
French, ex. Basque (53)	366	1.38
French Canadian (49)	72	0.27
German (3,478)	7,632	28.80
Greek (134)	254	0.96
Guyanese (23)	55	0.21
Hungarian (238)	993	3.75
Iranian (17)	32	0.12
Irish (773)	2,763	10.43
Italian (909)	2,209	8.34
Lithuanian (41)	85	0.32
Northern European (83)	83	0.31
Norwegian (14)	39	0.15
Pennsylvania German (800)	1,093	4.13
Polish (477)	1,458	5.50
Portuguese (0)	249	0.94
Romanian (68)	82	0.31
Russian (45)	321	1.21
Scotch-Irish (126)	233	0.88
Scottish (21)	257	0.97
Slovak (383)	1,204	4.54
Swedish (33)	120	0.45
Swiss (0)	24	0.09
Ukrainian (258)	684	2.58
Welsh (124)	417	1.57
West Indian, ex. Hispanic (144)	198	0.75
Barbadian (16)	27	0.10
Haitian (17)	17	0.06
Jamaican (17)	17	0.06
West Indian (94)	137	0.52
Yugoslavian (40)	40	0.15

Hispanic Origin	Population	%
Hispanic or Latino (of any race)	2,852	10.67
Central American, ex. Mexican	139	0.52
Costa Rican	5	0.02
Guatemalan	20	0.07
Honduran	30	0.11
Nicaraguan	19	0.07
Panamanian	13	0.05
Salvadoran	40	0.15
Other Central American	12	0.04
Cuban	55	0.21
Dominican Republic	536	2.00
Mexican	167	0.62
Puerto Rican	1,371	5.13
South American	386	1.44
Argentinean	11	0.04
Bolivian	6	0.02
Chilean	29	0.11
Colombian	149	0.56
Ecuadorian	97	0.36
Paraguayan	1	<0.01

*Notes: † The Census 2010 population figure is used to calculate the percentages in the Hispanic Origin and Race categories. Ancestry percentages are based on the 2006-2010 American Community Survey population (not shown); ‡ Numbers in parentheses indicate the number of people reporting a single ancestry; * Numbers in parentheses indicate the number of persons reporting this race alone, not in combination with any other race; Please refer to the Explanation of Data for more information.*

Peruvian	74	0.28
Uruguayan	3	0.01
Venezuelan	6	0.02
Other South American	10	0.04
Other Hispanic or Latino	198	0.74

Race*	Population	%
African-American/Black (1,530)	1,820	6.81
Not Hispanic (1,381)	1,573	5.88
Hispanic (149)	247	0.92
American Indian/Alaska Native (78)	160	0.60
Not Hispanic (30)	85	0.32
Hispanic (48)	75	0.28
Apache (3)	6	0.02
Blackfeet (1)	1	<0.01
Central American Ind. (2)	2	0.01
Cherokee (4)	21	0.08
Crow (0)	1	<0.01
Delaware (0)	7	0.03
Lumbee (1)	4	0.01
Mexican American Ind. (3)	3	0.01
Seminole (1)	1	<0.01
Sioux (0)	1	<0.01
South American Ind. (9)	15	0.06
Asian (1,108)	1,300	4.86
Not Hispanic (1,097)	1,273	4.76
Hispanic (11)	27	0.10
Bangladeshi (4)	5	0.02
Cambodian (1)	1	<0.01
Chinese, ex. Taiwanese (199)	229	0.86
Filipino (60)	78	0.29
Indian (443)	484	1.81
Indonesian (3)	10	0.04
Japanese (13)	27	0.10
Korean (60)	67	0.25
Laotian (0)	1	<0.01
Malaysian (3)	4	0.01
Nepalese (4)	5	0.02
Pakistani (28)	30	0.11
Taiwanese (1)	1	<0.01
Thai (8)	8	0.03
Vietnamese (248)	285	1.07
Hawaii Native/Pacific Islander (5)	36	0.13
Not Hispanic (4)	24	0.09
Hispanic (1)	12	0.04
Guamanian/Chamorro (1)	1	<0.01
Native Hawaiian (1)	11	0.04
Samoan (0)	6	0.02
White (22,162)	22,705	84.92
Not Hispanic (20,888)	21,250	79.47
Hispanic (1,274)	1,455	5.44

Whitemarsh

Place Type: Township
County: Montgomery
Population: 17,349†

Ancestry‡	Population	%
Albanian (9)	19	0.11
Alsatian (0)	11	0.06
American (902)	902	5.24
Arab (29)	92	0.53
Iraqi (11)	11	0.06
Other Arab (18)	81	0.47
Armenian (74)	96	0.56
Austrian (22)	236	1.37
Brazilian (19)	19	0.11
British (18)	33	0.19
Canadian (0)	18	0.10
Carpatho Rusyn (0)	7	0.04
Croatian (8)	22	0.13
Czech (0)	8	0.05
Czechoslovakian (13)	13	0.08
Danish (7)	61	0.35
Dutch (24)	148	0.86
Eastern European (136)	145	0.84
English (397)	1,902	11.05
European (287)	287	1.67
Finnish (0)	44	0.26
French, ex. Basque (30)	170	0.99
French Canadian (7)	7	0.04
German (820)	3,322	19.30
Greek (42)	66	0.38
Hungarian (70)	250	1.45
Irish (1,543)	4,414	25.64
Israeli (49)	49	0.28
Italian (1,406)	2,814	16.35
Lithuanian (38)	266	1.55
New Zealander (12)	12	0.07
Norwegian (28)	94	0.55
Pennsylvania German (18)	18	0.10
Polish (848)	1,956	11.36
Romanian (17)	55	0.32
Russian (730)	1,370	7.96
Scandinavian (0)	12	0.07
Scotch-Irish (176)	325	1.89
Scottish (136)	318	1.85
Serbian (5)	5	0.03
Slovak (22)	47	0.27
Swedish (57)	301	1.75
Swiss (10)	80	0.46
Ukrainian (116)	403	2.34
Welsh (18)	161	0.94
West Indian, ex. Hispanic (34)	104	0.60
Barbadian (24)	79	0.46
Jamaican (10)	25	0.15

Hispanic Origin	Population	%
Hispanic or Latino (of any race)	301	1.73
Central American, ex. Mexican	22	0.13
Costa Rican	4	0.02
Guatemalan	12	0.07
Nicaraguan	1	0.01
Panamanian	4	0.02
Salvadoran	1	0.01
Cuban	28	0.16
Dominican Republic	1	0.01
Mexican	86	0.50
Puerto Rican	83	0.48
South American	53	0.31
Argentinean	13	0.07
Bolivian	5	0.03
Chilean	1	0.01
Colombian	9	0.05
Ecuadorian	4	0.02
Paraguayan	1	0.01
Peruvian	10	0.06
Uruguayan	5	0.03
Venezuelan	5	0.03
Other Hispanic or Latino	28	0.16

Race*	Population	%
African-American/Black (604)	674	3.88
Not Hispanic (591)	653	3.76
Hispanic (13)	21	0.12
American Indian/Alaska Native (15)	48	0.28
Not Hispanic (14)	41	0.24
Hispanic (1)	7	0.04
Canadian/French Am. Ind. (0)	1	0.01
Central American Ind. (1)	1	0.01
Cherokee (0)	7	0.04
Cheyenne (1)	1	0.01
Chippewa (3)	4	0.02
Delaware (0)	2	0.01
Iroquois (4)	4	0.02
Mexican American Ind. (0)	1	0.01
Seminole (0)	1	0.01
Yaqui (0)	1	0.01
Asian (734)	849	4.89
Not Hispanic (732)	840	4.84
Hispanic (2)	9	0.05
Bangladeshi (6)	6	0.03
Burmese (6)	6	0.03
Cambodian (6)	8	0.05
Chinese, ex. Taiwanese (148)	195	1.12
Filipino (34)	58	0.33
Hmong (0)	1	0.01
Indian (173)	195	1.12
Indonesian (3)	3	0.02
Japanese (12)	22	0.13
Korean (256)	272	1.57
Nepalese (11)	12	0.07
Pakistani (13)	13	0.07
Sri Lankan (5)	5	0.03
Taiwanese (7)	11	0.06
Thai (6)	8	0.05
Vietnamese (20)	37	0.21
Hawaii Native/Pacific Islander (3)	8	0.05
Not Hispanic (3)	7	0.04
Hispanic (0)	1	0.01
Guamanian/Chamorro (0)	2	0.01
White (15,727)	15,908	91.69
Not Hispanic (15,512)	15,677	90.36
Hispanic (215)	231	1.33

Whitpain

Place Type: Township
County: Montgomery
Population: 18,875†

Ancestry‡	Population	%
African, Sub-Saharan (23)	23	0.12
African (9)	9	0.05
Ethiopian (14)	14	0.07
American (869)	869	4.62
Arab (109)	131	0.70
Arab (68)	68	0.36
Egyptian (41)	41	0.22
Other Arab (0)	22	0.12
Armenian (11)	55	0.29
Austrian (22)	155	0.82
Belgian (9)	23	0.12
British (0)	42	0.22
Canadian (16)	16	0.09
Croatian (10)	20	0.11
Czech (8)	66	0.35
Czechoslovakian (0)	22	0.12
Danish (0)	21	0.11
Dutch (42)	203	1.08
Eastern European (179)	192	1.02
English (414)	1,955	10.40
European (199)	288	1.53
French, ex. Basque (67)	377	2.00
French Canadian (0)	28	0.15
German (1,218)	3,851	20.48
Greek (59)	145	0.77
Hungarian (47)	221	1.18
Irish (1,496)	4,219	22.44
Italian (1,348)	2,947	15.67
Lithuanian (39)	201	1.07
Norwegian (19)	69	0.37
Pennsylvania German (53)	130	0.69
Polish (434)	1,347	7.16
Portuguese (0)	11	0.06
Romanian (72)	101	0.54
Russian (454)	948	5.04
Scotch-Irish (167)	377	2.00
Scottish (183)	511	2.72
Serbian (10)	20	0.11
Slovak (24)	116	0.62
Slovene (10)	10	0.05
Swedish (28)	150	0.80
Swiss (10)	76	0.40
Ukrainian (88)	166	0.88
Welsh (56)	289	1.54
West Indian, ex. Hispanic (224)	242	1.29
Bahamian (90)	90	0.48
Haitian (134)	134	0.71
Trinidadian/Tobagonian (0)	9	0.05
West Indian (0)	9	0.05
Yugoslavian (0)	25	0.13

Hispanic Origin	Population	%
Hispanic or Latino (of any race)	488	2.59
Central American, ex. Mexican	16	0.08
Costa Rican	4	0.02
Guatemalan	4	0.02
Honduran	1	0.01

*Notes: † The Census 2010 population figure is used to calculate the percentages in the Hispanic Origin and Race categories. Ancestry percentages are based on the 2006-2010 American Community Survey population (not shown); ‡ Numbers in parentheses indicate the number of people reporting a single ancestry; * Numbers in parentheses indicate the number of persons reporting this race alone, not in combination with any other race; Please refer to the Explanation of Data for more information.*

Nicaraguan	2	0.01
Panamanian	1	0.01
Salvadoran	3	0.02
Other Central American	1	0.01
Cuban	30	0.16
Dominican Republic	24	0.13
Mexican	100	0.53
Puerto Rican	150	0.79
South American	110	0.58
Argentinean	14	0.07
Bolivian	5	0.03
Chilean	5	0.03
Colombian	46	0.24
Ecuadorian	6	0.03
Paraguayan	8	0.04
Peruvian	6	0.03
Uruguayan	1	0.01
Venezuelan	18	0.10
Other South American	1	0.01
Other Hispanic or Latino	58	0.31

Race*	Population	%
African-American/Black (982)	1,077	5.71
Not Hispanic (963)	1,049	5.56
Hispanic (19)	28	0.15
American Indian/Alaska Native (10)	54	0.29
Not Hispanic (8)	48	0.25
Hispanic (2)	6	0.03
Blackfeet (0)	2	0.01
Canadian/French Am. Ind. (0)	1	0.01
Cherokee (0)	3	0.02
Cree (1)	1	0.01
Delaware (0)	6	0.03
Iroquois (0)	2	0.01
Potawatomi (0)	1	0.01
South American Ind. (0)	2	0.01
Asian (2,049)	2,169	11.49
Not Hispanic (2,048)	2,168	11.49
Hispanic (1)	1	0.01
Bangladeshi (5)	5	0.03
Burmese (4)	4	0.02
Cambodian (3)	7	0.04
Chinese, ex. Taiwanese (360)	388	2.06
Filipino (66)	100	0.53
Indian (422)	441	2.34
Japanese (29)	37	0.20
Korean (1,030)	1,056	5.59
Laotian (0)	1	0.01
Malaysian (3)	3	0.02
Nepalese (2)	2	0.01
Pakistani (21)	22	0.12
Sri Lankan (7)	7	0.04
Taiwanese (14)	18	0.10
Thai (3)	10	0.05
Vietnamese (45)	53	0.28
Hawaii Native/Pacific Islander (6)	9	0.05
Not Hispanic (6)	9	0.05
Guamanian/Chamorro (1)	1	0.01
Native Hawaiian (2)	2	0.01
White (15,450)	15,656	82.95
Not Hispanic (15,106)	15,293	81.02
Hispanic (344)	363	1.92

Wilkes-Barre

Place Type: City
County: Luzerne
Population: 41,498†

Ancestry‡	Population	%
African, Sub-Saharan (326)	343	0.82
African (246)	246	0.59
Cape Verdean (0)	17	0.04
Nigerian (80)	80	0.19
American (916)	916	2.20
Arab (327)	618	1.49
Arab (121)	121	0.29
Lebanese (138)	320	0.77
Palestinian (0)	14	0.03
Syrian (68)	163	0.39
Austrian (17)	142	0.34
Basque (11)	11	0.03
British (48)	95	0.23
Canadian (10)	17	0.04
Croatian (10)	21	0.05
Czech (31)	117	0.28
Czechoslovakian (83)	110	0.26
Danish (0)	61	0.15
Dutch (80)	644	1.55
Eastern European (24)	24	0.06
English (511)	2,186	5.26
European (52)	52	0.13
French, ex. Basque (31)	482	1.16
French Canadian (12)	30	0.07
German (1,424)	7,408	17.81
Greek (15)	225	0.54
Hungarian (168)	392	0.94
Iranian (0)	8	0.02
Irish (2,373)	9,075	21.82
Italian (1,570)	5,097	12.25
Lithuanian (372)	1,109	2.67
Norwegian (29)	40	0.10
Pennsylvania German (206)	442	1.06
Polish (3,182)	8,088	19.44
Portuguese (8)	33	0.08
Romanian (56)	87	0.21
Russian (404)	1,417	3.41
Scandinavian (9)	9	0.02
Scotch-Irish (79)	325	0.78
Scottish (36)	609	1.46
Slavic (29)	67	0.16
Slovak (630)	1,497	3.60
Swedish (19)	177	0.43
Swiss (0)	25	0.06
Ukrainian (264)	437	1.05
Welsh (313)	2,318	5.57
West Indian, ex. Hispanic (372)	409	0.98
Haitian (335)	335	0.81
Jamaican (25)	62	0.15
West Indian (12)	12	0.03
Yugoslavian (0)	10	0.02

Hispanic Origin	Population	%
Hispanic or Latino (of any race)	4,690	11.30
Central American, ex. Mexican	160	0.39
Costa Rican	7	0.02
Guatemalan	39	0.09
Honduran	67	0.16
Nicaraguan	11	0.03
Panamanian	7	0.02
Salvadoran	29	0.07
Cuban	91	0.22
Dominican Republic	608	1.47
Mexican	1,995	4.81
Puerto Rican	1,305	3.14
South American	186	0.45
Argentinean	29	0.07
Bolivian	1	<0.01
Chilean	3	0.01
Colombian	35	0.08
Ecuadorian	45	0.11
Peruvian	37	0.09
Uruguayan	33	0.08
Venezuelan	1	<0.01
Other South American	2	<0.01
Other Hispanic or Latino	345	0.83

Race*	Population	%
African-American/Black (4,519)	5,373	12.95
Not Hispanic (4,211)	4,902	11.81
Hispanic (308)	471	1.13
American Indian/Alaska Native (133)	358	0.86
Not Hispanic (45)	195	0.47
Hispanic (88)	163	0.39
Aleut *(Alaska Native)* (1)	1	<0.01
Apache (0)	8	0.02
Blackfeet (2)	11	0.03
Cherokee (4)	42	0.10
Cheyenne (1)	2	<0.01
Chippewa (1)	1	<0.01
Choctaw (0)	2	<0.01
Cree (1)	1	<0.01
Creek (0)	1	<0.01
Delaware (1)	4	0.01
Inupiat *(Alaska Native)* (1)	2	<0.01
Iroquois (3)	10	0.02
Mexican American Ind. (8)	15	0.04
Navajo (2)	4	0.01
Pueblo (1)	1	<0.01
Shoshone (0)	1	<0.01
Sioux (0)	2	<0.01
South American Ind. (3)	6	0.01
Spanish American Ind. (2)	2	<0.01
Asian (592)	716	1.73
Not Hispanic (579)	678	1.63
Hispanic (13)	38	0.09
Bangladeshi (9)	10	0.02
Cambodian (1)	2	<0.01
Chinese, ex. Taiwanese (108)	147	0.35
Filipino (56)	77	0.19
Hmong (1)	1	<0.01
Indian (110)	134	0.32
Indonesian (10)	15	0.04
Japanese (9)	17	0.04
Korean (27)	49	0.12
Laotian (1)	3	0.01
Pakistani (3)	7	0.02
Sri Lankan (1)	1	<0.01
Taiwanese (0)	2	<0.01
Thai (3)	11	0.03
Vietnamese (226)	231	0.56
Hawaii Native/Pacific Islander (12)	31	0.07
Not Hispanic (5)	15	0.04
Hispanic (7)	16	0.04
Fijian (0)	3	0.01
Guamanian/Chamorro (3)	3	0.01
Native Hawaiian (6)	11	0.03
Samoan (3)	8	0.02
White (32,866)	33,955	81.82
Not Hispanic (31,069)	31,856	76.77
Hispanic (1,797)	2,099	5.06

Wilkinsburg

Place Type: Borough
County: Allegheny
Population: 15,930†

Ancestry‡	Population	%
African, Sub-Saharan (699)	748	4.58
African (606)	655	4.01
Ethiopian (83)	83	0.51
Other Sub-Saharan African (10)	10	0.06
American (141)	141	0.86
Arab (96)	129	0.79
Arab (7)	7	0.04
Lebanese (11)	44	0.27
Moroccan (30)	30	0.18
Palestinian (20)	20	0.12
Syrian (28)	28	0.17
Australian (0)	10	0.06
Austrian (0)	40	0.24
Belgian (3)	3	0.02
Brazilian (0)	9	0.06
Canadian (10)	10	0.06
Croatian (0)	21	0.13
Czech (9)	9	0.06
Czechoslovakian (8)	51	0.31
Dutch (22)	83	0.51
Eastern European (22)	34	0.21
English (175)	373	2.28
European (54)	70	0.43
French, ex. Basque (108)	240	1.47
French Canadian (11)	11	0.07
German (338)	1,065	6.51
German Russian (8)	8	0.05
Greek (47)	99	0.61
Guyanese (32)	32	0.20
Hungarian (19)	90	0.55
Irish (235)	814	4.98

*Notes: † The Census 2010 population figure is used to calculate the percentages in the Hispanic Origin and Race categories. Ancestry percentages are based on the 2006-2010 American Community Survey population (not shown); ‡ Numbers in parentheses indicate the number of people reporting a single ancestry; * Numbers in parentheses indicate the number of persons reporting this race alone, not in combination with any other race; Please refer to the Explanation of Data for more information.*

Italian (367)	802	4.91
Lithuanian (41)	75	0.46
Norwegian (0)	25	0.15
Pennsylvania German (22)	36	0.22
Polish (156)	367	2.24
Portuguese (0)	34	0.21
Romanian (24)	24	0.15
Russian (107)	186	1.14
Scotch-Irish (70)	212	1.30
Scottish (98)	205	1.25
Serbian (0)	27	0.17
Slavic (0)	42	0.26
Slovak (54)	146	0.89
Slovene (0)	20	0.12
Swedish (21)	55	0.34
Ukrainian (9)	33	0.20
Welsh (0)	45	0.28
West Indian, ex. Hispanic (223)	302	1.85
Barbadian (16)	16	0.10
Haitian (41)	52	0.32
Jamaican (124)	166	1.02
West Indian (42)	68	0.42

Hispanic Origin	Population	%
Hispanic or Latino (of any race)	289	1.81
Central American, ex. Mexican	20	0.13
Costa Rican	3	0.02
Guatemalan	4	0.03
Honduran	1	0.01
Nicaraguan	3	0.02
Panamanian	5	0.03
Salvadoran	4	0.03
Cuban	24	0.15
Dominican Republic	5	0.03
Mexican	86	0.54
Puerto Rican	105	0.66
South American	19	0.12
Argentinean	1	0.01
Bolivian	2	0.01
Chilean	1	0.01
Colombian	6	0.04
Ecuadorian	2	0.01
Peruvian	1	0.01
Venezuelan	6	0.04
Other Hispanic or Latino	30	0.19

Race*	Population	%
African-American/Black (10,615)	11,047	69.35
Not Hispanic (10,514)	10,901	68.43
Hispanic (101)	146	0.92
American Indian/Alaska Native (67)	261	1.64
Not Hispanic (59)	237	1.49
Hispanic (8)	24	0.15
Aleut *(Alaska Native)* (0)	1	0.01
Apache (0)	3	0.02
Blackfeet (7)	14	0.09
Canadian/French Am. Ind. (0)	2	0.01
Cherokee (5)	54	0.34
Chickasaw (0)	3	0.02
Chippewa (0)	2	0.01
Choctaw (0)	3	0.02
Cree (0)	1	0.01
Creek (5)	13	0.08
Delaware (0)	1	0.01
Iroquois (1)	3	0.02
Mexican American Ind. (1)	1	0.01
Navajo (3)	4	0.03
Seminole (1)	6	0.04
Sioux (0)	2	0.01
South American Ind. (0)	1	0.01
Ute (0)	1	0.01
Asian (163)	218	1.37
Not Hispanic (161)	212	1.33
Hispanic (2)	6	0.04
Cambodian (1)	1	0.01
Chinese, ex. Taiwanese (36)	45	0.28
Filipino (13)	17	0.11
Indian (52)	71	0.45
Indonesian (2)	6	0.04
Japanese (6)	8	0.05
Korean (14)	22	0.14
Malaysian (1)	1	0.01
Nepalese (1)	1	0.01
Pakistani (9)	9	0.06
Sri Lankan (3)	3	0.02
Taiwanese (6)	6	0.04
Thai (2)	3	0.02
Vietnamese (0)	1	0.01
Hawaii Native/Pacific Islander (3)	11	0.07
Not Hispanic (3)	9	0.06
Hispanic (0)	2	0.01
Native Hawaiian (2)	5	0.03
Samoan (1)	3	0.02
White (4,510)	4,835	30.35
Not Hispanic (4,427)	4,730	29.69
Hispanic (83)	105	0.66

Williamsport

Place Type: City
County: Lycoming
Population: 29,381†

Ancestry‡	Population	%
African, Sub-Saharan (97)	104	0.35
African (97)	104	0.35
Alsatian (11)	11	0.04
American (1,585)	1,585	5.37
Arab (73)	149	0.50
Arab (19)	19	0.06
Lebanese (45)	88	0.30
Syrian (0)	33	0.11
Other Arab (9)	9	0.03
Australian (6)	6	0.02
Austrian (41)	101	0.34
British (22)	70	0.24
Canadian (12)	22	0.07
Celtic (18)	48	0.16
Czech (9)	77	0.26
Czechoslovakian (25)	33	0.11
Danish (8)	36	0.12
Dutch (217)	685	2.32
Eastern European (52)	52	0.18
English (693)	2,120	7.18
European (55)	66	0.22
Finnish (0)	12	0.04
French, ex. Basque (71)	442	1.50
French Canadian (0)	50	0.17
German (3,466)	9,074	30.75
Greek (3)	3	0.01
Guyanese (4)	4	0.01
Hungarian (25)	138	0.47
Irish (801)	4,707	15.95
Italian (1,356)	3,360	11.39
Lithuanian (8)	8	0.03
Northern European (23)	23	0.08
Norwegian (76)	232	0.79
Pennsylvania German (432)	823	2.79
Polish (527)	1,788	6.06
Portuguese (16)	32	0.11
Romanian (0)	112	0.38
Russian (20)	214	0.73
Scandinavian (0)	131	0.44
Scotch-Irish (207)	441	1.49
Scottish (122)	390	1.32
Slavic (9)	9	0.03
Slovak (38)	146	0.49
Slovene (0)	23	0.08
Swedish (58)	243	0.82
Ukrainian (51)	137	0.46
Welsh (69)	413	1.40
West Indian, ex. Hispanic (40)	73	0.25
Belizean (18)	18	0.06
Haitian (0)	33	0.11
Jamaican (18)	18	0.06
U.S. Virgin Islander (4)	4	0.01
Yugoslavian (24)	24	0.08

Hispanic Origin	Population	%
Hispanic or Latino (of any race)	771	2.62
Central American, ex. Mexican	38	0.13
Costa Rican	4	0.01
Guatemalan	3	0.01
Honduran	6	0.02
Nicaraguan	5	0.02
Panamanian	9	0.03
Salvadoran	9	0.03
Other Central American	2	0.01
Cuban	29	0.10
Dominican Republic	44	0.15
Mexican	169	0.58
Puerto Rican	364	1.24
South American	42	0.14
Argentinean	5	0.02
Chilean	3	0.01
Colombian	11	0.04
Ecuadorian	3	0.01
Paraguayan	3	0.01
Peruvian	6	0.02
Venezuelan	8	0.03
Other South American	3	0.01
Other Hispanic or Latino	85	0.29

Race*	Population	%
African-American/Black (3,970)	4,924	16.76
Not Hispanic (3,854)	4,741	16.14
Hispanic (116)	183	0.62
American Indian/Alaska Native (69)	302	1.03
Not Hispanic (62)	265	0.90
Hispanic (7)	37	0.13
Aleut *(Alaska Native)* (2)	2	0.01
Apache (4)	5	0.02
Blackfeet (2)	21	0.07
Canadian/French Am. Ind. (1)	3	0.01
Cherokee (2)	65	0.22
Chippewa (5)	6	0.02
Choctaw (0)	1	<0.01
Cree (0)	1	<0.01
Delaware (0)	4	0.01
Iroquois (3)	15	0.05
Lumbee (3)	3	0.01
Mexican American Ind. (0)	1	<0.01
Navajo (2)	4	0.01
Potawatomi (0)	1	<0.01
Sioux (2)	7	0.02
South American Ind. (0)	1	<0.01
Asian (219)	322	1.10
Not Hispanic (214)	302	1.03
Hispanic (5)	20	0.07
Bangladeshi (6)	6	0.02
Burmese (3)	3	0.01
Cambodian (2)	3	0.01
Chinese, ex. Taiwanese (46)	58	0.20
Filipino (38)	71	0.24
Indian (34)	52	0.18
Indonesian (3)	3	0.01
Japanese (6)	15	0.05
Korean (42)	63	0.21
Laotian (5)	6	0.02
Pakistani (2)	2	0.01
Sri Lankan (1)	1	<0.01
Taiwanese (1)	2	0.01
Thai (5)	5	0.02
Vietnamese (11)	17	0.06
Hawaii Native/Pacific Islander (5)	17	0.06
Not Hispanic (5)	10	0.03
Hispanic (0)	7	0.02
Guamanian/Chamorro (2)	4	0.01
Native Hawaiian (1)	6	0.02
White (23,735)	24,837	84.53
Not Hispanic (23,369)	24,378	82.97
Hispanic (366)	459	1.56

Willistown

Place Type: Township
County: Chester
Population: 10,497†

*Notes: † The Census 2010 population figure is used to calculate the percentages in the Hispanic Origin and Race categories. Ancestry percentages are based on the 2006-2010 American Community Survey population (not shown); ‡ Numbers in parentheses indicate the number of people reporting a single ancestry; * Numbers in parentheses indicate the number of persons reporting this race alone, not in combination with any other race; Please refer to the Explanation of Data for more information.*

Ancestry‡	Population	%
African, Sub-Saharan (40)	40	0.38
Kenyan (40)	40	0.38
Alsatian (7)	7	0.07
American (455)	455	4.34
Assyrian/Chaldean/Syriac (10)	10	0.10
Austrian (9)	35	0.33
Belgian (0)	88	0.84
Brazilian (0)	10	0.10
British (43)	75	0.72
Canadian (10)	32	0.31
Croatian (11)	21	0.20
Czech (11)	46	0.44
Danish (0)	99	0.95
Dutch (23)	225	2.15
Eastern European (33)	68	0.65
English (475)	2,014	19.23
European (112)	112	1.07
Finnish (0)	46	0.44
French, ex. Basque (36)	360	3.44
French Canadian (49)	49	0.47
German (502)	2,641	25.22
Greek (77)	134	1.28
Hungarian (14)	60	0.57
Irish (1,082)	3,147	30.05
Italian (736)	1,920	18.33
Lithuanian (10)	10	0.10
Norwegian (15)	42	0.40
Pennsylvania German (21)	53	0.51
Polish (187)	455	4.34
Portuguese (0)	10	0.10
Russian (69)	215	2.05
Scotch-Irish (245)	329	3.14
Scottish (126)	329	3.14
Slavic (0)	9	0.09
Slovak (0)	30	0.29
Slovene (0)	12	0.11
Swedish (10)	98	0.94
Swiss (0)	29	0.28
Ukrainian (41)	61	0.58
Welsh (8)	113	1.08

Hispanic Origin	Population	%
Hispanic or Latino (of any race)	159	1.51
Central American, ex. Mexican	5	0.05
Guatemalan	1	0.01
Honduran	2	0.02
Panamanian	2	0.02
Cuban	15	0.14
Mexican	54	0.51
Puerto Rican	29	0.28
South American	32	0.30
Argentinean	6	0.06
Chilean	10	0.10
Colombian	9	0.09
Peruvian	5	0.05
Venezuelan	2	0.02
Other Hispanic or Latino	24	0.23

Race*	Population	%
African-American/Black (217)	260	2.48
Not Hispanic (213)	254	2.42
Hispanic (4)	6	0.06
American Indian/Alaska Native (3)	26	0.25
Not Hispanic (3)	23	0.22
Hispanic (0)	3	0.03
Apache (1)	1	0.01
Cherokee (0)	2	0.02
Navajo (1)	1	0.01
Asian (381)	403	3.84
Not Hispanic (381)	403	3.84
Cambodian (1)	1	0.01
Chinese, ex. Taiwanese (65)	68	0.65
Filipino (9)	15	0.14
Indian (115)	126	1.20
Indonesian (4)	4	0.04
Japanese (12)	12	0.11
Korean (123)	125	1.19
Laotian (2)	2	0.02
Pakistani (8)	8	0.08
Sri Lankan (2)	2	0.02
Taiwanese (5)	5	0.05
Thai (4)	6	0.06
Vietnamese (25)	25	0.24
Hawaii Native/Pacific Islander (2)	3	0.03
Not Hispanic (2)	3	0.03
Native Hawaiian (2)	2	0.02
White (9,796)	9,867	94.00
Not Hispanic (9,661)	9,724	92.64
Hispanic (135)	143	1.36

Willow Grove

Place Type: CDP
County: Montgomery
Population: 15,726†

Ancestry‡	Population	%
African, Sub-Saharan (15)	15	0.09
African (15)	15	0.09
American (426)	426	2.59
Arab (38)	38	0.23
Arab (10)	10	0.06
Other Arab (28)	28	0.17
Austrian (20)	160	0.97
Belgian (0)	13	0.08
Brazilian (15)	15	0.09
British (23)	43	0.26
Canadian (0)	13	0.08
Croatian (10)	10	0.06
Czech (16)	31	0.19
Czechoslovakian (0)	9	0.05
Danish (0)	19	0.12
Dutch (35)	381	2.32
Eastern European (70)	93	0.57
English (438)	1,941	11.80
European (136)	158	0.96
French, ex. Basque (35)	285	1.73
French Canadian (0)	10	0.06
German (992)	4,208	25.57
Greek (54)	100	0.61
Hungarian (33)	219	1.33
Irish (1,358)	4,691	28.51
Italian (1,051)	2,945	17.90
Lithuanian (26)	108	0.66
Northern European (9)	9	0.05
Norwegian (7)	148	0.90
Pennsylvania German (33)	170	1.03
Polish (269)	1,008	6.13
Portuguese (17)	17	0.10
Romanian (20)	85	0.52
Russian (259)	374	2.27
Scandinavian (29)	42	0.26
Scotch-Irish (155)	397	2.41
Scottish (98)	426	2.59
Slavic (26)	68	0.41
Slovak (26)	46	0.28
Swedish (12)	134	0.81
Swiss (0)	16	0.10
Ukrainian (54)	201	1.22
Welsh (0)	245	1.49
West Indian, ex. Hispanic (138)	186	1.13
Haitian (0)	48	0.29
Jamaican (138)	138	0.84
Yugoslavian (0)	10	0.06

Hispanic Origin	Population	%
Hispanic or Latino (of any race)	548	3.48
Central American, ex. Mexican	73	0.46
Costa Rican	19	0.12
Guatemalan	32	0.20
Honduran	13	0.08
Nicaraguan	1	0.01
Panamanian	6	0.04
Salvadoran	2	0.01
Cuban	29	0.18
Dominican Republic	9	0.06
Mexican	96	0.61
Puerto Rican	209	1.33
South American	85	0.54
Argentinean	10	0.06
Chilean	2	0.01
Colombian	43	0.27
Ecuadorian	15	0.10
Peruvian	6	0.04
Uruguayan	5	0.03
Venezuelan	4	0.03
Other Hispanic or Latino	47	0.30

Race*	Population	%
African-American/Black (1,293)	1,507	9.58
Not Hispanic (1,269)	1,444	9.18
Hispanic (24)	63	0.40
American Indian/Alaska Native (36)	100	0.64
Not Hispanic (26)	72	0.46
Hispanic (10)	28	0.18
Apache (3)	5	0.03
Blackfeet (0)	8	0.05
Cherokee (11)	24	0.15
Iroquois (0)	8	0.05
Navajo (0)	1	0.01
Pueblo (0)	1	0.01
Seminole (0)	1	0.01
Sioux (0)	2	0.01
Asian (765)	871	5.54
Not Hispanic (762)	857	5.45
Hispanic (3)	14	0.09
Cambodian (22)	25	0.16
Chinese, ex. Taiwanese (92)	103	0.65
Filipino (60)	72	0.46
Indian (192)	218	1.39
Indonesian (0)	1	0.01
Japanese (17)	35	0.22
Korean (261)	273	1.74
Laotian (5)	5	0.03
Malaysian (1)	1	0.01
Nepalese (2)	2	0.01
Pakistani (6)	8	0.05
Sri Lankan (5)	5	0.03
Taiwanese (8)	12	0.08
Thai (8)	9	0.06
Vietnamese (57)	64	0.41
Hawaii Native/Pacific Islander (4)	25	0.16
Not Hispanic (3)	24	0.15
Hispanic (1)	1	0.01
Fijian (0)	1	0.01
Native Hawaiian (2)	5	0.03
Samoan (1)	5	0.03
White (13,099)	13,397	85.19
Not Hispanic (12,805)	13,044	82.95
Hispanic (294)	353	2.24

Willow Street

Place Type: CDP
County: Lancaster
Population: 7,578†

Ancestry‡	Population	%
American (468)	468	6.36
Arab (11)	29	0.39
Lebanese (0)	18	0.24
Syrian (11)	11	0.15
Armenian (28)	28	0.38
Austrian (0)	15	0.20
British (105)	135	1.84
Canadian (10)	25	0.34
Czech (38)	38	0.52
Dutch (43)	154	2.09
Eastern European (17)	17	0.23
English (445)	973	13.23
European (117)	132	1.79
French, ex. Basque (34)	134	1.82
German (1,841)	3,262	44.36
Hungarian (0)	34	0.46
Irish (251)	1,214	16.51
Italian (173)	474	6.45
Latvian (0)	19	0.26
Lithuanian (0)	24	0.33
Norwegian (14)	57	0.78

*Notes: † The Census 2010 population figure is used to calculate the percentages in the Hispanic Origin and Race categories. Ancestry percentages are based on the 2006-2010 American Community Survey population (not shown); ‡ Numbers in parentheses indicate the number of people reporting a single ancestry; * Numbers in parentheses indicate the number of persons reporting this race alone, not in combination with any other race; Please refer to the Explanation of Data for more information.*

Pennsylvania German (69)	69	0.94
Polish (58)	264	3.59
Portuguese (0)	19	0.26
Russian (0)	21	0.29
Scotch-Irish (96)	213	2.90
Scottish (30)	124	1.69
Slovak (15)	29	0.39
Swedish (63)	171	2.33
Swiss (109)	228	3.10
Ukrainian (33)	53	0.72

Hispanic Origin	Population	%
Hispanic or Latino (of any race)	189	2.49
Central American, ex. Mexican	7	0.09
Honduran	6	0.08
Salvadoran	1	0.01
Cuban	5	0.07
Dominican Republic	1	0.01
Mexican	8	0.11
Puerto Rican	146	1.93
South American	5	0.07
Colombian	2	0.03
Peruvian	2	0.03
Other South American	1	0.01
Other Hispanic or Latino	17	0.22

Race*	Population	%
African-American/Black (68)	91	1.20
Not Hispanic (55)	75	0.99
Hispanic (13)	16	0.21
American Indian/Alaska Native (6)	21	0.28
Not Hispanic (4)	18	0.24
Hispanic (2)	3	0.04
Cherokee (0)	7	0.09
Iroquois (0)	1	0.01
Navajo (1)	1	0.01
Sioux (1)	2	0.03
Asian (71)	78	1.03
Not Hispanic (71)	78	1.03
Burmese (3)	3	0.04
Cambodian (3)	3	0.04
Chinese, ex. Taiwanese (13)	16	0.21
Filipino (25)	29	0.38
Indian (9)	12	0.16
Japanese (11)	13	0.17
Korean (1)	1	0.01
Nepalese (3)	3	0.04
Vietnamese (0)	1	0.01
Hawaii Native/Pacific Islander (1)	8	0.11
Not Hispanic (1)	3	0.04
Hispanic (0)	5	0.07
Guamanian/Chamorro (1)	1	0.01
Native Hawaiian (0)	2	0.03
White (7,314)	7,364	97.18
Not Hispanic (7,217)	7,257	95.76
Hispanic (97)	107	1.41

Wilson

Place Type: Borough
County: Northampton
Population: 7,896†

Ancestry‡	Population	%
American (234)	234	2.96
Austrian (0)	18	0.23
Czech (0)	42	0.53
Czechoslovakian (0)	37	0.47
Danish (0)	10	0.13
Dutch (80)	381	4.82
English (123)	826	10.44
European (54)	54	0.68
Finnish (0)	36	0.46
French, ex. Basque (14)	165	2.09
French Canadian (0)	10	0.13
German (1,146)	2,990	37.79
German Russian (12)	12	0.15
Greek (36)	36	0.46
Hungarian (49)	342	4.32
Irish (93)	1,120	14.16
Italian (567)	1,418	17.92
Lithuanian (14)	14	0.18
Norwegian (13)	52	0.66
Pennsylvania German (244)	480	6.07
Polish (33)	342	4.32
Portuguese (16)	16	0.20
Russian (8)	50	0.63
Scotch-Irish (18)	162	2.05
Scottish (13)	190	2.40
Slovak (27)	61	0.77
Swedish (0)	29	0.37
Swiss (0)	10	0.13
Ukrainian (55)	155	1.96
Welsh (0)	127	1.61

Hispanic Origin	Population	%
Hispanic or Latino (of any race)	839	10.63
Central American, ex. Mexican	94	1.19
Costa Rican	17	0.22
Guatemalan	22	0.28
Honduran	22	0.28
Nicaraguan	3	0.04
Panamanian	13	0.16
Salvadoran	11	0.14
Other Central American	6	0.08
Cuban	11	0.14
Dominican Republic	39	0.49
Mexican	99	1.25
Puerto Rican	392	4.96
South American	126	1.60
Argentinean	13	0.16
Colombian	41	0.52
Ecuadorian	28	0.35
Peruvian	32	0.41
Uruguayan	1	0.01
Venezuelan	4	0.05
Other South American	7	0.09
Other Hispanic or Latino	78	0.99

Race*	Population	%
African-American/Black (516)	731	9.26
Not Hispanic (466)	628	7.95
Hispanic (50)	103	1.30
American Indian/Alaska Native (15)	99	1.25
Not Hispanic (13)	78	0.99
Hispanic (2)	21	0.27
Blackfeet (4)	4	0.05
Cherokee (4)	24	0.30
Chippewa (0)	3	0.04
Delaware (1)	8	0.10
Iroquois (2)	6	0.08
Mexican American Ind. (0)	2	0.03
South American Ind. (0)	3	0.04
Asian (164)	204	2.58
Not Hispanic (164)	200	2.53
Hispanic (0)	4	0.05
Bangladeshi (7)	7	0.09
Chinese, ex. Taiwanese (7)	8	0.10
Filipino (35)	40	0.51
Indian (74)	86	1.09
Indonesian (1)	3	0.04
Japanese (4)	9	0.11
Malaysian (1)	1	0.01
Pakistani (6)	6	0.08
Thai (4)	7	0.09
Vietnamese (24)	29	0.37
Hawaii Native/Pacific Islander (3)	14	0.18
Not Hispanic (3)	10	0.13
Hispanic (0)	4	0.05
Native Hawaiian (0)	2	0.03
Samoan (3)	5	0.06
White (6,639)	6,912	87.54
Not Hispanic (6,150)	6,347	80.38
Hispanic (489)	565	7.16

Windsor

Place Type: Township
County: York
Population: 17,504†

Ancestry‡	Population	%
African, Sub-Saharan (43)	43	0.26
African (43)	43	0.26
American (1,718)	1,718	10.24
Arab (0)	17	0.10
Lebanese (0)	17	0.10
Austrian (0)	86	0.51
British (39)	134	0.80
Canadian (16)	42	0.25
Croatian (17)	127	0.76
Czech (0)	447	2.67
Czechoslovakian (15)	40	0.24
Danish (0)	82	0.49
Dutch (143)	377	2.25
English (570)	1,647	9.82
European (194)	194	1.16
French, ex. Basque (27)	126	0.75
French Canadian (14)	14	0.08
German (3,721)	7,491	44.67
Greek (59)	59	0.35
Hungarian (0)	31	0.18
Irish (394)	2,350	14.01
Israeli (0)	9	0.05
Italian (399)	1,394	8.31
Lithuanian (35)	46	0.27
Norwegian (0)	41	0.24
Pennsylvania German (185)	202	1.20
Polish (59)	349	2.08
Portuguese (10)	73	0.44
Russian (21)	109	0.65
Scotch-Irish (96)	291	1.74
Scottish (87)	482	2.87
Slavic (0)	10	0.06
Slovak (56)	56	0.33
Slovene (10)	20	0.12
Swedish (30)	356	2.12
Swiss (12)	94	0.56
Ukrainian (10)	32	0.19
Welsh (23)	136	0.81

Hispanic Origin	Population	%
Hispanic or Latino (of any race)	373	2.13
Central American, ex. Mexican	22	0.13
Guatemalan	10	0.06
Honduran	3	0.02
Panamanian	6	0.03
Salvadoran	3	0.02
Cuban	4	0.02
Dominican Republic	19	0.11
Mexican	83	0.47
Puerto Rican	182	1.04
South American	30	0.17
Argentinean	2	0.01
Bolivian	1	0.01
Chilean	2	0.01
Colombian	14	0.08
Ecuadorian	1	0.01
Peruvian	7	0.04
Venezuelan	3	0.02
Other Hispanic or Latino	33	0.19

Race*	Population	%
African-American/Black (798)	931	5.32
Not Hispanic (762)	886	5.06
Hispanic (36)	45	0.26
American Indian/Alaska Native (24)	69	0.39
Not Hispanic (23)	64	0.37
Hispanic (1)	5	0.03
Apache (1)	1	0.01
Arapaho (1)	2	0.01
Blackfeet (1)	4	0.02
Cherokee (7)	26	0.15
Cheyenne (1)	1	0.01
Chippewa (1)	1	0.01
Crow (0)	1	0.01
Delaware (0)	1	0.01
Lumbee (0)	2	0.01
Mexican American Ind. (0)	1	0.01
Ottawa (1)	1	0.01
Sioux (0)	1	0.01

SECTION TWO

*Notes: † The Census 2010 population figure is used to calculate the percentages in the Hispanic Origin and Race categories. Ancestry percentages are based on the 2006-2010 American Community Survey population (not shown); ‡ Numbers in parentheses indicate the number of people reporting a single ancestry; * Numbers in parentheses indicate the number of persons reporting this race alone, not in combination with any other race; Please refer to the Explanation of Data for more information.*

Asian (249)	314	1.79
Not Hispanic (247)	310	1.77
Hispanic (2)	4	0.02
Cambodian (1)	1	0.01
Chinese, ex. Taiwanese (38)	40	0.23
Filipino (27)	51	0.29
Indian (68)	81	0.46
Japanese (4)	6	0.03
Korean (29)	47	0.27
Malaysian (0)	1	0.01
Pakistani (19)	19	0.11
Taiwanese (3)	3	0.02
Thai (5)	8	0.05
Vietnamese (49)	54	0.31
Hawaii Native/Pacific Islander (3)	19	0.11
Not Hispanic (2)	11	0.06
Hispanic (1)	8	0.05
Fijian (1)	1	0.01
Guamanian/Chamorro (1)	1	0.01
Native Hawaiian (0)	5	0.03
White (16,098)	16,334	93.32
Not Hispanic (15,875)	16,078	91.85
Hispanic (223)	256	1.46

Woodlyn

Place Type: CDP
County: Delaware
Population: 9,485†

Ancestry‡	Population	%
Albanian (0)	70	0.77
American (331)	331	3.65
Arab (6)	15	0.17
Lebanese (6)	6	0.07
Syrian (0)	9	0.10
Armenian (0)	5	0.06
Celtic (22)	22	0.24
Czech (0)	26	0.29
Danish (0)	11	0.12
Dutch (34)	192	2.12
English (72)	983	10.84
European (26)	26	0.29
Finnish (0)	130	1.43
French, ex. Basque (26)	153	1.69
German (331)	1,619	17.86
Greek (46)	72	0.79
Hungarian (61)	123	1.36
Irish (829)	3,434	37.87
Italian (822)	2,263	24.96
Lithuanian (41)	53	0.58
Norwegian (0)	40	0.44
Pennsylvania German (25)	58	0.64
Polish (146)	534	5.89
Russian (0)	63	0.69
Scotch-Irish (14)	155	1.71
Scottish (35)	164	1.81
Slavic (12)	12	0.13
Slovak (14)	26	0.29
Swedish (8)	37	0.41
Swiss (0)	38	0.42
Ukrainian (102)	157	1.73
Welsh (0)	146	1.61
West Indian, ex. Hispanic (7)	7	0.08
Bermudan (7)	7	0.08

Hispanic Origin	Population	%
Hispanic or Latino (of any race)	215	2.27
Central American, ex. Mexican	22	0.23
Costa Rican	6	0.06
Guatemalan	7	0.07
Honduran	1	0.01
Panamanian	1	0.01
Salvadoran	7	0.07
Cuban	6	0.06
Dominican Republic	8	0.08
Mexican	39	0.41
Puerto Rican	103	1.09
South American	21	0.22
Argentinean	7	0.07
Colombian	7	0.07
Ecuadorian	1	0.01
Peruvian	3	0.03
Uruguayan	1	0.01
Venezuelan	2	0.02
Other Hispanic or Latino	16	0.17

Race*	Population	%
African-American/Black (1,007)	1,111	11.71
Not Hispanic (987)	1,080	11.39
Hispanic (20)	31	0.33
American Indian/Alaska Native (15)	61	0.64
Not Hispanic (9)	50	0.53
Hispanic (6)	11	0.12
Blackfeet (0)	5	0.05
Cherokee (6)	21	0.22
Chippewa (0)	2	0.02
Choctaw (0)	2	0.02
Delaware (0)	1	0.01
Iroquois (0)	3	0.03
Lumbee (0)	2	0.02
Mexican American Ind. (2)	2	0.02
Navajo (0)	2	0.02
Spanish American Ind. (4)	4	0.04
Asian (121)	161	1.70
Not Hispanic (121)	161	1.70
Cambodian (14)	18	0.19
Chinese, ex. Taiwanese (24)	35	0.37
Filipino (17)	24	0.25
Indian (33)	36	0.38
Indonesian (0)	1	0.01
Japanese (5)	10	0.11
Korean (7)	8	0.08
Pakistani (3)	4	0.04
Thai (0)	6	0.06
Vietnamese (13)	24	0.25
Hawaii Native/Pacific Islander (0)	3	0.03
Not Hispanic (0)	3	0.03
White (8,111)	8,263	87.12
Not Hispanic (7,987)	8,123	85.64
Hispanic (124)	140	1.48

Worcester

Place Type: Township
County: Montgomery
Population: 9,750†

Ancestry‡	Population	%
Alsatian (0)	31	0.33
American (369)	369	3.93
Arab (58)	58	0.62
Egyptian (58)	58	0.62
Austrian (10)	43	0.46
Brazilian (0)	41	0.44
Croatian (11)	11	0.12
Czech (22)	89	0.95
Czechoslovakian (29)	47	0.50
Dutch (0)	67	0.71
English (213)	990	10.55
European (53)	149	1.59
French, ex. Basque (18)	229	2.44
German (456)	2,254	24.01
Greek (0)	27	0.29
Hungarian (11)	75	0.80
Irish (572)	2,429	25.88
Italian (935)	2,072	22.07
Lithuanian (29)	88	0.94
Norwegian (35)	70	0.75
Pennsylvania German (23)	34	0.36
Polish (195)	800	8.52
Romanian (15)	15	0.16
Russian (87)	285	3.04
Scotch-Irish (36)	107	1.14
Scottish (63)	233	2.48
Slavic (0)	67	0.71
Slovak (55)	85	0.91
Swedish (14)	175	1.86
Swiss (0)	70	0.75
Ukrainian (101)	209	2.23
Welsh (56)	212	2.26
West Indian, ex. Hispanic (12)	12	0.13
Haitian (12)	12	0.13

Hispanic Origin	Population	%
Hispanic or Latino (of any race)	159	1.63
Central American, ex. Mexican	15	0.15
Costa Rican	1	0.01
Guatemalan	12	0.12
Honduran	1	0.01
Salvadoran	1	0.01
Cuban	19	0.19
Dominican Republic	4	0.04
Mexican	50	0.51
Puerto Rican	28	0.29
South American	26	0.27
Argentinean	4	0.04
Bolivian	1	0.01
Chilean	5	0.05
Colombian	9	0.09
Ecuadorian	2	0.02
Paraguayan	2	0.02
Peruvian	2	0.02
Venezuelan	1	0.01
Other Hispanic or Latino	17	0.17

Race*	Population	%
African-American/Black (271)	306	3.14
Not Hispanic (266)	292	2.99
Hispanic (5)	14	0.14
American Indian/Alaska Native (1)	10	0.10
Not Hispanic (1)	6	0.06
Hispanic (0)	4	0.04
Cherokee (0)	3	0.03
Delaware (0)	1	0.01
Asian (1,000)	1,077	11.05
Not Hispanic (999)	1,076	11.04
Hispanic (1)	1	0.01
Bangladeshi (1)	5	0.05
Cambodian (3)	3	0.03
Chinese, ex. Taiwanese (253)	287	2.94
Filipino (18)	33	0.34
Indian (288)	309	3.17
Japanese (2)	3	0.03
Korean (365)	376	3.86
Nepalese (6)	6	0.06
Pakistani (12)	14	0.14
Sri Lankan (1)	2	0.02
Taiwanese (7)	8	0.08
Vietnamese (28)	30	0.31
Hawaii Native/Pacific Islander (2)	8	0.08
Not Hispanic (1)	7	0.07
Hispanic (1)	1	0.01
Guamanian/Chamorro (1)	1	0.01
Native Hawaiian (1)	2	0.02
White (8,312)	8,429	86.45
Not Hispanic (8,194)	8,299	85.12
Hispanic (118)	130	1.33

Wyomissing

Place Type: Borough
County: Berks
Population: 10,461†

Ancestry‡	Population	%
African, Sub-Saharan (0)	19	0.18
Cape Verdean (0)	19	0.18
American (482)	482	4.58
Arab (42)	60	0.57
Lebanese (42)	60	0.57
Australian (0)	31	0.29
Austrian (13)	78	0.74
British (24)	63	0.60
Czech (15)	42	0.40
Dutch (33)	307	2.92
English (184)	1,049	9.96
European (149)	149	1.42
French, ex. Basque (18)	244	2.32
French Canadian (0)	10	0.09

*Notes: † The Census 2010 population figure is used to calculate the percentages in the Hispanic Origin and Race categories. Ancestry percentages are based on the 2006-2010 American Community Survey population (not shown); ‡ Numbers in parentheses indicate the number of people reporting a single ancestry; * Numbers in parentheses indicate the number of persons reporting this race alone, not in combination with any other race; Please refer to the Explanation of Data for more information.*

Ancestry	Population	%
German (2,103)	3,718	35.32
Greek (92)	143	1.36
Hungarian (44)	179	1.70
Irish (446)	1,557	14.79
Italian (656)	1,495	14.20
Lithuanian (0)	57	0.54
Northern European (16)	16	0.15
Norwegian (15)	123	1.17
Pennsylvania German (134)	205	1.95
Polish (245)	860	8.17
Portuguese (8)	8	0.08
Romanian (30)	45	0.43
Russian (64)	165	1.57
Scandinavian (15)	62	0.59
Scotch-Irish (56)	111	1.05
Scottish (30)	258	2.45
Slavic (10)	10	0.09
Slovak (38)	95	0.90
Slovene (0)	25	0.24
Swedish (48)	104	0.99
Swiss (0)	15	0.14
Ukrainian (31)	99	0.94
Welsh (75)	333	3.16

Hispanic Origin	Population	%
Hispanic or Latino (of any race)	565	5.40
Central American, ex. Mexican	41	0.39
Costa Rican	5	0.05
Guatemalan	3	0.03
Honduran	15	0.14
Nicaraguan	6	0.06
Panamanian	1	0.01
Salvadoran	10	0.10
Other Central American	1	0.01
Cuban	15	0.14
Dominican Republic	93	0.89
Mexican	67	0.64
Puerto Rican	246	2.35
South American	70	0.67
Argentinean	21	0.20
Chilean	1	0.01
Colombian	9	0.09
Ecuadorian	31	0.30
Paraguayan	1	0.01
Peruvian	5	0.05
Venezuelan	2	0.02
Other Hispanic or Latino	33	0.32

Race*	Population	%
African-American/Black (246)	299	2.86
Not Hispanic (214)	257	2.46
Hispanic (32)	42	0.40
American Indian/Alaska Native (7)	31	0.30
Not Hispanic (3)	24	0.23
Hispanic (4)	7	0.07
Apache (0)	1	0.01
Cherokee (0)	2	0.02
Delaware (0)	2	0.02
Iroquois (0)	1	0.01
Potawatomi (0)	1	0.01
South American Ind. (1)	6	0.06
Asian (346)	403	3.85
Not Hispanic (344)	398	3.80
Hispanic (2)	5	0.05
Bangladeshi (1)	1	0.01
Chinese, ex. Taiwanese (72)	88	0.84
Filipino (20)	35	0.33
Indian (133)	149	1.42
Japanese (7)	13	0.12
Korean (22)	38	0.36
Malaysian (1)	1	0.01
Nepalese (17)	18	0.17
Pakistani (15)	15	0.14
Taiwanese (1)	1	0.01
Thai (3)	3	0.03
Vietnamese (43)	43	0.41
Hawaii Native/Pacific Islander (5)	11	0.11
Not Hispanic (5)	9	0.09
Hispanic (0)	2	0.02
Fijian (1)	1	0.01
Guamanian/Chamorro (3)	5	0.05
Native Hawaiian (1)	3	0.03
White (9,519)	9,661	92.35
Not Hispanic (9,206)	9,312	89.02
Hispanic (313)	349	3.34

Yeadon

Place Type: Borough
County: Delaware
Population: 11,443†

Ancestry‡	Population	%
African, Sub-Saharan (1,426)	1,504	13.11
African (370)	394	3.43
Ethiopian (71)	71	0.62
Ghanaian (99)	99	0.86
Liberian (612)	612	5.33
Nigerian (73)	109	0.95
Sierra Leonean (179)	197	1.72
Sudanese (22)	22	0.19
American (81)	81	0.71
Arab (6)	24	0.21
Arab (6)	6	0.05
Other Arab (0)	18	0.16
Dutch (0)	8	0.07
English (33)	110	0.96
European (0)	83	0.72
French, ex. Basque (38)	45	0.39
German (77)	197	1.72
Greek (30)	30	0.26
Irish (157)	219	1.91
Italian (170)	194	1.69
Lithuanian (0)	23	0.20
Norwegian (0)	23	0.20
Polish (0)	8	0.07
Russian (7)	23	0.20
Scotch-Irish (0)	7	0.06
Scottish (11)	45	0.39
Welsh (9)	17	0.15
West Indian, ex. Hispanic (586)	770	6.71
Belizean (13)	13	0.11
Haitian (61)	101	0.88
Jamaican (491)	571	4.98
Trinidadian/Tobagonian (0)	36	0.31
West Indian (21)	49	0.43

Hispanic Origin	Population	%
Hispanic or Latino (of any race)	216	1.89
Central American, ex. Mexican	22	0.19
Costa Rican	3	0.03
Honduran	4	0.03
Nicaraguan	4	0.03
Panamanian	11	0.10
Cuban	11	0.10
Dominican Republic	22	0.19
Mexican	13	0.11
Puerto Rican	108	0.94
South American	15	0.13
Bolivian	2	0.02
Colombian	1	0.01
Ecuadorian	6	0.05
Paraguayan	4	0.03
Venezuelan	2	0.02
Other Hispanic or Latino	25	0.22

Race*	Population	%
African-American/Black (10,141)	10,367	90.60
Not Hispanic (10,052)	10,244	89.52
Hispanic (89)	123	1.07
American Indian/Alaska Native (26)	121	1.06
Not Hispanic (24)	109	0.95
Hispanic (2)	12	0.10
Blackfeet (0)	5	0.04
Canadian/French Am. Ind. (0)	6	0.05
Cherokee (0)	27	0.24
Choctaw (0)	3	0.03
Creek (0)	1	0.01
Iroquois (0)	1	0.01
Menominee (0)	1	0.01
Mexican American Ind. (0)	1	0.01
Navajo (0)	3	0.03
Seminole (0)	3	0.03
Sioux (2)	5	0.04
South American Ind. (1)	3	0.03
Asian (88)	122	1.07
Not Hispanic (84)	116	1.01
Hispanic (4)	6	0.05
Cambodian (7)	10	0.09
Chinese, ex. Taiwanese (10)	13	0.11
Filipino (7)	16	0.14
Indian (13)	21	0.18
Japanese (1)	4	0.03
Korean (2)	8	0.07
Laotian (4)	4	0.03
Taiwanese (0)	2	0.02
Vietnamese (36)	41	0.36
Hawaii Native/Pacific Islander (7)	18	0.16
Not Hispanic (3)	14	0.12
Hispanic (4)	4	0.03
Guamanian/Chamorro (4)	5	0.04
Native Hawaiian (0)	1	0.01
White (861)	979	8.56
Not Hispanic (838)	939	8.21
Hispanic (23)	40	0.35

York

Place Type: City
County: York
Population: 43,718†

Ancestry‡	Population	%
African, Sub-Saharan (551)	647	1.48
African (408)	481	1.10
Ethiopian (50)	50	0.11
Ghanaian (32)	32	0.07
Nigerian (19)	19	0.04
Other Sub-Saharan African (42)	65	0.15
American (1,597)	1,597	3.66
Arab (67)	67	0.15
Arab (54)	54	0.12
Lebanese (13)	13	0.03
Austrian (10)	35	0.08
Belgian (0)	23	0.05
Brazilian (38)	83	0.19
British (8)	41	0.09
Croatian (0)	10	0.02
Czech (0)	21	0.05
Danish (8)	46	0.11
Dutch (170)	665	1.53
English (519)	1,504	3.45
European (80)	80	0.18
Finnish (0)	12	0.03
French, ex. Basque (47)	430	0.99
French Canadian (28)	52	0.12
German (4,096)	8,533	19.57
Greek (50)	100	0.23
Guyanese (11)	11	0.03
Hungarian (48)	130	0.30
Irish (909)	3,170	7.27
Italian (710)	2,161	4.96
Latvian (11)	11	0.03
Lithuanian (11)	63	0.14
Northern European (10)	10	0.02
Norwegian (20)	63	0.14
Pennsylvania German (311)	436	1.00
Polish (185)	947	2.17
Portuguese (0)	20	0.05
Romanian (46)	118	0.27
Russian (14)	82	0.19
Scotch-Irish (195)	564	1.29
Scottish (13)	274	0.63
Serbian (0)	17	0.04
Slovak (27)	51	0.12
Slovene (0)	11	0.03
Swedish (0)	77	0.18
Swiss (0)	11	0.03
Ukrainian (77)	111	0.25
Welsh (78)	284	0.65

*Notes: † The Census 2010 population figure is used to calculate the percentages in the Hispanic Origin and Race categories. Ancestry percentages are based on the 2006-2010 American Community Survey population (not shown); ‡ Numbers in parentheses indicate the number of people reporting a single ancestry; * Numbers in parentheses indicate the number of persons reporting this race alone, not in combination with any other race; Please refer to the Explanation of Data for more information.*

West Indian, ex. Hispanic (813)	949	2.18
Haitian (560)	560	1.28
Jamaican (221)	287	0.66
Trinidadian/Tobagonian (0)	24	0.06
West Indian (32)	78	0.18
Yugoslavian (0)	13	0.03

Hispanic Origin	Population	%
Hispanic or Latino (of any race)	12,458	28.50
Central American, ex. Mexican	282	0.65
Costa Rican	7	0.02
Guatemalan	23	0.05
Honduran	52	0.12
Nicaraguan	23	0.05
Panamanian	37	0.08
Salvadoran	131	0.30
Other Central American	9	0.02
Cuban	178	0.41
Dominican Republic	1,212	2.77
Mexican	1,482	3.39
Puerto Rican	8,440	19.31
South American	135	0.31
Argentinean	7	0.02
Bolivian	3	0.01
Chilean	4	0.01
Colombian	51	0.12
Ecuadorian	46	0.11
Paraguayan	2	<0.01
Peruvian	13	0.03
Uruguayan	7	0.02
Venezuelan	2	<0.01
Other Hispanic or Latino	729	1.67

Race*	Population	%
African-American/Black (12,248)	14,290	32.69
Not Hispanic (10,963)	12,458	28.50
Hispanic (1,285)	1,832	4.19
American Indian/Alaska Native (269)	686	1.57
Not Hispanic (99)	417	0.95
Hispanic (170)	269	0.62
Alaska Athabascan *(Ala. Nat.)* (1)	1	<0.01
Apache (2)	13	0.03
Blackfeet (8)	33	0.08
Central American Ind. (9)	11	0.03
Cherokee (16)	114	0.26
Cheyenne (1)	1	<0.01
Chippewa (1)	1	<0.01
Choctaw (1)	1	<0.01
Cree (1)	6	0.01
Creek (1)	5	0.01
Delaware (1)	1	<0.01
Iroquois (2)	8	0.02
Kiowa (0)	1	<0.01
Lumbee (0)	1	<0.01
Mexican American Ind. (6)	10	0.02
Navajo (1)	3	0.01
Potawatomi (2)	4	0.01
Sioux (4)	10	0.02
South American Ind. (12)	17	0.04
Spanish American Ind. (2)	3	0.01
Ute (0)	2	<0.01
Yaqui (1)	1	<0.01
Asian (541)	763	1.75
Not Hispanic (507)	661	1.51
Hispanic (34)	102	0.23
Bangladeshi (27)	33	0.08
Cambodian (105)	138	0.32
Chinese, ex. Taiwanese (70)	115	0.26
Filipino (23)	62	0.14
Indian (58)	108	0.25
Indonesian (0)	1	<0.01
Japanese (7)	33	0.08
Korean (23)	44	0.10
Laotian (21)	21	0.05
Malaysian (2)	2	<0.01
Nepalese (4)	4	0.01
Pakistani (15)	20	0.05
Sri Lankan (1)	2	<0.01
Taiwanese (2)	2	<0.01
Thai (2)	6	0.01
Vietnamese (142)	169	0.39
Hawaii Native/Pacific Islander (12)	81	0.19
Not Hispanic (4)	20	0.05
Hispanic (8)	61	0.14
Guamanian/Chamorro (1)	9	0.02
Native Hawaiian (8)	14	0.03
Samoan (0)	1	<0.01
White (22,398)	24,659	56.40
Not Hispanic (17,904)	19,452	44.49
Hispanic (4,494)	5,207	11.91

York

Place Type: Township
County: York
Population: 27,793†

Ancestry‡	Population	%
African, Sub-Saharan (229)	241	0.89
African (214)	226	0.83
Nigerian (15)	15	0.06
American (1,725)	1,725	6.34
Arab (0)	57	0.21
Egyptian (0)	16	0.06
Iraqi (0)	14	0.05
Lebanese (0)	27	0.10
Armenian (96)	96	0.35
Austrian (22)	66	0.24
Belgian (44)	57	0.21
Brazilian (0)	12	0.04
British (41)	122	0.45
Canadian (52)	70	0.26
Czech (12)	27	0.10
Czechoslovakian (38)	38	0.14
Danish (0)	42	0.15
Dutch (360)	915	3.36
Eastern European (19)	19	0.07
English (1,115)	2,718	9.98
European (175)	175	0.64
Finnish (0)	15	0.06
French, ex. Basque (145)	744	2.73
French Canadian (0)	26	0.10
German (6,797)	12,482	45.85
Greek (30)	91	0.33
Guyanese (41)	41	0.15
Hungarian (0)	35	0.13
Iranian (0)	36	0.13
Irish (848)	3,362	12.35
Italian (509)	1,455	5.34
Lithuanian (30)	85	0.31
Norwegian (62)	198	0.73
Pennsylvania German (128)	163	0.60
Polish (379)	1,049	3.85
Portuguese (16)	80	0.29
Romanian (0)	14	0.05
Russian (78)	258	0.95
Scandinavian (0)	17	0.06
Scotch-Irish (158)	719	2.64
Scottish (158)	433	1.59
Serbian (15)	27	0.10
Slovak (56)	149	0.55
Swedish (27)	369	1.36
Swiss (26)	182	0.67
Turkish (0)	16	0.06
Ukrainian (35)	40	0.15
Welsh (9)	258	0.95
West Indian, ex. Hispanic (10)	10	0.04
Jamaican (10)	10	0.04

Hispanic Origin	Population	%
Hispanic or Latino (of any race)	905	3.26
Central American, ex. Mexican	67	0.24
Costa Rican	3	0.01
Guatemalan	11	0.04
Honduran	8	0.03
Nicaraguan	8	0.03
Panamanian	6	0.02
Salvadoran	31	0.11
Cuban	40	0.14
Dominican Republic	46	0.17
Mexican	192	0.69
Puerto Rican	432	1.55
South American	80	0.29
Argentinean	5	0.02
Chilean	3	0.01
Colombian	29	0.10
Ecuadorian	4	0.01
Paraguayan	3	0.01
Peruvian	22	0.08
Uruguayan	4	0.01
Venezuelan	9	0.03
Other South American	1	<0.01
Other Hispanic or Latino	48	0.17

Race*	Population	%
African-American/Black (1,038)	1,239	4.46
Not Hispanic (979)	1,154	4.15
Hispanic (59)	85	0.31
American Indian/Alaska Native (48)	147	0.53
Not Hispanic (41)	134	0.48
Hispanic (7)	13	0.05
Apache (0)	4	0.01
Blackfeet (0)	6	0.02
Cherokee (9)	31	0.11
Chippewa (0)	2	0.01
Delaware (0)	2	0.01
Houma (1)	1	<0.01
Inupiat *(Alaska Native)* (2)	2	0.01
Lumbee (6)	6	0.02
Potawatomi (0)	3	0.01
Sioux (2)	5	0.02
Asian (635)	769	2.77
Not Hispanic (626)	749	2.69
Hispanic (9)	20	0.07
Bangladeshi (7)	7	0.03
Cambodian (6)	8	0.03
Chinese, ex. Taiwanese (143)	162	0.58
Filipino (36)	72	0.26
Indian (246)	266	0.96
Japanese (11)	24	0.09
Korean (90)	114	0.41
Laotian (1)	5	0.02
Pakistani (14)	20	0.07
Taiwanese (1)	1	<0.01
Thai (6)	12	0.04
Vietnamese (45)	49	0.18
Hawaii Native/Pacific Islander (6)	21	0.08
Not Hispanic (5)	17	0.06
Hispanic (1)	4	0.01
Guamanian/Chamorro (0)	2	0.01
Native Hawaiian (4)	11	0.04
Samoan (0)	1	<0.01
White (25,353)	25,745	92.63
Not Hispanic (24,847)	25,177	90.59
Hispanic (506)	568	2.04

*Notes: † The Census 2010 population figure is used to calculate the percentages in the Hispanic Origin and Race categories. Ancestry percentages are based on the 2006-2010 American Community Survey population (not shown); ‡ Numbers in parentheses indicate the number of people reporting a single ancestry; * Numbers in parentheses indicate the number of persons reporting this race alone, not in combination with any other race; Please refer to the Explanation of Data for more information.*

RHODE ISLAND

Place Type: State
Population: 1,052,567†

Ancestry‡	Population	%
Afghan (0)	11	<0.01
African, Sub-Saharan (25,727)	31,531	2.98
African (3,176)	4,050	0.38
Cape Verdean (15,528)	19,490	1.84
Ethiopian (145)	174	0.02
Ghanaian (826)	874	0.08
Kenyan (52)	52	<0.01
Liberian (2,834)	2,980	0.28
Nigerian (1,972)	2,106	0.20
Senegalese (201)	370	0.04
Sierra Leonean (37)	51	<0.01
South African (56)	128	0.01
Sudanese (71)	82	0.01
Ugandan (10)	10	<0.01
Other Sub-Saharan African (819)	1,164	0.11
Albanian (99)	249	0.02
Alsatian (17)	46	<0.01
American (22,938)	22,938	2.17
Arab (4,033)	8,762	0.83
Arab (374)	598	0.06
Egyptian (274)	513	0.05
Iraqi (76)	88	0.01
Jordanian (112)	177	0.02
Lebanese (1,390)	3,396	0.32
Moroccan (124)	169	0.02
Palestinian (0)	49	<0.01
Syrian (1,524)	3,519	0.33
Other Arab (159)	253	0.02
Armenian (3,856)	6,694	0.63
Assyrian/Chaldean/Syriac (57)	160	0.02
Australian (128)	272	0.03
Austrian (415)	2,125	0.20
Basque (0)	13	<0.01
Belgian (303)	1,120	0.11
Brazilian (1,179)	1,617	0.15
British (1,683)	3,451	0.33
Bulgarian (178)	193	0.02
Canadian (2,301)	5,044	0.48
Celtic (100)	226	0.02
Croatian (146)	330	0.03
Cypriot (9)	9	<0.01
Czech (345)	1,249	0.12
Czechoslovakian (154)	562	0.05
Danish (505)	2,127	0.20
Dutch (1,109)	5,604	0.53
Eastern European (1,245)	1,423	0.13
English (32,285)	135,087	12.79
Estonian (48)	89	0.01
European (3,347)	3,799	0.36
Finnish (349)	1,869	0.18
French, ex. Basque (35,908)	131,396	12.44
French Canadian (29,113)	52,379	4.96
German (11,914)	65,504	6.20
German Russian (43)	43	<0.01
Greek (2,944)	7,603	0.72
Guyanese (70)	83	0.01
Hungarian (698)	2,662	0.25
Icelander (0)	24	<0.01
Iranian (249)	380	0.04
Irish (59,231)	211,879	20.06
Israeli (87)	190	0.02
Italian (90,595)	202,100	19.13
Latvian (66)	127	0.01
Lithuanian (1,095)	4,291	0.41
Luxemburger (0)	73	0.01
Maltese (0)	65	0.01
New Zealander (14)	78	0.01
Northern European (454)	463	0.04
Norwegian (1,023)	4,523	0.43
Pennsylvania German (94)	233	0.02
Polish (12,786)	44,019	4.17
Portuguese (52,071)	101,178	9.58
Romanian (328)	741	0.07
Russian (4,270)	11,523	1.09
Scandinavian (370)	756	0.07
Scotch-Irish (5,491)	15,267	1.45
Scottish (5,057)	23,453	2.22
Serbian (48)	106	0.01
Slavic (32)	74	0.01
Slovak (358)	1,124	0.11
Slovene (30)	120	0.01
Swedish (4,270)	18,996	1.80
Swiss (250)	1,054	0.10
Turkish (369)	645	0.06
Ukrainian (973)	2,653	0.25
Welsh (463)	3,185	0.30
West Indian, ex. Hispanic (4,596)	6,025	0.57
Barbadian (336)	528	0.05
Belizean (292)	292	0.03
Bermudan (13)	37	<0.01
British West Indian (122)	188	0.02
Haitian (2,259)	2,477	0.23
Jamaican (785)	1,144	0.11
Trinidadian/Tobagonian (262)	327	0.03
U.S. Virgin Islander (86)	86	0.01
West Indian (441)	946	0.09
Yugoslavian (52)	201	0.02

Hispanic Origin	Population	%
Hispanic or Latino (of any race)	130,655	12.41
Central American, ex. Mexican	23,817	2.26
Costa Rican	242	0.02
Guatemalan	18,852	1.79
Honduran	1,250	0.12
Nicaraguan	267	0.03
Panamanian	359	0.03
Salvadoran	2,715	0.26
Other Central American	132	0.01
Cuban	1,640	0.16
Dominican Republic	35,008	3.33
Mexican	9,090	0.86
Puerto Rican	34,979	3.32
South American	14,013	1.33
Argentinean	471	0.04
Bolivian	1,912	0.18
Chilean	312	0.03
Colombian	8,283	0.79
Ecuadorian	1,128	0.11
Paraguayan	18	<0.01
Peruvian	1,067	0.10
Uruguayan	112	0.01
Venezuelan	643	0.06
Other South American	67	0.01
Other Hispanic or Latino	12,108	1.15

Race*	Population	%
African-American/Black (60,189)	77,754	7.39
Not Hispanic (51,560)	64,890	6.16
Hispanic (8,629)	12,864	1.22
American Indian/Alaska Native (6,058)	14,394	1.37
Not Hispanic (4,020)	10,580	1.01
Hispanic (2,038)	3,814	0.36
Alaska Athabascan *(Ala. Nat.)* (3)	7	<0.01
Aleut *(Alaska Native)* (0)	3	<0.01
Apache (14)	66	0.01
Blackfeet (61)	351	0.03
Canadian/French Am. Ind. (21)	94	0.01
Central American Ind. (151)	211	0.02
Cherokee (196)	987	0.09
Cheyenne (2)	8	<0.01
Chickasaw (9)	24	<0.01
Chippewa (23)	71	0.01
Choctaw (9)	50	<0.01
Colville (1)	1	<0.01
Comanche (5)	10	<0.01
Cree (10)	58	0.01
Creek (4)	23	<0.01
Crow (0)	8	<0.01
Delaware (8)	18	<0.01
Hopi (2)	8	<0.01
Houma (3)	4	<0.01
Inupiat *(Alaska Native)* (7)	11	<0.01
Iroquois (60)	278	0.03
Kiowa (1)	4	<0.01
Lumbee (15)	23	<0.01
Menominee (2)	6	<0.01
Mexican American Ind. (312)	447	0.04
Navajo (28)	73	0.01
Osage (1)	7	<0.01
Ottawa (1)	1	<0.01
Paiute (0)	2	<0.01
Pima (0)	1	<0.01
Potawatomi (6)	13	<0.01
Pueblo (12)	36	<0.01
Puget Sound Salish (1)	5	<0.01
Seminole (6)	43	<0.01
Shoshone (1)	12	<0.01
Sioux (54)	133	0.01
South American Ind. (200)	378	0.04
Spanish American Ind. (62)	94	0.01
Tlingit-Haida *(Alaska Native)* (1)	9	<0.01
Tohono O'Odham (7)	8	<0.01
Tsimshian *(Alaska Native)* (0)	1	<0.01
Ute (0)	3	<0.01
Yakama (0)	1	<0.01
Yaqui (3)	7	<0.01
Yuman (7)	8	<0.01
Yup'ik *(Alaska Native)* (6)	12	<0.01
Asian (30,457)	36,763	3.49
Not Hispanic (29,988)	35,535	3.38
Hispanic (469)	1,228	0.12
Bangladeshi (68)	83	0.01
Bhutanese (59)	72	0.01
Burmese (89)	108	0.01
Cambodian (5,176)	5,961	0.57
Chinese, ex. Taiwanese (6,574)	7,924	0.75
Filipino (2,621)	4,117	0.39
Hmong (909)	1,015	0.10
Indian (4,653)	5,645	0.54
Indonesian (52)	95	0.01
Japanese (639)	1,455	0.14
Korean (2,138)	2,658	0.25
Laotian (2,875)	3,380	0.32
Malaysian (50)	72	0.01
Nepalese (109)	128	0.01
Pakistani (604)	696	0.07
Sri Lankan (84)	106	0.01
Taiwanese (270)	325	0.03
Thai (351)	591	0.06
Vietnamese (1,326)	1,615	0.15
Hawaii Native/Pacific Islander (554)	2,260	0.21
Not Hispanic (305)	1,437	0.14
Hispanic (249)	823	0.08
Fijian (25)	37	<0.01
Guamanian/Chamorro (232)	360	0.03
Marshallese (11)	11	<0.01
Native Hawaiian (96)	397	0.04
Samoan (40)	93	0.01
Tongan (3)	10	<0.01
White (856,869)	882,280	83.82
Not Hispanic (803,685)	820,838	77.98
Hispanic (53,184)	61,442	5.84

*Notes: † The Census 2010 population figure is used to calculate the percentages in the Hispanic Origin and Race categories. Ancestry percentages are based on the 2006-2010 American Community Survey population (not shown); ‡ Numbers in parentheses indicate the number of people reporting a single ancestry; * Numbers in parentheses indicate the number of persons reporting this race alone, not in combination with any other race; Please refer to the Explanation of Data for more information.*

Barrington

Place Type: Town
County: Bristol
Population: 16,310†

Ancestry‡	Population	%
African, Sub-Saharan (14)	80	0.48
African (0)	11	0.07
Cape Verdean (14)	58	0.35
Sudanese (0)	11	0.07
Albanian (8)	28	0.17
Alsatian (11)	11	0.07
American (471)	471	2.85
Arab (30)	83	0.50
Arab (8)	8	0.05
Egyptian (2)	22	0.13
Lebanese (11)	40	0.24
Syrian (9)	13	0.08
Armenian (88)	139	0.84
Australian (0)	5	0.03
Austrian (45)	76	0.46
Brazilian (11)	11	0.07
British (21)	87	0.53
Canadian (46)	98	0.59
Croatian (0)	16	0.10
Czech (23)	41	0.25
Czechoslovakian (0)	12	0.07
Danish (29)	59	0.36
Dutch (20)	137	0.83
Eastern European (215)	215	1.30
English (916)	3,243	19.65
Estonian (12)	36	0.22
European (190)	204	1.24
Finnish (17)	26	0.16
French, ex. Basque (206)	1,181	7.16
French Canadian (157)	530	3.21
German (297)	1,464	8.87
Greek (199)	343	2.08
Hungarian (22)	97	0.59
Iranian (8)	16	0.10
Irish (1,302)	4,454	26.99
Israeli (12)	47	0.28
Italian (1,265)	3,422	20.74
Lithuanian (49)	88	0.53
Norwegian (35)	138	0.84
Polish (214)	614	3.72
Portuguese (545)	1,293	7.84
Russian (148)	379	2.30
Scotch-Irish (77)	332	2.01
Scottish (134)	511	3.10
Slovak (0)	12	0.07
Swedish (177)	670	4.06
Turkish (0)	23	0.14
Ukrainian (16)	74	0.45
Welsh (26)	141	0.85
West Indian, ex. Hispanic (20)	20	0.12
Haitian (10)	10	0.06
Trinidadian/Tobagonian (10)	10	0.06

Hispanic Origin	Population	%
Hispanic or Latino (of any race)	333	2.04
Central American, ex. Mexican	29	0.18
Costa Rican	1	0.01
Guatemalan	13	0.08
Honduran	7	0.04
Nicaraguan	1	0.01
Panamanian	1	0.01
Salvadoran	6	0.04
Cuban	35	0.21
Dominican Republic	22	0.13
Mexican	53	0.32
Puerto Rican	77	0.47
South American	83	0.51
Argentinean	16	0.10
Bolivian	4	0.02
Chilean	7	0.04
Colombian	31	0.19
Ecuadorian	5	0.03
Paraguayan	1	0.01
Peruvian	4	0.02
Uruguayan	1	0.01
Venezuelan	11	0.07
Other South American	3	0.02
Other Hispanic or Latino	34	0.21

Race*	Population	%
African-American/Black (80)	159	0.97
Not Hispanic (71)	144	0.88
Hispanic (9)	15	0.09
American Indian/Alaska Native (21)	90	0.55
Not Hispanic (19)	77	0.47
Hispanic (2)	13	0.08
Aleut *(Alaska Native)* (0)	1	0.01
Apache (1)	4	0.02
Blackfeet (0)	5	0.03
Central American Ind. (1)	1	0.01
Cherokee (0)	7	0.04
Chickasaw (4)	7	0.04
Chippewa (2)	2	0.01
Creek (0)	1	0.01
Iroquois (0)	1	0.01
Mexican American Ind. (1)	1	0.01
Potawatomi (0)	4	0.02
South American Ind. (0)	1	0.01
Tlingit-Haida *(Alaska Native)* (0)	3	0.02
Yup'ik *(Alaska Native)* (0)	1	0.01
Asian (451)	570	3.49
Not Hispanic (448)	556	3.41
Hispanic (3)	14	0.09
Bangladeshi (0)	2	0.01
Cambodian (4)	7	0.04
Chinese, ex. Taiwanese (197)	233	1.43
Filipino (27)	45	0.28
Indian (88)	124	0.76
Indonesian (3)	3	0.02
Japanese (16)	33	0.20
Korean (59)	67	0.41
Laotian (3)	5	0.03
Malaysian (0)	2	0.01
Pakistani (8)	14	0.09
Sri Lankan (4)	10	0.06
Taiwanese (7)	7	0.04
Thai (10)	10	0.06
Vietnamese (9)	13	0.08
Hawaii Native/Pacific Islander (0)	13	0.08
Not Hispanic (0)	7	0.04
Hispanic (0)	6	0.04
Native Hawaiian (0)	5	0.03
Samoan (0)	3	0.02
White (15,449)	15,659	96.01
Not Hispanic (15,202)	15,387	94.34
Hispanic (247)	272	1.67

Bristol

Place Type: Town
County: Bristol
Population: 22,954†

Ancestry‡	Population	%
African, Sub-Saharan (18)	18	0.08
African (15)	15	0.06
South African (3)	3	0.01
Albanian (2)	2	0.01
American (448)	448	1.93
Arab (23)	57	0.25
Lebanese (23)	27	0.12
Syrian (0)	20	0.09
Other Arab (0)	10	0.04
Armenian (0)	20	0.09
Assyrian/Chaldean/Syriac (0)	17	0.07
Austrian (10)	10	0.04
Belgian (0)	29	0.13
Brazilian (20)	20	0.09
British (46)	178	0.77
Canadian (11)	184	0.79
Celtic (11)	11	0.05
Croatian (0)	19	0.08
Czech (0)	26	0.11
Czechoslovakian (11)	47	0.20
Danish (61)	188	0.81
Dutch (0)	148	0.64
English (507)	2,645	11.41
European (136)	136	0.59
Finnish (11)	48	0.21
French, ex. Basque (378)	2,083	8.98
French Canadian (453)	990	4.27
German (379)	1,868	8.06
Greek (129)	310	1.34
Hungarian (10)	70	0.30
Irish (1,086)	4,823	20.80
Italian (1,843)	5,297	22.84
Lithuanian (0)	62	0.27
Northern European (36)	36	0.16
Norwegian (69)	170	0.73
Polish (267)	1,162	5.01
Portuguese (4,752)	7,346	31.68
Russian (49)	247	1.07
Scandinavian (5)	5	0.02
Scotch-Irish (209)	539	2.32
Scottish (263)	491	2.12
Slavic (0)	29	0.13
Slovak (18)	82	0.35
Swedish (62)	337	1.45
Ukrainian (0)	72	0.31
Welsh (9)	114	0.49
West Indian, ex. Hispanic (17)	17	0.07
Jamaican (17)	17	0.07

Hispanic Origin	Population	%
Hispanic or Latino (of any race)	462	2.01
Central American, ex. Mexican	47	0.20
Guatemalan	20	0.09
Honduran	8	0.03
Panamanian	5	0.02
Salvadoran	14	0.06
Cuban	24	0.10
Dominican Republic	22	0.10
Mexican	104	0.45
Puerto Rican	131	0.57
South American	73	0.32
Argentinean	11	0.05
Bolivian	1	<0.01
Chilean	14	0.06
Colombian	18	0.08
Ecuadorian	8	0.03
Paraguayan	2	0.01
Peruvian	7	0.03
Uruguayan	5	0.02
Venezuelan	7	0.03
Other Hispanic or Latino	61	0.27

Race*	Population	%
African-American/Black (194)	298	1.30
Not Hispanic (180)	270	1.18
Hispanic (14)	28	0.12
American Indian/Alaska Native (26)	150	0.65
Not Hispanic (24)	140	0.61
Hispanic (2)	10	0.04
Apache (0)	6	0.03
Blackfeet (0)	10	0.04
Canadian/French Am. Ind. (1)	4	0.02
Cherokee (2)	17	0.07
Cheyenne (0)	3	0.01
Chippewa (1)	2	0.01
Choctaw (0)	1	<0.01
Cree (0)	2	0.01
Delaware (1)	3	0.01
Houma (2)	2	0.01
Iroquois (1)	6	0.03
Mexican American Ind. (1)	3	0.01
Navajo (0)	4	0.02
Paiute (0)	1	<0.01
Sioux (0)	2	0.01
Asian (200)	275	1.20
Not Hispanic (193)	260	1.13
Hispanic (7)	15	0.07
Cambodian (7)	8	0.03
Chinese, ex. Taiwanese (53)	64	0.28

*Notes: † The Census 2010 population figure is used to calculate the percentages in the Hispanic Origin and Race categories. Ancestry percentages are based on the 2006-2010 American Community Survey population (not shown); ‡ Numbers in parentheses indicate the number of people reporting a single ancestry; * Numbers in parentheses indicate the number of persons reporting this race alone, not in combination with any other race; Please refer to the Explanation of Data for more information.*

Filipino (26)	49	0.21
Indian (35)	49	0.21
Japanese (10)	26	0.11
Korean (29)	37	0.16
Laotian (0)	1	<0.01
Malaysian (0)	1	<0.01
Pakistani (8)	8	0.03
Taiwanese (3)	3	0.01
Thai (1)	1	<0.01
Vietnamese (11)	13	0.06
Hawaii Native/Pacific Islander (1)	16	0.07
Not Hispanic (1)	15	0.07
Hispanic (0)	1	<0.01
Guamanian/Chamorro (0)	1	<0.01
Native Hawaiian (0)	2	0.01
Samoan (0)	1	<0.01
White (22,113)	22,415	97.65
Not Hispanic (21,790)	22,049	96.06
Hispanic (323)	366	1.59

Burrillville

Place Type: Town
County: Providence
Population: 15,955†

Ancestry‡	Population	%
African, Sub-Saharan (16)	16	0.10
African (16)	16	0.10
American (234)	234	1.47
Arab (30)	123	0.77
Lebanese (12)	12	0.08
Syrian (18)	111	0.70
Armenian (0)	22	0.14
Austrian (0)	13	0.08
Belgian (0)	12	0.08
British (13)	40	0.25
Canadian (115)	264	1.65
Czech (20)	47	0.29
Dutch (0)	14	0.09
English (672)	2,282	14.29
European (57)	57	0.36
Finnish (0)	26	0.16
French, ex. Basque (2,416)	5,117	32.04
French Canadian (1,709)	2,716	17.01
German (94)	853	5.34
Hungarian (15)	88	0.55
Irish (830)	3,566	22.33
Italian (660)	2,014	12.61
Lithuanian (25)	102	0.64
Northern European (43)	43	0.27
Norwegian (8)	37	0.23
Pennsylvania German (37)	37	0.23
Polish (225)	660	4.13
Portuguese (208)	557	3.49
Russian (27)	93	0.58
Scotch-Irish (96)	204	1.28
Scottish (198)	556	3.48
Slovak (21)	75	0.47
Swedish (127)	265	1.66
Ukrainian (0)	85	0.53
Welsh (0)	16	0.10

Hispanic Origin	Population	%
Hispanic or Latino (of any race)	265	1.66
Central American, ex. Mexican	22	0.14
Costa Rican	3	0.02
Guatemalan	10	0.06
Honduran	3	0.02
Nicaraguan	1	0.01
Panamanian	3	0.02
Salvadoran	2	0.01
Cuban	4	0.03
Dominican Republic	23	0.14
Mexican	60	0.38
Puerto Rican	73	0.46
South American	45	0.28
Argentinean	2	0.01
Bolivian	6	0.04
Chilean	3	0.02
Colombian	26	0.16
Ecuadorian	5	0.03
Paraguayan	1	0.01
Peruvian	2	0.01
Other Hispanic or Latino	38	0.24

Race*	Population	%
African-American/Black (78)	143	0.90
Not Hispanic (62)	124	0.78
Hispanic (16)	19	0.12
American Indian/Alaska Native (28)	95	0.60
Not Hispanic (17)	76	0.48
Hispanic (11)	19	0.12
Blackfeet (3)	7	0.04
Canadian/French Am. Ind. (0)	4	0.03
Cherokee (0)	7	0.04
Comanche (0)	2	0.01
Iroquois (0)	4	0.03
Lumbee (1)	1	0.01
Mexican American Ind. (5)	9	0.06
Puget Sound Salish (0)	1	0.01
Asian (59)	124	0.78
Not Hispanic (58)	117	0.73
Hispanic (1)	7	0.04
Bangladeshi (1)	2	0.01
Cambodian (4)	14	0.09
Chinese, ex. Taiwanese (15)	22	0.14
Filipino (8)	25	0.16
Hmong (0)	1	0.01
Indian (5)	9	0.06
Japanese (4)	25	0.16
Korean (3)	8	0.05
Laotian (10)	15	0.09
Taiwanese (3)	3	0.02
Thai (1)	1	0.01
Vietnamese (0)	4	0.03
Hawaii Native/Pacific Islander (3)	10	0.06
Not Hispanic (1)	6	0.04
Hispanic (2)	4	0.03
Guamanian/Chamorro (1)	1	0.01
Native Hawaiian (2)	6	0.04
Samoan (0)	1	0.01
White (15,498)	15,694	98.36
Not Hispanic (15,359)	15,529	97.33
Hispanic (139)	165	1.03

Central Falls

Place Type: City
County: Providence
Population: 19,376†

Ancestry‡	Population	%
African, Sub-Saharan (1,025)	1,308	6.75
African (13)	108	0.56
Cape Verdean (970)	1,158	5.97
Liberian (22)	22	0.11
Other Sub-Saharan African (20)	20	0.10
American (205)	205	1.06
Arab (182)	202	1.04
Lebanese (62)	62	0.32
Syrian (120)	140	0.72
Assyrian/Chaldean/Syriac (0)	20	0.10
Canadian (56)	85	0.44
Dutch (0)	8	0.04
English (84)	542	2.80
Finnish (0)	21	0.11
French, ex. Basque (479)	1,070	5.52
French Canadian (652)	852	4.39
German (10)	284	1.46
Hungarian (0)	20	0.10
Irish (404)	1,192	6.15
Italian (95)	369	1.90
Lithuanian (0)	11	0.06
Norwegian (0)	14	0.07
Polish (295)	589	3.04
Portuguese (1,375)	1,733	8.94
Scotch-Irish (23)	57	0.29
Scottish (0)	54	0.28
Swedish (17)	35	0.18
Welsh (0)	8	0.04
West Indian, ex. Hispanic (30)	30	0.15
Belizean (12)	12	0.06
Haitian (9)	9	0.05
Jamaican (9)	9	0.05

Hispanic Origin	Population	%
Hispanic or Latino (of any race)	11,685	60.31
Central American, ex. Mexican	3,060	15.79
Costa Rican	13	0.07
Guatemalan	2,574	13.28
Honduran	101	0.52
Nicaraguan	5	0.03
Panamanian	4	0.02
Salvadoran	358	1.85
Other Central American	5	0.03
Cuban	37	0.19
Dominican Republic	1,237	6.38
Mexican	1,341	6.92
Puerto Rican	2,878	14.85
South American	2,233	11.52
Argentinean	40	0.21
Bolivian	46	0.24
Chilean	7	0.04
Colombian	2,018	10.41
Ecuadorian	41	0.21
Peruvian	37	0.19
Uruguayan	1	0.01
Venezuelan	43	0.22
Other Hispanic or Latino	899	4.64

Race*	Population	%
African-American/Black (1,949)	2,547	13.15
Not Hispanic (1,413)	1,830	9.44
Hispanic (536)	717	3.70
American Indian/Alaska Native (183)	336	1.73
Not Hispanic (59)	142	0.73
Hispanic (124)	194	1.00
Alaska Athabascan *(Ala. Nat.)* (1)	1	0.01
Blackfeet (1)	4	0.02
Canadian/French Am. Ind. (0)	1	0.01
Central American Ind. (11)	12	0.06
Cherokee (2)	25	0.13
Choctaw (0)	2	0.01
Cree (1)	3	0.02
Iroquois (0)	2	0.01
Lumbee (1)	1	0.01
Mexican American Ind. (25)	27	0.14
Pueblo (1)	4	0.02
Seminole (0)	2	0.01
Sioux (1)	1	0.01
South American Ind. (6)	10	0.05
Spanish American Ind. (6)	9	0.05
Tohono O'Odham (2)	3	0.02
Asian (121)	189	0.98
Not Hispanic (98)	126	0.65
Hispanic (23)	63	0.33
Cambodian (14)	15	0.08
Chinese, ex. Taiwanese (31)	34	0.18
Filipino (7)	15	0.08
Indian (44)	56	0.29
Indonesian (0)	4	0.02
Japanese (1)	5	0.03
Korean (0)	5	0.03
Laotian (0)	1	0.01
Pakistani (1)	1	0.01
Thai (1)	1	0.01
Vietnamese (4)	5	0.03
Hawaii Native/Pacific Islander (18)	116	0.60
Not Hispanic (10)	67	0.35
Hispanic (8)	49	0.25
Guamanian/Chamorro (5)	6	0.03
Native Hawaiian (6)	8	0.04
Samoan (1)	2	0.01
White (10,258)	11,060	57.08
Not Hispanic (4,967)	5,235	27.02
Hispanic (5,291)	5,825	30.06

*Notes: † The Census 2010 population figure is used to calculate the percentages in the Hispanic Origin and Race categories. Ancestry percentages are based on the 2006-2010 American Community Survey population (not shown); ‡ Numbers in parentheses indicate the number of people reporting a single ancestry; * Numbers in parentheses indicate the number of persons reporting this race alone, not in combination with any other race; Please refer to the Explanation of Data for more information.*

Charlestown

Place Type: Town
County: Washington
Population: 7,827†

Ancestry‡	Population	%
African, Sub-Saharan (21)	40	0.51
Cape Verdean (0)	19	0.24
Ghanaian (21)	21	0.27
American (361)	361	4.58
Arab (42)	75	0.95
Egyptian (18)	51	0.65
Lebanese (12)	12	0.15
Other Arab (12)	12	0.15
Armenian (13)	25	0.32
Austrian (0)	29	0.37
Canadian (10)	67	0.85
Czech (0)	11	0.14
Czechoslovakian (10)	17	0.22
Danish (8)	42	0.53
Dutch (0)	9	0.11
English (604)	2,137	27.13
Finnish (0)	90	1.14
French, ex. Basque (158)	854	10.84
French Canadian (169)	271	3.44
German (177)	676	8.58
Greek (0)	21	0.27
Hungarian (0)	50	0.63
Irish (929)	2,483	31.53
Italian (510)	1,489	18.91
Lithuanian (10)	39	0.50
Norwegian (18)	39	0.50
Polish (162)	499	6.34
Portuguese (47)	282	3.58
Russian (30)	208	2.64
Scotch-Irish (101)	173	2.20
Scottish (22)	295	3.75
Slovak (12)	24	0.30
Slovene (0)	12	0.15
Swedish (31)	110	1.40
Ukrainian (0)	5	0.06
Welsh (27)	57	0.72

Hispanic Origin	Population	%
Hispanic or Latino (of any race)	127	1.62
Central American, ex. Mexican	9	0.11
Costa Rican	1	0.01
Guatemalan	6	0.08
Panamanian	2	0.03
Cuban	13	0.17
Dominican Republic	7	0.09
Mexican	13	0.17
Puerto Rican	52	0.66
South American	16	0.20
Bolivian	7	0.09
Chilean	2	0.03
Colombian	1	0.01
Ecuadorian	3	0.04
Peruvian	3	0.04
Other Hispanic or Latino	17	0.22

Race*	Population	%
African-American/Black (31)	81	1.03
Not Hispanic (29)	76	0.97
Hispanic (2)	5	0.06
American Indian/Alaska Native (150)	210	2.68
Not Hispanic (142)	197	2.52
Hispanic (8)	13	0.17
Apache (0)	2	0.03
Canadian/French Am. Ind. (0)	1	0.01
Cherokee (2)	7	0.09
Cree (1)	1	0.01
Creek (0)	1	0.01
Iroquois (1)	5	0.06
Navajo (0)	2	0.03
Asian (55)	102	1.30
Not Hispanic (55)	98	1.25
Hispanic (0)	4	0.05
Chinese, ex. Taiwanese (20)	28	0.36
Filipino (10)	36	0.46
Indian (5)	9	0.11
Japanese (3)	10	0.13
Korean (6)	6	0.08
Pakistani (2)	4	0.05
Thai (1)	1	0.01
Vietnamese (1)	8	0.10
Hawaii Native/Pacific Islander (2)	2	0.03
Not Hispanic (2)	2	0.03
Guamanian/Chamorro (1)	1	0.01
Native Hawaiian (1)	1	0.01
White (7,424)	7,543	96.37
Not Hispanic (7,347)	7,454	95.23
Hispanic (77)	89	1.14

Coventry

Place Type: Town
County: Kent
Population: 35,014†

Ancestry‡	Population	%
African, Sub-Saharan (47)	174	0.50
African (12)	12	0.03
Cape Verdean (35)	162	0.46
American (1,306)	1,306	3.73
Arab (30)	119	0.34
Lebanese (30)	100	0.29
Syrian (0)	19	0.05
Armenian (46)	76	0.22
Australian (0)	17	0.05
Austrian (10)	20	0.06
Belgian (0)	56	0.16
Brazilian (22)	22	0.06
British (59)	93	0.27
Canadian (103)	248	0.71
Czechoslovakian (0)	75	0.21
Danish (24)	98	0.28
Dutch (125)	232	0.66
Eastern European (15)	15	0.04
English (1,254)	5,459	15.58
European (125)	132	0.38
Finnish (16)	136	0.39
French, ex. Basque (2,309)	7,797	22.25
French Canadian (1,179)	2,444	6.97
German (579)	2,970	8.48
Greek (104)	299	0.85
Hungarian (0)	60	0.17
Iranian (16)	69	0.20
Irish (1,878)	8,121	23.18
Italian (2,856)	7,748	22.11
Lithuanian (45)	202	0.58
Maltese (0)	22	0.06
Norwegian (9)	39	0.11
Polish (562)	1,910	5.45
Portuguese (1,165)	3,429	9.79
Romanian (32)	43	0.12
Russian (77)	406	1.16
Scandinavian (18)	18	0.05
Scotch-Irish (192)	557	1.59
Scottish (166)	916	2.61
Swedish (271)	731	2.09
Swiss (30)	68	0.19
Turkish (20)	20	0.06
Ukrainian (42)	102	0.29
Welsh (18)	99	0.28
West Indian, ex. Hispanic (14)	14	0.04
Belizean (14)	14	0.04

Hispanic Origin	Population	%
Hispanic or Latino (of any race)	671	1.92
Central American, ex. Mexican	85	0.24
Costa Rican	4	0.01
Guatemalan	60	0.17
Honduran	11	0.03
Nicaraguan	2	0.01
Salvadoran	8	0.02
Cuban	36	0.10
Dominican Republic	107	0.31
Mexican	125	0.36
Puerto Rican	158	0.45
South American	87	0.25
Argentinean	10	0.03
Bolivian	7	0.02
Chilean	5	0.01
Colombian	29	0.08
Ecuadorian	14	0.04
Peruvian	5	0.01
Uruguayan	12	0.03
Other South American	5	0.01
Other Hispanic or Latino	73	0.21

Race*	Population	%
African-American/Black (226)	448	1.28
Not Hispanic (206)	391	1.12
Hispanic (20)	57	0.16
American Indian/Alaska Native (72)	194	0.55
Not Hispanic (58)	171	0.49
Hispanic (14)	23	0.07
Apache (0)	1	<0.01
Blackfeet (0)	6	0.02
Canadian/French Am. Ind. (0)	3	0.01
Cherokee (5)	23	0.07
Chippewa (0)	2	0.01
Creek (0)	2	0.01
Iroquois (0)	3	0.01
Lumbee (2)	2	0.01
Mexican American Ind. (2)	2	0.01
Ottawa (1)	1	<0.01
South American Ind. (2)	2	0.01
Yup'ik *(Alaska Native)* (1)	1	<0.01
Asian (264)	403	1.15
Not Hispanic (260)	393	1.12
Hispanic (4)	10	0.03
Cambodian (32)	33	0.09
Chinese, ex. Taiwanese (80)	103	0.29
Filipino (30)	78	0.22
Hmong (5)	5	0.01
Indian (45)	53	0.15
Japanese (7)	26	0.07
Korean (24)	37	0.11
Laotian (12)	14	0.04
Pakistani (1)	1	<0.01
Sri Lankan (1)	1	<0.01
Taiwanese (4)	5	0.01
Thai (6)	7	0.02
Vietnamese (11)	17	0.05
Hawaii Native/Pacific Islander (7)	32	0.09
Not Hispanic (5)	29	0.08
Hispanic (2)	3	0.01
Guamanian/Chamorro (3)	4	0.01
Native Hawaiian (0)	8	0.02
White (33,771)	34,225	97.75
Not Hispanic (33,361)	33,747	96.38
Hispanic (410)	478	1.37

Cranston

Place Type: City
County: Providence
Population: 80,387†

Ancestry‡	Population	%
African, Sub-Saharan (915)	1,263	1.57
African (68)	92	0.11
Cape Verdean (438)	739	0.92
Ghanaian (67)	67	0.08
Liberian (0)	8	0.01
Nigerian (277)	285	0.35
Sudanese (50)	50	0.06
Other Sub-Saharan African (15)	22	0.03
American (1,345)	1,345	1.67
Arab (432)	835	1.04
Arab (58)	71	0.09
Egyptian (0)	41	0.05
Lebanese (208)	368	0.46
Syrian (139)	306	0.38
Other Arab (27)	49	0.06
Armenian (1,174)	1,691	2.10
Austrian (27)	110	0.14

*Notes: † The Census 2010 population figure is used to calculate the percentages in the Hispanic Origin and Race categories. Ancestry percentages are based on the 2006-2010 American Community Survey population (not shown); ‡ Numbers in parentheses indicate the number of people reporting a single ancestry; * Numbers in parentheses indicate the number of persons reporting this race alone, not in combination with any other race; Please refer to the Explanation of Data for more information.*

Belgian (11)	39	0.05
Brazilian (60)	82	0.10
British (220)	341	0.42
Canadian (49)	136	0.17
Celtic (0)	10	0.01
Czech (28)	76	0.09
Czechoslovakian (19)	74	0.09
Danish (0)	77	0.10
Dutch (75)	383	0.48
Eastern European (69)	69	0.09
English (1,882)	8,453	10.49
European (93)	110	0.14
Finnish (40)	74	0.09
French, ex. Basque (1,282)	7,738	9.60
French Canadian (773)	2,296	2.85
German (580)	3,711	4.61
Greek (324)	882	1.09
Hungarian (71)	230	0.29
Icelander (0)	5	0.01
Iranian (64)	64	0.08
Irish (4,078)	16,799	20.85
Italian (15,322)	27,317	33.90
Latvian (9)	9	0.01
Lithuanian (27)	218	0.27
Northern European (0)	9	0.01
Norwegian (0)	140	0.17
Pennsylvania German (0)	9	0.01
Polish (554)	2,224	2.76
Portuguese (2,421)	5,508	6.84
Romanian (25)	63	0.08
Russian (304)	729	0.90
Scandinavian (43)	50	0.06
Scotch-Irish (182)	752	0.93
Scottish (270)	1,279	1.59
Slavic (22)	22	0.03
Slovak (18)	152	0.19
Slovene (0)	7	0.01
Swedish (492)	1,433	1.78
Swiss (0)	84	0.10
Ukrainian (137)	171	0.21
Welsh (38)	125	0.16
West Indian, ex. Hispanic (518)	687	0.85
Barbadian (21)	38	0.05
Haitian (419)	419	0.52
Jamaican (69)	177	0.22
Trinidadian/Tobagonian (0)	10	0.01
West Indian (9)	43	0.05

Hispanic Origin	Population	%
Hispanic or Latino (of any race)	8,709	10.83
Central American, ex. Mexican	1,247	1.55
Costa Rican	12	0.01
Guatemalan	998	1.24
Honduran	80	0.10
Nicaraguan	22	0.03
Panamanian	18	0.02
Salvadoran	111	0.14
Other Central American	6	0.01
Cuban	191	0.24
Dominican Republic	3,003	3.74
Mexican	488	0.61
Puerto Rican	1,638	2.04
South American	778	0.97
Argentinean	29	0.04
Bolivian	278	0.35
Chilean	12	0.01
Colombian	215	0.27
Ecuadorian	74	0.09
Paraguayan	1	<0.01
Peruvian	96	0.12
Uruguayan	15	0.02
Venezuelan	56	0.07
Other South American	2	<0.01
Other Hispanic or Latino	1,364	1.70

Race*	Population	%
African-American/Black (4,226)	5,251	6.53
Not Hispanic (3,654)	4,384	5.45
Hispanic (572)	867	1.08
American Indian/Alaska Native (256)	747	0.93
Not Hispanic (200)	581	0.72
Hispanic (56)	166	0.21
Aleut *(Alaska Native)* (0)	1	<0.01
Apache (2)	5	0.01
Blackfeet (1)	13	0.02
Canadian/French Am. Ind. (3)	5	0.01
Central American Ind. (1)	1	<0.01
Cherokee (4)	40	0.05
Cheyenne (0)	1	<0.01
Chippewa (1)	2	<0.01
Choctaw (0)	3	<0.01
Cree (1)	3	<0.01
Creek (0)	1	<0.01
Inupiat *(Alaska Native)* (0)	2	<0.01
Iroquois (3)	14	0.02
Lumbee (4)	6	0.01
Mexican American Ind. (7)	11	0.01
Pueblo (1)	6	0.01
Seminole (1)	9	0.01
Sioux (2)	4	<0.01
South American Ind. (6)	10	0.01
Spanish American Ind. (1)	1	<0.01
Yup'ik *(Alaska Native)* (2)	3	<0.01
Asian (4,156)	4,625	5.75
Not Hispanic (4,110)	4,533	5.64
Hispanic (46)	92	0.11
Bangladeshi (12)	14	0.02
Burmese (6)	6	0.01
Cambodian (1,396)	1,592	1.98
Chinese, ex. Taiwanese (978)	1,133	1.41
Filipino (430)	537	0.67
Hmong (63)	77	0.10
Indian (443)	521	0.65
Indonesian (6)	10	0.01
Japanese (32)	59	0.07
Korean (141)	173	0.22
Laotian (119)	162	0.20
Malaysian (4)	6	0.01
Nepalese (2)	2	<0.01
Pakistani (27)	29	0.04
Sri Lankan (1)	4	<0.01
Taiwanese (13)	16	0.02
Thai (16)	33	0.04
Vietnamese (203)	223	0.28
Hawaii Native/Pacific Islander (51)	129	0.16
Not Hispanic (33)	81	0.10
Hispanic (18)	48	0.06
Fijian (1)	1	<0.01
Guamanian/Chamorro (26)	37	0.05
Native Hawaiian (10)	31	0.04
Samoan (2)	11	0.01
White (65,858)	67,531	84.01
Not Hispanic (62,055)	63,167	78.58
Hispanic (3,803)	4,364	5.43

Cumberland Hill

Place Type: CDP
County: Providence
Population: 7,934†

Ancestry‡	Population	%
African, Sub-Saharan (71)	78	1.00
Cape Verdean (71)	78	1.00
Albanian (12)	12	0.15
American (115)	115	1.47
Arab (27)	143	1.83
Syrian (27)	143	1.83
Armenian (24)	62	0.79
Belgian (0)	14	0.18
British (39)	65	0.83
Canadian (81)	112	1.43
Danish (15)	15	0.19
Dutch (0)	115	1.47
Eastern European (15)	15	0.19
English (350)	1,188	15.19
European (11)	11	0.14
Finnish (0)	163	2.08
French, ex. Basque (618)	1,636	20.92
French Canadian (687)	1,161	14.85
German (54)	310	3.96
Greek (176)	226	2.89
Hungarian (92)	92	1.18
Irish (685)	1,627	20.81
Italian (432)	1,532	19.59
Norwegian (0)	11	0.14
Polish (81)	368	4.71
Portuguese (203)	547	6.99
Romanian (13)	13	0.17
Russian (10)	79	1.01
Scotch-Irish (0)	33	0.42
Scottish (11)	199	2.54
Swedish (49)	247	3.16
Ukrainian (15)	27	0.35
Welsh (21)	59	0.75

Hispanic Origin	Population	%
Hispanic or Latino (of any race)	207	2.61
Central American, ex. Mexican	21	0.26
Costa Rican	2	0.03
Guatemalan	15	0.19
Honduran	1	0.01
Panamanian	1	0.01
Salvadoran	2	0.03
Cuban	2	0.03
Dominican Republic	27	0.34
Mexican	18	0.23
Puerto Rican	53	0.67
South American	68	0.86
Argentinean	3	0.04
Chilean	2	0.03
Colombian	49	0.62
Ecuadorian	3	0.04
Peruvian	2	0.03
Venezuelan	9	0.11
Other Hispanic or Latino	18	0.23

Race*	Population	%
African-American/Black (99)	140	1.76
Not Hispanic (91)	130	1.64
Hispanic (8)	10	0.13
American Indian/Alaska Native (4)	18	0.23
Not Hispanic (4)	14	0.18
Hispanic (0)	4	0.05
Blackfeet (0)	1	0.01
Cherokee (0)	2	0.03
Chippewa (0)	1	0.01
Sioux (0)	1	0.01
South American Ind. (0)	4	0.05
Asian (229)	266	3.35
Not Hispanic (229)	266	3.35
Burmese (3)	3	0.04
Cambodian (5)	8	0.10
Chinese, ex. Taiwanese (62)	74	0.93
Filipino (24)	31	0.39
Hmong (1)	1	0.01
Indian (76)	78	0.98
Indonesian (0)	1	0.01
Japanese (2)	7	0.09
Korean (5)	11	0.14
Laotian (8)	11	0.14
Nepalese (3)	3	0.04
Pakistani (7)	7	0.09
Thai (2)	2	0.03
Vietnamese (24)	29	0.37
Hawaii Native/Pacific Islander (0)	1	0.01
Not Hispanic (0)	1	0.01
White (7,429)	7,530	94.91
Not Hispanic (7,299)	7,383	93.06
Hispanic (130)	147	1.85

Cumberland

Place Type: Town
County: Providence
Population: 33,506†

Ancestry‡	Population	%
African, Sub-Saharan (208)	260	0.78
African (42)	42	0.13

*Notes: † The Census 2010 population figure is used to calculate the percentages in the Hispanic Origin and Race categories. Ancestry percentages are based on the 2006-2010 American Community Survey population (not shown); ‡ Numbers in parentheses indicate the number of people reporting a single ancestry; * Numbers in parentheses indicate the number of persons reporting this race alone, not in combination with any other race; Please refer to the Explanation of Data for more information.*

Cape Verdean (156)	208	0.62
Other Sub-Saharan African (10)	10	0.03
Albanian (12)	51	0.15
American (687)	687	2.06
Arab (416)	830	2.49
Arab (65)	126	0.38
Lebanese (25)	84	0.25
Moroccan (9)	9	0.03
Syrian (317)	611	1.84
Armenian (64)	209	0.63
Assyrian/Chaldean/Syriac (0)	28	0.08
Austrian (12)	24	0.07
Belgian (13)	38	0.11
Brazilian (0)	12	0.04
British (59)	94	0.28
Canadian (153)	219	0.66
Celtic (0)	11	0.03
Croatian (0)	9	0.03
Czech (0)	20	0.06
Danish (35)	75	0.23
Dutch (18)	219	0.66
Eastern European (15)	15	0.05
English (1,113)	4,677	14.05
European (208)	257	0.77
Finnish (20)	183	0.55
French, ex. Basque (1,950)	6,277	18.85
French Canadian (1,922)	3,447	10.35
German (392)	1,798	5.40
Greek (228)	521	1.56
Hungarian (117)	176	0.53
Irish (2,345)	7,445	22.36
Italian (1,832)	5,108	15.34
Lithuanian (20)	59	0.18
Luxemburger (0)	42	0.13
Northern European (13)	13	0.04
Norwegian (10)	131	0.39
Polish (813)	2,423	7.28
Portuguese (2,912)	4,806	14.44
Romanian (13)	13	0.04
Russian (41)	178	0.53
Scandinavian (27)	27	0.08
Scotch-Irish (181)	462	1.39
Scottish (114)	963	2.89
Swedish (84)	597	1.79
Swiss (0)	15	0.05
Turkish (41)	41	0.12
Ukrainian (67)	104	0.31
Welsh (21)	106	0.32
West Indian, ex. Hispanic (11)	11	0.03
Jamaican (11)	11	0.03
Yugoslavian (0)	10	0.03

Hispanic Origin	Population	%
Hispanic or Latino (of any race)	1,496	4.46
Central American, ex. Mexican	163	0.49
Costa Rican	4	0.01
Guatemalan	138	0.41
Honduran	8	0.02
Panamanian	7	0.02
Salvadoran	6	0.02
Cuban	34	0.10
Dominican Republic	153	0.46
Mexican	82	0.24
Puerto Rican	369	1.10
South American	503	1.50
Argentinean	26	0.08
Bolivian	5	0.01
Chilean	7	0.02
Colombian	378	1.13
Ecuadorian	17	0.05
Peruvian	19	0.06
Venezuelan	47	0.14
Other South American	4	0.01
Other Hispanic or Latino	192	0.57

Race*	Population	%
African-American/Black (486)	719	2.15
Not Hispanic (446)	655	1.95
Hispanic (40)	64	0.19
American Indian/Alaska Native (84)	185	0.55
Not Hispanic (33)	123	0.37
Hispanic (51)	62	0.19
Alaska Athabascan *(Ala. Nat.)* (1)	3	0.01
Blackfeet (0)	3	0.01
Canadian/French Am. Ind. (0)	2	0.01
Cherokee (1)	15	0.04
Chippewa (0)	1	<0.01
Cree (0)	5	0.01
Iroquois (0)	7	0.02
Mexican American Ind. (7)	7	0.02
Sioux (0)	2	0.01
South American Ind. (0)	4	0.01
Yup'ik *(Alaska Native)* (0)	2	0.01
Asian (786)	936	2.79
Not Hispanic (781)	922	2.75
Hispanic (5)	14	0.04
Burmese (3)	4	0.01
Cambodian (14)	27	0.08
Chinese, ex. Taiwanese (146)	166	0.50
Filipino (41)	77	0.23
Hmong (1)	1	<0.01
Indian (415)	432	1.29
Indonesian (2)	4	0.01
Japanese (9)	33	0.10
Korean (26)	36	0.11
Laotian (18)	31	0.09
Nepalese (3)	3	0.01
Pakistani (29)	32	0.10
Taiwanese (4)	4	0.01
Thai (9)	13	0.04
Vietnamese (49)	55	0.16
Hawaii Native/Pacific Islander (11)	55	0.16
Not Hispanic (9)	38	0.11
Hispanic (2)	17	0.05
Guamanian/Chamorro (9)	14	0.04
Native Hawaiian (2)	6	0.02
White (31,102)	31,557	94.18
Not Hispanic (30,176)	30,553	91.19
Hispanic (926)	1,004	3.00

East Greenwich

Place Type: Town
County: Kent
Population: 13,146†

Ancestry‡	Population	%
African, Sub-Saharan (9)	19	0.14
South African (9)	19	0.14
American (768)	768	5.82
Arab (32)	132	1.00
Egyptian (19)	46	0.35
Lebanese (0)	38	0.29
Syrian (13)	38	0.29
Other Arab (0)	10	0.08
Armenian (28)	99	0.75
Austrian (54)	101	0.77
Belgian (7)	7	0.05
Brazilian (11)	21	0.16
British (60)	107	0.81
Canadian (64)	64	0.49
Danish (21)	57	0.43
Dutch (0)	119	0.90
Eastern European (99)	99	0.75
English (994)	2,960	22.45
European (43)	43	0.33
Finnish (20)	42	0.32
French, ex. Basque (90)	1,081	8.20
French Canadian (131)	364	2.76
German (304)	1,391	10.55
Greek (59)	117	0.89
Hungarian (27)	56	0.42
Iranian (45)	45	0.34
Irish (915)	3,167	24.02
Italian (1,001)	2,657	20.15
Latvian (0)	9	0.07
Lithuanian (8)	82	0.62
Northern European (58)	58	0.44
Norwegian (34)	114	0.86
Polish (189)	520	3.94
Portuguese (76)	392	2.97
Romanian (64)	75	0.57
Russian (254)	480	3.64
Scandinavian (46)	67	0.51
Scotch-Irish (101)	251	1.90
Scottish (78)	484	3.67
Serbian (0)	24	0.18
Slovak (0)	10	0.08
Swedish (237)	620	4.70
Turkish (9)	9	0.07
Ukrainian (47)	64	0.49
Welsh (23)	91	0.69
West Indian, ex. Hispanic (43)	43	0.33
Jamaican (43)	43	0.33

Hispanic Origin	Population	%
Hispanic or Latino (of any race)	227	1.73
Central American, ex. Mexican	19	0.14
Costa Rican	3	0.02
Guatemalan	12	0.09
Panamanian	1	0.01
Salvadoran	3	0.02
Cuban	22	0.17
Dominican Republic	37	0.28
Mexican	45	0.34
Puerto Rican	46	0.35
South American	32	0.24
Argentinean	9	0.07
Chilean	11	0.08
Colombian	4	0.03
Ecuadorian	5	0.04
Peruvian	1	0.01
Venezuelan	1	0.01
Other South American	1	0.01
Other Hispanic or Latino	26	0.20

Race*	Population	%
African-American/Black (107)	143	1.09
Not Hispanic (103)	132	1.00
Hispanic (4)	11	0.08
American Indian/Alaska Native (19)	70	0.53
Not Hispanic (15)	60	0.46
Hispanic (4)	10	0.08
Apache (0)	1	0.01
Blackfeet (0)	2	0.02
Cherokee (1)	15	0.11
Cree (0)	1	0.01
Iroquois (0)	4	0.03
Shoshone (0)	4	0.03
Sioux (1)	6	0.05
South American Ind. (1)	2	0.02
Yaqui (0)	1	0.01
Asian (538)	629	4.78
Not Hispanic (531)	621	4.72
Hispanic (7)	8	0.06
Cambodian (10)	10	0.08
Chinese, ex. Taiwanese (191)	214	1.63
Filipino (37)	53	0.40
Indian (147)	168	1.28
Indonesian (1)	2	0.02
Japanese (31)	49	0.37
Korean (39)	51	0.39
Laotian (11)	11	0.08
Malaysian (4)	4	0.03
Pakistani (29)	35	0.27
Taiwanese (13)	18	0.14
Thai (0)	1	0.01
Vietnamese (8)	14	0.11
Hawaii Native/Pacific Islander (2)	6	0.05
Not Hispanic (1)	5	0.04
Hispanic (1)	1	0.01
Guamanian/Chamorro (2)	4	0.03
Native Hawaiian (0)	1	0.01
White (12,255)	12,419	94.47
Not Hispanic (12,085)	12,238	93.09
Hispanic (170)	181	1.38

*Notes: † The Census 2010 population figure is used to calculate the percentages in the Hispanic Origin and Race categories. Ancestry percentages are based on the 2006-2010 American Community Survey population (not shown); ‡ Numbers in parentheses indicate the number of people reporting a single ancestry; * Numbers in parentheses indicate the number of persons reporting this race alone, not in combination with any other race; Please refer to the Explanation of Data for more information.*

East Providence

Place Type: City
County: Providence
Population: 47,037†

Ancestry‡	Population	%
African, Sub-Saharan (1,823)	2,631	5.54
African (144)	273	0.57
Cape Verdean (1,586)	2,265	4.77
Ghanaian (59)	59	0.12
Senegalese (34)	34	0.07
American (1,166)	1,166	2.46
Arab (128)	466	0.98
Lebanese (97)	317	0.67
Syrian (16)	134	0.28
Other Arab (15)	15	0.03
Armenian (89)	178	0.37
Austrian (28)	123	0.26
Belgian (0)	28	0.06
Brazilian (139)	185	0.39
British (38)	93	0.20
Canadian (65)	132	0.28
Celtic (0)	17	0.04
Croatian (0)	6	0.01
Czech (8)	67	0.14
Czechoslovakian (0)	12	0.03
Danish (0)	20	0.04
Dutch (30)	116	0.24
Eastern European (38)	44	0.09
English (1,018)	5,000	10.53
Estonian (0)	10	0.02
European (113)	118	0.25
Finnish (0)	42	0.09
French, ex. Basque (891)	4,910	10.34
French Canadian (774)	1,611	3.39
German (387)	2,231	4.70
Greek (87)	168	0.35
Hungarian (52)	141	0.30
Irish (2,547)	9,076	19.11
Italian (2,129)	6,806	14.33
Latvian (0)	13	0.03
Lithuanian (0)	136	0.29
Luxemburger (0)	12	0.03
Norwegian (17)	101	0.21
Polish (574)	1,504	3.17
Portuguese (10,545)	15,725	33.11
Romanian (25)	25	0.05
Russian (82)	295	0.62
Scandinavian (0)	28	0.06
Scotch-Irish (252)	677	1.43
Scottish (260)	1,309	2.76
Slovak (17)	26	0.05
Swedish (154)	803	1.69
Swiss (32)	42	0.09
Ukrainian (14)	82	0.17
Welsh (9)	163	0.34
West Indian, ex. Hispanic (179)	218	0.46
Haitian (23)	23	0.05
Jamaican (24)	63	0.13
Trinidadian/Tobagonian (88)	88	0.19
West Indian (44)	44	0.09

Hispanic Origin	Population	%
Hispanic or Latino (of any race)	1,913	4.07
Central American, ex. Mexican	215	0.46
Costa Rican	8	0.02
Guatemalan	123	0.26
Honduran	20	0.04
Nicaraguan	19	0.04
Panamanian	23	0.05
Salvadoran	17	0.04
Other Central American	5	0.01
Cuban	35	0.07
Dominican Republic	333	0.71
Mexican	147	0.31
Puerto Rican	695	1.48
South American	226	0.48
Argentinean	13	0.03
Bolivian	23	0.05
Chilean	5	0.01
Colombian	121	0.26
Ecuadorian	22	0.05
Peruvian	20	0.04
Venezuelan	21	0.04
Other South American	1	<0.01
Other Hispanic or Latino	262	0.56

Race*	Population	%
African-American/Black (2,709)	3,958	8.41
Not Hispanic (2,559)	3,683	7.83
Hispanic (150)	275	0.58
American Indian/Alaska Native (256)	749	1.59
Not Hispanic (220)	650	1.38
Hispanic (36)	99	0.21
Blackfeet (3)	15	0.03
Canadian/French Am. Ind. (4)	5	0.01
Central American Ind. (0)	5	0.01
Cherokee (11)	52	0.11
Chickasaw (2)	2	<0.01
Chippewa (0)	1	<0.01
Choctaw (1)	3	0.01
Cree (0)	2	<0.01
Creek (0)	2	<0.01
Delaware (1)	1	<0.01
Hopi (1)	2	<0.01
Iroquois (1)	16	0.03
Mexican American Ind. (6)	12	0.03
Navajo (0)	5	0.01
Pueblo (1)	2	<0.01
Seminole (1)	2	<0.01
Sioux (2)	4	0.01
South American Ind. (4)	14	0.03
Yuman (6)	6	0.01
Yup'ik *(Alaska Native)* (1)	1	<0.01
Asian (714)	940	2.00
Not Hispanic (708)	913	1.94
Hispanic (6)	27	0.06
Burmese (3)	3	0.01
Cambodian (21)	27	0.06
Chinese, ex. Taiwanese (223)	258	0.55
Filipino (83)	138	0.29
Indian (173)	195	0.41
Indonesian (1)	1	<0.01
Japanese (15)	44	0.09
Korean (63)	77	0.16
Laotian (5)	10	0.02
Malaysian (1)	1	<0.01
Nepalese (7)	7	0.01
Pakistani (18)	25	0.05
Sri Lankan (14)	14	0.03
Taiwanese (15)	18	0.04
Thai (25)	30	0.06
Vietnamese (34)	38	0.08
Hawaii Native/Pacific Islander (10)	112	0.24
Not Hispanic (7)	94	0.20
Hispanic (3)	18	0.04
Guamanian/Chamorro (5)	13	0.03
Native Hawaiian (1)	9	0.02
Samoan (0)	1	<0.01
White (39,525)	40,856	86.86
Not Hispanic (38,664)	39,808	84.63
Hispanic (861)	1,048	2.23

Glocester

Place Type: Town
County: Providence
Population: 9,746†

Ancestry‡	Population	%
African, Sub-Saharan (10)	26	0.27
Cape Verdean (0)	16	0.16
Senegalese (10)	10	0.10
American (202)	202	2.06
Arab (11)	89	0.91
Lebanese (11)	11	0.11
Moroccan (0)	31	0.32
Syrian (0)	47	0.48
Armenian (15)	15	0.15
Australian (0)	37	0.38
Austrian (0)	52	0.53
Belgian (0)	12	0.12
British (16)	16	0.16
Canadian (20)	50	0.51
Czech (0)	32	0.33
Danish (15)	24	0.24
Dutch (0)	40	0.41
Eastern European (14)	14	0.14
English (723)	2,278	23.23
European (24)	24	0.24
Finnish (0)	33	0.34
French, ex. Basque (655)	2,407	24.55
French Canadian (401)	863	8.80
German (215)	984	10.04
Greek (29)	175	1.78
Irish (305)	2,459	25.08
Italian (643)	1,763	17.98
Lithuanian (0)	12	0.12
Norwegian (9)	24	0.24
Polish (89)	394	4.02
Portuguese (238)	748	7.63
Russian (94)	94	0.96
Scandinavian (10)	21	0.21
Scotch-Irish (21)	167	1.70
Scottish (45)	182	1.86
Swedish (40)	341	3.48
Turkish (10)	10	0.10
Ukrainian (14)	35	0.36
Welsh (0)	66	0.67

Hispanic Origin	Population	%
Hispanic or Latino (of any race)	132	1.35
Central American, ex. Mexican	22	0.23
Guatemalan	18	0.18
Nicaraguan	1	0.01
Panamanian	2	0.02
Salvadoran	1	0.01
Cuban	5	0.05
Dominican Republic	8	0.08
Mexican	25	0.26
Puerto Rican	39	0.40
South American	16	0.16
Argentinean	2	0.02
Colombian	11	0.11
Peruvian	3	0.03
Other Hispanic or Latino	17	0.17

Race*	Population	%
African-American/Black (34)	67	0.69
Not Hispanic (28)	55	0.56
Hispanic (6)	12	0.12
American Indian/Alaska Native (10)	55	0.56
Not Hispanic (9)	49	0.50
Hispanic (1)	6	0.06
Blackfeet (0)	3	0.03
Canadian/French Am. Ind. (0)	1	0.01
Chippewa (0)	1	0.01
Cree (1)	1	0.01
Iroquois (0)	1	0.01
Mexican American Ind. (1)	2	0.02
Seminole (0)	1	0.01
Sioux (1)	2	0.02
Asian (62)	84	0.86
Not Hispanic (61)	82	0.84
Hispanic (1)	2	0.02
Cambodian (1)	3	0.03
Chinese, ex. Taiwanese (10)	10	0.10
Filipino (9)	17	0.17
Hmong (4)	4	0.04
Indian (20)	24	0.25
Japanese (1)	5	0.05
Korean (3)	3	0.03
Laotian (2)	2	0.02
Pakistani (2)	2	0.02
Vietnamese (7)	7	0.07
Hawaii Native/Pacific Islander (1)	5	0.05
Not Hispanic (1)	3	0.03
Hispanic (0)	2	0.02
Guamanian/Chamorro (1)	2	0.02

*Notes: † The Census 2010 population figure is used to calculate the percentages in the Hispanic Origin and Race categories. Ancestry percentages are based on the 2006-2010 American Community Survey population (not shown); ‡ Numbers in parentheses indicate the number of people reporting a single ancestry; * Numbers in parentheses indicate the number of persons reporting this race alone, not in combination with any other race; Please refer to the Explanation of Data for more information.*

Native Hawaiian (0)	1	0.01
White (9,498)	9,600	98.50
Not Hispanic (9,412)	9,496	97.43
Hispanic (86)	104	1.07

Greenville

Place Type: CDP
County: Providence
Population: 8,658†

Ancestry‡	Population	%
African, Sub-Saharan (112)	121	1.38
African (87)	87	0.99
Cape Verdean (25)	34	0.39
American (94)	94	1.07
Arab (40)	40	0.46
Syrian (40)	40	0.46
Armenian (44)	103	1.17
Austrian (0)	21	0.24
Belgian (24)	24	0.27
British (9)	48	0.55
Canadian (0)	54	0.62
Czech (21)	21	0.24
Danish (0)	25	0.29
English (376)	1,749	19.95
European (0)	27	0.31
French, ex. Basque (321)	1,482	16.90
French Canadian (382)	614	7.00
German (62)	466	5.32
Greek (0)	25	0.29
Irish (693)	2,340	26.69
Italian (1,352)	2,581	29.44
Lithuanian (0)	53	0.60
Norwegian (21)	99	1.13
Polish (150)	471	5.37
Portuguese (223)	657	7.49
Russian (19)	82	0.94
Scotch-Irish (62)	82	0.94
Scottish (69)	418	4.77
Serbian (23)	23	0.26
Slovak (13)	13	0.15
Swedish (45)	202	2.30
Swiss (20)	31	0.35
Ukrainian (12)	12	0.14
Welsh (0)	8	0.09

Hispanic Origin	Population	%
Hispanic or Latino (of any race)	125	1.44
Central American, ex. Mexican	12	0.14
Guatemalan	6	0.07
Panamanian	1	0.01
Salvadoran	4	0.05
Other Central American	1	0.01
Cuban	5	0.06
Dominican Republic	5	0.06
Mexican	35	0.40
Puerto Rican	28	0.32
South American	27	0.31
Argentinean	1	0.01
Bolivian	1	0.01
Chilean	1	0.01
Colombian	15	0.17
Ecuadorian	3	0.03
Peruvian	3	0.03
Venezuelan	3	0.03
Other Hispanic or Latino	13	0.15

Race*	Population	%
African-American/Black (68)	84	0.97
Not Hispanic (68)	83	0.96
Hispanic (0)	1	0.01
American Indian/Alaska Native (9)	27	0.31
Not Hispanic (7)	22	0.25
Hispanic (2)	5	0.06
Canadian/French Am. Ind. (2)	5	0.06
Cherokee (1)	7	0.08
Chippewa (0)	1	0.01
Mexican American Ind. (0)	1	0.01
South American Ind. (0)	2	0.02
Asian (76)	100	1.16
Not Hispanic (74)	98	1.13
Hispanic (2)	2	0.02
Cambodian (1)	1	0.01
Chinese, ex. Taiwanese (39)	43	0.50
Filipino (3)	4	0.05
Indian (12)	20	0.23
Japanese (4)	9	0.10
Korean (8)	12	0.14
Laotian (3)	4	0.05
Nepalese (3)	3	0.03
Vietnamese (1)	4	0.05
Hawaii Native/Pacific Islander (1)	2	0.02
Not Hispanic (1)	2	0.02
Guamanian/Chamorro (0)	1	0.01
White (8,404)	8,463	97.75
Not Hispanic (8,314)	8,365	96.62
Hispanic (90)	98	1.13

Hopkinton

Place Type: Town
County: Washington
Population: 8,188†

Ancestry‡	Population	%
Albanian (36)	36	0.44
American (389)	389	4.76
Arab (0)	93	1.14
Lebanese (0)	69	0.84
Syrian (0)	24	0.29
Armenian (0)	13	0.16
Austrian (0)	13	0.16
British (0)	45	0.55
Canadian (15)	15	0.18
Czech (15)	30	0.37
Czechoslovakian (0)	14	0.17
Danish (15)	15	0.18
Dutch (0)	28	0.34
English (617)	1,601	19.60
European (69)	69	0.84
Finnish (0)	28	0.34
French, ex. Basque (280)	1,606	19.66
French Canadian (133)	474	5.80
German (292)	859	10.52
Irish (413)	1,612	19.74
Italian (579)	1,570	19.22
Lithuanian (13)	53	0.65
Polish (29)	272	3.33
Portuguese (60)	270	3.31
Russian (14)	14	0.17
Scotch-Irish (65)	299	3.66
Scottish (49)	241	2.95
Slovak (0)	13	0.16
Swedish (63)	151	1.85
Swiss (0)	16	0.20
Welsh (0)	20	0.24
Yugoslavian (0)	13	0.16

Hispanic Origin	Population	%
Hispanic or Latino (of any race)	148	1.81
Central American, ex. Mexican	9	0.11
Costa Rican	3	0.04
Guatemalan	5	0.06
Nicaraguan	1	0.01
Cuban	8	0.10
Dominican Republic	15	0.18
Mexican	20	0.24
Puerto Rican	62	0.76
South American	18	0.22
Argentinean	3	0.04
Bolivian	3	0.04
Colombian	10	0.12
Ecuadorian	2	0.02
Other Hispanic or Latino	16	0.20

Race*	Population	%
African-American/Black (43)	102	1.25
Not Hispanic (39)	87	1.06
Hispanic (4)	15	0.18
American Indian/Alaska Native (73)	131	1.60
Not Hispanic (72)	127	1.55
Hispanic (1)	4	0.05
Blackfeet (1)	1	0.01
Cherokee (0)	1	0.01
Chippewa (0)	2	0.02
Inupiat *(Alaska Native)* (1)	1	0.01
Iroquois (1)	2	0.02
Lumbee (0)	1	0.01
Mexican American Ind. (1)	1	0.01
Sioux (2)	5	0.06
South American Ind. (1)	2	0.02
Asian (57)	88	1.07
Not Hispanic (57)	88	1.07
Chinese, ex. Taiwanese (9)	13	0.16
Filipino (13)	25	0.31
Indian (19)	23	0.28
Japanese (2)	10	0.12
Korean (8)	10	0.12
Laotian (1)	3	0.04
Pakistani (1)	1	0.01
Thai (1)	1	0.01
Vietnamese (2)	2	0.02
Hawaii Native/Pacific Islander (0)	2	0.02
Not Hispanic (0)	2	0.02
Native Hawaiian (0)	1	0.01
Samoan (0)	1	0.01
White (7,846)	7,959	97.20
Not Hispanic (7,749)	7,853	95.91
Hispanic (97)	106	1.29

Johnston

Place Type: Town
County: Providence
Population: 28,769†

Ancestry‡	Population	%
African, Sub-Saharan (48)	115	0.40
African (27)	27	0.09
Cape Verdean (0)	67	0.23
Nigerian (21)	21	0.07
American (327)	327	1.14
Arab (108)	394	1.37
Arab (0)	37	0.13
Lebanese (77)	223	0.78
Syrian (31)	134	0.47
Armenian (51)	221	0.77
Austrian (0)	13	0.05
Belgian (45)	108	0.38
Brazilian (23)	65	0.23
Canadian (0)	12	0.04
Czechoslovakian (0)	18	0.06
Danish (0)	21	0.07
Dutch (0)	23	0.08
English (559)	2,926	10.18
European (31)	31	0.11
Finnish (0)	22	0.08
French, ex. Basque (1,013)	4,342	15.10
French Canadian (448)	681	2.37
German (232)	913	3.18
Greek (74)	228	0.79
Hungarian (9)	77	0.27
Iranian (14)	14	0.05
Irish (831)	4,667	16.23
Italian (9,287)	14,729	51.23
Lithuanian (50)	180	0.63
Norwegian (0)	11	0.04
Polish (433)	1,344	4.67
Portuguese (955)	2,130	7.41
Romanian (0)	17	0.06
Russian (27)	65	0.23
Scotch-Irish (78)	168	0.58
Scottish (33)	286	0.99
Slovak (14)	59	0.21
Swedish (13)	263	0.91
Swiss (0)	29	0.10
Turkish (0)	16	0.06
Welsh (16)	23	0.08
West Indian, ex. Hispanic (39)	39	0.14

*Notes: † The Census 2010 population figure is used to calculate the percentages in the Hispanic Origin and Race categories. Ancestry percentages are based on the 2006-2010 American Community Survey population (not shown); ‡ Numbers in parentheses indicate the number of people reporting a single ancestry; * Numbers in parentheses indicate the number of persons reporting this race alone, not in combination with any other race; Please refer to the Explanation of Data for more information.*

British West Indian (16)	16	0.06
Haitian (9)	9	0.03
Jamaican (14)	14	0.05

Hispanic Origin	Population	%
Hispanic or Latino (of any race)	1,664	5.78
Central American, ex. Mexican	425	1.48
Costa Rican	1	<0.01
Guatemalan	383	1.33
Honduran	11	0.04
Nicaraguan	5	0.02
Panamanian	6	0.02
Salvadoran	19	0.07
Cuban	19	0.07
Dominican Republic	253	0.88
Mexican	113	0.39
Puerto Rican	367	1.28
South American	284	0.99
Argentinean	7	0.02
Bolivian	118	0.41
Chilean	1	<0.01
Colombian	111	0.39
Ecuadorian	20	0.07
Peruvian	20	0.07
Uruguayan	1	<0.01
Venezuelan	6	0.02
Other Hispanic or Latino	203	0.71

Race*	Population	%
African-American/Black (569)	767	2.67
Not Hispanic (520)	676	2.35
Hispanic (49)	91	0.32
American Indian/Alaska Native (42)	148	0.51
Not Hispanic (27)	119	0.41
Hispanic (15)	29	0.10
Blackfeet (0)	5	0.02
Canadian/French Am. Ind. (0)	2	0.01
Cherokee (0)	10	0.03
Iroquois (1)	11	0.04
Mexican American Ind. (2)	6	0.02
Seminole (0)	3	0.01
South American Ind. (0)	3	0.01
Spanish American Ind. (1)	1	<0.01
Asian (585)	685	2.38
Not Hispanic (580)	672	2.34
Hispanic (5)	13	0.05
Burmese (2)	2	0.01
Cambodian (53)	74	0.26
Chinese, ex. Taiwanese (89)	114	0.40
Filipino (34)	72	0.25
Hmong (38)	38	0.13
Indian (102)	115	0.40
Indonesian (1)	1	<0.01
Japanese (0)	3	0.01
Korean (26)	36	0.13
Laotian (145)	165	0.57
Malaysian (2)	2	0.01
Pakistani (19)	19	0.07
Taiwanese (3)	3	0.01
Thai (10)	16	0.06
Vietnamese (24)	27	0.09
Hawaii Native/Pacific Islander (17)	41	0.14
Not Hispanic (3)	23	0.08
Hispanic (14)	18	0.06
Guamanian/Chamorro (12)	15	0.05
Native Hawaiian (2)	14	0.05
Samoan (0)	1	<0.01
White (26,470)	26,896	93.49
Not Hispanic (25,570)	25,877	89.95
Hispanic (900)	1,019	3.54

Lincoln

Place Type: Town
County: Providence
Population: 21,105†

Ancestry‡	Population	%
African, Sub-Saharan (116)	196	0.93
Cape Verdean (116)	196	0.93
American (643)	643	3.04
Arab (361)	487	2.31
Lebanese (115)	177	0.84
Syrian (238)	302	1.43
Other Arab (8)	8	0.04
Armenian (59)	185	0.88
Assyrian/Chaldean/Syriac (57)	57	0.27
Austrian (0)	143	0.68
Belgian (0)	13	0.06
British (19)	29	0.14
Canadian (81)	132	0.63
Czech (10)	24	0.11
Dutch (50)	151	0.71
English (744)	3,099	14.67
European (31)	31	0.15
Finnish (10)	47	0.22
French, ex. Basque (1,239)	3,623	17.15
French Canadian (1,754)	2,483	11.76
German (164)	951	4.50
Greek (147)	208	0.98
Irish (1,289)	4,575	21.66
Italian (1,875)	4,213	19.95
Lithuanian (13)	139	0.66
Northern European (26)	26	0.12
Norwegian (13)	136	0.64
Polish (208)	1,212	5.74
Portuguese (1,066)	2,260	10.70
Russian (65)	295	1.40
Scandinavian (10)	67	0.32
Scotch-Irish (133)	438	2.07
Scottish (143)	585	2.77
Slovak (13)	13	0.06
Swedish (95)	314	1.49
Turkish (78)	151	0.71
Ukrainian (81)	165	0.78
Welsh (22)	138	0.65

Hispanic Origin	Population	%
Hispanic or Latino (of any race)	862	4.08
Central American, ex. Mexican	81	0.38
Costa Rican	3	0.01
Guatemalan	56	0.27
Honduran	9	0.04
Nicaraguan	2	0.01
Panamanian	2	0.01
Salvadoran	9	0.04
Cuban	20	0.09
Dominican Republic	110	0.52
Mexican	69	0.33
Puerto Rican	273	1.29
South American	230	1.09
Argentinean	19	0.09
Bolivian	5	0.02
Chilean	1	<0.01
Colombian	190	0.90
Paraguayan	1	<0.01
Peruvian	6	0.03
Venezuelan	7	0.03
Other South American	1	<0.01
Other Hispanic or Latino	79	0.37

Race*	Population	%
African-American/Black (355)	544	2.58
Not Hispanic (322)	491	2.33
Hispanic (33)	53	0.25
American Indian/Alaska Native (36)	130	0.62
Not Hispanic (24)	113	0.54
Hispanic (12)	17	0.08
Blackfeet (1)	5	0.02
Canadian/French Am. Ind. (0)	3	0.01
Cherokee (1)	9	0.04
Chippewa (0)	1	<0.01
Cree (3)	11	0.05
Iroquois (0)	3	0.01
Navajo (0)	2	0.01
Seminole (0)	1	<0.01
Sioux (1)	4	0.02
Asian (587)	701	3.32
Not Hispanic (580)	692	3.28
Hispanic (7)	9	0.04
Bangladeshi (7)	8	0.04
Burmese (2)	2	0.01
Cambodian (25)	28	0.13
Chinese, ex. Taiwanese (139)	152	0.72
Filipino (37)	66	0.31
Hmong (0)	1	<0.01
Indian (183)	203	0.96
Indonesian (1)	1	<0.01
Japanese (13)	19	0.09
Korean (37)	45	0.21
Laotian (19)	21	0.10
Malaysian (6)	6	0.03
Pakistani (55)	64	0.30
Sri Lankan (4)	6	0.03
Taiwanese (7)	8	0.04
Thai (2)	4	0.02
Vietnamese (29)	29	0.14
Hawaii Native/Pacific Islander (1)	12	0.06
Not Hispanic (0)	11	0.05
Hispanic (1)	1	<0.01
Guamanian/Chamorro (0)	2	0.01
Native Hawaiian (0)	5	0.02
Samoan (0)	2	0.01
White (19,362)	19,725	93.46
Not Hispanic (18,870)	19,182	90.89
Hispanic (492)	543	2.57

Middletown

Place Type: Town
County: Newport
Population: 16,150†

Ancestry‡	Population	%
African, Sub-Saharan (16)	35	0.21
African (16)	16	0.10
Cape Verdean (0)	19	0.12
American (389)	389	2.38
Arab (112)	215	1.31
Jordanian (112)	112	0.68
Lebanese (0)	68	0.42
Palestinian (0)	26	0.16
Syrian (0)	9	0.06
Armenian (10)	26	0.16
Australian (0)	10	0.06
Austrian (0)	14	0.09
Belgian (23)	23	0.14
Brazilian (92)	117	0.72
British (23)	77	0.47
Canadian (70)	70	0.43
Czech (0)	72	0.44
Czechoslovakian (39)	44	0.27
Danish (14)	60	0.37
Dutch (49)	185	1.13
Eastern European (45)	78	0.48
English (355)	2,357	14.41
European (29)	49	0.30
Finnish (51)	105	0.64
French, ex. Basque (199)	830	5.07
French Canadian (238)	419	2.56
German (368)	2,001	12.23
Greek (69)	171	1.05
Hungarian (0)	35	0.21
Irish (1,759)	4,750	29.03
Israeli (0)	11	0.07
Italian (625)	1,781	10.88
Lithuanian (0)	47	0.29
Norwegian (37)	93	0.57
Polish (130)	490	2.99
Portuguese (1,000)	1,757	10.74
Russian (36)	57	0.35
Scotch-Irish (64)	273	1.67
Scottish (64)	389	2.38
Slovak (45)	45	0.28
Swedish (99)	309	1.89
Turkish (5)	22	0.13
Ukrainian (34)	34	0.21
Welsh (11)	53	0.32
West Indian, ex. Hispanic (172)	225	1.38
Barbadian (78)	78	0.48

*Notes: † The Census 2010 population figure is used to calculate the percentages in the Hispanic Origin and Race categories. Ancestry percentages are based on the 2006-2010 American Community Survey population (not shown); ‡ Numbers in parentheses indicate the number of people reporting a single ancestry; * Numbers in parentheses indicate the number of persons reporting this race alone, not in combination with any other race; Please refer to the Explanation of Data for more information.*

Jamaican (94)	147	0.90

Hispanic Origin	Population	%
Hispanic or Latino (of any race)	763	4.72
Central American, ex. Mexican	113	0.70
Costa Rican	6	0.04
Guatemalan	40	0.25
Honduran	19	0.12
Nicaraguan	12	0.07
Panamanian	2	0.01
Salvadoran	30	0.19
Other Central American	4	0.02
Cuban	23	0.14
Dominican Republic	40	0.25
Mexican	151	0.93
Puerto Rican	267	1.65
South American	82	0.51
Argentinean	9	0.06
Bolivian	1	0.01
Chilean	13	0.08
Colombian	30	0.19
Ecuadorian	5	0.03
Peruvian	23	0.14
Venezuelan	1	0.01
Other Hispanic or Latino	87	0.54

Race*	Population	%
African-American/Black (728)	971	6.01
Not Hispanic (677)	875	5.42
Hispanic (51)	96	0.59
American Indian/Alaska Native (51)	168	1.04
Not Hispanic (39)	130	0.80
Hispanic (12)	38	0.24
Aleut *(Alaska Native)* (0)	1	0.01
Blackfeet (1)	4	0.02
Central American Ind. (0)	1	0.01
Cherokee (5)	17	0.11
Chippewa (0)	6	0.04
Choctaw (2)	2	0.01
Iroquois (1)	1	0.01
Puget Sound Salish (1)	1	0.01
Sioux (0)	1	0.01
South American Ind. (2)	3	0.02
Tohono O'Odham (1)	1	0.01
Asian (483)	695	4.30
Not Hispanic (479)	673	4.17
Hispanic (4)	22	0.14
Bangladeshi (4)	4	0.02
Cambodian (2)	4	0.02
Chinese, ex. Taiwanese (82)	104	0.64
Filipino (169)	266	1.65
Indian (44)	60	0.37
Japanese (34)	74	0.46
Korean (47)	76	0.47
Laotian (1)	1	0.01
Malaysian (4)	5	0.03
Pakistani (20)	20	0.12
Sri Lankan (3)	3	0.02
Taiwanese (13)	14	0.09
Thai (10)	17	0.11
Vietnamese (27)	36	0.22
Hawaii Native/Pacific Islander (21)	40	0.25
Not Hispanic (19)	34	0.21
Hispanic (2)	6	0.04
Guamanian/Chamorro (6)	10	0.06
Marshallese (11)	11	0.07
Native Hawaiian (3)	8	0.05
White (14,087)	14,530	89.97
Not Hispanic (13,662)	14,039	86.93
Hispanic (425)	491	3.04

Narragansett

Place Type: Town
County: Washington
Population: 15,868†

Ancestry‡	Population	%
African, Sub-Saharan (36)	36	0.22
Cape Verdean (36)	36	0.22
American (225)	225	1.40
Arab (59)	271	1.69
Arab (0)	41	0.26
Lebanese (59)	163	1.02
Syrian (0)	67	0.42
Armenian (100)	169	1.05
Austrian (22)	84	0.52
Belgian (0)	49	0.31
British (113)	113	0.70
Canadian (28)	89	0.56
Czech (20)	44	0.27
Dutch (19)	43	0.27
Eastern European (45)	45	0.28
English (526)	2,610	16.28
European (159)	159	0.99
Finnish (0)	32	0.20
French, ex. Basque (244)	1,517	9.46
French Canadian (239)	504	3.14
German (228)	1,389	8.66
Greek (16)	72	0.45
Hungarian (0)	37	0.23
Irish (2,437)	5,550	34.61
Italian (1,578)	3,670	22.89
Lithuanian (70)	200	1.25
Norwegian (10)	65	0.41
Pennsylvania German (31)	31	0.19
Polish (190)	698	4.35
Portuguese (306)	634	3.95
Romanian (0)	41	0.26
Russian (59)	328	2.05
Scandinavian (0)	17	0.11
Scotch-Irish (169)	495	3.09
Scottish (45)	429	2.68
Swedish (154)	558	3.48
Swiss (0)	88	0.55
Ukrainian (14)	61	0.38
Welsh (0)	75	0.47

Hispanic Origin	Population	%
Hispanic or Latino (of any race)	273	1.72
Central American, ex. Mexican	27	0.17
Costa Rican	1	0.01
Guatemalan	16	0.10
Honduran	4	0.03
Nicaraguan	3	0.02
Panamanian	3	0.02
Cuban	22	0.14
Dominican Republic	14	0.09
Mexican	36	0.23
Puerto Rican	95	0.60
South American	40	0.25
Argentinean	3	0.02
Bolivian	4	0.03
Chilean	7	0.04
Colombian	13	0.08
Ecuadorian	3	0.02
Peruvian	2	0.01
Venezuelan	8	0.05
Other Hispanic or Latino	39	0.25

Race*	Population	%
African-American/Black (131)	238	1.50
Not Hispanic (123)	212	1.34
Hispanic (8)	26	0.16
American Indian/Alaska Native (119)	213	1.34
Not Hispanic (115)	204	1.29
Hispanic (4)	9	0.06
Apache (0)	1	0.01
Blackfeet (1)	2	0.01
Canadian/French Am. Ind. (0)	2	0.01
Cherokee (0)	6	0.04
Cheyenne (0)	1	0.01
Chippewa (1)	1	0.01
Delaware (0)	1	0.01
Houma (1)	1	0.01
Iroquois (1)	10	0.06
Kiowa (1)	1	0.01
Navajo (0)	1	0.01
Sioux (1)	1	0.01
South American Ind. (0)	1	0.01
Tlingit-Haida *(Alaska Native)* (0)	1	0.01
Asian (131)	188	1.18
Not Hispanic (130)	185	1.17
Hispanic (1)	3	0.02
Cambodian (9)	11	0.07
Chinese, ex. Taiwanese (27)	40	0.25
Filipino (28)	45	0.28
Indian (19)	32	0.20
Indonesian (0)	2	0.01
Japanese (9)	14	0.09
Korean (11)	15	0.09
Laotian (2)	3	0.02
Pakistani (3)	3	0.02
Sri Lankan (2)	2	0.01
Taiwanese (7)	7	0.04
Thai (1)	3	0.02
Vietnamese (5)	11	0.07
Hawaii Native/Pacific Islander (4)	9	0.06
Not Hispanic (2)	5	0.03
Hispanic (2)	4	0.03
Native Hawaiian (2)	4	0.03
White (15,190)	15,381	96.93
Not Hispanic (15,005)	15,171	95.61
Hispanic (185)	210	1.32

Newport East

Place Type: CDP
County: Newport
Population: 11,769†

Ancestry‡	Population	%
African, Sub-Saharan (16)	35	0.30
African (16)	16	0.14
Cape Verdean (0)	19	0.16
American (260)	260	2.23
Arab (0)	77	0.66
Lebanese (0)	68	0.58
Syrian (0)	9	0.08
Armenian (0)	16	0.14
Australian (0)	10	0.09
Austrian (0)	14	0.12
Belgian (23)	23	0.20
Brazilian (92)	117	1.01
British (23)	77	0.66
Canadian (43)	43	0.37
Czech (0)	47	0.40
Czechoslovakian (39)	39	0.34
Danish (14)	60	0.52
Dutch (14)	93	0.80
Eastern European (31)	64	0.55
English (235)	1,740	14.95
European (29)	49	0.42
Finnish (51)	76	0.65
French, ex. Basque (178)	675	5.80
French Canadian (198)	308	2.65
German (187)	1,237	10.63
Greek (17)	81	0.70
Hungarian (0)	35	0.30
Irish (1,221)	3,245	27.89
Israeli (0)	11	0.09
Italian (483)	1,281	11.01
Lithuanian (0)	27	0.23
Norwegian (37)	62	0.53
Polish (96)	379	3.26
Portuguese (696)	1,217	10.46
Russian (7)	18	0.15
Scotch-Irish (56)	250	2.15
Scottish (64)	296	2.54
Slovak (14)	14	0.12
Swedish (64)	170	1.46
Turkish (5)	22	0.19
Ukrainian (34)	34	0.29
Welsh (11)	44	0.38
West Indian, ex. Hispanic (172)	225	1.93
Barbadian (78)	78	0.67
Jamaican (94)	147	1.26

Hispanic Origin	Population	%
Hispanic or Latino (of any race)	569	4.83

*Notes: † The Census 2010 population figure is used to calculate the percentages in the Hispanic Origin and Race categories. Ancestry percentages are based on the 2006-2010 American Community Survey population (not shown); ‡ Numbers in parentheses indicate the number of people reporting a single ancestry; * Numbers in parentheses indicate the number of persons reporting this race alone, not in combination with any other race; Please refer to the Explanation of Data for more information.*

Central American, ex. Mexican	69	0.59
Costa Rican	6	0.05
Guatemalan	26	0.22
Honduran	8	0.07
Nicaraguan	8	0.07
Panamanian	2	0.02
Salvadoran	19	0.16
Cuban	20	0.17
Dominican Republic	37	0.31
Mexican	85	0.72
Puerto Rican	227	1.93
South American	61	0.52
Argentinean	7	0.06
Bolivian	1	0.01
Chilean	7	0.06
Colombian	22	0.19
Ecuadorian	3	0.03
Peruvian	20	0.17
Venezuelan	1	0.01
Other Hispanic or Latino	70	0.59

Race*	Population	%
African-American/Black (588)	792	6.73
Not Hispanic (550)	713	6.06
Hispanic (38)	79	0.67
American Indian/Alaska Native (44)	139	1.18
Not Hispanic (32)	103	0.88
Hispanic (12)	36	0.31
Aleut *(Alaska Native)* (0)	1	0.01
Blackfeet (1)	4	0.03
Central American Ind. (0)	1	0.01
Cherokee (1)	10	0.08
Chippewa (0)	6	0.05
Choctaw (2)	2	0.02
Iroquois (1)	1	0.01
Puget Sound Salish (1)	1	0.01
Sioux (0)	1	0.01
South American Ind. (2)	3	0.03
Asian (352)	494	4.20
Not Hispanic (349)	479	4.07
Hispanic (3)	15	0.13
Cambodian (2)	2	0.02
Chinese, ex. Taiwanese (60)	73	0.62
Filipino (138)	208	1.77
Indian (29)	37	0.31
Japanese (17)	35	0.30
Korean (38)	60	0.51
Pakistani (11)	11	0.09
Taiwanese (9)	10	0.08
Thai (7)	11	0.09
Vietnamese (22)	31	0.26
Hawaii Native/Pacific Islander (19)	36	0.31
Not Hispanic (17)	31	0.26
Hispanic (2)	5	0.04
Guamanian/Chamorro (4)	8	0.07
Marshallese (11)	11	0.09
Native Hawaiian (3)	7	0.06
White (10,162)	10,493	89.16
Not Hispanic (9,852)	10,131	86.08
Hispanic (310)	362	3.08

Newport

Place Type: City
County: Newport
Population: 24,672†

Ancestry‡	Population	%
African, Sub-Saharan (401)	635	2.54
African (12)	57	0.23
Cape Verdean (389)	534	2.14
South African (0)	13	0.05
Other Sub-Saharan African (0)	31	0.12
Albanian (0)	13	0.05
American (528)	528	2.12
Arab (108)	295	1.18
Lebanese (76)	147	0.59
Syrian (32)	148	0.59
Armenian (15)	25	0.10
Australian (30)	38	0.15
Austrian (0)	50	0.20
Brazilian (21)	35	0.14
British (114)	124	0.50
Canadian (85)	135	0.54
Celtic (0)	15	0.06
Croatian (23)	70	0.28
Czech (40)	110	0.44
Danish (65)	187	0.75
Dutch (26)	365	1.46
English (1,372)	4,321	17.31
European (142)	165	0.66
Finnish (26)	43	0.17
French, ex. Basque (299)	1,638	6.56
French Canadian (302)	553	2.22
German (525)	2,843	11.39
German Russian (43)	43	0.17
Greek (116)	187	0.75
Hungarian (26)	78	0.31
Irish (1,995)	6,730	26.97
Italian (944)	3,308	13.25
Lithuanian (23)	187	0.75
Maltese (0)	15	0.06
Northern European (43)	43	0.17
Norwegian (24)	220	0.88
Polish (252)	1,136	4.55
Portuguese (791)	2,644	10.59
Romanian (0)	22	0.09
Russian (204)	548	2.20
Scandinavian (0)	29	0.12
Scotch-Irish (343)	573	2.30
Scottish (363)	1,060	4.25
Slovak (0)	27	0.11
Swedish (79)	370	1.48
Swiss (5)	83	0.33
Turkish (0)	16	0.06
Ukrainian (15)	74	0.30
Welsh (0)	62	0.25
West Indian, ex. Hispanic (24)	45	0.18
Bermudan (0)	10	0.04
Haitian (14)	25	0.10
Jamaican (10)	10	0.04

Hispanic Origin	Population	%
Hispanic or Latino (of any race)	2,062	8.36
Central American, ex. Mexican	463	1.88
Costa Rican	6	0.02
Guatemalan	305	1.24
Honduran	10	0.04
Nicaraguan	10	0.04
Panamanian	7	0.03
Salvadoran	125	0.51
Cuban	48	0.19
Dominican Republic	110	0.45
Mexican	260	1.05
Puerto Rican	826	3.35
South American	133	0.54
Argentinean	17	0.07
Bolivian	11	0.04
Chilean	12	0.05
Colombian	53	0.21
Ecuadorian	22	0.09
Peruvian	8	0.03
Uruguayan	1	<0.01
Venezuelan	8	0.03
Other South American	1	<0.01
Other Hispanic or Latino	222	0.90

Race*	Population	%
African-American/Black (1,710)	2,507	10.16
Not Hispanic (1,578)	2,249	9.12
Hispanic (132)	258	1.05
American Indian/Alaska Native (189)	542	2.20
Not Hispanic (161)	462	1.87
Hispanic (28)	80	0.32
Apache (1)	3	0.01
Blackfeet (4)	23	0.09
Canadian/French Am. Ind. (1)	5	0.02
Cherokee (8)	59	0.24
Chickasaw (1)	2	0.01
Chippewa (2)	2	0.01
Choctaw (1)	5	0.02
Cree (0)	3	0.01
Creek (0)	3	0.01
Iroquois (6)	15	0.06
Kiowa (0)	3	0.01
Lumbee (0)	1	<0.01
Mexican American Ind. (2)	5	0.02
Navajo (6)	10	0.04
Osage (0)	1	<0.01
Seminole (2)	3	0.01
Sioux (2)	5	0.02
South American Ind. (2)	5	0.02
Spanish American Ind. (2)	2	0.01
Yaqui (1)	1	<0.01
Asian (349)	578	2.34
Not Hispanic (334)	542	2.20
Hispanic (15)	36	0.15
Burmese (2)	3	0.01
Cambodian (2)	3	0.01
Chinese, ex. Taiwanese (60)	100	0.41
Filipino (134)	235	0.95
Indian (34)	43	0.17
Indonesian (1)	3	0.01
Japanese (40)	72	0.29
Korean (38)	60	0.24
Malaysian (0)	5	0.02
Nepalese (1)	2	0.01
Pakistani (7)	13	0.05
Taiwanese (0)	1	<0.01
Thai (5)	9	0.04
Vietnamese (12)	21	0.09
Hawaii Native/Pacific Islander (23)	95	0.39
Not Hispanic (11)	54	0.22
Hispanic (12)	41	0.17
Guamanian/Chamorro (17)	23	0.09
Native Hawaiian (1)	34	0.14
Samoan (3)	5	0.02
Tongan (1)	4	0.02
White (20,343)	21,399	86.73
Not Hispanic (19,360)	20,234	82.01
Hispanic (983)	1,165	4.72

North Kingstown

Place Type: Town
County: Washington
Population: 26,486†

Ancestry‡	Population	%
African, Sub-Saharan (16)	40	0.15
African (0)	9	0.03
Cape Verdean (16)	31	0.12
Albanian (14)	30	0.11
Alsatian (6)	6	0.02
American (769)	769	2.89
Arab (9)	34	0.13
Lebanese (0)	20	0.08
Syrian (0)	5	0.02
Other Arab (9)	9	0.03
Armenian (164)	287	1.08
Australian (7)	23	0.09
Austrian (0)	79	0.30
British (38)	181	0.68
Bulgarian (31)	31	0.12
Canadian (54)	170	0.64
Celtic (0)	12	0.05
Croatian (0)	8	0.03
Czech (0)	61	0.23
Danish (9)	102	0.38
Dutch (35)	219	0.82
Eastern European (30)	30	0.11
English (1,339)	5,536	20.80
Estonian (8)	8	0.03
European (163)	179	0.67
Finnish (20)	86	0.32
French, ex. Basque (608)	3,577	13.44
French Canadian (667)	1,394	5.24
German (495)	3,676	13.81
Greek (93)	102	0.38
Hungarian (8)	85	0.32

*Notes: † The Census 2010 population figure is used to calculate the percentages in the Hispanic Origin and Race categories. Ancestry percentages are based on the 2006-2010 American Community Survey population (not shown); ‡ Numbers in parentheses indicate the number of people reporting a single ancestry; * Numbers in parentheses indicate the number of persons reporting this race alone, not in combination with any other race; Please refer to the Explanation of Data for more information.*

Iranian (15)	21	0.08
Irish (2,543)	8,017	30.13
Italian (1,433)	4,628	17.39
Latvian (9)	19	0.07
Lithuanian (10)	164	0.62
Northern European (37)	37	0.14
Norwegian (87)	364	1.37
Polish (272)	1,248	4.69
Portuguese (399)	1,258	4.73
Romanian (16)	41	0.15
Russian (129)	320	1.20
Scandinavian (0)	11	0.04
Scotch-Irish (182)	537	2.02
Scottish (154)	848	3.19
Slovak (14)	57	0.21
Swedish (174)	754	2.83
Swiss (0)	12	0.05
Ukrainian (9)	36	0.14
Welsh (29)	105	0.39

Hispanic Origin	Population	%
Hispanic or Latino (of any race)	637	2.41
Central American, ex. Mexican	39	0.15
Costa Rican	2	0.01
Guatemalan	14	0.05
Honduran	7	0.03
Nicaraguan	4	0.02
Panamanian	4	0.02
Salvadoran	4	0.02
Other Central American	4	0.02
Cuban	31	0.12
Dominican Republic	44	0.17
Mexican	112	0.42
Puerto Rican	271	1.02
South American	88	0.33
Argentinean	6	0.02
Bolivian	10	0.04
Chilean	8	0.03
Colombian	33	0.12
Ecuadorian	7	0.03
Paraguayan	1	<0.01
Peruvian	13	0.05
Uruguayan	2	0.01
Venezuelan	8	0.03
Other Hispanic or Latino	52	0.20

Race*	Population	%
African-American/Black (267)	486	1.83
Not Hispanic (232)	420	1.59
Hispanic (35)	66	0.25
American Indian/Alaska Native (155)	341	1.29
Not Hispanic (135)	295	1.11
Hispanic (20)	46	0.17
Apache (2)	4	0.02
Blackfeet (3)	6	0.02
Cherokee (12)	25	0.09
Cheyenne (0)	1	<0.01
Chippewa (0)	1	<0.01
Choctaw (1)	1	<0.01
Inupiat *(Alaska Native)* (1)	1	<0.01
Iroquois (0)	2	0.01
Mexican American Ind. (5)	7	0.03
Potawatomi (1)	1	<0.01
Pueblo (1)	1	<0.01
Sioux (7)	7	0.03
South American Ind. (1)	5	0.02
Asian (356)	490	1.85
Not Hispanic (354)	477	1.80
Hispanic (2)	13	0.05
Cambodian (8)	12	0.05
Chinese, ex. Taiwanese (104)	148	0.56
Filipino (64)	93	0.35
Hmong (0)	1	<0.01
Indian (63)	81	0.31
Indonesian (2)	2	0.01
Japanese (31)	58	0.22
Korean (40)	62	0.23
Malaysian (1)	1	<0.01
Pakistani (4)	5	0.02
Sri Lankan (1)	1	<0.01
Taiwanese (4)	4	0.02
Thai (4)	16	0.06
Vietnamese (12)	20	0.08
Hawaii Native/Pacific Islander (9)	31	0.12
Not Hispanic (8)	26	0.10
Hispanic (1)	5	0.02
Fijian (2)	2	0.01
Guamanian/Chamorro (1)	2	0.01
Native Hawaiian (0)	16	0.06
Samoan (0)	1	<0.01
White (25,081)	25,524	96.37
Not Hispanic (24,654)	25,034	94.52
Hispanic (427)	490	1.85

North Providence

Place Type: Town
County: Providence
Population: 32,078†

Ancestry‡	Population	%
African, Sub-Saharan (382)	638	1.98
African (61)	61	0.19
Cape Verdean (221)	249	0.77
Kenyan (14)	14	0.04
Nigerian (51)	67	0.21
Senegalese (0)	106	0.33
Other Sub-Saharan African (35)	141	0.44
American (478)	478	1.48
Arab (257)	486	1.51
Arab (0)	31	0.10
Lebanese (120)	248	0.77
Syrian (137)	207	0.64
Armenian (194)	313	0.97
Australian (9)	9	0.03
Austrian (11)	103	0.32
Basque (0)	13	0.04
Belgian (35)	35	0.11
Brazilian (44)	44	0.14
British (0)	10	0.03
Canadian (94)	109	0.34
Croatian (0)	17	0.05
Danish (18)	48	0.15
Dutch (0)	84	0.26
English (463)	2,933	9.10
European (199)	199	0.62
Finnish (0)	100	0.31
French, ex. Basque (881)	3,689	11.44
French Canadian (804)	1,332	4.13
German (280)	1,105	3.43
Greek (109)	328	1.02
Hungarian (13)	91	0.28
Iranian (17)	17	0.05
Irish (1,447)	6,050	18.76
Italian (7,511)	12,717	39.44
Lithuanian (53)	176	0.55
Northern European (12)	12	0.04
Norwegian (12)	22	0.07
Polish (291)	1,070	3.32
Portuguese (1,064)	2,755	8.54
Russian (40)	99	0.31
Scotch-Irish (121)	329	1.02
Scottish (38)	390	1.21
Serbian (15)	15	0.05
Slavic (0)	13	0.04
Swedish (54)	400	1.24
Turkish (0)	36	0.11
Ukrainian (0)	31	0.10
Welsh (0)	46	0.14
West Indian, ex. Hispanic (125)	211	0.65
British West Indian (26)	26	0.08
Haitian (85)	171	0.53
Jamaican (14)	14	0.04

Hispanic Origin	Population	%
Hispanic or Latino (of any race)	2,447	7.63
Central American, ex. Mexican	273	0.85
Costa Rican	8	0.02
Guatemalan	227	0.71
Honduran	9	0.03
Nicaraguan	2	0.01
Panamanian	7	0.02
Salvadoran	20	0.06
Cuban	53	0.17
Dominican Republic	457	1.42
Mexican	138	0.43
Puerto Rican	644	2.01
South American	615	1.92
Argentinean	7	0.02
Bolivian	128	0.40
Chilean	4	0.01
Colombian	361	1.13
Ecuadorian	18	0.06
Peruvian	69	0.22
Uruguayan	1	<0.01
Venezuelan	20	0.06
Other South American	7	0.02
Other Hispanic or Latino	267	0.83

Race*	Population	%
African-American/Black (1,531)	1,903	5.93
Not Hispanic (1,412)	1,701	5.30
Hispanic (119)	202	0.63
American Indian/Alaska Native (109)	266	0.83
Not Hispanic (76)	199	0.62
Hispanic (33)	67	0.21
Apache (1)	3	0.01
Blackfeet (0)	8	0.02
Canadian/French Am. Ind. (2)	4	0.01
Central American Ind. (3)	3	0.01
Cherokee (2)	18	0.06
Chickasaw (1)	1	<0.01
Chippewa (0)	2	0.01
Choctaw (0)	1	<0.01
Comanche (0)	2	0.01
Cree (0)	1	<0.01
Creek (2)	2	0.01
Iroquois (1)	3	0.01
Mexican American Ind. (6)	9	0.03
Navajo (2)	5	0.02
Sioux (2)	2	0.01
South American Ind. (2)	6	0.02
Asian (727)	856	2.67
Not Hispanic (717)	829	2.58
Hispanic (10)	27	0.08
Burmese (1)	1	<0.01
Cambodian (28)	29	0.09
Chinese, ex. Taiwanese (177)	194	0.60
Filipino (90)	117	0.36
Hmong (8)	8	0.02
Indian (203)	229	0.71
Indonesian (3)	5	0.02
Japanese (7)	14	0.04
Korean (35)	48	0.15
Laotian (53)	62	0.19
Malaysian (2)	2	0.01
Pakistani (42)	45	0.14
Sri Lankan (6)	6	0.02
Taiwanese (4)	4	0.01
Thai (17)	25	0.08
Vietnamese (29)	35	0.11
Hawaii Native/Pacific Islander (8)	63	0.20
Not Hispanic (7)	47	0.15
Hispanic (1)	16	0.05
Fijian (0)	5	0.02
Guamanian/Chamorro (1)	6	0.02
Native Hawaiian (1)	6	0.02
Samoan (2)	3	0.01
White (27,918)	28,498	88.84
Not Hispanic (26,606)	27,009	84.20
Hispanic (1,312)	1,489	4.64

North Smithfield

Place Type: Town
County: Providence
Population: 11,967†

Ancestry‡	Population	%
African, Sub-Saharan (44)	44	0.37

*Notes: † The Census 2010 population figure is used to calculate the percentages in the Hispanic Origin and Race categories. Ancestry percentages are based on the 2006-2010 American Community Survey population (not shown); ‡ Numbers in parentheses indicate the number of people reporting a single ancestry; * Numbers in parentheses indicate the number of persons reporting this race alone, not in combination with any other race; Please refer to the Explanation of Data for more information.*

Ancestry	Population	%
Cape Verdean (44)	44	0.37
American (174)	174	1.48
Arab (50)	222	1.89
Lebanese (27)	134	1.14
Moroccan (13)	27	0.23
Syrian (10)	61	0.52
Armenian (9)	37	0.31
Austrian (0)	10	0.08
Belgian (8)	18	0.15
British (10)	19	0.16
Canadian (156)	168	1.43
Czech (0)	6	0.05
Dutch (10)	55	0.47
English (351)	1,275	10.83
European (16)	71	0.60
French, ex. Basque (1,907)	3,838	32.61
French Canadian (1,574)	1,990	16.91
German (153)	546	4.64
Greek (0)	23	0.20
Hungarian (0)	3	0.03
Irish (472)	2,061	17.51
Italian (651)	1,874	15.92
Lithuanian (0)	11	0.09
Norwegian (9)	15	0.13
Polish (299)	949	8.06
Portuguese (240)	554	4.71
Russian (0)	22	0.19
Scotch-Irish (61)	141	1.20
Scottish (67)	261	2.22
Swedish (33)	128	1.09
Swiss (25)	25	0.21
Ukrainian (16)	105	0.89
Welsh (0)	14	0.12
Yugoslavian (0)	8	0.07

Hispanic Origin	Population	%
Hispanic or Latino (of any race)	277	2.31
Central American, ex. Mexican	24	0.20
Costa Rican	1	0.01
Guatemalan	18	0.15
Panamanian	1	0.01
Salvadoran	4	0.03
Cuban	4	0.03
Dominican Republic	25	0.21
Mexican	34	0.28
Puerto Rican	96	0.80
South American	57	0.48
Argentinean	5	0.04
Chilean	4	0.03
Colombian	36	0.30
Ecuadorian	1	0.01
Peruvian	3	0.03
Venezuelan	8	0.07
Other Hispanic or Latino	37	0.31

Race*	Population	%
African-American/Black (65)	120	1.00
Not Hispanic (58)	105	0.88
Hispanic (7)	15	0.13
American Indian/Alaska Native (16)	55	0.46
Not Hispanic (14)	48	0.40
Hispanic (2)	7	0.06
Blackfeet (3)	7	0.06
Canadian/French Am. Ind. (1)	5	0.04
Cherokee (0)	4	0.03
Iroquois (1)	5	0.04
Menominee (1)	1	0.01
Shoshone (1)	1	0.01
South American Ind. (2)	5	0.04
Asian (123)	153	1.28
Not Hispanic (123)	152	1.27
Hispanic (0)	1	0.01
Bangladeshi (1)	1	0.01
Burmese (2)	2	0.02
Cambodian (3)	4	0.03
Chinese, ex. Taiwanese (22)	28	0.23
Filipino (7)	16	0.13
Indian (43)	48	0.40
Japanese (2)	10	0.08
Korean (8)	13	0.11
Laotian (12)	12	0.10
Pakistani (3)	4	0.03
Thai (4)	8	0.07
Vietnamese (11)	11	0.09
Hawaii Native/Pacific Islander (0)	3	0.03
Not Hispanic (0)	2	0.02
Hispanic (0)	1	0.01
Native Hawaiian (0)	2	0.02
White (11,559)	11,683	97.63
Not Hispanic (11,383)	11,476	95.90
Hispanic (176)	207	1.73

Pawtucket

Place Type: City
County: Providence
Population: 71,148†

Ancestry‡	Population	%
Afghan (0)	11	0.02
African, Sub-Saharan (10,244)	11,509	16.06
African (561)	766	1.07
Cape Verdean (7,836)	8,720	12.17
Ghanaian (244)	244	0.34
Kenyan (24)	24	0.03
Liberian (1,067)	1,075	1.50
Nigerian (221)	221	0.31
Senegalese (107)	170	0.24
Sudanese (21)	21	0.03
Other Sub-Saharan African (163)	268	0.37
American (1,293)	1,293	1.80
Arab (461)	780	1.09
Arab (80)	103	0.14
Jordanian (0)	65	0.09
Lebanese (86)	125	0.17
Palestinian (0)	23	0.03
Syrian (250)	419	0.58
Other Arab (45)	45	0.06
Armenian (182)	296	0.41
Austrian (9)	44	0.06
Belgian (0)	48	0.07
Brazilian (201)	261	0.36
British (64)	126	0.18
Canadian (133)	308	0.43
Czech (14)	23	0.03
Czechoslovakian (0)	20	0.03
Danish (14)	71	0.10
Dutch (51)	281	0.39
Eastern European (31)	35	0.05
English (1,494)	6,244	8.71
Estonian (9)	9	0.01
European (115)	115	0.16
Finnish (18)	68	0.09
French, ex. Basque (2,929)	9,245	12.90
French Canadian (1,910)	3,308	4.62
German (545)	2,638	3.68
Greek (358)	666	0.93
Hungarian (18)	54	0.08
Iranian (11)	20	0.03
Irish (2,877)	10,139	14.15
Israeli (11)	11	0.02
Italian (1,743)	4,982	6.95
Lithuanian (159)	194	0.27
Norwegian (9)	36	0.05
Pennsylvania German (0)	19	0.03
Polish (1,377)	3,075	4.29
Portuguese (5,138)	8,114	11.32
Romanian (9)	19	0.03
Russian (326)	532	0.74
Scandinavian (10)	10	0.01
Scotch-Irish (249)	807	1.13
Scottish (271)	1,129	1.58
Serbian (10)	17	0.02
Swedish (185)	828	1.16
Turkish (0)	20	0.03
Ukrainian (162)	223	0.31
Welsh (27)	95	0.13
West Indian, ex. Hispanic (393)	563	0.79
Barbadian (75)	90	0.13
Belizean (11)	11	0.02
British West Indian (12)	12	0.02
Haitian (211)	256	0.36
Jamaican (54)	106	0.15
Trinidadian/Tobagonian (10)	25	0.03
West Indian (20)	63	0.09

Hispanic Origin	Population	%
Hispanic or Latino (of any race)	14,042	19.74
Central American, ex. Mexican	1,909	2.68
Costa Rican	30	0.04
Guatemalan	1,301	1.83
Honduran	131	0.18
Nicaraguan	36	0.05
Panamanian	45	0.06
Salvadoran	344	0.48
Other Central American	22	0.03
Cuban	113	0.16
Dominican Republic	1,894	2.66
Mexican	798	1.12
Puerto Rican	4,729	6.65
South American	3,582	5.03
Argentinean	35	0.05
Bolivian	84	0.12
Chilean	30	0.04
Colombian	3,056	4.30
Ecuadorian	116	0.16
Peruvian	159	0.22
Uruguayan	14	0.02
Venezuelan	86	0.12
Other South American	2	<0.01
Other Hispanic or Latino	1,017	1.43

Race*	Population	%
African-American/Black (9,534)	12,251	17.22
Not Hispanic (8,667)	10,950	15.39
Hispanic (867)	1,301	1.83
American Indian/Alaska Native (445)	919	1.29
Not Hispanic (267)	645	0.91
Hispanic (178)	274	0.39
Apache (2)	6	0.01
Blackfeet (3)	14	0.02
Canadian/French Am. Ind. (2)	13	0.02
Central American Ind. (1)	4	0.01
Cherokee (25)	56	0.08
Chippewa (0)	7	0.01
Choctaw (0)	6	0.01
Cree (0)	3	<0.01
Inupiat *(Alaska Native)* (1)	2	<0.01
Iroquois (7)	13	0.02
Menominee (0)	1	<0.01
Mexican American Ind. (10)	13	0.02
Navajo (0)	1	<0.01
Paiute (0)	1	<0.01
Potawatomi (1)	1	<0.01
Sioux (5)	8	0.01
South American Ind. (8)	26	0.04
Spanish American Ind. (1)	5	0.01
Tlingit-Haida *(Alaska Native)* (0)	1	<0.01
Yaqui (0)	1	<0.01
Asian (1,073)	1,462	2.05
Not Hispanic (1,049)	1,384	1.95
Hispanic (24)	78	0.11
Bangladeshi (13)	14	0.02
Burmese (2)	3	<0.01
Cambodian (122)	157	0.22
Chinese, ex. Taiwanese (192)	271	0.38
Filipino (126)	201	0.28
Hmong (24)	25	0.04
Indian (243)	317	0.45
Indonesian (4)	4	0.01
Japanese (19)	45	0.06
Korean (39)	63	0.09
Laotian (39)	58	0.08
Nepalese (15)	15	0.02
Pakistani (52)	53	0.07
Sri Lankan (11)	12	0.02
Taiwanese (2)	2	<0.01
Thai (6)	10	0.01
Vietnamese (113)	123	0.17
Hawaii Native/Pacific Islander (54)	374	0.53

*Notes: † The Census 2010 population figure is used to calculate the percentages in the Hispanic Origin and Race categories. Ancestry percentages are based on the 2006-2010 American Community Survey population (not shown); ‡ Numbers in parentheses indicate the number of people reporting a single ancestry; * Numbers in parentheses indicate the number of persons reporting this race alone, not in combination with any other race; Please refer to the Explanation of Data for more information.*

Not Hispanic (32)	279	0.39
Hispanic (22)	95	0.13
Fijian (12)	14	0.02
Guamanian/Chamorro (11)	18	0.03
Native Hawaiian (12)	34	0.05
Samoan (4)	11	0.02
Tongan (1)	2	<0.01
White (47,289)	49,804	70.00
Not Hispanic (40,366)	41,972	58.99
Hispanic (6,923)	7,832	11.01

Portsmouth

Place Type: Town
County: Newport
Population: 17,389†

Ancestry‡	Population	%
African, Sub-Saharan (23)	107	0.62
Cape Verdean (0)	15	0.09
Other Sub-Saharan African (23)	92	0.53
American (805)	805	4.65
Arab (0)	28	0.16
Lebanese (0)	28	0.16
Armenian (14)	47	0.27
Austrian (32)	83	0.48
Brazilian (47)	122	0.70
British (14)	55	0.32
Canadian (17)	54	0.31
Celtic (15)	15	0.09
Croatian (18)	40	0.23
Czech (12)	12	0.07
Czechoslovakian (0)	14	0.08
Danish (0)	57	0.33
Dutch (10)	146	0.84
Eastern European (13)	13	0.08
English (715)	2,989	17.26
European (105)	152	0.88
Finnish (0)	13	0.08
French, ex. Basque (313)	1,564	9.03
French Canadian (354)	732	4.23
German (558)	2,097	12.11
Greek (96)	259	1.50
Hungarian (0)	49	0.28
Irish (1,623)	4,942	28.54
Italian (550)	1,894	10.94
Lithuanian (13)	118	0.68
Northern European (12)	12	0.07
Norwegian (27)	109	0.63
Polish (338)	1,072	6.19
Portuguese (1,341)	2,857	16.50
Romanian (0)	12	0.07
Russian (152)	351	2.03
Scandinavian (9)	9	0.05
Scotch-Irish (206)	526	3.04
Scottish (181)	630	3.64
Slovak (0)	23	0.13
Swedish (42)	252	1.46
Turkish (0)	22	0.13
Ukrainian (0)	32	0.18
Welsh (55)	169	0.98
West Indian, ex. Hispanic (18)	18	0.10
Jamaican (18)	18	0.10

Hispanic Origin	Population	%
Hispanic or Latino (of any race)	372	2.14
Central American, ex. Mexican	21	0.12
Costa Rican	3	0.02
Guatemalan	17	0.10
Panamanian	1	0.01
Cuban	25	0.14
Dominican Republic	22	0.13
Mexican	105	0.60
Puerto Rican	109	0.63
South American	33	0.19
Argentinean	3	0.02
Bolivian	6	0.03
Chilean	1	0.01
Colombian	5	0.03
Ecuadorian	5	0.03
Peruvian	6	0.03
Uruguayan	1	0.01
Venezuelan	6	0.03
Other Hispanic or Latino	57	0.33

Race*	Population	%
African-American/Black (234)	355	2.04
Not Hispanic (219)	314	1.81
Hispanic (15)	41	0.24
American Indian/Alaska Native (37)	109	0.63
Not Hispanic (29)	89	0.51
Hispanic (8)	20	0.12
Blackfeet (0)	2	0.01
Central American Ind. (3)	4	0.02
Cherokee (6)	23	0.13
Chippewa (0)	1	0.01
Colville (1)	1	0.01
Comanche (1)	1	0.01
Cree (0)	1	0.01
Inupiat *(Alaska Native)* (1)	1	0.01
Iroquois (1)	2	0.01
Mexican American Ind. (5)	5	0.03
Navajo (0)	5	0.03
Osage (1)	1	0.01
South American Ind. (0)	5	0.03
Asian (274)	405	2.33
Not Hispanic (270)	397	2.28
Hispanic (4)	8	0.05
Bangladeshi (2)	2	0.01
Cambodian (0)	2	0.01
Chinese, ex. Taiwanese (48)	57	0.33
Filipino (99)	153	0.88
Indian (11)	18	0.10
Japanese (21)	46	0.26
Korean (41)	59	0.34
Malaysian (0)	1	0.01
Pakistani (10)	15	0.09
Taiwanese (4)	9	0.05
Thai (6)	13	0.07
Vietnamese (23)	28	0.16
Hawaii Native/Pacific Islander (7)	17	0.10
Not Hispanic (7)	17	0.10
Guamanian/Chamorro (5)	7	0.04
Native Hawaiian (1)	3	0.02
Samoan (1)	1	0.01
White (16,445)	16,749	96.32
Not Hispanic (16,178)	16,451	94.61
Hispanic (267)	298	1.71

Providence

Place Type: City
County: Providence
Population: 178,042†

Ancestry‡	Population	%
African, Sub-Saharan (8,838)	10,380	5.82
African (1,736)	2,075	1.16
Cape Verdean (3,124)	4,015	2.25
Ethiopian (120)	149	0.08
Ghanaian (414)	462	0.26
Kenyan (14)	14	0.01
Liberian (1,600)	1,682	0.94
Nigerian (1,307)	1,388	0.78
Sierra Leonean (37)	51	0.03
South African (10)	41	0.02
Ugandan (10)	10	0.01
Other Sub-Saharan African (466)	493	0.28
Albanian (27)	39	0.02
Alsatian (0)	11	0.01
American (1,519)	1,519	0.85
Arab (404)	863	0.48
Arab (89)	102	0.06
Egyptian (44)	59	0.03
Iraqi (15)	27	0.02
Lebanese (202)	387	0.22
Moroccan (22)	22	0.01
Syrian (8)	190	0.11
Other Arab (24)	76	0.04
Armenian (703)	966	0.54
Assyrian/Chaldean/Syriac (0)	38	0.02
Australian (9)	32	0.02
Austrian (82)	344	0.19
Belgian (94)	185	0.10
Brazilian (103)	184	0.10
British (237)	714	0.40
Bulgarian (29)	29	0.02
Canadian (36)	401	0.22
Celtic (26)	42	0.02
Croatian (60)	78	0.04
Cypriot (9)	9	0.01
Czech (8)	145	0.08
Czechoslovakian (32)	76	0.04
Danish (42)	269	0.15
Dutch (163)	577	0.32
Eastern European (501)	609	0.34
English (1,779)	8,854	4.97
European (551)	642	0.36
Finnish (22)	91	0.05
French, ex. Basque (1,276)	6,529	3.66
French Canadian (1,346)	2,675	1.50
German (1,385)	6,538	3.67
Greek (291)	701	0.39
Guyanese (70)	83	0.05
Hungarian (95)	330	0.19
Icelander (0)	9	0.01
Iranian (48)	93	0.05
Irish (5,290)	17,079	9.58
Israeli (50)	97	0.05
Italian (9,544)	19,741	11.07
Latvian (12)	37	0.02
Lithuanian (113)	383	0.21
Northern European (94)	94	0.05
Norwegian (163)	666	0.37
Pennsylvania German (26)	26	0.01
Polish (1,161)	4,525	2.54
Portuguese (3,179)	5,586	3.13
Romanian (39)	147	0.08
Russian (1,124)	2,749	1.54
Scandinavian (48)	85	0.05
Scotch-Irish (453)	1,413	0.79
Scottish (548)	1,938	1.09
Serbian (0)	27	0.02
Slavic (10)	10	0.01
Slovak (14)	136	0.08
Slovene (30)	30	0.02
Swedish (299)	1,225	0.69
Swiss (19)	155	0.09
Turkish (183)	216	0.12
Ukrainian (60)	347	0.19
Welsh (69)	470	0.26
West Indian, ex. Hispanic (2,500)	3,133	1.76
Barbadian (162)	322	0.18
Belizean (255)	255	0.14
Bermudan (13)	27	0.02
British West Indian (36)	88	0.05
Haitian (1,226)	1,254	0.70
Jamaican (303)	370	0.21
Trinidadian/Tobagonian (137)	177	0.10
U.S. Virgin Islander (86)	86	0.05
West Indian (282)	554	0.31
Yugoslavian (11)	42	0.02

Hispanic Origin	Population	%
Hispanic or Latino (of any race)	67,835	38.10
Central American, ex. Mexican	14,630	8.22
Costa Rican	94	0.05
Guatemalan	11,930	6.70
Honduran	731	0.41
Nicaraguan	122	0.07
Panamanian	169	0.09
Salvadoran	1,503	0.84
Other Central American	81	0.05
Cuban	538	0.30
Dominican Republic	25,267	14.19
Mexican	3,188	1.79
Puerto Rican	14,847	8.34
South American	3,544	1.99
Argentinean	145	0.08
Bolivian	1,046	0.59

*Notes: † The Census 2010 population figure is used to calculate the percentages in the Hispanic Origin and Race categories. Ancestry percentages are based on the 2006-2010 American Community Survey population (not shown); ‡ Numbers in parentheses indicate the number of people reporting a single ancestry; * Numbers in parentheses indicate the number of persons reporting this race alone, not in combination with any other race; Please refer to the Explanation of Data for more information.*

Hispanic Origin	Population	%
Chilean	81	0.05
Colombian	969	0.54
Ecuadorian	629	0.35
Paraguayan	6	<0.01
Peruvian	404	0.23
Uruguayan	28	0.02
Venezuelan	200	0.11
Other South American	36	0.02
Other Hispanic or Latino	5,821	3.27

Race*	Population	%
African-American/Black (28,557)	34,496	19.38
Not Hispanic (23,399)	27,047	15.19
Hispanic (5,158)	7,449	4.18
American Indian/Alaska Native (2,412)	5,234	2.94
Not Hispanic (1,220)	3,066	1.72
Hispanic (1,192)	2,168	1.22
Alaska Athabascan *(Ala. Nat.)* (1)	3	<0.01
Apache (3)	22	0.01
Blackfeet (20)	99	0.06
Canadian/French Am. Ind. (3)	9	0.01
Central American Ind. (122)	168	0.09
Cherokee (60)	299	0.17
Chickasaw (1)	9	0.01
Chippewa (2)	9	0.01
Choctaw (1)	11	0.01
Cree (1)	2	<0.01
Creek (0)	2	<0.01
Delaware (0)	2	<0.01
Hopi (1)	6	<0.01
Houma (0)	1	<0.01
Inupiat *(Alaska Native)* (2)	3	<0.01
Iroquois (11)	58	0.03
Lumbee (1)	4	<0.01
Menominee (1)	2	<0.01
Mexican American Ind. (203)	293	0.16
Navajo (7)	17	0.01
Potawatomi (1)	2	<0.01
Pueblo (7)	22	0.01
Seminole (1)	18	0.01
Shoshone (0)	4	<0.01
Sioux (5)	24	0.01
South American Ind. (143)	225	0.13
Spanish American Ind. (49)	69	0.04
Tlingit-Haida *(Alaska Native)* (1)	1	<0.01
Tohono O'Odham (4)	4	<0.01
Tsimshian *(Alaska Native)* (0)	1	<0.01
Ute (0)	2	<0.01
Yaqui (2)	2	<0.01
Yup'ik *(Alaska Native)* (1)	3	<0.01
Asian (11,380)	13,128	7.37
Not Hispanic (11,153)	12,541	7.04
Hispanic (227)	587	0.33
Bangladeshi (21)	29	0.02
Bhutanese (59)	72	0.04
Burmese (52)	62	0.03
Cambodian (2,974)	3,339	1.88
Chinese, ex. Taiwanese (2,031)	2,512	1.41
Filipino (454)	702	0.39
Hmong (609)	673	0.38
Indian (1,312)	1,659	0.93
Indonesian (13)	24	0.01
Japanese (194)	476	0.27
Korean (1,005)	1,127	0.63
Laotian (1,052)	1,213	0.68
Malaysian (21)	25	0.01
Nepalese (75)	93	0.05
Pakistani (115)	142	0.08
Sri Lankan (19)	25	0.01
Taiwanese (140)	166	0.09
Thai (138)	241	0.14
Vietnamese (254)	334	0.19
Hawaii Native/Pacific Islander (222)	760	0.43
Not Hispanic (88)	341	0.19
Hispanic (134)	419	0.24
Fijian (2)	7	<0.01
Guamanian/Chamorro (87)	123	0.07
Native Hawaiian (35)	111	0.06
Samoan (26)	37	0.02
Tongan (1)	1	<0.01
White (88,623)	96,230	54.05
Not Hispanic (66,910)	70,447	39.57
Hispanic (21,713)	25,783	14.48

Richmond

Place Type: Town
County: Washington
Population: 7,708†

Ancestry‡	Population	%
Albanian (0)	12	0.16
American (224)	224	2.92
Arab (0)	14	0.18
Lebanese (0)	14	0.18
Austrian (16)	16	0.21
British (8)	8	0.10
Canadian (0)	30	0.39
Celtic (9)	9	0.12
Danish (24)	36	0.47
Dutch (11)	56	0.73
Eastern European (13)	13	0.17
English (471)	2,179	28.40
Estonian (10)	10	0.13
European (10)	10	0.13
Finnish (11)	11	0.14
French, ex. Basque (195)	1,413	18.42
French Canadian (208)	387	5.04
German (88)	651	8.49
Greek (0)	30	0.39
Hungarian (0)	49	0.64
Irish (515)	1,907	24.86
Italian (413)	1,433	18.68
Lithuanian (0)	31	0.40
Norwegian (12)	67	0.87
Polish (181)	548	7.14
Portuguese (245)	597	7.78
Russian (0)	75	0.98
Scandinavian (14)	14	0.18
Scotch-Irish (41)	78	1.02
Scottish (68)	343	4.47
Swedish (26)	258	3.36
Swiss (0)	33	0.43
Ukrainian (0)	13	0.17
Welsh (0)	54	0.70

Hispanic Origin	Population	%
Hispanic or Latino (of any race)	124	1.61
Central American, ex. Mexican	12	0.16
Costa Rican	5	0.06
Guatemalan	4	0.05
Honduran	2	0.03
Salvadoran	1	0.01
Cuban	4	0.05
Dominican Republic	15	0.19
Mexican	22	0.29
Puerto Rican	38	0.49
South American	11	0.14
Colombian	5	0.06
Ecuadorian	4	0.05
Peruvian	2	0.03
Other Hispanic or Latino	22	0.29

Race*	Population	%
African-American/Black (36)	83	1.08
Not Hispanic (33)	76	0.99
Hispanic (3)	7	0.09
American Indian/Alaska Native (42)	104	1.35
Not Hispanic (35)	92	1.19
Hispanic (7)	12	0.16
Blackfeet (0)	2	0.03
Canadian/French Am. Ind. (0)	3	0.04
Cherokee (1)	6	0.08
Choctaw (0)	3	0.04
Cree (0)	5	0.06
Iroquois (1)	3	0.04
Navajo (3)	3	0.04
Potawatomi (1)	1	0.01
Sioux (0)	1	0.01
Tlingit-Haida *(Alaska Native)* (0)	3	0.04
Asian (42)	63	0.82
Not Hispanic (42)	61	0.79
Hispanic (0)	2	0.03
Cambodian (0)	1	0.01
Chinese, ex. Taiwanese (12)	17	0.22
Filipino (6)	8	0.10
Indian (6)	14	0.18
Japanese (2)	5	0.06
Korean (11)	12	0.16
Taiwanese (3)	3	0.04
Vietnamese (1)	1	0.01
Hawaii Native/Pacific Islander (1)	2	0.03
Not Hispanic (1)	2	0.03
Native Hawaiian (1)	2	0.03
White (7,437)	7,544	97.87
Not Hispanic (7,356)	7,455	96.72
Hispanic (81)	89	1.15

Scituate

Place Type: Town
County: Providence
Population: 10,329†

Ancestry‡	Population	%
African, Sub-Saharan (8)	38	0.37
Cape Verdean (8)	38	0.37
American (470)	470	4.55
Arab (0)	19	0.18
Syrian (0)	19	0.18
Armenian (19)	46	0.45
Austrian (9)	9	0.09
Belgian (0)	29	0.28
British (35)	35	0.34
Canadian (28)	85	0.82
Czech (13)	39	0.38
Dutch (0)	244	2.36
Eastern European (33)	33	0.32
English (648)	2,915	28.20
European (13)	13	0.13
Finnish (0)	9	0.09
French, ex. Basque (377)	1,722	16.66
French Canadian (247)	621	6.01
German (77)	775	7.50
Greek (43)	53	0.51
Hungarian (31)	58	0.56
Irish (560)	2,447	23.67
Italian (1,314)	2,870	27.76
Lithuanian (0)	45	0.44
Northern European (18)	18	0.17
Norwegian (0)	137	1.33
Polish (22)	203	1.96
Portuguese (124)	634	6.13
Russian (0)	24	0.23
Scandinavian (0)	18	0.17
Scotch-Irish (35)	164	1.59
Scottish (0)	483	4.67
Slovak (9)	46	0.45
Swedish (42)	215	2.08
Swiss (0)	10	0.10
Ukrainian (9)	9	0.09
Welsh (0)	14	0.14
West Indian, ex. Hispanic (0)	40	0.39
Jamaican (0)	40	0.39

Hispanic Origin	Population	%
Hispanic or Latino (of any race)	123	1.19
Central American, ex. Mexican	21	0.20
Guatemalan	6	0.06
Nicaraguan	3	0.03
Salvadoran	11	0.11
Other Central American	1	0.01
Cuban	3	0.03
Dominican Republic	21	0.20
Mexican	13	0.13
Puerto Rican	26	0.25
South American	18	0.17
Chilean	1	0.01
Colombian	11	0.11
Peruvian	3	0.03

*Notes: † The Census 2010 population figure is used to calculate the percentages in the Hispanic Origin and Race categories. Ancestry percentages are based on the 2006-2010 American Community Survey population (not shown); ‡ Numbers in parentheses indicate the number of people reporting a single ancestry; * Numbers in parentheses indicate the number of persons reporting this race alone, not in combination with any other race; Please refer to the Explanation of Data for more information.*

Venezuelan	3	0.03
Other Hispanic or Latino	21	0.20

Race*	Population	%
African-American/Black (38)	64	0.62
Not Hispanic (37)	62	0.60
Hispanic (1)	2	0.02
American Indian/Alaska Native (18)	40	0.39
Not Hispanic (16)	38	0.37
Hispanic (2)	2	0.02
Apache (1)	2	0.02
Blackfeet (0)	2	0.02
Canadian/French Am. Ind. (1)	1	0.01
Cherokee (1)	2	0.02
Iroquois (0)	2	0.02
Mexican American Ind. (2)	2	0.02
Navajo (0)	2	0.02
Asian (68)	93	0.90
Not Hispanic (68)	89	0.86
Hispanic (0)	4	0.04
Cambodian (1)	1	0.01
Chinese, ex. Taiwanese (33)	42	0.41
Filipino (7)	14	0.14
Indian (5)	10	0.10
Indonesian (1)	1	0.01
Japanese (0)	5	0.05
Korean (9)	9	0.09
Vietnamese (8)	8	0.08
White (10,101)	10,170	98.46
Not Hispanic (10,009)	10,068	97.47
Hispanic (92)	102	0.99

Smithfield

Place Type: Town
County: Providence
Population: 21,430†

Ancestry‡	Population	%
African, Sub-Saharan (139)	166	0.77
African (87)	87	0.41
Cape Verdean (37)	61	0.28
Nigerian (15)	18	0.08
American (397)	397	1.85
Arab (67)	134	0.62
Arab (15)	15	0.07
Iraqi (3)	3	0.01
Lebanese (9)	61	0.28
Syrian (40)	55	0.26
Armenian (99)	186	0.87
Australian (0)	13	0.06
Austrian (0)	41	0.19
Belgian (24)	24	0.11
Brazilian (12)	12	0.06
British (23)	62	0.29
Canadian (43)	249	1.16
Czech (21)	36	0.17
Czechoslovakian (0)	14	0.07
Danish (4)	29	0.14
Dutch (15)	65	0.30
English (705)	3,421	15.93
European (48)	75	0.35
Finnish (16)	30	0.14
French, ex. Basque (660)	3,334	15.52
French Canadian (887)	1,836	8.55
German (185)	1,364	6.35
Greek (14)	107	0.50
Hungarian (0)	58	0.27
Irish (1,283)	5,473	25.48
Italian (2,896)	6,309	29.38
Latvian (15)	15	0.07
Lithuanian (25)	206	0.96
New Zealander (14)	14	0.07
Norwegian (46)	152	0.71
Polish (373)	1,320	6.15
Portuguese (401)	1,161	5.41
Russian (32)	208	0.97
Scotch-Irish (89)	206	0.96
Scottish (117)	696	3.24
Serbian (23)	23	0.11
Slovak (13)	13	0.06
Swedish (76)	351	1.63
Swiss (20)	41	0.19
Ukrainian (27)	56	0.26
Welsh (0)	47	0.22
West Indian, ex. Hispanic (30)	30	0.14
Haitian (29)	29	0.14
Jamaican (1)	1	<0.01

Hispanic Origin	Population	%
Hispanic or Latino (of any race)	466	2.17
Central American, ex. Mexican	59	0.28
Costa Rican	9	0.04
Guatemalan	29	0.14
Honduran	2	0.01
Nicaraguan	4	0.02
Panamanian	6	0.03
Salvadoran	8	0.04
Other Central American	1	<0.01
Cuban	18	0.08
Dominican Republic	40	0.19
Mexican	69	0.32
Puerto Rican	131	0.61
South American	101	0.47
Argentinean	5	0.02
Bolivian	7	0.03
Chilean	2	0.01
Colombian	51	0.24
Ecuadorian	18	0.08
Peruvian	13	0.06
Venezuelan	5	0.02
Other Hispanic or Latino	48	0.22

Race*	Population	%
African-American/Black (258)	329	1.54
Not Hispanic (252)	318	1.48
Hispanic (6)	11	0.05
American Indian/Alaska Native (32)	92	0.43
Not Hispanic (23)	74	0.35
Hispanic (9)	18	0.08
Blackfeet (1)	2	0.01
Canadian/French Am. Ind. (2)	5	0.02
Cherokee (1)	10	0.05
Chippewa (2)	5	0.02
Cree (0)	1	<0.01
Creek (0)	3	0.01
Iroquois (0)	1	<0.01
Mexican American Ind. (1)	2	0.01
Navajo (0)	2	0.01
Seminole (0)	1	<0.01
Sioux (0)	4	0.02
South American Ind. (4)	6	0.03
Asian (280)	357	1.67
Not Hispanic (275)	349	1.63
Hispanic (5)	8	0.04
Bangladeshi (1)	1	<0.01
Burmese (1)	1	<0.01
Cambodian (10)	11	0.05
Chinese, ex. Taiwanese (102)	121	0.56
Filipino (20)	27	0.13
Hmong (1)	1	<0.01
Indian (78)	97	0.45
Japanese (14)	23	0.11
Korean (16)	24	0.11
Laotian (4)	5	0.02
Malaysian (1)	2	0.01
Nepalese (3)	3	0.01
Pakistani (5)	6	0.03
Sri Lankan (6)	6	0.03
Thai (2)	2	0.01
Vietnamese (6)	15	0.07
Hawaii Native/Pacific Islander (8)	27	0.13
Not Hispanic (1)	13	0.06
Hispanic (7)	14	0.07
Guamanian/Chamorro (0)	5	0.02
Native Hawaiian (5)	8	0.04
White (20,507)	20,698	96.58
Not Hispanic (20,198)	20,355	94.98
Hispanic (309)	343	1.60

South Kingstown

Place Type: Town
County: Washington
Population: 30,639†

Ancestry‡	Population	%
African, Sub-Saharan (120)	182	0.60
African (12)	12	0.04
Cape Verdean (63)	99	0.33
Ethiopian (13)	13	0.04
Ghanaian (11)	11	0.04
Liberian (21)	21	0.07
Nigerian (0)	26	0.09
Albanian (0)	32	0.11
American (568)	568	1.88
Arab (36)	302	1.00
Arab (18)	18	0.06
Egyptian (9)	112	0.37
Lebanese (0)	59	0.20
Syrian (9)	113	0.37
Armenian (135)	229	0.76
Australian (0)	1	<0.01
Austrian (0)	180	0.60
Belgian (0)	36	0.12
Brazilian (64)	82	0.27
British (79)	110	0.36
Canadian (132)	223	0.74
Croatian (17)	17	0.06
Czech (16)	48	0.16
Czechoslovakian (0)	15	0.05
Danish (0)	199	0.66
Dutch (37)	226	0.75
English (1,567)	6,132	20.29
European (137)	137	0.45
Finnish (0)	29	0.10
French, ex. Basque (470)	2,199	7.28
French Canadian (552)	1,085	3.59
German (479)	3,510	11.61
Greek (51)	302	1.00
Hungarian (33)	189	0.63
Irish (2,307)	8,583	28.40
Israeli (9)	9	0.03
Italian (2,012)	5,310	17.57
Lithuanian (56)	162	0.54
Norwegian (97)	358	1.18
Pennsylvania German (0)	21	0.07
Polish (193)	1,090	3.61
Portuguese (490)	1,776	5.88
Romanian (14)	67	0.22
Russian (74)	355	1.17
Scandinavian (40)	40	0.13
Scotch-Irish (223)	816	2.70
Scottish (173)	1,097	3.63
Slovak (26)	46	0.15
Swedish (134)	1,034	3.42
Swiss (41)	93	0.31
Turkish (0)	13	0.04
Ukrainian (48)	136	0.45
Welsh (0)	233	0.77
West Indian, ex. Hispanic (84)	132	0.44
Haitian (84)	132	0.44
Yugoslavian (41)	76	0.25

Hispanic Origin	Population	%
Hispanic or Latino (of any race)	869	2.84
Central American, ex. Mexican	69	0.23
Costa Rican	5	0.02
Guatemalan	48	0.16
Honduran	3	0.01
Panamanian	6	0.02
Salvadoran	6	0.02
Other Central American	1	<0.01
Cuban	46	0.15
Dominican Republic	128	0.42
Mexican	140	0.46
Puerto Rican	226	0.74
South American	130	0.42
Argentinean	9	0.03
Bolivian	8	0.03

*Notes: † The Census 2010 population figure is used to calculate the percentages in the Hispanic Origin and Race categories. Ancestry percentages are based on the 2006-2010 American Community Survey population (not shown); ‡ Numbers in parentheses indicate the number of people reporting a single ancestry; * Numbers in parentheses indicate the number of persons reporting this race alone, not in combination with any other race; Please refer to the Explanation of Data for more information.*

Chilean	10	0.03
Colombian	72	0.23
Ecuadorian	9	0.03
Paraguayan	3	0.01
Peruvian	9	0.03
Uruguayan	1	<0.01
Venezuelan	9	0.03
Other Hispanic or Latino	130	0.42

Race*	Population	%
African-American/Black (669)	987	3.22
Not Hispanic (616)	905	2.95
Hispanic (53)	82	0.27
American Indian/Alaska Native (372)	649	2.12
Not Hispanic (338)	589	1.92
Hispanic (34)	60	0.20
Apache (1)	1	<0.01
Blackfeet (5)	7	0.02
Central American Ind. (2)	2	0.01
Cherokee (5)	24	0.08
Chippewa (0)	1	<0.01
Choctaw (0)	1	<0.01
Cree (1)	2	0.01
Creek (1)	2	0.01
Delaware (0)	1	<0.01
Inupiat *(Alaska Native)* (1)	1	<0.01
Iroquois (1)	7	0.02
Lumbee (2)	3	0.01
Menominee (0)	2	0.01
Mexican American Ind. (1)	4	0.01
Navajo (1)	1	<0.01
Potawatomi (1)	1	<0.01
Sioux (0)	1	<0.01
South American Ind. (1)	1	<0.01
Spanish American Ind. (1)	1	<0.01
Yaqui (0)	2	0.01
Yup'ik *(Alaska Native)* (1)	1	<0.01
Asian (815)	988	3.22
Not Hispanic (809)	970	3.17
Hispanic (6)	18	0.06
Bangladeshi (1)	1	<0.01
Burmese (1)	1	<0.01
Cambodian (36)	43	0.14
Chinese, ex. Taiwanese (317)	354	1.16
Filipino (38)	76	0.25
Hmong (7)	7	0.02
Indian (147)	160	0.52
Indonesian (5)	5	0.02
Japanese (31)	48	0.16
Korean (108)	131	0.43
Laotian (18)	28	0.09
Malaysian (1)	1	<0.01
Nepalese (3)	3	0.01
Pakistani (7)	7	0.02
Sri Lankan (8)	8	0.03
Taiwanese (4)	7	0.02
Thai (8)	18	0.06
Vietnamese (40)	51	0.17
Hawaii Native/Pacific Islander (9)	33	0.11
Not Hispanic (6)	22	0.07
Hispanic (3)	11	0.04
Guamanian/Chamorro (1)	5	0.02
Native Hawaiian (3)	11	0.04
White (27,837)	28,377	92.62
Not Hispanic (27,352)	27,829	90.83
Hispanic (485)	548	1.79

Tiverton

Place Type: CDP
County: Newport
Population: 7,557†

Ancestry‡	Population	%
African, Sub-Saharan (17)	66	0.90
Cape Verdean (17)	66	0.90
American (216)	216	2.96
Arab (43)	43	0.59
Egyptian (24)	24	0.33
Lebanese (11)	11	0.15
Syrian (8)	8	0.11
Austrian (0)	9	0.12
Brazilian (27)	27	0.37
British (18)	28	0.38
Bulgarian (80)	80	1.10
Czech (10)	22	0.30
Danish (0)	29	0.40
Dutch (7)	51	0.70
English (360)	1,200	16.45
European (10)	10	0.14
French, ex. Basque (226)	1,275	17.48
French Canadian (177)	370	5.07
German (76)	396	5.43
Greek (13)	55	0.75
Irish (306)	1,390	19.05
Italian (126)	479	6.57
Lithuanian (0)	8	0.11
Norwegian (0)	35	0.48
Polish (91)	443	6.07
Portuguese (1,441)	2,699	36.99
Russian (11)	21	0.29
Scotch-Irish (0)	74	1.01
Scottish (64)	182	2.49
Slovak (0)	31	0.42
Swedish (12)	59	0.81
Ukrainian (10)	10	0.14

Hispanic Origin	Population	%
Hispanic or Latino (of any race)	127	1.68
Central American, ex. Mexican	8	0.11
Guatemalan	2	0.03
Honduran	2	0.03
Nicaraguan	1	0.01
Salvadoran	3	0.04
Cuban	4	0.05
Dominican Republic	6	0.08
Mexican	39	0.52
Puerto Rican	47	0.62
South American	15	0.20
Argentinean	3	0.04
Colombian	8	0.11
Peruvian	2	0.03
Uruguayan	2	0.03
Other Hispanic or Latino	8	0.11

Race*	Population	%
African-American/Black (91)	145	1.92
Not Hispanic (82)	131	1.73
Hispanic (9)	14	0.19
American Indian/Alaska Native (10)	41	0.54
Not Hispanic (8)	36	0.48
Hispanic (2)	5	0.07
Blackfeet (0)	5	0.07
Central American Ind. (1)	1	0.01
Cherokee (1)	6	0.08
Shoshone (0)	1	0.01
South American Ind. (0)	1	0.01
Asian (77)	117	1.55
Not Hispanic (75)	114	1.51
Hispanic (2)	3	0.04
Cambodian (3)	4	0.05
Chinese, ex. Taiwanese (12)	13	0.17
Filipino (27)	47	0.62
Indian (22)	22	0.29
Japanese (4)	6	0.08
Korean (3)	7	0.09
Thai (3)	6	0.08
Vietnamese (3)	3	0.04
Hawaii Native/Pacific Islander (2)	10	0.13
Not Hispanic (2)	10	0.13
Native Hawaiian (2)	8	0.11
White (7,231)	7,345	97.19
Not Hispanic (7,142)	7,246	95.88
Hispanic (89)	99	1.31

Tiverton

Place Type: Town
County: Newport
Population: 15,780†

Ancestry‡	Population	%
African, Sub-Saharan (17)	66	0.42
Cape Verdean (17)	66	0.42
American (598)	598	3.82
Arab (43)	111	0.71
Egyptian (24)	24	0.15
Lebanese (11)	79	0.50
Syrian (8)	8	0.05
Austrian (0)	19	0.12
Brazilian (61)	61	0.39
British (47)	70	0.45
Bulgarian (80)	80	0.51
Canadian (46)	59	0.38
Czech (27)	39	0.25
Danish (0)	29	0.19
Dutch (16)	104	0.66
English (784)	2,933	18.71
European (10)	29	0.19
Finnish (0)	48	0.31
French, ex. Basque (589)	2,873	18.33
French Canadian (473)	971	6.19
German (174)	982	6.27
Greek (13)	147	0.94
Hungarian (0)	10	0.06
Irish (641)	2,703	17.25
Italian (225)	1,009	6.44
Lithuanian (12)	81	0.52
Norwegian (10)	81	0.52
Polish (248)	928	5.92
Portuguese (2,755)	5,574	35.56
Russian (31)	41	0.26
Scotch-Irish (0)	125	0.80
Scottish (92)	318	2.03
Slovak (19)	111	0.71
Swedish (22)	187	1.19
Swiss (0)	50	0.32
Ukrainian (10)	33	0.21
Welsh (15)	36	0.23
West Indian, ex. Hispanic (17)	17	0.11
Trinidadian/Tobagonian (17)	17	0.11

Hispanic Origin	Population	%
Hispanic or Latino (of any race)	190	1.20
Central American, ex. Mexican	14	0.09
Costa Rican	1	0.01
Guatemalan	6	0.04
Honduran	2	0.01
Nicaraguan	1	0.01
Panamanian	1	0.01
Salvadoran	3	0.02
Cuban	7	0.04
Dominican Republic	8	0.05
Mexican	49	0.31
Puerto Rican	70	0.44
South American	23	0.15
Argentinean	4	0.03
Colombian	14	0.09
Peruvian	2	0.01
Uruguayan	3	0.02
Other Hispanic or Latino	19	0.12

Race*	Population	%
African-American/Black (140)	221	1.40
Not Hispanic (126)	199	1.26
Hispanic (14)	22	0.14
American Indian/Alaska Native (22)	69	0.44
Not Hispanic (19)	63	0.40
Hispanic (3)	6	0.04
Blackfeet (0)	5	0.03
Central American Ind. (1)	1	0.01
Cherokee (1)	9	0.06
Delaware (0)	1	0.01
Iroquois (1)	2	0.01
Shoshone (0)	1	0.01
South American Ind. (0)	1	0.01
Asian (136)	202	1.28
Not Hispanic (134)	197	1.25
Hispanic (2)	5	0.03
Cambodian (4)	6	0.04
Chinese, ex. Taiwanese (20)	24	0.15

*Notes: † The Census 2010 population figure is used to calculate the percentages in the Hispanic Origin and Race categories. Ancestry percentages are based on the 2006-2010 American Community Survey population (not shown); ‡ Numbers in parentheses indicate the number of people reporting a single ancestry; * Numbers in parentheses indicate the number of persons reporting this race alone, not in combination with any other race; Please refer to the Explanation of Data for more information.*

Filipino (46)	75	0.48
Indian (24)	25	0.16
Indonesian (1)	1	0.01
Japanese (11)	17	0.11
Korean (6)	14	0.09
Taiwanese (1)	1	0.01
Thai (3)	6	0.04
Vietnamese (18)	19	0.12
Hawaii Native/Pacific Islander (3)	20	0.13
Not Hispanic (2)	19	0.12
Hispanic (1)	1	0.01
Guamanian/Chamorro (0)	1	0.01
Native Hawaiian (2)	9	0.06
White (15,235)	15,427	97.76
Not Hispanic (15,097)	15,273	96.79
Hispanic (138)	154	0.98

Valley Falls

Place Type: CDP
County: Providence
Population: 11,547†

Ancestry‡	Population	%
African, Sub-Saharan (72)	78	0.68
African (42)	42	0.36
Cape Verdean (20)	26	0.23
Other Sub-Saharan African (10)	10	0.09
American (267)	267	2.32
Arab (208)	275	2.39
Arab (65)	76	0.66
Lebanese (11)	11	0.10
Moroccan (9)	9	0.08
Syrian (123)	179	1.55
Armenian (0)	46	0.40
British (0)	9	0.08
Canadian (12)	12	0.10
Croatian (0)	9	0.08
Czech (0)	20	0.17
Danish (20)	44	0.38
Dutch (7)	46	0.40
English (220)	1,355	11.76
European (11)	11	0.10
Finnish (20)	20	0.17
French, ex. Basque (714)	2,261	19.63
French Canadian (354)	760	6.60
German (183)	578	5.02
Greek (10)	124	1.08
Hungarian (0)	10	0.09
Irish (630)	2,746	23.84
Italian (670)	1,732	15.04
Lithuanian (20)	47	0.41
Luxemburger (0)	42	0.36
Norwegian (0)	28	0.24
Polish (330)	804	6.98
Portuguese (1,976)	2,748	23.86
Russian (9)	49	0.43
Scandinavian (27)	27	0.23
Scotch-Irish (41)	79	0.69
Scottish (52)	398	3.46
Swedish (10)	58	0.50
Ukrainian (0)	13	0.11
Welsh (0)	15	0.13
West Indian, ex. Hispanic (11)	11	0.10
Jamaican (11)	11	0.10

Hispanic Origin	Population	%
Hispanic or Latino (of any race)	912	7.90
Central American, ex. Mexican	108	0.94
Costa Rican	2	0.02
Guatemalan	89	0.77
Honduran	7	0.06
Panamanian	6	0.05
Salvadoran	4	0.03
Cuban	14	0.12
Dominican Republic	79	0.68
Mexican	42	0.36
Puerto Rican	196	1.70
South American	358	3.10
Argentinean	13	0.11
Bolivian	2	0.02
Chilean	4	0.03
Colombian	287	2.49
Ecuadorian	13	0.11
Peruvian	7	0.06
Venezuelan	29	0.25
Other South American	3	0.03
Other Hispanic or Latino	115	1.00

Race*	Population	%
African-American/Black (222)	343	2.97
Not Hispanic (207)	314	2.72
Hispanic (15)	29	0.25
American Indian/Alaska Native (64)	116	1.00
Not Hispanic (22)	68	0.59
Hispanic (42)	48	0.42
Alaska Athabascan *(Ala. Nat.)* (1)	3	0.03
Blackfeet (0)	1	0.01
Canadian/French Am. Ind. (0)	2	0.02
Cherokee (1)	7	0.06
Cree (0)	5	0.04
Asian (102)	152	1.32
Not Hispanic (97)	139	1.20
Hispanic (5)	13	0.11
Cambodian (3)	7	0.06
Chinese, ex. Taiwanese (29)	33	0.29
Filipino (3)	13	0.11
Indian (22)	25	0.22
Japanese (0)	11	0.10
Korean (5)	5	0.04
Laotian (7)	13	0.11
Pakistani (9)	11	0.10
Thai (6)	10	0.09
Vietnamese (17)	18	0.16
Hawaii Native/Pacific Islander (2)	27	0.23
Not Hispanic (2)	20	0.17
Hispanic (0)	7	0.06
Guamanian/Chamorro (0)	5	0.04
Native Hawaiian (2)	3	0.03
White (10,586)	10,790	93.44
Not Hispanic (10,037)	10,198	88.32
Hispanic (549)	592	5.13

Wakefield-Peacedale

Place Type: CDP
County: Washington
Population: 8,487†

Ancestry‡	Population	%
African, Sub-Saharan (15)	40	0.44
Cape Verdean (15)	40	0.44
Albanian (0)	23	0.25
American (260)	260	2.88
Arab (0)	180	2.00
Egyptian (0)	90	1.00
Syrian (0)	90	1.00
Armenian (21)	87	0.96
Austrian (0)	12	0.13
Belgian (0)	17	0.19
British (14)	32	0.35
Canadian (13)	53	0.59
Czech (16)	16	0.18
Danish (0)	17	0.19
Dutch (13)	101	1.12
English (410)	2,400	26.60
European (48)	48	0.53
Finnish (0)	18	0.20
French, ex. Basque (144)	856	9.49
French Canadian (66)	238	2.64
German (104)	1,114	12.35
Greek (36)	195	2.16
Hungarian (12)	35	0.39
Irish (879)	3,059	33.91
Italian (550)	1,185	13.14
Lithuanian (12)	50	0.55
Norwegian (0)	119	1.32
Pennsylvania German (0)	21	0.23
Polish (0)	221	2.45
Portuguese (207)	598	6.63
Russian (43)	91	1.01
Scandinavian (40)	40	0.44
Scotch-Irish (59)	340	3.77
Scottish (30)	229	2.54
Slovak (0)	10	0.11
Swedish (21)	278	3.08
Swiss (17)	17	0.19
Ukrainian (29)	63	0.70
Welsh (0)	119	1.32
West Indian, ex. Hispanic (84)	132	1.46
Haitian (84)	132	1.46

Hispanic Origin	Population	%
Hispanic or Latino (of any race)	208	2.45
Central American, ex. Mexican	7	0.08
Costa Rican	1	0.01
Guatemalan	2	0.02
Panamanian	3	0.04
Other Central American	1	0.01
Cuban	5	0.06
Dominican Republic	15	0.18
Mexican	49	0.58
Puerto Rican	88	1.04
South American	23	0.27
Bolivian	1	0.01
Chilean	3	0.04
Colombian	10	0.12
Ecuadorian	3	0.04
Peruvian	1	0.01
Venezuelan	5	0.06
Other Hispanic or Latino	21	0.25

Race*	Population	%
African-American/Black (157)	297	3.50
Not Hispanic (147)	276	3.25
Hispanic (10)	21	0.25
American Indian/Alaska Native (221)	348	4.10
Not Hispanic (206)	321	3.78
Hispanic (15)	27	0.32
Blackfeet (1)	2	0.02
Cherokee (1)	9	0.11
Cree (1)	1	0.01
Creek (1)	1	0.01
Inupiat *(Alaska Native)* (1)	1	0.01
Iroquois (0)	1	0.01
Lumbee (1)	2	0.02
Mexican American Ind. (0)	1	0.01
Navajo (1)	1	0.01
Spanish American Ind. (1)	1	0.01
Yaqui (0)	2	0.02
Yup'ik *(Alaska Native)* (1)	1	0.01
Asian (118)	168	1.98
Not Hispanic (117)	163	1.92
Hispanic (1)	5	0.06
Burmese (1)	1	0.01
Cambodian (1)	3	0.04
Chinese, ex. Taiwanese (33)	38	0.45
Filipino (7)	19	0.22
Indian (21)	25	0.29
Indonesian (1)	1	0.01
Japanese (2)	6	0.07
Korean (15)	23	0.27
Laotian (4)	4	0.05
Malaysian (1)	1	0.01
Pakistani (2)	2	0.02
Sri Lankan (1)	1	0.01
Taiwanese (3)	4	0.05
Thai (2)	5	0.06
Vietnamese (20)	24	0.28
Hawaii Native/Pacific Islander (1)	12	0.14
Not Hispanic (1)	6	0.07
Hispanic (0)	6	0.07
Guamanian/Chamorro (0)	3	0.04
Native Hawaiian (1)	1	0.01
White (7,662)	7,878	92.82
Not Hispanic (7,548)	7,738	91.17
Hispanic (114)	140	1.65

*Notes: † The Census 2010 population figure is used to calculate the percentages in the Hispanic Origin and Race categories. Ancestry percentages are based on the 2006-2010 American Community Survey population (not shown); ‡ Numbers in parentheses indicate the number of people reporting a single ancestry; * Numbers in parentheses indicate the number of persons reporting this race alone, not in combination with any other race; Please refer to the Explanation of Data for more information.*

Warren

Place Type: Town
County: Bristol
Population: 10,611†

Ancestry‡	Population	%
African, Sub-Saharan (9)	19	0.18
Cape Verdean (9)	19	0.18
American (441)	441	4.08
Arab (23)	44	0.41
Lebanese (23)	44	0.41
Armenian (11)	25	0.23
Austrian (0)	8	0.07
Brazilian (12)	31	0.29
British (19)	28	0.26
Canadian (0)	44	0.41
Dutch (0)	8	0.07
English (299)	1,414	13.08
Estonian (9)	9	0.08
European (15)	15	0.14
French, ex. Basque (294)	1,706	15.78
French Canadian (242)	706	6.53
German (92)	764	7.07
Greek (93)	103	0.95
Hungarian (10)	45	0.42
Irish (411)	1,923	17.79
Israeli (0)	10	0.09
Italian (661)	1,919	17.75
Lithuanian (23)	91	0.84
Luxemburger (0)	9	0.08
Norwegian (25)	128	1.18
Polish (82)	401	3.71
Portuguese (2,130)	3,885	35.94
Russian (17)	100	0.92
Scandinavian (0)	29	0.27
Scotch-Irish (9)	143	1.32
Scottish (106)	460	4.25
Slovene (0)	9	0.08
Swedish (36)	206	1.91
Swiss (0)	6	0.06
Ukrainian (0)	16	0.15

Hispanic Origin	Population	%
Hispanic or Latino (of any race)	194	1.83
Central American, ex. Mexican	7	0.07
Guatemalan	6	0.06
Honduran	1	0.01
Cuban	8	0.08
Dominican Republic	16	0.15
Mexican	25	0.24
Puerto Rican	81	0.76
South American	26	0.25
Argentinean	2	0.02
Bolivian	2	0.02
Chilean	1	0.01
Colombian	10	0.09
Peruvian	8	0.08
Venezuelan	3	0.03
Other Hispanic or Latino	31	0.29

Race*	Population	%
African-American/Black (124)	186	1.75
Not Hispanic (112)	167	1.57
Hispanic (12)	19	0.18
American Indian/Alaska Native (33)	89	0.84
Not Hispanic (28)	80	0.75
Hispanic (5)	9	0.08
Blackfeet (0)	9	0.08
Cherokee (3)	11	0.10
Chickasaw (0)	1	0.01
Comanche (4)	4	0.04
Cree (1)	1	0.01
Crow (0)	2	0.02
Iroquois (0)	3	0.03
Mexican American Ind. (1)	1	0.01
Potawatomi (1)	2	0.02
Sioux (0)	3	0.03
South American Ind. (0)	1	0.01
Asian (65)	102	0.96
Not Hispanic (63)	98	0.92
Hispanic (2)	4	0.04
Burmese (2)	2	0.02
Cambodian (1)	2	0.02
Chinese, ex. Taiwanese (18)	23	0.22
Filipino (9)	25	0.24
Indian (6)	8	0.08
Indonesian (1)	1	0.01
Japanese (2)	10	0.09
Korean (8)	10	0.09
Laotian (1)	1	0.01
Pakistani (8)	9	0.08
Thai (2)	4	0.04
Vietnamese (4)	4	0.04
Hawaii Native/Pacific Islander (2)	11	0.10
Not Hispanic (2)	11	0.10
Fijian (1)	1	0.01
Native Hawaiian (0)	2	0.02
Samoan (1)	1	0.01
White (10,190)	10,347	97.51
Not Hispanic (10,060)	10,196	96.09
Hispanic (130)	151	1.42

Warwick

Place Type: City
County: Kent
Population: 82,672†

Ancestry‡	Population	%
African, Sub-Saharan (375)	555	0.66
African (144)	144	0.17
Cape Verdean (176)	338	0.40
Ethiopian (12)	12	0.01
Nigerian (43)	43	0.05
South African (0)	18	0.02
American (2,609)	2,609	3.12
Arab (172)	361	0.43
Egyptian (61)	61	0.07
Lebanese (31)	185	0.22
Moroccan (44)	44	0.05
Syrian (36)	71	0.08
Armenian (301)	540	0.65
Australian (0)	14	0.02
Austrian (11)	222	0.27
Belgian (9)	77	0.09
Brazilian (25)	39	0.05
British (88)	200	0.24
Bulgarian (0)	15	0.02
Canadian (222)	400	0.48
Celtic (10)	44	0.05
Czech (24)	50	0.06
Czechoslovakian (18)	33	0.04
Danish (66)	218	0.26
Dutch (184)	516	0.62
Eastern European (51)	78	0.09
English (3,392)	14,842	17.74
European (223)	231	0.28
Finnish (12)	211	0.25
French, ex. Basque (2,189)	12,183	14.56
French Canadian (1,075)	2,751	3.29
German (1,027)	6,303	7.53
Greek (79)	440	0.53
Hungarian (26)	211	0.25
Irish (7,608)	24,927	29.79
Israeli (5)	5	0.01
Italian (8,222)	19,973	23.87
Latvian (13)	13	0.02
Lithuanian (97)	424	0.51
Luxemburger (0)	10	0.01
Maltese (0)	28	0.03
New Zealander (0)	64	0.08
Northern European (25)	25	0.03
Norwegian (56)	263	0.31
Pennsylvania German (0)	33	0.04
Polish (861)	3,622	4.33
Portuguese (2,383)	6,472	7.73
Romanian (12)	27	0.03
Russian (504)	1,189	1.42
Scandinavian (46)	79	0.09
Scotch-Irish (679)	1,420	1.70
Scottish (517)	2,030	2.43
Slovak (59)	89	0.11
Slovene (0)	19	0.02
Swedish (534)	2,654	3.17
Swiss (27)	63	0.08
Turkish (23)	30	0.04
Ukrainian (45)	114	0.14
Welsh (31)	226	0.27
West Indian, ex. Hispanic (76)	76	0.09
Jamaican (56)	56	0.07
West Indian (20)	20	0.02

Hispanic Origin	Population	%
Hispanic or Latino (of any race)	2,827	3.42
Central American, ex. Mexican	303	0.37
Costa Rican	6	0.01
Guatemalan	227	0.27
Honduran	27	0.03
Panamanian	7	0.01
Salvadoran	36	0.04
Cuban	95	0.11
Dominican Republic	580	0.70
Mexican	337	0.41
Puerto Rican	789	0.95
South American	430	0.52
Argentinean	14	0.02
Bolivian	62	0.07
Chilean	37	0.04
Colombian	190	0.23
Ecuadorian	27	0.03
Peruvian	53	0.06
Uruguayan	18	0.02
Venezuelan	29	0.04
Other Hispanic or Latino	293	0.35

Race*	Population	%
African-American/Black (1,387)	2,034	2.46
Not Hispanic (1,228)	1,788	2.16
Hispanic (159)	246	0.30
American Indian/Alaska Native (235)	753	0.91
Not Hispanic (204)	689	0.83
Hispanic (31)	64	0.08
Apache (0)	1	<0.01
Blackfeet (2)	23	0.03
Canadian/French Am. Ind. (0)	4	<0.01
Central American Ind. (1)	1	<0.01
Cherokee (9)	56	0.07
Chippewa (6)	12	0.01
Choctaw (0)	4	<0.01
Comanche (0)	1	<0.01
Creek (0)	1	<0.01
Crow (0)	2	<0.01
Delaware (2)	2	<0.01
Iroquois (8)	32	0.04
Lumbee (1)	1	<0.01
Mexican American Ind. (6)	8	0.01
Navajo (5)	8	0.01
Seminole (0)	2	<0.01
Sioux (6)	17	0.02
South American Ind. (4)	10	0.01
Spanish American Ind. (1)	1	<0.01
Asian (1,864)	2,266	2.74
Not Hispanic (1,846)	2,216	2.68
Hispanic (18)	50	0.06
Burmese (9)	13	0.02
Cambodian (166)	217	0.26
Chinese, ex. Taiwanese (442)	522	0.63
Filipino (280)	394	0.48
Hmong (91)	100	0.12
Indian (311)	376	0.45
Indonesian (1)	8	0.01
Japanese (34)	60	0.07
Korean (168)	210	0.25
Laotian (55)	77	0.09
Malaysian (1)	6	0.01
Pakistani (62)	66	0.08
Sri Lankan (4)	7	0.01
Taiwanese (5)	8	0.01
Thai (29)	52	0.06

*Notes: † The Census 2010 population figure is used to calculate the percentages in the Hispanic Origin and Race categories. Ancestry percentages are based on the 2006-2010 American Community Survey population (not shown); ‡ Numbers in parentheses indicate the number of people reporting a single ancestry; * Numbers in parentheses indicate the number of persons reporting this race alone, not in combination with any other race; Please refer to the Explanation of Data for more information.*

Vietnamese (126)	145	0.18
Hawaii Native/Pacific Islander (20)	87	0.11
Not Hispanic (15)	75	0.09
Hispanic (5)	12	0.01
Fijian (4)	4	<0.01
Guamanian/Chamorro (13)	27	0.03
Native Hawaiian (2)	20	0.02
Samoan (0)	9	0.01
Tongan (0)	3	<0.01
White (76,643)	77,995	94.34
Not Hispanic (75,068)	76,169	92.13
Hispanic (1,575)	1,826	2.21

West Warwick

Place Type: Town
County: Kent
Population: 29,191†

Ancestry‡	Population	%
African, Sub-Saharan (138)	138	0.47
African (49)	49	0.17
Cape Verdean (59)	59	0.20
Liberian (15)	15	0.05
South African (15)	15	0.05
Alsatian (0)	9	0.03
American (673)	673	2.29
Arab (26)	42	0.14
Egyptian (11)	11	0.04
Lebanese (15)	15	0.05
Syrian (0)	16	0.05
Armenian (78)	198	0.67
Austrian (0)	7	0.02
Belgian (15)	28	0.10
Brazilian (44)	44	0.15
Canadian (98)	262	0.89
Celtic (29)	29	0.10
Croatian (0)	10	0.03
Czech (38)	90	0.31
Czechoslovakian (0)	36	0.12
Dutch (46)	237	0.81
English (1,128)	4,469	15.22
European (94)	94	0.32
Finnish (0)	48	0.16
French, ex. Basque (1,414)	5,269	17.95
French Canadian (957)	1,534	5.23
German (182)	1,685	5.74
Greek (21)	137	0.47
Hungarian (0)	45	0.15
Iranian (11)	11	0.04
Irish (1,790)	6,633	22.59
Italian (2,873)	7,021	23.92
Lithuanian (0)	91	0.31
Norwegian (24)	150	0.51
Polish (367)	1,513	5.15
Portuguese (1,953)	3,992	13.60
Russian (62)	158	0.54
Scandinavian (25)	61	0.21
Scotch-Irish (157)	523	1.78
Scottish (62)	425	1.45
Slovak (13)	13	0.04
Swedish (84)	640	2.18
Ukrainian (0)	33	0.11
Welsh (0)	59	0.20
West Indian, ex. Hispanic (70)	70	0.24
British West Indian (32)	32	0.11
Haitian (38)	38	0.13
Yugoslavian (0)	15	0.05

Hispanic Origin	Population	%
Hispanic or Latino (of any race)	1,453	4.98
Central American, ex. Mexican	134	0.46
Costa Rican	4	0.01
Guatemalan	86	0.29
Honduran	20	0.07
Nicaraguan	1	<0.01
Panamanian	5	0.02
Salvadoran	16	0.05
Other Central American	2	0.01
Cuban	35	0.12
Dominican Republic	196	0.67
Mexican	359	1.23
Puerto Rican	400	1.37
South American	151	0.52
Argentinean	11	0.04
Bolivian	13	0.04
Chilean	13	0.04
Colombian	48	0.16
Ecuadorian	16	0.05
Peruvian	22	0.08
Uruguayan	5	0.02
Venezuelan	23	0.08
Other Hispanic or Latino	178	0.61

Race*	Population	%
African-American/Black (635)	959	3.29
Not Hispanic (572)	861	2.95
Hispanic (63)	98	0.34
American Indian/Alaska Native (95)	326	1.12
Not Hispanic (63)	255	0.87
Hispanic (32)	71	0.24
Blackfeet (4)	14	0.05
Canadian/French Am. Ind. (0)	3	0.01
Cherokee (9)	31	0.11
Chippewa (0)	2	0.01
Choctaw (0)	1	<0.01
Cree (0)	5	0.02
Creek (0)	1	<0.01
Delaware (2)	2	0.01
Iroquois (4)	10	0.03
Mexican American Ind. (3)	6	0.02
Osage (0)	1	<0.01
Puget Sound Salish (0)	3	0.01
Sioux (1)	10	0.03
South American Ind. (1)	2	0.01
Asian (631)	773	2.65
Not Hispanic (628)	752	2.58
Hispanic (3)	21	0.07
Bangladeshi (4)	4	0.01
Cambodian (42)	55	0.19
Chinese, ex. Taiwanese (145)	161	0.55
Filipino (130)	180	0.62
Hmong (41)	48	0.16
Indian (88)	102	0.35
Japanese (21)	39	0.13
Korean (29)	39	0.13
Laotian (19)	29	0.10
Pakistani (38)	42	0.14
Taiwanese (6)	6	0.02
Thai (7)	8	0.03
Vietnamese (25)	28	0.10
Hawaii Native/Pacific Islander (10)	40	0.14
Not Hispanic (8)	33	0.11
Hispanic (2)	7	0.02
Guamanian/Chamorro (8)	10	0.03
Native Hawaiian (1)	6	0.02
Samoan (0)	1	<0.01
White (26,658)	27,276	93.44
Not Hispanic (25,831)	26,348	90.26
Hispanic (827)	928	3.18

Westerly

Place Type: CDP
County: Washington
Population: 17,936†

Ancestry‡	Population	%
African, Sub-Saharan (27)	56	0.32
African (8)	8	0.05
Cape Verdean (0)	29	0.17
South African (19)	19	0.11
American (383)	383	2.18
Arab (78)	128	0.73
Arab (9)	9	0.05
Egyptian (33)	33	0.19
Lebanese (0)	31	0.18
Moroccan (36)	36	0.21
Syrian (0)	19	0.11
Armenian (5)	20	0.11
Australian (12)	12	0.07
Austrian (7)	7	0.04
Belgian (0)	14	0.08
British (30)	86	0.49
Canadian (9)	17	0.10
Czech (0)	65	0.37
Dutch (0)	167	0.95
English (788)	2,523	14.37
European (5)	11	0.06
Finnish (16)	84	0.48
French, ex. Basque (350)	1,758	10.02
French Canadian (265)	734	4.18
German (323)	1,628	9.28
Hungarian (92)	103	0.59
Irish (777)	3,485	19.86
Italian (3,403)	6,300	35.89
Lithuanian (12)	17	0.10
Norwegian (55)	216	1.23
Pennsylvania German (0)	20	0.11
Polish (216)	884	5.04
Portuguese (308)	804	4.58
Romanian (0)	14	0.08
Russian (72)	284	1.62
Scotch-Irish (100)	248	1.41
Scottish (181)	785	4.47
Slovak (21)	27	0.15
Swedish (56)	268	1.53
Swiss (29)	29	0.17
Welsh (0)	42	0.24
West Indian, ex. Hispanic (48)	147	0.84
West Indian (48)	147	0.84

Hispanic Origin	Population	%
Hispanic or Latino (of any race)	582	3.24
Central American, ex. Mexican	36	0.20
Costa Rican	2	0.01
Guatemalan	15	0.08
Nicaraguan	6	0.03
Panamanian	7	0.04
Salvadoran	6	0.03
Cuban	6	0.03
Dominican Republic	29	0.16
Mexican	200	1.12
Puerto Rican	204	1.14
South American	42	0.23
Bolivian	3	0.02
Chilean	1	0.01
Colombian	10	0.06
Ecuadorian	10	0.06
Peruvian	12	0.07
Uruguayan	1	0.01
Venezuelan	4	0.02
Other South American	1	0.01
Other Hispanic or Latino	65	0.36

Race*	Population	%
African-American/Black (187)	339	1.89
Not Hispanic (168)	298	1.66
Hispanic (19)	41	0.23
American Indian/Alaska Native (97)	217	1.21
Not Hispanic (86)	189	1.05
Hispanic (11)	28	0.16
Apache (0)	3	0.02
Blackfeet (0)	8	0.04
Canadian/French Am. Ind. (0)	1	0.01
Cherokee (2)	11	0.06
Chippewa (3)	4	0.02
Choctaw (0)	1	0.01
Cree (0)	1	0.01
Delaware (2)	4	0.02
Iroquois (0)	3	0.02
Lumbee (1)	1	0.01
Mexican American Ind. (2)	2	0.01
Sioux (5)	7	0.04
South American Ind. (0)	3	0.02
Ute (0)	1	0.01
Yuman (1)	2	0.01
Asian (533)	658	3.67
Not Hispanic (527)	647	3.61
Hispanic (6)	11	0.06

*Notes: † The Census 2010 population figure is used to calculate the percentages in the Hispanic Origin and Race categories. Ancestry percentages are based on the 2006-2010 American Community Survey population (not shown); ‡ Numbers in parentheses indicate the number of people reporting a single ancestry; * Numbers in parentheses indicate the number of persons reporting this race alone, not in combination with any other race; Please refer to the Explanation of Data for more information.*

Cambodian (6)	6	0.03
Chinese, ex. Taiwanese (420)	449	2.50
Filipino (20)	65	0.36
Hmong (1)	4	0.02
Indian (35)	52	0.29
Indonesian (1)	6	0.03
Japanese (2)	22	0.12
Korean (14)	24	0.13
Laotian (12)	12	0.07
Pakistani (1)	1	0.01
Taiwanese (2)	5	0.03
Thai (4)	7	0.04
Vietnamese (2)	9	0.05
Hawaii Native/Pacific Islander (3)	13	0.07
Not Hispanic (3)	11	0.06
Hispanic (0)	2	0.01
Guamanian/Chamorro (2)	2	0.01
Native Hawaiian (0)	4	0.02
White (16,544)	16,876	94.09
Not Hispanic (16,237)	16,506	92.03
Hispanic (307)	370	2.06

Westerly

Place Type: Town
County: Washington
Population: 22,787†

Ancestry‡	Population	%
African, Sub-Saharan (67)	96	0.42
African (8)	8	0.03
Cape Verdean (40)	69	0.30
South African (19)	19	0.08
American (634)	634	2.76
Arab (78)	128	0.56
Arab (9)	9	0.04
Egyptian (33)	33	0.14
Lebanese (0)	31	0.14
Moroccan (36)	36	0.16
Syrian (0)	19	0.08
Armenian (5)	20	0.09
Australian (12)	12	0.05
Austrian (30)	49	0.21
Belgian (0)	25	0.11
British (67)	158	0.69
Canadian (18)	26	0.11
Czech (8)	82	0.36
Danish (19)	82	0.36
Dutch (0)	176	0.77
English (990)	3,505	15.27
European (54)	60	0.26
Finnish (16)	84	0.37
French, ex. Basque (503)	2,346	10.22
French Canadian (362)	864	3.76
German (471)	2,215	9.65
Hungarian (100)	111	0.48
Irish (1,191)	4,753	20.71
Italian (4,148)	7,569	32.98
Lithuanian (12)	26	0.11
Norwegian (55)	234	1.02
Pennsylvania German (0)	20	0.09
Polish (303)	1,209	5.27
Portuguese (339)	965	4.20
Romanian (0)	14	0.06
Russian (81)	364	1.59
Scotch-Irish (134)	456	1.99
Scottish (202)	977	4.26
Slovak (21)	27	0.12
Swedish (87)	513	2.24
Swiss (29)	29	0.13
Ukrainian (10)	35	0.15
Welsh (0)	105	0.46
West Indian, ex. Hispanic (48)	147	0.64
West Indian (48)	147	0.64

Hispanic Origin	Population	%
Hispanic or Latino (of any race)	651	2.86
Central American, ex. Mexican	45	0.20
Costa Rican	2	0.01
Guatemalan	19	0.08
Honduran	1	<0.01
Nicaraguan	6	0.03
Panamanian	7	0.03
Salvadoran	10	0.04
Cuban	6	0.03
Dominican Republic	33	0.14
Mexican	213	0.93
Puerto Rican	226	0.99
South American	48	0.21
Bolivian	3	0.01
Chilean	1	<0.01
Colombian	11	0.05
Ecuadorian	11	0.05
Paraguayan	2	0.01
Peruvian	14	0.06
Uruguayan	1	<0.01
Venezuelan	4	0.02
Other South American	1	<0.01
Other Hispanic or Latino	80	0.35

Race*	Population	%
African-American/Black (222)	401	1.76
Not Hispanic (201)	356	1.56
Hispanic (21)	45	0.20
American Indian/Alaska Native (158)	310	1.36
Not Hispanic (141)	274	1.20
Hispanic (17)	36	0.16
Apache (0)	3	0.01
Blackfeet (0)	9	0.04
Canadian/French Am. Ind. (0)	1	<0.01
Cherokee (3)	13	0.06
Chippewa (3)	4	0.02
Choctaw (0)	1	<0.01
Cree (0)	1	<0.01
Delaware (2)	5	0.02
Iroquois (0)	3	0.01
Lumbee (1)	1	<0.01
Mexican American Ind. (5)	5	0.02
Sioux (5)	7	0.03
South American Ind. (0)	3	0.01
Ute (0)	1	<0.01
Yuman (1)	2	0.01
Asian (567)	704	3.09
Not Hispanic (561)	693	3.04
Hispanic (6)	11	0.05
Cambodian (7)	7	0.03
Chinese, ex. Taiwanese (439)	469	2.06
Filipino (23)	70	0.31
Hmong (1)	4	0.02
Indian (36)	55	0.24
Indonesian (2)	7	0.03
Japanese (3)	25	0.11
Korean (20)	34	0.15
Laotian (13)	13	0.06
Pakistani (1)	1	<0.01
Taiwanese (2)	5	0.02
Thai (4)	7	0.03
Vietnamese (3)	10	0.04
Hawaii Native/Pacific Islander (3)	16	0.07
Not Hispanic (3)	14	0.06
Hispanic (0)	2	0.01
Guamanian/Chamorro (2)	3	0.01
Native Hawaiian (0)	4	0.02
White (21,171)	21,566	94.64
Not Hispanic (20,829)	21,157	92.85
Hispanic (342)	409	1.79

Woonsocket

Place Type: City
County: Providence
Population: 41,186†

Ancestry‡	Population	%
African, Sub-Saharan (557)	655	1.57
African (153)	170	0.41
Cape Verdean (111)	144	0.35
Ghanaian (10)	10	0.02
Liberian (109)	157	0.38
Nigerian (37)	37	0.09
Senegalese (50)	50	0.12
Other Sub-Saharan African (87)	87	0.21
Albanian (0)	6	0.01
Alsatian (0)	9	0.02
American (817)	817	1.96
Arab (253)	378	0.91
Arab (10)	15	0.04
Egyptian (53)	53	0.13
Iraqi (58)	58	0.14
Lebanese (39)	39	0.09
Syrian (93)	213	0.51
Armenian (38)	92	0.22
Australian (32)	32	0.08
Austrian (7)	26	0.06
Belgian (19)	101	0.24
Brazilian (155)	155	0.37
British (0)	33	0.08
Bulgarian (22)	22	0.05
Canadian (244)	360	0.86
Croatian (28)	40	0.10
Czech (0)	13	0.03
Danish (0)	14	0.03
Dutch (60)	141	0.34
English (587)	3,113	7.47
European (53)	68	0.16
Finnish (0)	11	0.03
French, ex. Basque (6,467)	12,573	30.16
French Canadian (5,298)	6,905	16.57
German (222)	1,210	2.90
Greek (25)	188	0.45
Hungarian (15)	41	0.10
Icelander (0)	10	0.02
Iranian (0)	10	0.02
Irish (1,172)	5,492	13.18
Italian (1,249)	4,571	10.97
Latvian (8)	12	0.03
Lithuanian (30)	70	0.17
Norwegian (39)	97	0.23
Polish (670)	1,892	4.54
Portuguese (413)	1,232	2.96
Romanian (79)	99	0.24
Russian (12)	134	0.32
Scandinavian (9)	9	0.02
Scotch-Irish (86)	292	0.70
Scottish (88)	434	1.04
Swedish (73)	434	1.04
Swiss (0)	9	0.02
Ukrainian (96)	243	0.58
Welsh (0)	82	0.20
West Indian, ex. Hispanic (129)	200	0.48
British West Indian (0)	14	0.03
Haitian (63)	63	0.15
Jamaican (48)	48	0.12
West Indian (18)	75	0.18

Hispanic Origin	Population	%
Hispanic or Latino (of any race)	5,845	14.19
Central American, ex. Mexican	154	0.37
Costa Rican	2	<0.01
Guatemalan	88	0.21
Honduran	19	0.05
Nicaraguan	1	<0.01
Panamanian	8	0.02
Salvadoran	36	0.09
Cuban	51	0.12
Dominican Republic	721	1.75
Mexican	287	0.70
Puerto Rican	4,117	10.00
South American	182	0.44
Bolivian	23	0.06
Chilean	2	<0.01
Colombian	110	0.27
Ecuadorian	16	0.04
Peruvian	16	0.04
Uruguayan	2	<0.01
Venezuelan	12	0.03
Other South American	1	<0.01
Other Hispanic or Latino	333	0.81

SECTION TWO

*Notes: † The Census 2010 population figure is used to calculate the percentages in the Hispanic Origin and Race categories. Ancestry percentages are based on the 2006-2010 American Community Survey population (not shown); ‡ Numbers in parentheses indicate the number of people reporting a single ancestry; * Numbers in parentheses indicate the number of persons reporting this race alone, not in combination with any other race; Please refer to the Explanation of Data for more information.*

Race*	Population	%
African-American/Black (2,621)	3,595	8.73
Not Hispanic (2,190)	2,981	7.24
Hispanic (431)	614	1.49
American Indian/Alaska Native (184)	596	1.45
Not Hispanic (110)	457	1.11
Hispanic (74)	139	0.34
Apache (0)	1	<0.01
Blackfeet (2)	23	0.06
Canadian/French Am. Ind. (1)	6	0.01
Central American Ind. (5)	8	0.02
Cherokee (13)	70	0.17
Cheyenne (2)	2	<0.01
Chippewa (3)	4	0.01
Cree (0)	1	<0.01
Creek (1)	1	<0.01
Iroquois (7)	18	0.04
Mexican American Ind. (4)	5	0.01
Navajo (2)	3	0.01
Osage (0)	3	0.01
Pima (0)	1	<0.01
Pueblo (1)	1	<0.01
Seminole (1)	1	<0.01
Shoshone (0)	1	<0.01
Sioux (7)	8	0.02
South American Ind. (7)	21	0.05
Spanish American Ind. (0)	1	<0.01
Asian (2,240)	2,584	6.27
Not Hispanic (2,216)	2,539	6.16
Hispanic (24)	45	0.11
Bangladeshi (1)	1	<0.01
Burmese (0)	1	<0.01
Cambodian (168)	202	0.49
Chinese, ex. Taiwanese (76)	127	0.31
Filipino (67)	126	0.31
Hmong (7)	12	0.03
Indian (219)	281	0.68
Indonesian (3)	4	0.01
Japanese (7)	33	0.08
Korean (11)	28	0.07
Laotian (1,255)	1,430	3.47
Pakistani (19)	21	0.05
Sri Lankan (0)	1	<0.01
Thai (18)	29	0.07
Vietnamese (210)	249	0.60
Hawaii Native/Pacific Islander (16)	60	0.15
Not Hispanic (13)	44	0.11
Hispanic (3)	16	0.04
Guamanian/Chamorro (13)	17	0.04
Native Hawaiian (0)	11	0.03
Samoan (0)	1	<0.01
White (32,011)	33,547	81.45
Not Hispanic (29,365)	30,539	74.15
Hispanic (2,646)	3,008	7.30

*Notes: † The Census 2010 population figure is used to calculate the percentages in the Hispanic Origin and Race categories. Ancestry percentages are based on the 2006-2010 American Community Survey population (not shown); ‡ Numbers in parentheses indicate the number of people reporting a single ancestry; * Numbers in parentheses indicate the number of persons reporting this race alone, not in combination with any other race; Please refer to the Explanation of Data for more information.*

SOUTH CAROLINA

Place Type: State
Population: 4,625,364†

Ancestry‡	Population	%
African, Sub-Saharan (34,418)	39,304	0.87
African (31,294)	35,276	0.78
Cape Verdean (284)	378	0.01
Ethiopian (396)	429	0.01
Ghanaian (149)	192	<0.01
Kenyan (190)	294	0.01
Liberian (120)	274	0.01
Nigerian (684)	699	0.02
Senegalese (40)	40	<0.01
Sierra Leonean (12)	12	<0.01
Somalian (149)	149	<0.01
South African (529)	853	0.02
Sudanese (123)	145	<0.01
Ugandan (28)	28	<0.01
Zimbabwean (12)	12	<0.01
Other Sub-Saharan African (408)	523	0.01
Albanian (666)	808	0.02
Alsatian (41)	113	<0.01
American (563,469)	563,469	12.49
Arab (6,867)	10,632	0.24
Arab (840)	1,113	0.02
Egyptian (1,310)	1,759	0.04
Iraqi (53)	64	<0.01
Jordanian (600)	615	0.01
Lebanese (2,240)	4,408	0.10
Moroccan (246)	395	0.01
Palestinian (302)	320	0.01
Syrian (453)	995	0.02
Other Arab (823)	963	0.02
Armenian (449)	1,024	0.02
Assyrian/Chaldean/Syriac (29)	94	<0.01
Australian (403)	684	0.02
Austrian (1,553)	5,711	0.13
Basque (81)	110	<0.01
Belgian (829)	2,062	0.05
Brazilian (1,883)	2,413	0.05
British (10,309)	18,348	0.41
Bulgarian (545)	769	0.02
Cajun (293)	768	0.02
Canadian (3,489)	6,175	0.14
Carpatho Rusyn (0)	27	<0.01
Celtic (457)	727	0.02
Croatian (716)	2,097	0.05
Cypriot (40)	40	<0.01
Czech (2,068)	7,444	0.17
Czechoslovakian (1,030)	2,098	0.05
Danish (1,792)	6,353	0.14
Dutch (10,485)	45,122	1.00
Eastern European (1,128)	1,405	0.03
English (206,463)	423,815	9.39
Estonian (84)	104	<0.01
European (32,834)	36,969	0.82
Finnish (1,799)	4,080	0.09
French, ex. Basque (23,340)	89,148	1.98
French Canadian (7,618)	15,434	0.34
German (163,825)	464,530	10.30
German Russian (106)	134	<0.01
Greek (6,918)	13,475	0.30
Guyanese (157)	365	0.01
Hungarian (3,699)	10,608	0.24
Icelander (128)	270	0.01
Iranian (1,167)	1,406	0.03
Irish (164,713)	435,909	9.66
Israeli (423)	596	0.01
Italian (47,931)	120,326	2.67
Latvian (388)	625	0.01
Lithuanian (1,248)	3,690	0.08
Luxemburger (11)	79	<0.01
Macedonian (79)	182	<0.01
Maltese (99)	210	<0.01
New Zealander (87)	116	<0.01
Northern European (1,703)	1,865	0.04
Norwegian (6,282)	17,246	0.38
Pennsylvania German (1,180)	1,877	0.04
Polish (20,963)	58,211	1.29
Portuguese (2,431)	5,466	0.12
Romanian (1,356)	2,497	0.06
Russian (6,201)	15,467	0.34
Scandinavian (1,900)	3,863	0.09
Scotch-Irish (91,658)	151,637	3.36
Scottish (39,005)	97,162	2.15
Serbian (425)	1,084	0.02
Slavic (478)	1,340	0.03
Slovak (1,943)	4,937	0.11
Slovene (407)	855	0.02
Soviet Union (12)	26	<0.01
Swedish (6,377)	23,186	0.51
Swiss (2,577)	8,780	0.19
Turkish (1,211)	1,758	0.04
Ukrainian (4,082)	7,313	0.16
Welsh (5,976)	22,370	0.50
West Indian, ex. Hispanic (7,193)	10,670	0.24
Bahamian (391)	581	0.01
Barbadian (193)	253	0.01
Belizean (103)	152	<0.01
Bermudan (171)	215	<0.01
British West Indian (174)	242	0.01
Dutch West Indian (109)	259	0.01
Haitian (1,029)	1,548	0.03
Jamaican (3,233)	4,323	0.10
Trinidadian/Tobagonian (888)	1,111	0.02
U.S. Virgin Islander (33)	38	<0.01
West Indian (836)	1,884	0.04
Other West Indian (33)	64	<0.01
Yugoslavian (427)	1,058	0.02

Hispanic Origin	Population	%
Hispanic or Latino (of any race)	235,682	5.10
Central American, ex. Mexican	26,290	0.57
Costa Rican	1,943	0.04
Guatemalan	8,883	0.19
Honduran	8,091	0.17
Nicaraguan	1,303	0.03
Panamanian	2,104	0.05
Salvadoran	3,830	0.08
Other Central American	136	<0.01
Cuban	5,955	0.13
Dominican Republic	3,018	0.07
Mexican	138,358	2.99
Puerto Rican	26,493	0.57
South American	17,856	0.39
Argentinean	1,439	0.03
Bolivian	493	0.01
Chilean	567	0.01
Colombian	9,436	0.20
Ecuadorian	1,602	0.03
Paraguayan	111	<0.01
Peruvian	1,908	0.04
Uruguayan	853	0.02
Venezuelan	1,315	0.03
Other South American	132	<0.01
Other Hispanic or Latino	17,712	0.38

Race*	Population	%
African-American/Black (1,290,684)	1,332,188	28.80
Not Hispanic (1,279,998)	1,316,691	28.47
Hispanic (10,686)	15,497	0.34
American Indian/Alaska Native (19,524)	42,171	0.91
Not Hispanic (16,614)	36,942	0.80
Hispanic (2,910)	5,229	0.11
Alaska Athabascan *(Ala. Nat.)* (26)	50	<0.01
Aleut *(Alaska Native)* (17)	40	<0.01
Apache (144)	366	0.01
Arapaho (3)	8	<0.01
Blackfeet (134)	937	0.02
Canadian/French Am. Ind. (34)	88	<0.01
Central American Ind. (114)	166	<0.01
Cherokee (3,126)	10,675	0.23
Cheyenne (13)	47	<0.01
Chickasaw (108)	201	<0.01
Chippewa (204)	388	0.01
Choctaw (218)	481	0.01
Colville (1)	2	<0.01
Comanche (46)	99	<0.01
Cree (19)	50	<0.01
Creek (196)	415	0.01
Crow (12)	63	<0.01
Delaware (26)	76	<0.01
Hopi (7)	18	<0.01
Houma (18)	26	<0.01
Inupiat *(Alaska Native)* (30)	63	<0.01
Iroquois (280)	575	0.01
Kiowa (12)	23	<0.01
Lumbee (1,585)	2,212	0.05
Menominee (6)	15	<0.01
Mexican American Ind. (936)	1,248	0.03
Navajo (152)	297	0.01
Osage (24)	45	<0.01
Ottawa (13)	25	<0.01
Paiute (3)	10	<0.01
Pima (7)	11	<0.01
Potawatomi (57)	83	<0.01
Pueblo (49)	72	<0.01
Puget Sound Salish (15)	25	<0.01
Seminole (51)	230	<0.01
Shoshone (4)	32	<0.01
Sioux (319)	688	0.01
South American Ind. (67)	186	<0.01
Spanish American Ind. (76)	97	<0.01
Tlingit-Haida *(Alaska Native)* (39)	62	<0.01
Tohono O'Odham (16)	20	<0.01
Tsimshian *(Alaska Native)* (3)	8	<0.01
Ute (8)	18	<0.01
Yakama (2)	9	<0.01
Yaqui (19)	32	<0.01
Yuman (4)	8	<0.01
Yup'ik *(Alaska Native)* (7)	12	<0.01
Asian (59,051)	75,674	1.64
Not Hispanic (58,307)	73,426	1.59
Hispanic (744)	2,248	0.05
Bangladeshi (214)	234	0.01
Bhutanese (5)	5	<0.01
Burmese (405)	425	0.01
Cambodian (1,334)	1,617	0.03
Chinese, ex. Taiwanese (9,279)	11,271	0.24
Filipino (10,053)	15,228	0.33
Hmong (1,135)	1,218	0.03
Indian (15,941)	17,961	0.39
Indonesian (177)	286	0.01
Japanese (2,413)	4,745	0.10
Korean (4,876)	7,162	0.15
Laotian (1,157)	1,432	0.03
Malaysian (56)	122	<0.01
Nepalese (140)	154	<0.01
Pakistani (986)	1,127	0.02
Sri Lankan (177)	212	<0.01
Taiwanese (369)	477	0.01
Thai (1,070)	1,797	0.04
Vietnamese (6,801)	7,840	0.17
Hawaii Native/Pacific Islander (2,706)	5,880	0.13
Not Hispanic (2,113)	4,709	0.10
Hispanic (593)	1,171	0.03
Fijian (12)	40	<0.01
Guamanian/Chamorro (1,046)	1,568	0.03
Marshallese (14)	18	<0.01
Native Hawaiian (570)	1,654	0.04
Samoan (225)	555	0.01
Tongan (27)	61	<0.01
White (3,060,000)	3,127,075	67.61
Not Hispanic (2,962,740)	3,017,747	65.24
Hispanic (97,260)	109,328	2.36

*Notes: † The Census 2010 population figure is used to calculate the percentages in the Hispanic Origin and Race categories. Ancestry percentages are based on the 2006-2010 American Community Survey population (not shown); ‡ Numbers in parentheses indicate the number of people reporting a single ancestry; * Numbers in parentheses indicate the number of persons reporting this race alone, not in combination with any other race; Please refer to the Explanation of Data for more information.*

Aiken

Place Type: City
County: Aiken
Population: 29,524†

Ancestry‡	Population	%
African, Sub-Saharan (48)	60	0.21
African (48)	60	0.21
Albanian (39)	39	0.14
American (2,948)	2,948	10.23
Arab (8)	102	0.35
Egyptian (0)	38	0.13
Lebanese (8)	54	0.19
Syrian (0)	10	0.03
Armenian (0)	55	0.19
Austrian (35)	89	0.31
Brazilian (0)	10	0.03
British (179)	251	0.87
Canadian (52)	206	0.72
Celtic (11)	20	0.07
Croatian (30)	81	0.28
Czech (27)	91	0.32
Danish (38)	50	0.17
Dutch (10)	227	0.79
English (1,777)	4,312	14.97
Estonian (7)	7	0.02
European (416)	443	1.54
Finnish (48)	48	0.17
French, ex. Basque (295)	755	2.62
French Canadian (42)	95	0.33
German (1,244)	3,803	13.20
Greek (81)	203	0.70
Hungarian (107)	143	0.50
Iranian (14)	14	0.05
Irish (957)	3,128	10.86
Italian (552)	1,216	4.22
Latvian (0)	12	0.04
Lithuanian (0)	16	0.06
Norwegian (79)	144	0.50
Polish (136)	474	1.65
Portuguese (19)	19	0.07
Romanian (69)	69	0.24
Russian (44)	125	0.43
Scandinavian (0)	58	0.20
Scotch-Irish (516)	1,053	3.66
Scottish (220)	625	2.17
Serbian (0)	20	0.07
Slavic (17)	17	0.06
Slovak (33)	54	0.19
Slovene (0)	8	0.03
Swedish (23)	218	0.76
Swiss (11)	107	0.37
Ukrainian (14)	37	0.13
Welsh (40)	186	0.65
West Indian, ex. Hispanic (5)	5	0.02
Jamaican (5)	5	0.02

Hispanic Origin	Population	%
Hispanic or Latino (of any race)	768	2.60
Central American, ex. Mexican	110	0.37
Costa Rican	10	0.03
Guatemalan	30	0.10
Honduran	35	0.12
Nicaraguan	1	<0.01
Panamanian	7	0.02
Salvadoran	27	0.09
Cuban	53	0.18
Dominican Republic	17	0.06
Mexican	279	0.94
Puerto Rican	164	0.56
South American	60	0.20
Argentinean	9	0.03
Bolivian	2	0.01
Chilean	8	0.03
Colombian	16	0.05
Ecuadorian	2	0.01
Paraguayan	1	<0.01
Peruvian	14	0.05
Venezuelan	8	0.03
Other Hispanic or Latino	85	0.29

Race*	Population	%
African-American/Black (8,401)	8,647	29.29
Not Hispanic (8,340)	8,563	29.00
Hispanic (61)	84	0.28
American Indian/Alaska Native (107)	225	0.76
Not Hispanic (98)	207	0.70
Hispanic (9)	18	0.06
Apache (1)	3	0.01
Blackfeet (0)	5	0.02
Cherokee (17)	50	0.17
Chippewa (7)	8	0.03
Choctaw (1)	2	0.01
Creek (1)	3	0.01
Delaware (0)	1	<0.01
Iroquois (6)	6	0.02
Lumbee (5)	9	0.03
Mexican American Ind. (1)	4	0.01
Navajo (2)	4	0.01
Pueblo (1)	1	<0.01
Sioux (0)	3	0.01
Spanish American Ind. (0)	1	<0.01
Tlingit-Haida *(Alaska Native)* (2)	2	0.01
Asian (567)	685	2.32
Not Hispanic (564)	671	2.27
Hispanic (3)	14	0.05
Bangladeshi (2)	2	0.01
Cambodian (1)	4	0.01
Chinese, ex. Taiwanese (88)	94	0.32
Filipino (94)	119	0.40
Indian (194)	216	0.73
Indonesian (1)	3	0.01
Japanese (53)	74	0.25
Korean (31)	56	0.19
Laotian (1)	3	0.01
Nepalese (12)	12	0.04
Pakistani (2)	2	0.01
Taiwanese (3)	5	0.02
Thai (4)	4	0.01
Vietnamese (67)	74	0.25
Hawaii Native/Pacific Islander (21)	44	0.15
Not Hispanic (21)	41	0.14
Hispanic (0)	3	0.01
Guamanian/Chamorro (0)	6	0.02
Native Hawaiian (14)	24	0.08
Samoan (0)	3	0.01
White (19,729)	20,095	68.06
Not Hispanic (19,324)	19,642	66.53
Hispanic (405)	453	1.53

Anderson

Place Type: City
County: Anderson
Population: 26,686†

Ancestry‡	Population	%
African, Sub-Saharan (68)	68	0.26
African (55)	55	0.21
Ethiopian (13)	13	0.05
American (2,520)	2,520	9.49
Arab (102)	162	0.61
Arab (41)	41	0.15
Lebanese (0)	60	0.23
Moroccan (8)	8	0.03
Other Arab (53)	53	0.20
Armenian (14)	14	0.05
Austrian (25)	66	0.25
British (34)	140	0.53
Canadian (14)	36	0.14
Czechoslovakian (25)	25	0.09
Danish (53)	78	0.29
Dutch (18)	234	0.88
English (1,254)	2,326	8.76
European (80)	87	0.33
Finnish (0)	8	0.03
French, ex. Basque (106)	315	1.19
French Canadian (37)	55	0.21
German (919)	2,283	8.59
Greek (45)	45	0.17
Hungarian (59)	160	0.60
Iranian (19)	19	0.07
Irish (1,392)	2,851	10.73
Italian (160)	761	2.86
Lithuanian (0)	63	0.24
Norwegian (0)	44	0.17
Polish (78)	132	0.50
Portuguese (29)	71	0.27
Romanian (0)	12	0.05
Russian (9)	9	0.03
Scotch-Irish (811)	1,231	4.63
Scottish (354)	701	2.64
Slovak (0)	20	0.08
Swedish (19)	61	0.23
Swiss (20)	126	0.47
Ukrainian (0)	16	0.06
Welsh (20)	84	0.32
West Indian, ex. Hispanic (280)	280	1.05
Bahamian (59)	59	0.22
British West Indian (14)	14	0.05
Haitian (207)	207	0.78

Hispanic Origin	Population	%
Hispanic or Latino (of any race)	1,089	4.08
Central American, ex. Mexican	80	0.30
Costa Rican	2	0.01
Guatemalan	17	0.06
Honduran	19	0.07
Nicaraguan	6	0.02
Panamanian	6	0.02
Salvadoran	30	0.11
Cuban	29	0.11
Dominican Republic	13	0.05
Mexican	579	2.17
Puerto Rican	173	0.65
South American	72	0.27
Bolivian	3	0.01
Chilean	2	0.01
Colombian	28	0.10
Ecuadorian	4	0.01
Paraguayan	2	0.01
Peruvian	25	0.09
Uruguayan	2	0.01
Venezuelan	6	0.02
Other Hispanic or Latino	143	0.54

Race*	Population	%
African-American/Black (8,959)	9,332	34.97
Not Hispanic (8,894)	9,239	34.62
Hispanic (65)	93	0.35
American Indian/Alaska Native (72)	201	0.75
Not Hispanic (63)	184	0.69
Hispanic (9)	17	0.06
Aleut *(Alaska Native)* (1)	3	0.01
Canadian/French Am. Ind. (0)	2	0.01
Cherokee (8)	59	0.22
Chippewa (1)	6	0.02
Choctaw (1)	1	<0.01
Comanche (1)	3	0.01
Creek (4)	6	0.02
Delaware (1)	1	<0.01
Lumbee (4)	4	0.01
Mexican American Ind. (2)	3	0.01
Navajo (1)	2	0.01
Ottawa (0)	1	<0.01
Potawatomi (1)	1	<0.01
Pueblo (1)	1	<0.01
Sioux (0)	3	0.01
Tsimshian *(Alaska Native)* (0)	1	<0.01
Asian (260)	316	1.18
Not Hispanic (253)	298	1.12
Hispanic (7)	18	0.07
Chinese, ex. Taiwanese (54)	60	0.22
Filipino (27)	36	0.13
Indian (79)	88	0.33
Indonesian (11)	12	0.04
Japanese (9)	22	0.08
Korean (18)	26	0.10
Laotian (3)	3	0.01

*Notes: † The Census 2010 population figure is used to calculate the percentages in the Hispanic Origin and Race categories. Ancestry percentages are based on the 2006-2010 American Community Survey population (not shown); ‡ Numbers in parentheses indicate the number of people reporting a single ancestry; * Numbers in parentheses indicate the number of persons reporting this race alone, not in combination with any other race; Please refer to the Explanation of Data for more information.*

Malaysian (1)	3	0.01
Nepalese (1)	3	0.01
Pakistani (8)	8	0.03
Sri Lankan (6)	6	0.02
Thai (4)	6	0.02
Vietnamese (22)	26	0.10
Hawaii Native/Pacific Islander (5)	17	0.06
Not Hispanic (4)	14	0.05
Hispanic (1)	3	0.01
Guamanian/Chamorro (0)	1	<0.01
Native Hawaiian (5)	5	0.02
Samoan (0)	5	0.02
White (16,382)	16,885	63.27
Not Hispanic (15,881)	16,324	61.17
Hispanic (501)	561	2.10

Beaufort

Place Type: City
County: Beaufort
Population: 12,361†

Ancestry‡	Population	%
African, Sub-Saharan (77)	108	0.86
African (62)	93	0.74
South African (15)	15	0.12
American (677)	677	5.42
Arab (14)	14	0.11
Lebanese (14)	14	0.11
Australian (23)	23	0.18
Austrian (0)	12	0.10
Basque (58)	58	0.46
Belgian (13)	32	0.26
Brazilian (8)	8	0.06
British (50)	50	0.40
Canadian (0)	30	0.24
Czech (0)	72	0.58
Danish (0)	42	0.34
Dutch (39)	128	1.02
Eastern European (2)	2	0.02
English (737)	1,729	13.84
European (78)	78	0.62
Finnish (0)	14	0.11
French, ex. Basque (147)	467	3.74
French Canadian (39)	80	0.64
German (386)	1,538	12.31
Greek (53)	79	0.63
Hungarian (14)	43	0.34
Iranian (11)	11	0.09
Irish (801)	1,801	14.42
Italian (154)	426	3.41
Latvian (78)	78	0.62
Lithuanian (5)	24	0.19
Macedonian (0)	7	0.06
Northern European (12)	12	0.10
Norwegian (36)	74	0.59
Polish (88)	308	2.47
Portuguese (0)	24	0.19
Russian (25)	88	0.70
Scandinavian (0)	8	0.06
Scotch-Irish (225)	545	4.36
Scottish (115)	356	2.85
Slavic (8)	8	0.06
Slovak (14)	42	0.34
Swedish (18)	124	0.99
Swiss (0)	38	0.30
Ukrainian (19)	22	0.18
Welsh (46)	67	0.54
West Indian, ex. Hispanic (70)	88	0.70
Bahamian (46)	46	0.37
Belizean (0)	10	0.08
Haitian (2)	2	0.02
Jamaican (22)	22	0.18
West Indian (0)	8	0.06
Yugoslavian (12)	12	0.10

Hispanic Origin	Population	%
Hispanic or Latino (of any race)	830	6.71
Central American, ex. Mexican	86	0.70
Costa Rican	9	0.07
Guatemalan	5	0.04
Honduran	50	0.40
Nicaraguan	3	0.02
Panamanian	9	0.07
Salvadoran	10	0.08
Cuban	29	0.23
Dominican Republic	22	0.18
Mexican	410	3.32
Puerto Rican	134	1.08
South American	49	0.40
Argentinean	5	0.04
Bolivian	2	0.02
Chilean	2	0.02
Colombian	14	0.11
Ecuadorian	8	0.06
Peruvian	12	0.10
Uruguayan	2	0.02
Venezuelan	4	0.03
Other Hispanic or Latino	100	0.81

Race*	Population	%
African-American/Black (3,176)	3,353	27.13
Not Hispanic (3,115)	3,254	26.32
Hispanic (61)	99	0.80
American Indian/Alaska Native (36)	120	0.97
Not Hispanic (29)	103	0.83
Hispanic (7)	17	0.14
Apache (0)	2	0.02
Blackfeet (0)	3	0.02
Canadian/French Am. Ind. (0)	1	0.01
Cherokee (7)	31	0.25
Chippewa (0)	2	0.02
Choctaw (1)	2	0.02
Creek (0)	1	0.01
Iroquois (0)	1	0.01
Lumbee (2)	2	0.02
Navajo (3)	3	0.02
Puget Sound Salish (1)	1	0.01
Seminole (0)	2	0.02
Shoshone (0)	1	0.01
Sioux (1)	1	0.01
Tlingit-Haida *(Alaska Native)* (0)	1	0.01
Yuman (1)	1	0.01
Yup'ik *(Alaska Native)* (0)	1	0.01
Asian (177)	260	2.10
Not Hispanic (171)	243	1.97
Hispanic (6)	17	0.14
Cambodian (1)	2	0.02
Chinese, ex. Taiwanese (28)	38	0.31
Filipino (64)	92	0.74
Hmong (1)	1	0.01
Indian (37)	38	0.31
Japanese (11)	25	0.20
Korean (9)	18	0.15
Laotian (0)	2	0.02
Thai (9)	15	0.12
Vietnamese (13)	13	0.11
Hawaii Native/Pacific Islander (17)	34	0.28
Not Hispanic (10)	27	0.22
Hispanic (7)	7	0.06
Guamanian/Chamorro (1)	5	0.04
Native Hawaiian (9)	19	0.15
Samoan (3)	6	0.05
White (8,300)	8,565	69.29
Not Hispanic (7,944)	8,147	65.91
Hispanic (356)	418	3.38

Bennettsville

Place Type: City
County: Marlboro
Population: 9,069†

Ancestry‡	Population	%
American (592)	592	6.35
Armenian (17)	17	0.18
British (0)	13	0.14
Dutch (0)	36	0.39
English (220)	341	3.66
European (35)	35	0.38
French, ex. Basque (34)	60	0.64
French Canadian (10)	10	0.11
German (174)	389	4.17
Irish (145)	262	2.81
Norwegian (0)	14	0.15
Polish (10)	18	0.19
Romanian (11)	11	0.12
Russian (0)	10	0.11
Scotch-Irish (121)	177	1.90
Scottish (51)	75	0.80
Swedish (10)	10	0.11
Turkish (39)	39	0.42
Welsh (0)	13	0.14
West Indian, ex. Hispanic (10)	38	0.41
Barbadian (0)	14	0.15
Jamaican (0)	14	0.15
Trinidadian/Tobagonian (10)	10	0.11

Hispanic Origin	Population	%
Hispanic or Latino (of any race)	148	1.63
Central American, ex. Mexican	14	0.15
Guatemalan	5	0.06
Honduran	3	0.03
Nicaraguan	4	0.04
Panamanian	2	0.02
Cuban	5	0.06
Dominican Republic	2	0.02
Mexican	63	0.69
Puerto Rican	37	0.41
South American	2	0.02
Peruvian	2	0.02
Other Hispanic or Latino	25	0.28

Race*	Population	%
African-American/Black (5,822)	5,878	64.81
Not Hispanic (5,798)	5,849	64.49
Hispanic (24)	29	0.32
American Indian/Alaska Native (76)	126	1.39
Not Hispanic (74)	124	1.37
Hispanic (2)	2	0.02
Blackfeet (0)	3	0.03
Cherokee (13)	27	0.30
Chippewa (1)	1	0.01
Iroquois (0)	1	0.01
Lumbee (15)	24	0.26
Mexican American Ind. (2)	2	0.02
Navajo (1)	1	0.01
Sioux (1)	1	0.01
Asian (36)	48	0.53
Not Hispanic (36)	48	0.53
Chinese, ex. Taiwanese (5)	7	0.08
Filipino (9)	9	0.10
Indian (11)	11	0.12
Japanese (2)	2	0.02
Korean (1)	7	0.08
Laotian (1)	1	0.01
Thai (2)	2	0.02
Vietnamese (3)	3	0.03
Hawaii Native/Pacific Islander (2)	11	0.12
Not Hispanic (2)	11	0.12
Native Hawaiian (1)	2	0.02
Samoan (1)	1	0.01
White (2,966)	3,048	33.61
Not Hispanic (2,908)	2,980	32.86
Hispanic (58)	68	0.75

Berea

Place Type: CDP
County: Greenville
Population: 14,295†

Ancestry‡	Population	%
African, Sub-Saharan (21)	62	0.48
African (21)	62	0.48
American (1,451)	1,451	11.22
Arab (111)	111	0.86
Arab (111)	111	0.86
Austrian (16)	29	0.22
Canadian (0)	10	0.08

*Notes: † The Census 2010 population figure is used to calculate the percentages in the Hispanic Origin and Race categories. Ancestry percentages are based on the 2006-2010 American Community Survey population (not shown); ‡ Numbers in parentheses indicate the number of people reporting a single ancestry; * Numbers in parentheses indicate the number of persons reporting this race alone, not in combination with any other race; Please refer to the Explanation of Data for more information.*

Czech (0)	30	0.23
Czechoslovakian (0)	18	0.14
Dutch (33)	100	0.77
English (392)	898	6.94
European (64)	75	0.58
French, ex. Basque (69)	137	1.06
French Canadian (0)	33	0.26
German (247)	1,020	7.89
Hungarian (9)	9	0.07
Irish (437)	1,117	8.64
Italian (94)	216	1.67
Lithuanian (0)	13	0.10
Norwegian (7)	19	0.15
Pennsylvania German (36)	51	0.39
Russian (10)	65	0.50
Scotch-Irish (233)	297	2.30
Scottish (133)	266	2.06
Swedish (0)	43	0.33
Swiss (0)	33	0.26
Welsh (9)	9	0.07
West Indian, ex. Hispanic (14)	14	0.11
Haitian (14)	14	0.11
Yugoslavian (0)	34	0.26

Hispanic Origin	Population	%
Hispanic or Latino (of any race)	3,630	25.39
Central American, ex. Mexican	954	6.67
Costa Rican	119	0.83
Guatemalan	248	1.73
Honduran	455	3.18
Nicaraguan	6	0.04
Panamanian	8	0.06
Salvadoran	116	0.81
Other Central American	2	0.01
Cuban	30	0.21
Dominican Republic	13	0.09
Mexican	2,021	14.14
Puerto Rican	105	0.73
South American	359	2.51
Argentinean	6	0.04
Chilean	2	0.01
Colombian	317	2.22
Ecuadorian	5	0.03
Peruvian	13	0.09
Uruguayan	3	0.02
Venezuelan	13	0.09
Other Hispanic or Latino	148	1.04

Race*	Population	%
African-American/Black (2,586)	2,724	19.06
Not Hispanic (2,553)	2,673	18.70
Hispanic (33)	51	0.36
American Indian/Alaska Native (73)	146	1.02
Not Hispanic (36)	76	0.53
Hispanic (37)	70	0.49
Blackfeet (3)	3	0.02
Central American Ind. (7)	7	0.05
Cherokee (13)	31	0.22
Chippewa (1)	1	0.01
Creek (0)	1	0.01
Iroquois (1)	4	0.03
Lumbee (1)	1	0.01
Mexican American Ind. (16)	20	0.14
Navajo (5)	5	0.03
Asian (177)	226	1.58
Not Hispanic (172)	214	1.50
Hispanic (5)	12	0.08
Chinese, ex. Taiwanese (15)	20	0.14
Filipino (17)	32	0.22
Indian (10)	18	0.13
Indonesian (1)	1	0.01
Japanese (0)	2	0.01
Korean (4)	4	0.03
Laotian (1)	3	0.02
Sri Lankan (3)	4	0.03
Thai (0)	3	0.02
Vietnamese (123)	130	0.91
Hawaii Native/Pacific Islander (1)	13	0.09
Not Hispanic (1)	13	0.09
Guamanian/Chamorro (1)	3	0.02
Native Hawaiian (0)	3	0.02
White (8,662)	8,976	62.79
Not Hispanic (7,694)	7,867	55.03
Hispanic (968)	1,109	7.76

Bluffton

Place Type: Town
County: Beaufort
Population: 12,530†

Ancestry‡	Population	%
African, Sub-Saharan (0)	9	0.08
Kenyan (0)	9	0.08
American (526)	526	4.89
Arab (12)	12	0.11
Iraqi (12)	12	0.11
Austrian (19)	37	0.34
Brazilian (13)	13	0.12
British (33)	44	0.41
Canadian (0)	47	0.44
Czech (59)	133	1.24
Danish (0)	27	0.25
Dutch (24)	226	2.10
Eastern European (8)	8	0.07
English (483)	1,037	9.65
European (56)	56	0.52
Finnish (76)	76	0.71
French, ex. Basque (56)	309	2.87
French Canadian (12)	24	0.22
German (520)	1,518	14.12
Greek (0)	11	0.10
Irish (388)	1,228	11.43
Israeli (12)	12	0.11
Italian (347)	890	8.28
Lithuanian (15)	37	0.34
Polish (146)	481	4.48
Portuguese (0)	10	0.09
Romanian (0)	37	0.34
Russian (59)	100	0.93
Scotch-Irish (60)	195	1.81
Scottish (84)	404	3.76
Swedish (0)	11	0.10
Swiss (9)	24	0.22
Ukrainian (18)	86	0.80
Welsh (0)	67	0.62
West Indian, ex. Hispanic (79)	79	0.74
Trinidadian/Tobagonian (79)	79	0.74
Yugoslavian (23)	28	0.26

Hispanic Origin	Population	%
Hispanic or Latino (of any race)	2,355	18.79
Central American, ex. Mexican	404	3.22
Costa Rican	77	0.61
Guatemalan	22	0.18
Honduran	210	1.68
Nicaraguan	38	0.30
Panamanian	5	0.04
Salvadoran	52	0.42
Cuban	31	0.25
Dominican Republic	33	0.26
Mexican	1,244	9.93
Puerto Rican	128	1.02
South American	345	2.75
Argentinean	64	0.51
Bolivian	55	0.44
Chilean	3	0.02
Colombian	59	0.47
Ecuadorian	8	0.06
Peruvian	21	0.17
Uruguayan	98	0.78
Venezuelan	37	0.30
Other Hispanic or Latino	170	1.36

Race*	Population	%
African-American/Black (2,025)	2,217	17.69
Not Hispanic (1,969)	2,125	16.96
Hispanic (56)	92	0.73
American Indian/Alaska Native (34)	109	0.87
Not Hispanic (19)	85	0.68
Hispanic (15)	24	0.19
Aleut *(Alaska Native)* (0)	1	0.01
Apache (1)	4	0.03
Blackfeet (0)	6	0.05
Cherokee (4)	25	0.20
Chippewa (2)	3	0.02
Colville (1)	1	0.01
Cree (0)	1	0.01
Creek (3)	5	0.04
Iroquois (0)	7	0.06
Lumbee (2)	2	0.02
Mexican American Ind. (8)	11	0.09
Osage (0)	1	0.01
Ottawa (0)	4	0.03
Seminole (0)	1	0.01
Sioux (1)	1	0.01
Spanish American Ind. (2)	2	0.02
Asian (245)	315	2.51
Not Hispanic (238)	295	2.35
Hispanic (7)	20	0.16
Burmese (3)	3	0.02
Chinese, ex. Taiwanese (47)	61	0.49
Filipino (43)	83	0.66
Indian (21)	29	0.23
Indonesian (1)	2	0.02
Japanese (9)	22	0.18
Korean (29)	32	0.26
Laotian (1)	1	0.01
Malaysian (0)	1	0.01
Taiwanese (0)	1	0.01
Thai (5)	5	0.04
Vietnamese (69)	74	0.59
Hawaii Native/Pacific Islander (6)	28	0.22
Not Hispanic (4)	17	0.14
Hispanic (2)	11	0.09
Guamanian/Chamorro (4)	9	0.07
Native Hawaiian (0)	8	0.06
Samoan (0)	3	0.02
White (8,950)	9,261	73.91
Not Hispanic (7,667)	7,887	62.94
Hispanic (1,283)	1,374	10.97

Boiling Springs

Place Type: CDP
County: Spartanburg
Population: 8,219†

Ancestry‡	Population	%
American (1,428)	1,428	17.31
Austrian (41)	57	0.69
Brazilian (63)	63	0.76
British (9)	9	0.11
Canadian (36)	36	0.44
Czech (17)	30	0.36
Dutch (0)	16	0.19
English (310)	632	7.66
European (0)	21	0.25
French, ex. Basque (36)	160	1.94
French Canadian (0)	29	0.35
German (128)	604	7.32
Greek (17)	60	0.73
Hungarian (9)	48	0.58
Irish (388)	1,069	12.96
Italian (34)	112	1.36
Norwegian (0)	43	0.52
Polish (85)	288	3.49
Russian (70)	87	1.05
Scotch-Irish (113)	172	2.09
Scottish (128)	191	2.32
Swedish (0)	28	0.34
Swiss (0)	49	0.59
Ukrainian (510)	510	6.18
Welsh (34)	34	0.41
Yugoslavian (16)	52	0.63

Hispanic Origin	Population	%
Hispanic or Latino (of any race)	350	4.26
Central American, ex. Mexican	38	0.46
Costa Rican	1	0.01

*Notes: † The Census 2010 population figure is used to calculate the percentages in the Hispanic Origin and Race categories. Ancestry percentages are based on the 2006-2010 American Community Survey population (not shown); ‡ Numbers in parentheses indicate the number of people reporting a single ancestry; * Numbers in parentheses indicate the number of persons reporting this race alone, not in combination with any other race; Please refer to the Explanation of Data for more information.*

Guatemalan	8	0.10
Honduran	14	0.17
Nicaraguan	5	0.06
Panamanian	7	0.09
Salvadoran	3	0.04
Cuban	7	0.09
Dominican Republic	2	0.02
Mexican	185	2.25
Puerto Rican	52	0.63
South American	38	0.46
Argentinean	1	0.01
Chilean	1	0.01
Colombian	26	0.32
Ecuadorian	1	0.01
Peruvian	8	0.10
Venezuelan	1	0.01
Other Hispanic or Latino	28	0.34

Race*	Population	%
African-American/Black (851)	908	11.05
Not Hispanic (838)	889	10.82
Hispanic (13)	19	0.23
American Indian/Alaska Native (25)	47	0.57
Not Hispanic (14)	32	0.39
Hispanic (11)	15	0.18
Apache (1)	4	0.05
Cherokee (3)	9	0.11
Chippewa (0)	1	0.01
Choctaw (1)	1	0.01
Hopi (1)	1	0.01
Lumbee (0)	2	0.02
Mexican American Ind. (3)	3	0.04
Yaqui (1)	3	0.04
Asian (307)	341	4.15
Not Hispanic (303)	335	4.08
Hispanic (4)	6	0.07
Cambodian (34)	37	0.45
Chinese, ex. Taiwanese (41)	43	0.52
Filipino (16)	22	0.27
Hmong (14)	14	0.17
Indian (84)	92	1.12
Indonesian (2)	4	0.05
Japanese (4)	6	0.07
Korean (10)	17	0.21
Laotian (27)	33	0.40
Pakistani (5)	6	0.07
Taiwanese (7)	7	0.09
Thai (11)	15	0.18
Vietnamese (16)	16	0.19
Hawaii Native/Pacific Islander (2)	7	0.09
Not Hispanic (2)	7	0.09
Native Hawaiian (1)	3	0.04
Samoan (0)	2	0.02
White (6,728)	6,838	83.20
Not Hispanic (6,593)	6,685	81.34
Hispanic (135)	153	1.86

Cayce

Place Type: City
County: Lexington
Population: 12,528[†]

Ancestry‡	Population	%
African, Sub-Saharan (82)	82	0.67
African (58)	58	0.47
Ghanaian (17)	17	0.14
Other Sub-Saharan African (7)	7	0.06
American (927)	927	7.52
Armenian (0)	13	0.11
Austrian (0)	9	0.07
British (0)	31	0.25
Cajun (0)	8	0.06
Canadian (10)	10	0.08
Czech (10)	26	0.21
Czechoslovakian (0)	9	0.07
Danish (12)	57	0.46
Dutch (28)	132	1.07
English (948)	1,454	11.80
European (75)	75	0.61
French, ex. Basque (99)	294	2.39
French Canadian (18)	18	0.15
German (508)	1,751	14.21
Greek (28)	50	0.41
Hungarian (8)	28	0.23
Irish (649)	1,493	12.12
Italian (81)	206	1.67
Latvian (25)	25	0.20
Lithuanian (0)	9	0.07
Norwegian (23)	55	0.45
Polish (49)	153	1.24
Portuguese (12)	12	0.10
Romanian (10)	10	0.08
Russian (29)	29	0.24
Scandinavian (0)	9	0.07
Scotch-Irish (321)	511	4.15
Scottish (209)	395	3.21
Swedish (30)	89	0.72
Welsh (10)	51	0.41
West Indian, ex. Hispanic (20)	20	0.16
Bermudan (20)	20	0.16

Hispanic Origin	Population	%
Hispanic or Latino (of any race)	539	4.30
Central American, ex. Mexican	78	0.62
Costa Rican	3	0.02
Guatemalan	25	0.20
Honduran	8	0.06
Nicaraguan	2	0.02
Panamanian	11	0.09
Salvadoran	29	0.23
Cuban	17	0.14
Dominican Republic	9	0.07
Mexican	277	2.21
Puerto Rican	94	0.75
South American	34	0.27
Argentinean	6	0.05
Chilean	1	0.01
Colombian	8	0.06
Ecuadorian	11	0.09
Peruvian	4	0.03
Uruguayan	1	0.01
Venezuelan	1	0.01
Other South American	2	0.02
Other Hispanic or Latino	30	0.24

Race*	Population	%
African-American/Black (3,150)	3,281	26.19
Not Hispanic (3,103)	3,220	25.70
Hispanic (47)	61	0.49
American Indian/Alaska Native (52)	142	1.13
Not Hispanic (47)	135	1.08
Hispanic (5)	7	0.06
Apache (1)	2	0.02
Blackfeet (1)	6	0.05
Central American Ind. (3)	3	0.02
Cherokee (4)	40	0.32
Choctaw (0)	1	0.01
Creek (0)	1	0.01
Crow (0)	1	0.01
Delaware (0)	1	0.01
Iroquois (0)	1	0.01
Lumbee (10)	15	0.12
Sioux (1)	1	0.01
South American Ind. (0)	1	0.01
Asian (236)	284	2.27
Not Hispanic (234)	278	2.22
Hispanic (2)	6	0.05
Burmese (19)	22	0.18
Cambodian (1)	2	0.02
Chinese, ex. Taiwanese (23)	32	0.26
Filipino (16)	26	0.21
Indian (126)	129	1.03
Japanese (10)	18	0.14
Korean (10)	14	0.11
Laotian (3)	3	0.02
Pakistani (1)	1	0.01
Taiwanese (5)	5	0.04
Thai (1)	4	0.03
Vietnamese (14)	19	0.15
Hawaii Native/Pacific Islander (9)	18	0.14
Not Hispanic (9)	18	0.14
Native Hawaiian (6)	9	0.07
Samoan (1)	2	0.02
White (8,522)	8,745	69.80
Not Hispanic (8,355)	8,552	68.26
Hispanic (167)	193	1.54

Charleston

Place Type: City
County: Charleston
Population: 120,083[†]

Ancestry‡	Population	%
African, Sub-Saharan (661)	754	0.65
African (544)	577	0.50
Ethiopian (11)	11	0.01
Nigerian (94)	94	0.08
South African (0)	49	0.04
Zimbabwean (12)	12	0.01
Other Sub-Saharan African (0)	11	0.01
Albanian (14)	14	0.01
American (12,018)	12,018	10.33
Arab (636)	878	0.75
Arab (37)	37	0.03
Egyptian (134)	134	0.12
Iraqi (10)	21	0.02
Jordanian (129)	140	0.12
Lebanese (243)	312	0.27
Moroccan (25)	53	0.05
Syrian (58)	146	0.13
Other Arab (0)	35	0.03
Armenian (46)	61	0.05
Australian (7)	15	0.01
Austrian (24)	182	0.16
Belgian (35)	57	0.05
Brazilian (10)	42	0.04
British (422)	801	0.69
Bulgarian (40)	40	0.03
Cajun (12)	45	0.04
Canadian (120)	194	0.17
Croatian (4)	12	0.01
Czech (81)	393	0.34
Czechoslovakian (13)	148	0.13
Danish (84)	204	0.18
Dutch (392)	1,301	1.12
Eastern European (42)	42	0.04
English (5,522)	14,530	12.49
Estonian (13)	26	0.02
European (1,287)	1,434	1.23
Finnish (35)	44	0.04
French, ex. Basque (735)	3,182	2.73
French Canadian (211)	397	0.34
German (4,276)	14,321	12.31
Greek (414)	882	0.76
Hungarian (36)	327	0.28
Iranian (93)	105	0.09
Irish (4,375)	12,396	10.65
Israeli (16)	16	0.01
Italian (1,692)	4,553	3.91
Latvian (0)	7	0.01
Lithuanian (108)	214	0.18
Macedonian (0)	14	0.01
New Zealander (0)	15	0.01
Northern European (132)	132	0.11
Norwegian (211)	734	0.63
Pennsylvania German (0)	19	0.02
Polish (835)	2,127	1.83
Portuguese (18)	109	0.09
Romanian (33)	94	0.08
Russian (512)	1,267	1.09
Scandinavian (109)	239	0.21
Scotch-Irish (2,233)	4,145	3.56
Scottish (1,610)	4,177	3.59
Serbian (0)	26	0.02
Slavic (0)	30	0.03
Slovak (48)	193	0.17
Slovene (9)	35	0.03
Swedish (325)	993	0.85

*Notes: † The Census 2010 population figure is used to calculate the percentages in the Hispanic Origin and Race categories. Ancestry percentages are based on the 2006-2010 American Community Survey population (not shown); ‡ Numbers in parentheses indicate the number of people reporting a single ancestry; * Numbers in parentheses indicate the number of persons reporting this race alone, not in combination with any other race; Please refer to the Explanation of Data for more information.*

Swiss (82)	297	0.26
Turkish (39)	39	0.03
Ukrainian (263)	408	0.35
Welsh (318)	909	0.78
West Indian, ex. Hispanic (172)	199	0.17
Bahamian (15)	15	0.01
Jamaican (132)	132	0.11
Trinidadian/Tobagonian (14)	14	0.01
West Indian (11)	38	0.03
Yugoslavian (14)	43	0.04

Hispanic Origin	Population	%
Hispanic or Latino (of any race)	3,451	2.87
Central American, ex. Mexican	296	0.25
Costa Rican	26	0.02
Guatemalan	93	0.08
Honduran	57	0.05
Nicaraguan	20	0.02
Panamanian	72	0.06
Salvadoran	25	0.02
Other Central American	3	<0.01
Cuban	150	0.12
Dominican Republic	55	0.05
Mexican	1,590	1.32
Puerto Rican	528	0.44
South American	477	0.40
Argentinean	83	0.07
Bolivian	62	0.05
Chilean	27	0.02
Colombian	126	0.10
Ecuadorian	83	0.07
Paraguayan	4	<0.01
Peruvian	51	0.04
Uruguayan	8	0.01
Venezuelan	30	0.02
Other South American	3	<0.01
Other Hispanic or Latino	355	0.30

Race*	Population	%
African-American/Black (30,491)	31,268	26.04
Not Hispanic (30,288)	30,973	25.79
Hispanic (203)	295	0.25
American Indian/Alaska Native (271)	753	0.63
Not Hispanic (235)	665	0.55
Hispanic (36)	88	0.07
Alaska Athabascan *(Ala. Nat.)* (0)	1	<0.01
Aleut *(Alaska Native)* (0)	1	<0.01
Apache (2)	6	<0.01
Blackfeet (2)	24	0.02
Canadian/French Am. Ind. (1)	4	<0.01
Central American Ind. (4)	7	0.01
Cherokee (54)	199	0.17
Cheyenne (0)	1	<0.01
Chickasaw (2)	5	<0.01
Chippewa (2)	6	<0.01
Choctaw (1)	12	0.01
Cree (0)	3	<0.01
Creek (6)	11	0.01
Crow (0)	2	<0.01
Inupiat *(Alaska Native)* (2)	7	0.01
Iroquois (4)	10	0.01
Kiowa (4)	4	<0.01
Lumbee (15)	19	0.02
Mexican American Ind. (6)	14	0.01
Navajo (1)	2	<0.01
Osage (0)	1	<0.01
Potawatomi (2)	5	<0.01
Pueblo (1)	1	<0.01
Puget Sound Salish (2)	3	<0.01
Seminole (0)	5	<0.01
Shoshone (0)	4	<0.01
Sioux (2)	9	0.01
South American Ind. (3)	6	<0.01
Ute (1)	2	<0.01
Asian (1,971)	2,557	2.13
Not Hispanic (1,950)	2,491	2.07
Hispanic (21)	66	0.05
Bangladeshi (6)	7	0.01
Bhutanese (1)	1	<0.01
Burmese (16)	16	0.01
Cambodian (10)	10	0.01
Chinese, ex. Taiwanese (405)	484	0.40
Filipino (316)	522	0.43
Hmong (1)	1	<0.01
Indian (564)	637	0.53
Indonesian (5)	7	0.01
Japanese (85)	158	0.13
Korean (162)	244	0.20
Malaysian (1)	4	<0.01
Nepalese (4)	5	<0.01
Pakistani (18)	20	0.02
Sri Lankan (18)	22	0.02
Taiwanese (36)	39	0.03
Thai (28)	49	0.04
Vietnamese (203)	243	0.20
Hawaii Native/Pacific Islander (122)	213	0.18
Not Hispanic (111)	192	0.16
Hispanic (11)	21	0.02
Fijian (1)	1	<0.01
Guamanian/Chamorro (21)	28	0.02
Marshallese (0)	1	<0.01
Native Hawaiian (17)	44	0.04
Samoan (6)	14	0.01
White (84,258)	85,755	71.41
Not Hispanic (82,427)	83,699	69.70
Hispanic (1,831)	2,056	1.71

Clemson

Place Type: City
County: Pickens
Population: 13,905†

Ancestry‡	Population	%
African, Sub-Saharan (92)	92	0.68
African (48)	48	0.35
Ghanaian (44)	44	0.32
American (1,104)	1,104	8.12
Arab (319)	332	2.44
Arab (39)	39	0.29
Egyptian (62)	62	0.46
Lebanese (0)	13	0.10
Other Arab (218)	218	1.60
Austrian (57)	117	0.86
British (251)	262	1.93
Canadian (26)	26	0.19
Carpatho Rusyn (0)	13	0.10
Czech (12)	47	0.35
Czechoslovakian (0)	20	0.15
Dutch (15)	83	0.61
English (807)	2,149	15.81
European (106)	121	0.89
French, ex. Basque (66)	298	2.19
French Canadian (13)	54	0.40
German (547)	1,950	14.34
Greek (28)	121	0.89
Hungarian (0)	13	0.10
Irish (592)	1,617	11.89
Italian (197)	450	3.31
Lithuanian (13)	64	0.47
Northern European (16)	16	0.12
Norwegian (23)	54	0.40
Pennsylvania German (0)	8	0.06
Polish (198)	433	3.18
Portuguese (0)	32	0.24
Russian (0)	43	0.32
Scandinavian (11)	11	0.08
Scotch-Irish (448)	807	5.94
Scottish (289)	484	3.56
Slovak (0)	26	0.19
Swedish (0)	45	0.33
Swiss (11)	93	0.68
Turkish (91)	91	0.67
Ukrainian (0)	69	0.51
Welsh (45)	165	1.21

Hispanic Origin	Population	%
Hispanic or Latino (of any race)	308	2.22
Central American, ex. Mexican	40	0.29
Costa Rican	9	0.06
Guatemalan	7	0.05
Honduran	6	0.04
Nicaraguan	5	0.04
Panamanian	4	0.03
Salvadoran	9	0.06
Cuban	28	0.20
Dominican Republic	6	0.04
Mexican	117	0.84
Puerto Rican	34	0.24
South American	51	0.37
Argentinean	4	0.03
Bolivian	1	0.01
Chilean	1	0.01
Colombian	20	0.14
Ecuadorian	9	0.06
Peruvian	11	0.08
Uruguayan	1	0.01
Venezuelan	4	0.03
Other Hispanic or Latino	32	0.23

Race*	Population	%
African-American/Black (1,437)	1,518	10.92
Not Hispanic (1,430)	1,506	10.83
Hispanic (7)	12	0.09
American Indian/Alaska Native (17)	59	0.42
Not Hispanic (13)	48	0.35
Hispanic (4)	11	0.08
Alaska Athabascan *(Ala. Nat.)* (0)	4	0.03
Apache (3)	3	0.02
Blackfeet (1)	1	0.01
Cherokee (2)	18	0.13
Choctaw (1)	1	0.01
Creek (2)	2	0.01
Lumbee (1)	1	0.01
Mexican American Ind. (1)	2	0.01
Navajo (1)	2	0.01
Seminole (1)	1	0.01
Tlingit-Haida *(Alaska Native)* (0)	1	0.01
Asian (1,127)	1,220	8.77
Not Hispanic (1,126)	1,209	8.69
Hispanic (1)	11	0.08
Bangladeshi (6)	6	0.04
Cambodian (7)	10	0.07
Chinese, ex. Taiwanese (445)	464	3.34
Filipino (24)	37	0.27
Indian (467)	483	3.47
Indonesian (2)	2	0.01
Japanese (22)	35	0.25
Korean (46)	53	0.38
Nepalese (4)	4	0.03
Pakistani (11)	17	0.12
Sri Lankan (29)	31	0.22
Taiwanese (11)	14	0.10
Thai (19)	22	0.16
Vietnamese (21)	25	0.18
Hawaii Native/Pacific Islander (1)	12	0.09
Not Hispanic (1)	10	0.07
Hispanic (0)	2	0.01
Native Hawaiian (1)	6	0.04
White (10,994)	11,186	80.45
Not Hispanic (10,822)	10,988	79.02
Hispanic (172)	198	1.42

Clinton

Place Type: City
County: Laurens
Population: 8,490†

Ancestry‡	Population	%
African, Sub-Saharan (24)	43	0.50
African (24)	43	0.50
American (1,197)	1,197	13.89
Arab (0)	12	0.14
Lebanese (0)	12	0.14
Australian (16)	16	0.19
Brazilian (12)	37	0.43
British (15)	30	0.35
Czech (0)	20	0.23
Czechoslovakian (6)	6	0.07

*Notes: † The Census 2010 population figure is used to calculate the percentages in the Hispanic Origin and Race categories. Ancestry percentages are based on the 2006-2010 American Community Survey population (not shown); ‡ Numbers in parentheses indicate the number of people reporting a single ancestry; * Numbers in parentheses indicate the number of persons reporting this race alone, not in combination with any other race; Please refer to the Explanation of Data for more information.*

Dutch (0)	20	0.23
English (290)	483	5.61
European (131)	131	1.52
French, ex. Basque (46)	103	1.20
German (319)	785	9.11
Greek (0)	8	0.09
Iranian (2)	2	0.02
Irish (173)	543	6.30
Italian (4)	25	0.29
Scandinavian (0)	8	0.09
Scotch-Irish (201)	311	3.61
Scottish (73)	172	2.00
Swedish (0)	21	0.24

Hispanic Origin	Population	%
Hispanic or Latino (of any race)	187	2.20
Central American, ex. Mexican	21	0.25
Guatemalan	11	0.13
Honduran	9	0.11
Nicaraguan	1	0.01
Cuban	5	0.06
Dominican Republic	1	0.01
Mexican	118	1.39
Puerto Rican	12	0.14
South American	5	0.06
Chilean	2	0.02
Colombian	1	0.01
Peruvian	1	0.01
Uruguayan	1	0.01
Other Hispanic or Latino	25	0.29

Race*	Population	%
African-American/Black (3,140)	3,230	38.04
Not Hispanic (3,121)	3,208	37.79
Hispanic (19)	22	0.26
American Indian/Alaska Native (19)	45	0.53
Not Hispanic (15)	39	0.46
Hispanic (4)	6	0.07
Blackfeet (1)	4	0.05
Cherokee (6)	12	0.14
Choctaw (1)	1	0.01
Crow (0)	1	0.01
Navajo (0)	2	0.02
Asian (48)	63	0.74
Not Hispanic (47)	60	0.71
Hispanic (1)	3	0.04
Chinese, ex. Taiwanese (4)	4	0.05
Filipino (2)	4	0.05
Indian (26)	26	0.31
Japanese (0)	1	0.01
Korean (5)	6	0.07
Vietnamese (6)	16	0.19
Hawaii Native/Pacific Islander (2)	5	0.06
Not Hispanic (2)	4	0.05
Hispanic (0)	1	0.01
Guamanian/Chamorro (1)	2	0.02
Native Hawaiian (0)	1	0.01
White (5,047)	5,158	60.75
Not Hispanic (4,998)	5,098	60.05
Hispanic (49)	60	0.71

Columbia

Place Type: City
County: Richland
Population: 129,272†

Ancestry‡	Population	%
African, Sub-Saharan (1,871)	2,206	1.73
African (1,606)	1,837	1.44
Cape Verdean (9)	9	0.01
Ethiopian (64)	64	0.05
Ghanaian (5)	5	<0.01
Kenyan (19)	72	0.06
Liberian (0)	51	0.04
Nigerian (39)	39	0.03
Sudanese (47)	47	0.04
Other Sub-Saharan African (82)	82	0.06
American (7,637)	7,637	5.98
Arab (321)	547	0.43
Arab (18)	38	0.03
Egyptian (24)	107	0.08
Iraqi (12)	12	0.01
Lebanese (104)	208	0.16
Moroccan (0)	12	0.01
Syrian (29)	36	0.03
Other Arab (134)	134	0.11
Armenian (25)	25	0.02
Assyrian/Chaldean/Syriac (0)	31	0.02
Australian (17)	30	0.02
Austrian (68)	154	0.12
Belgian (0)	60	0.05
Brazilian (11)	33	0.03
British (380)	762	0.60
Bulgarian (22)	57	0.04
Cajun (61)	130	0.10
Canadian (102)	214	0.17
Celtic (12)	39	0.03
Croatian (35)	55	0.04
Cypriot (11)	11	0.01
Czech (52)	246	0.19
Czechoslovakian (49)	107	0.08
Danish (106)	201	0.16
Dutch (271)	1,053	0.83
Eastern European (51)	76	0.06
English (5,522)	12,269	9.61
Estonian (9)	9	0.01
European (1,334)	1,415	1.11
Finnish (61)	149	0.12
French, ex. Basque (573)	2,527	1.98
French Canadian (139)	442	0.35
German (3,693)	12,047	9.44
Greek (566)	603	0.47
Hungarian (97)	311	0.24
Iranian (64)	81	0.06
Irish (4,142)	10,384	8.14
Israeli (12)	12	0.01
Italian (1,075)	2,784	2.18
Latvian (14)	27	0.02
Lithuanian (11)	113	0.09
Luxemburger (0)	51	0.04
New Zealander (13)	13	0.01
Northern European (99)	147	0.12
Norwegian (314)	742	0.58
Polish (547)	1,762	1.38
Portuguese (20)	113	0.09
Romanian (56)	82	0.06
Russian (217)	602	0.47
Scandinavian (56)	102	0.08
Scotch-Irish (2,850)	4,743	3.72
Scottish (1,294)	3,524	2.76
Serbian (83)	83	0.07
Slavic (71)	119	0.09
Slovak (49)	79	0.06
Slovene (28)	64	0.05
Swedish (140)	504	0.39
Swiss (11)	308	0.24
Turkish (34)	34	0.03
Ukrainian (75)	142	0.11
Welsh (234)	697	0.55
West Indian, ex. Hispanic (413)	643	0.50
Bahamian (97)	97	0.08
Belizean (0)	10	0.01
Haitian (53)	53	0.04
Jamaican (125)	227	0.18
Trinidadian/Tobagonian (54)	98	0.08
U.S. Virgin Islander (9)	9	0.01
West Indian (60)	134	0.11
Other West Indian (15)	15	0.01
Yugoslavian (47)	74	0.06

Hispanic Origin	Population	%
Hispanic or Latino (of any race)	5,622	4.35
Central American, ex. Mexican	473	0.37
Costa Rican	17	0.01
Guatemalan	136	0.11
Honduran	99	0.08
Nicaraguan	17	0.01
Panamanian	132	0.10
Salvadoran	72	0.06
Cuban	208	0.16
Dominican Republic	154	0.12
Mexican	2,423	1.87
Puerto Rican	1,337	1.03
South American	428	0.33
Argentinean	41	0.03
Bolivian	10	0.01
Chilean	15	0.01
Colombian	188	0.15
Ecuadorian	50	0.04
Paraguayan	4	<0.01
Peruvian	60	0.05
Uruguayan	5	<0.01
Venezuelan	53	0.04
Other South American	2	<0.01
Other Hispanic or Latino	599	0.46

Race*	Population	%
African-American/Black (54,537)	55,929	43.26
Not Hispanic (53,948)	55,158	42.67
Hispanic (589)	771	0.60
American Indian/Alaska Native (434)	1,141	0.88
Not Hispanic (363)	962	0.74
Hispanic (71)	179	0.14
Aleut *(Alaska Native)* (1)	1	<0.01
Apache (10)	19	0.01
Arapaho (1)	1	<0.01
Blackfeet (1)	39	0.03
Canadian/French Am. Ind. (1)	1	<0.01
Central American Ind. (3)	8	0.01
Cherokee (52)	256	0.20
Cheyenne (1)	5	<0.01
Chickasaw (4)	4	<0.01
Chippewa (5)	10	0.01
Choctaw (15)	34	0.03
Creek (1)	3	<0.01
Crow (1)	5	<0.01
Delaware (2)	2	<0.01
Hopi (0)	1	<0.01
Houma (0)	1	<0.01
Inupiat *(Alaska Native)* (0)	5	<0.01
Iroquois (1)	11	0.01
Lumbee (16)	26	0.02
Mexican American Ind. (13)	25	0.02
Navajo (13)	20	0.02
Osage (2)	3	<0.01
Ottawa (1)	1	<0.01
Paiute (1)	1	<0.01
Potawatomi (0)	2	<0.01
Pueblo (3)	4	<0.01
Seminole (5)	11	0.01
Shoshone (1)	1	<0.01
Sioux (15)	26	0.02
South American Ind. (2)	9	0.01
Spanish American Ind. (0)	3	<0.01
Tlingit-Haida *(Alaska Native)* (1)	1	<0.01
Yaqui (1)	1	<0.01
Yup'ik *(Alaska Native)* (2)	2	<0.01
Asian (2,879)	3,707	2.87
Not Hispanic (2,846)	3,610	2.79
Hispanic (33)	97	0.08
Bangladeshi (21)	21	0.02
Burmese (10)	11	0.01
Cambodian (20)	27	0.02
Chinese, ex. Taiwanese (685)	800	0.62
Filipino (292)	519	0.40
Hmong (18)	20	0.02
Indian (878)	953	0.74
Indonesian (15)	20	0.02
Japanese (95)	231	0.18
Korean (359)	536	0.41
Laotian (15)	21	0.02
Malaysian (1)	4	<0.01
Nepalese (20)	24	0.02
Pakistani (39)	44	0.03
Sri Lankan (13)	14	0.01
Taiwanese (32)	33	0.03
Thai (54)	70	0.05
Vietnamese (150)	196	0.15
Hawaii Native/Pacific Islander (164)	338	0.26

*Notes: † The Census 2010 population figure is used to calculate the percentages in the Hispanic Origin and Race categories. Ancestry percentages are based on the 2006-2010 American Community Survey population (not shown); ‡ Numbers in parentheses indicate the number of people reporting a single ancestry; * Numbers in parentheses indicate the number of persons reporting this race alone, not in combination with any other race; Please refer to the Explanation of Data for more information.*

Not Hispanic (150)	304	0.24
Hispanic (14)	34	0.03
Fijian (2)	6	<0.01
Guamanian/Chamorro (50)	71	0.05
Marshallese (1)	1	<0.01
Native Hawaiian (40)	116	0.09
Samoan (32)	56	0.04
Tongan (2)	5	<0.01
White (66,777)	68,681	53.13
Not Hispanic (64,062)	65,644	50.78
Hispanic (2,715)	3,037	2.35

Conway

Place Type: City
County: Horry
Population: 17,103†

Ancestry‡	Population	%
African, Sub-Saharan (34)	34	0.21
African (34)	34	0.21
American (2,427)	2,427	14.78
Arab (34)	70	0.43
Arab (26)	26	0.16
Lebanese (8)	26	0.16
Syrian (0)	18	0.11
Austrian (0)	11	0.07
British (80)	134	0.82
Canadian (24)	24	0.15
Croatian (0)	9	0.05
Czechoslovakian (10)	39	0.24
Danish (0)	11	0.07
Dutch (26)	74	0.45
Eastern European (7)	7	0.04
English (696)	1,434	8.73
European (87)	87	0.53
Finnish (0)	10	0.06
French, ex. Basque (25)	390	2.37
German (316)	1,492	9.08
Greek (27)	69	0.42
Hungarian (24)	59	0.36
Iranian (0)	15	0.09
Irish (725)	1,708	10.40
Italian (257)	850	5.18
Lithuanian (8)	8	0.05
Northern European (26)	26	0.16
Norwegian (0)	66	0.40
Polish (37)	224	1.36
Portuguese (0)	84	0.51
Romanian (0)	14	0.09
Russian (11)	89	0.54
Scandinavian (0)	5	0.03
Scotch-Irish (252)	421	2.56
Scottish (224)	593	3.61
Slavic (0)	91	0.55
Slovak (0)	9	0.05
Swedish (75)	116	0.71
Swiss (0)	14	0.09
Welsh (10)	144	0.88
West Indian, ex. Hispanic (58)	70	0.43
Jamaican (44)	56	0.34
Trinidadian/Tobagonian (14)	14	0.09

Hispanic Origin	Population	%
Hispanic or Latino (of any race)	500	2.92
Central American, ex. Mexican	47	0.27
Costa Rican	2	0.01
Guatemalan	12	0.07
Honduran	11	0.06
Nicaraguan	2	0.01
Panamanian	7	0.04
Salvadoran	13	0.08
Cuban	21	0.12
Dominican Republic	12	0.07
Mexican	199	1.16
Puerto Rican	105	0.61
South American	52	0.30
Argentinean	3	0.02
Bolivian	1	0.01
Chilean	6	0.04
Colombian	12	0.07
Ecuadorian	14	0.08
Peruvian	6	0.04
Uruguayan	4	0.02
Venezuelan	6	0.04
Other Hispanic or Latino	64	0.37

Race*	Population	%
African-American/Black (6,331)	6,506	38.04
Not Hispanic (6,251)	6,409	37.47
Hispanic (80)	97	0.57
American Indian/Alaska Native (38)	120	0.70
Not Hispanic (27)	105	0.61
Hispanic (11)	15	0.09
Apache (0)	1	0.01
Blackfeet (1)	1	0.01
Cherokee (7)	48	0.28
Cheyenne (0)	1	0.01
Chippewa (0)	2	0.01
Lumbee (9)	15	0.09
Mexican American Ind. (1)	1	0.01
Potawatomi (0)	2	0.01
Sioux (0)	1	0.01
Asian (117)	147	0.86
Not Hispanic (113)	139	0.81
Hispanic (4)	8	0.05
Cambodian (1)	1	0.01
Chinese, ex. Taiwanese (29)	35	0.20
Filipino (23)	35	0.20
Indian (26)	28	0.16
Japanese (18)	22	0.13
Korean (13)	19	0.11
Laotian (1)	1	0.01
Malaysian (1)	1	0.01
Pakistani (1)	1	0.01
Vietnamese (2)	2	0.01
Hawaii Native/Pacific Islander (7)	18	0.11
Not Hispanic (6)	12	0.07
Hispanic (1)	6	0.04
Native Hawaiian (4)	6	0.04
Samoan (2)	5	0.03
White (10,187)	10,387	60.73
Not Hispanic (9,981)	10,152	59.36
Hispanic (206)	235	1.37

Dentsville

Place Type: CDP
County: Richland
Population: 14,062†

Ancestry‡	Population	%
African, Sub-Saharan (492)	528	3.92
African (492)	528	3.92
American (714)	714	5.30
Austrian (24)	24	0.18
British (30)	30	0.22
Croatian (0)	35	0.26
Danish (0)	99	0.73
English (210)	353	2.62
European (79)	79	0.59
French, ex. Basque (0)	30	0.22
French Canadian (113)	136	1.01
German (171)	366	2.72
Greek (38)	38	0.28
Guyanese (0)	45	0.33
Hungarian (0)	35	0.26
Irish (203)	417	3.09
Italian (0)	153	1.14
Norwegian (0)	11	0.08
Polish (61)	87	0.65
Russian (16)	16	0.12
Scotch-Irish (104)	230	1.71
Scottish (39)	135	1.00
Swedish (0)	6	0.04
Ukrainian (0)	17	0.13
West Indian, ex. Hispanic (73)	80	0.59
Haitian (73)	73	0.54
Jamaican (0)	7	0.05

Hispanic Origin	Population	%
Hispanic or Latino (of any race)	752	5.35
Central American, ex. Mexican	130	0.92
Costa Rican	4	0.03
Guatemalan	45	0.32
Honduran	32	0.23
Nicaraguan	5	0.04
Panamanian	41	0.29
Salvadoran	3	0.02
Cuban	36	0.26
Dominican Republic	37	0.26
Mexican	306	2.18
Puerto Rican	164	1.17
South American	23	0.16
Chilean	2	0.01
Colombian	10	0.07
Ecuadorian	2	0.01
Paraguayan	1	0.01
Peruvian	3	0.02
Venezuelan	5	0.04
Other Hispanic or Latino	56	0.40

Race*	Population	%
African-American/Black (9,742)	9,980	70.97
Not Hispanic (9,603)	9,807	69.74
Hispanic (139)	173	1.23
American Indian/Alaska Native (39)	118	0.84
Not Hispanic (28)	101	0.72
Hispanic (11)	17	0.12
Apache (0)	1	0.01
Blackfeet (0)	7	0.05
Cherokee (4)	34	0.24
Chickasaw (0)	2	0.01
Comanche (0)	1	0.01
Mexican American Ind. (1)	1	0.01
Navajo (0)	1	0.01
Pueblo (0)	3	0.02
Seminole (0)	2	0.01
Sioux (1)	1	0.01
South American Ind. (0)	1	0.01
Spanish American Ind. (7)	8	0.06
Asian (387)	476	3.39
Not Hispanic (386)	470	3.34
Hispanic (1)	6	0.04
Bangladeshi (9)	9	0.06
Burmese (3)	3	0.02
Cambodian (3)	3	0.02
Chinese, ex. Taiwanese (17)	25	0.18
Filipino (38)	63	0.45
Indian (180)	189	1.34
Indonesian (0)	1	0.01
Japanese (13)	24	0.17
Korean (46)	59	0.42
Nepalese (2)	2	0.01
Pakistani (41)	42	0.30
Taiwanese (2)	3	0.02
Thai (2)	11	0.08
Vietnamese (24)	26	0.18
Hawaii Native/Pacific Islander (19)	38	0.27
Not Hispanic (17)	30	0.21
Hispanic (2)	8	0.06
Guamanian/Chamorro (7)	8	0.06
Native Hawaiian (3)	6	0.04
Samoan (2)	3	0.02
White (3,182)	3,413	24.27
Not Hispanic (2,977)	3,165	22.51
Hispanic (205)	248	1.76

Easley

Place Type: City
County: Pickens
Population: 19,993†

Ancestry‡	Population	%
African, Sub-Saharan (87)	117	0.59
African (57)	57	0.29
South African (30)	60	0.30
Albanian (13)	13	0.07
American (3,486)	3,486	17.68

*Notes: † The Census 2010 population figure is used to calculate the percentages in the Hispanic Origin and Race categories. Ancestry percentages are based on the 2006-2010 American Community Survey population (not shown); ‡ Numbers in parentheses indicate the number of people reporting a single ancestry; * Numbers in parentheses indicate the number of persons reporting this race alone, not in combination with any other race; Please refer to the Explanation of Data for more information.*

Arab (27)	27	0.14
Arab (27)	27	0.14
Brazilian (152)	170	0.86
British (38)	58	0.29
Canadian (15)	45	0.23
Croatian (8)	28	0.14
Czech (0)	32	0.16
Czechoslovakian (11)	11	0.06
Danish (0)	33	0.17
Dutch (23)	168	0.85
English (1,013)	2,067	10.48
European (22)	37	0.19
Finnish (63)	63	0.32
French, ex. Basque (57)	420	2.13
French Canadian (36)	47	0.24
German (904)	2,273	11.53
Greek (69)	90	0.46
Hungarian (0)	24	0.12
Irish (1,092)	2,513	12.74
Italian (255)	570	2.89
Norwegian (63)	159	0.81
Pennsylvania German (0)	28	0.14
Polish (64)	247	1.25
Romanian (0)	72	0.37
Russian (27)	61	0.31
Scotch-Irish (593)	1,120	5.68
Scottish (213)	608	3.08
Slavic (0)	17	0.09
Slovak (0)	12	0.06
Swedish (0)	53	0.27
Swiss (25)	74	0.38
Ukrainian (5)	23	0.12
Welsh (14)	62	0.31

Hispanic Origin	Population	%
Hispanic or Latino (of any race)	1,115	5.58
Central American, ex. Mexican	93	0.47
Costa Rican	19	0.10
Guatemalan	9	0.05
Honduran	33	0.17
Nicaraguan	15	0.08
Panamanian	2	0.01
Salvadoran	8	0.04
Other Central American	7	0.04
Cuban	13	0.07
Dominican Republic	13	0.07
Mexican	737	3.69
Puerto Rican	90	0.45
South American	92	0.46
Argentinean	1	0.01
Colombian	75	0.38
Ecuadorian	2	0.01
Peruvian	11	0.06
Venezuelan	3	0.02
Other Hispanic or Latino	77	0.39

Race*	Population	%
African-American/Black (2,277)	2,449	12.25
Not Hispanic (2,260)	2,425	12.13
Hispanic (17)	24	0.12
American Indian/Alaska Native (32)	121	0.61
Not Hispanic (28)	113	0.57
Hispanic (4)	8	0.04
Aleut *(Alaska Native)* (0)	1	0.01
Blackfeet (0)	2	0.01
Cherokee (5)	47	0.24
Cheyenne (0)	1	0.01
Chippewa (2)	2	0.01
Choctaw (2)	5	0.03
Iroquois (0)	2	0.01
Lumbee (1)	3	0.02
Navajo (1)	1	0.01
Potawatomi (0)	3	0.02
Seminole (1)	1	0.01
Sioux (0)	3	0.02
South American Ind. (0)	1	0.01
Spanish American Ind. (3)	3	0.02
Asian (154)	211	1.06
Not Hispanic (153)	198	0.99
Hispanic (1)	13	0.07
Cambodian (1)	1	0.01
Chinese, ex. Taiwanese (36)	44	0.22
Filipino (20)	34	0.17
Hmong (1)	1	0.01
Indian (43)	56	0.28
Indonesian (4)	4	0.02
Japanese (4)	13	0.07
Korean (21)	27	0.14
Laotian (0)	4	0.02
Pakistani (4)	4	0.02
Taiwanese (4)	4	0.02
Thai (3)	3	0.02
Vietnamese (9)	12	0.06
Hawaii Native/Pacific Islander (4)	15	0.08
Not Hispanic (4)	13	0.07
Hispanic (0)	2	0.01
Guamanian/Chamorro (3)	5	0.03
Native Hawaiian (1)	9	0.05
White (16,621)	16,949	84.77
Not Hispanic (16,114)	16,392	81.99
Hispanic (507)	557	2.79

Five Forks

Place Type: CDP
County: Greenville
Population: 14,140†

Ancestry‡	Population	%
African, Sub-Saharan (242)	242	1.84
African (25)	25	0.19
Ethiopian (217)	217	1.65
American (1,074)	1,074	8.18
Arab (43)	53	0.40
Egyptian (18)	18	0.14
Lebanese (25)	35	0.27
Austrian (0)	48	0.37
Belgian (0)	52	0.40
British (33)	119	0.91
Canadian (86)	123	0.94
Cypriot (14)	14	0.11
Danish (14)	55	0.42
Dutch (32)	217	1.65
Eastern European (67)	72	0.55
English (642)	1,836	13.98
European (306)	338	2.57
Finnish (10)	93	0.71
French, ex. Basque (107)	616	4.69
French Canadian (86)	302	2.30
German (1,001)	2,721	20.71
Greek (14)	74	0.56
Hungarian (0)	103	0.78
Icelander (0)	14	0.11
Irish (474)	2,058	15.67
Italian (506)	1,335	10.16
Lithuanian (0)	12	0.09
Macedonian (10)	10	0.08
Northern European (59)	59	0.45
Norwegian (41)	248	1.89
Polish (124)	494	3.76
Romanian (21)	21	0.16
Russian (43)	110	0.84
Scandinavian (0)	7	0.05
Scotch-Irish (224)	398	3.03
Scottish (198)	469	3.57
Slovak (25)	99	0.75
Swedish (97)	187	1.42
Swiss (34)	34	0.26
Turkish (63)	63	0.48
Ukrainian (43)	56	0.43
Welsh (32)	138	1.05

Hispanic Origin	Population	%
Hispanic or Latino (of any race)	597	4.22
Central American, ex. Mexican	52	0.37
Costa Rican	15	0.11
Guatemalan	10	0.07
Honduran	3	0.02
Nicaraguan	4	0.03
Panamanian	4	0.03
Salvadoran	16	0.11
Cuban	47	0.33
Dominican Republic	7	0.05
Mexican	183	1.29
Puerto Rican	85	0.60
South American	168	1.19
Argentinean	7	0.05
Bolivian	8	0.06
Chilean	9	0.06
Colombian	125	0.88
Paraguayan	1	0.01
Peruvian	4	0.03
Uruguayan	4	0.03
Venezuelan	9	0.06
Other South American	1	0.01
Other Hispanic or Latino	55	0.39

Race*	Population	%
African-American/Black (771)	833	5.89
Not Hispanic (763)	817	5.78
Hispanic (8)	16	0.11
American Indian/Alaska Native (32)	67	0.47
Not Hispanic (28)	62	0.44
Hispanic (4)	5	0.04
Apache (1)	2	0.01
Canadian/French Am. Ind. (0)	1	0.01
Cherokee (6)	17	0.12
Cheyenne (1)	1	0.01
Chickasaw (2)	2	0.01
Chippewa (0)	2	0.01
Choctaw (2)	2	0.01
Lumbee (3)	4	0.03
Ottawa (0)	1	0.01
Potawatomi (1)	1	0.01
Asian (616)	734	5.19
Not Hispanic (614)	724	5.12
Hispanic (2)	10	0.07
Bangladeshi (5)	5	0.04
Cambodian (2)	2	0.01
Chinese, ex. Taiwanese (154)	169	1.20
Filipino (51)	75	0.53
Indian (241)	254	1.80
Japanese (37)	55	0.39
Korean (63)	74	0.52
Malaysian (1)	2	0.01
Nepalese (3)	3	0.02
Pakistani (17)	17	0.12
Sri Lankan (1)	1	0.01
Taiwanese (0)	3	0.02
Thai (4)	6	0.04
Vietnamese (24)	32	0.23
Hawaii Native/Pacific Islander (1)	5	0.04
Not Hispanic (1)	5	0.04
Native Hawaiian (1)	2	0.01
White (12,366)	12,549	88.75
Not Hispanic (11,927)	12,091	85.51
Hispanic (439)	458	3.24

Florence

Place Type: City
County: Florence
Population: 37,056†

Ancestry‡	Population	%
African, Sub-Saharan (200)	200	0.56
African (200)	200	0.56
American (2,309)	2,309	6.41
Arab (29)	85	0.24
Lebanese (29)	29	0.08
Syrian (0)	56	0.16
Austrian (0)	37	0.10
British (88)	134	0.37
Canadian (32)	32	0.09
Croatian (0)	85	0.24
Czech (68)	113	0.31
Czechoslovakian (23)	23	0.06
Danish (12)	36	0.10
Dutch (26)	235	0.65
English (1,640)	2,974	8.26

*Notes: † The Census 2010 population figure is used to calculate the percentages in the Hispanic Origin and Race categories. Ancestry percentages are based on the 2006-2010 American Community Survey population (not shown); ‡ Numbers in parentheses indicate the number of people reporting a single ancestry; * Numbers in parentheses indicate the number of persons reporting this race alone, not in combination with any other race; Please refer to the Explanation of Data for more information.*

European (320)	320	0.89
Finnish (9)	9	0.02
French, ex. Basque (136)	646	1.79
French Canadian (43)	102	0.28
German (940)	2,640	7.33
Greek (125)	225	0.62
Hungarian (0)	32	0.09
Iranian (34)	34	0.09
Irish (899)	1,904	5.29
Italian (366)	650	1.80
Lithuanian (12)	12	0.03
Norwegian (96)	187	0.52
Polish (133)	505	1.40
Romanian (11)	80	0.22
Russian (33)	74	0.21
Scandinavian (0)	13	0.04
Scotch-Irish (1,421)	2,209	6.13
Scottish (346)	780	2.17
Serbian (14)	27	0.07
Slavic (0)	10	0.03
Slovak (9)	38	0.11
Swedish (0)	106	0.29
Swiss (11)	76	0.21
Turkish (10)	10	0.03
Ukrainian (16)	16	0.04
Welsh (16)	121	0.34
West Indian, ex. Hispanic (60)	85	0.24
Bahamian (0)	15	0.04
Dutch West Indian (14)	14	0.04
Jamaican (25)	25	0.07
Trinidadian/Tobagonian (0)	10	0.03
West Indian (21)	21	0.06
Yugoslavian (17)	17	0.05

Hispanic Origin	Population	%
Hispanic or Latino (of any race)	553	1.49
Central American, ex. Mexican	39	0.11
Costa Rican	15	0.04
Guatemalan	4	0.01
Honduran	4	0.01
Nicaraguan	1	<0.01
Panamanian	7	0.02
Salvadoran	8	0.02
Cuban	19	0.05
Dominican Republic	14	0.04
Mexican	238	0.64
Puerto Rican	147	0.40
South American	39	0.11
Argentinean	1	<0.01
Bolivian	3	0.01
Colombian	19	0.05
Ecuadorian	6	0.02
Peruvian	6	0.02
Uruguayan	2	0.01
Venezuelan	2	0.01
Other Hispanic or Latino	57	0.15

Race*	Population	%
African-American/Black (17,038)	17,351	46.82
Not Hispanic (16,972)	17,261	46.58
Hispanic (66)	90	0.24
American Indian/Alaska Native (106)	261	0.70
Not Hispanic (91)	240	0.65
Hispanic (15)	21	0.06
Apache (0)	1	<0.01
Blackfeet (0)	4	0.01
Canadian/French Am. Ind. (1)	1	<0.01
Cherokee (11)	49	0.13
Chippewa (1)	7	0.02
Choctaw (0)	2	0.01
Creek (2)	2	0.01
Delaware (0)	3	0.01
Lumbee (19)	29	0.08
Asian (680)	787	2.12
Not Hispanic (677)	782	2.11
Hispanic (3)	5	0.01
Burmese (3)	3	0.01
Cambodian (1)	1	<0.01
Chinese, ex. Taiwanese (160)	173	0.47
Filipino (133)	168	0.45
Indian (154)	165	0.45
Japanese (27)	39	0.11
Korean (59)	76	0.21
Laotian (5)	5	0.01
Malaysian (2)	2	0.01
Nepalese (7)	8	0.02
Pakistani (7)	11	0.03
Taiwanese (26)	29	0.08
Thai (12)	16	0.04
Vietnamese (69)	72	0.19
Hawaii Native/Pacific Islander (11)	39	0.11
Not Hispanic (11)	39	0.11
Fijian (0)	3	0.01
Guamanian/Chamorro (1)	2	0.01
Native Hawaiian (5)	9	0.02
Samoan (2)	8	0.02
White (18,535)	18,866	50.91
Not Hispanic (18,295)	18,595	50.18
Hispanic (240)	271	0.73

Forest Acres

Place Type: City
County: Richland
Population: 10,361†

Ancestry‡	Population	%
African, Sub-Saharan (51)	51	0.49
African (51)	51	0.49
American (1,416)	1,416	13.60
Arab (65)	124	1.19
Lebanese (21)	46	0.44
Syrian (0)	34	0.33
Other Arab (44)	44	0.42
Austrian (11)	11	0.11
Brazilian (28)	28	0.27
British (46)	81	0.78
Canadian (0)	18	0.17
Celtic (0)	13	0.12
Croatian (11)	22	0.21
Czech (11)	11	0.11
Czechoslovakian (0)	7	0.07
Danish (0)	12	0.12
Dutch (66)	161	1.55
English (1,111)	1,978	19.00
European (171)	201	1.93
Finnish (0)	20	0.19
French, ex. Basque (41)	435	4.18
French Canadian (27)	37	0.36
German (449)	1,319	12.67
Greek (29)	70	0.67
Hungarian (0)	39	0.37
Irish (383)	1,158	11.12
Italian (41)	136	1.31
Norwegian (0)	57	0.55
Pennsylvania German (0)	11	0.11
Polish (38)	183	1.76
Russian (10)	76	0.73
Scandinavian (0)	10	0.10
Scotch-Irish (663)	944	9.07
Scottish (188)	489	4.70
Swedish (0)	82	0.79
Swiss (0)	23	0.22
Ukrainian (48)	121	1.16
Welsh (9)	48	0.46
West Indian, ex. Hispanic (0)	10	0.10
Jamaican (0)	10	0.10

Hispanic Origin	Population	%
Hispanic or Latino (of any race)	313	3.02
Central American, ex. Mexican	49	0.47
Costa Rican	4	0.04
Guatemalan	13	0.13
Honduran	6	0.06
Nicaraguan	2	0.02
Panamanian	20	0.19
Salvadoran	4	0.04
Cuban	22	0.21
Dominican Republic	8	0.08
Mexican	77	0.74
Puerto Rican	78	0.75
South American	44	0.42
Bolivian	1	0.01
Chilean	4	0.04
Colombian	17	0.16
Ecuadorian	3	0.03
Peruvian	9	0.09
Venezuelan	7	0.07
Other South American	3	0.03
Other Hispanic or Latino	35	0.34

Race*	Population	%
African-American/Black (2,010)	2,127	20.53
Not Hispanic (1,983)	2,083	20.10
Hispanic (27)	44	0.42
American Indian/Alaska Native (22)	74	0.71
Not Hispanic (14)	61	0.59
Hispanic (8)	13	0.13
Apache (0)	1	0.01
Blackfeet (0)	5	0.05
Cherokee (5)	32	0.31
Chickasaw (0)	2	0.02
Chippewa (0)	2	0.02
Mexican American Ind. (1)	1	0.01
Potawatomi (1)	1	0.01
Seminole (1)	1	0.01
Tohono O'Odham (4)	4	0.04
Asian (155)	207	2.00
Not Hispanic (151)	199	1.92
Hispanic (4)	8	0.08
Burmese (7)	7	0.07
Chinese, ex. Taiwanese (23)	34	0.33
Filipino (18)	22	0.21
Hmong (7)	7	0.07
Indian (58)	66	0.64
Japanese (9)	20	0.19
Korean (18)	34	0.33
Pakistani (2)	2	0.02
Sri Lankan (1)	1	0.01
Thai (1)	6	0.06
Vietnamese (5)	7	0.07
Hawaii Native/Pacific Islander (6)	16	0.15
Not Hispanic (6)	14	0.14
Hispanic (0)	2	0.02
Guamanian/Chamorro (1)	3	0.03
Native Hawaiian (1)	6	0.06
Samoan (1)	1	0.01
White (7,875)	8,031	77.51
Not Hispanic (7,732)	7,856	75.82
Hispanic (143)	175	1.69

Fort Mill

Place Type: Town
County: York
Population: 10,811†

Ancestry‡	Population	%
African, Sub-Saharan (12)	12	0.12
South African (12)	12	0.12
American (785)	785	7.64
Arab (46)	46	0.45
Egyptian (46)	46	0.45
Austrian (9)	9	0.09
British (14)	41	0.40
Cajun (0)	25	0.24
Canadian (0)	11	0.11
Czech (0)	65	0.63
Czechoslovakian (6)	6	0.06
Danish (0)	13	0.13
Dutch (34)	89	0.87
Eastern European (18)	18	0.18
English (773)	1,384	13.47
European (144)	144	1.40
French, ex. Basque (29)	65	0.63
French Canadian (22)	53	0.52
German (664)	1,822	17.74
Greek (21)	71	0.69
Hungarian (13)	95	0.92
Irish (291)	1,207	11.75

*Notes: † The Census 2010 population figure is used to calculate the percentages in the Hispanic Origin and Race categories. Ancestry percentages are based on the 2006-2010 American Community Survey population (not shown); ‡ Numbers in parentheses indicate the number of people reporting a single ancestry; * Numbers in parentheses indicate the number of persons reporting this race alone, not in combination with any other race; Please refer to the Explanation of Data for more information.*

Italian (218)	570	5.55
Lithuanian (0)	83	0.81
Norwegian (31)	152	1.48
Pennsylvania German (40)	40	0.39
Polish (227)	485	4.72
Romanian (0)	7	0.07
Russian (19)	48	0.47
Scotch-Irish (245)	455	4.43
Scottish (161)	365	3.55
Slovene (0)	14	0.14
Swedish (31)	183	1.78
Welsh (11)	54	0.53

Hispanic Origin	Population	%
Hispanic or Latino (of any race)	313	2.90
Central American, ex. Mexican	44	0.41
Costa Rican	10	0.09
Guatemalan	8	0.07
Honduran	5	0.05
Nicaraguan	3	0.03
Panamanian	11	0.10
Salvadoran	6	0.06
Other Central American	1	0.01
Cuban	21	0.19
Dominican Republic	19	0.18
Mexican	82	0.76
Puerto Rican	87	0.80
South American	46	0.43
Argentinean	2	0.02
Colombian	25	0.23
Ecuadorian	4	0.04
Peruvian	14	0.13
Venezuelan	1	0.01
Other Hispanic or Latino	14	0.13

Race*	Population	%
African-American/Black (1,901)	2,029	18.77
Not Hispanic (1,881)	1,996	18.46
Hispanic (20)	33	0.31
American Indian/Alaska Native (40)	85	0.79
Not Hispanic (39)	79	0.73
Hispanic (1)	6	0.06
Apache (3)	4	0.04
Blackfeet (0)	4	0.04
Cherokee (1)	20	0.18
Chippewa (2)	4	0.04
Choctaw (0)	9	0.08
Creek (2)	2	0.02
Iroquois (0)	2	0.02
Lumbee (10)	11	0.10
Mexican American Ind. (0)	1	0.01
Navajo (4)	4	0.04
Sioux (0)	1	0.01
Asian (136)	179	1.66
Not Hispanic (136)	179	1.66
Burmese (0)	1	0.01
Cambodian (1)	3	0.03
Chinese, ex. Taiwanese (15)	18	0.17
Filipino (18)	27	0.25
Indian (44)	54	0.50
Indonesian (1)	1	0.01
Japanese (4)	7	0.06
Korean (12)	16	0.15
Laotian (1)	1	0.01
Pakistani (2)	6	0.06
Taiwanese (0)	3	0.03
Thai (2)	3	0.03
Vietnamese (22)	23	0.21
Hawaii Native/Pacific Islander (1)	4	0.04
Not Hispanic (0)	1	0.01
Hispanic (1)	3	0.03
Guamanian/Chamorro (1)	1	0.01
White (8,393)	8,595	79.50
Not Hispanic (8,236)	8,411	77.80
Hispanic (157)	184	1.70

Fountain Inn

Place Type: City
County: Greenville
Population: 7,799†

Ancestry‡	Population	%
American (555)	555	7.49
Austrian (0)	10	0.13
Dutch (11)	62	0.84
English (180)	596	8.04
French, ex. Basque (11)	122	1.65
French Canadian (29)	74	1.00
German (126)	512	6.91
Greek (45)	45	0.61
Irish (387)	773	10.43
Italian (45)	251	3.39
Norwegian (0)	10	0.13
Polish (23)	32	0.43
Russian (0)	11	0.15
Scotch-Irish (47)	267	3.60
Scottish (23)	102	1.38
Swedish (0)	20	0.27
Welsh (15)	42	0.57

Hispanic Origin	Population	%
Hispanic or Latino (of any race)	469	6.01
Central American, ex. Mexican	37	0.47
Costa Rican	1	0.01
Guatemalan	8	0.10
Honduran	25	0.32
Panamanian	2	0.03
Salvadoran	1	0.01
Cuban	11	0.14
Dominican Republic	17	0.22
Mexican	182	2.33
Puerto Rican	82	1.05
South American	116	1.49
Chilean	1	0.01
Colombian	72	0.92
Ecuadorian	32	0.41
Peruvian	8	0.10
Uruguayan	3	0.04
Other Hispanic or Latino	24	0.31

Race*	Population	%
African-American/Black (2,432)	2,531	32.45
Not Hispanic (2,416)	2,499	32.04
Hispanic (16)	32	0.41
American Indian/Alaska Native (22)	46	0.59
Not Hispanic (21)	45	0.58
Hispanic (1)	1	0.01
Blackfeet (0)	1	0.01
Canadian/French Am. Ind. (0)	4	0.05
Cherokee (9)	14	0.18
Choctaw (1)	1	0.01
Creek (0)	1	0.01
Mexican American Ind. (1)	1	0.01
Navajo (6)	7	0.09
Asian (23)	53	0.68
Not Hispanic (23)	52	0.67
Hispanic (0)	1	0.01
Chinese, ex. Taiwanese (0)	5	0.06
Filipino (8)	19	0.24
Hmong (1)	7	0.09
Indian (2)	2	0.03
Japanese (2)	7	0.09
Korean (10)	16	0.21
Hawaii Native/Pacific Islander (13)	27	0.35
Not Hispanic (13)	27	0.35
Guamanian/Chamorro (0)	4	0.05
Native Hawaiian (0)	3	0.04
Samoan (0)	1	0.01
Tongan (1)	3	0.04
White (4,965)	5,088	65.24
Not Hispanic (4,721)	4,833	61.97
Hispanic (244)	255	3.27

Gaffney

Place Type: City
County: Cherokee
Population: 12,414†

Ancestry‡	Population	%
African, Sub-Saharan (62)	62	0.50
African (62)	62	0.50
American (1,111)	1,111	8.89
Austrian (7)	7	0.06
British (35)	76	0.61
Bulgarian (5)	5	0.04
Dutch (0)	116	0.93
English (352)	484	3.87
European (19)	19	0.15
French, ex. Basque (125)	143	1.14
German (425)	781	6.25
Hungarian (9)	9	0.07
Irish (409)	710	5.68
Italian (46)	46	0.37
Polish (10)	28	0.22
Romanian (17)	17	0.14
Russian (17)	17	0.14
Scotch-Irish (369)	474	3.79
Scottish (72)	72	0.58
Welsh (38)	57	0.46
West Indian, ex. Hispanic (24)	36	0.29
West Indian (24)	36	0.29

Hispanic Origin	Population	%
Hispanic or Latino (of any race)	381	3.07
Central American, ex. Mexican	41	0.33
Costa Rican	3	0.02
Guatemalan	30	0.24
Honduran	1	0.01
Nicaraguan	2	0.02
Panamanian	4	0.03
Salvadoran	1	0.01
Cuban	4	0.03
Dominican Republic	6	0.05
Mexican	226	1.82
Puerto Rican	58	0.47
South American	14	0.11
Colombian	8	0.06
Paraguayan	1	0.01
Peruvian	3	0.02
Venezuelan	2	0.02
Other Hispanic or Latino	32	0.26

Race*	Population	%
African-American/Black (5,673)	5,811	46.81
Not Hispanic (5,639)	5,769	46.47
Hispanic (34)	42	0.34
American Indian/Alaska Native (31)	64	0.52
Not Hispanic (30)	62	0.50
Hispanic (1)	2	0.02
Blackfeet (0)	1	0.01
Cherokee (9)	19	0.15
Cheyenne (1)	1	0.01
Choctaw (1)	1	0.01
Inupiat *(Alaska Native)* (2)	2	0.02
Lumbee (3)	3	0.02
Pueblo (0)	4	0.03
Asian (108)	124	1.00
Not Hispanic (108)	122	0.98
Hispanic (0)	2	0.02
Chinese, ex. Taiwanese (11)	12	0.10
Filipino (15)	19	0.15
Indian (51)	57	0.46
Indonesian (1)	3	0.02
Japanese (6)	8	0.06
Korean (5)	5	0.04
Pakistani (5)	5	0.04
Thai (1)	1	0.01
Vietnamese (5)	5	0.04
Hawaii Native/Pacific Islander (11)	19	0.15
Not Hispanic (3)	9	0.07
Hispanic (8)	10	0.08
Guamanian/Chamorro (9)	12	0.10

*Notes: † The Census 2010 population figure is used to calculate the percentages in the Hispanic Origin and Race categories. Ancestry percentages are based on the 2006-2010 American Community Survey population (not shown); ‡ Numbers in parentheses indicate the number of people reporting a single ancestry; * Numbers in parentheses indicate the number of persons reporting this race alone, not in combination with any other race; Please refer to the Explanation of Data for more information.*

Native Hawaiian (1)	1	0.01
Samoan (1)	2	0.02
White (6,214)	6,383	51.42
Not Hispanic (6,073)	6,224	50.14
Hispanic (141)	159	1.28

Gantt

Place Type: CDP
County: Greenville
Population: 14,229†

Ancestry‡	Population	%
African, Sub-Saharan (101)	101	0.73
African (81)	81	0.58
Other Sub-Saharan African (20)	20	0.14
American (1,062)	1,062	7.65
Belgian (1)	1	0.01
Czech (0)	12	0.09
Dutch (0)	50	0.36
English (367)	736	5.30
European (90)	98	0.71
French, ex. Basque (13)	161	1.16
French Canadian (12)	40	0.29
German (134)	499	3.60
Greek (83)	93	0.67
Irish (213)	496	3.58
Italian (0)	44	0.32
Northern European (11)	11	0.08
Norwegian (34)	34	0.25
Polish (28)	128	0.92
Russian (0)	15	0.11
Scotch-Irish (77)	227	1.64
Scottish (22)	144	1.04
Slovak (10)	20	0.14
Swedish (15)	25	0.18
Swiss (0)	9	0.06
Welsh (0)	9	0.06
West Indian, ex. Hispanic (18)	36	0.26
West Indian (18)	36	0.26

Hispanic Origin	Population	%
Hispanic or Latino (of any race)	1,877	13.19
Central American, ex. Mexican	98	0.69
Costa Rican	4	0.03
Guatemalan	10	0.07
Honduran	59	0.41
Nicaraguan	2	0.01
Panamanian	5	0.04
Salvadoran	18	0.13
Cuban	14	0.10
Dominican Republic	9	0.06
Mexican	1,610	11.31
Puerto Rican	55	0.39
South American	25	0.18
Colombian	21	0.15
Ecuadorian	1	0.01
Peruvian	2	0.01
Venezuelan	1	0.01
Other Hispanic or Latino	66	0.46

Race*	Population	%
African-American/Black (8,418)	8,582	60.31
Not Hispanic (8,359)	8,499	59.73
Hispanic (59)	83	0.58
American Indian/Alaska Native (61)	107	0.75
Not Hispanic (24)	66	0.46
Hispanic (37)	41	0.29
Cherokee (1)	9	0.06
Cheyenne (0)	1	0.01
Chippewa (1)	1	0.01
Iroquois (1)	1	0.01
Lumbee (3)	6	0.04
Mexican American Ind. (29)	29	0.20
Sioux (1)	1	0.01
Asian (36)	47	0.33
Not Hispanic (32)	43	0.30
Hispanic (4)	4	0.03
Chinese, ex. Taiwanese (9)	9	0.06
Filipino (6)	13	0.09
Indian (1)	2	0.01
Japanese (2)	2	0.01
Korean (6)	7	0.05
Taiwanese (2)	2	0.01
Thai (2)	2	0.01
Vietnamese (6)	6	0.04
Hawaii Native/Pacific Islander (5)	11	0.08
Not Hispanic (4)	7	0.05
Hispanic (1)	4	0.03
Guamanian/Chamorro (2)	4	0.03
Native Hawaiian (3)	3	0.02
Samoan (0)	1	0.01
White (4,137)	4,347	30.55
Not Hispanic (3,756)	3,901	27.42
Hispanic (381)	446	3.13

Garden City

Place Type: CDP
County: Horry
Population: 9,209†

Ancestry‡	Population	%
African, Sub-Saharan (22)	22	0.25
African (22)	22	0.25
American (1,925)	1,925	21.72
Arab (11)	37	0.42
Lebanese (0)	26	0.29
Syrian (11)	11	0.12
Armenian (14)	14	0.16
Assyrian/Chaldean/Syriac (9)	9	0.10
Austrian (25)	25	0.28
Belgian (0)	13	0.15
British (41)	63	0.71
Canadian (46)	46	0.52
Czech (13)	26	0.29
Dutch (79)	153	1.73
Eastern European (20)	20	0.23
English (748)	1,474	16.63
European (14)	14	0.16
French, ex. Basque (260)	407	4.59
French Canadian (28)	28	0.32
German (638)	1,524	17.19
Greek (25)	69	0.78
Hungarian (88)	105	1.18
Irish (648)	1,578	17.80
Italian (314)	617	6.96
Lithuanian (0)	14	0.16
Norwegian (14)	14	0.16
Pennsylvania German (13)	13	0.15
Polish (92)	142	1.60
Portuguese (13)	13	0.15
Russian (27)	76	0.86
Scandinavian (13)	13	0.15
Scotch-Irish (213)	305	3.44
Scottish (102)	188	2.12
Slovak (0)	13	0.15
Swedish (0)	29	0.33
Swiss (13)	26	0.29
Ukrainian (119)	145	1.64
Welsh (12)	83	0.94
Yugoslavian (0)	25	0.28

Hispanic Origin	Population	%
Hispanic or Latino (of any race)	269	2.92
Central American, ex. Mexican	36	0.39
Costa Rican	1	0.01
Guatemalan	27	0.29
Honduran	7	0.08
Salvadoran	1	0.01
Cuban	10	0.11
Dominican Republic	2	0.02
Mexican	148	1.61
Puerto Rican	40	0.43
South American	14	0.15
Argentinean	1	0.01
Colombian	5	0.05
Ecuadorian	8	0.09
Other Hispanic or Latino	19	0.21

Race*	Population	%
African-American/Black (153)	203	2.20
Not Hispanic (144)	191	2.07
Hispanic (9)	12	0.13
American Indian/Alaska Native (25)	96	1.04
Not Hispanic (25)	96	1.04
Blackfeet (0)	3	0.03
Cherokee (11)	39	0.42
Chippewa (0)	2	0.02
Creek (1)	1	0.01
Iroquois (0)	1	0.01
Lumbee (3)	6	0.07
Sioux (1)	2	0.02
Asian (28)	49	0.53
Not Hispanic (28)	49	0.53
Cambodian (1)	1	0.01
Chinese, ex. Taiwanese (9)	11	0.12
Filipino (7)	9	0.10
Indian (6)	10	0.11
Japanese (1)	9	0.10
Thai (0)	2	0.02
Vietnamese (4)	6	0.07
Hawaii Native/Pacific Islander (13)	15	0.16
Not Hispanic (6)	7	0.08
Hispanic (7)	8	0.09
Guamanian/Chamorro (8)	9	0.10
White (8,776)	8,902	96.67
Not Hispanic (8,599)	8,719	94.68
Hispanic (177)	183	1.99

Georgetown

Place Type: City
County: Georgetown
Population: 9,163†

Ancestry‡	Population	%
African, Sub-Saharan (6)	6	0.06
African (6)	6	0.06
American (519)	519	5.58
Arab (0)	35	0.38
Lebanese (0)	35	0.38
Austrian (0)	55	0.59
British (21)	30	0.32
Dutch (22)	67	0.72
Eastern European (14)	14	0.15
English (467)	599	6.44
European (71)	71	0.76
French, ex. Basque (9)	42	0.45
French Canadian (11)	11	0.12
German (130)	457	4.91
Irish (224)	444	4.77
Italian (24)	94	1.01
Norwegian (43)	43	0.46
Polish (12)	33	0.35
Scotch-Irish (60)	112	1.20
Scottish (12)	102	1.10
Swedish (19)	59	0.63
Swiss (31)	65	0.70
Welsh (19)	25	0.27
West Indian, ex. Hispanic (8)	8	0.09
Jamaican (8)	8	0.09

Hispanic Origin	Population	%
Hispanic or Latino (of any race)	490	5.35
Central American, ex. Mexican	49	0.53
Guatemalan	21	0.23
Honduran	9	0.10
Panamanian	1	0.01
Salvadoran	18	0.20
Cuban	7	0.08
Mexican	372	4.06
Puerto Rican	41	0.45
South American	5	0.05
Colombian	5	0.05
Other Hispanic or Latino	16	0.17

Race*	Population	%
African-American/Black (5,192)	5,277	57.59
Not Hispanic (5,161)	5,236	57.14

*Notes: † The Census 2010 population figure is used to calculate the percentages in the Hispanic Origin and Race categories. Ancestry percentages are based on the 2006-2010 American Community Survey population (not shown); ‡ Numbers in parentheses indicate the number of people reporting a single ancestry; * Numbers in parentheses indicate the number of persons reporting this race alone, not in combination with any other race; Please refer to the Explanation of Data for more information.*

Hispanic (31)	41	0.45
American Indian/Alaska Native (20)	66	0.72
Not Hispanic (19)	64	0.70
Hispanic (1)	2	0.02
Blackfeet (0)	4	0.04
Cherokee (5)	22	0.24
Chickasaw (1)	1	0.01
Iroquois (0)	2	0.02
Lumbee (0)	5	0.05
Asian (60)	78	0.85
Not Hispanic (60)	77	0.84
Hispanic (0)	1	0.01
Chinese, ex. Taiwanese (21)	24	0.26
Filipino (9)	12	0.13
Indian (20)	26	0.28
Japanese (0)	1	0.01
Korean (5)	8	0.09
Thai (1)	3	0.03
Vietnamese (2)	2	0.02
Hawaii Native/Pacific Islander (5)	8	0.09
Not Hispanic (0)	1	0.01
Hispanic (5)	7	0.08
Native Hawaiian (5)	7	0.08
White (3,461)	3,530	38.52
Not Hispanic (3,325)	3,382	36.91
Hispanic (136)	148	1.62

Goose Creek

Place Type: City
County: Berkeley
Population: 35,938†

Ancestry‡	Population	%
African, Sub-Saharan (51)	51	0.15
African (51)	51	0.15
American (3,513)	3,513	10.10
Arab (65)	65	0.19
Other Arab (65)	65	0.19
Armenian (0)	2	0.01
Austrian (44)	44	0.13
Belgian (23)	25	0.07
Brazilian (278)	278	0.80
British (48)	209	0.60
Bulgarian (0)	9	0.03
Canadian (0)	61	0.18
Croatian (0)	19	0.05
Czech (67)	250	0.72
Czechoslovakian (9)	17	0.05
Danish (33)	53	0.15
Dutch (49)	289	0.83
English (999)	3,076	8.85
European (463)	477	1.37
Finnish (42)	54	0.16
French, ex. Basque (137)	827	2.38
French Canadian (48)	158	0.45
German (1,861)	5,005	14.40
Greek (20)	54	0.16
Hungarian (10)	73	0.21
Icelander (0)	13	0.04
Irish (1,427)	3,872	11.14
Italian (592)	1,471	4.23
Lithuanian (36)	36	0.10
Norwegian (72)	236	0.68
Polish (276)	681	1.96
Portuguese (13)	13	0.04
Romanian (0)	15	0.04
Russian (0)	54	0.16
Scandinavian (13)	42	0.12
Scotch-Irish (626)	1,156	3.33
Scottish (366)	1,333	3.83
Slavic (31)	91	0.26
Slovak (9)	42	0.12
Swedish (162)	288	0.83
Swiss (18)	60	0.17
Ukrainian (26)	38	0.11
Welsh (149)	330	0.95
West Indian, ex. Hispanic (0)	49	0.14
Belizean (0)	10	0.03
Haitian (0)	27	0.08
West Indian (0)	12	0.03

Hispanic Origin	Population	%
Hispanic or Latino (of any race)	2,203	6.13
Central American, ex. Mexican	268	0.75
Costa Rican	8	0.02
Guatemalan	67	0.19
Honduran	79	0.22
Nicaraguan	20	0.06
Panamanian	31	0.09
Salvadoran	63	0.18
Cuban	78	0.22
Dominican Republic	75	0.21
Mexican	841	2.34
Puerto Rican	448	1.25
South American	220	0.61
Argentinean	33	0.09
Bolivian	4	0.01
Chilean	8	0.02
Colombian	92	0.26
Ecuadorian	42	0.12
Peruvian	25	0.07
Uruguayan	2	0.01
Venezuelan	14	0.04
Other Hispanic or Latino	273	0.76

Race*	Population	%
African-American/Black (6,560)	7,065	19.66
Not Hispanic (6,460)	6,902	19.21
Hispanic (100)	163	0.45
American Indian/Alaska Native (184)	456	1.27
Not Hispanic (156)	412	1.15
Hispanic (28)	44	0.12
Aleut *(Alaska Native)* (3)	5	0.01
Apache (2)	2	0.01
Blackfeet (3)	17	0.05
Canadian/French Am. Ind. (2)	3	0.01
Central American Ind. (4)	6	0.02
Cherokee (41)	126	0.35
Chippewa (0)	5	0.01
Choctaw (1)	9	0.03
Comanche (5)	5	0.01
Creek (3)	7	0.02
Delaware (2)	4	0.01
Houma (3)	3	0.01
Inupiat *(Alaska Native)* (0)	1	<0.01
Iroquois (5)	10	0.03
Kiowa (1)	1	<0.01
Lumbee (13)	19	0.05
Mexican American Ind. (2)	4	0.01
Navajo (0)	4	0.01
Osage (0)	2	0.01
Potawatomi (2)	2	0.01
Seminole (1)	4	0.01
Sioux (1)	6	0.02
South American Ind. (3)	5	0.01
Spanish American Ind. (4)	4	0.01
Tlingit-Haida *(Alaska Native)* (0)	1	<0.01
Asian (1,340)	1,848	5.14
Not Hispanic (1,322)	1,795	4.99
Hispanic (18)	53	0.15
Cambodian (2)	4	0.01
Chinese, ex. Taiwanese (127)	188	0.52
Filipino (897)	1,210	3.37
Indian (81)	104	0.29
Indonesian (0)	1	<0.01
Japanese (45)	126	0.35
Korean (42)	74	0.21
Malaysian (0)	2	0.01
Pakistani (8)	9	0.03
Sri Lankan (4)	4	0.01
Taiwanese (0)	3	0.01
Thai (11)	26	0.07
Vietnamese (78)	105	0.29
Hawaii Native/Pacific Islander (47)	135	0.38
Not Hispanic (40)	123	0.34
Hispanic (7)	12	0.03
Fijian (0)	1	<0.01
Guamanian/Chamorro (5)	37	0.10
Native Hawaiian (12)	41	0.11
Samoan (8)	20	0.06
White (25,605)	26,717	74.34
Not Hispanic (24,501)	25,443	70.80
Hispanic (1,104)	1,274	3.54

Greenville

Place Type: City
County: Greenville
Population: 58,409†

Ancestry‡	Population	%
African, Sub-Saharan (275)	331	0.57
African (192)	228	0.39
Cape Verdean (30)	30	0.05
Nigerian (53)	53	0.09
South African (0)	20	0.03
American (6,496)	6,496	11.23
Arab (281)	420	0.73
Arab (95)	95	0.16
Egyptian (5)	5	0.01
Jordanian (98)	98	0.17
Lebanese (83)	222	0.38
Austrian (0)	64	0.11
Basque (0)	15	0.03
Brazilian (31)	31	0.05
British (197)	337	0.58
Bulgarian (6)	6	0.01
Canadian (84)	132	0.23
Celtic (29)	29	0.05
Croatian (13)	13	0.02
Czech (36)	114	0.20
Danish (31)	92	0.16
Dutch (257)	813	1.41
Eastern European (11)	11	0.02
English (3,230)	7,396	12.79
Estonian (6)	6	0.01
European (549)	601	1.04
French, ex. Basque (375)	1,290	2.23
French Canadian (133)	290	0.50
German (2,350)	6,981	12.07
Greek (107)	201	0.35
Hungarian (50)	117	0.20
Icelander (12)	12	0.02
Iranian (31)	51	0.09
Irish (1,602)	4,691	8.11
Italian (414)	1,445	2.50
Latvian (8)	22	0.04
Lithuanian (0)	12	0.02
Macedonian (6)	6	0.01
Maltese (0)	14	0.02
Northern European (24)	24	0.04
Norwegian (169)	494	0.85
Pennsylvania German (17)	17	0.03
Polish (262)	862	1.49
Portuguese (0)	22	0.04
Romanian (54)	79	0.14
Russian (74)	205	0.35
Scandinavian (58)	95	0.16
Scotch-Irish (1,520)	2,731	4.72
Scottish (718)	1,782	3.08
Serbian (7)	42	0.07
Slavic (41)	41	0.07
Slovak (10)	19	0.03
Slovene (0)	7	0.01
Swedish (148)	449	0.78
Swiss (74)	262	0.45
Turkish (0)	125	0.22
Ukrainian (32)	89	0.15
Welsh (106)	417	0.72
West Indian, ex. Hispanic (112)	182	0.31
Bahamian (2)	2	<0.01
Haitian (15)	24	0.04
Jamaican (61)	93	0.16
Trinidadian/Tobagonian (18)	18	0.03
West Indian (16)	35	0.06
Other West Indian (0)	10	0.02
Yugoslavian (9)	18	0.03

SECTION TWO

*Notes: † The Census 2010 population figure is used to calculate the percentages in the Hispanic Origin and Race categories. Ancestry percentages are based on the 2006-2010 American Community Survey population (not shown); ‡ Numbers in parentheses indicate the number of people reporting a single ancestry; * Numbers in parentheses indicate the number of persons reporting this race alone, not in combination with any other race; Please refer to the Explanation of Data for more information.*

Hispanic Origin	Population	%
Hispanic or Latino (of any race)	3,443	5.89
Central American, ex. Mexican	394	0.67
Costa Rican	42	0.07
Guatemalan	199	0.34
Honduran	80	0.14
Nicaraguan	15	0.03
Panamanian	7	0.01
Salvadoran	49	0.08
Other Central American	2	<0.01
Cuban	75	0.13
Dominican Republic	84	0.14
Mexican	1,692	2.90
Puerto Rican	337	0.58
South American	600	1.03
Argentinean	33	0.06
Bolivian	2	<0.01
Chilean	18	0.03
Colombian	427	0.73
Ecuadorian	18	0.03
Paraguayan	6	0.01
Peruvian	45	0.08
Uruguayan	15	0.03
Venezuelan	36	0.06
Other Hispanic or Latino	261	0.45

Race*	Population	%
African-American/Black (17,519)	18,069	30.94
Not Hispanic (17,377)	17,855	30.57
Hispanic (142)	214	0.37
American Indian/Alaska Native (148)	425	0.73
Not Hispanic (91)	334	0.57
Hispanic (57)	91	0.16
Apache (2)	6	0.01
Blackfeet (0)	10	0.02
Cherokee (15)	113	0.19
Chickasaw (0)	2	<0.01
Chippewa (0)	1	<0.01
Choctaw (8)	11	0.02
Comanche (0)	1	<0.01
Cree (0)	1	<0.01
Creek (0)	1	<0.01
Delaware (0)	1	<0.01
Iroquois (1)	4	0.01
Kiowa (0)	1	<0.01
Lumbee (3)	5	0.01
Mexican American Ind. (43)	47	0.08
Navajo (0)	2	<0.01
Seminole (0)	6	0.01
Sioux (4)	12	0.02
South American Ind. (0)	4	0.01
Spanish American Ind. (2)	2	<0.01
Yakama (0)	1	<0.01
Yaqui (2)	2	<0.01
Asian (793)	1,045	1.79
Not Hispanic (782)	1,006	1.72
Hispanic (11)	39	0.07
Bangladeshi (2)	5	0.01
Burmese (3)	3	0.01
Cambodian (1)	7	0.01
Chinese, ex. Taiwanese (130)	158	0.27
Filipino (81)	158	0.27
Hmong (1)	1	<0.01
Indian (233)	280	0.48
Indonesian (2)	5	0.01
Japanese (47)	82	0.14
Korean (139)	179	0.31
Laotian (3)	3	0.01
Nepalese (1)	1	<0.01
Pakistani (29)	30	0.05
Sri Lankan (4)	4	0.01
Taiwanese (5)	8	0.01
Thai (10)	18	0.03
Vietnamese (65)	72	0.12
Hawaii Native/Pacific Islander (54)	90	0.15
Not Hispanic (46)	70	0.12
Hispanic (8)	20	0.03
Guamanian/Chamorro (16)	22	0.04
Native Hawaiian (7)	23	0.04
Samoan (5)	12	0.02
Tongan (0)	2	<0.01
White (37,356)	38,214	65.42
Not Hispanic (35,776)	36,450	62.40
Hispanic (1,580)	1,764	3.02

Greenwood

Place Type: City
County: Greenwood
Population: 23,222†

Ancestry‡	Population	%
African, Sub-Saharan (161)	175	0.76
African (161)	175	0.76
American (2,681)	2,681	11.69
British (14)	14	0.06
Bulgarian (9)	9	0.04
Celtic (0)	16	0.07
Dutch (22)	302	1.32
Eastern European (0)	13	0.06
English (944)	1,533	6.68
European (159)	159	0.69
French, ex. Basque (22)	380	1.66
French Canadian (0)	16	0.07
German (640)	1,561	6.81
Irish (417)	1,244	5.42
Italian (129)	227	0.99
Lithuanian (0)	12	0.05
Norwegian (0)	8	0.03
Polish (0)	104	0.45
Russian (18)	18	0.08
Scandinavian (41)	41	0.18
Scotch-Irish (584)	893	3.89
Scottish (80)	239	1.04
Swedish (0)	30	0.13
Swiss (13)	22	0.10
West Indian, ex. Hispanic (35)	51	0.22
Jamaican (20)	20	0.09
West Indian (15)	31	0.14

Hispanic Origin	Population	%
Hispanic or Latino (of any race)	2,550	10.98
Central American, ex. Mexican	219	0.94
Costa Rican	20	0.09
Guatemalan	145	0.62
Honduran	44	0.19
Nicaraguan	4	0.02
Salvadoran	6	0.03
Cuban	17	0.07
Dominican Republic	4	0.02
Mexican	2,035	8.76
Puerto Rican	74	0.32
South American	49	0.21
Argentinean	3	0.01
Chilean	4	0.02
Colombian	19	0.08
Ecuadorian	15	0.06
Paraguayan	4	0.02
Peruvian	2	0.01
Venezuelan	2	0.01
Other Hispanic or Latino	152	0.65

Race*	Population	%
African-American/Black (10,389)	10,548	45.42
Not Hispanic (10,334)	10,468	45.08
Hispanic (55)	80	0.34
American Indian/Alaska Native (89)	160	0.69
Not Hispanic (48)	109	0.47
Hispanic (41)	51	0.22
Blackfeet (0)	1	<0.01
Cherokee (13)	28	0.12
Chickasaw (0)	1	<0.01
Choctaw (1)	1	<0.01
Creek (1)	2	0.01
Iroquois (1)	2	0.01
Lumbee (5)	9	0.04
Mexican American Ind. (14)	21	0.09
Seminole (1)	1	<0.01
Sioux (1)	1	<0.01
Tlingit-Haida *(Alaska Native)* (2)	2	0.01
Asian (235)	297	1.28
Not Hispanic (232)	291	1.25
Hispanic (3)	6	0.03
Cambodian (8)	9	0.04
Chinese, ex. Taiwanese (10)	14	0.06
Filipino (67)	75	0.32
Indian (37)	48	0.21
Indonesian (4)	4	0.02
Japanese (53)	59	0.25
Korean (5)	10	0.04
Pakistani (6)	8	0.03
Taiwanese (1)	1	<0.01
Thai (5)	5	0.02
Vietnamese (21)	25	0.11
Hawaii Native/Pacific Islander (15)	20	0.09
Not Hispanic (4)	7	0.03
Hispanic (11)	13	0.06
Guamanian/Chamorro (12)	12	0.05
Native Hawaiian (3)	4	0.02
White (10,367)	10,627	45.76
Not Hispanic (9,795)	9,958	42.88
Hispanic (572)	669	2.88

Greer

Place Type: City
County: Greenville
Population: 25,515†

Ancestry‡	Population	%
African, Sub-Saharan (181)	181	0.76
African (126)	126	0.53
Kenyan (46)	46	0.19
Nigerian (9)	9	0.04
American (3,533)	3,533	14.78
Arab (16)	16	0.07
Lebanese (13)	13	0.05
Palestinian (3)	3	0.01
Austrian (11)	28	0.12
Brazilian (14)	14	0.06
British (109)	118	0.49
Bulgarian (13)	13	0.05
Canadian (0)	66	0.28
Croatian (8)	8	0.03
Czech (10)	71	0.30
Czechoslovakian (17)	17	0.07
Danish (0)	25	0.10
Dutch (56)	214	0.90
English (960)	2,020	8.45
European (104)	116	0.49
Finnish (65)	76	0.32
French, ex. Basque (91)	235	0.98
French Canadian (34)	84	0.35
German (1,107)	2,862	11.97
Greek (18)	81	0.34
Hungarian (15)	57	0.24
Iranian (0)	27	0.11
Irish (1,042)	2,601	10.88
Italian (370)	1,163	4.86
Macedonian (0)	48	0.20
Norwegian (25)	104	0.44
Pennsylvania German (12)	26	0.11
Polish (213)	387	1.62
Portuguese (47)	47	0.20
Romanian (8)	24	0.10
Russian (15)	129	0.54
Scandinavian (11)	11	0.05
Scotch-Irish (272)	558	2.33
Scottish (157)	465	1.94
Serbian (9)	27	0.11
Slavic (28)	28	0.12
Slovak (29)	44	0.18
Swedish (34)	73	0.31
Swiss (0)	15	0.06
Ukrainian (0)	13	0.05
Welsh (57)	57	0.24
West Indian, ex. Hispanic (0)	11	0.05
Jamaican (0)	11	0.05

*Notes: † The Census 2010 population figure is used to calculate the percentages in the Hispanic Origin and Race categories. Ancestry percentages are based on the 2006-2010 American Community Survey population (not shown); ‡ Numbers in parentheses indicate the number of people reporting a single ancestry; * Numbers in parentheses indicate the number of persons reporting this race alone, not in combination with any other race; Please refer to the Explanation of Data for more information.*

Hispanic Origin	Population	%
Hispanic or Latino (of any race)	3,687	14.45
Central American, ex. Mexican	359	1.41
Costa Rican	28	0.11
Guatemalan	27	0.11
Honduran	191	0.75
Nicaraguan	13	0.05
Panamanian	4	0.02
Salvadoran	94	0.37
Other Central American	2	0.01
Cuban	73	0.29
Dominican Republic	73	0.29
Mexican	1,906	7.47
Puerto Rican	243	0.95
South American	836	3.28
Argentinean	9	0.04
Bolivian	8	0.03
Chilean	5	0.02
Colombian	695	2.72
Ecuadorian	22	0.09
Paraguayan	2	0.01
Peruvian	52	0.20
Uruguayan	24	0.09
Venezuelan	19	0.07
Other Hispanic or Latino	197	0.77

Race*	Population	%
African-American/Black (4,405)	4,683	18.35
Not Hispanic (4,339)	4,581	17.95
Hispanic (66)	102	0.40
American Indian/Alaska Native (67)	166	0.65
Not Hispanic (41)	121	0.47
Hispanic (26)	45	0.18
Apache (3)	5	0.02
Blackfeet (2)	7	0.03
Canadian/French Am. Ind. (1)	1	<0.01
Central American Ind. (2)	2	0.01
Cherokee (14)	43	0.17
Chippewa (0)	3	0.01
Choctaw (0)	1	<0.01
Comanche (0)	2	0.01
Creek (0)	2	0.01
Iroquois (2)	4	0.02
Lumbee (2)	3	0.01
Mexican American Ind. (1)	5	0.02
Potawatomi (1)	1	<0.01
Sioux (1)	1	<0.01
South American Ind. (1)	1	<0.01
Yaqui (1)	1	<0.01
Asian (570)	660	2.59
Not Hispanic (565)	642	2.52
Hispanic (5)	18	0.07
Bangladeshi (1)	1	<0.01
Burmese (11)	11	0.04
Cambodian (4)	8	0.03
Chinese, ex. Taiwanese (106)	115	0.45
Filipino (68)	88	0.34
Indian (141)	157	0.62
Japanese (25)	37	0.15
Korean (75)	93	0.36
Laotian (1)	2	0.01
Malaysian (0)	1	<0.01
Nepalese (4)	4	0.02
Pakistani (12)	13	0.05
Sri Lankan (5)	5	0.02
Taiwanese (2)	2	0.01
Thai (11)	17	0.07
Vietnamese (83)	83	0.33
Hawaii Native/Pacific Islander (14)	34	0.13
Not Hispanic (11)	26	0.10
Hispanic (3)	8	0.03
Guamanian/Chamorro (7)	15	0.06
Native Hawaiian (0)	4	0.02
Samoan (5)	8	0.03
White (18,071)	18,542	72.67
Not Hispanic (16,428)	16,774	65.74
Hispanic (1,643)	1,768	6.93

Hanahan

Place Type: City
County: Berkeley
Population: 17,997†

Ancestry‡	Population	%
African, Sub-Saharan (17)	17	0.10
African (12)	12	0.07
Nigerian (5)	5	0.03
American (1,387)	1,387	8.19
Arab (303)	318	1.88
Egyptian (274)	274	1.62
Moroccan (0)	15	0.09
Syrian (29)	29	0.17
Armenian (0)	3	0.02
Austrian (0)	12	0.07
Brazilian (183)	189	1.12
British (7)	35	0.21
Canadian (27)	41	0.24
Czech (12)	12	0.07
Danish (45)	57	0.34
Dutch (9)	121	0.71
English (575)	1,296	7.65
European (230)	240	1.42
French, ex. Basque (190)	829	4.89
French Canadian (40)	40	0.24
German (605)	2,084	12.30
Greek (107)	152	0.90
Hungarian (10)	29	0.17
Irish (814)	2,170	12.81
Israeli (1)	1	0.01
Italian (249)	813	4.80
Norwegian (15)	37	0.22
Polish (89)	177	1.04
Portuguese (124)	138	0.81
Romanian (10)	20	0.12
Russian (52)	62	0.37
Scotch-Irish (373)	568	3.35
Scottish (78)	508	3.00
Serbian (13)	13	0.08
Swedish (9)	68	0.40
Swiss (22)	46	0.27
Ukrainian (21)	43	0.25
Welsh (55)	67	0.40
West Indian, ex. Hispanic (14)	14	0.08
Jamaican (14)	14	0.08

Hispanic Origin	Population	%
Hispanic or Latino (of any race)	1,638	9.10
Central American, ex. Mexican	189	1.05
Costa Rican	13	0.07
Guatemalan	87	0.48
Honduran	51	0.28
Nicaraguan	7	0.04
Panamanian	4	0.02
Salvadoran	25	0.14
Other Central American	2	0.01
Cuban	19	0.11
Dominican Republic	25	0.14
Mexican	996	5.53
Puerto Rican	164	0.91
South American	90	0.50
Argentinean	8	0.04
Bolivian	5	0.03
Chilean	2	0.01
Colombian	43	0.24
Ecuadorian	12	0.07
Peruvian	13	0.07
Venezuelan	7	0.04
Other Hispanic or Latino	155	0.86

Race*	Population	%
African-American/Black (2,494)	2,673	14.85
Not Hispanic (2,443)	2,590	14.39
Hispanic (51)	83	0.46
American Indian/Alaska Native (110)	217	1.21
Not Hispanic (71)	162	0.90
Hispanic (39)	55	0.31
Apache (1)	5	0.03
Blackfeet (1)	5	0.03
Canadian/French Am. Ind. (1)	1	0.01
Central American Ind. (1)	1	0.01
Cherokee (21)	51	0.28
Chippewa (0)	1	0.01
Choctaw (0)	4	0.02
Comanche (0)	1	0.01
Cree (0)	3	0.02
Crow (0)	1	0.01
Iroquois (4)	5	0.03
Kiowa (1)	1	0.01
Lumbee (1)	2	0.01
Mexican American Ind. (10)	11	0.06
Navajo (2)	2	0.01
Osage (1)	4	0.02
Potawatomi (0)	1	0.01
Pueblo (0)	4	0.02
Puget Sound Salish (0)	2	0.01
Seminole (0)	2	0.01
Sioux (3)	6	0.03
Yup'ik *(Alaska Native)* (1)	1	0.01
Asian (620)	796	4.42
Not Hispanic (613)	775	4.31
Hispanic (7)	21	0.12
Cambodian (17)	17	0.09
Chinese, ex. Taiwanese (83)	102	0.57
Filipino (205)	315	1.75
Hmong (1)	3	0.02
Indian (49)	55	0.31
Indonesian (1)	2	0.01
Japanese (16)	26	0.14
Korean (22)	38	0.21
Laotian (2)	6	0.03
Pakistani (11)	13	0.07
Taiwanese (7)	10	0.06
Thai (10)	15	0.08
Vietnamese (168)	185	1.03
Hawaii Native/Pacific Islander (15)	38	0.21
Not Hispanic (12)	30	0.17
Hispanic (3)	8	0.04
Guamanian/Chamorro (11)	14	0.08
Native Hawaiian (3)	11	0.06
White (13,445)	13,902	77.25
Not Hispanic (12,748)	13,108	72.83
Hispanic (697)	794	4.41

Hartsville

Place Type: City
County: Darlington
Population: 7,764†

Ancestry‡	Population	%
African, Sub-Saharan (70)	70	0.90
African (70)	70	0.90
American (469)	469	6.01
Arab (16)	16	0.20
Lebanese (16)	16	0.20
Armenian (8)	8	0.10
Canadian (11)	11	0.14
Croatian (0)	7	0.09
Czech (0)	8	0.10
Dutch (8)	75	0.96
English (364)	732	9.38
French, ex. Basque (7)	37	0.47
German (174)	496	6.35
Irish (266)	566	7.25
Italian (69)	164	2.10
Norwegian (10)	10	0.13
Polish (14)	59	0.76
Russian (0)	12	0.15
Scandinavian (9)	9	0.12
Scotch-Irish (324)	348	4.46
Scottish (88)	231	2.96
Swedish (0)	10	0.13
Swiss (0)	5	0.06
Welsh (13)	15	0.19

Hispanic Origin	Population	%
Hispanic or Latino (of any race)	113	1.46

*Notes: † The Census 2010 population figure is used to calculate the percentages in the Hispanic Origin and Race categories. Ancestry percentages are based on the 2006-2010 American Community Survey population (not shown); ‡ Numbers in parentheses indicate the number of people reporting a single ancestry; * Numbers in parentheses indicate the number of persons reporting this race alone, not in combination with any other race; Please refer to the Explanation of Data for more information.*

Central American, ex. Mexican	4	0.05
Costa Rican	1	0.01
Guatemalan	2	0.03
Honduran	1	0.01
Cuban	9	0.12
Dominican Republic	7	0.09
Mexican	44	0.57
Puerto Rican	28	0.36
South American	14	0.18
Chilean	3	0.04
Colombian	3	0.04
Ecuadorian	1	0.01
Peruvian	3	0.04
Venezuelan	2	0.03
Other South American	2	0.03
Other Hispanic or Latino	7	0.09

Race*	Population	%
African-American/Black (3,598)	3,652	47.04
Not Hispanic (3,586)	3,630	46.75
Hispanic (12)	22	0.28
American Indian/Alaska Native (17)	47	0.61
Not Hispanic (16)	41	0.53
Hispanic (1)	6	0.08
Blackfeet (0)	1	0.01
Cherokee (6)	11	0.14
Delaware (0)	1	0.01
Lumbee (2)	6	0.08
South American Ind. (1)	2	0.03
Spanish American Ind. (0)	1	0.01
Asian (64)	75	0.97
Not Hispanic (63)	73	0.94
Hispanic (1)	2	0.03
Chinese, ex. Taiwanese (6)	10	0.13
Filipino (14)	16	0.21
Indian (27)	28	0.36
Japanese (6)	7	0.09
Korean (1)	1	0.01
Pakistani (8)	9	0.12
Hawaii Native/Pacific Islander (4)	9	0.12
Not Hispanic (4)	9	0.12
Guamanian/Chamorro (1)	2	0.03
Native Hawaiian (1)	2	0.03
White (3,960)	4,021	51.79
Not Hispanic (3,904)	3,963	51.04
Hispanic (56)	58	0.75

Hilton Head Island

Place Type: Town
County: Beaufort
Population: 37,099†

Ancestry‡	Population	%
African, Sub-Saharan (159)	212	0.58
African (27)	63	0.17
Cape Verdean (132)	149	0.41
Alsatian (0)	13	0.04
American (1,543)	1,543	4.20
Arab (32)	65	0.18
Arab (7)	20	0.05
Egyptian (10)	10	0.03
Lebanese (15)	24	0.07
Syrian (0)	11	0.03
Armenian (90)	119	0.32
Australian (0)	113	0.31
Austrian (80)	171	0.47
Belgian (40)	78	0.21
Brazilian (0)	9	0.02
British (235)	355	0.97
Bulgarian (98)	98	0.27
Cajun (25)	25	0.07
Canadian (37)	125	0.34
Czech (36)	207	0.56
Czechoslovakian (36)	36	0.10
Danish (21)	52	0.14
Dutch (222)	638	1.74
Eastern European (44)	44	0.12
English (2,862)	5,758	15.68
Estonian (22)	22	0.06
European (153)	174	0.47
Finnish (20)	64	0.17
French, ex. Basque (327)	1,259	3.43
French Canadian (79)	261	0.71
German (2,287)	6,412	17.46
Greek (42)	175	0.48
Guyanese (7)	7	0.02
Hungarian (118)	402	1.09
Icelander (9)	9	0.02
Irish (1,761)	5,247	14.29
Israeli (22)	51	0.14
Italian (1,174)	2,528	6.89
Latvian (14)	26	0.07
Lithuanian (44)	82	0.22
Northern European (9)	9	0.02
Norwegian (174)	339	0.92
Pennsylvania German (15)	25	0.07
Polish (586)	1,667	4.54
Portuguese (69)	106	0.29
Romanian (0)	34	0.09
Russian (233)	557	1.52
Scandinavian (26)	52	0.14
Scotch-Irish (624)	1,100	3.00
Scottish (269)	888	2.42
Slavic (0)	10	0.03
Slovak (121)	168	0.46
Slovene (32)	32	0.09
Swedish (227)	655	1.78
Swiss (51)	137	0.37
Turkish (60)	60	0.16
Ukrainian (66)	112	0.31
Welsh (73)	335	0.91
West Indian, ex. Hispanic (16)	26	0.07
Barbadian (0)	10	0.03
Bermudan (16)	16	0.04
Yugoslavian (0)	10	0.03

Hispanic Origin	Population	%
Hispanic or Latino (of any race)	5,861	15.80
Central American, ex. Mexican	729	1.97
Costa Rican	108	0.29
Guatemalan	124	0.33
Honduran	311	0.84
Nicaraguan	90	0.24
Panamanian	14	0.04
Salvadoran	82	0.22
Cuban	26	0.07
Dominican Republic	9	0.02
Mexican	4,034	10.87
Puerto Rican	100	0.27
South American	665	1.79
Argentinean	221	0.60
Bolivian	29	0.08
Chilean	9	0.02
Colombian	121	0.33
Ecuadorian	10	0.03
Paraguayan	3	0.01
Peruvian	26	0.07
Uruguayan	189	0.51
Venezuelan	53	0.14
Other South American	4	0.01
Other Hispanic or Latino	298	0.80

Race*	Population	%
African-American/Black (2,766)	2,930	7.90
Not Hispanic (2,690)	2,805	7.56
Hispanic (76)	125	0.34
American Indian/Alaska Native (57)	140	0.38
Not Hispanic (41)	104	0.28
Hispanic (16)	36	0.10
Aleut *(Alaska Native)* (0)	4	0.01
Apache (2)	2	0.01
Blackfeet (0)	5	0.01
Cherokee (4)	32	0.09
Choctaw (0)	2	0.01
Comanche (3)	3	0.01
Creek (0)	2	0.01
Delaware (0)	1	<0.01
Iroquois (0)	2	0.01
Kiowa (0)	1	<0.01
Mexican American Ind. (4)	4	0.01
Yaqui (1)	1	<0.01
Yuman (0)	1	<0.01
Asian (339)	422	1.14
Not Hispanic (331)	396	1.07
Hispanic (8)	26	0.07
Burmese (5)	5	0.01
Cambodian (2)	2	0.01
Chinese, ex. Taiwanese (115)	123	0.33
Filipino (36)	62	0.17
Indian (53)	58	0.16
Indonesian (5)	5	0.01
Japanese (34)	54	0.15
Korean (23)	29	0.08
Laotian (2)	4	0.01
Malaysian (6)	7	0.02
Pakistani (4)	4	0.01
Sri Lankan (3)	3	0.01
Taiwanese (1)	1	<0.01
Thai (7)	7	0.02
Vietnamese (33)	35	0.09
Hawaii Native/Pacific Islander (22)	38	0.10
Not Hispanic (2)	16	0.04
Hispanic (20)	22	0.06
Fijian (0)	3	0.01
Guamanian/Chamorro (20)	21	0.06
Marshallese (1)	1	<0.01
Native Hawaiian (0)	6	0.02
White (30,751)	31,150	83.96
Not Hispanic (27,888)	28,108	75.76
Hispanic (2,863)	3,042	8.20

Irmo

Place Type: Town
County: Richland
Population: 11,097†

Ancestry‡	Population	%
African, Sub-Saharan (148)	148	1.34
African (134)	134	1.21
Kenyan (14)	14	0.13
American (1,323)	1,323	11.94
Arab (58)	71	0.64
Arab (15)	15	0.14
Lebanese (31)	31	0.28
Syrian (12)	25	0.23
Austrian (0)	14	0.13
Belgian (21)	63	0.57
British (10)	10	0.09
Canadian (15)	15	0.14
Czech (0)	13	0.12
Danish (0)	34	0.31
Dutch (44)	218	1.97
English (527)	1,271	11.47
European (126)	126	1.14
French, ex. Basque (52)	397	3.58
French Canadian (14)	51	0.46
German (426)	1,620	14.61
Greek (0)	13	0.12
Hungarian (38)	52	0.47
Irish (424)	1,608	14.51
Italian (121)	277	2.50
Norwegian (54)	54	0.49
Polish (73)	300	2.71
Portuguese (0)	42	0.38
Romanian (45)	167	1.51
Scandinavian (0)	14	0.13
Scotch-Irish (288)	412	3.72
Scottish (244)	479	4.32
Swedish (0)	27	0.24
Swiss (0)	18	0.16
Welsh (19)	33	0.30
Yugoslavian (0)	24	0.22

Hispanic Origin	Population	%
Hispanic or Latino (of any race)	371	3.34
Central American, ex. Mexican	26	0.23
Costa Rican	3	0.03
Guatemalan	3	0.03

*Notes: † The Census 2010 population figure is used to calculate the percentages in the Hispanic Origin and Race categories. Ancestry percentages are based on the 2006-2010 American Community Survey population (not shown); ‡ Numbers in parentheses indicate the number of people reporting a single ancestry; * Numbers in parentheses indicate the number of persons reporting this race alone, not in combination with any other race; Please refer to the Explanation of Data for more information.*

Honduran	2	0.02
Nicaraguan	4	0.04
Panamanian	12	0.11
Salvadoran	2	0.02
Cuban	19	0.17
Dominican Republic	4	0.04
Mexican	102	0.92
Puerto Rican	103	0.93
South American	57	0.51
Argentinean	9	0.08
Chilean	4	0.04
Colombian	25	0.23
Ecuadorian	1	0.01
Paraguayan	1	0.01
Peruvian	11	0.10
Venezuelan	6	0.05
Other Hispanic or Latino	60	0.54

Race*	Population	%
African-American/Black (3,316)	3,482	31.38
Not Hispanic (3,277)	3,418	30.80
Hispanic (39)	64	0.58
American Indian/Alaska Native (41)	124	1.12
Not Hispanic (41)	116	1.05
Hispanic (0)	8	0.07
Apache (0)	1	0.01
Blackfeet (0)	2	0.02
Cherokee (10)	33	0.30
Choctaw (1)	1	0.01
Iroquois (0)	3	0.03
Lumbee (1)	2	0.02
Navajo (0)	1	0.01
Seminole (1)	2	0.02
Asian (178)	225	2.03
Not Hispanic (178)	217	1.96
Hispanic (0)	8	0.07
Cambodian (0)	1	0.01
Chinese, ex. Taiwanese (33)	37	0.33
Filipino (18)	27	0.24
Hmong (21)	21	0.19
Indian (48)	53	0.48
Japanese (8)	11	0.10
Korean (21)	32	0.29
Laotian (8)	12	0.11
Pakistani (10)	11	0.10
Taiwanese (2)	2	0.02
Thai (3)	6	0.05
Vietnamese (6)	6	0.05
Hawaii Native/Pacific Islander (0)	8	0.07
Not Hispanic (0)	7	0.06
Hispanic (0)	1	0.01
Native Hawaiian (0)	3	0.03
Samoan (0)	3	0.03
White (7,171)	7,400	66.68
Not Hispanic (6,981)	7,176	64.67
Hispanic (190)	224	2.02

Ladson

Place Type: CDP
County: Berkeley
Population: 13,790†

Ancestry‡	Population	%
African, Sub-Saharan (58)	69	0.49
African (58)	69	0.49
American (1,543)	1,543	10.89
Austrian (0)	12	0.08
Brazilian (0)	42	0.30
British (6)	6	0.04
Canadian (10)	10	0.07
Celtic (9)	9	0.06
Czech (0)	10	0.07
Danish (0)	10	0.07
Dutch (82)	171	1.21
English (519)	887	6.26
European (78)	78	0.55
French, ex. Basque (100)	536	3.78
German (588)	1,794	12.66
Greek (0)	12	0.08
Hungarian (29)	106	0.75
Irish (325)	928	6.55
Italian (138)	388	2.74
Lithuanian (0)	15	0.11
Norwegian (0)	90	0.64
Polish (206)	547	3.86
Russian (15)	15	0.11
Scandinavian (16)	69	0.49
Scotch-Irish (164)	437	3.08
Scottish (131)	279	1.97
Serbian (0)	38	0.27
Slovak (0)	10	0.07
Swedish (0)	58	0.41
Ukrainian (0)	17	0.12
Welsh (0)	56	0.40

Hispanic Origin	Population	%
Hispanic or Latino (of any race)	1,554	11.27
Central American, ex. Mexican	150	1.09
Costa Rican	9	0.07
Guatemalan	39	0.28
Honduran	22	0.16
Nicaraguan	3	0.02
Panamanian	16	0.12
Salvadoran	61	0.44
Cuban	38	0.28
Dominican Republic	36	0.26
Mexican	992	7.19
Puerto Rican	187	1.36
South American	59	0.43
Argentinean	3	0.02
Bolivian	1	0.01
Colombian	16	0.12
Ecuadorian	5	0.04
Peruvian	20	0.15
Uruguayan	12	0.09
Other South American	2	0.01
Other Hispanic or Latino	92	0.67

Race*	Population	%
African-American/Black (3,622)	3,861	28.00
Not Hispanic (3,532)	3,733	27.07
Hispanic (90)	128	0.93
American Indian/Alaska Native (111)	265	1.92
Not Hispanic (95)	234	1.70
Hispanic (16)	31	0.22
Alaska Athabascan *(Ala. Nat.)* (0)	2	0.01
Aleut *(Alaska Native)* (1)	2	0.01
Apache (1)	3	0.02
Blackfeet (3)	16	0.12
Cherokee (17)	73	0.53
Chickasaw (0)	3	0.02
Chippewa (1)	3	0.02
Choctaw (0)	4	0.03
Comanche (1)	1	0.01
Creek (1)	1	0.01
Delaware (1)	2	0.01
Iroquois (0)	7	0.05
Mexican American Ind. (7)	7	0.05
Navajo (0)	1	0.01
Osage (0)	1	0.01
Pueblo (1)	1	0.01
Seminole (0)	5	0.04
Sioux (12)	16	0.12
Asian (297)	401	2.91
Not Hispanic (286)	386	2.80
Hispanic (11)	15	0.11
Cambodian (2)	4	0.03
Chinese, ex. Taiwanese (19)	32	0.23
Filipino (207)	283	2.05
Hmong (4)	4	0.03
Indian (15)	19	0.14
Japanese (8)	14	0.10
Korean (16)	19	0.14
Thai (4)	8	0.06
Vietnamese (13)	14	0.10
Hawaii Native/Pacific Islander (8)	17	0.12
Not Hispanic (7)	15	0.11
Hispanic (1)	2	0.01
Fijian (0)	1	0.01
Guamanian/Chamorro (5)	6	0.04
Native Hawaiian (2)	7	0.05
Samoan (0)	1	0.01
White (8,484)	8,924	64.71
Not Hispanic (7,885)	8,255	59.86
Hispanic (599)	669	4.85

Lake Wylie

Place Type: CDP
County: York
Population: 8,841†

Ancestry‡	Population	%
American (689)	689	8.24
Arab (0)	118	1.41
Egyptian (0)	75	0.90
Syrian (0)	43	0.51
Armenian (0)	13	0.16
Austrian (0)	15	0.18
Belgian (23)	23	0.28
British (72)	72	0.86
Canadian (13)	13	0.16
Croatian (49)	83	0.99
Czech (15)	15	0.18
Czechoslovakian (0)	13	0.16
Danish (14)	14	0.17
Dutch (60)	231	2.76
English (621)	1,264	15.12
European (178)	178	2.13
French, ex. Basque (55)	361	4.32
German (679)	1,828	21.86
Hungarian (0)	11	0.13
Irish (548)	1,258	15.04
Italian (421)	674	8.06
Latvian (15)	15	0.18
Northern European (13)	13	0.16
Norwegian (11)	24	0.29
Polish (0)	70	0.84
Portuguese (8)	8	0.10
Romanian (0)	15	0.18
Russian (19)	34	0.41
Scandinavian (12)	12	0.14
Scotch-Irish (468)	600	7.18
Scottish (105)	255	3.05
Swedish (14)	43	0.51
Swiss (0)	72	0.86
Turkish (16)	16	0.19
Ukrainian (10)	10	0.12
Welsh (0)	14	0.17

Hispanic Origin	Population	%
Hispanic or Latino (of any race)	347	3.92
Central American, ex. Mexican	26	0.29
Costa Rican	10	0.11
Guatemalan	2	0.02
Honduran	3	0.03
Nicaraguan	1	0.01
Panamanian	2	0.02
Salvadoran	8	0.09
Cuban	29	0.33
Dominican Republic	24	0.27
Mexican	89	1.01
Puerto Rican	86	0.97
South American	70	0.79
Argentinean	6	0.07
Chilean	11	0.12
Colombian	29	0.33
Ecuadorian	12	0.14
Paraguayan	2	0.02
Peruvian	6	0.07
Uruguayan	1	0.01
Venezuelan	3	0.03
Other Hispanic or Latino	23	0.26

Race*	Population	%
African-American/Black (632)	687	7.77
Not Hispanic (613)	664	7.51
Hispanic (19)	23	0.26
American Indian/Alaska Native (26)	54	0.61

*Notes: † The Census 2010 population figure is used to calculate the percentages in the Hispanic Origin and Race categories. Ancestry percentages are based on the 2006-2010 American Community Survey population (not shown); ‡ Numbers in parentheses indicate the number of people reporting a single ancestry; * Numbers in parentheses indicate the number of persons reporting this race alone, not in combination with any other race; Please refer to the Explanation of Data for more information.*

Not Hispanic (19)	44	0.50
Hispanic (7)	10	0.11
Aleut *(Alaska Native)* (0)	1	0.01
Cherokee (5)	12	0.14
Creek (0)	3	0.03
Inupiat *(Alaska Native)* (1)	4	0.05
Iroquois (0)	1	0.01
Kiowa (0)	1	0.01
Lumbee (1)	1	0.01
Navajo (1)	1	0.01
Seminole (1)	3	0.03
South American Ind. (0)	1	0.01
Spanish American Ind. (1)	1	0.01
Asian (128)	172	1.95
Not Hispanic (126)	167	1.89
Hispanic (2)	5	0.06
Chinese, ex. Taiwanese (16)	26	0.29
Filipino (11)	17	0.19
Hmong (4)	4	0.05
Indian (32)	37	0.42
Indonesian (1)	1	0.01
Japanese (12)	26	0.29
Korean (10)	15	0.17
Taiwanese (0)	3	0.03
Thai (2)	6	0.07
Vietnamese (31)	36	0.41
Hawaii Native/Pacific Islander (10)	15	0.17
Not Hispanic (8)	12	0.14
Hispanic (2)	3	0.03
Guamanian/Chamorro (1)	1	0.01
Native Hawaiian (1)	2	0.02
Samoan (1)	1	0.01
White (7,842)	7,943	89.84
Not Hispanic (7,605)	7,689	86.97
Hispanic (237)	254	2.87

Lancaster

Place Type: City
County: Lancaster
Population: 8,526†

Ancestry‡	Population	%
African, Sub-Saharan (65)	119	1.44
African (10)	37	0.45
Liberian (55)	82	0.99
American (809)	809	9.77
Arab (0)	13	0.16
Moroccan (0)	13	0.16
Austrian (0)	7	0.08
Dutch (5)	62	0.75
English (269)	438	5.29
European (34)	34	0.41
French, ex. Basque (40)	72	0.87
German (166)	448	5.41
Irish (159)	385	4.65
Italian (33)	72	0.87
Polish (23)	102	1.23
Scotch-Irish (440)	583	7.04
Scottish (28)	76	0.92
Slovak (0)	3	0.04
Swedish (9)	9	0.11

Hispanic Origin	Population	%
Hispanic or Latino (of any race)	488	5.72
Central American, ex. Mexican	105	1.23
Guatemalan	12	0.14
Honduran	72	0.84
Nicaraguan	12	0.14
Panamanian	4	0.05
Salvadoran	5	0.06
Cuban	3	0.04
Dominican Republic	3	0.04
Mexican	322	3.78
Puerto Rican	10	0.12
South American	9	0.11
Argentinean	6	0.07
Uruguayan	3	0.04
Other Hispanic or Latino	36	0.42

Race*	Population	%
African-American/Black (4,378)	4,436	52.03
Not Hispanic (4,353)	4,402	51.63
Hispanic (25)	34	0.40
American Indian/Alaska Native (15)	41	0.48
Not Hispanic (15)	37	0.43
Hispanic (0)	4	0.05
Cherokee (0)	3	0.04
Cree (0)	1	0.01
Creek (1)	1	0.01
Hopi (0)	1	0.01
Lumbee (1)	2	0.02
Seminole (0)	1	0.01
Asian (79)	84	0.99
Not Hispanic (79)	84	0.99
Chinese, ex. Taiwanese (14)	15	0.18
Filipino (11)	11	0.13
Indian (37)	37	0.43
Indonesian (1)	1	0.01
Japanese (2)	3	0.04
Korean (2)	5	0.06
Thai (2)	2	0.02
Vietnamese (8)	10	0.12
Hawaii Native/Pacific Islander (1)	5	0.06
Not Hispanic (0)	4	0.05
Hispanic (1)	1	0.01
Guamanian/Chamorro (1)	3	0.04
Native Hawaiian (0)	2	0.02
Samoan (0)	2	0.02
White (3,664)	3,740	43.87
Not Hispanic (3,515)	3,572	41.90
Hispanic (149)	168	1.97

Laurens

Place Type: City
County: Laurens
Population: 9,139†

Ancestry‡	Population	%
African, Sub-Saharan (25)	25	0.27
African (25)	25	0.27
American (592)	592	6.39
British (14)	14	0.15
Canadian (0)	11	0.12
Danish (0)	45	0.49
Dutch (46)	96	1.04
English (681)	987	10.65
European (47)	47	0.51
French, ex. Basque (69)	103	1.11
French Canadian (0)	11	0.12
German (228)	529	5.71
Irish (229)	604	6.52
Italian (0)	41	0.44
Polish (55)	68	0.73
Scotch-Irish (164)	314	3.39
Scottish (85)	210	2.27
Ukrainian (0)	13	0.14
Welsh (10)	74	0.80
West Indian, ex. Hispanic (0)	72	0.78
British West Indian (0)	59	0.64
West Indian (0)	13	0.14

Hispanic Origin	Population	%
Hispanic or Latino (of any race)	524	5.73
Central American, ex. Mexican	144	1.58
Costa Rican	1	0.01
Guatemalan	133	1.46
Honduran	6	0.07
Nicaraguan	1	0.01
Panamanian	2	0.02
Salvadoran	1	0.01
Cuban	1	0.01
Dominican Republic	3	0.03
Mexican	283	3.10
Puerto Rican	37	0.40
South American	9	0.10
Colombian	7	0.08
Peruvian	1	0.01
Venezuelan	1	0.01
Other Hispanic or Latino	47	0.51

Race*	Population	%
African-American/Black (3,916)	3,986	43.62
Not Hispanic (3,879)	3,947	43.19
Hispanic (37)	39	0.43
American Indian/Alaska Native (24)	50	0.55
Not Hispanic (21)	46	0.50
Hispanic (3)	4	0.04
Apache (1)	1	0.01
Blackfeet (0)	4	0.04
Cherokee (9)	18	0.20
Iroquois (1)	1	0.01
Lumbee (1)	1	0.01
Sioux (0)	1	0.01
Spanish American Ind. (1)	1	0.01
Tsimshian *(Alaska Native)* (0)	2	0.02
Asian (27)	43	0.47
Not Hispanic (24)	39	0.43
Hispanic (3)	4	0.04
Chinese, ex. Taiwanese (4)	4	0.04
Filipino (2)	11	0.12
Hmong (1)	1	0.01
Indian (13)	14	0.15
Korean (1)	1	0.01
Thai (0)	1	0.01
Vietnamese (0)	3	0.03
Hawaii Native/Pacific Islander (2)	8	0.09
Not Hispanic (2)	7	0.08
Hispanic (0)	1	0.01
White (4,801)	4,890	53.51
Not Hispanic (4,587)	4,668	51.08
Hispanic (214)	222	2.43

Lexington

Place Type: Town
County: Lexington
Population: 17,870†

Ancestry‡	Population	%
African, Sub-Saharan (50)	58	0.35
African (50)	50	0.30
Ghanaian (0)	8	0.05
American (2,264)	2,264	13.80
Arab (36)	36	0.22
Lebanese (22)	22	0.13
Syrian (14)	14	0.09
Armenian (0)	33	0.20
Austrian (0)	13	0.08
British (45)	114	0.69
Bulgarian (50)	102	0.62
Canadian (51)	78	0.48
Celtic (12)	12	0.07
Czech (9)	35	0.21
Czechoslovakian (0)	15	0.09
Danish (0)	19	0.12
Dutch (93)	167	1.02
English (1,032)	2,212	13.48
European (173)	235	1.43
French, ex. Basque (87)	342	2.08
French Canadian (142)	158	0.96
German (613)	2,268	13.82
Greek (0)	25	0.15
Hungarian (0)	32	0.20
Irish (589)	2,043	12.45
Israeli (58)	110	0.67
Italian (285)	625	3.81
Lithuanian (10)	21	0.13
Norwegian (39)	96	0.59
Polish (137)	291	1.77
Russian (15)	38	0.23
Scandinavian (10)	89	0.54
Scotch-Irish (441)	745	4.54
Scottish (197)	488	2.97
Slovak (10)	34	0.21
Swedish (82)	182	1.11
Swiss (15)	45	0.27
Turkish (13)	13	0.08
Ukrainian (15)	29	0.18

*Notes: † The Census 2010 population figure is used to calculate the percentages in the Hispanic Origin and Race categories. Ancestry percentages are based on the 2006-2010 American Community Survey population (not shown); ‡ Numbers in parentheses indicate the number of people reporting a single ancestry; * Numbers in parentheses indicate the number of persons reporting this race alone, not in combination with any other race; Please refer to the Explanation of Data for more information.*

Welsh (44)	130	0.79
West Indian, ex. Hispanic (0)	8	0.05
Haitian (0)	8	0.05
Yugoslavian (16)	16	0.10

Hispanic Origin	Population	%
Hispanic or Latino (of any race)	631	3.53
Central American, ex. Mexican	67	0.37
Costa Rican	7	0.04
Guatemalan	16	0.09
Honduran	18	0.10
Nicaraguan	7	0.04
Panamanian	11	0.06
Salvadoran	8	0.04
Cuban	33	0.18
Dominican Republic	16	0.09
Mexican	218	1.22
Puerto Rican	170	0.95
South American	64	0.36
Argentinean	11	0.06
Bolivian	3	0.02
Chilean	2	0.01
Colombian	14	0.08
Ecuadorian	4	0.02
Peruvian	12	0.07
Uruguayan	1	0.01
Venezuelan	17	0.10
Other Hispanic or Latino	63	0.35

Race*	Population	%
African-American/Black (2,264)	2,393	13.39
Not Hispanic (2,237)	2,352	13.16
Hispanic (27)	41	0.23
American Indian/Alaska Native (48)	124	0.69
Not Hispanic (47)	117	0.65
Hispanic (1)	7	0.04
Blackfeet (0)	4	0.02
Cherokee (7)	35	0.20
Cheyenne (0)	1	0.01
Chippewa (0)	2	0.01
Choctaw (0)	1	0.01
Creek (3)	4	0.02
Inupiat *(Alaska Native)* (2)	2	0.01
Lumbee (5)	7	0.04
Mexican American Ind. (0)	3	0.02
Sioux (0)	1	0.01
South American Ind. (0)	1	0.01
Yup'ik *(Alaska Native)* (1)	1	0.01
Asian (665)	756	4.23
Not Hispanic (664)	750	4.20
Hispanic (1)	6	0.03
Cambodian (1)	3	0.02
Chinese, ex. Taiwanese (146)	165	0.92
Filipino (18)	43	0.24
Indian (367)	380	2.13
Japanese (22)	36	0.20
Korean (44)	64	0.36
Laotian (2)	4	0.02
Pakistani (3)	7	0.04
Taiwanese (6)	6	0.03
Thai (6)	11	0.06
Vietnamese (38)	47	0.26
Hawaii Native/Pacific Islander (6)	11	0.06
Not Hispanic (6)	11	0.06
Guamanian/Chamorro (3)	3	0.02
Native Hawaiian (0)	3	0.02
Samoan (1)	2	0.01
White (14,434)	14,644	81.95
Not Hispanic (14,027)	14,214	79.54
Hispanic (407)	430	2.41

Little River

Place Type: CDP
County: Horry
Population: 8,960†

Ancestry‡	Population	%
American (993)	993	11.45
Arab (22)	75	0.86
Lebanese (22)	75	0.86
Armenian (24)	66	0.76
Austrian (0)	48	0.55
Belgian (0)	19	0.22
British (56)	67	0.77
Canadian (16)	16	0.18
Czech (0)	46	0.53
Czechoslovakian (25)	25	0.29
Danish (9)	9	0.10
Dutch (53)	185	2.13
English (364)	1,232	14.20
European (85)	101	1.16
Finnish (0)	13	0.15
French, ex. Basque (97)	382	4.40
French Canadian (11)	11	0.13
German (545)	1,902	21.93
Greek (45)	45	0.52
Hungarian (85)	99	1.14
Iranian (6)	6	0.07
Irish (600)	1,797	20.71
Italian (401)	690	7.95
Lithuanian (15)	15	0.17
Norwegian (0)	15	0.17
Polish (152)	222	2.56
Romanian (14)	28	0.32
Russian (23)	51	0.59
Scotch-Irish (305)	516	5.95
Scottish (126)	364	4.20
Slovak (23)	23	0.27
Slovene (13)	13	0.15
Swedish (14)	66	0.76
Swiss (13)	27	0.31
Ukrainian (0)	11	0.13
Welsh (27)	106	1.22

Hispanic Origin	Population	%
Hispanic or Latino (of any race)	290	3.24
Central American, ex. Mexican	15	0.17
Costa Rican	3	0.03
Guatemalan	7	0.08
Honduran	1	0.01
Panamanian	1	0.01
Salvadoran	3	0.03
Cuban	12	0.13
Dominican Republic	5	0.06
Mexican	161	1.80
Puerto Rican	46	0.51
South American	24	0.27
Argentinean	1	0.01
Chilean	1	0.01
Colombian	7	0.08
Ecuadorian	8	0.09
Peruvian	1	0.01
Venezuelan	6	0.07
Other Hispanic or Latino	27	0.30

Race*	Population	%
African-American/Black (593)	642	7.17
Not Hispanic (587)	635	7.09
Hispanic (6)	7	0.08
American Indian/Alaska Native (48)	89	0.99
Not Hispanic (45)	85	0.95
Hispanic (3)	4	0.04
Apache (0)	2	0.02
Blackfeet (0)	5	0.06
Canadian/French Am. Ind. (0)	1	0.01
Cherokee (11)	25	0.28
Chippewa (0)	1	0.01
Cree (0)	3	0.03
Creek (0)	1	0.01
Inupiat *(Alaska Native)* (1)	1	0.01
Iroquois (5)	5	0.06
Lumbee (8)	9	0.10
Navajo (3)	3	0.03
Sioux (0)	1	0.01
Asian (77)	91	1.02
Not Hispanic (77)	91	1.02
Cambodian (1)	1	0.01
Chinese, ex. Taiwanese (25)	25	0.28
Filipino (5)	9	0.10
Indian (18)	18	0.20
Indonesian (5)	5	0.06
Japanese (1)	4	0.04
Korean (8)	10	0.11
Thai (2)	5	0.06
Vietnamese (12)	12	0.13
Hawaii Native/Pacific Islander (0)	10	0.11
Not Hispanic (0)	8	0.09
Hispanic (0)	2	0.02
Native Hawaiian (0)	3	0.03
Samoan (0)	1	0.01
White (7,978)	8,076	90.13
Not Hispanic (7,859)	7,945	88.67
Hispanic (119)	131	1.46

Mauldin

Place Type: City
County: Greenville
Population: 22,889†

Ancestry‡	Population	%
African, Sub-Saharan (118)	125	0.58
African (118)	125	0.58
American (3,443)	3,443	15.88
Arab (97)	112	0.52
Arab (13)	13	0.06
Jordanian (70)	70	0.32
Lebanese (14)	29	0.13
Austrian (0)	65	0.30
Basque (10)	10	0.05
British (94)	107	0.49
Canadian (37)	64	0.30
Croatian (38)	38	0.18
Czech (22)	107	0.49
Czechoslovakian (12)	28	0.13
Danish (0)	13	0.06
Dutch (47)	203	0.94
English (1,018)	2,292	10.57
European (157)	232	1.07
Finnish (16)	45	0.21
French, ex. Basque (48)	421	1.94
French Canadian (24)	98	0.45
German (696)	2,227	10.27
Greek (85)	114	0.53
Hungarian (25)	36	0.17
Iranian (11)	11	0.05
Irish (774)	2,411	11.12
Israeli (10)	10	0.05
Italian (166)	561	2.59
Lithuanian (13)	70	0.32
Northern European (12)	25	0.12
Norwegian (67)	115	0.53
Polish (99)	491	2.26
Portuguese (18)	81	0.37
Romanian (0)	38	0.18
Russian (12)	82	0.38
Scandinavian (20)	32	0.15
Scotch-Irish (344)	704	3.25
Scottish (197)	524	2.42
Slovak (58)	99	0.46
Slovene (72)	90	0.42
Swedish (0)	79	0.36
Swiss (16)	16	0.07
Ukrainian (0)	34	0.16
Welsh (0)	63	0.29
West Indian, ex. Hispanic (49)	66	0.30
Trinidadian/Tobagonian (49)	66	0.30
Yugoslavian (14)	30	0.14

Hispanic Origin	Population	%
Hispanic or Latino (of any race)	1,756	7.67
Central American, ex. Mexican	123	0.54
Costa Rican	15	0.07
Guatemalan	12	0.05
Honduran	27	0.12
Nicaraguan	27	0.12
Panamanian	14	0.06
Salvadoran	28	0.12
Cuban	73	0.32

*Notes: † The Census 2010 population figure is used to calculate the percentages in the Hispanic Origin and Race categories. Ancestry percentages are based on the 2006-2010 American Community Survey population (not shown); ‡ Numbers in parentheses indicate the number of people reporting a single ancestry; * Numbers in parentheses indicate the number of persons reporting this race alone, not in combination with any other race; Please refer to the Explanation of Data for more information.*

Dominican Republic	32	0.14
Mexican	514	2.25
Puerto Rican	214	0.93
South American	659	2.88
Argentinean	12	0.05
Bolivian	3	0.01
Chilean	13	0.06
Colombian	531	2.32
Ecuadorian	28	0.12
Paraguayan	1	<0.01
Peruvian	37	0.16
Uruguayan	10	0.04
Venezuelan	20	0.09
Other South American	4	0.02
Other Hispanic or Latino	141	0.62

Race*	Population	%
African-American/Black (5,152)	5,410	23.64
Not Hispanic (5,090)	5,311	23.20
Hispanic (62)	99	0.43
American Indian/Alaska Native (62)	130	0.57
Not Hispanic (45)	110	0.48
Hispanic (17)	20	0.09
Apache (2)	3	0.01
Blackfeet (0)	1	<0.01
Canadian/French Am. Ind. (0)	3	0.01
Central American Ind. (2)	2	0.01
Cherokee (11)	35	0.15
Cheyenne (0)	1	<0.01
Chippewa (0)	1	<0.01
Creek (1)	1	<0.01
Hopi (1)	1	<0.01
Iroquois (0)	1	<0.01
Lumbee (6)	9	0.04
Navajo (0)	1	<0.01
Potawatomi (2)	2	0.01
Seminole (0)	1	<0.01
Sioux (3)	3	0.01
Tlingit-Haida *(Alaska Native)* (0)	1	<0.01
Yaqui (1)	1	<0.01
Asian (808)	954	4.17
Not Hispanic (803)	935	4.08
Hispanic (5)	19	0.08
Cambodian (0)	2	0.01
Chinese, ex. Taiwanese (91)	116	0.51
Filipino (83)	125	0.55
Indian (328)	353	1.54
Indonesian (2)	2	0.01
Japanese (36)	40	0.17
Korean (51)	84	0.37
Laotian (4)	4	0.02
Nepalese (3)	3	0.01
Pakistani (22)	24	0.10
Sri Lankan (7)	7	0.03
Taiwanese (2)	2	0.01
Thai (12)	13	0.06
Vietnamese (130)	142	0.62
Hawaii Native/Pacific Islander (18)	45	0.20
Not Hispanic (16)	32	0.14
Hispanic (2)	13	0.06
Guamanian/Chamorro (2)	8	0.03
Native Hawaiian (7)	13	0.06
Samoan (0)	1	<0.01
White (15,731)	16,134	70.49
Not Hispanic (14,751)	15,053	65.77
Hispanic (980)	1,081	4.72

Moncks Corner

Place Type: Town
County: Berkeley
Population: 7,885†

Ancestry‡	Population	%
African, Sub-Saharan (53)	53	0.71
African (44)	44	0.59
South African (9)	9	0.12
American (862)	862	11.48
Belgian (0)	26	0.35
Dutch (37)	63	0.84
English (180)	347	4.62
European (123)	123	1.64
French, ex. Basque (11)	88	1.17
French Canadian (0)	20	0.27
German (219)	485	6.46
Irish (143)	396	5.27
Italian (47)	171	2.28
Lithuanian (15)	22	0.29
Polish (0)	32	0.43
Portuguese (6)	6	0.08
Scandinavian (13)	13	0.17
Scotch-Irish (25)	136	1.81
Scottish (7)	97	1.29
Swedish (37)	97	1.29
Swiss (0)	11	0.15
Welsh (11)	31	0.41

Hispanic Origin	Population	%
Hispanic or Latino (of any race)	400	5.07
Central American, ex. Mexican	17	0.22
Costa Rican	3	0.04
Guatemalan	2	0.03
Honduran	1	0.01
Nicaraguan	3	0.04
Panamanian	8	0.10
Cuban	3	0.04
Dominican Republic	3	0.04
Mexican	267	3.39
Puerto Rican	61	0.77
South American	14	0.18
Argentinean	5	0.06
Colombian	4	0.05
Ecuadorian	3	0.04
Paraguayan	1	0.01
Venezuelan	1	0.01
Other Hispanic or Latino	35	0.44

Race*	Population	%
African-American/Black (2,835)	2,933	37.20
Not Hispanic (2,811)	2,892	36.68
Hispanic (24)	41	0.52
American Indian/Alaska Native (37)	91	1.15
Not Hispanic (22)	66	0.84
Hispanic (15)	25	0.32
Apache (1)	1	0.01
Cherokee (3)	9	0.11
Chickasaw (0)	1	0.01
Chippewa (0)	1	0.01
Iroquois (2)	2	0.03
Lumbee (3)	6	0.08
Mexican American Ind. (7)	7	0.09
Sioux (1)	5	0.06
Spanish American Ind. (4)	4	0.05
Asian (42)	76	0.96
Not Hispanic (42)	75	0.95
Hispanic (0)	1	0.01
Bangladeshi (2)	2	0.03
Chinese, ex. Taiwanese (1)	8	0.10
Filipino (8)	23	0.29
Indian (30)	33	0.42
Japanese (0)	2	0.03
Korean (0)	6	0.08
Vietnamese (0)	3	0.04
Hawaii Native/Pacific Islander (2)	11	0.14
Not Hispanic (2)	11	0.14
Guamanian/Chamorro (2)	2	0.03
Native Hawaiian (0)	4	0.05
Samoan (0)	1	0.01
White (4,550)	4,672	59.25
Not Hispanic (4,471)	4,575	58.02
Hispanic (79)	97	1.23

Mount Pleasant

Place Type: Town
County: Charleston
Population: 67,843†

Ancestry‡	Population	%
African, Sub-Saharan (108)	171	0.27
African (32)	47	0.07
South African (60)	108	0.17
Other Sub-Saharan African (16)	16	0.02
American (7,092)	7,092	11.05
Arab (115)	299	0.47
Egyptian (0)	12	0.02
Lebanese (115)	287	0.45
Armenian (21)	49	0.08
Austrian (77)	215	0.33
Belgian (15)	36	0.06
British (203)	424	0.66
Bulgarian (29)	29	0.05
Canadian (63)	75	0.12
Celtic (17)	34	0.05
Croatian (4)	63	0.10
Czech (55)	295	0.46
Czechoslovakian (26)	71	0.11
Danish (30)	125	0.19
Dutch (310)	986	1.54
Eastern European (36)	56	0.09
English (4,029)	10,047	15.65
European (1,229)	1,383	2.15
Finnish (28)	112	0.17
French, ex. Basque (683)	2,855	4.45
French Canadian (115)	158	0.25
German (3,416)	11,137	17.35
Greek (231)	378	0.59
Hungarian (144)	422	0.66
Irish (4,437)	11,021	17.16
Israeli (10)	10	0.02
Italian (1,654)	4,378	6.82
Lithuanian (92)	175	0.27
Northern European (136)	136	0.21
Norwegian (117)	448	0.70
Pennsylvania German (0)	13	0.02
Polish (438)	1,755	2.73
Portuguese (55)	193	0.30
Romanian (54)	85	0.13
Russian (325)	704	1.10
Scandinavian (82)	219	0.34
Scotch-Irish (1,682)	2,909	4.53
Scottish (1,274)	3,089	4.81
Serbian (0)	55	0.09
Slavic (0)	31	0.05
Slovak (63)	146	0.23
Slovene (22)	22	0.03
Soviet Union (0)	14	0.02
Swedish (200)	951	1.48
Swiss (94)	254	0.40
Turkish (14)	14	0.02
Ukrainian (63)	240	0.37
Welsh (131)	560	0.87
Yugoslavian (0)	33	0.05

Hispanic Origin	Population	%
Hispanic or Latino (of any race)	1,850	2.73
Central American, ex. Mexican	138	0.20
Costa Rican	20	0.03
Guatemalan	53	0.08
Honduran	16	0.02
Nicaraguan	15	0.02
Panamanian	16	0.02
Salvadoran	18	0.03
Cuban	124	0.18
Dominican Republic	31	0.05
Mexican	734	1.08
Puerto Rican	254	0.37
South American	356	0.52
Argentinean	41	0.06
Bolivian	6	0.01
Chilean	36	0.05
Colombian	111	0.16
Ecuadorian	47	0.07
Paraguayan	8	0.01
Peruvian	59	0.09
Uruguayan	10	0.01
Venezuelan	36	0.05
Other South American	2	<0.01
Other Hispanic or Latino	213	0.31

*Notes: † The Census 2010 population figure is used to calculate the percentages in the Hispanic Origin and Race categories. Ancestry percentages are based on the 2006-2010 American Community Survey population (not shown); ‡ Numbers in parentheses indicate the number of people reporting a single ancestry; * Numbers in parentheses indicate the number of persons reporting this race alone, not in combination with any other race; Please refer to the Explanation of Data for more information.*

Race*	Population	%
African-American/Black (3,439)	3,701	5.46
Not Hispanic (3,403)	3,636	5.36
Hispanic (36)	65	0.10
American Indian/Alaska Native (166)	346	0.51
Not Hispanic (131)	288	0.42
Hispanic (35)	58	0.09
Blackfeet (2)	5	0.01
Canadian/French Am. Ind. (0)	2	<0.01
Central American Ind. (1)	1	<0.01
Cherokee (32)	93	0.14
Chickasaw (0)	2	<0.01
Chippewa (9)	9	0.01
Choctaw (4)	10	0.01
Comanche (3)	3	<0.01
Creek (2)	6	0.01
Delaware (2)	2	<0.01
Iroquois (6)	7	0.01
Lumbee (9)	14	0.02
Mexican American Ind. (18)	19	0.03
Navajo (1)	8	0.01
Osage (2)	2	<0.01
Potawatomi (0)	1	<0.01
Shoshone (0)	1	<0.01
Sioux (0)	2	<0.01
South American Ind. (1)	1	<0.01
Spanish American Ind. (1)	1	<0.01
Tlingit-Haida *(Alaska Native)* (1)	1	<0.01
Tsimshian *(Alaska Native)* (2)	2	<0.01
Asian (1,115)	1,418	2.09
Not Hispanic (1,103)	1,381	2.04
Hispanic (12)	37	0.05
Burmese (11)	11	0.02
Cambodian (15)	16	0.02
Chinese, ex. Taiwanese (296)	335	0.49
Filipino (120)	217	0.32
Hmong (1)	1	<0.01
Indian (282)	327	0.48
Indonesian (7)	13	0.02
Japanese (53)	88	0.13
Korean (109)	145	0.21
Laotian (6)	6	0.01
Malaysian (1)	5	0.01
Nepalese (6)	6	0.01
Pakistani (28)	29	0.04
Sri Lankan (5)	11	0.02
Taiwanese (14)	17	0.03
Thai (8)	12	0.02
Vietnamese (112)	134	0.20
Hawaii Native/Pacific Islander (25)	52	0.08
Not Hispanic (20)	44	0.06
Hispanic (5)	8	0.01
Guamanian/Chamorro (19)	29	0.04
Native Hawaiian (4)	10	0.01
Samoan (1)	9	0.01
Tongan (0)	1	<0.01
White (61,938)	62,618	92.30
Not Hispanic (60,653)	61,219	90.24
Hispanic (1,285)	1,399	2.06

Murrells Inlet

Place Type: CDP
County: Georgetown
Population: 7,547†

Ancestry‡	Population	%
American (733)	733	10.00
Austrian (12)	22	0.30
British (31)	31	0.42
Czechoslovakian (0)	9	0.12
Dutch (49)	96	1.31
Eastern European (19)	19	0.26
English (890)	1,429	19.49
European (62)	62	0.85
French, ex. Basque (49)	178	2.43
French Canadian (0)	77	1.05
German (331)	982	13.40
Hungarian (9)	48	0.65
Irish (591)	1,352	18.44
Italian (316)	439	5.99
Polish (141)	400	5.46
Russian (0)	43	0.59
Scotch-Irish (435)	616	8.40
Scottish (46)	120	1.64
Slovak (8)	8	0.11
Swedish (27)	80	1.09
Swiss (9)	18	0.25
Ukrainian (0)	9	0.12
Welsh (58)	67	0.91
Yugoslavian (0)	9	0.12

Hispanic Origin	Population	%
Hispanic or Latino (of any race)	168	2.23
Central American, ex. Mexican	12	0.16
Costa Rican	1	0.01
Guatemalan	1	0.01
Nicaraguan	3	0.04
Salvadoran	7	0.09
Cuban	8	0.11
Dominican Republic	8	0.11
Mexican	80	1.06
Puerto Rican	29	0.38
South American	20	0.27
Argentinean	3	0.04
Bolivian	1	0.01
Chilean	1	0.01
Colombian	3	0.04
Ecuadorian	1	0.01
Peruvian	3	0.04
Other South American	8	0.11
Other Hispanic or Latino	11	0.15

Race*	Population	%
African-American/Black (493)	524	6.94
Not Hispanic (491)	509	6.74
Hispanic (2)	15	0.20
American Indian/Alaska Native (22)	39	0.52
Not Hispanic (22)	39	0.52
Cherokee (11)	18	0.24
Iroquois (1)	4	0.05
Lumbee (4)	4	0.05
Seminole (2)	2	0.03
Sioux (0)	1	0.01
Asian (71)	82	1.09
Not Hispanic (71)	80	1.06
Hispanic (0)	2	0.03
Chinese, ex. Taiwanese (8)	9	0.12
Filipino (32)	35	0.46
Indian (16)	18	0.24
Japanese (1)	4	0.05
Korean (4)	4	0.05
Laotian (0)	1	0.01
Thai (2)	3	0.04
Vietnamese (3)	4	0.05
Hawaii Native/Pacific Islander (2)	7	0.09
Not Hispanic (2)	6	0.08
Hispanic (0)	1	0.01
Native Hawaiian (2)	4	0.05
Samoan (0)	1	0.01
White (6,842)	6,894	91.35
Not Hispanic (6,749)	6,785	89.90
Hispanic (93)	109	1.44

Myrtle Beach

Place Type: City
County: Horry
Population: 27,109†

Ancestry‡	Population	%
African, Sub-Saharan (37)	37	0.14
African (37)	37	0.14
Albanian (243)	243	0.91
Alsatian (0)	11	0.04
American (2,651)	2,651	9.93
Arab (141)	163	0.61
Lebanese (83)	83	0.31
Moroccan (58)	58	0.22
Other Arab (0)	22	0.08
Austrian (13)	50	0.19
Brazilian (0)	34	0.13
British (40)	50	0.19
Bulgarian (14)	30	0.11
Canadian (58)	58	0.22
Croatian (19)	43	0.16
Czech (8)	39	0.15
Danish (51)	66	0.25
Dutch (101)	401	1.50
English (1,287)	2,764	10.35
European (376)	410	1.54
Finnish (0)	27	0.10
French, ex. Basque (274)	768	2.88
French Canadian (110)	155	0.58
German (755)	2,495	9.35
Greek (64)	162	0.61
Hungarian (28)	71	0.27
Irish (890)	3,101	11.62
Israeli (15)	59	0.22
Italian (845)	1,796	6.73
Lithuanian (26)	46	0.17
New Zealander (17)	17	0.06
Norwegian (44)	164	0.61
Pennsylvania German (0)	16	0.06
Polish (150)	778	2.91
Portuguese (296)	357	1.34
Romanian (116)	116	0.43
Russian (17)	74	0.28
Scandinavian (8)	8	0.03
Scotch-Irish (577)	829	3.11
Scottish (222)	576	2.16
Serbian (0)	12	0.04
Slovak (11)	11	0.04
Slovene (11)	19	0.07
Swedish (36)	104	0.39
Swiss (21)	72	0.27
Ukrainian (31)	31	0.12
Welsh (88)	350	1.31
West Indian, ex. Hispanic (105)	108	0.40
Haitian (0)	3	0.01
Jamaican (105)	105	0.39

Hispanic Origin	Population	%
Hispanic or Latino (of any race)	3,708	13.68
Central American, ex. Mexican	628	2.32
Costa Rican	13	0.05
Guatemalan	384	1.42
Honduran	177	0.65
Nicaraguan	7	0.03
Panamanian	12	0.04
Salvadoran	35	0.13
Cuban	47	0.17
Dominican Republic	18	0.07
Mexican	2,412	8.90
Puerto Rican	211	0.78
South American	100	0.37
Argentinean	10	0.04
Bolivian	1	<0.01
Chilean	6	0.02
Colombian	32	0.12
Ecuadorian	16	0.06
Peruvian	11	0.04
Uruguayan	2	0.01
Venezuelan	22	0.08
Other Hispanic or Latino	292	1.08

Race*	Population	%
African-American/Black (3,764)	4,080	15.05
Not Hispanic (3,712)	3,982	14.69
Hispanic (52)	98	0.36
American Indian/Alaska Native (199)	352	1.30
Not Hispanic (139)	273	1.01
Hispanic (60)	79	0.29
Apache (5)	6	0.02
Blackfeet (1)	17	0.06
Central American Ind. (0)	4	0.01
Cherokee (51)	105	0.39
Chippewa (1)	4	0.01
Choctaw (0)	6	0.02

*Notes: † The Census 2010 population figure is used to calculate the percentages in the Hispanic Origin and Race categories. Ancestry percentages are based on the 2006-2010 American Community Survey population (not shown); ‡ Numbers in parentheses indicate the number of people reporting a single ancestry; * Numbers in parentheses indicate the number of persons reporting this race alone, not in combination with any other race; Please refer to the Explanation of Data for more information.*

Crow (0)	3	0.01
Iroquois (11)	23	0.08
Lumbee (12)	16	0.06
Mexican American Ind. (4)	4	0.01
Navajo (2)	3	0.01
Sioux (7)	11	0.04
South American Ind. (1)	1	<0.01
Asian (399)	624	2.30
Not Hispanic (397)	610	2.25
Hispanic (2)	14	0.05
Cambodian (0)	3	0.01
Chinese, ex. Taiwanese (78)	82	0.30
Filipino (58)	86	0.32
Indian (78)	91	0.34
Indonesian (4)	4	0.01
Japanese (24)	42	0.15
Korean (15)	19	0.07
Laotian (3)	4	0.01
Sri Lankan (1)	1	<0.01
Taiwanese (1)	1	<0.01
Thai (30)	36	0.13
Vietnamese (95)	99	0.37
Hawaii Native/Pacific Islander (81)	99	0.37
Not Hispanic (67)	80	0.30
Hispanic (14)	19	0.07
Guamanian/Chamorro (27)	27	0.10
Native Hawaiian (5)	10	0.04
Samoan (1)	1	<0.01
White (19,588)	20,254	74.71
Not Hispanic (18,380)	18,935	69.85
Hispanic (1,208)	1,319	4.87

Newberry

Place Type: City
County: Newberry
Population: 10,277†

Ancestry‡	Population	%
African, Sub-Saharan (52)	52	0.51
African (35)	35	0.34
Ghanaian (15)	15	0.15
South African (2)	2	0.02
American (1,159)	1,159	11.28
Arab (10)	10	0.10
Egyptian (10)	10	0.10
Belgian (11)	11	0.11
Danish (0)	21	0.20
Dutch (32)	70	0.68
English (357)	973	9.47
European (71)	71	0.69
Finnish (21)	21	0.20
French, ex. Basque (28)	210	2.04
German (484)	983	9.57
Greek (135)	149	1.45
Hungarian (20)	20	0.19
Irish (322)	653	6.36
Italian (0)	87	0.85
Norwegian (11)	13	0.13
Polish (0)	29	0.28
Romanian (0)	16	0.16
Russian (49)	121	1.18
Scotch-Irish (182)	308	3.00
Scottish (106)	311	3.03
Swedish (0)	16	0.16
Swiss (62)	84	0.82
Ukrainian (0)	23	0.22
Welsh (16)	165	1.61

Hispanic Origin	Population	%
Hispanic or Latino (of any race)	882	8.58
Central American, ex. Mexican	127	1.24
Costa Rican	3	0.03
Guatemalan	92	0.90
Honduran	5	0.05
Nicaraguan	24	0.23
Panamanian	2	0.02
Salvadoran	1	0.01
Cuban	11	0.11
Mexican	637	6.20
Puerto Rican	46	0.45
South American	13	0.13
Argentinean	1	0.01
Colombian	8	0.08
Ecuadorian	1	0.01
Peruvian	2	0.02
Venezuelan	1	0.01
Other Hispanic or Latino	48	0.47

Race*	Population	%
African-American/Black (4,683)	4,812	46.82
Not Hispanic (4,642)	4,757	46.29
Hispanic (41)	55	0.54
American Indian/Alaska Native (41)	76	0.74
Not Hispanic (25)	55	0.54
Hispanic (16)	21	0.20
Blackfeet (0)	1	0.01
Cherokee (11)	23	0.22
Chickasaw (0)	1	0.01
Lumbee (2)	2	0.02
Mexican American Ind. (5)	6	0.06
Pima (0)	1	0.01
Puget Sound Salish (0)	2	0.02
Tohono O'Odham (0)	1	0.01
Asian (63)	84	0.82
Not Hispanic (62)	78	0.76
Hispanic (1)	6	0.06
Chinese, ex. Taiwanese (11)	12	0.12
Filipino (6)	8	0.08
Indian (21)	22	0.21
Japanese (1)	1	0.01
Korean (1)	7	0.07
Laotian (3)	3	0.03
Nepalese (1)	1	0.01
Pakistani (2)	2	0.02
Thai (2)	2	0.02
Vietnamese (12)	17	0.17
Hawaii Native/Pacific Islander (13)	23	0.22
Not Hispanic (2)	9	0.09
Hispanic (11)	14	0.14
Guamanian/Chamorro (11)	13	0.13
Native Hawaiian (1)	2	0.02
White (4,669)	4,817	46.87
Not Hispanic (4,512)	4,628	45.03
Hispanic (157)	189	1.84

North Augusta

Place Type: City
County: Aiken
Population: 21,348†

Ancestry‡	Population	%
African, Sub-Saharan (198)	198	0.96
African (198)	198	0.96
American (3,308)	3,308	16.11
Arab (42)	42	0.20
Arab (25)	25	0.12
Lebanese (12)	12	0.06
Syrian (5)	5	0.02
Austrian (0)	52	0.25
Belgian (16)	37	0.18
British (46)	67	0.33
Croatian (0)	16	0.08
Czech (20)	26	0.13
Czechoslovakian (9)	9	0.04
Danish (0)	54	0.26
Dutch (58)	302	1.47
Eastern European (0)	10	0.05
English (1,709)	3,201	15.59
European (187)	222	1.08
French, ex. Basque (80)	607	2.96
French Canadian (53)	123	0.60
German (847)	2,261	11.01
German Russian (17)	17	0.08
Greek (23)	23	0.11
Guyanese (0)	9	0.04
Hungarian (13)	95	0.46
Irish (880)	2,237	10.89
Italian (113)	541	2.63
Latvian (0)	13	0.06
Northern European (14)	14	0.07
Norwegian (14)	48	0.23
Pennsylvania German (10)	10	0.05
Polish (57)	367	1.79
Portuguese (15)	33	0.16
Romanian (0)	13	0.06
Russian (36)	76	0.37
Scotch-Irish (363)	632	3.08
Scottish (179)	479	2.33
Slavic (8)	25	0.12
Slovak (10)	10	0.05
Slovene (10)	10	0.05
Swedish (8)	68	0.33
Swiss (16)	16	0.08
Ukrainian (48)	48	0.23
Welsh (31)	236	1.15
West Indian, ex. Hispanic (88)	88	0.43
Barbadian (26)	26	0.13
Belizean (30)	30	0.15
West Indian (32)	32	0.16
Yugoslavian (12)	12	0.06

Hispanic Origin	Population	%
Hispanic or Latino (of any race)	890	4.17
Central American, ex. Mexican	127	0.59
Costa Rican	61	0.29
Guatemalan	10	0.05
Honduran	21	0.10
Nicaraguan	9	0.04
Panamanian	8	0.04
Salvadoran	18	0.08
Cuban	18	0.08
Dominican Republic	5	0.02
Mexican	488	2.29
Puerto Rican	158	0.74
South American	31	0.15
Chilean	4	0.02
Colombian	9	0.04
Ecuadorian	14	0.07
Paraguayan	1	<0.01
Peruvian	2	0.01
Venezuelan	1	<0.01
Other Hispanic or Latino	63	0.30

Race*	Population	%
African-American/Black (4,362)	4,553	21.33
Not Hispanic (4,316)	4,496	21.06
Hispanic (46)	57	0.27
American Indian/Alaska Native (54)	158	0.74
Not Hispanic (44)	139	0.65
Hispanic (10)	19	0.09
Apache (0)	1	<0.01
Blackfeet (1)	4	0.02
Cherokee (10)	53	0.25
Chickasaw (4)	4	0.02
Choctaw (1)	1	<0.01
Comanche (2)	2	0.01
Creek (0)	9	0.04
Delaware (1)	1	<0.01
Iroquois (1)	1	<0.01
Lumbee (0)	3	0.01
Mexican American Ind. (1)	1	<0.01
Navajo (1)	3	0.01
Osage (0)	1	<0.01
Pueblo (1)	3	0.01
Seminole (0)	1	<0.01
Shoshone (0)	1	<0.01
Sioux (0)	7	0.03
South American Ind. (1)	1	<0.01
Spanish American Ind. (2)	2	0.01
Yakama (1)	1	<0.01
Asian (238)	336	1.57
Not Hispanic (236)	330	1.55
Hispanic (2)	6	0.03
Bangladeshi (1)	3	0.01
Burmese (4)	4	0.02
Chinese, ex. Taiwanese (47)	56	0.26
Filipino (28)	43	0.20
Indian (48)	70	0.33

*Notes: † The Census 2010 population figure is used to calculate the percentages in the Hispanic Origin and Race categories. Ancestry percentages are based on the 2006-2010 American Community Survey population (not shown); ‡ Numbers in parentheses indicate the number of people reporting a single ancestry; * Numbers in parentheses indicate the number of persons reporting this race alone, not in combination with any other race; Please refer to the Explanation of Data for more information.*

Japanese (14)	27	0.13
Korean (18)	38	0.18
Laotian (4)	5	0.02
Malaysian (1)	1	<0.01
Pakistani (2)	2	0.01
Thai (5)	10	0.05
Vietnamese (54)	58	0.27
Hawaii Native/Pacific Islander (8)	18	0.08
Not Hispanic (8)	18	0.08
Guamanian/Chamorro (2)	5	0.02
Native Hawaiian (6)	11	0.05
Samoan (0)	1	<0.01
White (15,837)	16,208	75.92
Not Hispanic (15,468)	15,776	73.90
Hispanic (369)	432	2.02

North Charleston

Place Type: City
County: Charleston
Population: 97,471†

Ancestry‡	Population	%
African, Sub-Saharan (632)	1,027	1.09
African (580)	951	1.01
Cape Verdean (7)	7	0.01
Ethiopian (21)	21	0.02
South African (0)	24	0.03
Sudanese (9)	9	0.01
Other Sub-Saharan African (15)	15	0.02
Albanian (14)	22	0.02
American (6,527)	6,527	6.91
Arab (30)	71	0.08
Arab (17)	33	0.03
Moroccan (0)	9	0.01
Syrian (0)	16	0.02
Other Arab (13)	13	0.01
Armenian (0)	20	0.02
Australian (40)	40	0.04
Austrian (46)	184	0.19
Belgian (22)	53	0.06
Brazilian (73)	73	0.08
British (57)	140	0.15
Canadian (100)	186	0.20
Croatian (0)	42	0.04
Czech (28)	120	0.13
Czechoslovakian (46)	46	0.05
Danish (20)	98	0.10
Dutch (66)	519	0.55
Eastern European (24)	24	0.03
English (2,397)	5,132	5.43
European (594)	792	0.84
Finnish (0)	22	0.02
French, ex. Basque (534)	1,585	1.68
French Canadian (231)	423	0.45
German (3,039)	7,850	8.30
Greek (55)	233	0.25
Guyanese (26)	32	0.03
Hungarian (54)	154	0.16
Irish (1,806)	5,476	5.79
Italian (693)	1,869	1.98
Latvian (0)	47	0.05
Macedonian (12)	12	0.01
New Zealander (18)	18	0.02
Northern European (48)	48	0.05
Norwegian (121)	321	0.34
Pennsylvania German (13)	41	0.04
Polish (364)	1,154	1.22
Portuguese (151)	242	0.26
Romanian (10)	65	0.07
Russian (124)	248	0.26
Scandinavian (79)	229	0.24
Scotch-Irish (635)	1,346	1.42
Scottish (383)	1,098	1.16
Slavic (11)	11	0.01
Slovak (34)	46	0.05
Slovene (0)	17	0.02
Swedish (109)	328	0.35
Swiss (0)	57	0.06
Turkish (101)	101	0.11
Ukrainian (36)	228	0.24
Welsh (66)	325	0.34
West Indian, ex. Hispanic (368)	504	0.53
British West Indian (37)	37	0.04
Dutch West Indian (46)	46	0.05
Haitian (27)	27	0.03
Jamaican (82)	136	0.14
Trinidadian/Tobagonian (101)	111	0.12
West Indian (75)	147	0.16
Yugoslavian (15)	43	0.05

Hispanic Origin	Population	%
Hispanic or Latino (of any race)	10,617	10.89
Central American, ex. Mexican	1,142	1.17
Costa Rican	24	0.02
Guatemalan	558	0.57
Honduran	264	0.27
Nicaraguan	59	0.06
Panamanian	84	0.09
Salvadoran	147	0.15
Other Central American	6	0.01
Cuban	151	0.15
Dominican Republic	95	0.10
Mexican	7,157	7.34
Puerto Rican	831	0.85
South American	433	0.44
Argentinean	58	0.06
Bolivian	38	0.04
Chilean	15	0.02
Colombian	143	0.15
Ecuadorian	41	0.04
Paraguayan	1	<0.01
Peruvian	82	0.08
Uruguayan	11	0.01
Venezuelan	41	0.04
Other South American	3	<0.01
Other Hispanic or Latino	808	0.83

Race*	Population	%
African-American/Black (45,964)	47,316	48.54
Not Hispanic (45,507)	46,648	47.86
Hispanic (457)	668	0.69
American Indian/Alaska Native (453)	1,029	1.06
Not Hispanic (333)	818	0.84
Hispanic (120)	211	0.22
Alaska Athabascan *(Ala. Nat.)* (2)	2	<0.01
Apache (4)	7	0.01
Blackfeet (2)	30	0.03
Central American Ind. (2)	3	<0.01
Cherokee (56)	246	0.25
Chippewa (2)	4	<0.01
Choctaw (3)	3	<0.01
Comanche (0)	7	0.01
Cree (2)	2	<0.01
Creek (3)	19	0.02
Crow (0)	5	0.01
Hopi (0)	1	<0.01
Houma (1)	1	<0.01
Inupiat *(Alaska Native)* (1)	3	<0.01
Iroquois (0)	14	0.01
Lumbee (33)	38	0.04
Menominee (1)	1	<0.01
Mexican American Ind. (50)	54	0.06
Navajo (4)	5	0.01
Osage (0)	2	<0.01
Potawatomi (1)	3	<0.01
Seminole (0)	5	0.01
Sioux (15)	34	0.03
South American Ind. (1)	1	<0.01
Spanish American Ind. (1)	3	<0.01
Tlingit-Haida *(Alaska Native)* (1)	1	<0.01
Tsimshian *(Alaska Native)* (1)	1	<0.01
Yaqui (1)	2	<0.01
Yuman (0)	1	<0.01
Asian (1,897)	2,485	2.55
Not Hispanic (1,871)	2,405	2.47
Hispanic (26)	80	0.08
Bangladeshi (9)	9	0.01
Burmese (11)	11	0.01
Cambodian (5)	6	0.01
Chinese, ex. Taiwanese (284)	364	0.37
Filipino (699)	969	0.99
Hmong (2)	2	<0.01
Indian (264)	306	0.31
Indonesian (5)	7	0.01
Japanese (71)	170	0.17
Korean (122)	207	0.21
Laotian (6)	11	0.01
Malaysian (1)	7	0.01
Nepalese (1)	1	<0.01
Pakistani (13)	14	0.01
Taiwanese (4)	8	0.01
Thai (26)	53	0.05
Vietnamese (286)	317	0.33
Hawaii Native/Pacific Islander (157)	288	0.30
Not Hispanic (119)	228	0.23
Hispanic (38)	60	0.06
Guamanian/Chamorro (76)	106	0.11
Marshallese (1)	1	<0.01
Native Hawaiian (29)	71	0.07
Samoan (12)	20	0.02
White (40,514)	42,441	43.54
Not Hispanic (36,945)	38,468	39.47
Hispanic (3,569)	3,973	4.08

North Myrtle Beach

Place Type: City
County: Horry
Population: 13,752†

Ancestry‡	Population	%
Alsatian (0)	14	0.10
American (1,507)	1,507	11.25
Arab (11)	24	0.18
Egyptian (11)	11	0.08
Lebanese (0)	13	0.10
Armenian (11)	11	0.08
Australian (155)	155	1.16
Austrian (21)	68	0.51
Belgian (14)	14	0.10
British (111)	219	1.63
Canadian (21)	48	0.36
Croatian (9)	45	0.34
Czech (32)	71	0.53
Danish (0)	29	0.22
Dutch (65)	171	1.28
Eastern European (36)	36	0.27
English (1,245)	2,531	18.89
European (50)	50	0.37
French, ex. Basque (119)	644	4.81
French Canadian (44)	88	0.66
German (573)	1,976	14.75
Greek (66)	66	0.49
Hungarian (41)	115	0.86
Icelander (0)	7	0.05
Irish (798)	2,151	16.06
Italian (249)	661	4.93
Lithuanian (58)	66	0.49
Norwegian (0)	66	0.49
Pennsylvania German (10)	10	0.07
Polish (111)	296	2.21
Portuguese (10)	10	0.07
Romanian (19)	19	0.14
Russian (26)	63	0.47
Scotch-Irish (534)	824	6.15
Scottish (293)	562	4.19
Serbian (13)	13	0.10
Slovak (40)	85	0.63
Swedish (0)	40	0.30
Swiss (38)	86	0.64
Welsh (21)	153	1.14
West Indian, ex. Hispanic (25)	25	0.19
Trinidadian/Tobagonian (25)	25	0.19

Hispanic Origin	Population	%
Hispanic or Latino (of any race)	871	6.33
Central American, ex. Mexican	307	2.23
Guatemalan	202	1.47
Honduran	29	0.21

*Notes: † The Census 2010 population figure is used to calculate the percentages in the Hispanic Origin and Race categories. Ancestry percentages are based on the 2006-2010 American Community Survey population (not shown); ‡ Numbers in parentheses indicate the number of people reporting a single ancestry; * Numbers in parentheses indicate the number of persons reporting this race alone, not in combination with any other race; Please refer to the Explanation of Data for more information.*

Panamanian	4	0.03
Salvadoran	72	0.52
Cuban	6	0.04
Dominican Republic	4	0.03
Mexican	341	2.48
Puerto Rican	58	0.42
South American	62	0.45
Argentinean	6	0.04
Bolivian	1	0.01
Chilean	1	0.01
Colombian	9	0.07
Ecuadorian	31	0.23
Peruvian	6	0.04
Uruguayan	1	0.01
Venezuelan	7	0.05
Other Hispanic or Latino	93	0.68

Race*	Population	%
African-American/Black (456)	536	3.90
Not Hispanic (445)	519	3.77
Hispanic (11)	17	0.12
American Indian/Alaska Native (75)	138	1.00
Not Hispanic (68)	126	0.92
Hispanic (7)	12	0.09
Apache (1)	1	0.01
Blackfeet (0)	1	0.01
Cherokee (13)	29	0.21
Chippewa (1)	3	0.02
Choctaw (1)	2	0.01
Creek (1)	2	0.01
Iroquois (9)	10	0.07
Lumbee (10)	10	0.07
Mexican American Ind. (1)	1	0.01
Navajo (0)	1	0.01
Osage (1)	1	0.01
Potawatomi (1)	1	0.01
Sioux (2)	2	0.01
Asian (128)	169	1.23
Not Hispanic (126)	166	1.21
Hispanic (2)	3	0.02
Bangladeshi (1)	1	0.01
Chinese, ex. Taiwanese (22)	22	0.16
Filipino (53)	76	0.55
Indian (5)	6	0.04
Japanese (4)	10	0.07
Korean (7)	12	0.09
Nepalese (1)	1	0.01
Pakistani (6)	6	0.04
Taiwanese (2)	2	0.01
Thai (18)	23	0.17
Vietnamese (6)	8	0.06
Hawaii Native/Pacific Islander (9)	20	0.15
Not Hispanic (9)	18	0.13
Hispanic (0)	2	0.01
Guamanian/Chamorro (5)	6	0.04
Native Hawaiian (3)	7	0.05
Samoan (1)	6	0.04
Tongan (0)	2	0.01
White (12,433)	12,614	91.72
Not Hispanic (12,065)	12,215	88.82
Hispanic (368)	399	2.90

Oak Grove

Place Type: CDP
County: Lexington
Population: 10,291†

Ancestry‡	Population	%
African, Sub-Saharan (98)	114	1.09
African (98)	114	1.09
American (1,279)	1,279	12.21
Arab (16)	16	0.15
Lebanese (16)	16	0.15
Austrian (0)	8	0.08
Brazilian (58)	58	0.55
Celtic (61)	61	0.58
Czech (0)	8	0.08
Danish (12)	24	0.23
Dutch (0)	14	0.13
English (816)	1,398	13.34
European (146)	159	1.52
French, ex. Basque (87)	198	1.89
French Canadian (36)	36	0.34
German (856)	1,839	17.55
Greek (0)	12	0.11
Hungarian (0)	11	0.10
Irish (610)	1,535	14.65
Italian (130)	238	2.27
Lithuanian (12)	12	0.11
Norwegian (11)	25	0.24
Polish (29)	105	1.00
Portuguese (0)	16	0.15
Romanian (0)	11	0.10
Russian (0)	11	0.10
Scotch-Irish (289)	376	3.59
Scottish (25)	121	1.15
Swedish (20)	31	0.30
Swiss (11)	94	0.90
Ukrainian (0)	24	0.23
Welsh (18)	78	0.74
West Indian, ex. Hispanic (12)	12	0.11
Jamaican (12)	12	0.11

Hispanic Origin	Population	%
Hispanic or Latino (of any race)	1,096	10.65
Central American, ex. Mexican	117	1.14
Costa Rican	1	0.01
Guatemalan	54	0.52
Honduran	44	0.43
Nicaraguan	6	0.06
Panamanian	2	0.02
Salvadoran	10	0.10
Cuban	21	0.20
Dominican Republic	1	0.01
Mexican	774	7.52
Puerto Rican	113	1.10
South American	26	0.25
Argentinean	11	0.11
Bolivian	1	0.01
Colombian	7	0.07
Ecuadorian	3	0.03
Venezuelan	4	0.04
Other Hispanic or Latino	44	0.43

Race*	Population	%
African-American/Black (1,158)	1,217	11.83
Not Hispanic (1,138)	1,183	11.50
Hispanic (20)	34	0.33
American Indian/Alaska Native (44)	101	0.98
Not Hispanic (38)	93	0.90
Hispanic (6)	8	0.08
Cherokee (8)	27	0.26
Chippewa (1)	3	0.03
Creek (1)	1	0.01
Iroquois (0)	1	0.01
Lumbee (2)	2	0.02
Mexican American Ind. (5)	6	0.06
Potawatomi (1)	1	0.01
Seminole (4)	5	0.05
Asian (161)	201	1.95
Not Hispanic (160)	198	1.92
Hispanic (1)	3	0.03
Bangladeshi (4)	4	0.04
Chinese, ex. Taiwanese (45)	52	0.51
Filipino (26)	27	0.26
Indian (40)	44	0.43
Japanese (5)	13	0.13
Korean (8)	24	0.23
Laotian (1)	1	0.01
Thai (2)	3	0.03
Vietnamese (25)	29	0.28
Hawaii Native/Pacific Islander (5)	8	0.08
Not Hispanic (4)	5	0.05
Hispanic (1)	3	0.03
Guamanian/Chamorro (2)	2	0.02
Native Hawaiian (0)	1	0.01
White (8,110)	8,268	80.34
Not Hispanic (7,713)	7,833	76.12
Hispanic (397)	435	4.23

Orangeburg

Place Type: City
County: Orangeburg
Population: 13,964†

Ancestry‡	Population	%
African, Sub-Saharan (163)	163	1.18
African (56)	56	0.40
Nigerian (13)	13	0.09
Senegalese (40)	40	0.29
Other Sub-Saharan African (54)	54	0.39
American (848)	848	6.12
Brazilian (18)	18	0.13
British (10)	10	0.07
Dutch (0)	57	0.41
English (297)	552	3.98
European (101)	101	0.73
French, ex. Basque (24)	105	0.76
French Canadian (0)	36	0.26
German (195)	523	3.77
German Russian (0)	15	0.11
Greek (0)	28	0.20
Irish (132)	340	2.45
Italian (0)	42	0.30
Norwegian (20)	37	0.27
Polish (34)	60	0.43
Scotch-Irish (132)	208	1.50
Scottish (4)	24	0.17
Swedish (14)	31	0.22
Swiss (14)	24	0.17
Turkish (0)	8	0.06
West Indian, ex. Hispanic (99)	154	1.11
Bahamian (0)	15	0.11
Jamaican (57)	57	0.41
Trinidadian/Tobagonian (42)	42	0.30
West Indian (0)	40	0.29

Hispanic Origin	Population	%
Hispanic or Latino (of any race)	266	1.90
Central American, ex. Mexican	30	0.21
Costa Rican	2	0.01
Guatemalan	1	0.01
Honduran	6	0.04
Nicaraguan	3	0.02
Panamanian	11	0.08
Salvadoran	7	0.05
Cuban	24	0.17
Dominican Republic	5	0.04
Mexican	101	0.72
Puerto Rican	70	0.50
South American	10	0.07
Argentinean	2	0.01
Chilean	1	0.01
Colombian	5	0.04
Peruvian	1	0.01
Venezuelan	1	0.01
Other Hispanic or Latino	26	0.19

Race*	Population	%
African-American/Black (10,479)	10,590	75.84
Not Hispanic (10,411)	10,504	75.22
Hispanic (68)	86	0.62
American Indian/Alaska Native (25)	76	0.54
Not Hispanic (24)	69	0.49
Hispanic (1)	7	0.05
Blackfeet (0)	2	0.01
Cherokee (2)	21	0.15
Chickasaw (0)	5	0.04
Choctaw (0)	1	0.01
Creek (0)	2	0.01
Delaware (1)	1	0.01
Sioux (0)	1	0.01
Asian (231)	256	1.83
Not Hispanic (231)	254	1.82
Hispanic (0)	2	0.01
Bangladeshi (4)	6	0.04
Chinese, ex. Taiwanese (40)	42	0.30
Filipino (18)	23	0.16
Indian (108)	120	0.86

*Notes: † The Census 2010 population figure is used to calculate the percentages in the Hispanic Origin and Race categories. Ancestry percentages are based on the 2006-2010 American Community Survey population (not shown); ‡ Numbers in parentheses indicate the number of people reporting a single ancestry; * Numbers in parentheses indicate the number of persons reporting this race alone, not in combination with any other race; Please refer to the Explanation of Data for more information.*

Indonesian (9)	9	0.06
Japanese (3)	3	0.02
Korean (2)	5	0.04
Malaysian (1)	1	0.01
Pakistani (12)	12	0.09
Sri Lankan (3)	3	0.02
Taiwanese (3)	3	0.02
Thai (2)	4	0.03
Vietnamese (24)	24	0.17
Hawaii Native/Pacific Islander (7)	12	0.09
Not Hispanic (7)	12	0.09
Guamanian/Chamorro (1)	4	0.03
Native Hawaiian (1)	1	0.01
Samoan (1)	2	0.01
White (2,977)	3,072	22.00
Not Hispanic (2,891)	2,971	21.28
Hispanic (86)	101	0.72

Parker

Place Type: CDP
County: Greenville
Population: 11,431†

Ancestry‡	Population	%
African, Sub-Saharan (29)	29	0.28
African (29)	29	0.28
American (1,501)	1,501	14.59
Belgian (0)	9	0.09
British (8)	12	0.12
Czech (0)	22	0.21
Dutch (0)	120	1.17
English (289)	580	5.64
European (36)	36	0.35
French, ex. Basque (0)	29	0.28
German (210)	664	6.46
Irish (533)	1,156	11.24
Italian (57)	67	0.65
Polish (15)	15	0.15
Russian (8)	14	0.14
Scotch-Irish (41)	122	1.19
Scottish (63)	79	0.77
Swedish (13)	13	0.13
Ukrainian (0)	6	0.06
West Indian, ex. Hispanic (0)	19	0.18
Dutch West Indian (0)	19	0.18

Hispanic Origin	Population	%
Hispanic or Latino (of any race)	2,373	20.76
Central American, ex. Mexican	436	3.81
Costa Rican	40	0.35
Guatemalan	245	2.14
Honduran	101	0.88
Nicaraguan	10	0.09
Panamanian	2	0.02
Salvadoran	38	0.33
Cuban	23	0.20
Dominican Republic	4	0.03
Mexican	1,581	13.83
Puerto Rican	69	0.60
South American	154	1.35
Argentinean	1	0.01
Chilean	2	0.02
Colombian	143	1.25
Ecuadorian	4	0.03
Peruvian	2	0.02
Uruguayan	2	0.02
Other Hispanic or Latino	106	0.93

Race*	Population	%
African-American/Black (2,475)	2,604	22.78
Not Hispanic (2,423)	2,542	22.24
Hispanic (52)	62	0.54
American Indian/Alaska Native (54)	122	1.07
Not Hispanic (35)	94	0.82
Hispanic (19)	28	0.24
Central American Ind. (4)	4	0.03
Cherokee (11)	36	0.31
Chippewa (0)	1	0.01
Choctaw (0)	2	0.02
Inupiat *(Alaska Native)* (1)	1	0.01
Mexican American Ind. (8)	9	0.08
Potawatomi (1)	1	0.01
Seminole (0)	1	0.01
Sioux (1)	1	0.01
Asian (51)	84	0.73
Not Hispanic (48)	75	0.66
Hispanic (3)	9	0.08
Chinese, ex. Taiwanese (4)	14	0.12
Filipino (3)	17	0.15
Indian (19)	21	0.18
Japanese (2)	7	0.06
Korean (0)	3	0.03
Pakistani (1)	1	0.01
Thai (0)	1	0.01
Vietnamese (19)	19	0.17
Hawaii Native/Pacific Islander (2)	23	0.20
Not Hispanic (2)	14	0.12
Hispanic (0)	9	0.08
Native Hawaiian (0)	9	0.08
Samoan (0)	5	0.04
White (7,083)	7,340	64.21
Not Hispanic (6,337)	6,517	57.01
Hispanic (746)	823	7.20

Port Royal

Place Type: Town
County: Beaufort
Population: 10,678†

Ancestry‡	Population	%
African, Sub-Saharan (20)	69	0.66
African (9)	50	0.48
Kenyan (11)	11	0.11
Other Sub-Saharan African (0)	8	0.08
Albanian (0)	15	0.14
American (651)	651	6.23
Arab (22)	56	0.54
Arab (0)	16	0.15
Lebanese (17)	17	0.16
Palestinian (0)	18	0.17
Other Arab (5)	5	0.05
Australian (0)	17	0.16
Austrian (0)	20	0.19
British (0)	50	0.48
Canadian (8)	55	0.53
Celtic (0)	5	0.05
Czech (0)	18	0.17
Czechoslovakian (0)	18	0.17
Dutch (45)	189	1.81
Eastern European (9)	9	0.09
English (364)	1,132	10.84
European (67)	67	0.64
Finnish (7)	7	0.07
French, ex. Basque (41)	202	1.93
French Canadian (64)	209	2.00
German (454)	2,001	19.16
Greek (0)	72	0.69
Guyanese (18)	18	0.17
Hungarian (2)	38	0.36
Irish (379)	1,890	18.10
Italian (201)	738	7.07
Latvian (10)	10	0.10
Lithuanian (0)	9	0.09
Maltese (0)	3	0.03
Norwegian (94)	161	1.54
Polish (17)	294	2.82
Portuguese (13)	40	0.38
Russian (11)	71	0.68
Scotch-Irish (136)	306	2.93
Scottish (69)	119	1.14
Slavic (0)	32	0.31
Slovak (0)	5	0.05
Swedish (24)	66	0.63
Swiss (0)	18	0.17
Ukrainian (0)	6	0.06
Welsh (13)	73	0.70
West Indian, ex. Hispanic (83)	138	1.32
Barbadian (33)	33	0.32
Haitian (40)	57	0.55
Jamaican (0)	36	0.34
Trinidadian/Tobagonian (0)	2	0.02
U.S. Virgin Islander (10)	10	0.10

Hispanic Origin	Population	%
Hispanic or Latino (of any race)	1,421	13.31
Central American, ex. Mexican	188	1.76
Costa Rican	8	0.07
Guatemalan	50	0.47
Honduran	58	0.54
Nicaraguan	18	0.17
Panamanian	10	0.09
Salvadoran	44	0.41
Cuban	50	0.47
Dominican Republic	75	0.70
Mexican	529	4.95
Puerto Rican	309	2.89
South American	128	1.20
Argentinean	5	0.05
Bolivian	3	0.03
Chilean	2	0.02
Colombian	46	0.43
Ecuadorian	26	0.24
Paraguayan	2	0.02
Peruvian	21	0.20
Venezuelan	21	0.20
Other South American	2	0.02
Other Hispanic or Latino	142	1.33

Race*	Population	%
African-American/Black (2,206)	2,405	22.52
Not Hispanic (2,105)	2,270	21.26
Hispanic (101)	135	1.26
American Indian/Alaska Native (63)	163	1.53
Not Hispanic (47)	130	1.22
Hispanic (16)	33	0.31
Blackfeet (0)	2	0.02
Central American Ind. (2)	2	0.02
Cherokee (6)	39	0.37
Chippewa (0)	1	0.01
Choctaw (5)	6	0.06
Comanche (0)	3	0.03
Creek (2)	4	0.04
Delaware (0)	2	0.02
Houma (1)	1	0.01
Inupiat *(Alaska Native)* (0)	1	0.01
Iroquois (0)	1	0.01
Kiowa (0)	1	0.01
Lumbee (0)	4	0.04
Menominee (2)	2	0.02
Mexican American Ind. (1)	1	0.01
Navajo (9)	11	0.10
Seminole (0)	1	0.01
Sioux (1)	3	0.03
South American Ind. (2)	3	0.03
Spanish American Ind. (5)	5	0.05
Yaqui (0)	1	0.01
Asian (263)	384	3.60
Not Hispanic (252)	352	3.30
Hispanic (11)	32	0.30
Burmese (1)	1	0.01
Cambodian (3)	4	0.04
Chinese, ex. Taiwanese (33)	49	0.46
Filipino (65)	129	1.21
Indian (45)	54	0.51
Japanese (29)	61	0.57
Korean (15)	27	0.25
Laotian (4)	4	0.04
Malaysian (1)	2	0.02
Nepalese (1)	1	0.01
Pakistani (0)	1	0.01
Sri Lankan (1)	1	0.01
Taiwanese (0)	2	0.02
Thai (9)	16	0.15
Vietnamese (35)	38	0.36
Hawaii Native/Pacific Islander (12)	53	0.50
Not Hispanic (11)	40	0.37
Hispanic (1)	13	0.12
Fijian (1)	1	0.01

SECTION TWO

*Notes: † The Census 2010 population figure is used to calculate the percentages in the Hispanic Origin and Race categories. Ancestry percentages are based on the 2006-2010 American Community Survey population (not shown); ‡ Numbers in parentheses indicate the number of people reporting a single ancestry; * Numbers in parentheses indicate the number of persons reporting this race alone, not in combination with any other race; Please refer to the Explanation of Data for more information.*

Guamanian/Chamorro (1)	8	0.07
Native Hawaiian (1)	19	0.18
Samoan (3)	9	0.08
White (7,346)	7,663	71.76
Not Hispanic (6,529)	6,778	63.48
Hispanic (817)	885	8.29

Powdersville

Place Type: CDP
County: Anderson
Population: 7,618†

Ancestry‡	Population	%
African, Sub-Saharan (0)	7	0.09
African (0)	7	0.09
American (1,319)	1,319	16.49
Australian (10)	10	0.13
Austrian (20)	20	0.25
British (22)	22	0.28
Croatian (0)	11	0.14
Danish (49)	67	0.84
Dutch (0)	91	1.14
English (430)	857	10.72
European (53)	70	0.88
French, ex. Basque (16)	66	0.83
French Canadian (12)	12	0.15
German (184)	916	11.45
Greek (10)	39	0.49
Hungarian (0)	59	0.74
Irish (650)	1,595	19.94
Italian (261)	389	4.86
Norwegian (45)	82	1.03
Polish (62)	165	2.06
Portuguese (0)	37	0.46
Scandinavian (8)	33	0.41
Scotch-Irish (144)	412	5.15
Scottish (122)	192	2.40
Swedish (0)	10	0.13
Swiss (19)	33	0.41
Welsh (43)	57	0.71

Hispanic Origin	Population	%
Hispanic or Latino (of any race)	278	3.65
Central American, ex. Mexican	16	0.21
Costa Rican	1	0.01
Guatemalan	2	0.03
Honduran	9	0.12
Nicaraguan	1	0.01
Panamanian	2	0.03
Salvadoran	1	0.01
Cuban	10	0.13
Dominican Republic	5	0.07
Mexican	127	1.67
Puerto Rican	37	0.49
South American	57	0.75
Argentinean	5	0.07
Colombian	46	0.60
Ecuadorian	2	0.03
Venezuelan	4	0.05
Other Hispanic or Latino	26	0.34

Race*	Population	%
African-American/Black (573)	631	8.28
Not Hispanic (569)	622	8.16
Hispanic (4)	9	0.12
American Indian/Alaska Native (23)	49	0.64
Not Hispanic (20)	46	0.60
Hispanic (3)	3	0.04
Apache (1)	1	0.01
Cherokee (4)	22	0.29
Chickasaw (0)	1	0.01
Creek (6)	6	0.08
Lumbee (0)	1	0.01
Seminole (2)	2	0.03
Asian (125)	142	1.86
Not Hispanic (125)	142	1.86
Chinese, ex. Taiwanese (16)	19	0.25
Filipino (1)	2	0.03
Indian (86)	94	1.23
Japanese (0)	1	0.01
Korean (8)	10	0.13
Laotian (0)	1	0.01
Malaysian (1)	1	0.01
Nepalese (0)	1	0.01
Vietnamese (11)	12	0.16
Hawaii Native/Pacific Islander (4)	8	0.11
Not Hispanic (4)	8	0.11
Guamanian/Chamorro (2)	3	0.04
Native Hawaiian (1)	4	0.05
Samoan (1)	1	0.01
White (6,648)	6,758	88.71
Not Hispanic (6,514)	6,597	86.60
Hispanic (134)	161	2.11

Red Bank

Place Type: CDP
County: Lexington
Population: 9,617†

Ancestry‡	Population	%
American (2,086)	2,086	20.69
Austrian (16)	16	0.16
British (33)	47	0.47
Canadian (9)	9	0.09
Dutch (13)	129	1.28
English (412)	692	6.86
European (29)	29	0.29
French, ex. Basque (147)	291	2.89
German (696)	1,732	17.18
Greek (62)	88	0.87
Hungarian (6)	28	0.28
Irish (265)	1,438	14.26
Italian (250)	755	7.49
Norwegian (47)	62	0.61
Polish (17)	70	0.69
Russian (0)	19	0.19
Scandinavian (11)	24	0.24
Scotch-Irish (140)	290	2.88
Scottish (49)	131	1.30
Swedish (45)	146	1.45
Welsh (0)	31	0.31
West Indian, ex. Hispanic (42)	42	0.42
Trinidadian/Tobagonian (42)	42	0.42

Hispanic Origin	Population	%
Hispanic or Latino (of any race)	382	3.97
Central American, ex. Mexican	11	0.11
Guatemalan	1	0.01
Honduran	6	0.06
Panamanian	4	0.04
Cuban	6	0.06
Dominican Republic	2	0.02
Mexican	247	2.57
Puerto Rican	83	0.86
South American	11	0.11
Argentinean	7	0.07
Colombian	1	0.01
Ecuadorian	1	0.01
Venezuelan	1	0.01
Other South American	1	0.01
Other Hispanic or Latino	22	0.23

Race*	Population	%
African-American/Black (991)	1,091	11.34
Not Hispanic (983)	1,071	11.14
Hispanic (8)	20	0.21
American Indian/Alaska Native (47)	102	1.06
Not Hispanic (44)	99	1.03
Hispanic (3)	3	0.03
Blackfeet (0)	1	0.01
Cherokee (18)	42	0.44
Choctaw (1)	1	0.01
Comanche (1)	1	0.01
Creek (2)	2	0.02
Crow (0)	1	0.01
Iroquois (2)	2	0.02
Lumbee (4)	5	0.05
Potawatomi (1)	1	0.01
Asian (53)	76	0.79
Not Hispanic (52)	71	0.74
Hispanic (1)	5	0.05
Chinese, ex. Taiwanese (3)	7	0.07
Filipino (24)	34	0.35
Indian (15)	18	0.19
Japanese (2)	3	0.03
Korean (4)	8	0.08
Pakistani (0)	2	0.02
Thai (0)	1	0.01
Vietnamese (3)	4	0.04
Hawaii Native/Pacific Islander (2)	3	0.03
Not Hispanic (0)	1	0.01
Hispanic (2)	2	0.02
Guamanian/Chamorro (2)	2	0.02
White (8,138)	8,306	86.37
Not Hispanic (7,990)	8,131	84.55
Hispanic (148)	175	1.82

Red Hill

Place Type: CDP
County: Horry
Population: 13,223†

Ancestry‡	Population	%
African, Sub-Saharan (29)	29	0.21
African (29)	29	0.21
American (2,336)	2,336	16.87
Arab (9)	35	0.25
Egyptian (0)	14	0.10
Lebanese (9)	9	0.07
Syrian (0)	12	0.09
Austrian (47)	47	0.34
British (28)	41	0.30
Canadian (44)	44	0.32
Croatian (0)	23	0.17
Czech (0)	34	0.25
Czechoslovakian (0)	32	0.23
Dutch (24)	233	1.68
Eastern European (25)	25	0.18
English (930)	1,922	13.88
European (0)	20	0.14
Finnish (0)	10	0.07
French, ex. Basque (118)	332	2.40
French Canadian (23)	80	0.58
German (722)	2,084	15.05
Greek (23)	23	0.17
Hungarian (11)	52	0.38
Icelander (78)	78	0.56
Irish (676)	1,901	13.73
Italian (318)	824	5.95
Latvian (27)	27	0.20
Lithuanian (12)	23	0.17
Norwegian (20)	97	0.70
Polish (184)	397	2.87
Portuguese (0)	27	0.20
Russian (20)	145	1.05
Scotch-Irish (145)	247	1.78
Scottish (183)	495	3.58
Slovak (0)	30	0.22
Slovene (0)	11	0.08
Swedish (22)	177	1.28
Swiss (30)	38	0.27
Ukrainian (10)	28	0.20
Welsh (26)	61	0.44
West Indian, ex. Hispanic (11)	11	0.08
Jamaican (11)	11	0.08

Hispanic Origin	Population	%
Hispanic or Latino (of any race)	1,130	8.55
Central American, ex. Mexican	84	0.64
Costa Rican	2	0.02
Guatemalan	26	0.20
Honduran	26	0.20
Nicaraguan	2	0.02
Panamanian	6	0.05
Salvadoran	19	0.14
Other Central American	3	0.02
Cuban	28	0.21

*Notes: † The Census 2010 population figure is used to calculate the percentages in the Hispanic Origin and Race categories. Ancestry percentages are based on the 2006-2010 American Community Survey population (not shown); ‡ Numbers in parentheses indicate the number of people reporting a single ancestry; * Numbers in parentheses indicate the number of persons reporting this race alone, not in combination with any other race; Please refer to the Explanation of Data for more information.*

Dominican Republic	8	0.06
Mexican	790	5.97
Puerto Rican	79	0.60
South American	60	0.45
Argentinean	13	0.10
Bolivian	4	0.03
Chilean	1	0.01
Colombian	22	0.17
Ecuadorian	9	0.07
Paraguayan	1	0.01
Peruvian	7	0.05
Uruguayan	2	0.02
Venezuelan	1	0.01
Other Hispanic or Latino	81	0.61

Race*	Population	%
African-American/Black (1,314)	1,453	10.99
Not Hispanic (1,290)	1,416	10.71
Hispanic (24)	37	0.28
American Indian/Alaska Native (60)	135	1.02
Not Hispanic (52)	111	0.84
Hispanic (8)	24	0.18
Apache (3)	4	0.03
Blackfeet (0)	2	0.02
Cherokee (12)	41	0.31
Chickasaw (3)	3	0.02
Choctaw (0)	3	0.02
Creek (3)	3	0.02
Iroquois (1)	1	0.01
Lumbee (13)	22	0.17
Menominee (0)	2	0.02
Mexican American Ind. (2)	2	0.02
Navajo (0)	2	0.02
South American Ind. (2)	2	0.02
Asian (161)	210	1.59
Not Hispanic (150)	193	1.46
Hispanic (11)	17	0.13
Chinese, ex. Taiwanese (14)	23	0.17
Filipino (51)	59	0.45
Indian (25)	28	0.21
Japanese (3)	13	0.10
Korean (35)	46	0.35
Laotian (8)	8	0.06
Thai (10)	16	0.12
Vietnamese (7)	7	0.05
Hawaii Native/Pacific Islander (9)	20	0.15
Not Hispanic (3)	13	0.10
Hispanic (6)	7	0.05
Guamanian/Chamorro (6)	6	0.05
Native Hawaiian (1)	7	0.05
White (10,779)	11,037	83.47
Not Hispanic (10,371)	10,567	79.91
Hispanic (408)	470	3.55

Rock Hill

Place Type: City
County: York
Population: 66,154†

Ancestry‡	Population	%
African, Sub-Saharan (491)	550	0.87
African (408)	467	0.74
Cape Verdean (65)	65	0.10
Other Sub-Saharan African (18)	18	0.03
American (3,840)	3,840	6.08
Arab (66)	81	0.13
Lebanese (29)	29	0.05
Syrian (24)	39	0.06
Other Arab (13)	13	0.02
Armenian (11)	11	0.02
Austrian (25)	108	0.17
Belgian (0)	10	0.02
Brazilian (26)	26	0.04
British (151)	291	0.46
Cajun (0)	11	0.02
Canadian (25)	49	0.08
Croatian (0)	9	0.01
Czech (64)	108	0.17
Czechoslovakian (0)	37	0.06
Danish (15)	109	0.17
Dutch (193)	730	1.16
Eastern European (15)	15	0.02
English (2,687)	5,454	8.64
European (580)	662	1.05
Finnish (46)	69	0.11
French, ex. Basque (214)	1,391	2.20
French Canadian (48)	104	0.16
German (2,423)	7,124	11.29
Greek (27)	93	0.15
Guyanese (8)	8	0.01
Hungarian (38)	72	0.11
Icelander (10)	24	0.04
Irish (1,873)	6,334	10.04
Italian (497)	1,636	2.59
Lithuanian (0)	39	0.06
Norwegian (42)	199	0.32
Pennsylvania German (9)	9	0.01
Polish (164)	525	0.83
Portuguese (45)	54	0.09
Russian (15)	24	0.04
Scandinavian (36)	36	0.06
Scotch-Irish (2,145)	3,164	5.01
Scottish (547)	1,401	2.22
Slavic (12)	12	0.02
Slovak (13)	46	0.07
Swedish (36)	222	0.35
Swiss (0)	93	0.15
Ukrainian (22)	81	0.13
Welsh (46)	376	0.60
West Indian, ex. Hispanic (0)	82	0.13
Jamaican (0)	52	0.08
West Indian (0)	30	0.05
Yugoslavian (17)	17	0.03

Hispanic Origin	Population	%
Hispanic or Latino (of any race)	3,761	5.69
Central American, ex. Mexican	421	0.64
Costa Rican	24	0.04
Guatemalan	63	0.10
Honduran	178	0.27
Nicaraguan	22	0.03
Panamanian	30	0.05
Salvadoran	100	0.15
Other Central American	4	0.01
Cuban	81	0.12
Dominican Republic	106	0.16
Mexican	2,002	3.03
Puerto Rican	465	0.70
South American	460	0.70
Argentinean	15	0.02
Bolivian	11	0.02
Chilean	18	0.03
Colombian	216	0.33
Ecuadorian	59	0.09
Paraguayan	1	<0.01
Peruvian	53	0.08
Uruguayan	69	0.10
Venezuelan	17	0.03
Other South American	1	<0.01
Other Hispanic or Latino	226	0.34

Race*	Population	%
African-American/Black (25,348)	26,236	39.66
Not Hispanic (25,148)	25,932	39.20
Hispanic (200)	304	0.46
American Indian/Alaska Native (322)	653	0.99
Not Hispanic (282)	595	0.90
Hispanic (40)	58	0.09
Alaska Athabascan *(Ala. Nat.)* (0)	1	<0.01
Apache (1)	2	<0.01
Arapaho (0)	1	<0.01
Blackfeet (1)	18	0.03
Central American Ind. (2)	2	<0.01
Cherokee (38)	117	0.18
Cheyenne (0)	1	<0.01
Chippewa (0)	1	<0.01
Choctaw (4)	7	0.01
Comanche (1)	1	<0.01
Creek (5)	14	0.02
Inupiat *(Alaska Native)* (1)	1	<0.01
Iroquois (4)	8	0.01
Lumbee (13)	17	0.03
Mexican American Ind. (10)	15	0.02
Navajo (0)	2	<0.01
Osage (4)	4	0.01
Puget Sound Salish (1)	1	<0.01
Seminole (1)	7	0.01
Shoshone (1)	1	<0.01
Sioux (1)	4	0.01
South American Ind. (0)	1	<0.01
Tlingit-Haida *(Alaska Native)* (5)	5	0.01
Tohono O'Odham (5)	5	0.01
Yup'ik *(Alaska Native)* (1)	1	<0.01
Asian (1,118)	1,372	2.07
Not Hispanic (1,113)	1,348	2.04
Hispanic (5)	24	0.04
Bangladeshi (3)	3	<0.01
Burmese (1)	1	<0.01
Cambodian (42)	55	0.08
Chinese, ex. Taiwanese (123)	170	0.26
Filipino (162)	213	0.32
Hmong (36)	37	0.06
Indian (222)	260	0.39
Indonesian (4)	5	0.01
Japanese (13)	43	0.06
Korean (64)	96	0.15
Laotian (19)	20	0.03
Malaysian (2)	4	0.01
Pakistani (16)	22	0.03
Sri Lankan (2)	2	<0.01
Taiwanese (4)	5	0.01
Thai (3)	17	0.03
Vietnamese (346)	384	0.58
Hawaii Native/Pacific Islander (69)	96	0.15
Not Hispanic (21)	42	0.06
Hispanic (48)	54	0.08
Fijian (0)	2	<0.01
Guamanian/Chamorro (57)	60	0.09
Native Hawaiian (2)	11	0.02
Samoan (4)	7	0.01
Tongan (3)	5	0.01
White (36,147)	37,269	56.34
Not Hispanic (34,594)	35,555	53.75
Hispanic (1,553)	1,714	2.59

Sangaree

Place Type: CDP
County: Berkeley
Population: 8,220†

Ancestry‡	Population	%
African, Sub-Saharan (22)	63	0.70
African (22)	57	0.63
Other Sub-Saharan African (0)	6	0.07
American (1,118)	1,118	12.40
British (29)	29	0.32
Czech (11)	29	0.32
Dutch (0)	91	1.01
English (667)	910	10.09
European (9)	9	0.10
French, ex. Basque (69)	206	2.28
French Canadian (35)	48	0.53
German (432)	1,160	12.86
Irish (449)	1,190	13.20
Italian (26)	118	1.31
Norwegian (27)	80	0.89
Polish (73)	207	2.30
Portuguese (0)	19	0.21
Scotch-Irish (68)	154	1.71
Scottish (75)	202	2.24
Slovak (49)	49	0.54
Swedish (14)	54	0.60
Swiss (11)	29	0.32
Ukrainian (22)	22	0.24
Welsh (0)	44	0.49
West Indian, ex. Hispanic (221)	221	2.45
Jamaican (221)	221	2.45

*Notes: † The Census 2010 population figure is used to calculate the percentages in the Hispanic Origin and Race categories. Ancestry percentages are based on the 2006-2010 American Community Survey population (not shown); ‡ Numbers in parentheses indicate the number of people reporting a single ancestry; * Numbers in parentheses indicate the number of persons reporting this race alone, not in combination with any other race; Please refer to the Explanation of Data for more information.*

Hispanic Origin	Population	%
Hispanic or Latino (of any race)	398	4.84
Central American, ex. Mexican	48	0.58
Guatemalan	16	0.19
Honduran	7	0.09
Nicaraguan	1	0.01
Panamanian	5	0.06
Salvadoran	18	0.22
Other Central American	1	0.01
Cuban	16	0.19
Dominican Republic	8	0.10
Mexican	159	1.93
Puerto Rican	111	1.35
South American	10	0.12
Bolivian	4	0.05
Chilean	1	0.01
Colombian	4	0.05
Venezuelan	1	0.01
Other Hispanic or Latino	46	0.56

Race*	Population	%
African-American/Black (1,937)	2,052	24.96
Not Hispanic (1,908)	2,017	24.54
Hispanic (29)	35	0.43
American Indian/Alaska Native (69)	149	1.81
Not Hispanic (61)	128	1.56
Hispanic (8)	21	0.26
Central American Ind. (0)	1	0.01
Cherokee (4)	20	0.24
Chickasaw (1)	1	0.01
Chippewa (1)	3	0.04
Choctaw (1)	1	0.01
Creek (5)	5	0.06
Houma (0)	1	0.01
Lumbee (9)	9	0.11
Mexican American Ind. (0)	1	0.01
Navajo (0)	2	0.02
Osage (0)	3	0.04
Sioux (2)	2	0.02
Asian (88)	138	1.68
Not Hispanic (87)	136	1.65
Hispanic (1)	2	0.02
Cambodian (1)	1	0.01
Chinese, ex. Taiwanese (6)	10	0.12
Filipino (51)	77	0.94
Indian (1)	6	0.07
Japanese (10)	23	0.28
Korean (3)	4	0.05
Pakistani (4)	4	0.05
Thai (3)	4	0.05
Vietnamese (6)	7	0.09
Hawaii Native/Pacific Islander (13)	26	0.32
Not Hispanic (13)	26	0.32
Guamanian/Chamorro (2)	2	0.02
Native Hawaiian (6)	14	0.17
Samoan (3)	3	0.04
White (5,787)	5,992	72.90
Not Hispanic (5,543)	5,727	69.67
Hispanic (244)	265	3.22

Sans Souci

Place Type: CDP
County: Greenville
Population: 7,869†

Ancestry‡	Population	%
American (1,118)	1,118	13.58
Austrian (35)	67	0.81
Canadian (9)	9	0.11
Czech (0)	7	0.09
Danish (0)	16	0.19
Dutch (16)	74	0.90
English (186)	549	6.67
European (79)	79	0.96
Finnish (0)	11	0.13
French, ex. Basque (65)	232	2.82
German (178)	575	6.99
Icelander (5)	5	0.06
Irish (206)	694	8.43
Israeli (28)	28	0.34
Italian (18)	81	0.98
Polish (51)	83	1.01
Portuguese (12)	21	0.26
Romanian (9)	18	0.22
Russian (11)	46	0.56
Scandinavian (8)	8	0.10
Scotch-Irish (86)	158	1.92
Scottish (34)	164	1.99
Slovak (8)	8	0.10
Swedish (0)	16	0.19
Swiss (11)	24	0.29
Ukrainian (10)	49	0.60
Welsh (0)	10	0.12

Hispanic Origin	Population	%
Hispanic or Latino (of any race)	1,345	17.09
Central American, ex. Mexican	512	6.51
Costa Rican	58	0.74
Guatemalan	328	4.17
Honduran	81	1.03
Nicaraguan	4	0.05
Panamanian	4	0.05
Salvadoran	34	0.43
Other Central American	3	0.04
Cuban	15	0.19
Dominican Republic	4	0.05
Mexican	587	7.46
Puerto Rican	73	0.93
South American	82	1.04
Argentinean	4	0.05
Chilean	3	0.04
Colombian	61	0.78
Ecuadorian	7	0.09
Peruvian	2	0.03
Uruguayan	1	0.01
Venezuelan	4	0.05
Other Hispanic or Latino	72	0.91

Race*	Population	%
African-American/Black (1,203)	1,316	16.72
Not Hispanic (1,179)	1,285	16.33
Hispanic (24)	31	0.39
American Indian/Alaska Native (137)	200	2.54
Not Hispanic (38)	91	1.16
Hispanic (99)	109	1.39
Apache (4)	4	0.05
Blackfeet (0)	1	0.01
Central American Ind. (10)	11	0.14
Cherokee (9)	34	0.43
Lumbee (2)	2	0.03
Mexican American Ind. (94)	102	1.30
Potawatomi (1)	1	0.01
Spanish American Ind. (0)	1	0.01
Asian (78)	96	1.22
Not Hispanic (74)	91	1.16
Hispanic (4)	5	0.06
Cambodian (4)	4	0.05
Chinese, ex. Taiwanese (7)	9	0.11
Filipino (3)	7	0.09
Indian (3)	7	0.09
Korean (8)	10	0.13
Malaysian (0)	3	0.04
Vietnamese (49)	49	0.62
Hawaii Native/Pacific Islander (5)	8	0.10
Not Hispanic (1)	4	0.05
Hispanic (4)	4	0.05
Guamanian/Chamorro (1)	1	0.01
Samoan (4)	4	0.05
White (5,468)	5,669	72.04
Not Hispanic (5,064)	5,212	66.23
Hispanic (404)	457	5.81

Seneca

Place Type: City
County: Oconee
Population: 8,102†

Ancestry‡	Population	%
American (845)	845	10.53
Arab (78)	78	0.97
Palestinian (78)	78	0.97
Brazilian (11)	11	0.14
British (18)	18	0.22
Czech (14)	14	0.17
Dutch (21)	68	0.85
English (414)	746	9.30
European (48)	48	0.60
French, ex. Basque (54)	133	1.66
German (275)	794	9.90
Hungarian (45)	90	1.12
Irish (308)	797	9.93
Italian (70)	198	2.47
Norwegian (0)	12	0.15
Polish (12)	47	0.59
Portuguese (8)	8	0.10
Russian (13)	13	0.16
Scandinavian (22)	22	0.27
Scotch-Irish (209)	361	4.50
Scottish (44)	139	1.73
Swedish (0)	6	0.07
Swiss (0)	14	0.17
Ukrainian (15)	15	0.19
Welsh (22)	53	0.66

Hispanic Origin	Population	%
Hispanic or Latino (of any race)	362	4.47
Central American, ex. Mexican	20	0.25
Costa Rican	1	0.01
Honduran	1	0.01
Panamanian	2	0.02
Salvadoran	16	0.20
Cuban	4	0.05
Dominican Republic	2	0.02
Mexican	272	3.36
Puerto Rican	27	0.33
South American	14	0.17
Argentinean	2	0.02
Colombian	6	0.07
Ecuadorian	1	0.01
Paraguayan	5	0.06
Other Hispanic or Latino	23	0.28

Race*	Population	%
African-American/Black (2,348)	2,470	30.49
Not Hispanic (2,329)	2,443	30.15
Hispanic (19)	27	0.33
American Indian/Alaska Native (22)	46	0.57
Not Hispanic (17)	39	0.48
Hispanic (5)	7	0.09
Cherokee (7)	20	0.25
Chickasaw (1)	1	0.01
Chippewa (2)	3	0.04
Delaware (1)	1	0.01
Lumbee (5)	5	0.06
Mexican American Ind. (1)	1	0.01
Asian (76)	102	1.26
Not Hispanic (74)	98	1.21
Hispanic (2)	4	0.05
Chinese, ex. Taiwanese (14)	16	0.20
Filipino (7)	14	0.17
Indian (28)	29	0.36
Japanese (0)	1	0.01
Korean (5)	8	0.10
Pakistani (4)	4	0.05
Taiwanese (1)	1	0.01
Thai (0)	3	0.04
Vietnamese (11)	12	0.15
Hawaii Native/Pacific Islander (1)	2	0.02
Not Hispanic (1)	2	0.02
Native Hawaiian (1)	2	0.02
White (5,288)	5,465	67.45
Not Hispanic (5,149)	5,300	65.42
Hispanic (139)	165	2.04

*Notes: † The Census 2010 population figure is used to calculate the percentages in the Hispanic Origin and Race categories. Ancestry percentages are based on the 2006-2010 American Community Survey population (not shown); ‡ Numbers in parentheses indicate the number of people reporting a single ancestry; * Numbers in parentheses indicate the number of persons reporting this race alone, not in combination with any other race; Please refer to the Explanation of Data for more information.*

Seven Oaks

Place Type: CDP
County: Lexington
Population: 15,144†

Ancestry‡	Population	%
African, Sub-Saharan (75)	75	0.46
African (75)	75	0.46
American (2,246)	2,246	13.75
Arab (40)	83	0.51
Arab (16)	16	0.10
Egyptian (0)	34	0.21
Lebanese (24)	24	0.15
Syrian (0)	9	0.06
Austrian (9)	18	0.11
British (25)	153	0.94
Bulgarian (0)	21	0.13
Canadian (52)	52	0.32
Czechoslovakian (0)	15	0.09
Danish (19)	153	0.94
Dutch (0)	64	0.39
Eastern European (8)	17	0.10
English (798)	1,904	11.66
European (138)	138	0.84
French, ex. Basque (26)	332	2.03
French Canadian (40)	92	0.56
German (674)	2,113	12.94
Greek (16)	65	0.40
Hungarian (34)	54	0.33
Irish (515)	1,586	9.71
Italian (54)	283	1.73
Lithuanian (0)	10	0.06
Northern European (19)	19	0.12
Norwegian (15)	41	0.25
Polish (30)	65	0.40
Romanian (0)	38	0.23
Russian (13)	75	0.46
Scandinavian (0)	47	0.29
Scotch-Irish (395)	760	4.65
Scottish (184)	340	2.08
Serbian (41)	41	0.25
Slovak (0)	12	0.07
Slovene (7)	7	0.04
Swedish (85)	151	0.92
Swiss (0)	11	0.07
Welsh (25)	93	0.57
West Indian, ex. Hispanic (131)	340	2.08
Bahamian (14)	47	0.29
Jamaican (117)	155	0.95
West Indian (0)	138	0.84

Hispanic Origin	Population	%
Hispanic or Latino (of any race)	572	3.78
Central American, ex. Mexican	54	0.36
Costa Rican	5	0.03
Guatemalan	17	0.11
Honduran	13	0.09
Nicaraguan	3	0.02
Panamanian	8	0.05
Salvadoran	8	0.05
Cuban	39	0.26
Dominican Republic	13	0.09
Mexican	227	1.50
Puerto Rican	129	0.85
South American	70	0.46
Argentinean	3	0.02
Chilean	8	0.05
Colombian	34	0.22
Ecuadorian	8	0.05
Peruvian	17	0.11
Other Hispanic or Latino	40	0.26

Race*	Population	%
African-American/Black (4,851)	5,119	33.80
Not Hispanic (4,810)	5,045	33.31
Hispanic (41)	74	0.49
American Indian/Alaska Native (40)	169	1.12
Not Hispanic (31)	150	0.99
Hispanic (9)	19	0.13
Apache (0)	1	0.01
Blackfeet (0)	2	0.01
Cherokee (10)	42	0.28
Cheyenne (2)	2	0.01
Chickasaw (0)	1	0.01
Chippewa (1)	3	0.02
Choctaw (0)	1	0.01
Comanche (2)	2	0.01
Delaware (0)	2	0.01
Iroquois (1)	1	0.01
Lumbee (1)	2	0.01
Mexican American Ind. (2)	2	0.01
Pueblo (5)	5	0.03
Seminole (0)	1	0.01
Sioux (1)	2	0.01
Asian (422)	527	3.48
Not Hispanic (417)	517	3.41
Hispanic (5)	10	0.07
Bangladeshi (6)	6	0.04
Burmese (3)	3	0.02
Cambodian (1)	1	0.01
Chinese, ex. Taiwanese (52)	74	0.49
Filipino (18)	39	0.26
Indian (224)	238	1.57
Japanese (15)	29	0.19
Korean (36)	41	0.27
Pakistani (0)	1	0.01
Sri Lankan (1)	1	0.01
Thai (9)	18	0.12
Vietnamese (35)	46	0.30
Hawaii Native/Pacific Islander (34)	53	0.35
Not Hispanic (32)	48	0.32
Hispanic (2)	5	0.03
Guamanian/Chamorro (16)	20	0.13
Native Hawaiian (3)	14	0.09
Samoan (0)	4	0.03
White (9,140)	9,435	62.30
Not Hispanic (8,891)	9,152	60.43
Hispanic (249)	283	1.87

Simpsonville

Place Type: City
County: Greenville
Population: 18,238†

Ancestry‡	Population	%
African, Sub-Saharan (143)	143	0.82
African (120)	120	0.68
Nigerian (23)	23	0.13
American (1,904)	1,904	10.86
Arab (324)	324	1.85
Arab (19)	19	0.11
Egyptian (224)	224	1.28
Other Arab (81)	81	0.46
British (51)	120	0.68
Canadian (48)	48	0.27
Croatian (0)	32	0.18
Czech (33)	33	0.19
Czechoslovakian (13)	13	0.07
Danish (16)	27	0.15
Dutch (36)	174	0.99
English (569)	1,640	9.35
European (196)	196	1.12
French, ex. Basque (126)	249	1.42
French Canadian (101)	113	0.64
German (700)	2,066	11.78
Greek (0)	90	0.51
Irish (571)	2,182	12.44
Italian (234)	550	3.14
Lithuanian (15)	33	0.19
Northern European (29)	29	0.17
Norwegian (11)	106	0.60
Polish (81)	290	1.65
Portuguese (13)	27	0.15
Russian (111)	111	0.63
Scotch-Irish (409)	584	3.33
Scottish (398)	543	3.10
Slovak (11)	51	0.29
Slovene (0)	15	0.09
Swedish (16)	177	1.01
Swiss (0)	27	0.15
Welsh (34)	180	1.03
West Indian, ex. Hispanic (8)	8	0.05
Haitian (8)	8	0.05
Yugoslavian (0)	18	0.10

Hispanic Origin	Population	%
Hispanic or Latino (of any race)	1,619	8.88
Central American, ex. Mexican	132	0.72
Costa Rican	17	0.09
Guatemalan	33	0.18
Honduran	43	0.24
Nicaraguan	14	0.08
Panamanian	5	0.03
Salvadoran	20	0.11
Cuban	85	0.47
Dominican Republic	47	0.26
Mexican	644	3.53
Puerto Rican	226	1.24
South American	345	1.89
Argentinean	12	0.07
Bolivian	3	0.02
Chilean	1	0.01
Colombian	268	1.47
Ecuadorian	22	0.12
Peruvian	23	0.13
Uruguayan	9	0.05
Venezuelan	7	0.04
Other Hispanic or Latino	140	0.77

Race*	Population	%
African-American/Black (3,000)	3,213	17.62
Not Hispanic (2,940)	3,128	17.15
Hispanic (60)	85	0.47
American Indian/Alaska Native (53)	140	0.77
Not Hispanic (37)	106	0.58
Hispanic (16)	34	0.19
Apache (2)	2	0.01
Blackfeet (0)	1	0.01
Central American Ind. (2)	2	0.01
Cherokee (13)	44	0.24
Chickasaw (0)	4	0.02
Chippewa (0)	1	0.01
Choctaw (1)	5	0.03
Creek (1)	3	0.02
Delaware (0)	4	0.02
Lumbee (9)	12	0.07
Mexican American Ind. (3)	3	0.02
Navajo (1)	3	0.02
Pueblo (1)	1	0.01
Spanish American Ind. (2)	2	0.01
Asian (231)	328	1.80
Not Hispanic (228)	314	1.72
Hispanic (3)	14	0.08
Bangladeshi (2)	2	0.01
Chinese, ex. Taiwanese (40)	44	0.24
Filipino (34)	63	0.35
Indian (67)	75	0.41
Japanese (7)	22	0.12
Korean (16)	36	0.20
Malaysian (1)	1	0.01
Nepalese (12)	12	0.07
Pakistani (4)	10	0.05
Taiwanese (1)	1	0.01
Thai (10)	13	0.07
Vietnamese (29)	29	0.16
Hawaii Native/Pacific Islander (20)	32	0.18
Not Hispanic (18)	30	0.16
Hispanic (2)	2	0.01
Guamanian/Chamorro (4)	5	0.03
Native Hawaiian (4)	7	0.04
Samoan (2)	7	0.04
Tongan (0)	1	0.01
White (13,798)	14,175	77.72
Not Hispanic (13,024)	13,333	73.11
Hispanic (774)	842	4.62

*Notes: † The Census 2010 population figure is used to calculate the percentages in the Hispanic Origin and Race categories. Ancestry percentages are based on the 2006-2010 American Community Survey population (not shown); ‡ Numbers in parentheses indicate the number of people reporting a single ancestry; * Numbers in parentheses indicate the number of persons reporting this race alone, not in combination with any other race; Please refer to the Explanation of Data for more information.*

Socastee

Place Type: CDP
County: Horry
Population: 19,952†

Ancestry‡	Population	%
African, Sub-Saharan (14)	32	0.19
African (14)	32	0.19
Albanian (43)	43	0.25
American (3,094)	3,094	18.09
Armenian (0)	17	0.10
Austrian (0)	12	0.07
British (62)	114	0.67
Bulgarian (11)	11	0.06
Canadian (29)	51	0.30
Croatian (0)	11	0.06
Czech (19)	37	0.22
Czechoslovakian (104)	115	0.67
Danish (0)	10	0.06
Dutch (84)	338	1.98
English (578)	1,503	8.79
European (5)	5	0.03
French, ex. Basque (161)	628	3.67
French Canadian (17)	30	0.18
German (1,023)	2,733	15.97
Greek (60)	144	0.84
Hungarian (17)	31	0.18
Irish (642)	2,418	14.13
Israeli (53)	53	0.31
Italian (585)	1,220	7.13
Lithuanian (19)	28	0.16
Norwegian (14)	45	0.26
Polish (120)	528	3.09
Portuguese (49)	66	0.39
Russian (22)	62	0.36
Scandinavian (0)	24	0.14
Scotch-Irish (197)	426	2.49
Scottish (125)	394	2.30
Slovak (10)	20	0.12
Slovene (0)	12	0.07
Soviet Union (12)	12	0.07
Swedish (42)	113	0.66
Swiss (18)	72	0.42
Ukrainian (29)	57	0.33
Welsh (42)	169	0.99
West Indian, ex. Hispanic (84)	84	0.49
Bermudan (57)	57	0.33
Jamaican (27)	27	0.16

Hispanic Origin	Population	%
Hispanic or Latino (of any race)	2,149	10.77
Central American, ex. Mexican	227	1.14
Costa Rican	7	0.04
Guatemalan	99	0.50
Honduran	60	0.30
Nicaraguan	16	0.08
Panamanian	7	0.04
Salvadoran	38	0.19
Cuban	22	0.11
Dominican Republic	17	0.09
Mexican	1,428	7.16
Puerto Rican	191	0.96
South American	62	0.31
Argentinean	2	0.01
Bolivian	1	0.01
Chilean	6	0.03
Colombian	28	0.14
Ecuadorian	3	0.02
Peruvian	11	0.06
Uruguayan	2	0.01
Venezuelan	7	0.04
Other South American	2	0.01
Other Hispanic or Latino	202	1.01

Race*	Population	%
African-American/Black (1,525)	1,792	8.98
Not Hispanic (1,482)	1,729	8.67
Hispanic (43)	63	0.32
American Indian/Alaska Native (116)	274	1.37
Not Hispanic (87)	232	1.16
Hispanic (29)	42	0.21
Apache (1)	5	0.03
Blackfeet (1)	6	0.03
Canadian/French Am. Ind. (2)	2	0.01
Cherokee (14)	67	0.34
Chickasaw (0)	1	0.01
Chippewa (2)	2	0.01
Choctaw (6)	8	0.04
Comanche (0)	1	0.01
Creek (1)	1	0.01
Inupiat *(Alaska Native)* (1)	1	0.01
Iroquois (3)	5	0.03
Lumbee (8)	12	0.06
Mexican American Ind. (11)	13	0.07
Navajo (1)	1	0.01
Seminole (1)	1	0.01
Sioux (7)	13	0.07
Spanish American Ind. (0)	2	0.01
Asian (362)	466	2.34
Not Hispanic (355)	446	2.24
Hispanic (7)	20	0.10
Cambodian (6)	6	0.03
Chinese, ex. Taiwanese (70)	85	0.43
Filipino (65)	105	0.53
Indian (11)	23	0.12
Indonesian (0)	1	0.01
Japanese (13)	15	0.08
Korean (14)	24	0.12
Laotian (1)	1	0.01
Pakistani (0)	1	0.01
Taiwanese (1)	2	0.01
Thai (29)	46	0.23
Vietnamese (127)	143	0.72
Hawaii Native/Pacific Islander (31)	55	0.28
Not Hispanic (15)	37	0.19
Hispanic (16)	18	0.09
Guamanian/Chamorro (18)	19	0.10
Native Hawaiian (1)	11	0.06
Samoan (0)	1	0.01
White (16,322)	16,852	84.46
Not Hispanic (15,399)	15,797	79.18
Hispanic (923)	1,055	5.29

Spartanburg

Place Type: City
County: Spartanburg
Population: 37,013†

Ancestry‡	Population	%
African, Sub-Saharan (272)	272	0.73
African (213)	213	0.57
Kenyan (36)	36	0.10
Other Sub-Saharan African (23)	23	0.06
American (2,311)	2,311	6.16
Arab (105)	121	0.32
Arab (21)	21	0.06
Lebanese (74)	90	0.24
Palestinian (10)	10	0.03
Armenian (13)	13	0.03
Austrian (14)	58	0.15
British (206)	285	0.76
Bulgarian (0)	13	0.03
Cajun (0)	24	0.06
Canadian (22)	22	0.06
Croatian (51)	65	0.17
Czech (32)	60	0.16
Czechoslovakian (1)	1	<0.01
Danish (0)	9	0.02
Dutch (43)	249	0.66
Eastern European (12)	12	0.03
English (1,816)	3,823	10.20
European (323)	470	1.25
French, ex. Basque (122)	542	1.45
French Canadian (43)	118	0.31
German (991)	2,416	6.44
German Russian (29)	29	0.08
Greek (55)	94	0.25
Hungarian (0)	20	0.05
Irish (748)	2,069	5.52
Italian (151)	495	1.32
Lithuanian (6)	6	0.02
Northern European (12)	12	0.03
Norwegian (16)	66	0.18
Pennsylvania German (8)	8	0.02
Polish (74)	250	0.67
Portuguese (17)	32	0.09
Russian (32)	93	0.25
Scandinavian (10)	10	0.03
Scotch-Irish (1,150)	1,602	4.27
Scottish (267)	1,087	2.90
Slovak (8)	14	0.04
Swedish (120)	260	0.69
Swiss (82)	125	0.33
Ukrainian (144)	157	0.42
Welsh (14)	35	0.09
West Indian, ex. Hispanic (67)	105	0.28
Barbadian (58)	58	0.15
Jamaican (9)	33	0.09
West Indian (0)	14	0.04

Hispanic Origin	Population	%
Hispanic or Latino (of any race)	1,264	3.42
Central American, ex. Mexican	122	0.33
Costa Rican	5	0.01
Guatemalan	33	0.09
Honduran	30	0.08
Nicaraguan	3	0.01
Panamanian	4	0.01
Salvadoran	37	0.10
Other Central American	10	0.03
Cuban	39	0.11
Dominican Republic	20	0.05
Mexican	570	1.54
Puerto Rican	242	0.65
South American	158	0.43
Argentinean	12	0.03
Bolivian	5	0.01
Chilean	5	0.01
Colombian	94	0.25
Ecuadorian	31	0.08
Peruvian	7	0.02
Venezuelan	4	0.01
Other Hispanic or Latino	113	0.31

Race*	Population	%
African-American/Black (18,255)	18,691	50.50
Not Hispanic (18,156)	18,535	50.08
Hispanic (99)	156	0.42
American Indian/Alaska Native (80)	271	0.73
Not Hispanic (68)	238	0.64
Hispanic (12)	33	0.09
Apache (2)	2	0.01
Blackfeet (1)	13	0.04
Cherokee (16)	75	0.20
Chickasaw (0)	3	0.01
Chippewa (3)	3	0.01
Choctaw (0)	4	0.01
Creek (0)	1	<0.01
Delaware (0)	1	<0.01
Iroquois (1)	2	0.01
Lumbee (11)	15	0.04
Mexican American Ind. (4)	8	0.02
Potawatomi (1)	1	<0.01
Sioux (0)	2	0.01
South American Ind. (0)	2	0.01
Tlingit-Haida *(Alaska Native)* (3)	3	0.01
Asian (667)	785	2.12
Not Hispanic (660)	767	2.07
Hispanic (7)	18	0.05
Cambodian (56)	71	0.19
Chinese, ex. Taiwanese (55)	74	0.20
Filipino (47)	68	0.18
Hmong (59)	61	0.16
Indian (172)	198	0.53
Japanese (6)	16	0.04
Korean (28)	40	0.11
Laotian (104)	112	0.30
Nepalese (9)	10	0.03

*Notes: † The Census 2010 population figure is used to calculate the percentages in the Hispanic Origin and Race categories. Ancestry percentages are based on the 2006-2010 American Community Survey population (not shown); ‡ Numbers in parentheses indicate the number of people reporting a single ancestry; * Numbers in parentheses indicate the number of persons reporting this race alone, not in combination with any other race; Please refer to the Explanation of Data for more information.*

Pakistani (24)	24	0.06
Thai (12)	18	0.05
Vietnamese (69)	78	0.21
Hawaii Native/Pacific Islander (14)	32	0.09
Not Hispanic (10)	24	0.06
Hispanic (4)	8	0.02
Guamanian/Chamorro (9)	13	0.04
Native Hawaiian (4)	10	0.03
White (16,877)	17,392	46.99
Not Hispanic (16,267)	16,691	45.09
Hispanic (610)	701	1.89

St. Andrews

Place Type: CDP
County: Richland
Population: 20,493†

Ancestry‡	Population	%
African, Sub-Saharan (354)	381	1.83
African (237)	264	1.27
Other Sub-Saharan African (117)	117	0.56
American (1,123)	1,123	5.39
Arab (0)	4	0.02
Lebanese (0)	2	0.01
Syrian (0)	2	0.01
Austrian (27)	70	0.34
Belgian (8)	8	0.04
British (15)	59	0.28
Canadian (0)	15	0.07
Dutch (27)	69	0.33
English (443)	1,087	5.22
European (52)	65	0.31
French, ex. Basque (47)	379	1.82
French Canadian (17)	31	0.15
German (447)	1,346	6.46
Greek (0)	177	0.85
Guyanese (0)	14	0.07
Hungarian (19)	30	0.14
Irish (230)	1,152	5.53
Italian (53)	325	1.56
Lithuanian (10)	19	0.09
Norwegian (65)	116	0.56
Pennsylvania German (12)	44	0.21
Polish (55)	82	0.39
Romanian (6)	6	0.03
Russian (0)	30	0.14
Scandinavian (13)	26	0.12
Scotch-Irish (153)	328	1.57
Scottish (77)	176	0.84
Slovak (0)	8	0.04
Swedish (0)	78	0.37
Swiss (10)	21	0.10
Turkish (0)	7	0.03
Ukrainian (9)	9	0.04
Welsh (0)	21	0.10
West Indian, ex. Hispanic (183)	183	0.88
Bahamian (24)	24	0.12
Haitian (41)	41	0.20
West Indian (118)	118	0.57
Yugoslavian (0)	35	0.17

Hispanic Origin	Population	%
Hispanic or Latino (of any race)	754	3.68
Central American, ex. Mexican	59	0.29
Costa Rican	3	0.01
Guatemalan	15	0.07
Honduran	10	0.05
Nicaraguan	3	0.01
Panamanian	20	0.10
Salvadoran	7	0.03
Other Central American	1	<0.01
Cuban	34	0.17
Dominican Republic	21	0.10
Mexican	324	1.58
Puerto Rican	205	1.00
South American	50	0.24
Bolivian	4	0.02
Chilean	2	0.01
Colombian	30	0.15
Ecuadorian	5	0.02
Peruvian	3	0.01
Venezuelan	6	0.03
Other Hispanic or Latino	61	0.30

Race*	Population	%
African-American/Black (13,474)	13,821	67.44
Not Hispanic (13,343)	13,649	66.60
Hispanic (131)	172	0.84
American Indian/Alaska Native (61)	199	0.97
Not Hispanic (51)	171	0.83
Hispanic (10)	28	0.14
Apache (0)	4	0.02
Blackfeet (0)	10	0.05
Central American Ind. (1)	2	0.01
Cherokee (6)	55	0.27
Chickasaw (0)	2	0.01
Chippewa (0)	1	<0.01
Choctaw (1)	5	0.02
Creek (0)	3	0.01
Lumbee (1)	1	<0.01
Mexican American Ind. (3)	3	0.01
Navajo (0)	4	0.02
Seminole (0)	1	<0.01
Shoshone (1)	1	<0.01
Sioux (1)	1	<0.01
Asian (400)	501	2.44
Not Hispanic (395)	487	2.38
Hispanic (5)	14	0.07
Bangladeshi (1)	1	<0.01
Bhutanese (4)	4	0.02
Burmese (138)	141	0.69
Chinese, ex. Taiwanese (40)	56	0.27
Filipino (22)	47	0.23
Hmong (9)	9	0.04
Indian (67)	82	0.40
Indonesian (2)	2	0.01
Japanese (12)	32	0.16
Korean (25)	39	0.19
Laotian (5)	5	0.02
Nepalese (1)	1	<0.01
Pakistani (7)	7	0.03
Taiwanese (1)	2	0.01
Thai (6)	7	0.03
Vietnamese (45)	49	0.24
Hawaii Native/Pacific Islander (19)	41	0.20
Not Hispanic (15)	34	0.17
Hispanic (4)	7	0.03
Fijian (3)	3	0.01
Guamanian/Chamorro (2)	5	0.02
Native Hawaiian (6)	18	0.09
Samoan (0)	1	<0.01
White (5,794)	6,102	29.78
Not Hispanic (5,516)	5,791	28.26
Hispanic (278)	311	1.52

Summerville

Place Type: Town
County: Dorchester
Population: 43,392†

Ancestry‡	Population	%
African, Sub-Saharan (180)	221	0.55
African (121)	130	0.32
Nigerian (44)	44	0.11
South African (15)	47	0.12
Albanian (0)	52	0.13
American (5,167)	5,167	12.79
Australian (16)	16	0.04
Austrian (0)	28	0.07
Belgian (164)	275	0.68
Brazilian (9)	9	0.02
British (106)	253	0.63
Cajun (9)	9	0.02
Canadian (8)	107	0.26
Croatian (21)	21	0.05
Czech (25)	110	0.27
Czechoslovakian (55)	80	0.20
Danish (32)	173	0.43
Dutch (172)	652	1.61
Eastern European (17)	17	0.04
English (1,885)	4,341	10.74
European (405)	405	1.00
Finnish (0)	27	0.07
French, ex. Basque (85)	1,381	3.42
French Canadian (99)	188	0.47
German (1,618)	6,379	15.79
Greek (79)	283	0.70
Hungarian (39)	72	0.18
Irish (1,450)	5,209	12.89
Israeli (23)	23	0.06
Italian (845)	2,309	5.71
Lithuanian (0)	69	0.17
Maltese (0)	11	0.03
Norwegian (79)	266	0.66
Polish (335)	941	2.33
Portuguese (8)	154	0.38
Russian (55)	153	0.38
Scandinavian (0)	25	0.06
Scotch-Irish (1,041)	1,594	3.94
Scottish (396)	1,027	2.54
Slavic (30)	116	0.29
Slovak (0)	56	0.14
Slovene (31)	49	0.12
Swedish (137)	384	0.95
Swiss (7)	52	0.13
Ukrainian (0)	114	0.28
Welsh (127)	322	0.80
West Indian, ex. Hispanic (95)	111	0.27
Belizean (34)	34	0.08
Jamaican (9)	25	0.06
Trinidadian/Tobagonian (52)	52	0.13

Hispanic Origin	Population	%
Hispanic or Latino (of any race)	2,165	4.99
Central American, ex. Mexican	251	0.58
Costa Rican	15	0.03
Guatemalan	34	0.08
Honduran	55	0.13
Nicaraguan	33	0.08
Panamanian	34	0.08
Salvadoran	75	0.17
Other Central American	5	0.01
Cuban	83	0.19
Dominican Republic	59	0.14
Mexican	836	1.93
Puerto Rican	529	1.22
South American	215	0.50
Argentinean	20	0.05
Bolivian	7	0.02
Chilean	5	0.01
Colombian	83	0.19
Ecuadorian	38	0.09
Peruvian	43	0.10
Venezuelan	13	0.03
Other South American	6	0.01
Other Hispanic or Latino	192	0.44

Race*	Population	%
African-American/Black (9,304)	9,956	22.94
Not Hispanic (9,158)	9,734	22.43
Hispanic (146)	222	0.51
American Indian/Alaska Native (173)	492	1.13
Not Hispanic (161)	441	1.02
Hispanic (12)	51	0.12
Alaska Athabascan *(Ala. Nat.)* (1)	3	0.01
Aleut *(Alaska Native)* (0)	1	<0.01
Apache (2)	6	0.01
Blackfeet (4)	27	0.06
Canadian/French Am. Ind. (0)	4	0.01
Central American Ind. (1)	1	<0.01
Cherokee (33)	121	0.28
Cheyenne (0)	1	<0.01
Chickasaw (4)	4	0.01
Chippewa (1)	4	0.01
Choctaw (5)	12	0.03
Comanche (4)	6	0.01
Cree (0)	1	<0.01
Creek (2)	6	0.01

*Notes: † The Census 2010 population figure is used to calculate the percentages in the Hispanic Origin and Race categories. Ancestry percentages are based on the 2006-2010 American Community Survey population (not shown); ‡ Numbers in parentheses indicate the number of people reporting a single ancestry; * Numbers in parentheses indicate the number of persons reporting this race alone, not in combination with any other race; Please refer to the Explanation of Data for more information.*

Delaware (0)	3	0.01
Houma (2)	2	<0.01
Iroquois (4)	14	0.03
Lumbee (4)	6	0.01
Mexican American Ind. (6)	7	0.02
Navajo (3)	6	0.01
Ottawa (1)	1	<0.01
Pima (1)	1	<0.01
Seminole (0)	5	0.01
Sioux (5)	18	0.04
Tlingit-Haida *(Alaska Native)* (0)	1	<0.01
Asian (657)	995	2.29
Not Hispanic (647)	954	2.20
Hispanic (10)	41	0.09
Cambodian (6)	6	0.01
Chinese, ex. Taiwanese (111)	138	0.32
Filipino (239)	407	0.94
Indian (127)	149	0.34
Indonesian (1)	4	0.01
Japanese (33)	96	0.22
Korean (34)	70	0.16
Laotian (1)	1	<0.01
Nepalese (4)	4	0.01
Pakistani (1)	2	<0.01
Taiwanese (0)	1	<0.01
Thai (22)	35	0.08
Vietnamese (66)	74	0.17
Hawaii Native/Pacific Islander (40)	94	0.22
Not Hispanic (38)	84	0.19
Hispanic (2)	10	0.02
Guamanian/Chamorro (8)	20	0.05
Native Hawaiian (13)	37	0.09
Samoan (0)	1	<0.01
White (31,271)	32,369	74.60
Not Hispanic (30,101)	31,037	71.53
Hispanic (1,170)	1,332	3.07

Sumter

Place Type: City
County: Sumter
Population: 40,524†

Ancestry‡	Population	%
African, Sub-Saharan (3,013)	3,075	7.62
African (2,997)	3,059	7.58
Ethiopian (5)	5	0.01
Nigerian (11)	11	0.03
American (2,026)	2,026	5.02
Arab (0)	70	0.17
Lebanese (0)	70	0.17
Australian (12)	12	0.03
Austrian (13)	13	0.03
British (58)	176	0.44
Cajun (46)	46	0.11
Canadian (0)	15	0.04
Croatian (10)	23	0.06
Czech (12)	51	0.13
Dutch (86)	252	0.62
Eastern European (30)	30	0.07
English (1,148)	2,537	6.29
European (308)	368	0.91
French, ex. Basque (129)	476	1.18
French Canadian (57)	141	0.35
German (796)	2,265	5.61
Greek (33)	97	0.24
Hungarian (34)	36	0.09
Irish (815)	1,977	4.90
Italian (343)	778	1.93
Lithuanian (15)	46	0.11
Maltese (0)	9	0.02
Northern European (0)	17	0.04
Norwegian (34)	72	0.18
Polish (148)	327	0.81
Portuguese (0)	22	0.05
Romanian (0)	5	0.01
Russian (32)	78	0.19
Scandinavian (0)	54	0.13
Scotch-Irish (647)	1,024	2.54
Scottish (304)	721	1.79
Serbian (0)	4	0.01
Slavic (0)	8	0.02
Slovak (0)	14	0.03
Swedish (26)	85	0.21
Turkish (30)	41	0.10
Welsh (58)	162	0.40
West Indian, ex. Hispanic (113)	187	0.46
Jamaican (83)	149	0.37
Trinidadian/Tobagonian (18)	18	0.04
West Indian (12)	20	0.05
Yugoslavian (0)	13	0.03

Hispanic Origin	Population	%
Hispanic or Latino (of any race)	1,467	3.62
Central American, ex. Mexican	177	0.44
Costa Rican	3	0.01
Guatemalan	73	0.18
Honduran	49	0.12
Nicaraguan	6	0.01
Panamanian	31	0.08
Salvadoran	15	0.04
Cuban	41	0.10
Dominican Republic	35	0.09
Mexican	718	1.77
Puerto Rican	317	0.78
South American	53	0.13
Argentinean	4	0.01
Chilean	3	0.01
Colombian	21	0.05
Ecuadorian	6	0.01
Peruvian	10	0.02
Uruguayan	2	<0.01
Venezuelan	7	0.02
Other Hispanic or Latino	126	0.31

Race*	Population	%
African-American/Black (19,889)	20,346	50.21
Not Hispanic (19,755)	20,156	49.74
Hispanic (134)	190	0.47
American Indian/Alaska Native (133)	341	0.84
Not Hispanic (101)	280	0.69
Hispanic (32)	61	0.15
Aleut *(Alaska Native)* (0)	1	<0.01
Apache (3)	4	0.01
Blackfeet (1)	3	0.01
Central American Ind. (3)	6	0.01
Cherokee (15)	75	0.19
Chickasaw (0)	3	0.01
Chippewa (1)	2	<0.01
Choctaw (1)	4	0.01
Comanche (1)	1	<0.01
Creek (0)	3	0.01
Delaware (0)	1	<0.01
Iroquois (1)	5	0.01
Lumbee (20)	28	0.07
Mexican American Ind. (0)	9	0.02
Navajo (1)	3	0.01
Pueblo (0)	1	<0.01
Seminole (0)	2	<0.01
Shoshone (0)	1	<0.01
Sioux (1)	2	<0.01
Tlingit-Haida *(Alaska Native)* (3)	3	0.01
Yakama (0)	4	0.01
Asian (654)	910	2.25
Not Hispanic (647)	880	2.17
Hispanic (7)	30	0.07
Burmese (3)	3	0.01
Cambodian (2)	4	0.01
Chinese, ex. Taiwanese (82)	108	0.27
Filipino (195)	283	0.70
Indian (156)	169	0.42
Indonesian (2)	6	0.01
Japanese (31)	79	0.19
Korean (57)	100	0.25
Laotian (4)	4	0.01
Malaysian (0)	1	<0.01
Pakistani (3)	4	0.01
Taiwanese (3)	9	0.02
Thai (31)	48	0.12
Vietnamese (61)	69	0.17
Hawaii Native/Pacific Islander (50)	89	0.22
Not Hispanic (48)	79	0.19
Hispanic (2)	10	0.02
Guamanian/Chamorro (31)	38	0.09
Native Hawaiian (13)	24	0.06
Samoan (4)	9	0.02
Tongan (1)	1	<0.01
White (18,359)	19,003	46.89
Not Hispanic (17,777)	18,324	45.22
Hispanic (582)	679	1.68

Taylors

Place Type: CDP
County: Greenville
Population: 21,617†

Ancestry‡	Population	%
African, Sub-Saharan (162)	162	0.75
African (13)	13	0.06
Somalian (149)	149	0.69
American (2,815)	2,815	13.01
Arab (42)	66	0.31
Lebanese (31)	40	0.18
Syrian (11)	11	0.05
Other Arab (0)	15	0.07
Armenian (19)	19	0.09
Austrian (0)	81	0.37
Brazilian (53)	53	0.24
British (163)	240	1.11
Cajun (11)	21	0.10
Canadian (20)	20	0.09
Czech (0)	22	0.10
Czechoslovakian (11)	11	0.05
Danish (0)	79	0.37
Dutch (53)	226	1.04
Eastern European (9)	9	0.04
English (1,062)	2,948	13.63
European (191)	210	0.97
Finnish (16)	16	0.07
French, ex. Basque (65)	422	1.95
French Canadian (26)	74	0.34
German (1,076)	3,167	14.64
Greek (35)	44	0.20
Guyanese (26)	26	0.12
Hungarian (0)	21	0.10
Iranian (55)	55	0.25
Irish (789)	2,773	12.82
Italian (175)	675	3.12
Latvian (12)	12	0.06
Lithuanian (0)	30	0.14
Northern European (18)	18	0.08
Norwegian (41)	189	0.87
Polish (155)	254	1.17
Portuguese (27)	27	0.12
Russian (21)	61	0.28
Scandinavian (9)	9	0.04
Scotch-Irish (495)	842	3.89
Scottish (244)	777	3.59
Slovak (28)	64	0.30
Swedish (78)	225	1.04
Swiss (0)	25	0.12
Turkish (43)	43	0.20
Ukrainian (37)	37	0.17
Welsh (52)	138	0.64
West Indian, ex. Hispanic (0)	46	0.21
Dutch West Indian (0)	13	0.06
Haitian (0)	33	0.15

Hispanic Origin	Population	%
Hispanic or Latino (of any race)	1,797	8.31
Central American, ex. Mexican	257	1.19
Costa Rican	23	0.11
Guatemalan	84	0.39
Honduran	51	0.24
Nicaraguan	16	0.07
Panamanian	3	0.01
Salvadoran	79	0.37
Other Central American	1	<0.01
Cuban	64	0.30

*Notes: † The Census 2010 population figure is used to calculate the percentages in the Hispanic Origin and Race categories. Ancestry percentages are based on the 2006-2010 American Community Survey population (not shown); ‡ Numbers in parentheses indicate the number of people reporting a single ancestry; * Numbers in parentheses indicate the number of persons reporting this race alone, not in combination with any other race; Please refer to the Explanation of Data for more information.*

Dominican Republic	46	0.21
Mexican	666	3.08
Puerto Rican	222	1.03
South American	393	1.82
Argentinean	4	0.02
Bolivian	2	0.01
Chilean	7	0.03
Colombian	329	1.52
Ecuadorian	2	0.01
Paraguayan	10	0.05
Peruvian	19	0.09
Uruguayan	8	0.04
Venezuelan	12	0.06
Other Hispanic or Latino	149	0.69

Race*	Population	%
African-American/Black (3,222)	3,443	15.93
Not Hispanic (3,176)	3,365	15.57
Hispanic (46)	78	0.36
American Indian/Alaska Native (35)	120	0.56
Not Hispanic (32)	111	0.51
Hispanic (3)	9	0.04
Apache (0)	2	0.01
Blackfeet (0)	2	0.01
Canadian/French Am. Ind. (0)	1	<0.01
Cherokee (11)	46	0.21
Chippewa (0)	1	<0.01
Choctaw (2)	5	0.02
Comanche (2)	2	0.01
Lumbee (2)	4	0.02
Mexican American Ind. (1)	2	0.01
Navajo (0)	2	0.01
Potawatomi (1)	1	<0.01
Sioux (0)	1	<0.01
South American Ind. (1)	1	<0.01
Ute (0)	1	<0.01
Asian (546)	632	2.92
Not Hispanic (542)	617	2.85
Hispanic (4)	15	0.07
Burmese (63)	63	0.29
Chinese, ex. Taiwanese (24)	40	0.19
Filipino (25)	51	0.24
Indian (42)	49	0.23
Indonesian (3)	3	0.01
Japanese (7)	19	0.09
Korean (26)	36	0.17
Pakistani (19)	19	0.09
Thai (2)	5	0.02
Vietnamese (329)	334	1.55
Hawaii Native/Pacific Islander (26)	42	0.19
Not Hispanic (19)	33	0.15
Hispanic (7)	9	0.04
Guamanian/Chamorro (8)	9	0.04
Native Hawaiian (1)	13	0.06
Samoan (2)	2	0.01
White (16,622)	17,018	78.73
Not Hispanic (15,693)	15,982	73.93
Hispanic (929)	1,036	4.79

Tega Cay

Place Type: City
County: York
Population: 7,620†

Ancestry‡	Population	%
American (380)	380	5.42
Arab (0)	36	0.51
Lebanese (0)	36	0.51
Austrian (33)	59	0.84
Belgian (0)	13	0.19
Brazilian (11)	11	0.16
British (29)	38	0.54
Croatian (51)	51	0.73
Danish (14)	25	0.36
Dutch (0)	52	0.74
English (373)	1,249	17.81
European (156)	156	2.22
Finnish (13)	13	0.19
French, ex. Basque (36)	202	2.88
French Canadian (0)	13	0.19
German (443)	1,654	23.58
Greek (0)	17	0.24
Hungarian (28)	83	1.18
Icelander (0)	22	0.31
Irish (480)	1,302	18.56
Italian (278)	709	10.11
Lithuanian (14)	14	0.20
New Zealander (24)	24	0.34
Norwegian (0)	34	0.48
Polish (13)	257	3.66
Romanian (11)	11	0.16
Russian (42)	114	1.63
Scotch-Irish (264)	448	6.39
Scottish (40)	411	5.86
Slovak (15)	28	0.40
Swedish (77)	175	2.50
Swiss (28)	122	1.74
Ukrainian (0)	26	0.37
Welsh (0)	88	1.25

Hispanic Origin	Population	%
Hispanic or Latino (of any race)	254	3.33
Central American, ex. Mexican	22	0.29
Costa Rican	1	0.01
Guatemalan	10	0.13
Honduran	6	0.08
Nicaraguan	1	0.01
Panamanian	4	0.05
Cuban	19	0.25
Dominican Republic	2	0.03
Mexican	101	1.33
Puerto Rican	34	0.45
South American	52	0.68
Argentinean	7	0.09
Bolivian	2	0.03
Chilean	8	0.10
Colombian	16	0.21
Ecuadorian	8	0.10
Peruvian	4	0.05
Uruguayan	1	0.01
Venezuelan	6	0.08
Other Hispanic or Latino	24	0.31

Race*	Population	%
African-American/Black (232)	266	3.49
Not Hispanic (227)	260	3.41
Hispanic (5)	6	0.08
American Indian/Alaska Native (17)	32	0.42
Not Hispanic (15)	28	0.37
Hispanic (2)	4	0.05
Alaska Athabascan *(Ala. Nat.)* (1)	1	0.01
Apache (0)	1	0.01
Cherokee (3)	12	0.16
Choctaw (3)	3	0.04
Delaware (1)	1	0.01
Lumbee (1)	1	0.01
South American Ind. (1)	1	0.01
Asian (151)	196	2.57
Not Hispanic (148)	189	2.48
Hispanic (3)	7	0.09
Burmese (1)	1	0.01
Cambodian (3)	3	0.04
Chinese, ex. Taiwanese (28)	29	0.38
Filipino (19)	34	0.45
Indian (62)	69	0.91
Japanese (0)	4	0.05
Korean (11)	17	0.22
Malaysian (2)	6	0.08
Taiwanese (4)	4	0.05
Thai (2)	2	0.03
Vietnamese (16)	24	0.31
Hawaii Native/Pacific Islander (10)	14	0.18
Not Hispanic (10)	14	0.18
Native Hawaiian (2)	3	0.04
White (7,058)	7,163	94.00
Not Hispanic (6,872)	6,958	91.31
Hispanic (186)	205	2.69

Union

Place Type: City
County: Union
Population: 8,393†

Ancestry‡	Population	%
African, Sub-Saharan (140)	150	1.77
African (140)	150	1.77
American (891)	891	10.50
Austrian (0)	9	0.11
British (33)	53	0.62
Canadian (0)	25	0.29
Dutch (0)	25	0.29
English (114)	352	4.15
European (70)	70	0.82
Finnish (7)	13	0.15
French, ex. Basque (75)	144	1.70
French Canadian (11)	11	0.13
German (166)	500	5.89
Greek (0)	17	0.20
Irish (190)	474	5.59
Italian (24)	71	0.84
Norwegian (44)	153	1.80
Polish (22)	70	0.82
Scotch-Irish (189)	245	2.89
Scottish (59)	216	2.55

Hispanic Origin	Population	%
Hispanic or Latino (of any race)	99	1.18
Central American, ex. Mexican	2	0.02
Guatemalan	2	0.02
Cuban	7	0.08
Mexican	48	0.57
Puerto Rican	22	0.26
South American	1	0.01
Colombian	1	0.01
Other Hispanic or Latino	19	0.23

Race*	Population	%
African-American/Black (3,948)	4,034	48.06
Not Hispanic (3,924)	4,000	47.66
Hispanic (24)	34	0.41
American Indian/Alaska Native (22)	44	0.52
Not Hispanic (22)	44	0.52
Cherokee (3)	13	0.15
Chippewa (3)	3	0.04
Choctaw (1)	1	0.01
Lumbee (1)	6	0.07
Seminole (0)	1	0.01
Asian (36)	49	0.58
Not Hispanic (36)	49	0.58
Chinese, ex. Taiwanese (2)	2	0.02
Filipino (6)	6	0.07
Indian (13)	18	0.21
Japanese (4)	5	0.06
Korean (4)	9	0.11
Nepalese (2)	2	0.02
Vietnamese (1)	2	0.02
Hawaii Native/Pacific Islander (0)	8	0.10
Not Hispanic (0)	6	0.07
Hispanic (0)	2	0.02
Fijian (0)	1	0.01
Guamanian/Chamorro (0)	3	0.04
White (4,238)	4,332	51.61
Not Hispanic (4,200)	4,284	51.04
Hispanic (38)	48	0.57

Wade Hampton

Place Type: CDP
County: Greenville
Population: 20,622†

Ancestry‡	Population	%
African, Sub-Saharan (47)	47	0.23
African (24)	24	0.12
Nigerian (23)	23	0.11
Albanian (0)	20	0.10
American (2,825)	2,825	13.91

*Notes: † The Census 2010 population figure is used to calculate the percentages in the Hispanic Origin and Race categories. Ancestry percentages are based on the 2006-2010 American Community Survey population (not shown); ‡ Numbers in parentheses indicate the number of people reporting a single ancestry; * Numbers in parentheses indicate the number of persons reporting this race alone, not in combination with any other race; Please refer to the Explanation of Data for more information.*

SECTION TWO

Arab (358)	418	2.06
Arab (0)	17	0.08
Egyptian (41)	41	0.20
Jordanian (153)	153	0.75
Lebanese (125)	168	0.83
Palestinian (39)	39	0.19
Austrian (0)	9	0.04
Belgian (0)	15	0.07
Brazilian (149)	149	0.73
British (48)	66	0.32
Canadian (0)	57	0.28
Croatian (20)	20	0.10
Czech (27)	38	0.19
Danish (0)	49	0.24
Dutch (96)	286	1.41
English (1,136)	2,748	13.53
European (310)	328	1.61
French, ex. Basque (125)	467	2.30
French Canadian (28)	52	0.26
German (816)	2,286	11.25
Greek (495)	524	2.58
Hungarian (0)	32	0.16
Iranian (10)	10	0.05
Irish (650)	1,973	9.71
Italian (176)	451	2.22
Lithuanian (0)	13	0.06
Northern European (13)	13	0.06
Norwegian (30)	115	0.57
Polish (254)	371	1.83
Portuguese (0)	68	0.33
Romanian (10)	10	0.05
Russian (9)	49	0.24
Scandinavian (19)	19	0.09
Scotch-Irish (422)	849	4.18
Scottish (244)	655	3.22
Slavic (10)	10	0.05
Slovak (33)	90	0.44
Swedish (29)	166	0.82
Swiss (37)	71	0.35
Turkish (57)	57	0.28
Ukrainian (0)	15	0.07
Welsh (94)	125	0.62
Yugoslavian (0)	29	0.14

Hispanic Origin	Population	%
Hispanic or Latino (of any race)	2,315	11.23
Central American, ex. Mexican	371	1.80
Costa Rican	34	0.16
Guatemalan	168	0.81
Honduran	86	0.42
Nicaraguan	13	0.06
Panamanian	2	0.01
Salvadoran	68	0.33
Cuban	41	0.20
Dominican Republic	53	0.26
Mexican	1,200	5.82
Puerto Rican	140	0.68
South American	374	1.81
Argentinean	1	<0.01
Bolivian	1	<0.01
Colombian	341	1.65
Ecuadorian	4	0.02
Paraguayan	2	0.01
Peruvian	11	0.05
Uruguayan	7	0.03
Venezuelan	7	0.03
Other Hispanic or Latino	136	0.66

Race*	Population	%
African-American/Black (2,100)	2,302	11.16
Not Hispanic (2,071)	2,255	10.93
Hispanic (29)	47	0.23
American Indian/Alaska Native (79)	156	0.76
Not Hispanic (59)	122	0.59
Hispanic (20)	34	0.16
Apache (0)	6	0.03
Blackfeet (0)	2	0.01
Canadian/French Am. Ind. (0)	1	<0.01
Central American Ind. (0)	1	<0.01
Cherokee (20)	49	0.24
Choctaw (1)	4	0.02
Creek (0)	1	<0.01
Lumbee (3)	8	0.04
Mexican American Ind. (9)	10	0.05
Pima (1)	1	<0.01
Potawatomi (1)	1	<0.01
Yakama (0)	1	<0.01
Yaqui (1)	1	<0.01
Asian (655)	754	3.66
Not Hispanic (653)	732	3.55
Hispanic (2)	22	0.11
Burmese (5)	5	0.02
Cambodian (2)	2	0.01
Chinese, ex. Taiwanese (56)	74	0.36
Filipino (37)	50	0.24
Indian (101)	115	0.56
Indonesian (1)	2	0.01
Japanese (12)	15	0.07
Korean (40)	62	0.30
Laotian (2)	2	0.01
Malaysian (1)	1	<0.01
Pakistani (27)	28	0.14
Sri Lankan (1)	1	<0.01
Taiwanese (2)	2	0.01
Thai (9)	13	0.06
Vietnamese (357)	369	1.79
Hawaii Native/Pacific Islander (30)	43	0.21
Not Hispanic (28)	36	0.17
Hispanic (2)	7	0.03
Guamanian/Chamorro (2)	3	0.01
Native Hawaiian (5)	11	0.05
Samoan (1)	1	<0.01
White (16,080)	16,461	79.82
Not Hispanic (15,161)	15,431	74.83
Hispanic (919)	1,030	4.99

West Columbia

Place Type: City
County: Lexington
Population: 14,988†

Ancestry‡	Population	%
African, Sub-Saharan (560)	560	3.82
African (521)	521	3.55
Sudanese (39)	39	0.27
American (1,729)	1,729	11.79
Arab (31)	31	0.21
Egyptian (24)	24	0.16
Lebanese (7)	7	0.05
Armenian (12)	12	0.08
Belgian (0)	5	0.03
British (36)	66	0.45
Bulgarian (0)	32	0.22
Canadian (8)	8	0.05
Danish (0)	39	0.27
Dutch (9)	126	0.86
Eastern European (5)	5	0.03
English (900)	1,653	11.27
European (90)	106	0.72
Finnish (10)	10	0.07
French, ex. Basque (76)	360	2.45
French Canadian (25)	25	0.17
German (727)	2,085	14.21
Greek (37)	37	0.25
Hungarian (0)	9	0.06
Iranian (27)	27	0.18
Irish (637)	1,554	10.59
Italian (76)	167	1.14
Latvian (8)	8	0.05
Norwegian (9)	56	0.38
Polish (61)	78	0.53
Portuguese (6)	15	0.10
Scotch-Irish (411)	677	4.62
Scottish (75)	248	1.69
Slovak (0)	9	0.06
Swedish (17)	68	0.46
Swiss (0)	24	0.16
Ukrainian (8)	17	0.12
Welsh (68)	113	0.77
West Indian, ex. Hispanic (26)	26	0.18
Belizean (26)	26	0.18

Hispanic Origin	Population	%
Hispanic or Latino (of any race)	2,174	14.50
Central American, ex. Mexican	328	2.19
Costa Rican	2	0.01
Guatemalan	263	1.75
Honduran	42	0.28
Nicaraguan	2	0.01
Panamanian	4	0.03
Salvadoran	15	0.10
Cuban	20	0.13
Dominican Republic	19	0.13
Mexican	1,561	10.41
Puerto Rican	83	0.55
South American	37	0.25
Argentinean	4	0.03
Chilean	1	0.01
Colombian	9	0.06
Ecuadorian	7	0.05
Paraguayan	2	0.01
Peruvian	5	0.03
Uruguayan	3	0.02
Venezuelan	5	0.03
Other South American	1	0.01
Other Hispanic or Latino	126	0.84

Race*	Population	%
African-American/Black (2,769)	2,935	19.58
Not Hispanic (2,676)	2,810	18.75
Hispanic (93)	125	0.83
American Indian/Alaska Native (119)	214	1.43
Not Hispanic (44)	120	0.80
Hispanic (75)	94	0.63
Apache (0)	1	0.01
Blackfeet (0)	3	0.02
Cherokee (12)	44	0.29
Cheyenne (1)	1	0.01
Chippewa (1)	1	0.01
Choctaw (1)	1	0.01
Iroquois (1)	1	0.01
Lumbee (1)	1	0.01
Mexican American Ind. (34)	49	0.33
Potawatomi (1)	1	0.01
Pueblo (2)	3	0.02
Seminole (1)	3	0.02
Sioux (1)	2	0.01
Spanish American Ind. (1)	2	0.01
Asian (271)	312	2.08
Not Hispanic (269)	307	2.05
Hispanic (2)	5	0.03
Bangladeshi (21)	22	0.15
Burmese (4)	4	0.03
Cambodian (1)	1	0.01
Chinese, ex. Taiwanese (86)	96	0.64
Filipino (12)	20	0.13
Indian (82)	86	0.57
Japanese (5)	8	0.05
Korean (11)	18	0.12
Laotian (10)	11	0.07
Pakistani (1)	1	0.01
Taiwanese (2)	2	0.01
Thai (4)	7	0.05
Vietnamese (28)	28	0.19
Hawaii Native/Pacific Islander (3)	11	0.07
Not Hispanic (1)	6	0.04
Hispanic (2)	5	0.03
Guamanian/Chamorro (2)	2	0.01
Native Hawaiian (0)	3	0.02
White (10,186)	10,464	69.82
Not Hispanic (9,579)	9,766	65.16
Hispanic (607)	698	4.66

Woodfield

Place Type: CDP
County: Richland
Population: 9,303†

*Notes: † The Census 2010 population figure is used to calculate the percentages in the Hispanic Origin and Race categories. Ancestry percentages are based on the 2006-2010 American Community Survey population (not shown); ‡ Numbers in parentheses indicate the number of people reporting a single ancestry; * Numbers in parentheses indicate the number of persons reporting this race alone, not in combination with any other race; Please refer to the Explanation of Data for more information.*

Ancestry[‡]	Population	%
African, Sub-Saharan (240)	355	3.53
African (240)	322	3.20
Ethiopian (0)	33	0.33
American (839)	839	8.34
Belgian (26)	26	0.26
British (10)	20	0.20
Danish (0)	7	0.07
Dutch (9)	25	0.25
English (205)	396	3.94
European (8)	29	0.29
French, ex. Basque (54)	77	0.77
French Canadian (0)	40	0.40
German (259)	488	4.85
Irish (90)	328	3.26
Italian (32)	61	0.61
Lithuanian (10)	10	0.10
Norwegian (10)	10	0.10
Polish (0)	23	0.23
Russian (9)	9	0.09
Scotch-Irish (185)	244	2.43
Scottish (39)	48	0.48
Swedish (0)	43	0.43
Swiss (10)	10	0.10
Welsh (11)	22	0.22
West Indian, ex. Hispanic (30)	101	1.00
Jamaican (30)	56	0.56
Trinidadian/Tobagonian (0)	27	0.27
West Indian (0)	18	0.18

Hispanic Origin	Population	%
Hispanic or Latino (of any race)	1,800	19.35
Central American, ex. Mexican	329	3.54
Costa Rican	10	0.11
Guatemalan	127	1.37
Honduran	111	1.19
Nicaraguan	13	0.14
Panamanian	54	0.58
Salvadoran	14	0.15
Cuban	17	0.18
Dominican Republic	23	0.25
Mexican	1,002	10.77
Puerto Rican	267	2.87
South American	44	0.47
Colombian	18	0.19
Ecuadorian	6	0.06
Peruvian	3	0.03
Venezuelan	13	0.14
Other South American	4	0.04
Other Hispanic or Latino	118	1.27

Race*	Population	%
African-American/Black (4,786)	4,973	53.46
Not Hispanic (4,685)	4,832	51.94
Hispanic (101)	141	1.52
American Indian/Alaska Native (62)	140	1.50
Not Hispanic (32)	92	0.99
Hispanic (30)	48	0.52
Blackfeet (0)	2	0.02
Central American Ind. (3)	3	0.03
Cherokee (11)	35	0.38
Choctaw (0)	1	0.01
Iroquois (1)	1	0.01
Lumbee (1)	1	0.01
Mexican American Ind. (10)	13	0.14
Navajo (3)	3	0.03
Pueblo (4)	4	0.04
Sioux (0)	2	0.02
South American Ind. (1)	1	0.01
Asian (292)	386	4.15
Not Hispanic (289)	364	3.91
Hispanic (3)	22	0.24
Bangladeshi (3)	3	0.03
Cambodian (3)	8	0.09
Chinese, ex. Taiwanese (29)	45	0.48
Filipino (60)	87	0.94
Indian (39)	50	0.54
Japanese (30)	50	0.54
Korean (77)	108	1.16
Pakistani (2)	2	0.02
Taiwanese (1)	1	0.01
Thai (4)	7	0.08
Vietnamese (34)	36	0.39
Hawaii Native/Pacific Islander (31)	65	0.70
Not Hispanic (28)	52	0.56
Hispanic (3)	13	0.14
Guamanian/Chamorro (15)	21	0.23
Native Hawaiian (5)	17	0.18
Samoan (3)	5	0.05
White (2,875)	3,122	33.56
Not Hispanic (2,246)	2,394	25.73
Hispanic (629)	728	7.83

York

Place Type: City
County: York
Population: 7,736[†]

Ancestry[‡]	Population	%
African, Sub-Saharan (27)	27	0.35
African (27)	27	0.35
American (653)	653	8.58
Canadian (16)	16	0.21
Czech (0)	10	0.13
Dutch (0)	83	1.09
English (298)	573	7.53
European (19)	19	0.25
French, ex. Basque (22)	46	0.60
French Canadian (11)	11	0.14
German (192)	479	6.29
Hungarian (0)	20	0.26
Irish (289)	764	10.04
Italian (117)	199	2.61
Norwegian (0)	20	0.26
Polish (6)	28	0.37
Portuguese (0)	28	0.37
Scotch-Irish (245)	457	6.00
Scottish (25)	39	0.51
Slovak (7)	46	0.60
Swedish (0)	17	0.22
Swiss (0)	12	0.16
Ukrainian (0)	20	0.26
Welsh (0)	20	0.26

Hispanic Origin	Population	%
Hispanic or Latino (of any race)	563	7.28
Central American, ex. Mexican	25	0.32
Costa Rican	5	0.06
Guatemalan	8	0.10
Honduran	9	0.12
Panamanian	1	0.01
Salvadoran	2	0.03
Cuban	12	0.16
Dominican Republic	10	0.13
Mexican	450	5.82
Puerto Rican	28	0.36
South American	4	0.05
Chilean	1	0.01
Colombian	2	0.03
Ecuadorian	1	0.01
Other Hispanic or Latino	34	0.44

Race*	Population	%
African-American/Black (2,968)	3,087	39.90
Not Hispanic (2,941)	3,053	39.46
Hispanic (27)	34	0.44
American Indian/Alaska Native (59)	102	1.32
Not Hispanic (35)	65	0.84
Hispanic (24)	37	0.48
Cherokee (3)	20	0.26
Creek (2)	2	0.03
Iroquois (3)	3	0.04
Lumbee (0)	1	0.01
Asian (44)	57	0.74
Not Hispanic (44)	53	0.69
Hispanic (0)	4	0.05
Cambodian (1)	1	0.01
Chinese, ex. Taiwanese (14)	14	0.18
Filipino (5)	6	0.08
Indian (5)	9	0.12
Japanese (0)	2	0.03
Korean (3)	4	0.05
Thai (6)	10	0.13
Vietnamese (10)	10	0.13
Hawaii Native/Pacific Islander (1)	3	0.04
Not Hispanic (1)	3	0.04
Native Hawaiian (0)	1	0.01
Samoan (1)	1	0.01
White (4,212)	4,352	56.26
Not Hispanic (4,011)	4,121	53.27
Hispanic (201)	231	2.99

*Notes: † The Census 2010 population figure is used to calculate the percentages in the Hispanic Origin and Race categories. Ancestry percentages are based on the 2006-2010 American Community Survey population (not shown); ‡ Numbers in parentheses indicate the number of people reporting a single ancestry; * Numbers in parentheses indicate the number of persons reporting this race alone, not in combination with any other race; Please refer to the Explanation of Data for more information.*

SOUTH DAKOTA

Place Type: State
Population: 814,180†

Ancestry‡	Population	%
Afghan (20)	20	<0.01
African, Sub-Saharan (3,016)	3,405	0.43
African (1,104)	1,271	0.16
Ethiopian (928)	934	0.12
Kenyan (68)	68	0.01
Liberian (84)	84	0.01
Nigerian (52)	93	0.01
Somalian (253)	253	0.03
South African (49)	71	0.01
Sudanese (340)	443	0.06
Ugandan (15)	15	<0.01
Other Sub-Saharan African (123)	173	0.02
Alsatian (16)	44	0.01
American (27,843)	27,843	3.48
Arab (777)	1,380	0.17
Arab (59)	127	0.02
Egyptian (2)	16	<0.01
Iraqi (81)	81	0.01
Jordanian (37)	41	0.01
Lebanese (223)	601	0.08
Moroccan (23)	23	<0.01
Palestinian (10)	10	<0.01
Syrian (152)	282	0.04
Other Arab (190)	199	0.02
Armenian (153)	238	0.03
Australian (35)	83	0.01
Austrian (296)	1,329	0.17
Basque (24)	58	0.01
Belgian (449)	1,683	0.21
Brazilian (36)	66	0.01
British (328)	1,023	0.13
Bulgarian (35)	111	0.01
Cajun (21)	27	<0.01
Canadian (187)	544	0.07
Carpatho Rusyn (0)	4	<0.01
Celtic (39)	122	0.02
Croatian (378)	641	0.08
Czech (6,398)	18,627	2.33
Czechoslovakian (873)	1,937	0.24
Danish (5,051)	18,778	2.35
Dutch (13,552)	38,184	4.78
Eastern European (39)	39	<0.01
English (13,724)	57,338	7.17
Estonian (33)	33	<0.01
European (5,143)	5,432	0.68
Finnish (1,394)	4,001	0.50
French, ex. Basque (2,638)	22,853	2.86
French Canadian (1,270)	4,471	0.56
German (159,183)	349,067	43.66
German Russian (65)	138	0.02
Greek (339)	1,025	0.13
Hungarian (309)	1,303	0.16
Icelander (60)	198	0.02
Iranian (0)	54	0.01
Irish (18,404)	88,995	11.13
Israeli (7)	23	<0.01
Italian (3,336)	10,084	1.26
Latvian (57)	147	0.02
Lithuanian (159)	584	0.07
Luxemburger (296)	782	0.10
Macedonian (15)	32	<0.01
Maltese (0)	19	<0.01
New Zealander (0)	3	<0.01
Northern European (448)	468	0.06
Norwegian (42,489)	119,341	14.93
Pennsylvania German (425)	719	0.09
Polish (2,966)	12,884	1.61
Portuguese (206)	591	0.07
Romanian (129)	247	0.03
Russian (1,964)	13,055	1.63
Scandinavian (3,965)	6,361	0.80
Scotch-Irish (2,667)	9,400	1.18
Scottish (2,336)	10,344	1.29
Serbian (159)	216	0.03
Slavic (24)	80	0.01
Slovak (118)	353	0.04
Slovene (53)	107	0.01
Swedish (6,298)	30,517	3.82
Swiss (548)	2,925	0.37
Turkish (44)	120	0.02
Ukrainian (732)	1,186	0.15
Welsh (784)	3,937	0.49
West Indian, ex. Hispanic (157)	363	0.05
Belizean (52)	88	0.01
Dutch West Indian (0)	3	<0.01
Haitian (28)	36	<0.01
Jamaican (59)	202	0.03
Trinidadian/Tobagonian (11)	17	<0.01
U.S. Virgin Islander (2)	2	<0.01
West Indian (5)	15	<0.01
Yugoslavian (577)	860	0.11

Hispanic Origin	Population	%
Hispanic or Latino (of any race)	22,119	2.72
Central American, ex. Mexican	2,891	0.36
Costa Rican	46	0.01
Guatemalan	1,620	0.20
Honduran	221	0.03
Nicaraguan	99	0.01
Panamanian	74	0.01
Salvadoran	780	0.10
Other Central American	51	0.01
Cuban	265	0.03
Dominican Republic	79	0.01
Mexican	13,839	1.70
Puerto Rican	1,483	0.18
South American	617	0.08
Argentinean	48	0.01
Bolivian	45	0.01
Chilean	79	0.01
Colombian	186	0.02
Ecuadorian	59	0.01
Paraguayan	14	<0.01
Peruvian	138	0.02
Uruguayan	12	<0.01
Venezuelan	25	<0.01
Other South American	11	<0.01
Other Hispanic or Latino	2,945	0.36

Race*	Population	%
African-American/Black (10,207)	14,705	1.81
Not Hispanic (9,959)	14,065	1.73
Hispanic (248)	640	0.08
American Indian/Alaska Native (71,817)	82,073	10.08
Not Hispanic (69,476)	78,770	9.67
Hispanic (2,341)	3,303	0.41
Alaska Athabascan *(Ala. Nat.)* (36)	45	0.01
Aleut *(Alaska Native)* (20)	37	<0.01
Apache (59)	103	0.01
Arapaho (156)	180	0.02
Blackfeet (81)	136	0.02
Canadian/French Am. Ind. (25)	51	0.01
Central American Ind. (8)	9	<0.01
Cherokee (155)	543	0.07
Cheyenne (263)	417	0.05
Chickasaw (14)	19	<0.01
Chippewa (576)	825	0.10
Choctaw (72)	151	0.02
Colville (7)	8	<0.01
Comanche (22)	31	<0.01
Cree (7)	24	<0.01
Creek (21)	51	0.01
Crow (66)	109	0.01
Delaware (4)	15	<0.01
Hopi (17)	29	<0.01
Inupiat *(Alaska Native)* (23)	31	<0.01
Iroquois (42)	101	0.01
Kiowa (15)	18	<0.01
Lumbee (8)	12	<0.01
Menominee (17)	24	<0.01
Mexican American Ind. (80)	102	0.01
Navajo (218)	300	0.04
Osage (10)	28	<0.01
Ottawa (10)	14	<0.01
Paiute (9)	10	<0.01
Pima (10)	17	<0.01
Potawatomi (40)	56	0.01
Pueblo (31)	41	0.01
Puget Sound Salish (7)	16	<0.01
Seminole (41)	58	0.01
Shoshone (29)	48	0.01
Sioux (55,948)	61,582	7.56
South American Ind. (9)	19	<0.01
Spanish American Ind. (5)	6	<0.01
Tlingit-Haida *(Alaska Native)* (14)	27	<0.01
Tohono O'Odham (5)	8	<0.01
Ute (14)	24	<0.01
Yakama (9)	11	<0.01
Yaqui (8)	15	<0.01
Yuman (14)	17	<0.01
Yup'ik *(Alaska Native)* (8)	9	<0.01
Asian (7,610)	10,216	1.25
Not Hispanic (7,553)	9,958	1.22
Hispanic (57)	258	0.03
Bangladeshi (41)	41	0.01
Bhutanese (67)	107	0.01
Burmese (654)	669	0.08
Cambodian (96)	125	0.02
Chinese, ex. Taiwanese (1,268)	1,534	0.19
Filipino (1,048)	1,864	0.23
Hmong (86)	94	0.01
Indian (1,152)	1,433	0.18
Indonesian (25)	46	0.01
Japanese (290)	696	0.09
Korean (834)	1,179	0.14
Laotian (372)	511	0.06
Malaysian (13)	18	<0.01
Nepalese (162)	209	0.03
Pakistani (91)	103	0.01
Sri Lankan (12)	12	<0.01
Taiwanese (25)	40	<0.01
Thai (149)	284	0.03
Vietnamese (762)	1,002	0.12
Hawaii Native/Pacific Islander (394)	920	0.11
Not Hispanic (313)	745	0.09
Hispanic (81)	175	0.02
Fijian (12)	16	<0.01
Guamanian/Chamorro (148)	216	0.03
Marshallese (1)	2	<0.01
Native Hawaiian (95)	336	0.04
Samoan (44)	91	0.01
Tongan (27)	46	0.01
White (699,392)	715,167	87.84
Not Hispanic (689,502)	703,177	86.37
Hispanic (9,890)	11,990	1.47

*Notes: † The Census 2010 population figure is used to calculate the percentages in the Hispanic Origin and Race categories. Ancestry percentages are based on the 2006-2010 American Community Survey population (not shown); ‡ Numbers in parentheses indicate the number of people reporting a single ancestry; * Numbers in parentheses indicate the number of persons reporting this race alone, not in combination with any other race; Please refer to the Explanation of Data for more information.*

Aberdeen

Place Type: City
County: Brown
Population: 26,091†

Ancestry‡	Population	%
African, Sub-Saharan (59)	59	0.23
Ethiopian (59)	59	0.23
American (1,014)	1,014	3.94
Arab (8)	8	0.03
Lebanese (8)	8	0.03
Armenian (9)	9	0.04
Austrian (0)	15	0.06
Belgian (17)	29	0.11
British (0)	15	0.06
Czech (90)	311	1.21
Czechoslovakian (10)	71	0.28
Danish (44)	296	1.15
Dutch (67)	535	2.08
English (334)	1,362	5.30
European (87)	98	0.38
Finnish (67)	261	1.02
French, ex. Basque (61)	663	2.58
French Canadian (25)	64	0.25
German (6,293)	13,450	52.31
German Russian (14)	27	0.11
Greek (14)	23	0.09
Hungarian (8)	20	0.08
Icelander (0)	12	0.05
Irish (710)	2,749	10.69
Italian (61)	147	0.57
Lithuanian (0)	20	0.08
Macedonian (0)	10	0.04
Northern European (21)	21	0.08
Norwegian (861)	3,665	14.25
Pennsylvania German (8)	16	0.06
Polish (210)	611	2.38
Portuguese (29)	41	0.16
Romanian (0)	10	0.04
Russian (56)	1,780	6.92
Scandinavian (124)	147	0.57
Scotch-Irish (98)	226	0.88
Scottish (69)	320	1.24
Swedish (225)	1,107	4.31
Swiss (13)	63	0.25
Ukrainian (0)	105	0.41
Welsh (28)	147	0.57
West Indian, ex. Hispanic (19)	38	0.15
Belizean (19)	38	0.15

Hispanic Origin	Population	%
Hispanic or Latino (of any race)	412	1.58
Central American, ex. Mexican	10	0.04
Costa Rican	1	<0.01
Guatemalan	5	0.02
Honduran	1	<0.01
Salvadoran	2	0.01
Other Central American	1	<0.01
Cuban	5	0.02
Mexican	239	0.92
Puerto Rican	76	0.29
South American	14	0.05
Argentinean	3	0.01
Colombian	6	0.02
Ecuadorian	3	0.01
Peruvian	1	<0.01
Venezuelan	1	<0.01
Other Hispanic or Latino	68	0.26

Race*	Population	%
African-American/Black (178)	307	1.18
Not Hispanic (171)	291	1.12
Hispanic (7)	16	0.06
American Indian/Alaska Native (945)	1,222	4.68
Not Hispanic (922)	1,176	4.51
Hispanic (23)	46	0.18
Alaska Athabascan *(Ala. Nat.)* (1)	2	0.01
Apache (1)	1	<0.01
Arapaho (0)	1	<0.01
Blackfeet (13)	17	0.07
Canadian/French Am. Ind. (0)	1	<0.01
Cherokee (2)	18	0.07
Cheyenne (3)	6	0.02
Chippewa (89)	106	0.41
Choctaw (1)	8	0.03
Cree (0)	1	<0.01
Crow (2)	3	0.01
Kiowa (2)	2	0.01
Menominee (1)	1	<0.01
Mexican American Ind. (1)	2	0.01
Navajo (11)	16	0.06
Pima (1)	1	<0.01
Potawatomi (0)	1	<0.01
Seminole (6)	6	0.02
Shoshone (2)	4	0.02
Sioux (504)	635	2.43
South American Ind. (0)	2	0.01
Spanish American Ind. (1)	1	<0.01
Asian (329)	402	1.54
Not Hispanic (327)	394	1.51
Hispanic (2)	8	0.03
Bangladeshi (4)	4	0.02
Chinese, ex. Taiwanese (81)	89	0.34
Filipino (27)	58	0.22
Hmong (10)	10	0.04
Indian (24)	42	0.16
Indonesian (1)	1	<0.01
Japanese (9)	18	0.07
Korean (119)	126	0.48
Laotian (4)	4	0.02
Pakistani (10)	12	0.05
Thai (3)	3	0.01
Vietnamese (27)	30	0.11
Hawaii Native/Pacific Islander (42)	68	0.26
Not Hispanic (42)	64	0.25
Hispanic (0)	4	0.02
Guamanian/Chamorro (1)	2	0.01
Marshallese (1)	1	<0.01
Native Hawaiian (7)	19	0.07
Samoan (13)	20	0.08
Tongan (14)	24	0.09
White (23,962)	24,451	93.71
Not Hispanic (23,759)	24,182	92.68
Hispanic (203)	269	1.03

Box Elder

Place Type: City
County: Pennington
Population: 7,800†

Ancestry‡	Population	%
American (302)	302	3.93
Austrian (0)	6	0.08
Belgian (40)	48	0.62
British (17)	60	0.78
Canadian (0)	37	0.48
Czech (23)	85	1.11
Czechoslovakian (11)	22	0.29
Danish (8)	48	0.62
Dutch (25)	140	1.82
English (316)	693	9.02
European (52)	84	1.09
Finnish (0)	7	0.09
French, ex. Basque (14)	291	3.79
French Canadian (10)	55	0.72
German (712)	2,476	32.21
Greek (0)	37	0.48
Hungarian (0)	21	0.27
Icelander (0)	8	0.10
Iranian (0)	8	0.10
Irish (240)	1,123	14.61
Italian (38)	398	5.18
Norwegian (163)	420	5.46
Polish (25)	145	1.89
Portuguese (0)	8	0.10
Romanian (0)	10	0.13
Russian (0)	68	0.88
Scandinavian (8)	8	0.10
Scotch-Irish (243)	305	3.97
Scottish (65)	374	4.87
Slovak (0)	6	0.08
Swedish (34)	168	2.19
Swiss (0)	13	0.17
Ukrainian (27)	42	0.55
Welsh (0)	44	0.57
West Indian, ex. Hispanic (8)	8	0.10
Jamaican (8)	8	0.10

Hispanic Origin	Population	%
Hispanic or Latino (of any race)	620	7.95
Central American, ex. Mexican	20	0.26
Guatemalan	2	0.03
Honduran	2	0.03
Panamanian	7	0.09
Salvadoran	9	0.12
Cuban	7	0.09
Dominican Republic	8	0.10
Mexican	352	4.51
Puerto Rican	117	1.50
South American	17	0.22
Argentinean	3	0.04
Bolivian	1	0.01
Colombian	5	0.06
Ecuadorian	5	0.06
Peruvian	2	0.03
Venezuelan	1	0.01
Other Hispanic or Latino	99	1.27

Race*	Population	%
African-American/Black (398)	558	7.15
Not Hispanic (382)	526	6.74
Hispanic (16)	32	0.41
American Indian/Alaska Native (347)	531	6.81
Not Hispanic (311)	462	5.92
Hispanic (36)	69	0.88
Alaska Athabascan *(Ala. Nat.)* (1)	1	0.01
Aleut *(Alaska Native)* (1)	3	0.04
Apache (1)	1	0.01
Blackfeet (0)	2	0.03
Canadian/French Am. Ind. (0)	2	0.03
Cherokee (2)	14	0.18
Cheyenne (11)	12	0.15
Chippewa (2)	14	0.18
Choctaw (1)	8	0.10
Comanche (1)	1	0.01
Creek (0)	2	0.03
Inupiat *(Alaska Native)* (1)	1	0.01
Iroquois (0)	1	0.01
Lumbee (1)	1	0.01
Navajo (8)	8	0.10
Potawatomi (0)	1	0.01
Seminole (0)	1	0.01
Shoshone (0)	1	0.01
Sioux (200)	279	3.58
Yuman (0)	1	0.01
Asian (171)	290	3.72
Not Hispanic (167)	274	3.51
Hispanic (4)	16	0.21
Cambodian (0)	1	0.01
Chinese, ex. Taiwanese (11)	28	0.36
Filipino (101)	147	1.88
Indian (8)	25	0.32
Japanese (11)	50	0.64
Korean (11)	22	0.28
Laotian (1)	1	0.01
Thai (17)	26	0.33
Vietnamese (5)	5	0.06
Hawaii Native/Pacific Islander (29)	51	0.65
Not Hispanic (29)	48	0.62
Hispanic (0)	3	0.04
Guamanian/Chamorro (23)	26	0.33
Native Hawaiian (2)	17	0.22
Samoan (1)	1	0.01
White (6,202)	6,628	84.97
Not Hispanic (5,901)	6,250	80.13
Hispanic (301)	378	4.85

*Notes: † The Census 2010 population figure is used to calculate the percentages in the Hispanic Origin and Race categories. Ancestry percentages are based on the 2006-2010 American Community Survey population (not shown); ‡ Numbers in parentheses indicate the number of people reporting a single ancestry; * Numbers in parentheses indicate the number of persons reporting this race alone, not in combination with any other race; Please refer to the Explanation of Data for more information.*

Brandon

Place Type: City
County: Minnehaha
Population: 8,785†

Ancestry‡	Population	%
American (239)	239	2.90
Arab (0)	32	0.39
Lebanese (0)	32	0.39
Belgian (14)	42	0.51
Czech (0)	72	0.87
Czechoslovakian (34)	55	0.67
Danish (42)	207	2.51
Dutch (279)	716	8.70
English (93)	704	8.55
European (16)	16	0.19
Finnish (6)	21	0.26
French, ex. Basque (30)	396	4.81
French Canadian (9)	74	0.90
German (1,450)	4,086	49.63
Greek (11)	11	0.13
Irish (91)	905	10.99
Italian (12)	209	2.54
Luxemburger (0)	10	0.12
Norwegian (510)	1,932	23.47
Polish (22)	42	0.51
Russian (0)	51	0.62
Scandinavian (31)	97	1.18
Scotch-Irish (0)	75	0.91
Scottish (0)	114	1.38
Swedish (91)	273	3.32
Welsh (0)	18	0.22

Hispanic Origin	Population	%
Hispanic or Latino (of any race)	105	1.20
Central American, ex. Mexican	12	0.14
Costa Rican	2	0.02
Guatemalan	1	0.01
Honduran	3	0.03
Nicaraguan	3	0.03
Salvadoran	3	0.03
Cuban	1	0.01
Dominican Republic	5	0.06
Mexican	57	0.65
Puerto Rican	7	0.08
South American	6	0.07
Colombian	5	0.06
Ecuadorian	1	0.01
Other Hispanic or Latino	17	0.19

Race*	Population	%
African-American/Black (52)	96	1.09
Not Hispanic (50)	94	1.07
Hispanic (2)	2	0.02
American Indian/Alaska Native (46)	79	0.90
Not Hispanic (41)	72	0.82
Hispanic (5)	7	0.08
Cherokee (0)	1	0.01
Chippewa (1)	2	0.02
Iroquois (0)	1	0.01
Mexican American Ind. (0)	1	0.01
Sioux (25)	42	0.48
Asian (52)	66	0.75
Not Hispanic (52)	65	0.74
Hispanic (0)	1	0.01
Cambodian (2)	3	0.03
Chinese, ex. Taiwanese (8)	8	0.09
Filipino (2)	7	0.08
Indian (2)	2	0.02
Japanese (2)	3	0.03
Korean (19)	22	0.25
Laotian (11)	13	0.15
Thai (1)	4	0.05
White (8,504)	8,606	97.96
Not Hispanic (8,442)	8,531	97.11
Hispanic (62)	75	0.85

Brookings

Place Type: City
County: Brookings
Population: 22,056†

Ancestry‡	Population	%
African, Sub-Saharan (121)	154	0.72
African (70)	103	0.48
Kenyan (8)	8	0.04
Somalian (43)	43	0.20
American (406)	406	1.89
Arab (32)	72	0.34
Arab (12)	12	0.06
Lebanese (20)	44	0.20
Syrian (0)	16	0.07
Austrian (0)	95	0.44
Belgian (13)	86	0.40
Brazilian (10)	10	0.05
British (12)	40	0.19
Canadian (12)	12	0.06
Celtic (0)	11	0.05
Croatian (0)	8	0.04
Czech (58)	357	1.66
Czechoslovakian (0)	15	0.07
Danish (100)	637	2.97
Dutch (237)	980	4.57
Eastern European (26)	26	0.12
English (358)	1,439	6.70
Estonian (13)	13	0.06
European (578)	620	2.89
Finnish (24)	177	0.82
French, ex. Basque (30)	467	2.18
French Canadian (19)	115	0.54
German (4,635)	10,250	47.75
Greek (9)	22	0.10
Hungarian (0)	32	0.15
Icelander (14)	14	0.07
Irish (586)	2,596	12.09
Italian (85)	183	0.85
Lithuanian (0)	11	0.05
Luxemburger (31)	53	0.25
Norwegian (1,635)	4,759	22.17
Pennsylvania German (7)	7	0.03
Polish (60)	242	1.13
Portuguese (11)	26	0.12
Russian (18)	92	0.43
Scandinavian (50)	108	0.50
Scotch-Irish (23)	342	1.59
Scottish (26)	280	1.30
Slovak (10)	22	0.10
Swedish (123)	1,213	5.65
Swiss (9)	41	0.19
Welsh (22)	113	0.53

Hispanic Origin	Population	%
Hispanic or Latino (of any race)	335	1.52
Central American, ex. Mexican	26	0.12
Costa Rican	1	<0.01
Guatemalan	7	0.03
Honduran	8	0.04
Salvadoran	10	0.05
Cuban	4	0.02
Dominican Republic	3	0.01
Mexican	207	0.94
Puerto Rican	12	0.05
South American	44	0.20
Argentinean	3	0.01
Bolivian	5	0.02
Chilean	4	0.02
Colombian	6	0.03
Peruvian	13	0.06
Uruguayan	9	0.04
Venezuelan	4	0.02
Other Hispanic or Latino	39	0.18

Race*	Population	%
African-American/Black (234)	340	1.54
Not Hispanic (232)	328	1.49
Hispanic (2)	12	0.05
American Indian/Alaska Native (217)	379	1.72
Not Hispanic (208)	356	1.61
Hispanic (9)	23	0.10
Apache (4)	4	0.02
Blackfeet (0)	2	0.01
Cherokee (2)	15	0.07
Cheyenne (1)	1	<0.01
Chippewa (8)	12	0.05
Cree (0)	1	<0.01
Creek (0)	1	<0.01
Iroquois (0)	1	<0.01
Lumbee (1)	1	<0.01
Menominee (4)	4	0.02
Navajo (4)	5	0.02
Ottawa (0)	2	0.01
Pima (0)	1	<0.01
Potawatomi (1)	1	<0.01
Sioux (131)	187	0.85
South American Ind. (0)	3	0.01
Yuman (1)	2	0.01
Asian (821)	931	4.22
Not Hispanic (818)	922	4.18
Hispanic (3)	9	0.04
Bangladeshi (19)	19	0.09
Chinese, ex. Taiwanese (277)	292	1.32
Filipino (33)	65	0.29
Indian (223)	241	1.09
Indonesian (2)	3	0.01
Japanese (20)	34	0.15
Korean (101)	120	0.54
Laotian (3)	3	0.01
Malaysian (4)	6	0.03
Nepalese (79)	88	0.40
Pakistani (5)	10	0.05
Sri Lankan (1)	1	<0.01
Taiwanese (2)	3	0.01
Thai (6)	8	0.04
Vietnamese (25)	30	0.14
Hawaii Native/Pacific Islander (8)	16	0.07
Not Hispanic (8)	14	0.06
Hispanic (0)	2	0.01
Guamanian/Chamorro (1)	1	<0.01
Native Hawaiian (4)	9	0.04
Samoan (1)	3	0.01
Tongan (1)	1	<0.01
White (20,305)	20,638	93.57
Not Hispanic (20,123)	20,431	92.63
Hispanic (182)	207	0.94

Huron

Place Type: City
County: Beadle
Population: 12,592†

Ancestry‡	Population	%
American (384)	384	3.17
Arab (0)	31	0.26
Lebanese (0)	31	0.26
Belgian (0)	10	0.08
British (0)	22	0.18
Czech (36)	106	0.88
Danish (117)	225	1.86
Dutch (51)	247	2.04
English (309)	1,059	8.74
European (393)	393	3.24
Finnish (0)	20	0.17
French, ex. Basque (22)	374	3.09
French Canadian (0)	43	0.35
German (2,424)	5,167	42.65
Greek (0)	19	0.16
Irish (194)	1,316	10.86
Italian (42)	81	0.67
Luxemburger (0)	16	0.13
Norwegian (445)	1,571	12.97
Pennsylvania German (23)	23	0.19
Polish (39)	384	3.17
Russian (0)	107	0.88
Scandinavian (36)	93	0.77
Scotch-Irish (11)	37	0.31

*Notes: † The Census 2010 population figure is used to calculate the percentages in the Hispanic Origin and Race categories. Ancestry percentages are based on the 2006-2010 American Community Survey population (not shown); ‡ Numbers in parentheses indicate the number of people reporting a single ancestry; * Numbers in parentheses indicate the number of persons reporting this race alone, not in combination with any other race; Please refer to the Explanation of Data for more information.*

Scottish (0)	70	0.58
Swedish (165)	509	4.20
Swiss (0)	177	1.46
Ukrainian (16)	16	0.13
Welsh (13)	138	1.14

Hispanic Origin	Population	%
Hispanic or Latino (of any race)	1,234	9.80
Central American, ex. Mexican	241	1.91
Guatemalan	172	1.37
Honduran	18	0.14
Nicaraguan	1	0.01
Panamanian	5	0.04
Salvadoran	34	0.27
Other Central American	11	0.09
Cuban	10	0.08
Dominican Republic	3	0.02
Mexican	649	5.15
Puerto Rican	208	1.65
South American	69	0.55
Chilean	3	0.02
Colombian	7	0.06
Peruvian	59	0.47
Other Hispanic or Latino	54	0.43

Race*	Population	%
African-American/Black (132)	244	1.94
Not Hispanic (106)	199	1.58
Hispanic (26)	45	0.36
American Indian/Alaska Native (153)	221	1.76
Not Hispanic (136)	199	1.58
Hispanic (17)	22	0.17
Canadian/French Am. Ind. (0)	1	0.01
Cherokee (2)	5	0.04
Chippewa (4)	5	0.04
Choctaw (1)	1	0.01
Comanche (1)	1	0.01
Navajo (0)	3	0.02
Sioux (87)	117	0.93
Asian (618)	637	5.06
Not Hispanic (618)	634	5.03
Hispanic (0)	3	0.02
Burmese (504)	515	4.09
Chinese, ex. Taiwanese (7)	8	0.06
Filipino (22)	31	0.25
Hmong (15)	20	0.16
Indian (8)	13	0.10
Japanese (2)	3	0.02
Korean (10)	11	0.09
Thai (1)	7	0.06
Vietnamese (4)	5	0.04
Hawaii Native/Pacific Islander (17)	25	0.20
Not Hispanic (8)	15	0.12
Hispanic (9)	10	0.08
Guamanian/Chamorro (10)	14	0.11
Native Hawaiian (2)	2	0.02
Tongan (4)	4	0.03
White (10,937)	11,159	88.62
Not Hispanic (10,319)	10,475	83.19
Hispanic (618)	684	5.43

Mitchell

Place Type: City
County: Davison
Population: 15,254†

Ancestry‡	Population	%
African, Sub-Saharan (0)	34	0.22
African (0)	12	0.08
South African (0)	22	0.15
American (690)	690	4.55
Arab (0)	62	0.41
Lebanese (0)	62	0.41
Belgian (0)	13	0.09
British (9)	9	0.06
Czech (235)	482	3.18
Czechoslovakian (19)	19	0.13
Danish (176)	461	3.04
Dutch (289)	855	5.64
English (255)	1,154	7.61
European (13)	13	0.09
Finnish (19)	52	0.34
French, ex. Basque (34)	456	3.01
French Canadian (54)	77	0.51
German (3,954)	7,574	49.94
Greek (7)	106	0.70
Hungarian (26)	26	0.17
Icelander (0)	10	0.07
Irish (298)	1,583	10.44
Italian (81)	192	1.27
Luxemburger (0)	14	0.09
Norwegian (517)	1,496	9.86
Polish (20)	182	1.20
Portuguese (12)	21	0.14
Russian (16)	236	1.56
Scandinavian (91)	148	0.98
Scotch-Irish (33)	110	0.73
Scottish (45)	160	1.05
Serbian (0)	8	0.05
Swedish (106)	468	3.09
Swiss (7)	43	0.28
Welsh (0)	68	0.45
West Indian, ex. Hispanic (18)	120	0.79
Jamaican (18)	120	0.79

Hispanic Origin	Population	%
Hispanic or Latino (of any race)	255	1.67
Central American, ex. Mexican	11	0.07
Guatemalan	9	0.06
Honduran	1	0.01
Salvadoran	1	0.01
Cuban	4	0.03
Dominican Republic	2	0.01
Mexican	167	1.09
Puerto Rican	31	0.20
South American	13	0.09
Chilean	3	0.02
Colombian	3	0.02
Ecuadorian	1	0.01
Peruvian	1	0.01
Venezuelan	3	0.02
Other South American	2	0.01
Other Hispanic or Latino	27	0.18

Race*	Population	%
African-American/Black (80)	162	1.06
Not Hispanic (70)	150	0.98
Hispanic (10)	12	0.08
American Indian/Alaska Native (451)	598	3.92
Not Hispanic (433)	571	3.74
Hispanic (18)	27	0.18
Apache (0)	1	0.01
Canadian/French Am. Ind. (0)	1	0.01
Cheyenne (4)	5	0.03
Chippewa (3)	3	0.02
Choctaw (1)	4	0.03
Cree (0)	2	0.01
Crow (1)	1	0.01
Iroquois (0)	1	0.01
Menominee (0)	1	0.01
Mexican American Ind. (2)	3	0.02
Navajo (5)	8	0.05
Potawatomi (0)	1	0.01
Sioux (261)	313	2.05
Asian (81)	114	0.75
Not Hispanic (79)	111	0.73
Hispanic (2)	3	0.02
Cambodian (11)	13	0.09
Chinese, ex. Taiwanese (13)	14	0.09
Filipino (17)	36	0.24
Indian (10)	12	0.08
Japanese (7)	10	0.07
Korean (12)	13	0.09
Laotian (0)	1	0.01
Pakistani (2)	2	0.01
Vietnamese (4)	6	0.04
Hawaii Native/Pacific Islander (11)	20	0.13
Not Hispanic (10)	18	0.12
Hispanic (1)	2	0.01
Guamanian/Chamorro (1)	1	0.01
Native Hawaiian (8)	10	0.07
White (14,279)	14,528	95.24
Not Hispanic (14,172)	14,384	94.30
Hispanic (107)	144	0.94

Pierre

Place Type: City
County: Hughes
Population: 13,646†

Ancestry‡	Population	%
African, Sub-Saharan (29)	29	0.21
Ethiopian (29)	29	0.21
American (510)	510	3.75
Belgian (21)	76	0.56
Brazilian (0)	15	0.11
British (0)	18	0.13
Czech (139)	464	3.41
Czechoslovakian (13)	52	0.38
Danish (52)	249	1.83
Dutch (16)	354	2.60
English (256)	1,439	10.58
European (107)	117	0.86
Finnish (0)	13	0.10
French, ex. Basque (53)	439	3.23
French Canadian (39)	47	0.35
German (2,702)	5,637	41.44
German Russian (10)	10	0.07
Hungarian (8)	29	0.21
Irish (396)	1,285	9.45
Italian (20)	83	0.61
Latvian (10)	10	0.07
Luxemburger (0)	18	0.13
Northern European (10)	10	0.07
Norwegian (760)	1,735	12.75
Polish (34)	207	1.52
Russian (0)	342	2.51
Scandinavian (17)	42	0.31
Scotch-Irish (72)	199	1.46
Scottish (0)	185	1.36
Slovene (8)	8	0.06
Swedish (183)	581	4.27
Swiss (8)	34	0.25
Welsh (0)	56	0.41

Hispanic Origin	Population	%
Hispanic or Latino (of any race)	259	1.90
Central American, ex. Mexican	6	0.04
Guatemalan	3	0.02
Honduran	2	0.01
Nicaraguan	1	0.01
Cuban	1	0.01
Mexican	183	1.34
Puerto Rican	21	0.15
South American	11	0.08
Argentinean	1	0.01
Colombian	7	0.05
Peruvian	1	0.01
Other South American	2	0.01
Other Hispanic or Latino	37	0.27

Race*	Population	%
African-American/Black (70)	130	0.95
Not Hispanic (70)	119	0.87
Hispanic (0)	11	0.08
American Indian/Alaska Native (1,494)	1,737	12.73
Not Hispanic (1,450)	1,656	12.14
Hispanic (44)	81	0.59
Apache (0)	2	0.01
Blackfeet (5)	9	0.07
Canadian/French Am. Ind. (4)	5	0.04
Cherokee (7)	10	0.07
Cheyenne (3)	14	0.10
Chippewa (37)	46	0.34
Choctaw (2)	3	0.02
Colville (1)	1	0.01
Hopi (0)	1	0.01
Iroquois (0)	3	0.02

*Notes: † The Census 2010 population figure is used to calculate the percentages in the Hispanic Origin and Race categories. Ancestry percentages are based on the 2006-2010 American Community Survey population (not shown); ‡ Numbers in parentheses indicate the number of people reporting a single ancestry; * Numbers in parentheses indicate the number of persons reporting this race alone, not in combination with any other race; Please refer to the Explanation of Data for more information.*

Lumbee (0)	1	0.01
Mexican American Ind. (2)	2	0.01
Navajo (3)	3	0.02
Pueblo (2)	2	0.01
Seminole (2)	4	0.03
Shoshone (0)	2	0.01
Sioux (862)	1,001	7.34
South American Ind. (1)	1	0.01
Yuman (6)	6	0.04
Asian (82)	119	0.87
Not Hispanic (81)	114	0.84
Hispanic (1)	5	0.04
Bangladeshi (1)	1	0.01
Cambodian (0)	3	0.02
Chinese, ex. Taiwanese (18)	20	0.15
Filipino (16)	26	0.19
Indian (22)	26	0.19
Indonesian (1)	2	0.01
Japanese (4)	5	0.04
Korean (8)	21	0.15
Pakistani (1)	1	0.01
Thai (1)	1	0.01
Vietnamese (8)	8	0.06
Hawaii Native/Pacific Islander (0)	5	0.04
Not Hispanic (0)	3	0.02
Hispanic (0)	2	0.01
Guamanian/Chamorro (0)	1	0.01
Native Hawaiian (0)	2	0.01
White (11,611)	11,898	87.19
Not Hispanic (11,509)	11,754	86.14
Hispanic (102)	144	1.06

Rapid City

Place Type: City
County: Pennington
Population: 67,956†

Ancestry‡	Population	%
African, Sub-Saharan (84)	92	0.14
African (59)	67	0.10
Kenyan (1)	1	<0.01
Sudanese (9)	9	0.01
Ugandan (15)	15	0.02
American (2,445)	2,445	3.70
Arab (13)	88	0.13
Arab (0)	35	0.05
Lebanese (13)	33	0.05
Syrian (0)	20	0.03
Australian (0)	11	0.02
Austrian (11)	216	0.33
Basque (0)	16	0.02
Belgian (81)	90	0.14
Brazilian (4)	8	0.01
British (74)	141	0.21
Bulgarian (0)	33	0.05
Canadian (7)	46	0.07
Celtic (12)	54	0.08
Croatian (31)	64	0.10
Czech (344)	1,081	1.63
Czechoslovakian (42)	175	0.26
Danish (219)	951	1.44
Dutch (366)	2,043	3.09
English (1,598)	6,807	10.29
European (555)	568	0.86
Finnish (67)	193	0.29
French, ex. Basque (213)	2,540	3.84
French Canadian (122)	399	0.60
German (9,198)	24,788	37.48
German Russian (14)	14	0.02
Greek (47)	201	0.30
Hungarian (41)	80	0.12
Irish (2,112)	9,442	14.27
Italian (498)	1,385	2.09
Lithuanian (30)	69	0.10
Luxemburger (35)	45	0.07
Maltese (0)	12	0.02
Northern European (89)	89	0.13
Norwegian (2,304)	7,457	11.27
Pennsylvania German (92)	174	0.26
Polish (194)	1,218	1.84
Portuguese (14)	105	0.16
Romanian (0)	21	0.03
Russian (52)	837	1.27
Scandinavian (400)	745	1.13
Scotch-Irish (584)	1,282	1.94
Scottish (392)	1,413	2.14
Serbian (5)	5	0.01
Slovak (11)	30	0.05
Swedish (415)	2,537	3.84
Swiss (25)	192	0.29
Turkish (2)	2	<0.01
Ukrainian (13)	78	0.12
Welsh (135)	403	0.61
West Indian, ex. Hispanic (0)	7	0.01
Jamaican (0)	7	0.01
Yugoslavian (10)	20	0.03

Hispanic Origin	Population	%
Hispanic or Latino (of any race)	2,816	4.14
Central American, ex. Mexican	63	0.09
Costa Rican	1	<0.01
Guatemalan	9	0.01
Honduran	4	0.01
Nicaraguan	2	<0.01
Panamanian	27	0.04
Salvadoran	20	0.03
Cuban	43	0.06
Dominican Republic	7	0.01
Mexican	1,949	2.87
Puerto Rican	234	0.34
South American	60	0.09
Bolivian	18	0.03
Chilean	7	0.01
Colombian	20	0.03
Ecuadorian	3	<0.01
Peruvian	4	0.01
Venezuelan	2	<0.01
Other South American	6	0.01
Other Hispanic or Latino	460	0.68

Race*	Population	%
African-American/Black (764)	1,447	2.13
Not Hispanic (734)	1,308	1.92
Hispanic (30)	139	0.20
American Indian/Alaska Native (8,416)	10,337	15.21
Not Hispanic (7,808)	9,470	13.94
Hispanic (608)	867	1.28
Alaska Athabascan *(Ala. Nat.)* (5)	6	0.01
Aleut *(Alaska Native)* (9)	13	0.02
Apache (6)	13	0.02
Arapaho (37)	41	0.06
Blackfeet (17)	26	0.04
Canadian/French Am. Ind. (1)	6	0.01
Central American Ind. (1)	1	<0.01
Cherokee (22)	78	0.11
Cheyenne (58)	95	0.14
Chickasaw (1)	3	<0.01
Chippewa (48)	77	0.11
Choctaw (6)	16	0.02
Colville (0)	1	<0.01
Comanche (4)	5	0.01
Cree (2)	6	0.01
Creek (9)	12	0.02
Crow (22)	33	0.05
Hopi (7)	8	0.01
Inupiat *(Alaska Native)* (5)	6	0.01
Iroquois (7)	19	0.03
Kiowa (2)	3	<0.01
Lumbee (1)	3	<0.01
Mexican American Ind. (10)	17	0.03
Navajo (44)	66	0.10
Osage (5)	8	0.01
Pima (3)	4	0.01
Potawatomi (5)	8	0.01
Pueblo (7)	13	0.02
Puget Sound Salish (1)	1	<0.01
Seminole (10)	10	0.01
Shoshone (10)	13	0.02
Sioux (5,471)	6,605	9.72
South American Ind. (2)	3	<0.01
Spanish American Ind. (1)	2	<0.01
Tlingit-Haida *(Alaska Native)* (1)	3	<0.01
Tohono O'Odham (1)	1	<0.01
Ute (3)	3	<0.01
Yaqui (2)	2	<0.01
Asian (795)	1,231	1.81
Not Hispanic (787)	1,190	1.75
Hispanic (8)	41	0.06
Bangladeshi (4)	4	0.01
Burmese (1)	1	<0.01
Cambodian (1)	2	<0.01
Chinese, ex. Taiwanese (164)	203	0.30
Filipino (171)	325	0.48
Hmong (8)	8	0.01
Indian (139)	170	0.25
Indonesian (8)	22	0.03
Japanese (55)	149	0.22
Korean (98)	145	0.21
Laotian (3)	6	0.01
Malaysian (1)	2	<0.01
Nepalese (5)	5	0.01
Pakistani (13)	13	0.02
Sri Lankan (2)	2	<0.01
Taiwanese (2)	5	0.01
Thai (30)	58	0.09
Vietnamese (51)	67	0.10
Hawaii Native/Pacific Islander (52)	148	0.22
Not Hispanic (48)	131	0.19
Hispanic (4)	17	0.03
Guamanian/Chamorro (11)	19	0.03
Native Hawaiian (24)	86	0.13
Samoan (3)	6	0.01
Tongan (4)	9	0.01
White (54,658)	57,089	84.01
Not Hispanic (53,412)	55,445	81.59
Hispanic (1,246)	1,644	2.42

Rapid Valley

Place Type: CDP
County: Pennington
Population: 8,260†

Ancestry‡	Population	%
American (419)	419	5.15
Armenian (0)	24	0.30
Czech (56)	107	1.32
Czechoslovakian (0)	11	0.14
Danish (13)	60	0.74
Dutch (50)	244	3.00
English (257)	608	7.48
European (21)	21	0.26
Finnish (11)	123	1.51
French, ex. Basque (57)	594	7.31
French Canadian (0)	74	0.91
German (1,273)	3,492	42.95
Hungarian (9)	17	0.21
Icelander (20)	20	0.25
Iranian (0)	15	0.18
Irish (178)	1,121	13.79
Italian (77)	329	4.05
Lithuanian (0)	16	0.20
Luxemburger (0)	12	0.15
Norwegian (177)	682	8.39
Polish (215)	495	6.09
Portuguese (36)	40	0.49
Romanian (0)	19	0.23
Russian (0)	137	1.69
Scandinavian (118)	173	2.13
Scotch-Irish (4)	301	3.70
Scottish (45)	101	1.24
Swedish (38)	148	1.82
Swiss (0)	11	0.14
Welsh (11)	45	0.55

Hispanic Origin	Population	%
Hispanic or Latino (of any race)	264	3.20
Central American, ex. Mexican	4	0.05
Guatemalan	3	0.04

*Notes: † The Census 2010 population figure is used to calculate the percentages in the Hispanic Origin and Race categories. Ancestry percentages are based on the 2006-2010 American Community Survey population (not shown); ‡ Numbers in parentheses indicate the number of people reporting a single ancestry; * Numbers in parentheses indicate the number of persons reporting this race alone, not in combination with any other race; Please refer to the Explanation of Data for more information.*

Panamanian	1	0.01
Cuban	3	0.04
Mexican	195	2.36
Puerto Rican	17	0.21
South American	4	0.05
Colombian	3	0.04
Ecuadorian	1	0.01
Other Hispanic or Latino	41	0.50

Race*	Population	%
African-American/Black (57)	110	1.33
Not Hispanic (57)	106	1.28
Hispanic (0)	4	0.05
American Indian/Alaska Native (349)	542	6.56
Not Hispanic (320)	489	5.92
Hispanic (29)	53	0.64
Arapaho (0)	1	0.01
Blackfeet (0)	3	0.04
Central American Ind. (0)	1	0.01
Cherokee (4)	11	0.13
Cheyenne (2)	4	0.05
Chippewa (3)	6	0.07
Choctaw (0)	1	0.01
Creek (1)	3	0.04
Inupiat *(Alaska Native)* (1)	3	0.04
Iroquois (0)	3	0.04
Mexican American Ind. (0)	4	0.05
Navajo (3)	3	0.04
Osage (0)	2	0.02
Potawatomi (1)	1	0.01
Pueblo (2)	2	0.02
Seminole (0)	1	0.01
Shoshone (1)	4	0.05
Sioux (255)	368	4.46
Ute (1)	1	0.01
Asian (71)	116	1.40
Not Hispanic (71)	116	1.40
Cambodian (1)	2	0.02
Chinese, ex. Taiwanese (3)	3	0.04
Filipino (40)	60	0.73
Indian (6)	6	0.07
Japanese (3)	11	0.13
Korean (12)	21	0.25
Taiwanese (1)	1	0.01
Thai (3)	9	0.11
Hawaii Native/Pacific Islander (6)	13	0.16
Not Hispanic (6)	12	0.15
Hispanic (0)	1	0.01
Guamanian/Chamorro (4)	6	0.07
Samoan (2)	6	0.07
White (7,431)	7,710	93.34
Not Hispanic (7,286)	7,528	91.14
Hispanic (145)	182	2.20

Sioux Falls

Place Type: City
County: Minnehaha
Population: 153,888†

Ancestry‡	Population	%
Afghan (20)	20	0.01
African, Sub-Saharan (2,469)	2,684	1.80
African (831)	867	0.58
Ethiopian (811)	811	0.54
Kenyan (59)	59	0.04
Liberian (84)	84	0.06
Nigerian (35)	76	0.05
Somalian (210)	210	0.14
Sudanese (316)	404	0.27
Other Sub-Saharan African (123)	173	0.12
Alsatian (13)	13	0.01
American (4,392)	4,392	2.95
Arab (425)	526	0.35
Arab (41)	57	0.04
Iraqi (35)	35	0.02
Jordanian (0)	4	<0.01
Lebanese (91)	160	0.11
Syrian (68)	80	0.05
Other Arab (190)	190	0.13
Armenian (142)	142	0.10
Australian (19)	56	0.04
Austrian (66)	143	0.10
Belgian (58)	393	0.26
Brazilian (6)	6	<0.01
British (43)	118	0.08
Canadian (34)	101	0.07
Croatian (187)	237	0.16
Czech (692)	2,644	1.78
Czechoslovakian (201)	367	0.25
Danish (979)	3,392	2.28
Dutch (4,162)	9,552	6.42
English (2,245)	9,585	6.44
European (581)	642	0.43
Finnish (99)	245	0.16
French, ex. Basque (426)	3,122	2.10
French Canadian (205)	889	0.60
German (28,677)	63,160	42.43
German Russian (0)	5	<0.01
Greek (82)	187	0.13
Hungarian (32)	182	0.12
Icelander (0)	10	0.01
Irish (4,144)	18,059	12.13
Italian (827)	2,166	1.46
Latvian (34)	64	0.04
Lithuanian (64)	226	0.15
Luxemburger (85)	207	0.14
Macedonian (15)	15	0.01
Northern European (168)	188	0.13
Norwegian (9,758)	24,722	16.61
Pennsylvania German (19)	60	0.04
Polish (605)	2,275	1.53
Portuguese (10)	88	0.06
Romanian (121)	169	0.11
Russian (489)	1,408	0.95
Scandinavian (814)	1,270	0.85
Scotch-Irish (295)	1,096	0.74
Scottish (449)	1,786	1.20
Serbian (143)	175	0.12
Slavic (0)	27	0.02
Slovak (52)	195	0.13
Slovene (0)	10	0.01
Swedish (1,131)	5,345	3.59
Swiss (86)	372	0.25
Turkish (42)	42	0.03
Ukrainian (427)	490	0.33
Welsh (143)	563	0.38
West Indian, ex. Hispanic (23)	55	0.04
Jamaican (12)	38	0.03
Trinidadian/Tobagonian (11)	17	0.01
Yugoslavian (507)	582	0.39

Hispanic Origin	Population	%
Hispanic or Latino (of any race)	6,827	4.44
Central American, ex. Mexican	1,903	1.24
Costa Rican	15	0.01
Guatemalan	1,063	0.69
Honduran	119	0.08
Nicaraguan	61	0.04
Panamanian	13	0.01
Salvadoran	608	0.40
Other Central American	24	0.02
Cuban	82	0.05
Dominican Republic	18	0.01
Mexican	3,452	2.24
Puerto Rican	330	0.21
South American	169	0.11
Argentinean	16	0.01
Bolivian	9	0.01
Chilean	26	0.02
Colombian	61	0.04
Ecuadorian	27	0.02
Paraguayan	6	<0.01
Peruvian	15	0.01
Uruguayan	3	<0.01
Venezuelan	5	<0.01
Other South American	1	<0.01
Other Hispanic or Latino	873	0.57

Race*	Population	%
African-American/Black (6,494)	8,135	5.29
Not Hispanic (6,412)	7,961	5.17
Hispanic (82)	174	0.11
American Indian/Alaska Native (4,092)	5,539	3.60
Not Hispanic (3,831)	5,118	3.33
Hispanic (261)	421	0.27
Alaska Athabascan *(Ala. Nat.)* (5)	7	<0.01
Aleut *(Alaska Native)* (1)	1	<0.01
Apache (0)	8	0.01
Arapaho (10)	14	0.01
Blackfeet (2)	12	0.01
Canadian/French Am. Ind. (2)	7	<0.01
Central American Ind. (6)	6	<0.01
Cherokee (26)	82	0.05
Cheyenne (15)	36	0.02
Chickasaw (3)	3	<0.01
Chippewa (62)	112	0.07
Choctaw (7)	13	0.01
Colville (1)	1	<0.01
Comanche (2)	4	<0.01
Cree (1)	1	<0.01
Creek (0)	9	0.01
Crow (7)	12	0.01
Delaware (0)	9	0.01
Hopi (1)	1	<0.01
Inupiat *(Alaska Native)* (1)	2	<0.01
Iroquois (1)	11	0.01
Kiowa (4)	6	<0.01
Lumbee (0)	1	<0.01
Menominee (4)	5	<0.01
Mexican American Ind. (39)	43	0.03
Navajo (17)	31	0.02
Osage (1)	3	<0.01
Ottawa (1)	1	<0.01
Paiute (1)	1	<0.01
Potawatomi (2)	4	<0.01
Seminole (1)	4	<0.01
Shoshone (2)	2	<0.01
Sioux (2,252)	2,830	1.84
South American Ind. (2)	3	<0.01
Spanish American Ind. (1)	1	<0.01
Tlingit-Haida *(Alaska Native)* (2)	3	<0.01
Ute (2)	7	<0.01
Yakama (0)	1	<0.01
Yaqui (0)	1	<0.01
Yup'ik *(Alaska Native)* (1)	2	<0.01
Asian (2,743)	3,468	2.25
Not Hispanic (2,724)	3,386	2.20
Hispanic (19)	82	0.05
Bangladeshi (8)	8	0.01
Bhutanese (66)	106	0.07
Burmese (128)	132	0.09
Cambodian (60)	71	0.05
Chinese, ex. Taiwanese (333)	419	0.27
Filipino (182)	332	0.22
Hmong (45)	48	0.03
Indian (475)	556	0.36
Indonesian (4)	6	<0.01
Japanese (78)	149	0.10
Korean (200)	304	0.20
Laotian (314)	419	0.27
Malaysian (4)	4	<0.01
Nepalese (73)	109	0.07
Pakistani (32)	33	0.02
Sri Lankan (3)	3	<0.01
Taiwanese (3)	7	<0.01
Thai (43)	77	0.05
Vietnamese (488)	610	0.40
Hawaii Native/Pacific Islander (131)	284	0.18
Not Hispanic (75)	187	0.12
Hispanic (56)	97	0.06
Fijian (8)	12	0.01
Guamanian/Chamorro (70)	95	0.06
Native Hawaiian (24)	80	0.05
Samoan (8)	16	0.01
Tongan (1)	2	<0.01
White (133,572)	137,010	89.03
Not Hispanic (130,577)	133,542	86.78

*Notes: † The Census 2010 population figure is used to calculate the percentages in the Hispanic Origin and Race categories. Ancestry percentages are based on the 2006-2010 American Community Survey population (not shown); ‡ Numbers in parentheses indicate the number of people reporting a single ancestry; * Numbers in parentheses indicate the number of persons reporting this race alone, not in combination with any other race; Please refer to the Explanation of Data for more information.*

Hispanic (2,995)	3,468	2.25

Spearfish

Place Type: City
County: Lawrence
Population: 10,494†

Ancestry‡	Population	%
American (499)	499	4.89
Arab (0)	8	0.08
Syrian (0)	8	0.08
Austrian (0)	129	1.27
Belgian (8)	8	0.08
Croatian (8)	8	0.08
Czech (28)	204	2.00
Czechoslovakian (0)	17	0.17
Danish (24)	149	1.46
Dutch (72)	247	2.42
English (150)	1,066	10.46
European (26)	30	0.29
Finnish (11)	74	0.73
French, ex. Basque (113)	407	3.99
French Canadian (23)	111	1.09
German (2,283)	4,910	48.16
Hungarian (13)	22	0.22
Irish (172)	1,346	13.20
Italian (164)	281	2.76
Luxemburger (0)	13	0.13
Norwegian (346)	1,098	10.77
Pennsylvania German (11)	23	0.23
Polish (29)	182	1.79
Russian (8)	189	1.85
Scandinavian (21)	57	0.56
Scotch-Irish (71)	170	1.67
Scottish (25)	148	1.45
Swedish (90)	397	3.89
Swiss (11)	45	0.44
Turkish (0)	72	0.71
Ukrainian (16)	16	0.16
Welsh (23)	213	2.09

Hispanic Origin	Population	%
Hispanic or Latino (of any race)	287	2.73
Central American, ex. Mexican	8	0.08
Honduran	3	0.03
Panamanian	2	0.02
Salvadoran	3	0.03
Mexican	209	1.99
Puerto Rican	17	0.16
South American	11	0.10
Colombian	5	0.05
Peruvian	1	0.01
Venezuelan	5	0.05
Other Hispanic or Latino	42	0.40

Race*	Population	%
African-American/Black (43)	82	0.78
Not Hispanic (41)	70	0.67
Hispanic (2)	12	0.11
American Indian/Alaska Native (215)	367	3.50
Not Hispanic (199)	335	3.19
Hispanic (16)	32	0.30
Apache (3)	4	0.04
Cherokee (0)	8	0.08
Cheyenne (6)	16	0.15
Chippewa (1)	4	0.04
Choctaw (0)	1	0.01
Cree (1)	2	0.02
Crow (0)	2	0.02
Hopi (2)	4	0.04
Inupiat *(Alaska Native)* (1)	1	0.01
Iroquois (2)	2	0.02
Lumbee (1)	1	0.01
Mexican American Ind. (1)	2	0.02
Navajo (5)	6	0.06
Sioux (130)	212	2.02
Yuman (2)	2	0.02
Asian (116)	158	1.51
Not Hispanic (116)	153	1.46
Hispanic (0)	5	0.05
Bangladeshi (2)	2	0.02
Cambodian (1)	1	0.01
Chinese, ex. Taiwanese (43)	45	0.43
Filipino (13)	25	0.24
Indian (6)	15	0.14
Japanese (5)	14	0.13
Korean (16)	23	0.22
Malaysian (1)	1	0.01
Pakistani (8)	8	0.08
Taiwanese (5)	5	0.05
Thai (2)	4	0.04
Vietnamese (6)	6	0.06
Hawaii Native/Pacific Islander (2)	11	0.10
Not Hispanic (2)	9	0.09
Hispanic (0)	2	0.02
Guamanian/Chamorro (0)	1	0.01
Marshallese (0)	1	0.01
Native Hawaiian (1)	4	0.04
Samoan (1)	3	0.03
White (9,815)	10,050	95.77
Not Hispanic (9,640)	9,840	93.77
Hispanic (175)	210	2.00

Vermillion

Place Type: City
County: Clay
Population: 10,571†

Ancestry‡	Population	%
African, Sub-Saharan (16)	16	0.15
African (10)	10	0.10
Ethiopian (6)	6	0.06
American (108)	108	1.03
Arab (0)	9	0.09
Other Arab (0)	9	0.09
Belgian (8)	17	0.16
Brazilian (9)	9	0.09
British (0)	39	0.37
Croatian (0)	18	0.17
Czech (29)	238	2.26
Danish (75)	208	1.98
Dutch (135)	436	4.15
English (300)	932	8.86
European (139)	139	1.32
Finnish (0)	26	0.25
French, ex. Basque (89)	322	3.06
French Canadian (55)	66	0.63
German (1,744)	4,673	44.43
German Russian (0)	7	0.07
Greek (0)	21	0.20
Hungarian (0)	17	0.16
Irish (480)	1,755	16.69
Italian (45)	155	1.47
Lithuanian (0)	15	0.14
Northern European (22)	22	0.21
Norwegian (382)	1,555	14.79
Pennsylvania German (17)	17	0.16
Polish (13)	223	2.12
Portuguese (0)	11	0.10
Russian (19)	110	1.05
Scandinavian (173)	215	2.04
Scotch-Irish (63)	324	3.08
Scottish (67)	175	1.66
Swedish (78)	477	4.54
Swiss (0)	45	0.43
Ukrainian (0)	12	0.11
Welsh (11)	73	0.69
West Indian, ex. Hispanic (12)	12	0.11
Jamaican (12)	12	0.11

Hispanic Origin	Population	%
Hispanic or Latino (of any race)	256	2.42
Central American, ex. Mexican	11	0.10
Costa Rican	3	0.03
Guatemalan	2	0.02
Honduran	2	0.02
Nicaraguan	1	0.01
Panamanian	1	0.01
Salvadoran	2	0.02
Cuban	7	0.07
Dominican Republic	3	0.03
Mexican	161	1.52
Puerto Rican	35	0.33
South American	20	0.19
Argentinean	12	0.11
Bolivian	1	0.01
Chilean	2	0.02
Colombian	1	0.01
Paraguayan	1	0.01
Peruvian	3	0.03
Other Hispanic or Latino	19	0.18

Race*	Population	%
African-American/Black (176)	266	2.52
Not Hispanic (170)	252	2.38
Hispanic (6)	14	0.13
American Indian/Alaska Native (377)	507	4.80
Not Hispanic (356)	470	4.45
Hispanic (21)	37	0.35
Alaska Athabascan *(Ala. Nat.)* (3)	3	0.03
Aleut *(Alaska Native)* (0)	4	0.04
Arapaho (2)	2	0.02
Blackfeet (0)	1	0.01
Cherokee (3)	10	0.09
Cheyenne (8)	8	0.08
Chippewa (3)	4	0.04
Choctaw (2)	4	0.04
Hopi (0)	1	0.01
Iroquois (1)	3	0.03
Menominee (1)	1	0.01
Mexican American Ind. (1)	1	0.01
Navajo (6)	6	0.06
Potawatomi (0)	1	0.01
Pueblo (0)	1	0.01
Sioux (245)	296	2.80
Asian (221)	266	2.52
Not Hispanic (220)	262	2.48
Hispanic (1)	4	0.04
Chinese, ex. Taiwanese (103)	110	1.04
Filipino (19)	36	0.34
Indian (44)	50	0.47
Japanese (8)	16	0.15
Korean (22)	27	0.26
Laotian (0)	1	0.01
Malaysian (1)	1	0.01
Nepalese (2)	2	0.02
Sri Lankan (1)	1	0.01
Taiwanese (1)	3	0.03
Thai (0)	1	0.01
Vietnamese (8)	11	0.10
Hawaii Native/Pacific Islander (4)	8	0.08
Not Hispanic (3)	7	0.07
Hispanic (1)	1	0.01
Fijian (1)	1	0.01
Guamanian/Chamorro (0)	1	0.01
Native Hawaiian (0)	1	0.01
Samoan (2)	3	0.03
White (9,469)	9,722	91.97
Not Hispanic (9,329)	9,541	90.26
Hispanic (140)	181	1.71

Watertown

Place Type: City
County: Codington
Population: 21,482†

Ancestry‡	Population	%
American (746)	746	3.50
Arab (20)	35	0.16
Lebanese (8)	23	0.11
Syrian (12)	12	0.06
Armenian (0)	26	0.12
Belgian (0)	68	0.32
British (0)	15	0.07
Canadian (0)	14	0.07
Czech (98)	243	1.14
Czechoslovakian (0)	46	0.22

*Notes: † The Census 2010 population figure is used to calculate the percentages in the Hispanic Origin and Race categories. Ancestry percentages are based on the 2006-2010 American Community Survey population (not shown); ‡ Numbers in parentheses indicate the number of people reporting a single ancestry; * Numbers in parentheses indicate the number of persons reporting this race alone, not in combination with any other race; Please refer to the Explanation of Data for more information.*

Danish (95)	514	2.41
Dutch (204)	873	4.10
English (301)	1,334	6.26
European (175)	175	0.82
Finnish (62)	151	0.71
French, ex. Basque (62)	586	2.75
French Canadian (21)	61	0.29
German (5,363)	11,335	53.17
Greek (39)	39	0.18
Hungarian (0)	16	0.08
Icelander (0)	5	0.02
Irish (333)	1,894	8.88
Italian (53)	106	0.50
Luxemburger (9)	9	0.04
Norwegian (1,394)	4,938	23.16
Polish (146)	403	1.89
Russian (15)	250	1.17
Scandinavian (64)	105	0.49
Scotch-Irish (93)	312	1.46
Scottish (37)	127	0.60
Swedish (175)	743	3.49
Swiss (0)	26	0.12
Welsh (0)	42	0.20
Yugoslavian (8)	24	0.11

Hispanic Origin	Population	%
Hispanic or Latino (of any race)	345	1.61
Central American, ex. Mexican	9	0.04
Costa Rican	2	0.01
Guatemalan	2	0.01
Honduran	1	<0.01
Nicaraguan	2	0.01
Salvadoran	2	0.01
Cuban	1	<0.01
Dominican Republic	2	0.01
Mexican	268	1.25
Puerto Rican	8	0.04
South American	11	0.05
Colombian	3	0.01
Peruvian	7	0.03
Venezuelan	1	<0.01
Other Hispanic or Latino	46	0.21

Race*	Population	%
African-American/Black (81)	147	0.68
Not Hispanic (76)	137	0.64
Hispanic (5)	10	0.05
American Indian/Alaska Native (510)	669	3.11
Not Hispanic (481)	625	2.91
Hispanic (29)	44	0.20
Alaska Athabascan *(Ala. Nat.)* (6)	6	0.03
Aleut *(Alaska Native)* (1)	1	<0.01
Apache (0)	1	<0.01
Cherokee (2)	11	0.05
Cheyenne (0)	1	<0.01
Chippewa (8)	13	0.06
Crow (0)	1	<0.01
Hopi (1)	1	<0.01
Inupiat *(Alaska Native)* (0)	1	<0.01
Menominee (0)	1	<0.01
Mexican American Ind. (3)	3	0.01
Navajo (0)	2	0.01
Potawatomi (2)	2	0.01
Sioux (341)	428	1.99
Ute (0)	1	<0.01
Asian (108)	179	0.83
Not Hispanic (108)	176	0.82
Hispanic (0)	3	0.01
Cambodian (0)	3	0.01
Chinese, ex. Taiwanese (18)	21	0.10
Filipino (36)	66	0.31
Indian (11)	13	0.06
Indonesian (1)	1	<0.01
Japanese (6)	8	0.04
Korean (15)	18	0.08
Laotian (0)	2	0.01
Nepalese (2)	2	0.01
Thai (3)	3	0.01
Vietnamese (14)	37	0.17
Hawaii Native/Pacific Islander (0)	3	0.01
Not Hispanic (0)	3	0.01
Guamanian/Chamorro (0)	1	<0.01
Samoan (0)	2	0.01
White (20,361)	20,647	96.11
Not Hispanic (20,206)	20,461	95.25
Hispanic (155)	186	0.87

Yankton

Place Type: City
County: Yankton
Population: 14,454†

Ancestry‡	Population	%
African, Sub-Saharan (40)	40	0.28
African (40)	40	0.28
American (529)	529	3.71
Arab (74)	88	0.62
Iraqi (46)	46	0.32
Lebanese (0)	14	0.10
Moroccan (18)	18	0.13
Palestinian (10)	10	0.07
Austrian (0)	62	0.44
Belgian (0)	24	0.17
British (0)	9	0.06
Croatian (6)	6	0.04
Czech (354)	752	5.28
Czechoslovakian (35)	56	0.39
Danish (103)	464	3.26
Dutch (104)	391	2.75
English (281)	940	6.60
European (24)	24	0.17
Finnish (8)	15	0.11
French, ex. Basque (33)	286	2.01
French Canadian (26)	84	0.59
German (3,403)	6,889	48.37
Greek (26)	62	0.44
Hungarian (0)	7	0.05
Irish (259)	1,477	10.37
Italian (13)	146	1.03
Lithuanian (13)	13	0.09
Luxemburger (10)	17	0.12
Northern European (12)	12	0.08
Norwegian (756)	2,273	15.96
Polish (56)	222	1.56
Russian (0)	127	0.89
Scandinavian (20)	20	0.14
Scotch-Irish (36)	107	0.75
Scottish (36)	152	1.07
Slovene (0)	22	0.15
Swedish (124)	649	4.56
Swiss (13)	71	0.50
Ukrainian (6)	6	0.04
Welsh (16)	73	0.51
Yugoslavian (0)	47	0.33

Hispanic Origin	Population	%
Hispanic or Latino (of any race)	494	3.42
Central American, ex. Mexican	21	0.15
Guatemalan	12	0.08
Honduran	6	0.04
Salvadoran	3	0.02
Cuban	10	0.07
Dominican Republic	2	0.01
Mexican	378	2.62
Puerto Rican	27	0.19
South American	14	0.10
Argentinean	1	0.01
Chilean	5	0.03
Colombian	7	0.05
Peruvian	1	0.01
Other Hispanic or Latino	42	0.29

Race*	Population	%
African-American/Black (299)	374	2.59
Not Hispanic (286)	358	2.48
Hispanic (13)	16	0.11
American Indian/Alaska Native (327)	438	3.03
Not Hispanic (297)	401	2.77
Hispanic (30)	37	0.26
Arapaho (4)	4	0.03
Cherokee (5)	8	0.06
Cheyenne (0)	1	0.01
Chippewa (4)	5	0.03
Choctaw (0)	4	0.03
Osage (0)	2	0.01
Potawatomi (0)	1	0.01
Sioux (237)	289	2.00
Asian (96)	125	0.86
Not Hispanic (95)	124	0.86
Hispanic (1)	1	0.01
Bangladeshi (3)	3	0.02
Cambodian (1)	3	0.02
Chinese, ex. Taiwanese (20)	24	0.17
Filipino (17)	27	0.19
Indian (12)	14	0.10
Japanese (0)	2	0.01
Korean (11)	11	0.08
Laotian (1)	2	0.01
Pakistani (0)	1	0.01
Thai (3)	5	0.03
Vietnamese (23)	26	0.18
Hawaii Native/Pacific Islander (5)	10	0.07
Not Hispanic (4)	9	0.06
Hispanic (1)	1	0.01
Guamanian/Chamorro (0)	1	0.01
Native Hawaiian (1)	5	0.03
Samoan (1)	2	0.01
White (13,312)	13,523	93.56
Not Hispanic (13,087)	13,257	91.72
Hispanic (225)	266	1.84

*Notes: † The Census 2010 population figure is used to calculate the percentages in the Hispanic Origin and Race categories. Ancestry percentages are based on the 2006-2010 American Community Survey population (not shown); ‡ Numbers in parentheses indicate the number of people reporting a single ancestry; * Numbers in parentheses indicate the number of persons reporting this race alone, not in combination with any other race; Please refer to the Explanation of Data for more information.*

TENNESSEE

Place Type: State
Population: 6,346,105†

Ancestry‡	Population	%
Afghan (329)	329	0.01
African, Sub-Saharan (36,125)	40,669	0.65
African (22,946)	26,128	0.42
Cape Verdean (24)	78	<0.01
Ethiopian (2,909)	3,171	0.05
Ghanaian (467)	554	0.01
Kenyan (739)	755	0.01
Liberian (438)	551	0.01
Nigerian (2,243)	2,540	0.04
Senegalese (37)	54	<0.01
Sierra Leonean (116)	127	<0.01
Somalian (2,080)	2,211	0.04
South African (595)	797	0.01
Sudanese (1,320)	1,386	0.02
Ugandan (30)	30	<0.01
Zimbabwean (140)	160	<0.01
Other Sub-Saharan African (2,041)	2,127	0.03
Albanian (202)	272	<0.01
Alsatian (21)	25	<0.01
American (1,075,817)	1,075,817	17.25
Arab (16,875)	22,034	0.35
Arab (2,817)	3,630	0.06
Egyptian (4,027)	4,302	0.07
Iraqi (2,058)	2,559	0.04
Jordanian (792)	894	0.01
Lebanese (2,350)	4,277	0.07
Moroccan (87)	146	<0.01
Palestinian (1,042)	1,278	0.02
Syrian (324)	1,025	0.02
Other Arab (3,378)	3,923	0.06
Armenian (803)	1,348	0.02
Assyrian/Chaldean/Syriac (78)	177	<0.01
Australian (680)	1,029	0.02
Austrian (1,813)	6,067	0.10
Basque (80)	146	<0.01
Belgian (1,042)	2,654	0.04
Brazilian (806)	1,288	0.02
British (15,653)	26,831	0.43
Bulgarian (295)	362	0.01
Cajun (827)	1,556	0.02
Canadian (3,829)	6,232	0.10
Carpatho Rusyn (0)	51	<0.01
Celtic (568)	910	0.01
Croatian (813)	1,689	0.03
Cypriot (16)	16	<0.01
Czech (2,954)	9,921	0.16
Czechoslovakian (927)	2,123	0.03
Danish (2,587)	9,312	0.15
Dutch (17,860)	84,418	1.35
Eastern European (1,971)	2,311	0.04
English (333,676)	655,572	10.51
Estonian (160)	200	<0.01
European (51,743)	58,594	0.94
Finnish (1,326)	3,989	0.06
French, ex. Basque (28,041)	113,844	1.83
French Canadian (7,576)	15,974	0.26
German (224,301)	655,948	10.52
German Russian (50)	174	<0.01
Greek (5,332)	11,234	0.18
Guyanese (279)	499	0.01
Hungarian (4,275)	12,297	0.20
Icelander (178)	355	0.01
Iranian (2,889)	3,176	0.05
Irish (266,350)	704,259	11.30
Israeli (411)	585	0.01
Italian (50,834)	129,067	2.07
Latvian (290)	666	0.01
Lithuanian (1,196)	4,522	0.07
Luxemburger (35)	178	<0.01
Macedonian (66)	127	<0.01
Maltese (40)	113	<0.01
New Zealander (229)	327	0.01
Northern European (2,278)	2,477	0.04
Norwegian (10,311)	27,199	0.44
Pennsylvania German (845)	1,594	0.03
Polish (21,457)	64,764	1.04
Portuguese (2,302)	5,608	0.09
Romanian (2,243)	3,962	0.06
Russian (7,368)	18,228	0.29
Scandinavian (2,319)	5,027	0.08
Scotch-Irish (110,210)	199,359	3.20
Scottish (59,429)	140,810	2.26
Serbian (335)	825	0.01
Slavic (736)	1,522	0.02
Slovak (1,491)	3,915	0.06
Slovene (236)	817	0.01
Soviet Union (24)	24	<0.01
Swedish (9,773)	35,031	0.56
Swiss (3,020)	11,563	0.19
Turkish (955)	1,396	0.02
Ukrainian (3,842)	7,311	0.12
Welsh (9,903)	34,433	0.55
West Indian, ex. Hispanic (4,599)	8,270	0.13
Bahamian (220)	418	0.01
Barbadian (156)	221	<0.01
Belizean (151)	161	<0.01
Bermudan (18)	18	<0.01
British West Indian (147)	209	<0.01
Dutch West Indian (310)	1,701	0.03
Haitian (1,296)	1,733	0.03
Jamaican (1,104)	2,092	0.03
Trinidadian/Tobagonian (242)	345	0.01
U.S. Virgin Islander (79)	81	<0.01
West Indian (847)	1,262	0.02
Other West Indian (29)	29	<0.01
Yugoslavian (2,548)	3,465	0.06

Hispanic Origin	Population	%
Hispanic or Latino (of any race)	290,059	4.57
Central American, ex. Mexican	36,856	0.58
Costa Rican	1,045	0.02
Guatemalan	14,323	0.23
Honduran	9,455	0.15
Nicaraguan	1,339	0.02
Panamanian	1,915	0.03
Salvadoran	8,570	0.14
Other Central American	209	<0.01
Cuban	7,773	0.12
Dominican Republic	2,113	0.03
Mexican	186,615	2.94
Puerto Rican	21,060	0.33
South American	11,039	0.17
Argentinean	1,028	0.02
Bolivian	351	0.01
Chilean	774	0.01
Colombian	3,695	0.06
Ecuadorian	1,151	0.02
Paraguayan	108	<0.01
Peruvian	1,918	0.03
Uruguayan	214	<0.01
Venezuelan	1,667	0.03
Other South American	133	<0.01
Other Hispanic or Latino	24,603	0.39

Race*	Population	%
African-American/Black (1,057,315)	1,107,178	17.45
Not Hispanic (1,049,391)	1,094,696	17.25
Hispanic (7,924)	12,482	0.20
American Indian/Alaska Native (19,994)	54,874	0.86
Not Hispanic (16,302)	47,888	0.75
Hispanic (3,692)	6,986	0.11
Alaska Athabascan *(Ala. Nat.)* (28)	43	<0.01
Aleut *(Alaska Native)* (47)	70	<0.01
Apache (263)	752	0.01
Arapaho (20)	34	<0.01
Blackfeet (171)	1,251	0.02
Canadian/French Am. Ind. (53)	143	<0.01
Central American Ind. (157)	242	<0.01
Cherokee (5,327)	19,938	0.31
Cheyenne (41)	127	<0.01
Chickasaw (172)	437	0.01
Chippewa (428)	780	0.01
Choctaw (730)	1,659	0.03
Colville (6)	8	<0.01
Comanche (46)	135	<0.01
Cree (21)	100	<0.01
Creek (309)	709	0.01
Crow (22)	91	<0.01
Delaware (84)	150	<0.01
Hopi (16)	42	<0.01
Houma (51)	72	<0.01
Inupiat *(Alaska Native)* (37)	74	<0.01
Iroquois (308)	683	0.01
Kiowa (28)	54	<0.01
Lumbee (275)	409	0.01
Menominee (18)	27	<0.01
Mexican American Ind. (1,061)	1,448	0.02
Navajo (228)	415	0.01
Osage (58)	123	<0.01
Ottawa (54)	100	<0.01
Paiute (34)	55	<0.01
Pima (25)	28	<0.01
Potawatomi (133)	227	<0.01
Pueblo (61)	105	<0.01
Puget Sound Salish (22)	52	<0.01
Seminole (81)	217	<0.01
Shoshone (13)	38	<0.01
Sioux (338)	837	0.01
South American Ind. (102)	238	<0.01
Spanish American Ind. (163)	195	<0.01
Tlingit-Haida *(Alaska Native)* (49)	68	<0.01
Tohono O'Odham (13)	27	<0.01
Tsimshian *(Alaska Native)* (3)	14	<0.01
Ute (22)	47	<0.01
Yakama (7)	11	<0.01
Yaqui (22)	45	<0.01
Yuman (5)	8	<0.01
Yup'ik *(Alaska Native)* (33)	41	<0.01
Asian (91,242)	113,398	1.79
Not Hispanic (90,311)	110,618	1.74
Hispanic (931)	2,780	0.04
Bangladeshi (481)	521	0.01
Bhutanese (463)	498	0.01
Burmese (1,252)	1,324	0.02
Cambodian (1,587)	1,949	0.03
Chinese, ex. Taiwanese (14,605)	17,422	0.27
Filipino (9,247)	14,409	0.23
Hmong (363)	400	0.01
Indian (23,900)	26,619	0.42
Indonesian (332)	484	0.01
Japanese (3,962)	6,955	0.11
Korean (9,818)	13,245	0.21
Laotian (6,336)	7,276	0.11
Malaysian (289)	390	0.01
Nepalese (193)	220	<0.01
Pakistani (1,934)	2,243	0.04
Sri Lankan (164)	214	<0.01
Taiwanese (777)	935	0.01
Thai (1,373)	2,183	0.03
Vietnamese (10,033)	11,351	0.18
Hawaii Native/Pacific Islander (3,642)	7,785	0.12
Not Hispanic (2,767)	6,070	0.10
Hispanic (875)	1,715	0.03
Fijian (21)	39	<0.01
Guamanian/Chamorro (1,507)	2,124	0.03
Marshallese (40)	42	<0.01
Native Hawaiian (771)	2,224	0.04
Samoan (516)	1,022	0.02
Tongan (26)	59	<0.01
White (4,921,948)	5,019,639	79.10
Not Hispanic (4,800,782)	4,882,031	76.93
Hispanic (121,166)	137,608	2.17

*Notes: † The Census 2010 population figure is used to calculate the percentages in the Hispanic Origin and Race categories. Ancestry percentages are based on the 2006-2010 American Community Survey population (not shown); ‡ Numbers in parentheses indicate the number of people reporting a single ancestry; * Numbers in parentheses indicate the number of persons reporting this race alone, not in combination with any other race; Please refer to the Explanation of Data for more information.*

Alcoa

Place Type: City
County: Blount
Population: 8,449†

Ancestry‡	Population	%
African, Sub-Saharan (105)	121	1.43
African (105)	121	1.43
American (1,276)	1,276	15.06
British (12)	12	0.14
Czech (13)	35	0.41
Danish (11)	11	0.13
Dutch (17)	111	1.31
English (585)	1,071	12.64
European (48)	64	0.76
French, ex. Basque (10)	130	1.53
German (398)	1,161	13.70
Hungarian (0)	132	1.56
Iranian (0)	14	0.17
Irish (433)	1,073	12.66
Italian (61)	73	0.86
Polish (8)	76	0.90
Portuguese (0)	11	0.13
Romanian (8)	17	0.20
Russian (0)	15	0.18
Scotch-Irish (439)	660	7.79
Scottish (50)	115	1.36
Swedish (27)	27	0.32
Swiss (0)	79	0.93
Welsh (13)	13	0.15
West Indian, ex. Hispanic (0)	114	1.35
Dutch West Indian (0)	114	1.35

Hispanic Origin	Population	%
Hispanic or Latino (of any race)	575	6.81
Central American, ex. Mexican	72	0.85
Guatemalan	9	0.11
Honduran	21	0.25
Panamanian	5	0.06
Salvadoran	37	0.44
Cuban	13	0.15
Dominican Republic	8	0.09
Mexican	410	4.85
Puerto Rican	23	0.27
South American	10	0.12
Argentinean	3	0.04
Colombian	1	0.01
Peruvian	6	0.07
Other Hispanic or Latino	39	0.46

Race*	Population	%
African-American/Black (1,181)	1,324	15.67
Not Hispanic (1,163)	1,299	15.37
Hispanic (18)	25	0.30
American Indian/Alaska Native (18)	75	0.89
Not Hispanic (11)	58	0.69
Hispanic (7)	17	0.20
Blackfeet (0)	3	0.04
Central American Ind. (1)	1	0.01
Cherokee (6)	31	0.37
Cree (0)	1	0.01
Creek (0)	2	0.02
Mexican American Ind. (0)	7	0.08
Seminole (0)	1	0.01
Asian (40)	59	0.70
Not Hispanic (39)	55	0.65
Hispanic (1)	4	0.05
Chinese, ex. Taiwanese (1)	5	0.06
Filipino (4)	6	0.07
Indian (14)	15	0.18
Japanese (4)	8	0.09
Korean (6)	8	0.09
Laotian (1)	1	0.01
Thai (3)	4	0.05
Vietnamese (7)	7	0.08
Hawaii Native/Pacific Islander (1)	4	0.05
Not Hispanic (1)	3	0.04
Hispanic (0)	1	0.01
Guamanian/Chamorro (0)	1	0.01
Native Hawaiian (1)	1	0.01
White (6,683)	6,877	81.39
Not Hispanic (6,451)	6,622	78.38
Hispanic (232)	255	3.02

Arlington

Place Type: Town
County: Shelby
Population: 11,517†

Ancestry‡	Population	%
American (1,249)	1,249	12.58
Arab (59)	87	0.88
Lebanese (59)	87	0.88
British (10)	10	0.10
Cajun (0)	35	0.35
Canadian (0)	20	0.20
Danish (0)	15	0.15
Dutch (7)	211	2.13
English (787)	1,361	13.71
European (161)	161	1.62
French, ex. Basque (21)	131	1.32
French Canadian (0)	9	0.09
German (541)	1,284	12.94
Greek (0)	27	0.27
Hungarian (0)	16	0.16
Irish (288)	1,120	11.28
Italian (109)	350	3.53
Macedonian (0)	17	0.17
Northern European (8)	8	0.08
Norwegian (0)	43	0.43
Polish (21)	102	1.03
Portuguese (0)	12	0.12
Russian (63)	87	0.88
Scandinavian (12)	12	0.12
Scotch-Irish (169)	407	4.10
Scottish (132)	261	2.63
Swedish (0)	8	0.08
Swiss (0)	17	0.17
Welsh (10)	20	0.20

Hispanic Origin	Population	%
Hispanic or Latino (of any race)	343	2.98
Central American, ex. Mexican	30	0.26
Costa Rican	1	0.01
Guatemalan	11	0.10
Honduran	7	0.06
Nicaraguan	4	0.03
Panamanian	7	0.06
Cuban	14	0.12
Mexican	175	1.52
Puerto Rican	59	0.51
South American	24	0.21
Colombian	12	0.10
Ecuadorian	1	0.01
Venezuelan	11	0.10
Other Hispanic or Latino	41	0.36

Race*	Population	%
African-American/Black (1,594)	1,690	14.67
Not Hispanic (1,583)	1,669	14.49
Hispanic (11)	21	0.18
American Indian/Alaska Native (19)	79	0.69
Not Hispanic (17)	74	0.64
Hispanic (2)	5	0.04
Cherokee (9)	39	0.34
Chickasaw (0)	1	0.01
Potawatomi (1)	1	0.01
Seminole (0)	2	0.02
South American Ind. (0)	1	0.01
Asian (207)	317	2.75
Not Hispanic (206)	313	2.72
Hispanic (1)	4	0.03
Cambodian (2)	4	0.03
Chinese, ex. Taiwanese (55)	61	0.53
Filipino (32)	66	0.57
Indian (36)	43	0.37
Japanese (9)	19	0.16
Korean (17)	29	0.25
Laotian (3)	3	0.03
Pakistani (7)	7	0.06
Thai (2)	6	0.05
Vietnamese (41)	55	0.48
Hawaii Native/Pacific Islander (2)	5	0.04
Not Hispanic (2)	5	0.04
Native Hawaiian (0)	2	0.02
White (9,356)	9,569	83.09
Not Hispanic (9,141)	9,329	81.00
Hispanic (215)	240	2.08

Athens

Place Type: City
County: McMinn
Population: 13,458†

Ancestry‡	Population	%
African, Sub-Saharan (0)	14	0.10
African (0)	14	0.10
American (1,553)	1,553	11.51
Armenian (77)	77	0.57
Brazilian (0)	14	0.10
British (0)	41	0.30
Czech (0)	15	0.11
Danish (0)	81	0.60
Dutch (29)	334	2.48
Eastern European (26)	26	0.19
English (782)	1,257	9.32
European (32)	32	0.24
French, ex. Basque (33)	162	1.20
French Canadian (37)	37	0.27
German (581)	1,610	11.93
Greek (24)	24	0.18
Hungarian (55)	57	0.42
Iranian (76)	76	0.56
Irish (687)	1,730	12.82
Italian (32)	223	1.65
Norwegian (9)	54	0.40
Polish (114)	269	1.99
Portuguese (23)	23	0.17
Scandinavian (16)	16	0.12
Scotch-Irish (197)	539	4.00
Scottish (121)	466	3.45
Slovak (0)	5	0.04
Swedish (11)	46	0.34
Ukrainian (13)	65	0.48
Welsh (14)	27	0.20
Yugoslavian (12)	27	0.20

Hispanic Origin	Population	%
Hispanic or Latino (of any race)	709	5.27
Central American, ex. Mexican	58	0.43
Costa Rican	5	0.04
Guatemalan	31	0.23
Honduran	14	0.10
Salvadoran	8	0.06
Cuban	18	0.13
Dominican Republic	20	0.15
Mexican	418	3.11
Puerto Rican	38	0.28
South American	100	0.74
Argentinean	1	0.01
Bolivian	1	0.01
Chilean	1	0.01
Colombian	95	0.71
Ecuadorian	2	0.01
Other Hispanic or Latino	57	0.42

Race*	Population	%
African-American/Black (1,093)	1,306	9.70
Not Hispanic (1,073)	1,269	9.43
Hispanic (20)	37	0.27
American Indian/Alaska Native (47)	155	1.15
Not Hispanic (41)	142	1.06
Hispanic (6)	13	0.10
Apache (0)	3	0.02
Blackfeet (1)	4	0.03
Cherokee (24)	81	0.60
Chippewa (2)	4	0.03

*Notes: † The Census 2010 population figure is used to calculate the percentages in the Hispanic Origin and Race categories. Ancestry percentages are based on the 2006-2010 American Community Survey population (not shown); ‡ Numbers in parentheses indicate the number of people reporting a single ancestry; * Numbers in parentheses indicate the number of persons reporting this race alone, not in combination with any other race; Please refer to the Explanation of Data for more information.*

Choctaw (2)	4	0.03
Mexican American Ind. (0)	1	0.01
Shoshone (1)	1	0.01
Yaqui (0)	1	0.01
Asian (221)	269	2.00
Not Hispanic (218)	263	1.95
Hispanic (3)	6	0.04
Chinese, ex. Taiwanese (14)	14	0.10
Filipino (22)	38	0.28
Hmong (1)	1	0.01
Indian (72)	80	0.59
Indonesian (4)	4	0.03
Japanese (45)	52	0.39
Korean (12)	15	0.11
Laotian (35)	37	0.27
Pakistani (2)	3	0.02
Taiwanese (2)	2	0.01
Thai (2)	5	0.04
Vietnamese (10)	11	0.08
Hawaii Native/Pacific Islander (6)	10	0.07
Not Hispanic (6)	7	0.05
Hispanic (0)	3	0.02
Native Hawaiian (5)	6	0.04
Samoan (0)	2	0.01
White (11,375)	11,746	87.28
Not Hispanic (11,065)	11,377	84.54
Hispanic (310)	369	2.74

Atoka

Place Type: Town
County: Tipton
Population: 8,387†

Ancestry‡	Population	%
American (1,739)	1,739	22.79
British (28)	60	0.79
Czech (45)	63	0.83
Danish (0)	14	0.18
Dutch (27)	132	1.73
English (405)	826	10.83
European (76)	76	1.00
Finnish (11)	11	0.14
French, ex. Basque (50)	335	4.39
French Canadian (19)	30	0.39
German (405)	1,182	15.49
Hungarian (0)	71	0.93
Irish (622)	1,269	16.63
Italian (129)	286	3.75
Norwegian (23)	42	0.55
Polish (35)	35	0.46
Russian (24)	24	0.31
Scandinavian (31)	44	0.58
Scotch-Irish (155)	242	3.17
Scottish (55)	68	0.89
Swedish (0)	95	1.25
Swiss (0)	30	0.39

Hispanic Origin	Population	%
Hispanic or Latino (of any race)	222	2.65
Central American, ex. Mexican	13	0.16
Costa Rican	4	0.05
Guatemalan	3	0.04
Honduran	2	0.02
Panamanian	2	0.02
Salvadoran	2	0.02
Cuban	18	0.21
Mexican	125	1.49
Puerto Rican	18	0.21
South American	7	0.08
Argentinean	2	0.02
Colombian	3	0.04
Peruvian	1	0.01
Venezuelan	1	0.01
Other Hispanic or Latino	41	0.49

Race*	Population	%
African-American/Black (921)	1,000	11.92
Not Hispanic (918)	992	11.83
Hispanic (3)	8	0.10
American Indian/Alaska Native (42)	95	1.13
Not Hispanic (41)	89	1.06
Hispanic (1)	6	0.07
Apache (0)	3	0.04
Blackfeet (1)	2	0.02
Cherokee (7)	35	0.42
Choctaw (5)	12	0.14
Comanche (2)	2	0.02
Creek (1)	1	0.01
Iroquois (6)	6	0.07
Sioux (0)	2	0.02
South American Ind. (2)	3	0.04
Asian (114)	168	2.00
Not Hispanic (108)	158	1.88
Hispanic (6)	10	0.12
Cambodian (3)	5	0.06
Chinese, ex. Taiwanese (8)	13	0.16
Filipino (51)	80	0.95
Indian (1)	4	0.05
Indonesian (1)	1	0.01
Japanese (13)	26	0.31
Korean (11)	11	0.13
Taiwanese (7)	7	0.08
Thai (0)	3	0.04
Vietnamese (14)	18	0.21
Hawaii Native/Pacific Islander (10)	21	0.25
Not Hispanic (10)	21	0.25
Guamanian/Chamorro (2)	5	0.06
Native Hawaiian (2)	5	0.06
White (7,089)	7,244	86.37
Not Hispanic (6,933)	7,061	84.19
Hispanic (156)	183	2.18

Bartlett

Place Type: City
County: Shelby
Population: 54,613†

Ancestry‡	Population	%
African, Sub-Saharan (37)	170	0.32
African (8)	86	0.16
Ghanaian (29)	84	0.16
American (4,726)	4,726	8.96
Arab (171)	171	0.32
Iraqi (14)	14	0.03
Palestinian (142)	142	0.27
Syrian (15)	15	0.03
Assyrian/Chaldean/Syriac (39)	39	0.07
Australian (14)	26	0.05
Austrian (27)	71	0.13
Belgian (0)	19	0.04
British (81)	288	0.55
Bulgarian (38)	38	0.07
Cajun (41)	41	0.08
Canadian (16)	51	0.10
Czech (29)	75	0.14
Czechoslovakian (15)	15	0.03
Danish (83)	176	0.33
Dutch (200)	820	1.55
English (3,052)	6,226	11.80
European (958)	1,072	2.03
Finnish (0)	16	0.03
French, ex. Basque (257)	980	1.86
French Canadian (44)	166	0.31
German (2,541)	7,064	13.39
German Russian (0)	20	0.04
Greek (70)	182	0.34
Hungarian (52)	90	0.17
Iranian (48)	48	0.09
Irish (2,940)	7,321	13.88
Italian (945)	1,965	3.72
Lithuanian (0)	56	0.11
Northern European (8)	8	0.02
Norwegian (93)	332	0.63
Pennsylvania German (13)	50	0.09
Polish (232)	670	1.27
Romanian (11)	16	0.03
Russian (73)	243	0.46
Scandinavian (58)	58	0.11
Scotch-Irish (1,128)	2,273	4.31
Scottish (754)	1,543	2.92
Serbian (8)	59	0.11
Slovak (0)	45	0.09
Swedish (335)	860	1.63
Swiss (0)	107	0.20
Turkish (0)	33	0.06
Ukrainian (0)	51	0.10
Welsh (156)	327	0.62
West Indian, ex. Hispanic (57)	87	0.16
Bahamian (7)	22	0.04
Dutch West Indian (16)	31	0.06
Jamaican (15)	15	0.03
Trinidadian/Tobagonian (19)	19	0.04
Yugoslavian (0)	9	0.02

Hispanic Origin	Population	%
Hispanic or Latino (of any race)	1,470	2.69
Central American, ex. Mexican	136	0.25
Costa Rican	7	0.01
Guatemalan	14	0.03
Honduran	44	0.08
Nicaraguan	8	0.01
Panamanian	21	0.04
Salvadoran	42	0.08
Cuban	33	0.06
Dominican Republic	18	0.03
Mexican	804	1.47
Puerto Rican	194	0.36
South American	142	0.26
Argentinean	14	0.03
Bolivian	13	0.02
Chilean	5	0.01
Colombian	44	0.08
Ecuadorian	1	<0.01
Paraguayan	1	<0.01
Peruvian	29	0.05
Uruguayan	7	0.01
Venezuelan	28	0.05
Other Hispanic or Latino	143	0.26

Race*	Population	%
African-American/Black (8,771)	9,128	16.71
Not Hispanic (8,721)	9,038	16.55
Hispanic (50)	90	0.16
American Indian/Alaska Native (138)	329	0.60
Not Hispanic (116)	290	0.53
Hispanic (22)	39	0.07
Apache (4)	4	0.01
Blackfeet (0)	4	0.01
Cherokee (33)	119	0.22
Cheyenne (0)	2	<0.01
Chickasaw (0)	4	0.01
Chippewa (2)	2	<0.01
Choctaw (2)	14	0.03
Creek (5)	9	0.02
Houma (0)	1	<0.01
Iroquois (7)	7	0.01
Lumbee (1)	3	0.01
Menominee (1)	1	<0.01
Mexican American Ind. (2)	4	0.01
Navajo (1)	4	0.01
Potawatomi (1)	1	<0.01
Sioux (1)	5	0.01
South American Ind. (1)	1	<0.01
Spanish American Ind. (0)	2	<0.01
Tlingit-Haida *(Alaska Native)* (1)	1	<0.01
Ute (1)	4	0.01
Asian (1,368)	1,730	3.17
Not Hispanic (1,350)	1,671	3.06
Hispanic (18)	59	0.11
Bangladeshi (20)	22	0.04
Cambodian (51)	60	0.11
Chinese, ex. Taiwanese (258)	314	0.57
Filipino (369)	453	0.83
Hmong (21)	22	0.04
Indian (125)	133	0.24
Indonesian (0)	1	<0.01
Japanese (51)	140	0.26
Korean (89)	132	0.24

*Notes: † The Census 2010 population figure is used to calculate the percentages in the Hispanic Origin and Race categories. Ancestry percentages are based on the 2006-2010 American Community Survey population (not shown); ‡ Numbers in parentheses indicate the number of people reporting a single ancestry; * Numbers in parentheses indicate the number of persons reporting this race alone, not in combination with any other race; Please refer to the Explanation of Data for more information.*

Laotian (24)	33	0.06
Malaysian (4)	5	0.01
Pakistani (48)	55	0.10
Taiwanese (5)	7	0.01
Thai (17)	25	0.05
Vietnamese (250)	281	0.51
Hawaii Native/Pacific Islander (22)	62	0.11
Not Hispanic (20)	50	0.09
Hispanic (2)	12	0.02
Guamanian/Chamorro (7)	10	0.02
Marshallese (4)	4	0.01
Native Hawaiian (5)	22	0.04
Samoan (1)	10	0.02
Tongan (0)	1	<0.01
White (42,975)	43,711	80.04
Not Hispanic (42,158)	42,773	78.32
Hispanic (817)	938	1.72

Bloomingdale

Place Type: CDP
County: Sullivan
Population: 9,888†

Ancestry‡	Population	%
American (2,773)	2,773	28.46
Arab (9)	9	0.09
Lebanese (9)	9	0.09
British (41)	41	0.42
Danish (9)	19	0.20
Dutch (32)	113	1.16
English (453)	961	9.86
European (43)	43	0.44
French, ex. Basque (40)	162	1.66
French Canadian (21)	21	0.22
German (245)	794	8.15
Hungarian (8)	28	0.29
Irish (532)	1,082	11.11
Italian (22)	50	0.51
Polish (23)	31	0.32
Portuguese (8)	8	0.08
Scandinavian (0)	30	0.31
Scotch-Irish (227)	331	3.40
Scottish (79)	185	1.90
Swedish (8)	17	0.17
Swiss (0)	25	0.26
Ukrainian (0)	10	0.10

Hispanic Origin	Population	%
Hispanic or Latino (of any race)	127	1.28
Central American, ex. Mexican	13	0.13
Costa Rican	1	0.01
Guatemalan	3	0.03
Honduran	2	0.02
Nicaraguan	2	0.02
Other Central American	5	0.05
Cuban	7	0.07
Mexican	84	0.85
Puerto Rican	8	0.08
South American	3	0.03
Colombian	2	0.02
Peruvian	1	0.01
Other Hispanic or Latino	12	0.12

Race*	Population	%
African-American/Black (69)	132	1.33
Not Hispanic (67)	128	1.29
Hispanic (2)	4	0.04
American Indian/Alaska Native (31)	85	0.86
Not Hispanic (31)	82	0.83
Hispanic (0)	3	0.03
Apache (0)	1	0.01
Cherokee (13)	45	0.46
Choctaw (0)	1	0.01
Crow (1)	1	0.01
Puget Sound Salish (3)	3	0.03
South American Ind. (1)	1	0.01
Asian (25)	38	0.38
Not Hispanic (25)	37	0.37
Hispanic (0)	1	0.01
Chinese, ex. Taiwanese (4)	4	0.04
Filipino (8)	11	0.11
Indian (4)	7	0.07
Japanese (0)	1	0.01
Korean (1)	4	0.04
Vietnamese (8)	8	0.08
Hawaii Native/Pacific Islander (0)	2	0.02
Not Hispanic (0)	2	0.02
White (9,575)	9,703	98.13
Not Hispanic (9,508)	9,632	97.41
Hispanic (67)	71	0.72

Brentwood

Place Type: City
County: Williamson
Population: 37,060†

Ancestry‡	Population	%
African, Sub-Saharan (131)	170	0.48
African (23)	55	0.16
Nigerian (14)	14	0.04
South African (51)	58	0.16
Other Sub-Saharan African (43)	43	0.12
American (2,704)	2,704	7.65
Arab (199)	331	0.94
Arab (8)	8	0.02
Iraqi (23)	23	0.07
Jordanian (33)	91	0.26
Lebanese (104)	120	0.34
Palestinian (31)	89	0.25
Armenian (61)	61	0.17
Australian (93)	103	0.29
Austrian (0)	44	0.12
Belgian (0)	12	0.03
British (201)	294	0.83
Bulgarian (0)	16	0.05
Canadian (37)	67	0.19
Celtic (14)	41	0.12
Croatian (11)	70	0.20
Czech (63)	187	0.53
Czechoslovakian (0)	6	0.02
Danish (19)	108	0.31
Dutch (108)	365	1.03
Eastern European (26)	50	0.14
English (2,680)	6,201	17.55
European (665)	687	1.94
Finnish (30)	166	0.47
French, ex. Basque (230)	1,299	3.68
French Canadian (87)	142	0.40
German (2,349)	7,065	20.00
Greek (17)	217	0.61
Guyanese (0)	37	0.10
Hungarian (61)	144	0.41
Iranian (253)	253	0.72
Irish (1,730)	5,153	14.58
Italian (423)	1,680	4.76
Latvian (0)	36	0.10
Lithuanian (0)	92	0.26
Maltese (14)	14	0.04
Northern European (78)	95	0.27
Norwegian (40)	195	0.55
Pennsylvania German (39)	39	0.11
Polish (287)	1,098	3.11
Portuguese (9)	116	0.33
Romanian (41)	41	0.12
Russian (211)	310	0.88
Scandinavian (39)	158	0.45
Scotch-Irish (1,063)	1,730	4.90
Scottish (724)	1,926	5.45
Serbian (12)	12	0.03
Slavic (21)	21	0.06
Slovak (49)	58	0.16
Slovene (0)	12	0.03
Swedish (153)	453	1.28
Swiss (58)	227	0.64
Turkish (10)	10	0.03
Ukrainian (27)	80	0.23
Welsh (199)	448	1.27
West Indian, ex. Hispanic (89)	121	0.34
Haitian (30)	62	0.18
Jamaican (45)	45	0.13
U.S. Virgin Islander (14)	14	0.04
Yugoslavian (8)	54	0.15

Hispanic Origin	Population	%
Hispanic or Latino (of any race)	785	2.12
Central American, ex. Mexican	55	0.15
Costa Rican	9	0.02
Guatemalan	12	0.03
Honduran	5	0.01
Nicaraguan	12	0.03
Panamanian	13	0.04
Salvadoran	4	0.01
Cuban	58	0.16
Dominican Republic	10	0.03
Mexican	366	0.99
Puerto Rican	79	0.21
South American	129	0.35
Argentinean	17	0.05
Bolivian	1	<0.01
Chilean	16	0.04
Colombian	55	0.15
Ecuadorian	18	0.05
Peruvian	10	0.03
Venezuelan	12	0.03
Other Hispanic or Latino	88	0.24

Race*	Population	%
African-American/Black (1,099)	1,224	3.30
Not Hispanic (1,077)	1,187	3.20
Hispanic (22)	37	0.10
American Indian/Alaska Native (59)	177	0.48
Not Hispanic (57)	172	0.46
Hispanic (2)	5	0.01
Alaska Athabascan *(Ala. Nat.)* (0)	1	<0.01
Aleut *(Alaska Native)* (1)	3	0.01
Blackfeet (0)	3	0.01
Canadian/French Am. Ind. (1)	1	<0.01
Cherokee (11)	43	0.12
Chickasaw (0)	2	0.01
Choctaw (1)	10	0.03
Comanche (0)	2	0.01
Creek (4)	5	0.01
Iroquois (0)	5	0.01
Lumbee (0)	2	0.01
Navajo (0)	1	<0.01
Osage (3)	3	0.01
Paiute (1)	1	<0.01
Potawatomi (1)	1	<0.01
Pueblo (0)	1	<0.01
Seminole (0)	1	<0.01
Sioux (0)	2	0.01
South American Ind. (1)	1	<0.01
Asian (1,851)	2,181	5.89
Not Hispanic (1,847)	2,171	5.86
Hispanic (4)	10	0.03
Burmese (1)	1	<0.01
Chinese, ex. Taiwanese (468)	524	1.41
Filipino (40)	91	0.25
Indian (646)	688	1.86
Indonesian (0)	5	0.01
Japanese (89)	130	0.35
Korean (374)	411	1.11
Laotian (22)	29	0.08
Malaysian (1)	1	<0.01
Nepalese (2)	2	0.01
Pakistani (51)	65	0.18
Sri Lankan (6)	10	0.03
Taiwanese (32)	35	0.09
Thai (7)	21	0.06
Vietnamese (60)	82	0.22
Hawaii Native/Pacific Islander (8)	23	0.06
Not Hispanic (8)	23	0.06
Native Hawaiian (1)	4	0.01
Samoan (2)	2	0.01
Tongan (1)	1	<0.01
White (33,344)	33,865	91.38
Not Hispanic (32,740)	33,217	89.63
Hispanic (604)	648	1.75

*Notes: † The Census 2010 population figure is used to calculate the percentages in the Hispanic Origin and Race categories. Ancestry percentages are based on the 2006-2010 American Community Survey population (not shown); ‡ Numbers in parentheses indicate the number of people reporting a single ancestry; * Numbers in parentheses indicate the number of persons reporting this race alone, not in combination with any other race; Please refer to the Explanation of Data for more information.*

Bristol

Place Type: City
County: Sullivan
Population: 26,702†

Ancestry‡	Population	%
African, Sub-Saharan (10)	17	0.06
African (10)	17	0.06
Albanian (8)	8	0.03
Alsatian (9)	9	0.03
American (6,121)	6,121	23.16
Arab (5)	18	0.07
Lebanese (5)	18	0.07
Australian (12)	12	0.05
Austrian (0)	30	0.11
Brazilian (37)	37	0.14
British (90)	161	0.61
Canadian (11)	11	0.04
Croatian (0)	14	0.05
Czech (9)	9	0.03
Czechoslovakian (33)	33	0.12
Danish (0)	8	0.03
Dutch (142)	629	2.38
Eastern European (17)	35	0.13
English (1,746)	3,284	12.43
European (375)	381	1.44
French, ex. Basque (144)	425	1.61
French Canadian (0)	10	0.04
German (1,206)	3,693	13.97
Greek (18)	79	0.30
Hungarian (48)	80	0.30
Iranian (13)	13	0.05
Irish (1,125)	3,334	12.62
Italian (269)	411	1.56
Northern European (13)	13	0.05
Norwegian (7)	86	0.33
Polish (86)	168	0.64
Russian (65)	87	0.33
Scandinavian (70)	124	0.47
Scotch-Irish (696)	1,166	4.41
Scottish (286)	717	2.71
Slavic (9)	9	0.03
Swedish (89)	179	0.68
Swiss (0)	12	0.05
Welsh (34)	145	0.55
West Indian, ex. Hispanic (79)	119	0.45
Dutch West Indian (2)	17	0.06
Haitian (63)	88	0.33
Jamaican (14)	14	0.05
Yugoslavian (37)	37	0.14

Hispanic Origin	Population	%
Hispanic or Latino (of any race)	502	1.88
Central American, ex. Mexican	50	0.19
Costa Rican	5	0.02
Guatemalan	20	0.07
Honduran	15	0.06
Nicaraguan	1	<0.01
Panamanian	1	<0.01
Salvadoran	8	0.03
Cuban	14	0.05
Dominican Republic	3	0.01
Mexican	294	1.10
Puerto Rican	57	0.21
South American	30	0.11
Argentinean	2	0.01
Bolivian	1	<0.01
Chilean	3	0.01
Colombian	6	0.02
Ecuadorian	2	0.01
Peruvian	10	0.04
Uruguayan	2	0.01
Venezuelan	4	0.01
Other Hispanic or Latino	54	0.20

Race*	Population	%
African-American/Black (904)	1,079	4.04
Not Hispanic (884)	1,053	3.94
Hispanic (20)	26	0.10
American Indian/Alaska Native (83)	218	0.82
Not Hispanic (72)	203	0.76
Hispanic (11)	15	0.06
Apache (0)	1	<0.01
Blackfeet (0)	2	0.01
Central American Ind. (0)	1	<0.01
Cherokee (25)	97	0.36
Cheyenne (0)	2	0.01
Choctaw (1)	4	0.01
Creek (3)	4	0.01
Houma (1)	1	<0.01
Navajo (1)	1	<0.01
Paiute (4)	4	0.01
Potawatomi (1)	1	<0.01
Seminole (1)	1	<0.01
Sioux (1)	4	0.01
South American Ind. (2)	3	0.01
Asian (193)	262	0.98
Not Hispanic (193)	258	0.97
Hispanic (0)	4	0.01
Chinese, ex. Taiwanese (50)	58	0.22
Filipino (17)	28	0.10
Indian (59)	68	0.25
Indonesian (0)	1	<0.01
Japanese (7)	17	0.06
Korean (17)	34	0.13
Laotian (2)	2	0.01
Pakistani (1)	1	<0.01
Thai (3)	6	0.02
Vietnamese (35)	35	0.13
Hawaii Native/Pacific Islander (4)	19	0.07
Not Hispanic (4)	15	0.06
Hispanic (0)	4	0.01
Guamanian/Chamorro (0)	2	0.01
Native Hawaiian (2)	5	0.02
Samoan (0)	2	0.01
White (24,913)	25,276	94.66
Not Hispanic (24,671)	25,005	93.64
Hispanic (242)	271	1.01

Brownsville

Place Type: City
County: Haywood
Population: 10,292†

Ancestry‡	Population	%
African, Sub-Saharan (101)	131	1.26
African (101)	131	1.26
American (1,100)	1,100	10.59
Danish (0)	34	0.33
English (309)	587	5.65
European (0)	13	0.13
French, ex. Basque (14)	100	0.96
French Canadian (47)	47	0.45
German (158)	448	4.31
Irish (173)	551	5.30
Italian (68)	166	1.60
Pennsylvania German (22)	22	0.21
Polish (20)	94	0.90
Scotch-Irish (21)	54	0.52
Scottish (0)	64	0.62
Swedish (36)	50	0.48
Ukrainian (9)	9	0.09
Welsh (0)	15	0.14

Hispanic Origin	Population	%
Hispanic or Latino (of any race)	481	4.67
Central American, ex. Mexican	23	0.22
Honduran	8	0.08
Nicaraguan	5	0.05
Panamanian	1	0.01
Salvadoran	9	0.09
Cuban	7	0.07
Mexican	414	4.02
Puerto Rican	5	0.05
South American	7	0.07
Ecuadorian	3	0.03
Peruvian	4	0.04
Other Hispanic or Latino	25	0.24

Race*	Population	%
African-American/Black (6,654)	6,730	65.39
Not Hispanic (6,631)	6,699	65.09
Hispanic (23)	31	0.30
American Indian/Alaska Native (21)	54	0.52
Not Hispanic (17)	49	0.48
Hispanic (4)	5	0.05
Blackfeet (1)	2	0.02
Cherokee (5)	18	0.17
Choctaw (0)	3	0.03
Creek (1)	7	0.07
Mexican American Ind. (2)	2	0.02
Sioux (0)	1	0.01
Asian (11)	17	0.17
Not Hispanic (11)	15	0.15
Hispanic (0)	2	0.02
Chinese, ex. Taiwanese (4)	4	0.04
Filipino (3)	5	0.05
Indian (0)	1	0.01
Korean (1)	1	0.01
Vietnamese (3)	3	0.03
Hawaii Native/Pacific Islander (0)	2	0.02
Not Hispanic (0)	2	0.02
Samoan (0)	1	0.01
White (3,176)	3,249	31.57
Not Hispanic (3,056)	3,113	30.25
Hispanic (120)	136	1.32

Chattanooga

Place Type: City
County: Hamilton
Population: 167,674†

Ancestry‡	Population	%
African, Sub-Saharan (1,344)	1,478	0.90
African (1,038)	1,142	0.69
Ethiopian (72)	72	0.04
Kenyan (20)	20	0.01
Liberian (53)	53	0.03
Nigerian (71)	71	0.04
South African (42)	72	0.04
Other Sub-Saharan African (48)	48	0.03
Albanian (50)	50	0.03
American (21,415)	21,415	13.02
Arab (282)	455	0.28
Arab (112)	112	0.07
Egyptian (32)	49	0.03
Jordanian (18)	18	0.01
Lebanese (52)	137	0.08
Palestinian (29)	29	0.02
Syrian (0)	55	0.03
Other Arab (39)	55	0.03
Armenian (97)	97	0.06
Australian (14)	14	0.01
Austrian (25)	66	0.04
Belgian (50)	104	0.06
Brazilian (44)	44	0.03
British (488)	762	0.46
Bulgarian (13)	13	0.01
Cajun (29)	29	0.02
Canadian (140)	250	0.15
Celtic (0)	24	0.01
Croatian (11)	11	0.01
Czech (51)	121	0.07
Czechoslovakian (32)	109	0.07
Danish (116)	233	0.14
Dutch (602)	2,043	1.24
Eastern European (43)	43	0.03
English (5,574)	13,275	8.07
European (1,650)	1,989	1.21
Finnish (80)	116	0.07
French, ex. Basque (614)	2,708	1.65
French Canadian (140)	351	0.21
German (4,621)	13,157	8.00
German Russian (20)	20	0.01
Greek (86)	129	0.08
Guyanese (43)	43	0.03
Hungarian (80)	179	0.11

*Notes: † The Census 2010 population figure is used to calculate the percentages in the Hispanic Origin and Race categories. Ancestry percentages are based on the 2006-2010 American Community Survey population (not shown); ‡ Numbers in parentheses indicate the number of people reporting a single ancestry; * Numbers in parentheses indicate the number of persons reporting this race alone, not in combination with any other race; Please refer to the Explanation of Data for more information.*

Icelander (24)	24	0.01
Iranian (75)	75	0.05
Irish (5,226)	14,012	8.52
Israeli (12)	30	0.02
Italian (1,051)	2,688	1.63
Lithuanian (110)	118	0.07
Northern European (79)	79	0.05
Norwegian (518)	710	0.43
Pennsylvania German (30)	30	0.02
Polish (541)	1,434	0.87
Portuguese (69)	152	0.09
Romanian (123)	154	0.09
Russian (221)	424	0.26
Scandinavian (113)	155	0.09
Scotch-Irish (2,305)	4,509	2.74
Scottish (1,197)	3,484	2.12
Serbian (24)	42	0.03
Slavic (0)	2	<0.01
Slovak (113)	184	0.11
Slovene (17)	85	0.05
Swedish (252)	801	0.49
Swiss (142)	441	0.27
Turkish (0)	58	0.04
Ukrainian (58)	80	0.05
Welsh (185)	874	0.53
West Indian, ex. Hispanic (306)	385	0.23
Dutch West Indian (0)	17	0.01
Haitian (127)	127	0.08
Jamaican (98)	113	0.07
West Indian (81)	128	0.08

Hispanic Origin	Population	%
Hispanic or Latino (of any race)	9,225	5.50
Central American, ex. Mexican	2,990	1.78
Costa Rican	17	0.01
Guatemalan	2,633	1.57
Honduran	120	0.07
Nicaraguan	33	0.02
Panamanian	38	0.02
Salvadoran	146	0.09
Other Central American	3	<0.01
Cuban	266	0.16
Dominican Republic	70	0.04
Mexican	4,180	2.49
Puerto Rican	495	0.30
South American	344	0.21
Argentinean	26	0.02
Bolivian	12	0.01
Chilean	22	0.01
Colombian	117	0.07
Ecuadorian	57	0.03
Paraguayan	6	<0.01
Peruvian	44	0.03
Uruguayan	2	<0.01
Venezuelan	52	0.03
Other South American	6	<0.01
Other Hispanic or Latino	880	0.52

Race*	Population	%
African-American/Black (58,507)	60,205	35.91
Not Hispanic (58,256)	59,817	35.67
Hispanic (251)	388	0.23
American Indian/Alaska Native (647)	1,666	0.99
Not Hispanic (409)	1,230	0.73
Hispanic (238)	436	0.26
Alaska Athabascan *(Ala. Nat.)* (1)	1	<0.01
Aleut *(Alaska Native)* (1)	1	<0.01
Apache (5)	12	0.01
Blackfeet (3)	41	0.02
Canadian/French Am. Ind. (0)	2	<0.01
Central American Ind. (16)	46	0.03
Cherokee (112)	466	0.28
Cheyenne (0)	1	<0.01
Chickasaw (2)	4	<0.01
Chippewa (9)	18	0.01
Choctaw (11)	39	0.02
Comanche (2)	3	<0.01
Cree (0)	1	<0.01
Creek (7)	23	0.01
Crow (0)	1	<0.01
Delaware (1)	2	<0.01
Inupiat *(Alaska Native)* (1)	1	<0.01
Iroquois (2)	12	0.01
Lumbee (7)	8	<0.01
Menominee (1)	1	<0.01
Mexican American Ind. (134)	158	0.09
Navajo (5)	11	0.01
Osage (0)	2	<0.01
Ottawa (0)	3	<0.01
Pima (1)	1	<0.01
Pueblo (1)	1	<0.01
Puget Sound Salish (0)	1	<0.01
Seminole (4)	7	<0.01
Sioux (8)	26	0.02
South American Ind. (0)	4	<0.01
Spanish American Ind. (4)	4	<0.01
Asian (3,306)	3,820	2.28
Not Hispanic (3,273)	3,751	2.24
Hispanic (33)	69	0.04
Bangladeshi (3)	3	<0.01
Burmese (16)	16	0.01
Cambodian (76)	107	0.06
Chinese, ex. Taiwanese (372)	449	0.27
Filipino (269)	378	0.23
Hmong (1)	3	<0.01
Indian (1,433)	1,520	0.91
Indonesian (9)	15	0.01
Japanese (109)	184	0.11
Korean (306)	369	0.22
Laotian (50)	69	0.04
Malaysian (3)	3	<0.01
Nepalese (4)	4	<0.01
Pakistani (108)	120	0.07
Sri Lankan (2)	4	<0.01
Taiwanese (43)	49	0.03
Thai (41)	58	0.03
Vietnamese (313)	355	0.21
Hawaii Native/Pacific Islander (182)	304	0.18
Not Hispanic (79)	166	0.10
Hispanic (103)	138	0.08
Fijian (1)	4	<0.01
Guamanian/Chamorro (137)	160	0.10
Marshallese (1)	1	<0.01
Native Hawaiian (15)	39	0.02
Samoan (8)	32	0.02
White (97,202)	99,762	59.50
Not Hispanic (93,698)	95,846	57.16
Hispanic (3,504)	3,916	2.34

Clarksville

Place Type: City
County: Montgomery
Population: 132,929†

Ancestry‡	Population	%
African, Sub-Saharan (864)	1,020	0.81
African (836)	992	0.79
Cape Verdean (10)	10	0.01
Other Sub-Saharan African (18)	18	0.01
American (12,832)	12,832	10.17
Arab (217)	345	0.27
Arab (0)	24	0.02
Iraqi (43)	43	0.03
Jordanian (32)	32	0.03
Lebanese (27)	79	0.06
Moroccan (18)	18	0.01
Palestinian (97)	97	0.08
Syrian (0)	52	0.04
Armenian (30)	118	0.09
Assyrian/Chaldean/Syriac (0)	12	0.01
Australian (35)	63	0.05
Austrian (50)	121	0.10
Basque (10)	10	0.01
Belgian (0)	10	0.01
British (132)	181	0.14
Cajun (4)	17	0.01
Canadian (28)	70	0.06
Croatian (16)	26	0.02
Czech (144)	285	0.23
Czechoslovakian (8)	60	0.05
Danish (127)	320	0.25
Dutch (214)	1,256	1.00
Eastern European (13)	13	0.01
English (4,742)	9,213	7.30
European (749)	777	0.62
Finnish (34)	123	0.10
French, ex. Basque (1,245)	2,701	2.14
French Canadian (222)	521	0.41
German (7,528)	16,023	12.70
German Russian (0)	18	0.01
Greek (163)	300	0.24
Guyanese (76)	142	0.11
Hungarian (149)	326	0.26
Irish (6,580)	13,901	11.02
Italian (1,574)	3,805	3.02
Latvian (10)	10	0.01
Lithuanian (55)	128	0.10
Norwegian (306)	863	0.68
Pennsylvania German (32)	32	0.03
Polish (612)	1,781	1.41
Portuguese (148)	234	0.19
Russian (177)	338	0.27
Scandinavian (31)	162	0.13
Scotch-Irish (1,193)	2,518	2.00
Scottish (1,059)	2,478	1.96
Slavic (57)	57	0.05
Slovak (29)	193	0.15
Swedish (129)	756	0.60
Swiss (54)	176	0.14
Turkish (20)	44	0.03
Ukrainian (75)	181	0.14
Welsh (343)	786	0.62
West Indian, ex. Hispanic (290)	569	0.45
Belizean (7)	17	0.01
British West Indian (40)	40	0.03
Dutch West Indian (0)	17	0.01
Haitian (97)	180	0.14
Jamaican (114)	174	0.14
West Indian (32)	141	0.11
Yugoslavian (0)	38	0.03

Hispanic Origin	Population	%
Hispanic or Latino (of any race)	12,302	9.25
Central American, ex. Mexican	981	0.74
Costa Rican	34	0.03
Guatemalan	94	0.07
Honduran	113	0.09
Nicaraguan	42	0.03
Panamanian	588	0.44
Salvadoran	106	0.08
Other Central American	4	<0.01
Cuban	308	0.23
Dominican Republic	297	0.22
Mexican	5,425	4.08
Puerto Rican	3,957	2.98
South American	402	0.30
Argentinean	21	0.02
Bolivian	17	0.01
Chilean	17	0.01
Colombian	166	0.12
Ecuadorian	60	0.05
Peruvian	85	0.06
Uruguayan	1	<0.01
Venezuelan	24	0.02
Other South American	11	0.01
Other Hispanic or Latino	932	0.70

Race*	Population	%
African-American/Black (30,798)	34,448	25.91
Not Hispanic (29,872)	32,869	24.73
Hispanic (926)	1,579	1.19
American Indian/Alaska Native (807)	2,302	1.73
Not Hispanic (616)	1,818	1.37
Hispanic (191)	484	0.36
Alaska Athabascan *(Ala. Nat.)* (4)	6	<0.01
Aleut *(Alaska Native)* (2)	2	<0.01
Apache (31)	58	0.04
Blackfeet (6)	60	0.05
Canadian/French Am. Ind. (2)	6	<0.01

*Notes: † The Census 2010 population figure is used to calculate the percentages in the Hispanic Origin and Race categories. Ancestry percentages are based on the 2006-2010 American Community Survey population (not shown); ‡ Numbers in parentheses indicate the number of people reporting a single ancestry; * Numbers in parentheses indicate the number of persons reporting this race alone, not in combination with any other race; Please refer to the Explanation of Data for more information.*

Central American Ind. (2)	3	<0.01
Cherokee (121)	633	0.48
Cheyenne (2)	5	<0.01
Chickasaw (11)	24	0.02
Chippewa (29)	53	0.04
Choctaw (22)	54	0.04
Colville (1)	1	<0.01
Comanche (6)	16	0.01
Cree (4)	10	0.01
Creek (8)	28	0.02
Crow (0)	4	<0.01
Delaware (2)	12	0.01
Hopi (1)	3	<0.01
Houma (6)	6	<0.01
Inupiat *(Alaska Native)* (6)	11	0.01
Iroquois (19)	40	0.03
Kiowa (2)	5	<0.01
Lumbee (22)	27	0.02
Mexican American Ind. (30)	49	0.04
Navajo (47)	74	0.06
Osage (2)	3	<0.01
Paiute (1)	5	<0.01
Pima (10)	10	0.01
Potawatomi (5)	11	0.01
Pueblo (5)	12	0.01
Puget Sound Salish (1)	2	<0.01
Seminole (2)	9	0.01
Shoshone (2)	6	<0.01
Sioux (31)	50	0.04
South American Ind. (10)	28	0.02
Spanish American Ind. (8)	10	0.01
Tlingit-Haida *(Alaska Native)* (3)	4	<0.01
Tsimshian *(Alaska Native)* (1)	1	<0.01
Ute (2)	2	<0.01
Yakama (0)	2	<0.01
Yaqui (6)	8	0.01
Yup'ik *(Alaska Native)* (4)	4	<0.01
Asian (3,093)	5,026	3.78
Not Hispanic (3,011)	4,693	3.53
Hispanic (82)	333	0.25
Bangladeshi (16)	16	0.01
Burmese (2)	2	<0.01
Cambodian (15)	22	0.02
Chinese, ex. Taiwanese (229)	406	0.31
Filipino (606)	1,139	0.86
Hmong (8)	10	0.01
Indian (408)	496	0.37
Indonesian (13)	24	0.02
Japanese (159)	435	0.33
Korean (1,204)	1,977	1.49
Laotian (33)	42	0.03
Malaysian (8)	19	0.01
Nepalese (16)	16	0.01
Pakistani (23)	37	0.03
Sri Lankan (5)	6	<0.01
Taiwanese (6)	13	0.01
Thai (83)	175	0.13
Vietnamese (157)	214	0.16
Hawaii Native/Pacific Islander (628)	1,076	0.81
Not Hispanic (586)	926	0.70
Hispanic (42)	150	0.11
Fijian (5)	10	0.01
Guamanian/Chamorro (233)	333	0.25
Marshallese (16)	16	0.01
Native Hawaiian (101)	273	0.21
Samoan (155)	232	0.17
Tongan (6)	11	0.01
White (87,135)	92,740	69.77
Not Hispanic (81,165)	85,569	64.37
Hispanic (5,970)	7,171	5.39

Cleveland

Place Type: City
County: Bradley
Population: 41,285†

Ancestry‡	Population	%
African, Sub-Saharan (104)	269	0.66
African (51)	154	0.38
Cape Verdean (0)	42	0.10
Nigerian (32)	52	0.13
Zimbabwean (21)	21	0.05
American (4,470)	4,470	11.04
Australian (9)	9	0.02
Austrian (10)	56	0.14
Belgian (0)	49	0.12
Brazilian (27)	27	0.07
British (88)	179	0.44
Cajun (43)	43	0.11
Celtic (0)	24	0.06
Czech (0)	43	0.11
Danish (8)	21	0.05
Dutch (162)	895	2.21
English (1,674)	4,073	10.06
European (566)	619	1.53
Finnish (0)	48	0.12
French, ex. Basque (220)	1,031	2.55
French Canadian (24)	77	0.19
German (1,453)	4,614	11.39
Greek (19)	70	0.17
Hungarian (12)	21	0.05
Irish (1,742)	4,909	12.12
Italian (467)	964	2.38
New Zealander (10)	10	0.02
Northern European (47)	47	0.12
Norwegian (53)	213	0.53
Polish (96)	486	1.20
Romanian (58)	58	0.14
Russian (58)	194	0.48
Scotch-Irish (1,009)	1,681	4.15
Scottish (673)	1,459	3.60
Serbian (11)	11	0.03
Slavic (0)	41	0.10
Slovak (0)	14	0.03
Slovene (0)	14	0.03
Swedish (49)	218	0.54
Swiss (20)	59	0.15
Turkish (0)	12	0.03
Ukrainian (83)	83	0.20
Welsh (74)	216	0.53
West Indian, ex. Hispanic (72)	126	0.31
Bahamian (24)	24	0.06
Haitian (30)	30	0.07
Jamaican (18)	72	0.18
Yugoslavian (151)	151	0.37

Hispanic Origin	Population	%
Hispanic or Latino (of any race)	3,106	7.52
Central American, ex. Mexican	297	0.72
Costa Rican	9	0.02
Guatemalan	143	0.35
Honduran	102	0.25
Nicaraguan	5	0.01
Panamanian	13	0.03
Salvadoran	25	0.06
Cuban	58	0.14
Dominican Republic	60	0.15
Mexican	1,936	4.69
Puerto Rican	336	0.81
South American	188	0.46
Argentinean	18	0.04
Bolivian	1	<0.01
Chilean	37	0.09
Colombian	52	0.13
Ecuadorian	37	0.09
Paraguayan	1	<0.01
Peruvian	24	0.06
Uruguayan	5	0.01
Venezuelan	12	0.03
Other South American	1	<0.01
Other Hispanic or Latino	231	0.56

Race*	Population	%
African-American/Black (3,048)	3,529	8.55
Not Hispanic (2,975)	3,415	8.27
Hispanic (73)	114	0.28
American Indian/Alaska Native (165)	461	1.12
Not Hispanic (107)	370	0.90
Hispanic (58)	91	0.22
Apache (2)	5	0.01
Blackfeet (0)	8	0.02
Cherokee (36)	172	0.42
Chickasaw (0)	2	<0.01
Chippewa (3)	4	0.01
Choctaw (2)	9	0.02
Cree (0)	1	<0.01
Creek (2)	7	0.02
Hopi (0)	2	<0.01
Iroquois (2)	6	0.01
Kiowa (1)	3	0.01
Lumbee (2)	3	0.01
Mexican American Ind. (40)	51	0.12
Navajo (4)	7	0.02
Pueblo (1)	2	<0.01
Puget Sound Salish (0)	1	<0.01
Seminole (1)	1	<0.01
Sioux (0)	2	<0.01
South American Ind. (0)	1	<0.01
Spanish American Ind. (0)	4	0.01
Tlingit-Haida *(Alaska Native)* (1)	1	<0.01
Yaqui (1)	1	<0.01
Asian (630)	747	1.81
Not Hispanic (618)	717	1.74
Hispanic (12)	30	0.07
Bangladeshi (1)	1	<0.01
Burmese (1)	1	<0.01
Cambodian (2)	3	0.01
Chinese, ex. Taiwanese (89)	108	0.26
Filipino (42)	71	0.17
Indian (301)	325	0.79
Indonesian (8)	8	0.02
Japanese (16)	40	0.10
Korean (47)	58	0.14
Laotian (2)	6	0.01
Malaysian (3)	3	0.01
Nepalese (15)	15	0.04
Pakistani (12)	13	0.03
Sri Lankan (2)	7	0.02
Taiwanese (2)	2	<0.01
Thai (2)	4	0.01
Vietnamese (63)	68	0.16
Hawaii Native/Pacific Islander (35)	62	0.15
Not Hispanic (31)	56	0.14
Hispanic (4)	6	0.01
Guamanian/Chamorro (7)	8	0.02
Native Hawaiian (7)	14	0.03
Samoan (1)	5	0.01
White (34,624)	35,537	86.08
Not Hispanic (33,612)	34,339	83.18
Hispanic (1,012)	1,198	2.90

Clinton

Place Type: City
County: Anderson
Population: 9,841†

Ancestry‡	Population	%
American (2,160)	2,160	22.17
Austrian (52)	62	0.64
Dutch (38)	311	3.19
English (767)	1,250	12.83
European (134)	160	1.64
French, ex. Basque (42)	145	1.49
German (392)	1,194	12.25
Greek (19)	19	0.19
Hungarian (9)	24	0.25
Irish (642)	1,644	16.87
Italian (21)	195	2.00
Lithuanian (0)	12	0.12
Norwegian (0)	17	0.17
Polish (14)	23	0.24
Portuguese (0)	8	0.08
Romanian (58)	124	1.27
Russian (0)	19	0.19
Scandinavian (25)	74	0.76
Scotch-Irish (159)	295	3.03
Scottish (168)	308	3.16
Swedish (11)	72	0.74

*Notes: † The Census 2010 population figure is used to calculate the percentages in the Hispanic Origin and Race categories. Ancestry percentages are based on the 2006-2010 American Community Survey population (not shown); ‡ Numbers in parentheses indicate the number of people reporting a single ancestry; * Numbers in parentheses indicate the number of persons reporting this race alone, not in combination with any other race; Please refer to the Explanation of Data for more information.*

Swiss (0)	9	0.09
Welsh (35)	111	1.14

Hispanic Origin	Population	%
Hispanic or Latino (of any race)	168	1.71
Central American, ex. Mexican	9	0.09
Costa Rican	1	0.01
Guatemalan	4	0.04
Honduran	1	0.01
Panamanian	2	0.02
Salvadoran	1	0.01
Cuban	5	0.05
Mexican	107	1.09
Puerto Rican	17	0.17
South American	12	0.12
Argentinean	1	0.01
Chilean	1	0.01
Colombian	10	0.10
Other Hispanic or Latino	18	0.18

Race*	Population	%
African-American/Black (199)	295	3.00
Not Hispanic (193)	286	2.91
Hispanic (6)	9	0.09
American Indian/Alaska Native (33)	98	1.00
Not Hispanic (31)	90	0.91
Hispanic (2)	8	0.08
Blackfeet (0)	6	0.06
Central American Ind. (1)	1	0.01
Cherokee (13)	50	0.51
Chippewa (2)	2	0.02
Choctaw (2)	4	0.04
Lumbee (1)	1	0.01
Navajo (1)	1	0.01
Seminole (0)	1	0.01
Sioux (2)	8	0.08
Asian (50)	74	0.75
Not Hispanic (50)	72	0.73
Hispanic (0)	2	0.02
Cambodian (0)	1	0.01
Chinese, ex. Taiwanese (4)	13	0.13
Filipino (6)	15	0.15
Indian (19)	23	0.23
Japanese (3)	5	0.05
Korean (3)	9	0.09
Pakistani (4)	4	0.04
Taiwanese (2)	2	0.02
Vietnamese (2)	4	0.04
Hawaii Native/Pacific Islander (4)	8	0.08
Not Hispanic (3)	6	0.06
Hispanic (1)	2	0.02
Guamanian/Chamorro (1)	2	0.02
Samoan (3)	3	0.03
White (9,341)	9,519	96.73
Not Hispanic (9,225)	9,389	95.41
Hispanic (116)	130	1.32

Collegedale

Place Type: City
County: Hamilton
Population: 8,282†

Ancestry‡	Population	%
African, Sub-Saharan (34)	45	0.57
African (13)	14	0.18
Nigerian (0)	10	0.13
South African (21)	21	0.26
American (1,161)	1,161	14.63
Armenian (0)	10	0.13
Austrian (0)	16	0.20
Belgian (9)	9	0.11
Brazilian (0)	13	0.16
British (63)	114	1.44
Canadian (34)	51	0.64
Danish (17)	56	0.71
Dutch (25)	50	0.63
English (665)	1,075	13.54
European (155)	215	2.71
French, ex. Basque (61)	359	4.52
French Canadian (11)	25	0.31
German (409)	1,307	16.47
Greek (0)	46	0.58
Hungarian (11)	28	0.35
Irish (435)	1,098	13.83
Italian (31)	106	1.34
Lithuanian (0)	8	0.10
Norwegian (34)	75	0.94
Polish (11)	87	1.10
Romanian (0)	42	0.53
Russian (0)	1	0.01
Scandinavian (8)	17	0.21
Scotch-Irish (80)	125	1.57
Scottish (12)	97	1.22
Swedish (65)	245	3.09
Swiss (0)	86	1.08
Ukrainian (0)	5	0.06
Welsh (14)	26	0.33
West Indian, ex. Hispanic (196)	240	3.02
Barbadian (0)	10	0.13
British West Indian (0)	21	0.26
Haitian (137)	137	1.73
Jamaican (24)	36	0.45
Trinidadian/Tobagonian (18)	19	0.24
West Indian (17)	17	0.21
Yugoslavian (85)	85	1.07

Hispanic Origin	Population	%
Hispanic or Latino (of any race)	1,027	12.40
Central American, ex. Mexican	77	0.93
Costa Rican	5	0.06
Guatemalan	23	0.28
Honduran	19	0.23
Nicaraguan	3	0.04
Panamanian	7	0.08
Salvadoran	16	0.19
Other Central American	4	0.05
Cuban	58	0.70
Dominican Republic	98	1.18
Mexican	162	1.96
Puerto Rican	142	1.71
South American	151	1.82
Argentinean	12	0.14
Bolivian	1	0.01
Chilean	11	0.13
Colombian	47	0.57
Ecuadorian	13	0.16
Peruvian	47	0.57
Uruguayan	8	0.10
Venezuelan	12	0.14
Other Hispanic or Latino	339	4.09

Race*	Population	%
African-American/Black (603)	658	7.94
Not Hispanic (550)	593	7.16
Hispanic (53)	65	0.78
American Indian/Alaska Native (37)	110	1.33
Not Hispanic (29)	89	1.07
Hispanic (8)	21	0.25
Apache (1)	6	0.07
Central American Ind. (0)	1	0.01
Cherokee (9)	43	0.52
Chippewa (2)	2	0.02
Choctaw (0)	2	0.02
Cree (0)	2	0.02
Creek (4)	5	0.06
Crow (0)	1	0.01
Iroquois (0)	2	0.02
Kiowa (1)	2	0.02
Mexican American Ind. (3)	5	0.06
Sioux (1)	2	0.02
South American Ind. (1)	1	0.01
Asian (336)	383	4.62
Not Hispanic (334)	377	4.55
Hispanic (2)	6	0.07
Cambodian (2)	3	0.04
Chinese, ex. Taiwanese (29)	38	0.46
Filipino (36)	58	0.70
Indian (42)	50	0.60
Indonesian (3)	3	0.04
Japanese (9)	19	0.23
Korean (55)	55	0.66
Laotian (5)	5	0.06
Taiwanese (1)	1	0.01
Thai (5)	5	0.06
Vietnamese (10)	10	0.12
Hawaii Native/Pacific Islander (25)	33	0.40
Not Hispanic (20)	21	0.25
Hispanic (5)	12	0.14
Guamanian/Chamorro (7)	7	0.08
Marshallese (5)	5	0.06
Native Hawaiian (10)	10	0.12
White (6,791)	6,960	84.04
Not Hispanic (6,173)	6,298	76.04
Hispanic (618)	662	7.99

Collierville

Place Type: Town
County: Shelby
Population: 43,965†

Ancestry‡	Population	%
African, Sub-Saharan (37)	105	0.25
African (37)	93	0.22
South African (0)	12	0.03
Albanian (0)	10	0.02
American (4,671)	4,671	11.13
Arab (125)	215	0.51
Arab (51)	81	0.19
Lebanese (0)	38	0.09
Palestinian (54)	54	0.13
Other Arab (20)	42	0.10
Armenian (12)	12	0.03
Australian (0)	11	0.03
Austrian (10)	10	0.02
Belgian (7)	18	0.04
Brazilian (91)	91	0.22
British (84)	166	0.40
Canadian (78)	112	0.27
Croatian (12)	25	0.06
Czech (50)	93	0.22
Czechoslovakian (16)	36	0.09
Danish (40)	128	0.30
Dutch (201)	748	1.78
Eastern European (11)	11	0.03
English (2,901)	5,642	13.44
European (530)	639	1.52
Finnish (0)	53	0.13
French, ex. Basque (167)	1,199	2.86
French Canadian (163)	213	0.51
German (2,610)	7,050	16.79
Greek (106)	162	0.39
Hungarian (51)	158	0.38
Irish (2,024)	5,787	13.78
Italian (737)	1,841	4.39
Lithuanian (8)	8	0.02
Northern European (24)	24	0.06
Norwegian (157)	521	1.24
Polish (185)	847	2.02
Portuguese (36)	36	0.09
Russian (142)	315	0.75
Scandinavian (28)	49	0.12
Scotch-Irish (1,084)	1,808	4.31
Scottish (376)	921	2.19
Slavic (0)	11	0.03
Slovak (6)	59	0.14
Swedish (152)	489	1.16
Swiss (36)	132	0.31
Ukrainian (18)	59	0.14
Welsh (59)	342	0.81
West Indian, ex. Hispanic (34)	49	0.12
Barbadian (18)	33	0.08
Jamaican (16)	16	0.04

Hispanic Origin	Population	%
Hispanic or Latino (of any race)	1,154	2.62
Central American, ex. Mexican	96	0.22
Costa Rican	14	0.03
Guatemalan	31	0.07

*Notes: † The Census 2010 population figure is used to calculate the percentages in the Hispanic Origin and Race categories. Ancestry percentages are based on the 2006-2010 American Community Survey population (not shown); ‡ Numbers in parentheses indicate the number of people reporting a single ancestry; * Numbers in parentheses indicate the number of persons reporting this race alone, not in combination with any other race; Please refer to the Explanation of Data for more information.*

Honduran	17	0.04
Nicaraguan	4	0.01
Panamanian	9	0.02
Salvadoran	21	0.05
Cuban	40	0.09
Dominican Republic	18	0.04
Mexican	687	1.56
Puerto Rican	105	0.24
South American	94	0.21
Argentinean	18	0.04
Bolivian	8	0.02
Chilean	1	<0.01
Colombian	19	0.04
Ecuadorian	8	0.02
Peruvian	19	0.04
Venezuelan	19	0.04
Other South American	2	<0.01
Other Hispanic or Latino	114	0.26

Race*	Population	%
African-American/Black (4,771)	4,933	11.22
Not Hispanic (4,740)	4,873	11.08
Hispanic (31)	60	0.14
American Indian/Alaska Native (69)	216	0.49
Not Hispanic (64)	201	0.46
Hispanic (5)	15	0.03
Apache (0)	5	0.01
Blackfeet (0)	8	0.02
Canadian/French Am. Ind. (0)	2	<0.01
Cherokee (20)	53	0.12
Cheyenne (0)	1	<0.01
Chickasaw (2)	7	0.02
Chippewa (0)	3	0.01
Choctaw (5)	15	0.03
Colville (1)	1	<0.01
Delaware (3)	3	0.01
Iroquois (0)	1	<0.01
Mexican American Ind. (0)	1	<0.01
Navajo (1)	1	<0.01
Osage (0)	1	<0.01
Potawatomi (1)	1	<0.01
Sioux (2)	9	0.02
South American Ind. (2)	2	<0.01
Tsimshian *(Alaska Native)* (0)	4	0.01
Asian (3,123)	3,422	7.78
Not Hispanic (3,111)	3,383	7.69
Hispanic (12)	39	0.09
Bangladeshi (4)	5	0.01
Burmese (4)	4	0.01
Cambodian (3)	7	0.02
Chinese, ex. Taiwanese (523)	569	1.29
Filipino (84)	130	0.30
Indian (1,538)	1,599	3.64
Indonesian (9)	11	0.03
Japanese (52)	93	0.21
Korean (472)	510	1.16
Laotian (10)	11	0.03
Malaysian (3)	10	0.02
Pakistani (202)	221	0.50
Sri Lankan (6)	12	0.03
Taiwanese (9)	9	0.02
Thai (12)	18	0.04
Vietnamese (114)	135	0.31
Hawaii Native/Pacific Islander (13)	25	0.06
Not Hispanic (12)	24	0.05
Hispanic (1)	1	<0.01
Guamanian/Chamorro (2)	3	0.01
Native Hawaiian (7)	16	0.04
Samoan (3)	3	0.01
White (35,035)	35,496	80.74
Not Hispanic (34,344)	34,731	79.00
Hispanic (691)	765	1.74

Columbia

Place Type: City
County: Maury
Population: 34,681†

Ancestry‡	Population	%
African, Sub-Saharan (56)	56	0.16
African (56)	56	0.16
American (6,485)	6,485	18.81
Arab (21)	21	0.06
Other Arab (21)	21	0.06
Australian (0)	12	0.03
British (38)	106	0.31
Canadian (14)	50	0.15
Czech (0)	22	0.06
Dutch (44)	246	0.71
Eastern European (11)	11	0.03
English (1,724)	3,301	9.57
European (155)	155	0.45
French, ex. Basque (291)	985	2.86
French Canadian (69)	162	0.47
German (919)	3,100	8.99
Greek (36)	72	0.21
Hungarian (25)	25	0.07
Irish (1,238)	3,754	10.89
Italian (266)	735	2.13
Lithuanian (0)	20	0.06
Norwegian (114)	211	0.61
Polish (132)	374	1.08
Portuguese (0)	11	0.03
Russian (16)	16	0.05
Scandinavian (11)	24	0.07
Scotch-Irish (416)	691	2.00
Scottish (430)	850	2.47
Swedish (25)	94	0.27
Swiss (21)	33	0.10
Ukrainian (0)	70	0.20
Welsh (87)	303	0.88
West Indian, ex. Hispanic (17)	17	0.05
Jamaican (17)	17	0.05
Yugoslavian (53)	53	0.15

Hispanic Origin	Population	%
Hispanic or Latino (of any race)	2,433	7.02
Central American, ex. Mexican	155	0.45
Costa Rican	10	0.03
Guatemalan	95	0.27
Honduran	9	0.03
Nicaraguan	15	0.04
Panamanian	8	0.02
Salvadoran	18	0.05
Cuban	70	0.20
Dominican Republic	44	0.13
Mexican	1,846	5.32
Puerto Rican	152	0.44
South American	67	0.19
Argentinean	6	0.02
Bolivian	1	<0.01
Chilean	4	0.01
Colombian	28	0.08
Ecuadorian	7	0.02
Paraguayan	4	0.01
Peruvian	11	0.03
Venezuelan	6	0.02
Other Hispanic or Latino	99	0.29

Race*	Population	%
African-American/Black (7,205)	7,702	22.21
Not Hispanic (7,153)	7,628	21.99
Hispanic (52)	74	0.21
American Indian/Alaska Native (109)	284	0.82
Not Hispanic (87)	242	0.70
Hispanic (22)	42	0.12
Apache (1)	2	0.01
Blackfeet (6)	19	0.05
Central American Ind. (0)	1	<0.01
Cherokee (26)	83	0.24
Cheyenne (0)	1	<0.01
Chickasaw (1)	3	0.01
Chippewa (7)	7	0.02
Choctaw (3)	9	0.03
Cree (1)	2	0.01
Creek (1)	4	0.01
Houma (0)	2	0.01
Iroquois (1)	4	0.01
Lumbee (4)	5	0.01
Mexican American Ind. (8)	9	0.03
Navajo (4)	4	0.01
Potawatomi (0)	1	<0.01
Seminole (0)	1	<0.01
Sioux (1)	3	0.01
South American Ind. (1)	4	0.01
Asian (267)	359	1.04
Not Hispanic (265)	344	0.99
Hispanic (2)	15	0.04
Chinese, ex. Taiwanese (32)	38	0.11
Filipino (53)	81	0.23
Indian (111)	124	0.36
Indonesian (1)	3	0.01
Japanese (10)	18	0.05
Korean (11)	18	0.05
Laotian (1)	8	0.02
Sri Lankan (4)	4	0.01
Thai (1)	2	0.01
Vietnamese (27)	29	0.08
Hawaii Native/Pacific Islander (5)	16	0.05
Not Hispanic (5)	13	0.04
Hispanic (0)	3	0.01
Native Hawaiian (1)	3	0.01
Samoan (2)	3	0.01
White (25,005)	25,793	74.37
Not Hispanic (24,038)	24,665	71.12
Hispanic (967)	1,128	3.25

Cookeville

Place Type: City
County: Putnam
Population: 30,435†

Ancestry‡	Population	%
African, Sub-Saharan (53)	53	0.18
Nigerian (10)	10	0.03
South African (20)	20	0.07
Other Sub-Saharan African (23)	23	0.08
American (8,005)	8,005	26.93
Arab (0)	15	0.05
Lebanese (0)	15	0.05
Armenian (0)	10	0.03
Assyrian/Chaldean/Syriac (0)	16	0.05
Austrian (0)	30	0.10
Belgian (0)	10	0.03
Brazilian (12)	12	0.04
British (155)	246	0.83
Cajun (21)	21	0.07
Canadian (73)	91	0.31
Czech (0)	21	0.07
Czechoslovakian (0)	7	0.02
Danish (0)	13	0.04
Dutch (43)	201	0.68
Eastern European (50)	50	0.17
English (1,406)	2,657	8.94
European (274)	321	1.08
Finnish (7)	7	0.02
French, ex. Basque (138)	369	1.24
French Canadian (49)	64	0.22
German (742)	2,259	7.60
Greek (11)	28	0.09
Hungarian (30)	76	0.26
Irish (1,201)	3,057	10.29
Italian (268)	508	1.71
Norwegian (29)	81	0.27
Polish (130)	462	1.55
Portuguese (35)	35	0.12
Romanian (0)	21	0.07
Russian (11)	60	0.20
Scandinavian (0)	21	0.07
Scotch-Irish (560)	910	3.06
Scottish (214)	477	1.60
Slovak (0)	57	0.19
Swedish (37)	146	0.49
Swiss (0)	9	0.03
Turkish (6)	6	0.02
Ukrainian (0)	12	0.04
Welsh (4)	66	0.22

SECTION TWO

*Notes: † The Census 2010 population figure is used to calculate the percentages in the Hispanic Origin and Race categories. Ancestry percentages are based on the 2006-2010 American Community Survey population (not shown); ‡ Numbers in parentheses indicate the number of people reporting a single ancestry; * Numbers in parentheses indicate the number of persons reporting this race alone, not in combination with any other race; Please refer to the Explanation of Data for more information.*

West Indian, ex. Hispanic (1)	1	<0.01
Jamaican (1)	1	<0.01

Hispanic Origin	Population	%
Hispanic or Latino (of any race)	2,132	7.01
Central American, ex. Mexican	652	2.14
Costa Rican	8	0.03
Guatemalan	564	1.85
Honduran	34	0.11
Nicaraguan	13	0.04
Panamanian	9	0.03
Salvadoran	24	0.08
Cuban	49	0.16
Dominican Republic	10	0.03
Mexican	1,106	3.63
Puerto Rican	101	0.33
South American	39	0.13
Argentinean	3	0.01
Chilean	2	0.01
Colombian	19	0.06
Ecuadorian	3	0.01
Peruvian	11	0.04
Venezuelan	1	<0.01
Other Hispanic or Latino	175	0.57

Race*	Population	%
African-American/Black (1,029)	1,292	4.25
Not Hispanic (1,005)	1,252	4.11
Hispanic (24)	40	0.13
American Indian/Alaska Native (171)	346	1.14
Not Hispanic (105)	259	0.85
Hispanic (66)	87	0.29
Aleut *(Alaska Native)* (0)	1	<0.01
Apache (1)	2	0.01
Blackfeet (2)	4	0.01
Canadian/French Am. Ind. (0)	2	0.01
Central American Ind. (7)	8	0.03
Cherokee (35)	116	0.38
Cheyenne (0)	1	<0.01
Chickasaw (2)	2	0.01
Chippewa (1)	3	0.01
Choctaw (1)	1	<0.01
Creek (1)	6	0.02
Crow (0)	1	<0.01
Inupiat *(Alaska Native)* (0)	1	<0.01
Iroquois (1)	1	<0.01
Lumbee (10)	11	0.04
Mexican American Ind. (32)	35	0.11
Navajo (2)	3	0.01
Ottawa (1)	1	<0.01
Potawatomi (1)	1	<0.01
Sioux (3)	15	0.05
South American Ind. (1)	1	<0.01
Ute (1)	1	<0.01
Yup'ik *(Alaska Native)* (4)	4	0.01
Asian (620)	750	2.46
Not Hispanic (618)	740	2.43
Hispanic (2)	10	0.03
Bangladeshi (7)	8	0.03
Cambodian (0)	1	<0.01
Chinese, ex. Taiwanese (115)	131	0.43
Filipino (58)	92	0.30
Indian (283)	302	0.99
Japanese (18)	35	0.11
Korean (44)	54	0.18
Laotian (4)	5	0.02
Nepalese (1)	1	<0.01
Pakistani (5)	5	0.02
Sri Lankan (4)	4	0.01
Taiwanese (7)	7	0.02
Thai (15)	21	0.07
Vietnamese (45)	50	0.16
Hawaii Native/Pacific Islander (22)	39	0.13
Not Hispanic (9)	24	0.08
Hispanic (13)	15	0.05
Guamanian/Chamorro (14)	15	0.05
Native Hawaiian (7)	13	0.04
Samoan (0)	6	0.02
White (26,738)	27,317	89.76
Not Hispanic (26,048)	26,512	87.11
Hispanic (690)	805	2.64

Covington

Place Type: City
County: Tipton
Population: 9,038†

Ancestry‡	Population	%
African, Sub-Saharan (73)	73	0.81
African (73)	73	0.81
American (1,933)	1,933	21.44
Arab (31)	31	0.34
Arab (31)	31	0.34
British (25)	36	0.40
Czech (11)	11	0.12
Dutch (8)	42	0.47
English (297)	550	6.10
French, ex. Basque (0)	33	0.37
German (91)	259	2.87
Irish (276)	521	5.78
Italian (161)	189	2.10
Lithuanian (4)	4	0.04
Russian (0)	16	0.18
Scotch-Irish (33)	109	1.21
Scottish (1)	49	0.54
Swedish (30)	38	0.42
Swiss (0)	3	0.03
Welsh (0)	22	0.24

Hispanic Origin	Population	%
Hispanic or Latino (of any race)	106	1.17
Central American, ex. Mexican	4	0.04
Nicaraguan	3	0.03
Salvadoran	1	0.01
Cuban	2	0.02
Dominican Republic	1	0.01
Mexican	75	0.83
Puerto Rican	7	0.08
South American	2	0.02
Venezuelan	2	0.02
Other Hispanic or Latino	15	0.17

Race*	Population	%
African-American/Black (4,612)	4,692	51.91
Not Hispanic (4,595)	4,675	51.73
Hispanic (17)	17	0.19
American Indian/Alaska Native (27)	67	0.74
Not Hispanic (24)	64	0.71
Hispanic (3)	3	0.03
Apache (1)	2	0.02
Blackfeet (0)	3	0.03
Cherokee (10)	24	0.27
Choctaw (1)	1	0.01
Asian (28)	43	0.48
Not Hispanic (28)	40	0.44
Hispanic (0)	3	0.03
Cambodian (11)	11	0.12
Chinese, ex. Taiwanese (6)	7	0.08
Filipino (2)	6	0.07
Indian (5)	7	0.08
Japanese (1)	5	0.06
Korean (1)	2	0.02
Thai (2)	2	0.02
Hawaii Native/Pacific Islander (4)	8	0.09
Not Hispanic (4)	8	0.09
Guamanian/Chamorro (3)	3	0.03
Native Hawaiian (1)	1	0.01
White (4,204)	4,296	47.53
Not Hispanic (4,157)	4,242	46.94
Hispanic (47)	54	0.60

Crossville

Place Type: City
County: Cumberland
Population: 10,795†

Ancestry‡	Population	%
American (2,255)	2,255	21.22
British (0)	15	0.14
Czech (14)	26	0.24
Danish (0)	23	0.22
Dutch (108)	197	1.85
Eastern European (14)	14	0.13
English (868)	1,609	15.14
European (107)	107	1.01
French, ex. Basque (12)	208	1.96
French Canadian (30)	54	0.51
German (353)	1,135	10.68
Greek (0)	43	0.40
Hungarian (0)	67	0.63
Irish (358)	1,205	11.34
Italian (12)	159	1.50
Norwegian (0)	15	0.14
Polish (77)	155	1.46
Russian (17)	79	0.74
Scandinavian (14)	14	0.13
Scotch-Irish (107)	215	2.02
Scottish (125)	247	2.32
Slovak (59)	75	0.71
Swedish (41)	64	0.60
Welsh (26)	26	0.24

Hispanic Origin	Population	%
Hispanic or Latino (of any race)	597	5.53
Central American, ex. Mexican	75	0.69
Guatemalan	60	0.56
Honduran	10	0.09
Salvadoran	5	0.05
Cuban	14	0.13
Mexican	401	3.71
Puerto Rican	39	0.36
South American	14	0.13
Colombian	7	0.06
Peruvian	4	0.04
Venezuelan	3	0.03
Other Hispanic or Latino	54	0.50

Race*	Population	%
African-American/Black (53)	96	0.89
Not Hispanic (44)	78	0.72
Hispanic (9)	18	0.17
American Indian/Alaska Native (61)	117	1.08
Not Hispanic (49)	103	0.95
Hispanic (12)	14	0.13
Blackfeet (0)	2	0.02
Cherokee (24)	46	0.43
Chippewa (1)	2	0.02
Choctaw (2)	5	0.05
Comanche (0)	1	0.01
Creek (0)	2	0.02
Iroquois (0)	2	0.02
Kiowa (1)	1	0.01
Lumbee (0)	3	0.03
Osage (1)	1	0.01
Sioux (2)	5	0.05
Asian (99)	118	1.09
Not Hispanic (98)	115	1.07
Hispanic (1)	3	0.03
Chinese, ex. Taiwanese (28)	30	0.28
Filipino (11)	14	0.13
Indian (36)	39	0.36
Japanese (2)	6	0.06
Korean (3)	5	0.05
Thai (4)	4	0.04
Vietnamese (13)	13	0.12
Hawaii Native/Pacific Islander (23)	27	0.25
Not Hispanic (12)	12	0.11
Hispanic (11)	15	0.14
Guamanian/Chamorro (17)	17	0.16
White (10,093)	10,238	94.84
Not Hispanic (9,882)	9,986	92.51
Hispanic (211)	252	2.33

Dickson

Place Type: City
County: Dickson
Population: 14,538†

*Notes: † The Census 2010 population figure is used to calculate the percentages in the Hispanic Origin and Race categories. Ancestry percentages are based on the 2006-2010 American Community Survey population (not shown); ‡ Numbers in parentheses indicate the number of people reporting a single ancestry; * Numbers in parentheses indicate the number of persons reporting this race alone, not in combination with any other race; Please refer to the Explanation of Data for more information.*

Ancestry‡	Population	%
African, Sub-Saharan (0)	33	0.23
African (0)	33	0.23
American (2,207)	2,207	15.43
Arab (35)	35	0.24
Arab (35)	35	0.24
Belgian (0)	12	0.08
British (9)	23	0.16
Canadian (56)	56	0.39
Czech (13)	13	0.09
Czechoslovakian (2)	2	0.01
Dutch (13)	218	1.52
English (956)	2,602	18.20
European (35)	58	0.41
Finnish (10)	10	0.07
French, ex. Basque (15)	320	2.24
French Canadian (4)	4	0.03
German (453)	1,694	11.85
Irish (993)	2,706	18.92
Italian (220)	398	2.78
Northern European (25)	33	0.23
Norwegian (18)	44	0.31
Polish (0)	33	0.23
Russian (9)	18	0.13
Scotch-Irish (339)	556	3.89
Scottish (113)	311	2.17
Slovak (11)	11	0.08
Swedish (34)	34	0.24
Welsh (21)	71	0.50
West Indian, ex. Hispanic (10)	10	0.07
Bahamian (10)	10	0.07

Hispanic Origin	Population	%
Hispanic or Latino (of any race)	866	5.96
Central American, ex. Mexican	28	0.19
Guatemalan	15	0.10
Panamanian	1	0.01
Salvadoran	12	0.08
Cuban	25	0.17
Dominican Republic	1	0.01
Mexican	674	4.64
Puerto Rican	61	0.42
South American	7	0.05
Argentinean	1	0.01
Chilean	1	0.01
Colombian	3	0.02
Peruvian	1	0.01
Other South American	1	0.01
Other Hispanic or Latino	70	0.48

Race*	Population	%
African-American/Black (1,280)	1,537	10.57
Not Hispanic (1,266)	1,501	10.32
Hispanic (14)	36	0.25
American Indian/Alaska Native (51)	138	0.95
Not Hispanic (46)	125	0.86
Hispanic (5)	13	0.09
Blackfeet (2)	4	0.03
Canadian/French Am. Ind. (3)	3	0.02
Cherokee (9)	31	0.21
Cheyenne (0)	2	0.01
Choctaw (8)	8	0.06
Crow (1)	1	0.01
Delaware (3)	3	0.02
Iroquois (0)	6	0.04
Kiowa (0)	1	0.01
Menominee (2)	2	0.01
Mexican American Ind. (5)	6	0.04
Navajo (1)	2	0.01
Pueblo (0)	1	0.01
Tlingit-Haida *(Alaska Native)* (1)	1	0.01
Asian (119)	148	1.02
Not Hispanic (108)	133	0.91
Hispanic (11)	15	0.10
Cambodian (8)	8	0.06
Chinese, ex. Taiwanese (11)	15	0.10
Filipino (20)	26	0.18
Indian (57)	59	0.41
Indonesian (1)	1	0.01
Japanese (0)	1	0.01
Korean (14)	27	0.19
Vietnamese (7)	7	0.05
Hawaii Native/Pacific Islander (13)	20	0.14
Not Hispanic (12)	15	0.10
Hispanic (1)	5	0.03
Guamanian/Chamorro (8)	8	0.06
Native Hawaiian (0)	4	0.03
Samoan (5)	6	0.04
White (12,230)	12,597	86.65
Not Hispanic (11,893)	12,205	83.95
Hispanic (337)	392	2.70

Dyersburg

Place Type: City
County: Dyer
Population: 17,145†

Ancestry‡	Population	%
African, Sub-Saharan (262)	297	1.73
African (262)	297	1.73
American (2,004)	2,004	11.64
Arab (65)	65	0.38
Arab (9)	9	0.05
Iraqi (21)	21	0.12
Other Arab (35)	35	0.20
Austrian (0)	10	0.06
British (68)	68	0.40
Dutch (20)	213	1.24
English (436)	1,033	6.00
European (94)	94	0.55
French, ex. Basque (33)	146	0.85
French Canadian (32)	32	0.19
German (305)	978	5.68
Iranian (25)	25	0.15
Irish (540)	1,271	7.38
Italian (17)	34	0.20
Norwegian (28)	28	0.16
Polish (0)	174	1.01
Russian (23)	23	0.13
Scotch-Irish (151)	233	1.35
Scottish (43)	132	0.77
Swedish (0)	23	0.13
Welsh (14)	14	0.08
West Indian, ex. Hispanic (0)	14	0.08
Dutch West Indian (0)	14	0.08

Hispanic Origin	Population	%
Hispanic or Latino (of any race)	513	2.99
Central American, ex. Mexican	14	0.08
Guatemalan	3	0.02
Honduran	3	0.02
Panamanian	3	0.02
Salvadoran	5	0.03
Cuban	3	0.02
Dominican Republic	2	0.01
Mexican	389	2.27
Puerto Rican	44	0.26
South American	14	0.08
Argentinean	5	0.03
Colombian	3	0.02
Ecuadorian	4	0.02
Peruvian	1	0.01
Other South American	1	0.01
Other Hispanic or Latino	47	0.27

Race*	Population	%
African-American/Black (4,442)	4,696	27.39
Not Hispanic (4,404)	4,652	27.13
Hispanic (38)	44	0.26
American Indian/Alaska Native (32)	107	0.62
Not Hispanic (25)	95	0.55
Hispanic (7)	12	0.07
Apache (1)	3	0.02
Cherokee (3)	20	0.12
Chickasaw (0)	2	0.01
Choctaw (1)	3	0.02
Kiowa (0)	1	0.01
Navajo (0)	1	0.01
Tohono O'Odham (2)	5	0.03
Asian (130)	160	0.93
Not Hispanic (130)	155	0.90
Hispanic (0)	5	0.03
Chinese, ex. Taiwanese (29)	32	0.19
Filipino (37)	43	0.25
Indian (33)	45	0.26
Japanese (4)	6	0.03
Korean (11)	12	0.07
Nepalese (2)	2	0.01
Pakistani (5)	5	0.03
Thai (1)	1	0.01
Vietnamese (3)	6	0.03
Hawaii Native/Pacific Islander (4)	7	0.04
Not Hispanic (4)	7	0.04
Guamanian/Chamorro (1)	1	0.01
Native Hawaiian (1)	3	0.02
Samoan (2)	2	0.01
White (11,923)	12,277	71.61
Not Hispanic (11,730)	12,031	70.17
Hispanic (193)	246	1.43

East Ridge

Place Type: City
County: Hamilton
Population: 20,979†

Ancestry‡	Population	%
African, Sub-Saharan (35)	35	0.17
Kenyan (35)	35	0.17
American (3,997)	3,997	19.24
Arab (22)	22	0.11
Other Arab (22)	22	0.11
Australian (34)	34	0.16
Brazilian (0)	14	0.07
British (21)	69	0.33
Canadian (0)	11	0.05
Czech (0)	43	0.21
Czechoslovakian (14)	14	0.07
Dutch (62)	253	1.22
Eastern European (12)	12	0.06
English (996)	2,520	12.13
European (80)	93	0.45
French, ex. Basque (19)	242	1.16
French Canadian (43)	43	0.21
German (633)	2,354	11.33
Greek (15)	27	0.13
Irish (1,135)	2,989	14.39
Italian (45)	213	1.03
Norwegian (41)	50	0.24
Polish (107)	325	1.56
Portuguese (22)	55	0.26
Russian (59)	71	0.34
Scandinavian (0)	10	0.05
Scotch-Irish (334)	464	2.23
Scottish (169)	855	4.11
Slovak (9)	9	0.04
Swedish (18)	92	0.44
Swiss (0)	40	0.19
Ukrainian (12)	12	0.06
Welsh (14)	89	0.43
West Indian, ex. Hispanic (17)	30	0.14
Bahamian (17)	30	0.14
Yugoslavian (674)	692	3.33

Hispanic Origin	Population	%
Hispanic or Latino (of any race)	1,050	5.01
Central American, ex. Mexican	329	1.57
Costa Rican	3	0.01
Guatemalan	287	1.37
Honduran	11	0.05
Nicaraguan	4	0.02
Panamanian	1	<0.01
Salvadoran	21	0.10
Other Central American	2	0.01
Cuban	22	0.10
Dominican Republic	3	0.01
Mexican	495	2.36
Puerto Rican	71	0.34
South American	28	0.13

*Notes: † The Census 2010 population figure is used to calculate the percentages in the Hispanic Origin and Race categories. Ancestry percentages are based on the 2006-2010 American Community Survey population (not shown); ‡ Numbers in parentheses indicate the number of people reporting a single ancestry; * Numbers in parentheses indicate the number of persons reporting this race alone, not in combination with any other race; Please refer to the Explanation of Data for more information.*

Argentinean	2	0.01
Bolivian	4	0.02
Chilean	1	<0.01
Colombian	4	0.02
Ecuadorian	12	0.06
Paraguayan	3	0.01
Peruvian	2	0.01
Other Hispanic or Latino	102	0.49

Race*	Population	%
African-American/Black (2,071)	2,234	10.65
Not Hispanic (2,050)	2,199	10.48
Hispanic (21)	35	0.17
American Indian/Alaska Native (102)	262	1.25
Not Hispanic (55)	190	0.91
Hispanic (47)	72	0.34
Aleut *(Alaska Native)* (0)	1	<0.01
Apache (1)	5	0.02
Central American Ind. (19)	19	0.09
Cherokee (24)	93	0.44
Cheyenne (1)	1	<0.01
Chippewa (2)	7	0.03
Choctaw (2)	2	0.01
Creek (1)	4	0.02
Iroquois (1)	7	0.03
Kiowa (1)	1	<0.01
Mexican American Ind. (24)	28	0.13
Ottawa (1)	1	<0.01
Seminole (0)	1	<0.01
Sioux (2)	4	0.02
South American Ind. (1)	4	0.02
Asian (372)	455	2.17
Not Hispanic (372)	448	2.14
Hispanic (0)	7	0.03
Cambodian (53)	54	0.26
Chinese, ex. Taiwanese (56)	59	0.28
Filipino (24)	36	0.17
Indian (117)	134	0.64
Indonesian (5)	5	0.02
Japanese (7)	18	0.09
Korean (24)	35	0.17
Laotian (31)	42	0.20
Pakistani (9)	12	0.06
Sri Lankan (1)	1	<0.01
Taiwanese (4)	4	0.02
Thai (9)	10	0.05
Vietnamese (29)	32	0.15
Hawaii Native/Pacific Islander (33)	49	0.23
Not Hispanic (4)	11	0.05
Hispanic (29)	38	0.18
Guamanian/Chamorro (32)	37	0.18
Native Hawaiian (0)	10	0.05
Samoan (1)	2	0.01
White (17,497)	17,853	85.10
Not Hispanic (17,086)	17,378	82.84
Hispanic (411)	475	2.26

Elizabethton

Place Type: City
County: Carter
Population: 14,176†

Ancestry‡	Population	%
African, Sub-Saharan (36)	36	0.25
African (21)	21	0.15
South African (8)	8	0.06
Other Sub-Saharan African (7)	7	0.05
American (3,272)	3,272	22.87
British (22)	22	0.15
Cajun (1)	1	0.01
Canadian (0)	12	0.08
Czech (62)	62	0.43
Danish (0)	25	0.17
Dutch (56)	369	2.58
English (805)	1,205	8.42
European (102)	109	0.76
Finnish (11)	48	0.34
French, ex. Basque (110)	271	1.89
French Canadian (0)	44	0.31
German (797)	2,008	14.04
Greek (10)	56	0.39
Hungarian (11)	17	0.12
Irish (697)	1,807	12.63
Italian (158)	278	1.94
Pennsylvania German (0)	12	0.08
Polish (22)	45	0.31
Portuguese (0)	13	0.09
Scandinavian (13)	39	0.27
Scotch-Irish (391)	579	4.05
Scottish (256)	456	3.19
Swedish (44)	81	0.57
Swiss (0)	20	0.14
Welsh (8)	29	0.20

Hispanic Origin	Population	%
Hispanic or Latino (of any race)	281	1.98
Central American, ex. Mexican	5	0.04
Guatemalan	2	0.01
Honduran	1	0.01
Salvadoran	2	0.01
Cuban	7	0.05
Dominican Republic	3	0.02
Mexican	178	1.26
Puerto Rican	30	0.21
South American	15	0.11
Argentinean	3	0.02
Chilean	4	0.03
Colombian	5	0.04
Peruvian	3	0.02
Other Hispanic or Latino	43	0.30

Race*	Population	%
African-American/Black (440)	543	3.83
Not Hispanic (436)	535	3.77
Hispanic (4)	8	0.06
American Indian/Alaska Native (14)	88	0.62
Not Hispanic (14)	81	0.57
Hispanic (0)	7	0.05
Blackfeet (0)	1	0.01
Cherokee (6)	50	0.35
Choctaw (0)	2	0.01
Lumbee (1)	3	0.02
Navajo (0)	1	0.01
Sioux (1)	1	0.01
Asian (90)	110	0.78
Not Hispanic (90)	108	0.76
Hispanic (0)	2	0.01
Chinese, ex. Taiwanese (12)	16	0.11
Filipino (19)	25	0.18
Indian (24)	30	0.21
Indonesian (2)	2	0.01
Japanese (4)	6	0.04
Korean (1)	2	0.01
Laotian (17)	17	0.12
Taiwanese (0)	1	0.01
Thai (3)	3	0.02
Vietnamese (2)	2	0.01
Hawaii Native/Pacific Islander (3)	10	0.07
Not Hispanic (3)	8	0.06
Hispanic (0)	2	0.01
Native Hawaiian (2)	8	0.06
White (13,332)	13,538	95.50
Not Hispanic (13,148)	13,324	93.99
Hispanic (184)	214	1.51

Fairview

Place Type: City
County: Williamson
Population: 7,720†

Ancestry‡	Population	%
American (1,107)	1,107	14.76
Arab (50)	55	0.73
Iraqi (50)	50	0.67
Palestinian (0)	5	0.07
Celtic (0)	17	0.23
Czech (32)	32	0.43
Dutch (16)	124	1.65
English (934)	1,637	21.83
European (164)	194	2.59
French, ex. Basque (49)	258	3.44
German (385)	936	12.48
Greek (11)	11	0.15
Hungarian (0)	11	0.15
Iranian (49)	49	0.65
Irish (388)	1,102	14.69
Italian (58)	339	4.52
Norwegian (8)	49	0.65
Polish (33)	80	1.07
Portuguese (0)	13	0.17
Scotch-Irish (43)	287	3.83
Scottish (41)	157	2.09
Swedish (16)	115	1.53
Swiss (0)	5	0.07
Ukrainian (0)	42	0.56
Welsh (27)	136	1.81
West Indian, ex. Hispanic (5)	5	0.07
U.S. Virgin Islander (5)	5	0.07

Hispanic Origin	Population	%
Hispanic or Latino (of any race)	217	2.81
Central American, ex. Mexican	6	0.08
Costa Rican	2	0.03
Guatemalan	1	0.01
Honduran	2	0.03
Nicaraguan	1	0.01
Cuban	10	0.13
Dominican Republic	3	0.04
Mexican	151	1.96
Puerto Rican	27	0.35
South American	11	0.14
Argentinean	1	0.01
Chilean	2	0.03
Colombian	2	0.03
Paraguayan	1	0.01
Peruvian	3	0.04
Venezuelan	2	0.03
Other Hispanic or Latino	9	0.12

Race*	Population	%
African-American/Black (83)	120	1.55
Not Hispanic (80)	108	1.40
Hispanic (3)	12	0.16
American Indian/Alaska Native (33)	59	0.76
Not Hispanic (29)	52	0.67
Hispanic (4)	7	0.09
Apache (1)	1	0.01
Blackfeet (0)	1	0.01
Cherokee (7)	16	0.21
Choctaw (1)	1	0.01
Delaware (1)	1	0.01
Hopi (1)	1	0.01
Iroquois (3)	7	0.09
Lumbee (1)	1	0.01
Seminole (3)	4	0.05
Shoshone (1)	1	0.01
Asian (48)	67	0.87
Not Hispanic (47)	66	0.85
Hispanic (1)	1	0.01
Cambodian (1)	3	0.04
Chinese, ex. Taiwanese (10)	11	0.14
Filipino (6)	10	0.13
Indian (12)	16	0.21
Japanese (1)	2	0.03
Korean (8)	12	0.16
Laotian (0)	2	0.03
Malaysian (0)	1	0.01
Pakistani (4)	4	0.05
Thai (0)	1	0.01
Vietnamese (2)	2	0.03
Hawaii Native/Pacific Islander (7)	13	0.17
Not Hispanic (7)	10	0.13
Hispanic (0)	3	0.04
Native Hawaiian (4)	10	0.13
White (7,392)	7,493	97.06
Not Hispanic (7,262)	7,334	95.00
Hispanic (130)	159	2.06

*Notes: † The Census 2010 population figure is used to calculate the percentages in the Hispanic Origin and Race categories. Ancestry percentages are based on the 2006-2010 American Community Survey population (not shown); ‡ Numbers in parentheses indicate the number of people reporting a single ancestry; * Numbers in parentheses indicate the number of persons reporting this race alone, not in combination with any other race; Please refer to the Explanation of Data for more information.*

Farragut

Place Type: Town
County: Knox
Population: 20,676†

Ancestry‡	Population	%
African, Sub-Saharan (0)	13	0.06
African (0)	13	0.06
American (2,203)	2,203	10.93
Arab (101)	144	0.71
Lebanese (101)	144	0.71
Belgian (6)	13	0.06
British (129)	363	1.80
Canadian (13)	13	0.06
Croatian (14)	47	0.23
Danish (11)	31	0.15
Dutch (70)	367	1.82
Eastern European (15)	15	0.07
English (1,725)	3,494	17.34
European (350)	359	1.78
Finnish (13)	24	0.12
French, ex. Basque (96)	563	2.79
French Canadian (34)	110	0.55
German (1,621)	4,497	22.31
Greek (18)	18	0.09
Hungarian (0)	62	0.31
Iranian (132)	132	0.65
Irish (791)	2,848	14.13
Italian (273)	817	4.05
Northern European (18)	18	0.09
Norwegian (137)	397	1.97
Polish (194)	422	2.09
Portuguese (0)	15	0.07
Russian (0)	13	0.06
Scotch-Irish (755)	1,329	6.59
Scottish (224)	722	3.58
Serbian (17)	17	0.08
Slovak (0)	24	0.12
Slovene (13)	61	0.30
Swedish (96)	192	0.95
Swiss (10)	158	0.78
Turkish (52)	52	0.26
Ukrainian (10)	24	0.12
Welsh (26)	177	0.88

Hispanic Origin	Population	%
Hispanic or Latino (of any race)	513	2.48
Central American, ex. Mexican	42	0.20
Costa Rican	3	0.01
Guatemalan	18	0.09
Honduran	4	0.02
Nicaraguan	2	0.01
Panamanian	7	0.03
Salvadoran	8	0.04
Cuban	33	0.16
Dominican Republic	6	0.03
Mexican	213	1.03
Puerto Rican	71	0.34
South American	74	0.36
Argentinean	9	0.04
Bolivian	3	0.01
Chilean	6	0.03
Colombian	27	0.13
Ecuadorian	4	0.02
Peruvian	10	0.05
Venezuelan	15	0.07
Other Hispanic or Latino	74	0.36

Race*	Population	%
African-American/Black (397)	465	2.25
Not Hispanic (390)	452	2.19
Hispanic (7)	13	0.06
American Indian/Alaska Native (39)	114	0.55
Not Hispanic (35)	101	0.49
Hispanic (4)	13	0.06
Alaska Athabascan *(Ala. Nat.)* (2)	2	0.01
Apache (2)	4	0.02
Cherokee (8)	37	0.18
Chickasaw (1)	1	<0.01
Chippewa (0)	5	0.02
Choctaw (4)	6	0.03
Creek (6)	7	0.03
Inupiat *(Alaska Native)* (1)	1	<0.01
Iroquois (3)	7	0.03
Navajo (1)	2	0.01
Osage (0)	1	<0.01
Potawatomi (3)	3	0.01
Pueblo (1)	1	<0.01
Sioux (0)	1	<0.01
Asian (1,116)	1,256	6.07
Not Hispanic (1,114)	1,240	6.00
Hispanic (2)	16	0.08
Bangladeshi (5)	5	0.02
Cambodian (2)	2	0.01
Chinese, ex. Taiwanese (306)	335	1.62
Filipino (65)	104	0.50
Indian (323)	343	1.66
Indonesian (2)	2	0.01
Japanese (40)	65	0.31
Korean (167)	180	0.87
Laotian (0)	1	<0.01
Malaysian (0)	2	0.01
Pakistani (48)	54	0.26
Sri Lankan (3)	3	0.01
Taiwanese (40)	43	0.21
Thai (17)	19	0.09
Vietnamese (57)	67	0.32
Hawaii Native/Pacific Islander (4)	20	0.10
Not Hispanic (3)	16	0.08
Hispanic (1)	4	0.02
Native Hawaiian (4)	12	0.06
White (18,732)	18,995	91.87
Not Hispanic (18,357)	18,581	89.87
Hispanic (375)	414	2.00

Franklin

Place Type: City
County: Williamson
Population: 62,487†

Ancestry‡	Population	%
African, Sub-Saharan (196)	196	0.33
Kenyan (79)	79	0.13
Nigerian (24)	24	0.04
South African (73)	73	0.12
Other Sub-Saharan African (20)	20	0.03
American (4,116)	4,116	6.87
Arab (45)	116	0.19
Arab (30)	30	0.05
Egyptian (15)	15	0.03
Lebanese (0)	56	0.09
Syrian (0)	15	0.03
Armenian (14)	14	0.02
Austrian (27)	191	0.32
Belgian (0)	53	0.09
Brazilian (16)	16	0.03
British (196)	583	0.97
Bulgarian (75)	75	0.13
Canadian (114)	173	0.29
Celtic (39)	39	0.07
Croatian (0)	38	0.06
Czech (13)	148	0.25
Danish (44)	111	0.19
Dutch (224)	923	1.54
Eastern European (34)	46	0.08
English (4,491)	10,567	17.64
Estonian (29)	29	0.05
European (1,303)	1,490	2.49
Finnish (28)	128	0.21
French, ex. Basque (459)	2,100	3.51
French Canadian (126)	217	0.36
German (2,669)	9,352	15.61
Greek (29)	115	0.19
Hungarian (119)	304	0.51
Iranian (182)	182	0.30
Irish (2,827)	7,971	13.31
Israeli (23)	23	0.04
Italian (1,022)	3,029	5.06
Latvian (7)	9	0.02
Lithuanian (79)	111	0.19
New Zealander (24)	24	0.04
Northern European (62)	62	0.10
Norwegian (228)	725	1.21
Pennsylvania German (15)	43	0.07
Polish (335)	1,195	1.99
Portuguese (52)	105	0.18
Romanian (0)	31	0.05
Russian (114)	267	0.45
Scandinavian (48)	80	0.13
Scotch-Irish (1,878)	3,235	5.40
Scottish (852)	2,309	3.85
Serbian (0)	51	0.09
Slavic (13)	28	0.05
Slovak (25)	79	0.13
Slovene (12)	35	0.06
Swedish (159)	608	1.01
Swiss (69)	300	0.50
Turkish (181)	181	0.30
Ukrainian (138)	202	0.34
Welsh (54)	523	0.87
West Indian, ex. Hispanic (52)	113	0.19
Belizean (20)	20	0.03
Jamaican (13)	74	0.12
West Indian (19)	19	0.03
Yugoslavian (35)	35	0.06

Hispanic Origin	Population	%
Hispanic or Latino (of any race)	4,759	7.62
Central American, ex. Mexican	245	0.39
Costa Rican	17	0.03
Guatemalan	83	0.13
Honduran	79	0.13
Nicaraguan	21	0.03
Panamanian	16	0.03
Salvadoran	23	0.04
Other Central American	6	0.01
Cuban	138	0.22
Dominican Republic	22	0.04
Mexican	3,536	5.66
Puerto Rican	214	0.34
South American	302	0.48
Argentinean	16	0.03
Bolivian	10	0.02
Chilean	9	0.01
Colombian	121	0.19
Ecuadorian	16	0.03
Paraguayan	1	<0.01
Peruvian	69	0.11
Uruguayan	8	0.01
Venezuelan	46	0.07
Other South American	6	0.01
Other Hispanic or Latino	302	0.48

Race*	Population	%
African-American/Black (4,210)	4,575	7.32
Not Hispanic (4,157)	4,496	7.20
Hispanic (53)	79	0.13
American Indian/Alaska Native (147)	409	0.65
Not Hispanic (123)	346	0.55
Hispanic (24)	63	0.10
Apache (3)	7	0.01
Blackfeet (8)	14	0.02
Cherokee (32)	113	0.18
Chickasaw (4)	7	0.01
Chippewa (4)	10	0.02
Choctaw (13)	19	0.03
Comanche (0)	6	0.01
Cree (1)	2	<0.01
Creek (4)	6	0.01
Delaware (2)	3	<0.01
Hopi (0)	1	<0.01
Iroquois (3)	6	0.01
Lumbee (0)	1	<0.01
Mexican American Ind. (5)	6	0.01
Navajo (1)	10	0.02
Osage (2)	3	<0.01
Ottawa (1)	6	0.01
Pueblo (1)	2	<0.01

SECTION TWO

*Notes: † The Census 2010 population figure is used to calculate the percentages in the Hispanic Origin and Race categories. Ancestry percentages are based on the 2006-2010 American Community Survey population (not shown); ‡ Numbers in parentheses indicate the number of people reporting a single ancestry; * Numbers in parentheses indicate the number of persons reporting this race alone, not in combination with any other race; Please refer to the Explanation of Data for more information.*

Sioux (2)	6	0.01
South American Ind. (1)	1	<0.01
Yaqui (0)	1	<0.01
Asian (2,360)	2,732	4.37
Not Hispanic (2,352)	2,700	4.32
Hispanic (8)	32	0.05
Bangladeshi (8)	8	0.01
Burmese (26)	26	0.04
Cambodian (3)	3	<0.01
Chinese, ex. Taiwanese (399)	439	0.70
Filipino (118)	185	0.30
Hmong (1)	1	<0.01
Indian (931)	973	1.56
Indonesian (10)	10	0.02
Japanese (198)	255	0.41
Korean (501)	589	0.94
Laotian (17)	26	0.04
Malaysian (2)	2	<0.01
Nepalese (2)	2	<0.01
Pakistani (31)	38	0.06
Sri Lankan (4)	6	0.01
Taiwanese (11)	19	0.03
Thai (6)	12	0.02
Vietnamese (41)	61	0.10
Hawaii Native/Pacific Islander (21)	64	0.10
Not Hispanic (21)	63	0.10
Hispanic (0)	1	<0.01
Guamanian/Chamorro (5)	6	0.01
Native Hawaiian (2)	16	0.03
Samoan (3)	17	0.03
White (52,713)	53,681	85.91
Not Hispanic (50,104)	50,900	81.46
Hispanic (2,609)	2,781	4.45

Gallatin

Place Type: City
County: Sumner
Population: 30,278†

Ancestry‡	Population	%
African, Sub-Saharan (257)	257	0.88
African (72)	72	0.25
Ethiopian (17)	17	0.06
Sudanese (104)	104	0.36
Other Sub-Saharan African (64)	64	0.22
American (3,278)	3,278	11.27
Arab (107)	107	0.37
Arab (84)	84	0.29
Jordanian (23)	23	0.08
Belgian (9)	9	0.03
British (108)	108	0.37
Canadian (0)	18	0.06
Czech (11)	31	0.11
Danish (0)	43	0.15
Dutch (137)	444	1.53
English (1,765)	3,386	11.64
European (169)	221	0.76
Finnish (0)	11	0.04
French, ex. Basque (172)	687	2.36
French Canadian (228)	240	0.83
German (1,070)	3,883	13.35
Greek (28)	51	0.18
Hungarian (0)	24	0.08
Irish (1,483)	3,902	13.42
Italian (164)	618	2.12
Norwegian (50)	84	0.29
Pennsylvania German (0)	10	0.03
Polish (100)	299	1.03
Portuguese (28)	65	0.22
Romanian (25)	78	0.27
Russian (0)	53	0.18
Scandinavian (0)	21	0.07
Scotch-Irish (459)	941	3.24
Scottish (213)	681	2.34
Slovene (0)	15	0.05
Swedish (68)	134	0.46
Swiss (13)	41	0.14
Ukrainian (35)	44	0.15
Welsh (113)	234	0.80
West Indian, ex. Hispanic (0)	18	0.06
Haitian (0)	18	0.06
Yugoslavian (12)	12	0.04

Hispanic Origin	Population	%
Hispanic or Latino (of any race)	2,434	8.04
Central American, ex. Mexican	327	1.08
Costa Rican	36	0.12
Guatemalan	32	0.11
Honduran	54	0.18
Nicaraguan	6	0.02
Panamanian	12	0.04
Salvadoran	176	0.58
Other Central American	11	0.04
Cuban	38	0.13
Dominican Republic	16	0.05
Mexican	1,742	5.75
Puerto Rican	113	0.37
South American	39	0.13
Argentinean	2	0.01
Chilean	3	0.01
Colombian	12	0.04
Ecuadorian	8	0.03
Peruvian	9	0.03
Venezuelan	5	0.02
Other Hispanic or Latino	159	0.53

Race*	Population	%
African-American/Black (4,442)	4,804	15.87
Not Hispanic (4,417)	4,736	15.64
Hispanic (25)	68	0.22
American Indian/Alaska Native (88)	217	0.72
Not Hispanic (72)	197	0.65
Hispanic (16)	20	0.07
Apache (3)	6	0.02
Blackfeet (0)	3	0.01
Canadian/French Am. Ind. (1)	1	<0.01
Cherokee (15)	51	0.17
Cheyenne (0)	1	<0.01
Chippewa (7)	7	0.02
Choctaw (1)	1	<0.01
Comanche (2)	4	0.01
Cree (0)	1	<0.01
Creek (0)	4	0.01
Houma (1)	2	0.01
Iroquois (3)	5	0.02
Lumbee (1)	1	<0.01
Mexican American Ind. (1)	3	0.01
Navajo (0)	1	<0.01
Osage (2)	4	0.01
Ottawa (3)	3	0.01
Pueblo (0)	4	0.01
Seminole (1)	2	0.01
Sioux (0)	5	0.02
Tlingit-Haida *(Alaska Native)* (1)	1	<0.01
Asian (231)	302	1.00
Not Hispanic (224)	288	0.95
Hispanic (7)	14	0.05
Burmese (1)	1	<0.01
Cambodian (3)	3	0.01
Chinese, ex. Taiwanese (30)	39	0.13
Filipino (45)	66	0.22
Indian (48)	59	0.19
Indonesian (0)	3	0.01
Japanese (16)	27	0.09
Korean (30)	36	0.12
Laotian (9)	11	0.04
Malaysian (1)	1	<0.01
Pakistani (8)	10	0.03
Sri Lankan (1)	1	<0.01
Thai (4)	6	0.02
Vietnamese (29)	30	0.10
Hawaii Native/Pacific Islander (45)	65	0.21
Not Hispanic (27)	41	0.14
Hispanic (18)	24	0.08
Guamanian/Chamorro (34)	38	0.13
Native Hawaiian (9)	15	0.05
Samoan (1)	3	0.01
White (23,515)	24,053	79.44
Not Hispanic (22,558)	22,974	75.88
Hispanic (957)	1,079	3.56

Germantown

Place Type: City
County: Shelby
Population: 38,844†

Ancestry‡	Population	%
African, Sub-Saharan (39)	62	0.16
African (0)	14	0.04
South African (39)	48	0.12
American (4,874)	4,874	12.61
Arab (185)	275	0.71
Arab (51)	105	0.27
Lebanese (93)	116	0.30
Palestinian (15)	28	0.07
Syrian (26)	26	0.07
Australian (106)	137	0.35
Austrian (47)	157	0.41
Belgian (0)	16	0.04
Brazilian (14)	32	0.08
British (396)	494	1.28
Cajun (10)	10	0.03
Canadian (9)	22	0.06
Czech (94)	227	0.59
Czechoslovakian (0)	9	0.02
Danish (0)	169	0.44
Dutch (258)	579	1.50
Eastern European (129)	129	0.33
English (2,937)	6,806	17.61
European (639)	774	2.00
French, ex. Basque (212)	1,200	3.10
French Canadian (31)	136	0.35
German (1,647)	5,355	13.85
Greek (220)	287	0.74
Hungarian (37)	119	0.31
Iranian (24)	51	0.13
Irish (2,478)	5,845	15.12
Italian (944)	2,208	5.71
Lithuanian (23)	112	0.29
New Zealander (0)	9	0.02
Northern European (16)	16	0.04
Norwegian (61)	396	1.02
Polish (381)	1,083	2.80
Portuguese (39)	69	0.18
Romanian (13)	21	0.05
Russian (349)	578	1.50
Scandinavian (24)	90	0.23
Scotch-Irish (1,119)	1,936	5.01
Scottish (870)	1,937	5.01
Slovak (0)	98	0.25
Swedish (106)	543	1.40
Swiss (25)	103	0.27
Ukrainian (58)	74	0.19
Welsh (64)	225	0.58
West Indian, ex. Hispanic (14)	27	0.07
Jamaican (14)	27	0.07

Hispanic Origin	Population	%
Hispanic or Latino (of any race)	733	1.89
Central American, ex. Mexican	49	0.13
Costa Rican	3	0.01
Guatemalan	16	0.04
Honduran	8	0.02
Nicaraguan	6	0.02
Panamanian	2	0.01
Salvadoran	14	0.04
Cuban	66	0.17
Dominican Republic	8	0.02
Mexican	291	0.75
Puerto Rican	81	0.21
South American	145	0.37
Argentinean	20	0.05
Bolivian	9	0.02
Chilean	6	0.02
Colombian	30	0.08
Ecuadorian	4	0.01
Paraguayan	4	0.01
Peruvian	24	0.06

*Notes: † The Census 2010 population figure is used to calculate the percentages in the Hispanic Origin and Race categories. Ancestry percentages are based on the 2006-2010 American Community Survey population (not shown); ‡ Numbers in parentheses indicate the number of people reporting a single ancestry; * Numbers in parentheses indicate the number of persons reporting this race alone, not in combination with any other race; Please refer to the Explanation of Data for more information.*

Uruguayan	7	0.02
Venezuelan	41	0.11
Other Hispanic or Latino	93	0.24

Race*	Population	%
African-American/Black (1,387)	1,464	3.77
Not Hispanic (1,381)	1,457	3.75
Hispanic (6)	7	0.02
American Indian/Alaska Native (83)	168	0.43
Not Hispanic (71)	150	0.39
Hispanic (12)	18	0.05
Apache (2)	4	0.01
Blackfeet (4)	5	0.01
Cherokee (12)	44	0.11
Chickasaw (4)	6	0.02
Chippewa (5)	5	0.01
Choctaw (6)	15	0.04
Creek (4)	4	0.01
Kiowa (1)	1	<0.01
Mexican American Ind. (1)	1	<0.01
Osage (1)	1	<0.01
Ottawa (1)	1	<0.01
Potawatomi (6)	6	0.02
South American Ind. (1)	1	<0.01
Asian (2,002)	2,245	5.78
Not Hispanic (1,994)	2,230	5.74
Hispanic (8)	15	0.04
Bangladeshi (42)	42	0.11
Burmese (5)	5	0.01
Cambodian (5)	5	0.01
Chinese, ex. Taiwanese (527)	571	1.47
Filipino (56)	90	0.23
Indian (691)	737	1.90
Indonesian (2)	2	0.01
Japanese (113)	153	0.39
Korean (258)	291	0.75
Laotian (3)	3	0.01
Malaysian (2)	4	0.01
Pakistani (117)	125	0.32
Taiwanese (58)	66	0.17
Thai (15)	17	0.04
Vietnamese (67)	75	0.19
Hawaii Native/Pacific Islander (7)	38	0.10
Not Hispanic (7)	38	0.10
Guamanian/Chamorro (5)	9	0.02
Native Hawaiian (0)	3	0.01
White (34,783)	35,132	90.44
Not Hispanic (34,233)	34,549	88.94
Hispanic (550)	583	1.50

Goodlettsville

Place Type: City
County: Davidson
Population: 15,921†

Ancestry‡	Population	%
African, Sub-Saharan (31)	31	0.20
African (31)	31	0.20
American (2,367)	2,367	15.32
Arab (150)	480	3.11
Arab (11)	11	0.07
Iraqi (56)	221	1.43
Jordanian (77)	77	0.50
Syrian (6)	6	0.04
Other Arab (0)	165	1.07
Austrian (0)	9	0.06
British (23)	47	0.30
Cajun (14)	14	0.09
Canadian (14)	14	0.09
Czech (17)	24	0.16
Danish (0)	16	0.10
Dutch (37)	211	1.37
English (1,088)	2,094	13.56
Estonian (0)	9	0.06
European (118)	130	0.84
Finnish (0)	13	0.08
French, ex. Basque (34)	273	1.77
German (578)	1,658	10.73
Hungarian (0)	5	0.03
Irish (711)	1,644	10.64
Italian (163)	255	1.65
Norwegian (7)	104	0.67
Polish (74)	287	1.86
Russian (57)	110	0.71
Scandinavian (16)	16	0.10
Scotch-Irish (380)	566	3.66
Scottish (139)	403	2.61
Swedish (0)	129	0.84
Swiss (12)	28	0.18
Welsh (44)	95	0.61
West Indian, ex. Hispanic (36)	36	0.23
Jamaican (7)	7	0.05
Trinidadian/Tobagonian (29)	29	0.19
Yugoslavian (0)	9	0.06

Hispanic Origin	Population	%
Hispanic or Latino (of any race)	638	4.01
Central American, ex. Mexican	87	0.55
Costa Rican	9	0.06
Guatemalan	19	0.12
Honduran	5	0.03
Nicaraguan	5	0.03
Panamanian	3	0.02
Salvadoran	46	0.29
Cuban	44	0.28
Dominican Republic	15	0.09
Mexican	345	2.17
Puerto Rican	68	0.43
South American	30	0.19
Colombian	12	0.08
Ecuadorian	4	0.03
Uruguayan	1	0.01
Venezuelan	10	0.06
Other South American	3	0.02
Other Hispanic or Latino	49	0.31

Race*	Population	%
African-American/Black (2,950)	3,132	19.67
Not Hispanic (2,928)	3,091	19.41
Hispanic (22)	41	0.26
American Indian/Alaska Native (39)	135	0.85
Not Hispanic (27)	108	0.68
Hispanic (12)	27	0.17
Apache (0)	1	0.01
Blackfeet (0)	1	0.01
Canadian/French Am. Ind. (0)	1	0.01
Cherokee (11)	41	0.26
Cheyenne (0)	1	0.01
Chippewa (0)	2	0.01
Choctaw (1)	1	0.01
Iroquois (0)	1	0.01
Lumbee (1)	1	0.01
Mexican American Ind. (8)	9	0.06
Ottawa (0)	1	0.01
Pueblo (2)	2	0.01
Sioux (0)	5	0.03
Yaqui (2)	2	0.01
Asian (390)	462	2.90
Not Hispanic (385)	445	2.80
Hispanic (5)	17	0.11
Bangladeshi (6)	6	0.04
Cambodian (10)	10	0.06
Chinese, ex. Taiwanese (66)	82	0.52
Filipino (22)	36	0.23
Indian (175)	178	1.12
Indonesian (1)	1	0.01
Japanese (11)	22	0.14
Korean (46)	59	0.37
Laotian (12)	13	0.08
Malaysian (2)	2	0.01
Nepalese (2)	2	0.01
Pakistani (8)	9	0.06
Thai (2)	6	0.04
Vietnamese (16)	18	0.11
Hawaii Native/Pacific Islander (17)	33	0.21
Not Hispanic (17)	32	0.20
Hispanic (0)	1	0.01
Native Hawaiian (3)	6	0.04
Samoan (0)	5	0.03
White (11,891)	12,214	76.72
Not Hispanic (11,612)	11,887	74.66
Hispanic (279)	327	2.05

Greeneville

Place Type: Town
County: Greene
Population: 15,062†

Ancestry‡	Population	%
African, Sub-Saharan (331)	331	2.18
African (331)	331	2.18
American (2,066)	2,066	13.60
Arab (9)	29	0.19
Lebanese (9)	29	0.19
British (13)	43	0.28
Canadian (0)	17	0.11
Czech (0)	36	0.24
Danish (16)	24	0.16
Dutch (24)	283	1.86
English (1,782)	3,171	20.88
European (28)	28	0.18
French, ex. Basque (68)	176	1.16
French Canadian (55)	55	0.36
German (635)	1,975	13.00
Hungarian (56)	142	0.93
Irish (838)	1,918	12.63
Italian (186)	379	2.50
Lithuanian (0)	12	0.08
Norwegian (16)	31	0.20
Polish (58)	105	0.69
Portuguese (20)	74	0.49
Scandinavian (0)	12	0.08
Scotch-Irish (391)	596	3.92
Scottish (174)	470	3.09
Slavic (13)	13	0.09
Slovak (7)	7	0.05
Swedish (72)	93	0.61
Welsh (12)	24	0.16

Hispanic Origin	Population	%
Hispanic or Latino (of any race)	662	4.40
Central American, ex. Mexican	18	0.12
Guatemalan	10	0.07
Honduran	3	0.02
Panamanian	1	0.01
Salvadoran	4	0.03
Cuban	8	0.05
Mexican	529	3.51
Puerto Rican	47	0.31
South American	23	0.15
Argentinean	2	0.01
Chilean	6	0.04
Colombian	13	0.09
Peruvian	1	0.01
Other South American	1	0.01
Other Hispanic or Latino	37	0.25

Race*	Population	%
African-American/Black (837)	979	6.50
Not Hispanic (825)	958	6.36
Hispanic (12)	21	0.14
American Indian/Alaska Native (35)	141	0.94
Not Hispanic (27)	127	0.84
Hispanic (8)	14	0.09
Aleut *(Alaska Native)* (0)	3	0.02
Apache (1)	2	0.01
Blackfeet (0)	4	0.03
Cherokee (9)	50	0.33
Chippewa (1)	1	0.01
Iroquois (1)	7	0.05
Mexican American Ind. (0)	1	0.01
Navajo (0)	1	0.01
Potawatomi (1)	1	0.01
Seminole (0)	1	0.01
Asian (121)	140	0.93
Not Hispanic (121)	140	0.93
Chinese, ex. Taiwanese (22)	22	0.15
Filipino (9)	10	0.07

*Notes: † The Census 2010 population figure is used to calculate the percentages in the Hispanic Origin and Race categories. Ancestry percentages are based on the 2006-2010 American Community Survey population (not shown); ‡ Numbers in parentheses indicate the number of people reporting a single ancestry; * Numbers in parentheses indicate the number of persons reporting this race alone, not in combination with any other race; Please refer to the Explanation of Data for more information.*

Indian (34)	45	0.30
Japanese (32)	34	0.23
Korean (1)	4	0.03
Laotian (3)	3	0.02
Taiwanese (1)	1	0.01
Thai (7)	9	0.06
Vietnamese (10)	10	0.07
Hawaii Native/Pacific Islander (3)	17	0.11
Not Hispanic (1)	11	0.07
Hispanic (2)	6	0.04
Guamanian/Chamorro (1)	3	0.02
Native Hawaiian (2)	13	0.09
White (13,418)	13,686	90.86
Not Hispanic (13,186)	13,395	88.93
Hispanic (232)	291	1.93

Harrison

Place Type: CDP
County: Hamilton
Population: 7,769†

Ancestry‡	Population	%
American (1,486)	1,486	18.77
Armenian (0)	17	0.21
Austrian (11)	52	0.66
British (21)	21	0.27
Bulgarian (0)	28	0.35
Czech (0)	19	0.24
Dutch (13)	63	0.80
English (259)	882	11.14
European (23)	23	0.29
French, ex. Basque (33)	94	1.19
German (196)	871	11.00
Irish (340)	1,151	14.54
Italian (13)	71	0.90
Lithuanian (14)	14	0.18
Norwegian (0)	71	0.90
Polish (0)	10	0.13
Romanian (0)	10	0.13
Scotch-Irish (224)	354	4.47
Scottish (176)	235	2.97
Slovak (17)	17	0.21
Swedish (0)	14	0.18
Welsh (0)	60	0.76

Hispanic Origin	Population	%
Hispanic or Latino (of any race)	184	2.37
Central American, ex. Mexican	14	0.18
Costa Rican	3	0.04
Guatemalan	3	0.04
Honduran	2	0.03
Panamanian	2	0.03
Salvadoran	4	0.05
Cuban	6	0.08
Dominican Republic	9	0.12
Mexican	74	0.95
Puerto Rican	38	0.49
South American	28	0.36
Bolivian	7	0.09
Chilean	2	0.03
Colombian	2	0.03
Peruvian	11	0.14
Venezuelan	6	0.08
Other Hispanic or Latino	15	0.19

Race*	Population	%
African-American/Black (1,540)	1,625	20.92
Not Hispanic (1,532)	1,617	20.81
Hispanic (8)	8	0.10
American Indian/Alaska Native (13)	66	0.85
Not Hispanic (13)	63	0.81
Hispanic (0)	3	0.04
Canadian/French Am. Ind. (0)	3	0.04
Cherokee (7)	26	0.33
Chippewa (1)	1	0.01
Kiowa (1)	2	0.03
Mexican American Ind. (0)	1	0.01
Ottawa (0)	2	0.03
South American Ind. (0)	1	0.01
Asian (91)	126	1.62
Not Hispanic (90)	124	1.60
Hispanic (1)	2	0.03
Cambodian (1)	2	0.03
Chinese, ex. Taiwanese (25)	31	0.40
Filipino (28)	38	0.49
Indian (9)	10	0.13
Japanese (7)	8	0.10
Korean (8)	14	0.18
Pakistani (1)	5	0.06
Taiwanese (6)	6	0.08
Vietnamese (5)	6	0.08
Hawaii Native/Pacific Islander (4)	6	0.08
Not Hispanic (4)	6	0.08
Guamanian/Chamorro (2)	2	0.03
Native Hawaiian (0)	1	0.01
White (5,885)	6,046	77.82
Not Hispanic (5,783)	5,930	76.33
Hispanic (102)	116	1.49

Hartsville-Trousdale County

Place Type: Consolidated Government
County: Trousdale
Population: 7,870†

Ancestry‡	Population	%
American (1,375)	1,375	17.74
British (0)	37	0.48
Canadian (5)	5	0.06
Czech (0)	16	0.21
Danish (0)	6	0.08
Dutch (0)	33	0.43
English (686)	1,032	13.31
European (93)	93	1.20
French, ex. Basque (39)	231	2.98
French Canadian (4)	4	0.05
German (240)	1,024	13.21
Irish (394)	986	12.72
Italian (5)	64	0.83
Norwegian (55)	107	1.38
Polish (103)	122	1.57
Scotch-Irish (117)	203	2.62
Scottish (12)	81	1.05
Swedish (0)	27	0.35
Welsh (0)	23	0.30

Hispanic Origin	Population	%
Hispanic or Latino (of any race)	198	2.52
Central American, ex. Mexican	1	0.01
Honduran	1	0.01
Cuban	2	0.03
Mexican	162	2.06
Puerto Rican	5	0.06
South American	2	0.03
Peruvian	1	0.01
Uruguayan	1	0.01
Other Hispanic or Latino	26	0.33

Race*	Population	%
African-American/Black (754)	824	10.47
Not Hispanic (748)	818	10.39
Hispanic (6)	6	0.08
American Indian/Alaska Native (33)	76	0.97
Not Hispanic (23)	64	0.81
Hispanic (10)	12	0.15
Blackfeet (0)	1	0.01
Central American Ind. (1)	1	0.01
Cherokee (12)	25	0.32
Cheyenne (0)	1	0.01
Chickasaw (0)	1	0.01
Choctaw (0)	5	0.06
Hopi (0)	1	0.01
Iroquois (0)	1	0.01
Mexican American Ind. (0)	1	0.01
Osage (0)	1	0.01
Sioux (1)	1	0.01
Yaqui (0)	1	0.01
Asian (18)	23	0.29
Not Hispanic (18)	22	0.28
Hispanic (0)	1	0.01
Chinese, ex. Taiwanese (6)	6	0.08
Filipino (8)	8	0.10
Indian (1)	2	0.03
Japanese (0)	1	0.01
Korean (2)	2	0.03
Thai (1)	1	0.01
Hawaii Native/Pacific Islander (1)	2	0.03
Not Hispanic (1)	2	0.03
Native Hawaiian (1)	1	0.01
White (6,852)	6,988	88.79
Not Hispanic (6,761)	6,877	87.38
Hispanic (91)	111	1.41

Hendersonville

Place Type: City
County: Sumner
Population: 51,372†

Ancestry‡	Population	%
African, Sub-Saharan (104)	104	0.21
African (76)	76	0.15
Nigerian (28)	28	0.06
American (6,053)	6,053	12.17
Arab (201)	429	0.86
Arab (16)	16	0.03
Egyptian (138)	138	0.28
Lebanese (33)	127	0.26
Syrian (0)	134	0.27
Other Arab (14)	14	0.03
Armenian (24)	24	0.05
Australian (28)	44	0.09
Austrian (65)	213	0.43
Belgian (0)	28	0.06
British (271)	353	0.71
Cajun (12)	12	0.02
Canadian (52)	79	0.16
Celtic (0)	17	0.03
Croatian (10)	18	0.04
Czech (19)	86	0.17
Czechoslovakian (0)	19	0.04
Danish (10)	40	0.08
Dutch (203)	789	1.59
Eastern European (15)	29	0.06
English (3,506)	7,042	14.16
European (889)	1,059	2.13
French, ex. Basque (386)	1,626	3.27
French Canadian (51)	143	0.29
German (2,364)	7,808	15.70
Greek (35)	72	0.14
Guyanese (11)	11	0.02
Hungarian (31)	116	0.23
Icelander (53)	53	0.11
Iranian (11)	11	0.02
Irish (2,887)	7,171	14.42
Italian (737)	1,942	3.91
Lithuanian (16)	97	0.20
Macedonian (37)	37	0.07
New Zealander (43)	43	0.09
Northern European (23)	23	0.05
Norwegian (97)	346	0.70
Pennsylvania German (19)	19	0.04
Polish (327)	985	1.98
Portuguese (11)	72	0.14
Romanian (123)	123	0.25
Russian (21)	196	0.39
Scandinavian (111)	180	0.36
Scotch-Irish (961)	1,865	3.75
Scottish (547)	1,369	2.75
Slavic (0)	31	0.06
Slovak (21)	43	0.09
Swedish (112)	544	1.09
Swiss (77)	191	0.38
Ukrainian (112)	112	0.23
Welsh (65)	379	0.76
West Indian, ex. Hispanic (195)	210	0.42
British West Indian (47)	47	0.09

*Notes: † The Census 2010 population figure is used to calculate the percentages in the Hispanic Origin and Race categories. Ancestry percentages are based on the 2006-2010 American Community Survey population (not shown); ‡ Numbers in parentheses indicate the number of people reporting a single ancestry; * Numbers in parentheses indicate the number of persons reporting this race alone, not in combination with any other race; Please refer to the Explanation of Data for more information.*

Jamaican (0)	15	0.03
Trinidadian/Tobagonian (7)	7	0.01
West Indian (141)	141	0.28

Hispanic Origin	Population	%
Hispanic or Latino (of any race)	1,860	3.62
Central American, ex. Mexican	258	0.50
Costa Rican	51	0.10
Guatemalan	55	0.11
Honduran	16	0.03
Nicaraguan	14	0.03
Panamanian	23	0.04
Salvadoran	99	0.19
Cuban	60	0.12
Dominican Republic	14	0.03
Mexican	1,045	2.03
Puerto Rican	181	0.35
South American	163	0.32
Argentinean	8	0.02
Bolivian	1	<0.01
Chilean	5	0.01
Colombian	60	0.12
Ecuadorian	10	0.02
Peruvian	36	0.07
Uruguayan	1	<0.01
Venezuelan	40	0.08
Other South American	2	<0.01
Other Hispanic or Latino	139	0.27

Race*	Population	%
African-American/Black (3,225)	3,601	7.01
Not Hispanic (3,188)	3,523	6.86
Hispanic (37)	78	0.15
American Indian/Alaska Native (168)	466	0.91
Not Hispanic (154)	430	0.84
Hispanic (14)	36	0.07
Aleut *(Alaska Native)* (1)	1	<0.01
Apache (0)	1	<0.01
Blackfeet (3)	16	0.03
Canadian/French Am. Ind. (2)	4	0.01
Central American Ind. (4)	4	0.01
Cherokee (40)	160	0.31
Chickasaw (2)	4	0.01
Chippewa (4)	5	0.01
Choctaw (12)	30	0.06
Comanche (0)	1	<0.01
Cree (1)	1	<0.01
Creek (3)	9	0.02
Crow (0)	1	<0.01
Delaware (0)	2	<0.01
Inupiat *(Alaska Native)* (0)	4	0.01
Iroquois (6)	17	0.03
Kiowa (0)	1	<0.01
Lumbee (1)	3	0.01
Mexican American Ind. (1)	4	0.01
Navajo (0)	2	<0.01
Osage (0)	1	<0.01
Ottawa (3)	3	0.01
Paiute (1)	3	0.01
Potawatomi (6)	6	0.01
Puget Sound Salish (1)	1	<0.01
Shoshone (1)	1	<0.01
Sioux (9)	12	0.02
South American Ind. (2)	2	<0.01
Tlingit-Haida *(Alaska Native)* (0)	1	<0.01
Asian (812)	1,062	2.07
Not Hispanic (808)	1,046	2.04
Hispanic (4)	16	0.03
Bangladeshi (4)	4	0.01
Burmese (10)	10	0.02
Cambodian (5)	5	0.01
Chinese, ex. Taiwanese (134)	162	0.32
Filipino (156)	228	0.44
Indian (170)	193	0.38
Indonesian (2)	4	0.01
Japanese (40)	79	0.15
Korean (122)	170	0.33
Laotian (5)	9	0.02
Pakistani (10)	15	0.03
Sri Lankan (3)	3	0.01
Taiwanese (2)	4	0.01
Thai (15)	29	0.06
Vietnamese (100)	112	0.22
Hawaii Native/Pacific Islander (35)	83	0.16
Not Hispanic (35)	76	0.15
Hispanic (0)	7	0.01
Fijian (2)	2	<0.01
Guamanian/Chamorro (17)	27	0.05
Native Hawaiian (6)	22	0.04
Samoan (2)	5	0.01
White (45,537)	46,426	90.37
Not Hispanic (44,478)	45,214	88.01
Hispanic (1,059)	1,212	2.36

Humboldt

Place Type: City
County: Gibson
Population: 8,452†

Ancestry‡	Population	%
African, Sub-Saharan (219)	231	2.69
African (219)	231	2.69
American (849)	849	9.89
Arab (7)	7	0.08
Arab (7)	7	0.08
Dutch (18)	116	1.35
English (270)	430	5.01
European (112)	112	1.31
French, ex. Basque (34)	88	1.03
German (47)	184	2.14
Irish (401)	882	10.28
Italian (43)	95	1.11
Polish (0)	47	0.55
Portuguese (19)	19	0.22
Scandinavian (5)	5	0.06
Scotch-Irish (110)	127	1.48
Scottish (14)	41	0.48
Welsh (0)	8	0.09
West Indian, ex. Hispanic (61)	61	0.71
Bahamian (17)	17	0.20
West Indian (44)	44	0.51

Hispanic Origin	Population	%
Hispanic or Latino (of any race)	264	3.12
Central American, ex. Mexican	3	0.04
Guatemalan	1	0.01
Salvadoran	2	0.02
Dominican Republic	1	0.01
Mexican	206	2.44
Puerto Rican	17	0.20
South American	8	0.09
Colombian	1	0.01
Ecuadorian	7	0.08
Other Hispanic or Latino	29	0.34

Race*	Population	%
African-American/Black (4,045)	4,100	48.51
Not Hispanic (4,031)	4,078	48.25
Hispanic (14)	22	0.26
American Indian/Alaska Native (11)	46	0.54
Not Hispanic (11)	41	0.49
Hispanic (0)	5	0.06
Apache (0)	1	0.01
Cherokee (2)	15	0.18
Choctaw (0)	2	0.02
Puget Sound Salish (0)	1	0.01
Sioux (0)	2	0.02
Asian (13)	20	0.24
Not Hispanic (13)	20	0.24
Chinese, ex. Taiwanese (4)	7	0.08
Filipino (3)	5	0.06
Indian (1)	6	0.07
Korean (0)	2	0.02
Thai (2)	2	0.02
Hawaii Native/Pacific Islander (2)	2	0.02
Hispanic (2)	2	0.02
Native Hawaiian (2)	2	0.02
White (4,142)	4,220	49.93
Not Hispanic (4,057)	4,119	48.73
Hispanic (85)	101	1.19

Jackson

Place Type: City
County: Madison
Population: 65,211†

Ancestry‡	Population	%
African, Sub-Saharan (1,988)	2,253	3.50
African (1,952)	2,217	3.44
Ethiopian (25)	25	0.04
Liberian (11)	11	0.02
American (6,752)	6,752	10.48
Arab (167)	185	0.29
Arab (79)	79	0.12
Egyptian (9)	19	0.03
Lebanese (63)	71	0.11
Palestinian (16)	16	0.02
Armenian (0)	41	0.06
Australian (15)	34	0.05
Belgian (22)	38	0.06
British (44)	141	0.22
Canadian (10)	26	0.04
Croatian (0)	18	0.03
Czech (0)	37	0.06
Czechoslovakian (8)	49	0.08
Danish (7)	57	0.09
Dutch (161)	487	0.76
Eastern European (18)	18	0.03
English (2,403)	4,280	6.64
European (598)	653	1.01
French, ex. Basque (230)	786	1.22
French Canadian (10)	51	0.08
German (1,417)	3,912	6.07
Greek (47)	83	0.13
Hungarian (11)	17	0.03
Iranian (27)	27	0.04
Irish (2,110)	4,498	6.98
Italian (411)	964	1.50
Lithuanian (9)	51	0.08
Norwegian (86)	170	0.26
Polish (82)	427	0.66
Portuguese (9)	9	0.01
Romanian (0)	13	0.02
Russian (153)	163	0.25
Scandinavian (14)	14	0.02
Scotch-Irish (1,217)	1,815	2.82
Scottish (617)	1,104	1.71
Slovak (13)	71	0.11
Swedish (147)	345	0.54
Swiss (40)	115	0.18
Ukrainian (86)	86	0.13
Welsh (53)	159	0.25
West Indian, ex. Hispanic (6)	13	0.02
Jamaican (6)	13	0.02

Hispanic Origin	Population	%
Hispanic or Latino (of any race)	2,592	3.97
Central American, ex. Mexican	242	0.37
Costa Rican	8	0.01
Guatemalan	38	0.06
Honduran	166	0.25
Nicaraguan	3	<0.01
Panamanian	7	0.01
Salvadoran	20	0.03
Cuban	38	0.06
Dominican Republic	7	0.01
Mexican	1,882	2.89
Puerto Rican	158	0.24
South American	76	0.12
Argentinean	7	0.01
Chilean	8	0.01
Colombian	22	0.03
Ecuadorian	8	0.01
Peruvian	17	0.03
Venezuelan	10	0.02
Other South American	4	0.01
Other Hispanic or Latino	189	0.29

*Notes: † The Census 2010 population figure is used to calculate the percentages in the Hispanic Origin and Race categories. Ancestry percentages are based on the 2006-2010 American Community Survey population (not shown); ‡ Numbers in parentheses indicate the number of people reporting a single ancestry; * Numbers in parentheses indicate the number of persons reporting this race alone, not in combination with any other race; Please refer to the Explanation of Data for more information.*

Race*	Population	%
African-American/Black (29,802)	30,386	46.60
Not Hispanic (29,705)	30,234	46.36
Hispanic (97)	152	0.23
American Indian/Alaska Native (103)	314	0.48
Not Hispanic (84)	281	0.43
Hispanic (19)	33	0.05
Apache (0)	3	<0.01
Blackfeet (0)	7	0.01
Canadian/French Am. Ind. (0)	1	<0.01
Central American Ind. (0)	5	0.01
Cherokee (18)	111	0.17
Cheyenne (0)	2	<0.01
Chickasaw (1)	1	<0.01
Chippewa (2)	4	0.01
Choctaw (5)	22	0.03
Creek (3)	6	0.01
Crow (0)	4	0.01
Iroquois (2)	2	<0.01
Mexican American Ind. (13)	15	0.02
Navajo (2)	6	0.01
Potawatomi (2)	4	0.01
Seminole (0)	1	<0.01
Shoshone (0)	4	0.01
Sioux (1)	5	0.01
Asian (757)	948	1.45
Not Hispanic (738)	915	1.40
Hispanic (19)	33	0.05
Cambodian (15)	18	0.03
Chinese, ex. Taiwanese (125)	155	0.24
Filipino (148)	188	0.29
Indian (192)	231	0.35
Japanese (56)	81	0.12
Korean (57)	73	0.11
Laotian (3)	3	<0.01
Malaysian (1)	2	<0.01
Pakistani (19)	24	0.04
Sri Lankan (2)	2	<0.01
Taiwanese (2)	3	<0.01
Thai (9)	13	0.02
Vietnamese (93)	107	0.16
Hawaii Native/Pacific Islander (19)	45	0.07
Not Hispanic (16)	39	0.06
Hispanic (3)	6	0.01
Guamanian/Chamorro (13)	17	0.03
Native Hawaiian (4)	13	0.02
Samoan (2)	5	0.01
White (32,092)	32,876	50.41
Not Hispanic (31,192)	31,862	48.86
Hispanic (900)	1,014	1.55

Jefferson City

Place Type: City
County: Jefferson
Population: 8,047†

Ancestry‡	Population	%
American (2,529)	2,529	31.24
British (0)	58	0.72
Canadian (0)	12	0.15
Dutch (0)	26	0.32
English (297)	614	7.58
European (39)	39	0.48
Finnish (10)	10	0.12
French, ex. Basque (31)	127	1.57
French Canadian (11)	43	0.53
German (385)	1,199	14.81
Greek (0)	9	0.11
Hungarian (0)	17	0.21
Icelander (8)	8	0.10
Irish (379)	870	10.75
Italian (65)	167	2.06
Norwegian (27)	55	0.68
Polish (0)	46	0.57
Portuguese (0)	7	0.09
Romanian (0)	12	0.15
Scotch-Irish (235)	371	4.58
Scottish (159)	334	4.13
Swedish (23)	40	0.49
Swiss (15)	49	0.61
Turkish (0)	7	0.09
Ukrainian (0)	12	0.15
Welsh (9)	97	1.20

Hispanic Origin	Population	%
Hispanic or Latino (of any race)	619	7.69
Central American, ex. Mexican	6	0.07
Guatemalan	4	0.05
Honduran	2	0.02
Cuban	9	0.11
Dominican Republic	1	0.01
Mexican	490	6.09
Puerto Rican	28	0.35
South American	7	0.09
Argentinean	1	0.01
Peruvian	1	0.01
Venezuelan	5	0.06
Other Hispanic or Latino	78	0.97

Race*	Population	%
African-American/Black (473)	543	6.75
Not Hispanic (465)	525	6.52
Hispanic (8)	18	0.22
American Indian/Alaska Native (44)	101	1.26
Not Hispanic (34)	86	1.07
Hispanic (10)	15	0.19
Cherokee (12)	41	0.51
Choctaw (8)	9	0.11
Iroquois (1)	1	0.01
Lumbee (8)	8	0.10
Pima (1)	1	0.01
Seminole (2)	2	0.02
Sioux (0)	2	0.02
Asian (98)	121	1.50
Not Hispanic (98)	121	1.50
Chinese, ex. Taiwanese (20)	22	0.27
Filipino (7)	10	0.12
Indian (1)	4	0.05
Japanese (14)	17	0.21
Korean (25)	36	0.45
Taiwanese (6)	6	0.07
Vietnamese (15)	18	0.22
Hawaii Native/Pacific Islander (7)	19	0.24
Not Hispanic (7)	19	0.24
Native Hawaiian (0)	4	0.05
White (6,993)	7,142	88.75
Not Hispanic (6,669)	6,793	84.42
Hispanic (324)	349	4.34

Johnson City

Place Type: City
County: Washington
Population: 63,152†

Ancestry‡	Population	%
African, Sub-Saharan (305)	437	0.71
African (143)	228	0.37
Kenyan (9)	9	0.01
Liberian (63)	110	0.18
Nigerian (38)	38	0.06
South African (14)	14	0.02
Other Sub-Saharan African (38)	38	0.06
Alsatian (12)	12	0.02
American (16,607)	16,607	26.89
Arab (162)	184	0.30
Arab (88)	88	0.14
Jordanian (9)	9	0.01
Lebanese (65)	87	0.14
Austrian (56)	68	0.11
Belgian (24)	52	0.08
Brazilian (30)	30	0.05
British (334)	420	0.68
Cajun (0)	7	0.01
Canadian (104)	127	0.21
Celtic (75)	75	0.12
Croatian (21)	50	0.08
Czech (0)	59	0.10
Czechoslovakian (0)	17	0.03
Danish (48)	72	0.12
Dutch (176)	842	1.36
English (3,651)	7,639	12.37
European (552)	644	1.04
Finnish (0)	80	0.13
French, ex. Basque (257)	1,205	1.95
French Canadian (36)	91	0.15
German (2,559)	7,904	12.80
Greek (36)	199	0.32
Hungarian (29)	78	0.13
Iranian (11)	11	0.02
Irish (2,518)	7,291	11.81
Italian (477)	1,218	1.97
Lithuanian (34)	128	0.21
Luxemburger (0)	21	0.03
Northern European (78)	78	0.13
Norwegian (86)	312	0.51
Pennsylvania German (0)	31	0.05
Polish (142)	551	0.89
Portuguese (14)	46	0.07
Romanian (0)	11	0.02
Russian (51)	173	0.28
Scandinavian (19)	44	0.07
Scotch-Irish (1,726)	2,740	4.44
Scottish (869)	2,152	3.48
Serbian (12)	12	0.02
Slovak (0)	19	0.03
Swedish (139)	320	0.52
Swiss (25)	100	0.16
Turkish (13)	13	0.02
Ukrainian (116)	207	0.34
Welsh (42)	418	0.68
West Indian, ex. Hispanic (17)	50	0.08
Haitian (17)	50	0.08
Yugoslavian (0)	13	0.02

Hispanic Origin	Population	%
Hispanic or Latino (of any race)	2,656	4.21
Central American, ex. Mexican	234	0.37
Costa Rican	13	0.02
Guatemalan	55	0.09
Honduran	62	0.10
Nicaraguan	30	0.05
Panamanian	18	0.03
Salvadoran	52	0.08
Other Central American	4	0.01
Cuban	85	0.13
Dominican Republic	31	0.05
Mexican	1,651	2.61
Puerto Rican	265	0.42
South American	164	0.26
Argentinean	22	0.03
Bolivian	4	0.01
Chilean	10	0.02
Colombian	39	0.06
Ecuadorian	34	0.05
Paraguayan	2	<0.01
Peruvian	23	0.04
Venezuelan	30	0.05
Other Hispanic or Latino	226	0.36

Race*	Population	%
African-American/Black (4,183)	4,949	7.84
Not Hispanic (4,108)	4,804	7.61
Hispanic (75)	145	0.23
American Indian/Alaska Native (216)	556	0.88
Not Hispanic (185)	497	0.79
Hispanic (31)	59	0.09
Apache (1)	5	0.01
Blackfeet (3)	15	0.02
Central American Ind. (0)	1	<0.01
Cherokee (73)	221	0.35
Cheyenne (0)	2	<0.01
Chickasaw (9)	9	0.01
Chippewa (0)	10	0.02
Choctaw (5)	12	0.02
Comanche (0)	1	<0.01
Creek (1)	4	0.01
Inupiat *(Alaska Native)* (2)	2	<0.01

*Notes: † The Census 2010 population figure is used to calculate the percentages in the Hispanic Origin and Race categories. Ancestry percentages are based on the 2006-2010 American Community Survey population (not shown); ‡ Numbers in parentheses indicate the number of people reporting a single ancestry; * Numbers in parentheses indicate the number of persons reporting this race alone, not in combination with any other race; Please refer to the Explanation of Data for more information.*

Iroquois (0)	1	<0.01
Lumbee (1)	5	0.01
Mexican American Ind. (4)	9	0.01
Navajo (5)	5	0.01
Paiute (1)	1	<0.01
Potawatomi (2)	5	0.01
Seminole (0)	3	<0.01
Shoshone (0)	2	<0.01
Sioux (6)	11	0.02
South American Ind. (1)	1	<0.01
Tlingit-Haida *(Alaska Native)* (1)	2	<0.01
Yakama (1)	1	<0.01
Asian (1,241)	1,482	2.35
Not Hispanic (1,239)	1,467	2.32
Hispanic (2)	15	0.02
Bangladeshi (7)	7	0.01
Burmese (5)	5	0.01
Cambodian (3)	4	0.01
Chinese, ex. Taiwanese (324)	363	0.57
Filipino (104)	169	0.27
Hmong (8)	8	0.01
Indian (438)	476	0.75
Indonesian (7)	7	0.01
Japanese (43)	68	0.11
Korean (68)	119	0.19
Laotian (3)	3	<0.01
Malaysian (1)	1	<0.01
Nepalese (4)	4	0.01
Pakistani (54)	54	0.09
Sri Lankan (1)	3	<0.01
Taiwanese (14)	18	0.03
Thai (13)	22	0.03
Vietnamese (94)	105	0.17
Hawaii Native/Pacific Islander (20)	73	0.12
Not Hispanic (11)	54	0.09
Hispanic (9)	19	0.03
Guamanian/Chamorro (6)	23	0.04
Native Hawaiian (4)	17	0.03
Samoan (3)	8	0.01
White (54,893)	56,211	89.01
Not Hispanic (53,693)	54,809	86.79
Hispanic (1,200)	1,402	2.22

Kingsport

Place Type: City
County: Sullivan
Population: 48,205†

Ancestry‡	Population	%
African, Sub-Saharan (134)	163	0.34
African (119)	148	0.31
Other Sub-Saharan African (15)	15	0.03
American (12,357)	12,357	25.82
Arab (145)	170	0.36
Arab (64)	64	0.13
Egyptian (55)	55	0.11
Jordanian (17)	17	0.04
Lebanese (9)	26	0.05
Syrian (0)	8	0.02
Armenian (44)	44	0.09
Austrian (20)	37	0.08
Belgian (11)	42	0.09
Brazilian (23)	23	0.05
British (188)	225	0.47
Cajun (53)	53	0.11
Canadian (37)	37	0.08
Celtic (0)	11	0.02
Czech (9)	87	0.18
Czechoslovakian (0)	39	0.08
Danish (43)	145	0.30
Dutch (262)	796	1.66
English (3,484)	6,449	13.48
European (396)	449	0.94
French, ex. Basque (235)	870	1.82
French Canadian (93)	98	0.20
German (1,864)	5,267	11.01
Greek (9)	24	0.05
Hungarian (0)	44	0.09
Irish (2,826)	6,173	12.90
Italian (457)	1,125	2.35
Northern European (10)	20	0.04
Norwegian (49)	136	0.28
Pennsylvania German (14)	27	0.06
Polish (142)	398	0.83
Romanian (0)	7	0.01
Russian (28)	43	0.09
Scandinavian (9)	30	0.06
Scotch-Irish (1,369)	2,197	4.59
Scottish (677)	1,596	3.34
Serbian (0)	47	0.10
Slovak (0)	66	0.14
Swedish (34)	201	0.42
Swiss (12)	59	0.12
Welsh (89)	300	0.63
West Indian, ex. Hispanic (16)	16	0.03
Jamaican (16)	16	0.03
Yugoslavian (82)	82	0.17

Hispanic Origin	Population	%
Hispanic or Latino (of any race)	1,036	2.15
Central American, ex. Mexican	49	0.10
Costa Rican	3	0.01
Guatemalan	12	0.02
Honduran	11	0.02
Nicaraguan	9	0.02
Panamanian	1	<0.01
Salvadoran	13	0.03
Cuban	33	0.07
Dominican Republic	6	0.01
Mexican	716	1.49
Puerto Rican	93	0.19
South American	49	0.10
Argentinean	4	0.01
Bolivian	1	<0.01
Chilean	1	<0.01
Colombian	12	0.02
Ecuadorian	2	<0.01
Peruvian	15	0.03
Uruguayan	1	<0.01
Venezuelan	13	0.03
Other Hispanic or Latino	90	0.19

Race*	Population	%
African-American/Black (1,954)	2,423	5.03
Not Hispanic (1,926)	2,364	4.90
Hispanic (28)	59	0.12
American Indian/Alaska Native (126)	406	0.84
Not Hispanic (112)	375	0.78
Hispanic (14)	31	0.06
Apache (2)	7	0.01
Blackfeet (0)	12	0.02
Canadian/French Am. Ind. (1)	2	<0.01
Cherokee (46)	170	0.35
Chickasaw (0)	2	<0.01
Chippewa (2)	10	0.02
Choctaw (7)	11	0.02
Creek (0)	3	0.01
Delaware (0)	5	0.01
Iroquois (0)	3	0.01
Lumbee (10)	10	0.02
Mexican American Ind. (2)	3	0.01
Navajo (5)	5	0.01
Potawatomi (1)	4	0.01
Sioux (1)	2	<0.01
South American Ind. (1)	2	<0.01
Asian (483)	593	1.23
Not Hispanic (481)	585	1.21
Hispanic (2)	8	0.02
Chinese, ex. Taiwanese (168)	183	0.38
Filipino (52)	76	0.16
Indian (173)	199	0.41
Indonesian (1)	1	<0.01
Japanese (8)	25	0.05
Korean (39)	50	0.10
Laotian (2)	6	0.01
Pakistani (4)	4	0.01
Taiwanese (7)	9	0.02
Thai (4)	7	0.01
Vietnamese (16)	26	0.05
Hawaii Native/Pacific Islander (14)	35	0.07
Not Hispanic (13)	34	0.07
Hispanic (1)	1	<0.01
Guamanian/Chamorro (2)	3	0.01
Marshallese (3)	3	0.01
Native Hawaiian (4)	15	0.03
Samoan (2)	2	<0.01
White (44,308)	45,143	93.65
Not Hispanic (43,798)	44,547	92.41
Hispanic (510)	596	1.24

Knoxville

Place Type: City
County: Knox
Population: 178,874†

Ancestry‡	Population	%
African, Sub-Saharan (2,348)	2,605	1.46
African (1,983)	2,215	1.24
Ethiopian (22)	22	0.01
Kenyan (65)	65	0.04
Liberian (89)	89	0.05
Nigerian (24)	24	0.01
Senegalese (28)	28	0.02
South African (0)	25	0.01
Zimbabwean (28)	28	0.02
Other Sub-Saharan African (109)	109	0.06
Albanian (11)	11	0.01
American (19,205)	19,205	10.78
Arab (646)	792	0.44
Arab (250)	311	0.17
Egyptian (85)	93	0.05
Iraqi (35)	35	0.02
Jordanian (7)	7	<0.01
Lebanese (50)	80	0.04
Palestinian (89)	89	0.05
Syrian (0)	32	0.02
Other Arab (130)	145	0.08
Armenian (49)	49	0.03
Australian (10)	28	0.02
Austrian (104)	417	0.23
Belgian (95)	140	0.08
Brazilian (0)	20	0.01
British (661)	1,053	0.59
Bulgarian (0)	7	<0.01
Canadian (307)	386	0.22
Celtic (18)	41	0.02
Croatian (12)	72	0.04
Czech (103)	393	0.22
Czechoslovakian (35)	98	0.05
Danish (60)	370	0.21
Dutch (586)	2,933	1.65
Eastern European (65)	65	0.04
English (13,468)	27,870	15.64
European (1,959)	2,161	1.21
Finnish (24)	122	0.07
French, ex. Basque (782)	3,911	2.19
French Canadian (293)	511	0.29
German (9,829)	26,566	14.91
German Russian (0)	22	0.01
Greek (347)	730	0.41
Guyanese (0)	13	0.01
Hungarian (139)	442	0.25
Icelander (19)	19	0.01
Iranian (155)	169	0.09
Irish (7,589)	20,484	11.49
Italian (1,501)	4,053	2.27
Latvian (0)	11	0.01
Lithuanian (25)	679	0.38
Luxemburger (0)	12	0.01
Macedonian (0)	21	0.01
Northern European (85)	117	0.07
Norwegian (419)	1,155	0.65
Pennsylvania German (16)	16	0.01
Polish (785)	2,364	1.33
Portuguese (63)	114	0.06
Romanian (73)	103	0.06
Russian (264)	777	0.44
Scandinavian (38)	173	0.10

*Notes: † The Census 2010 population figure is used to calculate the percentages in the Hispanic Origin and Race categories. Ancestry percentages are based on the 2006-2010 American Community Survey population (not shown); ‡ Numbers in parentheses indicate the number of people reporting a single ancestry; * Numbers in parentheses indicate the number of persons reporting this race alone, not in combination with any other race; Please refer to the Explanation of Data for more information.*

Scotch-Irish (4,096)	7,606	4.27
Scottish (1,920)	5,075	2.85
Serbian (22)	22	0.01
Slavic (13)	44	0.02
Slovak (46)	97	0.05
Slovene (0)	16	0.01
Swedish (478)	1,700	0.95
Swiss (80)	535	0.30
Turkish (70)	113	0.06
Ukrainian (252)	469	0.26
Welsh (524)	1,534	0.86
West Indian, ex. Hispanic (90)	260	0.15
Belizean (2)	2	<0.01
Dutch West Indian (10)	75	0.04
Haitian (0)	40	0.02
Jamaican (25)	61	0.03
West Indian (53)	82	0.05
Yugoslavian (128)	174	0.10

Hispanic Origin	Population	%
Hispanic or Latino (of any race)	8,206	4.59
Central American, ex. Mexican	1,294	0.72
Costa Rican	20	0.01
Guatemalan	695	0.39
Honduran	354	0.20
Nicaraguan	35	0.02
Panamanian	60	0.03
Salvadoran	129	0.07
Other Central American	1	<0.01
Cuban	248	0.14
Dominican Republic	39	0.02
Mexican	4,960	2.77
Puerto Rican	611	0.34
South American	390	0.22
Argentinean	42	0.02
Bolivian	28	0.02
Chilean	32	0.02
Colombian	150	0.08
Ecuadorian	33	0.02
Paraguayan	3	<0.01
Peruvian	55	0.03
Uruguayan	4	<0.01
Venezuelan	41	0.02
Other South American	2	<0.01
Other Hispanic or Latino	664	0.37

Race*	Population	%
African-American/Black (30,567)	33,167	18.54
Not Hispanic (30,257)	32,665	18.26
Hispanic (310)	502	0.28
American Indian/Alaska Native (631)	1,859	1.04
Not Hispanic (496)	1,622	0.91
Hispanic (135)	237	0.13
Alaska Athabascan *(Ala. Nat.)* (2)	2	<0.01
Aleut *(Alaska Native)* (1)	1	<0.01
Apache (4)	18	0.01
Blackfeet (4)	42	0.02
Central American Ind. (13)	20	0.01
Cherokee (177)	717	0.40
Cheyenne (1)	3	<0.01
Chickasaw (6)	12	0.01
Chippewa (22)	36	0.02
Choctaw (19)	42	0.02
Comanche (0)	1	<0.01
Creek (3)	9	0.01
Crow (3)	6	<0.01
Delaware (4)	6	<0.01
Hopi (1)	3	<0.01
Houma (3)	6	<0.01
Inupiat *(Alaska Native)* (1)	1	<0.01
Iroquois (3)	19	0.01
Lumbee (13)	24	0.01
Menominee (3)	6	<0.01
Mexican American Ind. (53)	59	0.03
Navajo (6)	13	0.01
Osage (3)	7	<0.01
Ottawa (2)	4	<0.01
Potawatomi (1)	2	<0.01
Puget Sound Salish (0)	6	<0.01
Seminole (0)	6	<0.01
Sioux (4)	15	0.01
South American Ind. (6)	8	<0.01
Spanish American Ind. (6)	6	<0.01
Ute (1)	1	<0.01
Yaqui (0)	3	<0.01
Yup'ik *(Alaska Native)* (1)	1	<0.01
Asian (2,943)	3,721	2.08
Not Hispanic (2,875)	3,593	2.01
Hispanic (68)	128	0.07
Bangladeshi (23)	23	0.01
Burmese (38)	39	0.02
Cambodian (26)	43	0.02
Chinese, ex. Taiwanese (763)	860	0.48
Filipino (269)	457	0.26
Hmong (2)	2	<0.01
Indian (660)	745	0.42
Indonesian (44)	60	0.03
Japanese (131)	237	0.13
Korean (386)	484	0.27
Laotian (20)	23	0.01
Malaysian (11)	17	0.01
Nepalese (20)	22	0.01
Pakistani (54)	62	0.03
Sri Lankan (15)	16	0.01
Taiwanese (42)	50	0.03
Thai (43)	53	0.03
Vietnamese (286)	336	0.19
Hawaii Native/Pacific Islander (277)	420	0.23
Not Hispanic (198)	323	0.18
Hispanic (79)	97	0.05
Fijian (0)	2	<0.01
Guamanian/Chamorro (122)	135	0.08
Native Hawaiian (38)	83	0.05
Samoan (21)	31	0.02
Tongan (0)	2	<0.01
White (136,097)	140,108	78.33
Not Hispanic (132,641)	136,185	76.13
Hispanic (3,456)	3,923	2.19

La Vergne

Place Type: City
County: Rutherford
Population: 32,588†

Ancestry‡	Population	%
African, Sub-Saharan (180)	191	0.63
African (87)	98	0.32
Sudanese (93)	93	0.31
American (6,573)	6,573	21.65
Arab (91)	100	0.33
Iraqi (64)	73	0.24
Lebanese (9)	9	0.03
Syrian (11)	11	0.04
Other Arab (7)	7	0.02
Austrian (0)	44	0.14
Belgian (0)	83	0.27
British (22)	45	0.15
Canadian (65)	87	0.29
Celtic (14)	14	0.05
Croatian (0)	53	0.17
Czech (21)	38	0.13
Danish (0)	15	0.05
Dutch (113)	355	1.17
English (945)	1,839	6.06
European (130)	143	0.47
Finnish (9)	31	0.10
French, ex. Basque (35)	495	1.63
French Canadian (29)	73	0.24
German (1,015)	2,703	8.90
Greek (23)	23	0.08
Guyanese (28)	28	0.09
Hungarian (14)	24	0.08
Irish (874)	2,901	9.55
Italian (273)	574	1.89
Lithuanian (16)	42	0.14
Norwegian (99)	151	0.50
Pennsylvania German (20)	20	0.07
Polish (97)	290	0.95
Portuguese (0)	3	0.01
Romanian (0)	13	0.04
Russian (0)	52	0.17
Scandinavian (4)	4	0.01
Scotch-Irish (212)	576	1.90
Scottish (181)	462	1.52
Slovak (0)	9	0.03
Swedish (32)	103	0.34
Swiss (14)	28	0.09
Ukrainian (20)	49	0.16
Welsh (56)	105	0.35
West Indian, ex. Hispanic (30)	39	0.13
Dutch West Indian (0)	9	0.03
Jamaican (21)	21	0.07
West Indian (9)	9	0.03
Yugoslavian (32)	32	0.11

Hispanic Origin	Population	%
Hispanic or Latino (of any race)	4,239	13.01
Central American, ex. Mexican	906	2.78
Costa Rican	33	0.10
Guatemalan	170	0.52
Honduran	169	0.52
Nicaraguan	47	0.14
Panamanian	22	0.07
Salvadoran	460	1.41
Other Central American	5	0.02
Cuban	92	0.28
Dominican Republic	34	0.10
Mexican	2,253	6.91
Puerto Rican	473	1.45
South American	215	0.66
Argentinean	1	<0.01
Bolivian	4	0.01
Chilean	4	0.01
Colombian	41	0.13
Ecuadorian	67	0.21
Peruvian	72	0.22
Venezuelan	26	0.08
Other Hispanic or Latino	266	0.82

Race*	Population	%
African-American/Black (7,491)	8,052	24.71
Not Hispanic (7,393)	7,897	24.23
Hispanic (98)	155	0.48
American Indian/Alaska Native (113)	283	0.87
Not Hispanic (59)	203	0.62
Hispanic (54)	80	0.25
Alaska Athabascan *(Ala. Nat.)* (1)	1	<0.01
Aleut *(Alaska Native)* (1)	5	0.02
Apache (0)	4	0.01
Blackfeet (1)	16	0.05
Canadian/French Am. Ind. (1)	1	<0.01
Central American Ind. (5)	5	0.02
Cherokee (12)	67	0.21
Cheyenne (0)	1	<0.01
Chickasaw (0)	1	<0.01
Chippewa (1)	3	0.01
Choctaw (5)	6	0.02
Comanche (1)	6	0.02
Creek (1)	1	<0.01
Houma (0)	1	<0.01
Iroquois (2)	2	0.01
Menominee (0)	1	<0.01
Mexican American Ind. (8)	12	0.04
Navajo (0)	1	<0.01
Osage (0)	3	0.01
Ottawa (2)	2	0.01
Sioux (1)	4	0.01
South American Ind. (1)	4	0.01
Spanish American Ind. (21)	21	0.06
Asian (1,060)	1,262	3.87
Not Hispanic (1,052)	1,225	3.76
Hispanic (8)	37	0.11
Bangladeshi (3)	3	0.01
Burmese (13)	13	0.04
Cambodian (21)	31	0.10
Chinese, ex. Taiwanese (39)	56	0.17
Filipino (87)	140	0.43
Hmong (6)	6	0.02
Indian (91)	121	0.37

*Notes: † The Census 2010 population figure is used to calculate the percentages in the Hispanic Origin and Race categories. Ancestry percentages are based on the 2006-2010 American Community Survey population (not shown); ‡ Numbers in parentheses indicate the number of people reporting a single ancestry; * Numbers in parentheses indicate the number of persons reporting this race alone, not in combination with any other race; Please refer to the Explanation of Data for more information.*

Indonesian (1)	2	0.01
Japanese (23)	39	0.12
Korean (31)	47	0.14
Laotian (545)	612	1.88
Malaysian (1)	1	<0.01
Pakistani (11)	13	0.04
Taiwanese (2)	3	0.01
Thai (37)	54	0.17
Vietnamese (50)	58	0.18
Hawaii Native/Pacific Islander (27)	69	0.21
Not Hispanic (25)	52	0.16
Hispanic (2)	17	0.05
Guamanian/Chamorro (20)	21	0.06
Native Hawaiian (3)	11	0.03
Samoan (1)	4	0.01
White (20,529)	21,379	65.60
Not Hispanic (19,015)	19,677	60.38
Hispanic (1,514)	1,702	5.22

Lakeland

Place Type: City
County: Shelby
Population: 12,430†

Ancestry‡	Population	%
American (1,135)	1,135	9.87
Arab (25)	25	0.22
Arab (10)	10	0.09
Lebanese (15)	15	0.13
Assyrian/Chaldean/Syriac (25)	44	0.38
British (0)	8	0.07
Canadian (36)	62	0.54
Croatian (34)	34	0.30
Czech (15)	33	0.29
Danish (0)	41	0.36
Dutch (62)	165	1.43
Eastern European (13)	13	0.11
English (578)	1,827	15.88
European (130)	130	1.13
French, ex. Basque (53)	314	2.73
French Canadian (52)	92	0.80
German (339)	1,174	10.21
Irish (731)	2,084	18.12
Italian (207)	466	4.05
Latvian (39)	39	0.34
Norwegian (0)	27	0.23
Polish (73)	87	0.76
Russian (57)	92	0.80
Scotch-Irish (306)	489	4.25
Scottish (106)	204	1.77
Slavic (0)	7	0.06
Slovak (0)	33	0.29
Swedish (25)	178	1.55
Ukrainian (13)	13	0.11
Welsh (0)	30	0.26

Hispanic Origin	Population	%
Hispanic or Latino (of any race)	424	3.41
Central American, ex. Mexican	19	0.15
Guatemalan	1	0.01
Honduran	13	0.10
Nicaraguan	1	0.01
Salvadoran	4	0.03
Cuban	7	0.06
Dominican Republic	1	0.01
Mexican	280	2.25
Puerto Rican	43	0.35
South American	18	0.14
Argentinean	1	0.01
Chilean	2	0.02
Colombian	6	0.05
Ecuadorian	2	0.02
Peruvian	2	0.02
Uruguayan	1	0.01
Venezuelan	4	0.03
Other Hispanic or Latino	56	0.45

Race*	Population	%
African-American/Black (1,163)	1,231	9.90
Not Hispanic (1,159)	1,216	9.78
Hispanic (4)	15	0.12
American Indian/Alaska Native (30)	81	0.65
Not Hispanic (27)	70	0.56
Hispanic (3)	11	0.09
Apache (0)	4	0.03
Blackfeet (1)	1	0.01
Cherokee (6)	21	0.17
Chickasaw (0)	2	0.02
Chippewa (0)	2	0.02
Choctaw (10)	13	0.10
Mexican American Ind. (2)	3	0.02
Potawatomi (0)	1	0.01
Spanish American Ind. (1)	1	0.01
Asian (553)	632	5.08
Not Hispanic (551)	624	5.02
Hispanic (2)	8	0.06
Cambodian (9)	10	0.08
Chinese, ex. Taiwanese (157)	171	1.38
Filipino (54)	83	0.67
Indian (142)	154	1.24
Indonesian (1)	2	0.02
Japanese (4)	7	0.06
Korean (52)	62	0.50
Laotian (12)	16	0.13
Malaysian (2)	2	0.02
Pakistani (27)	30	0.24
Taiwanese (5)	9	0.07
Thai (1)	1	0.01
Vietnamese (72)	85	0.68
Hawaii Native/Pacific Islander (1)	7	0.06
Not Hispanic (1)	6	0.05
Hispanic (0)	1	0.01
Guamanian/Chamorro (0)	1	0.01
Samoan (1)	3	0.02
White (10,358)	10,510	84.55
Not Hispanic (10,109)	10,239	82.37
Hispanic (249)	271	2.18

Lawrenceburg

Place Type: City
County: Lawrence
Population: 10,428†

Ancestry‡	Population	%
African, Sub-Saharan (14)	14	0.13
African (14)	14	0.13
American (1,481)	1,481	14.21
Austrian (24)	24	0.23
British (56)	56	0.54
Cajun (0)	87	0.83
Canadian (49)	49	0.47
Celtic (0)	13	0.12
Croatian (0)	17	0.16
Danish (16)	37	0.35
Dutch (62)	194	1.86
English (521)	792	7.60
European (85)	96	0.92
Finnish (0)	17	0.16
French, ex. Basque (106)	326	3.13
French Canadian (0)	33	0.32
German (367)	1,171	11.23
Greek (0)	39	0.37
Hungarian (46)	46	0.44
Irish (647)	1,259	12.08
Israeli (17)	17	0.16
Italian (185)	294	2.82
Norwegian (25)	83	0.80
Polish (59)	120	1.15
Portuguese (0)	24	0.23
Scotch-Irish (368)	475	4.56
Scottish (38)	84	0.81
Slovak (21)	46	0.44
Slovene (0)	17	0.16
Swedish (0)	39	0.37
Ukrainian (0)	30	0.29
Welsh (28)	40	0.38

Hispanic Origin	Population	%
Hispanic or Latino (of any race)	322	3.09
Central American, ex. Mexican	13	0.12
Guatemalan	2	0.02
Honduran	8	0.08
Nicaraguan	2	0.02
Other Central American	1	0.01
Cuban	11	0.11
Mexican	232	2.22
Puerto Rican	37	0.35
South American	1	0.01
Venezuelan	1	0.01
Other Hispanic or Latino	28	0.27

Race*	Population	%
African-American/Black (467)	601	5.76
Not Hispanic (463)	581	5.57
Hispanic (4)	20	0.19
American Indian/Alaska Native (48)	160	1.53
Not Hispanic (42)	142	1.36
Hispanic (6)	18	0.17
Apache (1)	1	0.01
Blackfeet (0)	1	0.01
Cherokee (14)	59	0.57
Chickasaw (2)	2	0.02
Choctaw (2)	6	0.06
Creek (2)	3	0.03
Sioux (2)	3	0.03
Asian (55)	79	0.76
Not Hispanic (55)	73	0.70
Hispanic (0)	6	0.06
Chinese, ex. Taiwanese (8)	8	0.08
Filipino (9)	13	0.12
Indian (25)	34	0.33
Japanese (2)	2	0.02
Korean (3)	8	0.08
Thai (6)	6	0.06
Vietnamese (0)	6	0.06
Hawaii Native/Pacific Islander (0)	4	0.04
Not Hispanic (0)	2	0.02
Hispanic (0)	2	0.02
Samoan (0)	1	0.01
White (9,474)	9,732	93.33
Not Hispanic (9,312)	9,531	91.40
Hispanic (162)	201	1.93

Lebanon

Place Type: City
County: Wilson
Population: 26,190†

Ancestry‡	Population	%
African, Sub-Saharan (39)	39	0.15
African (39)	39	0.15
American (4,321)	4,321	17.15
Arab (120)	149	0.59
Arab (12)	41	0.16
Lebanese (12)	12	0.05
Syrian (96)	96	0.38
Armenian (0)	14	0.06
Australian (16)	16	0.06
Austrian (16)	28	0.11
Brazilian (23)	23	0.09
British (62)	92	0.37
Cajun (16)	16	0.06
Canadian (19)	30	0.12
Czech (0)	13	0.05
Czechoslovakian (0)	9	0.04
Danish (0)	28	0.11
Dutch (112)	370	1.47
English (1,031)	2,087	8.29
European (171)	188	0.75
Finnish (0)	9	0.04
French, ex. Basque (182)	662	2.63
French Canadian (16)	31	0.12
German (769)	1,992	7.91
Greek (0)	14	0.06
Irish (749)	2,057	8.17
Italian (247)	529	2.10

*Notes: † The Census 2010 population figure is used to calculate the percentages in the Hispanic Origin and Race categories. Ancestry percentages are based on the 2006-2010 American Community Survey population (not shown); ‡ Numbers in parentheses indicate the number of people reporting a single ancestry; * Numbers in parentheses indicate the number of persons reporting this race alone, not in combination with any other race; Please refer to the Explanation of Data for more information.*

Latvian (0)	18	0.07
Northern European (8)	8	0.03
Norwegian (12)	30	0.12
Polish (55)	227	0.90
Russian (10)	33	0.13
Scandinavian (23)	23	0.09
Scotch-Irish (329)	684	2.72
Scottish (160)	348	1.38
Slavic (0)	13	0.05
Slovak (0)	8	0.03
Swedish (12)	95	0.38
Swiss (0)	40	0.16
Ukrainian (0)	18	0.07
Welsh (44)	286	1.14

Hispanic Origin	Population	%
Hispanic or Latino (of any race)	1,630	6.22
Central American, ex. Mexican	131	0.50
Guatemalan	71	0.27
Honduran	12	0.05
Nicaraguan	7	0.03
Panamanian	8	0.03
Salvadoran	33	0.13
Cuban	36	0.14
Dominican Republic	7	0.03
Mexican	1,232	4.70
Puerto Rican	74	0.28
South American	31	0.12
Argentinean	2	0.01
Colombian	6	0.02
Ecuadorian	5	0.02
Paraguayan	1	<0.01
Peruvian	15	0.06
Uruguayan	1	<0.01
Venezuelan	1	<0.01
Other Hispanic or Latino	119	0.45

Race*	Population	%
African-American/Black (3,138)	3,451	13.18
Not Hispanic (3,120)	3,420	13.06
Hispanic (18)	31	0.12
American Indian/Alaska Native (73)	234	0.89
Not Hispanic (69)	213	0.81
Hispanic (4)	21	0.08
Blackfeet (0)	9	0.03
Central American Ind. (2)	3	0.01
Cherokee (22)	85	0.32
Chickasaw (2)	2	0.01
Chippewa (1)	4	0.02
Choctaw (2)	3	0.01
Comanche (0)	1	<0.01
Creek (6)	9	0.03
Iroquois (0)	1	<0.01
Lumbee (2)	2	0.01
Mexican American Ind. (1)	6	0.02
Navajo (2)	5	0.02
Ottawa (2)	2	0.01
Pima (1)	1	<0.01
Potawatomi (1)	3	0.01
Pueblo (0)	1	<0.01
Puget Sound Salish (0)	3	0.01
Seminole (0)	2	0.01
Sioux (0)	2	0.01
Spanish American Ind. (0)	3	0.01
Tohono O'Odham (2)	2	0.01
Asian (340)	408	1.56
Not Hispanic (338)	400	1.53
Hispanic (2)	8	0.03
Cambodian (2)	3	0.01
Chinese, ex. Taiwanese (43)	58	0.22
Filipino (27)	43	0.16
Hmong (2)	2	0.01
Indian (166)	173	0.66
Indonesian (2)	2	0.01
Japanese (7)	17	0.06
Korean (32)	42	0.16
Laotian (12)	12	0.05
Pakistani (1)	1	<0.01
Thai (7)	10	0.04
Vietnamese (23)	31	0.12
Hawaii Native/Pacific Islander (7)	25	0.10
Not Hispanic (7)	21	0.08
Hispanic (0)	4	0.02
Guamanian/Chamorro (2)	2	0.01
Native Hawaiian (3)	16	0.06
Samoan (0)	1	<0.01
White (21,143)	21,658	82.70
Not Hispanic (20,520)	20,944	79.97
Hispanic (623)	714	2.73

Lenoir City

Place Type: City
County: Loudon
Population: 8,642†

Ancestry‡	Population	%
American (2,398)	2,398	28.68
British (18)	18	0.22
Dutch (73)	249	2.98
English (467)	682	8.16
French, ex. Basque (66)	216	2.58
German (176)	1,041	12.45
Irish (376)	948	11.34
Italian (36)	138	1.65
Norwegian (34)	75	0.90
Polish (8)	144	1.72
Scotch-Irish (135)	277	3.31
Scottish (60)	294	3.52
Swedish (9)	9	0.11
Welsh (0)	77	0.92
West Indian, ex. Hispanic (0)	36	0.43
Dutch West Indian (0)	36	0.43

Hispanic Origin	Population	%
Hispanic or Latino (of any race)	1,515	17.53
Central American, ex. Mexican	338	3.91
Guatemalan	213	2.46
Honduran	43	0.50
Nicaraguan	1	0.01
Panamanian	5	0.06
Salvadoran	75	0.87
Other Central American	1	0.01
Cuban	5	0.06
Mexican	1,048	12.13
Puerto Rican	27	0.31
South American	8	0.09
Colombian	3	0.03
Ecuadorian	1	0.01
Peruvian	4	0.05
Other Hispanic or Latino	89	1.03

Race*	Population	%
African-American/Black (135)	208	2.41
Not Hispanic (127)	193	2.23
Hispanic (8)	15	0.17
American Indian/Alaska Native (39)	76	0.88
Not Hispanic (22)	52	0.60
Hispanic (17)	24	0.28
Blackfeet (0)	7	0.08
Cherokee (8)	21	0.24
Creek (0)	1	0.01
Iroquois (1)	1	0.01
Kiowa (1)	1	0.01
Mexican American Ind. (0)	4	0.05
Pima (0)	1	0.01
Sioux (1)	1	0.01
Asian (53)	69	0.80
Not Hispanic (53)	64	0.74
Hispanic (0)	5	0.06
Chinese, ex. Taiwanese (7)	7	0.08
Filipino (14)	21	0.24
Indian (5)	5	0.06
Indonesian (8)	8	0.09
Japanese (1)	4	0.05
Korean (12)	12	0.14
Taiwanese (1)	1	0.01
Thai (1)	5	0.06
Vietnamese (3)	3	0.03
Hawaii Native/Pacific Islander (24)	31	0.36
Not Hispanic (10)	16	0.19
Hispanic (14)	15	0.17
Guamanian/Chamorro (14)	14	0.16
Native Hawaiian (1)	8	0.09
Samoan (1)	1	0.01
White (7,543)	7,690	88.98
Not Hispanic (6,803)	6,911	79.97
Hispanic (740)	779	9.01

Lewisburg

Place Type: City
County: Marshall
Population: 11,100†

Ancestry‡	Population	%
American (2,965)	2,965	27.07
Canadian (19)	25	0.23
Croatian (9)	9	0.08
Dutch (10)	140	1.28
English (352)	605	5.52
European (36)	36	0.33
French, ex. Basque (68)	128	1.17
French Canadian (0)	21	0.19
German (242)	1,079	9.85
Hungarian (0)	8	0.07
Irish (640)	1,294	11.81
Italian (43)	176	1.61
Lithuanian (9)	9	0.08
Norwegian (25)	25	0.23
Polish (0)	26	0.24
Portuguese (0)	10	0.09
Scotch-Irish (93)	205	1.87
Scottish (108)	199	1.82
Swedish (22)	34	0.31
Swiss (9)	9	0.08
Ukrainian (0)	13	0.12
Welsh (0)	9	0.08
West Indian, ex. Hispanic (29)	29	0.26
Belizean (29)	29	0.26

Hispanic Origin	Population	%
Hispanic or Latino (of any race)	863	7.77
Central American, ex. Mexican	49	0.44
Guatemalan	27	0.24
Honduran	5	0.05
Nicaraguan	1	0.01
Panamanian	4	0.04
Salvadoran	12	0.11
Cuban	5	0.05
Mexican	701	6.32
Puerto Rican	53	0.48
South American	23	0.21
Chilean	7	0.06
Colombian	6	0.05
Peruvian	7	0.06
Uruguayan	3	0.03
Other Hispanic or Latino	32	0.29

Race*	Population	%
African-American/Black (1,517)	1,688	15.21
Not Hispanic (1,502)	1,662	14.97
Hispanic (15)	26	0.23
American Indian/Alaska Native (24)	66	0.59
Not Hispanic (23)	64	0.58
Hispanic (1)	2	0.02
Blackfeet (0)	2	0.02
Cherokee (6)	26	0.23
Chickasaw (0)	1	0.01
Creek (1)	1	0.01
Crow (0)	1	0.01
Iroquois (0)	1	0.01
Lumbee (3)	3	0.03
Sioux (0)	4	0.04
Asian (76)	107	0.96
Not Hispanic (76)	106	0.95
Hispanic (0)	1	0.01
Chinese, ex. Taiwanese (12)	17	0.15
Filipino (9)	21	0.19
Indian (30)	33	0.30

*Notes: † The Census 2010 population figure is used to calculate the percentages in the Hispanic Origin and Race categories. Ancestry percentages are based on the 2006-2010 American Community Survey population (not shown); ‡ Numbers in parentheses indicate the number of people reporting a single ancestry; * Numbers in parentheses indicate the number of persons reporting this race alone, not in combination with any other race; Please refer to the Explanation of Data for more information.*

Indonesian (1)	3	0.03
Japanese (6)	8	0.07
Korean (1)	1	0.01
Laotian (2)	3	0.03
Thai (7)	9	0.08
Vietnamese (5)	5	0.05
Hawaii Native/Pacific Islander (5)	11	0.10
Not Hispanic (1)	7	0.06
Hispanic (4)	4	0.04
Guamanian/Chamorro (5)	5	0.05
Native Hawaiian (0)	6	0.05
White (8,693)	8,977	80.87
Not Hispanic (8,388)	8,613	77.59
Hispanic (305)	364	3.28

Lexington

Place Type: City
County: Henderson
Population: 7,652†

Ancestry‡	Population	%
African, Sub-Saharan (45)	45	0.59
African (45)	45	0.59
American (1,251)	1,251	16.37
British (19)	19	0.25
Celtic (0)	8	0.10
English (498)	741	9.70
European (63)	63	0.82
French, ex. Basque (52)	237	3.10
German (179)	604	7.90
Irish (431)	964	12.62
Italian (47)	166	2.17
Norwegian (0)	35	0.46
Portuguese (5)	5	0.07
Scotch-Irish (155)	164	2.15
Scottish (17)	84	1.10
Swedish (0)	13	0.17
Swiss (13)	13	0.17
Welsh (0)	11	0.14

Hispanic Origin	Population	%
Hispanic or Latino (of any race)	250	3.27
Central American, ex. Mexican	14	0.18
Costa Rican	1	0.01
Guatemalan	9	0.12
Honduran	3	0.04
Nicaraguan	1	0.01
Cuban	1	0.01
Dominican Republic	1	0.01
Mexican	162	2.12
Puerto Rican	10	0.13
Other Hispanic or Latino	62	0.81

Race*	Population	%
African-American/Black (1,098)	1,289	16.85
Not Hispanic (1,091)	1,277	16.69
Hispanic (7)	12	0.16
American Indian/Alaska Native (15)	44	0.58
Not Hispanic (12)	38	0.50
Hispanic (3)	6	0.08
Blackfeet (0)	4	0.05
Cherokee (6)	19	0.25
Chippewa (1)	1	0.01
Choctaw (0)	3	0.04
Houma (2)	2	0.03
Mexican American Ind. (3)	3	0.04
Asian (36)	40	0.52
Not Hispanic (36)	40	0.52
Chinese, ex. Taiwanese (9)	9	0.12
Filipino (6)	6	0.08
Indian (9)	11	0.14
Indonesian (1)	1	0.01
Korean (4)	4	0.05
Laotian (1)	2	0.03
Vietnamese (5)	6	0.08
Hawaii Native/Pacific Islander (0)	1	0.01
Not Hispanic (0)	1	0.01
Native Hawaiian (0)	1	0.01
White (6,161)	6,378	83.35
Not Hispanic (6,038)	6,242	81.57
Hispanic (123)	136	1.78

Manchester

Place Type: City
County: Coffee
Population: 10,102†

Ancestry‡	Population	%
African, Sub-Saharan (9)	9	0.09
African (9)	9	0.09
American (3,290)	3,290	33.24
Australian (12)	12	0.12
British (16)	44	0.44
Cypriot (11)	11	0.11
Dutch (38)	146	1.47
English (543)	1,086	10.97
European (140)	140	1.41
French, ex. Basque (13)	148	1.50
German (313)	969	9.79
Greek (74)	74	0.75
Iranian (9)	9	0.09
Irish (428)	1,061	10.72
Italian (22)	87	0.88
Norwegian (0)	35	0.35
Pennsylvania German (0)	14	0.14
Polish (66)	170	1.72
Russian (0)	11	0.11
Scotch-Irish (73)	160	1.62
Scottish (51)	122	1.23
Serbian (6)	24	0.24
Swedish (0)	27	0.27
Welsh (0)	70	0.71

Hispanic Origin	Population	%
Hispanic or Latino (of any race)	710	7.03
Central American, ex. Mexican	25	0.25
Guatemalan	10	0.10
Honduran	5	0.05
Nicaraguan	4	0.04
Panamanian	1	0.01
Salvadoran	5	0.05
Cuban	20	0.20
Mexican	586	5.80
Puerto Rican	31	0.31
South American	14	0.14
Ecuadorian	4	0.04
Peruvian	7	0.07
Venezuelan	3	0.03
Other Hispanic or Latino	34	0.34

Race*	Population	%
African-American/Black (347)	460	4.55
Not Hispanic (342)	451	4.46
Hispanic (5)	9	0.09
American Indian/Alaska Native (21)	73	0.72
Not Hispanic (19)	63	0.62
Hispanic (2)	10	0.10
Apache (0)	1	0.01
Blackfeet (0)	2	0.02
Cherokee (4)	26	0.26
Cheyenne (0)	1	0.01
Chippewa (2)	4	0.04
Creek (1)	3	0.03
Crow (1)	1	0.01
Iroquois (1)	1	0.01
Navajo (2)	3	0.03
Potawatomi (1)	1	0.01
Sioux (0)	1	0.01
Asian (116)	138	1.37
Not Hispanic (114)	135	1.34
Hispanic (2)	3	0.03
Cambodian (7)	7	0.07
Chinese, ex. Taiwanese (16)	17	0.17
Filipino (8)	13	0.13
Hmong (2)	2	0.02
Indian (27)	29	0.29
Japanese (21)	21	0.21
Korean (6)	13	0.13
Laotian (4)	4	0.04
Taiwanese (6)	6	0.06
Thai (0)	4	0.04
Vietnamese (11)	13	0.13
Hawaii Native/Pacific Islander (8)	17	0.17
Not Hispanic (5)	12	0.12
Hispanic (3)	5	0.05
Guamanian/Chamorro (5)	8	0.08
Native Hawaiian (2)	5	0.05
Samoan (0)	1	0.01
White (9,135)	9,328	92.34
Not Hispanic (8,739)	8,908	88.18
Hispanic (396)	420	4.16

Martin

Place Type: City
County: Weakley
Population: 11,473†

Ancestry‡	Population	%
American (1,529)	1,529	13.80
Arab (211)	229	2.07
Arab (0)	18	0.16
Egyptian (211)	211	1.90
Brazilian (0)	2	0.02
British (0)	18	0.16
Danish (0)	17	0.15
Dutch (12)	61	0.55
English (506)	1,066	9.62
European (53)	57	0.51
French, ex. Basque (51)	131	1.18
German (347)	1,121	10.11
Hungarian (13)	44	0.40
Irish (477)	1,168	10.54
Israeli (0)	52	0.47
Italian (57)	159	1.43
Norwegian (0)	14	0.13
Polish (20)	89	0.80
Russian (0)	8	0.07
Scotch-Irish (174)	354	3.19
Scottish (65)	140	1.26
Slovak (13)	13	0.12
Swedish (0)	30	0.27
Turkish (28)	28	0.25
Welsh (13)	38	0.34

Hispanic Origin	Population	%
Hispanic or Latino (of any race)	258	2.25
Central American, ex. Mexican	17	0.15
Guatemalan	3	0.03
Honduran	7	0.06
Nicaraguan	2	0.02
Panamanian	3	0.03
Salvadoran	2	0.02
Cuban	2	0.02
Dominican Republic	1	0.01
Mexican	173	1.51
Puerto Rican	23	0.20
South American	14	0.12
Argentinean	5	0.04
Colombian	6	0.05
Ecuadorian	1	0.01
Venezuelan	2	0.02
Other Hispanic or Latino	28	0.24

Race*	Population	%
African-American/Black (1,936)	2,040	17.78
Not Hispanic (1,922)	2,015	17.56
Hispanic (14)	25	0.22
American Indian/Alaska Native (22)	78	0.68
Not Hispanic (20)	70	0.61
Hispanic (2)	8	0.07
Alaska Athabascan *(Ala. Nat.)* (0)	2	0.02
Cherokee (5)	26	0.23
Chickasaw (0)	1	0.01
Choctaw (0)	2	0.02
Cree (0)	1	0.01
Creek (2)	2	0.02
Iroquois (0)	1	0.01

*Notes: † The Census 2010 population figure is used to calculate the percentages in the Hispanic Origin and Race categories. Ancestry percentages are based on the 2006-2010 American Community Survey population (not shown); ‡ Numbers in parentheses indicate the number of people reporting a single ancestry; * Numbers in parentheses indicate the number of persons reporting this race alone, not in combination with any other race; Please refer to the Explanation of Data for more information.*

Mexican American Ind. (0)	1	0.01
Ottawa (0)	1	0.01
Yaqui (1)	1	0.01
Asian (329)	388	3.38
Not Hispanic (326)	379	3.30
Hispanic (3)	9	0.08
Cambodian (2)	2	0.02
Chinese, ex. Taiwanese (53)	62	0.54
Filipino (35)	41	0.36
Indian (64)	72	0.63
Japanese (16)	24	0.21
Korean (122)	130	1.13
Taiwanese (17)	19	0.17
Thai (12)	14	0.12
Vietnamese (2)	3	0.03
Hawaii Native/Pacific Islander (5)	19	0.17
Not Hispanic (5)	17	0.15
Hispanic (0)	2	0.02
Guamanian/Chamorro (0)	4	0.03
Native Hawaiian (1)	9	0.08
Samoan (0)	1	0.01
Tongan (2)	3	0.03
White (8,899)	9,080	79.14
Not Hispanic (8,754)	8,915	77.70
Hispanic (145)	165	1.44

Maryville

Place Type: City
County: Blount
Population: 27,465†

Ancestry‡	Population	%
African, Sub-Saharan (181)	181	0.67
African (21)	21	0.08
Sudanese (160)	160	0.59
American (3,160)	3,160	11.74
Arab (129)	171	0.64
Arab (8)	17	0.06
Lebanese (121)	154	0.57
Armenian (14)	14	0.05
Austrian (0)	32	0.12
Belgian (14)	32	0.12
British (108)	217	0.81
Cajun (20)	34	0.13
Canadian (27)	27	0.10
Croatian (0)	7	0.03
Czech (13)	95	0.35
Czechoslovakian (0)	13	0.05
Danish (33)	33	0.12
Dutch (103)	442	1.64
Eastern European (24)	36	0.13
English (1,810)	3,885	14.43
European (450)	456	1.69
French, ex. Basque (110)	597	2.22
French Canadian (44)	86	0.32
German (1,393)	4,138	15.37
Greek (0)	49	0.18
Hungarian (41)	125	0.46
Iranian (0)	14	0.05
Irish (1,231)	3,816	14.17
Italian (451)	1,014	3.77
Latvian (0)	24	0.09
Lithuanian (13)	22	0.08
Macedonian (10)	10	0.04
Northern European (47)	47	0.17
Norwegian (25)	150	0.56
Pennsylvania German (11)	29	0.11
Polish (134)	433	1.61
Portuguese (0)	26	0.10
Romanian (0)	52	0.19
Russian (54)	177	0.66
Scandinavian (28)	45	0.17
Scotch-Irish (1,122)	1,912	7.10
Scottish (223)	694	2.58
Slovene (11)	11	0.04
Swedish (87)	345	1.28
Swiss (22)	102	0.38
Ukrainian (52)	120	0.45
Welsh (133)	354	1.31
West Indian, ex. Hispanic (30)	44	0.16
Belizean (20)	20	0.07
Dutch West Indian (10)	24	0.09
Yugoslavian (12)	12	0.04

Hispanic Origin	Population	%
Hispanic or Latino (of any race)	867	3.16
Central American, ex. Mexican	70	0.25
Costa Rican	2	0.01
Guatemalan	22	0.08
Honduran	14	0.05
Nicaraguan	9	0.03
Panamanian	12	0.04
Salvadoran	11	0.04
Cuban	36	0.13
Dominican Republic	9	0.03
Mexican	574	2.09
Puerto Rican	58	0.21
South American	38	0.14
Argentinean	3	0.01
Bolivian	1	<0.01
Colombian	17	0.06
Ecuadorian	1	<0.01
Peruvian	8	0.03
Uruguayan	1	<0.01
Venezuelan	4	0.01
Other South American	3	0.01
Other Hispanic or Latino	82	0.30

Race*	Population	%
African-American/Black (887)	1,093	3.98
Not Hispanic (874)	1,063	3.87
Hispanic (13)	30	0.11
American Indian/Alaska Native (92)	253	0.92
Not Hispanic (68)	215	0.78
Hispanic (24)	38	0.14
Apache (5)	8	0.03
Blackfeet (0)	7	0.03
Cherokee (27)	138	0.50
Chickasaw (0)	1	<0.01
Chippewa (0)	2	0.01
Choctaw (1)	2	0.01
Creek (1)	4	0.01
Delaware (1)	1	<0.01
Iroquois (2)	3	0.01
Mexican American Ind. (17)	17	0.06
Potawatomi (1)	1	<0.01
Sioux (0)	1	<0.01
Spanish American Ind. (1)	1	<0.01
Tlingit-Haida *(Alaska Native)* (1)	2	0.01
Asian (420)	531	1.93
Not Hispanic (417)	524	1.91
Hispanic (3)	7	0.03
Cambodian (1)	1	<0.01
Chinese, ex. Taiwanese (59)	81	0.29
Filipino (36)	57	0.21
Indian (54)	61	0.22
Indonesian (2)	2	0.01
Japanese (196)	224	0.82
Korean (17)	42	0.15
Laotian (3)	3	0.01
Malaysian (1)	1	<0.01
Taiwanese (4)	4	0.01
Thai (5)	14	0.05
Vietnamese (19)	23	0.08
Hawaii Native/Pacific Islander (9)	23	0.08
Not Hispanic (9)	21	0.08
Hispanic (0)	2	0.01
Guamanian/Chamorro (6)	8	0.03
Native Hawaiian (2)	12	0.04
Samoan (1)	1	<0.01
Tongan (0)	2	0.01
White (25,266)	25,722	93.65
Not Hispanic (24,764)	25,164	91.62
Hispanic (502)	558	2.03

McMinnville

Place Type: City
County: Warren
Population: 13,605†

Ancestry‡	Population	%
American (4,258)	4,258	31.60
British (12)	12	0.09
Czech (0)	8	0.06
Danish (0)	11	0.08
Dutch (0)	68	0.50
English (678)	1,175	8.72
European (259)	259	1.92
Finnish (8)	8	0.06
French, ex. Basque (54)	127	0.94
German (301)	754	5.60
Irish (276)	852	6.32
Italian (16)	132	0.98
Norwegian (16)	27	0.20
Polish (0)	119	0.88
Russian (0)	96	0.71
Scotch-Irish (231)	319	2.37
Scottish (84)	197	1.46
Slovak (0)	35	0.26
Swedish (10)	33	0.24
Swiss (9)	18	0.13
Turkish (0)	15	0.11
Welsh (0)	38	0.28

Hispanic Origin	Population	%
Hispanic or Latino (of any race)	1,627	11.96
Central American, ex. Mexican	24	0.18
Guatemalan	14	0.10
Honduran	5	0.04
Salvadoran	5	0.04
Cuban	31	0.23
Dominican Republic	1	0.01
Mexican	1,458	10.72
Puerto Rican	57	0.42
South American	9	0.07
Bolivian	1	0.01
Colombian	3	0.02
Ecuadorian	1	0.01
Peruvian	3	0.02
Venezuelan	1	0.01
Other Hispanic or Latino	47	0.35

Race*	Population	%
African-American/Black (582)	688	5.06
Not Hispanic (553)	651	4.79
Hispanic (29)	37	0.27
American Indian/Alaska Native (49)	120	0.88
Not Hispanic (39)	105	0.77
Hispanic (10)	15	0.11
Aleut *(Alaska Native)* (1)	2	0.01
Apache (0)	1	0.01
Blackfeet (0)	1	0.01
Cherokee (14)	43	0.32
Cheyenne (0)	2	0.01
Chickasaw (0)	1	0.01
Choctaw (2)	4	0.03
Comanche (0)	2	0.01
Iroquois (0)	1	0.01
Lumbee (0)	1	0.01
Mexican American Ind. (5)	5	0.04
Navajo (0)	1	0.01
Potawatomi (1)	1	0.01
Shoshone (0)	1	0.01
Sioux (1)	2	0.01
Asian (127)	156	1.15
Not Hispanic (127)	154	1.13
Hispanic (0)	2	0.01
Chinese, ex. Taiwanese (15)	17	0.12
Filipino (16)	26	0.19
Indian (36)	41	0.30
Japanese (23)	28	0.21
Korean (0)	1	0.01
Laotian (1)	3	0.02
Thai (1)	1	0.01

*Notes: † The Census 2010 population figure is used to calculate the percentages in the Hispanic Origin and Race categories. Ancestry percentages are based on the 2006-2010 American Community Survey population (not shown); ‡ Numbers in parentheses indicate the number of people reporting a single ancestry; * Numbers in parentheses indicate the number of persons reporting this race alone, not in combination with any other race; Please refer to the Explanation of Data for more information.*

Vietnamese (32)	39	0.29
Hawaii Native/Pacific Islander (5)	13	0.10
Not Hispanic (5)	10	0.07
Hispanic (0)	3	0.02
Guamanian/Chamorro (1)	2	0.01
Native Hawaiian (1)	3	0.02
Samoan (3)	4	0.03
White (11,521)	11,805	86.77
Not Hispanic (11,038)	11,236	82.59
Hispanic (483)	569	4.18

Memphis

Place Type: City
County: Shelby
Population: 646,889†

Ancestry‡	Population	%
Afghan (35)	35	0.01
African, Sub-Saharan (9,093)	9,640	1.47
African (6,399)	6,705	1.02
Cape Verdean (14)	14	<0.01
Ethiopian (622)	709	0.11
Ghanaian (132)	132	0.02
Kenyan (210)	210	0.03
Liberian (11)	11	<0.01
Nigerian (424)	481	0.07
Senegalese (0)	17	<0.01
Somalian (116)	116	0.02
South African (33)	33	0.01
Sudanese (156)	171	0.03
Ugandan (9)	9	<0.01
Zimbabwean (59)	79	0.01
Other Sub-Saharan African (908)	953	0.15
American (32,233)	32,233	4.92
Arab (1,614)	1,931	0.29
Arab (719)	807	0.12
Egyptian (122)	122	0.02
Iraqi (156)	156	0.02
Jordanian (98)	98	0.01
Lebanese (202)	282	0.04
Moroccan (20)	31	<0.01
Palestinian (167)	224	0.03
Syrian (15)	84	0.01
Other Arab (115)	127	0.02
Armenian (28)	76	0.01
Australian (18)	51	0.01
Austrian (108)	338	0.05
Belgian (19)	94	0.01
Brazilian (90)	242	0.04
British (931)	1,756	0.27
Cajun (21)	45	0.01
Canadian (71)	117	0.02
Celtic (23)	37	0.01
Croatian (129)	140	0.02
Czech (113)	471	0.07
Czechoslovakian (42)	88	0.01
Danish (137)	547	0.08
Dutch (623)	3,241	0.49
Eastern European (452)	463	0.07
English (15,241)	33,489	5.11
Estonian (0)	12	<0.01
European (3,548)	4,012	0.61
Finnish (33)	112	0.02
French, ex. Basque (1,616)	6,875	1.05
French Canadian (295)	813	0.12
German (8,451)	28,260	4.32
Greek (485)	985	0.15
Hungarian (145)	471	0.07
Icelander (27)	77	0.01
Iranian (174)	259	0.04
Irish (12,827)	34,871	5.32
Israeli (37)	37	0.01
Italian (4,754)	9,939	1.52
Latvian (36)	121	0.02
Lithuanian (158)	356	0.05
Maltese (0)	17	<0.01
New Zealander (39)	92	0.01
Northern European (179)	195	0.03
Norwegian (413)	1,242	0.19
Pennsylvania German (9)	28	<0.01
Polish (1,717)	3,834	0.59
Portuguese (53)	257	0.04
Romanian (97)	143	0.02
Russian (518)	1,581	0.24
Scandinavian (186)	319	0.05
Scotch-Irish (6,074)	10,576	1.61
Scottish (3,106)	7,654	1.17
Serbian (29)	39	0.01
Slavic (19)	84	0.01
Slovak (95)	286	0.04
Slovene (51)	61	0.01
Swedish (681)	1,981	0.30
Swiss (164)	556	0.08
Turkish (55)	82	0.01
Ukrainian (251)	439	0.07
Welsh (668)	1,935	0.30
West Indian, ex. Hispanic (367)	670	0.10
Bahamian (24)	35	0.01
Dutch West Indian (0)	13	<0.01
Haitian (93)	110	0.02
Jamaican (188)	369	0.06
Trinidadian/Tobagonian (30)	91	0.01
U.S. Virgin Islander (32)	32	<0.01
West Indian (0)	20	<0.01
Yugoslavian (37)	136	0.02

Hispanic Origin	Population	%
Hispanic or Latino (of any race)	41,994	6.49
Central American, ex. Mexican	4,881	0.75
Costa Rican	61	0.01
Guatemalan	1,680	0.26
Honduran	1,895	0.29
Nicaraguan	166	0.03
Panamanian	147	0.02
Salvadoran	902	0.14
Other Central American	30	<0.01
Cuban	679	0.10
Dominican Republic	182	0.03
Mexican	30,799	4.76
Puerto Rican	1,169	0.18
South American	1,051	0.16
Argentinean	125	0.02
Bolivian	22	<0.01
Chilean	72	0.01
Colombian	356	0.06
Ecuadorian	51	0.01
Paraguayan	13	<0.01
Peruvian	147	0.02
Uruguayan	41	0.01
Venezuelan	207	0.03
Other South American	17	<0.01
Other Hispanic or Latino	3,233	0.50

Race*	Population	%
African-American/Black (409,687)	414,928	64.14
Not Hispanic (408,075)	412,759	63.81
Hispanic (1,612)	2,169	0.34
American Indian/Alaska Native (1,549)	3,991	0.62
Not Hispanic (1,186)	3,357	0.52
Hispanic (363)	634	0.10
Alaska Athabascan *(Ala. Nat.)* (1)	3	<0.01
Aleut *(Alaska Native)* (4)	5	<0.01
Apache (21)	55	0.01
Arapaho (3)	8	<0.01
Blackfeet (14)	101	0.02
Canadian/French Am. Ind. (1)	2	<0.01
Central American Ind. (4)	11	<0.01
Cherokee (209)	931	0.14
Cheyenne (1)	3	<0.01
Chickasaw (14)	45	0.01
Chippewa (10)	28	<0.01
Choctaw (84)	205	0.03
Colville (1)	2	<0.01
Comanche (3)	8	<0.01
Cree (1)	6	<0.01
Creek (10)	37	0.01
Crow (1)	5	<0.01
Delaware (1)	1	<0.01
Houma (0)	1	<0.01
Inupiat *(Alaska Native)* (1)	2	<0.01
Iroquois (24)	33	0.01
Kiowa (1)	1	<0.01
Lumbee (9)	9	<0.01
Mexican American Ind. (99)	133	0.02
Navajo (15)	26	<0.01
Osage (3)	10	<0.01
Ottawa (1)	1	<0.01
Paiute (4)	8	<0.01
Pima (2)	2	<0.01
Potawatomi (7)	10	<0.01
Pueblo (10)	19	<0.01
Puget Sound Salish (3)	6	<0.01
Seminole (9)	13	<0.01
Sioux (19)	48	0.01
South American Ind. (3)	13	<0.01
Spanish American Ind. (0)	5	<0.01
Tlingit-Haida *(Alaska Native)* (10)	10	<0.01
Tsimshian *(Alaska Native)* (1)	1	<0.01
Yakama (3)	3	<0.01
Yaqui (5)	6	<0.01
Asian (10,146)	12,096	1.87
Not Hispanic (10,067)	11,841	1.83
Hispanic (79)	255	0.04
Bangladeshi (60)	61	0.01
Bhutanese (36)	36	0.01
Burmese (21)	24	<0.01
Cambodian (483)	548	0.08
Chinese, ex. Taiwanese (1,893)	2,207	0.34
Filipino (767)	1,108	0.17
Hmong (39)	41	0.01
Indian (2,582)	2,894	0.45
Indonesian (27)	42	0.01
Japanese (260)	488	0.08
Korean (501)	713	0.11
Laotian (256)	299	0.05
Malaysian (10)	17	<0.01
Nepalese (31)	35	0.01
Pakistani (254)	280	0.04
Sri Lankan (29)	36	0.01
Taiwanese (77)	96	0.01
Thai (87)	154	0.02
Vietnamese (2,347)	2,515	0.39
Hawaii Native/Pacific Islander (300)	726	0.11
Not Hispanic (159)	456	0.07
Hispanic (141)	270	0.04
Fijian (2)	2	<0.01
Guamanian/Chamorro (153)	243	0.04
Marshallese (1)	2	<0.01
Native Hawaiian (63)	215	0.03
Samoan (34)	87	0.01
Tongan (4)	15	<0.01
White (190,120)	196,701	30.41
Not Hispanic (177,735)	182,870	28.27
Hispanic (12,385)	13,831	2.14

Middle Valley

Place Type: CDP
County: Hamilton
Population: 12,684†

Ancestry‡	Population	%
African, Sub-Saharan (240)	240	1.87
African (240)	240	1.87
American (2,770)	2,770	21.55
Arab (0)	8	0.06
Lebanese (0)	8	0.06
Armenian (0)	20	0.16
British (10)	10	0.08
Dutch (63)	199	1.55
English (429)	936	7.28
European (192)	192	1.49
Finnish (11)	11	0.09
French, ex. Basque (57)	211	1.64
German (461)	1,200	9.34
Greek (0)	13	0.10
Iranian (8)	8	0.06
Irish (1,051)	2,062	16.04
Italian (78)	191	1.49

*Notes: † The Census 2010 population figure is used to calculate the percentages in the Hispanic Origin and Race categories. Ancestry percentages are based on the 2006-2010 American Community Survey population (not shown); ‡ Numbers in parentheses indicate the number of people reporting a single ancestry; * Numbers in parentheses indicate the number of persons reporting this race alone, not in combination with any other race; Please refer to the Explanation of Data for more information.*

Lithuanian (11)	19	0.15
Northern European (46)	46	0.36
Norwegian (12)	84	0.65
Pennsylvania German (10)	10	0.08
Polish (76)	155	1.21
Portuguese (0)	11	0.09
Romanian (14)	14	0.11
Russian (44)	44	0.34
Scandinavian (0)	15	0.12
Scotch-Irish (328)	553	4.30
Scottish (138)	189	1.47
Slovak (10)	10	0.08
Swedish (9)	9	0.07
Swiss (9)	9	0.07
Welsh (47)	118	0.92
Yugoslavian (52)	52	0.40

Hispanic Origin	Population	%
Hispanic or Latino (of any race)	215	1.70
Central American, ex. Mexican	12	0.09
Costa Rican	2	0.02
Guatemalan	7	0.06
Honduran	2	0.02
Nicaraguan	1	0.01
Cuban	5	0.04
Mexican	134	1.06
Puerto Rican	24	0.19
South American	19	0.15
Argentinean	7	0.06
Bolivian	1	0.01
Colombian	3	0.02
Peruvian	4	0.03
Venezuelan	1	0.01
Other South American	3	0.02
Other Hispanic or Latino	21	0.17

Race*	Population	%
African-American/Black (285)	320	2.52
Not Hispanic (285)	320	2.52
American Indian/Alaska Native (38)	85	0.67
Not Hispanic (36)	83	0.65
Hispanic (2)	2	0.02
Apache (0)	5	0.04
Blackfeet (0)	2	0.02
Cherokee (8)	36	0.28
Choctaw (1)	1	0.01
Creek (1)	1	0.01
Lumbee (6)	6	0.05
Mexican American Ind. (1)	1	0.01
Navajo (0)	1	0.01
Osage (2)	2	0.02
Potawatomi (0)	5	0.04
Sioux (3)	4	0.03
Asian (252)	294	2.32
Not Hispanic (250)	289	2.28
Hispanic (2)	5	0.04
Cambodian (3)	3	0.02
Chinese, ex. Taiwanese (41)	51	0.40
Filipino (16)	29	0.23
Hmong (1)	2	0.02
Indian (71)	80	0.63
Indonesian (2)	2	0.02
Japanese (24)	26	0.20
Korean (14)	23	0.18
Pakistani (16)	16	0.13
Taiwanese (3)	3	0.02
Thai (7)	8	0.06
Vietnamese (45)	45	0.35
Hawaii Native/Pacific Islander (1)	12	0.09
Not Hispanic (1)	10	0.08
Hispanic (0)	2	0.02
Native Hawaiian (0)	4	0.03
Samoan (1)	8	0.06
White (11,914)	12,041	94.93
Not Hispanic (11,769)	11,885	93.70
Hispanic (145)	156	1.23

Milan

Place Type: City
County: Gibson
Population: 7,851†

Ancestry‡	Population	%
African, Sub-Saharan (0)	16	0.21
African (0)	16	0.21
American (809)	809	10.38
Arab (63)	63	0.81
Palestinian (63)	63	0.81
British (13)	117	1.50
Cajun (0)	24	0.31
Dutch (17)	62	0.80
English (473)	659	8.45
European (10)	10	0.13
French, ex. Basque (0)	8	0.10
German (248)	650	8.34
Irish (350)	891	11.43
Italian (50)	86	1.10
Norwegian (83)	95	1.22
Polish (26)	82	1.05
Russian (0)	31	0.40
Scotch-Irish (84)	221	2.83
Scottish (88)	184	2.36
Swedish (0)	12	0.15
Welsh (15)	28	0.36

Hispanic Origin	Population	%
Hispanic or Latino (of any race)	200	2.55
Central American, ex. Mexican	14	0.18
Guatemalan	1	0.01
Honduran	7	0.09
Salvadoran	6	0.08
Cuban	2	0.03
Dominican Republic	1	0.01
Mexican	138	1.76
Puerto Rican	10	0.13
South American	13	0.17
Chilean	4	0.05
Colombian	6	0.08
Venezuelan	3	0.04
Other Hispanic or Latino	22	0.28

Race*	Population	%
African-American/Black (1,792)	1,922	24.48
Not Hispanic (1,782)	1,906	24.28
Hispanic (10)	16	0.20
American Indian/Alaska Native (26)	50	0.64
Not Hispanic (25)	49	0.62
Hispanic (1)	1	0.01
Apache (1)	1	0.01
Cherokee (9)	18	0.23
Chickasaw (1)	2	0.03
Choctaw (2)	2	0.03
Creek (1)	1	0.01
Potawatomi (1)	1	0.01
Puget Sound Salish (0)	3	0.04
Sioux (3)	4	0.05
Asian (28)	34	0.43
Not Hispanic (28)	32	0.41
Hispanic (0)	2	0.03
Chinese, ex. Taiwanese (4)	4	0.05
Filipino (2)	2	0.03
Hmong (8)	8	0.10
Indian (2)	2	0.03
Japanese (3)	5	0.06
Korean (1)	3	0.04
Laotian (4)	4	0.05
Thai (1)	2	0.03
Vietnamese (3)	3	0.04
Hawaii Native/Pacific Islander (0)	2	0.03
Not Hispanic (0)	2	0.03
Native Hawaiian (0)	1	0.01
White (5,769)	5,918	75.38
Not Hispanic (5,666)	5,802	73.90
Hispanic (103)	116	1.48

Millington

Place Type: City
County: Shelby
Population: 10,176†

Ancestry‡	Population	%
American (1,982)	1,982	19.15
Austrian (13)	78	0.75
Belgian (0)	12	0.12
British (0)	36	0.35
Cajun (0)	35	0.34
Canadian (42)	42	0.41
Croatian (34)	34	0.33
Czech (0)	12	0.12
Danish (0)	9	0.09
Dutch (0)	48	0.46
English (514)	680	6.57
European (96)	96	0.93
French, ex. Basque (25)	198	1.91
German (343)	826	7.98
Greek (0)	26	0.25
Hungarian (0)	18	0.17
Irish (449)	1,038	10.03
Italian (231)	363	3.51
Norwegian (15)	39	0.38
Polish (26)	157	1.52
Russian (0)	16	0.15
Scandinavian (0)	35	0.34
Scotch-Irish (137)	205	1.98
Scottish (88)	217	2.10
Serbian (12)	12	0.12
Swedish (12)	12	0.12
Ukrainian (20)	20	0.19
Welsh (26)	47	0.45
West Indian, ex. Hispanic (16)	16	0.15
Jamaican (16)	16	0.15
Yugoslavian (0)	28	0.27

Hispanic Origin	Population	%
Hispanic or Latino (of any race)	600	5.90
Central American, ex. Mexican	36	0.35
Costa Rican	3	0.03
Guatemalan	12	0.12
Honduran	8	0.08
Nicaraguan	4	0.04
Panamanian	4	0.04
Salvadoran	5	0.05
Cuban	10	0.10
Dominican Republic	5	0.05
Mexican	401	3.94
Puerto Rican	57	0.56
South American	18	0.18
Argentinean	1	0.01
Bolivian	1	0.01
Chilean	1	0.01
Colombian	5	0.05
Ecuadorian	1	0.01
Peruvian	4	0.04
Venezuelan	5	0.05
Other Hispanic or Latino	73	0.72

Race*	Population	%
African-American/Black (2,610)	2,766	27.18
Not Hispanic (2,585)	2,718	26.71
Hispanic (25)	48	0.47
American Indian/Alaska Native (62)	152	1.49
Not Hispanic (60)	148	1.45
Hispanic (2)	4	0.04
Alaska Athabascan *(Ala. Nat.)* (1)	2	0.02
Apache (5)	5	0.05
Blackfeet (1)	3	0.03
Cherokee (14)	53	0.52
Choctaw (4)	5	0.05
Creek (0)	1	0.01
Mexican American Ind. (1)	1	0.01
Sioux (2)	5	0.05
Asian (241)	326	3.20
Not Hispanic (235)	310	3.05
Hispanic (6)	16	0.16

*Notes: † The Census 2010 population figure is used to calculate the percentages in the Hispanic Origin and Race categories. Ancestry percentages are based on the 2006-2010 American Community Survey population (not shown); ‡ Numbers in parentheses indicate the number of people reporting a single ancestry; * Numbers in parentheses indicate the number of persons reporting this race alone, not in combination with any other race; Please refer to the Explanation of Data for more information.*

Burmese (4)	4	0.04
Chinese, ex. Taiwanese (30)	38	0.37
Filipino (139)	182	1.79
Indian (18)	23	0.23
Japanese (10)	25	0.25
Korean (18)	27	0.27
Laotian (1)	1	0.01
Malaysian (0)	2	0.02
Taiwanese (2)	3	0.03
Thai (3)	3	0.03
Vietnamese (5)	12	0.12
Hawaii Native/Pacific Islander (19)	44	0.43
Not Hispanic (19)	41	0.40
Hispanic (0)	3	0.03
Guamanian/Chamorro (4)	9	0.09
Native Hawaiian (6)	18	0.18
Samoan (3)	8	0.08
White (6,638)	6,903	67.84
Not Hispanic (6,398)	6,633	65.18
Hispanic (240)	270	2.65

Morristown

Place Type: City
County: Hamblen
Population: 29,137†

Ancestry‡	Population	%
African, Sub-Saharan (22)	39	0.14
African (22)	39	0.14
American (6,330)	6,330	22.02
Belgian (0)	11	0.04
British (87)	169	0.59
Canadian (35)	35	0.12
Czech (19)	69	0.24
Czechoslovakian (25)	25	0.09
Danish (32)	32	0.11
Dutch (74)	388	1.35
Eastern European (11)	11	0.04
English (1,222)	2,429	8.45
European (164)	164	0.57
Finnish (0)	12	0.04
French, ex. Basque (128)	596	2.07
French Canadian (0)	72	0.25
German (847)	2,516	8.75
Greek (34)	34	0.12
Hungarian (53)	73	0.25
Irish (844)	2,338	8.13
Italian (56)	172	0.60
Norwegian (0)	8	0.03
Polish (41)	160	0.56
Scotch-Irish (563)	1,010	3.51
Scottish (103)	219	0.76
Swedish (16)	91	0.32
Swiss (0)	15	0.05
Welsh (12)	144	0.50
West Indian, ex. Hispanic (19)	19	0.07
Dutch West Indian (19)	19	0.07

Hispanic Origin	Population	%
Hispanic or Latino (of any race)	5,743	19.71
Central American, ex. Mexican	649	2.23
Costa Rican	4	0.01
Guatemalan	508	1.74
Honduran	61	0.21
Nicaraguan	19	0.07
Panamanian	11	0.04
Salvadoran	45	0.15
Other Central American	1	<0.01
Cuban	45	0.15
Dominican Republic	10	0.03
Mexican	4,600	15.79
Puerto Rican	146	0.50
South American	28	0.10
Argentinean	2	0.01
Bolivian	2	0.01
Chilean	3	0.01
Colombian	5	0.02
Ecuadorian	2	0.01
Peruvian	5	0.02
Venezuelan	8	0.03
Other South American	1	<0.01
Other Hispanic or Latino	265	0.91

Race*	Population	%
African-American/Black (1,945)	2,392	8.21
Not Hispanic (1,827)	2,239	7.68
Hispanic (118)	153	0.53
American Indian/Alaska Native (146)	309	1.06
Not Hispanic (54)	201	0.69
Hispanic (92)	108	0.37
Apache (0)	7	0.02
Blackfeet (1)	6	0.02
Cherokee (25)	75	0.26
Cheyenne (0)	2	0.01
Cree (0)	1	<0.01
Houma (0)	1	<0.01
Mexican American Ind. (40)	41	0.14
Potawatomi (0)	1	<0.01
Seminole (0)	2	0.01
Sioux (0)	1	<0.01
South American Ind. (1)	2	0.01
Spanish American Ind. (17)	17	0.06
Asian (250)	305	1.05
Not Hispanic (233)	283	0.97
Hispanic (17)	22	0.08
Bangladeshi (2)	3	0.01
Burmese (1)	2	0.01
Cambodian (10)	11	0.04
Chinese, ex. Taiwanese (23)	28	0.10
Filipino (53)	65	0.22
Indian (85)	91	0.31
Indonesian (1)	2	0.01
Japanese (38)	43	0.15
Korean (5)	17	0.06
Laotian (0)	1	<0.01
Pakistani (6)	6	0.02
Taiwanese (1)	1	<0.01
Thai (1)	3	0.01
Vietnamese (22)	22	0.08
Hawaii Native/Pacific Islander (44)	65	0.22
Not Hispanic (44)	64	0.22
Hispanic (0)	1	<0.01
Guamanian/Chamorro (24)	31	0.11
Native Hawaiian (3)	6	0.02
Samoan (1)	1	<0.01
White (22,504)	23,250	79.80
Not Hispanic (20,637)	21,164	72.64
Hispanic (1,867)	2,086	7.16

Mount Juliet

Place Type: City
County: Wilson
Population: 23,671†

Ancestry‡	Population	%
African, Sub-Saharan (141)	141	0.64
African (38)	38	0.17
Ethiopian (34)	34	0.16
Ghanaian (51)	51	0.23
Nigerian (8)	8	0.04
South African (10)	10	0.05
American (3,357)	3,357	15.31
Arab (104)	104	0.47
Egyptian (33)	33	0.15
Lebanese (71)	71	0.32
Australian (15)	15	0.07
Austrian (15)	15	0.07
British (66)	106	0.48
Bulgarian (8)	8	0.04
Cajun (11)	21	0.10
Czech (59)	71	0.32
Danish (16)	16	0.07
Dutch (91)	488	2.23
English (1,475)	2,642	12.05
European (173)	215	0.98
Finnish (0)	55	0.25
French, ex. Basque (122)	565	2.58
French Canadian (28)	132	0.60
German (888)	3,349	15.28
Greek (29)	29	0.13
Hungarian (0)	107	0.49
Iranian (16)	16	0.07
Irish (900)	3,015	13.75
Italian (369)	1,087	4.96
Lithuanian (0)	6	0.03
Norwegian (81)	377	1.72
Polish (75)	361	1.65
Portuguese (0)	23	0.10
Russian (12)	21	0.10
Scandinavian (0)	28	0.13
Scotch-Irish (517)	700	3.19
Scottish (251)	481	2.19
Slovak (0)	12	0.05
Swedish (23)	403	1.84
Swiss (0)	58	0.26
Ukrainian (0)	8	0.04
Welsh (3)	109	0.50
West Indian, ex. Hispanic (82)	82	0.37
Haitian (20)	20	0.09
Trinidadian/Tobagonian (55)	55	0.25
West Indian (7)	7	0.03

Hispanic Origin	Population	%
Hispanic or Latino (of any race)	785	3.32
Central American, ex. Mexican	67	0.28
Costa Rican	6	0.03
Guatemalan	23	0.10
Honduran	6	0.03
Nicaraguan	12	0.05
Panamanian	8	0.03
Salvadoran	12	0.05
Cuban	27	0.11
Dominican Republic	10	0.04
Mexican	475	2.01
Puerto Rican	78	0.33
South American	54	0.23
Argentinean	11	0.05
Bolivian	1	<0.01
Chilean	4	0.02
Colombian	24	0.10
Ecuadorian	5	0.02
Paraguayan	1	<0.01
Peruvian	5	0.02
Venezuelan	3	0.01
Other Hispanic or Latino	74	0.31

Race*	Population	%
African-American/Black (1,587)	1,784	7.54
Not Hispanic (1,577)	1,753	7.41
Hispanic (10)	31	0.13
American Indian/Alaska Native (103)	246	1.04
Not Hispanic (89)	220	0.93
Hispanic (14)	26	0.11
Apache (1)	1	<0.01
Blackfeet (0)	3	0.01
Canadian/French Am. Ind. (0)	2	0.01
Cherokee (13)	76	0.32
Chippewa (10)	11	0.05
Choctaw (8)	12	0.05
Colville (1)	1	<0.01
Comanche (0)	1	<0.01
Creek (3)	11	0.05
Crow (2)	2	0.01
Delaware (0)	2	0.01
Houma (3)	3	0.01
Iroquois (4)	4	0.02
Lumbee (1)	1	<0.01
Mexican American Ind. (3)	3	0.01
Navajo (1)	2	0.01
Ottawa (3)	3	0.01
Paiute (0)	4	0.02
Potawatomi (3)	5	0.02
Seminole (1)	1	<0.01
Sioux (1)	2	0.01
Tlingit-Haida *(Alaska Native)* (1)	1	<0.01
Yup'ik *(Alaska Native)* (1)	2	0.01
Asian (584)	721	3.05
Not Hispanic (578)	707	2.99

*Notes: † The Census 2010 population figure is used to calculate the percentages in the Hispanic Origin and Race categories. Ancestry percentages are based on the 2006-2010 American Community Survey population (not shown); ‡ Numbers in parentheses indicate the number of people reporting a single ancestry; * Numbers in parentheses indicate the number of persons reporting this race alone, not in combination with any other race; Please refer to the Explanation of Data for more information.*

SECTION TWO

Hispanic (6)	14	0.06
Cambodian (0)	1	<0.01
Chinese, ex. Taiwanese (95)	112	0.47
Filipino (85)	132	0.56
Indian (231)	241	1.02
Indonesian (1)	3	0.01
Japanese (15)	37	0.16
Korean (84)	98	0.41
Laotian (13)	17	0.07
Malaysian (0)	4	0.02
Pakistani (0)	6	0.03
Sri Lankan (0)	1	<0.01
Taiwanese (2)	2	0.01
Thai (6)	13	0.05
Vietnamese (25)	41	0.17
Hawaii Native/Pacific Islander (12)	35	0.15
Not Hispanic (8)	27	0.11
Hispanic (4)	8	0.03
Guamanian/Chamorro (4)	7	0.03
Native Hawaiian (2)	10	0.04
Samoan (0)	3	0.01
White (20,575)	21,014	88.78
Not Hispanic (20,179)	20,564	86.87
Hispanic (396)	450	1.90

Murfreesboro

Place Type: City
County: Rutherford
Population: 108,755†

Ancestry‡	Population	%
Afghan (8)	8	0.01
African, Sub-Saharan (381)	604	0.59
African (320)	543	0.53
Ethiopian (8)	8	0.01
Nigerian (39)	39	0.04
South African (14)	14	0.01
American (13,352)	13,352	13.01
Arab (347)	427	0.42
Arab (217)	217	0.21
Egyptian (21)	21	0.02
Iraqi (17)	17	0.02
Jordanian (26)	26	0.03
Lebanese (51)	101	0.10
Palestinian (15)	28	0.03
Other Arab (0)	17	0.02
Australian (0)	10	0.01
Austrian (36)	115	0.11
Basque (13)	13	0.01
Belgian (60)	67	0.07
Brazilian (0)	29	0.03
British (487)	607	0.59
Cajun (94)	94	0.09
Canadian (82)	123	0.12
Celtic (13)	13	0.01
Croatian (8)	22	0.02
Czech (89)	254	0.25
Czechoslovakian (27)	75	0.07
Danish (37)	353	0.34
Dutch (337)	1,335	1.30
English (4,668)	10,205	9.95
European (1,418)	1,602	1.56
Finnish (14)	79	0.08
French, ex. Basque (511)	2,667	2.60
French Canadian (172)	310	0.30
German (4,426)	12,226	11.92
German Russian (9)	9	0.01
Greek (64)	138	0.13
Guyanese (16)	61	0.06
Hungarian (79)	216	0.21
Iranian (21)	36	0.04
Irish (3,897)	11,616	11.32
Italian (968)	2,930	2.86
Latvian (11)	11	0.01
Lithuanian (16)	22	0.02
Luxemburger (0)	41	0.04
Macedonian (0)	9	0.01
Maltese (26)	26	0.03
Northern European (17)	17	0.02
Norwegian (122)	455	0.44
Pennsylvania German (11)	11	0.01
Polish (512)	1,593	1.55
Portuguese (21)	37	0.04
Romanian (76)	98	0.10
Russian (163)	454	0.44
Scandinavian (115)	246	0.24
Scotch-Irish (2,143)	3,807	3.71
Scottish (1,019)	2,609	2.54
Slavic (215)	244	0.24
Slovak (150)	202	0.20
Slovene (18)	18	0.02
Swedish (229)	642	0.63
Swiss (94)	135	0.13
Turkish (26)	26	0.03
Ukrainian (21)	189	0.18
Welsh (247)	795	0.77
West Indian, ex. Hispanic (51)	79	0.08
Dutch West Indian (15)	43	0.04
Trinidadian/Tobagonian (6)	6	0.01
West Indian (30)	30	0.03
Yugoslavian (8)	38	0.04

Hispanic Origin	Population	%
Hispanic or Latino (of any race)	6,453	5.93
Central American, ex. Mexican	706	0.65
Costa Rican	16	0.01
Guatemalan	299	0.27
Honduran	85	0.08
Nicaraguan	73	0.07
Panamanian	43	0.04
Salvadoran	185	0.17
Other Central American	5	<0.01
Cuban	183	0.17
Dominican Republic	76	0.07
Mexican	4,005	3.68
Puerto Rican	541	0.50
South American	407	0.37
Argentinean	28	0.03
Bolivian	9	0.01
Chilean	20	0.02
Colombian	192	0.18
Ecuadorian	28	0.03
Paraguayan	4	<0.01
Peruvian	62	0.06
Uruguayan	10	0.01
Venezuelan	54	0.05
Other Hispanic or Latino	535	0.49

Race*	Population	%
African-American/Black (16,510)	18,066	16.61
Not Hispanic (16,333)	17,778	16.35
Hispanic (177)	288	0.26
American Indian/Alaska Native (378)	993	0.91
Not Hispanic (292)	830	0.76
Hispanic (86)	163	0.15
Alaska Athabascan *(Ala. Nat.)* (1)	1	<0.01
Apache (4)	13	0.01
Blackfeet (3)	40	0.04
Canadian/French Am. Ind. (1)	4	<0.01
Central American Ind. (1)	1	<0.01
Cherokee (75)	260	0.24
Chickasaw (2)	5	<0.01
Chippewa (21)	27	0.02
Choctaw (14)	30	0.03
Comanche (1)	3	<0.01
Creek (5)	14	0.01
Crow (0)	4	<0.01
Delaware (0)	3	<0.01
Houma (9)	9	0.01
Inupiat *(Alaska Native)* (1)	1	<0.01
Iroquois (5)	6	0.01
Lumbee (4)	8	0.01
Mexican American Ind. (19)	26	0.02
Navajo (9)	16	0.01
Osage (1)	1	<0.01
Ottawa (2)	6	0.01
Pima (2)	2	<0.01
Potawatomi (1)	1	<0.01
Pueblo (6)	6	0.01
Seminole (2)	8	0.01
Sioux (4)	16	0.01
South American Ind. (3)	5	<0.01
Tlingit-Haida *(Alaska Native)* (3)	3	<0.01
Tohono O'Odham (1)	2	<0.01
Yaqui (0)	3	<0.01
Asian (3,658)	4,458	4.10
Not Hispanic (3,628)	4,371	4.02
Hispanic (30)	87	0.08
Bangladeshi (4)	4	<0.01
Burmese (10)	11	0.01
Cambodian (25)	35	0.03
Chinese, ex. Taiwanese (328)	417	0.38
Filipino (244)	428	0.39
Hmong (50)	55	0.05
Indian (655)	732	0.67
Indonesian (19)	24	0.02
Japanese (233)	343	0.32
Korean (233)	313	0.29
Laotian (1,395)	1,581	1.45
Malaysian (8)	15	0.01
Nepalese (1)	1	<0.01
Pakistani (43)	52	0.05
Sri Lankan (5)	5	<0.01
Taiwanese (15)	23	0.02
Thai (58)	109	0.10
Vietnamese (120)	164	0.15
Hawaii Native/Pacific Islander (47)	153	0.14
Not Hispanic (43)	127	0.12
Hispanic (4)	26	0.02
Fijian (0)	1	<0.01
Guamanian/Chamorro (20)	34	0.03
Native Hawaiian (8)	40	0.04
Samoan (11)	24	0.02
Tongan (1)	1	<0.01
White (82,240)	84,707	77.89
Not Hispanic (79,471)	81,555	74.99
Hispanic (2,769)	3,152	2.90

Nashville-Davidson

Place Type: Metropolitan Government
County: Davidson
Population: 601,222†

Ancestry‡	Population	%
Afghan (266)	266	0.05
African, Sub-Saharan (9,989)	11,035	1.88
African (3,322)	3,804	0.65
Ethiopian (1,675)	1,850	0.31
Ghanaian (209)	241	0.04
Kenyan (272)	288	0.05
Liberian (126)	141	0.02
Nigerian (1,358)	1,462	0.25
Sierra Leonean (116)	127	0.02
Somalian (1,749)	1,880	0.32
South African (13)	52	0.01
Sudanese (653)	653	0.11
Ugandan (21)	21	<0.01
Other Sub-Saharan African (475)	516	0.09
Albanian (51)	51	0.01
American (58,785)	58,785	10.00
Arab (8,161)	9,538	1.62
Arab (615)	890	0.15
Egyptian (2,987)	3,050	0.52
Iraqi (1,428)	1,707	0.29
Jordanian (227)	249	0.04
Lebanese (235)	524	0.09
Moroccan (27)	40	0.01
Palestinian (194)	206	0.04
Syrian (79)	230	0.04
Other Arab (2,369)	2,642	0.45
Armenian (121)	284	0.05
Australian (89)	125	0.02
Austrian (247)	904	0.15
Basque (5)	43	0.01
Belgian (111)	319	0.05
Brazilian (226)	285	0.05
British (1,797)	3,331	0.57
Bulgarian (12)	12	<0.01

*Notes: † The Census 2010 population figure is used to calculate the percentages in the Hispanic Origin and Race categories. Ancestry percentages are based on the 2006-2010 American Community Survey population (not shown); ‡ Numbers in parentheses indicate the number of people reporting a single ancestry; * Numbers in parentheses indicate the number of persons reporting this race alone, not in combination with any other race; Please refer to the Explanation of Data for more information.*

Cajun (37)	71	0.01
Canadian (501)	711	0.12
Carpatho Rusyn (0)	30	0.01
Celtic (44)	52	0.01
Croatian (172)	354	0.06
Czech (270)	1,226	0.21
Czechoslovakian (43)	136	0.02
Danish (291)	959	0.16
Dutch (1,501)	6,654	1.13
Eastern European (392)	415	0.07
English (21,871)	52,395	8.91
Estonian (39)	50	0.01
European (5,148)	5,959	1.01
Finnish (220)	613	0.10
French, ex. Basque (2,271)	11,069	1.88
French Canadian (516)	1,285	0.22
German (17,838)	57,440	9.77
German Russian (0)	15	<0.01
Greek (575)	1,199	0.20
Guyanese (79)	107	0.02
Hungarian (486)	1,567	0.27
Icelander (0)	23	<0.01
Iranian (976)	1,008	0.17
Irish (19,033)	54,980	9.35
Israeli (300)	329	0.06
Italian (5,181)	13,591	2.31
Latvian (17)	73	0.01
Lithuanian (57)	588	0.10
Luxemburger (0)	44	0.01
New Zealander (51)	51	0.01
Northern European (280)	290	0.05
Norwegian (1,011)	2,886	0.49
Pennsylvania German (27)	40	0.01
Polish (1,858)	6,574	1.12
Portuguese (248)	655	0.11
Romanian (505)	628	0.11
Russian (1,329)	3,447	0.59
Scandinavian (189)	333	0.06
Scotch-Irish (9,185)	18,192	3.09
Scottish (5,096)	13,002	2.21
Serbian (102)	155	0.03
Slavic (43)	128	0.02
Slovak (201)	395	0.07
Slovene (0)	51	0.01
Swedish (835)	3,661	0.62
Swiss (366)	1,234	0.21
Turkish (234)	254	0.04
Ukrainian (485)	1,119	0.19
Welsh (949)	3,812	0.65
West Indian, ex. Hispanic (1,023)	1,493	0.25
Bahamian (121)	121	0.02
Barbadian (48)	76	0.01
Belizean (42)	42	0.01
British West Indian (47)	47	0.01
Dutch West Indian (0)	60	0.01
Haitian (349)	416	0.07
Jamaican (172)	367	0.06
Trinidadian/Tobagonian (46)	78	0.01
U.S. Virgin Islander (28)	28	<0.01
West Indian (156)	244	0.04
Other West Indian (14)	14	<0.01
Yugoslavian (748)	940	0.16

Hispanic Origin	Population	%
Hispanic or Latino (of any race)	60,390	10.04
Central American, ex. Mexican	11,180	1.86
Costa Rican	252	0.04
Guatemalan	3,140	0.52
Honduran	3,018	0.50
Nicaraguan	374	0.06
Panamanian	212	0.04
Salvadoran	4,121	0.69
Other Central American	63	0.01
Cuban	1,716	0.29
Dominican Republic	355	0.06
Mexican	36,877	6.13
Puerto Rican	3,076	0.51
South American	2,204	0.37
Argentinean	162	0.03
Bolivian	66	0.01
Chilean	160	0.03
Colombian	732	0.12
Ecuadorian	306	0.05
Paraguayan	12	<0.01
Peruvian	375	0.06
Uruguayan	25	<0.01
Venezuelan	349	0.06
Other South American	17	<0.01
Other Hispanic or Latino	4,982	0.83

Race*	Population	%
African-American/Black (170,907)	177,894	29.59
Not Hispanic (169,272)	175,416	29.18
Hispanic (1,635)	2,478	0.41
American Indian/Alaska Native (2,047)	5,520	0.92
Not Hispanic (1,418)	4,219	0.70
Hispanic (629)	1,301	0.22
Alaska Athabascan *(Ala. Nat.)* (2)	2	<0.01
Aleut *(Alaska Native)* (3)	7	<0.01
Apache (30)	60	0.01
Arapaho (13)	17	<0.01
Blackfeet (9)	126	0.02
Canadian/French Am. Ind. (11)	23	<0.01
Central American Ind. (26)	39	0.01
Cherokee (338)	1,467	0.24
Cheyenne (9)	16	<0.01
Chickasaw (24)	64	0.01
Chippewa (28)	54	0.01
Choctaw (67)	155	0.03
Colville (0)	1	<0.01
Comanche (3)	19	<0.01
Cree (3)	20	<0.01
Creek (31)	73	0.01
Crow (2)	7	<0.01
Delaware (0)	3	<0.01
Hopi (3)	4	<0.01
Houma (5)	5	<0.01
Inupiat *(Alaska Native)* (2)	6	<0.01
Iroquois (27)	55	0.01
Kiowa (5)	7	<0.01
Lumbee (20)	28	<0.01
Menominee (1)	3	<0.01
Mexican American Ind. (120)	224	0.04
Navajo (11)	23	<0.01
Osage (5)	9	<0.01
Ottawa (7)	11	<0.01
Paiute (4)	5	<0.01
Pima (2)	3	<0.01
Potawatomi (4)	15	<0.01
Pueblo (4)	7	<0.01
Puget Sound Salish (6)	9	<0.01
Seminole (8)	33	0.01
Shoshone (1)	1	<0.01
Sioux (42)	100	0.02
South American Ind. (19)	60	0.01
Spanish American Ind. (14)	20	<0.01
Tlingit-Haida *(Alaska Native)* (3)	4	<0.01
Tohono O'Odham (1)	1	<0.01
Ute (1)	1	<0.01
Yakama (1)	2	<0.01
Yaqui (0)	2	<0.01
Yup'ik *(Alaska Native)* (5)	5	<0.01
Asian (18,641)	22,739	3.78
Not Hispanic (18,497)	22,251	3.70
Hispanic (144)	488	0.08
Bangladeshi (136)	159	0.03
Bhutanese (427)	462	0.08
Burmese (843)	883	0.15
Cambodian (521)	641	0.11
Chinese, ex. Taiwanese (2,520)	2,982	0.50
Filipino (1,100)	1,759	0.29
Hmong (20)	28	<0.01
Indian (4,168)	4,691	0.78
Indonesian (42)	54	0.01
Japanese (510)	886	0.15
Korean (1,611)	2,052	0.34
Laotian (1,837)	2,115	0.35
Malaysian (177)	195	0.03
Nepalese (67)	85	0.01
Pakistani (360)	417	0.07
Sri Lankan (38)	51	0.01
Taiwanese (126)	151	0.03
Thai (299)	450	0.07
Vietnamese (2,774)	2,986	0.50
Hawaii Native/Pacific Islander (376)	997	0.17
Not Hispanic (275)	757	0.13
Hispanic (101)	240	0.04
Fijian (7)	12	<0.01
Guamanian/Chamorro (134)	198	0.03
Native Hawaiian (75)	205	0.03
Samoan (79)	156	0.03
Tongan (2)	5	<0.01
White (363,611)	376,470	62.62
Not Hispanic (338,782)	348,544	57.97
Hispanic (24,829)	27,926	4.64

Oak Ridge

Place Type: City
County: Anderson
Population: 29,330†

Ancestry‡	Population	%
African, Sub-Saharan (119)	119	0.41
African (59)	59	0.20
Nigerian (49)	49	0.17
Other Sub-Saharan African (11)	11	0.04
American (4,368)	4,368	15.10
Arab (21)	44	0.15
Egyptian (21)	21	0.07
Lebanese (0)	14	0.05
Palestinian (0)	9	0.03
Austrian (16)	25	0.09
Belgian (0)	4	0.01
British (129)	172	0.59
Cajun (22)	32	0.11
Canadian (49)	94	0.32
Croatian (20)	20	0.07
Czech (34)	79	0.27
Czechoslovakian (16)	36	0.12
Danish (0)	32	0.11
Dutch (81)	604	2.09
English (1,422)	3,758	12.99
European (398)	448	1.55
French, ex. Basque (174)	706	2.44
French Canadian (97)	129	0.45
German (1,569)	4,082	14.11
Greek (60)	93	0.32
Hungarian (72)	217	0.75
Irish (1,427)	3,874	13.39
Italian (430)	841	2.91
Lithuanian (0)	17	0.06
New Zealander (8)	8	0.03
Northern European (21)	21	0.07
Norwegian (85)	296	1.02
Polish (196)	814	2.81
Portuguese (0)	19	0.07
Romanian (42)	50	0.17
Russian (194)	286	0.99
Scandinavian (12)	39	0.13
Scotch-Irish (726)	1,453	5.02
Scottish (491)	867	3.00
Slovak (30)	83	0.29
Slovene (0)	106	0.37
Swedish (32)	182	0.63
Swiss (7)	112	0.39
Turkish (15)	15	0.05
Ukrainian (4)	53	0.18
Welsh (88)	312	1.08
West Indian, ex. Hispanic (0)	26	0.09
Dutch West Indian (0)	26	0.09

Hispanic Origin	Population	%
Hispanic or Latino (of any race)	1,348	4.60
Central American, ex. Mexican	145	0.49
Costa Rican	2	0.01
Guatemalan	22	0.08
Honduran	82	0.28
Panamanian	16	0.05
Salvadoran	18	0.06

*Notes: † The Census 2010 population figure is used to calculate the percentages in the Hispanic Origin and Race categories. Ancestry percentages are based on the 2006-2010 American Community Survey population (not shown); ‡ Numbers in parentheses indicate the number of people reporting a single ancestry; * Numbers in parentheses indicate the number of persons reporting this race alone, not in combination with any other race; Please refer to the Explanation of Data for more information.*

Other Central American	5	0.02
Cuban	22	0.08
Dominican Republic	5	0.02
Mexican	859	2.93
Puerto Rican	80	0.27
South American	87	0.30
Argentinean	22	0.08
Bolivian	2	0.01
Chilean	6	0.02
Colombian	22	0.08
Ecuadorian	9	0.03
Peruvian	10	0.03
Uruguayan	1	<0.01
Venezuelan	13	0.04
Other South American	2	0.01
Other Hispanic or Latino	150	0.51

Race*	Population	%
African-American/Black (2,381)	2,841	9.69
Not Hispanic (2,362)	2,798	9.54
Hispanic (19)	43	0.15
American Indian/Alaska Native (108)	382	1.30
Not Hispanic (87)	340	1.16
Hispanic (21)	42	0.14
Alaska Athabascan *(Ala. Nat.)* (0)	1	<0.01
Apache (0)	4	0.01
Blackfeet (0)	2	0.01
Central American Ind. (1)	1	<0.01
Cherokee (46)	166	0.57
Chickasaw (1)	6	0.02
Chippewa (4)	7	0.02
Choctaw (0)	6	0.02
Comanche (0)	1	<0.01
Cree (0)	1	<0.01
Creek (0)	2	0.01
Crow (1)	3	0.01
Delaware (1)	1	<0.01
Inupiat *(Alaska Native)* (0)	2	0.01
Iroquois (1)	2	0.01
Mexican American Ind. (7)	10	0.03
Navajo (1)	1	<0.01
Paiute (1)	1	<0.01
Seminole (1)	2	0.01
Sioux (6)	11	0.04
South American Ind. (4)	4	0.01
Yaqui (2)	3	0.01
Yuman (0)	3	0.01
Asian (732)	899	3.07
Not Hispanic (725)	885	3.02
Hispanic (7)	14	0.05
Bangladeshi (19)	19	0.06
Burmese (2)	2	0.01
Cambodian (2)	2	0.01
Chinese, ex. Taiwanese (308)	344	1.17
Filipino (59)	104	0.35
Hmong (7)	7	0.02
Indian (133)	149	0.51
Indonesian (2)	6	0.02
Japanese (30)	67	0.23
Korean (56)	76	0.26
Malaysian (1)	2	0.01
Nepalese (8)	8	0.03
Pakistani (12)	12	0.04
Sri Lankan (2)	2	0.01
Taiwanese (20)	21	0.07
Thai (9)	18	0.06
Vietnamese (47)	57	0.19
Hawaii Native/Pacific Islander (9)	37	0.13
Not Hispanic (8)	33	0.11
Hispanic (1)	4	0.01
Guamanian/Chamorro (0)	7	0.02
Native Hawaiian (4)	18	0.06
Samoan (3)	5	0.02
Tongan (1)	1	<0.01
White (24,619)	25,455	86.79
Not Hispanic (23,978)	24,723	84.29
Hispanic (641)	732	2.50

Paris

Place Type: City
County: Henry
Population: 10,156†

Ancestry‡	Population	%
African, Sub-Saharan (0)	92	0.91
African (0)	92	0.91
American (1,531)	1,531	15.18
British (7)	7	0.07
Croatian (0)	16	0.16
Czech (0)	9	0.09
Danish (0)	29	0.29
Dutch (33)	140	1.39
English (442)	1,078	10.69
European (25)	25	0.25
French, ex. Basque (55)	189	1.87
French Canadian (51)	75	0.74
German (373)	1,176	11.66
Greek (115)	115	1.14
Irish (350)	1,324	13.13
Italian (126)	363	3.60
Lithuanian (0)	12	0.12
Northern European (0)	7	0.07
Norwegian (0)	81	0.80
Polish (20)	75	0.74
Portuguese (0)	13	0.13
Scotch-Irish (223)	302	3.00
Scottish (84)	193	1.91
Swedish (76)	174	1.73
Welsh (11)	62	0.61
West Indian, ex. Hispanic (0)	31	0.31
Dutch West Indian (0)	31	0.31
Yugoslavian (0)	17	0.17

Hispanic Origin	Population	%
Hispanic or Latino (of any race)	166	1.63
Central American, ex. Mexican	1	0.01
Costa Rican	1	0.01
Cuban	5	0.05
Dominican Republic	2	0.02
Mexican	94	0.93
Puerto Rican	19	0.19
South American	7	0.07
Chilean	3	0.03
Colombian	2	0.02
Peruvian	1	0.01
Venezuelan	1	0.01
Other Hispanic or Latino	38	0.37

Race*	Population	%
African-American/Black (1,955)	2,133	21.00
Not Hispanic (1,941)	2,112	20.80
Hispanic (14)	21	0.21
American Indian/Alaska Native (35)	83	0.82
Not Hispanic (31)	78	0.77
Hispanic (4)	5	0.05
Apache (0)	2	0.02
Blackfeet (2)	9	0.09
Cherokee (11)	33	0.32
Chickasaw (0)	1	0.01
Chippewa (0)	2	0.02
Choctaw (1)	1	0.01
Potawatomi (1)	1	0.01
Sioux (1)	3	0.03
Asian (65)	80	0.79
Not Hispanic (65)	79	0.78
Hispanic (0)	1	0.01
Chinese, ex. Taiwanese (18)	18	0.18
Filipino (10)	19	0.19
Indian (14)	14	0.14
Japanese (9)	11	0.11
Korean (4)	8	0.08
Malaysian (0)	6	0.06
Vietnamese (4)	4	0.04
Hawaii Native/Pacific Islander (1)	1	0.01
Not Hispanic (1)	1	0.01
White (7,819)	8,047	79.23
Not Hispanic (7,723)	7,938	78.16
Hispanic (96)	109	1.07

Portland

Place Type: City
County: Sumner
Population: 11,480†

Ancestry‡	Population	%
American (1,614)	1,614	14.71
British (90)	135	1.23
Canadian (15)	15	0.14
Czech (0)	22	0.20
Dutch (156)	217	1.98
English (663)	1,124	10.24
European (154)	154	1.40
Finnish (0)	10	0.09
French, ex. Basque (37)	302	2.75
French Canadian (0)	83	0.76
German (549)	1,435	13.08
Hungarian (16)	16	0.15
Irish (724)	1,578	14.38
Italian (158)	525	4.78
Norwegian (26)	72	0.66
Polish (70)	140	1.28
Portuguese (0)	138	1.26
Scotch-Irish (254)	312	2.84
Scottish (78)	333	3.03
Slovene (0)	14	0.13
Swiss (0)	27	0.25
Welsh (0)	30	0.27

Hispanic Origin	Population	%
Hispanic or Latino (of any race)	452	3.94
Central American, ex. Mexican	37	0.32
Costa Rican	1	0.01
Guatemalan	14	0.12
Honduran	7	0.06
Nicaraguan	1	0.01
Panamanian	6	0.05
Salvadoran	8	0.07
Cuban	8	0.07
Dominican Republic	8	0.07
Mexican	319	2.78
Puerto Rican	47	0.41
South American	9	0.08
Bolivian	2	0.02
Colombian	3	0.03
Ecuadorian	1	0.01
Peruvian	2	0.02
Uruguayan	1	0.01
Other Hispanic or Latino	24	0.21

Race*	Population	%
African-American/Black (401)	503	4.38
Not Hispanic (388)	487	4.24
Hispanic (13)	16	0.14
American Indian/Alaska Native (35)	85	0.74
Not Hispanic (19)	60	0.52
Hispanic (16)	25	0.22
Apache (0)	1	0.01
Blackfeet (0)	1	0.01
Central American Ind. (3)	3	0.03
Cherokee (8)	38	0.33
Chickasaw (0)	2	0.02
Chippewa (1)	2	0.02
Choctaw (0)	6	0.05
Creek (0)	3	0.03
Iroquois (2)	3	0.03
Mexican American Ind. (11)	12	0.10
Sioux (1)	4	0.03
Asian (62)	92	0.80
Not Hispanic (62)	83	0.72
Hispanic (0)	9	0.08
Cambodian (1)	1	0.01
Chinese, ex. Taiwanese (11)	16	0.14
Filipino (16)	26	0.23
Indian (17)	17	0.15
Japanese (4)	12	0.10
Korean (3)	5	0.04

*Notes: † The Census 2010 population figure is used to calculate the percentages in the Hispanic Origin and Race categories. Ancestry percentages are based on the 2006-2010 American Community Survey population (not shown); ‡ Numbers in parentheses indicate the number of people reporting a single ancestry; * Numbers in parentheses indicate the number of persons reporting this race alone, not in combination with any other race; Please refer to the Explanation of Data for more information.*

Taiwanese (0)	2	0.02
Thai (1)	1	0.01
Vietnamese (7)	8	0.07
Hawaii Native/Pacific Islander (6)	10	0.09
Not Hispanic (5)	5	0.04
Hispanic (1)	5	0.04
Guamanian/Chamorro (4)	4	0.03
Native Hawaiian (1)	4	0.03
Samoan (1)	2	0.02
White (10,605)	10,798	94.06
Not Hispanic (10,387)	10,546	91.86
Hispanic (218)	252	2.20

Pulaski

Place Type: City
County: Giles
Population: 7,870†

Ancestry‡	Population	%
African, Sub-Saharan (33)	51	0.65
African (33)	51	0.65
American (1,455)	1,455	18.43
Czechoslovakian (0)	9	0.11
Dutch (13)	97	1.23
English (334)	612	7.75
European (23)	23	0.29
French, ex. Basque (17)	67	0.85
French Canadian (34)	43	0.54
German (44)	218	2.76
Greek (12)	12	0.15
Hungarian (18)	18	0.23
Irish (295)	546	6.92
Italian (0)	7	0.09
Norwegian (14)	14	0.18
Polish (12)	12	0.15
Scotch-Irish (88)	134	1.70
Scottish (77)	156	1.98
Swedish (66)	120	1.52

Hispanic Origin	Population	%
Hispanic or Latino (of any race)	169	2.15
Central American, ex. Mexican	14	0.18
Guatemalan	11	0.14
Panamanian	2	0.03
Salvadoran	1	0.01
Cuban	3	0.04
Dominican Republic	5	0.06
Mexican	106	1.35
Puerto Rican	13	0.17
South American	3	0.04
Argentinean	1	0.01
Colombian	1	0.01
Uruguayan	1	0.01
Other Hispanic or Latino	25	0.32

Race*	Population	%
African-American/Black (1,920)	2,050	26.05
Not Hispanic (1,918)	2,041	25.93
Hispanic (2)	9	0.11
American Indian/Alaska Native (15)	56	0.71
Not Hispanic (11)	49	0.62
Hispanic (4)	7	0.09
Blackfeet (1)	3	0.04
Cherokee (2)	18	0.23
Cree (0)	3	0.04
Creek (0)	2	0.03
Crow (0)	1	0.01
Mexican American Ind. (3)	3	0.04
Sioux (1)	2	0.03
Asian (45)	82	1.04
Not Hispanic (43)	79	1.00
Hispanic (2)	3	0.04
Chinese, ex. Taiwanese (11)	12	0.15
Filipino (3)	14	0.18
Indian (16)	22	0.28
Japanese (1)	1	0.01
Korean (8)	10	0.13
Sri Lankan (1)	1	0.01
Thai (1)	5	0.06
Vietnamese (2)	9	0.11
Hawaii Native/Pacific Islander (7)	16	0.20
Not Hispanic (4)	11	0.14
Hispanic (3)	5	0.06
Guamanian/Chamorro (3)	3	0.04
White (5,589)	5,780	73.44
Not Hispanic (5,513)	5,686	72.25
Hispanic (76)	94	1.19

Red Bank

Place Type: City
County: Hamilton
Population: 11,651†

Ancestry‡	Population	%
African, Sub-Saharan (69)	69	0.59
African (69)	69	0.59
American (2,210)	2,210	18.95
Belgian (9)	46	0.39
British (24)	39	0.33
Danish (18)	28	0.24
Dutch (35)	199	1.71
English (455)	1,311	11.24
European (76)	76	0.65
French, ex. Basque (53)	316	2.71
French Canadian (41)	41	0.35
German (492)	1,543	13.23
Hungarian (0)	33	0.28
Irish (544)	1,590	13.64
Israeli (0)	26	0.22
Italian (184)	318	2.73
Norwegian (12)	42	0.36
Polish (28)	140	1.20
Portuguese (24)	24	0.21
Russian (19)	19	0.16
Scandinavian (0)	54	0.46
Scotch-Irish (321)	784	6.72
Scottish (213)	327	2.80
Swedish (0)	14	0.12
Swiss (0)	24	0.21
Welsh (15)	101	0.87
Yugoslavian (0)	16	0.14

Hispanic Origin	Population	%
Hispanic or Latino (of any race)	752	6.45
Central American, ex. Mexican	86	0.74
Costa Rican	1	0.01
Guatemalan	61	0.52
Honduran	3	0.03
Panamanian	4	0.03
Salvadoran	17	0.15
Cuban	18	0.15
Dominican Republic	4	0.03
Mexican	543	4.66
Puerto Rican	36	0.31
South American	22	0.19
Argentinean	1	0.01
Chilean	1	0.01
Ecuadorian	13	0.11
Peruvian	4	0.03
Venezuelan	3	0.03
Other Hispanic or Latino	43	0.37

Race*	Population	%
African-American/Black (869)	984	8.45
Not Hispanic (854)	956	8.21
Hispanic (15)	28	0.24
American Indian/Alaska Native (41)	116	1.00
Not Hispanic (37)	109	0.94
Hispanic (4)	7	0.06
Aleut *(Alaska Native)* (1)	1	0.01
Blackfeet (2)	3	0.03
Cherokee (17)	51	0.44
Chickasaw (1)	1	0.01
Chippewa (1)	5	0.04
Choctaw (1)	1	0.01
Inupiat *(Alaska Native)* (1)	1	0.01
Kiowa (0)	1	0.01
Lumbee (0)	3	0.03
Mexican American Ind. (5)	6	0.05
Navajo (0)	2	0.02
Seminole (0)	2	0.02
Sioux (1)	2	0.02
Asian (153)	189	1.62
Not Hispanic (151)	186	1.60
Hispanic (2)	3	0.03
Cambodian (4)	4	0.03
Chinese, ex. Taiwanese (40)	41	0.35
Filipino (10)	20	0.17
Indian (27)	28	0.24
Indonesian (0)	1	0.01
Japanese (3)	9	0.08
Korean (17)	20	0.17
Laotian (9)	9	0.08
Nepalese (1)	1	0.01
Pakistani (2)	2	0.02
Taiwanese (2)	2	0.02
Thai (9)	9	0.08
Vietnamese (19)	22	0.19
Hawaii Native/Pacific Islander (9)	17	0.15
Not Hispanic (8)	15	0.13
Hispanic (1)	2	0.02
Guamanian/Chamorro (2)	3	0.03
Native Hawaiian (6)	9	0.08
White (9,907)	10,137	87.01
Not Hispanic (9,630)	9,832	84.39
Hispanic (277)	305	2.62

Ripley

Place Type: City
County: Lauderdale
Population: 8,445†

Ancestry‡	Population	%
African, Sub-Saharan (23)	23	0.27
African (23)	23	0.27
American (577)	577	6.89
Arab (6)	6	0.07
Egyptian (6)	6	0.07
Austrian (11)	11	0.13
British (11)	24	0.29
English (167)	225	2.69
European (49)	49	0.59
French, ex. Basque (9)	9	0.11
German (20)	246	2.94
Irish (125)	372	4.44
Italian (8)	58	0.69
Luxemburger (11)	11	0.13
Polish (0)	38	0.45
Russian (0)	12	0.14
Scotch-Irish (133)	192	2.29
Scottish (34)	76	0.91
Serbian (20)	20	0.24

Hispanic Origin	Population	%
Hispanic or Latino (of any race)	134	1.59
Central American, ex. Mexican	5	0.06
Guatemalan	3	0.04
Panamanian	1	0.01
Salvadoran	1	0.01
Cuban	2	0.02
Mexican	110	1.30
Puerto Rican	3	0.04
South American	1	0.01
Peruvian	1	0.01
Other Hispanic or Latino	13	0.15

Race*	Population	%
African-American/Black (4,535)	4,619	54.70
Not Hispanic (4,512)	4,593	54.39
Hispanic (23)	26	0.31
American Indian/Alaska Native (14)	36	0.43
Not Hispanic (13)	35	0.41
Hispanic (1)	1	0.01
Cherokee (2)	11	0.13
Choctaw (6)	9	0.11
Asian (34)	59	0.70
Not Hispanic (33)	54	0.64

*Notes: † The Census 2010 population figure is used to calculate the percentages in the Hispanic Origin and Race categories. Ancestry percentages are based on the 2006-2010 American Community Survey population (not shown); ‡ Numbers in parentheses indicate the number of people reporting a single ancestry; * Numbers in parentheses indicate the number of persons reporting this race alone, not in combination with any other race; Please refer to the Explanation of Data for more information.*

Hispanic (1)	5	0.06
Chinese, ex. Taiwanese (8)	14	0.17
Filipino (4)	9	0.11
Indian (16)	16	0.19
Japanese (4)	4	0.05
Korean (2)	3	0.04
Pakistani (0)	4	0.05
Thai (0)	1	0.01
Vietnamese (0)	1	0.01
Hawaii Native/Pacific Islander (3)	8	0.09
Not Hispanic (0)	4	0.05
Hispanic (3)	4	0.05
Guamanian/Chamorro (3)	4	0.05
Samoan (0)	1	0.01
White (3,680)	3,782	44.78
Not Hispanic (3,630)	3,724	44.10
Hispanic (50)	58	0.69

Sevierville

Place Type: City
County: Sevier
Population: 14,807†

Ancestry‡	Population	%
American (3,710)	3,710	25.63
British (53)	67	0.46
Canadian (0)	16	0.11
Czech (19)	25	0.17
Czechoslovakian (67)	67	0.46
Danish (0)	35	0.24
Dutch (30)	174	1.20
English (662)	1,693	11.69
European (34)	34	0.23
Finnish (29)	29	0.20
French, ex. Basque (67)	259	1.79
French Canadian (11)	72	0.50
German (554)	1,776	12.27
Hungarian (0)	77	0.53
Irish (479)	1,606	11.09
Italian (56)	247	1.71
Lithuanian (14)	14	0.10
Norwegian (48)	48	0.33
Polish (38)	274	1.89
Russian (87)	87	0.60
Scotch-Irish (470)	829	5.73
Scottish (223)	420	2.90
Swedish (0)	71	0.49
Welsh (0)	34	0.23
West Indian, ex. Hispanic (0)	10	0.07
Jamaican (0)	10	0.07

Hispanic Origin	Population	%
Hispanic or Latino (of any race)	1,518	10.25
Central American, ex. Mexican	432	2.92
Costa Rican	23	0.16
Guatemalan	37	0.25
Honduran	339	2.29
Nicaraguan	4	0.03
Panamanian	3	0.02
Salvadoran	26	0.18
Cuban	52	0.35
Dominican Republic	5	0.03
Mexican	799	5.40
Puerto Rican	65	0.44
South American	60	0.41
Argentinean	5	0.03
Chilean	10	0.07
Colombian	14	0.09
Ecuadorian	7	0.05
Paraguayan	2	0.01
Peruvian	3	0.02
Uruguayan	17	0.11
Venezuelan	2	0.01
Other Hispanic or Latino	105	0.71

Race*	Population	%
African-American/Black (227)	303	2.05
Not Hispanic (208)	279	1.88
Hispanic (19)	24	0.16
American Indian/Alaska Native (82)	150	1.01
Not Hispanic (68)	134	0.90
Hispanic (14)	16	0.11
Aleut *(Alaska Native)* (0)	1	0.01
Apache (4)	4	0.03
Blackfeet (1)	5	0.03
Cherokee (37)	72	0.49
Chippewa (0)	1	0.01
Choctaw (1)	3	0.02
Creek (0)	1	0.01
Crow (0)	1	0.01
Lumbee (2)	2	0.01
Mexican American Ind. (2)	2	0.01
Sioux (0)	2	0.01
South American Ind. (2)	2	0.01
Asian (187)	241	1.63
Not Hispanic (184)	237	1.60
Hispanic (3)	4	0.03
Bangladeshi (0)	4	0.03
Burmese (1)	1	0.01
Chinese, ex. Taiwanese (27)	31	0.21
Filipino (17)	22	0.15
Hmong (2)	2	0.01
Indian (88)	98	0.66
Indonesian (11)	11	0.07
Japanese (4)	9	0.06
Korean (3)	10	0.07
Laotian (1)	1	0.01
Nepalese (1)	1	0.01
Pakistani (2)	4	0.03
Taiwanese (1)	1	0.01
Thai (6)	7	0.05
Vietnamese (20)	20	0.14
Hawaii Native/Pacific Islander (2)	11	0.07
Not Hispanic (2)	10	0.07
Hispanic (0)	1	0.01
Guamanian/Chamorro (0)	2	0.01
Native Hawaiian (1)	6	0.04
White (13,165)	13,392	90.44
Not Hispanic (12,617)	12,790	86.38
Hispanic (548)	602	4.07

Seymour

Place Type: CDP
County: Sevier
Population: 10,919†

Ancestry‡	Population	%
American (1,863)	1,863	17.95
Arab (0)	11	0.11
Other Arab (0)	11	0.11
Austrian (16)	16	0.15
British (40)	107	1.03
Czechoslovakian (12)	12	0.12
Danish (16)	16	0.15
Dutch (24)	260	2.51
English (784)	1,565	15.08
European (116)	130	1.25
Finnish (11)	11	0.11
French, ex. Basque (141)	258	2.49
French Canadian (8)	8	0.08
German (542)	1,475	14.21
Greek (9)	30	0.29
Hungarian (17)	32	0.31
Irish (626)	1,605	15.47
Italian (189)	283	2.73
Lithuanian (0)	15	0.14
Norwegian (36)	36	0.35
Polish (64)	209	2.01
Portuguese (0)	12	0.12
Russian (0)	29	0.28
Scandinavian (11)	11	0.11
Scotch-Irish (144)	319	3.07
Scottish (156)	269	2.59
Serbian (0)	13	0.13
Slovak (0)	11	0.11
Swedish (12)	35	0.34
Welsh (112)	188	1.81
West Indian, ex. Hispanic (0)	14	0.13
Dutch West Indian (0)	14	0.13

Hispanic Origin	Population	%
Hispanic or Latino (of any race)	188	1.72
Central American, ex. Mexican	8	0.07
Costa Rican	1	0.01
Honduran	5	0.05
Panamanian	1	0.01
Salvadoran	1	0.01
Cuban	29	0.27
Mexican	77	0.71
Puerto Rican	37	0.34
South American	15	0.14
Colombian	9	0.08
Venezuelan	6	0.05
Other Hispanic or Latino	22	0.20

Race*	Population	%
African-American/Black (77)	115	1.05
Not Hispanic (73)	109	1.00
Hispanic (4)	6	0.05
American Indian/Alaska Native (18)	56	0.51
Not Hispanic (12)	40	0.37
Hispanic (6)	16	0.15
Aleut *(Alaska Native)* (2)	2	0.02
Apache (1)	9	0.08
Blackfeet (0)	5	0.05
Cherokee (3)	14	0.13
Chippewa (1)	1	0.01
Lumbee (0)	1	0.01
Mexican American Ind. (2)	4	0.04
Pueblo (1)	1	0.01
South American Ind. (2)	2	0.02
Asian (61)	97	0.89
Not Hispanic (61)	92	0.84
Hispanic (0)	5	0.05
Chinese, ex. Taiwanese (14)	17	0.16
Filipino (14)	29	0.27
Indian (12)	13	0.12
Indonesian (2)	2	0.02
Japanese (2)	15	0.14
Korean (4)	8	0.07
Laotian (1)	1	0.01
Thai (1)	4	0.04
Vietnamese (4)	7	0.06
Hawaii Native/Pacific Islander (1)	7	0.06
Not Hispanic (1)	5	0.05
Hispanic (0)	2	0.02
Guamanian/Chamorro (0)	1	0.01
Native Hawaiian (1)	4	0.04
White (10,611)	10,724	98.21
Not Hispanic (10,477)	10,573	96.83
Hispanic (134)	151	1.38

Shelbyville

Place Type: City
County: Bedford
Population: 20,335†

Ancestry‡	Population	%
African, Sub-Saharan (446)	446	2.26
Ethiopian (242)	242	1.22
Kenyan (32)	32	0.16
Somalian (172)	172	0.87
American (5,828)	5,828	29.48
Belgian (0)	12	0.06
British (13)	13	0.07
Czech (0)	21	0.11
Dutch (37)	125	0.63
English (643)	1,262	6.38
European (49)	96	0.49
Finnish (0)	27	0.14
French, ex. Basque (40)	174	0.88
French Canadian (11)	27	0.14
German (407)	1,023	5.17
Greek (0)	14	0.07
Irish (464)	1,186	6.00
Italian (31)	85	0.43
Norwegian (17)	41	0.21

*Notes: † The Census 2010 population figure is used to calculate the percentages in the Hispanic Origin and Race categories. Ancestry percentages are based on the 2006-2010 American Community Survey population (not shown); ‡ Numbers in parentheses indicate the number of people reporting a single ancestry; * Numbers in parentheses indicate the number of persons reporting this race alone, not in combination with any other race; Please refer to the Explanation of Data for more information.*

Polish (30)	90	0.46
Russian (0)	64	0.32
Scotch-Irish (138)	277	1.40
Scottish (123)	264	1.34
Swedish (29)	86	0.44
Ukrainian (30)	94	0.48
Welsh (0)	31	0.16
Yugoslavian (0)	9	0.05

Hispanic Origin	Population	%
Hispanic or Latino (of any race)	4,127	20.30
Central American, ex. Mexican	391	1.92
Costa Rican	5	0.02
Guatemalan	315	1.55
Honduran	15	0.07
Nicaraguan	7	0.03
Panamanian	2	0.01
Salvadoran	30	0.15
Other Central American	17	0.08
Cuban	17	0.08
Dominican Republic	7	0.03
Mexican	3,427	16.85
Puerto Rican	31	0.15
South American	18	0.09
Argentinean	4	0.02
Colombian	6	0.03
Ecuadorian	4	0.02
Peruvian	1	<0.01
Venezuelan	3	0.01
Other Hispanic or Latino	236	1.16

Race*	Population	%
African-American/Black (2,860)	3,188	15.68
Not Hispanic (2,757)	3,068	15.09
Hispanic (103)	120	0.59
American Indian/Alaska Native (104)	211	1.04
Not Hispanic (37)	130	0.64
Hispanic (67)	81	0.40
Aleut *(Alaska Native)* (1)	1	<0.01
Apache (0)	4	0.02
Blackfeet (0)	4	0.02
Central American Ind. (16)	17	0.08
Cherokee (12)	53	0.26
Cheyenne (0)	8	0.04
Chickasaw (1)	2	0.01
Choctaw (0)	3	0.01
Creek (0)	3	0.01
Iroquois (2)	3	0.01
Mexican American Ind. (38)	39	0.19
Navajo (0)	1	<0.01
Potawatomi (1)	1	<0.01
Seminole (1)	1	<0.01
Sioux (0)	1	<0.01
Spanish American Ind. (2)	3	0.01
Asian (141)	186	0.91
Not Hispanic (131)	172	0.85
Hispanic (10)	14	0.07
Cambodian (2)	2	0.01
Chinese, ex. Taiwanese (13)	19	0.09
Filipino (22)	37	0.18
Indian (63)	72	0.35
Japanese (16)	24	0.12
Korean (9)	11	0.05
Laotian (4)	6	0.03
Taiwanese (1)	1	<0.01
Vietnamese (8)	9	0.04
Hawaii Native/Pacific Islander (40)	55	0.27
Not Hispanic (28)	37	0.18
Hispanic (12)	18	0.09
Guamanian/Chamorro (17)	23	0.11
Native Hawaiian (6)	12	0.06
Samoan (17)	18	0.09
White (13,886)	14,516	71.38
Not Hispanic (12,803)	13,201	64.92
Hispanic (1,083)	1,315	6.47

Signal Mountain

Place Type: Town
County: Hamilton
Population: 7,554†

Ancestry‡	Population	%
African, Sub-Saharan (70)	70	0.94
South African (70)	70	0.94
American (1,099)	1,099	14.69
Australian (21)	21	0.28
Belgian (61)	61	0.82
British (92)	92	1.23
Canadian (11)	23	0.31
Danish (11)	11	0.15
Dutch (0)	58	0.78
Eastern European (24)	24	0.32
English (787)	1,670	22.32
European (244)	258	3.45
French, ex. Basque (22)	174	2.33
French Canadian (10)	10	0.13
German (288)	959	12.82
Hungarian (14)	14	0.19
Irish (568)	1,094	14.62
Italian (75)	175	2.34
Norwegian (115)	153	2.05
Polish (81)	188	2.51
Russian (0)	27	0.36
Scotch-Irish (397)	709	9.48
Scottish (103)	446	5.96
Swedish (12)	88	1.18
Swiss (12)	25	0.33
Welsh (33)	97	1.30

Hispanic Origin	Population	%
Hispanic or Latino (of any race)	120	1.59
Central American, ex. Mexican	9	0.12
Guatemalan	4	0.05
Honduran	1	0.01
Nicaraguan	1	0.01
Panamanian	2	0.03
Salvadoran	1	0.01
Cuban	15	0.20
Mexican	51	0.68
Puerto Rican	10	0.13
South American	21	0.28
Argentinean	3	0.04
Bolivian	1	0.01
Colombian	2	0.03
Ecuadorian	3	0.04
Paraguayan	1	0.01
Peruvian	4	0.05
Uruguayan	1	0.01
Venezuelan	6	0.08
Other Hispanic or Latino	14	0.19

Race*	Population	%
African-American/Black (19)	28	0.37
Not Hispanic (19)	28	0.37
American Indian/Alaska Native (10)	48	0.64
Not Hispanic (9)	41	0.54
Hispanic (1)	7	0.09
Blackfeet (0)	1	0.01
Cherokee (4)	21	0.28
Creek (0)	2	0.03
Lumbee (3)	3	0.04
Mexican American Ind. (0)	2	0.03
Asian (58)	81	1.07
Not Hispanic (58)	81	1.07
Cambodian (1)	3	0.04
Chinese, ex. Taiwanese (13)	17	0.23
Filipino (13)	17	0.23
Indian (14)	16	0.21
Japanese (0)	4	0.05
Korean (3)	7	0.09
Taiwanese (4)	4	0.05
Vietnamese (10)	10	0.13
Hawaii Native/Pacific Islander (7)	11	0.15
Not Hispanic (6)	10	0.13
Hispanic (1)	1	0.01
Guamanian/Chamorro (1)	2	0.03
Native Hawaiian (4)	7	0.09
White (7,363)	7,437	98.45
Not Hispanic (7,268)	7,335	97.10
Hispanic (95)	102	1.35

Smyrna

Place Type: Town
County: Rutherford
Population: 39,974†

Ancestry‡	Population	%
African, Sub-Saharan (63)	78	0.20
African (63)	63	0.17
South African (0)	15	0.04
American (7,890)	7,890	20.71
Arab (138)	314	0.82
Arab (15)	41	0.11
Egyptian (78)	126	0.33
Iraqi (0)	48	0.13
Jordanian (0)	12	0.03
Lebanese (0)	17	0.04
Moroccan (0)	13	0.03
Syrian (0)	12	0.03
Other Arab (45)	45	0.12
Armenian (13)	24	0.06
Brazilian (10)	23	0.06
British (119)	119	0.31
Bulgarian (0)	9	0.02
Cajun (0)	15	0.04
Canadian (24)	54	0.14
Czech (65)	113	0.30
Danish (8)	51	0.13
Dutch (102)	523	1.37
Eastern European (9)	9	0.02
English (1,675)	3,077	8.08
European (470)	500	1.31
Finnish (20)	54	0.14
French, ex. Basque (299)	1,096	2.88
French Canadian (84)	185	0.49
German (1,101)	3,934	10.32
Greek (51)	85	0.22
Hungarian (19)	47	0.12
Irish (1,775)	4,368	11.46
Italian (407)	1,092	2.87
Lithuanian (0)	17	0.04
Northern European (0)	13	0.03
Norwegian (42)	150	0.39
Polish (112)	453	1.19
Portuguese (0)	15	0.04
Russian (0)	6	0.02
Scandinavian (0)	14	0.04
Scotch-Irish (332)	968	2.54
Scottish (306)	643	1.69
Serbian (0)	11	0.03
Slovak (0)	14	0.04
Swedish (44)	84	0.22
Swiss (0)	23	0.06
Welsh (51)	150	0.39
West Indian, ex. Hispanic (246)	246	0.65
Haitian (235)	235	0.62
West Indian (11)	11	0.03

Hispanic Origin	Population	%
Hispanic or Latino (of any race)	4,286	10.72
Central American, ex. Mexican	880	2.20
Costa Rican	7	0.02
Guatemalan	387	0.97
Honduran	98	0.25
Nicaraguan	14	0.04
Panamanian	14	0.04
Salvadoran	358	0.90
Other Central American	2	0.01
Cuban	58	0.15
Dominican Republic	19	0.05
Mexican	2,697	6.75
Puerto Rican	249	0.62
South American	94	0.24
Argentinean	7	0.02

*Notes: † The Census 2010 population figure is used to calculate the percentages in the Hispanic Origin and Race categories. Ancestry percentages are based on the 2006-2010 American Community Survey population (not shown); ‡ Numbers in parentheses indicate the number of people reporting a single ancestry; * Numbers in parentheses indicate the number of persons reporting this race alone, not in combination with any other race; Please refer to the Explanation of Data for more information.*

Bolivian	12	0.03
Chilean	3	0.01
Colombian	20	0.05
Ecuadorian	6	0.02
Peruvian	37	0.09
Uruguayan	1	<0.01
Venezuelan	7	0.02
Other South American	1	<0.01
Other Hispanic or Latino	289	0.72

Race*	Population	%
African-American/Black (4,480)	5,011	12.54
Not Hispanic (4,422)	4,910	12.28
Hispanic (58)	101	0.25
American Indian/Alaska Native (236)	480	1.20
Not Hispanic (119)	335	0.84
Hispanic (117)	145	0.36
Alaska Athabascan *(Ala. Nat.)* (0)	1	<0.01
Apache (0)	2	0.01
Blackfeet (0)	8	0.02
Cherokee (37)	124	0.31
Chippewa (3)	4	0.01
Choctaw (10)	21	0.05
Comanche (1)	1	<0.01
Creek (1)	7	0.02
Crow (1)	3	0.01
Delaware (0)	2	0.01
Hopi (1)	1	<0.01
Houma (1)	1	<0.01
Iroquois (3)	6	0.02
Kiowa (2)	3	0.01
Lumbee (4)	6	0.02
Mexican American Ind. (8)	10	0.03
Navajo (5)	5	0.01
Ottawa (0)	1	<0.01
Potawatomi (0)	1	<0.01
Pueblo (0)	1	<0.01
Seminole (1)	2	0.01
Spanish American Ind. (63)	65	0.16
Tsimshian *(Alaska Native)* (0)	1	<0.01
Yup'ik *(Alaska Native)* (1)	2	0.01
Asian (1,739)	1,962	4.91
Not Hispanic (1,716)	1,916	4.79
Hispanic (23)	46	0.12
Bangladeshi (5)	5	0.01
Burmese (218)	241	0.60
Cambodian (11)	18	0.05
Chinese, ex. Taiwanese (66)	86	0.22
Filipino (158)	227	0.57
Hmong (13)	15	0.04
Indian (266)	325	0.81
Indonesian (1)	1	<0.01
Japanese (20)	47	0.12
Korean (55)	77	0.19
Laotian (666)	707	1.77
Nepalese (4)	4	0.01
Pakistani (16)	17	0.04
Taiwanese (3)	3	0.01
Thai (44)	55	0.14
Vietnamese (76)	85	0.21
Hawaii Native/Pacific Islander (32)	72	0.18
Not Hispanic (22)	41	0.10
Hispanic (10)	31	0.08
Guamanian/Chamorro (23)	30	0.08
Native Hawaiian (5)	14	0.04
Samoan (3)	5	0.01
White (29,982)	30,955	77.44
Not Hispanic (28,527)	29,285	73.26
Hispanic (1,455)	1,670	4.18

Soddy-Daisy

Place Type: City
County: Hamilton
Population: 12,714†

Ancestry‡	Population	%
American (3,348)	3,348	27.02
British (14)	14	0.11
Danish (16)	93	0.75
Dutch (0)	291	2.35
English (667)	1,471	11.87
European (40)	77	0.62
French, ex. Basque (47)	231	1.86
French Canadian (7)	7	0.06
German (336)	1,244	10.04
Hungarian (12)	12	0.10
Irish (889)	2,248	18.14
Italian (58)	187	1.51
Norwegian (10)	37	0.30
Polish (44)	103	0.83
Romanian (24)	96	0.77
Russian (37)	64	0.52
Scotch-Irish (104)	296	2.39
Scottish (104)	196	1.58
Swedish (29)	103	0.83
Swiss (0)	13	0.10
Ukrainian (0)	23	0.19
Welsh (60)	208	1.68
West Indian, ex. Hispanic (10)	68	0.55
Dutch West Indian (0)	58	0.47
West Indian (10)	10	0.08

Hispanic Origin	Population	%
Hispanic or Latino (of any race)	205	1.61
Central American, ex. Mexican	9	0.07
Guatemalan	2	0.02
Honduran	6	0.05
Panamanian	1	0.01
Cuban	12	0.09
Mexican	144	1.13
Puerto Rican	10	0.08
South American	10	0.08
Bolivian	7	0.06
Chilean	1	0.01
Colombian	2	0.02
Other Hispanic or Latino	20	0.16

Race*	Population	%
African-American/Black (88)	113	0.89
Not Hispanic (83)	108	0.85
Hispanic (5)	5	0.04
American Indian/Alaska Native (50)	133	1.05
Not Hispanic (42)	125	0.98
Hispanic (8)	8	0.06
Apache (1)	1	0.01
Cherokee (15)	52	0.41
Cheyenne (0)	1	0.01
Choctaw (1)	5	0.04
Comanche (0)	3	0.02
Creek (0)	1	0.01
Hopi (0)	3	0.02
Iroquois (3)	3	0.02
Mexican American Ind. (3)	3	0.02
Potawatomi (2)	3	0.02
Seminole (1)	1	0.01
Sioux (1)	5	0.04
Tohono O'Odham (0)	4	0.03
Asian (41)	61	0.48
Not Hispanic (41)	61	0.48
Cambodian (0)	1	0.01
Chinese, ex. Taiwanese (6)	6	0.05
Filipino (4)	5	0.04
Indian (6)	9	0.07
Indonesian (0)	1	0.01
Japanese (4)	5	0.04
Korean (13)	19	0.15
Vietnamese (5)	6	0.05
Hawaii Native/Pacific Islander (1)	6	0.05
Not Hispanic (1)	6	0.05
Guamanian/Chamorro (1)	1	0.01
Native Hawaiian (0)	1	0.01
White (12,325)	12,455	97.96
Not Hispanic (12,206)	12,329	96.97
Hispanic (119)	126	0.99

Spring Hill

Place Type: City
County: Williamson
Population: 29,036†

Ancestry‡	Population	%
Afghan (20)	20	0.08
African, Sub-Saharan (33)	67	0.26
African (0)	11	0.04
Cape Verdean (0)	12	0.05
Liberian (8)	8	0.03
South African (16)	27	0.11
Zimbabwean (9)	9	0.04
American (2,384)	2,384	9.38
Arab (0)	41	0.16
Egyptian (0)	8	0.03
Lebanese (0)	33	0.13
Austrian (13)	30	0.12
British (32)	96	0.38
Canadian (37)	44	0.17
Croatian (27)	27	0.11
Czech (8)	105	0.41
Czechoslovakian (0)	19	0.07
Dutch (55)	403	1.59
English (1,944)	4,389	17.27
Estonian (32)	32	0.13
European (285)	353	1.39
Finnish (0)	15	0.06
French, ex. Basque (179)	837	3.29
French Canadian (64)	243	0.96
German (1,752)	5,245	20.64
Greek (25)	249	0.98
Hungarian (0)	74	0.29
Iranian (68)	68	0.27
Irish (1,423)	4,312	16.97
Italian (430)	1,624	6.39
Lithuanian (0)	27	0.11
New Zealander (9)	9	0.04
Norwegian (184)	358	1.41
Pennsylvania German (12)	12	0.05
Polish (238)	810	3.19
Portuguese (31)	43	0.17
Romanian (24)	24	0.09
Russian (70)	202	0.79
Scotch-Irish (266)	553	2.18
Scottish (203)	915	3.60
Serbian (11)	11	0.04
Slavic (11)	22	0.09
Swedish (71)	452	1.78
Swiss (0)	9	0.04
Ukrainian (109)	163	0.64
Welsh (44)	289	1.14
West Indian, ex. Hispanic (26)	26	0.10
British West Indian (13)	13	0.05
Jamaican (13)	13	0.05

Hispanic Origin	Population	%
Hispanic or Latino (of any race)	1,640	5.65
Central American, ex. Mexican	138	0.48
Costa Rican	7	0.02
Guatemalan	22	0.08
Honduran	50	0.17
Nicaraguan	16	0.06
Panamanian	14	0.05
Salvadoran	29	0.10
Cuban	93	0.32
Dominican Republic	32	0.11
Mexican	895	3.08
Puerto Rican	216	0.74
South American	151	0.52
Argentinean	12	0.04
Bolivian	4	0.01
Chilean	17	0.06
Colombian	52	0.18
Ecuadorian	13	0.04
Paraguayan	1	<0.01
Peruvian	27	0.09
Uruguayan	3	0.01
Venezuelan	22	0.08

*Notes: † The Census 2010 population figure is used to calculate the percentages in the Hispanic Origin and Race categories. Ancestry percentages are based on the 2006-2010 American Community Survey population (not shown); ‡ Numbers in parentheses indicate the number of people reporting a single ancestry; * Numbers in parentheses indicate the number of persons reporting this race alone, not in combination with any other race; Please refer to the Explanation of Data for more information.*

Other Hispanic or Latino	115	0.40

Race*	Population	%
African-American/Black (1,564)	1,792	6.17
Not Hispanic (1,546)	1,757	6.05
Hispanic (18)	35	0.12
American Indian/Alaska Native (69)	199	0.69
Not Hispanic (52)	167	0.58
Hispanic (17)	32	0.11
Blackfeet (0)	3	0.01
Cherokee (17)	57	0.20
Chickasaw (3)	4	0.01
Chippewa (6)	11	0.04
Choctaw (3)	11	0.04
Cree (0)	1	<0.01
Creek (1)	5	0.02
Crow (1)	1	<0.01
Delaware (1)	2	0.01
Houma (1)	1	<0.01
Lumbee (1)	1	<0.01
Mexican American Ind. (3)	4	0.01
Navajo (1)	1	<0.01
Paiute (1)	1	<0.01
Potawatomi (1)	1	<0.01
Seminole (1)	4	0.01
Sioux (0)	5	0.02
South American Ind. (0)	6	0.02
Ute (0)	8	0.03
Asian (476)	622	2.14
Not Hispanic (467)	604	2.08
Hispanic (9)	18	0.06
Bangladeshi (6)	6	0.02
Burmese (5)	5	0.02
Cambodian (9)	9	0.03
Chinese, ex. Taiwanese (88)	109	0.38
Filipino (78)	106	0.37
Indian (92)	109	0.38
Japanese (24)	48	0.17
Korean (56)	89	0.31
Laotian (3)	5	0.02
Malaysian (2)	4	0.01
Nepalese (2)	2	0.01
Pakistani (2)	3	0.01
Taiwanese (1)	1	<0.01
Thai (17)	28	0.10
Vietnamese (67)	80	0.28
Hawaii Native/Pacific Islander (48)	88	0.30
Not Hispanic (39)	74	0.25
Hispanic (9)	14	0.05
Fijian (1)	3	0.01
Guamanian/Chamorro (11)	16	0.06
Native Hawaiian (10)	22	0.08
Samoan (21)	38	0.13
White (25,883)	26,400	90.92
Not Hispanic (24,815)	25,232	86.90
Hispanic (1,068)	1,168	4.02

Springfield

Place Type: City
County: Robertson
Population: 16,440†

Ancestry‡	Population	%
African, Sub-Saharan (84)	92	0.57
African (84)	92	0.57
American (2,979)	2,979	18.51
Arab (21)	21	0.13
Other Arab (21)	21	0.13
Armenian (48)	48	0.30
Austrian (0)	8	0.05
British (15)	15	0.09
Canadian (7)	14	0.09
Czech (0)	15	0.09
Czechoslovakian (8)	8	0.05
Dutch (10)	114	0.71
English (645)	1,314	8.16
European (163)	163	1.01
French, ex. Basque (0)	103	0.64
French Canadian (0)	7	0.04
German (415)	1,128	7.01
Greek (15)	37	0.23
Hungarian (0)	8	0.05
Iranian (25)	25	0.16
Irish (425)	1,369	8.50
Italian (47)	147	0.91
Northern European (0)	6	0.04
Norwegian (0)	16	0.10
Polish (44)	101	0.63
Romanian (12)	12	0.07
Scandinavian (27)	27	0.17
Scotch-Irish (92)	223	1.39
Scottish (90)	191	1.19
Slavic (4)	4	0.02
Swedish (36)	47	0.29
Welsh (22)	132	0.82
West Indian, ex. Hispanic (15)	24	0.15
Jamaican (0)	9	0.06
Other West Indian (15)	15	0.09

Hispanic Origin	Population	%
Hispanic or Latino (of any race)	2,540	15.45
Central American, ex. Mexican	319	1.94
Costa Rican	4	0.02
Guatemalan	120	0.73
Honduran	95	0.58
Nicaraguan	10	0.06
Panamanian	4	0.02
Salvadoran	86	0.52
Cuban	12	0.07
Dominican Republic	3	0.02
Mexican	2,016	12.26
Puerto Rican	60	0.36
South American	11	0.07
Chilean	1	0.01
Colombian	4	0.02
Peruvian	2	0.01
Venezuelan	2	0.01
Other South American	2	0.01
Other Hispanic or Latino	119	0.72

Race*	Population	%
African-American/Black (3,894)	4,064	24.72
Not Hispanic (3,852)	4,007	24.37
Hispanic (42)	57	0.35
American Indian/Alaska Native (62)	154	0.94
Not Hispanic (37)	121	0.74
Hispanic (25)	33	0.20
Apache (1)	1	0.01
Blackfeet (1)	4	0.02
Cherokee (13)	47	0.29
Chippewa (2)	2	0.01
Choctaw (0)	2	0.01
Cree (0)	1	0.01
Creek (0)	8	0.05
Iroquois (1)	3	0.02
Mexican American Ind. (9)	9	0.05
Potawatomi (0)	2	0.01
Sioux (1)	5	0.03
Spanish American Ind. (7)	8	0.05
Asian (106)	138	0.84
Not Hispanic (105)	133	0.81
Hispanic (1)	5	0.03
Cambodian (4)	4	0.02
Chinese, ex. Taiwanese (20)	21	0.13
Filipino (14)	17	0.10
Indian (30)	32	0.19
Japanese (1)	10	0.06
Korean (23)	31	0.19
Laotian (3)	3	0.02
Taiwanese (1)	1	0.01
Vietnamese (8)	9	0.05
Hawaii Native/Pacific Islander (17)	21	0.13
Not Hispanic (2)	4	0.02
Hispanic (15)	17	0.10
Guamanian/Chamorro (9)	10	0.06
Native Hawaiian (2)	2	0.01
Samoan (0)	2	0.01
White (10,826)	11,119	67.63
Not Hispanic (9,654)	9,857	59.96
Hispanic (1,172)	1,262	7.68

Tullahoma

Place Type: City
County: Coffee
Population: 18,655†

Ancestry‡	Population	%
African, Sub-Saharan (23)	37	0.20
African (0)	14	0.08
Somalian (23)	23	0.12
American (2,962)	2,962	15.96
Austrian (20)	20	0.11
Belgian (0)	13	0.07
British (170)	170	0.92
Canadian (11)	11	0.06
Dutch (75)	430	2.32
English (1,806)	3,009	16.21
European (182)	182	0.98
French, ex. Basque (97)	604	3.25
French Canadian (47)	136	0.73
German (603)	2,450	13.20
Hungarian (12)	45	0.24
Iranian (25)	25	0.13
Irish (876)	3,010	16.22
Italian (213)	790	4.26
Norwegian (43)	222	1.20
Polish (10)	121	0.65
Portuguese (19)	96	0.52
Russian (9)	22	0.12
Scandinavian (0)	56	0.30
Scotch-Irish (290)	826	4.45
Scottish (314)	617	3.32
Swedish (38)	259	1.40
Swiss (0)	116	0.62
Ukrainian (0)	20	0.11
Welsh (0)	74	0.40
West Indian, ex. Hispanic (0)	11	0.06
Dutch West Indian (0)	11	0.06
Yugoslavian (15)	15	0.08

Hispanic Origin	Population	%
Hispanic or Latino (of any race)	577	3.09
Central American, ex. Mexican	44	0.24
Costa Rican	1	0.01
Guatemalan	4	0.02
Honduran	5	0.03
Panamanian	6	0.03
Salvadoran	28	0.15
Cuban	11	0.06
Dominican Republic	4	0.02
Mexican	409	2.19
Puerto Rican	34	0.18
South American	20	0.11
Colombian	1	0.01
Ecuadorian	4	0.02
Peruvian	14	0.08
Venezuelan	1	0.01
Other Hispanic or Latino	55	0.29

Race*	Population	%
African-American/Black (1,306)	1,580	8.47
Not Hispanic (1,293)	1,554	8.33
Hispanic (13)	26	0.14
American Indian/Alaska Native (44)	145	0.78
Not Hispanic (37)	126	0.68
Hispanic (7)	19	0.10
Apache (1)	2	0.01
Blackfeet (1)	4	0.02
Cherokee (11)	51	0.27
Chippewa (3)	4	0.02
Choctaw (5)	13	0.07
Iroquois (1)	1	0.01
Mexican American Ind. (3)	5	0.03
Navajo (4)	6	0.03
Ottawa (0)	1	0.01
Shoshone (0)	1	0.01
Tlingit-Haida *(Alaska Native)* (0)	2	0.01
Asian (215)	271	1.45

*Notes: † The Census 2010 population figure is used to calculate the percentages in the Hispanic Origin and Race categories. Ancestry percentages are based on the 2006-2010 American Community Survey population (not shown); ‡ Numbers in parentheses indicate the number of people reporting a single ancestry; * Numbers in parentheses indicate the number of persons reporting this race alone, not in combination with any other race; Please refer to the Explanation of Data for more information.*

Not Hispanic (214)	269	1.44
Hispanic (1)	2	0.01
Bangladeshi (11)	11	0.06
Chinese, ex. Taiwanese (49)	52	0.28
Filipino (28)	44	0.24
Indian (50)	55	0.29
Indonesian (1)	1	0.01
Japanese (23)	35	0.19
Korean (9)	19	0.10
Laotian (2)	2	0.01
Malaysian (1)	1	0.01
Pakistani (0)	1	0.01
Taiwanese (8)	8	0.04
Thai (3)	4	0.02
Vietnamese (30)	34	0.18
Hawaii Native/Pacific Islander (6)	17	0.09
Not Hispanic (6)	17	0.09
Guamanian/Chamorro (4)	8	0.04
Native Hawaiian (1)	5	0.03
Samoan (1)	3	0.02
White (16,426)	16,865	90.40
Not Hispanic (16,126)	16,503	88.46
Hispanic (300)	362	1.94

Union City

Place Type: City
County: Obion
Population: 10,895†

Ancestry‡	Population	%
American (1,975)	1,975	18.13
Arab (47)	47	0.43
Lebanese (47)	47	0.43
Brazilian (22)	22	0.20
British (16)	16	0.15
Czech (24)	24	0.22
Czechoslovakian (8)	8	0.07
Dutch (31)	178	1.63
English (491)	996	9.14
European (55)	55	0.50
French, ex. Basque (14)	45	0.41
French Canadian (6)	6	0.06
German (83)	677	6.21
Irish (321)	1,077	9.88
Italian (60)	166	1.52
Norwegian (0)	57	0.52
Polish (0)	5	0.05
Portuguese (0)	16	0.15
Scotch-Irish (221)	417	3.83
Scottish (35)	106	0.97
Swedish (9)	47	0.43
Welsh (14)	14	0.13

Hispanic Origin	Population	%
Hispanic or Latino (of any race)	563	5.17
Central American, ex. Mexican	37	0.34
Guatemalan	23	0.21
Honduran	5	0.05
Nicaraguan	5	0.05
Panamanian	2	0.02
Salvadoran	2	0.02
Cuban	10	0.09
Mexican	474	4.35
Puerto Rican	16	0.15
South American	7	0.06
Argentinean	1	0.01
Paraguayan	1	0.01
Peruvian	1	0.01
Venezuelan	4	0.04
Other Hispanic or Latino	19	0.17

Race*	Population	%
African-American/Black (2,583)	2,713	24.90
Not Hispanic (2,571)	2,690	24.69
Hispanic (12)	23	0.21
American Indian/Alaska Native (18)	55	0.50
Not Hispanic (15)	49	0.45
Hispanic (3)	6	0.06
Central American Ind. (1)	1	0.01
Cherokee (4)	12	0.11
Chippewa (1)	1	0.01
Choctaw (0)	2	0.02
Creek (1)	1	0.01
Crow (0)	1	0.01
Iroquois (1)	1	0.01
Sioux (0)	3	0.03
Asian (44)	53	0.49
Not Hispanic (43)	51	0.47
Hispanic (1)	2	0.02
Chinese, ex. Taiwanese (5)	8	0.07
Filipino (8)	10	0.09
Indian (3)	3	0.03
Indonesian (1)	1	0.01
Japanese (1)	1	0.01
Korean (2)	4	0.04
Pakistani (0)	4	0.04
Vietnamese (24)	24	0.22
Hawaii Native/Pacific Islander (6)	6	0.06
Not Hispanic (2)	2	0.02
Hispanic (4)	4	0.04
Guamanian/Chamorro (4)	4	0.04
Native Hawaiian (2)	2	0.02
White (7,748)	7,915	72.65
Not Hispanic (7,543)	7,688	70.56
Hispanic (205)	227	2.08

White House

Place Type: City
County: Sumner
Population: 10,255†

Ancestry‡	Population	%
American (1,649)	1,649	16.89
British (28)	87	0.89
Dutch (26)	126	1.29
English (914)	1,438	14.73
European (129)	223	2.28
French, ex. Basque (49)	74	0.76
French Canadian (40)	61	0.62
German (466)	1,271	13.02
Greek (0)	68	0.70
Hungarian (16)	16	0.16
Irish (364)	1,607	16.46
Italian (85)	177	1.81
Norwegian (10)	84	0.86
Polish (19)	62	0.63
Russian (16)	32	0.33
Scotch-Irish (384)	539	5.52
Scottish (193)	363	3.72
Slovak (43)	43	0.44
Swedish (58)	136	1.39
Swiss (0)	32	0.33
Welsh (17)	17	0.17
West Indian, ex. Hispanic (0)	21	0.22
Dutch West Indian (0)	21	0.22

Hispanic Origin	Population	%
Hispanic or Latino (of any race)	284	2.77
Central American, ex. Mexican	28	0.27
Costa Rican	1	0.01
Guatemalan	7	0.07
Honduran	9	0.09
Nicaraguan	4	0.04
Panamanian	1	0.01
Salvadoran	6	0.06
Cuban	25	0.24
Dominican Republic	6	0.06
Mexican	170	1.66
Puerto Rican	11	0.11
South American	19	0.19
Argentinean	2	0.02
Chilean	3	0.03
Colombian	6	0.06
Ecuadorian	2	0.02
Paraguayan	1	0.01
Peruvian	2	0.02
Venezuelan	3	0.03
Other Hispanic or Latino	25	0.24

Race*	Population	%
African-American/Black (179)	229	2.23
Not Hispanic (175)	218	2.13
Hispanic (4)	11	0.11
American Indian/Alaska Native (16)	62	0.60
Not Hispanic (14)	57	0.56
Hispanic (2)	5	0.05
Cherokee (7)	21	0.20
Chippewa (0)	5	0.05
Choctaw (1)	8	0.08
Creek (1)	1	0.01
Sioux (0)	3	0.03
South American Ind. (1)	1	0.01
Tohono O'Odham (1)	4	0.04
Asian (86)	120	1.17
Not Hispanic (85)	115	1.12
Hispanic (1)	5	0.05
Chinese, ex. Taiwanese (25)	28	0.27
Filipino (6)	12	0.12
Indian (14)	15	0.15
Japanese (3)	8	0.08
Korean (13)	23	0.22
Laotian (1)	1	0.01
Malaysian (1)	1	0.01
Vietnamese (23)	26	0.25
Hawaii Native/Pacific Islander (9)	13	0.13
Not Hispanic (9)	13	0.13
Guamanian/Chamorro (1)	2	0.02
Native Hawaiian (1)	1	0.01
Samoan (6)	6	0.06
White (9,734)	9,859	96.14
Not Hispanic (9,565)	9,675	94.34
Hispanic (169)	184	1.79

Winchester

Place Type: City
County: Franklin
Population: 8,530†

Ancestry‡	Population	%
American (1,405)	1,405	16.67
Belgian (0)	14	0.17
British (39)	70	0.83
Danish (0)	29	0.34
Dutch (15)	118	1.40
English (982)	1,380	16.37
European (27)	27	0.32
French, ex. Basque (55)	189	2.24
French Canadian (0)	140	1.66
German (232)	1,007	11.95
Icelander (0)	41	0.49
Irish (372)	1,244	14.76
Italian (64)	117	1.39
Lithuanian (17)	45	0.53
Northern European (21)	21	0.25
Norwegian (0)	14	0.17
Polish (90)	188	2.23
Russian (28)	110	1.30
Scandinavian (0)	35	0.42
Scotch-Irish (239)	347	4.12
Scottish (0)	74	0.88
Swedish (11)	49	0.58
Swiss (29)	42	0.50
Welsh (0)	32	0.38

Hispanic Origin	Population	%
Hispanic or Latino (of any race)	299	3.51
Central American, ex. Mexican	22	0.26
Guatemalan	12	0.14
Honduran	10	0.12
Cuban	2	0.02
Mexican	237	2.78
Puerto Rican	17	0.20
South American	1	0.01
Uruguayan	1	0.01
Other Hispanic or Latino	20	0.23

Race*	Population	%
African-American/Black (955)	1,035	12.13

*Notes: † The Census 2010 population figure is used to calculate the percentages in the Hispanic Origin and Race categories. Ancestry percentages are based on the 2006-2010 American Community Survey population (not shown); ‡ Numbers in parentheses indicate the number of people reporting a single ancestry; * Numbers in parentheses indicate the number of persons reporting this race alone, not in combination with any other race; Please refer to the Explanation of Data for more information.*

Not Hispanic (944)	1,021	11.97
Hispanic (11)	14	0.16
American Indian/Alaska Native (31)	93	1.09
Not Hispanic (30)	90	1.06
Hispanic (1)	3	0.04
Apache (0)	2	0.02
Blackfeet (1)	1	0.01
Cherokee (9)	46	0.54
Chippewa (2)	2	0.02
Choctaw (6)	6	0.07
Iroquois (1)	1	0.01
Sioux (2)	4	0.05
Asian (111)	130	1.52
Not Hispanic (111)	130	1.52
Chinese, ex. Taiwanese (13)	18	0.21
Filipino (14)	17	0.20
Indian (47)	50	0.59
Japanese (13)	18	0.21
Korean (7)	8	0.09
Laotian (4)	4	0.05
Pakistani (0)	1	0.01
Vietnamese (4)	4	0.05
Hawaii Native/Pacific Islander (3)	4	0.05
Not Hispanic (2)	2	0.02
Hispanic (1)	2	0.02
Guamanian/Chamorro (1)	2	0.02
Marshallese (1)	1	0.01
Native Hawaiian (1)	1	0.01
White (7,106)	7,272	85.25
Not Hispanic (6,986)	7,131	83.60
Hispanic (120)	141	1.65

*Notes: † The Census 2010 population figure is used to calculate the percentages in the Hispanic Origin and Race categories. Ancestry percentages are based on the 2006-2010 American Community Survey population (not shown); ‡ Numbers in parentheses indicate the number of people reporting a single ancestry; * Numbers in parentheses indicate the number of persons reporting this race alone, not in combination with any other race; Please refer to the Explanation of Data for more information.*

SECTION TWO

TEXAS

Place Type: State
Population: 25,145,561†

Ancestry‡	Population	%
Afghan (1,945)	2,204	0.01
African, Sub-Saharan (197,952)	227,737	0.94
African (118,284)	139,942	0.58
Cape Verdean (151)	514	<0.01
Ethiopian (11,459)	11,989	0.05
Ghanaian (2,757)	2,981	0.01
Kenyan (5,435)	5,989	0.02
Liberian (1,671)	1,729	0.01
Nigerian (38,958)	42,529	0.17
Senegalese (262)	380	<0.01
Sierra Leonean (827)	954	<0.01
Somalian (3,339)	3,601	0.01
South African (2,814)	3,814	0.02
Sudanese (3,096)	3,279	0.01
Ugandan (194)	226	<0.01
Zimbabwean (616)	686	<0.01
Other Sub-Saharan African (8,089)	9,124	0.04
Albanian (4,256)	4,654	0.02
Alsatian (1,028)	2,796	0.01
American (1,367,253)	1,367,253	5.62
Arab (63,551)	91,635	0.38
Arab (12,499)	16,323	0.07
Egyptian (6,268)	7,521	0.03
Iraqi (3,386)	3,770	0.02
Jordanian (4,397)	5,296	0.02
Lebanese (17,743)	31,584	0.13
Moroccan (2,033)	2,627	0.01
Palestinian (4,896)	6,557	0.03
Syrian (4,362)	7,835	0.03
Other Arab (7,967)	10,122	0.04
Armenian (2,951)	5,754	0.02
Assyrian/Chaldean/Syriac (202)	406	<0.01
Australian (3,414)	5,952	0.02
Austrian (6,881)	26,496	0.11
Basque (927)	1,959	0.01
Belgian (4,274)	12,067	0.05
Brazilian (8,543)	12,012	0.05
British (46,044)	82,805	0.34
Bulgarian (1,789)	2,749	0.01
Cajun (13,176)	23,705	0.10
Canadian (18,156)	31,732	0.13
Carpatho Rusyn (15)	107	<0.01
Celtic (2,117)	3,860	0.02
Croatian (3,923)	9,186	0.04
Cypriot (137)	137	<0.01
Czech (85,425)	215,461	0.89
Czechoslovakian (13,499)	24,660	0.10
Danish (15,461)	52,181	0.21
Dutch (54,273)	242,507	1.00
Eastern European (9,023)	10,443	0.04
English (726,110)	1,774,733	7.30
Estonian (407)	977	<0.01
European (153,576)	181,386	0.75
Finnish (5,042)	15,486	0.06
French, ex. Basque (138,065)	579,204	2.38
French Canadian (37,890)	73,747	0.30
German (977,227)	2,670,955	10.99
German Russian (393)	869	<0.01
Greek (18,728)	43,145	0.18
Guyanese (1,552)	1,935	0.01
Hungarian (12,256)	36,107	0.15
Icelander (704)	1,835	0.01
Iranian (25,638)	29,906	0.12
Irish (577,350)	1,911,738	7.86
Israeli (4,651)	6,005	0.02
Italian (165,286)	466,610	1.92
Latvian (849)	2,300	0.01
Lithuanian (4,945)	15,098	0.06
Luxemburger (383)	1,129	<0.01
Macedonian (790)	1,066	<0.01
Maltese (553)	1,084	<0.01
New Zealander (597)	1,131	<0.01
Northern European (9,061)	10,021	0.04
Norwegian (46,555)	132,828	0.55
Pennsylvania German (2,514)	4,717	0.02
Polish (95,467)	278,519	1.15
Portuguese (8,357)	26,974	0.11
Romanian (9,851)	15,958	0.07
Russian (32,686)	81,869	0.34
Scandinavian (10,681)	23,366	0.10
Scotch-Irish (182,405)	402,443	1.66
Scottish (139,877)	389,832	1.60
Serbian (1,879)	3,567	0.01
Slavic (1,857)	4,227	0.02
Slovak (3,701)	10,918	0.04
Slovene (1,662)	4,306	0.02
Soviet Union (0)	25	<0.01
Swedish (44,664)	158,259	0.65
Swiss (7,601)	33,911	0.14
Turkish (6,808)	9,221	0.04
Ukrainian (8,660)	19,625	0.08
Welsh (25,258)	102,101	0.42
West Indian, ex. Hispanic (35,339)	61,097	0.25
Bahamian (643)	1,010	<0.01
Barbadian (657)	1,268	0.01
Belizean (3,036)	3,677	0.02
Bermudan (403)	481	<0.01
British West Indian (1,408)	2,023	0.01
Dutch West Indian (3,466)	15,988	0.07
Haitian (3,894)	5,240	0.02
Jamaican (12,999)	18,540	0.08
Trinidadian/Tobagonian (3,833)	5,278	0.02
U.S. Virgin Islander (209)	436	<0.01
West Indian (4,651)	6,883	0.03
Other West Indian (140)	273	<0.01
Yugoslavian (7,230)	11,289	0.05

Hispanic Origin	Population	%
Hispanic or Latino (of any race)	9,460,921	37.62
Central American, ex. Mexican	420,683	1.67
Costa Rican	6,982	0.03
Guatemalan	66,244	0.26
Honduran	88,389	0.35
Nicaraguan	19,817	0.08
Panamanian	13,994	0.06
Salvadoran	222,599	0.89
Other Central American	2,658	0.01
Cuban	46,541	0.19
Dominican Republic	13,353	0.05
Mexican	7,951,193	31.62
Puerto Rican	130,576	0.52
South American	133,808	0.53
Argentinean	13,831	0.06
Bolivian	4,913	0.02
Chilean	6,282	0.02
Colombian	50,810	0.20
Ecuadorian	10,793	0.04
Paraguayan	763	<0.01
Peruvian	22,605	0.09
Uruguayan	2,566	0.01
Venezuelan	20,162	0.08
Other South American	1,083	<0.01
Other Hispanic or Latino	764,767	3.04

Race*	Population	%
African-American/Black (2,979,598)	3,168,469	12.60
Not Hispanic (2,886,825)	3,019,318	12.01
Hispanic (92,773)	149,151	0.59
American Indian/Alaska Native (170,972)	315,264	1.25
Not Hispanic (80,586)	178,127	0.71
Hispanic (90,386)	137,137	0.55
Alaska Athabascan *(Ala. Nat.)* (183)	296	<0.01
Aleut *(Alaska Native)* (159)	259	<0.01
Apache (4,729)	9,529	0.04
Arapaho (112)	283	<0.01
Blackfeet (738)	3,744	0.01
Canadian/French Am. Ind. (302)	658	<0.01
Central American Ind. (1,266)	2,072	0.01
Cherokee (17,084)	50,954	0.20
Cheyenne (263)	628	<0.01
Chickasaw (3,861)	6,836	0.03
Chippewa (1,164)	2,098	0.01
Choctaw (12,722)	24,024	0.10
Colville (43)	76	<0.01
Comanche (1,647)	3,989	0.02
Cree (104)	303	<0.01
Creek (2,302)	4,823	0.02
Crow (119)	312	<0.01
Delaware (478)	849	<0.01
Hopi (154)	359	<0.01
Houma (213)	377	<0.01
Inupiat *(Alaska Native)* (173)	317	<0.01
Iroquois (751)	1,764	0.01
Kiowa (540)	895	<0.01
Lumbee (403)	642	<0.01
Menominee (53)	109	<0.01
Mexican American Ind. (14,435)	20,349	0.08
Navajo (2,759)	4,269	0.02
Osage (739)	1,535	0.01
Ottawa (282)	415	<0.01
Paiute (130)	216	<0.01
Pima (150)	250	<0.01
Potawatomi (1,373)	2,099	0.01
Pueblo (1,904)	2,599	0.01
Puget Sound Salish (77)	121	<0.01
Seminole (585)	1,496	0.01
Shoshone (148)	267	<0.01
Sioux (1,936)	3,951	0.02
South American Ind. (707)	1,644	0.01
Spanish American Ind. (1,214)	1,845	0.01
Tlingit-Haida *(Alaska Native)* (182)	290	<0.01
Tohono O'Odham (164)	252	<0.01
Tsimshian *(Alaska Native)* (13)	35	<0.01
Ute (113)	216	<0.01
Yakama (45)	83	<0.01
Yaqui (374)	736	<0.01
Yuman (94)	160	<0.01
Yup'ik *(Alaska Native)* (84)	120	<0.01
Asian (964,596)	1,110,666	4.42
Not Hispanic (948,426)	1,063,715	4.23
Hispanic (16,170)	46,951	0.19
Bangladeshi (8,060)	8,930	0.04
Bhutanese (1,823)	2,275	0.01
Burmese (9,800)	10,451	0.04
Cambodian (12,056)	14,347	0.06
Chinese, ex. Taiwanese (141,823)	166,837	0.66
Filipino (103,074)	137,713	0.55
Hmong (777)	920	<0.01
Indian (245,981)	269,327	1.07
Indonesian (3,833)	5,244	0.02
Japanese (18,360)	37,715	0.15
Korean (67,750)	85,332	0.34
Laotian (13,298)	15,784	0.06
Malaysian (1,396)	2,048	0.01
Nepalese (6,755)	7,513	0.03
Pakistani (53,901)	59,678	0.24
Sri Lankan (2,536)	2,916	0.01
Taiwanese (14,175)	16,555	0.07
Thai (11,049)	16,472	0.07
Vietnamese (210,913)	227,968	0.91
Hawaii Native/Pacific Islander (21,656)	47,646	0.19
Not Hispanic (17,920)	34,506	0.14
Hispanic (3,736)	13,140	0.05
Fijian (308)	454	<0.01
Guamanian/Chamorro (6,591)	10,167	0.04
Marshallese (471)	550	<0.01
Native Hawaiian (4,794)	13,192	0.05
Samoan (2,918)	5,490	0.02
Tongan (1,836)	2,287	0.01
White (17,701,552)	18,276,506	72.68
Not Hispanic (11,397,345)	11,669,272	46.41
Hispanic (6,304,207)	6,607,234	26.28

*Notes: † The Census 2010 population figure is used to calculate the percentages in the Hispanic Origin and Race categories. Ancestry percentages are based on the 2006-2010 American Community Survey population (not shown); ‡ Numbers in parentheses indicate the number of people reporting a single ancestry; * Numbers in parentheses indicate the number of persons reporting this race alone, not in combination with any other race; Please refer to the Explanation of Data for more information.*

Abilene

Place Type: City
County: Taylor
Population: 117,063†

Ancestry‡	Population	%
African, Sub-Saharan (853)	985	0.84
African (706)	838	0.72
Kenyan (20)	20	0.02
Liberian (111)	111	0.10
Nigerian (16)	16	0.01
Albanian (221)	221	0.19
American (6,746)	6,746	5.78
Arab (66)	119	0.10
Arab (6)	6	0.01
Egyptian (12)	12	0.01
Lebanese (12)	19	0.02
Syrian (36)	67	0.06
Other Arab (0)	15	0.01
Assyrian/Chaldean/Syriac (9)	9	0.01
Australian (29)	29	0.02
Austrian (51)	88	0.08
Belgian (20)	36	0.03
Brazilian (51)	61	0.05
British (268)	564	0.48
Cajun (121)	136	0.12
Canadian (115)	221	0.19
Celtic (38)	51	0.04
Czech (73)	416	0.36
Czechoslovakian (41)	71	0.06
Danish (35)	201	0.17
Dutch (175)	1,200	1.03
English (4,906)	10,274	8.81
European (430)	525	0.45
Finnish (10)	86	0.07
French, ex. Basque (700)	2,864	2.46
French Canadian (82)	243	0.21
German (6,069)	15,782	13.53
German Russian (29)	63	0.05
Greek (110)	208	0.18
Hungarian (42)	109	0.09
Iranian (31)	45	0.04
Irish (3,583)	11,549	9.90
Israeli (10)	10	0.01
Italian (587)	1,725	1.48
Lithuanian (0)	16	0.01
Northern European (66)	94	0.08
Norwegian (343)	718	0.62
Pennsylvania German (8)	8	0.01
Polish (384)	913	0.78
Portuguese (40)	237	0.20
Romanian (0)	56	0.05
Russian (49)	260	0.22
Scandinavian (189)	353	0.30
Scotch-Irish (1,302)	2,845	2.44
Scottish (1,120)	2,530	2.17
Slavic (0)	17	0.01
Slovak (14)	91	0.08
Slovene (0)	10	0.01
Swedish (113)	707	0.61
Swiss (7)	129	0.11
Turkish (0)	36	0.03
Ukrainian (21)	39	0.03
Welsh (156)	622	0.53
West Indian, ex. Hispanic (90)	188	0.16
British West Indian (10)	10	0.01
Dutch West Indian (0)	52	0.04
Haitian (14)	14	0.01
Jamaican (25)	71	0.06
Trinidadian/Tobagonian (22)	22	0.02
West Indian (19)	19	0.02
Yugoslavian (18)	27	0.02

Hispanic Origin	Population	%
Hispanic or Latino (of any race)	28,666	24.49
Central American, ex. Mexican	394	0.34
Costa Rican	9	0.01
Guatemalan	41	0.04
Honduran	56	0.05
Nicaraguan	119	0.10
Panamanian	57	0.05
Salvadoran	111	0.09
Other Central American	1	<0.01
Cuban	107	0.09
Dominican Republic	49	0.04
Mexican	22,897	19.56
Puerto Rican	569	0.49
South American	197	0.17
Argentinean	15	0.01
Bolivian	5	<0.01
Chilean	6	0.01
Colombian	66	0.06
Ecuadorian	24	0.02
Paraguayan	2	<0.01
Peruvian	51	0.04
Uruguayan	6	0.01
Venezuelan	17	0.01
Other South American	5	<0.01
Other Hispanic or Latino	4,453	3.80

Race*	Population	%
African-American/Black (11,209)	12,731	10.88
Not Hispanic (10,638)	11,726	10.02
Hispanic (571)	1,005	0.86
American Indian/Alaska Native (797)	1,601	1.37
Not Hispanic (448)	1,069	0.91
Hispanic (349)	532	0.45
Aleut *(Alaska Native)* (4)	5	<0.01
Apache (50)	93	0.08
Blackfeet (12)	37	0.03
Canadian/French Am. Ind. (3)	3	<0.01
Central American Ind. (0)	1	<0.01
Cherokee (84)	290	0.25
Cheyenne (2)	6	0.01
Chickasaw (20)	35	0.03
Chippewa (1)	7	0.01
Choctaw (55)	129	0.11
Comanche (2)	20	0.02
Creek (6)	19	0.02
Crow (2)	2	<0.01
Delaware (3)	3	<0.01
Hopi (4)	4	<0.01
Inupiat *(Alaska Native)* (10)	12	0.01
Iroquois (3)	17	0.01
Kiowa (4)	5	<0.01
Lumbee (1)	1	<0.01
Menominee (0)	1	<0.01
Mexican American Ind. (38)	55	0.05
Navajo (26)	35	0.03
Osage (1)	4	<0.01
Potawatomi (5)	9	0.01
Pueblo (6)	9	0.01
Puget Sound Salish (1)	2	<0.01
Seminole (3)	11	0.01
Sioux (15)	24	0.02
South American Ind. (1)	2	<0.01
Spanish American Ind. (3)	5	<0.01
Tohono O'Odham (1)	1	<0.01
Tsimshian *(Alaska Native)* (1)	1	<0.01
Yakama (1)	1	<0.01
Yaqui (2)	4	<0.01
Yuman (0)	3	<0.01
Yup'ik *(Alaska Native)* (0)	1	<0.01
Asian (1,952)	2,756	2.35
Not Hispanic (1,865)	2,501	2.14
Hispanic (87)	255	0.22
Bangladeshi (3)	3	<0.01
Bhutanese (122)	158	0.13
Burmese (0)	1	<0.01
Cambodian (104)	117	0.10
Chinese, ex. Taiwanese (267)	366	0.31
Filipino (505)	801	0.68
Hmong (2)	2	<0.01
Indian (202)	279	0.24
Indonesian (2)	2	<0.01
Japanese (94)	228	0.19
Korean (152)	255	0.22
Laotian (12)	14	0.01
Malaysian (6)	10	0.01
Nepalese (81)	110	0.09
Pakistani (26)	29	0.02
Taiwanese (6)	7	0.01
Thai (101)	168	0.14
Vietnamese (138)	182	0.16
Hawaii Native/Pacific Islander (111)	259	0.22
Not Hispanic (94)	200	0.17
Hispanic (17)	59	0.05
Guamanian/Chamorro (59)	85	0.07
Native Hawaiian (21)	89	0.08
Samoan (8)	20	0.02
Tongan (2)	2	<0.01
White (88,352)	91,716	78.35
Not Hispanic (73,016)	74,985	64.06
Hispanic (15,336)	16,731	14.29

Addison

Place Type: Town
County: Dallas
Population: 13,056†

Ancestry‡	Population	%
African, Sub-Saharan (189)	210	1.60
African (40)	61	0.46
Kenyan (66)	66	0.50
Nigerian (83)	83	0.63
American (1,300)	1,300	9.89
Arab (67)	91	0.69
Egyptian (44)	44	0.33
Lebanese (23)	47	0.36
Armenian (29)	104	0.79
Austrian (0)	22	0.17
Belgian (38)	38	0.29
Brazilian (58)	97	0.74
British (47)	68	0.52
Cajun (22)	22	0.17
Croatian (0)	24	0.18
Czech (0)	35	0.27
Czechoslovakian (0)	15	0.11
Danish (11)	19	0.14
Dutch (28)	133	1.01
English (286)	1,009	7.68
European (269)	306	2.33
Finnish (10)	10	0.08
French, ex. Basque (90)	303	2.30
French Canadian (16)	27	0.21
German (428)	1,175	8.94
Greek (0)	10	0.08
Iranian (22)	22	0.17
Irish (255)	1,005	7.64
Italian (210)	520	3.96
Latvian (0)	11	0.08
Lithuanian (0)	50	0.38
Maltese (12)	12	0.09
Norwegian (77)	136	1.03
Polish (125)	208	1.58
Portuguese (43)	60	0.46
Romanian (39)	65	0.49
Russian (119)	149	1.13
Scandinavian (5)	5	0.04
Scotch-Irish (36)	104	0.79
Scottish (144)	335	2.55
Slovak (18)	28	0.21
Swedish (29)	88	0.67
Turkish (14)	14	0.11
Welsh (0)	16	0.12
West Indian, ex. Hispanic (35)	123	0.94
Dutch West Indian (35)	68	0.52
Jamaican (0)	55	0.42

Hispanic Origin	Population	%
Hispanic or Latino (of any race)	3,290	25.20
Central American, ex. Mexican	419	3.21
Costa Rican	6	0.05
Guatemalan	42	0.32
Honduran	58	0.44
Nicaraguan	25	0.19
Panamanian	14	0.11
Salvadoran	273	2.09

*Notes: † The Census 2010 population figure is used to calculate the percentages in the Hispanic Origin and Race categories. Ancestry percentages are based on the 2006-2010 American Community Survey population (not shown); ‡ Numbers in parentheses indicate the number of people reporting a single ancestry; * Numbers in parentheses indicate the number of persons reporting this race alone, not in combination with any other race; Please refer to the Explanation of Data for more information.*

Other Central American	1	0.01
Cuban	26	0.20
Dominican Republic	8	0.06
Mexican	2,359	18.07
Puerto Rican	88	0.67
South American	180	1.38
Argentinean	10	0.08
Bolivian	8	0.06
Chilean	4	0.03
Colombian	73	0.56
Ecuadorian	9	0.07
Paraguayan	1	0.01
Peruvian	44	0.34
Uruguayan	1	0.01
Venezuelan	30	0.23
Other Hispanic or Latino	210	1.61

Race*	Population	%
African-American/Black (1,547)	1,668	12.78
Not Hispanic (1,498)	1,575	12.06
Hispanic (49)	93	0.71
American Indian/Alaska Native (51)	158	1.21
Not Hispanic (39)	100	0.77
Hispanic (12)	58	0.44
Apache (2)	3	0.02
Blackfeet (2)	3	0.02
Central American Ind. (0)	7	0.05
Cherokee (5)	28	0.21
Cheyenne (0)	1	0.01
Chickasaw (4)	6	0.05
Choctaw (11)	15	0.11
Cree (0)	1	0.01
Creek (0)	3	0.02
Houma (0)	1	0.01
Iroquois (0)	1	0.01
Mexican American Ind. (0)	7	0.05
Navajo (1)	1	0.01
Potawatomi (1)	2	0.02
Sioux (1)	2	0.02
Tohono O'Odham (4)	4	0.03
Asian (969)	1,107	8.48
Not Hispanic (964)	1,075	8.23
Hispanic (5)	32	0.25
Bangladeshi (7)	8	0.06
Cambodian (8)	10	0.08
Chinese, ex. Taiwanese (93)	117	0.90
Filipino (56)	84	0.64
Indian (392)	420	3.22
Indonesian (9)	11	0.08
Japanese (22)	40	0.31
Korean (171)	187	1.43
Laotian (4)	9	0.07
Malaysian (1)	6	0.05
Nepalese (28)	30	0.23
Pakistani (16)	21	0.16
Sri Lankan (6)	7	0.05
Taiwanese (17)	21	0.16
Thai (17)	21	0.16
Vietnamese (86)	101	0.77
Hawaii Native/Pacific Islander (5)	31	0.24
Not Hispanic (5)	25	0.19
Hispanic (0)	6	0.05
Fijian (1)	1	0.01
Guamanian/Chamorro (1)	3	0.02
Native Hawaiian (3)	10	0.08
White (8,840)	9,232	70.71
Not Hispanic (6,991)	7,175	54.96
Hispanic (1,849)	2,057	15.76

Alamo

Place Type: City
County: Hidalgo
Population: 18,353†

Ancestry‡	Population	%
American (168)	168	0.94
Austrian (12)	12	0.07
British (11)	43	0.24
Canadian (21)	21	0.12
Czech (56)	81	0.45
Danish (19)	19	0.11
Dutch (71)	167	0.94
English (85)	506	2.84
European (30)	30	0.17
Finnish (10)	10	0.06
French, ex. Basque (29)	60	0.34
French Canadian (0)	7	0.04
German (465)	1,042	5.85
Hungarian (10)	10	0.06
Irish (140)	376	2.11
Italian (50)	93	0.52
Norwegian (39)	115	0.65
Pennsylvania German (0)	44	0.25
Polish (75)	100	0.56
Scandinavian (15)	15	0.08
Scotch-Irish (0)	147	0.83
Scottish (62)	140	0.79
Swedish (11)	66	0.37
Swiss (0)	48	0.27

Hispanic Origin	Population	%
Hispanic or Latino (of any race)	15,528	84.61
Central American, ex. Mexican	63	0.34
Costa Rican	17	0.09
Guatemalan	4	0.02
Honduran	20	0.11
Nicaraguan	9	0.05
Salvadoran	9	0.05
Other Central American	4	0.02
Cuban	9	0.05
Dominican Republic	5	0.03
Mexican	14,094	76.79
Puerto Rican	22	0.12
South American	8	0.04
Bolivian	2	0.01
Colombian	2	0.01
Venezuelan	4	0.02
Other Hispanic or Latino	1,327	7.23

Race*	Population	%
African-American/Black (83)	88	0.48
Not Hispanic (36)	36	0.20
Hispanic (47)	52	0.28
American Indian/Alaska Native (56)	87	0.47
Not Hispanic (12)	34	0.19
Hispanic (44)	53	0.29
Canadian/French Am. Ind. (1)	1	0.01
Cherokee (4)	13	0.07
Choctaw (1)	2	0.01
Mexican American Ind. (8)	9	0.05
Puget Sound Salish (1)	1	0.01
Yaqui (0)	5	0.03
Asian (26)	39	0.21
Not Hispanic (17)	23	0.13
Hispanic (9)	16	0.09
Chinese, ex. Taiwanese (3)	4	0.02
Filipino (7)	8	0.04
Indian (9)	10	0.05
Japanese (0)	1	0.01
Thai (3)	3	0.02
Vietnamese (4)	9	0.05
Hawaii Native/Pacific Islander (1)	9	0.05
Not Hispanic (0)	1	0.01
Hispanic (1)	8	0.04
Guamanian/Chamorro (0)	2	0.01
Native Hawaiian (0)	1	0.01
White (15,959)	16,136	87.92
Not Hispanic (2,722)	2,745	14.96
Hispanic (13,237)	13,391	72.96

Aldine

Place Type: CDP
County: Harris
Population: 15,869†

Ancestry‡	Population	%
African, Sub-Saharan (0)	22	0.16
African (0)	22	0.16
American (429)	429	3.03
Canadian (10)	10	0.07
Czech (10)	10	0.07
Dutch (0)	88	0.62
English (103)	229	1.62
European (48)	48	0.34
French, ex. Basque (7)	29	0.20
French Canadian (49)	49	0.35
German (143)	567	4.01
Irish (134)	370	2.61
Italian (40)	115	0.81
Norwegian (15)	15	0.11
Polish (19)	53	0.37
Scotch-Irish (6)	12	0.08
Scottish (0)	9	0.06
Swedish (0)	17	0.12

Hispanic Origin	Population	%
Hispanic or Latino (of any race)	13,036	82.15
Central American, ex. Mexican	1,173	7.39
Costa Rican	5	0.03
Guatemalan	145	0.91
Honduran	402	2.53
Nicaraguan	14	0.09
Panamanian	5	0.03
Salvadoran	597	3.76
Other Central American	5	0.03
Cuban	28	0.18
Dominican Republic	3	0.02
Mexican	11,093	69.90
Puerto Rican	43	0.27
South American	38	0.24
Argentinean	1	0.01
Chilean	8	0.05
Colombian	15	0.09
Ecuadorian	5	0.03
Peruvian	7	0.04
Uruguayan	2	0.01
Other Hispanic or Latino	658	4.15

Race*	Population	%
African-American/Black (454)	550	3.47
Not Hispanic (403)	446	2.81
Hispanic (51)	104	0.66
American Indian/Alaska Native (151)	210	1.32
Not Hispanic (13)	37	0.23
Hispanic (138)	173	1.09
Blackfeet (0)	1	0.01
Central American Ind. (4)	9	0.06
Cherokee (3)	8	0.05
Chippewa (1)	1	0.01
Choctaw (0)	2	0.01
Cree (0)	1	0.01
Mexican American Ind. (21)	24	0.15
Sioux (1)	1	0.01
Spanish American Ind. (5)	5	0.03
Asian (312)	356	2.24
Not Hispanic (279)	306	1.93
Hispanic (33)	50	0.32
Cambodian (3)	3	0.02
Chinese, ex. Taiwanese (9)	18	0.11
Filipino (22)	30	0.19
Indian (39)	46	0.29
Japanese (3)	11	0.07
Laotian (62)	66	0.42
Vietnamese (153)	159	1.00
Hawaii Native/Pacific Islander (1)	13	0.08
Not Hispanic (0)	6	0.04
Hispanic (1)	7	0.04
Guamanian/Chamorro (1)	1	0.01
Native Hawaiian (0)	5	0.03
White (9,311)	9,897	62.37
Not Hispanic (2,026)	2,096	13.21
Hispanic (7,285)	7,801	49.16

Alice

Place Type: City
County: Jim Wells
Population: 19,104†

*Notes: † The Census 2010 population figure is used to calculate the percentages in the Hispanic Origin and Race categories. Ancestry percentages are based on the 2006-2010 American Community Survey population (not shown); ‡ Numbers in parentheses indicate the number of people reporting a single ancestry; * Numbers in parentheses indicate the number of persons reporting this race alone, not in combination with any other race; Please refer to the Explanation of Data for more information.*

Ancestry‡	Population	%
American (694)	694	3.63
Czech (0)	9	0.05
Czechoslovakian (9)	9	0.05
Danish (0)	10	0.05
Dutch (53)	114	0.60
English (123)	305	1.59
French, ex. Basque (7)	140	0.73
German (269)	896	4.68
Greek (18)	18	0.09
Irish (213)	599	3.13
Italian (0)	75	0.39
Norwegian (0)	66	0.34
Polish (10)	10	0.05
Scotch-Irish (39)	72	0.38
Scottish (39)	39	0.20
Swedish (0)	86	0.45
Swiss (0)	16	0.08
Welsh (0)	47	0.25
West Indian, ex. Hispanic (72)	72	0.38
Dutch West Indian (72)	72	0.38

Hispanic Origin	Population	%
Hispanic or Latino (of any race)	16,259	85.11
Central American, ex. Mexican	32	0.17
Guatemalan	7	0.04
Honduran	12	0.06
Panamanian	3	0.02
Salvadoran	10	0.05
Cuban	6	0.03
Dominican Republic	1	0.01
Mexican	13,187	69.03
Puerto Rican	21	0.11
South American	34	0.18
Argentinean	2	0.01
Bolivian	2	0.01
Colombian	9	0.05
Ecuadorian	4	0.02
Paraguayan	1	0.01
Peruvian	2	0.01
Venezuelan	14	0.07
Other Hispanic or Latino	2,978	15.59

Race*	Population	%
African-American/Black (152)	185	0.97
Not Hispanic (111)	113	0.59
Hispanic (41)	72	0.38
American Indian/Alaska Native (139)	206	1.08
Not Hispanic (36)	47	0.25
Hispanic (103)	159	0.83
Apache (40)	46	0.24
Cherokee (0)	8	0.04
Chippewa (0)	6	0.03
Choctaw (8)	8	0.04
Comanche (0)	1	0.01
Mexican American Ind. (5)	8	0.04
Navajo (6)	7	0.04
Ottawa (0)	4	0.02
Potawatomi (3)	3	0.02
Sioux (0)	1	0.01
Spanish American Ind. (2)	3	0.02
Asian (109)	160	0.84
Not Hispanic (102)	119	0.62
Hispanic (7)	41	0.21
Cambodian (4)	5	0.03
Chinese, ex. Taiwanese (1)	5	0.03
Filipino (35)	48	0.25
Indian (29)	36	0.19
Japanese (1)	3	0.02
Korean (11)	15	0.08
Pakistani (15)	19	0.10
Thai (0)	1	0.01
Vietnamese (13)	13	0.07
Hawaii Native/Pacific Islander (2)	10	0.05
Not Hispanic (1)	1	0.01
Hispanic (1)	9	0.05
Guamanian/Chamorro (1)	1	0.01
Native Hawaiian (0)	4	0.02
Samoan (1)	1	0.01
White (16,565)	16,835	88.12
Not Hispanic (2,545)	2,573	13.47
Hispanic (14,020)	14,262	74.65

Allen

Place Type: City
County: Collin
Population: 84,246†

Ancestry‡	Population	%
Afghan (35)	35	0.04
African, Sub-Saharan (1,093)	1,174	1.51
African (665)	714	0.92
Nigerian (197)	217	0.28
Sierra Leonean (50)	50	0.06
Sudanese (181)	181	0.23
Other Sub-Saharan African (0)	12	0.02
American (3,840)	3,840	4.93
Arab (1,006)	1,321	1.70
Arab (128)	128	0.16
Egyptian (95)	127	0.16
Jordanian (8)	8	0.01
Lebanese (94)	305	0.39
Moroccan (0)	11	0.01
Palestinian (152)	152	0.20
Syrian (46)	107	0.14
Other Arab (483)	483	0.62
Armenian (9)	9	0.01
Austrian (29)	320	0.41
Belgian (16)	16	0.02
British (329)	537	0.69
Cajun (27)	69	0.09
Canadian (179)	477	0.61
Celtic (14)	28	0.04
Croatian (13)	54	0.07
Czech (210)	570	0.73
Czechoslovakian (16)	36	0.05
Danish (32)	292	0.38
Dutch (310)	1,465	1.88
Eastern European (107)	148	0.19
English (3,171)	8,657	11.12
European (1,288)	1,371	1.76
Finnish (28)	39	0.05
French, ex. Basque (466)	2,543	3.27
French Canadian (110)	396	0.51
German (4,355)	13,165	16.91
Greek (30)	274	0.35
Guyanese (18)	18	0.02
Hungarian (77)	224	0.29
Iranian (442)	501	0.64
Irish (2,486)	8,695	11.17
Israeli (15)	15	0.02
Italian (802)	3,160	4.06
Latvian (0)	8	0.01
Lithuanian (8)	126	0.16
Macedonian (6)	27	0.03
Maltese (0)	45	0.06
New Zealander (10)	10	0.01
Northern European (96)	96	0.12
Norwegian (162)	670	0.86
Pennsylvania German (7)	31	0.04
Polish (631)	1,792	2.30
Portuguese (28)	70	0.09
Romanian (0)	45	0.06
Russian (252)	508	0.65
Scandinavian (46)	94	0.12
Scotch-Irish (752)	1,553	2.00
Scottish (601)	2,226	2.86
Serbian (0)	21	0.03
Slavic (7)	35	0.04
Slovak (19)	38	0.05
Slovene (0)	7	0.01
Swedish (476)	1,321	1.70
Swiss (109)	279	0.36
Turkish (78)	78	0.10
Ukrainian (14)	126	0.16
Welsh (182)	549	0.71
West Indian, ex. Hispanic (201)	232	0.30
British West Indian (24)	24	0.03
Jamaican (45)	62	0.08
Trinidadian/Tobagonian (95)	109	0.14
West Indian (37)	37	0.05
Yugoslavian (14)	28	0.04

Hispanic Origin	Population	%
Hispanic or Latino (of any race)	9,443	11.21
Central American, ex. Mexican	711	0.84
Costa Rican	48	0.06
Guatemalan	139	0.16
Honduran	126	0.15
Nicaraguan	55	0.07
Panamanian	79	0.09
Salvadoran	261	0.31
Other Central American	3	<0.01
Cuban	181	0.21
Dominican Republic	65	0.08
Mexican	6,575	7.80
Puerto Rican	488	0.58
South American	713	0.85
Argentinean	72	0.09
Bolivian	26	0.03
Chilean	54	0.06
Colombian	204	0.24
Ecuadorian	63	0.07
Paraguayan	7	0.01
Peruvian	192	0.23
Uruguayan	18	0.02
Venezuelan	75	0.09
Other South American	2	<0.01
Other Hispanic or Latino	710	0.84

Race*	Population	%
African-American/Black (7,071)	7,743	9.19
Not Hispanic (6,891)	7,437	8.83
Hispanic (180)	306	0.36
American Indian/Alaska Native (460)	1,008	1.20
Not Hispanic (372)	806	0.96
Hispanic (88)	202	0.24
Apache (8)	24	0.03
Arapaho (2)	2	<0.01
Blackfeet (2)	9	0.01
Canadian/French Am. Ind. (1)	1	<0.01
Central American Ind. (6)	6	0.01
Cherokee (66)	211	0.25
Cheyenne (0)	1	<0.01
Chickasaw (30)	62	0.07
Chippewa (6)	9	0.01
Choctaw (88)	160	0.19
Comanche (9)	15	0.02
Creek (11)	33	0.04
Delaware (2)	2	<0.01
Houma (3)	3	<0.01
Iroquois (3)	16	0.02
Kiowa (1)	2	<0.01
Lumbee (5)	5	0.01
Mexican American Ind. (13)	14	0.02
Navajo (5)	16	0.02
Osage (8)	26	0.03
Potawatomi (16)	20	0.02
Pueblo (2)	7	0.01
Seminole (2)	3	<0.01
Shoshone (1)	1	<0.01
Sioux (7)	10	0.01
South American Ind. (1)	14	0.02
Spanish American Ind. (2)	2	<0.01
Ute (0)	1	<0.01
Yaqui (1)	1	<0.01
Asian (10,837)	11,962	14.20
Not Hispanic (10,772)	11,802	14.01
Hispanic (65)	160	0.19
Bangladeshi (373)	395	0.47
Burmese (11)	12	0.01
Cambodian (79)	87	0.10
Chinese, ex. Taiwanese (1,964)	2,184	2.59
Filipino (848)	1,044	1.24
Hmong (16)	16	0.02
Indian (3,731)	3,923	4.66
Indonesian (25)	40	0.05
Japanese (138)	254	0.30
Korean (822)	953	1.13

*Notes: † The Census 2010 population figure is used to calculate the percentages in the Hispanic Origin and Race categories. Ancestry percentages are based on the 2006-2010 American Community Survey population (not shown); ‡ Numbers in parentheses indicate the number of people reporting a single ancestry; * Numbers in parentheses indicate the number of persons reporting this race alone, not in combination with any other race; Please refer to the Explanation of Data for more information.*

Laotian (41)	53	0.06
Malaysian (9)	18	0.02
Nepalese (34)	35	0.04
Pakistani (633)	696	0.83
Sri Lankan (30)	41	0.05
Taiwanese (174)	198	0.24
Thai (108)	159	0.19
Vietnamese (1,454)	1,584	1.88
Hawaii Native/Pacific Islander (47)	125	0.15
Not Hispanic (40)	103	0.12
Hispanic (7)	22	0.03
Fijian (2)	4	<0.01
Guamanian/Chamorro (20)	38	0.05
Native Hawaiian (6)	17	0.02
Samoan (8)	17	0.02
White (60,666)	62,786	74.53
Not Hispanic (54,690)	56,309	66.84
Hispanic (5,976)	6,477	7.69

Alton

Place Type: City
County: Hidalgo
Population: 12,341†

Ancestry‡	Population	%
American (33)	33	0.27
English (59)	90	0.75
Irish (0)	106	0.88
Swedish (11)	11	0.09
Welsh (10)	10	0.08

Hispanic Origin	Population	%
Hispanic or Latino (of any race)	11,554	93.62
Central American, ex. Mexican	21	0.17
Guatemalan	2	0.02
Honduran	14	0.11
Nicaraguan	1	0.01
Salvadoran	4	0.03
Cuban	6	0.05
Mexican	11,325	91.77
Puerto Rican	10	0.08
South American	3	0.02
Colombian	1	0.01
Ecuadorian	2	0.02
Other Hispanic or Latino	189	1.53

Race*	Population	%
African-American/Black (25)	27	0.22
Not Hispanic (19)	19	0.15
Hispanic (6)	8	0.06
American Indian/Alaska Native (12)	19	0.15
Not Hispanic (6)	6	0.05
Hispanic (6)	13	0.11
Blackfeet (1)	1	0.01
Choctaw (5)	5	0.04
Asian (7)	8	0.06
Not Hispanic (4)	4	0.03
Hispanic (3)	4	0.03
Filipino (4)	4	0.03
Indian (3)	3	0.02
Japanese (0)	1	0.01
Hawaii Native/Pacific Islander (9)	9	0.07
Hispanic (9)	9	0.07
Guamanian/Chamorro (8)	8	0.06
Tongan (1)	1	0.01
White (11,973)	12,067	97.78
Not Hispanic (756)	757	6.13
Hispanic (11,217)	11,310	91.65

Alvin

Place Type: City
County: Brazoria
Population: 24,236†

Ancestry‡	Population	%
African, Sub-Saharan (51)	61	0.25
African (47)	57	0.23
Nigerian (4)	4	0.02
American (2,337)	2,337	9.53
Arab (66)	99	0.40
Lebanese (66)	99	0.40
Australian (29)	87	0.35
Austrian (18)	18	0.07
Belgian (0)	18	0.07
Brazilian (0)	29	0.12
British (52)	52	0.21
Cajun (51)	68	0.28
Canadian (14)	25	0.10
Croatian (0)	13	0.05
Czech (91)	271	1.11
Czechoslovakian (7)	55	0.22
Danish (85)	194	0.79
Dutch (95)	559	2.28
English (904)	1,955	7.98
European (220)	229	0.93
French, ex. Basque (310)	1,108	4.52
French Canadian (49)	113	0.46
German (1,117)	3,157	12.88
Greek (44)	103	0.42
Hungarian (17)	118	0.48
Irish (793)	2,628	10.72
Italian (221)	513	2.09
Norwegian (51)	149	0.61
Polish (109)	401	1.64
Russian (43)	71	0.29
Scandinavian (25)	25	0.10
Scotch-Irish (157)	375	1.53
Scottish (115)	320	1.31
Swedish (56)	73	0.30
Swiss (11)	46	0.19
Welsh (15)	64	0.26
West Indian, ex. Hispanic (0)	13	0.05
West Indian (0)	13	0.05
Yugoslavian (10)	10	0.04

Hispanic Origin	Population	%
Hispanic or Latino (of any race)	8,767	36.17
Central American, ex. Mexican	311	1.28
Costa Rican	4	0.02
Guatemalan	41	0.17
Honduran	63	0.26
Nicaraguan	24	0.10
Panamanian	6	0.02
Salvadoran	173	0.71
Cuban	26	0.11
Dominican Republic	13	0.05
Mexican	7,407	30.56
Puerto Rican	110	0.45
South American	65	0.27
Argentinean	5	0.02
Chilean	1	<0.01
Colombian	20	0.08
Ecuadorian	2	0.01
Peruvian	20	0.08
Venezuelan	17	0.07
Other Hispanic or Latino	835	3.45

Race*	Population	%
African-American/Black (744)	861	3.55
Not Hispanic (700)	781	3.22
Hispanic (44)	80	0.33
American Indian/Alaska Native (137)	282	1.16
Not Hispanic (84)	186	0.77
Hispanic (53)	96	0.40
Apache (1)	4	0.02
Blackfeet (0)	4	0.02
Cherokee (28)	57	0.24
Cheyenne (0)	1	<0.01
Chickasaw (1)	4	0.02
Chippewa (0)	2	0.01
Choctaw (6)	8	0.03
Colville (0)	1	<0.01
Comanche (4)	12	0.05
Cree (2)	2	0.01
Creek (0)	3	0.01
Crow (0)	1	<0.01
Hopi (1)	1	<0.01
Houma (1)	2	0.01
Mexican American Ind. (13)	22	0.09
Navajo (0)	1	<0.01
Osage (4)	4	0.02
Potawatomi (5)	5	0.02
Sioux (2)	7	0.03
Tlingit-Haida *(Alaska Native)* (1)	1	<0.01
Yaqui (7)	7	0.03
Asian (215)	280	1.16
Not Hispanic (205)	243	1.00
Hispanic (10)	37	0.15
Bangladeshi (5)	5	0.02
Cambodian (19)	22	0.09
Chinese, ex. Taiwanese (23)	25	0.10
Filipino (26)	38	0.16
Indian (33)	49	0.20
Indonesian (2)	2	0.01
Japanese (7)	14	0.06
Korean (4)	8	0.03
Laotian (0)	5	0.02
Pakistani (65)	67	0.28
Thai (2)	6	0.02
Vietnamese (13)	18	0.07
Hawaii Native/Pacific Islander (6)	18	0.07
Not Hispanic (4)	11	0.05
Hispanic (2)	7	0.03
Guamanian/Chamorro (0)	1	<0.01
Native Hawaiian (1)	4	0.02
Samoan (3)	6	0.02
White (19,250)	19,820	81.78
Not Hispanic (14,220)	14,436	59.56
Hispanic (5,030)	5,384	22.21

Amarillo

Place Type: City
County: Potter
Population: 190,695†

Ancestry‡	Population	%
African, Sub-Saharan (1,522)	1,700	0.91
African (887)	1,049	0.56
Ethiopian (77)	77	0.04
Ghanaian (0)	16	0.01
Liberian (6)	6	<0.01
Senegalese (73)	73	0.04
Somalian (194)	194	0.10
South African (9)	9	<0.01
Sudanese (244)	244	0.13
Other Sub-Saharan African (32)	32	0.02
Alsatian (0)	9	<0.01
American (12,934)	12,934	6.91
Arab (124)	196	0.10
Egyptian (6)	29	0.02
Lebanese (100)	149	0.08
Other Arab (18)	18	0.01
Armenian (26)	38	0.02
Australian (60)	69	0.04
Austrian (67)	92	0.05
Basque (9)	9	<0.01
Belgian (19)	91	0.05
Brazilian (59)	59	0.03
British (311)	600	0.32
Cajun (21)	21	0.01
Canadian (160)	249	0.13
Celtic (13)	13	0.01
Croatian (54)	87	0.05
Czech (242)	736	0.39
Czechoslovakian (62)	134	0.07
Danish (156)	567	0.30
Dutch (731)	2,642	1.41
Eastern European (33)	56	0.03
English (7,124)	16,417	8.77
European (1,005)	1,159	0.62
Finnish (36)	63	0.03
French, ex. Basque (1,022)	4,513	2.41
French Canadian (177)	260	0.14
German (10,759)	24,512	13.09
German Russian (7)	7	<0.01
Greek (148)	299	0.16
Hungarian (62)	108	0.06

SECTION TWO

*Notes: † The Census 2010 population figure is used to calculate the percentages in the Hispanic Origin and Race categories. Ancestry percentages are based on the 2006-2010 American Community Survey population (not shown); ‡ Numbers in parentheses indicate the number of people reporting a single ancestry; * Numbers in parentheses indicate the number of persons reporting this race alone, not in combination with any other race; Please refer to the Explanation of Data for more information.*

Iranian (401)	414	0.22
Irish (6,111)	17,692	9.45
Italian (1,343)	3,275	1.75
Lithuanian (13)	13	0.01
Luxemburger (0)	9	<0.01
Northern European (83)	83	0.04
Norwegian (356)	1,320	0.71
Pennsylvania German (7)	20	0.01
Polish (589)	1,254	0.67
Portuguese (17)	106	0.06
Romanian (15)	25	0.01
Russian (221)	373	0.20
Scandinavian (99)	208	0.11
Scotch-Irish (1,924)	3,584	1.91
Scottish (1,534)	3,505	1.87
Serbian (95)	95	0.05
Slavic (0)	30	0.02
Slovak (0)	16	0.01
Slovene (0)	10	0.01
Swedish (510)	1,028	0.55
Swiss (113)	323	0.17
Ukrainian (65)	138	0.07
Welsh (192)	813	0.43
West Indian, ex. Hispanic (133)	483	0.26
Dutch West Indian (93)	332	0.18
Jamaican (27)	129	0.07
U.S. Virgin Islander (6)	6	<0.01
West Indian (7)	16	0.01
Yugoslavian (81)	117	0.06

Hispanic Origin	Population	%
Hispanic or Latino (of any race)	54,881	28.78
Central American, ex. Mexican	560	0.29
Costa Rican	11	0.01
Guatemalan	88	0.05
Honduran	137	0.07
Nicaraguan	22	0.01
Panamanian	38	0.02
Salvadoran	261	0.14
Other Central American	3	<0.01
Cuban	249	0.13
Dominican Republic	31	0.02
Mexican	47,195	24.75
Puerto Rican	318	0.17
South American	193	0.10
Argentinean	12	0.01
Bolivian	4	<0.01
Chilean	41	0.02
Colombian	55	0.03
Ecuadorian	20	0.01
Peruvian	33	0.02
Uruguayan	6	<0.01
Venezuelan	20	0.01
Other South American	2	<0.01
Other Hispanic or Latino	6,335	3.32

Race*	Population	%
African-American/Black (12,632)	14,539	7.62
Not Hispanic (11,977)	13,352	7.00
Hispanic (655)	1,187	0.62
American Indian/Alaska Native (1,480)	2,841	1.49
Not Hispanic (928)	1,891	0.99
Hispanic (552)	950	0.50
Alaska Athabascan *(Ala. Nat.)* (0)	1	<0.01
Aleut *(Alaska Native)* (1)	4	<0.01
Apache (62)	125	0.07
Arapaho (1)	8	<0.01
Blackfeet (9)	25	0.01
Canadian/French Am. Ind. (0)	2	<0.01
Cherokee (194)	573	0.30
Cheyenne (10)	22	0.01
Chickasaw (50)	88	0.05
Chippewa (8)	14	0.01
Choctaw (199)	327	0.17
Comanche (15)	63	0.03
Cree (2)	2	<0.01
Creek (40)	60	0.03
Crow (1)	2	<0.01
Delaware (7)	14	0.01
Hopi (1)	2	<0.01
Houma (0)	1	<0.01
Inupiat *(Alaska Native)* (2)	4	<0.01
Iroquois (2)	5	<0.01
Kiowa (17)	23	0.01
Lumbee (2)	2	<0.01
Menominee (1)	1	<0.01
Mexican American Ind. (73)	112	0.06
Navajo (62)	95	0.05
Osage (4)	15	0.01
Ottawa (1)	2	<0.01
Paiute (0)	1	<0.01
Pima (0)	3	<0.01
Potawatomi (22)	32	0.02
Pueblo (16)	27	0.01
Seminole (8)	11	0.01
Shoshone (1)	1	<0.01
Sioux (24)	46	0.02
South American Ind. (2)	8	<0.01
Spanish American Ind. (13)	19	0.01
Tlingit-Haida *(Alaska Native)* (5)	6	<0.01
Tohono O'Odham (2)	2	<0.01
Ute (5)	10	0.01
Yaqui (0)	1	<0.01
Yuman (0)	3	<0.01
Yup'ik *(Alaska Native)* (2)	2	<0.01
Asian (6,072)	6,883	3.61
Not Hispanic (5,883)	6,504	3.41
Hispanic (189)	379	0.20
Bangladeshi (30)	30	0.02
Burmese (1,611)	1,679	0.88
Cambodian (11)	19	0.01
Chinese, ex. Taiwanese (273)	353	0.19
Filipino (258)	393	0.21
Indian (617)	751	0.39
Indonesian (6)	14	0.01
Japanese (68)	159	0.08
Korean (123)	176	0.09
Laotian (1,036)	1,195	0.63
Malaysian (5)	8	<0.01
Nepalese (5)	6	<0.01
Pakistani (63)	68	0.04
Sri Lankan (2)	2	<0.01
Taiwanese (6)	7	<0.01
Thai (141)	181	0.09
Vietnamese (1,494)	1,654	0.87
Hawaii Native/Pacific Islander (90)	248	0.13
Not Hispanic (62)	166	0.09
Hispanic (28)	82	0.04
Guamanian/Chamorro (20)	28	0.01
Marshallese (1)	1	<0.01
Native Hawaiian (33)	83	0.04
Samoan (31)	55	0.03
White (146,867)	151,640	79.52
Not Hispanic (113,929)	116,456	61.07
Hispanic (32,938)	35,184	18.45

Andrews

Place Type: City
County: Andrews
Population: 11,088†

Ancestry‡	Population	%
American (836)	836	7.94
Austrian (0)	14	0.13
Canadian (63)	63	0.60
Czechoslovakian (41)	41	0.39
Danish (0)	7	0.07
Dutch (24)	137	1.30
English (360)	656	6.23
European (36)	36	0.34
French, ex. Basque (123)	288	2.74
French Canadian (22)	22	0.21
German (186)	439	4.17
Irish (285)	1,116	10.60
Italian (0)	22	0.21
Northern European (13)	13	0.12
Polish (0)	26	0.25
Scandinavian (0)	31	0.29
Scotch-Irish (66)	80	0.76
Scottish (59)	303	2.88
Swedish (0)	20	0.19
Welsh (15)	36	0.34
West Indian, ex. Hispanic (0)	62	0.59
Dutch West Indian (0)	62	0.59

Hispanic Origin	Population	%
Hispanic or Latino (of any race)	5,566	50.20
Central American, ex. Mexican	15	0.14
Guatemalan	3	0.03
Honduran	1	0.01
Nicaraguan	1	0.01
Salvadoran	10	0.09
Cuban	4	0.04
Mexican	4,968	44.81
Puerto Rican	18	0.16
South American	3	0.03
Colombian	2	0.02
Ecuadorian	1	0.01
Other Hispanic or Latino	558	5.03

Race*	Population	%
African-American/Black (206)	265	2.39
Not Hispanic (183)	222	2.00
Hispanic (23)	43	0.39
American Indian/Alaska Native (105)	155	1.40
Not Hispanic (70)	103	0.93
Hispanic (35)	52	0.47
Apache (9)	10	0.09
Blackfeet (1)	2	0.02
Central American Ind. (1)	1	0.01
Cherokee (11)	27	0.24
Chickasaw (0)	3	0.03
Choctaw (5)	6	0.05
Comanche (6)	9	0.08
Creek (0)	1	0.01
Iroquois (1)	1	0.01
Lumbee (3)	4	0.04
Mexican American Ind. (5)	8	0.07
Navajo (3)	3	0.03
Osage (0)	3	0.03
Potawatomi (3)	3	0.03
Pueblo (1)	1	0.01
Sioux (4)	8	0.07
Yaqui (1)	4	0.04
Yup'ik *(Alaska Native)* (1)	1	0.01
Asian (75)	96	0.87
Not Hispanic (69)	82	0.74
Hispanic (6)	14	0.13
Chinese, ex. Taiwanese (2)	6	0.05
Filipino (28)	39	0.35
Hmong (1)	1	0.01
Indian (6)	7	0.06
Japanese (1)	2	0.02
Korean (2)	4	0.04
Laotian (1)	1	0.01
Pakistani (6)	6	0.05
Vietnamese (27)	29	0.26
Hawaii Native/Pacific Islander (1)	4	0.04
Not Hispanic (1)	3	0.03
Hispanic (0)	1	0.01
Native Hawaiian (1)	4	0.04
White (8,750)	8,965	80.85
Not Hispanic (5,101)	5,176	46.68
Hispanic (3,649)	3,789	34.17

Angleton

Place Type: City
County: Brazoria
Population: 18,862†

Ancestry‡	Population	%
African, Sub-Saharan (47)	111	0.59
African (18)	18	0.10
Nigerian (29)	93	0.49
American (1,053)	1,053	5.59
Arab (6)	6	0.03
Syrian (6)	6	0.03
Austrian (0)	28	0.15

*Notes: † The Census 2010 population figure is used to calculate the percentages in the Hispanic Origin and Race categories. Ancestry percentages are based on the 2006-2010 American Community Survey population (not shown); ‡ Numbers in parentheses indicate the number of people reporting a single ancestry; * Numbers in parentheses indicate the number of persons reporting this race alone, not in combination with any other race; Please refer to the Explanation of Data for more information.*

British (26)	69	0.37
Cajun (9)	9	0.05
Czech (220)	548	2.91
Czechoslovakian (9)	61	0.32
Danish (11)	11	0.06
Dutch (45)	265	1.41
English (422)	1,303	6.91
European (154)	166	0.88
French, ex. Basque (222)	729	3.87
French Canadian (23)	23	0.12
German (1,239)	3,228	17.12
Greek (46)	46	0.24
Hungarian (0)	21	0.11
Irish (587)	2,331	12.36
Italian (78)	261	1.38
Norwegian (31)	73	0.39
Polish (31)	134	0.71
Portuguese (12)	62	0.33
Romanian (27)	47	0.25
Russian (0)	14	0.07
Scandinavian (0)	64	0.34
Scotch-Irish (232)	424	2.25
Scottish (64)	231	1.23
Slavic (11)	11	0.06
Swedish (0)	241	1.28
Swiss (0)	10	0.05
Welsh (12)	47	0.25
West Indian, ex. Hispanic (39)	39	0.21
Jamaican (7)	7	0.04
Trinidadian/Tobagonian (18)	18	0.10
West Indian (14)	14	0.07

Hispanic Origin	Population	%
Hispanic or Latino (of any race)	5,746	30.46
Central American, ex. Mexican	148	0.78
Costa Rican	1	0.01
Guatemalan	55	0.29
Honduran	11	0.06
Nicaraguan	18	0.10
Panamanian	11	0.06
Salvadoran	47	0.25
Other Central American	5	0.03
Cuban	11	0.06
Mexican	4,945	26.22
Puerto Rican	59	0.31
South American	32	0.17
Argentinean	1	0.01
Bolivian	1	0.01
Chilean	9	0.05
Colombian	7	0.04
Ecuadorian	8	0.04
Peruvian	1	0.01
Venezuelan	5	0.03
Other Hispanic or Latino	551	2.92

Race*	Population	%
African-American/Black (2,345)	2,556	13.55
Not Hispanic (2,282)	2,432	12.89
Hispanic (63)	124	0.66
American Indian/Alaska Native (105)	215	1.14
Not Hispanic (58)	146	0.77
Hispanic (47)	69	0.37
Aleut *(Alaska Native)* (1)	1	0.01
Apache (2)	5	0.03
Blackfeet (5)	11	0.06
Canadian/French Am. Ind. (1)	2	0.01
Cherokee (6)	29	0.15
Cheyenne (1)	1	0.01
Chickasaw (1)	2	0.01
Chippewa (1)	1	0.01
Choctaw (15)	31	0.16
Comanche (0)	4	0.02
Creek (1)	8	0.04
Hopi (1)	1	0.01
Iroquois (0)	2	0.01
Mexican American Ind. (8)	8	0.04
Navajo (1)	1	0.01
Osage (0)	6	0.03
Ottawa (1)	1	0.01
Potawatomi (2)	2	0.01
Seminole (0)	2	0.01
Sioux (3)	7	0.04
Tlingit-Haida *(Alaska Native)* (0)	2	0.01
Yaqui (1)	1	0.01
Asian (202)	264	1.40
Not Hispanic (196)	246	1.30
Hispanic (6)	18	0.10
Cambodian (8)	8	0.04
Chinese, ex. Taiwanese (27)	30	0.16
Filipino (29)	47	0.25
Indian (37)	45	0.24
Indonesian (0)	1	0.01
Japanese (10)	18	0.10
Korean (6)	20	0.11
Laotian (2)	2	0.01
Nepalese (5)	5	0.03
Pakistani (1)	1	0.01
Taiwanese (2)	2	0.01
Thai (2)	7	0.04
Vietnamese (63)	67	0.36
Hawaii Native/Pacific Islander (6)	16	0.08
Not Hispanic (3)	9	0.05
Hispanic (3)	7	0.04
Guamanian/Chamorro (3)	3	0.02
Native Hawaiian (3)	6	0.03
Samoan (0)	4	0.02
White (13,523)	14,018	74.32
Not Hispanic (10,277)	10,543	55.90
Hispanic (3,246)	3,475	18.42

Anna

Place Type: City
County: Collin
Population: 8,249†

Ancestry‡	Population	%
African, Sub-Saharan (21)	31	0.43
Kenyan (7)	7	0.10
Other Sub-Saharan African (14)	24	0.33
American (809)	809	11.24
Austrian (0)	7	0.10
British (54)	81	1.13
Cajun (20)	20	0.28
Czech (21)	40	0.56
Danish (3)	5	0.07
Dutch (14)	101	1.40
English (236)	529	7.35
European (48)	55	0.76
French, ex. Basque (25)	110	1.53
French Canadian (0)	17	0.24
German (487)	871	12.10
Greek (16)	47	0.65
Hungarian (44)	44	0.61
Iranian (14)	14	0.19
Irish (185)	596	8.28
Italian (386)	455	6.32
Lithuanian (0)	10	0.14
Norwegian (76)	155	2.15
Polish (79)	196	2.72
Portuguese (0)	29	0.40
Romanian (0)	10	0.14
Russian (0)	10	0.14
Scandinavian (11)	28	0.39
Scotch-Irish (63)	130	1.81
Scottish (32)	109	1.51
Serbian (10)	10	0.14
Slavic (3)	35	0.49
Slovak (0)	15	0.21
Swedish (32)	56	0.78
Welsh (0)	11	0.15

Hispanic Origin	Population	%
Hispanic or Latino (of any race)	1,725	20.91
Central American, ex. Mexican	60	0.73
Guatemalan	3	0.04
Honduran	14	0.17
Nicaraguan	1	0.01
Panamanian	4	0.05
Salvadoran	38	0.46
Cuban	2	0.02
Dominican Republic	1	0.01
Mexican	1,286	15.59
Puerto Rican	39	0.47
South American	37	0.45
Argentinean	6	0.07
Bolivian	1	0.01
Colombian	8	0.10
Peruvian	19	0.23
Venezuelan	1	0.01
Other South American	2	0.02
Other Hispanic or Latino	300	3.64

Race*	Population	%
African-American/Black (632)	716	8.68
Not Hispanic (602)	673	8.16
Hispanic (30)	43	0.52
American Indian/Alaska Native (90)	172	2.09
Not Hispanic (72)	144	1.75
Hispanic (18)	28	0.34
Apache (2)	3	0.04
Blackfeet (0)	4	0.05
Cherokee (14)	42	0.51
Chickasaw (5)	11	0.13
Chippewa (2)	2	0.02
Choctaw (13)	25	0.30
Creek (10)	13	0.16
Iroquois (1)	1	0.01
Mexican American Ind. (3)	3	0.04
Navajo (0)	1	0.01
Osage (3)	3	0.04
Pima (0)	1	0.01
Potawatomi (3)	3	0.04
Seminole (4)	4	0.05
Sioux (0)	2	0.02
Tohono O'Odham (0)	1	0.01
Asian (70)	117	1.42
Not Hispanic (68)	111	1.35
Hispanic (2)	6	0.07
Bangladeshi (1)	5	0.06
Cambodian (0)	1	0.01
Chinese, ex. Taiwanese (2)	6	0.07
Filipino (28)	47	0.57
Hmong (5)	5	0.06
Indian (3)	8	0.10
Indonesian (1)	1	0.01
Japanese (6)	12	0.15
Korean (2)	4	0.05
Thai (5)	7	0.08
Vietnamese (5)	9	0.11
Hawaii Native/Pacific Islander (4)	23	0.28
Not Hispanic (4)	22	0.27
Hispanic (0)	1	0.01
Guamanian/Chamorro (1)	4	0.05
Native Hawaiian (0)	2	0.02
Samoan (0)	6	0.07
White (6,471)	6,728	81.56
Not Hispanic (5,588)	5,765	69.89
Hispanic (883)	963	11.67

Aransas Pass

Place Type: City
County: San Patricio
Population: 8,204†

Ancestry‡	Population	%
African, Sub-Saharan (12)	12	0.14
African (12)	12	0.14
American (342)	342	4.13
Belgian (0)	20	0.24
British (9)	31	0.37
Czech (52)	137	1.65
Dutch (0)	255	3.08
English (175)	808	9.76
European (23)	23	0.28
French, ex. Basque (24)	184	2.22
German (346)	1,150	13.89
Greek (0)	11	0.13
Irish (269)	907	10.95

*Notes: † The Census 2010 population figure is used to calculate the percentages in the Hispanic Origin and Race categories. Ancestry percentages are based on the 2006-2010 American Community Survey population (not shown); ‡ Numbers in parentheses indicate the number of people reporting a single ancestry; * Numbers in parentheses indicate the number of persons reporting this race alone, not in combination with any other race; Please refer to the Explanation of Data for more information.*

SECTION TWO

Ancestry (continued)	Population	%
Italian (28)	250	3.02
Norwegian (3)	95	1.15
Polish (27)	232	2.80
Russian (0)	26	0.31
Scandinavian (0)	10	0.12
Scotch-Irish (17)	129	1.56
Scottish (0)	108	1.30
Swedish (10)	10	0.12
Welsh (0)	91	1.10

Hispanic Origin	Population	%
Hispanic or Latino (of any race)	3,278	39.96
Central American, ex. Mexican	21	0.26
Costa Rican	1	0.01
Guatemalan	6	0.07
Honduran	3	0.04
Panamanian	1	0.01
Salvadoran	10	0.12
Cuban	7	0.09
Mexican	2,767	33.73
Puerto Rican	25	0.30
South American	12	0.15
Colombian	11	0.13
Peruvian	1	0.01
Other Hispanic or Latino	446	5.44

Race*	Population	%
African-American/Black (251)	316	3.85
Not Hispanic (228)	263	3.21
Hispanic (23)	53	0.65
American Indian/Alaska Native (63)	124	1.51
Not Hispanic (34)	73	0.89
Hispanic (29)	51	0.62
Apache (3)	6	0.07
Central American Ind. (1)	4	0.05
Cherokee (12)	31	0.38
Choctaw (1)	2	0.02
Comanche (1)	3	0.04
Cree (1)	1	0.01
Iroquois (0)	1	0.01
Mexican American Ind. (5)	5	0.06
Paiute (0)	1	0.01
Shoshone (0)	1	0.01
Sioux (0)	3	0.04
Asian (79)	116	1.41
Not Hispanic (78)	104	1.27
Hispanic (1)	12	0.15
Burmese (0)	1	0.01
Cambodian (2)	3	0.04
Chinese, ex. Taiwanese (7)	10	0.12
Filipino (23)	38	0.46
Indian (23)	28	0.34
Japanese (2)	5	0.06
Korean (0)	7	0.09
Pakistani (0)	1	0.01
Taiwanese (2)	2	0.02
Vietnamese (15)	17	0.21
Hawaii Native/Pacific Islander (10)	15	0.18
Not Hispanic (9)	13	0.16
Hispanic (1)	2	0.02
Native Hawaiian (6)	10	0.12
Samoan (1)	1	0.01
White (6,942)	7,136	86.98
Not Hispanic (4,472)	4,554	55.51
Hispanic (2,470)	2,582	31.47

Arlington

Place Type: City
County: Tarrant
Population: 365,438†

Ancestry‡	Population	%
Afghan (35)	35	0.01
African, Sub-Saharan (7,899)	8,945	2.49
African (4,120)	4,720	1.31
Ethiopian (269)	421	0.12
Ghanaian (447)	478	0.13
Kenyan (891)	913	0.25
Liberian (123)	135	0.04
Nigerian (1,692)	1,737	0.48
Sierra Leonean (0)	16	<0.01
Somalian (73)	214	0.06
South African (59)	71	0.02
Sudanese (11)	11	<0.01
Other Sub-Saharan African (214)	229	0.06
Albanian (45)	45	0.01
American (18,145)	18,145	5.05
Arab (3,287)	3,607	1.00
Arab (630)	687	0.19
Egyptian (244)	244	0.07
Iraqi (652)	652	0.18
Jordanian (787)	787	0.22
Lebanese (278)	438	0.12
Moroccan (6)	6	<0.01
Palestinian (40)	70	0.02
Syrian (259)	300	0.08
Other Arab (391)	423	0.12
Armenian (27)	55	0.02
Assyrian/Chaldean/Syriac (0)	10	<0.01
Australian (189)	203	0.06
Austrian (333)	540	0.15
Belgian (60)	172	0.05
Brazilian (0)	27	0.01
British (934)	1,509	0.42
Bulgarian (118)	178	0.05
Cajun (56)	106	0.03
Canadian (195)	345	0.10
Celtic (41)	145	0.04
Croatian (31)	90	0.03
Czech (1,021)	2,426	0.67
Czechoslovakian (145)	345	0.10
Danish (307)	701	0.20
Dutch (692)	3,739	1.04
Eastern European (129)	146	0.04
English (9,343)	25,578	7.12
European (3,542)	4,105	1.14
Finnish (147)	190	0.05
French, ex. Basque (1,647)	7,574	2.11
French Canadian (392)	971	0.27
German (12,804)	38,903	10.82
German Russian (14)	50	0.01
Greek (273)	744	0.21
Guyanese (7)	7	<0.01
Hungarian (149)	526	0.15
Icelander (15)	64	0.02
Iranian (972)	1,042	0.29
Irish (10,097)	30,767	8.56
Israeli (75)	91	0.03
Italian (2,790)	8,025	2.23
Latvian (20)	20	0.01
Lithuanian (81)	264	0.07
Luxemburger (20)	20	0.01
Maltese (16)	16	<0.01
Northern European (133)	149	0.04
Norwegian (903)	2,595	0.72
Pennsylvania German (0)	25	0.01
Polish (1,310)	3,822	1.06
Portuguese (223)	463	0.13
Romanian (196)	228	0.06
Russian (396)	1,129	0.31
Scandinavian (151)	222	0.06
Scotch-Irish (3,372)	6,774	1.88
Scottish (2,103)	6,592	1.83
Serbian (4)	4	<0.01
Slavic (35)	76	0.02
Slovak (54)	183	0.05
Slovene (24)	24	0.01
Swedish (441)	1,935	0.54
Swiss (134)	572	0.16
Turkish (105)	197	0.05
Ukrainian (102)	219	0.06
Welsh (554)	1,699	0.47
West Indian, ex. Hispanic (366)	846	0.24
Barbadian (0)	19	0.01
Belizean (56)	95	0.03
British West Indian (0)	16	<0.01
Dutch West Indian (19)	54	0.02
Haitian (0)	63	0.02
Jamaican (228)	447	0.12
Trinidadian/Tobagonian (47)	47	0.01
U.S. Virgin Islander (16)	16	<0.01
West Indian (0)	80	0.02
Other West Indian (0)	9	<0.01
Yugoslavian (132)	185	0.05

Hispanic Origin	Population	%
Hispanic or Latino (of any race)	100,269	27.44
Central American, ex. Mexican	5,002	1.37
Costa Rican	134	0.04
Guatemalan	605	0.17
Honduran	835	0.23
Nicaraguan	236	0.06
Panamanian	240	0.07
Salvadoran	2,938	0.80
Other Central American	14	<0.01
Cuban	532	0.15
Dominican Republic	323	0.09
Mexican	82,834	22.67
Puerto Rican	3,251	0.89
South American	1,935	0.53
Argentinean	187	0.05
Bolivian	46	0.01
Chilean	72	0.02
Colombian	781	0.21
Ecuadorian	273	0.07
Paraguayan	5	<0.01
Peruvian	383	0.10
Uruguayan	26	0.01
Venezuelan	151	0.04
Other South American	11	<0.01
Other Hispanic or Latino	6,392	1.75

Race*	Population	%
African-American/Black (68,792)	73,417	20.09
Not Hispanic (67,087)	70,620	19.32
Hispanic (1,705)	2,797	0.77
American Indian/Alaska Native (2,439)	5,218	1.43
Not Hispanic (1,338)	3,262	0.89
Hispanic (1,101)	1,956	0.54
Alaska Athabascan *(Ala. Nat.)* (1)	1	<0.01
Aleut *(Alaska Native)* (7)	12	<0.01
Apache (48)	124	0.03
Arapaho (11)	19	0.01
Blackfeet (18)	90	0.02
Canadian/French Am. Ind. (9)	16	<0.01
Central American Ind. (5)	8	<0.01
Cherokee (297)	974	0.27
Cheyenne (6)	12	<0.01
Chickasaw (76)	130	0.04
Chippewa (40)	53	0.01
Choctaw (205)	462	0.13
Comanche (31)	62	0.02
Cree (0)	7	<0.01
Creek (53)	136	0.04
Crow (1)	1	<0.01
Delaware (9)	15	<0.01
Hopi (1)	3	<0.01
Houma (12)	19	0.01
Inupiat *(Alaska Native)* (6)	13	<0.01
Iroquois (9)	39	0.01
Kiowa (17)	33	0.01
Lumbee (11)	14	<0.01
Menominee (1)	2	<0.01
Mexican American Ind. (172)	276	0.08
Navajo (51)	79	0.02
Osage (6)	9	<0.01
Ottawa (4)	6	<0.01
Paiute (4)	10	<0.01
Pima (8)	9	<0.01
Potawatomi (22)	32	0.01
Pueblo (10)	19	0.01
Puget Sound Salish (1)	1	<0.01
Seminole (11)	16	<0.01
Shoshone (1)	3	<0.01
Sioux (20)	62	0.02
South American Ind. (8)	39	0.01
Spanish American Ind. (18)	25	0.01
Tlingit-Haida *(Alaska Native)* (2)	3	<0.01
Tohono O'Odham (1)	2	<0.01

*Notes: † The Census 2010 population figure is used to calculate the percentages in the Hispanic Origin and Race categories. Ancestry percentages are based on the 2006-2010 American Community Survey population (not shown); ‡ Numbers in parentheses indicate the number of people reporting a single ancestry; * Numbers in parentheses indicate the number of persons reporting this race alone, not in combination with any other race; Please refer to the Explanation of Data for more information.*

Yakama (3)	3	<0.01
Yaqui (2)	4	<0.01
Yuman (7)	8	<0.01
Yup'ik *(Alaska Native)* (0)	1	<0.01
Asian (24,826)	27,745	7.59
Not Hispanic (24,564)	27,092	7.41
Hispanic (262)	653	0.18
Bangladeshi (322)	351	0.10
Burmese (15)	17	<0.01
Cambodian (166)	218	0.06
Chinese, ex. Taiwanese (2,351)	2,797	0.77
Filipino (1,422)	2,056	0.56
Hmong (46)	51	0.01
Indian (3,349)	3,749	1.03
Indonesian (102)	139	0.04
Japanese (260)	616	0.17
Korean (1,078)	1,320	0.36
Laotian (177)	237	0.06
Malaysian (37)	55	0.02
Nepalese (258)	275	0.08
Pakistani (1,055)	1,174	0.32
Sri Lankan (98)	113	0.03
Taiwanese (339)	389	0.11
Thai (316)	420	0.11
Vietnamese (12,602)	13,105	3.59
Hawaii Native/Pacific Islander (410)	885	0.24
Not Hispanic (373)	723	0.20
Hispanic (37)	162	0.04
Fijian (2)	2	<0.01
Guamanian/Chamorro (77)	148	0.04
Marshallese (3)	3	<0.01
Native Hawaiian (81)	231	0.06
Samoan (127)	179	0.05
Tongan (58)	67	0.02
White (215,588)	225,760	61.78
Not Hispanic (164,022)	170,093	46.54
Hispanic (51,566)	55,667	15.23

Atascocita

Place Type: CDP
County: Harris
Population: 65,844†

Ancestry‡	Population	%
Afghan (117)	135	0.22
African, Sub-Saharan (990)	1,236	2.00
African (973)	1,204	1.95
Nigerian (17)	17	0.03
South African (0)	15	0.02
Albanian (10)	10	0.02
American (4,702)	4,702	7.61
Arab (84)	106	0.17
Arab (10)	10	0.02
Egyptian (22)	31	0.05
Lebanese (29)	42	0.07
Palestinian (12)	12	0.02
Syrian (11)	11	0.02
Armenian (10)	10	0.02
Assyrian/Chaldean/Syriac (0)	10	0.02
Australian (0)	22	0.04
Austrian (0)	40	0.06
British (94)	133	0.22
Cajun (108)	207	0.34
Canadian (277)	334	0.54
Celtic (0)	9	0.01
Croatian (0)	9	0.01
Czech (85)	162	0.26
Czechoslovakian (11)	57	0.09
Danish (109)	298	0.48
Dutch (103)	654	1.06
Eastern European (13)	13	0.02
English (1,372)	4,062	6.58
European (279)	347	0.56
Finnish (25)	69	0.11
French, ex. Basque (657)	2,492	4.04
French Canadian (146)	341	0.55
German (1,885)	6,604	10.69
Greek (46)	140	0.23
Hungarian (68)	83	0.13
Iranian (66)	66	0.11
Irish (1,721)	5,970	9.67
Italian (703)	1,739	2.82
Lithuanian (22)	31	0.05
Northern European (31)	31	0.05
Norwegian (107)	369	0.60
Polish (379)	926	1.50
Portuguese (53)	122	0.20
Romanian (273)	298	0.48
Russian (61)	170	0.28
Scandinavian (9)	23	0.04
Scotch-Irish (384)	850	1.38
Scottish (541)	1,238	2.00
Serbian (13)	25	0.04
Slovak (14)	95	0.15
Slovene (0)	24	0.04
Swedish (83)	455	0.74
Swiss (9)	9	0.01
Turkish (8)	8	0.01
Ukrainian (45)	45	0.07
Welsh (79)	156	0.25
West Indian, ex. Hispanic (227)	271	0.44
Barbadian (15)	15	0.02
British West Indian (16)	16	0.03
Haitian (0)	9	0.01
Jamaican (196)	209	0.34
West Indian (0)	22	0.04
Yugoslavian (0)	32	0.05

Hispanic Origin	Population	%
Hispanic or Latino (of any race)	15,027	22.82
Central American, ex. Mexican	1,072	1.63
Costa Rican	52	0.08
Guatemalan	164	0.25
Honduran	190	0.29
Nicaraguan	115	0.17
Panamanian	55	0.08
Salvadoran	490	0.74
Other Central American	6	0.01
Cuban	167	0.25
Dominican Republic	99	0.15
Mexican	10,663	16.19
Puerto Rican	500	0.76
South American	842	1.28
Argentinean	97	0.15
Bolivian	8	0.01
Chilean	47	0.07
Colombian	289	0.44
Ecuadorian	114	0.17
Paraguayan	2	<0.01
Peruvian	110	0.17
Uruguayan	13	0.02
Venezuelan	160	0.24
Other South American	2	<0.01
Other Hispanic or Latino	1,684	2.56

Race*	Population	%
African-American/Black (12,633)	13,275	20.16
Not Hispanic (12,300)	12,771	19.40
Hispanic (333)	504	0.77
American Indian/Alaska Native (297)	637	0.97
Not Hispanic (169)	434	0.66
Hispanic (128)	203	0.31
Apache (10)	13	0.02
Blackfeet (3)	11	0.02
Central American Ind. (10)	21	0.03
Cherokee (39)	146	0.22
Cheyenne (1)	1	<0.01
Chickasaw (6)	9	0.01
Chippewa (0)	1	<0.01
Choctaw (18)	39	0.06
Comanche (6)	9	0.01
Cree (1)	1	<0.01
Creek (13)	15	0.02
Delaware (0)	1	<0.01
Hopi (0)	2	<0.01
Houma (2)	2	<0.01
Inupiat *(Alaska Native)* (1)	1	<0.01
Kiowa (1)	1	<0.01
Lumbee (2)	2	<0.01
Mexican American Ind. (13)	20	0.03
Osage (0)	1	<0.01
Ottawa (5)	5	0.01
Pueblo (1)	6	0.01
Seminole (0)	1	<0.01
Sioux (2)	12	0.02
South American Ind. (0)	2	<0.01
Spanish American Ind. (1)	1	<0.01
Tlingit-Haida *(Alaska Native)* (0)	1	<0.01
Ute (3)	3	<0.01
Yaqui (1)	1	<0.01
Asian (1,872)	2,429	3.69
Not Hispanic (1,826)	2,280	3.46
Hispanic (46)	149	0.23
Bangladeshi (11)	11	0.02
Cambodian (32)	44	0.07
Chinese, ex. Taiwanese (270)	354	0.54
Filipino (414)	569	0.86
Indian (285)	346	0.53
Indonesian (5)	17	0.03
Japanese (53)	133	0.20
Korean (82)	127	0.19
Laotian (8)	14	0.02
Malaysian (2)	4	0.01
Pakistani (165)	202	0.31
Sri Lankan (9)	9	0.01
Taiwanese (13)	17	0.03
Thai (42)	62	0.09
Vietnamese (375)	436	0.66
Hawaii Native/Pacific Islander (169)	269	0.41
Not Hispanic (150)	236	0.36
Hispanic (19)	33	0.05
Fijian (9)	9	0.01
Guamanian/Chamorro (69)	90	0.14
Native Hawaiian (37)	76	0.12
Samoan (2)	17	0.03
Tongan (24)	24	0.04
White (44,618)	46,184	70.14
Not Hispanic (35,188)	36,063	54.77
Hispanic (9,430)	10,121	15.37

Athens

Place Type: City
County: Henderson
Population: 12,710†

Ancestry‡	Population	%
American (1,788)	1,788	14.13
Arab (9)	9	0.07
Other Arab (9)	9	0.07
Austrian (0)	17	0.13
British (0)	23	0.18
Czechoslovakian (16)	16	0.13
Danish (0)	6	0.05
Dutch (14)	126	1.00
English (462)	902	7.13
European (43)	68	0.54
Finnish (0)	9	0.07
French, ex. Basque (28)	239	1.89
German (457)	842	6.65
Hungarian (13)	35	0.28
Iranian (36)	36	0.28
Irish (303)	778	6.15
Italian (66)	89	0.70
Norwegian (16)	36	0.28
Polish (0)	60	0.47
Russian (0)	31	0.25
Scotch-Irish (130)	228	1.80
Scottish (63)	175	1.38
Swedish (30)	50	0.40
Turkish (0)	8	0.06
Ukrainian (0)	7	0.06
Welsh (0)	47	0.37
West Indian, ex. Hispanic (16)	29	0.23
Jamaican (16)	16	0.13
West Indian (0)	13	0.10

Hispanic Origin	Population	%
Hispanic or Latino (of any race)	3,397	26.73

*Notes: † The Census 2010 population figure is used to calculate the percentages in the Hispanic Origin and Race categories. Ancestry percentages are based on the 2006-2010 American Community Survey population (not shown); ‡ Numbers in parentheses indicate the number of people reporting a single ancestry; * Numbers in parentheses indicate the number of persons reporting this race alone, not in combination with any other race; Please refer to the Explanation of Data for more information.*

Central American, ex. Mexican	105	0.83
Guatemalan	5	0.04
Honduran	66	0.52
Salvadoran	34	0.27
Cuban	8	0.06
Dominican Republic	1	0.01
Mexican	3,048	23.98
Puerto Rican	11	0.09
South American	8	0.06
Argentinean	2	0.02
Bolivian	1	0.01
Chilean	1	0.01
Colombian	3	0.02
Venezuelan	1	0.01
Other Hispanic or Latino	216	1.70

Race*	Population	%
African-American/Black (2,256)	2,369	18.64
Not Hispanic (2,216)	2,301	18.10
Hispanic (40)	68	0.54
American Indian/Alaska Native (63)	127	1.00
Not Hispanic (39)	90	0.71
Hispanic (24)	37	0.29
Apache (1)	2	0.02
Blackfeet (0)	4	0.03
Cherokee (20)	34	0.27
Cheyenne (0)	1	0.01
Chickasaw (0)	2	0.02
Chippewa (1)	1	0.01
Choctaw (5)	7	0.06
Mexican American Ind. (6)	6	0.05
Osage (0)	5	0.04
Asian (77)	87	0.68
Not Hispanic (75)	83	0.65
Hispanic (2)	4	0.03
Cambodian (6)	6	0.05
Chinese, ex. Taiwanese (11)	16	0.13
Filipino (23)	24	0.19
Indian (19)	23	0.18
Japanese (1)	4	0.03
Korean (1)	2	0.02
Pakistani (6)	6	0.05
Thai (1)	1	0.01
Vietnamese (4)	8	0.06
Hawaii Native/Pacific Islander (3)	12	0.09
Not Hispanic (3)	12	0.09
Guamanian/Chamorro (1)	1	0.01
Marshallese (0)	1	0.01
Native Hawaiian (1)	8	0.06
Samoan (1)	1	0.01
White (8,305)	8,534	67.14
Not Hispanic (6,835)	6,970	54.84
Hispanic (1,470)	1,564	12.31

Austin

Place Type: City
County: Travis
Population: 790,390†

Ancestry‡	Population	%
African, Sub-Saharan (4,239)	4,779	0.63
African (1,942)	2,290	0.30
Cape Verdean (0)	13	<0.01
Ethiopian (516)	530	0.07
Ghanaian (124)	124	0.02
Kenyan (172)	172	0.02
Liberian (149)	158	0.02
Nigerian (969)	1,038	0.14
South African (202)	258	0.03
Sudanese (11)	11	<0.01
Other Sub-Saharan African (154)	185	0.02
Albanian (29)	58	0.01
Alsatian (37)	102	0.01
American (24,492)	24,492	3.21
Arab (2,510)	4,508	0.59
Arab (409)	593	0.08
Egyptian (136)	186	0.02
Iraqi (103)	150	0.02
Jordanian (114)	202	0.03
Lebanese (1,010)	2,130	0.28
Moroccan (111)	155	0.02
Palestinian (101)	182	0.02
Syrian (196)	384	0.05
Other Arab (330)	526	0.07
Armenian (176)	319	0.04
Assyrian/Chaldean/Syriac (6)	13	<0.01
Australian (176)	356	0.05
Austrian (410)	1,482	0.19
Basque (121)	148	0.02
Belgian (341)	723	0.09
Brazilian (771)	966	0.13
British (2,601)	4,770	0.62
Bulgarian (195)	231	0.03
Cajun (337)	660	0.09
Canadian (1,193)	1,759	0.23
Carpatho Rusyn (15)	28	<0.01
Celtic (179)	302	0.04
Croatian (157)	606	0.08
Cypriot (15)	15	<0.01
Czech (2,548)	7,696	1.01
Czechoslovakian (346)	839	0.11
Danish (644)	2,849	0.37
Dutch (1,831)	7,521	0.98
Eastern European (1,053)	1,156	0.15
English (21,689)	70,206	9.19
Estonian (16)	136	0.02
European (8,147)	9,853	1.29
Finnish (252)	802	0.10
French, ex. Basque (3,920)	21,636	2.83
French Canadian (1,433)	2,998	0.39
German (31,349)	97,420	12.75
German Russian (17)	17	<0.01
Greek (958)	2,359	0.31
Guyanese (165)	188	0.02
Hungarian (633)	1,960	0.26
Icelander (41)	139	0.02
Iranian (1,445)	1,872	0.24
Irish (17,996)	66,161	8.66
Israeli (412)	519	0.07
Italian (7,067)	21,105	2.76
Latvian (70)	215	0.03
Lithuanian (214)	1,213	0.16
Luxemburger (67)	101	0.01
Macedonian (67)	76	0.01
Maltese (14)	14	<0.01
New Zealander (49)	49	0.01
Northern European (696)	837	0.11
Norwegian (2,047)	6,273	0.82
Pennsylvania German (100)	218	0.03
Polish (3,698)	12,686	1.66
Portuguese (418)	1,256	0.16
Romanian (592)	947	0.12
Russian (2,390)	6,655	0.87
Scandinavian (687)	1,413	0.18
Scotch-Irish (8,674)	18,418	2.41
Scottish (5,976)	18,914	2.48
Serbian (81)	336	0.04
Slavic (153)	289	0.04
Slovak (154)	732	0.10
Slovene (147)	415	0.05
Swedish (2,386)	8,572	1.12
Swiss (444)	2,023	0.26
Turkish (636)	820	0.11
Ukrainian (475)	1,008	0.13
Welsh (1,083)	5,568	0.73
West Indian, ex. Hispanic (653)	1,216	0.16
Bahamian (0)	20	<0.01
Barbadian (31)	59	0.01
Belizean (32)	74	0.01
British West Indian (7)	36	<0.01
Dutch West Indian (104)	255	0.03
Haitian (66)	117	0.02
Jamaican (304)	416	0.05
Trinidadian/Tobagonian (55)	142	0.02
West Indian (49)	79	0.01
Other West Indian (5)	18	<0.01
Yugoslavian (334)	433	0.06

Hispanic Origin	Population	%
Hispanic or Latino (of any race)	277,707	35.14
Central American, ex. Mexican	13,423	1.70
Costa Rican	312	0.04
Guatemalan	3,007	0.38
Honduran	4,503	0.57
Nicaraguan	1,041	0.13
Panamanian	607	0.08
Salvadoran	3,811	0.48
Other Central American	142	0.02
Cuban	3,163	0.40
Dominican Republic	366	0.05
Mexican	229,865	29.08
Puerto Rican	4,055	0.51
South American	5,002	0.63
Argentinean	600	0.08
Bolivian	244	0.03
Chilean	340	0.04
Colombian	1,619	0.20
Ecuadorian	390	0.05
Paraguayan	50	0.01
Peruvian	804	0.10
Uruguayan	77	0.01
Venezuelan	823	0.10
Other South American	55	0.01
Other Hispanic or Latino	21,833	2.76

Race*	Population	%
African-American/Black (64,406)	71,130	9.00
Not Hispanic (60,760)	65,227	8.25
Hispanic (3,646)	5,903	0.75
American Indian/Alaska Native (6,901)	12,725	1.61
Not Hispanic (1,967)	5,512	0.70
Hispanic (4,934)	7,213	0.91
Alaska Athabascan *(Ala. Nat.)* (1)	10	<0.01
Aleut *(Alaska Native)* (4)	7	<0.01
Apache (155)	329	0.04
Arapaho (2)	7	<0.01
Blackfeet (30)	147	0.02
Canadian/French Am. Ind. (8)	24	<0.01
Central American Ind. (55)	92	0.01
Cherokee (439)	1,686	0.21
Cheyenne (9)	19	<0.01
Chickasaw (78)	191	0.02
Chippewa (42)	86	0.01
Choctaw (252)	559	0.07
Colville (1)	2	<0.01
Comanche (43)	123	0.02
Cree (11)	18	<0.01
Creek (52)	168	0.02
Crow (5)	15	<0.01
Delaware (17)	22	<0.01
Hopi (4)	16	<0.01
Houma (7)	8	<0.01
Inupiat *(Alaska Native)* (4)	18	<0.01
Iroquois (38)	89	0.01
Kiowa (5)	16	<0.01
Lumbee (19)	28	<0.01
Menominee (4)	6	<0.01
Mexican American Ind. (716)	1,006	0.13
Navajo (92)	164	0.02
Osage (22)	45	0.01
Ottawa (3)	10	<0.01
Paiute (10)	11	<0.01
Pima (6)	6	<0.01
Potawatomi (39)	66	0.01
Pueblo (31)	48	0.01
Puget Sound Salish (1)	1	<0.01
Seminole (6)	28	<0.01
Shoshone (7)	14	<0.01
Sioux (63)	124	0.02
South American Ind. (49)	114	0.01
Spanish American Ind. (69)	103	0.01
Tlingit-Haida *(Alaska Native)* (11)	18	<0.01
Tohono O'Odham (4)	9	<0.01
Tsimshian *(Alaska Native)* (0)	1	<0.01
Ute (5)	11	<0.01
Yakama (1)	5	<0.01
Yaqui (14)	34	<0.01
Yuman (9)	9	<0.01

*Notes: † The Census 2010 population figure is used to calculate the percentages in the Hispanic Origin and Race categories. Ancestry percentages are based on the 2006-2010 American Community Survey population (not shown); ‡ Numbers in parentheses indicate the number of people reporting a single ancestry; * Numbers in parentheses indicate the number of persons reporting this race alone, not in combination with any other race; Please refer to the Explanation of Data for more information.*

Yup'ik *(Alaska Native)* (6)	6	<0.01
Asian (49,864)	57,893	7.32
Not Hispanic (49,159)	55,842	7.07
Hispanic (705)	2,051	0.26
Bangladeshi (479)	521	0.07
Bhutanese (58)	107	0.01
Burmese (447)	492	0.06
Cambodian (243)	291	0.04
Chinese, ex. Taiwanese (10,024)	11,810	1.49
Filipino (2,698)	4,214	0.53
Hmong (14)	18	<0.01
Indian (14,885)	16,162	2.04
Indonesian (248)	354	0.04
Japanese (1,211)	2,433	0.31
Korean (5,490)	6,564	0.83
Laotian (155)	197	0.02
Malaysian (99)	149	0.02
Nepalese (284)	353	0.04
Pakistani (1,797)	2,030	0.26
Sri Lankan (215)	244	0.03
Taiwanese (1,423)	1,683	0.21
Thai (615)	929	0.12
Vietnamese (7,575)	8,430	1.07
Hawaii Native/Pacific Islander (529)	1,506	0.19
Not Hispanic (401)	1,075	0.14
Hispanic (128)	431	0.05
Fijian (4)	7	<0.01
Guamanian/Chamorro (135)	274	0.03
Marshallese (2)	2	<0.01
Native Hawaiian (187)	535	0.07
Samoan (60)	129	0.02
Tongan (23)	44	0.01
White (539,760)	562,451	71.16
Not Hispanic (385,271)	397,176	50.25
Hispanic (154,489)	165,275	20.91

Azle

Place Type: City
County: Tarrant
Population: 10,947†

Ancestry‡	Population	%
African, Sub-Saharan (0)	17	0.16
African (0)	17	0.16
American (1,407)	1,407	13.07
Arab (0)	7	0.07
Lebanese (0)	7	0.07
Austrian (0)	51	0.47
Belgian (11)	11	0.10
Brazilian (37)	37	0.34
British (29)	37	0.34
Canadian (0)	9	0.08
Czech (54)	164	1.52
Czechoslovakian (13)	13	0.12
Danish (37)	37	0.34
Dutch (60)	341	3.17
English (775)	1,464	13.59
European (119)	127	1.18
French, ex. Basque (5)	180	1.67
French Canadian (22)	54	0.50
German (688)	1,580	14.67
Hungarian (0)	80	0.74
Irish (516)	1,631	15.15
Italian (145)	275	2.55
Norwegian (18)	68	0.63
Polish (73)	147	1.37
Russian (15)	33	0.31
Scotch-Irish (151)	252	2.34
Scottish (235)	348	3.23
Slovak (0)	6	0.06
Swedish (28)	180	1.67
Swiss (15)	27	0.25
Ukrainian (15)	15	0.14
Welsh (0)	12	0.11
West Indian, ex. Hispanic (9)	9	0.08
Dutch West Indian (9)	9	0.08

Hispanic Origin	Population	%
Hispanic or Latino (of any race)	901	8.23
Central American, ex. Mexican	22	0.20
Costa Rican	2	0.02
Guatemalan	1	0.01
Nicaraguan	2	0.02
Panamanian	11	0.10
Salvadoran	6	0.05
Cuban	4	0.04
Dominican Republic	1	0.01
Mexican	775	7.08
Puerto Rican	19	0.17
South American	5	0.05
Colombian	3	0.03
Peruvian	1	0.01
Venezuelan	1	0.01
Other Hispanic or Latino	75	0.69

Race*	Population	%
African-American/Black (73)	102	0.93
Not Hispanic (62)	91	0.83
Hispanic (11)	11	0.10
American Indian/Alaska Native (102)	202	1.85
Not Hispanic (90)	185	1.69
Hispanic (12)	17	0.16
Apache (0)	1	0.01
Blackfeet (1)	6	0.05
Cherokee (27)	55	0.50
Chickasaw (7)	14	0.13
Chippewa (1)	1	0.01
Choctaw (12)	18	0.16
Creek (3)	5	0.05
Houma (0)	2	0.02
Mexican American Ind. (4)	8	0.07
Navajo (0)	1	0.01
Ottawa (6)	6	0.05
Potawatomi (0)	3	0.03
Pueblo (0)	2	0.02
Sioux (2)	6	0.05
Spanish American Ind. (1)	1	0.01
Yaqui (1)	1	0.01
Asian (73)	110	1.00
Not Hispanic (70)	104	0.95
Hispanic (3)	6	0.05
Chinese, ex. Taiwanese (9)	12	0.11
Filipino (19)	33	0.30
Indian (4)	10	0.09
Japanese (3)	9	0.08
Korean (5)	9	0.08
Laotian (2)	5	0.05
Nepalese (6)	7	0.06
Pakistani (1)	4	0.04
Thai (4)	9	0.08
Vietnamese (10)	13	0.12
Hawaii Native/Pacific Islander (2)	4	0.04
Not Hispanic (2)	4	0.04
Guamanian/Chamorro (0)	1	0.01
Native Hawaiian (2)	3	0.03
White (10,147)	10,365	94.68
Not Hispanic (9,654)	9,815	89.66
Hispanic (493)	550	5.02

Bacliff

Place Type: CDP
County: Galveston
Population: 8,619†

Ancestry‡	Population	%
African, Sub-Saharan (0)	31	0.43
African (0)	31	0.43
Albanian (45)	45	0.62
American (646)	646	8.88
Austrian (19)	54	0.74
British (47)	67	0.92
Croatian (0)	9	0.12
Czech (0)	59	0.81
Dutch (24)	294	4.04
English (127)	532	7.31
European (31)	50	0.69
French, ex. Basque (177)	494	6.79
German (164)	775	10.65
Hungarian (0)	70	0.96
Irish (330)	1,092	15.01
Italian (37)	194	2.67
Lithuanian (20)	40	0.55
Maltese (0)	8	0.11
Northern European (0)	13	0.18
Norwegian (81)	81	1.11
Polish (43)	120	1.65
Russian (14)	29	0.40
Scotch-Irish (26)	94	1.29
Scottish (0)	80	1.10
Slovak (0)	12	0.16
Swedish (0)	114	1.57
Welsh (0)	9	0.12
Yugoslavian (66)	81	1.11

Hispanic Origin	Population	%
Hispanic or Latino (of any race)	3,196	37.08
Central American, ex. Mexican	151	1.75
Costa Rican	1	0.01
Guatemalan	31	0.36
Honduran	26	0.30
Nicaraguan	5	0.06
Panamanian	1	0.01
Salvadoran	87	1.01
Cuban	23	0.27
Dominican Republic	5	0.06
Mexican	2,782	32.28
Puerto Rican	35	0.41
South American	28	0.32
Argentinean	2	0.02
Bolivian	3	0.03
Colombian	14	0.16
Ecuadorian	2	0.02
Paraguayan	3	0.03
Uruguayan	1	0.01
Venezuelan	3	0.03
Other Hispanic or Latino	172	2.00

Race*	Population	%
African-American/Black (300)	352	4.08
Not Hispanic (283)	312	3.62
Hispanic (17)	40	0.46
American Indian/Alaska Native (65)	121	1.40
Not Hispanic (46)	83	0.96
Hispanic (19)	38	0.44
Aleut *(Alaska Native)* (0)	3	0.03
Apache (2)	10	0.12
Blackfeet (0)	5	0.06
Central American Ind. (2)	2	0.02
Cherokee (5)	21	0.24
Cheyenne (0)	2	0.02
Chippewa (0)	2	0.02
Choctaw (4)	4	0.05
Comanche (0)	3	0.03
Creek (1)	4	0.05
Iroquois (1)	3	0.03
Mexican American Ind. (1)	2	0.02
Ottawa (4)	4	0.05
Potawatomi (1)	1	0.01
Sioux (3)	3	0.03
Spanish American Ind. (1)	1	0.01
Asian (243)	281	3.26
Not Hispanic (237)	253	2.94
Hispanic (6)	28	0.32
Chinese, ex. Taiwanese (16)	18	0.21
Filipino (10)	17	0.20
Indian (31)	39	0.45
Indonesian (1)	2	0.02
Korean (10)	11	0.13
Thai (0)	1	0.01
Vietnamese (168)	180	2.09
Hawaii Native/Pacific Islander (6)	19	0.22
Not Hispanic (6)	11	0.13
Hispanic (0)	8	0.09
Guamanian/Chamorro (5)	7	0.08
Native Hawaiian (0)	3	0.03
Samoan (1)	1	0.01
White (6,403)	6,615	76.75
Not Hispanic (4,741)	4,826	55.99

*Notes: † The Census 2010 population figure is used to calculate the percentages in the Hispanic Origin and Race categories. Ancestry percentages are based on the 2006-2010 American Community Survey population (not shown); ‡ Numbers in parentheses indicate the number of people reporting a single ancestry; * Numbers in parentheses indicate the number of persons reporting this race alone, not in combination with any other race; Please refer to the Explanation of Data for more information.*

Hispanic (1,662)	1,789	20.76

Balch Springs

Place Type: City
County: Dallas
Population: 23,728†

Ancestry‡	Population	%
African, Sub-Saharan (240)	328	1.44
African (78)	122	0.54
Kenyan (59)	59	0.26
Nigerian (103)	147	0.65
American (3,815)	3,815	16.75
Arab (12)	12	0.05
Arab (12)	12	0.05
Brazilian (0)	10	0.04
British (0)	16	0.07
Czech (0)	13	0.06
Dutch (10)	60	0.26
English (288)	677	2.97
European (25)	25	0.11
French, ex. Basque (21)	84	0.37
German (251)	836	3.67
Greek (8)	8	0.04
Irish (175)	600	2.63
Italian (68)	103	0.45
Norwegian (12)	12	0.05
Polish (11)	11	0.05
Romanian (31)	31	0.14
Scotch-Irish (8)	91	0.40
Scottish (17)	46	0.20
Swedish (19)	42	0.18
Welsh (0)	14	0.06
West Indian, ex. Hispanic (54)	54	0.24
Jamaican (54)	54	0.24

Hispanic Origin	Population	%
Hispanic or Latino (of any race)	10,870	45.81
Central American, ex. Mexican	480	2.02
Costa Rican	13	0.05
Guatemalan	53	0.22
Honduran	95	0.40
Nicaraguan	17	0.07
Panamanian	10	0.04
Salvadoran	291	1.23
Other Central American	1	<0.01
Cuban	53	0.22
Dominican Republic	17	0.07
Mexican	9,703	40.89
Puerto Rican	61	0.26
South American	69	0.29
Argentinean	6	0.03
Chilean	10	0.04
Colombian	20	0.08
Ecuadorian	3	0.01
Peruvian	18	0.08
Uruguayan	1	<0.01
Venezuelan	7	0.03
Other South American	4	0.02
Other Hispanic or Latino	487	2.05

Race*	Population	%
African-American/Black (5,755)	6,060	25.54
Not Hispanic (5,621)	5,834	24.59
Hispanic (134)	226	0.95
American Indian/Alaska Native (330)	491	2.07
Not Hispanic (115)	226	0.95
Hispanic (215)	265	1.12
Apache (2)	7	0.03
Blackfeet (0)	3	0.01
Central American Ind. (0)	4	0.02
Cherokee (16)	57	0.24
Chickasaw (7)	8	0.03
Chippewa (2)	2	0.01
Choctaw (33)	55	0.23
Comanche (1)	1	<0.01
Creek (12)	15	0.06
Mexican American Ind. (27)	37	0.16
Navajo (1)	5	0.02
Potawatomi (2)	2	0.01
Pueblo (4)	4	0.02
Seminole (0)	1	<0.01
Shoshone (0)	2	0.01
Sioux (1)	3	0.01
Ute (3)	3	0.01
Yup'ik *(Alaska Native)* (1)	1	<0.01
Asian (209)	277	1.17
Not Hispanic (200)	244	1.03
Hispanic (9)	33	0.14
Cambodian (8)	10	0.04
Chinese, ex. Taiwanese (4)	15	0.06
Filipino (41)	61	0.26
Indian (57)	62	0.26
Japanese (2)	5	0.02
Korean (18)	19	0.08
Laotian (2)	3	0.01
Nepalese (7)	10	0.04
Pakistani (13)	16	0.07
Taiwanese (4)	5	0.02
Thai (7)	13	0.05
Vietnamese (34)	42	0.18
Hawaii Native/Pacific Islander (3)	26	0.11
Not Hispanic (2)	10	0.04
Hispanic (1)	16	0.07
Guamanian/Chamorro (1)	1	<0.01
Native Hawaiian (1)	14	0.06
White (12,027)	12,659	53.35
Not Hispanic (6,577)	6,838	28.82
Hispanic (5,450)	5,821	24.53

Bay City

Place Type: City
County: Matagorda
Population: 17,614†

Ancestry‡	Population	%
African, Sub-Saharan (0)	15	0.08
African (0)	15	0.08
American (892)	892	5.05
Austrian (0)	32	0.18
British (37)	108	0.61
Cajun (13)	13	0.07
Czech (422)	880	4.98
Czechoslovakian (24)	24	0.14
Danish (67)	126	0.71
Dutch (5)	127	0.72
English (457)	1,152	6.52
European (59)	59	0.33
French, ex. Basque (33)	384	2.17
French Canadian (19)	32	0.18
German (674)	1,999	11.31
Icelander (14)	14	0.08
Irish (358)	1,170	6.62
Italian (71)	333	1.88
Norwegian (0)	25	0.14
Polish (13)	97	0.55
Romanian (0)	7	0.04
Russian (0)	7	0.04
Scotch-Irish (106)	294	1.66
Scottish (82)	198	1.12
Swedish (8)	57	0.32
Ukrainian (0)	50	0.28
Welsh (0)	67	0.38
West Indian, ex. Hispanic (8)	14	0.08
Dutch West Indian (0)	6	0.03
Jamaican (8)	8	0.05

Hispanic Origin	Population	%
Hispanic or Latino (of any race)	7,639	43.37
Central American, ex. Mexican	69	0.39
Guatemalan	29	0.16
Honduran	18	0.10
Panamanian	3	0.02
Salvadoran	19	0.11
Cuban	1	0.01
Dominican Republic	2	0.01
Mexican	6,808	38.65
Puerto Rican	31	0.18
South American	8	0.05
Argentinean	2	0.01
Colombian	2	0.01
Venezuelan	4	0.02
Other Hispanic or Latino	720	4.09

Race*	Population	%
African-American/Black (2,818)	2,940	16.69
Not Hispanic (2,731)	2,811	15.96
Hispanic (87)	129	0.73
American Indian/Alaska Native (121)	204	1.16
Not Hispanic (47)	89	0.51
Hispanic (74)	115	0.65
Apache (1)	3	0.02
Blackfeet (1)	1	0.01
Canadian/French Am. Ind. (0)	1	0.01
Cherokee (9)	30	0.17
Cheyenne (1)	1	0.01
Chickasaw (0)	1	0.01
Chippewa (0)	1	0.01
Choctaw (14)	15	0.09
Comanche (2)	2	0.01
Creek (1)	3	0.02
Delaware (1)	1	0.01
Mexican American Ind. (5)	5	0.03
Navajo (3)	7	0.04
Osage (1)	1	0.01
Ottawa (0)	1	0.01
Pueblo (0)	1	0.01
Sioux (0)	1	0.01
Asian (144)	207	1.18
Not Hispanic (133)	165	0.94
Hispanic (11)	42	0.24
Cambodian (4)	4	0.02
Chinese, ex. Taiwanese (4)	9	0.05
Filipino (25)	53	0.30
Indian (72)	84	0.48
Japanese (3)	13	0.07
Korean (5)	7	0.04
Pakistani (1)	4	0.02
Sri Lankan (0)	1	0.01
Vietnamese (25)	25	0.14
Hawaii Native/Pacific Islander (5)	30	0.17
Not Hispanic (4)	14	0.08
Hispanic (1)	16	0.09
Guamanian/Chamorro (1)	4	0.02
Native Hawaiian (1)	4	0.02
Samoan (0)	2	0.01
Tongan (0)	1	0.01
White (11,395)	11,733	66.61
Not Hispanic (6,891)	7,016	39.83
Hispanic (4,504)	4,717	26.78

Baytown

Place Type: City
County: Harris
Population: 71,802†

Ancestry‡	Population	%
African, Sub-Saharan (837)	1,067	1.52
African (837)	1,067	1.52
American (4,397)	4,397	6.24
Arab (110)	267	0.38
Egyptian (74)	143	0.20
Lebanese (17)	17	0.02
Syrian (0)	88	0.12
Other Arab (19)	19	0.03
Austrian (0)	30	0.04
Belgian (13)	41	0.06
Brazilian (15)	15	0.02
British (208)	224	0.32
Cajun (51)	75	0.11
Canadian (8)	8	0.01
Czech (331)	660	0.94
Czechoslovakian (68)	142	0.20
Danish (43)	81	0.12
Dutch (110)	580	0.82
English (1,930)	4,323	6.14
European (388)	505	0.72

*Notes: † The Census 2010 population figure is used to calculate the percentages in the Hispanic Origin and Race categories. Ancestry percentages are based on the 2006-2010 American Community Survey population (not shown); ‡ Numbers in parentheses indicate the number of people reporting a single ancestry; * Numbers in parentheses indicate the number of persons reporting this race alone, not in combination with any other race; Please refer to the Explanation of Data for more information.*

French, ex. Basque (700)	1,878	2.67
French Canadian (224)	277	0.39
German (1,546)	5,046	7.16
Greek (0)	35	0.05
Hungarian (240)	298	0.42
Icelander (96)	96	0.14
Iranian (25)	25	0.04
Irish (1,359)	4,347	6.17
Italian (340)	752	1.07
Norwegian (134)	233	0.33
Pennsylvania German (19)	19	0.03
Polish (148)	458	0.65
Portuguese (0)	5	0.01
Romanian (18)	18	0.03
Russian (0)	71	0.10
Scandinavian (9)	94	0.13
Scotch-Irish (360)	934	1.33
Scottish (383)	911	1.29
Slavic (10)	20	0.03
Slovene (0)	7	0.01
Swedish (63)	391	0.56
Swiss (0)	22	0.03
Ukrainian (12)	25	0.04
Welsh (48)	221	0.31
West Indian, ex. Hispanic (662)	727	1.03
British West Indian (171)	171	0.24
Dutch West Indian (0)	12	0.02
Jamaican (61)	61	0.09
Trinidadian/Tobagonian (131)	184	0.26
West Indian (299)	299	0.42
Yugoslavian (97)	154	0.22

Hispanic Origin	Population	%
Hispanic or Latino (of any race)	31,156	43.39
Central American, ex. Mexican	553	0.77
Costa Rican	2	<0.01
Guatemalan	120	0.17
Honduran	146	0.20
Nicaraguan	34	0.05
Panamanian	15	0.02
Salvadoran	229	0.32
Other Central American	7	0.01
Cuban	104	0.14
Dominican Republic	68	0.09
Mexican	28,015	39.02
Puerto Rican	310	0.43
South American	171	0.24
Argentinean	23	0.03
Bolivian	10	0.01
Chilean	34	0.05
Colombian	48	0.07
Ecuadorian	7	0.01
Peruvian	11	0.02
Uruguayan	8	0.01
Venezuelan	30	0.04
Other Hispanic or Latino	1,935	2.69

Race*	Population	%
African-American/Black (11,101)	11,698	16.29
Not Hispanic (10,759)	11,181	15.57
Hispanic (342)	517	0.72
American Indian/Alaska Native (458)	770	1.07
Not Hispanic (180)	341	0.47
Hispanic (278)	429	0.60
Apache (1)	8	0.01
Arapaho (1)	1	<0.01
Blackfeet (0)	3	<0.01
Canadian/French Am. Ind. (1)	4	0.01
Central American Ind. (5)	11	0.02
Cherokee (36)	78	0.11
Chickasaw (8)	13	0.02
Chippewa (6)	11	0.02
Choctaw (16)	23	0.03
Comanche (6)	14	0.02
Creek (5)	7	0.01
Houma (2)	2	<0.01
Iroquois (0)	1	<0.01
Lumbee (1)	1	<0.01
Mexican American Ind. (46)	65	0.09
Navajo (5)	5	0.01
Osage (1)	1	<0.01
Potawatomi (2)	2	<0.01
Puget Sound Salish (2)	2	<0.01
Seminole (1)	7	0.01
Sioux (4)	16	0.02
Spanish American Ind. (1)	1	<0.01
Yaqui (0)	2	<0.01
Asian (1,052)	1,261	1.76
Not Hispanic (1,022)	1,177	1.64
Hispanic (30)	84	0.12
Bangladeshi (20)	27	0.04
Cambodian (12)	14	0.02
Chinese, ex. Taiwanese (64)	82	0.11
Filipino (349)	397	0.55
Hmong (3)	3	<0.01
Indian (301)	323	0.45
Indonesian (9)	9	0.01
Japanese (8)	21	0.03
Korean (45)	61	0.08
Laotian (3)	5	0.01
Malaysian (3)	3	<0.01
Nepalese (6)	6	0.01
Pakistani (73)	78	0.11
Sri Lankan (0)	2	<0.01
Taiwanese (2)	7	0.01
Thai (16)	29	0.04
Vietnamese (109)	118	0.16
Hawaii Native/Pacific Islander (34)	156	0.22
Not Hispanic (24)	89	0.12
Hispanic (10)	67	0.09
Guamanian/Chamorro (3)	10	0.01
Native Hawaiian (13)	29	0.04
Samoan (6)	15	0.02
Tongan (4)	11	0.02
White (45,150)	46,726	65.08
Not Hispanic (27,803)	28,384	39.53
Hispanic (17,347)	18,342	25.55

Beaumont

Place Type: City
County: Jefferson
Population: 118,296†

Ancestry‡	Population	%
African, Sub-Saharan (974)	1,303	1.12
African (642)	906	0.78
Ethiopian (6)	6	0.01
Nigerian (140)	205	0.18
South African (17)	17	0.01
Other Sub-Saharan African (169)	169	0.15
Albanian (247)	247	0.21
American (4,148)	4,148	3.57
Arab (107)	283	0.24
Lebanese (60)	165	0.14
Moroccan (0)	19	0.02
Palestinian (0)	9	0.01
Syrian (27)	70	0.06
Other Arab (20)	20	0.02
Australian (9)	9	0.01
Austrian (37)	53	0.05
Belgian (0)	17	0.01
Brazilian (0)	67	0.06
British (63)	116	0.10
Cajun (313)	616	0.53
Canadian (27)	210	0.18
Celtic (31)	31	0.03
Croatian (22)	22	0.02
Czech (101)	255	0.22
Czechoslovakian (87)	87	0.07
Danish (71)	152	0.13
Dutch (230)	830	0.72
English (2,883)	6,452	5.56
European (754)	889	0.77
Finnish (9)	20	0.02
French, ex. Basque (2,043)	6,139	5.29
French Canadian (574)	945	0.81
German (2,772)	7,580	6.53
German Russian (16)	16	0.01
Greek (97)	294	0.25
Hungarian (26)	73	0.06
Iranian (17)	79	0.07
Irish (1,859)	6,718	5.79
Israeli (35)	44	0.04
Italian (1,157)	2,670	2.30
Latvian (18)	39	0.03
Lithuanian (11)	35	0.03
New Zealander (16)	62	0.05
Northern European (55)	55	0.05
Norwegian (202)	489	0.42
Polish (175)	691	0.60
Portuguese (7)	58	0.05
Romanian (0)	21	0.02
Russian (37)	391	0.34
Scandinavian (76)	112	0.10
Scotch-Irish (913)	1,826	1.57
Scottish (268)	1,076	0.93
Slovak (61)	101	0.09
Swedish (94)	566	0.49
Swiss (0)	106	0.09
Turkish (64)	64	0.06
Ukrainian (11)	51	0.04
Welsh (146)	619	0.53
West Indian, ex. Hispanic (38)	106	0.09
Haitian (0)	17	0.01
Jamaican (12)	63	0.05
West Indian (26)	26	0.02
Yugoslavian (14)	31	0.03

Hispanic Origin	Population	%
Hispanic or Latino (of any race)	15,898	13.44
Central American, ex. Mexican	664	0.56
Costa Rican	4	<0.01
Guatemalan	208	0.18
Honduran	201	0.17
Nicaraguan	59	0.05
Panamanian	45	0.04
Salvadoran	146	0.12
Other Central American	1	<0.01
Cuban	213	0.18
Dominican Republic	39	0.03
Mexican	13,333	11.27
Puerto Rican	302	0.26
South American	245	0.21
Argentinean	29	0.02
Bolivian	13	0.01
Chilean	26	0.02
Colombian	64	0.05
Ecuadorian	11	0.01
Paraguayan	1	<0.01
Peruvian	41	0.03
Venezuelan	60	0.05
Other Hispanic or Latino	1,102	0.93

Race*	Population	%
African-American/Black (55,931)	57,126	48.29
Not Hispanic (55,489)	56,478	47.74
Hispanic (442)	648	0.55
American Indian/Alaska Native (653)	1,192	1.01
Not Hispanic (360)	779	0.66
Hispanic (293)	413	0.35
Alaska Athabascan *(Ala. Nat.)* (1)	1	<0.01
Apache (13)	20	0.02
Blackfeet (9)	29	0.02
Canadian/French Am. Ind. (1)	4	<0.01
Central American Ind. (2)	4	<0.01
Cherokee (61)	178	0.15
Cheyenne (0)	1	<0.01
Chickasaw (5)	7	0.01
Chippewa (0)	1	<0.01
Choctaw (18)	56	0.05
Comanche (10)	15	0.01
Creek (3)	12	0.01
Delaware (0)	1	<0.01
Houma (4)	7	0.01
Inupiat *(Alaska Native)* (0)	2	<0.01
Iroquois (1)	9	0.01
Kiowa (0)	1	<0.01
Lumbee (1)	1	<0.01
Mexican American Ind. (26)	50	0.04

*Notes: † The Census 2010 population figure is used to calculate the percentages in the Hispanic Origin and Race categories. Ancestry percentages are based on the 2006-2010 American Community Survey population (not shown); ‡ Numbers in parentheses indicate the number of people reporting a single ancestry; * Numbers in parentheses indicate the number of persons reporting this race alone, not in combination with any other race; Please refer to the Explanation of Data for more information.*

Navajo (2)	4	<0.01
Osage (1)	3	<0.01
Paiute (0)	3	<0.01
Pima (2)	2	<0.01
Potawatomi (4)	5	<0.01
Pueblo (0)	1	<0.01
Seminole (1)	2	<0.01
Sioux (2)	11	0.01
South American Ind. (0)	1	<0.01
Spanish American Ind. (6)	6	0.01
Tlingit-Haida *(Alaska Native)* (1)	1	<0.01
Tohono O'Odham (2)	3	<0.01
Yakama (1)	2	<0.01
Yaqui (2)	5	<0.01
Yuman (1)	1	<0.01
Yup'ik *(Alaska Native)* (1)	1	<0.01
Asian (3,893)	4,310	3.64
Not Hispanic (3,850)	4,194	3.55
Hispanic (43)	116	0.10
Bangladeshi (40)	46	0.04
Burmese (19)	19	0.02
Cambodian (24)	40	0.03
Chinese, ex. Taiwanese (345)	435	0.37
Filipino (670)	792	0.67
Indian (1,024)	1,104	0.93
Indonesian (1)	7	0.01
Japanese (25)	81	0.07
Korean (88)	106	0.09
Laotian (6)	6	0.01
Malaysian (7)	10	0.01
Nepalese (59)	59	0.05
Pakistani (229)	258	0.22
Sri Lankan (9)	13	0.01
Taiwanese (24)	28	0.02
Thai (40)	56	0.05
Vietnamese (1,084)	1,162	0.98
Hawaii Native/Pacific Islander (34)	150	0.13
Not Hispanic (25)	101	0.09
Hispanic (9)	49	0.04
Fijian (1)	1	<0.01
Guamanian/Chamorro (7)	21	0.02
Native Hawaiian (10)	57	0.05
Samoan (4)	9	0.01
White (47,044)	48,837	41.28
Not Hispanic (41,041)	42,218	35.69
Hispanic (6,003)	6,619	5.60

Bedford

Place Type: City
County: Tarrant
Population: 46,979†

Ancestry‡	Population	%
Afghan (32)	50	0.11
African, Sub-Saharan (977)	1,079	2.30
African (258)	348	0.74
Ethiopian (86)	86	0.18
Liberian (9)	9	0.02
South African (12)	24	0.05
Other Sub-Saharan African (612)	612	1.30
Albanian (182)	182	0.39
American (3,259)	3,259	6.94
Arab (185)	207	0.44
Arab (133)	133	0.28
Egyptian (0)	10	0.02
Jordanian (28)	28	0.06
Lebanese (24)	36	0.08
Armenian (0)	8	0.02
Austrian (17)	113	0.24
Basque (21)	21	0.04
Belgian (0)	26	0.06
Brazilian (137)	172	0.37
British (133)	239	0.51
Bulgarian (81)	81	0.17
Canadian (24)	49	0.10
Croatian (48)	85	0.18
Czech (126)	342	0.73
Czechoslovakian (65)	80	0.17
Danish (25)	103	0.22
Dutch (304)	1,161	2.47
Eastern European (28)	28	0.06
English (2,671)	6,657	14.17
European (1,078)	1,218	2.59
Finnish (0)	25	0.05
French, ex. Basque (302)	1,445	3.08
French Canadian (103)	210	0.45
German (2,734)	8,470	18.03
German Russian (0)	11	0.02
Greek (152)	186	0.40
Hungarian (0)	243	0.52
Iranian (8)	8	0.02
Irish (1,512)	5,773	12.29
Italian (464)	1,318	2.81
Latvian (13)	13	0.03
Lithuanian (46)	107	0.23
Northern European (35)	35	0.07
Norwegian (273)	628	1.34
Pennsylvania German (13)	38	0.08
Polish (404)	1,265	2.69
Portuguese (18)	128	0.27
Russian (48)	364	0.77
Scandinavian (12)	34	0.07
Scotch-Irish (555)	1,665	3.54
Scottish (479)	1,343	2.86
Serbian (0)	20	0.04
Slavic (0)	23	0.05
Slovak (19)	53	0.11
Swedish (171)	580	1.23
Swiss (14)	102	0.22
Turkish (12)	12	0.03
Ukrainian (0)	85	0.18
Welsh (60)	449	0.96
West Indian, ex. Hispanic (46)	76	0.16
Bermudan (8)	8	0.02
Dutch West Indian (5)	5	0.01
Haitian (21)	21	0.04
Jamaican (12)	12	0.03
West Indian (0)	17	0.04
Other West Indian (0)	13	0.03
Yugoslavian (48)	70	0.15

Hispanic Origin	Population	%
Hispanic or Latino (of any race)	5,881	12.52
Central American, ex. Mexican	306	0.65
Costa Rican	19	0.04
Guatemalan	31	0.07
Honduran	38	0.08
Nicaraguan	16	0.03
Panamanian	35	0.07
Salvadoran	165	0.35
Other Central American	2	<0.01
Cuban	97	0.21
Dominican Republic	32	0.07
Mexican	4,140	8.81
Puerto Rican	511	1.09
South American	250	0.53
Argentinean	31	0.07
Bolivian	6	0.01
Chilean	22	0.05
Colombian	67	0.14
Ecuadorian	30	0.06
Peruvian	59	0.13
Uruguayan	2	<0.01
Venezuelan	32	0.07
Other South American	1	<0.01
Other Hispanic or Latino	545	1.16

Race*	Population	%
African-American/Black (3,277)	3,709	7.90
Not Hispanic (3,175)	3,536	7.53
Hispanic (102)	173	0.37
American Indian/Alaska Native (264)	610	1.30
Not Hispanic (205)	499	1.06
Hispanic (59)	111	0.24
Apache (7)	15	0.03
Blackfeet (0)	3	0.01
Canadian/French Am. Ind. (0)	1	<0.01
Cherokee (47)	143	0.30
Chickasaw (12)	19	0.04
Chippewa (5)	10	0.02
Choctaw (42)	77	0.16
Comanche (7)	12	0.03
Creek (11)	24	0.05
Delaware (0)	2	<0.01
Hopi (1)	1	<0.01
Houma (1)	1	<0.01
Inupiat *(Alaska Native)* (0)	1	<0.01
Iroquois (3)	5	0.01
Kiowa (2)	2	<0.01
Lumbee (1)	2	<0.01
Menominee (0)	1	<0.01
Mexican American Ind. (12)	17	0.04
Navajo (6)	11	0.02
Osage (3)	10	0.02
Ottawa (1)	1	<0.01
Potawatomi (8)	12	0.03
Seminole (1)	2	<0.01
Sioux (5)	13	0.03
South American Ind. (2)	4	0.01
Tlingit-Haida *(Alaska Native)* (5)	5	0.01
Yaqui (0)	4	0.01
Yup'ik *(Alaska Native)* (0)	1	<0.01
Asian (2,082)	2,452	5.22
Not Hispanic (2,066)	2,384	5.07
Hispanic (16)	68	0.14
Bangladeshi (13)	18	0.04
Burmese (4)	5	0.01
Cambodian (17)	24	0.05
Chinese, ex. Taiwanese (217)	286	0.61
Filipino (190)	274	0.58
Hmong (2)	3	0.01
Indian (564)	625	1.33
Indonesian (12)	16	0.03
Japanese (61)	117	0.25
Korean (297)	336	0.72
Laotian (77)	97	0.21
Malaysian (1)	1	<0.01
Nepalese (61)	62	0.13
Pakistani (172)	203	0.43
Sri Lankan (6)	9	0.02
Taiwanese (21)	27	0.06
Thai (43)	70	0.15
Vietnamese (211)	257	0.55
Hawaii Native/Pacific Islander (166)	242	0.52
Not Hispanic (165)	227	0.48
Hispanic (1)	15	0.03
Guamanian/Chamorro (10)	20	0.04
Native Hawaiian (7)	38	0.08
Samoan (18)	24	0.05
Tongan (112)	130	0.28
White (38,100)	39,210	83.46
Not Hispanic (34,511)	35,293	75.13
Hispanic (3,589)	3,917	8.34

Beeville

Place Type: City
County: Bee
Population: 12,863†

Ancestry‡	Population	%
African, Sub-Saharan (18)	18	0.13
African (18)	18	0.13
American (168)	168	1.26
Arab (0)	10	0.07
Arab (0)	10	0.07
British (3)	10	0.07
Canadian (27)	42	0.31
Czech (38)	97	0.73
Dutch (0)	68	0.51
English (237)	729	5.46
European (11)	14	0.10
French, ex. Basque (0)	117	0.88
French Canadian (0)	10	0.07
German (622)	1,514	11.35
Irish (151)	921	6.90
Italian (0)	91	0.68
Norwegian (47)	74	0.55
Polish (19)	53	0.40

*Notes: † The Census 2010 population figure is used to calculate the percentages in the Hispanic Origin and Race categories. Ancestry percentages are based on the 2006-2010 American Community Survey population (not shown); ‡ Numbers in parentheses indicate the number of people reporting a single ancestry; * Numbers in parentheses indicate the number of persons reporting this race alone, not in combination with any other race; Please refer to the Explanation of Data for more information.*

Russian (1)	2	0.01
Scandinavian (0)	42	0.31
Scotch-Irish (19)	212	1.59
Scottish (30)	298	2.23
Swiss (7)	30	0.22
Welsh (0)	49	0.37
West Indian, ex. Hispanic (4)	4	0.03
Jamaican (4)	4	0.03

Hispanic Origin	Population	%
Hispanic or Latino (of any race)	9,251	71.92
Central American, ex. Mexican	22	0.17
Guatemalan	2	0.02
Honduran	5	0.04
Panamanian	6	0.05
Salvadoran	9	0.07
Cuban	7	0.05
Mexican	7,428	57.75
Puerto Rican	36	0.28
South American	18	0.14
Argentinean	2	0.02
Colombian	10	0.08
Peruvian	2	0.02
Venezuelan	4	0.03
Other Hispanic or Latino	1,740	13.53

Race*	Population	%
African-American/Black (346)	414	3.22
Not Hispanic (301)	325	2.53
Hispanic (45)	89	0.69
American Indian/Alaska Native (95)	171	1.33
Not Hispanic (32)	69	0.54
Hispanic (63)	102	0.79
Apache (8)	15	0.12
Blackfeet (0)	2	0.02
Canadian/French Am. Ind. (0)	1	0.01
Cherokee (9)	16	0.12
Choctaw (1)	2	0.02
Comanche (2)	2	0.02
Cree (0)	1	0.01
Creek (1)	2	0.02
Mexican American Ind. (4)	6	0.05
Navajo (1)	1	0.01
Pueblo (0)	1	0.01
Sioux (6)	7	0.05
Spanish American Ind. (0)	1	0.01
Yup'ik *(Alaska Native)* (1)	1	0.01
Asian (113)	151	1.17
Not Hispanic (109)	132	1.03
Hispanic (4)	19	0.15
Cambodian (1)	1	0.01
Chinese, ex. Taiwanese (14)	16	0.12
Filipino (67)	88	0.68
Indian (7)	17	0.13
Japanese (5)	10	0.08
Korean (4)	4	0.03
Pakistani (1)	1	0.01
Vietnamese (9)	9	0.07
Hawaii Native/Pacific Islander (11)	22	0.17
Not Hispanic (4)	14	0.11
Hispanic (7)	8	0.06
Guamanian/Chamorro (5)	8	0.06
Native Hawaiian (3)	4	0.03
Samoan (1)	1	0.01
White (10,173)	10,560	82.10
Not Hispanic (3,046)	3,141	24.42
Hispanic (7,127)	7,419	57.68

Bellaire

Place Type: City
County: Harris
Population: 16,855†

Ancestry‡	Population	%
African, Sub-Saharan (53)	116	0.70
South African (34)	61	0.37
Other Sub-Saharan African (19)	55	0.33
American (1,153)	1,153	6.97
Arab (82)	111	0.67
Egyptian (31)	60	0.36
Lebanese (51)	51	0.31
Armenian (4)	9	0.05
Australian (0)	21	0.13
Austrian (13)	68	0.41
Basque (0)	17	0.10
Belgian (35)	35	0.21
Brazilian (12)	12	0.07
British (81)	267	1.61
Bulgarian (36)	36	0.22
Cajun (13)	13	0.08
Canadian (58)	58	0.35
Croatian (0)	33	0.20
Czech (115)	201	1.21
Czechoslovakian (12)	31	0.19
Danish (40)	102	0.62
Dutch (28)	191	1.15
Eastern European (180)	207	1.25
English (779)	2,329	14.07
European (261)	288	1.74
Finnish (0)	27	0.16
French, ex. Basque (132)	719	4.34
French Canadian (21)	21	0.13
German (841)	2,774	16.76
Greek (35)	86	0.52
Hungarian (15)	80	0.48
Iranian (10)	31	0.19
Irish (631)	1,768	10.68
Italian (316)	745	4.50
Lithuanian (11)	46	0.28
Northern European (58)	58	0.35
Norwegian (26)	275	1.66
Pennsylvania German (0)	12	0.07
Polish (139)	461	2.79
Portuguese (16)	30	0.18
Romanian (0)	81	0.49
Russian (289)	534	3.23
Scandinavian (11)	22	0.13
Scotch-Irish (132)	544	3.29
Scottish (135)	483	2.92
Serbian (35)	35	0.21
Slovak (0)	33	0.20
Swedish (37)	236	1.43
Swiss (62)	111	0.67
Ukrainian (9)	112	0.68
Welsh (0)	111	0.67
Yugoslavian (0)	10	0.06

Hispanic Origin	Population	%
Hispanic or Latino (of any race)	1,595	9.46
Central American, ex. Mexican	99	0.59
Costa Rican	8	0.05
Guatemalan	22	0.13
Honduran	20	0.12
Nicaraguan	14	0.08
Panamanian	12	0.07
Salvadoran	23	0.14
Cuban	100	0.59
Dominican Republic	7	0.04
Mexican	880	5.22
Puerto Rican	70	0.42
South American	284	1.68
Argentinean	61	0.36
Bolivian	13	0.08
Chilean	10	0.06
Colombian	87	0.52
Ecuadorian	26	0.15
Paraguayan	6	0.04
Peruvian	32	0.19
Uruguayan	13	0.08
Venezuelan	33	0.20
Other South American	3	0.02
Other Hispanic or Latino	155	0.92

Race*	Population	%
African-American/Black (277)	339	2.01
Not Hispanic (274)	324	1.92
Hispanic (3)	15	0.09
American Indian/Alaska Native (40)	109	0.65
Not Hispanic (23)	89	0.53
Hispanic (17)	20	0.12
Central American Ind. (0)	1	0.01
Cherokee (3)	22	0.13
Chickasaw (3)	3	0.02
Choctaw (6)	18	0.11
Crow (0)	1	0.01
Mexican American Ind. (3)	3	0.02
Seminole (4)	4	0.02
South American Ind. (0)	2	0.01
Asian (2,384)	2,627	15.59
Not Hispanic (2,374)	2,593	15.38
Hispanic (10)	34	0.20
Burmese (2)	2	0.01
Cambodian (1)	4	0.02
Chinese, ex. Taiwanese (1,073)	1,189	7.05
Filipino (77)	115	0.68
Indian (527)	568	3.37
Indonesian (15)	19	0.11
Japanese (34)	63	0.37
Korean (118)	162	0.96
Laotian (1)	2	0.01
Malaysian (1)	1	0.01
Pakistani (59)	65	0.39
Sri Lankan (1)	2	0.01
Taiwanese (162)	182	1.08
Thai (11)	18	0.11
Vietnamese (215)	256	1.52
Hawaii Native/Pacific Islander (2)	19	0.11
Not Hispanic (1)	15	0.09
Hispanic (1)	4	0.02
Fijian (1)	1	0.01
Guamanian/Chamorro (1)	1	0.01
Native Hawaiian (0)	5	0.03
White (13,483)	13,817	81.98
Not Hispanic (12,242)	12,510	74.22
Hispanic (1,241)	1,307	7.75

Bellmead

Place Type: City
County: McLennan
Population: 9,901†

Ancestry‡	Population	%
American (1,434)	1,434	14.73
Arab (0)	7	0.07
Lebanese (0)	7	0.07
Australian (7)	7	0.07
Czech (117)	234	2.40
Czechoslovakian (36)	45	0.46
Dutch (67)	113	1.16
English (135)	396	4.07
French, ex. Basque (21)	36	0.37
French Canadian (0)	31	0.32
German (737)	1,281	13.16
Irish (172)	765	7.86
Italian (0)	64	0.66
Polish (25)	25	0.26
Russian (0)	32	0.33
Scotch-Irish (24)	107	1.10
Scottish (12)	77	0.79
Swedish (16)	63	0.65
Welsh (8)	8	0.08
West Indian, ex. Hispanic (22)	22	0.23
Dutch West Indian (22)	22	0.23

Hispanic Origin	Population	%
Hispanic or Latino (of any race)	3,742	37.79
Central American, ex. Mexican	44	0.44
Honduran	1	0.01
Nicaraguan	17	0.17
Panamanian	1	0.01
Salvadoran	25	0.25
Mexican	3,389	34.23
Puerto Rican	34	0.34
South American	3	0.03
Ecuadorian	1	0.01
Venezuelan	1	0.01
Other South American	1	0.01
Other Hispanic or Latino	272	2.75

SECTION TWO

*Notes: † The Census 2010 population figure is used to calculate the percentages in the Hispanic Origin and Race categories. Ancestry percentages are based on the 2006-2010 American Community Survey population (not shown); ‡ Numbers in parentheses indicate the number of people reporting a single ancestry; * Numbers in parentheses indicate the number of persons reporting this race alone, not in combination with any other race; Please refer to the Explanation of Data for more information.*

Race*	Population	%
African-American/Black (1,735)	1,854	18.73
Not Hispanic (1,703)	1,791	18.09
Hispanic (32)	63	0.64
American Indian/Alaska Native (98)	164	1.66
Not Hispanic (35)	85	0.86
Hispanic (63)	79	0.80
Apache (3)	3	0.03
Blackfeet (0)	1	0.01
Central American Ind. (0)	1	0.01
Cherokee (7)	19	0.19
Choctaw (7)	9	0.09
Comanche (1)	2	0.02
Creek (0)	4	0.04
Delaware (0)	1	0.01
Iroquois (0)	2	0.02
Mexican American Ind. (8)	14	0.14
Pueblo (4)	4	0.04
Asian (67)	96	0.97
Not Hispanic (63)	78	0.79
Hispanic (4)	18	0.18
Cambodian (1)	3	0.03
Chinese, ex. Taiwanese (15)	16	0.16
Filipino (7)	9	0.09
Indian (21)	27	0.27
Japanese (2)	3	0.03
Korean (4)	10	0.10
Vietnamese (16)	17	0.17
Hawaii Native/Pacific Islander (0)	13	0.13
Not Hispanic (0)	5	0.05
Hispanic (0)	8	0.08
Native Hawaiian (0)	5	0.05
White (5,594)	5,844	59.02
Not Hispanic (4,204)	4,339	43.82
Hispanic (1,390)	1,505	15.20

Belton

Place Type: City
County: Bell
Population: 18,216†

Ancestry‡	Population	%
African, Sub-Saharan (48)	48	0.27
African (31)	31	0.17
Ethiopian (17)	17	0.10
American (1,242)	1,242	6.96
Arab (61)	61	0.34
Arab (51)	51	0.29
Syrian (10)	10	0.06
Australian (22)	42	0.24
Austrian (0)	17	0.10
British (44)	128	0.72
Cajun (0)	19	0.11
Canadian (0)	30	0.17
Czech (139)	244	1.37
Czechoslovakian (11)	11	0.06
Dutch (28)	119	0.67
English (1,740)	2,664	14.93
European (127)	127	0.71
French, ex. Basque (115)	383	2.15
French Canadian (16)	72	0.40
German (1,213)	2,888	16.18
Greek (21)	48	0.27
Hungarian (20)	20	0.11
Irish (694)	1,924	10.78
Italian (138)	383	2.15
New Zealander (0)	17	0.10
Northern European (7)	7	0.04
Norwegian (0)	8	0.04
Pennsylvania German (10)	10	0.06
Polish (89)	129	0.72
Portuguese (10)	10	0.06
Russian (57)	57	0.32
Scandinavian (12)	24	0.13
Scotch-Irish (208)	559	3.13
Scottish (138)	417	2.34
Swedish (22)	51	0.29
Swiss (0)	30	0.17
Turkish (72)	72	0.40
Ukrainian (0)	14	0.08
Welsh (13)	85	0.48
West Indian, ex. Hispanic (5)	5	0.03
Jamaican (5)	5	0.03
Yugoslavian (20)	20	0.11

Hispanic Origin	Population	%
Hispanic or Latino (of any race)	5,293	29.06
Central American, ex. Mexican	74	0.41
Costa Rican	5	0.03
Guatemalan	38	0.21
Honduran	7	0.04
Nicaraguan	1	0.01
Panamanian	5	0.03
Salvadoran	18	0.10
Cuban	15	0.08
Dominican Republic	10	0.05
Mexican	4,668	25.63
Puerto Rican	140	0.77
South American	32	0.18
Argentinean	2	0.01
Bolivian	1	0.01
Chilean	1	0.01
Colombian	16	0.09
Ecuadorian	1	0.01
Peruvian	8	0.04
Uruguayan	1	0.01
Venezuelan	2	0.01
Other Hispanic or Latino	354	1.94

Race*	Population	%
African-American/Black (1,476)	1,687	9.26
Not Hispanic (1,394)	1,569	8.61
Hispanic (82)	118	0.65
American Indian/Alaska Native (158)	277	1.52
Not Hispanic (84)	169	0.93
Hispanic (74)	108	0.59
Apache (0)	11	0.06
Arapaho (0)	1	0.01
Blackfeet (1)	6	0.03
Cherokee (13)	40	0.22
Cheyenne (0)	1	0.01
Chickasaw (4)	4	0.02
Chippewa (2)	3	0.02
Choctaw (9)	20	0.11
Comanche (2)	4	0.02
Creek (6)	9	0.05
Menominee (0)	1	0.01
Mexican American Ind. (7)	7	0.04
Navajo (2)	3	0.02
Potawatomi (0)	2	0.01
Seminole (1)	1	0.01
Sioux (6)	9	0.05
Spanish American Ind. (1)	1	0.01
Yakama (1)	1	0.01
Yaqui (1)	1	0.01
Asian (292)	380	2.09
Not Hispanic (283)	352	1.93
Hispanic (9)	28	0.15
Burmese (5)	5	0.03
Chinese, ex. Taiwanese (49)	62	0.34
Filipino (49)	68	0.37
Indian (80)	84	0.46
Indonesian (1)	2	0.01
Japanese (4)	18	0.10
Korean (54)	82	0.45
Pakistani (6)	6	0.03
Sri Lankan (4)	4	0.02
Thai (2)	7	0.04
Vietnamese (25)	34	0.19
Hawaii Native/Pacific Islander (35)	70	0.38
Not Hispanic (27)	49	0.27
Hispanic (8)	21	0.12
Guamanian/Chamorro (25)	41	0.23
Native Hawaiian (4)	11	0.06
Samoan (4)	6	0.03
White (13,564)	14,026	77.00
Not Hispanic (10,816)	11,087	60.86
Hispanic (2,748)	2,939	16.13

Benbrook

Place Type: City
County: Tarrant
Population: 21,234†

Ancestry‡	Population	%
African, Sub-Saharan (74)	74	0.35
African (74)	74	0.35
Albanian (125)	125	0.59
American (2,846)	2,846	13.52
Arab (89)	99	0.47
Lebanese (0)	10	0.05
Palestinian (8)	8	0.04
Syrian (81)	81	0.38
Australian (11)	11	0.05
Austrian (42)	63	0.30
British (127)	187	0.89
Canadian (14)	38	0.18
Czech (60)	98	0.47
Czechoslovakian (34)	45	0.21
Danish (18)	42	0.20
Dutch (156)	502	2.39
English (1,286)	2,894	13.75
European (414)	426	2.02
Finnish (55)	146	0.69
French, ex. Basque (114)	602	2.86
French Canadian (55)	65	0.31
German (1,252)	3,287	15.62
Hungarian (18)	48	0.23
Iranian (12)	12	0.06
Irish (891)	2,425	11.52
Italian (240)	474	2.25
Luxemburger (6)	6	0.03
Northern European (75)	75	0.36
Norwegian (113)	265	1.26
Pennsylvania German (0)	9	0.04
Polish (101)	290	1.38
Romanian (41)	41	0.19
Russian (10)	56	0.27
Scandinavian (38)	45	0.21
Scotch-Irish (313)	851	4.04
Scottish (188)	440	2.09
Slavic (0)	9	0.04
Slovene (10)	20	0.10
Swedish (123)	284	1.35
Swiss (0)	68	0.32
Ukrainian (30)	52	0.25
Welsh (44)	91	0.43
West Indian, ex. Hispanic (0)	43	0.20
Dutch West Indian (0)	37	0.18
Trinidadian/Tobagonian (0)	6	0.03

Hispanic Origin	Population	%
Hispanic or Latino (of any race)	2,373	11.18
Central American, ex. Mexican	66	0.31
Guatemalan	13	0.06
Honduran	7	0.03
Nicaraguan	24	0.11
Panamanian	7	0.03
Salvadoran	14	0.07
Other Central American	1	<0.01
Cuban	42	0.20
Dominican Republic	2	0.01
Mexican	1,960	9.23
Puerto Rican	63	0.30
South American	59	0.28
Argentinean	4	0.02
Chilean	2	0.01
Colombian	30	0.14
Ecuadorian	2	0.01
Peruvian	11	0.05
Uruguayan	2	0.01
Venezuelan	8	0.04
Other Hispanic or Latino	181	0.85

Race*	Population	%
African-American/Black (1,130)	1,270	5.98
Not Hispanic (1,085)	1,198	5.64
Hispanic (45)	72	0.34

*Notes: † The Census 2010 population figure is used to calculate the percentages in the Hispanic Origin and Race categories. Ancestry percentages are based on the 2006-2010 American Community Survey population (not shown); ‡ Numbers in parentheses indicate the number of people reporting a single ancestry; * Numbers in parentheses indicate the number of persons reporting this race alone, not in combination with any other race; Please refer to the Explanation of Data for more information.*

American Indian/Alaska Native (126)	259	1.22
Not Hispanic (107)	221	1.04
Hispanic (19)	38	0.18
Apache (1)	2	0.01
Blackfeet (2)	4	0.02
Cherokee (29)	62	0.29
Chickasaw (7)	11	0.05
Chippewa (1)	1	<0.01
Choctaw (26)	40	0.19
Comanche (1)	7	0.03
Creek (7)	7	0.03
Delaware (0)	1	<0.01
Hopi (0)	2	0.01
Mexican American Ind. (2)	5	0.02
Navajo (0)	3	0.01
Osage (1)	1	<0.01
Ottawa (2)	2	0.01
Potawatomi (2)	4	0.02
Pueblo (2)	4	0.02
Sioux (1)	2	0.01
South American Ind. (0)	1	<0.01
Tohono O'Odham (1)	1	<0.01
Asian (409)	535	2.52
Not Hispanic (393)	507	2.39
Hispanic (16)	28	0.13
Bangladeshi (1)	1	<0.01
Burmese (0)	2	0.01
Cambodian (6)	9	0.04
Chinese, ex. Taiwanese (52)	73	0.34
Filipino (71)	97	0.46
Hmong (1)	1	<0.01
Indian (88)	97	0.46
Indonesian (1)	1	<0.01
Japanese (21)	47	0.22
Korean (77)	101	0.48
Laotian (1)	1	<0.01
Malaysian (1)	1	<0.01
Nepalese (12)	12	0.06
Pakistani (8)	9	0.04
Sri Lankan (1)	3	0.01
Taiwanese (11)	13	0.06
Thai (18)	25	0.12
Vietnamese (18)	36	0.17
Hawaii Native/Pacific Islander (15)	40	0.19
Not Hispanic (13)	26	0.12
Hispanic (2)	14	0.07
Guamanian/Chamorro (7)	21	0.10
Native Hawaiian (4)	10	0.05
Samoan (3)	3	0.01
White (18,423)	18,844	88.74
Not Hispanic (16,931)	17,223	81.11
Hispanic (1,492)	1,621	7.63

Big Spring

Place Type: City
County: Howard
Population: 27,282†

Ancestry‡	Population	%
African, Sub-Saharan (124)	124	0.47
African (87)	87	0.33
Nigerian (18)	18	0.07
Somalian (9)	9	0.03
Other Sub-Saharan African (10)	10	0.04
American (1,244)	1,244	4.68
Arab (43)	52	0.20
Arab (15)	15	0.06
Lebanese (28)	37	0.14
Armenian (8)	8	0.03
British (44)	59	0.22
Bulgarian (0)	59	0.22
Cajun (6)	6	0.02
Canadian (20)	20	0.08
Czech (49)	94	0.35
Czechoslovakian (110)	110	0.41
Danish (14)	123	0.46
Dutch (42)	191	0.72
English (858)	1,745	6.57
European (43)	86	0.32
Finnish (0)	13	0.05
French, ex. Basque (149)	484	1.82
French Canadian (30)	30	0.11
German (703)	2,228	8.39
Greek (0)	23	0.09
Hungarian (10)	10	0.04
Irish (975)	2,505	9.43
Israeli (11)	11	0.04
Italian (19)	184	0.69
Lithuanian (23)	23	0.09
Macedonian (0)	27	0.10
Norwegian (22)	44	0.17
Pennsylvania German (0)	7	0.03
Polish (22)	104	0.39
Russian (0)	19	0.07
Scandinavian (6)	6	0.02
Scotch-Irish (173)	354	1.33
Scottish (239)	508	1.91
Slavic (35)	35	0.13
Swedish (20)	75	0.28
Ukrainian (237)	237	0.89
Welsh (47)	58	0.22
West Indian, ex. Hispanic (39)	150	0.56
Belizean (9)	9	0.03
Dutch West Indian (0)	111	0.42
Haitian (11)	11	0.04
Jamaican (9)	9	0.03
West Indian (10)	10	0.04

Hispanic Origin	Population	%
Hispanic or Latino (of any race)	11,751	43.07
Central American, ex. Mexican	36	0.13
Costa Rican	5	0.02
Guatemalan	5	0.02
Honduran	5	0.02
Nicaraguan	16	0.06
Panamanian	1	<0.01
Salvadoran	4	0.01
Cuban	22	0.08
Dominican Republic	3	0.01
Mexican	8,291	30.39
Puerto Rican	71	0.26
South American	15	0.05
Argentinean	3	0.01
Bolivian	2	0.01
Colombian	4	0.01
Peruvian	2	0.01
Uruguayan	2	0.01
Venezuelan	2	0.01
Other Hispanic or Latino	3,313	12.14

Race*	Population	%
African-American/Black (2,123)	2,335	8.56
Not Hispanic (2,030)	2,155	7.90
Hispanic (93)	180	0.66
American Indian/Alaska Native (246)	384	1.41
Not Hispanic (173)	245	0.90
Hispanic (73)	139	0.51
Apache (13)	16	0.06
Blackfeet (2)	2	0.01
Central American Ind. (0)	1	<0.01
Cherokee (27)	58	0.21
Cheyenne (0)	5	0.02
Chickasaw (13)	14	0.05
Chippewa (1)	2	0.01
Choctaw (11)	14	0.05
Comanche (4)	4	0.01
Creek (8)	11	0.04
Menominee (2)	2	0.01
Mexican American Ind. (15)	19	0.07
Navajo (7)	11	0.04
Pima (2)	3	0.01
Seminole (0)	3	0.01
Shoshone (1)	1	<0.01
Sioux (7)	11	0.04
Ute (0)	1	<0.01
Asian (248)	331	1.21
Not Hispanic (237)	297	1.09
Hispanic (11)	34	0.12
Burmese (1)	1	<0.01
Cambodian (1)	2	0.01
Chinese, ex. Taiwanese (42)	65	0.24
Filipino (34)	51	0.19
Hmong (1)	1	<0.01
Indian (39)	48	0.18
Japanese (4)	12	0.04
Korean (8)	19	0.07
Laotian (1)	1	<0.01
Pakistani (5)	5	0.02
Taiwanese (4)	4	0.01
Thai (3)	3	0.01
Vietnamese (18)	22	0.08
Hawaii Native/Pacific Islander (11)	49	0.18
Not Hispanic (9)	31	0.11
Hispanic (2)	18	0.07
Guamanian/Chamorro (0)	1	<0.01
Native Hawaiian (1)	33	0.12
Samoan (0)	16	0.06
Tongan (5)	17	0.06
White (19,013)	19,525	71.57
Not Hispanic (12,742)	12,973	47.55
Hispanic (6,271)	6,552	24.02

Boerne

Place Type: City
County: Kendall
Population: 10,471†

Ancestry‡	Population	%
Alsatian (0)	58	0.60
American (374)	374	3.87
Arab (14)	59	0.61
Lebanese (14)	59	0.61
Belgian (10)	10	0.10
British (43)	105	1.09
Canadian (13)	13	0.13
Czech (14)	43	0.44
Czechoslovakian (0)	27	0.28
Danish (0)	12	0.12
Dutch (10)	137	1.42
English (815)	1,634	16.91
European (33)	54	0.56
Finnish (0)	9	0.09
French, ex. Basque (53)	324	3.35
French Canadian (27)	116	1.20
German (1,183)	2,886	29.86
Greek (16)	16	0.17
Hungarian (0)	9	0.09
Irish (226)	1,413	14.62
Italian (94)	239	2.47
Lithuanian (7)	7	0.07
Norwegian (64)	122	1.26
Polish (135)	290	3.00
Russian (51)	69	0.71
Scandinavian (0)	11	0.11
Scotch-Irish (31)	224	2.32
Scottish (218)	386	3.99
Swedish (43)	226	2.34
Swiss (13)	46	0.48
Welsh (31)	41	0.42

Hispanic Origin	Population	%
Hispanic or Latino (of any race)	2,381	22.74
Central American, ex. Mexican	138	1.32
Costa Rican	1	0.01
Guatemalan	81	0.77
Honduran	18	0.17
Nicaraguan	14	0.13
Panamanian	3	0.03
Salvadoran	20	0.19
Other Central American	1	0.01
Cuban	11	0.11
Dominican Republic	4	0.04
Mexican	2,003	19.13
Puerto Rican	56	0.53
South American	10	0.10
Argentinean	2	0.02
Colombian	3	0.03
Peruvian	4	0.04

*Notes: † The Census 2010 population figure is used to calculate the percentages in the Hispanic Origin and Race categories. Ancestry percentages are based on the 2006-2010 American Community Survey population (not shown); ‡ Numbers in parentheses indicate the number of people reporting a single ancestry; * Numbers in parentheses indicate the number of persons reporting this race alone, not in combination with any other race; Please refer to the Explanation of Data for more information.*

Venezuelan	1	0.01
Other Hispanic or Latino	159	1.52

Race*	Population	%
African-American/Black (61)	88	0.84
Not Hispanic (53)	69	0.66
Hispanic (8)	19	0.18
American Indian/Alaska Native (39)	99	0.95
Not Hispanic (28)	83	0.79
Hispanic (11)	16	0.15
Apache (2)	2	0.02
Blackfeet (1)	6	0.06
Cherokee (6)	27	0.26
Chickasaw (3)	5	0.05
Choctaw (2)	5	0.05
Comanche (2)	2	0.02
Creek (2)	2	0.02
Houma (1)	1	0.01
Mexican American Ind. (2)	3	0.03
Navajo (0)	3	0.03
Osage (1)	1	0.01
Sioux (2)	2	0.02
Tlingit-Haida *(Alaska Native)* (0)	2	0.02
Asian (85)	129	1.23
Not Hispanic (80)	118	1.13
Hispanic (5)	11	0.11
Cambodian (3)	3	0.03
Chinese, ex. Taiwanese (10)	11	0.11
Filipino (18)	37	0.35
Indian (13)	13	0.12
Japanese (8)	17	0.16
Korean (4)	9	0.09
Pakistani (0)	1	0.01
Sri Lankan (7)	7	0.07
Thai (3)	3	0.03
Vietnamese (16)	17	0.16
Hawaii Native/Pacific Islander (10)	12	0.11
Not Hispanic (6)	8	0.08
Hispanic (4)	4	0.04
Guamanian/Chamorro (5)	5	0.05
Native Hawaiian (2)	4	0.04
White (9,455)	9,626	91.93
Not Hispanic (7,807)	7,913	75.57
Hispanic (1,648)	1,713	16.36

Bonham

Place Type: City
County: Fannin
Population: 10,127†

Ancestry‡	Population	%
African, Sub-Saharan (77)	129	1.26
African (77)	129	1.26
American (1,042)	1,042	10.21
Austrian (0)	148	1.45
British (7)	22	0.22
Cajun (0)	13	0.13
Czech (2)	20	0.20
Danish (0)	9	0.09
Dutch (12)	32	0.31
English (248)	602	5.90
European (90)	90	0.88
Finnish (0)	8	0.08
French, ex. Basque (40)	320	3.13
German (417)	1,370	13.42
Irish (549)	944	9.25
Italian (59)	114	1.12
Norwegian (2)	13	0.13
Polish (0)	18	0.18
Russian (0)	11	0.11
Scotch-Irish (197)	233	2.28
Scottish (13)	81	0.79
Swedish (62)	88	0.86
West Indian, ex. Hispanic (0)	16	0.16
Dutch West Indian (0)	16	0.16

Hispanic Origin	Population	%
Hispanic or Latino (of any race)	1,560	15.40
Central American, ex. Mexican	32	0.32
Costa Rican	3	0.03
Honduran	21	0.21
Panamanian	2	0.02
Salvadoran	2	0.02
Other Central American	4	0.04
Cuban	6	0.06
Mexican	915	9.04
Puerto Rican	19	0.19
South American	1	0.01
Colombian	1	0.01
Other Hispanic or Latino	587	5.80

Race*	Population	%
African-American/Black (1,500)	1,564	15.44
Not Hispanic (1,472)	1,534	15.15
Hispanic (28)	30	0.30
American Indian/Alaska Native (98)	161	1.59
Not Hispanic (73)	128	1.26
Hispanic (25)	33	0.33
Apache (3)	7	0.07
Arapaho (1)	1	0.01
Blackfeet (0)	2	0.02
Cherokee (13)	29	0.29
Cheyenne (1)	1	0.01
Chickasaw (2)	4	0.04
Chippewa (1)	1	0.01
Choctaw (21)	40	0.39
Comanche (1)	4	0.04
Creek (0)	2	0.02
Iroquois (0)	1	0.01
Mexican American Ind. (6)	7	0.07
Navajo (2)	2	0.02
Potawatomi (1)	1	0.01
Sioux (0)	3	0.03
Yuman (1)	1	0.01
Yup'ik *(Alaska Native)* (1)	1	0.01
Asian (45)	70	0.69
Not Hispanic (43)	65	0.64
Hispanic (2)	5	0.05
Cambodian (2)	2	0.02
Chinese, ex. Taiwanese (2)	5	0.05
Filipino (7)	19	0.19
Indian (6)	10	0.10
Japanese (2)	6	0.06
Korean (4)	5	0.05
Thai (2)	3	0.03
Vietnamese (5)	6	0.06
Hawaii Native/Pacific Islander (1)	7	0.07
Not Hispanic (0)	3	0.03
Hispanic (1)	4	0.04
Guamanian/Chamorro (1)	4	0.04
Native Hawaiian (0)	2	0.02
White (7,635)	7,805	77.07
Not Hispanic (6,831)	6,969	68.82
Hispanic (804)	836	8.26

Borger

Place Type: City
County: Hutchinson
Population: 13,251†

Ancestry‡	Population	%
African, Sub-Saharan (8)	28	0.21
African (8)	28	0.21
Albanian (39)	39	0.30
American (889)	889	6.73
Arab (9)	9	0.07
Other Arab (9)	9	0.07
Austrian (15)	26	0.20
Belgian (19)	19	0.14
British (10)	18	0.14
Canadian (0)	10	0.08
Czech (24)	76	0.57
Danish (9)	9	0.07
Dutch (17)	142	1.07
English (641)	1,457	11.02
European (78)	78	0.59
French, ex. Basque (36)	354	2.68
French Canadian (0)	48	0.36
German (647)	1,441	10.90
Greek (9)	9	0.07
Hungarian (0)	23	0.17
Irish (718)	2,166	16.39
Italian (31)	85	0.64
Norwegian (34)	69	0.52
Polish (13)	101	0.76
Romanian (0)	46	0.35
Russian (10)	10	0.08
Scandinavian (0)	13	0.10
Scotch-Irish (72)	256	1.94
Scottish (71)	159	1.20
Swedish (14)	37	0.28
Swiss (0)	14	0.11
Welsh (37)	72	0.54
West Indian, ex. Hispanic (60)	80	0.61
Dutch West Indian (60)	80	0.61
Yugoslavian (0)	11	0.08

Hispanic Origin	Population	%
Hispanic or Latino (of any race)	3,616	27.29
Central American, ex. Mexican	22	0.17
Honduran	12	0.09
Panamanian	1	0.01
Salvadoran	9	0.07
Cuban	5	0.04
Mexican	3,255	24.56
Puerto Rican	19	0.14
South American	20	0.15
Argentinean	1	0.01
Colombian	4	0.03
Peruvian	2	0.02
Venezuelan	13	0.10
Other Hispanic or Latino	295	2.23

Race*	Population	%
African-American/Black (479)	571	4.31
Not Hispanic (439)	511	3.86
Hispanic (40)	60	0.45
American Indian/Alaska Native (231)	403	3.04
Not Hispanic (178)	305	2.30
Hispanic (53)	98	0.74
Aleut *(Alaska Native)* (1)	1	0.01
Apache (0)	18	0.14
Arapaho (1)	1	0.01
Blackfeet (1)	2	0.02
Canadian/French Am. Ind. (0)	5	0.04
Cherokee (62)	117	0.88
Chickasaw (8)	17	0.13
Chippewa (1)	1	0.01
Choctaw (56)	82	0.62
Comanche (4)	5	0.04
Creek (1)	2	0.02
Delaware (2)	4	0.03
Hopi (0)	1	0.01
Iroquois (3)	4	0.03
Lumbee (0)	1	0.01
Mexican American Ind. (9)	18	0.14
Navajo (4)	5	0.04
Osage (4)	8	0.06
Pima (0)	1	0.01
Potawatomi (6)	10	0.08
Seminole (3)	3	0.02
Sioux (3)	6	0.05
Spanish American Ind. (4)	5	0.04
Yaqui (0)	1	0.01
Asian (64)	92	0.69
Not Hispanic (64)	83	0.63
Hispanic (0)	9	0.07
Chinese, ex. Taiwanese (8)	10	0.08
Filipino (22)	29	0.22
Indian (13)	14	0.11
Japanese (6)	9	0.07
Korean (6)	14	0.11
Vietnamese (6)	6	0.05
Hawaii Native/Pacific Islander (5)	20	0.15
Not Hispanic (3)	9	0.07
Hispanic (2)	11	0.08
Guamanian/Chamorro (2)	7	0.05
Native Hawaiian (1)	3	0.02

*Notes: † The Census 2010 population figure is used to calculate the percentages in the Hispanic Origin and Race categories. Ancestry percentages are based on the 2006-2010 American Community Survey population (not shown); ‡ Numbers in parentheses indicate the number of people reporting a single ancestry; * Numbers in parentheses indicate the number of persons reporting this race alone, not in combination with any other race; Please refer to the Explanation of Data for more information.*

	Population	%
White (10,675)	11,069	83.53
Not Hispanic (8,715)	8,931	67.40
Hispanic (1,960)	2,138	16.13

Brenham

Place Type: City
County: Washington
Population: 15,716†

Ancestry‡	Population	%
African, Sub-Saharan (31)	80	0.52
African (16)	65	0.42
Nigerian (15)	15	0.10
American (491)	491	3.20
Arab (0)	11	0.07
Syrian (0)	11	0.07
Australian (0)	41	0.27
Austrian (20)	20	0.13
Belgian (11)	11	0.07
Bulgarian (9)	9	0.06
Czech (78)	299	1.95
Czechoslovakian (10)	10	0.07
Danish (10)	100	0.65
Dutch (10)	98	0.64
English (309)	957	6.23
European (36)	36	0.23
French, ex. Basque (35)	167	1.09
French Canadian (8)	14	0.09
German (1,795)	2,846	18.53
Greek (22)	80	0.52
Irish (262)	934	6.08
Italian (66)	317	2.06
Norwegian (14)	14	0.09
Polish (298)	404	2.63
Russian (0)	15	0.10
Scotch-Irish (164)	247	1.61
Scottish (89)	268	1.75
Swedish (33)	99	0.64
Swiss (0)	11	0.07
Ukrainian (0)	21	0.14
Welsh (0)	73	0.48
West Indian, ex. Hispanic (36)	49	0.32
Dutch West Indian (15)	28	0.18
Trinidadian/Tobagonian (21)	21	0.14

Hispanic Origin	Population	%
Hispanic or Latino (of any race)	2,397	15.25
Central American, ex. Mexican	148	0.94
Costa Rican	1	0.01
Guatemalan	15	0.10
Honduran	55	0.35
Nicaraguan	4	0.03
Salvadoran	73	0.46
Cuban	17	0.11
Dominican Republic	1	0.01
Mexican	1,951	12.41
Puerto Rican	37	0.24
South American	24	0.15
Argentinean	8	0.05
Chilean	1	0.01
Colombian	7	0.04
Peruvian	4	0.03
Venezuelan	4	0.03
Other Hispanic or Latino	219	1.39

Race*	Population	%
African-American/Black (3,724)	3,866	24.60
Not Hispanic (3,656)	3,751	23.87
Hispanic (68)	115	0.73
American Indian/Alaska Native (46)	101	0.64
Not Hispanic (27)	75	0.48
Hispanic (19)	26	0.17
Aleut *(Alaska Native)* (1)	1	0.01
Apache (0)	1	0.01
Blackfeet (0)	1	0.01
Cherokee (3)	17	0.11
Chickasaw (0)	1	0.01
Chippewa (0)	1	0.01
Choctaw (6)	7	0.04
Creek (1)	1	0.01
Inupiat *(Alaska Native)* (0)	1	0.01
Lumbee (2)	2	0.01
Mexican American Ind. (1)	1	0.01
Osage (1)	2	0.01
Potawatomi (1)	1	0.01
Seminole (0)	5	0.03
Sioux (0)	1	0.01
South American Ind. (0)	1	0.01
Spanish American Ind. (1)	1	0.01
Asian (289)	327	2.08
Not Hispanic (277)	302	1.92
Hispanic (12)	25	0.16
Bangladeshi (5)	8	0.05
Cambodian (11)	11	0.07
Chinese, ex. Taiwanese (8)	15	0.10
Filipino (31)	38	0.24
Indian (34)	47	0.30
Japanese (3)	5	0.03
Korean (4)	5	0.03
Laotian (2)	9	0.06
Pakistani (5)	5	0.03
Sri Lankan (1)	1	0.01
Taiwanese (2)	4	0.03
Thai (4)	4	0.03
Vietnamese (163)	169	1.08
Hawaii Native/Pacific Islander (7)	22	0.14
Not Hispanic (6)	16	0.10
Hispanic (1)	6	0.04
Fijian (0)	1	0.01
Guamanian/Chamorro (3)	5	0.03
Native Hawaiian (2)	6	0.04
Samoan (1)	2	0.01
White (10,468)	10,680	67.96
Not Hispanic (9,186)	9,309	59.23
Hispanic (1,282)	1,371	8.72

Bridge City

Place Type: City
County: Orange
Population: 7,840†

Ancestry‡	Population	%
American (726)	726	9.12
Brazilian (4)	4	0.05
British (0)	85	1.07
Cajun (101)	134	1.68
Canadian (0)	24	0.30
Czech (0)	7	0.09
Czechoslovakian (6)	6	0.08
Dutch (103)	363	4.56
English (318)	656	8.24
French, ex. Basque (609)	1,384	17.38
French Canadian (407)	552	6.93
German (273)	714	8.97
Irish (548)	1,425	17.90
Italian (95)	285	3.58
Lithuanian (0)	15	0.19
Polish (12)	12	0.15
Romanian (21)	21	0.26
Russian (0)	64	0.80
Scandinavian (0)	10	0.13
Scotch-Irish (54)	114	1.43
Scottish (42)	126	1.58
Swedish (0)	37	0.46
Swiss (15)	15	0.19
Ukrainian (24)	24	0.30

Hispanic Origin	Population	%
Hispanic or Latino (of any race)	556	7.09
Central American, ex. Mexican	27	0.34
Guatemalan	6	0.08
Honduran	8	0.10
Nicaraguan	6	0.08
Panamanian	1	0.01
Salvadoran	6	0.08
Cuban	5	0.06
Dominican Republic	1	0.01
Mexican	462	5.89
Puerto Rican	9	0.11
South American	5	0.06
Chilean	2	0.03
Peruvian	3	0.04
Other Hispanic or Latino	47	0.60

Race*	Population	%
African-American/Black (26)	40	0.51
Not Hispanic (20)	34	0.43
Hispanic (6)	6	0.08
American Indian/Alaska Native (35)	88	1.12
Not Hispanic (22)	74	0.94
Hispanic (13)	14	0.18
Apache (3)	4	0.05
Blackfeet (0)	3	0.04
Cherokee (4)	21	0.27
Cheyenne (0)	1	0.01
Chickasaw (0)	1	0.01
Chippewa (0)	1	0.01
Choctaw (8)	16	0.20
Comanche (2)	3	0.04
Creek (0)	1	0.01
Delaware (0)	3	0.04
Iroquois (1)	2	0.03
Navajo (0)	1	0.01
Osage (0)	1	0.01
Spanish American Ind. (2)	2	0.03
Asian (154)	195	2.49
Not Hispanic (154)	189	2.41
Hispanic (0)	6	0.08
Cambodian (7)	9	0.11
Chinese, ex. Taiwanese (9)	9	0.11
Filipino (16)	39	0.50
Indian (12)	18	0.23
Japanese (8)	16	0.20
Korean (1)	1	0.01
Pakistani (5)	5	0.06
Sri Lankan (0)	1	0.01
Vietnamese (85)	92	1.17
Hawaii Native/Pacific Islander (0)	9	0.11
Not Hispanic (0)	7	0.09
Hispanic (0)	2	0.03
Native Hawaiian (0)	4	0.05
White (7,284)	7,430	94.77
Not Hispanic (6,982)	7,079	90.29
Hispanic (302)	351	4.48

Brownfield

Place Type: City
County: Terry
Population: 9,657†

Ancestry‡	Population	%
American (618)	618	6.51
British (35)	35	0.37
Dutch (8)	136	1.43
English (241)	498	5.24
European (111)	111	1.17
French, ex. Basque (31)	63	0.66
German (241)	477	5.02
Greek (0)	10	0.11
Irish (218)	419	4.41
Italian (93)	116	1.22
Norwegian (23)	53	0.56
Scotch-Irish (106)	306	3.22
Scottish (15)	48	0.51
Swedish (0)	16	0.17
Welsh (0)	8	0.08
West Indian, ex. Hispanic (15)	46	0.48
Dutch West Indian (0)	31	0.33
Jamaican (15)	15	0.16

Hispanic Origin	Population	%
Hispanic or Latino (of any race)	5,010	51.88
Central American, ex. Mexican	10	0.10
Guatemalan	3	0.03
Honduran	5	0.05
Salvadoran	2	0.02
Cuban	7	0.07

*Notes: † The Census 2010 population figure is used to calculate the percentages in the Hispanic Origin and Race categories. Ancestry percentages are based on the 2006-2010 American Community Survey population (not shown); ‡ Numbers in parentheses indicate the number of people reporting a single ancestry; * Numbers in parentheses indicate the number of persons reporting this race alone, not in combination with any other race; Please refer to the Explanation of Data for more information.*

Dominican Republic	2	0.02
Mexican	4,296	44.49
Puerto Rican	15	0.16
South American	2	0.02
Colombian	2	0.02
Other Hispanic or Latino	678	7.02

Race*	Population	%
African-American/Black (578)	627	6.49
Not Hispanic (540)	571	5.91
Hispanic (38)	56	0.58
American Indian/Alaska Native (69)	116	1.20
Not Hispanic (21)	36	0.37
Hispanic (48)	80	0.83
Apache (3)	4	0.04
Blackfeet (0)	1	0.01
Cherokee (1)	6	0.06
Chickasaw (1)	1	0.01
Choctaw (9)	10	0.10
Inupiat *(Alaska Native)* (0)	1	0.01
Mexican American Ind. (6)	14	0.14
Navajo (1)	1	0.01
Osage (0)	1	0.01
Sioux (0)	1	0.01
Asian (21)	43	0.45
Not Hispanic (19)	22	0.23
Hispanic (2)	21	0.22
Chinese, ex. Taiwanese (4)	5	0.05
Filipino (7)	11	0.11
Indian (2)	13	0.13
Japanese (2)	2	0.02
Korean (3)	4	0.04
Thai (0)	1	0.01
Vietnamese (2)	2	0.02
Hawaii Native/Pacific Islander (0)	13	0.13
Not Hispanic (0)	5	0.05
Hispanic (0)	8	0.08
White (7,691)	7,908	81.89
Not Hispanic (4,004)	4,058	42.02
Hispanic (3,687)	3,850	39.87

Brownsville

Place Type: City
County: Cameron
Population: 175,023†

Ancestry‡	Population	%
African, Sub-Saharan (9)	75	0.04
African (0)	66	0.04
Other Sub-Saharan African (9)	9	0.01
American (2,194)	2,194	1.29
Arab (118)	137	0.08
Egyptian (46)	46	0.03
Lebanese (72)	72	0.04
Syrian (0)	19	0.01
Australian (0)	8	<0.01
Austrian (10)	62	0.04
Basque (0)	7	<0.01
Brazilian (8)	8	<0.01
British (60)	156	0.09
Cajun (0)	31	0.02
Canadian (26)	34	0.02
Croatian (8)	8	<0.01
Czech (68)	81	0.05
Czechoslovakian (28)	87	0.05
Danish (9)	89	0.05
Dutch (81)	266	0.16
English (454)	1,380	0.81
European (49)	84	0.05
Finnish (10)	33	0.02
French, ex. Basque (161)	679	0.40
French Canadian (49)	98	0.06
German (654)	2,318	1.37
Greek (0)	68	0.04
Hungarian (0)	70	0.04
Iranian (87)	124	0.07
Irish (467)	1,491	0.88
Italian (192)	544	0.32
Latvian (0)	9	0.01
Lithuanian (6)	6	<0.01
Northern European (0)	11	0.01
Norwegian (57)	108	0.06
Polish (134)	434	0.26
Portuguese (29)	47	0.03
Romanian (43)	68	0.04
Russian (20)	70	0.04
Scandinavian (9)	27	0.02
Scotch-Irish (200)	524	0.31
Scottish (137)	381	0.22
Swedish (22)	259	0.15
Swiss (0)	11	0.01
Ukrainian (10)	35	0.02
Welsh (104)	173	0.10
West Indian, ex. Hispanic (38)	38	0.02
Jamaican (38)	38	0.02
Yugoslavian (10)	10	0.01

Hispanic Origin	Population	%
Hispanic or Latino (of any race)	163,109	93.19
Central American, ex. Mexican	725	0.41
Costa Rican	21	0.01
Guatemalan	94	0.05
Honduran	260	0.15
Nicaraguan	104	0.06
Panamanian	16	0.01
Salvadoran	222	0.13
Other Central American	8	<0.01
Cuban	240	0.14
Dominican Republic	53	0.03
Mexican	150,945	86.24
Puerto Rican	459	0.26
South American	363	0.21
Argentinean	63	0.04
Bolivian	10	0.01
Chilean	25	0.01
Colombian	124	0.07
Ecuadorian	26	0.01
Paraguayan	9	0.01
Peruvian	54	0.03
Uruguayan	20	0.01
Venezuelan	31	0.02
Other South American	1	<0.01
Other Hispanic or Latino	10,324	5.90

Race*	Population	%
African-American/Black (709)	927	0.53
Not Hispanic (332)	387	0.22
Hispanic (377)	540	0.31
American Indian/Alaska Native (614)	882	0.50
Not Hispanic (120)	192	0.11
Hispanic (494)	690	0.39
Aleut *(Alaska Native)* (1)	1	<0.01
Apache (30)	56	0.03
Arapaho (0)	1	<0.01
Blackfeet (0)	5	<0.01
Canadian/French Am. Ind. (2)	3	<0.01
Central American Ind. (4)	5	<0.01
Cherokee (26)	46	0.03
Cheyenne (2)	2	<0.01
Chickasaw (2)	7	<0.01
Chippewa (1)	1	<0.01
Choctaw (5)	14	0.01
Comanche (5)	7	<0.01
Creek (7)	9	0.01
Inupiat *(Alaska Native)* (2)	2	<0.01
Iroquois (1)	3	<0.01
Mexican American Ind. (78)	99	0.06
Navajo (7)	11	0.01
Osage (1)	1	<0.01
Pueblo (6)	6	<0.01
Seminole (5)	5	<0.01
Sioux (4)	10	0.01
South American Ind. (1)	6	<0.01
Spanish American Ind. (5)	6	<0.01
Yaqui (2)	2	<0.01
Asian (1,189)	1,459	0.83
Not Hispanic (1,091)	1,198	0.68
Hispanic (98)	261	0.15
Bangladeshi (8)	10	0.01
Chinese, ex. Taiwanese (128)	176	0.10
Filipino (455)	532	0.30
Hmong (1)	6	<0.01
Indian (246)	286	0.16
Indonesian (3)	7	<0.01
Japanese (39)	69	0.04
Korean (104)	116	0.07
Laotian (1)	2	<0.01
Pakistani (76)	77	0.04
Sri Lankan (4)	4	<0.01
Taiwanese (14)	16	0.01
Thai (3)	9	0.01
Vietnamese (79)	87	0.05
Hawaii Native/Pacific Islander (38)	101	0.06
Not Hispanic (24)	36	0.02
Hispanic (14)	65	0.04
Guamanian/Chamorro (7)	11	0.01
Native Hawaiian (15)	40	0.02
Samoan (8)	8	<0.01
Tongan (0)	1	<0.01
White (153,987)	156,312	89.31
Not Hispanic (10,027)	10,245	5.85
Hispanic (143,960)	146,067	83.46

Brownwood

Place Type: City
County: Brown
Population: 19,288†

Ancestry‡	Population	%
American (1,774)	1,774	9.12
Belgian (8)	32	0.16
British (33)	62	0.32
Cajun (15)	51	0.26
Canadian (0)	8	0.04
Celtic (13)	13	0.07
Czech (52)	105	0.54
Czechoslovakian (0)	10	0.05
Danish (5)	17	0.09
Dutch (46)	227	1.17
English (2,828)	3,695	19.01
European (16)	16	0.08
French, ex. Basque (94)	528	2.72
French Canadian (55)	94	0.48
German (851)	2,087	10.73
Greek (19)	19	0.10
Irish (911)	1,953	10.05
Italian (167)	397	2.04
Norwegian (83)	107	0.55
Polish (11)	263	1.35
Portuguese (10)	10	0.05
Scandinavian (11)	11	0.06
Scotch-Irish (299)	530	2.73
Scottish (319)	406	2.09
Slovene (0)	34	0.17
Swedish (5)	27	0.14
Swiss (8)	18	0.09
Welsh (39)	83	0.43
West Indian, ex. Hispanic (0)	19	0.10
Dutch West Indian (0)	19	0.10

Hispanic Origin	Population	%
Hispanic or Latino (of any race)	4,990	25.87
Central American, ex. Mexican	16	0.08
Guatemalan	2	0.01
Honduran	1	0.01
Nicaraguan	1	0.01
Salvadoran	12	0.06
Cuban	8	0.04
Mexican	4,541	23.54
Puerto Rican	52	0.27
South American	10	0.05
Argentinean	2	0.01
Chilean	1	0.01
Colombian	1	0.01
Peruvian	3	0.02
Venezuelan	3	0.02
Other Hispanic or Latino	363	1.88

*Notes: † The Census 2010 population figure is used to calculate the percentages in the Hispanic Origin and Race categories. Ancestry percentages are based on the 2006-2010 American Community Survey population (not shown); ‡ Numbers in parentheses indicate the number of people reporting a single ancestry; * Numbers in parentheses indicate the number of persons reporting this race alone, not in combination with any other race; Please refer to the Explanation of Data for more information.*

Race*	Population	%
African-American/Black (956)	1,113	5.77
Not Hispanic (895)	1,029	5.33
Hispanic (61)	84	0.44
American Indian/Alaska Native (99)	208	1.08
Not Hispanic (78)	170	0.88
Hispanic (21)	38	0.20
Alaska Athabascan *(Ala. Nat.)* (1)	1	0.01
Apache (5)	7	0.04
Blackfeet (1)	2	0.01
Canadian/French Am. Ind. (0)	1	0.01
Cherokee (10)	34	0.18
Cheyenne (0)	4	0.02
Chickasaw (5)	5	0.03
Chippewa (1)	1	0.01
Choctaw (11)	25	0.13
Comanche (5)	6	0.03
Cree (1)	1	0.01
Delaware (0)	3	0.02
Iroquois (0)	1	0.01
Kiowa (0)	1	0.01
Mexican American Ind. (1)	2	0.01
Navajo (0)	1	0.01
Potawatomi (2)	3	0.02
Pueblo (1)	1	0.01
Seminole (0)	1	0.01
Shoshone (2)	3	0.02
Sioux (0)	1	0.01
Spanish American Ind. (0)	4	0.02
Tsimshian *(Alaska Native)* (1)	5	0.03
Yuman (1)	1	0.01
Asian (95)	128	0.66
Not Hispanic (93)	114	0.59
Hispanic (2)	14	0.07
Bangladeshi (0)	4	0.02
Cambodian (7)	7	0.04
Chinese, ex. Taiwanese (12)	16	0.08
Filipino (17)	25	0.13
Indian (11)	16	0.08
Japanese (2)	8	0.04
Korean (8)	11	0.06
Taiwanese (6)	6	0.03
Thai (5)	7	0.04
Vietnamese (19)	23	0.12
Hawaii Native/Pacific Islander (4)	16	0.08
Not Hispanic (4)	10	0.05
Hispanic (0)	6	0.03
Guamanian/Chamorro (2)	3	0.02
Native Hawaiian (1)	5	0.03
Samoan (1)	4	0.02
White (15,977)	16,398	85.02
Not Hispanic (12,947)	13,195	68.41
Hispanic (3,030)	3,203	16.61

Brushy Creek

Place Type: CDP
County: Williamson
Population: 21,764†

Ancestry‡	Population	%
African, Sub-Saharan (67)	82	0.37
African (67)	82	0.37
American (873)	873	3.94
Arab (83)	174	0.78
Arab (0)	14	0.06
Lebanese (61)	111	0.50
Palestinian (22)	49	0.22
Austrian (13)	39	0.18
Brazilian (0)	26	0.12
British (75)	207	0.93
Canadian (0)	125	0.56
Croatian (0)	20	0.09
Czech (122)	582	2.62
Czechoslovakian (23)	58	0.26
Danish (90)	195	0.88
Dutch (76)	523	2.36
Eastern European (75)	75	0.34
English (728)	2,582	11.64
European (400)	444	2.00
Finnish (0)	27	0.12
French, ex. Basque (124)	887	4.00
French Canadian (55)	104	0.47
German (1,321)	4,396	19.83
Greek (19)	74	0.33
Hungarian (8)	8	0.04
Iranian (53)	107	0.48
Irish (447)	2,035	9.18
Italian (118)	966	4.36
Lithuanian (0)	129	0.58
Northern European (13)	13	0.06
Norwegian (92)	350	1.58
Pennsylvania German (0)	8	0.04
Polish (180)	593	2.67
Portuguese (0)	61	0.28
Romanian (40)	59	0.27
Russian (39)	416	1.88
Scandinavian (62)	62	0.28
Scotch-Irish (502)	861	3.88
Scottish (275)	813	3.67
Serbian (0)	22	0.10
Slovak (0)	58	0.26
Slovene (25)	25	0.11
Swedish (99)	594	2.68
Swiss (31)	153	0.69
Turkish (9)	9	0.04
Ukrainian (43)	68	0.31
Welsh (25)	140	0.63
West Indian, ex. Hispanic (15)	30	0.14
Jamaican (15)	30	0.14
Yugoslavian (0)	13	0.06

Hispanic Origin	Population	%
Hispanic or Latino (of any race)	2,856	13.12
Central American, ex. Mexican	125	0.57
Costa Rican	3	0.01
Guatemalan	13	0.06
Honduran	23	0.11
Nicaraguan	15	0.07
Panamanian	17	0.08
Salvadoran	54	0.25
Cuban	45	0.21
Dominican Republic	3	0.01
Mexican	2,138	9.82
Puerto Rican	112	0.51
South American	183	0.84
Argentinean	30	0.14
Bolivian	14	0.06
Chilean	16	0.07
Colombian	57	0.26
Ecuadorian	18	0.08
Paraguayan	1	<0.01
Peruvian	22	0.10
Uruguayan	5	0.02
Venezuelan	20	0.09
Other Hispanic or Latino	250	1.15

Race*	Population	%
African-American/Black (892)	1,064	4.89
Not Hispanic (848)	986	4.53
Hispanic (44)	78	0.36
American Indian/Alaska Native (115)	263	1.21
Not Hispanic (74)	177	0.81
Hispanic (41)	86	0.40
Alaska Athabascan *(Ala. Nat.)* (1)	1	<0.01
Apache (8)	10	0.05
Cherokee (17)	54	0.25
Chickasaw (7)	14	0.06
Choctaw (6)	7	0.03
Creek (10)	10	0.05
Houma (0)	2	0.01
Inupiat *(Alaska Native)* (0)	4	0.02
Mexican American Ind. (2)	3	0.01
Navajo (1)	1	<0.01
Potawatomi (6)	7	0.03
Seminole (1)	1	<0.01
Sioux (4)	13	0.06
South American Ind. (0)	5	0.02
Yaqui (0)	1	<0.01
Yuman (0)	1	<0.01
Yup'ik *(Alaska Native)* (3)	3	0.01
Asian (2,622)	2,913	13.38
Not Hispanic (2,604)	2,861	13.15
Hispanic (18)	52	0.24
Bangladeshi (60)	67	0.31
Cambodian (10)	10	0.05
Chinese, ex. Taiwanese (564)	641	2.95
Filipino (90)	150	0.69
Indian (1,102)	1,145	5.26
Indonesian (10)	10	0.05
Japanese (63)	109	0.50
Korean (251)	291	1.34
Laotian (1)	5	0.02
Malaysian (6)	8	0.04
Nepalese (3)	4	0.02
Pakistani (112)	115	0.53
Sri Lankan (8)	8	0.04
Taiwanese (29)	38	0.17
Thai (17)	33	0.15
Vietnamese (214)	244	1.12
Hawaii Native/Pacific Islander (28)	74	0.34
Not Hispanic (26)	62	0.28
Hispanic (2)	12	0.06
Guamanian/Chamorro (5)	11	0.05
Native Hawaiian (13)	37	0.17
Samoan (5)	14	0.06
White (16,910)	17,498	80.40
Not Hispanic (14,831)	15,257	70.10
Hispanic (2,079)	2,241	10.30

Bryan

Place Type: City
County: Brazos
Population: 76,201†

Ancestry‡	Population	%
African, Sub-Saharan (282)	491	0.67
African (201)	410	0.56
Nigerian (68)	68	0.09
Other Sub-Saharan African (13)	13	0.02
American (2,342)	2,342	3.19
Arab (115)	202	0.27
Egyptian (59)	59	0.08
Lebanese (24)	94	0.13
Palestinian (17)	17	0.02
Syrian (0)	17	0.02
Other Arab (15)	15	0.02
Armenian (0)	16	0.02
Austrian (0)	139	0.19
Belgian (0)	18	0.02
British (78)	268	0.36
Croatian (10)	71	0.10
Czech (590)	1,405	1.91
Czechoslovakian (62)	147	0.20
Danish (32)	195	0.27
Dutch (210)	687	0.93
Eastern European (9)	9	0.01
English (1,952)	5,155	7.01
European (243)	300	0.41
Finnish (12)	46	0.06
French, ex. Basque (231)	1,866	2.54
French Canadian (78)	164	0.22
German (3,005)	8,908	12.11
Greek (0)	112	0.15
Hungarian (20)	47	0.06
Icelander (0)	17	0.02
Iranian (69)	69	0.09
Irish (1,490)	5,523	7.51
Israeli (0)	23	0.03
Italian (765)	2,032	2.76
Latvian (16)	16	0.02
Lithuanian (10)	25	0.03
Northern European (22)	22	0.03
Norwegian (6)	278	0.38
Pennsylvania German (21)	21	0.03
Polish (315)	1,057	1.44
Portuguese (0)	44	0.06
Romanian (9)	9	0.01

*Notes: † The Census 2010 population figure is used to calculate the percentages in the Hispanic Origin and Race categories. Ancestry percentages are based on the 2006-2010 American Community Survey population (not shown); ‡ Numbers in parentheses indicate the number of people reporting a single ancestry; * Numbers in parentheses indicate the number of persons reporting this race alone, not in combination with any other race; Please refer to the Explanation of Data for more information.*

Russian (54)	54	0.07
Scandinavian (0)	63	0.09
Scotch-Irish (737)	1,622	2.21
Scottish (387)	1,308	1.78
Serbian (23)	23	0.03
Swedish (67)	497	0.68
Swiss (0)	150	0.20
Ukrainian (15)	49	0.07
Welsh (105)	266	0.36
West Indian, ex. Hispanic (41)	145	0.20
British West Indian (33)	33	0.04
Dutch West Indian (8)	42	0.06
Jamaican (0)	28	0.04
West Indian (0)	42	0.06
Yugoslavian (0)	13	0.02

Hispanic Origin	Population	%
Hispanic or Latino (of any race)	27,617	36.24
Central American, ex. Mexican	649	0.85
Costa Rican	12	0.02
Guatemalan	189	0.25
Honduran	169	0.22
Nicaraguan	16	0.02
Panamanian	17	0.02
Salvadoran	241	0.32
Other Central American	5	0.01
Cuban	99	0.13
Dominican Republic	17	0.02
Mexican	24,699	32.41
Puerto Rican	228	0.30
South American	189	0.25
Argentinean	22	0.03
Bolivian	22	0.03
Chilean	11	0.01
Colombian	42	0.06
Ecuadorian	18	0.02
Paraguayan	1	<0.01
Peruvian	36	0.05
Uruguayan	3	<0.01
Venezuelan	34	0.04
Other Hispanic or Latino	1,736	2.28

Race*	Population	%
African-American/Black (13,748)	14,374	18.86
Not Hispanic (13,406)	13,858	18.19
Hispanic (342)	516	0.68
American Indian/Alaska Native (420)	814	1.07
Not Hispanic (175)	421	0.55
Hispanic (245)	393	0.52
Apache (0)	8	0.01
Arapaho (2)	5	0.01
Blackfeet (1)	8	0.01
Canadian/French Am. Ind. (0)	1	<0.01
Central American Ind. (12)	12	0.02
Cherokee (45)	137	0.18
Chickasaw (6)	10	0.01
Chippewa (1)	2	<0.01
Choctaw (26)	49	0.06
Comanche (3)	8	0.01
Cree (0)	1	<0.01
Creek (8)	13	0.02
Crow (1)	1	<0.01
Delaware (0)	1	<0.01
Houma (0)	1	<0.01
Inupiat *(Alaska Native)* (1)	1	<0.01
Iroquois (0)	2	<0.01
Kiowa (2)	4	0.01
Lumbee (1)	2	<0.01
Mexican American Ind. (36)	48	0.06
Navajo (4)	9	0.01
Osage (2)	4	0.01
Potawatomi (5)	6	0.01
Pueblo (0)	1	<0.01
Seminole (0)	1	<0.01
Shoshone (1)	1	<0.01
Sioux (4)	11	0.01
South American Ind. (3)	5	0.01
Spanish American Ind. (1)	3	<0.01
Tlingit-Haida *(Alaska Native)* (4)	4	0.01
Yaqui (0)	4	0.01
Yup'ik *(Alaska Native)* (1)	1	<0.01
Asian (1,313)	1,623	2.13
Not Hispanic (1,278)	1,487	1.95
Hispanic (35)	136	0.18
Bangladeshi (14)	15	0.02
Cambodian (17)	20	0.03
Chinese, ex. Taiwanese (192)	228	0.30
Filipino (94)	157	0.21
Hmong (1)	1	<0.01
Indian (549)	582	0.76
Indonesian (4)	6	0.01
Japanese (37)	96	0.13
Korean (117)	153	0.20
Laotian (5)	5	0.01
Malaysian (5)	7	0.01
Nepalese (6)	6	0.01
Pakistani (50)	59	0.08
Sri Lankan (10)	11	0.01
Taiwanese (10)	16	0.02
Thai (14)	29	0.04
Vietnamese (155)	171	0.22
Hawaii Native/Pacific Islander (52)	101	0.13
Not Hispanic (40)	65	0.09
Hispanic (12)	36	0.05
Fijian (1)	1	<0.01
Guamanian/Chamorro (22)	28	0.04
Native Hawaiian (11)	29	0.04
Samoan (4)	7	0.01
Tongan (6)	6	0.01
White (48,939)	50,613	66.42
Not Hispanic (32,772)	33,493	43.95
Hispanic (16,167)	17,120	22.47

Burkburnett

Place Type: City
County: Wichita
Population: 10,811†

Ancestry‡	Population	%
American (2,372)	2,372	21.99
Arab (11)	11	0.10
Other Arab (11)	11	0.10
British (17)	58	0.54
Cajun (16)	16	0.15
Czech (11)	11	0.10
Czechoslovakian (13)	13	0.12
Danish (25)	25	0.23
Dutch (22)	203	1.88
English (536)	936	8.68
European (91)	103	0.95
French, ex. Basque (63)	295	2.74
French Canadian (56)	189	1.75
German (710)	1,622	15.04
Hungarian (0)	12	0.11
Irish (837)	1,863	17.27
Italian (193)	313	2.90
Norwegian (54)	176	1.63
Polish (58)	205	1.90
Portuguese (14)	14	0.13
Scotch-Irish (129)	179	1.66
Scottish (124)	255	2.36
Slovak (14)	32	0.30
Swedish (6)	67	0.62
Welsh (23)	96	0.89
West Indian, ex. Hispanic (0)	12	0.11
Dutch West Indian (0)	12	0.11

Hispanic Origin	Population	%
Hispanic or Latino (of any race)	879	8.13
Central American, ex. Mexican	17	0.16
Costa Rican	1	0.01
Guatemalan	4	0.04
Honduran	1	0.01
Panamanian	3	0.03
Salvadoran	8	0.07
Cuban	9	0.08
Dominican Republic	1	0.01
Mexican	695	6.43
Puerto Rican	54	0.50
South American	17	0.16
Colombian	3	0.03
Peruvian	9	0.08
Uruguayan	1	0.01
Venezuelan	2	0.02
Other South American	2	0.02
Other Hispanic or Latino	86	0.80

Race*	Population	%
African-American/Black (287)	338	3.13
Not Hispanic (282)	328	3.03
Hispanic (5)	10	0.09
American Indian/Alaska Native (139)	229	2.12
Not Hispanic (113)	187	1.73
Hispanic (26)	42	0.39
Apache (4)	8	0.07
Blackfeet (0)	2	0.02
Cherokee (20)	41	0.38
Cheyenne (0)	1	0.01
Chickasaw (9)	21	0.19
Choctaw (34)	54	0.50
Comanche (6)	8	0.07
Creek (3)	3	0.03
Kiowa (11)	14	0.13
Mexican American Ind. (5)	11	0.10
Navajo (1)	1	0.01
Ottawa (1)	1	0.01
Potawatomi (1)	1	0.01
Seminole (1)	2	0.02
Sioux (3)	10	0.09
South American Ind. (1)	1	0.01
Tlingit-Haida *(Alaska Native)* (1)	1	0.01
Asian (110)	162	1.50
Not Hispanic (103)	148	1.37
Hispanic (7)	14	0.13
Chinese, ex. Taiwanese (7)	15	0.14
Filipino (40)	64	0.59
Indian (4)	4	0.04
Japanese (15)	35	0.32
Korean (22)	25	0.23
Laotian (2)	2	0.02
Pakistani (1)	1	0.01
Taiwanese (3)	3	0.03
Thai (2)	4	0.04
Vietnamese (10)	10	0.09
Hawaii Native/Pacific Islander (2)	13	0.12
Not Hispanic (2)	13	0.12
Native Hawaiian (1)	8	0.07
Samoan (1)	1	0.01
White (9,860)	10,079	93.23
Not Hispanic (9,261)	9,420	87.13
Hispanic (599)	659	6.10

Burleson

Place Type: City
County: Johnson
Population: 36,690†

Ancestry‡	Population	%
African, Sub-Saharan (115)	115	0.34
African (115)	115	0.34
American (3,266)	3,266	9.56
Arab (15)	24	0.07
Lebanese (0)	9	0.03
Palestinian (15)	15	0.04
Australian (25)	25	0.07
Austrian (14)	66	0.19
Belgian (12)	49	0.14
Brazilian (19)	57	0.17
British (31)	109	0.32
Cajun (8)	19	0.06
Canadian (16)	77	0.23
Celtic (0)	11	0.03
Czech (106)	313	0.92
Czechoslovakian (21)	21	0.06
Danish (16)	84	0.25
Dutch (190)	991	2.90
English (3,084)	6,727	19.69
European (319)	329	0.96

*Notes: † The Census 2010 population figure is used to calculate the percentages in the Hispanic Origin and Race categories. Ancestry percentages are based on the 2006-2010 American Community Survey population (not shown); ‡ Numbers in parentheses indicate the number of people reporting a single ancestry; * Numbers in parentheses indicate the number of persons reporting this race alone, not in combination with any other race; Please refer to the Explanation of Data for more information.*

Ancestry	Population	%
Finnish (24)	59	0.17
French, ex. Basque (250)	984	2.88
French Canadian (60)	157	0.46
German (1,607)	5,883	17.22
Greek (21)	21	0.06
Hungarian (56)	115	0.34
Irish (1,301)	5,027	14.71
Italian (256)	793	2.32
Lithuanian (0)	8	0.02
Norwegian (69)	193	0.56
Polish (260)	743	2.17
Portuguese (9)	27	0.08
Romanian (0)	26	0.08
Russian (10)	64	0.19
Scandinavian (11)	23	0.07
Scotch-Irish (341)	807	2.36
Scottish (286)	865	2.53
Swedish (87)	441	1.29
Swiss (15)	15	0.04
Ukrainian (0)	12	0.04
Welsh (44)	183	0.54
West Indian, ex. Hispanic (44)	70	0.20
Belizean (44)	44	0.13
Dutch West Indian (0)	26	0.08

Hispanic Origin	Population	%
Hispanic or Latino (of any race)	4,219	11.50
Central American, ex. Mexican	116	0.32
Costa Rican	16	0.04
Guatemalan	37	0.10
Honduran	15	0.04
Nicaraguan	13	0.04
Panamanian	10	0.03
Salvadoran	25	0.07
Cuban	25	0.07
Dominican Republic	16	0.04
Mexican	3,461	9.43
Puerto Rican	180	0.49
South American	104	0.28
Argentinean	18	0.05
Chilean	3	0.01
Colombian	19	0.05
Ecuadorian	12	0.03
Peruvian	35	0.10
Venezuelan	16	0.04
Other South American	1	<0.01
Other Hispanic or Latino	317	0.86

Race*	Population	%
African-American/Black (862)	1,052	2.87
Not Hispanic (831)	990	2.70
Hispanic (31)	62	0.17
American Indian/Alaska Native (198)	441	1.20
Not Hispanic (156)	359	0.98
Hispanic (42)	82	0.22
Apache (3)	13	0.04
Blackfeet (1)	3	0.01
Canadian/French Am. Ind. (0)	4	0.01
Central American Ind. (5)	6	0.02
Cherokee (45)	137	0.37
Chickasaw (11)	15	0.04
Chippewa (0)	3	0.01
Choctaw (34)	61	0.17
Comanche (6)	12	0.03
Cree (1)	1	<0.01
Creek (5)	7	0.02
Delaware (1)	1	<0.01
Houma (0)	1	<0.01
Inupiat *(Alaska Native)* (1)	1	<0.01
Iroquois (5)	7	0.02
Kiowa (0)	2	0.01
Mexican American Ind. (6)	7	0.02
Navajo (1)	4	0.01
Potawatomi (0)	3	0.01
Pueblo (1)	2	0.01
Seminole (4)	4	0.01
Shoshone (0)	1	<0.01
Sioux (7)	10	0.03
South American Ind. (6)	8	0.02
Spanish American Ind. (1)	1	<0.01
Asian (388)	563	1.53
Not Hispanic (375)	520	1.42
Hispanic (13)	43	0.12
Bangladeshi (5)	5	0.01
Cambodian (9)	11	0.03
Chinese, ex. Taiwanese (66)	82	0.22
Filipino (61)	104	0.28
Hmong (7)	7	0.02
Indian (65)	81	0.22
Indonesian (2)	6	0.02
Japanese (19)	40	0.11
Korean (43)	63	0.17
Laotian (12)	13	0.04
Malaysian (2)	3	0.01
Nepalese (16)	16	0.04
Pakistani (17)	22	0.06
Thai (13)	23	0.06
Vietnamese (43)	63	0.17
Hawaii Native/Pacific Islander (11)	49	0.13
Not Hispanic (10)	39	0.11
Hispanic (1)	10	0.03
Guamanian/Chamorro (3)	15	0.04
Native Hawaiian (5)	18	0.05
White (33,256)	34,026	92.74
Not Hispanic (30,535)	31,056	84.64
Hispanic (2,721)	2,970	8.09

Canyon Lake

Place Type: CDP
County: Comal
Population: 21,262†

Ancestry‡	Population	%
Alsatian (0)	15	0.08
American (1,798)	1,798	9.00
Arab (13)	13	0.07
Lebanese (13)	13	0.07
Armenian (24)	47	0.24
Austrian (0)	73	0.37
Belgian (0)	12	0.06
British (202)	248	1.24
Cajun (12)	34	0.17
Canadian (97)	114	0.57
Croatian (0)	12	0.06
Czech (87)	112	0.56
Czechoslovakian (16)	53	0.27
Danish (12)	53	0.27
Dutch (92)	383	1.92
English (1,136)	3,215	16.10
European (147)	147	0.74
Finnish (58)	158	0.79
French, ex. Basque (197)	987	4.94
French Canadian (57)	126	0.63
German (2,018)	5,242	26.25
Greek (0)	25	0.13
Hungarian (67)	268	1.34
Icelander (0)	28	0.14
Irish (993)	2,978	14.91
Italian (166)	474	2.37
Lithuanian (12)	12	0.06
Norwegian (83)	285	1.43
Pennsylvania German (0)	54	0.27
Polish (137)	635	3.18
Portuguese (0)	72	0.36
Russian (23)	109	0.55
Scandinavian (0)	12	0.06
Scotch-Irish (107)	738	3.69
Scottish (133)	519	2.60
Swedish (116)	312	1.56
Swiss (14)	116	0.58
Turkish (0)	16	0.08
Ukrainian (0)	22	0.11
Welsh (46)	175	0.88

Hispanic Origin	Population	%
Hispanic or Latino (of any race)	2,842	13.37
Central American, ex. Mexican	61	0.29
Costa Rican	3	0.01
Guatemalan	13	0.06
Honduran	10	0.05
Nicaraguan	5	0.02
Panamanian	19	0.09
Salvadoran	11	0.05
Cuban	34	0.16
Dominican Republic	2	0.01
Mexican	2,315	10.89
Puerto Rican	90	0.42
South American	32	0.15
Argentinean	1	<0.01
Bolivian	1	<0.01
Chilean	5	0.02
Colombian	16	0.08
Peruvian	8	0.04
Venezuelan	1	<0.01
Other Hispanic or Latino	308	1.45

Race*	Population	%
African-American/Black (142)	200	0.94
Not Hispanic (133)	175	0.82
Hispanic (9)	25	0.12
American Indian/Alaska Native (139)	323	1.52
Not Hispanic (98)	249	1.17
Hispanic (41)	74	0.35
Apache (3)	5	0.02
Blackfeet (3)	10	0.05
Canadian/French Am. Ind. (0)	1	<0.01
Cherokee (28)	93	0.44
Cheyenne (0)	3	0.01
Chickasaw (2)	3	0.01
Chippewa (4)	5	0.02
Choctaw (7)	26	0.12
Comanche (2)	7	0.03
Cree (1)	1	<0.01
Creek (1)	6	0.03
Crow (0)	3	0.01
Lumbee (1)	1	<0.01
Mexican American Ind. (4)	7	0.03
Navajo (2)	4	0.02
Osage (5)	11	0.05
Potawatomi (0)	2	0.01
Sioux (5)	11	0.05
Spanish American Ind. (0)	1	<0.01
Yuman (0)	1	<0.01
Asian (103)	183	0.86
Not Hispanic (99)	162	0.76
Hispanic (4)	21	0.10
Cambodian (4)	4	0.02
Chinese, ex. Taiwanese (7)	20	0.09
Filipino (30)	48	0.23
Indian (14)	17	0.08
Indonesian (1)	2	0.01
Japanese (16)	33	0.16
Korean (11)	29	0.14
Thai (4)	6	0.03
Vietnamese (10)	14	0.07
Hawaii Native/Pacific Islander (11)	25	0.12
Not Hispanic (7)	21	0.10
Hispanic (4)	4	0.02
Guamanian/Chamorro (3)	7	0.03
Marshallese (3)	3	0.01
Native Hawaiian (4)	5	0.02
Samoan (0)	2	0.01
White (19,711)	20,127	94.66
Not Hispanic (17,779)	18,044	84.87
Hispanic (1,932)	2,083	9.80

Canyon

Place Type: City
County: Randall
Population: 13,303†

Ancestry‡	Population	%
African, Sub-Saharan (89)	112	0.85
African (72)	95	0.73
Ethiopian (17)	17	0.13
American (872)	872	6.65
Arab (23)	23	0.18
Jordanian (10)	10	0.08

*Notes: † The Census 2010 population figure is used to calculate the percentages in the Hispanic Origin and Race categories. Ancestry percentages are based on the 2006-2010 American Community Survey population (not shown); ‡ Numbers in parentheses indicate the number of people reporting a single ancestry; * Numbers in parentheses indicate the number of persons reporting this race alone, not in combination with any other race; Please refer to the Explanation of Data for more information.*

Lebanese (13)	13	0.10
Austrian (0)	8	0.06
Bulgarian (7)	7	0.05
Canadian (10)	29	0.22
Czech (81)	163	1.24
Czechoslovakian (0)	8	0.06
Dutch (17)	99	0.76
English (767)	1,654	12.62
European (44)	44	0.34
French, ex. Basque (38)	251	1.92
French Canadian (34)	34	0.26
German (1,252)	2,762	21.08
Greek (40)	40	0.31
Hungarian (0)	57	0.44
Irish (785)	1,815	13.85
Italian (73)	354	2.70
Latvian (17)	17	0.13
Norwegian (0)	39	0.30
Polish (79)	162	1.24
Portuguese (0)	3	0.02
Russian (12)	12	0.09
Scotch-Irish (227)	515	3.93
Scottish (71)	411	3.14
Swedish (74)	177	1.35
Swiss (0)	28	0.21
Ukrainian (7)	17	0.13
Welsh (0)	63	0.48
West Indian, ex. Hispanic (18)	108	0.82
Dutch West Indian (0)	90	0.69
Jamaican (18)	18	0.14
Yugoslavian (0)	13	0.10

Hispanic Origin	Population	%
Hispanic or Latino (of any race)	2,088	15.70
Central American, ex. Mexican	19	0.14
Costa Rican	1	0.01
Guatemalan	5	0.04
Honduran	2	0.02
Nicaraguan	6	0.05
Panamanian	3	0.02
Salvadoran	2	0.02
Cuban	4	0.03
Dominican Republic	4	0.03
Mexican	1,717	12.91
Puerto Rican	23	0.17
South American	33	0.25
Argentinean	1	0.01
Bolivian	5	0.04
Chilean	1	0.01
Colombian	13	0.10
Ecuadorian	10	0.08
Peruvian	3	0.02
Other Hispanic or Latino	288	2.16

Race*	Population	%
African-American/Black (313)	365	2.74
Not Hispanic (291)	331	2.49
Hispanic (22)	34	0.26
American Indian/Alaska Native (91)	163	1.23
Not Hispanic (66)	117	0.88
Hispanic (25)	46	0.35
Apache (3)	10	0.08
Cherokee (11)	22	0.17
Cheyenne (1)	2	0.02
Chickasaw (1)	3	0.02
Chippewa (1)	1	0.01
Choctaw (14)	29	0.22
Comanche (2)	4	0.03
Kiowa (0)	2	0.02
Mexican American Ind. (2)	3	0.02
Navajo (3)	4	0.03
Potawatomi (1)	5	0.04
Seminole (0)	2	0.02
Ute (0)	1	0.01
Asian (233)	270	2.03
Not Hispanic (231)	263	1.98
Hispanic (2)	7	0.05
Bangladeshi (3)	3	0.02
Chinese, ex. Taiwanese (72)	77	0.58
Filipino (10)	21	0.16
Indian (38)	40	0.30
Indonesian (2)	2	0.02
Japanese (5)	13	0.10
Korean (26)	30	0.23
Laotian (11)	13	0.10
Malaysian (1)	2	0.02
Nepalese (3)	3	0.02
Pakistani (9)	10	0.08
Taiwanese (8)	8	0.06
Thai (12)	13	0.10
Vietnamese (18)	21	0.16
Hawaii Native/Pacific Islander (10)	16	0.12
Not Hispanic (7)	10	0.08
Hispanic (3)	6	0.05
Native Hawaiian (3)	5	0.04
Samoan (3)	3	0.02
White (11,770)	12,019	90.35
Not Hispanic (10,488)	10,608	79.74
Hispanic (1,282)	1,411	10.61

Carrollton

Place Type: City
County: Denton
Population: 119,097†

Ancestry‡	Population	%
African, Sub-Saharan (1,049)	1,387	1.18
African (513)	823	0.70
Ethiopian (432)	432	0.37
Kenyan (10)	10	0.01
Nigerian (88)	88	0.07
Other Sub-Saharan African (6)	34	0.03
Alsatian (0)	8	0.01
American (5,986)	5,986	5.09
Arab (445)	757	0.64
Arab (249)	249	0.21
Egyptian (58)	108	0.09
Iraqi (19)	19	0.02
Jordanian (0)	42	0.04
Lebanese (119)	245	0.21
Palestinian (0)	94	0.08
Austrian (21)	107	0.09
Basque (0)	7	0.01
Belgian (16)	63	0.05
Brazilian (164)	201	0.17
British (265)	638	0.54
Bulgarian (45)	45	0.04
Cajun (21)	49	0.04
Canadian (84)	172	0.15
Celtic (21)	21	0.02
Croatian (14)	32	0.03
Czech (320)	768	0.65
Czechoslovakian (108)	177	0.15
Danish (93)	335	0.28
Dutch (391)	1,376	1.17
Eastern European (95)	95	0.08
English (3,783)	10,463	8.89
European (995)	1,183	1.00
Finnish (40)	192	0.16
French, ex. Basque (477)	2,851	2.42
French Canadian (124)	267	0.23
German (5,283)	14,314	12.16
Greek (39)	180	0.15
Hungarian (93)	178	0.15
Iranian (178)	212	0.18
Irish (3,313)	10,522	8.94
Israeli (11)	56	0.05
Italian (862)	2,528	2.15
Latvian (21)	32	0.03
Lithuanian (48)	192	0.16
Macedonian (0)	9	0.01
Northern European (73)	73	0.06
Norwegian (191)	860	0.73
Pennsylvania German (29)	29	0.02
Polish (492)	1,718	1.46
Portuguese (48)	134	0.11
Romanian (13)	43	0.04
Russian (199)	476	0.40
Scandinavian (102)	148	0.13
Scotch-Irish (870)	2,267	1.93
Scottish (480)	2,024	1.72
Serbian (43)	96	0.08
Slovak (10)	18	0.02
Slovene (50)	91	0.08
Swedish (540)	1,318	1.12
Swiss (59)	337	0.29
Turkish (7)	42	0.04
Ukrainian (62)	204	0.17
Welsh (147)	563	0.48
West Indian, ex. Hispanic (214)	375	0.32
Dutch West Indian (0)	116	0.10
Haitian (15)	15	0.01
Jamaican (131)	176	0.15
Trinidadian/Tobagonian (35)	35	0.03
West Indian (33)	33	0.03

Hispanic Origin	Population	%
Hispanic or Latino (of any race)	35,710	29.98
Central American, ex. Mexican	4,295	3.61
Costa Rican	81	0.07
Guatemalan	384	0.32
Honduran	519	0.44
Nicaraguan	208	0.17
Panamanian	53	0.04
Salvadoran	3,034	2.55
Other Central American	16	0.01
Cuban	372	0.31
Dominican Republic	80	0.07
Mexican	27,195	22.83
Puerto Rican	654	0.55
South American	1,165	0.98
Argentinean	77	0.06
Bolivian	43	0.04
Chilean	51	0.04
Colombian	425	0.36
Ecuadorian	141	0.12
Paraguayan	5	<0.01
Peruvian	287	0.24
Uruguayan	28	0.02
Venezuelan	90	0.08
Other South American	18	0.02
Other Hispanic or Latino	1,949	1.64

Race*	Population	%
African-American/Black (10,001)	11,031	9.26
Not Hispanic (9,631)	10,418	8.75
Hispanic (370)	613	0.51
American Indian/Alaska Native (758)	1,468	1.23
Not Hispanic (378)	877	0.74
Hispanic (380)	591	0.50
Alaska Athabascan *(Ala. Nat.)* (1)	2	<0.01
Aleut *(Alaska Native)* (2)	2	<0.01
Apache (10)	24	0.02
Arapaho (1)	1	<0.01
Blackfeet (0)	9	0.01
Canadian/French Am. Ind. (2)	2	<0.01
Central American Ind. (6)	8	0.01
Cherokee (88)	227	0.19
Cheyenne (0)	1	<0.01
Chickasaw (27)	47	0.04
Chippewa (4)	8	0.01
Choctaw (76)	120	0.10
Comanche (9)	27	0.02
Creek (11)	37	0.03
Delaware (4)	8	0.01
Hopi (5)	7	0.01
Inupiat *(Alaska Native)* (1)	2	<0.01
Iroquois (1)	4	<0.01
Kiowa (6)	6	0.01
Mexican American Ind. (120)	136	0.11
Navajo (21)	28	0.02
Osage (3)	6	0.01
Ottawa (1)	1	<0.01
Paiute (0)	4	<0.01
Potawatomi (14)	25	0.02
Pueblo (3)	6	0.01
Seminole (1)	6	0.01
Sioux (14)	24	0.02
South American Ind. (4)	11	0.01

*Notes: † The Census 2010 population figure is used to calculate the percentages in the Hispanic Origin and Race categories. Ancestry percentages are based on the 2006-2010 American Community Survey population (not shown); ‡ Numbers in parentheses indicate the number of people reporting a single ancestry; * Numbers in parentheses indicate the number of persons reporting this race alone, not in combination with any other race; Please refer to the Explanation of Data for more information.*

Spanish American Ind. (2)	4	<0.01
Tohono O'Odham (1)	3	<0.01
Yaqui (12)	13	0.01
Asian (16,008)	17,278	14.51
Not Hispanic (15,917)	16,994	14.27
Hispanic (91)	284	0.24
Bangladeshi (118)	128	0.11
Burmese (36)	38	0.03
Cambodian (819)	906	0.76
Chinese, ex. Taiwanese (930)	1,182	0.99
Filipino (513)	663	0.56
Hmong (1)	1	<0.01
Indian (4,575)	4,980	4.18
Indonesian (51)	64	0.05
Japanese (158)	288	0.24
Korean (2,537)	2,676	2.25
Laotian (45)	56	0.05
Malaysian (3)	6	0.01
Nepalese (20)	22	0.02
Pakistani (2,172)	2,374	1.99
Sri Lankan (26)	26	0.02
Taiwanese (104)	130	0.11
Thai (81)	141	0.12
Vietnamese (3,208)	3,430	2.88
Hawaii Native/Pacific Islander (36)	157	0.13
Not Hispanic (32)	115	0.10
Hispanic (4)	42	0.04
Fijian (1)	3	<0.01
Guamanian/Chamorro (10)	12	0.01
Native Hawaiian (10)	53	0.04
Samoan (2)	10	0.01
Tongan (1)	4	<0.01
White (75,777)	78,741	66.12
Not Hispanic (55,083)	56,719	47.62
Hispanic (20,694)	22,022	18.49

Cedar Hill

Place Type: City
County: Dallas
Population: 45,028†

Ancestry‡	Population	%
African, Sub-Saharan (561)	692	1.63
African (411)	477	1.12
Ghanaian (40)	40	0.09
Nigerian (110)	175	0.41
American (1,508)	1,508	3.55
Arab (14)	53	0.12
Lebanese (14)	53	0.12
Armenian (8)	21	0.05
Austrian (18)	32	0.08
Belgian (16)	16	0.04
British (36)	77	0.18
Cajun (0)	16	0.04
Canadian (40)	40	0.09
Croatian (0)	9	0.02
Czech (26)	137	0.32
Danish (0)	11	0.03
Dutch (80)	310	0.73
English (669)	1,910	4.50
European (243)	286	0.67
French, ex. Basque (201)	932	2.20
French Canadian (75)	91	0.21
German (918)	2,285	5.38
Greek (14)	31	0.07
Hungarian (0)	56	0.13
Iranian (14)	14	0.03
Irish (766)	2,575	6.07
Italian (117)	342	0.81
Northern European (10)	10	0.02
Norwegian (51)	169	0.40
Polish (104)	253	0.60
Romanian (0)	31	0.07
Russian (52)	83	0.20
Scandinavian (23)	23	0.05
Scotch-Irish (245)	389	0.92
Scottish (159)	363	0.86
Slovak (30)	30	0.07
Swedish (76)	218	0.51
Swiss (19)	35	0.08
Turkish (26)	26	0.06
Welsh (58)	111	0.26
West Indian, ex. Hispanic (91)	140	0.33
Bermudan (45)	45	0.11
Jamaican (46)	77	0.18
West Indian (0)	18	0.04
Yugoslavian (12)	12	0.03

Hispanic Origin	Population	%
Hispanic or Latino (of any race)	8,405	18.67
Central American, ex. Mexican	373	0.83
Costa Rican	6	0.01
Guatemalan	50	0.11
Honduran	52	0.12
Nicaraguan	14	0.03
Panamanian	29	0.06
Salvadoran	212	0.47
Other Central American	10	0.02
Cuban	55	0.12
Dominican Republic	28	0.06
Mexican	7,066	15.69
Puerto Rican	228	0.51
South American	119	0.26
Argentinean	11	0.02
Bolivian	2	<0.01
Chilean	2	<0.01
Colombian	51	0.11
Ecuadorian	8	0.02
Paraguayan	6	0.01
Peruvian	22	0.05
Uruguayan	1	<0.01
Venezuelan	14	0.03
Other South American	2	<0.01
Other Hispanic or Latino	536	1.19

Race*	Population	%
African-American/Black (23,382)	24,088	53.50
Not Hispanic (23,146)	23,658	52.54
Hispanic (236)	430	0.95
American Indian/Alaska Native (223)	543	1.21
Not Hispanic (134)	389	0.86
Hispanic (89)	154	0.34
Apache (13)	25	0.06
Blackfeet (0)	10	0.02
Central American Ind. (4)	4	0.01
Cherokee (30)	92	0.20
Chickasaw (4)	11	0.02
Chippewa (4)	5	0.01
Choctaw (18)	47	0.10
Comanche (1)	11	0.02
Creek (16)	20	0.04
Hopi (0)	5	0.01
Houma (1)	2	<0.01
Inupiat *(Alaska Native)* (0)	1	<0.01
Iroquois (1)	2	<0.01
Kiowa (2)	5	0.01
Lumbee (0)	5	0.01
Mexican American Ind. (18)	27	0.06
Navajo (5)	9	0.02
Potawatomi (1)	3	0.01
Pueblo (1)	1	<0.01
Seminole (0)	3	0.01
Shoshone (0)	1	<0.01
Sioux (1)	3	0.01
South American Ind. (0)	2	<0.01
Spanish American Ind. (2)	2	<0.01
Tlingit-Haida *(Alaska Native)* (0)	1	<0.01
Yaqui (0)	1	<0.01
Asian (908)	1,121	2.49
Not Hispanic (893)	1,076	2.39
Hispanic (15)	45	0.10
Bangladeshi (4)	4	0.01
Burmese (12)	12	0.03
Cambodian (1)	4	0.01
Chinese, ex. Taiwanese (100)	151	0.34
Filipino (255)	319	0.71
Hmong (37)	37	0.08
Indian (145)	170	0.38
Indonesian (5)	5	0.01
Japanese (11)	43	0.10
Korean (40)	67	0.15
Laotian (35)	45	0.10
Malaysian (0)	3	0.01
Nepalese (7)	9	0.02
Pakistani (38)	44	0.10
Taiwanese (3)	3	0.01
Thai (10)	19	0.04
Vietnamese (169)	185	0.41
Hawaii Native/Pacific Islander (23)	46	0.10
Not Hispanic (18)	38	0.08
Hispanic (5)	8	0.02
Guamanian/Chamorro (6)	9	0.02
Native Hawaiian (13)	23	0.05
Samoan (1)	2	<0.01
White (15,934)	16,879	37.49
Not Hispanic (11,604)	12,207	27.11
Hispanic (4,330)	4,672	10.38

Cedar Park

Place Type: City
County: Williamson
Population: 48,937†

Ancestry‡	Population	%
African, Sub-Saharan (265)	432	0.96
African (75)	147	0.33
Kenyan (20)	20	0.04
Nigerian (140)	235	0.52
South African (30)	30	0.07
Albanian (92)	92	0.20
Alsatian (17)	17	0.04
American (2,808)	2,808	6.26
Arab (40)	189	0.42
Lebanese (22)	171	0.38
Palestinian (18)	18	0.04
Austrian (52)	209	0.47
Belgian (37)	93	0.21
Brazilian (53)	126	0.28
British (51)	188	0.42
Cajun (87)	171	0.38
Canadian (31)	151	0.34
Czech (91)	770	1.72
Czechoslovakian (30)	59	0.13
Danish (101)	217	0.48
Dutch (148)	704	1.57
Eastern European (31)	31	0.07
English (1,948)	4,475	9.97
European (644)	756	1.68
Finnish (17)	82	0.18
French, ex. Basque (434)	1,682	3.75
French Canadian (89)	416	0.93
German (3,157)	9,296	20.71
Greek (12)	87	0.19
Hungarian (27)	97	0.22
Iranian (41)	41	0.09
Irish (1,416)	5,088	11.34
Italian (563)	1,459	3.25
Lithuanian (23)	58	0.13
Luxemburger (28)	64	0.14
Maltese (15)	15	0.03
Norwegian (209)	721	1.61
Polish (348)	968	2.16
Portuguese (17)	72	0.16
Romanian (15)	15	0.03
Russian (126)	443	0.99
Scandinavian (30)	46	0.10
Scotch-Irish (308)	618	1.38
Scottish (215)	864	1.92
Slavic (0)	12	0.03
Slovak (27)	40	0.09
Slovene (11)	22	0.05
Swedish (158)	877	1.95
Swiss (17)	117	0.26
Turkish (11)	11	0.02
Ukrainian (36)	74	0.16
Welsh (98)	290	0.65
West Indian, ex. Hispanic (89)	165	0.37
Dutch West Indian (0)	34	0.08

SECTION TWO

*Notes: † The Census 2010 population figure is used to calculate the percentages in the Hispanic Origin and Race categories. Ancestry percentages are based on the 2006-2010 American Community Survey population (not shown); ‡ Numbers in parentheses indicate the number of people reporting a single ancestry; * Numbers in parentheses indicate the number of persons reporting this race alone, not in combination with any other race; Please refer to the Explanation of Data for more information.*

Jamaican (83)	125	0.28
West Indian (6)	6	0.01

Hispanic Origin	Population	%
Hispanic or Latino (of any race)	9,279	18.96
Central American, ex. Mexican	343	0.70
Costa Rican	17	0.03
Guatemalan	47	0.10
Honduran	57	0.12
Nicaraguan	16	0.03
Panamanian	58	0.12
Salvadoran	138	0.28
Other Central American	10	0.02
Cuban	104	0.21
Dominican Republic	34	0.07
Mexican	7,275	14.87
Puerto Rican	352	0.72
South American	390	0.80
Argentinean	27	0.06
Bolivian	22	0.04
Chilean	35	0.07
Colombian	153	0.31
Ecuadorian	23	0.05
Paraguayan	7	0.01
Peruvian	82	0.17
Uruguayan	5	0.01
Venezuelan	36	0.07
Other Hispanic or Latino	781	1.60

Race*	Population	%
African-American/Black (2,102)	2,564	5.24
Not Hispanic (1,985)	2,342	4.79
Hispanic (117)	222	0.45
American Indian/Alaska Native (232)	580	1.19
Not Hispanic (152)	420	0.86
Hispanic (80)	160	0.33
Apache (9)	16	0.03
Blackfeet (0)	1	<0.01
Central American Ind. (0)	4	0.01
Cherokee (31)	130	0.27
Cheyenne (4)	5	0.01
Chickasaw (0)	6	0.01
Chippewa (5)	7	0.01
Choctaw (28)	65	0.13
Comanche (5)	22	0.04
Creek (1)	9	0.02
Crow (0)	1	<0.01
Delaware (3)	5	0.01
Hopi (1)	2	<0.01
Inupiat *(Alaska Native)* (0)	1	<0.01
Iroquois (6)	8	0.02
Kiowa (0)	2	<0.01
Mexican American Ind. (5)	8	0.02
Navajo (3)	5	0.01
Osage (0)	3	0.01
Ottawa (0)	1	<0.01
Potawatomi (2)	5	0.01
Pueblo (3)	6	0.01
Puget Sound Salish (9)	9	0.02
Seminole (0)	5	0.01
Sioux (8)	14	0.03
South American Ind. (0)	5	0.01
Spanish American Ind. (0)	1	<0.01
Tsimshian *(Alaska Native)* (0)	1	<0.01
Asian (2,483)	3,071	6.28
Not Hispanic (2,439)	2,930	5.99
Hispanic (44)	141	0.29
Bangladeshi (17)	20	0.04
Burmese (2)	2	<0.01
Cambodian (31)	46	0.09
Chinese, ex. Taiwanese (313)	422	0.86
Filipino (231)	410	0.84
Indian (803)	853	1.74
Indonesian (30)	38	0.08
Japanese (69)	161	0.33
Korean (255)	339	0.69
Laotian (21)	25	0.05
Malaysian (4)	5	0.01
Nepalese (0)	1	<0.01
Pakistani (52)	56	0.11
Sri Lankan (2)	8	0.02
Taiwanese (32)	43	0.09
Thai (47)	75	0.15
Vietnamese (464)	543	1.11
Hawaii Native/Pacific Islander (43)	137	0.28
Not Hispanic (34)	122	0.25
Hispanic (9)	15	0.03
Fijian (0)	1	<0.01
Guamanian/Chamorro (8)	18	0.04
Native Hawaiian (27)	81	0.17
Samoan (1)	12	0.02
Tongan (1)	5	0.01
White (39,817)	41,319	84.43
Not Hispanic (33,909)	34,888	71.29
Hispanic (5,908)	6,431	13.14

Channelview

Place Type: CDP
County: Harris
Population: 38,289†

Ancestry‡	Population	%
African, Sub-Saharan (125)	125	0.33
African (34)	34	0.09
Nigerian (91)	91	0.24
American (1,319)	1,319	3.47
British (13)	13	0.03
Canadian (11)	11	0.03
Czech (36)	93	0.24
Dutch (83)	236	0.62
English (406)	1,097	2.89
European (28)	28	0.07
French, ex. Basque (360)	755	1.99
French Canadian (0)	47	0.12
German (605)	1,376	3.62
Greek (17)	40	0.11
Irish (399)	1,250	3.29
Italian (45)	111	0.29
Norwegian (22)	56	0.15
Polish (102)	129	0.34
Portuguese (0)	36	0.09
Russian (0)	63	0.17
Scotch-Irish (229)	424	1.12
Scottish (103)	307	0.81
Slavic (0)	30	0.08
Swedish (12)	74	0.19
Swiss (0)	28	0.07
Welsh (16)	26	0.07
West Indian, ex. Hispanic (30)	30	0.08
Trinidadian/Tobagonian (30)	30	0.08

Hispanic Origin	Population	%
Hispanic or Latino (of any race)	23,100	60.33
Central American, ex. Mexican	1,465	3.83
Costa Rican	12	0.03
Guatemalan	163	0.43
Honduran	359	0.94
Nicaraguan	38	0.10
Panamanian	3	0.01
Salvadoran	888	2.32
Other Central American	2	0.01
Cuban	56	0.15
Dominican Republic	35	0.09
Mexican	19,822	51.77
Puerto Rican	177	0.46
South American	159	0.42
Argentinean	22	0.06
Bolivian	7	0.02
Chilean	15	0.04
Colombian	85	0.22
Ecuadorian	3	0.01
Peruvian	14	0.04
Uruguayan	7	0.02
Venezuelan	6	0.02
Other Hispanic or Latino	1,386	3.62

Race*	Population	%
African-American/Black (5,861)	6,091	15.91
Not Hispanic (5,671)	5,804	15.16
Hispanic (190)	287	0.75
American Indian/Alaska Native (309)	517	1.35
Not Hispanic (95)	197	0.51
Hispanic (214)	320	0.84
Apache (2)	15	0.04
Blackfeet (0)	2	0.01
Canadian/French Am. Ind. (0)	1	<0.01
Central American Ind. (4)	5	0.01
Cherokee (22)	76	0.20
Chickasaw (2)	2	0.01
Choctaw (4)	13	0.03
Comanche (4)	8	0.02
Cree (1)	1	<0.01
Creek (1)	4	0.01
Crow (3)	3	0.01
Delaware (4)	4	0.01
Hopi (4)	4	0.01
Iroquois (6)	6	0.02
Mexican American Ind. (47)	77	0.20
Navajo (7)	7	0.02
Osage (2)	2	0.01
Ottawa (1)	1	<0.01
Potawatomi (0)	1	<0.01
Pueblo (2)	4	0.01
Sioux (2)	3	0.01
Spanish American Ind. (1)	1	<0.01
Yuman (1)	1	<0.01
Asian (615)	746	1.95
Not Hispanic (592)	664	1.73
Hispanic (23)	82	0.21
Bangladeshi (8)	8	0.02
Cambodian (19)	21	0.05
Chinese, ex. Taiwanese (55)	83	0.22
Filipino (174)	210	0.55
Indian (61)	82	0.21
Japanese (4)	15	0.04
Korean (7)	20	0.05
Laotian (0)	3	0.01
Malaysian (1)	5	0.01
Pakistani (4)	6	0.02
Taiwanese (0)	1	<0.01
Thai (3)	6	0.02
Vietnamese (242)	265	0.69
Hawaii Native/Pacific Islander (23)	105	0.27
Not Hispanic (14)	37	0.10
Hispanic (9)	68	0.18
Guamanian/Chamorro (0)	9	0.02
Native Hawaiian (1)	13	0.03
Samoan (1)	4	0.01
Tongan (7)	7	0.02
White (21,391)	22,574	58.96
Not Hispanic (8,483)	8,709	22.75
Hispanic (12,908)	13,865	36.21

Cibolo

Place Type: City
County: Guadalupe
Population: 15,349†

Ancestry‡	Population	%
African, Sub-Saharan (20)	116	0.89
African (8)	104	0.80
Zimbabwean (12)	12	0.09
American (611)	611	4.69
Australian (32)	32	0.25
Basque (7)	7	0.05
Belgian (8)	26	0.20
British (10)	29	0.22
Canadian (7)	7	0.05
Croatian (0)	45	0.35
Czech (0)	84	0.64
Czechoslovakian (12)	22	0.17
Danish (27)	27	0.21
Dutch (0)	61	0.47
English (424)	1,283	9.84
European (54)	54	0.41
Finnish (0)	25	0.19
French, ex. Basque (64)	603	4.63
French Canadian (63)	109	0.84

*Notes: † The Census 2010 population figure is used to calculate the percentages in the Hispanic Origin and Race categories. Ancestry percentages are based on the 2006-2010 American Community Survey population (not shown); ‡ Numbers in parentheses indicate the number of people reporting a single ancestry; * Numbers in parentheses indicate the number of persons reporting this race alone, not in combination with any other race; Please refer to the Explanation of Data for more information.*

German (797)	2,614	20.05
Greek (10)	21	0.16
Iranian (12)	49	0.38
Irish (242)	1,313	10.07
Italian (97)	362	2.78
Maltese (7)	12	0.09
Northern European (0)	5	0.04
Norwegian (23)	170	1.30
Polish (50)	224	1.72
Portuguese (51)	51	0.39
Russian (0)	113	0.87
Scotch-Irish (151)	484	3.71
Scottish (92)	291	2.23
Swedish (19)	111	0.85
Swiss (0)	21	0.16
Ukrainian (0)	15	0.12
Welsh (19)	92	0.71
West Indian, ex. Hispanic (71)	113	0.87
Bermudan (17)	17	0.13
Dutch West Indian (13)	13	0.10
Jamaican (12)	54	0.41
West Indian (29)	29	0.22

Hispanic Origin	Population	%
Hispanic or Latino (of any race)	3,626	23.62
Central American, ex. Mexican	154	1.00
Costa Rican	5	0.03
Guatemalan	32	0.21
Honduran	15	0.10
Nicaraguan	18	0.12
Panamanian	53	0.35
Salvadoran	27	0.18
Other Central American	4	0.03
Cuban	34	0.22
Dominican Republic	16	0.10
Mexican	2,637	17.18
Puerto Rican	337	2.20
South American	111	0.72
Argentinean	5	0.03
Bolivian	1	0.01
Chilean	4	0.03
Colombian	60	0.39
Ecuadorian	19	0.12
Peruvian	10	0.07
Venezuelan	11	0.07
Other South American	1	0.01
Other Hispanic or Latino	337	2.20

Race*	Population	%
African-American/Black (2,134)	2,414	15.73
Not Hispanic (2,008)	2,221	14.47
Hispanic (126)	193	1.26
American Indian/Alaska Native (82)	205	1.34
Not Hispanic (58)	140	0.91
Hispanic (24)	65	0.42
Aleut *(Alaska Native)* (1)	1	0.01
Apache (5)	6	0.04
Blackfeet (0)	3	0.02
Canadian/French Am. Ind. (0)	1	0.01
Cherokee (12)	30	0.20
Chippewa (2)	2	0.01
Choctaw (7)	11	0.07
Creek (0)	2	0.01
Hopi (1)	1	0.01
Inupiat *(Alaska Native)* (2)	2	0.01
Iroquois (0)	2	0.01
Lumbee (3)	3	0.02
Mexican American Ind. (4)	11	0.07
Navajo (2)	8	0.05
Potawatomi (1)	1	0.01
Pueblo (0)	1	0.01
Seminole (0)	5	0.03
Sioux (1)	5	0.03
South American Ind. (1)	1	0.01
Asian (462)	757	4.93
Not Hispanic (441)	685	4.46
Hispanic (21)	72	0.47
Cambodian (8)	10	0.07
Chinese, ex. Taiwanese (24)	58	0.38
Filipino (216)	320	2.08
Indian (22)	23	0.15
Japanese (29)	80	0.52
Korean (71)	133	0.87
Laotian (2)	2	0.01
Pakistani (4)	4	0.03
Taiwanese (6)	17	0.11
Thai (23)	43	0.28
Vietnamese (47)	64	0.42
Hawaii Native/Pacific Islander (46)	89	0.58
Not Hispanic (42)	79	0.51
Hispanic (4)	10	0.07
Guamanian/Chamorro (9)	22	0.14
Native Hawaiian (11)	28	0.18
Samoan (14)	20	0.13
Tongan (2)	2	0.01
White (11,282)	11,879	77.39
Not Hispanic (8,666)	9,076	59.13
Hispanic (2,616)	2,803	18.26

Cinco Ranch

Place Type: CDP
County: Fort Bend
Population: 18,274†

Ancestry‡	Population	%
African, Sub-Saharan (122)	168	0.93
African (101)	147	0.81
Nigerian (21)	21	0.12
American (1,351)	1,351	7.45
Arab (46)	80	0.44
Arab (13)	13	0.07
Egyptian (11)	11	0.06
Lebanese (0)	21	0.12
Syrian (0)	13	0.07
Other Arab (22)	22	0.12
Armenian (16)	16	0.09
Australian (46)	46	0.25
Austrian (0)	38	0.21
Brazilian (76)	127	0.70
British (208)	320	1.76
Cajun (13)	40	0.22
Canadian (72)	86	0.47
Croatian (0)	42	0.23
Czech (45)	134	0.74
Czechoslovakian (11)	34	0.19
Danish (14)	56	0.31
Dutch (79)	320	1.76
English (873)	2,465	13.59
European (95)	122	0.67
Finnish (52)	90	0.50
French, ex. Basque (246)	665	3.67
French Canadian (118)	164	0.90
German (900)	2,839	15.65
Greek (46)	84	0.46
Hungarian (12)	22	0.12
Iranian (208)	234	1.29
Irish (353)	1,679	9.26
Italian (369)	750	4.13
Lithuanian (14)	14	0.08
Maltese (17)	17	0.09
New Zealander (0)	115	0.63
Northern European (19)	19	0.10
Norwegian (276)	350	1.93
Polish (127)	368	2.03
Portuguese (49)	152	0.84
Romanian (26)	56	0.31
Russian (116)	177	0.98
Scandinavian (0)	34	0.19
Scotch-Irish (50)	326	1.80
Scottish (240)	537	2.96
Slavic (9)	9	0.05
Slovene (17)	26	0.14
Swedish (103)	250	1.38
Swiss (0)	118	0.65
Ukrainian (72)	112	0.62
Welsh (22)	177	0.98
West Indian, ex. Hispanic (33)	77	0.42
Jamaican (33)	33	0.18
West Indian (0)	44	0.24
Yugoslavian (13)	55	0.30

Hispanic Origin	Population	%
Hispanic or Latino (of any race)	2,349	12.85
Central American, ex. Mexican	171	0.94
Costa Rican	21	0.11
Guatemalan	31	0.17
Honduran	31	0.17
Nicaraguan	20	0.11
Panamanian	11	0.06
Salvadoran	56	0.31
Other Central American	1	0.01
Cuban	98	0.54
Dominican Republic	19	0.10
Mexican	1,001	5.48
Puerto Rican	80	0.44
South American	757	4.14
Argentinean	83	0.45
Bolivian	16	0.09
Chilean	9	0.05
Colombian	267	1.46
Ecuadorian	23	0.13
Paraguayan	3	0.02
Peruvian	92	0.50
Uruguayan	8	0.04
Venezuelan	250	1.37
Other South American	6	0.03
Other Hispanic or Latino	223	1.22

Race*	Population	%
African-American/Black (658)	773	4.23
Not Hispanic (634)	719	3.93
Hispanic (24)	54	0.30
American Indian/Alaska Native (65)	151	0.83
Not Hispanic (38)	101	0.55
Hispanic (27)	50	0.27
Apache (2)	4	0.02
Cherokee (8)	33	0.18
Chickasaw (3)	8	0.04
Choctaw (7)	14	0.08
Inupiat *(Alaska Native)* (0)	1	0.01
Iroquois (1)	2	0.01
Mexican American Ind. (1)	3	0.02
Osage (2)	2	0.01
South American Ind. (0)	2	0.01
Spanish American Ind. (4)	4	0.02
Asian (2,371)	2,602	14.24
Not Hispanic (2,343)	2,549	13.95
Hispanic (28)	53	0.29
Bangladeshi (12)	12	0.07
Burmese (5)	9	0.05
Cambodian (8)	8	0.04
Chinese, ex. Taiwanese (670)	710	3.89
Filipino (130)	170	0.93
Indian (798)	849	4.65
Indonesian (25)	27	0.15
Japanese (60)	107	0.59
Korean (219)	240	1.31
Laotian (1)	3	0.02
Malaysian (14)	15	0.08
Pakistani (123)	134	0.73
Sri Lankan (8)	12	0.07
Taiwanese (21)	22	0.12
Thai (13)	16	0.09
Vietnamese (190)	208	1.14
Hawaii Native/Pacific Islander (7)	25	0.14
Not Hispanic (6)	13	0.07
Hispanic (1)	12	0.07
Fijian (1)	1	0.01
Guamanian/Chamorro (1)	2	0.01
Native Hawaiian (3)	8	0.04
Samoan (2)	2	0.01
White (14,333)	14,698	80.43
Not Hispanic (12,537)	12,803	70.06
Hispanic (1,796)	1,895	10.37

*Notes: † The Census 2010 population figure is used to calculate the percentages in the Hispanic Origin and Race categories. Ancestry percentages are based on the 2006-2010 American Community Survey population (not shown); ‡ Numbers in parentheses indicate the number of people reporting a single ancestry; * Numbers in parentheses indicate the number of persons reporting this race alone, not in combination with any other race; Please refer to the Explanation of Data for more information.*

Cleburne

Place Type: City
County: Johnson
Population: 29,337†

Ancestry‡	Population	%
African, Sub-Saharan (34)	34	0.12
African (23)	23	0.08
Ugandan (11)	11	0.04
American (1,910)	1,910	6.58
Austrian (0)	21	0.07
Brazilian (36)	36	0.12
British (20)	55	0.19
Cajun (7)	7	0.02
Croatian (12)	12	0.04
Czech (64)	201	0.69
Czechoslovakian (0)	7	0.02
Dutch (68)	601	2.07
English (2,257)	4,965	17.11
European (71)	71	0.24
Finnish (0)	18	0.06
French, ex. Basque (121)	630	2.17
French Canadian (42)	87	0.30
German (1,281)	4,663	16.07
Greek (0)	18	0.06
Hungarian (30)	51	0.18
Irish (1,169)	4,426	15.25
Italian (103)	356	1.23
New Zealander (13)	28	0.10
Norwegian (64)	127	0.44
Pennsylvania German (0)	37	0.13
Polish (4)	81	0.28
Portuguese (9)	23	0.08
Russian (18)	67	0.23
Scandinavian (0)	20	0.07
Scotch-Irish (288)	663	2.28
Scottish (281)	803	2.77
Swedish (56)	172	0.59
Swiss (0)	10	0.03
Turkish (15)	15	0.05
Ukrainian (8)	44	0.15
Welsh (27)	106	0.37
West Indian, ex. Hispanic (14)	54	0.19
Dutch West Indian (14)	54	0.19

Hispanic Origin	Population	%
Hispanic or Latino (of any race)	7,959	27.13
Central American, ex. Mexican	129	0.44
Costa Rican	8	0.03
Guatemalan	24	0.08
Honduran	55	0.19
Nicaraguan	2	0.01
Panamanian	4	0.01
Salvadoran	31	0.11
Other Central American	5	0.02
Cuban	24	0.08
Dominican Republic	5	0.02
Mexican	7,160	24.41
Puerto Rican	144	0.49
South American	60	0.20
Argentinean	1	<0.01
Colombian	13	0.04
Ecuadorian	2	0.01
Peruvian	8	0.03
Venezuelan	35	0.12
Other South American	1	<0.01
Other Hispanic or Latino	437	1.49

Race*	Population	%
African-American/Black (1,290)	1,505	5.13
Not Hispanic (1,238)	1,416	4.83
Hispanic (52)	89	0.30
American Indian/Alaska Native (201)	326	1.11
Not Hispanic (112)	216	0.74
Hispanic (89)	110	0.37
Alaska Athabascan *(Ala. Nat.)* (0)	1	<0.01
Apache (4)	9	0.03
Blackfeet (1)	6	0.02
Cherokee (29)	52	0.18
Cheyenne (1)	1	<0.01
Chickasaw (9)	10	0.03
Choctaw (15)	24	0.08
Comanche (2)	4	0.01
Creek (2)	7	0.02
Iroquois (1)	5	0.02
Mexican American Ind. (10)	15	0.05
Navajo (3)	4	0.01
Osage (4)	4	0.01
Paiute (0)	1	<0.01
Potawatomi (3)	3	0.01
Seminole (3)	8	0.03
Sioux (9)	15	0.05
Spanish American Ind. (0)	1	<0.01
Yaqui (0)	1	<0.01
Yup'ik *(Alaska Native)* (0)	3	0.01
Asian (147)	243	0.83
Not Hispanic (146)	217	0.74
Hispanic (1)	26	0.09
Chinese, ex. Taiwanese (36)	44	0.15
Filipino (24)	47	0.16
Indian (31)	54	0.18
Japanese (7)	30	0.10
Korean (16)	28	0.10
Nepalese (4)	4	0.01
Pakistani (3)	4	0.01
Thai (3)	4	0.01
Vietnamese (14)	16	0.05
Hawaii Native/Pacific Islander (91)	128	0.44
Not Hispanic (86)	114	0.39
Hispanic (5)	14	0.05
Guamanian/Chamorro (0)	3	0.01
Marshallese (44)	56	0.19
Native Hawaiian (20)	31	0.11
Samoan (1)	6	0.02
White (24,159)	24,775	84.45
Not Hispanic (19,406)	19,725	67.24
Hispanic (4,753)	5,050	17.21

Cleveland

Place Type: City
County: Liberty
Population: 7,675†

Ancestry‡	Population	%
American (445)	445	5.68
Cajun (22)	22	0.28
Czech (0)	45	0.57
Dutch (0)	29	0.37
English (160)	262	3.34
European (106)	120	1.53
French, ex. Basque (19)	203	2.59
German (187)	683	8.72
Irish (138)	767	9.79
Italian (52)	76	0.97
Norwegian (11)	11	0.14
Polish (0)	62	0.79
Scotch-Irish (20)	36	0.46
Scottish (42)	135	1.72
Swedish (18)	18	0.23
Welsh (40)	49	0.63
West Indian, ex. Hispanic (10)	10	0.13
Dutch West Indian (10)	10	0.13

Hispanic Origin	Population	%
Hispanic or Latino (of any race)	2,131	27.77
Central American, ex. Mexican	33	0.43
Guatemalan	6	0.08
Honduran	5	0.07
Panamanian	1	0.01
Salvadoran	21	0.27
Cuban	4	0.05
Mexican	1,908	24.86
Puerto Rican	17	0.22
South American	7	0.09
Colombian	3	0.04
Ecuadorian	4	0.05
Other Hispanic or Latino	162	2.11

Race*	Population	%
African-American/Black (1,845)	1,920	25.02
Not Hispanic (1,819)	1,873	24.40
Hispanic (26)	47	0.61
American Indian/Alaska Native (45)	104	1.36
Not Hispanic (12)	37	0.48
Hispanic (33)	67	0.87
Blackfeet (0)	2	0.03
Cherokee (1)	12	0.16
Cheyenne (0)	1	0.01
Choctaw (1)	1	0.01
Hopi (0)	2	0.03
Lumbee (1)	1	0.01
Mexican American Ind. (2)	3	0.04
Osage (0)	1	0.01
Sioux (1)	1	0.01
South American Ind. (0)	1	0.01
Asian (101)	126	1.64
Not Hispanic (99)	115	1.50
Hispanic (2)	11	0.14
Bangladeshi (3)	3	0.04
Cambodian (1)	5	0.07
Chinese, ex. Taiwanese (11)	13	0.17
Filipino (7)	9	0.12
Indian (15)	19	0.25
Japanese (2)	13	0.17
Korean (1)	3	0.04
Pakistani (44)	46	0.60
Vietnamese (2)	2	0.03
Hawaii Native/Pacific Islander (1)	3	0.04
Not Hispanic (1)	3	0.04
Native Hawaiian (1)	1	0.01
White (4,537)	4,701	61.25
Not Hispanic (3,510)	3,594	46.83
Hispanic (1,027)	1,107	14.42

Cloverleaf

Place Type: CDP
County: Harris
Population: 22,942†

Ancestry‡	Population	%
African, Sub-Saharan (503)	503	2.20
African (461)	461	2.02
Nigerian (42)	42	0.18
American (569)	569	2.49
Arab (132)	132	0.58
Arab (79)	79	0.35
Palestinian (53)	53	0.23
Austrian (0)	15	0.07
Croatian (0)	44	0.19
Czech (3)	33	0.14
Czechoslovakian (15)	30	0.13
Dutch (0)	130	0.57
Eastern European (0)	7	0.03
English (268)	563	2.46
European (17)	17	0.07
French, ex. Basque (15)	119	0.52
French Canadian (77)	77	0.34
German (178)	406	1.78
Greek (82)	82	0.36
Irish (82)	595	2.60
Italian (79)	79	0.35
Lithuanian (12)	12	0.05
Norwegian (18)	18	0.08
Polish (10)	50	0.22
Scotch-Irish (101)	177	0.77
Scottish (24)	43	0.19
Serbian (0)	10	0.04
Swedish (9)	42	0.18
Swiss (13)	13	0.06
Welsh (24)	34	0.15

Hispanic Origin	Population	%
Hispanic or Latino (of any race)	15,636	68.15
Central American, ex. Mexican	1,177	5.13
Costa Rican	12	0.05
Guatemalan	120	0.52
Honduran	290	1.26

*Notes: † The Census 2010 population figure is used to calculate the percentages in the Hispanic Origin and Race categories. Ancestry percentages are based on the 2006-2010 American Community Survey population (not shown); ‡ Numbers in parentheses indicate the number of people reporting a single ancestry; * Numbers in parentheses indicate the number of persons reporting this race alone, not in combination with any other race; Please refer to the Explanation of Data for more information.*

Nicaraguan	32	0.14
Panamanian	6	0.03
Salvadoran	700	3.05
Other Central American	17	0.07
Cuban	18	0.08
Dominican Republic	2	0.01
Mexican	13,431	58.54
Puerto Rican	60	0.26
South American	61	0.27
Argentinean	4	0.02
Chilean	6	0.03
Colombian	35	0.15
Ecuadorian	5	0.02
Peruvian	5	0.02
Venezuelan	6	0.03
Other Hispanic or Latino	887	3.87

Race*	Population	%
African-American/Black (2,414)	2,514	10.96
Not Hispanic (2,310)	2,364	10.30
Hispanic (104)	150	0.65
American Indian/Alaska Native (207)	291	1.27
Not Hispanic (32)	76	0.33
Hispanic (175)	215	0.94
Apache (0)	1	<0.01
Blackfeet (0)	4	0.02
Central American Ind. (1)	1	<0.01
Cherokee (11)	29	0.13
Chippewa (1)	1	<0.01
Choctaw (4)	11	0.05
Comanche (1)	1	<0.01
Creek (1)	1	<0.01
Mexican American Ind. (38)	46	0.20
Navajo (5)	6	0.03
Pueblo (1)	2	0.01
Seminole (0)	1	<0.01
Shoshone (1)	1	<0.01
South American Ind. (6)	8	0.03
Spanish American Ind. (2)	4	0.02
Asian (278)	344	1.50
Not Hispanic (270)	312	1.36
Hispanic (8)	32	0.14
Bangladeshi (11)	11	0.05
Chinese, ex. Taiwanese (29)	37	0.16
Filipino (72)	95	0.41
Indian (85)	86	0.37
Indonesian (1)	3	0.01
Japanese (4)	11	0.05
Korean (5)	12	0.05
Laotian (1)	1	<0.01
Thai (4)	4	0.02
Vietnamese (55)	57	0.25
Hawaii Native/Pacific Islander (6)	29	0.13
Not Hispanic (4)	13	0.06
Hispanic (2)	16	0.07
Guamanian/Chamorro (3)	4	0.02
Native Hawaiian (2)	7	0.03
White (14,033)	14,755	64.31
Not Hispanic (4,531)	4,636	20.21
Hispanic (9,502)	10,119	44.11

Clute

Place Type: City
County: Brazoria
Population: 11,211†

Ancestry‡	Population	%
American (418)	418	3.77
Austrian (0)	11	0.10
British (0)	12	0.11
Cajun (0)	14	0.13
Canadian (10)	20	0.18
Celtic (12)	12	0.11
Czech (40)	121	1.09
Dutch (0)	15	0.14
English (208)	523	4.72
European (24)	24	0.22
French, ex. Basque (53)	251	2.26
French Canadian (11)	55	0.50
German (268)	1,070	9.65
Greek (9)	9	0.08
Irish (243)	908	8.19
Italian (29)	108	0.97
Norwegian (0)	26	0.23
Polish (10)	91	0.82
Scotch-Irish (35)	82	0.74
Scottish (82)	198	1.79
Swedish (28)	186	1.68
Ukrainian (0)	5	0.05
Welsh (8)	40	0.36

Hispanic Origin	Population	%
Hispanic or Latino (of any race)	6,006	53.57
Central American, ex. Mexican	116	1.03
Costa Rican	3	0.03
Guatemalan	45	0.40
Honduran	26	0.23
Nicaraguan	16	0.14
Panamanian	1	0.01
Salvadoran	25	0.22
Cuban	3	0.03
Mexican	5,374	47.94
Puerto Rican	51	0.45
South American	55	0.49
Argentinean	8	0.07
Bolivian	2	0.02
Chilean	4	0.04
Colombian	17	0.15
Ecuadorian	14	0.12
Peruvian	4	0.04
Venezuelan	6	0.05
Other Hispanic or Latino	407	3.63

Race*	Population	%
African-American/Black (1,172)	1,275	11.37
Not Hispanic (1,124)	1,198	10.69
Hispanic (48)	77	0.69
American Indian/Alaska Native (100)	180	1.61
Not Hispanic (19)	59	0.53
Hispanic (81)	121	1.08
Apache (0)	4	0.04
Blackfeet (0)	1	0.01
Cherokee (6)	19	0.17
Chickasaw (0)	2	0.02
Choctaw (2)	8	0.07
Creek (0)	1	0.01
Mexican American Ind. (19)	26	0.23
Osage (2)	2	0.02
Ottawa (1)	1	0.01
Potawatomi (1)	3	0.03
Pueblo (0)	2	0.02
Puget Sound Salish (0)	1	0.01
Sioux (0)	1	0.01
Asian (81)	93	0.83
Not Hispanic (64)	73	0.65
Hispanic (17)	20	0.18
Cambodian (6)	6	0.05
Chinese, ex. Taiwanese (7)	8	0.07
Filipino (10)	11	0.10
Indian (22)	25	0.22
Japanese (1)	2	0.02
Korean (3)	5	0.04
Pakistani (8)	8	0.07
Taiwanese (3)	3	0.03
Thai (1)	1	0.01
Vietnamese (20)	21	0.19
Hawaii Native/Pacific Islander (1)	5	0.04
Not Hispanic (1)	4	0.04
Hispanic (0)	1	0.01
Samoan (1)	2	0.02
White (7,755)	8,059	71.88
Not Hispanic (3,874)	3,973	35.44
Hispanic (3,881)	4,086	36.45

College Station

Place Type: City
County: Brazos
Population: 93,857†

Ancestry‡	Population	%
African, Sub-Saharan (506)	537	0.61
African (304)	327	0.37
Ethiopian (15)	15	0.02
Nigerian (112)	112	0.13
Senegalese (0)	8	0.01
Sudanese (14)	14	0.02
Other Sub-Saharan African (61)	61	0.07
American (3,108)	3,108	3.51
Arab (365)	425	0.48
Arab (47)	58	0.07
Egyptian (78)	78	0.09
Iraqi (14)	14	0.02
Jordanian (17)	17	0.02
Lebanese (109)	158	0.18
Palestinian (66)	66	0.07
Other Arab (34)	34	0.04
Armenian (0)	44	0.05
Australian (14)	14	0.02
Austrian (16)	103	0.12
Basque (29)	29	0.03
Belgian (22)	44	0.05
Brazilian (52)	52	0.06
British (274)	527	0.60
Bulgarian (13)	20	0.02
Cajun (25)	46	0.05
Canadian (64)	173	0.20
Croatian (49)	56	0.06
Cypriot (8)	8	0.01
Czech (884)	2,125	2.40
Czechoslovakian (50)	146	0.16
Danish (62)	184	0.21
Dutch (293)	1,441	1.63
Eastern European (36)	36	0.04
English (3,383)	9,704	10.96
European (740)	935	1.06
Finnish (36)	64	0.07
French, ex. Basque (479)	2,360	2.67
French Canadian (86)	192	0.22
German (6,195)	16,002	18.07
Greek (98)	280	0.32
Hungarian (75)	222	0.25
Icelander (0)	15	0.02
Iranian (80)	116	0.13
Irish (2,093)	8,389	9.47
Israeli (0)	12	0.01
Italian (949)	2,415	2.73
Lithuanian (13)	76	0.09
Luxemburger (0)	15	0.02
Macedonian (7)	7	0.01
New Zealander (0)	14	0.02
Northern European (28)	42	0.05
Norwegian (369)	1,121	1.27
Polish (786)	2,146	2.42
Portuguese (63)	145	0.16
Romanian (7)	7	0.01
Russian (404)	743	0.84
Scandinavian (61)	101	0.11
Scotch-Irish (1,111)	2,796	3.16
Scottish (717)	2,467	2.79
Serbian (36)	36	0.04
Slavic (0)	29	0.03
Slovak (0)	33	0.04
Slovene (0)	21	0.02
Swedish (428)	1,190	1.34
Swiss (39)	74	0.08
Turkish (79)	96	0.11
Ukrainian (121)	220	0.25
Welsh (206)	539	0.61
West Indian, ex. Hispanic (63)	93	0.11
Belizean (13)	13	0.01
Dutch West Indian (0)	8	0.01
Jamaican (50)	72	0.08
Yugoslavian (20)	20	0.02

Hispanic Origin	Population	%
Hispanic or Latino (of any race)	13,165	14.03
Central American, ex. Mexican	881	0.94
Costa Rican	49	0.05
Guatemalan	419	0.45

*Notes: † The Census 2010 population figure is used to calculate the percentages in the Hispanic Origin and Race categories. Ancestry percentages are based on the 2006-2010 American Community Survey population (not shown); ‡ Numbers in parentheses indicate the number of people reporting a single ancestry; * Numbers in parentheses indicate the number of persons reporting this race alone, not in combination with any other race; Please refer to the Explanation of Data for more information.*

Honduran	76	0.08
Nicaraguan	44	0.05
Panamanian	82	0.09
Salvadoran	191	0.20
Other Central American	20	0.02
Cuban	189	0.20
Dominican Republic	55	0.06
Mexican	9,773	10.41
Puerto Rican	328	0.35
South American	802	0.85
Argentinean	61	0.06
Bolivian	40	0.04
Chilean	64	0.07
Colombian	277	0.30
Ecuadorian	63	0.07
Paraguayan	7	0.01
Peruvian	113	0.12
Uruguayan	15	0.02
Venezuelan	160	0.17
Other South American	2	<0.01
Other Hispanic or Latino	1,137	1.21

Race*	Population	%
African-American/Black (6,383)	6,905	7.36
Not Hispanic (6,161)	6,571	7.00
Hispanic (222)	334	0.36
American Indian/Alaska Native (369)	796	0.85
Not Hispanic (247)	577	0.61
Hispanic (122)	219	0.23
Alaska Athabascan *(Ala. Nat.)* (0)	1	<0.01
Aleut *(Alaska Native)* (0)	2	<0.01
Apache (9)	27	0.03
Arapaho (1)	1	<0.01
Blackfeet (1)	6	0.01
Canadian/French Am. Ind. (1)	5	0.01
Central American Ind. (17)	17	0.02
Cherokee (65)	180	0.19
Cheyenne (2)	2	<0.01
Chickasaw (9)	18	0.02
Chippewa (6)	8	0.01
Choctaw (47)	80	0.09
Comanche (2)	5	0.01
Cree (1)	2	<0.01
Creek (9)	19	0.02
Delaware (2)	4	<0.01
Houma (0)	1	<0.01
Iroquois (3)	7	0.01
Kiowa (0)	1	<0.01
Lumbee (0)	1	<0.01
Menominee (0)	1	<0.01
Mexican American Ind. (17)	23	0.02
Navajo (5)	7	0.01
Osage (3)	4	<0.01
Potawatomi (4)	8	0.01
Pueblo (3)	3	<0.01
Seminole (1)	3	<0.01
Sioux (2)	5	0.01
South American Ind. (1)	5	0.01
Spanish American Ind. (0)	1	<0.01
Yaqui (1)	1	<0.01
Yup'ik *(Alaska Native)* (4)	4	<0.01
Asian (8,576)	9,492	10.11
Not Hispanic (8,518)	9,354	9.97
Hispanic (58)	138	0.15
Bangladeshi (81)	87	0.09
Bhutanese (1)	1	<0.01
Burmese (3)	3	<0.01
Cambodian (16)	23	0.02
Chinese, ex. Taiwanese (2,668)	2,875	3.06
Filipino (242)	392	0.42
Hmong (2)	2	<0.01
Indian (2,231)	2,364	2.52
Indonesian (58)	64	0.07
Japanese (128)	258	0.27
Korean (1,484)	1,593	1.70
Laotian (5)	5	0.01
Malaysian (31)	37	0.04
Nepalese (42)	42	0.04
Pakistani (385)	416	0.44
Sri Lankan (51)	54	0.06
Taiwanese (365)	386	0.41
Thai (69)	82	0.09
Vietnamese (530)	635	0.68
Hawaii Native/Pacific Islander (59)	181	0.19
Not Hispanic (36)	146	0.16
Hispanic (23)	35	0.04
Guamanian/Chamorro (25)	33	0.04
Native Hawaiian (16)	56	0.06
Samoan (11)	24	0.03
White (72,502)	74,456	79.33
Not Hispanic (64,060)	65,390	69.67
Hispanic (8,442)	9,066	9.66

Colleyville

Place Type: City
County: Tarrant
Population: 22,807†

Ancestry‡	Population	%
African, Sub-Saharan (22)	22	0.10
African (22)	22	0.10
American (2,157)	2,157	9.71
Arab (176)	235	1.06
Egyptian (143)	143	0.64
Lebanese (19)	69	0.31
Syrian (0)	9	0.04
Other Arab (14)	14	0.06
Armenian (36)	44	0.20
Basque (12)	24	0.11
Brazilian (30)	62	0.28
British (209)	246	1.11
Canadian (25)	57	0.26
Celtic (0)	11	0.05
Croatian (0)	12	0.05
Czech (40)	263	1.18
Czechoslovakian (0)	53	0.24
Danish (81)	212	0.95
Dutch (56)	183	0.82
Eastern European (4)	4	0.02
English (1,463)	3,582	16.12
European (538)	562	2.53
Finnish (18)	18	0.08
French, ex. Basque (267)	727	3.27
French Canadian (43)	77	0.35
German (1,756)	4,928	22.18
Greek (28)	57	0.26
Hungarian (0)	25	0.11
Icelander (8)	17	0.08
Iranian (14)	14	0.06
Irish (757)	3,003	13.52
Italian (280)	1,065	4.79
Lithuanian (34)	65	0.29
Northern European (11)	11	0.05
Norwegian (89)	359	1.62
Polish (111)	337	1.52
Portuguese (0)	49	0.22
Romanian (62)	149	0.67
Russian (193)	311	1.40
Scandinavian (49)	60	0.27
Scotch-Irish (183)	307	1.38
Scottish (213)	650	2.93
Serbian (10)	10	0.05
Slavic (0)	25	0.11
Slovak (22)	54	0.24
Swedish (165)	469	2.11
Swiss (0)	134	0.60
Turkish (10)	20	0.09
Ukrainian (28)	54	0.24
Welsh (72)	510	2.30
Yugoslavian (27)	63	0.28

Hispanic Origin	Population	%
Hispanic or Latino (of any race)	1,168	5.12
Central American, ex. Mexican	47	0.21
Costa Rican	10	0.04
Guatemalan	11	0.05
Nicaraguan	11	0.05
Panamanian	8	0.04
Salvadoran	6	0.03
Other Central American	1	<0.01
Cuban	51	0.22
Dominican Republic	10	0.04
Mexican	756	3.31
Puerto Rican	92	0.40
South American	103	0.45
Argentinean	4	0.02
Bolivian	7	0.03
Chilean	3	0.01
Colombian	50	0.22
Ecuadorian	10	0.04
Peruvian	20	0.09
Uruguayan	2	0.01
Venezuelan	7	0.03
Other Hispanic or Latino	109	0.48

Race*	Population	%
African-American/Black (450)	505	2.21
Not Hispanic (442)	493	2.16
Hispanic (8)	12	0.05
American Indian/Alaska Native (106)	220	0.96
Not Hispanic (101)	207	0.91
Hispanic (5)	13	0.06
Apache (0)	2	0.01
Blackfeet (0)	2	0.01
Cherokee (30)	58	0.25
Chickasaw (13)	15	0.07
Chippewa (1)	8	0.04
Choctaw (12)	32	0.14
Comanche (4)	4	0.02
Cree (1)	1	<0.01
Creek (4)	10	0.04
Mexican American Ind. (1)	1	<0.01
Navajo (3)	3	0.01
Osage (1)	3	0.01
Ottawa (0)	1	<0.01
Potawatomi (3)	4	0.02
Sioux (5)	5	0.02
Asian (1,351)	1,579	6.92
Not Hispanic (1,339)	1,547	6.78
Hispanic (12)	32	0.14
Bangladeshi (2)	2	0.01
Burmese (1)	1	<0.01
Chinese, ex. Taiwanese (190)	227	1.00
Filipino (75)	117	0.51
Indian (495)	540	2.37
Indonesian (3)	14	0.06
Japanese (26)	56	0.25
Korean (129)	144	0.63
Laotian (10)	10	0.04
Malaysian (2)	6	0.03
Pakistani (187)	212	0.93
Sri Lankan (4)	4	0.02
Taiwanese (19)	19	0.08
Thai (5)	11	0.05
Vietnamese (141)	164	0.72
Hawaii Native/Pacific Islander (3)	23	0.10
Not Hispanic (2)	21	0.09
Hispanic (1)	2	0.01
Fijian (1)	1	<0.01
Guamanian/Chamorro (1)	2	0.01
Native Hawaiian (0)	8	0.04
Samoan (1)	2	0.01
Tongan (0)	1	<0.01
White (20,267)	20,668	90.62
Not Hispanic (19,365)	19,692	86.34
Hispanic (902)	976	4.28

Commerce

Place Type: City
County: Hunt
Population: 8,078†

Ancestry‡	Population	%
African, Sub-Saharan (130)	146	1.80
African (98)	114	1.41
Nigerian (32)	32	0.40
American (264)	264	3.26
Arab (16)	16	0.20

*Notes: † The Census 2010 population figure is used to calculate the percentages in the Hispanic Origin and Race categories. Ancestry percentages are based on the 2006-2010 American Community Survey population (not shown); ‡ Numbers in parentheses indicate the number of people reporting a single ancestry; * Numbers in parentheses indicate the number of persons reporting this race alone, not in combination with any other race; Please refer to the Explanation of Data for more information.*

Arab (16)	16	0.20
Australian (15)	15	0.19
Brazilian (0)	10	0.12
British (0)	7	0.09
Czech (15)	16	0.20
Czechoslovakian (12)	12	0.15
Danish (0)	6	0.07
Dutch (8)	169	2.09
English (214)	486	6.00
European (6)	22	0.27
French, ex. Basque (40)	188	2.32
French Canadian (0)	64	0.79
German (260)	902	11.14
Hungarian (41)	52	0.64
Iranian (27)	27	0.33
Irish (537)	1,661	20.51
Italian (19)	122	1.51
Norwegian (22)	45	0.56
Polish (31)	123	1.52
Portuguese (0)	96	1.19
Scotch-Irish (143)	210	2.59
Scottish (19)	108	1.33
Slovak (0)	11	0.14
Swedish (0)	43	0.53
Ukrainian (0)	17	0.21
Welsh (0)	41	0.51
West Indian, ex. Hispanic (0)	47	0.58
Jamaican (0)	47	0.58

Hispanic Origin	Population	%
Hispanic or Latino (of any race)	894	11.07
Central American, ex. Mexican	23	0.28
Guatemalan	7	0.09
Honduran	7	0.09
Nicaraguan	1	0.01
Panamanian	1	0.01
Salvadoran	7	0.09
Cuban	8	0.10
Dominican Republic	1	0.01
Mexican	756	9.36
Puerto Rican	25	0.31
South American	9	0.11
Ecuadorian	1	0.01
Paraguayan	5	0.06
Peruvian	3	0.04
Other Hispanic or Latino	72	0.89

Race*	Population	%
African-American/Black (1,744)	1,851	22.91
Not Hispanic (1,707)	1,802	22.31
Hispanic (37)	49	0.61
American Indian/Alaska Native (62)	146	1.81
Not Hispanic (53)	121	1.50
Hispanic (9)	25	0.31
Alaska Athabascan *(Ala. Nat.)* (0)	1	0.01
Apache (1)	4	0.05
Blackfeet (1)	3	0.04
Cherokee (9)	23	0.28
Chickasaw (1)	1	0.01
Choctaw (7)	16	0.20
Creek (2)	5	0.06
Mexican American Ind. (1)	6	0.07
Navajo (0)	1	0.01
Pueblo (1)	2	0.02
Tlingit-Haida *(Alaska Native)* (0)	1	0.01
Asian (403)	445	5.51
Not Hispanic (400)	440	5.45
Hispanic (3)	5	0.06
Bangladeshi (7)	7	0.09
Cambodian (14)	14	0.17
Chinese, ex. Taiwanese (48)	66	0.82
Filipino (8)	10	0.12
Indian (262)	262	3.24
Indonesian (1)	1	0.01
Japanese (3)	5	0.06
Korean (5)	5	0.06
Laotian (0)	1	0.01
Malaysian (0)	8	0.10
Nepalese (6)	6	0.07
Taiwanese (10)	11	0.14
Thai (7)	8	0.10
Vietnamese (26)	32	0.40
Hawaii Native/Pacific Islander (50)	61	0.76
Not Hispanic (50)	60	0.74
Hispanic (0)	1	0.01
Guamanian/Chamorro (0)	1	0.01
Native Hawaiian (15)	15	0.19
Samoan (5)	6	0.07
White (5,210)	5,412	67.00
Not Hispanic (4,797)	4,935	61.09
Hispanic (413)	477	5.90

Conroe

Place Type: City
County: Montgomery
Population: 56,207†

Ancestry‡	Population	%
African, Sub-Saharan (44)	213	0.40
African (12)	181	0.34
Nigerian (32)	32	0.06
American (2,924)	2,924	5.49
Arab (105)	105	0.20
Arab (9)	9	0.02
Egyptian (52)	52	0.10
Moroccan (44)	44	0.08
Austrian (13)	13	0.02
Brazilian (0)	10	0.02
British (121)	136	0.26
Cajun (24)	33	0.06
Canadian (90)	90	0.17
Celtic (18)	30	0.06
Croatian (36)	44	0.08
Czech (172)	526	0.99
Czechoslovakian (22)	22	0.04
Danish (28)	52	0.10
Dutch (59)	478	0.90
English (2,005)	4,847	9.10
European (231)	290	0.54
Finnish (12)	36	0.07
French, ex. Basque (332)	1,918	3.60
French Canadian (31)	271	0.51
German (2,599)	6,497	12.20
Greek (0)	19	0.04
Hungarian (0)	33	0.06
Icelander (18)	18	0.03
Irish (1,590)	4,407	8.27
Israeli (12)	12	0.02
Italian (391)	1,210	2.27
Lithuanian (0)	10	0.02
Northern European (13)	13	0.02
Norwegian (82)	272	0.51
Pennsylvania German (20)	20	0.04
Polish (154)	485	0.91
Portuguese (30)	217	0.41
Romanian (0)	25	0.05
Russian (56)	99	0.19
Scandinavian (0)	34	0.06
Scotch-Irish (304)	745	1.40
Scottish (296)	1,098	2.06
Slovak (0)	8	0.02
Swedish (18)	349	0.66
Swiss (6)	38	0.07
Turkish (0)	24	0.05
Ukrainian (17)	17	0.03
Welsh (107)	335	0.63
West Indian, ex. Hispanic (26)	72	0.14
Jamaican (26)	72	0.14
Yugoslavian (28)	45	0.08

Hispanic Origin	Population	%
Hispanic or Latino (of any race)	21,661	38.54
Central American, ex. Mexican	3,475	6.18
Costa Rican	11	0.02
Guatemalan	178	0.32
Honduran	1,766	3.14
Nicaraguan	72	0.13
Panamanian	19	0.03
Salvadoran	1,415	2.52
Other Central American	14	0.02
Cuban	93	0.17
Dominican Republic	24	0.04
Mexican	16,452	29.27
Puerto Rican	268	0.48
South American	233	0.41
Argentinean	31	0.06
Bolivian	5	0.01
Chilean	20	0.04
Colombian	83	0.15
Ecuadorian	20	0.04
Peruvian	32	0.06
Uruguayan	1	<0.01
Venezuelan	41	0.07
Other Hispanic or Latino	1,116	1.99

Race*	Population	%
African-American/Black (5,808)	6,183	11.00
Not Hispanic (5,552)	5,826	10.37
Hispanic (256)	357	0.64
American Indian/Alaska Native (688)	1,091	1.94
Not Hispanic (178)	377	0.67
Hispanic (510)	714	1.27
Apache (5)	12	0.02
Arapaho (0)	1	<0.01
Blackfeet (2)	8	0.01
Canadian/French Am. Ind. (1)	2	<0.01
Central American Ind. (5)	13	0.02
Cherokee (56)	137	0.24
Cheyenne (2)	3	0.01
Chickasaw (3)	5	0.01
Chippewa (5)	7	0.01
Choctaw (14)	34	0.06
Comanche (1)	7	0.01
Creek (3)	4	0.01
Delaware (3)	5	0.01
Inupiat *(Alaska Native)* (1)	1	<0.01
Iroquois (2)	8	0.01
Lumbee (3)	3	0.01
Mexican American Ind. (63)	78	0.14
Navajo (1)	3	0.01
Osage (0)	1	<0.01
Ottawa (0)	2	<0.01
Potawatomi (1)	2	<0.01
Seminole (0)	3	0.01
Sioux (4)	6	0.01
South American Ind. (0)	1	<0.01
Spanish American Ind. (2)	14	0.02
Asian (1,024)	1,268	2.26
Not Hispanic (988)	1,150	2.05
Hispanic (36)	118	0.21
Bangladeshi (9)	9	0.02
Burmese (0)	1	<0.01
Cambodian (19)	34	0.06
Chinese, ex. Taiwanese (135)	180	0.32
Filipino (281)	343	0.61
Hmong (5)	5	0.01
Indian (183)	218	0.39
Indonesian (4)	6	0.01
Japanese (20)	45	0.08
Korean (40)	61	0.11
Laotian (10)	11	0.02
Nepalese (4)	4	0.01
Pakistani (47)	57	0.10
Sri Lankan (10)	10	0.02
Taiwanese (8)	14	0.02
Thai (21)	26	0.05
Vietnamese (175)	211	0.38
Hawaii Native/Pacific Islander (23)	97	0.17
Not Hispanic (13)	57	0.10
Hispanic (10)	40	0.07
Guamanian/Chamorro (8)	14	0.02
Native Hawaiian (8)	25	0.04
Samoan (1)	4	0.01
White (39,149)	40,682	72.38
Not Hispanic (27,147)	27,684	49.25
Hispanic (12,002)	12,998	23.13

*Notes: † The Census 2010 population figure is used to calculate the percentages in the Hispanic Origin and Race categories. Ancestry percentages are based on the 2006-2010 American Community Survey population (not shown); ‡ Numbers in parentheses indicate the number of people reporting a single ancestry; * Numbers in parentheses indicate the number of persons reporting this race alone, not in combination with any other race; Please refer to the Explanation of Data for more information.*

Converse

Place Type: City
County: Bexar
Population: 18,198†

Ancestry‡	Population	%
African, Sub-Saharan (116)	226	1.33
African (116)	226	1.33
American (525)	525	3.10
Basque (12)	12	0.07
British (22)	22	0.13
Canadian (12)	12	0.07
Czech (37)	55	0.32
Czechoslovakian (11)	25	0.15
Danish (0)	31	0.18
Dutch (341)	845	4.98
English (255)	768	4.53
European (40)	53	0.31
Finnish (47)	82	0.48
French, ex. Basque (86)	445	2.62
French Canadian (73)	124	0.73
German (1,120)	2,799	16.51
Greek (12)	23	0.14
Hungarian (54)	78	0.46
Irish (382)	1,326	7.82
Italian (49)	345	2.04
Lithuanian (17)	30	0.18
Norwegian (32)	47	0.28
Polish (68)	322	1.90
Portuguese (17)	17	0.10
Scandinavian (20)	20	0.12
Scotch-Irish (52)	249	1.47
Scottish (84)	239	1.41
Swedish (65)	242	1.43
Welsh (14)	36	0.21
West Indian, ex. Hispanic (79)	249	1.47
Bahamian (38)	38	0.22
Dutch West Indian (28)	62	0.37
Haitian (0)	110	0.65
Jamaican (13)	21	0.12
Trinidadian/Tobagonian (0)	18	0.11
Yugoslavian (0)	20	0.12

Hispanic Origin	Population	%
Hispanic or Latino (of any race)	6,861	37.70
Central American, ex. Mexican	252	1.38
Costa Rican	9	0.05
Guatemalan	59	0.32
Honduran	35	0.19
Nicaraguan	20	0.11
Panamanian	68	0.37
Salvadoran	61	0.34
Cuban	21	0.12
Dominican Republic	20	0.11
Mexican	5,425	29.81
Puerto Rican	435	2.39
South American	80	0.44
Argentinean	4	0.02
Bolivian	7	0.04
Chilean	3	0.02
Colombian	32	0.18
Ecuadorian	16	0.09
Peruvian	13	0.07
Uruguayan	2	0.01
Venezuelan	3	0.02
Other Hispanic or Latino	628	3.45

Race*	Population	%
African-American/Black (3,836)	4,302	23.64
Not Hispanic (3,600)	3,930	21.60
Hispanic (236)	372	2.04
American Indian/Alaska Native (119)	263	1.45
Not Hispanic (54)	154	0.85
Hispanic (65)	109	0.60
Alaska Athabascan *(Ala. Nat.)* (1)	2	0.01
Apache (10)	18	0.10
Blackfeet (1)	4	0.02
Canadian/French Am. Ind. (0)	4	0.02
Cherokee (6)	44	0.24
Chickasaw (4)	5	0.03
Chippewa (3)	4	0.02
Choctaw (2)	11	0.06
Creek (1)	7	0.04
Lumbee (1)	2	0.01
Mexican American Ind. (9)	11	0.06
Navajo (0)	7	0.04
Ottawa (1)	1	0.01
Pima (1)	1	0.01
Pueblo (1)	1	0.01
Sioux (2)	7	0.04
Spanish American Ind. (2)	2	0.01
Asian (436)	671	3.69
Not Hispanic (416)	596	3.28
Hispanic (20)	75	0.41
Cambodian (2)	3	0.02
Chinese, ex. Taiwanese (14)	27	0.15
Filipino (185)	278	1.53
Indian (27)	43	0.24
Indonesian (1)	3	0.02
Japanese (27)	61	0.34
Korean (62)	107	0.59
Laotian (2)	2	0.01
Pakistani (9)	10	0.05
Taiwanese (1)	5	0.03
Thai (29)	43	0.24
Vietnamese (62)	74	0.41
Hawaii Native/Pacific Islander (71)	125	0.69
Not Hispanic (66)	106	0.58
Hispanic (5)	19	0.10
Guamanian/Chamorro (34)	46	0.25
Marshallese (6)	6	0.03
Native Hawaiian (15)	27	0.15
Samoan (10)	26	0.14
Tongan (0)	1	0.01
White (11,248)	11,937	65.60
Not Hispanic (6,653)	7,045	38.71
Hispanic (4,595)	4,892	26.88

Coppell

Place Type: City
County: Dallas
Population: 38,659†

Ancestry‡	Population	%
African, Sub-Saharan (300)	300	0.78
African (40)	40	0.10
Nigerian (101)	101	0.26
Zimbabwean (82)	82	0.21
Other Sub-Saharan African (77)	77	0.20
Albanian (41)	41	0.11
American (2,756)	2,756	7.19
Arab (32)	63	0.16
Egyptian (7)	7	0.02
Jordanian (0)	10	0.03
Lebanese (25)	46	0.12
Armenian (10)	20	0.05
Assyrian/Chaldean/Syriac (0)	10	0.03
Austrian (0)	24	0.06
Belgian (18)	26	0.07
Brazilian (14)	14	0.04
British (103)	263	0.69
Bulgarian (58)	70	0.18
Cajun (10)	24	0.06
Canadian (28)	54	0.14
Celtic (13)	23	0.06
Czech (53)	303	0.79
Czechoslovakian (53)	63	0.16
Danish (108)	275	0.72
Dutch (291)	702	1.83
Eastern European (23)	23	0.06
English (1,804)	5,158	13.46
European (390)	441	1.15
Finnish (23)	65	0.17
French, ex. Basque (330)	1,567	4.09
French Canadian (23)	52	0.14
German (2,138)	6,337	16.53
German Russian (12)	12	0.03
Greek (67)	141	0.37
Hungarian (0)	147	0.38
Iranian (292)	292	0.76
Irish (1,316)	4,112	10.73
Israeli (13)	27	0.07
Italian (754)	2,095	5.47
Latvian (37)	103	0.27
Lithuanian (37)	45	0.12
Luxemburger (0)	7	0.02
Northern European (27)	27	0.07
Norwegian (162)	425	1.11
Pennsylvania German (9)	19	0.05
Polish (320)	769	2.01
Portuguese (9)	23	0.06
Romanian (0)	71	0.19
Russian (145)	360	0.94
Scandinavian (10)	46	0.12
Scotch-Irish (571)	1,098	2.86
Scottish (271)	1,021	2.66
Serbian (13)	52	0.14
Slavic (0)	12	0.03
Slovak (22)	77	0.20
Slovene (24)	58	0.15
Swedish (100)	368	0.96
Swiss (31)	181	0.47
Turkish (39)	39	0.10
Ukrainian (29)	88	0.23
Welsh (70)	272	0.71
West Indian, ex. Hispanic (20)	57	0.15
Dutch West Indian (0)	16	0.04
Jamaican (20)	41	0.11
Yugoslavian (0)	10	0.03

Hispanic Origin	Population	%
Hispanic or Latino (of any race)	4,365	11.29
Central American, ex. Mexican	198	0.51
Costa Rican	10	0.03
Guatemalan	52	0.13
Honduran	19	0.05
Nicaraguan	29	0.08
Panamanian	21	0.05
Salvadoran	67	0.17
Cuban	98	0.25
Dominican Republic	41	0.11
Mexican	3,101	8.02
Puerto Rican	192	0.50
South American	431	1.11
Argentinean	33	0.09
Bolivian	14	0.04
Chilean	15	0.04
Colombian	116	0.30
Ecuadorian	33	0.09
Paraguayan	2	0.01
Peruvian	115	0.30
Uruguayan	14	0.04
Venezuelan	88	0.23
Other South American	1	<0.01
Other Hispanic or Latino	304	0.79

Race*	Population	%
African-American/Black (1,730)	1,943	5.03
Not Hispanic (1,694)	1,857	4.80
Hispanic (36)	86	0.22
American Indian/Alaska Native (164)	391	1.01
Not Hispanic (111)	312	0.81
Hispanic (53)	79	0.20
Alaska Athabascan *(Ala. Nat.)* (1)	3	0.01
Apache (4)	7	0.02
Blackfeet (0)	6	0.02
Cherokee (30)	97	0.25
Chickasaw (12)	15	0.04
Chippewa (0)	3	0.01
Choctaw (18)	33	0.09
Comanche (0)	2	0.01
Creek (1)	4	0.01
Crow (0)	1	<0.01
Delaware (0)	1	<0.01
Inupiat *(Alaska Native)* (1)	1	<0.01
Iroquois (0)	6	0.02
Kiowa (3)	3	0.01
Lumbee (0)	2	0.01

*Notes: † The Census 2010 population figure is used to calculate the percentages in the Hispanic Origin and Race categories. Ancestry percentages are based on the 2006-2010 American Community Survey population (not shown); ‡ Numbers in parentheses indicate the number of people reporting a single ancestry; * Numbers in parentheses indicate the number of persons reporting this race alone, not in combination with any other race; Please refer to the Explanation of Data for more information.*

Mexican American Ind. (2)	3	0.01
Navajo (2)	2	0.01
Osage (2)	8	0.02
Paiute (1)	1	<0.01
Potawatomi (4)	9	0.02
Seminole (0)	3	0.01
Sioux (1)	3	0.01
South American Ind. (3)	4	0.01
Asian (6,133)	6,637	17.17
Not Hispanic (6,120)	6,573	17.00
Hispanic (13)	64	0.17
Bangladeshi (28)	31	0.08
Burmese (11)	11	0.03
Cambodian (31)	36	0.09
Chinese, ex. Taiwanese (918)	1,058	2.74
Filipino (191)	252	0.65
Hmong (2)	2	0.01
Indian (2,585)	2,709	7.01
Indonesian (20)	35	0.09
Japanese (264)	350	0.91
Korean (1,192)	1,239	3.20
Laotian (6)	13	0.03
Malaysian (1)	8	0.02
Nepalese (44)	47	0.12
Pakistani (232)	252	0.65
Sri Lankan (32)	34	0.09
Taiwanese (83)	105	0.27
Thai (61)	76	0.20
Vietnamese (315)	357	0.92
Hawaii Native/Pacific Islander (21)	71	0.18
Not Hispanic (17)	60	0.16
Hispanic (4)	11	0.03
Guamanian/Chamorro (2)	6	0.02
Native Hawaiian (0)	15	0.04
Samoan (4)	8	0.02
Tongan (9)	9	0.02
White (28,517)	29,340	75.89
Not Hispanic (25,537)	26,155	67.66
Hispanic (2,980)	3,185	8.24

Copperas Cove

Place Type: City
County: Coryell
Population: 32,032†

Ancestry‡	Population	%
African, Sub-Saharan (315)	377	1.19
African (236)	298	0.94
Ethiopian (79)	79	0.25
American (1,687)	1,687	5.34
Arab (38)	131	0.41
Egyptian (0)	10	0.03
Lebanese (5)	5	0.02
Syrian (33)	116	0.37
Armenian (0)	7	0.02
Australian (0)	13	0.04
Austrian (0)	40	0.13
Belgian (0)	70	0.22
Brazilian (20)	20	0.06
British (85)	138	0.44
Cajun (43)	133	0.42
Canadian (14)	14	0.04
Croatian (0)	7	0.02
Czech (107)	176	0.56
Czechoslovakian (8)	8	0.03
Danish (55)	104	0.33
Dutch (97)	352	1.11
English (2,527)	3,366	10.65
European (110)	144	0.46
Finnish (0)	37	0.12
French, ex. Basque (256)	847	2.68
French Canadian (40)	98	0.31
German (3,133)	5,957	18.85
German Russian (10)	10	0.03
Greek (0)	12	0.04
Hungarian (0)	41	0.13
Irish (1,115)	3,169	10.03
Italian (340)	864	2.73
Lithuanian (0)	17	0.05
Norwegian (249)	299	0.95
Pennsylvania German (0)	11	0.03
Polish (366)	802	2.54
Portuguese (9)	14	0.04
Romanian (0)	17	0.05
Russian (19)	202	0.64
Scandinavian (0)	51	0.16
Scotch-Irish (230)	370	1.17
Scottish (203)	498	1.58
Serbian (0)	22	0.07
Slovak (29)	29	0.09
Slovene (9)	9	0.03
Swedish (9)	280	0.89
Swiss (27)	42	0.13
Ukrainian (7)	7	0.02
Welsh (16)	165	0.52
West Indian, ex. Hispanic (39)	66	0.21
Haitian (16)	16	0.05
Jamaican (23)	39	0.12
West Indian (0)	11	0.03
Yugoslavian (28)	36	0.11

Hispanic Origin	Population	%
Hispanic or Latino (of any race)	4,811	15.02
Central American, ex. Mexican	283	0.88
Costa Rican	6	0.02
Guatemalan	28	0.09
Honduran	32	0.10
Nicaraguan	14	0.04
Panamanian	157	0.49
Salvadoran	45	0.14
Other Central American	1	<0.01
Cuban	69	0.22
Dominican Republic	85	0.27
Mexican	2,789	8.71
Puerto Rican	1,093	3.41
South American	103	0.32
Argentinean	8	0.02
Bolivian	3	0.01
Chilean	2	0.01
Colombian	44	0.14
Ecuadorian	18	0.06
Peruvian	15	0.05
Uruguayan	1	<0.01
Venezuelan	10	0.03
Other South American	2	0.01
Other Hispanic or Latino	389	1.21

Race*	Population	%
African-American/Black (5,767)	6,899	21.54
Not Hispanic (5,489)	6,416	20.03
Hispanic (278)	483	1.51
American Indian/Alaska Native (284)	696	2.17
Not Hispanic (213)	540	1.69
Hispanic (71)	156	0.49
Alaska Athabascan *(Ala. Nat.)* (1)	1	<0.01
Apache (21)	26	0.08
Blackfeet (3)	18	0.06
Central American Ind. (2)	2	0.01
Cherokee (37)	147	0.46
Cheyenne (0)	2	0.01
Chickasaw (11)	16	0.05
Chippewa (3)	7	0.02
Choctaw (16)	53	0.17
Colville (1)	3	0.01
Comanche (5)	9	0.03
Creek (5)	9	0.03
Hopi (0)	5	0.02
Houma (1)	1	<0.01
Iroquois (6)	7	0.02
Kiowa (2)	2	0.01
Lumbee (9)	13	0.04
Mexican American Ind. (10)	13	0.04
Navajo (12)	24	0.07
Paiute (2)	4	0.01
Pueblo (10)	14	0.04
Seminole (0)	1	<0.01
Sioux (5)	18	0.06
South American Ind. (4)	7	0.02
Tlingit-Haida *(Alaska Native)* (5)	5	0.02
Yaqui (3)	3	0.01
Yup'ik *(Alaska Native)* (1)	1	<0.01
Asian (949)	1,562	4.88
Not Hispanic (888)	1,394	4.35
Hispanic (61)	168	0.52
Burmese (2)	2	0.01
Cambodian (13)	13	0.04
Chinese, ex. Taiwanese (51)	99	0.31
Filipino (264)	430	1.34
Hmong (7)	7	0.02
Indian (42)	74	0.23
Indonesian (2)	2	0.01
Japanese (72)	187	0.58
Korean (347)	546	1.70
Laotian (1)	2	0.01
Malaysian (0)	1	<0.01
Pakistani (3)	9	0.03
Taiwanese (5)	6	0.02
Thai (36)	84	0.26
Vietnamese (72)	95	0.30
Hawaii Native/Pacific Islander (346)	547	1.71
Not Hispanic (330)	490	1.53
Hispanic (16)	57	0.18
Guamanian/Chamorro (114)	180	0.56
Native Hawaiian (47)	123	0.38
Samoan (89)	117	0.37
Tongan (5)	9	0.03
White (21,206)	23,023	71.88
Not Hispanic (18,654)	20,013	62.48
Hispanic (2,552)	3,010	9.40

Corinth

Place Type: City
County: Denton
Population: 19,935†

Ancestry‡	Population	%
African, Sub-Saharan (55)	85	0.46
African (0)	15	0.08
Nigerian (55)	70	0.38
American (1,199)	1,199	6.45
Arab (0)	51	0.27
Lebanese (0)	13	0.07
Other Arab (0)	38	0.20
Austrian (0)	6	0.03
Belgian (55)	67	0.36
Brazilian (0)	19	0.10
British (104)	120	0.65
Cajun (14)	14	0.08
Canadian (45)	45	0.24
Croatian (0)	14	0.08
Czech (77)	131	0.70
Czechoslovakian (0)	83	0.45
Danish (37)	261	1.40
Dutch (49)	162	0.87
English (934)	2,756	14.83
Estonian (0)	17	0.09
European (174)	223	1.20
Finnish (0)	16	0.09
French, ex. Basque (188)	702	3.78
French Canadian (63)	261	1.40
German (1,800)	4,131	22.22
Greek (12)	112	0.60
Hungarian (0)	52	0.28
Irish (551)	2,349	12.64
Italian (116)	793	4.27
Maltese (23)	23	0.12
Northern European (10)	10	0.05
Norwegian (105)	321	1.73
Polish (183)	592	3.18
Portuguese (0)	87	0.47
Romanian (13)	13	0.07
Russian (74)	135	0.73
Scotch-Irish (122)	691	3.72
Scottish (166)	493	2.65
Swedish (9)	62	0.33
Swiss (3)	67	0.36
Ukrainian (47)	73	0.39
Welsh (0)	83	0.45

SECTION TWO

*Notes: † The Census 2010 population figure is used to calculate the percentages in the Hispanic Origin and Race categories. Ancestry percentages are based on the 2006-2010 American Community Survey population (not shown); ‡ Numbers in parentheses indicate the number of people reporting a single ancestry; * Numbers in parentheses indicate the number of persons reporting this race alone, not in combination with any other race; Please refer to the Explanation of Data for more information.*

Hispanic Origin	Population	%
Hispanic or Latino (of any race)	2,346	11.77
Central American, ex. Mexican	111	0.56
Costa Rican	2	0.01
Guatemalan	29	0.15
Honduran	9	0.05
Nicaraguan	2	0.01
Panamanian	14	0.07
Salvadoran	55	0.28
Cuban	26	0.13
Dominican Republic	16	0.08
Mexican	1,723	8.64
Puerto Rican	114	0.57
South American	120	0.60
Argentinean	21	0.11
Bolivian	3	0.02
Chilean	12	0.06
Colombian	36	0.18
Ecuadorian	4	0.02
Peruvian	25	0.13
Uruguayan	1	0.01
Venezuelan	15	0.08
Other South American	3	0.02
Other Hispanic or Latino	236	1.18

Race*	Population	%
African-American/Black (1,142)	1,301	6.53
Not Hispanic (1,122)	1,245	6.25
Hispanic (20)	56	0.28
American Indian/Alaska Native (167)	328	1.65
Not Hispanic (144)	285	1.43
Hispanic (23)	43	0.22
Apache (4)	9	0.05
Blackfeet (1)	2	0.01
Cherokee (45)	97	0.49
Chickasaw (13)	18	0.09
Chippewa (1)	1	0.01
Choctaw (29)	49	0.25
Comanche (4)	6	0.03
Creek (5)	6	0.03
Hopi (1)	3	0.02
Iroquois (1)	1	0.01
Kiowa (0)	1	0.01
Menominee (0)	1	0.01
Mexican American Ind. (4)	6	0.03
Osage (1)	7	0.04
Paiute (0)	3	0.02
Potawatomi (1)	2	0.01
Pueblo (0)	2	0.01
Sioux (4)	4	0.02
South American Ind. (1)	1	0.01
Asian (529)	703	3.53
Not Hispanic (527)	670	3.36
Hispanic (2)	33	0.17
Bangladeshi (3)	3	0.02
Cambodian (18)	24	0.12
Chinese, ex. Taiwanese (71)	93	0.47
Filipino (69)	105	0.53
Indian (127)	142	0.71
Indonesian (6)	12	0.06
Japanese (20)	56	0.28
Korean (101)	118	0.59
Laotian (3)	3	0.02
Malaysian (1)	4	0.02
Pakistani (48)	59	0.30
Sri Lankan (1)	1	0.01
Taiwanese (2)	4	0.02
Thai (16)	19	0.10
Vietnamese (30)	42	0.21
Hawaii Native/Pacific Islander (9)	52	0.26
Not Hispanic (9)	46	0.23
Hispanic (0)	6	0.03
Fijian (0)	3	0.02
Guamanian/Chamorro (4)	4	0.02
Native Hawaiian (2)	21	0.11
Samoan (0)	4	0.02
White (16,880)	17,388	87.22
Not Hispanic (15,363)	15,723	78.87
Hispanic (1,517)	1,665	8.35

Corpus Christi

Place Type: City
County: Nueces
Population: 305,215†

Ancestry‡	Population	%
African, Sub-Saharan (571)	665	0.22
African (186)	261	0.09
Ethiopian (18)	18	0.01
Ghanaian (15)	15	0.01
Kenyan (37)	37	0.01
Nigerian (281)	300	0.10
Somalian (34)	34	0.01
Alsatian (11)	32	0.01
American (10,626)	10,626	3.55
Arab (701)	1,016	0.34
Arab (228)	263	0.09
Egyptian (9)	9	<0.01
Jordanian (0)	9	<0.01
Lebanese (317)	562	0.19
Syrian (132)	149	0.05
Other Arab (15)	24	0.01
Armenian (11)	28	0.01
Australian (0)	38	0.01
Austrian (93)	340	0.11
Basque (0)	12	<0.01
Belgian (79)	121	0.04
Brazilian (58)	281	0.09
British (371)	631	0.21
Cajun (90)	139	0.05
Canadian (209)	419	0.14
Celtic (25)	70	0.02
Croatian (115)	153	0.05
Cypriot (7)	7	<0.01
Czech (1,057)	2,403	0.80
Czechoslovakian (213)	546	0.18
Danish (204)	481	0.16
Dutch (399)	2,306	0.77
Eastern European (46)	46	0.02
English (5,440)	15,937	5.32
European (1,015)	1,223	0.41
Finnish (74)	180	0.06
French, ex. Basque (1,145)	5,816	1.94
French Canadian (521)	931	0.31
German (10,487)	29,575	9.88
German Russian (0)	13	<0.01
Greek (240)	661	0.22
Guyanese (91)	100	0.03
Hungarian (30)	133	0.04
Iranian (136)	136	0.05
Irish (5,509)	18,284	6.11
Israeli (0)	10	<0.01
Italian (1,750)	5,033	1.68
Latvian (31)	31	0.01
Lithuanian (58)	212	0.07
Luxemburger (0)	21	0.01
Maltese (14)	14	<0.01
Northern European (79)	79	0.03
Norwegian (472)	1,365	0.46
Pennsylvania German (0)	11	<0.01
Polish (1,117)	3,374	1.13
Portuguese (39)	213	0.07
Romanian (128)	164	0.05
Russian (219)	975	0.33
Scandinavian (40)	91	0.03
Scotch-Irish (1,805)	4,241	1.42
Scottish (1,390)	4,071	1.36
Serbian (132)	143	0.05
Slavic (51)	67	0.02
Slovak (79)	133	0.04
Slovene (12)	12	<0.01
Swedish (472)	1,751	0.58
Swiss (25)	203	0.07
Turkish (31)	31	0.01
Ukrainian (64)	142	0.05
Welsh (108)	706	0.24
West Indian, ex. Hispanic (320)	484	0.16
British West Indian (12)	12	<0.01
Dutch West Indian (11)	121	0.04
Haitian (188)	188	0.06
Jamaican (28)	82	0.03
Trinidadian/Tobagonian (46)	46	0.02
Other West Indian (35)	35	0.01
Yugoslavian (25)	36	0.01

Hispanic Origin	Population	%
Hispanic or Latino (of any race)	182,181	59.69
Central American, ex. Mexican	978	0.32
Costa Rican	31	0.01
Guatemalan	204	0.07
Honduran	202	0.07
Nicaraguan	60	0.02
Panamanian	119	0.04
Salvadoran	354	0.12
Other Central American	8	<0.01
Cuban	483	0.16
Dominican Republic	87	0.03
Mexican	148,800	48.75
Puerto Rican	1,248	0.41
South American	832	0.27
Argentinean	74	0.02
Bolivian	31	0.01
Chilean	82	0.03
Colombian	304	0.10
Ecuadorian	57	0.02
Paraguayan	4	<0.01
Peruvian	121	0.04
Uruguayan	10	<0.01
Venezuelan	139	0.05
Other South American	10	<0.01
Other Hispanic or Latino	29,753	9.75

Race*	Population	%
African-American/Black (13,254)	14,997	4.91
Not Hispanic (11,912)	12,880	4.22
Hispanic (1,342)	2,117	0.69
American Indian/Alaska Native (1,940)	3,499	1.15
Not Hispanic (792)	1,670	0.55
Hispanic (1,148)	1,829	0.60
Alaska Athabascan *(Ala. Nat.)* (2)	5	<0.01
Aleut *(Alaska Native)* (1)	1	<0.01
Apache (134)	239	0.08
Arapaho (6)	7	<0.01
Blackfeet (5)	35	0.01
Canadian/French Am. Ind. (5)	11	<0.01
Central American Ind. (4)	4	<0.01
Cherokee (168)	502	0.16
Cheyenne (1)	7	<0.01
Chickasaw (18)	36	0.01
Chippewa (15)	27	0.01
Choctaw (104)	190	0.06
Colville (0)	3	<0.01
Comanche (4)	37	0.01
Cree (0)	1	<0.01
Creek (21)	43	0.01
Crow (2)	5	<0.01
Delaware (4)	9	<0.01
Hopi (4)	7	<0.01
Houma (4)	4	<0.01
Inupiat *(Alaska Native)* (4)	7	<0.01
Iroquois (8)	23	0.01
Kiowa (2)	3	<0.01
Lumbee (6)	10	<0.01
Menominee (3)	3	<0.01
Mexican American Ind. (163)	242	0.08
Navajo (41)	54	0.02
Osage (9)	19	0.01
Ottawa (4)	4	<0.01
Paiute (0)	1	<0.01
Pima (1)	8	<0.01
Potawatomi (20)	36	0.01
Pueblo (1)	9	<0.01
Puget Sound Salish (3)	4	<0.01
Seminole (10)	17	0.01
Shoshone (3)	3	<0.01
Sioux (10)	33	0.01
South American Ind. (2)	7	<0.01
Spanish American Ind. (6)	13	<0.01

*Notes: † The Census 2010 population figure is used to calculate the percentages in the Hispanic Origin and Race categories. Ancestry percentages are based on the 2006-2010 American Community Survey population (not shown); ‡ Numbers in parentheses indicate the number of people reporting a single ancestry; * Numbers in parentheses indicate the number of persons reporting this race alone, not in combination with any other race; Please refer to the Explanation of Data for more information.*

Tlingit-Haida *(Alaska Native)* (1)	6	<0.01
Tohono O'Odham (0)	1	<0.01
Ute (0)	2	<0.01
Yaqui (6)	11	<0.01
Asian (5,613)	7,145	2.34
Not Hispanic (5,398)	6,417	2.10
Hispanic (215)	728	0.24
Bangladeshi (9)	9	<0.01
Burmese (3)	3	<0.01
Cambodian (17)	27	0.01
Chinese, ex. Taiwanese (560)	667	0.22
Filipino (2,379)	3,093	1.01
Hmong (1)	3	<0.01
Indian (878)	1,013	0.33
Indonesian (29)	44	0.01
Japanese (178)	411	0.13
Korean (466)	616	0.20
Laotian (36)	58	0.02
Malaysian (1)	5	<0.01
Nepalese (2)	2	<0.01
Pakistani (144)	159	0.05
Sri Lankan (0)	2	<0.01
Taiwanese (44)	45	0.01
Thai (97)	167	0.05
Vietnamese (600)	674	0.22
Hawaii Native/Pacific Islander (261)	557	0.18
Not Hispanic (204)	380	0.12
Hispanic (57)	177	0.06
Guamanian/Chamorro (56)	90	0.03
Marshallese (0)	1	<0.01
Native Hawaiian (81)	173	0.06
Samoan (53)	91	0.03
Tongan (1)	1	<0.01
White (246,988)	253,562	83.08
Not Hispanic (101,593)	104,028	34.08
Hispanic (145,395)	149,534	48.99

Corsicana

Place Type: City
County: Navarro
Population: 23,770†

Ancestry‡	Population	%
African, Sub-Saharan (127)	139	0.58
African (127)	139	0.58
Albanian (16)	16	0.07
American (1,300)	1,300	5.42
Arab (10)	39	0.16
Arab (10)	10	0.04
Other Arab (0)	29	0.12
Austrian (0)	33	0.14
Belgian (10)	10	0.04
British (7)	7	0.03
Cajun (0)	10	0.04
Czech (47)	77	0.32
Dutch (0)	134	0.56
English (652)	1,447	6.03
European (31)	31	0.13
French, ex. Basque (69)	196	0.82
French Canadian (13)	13	0.05
German (434)	1,552	6.47
Greek (0)	9	0.04
Hungarian (23)	56	0.23
Irish (583)	1,963	8.18
Italian (31)	150	0.62
Norwegian (56)	224	0.93
Polish (52)	181	0.75
Romanian (0)	12	0.05
Russian (0)	34	0.14
Scotch-Irish (200)	267	1.11
Scottish (122)	249	1.04
Swedish (194)	313	1.30
Welsh (75)	110	0.46

Hispanic Origin	Population	%
Hispanic or Latino (of any race)	7,391	31.09
Central American, ex. Mexican	97	0.41
Guatemalan	18	0.08
Honduran	10	0.04
Panamanian	3	0.01
Salvadoran	66	0.28
Cuban	10	0.04
Dominican Republic	2	0.01
Mexican	6,795	28.59
Puerto Rican	43	0.18
South American	18	0.08
Argentinean	2	0.01
Chilean	1	<0.01
Colombian	3	0.01
Ecuadorian	3	0.01
Peruvian	1	<0.01
Uruguayan	4	0.02
Venezuelan	4	0.02
Other Hispanic or Latino	426	1.79

Race*	Population	%
African-American/Black (4,960)	5,186	21.82
Not Hispanic (4,874)	5,011	21.08
Hispanic (86)	175	0.74
American Indian/Alaska Native (139)	275	1.16
Not Hispanic (63)	159	0.67
Hispanic (76)	116	0.49
Alaska Athabascan *(Ala. Nat.)* (1)	5	0.02
Apache (4)	10	0.04
Arapaho (1)	6	0.03
Central American Ind. (2)	2	0.01
Cherokee (8)	35	0.15
Cheyenne (1)	1	<0.01
Chickasaw (0)	2	0.01
Choctaw (13)	29	0.12
Comanche (0)	1	<0.01
Creek (0)	5	0.02
Crow (2)	2	0.01
Hopi (1)	1	<0.01
Kiowa (1)	1	<0.01
Lumbee (2)	2	0.01
Mexican American Ind. (14)	22	0.09
Navajo (1)	1	<0.01
Osage (0)	1	<0.01
Pima (0)	1	<0.01
Potawatomi (0)	7	0.03
Puget Sound Salish (1)	1	<0.01
Spanish American Ind. (1)	1	<0.01
Tohono O'Odham (0)	7	0.03
Asian (166)	208	0.88
Not Hispanic (160)	184	0.77
Hispanic (6)	24	0.10
Bangladeshi (3)	3	0.01
Cambodian (6)	7	0.03
Chinese, ex. Taiwanese (15)	28	0.12
Filipino (12)	18	0.08
Indian (46)	53	0.22
Japanese (7)	10	0.04
Korean (15)	19	0.08
Nepalese (7)	7	0.03
Pakistani (9)	11	0.05
Sri Lankan (2)	2	0.01
Thai (1)	5	0.02
Vietnamese (31)	33	0.14
Hawaii Native/Pacific Islander (305)	335	1.41
Not Hispanic (303)	326	1.37
Hispanic (2)	9	0.04
Guamanian/Chamorro (11)	12	0.05
Marshallese (0)	1	<0.01
Native Hawaiian (6)	15	0.06
Samoan (3)	3	0.01
Tongan (0)	1	<0.01
White (13,804)	14,250	59.95
Not Hispanic (10,707)	10,916	45.92
Hispanic (3,097)	3,334	14.03

Crowley

Place Type: City
County: Tarrant
Population: 12,838†

Ancestry‡	Population	%
African, Sub-Saharan (83)	83	0.70
Nigerian (83)	83	0.70
American (1,823)	1,823	15.33
Basque (0)	23	0.19
British (52)	60	0.50
Canadian (0)	19	0.16
Celtic (8)	8	0.07
Czech (19)	86	0.72
Danish (30)	57	0.48
Dutch (66)	170	1.43
English (516)	982	8.26
European (36)	60	0.50
French, ex. Basque (7)	212	1.78
French Canadian (0)	39	0.33
German (601)	1,510	12.69
Iranian (8)	8	0.07
Irish (441)	1,120	9.42
Italian (206)	388	3.26
Lithuanian (34)	34	0.29
Luxemburger (7)	7	0.06
Norwegian (15)	40	0.34
Polish (32)	126	1.06
Portuguese (44)	76	0.64
Russian (0)	16	0.13
Scandinavian (37)	37	0.31
Scotch-Irish (210)	289	2.43
Scottish (195)	348	2.93
Swedish (121)	255	2.14
Swiss (8)	24	0.20
Ukrainian (11)	11	0.09
Welsh (0)	43	0.36
West Indian, ex. Hispanic (0)	9	0.08
Dutch West Indian (0)	9	0.08

Hispanic Origin	Population	%
Hispanic or Latino (of any race)	1,954	15.22
Central American, ex. Mexican	52	0.41
Costa Rican	2	0.02
Guatemalan	9	0.07
Honduran	2	0.02
Nicaraguan	6	0.05
Panamanian	7	0.05
Salvadoran	22	0.17
Other Central American	4	0.03
Cuban	11	0.09
Dominican Republic	1	0.01
Mexican	1,623	12.64
Puerto Rican	77	0.60
South American	48	0.37
Argentinean	8	0.06
Colombian	13	0.10
Ecuadorian	8	0.06
Peruvian	11	0.09
Venezuelan	8	0.06
Other Hispanic or Latino	142	1.11

Race*	Population	%
African-American/Black (1,703)	1,829	14.25
Not Hispanic (1,667)	1,774	13.82
Hispanic (36)	55	0.43
American Indian/Alaska Native (97)	218	1.70
Not Hispanic (81)	172	1.34
Hispanic (16)	46	0.36
Apache (3)	5	0.04
Blackfeet (0)	4	0.03
Cherokee (15)	44	0.34
Chickasaw (9)	11	0.09
Choctaw (18)	36	0.28
Comanche (0)	4	0.03
Creek (0)	1	0.01
Kiowa (0)	2	0.02
Menominee (1)	1	0.01
Mexican American Ind. (2)	4	0.03
Navajo (1)	1	0.01
Osage (0)	4	0.03
Potawatomi (9)	9	0.07
Seminole (1)	1	0.01
Sioux (3)	6	0.05
Yaqui (1)	1	0.01
Asian (197)	258	2.01
Not Hispanic (187)	240	1.87

SECTION TWO

*Notes: † The Census 2010 population figure is used to calculate the percentages in the Hispanic Origin and Race categories. Ancestry percentages are based on the 2006-2010 American Community Survey population (not shown); ‡ Numbers in parentheses indicate the number of people reporting a single ancestry; * Numbers in parentheses indicate the number of persons reporting this race alone, not in combination with any other race; Please refer to the Explanation of Data for more information.*

	Population	%
Hispanic (10)	18	0.14
Burmese (20)	21	0.16
Cambodian (5)	5	0.04
Chinese, ex. Taiwanese (13)	23	0.18
Filipino (42)	63	0.49
Indian (18)	30	0.23
Japanese (8)	15	0.12
Korean (21)	34	0.26
Laotian (0)	3	0.02
Nepalese (2)	2	0.02
Pakistani (3)	3	0.02
Taiwanese (0)	1	0.01
Thai (6)	7	0.05
Vietnamese (31)	39	0.30
Hawaii Native/Pacific Islander (10)	25	0.19
Not Hispanic (10)	24	0.19
Hispanic (0)	1	0.01
Guamanian/Chamorro (0)	2	0.02
Native Hawaiian (8)	13	0.10
Samoan (0)	1	0.01
White (9,816)	10,165	79.18
Not Hispanic (8,686)	8,886	69.22
Hispanic (1,130)	1,279	9.96

Dalhart

Place Type: City
County: Dallam
Population: 7,930†

Ancestry‡	Population	%
American (364)	364	4.75
Arab (0)	35	0.46
Lebanese (0)	35	0.46
Belgian (0)	7	0.09
British (0)	32	0.42
Czech (0)	52	0.68
Danish (0)	6	0.08
Dutch (8)	147	1.92
English (410)	911	11.89
European (50)	62	0.81
French, ex. Basque (42)	231	3.01
French Canadian (9)	18	0.23
German (571)	1,475	19.25
Irish (268)	1,030	13.44
Italian (9)	104	1.36
Norwegian (32)	55	0.72
Polish (11)	16	0.21
Portuguese (16)	21	0.27
Russian (12)	42	0.55
Scotch-Irish (35)	202	2.64
Scottish (53)	141	1.84
Swedish (38)	180	2.35
Welsh (0)	14	0.18

Hispanic Origin	Population	%
Hispanic or Latino (of any race)	2,697	34.01
Central American, ex. Mexican	28	0.35
Guatemalan	23	0.29
Honduran	2	0.03
Panamanian	3	0.04
Cuban	4	0.05
Mexican	2,193	27.65
Puerto Rican	6	0.08
South American	11	0.14
Argentinean	2	0.03
Chilean	1	0.01
Colombian	1	0.01
Ecuadorian	6	0.08
Venezuelan	1	0.01
Other Hispanic or Latino	455	5.74

Race*	Population	%
African-American/Black (97)	131	1.65
Not Hispanic (93)	110	1.39
Hispanic (4)	21	0.26
American Indian/Alaska Native (74)	117	1.48
Not Hispanic (33)	73	0.92
Hispanic (41)	44	0.55
Apache (5)	7	0.09
Arapaho (1)	1	0.01
Cherokee (8)	18	0.23
Cheyenne (1)	1	0.01
Chickasaw (0)	1	0.01
Chippewa (1)	1	0.01
Choctaw (1)	5	0.06
Comanche (1)	4	0.05
Creek (2)	2	0.03
Kiowa (2)	2	0.03
Mexican American Ind. (6)	6	0.08
Navajo (2)	2	0.03
Osage (1)	1	0.01
Potawatomi (5)	5	0.06
Spanish American Ind. (3)	3	0.04
Asian (54)	65	0.82
Not Hispanic (50)	57	0.72
Hispanic (4)	8	0.10
Chinese, ex. Taiwanese (1)	1	0.01
Filipino (10)	11	0.14
Hmong (3)	4	0.05
Indian (30)	30	0.38
Japanese (1)	2	0.03
Korean (1)	2	0.03
Laotian (4)	4	0.05
Vietnamese (2)	2	0.03
Hawaii Native/Pacific Islander (8)	8	0.10
Not Hispanic (8)	8	0.10
Guamanian/Chamorro (3)	3	0.04
Native Hawaiian (5)	5	0.06
White (6,665)	6,845	86.32
Not Hispanic (4,963)	5,017	63.27
Hispanic (1,702)	1,828	23.05

Dallas

Place Type: City
County: Dallas
Population: 1,197,816†

Ancestry‡	Population	%
Afghan (86)	86	0.01
African, Sub-Saharan (18,211)	19,903	1.68
African (9,844)	10,746	0.91
Cape Verdean (15)	15	<0.01
Ethiopian (2,590)	2,719	0.23
Ghanaian (205)	205	0.02
Kenyan (377)	409	0.03
Liberian (287)	307	0.03
Nigerian (2,216)	2,477	0.21
Senegalese (12)	12	<0.01
Sierra Leonean (66)	100	0.01
Somalian (780)	780	0.07
South African (319)	465	0.04
Sudanese (491)	491	0.04
Ugandan (10)	10	<0.01
Zimbabwean (60)	90	0.01
Other Sub-Saharan African (939)	1,077	0.09
Albanian (428)	481	0.04
Alsatian (0)	37	<0.01
American (33,684)	33,684	2.84
Arab (2,498)	3,820	0.32
Arab (192)	339	0.03
Egyptian (197)	256	0.02
Iraqi (250)	250	0.02
Jordanian (125)	136	0.01
Lebanese (1,016)	1,717	0.14
Moroccan (125)	125	0.01
Palestinian (337)	500	0.04
Syrian (71)	192	0.02
Other Arab (185)	305	0.03
Armenian (72)	387	0.03
Assyrian/Chaldean/Syriac (35)	35	<0.01
Australian (95)	149	0.01
Austrian (393)	1,538	0.13
Basque (0)	62	0.01
Belgian (141)	346	0.03
Brazilian (715)	850	0.07
British (2,493)	4,910	0.41
Bulgarian (123)	226	0.02
Cajun (246)	444	0.04
Canadian (490)	883	0.07
Carpatho Rusyn (0)	12	<0.01
Celtic (65)	132	0.01
Croatian (276)	487	0.04
Czech (1,553)	4,600	0.39
Czechoslovakian (340)	611	0.05
Danish (700)	1,958	0.16
Dutch (1,531)	6,964	0.59
Eastern European (1,274)	1,384	0.12
English (25,908)	64,225	5.41
Estonian (28)	64	0.01
European (8,814)	10,354	0.87
Finnish (179)	571	0.05
French, ex. Basque (4,223)	17,325	1.46
French Canadian (696)	1,729	0.15
German (23,682)	73,347	6.18
German Russian (0)	30	<0.01
Greek (1,036)	2,251	0.19
Guyanese (51)	62	0.01
Hungarian (754)	1,814	0.15
Icelander (17)	29	<0.01
Iranian (1,811)	2,012	0.17
Irish (17,257)	57,324	4.83
Israeli (858)	947	0.08
Italian (6,578)	17,246	1.45
Latvian (44)	180	0.02
Lithuanian (141)	573	0.05
Luxemburger (0)	64	0.01
Macedonian (52)	70	0.01
New Zealander (123)	132	0.01
Northern European (579)	596	0.05
Norwegian (1,593)	4,919	0.41
Pennsylvania German (35)	100	0.01
Polish (3,445)	10,063	0.85
Portuguese (266)	825	0.07
Romanian (542)	1,061	0.09
Russian (3,815)	7,373	0.62
Scandinavian (332)	958	0.08
Scotch-Irish (7,441)	15,332	1.29
Scottish (5,450)	15,251	1.28
Serbian (41)	92	0.01
Slavic (103)	139	0.01
Slovak (109)	397	0.03
Slovene (46)	87	0.01
Swedish (1,801)	6,140	0.52
Swiss (311)	1,387	0.12
Turkish (567)	625	0.05
Ukrainian (383)	999	0.08
Welsh (970)	4,109	0.35
West Indian, ex. Hispanic (1,518)	2,173	0.18
Bahamian (12)	12	<0.01
Barbadian (95)	129	0.01
Belizean (279)	335	0.03
British West Indian (86)	113	0.01
Dutch West Indian (33)	173	0.01
Haitian (308)	350	0.03
Jamaican (526)	761	0.06
Trinidadian/Tobagonian (129)	200	0.02
West Indian (35)	85	0.01
Other West Indian (15)	15	<0.01
Yugoslavian (458)	702	0.06

Hispanic Origin	Population	%
Hispanic or Latino (of any race)	507,309	42.35
Central American, ex. Mexican	28,798	2.40
Costa Rican	462	0.04
Guatemalan	4,238	0.35
Honduran	6,890	0.58
Nicaraguan	816	0.07
Panamanian	458	0.04
Salvadoran	15,696	1.31
Other Central American	238	0.02
Cuban	2,322	0.19
Dominican Republic	530	0.04
Mexican	439,460	36.69
Puerto Rican	3,643	0.30
South American	5,683	0.47
Argentinean	599	0.05
Bolivian	301	0.03
Chilean	283	0.02

*Notes: † The Census 2010 population figure is used to calculate the percentages in the Hispanic Origin and Race categories. Ancestry percentages are based on the 2006-2010 American Community Survey population (not shown); ‡ Numbers in parentheses indicate the number of people reporting a single ancestry; * Numbers in parentheses indicate the number of persons reporting this race alone, not in combination with any other race; Please refer to the Explanation of Data for more information.*

Colombian	1,563	0.13
Ecuadorian	412	0.03
Paraguayan	74	0.01
Peruvian	1,725	0.14
Uruguayan	103	0.01
Venezuelan	548	0.05
Other South American	75	0.01
Other Hispanic or Latino	26,873	2.24

Race*	Population	%
African-American/Black (298,993)	308,087	25.72
Not Hispanic (294,159)	300,502	25.09
Hispanic (4,834)	7,585	0.63
American Indian/Alaska Native (8,099)	14,114	1.18
Not Hispanic (3,167)	7,020	0.59
Hispanic (4,932)	7,094	0.59
Alaska Athabascan *(Ala. Nat.)* (10)	11	<0.01
Aleut *(Alaska Native)* (6)	12	<0.01
Apache (115)	225	0.02
Arapaho (8)	14	<0.01
Blackfeet (17)	134	0.01
Canadian/French Am. Ind. (7)	20	<0.01
Central American Ind. (47)	83	0.01
Cherokee (533)	1,684	0.14
Cheyenne (14)	22	<0.01
Chickasaw (170)	284	0.02
Chippewa (47)	73	0.01
Choctaw (594)	1,030	0.09
Colville (1)	2	<0.01
Comanche (91)	178	0.01
Cree (1)	4	<0.01
Creek (104)	251	0.02
Crow (4)	12	<0.01
Delaware (15)	28	<0.01
Hopi (13)	23	<0.01
Houma (3)	4	<0.01
Inupiat *(Alaska Native)* (5)	12	<0.01
Iroquois (13)	36	<0.01
Kiowa (52)	72	0.01
Lumbee (11)	17	<0.01
Mexican American Ind. (1,084)	1,495	0.12
Navajo (145)	197	0.02
Osage (29)	55	<0.01
Ottawa (7)	10	<0.01
Paiute (5)	6	<0.01
Pima (14)	21	<0.01
Potawatomi (78)	104	0.01
Pueblo (53)	71	0.01
Puget Sound Salish (0)	3	<0.01
Seminole (36)	104	0.01
Shoshone (2)	5	<0.01
Sioux (112)	175	0.01
South American Ind. (55)	86	0.01
Spanish American Ind. (97)	127	0.01
Tlingit-Haida *(Alaska Native)* (8)	16	<0.01
Tohono O'Odham (22)	37	<0.01
Tsimshian *(Alaska Native)* (1)	1	<0.01
Ute (1)	5	<0.01
Yakama (3)	6	<0.01
Yaqui (20)	28	<0.01
Yuman (4)	4	<0.01
Yup'ik *(Alaska Native)* (1)	2	<0.01
Asian (34,263)	39,508	3.30
Not Hispanic (33,609)	37,744	3.15
Hispanic (654)	1,764	0.15
Bangladeshi (336)	373	0.03
Bhutanese (526)	614	0.05
Burmese (2,015)	2,127	0.18
Cambodian (863)	992	0.08
Chinese, ex. Taiwanese (5,608)	6,608	0.55
Filipino (2,442)	3,387	0.28
Hmong (14)	25	<0.01
Indian (7,313)	8,314	0.69
Indonesian (125)	178	0.01
Japanese (747)	1,337	0.11
Korean (3,218)	3,760	0.31
Laotian (960)	1,114	0.09
Malaysian (50)	81	0.01
Nepalese (288)	335	0.03
Pakistani (1,027)	1,152	0.10
Sri Lankan (80)	103	0.01
Taiwanese (549)	621	0.05
Thai (686)	868	0.07
Vietnamese (5,739)	6,307	0.53
Hawaii Native/Pacific Islander (482)	1,549	0.13
Not Hispanic (311)	855	0.07
Hispanic (171)	694	0.06
Fijian (19)	21	<0.01
Guamanian/Chamorro (173)	262	0.02
Marshallese (6)	7	<0.01
Native Hawaiian (125)	371	0.03
Samoan (68)	174	0.01
Tongan (8)	19	<0.01
White (607,415)	633,355	52.88
Not Hispanic (345,205)	354,625	29.61
Hispanic (262,210)	278,730	23.27

DeSoto

Place Type: City
County: Dallas
Population: 49,047†

Ancestry‡	Population	%
African, Sub-Saharan (852)	1,059	2.27
African (505)	700	1.50
Cape Verdean (0)	12	0.03
Kenyan (187)	187	0.40
Nigerian (100)	100	0.21
Sierra Leonean (14)	14	0.03
Zimbabwean (46)	46	0.10
American (1,288)	1,288	2.76
Arab (182)	220	0.47
Arab (73)	73	0.16
Lebanese (6)	44	0.09
Palestinian (103)	103	0.22
Austrian (0)	36	0.08
British (54)	63	0.14
Canadian (27)	91	0.20
Czech (52)	106	0.23
Czechoslovakian (26)	33	0.07
Danish (91)	124	0.27
Dutch (160)	382	0.82
Eastern European (15)	15	0.03
English (761)	1,569	3.37
European (60)	83	0.18
Finnish (8)	8	0.02
French, ex. Basque (157)	501	1.07
French Canadian (49)	61	0.13
German (873)	1,930	4.14
Greek (16)	16	0.03
Hungarian (46)	77	0.17
Iranian (0)	32	0.07
Irish (599)	1,512	3.24
Italian (129)	368	0.79
Lithuanian (0)	10	0.02
Norwegian (18)	107	0.23
Pennsylvania German (11)	11	0.02
Polish (62)	228	0.49
Portuguese (0)	12	0.03
Romanian (0)	14	0.03
Russian (26)	26	0.06
Scandinavian (10)	22	0.05
Scotch-Irish (171)	344	0.74
Scottish (215)	419	0.90
Slavic (11)	11	0.02
Slovak (0)	10	0.02
Swedish (7)	90	0.19
Ukrainian (21)	21	0.05
Welsh (58)	118	0.25
West Indian, ex. Hispanic (193)	204	0.44
Belizean (125)	125	0.27
British West Indian (14)	14	0.03
Dutch West Indian (7)	7	0.02
Haitian (14)	14	0.03
Jamaican (8)	8	0.02
Trinidadian/Tobagonian (14)	25	0.05
West Indian (11)	11	0.02
Yugoslavian (8)	8	0.02

Hispanic Origin	Population	%
Hispanic or Latino (of any race)	5,914	12.06
Central American, ex. Mexican	241	0.49
Costa Rican	2	<0.01
Guatemalan	28	0.06
Honduran	31	0.06
Nicaraguan	10	0.02
Panamanian	40	0.08
Salvadoran	130	0.27
Cuban	38	0.08
Dominican Republic	18	0.04
Mexican	4,928	10.05
Puerto Rican	165	0.34
South American	74	0.15
Argentinean	16	0.03
Chilean	11	0.02
Colombian	32	0.07
Ecuadorian	1	<0.01
Paraguayan	1	<0.01
Peruvian	8	0.02
Venezuelan	4	0.01
Other South American	1	<0.01
Other Hispanic or Latino	450	0.92

Race*	Population	%
African-American/Black (33,648)	34,276	69.88
Not Hispanic (33,337)	33,823	68.96
Hispanic (311)	453	0.92
American Indian/Alaska Native (200)	441	0.90
Not Hispanic (111)	297	0.61
Hispanic (89)	144	0.29
Apache (4)	15	0.03
Blackfeet (0)	8	0.02
Central American Ind. (0)	3	0.01
Cherokee (21)	66	0.13
Chickasaw (6)	9	0.02
Choctaw (6)	22	0.04
Comanche (2)	6	0.01
Creek (9)	19	0.04
Crow (3)	3	0.01
Delaware (0)	2	<0.01
Lumbee (0)	3	0.01
Mexican American Ind. (16)	27	0.06
Navajo (2)	7	0.01
Osage (2)	4	0.01
Ottawa (2)	2	<0.01
Potawatomi (1)	1	<0.01
Seminole (1)	5	0.01
Sioux (0)	2	<0.01
South American Ind. (1)	4	0.01
Spanish American Ind. (1)	1	<0.01
Yuman (3)	3	0.01
Asian (454)	595	1.21
Not Hispanic (446)	559	1.14
Hispanic (8)	36	0.07
Bangladeshi (1)	3	0.01
Chinese, ex. Taiwanese (85)	109	0.22
Filipino (100)	131	0.27
Hmong (2)	2	<0.01
Indian (107)	120	0.24
Indonesian (0)	3	0.01
Japanese (14)	24	0.05
Korean (48)	69	0.14
Laotian (1)	2	<0.01
Malaysian (0)	1	<0.01
Nepalese (3)	3	0.01
Pakistani (13)	13	0.03
Taiwanese (1)	3	0.01
Thai (1)	5	0.01
Vietnamese (56)	63	0.13
Hawaii Native/Pacific Islander (22)	44	0.09
Not Hispanic (22)	41	0.08
Hispanic (0)	3	0.01
Guamanian/Chamorro (5)	6	0.01
Native Hawaiian (8)	15	0.03
Samoan (1)	4	0.01
White (11,358)	11,994	24.45
Not Hispanic (8,542)	8,983	18.32
Hispanic (2,816)	3,011	6.14

*Notes: † The Census 2010 population figure is used to calculate the percentages in the Hispanic Origin and Race categories. Ancestry percentages are based on the 2006-2010 American Community Survey population (not shown); ‡ Numbers in parentheses indicate the number of people reporting a single ancestry; * Numbers in parentheses indicate the number of persons reporting this race alone, not in combination with any other race; Please refer to the Explanation of Data for more information.*

Deer Park

Place Type: City
County: Harris
Population: 32,010†

Ancestry‡	Population	%
African, Sub-Saharan (12)	12	0.04
African (12)	12	0.04
American (3,242)	3,242	10.38
Australian (0)	27	0.09
Austrian (39)	104	0.33
Belgian (10)	10	0.03
British (41)	41	0.13
Cajun (89)	198	0.63
Celtic (0)	11	0.04
Czech (124)	297	0.95
Czechoslovakian (91)	101	0.32
Danish (25)	124	0.40
Dutch (41)	329	1.05
English (1,073)	2,808	8.99
European (566)	566	1.81
French, ex. Basque (335)	1,197	3.83
French Canadian (29)	45	0.14
German (1,366)	3,935	12.60
Greek (33)	145	0.46
Hungarian (9)	69	0.22
Irish (1,486)	4,016	12.85
Italian (299)	505	1.62
Lithuanian (0)	9	0.03
Northern European (15)	32	0.10
Norwegian (22)	161	0.52
Polish (198)	515	1.65
Portuguese (0)	11	0.04
Russian (0)	20	0.06
Scandinavian (20)	41	0.13
Scotch-Irish (298)	682	2.18
Scottish (194)	543	1.74
Slavic (20)	76	0.24
Slovak (17)	17	0.05
Swedish (28)	94	0.30
Swiss (7)	7	0.02
Welsh (74)	105	0.34
West Indian, ex. Hispanic (46)	62	0.20
Dutch West Indian (0)	16	0.05
Jamaican (46)	46	0.15

Hispanic Origin	Population	%
Hispanic or Latino (of any race)	8,418	26.30
Central American, ex. Mexican	280	0.87
Costa Rican	16	0.05
Guatemalan	43	0.13
Honduran	55	0.17
Nicaraguan	14	0.04
Panamanian	3	0.01
Salvadoran	144	0.45
Other Central American	5	0.02
Cuban	61	0.19
Dominican Republic	5	0.02
Mexican	7,050	22.02
Puerto Rican	124	0.39
South American	111	0.35
Argentinean	8	0.02
Bolivian	11	0.03
Chilean	1	<0.01
Colombian	37	0.12
Ecuadorian	1	<0.01
Peruvian	15	0.05
Venezuelan	37	0.12
Other South American	1	<0.01
Other Hispanic or Latino	787	2.46

Race*	Population	%
African-American/Black (475)	611	1.91
Not Hispanic (426)	527	1.65
Hispanic (49)	84	0.26
American Indian/Alaska Native (225)	367	1.15
Not Hispanic (107)	211	0.66
Hispanic (118)	156	0.49
Apache (10)	18	0.06
Arapaho (1)	1	<0.01
Blackfeet (1)	1	<0.01
Canadian/French Am. Ind. (1)	1	<0.01
Central American Ind. (1)	1	<0.01
Cherokee (21)	56	0.17
Cheyenne (0)	3	0.01
Chickasaw (4)	9	0.03
Chippewa (1)	2	0.01
Choctaw (17)	33	0.10
Cree (0)	1	<0.01
Creek (4)	4	0.01
Inupiat *(Alaska Native)* (1)	1	<0.01
Iroquois (2)	3	0.01
Mexican American Ind. (7)	12	0.04
Navajo (4)	12	0.04
Osage (1)	4	0.01
Ottawa (3)	3	0.01
Paiute (3)	3	0.01
Potawatomi (3)	3	0.01
Sioux (3)	7	0.02
Yaqui (2)	2	0.01
Yuman (1)	1	<0.01
Asian (482)	627	1.96
Not Hispanic (461)	555	1.73
Hispanic (21)	72	0.22
Bangladeshi (3)	5	0.02
Cambodian (20)	20	0.06
Chinese, ex. Taiwanese (35)	53	0.17
Filipino (82)	106	0.33
Indian (113)	149	0.47
Indonesian (3)	3	0.01
Japanese (9)	39	0.12
Korean (59)	82	0.26
Laotian (3)	5	0.02
Pakistani (39)	52	0.16
Thai (5)	8	0.02
Vietnamese (74)	94	0.29
Hawaii Native/Pacific Islander (26)	73	0.23
Not Hispanic (18)	55	0.17
Hispanic (8)	18	0.06
Guamanian/Chamorro (8)	9	0.03
Native Hawaiian (14)	37	0.12
Samoan (0)	2	0.01
White (27,602)	28,234	88.20
Not Hispanic (22,257)	22,532	70.39
Hispanic (5,345)	5,702	17.81

Del Rio

Place Type: City
County: Val Verde
Population: 35,591†

Ancestry‡	Population	%
American (1,391)	1,391	3.95
British (33)	82	0.23
Dutch (71)	178	0.51
English (311)	816	2.32
European (82)	108	0.31
French, ex. Basque (23)	217	0.62
French Canadian (31)	43	0.12
German (489)	1,183	3.36
Irish (169)	788	2.24
Italian (195)	481	1.37
Norwegian (32)	52	0.15
Polish (45)	135	0.38
Portuguese (62)	89	0.25
Russian (0)	4	0.01
Scotch-Irish (134)	231	0.66
Scottish (31)	141	0.40
Swedish (14)	68	0.19
Swiss (15)	92	0.26
Ukrainian (0)	16	0.05
Welsh (0)	15	0.04
West Indian, ex. Hispanic (4)	4	0.01
Barbadian (4)	4	0.01

Hispanic Origin	Population	%
Hispanic or Latino (of any race)	29,927	84.09
Central American, ex. Mexican	145	0.41
Costa Rican	11	0.03
Guatemalan	23	0.06
Honduran	60	0.17
Nicaraguan	6	0.02
Panamanian	10	0.03
Salvadoran	35	0.10
Cuban	23	0.06
Dominican Republic	17	0.05
Mexican	27,626	77.62
Puerto Rican	184	0.52
South American	46	0.13
Argentinean	1	<0.01
Colombian	13	0.04
Ecuadorian	6	0.02
Paraguayan	5	0.01
Peruvian	10	0.03
Venezuelan	11	0.03
Other Hispanic or Latino	1,886	5.30

Race*	Population	%
African-American/Black (528)	660	1.85
Not Hispanic (398)	435	1.22
Hispanic (130)	225	0.63
American Indian/Alaska Native (179)	287	0.81
Not Hispanic (59)	101	0.28
Hispanic (120)	186	0.52
Apache (3)	17	0.05
Blackfeet (0)	1	<0.01
Central American Ind. (3)	3	0.01
Cherokee (23)	32	0.09
Chickasaw (3)	4	0.01
Choctaw (14)	23	0.06
Comanche (4)	4	0.01
Creek (3)	3	0.01
Iroquois (0)	3	0.01
Menominee (3)	3	0.01
Mexican American Ind. (19)	27	0.08
Navajo (5)	9	0.03
Osage (2)	3	0.01
Pima (0)	1	<0.01
Pueblo (2)	2	0.01
Puget Sound Salish (1)	1	<0.01
Seminole (4)	14	0.04
Sioux (4)	8	0.02
South American Ind. (0)	1	<0.01
Asian (172)	261	0.73
Not Hispanic (145)	194	0.55
Hispanic (27)	67	0.19
Chinese, ex. Taiwanese (8)	23	0.06
Filipino (75)	111	0.31
Indian (13)	20	0.06
Japanese (15)	24	0.07
Korean (31)	51	0.14
Malaysian (0)	1	<0.01
Taiwanese (0)	3	0.01
Thai (9)	12	0.03
Vietnamese (9)	13	0.04
Hawaii Native/Pacific Islander (36)	66	0.19
Not Hispanic (30)	40	0.11
Hispanic (6)	26	0.07
Guamanian/Chamorro (12)	14	0.04
Native Hawaiian (8)	25	0.07
Samoan (12)	13	0.04
White (30,126)	30,779	86.48
Not Hispanic (4,898)	4,999	14.05
Hispanic (25,228)	25,780	72.43

Denison

Place Type: City
County: Grayson
Population: 22,682†

Ancestry‡	Population	%
African, Sub-Saharan (134)	354	1.56
African (125)	345	1.52
Ugandan (9)	9	0.04
American (2,320)	2,320	10.21
Arab (0)	98	0.43
Arab (0)	56	0.25

*Notes: † The Census 2010 population figure is used to calculate the percentages in the Hispanic Origin and Race categories. Ancestry percentages are based on the 2006-2010 American Community Survey population (not shown); ‡ Numbers in parentheses indicate the number of people reporting a single ancestry; * Numbers in parentheses indicate the number of persons reporting this race alone, not in combination with any other race; Please refer to the Explanation of Data for more information.*

Lebanese (0)	42	0.18
Austrian (10)	57	0.25
British (23)	68	0.30
Cajun (12)	12	0.05
Canadian (0)	6	0.03
Czech (115)	206	0.91
Dutch (112)	555	2.44
English (1,347)	2,680	11.79
European (142)	147	0.65
French, ex. Basque (106)	621	2.73
French Canadian (75)	93	0.41
German (678)	2,278	10.02
Greek (0)	60	0.26
Hungarian (13)	13	0.06
Irish (641)	3,306	14.55
Italian (187)	409	1.80
Norwegian (19)	40	0.18
Pennsylvania German (0)	10	0.04
Polish (27)	81	0.36
Portuguese (0)	116	0.51
Russian (8)	24	0.11
Scotch-Irish (360)	621	2.73
Scottish (109)	364	1.60
Swedish (49)	149	0.66
Ukrainian (0)	13	0.06
Welsh (17)	74	0.33
West Indian, ex. Hispanic (0)	64	0.28
Dutch West Indian (0)	64	0.28

Hispanic Origin	Population	%
Hispanic or Latino (of any race)	1,996	8.80
Central American, ex. Mexican	39	0.17
Guatemalan	2	0.01
Honduran	6	0.03
Panamanian	3	0.01
Salvadoran	28	0.12
Cuban	9	0.04
Dominican Republic	1	<0.01
Mexican	1,731	7.63
Puerto Rican	71	0.31
South American	14	0.06
Argentinean	1	<0.01
Chilean	1	<0.01
Colombian	3	0.01
Peruvian	1	<0.01
Venezuelan	8	0.04
Other Hispanic or Latino	131	0.58

Race*	Population	%
African-American/Black (2,104)	2,365	10.43
Not Hispanic (2,066)	2,293	10.11
Hispanic (38)	72	0.32
American Indian/Alaska Native (467)	823	3.63
Not Hispanic (411)	746	3.29
Hispanic (56)	77	0.34
Apache (1)	4	0.02
Blackfeet (1)	3	0.01
Cherokee (59)	151	0.67
Chickasaw (46)	95	0.42
Chippewa (0)	6	0.03
Choctaw (170)	271	1.19
Comanche (3)	5	0.02
Creek (14)	29	0.13
Delaware (0)	2	0.01
Hopi (0)	3	0.01
Iroquois (3)	3	0.01
Kiowa (4)	5	0.02
Mexican American Ind. (3)	3	0.01
Navajo (2)	5	0.02
Osage (0)	1	<0.01
Paiute (1)	1	<0.01
Potawatomi (0)	6	0.03
Seminole (1)	2	0.01
Shoshone (1)	1	<0.01
Sioux (0)	3	0.01
Spanish American Ind. (1)	1	<0.01
Tohono O'Odham (0)	3	0.01
Asian (133)	189	0.83
Not Hispanic (133)	185	0.82
Hispanic (0)	4	0.02
Cambodian (1)	1	<0.01
Chinese, ex. Taiwanese (12)	16	0.07
Filipino (20)	39	0.17
Hmong (3)	3	0.01
Indian (28)	36	0.16
Japanese (12)	13	0.06
Korean (0)	8	0.04
Nepalese (12)	12	0.05
Pakistani (21)	22	0.10
Taiwanese (1)	1	<0.01
Thai (4)	8	0.04
Vietnamese (6)	19	0.08
Hawaii Native/Pacific Islander (16)	34	0.15
Not Hispanic (15)	29	0.13
Hispanic (1)	5	0.02
Guamanian/Chamorro (4)	5	0.02
Native Hawaiian (12)	21	0.09
White (18,660)	19,330	85.22
Not Hispanic (17,461)	18,015	79.42
Hispanic (1,199)	1,315	5.80

Denton

Place Type: City
County: Denton
Population: 113,383†

Ancestry‡	Population	%
African, Sub-Saharan (1,445)	1,748	1.60
African (664)	862	0.79
Ethiopian (98)	115	0.11
Ghanaian (38)	38	0.03
Kenyan (338)	338	0.31
Nigerian (225)	297	0.27
South African (26)	42	0.04
Ugandan (12)	12	0.01
Other Sub-Saharan African (44)	44	0.04
Albanian (41)	41	0.04
Alsatian (10)	10	0.01
American (4,454)	4,454	4.08
Arab (245)	535	0.49
Arab (110)	120	0.11
Egyptian (20)	29	0.03
Iraqi (15)	39	0.04
Lebanese (48)	121	0.11
Palestinian (0)	43	0.04
Syrian (19)	80	0.07
Other Arab (33)	103	0.09
Armenian (39)	69	0.06
Assyrian/Chaldean/Syriac (24)	35	0.03
Austrian (54)	228	0.21
Belgian (16)	106	0.10
Brazilian (56)	74	0.07
British (351)	668	0.61
Bulgarian (26)	26	0.02
Cajun (37)	85	0.08
Canadian (109)	143	0.13
Celtic (13)	23	0.02
Croatian (7)	122	0.11
Czech (211)	760	0.70
Czechoslovakian (186)	238	0.22
Danish (73)	148	0.14
Dutch (321)	1,585	1.45
Eastern European (51)	51	0.05
English (4,229)	11,462	10.50
European (1,110)	1,478	1.35
Finnish (55)	101	0.09
French, ex. Basque (632)	3,036	2.78
French Canadian (347)	469	0.43
German (5,625)	17,978	16.46
Greek (21)	117	0.11
Guyanese (0)	10	0.01
Hungarian (31)	89	0.08
Icelander (6)	12	0.01
Iranian (158)	188	0.17
Irish (3,285)	12,133	11.11
Italian (1,217)	3,231	2.96
Lithuanian (43)	126	0.12
Northern European (32)	32	0.03
Norwegian (501)	1,475	1.35
Pennsylvania German (10)	20	0.02
Polish (381)	1,623	1.49
Portuguese (163)	242	0.22
Romanian (93)	93	0.09
Russian (143)	465	0.43
Scandinavian (97)	243	0.22
Scotch-Irish (1,235)	3,013	2.76
Scottish (910)	2,815	2.58
Serbian (21)	21	0.02
Slavic (22)	43	0.04
Slovak (0)	16	0.01
Slovene (16)	62	0.06
Swedish (226)	962	0.88
Swiss (43)	187	0.17
Turkish (67)	109	0.10
Ukrainian (11)	96	0.09
Welsh (295)	1,030	0.94
West Indian, ex. Hispanic (145)	407	0.37
Bahamian (0)	60	0.05
Belizean (0)	22	0.02
British West Indian (0)	18	0.02
Dutch West Indian (0)	9	0.01
Haitian (22)	22	0.02
Jamaican (112)	197	0.18
Trinidadian/Tobagonian (11)	11	0.01
West Indian (0)	68	0.06
Yugoslavian (11)	11	0.01

Hispanic Origin	Population	%
Hispanic or Latino (of any race)	24,071	21.23
Central American, ex. Mexican	1,336	1.18
Costa Rican	27	0.02
Guatemalan	458	0.40
Honduran	187	0.16
Nicaraguan	58	0.05
Panamanian	85	0.07
Salvadoran	505	0.45
Other Central American	16	0.01
Cuban	158	0.14
Dominican Republic	60	0.05
Mexican	18,766	16.55
Puerto Rican	621	0.55
South American	742	0.65
Argentinean	46	0.04
Bolivian	37	0.03
Chilean	25	0.02
Colombian	322	0.28
Ecuadorian	43	0.04
Paraguayan	2	<0.01
Peruvian	176	0.16
Uruguayan	1	<0.01
Venezuelan	78	0.07
Other South American	12	0.01
Other Hispanic or Latino	2,388	2.11

Race*	Population	%
African-American/Black (11,734)	12,975	11.44
Not Hispanic (11,370)	12,337	10.88
Hispanic (364)	638	0.56
American Indian/Alaska Native (871)	1,894	1.67
Not Hispanic (569)	1,350	1.19
Hispanic (302)	544	0.48
Alaska Athabascan *(Ala. Nat.)* (1)	2	<0.01
Aleut *(Alaska Native)* (1)	1	<0.01
Apache (10)	20	0.02
Arapaho (1)	1	<0.01
Blackfeet (10)	27	0.02
Canadian/French Am. Ind. (4)	8	0.01
Central American Ind. (1)	8	0.01
Cherokee (156)	406	0.36
Cheyenne (0)	1	<0.01
Chickasaw (49)	79	0.07
Chippewa (7)	19	0.02
Choctaw (89)	193	0.17
Comanche (17)	38	0.03
Cree (0)	2	<0.01
Creek (17)	39	0.03
Crow (0)	1	<0.01
Delaware (0)	3	<0.01
Hopi (0)	5	<0.01

SECTION TWO

*Notes: † The Census 2010 population figure is used to calculate the percentages in the Hispanic Origin and Race categories. Ancestry percentages are based on the 2006-2010 American Community Survey population (not shown); ‡ Numbers in parentheses indicate the number of people reporting a single ancestry; * Numbers in parentheses indicate the number of persons reporting this race alone, not in combination with any other race; Please refer to the Explanation of Data for more information.*

Inupiat *(Alaska Native)* (0)	1	<0.01
Iroquois (3)	12	0.01
Kiowa (19)	23	0.02
Menominee (1)	1	<0.01
Mexican American Ind. (72)	113	0.10
Navajo (23)	34	0.03
Osage (2)	4	<0.01
Ottawa (2)	3	<0.01
Pima (1)	1	<0.01
Potawatomi (16)	22	0.02
Pueblo (7)	14	0.01
Puget Sound Salish (0)	1	<0.01
Seminole (1)	6	0.01
Shoshone (1)	1	<0.01
Sioux (12)	21	0.02
South American Ind. (2)	8	0.01
Spanish American Ind. (3)	3	<0.01
Tohono O'Odham (0)	1	<0.01
Yup'ik *(Alaska Native)* (2)	3	<0.01
Asian (4,670)	5,617	4.95
Not Hispanic (4,597)	5,401	4.76
Hispanic (73)	216	0.19
Bangladeshi (58)	65	0.06
Burmese (3)	6	0.01
Cambodian (17)	24	0.02
Chinese, ex. Taiwanese (1,000)	1,163	1.03
Filipino (330)	553	0.49
Hmong (7)	8	0.01
Indian (1,127)	1,234	1.09
Indonesian (15)	24	0.02
Japanese (186)	323	0.28
Korean (625)	749	0.66
Laotian (24)	29	0.03
Malaysian (19)	24	0.02
Nepalese (175)	189	0.17
Pakistani (119)	144	0.13
Sri Lankan (32)	32	0.03
Taiwanese (195)	217	0.19
Thai (153)	209	0.18
Vietnamese (367)	447	0.39
Hawaii Native/Pacific Islander (116)	276	0.24
Not Hispanic (104)	229	0.20
Hispanic (12)	47	0.04
Fijian (1)	1	<0.01
Guamanian/Chamorro (52)	78	0.07
Native Hawaiian (19)	51	0.04
Samoan (8)	18	0.02
Tongan (0)	4	<0.01
White (83,705)	86,843	76.59
Not Hispanic (70,190)	72,207	63.68
Hispanic (13,515)	14,636	12.91

Dickinson

Place Type: City
County: Galveston
Population: 18,680†

Ancestry‡	Population	%
African, Sub-Saharan (59)	59	0.32
African (59)	59	0.32
Albanian (171)	171	0.92
American (1,103)	1,103	5.96
Arab (0)	24	0.13
Syrian (0)	24	0.13
Austrian (0)	33	0.18
British (42)	42	0.23
Cajun (30)	51	0.28
Canadian (0)	25	0.14
Czech (143)	414	2.24
Czechoslovakian (47)	73	0.39
Danish (21)	85	0.46
Dutch (16)	151	0.82
English (696)	1,443	7.80
European (206)	206	1.11
French, ex. Basque (74)	467	2.53
French Canadian (50)	165	0.89
German (978)	2,754	14.89
Greek (9)	37	0.20
Hungarian (0)	36	0.19
Irish (454)	1,771	9.58
Italian (428)	925	5.00
Norwegian (20)	81	0.44
Polish (33)	131	0.71
Portuguese (0)	20	0.11
Russian (68)	90	0.49
Scotch-Irish (222)	450	2.43
Scottish (23)	200	1.08
Slovak (0)	15	0.08
Swedish (29)	29	0.16
Swiss (0)	36	0.19
Turkish (0)	11	0.06
Welsh (25)	143	0.77
West Indian, ex. Hispanic (90)	158	0.85
Belizean (18)	36	0.19
Dutch West Indian (0)	31	0.17
Jamaican (72)	91	0.49

Hispanic Origin	Population	%
Hispanic or Latino (of any race)	6,106	32.69
Central American, ex. Mexican	181	0.97
Costa Rican	5	0.03
Guatemalan	27	0.14
Honduran	53	0.28
Nicaraguan	4	0.02
Salvadoran	90	0.48
Other Central American	2	0.01
Cuban	37	0.20
Mexican	5,327	28.52
Puerto Rican	95	0.51
South American	45	0.24
Argentinean	8	0.04
Bolivian	3	0.02
Chilean	8	0.04
Colombian	15	0.08
Ecuadorian	1	0.01
Peruvian	7	0.04
Venezuelan	3	0.02
Other Hispanic or Latino	421	2.25

Race*	Population	%
African-American/Black (2,148)	2,323	12.44
Not Hispanic (2,087)	2,199	11.77
Hispanic (61)	124	0.66
American Indian/Alaska Native (102)	198	1.06
Not Hispanic (57)	129	0.69
Hispanic (45)	69	0.37
Apache (1)	4	0.02
Blackfeet (1)	4	0.02
Cherokee (10)	30	0.16
Chickasaw (3)	3	0.02
Choctaw (0)	1	0.01
Creek (3)	4	0.02
Delaware (1)	1	0.01
Inupiat *(Alaska Native)* (1)	1	0.01
Iroquois (0)	1	0.01
Mexican American Ind. (4)	10	0.05
Navajo (1)	1	0.01
Osage (4)	4	0.02
Seminole (0)	2	0.01
Sioux (0)	2	0.01
Spanish American Ind. (1)	2	0.01
Yaqui (0)	3	0.02
Asian (364)	448	2.40
Not Hispanic (350)	412	2.21
Hispanic (14)	36	0.19
Bangladeshi (0)	8	0.04
Cambodian (4)	4	0.02
Chinese, ex. Taiwanese (22)	35	0.19
Filipino (48)	67	0.36
Indian (33)	53	0.28
Indonesian (2)	3	0.02
Japanese (17)	31	0.17
Korean (5)	10	0.05
Laotian (1)	1	0.01
Pakistani (10)	13	0.07
Sri Lankan (2)	2	0.01
Taiwanese (0)	1	0.01
Thai (5)	10	0.05
Vietnamese (193)	207	1.11
Hawaii Native/Pacific Islander (9)	29	0.16
Not Hispanic (9)	22	0.12
Hispanic (0)	7	0.04
Guamanian/Chamorro (1)	1	0.01
Native Hawaiian (6)	16	0.09
Samoan (1)	1	0.01
Tongan (1)	1	0.01
White (13,169)	13,657	73.11
Not Hispanic (9,770)	9,983	53.44
Hispanic (3,399)	3,674	19.67

Donna

Place Type: City
County: Hidalgo
Population: 15,798†

Ancestry‡	Population	%
American (193)	193	1.22
Austrian (7)	14	0.09
Belgian (9)	9	0.06
Canadian (23)	23	0.15
Croatian (0)	7	0.04
Czech (21)	21	0.13
Danish (10)	10	0.06
Dutch (20)	37	0.23
English (126)	267	1.69
French, ex. Basque (22)	64	0.41
French Canadian (14)	14	0.09
German (415)	700	4.43
Irish (43)	393	2.49
Italian (27)	42	0.27
Norwegian (93)	93	0.59
Polish (24)	43	0.27
Scotch-Irish (0)	14	0.09
Scottish (0)	26	0.16
Swedish (0)	19	0.12
Swiss (7)	14	0.09
Ukrainian (7)	7	0.04
Welsh (0)	44	0.28

Hispanic Origin	Population	%
Hispanic or Latino (of any race)	14,578	92.28
Central American, ex. Mexican	51	0.32
Guatemalan	8	0.05
Honduran	24	0.15
Nicaraguan	8	0.05
Panamanian	1	0.01
Salvadoran	10	0.06
Cuban	7	0.04
Mexican	13,366	84.61
Puerto Rican	14	0.09
South American	9	0.06
Colombian	1	0.01
Peruvian	2	0.01
Uruguayan	5	0.03
Venezuelan	1	0.01
Other Hispanic or Latino	1,131	7.16

Race*	Population	%
African-American/Black (65)	80	0.51
Not Hispanic (17)	21	0.13
Hispanic (48)	59	0.37
American Indian/Alaska Native (40)	62	0.39
Not Hispanic (9)	17	0.11
Hispanic (31)	45	0.28
Apache (1)	2	0.01
Central American Ind. (3)	3	0.02
Cherokee (1)	1	0.01
Chickasaw (1)	1	0.01
Mexican American Ind. (6)	8	0.05
Asian (29)	43	0.27
Not Hispanic (19)	21	0.13
Hispanic (10)	22	0.14
Chinese, ex. Taiwanese (0)	1	0.01
Filipino (14)	16	0.10
Indian (11)	11	0.07
Korean (0)	1	0.01
Laotian (3)	3	0.02
Pakistani (1)	2	0.01

*Notes: † The Census 2010 population figure is used to calculate the percentages in the Hispanic Origin and Race categories. Ancestry percentages are based on the 2006-2010 American Community Survey population (not shown); ‡ Numbers in parentheses indicate the number of people reporting a single ancestry; * Numbers in parentheses indicate the number of persons reporting this race alone, not in combination with any other race; Please refer to the Explanation of Data for more information.*

Hawaii Native/Pacific Islander (0)	3	0.02
Hispanic (0)	3	0.02
Samoan (0)	2	0.01
White (13,646)	13,867	87.78
Not Hispanic (1,152)	1,166	7.38
Hispanic (12,494)	12,701	80.40

Dumas

Place Type: City
County: Moore
Population: 14,691†

Ancestry‡	Population	%
African, Sub-Saharan (42)	42	0.30
African (7)	7	0.05
Sudanese (35)	35	0.25
American (725)	725	5.10
British (12)	12	0.08
Canadian (49)	49	0.34
Czech (0)	56	0.39
Danish (13)	28	0.20
Dutch (36)	174	1.22
English (366)	776	5.46
French, ex. Basque (40)	242	1.70
French Canadian (0)	15	0.11
German (724)	1,717	12.07
Hungarian (9)	9	0.06
Iranian (32)	32	0.23
Irish (375)	1,239	8.71
Italian (18)	60	0.42
Norwegian (10)	80	0.56
Polish (49)	164	1.15
Scandinavian (0)	7	0.05
Scotch-Irish (125)	217	1.53
Scottish (69)	198	1.39
Swedish (0)	34	0.24
Welsh (15)	33	0.23

Hispanic Origin	Population	%
Hispanic or Latino (of any race)	7,422	50.52
Central American, ex. Mexican	49	0.33
Guatemalan	31	0.21
Honduran	9	0.06
Salvadoran	9	0.06
Cuban	6	0.04
Mexican	6,748	45.93
Puerto Rican	14	0.10
South American	30	0.20
Chilean	26	0.18
Colombian	3	0.02
Peruvian	1	0.01
Other Hispanic or Latino	575	3.91

Race*	Population	%
African-American/Black (291)	330	2.25
Not Hispanic (250)	271	1.84
Hispanic (41)	59	0.40
American Indian/Alaska Native (138)	211	1.44
Not Hispanic (71)	125	0.85
Hispanic (67)	86	0.59
Apache (1)	1	0.01
Blackfeet (0)	5	0.03
Cherokee (16)	33	0.22
Cheyenne (5)	5	0.03
Chickasaw (3)	5	0.03
Chippewa (0)	2	0.01
Choctaw (19)	28	0.19
Comanche (1)	1	0.01
Cree (0)	1	0.01
Creek (2)	6	0.04
Delaware (0)	1	0.01
Iroquois (0)	1	0.01
Kiowa (3)	3	0.02
Mexican American Ind. (15)	15	0.10
Navajo (4)	4	0.03
Osage (2)	2	0.01
Pueblo (7)	8	0.05
Sioux (0)	1	0.01
Asian (685)	729	4.96
Not Hispanic (675)	701	4.77
Hispanic (10)	28	0.19
Bhutanese (5)	5	0.03
Burmese (490)	507	3.45
Chinese, ex. Taiwanese (5)	7	0.05
Filipino (16)	27	0.18
Indian (23)	38	0.26
Japanese (0)	4	0.03
Korean (2)	6	0.04
Laotian (81)	84	0.57
Thai (31)	31	0.21
Vietnamese (8)	11	0.07
Hawaii Native/Pacific Islander (6)	23	0.16
Not Hispanic (6)	7	0.05
Hispanic (0)	16	0.11
Guamanian/Chamorro (0)	4	0.03
Native Hawaiian (0)	11	0.07
Samoan (6)	6	0.04
White (11,009)	11,243	76.53
Not Hispanic (6,124)	6,209	42.26
Hispanic (4,885)	5,034	34.27

Duncanville

Place Type: City
County: Dallas
Population: 38,524†

Ancestry‡	Population	%
African, Sub-Saharan (110)	224	0.59
African (77)	191	0.51
Ethiopian (12)	12	0.03
Kenyan (21)	21	0.06
Albanian (0)	35	0.09
American (1,831)	1,831	4.85
Arab (21)	21	0.06
Lebanese (21)	21	0.06
Austrian (16)	16	0.04
Brazilian (21)	21	0.06
British (77)	121	0.32
Canadian (0)	30	0.08
Czech (21)	152	0.40
Czechoslovakian (44)	79	0.21
Danish (0)	109	0.29
Dutch (82)	361	0.96
English (1,095)	2,221	5.88
European (348)	401	1.06
Finnish (0)	22	0.06
French, ex. Basque (67)	714	1.89
French Canadian (49)	66	0.17
German (798)	2,774	7.34
Greek (0)	49	0.13
Hungarian (12)	12	0.03
Irish (562)	2,014	5.33
Italian (94)	240	0.64
Lithuanian (0)	8	0.02
Northern European (14)	14	0.04
Norwegian (73)	195	0.52
Polish (115)	228	0.60
Portuguese (15)	15	0.04
Scandinavian (12)	79	0.21
Scotch-Irish (287)	730	1.93
Scottish (182)	325	0.86
Serbian (11)	11	0.03
Slovak (12)	12	0.03
Swedish (58)	182	0.48
Swiss (105)	131	0.35
Welsh (18)	104	0.28
West Indian, ex. Hispanic (52)	52	0.14
Dutch West Indian (10)	10	0.03
Jamaican (14)	14	0.04
West Indian (28)	28	0.07
Yugoslavian (20)	20	0.05

Hispanic Origin	Population	%
Hispanic or Latino (of any race)	13,480	34.99
Central American, ex. Mexican	604	1.57
Costa Rican	10	0.03
Guatemalan	116	0.30
Honduran	64	0.17
Nicaraguan	29	0.08
Panamanian	34	0.09
Salvadoran	347	0.90
Other Central American	4	0.01
Cuban	48	0.12
Dominican Republic	25	0.06
Mexican	11,972	31.08
Puerto Rican	135	0.35
South American	137	0.36
Argentinean	24	0.06
Bolivian	4	0.01
Chilean	11	0.03
Colombian	57	0.15
Ecuadorian	13	0.03
Peruvian	17	0.04
Uruguayan	2	0.01
Venezuelan	9	0.02
Other Hispanic or Latino	559	1.45

Race*	Population	%
African-American/Black (11,478)	11,837	30.73
Not Hispanic (11,331)	11,586	30.07
Hispanic (147)	251	0.65
American Indian/Alaska Native (282)	529	1.37
Not Hispanic (113)	288	0.75
Hispanic (169)	241	0.63
Alaska Athabascan *(Ala. Nat.)* (0)	3	0.01
Apache (3)	6	0.02
Blackfeet (0)	1	<0.01
Canadian/French Am. Ind. (0)	1	<0.01
Central American Ind. (3)	6	0.02
Cherokee (20)	73	0.19
Cheyenne (1)	4	0.01
Chickasaw (4)	12	0.03
Chippewa (0)	2	0.01
Choctaw (31)	44	0.11
Creek (7)	23	0.06
Crow (3)	3	0.01
Iroquois (1)	6	0.02
Kiowa (1)	1	<0.01
Lumbee (0)	2	0.01
Mexican American Ind. (26)	30	0.08
Navajo (3)	12	0.03
Ottawa (1)	2	0.01
Potawatomi (2)	2	0.01
Seminole (0)	4	0.01
Sioux (3)	10	0.03
South American Ind. (5)	9	0.02
Spanish American Ind. (0)	5	0.01
Tohono O'Odham (3)	3	0.01
Yaqui (0)	1	<0.01
Yuman (2)	2	0.01
Asian (647)	789	2.05
Not Hispanic (637)	747	1.94
Hispanic (10)	42	0.11
Bangladeshi (5)	8	0.02
Cambodian (20)	22	0.06
Chinese, ex. Taiwanese (72)	87	0.23
Filipino (142)	180	0.47
Hmong (28)	31	0.08
Indian (56)	89	0.23
Indonesian (8)	12	0.03
Japanese (26)	47	0.12
Korean (60)	84	0.22
Laotian (63)	68	0.18
Nepalese (9)	9	0.02
Pakistani (4)	6	0.02
Sri Lankan (1)	2	0.01
Thai (10)	13	0.03
Vietnamese (110)	119	0.31
Hawaii Native/Pacific Islander (24)	48	0.12
Not Hispanic (10)	19	0.05
Hispanic (14)	29	0.08
Guamanian/Chamorro (9)	9	0.02
Native Hawaiian (12)	23	0.06
Samoan (0)	5	0.01
White (19,421)	20,219	52.48
Not Hispanic (12,461)	12,812	33.26
Hispanic (6,960)	7,407	19.23

*Notes: † The Census 2010 population figure is used to calculate the percentages in the Hispanic Origin and Race categories. Ancestry percentages are based on the 2006-2010 American Community Survey population (not shown); ‡ Numbers in parentheses indicate the number of people reporting a single ancestry; * Numbers in parentheses indicate the number of persons reporting this race alone, not in combination with any other race; Please refer to the Explanation of Data for more information.*

Eagle Pass

Place Type: City
County: Maverick
Population: 26,248†

Ancestry‡	Population	%
African, Sub-Saharan (0)	10	0.04
South African (0)	10	0.04
American (223)	223	0.88
Arab (9)	24	0.09
Egyptian (9)	24	0.09
Armenian (0)	8	0.03
Canadian (16)	16	0.06
Celtic (35)	50	0.20
English (41)	55	0.22
European (0)	10	0.04
French, ex. Basque (0)	7	0.03
French Canadian (0)	14	0.05
German (103)	320	1.26
Greek (0)	8	0.03
Irish (49)	145	0.57
Italian (6)	37	0.15
Norwegian (13)	26	0.10
Portuguese (0)	18	0.07
Scotch-Irish (116)	167	0.66
Swedish (0)	19	0.07
Swiss (0)	79	0.31

Hispanic Origin	Population	%
Hispanic or Latino (of any race)	25,065	95.49
Central American, ex. Mexican	29	0.11
Guatemalan	3	0.01
Honduran	2	0.01
Nicaraguan	7	0.03
Panamanian	4	0.02
Salvadoran	10	0.04
Other Central American	3	0.01
Cuban	8	0.03
Dominican Republic	9	0.03
Mexican	23,574	89.81
Puerto Rican	106	0.40
South American	44	0.17
Argentinean	8	0.03
Chilean	9	0.03
Colombian	10	0.04
Ecuadorian	2	0.01
Paraguayan	1	<0.01
Peruvian	10	0.04
Uruguayan	4	0.02
Other Hispanic or Latino	1,295	4.93

Race*	Population	%
African-American/Black (70)	113	0.43
Not Hispanic (30)	41	0.16
Hispanic (40)	72	0.27
American Indian/Alaska Native (96)	126	0.48
Not Hispanic (38)	51	0.19
Hispanic (58)	75	0.29
Cherokee (1)	1	<0.01
Chickasaw (0)	1	<0.01
Chippewa (2)	2	0.01
Choctaw (1)	1	<0.01
Mexican American Ind. (20)	27	0.10
Potawatomi (1)	1	<0.01
Pueblo (2)	2	0.01
Seminole (5)	5	0.02
Ute (3)	3	0.01
Asian (145)	185	0.70
Not Hispanic (117)	127	0.48
Hispanic (28)	58	0.22
Chinese, ex. Taiwanese (14)	24	0.09
Filipino (62)	73	0.28
Indian (34)	42	0.16
Indonesian (1)	1	<0.01
Japanese (10)	16	0.06
Korean (11)	11	0.04
Laotian (0)	3	0.01
Thai (0)	3	0.01
Vietnamese (4)	5	0.02
Hawaii Native/Pacific Islander (1)	6	0.02
Hispanic (1)	6	0.02
Guamanian/Chamorro (1)	1	<0.01
Samoan (0)	1	<0.01
White (23,115)	23,443	89.31
Not Hispanic (953)	974	3.71
Hispanic (22,162)	22,469	85.60

Edinburg

Place Type: City
County: Hidalgo
Population: 77,100†

Ancestry‡	Population	%
African, Sub-Saharan (182)	216	0.30
African (144)	164	0.23
Ghanaian (29)	29	0.04
Other Sub-Saharan African (9)	23	0.03
American (737)	737	1.01
Arab (60)	60	0.08
Arab (9)	9	0.01
Egyptian (14)	14	0.02
Lebanese (23)	23	0.03
Palestinian (14)	14	0.02
Armenian (17)	17	0.02
Basque (62)	62	0.09
Belgian (10)	10	0.01
Brazilian (5)	23	0.03
British (39)	53	0.07
Canadian (0)	22	0.03
Czech (0)	91	0.13
Czechoslovakian (0)	14	0.02
Danish (0)	19	0.03
Dutch (80)	186	0.26
English (268)	808	1.11
European (32)	164	0.23
French, ex. Basque (157)	484	0.67
French Canadian (48)	48	0.07
German (569)	1,810	2.49
Greek (0)	99	0.14
Iranian (74)	74	0.10
Irish (150)	1,184	1.63
Italian (164)	604	0.83
Lithuanian (91)	91	0.13
Northern European (19)	19	0.03
Norwegian (16)	52	0.07
Polish (78)	193	0.27
Portuguese (6)	20	0.03
Romanian (12)	21	0.03
Russian (42)	52	0.07
Scandinavian (13)	53	0.07
Scotch-Irish (112)	232	0.32
Scottish (13)	355	0.49
Slovak (10)	10	0.01
Swedish (45)	82	0.11
Turkish (28)	28	0.04
Ukrainian (17)	17	0.02
Welsh (9)	36	0.05
West Indian, ex. Hispanic (11)	11	0.02
Jamaican (11)	11	0.02

Hispanic Origin	Population	%
Hispanic or Latino (of any race)	67,989	88.18
Central American, ex. Mexican	365	0.47
Costa Rican	12	0.02
Guatemalan	93	0.12
Honduran	106	0.14
Nicaraguan	42	0.05
Panamanian	14	0.02
Salvadoran	90	0.12
Other Central American	8	0.01
Cuban	75	0.10
Dominican Republic	41	0.05
Mexican	63,294	82.09
Puerto Rican	244	0.32
South American	243	0.32
Argentinean	32	0.04
Bolivian	8	0.01
Chilean	11	0.01
Colombian	79	0.10
Ecuadorian	31	0.04
Paraguayan	2	<0.01
Peruvian	42	0.05
Uruguayan	5	0.01
Venezuelan	33	0.04
Other Hispanic or Latino	3,727	4.83

Race*	Population	%
African-American/Black (1,223)	1,411	1.83
Not Hispanic (1,033)	1,083	1.40
Hispanic (190)	328	0.43
American Indian/Alaska Native (318)	528	0.68
Not Hispanic (59)	101	0.13
Hispanic (259)	427	0.55
Alaska Athabascan *(Ala. Nat.)* (1)	1	<0.01
Apache (18)	39	0.05
Blackfeet (1)	4	0.01
Canadian/French Am. Ind. (1)	1	<0.01
Cherokee (16)	43	0.06
Chickasaw (0)	5	0.01
Choctaw (2)	8	0.01
Comanche (2)	3	<0.01
Creek (1)	1	<0.01
Iroquois (0)	1	<0.01
Mexican American Ind. (16)	39	0.05
Navajo (1)	1	<0.01
Osage (1)	5	0.01
Ottawa (3)	3	<0.01
Sioux (2)	3	<0.01
South American Ind. (1)	2	<0.01
Spanish American Ind. (4)	5	0.01
Yaqui (0)	6	0.01
Asian (1,672)	1,846	2.39
Not Hispanic (1,618)	1,700	2.20
Hispanic (54)	146	0.19
Bangladeshi (5)	5	0.01
Burmese (1)	1	<0.01
Cambodian (11)	12	0.02
Chinese, ex. Taiwanese (107)	135	0.18
Filipino (949)	1,004	1.30
Indian (335)	377	0.49
Indonesian (1)	5	0.01
Japanese (23)	51	0.07
Korean (72)	88	0.11
Malaysian (0)	5	0.01
Nepalese (5)	5	0.01
Pakistani (27)	28	0.04
Taiwanese (3)	5	0.01
Thai (3)	6	0.01
Vietnamese (67)	80	0.10
Hawaii Native/Pacific Islander (13)	57	0.07
Not Hispanic (7)	18	0.02
Hispanic (6)	39	0.05
Guamanian/Chamorro (2)	12	0.02
Native Hawaiian (5)	18	0.02
Samoan (3)	14	0.02
Tongan (1)	1	<0.01
White (65,744)	66,709	86.52
Not Hispanic (6,177)	6,310	8.18
Hispanic (59,567)	60,399	78.34

Eidson Road

Place Type: CDP
County: Maverick
Population: 8,960†

Ancestry‡	Population	%
Irish (0)	14	0.14

Hispanic Origin	Population	%
Hispanic or Latino (of any race)	8,864	98.93
Central American, ex. Mexican	2	0.02
Honduran	1	0.01
Salvadoran	1	0.01
Mexican	8,849	98.76
Puerto Rican	10	0.11
Other Hispanic or Latino	3	0.03

*Notes: † The Census 2010 population figure is used to calculate the percentages in the Hispanic Origin and Race categories. Ancestry percentages are based on the 2006-2010 American Community Survey population (not shown); ‡ Numbers in parentheses indicate the number of people reporting a single ancestry; * Numbers in parentheses indicate the number of persons reporting this race alone, not in combination with any other race; Please refer to the Explanation of Data for more information.*

Race*	Population	%
African-American/Black (9)	18	0.20
Not Hispanic (9)	10	0.11
Hispanic (0)	8	0.09
American Indian/Alaska Native (41)	46	0.51
Not Hispanic (38)	43	0.48
Hispanic (3)	3	0.03
Mexican American Ind. (2)	2	0.02
Seminole (3)	3	0.03
Asian (2)	3	0.03
Not Hispanic (1)	1	0.01
Hispanic (1)	2	0.02
Chinese, ex. Taiwanese (0)	1	0.01
Indian (1)	1	0.01
Japanese (1)	1	0.01
White (8,859)	8,887	99.19
Not Hispanic (42)	44	0.49
Hispanic (8,817)	8,843	98.69

El Campo

Place Type: City
County: Wharton
Population: 11,602†

Ancestry‡	Population	%
African, Sub-Saharan (97)	97	0.84
African (97)	97	0.84
American (264)	264	2.29
Austrian (0)	42	0.36
British (6)	71	0.62
Canadian (12)	12	0.10
Czech (673)	1,063	9.22
Danish (116)	309	2.68
Dutch (29)	58	0.50
English (113)	343	2.97
French, ex. Basque (43)	267	2.31
French Canadian (0)	24	0.21
German (466)	1,747	15.15
Greek (0)	42	0.36
Irish (134)	831	7.20
Italian (15)	167	1.45
Norwegian (0)	97	0.84
Polish (70)	237	2.05
Russian (0)	18	0.16
Scotch-Irish (99)	321	2.78
Scottish (38)	90	0.78
Swedish (97)	213	1.85
Welsh (0)	34	0.29

Hispanic Origin	Population	%
Hispanic or Latino (of any race)	5,449	46.97
Central American, ex. Mexican	47	0.41
Guatemalan	15	0.13
Honduran	8	0.07
Nicaraguan	2	0.02
Panamanian	7	0.06
Salvadoran	14	0.12
Other Central American	1	0.01
Cuban	18	0.16
Dominican Republic	1	0.01
Mexican	4,802	41.39
Puerto Rican	13	0.11
South American	6	0.05
Colombian	3	0.03
Peruvian	2	0.02
Venezuelan	1	0.01
Other Hispanic or Latino	562	4.84

Race*	Population	%
African-American/Black (1,263)	1,308	11.27
Not Hispanic (1,206)	1,226	10.57
Hispanic (57)	82	0.71
American Indian/Alaska Native (33)	64	0.55
Not Hispanic (9)	30	0.26
Hispanic (24)	34	0.29
Apache (1)	2	0.02
Canadian/French Am. Ind. (4)	5	0.04
Cherokee (2)	6	0.05
Choctaw (1)	8	0.07
Iroquois (0)	2	0.02
Mexican American Ind. (8)	10	0.09
Sioux (1)	1	0.01
South American Ind. (1)	3	0.03
Asian (58)	76	0.66
Not Hispanic (56)	64	0.55
Hispanic (2)	12	0.10
Cambodian (1)	1	0.01
Chinese, ex. Taiwanese (19)	21	0.18
Filipino (1)	1	0.01
Indian (18)	21	0.18
Japanese (1)	3	0.03
Korean (0)	6	0.05
Pakistani (7)	7	0.06
Sri Lankan (1)	1	0.01
Taiwanese (0)	2	0.02
Thai (1)	1	0.01
Vietnamese (5)	7	0.06
Hawaii Native/Pacific Islander (1)	2	0.02
Not Hispanic (1)	1	0.01
Hispanic (0)	1	0.01
Guamanian/Chamorro (1)	1	0.01
White (8,829)	9,011	77.67
Not Hispanic (4,827)	4,875	42.02
Hispanic (4,002)	4,136	35.65

El Paso

Place Type: City
County: El Paso
Population: 649,121†

Ancestry‡	Population	%
African, Sub-Saharan (1,054)	1,582	0.25
African (546)	964	0.15
Cape Verdean (19)	27	<0.01
Ethiopian (3)	5	<0.01
Kenyan (12)	12	<0.01
Liberian (13)	13	<0.01
Nigerian (432)	523	0.08
Somalian (29)	29	<0.01
South African (0)	7	<0.01
Other Sub-Saharan African (0)	2	<0.01
Albanian (12)	12	<0.01
Alsatian (0)	14	<0.01
American (22,367)	22,367	3.56
Arab (1,864)	2,973	0.47
Arab (318)	569	0.09
Egyptian (49)	70	0.01
Jordanian (25)	25	<0.01
Lebanese (879)	1,419	0.23
Palestinian (28)	110	0.02
Syrian (554)	718	0.11
Other Arab (11)	62	0.01
Armenian (23)	111	0.02
Assyrian/Chaldean/Syriac (36)	36	0.01
Australian (8)	8	<0.01
Austrian (214)	532	0.08
Basque (14)	14	<0.01
Belgian (46)	128	0.02
Brazilian (53)	188	0.03
British (442)	743	0.12
Bulgarian (11)	11	<0.01
Cajun (1)	24	<0.01
Canadian (272)	413	0.07
Celtic (13)	23	<0.01
Croatian (24)	66	0.01
Cypriot (23)	23	<0.01
Czech (202)	565	0.09
Czechoslovakian (48)	126	0.02
Danish (239)	807	0.13
Dutch (357)	1,715	0.27
Eastern European (69)	105	0.02
English (4,732)	14,883	2.37
Estonian (13)	13	<0.01
European (1,424)	1,983	0.32
Finnish (62)	200	0.03
French, ex. Basque (830)	4,709	0.75
French Canadian (252)	526	0.08
German (9,067)	25,193	4.01
German Russian (10)	10	<0.01
Greek (183)	285	0.05
Guyanese (25)	25	<0.01
Hungarian (100)	495	0.08
Iranian (217)	407	0.06
Irish (4,337)	16,455	2.62
Israeli (64)	77	0.01
Italian (2,382)	6,670	1.06
Latvian (0)	9	<0.01
Lithuanian (74)	208	0.03
Luxemburger (0)	19	<0.01
New Zealander (9)	9	<0.01
Northern European (165)	191	0.03
Norwegian (408)	1,239	0.20
Pennsylvania German (70)	126	0.02
Polish (1,103)	3,190	0.51
Portuguese (132)	390	0.06
Romanian (31)	129	0.02
Russian (258)	876	0.14
Scandinavian (54)	109	0.02
Scotch-Irish (1,254)	3,199	0.51
Scottish (717)	3,254	0.52
Serbian (12)	12	<0.01
Slavic (47)	55	0.01
Slovak (43)	273	0.04
Slovene (18)	40	0.01
Swedish (374)	1,689	0.27
Swiss (110)	448	0.07
Turkish (9)	39	0.01
Ukrainian (199)	277	0.04
Welsh (200)	895	0.14
West Indian, ex. Hispanic (441)	776	0.12
British West Indian (38)	38	0.01
Dutch West Indian (0)	72	0.01
Haitian (122)	217	0.03
Jamaican (214)	309	0.05
West Indian (67)	140	0.02
Yugoslavian (13)	38	0.01

Hispanic Origin	Population	%
Hispanic or Latino (of any race)	523,721	80.68
Central American, ex. Mexican	2,313	0.36
Costa Rican	95	0.01
Guatemalan	432	0.07
Honduran	302	0.05
Nicaraguan	288	0.04
Panamanian	551	0.08
Salvadoran	625	0.10
Other Central American	20	<0.01
Cuban	737	0.11
Dominican Republic	385	0.06
Mexican	486,186	74.90
Puerto Rican	5,793	0.89
South American	1,676	0.26
Argentinean	240	0.04
Bolivian	72	0.01
Chilean	111	0.02
Colombian	578	0.09
Ecuadorian	174	0.03
Paraguayan	15	<0.01
Peruvian	293	0.05
Uruguayan	24	<0.01
Venezuelan	161	0.02
Other South American	8	<0.01
Other Hispanic or Latino	26,631	4.10

Race*	Population	%
African-American/Black (22,006)	26,196	4.04
Not Hispanic (18,155)	20,267	3.12
Hispanic (3,851)	5,929	0.91
American Indian/Alaska Native (4,757)	7,204	1.11
Not Hispanic (1,633)	2,702	0.42
Hispanic (3,124)	4,502	0.69
Alaska Athabascan *(Ala. Nat.)* (9)	11	<0.01
Aleut *(Alaska Native)* (3)	3	<0.01
Apache (237)	431	0.07
Arapaho (3)	5	<0.01
Blackfeet (16)	70	0.01
Canadian/French Am. Ind. (8)	13	<0.01
Central American Ind. (3)	13	<0.01

*Notes: † The Census 2010 population figure is used to calculate the percentages in the Hispanic Origin and Race categories. Ancestry percentages are based on the 2006-2010 American Community Survey population (not shown); ‡ Numbers in parentheses indicate the number of people reporting a single ancestry; * Numbers in parentheses indicate the number of persons reporting this race alone, not in combination with any other race; Please refer to the Explanation of Data for more information.*

Cherokee (170)	542	0.08
Cheyenne (8)	14	<0.01
Chickasaw (25)	44	0.01
Chippewa (21)	39	0.01
Choctaw (51)	119	0.02
Colville (7)	8	<0.01
Comanche (18)	39	0.01
Cree (1)	1	<0.01
Creek (25)	53	0.01
Crow (0)	6	<0.01
Delaware (2)	2	<0.01
Hopi (13)	22	<0.01
Houma (2)	3	<0.01
Inupiat *(Alaska Native)* (10)	14	<0.01
Iroquois (8)	21	<0.01
Kiowa (3)	5	<0.01
Lumbee (24)	38	0.01
Mexican American Ind. (339)	497	0.08
Navajo (175)	239	0.04
Osage (2)	5	<0.01
Ottawa (11)	11	<0.01
Paiute (6)	9	<0.01
Pima (9)	16	<0.01
Potawatomi (7)	18	<0.01
Pueblo (735)	861	0.13
Puget Sound Salish (2)	4	<0.01
Seminole (3)	14	<0.01
Shoshone (1)	6	<0.01
Sioux (41)	77	0.01
South American Ind. (7)	29	<0.01
Spanish American Ind. (35)	50	0.01
Tlingit-Haida *(Alaska Native)* (11)	18	<0.01
Tohono O'Odham (2)	6	<0.01
Tsimshian *(Alaska Native)* (0)	6	<0.01
Ute (3)	6	<0.01
Yakama (3)	6	<0.01
Yaqui (43)	79	0.01
Yuman (4)	4	<0.01
Asian (7,723)	11,365	1.75
Not Hispanic (7,092)	9,131	1.41
Hispanic (631)	2,234	0.34
Bangladeshi (48)	54	0.01
Bhutanese (6)	6	<0.01
Burmese (29)	31	<0.01
Cambodian (16)	23	<0.01
Chinese, ex. Taiwanese (1,038)	1,529	0.24
Filipino (1,746)	2,620	0.40
Hmong (7)	9	<0.01
Indian (1,108)	1,366	0.21
Indonesian (26)	40	0.01
Japanese (814)	1,614	0.25
Korean (1,696)	2,461	0.38
Laotian (31)	49	0.01
Malaysian (6)	11	<0.01
Nepalese (18)	20	<0.01
Pakistani (82)	109	0.02
Sri Lankan (19)	20	<0.01
Taiwanese (180)	198	0.03
Thai (104)	177	0.03
Vietnamese (470)	636	0.10
Hawaii Native/Pacific Islander (909)	1,647	0.25
Not Hispanic (737)	1,119	0.17
Hispanic (172)	528	0.08
Fijian (1)	8	<0.01
Guamanian/Chamorro (342)	530	0.08
Marshallese (5)	5	<0.01
Native Hawaiian (153)	376	0.06
Samoan (195)	290	0.04
Tongan (6)	6	<0.01
White (524,764)	539,737	83.15
Not Hispanic (92,426)	96,505	14.87
Hispanic (432,338)	443,232	68.28

Elgin

Place Type: City
County: Bastrop
Population: 8,135†

Ancestry‡	Population	%
African, Sub-Saharan (63)	68	0.84
African (63)	68	0.84
American (94)	94	1.16
Arab (0)	11	0.14
Lebanese (0)	11	0.14
Cajun (13)	49	0.60
Celtic (7)	7	0.09
Czech (0)	154	1.89
Czechoslovakian (28)	28	0.34
Dutch (17)	41	0.50
English (162)	295	3.63
European (23)	23	0.28
Finnish (0)	38	0.47
French, ex. Basque (10)	145	1.78
French Canadian (11)	11	0.14
German (729)	1,286	15.81
Irish (87)	669	8.23
Italian (0)	8	0.10
Northern European (9)	9	0.11
Polish (65)	146	1.80
Portuguese (0)	8	0.10
Romanian (0)	13	0.16
Russian (0)	37	0.45
Scotch-Irish (74)	123	1.51
Scottish (50)	68	0.84
Slovak (0)	12	0.15
Swedish (126)	180	2.21
Swiss (0)	6	0.07

Hispanic Origin	Population	%
Hispanic or Latino (of any race)	3,715	45.67
Central American, ex. Mexican	46	0.57
Costa Rican	2	0.02
Guatemalan	4	0.05
Honduran	19	0.23
Nicaraguan	5	0.06
Panamanian	1	0.01
Salvadoran	15	0.18
Cuban	8	0.10
Dominican Republic	3	0.04
Mexican	3,350	41.18
Puerto Rican	27	0.33
South American	11	0.14
Argentinean	1	0.01
Colombian	4	0.05
Ecuadorian	2	0.02
Peruvian	3	0.04
Venezuelan	1	0.01
Other Hispanic or Latino	270	3.32

Race*	Population	%
African-American/Black (1,407)	1,544	18.98
Not Hispanic (1,353)	1,432	17.60
Hispanic (54)	112	1.38
American Indian/Alaska Native (82)	160	1.97
Not Hispanic (21)	56	0.69
Hispanic (61)	104	1.28
Apache (2)	7	0.09
Blackfeet (0)	1	0.01
Cherokee (8)	23	0.28
Cheyenne (0)	3	0.04
Comanche (2)	2	0.02
Creek (0)	5	0.06
Mexican American Ind. (7)	7	0.09
Navajo (1)	1	0.01
Pueblo (1)	1	0.01
Sioux (2)	6	0.07
Asian (40)	71	0.87
Not Hispanic (38)	56	0.69
Hispanic (2)	15	0.18
Cambodian (3)	3	0.04
Chinese, ex. Taiwanese (2)	4	0.05
Filipino (15)	20	0.25
Indian (7)	7	0.09
Japanese (1)	8	0.10
Korean (3)	10	0.12
Pakistani (3)	5	0.06
Taiwanese (2)	2	0.02
Thai (1)	2	0.02
Vietnamese (1)	3	0.04
Hawaii Native/Pacific Islander (16)	21	0.26
Not Hispanic (7)	7	0.09
Hispanic (9)	14	0.17
Guamanian/Chamorro (4)	4	0.05
Native Hawaiian (7)	12	0.15
White (4,648)	4,895	60.17
Not Hispanic (2,869)	2,982	36.66
Hispanic (1,779)	1,913	23.52

Ennis

Place Type: City
County: Ellis
Population: 18,513†

Ancestry‡	Population	%
Albanian (48)	48	0.26
American (890)	890	4.87
Arab (0)	13	0.07
Lebanese (0)	13	0.07
Armenian (12)	73	0.40
Belgian (7)	7	0.04
British (13)	13	0.07
Cajun (0)	7	0.04
Canadian (0)	21	0.11
Czech (542)	946	5.18
Czechoslovakian (138)	171	0.94
Dutch (47)	262	1.43
English (419)	1,048	5.74
European (50)	50	0.27
French, ex. Basque (44)	336	1.84
French Canadian (36)	108	0.59
German (531)	1,827	10.00
Hungarian (60)	71	0.39
Irish (699)	1,609	8.81
Italian (20)	118	0.65
Lithuanian (0)	13	0.07
New Zealander (19)	19	0.10
Norwegian (0)	19	0.10
Polish (12)	38	0.21
Scotch-Irish (68)	260	1.42
Scottish (210)	456	2.50
Slovak (0)	107	0.59
Swedish (0)	74	0.41
Welsh (0)	27	0.15

Hispanic Origin	Population	%
Hispanic or Latino (of any race)	7,456	40.27
Central American, ex. Mexican	51	0.28
Costa Rican	1	0.01
Guatemalan	3	0.02
Honduran	6	0.03
Nicaraguan	1	0.01
Panamanian	2	0.01
Salvadoran	38	0.21
Cuban	13	0.07
Dominican Republic	1	0.01
Mexican	6,896	37.25
Puerto Rican	22	0.12
South American	21	0.11
Argentinean	1	0.01
Chilean	4	0.02
Colombian	2	0.01
Ecuadorian	2	0.01
Peruvian	3	0.02
Venezuelan	9	0.05
Other Hispanic or Latino	452	2.44

Race*	Population	%
African-American/Black (2,605)	2,742	14.81
Not Hispanic (2,549)	2,636	14.24
Hispanic (56)	106	0.57
American Indian/Alaska Native (129)	206	1.11
Not Hispanic (45)	87	0.47
Hispanic (84)	119	0.64
Apache (0)	8	0.04
Blackfeet (2)	3	0.02
Cherokee (11)	27	0.15
Chickasaw (1)	1	0.01

*Notes: † The Census 2010 population figure is used to calculate the percentages in the Hispanic Origin and Race categories. Ancestry percentages are based on the 2006-2010 American Community Survey population (not shown); ‡ Numbers in parentheses indicate the number of people reporting a single ancestry; * Numbers in parentheses indicate the number of persons reporting this race alone, not in combination with any other race; Please refer to the Explanation of Data for more information.*

Choctaw (7)	16	0.09
Comanche (0)	1	0.01
Creek (0)	3	0.02
Mexican American Ind. (8)	8	0.04
Navajo (0)	1	0.01
Potawatomi (3)	3	0.02
Pueblo (1)	1	0.01
Seminole (1)	2	0.01
Spanish American Ind. (2)	5	0.03
Tlingit-Haida *(Alaska Native)* (0)	1	0.01
Yaqui (0)	4	0.02
Asian (98)	129	0.70
Not Hispanic (96)	109	0.59
Hispanic (2)	20	0.11
Bangladeshi (1)	1	0.01
Chinese, ex. Taiwanese (23)	27	0.15
Filipino (20)	24	0.13
Hmong (5)	5	0.03
Indian (15)	27	0.15
Japanese (3)	7	0.04
Korean (5)	6	0.03
Nepalese (4)	4	0.02
Pakistani (5)	8	0.04
Sri Lankan (1)	4	0.02
Taiwanese (2)	2	0.01
Thai (1)	5	0.03
Vietnamese (7)	9	0.05
Hawaii Native/Pacific Islander (32)	49	0.26
Not Hispanic (31)	37	0.20
Hispanic (1)	12	0.06
Guamanian/Chamorro (0)	1	0.01
Native Hawaiian (9)	11	0.06
Samoan (1)	2	0.01
White (11,943)	12,313	66.51
Not Hispanic (8,183)	8,301	44.84
Hispanic (3,760)	4,012	21.67

Euless

Place Type: City
County: Tarrant
Population: 51,277†

Ancestry‡	Population	%
African, Sub-Saharan (1,691)	1,739	3.46
African (391)	416	0.83
Ethiopian (53)	53	0.11
Ghanaian (19)	19	0.04
Kenyan (72)	72	0.14
Liberian (256)	256	0.51
Nigerian (75)	98	0.19
Somalian (79)	79	0.16
South African (31)	31	0.06
Sudanese (518)	518	1.03
Other Sub-Saharan African (197)	197	0.39
Albanian (8)	32	0.06
American (2,465)	2,465	4.90
Arab (269)	293	0.58
Arab (45)	59	0.12
Egyptian (46)	46	0.09
Iraqi (49)	49	0.10
Jordanian (14)	14	0.03
Lebanese (25)	35	0.07
Palestinian (90)	90	0.18
Armenian (20)	20	0.04
Australian (0)	16	0.03
Austrian (33)	184	0.37
Belgian (0)	15	0.03
Brazilian (50)	50	0.10
British (134)	182	0.36
Canadian (94)	175	0.35
Celtic (12)	12	0.02
Czech (82)	269	0.53
Czechoslovakian (46)	46	0.09
Danish (32)	119	0.24
Dutch (148)	867	1.72
Eastern European (0)	14	0.03
English (1,504)	4,210	8.37
European (344)	433	0.86
Finnish (18)	32	0.06
French, ex. Basque (269)	1,447	2.88
French Canadian (82)	233	0.46
German (2,264)	7,400	14.71
Greek (15)	203	0.40
Guyanese (17)	17	0.03
Hungarian (21)	117	0.23
Iranian (11)	11	0.02
Irish (1,506)	5,205	10.35
Italian (573)	1,750	3.48
Lithuanian (11)	27	0.05
Luxemburger (0)	14	0.03
Norwegian (70)	435	0.86
Polish (443)	860	1.71
Portuguese (25)	98	0.19
Romanian (0)	36	0.07
Russian (45)	168	0.33
Scandinavian (47)	56	0.11
Scotch-Irish (600)	1,084	2.16
Scottish (335)	1,144	2.27
Slavic (28)	74	0.15
Slovak (12)	20	0.04
Slovene (12)	23	0.05
Swedish (150)	519	1.03
Swiss (33)	216	0.43
Turkish (26)	26	0.05
Ukrainian (19)	39	0.08
Welsh (58)	372	0.74
West Indian, ex. Hispanic (81)	248	0.49
Dutch West Indian (29)	170	0.34
Jamaican (30)	30	0.06
Trinidadian/Tobagonian (22)	22	0.04
West Indian (0)	26	0.05
Yugoslavian (0)	15	0.03

Hispanic Origin	Population	%
Hispanic or Latino (of any race)	9,719	18.95
Central American, ex. Mexican	596	1.16
Costa Rican	17	0.03
Guatemalan	89	0.17
Honduran	60	0.12
Nicaraguan	29	0.06
Panamanian	28	0.05
Salvadoran	372	0.73
Other Central American	1	<0.01
Cuban	125	0.24
Dominican Republic	61	0.12
Mexican	6,897	13.45
Puerto Rican	916	1.79
South American	422	0.82
Argentinean	59	0.12
Bolivian	12	0.02
Chilean	19	0.04
Colombian	128	0.25
Ecuadorian	74	0.14
Peruvian	80	0.16
Uruguayan	3	0.01
Venezuelan	41	0.08
Other South American	6	0.01
Other Hispanic or Latino	702	1.37

Race*	Population	%
African-American/Black (5,497)	6,152	12.00
Not Hispanic (5,315)	5,828	11.37
Hispanic (182)	324	0.63
American Indian/Alaska Native (330)	737	1.44
Not Hispanic (241)	564	1.10
Hispanic (89)	173	0.34
Aleut *(Alaska Native)* (3)	3	0.01
Apache (6)	21	0.04
Blackfeet (1)	7	0.01
Canadian/French Am. Ind. (0)	4	0.01
Cherokee (60)	152	0.30
Cheyenne (3)	3	0.01
Chickasaw (6)	17	0.03
Chippewa (6)	8	0.02
Choctaw (46)	90	0.18
Comanche (6)	21	0.04
Cree (1)	1	<0.01
Creek (10)	18	0.04
Delaware (5)	6	0.01
Hopi (0)	1	<0.01
Inupiat *(Alaska Native)* (0)	1	<0.01
Iroquois (8)	19	0.04
Kiowa (2)	3	0.01
Lumbee (0)	3	0.01
Mexican American Ind. (10)	25	0.05
Navajo (3)	4	0.01
Osage (2)	6	0.01
Paiute (2)	2	<0.01
Potawatomi (9)	11	0.02
Pueblo (1)	1	<0.01
Seminole (4)	7	0.01
Sioux (2)	10	0.02
South American Ind. (11)	14	0.03
Spanish American Ind. (5)	5	0.01
Tlingit-Haida *(Alaska Native)* (1)	2	<0.01
Asian (5,301)	5,846	11.40
Not Hispanic (5,232)	5,715	11.15
Hispanic (69)	131	0.26
Bangladeshi (68)	78	0.15
Burmese (4)	4	0.01
Cambodian (28)	48	0.09
Chinese, ex. Taiwanese (310)	364	0.71
Filipino (331)	421	0.82
Hmong (7)	7	0.01
Indian (1,638)	1,829	3.57
Indonesian (22)	29	0.06
Japanese (71)	126	0.25
Korean (314)	352	0.69
Laotian (355)	392	0.76
Malaysian (8)	11	0.02
Nepalese (318)	338	0.66
Pakistani (969)	1,097	2.14
Sri Lankan (18)	19	0.04
Taiwanese (30)	39	0.08
Thai (89)	121	0.24
Vietnamese (413)	451	0.88
Hawaii Native/Pacific Islander (1,101)	1,247	2.43
Not Hispanic (1,078)	1,196	2.33
Hispanic (23)	51	0.10
Fijian (3)	5	0.01
Guamanian/Chamorro (12)	25	0.05
Marshallese (1)	1	<0.01
Native Hawaiian (64)	97	0.19
Samoan (74)	102	0.20
Tongan (826)	885	1.73
White (33,833)	35,333	68.91
Not Hispanic (28,345)	29,327	57.19
Hispanic (5,488)	6,006	11.71

Fabens

Place Type: CDP
County: El Paso
Population: 8,257†

Ancestry‡	Population	%
American (241)	241	3.27
Danish (16)	16	0.22
English (18)	18	0.24
German (0)	20	0.27
Swiss (0)	20	0.27

Hispanic Origin	Population	%
Hispanic or Latino (of any race)	7,993	96.80
Central American, ex. Mexican	7	0.08
Nicaraguan	2	0.02
Panamanian	1	0.01
Salvadoran	4	0.05
Mexican	7,485	90.65
Puerto Rican	22	0.27
South American	1	0.01
Colombian	1	0.01
Other Hispanic or Latino	478	5.79

Race*	Population	%
African-American/Black (33)	51	0.62
Not Hispanic (6)	7	0.08
Hispanic (27)	44	0.53
American Indian/Alaska Native (46)	53	0.64

*Notes: † The Census 2010 population figure is used to calculate the percentages in the Hispanic Origin and Race categories. Ancestry percentages are based on the 2006-2010 American Community Survey population (not shown); ‡ Numbers in parentheses indicate the number of people reporting a single ancestry; * Numbers in parentheses indicate the number of persons reporting this race alone, not in combination with any other race; Please refer to the Explanation of Data for more information.*

SECTION TWO

Not Hispanic (4)	6	0.07
Hispanic (42)	47	0.57
Choctaw (2)	2	0.02
Mexican American Ind. (7)	7	0.08
Pueblo (6)	7	0.08
Asian (23)	33	0.40
Not Hispanic (6)	9	0.11
Hispanic (17)	24	0.29
Chinese, ex. Taiwanese (1)	4	0.05
Filipino (10)	15	0.18
Indian (6)	8	0.10
Hawaii Native/Pacific Islander (3)	4	0.05
Hispanic (3)	4	0.05
Samoan (0)	4	0.05
White (7,085)	7,202	87.22
Not Hispanic (240)	246	2.98
Hispanic (6,845)	6,956	84.24

Farmers Branch

Place Type: City
County: Dallas
Population: 28,616†

Ancestry‡	Population	%
African, Sub-Saharan (14)	26	0.09
African (0)	12	0.04
Ethiopian (14)	14	0.05
Albanian (204)	204	0.72
American (2,023)	2,023	7.18
Arab (12)	40	0.14
Lebanese (12)	12	0.04
Syrian (0)	28	0.10
Austrian (0)	43	0.15
British (84)	166	0.59
Canadian (20)	20	0.07
Czech (73)	141	0.50
Czechoslovakian (33)	67	0.24
Danish (0)	22	0.08
Dutch (66)	283	1.00
English (1,616)	3,587	12.74
European (146)	167	0.59
French, ex. Basque (139)	591	2.10
French Canadian (28)	116	0.41
German (823)	2,382	8.46
Greek (48)	48	0.17
Hungarian (107)	107	0.38
Iranian (41)	41	0.15
Irish (490)	1,811	6.43
Italian (350)	659	2.34
Lithuanian (0)	38	0.13
Norwegian (132)	263	0.93
Polish (36)	215	0.76
Portuguese (37)	37	0.13
Romanian (20)	20	0.07
Russian (31)	108	0.38
Scandinavian (39)	39	0.14
Scotch-Irish (332)	538	1.91
Scottish (87)	273	0.97
Serbian (11)	42	0.15
Swedish (25)	161	0.57
Swiss (0)	53	0.19
Ukrainian (8)	8	0.03
Welsh (30)	86	0.31
West Indian, ex. Hispanic (0)	33	0.12
Dutch West Indian (0)	33	0.12
Yugoslavian (38)	38	0.13

Hispanic Origin	Population	%
Hispanic or Latino (of any race)	12,984	45.37
Central American, ex. Mexican	1,683	5.88
Costa Rican	12	0.04
Guatemalan	113	0.39
Honduran	134	0.47
Nicaraguan	56	0.20
Panamanian	13	0.05
Salvadoran	1,347	4.71
Other Central American	8	0.03
Cuban	72	0.25
Dominican Republic	6	0.02
Mexican	10,258	35.85
Puerto Rican	97	0.34
South American	249	0.87
Argentinean	26	0.09
Bolivian	19	0.07
Chilean	8	0.03
Colombian	103	0.36
Ecuadorian	18	0.06
Peruvian	55	0.19
Uruguayan	6	0.02
Venezuelan	12	0.04
Other South American	2	0.01
Other Hispanic or Latino	619	2.16

Race*	Population	%
African-American/Black (1,365)	1,539	5.38
Not Hispanic (1,280)	1,401	4.90
Hispanic (85)	138	0.48
American Indian/Alaska Native (206)	352	1.23
Not Hispanic (93)	202	0.71
Hispanic (113)	150	0.52
Aleut *(Alaska Native)* (1)	2	0.01
Apache (2)	4	0.01
Blackfeet (1)	2	0.01
Canadian/French Am. Ind. (2)	2	0.01
Central American Ind. (0)	2	0.01
Cherokee (23)	59	0.21
Cheyenne (1)	2	0.01
Chickasaw (7)	12	0.04
Choctaw (26)	40	0.14
Comanche (0)	2	0.01
Creek (2)	3	0.01
Delaware (2)	2	0.01
Kiowa (1)	4	0.01
Mexican American Ind. (10)	14	0.05
Navajo (2)	2	0.01
Osage (5)	5	0.02
Potawatomi (0)	2	0.01
Pueblo (2)	4	0.01
Seminole (0)	1	<0.01
Sioux (0)	3	0.01
South American Ind. (1)	1	<0.01
Tohono O'Odham (0)	1	<0.01
Yaqui (1)	2	0.01
Asian (1,249)	1,435	5.01
Not Hispanic (1,236)	1,371	4.79
Hispanic (13)	64	0.22
Bangladeshi (1)	1	<0.01
Cambodian (34)	38	0.13
Chinese, ex. Taiwanese (76)	102	0.36
Filipino (86)	132	0.46
Hmong (0)	1	<0.01
Indian (300)	332	1.16
Indonesian (4)	7	0.02
Japanese (26)	40	0.14
Korean (292)	318	1.11
Laotian (6)	8	0.03
Malaysian (1)	2	0.01
Nepalese (1)	1	<0.01
Pakistani (20)	23	0.08
Taiwanese (14)	20	0.07
Thai (27)	35	0.12
Vietnamese (320)	331	1.16
Hawaii Native/Pacific Islander (12)	34	0.12
Not Hispanic (2)	12	0.04
Hispanic (10)	22	0.08
Guamanian/Chamorro (1)	4	0.01
Native Hawaiian (11)	15	0.05
Samoan (0)	1	<0.01
White (21,017)	21,723	75.91
Not Hispanic (12,648)	12,934	45.20
Hispanic (8,369)	8,789	30.71

Flower Mound

Place Type: Town
County: Denton
Population: 64,669†

Ancestry‡	Population	%
Afghan (31)	88	0.14
African, Sub-Saharan (568)	648	1.03
African (216)	263	0.42
Nigerian (222)	222	0.35
Somalian (39)	39	0.06
South African (91)	124	0.20
American (3,564)	3,564	5.65
Arab (271)	442	0.70
Egyptian (71)	71	0.11
Lebanese (128)	258	0.41
Syrian (54)	71	0.11
Other Arab (18)	42	0.07
Armenian (22)	39	0.06
Australian (13)	39	0.06
Austrian (63)	617	0.98
Belgian (22)	50	0.08
British (348)	521	0.83
Canadian (170)	232	0.37
Celtic (13)	115	0.18
Croatian (0)	114	0.18
Czech (99)	817	1.30
Czechoslovakian (0)	12	0.02
Danish (94)	337	0.53
Dutch (447)	956	1.52
Eastern European (43)	43	0.07
English (3,395)	9,119	14.46
European (1,137)	1,231	1.95
Finnish (74)	121	0.19
French, ex. Basque (516)	2,713	4.30
French Canadian (322)	618	0.98
German (4,988)	14,510	23.01
Greek (69)	127	0.20
Guyanese (0)	7	0.01
Hungarian (84)	325	0.52
Iranian (25)	25	0.04
Irish (2,431)	8,819	13.99
Italian (943)	3,180	5.04
Latvian (27)	50	0.08
Lithuanian (28)	204	0.32
Norwegian (522)	1,286	2.04
Polish (480)	1,727	2.74
Portuguese (32)	173	0.27
Romanian (11)	35	0.06
Russian (232)	453	0.72
Scandinavian (36)	251	0.40
Scotch-Irish (632)	1,539	2.44
Scottish (606)	1,778	2.82
Serbian (56)	90	0.14
Slavic (27)	27	0.04
Slovak (85)	126	0.20
Slovene (15)	15	0.02
Swedish (245)	1,258	2.00
Swiss (63)	225	0.36
Ukrainian (11)	39	0.06
Welsh (187)	545	0.86
West Indian, ex. Hispanic (18)	34	0.05
Belizean (0)	12	0.02
Dutch West Indian (0)	4	0.01
Jamaican (18)	18	0.03
Yugoslavian (37)	113	0.18

Hispanic Origin	Population	%
Hispanic or Latino (of any race)	5,433	8.40
Central American, ex. Mexican	282	0.44
Costa Rican	35	0.05
Guatemalan	80	0.12
Honduran	38	0.06
Nicaraguan	31	0.05
Panamanian	29	0.04
Salvadoran	63	0.10
Other Central American	6	0.01
Cuban	184	0.28
Dominican Republic	43	0.07
Mexican	3,605	5.57
Puerto Rican	348	0.54
South American	425	0.66
Argentinean	43	0.07
Bolivian	18	0.03
Chilean	20	0.03

*Notes: † The Census 2010 population figure is used to calculate the percentages in the Hispanic Origin and Race categories. Ancestry percentages are based on the 2006-2010 American Community Survey population (not shown); ‡ Numbers in parentheses indicate the number of people reporting a single ancestry; * Numbers in parentheses indicate the number of persons reporting this race alone, not in combination with any other race; Please refer to the Explanation of Data for more information.*

Colombian	119	0.18
Ecuadorian	48	0.07
Paraguayan	6	0.01
Peruvian	109	0.17
Uruguayan	2	<0.01
Venezuelan	56	0.09
Other South American	4	0.01
Other Hispanic or Latino	546	0.84

Race*	Population	%
African-American/Black (2,061)	2,384	3.69
Not Hispanic (1,994)	2,259	3.49
Hispanic (67)	125	0.19
American Indian/Alaska Native (341)	693	1.07
Not Hispanic (281)	562	0.87
Hispanic (60)	131	0.20
Alaska Athabascan *(Ala. Nat.)* (1)	1	<0.01
Apache (5)	19	0.03
Arapaho (4)	4	0.01
Blackfeet (0)	8	0.01
Canadian/French Am. Ind. (1)	1	<0.01
Central American Ind. (1)	1	<0.01
Cherokee (80)	203	0.31
Cheyenne (1)	4	0.01
Chickasaw (25)	32	0.05
Chippewa (0)	9	0.01
Choctaw (39)	76	0.12
Comanche (9)	13	0.02
Creek (2)	6	0.01
Delaware (4)	4	0.01
Inupiat *(Alaska Native)* (1)	1	<0.01
Iroquois (5)	8	0.01
Menominee (2)	2	<0.01
Mexican American Ind. (5)	8	0.01
Navajo (9)	14	0.02
Osage (3)	3	<0.01
Ottawa (0)	3	<0.01
Pima (4)	4	0.01
Potawatomi (5)	6	0.01
Seminole (2)	2	<0.01
Sioux (7)	9	0.01
South American Ind. (2)	2	<0.01
Tlingit-Haida *(Alaska Native)* (0)	2	<0.01
Tsimshian *(Alaska Native)* (1)	1	<0.01
Yakama (1)	1	<0.01
Yaqui (0)	4	0.01
Asian (5,540)	6,181	9.56
Not Hispanic (5,521)	6,077	9.40
Hispanic (19)	104	0.16
Bangladeshi (23)	26	0.04
Burmese (5)	5	0.01
Cambodian (20)	20	0.03
Chinese, ex. Taiwanese (586)	726	1.12
Filipino (218)	359	0.56
Hmong (1)	2	<0.01
Indian (2,653)	2,776	4.29
Indonesian (15)	20	0.03
Japanese (85)	212	0.33
Korean (1,073)	1,182	1.83
Laotian (14)	15	0.02
Malaysian (4)	13	0.02
Nepalese (30)	33	0.05
Pakistani (200)	221	0.34
Sri Lankan (61)	69	0.11
Taiwanese (41)	54	0.08
Thai (41)	59	0.09
Vietnamese (346)	392	0.61
Hawaii Native/Pacific Islander (37)	116	0.18
Not Hispanic (36)	103	0.16
Hispanic (1)	13	0.02
Fijian (1)	1	<0.01
Guamanian/Chamorro (4)	11	0.02
Marshallese (4)	4	0.01
Native Hawaiian (18)	68	0.11
Samoan (6)	9	0.01
Tongan (2)	6	0.01
White (54,249)	55,471	85.78
Not Hispanic (50,270)	51,179	79.14
Hispanic (3,979)	4,292	6.64

Forest Hill

Place Type: City
County: Tarrant
Population: 12,355†

Ancestry‡	Population	%
African, Sub-Saharan (360)	370	2.97
African (310)	320	2.57
Nigerian (50)	50	0.40
American (244)	244	1.96
Arab (9)	17	0.14
Iraqi (9)	9	0.07
Palestinian (0)	8	0.06
Celtic (0)	10	0.08
Czechoslovakian (0)	10	0.08
Dutch (0)	19	0.15
English (45)	197	1.58
French, ex. Basque (9)	106	0.85
French Canadian (10)	19	0.15
German (94)	275	2.21
Irish (52)	248	1.99
Israeli (22)	22	0.18
Italian (10)	20	0.16
Polish (14)	28	0.22
Scotch-Irish (13)	52	0.42
Scottish (8)	8	0.06
Swedish (10)	39	0.31
Welsh (0)	9	0.07
West Indian, ex. Hispanic (8)	27	0.22
Dutch West Indian (0)	9	0.07
Haitian (8)	8	0.06
Jamaican (0)	10	0.08

Hispanic Origin	Population	%
Hispanic or Latino (of any race)	4,715	38.16
Central American, ex. Mexican	76	0.62
Guatemalan	12	0.10
Honduran	37	0.30
Nicaraguan	2	0.02
Panamanian	3	0.02
Salvadoran	22	0.18
Cuban	5	0.04
Dominican Republic	7	0.06
Mexican	4,414	35.73
Puerto Rican	27	0.22
South American	10	0.08
Argentinean	4	0.03
Chilean	4	0.03
Peruvian	2	0.02
Other Hispanic or Latino	176	1.42

Race*	Population	%
African-American/Black (5,988)	6,124	49.57
Not Hispanic (5,938)	6,046	48.94
Hispanic (50)	78	0.63
American Indian/Alaska Native (66)	131	1.06
Not Hispanic (29)	83	0.67
Hispanic (37)	48	0.39
Apache (1)	16	0.13
Blackfeet (1)	6	0.05
Cherokee (2)	18	0.15
Chickasaw (2)	2	0.02
Choctaw (4)	8	0.06
Creek (1)	2	0.02
Mexican American Ind. (11)	13	0.11
Navajo (0)	1	0.01
Potawatomi (2)	2	0.02
Seminole (0)	1	0.01
Asian (73)	97	0.79
Not Hispanic (68)	81	0.66
Hispanic (5)	16	0.13
Chinese, ex. Taiwanese (5)	11	0.09
Filipino (7)	16	0.13
Indian (5)	10	0.08
Japanese (0)	1	0.01
Korean (1)	1	0.01
Laotian (0)	1	0.01
Nepalese (0)	1	0.01
Vietnamese (53)	55	0.45
Hawaii Native/Pacific Islander (5)	21	0.17
Not Hispanic (5)	11	0.09
Hispanic (0)	10	0.08
Guamanian/Chamorro (1)	5	0.04
Native Hawaiian (0)	3	0.02
Samoan (4)	9	0.07
White (3,589)	3,813	30.86
Not Hispanic (1,441)	1,533	12.41
Hispanic (2,148)	2,280	18.45

Forney

Place Type: City
County: Kaufman
Population: 14,661†

Ancestry‡	Population	%
African, Sub-Saharan (58)	115	0.87
African (6)	63	0.48
Zimbabwean (52)	52	0.40
American (829)	829	6.30
Arab (12)	12	0.09
Lebanese (12)	12	0.09
Austrian (12)	12	0.09
British (18)	26	0.20
Cajun (0)	6	0.05
Czech (34)	136	1.03
Czechoslovakian (6)	22	0.17
Danish (0)	6	0.05
Dutch (34)	189	1.44
English (721)	1,648	12.52
European (61)	61	0.46
French, ex. Basque (115)	430	3.27
French Canadian (43)	103	0.78
German (890)	2,189	16.63
Irish (452)	1,664	12.64
Italian (257)	570	4.33
Norwegian (7)	61	0.46
Polish (10)	69	0.52
Russian (11)	33	0.25
Scandinavian (7)	7	0.05
Scotch-Irish (190)	335	2.55
Scottish (61)	213	1.62
Swedish (20)	56	0.43
Swiss (5)	5	0.04
Welsh (77)	107	0.81
West Indian, ex. Hispanic (8)	87	0.66
Belizean (8)	26	0.20
Dutch West Indian (0)	61	0.46
Yugoslavian (8)	8	0.06

Hispanic Origin	Population	%
Hispanic or Latino (of any race)	2,342	15.97
Central American, ex. Mexican	60	0.41
Costa Rican	5	0.03
Guatemalan	3	0.02
Honduran	10	0.07
Nicaraguan	1	0.01
Panamanian	8	0.05
Salvadoran	32	0.22
Other Central American	1	0.01
Cuban	12	0.08
Dominican Republic	6	0.04
Mexican	1,909	13.02
Puerto Rican	63	0.43
South American	56	0.38
Argentinean	5	0.03
Chilean	12	0.08
Colombian	13	0.09
Ecuadorian	2	0.01
Peruvian	18	0.12
Venezuelan	2	0.01
Other South American	4	0.03
Other Hispanic or Latino	236	1.61

Race*	Population	%
African-American/Black (1,463)	1,561	10.65
Not Hispanic (1,433)	1,515	10.33
Hispanic (30)	46	0.31
American Indian/Alaska Native (108)	201	1.37

SECTION TWO

*Notes: † The Census 2010 population figure is used to calculate the percentages in the Hispanic Origin and Race categories. Ancestry percentages are based on the 2006-2010 American Community Survey population (not shown); ‡ Numbers in parentheses indicate the number of people reporting a single ancestry; * Numbers in parentheses indicate the number of persons reporting this race alone, not in combination with any other race; Please refer to the Explanation of Data for more information.*

Not Hispanic (88)	145	0.99
Hispanic (20)	56	0.38
Aleut *(Alaska Native)* (5)	5	0.03
Apache (0)	4	0.03
Blackfeet (0)	3	0.02
Canadian/French Am. Ind. (2)	2	0.01
Central American Ind. (2)	2	0.01
Cherokee (20)	39	0.27
Chickasaw (7)	9	0.06
Chippewa (0)	1	0.01
Choctaw (25)	31	0.21
Comanche (4)	9	0.06
Creek (1)	8	0.05
Iroquois (0)	4	0.03
Kiowa (1)	4	0.03
Lumbee (0)	3	0.02
Mexican American Ind. (2)	6	0.04
Navajo (0)	2	0.01
Paiute (1)	1	0.01
Potawatomi (0)	1	0.01
Pueblo (0)	4	0.03
Seminole (1)	1	0.01
Sioux (1)	1	0.01
Yaqui (1)	1	0.01
Asian (157)	227	1.55
Not Hispanic (154)	214	1.46
Hispanic (3)	13	0.09
Burmese (0)	4	0.03
Cambodian (5)	5	0.03
Chinese, ex. Taiwanese (14)	25	0.17
Filipino (34)	57	0.39
Indian (32)	41	0.28
Japanese (5)	14	0.10
Korean (7)	14	0.10
Laotian (5)	7	0.05
Nepalese (3)	3	0.02
Pakistani (14)	14	0.10
Thai (6)	6	0.04
Vietnamese (27)	44	0.30
Hawaii Native/Pacific Islander (3)	16	0.11
Not Hispanic (2)	14	0.10
Hispanic (1)	2	0.01
Guamanian/Chamorro (2)	6	0.04
Native Hawaiian (0)	4	0.03
Samoan (1)	3	0.02
Tongan (0)	1	0.01
White (11,841)	12,132	82.75
Not Hispanic (10,442)	10,607	72.35
Hispanic (1,399)	1,525	10.40

Fort Bliss

Place Type: CDP
County: El Paso
Population: 8,591†

Ancestry‡	Population	%
African, Sub-Saharan (34)	65	0.73
African (18)	44	0.50
Nigerian (16)	21	0.24
American (618)	618	6.97
Arab (0)	39	0.44
Lebanese (0)	39	0.44
British (0)	32	0.36
Canadian (0)	42	0.47
Celtic (0)	12	0.14
Czechoslovakian (11)	11	0.12
Dutch (159)	295	3.33
English (79)	408	4.60
European (92)	130	1.47
Finnish (0)	8	0.09
French, ex. Basque (11)	112	1.26
French Canadian (0)	22	0.25
German (360)	1,188	13.40
Greek (8)	8	0.09
Hungarian (14)	24	0.27
Irish (366)	1,037	11.70
Italian (253)	473	5.34
Macedonian (9)	9	0.10
Norwegian (13)	32	0.36
Polish (8)	200	2.26
Russian (0)	96	1.08
Scotch-Irish (31)	144	1.62
Scottish (60)	216	2.44
Slovak (0)	9	0.10
Swedish (0)	63	0.71
Ukrainian (18)	31	0.35
Welsh (9)	50	0.56
West Indian, ex. Hispanic (45)	57	0.64
Haitian (29)	41	0.46
West Indian (16)	16	0.18
Yugoslavian (8)	8	0.09

Hispanic Origin	Population	%
Hispanic or Latino (of any race)	1,573	18.31
Central American, ex. Mexican	85	0.99
Costa Rican	1	0.01
Guatemalan	8	0.09
Honduran	13	0.15
Nicaraguan	11	0.13
Panamanian	37	0.43
Salvadoran	14	0.16
Other Central American	1	0.01
Cuban	26	0.30
Dominican Republic	25	0.29
Mexican	929	10.81
Puerto Rican	301	3.50
South American	56	0.65
Argentinean	2	0.02
Bolivian	3	0.03
Chilean	3	0.03
Colombian	31	0.36
Ecuadorian	4	0.05
Peruvian	12	0.14
Venezuelan	1	0.01
Other Hispanic or Latino	151	1.76

Race*	Population	%
African-American/Black (1,245)	1,424	16.58
Not Hispanic (1,163)	1,295	15.07
Hispanic (82)	129	1.50
American Indian/Alaska Native (137)	249	2.90
Not Hispanic (115)	204	2.37
Hispanic (22)	45	0.52
Apache (2)	6	0.07
Blackfeet (1)	3	0.03
Central American Ind. (1)	1	0.01
Cherokee (7)	44	0.51
Choctaw (1)	4	0.05
Comanche (1)	1	0.01
Hopi (1)	1	0.01
Inupiat *(Alaska Native)* (3)	3	0.03
Iroquois (1)	3	0.03
Kiowa (1)	1	0.01
Lumbee (7)	9	0.10
Mexican American Ind. (3)	4	0.05
Navajo (10)	15	0.17
Ottawa (2)	2	0.02
Pima (0)	2	0.02
Pueblo (3)	6	0.07
Shoshone (0)	1	0.01
Sioux (4)	7	0.08
Tlingit-Haida *(Alaska Native)* (2)	2	0.02
Yuman (0)	1	0.01
Asian (208)	334	3.89
Not Hispanic (197)	298	3.47
Hispanic (11)	36	0.42
Bangladeshi (2)	2	0.02
Cambodian (2)	2	0.02
Chinese, ex. Taiwanese (4)	13	0.15
Filipino (94)	142	1.65
Hmong (4)	6	0.07
Indian (19)	26	0.30
Japanese (9)	31	0.36
Korean (41)	75	0.87
Laotian (13)	13	0.15
Thai (8)	9	0.10
Vietnamese (6)	10	0.12
Hawaii Native/Pacific Islander (30)	57	0.66
Not Hispanic (27)	52	0.61
Hispanic (3)	5	0.06
Fijian (0)	1	0.01
Guamanian/Chamorro (12)	18	0.21
Native Hawaiian (3)	11	0.13
Samoan (7)	9	0.10
White (6,148)	6,491	75.56
Not Hispanic (5,227)	5,460	63.55
Hispanic (921)	1,031	12.00

Fort Hood

Place Type: CDP
County: Bell
Population: 29,589†

Ancestry‡	Population	%
African, Sub-Saharan (319)	418	1.21
African (319)	418	1.21
American (748)	748	2.17
Arab (14)	21	0.06
Egyptian (14)	14	0.04
Palestinian (0)	7	0.02
Armenian (7)	7	0.02
Austrian (0)	13	0.04
Belgian (0)	9	0.03
British (48)	140	0.41
Cajun (49)	143	0.42
Canadian (101)	110	0.32
Croatian (18)	33	0.10
Czech (0)	55	0.16
Czechoslovakian (0)	12	0.03
Danish (0)	50	0.15
Dutch (37)	211	0.61
English (1,024)	1,852	5.38
European (131)	175	0.51
Finnish (0)	15	0.04
French, ex. Basque (210)	841	2.44
French Canadian (67)	163	0.47
German (1,796)	5,027	14.59
Greek (12)	106	0.31
Hungarian (33)	95	0.28
Irish (656)	2,781	8.07
Italian (387)	1,270	3.69
Latvian (0)	3	0.01
Lithuanian (7)	30	0.09
Northern European (26)	26	0.08
Norwegian (83)	218	0.63
Polish (280)	594	1.72
Portuguese (46)	168	0.49
Romanian (0)	3	0.01
Russian (34)	54	0.16
Scandinavian (23)	39	0.11
Scotch-Irish (224)	492	1.43
Scottish (124)	262	0.76
Slovak (0)	46	0.13
Swedish (28)	112	0.33
Swiss (0)	54	0.16
Ukrainian (0)	15	0.04
Welsh (0)	102	0.30
West Indian, ex. Hispanic (123)	197	0.57
British West Indian (24)	24	0.07
Dutch West Indian (0)	63	0.18
Jamaican (46)	57	0.17
Trinidadian/Tobagonian (42)	42	0.12
West Indian (11)	11	0.03

Hispanic Origin	Population	%
Hispanic or Latino (of any race)	5,923	20.02
Central American, ex. Mexican	287	0.97
Costa Rican	17	0.06
Guatemalan	33	0.11
Honduran	38	0.13
Nicaraguan	28	0.09
Panamanian	94	0.32
Salvadoran	71	0.24
Other Central American	6	0.02
Cuban	89	0.30
Dominican Republic	85	0.29
Mexican	3,613	12.21
Puerto Rican	1,240	4.19

*Notes: † The Census 2010 population figure is used to calculate the percentages in the Hispanic Origin and Race categories. Ancestry percentages are based on the 2006-2010 American Community Survey population (not shown); ‡ Numbers in parentheses indicate the number of people reporting a single ancestry; * Numbers in parentheses indicate the number of persons reporting this race alone, not in combination with any other race; Please refer to the Explanation of Data for more information.*

South American	180	0.61
Argentinean	10	0.03
Bolivian	2	0.01
Chilean	7	0.02
Colombian	77	0.26
Ecuadorian	37	0.13
Paraguayan	1	<0.01
Peruvian	30	0.10
Uruguayan	1	<0.01
Venezuelan	14	0.05
Other South American	1	<0.01
Other Hispanic or Latino	429	1.45

Race*	Population	%
African-American/Black (5,272)	6,268	21.18
Not Hispanic (4,955)	5,660	19.13
Hispanic (317)	608	2.05
American Indian/Alaska Native (383)	830	2.81
Not Hispanic (248)	574	1.94
Hispanic (135)	256	0.87
Alaska Athabascan *(Ala. Nat.)* (4)	12	0.04
Apache (12)	34	0.11
Blackfeet (7)	25	0.08
Canadian/French Am. Ind. (2)	2	0.01
Central American Ind. (1)	1	<0.01
Cherokee (33)	169	0.57
Cheyenne (5)	10	0.03
Chickasaw (4)	8	0.03
Chippewa (7)	9	0.03
Choctaw (10)	37	0.13
Colville (4)	4	0.01
Comanche (3)	3	0.01
Cree (1)	2	0.01
Creek (5)	7	0.02
Crow (6)	7	0.02
Delaware (0)	3	0.01
Houma (0)	1	<0.01
Inupiat *(Alaska Native)* (5)	5	0.02
Iroquois (3)	9	0.03
Kiowa (6)	7	0.02
Lumbee (6)	11	0.04
Menominee (1)	2	0.01
Mexican American Ind. (20)	34	0.11
Navajo (43)	60	0.20
Osage (0)	6	0.02
Pima (4)	4	0.01
Potawatomi (6)	9	0.03
Pueblo (2)	3	0.01
Puget Sound Salish (1)	1	<0.01
Seminole (0)	6	0.02
Sioux (16)	35	0.12
South American Ind. (5)	16	0.05
Spanish American Ind. (1)	7	0.02
Tlingit-Haida *(Alaska Native)* (5)	5	0.02
Tohono O'Odham (1)	1	<0.01
Yakama (1)	1	<0.01
Yaqui (6)	6	0.02
Yup'ik *(Alaska Native)* (1)	3	0.01
Asian (663)	1,191	4.03
Not Hispanic (620)	1,048	3.54
Hispanic (43)	143	0.48
Burmese (3)	5	0.02
Cambodian (17)	22	0.07
Chinese, ex. Taiwanese (28)	66	0.22
Filipino (335)	595	2.01
Hmong (6)	6	0.02
Indian (22)	40	0.14
Indonesian (3)	5	0.02
Japanese (27)	94	0.32
Korean (128)	248	0.84
Laotian (9)	15	0.05
Nepalese (1)	1	<0.01
Pakistani (1)	3	0.01
Sri Lankan (1)	4	0.01
Taiwanese (2)	4	0.01
Thai (8)	26	0.09
Vietnamese (42)	64	0.22
Hawaii Native/Pacific Islander (525)	716	2.42
Not Hispanic (493)	636	2.15
Hispanic (32)	80	0.27
Fijian (7)	8	0.03
Guamanian/Chamorro (187)	226	0.76
Marshallese (26)	26	0.09
Native Hawaiian (33)	115	0.39
Samoan (103)	156	0.53
Tongan (8)	15	0.05
White (18,933)	20,433	69.06
Not Hispanic (16,008)	17,069	57.69
Hispanic (2,925)	3,364	11.37

Fort Stockton

Place Type: City
County: Pecos
Population: 8,283†

Ancestry‡	Population	%
American (320)	320	3.99
Armenian (11)	11	0.14
British (16)	16	0.20
Canadian (26)	26	0.32
Czech (0)	6	0.07
Danish (0)	14	0.17
Dutch (5)	28	0.35
English (53)	184	2.30
European (31)	31	0.39
French, ex. Basque (12)	25	0.31
French Canadian (7)	22	0.27
German (124)	259	3.23
Irish (80)	220	2.74
Italian (8)	8	0.10
Norwegian (0)	8	0.10
Polish (7)	7	0.09
Scotch-Irish (42)	46	0.57
Scottish (32)	32	0.40
Swedish (11)	43	0.54
Welsh (0)	11	0.14

Hispanic Origin	Population	%
Hispanic or Latino (of any race)	6,103	73.68
Central American, ex. Mexican	2	0.02
Guatemalan	1	0.01
Salvadoran	1	0.01
Cuban	3	0.04
Dominican Republic	1	0.01
Mexican	5,235	63.20
Puerto Rican	29	0.35
South American	2	0.02
Colombian	1	0.01
Ecuadorian	1	0.01
Other Hispanic or Latino	831	10.03

Race*	Population	%
African-American/Black (174)	202	2.44
Not Hispanic (159)	174	2.10
Hispanic (15)	28	0.34
American Indian/Alaska Native (59)	90	1.09
Not Hispanic (24)	35	0.42
Hispanic (35)	55	0.66
Apache (3)	3	0.04
Canadian/French Am. Ind. (1)	1	0.01
Cherokee (5)	14	0.17
Chickasaw (1)	1	0.01
Choctaw (1)	1	0.01
Comanche (2)	3	0.04
Mexican American Ind. (1)	2	0.02
Navajo (3)	5	0.06
Seminole (1)	3	0.04
Asian (69)	102	1.23
Not Hispanic (64)	79	0.95
Hispanic (5)	23	0.28
Burmese (8)	8	0.10
Chinese, ex. Taiwanese (0)	3	0.04
Filipino (5)	6	0.07
Indian (31)	42	0.51
Korean (3)	3	0.04
Laotian (2)	3	0.04
Thai (3)	9	0.11
Vietnamese (6)	7	0.08
Hawaii Native/Pacific Islander (3)	11	0.13
Not Hispanic (3)	7	0.08
Hispanic (0)	4	0.05
Guamanian/Chamorro (1)	4	0.05
Native Hawaiian (0)	4	0.05
Tongan (1)	1	0.01
White (6,573)	6,717	81.09
Not Hispanic (1,881)	1,907	23.02
Hispanic (4,692)	4,810	58.07

Fort Worth

Place Type: City
County: Tarrant
Population: 741,206†

Ancestry‡	Population	%
Afghan (218)	235	0.03
African, Sub-Saharan (17,470)	18,558	2.63
African (15,369)	16,247	2.30
Cape Verdean (0)	17	<0.01
Ethiopian (154)	171	0.02
Ghanaian (40)	40	0.01
Kenyan (94)	94	0.01
Liberian (76)	76	0.01
Nigerian (448)	466	0.07
Sierra Leonean (0)	14	<0.01
Somalian (194)	209	0.03
South African (129)	175	0.02
Sudanese (164)	164	0.02
Zimbabwean (11)	41	0.01
Other Sub-Saharan African (791)	844	0.12
Albanian (247)	254	0.04
American (48,874)	48,874	6.93
Arab (1,186)	1,628	0.23
Arab (249)	335	0.05
Egyptian (129)	129	0.02
Iraqi (77)	77	0.01
Jordanian (72)	100	0.01
Lebanese (229)	394	0.06
Moroccan (15)	22	<0.01
Palestinian (110)	153	0.02
Syrian (73)	116	0.02
Other Arab (232)	302	0.04
Armenian (122)	163	0.02
Australian (86)	195	0.03
Austrian (233)	665	0.09
Basque (34)	34	<0.01
Belgian (60)	94	0.01
Brazilian (279)	348	0.05
British (1,067)	1,934	0.27
Bulgarian (143)	152	0.02
Cajun (161)	219	0.03
Canadian (606)	1,026	0.15
Celtic (62)	136	0.02
Croatian (229)	384	0.05
Czech (1,066)	3,259	0.46
Czechoslovakian (222)	546	0.08
Danish (323)	1,378	0.20
Dutch (1,490)	6,572	0.93
Eastern European (202)	258	0.04
English (19,985)	50,261	7.13
Estonian (0)	11	<0.01
European (6,788)	7,768	1.10
Finnish (64)	288	0.04
French, ex. Basque (2,599)	12,534	1.78
French Canadian (646)	1,451	0.21
German (22,573)	65,149	9.24
Greek (673)	1,211	0.17
Guyanese (22)	32	<0.01
Hungarian (366)	727	0.10
Icelander (49)	49	0.01
Iranian (330)	398	0.06
Irish (17,425)	52,236	7.41
Israeli (58)	162	0.02
Italian (4,543)	13,182	1.87
Latvian (15)	39	0.01
Lithuanian (69)	518	0.07
Luxemburger (16)	55	0.01
Northern European (292)	301	0.04
Norwegian (1,467)	4,959	0.70

*Notes: † The Census 2010 population figure is used to calculate the percentages in the Hispanic Origin and Race categories. Ancestry percentages are based on the 2006-2010 American Community Survey population (not shown); ‡ Numbers in parentheses indicate the number of people reporting a single ancestry; * Numbers in parentheses indicate the number of persons reporting this race alone, not in combination with any other race; Please refer to the Explanation of Data for more information.*

Pennsylvania German (13)	48	0.01
Polish (2,581)	7,162	1.02
Portuguese (251)	750	0.11
Romanian (328)	594	0.08
Russian (934)	2,166	0.31
Scandinavian (318)	762	0.11
Scotch-Irish (5,648)	11,727	1.66
Scottish (5,020)	12,780	1.81
Serbian (148)	185	0.03
Slavic (40)	87	0.01
Slovak (121)	377	0.05
Slovene (41)	74	0.01
Swedish (1,581)	4,965	0.70
Swiss (279)	1,038	0.15
Turkish (69)	210	0.03
Ukrainian (385)	684	0.10
Welsh (721)	3,065	0.43
West Indian, ex. Hispanic (771)	1,418	0.20
Barbadian (0)	47	0.01
Belizean (31)	41	0.01
Dutch West Indian (82)	435	0.06
Haitian (148)	198	0.03
Jamaican (403)	560	0.08
Trinidadian/Tobagonian (61)	61	0.01
West Indian (46)	76	0.01
Yugoslavian (830)	897	0.13

Hispanic Origin	Population	%
Hispanic or Latino (of any race)	252,468	34.06
Central American, ex. Mexican	6,855	0.92
Costa Rican	183	0.02
Guatemalan	1,280	0.17
Honduran	1,820	0.25
Nicaraguan	372	0.05
Panamanian	419	0.06
Salvadoran	2,729	0.37
Other Central American	52	0.01
Cuban	1,495	0.20
Dominican Republic	470	0.06
Mexican	219,653	29.63
Puerto Rican	5,650	0.76
South American	3,014	0.41
Argentinean	436	0.06
Bolivian	89	0.01
Chilean	153	0.02
Colombian	1,093	0.15
Ecuadorian	344	0.05
Paraguayan	17	<0.01
Peruvian	473	0.06
Uruguayan	31	<0.01
Venezuelan	339	0.05
Other South American	39	0.01
Other Hispanic or Latino	15,331	2.07

Race*	Population	%
African-American/Black (140,133)	147,411	19.89
Not Hispanic (136,941)	142,352	19.21
Hispanic (3,192)	5,059	0.68
American Indian/Alaska Native (4,762)	9,188	1.24
Not Hispanic (2,481)	5,723	0.77
Hispanic (2,281)	3,465	0.47
Alaska Athabascan *(Ala. Nat.)* (11)	18	<0.01
Aleut *(Alaska Native)* (2)	5	<0.01
Apache (115)	225	0.03
Arapaho (4)	9	<0.01
Blackfeet (25)	119	0.02
Canadian/French Am. Ind. (14)	25	<0.01
Central American Ind. (18)	34	<0.01
Cherokee (529)	1,675	0.23
Cheyenne (10)	13	<0.01
Chickasaw (147)	277	0.04
Chippewa (48)	76	0.01
Choctaw (319)	717	0.10
Comanche (84)	163	0.02
Cree (6)	13	<0.01
Creek (74)	189	0.03
Crow (11)	17	<0.01
Delaware (12)	19	<0.01
Hopi (3)	11	<0.01
Houma (13)	18	<0.01
Inupiat *(Alaska Native)* (5)	10	<0.01
Iroquois (22)	61	0.01
Kiowa (37)	61	0.01
Lumbee (14)	29	<0.01
Menominee (0)	1	<0.01
Mexican American Ind. (536)	715	0.10
Navajo (73)	124	0.02
Osage (23)	54	0.01
Ottawa (4)	5	<0.01
Paiute (8)	9	<0.01
Pima (6)	10	<0.01
Potawatomi (46)	58	0.01
Pueblo (19)	38	0.01
Puget Sound Salish (2)	4	<0.01
Seminole (26)	67	0.01
Shoshone (3)	4	<0.01
Sioux (96)	165	0.02
South American Ind. (33)	52	0.01
Spanish American Ind. (15)	25	<0.01
Tlingit-Haida *(Alaska Native)* (10)	11	<0.01
Tohono O'Odham (26)	28	<0.01
Tsimshian *(Alaska Native)* (0)	1	<0.01
Ute (8)	10	<0.01
Yakama (0)	1	<0.01
Yaqui (8)	16	<0.01
Yuman (3)	6	<0.01
Yup'ik *(Alaska Native)* (0)	5	<0.01
Asian (27,615)	32,411	4.37
Not Hispanic (27,095)	30,971	4.18
Hispanic (520)	1,440	0.19
Bangladeshi (258)	302	0.04
Bhutanese (295)	343	0.05
Burmese (730)	791	0.11
Cambodian (542)	679	0.09
Chinese, ex. Taiwanese (1,835)	2,545	0.34
Filipino (2,468)	3,715	0.50
Hmong (108)	132	0.02
Indian (4,733)	5,467	0.74
Indonesian (79)	128	0.02
Japanese (520)	1,187	0.16
Korean (2,048)	2,523	0.34
Laotian (2,686)	3,009	0.41
Malaysian (58)	64	0.01
Nepalese (502)	594	0.08
Pakistani (949)	1,081	0.15
Sri Lankan (82)	106	0.01
Taiwanese (126)	172	0.02
Thai (487)	756	0.10
Vietnamese (7,605)	8,223	1.11
Hawaii Native/Pacific Islander (746)	1,651	0.22
Not Hispanic (615)	1,237	0.17
Hispanic (131)	414	0.06
Fijian (9)	23	<0.01
Guamanian/Chamorro (153)	283	0.04
Native Hawaiian (180)	494	0.07
Samoan (89)	216	0.03
Tongan (207)	250	0.03
White (452,885)	472,242	63.71
Not Hispanic (309,312)	318,763	43.01
Hispanic (143,573)	153,479	20.71

Four Corners

Place Type: CDP
County: Fort Bend
Population: 12,382†

Ancestry‡	Population	%
Afghan (0)	8	0.06
African, Sub-Saharan (1,102)	1,332	10.81
African (263)	367	2.98
Nigerian (830)	956	7.76
Other Sub-Saharan African (9)	9	0.07
American (323)	323	2.62
Arab (11)	22	0.18
Moroccan (11)	22	0.18
Austrian (0)	15	0.12
Canadian (16)	30	0.24
Dutch (46)	54	0.44
English (226)	530	4.30
European (21)	35	0.28
French, ex. Basque (9)	20	0.16
French Canadian (4)	4	0.03
German (81)	314	2.55
Greek (56)	72	0.58
Irish (0)	200	1.62
Italian (0)	33	0.27
Polish (0)	29	0.24
Russian (0)	43	0.35
Scottish (0)	34	0.28
West Indian, ex. Hispanic (207)	238	1.93
Jamaican (207)	218	1.77
U.S. Virgin Islander (0)	10	0.08
West Indian (0)	10	0.08

Hispanic Origin	Population	%
Hispanic or Latino (of any race)	3,145	25.40
Central American, ex. Mexican	580	4.68
Costa Rican	7	0.06
Guatemalan	100	0.81
Honduran	62	0.50
Nicaraguan	14	0.11
Panamanian	6	0.05
Salvadoran	390	3.15
Other Central American	1	0.01
Cuban	19	0.15
Dominican Republic	24	0.19
Mexican	1,969	15.90
Puerto Rican	67	0.54
South American	211	1.70
Argentinean	14	0.11
Bolivian	8	0.06
Colombian	111	0.90
Ecuadorian	14	0.11
Peruvian	35	0.28
Uruguayan	2	0.02
Venezuelan	27	0.22
Other Hispanic or Latino	275	2.22

Race*	Population	%
African-American/Black (3,861)	3,992	32.24
Not Hispanic (3,794)	3,893	31.44
Hispanic (67)	99	0.80
American Indian/Alaska Native (44)	97	0.78
Not Hispanic (21)	46	0.37
Hispanic (23)	51	0.41
Cherokee (10)	11	0.09
Chickasaw (5)	5	0.04
Choctaw (2)	4	0.03
Cree (1)	2	0.02
Delaware (0)	1	0.01
Mexican American Ind. (7)	17	0.14
Pueblo (1)	1	0.01
Asian (4,286)	4,495	36.30
Not Hispanic (4,277)	4,457	36.00
Hispanic (9)	38	0.31
Bangladeshi (44)	49	0.40
Cambodian (10)	12	0.10
Chinese, ex. Taiwanese (428)	472	3.81
Filipino (513)	541	4.37
Indian (1,146)	1,248	10.08
Indonesian (6)	6	0.05
Japanese (0)	3	0.02
Korean (13)	16	0.13
Laotian (3)	7	0.06
Malaysian (5)	5	0.04
Pakistani (839)	912	7.37
Sri Lankan (1)	3	0.02
Taiwanese (31)	33	0.27
Thai (11)	12	0.10
Vietnamese (1,068)	1,134	9.16
Hawaii Native/Pacific Islander (3)	4	0.03
Not Hispanic (2)	2	0.02
Hispanic (1)	2	0.02
Guamanian/Chamorro (1)	1	0.01
Native Hawaiian (1)	1	0.01
White (2,303)	2,568	20.74
Not Hispanic (846)	994	8.03
Hispanic (1,457)	1,574	12.71

*Notes: † The Census 2010 population figure is used to calculate the percentages in the Hispanic Origin and Race categories. Ancestry percentages are based on the 2006-2010 American Community Survey population (not shown); ‡ Numbers in parentheses indicate the number of people reporting a single ancestry; * Numbers in parentheses indicate the number of persons reporting this race alone, not in combination with any other race; Please refer to the Explanation of Data for more information.*

Fredericksburg

Place Type: City
County: Gillespie
Population: 10,530†

Ancestry‡	Population	%
American (473)	473	4.56
Arab (0)	65	0.63
Lebanese (0)	50	0.48
Syrian (0)	15	0.14
Austrian (15)	55	0.53
Brazilian (14)	52	0.50
British (21)	105	1.01
Czech (30)	100	0.96
Czechoslovakian (9)	19	0.18
Danish (0)	47	0.45
Dutch (53)	249	2.40
English (310)	1,136	10.96
European (40)	40	0.39
French, ex. Basque (34)	283	2.73
German (2,573)	4,222	40.74
Greek (10)	22	0.21
Irish (441)	1,329	12.82
Italian (0)	170	1.64
Norwegian (22)	70	0.68
Polish (23)	70	0.68
Portuguese (0)	12	0.12
Russian (0)	32	0.31
Scandinavian (0)	8	0.08
Scotch-Irish (144)	402	3.88
Scottish (108)	345	3.33
Slavic (0)	9	0.09
Swedish (21)	110	1.06
Swiss (0)	28	0.27
Welsh (32)	73	0.70

Hispanic Origin	Population	%
Hispanic or Latino (of any race)	2,248	21.35
Central American, ex. Mexican	23	0.22
Guatemalan	5	0.05
Honduran	13	0.12
Panamanian	1	0.01
Salvadoran	4	0.04
Cuban	5	0.05
Dominican Republic	1	0.01
Mexican	1,989	18.89
Puerto Rican	20	0.19
South American	14	0.13
Argentinean	1	0.01
Bolivian	1	0.01
Colombian	7	0.07
Ecuadorian	3	0.03
Peruvian	1	0.01
Venezuelan	1	0.01
Other Hispanic or Latino	196	1.86

Race*	Population	%
African-American/Black (51)	70	0.66
Not Hispanic (24)	38	0.36
Hispanic (27)	32	0.30
American Indian/Alaska Native (67)	108	1.03
Not Hispanic (33)	64	0.61
Hispanic (34)	44	0.42
Aleut *(Alaska Native)* (1)	1	0.01
Apache (0)	1	0.01
Cherokee (10)	18	0.17
Chickasaw (2)	4	0.04
Choctaw (2)	7	0.07
Comanche (0)	1	0.01
Creek (1)	3	0.03
Iroquois (1)	3	0.03
Mexican American Ind. (6)	7	0.07
Navajo (4)	5	0.05
Osage (2)	2	0.02
Sioux (1)	2	0.02
Spanish American Ind. (2)	3	0.03
Asian (63)	76	0.72
Not Hispanic (63)	74	0.70
Hispanic (0)	2	0.02
Cambodian (2)	2	0.02
Chinese, ex. Taiwanese (2)	3	0.03
Filipino (13)	14	0.13
Indian (24)	27	0.26
Japanese (1)	3	0.03
Korean (5)	9	0.09
Laotian (2)	2	0.02
Vietnamese (14)	14	0.13
Hawaii Native/Pacific Islander (3)	6	0.06
Not Hispanic (3)	5	0.05
Hispanic (0)	1	0.01
Guamanian/Chamorro (1)	1	0.01
Native Hawaiian (2)	3	0.03
White (9,531)	9,636	91.51
Not Hispanic (8,081)	8,144	77.34
Hispanic (1,450)	1,492	14.17

Freeport

Place Type: City
County: Brazoria
Population: 12,049†

Ancestry‡	Population	%
American (403)	403	3.31
Czech (0)	170	1.40
Czechoslovakian (11)	37	0.30
Dutch (23)	109	0.89
English (85)	414	3.40
European (16)	16	0.13
French, ex. Basque (104)	313	2.57
German (179)	742	6.09
Irish (242)	622	5.11
Italian (49)	49	0.40
Polish (38)	337	2.77
Scotch-Irish (76)	207	1.70
Scottish (0)	10	0.08
Swedish (38)	70	0.57
Swiss (0)	8	0.07
West Indian, ex. Hispanic (0)	11	0.09
Jamaican (0)	11	0.09

Hispanic Origin	Population	%
Hispanic or Latino (of any race)	7,223	59.95
Central American, ex. Mexican	169	1.40
Guatemalan	29	0.24
Honduran	20	0.17
Nicaraguan	54	0.45
Panamanian	3	0.02
Salvadoran	63	0.52
Cuban	8	0.07
Mexican	6,278	52.10
Puerto Rican	27	0.22
South American	4	0.03
Colombian	2	0.02
Peruvian	1	0.01
Venezuelan	1	0.01
Other Hispanic or Latino	737	6.12

Race*	Population	%
African-American/Black (1,467)	1,665	13.82
Not Hispanic (1,353)	1,476	12.25
Hispanic (114)	189	1.57
American Indian/Alaska Native (95)	186	1.54
Not Hispanic (29)	73	0.61
Hispanic (66)	113	0.94
Apache (5)	6	0.05
Blackfeet (0)	5	0.04
Cherokee (9)	41	0.34
Chickasaw (2)	2	0.02
Chippewa (1)	1	0.01
Choctaw (5)	14	0.12
Comanche (0)	5	0.04
Delaware (3)	3	0.02
Mexican American Ind. (17)	18	0.15
Ottawa (2)	2	0.02
Seminole (0)	1	0.01
Shoshone (0)	5	0.04
Sioux (0)	6	0.05
South American Ind. (1)	2	0.02
Asian (60)	103	0.85
Not Hispanic (56)	89	0.74
Hispanic (4)	14	0.12
Cambodian (8)	8	0.07
Filipino (5)	25	0.21
Indian (28)	31	0.26
Japanese (1)	11	0.09
Laotian (1)	4	0.03
Vietnamese (17)	22	0.18
Hawaii Native/Pacific Islander (1)	17	0.14
Not Hispanic (1)	12	0.10
Hispanic (0)	5	0.04
Native Hawaiian (1)	15	0.12
White (7,829)	8,282	68.74
Not Hispanic (3,190)	3,356	27.85
Hispanic (4,639)	4,926	40.88

Fresno

Place Type: CDP
County: Fort Bend
Population: 19,069†

Ancestry‡	Population	%
African, Sub-Saharan (458)	458	2.76
African (199)	199	1.20
Nigerian (259)	259	1.56
American (475)	475	2.86
British (0)	14	0.08
Cajun (10)	10	0.06
Dutch (0)	16	0.10
English (106)	227	1.37
European (6)	6	0.04
French, ex. Basque (215)	245	1.47
German (110)	411	2.47
Irish (125)	403	2.43
Italian (111)	111	0.67
Polish (0)	61	0.37
Russian (24)	24	0.14
Scotch-Irish (25)	25	0.15
Scottish (0)	69	0.42
Swedish (0)	9	0.05
West Indian, ex. Hispanic (236)	317	1.91
British West Indian (6)	6	0.04
Jamaican (43)	102	0.61
Trinidadian/Tobagonian (103)	103	0.62
West Indian (84)	106	0.64

Hispanic Origin	Population	%
Hispanic or Latino (of any race)	6,318	33.13
Central American, ex. Mexican	659	3.46
Costa Rican	4	0.02
Guatemalan	48	0.25
Honduran	101	0.53
Nicaraguan	23	0.12
Panamanian	29	0.15
Salvadoran	451	2.37
Other Central American	3	0.02
Cuban	21	0.11
Dominican Republic	23	0.12
Mexican	5,129	26.90
Puerto Rican	54	0.28
South American	43	0.23
Bolivian	1	0.01
Colombian	28	0.15
Ecuadorian	3	0.02
Peruvian	4	0.02
Venezuelan	6	0.03
Other South American	1	0.01
Other Hispanic or Latino	389	2.04

Race*	Population	%
African-American/Black (11,387)	11,692	61.31
Not Hispanic (11,225)	11,455	60.07
Hispanic (162)	237	1.24
American Indian/Alaska Native (120)	245	1.28
Not Hispanic (15)	89	0.47
Hispanic (105)	156	0.82
Apache (0)	1	0.01
Arapaho (0)	1	0.01

SECTION TWO

*Notes: † The Census 2010 population figure is used to calculate the percentages in the Hispanic Origin and Race categories. Ancestry percentages are based on the 2006-2010 American Community Survey population (not shown); ‡ Numbers in parentheses indicate the number of people reporting a single ancestry; * Numbers in parentheses indicate the number of persons reporting this race alone, not in combination with any other race; Please refer to the Explanation of Data for more information.*

Blackfeet (0)	3	0.02
Central American Ind. (0)	1	0.01
Cherokee (0)	24	0.13
Cheyenne (1)	1	0.01
Chickasaw (1)	1	0.01
Choctaw (1)	9	0.05
Creek (1)	4	0.02
Mexican American Ind. (25)	32	0.17
Spanish American Ind. (6)	6	0.03
Yaqui (0)	1	0.01
Asian (185)	284	1.49
Not Hispanic (181)	244	1.28
Hispanic (4)	40	0.21
Cambodian (11)	14	0.07
Chinese, ex. Taiwanese (13)	23	0.12
Filipino (41)	80	0.42
Indian (36)	48	0.25
Indonesian (5)	5	0.03
Japanese (3)	9	0.05
Korean (2)	9	0.05
Pakistani (14)	19	0.10
Taiwanese (0)	2	0.01
Thai (9)	10	0.05
Vietnamese (43)	51	0.27
Hawaii Native/Pacific Islander (4)	23	0.12
Not Hispanic (2)	14	0.07
Hispanic (2)	9	0.05
Guamanian/Chamorro (0)	2	0.01
Native Hawaiian (0)	1	0.01
White (3,568)	3,955	20.74
Not Hispanic (1,011)	1,201	6.30
Hispanic (2,557)	2,754	14.44

Friendswood

Place Type: City
County: Galveston
Population: 35,805†

Ancestry‡	Population	%
African, Sub-Saharan (73)	73	0.21
African (73)	73	0.21
Alsatian (12)	26	0.07
American (2,359)	2,359	6.78
Arab (0)	8	0.02
Lebanese (0)	8	0.02
Armenian (0)	8	0.02
Australian (0)	10	0.03
Austrian (0)	58	0.17
Belgian (49)	60	0.17
Brazilian (0)	24	0.07
British (83)	245	0.70
Cajun (100)	109	0.31
Czech (163)	523	1.50
Czechoslovakian (24)	78	0.22
Danish (79)	163	0.47
Dutch (134)	595	1.71
Eastern European (22)	22	0.06
English (1,564)	4,295	12.35
European (593)	790	2.27
Finnish (0)	39	0.11
French, ex. Basque (362)	1,562	4.49
French Canadian (115)	129	0.37
German (2,246)	7,933	22.81
Greek (56)	101	0.29
Hungarian (16)	153	0.44
Iranian (0)	14	0.04
Irish (1,443)	5,233	15.05
Israeli (8)	8	0.02
Italian (641)	1,764	5.07
Lithuanian (0)	8	0.02
Macedonian (22)	22	0.06
Northern European (19)	19	0.05
Norwegian (100)	338	0.97
Pennsylvania German (29)	29	0.08
Polish (230)	646	1.86
Portuguese (52)	98	0.28
Russian (83)	170	0.49
Scandinavian (41)	122	0.35
Scotch-Irish (624)	1,111	3.20
Scottish (292)	1,004	2.89
Slavic (5)	15	0.04
Slovak (56)	94	0.27
Slovene (0)	9	0.03
Swedish (125)	642	1.85
Swiss (0)	105	0.30
Turkish (0)	10	0.03
Ukrainian (86)	146	0.42
Welsh (67)	383	1.10
West Indian, ex. Hispanic (14)	14	0.04
Dutch West Indian (14)	14	0.04
Yugoslavian (0)	18	0.05

Hispanic Origin	Population	%
Hispanic or Latino (of any race)	4,470	12.48
Central American, ex. Mexican	323	0.90
Costa Rican	19	0.05
Guatemalan	38	0.11
Honduran	48	0.13
Nicaraguan	20	0.06
Panamanian	14	0.04
Salvadoran	184	0.51
Cuban	114	0.32
Dominican Republic	18	0.05
Mexican	3,295	9.20
Puerto Rican	168	0.47
South American	219	0.61
Argentinean	31	0.09
Bolivian	16	0.04
Chilean	11	0.03
Colombian	54	0.15
Ecuadorian	7	0.02
Paraguayan	4	0.01
Peruvian	38	0.11
Uruguayan	10	0.03
Venezuelan	43	0.12
Other South American	5	0.01
Other Hispanic or Latino	333	0.93

Race*	Population	%
African-American/Black (1,232)	1,400	3.91
Not Hispanic (1,184)	1,337	3.73
Hispanic (48)	63	0.18
American Indian/Alaska Native (154)	366	1.02
Not Hispanic (95)	266	0.74
Hispanic (59)	100	0.28
Apache (3)	16	0.04
Blackfeet (0)	9	0.03
Central American Ind. (1)	3	0.01
Cherokee (16)	75	0.21
Chickasaw (5)	8	0.02
Chippewa (0)	1	<0.01
Choctaw (17)	32	0.09
Comanche (1)	1	<0.01
Cree (1)	1	<0.01
Creek (4)	7	0.02
Delaware (3)	3	0.01
Houma (1)	1	<0.01
Inupiat *(Alaska Native)* (0)	2	0.01
Iroquois (1)	1	<0.01
Lumbee (3)	5	0.01
Mexican American Ind. (4)	10	0.03
Navajo (3)	7	0.02
Ottawa (1)	2	0.01
Potawatomi (4)	10	0.03
Pueblo (4)	4	0.01
Puget Sound Salish (1)	1	<0.01
Sioux (0)	4	0.01
Spanish American Ind. (9)	10	0.03
Asian (1,735)	1,994	5.57
Not Hispanic (1,720)	1,943	5.43
Hispanic (15)	51	0.14
Bangladeshi (11)	12	0.03
Burmese (5)	5	0.01
Cambodian (22)	30	0.08
Chinese, ex. Taiwanese (228)	272	0.76
Filipino (112)	167	0.47
Indian (499)	545	1.52
Indonesian (4)	10	0.03
Japanese (24)	52	0.15
Korean (38)	67	0.19
Laotian (4)	4	0.01
Malaysian (1)	1	<0.01
Pakistani (169)	182	0.51
Sri Lankan (8)	8	0.02
Taiwanese (18)	19	0.05
Thai (9)	16	0.04
Vietnamese (502)	542	1.51
Hawaii Native/Pacific Islander (19)	50	0.14
Not Hispanic (17)	38	0.11
Hispanic (2)	12	0.03
Guamanian/Chamorro (5)	9	0.03
Native Hawaiian (6)	21	0.06
Samoan (1)	4	0.01
Tongan (0)	1	<0.01
White (31,016)	31,673	88.46
Not Hispanic (27,733)	28,214	78.80
Hispanic (3,283)	3,459	9.66

Frisco

Place Type: City
County: Collin
Population: 116,989†

Ancestry‡	Population	%
Afghan (76)	76	0.07
African, Sub-Saharan (688)	803	0.78
African (336)	379	0.37
Kenyan (46)	88	0.09
Nigerian (160)	182	0.18
South African (5)	5	<0.01
Sudanese (0)	8	0.01
Zimbabwean (83)	83	0.08
Other Sub-Saharan African (58)	58	0.06
Albanian (210)	210	0.20
American (6,093)	6,093	5.91
Arab (776)	1,153	1.12
Arab (36)	56	0.05
Egyptian (196)	230	0.22
Iraqi (16)	16	0.02
Jordanian (29)	29	0.03
Lebanese (341)	589	0.57
Syrian (37)	85	0.08
Other Arab (121)	148	0.14
Armenian (0)	45	0.04
Australian (68)	107	0.10
Austrian (0)	122	0.12
Basque (6)	6	0.01
Belgian (61)	115	0.11
Brazilian (61)	61	0.06
British (381)	735	0.71
Bulgarian (56)	56	0.05
Canadian (159)	195	0.19
Croatian (36)	104	0.10
Czech (358)	971	0.94
Czechoslovakian (26)	52	0.05
Danish (46)	200	0.19
Dutch (524)	1,685	1.63
Eastern European (33)	33	0.03
English (4,452)	11,526	11.17
Estonian (0)	11	0.01
European (1,635)	1,954	1.89
Finnish (0)	29	0.03
French, ex. Basque (850)	2,938	2.85
French Canadian (186)	425	0.41
German (5,120)	17,003	16.48
German Russian (0)	13	0.01
Greek (263)	464	0.45
Hungarian (161)	430	0.42
Iranian (1,030)	1,039	1.01
Irish (2,763)	11,865	11.50
Italian (1,585)	5,798	5.62
Lithuanian (42)	125	0.12
Maltese (2)	5	<0.01
Northern European (79)	90	0.09
Norwegian (484)	1,322	1.28
Pennsylvania German (47)	47	0.05
Polish (873)	2,782	2.70
Portuguese (86)	287	0.28

*Notes: † The Census 2010 population figure is used to calculate the percentages in the Hispanic Origin and Race categories. Ancestry percentages are based on the 2006-2010 American Community Survey population (not shown); ‡ Numbers in parentheses indicate the number of people reporting a single ancestry; * Numbers in parentheses indicate the number of persons reporting this race alone, not in combination with any other race; Please refer to the Explanation of Data for more information.*

Romanian (200)	222	0.22
Russian (403)	969	0.94
Scandinavian (129)	249	0.24
Scotch-Irish (1,057)	2,624	2.54
Scottish (764)	2,447	2.37
Slavic (0)	12	0.01
Slovak (31)	106	0.10
Slovene (21)	21	0.02
Swedish (208)	1,067	1.03
Swiss (47)	244	0.24
Turkish (59)	74	0.07
Ukrainian (49)	167	0.16
Welsh (153)	563	0.55
West Indian, ex. Hispanic (147)	290	0.28
Bahamian (0)	59	0.06
British West Indian (17)	17	0.02
Dutch West Indian (16)	61	0.06
Jamaican (93)	128	0.12
Trinidadian/Tobagonian (21)	21	0.02
West Indian (0)	4	<0.01
Yugoslavian (0)	29	0.03

Hispanic Origin	Population	%
Hispanic or Latino (of any race)	14,154	12.10
Central American, ex. Mexican	680	0.58
Costa Rican	28	0.02
Guatemalan	134	0.11
Honduran	107	0.09
Nicaraguan	80	0.07
Panamanian	58	0.05
Salvadoran	266	0.23
Other Central American	7	0.01
Cuban	336	0.29
Dominican Republic	135	0.12
Mexican	9,799	8.38
Puerto Rican	782	0.67
South American	1,197	1.02
Argentinean	111	0.09
Bolivian	29	0.02
Chilean	48	0.04
Colombian	388	0.33
Ecuadorian	125	0.11
Paraguayan	13	0.01
Peruvian	250	0.21
Uruguayan	15	0.01
Venezuelan	199	0.17
Other South American	19	0.02
Other Hispanic or Latino	1,225	1.05

Race*	Population	%
African-American/Black (9,459)	10,497	8.97
Not Hispanic (9,182)	10,045	8.59
Hispanic (277)	452	0.39
American Indian/Alaska Native (586)	1,311	1.12
Not Hispanic (453)	1,034	0.88
Hispanic (133)	277	0.24
Aleut *(Alaska Native)* (1)	1	<0.01
Apache (8)	29	0.02
Arapaho (0)	3	<0.01
Blackfeet (4)	18	0.02
Central American Ind. (1)	6	0.01
Cherokee (92)	284	0.24
Chickasaw (39)	67	0.06
Chippewa (8)	11	0.01
Choctaw (116)	199	0.17
Comanche (8)	12	0.01
Creek (17)	45	0.04
Delaware (2)	6	0.01
Houma (1)	4	<0.01
Iroquois (6)	18	0.02
Lumbee (1)	2	<0.01
Mexican American Ind. (19)	35	0.03
Navajo (13)	22	0.02
Osage (2)	4	<0.01
Ottawa (1)	3	<0.01
Potawatomi (8)	9	0.01
Pueblo (0)	6	0.01
Puget Sound Salish (0)	1	<0.01
Seminole (8)	10	0.01
Sioux (11)	19	0.02
South American Ind. (7)	9	0.01
Spanish American Ind. (4)	5	<0.01
Tlingit-Haida *(Alaska Native)* (0)	5	<0.01
Tohono O'Odham (1)	1	<0.01
Tsimshian *(Alaska Native)* (0)	3	<0.01
Ute (1)	1	<0.01
Yaqui (0)	3	<0.01
Asian (11,664)	13,331	11.40
Not Hispanic (11,568)	13,056	11.16
Hispanic (96)	275	0.24
Bangladeshi (102)	114	0.10
Burmese (2)	4	<0.01
Cambodian (73)	101	0.09
Chinese, ex. Taiwanese (1,644)	2,016	1.72
Filipino (1,081)	1,432	1.22
Hmong (20)	20	0.02
Indian (4,772)	4,984	4.26
Indonesian (40)	67	0.06
Japanese (152)	356	0.30
Korean (1,057)	1,269	1.08
Laotian (59)	65	0.06
Malaysian (27)	33	0.03
Nepalese (31)	31	0.03
Pakistani (690)	747	0.64
Sri Lankan (35)	38	0.03
Taiwanese (164)	206	0.18
Thai (70)	130	0.11
Vietnamese (1,236)	1,415	1.21
Hawaii Native/Pacific Islander (51)	196	0.17
Not Hispanic (47)	172	0.15
Hispanic (4)	24	0.02
Fijian (4)	4	<0.01
Guamanian/Chamorro (21)	46	0.04
Marshallese (3)	3	<0.01
Native Hawaiian (9)	71	0.06
Samoan (2)	18	0.02
Tongan (1)	1	<0.01
White (87,706)	90,910	77.71
Not Hispanic (78,566)	80,972	69.21
Hispanic (9,140)	9,938	8.49

Gainesville

Place Type: City
County: Cooke
Population: 16,002†

Ancestry‡	Population	%
African, Sub-Saharan (49)	49	0.31
African (40)	40	0.25
Other Sub-Saharan African (9)	9	0.06
American (1,043)	1,043	6.50
Arab (48)	48	0.30
Jordanian (13)	13	0.08
Syrian (35)	35	0.22
Austrian (8)	23	0.14
British (0)	11	0.07
Canadian (0)	11	0.07
Czech (0)	27	0.17
Danish (0)	32	0.20
Dutch (8)	161	1.00
English (657)	1,229	7.66
European (37)	37	0.23
French, ex. Basque (51)	311	1.94
French Canadian (21)	21	0.13
German (880)	1,999	12.46
Irish (456)	1,798	11.20
Italian (145)	200	1.25
Norwegian (73)	94	0.59
Polish (126)	175	1.09
Russian (0)	11	0.07
Scotch-Irish (244)	466	2.90
Scottish (102)	174	1.08
Swedish (0)	54	0.34
Swiss (0)	23	0.14
Welsh (8)	88	0.55
West Indian, ex. Hispanic (17)	113	0.70
Dutch West Indian (17)	113	0.70

Hispanic Origin	Population	%
Hispanic or Latino (of any race)	4,521	28.25
Central American, ex. Mexican	74	0.46
Costa Rican	1	0.01
Guatemalan	26	0.16
Honduran	5	0.03
Nicaraguan	7	0.04
Panamanian	1	0.01
Salvadoran	34	0.21
Cuban	3	0.02
Mexican	4,129	25.80
Puerto Rican	43	0.27
South American	22	0.14
Argentinean	7	0.04
Colombian	12	0.07
Venezuelan	3	0.02
Other Hispanic or Latino	250	1.56

Race*	Population	%
African-American/Black (820)	1,028	6.42
Not Hispanic (789)	968	6.05
Hispanic (31)	60	0.37
American Indian/Alaska Native (210)	343	2.14
Not Hispanic (146)	262	1.64
Hispanic (64)	81	0.51
Alaska Athabascan *(Ala. Nat.)* (3)	3	0.02
Apache (1)	4	0.02
Blackfeet (0)	1	0.01
Cherokee (26)	78	0.49
Chickasaw (26)	35	0.22
Choctaw (24)	42	0.26
Comanche (1)	7	0.04
Creek (3)	4	0.02
Delaware (1)	4	0.02
Iroquois (0)	4	0.02
Mexican American Ind. (18)	19	0.12
Navajo (1)	3	0.02
Osage (0)	1	0.01
Pima (1)	1	0.01
Potawatomi (9)	9	0.06
Pueblo (1)	1	0.01
Seminole (1)	1	0.01
Sioux (6)	8	0.05
Yaqui (2)	2	0.01
Asian (202)	241	1.51
Not Hispanic (193)	212	1.32
Hispanic (9)	29	0.18
Bangladeshi (1)	1	0.01
Cambodian (7)	9	0.06
Chinese, ex. Taiwanese (30)	36	0.22
Filipino (31)	48	0.30
Indian (71)	78	0.49
Indonesian (1)	1	0.01
Japanese (4)	4	0.02
Korean (15)	16	0.10
Laotian (2)	5	0.03
Nepalese (2)	2	0.01
Pakistani (8)	8	0.05
Thai (1)	2	0.01
Vietnamese (23)	24	0.15
Hawaii Native/Pacific Islander (15)	18	0.11
Not Hispanic (15)	16	0.10
Hispanic (0)	2	0.01
Native Hawaiian (3)	5	0.03
Samoan (11)	11	0.07
White (11,960)	12,434	77.70
Not Hispanic (10,019)	10,295	64.34
Hispanic (1,941)	2,139	13.37

Galena Park

Place Type: City
County: Harris
Population: 10,887†

Ancestry‡	Population	%
American (261)	261	2.42
British (18)	18	0.17
Czech (14)	76	0.70
Dutch (0)	17	0.16

*Notes: † The Census 2010 population figure is used to calculate the percentages in the Hispanic Origin and Race categories. Ancestry percentages are based on the 2006-2010 American Community Survey population (not shown); ‡ Numbers in parentheses indicate the number of people reporting a single ancestry; * Numbers in parentheses indicate the number of persons reporting this race alone, not in combination with any other race; Please refer to the Explanation of Data for more information.*

English (52)	287	2.66
French, ex. Basque (42)	42	0.39
German (87)	193	1.79
Irish (199)	279	2.58
Italian (29)	47	0.44
Polish (32)	32	0.30
Scotch-Irish (66)	134	1.24
Scottish (0)	15	0.14
West Indian, ex. Hispanic (16)	16	0.15
U.S. Virgin Islander (16)	16	0.15

Hispanic Origin	Population	%
Hispanic or Latino (of any race)	8,860	81.38
Central American, ex. Mexican	255	2.34
Costa Rican	7	0.06
Guatemalan	14	0.13
Honduran	51	0.47
Nicaraguan	6	0.06
Salvadoran	177	1.63
Cuban	5	0.05
Dominican Republic	5	0.05
Mexican	8,161	74.96
Puerto Rican	22	0.20
South American	30	0.28
Argentinean	1	0.01
Chilean	2	0.02
Colombian	8	0.07
Ecuadorian	1	0.01
Peruvian	17	0.16
Venezuelan	1	0.01
Other Hispanic or Latino	382	3.51

Race*	Population	%
African-American/Black (745)	764	7.02
Not Hispanic (719)	730	6.71
Hispanic (26)	34	0.31
American Indian/Alaska Native (86)	128	1.18
Not Hispanic (13)	22	0.20
Hispanic (73)	106	0.97
Cherokee (1)	2	0.02
Chickasaw (2)	2	0.02
Choctaw (1)	1	0.01
Mexican American Ind. (22)	23	0.21
South American Ind. (5)	5	0.05
Spanish American Ind. (1)	1	0.01
Yaqui (2)	2	0.02
Yuman (1)	5	0.05
Asian (11)	21	0.19
Not Hispanic (10)	15	0.14
Hispanic (1)	6	0.06
Cambodian (2)	2	0.02
Chinese, ex. Taiwanese (2)	5	0.05
Filipino (2)	5	0.05
Indian (1)	1	0.01
Korean (2)	2	0.02
Hawaii Native/Pacific Islander (1)	12	0.11
Not Hispanic (1)	4	0.04
Hispanic (0)	8	0.07
Fijian (0)	3	0.03
Guamanian/Chamorro (0)	2	0.02
Native Hawaiian (1)	1	0.01
White (6,946)	7,265	66.73
Not Hispanic (1,240)	1,259	11.56
Hispanic (5,706)	6,006	55.17

Galveston

Place Type: City
County: Galveston
Population: 47,743†

Ancestry‡	Population	%
African, Sub-Saharan (299)	373	0.75
African (247)	321	0.64
Ethiopian (13)	13	0.03
Nigerian (27)	27	0.05
South African (12)	12	0.02
Alsatian (10)	10	0.02
American (2,202)	2,202	4.40
Arab (84)	84	0.17
Arab (6)	6	0.01
Egyptian (63)	63	0.13
Palestinian (15)	15	0.03
Armenian (0)	19	0.04
Australian (13)	38	0.08
Austrian (26)	288	0.58
British (127)	308	0.62
Cajun (28)	163	0.33
Canadian (9)	40	0.08
Croatian (33)	33	0.07
Czech (148)	361	0.72
Czechoslovakian (9)	71	0.14
Danish (28)	71	0.14
Dutch (82)	583	1.17
Eastern European (96)	96	0.19
English (1,115)	3,305	6.61
European (371)	416	0.83
Finnish (0)	10	0.02
French, ex. Basque (224)	1,442	2.88
French Canadian (142)	219	0.44
German (2,009)	5,639	11.28
Greek (65)	107	0.21
Guyanese (10)	10	0.02
Hungarian (67)	76	0.15
Iranian (79)	79	0.16
Irish (1,303)	5,213	10.43
Italian (773)	1,972	3.94
Latvian (0)	9	0.02
Lithuanian (23)	66	0.13
Northern European (55)	70	0.14
Norwegian (122)	331	0.66
Polish (176)	906	1.81
Portuguese (75)	114	0.23
Romanian (23)	35	0.07
Russian (142)	427	0.85
Scandinavian (0)	58	0.12
Scotch-Irish (426)	827	1.65
Scottish (249)	660	1.32
Slavic (12)	41	0.08
Slovene (12)	12	0.02
Swedish (209)	489	0.98
Swiss (42)	122	0.24
Ukrainian (48)	68	0.14
Welsh (98)	364	0.73
West Indian, ex. Hispanic (132)	150	0.30
Dutch West Indian (11)	21	0.04
Haitian (39)	39	0.08
Jamaican (21)	21	0.04
Trinidadian/Tobagonian (61)	69	0.14
Yugoslavian (11)	11	0.02

Hispanic Origin	Population	%
Hispanic or Latino (of any race)	14,925	31.26
Central American, ex. Mexican	1,599	3.35
Costa Rican	30	0.06
Guatemalan	271	0.57
Honduran	438	0.92
Nicaraguan	47	0.10
Panamanian	25	0.05
Salvadoran	780	1.63
Other Central American	8	0.02
Cuban	101	0.21
Dominican Republic	13	0.03
Mexican	11,605	24.31
Puerto Rican	198	0.41
South American	240	0.50
Argentinean	20	0.04
Bolivian	10	0.02
Chilean	39	0.08
Colombian	68	0.14
Ecuadorian	14	0.03
Paraguayan	1	<0.01
Peruvian	62	0.13
Uruguayan	2	<0.01
Venezuelan	23	0.05
Other South American	1	<0.01
Other Hispanic or Latino	1,169	2.45

Race*	Population	%
African-American/Black (9,145)	9,543	19.99
Not Hispanic (8,895)	9,149	19.16
Hispanic (250)	394	0.83
American Indian/Alaska Native (410)	777	1.63
Not Hispanic (205)	462	0.97
Hispanic (205)	315	0.66
Aleut *(Alaska Native)* (1)	1	<0.01
Apache (14)	25	0.05
Blackfeet (3)	6	0.01
Canadian/French Am. Ind. (1)	3	0.01
Central American Ind. (4)	6	0.01
Cherokee (33)	131	0.27
Cheyenne (0)	1	<0.01
Chickasaw (6)	10	0.02
Chippewa (1)	2	<0.01
Choctaw (17)	47	0.10
Comanche (0)	2	<0.01
Creek (7)	7	0.01
Delaware (0)	2	<0.01
Hopi (1)	1	<0.01
Inupiat *(Alaska Native)* (0)	2	<0.01
Iroquois (2)	3	0.01
Mexican American Ind. (20)	39	0.08
Navajo (2)	2	<0.01
Osage (2)	9	0.02
Ottawa (1)	1	<0.01
Paiute (5)	7	0.01
Potawatomi (0)	1	<0.01
Pueblo (9)	9	0.02
Seminole (1)	1	<0.01
Shoshone (1)	1	<0.01
Sioux (6)	9	0.02
South American Ind. (1)	5	0.01
Spanish American Ind. (3)	4	0.01
Tlingit-Haida *(Alaska Native)* (0)	1	<0.01
Ute (1)	1	<0.01
Yuman (1)	1	<0.01
Asian (1,512)	1,744	3.65
Not Hispanic (1,479)	1,655	3.47
Hispanic (33)	89	0.19
Bangladeshi (4)	7	0.01
Burmese (1)	3	0.01
Cambodian (13)	13	0.03
Chinese, ex. Taiwanese (343)	378	0.79
Filipino (315)	393	0.82
Hmong (1)	3	0.01
Indian (402)	438	0.92
Indonesian (4)	5	0.01
Japanese (57)	83	0.17
Korean (69)	94	0.20
Laotian (2)	3	0.01
Malaysian (1)	1	<0.01
Pakistani (39)	47	0.10
Sri Lankan (11)	11	0.02
Taiwanese (17)	17	0.04
Thai (22)	26	0.05
Vietnamese (164)	182	0.38
Hawaii Native/Pacific Islander (23)	76	0.16
Not Hispanic (23)	53	0.11
Hispanic (0)	23	0.05
Fijian (1)	1	<0.01
Guamanian/Chamorro (7)	14	0.03
Native Hawaiian (6)	33	0.07
Samoan (1)	1	<0.01
White (29,835)	31,194	65.34
Not Hispanic (21,500)	22,091	46.27
Hispanic (8,335)	9,103	19.07

Garland

Place Type: City
County: Dallas
Population: 226,876†

Ancestry‡	Population	%
Afghan (114)	114	0.05
African, Sub-Saharan (3,458)	4,107	1.84
African (1,193)	1,408	0.63
Ethiopian (863)	863	0.39
Kenyan (35)	35	0.02
Liberian (65)	65	0.03

*Notes: † The Census 2010 population figure is used to calculate the percentages in the Hispanic Origin and Race categories. Ancestry percentages are based on the 2006-2010 American Community Survey population (not shown); ‡ Numbers in parentheses indicate the number of people reporting a single ancestry; * Numbers in parentheses indicate the number of persons reporting this race alone, not in combination with any other race; Please refer to the Explanation of Data for more information.*

Nigerian (939)	1,291	0.58
Sierra Leonean (97)	97	0.04
South African (0)	45	0.02
Sudanese (7)	26	0.01
Ugandan (63)	63	0.03
Zimbabwean (79)	79	0.04
Other Sub-Saharan African (117)	135	0.06
Albanian (30)	30	0.01
Alsatian (0)	29	0.01
American (8,029)	8,029	3.60
Arab (618)	1,307	0.59
Arab (125)	280	0.13
Egyptian (80)	95	0.04
Iraqi (53)	53	0.02
Jordanian (16)	87	0.04
Lebanese (123)	471	0.21
Moroccan (14)	25	0.01
Palestinian (61)	61	0.03
Syrian (53)	91	0.04
Other Arab (93)	144	0.06
Armenian (36)	36	0.02
Australian (0)	39	0.02
Austrian (78)	174	0.08
Belgian (34)	34	0.02
Brazilian (45)	87	0.04
British (205)	491	0.22
Bulgarian (0)	52	0.02
Cajun (37)	103	0.05
Canadian (61)	177	0.08
Celtic (27)	27	0.01
Croatian (0)	11	<0.01
Czech (379)	1,038	0.47
Czechoslovakian (119)	182	0.08
Danish (249)	467	0.21
Dutch (341)	2,101	0.94
Eastern European (166)	166	0.07
English (5,835)	14,518	6.51
Estonian (11)	11	<0.01
European (1,156)	1,378	0.62
Finnish (30)	100	0.04
French, ex. Basque (942)	5,340	2.40
French Canadian (162)	427	0.19
German (5,131)	18,498	8.30
Greek (213)	440	0.20
Hungarian (124)	458	0.21
Iranian (125)	125	0.06
Irish (4,212)	15,483	6.94
Italian (1,018)	3,986	1.79
Lithuanian (23)	49	0.02
Macedonian (16)	16	0.01
Northern European (98)	98	0.04
Norwegian (349)	1,116	0.50
Pennsylvania German (62)	73	0.03
Polish (765)	1,947	0.87
Portuguese (129)	506	0.23
Romanian (83)	104	0.05
Russian (147)	538	0.24
Scandinavian (65)	190	0.09
Scotch-Irish (1,570)	3,317	1.49
Scottish (889)	2,498	1.12
Serbian (8)	8	<0.01
Slavic (0)	41	0.02
Slovak (13)	34	0.02
Slovene (0)	15	0.01
Swedish (320)	1,359	0.61
Swiss (147)	336	0.15
Turkish (36)	55	0.02
Ukrainian (75)	244	0.11
Welsh (199)	780	0.35
West Indian, ex. Hispanic (444)	1,100	0.49
Belizean (10)	30	0.01
British West Indian (47)	196	0.09
Dutch West Indian (25)	121	0.05
Haitian (13)	26	0.01
Jamaican (251)	445	0.20
Trinidadian/Tobagonian (43)	163	0.07
West Indian (55)	119	0.05
Yugoslavian (159)	276	0.12

Hispanic Origin	Population	%
Hispanic or Latino (of any race)	85,784	37.81
Central American, ex. Mexican	7,792	3.43
Costa Rican	134	0.06
Guatemalan	1,656	0.73
Honduran	1,058	0.47
Nicaraguan	151	0.07
Panamanian	113	0.05
Salvadoran	4,627	2.04
Other Central American	53	0.02
Cuban	399	0.18
Dominican Republic	105	0.05
Mexican	70,016	30.86
Puerto Rican	912	0.40
South American	1,580	0.70
Argentinean	128	0.06
Bolivian	77	0.03
Chilean	43	0.02
Colombian	576	0.25
Ecuadorian	146	0.06
Paraguayan	3	<0.01
Peruvian	493	0.22
Uruguayan	29	0.01
Venezuelan	76	0.03
Other South American	9	<0.01
Other Hispanic or Latino	4,980	2.20

Race*	Population	%
African-American/Black (32,980)	35,068	15.46
Not Hispanic (32,164)	33,685	14.85
Hispanic (816)	1,383	0.61
American Indian/Alaska Native (1,851)	3,288	1.45
Not Hispanic (789)	1,738	0.77
Hispanic (1,062)	1,550	0.68
Alaska Athabascan *(Ala. Nat.)* (3)	6	<0.01
Apache (27)	60	0.03
Blackfeet (9)	51	0.02
Canadian/French Am. Ind. (2)	6	<0.01
Central American Ind. (8)	9	<0.01
Cherokee (168)	475	0.21
Cheyenne (8)	12	0.01
Chickasaw (43)	90	0.04
Chippewa (6)	22	0.01
Choctaw (182)	293	0.13
Comanche (18)	29	0.01
Cree (0)	1	<0.01
Creek (32)	51	0.02
Crow (0)	5	<0.01
Delaware (8)	9	<0.01
Hopi (1)	5	<0.01
Inupiat *(Alaska Native)* (6)	6	<0.01
Iroquois (5)	7	<0.01
Kiowa (4)	6	<0.01
Lumbee (1)	3	<0.01
Menominee (2)	2	<0.01
Mexican American Ind. (143)	187	0.08
Navajo (33)	44	0.02
Osage (4)	13	0.01
Ottawa (3)	6	<0.01
Paiute (1)	1	<0.01
Potawatomi (15)	23	0.01
Pueblo (12)	13	0.01
Puget Sound Salish (1)	1	<0.01
Seminole (6)	21	0.01
Shoshone (0)	1	<0.01
Sioux (16)	24	0.01
South American Ind. (6)	16	0.01
Spanish American Ind. (21)	24	0.01
Tohono O'Odham (5)	7	<0.01
Yaqui (3)	4	<0.01
Yup'ik *(Alaska Native)* (1)	3	<0.01
Asian (21,352)	23,007	10.14
Not Hispanic (21,162)	22,492	9.91
Hispanic (190)	515	0.23
Bangladeshi (124)	138	0.06
Burmese (39)	44	0.02
Cambodian (533)	615	0.27
Chinese, ex. Taiwanese (1,606)	2,002	0.88
Filipino (1,678)	1,996	0.88
Hmong (5)	6	<0.01
Indian (3,985)	4,358	1.92
Indonesian (12)	19	0.01
Japanese (94)	224	0.10
Korean (823)	948	0.42
Laotian (622)	691	0.30
Malaysian (5)	9	<0.01
Nepalese (10)	10	<0.01
Pakistani (512)	572	0.25
Sri Lankan (13)	21	0.01
Taiwanese (96)	115	0.05
Thai (154)	196	0.09
Vietnamese (10,373)	10,877	4.79
Hawaii Native/Pacific Islander (93)	422	0.19
Not Hispanic (65)	228	0.10
Hispanic (28)	194	0.09
Fijian (0)	6	<0.01
Guamanian/Chamorro (27)	72	0.03
Native Hawaiian (38)	114	0.05
Samoan (11)	31	0.01
Tongan (0)	2	<0.01
White (130,368)	136,442	60.14
Not Hispanic (83,259)	85,855	37.84
Hispanic (47,109)	50,587	22.30

Gatesville

Place Type: City
County: Coryell
Population: 15,751†

Ancestry‡	Population	%
African, Sub-Saharan (104)	104	0.67
African (104)	104	0.67
American (1,038)	1,038	6.68
Arab (27)	32	0.21
Lebanese (0)	5	0.03
Moroccan (27)	27	0.17
Austrian (0)	7	0.05
British (19)	31	0.20
Canadian (10)	10	0.06
Celtic (1)	1	0.01
Czech (88)	235	1.51
Czechoslovakian (0)	14	0.09
Danish (11)	196	1.26
Dutch (1)	80	0.51
English (1,146)	1,714	11.03
European (116)	166	1.07
French, ex. Basque (22)	390	2.51
French Canadian (10)	103	0.66
German (679)	2,050	13.19
Greek (1)	1	0.01
Hungarian (1)	3	0.02
Irish (522)	1,776	11.43
Italian (91)	298	1.92
Norwegian (53)	100	0.64
Polish (126)	234	1.51
Portuguese (3)	4	0.03
Russian (0)	107	0.69
Scandinavian (74)	74	0.48
Scotch-Irish (109)	344	2.21
Scottish (212)	446	2.87
Serbian (32)	32	0.21
Swedish (21)	154	0.99
Swiss (0)	1	0.01
Welsh (10)	88	0.57
West Indian, ex. Hispanic (75)	85	0.55
Dutch West Indian (0)	10	0.06
Jamaican (75)	75	0.48

Hispanic Origin	Population	%
Hispanic or Latino (of any race)	2,699	17.14
Central American, ex. Mexican	33	0.21
Costa Rican	1	0.01
Guatemalan	6	0.04
Honduran	7	0.04
Nicaraguan	1	0.01
Salvadoran	14	0.09
Other Central American	4	0.03
Cuban	17	0.11
Dominican Republic	2	0.01

*Notes: † The Census 2010 population figure is used to calculate the percentages in the Hispanic Origin and Race categories. Ancestry percentages are based on the 2006-2010 American Community Survey population (not shown); ‡ Numbers in parentheses indicate the number of people reporting a single ancestry; * Numbers in parentheses indicate the number of persons reporting this race alone, not in combination with any other race; Please refer to the Explanation of Data for more information.*

Mexican	2,275	14.44
Puerto Rican	42	0.27
South American	3	0.02
Colombian	2	0.01
Venezuelan	1	0.01
Other Hispanic or Latino	327	2.08

Race*	Population	%
African-American/Black (3,155)	3,232	20.52
Not Hispanic (3,127)	3,189	20.25
Hispanic (28)	43	0.27
American Indian/Alaska Native (83)	170	1.08
Not Hispanic (46)	111	0.70
Hispanic (37)	59	0.37
Aleut *(Alaska Native)* (0)	1	0.01
Apache (5)	7	0.04
Arapaho (1)	3	0.02
Central American Ind. (2)	2	0.01
Cherokee (10)	37	0.23
Chickasaw (1)	2	0.01
Chippewa (0)	1	0.01
Choctaw (4)	14	0.09
Comanche (0)	1	0.01
Creek (2)	2	0.01
Hopi (5)	5	0.03
Iroquois (0)	2	0.01
Mexican American Ind. (1)	1	0.01
Sioux (0)	1	0.01
South American Ind. (0)	2	0.01
Spanish American Ind. (1)	5	0.03
Asian (79)	107	0.68
Not Hispanic (76)	100	0.63
Hispanic (3)	7	0.04
Cambodian (12)	12	0.08
Chinese, ex. Taiwanese (6)	6	0.04
Filipino (7)	19	0.12
Indian (10)	11	0.07
Japanese (3)	6	0.04
Korean (9)	12	0.08
Thai (1)	5	0.03
Vietnamese (9)	15	0.10
Hawaii Native/Pacific Islander (4)	5	0.03
Not Hispanic (1)	1	0.01
Hispanic (3)	4	0.03
Guamanian/Chamorro (2)	2	0.01
Native Hawaiian (2)	2	0.01
Samoan (0)	1	0.01
White (11,149)	11,383	72.27
Not Hispanic (9,578)	9,713	61.67
Hispanic (1,571)	1,670	10.60

Georgetown

Place Type: City
County: Williamson
Population: 47,400†

Ancestry‡	Population	%
African, Sub-Saharan (28)	37	0.08
African (20)	29	0.07
Nigerian (8)	8	0.02
American (2,231)	2,231	5.06
Arab (36)	112	0.25
Arab (16)	46	0.10
Lebanese (20)	66	0.15
Armenian (10)	10	0.02
Austrian (0)	48	0.11
Basque (0)	12	0.03
Belgian (29)	29	0.07
Brazilian (19)	40	0.09
British (180)	302	0.68
Cajun (0)	37	0.08
Canadian (5)	75	0.17
Croatian (36)	45	0.10
Czech (275)	723	1.64
Czechoslovakian (66)	135	0.31
Danish (119)	326	0.74
Dutch (218)	675	1.53
Eastern European (0)	9	0.02
English (2,586)	6,356	14.41
European (588)	741	1.68
Finnish (43)	79	0.18
French, ex. Basque (273)	1,330	3.02
French Canadian (170)	198	0.45
German (3,201)	9,336	21.17
Greek (26)	50	0.11
Hungarian (82)	134	0.30
Iranian (22)	22	0.05
Irish (1,577)	5,177	11.74
Italian (373)	1,142	2.59
Lithuanian (0)	14	0.03
Northern European (52)	52	0.12
Norwegian (207)	530	1.20
Pennsylvania German (0)	16	0.04
Polish (134)	616	1.40
Portuguese (43)	162	0.37
Romanian (23)	32	0.07
Russian (37)	130	0.29
Scandinavian (0)	114	0.26
Scotch-Irish (497)	1,159	2.63
Scottish (506)	1,580	3.58
Serbian (0)	33	0.07
Slavic (17)	17	0.04
Slovak (23)	23	0.05
Swedish (307)	837	1.90
Swiss (43)	126	0.29
Turkish (11)	11	0.02
Ukrainian (24)	63	0.14
Welsh (111)	502	1.14
West Indian, ex. Hispanic (31)	38	0.09
Jamaican (28)	35	0.08
Trinidadian/Tobagonian (3)	3	0.01

Hispanic Origin	Population	%
Hispanic or Latino (of any race)	10,317	21.77
Central American, ex. Mexican	192	0.41
Costa Rican	5	0.01
Guatemalan	54	0.11
Honduran	50	0.11
Nicaraguan	27	0.06
Panamanian	19	0.04
Salvadoran	37	0.08
Cuban	42	0.09
Dominican Republic	21	0.04
Mexican	8,798	18.56
Puerto Rican	295	0.62
South American	185	0.39
Argentinean	10	0.02
Bolivian	13	0.03
Chilean	9	0.02
Colombian	74	0.16
Ecuadorian	9	0.02
Peruvian	32	0.07
Uruguayan	4	0.01
Venezuelan	31	0.07
Other South American	3	0.01
Other Hispanic or Latino	784	1.65

Race*	Population	%
African-American/Black (1,746)	2,068	4.36
Not Hispanic (1,620)	1,831	3.86
Hispanic (126)	237	0.50
American Indian/Alaska Native (270)	576	1.22
Not Hispanic (135)	345	0.73
Hispanic (135)	231	0.49
Aleut *(Alaska Native)* (1)	4	0.01
Apache (8)	17	0.04
Blackfeet (3)	15	0.03
Central American Ind. (0)	1	<0.01
Cherokee (41)	115	0.24
Cheyenne (0)	6	0.01
Chickasaw (6)	15	0.03
Chippewa (3)	4	0.01
Choctaw (21)	47	0.10
Comanche (4)	12	0.03
Creek (2)	9	0.02
Delaware (3)	3	0.01
Inupiat *(Alaska Native)* (1)	1	<0.01
Iroquois (3)	3	0.01
Kiowa (1)	1	<0.01
Mexican American Ind. (22)	31	0.07
Navajo (1)	5	0.01
Potawatomi (5)	15	0.03
Seminole (3)	7	0.01
Sioux (7)	11	0.02
South American Ind. (8)	19	0.04
Spanish American Ind. (5)	6	0.01
Asian (488)	726	1.53
Not Hispanic (481)	662	1.40
Hispanic (7)	64	0.14
Bangladeshi (1)	3	0.01
Cambodian (18)	23	0.05
Chinese, ex. Taiwanese (94)	143	0.30
Filipino (77)	143	0.30
Hmong (6)	6	0.01
Indian (81)	105	0.22
Indonesian (1)	7	0.01
Japanese (25)	68	0.14
Korean (56)	88	0.19
Laotian (0)	1	<0.01
Malaysian (4)	5	0.01
Nepalese (1)	1	<0.01
Pakistani (31)	45	0.09
Sri Lankan (9)	9	0.02
Taiwanese (1)	1	<0.01
Thai (6)	8	0.02
Vietnamese (30)	47	0.10
Hawaii Native/Pacific Islander (40)	86	0.18
Not Hispanic (37)	64	0.14
Hispanic (3)	22	0.05
Fijian (0)	2	<0.01
Guamanian/Chamorro (13)	18	0.04
Native Hawaiian (13)	27	0.06
Samoan (2)	5	0.01
White (40,866)	41,793	88.17
Not Hispanic (34,188)	34,731	73.27
Hispanic (6,678)	7,062	14.90

Glenn Heights

Place Type: City
County: Dallas
Population: 11,278†

Ancestry‡	Population	%
African, Sub-Saharan (143)	232	2.21
African (106)	195	1.86
Nigerian (37)	37	0.35
American (410)	410	3.91
Arab (48)	82	0.78
Arab (0)	17	0.16
Palestinian (29)	29	0.28
Syrian (19)	36	0.34
Austrian (0)	13	0.12
Cajun (16)	16	0.15
Croatian (0)	10	0.10
Dutch (11)	69	0.66
English (191)	579	5.52
European (24)	24	0.23
French, ex. Basque (15)	43	0.41
German (122)	425	4.05
Hungarian (9)	25	0.24
Irish (227)	558	5.32
Italian (41)	82	0.78
Polish (13)	13	0.12
Russian (0)	23	0.22
Scotch-Irish (23)	63	0.60
Scottish (46)	109	1.04
Slovak (22)	22	0.21
Swiss (0)	13	0.12
Welsh (0)	12	0.11

Hispanic Origin	Population	%
Hispanic or Latino (of any race)	2,502	22.18
Central American, ex. Mexican	89	0.79
Guatemalan	11	0.10
Honduran	12	0.11
Nicaraguan	19	0.17
Panamanian	6	0.05
Salvadoran	41	0.36

*Notes: † The Census 2010 population figure is used to calculate the percentages in the Hispanic Origin and Race categories. Ancestry percentages are based on the 2006-2010 American Community Survey population (not shown); ‡ Numbers in parentheses indicate the number of people reporting a single ancestry; * Numbers in parentheses indicate the number of persons reporting this race alone, not in combination with any other race; Please refer to the Explanation of Data for more information.*

Cuban	11	0.10
Dominican Republic	6	0.05
Mexican	2,156	19.12
Puerto Rican	60	0.53
South American	27	0.24
Colombian	19	0.17
Ecuadorian	3	0.03
Peruvian	5	0.04
Other Hispanic or Latino	153	1.36

Race*	Population	%
African-American/Black (5,644)	5,824	51.64
Not Hispanic (5,598)	5,735	50.85
Hispanic (46)	89	0.79
American Indian/Alaska Native (71)	171	1.52
Not Hispanic (53)	139	1.23
Hispanic (18)	32	0.28
Apache (1)	2	0.02
Blackfeet (1)	1	0.01
Central American Ind. (0)	1	0.01
Cherokee (10)	24	0.21
Choctaw (13)	23	0.20
Comanche (1)	1	0.01
Creek (4)	8	0.07
Navajo (2)	10	0.09
Potawatomi (4)	4	0.04
Pueblo (4)	6	0.05
Seminole (0)	1	0.01
Asian (68)	100	0.89
Not Hispanic (64)	93	0.82
Hispanic (4)	7	0.06
Chinese, ex. Taiwanese (0)	1	0.01
Filipino (23)	31	0.27
Indian (11)	19	0.17
Indonesian (1)	1	0.01
Japanese (1)	3	0.03
Korean (13)	18	0.16
Nepalese (8)	8	0.07
Taiwanese (1)	1	0.01
Vietnamese (10)	10	0.09
Hawaii Native/Pacific Islander (4)	8	0.07
Not Hispanic (4)	8	0.07
Guamanian/Chamorro (3)	3	0.03
Native Hawaiian (1)	1	0.01
Samoan (0)	4	0.04
White (4,107)	4,340	38.48
Not Hispanic (2,844)	3,008	26.67
Hispanic (1,263)	1,332	11.81

Graham

Place Type: City
County: Young
Population: 8,903†

Ancestry‡	Population	%
American (966)	966	10.96
Belgian (0)	11	0.12
British (17)	17	0.19
Canadian (12)	12	0.14
Czech (117)	137	1.55
Dutch (9)	180	2.04
English (485)	907	10.29
French, ex. Basque (26)	202	2.29
French Canadian (0)	39	0.44
German (158)	1,107	12.56
Hungarian (0)	24	0.27
Irish (241)	1,174	13.32
Italian (35)	47	0.53
Polish (28)	28	0.32
Scandinavian (12)	12	0.14
Scotch-Irish (86)	97	1.10
Scottish (92)	133	1.51
Slovak (0)	26	0.29
Swedish (6)	19	0.22
Swiss (0)	42	0.48
Welsh (11)	180	2.04

Hispanic Origin	Population	%
Hispanic or Latino (of any race)	1,821	20.45
Central American, ex. Mexican	23	0.26
Guatemalan	16	0.18
Honduran	2	0.02
Nicaraguan	4	0.04
Panamanian	1	0.01
Cuban	1	0.01
Mexican	1,641	18.43
Puerto Rican	6	0.07
South American	7	0.08
Argentinean	1	0.01
Colombian	1	0.01
Peruvian	5	0.06
Other Hispanic or Latino	143	1.61

Race*	Population	%
African-American/Black (107)	151	1.70
Not Hispanic (97)	128	1.44
Hispanic (10)	23	0.26
American Indian/Alaska Native (82)	121	1.36
Not Hispanic (44)	75	0.84
Hispanic (38)	46	0.52
Central American Ind. (4)	4	0.04
Cherokee (27)	39	0.44
Chickasaw (0)	1	0.01
Chippewa (1)	1	0.01
Choctaw (2)	9	0.10
Comanche (6)	10	0.11
Crow (1)	1	0.01
Inupiat *(Alaska Native)* (2)	2	0.02
Iroquois (1)	1	0.01
Kiowa (0)	1	0.01
Mexican American Ind. (1)	5	0.06
Navajo (2)	2	0.02
Potawatomi (0)	1	0.01
Asian (46)	71	0.80
Not Hispanic (36)	53	0.60
Hispanic (10)	18	0.20
Chinese, ex. Taiwanese (15)	21	0.24
Filipino (5)	17	0.19
Indian (7)	7	0.08
Japanese (1)	7	0.08
Korean (4)	12	0.13
Pakistani (0)	2	0.02
Thai (1)	1	0.01
Vietnamese (10)	12	0.13
Hawaii Native/Pacific Islander (4)	15	0.17
Not Hispanic (4)	8	0.09
Hispanic (0)	7	0.08
Native Hawaiian (0)	7	0.08
Samoan (4)	4	0.04
White (7,849)	7,999	89.85
Not Hispanic (6,819)	6,890	77.39
Hispanic (1,030)	1,109	12.46

Granbury

Place Type: City
County: Hood
Population: 7,978†

Ancestry‡	Population	%
American (590)	590	7.61
Austrian (25)	25	0.32
Canadian (6)	6	0.08
Czech (26)	45	0.58
Danish (33)	33	0.43
Dutch (43)	210	2.71
English (337)	725	9.35
European (94)	114	1.47
French, ex. Basque (12)	276	3.56
German (633)	1,075	13.86
Greek (30)	30	0.39
Hungarian (0)	19	0.24
Iranian (10)	10	0.13
Irish (379)	1,106	14.26
Italian (27)	254	3.27
Lithuanian (0)	8	0.10
Norwegian (48)	116	1.50
Scotch-Irish (144)	245	3.16
Scottish (25)	259	3.34
Swedish (19)	58	0.75
Welsh (19)	116	1.50

Hispanic Origin	Population	%
Hispanic or Latino (of any race)	684	8.57
Central American, ex. Mexican	2	0.03
Salvadoran	2	0.03
Cuban	9	0.11
Mexican	582	7.30
Puerto Rican	25	0.31
South American	13	0.16
Colombian	3	0.04
Ecuadorian	1	0.01
Peruvian	3	0.04
Venezuelan	6	0.08
Other Hispanic or Latino	53	0.66

Race*	Population	%
African-American/Black (57)	79	0.99
Not Hispanic (53)	70	0.88
Hispanic (4)	9	0.11
American Indian/Alaska Native (57)	104	1.30
Not Hispanic (46)	89	1.12
Hispanic (11)	15	0.19
Apache (3)	5	0.06
Cherokee (11)	18	0.23
Cheyenne (0)	1	0.01
Chickasaw (2)	4	0.05
Choctaw (8)	13	0.16
Comanche (2)	3	0.04
Creek (2)	4	0.05
Iroquois (0)	2	0.03
Mexican American Ind. (3)	3	0.04
Navajo (1)	5	0.06
Seminole (1)	1	0.01
Sioux (4)	12	0.15
South American Ind. (1)	1	0.01
Asian (90)	101	1.27
Not Hispanic (90)	99	1.24
Hispanic (0)	2	0.03
Chinese, ex. Taiwanese (1)	3	0.04
Filipino (9)	12	0.15
Indian (31)	33	0.41
Japanese (7)	13	0.16
Korean (20)	21	0.26
Pakistani (6)	6	0.08
Sri Lankan (1)	1	0.01
Taiwanese (4)	4	0.05
Thai (3)	4	0.05
Vietnamese (5)	5	0.06
Hawaii Native/Pacific Islander (1)	3	0.04
Not Hispanic (1)	3	0.04
Native Hawaiian (0)	2	0.03
Tongan (1)	1	0.01
White (7,479)	7,601	95.27
Not Hispanic (7,030)	7,100	88.99
Hispanic (449)	501	6.28

Grand Prairie

Place Type: City
County: Dallas
Population: 175,396†

Ancestry‡	Population	%
Afghan (27)	27	0.02
African, Sub-Saharan (3,407)	3,688	2.22
African (1,191)	1,257	0.76
Cape Verdean (13)	29	0.02
Ghanaian (201)	201	0.12
Kenyan (351)	400	0.24
Liberian (0)	11	0.01
Nigerian (1,459)	1,571	0.95
Other Sub-Saharan African (192)	219	0.13
American (7,642)	7,642	4.61
Arab (550)	605	0.36
Arab (171)	201	0.12
Egyptian (20)	20	0.01
Jordanian (147)	147	0.09
Lebanese (121)	146	0.09

SECTION TWO

*Notes: † The Census 2010 population figure is used to calculate the percentages in the Hispanic Origin and Race categories. Ancestry percentages are based on the 2006-2010 American Community Survey population (not shown); ‡ Numbers in parentheses indicate the number of people reporting a single ancestry; * Numbers in parentheses indicate the number of persons reporting this race alone, not in combination with any other race; Please refer to the Explanation of Data for more information.*

Palestinian (34)	34	0.02
Syrian (33)	33	0.02
Other Arab (24)	24	0.01
Armenian (0)	40	0.02
Australian (20)	31	0.02
Austrian (20)	203	0.12
Belgian (54)	156	0.09
Brazilian (93)	108	0.07
British (100)	231	0.14
Cajun (39)	68	0.04
Canadian (54)	112	0.07
Czech (196)	532	0.32
Czechoslovakian (40)	56	0.03
Danish (25)	178	0.11
Dutch (154)	990	0.60
Eastern European (36)	36	0.02
English (3,766)	8,014	4.83
European (742)	969	0.58
Finnish (14)	71	0.04
French, ex. Basque (672)	2,872	1.73
French Canadian (46)	241	0.15
German (3,440)	11,199	6.76
Greek (33)	182	0.11
Hungarian (39)	104	0.06
Iranian (88)	150	0.09
Irish (3,093)	9,280	5.60
Israeli (0)	13	0.01
Italian (852)	2,652	1.60
Lithuanian (28)	70	0.04
Northern European (63)	63	0.04
Norwegian (215)	764	0.46
Pennsylvania German (11)	11	0.01
Polish (339)	1,283	0.77
Portuguese (109)	236	0.14
Romanian (11)	11	0.01
Russian (51)	117	0.07
Scandinavian (29)	82	0.05
Scotch-Irish (492)	1,276	0.77
Scottish (671)	1,738	1.05
Slavic (11)	20	0.01
Slovak (0)	11	0.01
Slovene (10)	30	0.02
Swedish (232)	672	0.41
Swiss (19)	117	0.07
Ukrainian (0)	67	0.04
Welsh (71)	334	0.20
West Indian, ex. Hispanic (327)	597	0.36
Belizean (45)	56	0.03
British West Indian (9)	9	0.01
Dutch West Indian (11)	142	0.09
Haitian (92)	92	0.06
Jamaican (96)	197	0.12
Trinidadian/Tobagonian (15)	15	0.01
West Indian (51)	78	0.05
Other West Indian (8)	8	<0.01

Hispanic Origin	Population	%
Hispanic or Latino (of any race)	74,893	42.70
Central American, ex. Mexican	4,345	2.48
Costa Rican	65	0.04
Guatemalan	377	0.21
Honduran	484	0.28
Nicaraguan	242	0.14
Panamanian	113	0.06
Salvadoran	3,043	1.73
Other Central American	21	0.01
Cuban	300	0.17
Dominican Republic	128	0.07
Mexican	63,100	35.98
Puerto Rican	1,500	0.86
South American	919	0.52
Argentinean	196	0.11
Bolivian	5	<0.01
Chilean	32	0.02
Colombian	300	0.17
Ecuadorian	117	0.07
Paraguayan	1	<0.01
Peruvian	177	0.10
Uruguayan	11	0.01
Venezuelan	70	0.04
Other South American	10	0.01
Other Hispanic or Latino	4,601	2.62

Race*	Population	%
African-American/Black (35,390)	37,433	21.34
Not Hispanic (34,436)	35,887	20.46
Hispanic (954)	1,546	0.88
American Indian/Alaska Native (1,483)	2,521	1.44
Not Hispanic (709)	1,372	0.78
Hispanic (774)	1,149	0.66
Alaska Athabascan *(Ala. Nat.)* (1)	1	<0.01
Apache (55)	96	0.05
Arapaho (1)	3	<0.01
Blackfeet (3)	17	0.01
Canadian/French Am. Ind. (0)	2	<0.01
Central American Ind. (0)	4	<0.01
Cherokee (99)	305	0.17
Cheyenne (5)	8	<0.01
Chickasaw (30)	43	0.02
Chippewa (7)	12	0.01
Choctaw (132)	215	0.12
Colville (0)	3	<0.01
Comanche (23)	38	0.02
Cree (1)	2	<0.01
Creek (26)	47	0.03
Hopi (0)	4	<0.01
Houma (2)	3	<0.01
Inupiat *(Alaska Native)* (1)	2	<0.01
Iroquois (5)	25	0.01
Kiowa (20)	38	0.02
Lumbee (5)	7	<0.01
Menominee (1)	1	<0.01
Mexican American Ind. (109)	149	0.08
Navajo (42)	64	0.04
Osage (3)	4	<0.01
Ottawa (1)	1	<0.01
Potawatomi (7)	13	0.01
Pueblo (6)	11	0.01
Puget Sound Salish (0)	6	<0.01
Seminole (2)	12	0.01
Shoshone (6)	7	<0.01
Sioux (30)	41	0.02
South American Ind. (5)	10	0.01
Spanish American Ind. (21)	35	0.02
Tlingit-Haida *(Alaska Native)* (0)	1	<0.01
Tohono O'Odham (0)	1	<0.01
Yaqui (0)	5	<0.01
Yuman (6)	6	<0.01
Yup'ik *(Alaska Native)* (3)	3	<0.01
Asian (11,475)	12,640	7.21
Not Hispanic (11,329)	12,179	6.94
Hispanic (146)	461	0.26
Bangladeshi (67)	77	0.04
Burmese (2)	4	<0.01
Cambodian (69)	83	0.05
Chinese, ex. Taiwanese (615)	781	0.45
Filipino (1,324)	1,634	0.93
Hmong (86)	89	0.05
Indian (1,477)	1,650	0.94
Indonesian (43)	49	0.03
Japanese (110)	225	0.13
Korean (346)	461	0.26
Laotian (703)	779	0.44
Malaysian (4)	10	0.01
Nepalese (85)	97	0.06
Pakistani (173)	205	0.12
Taiwanese (41)	48	0.03
Thai (68)	125	0.07
Vietnamese (5,860)	6,135	3.50
Hawaii Native/Pacific Islander (179)	348	0.20
Not Hispanic (129)	240	0.14
Hispanic (50)	108	0.06
Fijian (4)	4	<0.01
Guamanian/Chamorro (47)	66	0.04
Marshallese (2)	3	<0.01
Native Hawaiian (51)	96	0.05
Samoan (29)	41	0.02
Tongan (26)	34	0.02
White (92,271)	96,837	55.21
Not Hispanic (51,058)	53,143	30.30
Hispanic (41,213)	43,694	24.91

Grapevine

Place Type: City
County: Tarrant
Population: 46,334†

Ancestry‡	Population	%
African, Sub-Saharan (112)	112	0.25
African (112)	112	0.25
American (3,543)	3,543	7.78
Arab (219)	272	0.60
Arab (10)	10	0.02
Egyptian (18)	18	0.04
Lebanese (95)	139	0.31
Other Arab (96)	105	0.23
Australian (34)	34	0.07
Austrian (24)	49	0.11
Basque (0)	9	0.02
Belgian (0)	37	0.08
Brazilian (36)	36	0.08
British (203)	310	0.68
Canadian (7)	7	0.02
Czech (122)	318	0.70
Czechoslovakian (10)	35	0.08
Danish (63)	454	1.00
Dutch (109)	913	2.00
English (2,196)	6,645	14.59
European (903)	1,020	2.24
Finnish (52)	83	0.18
French, ex. Basque (457)	1,883	4.13
French Canadian (138)	189	0.41
German (3,233)	8,703	19.11
Greek (58)	105	0.23
Hungarian (35)	112	0.25
Iranian (3)	16	0.04
Irish (1,652)	5,730	12.58
Italian (525)	1,693	3.72
Latvian (0)	24	0.05
Lithuanian (51)	130	0.29
Maltese (0)	6	0.01
Norwegian (133)	413	0.91
Pennsylvania German (17)	17	0.04
Polish (404)	1,069	2.35
Portuguese (27)	39	0.09
Romanian (11)	41	0.09
Russian (156)	469	1.03
Scandinavian (23)	120	0.26
Scotch-Irish (378)	1,172	2.57
Scottish (468)	1,383	3.04
Serbian (8)	8	0.02
Slavic (0)	6	0.01
Slovak (12)	21	0.05
Slovene (0)	31	0.07
Swedish (170)	911	2.00
Swiss (36)	167	0.37
Turkish (30)	68	0.15
Ukrainian (106)	139	0.31
Welsh (56)	233	0.51
West Indian, ex. Hispanic (88)	88	0.19
Belizean (60)	60	0.13
British West Indian (19)	19	0.04
Jamaican (9)	9	0.02
Yugoslavian (0)	39	0.09

Hispanic Origin	Population	%
Hispanic or Latino (of any race)	8,324	17.97
Central American, ex. Mexican	312	0.67
Costa Rican	22	0.05
Guatemalan	52	0.11
Honduran	30	0.06
Nicaraguan	20	0.04
Panamanian	10	0.02
Salvadoran	177	0.38
Other Central American	1	<0.01
Cuban	93	0.20
Dominican Republic	38	0.08
Mexican	6,732	14.53
Puerto Rican	346	0.75

*Notes: † The Census 2010 population figure is used to calculate the percentages in the Hispanic Origin and Race categories. Ancestry percentages are based on the 2006-2010 American Community Survey population (not shown); ‡ Numbers in parentheses indicate the number of people reporting a single ancestry; * Numbers in parentheses indicate the number of persons reporting this race alone, not in combination with any other race; Please refer to the Explanation of Data for more information.*

South American	304	0.66
Argentinean	23	0.05
Bolivian	13	0.03
Chilean	24	0.05
Colombian	108	0.23
Ecuadorian	54	0.12
Peruvian	41	0.09
Uruguayan	3	0.01
Venezuelan	32	0.07
Other South American	6	0.01
Other Hispanic or Latino	499	1.08

Race*	Population	%
African-American/Black (1,547)	1,776	3.83
Not Hispanic (1,468)	1,649	3.56
Hispanic (79)	127	0.27
American Indian/Alaska Native (307)	591	1.28
Not Hispanic (206)	430	0.93
Hispanic (101)	161	0.35
Apache (6)	9	0.02
Blackfeet (1)	8	0.02
Canadian/French Am. Ind. (0)	4	0.01
Cherokee (45)	145	0.31
Cheyenne (1)	2	<0.01
Chickasaw (21)	28	0.06
Chippewa (3)	4	0.01
Choctaw (38)	58	0.13
Comanche (4)	9	0.02
Creek (7)	11	0.02
Iroquois (2)	4	0.01
Kiowa (1)	4	0.01
Mexican American Ind. (17)	31	0.07
Navajo (1)	3	0.01
Osage (2)	7	0.02
Ottawa (0)	1	<0.01
Pima (0)	3	0.01
Potawatomi (10)	10	0.02
Pueblo (2)	4	0.01
Seminole (0)	5	0.01
Sioux (6)	7	0.02
Spanish American Ind. (5)	8	0.02
Yaqui (1)	1	<0.01
Yup'ik *(Alaska Native)* (1)	1	<0.01
Asian (2,067)	2,449	5.29
Not Hispanic (2,045)	2,378	5.13
Hispanic (22)	71	0.15
Bangladeshi (27)	30	0.06
Burmese (6)	6	0.01
Cambodian (2)	3	0.01
Chinese, ex. Taiwanese (386)	475	1.03
Filipino (119)	194	0.42
Indian (666)	732	1.58
Indonesian (10)	12	0.03
Japanese (66)	146	0.32
Korean (313)	355	0.77
Laotian (23)	25	0.05
Malaysian (10)	13	0.03
Nepalese (7)	10	0.02
Pakistani (129)	149	0.32
Sri Lankan (2)	4	0.01
Taiwanese (40)	41	0.09
Thai (42)	51	0.11
Vietnamese (132)	156	0.34
Hawaii Native/Pacific Islander (83)	159	0.34
Not Hispanic (76)	124	0.27
Hispanic (7)	35	0.08
Guamanian/Chamorro (16)	19	0.04
Native Hawaiian (18)	60	0.13
Samoan (2)	8	0.02
Tongan (45)	60	0.13
White (37,577)	38,477	83.04
Not Hispanic (33,456)	34,062	73.51
Hispanic (4,121)	4,415	9.53

Greatwood

Place Type: CDP
County: Fort Bend
Population: 11,538†

Ancestry‡	Population	%
African, Sub-Saharan (163)	163	1.39
African (26)	26	0.22
Nigerian (109)	109	0.93
Other Sub-Saharan African (28)	28	0.24
American (796)	796	6.78
Arab (28)	58	0.49
Egyptian (4)	4	0.03
Lebanese (15)	35	0.30
Other Arab (9)	19	0.16
Armenian (0)	53	0.45
Assyrian/Chaldean/Syriac (0)	53	0.45
Australian (0)	18	0.15
Austrian (4)	4	0.03
Belgian (0)	13	0.11
British (51)	77	0.66
Cajun (38)	47	0.40
Croatian (25)	73	0.62
Czech (76)	346	2.95
Czechoslovakian (19)	19	0.16
Danish (0)	24	0.20
Dutch (20)	70	0.60
Eastern European (30)	30	0.26
English (514)	1,239	10.56
European (172)	172	1.47
Finnish (8)	52	0.44
French, ex. Basque (146)	680	5.79
French Canadian (24)	122	1.04
German (962)	2,374	20.23
Iranian (27)	27	0.23
Irish (428)	1,537	13.10
Italian (103)	534	4.55
Lithuanian (20)	64	0.55
Norwegian (0)	61	0.52
Polish (171)	315	2.68
Portuguese (11)	36	0.31
Russian (46)	46	0.39
Scotch-Irish (140)	353	3.01
Scottish (140)	265	2.26
Swedish (12)	31	0.26
Swiss (22)	47	0.40
Ukrainian (0)	9	0.08
Welsh (8)	125	1.07
West Indian, ex. Hispanic (8)	8	0.07
Haitian (8)	8	0.07

Hispanic Origin	Population	%
Hispanic or Latino (of any race)	1,221	10.58
Central American, ex. Mexican	98	0.85
Costa Rican	5	0.04
Guatemalan	10	0.09
Honduran	18	0.16
Nicaraguan	19	0.16
Panamanian	12	0.10
Salvadoran	34	0.29
Cuban	73	0.63
Dominican Republic	5	0.04
Mexican	708	6.14
Puerto Rican	64	0.55
South American	180	1.56
Argentinean	22	0.19
Bolivian	5	0.04
Chilean	4	0.03
Colombian	61	0.53
Ecuadorian	19	0.16
Peruvian	23	0.20
Uruguayan	4	0.03
Venezuelan	42	0.36
Other Hispanic or Latino	93	0.81

Race*	Population	%
African-American/Black (927)	976	8.46
Not Hispanic (901)	941	8.16
Hispanic (26)	35	0.30
American Indian/Alaska Native (23)	57	0.49
Not Hispanic (22)	51	0.44
Hispanic (1)	6	0.05
Apache (1)	3	0.03
Cherokee (6)	13	0.11
Choctaw (2)	4	0.03
Comanche (0)	3	0.03
Creek (4)	4	0.03
Lumbee (0)	1	0.01
Mexican American Ind. (0)	1	0.01
Sioux (1)	1	0.01
South American Ind. (0)	1	0.01
Asian (1,188)	1,343	11.64
Not Hispanic (1,177)	1,306	11.32
Hispanic (11)	37	0.32
Bangladeshi (6)	6	0.05
Bhutanese (0)	4	0.03
Chinese, ex. Taiwanese (239)	287	2.49
Filipino (111)	142	1.23
Indian (321)	350	3.03
Japanese (11)	21	0.18
Korean (34)	48	0.42
Laotian (1)	1	0.01
Malaysian (7)	8	0.07
Pakistani (99)	110	0.95
Sri Lankan (3)	6	0.05
Taiwanese (27)	40	0.35
Thai (17)	17	0.15
Vietnamese (249)	274	2.37
Hawaii Native/Pacific Islander (0)	18	0.16
Not Hispanic (0)	17	0.15
Hispanic (0)	1	0.01
Guamanian/Chamorro (0)	4	0.03
Native Hawaiian (0)	5	0.04
White (8,949)	9,174	79.51
Not Hispanic (8,011)	8,163	70.75
Hispanic (938)	1,011	8.76

Greenville

Place Type: City
County: Hunt
Population: 25,557†

Ancestry‡	Population	%
African, Sub-Saharan (63)	132	0.52
African (63)	132	0.52
American (1,485)	1,485	5.84
Austrian (13)	41	0.16
British (36)	78	0.31
Cajun (0)	8	0.03
Czech (0)	25	0.10
Czechoslovakian (7)	7	0.03
Danish (0)	65	0.26
Dutch (10)	237	0.93
English (1,068)	2,208	8.69
European (212)	212	0.83
Finnish (0)	10	0.04
French, ex. Basque (82)	394	1.55
French Canadian (10)	84	0.33
German (949)	3,088	12.15
Greek (0)	52	0.20
Hungarian (48)	240	0.94
Irish (1,150)	3,284	12.92
Italian (226)	417	1.64
New Zealander (17)	17	0.07
Norwegian (10)	90	0.35
Pennsylvania German (0)	10	0.04
Polish (50)	195	0.77
Portuguese (43)	43	0.17
Romanian (0)	14	0.06
Russian (5)	5	0.02
Scandinavian (0)	7	0.03
Scotch-Irish (448)	685	2.70
Scottish (144)	358	1.41
Slovak (16)	30	0.12
Swedish (7)	21	0.08
Swiss (15)	29	0.11
Welsh (31)	56	0.22
West Indian, ex. Hispanic (0)	7	0.03
Dutch West Indian (0)	7	0.03

Hispanic Origin	Population	%
Hispanic or Latino (of any race)	5,733	22.43
Central American, ex. Mexican	134	0.52
Guatemalan	36	0.14

SECTION TWO

*Notes: † The Census 2010 population figure is used to calculate the percentages in the Hispanic Origin and Race categories. Ancestry percentages are based on the 2006-2010 American Community Survey population (not shown); ‡ Numbers in parentheses indicate the number of people reporting a single ancestry; * Numbers in parentheses indicate the number of persons reporting this race alone, not in combination with any other race; Please refer to the Explanation of Data for more information.*

	Population	%
Honduran	25	0.10
Nicaraguan	10	0.04
Panamanian	14	0.05
Salvadoran	49	0.19
Cuban	14	0.05
Dominican Republic	3	0.01
Mexican	5,139	20.11
Puerto Rican	87	0.34
South American	41	0.16
Argentinean	2	0.01
Chilean	1	<0.01
Colombian	30	0.12
Ecuadorian	3	0.01
Peruvian	5	0.02
Other Hispanic or Latino	315	1.23

Race*	Population	%
African-American/Black (4,282)	4,542	17.77
Not Hispanic (4,197)	4,405	17.24
Hispanic (85)	137	0.54
American Indian/Alaska Native (226)	466	1.82
Not Hispanic (135)	302	1.18
Hispanic (91)	164	0.64
Apache (6)	13	0.05
Arapaho (0)	1	<0.01
Blackfeet (4)	6	0.02
Central American Ind. (0)	1	<0.01
Cherokee (24)	72	0.28
Cheyenne (0)	2	0.01
Chickasaw (5)	8	0.03
Chippewa (1)	1	<0.01
Choctaw (29)	58	0.23
Comanche (4)	5	0.02
Creek (5)	10	0.04
Hopi (4)	4	0.02
Inupiat *(Alaska Native)* (0)	7	0.03
Iroquois (1)	2	0.01
Kiowa (0)	2	0.01
Lumbee (1)	1	<0.01
Mexican American Ind. (24)	28	0.11
Navajo (4)	6	0.02
Osage (1)	1	<0.01
Potawatomi (4)	4	0.02
Puget Sound Salish (1)	1	<0.01
Seminole (0)	12	0.05
Shoshone (4)	6	0.02
Sioux (2)	3	0.01
Spanish American Ind. (5)	5	0.02
Ute (0)	1	<0.01
Asian (274)	351	1.37
Not Hispanic (262)	319	1.25
Hispanic (12)	32	0.13
Bangladeshi (4)	4	0.02
Cambodian (1)	3	0.01
Chinese, ex. Taiwanese (31)	39	0.15
Filipino (47)	71	0.28
Indian (116)	134	0.52
Indonesian (1)	1	<0.01
Japanese (5)	8	0.03
Korean (17)	25	0.10
Laotian (3)	6	0.02
Malaysian (2)	2	0.01
Nepalese (7)	7	0.03
Pakistani (4)	5	0.02
Taiwanese (3)	3	0.01
Thai (13)	16	0.06
Vietnamese (10)	11	0.04
Hawaii Native/Pacific Islander (74)	88	0.34
Not Hispanic (64)	73	0.29
Hispanic (10)	15	0.06
Fijian (0)	14	0.05
Guamanian/Chamorro (3)	5	0.02
Native Hawaiian (1)	6	0.02
Samoan (0)	15	0.06
White (17,498)	18,088	70.78
Not Hispanic (14,746)	15,076	58.99
Hispanic (2,752)	3,012	11.79

Groves

Place Type: City
County: Jefferson
Population: 16,144†

Ancestry‡	Population	%
African, Sub-Saharan (32)	32	0.20
African (32)	32	0.20
American (1,042)	1,042	6.52
Basque (0)	17	0.11
British (93)	93	0.58
Cajun (254)	359	2.25
Czech (15)	26	0.16
Dutch (43)	104	0.65
English (409)	1,373	8.59
European (75)	82	0.51
Finnish (20)	30	0.19
French, ex. Basque (1,642)	3,431	21.46
French Canadian (383)	518	3.24
German (252)	1,143	7.15
Greek (9)	9	0.06
Iranian (172)	172	1.08
Irish (581)	2,148	13.44
Italian (186)	587	3.67
Norwegian (11)	66	0.41
Pennsylvania German (0)	37	0.23
Polish (82)	296	1.85
Portuguese (10)	10	0.06
Scandinavian (0)	12	0.08
Scotch-Irish (66)	188	1.18
Scottish (100)	235	1.47
Swedish (0)	72	0.45

Hispanic Origin	Population	%
Hispanic or Latino (of any race)	2,639	16.35
Central American, ex. Mexican	165	1.02
Guatemalan	12	0.07
Honduran	72	0.45
Nicaraguan	51	0.32
Panamanian	8	0.05
Salvadoran	22	0.14
Cuban	17	0.11
Dominican Republic	1	0.01
Mexican	2,156	13.35
Puerto Rican	71	0.44
South American	38	0.24
Argentinean	4	0.02
Chilean	5	0.03
Colombian	12	0.07
Peruvian	1	0.01
Uruguayan	5	0.03
Venezuelan	10	0.06
Other South American	1	0.01
Other Hispanic or Latino	191	1.18

Race*	Population	%
African-American/Black (666)	751	4.65
Not Hispanic (651)	706	4.37
Hispanic (15)	45	0.28
American Indian/Alaska Native (47)	134	0.83
Not Hispanic (32)	87	0.54
Hispanic (15)	47	0.29
Alaska Athabascan *(Ala. Nat.)* (0)	1	0.01
Apache (0)	3	0.02
Blackfeet (0)	1	0.01
Canadian/French Am. Ind. (0)	4	0.02
Central American Ind. (1)	2	0.01
Cherokee (6)	25	0.15
Chickasaw (1)	3	0.02
Choctaw (3)	5	0.03
Comanche (1)	1	0.01
Creek (1)	2	0.01
Houma (0)	3	0.02
Lumbee (1)	1	0.01
Mexican American Ind. (2)	9	0.06
Navajo (1)	1	0.01
Potawatomi (1)	3	0.02
Seminole (1)	1	0.01
Sioux (1)	1	0.01
Spanish American Ind. (1)	1	0.01
Asian (484)	543	3.36
Not Hispanic (482)	527	3.26
Hispanic (2)	16	0.10
Cambodian (4)	6	0.04
Chinese, ex. Taiwanese (4)	8	0.05
Filipino (60)	80	0.50
Indian (98)	111	0.69
Japanese (6)	13	0.08
Korean (6)	8	0.05
Pakistani (13)	20	0.12
Thai (1)	7	0.04
Vietnamese (274)	286	1.77
Hawaii Native/Pacific Islander (5)	15	0.09
Not Hispanic (5)	14	0.09
Hispanic (0)	1	0.01
Native Hawaiian (3)	6	0.04
White (13,845)	14,120	87.46
Not Hispanic (12,174)	12,310	76.25
Hispanic (1,671)	1,810	11.21

Haltom City

Place Type: City
County: Tarrant
Population: 42,409†

Ancestry‡	Population	%
African, Sub-Saharan (24)	46	0.11
African (9)	31	0.07
Kenyan (7)	7	0.02
Other Sub-Saharan African (8)	8	0.02
Albanian (0)	30	0.07
American (5,144)	5,144	12.34
Arab (10)	20	0.05
Arab (10)	20	0.05
Austrian (0)	33	0.08
Belgian (15)	15	0.04
British (51)	57	0.14
Cajun (0)	6	0.01
Canadian (12)	38	0.09
Celtic (24)	24	0.06
Czech (98)	260	0.62
Czechoslovakian (29)	29	0.07
Danish (20)	97	0.23
Dutch (25)	155	0.37
English (1,338)	2,543	6.10
European (218)	218	0.52
Finnish (34)	272	0.65
French, ex. Basque (110)	393	0.94
French Canadian (42)	75	0.18
German (1,208)	3,316	7.96
Greek (23)	74	0.18
Hungarian (6)	23	0.06
Irish (1,087)	2,989	7.17
Italian (194)	411	0.99
Latvian (8)	8	0.02
Norwegian (44)	97	0.23
Pennsylvania German (5)	5	0.01
Polish (112)	342	0.82
Portuguese (81)	81	0.19
Romanian (9)	9	0.02
Russian (87)	129	0.31
Scandinavian (12)	12	0.03
Scotch-Irish (297)	657	1.58
Scottish (338)	680	1.63
Slovak (17)	34	0.08
Swedish (11)	131	0.31
Swiss (0)	40	0.10
Ukrainian (13)	13	0.03
Welsh (51)	159	0.38
West Indian, ex. Hispanic (226)	234	0.56
Bermudan (196)	196	0.47
Dutch West Indian (10)	18	0.04
Jamaican (20)	20	0.05

Hispanic Origin	Population	%
Hispanic or Latino (of any race)	16,515	38.94
Central American, ex. Mexican	681	1.61
Costa Rican	6	0.01

*Notes: † The Census 2010 population figure is used to calculate the percentages in the Hispanic Origin and Race categories. Ancestry percentages are based on the 2006-2010 American Community Survey population (not shown); ‡ Numbers in parentheses indicate the number of people reporting a single ancestry; * Numbers in parentheses indicate the number of persons reporting this race alone, not in combination with any other race; Please refer to the Explanation of Data for more information.*

Guatemalan	92	0.22
Honduran	125	0.29
Nicaraguan	21	0.05
Panamanian	14	0.03
Salvadoran	422	1.00
Other Central American	1	<0.01
Cuban	66	0.16
Dominican Republic	19	0.04
Mexican	14,291	33.70
Puerto Rican	231	0.54
South American	131	0.31
Argentinean	28	0.07
Bolivian	2	<0.01
Chilean	7	0.02
Colombian	35	0.08
Ecuadorian	10	0.02
Peruvian	40	0.09
Uruguayan	1	<0.01
Venezuelan	8	0.02
Other Hispanic or Latino	1,096	2.58

Race*	Population	%
African-American/Black (1,776)	2,047	4.83
Not Hispanic (1,681)	1,877	4.43
Hispanic (95)	170	0.40
American Indian/Alaska Native (391)	696	1.64
Not Hispanic (164)	364	0.86
Hispanic (227)	332	0.78
Aleut *(Alaska Native)* (1)	1	<0.01
Apache (12)	24	0.06
Blackfeet (1)	11	0.03
Canadian/French Am. Ind. (4)	4	0.01
Central American Ind. (3)	3	0.01
Cherokee (27)	103	0.24
Cheyenne (1)	1	<0.01
Chickasaw (6)	9	0.02
Chippewa (3)	6	0.01
Choctaw (32)	58	0.14
Comanche (6)	11	0.03
Cree (0)	4	0.01
Creek (21)	43	0.10
Hopi (0)	2	<0.01
Houma (7)	7	0.02
Inupiat *(Alaska Native)* (0)	3	0.01
Iroquois (6)	10	0.02
Kiowa (5)	6	0.01
Menominee (1)	1	<0.01
Mexican American Ind. (25)	54	0.13
Navajo (3)	4	0.01
Osage (0)	2	<0.01
Ottawa (0)	1	<0.01
Potawatomi (4)	4	0.01
Pueblo (0)	3	0.01
Seminole (0)	4	0.01
Shoshone (0)	1	<0.01
Sioux (3)	9	0.02
Spanish American Ind. (0)	1	<0.01
Yaqui (2)	2	<0.01
Asian (3,437)	3,670	8.65
Not Hispanic (3,392)	3,577	8.43
Hispanic (45)	93	0.22
Bangladeshi (9)	12	0.03
Bhutanese (10)	26	0.06
Burmese (14)	15	0.04
Cambodian (38)	46	0.11
Chinese, ex. Taiwanese (74)	106	0.25
Filipino (101)	155	0.37
Hmong (12)	18	0.04
Indian (274)	318	0.75
Indonesian (0)	2	<0.01
Japanese (15)	44	0.10
Korean (35)	44	0.10
Laotian (908)	976	2.30
Nepalese (58)	85	0.20
Pakistani (40)	47	0.11
Sri Lankan (15)	16	0.04
Taiwanese (6)	8	0.02
Thai (72)	104	0.25
Vietnamese (1,555)	1,623	3.83
Hawaii Native/Pacific Islander (97)	148	0.35
Not Hispanic (87)	119	0.28
Hispanic (10)	29	0.07
Guamanian/Chamorro (20)	21	0.05
Marshallese (4)	4	0.01
Native Hawaiian (16)	33	0.08
Samoan (4)	5	0.01
Tongan (12)	19	0.04
White (28,194)	29,340	69.18
Not Hispanic (19,967)	20,464	48.25
Hispanic (8,227)	8,876	20.93

Harker Heights

Place Type: City
County: Bell
Population: 26,700†

Ancestry‡	Population	%
African, Sub-Saharan (184)	236	0.95
African (83)	109	0.44
Cape Verdean (33)	43	0.17
Liberian (0)	6	0.02
Nigerian (68)	78	0.31
American (1,097)	1,097	4.41
Arab (9)	45	0.18
Lebanese (9)	29	0.12
Moroccan (0)	16	0.06
Austrian (0)	5	0.02
Brazilian (0)	10	0.04
British (29)	29	0.12
Canadian (0)	9	0.04
Croatian (0)	58	0.23
Czech (26)	101	0.41
Czechoslovakian (0)	11	0.04
Danish (35)	62	0.25
Dutch (84)	175	0.70
Eastern European (9)	9	0.04
English (550)	1,197	4.81
European (363)	418	1.68
French, ex. Basque (133)	429	1.72
French Canadian (232)	291	1.17
German (1,335)	3,008	12.09
Greek (16)	28	0.11
Guyanese (22)	22	0.09
Hungarian (0)	9	0.04
Irish (408)	1,545	6.21
Israeli (0)	11	0.04
Italian (219)	722	2.90
Lithuanian (5)	5	0.02
Northern European (37)	37	0.15
Norwegian (77)	189	0.76
Polish (153)	238	0.96
Portuguese (31)	70	0.28
Russian (35)	43	0.17
Scandinavian (13)	13	0.05
Scotch-Irish (163)	446	1.79
Scottish (47)	283	1.14
Slovak (11)	40	0.16
Swedish (11)	262	1.05
Ukrainian (0)	19	0.08
Welsh (0)	21	0.08
West Indian, ex. Hispanic (110)	145	0.58
Barbadian (0)	6	0.02
Haitian (20)	20	0.08
Jamaican (38)	38	0.15
West Indian (52)	81	0.33
Yugoslavian (26)	26	0.10

Hispanic Origin	Population	%
Hispanic or Latino (of any race)	4,920	18.43
Central American, ex. Mexican	326	1.22
Costa Rican	4	0.01
Guatemalan	18	0.07
Honduran	65	0.24
Nicaraguan	14	0.05
Panamanian	185	0.69
Salvadoran	39	0.15
Other Central American	1	<0.01
Cuban	50	0.19
Dominican Republic	63	0.24
Mexican	3,235	12.12
Puerto Rican	913	3.42
South American	103	0.39
Argentinean	2	0.01
Bolivian	2	0.01
Colombian	44	0.16
Ecuadorian	13	0.05
Peruvian	30	0.11
Uruguayan	1	<0.01
Venezuelan	10	0.04
Other South American	1	<0.01
Other Hispanic or Latino	230	0.86

Race*	Population	%
African-American/Black (5,332)	6,107	22.87
Not Hispanic (5,084)	5,690	21.31
Hispanic (248)	417	1.56
American Indian/Alaska Native (261)	593	2.22
Not Hispanic (136)	380	1.42
Hispanic (125)	213	0.80
Apache (4)	21	0.08
Blackfeet (3)	13	0.05
Canadian/French Am. Ind. (0)	1	<0.01
Cherokee (41)	118	0.44
Chickasaw (2)	2	0.01
Chippewa (5)	14	0.05
Choctaw (6)	19	0.07
Colville (0)	1	<0.01
Comanche (7)	7	0.03
Cree (2)	3	0.01
Creek (5)	9	0.03
Delaware (5)	6	0.02
Iroquois (4)	4	0.01
Kiowa (1)	5	0.02
Lumbee (0)	1	<0.01
Mexican American Ind. (4)	12	0.04
Navajo (9)	14	0.05
Osage (0)	3	0.01
Ottawa (1)	1	<0.01
Pueblo (5)	5	0.02
Seminole (0)	5	0.02
Shoshone (1)	1	<0.01
Sioux (4)	8	0.03
South American Ind. (4)	16	0.06
Spanish American Ind. (0)	5	0.02
Asian (1,029)	1,568	5.87
Not Hispanic (1,004)	1,459	5.46
Hispanic (25)	109	0.41
Burmese (2)	2	0.01
Cambodian (19)	26	0.10
Chinese, ex. Taiwanese (60)	125	0.47
Filipino (244)	399	1.49
Hmong (0)	2	0.01
Indian (87)	106	0.40
Indonesian (0)	3	0.01
Japanese (41)	163	0.61
Korean (403)	563	2.11
Laotian (4)	7	0.03
Nepalese (3)	5	0.02
Pakistani (38)	45	0.17
Sri Lankan (1)	3	0.01
Taiwanese (8)	9	0.03
Thai (21)	47	0.18
Vietnamese (60)	86	0.32
Hawaii Native/Pacific Islander (230)	394	1.48
Not Hispanic (224)	347	1.30
Hispanic (6)	47	0.18
Guamanian/Chamorro (89)	134	0.50
Marshallese (0)	1	<0.01
Native Hawaiian (14)	65	0.24
Samoan (71)	124	0.46
Tongan (6)	7	0.03
White (16,800)	18,097	67.78
Not Hispanic (14,145)	15,090	56.52
Hispanic (2,655)	3,007	11.26

*Notes: † The Census 2010 population figure is used to calculate the percentages in the Hispanic Origin and Race categories. Ancestry percentages are based on the 2006-2010 American Community Survey population (not shown); ‡ Numbers in parentheses indicate the number of people reporting a single ancestry; * Numbers in parentheses indicate the number of persons reporting this race alone, not in combination with any other race; Please refer to the Explanation of Data for more information.*

Harlingen

Place Type: City
County: Cameron
Population: 64,849†

Ancestry‡	Population	%
African, Sub-Saharan (214)	214	0.33
African (27)	27	0.04
Nigerian (187)	187	0.29
American (1,303)	1,303	2.03
Arab (25)	48	0.07
Lebanese (0)	23	0.04
Moroccan (25)	25	0.04
Armenian (6)	6	0.01
Australian (7)	16	0.02
Austrian (0)	9	0.01
Basque (0)	7	0.01
Belgian (13)	27	0.04
British (84)	91	0.14
Canadian (0)	21	0.03
Croatian (0)	36	0.06
Czech (148)	181	0.28
Czechoslovakian (7)	7	0.01
Danish (27)	139	0.22
Dutch (69)	174	0.27
English (1,141)	2,314	3.61
European (65)	85	0.13
French, ex. Basque (279)	686	1.07
French Canadian (17)	17	0.03
German (1,990)	3,545	5.52
Greek (9)	22	0.03
Hungarian (35)	142	0.22
Iranian (32)	32	0.05
Irish (646)	1,851	2.88
Italian (93)	336	0.52
Lithuanian (13)	13	0.02
Luxemburger (11)	11	0.02
Norwegian (97)	211	0.33
Pennsylvania German (7)	8	0.01
Polish (171)	301	0.47
Portuguese (9)	23	0.04
Russian (39)	74	0.12
Scandinavian (8)	65	0.10
Scotch-Irish (163)	471	0.73
Scottish (366)	503	0.78
Slovak (7)	15	0.02
Swedish (37)	170	0.26
Swiss (34)	69	0.11
Turkish (0)	18	0.03
Ukrainian (26)	33	0.05
Welsh (49)	86	0.13
West Indian, ex. Hispanic (3)	32	0.05
Haitian (3)	5	0.01
Jamaican (0)	27	0.04

Hispanic Origin	Population	%
Hispanic or Latino (of any race)	51,581	79.54
Central American, ex. Mexican	428	0.66
Costa Rican	9	0.01
Guatemalan	78	0.12
Honduran	87	0.13
Nicaraguan	59	0.09
Panamanian	24	0.04
Salvadoran	166	0.26
Other Central American	5	0.01
Cuban	57	0.09
Dominican Republic	19	0.03
Mexican	45,357	69.94
Puerto Rican	292	0.45
South American	187	0.29
Argentinean	18	0.03
Bolivian	8	0.01
Chilean	11	0.02
Colombian	57	0.09
Ecuadorian	24	0.04
Paraguayan	14	0.02
Peruvian	32	0.05
Uruguayan	6	0.01
Venezuelan	17	0.03
Other Hispanic or Latino	5,241	8.08

Race*	Population	%
African-American/Black (632)	777	1.20
Not Hispanic (432)	483	0.74
Hispanic (200)	294	0.45
American Indian/Alaska Native (305)	526	0.81
Not Hispanic (80)	146	0.23
Hispanic (225)	380	0.59
Alaska Athabascan *(Ala. Nat.)* (3)	3	<0.01
Apache (18)	37	0.06
Arapaho (0)	1	<0.01
Blackfeet (2)	4	0.01
Canadian/French Am. Ind. (2)	4	0.01
Central American Ind. (1)	1	<0.01
Cherokee (18)	49	0.08
Chickasaw (9)	17	0.03
Chippewa (2)	3	<0.01
Choctaw (5)	14	0.02
Comanche (0)	3	<0.01
Cree (1)	1	<0.01
Creek (2)	2	<0.01
Delaware (1)	1	<0.01
Iroquois (1)	1	<0.01
Lumbee (1)	1	<0.01
Mexican American Ind. (23)	47	0.07
Navajo (1)	1	<0.01
Osage (0)	4	0.01
Pueblo (3)	6	0.01
Sioux (4)	5	0.01
Spanish American Ind. (4)	9	0.01
Yakama (1)	1	<0.01
Yaqui (0)	2	<0.01
Yuman (1)	1	<0.01
Asian (852)	1,019	1.57
Not Hispanic (814)	888	1.37
Hispanic (38)	131	0.20
Burmese (1)	2	<0.01
Cambodian (3)	3	<0.01
Chinese, ex. Taiwanese (80)	96	0.15
Filipino (495)	559	0.86
Indian (110)	125	0.19
Indonesian (1)	1	<0.01
Japanese (33)	65	0.10
Korean (22)	41	0.06
Malaysian (1)	2	<0.01
Pakistani (12)	12	0.02
Sri Lankan (2)	2	<0.01
Taiwanese (5)	7	0.01
Thai (5)	5	0.01
Vietnamese (66)	74	0.11
Hawaii Native/Pacific Islander (34)	69	0.11
Not Hispanic (27)	38	0.06
Hispanic (7)	31	0.05
Guamanian/Chamorro (19)	22	0.03
Native Hawaiian (11)	35	0.05
Samoan (1)	1	<0.01
Tongan (0)	1	<0.01
White (56,583)	57,645	88.89
Not Hispanic (11,681)	11,844	18.26
Hispanic (44,902)	45,801	70.63

Henderson

Place Type: City
County: Rusk
Population: 13,712†

Ancestry‡	Population	%
African, Sub-Saharan (34)	34	0.26
Sudanese (18)	18	0.14
Other Sub-Saharan African (16)	16	0.12
American (1,579)	1,579	11.95
Arab (0)	17	0.13
Palestinian (0)	17	0.13
Australian (11)	11	0.08
Brazilian (9)	9	0.07
British (11)	11	0.08
Cajun (19)	19	0.14
Czech (16)	62	0.47
Danish (0)	13	0.10
Dutch (17)	51	0.39
Eastern European (12)	12	0.09
English (888)	1,335	10.10
Estonian (0)	21	0.16
European (42)	42	0.32
French, ex. Basque (127)	426	3.22
French Canadian (0)	14	0.11
German (401)	1,187	8.98
Irish (497)	1,385	10.48
Italian (66)	244	1.85
Northern European (18)	18	0.14
Norwegian (31)	101	0.76
Polish (59)	191	1.45
Portuguese (0)	43	0.33
Scotch-Irish (127)	189	1.43
Scottish (108)	124	0.94
Swedish (0)	55	0.42
Welsh (44)	54	0.41
West Indian, ex. Hispanic (0)	11	0.08
Dutch West Indian (0)	11	0.08

Hispanic Origin	Population	%
Hispanic or Latino (of any race)	2,474	18.04
Central American, ex. Mexican	185	1.35
Costa Rican	2	0.01
Guatemalan	4	0.03
Honduran	10	0.07
Panamanian	1	0.01
Salvadoran	168	1.23
Dominican Republic	2	0.01
Mexican	2,138	15.59
Puerto Rican	25	0.18
South American	4	0.03
Bolivian	3	0.02
Colombian	1	0.01
Other Hispanic or Latino	120	0.88

Race*	Population	%
African-American/Black (3,275)	3,376	24.62
Not Hispanic (3,255)	3,337	24.34
Hispanic (20)	39	0.28
American Indian/Alaska Native (58)	106	0.77
Not Hispanic (26)	60	0.44
Hispanic (32)	46	0.34
Apache (0)	1	0.01
Blackfeet (0)	1	0.01
Cherokee (3)	17	0.12
Chickasaw (2)	2	0.01
Chippewa (2)	8	0.06
Choctaw (8)	10	0.07
Lumbee (0)	2	0.01
Mexican American Ind. (5)	5	0.04
Potawatomi (0)	1	0.01
Asian (101)	129	0.94
Not Hispanic (91)	109	0.79
Hispanic (10)	20	0.15
Bangladeshi (4)	4	0.03
Burmese (2)	2	0.01
Cambodian (8)	11	0.08
Chinese, ex. Taiwanese (11)	18	0.13
Filipino (26)	31	0.23
Indian (23)	33	0.24
Japanese (1)	2	0.01
Korean (3)	8	0.06
Sri Lankan (1)	1	0.01
Taiwanese (1)	1	0.01
Vietnamese (16)	18	0.13
Hawaii Native/Pacific Islander (11)	27	0.20
Not Hispanic (6)	9	0.07
Hispanic (5)	18	0.13
Native Hawaiian (0)	4	0.03
Samoan (5)	5	0.04
Tongan (4)	4	0.03
White (8,845)	9,063	66.10
Not Hispanic (7,711)	7,831	57.11
Hispanic (1,134)	1,232	8.98

*Notes: † The Census 2010 population figure is used to calculate the percentages in the Hispanic Origin and Race categories. Ancestry percentages are based on the 2006-2010 American Community Survey population (not shown); ‡ Numbers in parentheses indicate the number of people reporting a single ancestry; * Numbers in parentheses indicate the number of persons reporting this race alone, not in combination with any other race; Please refer to the Explanation of Data for more information.*

Hereford

Place Type: City
County: Deaf Smith
Population: 15,370†

Ancestry‡	Population	%
African, Sub-Saharan (23)	23	0.15
South African (23)	23	0.15
American (574)	574	3.80
Belgian (14)	14	0.09
Canadian (8)	8	0.05
Croatian (0)	35	0.23
Czech (0)	13	0.09
Dutch (0)	51	0.34
English (241)	480	3.18
European (26)	26	0.17
French, ex. Basque (39)	217	1.44
French Canadian (15)	15	0.10
German (735)	1,339	8.87
Greek (14)	36	0.24
Hungarian (8)	8	0.05
Irish (303)	855	5.66
Italian (0)	79	0.52
Norwegian (8)	36	0.24
Polish (0)	38	0.25
Portuguese (6)	6	0.04
Scotch-Irish (83)	120	0.79
Scottish (17)	112	0.74
Swiss (0)	7	0.05
Welsh (0)	15	0.10
West Indian, ex. Hispanic (0)	7	0.05
Dutch West Indian (0)	7	0.05

Hispanic Origin	Population	%
Hispanic or Latino (of any race)	11,019	71.69
Central American, ex. Mexican	102	0.66
Costa Rican	4	0.03
Guatemalan	64	0.42
Nicaraguan	1	0.01
Salvadoran	27	0.18
Other Central American	6	0.04
Cuban	11	0.07
Mexican	9,609	62.52
Puerto Rican	7	0.05
South American	2	0.01
Argentinean	1	0.01
Ecuadorian	1	0.01
Other Hispanic or Latino	1,288	8.38

Race*	Population	%
African-American/Black (220)	264	1.72
Not Hispanic (139)	170	1.11
Hispanic (81)	94	0.61
American Indian/Alaska Native (149)	228	1.48
Not Hispanic (37)	67	0.44
Hispanic (112)	161	1.05
Apache (3)	9	0.06
Cherokee (4)	12	0.08
Chickasaw (4)	4	0.03
Choctaw (6)	9	0.06
Comanche (1)	2	0.01
Creek (2)	3	0.02
Lumbee (0)	2	0.01
Mexican American Ind. (26)	28	0.18
Navajo (10)	10	0.07
Osage (0)	1	0.01
Ottawa (3)	3	0.02
Pima (2)	2	0.01
Pueblo (1)	1	0.01
Sioux (6)	7	0.05
Asian (53)	70	0.46
Not Hispanic (48)	52	0.34
Hispanic (5)	18	0.12
Cambodian (4)	4	0.03
Filipino (13)	17	0.11
Indian (16)	23	0.15
Korean (2)	4	0.03
Laotian (5)	5	0.03
Thai (6)	7	0.05
Vietnamese (7)	8	0.05
Hawaii Native/Pacific Islander (2)	16	0.10
Not Hispanic (2)	9	0.06
Hispanic (0)	7	0.05
Guamanian/Chamorro (1)	1	0.01
Native Hawaiian (1)	3	0.02
White (11,856)	12,190	79.31
Not Hispanic (4,041)	4,105	26.71
Hispanic (7,815)	8,085	52.60

Hewitt

Place Type: City
County: McLennan
Population: 13,549†

Ancestry‡	Population	%
African, Sub-Saharan (116)	116	0.89
African (18)	18	0.14
Nigerian (88)	88	0.68
South African (10)	10	0.08
American (717)	717	5.51
Austrian (5)	14	0.11
Brazilian (0)	28	0.22
British (23)	23	0.18
Canadian (0)	7	0.05
Czech (50)	154	1.18
Danish (10)	17	0.13
Dutch (20)	162	1.24
English (883)	1,799	13.82
European (114)	114	0.88
Finnish (0)	67	0.51
French, ex. Basque (92)	314	2.41
French Canadian (91)	139	1.07
German (767)	2,445	18.78
Greek (6)	25	0.19
Hungarian (10)	19	0.15
Irish (588)	1,843	14.15
Italian (101)	482	3.70
Norwegian (22)	149	1.14
Pennsylvania German (22)	22	0.17
Polish (12)	79	0.61
Russian (0)	9	0.07
Scandinavian (7)	7	0.05
Scotch-Irish (175)	274	2.10
Scottish (101)	315	2.42
Serbian (0)	8	0.06
Swedish (62)	115	0.88
Swiss (0)	25	0.19
Ukrainian (13)	13	0.10
Welsh (12)	18	0.14
West Indian, ex. Hispanic (75)	75	0.58
Barbadian (10)	10	0.08
Jamaican (9)	9	0.07
West Indian (56)	56	0.43
Yugoslavian (20)	20	0.15

Hispanic Origin	Population	%
Hispanic or Latino (of any race)	1,934	14.27
Central American, ex. Mexican	27	0.20
Costa Rican	1	0.01
Guatemalan	2	0.01
Honduran	7	0.05
Nicaraguan	2	0.01
Panamanian	4	0.03
Salvadoran	11	0.08
Cuban	6	0.04
Dominican Republic	5	0.04
Mexican	1,559	11.51
Puerto Rican	120	0.89
South American	26	0.19
Chilean	5	0.04
Colombian	13	0.10
Ecuadorian	5	0.04
Peruvian	2	0.01
Uruguayan	1	0.01
Other Hispanic or Latino	191	1.41

Race*	Population	%
African-American/Black (1,145)	1,239	9.14
Not Hispanic (1,126)	1,205	8.89
Hispanic (19)	34	0.25
American Indian/Alaska Native (49)	133	0.98
Not Hispanic (36)	98	0.72
Hispanic (13)	35	0.26
Blackfeet (1)	2	0.01
Cherokee (12)	42	0.31
Cheyenne (0)	1	0.01
Chickasaw (3)	3	0.02
Chippewa (0)	1	0.01
Choctaw (2)	12	0.09
Creek (1)	4	0.03
Iroquois (2)	2	0.01
Mexican American Ind. (1)	3	0.02
Navajo (2)	2	0.01
Potawatomi (2)	2	0.01
Pueblo (0)	1	0.01
Seminole (1)	1	0.01
Sioux (0)	2	0.01
South American Ind. (1)	1	0.01
Spanish American Ind. (3)	3	0.02
Tlingit-Haida *(Alaska Native)* (5)	5	0.04
Yaqui (1)	1	0.01
Asian (440)	532	3.93
Not Hispanic (433)	509	3.76
Hispanic (7)	23	0.17
Chinese, ex. Taiwanese (58)	70	0.52
Filipino (62)	87	0.64
Indian (68)	71	0.52
Indonesian (3)	4	0.03
Japanese (8)	23	0.17
Korean (31)	40	0.30
Laotian (1)	1	0.01
Pakistani (46)	50	0.37
Sri Lankan (2)	2	0.01
Thai (21)	31	0.23
Vietnamese (123)	125	0.92
Hawaii Native/Pacific Islander (10)	13	0.10
Not Hispanic (10)	13	0.10
Guamanian/Chamorro (1)	1	0.01
Marshallese (1)	1	0.01
Native Hawaiian (8)	11	0.08
White (10,928)	11,235	82.92
Not Hispanic (9,780)	9,989	73.72
Hispanic (1,148)	1,246	9.20

Hidalgo

Place Type: City
County: Hidalgo
Population: 11,198†

Ancestry‡	Population	%
American (63)	63	0.60
Armenian (0)	37	0.35
Czech (11)	28	0.27
German (21)	38	0.36
Russian (31)	31	0.29
Scottish (0)	8	0.08

Hispanic Origin	Population	%
Hispanic or Latino (of any race)	11,015	98.37
Central American, ex. Mexican	19	0.17
Guatemalan	2	0.02
Honduran	10	0.09
Panamanian	1	0.01
Salvadoran	6	0.05
Cuban	4	0.04
Dominican Republic	3	0.03
Mexican	10,804	96.48
Puerto Rican	7	0.06
South American	6	0.05
Colombian	4	0.04
Peruvian	2	0.02
Other Hispanic or Latino	172	1.54

Race*	Population	%
African-American/Black (24)	37	0.33
Not Hispanic (10)	10	0.09
Hispanic (14)	27	0.24

*Notes: † The Census 2010 population figure is used to calculate the percentages in the Hispanic Origin and Race categories. Ancestry percentages are based on the 2006-2010 American Community Survey population (not shown); ‡ Numbers in parentheses indicate the number of people reporting a single ancestry; * Numbers in parentheses indicate the number of persons reporting this race alone, not in combination with any other race; Please refer to the Explanation of Data for more information.*

American Indian/Alaska Native (12)	14	0.13
Not Hispanic (1)	1	0.01
Hispanic (11)	13	0.12
Apache (1)	1	0.01
Mexican American Ind. (4)	4	0.04
Asian (2)	8	0.07
Not Hispanic (1)	2	0.02
Hispanic (1)	6	0.05
Chinese, ex. Taiwanese (0)	1	0.01
Filipino (0)	1	0.01
Indian (2)	4	0.04
Japanese (0)	3	0.03
Hawaii Native/Pacific Islander (1)	5	0.04
Not Hispanic (1)	4	0.04
Hispanic (0)	1	0.01
Guamanian/Chamorro (0)	1	0.01
Samoan (1)	2	0.02
White (10,528)	10,601	94.67
Not Hispanic (165)	169	1.51
Hispanic (10,363)	10,432	93.16

Highland Park

Place Type: Town
County: Dallas
Population: 8,564†

Ancestry‡	Population	%
American (510)	510	5.98
Arab (22)	78	0.91
Egyptian (9)	36	0.42
Iraqi (13)	13	0.15
Lebanese (0)	29	0.34
Austrian (0)	53	0.62
British (96)	250	2.93
Cajun (0)	25	0.29
Celtic (0)	10	0.12
Czech (29)	29	0.34
Czechoslovakian (9)	9	0.11
Danish (31)	41	0.48
Dutch (14)	67	0.79
Eastern European (21)	21	0.25
English (942)	2,447	28.68
European (111)	111	1.30
French, ex. Basque (80)	502	5.88
German (346)	1,321	15.48
Greek (10)	30	0.35
Hungarian (17)	33	0.39
Iranian (61)	61	0.72
Irish (414)	1,563	18.32
Italian (79)	277	3.25
Lithuanian (48)	111	1.30
Northern European (37)	37	0.43
Norwegian (9)	85	1.00
Polish (31)	280	3.28
Romanian (0)	146	1.71
Russian (37)	91	1.07
Scandinavian (10)	10	0.12
Scotch-Irish (299)	406	4.76
Scottish (230)	585	6.86
Serbian (12)	41	0.48
Swedish (59)	150	1.76
Swiss (10)	42	0.49
Welsh (31)	149	1.75

Hispanic Origin	Population	%
Hispanic or Latino (of any race)	343	4.01
Central American, ex. Mexican	33	0.39
Costa Rican	3	0.04
Guatemalan	6	0.07
Honduran	13	0.15
Nicaraguan	4	0.05
Salvadoran	7	0.08
Cuban	3	0.04
Dominican Republic	7	0.08
Mexican	214	2.50
Puerto Rican	20	0.23
South American	27	0.32
Argentinean	2	0.02
Bolivian	3	0.04
Chilean	2	0.02
Colombian	9	0.11
Ecuadorian	4	0.05
Peruvian	3	0.04
Uruguayan	1	0.01
Venezuelan	3	0.04
Other Hispanic or Latino	39	0.46

Race*	Population	%
African-American/Black (42)	47	0.55
Not Hispanic (32)	36	0.42
Hispanic (10)	11	0.13
American Indian/Alaska Native (22)	58	0.68
Not Hispanic (19)	53	0.62
Hispanic (3)	5	0.06
Apache (1)	1	0.01
Cherokee (13)	26	0.30
Chickasaw (0)	4	0.05
Choctaw (2)	11	0.13
Cree (1)	1	0.01
Creek (1)	2	0.02
Delaware (0)	1	0.01
Osage (1)	1	0.01
Sioux (0)	3	0.04
Asian (241)	282	3.29
Not Hispanic (241)	278	3.25
Hispanic (0)	4	0.05
Burmese (0)	1	0.01
Chinese, ex. Taiwanese (94)	101	1.18
Filipino (9)	12	0.14
Indian (49)	61	0.71
Indonesian (1)	2	0.02
Japanese (14)	20	0.23
Korean (18)	29	0.34
Pakistani (15)	15	0.18
Taiwanese (2)	5	0.06
Thai (4)	7	0.08
Vietnamese (21)	27	0.32
White (8,082)	8,170	95.40
Not Hispanic (7,842)	7,915	92.42
Hispanic (240)	255	2.98

Highland Village

Place Type: City
County: Denton
Population: 15,056†

Ancestry‡	Population	%
African, Sub-Saharan (47)	47	0.32
Nigerian (19)	19	0.13
South African (19)	19	0.13
Zimbabwean (9)	9	0.06
American (1,052)	1,052	7.16
Arab (118)	186	1.27
Arab (0)	17	0.12
Egyptian (109)	109	0.74
Lebanese (0)	51	0.35
Other Arab (9)	9	0.06
Armenian (30)	53	0.36
Austrian (0)	11	0.07
Belgian (0)	23	0.16
Brazilian (48)	61	0.41
British (32)	127	0.86
Cajun (22)	22	0.15
Canadian (32)	52	0.35
Croatian (0)	34	0.23
Cypriot (14)	14	0.10
Czech (7)	77	0.52
Czechoslovakian (10)	10	0.07
Danish (0)	61	0.41
Dutch (86)	537	3.65
Eastern European (9)	9	0.06
English (1,092)	2,638	17.94
European (226)	312	2.12
Finnish (0)	30	0.20
French, ex. Basque (161)	786	5.35
French Canadian (29)	101	0.69
German (944)	3,284	22.34
Greek (29)	104	0.71
Hungarian (26)	82	0.56
Irish (753)	2,524	17.17
Italian (111)	412	2.80
Lithuanian (19)	54	0.37
Luxemburger (12)	12	0.08
Northern European (8)	12	0.08
Norwegian (158)	397	2.70
Polish (116)	358	2.44
Portuguese (14)	27	0.18
Russian (75)	167	1.14
Scandinavian (34)	45	0.31
Scotch-Irish (164)	432	2.94
Scottish (150)	456	3.10
Slovak (16)	46	0.31
Swedish (81)	317	2.16
Swiss (0)	119	0.81
Welsh (67)	188	1.28
West Indian, ex. Hispanic (14)	20	0.14
Jamaican (14)	20	0.14
Yugoslavian (102)	102	0.69

Hispanic Origin	Population	%
Hispanic or Latino (of any race)	953	6.33
Central American, ex. Mexican	64	0.43
Costa Rican	4	0.03
Guatemalan	14	0.09
Honduran	4	0.03
Nicaraguan	7	0.05
Panamanian	12	0.08
Salvadoran	23	0.15
Cuban	52	0.35
Dominican Republic	26	0.17
Mexican	590	3.92
Puerto Rican	59	0.39
South American	78	0.52
Argentinean	7	0.05
Bolivian	2	0.01
Chilean	7	0.05
Colombian	24	0.16
Ecuadorian	2	0.01
Peruvian	28	0.19
Uruguayan	4	0.03
Venezuelan	4	0.03
Other Hispanic or Latino	84	0.56

Race*	Population	%
African-American/Black (389)	457	3.04
Not Hispanic (376)	436	2.90
Hispanic (13)	21	0.14
American Indian/Alaska Native (59)	137	0.91
Not Hispanic (43)	112	0.74
Hispanic (16)	25	0.17
Alaska Athabascan *(Ala. Nat.)* (1)	1	0.01
Apache (2)	3	0.02
Blackfeet (1)	6	0.04
Canadian/French Am. Ind. (3)	3	0.02
Cherokee (13)	32	0.21
Chickasaw (4)	15	0.10
Chippewa (0)	1	0.01
Choctaw (3)	24	0.16
Comanche (1)	1	0.01
Creek (2)	6	0.04
Hopi (0)	1	0.01
Iroquois (2)	2	0.01
Mexican American Ind. (7)	8	0.05
Sioux (4)	5	0.03
Asian (468)	611	4.06
Not Hispanic (465)	595	3.95
Hispanic (3)	16	0.11
Chinese, ex. Taiwanese (65)	91	0.60
Filipino (32)	61	0.41
Indian (217)	244	1.62
Indonesian (2)	3	0.02
Japanese (23)	53	0.35
Korean (52)	71	0.47
Malaysian (2)	2	0.01
Nepalese (1)	2	0.01
Pakistani (12)	15	0.10
Taiwanese (11)	11	0.07
Thai (0)	1	0.01

*Notes: † The Census 2010 population figure is used to calculate the percentages in the Hispanic Origin and Race categories. Ancestry percentages are based on the 2006-2010 American Community Survey population (not shown); ‡ Numbers in parentheses indicate the number of people reporting a single ancestry; * Numbers in parentheses indicate the number of persons reporting this race alone, not in combination with any other race; Please refer to the Explanation of Data for more information.*

Vietnamese (40)	47	0.31
Hawaii Native/Pacific Islander (15)	35	0.23
Not Hispanic (12)	31	0.21
Hispanic (3)	4	0.03
Guamanian/Chamorro (4)	4	0.03
Native Hawaiian (4)	14	0.09
Samoan (0)	3	0.02
White (13,649)	13,927	92.50
Not Hispanic (12,927)	13,159	87.40
Hispanic (722)	768	5.10

Highlands

Place Type: CDP
County: Harris
Population: 7,522†

Ancestry‡	Population	%
American (763)	763	9.59
Arab (0)	12	0.15
Lebanese (0)	12	0.15
Cajun (0)	14	0.18
Canadian (0)	12	0.15
Czech (47)	113	1.42
Dutch (36)	73	0.92
English (85)	311	3.91
European (201)	201	2.53
French, ex. Basque (63)	235	2.95
French Canadian (0)	17	0.21
German (179)	968	12.17
Greek (12)	37	0.47
Irish (382)	847	10.65
Italian (149)	184	2.31
Norwegian (46)	46	0.58
Polish (50)	100	1.26
Scotch-Irish (26)	102	1.28
Scottish (130)	289	3.63
Slovak (0)	13	0.16
Swedish (0)	22	0.28
Welsh (0)	26	0.33

Hispanic Origin	Population	%
Hispanic or Latino (of any race)	1,867	24.82
Central American, ex. Mexican	53	0.70
Guatemalan	8	0.11
Honduran	22	0.29
Nicaraguan	2	0.03
Salvadoran	21	0.28
Cuban	4	0.05
Mexican	1,647	21.90
Puerto Rican	13	0.17
South American	4	0.05
Colombian	2	0.03
Venezuelan	2	0.03
Other Hispanic or Latino	146	1.94

Race*	Population	%
African-American/Black (236)	274	3.64
Not Hispanic (229)	259	3.44
Hispanic (7)	15	0.20
American Indian/Alaska Native (69)	108	1.44
Not Hispanic (40)	68	0.90
Hispanic (29)	40	0.53
Apache (0)	2	0.03
Blackfeet (1)	6	0.08
Canadian/French Am. Ind. (0)	1	0.01
Cherokee (5)	12	0.16
Choctaw (8)	12	0.16
Creek (2)	2	0.03
Crow (0)	1	0.01
Delaware (0)	2	0.03
Mexican American Ind. (12)	14	0.19
Navajo (2)	2	0.03
Osage (3)	3	0.04
Sioux (4)	4	0.05
South American Ind. (2)	4	0.05
Asian (27)	40	0.53
Not Hispanic (27)	34	0.45
Hispanic (0)	6	0.08
Chinese, ex. Taiwanese (2)	2	0.03
Filipino (11)	14	0.19
Indian (1)	1	0.01
Indonesian (1)	1	0.01
Japanese (3)	4	0.05
Pakistani (2)	3	0.04
Vietnamese (4)	7	0.09
Hawaii Native/Pacific Islander (0)	4	0.05
Not Hispanic (0)	3	0.04
Hispanic (0)	1	0.01
Native Hawaiian (0)	1	0.01
White (6,330)	6,487	86.24
Not Hispanic (5,280)	5,347	71.08
Hispanic (1,050)	1,140	15.16

Hillsboro

Place Type: City
County: Hill
Population: 8,456†

Ancestry‡	Population	%
African, Sub-Saharan (38)	71	0.83
African (38)	71	0.83
American (504)	504	5.92
British (19)	19	0.22
Czech (33)	40	0.47
Dutch (11)	60	0.70
English (248)	476	5.59
European (32)	32	0.38
French, ex. Basque (0)	102	1.20
French Canadian (0)	10	0.12
German (385)	744	8.74
Hungarian (75)	75	0.88
Irish (238)	608	7.14
Italian (107)	123	1.44
Norwegian (85)	96	1.13
Polish (0)	9	0.11
Scotch-Irish (131)	186	2.18
Scottish (65)	129	1.52
Swedish (39)	51	0.60
Welsh (32)	46	0.54
West Indian, ex. Hispanic (28)	28	0.33
Haitian (28)	28	0.33

Hispanic Origin	Population	%
Hispanic or Latino (of any race)	3,306	39.10
Central American, ex. Mexican	18	0.21
Guatemalan	1	0.01
Honduran	8	0.09
Nicaraguan	1	0.01
Panamanian	2	0.02
Salvadoran	6	0.07
Cuban	8	0.09
Mexican	3,084	36.47
Puerto Rican	42	0.50
South American	8	0.09
Argentinean	5	0.06
Chilean	1	0.01
Ecuadorian	1	0.01
Peruvian	1	0.01
Other Hispanic or Latino	146	1.73

Race*	Population	%
African-American/Black (1,230)	1,333	15.76
Not Hispanic (1,206)	1,290	15.26
Hispanic (24)	43	0.51
American Indian/Alaska Native (44)	73	0.86
Not Hispanic (26)	44	0.52
Hispanic (18)	29	0.34
Apache (2)	4	0.05
Central American Ind. (1)	1	0.01
Cherokee (7)	16	0.19
Choctaw (4)	4	0.05
Comanche (1)	1	0.01
Iroquois (3)	3	0.04
Mexican American Ind. (7)	7	0.08
Osage (1)	1	0.01
Pueblo (1)	1	0.01
Seminole (1)	1	0.01
Sioux (1)	2	0.02
Asian (41)	56	0.66
Not Hispanic (38)	48	0.57
Hispanic (3)	8	0.09
Chinese, ex. Taiwanese (10)	10	0.12
Filipino (4)	14	0.17
Indian (3)	3	0.04
Japanese (2)	3	0.04
Korean (11)	12	0.14
Malaysian (1)	1	0.01
Nepalese (3)	3	0.04
Pakistani (1)	1	0.01
Taiwanese (0)	2	0.02
Vietnamese (3)	4	0.05
Hawaii Native/Pacific Islander (1)	5	0.06
Not Hispanic (1)	2	0.02
Hispanic (0)	3	0.04
Native Hawaiian (1)	1	0.01
Samoan (0)	1	0.01
White (5,557)	5,746	67.95
Not Hispanic (3,765)	3,866	45.72
Hispanic (1,792)	1,880	22.23

Hondo

Place Type: City
County: Medina
Population: 8,803†

Ancestry‡	Population	%
African, Sub-Saharan (88)	88	1.01
African (88)	88	1.01
Alsatian (18)	77	0.88
American (731)	731	8.39
Belgian (16)	16	0.18
British (6)	64	0.73
Canadian (0)	18	0.21
Czech (39)	70	0.80
Dutch (14)	14	0.16
English (86)	264	3.03
French, ex. Basque (7)	117	1.34
French Canadian (0)	33	0.38
German (687)	1,313	15.07
Irish (109)	228	2.62
Italian (93)	209	2.40
Lithuanian (12)	12	0.14
Northern European (41)	41	0.47
Norwegian (0)	19	0.22
Polish (9)	38	0.44
Scotch-Irish (78)	135	1.55
Scottish (0)	105	1.20
Swedish (0)	12	0.14
Welsh (10)	29	0.33
West Indian, ex. Hispanic (0)	10	0.11
Dutch West Indian (0)	10	0.11

Hispanic Origin	Population	%
Hispanic or Latino (of any race)	5,587	63.47
Central American, ex. Mexican	66	0.75
Guatemalan	15	0.17
Honduran	22	0.25
Panamanian	12	0.14
Salvadoran	17	0.19
Cuban	4	0.05
Dominican Republic	5	0.06
Mexican	4,780	54.30
Puerto Rican	13	0.15
South American	1	0.01
Colombian	1	0.01
Other Hispanic or Latino	718	8.16

Race*	Population	%
African-American/Black (696)	731	8.30
Not Hispanic (652)	668	7.59
Hispanic (44)	63	0.72
American Indian/Alaska Native (56)	95	1.08
Not Hispanic (17)	36	0.41
Hispanic (39)	59	0.67
Apache (6)	12	0.14
Cherokee (0)	10	0.11
Chickasaw (3)	3	0.03

SECTION TWO

*Notes: † The Census 2010 population figure is used to calculate the percentages in the Hispanic Origin and Race categories. Ancestry percentages are based on the 2006-2010 American Community Survey population (not shown); ‡ Numbers in parentheses indicate the number of people reporting a single ancestry; * Numbers in parentheses indicate the number of persons reporting this race alone, not in combination with any other race; Please refer to the Explanation of Data for more information.*

Chippewa (0)	4	0.05
Choctaw (4)	5	0.06
Kiowa (0)	2	0.02
Navajo (1)	1	0.01
Yaqui (1)	3	0.03
Asian (135)	151	1.72
Not Hispanic (129)	140	1.59
Hispanic (6)	11	0.12
Cambodian (1)	3	0.03
Chinese, ex. Taiwanese (86)	86	0.98
Filipino (11)	12	0.14
Indian (16)	19	0.22
Japanese (1)	6	0.07
Korean (1)	4	0.05
Pakistani (1)	1	0.01
Thai (0)	1	0.01
Vietnamese (9)	10	0.11
Hawaii Native/Pacific Islander (1)	6	0.07
Not Hispanic (0)	4	0.05
Hispanic (1)	2	0.02
Guamanian/Chamorro (0)	4	0.05
Native Hawaiian (1)	1	0.01
White (7,127)	7,263	82.51
Not Hispanic (2,364)	2,408	27.35
Hispanic (4,763)	4,855	55.15

Horizon City

Place Type: City
County: El Paso
Population: 16,735†

Ancestry‡	Population	%
African, Sub-Saharan (24)	24	0.16
African (24)	24	0.16
American (717)	717	4.92
Canadian (0)	14	0.10
Celtic (0)	12	0.08
Czech (10)	32	0.22
Danish (0)	61	0.42
Dutch (14)	14	0.10
English (94)	212	1.46
European (26)	37	0.25
Finnish (0)	15	0.10
French, ex. Basque (98)	262	1.80
German (168)	529	3.63
Iranian (0)	19	0.13
Irish (79)	252	1.73
Italian (25)	36	0.25
Norwegian (63)	82	0.56
Polish (83)	226	1.55
Russian (0)	33	0.23
Scotch-Irish (67)	81	0.56
Scottish (35)	44	0.30
Swedish (0)	12	0.08
West Indian, ex. Hispanic (118)	118	0.81
Haitian (118)	118	0.81

Hispanic Origin	Population	%
Hispanic or Latino (of any race)	14,373	85.89
Central American, ex. Mexican	52	0.31
Costa Rican	3	0.02
Guatemalan	8	0.05
Honduran	6	0.04
Nicaraguan	8	0.05
Panamanian	4	0.02
Salvadoran	23	0.14
Cuban	8	0.05
Dominican Republic	17	0.10
Mexican	13,507	80.71
Puerto Rican	139	0.83
South American	25	0.15
Argentinean	1	0.01
Chilean	2	0.01
Colombian	16	0.10
Ecuadorian	1	0.01
Paraguayan	1	0.01
Peruvian	3	0.02
Venezuelan	1	0.01
Other Hispanic or Latino	625	3.73

Race*	Population	%
African-American/Black (390)	481	2.87
Not Hispanic (299)	332	1.98
Hispanic (91)	149	0.89
American Indian/Alaska Native (94)	140	0.84
Not Hispanic (32)	45	0.27
Hispanic (62)	95	0.57
Apache (4)	6	0.04
Cherokee (2)	6	0.04
Choctaw (1)	4	0.02
Mexican American Ind. (10)	14	0.08
Navajo (1)	1	0.01
Potawatomi (1)	1	0.01
Pueblo (30)	36	0.22
South American Ind. (2)	2	0.01
Yaqui (1)	1	0.01
Asian (76)	121	0.72
Not Hispanic (65)	90	0.54
Hispanic (11)	31	0.19
Chinese, ex. Taiwanese (9)	9	0.05
Filipino (24)	40	0.24
Indian (7)	11	0.07
Japanese (5)	18	0.11
Korean (7)	20	0.12
Malaysian (1)	1	0.01
Pakistani (2)	2	0.01
Taiwanese (3)	3	0.02
Vietnamese (16)	16	0.10
Hawaii Native/Pacific Islander (13)	17	0.10
Not Hispanic (9)	10	0.06
Hispanic (4)	7	0.04
Guamanian/Chamorro (6)	7	0.04
Native Hawaiian (1)	3	0.02
Samoan (6)	6	0.04
White (13,610)	13,977	83.52
Not Hispanic (1,890)	1,940	11.59
Hispanic (11,720)	12,037	71.93

Houston

Place Type: City
County: Harris
Population: 2,099,451†

Ancestry‡	Population	%
Afghan (208)	224	0.01
African, Sub-Saharan (37,939)	41,757	2.02
African (22,153)	24,810	1.20
Cape Verdean (24)	66	<0.01
Ethiopian (2,287)	2,393	0.12
Ghanaian (172)	271	0.01
Kenyan (316)	331	0.02
Liberian (311)	311	0.02
Nigerian (8,315)	8,818	0.43
Senegalese (128)	144	0.01
Sierra Leonean (219)	235	0.01
Somalian (784)	784	0.04
South African (567)	594	0.03
Sudanese (512)	541	0.03
Zimbabwean (0)	10	<0.01
Other Sub-Saharan African (2,151)	2,449	0.12
Albanian (555)	615	0.03
Alsatian (27)	72	<0.01
American (54,678)	54,678	2.64
Arab (10,451)	13,350	0.65
Arab (2,522)	3,016	0.15
Egyptian (607)	732	0.04
Iraqi (532)	532	0.03
Jordanian (397)	595	0.03
Lebanese (2,741)	3,912	0.19
Moroccan (684)	765	0.04
Palestinian (617)	949	0.05
Syrian (704)	988	0.05
Other Arab (1,647)	1,861	0.09
Armenian (526)	834	0.04
Assyrian/Chaldean/Syriac (15)	52	<0.01
Australian (409)	690	0.03
Austrian (689)	2,488	0.12
Basque (83)	228	0.01
Belgian (448)	887	0.04
Brazilian (975)	1,370	0.07
British (4,411)	7,594	0.37
Bulgarian (148)	168	0.01
Cajun (598)	1,358	0.07
Canadian (1,560)	2,415	0.12
Celtic (105)	164	0.01
Croatian (274)	518	0.03
Czech (4,205)	11,531	0.56
Czechoslovakian (850)	1,568	0.08
Danish (990)	3,200	0.15
Dutch (3,008)	10,740	0.52
Eastern European (1,444)	1,613	0.08
English (36,169)	92,025	4.45
Estonian (89)	171	0.01
European (11,382)	13,040	0.63
Finnish (324)	936	0.05
French, ex. Basque (9,259)	35,661	1.72
French Canadian (2,187)	4,357	0.21
German (42,181)	122,874	5.94
German Russian (73)	142	0.01
Greek (2,765)	5,132	0.25
Guyanese (434)	510	0.02
Hungarian (832)	2,396	0.12
Icelander (25)	119	0.01
Iranian (4,125)	4,582	0.22
Irish (26,408)	84,899	4.11
Israeli (888)	1,071	0.05
Italian (12,614)	31,661	1.53
Latvian (167)	344	0.02
Lithuanian (509)	1,489	0.07
Luxemburger (0)	76	<0.01
Macedonian (0)	23	<0.01
Maltese (39)	88	<0.01
New Zealander (123)	144	0.01
Northern European (949)	997	0.05
Norwegian (2,592)	6,888	0.33
Pennsylvania German (69)	120	0.01
Polish (7,002)	19,181	0.93
Portuguese (668)	1,699	0.08
Romanian (1,998)	2,664	0.13
Russian (4,690)	9,363	0.45
Scandinavian (801)	1,548	0.07
Scotch-Irish (9,321)	21,460	1.04
Scottish (7,503)	21,995	1.06
Serbian (222)	309	0.01
Slavic (160)	242	0.01
Slovak (361)	775	0.04
Slovene (87)	233	0.01
Swedish (2,322)	7,900	0.38
Swiss (823)	2,669	0.13
Turkish (1,799)	2,090	0.10
Ukrainian (914)	1,858	0.09
Welsh (1,643)	5,944	0.29
West Indian, ex. Hispanic (7,115)	9,005	0.44
Bahamian (118)	165	0.01
Barbadian (71)	71	<0.01
Belizean (1,400)	1,482	0.07
Bermudan (0)	19	<0.01
British West Indian (83)	130	0.01
Dutch West Indian (107)	157	0.01
Haitian (1,099)	1,438	0.07
Jamaican (2,163)	2,897	0.14
Trinidadian/Tobagonian (830)	1,106	0.05
West Indian (1,223)	1,453	0.07
Other West Indian (21)	87	<0.01
Yugoslavian (1,065)	1,287	0.06

Hispanic Origin	Population	%
Hispanic or Latino (of any race)	919,668	43.81
Central American, ex. Mexican	140,815	6.71
Costa Rican	923	0.04
Guatemalan	25,205	1.20
Honduran	32,807	1.56
Nicaraguan	4,226	0.20
Panamanian	1,076	0.05
Salvadoran	75,907	3.62
Other Central American	671	0.03
Cuban	7,663	0.37
Dominican Republic	1,876	0.09

*Notes: † The Census 2010 population figure is used to calculate the percentages in the Hispanic Origin and Race categories. Ancestry percentages are based on the 2006-2010 American Community Survey population (not shown); ‡ Numbers in parentheses indicate the number of people reporting a single ancestry; * Numbers in parentheses indicate the number of persons reporting this race alone, not in combination with any other race; Please refer to the Explanation of Data for more information.*

Mexican	673,093	32.06
Puerto Rican	9,290	0.44
South American	24,040	1.15
Argentinean	2,440	0.12
Bolivian	958	0.05
Chilean	934	0.04
Colombian	10,226	0.49
Ecuadorian	1,557	0.07
Paraguayan	119	0.01
Peruvian	3,237	0.15
Uruguayan	642	0.03
Venezuelan	3,770	0.18
Other South American	157	0.01
Other Hispanic or Latino	62,891	3.00

Race*	Population	%
African-American/Black (498,466)	514,217	24.49
Not Hispanic (485,956)	495,792	23.62
Hispanic (12,510)	18,425	0.88
American Indian/Alaska Native (14,997)	25,521	1.22
Not Hispanic (3,528)	8,735	0.42
Hispanic (11,469)	16,786	0.80
Alaska Athabascan *(Ala. Nat.)* (4)	7	<0.01
Aleut *(Alaska Native)* (7)	9	<0.01
Apache (140)	319	0.02
Arapaho (1)	10	<0.01
Blackfeet (36)	179	0.01
Canadian/French Am. Ind. (16)	49	<0.01
Central American Ind. (567)	876	0.04
Cherokee (648)	2,120	0.10
Cheyenne (12)	22	<0.01
Chickasaw (95)	168	0.01
Chippewa (49)	90	<0.01
Choctaw (291)	697	0.03
Colville (0)	1	<0.01
Comanche (58)	151	0.01
Cree (5)	17	<0.01
Creek (85)	192	0.01
Crow (2)	9	<0.01
Delaware (27)	49	<0.01
Hopi (4)	16	<0.01
Houma (8)	16	<0.01
Inupiat *(Alaska Native)* (7)	14	<0.01
Iroquois (52)	107	0.01
Kiowa (9)	24	<0.01
Lumbee (12)	14	<0.01
Menominee (1)	1	<0.01
Mexican American Ind. (2,579)	3,570	0.17
Navajo (110)	172	0.01
Osage (32)	84	<0.01
Ottawa (5)	12	<0.01
Paiute (12)	17	<0.01
Pima (14)	17	<0.01
Potawatomi (38)	63	<0.01
Pueblo (53)	93	<0.01
Puget Sound Salish (1)	5	<0.01
Seminole (30)	67	<0.01
Shoshone (6)	8	<0.01
Sioux (80)	184	0.01
South American Ind. (97)	206	0.01
Spanish American Ind. (282)	421	0.02
Tlingit-Haida *(Alaska Native)* (3)	13	<0.01
Tohono O'Odham (7)	11	<0.01
Tsimshian *(Alaska Native)* (1)	4	<0.01
Ute (5)	10	<0.01
Yakama (1)	3	<0.01
Yaqui (18)	33	<0.01
Yuman (12)	14	<0.01
Yup'ik *(Alaska Native)* (0)	1	<0.01
Asian (126,378)	139,960	6.67
Not Hispanic (124,859)	135,594	6.46
Hispanic (1,519)	4,366	0.21
Bangladeshi (765)	847	0.04
Bhutanese (633)	788	0.04
Burmese (1,385)	1,460	0.07
Cambodian (849)	1,050	0.05
Chinese, ex. Taiwanese (25,246)	28,268	1.35
Filipino (8,999)	11,140	0.53
Hmong (17)	22	<0.01
Indian (26,289)	29,128	1.39
Indonesian (718)	888	0.04
Japanese (2,346)	3,463	0.16
Korean (6,568)	7,578	0.36
Laotian (236)	351	0.02
Malaysian (184)	260	0.01
Nepalese (833)	995	0.05
Pakistani (7,406)	8,258	0.39
Sri Lankan (286)	324	0.02
Taiwanese (2,505)	2,910	0.14
Thai (1,106)	1,462	0.07
Vietnamese (34,838)	37,178	1.77
Hawaii Native/Pacific Islander (1,153)	3,341	0.16
Not Hispanic (711)	1,887	0.09
Hispanic (442)	1,454	0.07
Fijian (42)	56	<0.01
Guamanian/Chamorro (500)	693	0.03
Marshallese (2)	3	<0.01
Native Hawaiian (241)	713	0.03
Samoan (115)	261	0.01
Tongan (13)	26	<0.01
White (1,060,491)	1,116,036	53.16
Not Hispanic (537,901)	555,181	26.44
Hispanic (522,590)	560,855	26.71

Humble

Place Type: City
County: Harris
Population: 15,133†

Ancestry‡	Population	%
African, Sub-Saharan (236)	236	1.58
African (236)	236	1.58
American (1,000)	1,000	6.68
Arab (9)	9	0.06
Syrian (9)	9	0.06
Cajun (22)	22	0.15
Canadian (0)	62	0.41
Czech (36)	98	0.65
Danish (0)	9	0.06
Dutch (22)	143	0.95
English (266)	528	3.52
French, ex. Basque (38)	175	1.17
French Canadian (9)	33	0.22
German (704)	1,312	8.76
Greek (25)	30	0.20
Hungarian (13)	29	0.19
Irish (521)	1,298	8.67
Italian (39)	111	0.74
Polish (15)	55	0.37
Portuguese (0)	35	0.23
Russian (0)	7	0.05
Scotch-Irish (126)	243	1.62
Scottish (94)	260	1.74
Swedish (9)	28	0.19
Welsh (0)	40	0.27
Yugoslavian (14)	14	0.09

Hispanic Origin	Population	%
Hispanic or Latino (of any race)	6,234	41.19
Central American, ex. Mexican	629	4.16
Costa Rican	19	0.13
Guatemalan	176	1.16
Honduran	169	1.12
Nicaraguan	46	0.30
Panamanian	18	0.12
Salvadoran	197	1.30
Other Central American	4	0.03
Cuban	45	0.30
Dominican Republic	25	0.17
Mexican	4,975	32.88
Puerto Rican	81	0.54
South American	96	0.63
Argentinean	5	0.03
Bolivian	3	0.02
Chilean	13	0.09
Colombian	19	0.13
Ecuadorian	12	0.08
Peruvian	23	0.15
Uruguayan	4	0.03
Venezuelan	14	0.09
Other South American	3	0.02
Other Hispanic or Latino	383	2.53

Race*	Population	%
African-American/Black (3,276)	3,401	22.47
Not Hispanic (3,193)	3,274	21.63
Hispanic (83)	127	0.84
American Indian/Alaska Native (118)	191	1.26
Not Hispanic (45)	74	0.49
Hispanic (73)	117	0.77
Apache (1)	2	0.01
Blackfeet (1)	1	0.01
Cherokee (19)	36	0.24
Cheyenne (1)	2	0.01
Chippewa (1)	2	0.01
Choctaw (6)	13	0.09
Iroquois (1)	2	0.01
Mexican American Ind. (23)	24	0.16
Navajo (0)	3	0.02
Potawatomi (1)	1	0.01
Spanish American Ind. (2)	2	0.01
Asian (413)	479	3.17
Not Hispanic (399)	435	2.87
Hispanic (14)	44	0.29
Cambodian (3)	5	0.03
Chinese, ex. Taiwanese (32)	49	0.32
Filipino (78)	91	0.60
Indian (75)	88	0.58
Indonesian (4)	4	0.03
Japanese (4)	7	0.05
Korean (7)	13	0.09
Laotian (1)	5	0.03
Nepalese (23)	24	0.16
Pakistani (34)	35	0.23
Sri Lankan (0)	1	0.01
Thai (2)	2	0.01
Vietnamese (117)	129	0.85
Hawaii Native/Pacific Islander (145)	186	1.23
Not Hispanic (129)	150	0.99
Hispanic (16)	36	0.24
Guamanian/Chamorro (31)	39	0.26
Native Hawaiian (17)	24	0.16
Samoan (2)	2	0.01
White (8,168)	8,642	57.11
Not Hispanic (4,964)	5,079	33.56
Hispanic (3,204)	3,563	23.54

Huntsville

Place Type: City
County: Walker
Population: 38,548†

Ancestry‡	Population	%
African, Sub-Saharan (99)	130	0.34
African (46)	77	0.20
Kenyan (36)	36	0.10
Nigerian (17)	17	0.04
Albanian (15)	15	0.04
American (4,075)	4,075	10.78
Arab (49)	59	0.16
Arab (0)	10	0.03
Egyptian (12)	12	0.03
Lebanese (7)	7	0.02
Moroccan (20)	20	0.05
Other Arab (10)	10	0.03
Austrian (12)	55	0.15
Belgian (0)	9	0.02
British (93)	132	0.35
Cajun (15)	40	0.11
Canadian (21)	39	0.10
Croatian (11)	11	0.03
Czech (136)	598	1.58
Czechoslovakian (19)	25	0.07
Danish (57)	99	0.26
Dutch (128)	242	0.64
Eastern European (43)	43	0.11
English (1,326)	3,039	8.04
European (121)	199	0.53

*Notes: † The Census 2010 population figure is used to calculate the percentages in the Hispanic Origin and Race categories. Ancestry percentages are based on the 2006-2010 American Community Survey population (not shown); ‡ Numbers in parentheses indicate the number of people reporting a single ancestry; * Numbers in parentheses indicate the number of persons reporting this race alone, not in combination with any other race; Please refer to the Explanation of Data for more information.*

SECTION TWO

Ancestry	Population	%
Finnish (7)	29	0.08
French, ex. Basque (172)	606	1.60
French Canadian (55)	106	0.28
German (1,925)	4,564	12.07
Greek (18)	18	0.05
Hungarian (0)	6	0.02
Iranian (10)	10	0.03
Irish (1,484)	3,277	8.67
Italian (418)	712	1.88
Norwegian (81)	198	0.52
Polish (96)	332	0.88
Portuguese (0)	10	0.03
Russian (63)	116	0.31
Scandinavian (0)	9	0.02
Scotch-Irish (346)	674	1.78
Scottish (268)	713	1.89
Slovak (0)	13	0.03
Slovene (17)	17	0.04
Swedish (185)	314	0.83
Swiss (12)	41	0.11
Welsh (66)	248	0.66
West Indian, ex. Hispanic (0)	18	0.05
Jamaican (0)	18	0.05

Hispanic Origin	Population	%
Hispanic or Latino (of any race)	7,211	18.71
Central American, ex. Mexican	460	1.19
Costa Rican	3	0.01
Guatemalan	19	0.05
Honduran	48	0.12
Nicaraguan	7	0.02
Panamanian	14	0.04
Salvadoran	365	0.95
Other Central American	4	0.01
Cuban	62	0.16
Dominican Republic	15	0.04
Mexican	5,759	14.94
Puerto Rican	121	0.31
South American	98	0.25
Argentinean	7	0.02
Bolivian	7	0.02
Chilean	2	0.01
Colombian	36	0.09
Ecuadorian	15	0.04
Paraguayan	1	<0.01
Peruvian	14	0.04
Venezuelan	15	0.04
Other South American	1	<0.01
Other Hispanic or Latino	696	1.81

Race*	Population	%
African-American/Black (9,799)	10,127	26.27
Not Hispanic (9,695)	9,955	25.82
Hispanic (104)	172	0.45
American Indian/Alaska Native (160)	332	0.86
Not Hispanic (88)	223	0.58
Hispanic (72)	109	0.28
Apache (5)	7	0.02
Blackfeet (2)	5	0.01
Cherokee (20)	85	0.22
Cheyenne (0)	1	<0.01
Chickasaw (2)	5	0.01
Choctaw (7)	16	0.04
Comanche (3)	7	0.02
Creek (1)	5	0.01
Crow (0)	4	0.01
Iroquois (0)	1	<0.01
Kiowa (1)	2	0.01
Mexican American Ind. (7)	9	0.02
Navajo (4)	4	0.01
Osage (0)	3	0.01
Paiute (0)	2	0.01
Potawatomi (2)	2	0.01
Seminole (0)	1	<0.01
Shoshone (1)	1	<0.01
Sioux (0)	5	0.01
South American Ind. (2)	2	0.01
Spanish American Ind. (5)	7	0.02
Ute (2)	2	0.01
Asian (523)	657	1.70
Not Hispanic (511)	618	1.60
Hispanic (12)	39	0.10
Bangladeshi (4)	4	0.01
Burmese (0)	1	<0.01
Cambodian (13)	13	0.03
Chinese, ex. Taiwanese (109)	124	0.32
Filipino (84)	123	0.32
Indian (96)	115	0.30
Indonesian (4)	5	0.01
Japanese (23)	55	0.14
Korean (52)	65	0.17
Laotian (4)	4	0.01
Malaysian (1)	2	0.01
Nepalese (4)	6	0.02
Pakistani (13)	17	0.04
Sri Lankan (8)	8	0.02
Taiwanese (9)	12	0.03
Thai (9)	12	0.03
Vietnamese (64)	66	0.17
Hawaii Native/Pacific Islander (21)	47	0.12
Not Hispanic (16)	33	0.09
Hispanic (5)	14	0.04
Guamanian/Chamorro (9)	10	0.03
Native Hawaiian (6)	19	0.05
Samoan (0)	4	0.01
White (24,152)	24,874	64.53
Not Hispanic (20,537)	20,924	54.28
Hispanic (3,615)	3,950	10.25

Hurst

Place Type: City
County: Tarrant
Population: 37,337†

Ancestry‡	Population	%
African, Sub-Saharan (187)	187	0.50
African (89)	89	0.24
Nigerian (98)	98	0.26
American (3,897)	3,897	10.49
Arab (502)	533	1.44
Arab (356)	367	0.99
Egyptian (77)	77	0.21
Iraqi (12)	12	0.03
Jordanian (33)	33	0.09
Lebanese (15)	27	0.07
Palestinian (0)	8	0.02
Other Arab (9)	9	0.02
Austrian (0)	43	0.12
British (115)	130	0.35
Cajun (0)	10	0.03
Canadian (46)	108	0.29
Celtic (0)	17	0.05
Czech (86)	145	0.39
Czechoslovakian (0)	50	0.13
Danish (19)	71	0.19
Dutch (101)	456	1.23
English (1,880)	4,776	12.86
European (417)	438	1.18
Finnish (39)	45	0.12
French, ex. Basque (204)	1,260	3.39
French Canadian (14)	72	0.19
German (2,059)	6,109	16.45
Greek (56)	128	0.34
Hungarian (24)	67	0.18
Iranian (106)	106	0.29
Irish (1,366)	3,810	10.26
Italian (288)	1,274	3.43
Latvian (0)	48	0.13
Maltese (20)	20	0.05
Northern European (18)	18	0.05
Norwegian (179)	297	0.80
Pennsylvania German (0)	8	0.02
Polish (158)	386	1.04
Portuguese (16)	16	0.04
Russian (94)	109	0.29
Scandinavian (35)	92	0.25
Scotch-Irish (536)	1,020	2.75
Scottish (513)	1,264	3.40
Serbian (5)	5	0.01
Slavic (0)	17	0.05
Slovak (22)	61	0.16
Slovene (10)	10	0.03
Swedish (135)	512	1.38
Swiss (11)	61	0.16
Ukrainian (51)	92	0.25
Welsh (100)	266	0.72
West Indian, ex. Hispanic (134)	161	0.43
British West Indian (27)	27	0.07
Dutch West Indian (9)	36	0.10
Trinidadian/Tobagonian (98)	98	0.26
Yugoslavian (8)	8	0.02

Hispanic Origin	Population	%
Hispanic or Latino (of any race)	7,510	20.11
Central American, ex. Mexican	454	1.22
Costa Rican	7	0.02
Guatemalan	30	0.08
Honduran	99	0.27
Nicaraguan	8	0.02
Panamanian	17	0.05
Salvadoran	282	0.76
Other Central American	11	0.03
Cuban	57	0.15
Dominican Republic	34	0.09
Mexican	5,899	15.80
Puerto Rican	328	0.88
South American	141	0.38
Argentinean	33	0.09
Bolivian	2	0.01
Chilean	10	0.03
Colombian	51	0.14
Ecuadorian	7	0.02
Peruvian	21	0.06
Venezuelan	17	0.05
Other Hispanic or Latino	597	1.60

Race*	Population	%
African-American/Black (2,105)	2,421	6.48
Not Hispanic (2,015)	2,275	6.09
Hispanic (90)	146	0.39
American Indian/Alaska Native (245)	544	1.46
Not Hispanic (187)	431	1.15
Hispanic (58)	113	0.30
Aleut *(Alaska Native)* (1)	2	0.01
Apache (8)	12	0.03
Blackfeet (2)	7	0.02
Cherokee (49)	145	0.39
Chickasaw (11)	24	0.06
Choctaw (50)	74	0.20
Comanche (7)	10	0.03
Cree (1)	1	<0.01
Creek (4)	20	0.05
Delaware (1)	5	0.01
Hopi (0)	1	<0.01
Iroquois (1)	2	0.01
Kiowa (2)	2	0.01
Lumbee (5)	5	0.01
Mexican American Ind. (13)	16	0.04
Navajo (1)	2	0.01
Osage (1)	4	0.01
Potawatomi (2)	8	0.02
Pueblo (0)	3	0.01
Seminole (0)	2	0.01
Sioux (6)	7	0.02
Asian (865)	1,112	2.98
Not Hispanic (852)	1,063	2.85
Hispanic (13)	49	0.13
Bangladeshi (16)	21	0.06
Burmese (2)	2	0.01
Cambodian (11)	11	0.03
Chinese, ex. Taiwanese (85)	124	0.33
Filipino (83)	129	0.35
Indian (192)	221	0.59
Indonesian (5)	8	0.02
Japanese (28)	72	0.19
Korean (90)	119	0.32
Laotian (24)	42	0.11
Malaysian (1)	1	<0.01
Nepalese (16)	16	0.04

*Notes: † The Census 2010 population figure is used to calculate the percentages in the Hispanic Origin and Race categories. Ancestry percentages are based on the 2006-2010 American Community Survey population (not shown); ‡ Numbers in parentheses indicate the number of people reporting a single ancestry; * Numbers in parentheses indicate the number of persons reporting this race alone, not in combination with any other race; Please refer to the Explanation of Data for more information.*

Pakistani (41)	53	0.14
Taiwanese (7)	9	0.02
Thai (26)	44	0.12
Vietnamese (195)	212	0.57
Hawaii Native/Pacific Islander (130)	203	0.54
Not Hispanic (128)	188	0.50
Hispanic (2)	15	0.04
Fijian (2)	2	0.01
Guamanian/Chamorro (2)	5	0.01
Marshallese (1)	1	<0.01
Native Hawaiian (20)	36	0.10
Samoan (9)	21	0.06
Tongan (61)	72	0.19
White (30,191)	31,173	83.49
Not Hispanic (25,883)	26,505	70.99
Hispanic (4,308)	4,668	12.50

Hutto

Place Type: City
County: Williamson
Population: 14,698†

Ancestry‡	Population	%
African, Sub-Saharan (101)	101	0.82
African (101)	101	0.82
American (942)	942	7.65
Arab (9)	22	0.18
Lebanese (9)	22	0.18
Austrian (0)	6	0.05
Basque (24)	24	0.20
Belgian (0)	33	0.27
British (14)	14	0.11
Croatian (0)	31	0.25
Czech (80)	419	3.40
Dutch (86)	174	1.41
English (311)	1,116	9.07
European (106)	204	1.66
French, ex. Basque (59)	227	1.84
French Canadian (11)	57	0.46
German (636)	2,197	17.85
Greek (69)	69	0.56
Hungarian (5)	36	0.29
Irish (320)	1,151	9.35
Italian (302)	743	6.04
Northern European (11)	11	0.09
Norwegian (24)	77	0.63
Polish (55)	272	2.21
Russian (5)	13	0.11
Scotch-Irish (49)	304	2.47
Scottish (25)	165	1.34
Swedish (153)	338	2.75
Welsh (0)	166	1.35
West Indian, ex. Hispanic (16)	27	0.22
Barbadian (16)	16	0.13
Jamaican (0)	11	0.09

Hispanic Origin	Population	%
Hispanic or Latino (of any race)	4,534	30.85
Central American, ex. Mexican	147	1.00
Costa Rican	4	0.03
Guatemalan	29	0.20
Honduran	20	0.14
Nicaraguan	13	0.09
Panamanian	17	0.12
Salvadoran	63	0.43
Other Central American	1	0.01
Cuban	70	0.48
Dominican Republic	15	0.10
Mexican	3,800	25.85
Puerto Rican	157	1.07
South American	48	0.33
Argentinean	3	0.02
Bolivian	1	0.01
Chilean	1	0.01
Colombian	25	0.17
Ecuadorian	2	0.01
Peruvian	8	0.05
Venezuelan	8	0.05
Other Hispanic or Latino	297	2.02

Race*	Population	%
African-American/Black (2,108)	2,343	15.94
Not Hispanic (1,997)	2,185	14.87
Hispanic (111)	158	1.07
American Indian/Alaska Native (119)	245	1.67
Not Hispanic (41)	126	0.86
Hispanic (78)	119	0.81
Apache (0)	8	0.05
Blackfeet (0)	5	0.03
Cherokee (12)	49	0.33
Chickasaw (1)	10	0.07
Choctaw (8)	18	0.12
Comanche (0)	4	0.03
Cree (1)	1	0.01
Creek (1)	1	0.01
Hopi (3)	3	0.02
Houma (4)	4	0.03
Iroquois (1)	2	0.01
Lumbee (0)	2	0.01
Mexican American Ind. (7)	11	0.07
Navajo (1)	6	0.04
Ottawa (0)	2	0.01
Pima (0)	1	0.01
South American Ind. (2)	2	0.01
Tlingit-Haida *(Alaska Native)* (2)	2	0.01
Yaqui (1)	2	0.01
Asian (202)	346	2.35
Not Hispanic (190)	307	2.09
Hispanic (12)	39	0.27
Bangladeshi (0)	2	0.01
Cambodian (13)	21	0.14
Chinese, ex. Taiwanese (9)	19	0.13
Filipino (52)	94	0.64
Indian (26)	35	0.24
Indonesian (4)	6	0.04
Japanese (8)	20	0.14
Korean (6)	37	0.25
Laotian (4)	5	0.03
Pakistani (11)	11	0.07
Taiwanese (1)	3	0.02
Thai (5)	13	0.09
Vietnamese (52)	66	0.45
Hawaii Native/Pacific Islander (12)	56	0.38
Not Hispanic (9)	42	0.29
Hispanic (3)	14	0.10
Fijian (3)	3	0.02
Guamanian/Chamorro (1)	11	0.07
Native Hawaiian (3)	23	0.16
Samoan (3)	6	0.04
White (10,563)	11,082	75.40
Not Hispanic (7,553)	7,866	53.52
Hispanic (3,010)	3,216	21.88

Ingleside

Place Type: City
County: San Patricio
Population: 9,387†

Ancestry‡	Population	%
American (398)	398	4.19
Austrian (10)	20	0.21
Canadian (20)	20	0.21
Croatian (13)	24	0.25
Czech (37)	117	1.23
Danish (0)	15	0.16
Dutch (0)	161	1.69
English (212)	668	7.03
European (161)	161	1.69
French, ex. Basque (23)	178	1.87
French Canadian (11)	11	0.12
German (343)	1,367	14.39
Greek (8)	8	0.08
Hungarian (0)	10	0.11
Irish (407)	1,338	14.08
Italian (0)	168	1.77
Norwegian (0)	5	0.05
Polish (124)	237	2.49
Russian (0)	8	0.08
Scotch-Irish (49)	176	1.85
Scottish (71)	162	1.70
Slavic (9)	9	0.09
Swedish (0)	15	0.16
Ukrainian (14)	14	0.15
Welsh (19)	57	0.60
Yugoslavian (0)	87	0.92

Hispanic Origin	Population	%
Hispanic or Latino (of any race)	3,834	40.84
Central American, ex. Mexican	19	0.20
Guatemalan	4	0.04
Honduran	9	0.10
Panamanian	6	0.06
Cuban	13	0.14
Dominican Republic	8	0.09
Mexican	3,243	34.55
Puerto Rican	37	0.39
South American	21	0.22
Argentinean	2	0.02
Chilean	2	0.02
Colombian	10	0.11
Ecuadorian	1	0.01
Paraguayan	1	0.01
Peruvian	2	0.02
Venezuelan	3	0.03
Other Hispanic or Latino	493	5.25

Race*	Population	%
African-American/Black (175)	235	2.50
Not Hispanic (164)	209	2.23
Hispanic (11)	26	0.28
American Indian/Alaska Native (60)	122	1.30
Not Hispanic (39)	73	0.78
Hispanic (21)	49	0.52
Apache (3)	16	0.17
Blackfeet (0)	4	0.04
Cherokee (1)	16	0.17
Chippewa (0)	4	0.04
Choctaw (8)	9	0.10
Comanche (0)	3	0.03
Inupiat *(Alaska Native)* (1)	1	0.01
Iroquois (4)	4	0.04
Mexican American Ind. (4)	4	0.04
Navajo (8)	8	0.09
Pueblo (0)	1	0.01
Sioux (1)	1	0.01
Asian (198)	273	2.91
Not Hispanic (185)	238	2.54
Hispanic (13)	35	0.37
Cambodian (5)	5	0.05
Chinese, ex. Taiwanese (12)	17	0.18
Filipino (86)	134	1.43
Indian (51)	56	0.60
Indonesian (1)	1	0.01
Japanese (10)	17	0.18
Korean (4)	11	0.12
Laotian (2)	5	0.05
Thai (10)	10	0.11
Vietnamese (5)	7	0.07
Hawaii Native/Pacific Islander (7)	13	0.14
Not Hispanic (7)	13	0.14
Guamanian/Chamorro (5)	5	0.05
Native Hawaiian (1)	6	0.06
White (7,853)	8,152	86.84
Not Hispanic (5,021)	5,140	54.76
Hispanic (2,832)	3,012	32.09

Irving

Place Type: City
County: Dallas
Population: 216,290†

Ancestry‡	Population	%
African, Sub-Saharan (3,964)	4,601	2.19
African (2,106)	2,360	1.12
Ethiopian (180)	236	0.11
Ghanaian (21)	21	0.01
Kenyan (237)	284	0.14

*Notes: † The Census 2010 population figure is used to calculate the percentages in the Hispanic Origin and Race categories. Ancestry percentages are based on the 2006-2010 American Community Survey population (not shown); ‡ Numbers in parentheses indicate the number of people reporting a single ancestry; * Numbers in parentheses indicate the number of persons reporting this race alone, not in combination with any other race; Please refer to the Explanation of Data for more information.*

Liberian (11)	11	0.01
Nigerian (666)	789	0.38
Sierra Leonean (0)	10	<0.01
Somalian (514)	514	0.24
South African (12)	24	0.01
Sudanese (195)	229	0.11
Zimbabwean (4)	4	<0.01
Other Sub-Saharan African (18)	119	0.06
Albanian (11)	34	0.02
Alsatian (11)	11	0.01
American (8,519)	8,519	4.06
Arab (1,284)	1,418	0.68
Arab (459)	472	0.22
Egyptian (24)	41	0.02
Iraqi (401)	401	0.19
Jordanian (129)	129	0.06
Lebanese (139)	167	0.08
Moroccan (33)	44	0.02
Palestinian (21)	21	0.01
Other Arab (78)	143	0.07
Armenian (40)	62	0.03
Austrian (34)	125	0.06
Basque (15)	15	0.01
Belgian (0)	35	0.02
Brazilian (75)	90	0.04
British (506)	628	0.30
Bulgarian (15)	31	0.01
Cajun (13)	57	0.03
Canadian (93)	126	0.06
Celtic (19)	32	0.02
Croatian (8)	69	0.03
Czech (472)	977	0.47
Czechoslovakian (126)	244	0.12
Danish (90)	436	0.21
Dutch (343)	2,132	1.02
Eastern European (60)	60	0.03
English (3,720)	11,453	5.45
European (1,086)	1,217	0.58
Finnish (223)	373	0.18
French, ex. Basque (621)	3,273	1.56
French Canadian (342)	488	0.23
German (5,110)	16,323	7.77
Greek (139)	347	0.17
Hungarian (133)	325	0.15
Icelander (0)	10	<0.01
Iranian (384)	498	0.24
Irish (3,595)	13,068	6.22
Italian (1,229)	3,759	1.79
Lithuanian (58)	99	0.05
Luxemburger (12)	25	0.01
Macedonian (0)	35	0.02
Northern European (65)	78	0.04
Norwegian (205)	525	0.25
Polish (368)	1,331	0.63
Portuguese (99)	192	0.09
Romanian (119)	157	0.07
Russian (293)	628	0.30
Scandinavian (37)	118	0.06
Scotch-Irish (1,195)	2,863	1.36
Scottish (805)	2,531	1.21
Serbian (121)	121	0.06
Slavic (20)	20	0.01
Slovak (0)	67	0.03
Slovene (7)	15	0.01
Swedish (205)	873	0.42
Swiss (6)	215	0.10
Turkish (56)	105	0.05
Ukrainian (46)	137	0.07
Welsh (55)	671	0.32
West Indian, ex. Hispanic (159)	272	0.13
British West Indian (8)	8	<0.01
Dutch West Indian (11)	70	0.03
Haitian (11)	11	0.01
Jamaican (91)	122	0.06
Trinidadian/Tobagonian (25)	25	0.01
West Indian (13)	36	0.02
Yugoslavian (111)	145	0.07

Hispanic Origin	Population	%
Hispanic or Latino (of any race)	88,967	41.13
Central American, ex. Mexican	15,203	7.03
Costa Rican	92	0.04
Guatemalan	644	0.30
Honduran	1,547	0.72
Nicaraguan	186	0.09
Panamanian	123	0.06
Salvadoran	12,544	5.80
Other Central American	67	0.03
Cuban	359	0.17
Dominican Republic	196	0.09
Mexican	64,396	29.77
Puerto Rican	1,176	0.54
South American	2,388	1.10
Argentinean	803	0.37
Bolivian	57	0.03
Chilean	84	0.04
Colombian	456	0.21
Ecuadorian	136	0.06
Paraguayan	15	0.01
Peruvian	538	0.25
Uruguayan	35	0.02
Venezuelan	245	0.11
Other South American	19	0.01
Other Hispanic or Latino	5,249	2.43

Race*	Population	%
African-American/Black (26,522)	28,590	13.22
Not Hispanic (25,550)	27,075	12.52
Hispanic (972)	1,515	0.70
American Indian/Alaska Native (1,878)	3,254	1.50
Not Hispanic (807)	1,722	0.80
Hispanic (1,071)	1,532	0.71
Alaska Athabascan *(Ala. Nat.)* (1)	2	<0.01
Aleut *(Alaska Native)* (4)	4	<0.01
Apache (24)	52	0.02
Blackfeet (3)	23	0.01
Canadian/French Am. Ind. (2)	3	<0.01
Central American Ind. (17)	22	0.01
Cherokee (125)	428	0.20
Cheyenne (3)	10	<0.01
Chickasaw (25)	46	0.02
Chippewa (7)	25	0.01
Choctaw (130)	258	0.12
Colville (0)	3	<0.01
Comanche (29)	52	0.02
Cree (0)	1	<0.01
Creek (16)	41	0.02
Delaware (5)	8	<0.01
Houma (1)	1	<0.01
Inupiat *(Alaska Native)* (1)	1	<0.01
Iroquois (7)	17	0.01
Kiowa (16)	19	0.01
Lumbee (4)	7	<0.01
Menominee (0)	1	<0.01
Mexican American Ind. (135)	175	0.08
Navajo (60)	78	0.04
Osage (6)	9	<0.01
Ottawa (2)	2	<0.01
Pima (5)	6	<0.01
Potawatomi (13)	15	0.01
Pueblo (7)	9	<0.01
Puget Sound Salish (1)	2	<0.01
Seminole (5)	13	0.01
Shoshone (2)	5	<0.01
Sioux (13)	33	0.02
South American Ind. (15)	19	0.01
Spanish American Ind. (13)	25	0.01
Ute (3)	5	<0.01
Yakama (2)	3	<0.01
Yaqui (3)	8	<0.01
Yuman (0)	1	<0.01
Asian (30,359)	32,212	14.89
Not Hispanic (30,161)	31,808	14.71
Hispanic (198)	404	0.19
Bangladeshi (549)	605	0.28
Bhutanese (5)	5	<0.01
Burmese (33)	43	0.02
Cambodian (85)	108	0.05
Chinese, ex. Taiwanese (1,424)	1,677	0.78
Filipino (859)	1,112	0.51
Hmong (23)	24	0.01
Indian (17,403)	18,025	8.33
Indonesian (99)	123	0.06
Japanese (466)	651	0.30
Korean (3,081)	3,261	1.51
Laotian (415)	453	0.21
Malaysian (27)	39	0.02
Nepalese (1,507)	1,590	0.74
Pakistani (1,152)	1,252	0.58
Sri Lankan (54)	57	0.03
Taiwanese (142)	172	0.08
Thai (257)	315	0.15
Vietnamese (1,974)	2,120	0.98
Hawaii Native/Pacific Islander (255)	473	0.22
Not Hispanic (221)	361	0.17
Hispanic (34)	112	0.05
Fijian (3)	4	<0.01
Guamanian/Chamorro (41)	72	0.03
Native Hawaiian (50)	104	0.05
Samoan (29)	45	0.02
Tongan (23)	29	0.01
White (114,779)	120,665	55.79
Not Hispanic (66,559)	69,131	31.96
Hispanic (48,220)	51,534	23.83

Jacinto City

Place Type: City
County: Harris
Population: 10,553†

Ancestry‡	Population	%
American (241)	241	2.30
Danish (17)	17	0.16
Dutch (0)	46	0.44
English (148)	193	1.84
French, ex. Basque (0)	26	0.25
German (107)	251	2.40
Greek (77)	77	0.74
Irish (108)	234	2.24
Italian (22)	51	0.49
Norwegian (0)	31	0.30
Scotch-Irish (16)	16	0.15
Scottish (0)	16	0.15

Hispanic Origin	Population	%
Hispanic or Latino (of any race)	8,856	83.92
Central American, ex. Mexican	260	2.46
Guatemalan	24	0.23
Honduran	53	0.50
Nicaraguan	25	0.24
Salvadoran	156	1.48
Other Central American	2	0.02
Cuban	9	0.09
Dominican Republic	2	0.02
Mexican	8,086	76.62
Puerto Rican	22	0.21
South American	13	0.12
Argentinean	1	0.01
Chilean	1	0.01
Colombian	11	0.10
Other Hispanic or Latino	464	4.40

Race*	Population	%
African-American/Black (371)	391	3.71
Not Hispanic (329)	333	3.16
Hispanic (42)	58	0.55
American Indian/Alaska Native (118)	172	1.63
Not Hispanic (14)	28	0.27
Hispanic (104)	144	1.36
Apache (2)	4	0.04
Blackfeet (0)	2	0.02
Central American Ind. (0)	1	0.01
Cherokee (7)	10	0.09
Cheyenne (0)	1	0.01
Chippewa (1)	1	0.01
Comanche (0)	4	0.04
Mexican American Ind. (15)	26	0.25
Seminole (1)	2	0.02
Sioux (0)	1	0.01

*Notes: † The Census 2010 population figure is used to calculate the percentages in the Hispanic Origin and Race categories. Ancestry percentages are based on the 2006-2010 American Community Survey population (not shown); ‡ Numbers in parentheses indicate the number of people reporting a single ancestry; * Numbers in parentheses indicate the number of persons reporting this race alone, not in combination with any other race; Please refer to the Explanation of Data for more information.*

South American Ind. (0)	1	0.01
Yaqui (0)	1	0.01
Asian (24)	49	0.46
Not Hispanic (23)	29	0.27
Hispanic (1)	20	0.19
Cambodian (2)	2	0.02
Chinese, ex. Taiwanese (1)	3	0.03
Filipino (2)	8	0.08
Indian (13)	15	0.14
Indonesian (1)	4	0.04
Japanese (1)	6	0.06
Korean (3)	5	0.05
Vietnamese (1)	1	0.01
Hawaii Native/Pacific Islander (0)	5	0.05
Not Hispanic (0)	3	0.03
Hispanic (0)	2	0.02
Native Hawaiian (0)	3	0.03
White (6,788)	7,118	67.45
Not Hispanic (1,294)	1,320	12.51
Hispanic (5,494)	5,798	54.94

Jacksonville

Place Type: City
County: Cherokee
Population: 14,544†

Ancestry‡	Population	%
African, Sub-Saharan (160)	160	1.11
African (160)	160	1.11
American (1,114)	1,114	7.74
Arab (0)	22	0.15
Other Arab (0)	22	0.15
British (74)	91	0.63
Czech (10)	58	0.40
Danish (29)	29	0.20
Dutch (0)	115	0.80
English (472)	1,175	8.16
European (41)	41	0.28
French, ex. Basque (26)	160	1.11
German (179)	799	5.55
Hungarian (0)	9	0.06
Irish (299)	962	6.68
Italian (46)	87	0.60
Norwegian (0)	11	0.08
Russian (0)	271	1.88
Scotch-Irish (92)	219	1.52
Scottish (104)	356	2.47
Swedish (10)	37	0.26
Welsh (0)	10	0.07

Hispanic Origin	Population	%
Hispanic or Latino (of any race)	4,986	34.28
Central American, ex. Mexican	71	0.49
Guatemalan	43	0.30
Honduran	10	0.07
Nicaraguan	9	0.06
Salvadoran	9	0.06
Cuban	2	0.01
Dominican Republic	2	0.01
Mexican	4,702	32.33
Puerto Rican	26	0.18
South American	9	0.06
Colombian	3	0.02
Ecuadorian	1	0.01
Peruvian	4	0.03
Venezuelan	1	0.01
Other Hispanic or Latino	174	1.20

Race*	Population	%
African-American/Black (3,251)	3,377	23.22
Not Hispanic (3,195)	3,296	22.66
Hispanic (56)	81	0.56
American Indian/Alaska Native (116)	211	1.45
Not Hispanic (24)	71	0.49
Hispanic (92)	140	0.96
Apache (0)	2	0.01
Blackfeet (0)	1	0.01
Cherokee (8)	22	0.15
Chickasaw (0)	4	0.03
Choctaw (10)	12	0.08
Creek (0)	2	0.01
Mexican American Ind. (27)	67	0.46
Navajo (1)	1	0.01
Asian (124)	150	1.03
Not Hispanic (121)	141	0.97
Hispanic (3)	9	0.06
Cambodian (13)	17	0.12
Chinese, ex. Taiwanese (29)	32	0.22
Filipino (33)	42	0.29
Indian (16)	21	0.14
Japanese (4)	6	0.04
Korean (7)	8	0.06
Taiwanese (2)	3	0.02
Vietnamese (7)	7	0.05
Hawaii Native/Pacific Islander (7)	15	0.10
Not Hispanic (4)	6	0.04
Hispanic (3)	9	0.06
Guamanian/Chamorro (7)	8	0.06
Native Hawaiian (0)	4	0.03
White (7,685)	7,996	54.98
Not Hispanic (6,030)	6,187	42.54
Hispanic (1,655)	1,809	12.44

Jasper

Place Type: City
County: Jasper
Population: 7,590†

Ancestry‡	Population	%
African, Sub-Saharan (66)	66	0.88
African (66)	66	0.88
American (656)	656	8.70
British (17)	17	0.23
Cajun (26)	52	0.69
Croatian (0)	6	0.08
Czech (15)	15	0.20
Danish (0)	19	0.25
Dutch (12)	66	0.88
English (151)	390	5.18
European (62)	62	0.82
Finnish (8)	8	0.11
French, ex. Basque (39)	309	4.10
French Canadian (0)	12	0.16
German (204)	1,054	13.99
Irish (199)	733	9.73
Italian (0)	14	0.19
Norwegian (0)	21	0.28
Polish (7)	14	0.19
Portuguese (0)	11	0.15
Russian (0)	13	0.17
Scotch-Irish (7)	75	1.00
Scottish (40)	103	1.37
Swedish (0)	6	0.08
Swiss (0)	11	0.15
Yugoslavian (0)	6	0.08

Hispanic Origin	Population	%
Hispanic or Latino (of any race)	822	10.83
Central American, ex. Mexican	3	0.04
Honduran	3	0.04
Cuban	1	0.01
Mexican	748	9.86
Puerto Rican	6	0.08
South American	11	0.14
Argentinean	7	0.09
Colombian	3	0.04
Ecuadorian	1	0.01
Other Hispanic or Latino	53	0.70

Race*	Population	%
African-American/Black (3,372)	3,456	45.53
Not Hispanic (3,357)	3,430	45.19
Hispanic (15)	26	0.34
American Indian/Alaska Native (28)	56	0.74
Not Hispanic (23)	46	0.61
Hispanic (5)	10	0.13
Blackfeet (0)	3	0.04
Cherokee (3)	8	0.11
Chickasaw (0)	4	0.05
Choctaw (0)	1	0.01
Houma (1)	1	0.01
Kiowa (0)	1	0.01
Ottawa (3)	3	0.04
Potawatomi (0)	1	0.01
Asian (111)	123	1.62
Not Hispanic (111)	122	1.61
Hispanic (0)	1	0.01
Cambodian (3)	3	0.04
Chinese, ex. Taiwanese (8)	9	0.12
Filipino (26)	31	0.41
Indian (40)	41	0.54
Indonesian (1)	1	0.01
Japanese (0)	1	0.01
Korean (13)	13	0.17
Laotian (1)	4	0.05
Pakistani (11)	11	0.14
Thai (2)	2	0.03
Vietnamese (2)	2	0.03
Hawaii Native/Pacific Islander (0)	3	0.04
Not Hispanic (0)	3	0.04
Samoan (0)	2	0.03
White (3,473)	3,601	47.44
Not Hispanic (3,177)	3,251	42.83
Hispanic (296)	350	4.61

Jersey Village

Place Type: City
County: Harris
Population: 7,620†

Ancestry‡	Population	%
American (359)	359	4.82
Arab (87)	98	1.32
Arab (0)	11	0.15
Lebanese (5)	5	0.07
Palestinian (34)	34	0.46
Other Arab (48)	48	0.64
British (20)	20	0.27
Celtic (15)	26	0.35
Croatian (0)	11	0.15
Czech (104)	228	3.06
Dutch (0)	85	1.14
English (170)	741	9.95
European (113)	113	1.52
French, ex. Basque (100)	260	3.49
German (527)	1,498	20.11
Hungarian (0)	23	0.31
Iranian (20)	20	0.27
Irish (186)	578	7.76
Israeli (11)	22	0.30
Italian (230)	380	5.10
Northern European (19)	19	0.26
Norwegian (12)	75	1.01
Polish (88)	209	2.81
Romanian (3)	3	0.04
Russian (0)	28	0.38
Scotch-Irish (119)	272	3.65
Scottish (42)	183	2.46
Slovak (47)	47	0.63
Swedish (28)	38	0.51
Swiss (28)	39	0.52
Welsh (19)	19	0.26
West Indian, ex. Hispanic (35)	35	0.47
Jamaican (35)	35	0.47

Hispanic Origin	Population	%
Hispanic or Latino (of any race)	1,109	14.55
Central American, ex. Mexican	91	1.19
Costa Rican	3	0.04
Guatemalan	6	0.08
Honduran	8	0.10
Nicaraguan	19	0.25
Salvadoran	55	0.72
Cuban	26	0.34
Dominican Republic	3	0.04
Mexican	751	9.86
Puerto Rican	35	0.46

*Notes: † The Census 2010 population figure is used to calculate the percentages in the Hispanic Origin and Race categories. Ancestry percentages are based on the 2006-2010 American Community Survey population (not shown); ‡ Numbers in parentheses indicate the number of people reporting a single ancestry; * Numbers in parentheses indicate the number of persons reporting this race alone, not in combination with any other race; Please refer to the Explanation of Data for more information.*

South American	101	1.33
Argentinean	7	0.09
Bolivian	3	0.04
Chilean	1	0.01
Colombian	40	0.52
Ecuadorian	13	0.17
Peruvian	11	0.14
Uruguayan	6	0.08
Venezuelan	20	0.26
Other Hispanic or Latino	102	1.34

Race*	Population	%
African-American/Black (631)	680	8.92
Not Hispanic (618)	649	8.52
Hispanic (13)	31	0.41
American Indian/Alaska Native (29)	58	0.76
Not Hispanic (21)	45	0.59
Hispanic (8)	13	0.17
Apache (1)	3	0.04
Blackfeet (0)	1	0.01
Cherokee (7)	15	0.20
Chickasaw (1)	1	0.01
Chippewa (0)	1	0.01
Choctaw (4)	4	0.05
Creek (0)	5	0.07
Mexican American Ind. (0)	2	0.03
Osage (1)	1	0.01
Seminole (0)	1	0.01
South American Ind. (0)	1	0.01
Asian (663)	722	9.48
Not Hispanic (657)	706	9.27
Hispanic (6)	16	0.21
Bangladeshi (1)	1	0.01
Cambodian (11)	11	0.14
Chinese, ex. Taiwanese (140)	153	2.01
Filipino (28)	33	0.43
Indian (154)	170	2.23
Indonesian (6)	7	0.09
Japanese (8)	12	0.16
Korean (36)	43	0.56
Laotian (8)	11	0.14
Nepalese (7)	7	0.09
Pakistani (19)	23	0.30
Sri Lankan (1)	1	0.01
Taiwanese (14)	19	0.25
Thai (1)	2	0.03
Vietnamese (200)	218	2.86
Hawaii Native/Pacific Islander (0)	4	0.05
Not Hispanic (0)	3	0.04
Hispanic (0)	1	0.01
White (5,813)	5,943	77.99
Not Hispanic (5,096)	5,188	68.08
Hispanic (717)	755	9.91

Jollyville

Place Type: CDP
County: Williamson
Population: 16,151†

Ancestry‡	Population	%
African, Sub-Saharan (118)	217	1.35
African (65)	65	0.40
Ghanaian (53)	53	0.33
Somalian (0)	45	0.28
South African (0)	54	0.34
American (585)	585	3.64
Arab (11)	40	0.25
Iraqi (11)	23	0.14
Palestinian (0)	17	0.11
Austrian (17)	87	0.54
Belgian (0)	20	0.12
British (19)	98	0.61
Cajun (30)	30	0.19
Canadian (5)	60	0.37
Celtic (0)	16	0.10
Croatian (50)	50	0.31
Czech (82)	306	1.90
Czechoslovakian (10)	10	0.06
Danish (0)	16	0.10
Dutch (65)	245	1.52
Eastern European (18)	18	0.11
English (558)	2,038	12.67
European (261)	377	2.34
Finnish (16)	77	0.48
French, ex. Basque (114)	632	3.93
French Canadian (62)	143	0.89
German (784)	2,744	17.07
Greek (0)	33	0.21
Hungarian (16)	16	0.10
Iranian (5)	5	0.03
Irish (329)	1,748	10.87
Israeli (30)	85	0.53
Italian (194)	592	3.68
Latvian (0)	41	0.25
Lithuanian (16)	28	0.17
Northern European (100)	100	0.62
Norwegian (123)	244	1.52
Polish (85)	333	2.07
Portuguese (17)	29	0.18
Romanian (58)	58	0.36
Russian (0)	163	1.01
Scandinavian (0)	26	0.16
Scotch-Irish (124)	549	3.41
Scottish (107)	597	3.71
Swedish (139)	347	2.16
Swiss (17)	73	0.45
Turkish (22)	22	0.14
Ukrainian (49)	66	0.41
Welsh (0)	104	0.65
Yugoslavian (59)	59	0.37

Hispanic Origin	Population	%
Hispanic or Latino (of any race)	2,758	17.08
Central American, ex. Mexican	128	0.79
Costa Rican	12	0.07
Guatemalan	18	0.11
Honduran	23	0.14
Nicaraguan	21	0.13
Panamanian	33	0.20
Salvadoran	21	0.13
Cuban	16	0.10
Dominican Republic	14	0.09
Mexican	2,141	13.26
Puerto Rican	85	0.53
South American	118	0.73
Argentinean	18	0.11
Bolivian	16	0.10
Chilean	5	0.03
Colombian	33	0.20
Ecuadorian	3	0.02
Peruvian	26	0.16
Venezuelan	17	0.11
Other Hispanic or Latino	256	1.59

Race*	Population	%
African-American/Black (1,000)	1,161	7.19
Not Hispanic (927)	1,040	6.44
Hispanic (73)	121	0.75
American Indian/Alaska Native (102)	256	1.59
Not Hispanic (57)	165	1.02
Hispanic (45)	91	0.56
Apache (1)	4	0.02
Arapaho (1)	1	0.01
Blackfeet (1)	4	0.02
Canadian/French Am. Ind. (1)	2	0.01
Cherokee (23)	54	0.33
Chickasaw (0)	4	0.02
Choctaw (5)	16	0.10
Comanche (0)	1	0.01
Creek (0)	2	0.01
Hopi (0)	1	0.01
Iroquois (1)	1	0.01
Lumbee (0)	1	0.01
Mexican American Ind. (6)	15	0.09
Navajo (4)	4	0.02
Osage (1)	4	0.02
Potawatomi (0)	2	0.01
Pueblo (0)	1	0.01
Puget Sound Salish (1)	1	0.01
Seminole (0)	1	0.01
Sioux (6)	8	0.05
South American Ind. (0)	4	0.02
Spanish American Ind. (0)	3	0.02
Ute (0)	3	0.02
Asian (1,406)	1,635	10.12
Not Hispanic (1,391)	1,574	9.75
Hispanic (15)	61	0.38
Bangladeshi (14)	14	0.09
Cambodian (7)	8	0.05
Chinese, ex. Taiwanese (432)	508	3.15
Filipino (72)	127	0.79
Indian (312)	342	2.12
Indonesian (10)	15	0.09
Japanese (31)	74	0.46
Korean (107)	129	0.80
Laotian (6)	11	0.07
Pakistani (49)	54	0.33
Sri Lankan (21)	24	0.15
Taiwanese (58)	87	0.54
Thai (24)	31	0.19
Vietnamese (188)	214	1.32
Hawaii Native/Pacific Islander (15)	42	0.26
Not Hispanic (14)	37	0.23
Hispanic (1)	5	0.03
Fijian (1)	1	0.01
Guamanian/Chamorro (3)	6	0.04
Native Hawaiian (9)	21	0.13
Samoan (0)	1	0.01
White (12,375)	12,887	79.79
Not Hispanic (10,596)	10,940	67.74
Hispanic (1,779)	1,947	12.05

Katy

Place Type: City
County: Harris
Population: 14,102†

Ancestry‡	Population	%
African, Sub-Saharan (38)	38	0.28
Nigerian (38)	38	0.28
American (2,047)	2,047	15.31
Austrian (0)	6	0.04
British (13)	13	0.10
Canadian (29)	29	0.22
Croatian (6)	12	0.09
Czech (125)	219	1.64
Czechoslovakian (9)	16	0.12
Danish (36)	36	0.27
Dutch (0)	83	0.62
English (560)	1,259	9.42
European (158)	164	1.23
French, ex. Basque (46)	200	1.50
French Canadian (23)	59	0.44
German (883)	1,580	11.82
Greek (14)	47	0.35
Hungarian (14)	101	0.76
Irish (374)	1,124	8.41
Italian (120)	518	3.87
Lithuanian (37)	37	0.28
Northern European (6)	6	0.04
Norwegian (23)	149	1.11
Polish (101)	164	1.23
Russian (14)	50	0.37
Scotch-Irish (119)	246	1.84
Scottish (49)	153	1.14
Swedish (7)	133	0.99
Swiss (0)	10	0.07
Welsh (15)	70	0.52

Hispanic Origin	Population	%
Hispanic or Latino (of any race)	4,092	29.02
Central American, ex. Mexican	317	2.25
Guatemalan	62	0.44
Honduran	47	0.33
Nicaraguan	18	0.13
Panamanian	2	0.01
Salvadoran	185	1.31
Other Central American	3	0.02

*Notes: † The Census 2010 population figure is used to calculate the percentages in the Hispanic Origin and Race categories. Ancestry percentages are based on the 2006-2010 American Community Survey population (not shown); ‡ Numbers in parentheses indicate the number of people reporting a single ancestry; * Numbers in parentheses indicate the number of persons reporting this race alone, not in combination with any other race; Please refer to the Explanation of Data for more information.*

Cuban	54	0.38
Dominican Republic	6	0.04
Mexican	3,322	23.56
Puerto Rican	65	0.46
South American	117	0.83
Argentinean	6	0.04
Bolivian	2	0.01
Chilean	1	0.01
Colombian	60	0.43
Ecuadorian	12	0.09
Peruvian	20	0.14
Uruguayan	7	0.05
Venezuelan	9	0.06
Other Hispanic or Latino	211	1.50

Race*	Population	%
African-American/Black (742)	836	5.93
Not Hispanic (713)	781	5.54
Hispanic (29)	55	0.39
American Indian/Alaska Native (86)	184	1.30
Not Hispanic (36)	103	0.73
Hispanic (50)	81	0.57
Apache (0)	3	0.02
Arapaho (1)	1	0.01
Blackfeet (0)	1	0.01
Cherokee (3)	20	0.14
Choctaw (2)	10	0.07
Creek (2)	8	0.06
Iroquois (4)	4	0.03
Kiowa (0)	2	0.01
Mexican American Ind. (8)	21	0.15
Navajo (1)	1	0.01
Osage (1)	1	0.01
Ottawa (1)	1	0.01
Potawatomi (1)	1	0.01
Seminole (1)	7	0.05
Sioux (0)	3	0.02
South American Ind. (0)	2	0.01
Tlingit-Haida *(Alaska Native)* (1)	4	0.03
Asian (218)	289	2.05
Not Hispanic (207)	270	1.91
Hispanic (11)	19	0.13
Burmese (1)	3	0.02
Cambodian (5)	5	0.04
Chinese, ex. Taiwanese (29)	47	0.33
Filipino (38)	46	0.33
Indian (49)	55	0.39
Indonesian (10)	11	0.08
Japanese (2)	19	0.13
Korean (6)	16	0.11
Nepalese (0)	1	0.01
Pakistani (38)	38	0.27
Taiwanese (1)	1	0.01
Thai (3)	4	0.03
Vietnamese (30)	33	0.23
Hawaii Native/Pacific Islander (0)	16	0.11
Not Hispanic (0)	10	0.07
Hispanic (0)	6	0.04
Native Hawaiian (0)	12	0.09
White (11,294)	11,661	82.69
Not Hispanic (8,854)	9,015	63.93
Hispanic (2,440)	2,646	18.76

Keller

Place Type: City
County: Tarrant
Population: 39,627†

Ancestry‡	Population	%
African, Sub-Saharan (64)	64	0.17
African (43)	43	0.11
Ghanaian (10)	10	0.03
Ugandan (11)	11	0.03
American (3,729)	3,729	9.97
Arab (74)	246	0.66
Lebanese (74)	246	0.66
Australian (48)	62	0.17
Austrian (11)	83	0.22
Brazilian (59)	84	0.22
British (270)	343	0.92
Cajun (0)	50	0.13
Canadian (241)	263	0.70
Croatian (12)	12	0.03
Czech (102)	548	1.47
Czechoslovakian (125)	194	0.52
Danish (12)	123	0.33
Dutch (354)	987	2.64
English (2,140)	5,830	15.59
European (646)	740	1.98
Finnish (8)	35	0.09
French, ex. Basque (399)	1,564	4.18
French Canadian (47)	233	0.62
German (2,450)	7,865	21.03
Greek (123)	223	0.60
Hungarian (49)	338	0.90
Iranian (33)	33	0.09
Irish (1,619)	5,683	15.19
Italian (637)	2,206	5.90
Lithuanian (14)	38	0.10
Northern European (83)	83	0.22
Norwegian (280)	864	2.31
Pennsylvania German (18)	18	0.05
Polish (220)	1,067	2.85
Portuguese (15)	118	0.32
Romanian (13)	33	0.09
Russian (100)	318	0.85
Scandinavian (10)	10	0.03
Scotch-Irish (464)	976	2.61
Scottish (438)	1,575	4.21
Slovak (0)	110	0.29
Slovene (0)	58	0.16
Swedish (278)	592	1.58
Swiss (10)	116	0.31
Turkish (0)	16	0.04
Ukrainian (0)	153	0.41
Welsh (66)	290	0.78
West Indian, ex. Hispanic (0)	28	0.07
Jamaican (0)	10	0.03
West Indian (0)	18	0.05
Yugoslavian (0)	37	0.10

Hispanic Origin	Population	%
Hispanic or Latino (of any race)	2,924	7.38
Central American, ex. Mexican	142	0.36
Costa Rican	13	0.03
Guatemalan	23	0.06
Honduran	13	0.03
Nicaraguan	15	0.04
Panamanian	31	0.08
Salvadoran	46	0.12
Other Central American	1	<0.01
Cuban	118	0.30
Dominican Republic	8	0.02
Mexican	1,979	4.99
Puerto Rican	193	0.49
South American	214	0.54
Argentinean	15	0.04
Bolivian	3	0.01
Chilean	18	0.05
Colombian	73	0.18
Ecuadorian	30	0.08
Paraguayan	2	0.01
Peruvian	23	0.06
Venezuelan	46	0.12
Other South American	4	0.01
Other Hispanic or Latino	270	0.68

Race*	Population	%
African-American/Black (945)	1,109	2.80
Not Hispanic (910)	1,035	2.61
Hispanic (35)	74	0.19
American Indian/Alaska Native (197)	425	1.07
Not Hispanic (167)	357	0.90
Hispanic (30)	68	0.17
Alaska Athabascan *(Ala. Nat.)* (0)	1	<0.01
Apache (0)	2	0.01
Blackfeet (0)	1	<0.01
Central American Ind. (1)	4	0.01
Cherokee (54)	131	0.33
Chickasaw (15)	27	0.07
Chippewa (0)	3	0.01
Choctaw (40)	70	0.18
Comanche (0)	5	0.01
Creek (5)	8	0.02
Crow (1)	2	0.01
Delaware (1)	1	<0.01
Iroquois (2)	2	0.01
Mexican American Ind. (10)	16	0.04
Navajo (1)	7	0.02
Osage (1)	7	0.02
Ottawa (3)	3	0.01
Potawatomi (1)	2	0.01
Pueblo (0)	3	0.01
Seminole (5)	6	0.02
Sioux (3)	5	0.01
South American Ind. (1)	1	<0.01
Asian (1,496)	1,871	4.72
Not Hispanic (1,482)	1,807	4.56
Hispanic (14)	64	0.16
Bangladeshi (23)	29	0.07
Burmese (6)	7	0.02
Cambodian (14)	15	0.04
Chinese, ex. Taiwanese (172)	231	0.58
Filipino (117)	202	0.51
Hmong (0)	1	<0.01
Indian (423)	494	1.25
Indonesian (9)	13	0.03
Japanese (44)	126	0.32
Korean (162)	218	0.55
Laotian (59)	70	0.18
Malaysian (1)	1	<0.01
Nepalese (5)	5	0.01
Pakistani (70)	80	0.20
Sri Lankan (0)	4	0.01
Taiwanese (8)	11	0.03
Thai (55)	81	0.20
Vietnamese (258)	302	0.76
Hawaii Native/Pacific Islander (35)	94	0.24
Not Hispanic (32)	85	0.21
Hispanic (3)	9	0.02
Fijian (1)	1	<0.01
Guamanian/Chamorro (10)	15	0.04
Marshallese (2)	2	0.01
Native Hawaiian (2)	27	0.07
Samoan (8)	18	0.05
Tongan (5)	10	0.03
White (35,506)	36,281	91.56
Not Hispanic (33,433)	33,993	85.78
Hispanic (2,073)	2,288	5.77

Kerrville

Place Type: City
County: Kerr
Population: 22,347†

Ancestry‡	Population	%
African, Sub-Saharan (0)	13	0.06
African (0)	13	0.06
American (883)	883	3.98
Arab (22)	35	0.16
Lebanese (0)	13	0.06
Palestinian (22)	22	0.10
Australian (0)	14	0.06
Austrian (31)	31	0.14
British (61)	125	0.56
Cajun (41)	41	0.18
Czech (30)	139	0.63
Czechoslovakian (0)	18	0.08
Danish (0)	59	0.27
Dutch (42)	186	0.84
Eastern European (10)	10	0.05
English (923)	2,619	11.81
European (71)	84	0.38
Finnish (7)	47	0.21
French, ex. Basque (156)	937	4.23
French Canadian (14)	56	0.25
German (2,245)	5,189	23.41
Greek (20)	106	0.48

*Notes: † The Census 2010 population figure is used to calculate the percentages in the Hispanic Origin and Race categories. Ancestry percentages are based on the 2006-2010 American Community Survey population (not shown); ‡ Numbers in parentheses indicate the number of people reporting a single ancestry; * Numbers in parentheses indicate the number of persons reporting this race alone, not in combination with any other race; Please refer to the Explanation of Data for more information.*

Hungarian (42)	50	0.23
Iranian (110)	110	0.50
Irish (974)	2,886	13.02
Italian (88)	473	2.13
Lithuanian (2)	52	0.23
Northern European (29)	29	0.13
Norwegian (116)	314	1.42
Polish (107)	278	1.25
Portuguese (0)	10	0.05
Russian (34)	46	0.21
Scandinavian (0)	4	0.02
Scotch-Irish (467)	958	4.32
Scottish (312)	659	2.97
Slovene (15)	15	0.07
Swedish (59)	211	0.95
Swiss (21)	48	0.22
Turkish (0)	8	0.04
Ukrainian (10)	10	0.05
Welsh (62)	116	0.52
West Indian, ex. Hispanic (0)	29	0.13
Dutch West Indian (0)	11	0.05
Jamaican (0)	18	0.08

Hispanic Origin	Population	%
Hispanic or Latino (of any race)	6,124	27.40
Central American, ex. Mexican	47	0.21
Costa Rican	3	0.01
Guatemalan	11	0.05
Honduran	16	0.07
Nicaraguan	1	<0.01
Panamanian	9	0.04
Salvadoran	7	0.03
Cuban	20	0.09
Dominican Republic	8	0.04
Mexican	5,387	24.11
Puerto Rican	33	0.15
South American	30	0.13
Argentinean	4	0.02
Chilean	2	0.01
Colombian	9	0.04
Ecuadorian	5	0.02
Peruvian	5	0.02
Uruguayan	1	<0.01
Venezuelan	4	0.02
Other Hispanic or Latino	599	2.68

Race*	Population	%
African-American/Black (687)	803	3.59
Not Hispanic (575)	654	2.93
Hispanic (112)	149	0.67
American Indian/Alaska Native (124)	376	1.68
Not Hispanic (68)	176	0.79
Hispanic (56)	200	0.89
Apache (9)	19	0.09
Blackfeet (0)	5	0.02
Cherokee (9)	36	0.16
Cheyenne (1)	1	<0.01
Chickasaw (5)	5	0.02
Chippewa (2)	2	0.01
Choctaw (11)	25	0.11
Comanche (1)	5	0.02
Cree (1)	3	0.01
Creek (2)	2	0.01
Hopi (1)	1	<0.01
Iroquois (1)	3	0.01
Mexican American Ind. (5)	11	0.05
Navajo (3)	6	0.03
Osage (0)	3	0.01
Pima (0)	4	0.02
Potawatomi (0)	3	0.01
Seminole (1)	3	0.01
Sioux (5)	10	0.04
Tlingit-Haida *(Alaska Native)* (1)	1	<0.01
Yaqui (0)	1	<0.01
Asian (208)	285	1.28
Not Hispanic (205)	257	1.15
Hispanic (3)	28	0.13
Burmese (4)	4	0.02
Cambodian (7)	10	0.04
Chinese, ex. Taiwanese (32)	39	0.17
Filipino (43)	67	0.30
Indian (28)	30	0.13
Japanese (8)	19	0.09
Korean (5)	18	0.08
Laotian (4)	6	0.03
Malaysian (1)	1	<0.01
Pakistani (0)	1	<0.01
Taiwanese (13)	13	0.06
Thai (4)	6	0.03
Vietnamese (49)	53	0.24
Hawaii Native/Pacific Islander (12)	26	0.12
Not Hispanic (7)	18	0.08
Hispanic (5)	8	0.04
Guamanian/Chamorro (0)	2	0.01
Native Hawaiian (9)	14	0.06
Samoan (3)	6	0.03
White (19,277)	19,754	88.40
Not Hispanic (15,115)	15,342	68.65
Hispanic (4,162)	4,412	19.74

Kilgore

Place Type: City
County: Gregg
Population: 12,975†

Ancestry‡	Population	%
African, Sub-Saharan (20)	27	0.21
African (20)	27	0.21
American (1,953)	1,953	15.37
Austrian (13)	13	0.10
Belgian (0)	31	0.24
British (17)	17	0.13
Cajun (24)	24	0.19
Canadian (12)	12	0.09
Czech (0)	125	0.98
Danish (0)	10	0.08
Dutch (0)	72	0.57
English (459)	1,241	9.77
European (64)	64	0.50
French, ex. Basque (216)	497	3.91
French Canadian (23)	23	0.18
German (452)	1,307	10.29
Hungarian (36)	76	0.60
Irish (411)	1,658	13.05
Italian (41)	59	0.46
Lithuanian (13)	13	0.10
Norwegian (0)	31	0.24
Polish (101)	309	2.43
Portuguese (19)	19	0.15
Russian (32)	32	0.25
Scandinavian (83)	83	0.65
Scotch-Irish (287)	456	3.59
Scottish (43)	148	1.16
Swedish (13)	46	0.36
Welsh (29)	72	0.57

Hispanic Origin	Population	%
Hispanic or Latino (of any race)	2,568	19.79
Central American, ex. Mexican	38	0.29
Costa Rican	1	0.01
Honduran	12	0.09
Nicaraguan	1	0.01
Panamanian	4	0.03
Salvadoran	20	0.15
Cuban	10	0.08
Mexican	2,399	18.49
Puerto Rican	16	0.12
South American	7	0.05
Argentinean	1	0.01
Bolivian	1	0.01
Colombian	1	0.01
Ecuadorian	1	0.01
Peruvian	2	0.02
Venezuelan	1	0.01
Other Hispanic or Latino	98	0.76

Race*	Population	%
African-American/Black (1,751)	1,866	14.38
Not Hispanic (1,717)	1,812	13.97
Hispanic (34)	54	0.42
American Indian/Alaska Native (92)	177	1.36
Not Hispanic (56)	131	1.01
Hispanic (36)	46	0.35
Apache (5)	7	0.05
Blackfeet (0)	6	0.05
Central American Ind. (5)	5	0.04
Cherokee (11)	56	0.43
Chickasaw (2)	3	0.02
Choctaw (17)	28	0.22
Comanche (3)	8	0.06
Creek (0)	1	0.01
Crow (0)	6	0.05
Houma (4)	4	0.03
Mexican American Ind. (3)	4	0.03
Navajo (1)	1	0.01
Potawatomi (2)	2	0.02
Pueblo (0)	3	0.02
Seminole (1)	1	0.01
Sioux (0)	4	0.03
Tlingit-Haida *(Alaska Native)* (0)	1	0.01
Yuman (1)	1	0.01
Asian (144)	175	1.35
Not Hispanic (144)	168	1.29
Hispanic (0)	7	0.05
Bangladeshi (1)	4	0.03
Cambodian (22)	25	0.19
Chinese, ex. Taiwanese (20)	21	0.16
Filipino (5)	7	0.05
Indian (49)	53	0.41
Indonesian (2)	2	0.02
Japanese (8)	19	0.15
Korean (14)	17	0.13
Laotian (1)	1	0.01
Malaysian (1)	1	0.01
Nepalese (5)	5	0.04
Pakistani (4)	4	0.03
Vietnamese (5)	5	0.04
Hawaii Native/Pacific Islander (10)	19	0.15
Not Hispanic (10)	15	0.12
Hispanic (0)	4	0.03
Guamanian/Chamorro (0)	1	0.01
White (9,283)	9,548	73.59
Not Hispanic (8,277)	8,447	65.10
Hispanic (1,006)	1,101	8.49

Killeen

Place Type: City
County: Bell
Population: 127,921†

Ancestry‡	Population	%
African, Sub-Saharan (613)	1,002	0.83
African (561)	859	0.72
Ghanaian (9)	9	0.01
Nigerian (13)	88	0.07
Other Sub-Saharan African (30)	46	0.04
American (3,222)	3,222	2.68
Arab (257)	353	0.29
Arab (80)	146	0.12
Egyptian (17)	17	0.01
Iraqi (36)	36	0.03
Lebanese (26)	26	0.02
Other Arab (98)	128	0.11
Australian (15)	15	0.01
Austrian (26)	26	0.02
Belgian (4)	4	<0.01
Brazilian (45)	45	0.04
British (75)	266	0.22
Canadian (59)	76	0.06
Croatian (47)	61	0.05
Czech (83)	352	0.29
Czechoslovakian (23)	92	0.08
Danish (8)	39	0.03
Dutch (101)	633	0.53
English (1,576)	3,712	3.09
European (820)	983	0.82
Finnish (10)	40	0.03
French, ex. Basque (339)	1,543	1.29

*Notes: † The Census 2010 population figure is used to calculate the percentages in the Hispanic Origin and Race categories. Ancestry percentages are based on the 2006-2010 American Community Survey population (not shown); ‡ Numbers in parentheses indicate the number of people reporting a single ancestry; * Numbers in parentheses indicate the number of persons reporting this race alone, not in combination with any other race; Please refer to the Explanation of Data for more information.*

Ancestry	Population	%
French Canadian (65)	303	0.25
German (4,178)	10,276	8.56
German Russian (16)	16	0.01
Greek (46)	124	0.10
Guyanese (31)	64	0.05
Hungarian (17)	63	0.05
Irish (1,254)	5,331	4.44
Israeli (17)	40	0.03
Italian (710)	2,500	2.08
Lithuanian (25)	51	0.04
Macedonian (9)	12	0.01
Maltese (47)	47	0.04
New Zealander (0)	16	0.01
Norwegian (185)	429	0.36
Pennsylvania German (0)	13	0.01
Polish (547)	1,350	1.12
Portuguese (25)	103	0.09
Romanian (0)	102	0.08
Russian (75)	224	0.19
Scandinavian (0)	48	0.04
Scotch-Irish (340)	1,263	1.05
Scottish (210)	1,096	0.91
Serbian (5)	5	<0.01
Slovak (11)	44	0.04
Swedish (58)	350	0.29
Swiss (12)	29	0.02
Turkish (27)	27	0.02
Ukrainian (10)	22	0.02
Welsh (16)	202	0.17
West Indian, ex. Hispanic (948)	1,227	1.02
Belizean (51)	62	0.05
Bermudan (14)	14	0.01
Dutch West Indian (26)	26	0.02
Haitian (0)	4	<0.01
Jamaican (554)	671	0.56
Trinidadian/Tobagonian (62)	62	0.05
U.S. Virgin Islander (54)	54	0.04
West Indian (187)	334	0.28
Yugoslavian (26)	121	0.10

Hispanic Origin	Population	%
Hispanic or Latino (of any race)	29,345	22.94
Central American, ex. Mexican	1,758	1.37
Costa Rican	25	0.02
Guatemalan	156	0.12
Honduran	167	0.13
Nicaraguan	126	0.10
Panamanian	998	0.78
Salvadoran	273	0.21
Other Central American	13	0.01
Cuban	345	0.27
Dominican Republic	479	0.37
Mexican	16,321	12.76
Puerto Rican	8,117	6.35
South American	746	0.58
Argentinean	39	0.03
Bolivian	4	<0.01
Chilean	24	0.02
Colombian	264	0.21
Ecuadorian	135	0.11
Paraguayan	4	<0.01
Peruvian	227	0.18
Uruguayan	3	<0.01
Venezuelan	44	0.03
Other South American	2	<0.01
Other Hispanic or Latino	1,579	1.23

Race*	Population	%
African-American/Black (43,610)	48,448	37.87
Not Hispanic (41,301)	44,874	35.08
Hispanic (2,309)	3,574	2.79
American Indian/Alaska Native (1,041)	2,550	1.99
Not Hispanic (635)	1,720	1.34
Hispanic (406)	830	0.65
Alaska Athabascan *(Ala. Nat.)* (4)	6	<0.01
Aleut *(Alaska Native)* (4)	7	0.01
Apache (39)	81	0.06
Arapaho (5)	12	0.01
Blackfeet (13)	66	0.05
Canadian/French Am. Ind. (2)	5	<0.01
Central American Ind. (9)	16	0.01
Cherokee (96)	388	0.30
Cheyenne (0)	5	<0.01
Chickasaw (9)	29	0.02
Chippewa (11)	26	0.02
Choctaw (67)	139	0.11
Colville (4)	8	0.01
Comanche (7)	24	0.02
Cree (1)	5	<0.01
Creek (8)	20	0.02
Crow (2)	5	<0.01
Delaware (2)	8	0.01
Hopi (2)	5	<0.01
Inupiat *(Alaska Native)* (11)	14	0.01
Iroquois (12)	22	0.02
Kiowa (5)	6	<0.01
Lumbee (10)	20	0.02
Menominee (2)	5	<0.01
Mexican American Ind. (41)	74	0.06
Navajo (88)	114	0.09
Osage (0)	3	<0.01
Ottawa (6)	9	0.01
Paiute (1)	2	<0.01
Potawatomi (5)	15	0.01
Pueblo (10)	14	0.01
Seminole (6)	22	0.02
Shoshone (0)	2	<0.01
Sioux (32)	64	0.05
South American Ind. (19)	57	0.04
Spanish American Ind. (1)	1	<0.01
Tlingit-Haida *(Alaska Native)* (4)	9	0.01
Tohono O'Odham (3)	3	<0.01
Ute (0)	2	<0.01
Yaqui (0)	2	<0.01
Asian (5,102)	7,701	6.02
Not Hispanic (4,835)	6,889	5.39
Hispanic (267)	812	0.63
Bangladeshi (16)	16	0.01
Burmese (9)	9	0.01
Cambodian (30)	54	0.04
Chinese, ex. Taiwanese (173)	382	0.30
Filipino (1,614)	2,395	1.87
Hmong (8)	8	0.01
Indian (244)	374	0.29
Indonesian (15)	21	0.02
Japanese (195)	575	0.45
Korean (1,961)	2,978	2.33
Laotian (41)	55	0.04
Malaysian (5)	9	0.01
Nepalese (7)	12	0.01
Pakistani (88)	114	0.09
Sri Lankan (1)	1	<0.01
Taiwanese (14)	21	0.02
Thai (128)	227	0.18
Vietnamese (363)	505	0.39
Hawaii Native/Pacific Islander (1,733)	2,549	1.99
Not Hispanic (1,614)	2,209	1.73
Hispanic (119)	340	0.27
Fijian (8)	18	0.01
Guamanian/Chamorro (840)	1,077	0.84
Marshallese (7)	9	0.01
Native Hawaiian (191)	474	0.37
Samoan (415)	565	0.44
Tongan (17)	29	0.02
White (57,736)	64,054	50.07
Not Hispanic (44,233)	48,583	37.98
Hispanic (13,503)	15,471	12.09

Kingsville

Place Type: City
County: Kleberg
Population: 26,213†

Ancestry‡	Population	%
African, Sub-Saharan (0)	7	0.03
African (0)	7	0.03
American (893)	893	3.46
British (9)	60	0.23
Canadian (14)	74	0.29
Celtic (12)	12	0.05
Czech (50)	140	0.54
Czechoslovakian (9)	9	0.03
Dutch (0)	17	0.07
English (294)	781	3.03
European (86)	140	0.54
Finnish (3)	13	0.05
French, ex. Basque (13)	223	0.86
French Canadian (0)	15	0.06
German (744)	1,923	7.45
Greek (0)	28	0.11
Iranian (7)	7	0.03
Irish (265)	1,270	4.92
Italian (102)	203	0.79
Norwegian (14)	33	0.13
Polish (78)	95	0.37
Portuguese (0)	4	0.02
Russian (0)	26	0.10
Scandinavian (12)	22	0.09
Scotch-Irish (76)	281	1.09
Scottish (120)	203	0.79
Swedish (21)	64	0.25
Swiss (0)	22	0.09
Ukrainian (14)	14	0.05
Welsh (0)	51	0.20
West Indian, ex. Hispanic (27)	27	0.10
Haitian (17)	17	0.07
Trinidadian/Tobagonian (10)	10	0.04
Yugoslavian (7)	7	0.03

Hispanic Origin	Population	%
Hispanic or Latino (of any race)	18,726	71.44
Central American, ex. Mexican	69	0.26
Costa Rican	3	0.01
Guatemalan	13	0.05
Honduran	28	0.11
Nicaraguan	1	<0.01
Panamanian	7	0.03
Salvadoran	17	0.06
Cuban	20	0.08
Dominican Republic	6	0.02
Mexican	15,711	59.94
Puerto Rican	150	0.57
South American	46	0.18
Argentinean	6	0.02
Bolivian	5	0.02
Chilean	1	<0.01
Colombian	8	0.03
Ecuadorian	9	0.03
Peruvian	7	0.03
Venezuelan	10	0.04
Other Hispanic or Latino	2,724	10.39

Race*	Population	%
African-American/Black (1,151)	1,316	5.02
Not Hispanic (1,039)	1,108	4.23
Hispanic (112)	208	0.79
American Indian/Alaska Native (176)	302	1.15
Not Hispanic (39)	81	0.31
Hispanic (137)	221	0.84
Apache (17)	32	0.12
Blackfeet (0)	1	<0.01
Canadian/French Am. Ind. (1)	1	<0.01
Central American Ind. (2)	3	0.01
Cherokee (11)	32	0.12
Chickasaw (4)	4	0.02
Chippewa (6)	6	0.02
Choctaw (7)	9	0.03
Comanche (1)	13	0.05
Creek (1)	1	<0.01
Inupiat *(Alaska Native)* (0)	1	<0.01
Iroquois (1)	1	<0.01
Mexican American Ind. (30)	45	0.17
Navajo (0)	2	0.01
Ottawa (1)	1	<0.01
Potawatomi (0)	2	0.01
Pueblo (1)	1	<0.01
Sioux (0)	2	0.01
South American Ind. (1)	1	<0.01
Asian (699)	798	3.04

*Notes: † The Census 2010 population figure is used to calculate the percentages in the Hispanic Origin and Race categories. Ancestry percentages are based on the 2006-2010 American Community Survey population (not shown); ‡ Numbers in parentheses indicate the number of people reporting a single ancestry; * Numbers in parentheses indicate the number of persons reporting this race alone, not in combination with any other race; Please refer to the Explanation of Data for more information.*

Not Hispanic (670)	731	2.79
Hispanic (29)	67	0.26
Bangladeshi (5)	5	0.02
Cambodian (3)	5	0.02
Chinese, ex. Taiwanese (69)	76	0.29
Filipino (152)	209	0.80
Indian (339)	351	1.34
Indonesian (2)	2	0.01
Japanese (16)	33	0.13
Korean (22)	22	0.08
Malaysian (1)	1	<0.01
Nepalese (1)	1	<0.01
Pakistani (5)	5	0.02
Sri Lankan (3)	5	0.02
Taiwanese (11)	13	0.05
Thai (7)	14	0.05
Vietnamese (43)	48	0.18
Hawaii Native/Pacific Islander (33)	47	0.18
Not Hispanic (24)	31	0.12
Hispanic (9)	16	0.06
Guamanian/Chamorro (5)	7	0.03
Native Hawaiian (10)	10	0.04
Samoan (7)	8	0.03
White (20,550)	21,128	80.60
Not Hispanic (5,522)	5,670	21.63
Hispanic (15,028)	15,458	58.97

Kirby

Place Type: City
County: Bexar
Population: 8,000†

Ancestry‡	Population	%
American (209)	209	2.58
Cajun (38)	52	0.64
Canadian (30)	30	0.37
Czech (57)	78	0.96
Danish (13)	108	1.33
Dutch (0)	96	1.18
English (90)	300	3.70
European (25)	25	0.31
French, ex. Basque (14)	210	2.59
French Canadian (10)	10	0.12
German (475)	1,245	15.34
Irish (129)	442	5.45
Italian (78)	110	1.36
Norwegian (0)	138	1.70
Polish (143)	377	4.65
Portuguese (10)	10	0.12
Scotch-Irish (27)	183	2.25
Scottish (49)	125	1.54
Swedish (0)	29	0.36
Swiss (0)	25	0.31
Welsh (0)	14	0.17
West Indian, ex. Hispanic (39)	39	0.48
Barbadian (39)	39	0.48

Hispanic Origin	Population	%
Hispanic or Latino (of any race)	4,207	52.59
Central American, ex. Mexican	59	0.74
Costa Rican	9	0.11
Guatemalan	6	0.08
Honduran	3	0.04
Nicaraguan	10	0.13
Panamanian	15	0.19
Salvadoran	16	0.20
Cuban	13	0.16
Dominican Republic	4	0.05
Mexican	3,606	45.08
Puerto Rican	114	1.43
South American	21	0.26
Bolivian	5	0.06
Chilean	2	0.03
Colombian	10	0.13
Ecuadorian	1	0.01
Peruvian	3	0.04
Other Hispanic or Latino	390	4.88

Race*	Population	%
African-American/Black (1,164)	1,252	15.65
Not Hispanic (1,124)	1,184	14.80
Hispanic (40)	68	0.85
American Indian/Alaska Native (84)	128	1.60
Not Hispanic (26)	62	0.78
Hispanic (58)	66	0.83
Alaska Athabascan *(Ala. Nat.)* (1)	1	0.01
Apache (6)	6	0.08
Blackfeet (0)	1	0.01
Canadian/French Am. Ind. (1)	1	0.01
Cherokee (5)	12	0.15
Chippewa (1)	1	0.01
Choctaw (0)	1	0.01
Comanche (4)	4	0.05
Creek (3)	3	0.04
Delaware (2)	5	0.06
Iroquois (0)	3	0.04
Kiowa (0)	1	0.01
Sioux (1)	2	0.03
Asian (130)	181	2.26
Not Hispanic (124)	166	2.08
Hispanic (6)	15	0.19
Burmese (3)	3	0.04
Chinese, ex. Taiwanese (0)	1	0.01
Filipino (30)	50	0.63
Indian (4)	10	0.13
Indonesian (1)	1	0.01
Japanese (6)	14	0.18
Korean (22)	41	0.51
Laotian (35)	35	0.44
Pakistani (1)	1	0.01
Thai (3)	3	0.04
Vietnamese (19)	19	0.24
Hawaii Native/Pacific Islander (25)	42	0.53
Not Hispanic (16)	23	0.29
Hispanic (9)	19	0.24
Guamanian/Chamorro (1)	2	0.03
Native Hawaiian (13)	27	0.34
Samoan (8)	12	0.15
White (5,050)	5,239	65.49
Not Hispanic (2,382)	2,462	30.78
Hispanic (2,668)	2,777	34.71

Kyle

Place Type: City
County: Hays
Population: 28,016†

Ancestry‡	Population	%
American (483)	483	2.01
Arab (13)	23	0.10
Lebanese (0)	10	0.04
Moroccan (13)	13	0.05
Austrian (0)	26	0.11
British (14)	107	0.44
Cajun (31)	63	0.26
Canadian (19)	83	0.34
Croatian (13)	13	0.05
Czech (159)	377	1.57
Czechoslovakian (9)	9	0.04
Danish (0)	43	0.18
Dutch (66)	534	2.22
English (499)	1,608	6.68
European (88)	121	0.50
Finnish (0)	9	0.04
French, ex. Basque (145)	702	2.92
French Canadian (14)	98	0.41
German (1,052)	3,830	15.92
Greek (0)	26	0.11
Hungarian (0)	6	0.02
Irish (676)	1,856	7.71
Italian (81)	325	1.35
Northern European (11)	11	0.05
Norwegian (42)	77	0.32
Pennsylvania German (0)	27	0.11
Polish (121)	464	1.93
Romanian (0)	9	0.04
Russian (0)	81	0.34
Scandinavian (11)	26	0.11
Scotch-Irish (267)	524	2.18
Scottish (218)	564	2.34
Swedish (114)	368	1.53
Swiss (11)	33	0.14
Welsh (38)	133	0.55
West Indian, ex. Hispanic (179)	179	0.74
Jamaican (179)	179	0.74

Hispanic Origin	Population	%
Hispanic or Latino (of any race)	12,979	46.33
Central American, ex. Mexican	319	1.14
Costa Rican	10	0.04
Guatemalan	61	0.22
Honduran	92	0.33
Nicaraguan	50	0.18
Panamanian	19	0.07
Salvadoran	84	0.30
Other Central American	3	0.01
Cuban	38	0.14
Dominican Republic	7	0.02
Mexican	11,102	39.63
Puerto Rican	238	0.85
South American	109	0.39
Argentinean	9	0.03
Bolivian	4	0.01
Chilean	5	0.02
Colombian	35	0.12
Ecuadorian	10	0.04
Peruvian	21	0.07
Uruguayan	1	<0.01
Venezuelan	21	0.07
Other South American	3	0.01
Other Hispanic or Latino	1,166	4.16

Race*	Population	%
African-American/Black (1,557)	1,838	6.56
Not Hispanic (1,428)	1,612	5.75
Hispanic (129)	226	0.81
American Indian/Alaska Native (230)	438	1.56
Not Hispanic (86)	201	0.72
Hispanic (144)	237	0.85
Apache (13)	14	0.05
Blackfeet (0)	5	0.02
Canadian/French Am. Ind. (0)	1	<0.01
Central American Ind. (1)	1	<0.01
Cherokee (33)	79	0.28
Chickasaw (2)	6	0.02
Chippewa (0)	2	0.01
Choctaw (13)	26	0.09
Comanche (5)	10	0.04
Creek (2)	9	0.03
Houma (1)	3	0.01
Iroquois (1)	1	<0.01
Kiowa (6)	6	0.02
Mexican American Ind. (16)	20	0.07
Navajo (2)	4	0.01
Seminole (0)	3	0.01
Sioux (1)	3	0.01
South American Ind. (4)	5	0.02
Tlingit-Haida *(Alaska Native)* (0)	2	0.01
Yaqui (1)	1	<0.01
Yuman (1)	1	<0.01
Asian (316)	518	1.85
Not Hispanic (286)	432	1.54
Hispanic (30)	86	0.31
Bangladeshi (2)	2	0.01
Cambodian (17)	17	0.06
Chinese, ex. Taiwanese (27)	41	0.15
Filipino (101)	165	0.59
Hmong (0)	2	0.01
Indian (35)	44	0.16
Indonesian (5)	8	0.03
Japanese (15)	53	0.19
Korean (34)	65	0.23
Laotian (5)	7	0.02
Malaysian (1)	1	<0.01
Pakistani (18)	19	0.07
Taiwanese (2)	4	0.01

*Notes: † The Census 2010 population figure is used to calculate the percentages in the Hispanic Origin and Race categories. Ancestry percentages are based on the 2006-2010 American Community Survey population (not shown); ‡ Numbers in parentheses indicate the number of people reporting a single ancestry; * Numbers in parentheses indicate the number of persons reporting this race alone, not in combination with any other race; Please refer to the Explanation of Data for more information.*

Thai (13)	35	0.12
Vietnamese (30)	45	0.16
Hawaii Native/Pacific Islander (12)	60	0.21
Not Hispanic (10)	43	0.15
Hispanic (2)	17	0.06
Guamanian/Chamorro (4)	16	0.06
Native Hawaiian (5)	29	0.10
Samoan (0)	2	0.01
Tongan (1)	2	0.01
White (20,882)	21,773	77.72
Not Hispanic (12,733)	13,120	46.83
Hispanic (8,149)	8,653	30.89

La Homa

Place Type: CDP
County: Hidalgo
Population: 11,985†

Ancestry‡	Population	%
American (38)	38	0.26
Canadian (21)	34	0.24
Dutch (17)	34	0.24
English (31)	103	0.72
French, ex. Basque (0)	8	0.06
German (54)	146	1.02
Irish (0)	170	1.18
Italian (0)	8	0.06
Swiss (0)	8	0.06

Hispanic Origin	Population	%
Hispanic or Latino (of any race)	11,632	97.05
Central American, ex. Mexican	12	0.10
Honduran	8	0.07
Nicaraguan	2	0.02
Salvadoran	2	0.02
Cuban	2	0.02
Mexican	11,348	94.69
Puerto Rican	7	0.06
South American	1	0.01
Chilean	1	0.01
Other Hispanic or Latino	262	2.19

Race*	Population	%
African-American/Black (8)	17	0.14
Not Hispanic (2)	3	0.03
Hispanic (6)	14	0.12
American Indian/Alaska Native (3)	19	0.16
Not Hispanic (3)	3	0.03
Hispanic (0)	16	0.13
Choctaw (1)	1	0.01
Comanche (1)	1	0.01
Sioux (0)	1	0.01
Asian (7)	14	0.12
Not Hispanic (4)	4	0.03
Hispanic (3)	10	0.08
Indian (3)	10	0.08
Japanese (2)	2	0.02
Korean (2)	2	0.02
Hawaii Native/Pacific Islander (0)	1	0.01
Hispanic (0)	1	0.01
Native Hawaiian (0)	1	0.01
White (11,832)	11,882	99.14
Not Hispanic (343)	344	2.87
Hispanic (11,489)	11,538	96.27

La Marque

Place Type: City
County: Galveston
Population: 14,509†

Ancestry‡	Population	%
African, Sub-Saharan (66)	66	0.45
African (66)	66	0.45
American (718)	718	4.94
Austrian (0)	10	0.07
Cajun (0)	11	0.08
Czech (38)	134	0.92
Czechoslovakian (10)	20	0.14
Dutch (9)	86	0.59
English (327)	840	5.78
European (118)	172	1.18
French, ex. Basque (192)	698	4.80
French Canadian (0)	9	0.06
German (397)	1,155	7.94
Greek (0)	14	0.10
Hungarian (15)	42	0.29
Irish (270)	1,220	8.39
Italian (113)	258	1.77
Norwegian (16)	37	0.25
Polish (138)	279	1.92
Russian (8)	68	0.47
Scotch-Irish (117)	242	1.66
Scottish (96)	142	0.98
Swedish (54)	97	0.67
Swiss (8)	8	0.06
Welsh (18)	33	0.23
West Indian, ex. Hispanic (42)	42	0.29
Bahamian (31)	31	0.21
Haitian (11)	11	0.08
Yugoslavian (10)	31	0.21

Hispanic Origin	Population	%
Hispanic or Latino (of any race)	3,271	22.54
Central American, ex. Mexican	165	1.14
Costa Rican	15	0.10
Guatemalan	13	0.09
Honduran	44	0.30
Panamanian	4	0.03
Salvadoran	89	0.61
Cuban	14	0.10
Mexican	2,785	19.19
Puerto Rican	51	0.35
South American	13	0.09
Bolivian	1	0.01
Chilean	2	0.01
Colombian	6	0.04
Peruvian	1	0.01
Venezuelan	3	0.02
Other Hispanic or Latino	243	1.67

Race*	Population	%
African-American/Black (5,325)	5,476	37.74
Not Hispanic (5,256)	5,366	36.98
Hispanic (69)	110	0.76
American Indian/Alaska Native (112)	201	1.39
Not Hispanic (64)	127	0.88
Hispanic (48)	74	0.51
Apache (4)	11	0.08
Blackfeet (3)	4	0.03
Cherokee (19)	30	0.21
Chickasaw (2)	4	0.03
Chippewa (1)	1	0.01
Choctaw (2)	10	0.07
Comanche (0)	4	0.03
Houma (0)	1	0.01
Inupiat *(Alaska Native)* (1)	1	0.01
Lumbee (1)	1	0.01
Mexican American Ind. (10)	11	0.08
Ottawa (1)	1	0.01
Pima (1)	1	0.01
Sioux (3)	5	0.03
South American Ind. (0)	1	0.01
Yaqui (1)	1	0.01
Asian (102)	137	0.94
Not Hispanic (90)	113	0.78
Hispanic (12)	24	0.17
Cambodian (6)	6	0.04
Chinese, ex. Taiwanese (11)	18	0.12
Filipino (45)	63	0.43
Indian (4)	5	0.03
Japanese (6)	8	0.06
Korean (1)	7	0.05
Pakistani (5)	5	0.03
Taiwanese (0)	1	0.01
Thai (1)	3	0.02
Vietnamese (20)	28	0.19
Hawaii Native/Pacific Islander (7)	17	0.12
Not Hispanic (4)	13	0.09
Hispanic (3)	4	0.03
Fijian (1)	1	0.01
Native Hawaiian (4)	4	0.03
Samoan (0)	4	0.03
White (7,620)	7,913	54.54
Not Hispanic (5,621)	5,780	39.84
Hispanic (1,999)	2,133	14.70

La Porte

Place Type: City
County: Harris
Population: 33,800†

Ancestry‡	Population	%
African, Sub-Saharan (50)	50	0.15
African (50)	50	0.15
American (3,267)	3,267	9.80
Arab (53)	81	0.24
Egyptian (30)	30	0.09
Lebanese (23)	51	0.15
British (38)	51	0.15
Cajun (137)	216	0.65
Canadian (5)	37	0.11
Celtic (0)	11	0.03
Czech (80)	397	1.19
Czechoslovakian (59)	68	0.20
Danish (0)	27	0.08
Dutch (136)	379	1.14
English (1,291)	3,232	9.70
European (1,001)	1,135	3.41
Finnish (8)	25	0.08
French, ex. Basque (369)	1,231	3.69
French Canadian (59)	192	0.58
German (1,614)	4,897	14.69
Greek (24)	24	0.07
Hungarian (27)	52	0.16
Iranian (15)	53	0.16
Irish (700)	3,036	9.11
Italian (287)	635	1.91
Lithuanian (5)	45	0.14
New Zealander (0)	27	0.08
Northern European (32)	32	0.10
Norwegian (53)	139	0.42
Polish (88)	381	1.14
Portuguese (0)	50	0.15
Romanian (26)	39	0.12
Russian (22)	22	0.07
Scandinavian (10)	193	0.58
Scotch-Irish (157)	412	1.24
Scottish (302)	667	2.00
Swedish (23)	192	0.58
Swiss (0)	35	0.11
Turkish (0)	48	0.14
Ukrainian (7)	7	0.02
Welsh (58)	196	0.59
West Indian, ex. Hispanic (109)	109	0.33
Trinidadian/Tobagonian (8)	8	0.02
West Indian (101)	101	0.30
Yugoslavian (13)	32	0.10

Hispanic Origin	Population	%
Hispanic or Latino (of any race)	9,932	29.38
Central American, ex. Mexican	322	0.95
Costa Rican	10	0.03
Guatemalan	75	0.22
Honduran	68	0.20
Nicaraguan	22	0.07
Panamanian	13	0.04
Salvadoran	131	0.39
Other Central American	3	0.01
Cuban	101	0.30
Dominican Republic	8	0.02
Mexican	8,230	24.35
Puerto Rican	175	0.52
South American	134	0.40
Argentinean	13	0.04
Chilean	7	0.02
Colombian	55	0.16
Ecuadorian	5	0.01

*Notes: † The Census 2010 population figure is used to calculate the percentages in the Hispanic Origin and Race categories. Ancestry percentages are based on the 2006-2010 American Community Survey population (not shown); ‡ Numbers in parentheses indicate the number of people reporting a single ancestry; * Numbers in parentheses indicate the number of persons reporting this race alone, not in combination with any other race; Please refer to the Explanation of Data for more information.*

	Population	%
Peruvian	17	0.05
Uruguayan	8	0.02
Venezuelan	29	0.09
Other Hispanic or Latino	962	2.85

Race*	Population	%
African-American/Black (2,100)	2,358	6.98
Not Hispanic (2,003)	2,193	6.49
Hispanic (97)	165	0.49
American Indian/Alaska Native (211)	423	1.25
Not Hispanic (139)	303	0.90
Hispanic (72)	120	0.36
Apache (2)	8	0.02
Blackfeet (0)	3	0.01
Central American Ind. (0)	2	0.01
Cherokee (23)	99	0.29
Cheyenne (1)	1	<0.01
Chickasaw (0)	6	0.02
Chippewa (0)	1	<0.01
Choctaw (17)	49	0.14
Comanche (4)	10	0.03
Creek (3)	8	0.02
Delaware (1)	1	<0.01
Iroquois (3)	4	0.01
Mexican American Ind. (23)	28	0.08
Navajo (17)	23	0.07
Osage (7)	13	0.04
Ottawa (4)	4	0.01
Pima (0)	2	0.01
Potawatomi (7)	11	0.03
Puget Sound Salish (1)	1	<0.01
Shoshone (2)	2	0.01
Sioux (4)	6	0.02
Spanish American Ind. (0)	1	<0.01
Asian (411)	566	1.67
Not Hispanic (387)	499	1.48
Hispanic (24)	67	0.20
Cambodian (14)	17	0.05
Chinese, ex. Taiwanese (22)	39	0.12
Filipino (66)	98	0.29
Indian (92)	115	0.34
Indonesian (1)	4	0.01
Japanese (17)	41	0.12
Korean (45)	61	0.18
Laotian (7)	11	0.03
Malaysian (1)	1	<0.01
Pakistani (3)	6	0.02
Taiwanese (1)	2	0.01
Thai (6)	7	0.02
Vietnamese (118)	132	0.39
Hawaii Native/Pacific Islander (37)	69	0.20
Not Hispanic (30)	49	0.14
Hispanic (7)	20	0.06
Guamanian/Chamorro (16)	17	0.05
Native Hawaiian (14)	23	0.07
Samoan (3)	12	0.04
White (27,063)	27,861	82.43
Not Hispanic (20,802)	21,238	62.83
Hispanic (6,261)	6,623	19.59

Lackland AFB

Place Type: CDP
County: Bexar
Population: 9,918†

Ancestry‡	Population	%
Afghan (25)	55	0.73
African, Sub-Saharan (43)	43	0.57
African (43)	43	0.57
American (48)	48	0.63
Arab (63)	66	0.87
Arab (55)	58	0.76
Iraqi (8)	8	0.11
Belgian (0)	22	0.29
British (36)	36	0.47
Cajun (0)	19	0.25
Canadian (12)	24	0.32
Croatian (0)	9	0.12
Czech (18)	18	0.24
Czechoslovakian (3)	3	0.04
Danish (0)	32	0.42
Dutch (19)	73	0.96
English (248)	663	8.74
Finnish (7)	7	0.09
French, ex. Basque (111)	268	3.53
French Canadian (69)	144	1.90
German (812)	1,841	24.27
Greek (0)	10	0.13
Hungarian (0)	6	0.08
Irish (421)	1,205	15.89
Italian (103)	438	5.77
Lithuanian (12)	53	0.70
Norwegian (47)	175	2.31
Polish (71)	228	3.01
Portuguese (0)	65	0.86
Romanian (29)	55	0.73
Russian (29)	60	0.79
Scandinavian (0)	25	0.33
Scotch-Irish (0)	6	0.08
Scottish (128)	306	4.03
Slavic (0)	30	0.40
Swedish (28)	78	1.03
Swiss (0)	18	0.24
Ukrainian (12)	22	0.29
Welsh (0)	57	0.75
West Indian, ex. Hispanic (39)	39	0.51
British West Indian (15)	15	0.20
Jamaican (12)	12	0.16
Trinidadian/Tobagonian (3)	3	0.04
West Indian (9)	9	0.12

Hispanic Origin	Population	%
Hispanic or Latino (of any race)	769	7.75
Central American, ex. Mexican	3	0.03
Guatemalan	1	0.01
Honduran	1	0.01
Salvadoran	1	0.01
Cuban	8	0.08
Dominican Republic	8	0.08
Mexican	262	2.64
Puerto Rican	95	0.96
South American	54	0.54
Bolivian	1	0.01
Chilean	4	0.04
Colombian	25	0.25
Ecuadorian	10	0.10
Peruvian	14	0.14
Other Hispanic or Latino	339	3.42

Race*	Population	%
African-American/Black (1,590)	1,629	16.42
Not Hispanic (1,575)	1,600	16.13
Hispanic (15)	29	0.29
American Indian/Alaska Native (49)	61	0.62
Not Hispanic (49)	60	0.60
Hispanic (0)	1	0.01
Cherokee (1)	4	0.04
Cheyenne (0)	4	0.04
Choctaw (1)	1	0.01
Inupiat *(Alaska Native)* (1)	1	0.01
Lumbee (1)	1	0.01
Asian (180)	203	2.05
Not Hispanic (175)	197	1.99
Hispanic (5)	6	0.06
Chinese, ex. Taiwanese (11)	14	0.14
Filipino (36)	43	0.43
Indian (46)	50	0.50
Japanese (4)	8	0.08
Korean (14)	20	0.20
Thai (2)	2	0.02
Vietnamese (1)	1	0.01
Hawaii Native/Pacific Islander (151)	160	1.61
Not Hispanic (150)	159	1.60
Hispanic (1)	1	0.01
Guamanian/Chamorro (10)	11	0.11
Native Hawaiian (122)	128	1.29
Samoan (3)	3	0.03
White (7,086)	7,170	72.29
Not Hispanic (6,871)	6,936	69.93
Hispanic (215)	234	2.36

Lake Jackson

Place Type: City
County: Brazoria
Population: 26,849†

Ancestry‡	Population	%
African, Sub-Saharan (13)	37	0.14
African (13)	37	0.14
American (1,611)	1,611	5.97
Arab (0)	11	0.04
Iraqi (0)	11	0.04
Armenian (0)	11	0.04
Australian (17)	17	0.06
Austrian (21)	51	0.19
Belgian (0)	7	0.03
Brazilian (219)	277	1.03
British (36)	94	0.35
Cajun (81)	118	0.44
Canadian (110)	126	0.47
Croatian (32)	51	0.19
Czech (190)	417	1.54
Czechoslovakian (39)	48	0.18
Danish (0)	16	0.06
Dutch (158)	488	1.81
English (1,298)	3,493	12.94
European (140)	285	1.06
Finnish (0)	7	0.03
French, ex. Basque (194)	1,560	5.78
French Canadian (139)	186	0.69
German (1,610)	4,488	16.62
Greek (51)	77	0.29
Hungarian (0)	226	0.84
Irish (1,076)	3,672	13.60
Italian (201)	911	3.37
Lithuanian (0)	54	0.20
Norwegian (109)	247	0.91
Pennsylvania German (0)	39	0.14
Polish (70)	506	1.87
Portuguese (0)	85	0.31
Romanian (17)	35	0.13
Russian (47)	176	0.65
Scandinavian (0)	8	0.03
Scotch-Irish (398)	695	2.57
Scottish (410)	1,048	3.88
Serbian (44)	44	0.16
Slavic (0)	18	0.07
Slovak (12)	12	0.04
Slovene (20)	20	0.07
Swedish (104)	219	0.81
Swiss (41)	220	0.81
Ukrainian (0)	21	0.08
Welsh (58)	207	0.77
West Indian, ex. Hispanic (0)	44	0.16
Belizean (0)	44	0.16
Yugoslavian (0)	12	0.04

Hispanic Origin	Population	%
Hispanic or Latino (of any race)	5,513	20.53
Central American, ex. Mexican	104	0.39
Costa Rican	11	0.04
Guatemalan	27	0.10
Honduran	9	0.03
Nicaraguan	14	0.05
Panamanian	7	0.03
Salvadoran	36	0.13
Cuban	30	0.11
Dominican Republic	8	0.03
Mexican	4,585	17.08
Puerto Rican	99	0.37
South American	142	0.53
Argentinean	9	0.03
Bolivian	11	0.04
Chilean	9	0.03
Colombian	49	0.18
Ecuadorian	29	0.11
Paraguayan	2	0.01
Peruvian	18	0.07

*Notes: † The Census 2010 population figure is used to calculate the percentages in the Hispanic Origin and Race categories. Ancestry percentages are based on the 2006-2010 American Community Survey population (not shown); ‡ Numbers in parentheses indicate the number of people reporting a single ancestry; * Numbers in parentheses indicate the number of persons reporting this race alone, not in combination with any other race; Please refer to the Explanation of Data for more information.*

Venezuelan	15	0.06
Other Hispanic or Latino	545	2.03

Race*	Population	%
African-American/Black (1,370)	1,558	5.80
Not Hispanic (1,312)	1,452	5.41
Hispanic (58)	106	0.39
American Indian/Alaska Native (140)	285	1.06
Not Hispanic (105)	220	0.82
Hispanic (35)	65	0.24
Apache (3)	6	0.02
Blackfeet (1)	2	0.01
Canadian/French Am. Ind. (0)	2	0.01
Cherokee (22)	64	0.24
Cheyenne (1)	1	<0.01
Chickasaw (8)	8	0.03
Chippewa (4)	5	0.02
Choctaw (10)	31	0.12
Colville (1)	1	<0.01
Comanche (2)	13	0.05
Creek (4)	8	0.03
Mexican American Ind. (2)	2	0.01
Navajo (0)	1	<0.01
Osage (0)	3	0.01
Ottawa (0)	2	0.01
Pima (0)	1	<0.01
Potawatomi (1)	1	<0.01
Pueblo (1)	6	0.02
Tlingit-Haida *(Alaska Native)* (1)	1	<0.01
Ute (0)	1	<0.01
Asian (842)	951	3.54
Not Hispanic (831)	920	3.43
Hispanic (11)	31	0.12
Bangladeshi (14)	16	0.06
Burmese (2)	2	0.01
Cambodian (9)	9	0.03
Chinese, ex. Taiwanese (165)	184	0.69
Filipino (129)	151	0.56
Indian (201)	212	0.79
Indonesian (3)	7	0.03
Japanese (50)	65	0.24
Korean (48)	74	0.28
Pakistani (34)	37	0.14
Taiwanese (16)	19	0.07
Thai (4)	10	0.04
Vietnamese (147)	157	0.58
Hawaii Native/Pacific Islander (10)	28	0.10
Not Hispanic (8)	21	0.08
Hispanic (2)	7	0.03
Guamanian/Chamorro (1)	1	<0.01
Native Hawaiian (6)	18	0.07
Samoan (0)	2	0.01
White (22,649)	23,241	86.56
Not Hispanic (18,710)	19,029	70.87
Hispanic (3,939)	4,212	15.69

Lakeway

Place Type: City
County: Travis
Population: 11,391†

Ancestry‡	Population	%
American (1,270)	1,270	11.84
Arab (21)	21	0.20
Lebanese (21)	21	0.20
Armenian (8)	8	0.07
Austrian (0)	37	0.34
Brazilian (15)	22	0.21
British (60)	89	0.83
Canadian (0)	13	0.12
Czech (15)	49	0.46
Czechoslovakian (25)	25	0.23
Danish (84)	202	1.88
Dutch (50)	254	2.37
English (579)	1,976	18.42
Estonian (52)	52	0.48
European (211)	285	2.66
Finnish (14)	42	0.39
French, ex. Basque (60)	435	4.06
French Canadian (68)	112	1.04
German (854)	2,468	23.01
Greek (13)	57	0.53
Hungarian (0)	16	0.15
Iranian (9)	9	0.08
Irish (346)	1,350	12.59
Italian (248)	428	3.99
Latvian (21)	21	0.20
Lithuanian (24)	24	0.22
Northern European (41)	41	0.38
Norwegian (66)	190	1.77
Polish (26)	216	2.01
Russian (11)	22	0.21
Scandinavian (0)	54	0.50
Scotch-Irish (189)	294	2.74
Scottish (125)	411	3.83
Swedish (72)	395	3.68
Swiss (12)	56	0.52
Welsh (35)	230	2.14

Hispanic Origin	Population	%
Hispanic or Latino (of any race)	836	7.34
Central American, ex. Mexican	40	0.35
Costa Rican	10	0.09
Guatemalan	11	0.10
Honduran	1	0.01
Nicaraguan	7	0.06
Panamanian	4	0.04
Salvadoran	4	0.04
Other Central American	3	0.03
Cuban	21	0.18
Dominican Republic	2	0.02
Mexican	575	5.05
Puerto Rican	25	0.22
South American	68	0.60
Argentinean	23	0.20
Chilean	1	0.01
Colombian	15	0.13
Ecuadorian	13	0.11
Peruvian	3	0.03
Venezuelan	13	0.11
Other Hispanic or Latino	105	0.92

Race*	Population	%
African-American/Black (111)	155	1.36
Not Hispanic (106)	145	1.27
Hispanic (5)	10	0.09
American Indian/Alaska Native (30)	125	1.10
Not Hispanic (22)	105	0.92
Hispanic (8)	20	0.18
Apache (1)	4	0.04
Blackfeet (0)	2	0.02
Cherokee (3)	40	0.35
Chickasaw (2)	3	0.03
Choctaw (1)	4	0.04
Comanche (0)	3	0.03
Creek (2)	4	0.04
Iroquois (1)	4	0.04
Mexican American Ind. (1)	2	0.02
Osage (0)	6	0.05
Pueblo (0)	1	0.01
Yakama (0)	1	0.01
Asian (368)	451	3.96
Not Hispanic (364)	434	3.81
Hispanic (4)	17	0.15
Bangladeshi (10)	10	0.09
Cambodian (1)	1	0.01
Chinese, ex. Taiwanese (87)	108	0.95
Filipino (18)	31	0.27
Indian (101)	108	0.95
Japanese (13)	32	0.28
Korean (23)	35	0.31
Malaysian (1)	1	0.01
Pakistani (29)	29	0.25
Taiwanese (8)	12	0.11
Thai (5)	11	0.10
Vietnamese (61)	72	0.63
Hawaii Native/Pacific Islander (3)	12	0.11
Not Hispanic (3)	11	0.10
Hispanic (0)	1	0.01
Guamanian/Chamorro (1)	1	0.01
Native Hawaiian (1)	8	0.07
White (10,521)	10,741	94.29
Not Hispanic (9,883)	10,043	88.17
Hispanic (638)	698	6.13

Lamesa

Place Type: City
County: Dawson
Population: 9,422†

Ancestry‡	Population	%
African, Sub-Saharan (94)	94	1.00
African (94)	94	1.00
American (433)	433	4.62
Czech (0)	34	0.36
Dutch (15)	23	0.25
English (400)	514	5.49
French, ex. Basque (8)	42	0.45
German (423)	721	7.70
Irish (408)	532	5.68
Italian (0)	36	0.38
Northern European (13)	13	0.14
Norwegian (11)	11	0.12
Portuguese (0)	12	0.13
Scotch-Irish (47)	57	0.61
Scottish (40)	54	0.58
Swedish (12)	25	0.27
Welsh (0)	26	0.28

Hispanic Origin	Population	%
Hispanic or Latino (of any race)	5,530	58.69
Central American, ex. Mexican	8	0.08
Guatemalan	6	0.06
Honduran	1	0.01
Salvadoran	1	0.01
Cuban	2	0.02
Mexican	4,657	49.43
Puerto Rican	14	0.15
South American	1	0.01
Argentinean	1	0.01
Other Hispanic or Latino	848	9.00

Race*	Population	%
African-American/Black (432)	483	5.13
Not Hispanic (401)	426	4.52
Hispanic (31)	57	0.60
American Indian/Alaska Native (69)	94	1.00
Not Hispanic (20)	35	0.37
Hispanic (49)	59	0.63
Apache (6)	6	0.06
Cherokee (3)	13	0.14
Chickasaw (5)	8	0.08
Choctaw (3)	3	0.03
Comanche (0)	1	0.01
Iroquois (1)	2	0.02
Kiowa (1)	1	0.01
Mexican American Ind. (3)	3	0.03
Navajo (1)	1	0.01
Tohono O'Odham (2)	2	0.02
Yup'ik *(Alaska Native)* (1)	1	0.01
Asian (42)	58	0.62
Not Hispanic (39)	50	0.53
Hispanic (3)	8	0.08
Chinese, ex. Taiwanese (7)	11	0.12
Filipino (16)	22	0.23
Indian (6)	8	0.08
Japanese (0)	6	0.06
Korean (5)	8	0.08
Thai (4)	4	0.04
Vietnamese (3)	3	0.03
Hawaii Native/Pacific Islander (6)	20	0.21
Not Hispanic (2)	9	0.10
Hispanic (4)	11	0.12
Guamanian/Chamorro (2)	2	0.02
Native Hawaiian (2)	11	0.12
Samoan (0)	2	0.02
White (7,595)	7,787	82.65
Not Hispanic (3,374)	3,415	36.24

SECTION TWO

*Notes: † The Census 2010 population figure is used to calculate the percentages in the Hispanic Origin and Race categories. Ancestry percentages are based on the 2006-2010 American Community Survey population (not shown); ‡ Numbers in parentheses indicate the number of people reporting a single ancestry; * Numbers in parentheses indicate the number of persons reporting this race alone, not in combination with any other race; Please refer to the Explanation of Data for more information.*

Hispanic (4,221)	4,372	46.40

Lancaster

Place Type: City
County: Dallas
Population: 36,361†

Ancestry‡	Population	%
African, Sub-Saharan (328)	358	1.05
African (205)	235	0.69
Ghanaian (9)	9	0.03
Nigerian (40)	40	0.12
Other Sub-Saharan African (74)	74	0.22
American (1,004)	1,004	2.94
Arab (55)	55	0.16
Arab (55)	55	0.16
Austrian (12)	12	0.04
British (57)	66	0.19
Czech (7)	13	0.04
Czechoslovakian (9)	9	0.03
Dutch (2)	212	0.62
English (349)	899	2.63
European (41)	49	0.14
French, ex. Basque (77)	151	0.44
German (311)	724	2.12
Greek (11)	11	0.03
Irish (514)	1,219	3.57
Italian (22)	103	0.30
Norwegian (8)	47	0.14
Polish (11)	80	0.23
Romanian (9)	9	0.03
Russian (0)	6	0.02
Scandinavian (10)	10	0.03
Scotch-Irish (97)	227	0.66
Scottish (46)	152	0.44
Swedish (26)	40	0.12
Welsh (0)	89	0.26
West Indian, ex. Hispanic (24)	49	0.14
Jamaican (9)	34	0.10
West Indian (15)	15	0.04
Yugoslavian (14)	14	0.04

Hispanic Origin	Population	%
Hispanic or Latino (of any race)	6,164	16.95
Central American, ex. Mexican	251	0.69
Costa Rican	4	0.01
Guatemalan	13	0.04
Honduran	21	0.06
Nicaraguan	9	0.02
Panamanian	9	0.02
Salvadoran	183	0.50
Other Central American	12	0.03
Cuban	18	0.05
Dominican Republic	5	0.01
Mexican	5,304	14.59
Puerto Rican	130	0.36
South American	42	0.12
Argentinean	6	0.02
Bolivian	3	0.01
Colombian	20	0.06
Ecuadorian	7	0.02
Peruvian	3	0.01
Venezuelan	3	0.01
Other Hispanic or Latino	414	1.14

Race*	Population	%
African-American/Black (24,997)	25,497	70.12
Not Hispanic (24,827)	25,217	69.35
Hispanic (170)	280	0.77
American Indian/Alaska Native (128)	340	0.94
Not Hispanic (64)	234	0.64
Hispanic (64)	106	0.29
Apache (2)	8	0.02
Arapaho (0)	3	0.01
Blackfeet (0)	10	0.03
Cherokee (6)	51	0.14
Chickasaw (2)	2	0.01
Chippewa (1)	3	0.01
Choctaw (16)	39	0.11
Creek (1)	3	0.01
Iroquois (1)	1	<0.01
Mexican American Ind. (6)	12	0.03
Navajo (1)	4	0.01
Pueblo (5)	5	0.01
Tohono O'Odham (0)	1	<0.01
Yakama (1)	1	<0.01
Asian (106)	203	0.56
Not Hispanic (99)	184	0.51
Hispanic (7)	19	0.05
Cambodian (4)	4	0.01
Chinese, ex. Taiwanese (11)	20	0.06
Filipino (27)	54	0.15
Hmong (1)	1	<0.01
Indian (14)	33	0.09
Indonesian (1)	1	<0.01
Japanese (3)	15	0.04
Korean (13)	26	0.07
Laotian (8)	8	0.02
Pakistani (5)	5	0.01
Sri Lankan (1)	1	<0.01
Thai (4)	15	0.04
Vietnamese (7)	12	0.03
Hawaii Native/Pacific Islander (13)	35	0.10
Not Hispanic (10)	28	0.08
Hispanic (3)	7	0.02
Fijian (1)	2	0.01
Guamanian/Chamorro (2)	2	0.01
Native Hawaiian (2)	9	0.02
Samoan (7)	8	0.02
Tongan (0)	1	<0.01
White (7,409)	7,906	21.74
Not Hispanic (4,689)	5,006	13.77
Hispanic (2,720)	2,900	7.98

Laredo

Place Type: City
County: Webb
Population: 236,091†

Ancestry‡	Population	%
African, Sub-Saharan (0)	8	<0.01
African (0)	8	<0.01
Alsatian (0)	32	0.01
American (2,212)	2,212	0.98
Arab (166)	329	0.15
Arab (10)	50	0.02
Egyptian (8)	8	<0.01
Lebanese (104)	161	0.07
Other Arab (44)	110	0.05
Armenian (0)	97	0.04
Austrian (8)	51	0.02
Basque (0)	10	<0.01
British (13)	26	0.01
Cajun (0)	17	0.01
Canadian (22)	22	0.01
Czech (5)	26	0.01
Czechoslovakian (8)	8	<0.01
Dutch (0)	120	0.05
English (168)	760	0.34
European (138)	218	0.10
French, ex. Basque (46)	727	0.32
French Canadian (7)	57	0.03
German (427)	2,538	1.12
Greek (23)	93	0.04
Hungarian (0)	21	0.01
Icelander (0)	12	0.01
Iranian (49)	49	0.02
Irish (415)	1,749	0.77
Italian (91)	584	0.26
Lithuanian (13)	13	0.01
Maltese (0)	12	0.01
Norwegian (12)	30	0.01
Polish (136)	458	0.20
Portuguese (0)	180	0.08
Romanian (0)	128	0.06
Russian (37)	153	0.07
Scotch-Irish (122)	188	0.08
Scottish (117)	274	0.12
Slovene (40)	40	0.02
Swedish (25)	61	0.03
Swiss (12)	168	0.07
Welsh (0)	39	0.02
West Indian, ex. Hispanic (8)	43	0.02
Haitian (8)	23	0.01
Jamaican (0)	20	0.01
Yugoslavian (58)	58	0.03

Hispanic Origin	Population	%
Hispanic or Latino (of any race)	225,750	95.62
Central American, ex. Mexican	966	0.41
Costa Rican	22	0.01
Guatemalan	209	0.09
Honduran	370	0.16
Nicaraguan	73	0.03
Panamanian	25	0.01
Salvadoran	261	0.11
Other Central American	6	<0.01
Cuban	223	0.09
Dominican Republic	57	0.02
Mexican	205,079	86.86
Puerto Rican	831	0.35
South American	332	0.14
Argentinean	35	0.01
Bolivian	16	0.01
Chilean	25	0.01
Colombian	106	0.04
Ecuadorian	41	0.02
Paraguayan	1	<0.01
Peruvian	54	0.02
Uruguayan	9	<0.01
Venezuelan	45	0.02
Other Hispanic or Latino	18,262	7.74

Race*	Population	%
African-American/Black (1,110)	1,406	0.60
Not Hispanic (478)	538	0.23
Hispanic (632)	868	0.37
American Indian/Alaska Native (965)	1,287	0.55
Not Hispanic (87)	149	0.06
Hispanic (878)	1,138	0.48
Alaska Athabascan *(Ala. Nat.)* (1)	2	<0.01
Apache (17)	26	0.01
Blackfeet (0)	1	<0.01
Canadian/French Am. Ind. (1)	1	<0.01
Central American Ind. (2)	2	<0.01
Cherokee (21)	36	0.02
Cheyenne (0)	1	<0.01
Chickasaw (6)	7	<0.01
Choctaw (7)	12	0.01
Comanche (6)	7	<0.01
Creek (1)	1	<0.01
Inupiat *(Alaska Native)* (0)	1	<0.01
Iroquois (0)	1	<0.01
Mexican American Ind. (129)	167	0.07
Navajo (4)	9	<0.01
Osage (1)	2	<0.01
Ottawa (2)	2	<0.01
Pueblo (4)	4	<0.01
Seminole (3)	4	<0.01
Shoshone (3)	3	<0.01
Sioux (6)	11	<0.01
South American Ind. (0)	4	<0.01
Spanish American Ind. (12)	16	0.01
Tohono O'Odham (1)	1	<0.01
Ute (4)	7	<0.01
Yaqui (0)	1	<0.01
Yuman (5)	5	<0.01
Asian (1,454)	1,813	0.77
Not Hispanic (1,313)	1,427	0.60
Hispanic (141)	386	0.16
Bangladeshi (6)	6	<0.01
Burmese (15)	16	0.01
Cambodian (2)	6	<0.01
Chinese, ex. Taiwanese (161)	208	0.09
Filipino (498)	556	0.24
Indian (272)	350	0.15
Indonesian (0)	1	<0.01
Japanese (94)	115	0.05

*Notes: † The Census 2010 population figure is used to calculate the percentages in the Hispanic Origin and Race categories. Ancestry percentages are based on the 2006-2010 American Community Survey population (not shown); ‡ Numbers in parentheses indicate the number of people reporting a single ancestry; * Numbers in parentheses indicate the number of persons reporting this race alone, not in combination with any other race; Please refer to the Explanation of Data for more information.*

Korean (188)	222	0.09
Laotian (1)	4	<0.01
Pakistani (6)	8	<0.01
Sri Lankan (2)	3	<0.01
Taiwanese (27)	29	0.01
Thai (5)	12	0.01
Vietnamese (147)	164	0.07
Hawaii Native/Pacific Islander (29)	83	0.04
Not Hispanic (11)	24	0.01
Hispanic (18)	59	0.02
Guamanian/Chamorro (8)	15	0.01
Native Hawaiian (12)	25	0.01
Samoan (7)	14	0.01
White (207,067)	210,309	89.08
Not Hispanic (8,086)	8,285	3.51
Hispanic (198,981)	202,024	85.57

League City

Place Type: City
County: Galveston
Population: 83,560†

Ancestry‡	Population	%
African, Sub-Saharan (707)	822	1.07
African (229)	309	0.40
Cape Verdean (12)	12	0.02
Ethiopian (221)	221	0.29
Ghanaian (15)	15	0.02
Nigerian (204)	204	0.27
Somalian (0)	10	0.01
South African (26)	51	0.07
American (3,520)	3,520	4.59
Arab (337)	425	0.55
Egyptian (0)	24	0.03
Iraqi (9)	26	0.03
Jordanian (269)	269	0.35
Lebanese (47)	85	0.11
Syrian (12)	12	0.02
Other Arab (0)	9	0.01
Armenian (22)	54	0.07
Austrian (73)	226	0.29
Belgian (0)	14	0.02
Brazilian (51)	67	0.09
British (179)	548	0.71
Bulgarian (8)	8	0.01
Cajun (140)	176	0.23
Canadian (342)	599	0.78
Croatian (12)	34	0.04
Czech (237)	871	1.13
Czechoslovakian (106)	135	0.18
Danish (128)	287	0.37
Dutch (132)	781	1.02
Eastern European (51)	83	0.11
English (2,865)	7,924	10.32
European (1,335)	1,449	1.89
Finnish (28)	83	0.11
French, ex. Basque (1,174)	4,085	5.32
French Canadian (207)	630	0.82
German (4,272)	13,204	17.20
German Russian (10)	10	0.01
Greek (178)	368	0.48
Hungarian (124)	477	0.62
Iranian (180)	292	0.38
Irish (2,733)	8,992	11.71
Israeli (383)	383	0.50
Italian (1,420)	4,368	5.69
Lithuanian (98)	122	0.16
Northern European (15)	56	0.07
Norwegian (502)	716	0.93
Polish (562)	1,898	2.47
Portuguese (88)	283	0.37
Romanian (0)	18	0.02
Russian (189)	337	0.44
Scandinavian (88)	141	0.18
Scotch-Irish (693)	1,859	2.42
Scottish (640)	2,070	2.70
Slovak (43)	97	0.13
Slovene (10)	10	0.01
Swedish (131)	648	0.84
Swiss (47)	55	0.07
Turkish (17)	17	0.02
Ukrainian (35)	111	0.14
Welsh (173)	472	0.61
West Indian, ex. Hispanic (103)	257	0.33
Dutch West Indian (0)	69	0.09
Haitian (74)	74	0.10
Jamaican (29)	48	0.06
Trinidadian/Tobagonian (0)	37	0.05
West Indian (0)	29	0.04
Yugoslavian (32)	59	0.08

Hispanic Origin	Population	%
Hispanic or Latino (of any race)	14,446	17.29
Central American, ex. Mexican	1,065	1.27
Costa Rican	33	0.04
Guatemalan	142	0.17
Honduran	158	0.19
Nicaraguan	73	0.09
Panamanian	58	0.07
Salvadoran	585	0.70
Other Central American	16	0.02
Cuban	230	0.28
Dominican Republic	77	0.09
Mexican	10,148	12.14
Puerto Rican	733	0.88
South American	749	0.90
Argentinean	78	0.09
Bolivian	67	0.08
Chilean	29	0.03
Colombian	218	0.26
Ecuadorian	47	0.06
Paraguayan	2	<0.01
Peruvian	117	0.14
Uruguayan	8	0.01
Venezuelan	173	0.21
Other South American	10	0.01
Other Hispanic or Latino	1,444	1.73

Race*	Population	%
African-American/Black (5,946)	6,553	7.84
Not Hispanic (5,791)	6,247	7.48
Hispanic (155)	306	0.37
American Indian/Alaska Native (363)	808	0.97
Not Hispanic (246)	601	0.72
Hispanic (117)	207	0.25
Alaska Athabascan *(Ala. Nat.)* (2)	6	0.01
Aleut *(Alaska Native)* (1)	2	<0.01
Apache (8)	23	0.03
Blackfeet (4)	21	0.03
Canadian/French Am. Ind. (1)	3	<0.01
Central American Ind. (2)	7	0.01
Cherokee (46)	158	0.19
Cheyenne (3)	3	<0.01
Chickasaw (9)	15	0.02
Chippewa (3)	9	0.01
Choctaw (31)	59	0.07
Comanche (5)	8	0.01
Cree (0)	1	<0.01
Creek (7)	20	0.02
Delaware (1)	2	<0.01
Hopi (0)	1	<0.01
Houma (2)	4	<0.01
Inupiat *(Alaska Native)* (2)	3	<0.01
Iroquois (2)	4	<0.01
Kiowa (1)	1	<0.01
Lumbee (3)	6	0.01
Menominee (0)	1	<0.01
Mexican American Ind. (9)	17	0.02
Navajo (3)	7	0.01
Osage (1)	3	<0.01
Paiute (0)	3	<0.01
Pima (1)	1	<0.01
Potawatomi (2)	7	0.01
Pueblo (7)	14	0.02
Seminole (6)	11	0.01
Sioux (3)	10	0.01
South American Ind. (1)	2	<0.01
Spanish American Ind. (6)	6	0.01
Tlingit-Haida *(Alaska Native)* (2)	2	<0.01
Asian (4,506)	5,360	6.41
Not Hispanic (4,453)	5,167	6.18
Hispanic (53)	193	0.23
Bangladeshi (29)	33	0.04
Burmese (2)	2	<0.01
Cambodian (61)	70	0.08
Chinese, ex. Taiwanese (733)	857	1.03
Filipino (632)	846	1.01
Indian (1,235)	1,361	1.63
Indonesian (7)	19	0.02
Japanese (79)	180	0.22
Korean (201)	295	0.35
Laotian (7)	8	0.01
Malaysian (1)	1	<0.01
Nepalese (6)	10	0.01
Pakistani (256)	298	0.36
Sri Lankan (13)	13	0.02
Taiwanese (21)	24	0.03
Thai (46)	79	0.09
Vietnamese (1,033)	1,141	1.37
Hawaii Native/Pacific Islander (49)	133	0.16
Not Hispanic (42)	112	0.13
Hispanic (7)	21	0.03
Fijian (2)	3	<0.01
Guamanian/Chamorro (15)	21	0.03
Native Hawaiian (12)	31	0.04
Samoan (8)	14	0.02
White (66,408)	68,534	82.02
Not Hispanic (56,977)	58,291	69.76
Hispanic (9,431)	10,243	12.26

Leander

Place Type: City
County: Williamson
Population: 26,521†

Ancestry‡	Population	%
African, Sub-Saharan (166)	200	0.86
African (166)	200	0.86
American (1,131)	1,131	4.86
Arab (70)	70	0.30
Egyptian (67)	67	0.29
Lebanese (3)	3	0.01
Australian (0)	21	0.09
Austrian (26)	26	0.11
British (25)	67	0.29
Canadian (0)	9	0.04
Celtic (0)	23	0.10
Croatian (11)	19	0.08
Czech (166)	551	2.37
Czechoslovakian (0)	4	0.02
Danish (13)	42	0.18
Dutch (0)	188	0.81
English (855)	2,055	8.82
European (164)	197	0.85
Finnish (0)	21	0.09
French, ex. Basque (108)	817	3.51
French Canadian (83)	139	0.60
German (1,790)	5,409	23.22
Greek (0)	37	0.16
Iranian (40)	47	0.20
Irish (577)	3,005	12.90
Italian (289)	1,107	4.75
Lithuanian (0)	34	0.15
Northern European (26)	26	0.11
Norwegian (40)	178	0.76
Polish (154)	783	3.36
Portuguese (4)	97	0.42
Russian (19)	45	0.19
Scandinavian (65)	65	0.28
Scotch-Irish (587)	1,216	5.22
Scottish (363)	818	3.51
Swedish (61)	351	1.51
Swiss (0)	15	0.06
Turkish (30)	30	0.13
Ukrainian (0)	36	0.15
Welsh (9)	71	0.30
West Indian, ex. Hispanic (78)	94	0.40
British West Indian (22)	22	0.09

SECTION TWO

*Notes: † The Census 2010 population figure is used to calculate the percentages in the Hispanic Origin and Race categories. Ancestry percentages are based on the 2006-2010 American Community Survey population (not shown); ‡ Numbers in parentheses indicate the number of people reporting a single ancestry; * Numbers in parentheses indicate the number of persons reporting this race alone, not in combination with any other race; Please refer to the Explanation of Data for more information.*

Jamaican (33)	49	0.21
U.S. Virgin Islander (14)	14	0.06
West Indian (9)	9	0.04

Hispanic Origin	Population	%
Hispanic or Latino (of any race)	6,500	24.51
Central American, ex. Mexican	249	0.94
Costa Rican	17	0.06
Guatemalan	33	0.12
Honduran	37	0.14
Nicaraguan	18	0.07
Panamanian	45	0.17
Salvadoran	94	0.35
Other Central American	5	0.02
Cuban	75	0.28
Dominican Republic	10	0.04
Mexican	5,328	20.09
Puerto Rican	219	0.83
South American	131	0.49
Argentinean	9	0.03
Bolivian	2	0.01
Chilean	17	0.06
Colombian	40	0.15
Ecuadorian	10	0.04
Peruvian	34	0.13
Venezuelan	17	0.06
Other South American	2	0.01
Other Hispanic or Latino	488	1.84

Race*	Population	%
African-American/Black (1,270)	1,544	5.82
Not Hispanic (1,171)	1,383	5.21
Hispanic (99)	161	0.61
American Indian/Alaska Native (183)	428	1.61
Not Hispanic (109)	279	1.05
Hispanic (74)	149	0.56
Apache (8)	15	0.06
Blackfeet (0)	10	0.04
Canadian/French Am. Ind. (1)	1	<0.01
Cherokee (29)	90	0.34
Chickasaw (6)	10	0.04
Chippewa (5)	8	0.03
Choctaw (27)	43	0.16
Comanche (0)	8	0.03
Creek (2)	2	0.01
Delaware (0)	1	<0.01
Hopi (0)	1	<0.01
Inupiat *(Alaska Native)* (2)	2	0.01
Iroquois (0)	2	0.01
Kiowa (2)	2	0.01
Lumbee (2)	3	0.01
Mexican American Ind. (10)	14	0.05
Navajo (4)	4	0.02
Osage (1)	1	<0.01
Ottawa (1)	1	<0.01
Pima (0)	3	0.01
Potawatomi (1)	3	0.01
Pueblo (1)	3	0.01
Seminole (0)	1	<0.01
Sioux (3)	9	0.03
South American Ind. (0)	3	0.01
Asian (629)	925	3.49
Not Hispanic (592)	828	3.12
Hispanic (37)	97	0.37
Bangladeshi (4)	4	0.02
Burmese (1)	1	<0.01
Cambodian (22)	24	0.09
Chinese, ex. Taiwanese (51)	91	0.34
Filipino (152)	245	0.92
Hmong (6)	8	0.03
Indian (90)	113	0.43
Indonesian (1)	1	<0.01
Japanese (23)	91	0.34
Korean (42)	97	0.37
Laotian (1)	1	<0.01
Malaysian (17)	17	0.06
Pakistani (27)	32	0.12
Sri Lankan (10)	11	0.04
Taiwanese (7)	10	0.04
Thai (20)	30	0.11
Vietnamese (125)	148	0.56
Hawaii Native/Pacific Islander (25)	73	0.28
Not Hispanic (22)	52	0.20
Hispanic (3)	21	0.08
Guamanian/Chamorro (2)	14	0.05
Native Hawaiian (8)	25	0.09
Samoan (10)	18	0.07
White (21,283)	22,268	83.96
Not Hispanic (17,459)	18,035	68.00
Hispanic (3,824)	4,233	15.96

Leon Valley

Place Type: City
County: Bexar
Population: 10,151†

Ancestry‡	Population	%
American (448)	448	4.50
Austrian (0)	18	0.18
Belgian (0)	60	0.60
British (27)	58	0.58
Czech (8)	29	0.29
Czechoslovakian (54)	77	0.77
Dutch (23)	82	0.82
English (255)	866	8.70
European (72)	72	0.72
French, ex. Basque (0)	217	2.18
German (402)	1,201	12.07
Greek (0)	41	0.41
Hungarian (0)	28	0.28
Irish (223)	642	6.45
Italian (134)	296	2.97
Lithuanian (0)	10	0.10
Northern European (11)	11	0.11
Norwegian (0)	23	0.23
Polish (47)	190	1.91
Romanian (0)	17	0.17
Russian (40)	40	0.40
Scotch-Irish (81)	242	2.43
Scottish (27)	119	1.20
Swedish (0)	44	0.44
Swiss (10)	33	0.33
Turkish (29)	48	0.48
Welsh (0)	78	0.78

Hispanic Origin	Population	%
Hispanic or Latino (of any race)	5,707	56.22
Central American, ex. Mexican	69	0.68
Costa Rican	3	0.03
Guatemalan	17	0.17
Honduran	13	0.13
Nicaraguan	1	0.01
Panamanian	15	0.15
Salvadoran	20	0.20
Cuban	13	0.13
Dominican Republic	20	0.20
Mexican	4,951	48.77
Puerto Rican	92	0.91
South American	80	0.79
Argentinean	8	0.08
Bolivian	6	0.06
Chilean	1	0.01
Colombian	31	0.31
Ecuadorian	1	0.01
Peruvian	27	0.27
Venezuelan	6	0.06
Other Hispanic or Latino	482	4.75

Race*	Population	%
African-American/Black (404)	470	4.63
Not Hispanic (355)	396	3.90
Hispanic (49)	74	0.73
American Indian/Alaska Native (58)	120	1.18
Not Hispanic (20)	49	0.48
Hispanic (38)	71	0.70
Apache (2)	8	0.08
Blackfeet (0)	1	0.01
Central American Ind. (0)	1	0.01
Cherokee (7)	19	0.19
Chickasaw (4)	5	0.05
Chippewa (2)	2	0.02
Choctaw (0)	1	0.01
Comanche (1)	1	0.01
Iroquois (1)	2	0.02
Mexican American Ind. (5)	5	0.05
Navajo (2)	2	0.02
Pueblo (1)	1	0.01
South American Ind. (1)	2	0.02
Yaqui (0)	2	0.02
Asian (377)	458	4.51
Not Hispanic (359)	410	4.04
Hispanic (18)	48	0.47
Bangladeshi (1)	1	0.01
Cambodian (7)	7	0.07
Chinese, ex. Taiwanese (62)	76	0.75
Filipino (149)	177	1.74
Indian (57)	68	0.67
Indonesian (1)	1	0.01
Japanese (10)	22	0.22
Korean (15)	24	0.24
Laotian (1)	4	0.04
Nepalese (3)	3	0.03
Pakistani (8)	8	0.08
Taiwanese (2)	2	0.02
Thai (16)	27	0.27
Vietnamese (33)	35	0.34
Hawaii Native/Pacific Islander (19)	24	0.24
Not Hispanic (19)	20	0.20
Hispanic (0)	4	0.04
Guamanian/Chamorro (12)	12	0.12
Native Hawaiian (1)	5	0.05
Samoan (2)	2	0.02
White (8,220)	8,435	83.10
Not Hispanic (3,565)	3,661	36.07
Hispanic (4,655)	4,774	47.03

Levelland

Place Type: City
County: Hockley
Population: 13,542†

Ancestry‡	Population	%
American (964)	964	7.17
Austrian (29)	41	0.30
British (12)	52	0.39
Canadian (7)	7	0.05
Czechoslovakian (0)	7	0.05
Dutch (8)	151	1.12
English (347)	790	5.88
European (80)	91	0.68
French, ex. Basque (52)	299	2.22
French Canadian (11)	18	0.13
German (415)	1,130	8.40
Hungarian (16)	16	0.12
Irish (312)	810	6.02
Italian (72)	177	1.32
Norwegian (18)	30	0.22
Polish (27)	29	0.22
Portuguese (10)	10	0.07
Russian (7)	22	0.16
Scandinavian (9)	9	0.07
Scotch-Irish (186)	340	2.53
Scottish (28)	209	1.55
Swedish (11)	21	0.16
Ukrainian (0)	8	0.06
Welsh (30)	49	0.36
West Indian, ex. Hispanic (12)	12	0.09
Trinidadian/Tobagonian (12)	12	0.09
Yugoslavian (0)	9	0.07

Hispanic Origin	Population	%
Hispanic or Latino (of any race)	6,523	48.17
Central American, ex. Mexican	10	0.07
Guatemalan	4	0.03
Honduran	3	0.02
Salvadoran	3	0.02
Cuban	2	0.01
Dominican Republic	7	0.05

*Notes: † The Census 2010 population figure is used to calculate the percentages in the Hispanic Origin and Race categories. Ancestry percentages are based on the 2006-2010 American Community Survey population (not shown); ‡ Numbers in parentheses indicate the number of people reporting a single ancestry; * Numbers in parentheses indicate the number of persons reporting this race alone, not in combination with any other race; Please refer to the Explanation of Data for more information.*

Mexican	5,699	42.08
Puerto Rican	12	0.09
Other Hispanic or Latino	793	5.86

Race*	Population	%
African-American/Black (692)	751	5.55
Not Hispanic (668)	702	5.18
Hispanic (24)	49	0.36
American Indian/Alaska Native (123)	193	1.43
Not Hispanic (41)	74	0.55
Hispanic (82)	119	0.88
Apache (7)	12	0.09
Arapaho (1)	3	0.02
Cherokee (7)	16	0.12
Chickasaw (2)	3	0.02
Chippewa (0)	1	0.01
Choctaw (5)	15	0.11
Comanche (0)	3	0.02
Creek (6)	9	0.07
Hopi (0)	4	0.03
Mexican American Ind. (18)	22	0.16
Pima (1)	2	0.01
Potawatomi (1)	1	0.01
Seminole (0)	3	0.02
Shoshone (1)	1	0.01
Yup'ik *(Alaska Native)* (2)	2	0.01
Asian (51)	75	0.55
Not Hispanic (49)	55	0.41
Hispanic (2)	20	0.15
Chinese, ex. Taiwanese (7)	11	0.08
Filipino (11)	15	0.11
Indian (13)	23	0.17
Indonesian (0)	1	0.01
Japanese (2)	7	0.05
Korean (2)	3	0.02
Thai (4)	6	0.04
Vietnamese (7)	8	0.06
Hawaii Native/Pacific Islander (4)	10	0.07
Not Hispanic (3)	3	0.02
Hispanic (1)	7	0.05
Native Hawaiian (3)	8	0.06
White (10,222)	10,526	77.73
Not Hispanic (6,146)	6,228	45.99
Hispanic (4,076)	4,298	31.74

Lewisville

Place Type: City
County: Denton
Population: 95,290†

Ancestry‡	Population	%
African, Sub-Saharan (1,392)	1,747	1.88
African (309)	436	0.47
Kenyan (220)	349	0.38
Nigerian (811)	882	0.95
Senegalese (0)	28	0.03
Zimbabwean (12)	12	0.01
Other Sub-Saharan African (40)	40	0.04
American (3,702)	3,702	3.98
Arab (330)	632	0.68
Arab (126)	163	0.18
Egyptian (52)	57	0.06
Lebanese (53)	147	0.16
Syrian (84)	250	0.27
Other Arab (15)	15	0.02
Armenian (109)	109	0.12
Assyrian/Chaldean/Syriac (16)	34	0.04
Australian (0)	8	0.01
Austrian (0)	50	0.05
Basque (0)	13	0.01
Belgian (13)	60	0.06
Brazilian (133)	144	0.15
British (126)	292	0.31
Bulgarian (0)	19	0.02
Cajun (55)	55	0.06
Canadian (64)	127	0.14
Croatian (4)	76	0.08
Czech (126)	319	0.34
Czechoslovakian (52)	162	0.17
Danish (233)	437	0.47
Dutch (361)	1,652	1.78
Eastern European (20)	32	0.03
English (2,933)	8,696	9.36
European (868)	1,154	1.24
Finnish (0)	8	0.01
French, ex. Basque (451)	2,490	2.68
French Canadian (190)	419	0.45
German (3,623)	12,431	13.38
Greek (91)	344	0.37
Hungarian (111)	313	0.34
Iranian (152)	163	0.18
Irish (2,740)	9,114	9.81
Israeli (18)	54	0.06
Italian (789)	2,194	2.36
Lithuanian (47)	59	0.06
Macedonian (16)	16	0.02
Norwegian (348)	1,067	1.15
Polish (441)	1,305	1.40
Portuguese (137)	237	0.26
Romanian (249)	258	0.28
Russian (271)	572	0.62
Scandinavian (104)	164	0.18
Scotch-Irish (595)	1,654	1.78
Scottish (579)	1,856	2.00
Serbian (13)	48	0.05
Slavic (0)	26	0.03
Slovak (0)	20	0.02
Swedish (121)	860	0.93
Swiss (44)	180	0.19
Turkish (34)	34	0.04
Ukrainian (95)	152	0.16
Welsh (95)	574	0.62
West Indian, ex. Hispanic (75)	92	0.10
Barbadian (21)	21	0.02
British West Indian (19)	19	0.02
Dutch West Indian (7)	7	0.01
Jamaican (0)	17	0.02
Trinidadian/Tobagonian (28)	28	0.03
Yugoslavian (152)	162	0.17

Hispanic Origin	Population	%
Hispanic or Latino (of any race)	27,783	29.16
Central American, ex. Mexican	1,675	1.76
Costa Rican	30	0.03
Guatemalan	239	0.25
Honduran	271	0.28
Nicaraguan	91	0.10
Panamanian	57	0.06
Salvadoran	972	1.02
Other Central American	15	0.02
Cuban	222	0.23
Dominican Republic	101	0.11
Mexican	22,886	24.02
Puerto Rican	701	0.74
South American	639	0.67
Argentinean	71	0.07
Bolivian	18	0.02
Chilean	52	0.05
Colombian	203	0.21
Ecuadorian	37	0.04
Paraguayan	1	<0.01
Peruvian	138	0.14
Uruguayan	13	0.01
Venezuelan	94	0.10
Other South American	12	0.01
Other Hispanic or Latino	1,559	1.64

Race*	Population	%
African-American/Black (10,661)	11,751	12.33
Not Hispanic (10,370)	11,227	11.78
Hispanic (291)	524	0.55
American Indian/Alaska Native (623)	1,338	1.40
Not Hispanic (347)	873	0.92
Hispanic (276)	465	0.49
Aleut *(Alaska Native)* (1)	3	<0.01
Apache (6)	21	0.02
Blackfeet (6)	16	0.02
Central American Ind. (3)	5	0.01
Cherokee (56)	250	0.26
Chickasaw (26)	61	0.06
Chippewa (1)	8	0.01
Choctaw (54)	119	0.12
Comanche (4)	20	0.02
Creek (10)	19	0.02
Crow (3)	5	0.01
Delaware (3)	4	<0.01
Hopi (1)	3	<0.01
Houma (1)	1	<0.01
Iroquois (2)	7	0.01
Kiowa (6)	8	0.01
Mexican American Ind. (27)	45	0.05
Navajo (11)	11	0.01
Osage (2)	10	0.01
Ottawa (0)	1	<0.01
Potawatomi (12)	16	0.02
Pueblo (3)	9	0.01
Seminole (2)	7	0.01
Sioux (5)	12	0.01
South American Ind. (2)	12	0.01
Tlingit-Haida *(Alaska Native)* (1)	2	<0.01
Yaqui (0)	1	<0.01
Yuman (3)	3	<0.01
Asian (7,392)	8,179	8.58
Not Hispanic (7,325)	7,999	8.39
Hispanic (67)	180	0.19
Bangladeshi (62)	65	0.07
Burmese (911)	942	0.99
Cambodian (115)	134	0.14
Chinese, ex. Taiwanese (514)	615	0.65
Filipino (373)	554	0.58
Hmong (1)	3	<0.01
Indian (2,314)	2,495	2.62
Indonesian (11)	17	0.02
Japanese (76)	187	0.20
Korean (1,220)	1,333	1.40
Laotian (34)	42	0.04
Malaysian (5)	11	0.01
Nepalese (55)	56	0.06
Pakistani (440)	487	0.51
Sri Lankan (16)	19	0.02
Taiwanese (39)	45	0.05
Thai (71)	94	0.10
Vietnamese (891)	962	1.01
Hawaii Native/Pacific Islander (67)	170	0.18
Not Hispanic (59)	139	0.15
Hispanic (8)	31	0.03
Fijian (1)	1	<0.01
Guamanian/Chamorro (16)	31	0.03
Native Hawaiian (11)	42	0.04
Samoan (15)	19	0.02
Tongan (2)	2	<0.01
White (62,263)	64,826	68.03
Not Hispanic (47,280)	48,905	51.32
Hispanic (14,983)	15,921	16.71

Liberty

Place Type: City
County: Liberty
Population: 8,397†

Ancestry‡	Population	%
African, Sub-Saharan (0)	35	0.42
African (0)	35	0.42
American (447)	447	5.32
British (12)	12	0.14
Cajun (0)	8	0.10
Czech (11)	142	1.69
Danish (0)	23	0.27
English (307)	712	8.47
European (21)	21	0.25
French, ex. Basque (96)	541	6.44
French Canadian (22)	54	0.64
German (206)	1,054	12.54
Irish (319)	1,206	14.35
Italian (75)	201	2.39
Norwegian (29)	92	1.09
Polish (43)	196	2.33
Portuguese (12)	12	0.14

*Notes: † The Census 2010 population figure is used to calculate the percentages in the Hispanic Origin and Race categories. Ancestry percentages are based on the 2006-2010 American Community Survey population (not shown); ‡ Numbers in parentheses indicate the number of people reporting a single ancestry; * Numbers in parentheses indicate the number of persons reporting this race alone, not in combination with any other race; Please refer to the Explanation of Data for more information.*

Russian (0)	13	0.15
Scotch-Irish (53)	259	3.08
Scottish (38)	70	0.83
Swedish (0)	34	0.40
Welsh (0)	24	0.29
West Indian, ex. Hispanic (26)	162	1.93
Dutch West Indian (0)	103	1.23
Jamaican (26)	59	0.70

Hispanic Origin	Population	%
Hispanic or Latino (of any race)	1,949	23.21
Central American, ex. Mexican	20	0.24
Costa Rican	1	0.01
Guatemalan	6	0.07
Honduran	7	0.08
Salvadoran	6	0.07
Cuban	3	0.04
Mexican	1,816	21.63
Puerto Rican	4	0.05
South American	8	0.10
Argentinean	2	0.02
Ecuadorian	1	0.01
Venezuelan	5	0.06
Other Hispanic or Latino	98	1.17

Race*	Population	%
African-American/Black (1,119)	1,190	14.17
Not Hispanic (1,100)	1,163	13.85
Hispanic (19)	27	0.32
American Indian/Alaska Native (23)	60	0.71
Not Hispanic (17)	52	0.62
Hispanic (6)	8	0.10
Canadian/French Am. Ind. (0)	1	0.01
Cherokee (3)	12	0.14
Chickasaw (2)	2	0.02
Choctaw (2)	3	0.04
Comanche (2)	2	0.02
Kiowa (0)	1	0.01
Mexican American Ind. (1)	1	0.01
Potawatomi (1)	1	0.01
Sioux (0)	1	0.01
Asian (53)	77	0.92
Not Hispanic (53)	71	0.85
Hispanic (0)	6	0.07
Cambodian (2)	2	0.02
Chinese, ex. Taiwanese (10)	11	0.13
Filipino (13)	24	0.29
Indian (19)	24	0.29
Japanese (0)	4	0.05
Korean (1)	2	0.02
Pakistani (2)	2	0.02
Thai (1)	1	0.01
Vietnamese (5)	5	0.06
Hawaii Native/Pacific Islander (3)	13	0.15
Not Hispanic (3)	12	0.14
Hispanic (0)	1	0.01
Guamanian/Chamorro (0)	2	0.02
Native Hawaiian (3)	7	0.08
Samoan (0)	2	0.02
White (5,899)	6,048	72.03
Not Hispanic (5,155)	5,252	62.55
Hispanic (744)	796	9.48

Little Elm

Place Type: City
County: Denton
Population: 25,898†

Ancestry‡	Population	%
African, Sub-Saharan (156)	156	0.70
African (42)	42	0.19
Kenyan (71)	71	0.32
Sierra Leonean (30)	30	0.14
Other Sub-Saharan African (13)	13	0.06
American (1,178)	1,178	5.31
Arab (0)	9	0.04
Other Arab (0)	9	0.04
Australian (0)	10	0.05
Austrian (0)	59	0.27
Belgian (23)	23	0.10
Brazilian (163)	163	0.73
British (57)	144	0.65
Cajun (44)	44	0.20
Canadian (9)	42	0.19
Croatian (0)	9	0.04
Czech (122)	196	0.88
Czechoslovakian (7)	7	0.03
Danish (16)	60	0.27
Dutch (48)	317	1.43
English (941)	2,109	9.50
European (225)	238	1.07
Finnish (11)	31	0.14
French, ex. Basque (184)	582	2.62
French Canadian (26)	31	0.14
German (855)	3,306	14.89
Greek (41)	101	0.45
Guyanese (0)	10	0.05
Hungarian (34)	45	0.20
Iranian (0)	9	0.04
Irish (684)	2,117	9.54
Italian (292)	778	3.50
Lithuanian (10)	10	0.05
Norwegian (73)	437	1.97
Polish (100)	395	1.78
Portuguese (39)	84	0.38
Romanian (41)	41	0.18
Russian (30)	153	0.69
Scotch-Irish (86)	359	1.62
Scottish (95)	435	1.96
Serbian (0)	9	0.04
Slavic (0)	39	0.18
Slovak (16)	16	0.07
Slovene (0)	11	0.05
Swedish (111)	239	1.08
Swiss (9)	9	0.04
Ukrainian (6)	20	0.09
Welsh (66)	148	0.67
West Indian, ex. Hispanic (82)	98	0.44
Dutch West Indian (36)	36	0.16
Haitian (10)	10	0.05
Jamaican (15)	31	0.14
Trinidadian/Tobagonian (10)	10	0.05
West Indian (11)	11	0.05
Yugoslavian (118)	118	0.53

Hispanic Origin	Population	%
Hispanic or Latino (of any race)	6,228	24.05
Central American, ex. Mexican	807	3.12
Costa Rican	12	0.05
Guatemalan	144	0.56
Honduran	111	0.43
Nicaraguan	73	0.28
Panamanian	22	0.08
Salvadoran	444	1.71
Other Central American	1	<0.01
Cuban	104	0.40
Dominican Republic	32	0.12
Mexican	4,208	16.25
Puerto Rican	261	1.01
South American	304	1.17
Argentinean	31	0.12
Bolivian	9	0.03
Chilean	15	0.06
Colombian	105	0.41
Ecuadorian	22	0.08
Peruvian	50	0.19
Uruguayan	1	<0.01
Venezuelan	69	0.27
Other South American	2	0.01
Other Hispanic or Latino	512	1.98

Race*	Population	%
African-American/Black (3,698)	4,065	15.70
Not Hispanic (3,621)	3,926	15.16
Hispanic (77)	139	0.54
American Indian/Alaska Native (205)	412	1.59
Not Hispanic (148)	306	1.18
Hispanic (57)	106	0.41
Apache (2)	4	0.02
Blackfeet (4)	21	0.08
Canadian/French Am. Ind. (2)	3	0.01
Central American Ind. (0)	1	<0.01
Cherokee (22)	66	0.25
Cheyenne (0)	3	0.01
Chickasaw (16)	19	0.07
Chippewa (3)	5	0.02
Choctaw (39)	56	0.22
Comanche (2)	4	0.02
Cree (0)	1	<0.01
Creek (1)	12	0.05
Iroquois (2)	8	0.03
Kiowa (1)	1	<0.01
Mexican American Ind. (4)	8	0.03
Navajo (1)	1	<0.01
Paiute (1)	1	<0.01
Potawatomi (2)	2	0.01
Pueblo (4)	5	0.02
Seminole (1)	1	<0.01
Sioux (1)	2	0.01
South American Ind. (2)	3	0.01
Tlingit-Haida *(Alaska Native)* (1)	1	<0.01
Ute (2)	2	0.01
Asian (904)	1,152	4.45
Not Hispanic (885)	1,091	4.21
Hispanic (19)	61	0.24
Bangladeshi (7)	8	0.03
Cambodian (50)	61	0.24
Chinese, ex. Taiwanese (87)	116	0.45
Filipino (120)	189	0.73
Hmong (5)	5	0.02
Indian (200)	228	0.88
Indonesian (0)	6	0.02
Japanese (15)	48	0.19
Korean (67)	103	0.40
Laotian (18)	33	0.13
Malaysian (4)	6	0.02
Nepalese (1)	1	<0.01
Pakistani (99)	105	0.41
Sri Lankan (2)	2	0.01
Thai (25)	38	0.15
Vietnamese (170)	199	0.77
Hawaii Native/Pacific Islander (13)	48	0.19
Not Hispanic (12)	39	0.15
Hispanic (1)	9	0.03
Guamanian/Chamorro (5)	6	0.02
Native Hawaiian (8)	34	0.13
White (17,949)	18,720	72.28
Not Hispanic (14,326)	14,858	57.37
Hispanic (3,623)	3,862	14.91

Live Oak

Place Type: City
County: Bexar
Population: 13,131†

Ancestry‡	Population	%
African, Sub-Saharan (100)	100	0.80
African (100)	100	0.80
American (459)	459	3.69
British (40)	63	0.51
Canadian (23)	23	0.19
Czech (0)	111	0.89
Czechoslovakian (0)	16	0.13
Danish (0)	42	0.34
Dutch (10)	255	2.05
English (398)	915	7.37
European (62)	71	0.57
Finnish (0)	12	0.10
French, ex. Basque (64)	182	1.47
French Canadian (38)	134	1.08
German (660)	1,967	15.83
Greek (8)	8	0.06
Irish (319)	1,331	10.71
Italian (79)	344	2.77
Lithuanian (0)	11	0.09
Norwegian (41)	237	1.91
Polish (117)	408	3.28
Scotch-Irish (110)	262	2.11

*Notes: † The Census 2010 population figure is used to calculate the percentages in the Hispanic Origin and Race categories. Ancestry percentages are based on the 2006-2010 American Community Survey population (not shown); ‡ Numbers in parentheses indicate the number of people reporting a single ancestry; * Numbers in parentheses indicate the number of persons reporting this race alone, not in combination with any other race; Please refer to the Explanation of Data for more information.*

Scottish (55)	188	1.51
Slovak (17)	52	0.42
Swedish (0)	45	0.36
Swiss (30)	60	0.48
Welsh (0)	80	0.64
Yugoslavian (0)	23	0.19

Hispanic Origin	Population	%
Hispanic or Latino (of any race)	4,594	34.99
Central American, ex. Mexican	122	0.93
Costa Rican	2	0.02
Guatemalan	27	0.21
Honduran	10	0.08
Nicaraguan	23	0.18
Panamanian	34	0.26
Salvadoran	24	0.18
Other Central American	2	0.02
Cuban	29	0.22
Dominican Republic	13	0.10
Mexican	3,500	26.65
Puerto Rican	261	1.99
South American	66	0.50
Argentinean	12	0.09
Bolivian	5	0.04
Chilean	2	0.02
Colombian	21	0.16
Ecuadorian	11	0.08
Peruvian	14	0.11
Venezuelan	1	0.01
Other Hispanic or Latino	603	4.59

Race*	Population	%
African-American/Black (1,753)	1,993	15.18
Not Hispanic (1,657)	1,842	14.03
Hispanic (96)	151	1.15
American Indian/Alaska Native (66)	194	1.48
Not Hispanic (29)	106	0.81
Hispanic (37)	88	0.67
Apache (3)	6	0.05
Arapaho (1)	3	0.02
Blackfeet (0)	1	0.01
Cherokee (6)	44	0.34
Cheyenne (1)	1	0.01
Chippewa (1)	1	0.01
Choctaw (6)	11	0.08
Comanche (3)	3	0.02
Cree (0)	1	0.01
Creek (1)	2	0.02
Hopi (0)	1	0.01
Iroquois (0)	3	0.02
Mexican American Ind. (4)	9	0.07
Osage (0)	2	0.02
Potawatomi (2)	2	0.02
Pueblo (0)	2	0.02
Seminole (0)	1	0.01
Sioux (4)	6	0.05
South American Ind. (1)	1	0.01
Spanish American Ind. (2)	4	0.03
Tlingit-Haida *(Alaska Native)* (1)	1	0.01
Yaqui (2)	10	0.08
Asian (474)	663	5.05
Not Hispanic (451)	595	4.53
Hispanic (23)	68	0.52
Cambodian (0)	2	0.02
Chinese, ex. Taiwanese (15)	33	0.25
Filipino (150)	212	1.61
Indian (33)	41	0.31
Indonesian (2)	5	0.04
Japanese (35)	82	0.62
Korean (59)	100	0.76
Laotian (1)	1	0.01
Malaysian (1)	1	0.01
Pakistani (8)	9	0.07
Taiwanese (1)	1	0.01
Thai (31)	37	0.28
Vietnamese (132)	145	1.10
Hawaii Native/Pacific Islander (49)	97	0.74
Not Hispanic (36)	76	0.58
Hispanic (13)	21	0.16
Guamanian/Chamorro (21)	31	0.24
Native Hawaiian (19)	52	0.40
Samoan (2)	9	0.07
White (9,305)	9,807	74.69
Not Hispanic (5,972)	6,272	47.76
Hispanic (3,333)	3,535	26.92

Lockhart

Place Type: City
County: Caldwell
Population: 12,698†

Ancestry‡	Population	%
African, Sub-Saharan (0)	10	0.08
Nigerian (0)	10	0.08
American (362)	362	2.86
Arab (9)	19	0.15
Jordanian (9)	9	0.07
Lebanese (0)	10	0.08
Assyrian/Chaldean/Syriac (9)	9	0.07
British (0)	44	0.35
Czech (29)	29	0.23
Dutch (6)	93	0.73
English (227)	620	4.90
European (139)	139	1.10
French, ex. Basque (71)	285	2.25
French Canadian (38)	51	0.40
German (522)	1,637	12.93
Irish (341)	1,325	10.47
Italian (57)	255	2.01
Norwegian (21)	175	1.38
Polish (31)	129	1.02
Scotch-Irish (149)	207	1.64
Scottish (32)	163	1.29
Swedish (19)	166	1.31
Swiss (0)	23	0.18
Welsh (0)	37	0.29
West Indian, ex. Hispanic (10)	10	0.08
Jamaican (10)	10	0.08
Yugoslavian (0)	10	0.08

Hispanic Origin	Population	%
Hispanic or Latino (of any race)	6,483	51.06
Central American, ex. Mexican	15	0.12
Guatemalan	4	0.03
Honduran	1	0.01
Nicaraguan	2	0.02
Salvadoran	8	0.06
Cuban	16	0.13
Dominican Republic	3	0.02
Mexican	5,763	45.39
Puerto Rican	91	0.72
South American	20	0.16
Argentinean	5	0.04
Chilean	5	0.04
Colombian	2	0.02
Ecuadorian	6	0.05
Venezuelan	2	0.02
Other Hispanic or Latino	575	4.53

Race*	Population	%
African-American/Black (1,189)	1,268	9.99
Not Hispanic (1,137)	1,178	9.28
Hispanic (52)	90	0.71
American Indian/Alaska Native (102)	179	1.41
Not Hispanic (27)	69	0.54
Hispanic (75)	110	0.87
Apache (8)	10	0.08
Blackfeet (0)	3	0.02
Cherokee (2)	19	0.15
Chickasaw (0)	1	0.01
Chippewa (0)	1	0.01
Choctaw (6)	15	0.12
Comanche (0)	6	0.05
Creek (1)	1	0.01
Iroquois (1)	1	0.01
Mexican American Ind. (7)	7	0.06
Asian (56)	92	0.72
Not Hispanic (50)	71	0.56
Hispanic (6)	21	0.17
Cambodian (5)	6	0.05
Chinese, ex. Taiwanese (5)	8	0.06
Filipino (11)	30	0.24
Indian (7)	8	0.06
Japanese (2)	10	0.08
Korean (4)	7	0.06
Malaysian (6)	9	0.07
Pakistani (0)	2	0.02
Vietnamese (12)	12	0.09
Hawaii Native/Pacific Islander (2)	8	0.06
Not Hispanic (1)	3	0.02
Hispanic (1)	5	0.04
Guamanian/Chamorro (0)	1	0.01
Native Hawaiian (1)	2	0.02
White (9,275)	9,587	75.50
Not Hispanic (4,877)	4,977	39.20
Hispanic (4,398)	4,610	36.30

Longview

Place Type: City
County: Gregg
Population: 80,455†

Ancestry‡	Population	%
African, Sub-Saharan (284)	382	0.48
African (209)	307	0.39
Kenyan (53)	53	0.07
Nigerian (22)	22	0.03
American (9,691)	9,691	12.23
Arab (186)	207	0.26
Lebanese (107)	128	0.16
Moroccan (10)	10	0.01
Other Arab (69)	69	0.09
Armenian (8)	8	0.01
Australian (0)	8	0.01
Austrian (8)	34	0.04
Belgian (7)	20	0.03
British (176)	271	0.34
Cajun (55)	98	0.12
Canadian (44)	136	0.17
Croatian (9)	9	0.01
Czech (263)	564	0.71
Czechoslovakian (42)	111	0.14
Danish (26)	202	0.25
Dutch (167)	911	1.15
Eastern European (15)	23	0.03
English (3,708)	7,291	9.20
European (435)	435	0.55
Finnish (12)	12	0.02
French, ex. Basque (1,201)	3,135	3.96
French Canadian (180)	342	0.43
German (2,739)	7,767	9.80
Greek (60)	81	0.10
Hungarian (0)	46	0.06
Icelander (29)	66	0.08
Iranian (0)	56	0.07
Irish (3,142)	8,137	10.27
Italian (593)	1,349	1.70
Latvian (11)	11	0.01
Macedonian (55)	55	0.07
New Zealander (0)	15	0.02
Norwegian (302)	512	0.65
Polish (376)	755	0.95
Portuguese (9)	34	0.04
Romanian (24)	24	0.03
Russian (18)	68	0.09
Scandinavian (21)	59	0.07
Scotch-Irish (673)	1,441	1.82
Scottish (896)	1,720	2.17
Slovak (40)	99	0.12
Swedish (53)	333	0.42
Swiss (9)	165	0.21
Ukrainian (36)	98	0.12
Welsh (84)	665	0.84
West Indian, ex. Hispanic (11)	26	0.03
Haitian (0)	15	0.02
West Indian (11)	11	0.01
Yugoslavian (25)	25	0.03

*Notes: † The Census 2010 population figure is used to calculate the percentages in the Hispanic Origin and Race categories. Ancestry percentages are based on the 2006-2010 American Community Survey population (not shown); ‡ Numbers in parentheses indicate the number of people reporting a single ancestry; * Numbers in parentheses indicate the number of persons reporting this race alone, not in combination with any other race; Please refer to the Explanation of Data for more information.*

Hispanic Origin	Population	%
Hispanic or Latino (of any race)	14,460	17.97
Central American, ex. Mexican	427	0.53
Costa Rican	11	0.01
Guatemalan	91	0.11
Honduran	81	0.10
Nicaraguan	10	0.01
Panamanian	19	0.02
Salvadoran	208	0.26
Other Central American	7	0.01
Cuban	55	0.07
Dominican Republic	18	0.02
Mexican	12,911	16.05
Puerto Rican	114	0.14
South American	134	0.17
Argentinean	22	0.03
Bolivian	2	<0.01
Chilean	10	0.01
Colombian	47	0.06
Ecuadorian	6	0.01
Paraguayan	3	<0.01
Peruvian	23	0.03
Uruguayan	4	<0.01
Venezuelan	14	0.02
Other South American	3	<0.01
Other Hispanic or Latino	801	1.00

Race*	Population	%
African-American/Black (18,453)	19,245	23.92
Not Hispanic (18,190)	18,826	23.40
Hispanic (263)	419	0.52
American Indian/Alaska Native (437)	919	1.14
Not Hispanic (292)	662	0.82
Hispanic (145)	257	0.32
Alaska Athabascan *(Ala. Nat.)* (3)	3	<0.01
Aleut *(Alaska Native)* (0)	1	<0.01
Apache (6)	15	0.02
Blackfeet (2)	8	0.01
Canadian/French Am. Ind. (2)	3	<0.01
Central American Ind. (0)	1	<0.01
Cherokee (53)	218	0.27
Cheyenne (0)	4	<0.01
Chickasaw (11)	14	0.02
Chippewa (0)	2	<0.01
Choctaw (60)	103	0.13
Comanche (7)	9	0.01
Creek (14)	17	0.02
Delaware (1)	4	<0.01
Hopi (2)	2	<0.01
Houma (0)	3	<0.01
Inupiat *(Alaska Native)* (2)	2	<0.01
Iroquois (0)	6	0.01
Lumbee (0)	3	<0.01
Mexican American Ind. (36)	52	0.06
Navajo (5)	9	0.01
Osage (2)	5	0.01
Potawatomi (7)	20	0.02
Pueblo (1)	1	<0.01
Puget Sound Salish (1)	1	<0.01
Seminole (0)	1	<0.01
Sioux (4)	10	0.01
South American Ind. (0)	1	<0.01
Spanish American Ind. (1)	1	<0.01
Tlingit-Haida *(Alaska Native)* (2)	4	<0.01
Tohono O'Odham (1)	1	<0.01
Ute (1)	1	<0.01
Yakama (0)	1	<0.01
Yuman (0)	2	<0.01
Asian (1,088)	1,365	1.70
Not Hispanic (1,063)	1,295	1.61
Hispanic (25)	70	0.09
Bangladeshi (3)	3	<0.01
Cambodian (29)	31	0.04
Chinese, ex. Taiwanese (131)	179	0.22
Filipino (120)	185	0.23
Indian (280)	303	0.38
Indonesian (7)	7	0.01
Japanese (24)	52	0.06
Korean (115)	158	0.20
Laotian (5)	13	0.02
Malaysian (1)	4	<0.01
Nepalese (7)	8	0.01
Pakistani (74)	89	0.11
Sri Lankan (4)	4	<0.01
Taiwanese (9)	9	0.01
Thai (20)	41	0.05
Vietnamese (188)	210	0.26
Hawaii Native/Pacific Islander (38)	96	0.12
Not Hispanic (21)	55	0.07
Hispanic (17)	41	0.05
Guamanian/Chamorro (17)	21	0.03
Marshallese (0)	1	<0.01
Native Hawaiian (11)	40	0.05
Samoan (9)	18	0.02
White (50,941)	52,504	65.26
Not Hispanic (45,230)	46,183	57.40
Hispanic (5,711)	6,321	7.86

Lubbock

Place Type: City
County: Lubbock
Population: 229,573[†]

Ancestry[‡]	Population	%
Afghan (0)	14	0.01
African, Sub-Saharan (628)	800	0.36
African (483)	647	0.29
Ghanaian (19)	19	0.01
Nigerian (126)	126	0.06
South African (0)	8	<0.01
Albanian (12)	26	0.01
American (13,599)	13,599	6.12
Arab (462)	763	0.34
Arab (14)	104	0.05
Egyptian (32)	32	0.01
Iraqi (0)	4	<0.01
Lebanese (308)	456	0.21
Palestinian (23)	23	0.01
Syrian (28)	55	0.02
Other Arab (57)	89	0.04
Armenian (31)	44	0.02
Assyrian/Chaldean/Syriac (10)	10	<0.01
Australian (11)	63	0.03
Austrian (82)	529	0.24
Basque (14)	14	0.01
Belgian (12)	74	0.03
Brazilian (72)	72	0.03
British (653)	1,274	0.57
Bulgarian (0)	36	0.02
Cajun (21)	72	0.03
Canadian (60)	139	0.06
Celtic (0)	30	0.01
Croatian (0)	67	0.03
Czech (405)	1,266	0.57
Czechoslovakian (60)	123	0.06
Danish (181)	685	0.31
Dutch (720)	2,473	1.11
Eastern European (50)	90	0.04
English (7,923)	19,524	8.78
European (1,892)	2,023	0.91
Finnish (35)	108	0.05
French, ex. Basque (1,008)	4,891	2.20
French Canadian (137)	269	0.12
German (10,617)	25,521	11.48
German Russian (0)	47	0.02
Greek (106)	207	0.09
Hungarian (34)	164	0.07
Icelander (23)	46	0.02
Iranian (80)	96	0.04
Irish (7,171)	21,166	9.52
Israeli (0)	12	0.01
Italian (1,361)	3,236	1.46
Latvian (10)	10	<0.01
Lithuanian (82)	202	0.09
New Zealander (31)	46	0.02
Northern European (23)	29	0.01
Norwegian (458)	1,301	0.59
Pennsylvania German (9)	9	<0.01
Polish (462)	2,003	0.90
Portuguese (103)	229	0.10
Romanian (96)	136	0.06
Russian (138)	583	0.26
Scandinavian (163)	257	0.12
Scotch-Irish (2,556)	5,240	2.36
Scottish (2,202)	5,187	2.33
Slavic (31)	81	0.04
Slovak (36)	64	0.03
Slovene (14)	14	0.01
Swedish (435)	1,409	0.63
Swiss (14)	367	0.17
Turkish (41)	41	0.02
Ukrainian (34)	110	0.05
Welsh (482)	1,248	0.56
West Indian, ex. Hispanic (77)	408	0.18
Belizean (18)	42	0.02
Bermudan (12)	12	0.01
Dutch West Indian (47)	249	0.11
Haitian (0)	34	0.02
West Indian (0)	71	0.03
Yugoslavian (67)	158	0.07

Hispanic Origin	Population	%
Hispanic or Latino (of any race)	73,625	32.07
Central American, ex. Mexican	490	0.21
Costa Rican	34	0.01
Guatemalan	93	0.04
Honduran	89	0.04
Nicaraguan	79	0.03
Panamanian	38	0.02
Salvadoran	155	0.07
Other Central American	2	<0.01
Cuban	207	0.09
Dominican Republic	48	0.02
Mexican	60,977	26.56
Puerto Rican	490	0.21
South American	400	0.17
Argentinean	43	0.02
Bolivian	25	0.01
Chilean	16	0.01
Colombian	160	0.07
Ecuadorian	50	0.02
Paraguayan	3	<0.01
Peruvian	62	0.03
Uruguayan	1	<0.01
Venezuelan	36	0.02
Other South American	4	<0.01
Other Hispanic or Latino	11,013	4.80

Race*	Population	%
African-American/Black (19,647)	21,302	9.28
Not Hispanic (18,744)	19,807	8.63
Hispanic (903)	1,495	0.65
American Indian/Alaska Native (1,698)	2,938	1.28
Not Hispanic (845)	1,641	0.71
Hispanic (853)	1,297	0.56
Apache (96)	174	0.08
Arapaho (1)	3	<0.01
Blackfeet (6)	25	0.01
Canadian/French Am. Ind. (5)	7	<0.01
Central American Ind. (4)	5	<0.01
Cherokee (162)	452	0.20
Cheyenne (2)	8	<0.01
Chickasaw (57)	89	0.04
Chippewa (6)	11	<0.01
Choctaw (149)	261	0.11
Comanche (37)	73	0.03
Cree (1)	4	<0.01
Creek (17)	30	0.01
Crow (0)	1	<0.01
Delaware (3)	9	<0.01
Hopi (0)	2	<0.01
Houma (4)	4	<0.01
Iroquois (13)	30	0.01
Kiowa (1)	1	<0.01
Lumbee (1)	3	<0.01
Menominee (1)	1	<0.01
Mexican American Ind. (57)	76	0.03
Navajo (49)	73	0.03
Osage (7)	13	0.01

*Notes: † The Census 2010 population figure is used to calculate the percentages in the Hispanic Origin and Race categories. Ancestry percentages are based on the 2006-2010 American Community Survey population (not shown); ‡ Numbers in parentheses indicate the number of people reporting a single ancestry; * Numbers in parentheses indicate the number of persons reporting this race alone, not in combination with any other race; Please refer to the Explanation of Data for more information.*

Paiute (1)	1	<0.01
Pima (1)	3	<0.01
Potawatomi (31)	50	0.02
Pueblo (11)	21	0.01
Seminole (9)	11	<0.01
Shoshone (2)	10	<0.01
Sioux (29)	39	0.02
South American Ind. (0)	1	<0.01
Spanish American Ind. (6)	17	0.01
Tsimshian *(Alaska Native)* (1)	1	<0.01
Ute (0)	2	<0.01
Yakama (0)	1	<0.01
Yaqui (11)	14	0.01
Asian (5,559)	6,664	2.90
Not Hispanic (5,471)	6,313	2.75
Hispanic (88)	351	0.15
Bangladeshi (44)	47	0.02
Burmese (4)	4	<0.01
Cambodian (31)	35	0.02
Chinese, ex. Taiwanese (973)	1,120	0.49
Filipino (1,176)	1,393	0.61
Hmong (7)	7	<0.01
Indian (1,546)	1,698	0.74
Indonesian (29)	36	0.02
Japanese (94)	283	0.12
Korean (464)	610	0.27
Laotian (23)	40	0.02
Malaysian (18)	22	0.01
Nepalese (80)	89	0.04
Pakistani (119)	128	0.06
Sri Lankan (56)	61	0.03
Taiwanese (50)	64	0.03
Thai (101)	147	0.06
Vietnamese (461)	552	0.24
Hawaii Native/Pacific Islander (172)	420	0.18
Not Hispanic (147)	338	0.15
Hispanic (25)	82	0.04
Fijian (4)	4	<0.01
Guamanian/Chamorro (44)	67	0.03
Native Hawaiian (22)	81	0.04
Samoan (22)	49	0.02
Tongan (7)	10	<0.01
White (174,014)	178,875	77.92
Not Hispanic (127,915)	130,123	56.68
Hispanic (46,099)	48,752	21.24

Lufkin

Place Type: City
County: Angelina
Population: 35,067†

Ancestry‡	Population	%
African, Sub-Saharan (552)	608	1.75
African (535)	591	1.70
Ghanaian (17)	17	0.05
American (2,580)	2,580	7.44
Arab (47)	47	0.14
Egyptian (16)	16	0.05
Lebanese (31)	31	0.09
Austrian (0)	14	0.04
British (37)	37	0.11
Cajun (14)	78	0.22
Canadian (17)	147	0.42
Croatian (0)	15	0.04
Czech (12)	64	0.18
Czechoslovakian (9)	9	0.03
Danish (19)	58	0.17
Dutch (55)	370	1.07
English (1,105)	2,584	7.45
European (177)	208	0.60
French, ex. Basque (263)	779	2.25
French Canadian (23)	116	0.33
German (1,403)	3,089	8.90
Hungarian (0)	11	0.03
Irish (946)	2,631	7.58
Italian (89)	247	0.71
Lithuanian (0)	10	0.03
Norwegian (80)	195	0.56
Polish (81)	359	1.03
Scandinavian (13)	32	0.09
Scotch-Irish (348)	589	1.70
Scottish (234)	590	1.70
Swedish (16)	90	0.26
Welsh (14)	130	0.37
West Indian, ex. Hispanic (0)	20	0.06
Jamaican (0)	20	0.06
Yugoslavian (8)	8	0.02

Hispanic Origin	Population	%
Hispanic or Latino (of any race)	8,464	24.14
Central American, ex. Mexican	255	0.73
Costa Rican	1	<0.01
Guatemalan	7	0.02
Honduran	44	0.13
Nicaraguan	2	0.01
Panamanian	10	0.03
Salvadoran	190	0.54
Other Central American	1	<0.01
Cuban	25	0.07
Dominican Republic	4	0.01
Mexican	7,615	21.72
Puerto Rican	52	0.15
South American	48	0.14
Argentinean	3	0.01
Bolivian	2	0.01
Chilean	4	0.01
Colombian	17	0.05
Ecuadorian	2	0.01
Peruvian	19	0.05
Venezuelan	1	<0.01
Other Hispanic or Latino	465	1.33

Race*	Population	%
African-American/Black (9,603)	9,929	28.31
Not Hispanic (9,480)	9,724	27.73
Hispanic (123)	205	0.58
American Indian/Alaska Native (163)	304	0.87
Not Hispanic (89)	191	0.54
Hispanic (74)	113	0.32
Alaska Athabascan *(Ala. Nat.)* (2)	3	0.01
Apache (2)	7	0.02
Blackfeet (2)	6	0.02
Central American Ind. (0)	7	0.02
Cherokee (20)	53	0.15
Cheyenne (0)	1	<0.01
Chickasaw (6)	6	0.02
Chippewa (4)	4	0.01
Choctaw (11)	16	0.05
Comanche (2)	3	0.01
Cree (0)	3	0.01
Creek (3)	7	0.02
Delaware (1)	1	<0.01
Hopi (1)	5	0.01
Iroquois (1)	1	<0.01
Mexican American Ind. (22)	29	0.08
Navajo (2)	4	0.01
Osage (1)	1	<0.01
Ottawa (0)	1	<0.01
Pima (2)	2	0.01
Potawatomi (3)	3	0.01
Sioux (0)	3	0.01
Asian (579)	693	1.98
Not Hispanic (559)	634	1.81
Hispanic (20)	59	0.17
Cambodian (27)	31	0.09
Chinese, ex. Taiwanese (56)	73	0.21
Filipino (100)	117	0.33
Indian (242)	266	0.76
Indonesian (1)	1	<0.01
Japanese (4)	13	0.04
Korean (17)	32	0.09
Laotian (0)	1	<0.01
Nepalese (7)	7	0.02
Pakistani (40)	45	0.13
Thai (0)	1	<0.01
Vietnamese (59)	67	0.19
Hawaii Native/Pacific Islander (6)	25	0.07
Not Hispanic (5)	17	0.05
Hispanic (1)	8	0.02
Guamanian/Chamorro (3)	8	0.02
Native Hawaiian (3)	5	0.01
Samoan (0)	6	0.02
White (19,888)	20,506	58.48
Not Hispanic (16,029)	16,364	46.66
Hispanic (3,859)	4,142	11.81

Lumberton

Place Type: City
County: Hardin
Population: 11,943†

Ancestry‡	Population	%
African, Sub-Saharan (12)	12	0.11
African (12)	12	0.11
American (1,032)	1,032	9.11
Brazilian (16)	50	0.44
British (0)	4	0.04
Cajun (102)	178	1.57
Czech (9)	91	0.80
Czechoslovakian (16)	16	0.14
Danish (0)	8	0.07
Dutch (15)	102	0.90
English (438)	971	8.57
European (162)	185	1.63
French, ex. Basque (406)	1,057	9.33
French Canadian (140)	288	2.54
German (584)	1,840	16.24
Greek (0)	14	0.12
Hungarian (0)	18	0.16
Irish (609)	2,126	18.76
Italian (261)	605	5.34
Lithuanian (13)	13	0.11
Norwegian (12)	38	0.34
Polish (24)	42	0.37
Russian (9)	9	0.08
Scotch-Irish (124)	379	3.34
Scottish (25)	158	1.39
Swedish (6)	25	0.22
Ukrainian (0)	23	0.20
Welsh (0)	87	0.77
West Indian, ex. Hispanic (11)	11	0.10
Dutch West Indian (11)	11	0.10

Hispanic Origin	Population	%
Hispanic or Latino (of any race)	567	4.75
Central American, ex. Mexican	36	0.30
Costa Rican	3	0.03
Guatemalan	3	0.03
Honduran	7	0.06
Nicaraguan	5	0.04
Panamanian	5	0.04
Salvadoran	13	0.11
Cuban	7	0.06
Dominican Republic	1	0.01
Mexican	412	3.45
Puerto Rican	17	0.14
South American	30	0.25
Argentinean	1	0.01
Bolivian	1	0.01
Chilean	1	0.01
Colombian	7	0.06
Peruvian	1	0.01
Venezuelan	19	0.16
Other Hispanic or Latino	64	0.54

Race*	Population	%
African-American/Black (53)	80	0.67
Not Hispanic (50)	73	0.61
Hispanic (3)	7	0.06
American Indian/Alaska Native (39)	102	0.85
Not Hispanic (35)	93	0.78
Hispanic (4)	9	0.08
Aleut *(Alaska Native)* (1)	1	0.01
Apache (0)	1	0.01
Blackfeet (1)	3	0.03
Cherokee (7)	26	0.22
Chickasaw (1)	2	0.02
Chippewa (2)	2	0.02

SECTION TWO

*Notes: † The Census 2010 population figure is used to calculate the percentages in the Hispanic Origin and Race categories. Ancestry percentages are based on the 2006-2010 American Community Survey population (not shown); ‡ Numbers in parentheses indicate the number of people reporting a single ancestry; * Numbers in parentheses indicate the number of persons reporting this race alone, not in combination with any other race; Please refer to the Explanation of Data for more information.*

Choctaw (6)	11	0.09
Creek (0)	1	0.01
Mexican American Ind. (2)	2	0.02
Potawatomi (1)	1	0.01
Seminole (0)	1	0.01
Sioux (0)	2	0.02
Yakama (1)	1	0.01
Asian (82)	121	1.01
Not Hispanic (82)	115	0.96
Hispanic (0)	6	0.05
Bangladeshi (10)	10	0.08
Cambodian (15)	15	0.13
Chinese, ex. Taiwanese (11)	16	0.13
Filipino (15)	23	0.19
Indian (3)	5	0.04
Japanese (1)	19	0.16
Korean (7)	10	0.08
Taiwanese (2)	2	0.02
Thai (2)	3	0.03
Vietnamese (12)	12	0.10
Hawaii Native/Pacific Islander (0)	3	0.03
Not Hispanic (0)	3	0.03
White (11,501)	11,648	97.53
Not Hispanic (11,096)	11,203	93.80
Hispanic (405)	445	3.73

Mansfield

Place Type: City
County: Tarrant
Population: 56,368†

Ancestry‡	Population	%
African, Sub-Saharan (795)	840	1.65
African (306)	349	0.69
Ghanaian (2)	4	0.01
Nigerian (478)	478	0.94
Zimbabwean (9)	9	0.02
Albanian (332)	332	0.65
American (4,008)	4,008	7.87
Arab (235)	242	0.48
Arab (38)	45	0.09
Lebanese (75)	75	0.15
Palestinian (95)	95	0.19
Other Arab (27)	27	0.05
Armenian (0)	8	0.02
Austrian (0)	50	0.10
Basque (11)	11	0.02
Belgian (0)	40	0.08
Brazilian (14)	14	0.03
British (114)	159	0.31
Cajun (82)	82	0.16
Canadian (25)	128	0.25
Czech (99)	336	0.66
Czechoslovakian (22)	54	0.11
Danish (0)	48	0.09
Dutch (231)	863	1.69
Eastern European (13)	41	0.08
English (1,990)	5,066	9.94
European (851)	1,067	2.09
Finnish (0)	14	0.03
French, ex. Basque (369)	1,470	2.89
French Canadian (48)	124	0.24
German (2,666)	7,656	15.03
Greek (33)	161	0.32
Guyanese (37)	37	0.07
Hungarian (79)	113	0.22
Iranian (6)	6	0.01
Irish (1,437)	5,204	10.22
Italian (408)	1,730	3.40
Lithuanian (10)	19	0.04
Macedonian (309)	309	0.61
Northern European (55)	55	0.11
Norwegian (147)	386	0.76
Pennsylvania German (0)	21	0.04
Polish (185)	636	1.25
Portuguese (0)	27	0.05
Russian (149)	149	0.29
Scandinavian (63)	140	0.27
Scotch-Irish (480)	1,262	2.48
Scottish (342)	1,052	2.07
Slovene (20)	60	0.12
Swedish (193)	590	1.16
Swiss (29)	73	0.14
Turkish (32)	41	0.08
Ukrainian (108)	108	0.21
Welsh (45)	251	0.49
West Indian, ex. Hispanic (21)	97	0.19
Jamaican (0)	10	0.02
Trinidadian/Tobagonian (12)	41	0.08
West Indian (9)	46	0.09
Yugoslavian (10)	17	0.03

Hispanic Origin	Population	%
Hispanic or Latino (of any race)	8,689	15.41
Central American, ex. Mexican	295	0.52
Costa Rican	20	0.04
Guatemalan	57	0.10
Honduran	47	0.08
Nicaraguan	24	0.04
Panamanian	29	0.05
Salvadoran	117	0.21
Other Central American	1	<0.01
Cuban	86	0.15
Dominican Republic	50	0.09
Mexican	6,914	12.27
Puerto Rican	402	0.71
South American	288	0.51
Argentinean	12	0.02
Bolivian	15	0.03
Chilean	8	0.01
Colombian	80	0.14
Ecuadorian	49	0.09
Paraguayan	2	<0.01
Peruvian	93	0.16
Uruguayan	2	<0.01
Venezuelan	21	0.04
Other South American	6	0.01
Other Hispanic or Latino	654	1.16

Race*	Population	%
African-American/Black (7,982)	8,540	15.15
Not Hispanic (7,851)	8,336	14.79
Hispanic (131)	204	0.36
American Indian/Alaska Native (315)	686	1.22
Not Hispanic (207)	512	0.91
Hispanic (108)	174	0.31
Aleut *(Alaska Native)* (1)	1	<0.01
Apache (1)	12	0.02
Arapaho (0)	1	<0.01
Blackfeet (1)	7	0.01
Central American Ind. (0)	1	<0.01
Cherokee (43)	142	0.25
Cheyenne (1)	2	<0.01
Chickasaw (15)	39	0.07
Chippewa (2)	4	0.01
Choctaw (49)	72	0.13
Comanche (3)	19	0.03
Creek (13)	24	0.04
Delaware (1)	5	0.01
Houma (0)	1	<0.01
Kiowa (3)	5	0.01
Lumbee (1)	1	<0.01
Mexican American Ind. (23)	25	0.04
Navajo (2)	4	0.01
Osage (0)	5	0.01
Ottawa (1)	1	<0.01
Potawatomi (7)	9	0.02
Pueblo (1)	1	<0.01
Seminole (0)	3	0.01
Shoshone (1)	1	<0.01
Sioux (8)	21	0.04
South American Ind. (6)	6	0.01
Ute (0)	2	<0.01
Yaqui (1)	1	<0.01
Yuman (0)	5	0.01
Asian (2,094)	2,590	4.59
Not Hispanic (2,063)	2,511	4.45
Hispanic (31)	79	0.14
Bangladeshi (11)	11	0.02
Burmese (1)	6	0.01
Cambodian (14)	19	0.03
Chinese, ex. Taiwanese (173)	229	0.41
Filipino (243)	366	0.65
Indian (366)	413	0.73
Indonesian (3)	11	0.02
Japanese (33)	99	0.18
Korean (145)	195	0.35
Laotian (21)	34	0.06
Malaysian (1)	2	<0.01
Nepalese (2)	4	0.01
Pakistani (125)	140	0.25
Sri Lankan (15)	19	0.03
Taiwanese (16)	17	0.03
Thai (18)	26	0.05
Vietnamese (842)	908	1.61
Hawaii Native/Pacific Islander (44)	109	0.19
Not Hispanic (43)	99	0.18
Hispanic (1)	10	0.02
Fijian (1)	1	<0.01
Guamanian/Chamorro (11)	25	0.04
Marshallese (1)	1	<0.01
Native Hawaiian (10)	44	0.08
Samoan (1)	1	<0.01
Tongan (18)	18	0.03
White (41,445)	42,833	75.99
Not Hispanic (36,292)	37,284	66.14
Hispanic (5,153)	5,549	9.84

Marshall

Place Type: City
County: Harrison
Population: 23,523†

Ancestry‡	Population	%
African, Sub-Saharan (220)	480	2.05
African (203)	463	1.98
South African (17)	17	0.07
American (2,239)	2,239	9.57
Arab (194)	194	0.83
Arab (80)	80	0.34
Egyptian (37)	37	0.16
Lebanese (77)	77	0.33
British (48)	48	0.21
Cajun (0)	26	0.11
Czech (121)	130	0.56
Dutch (88)	224	0.96
English (446)	1,244	5.32
Estonian (18)	18	0.08
European (42)	42	0.18
Finnish (44)	54	0.23
French, ex. Basque (134)	411	1.76
French Canadian (0)	29	0.12
German (504)	1,719	7.35
Greek (0)	16	0.07
Irish (471)	1,294	5.53
Italian (246)	397	1.70
Norwegian (18)	37	0.16
Polish (31)	74	0.32
Portuguese (13)	13	0.06
Scandinavian (0)	19	0.08
Scotch-Irish (277)	515	2.20
Scottish (194)	337	1.44
Swedish (60)	108	0.46
Welsh (8)	31	0.13
West Indian, ex. Hispanic (10)	50	0.21
Jamaican (10)	38	0.16
West Indian (0)	12	0.05

Hispanic Origin	Population	%
Hispanic or Latino (of any race)	3,997	16.99
Central American, ex. Mexican	38	0.16
Costa Rican	1	<0.01
Guatemalan	13	0.06
Honduran	8	0.03
Nicaraguan	4	0.02
Salvadoran	12	0.05
Cuban	14	0.06
Dominican Republic	5	0.02

*Notes: † The Census 2010 population figure is used to calculate the percentages in the Hispanic Origin and Race categories. Ancestry percentages are based on the 2006-2010 American Community Survey population (not shown); ‡ Numbers in parentheses indicate the number of people reporting a single ancestry; * Numbers in parentheses indicate the number of persons reporting this race alone, not in combination with any other race; Please refer to the Explanation of Data for more information.*

Mexican	3,731	15.86
Puerto Rican	44	0.19
South American	22	0.09
Argentinean	1	<0.01
Colombian	14	0.06
Ecuadorian	3	0.01
Venezuelan	4	0.02
Other Hispanic or Latino	143	0.61

Race*	Population	%
African-American/Black (9,018)	9,223	39.21
Not Hispanic (8,959)	9,137	38.84
Hispanic (59)	86	0.37
American Indian/Alaska Native (190)	283	1.20
Not Hispanic (72)	157	0.67
Hispanic (118)	126	0.54
Apache (3)	5	0.02
Blackfeet (0)	3	0.01
Canadian/French Am. Ind. (3)	3	0.01
Cherokee (16)	41	0.17
Chickasaw (0)	2	0.01
Chippewa (1)	2	0.01
Choctaw (7)	15	0.06
Comanche (2)	4	0.02
Creek (0)	6	0.03
Iroquois (1)	1	<0.01
Kiowa (1)	1	<0.01
Lumbee (1)	1	<0.01
Mexican American Ind. (29)	36	0.15
Navajo (4)	5	0.02
Osage (0)	3	0.01
Pueblo (4)	4	0.02
Seminole (0)	5	0.02
Sioux (5)	6	0.03
Spanish American Ind. (3)	3	0.01
Asian (186)	223	0.95
Not Hispanic (185)	214	0.91
Hispanic (1)	9	0.04
Cambodian (57)	59	0.25
Chinese, ex. Taiwanese (22)	24	0.10
Filipino (9)	20	0.09
Indian (39)	43	0.18
Japanese (2)	5	0.02
Korean (10)	19	0.08
Malaysian (2)	2	0.01
Nepalese (0)	1	<0.01
Pakistani (2)	2	0.01
Thai (8)	10	0.04
Vietnamese (31)	31	0.13
Hawaii Native/Pacific Islander (9)	26	0.11
Not Hispanic (9)	16	0.07
Hispanic (0)	10	0.04
Guamanian/Chamorro (5)	5	0.02
Native Hawaiian (2)	14	0.06
Samoan (0)	3	0.01
White (11,282)	11,604	49.33
Not Hispanic (10,024)	10,227	43.48
Hispanic (1,258)	1,377	5.85

McAllen

Place Type: City
County: Hidalgo
Population: 129,877†

Ancestry‡	Population	%
African, Sub-Saharan (49)	59	0.05
African (24)	34	0.03
Nigerian (25)	25	0.02
American (1,435)	1,435	1.14
Arab (197)	516	0.41
Arab (28)	137	0.11
Egyptian (11)	11	0.01
Lebanese (109)	257	0.20
Moroccan (0)	16	0.01
Palestinian (0)	19	0.02
Other Arab (49)	76	0.06
Armenian (0)	12	0.01
Assyrian/Chaldean/Syriac (0)	48	0.04
Australian (0)	7	0.01
Austrian (64)	72	0.06
Belgian (0)	10	0.01
Brazilian (13)	13	0.01
British (67)	184	0.15
Bulgarian (30)	30	0.02
Canadian (47)	142	0.11
Celtic (12)	71	0.06
Croatian (0)	13	0.01
Czech (10)	157	0.13
Czechoslovakian (13)	17	0.01
Danish (0)	119	0.09
Dutch (65)	288	0.23
Eastern European (84)	84	0.07
English (861)	2,415	1.92
Estonian (15)	42	0.03
European (231)	276	0.22
Finnish (0)	26	0.02
French, ex. Basque (117)	1,007	0.80
French Canadian (56)	133	0.11
German (1,719)	5,717	4.55
Greek (49)	68	0.05
Guyanese (0)	68	0.05
Hungarian (31)	54	0.04
Iranian (19)	19	0.02
Irish (877)	2,699	2.15
Israeli (0)	23	0.02
Italian (155)	1,293	1.03
Latvian (31)	99	0.08
Northern European (14)	14	0.01
Norwegian (128)	352	0.28
Polish (143)	602	0.48
Portuguese (13)	66	0.05
Romanian (20)	20	0.02
Russian (27)	220	0.18
Scandinavian (303)	412	0.33
Scotch-Irish (207)	666	0.53
Scottish (164)	551	0.44
Slovene (7)	20	0.02
Swedish (105)	531	0.42
Swiss (93)	196	0.16
Turkish (11)	24	0.02
Ukrainian (0)	8	0.01
Welsh (19)	124	0.10
West Indian, ex. Hispanic (27)	99	0.08
Haitian (0)	72	0.06
Jamaican (27)	27	0.02
Yugoslavian (13)	13	0.01

Hispanic Origin	Population	%
Hispanic or Latino (of any race)	109,910	84.63
Central American, ex. Mexican	609	0.47
Costa Rican	29	0.02
Guatemalan	112	0.09
Honduran	147	0.11
Nicaraguan	68	0.05
Panamanian	55	0.04
Salvadoran	192	0.15
Other Central American	6	<0.01
Cuban	328	0.25
Dominican Republic	191	0.15
Mexican	100,963	77.74
Puerto Rican	574	0.44
South American	817	0.63
Argentinean	137	0.11
Bolivian	29	0.02
Chilean	59	0.05
Colombian	253	0.19
Ecuadorian	44	0.03
Paraguayan	11	0.01
Peruvian	161	0.12
Uruguayan	14	0.01
Venezuelan	100	0.08
Other South American	9	0.01
Other Hispanic or Latino	6,428	4.95

Race*	Population	%
African-American/Black (1,215)	1,507	1.16
Not Hispanic (833)	948	0.73
Hispanic (382)	559	0.43
American Indian/Alaska Native (487)	768	0.59
Not Hispanic (120)	231	0.18
Hispanic (367)	537	0.41
Apache (25)	40	0.03
Arapaho (2)	2	<0.01
Blackfeet (2)	8	0.01
Canadian/French Am. Ind. (0)	1	<0.01
Central American Ind. (3)	3	<0.01
Cherokee (34)	62	0.05
Chickasaw (4)	4	<0.01
Chippewa (0)	2	<0.01
Choctaw (7)	22	0.02
Comanche (1)	5	<0.01
Cree (0)	2	<0.01
Creek (3)	5	<0.01
Iroquois (4)	5	<0.01
Mexican American Ind. (34)	67	0.05
Navajo (2)	4	<0.01
Osage (6)	8	0.01
Ottawa (1)	1	<0.01
Potawatomi (0)	1	<0.01
Pueblo (1)	2	<0.01
Seminole (0)	1	<0.01
Shoshone (1)	1	<0.01
Sioux (2)	2	<0.01
South American Ind. (3)	9	0.01
Spanish American Ind. (3)	6	<0.01
Tlingit-Haida *(Alaska Native)* (1)	1	<0.01
Asian (3,372)	3,772	2.90
Not Hispanic (3,288)	3,500	2.69
Hispanic (84)	272	0.21
Bangladeshi (11)	12	0.01
Cambodian (3)	6	<0.01
Chinese, ex. Taiwanese (302)	368	0.28
Filipino (1,724)	1,852	1.43
Hmong (0)	1	<0.01
Indian (573)	651	0.50
Indonesian (3)	6	<0.01
Japanese (130)	177	0.14
Korean (286)	309	0.24
Laotian (5)	5	<0.01
Malaysian (1)	4	<0.01
Nepalese (6)	6	<0.01
Pakistani (52)	54	0.04
Sri Lankan (4)	4	<0.01
Taiwanese (28)	29	0.02
Thai (4)	16	0.01
Vietnamese (159)	185	0.14
Hawaii Native/Pacific Islander (25)	92	0.07
Not Hispanic (17)	36	0.03
Hispanic (8)	56	0.04
Fijian (0)	1	<0.01
Guamanian/Chamorro (12)	23	0.02
Native Hawaiian (8)	24	0.02
Samoan (1)	7	0.01
Tongan (0)	4	<0.01
White (108,913)	111,011	85.47
Not Hispanic (15,193)	15,531	11.96
Hispanic (93,720)	95,480	73.52

McKinney

Place Type: City
County: Collin
Population: 131,117†

Ancestry‡	Population	%
Afghan (119)	119	0.10
African, Sub-Saharan (1,313)	1,567	1.32
African (771)	987	0.83
Ethiopian (57)	57	0.05
Ghanaian (28)	28	0.02
Kenyan (256)	275	0.23
Liberian (6)	6	0.01
Nigerian (145)	145	0.12
Zimbabwean (50)	50	0.04
Other Sub-Saharan African (0)	19	0.02
American (11,945)	11,945	10.07
Arab (196)	260	0.22
Arab (59)	59	0.05
Iraqi (33)	33	0.03

*Notes: † The Census 2010 population figure is used to calculate the percentages in the Hispanic Origin and Race categories. Ancestry percentages are based on the 2006-2010 American Community Survey population (not shown); ‡ Numbers in parentheses indicate the number of people reporting a single ancestry; * Numbers in parentheses indicate the number of persons reporting this race alone, not in combination with any other race; Please refer to the Explanation of Data for more information.*

SECTION TWO

Lebanese (95)	124	0.10
Syrian (9)	44	0.04
Armenian (11)	21	0.02
Australian (46)	91	0.08
Austrian (85)	130	0.11
Belgian (66)	261	0.22
Brazilian (35)	76	0.06
British (320)	593	0.50
Cajun (64)	98	0.08
Canadian (259)	417	0.35
Celtic (12)	12	0.01
Croatian (23)	115	0.10
Czech (281)	944	0.80
Czechoslovakian (60)	108	0.09
Danish (131)	565	0.48
Dutch (324)	1,573	1.33
Eastern European (56)	56	0.05
English (4,817)	13,073	11.02
European (1,424)	1,613	1.36
Finnish (82)	199	0.17
French, ex. Basque (690)	3,975	3.35
French Canadian (294)	481	0.41
German (5,536)	18,542	15.63
Greek (174)	373	0.31
Hungarian (75)	380	0.32
Iranian (353)	464	0.39
Irish (3,788)	12,923	10.89
Israeli (36)	61	0.05
Italian (1,683)	4,569	3.85
Latvian (0)	18	0.02
Lithuanian (37)	123	0.10
Luxemburger (0)	22	0.02
Macedonian (0)	8	0.01
New Zealander (6)	24	0.02
Northern European (13)	13	0.01
Norwegian (328)	1,376	1.16
Pennsylvania German (8)	16	0.01
Polish (634)	2,491	2.10
Portuguese (98)	206	0.17
Romanian (38)	76	0.06
Russian (217)	703	0.59
Scandinavian (198)	376	0.32
Scotch-Irish (1,017)	2,431	2.05
Scottish (1,289)	3,607	3.04
Serbian (14)	14	0.01
Slavic (27)	105	0.09
Slovak (6)	41	0.03
Slovene (0)	76	0.06
Swedish (329)	1,263	1.06
Swiss (38)	141	0.12
Turkish (13)	13	0.01
Ukrainian (144)	251	0.21
Welsh (189)	828	0.70
West Indian, ex. Hispanic (208)	385	0.32
Bahamian (14)	55	0.05
Barbadian (20)	20	0.02
British West Indian (16)	16	0.01
Dutch West Indian (0)	27	0.02
Haitian (12)	12	0.01
Jamaican (71)	169	0.14
Trinidadian/Tobagonian (16)	16	0.01
West Indian (59)	70	0.06
Yugoslavian (43)	127	0.11

Hispanic Origin	Population	%
Hispanic or Latino (of any race)	24,406	18.61
Central American, ex. Mexican	1,270	0.97
Costa Rican	26	0.02
Guatemalan	178	0.14
Honduran	286	0.22
Nicaraguan	88	0.07
Panamanian	106	0.08
Salvadoran	578	0.44
Other Central American	8	0.01
Cuban	290	0.22
Dominican Republic	103	0.08
Mexican	18,917	14.43
Puerto Rican	839	0.64
South American	1,054	0.80
Argentinean	63	0.05
Bolivian	43	0.03
Chilean	46	0.04
Colombian	359	0.27
Ecuadorian	114	0.09
Paraguayan	6	<0.01
Peruvian	212	0.16
Uruguayan	18	0.01
Venezuelan	166	0.13
Other South American	27	0.02
Other Hispanic or Latino	1,933	1.47

Race*	Population	%
African-American/Black (13,751)	15,118	11.53
Not Hispanic (13,416)	14,507	11.06
Hispanic (335)	611	0.47
American Indian/Alaska Native (930)	1,865	1.42
Not Hispanic (604)	1,332	1.02
Hispanic (326)	533	0.41
Apache (26)	41	0.03
Arapaho (0)	2	<0.01
Blackfeet (1)	27	0.02
Central American Ind. (1)	5	<0.01
Cherokee (122)	393	0.30
Cheyenne (3)	3	<0.01
Chickasaw (56)	102	0.08
Chippewa (1)	9	0.01
Choctaw (142)	238	0.18
Comanche (4)	23	0.02
Creek (26)	55	0.04
Crow (1)	1	<0.01
Delaware (3)	11	0.01
Hopi (1)	3	<0.01
Houma (0)	2	<0.01
Iroquois (10)	18	0.01
Kiowa (8)	11	0.01
Lumbee (7)	9	0.01
Mexican American Ind. (45)	66	0.05
Navajo (2)	5	<0.01
Osage (3)	12	0.01
Ottawa (2)	2	<0.01
Paiute (1)	2	<0.01
Potawatomi (22)	31	0.02
Pueblo (5)	5	<0.01
Puget Sound Salish (0)	2	<0.01
Seminole (2)	12	0.01
Shoshone (0)	1	<0.01
Sioux (5)	17	0.01
South American Ind. (2)	6	<0.01
Spanish American Ind. (8)	10	0.01
Tohono O'Odham (0)	1	<0.01
Ute (0)	3	<0.01
Asian (5,325)	6,606	5.04
Not Hispanic (5,244)	6,352	4.84
Hispanic (81)	254	0.19
Bangladeshi (133)	137	0.10
Burmese (4)	6	<0.01
Cambodian (75)	93	0.07
Chinese, ex. Taiwanese (882)	1,132	0.86
Filipino (887)	1,204	0.92
Hmong (2)	5	<0.01
Indian (1,287)	1,423	1.09
Indonesian (33)	49	0.04
Japanese (124)	324	0.25
Korean (526)	709	0.54
Laotian (45)	74	0.06
Malaysian (3)	4	<0.01
Nepalese (44)	47	0.04
Pakistani (254)	299	0.23
Sri Lankan (19)	21	0.02
Taiwanese (92)	104	0.08
Thai (65)	124	0.09
Vietnamese (620)	763	0.58
Hawaii Native/Pacific Islander (95)	251	0.19
Not Hispanic (81)	192	0.15
Hispanic (14)	59	0.04
Fijian (9)	10	0.01
Guamanian/Chamorro (25)	42	0.03
Native Hawaiian (34)	108	0.08
Samoan (14)	37	0.03
Tongan (1)	2	<0.01
White (98,090)	101,590	77.48
Not Hispanic (84,547)	86,824	66.22
Hispanic (13,543)	14,766	11.26

Mercedes

Place Type: City
County: Hidalgo
Population: 15,570†

Ancestry‡	Population	%
American (283)	283	1.84
Arab (0)	46	0.30
Syrian (0)	46	0.30
Belgian (0)	21	0.14
Canadian (94)	111	0.72
Dutch (0)	27	0.18
English (30)	126	0.82
Finnish (14)	14	0.09
French, ex. Basque (35)	124	0.81
French Canadian (61)	61	0.40
German (158)	412	2.68
Irish (51)	115	0.75
Italian (9)	36	0.23
Norwegian (0)	15	0.10
Polish (29)	64	0.42
Scotch-Irish (3)	12	0.08
Scottish (32)	48	0.31
Swedish (0)	9	0.06
Swiss (0)	8	0.05
Ukrainian (24)	32	0.21
Welsh (0)	7	0.05

Hispanic Origin	Population	%
Hispanic or Latino (of any race)	14,302	91.86
Central American, ex. Mexican	27	0.17
Guatemalan	15	0.10
Honduran	3	0.02
Nicaraguan	1	0.01
Salvadoran	8	0.05
Cuban	10	0.06
Mexican	12,934	83.07
Puerto Rican	17	0.11
South American	4	0.03
Bolivian	1	0.01
Ecuadorian	1	0.01
Other South American	2	0.01
Other Hispanic or Latino	1,310	8.41

Race*	Population	%
African-American/Black (37)	78	0.50
Not Hispanic (8)	21	0.13
Hispanic (29)	57	0.37
American Indian/Alaska Native (87)	144	0.92
Not Hispanic (17)	30	0.19
Hispanic (70)	114	0.73
Apache (3)	3	0.02
Cherokee (7)	18	0.12
Chickasaw (1)	1	0.01
Mexican American Ind. (12)	13	0.08
Osage (0)	1	0.01
Shoshone (1)	1	0.01
Sioux (5)	5	0.03
Spanish American Ind. (1)	2	0.01
Asian (8)	28	0.18
Not Hispanic (5)	7	0.04
Hispanic (3)	21	0.13
Chinese, ex. Taiwanese (1)	2	0.01
Filipino (4)	7	0.04
Indian (2)	6	0.04
Japanese (0)	3	0.02
Korean (0)	6	0.04
Hawaii Native/Pacific Islander (10)	15	0.10
Not Hispanic (5)	7	0.04
Hispanic (5)	8	0.05
Guamanian/Chamorro (4)	4	0.03
Native Hawaiian (3)	5	0.03
White (13,278)	13,544	86.99
Not Hispanic (1,205)	1,227	7.88
Hispanic (12,073)	12,317	79.11

*Notes: † The Census 2010 population figure is used to calculate the percentages in the Hispanic Origin and Race categories. Ancestry percentages are based on the 2006-2010 American Community Survey population (not shown); ‡ Numbers in parentheses indicate the number of people reporting a single ancestry; * Numbers in parentheses indicate the number of persons reporting this race alone, not in combination with any other race; Please refer to the Explanation of Data for more information.*

Mesquite

Place Type: City
County: Dallas
Population: 139,824†

Ancestry‡	Population	%
Afghan (57)	57	0.04
African, Sub-Saharan (2,025)	2,108	1.55
African (1,281)	1,318	0.97
Cape Verdean (0)	23	0.02
Ethiopian (118)	118	0.09
Ghanaian (227)	227	0.17
Kenyan (34)	34	0.03
Nigerian (365)	388	0.29
Alsatian (12)	12	0.01
American (17,131)	17,131	12.60
Arab (756)	944	0.69
Arab (182)	182	0.13
Egyptian (27)	27	0.02
Iraqi (24)	116	0.09
Jordanian (176)	176	0.13
Lebanese (75)	95	0.07
Palestinian (137)	198	0.15
Syrian (0)	15	0.01
Other Arab (135)	135	0.10
Armenian (11)	11	0.01
Austrian (0)	24	0.02
Belgian (0)	49	0.04
Brazilian (226)	287	0.21
British (110)	212	0.16
Cajun (0)	6	<0.01
Canadian (188)	213	0.16
Croatian (35)	35	0.03
Czech (287)	586	0.43
Czechoslovakian (127)	142	0.10
Danish (82)	157	0.12
Dutch (186)	939	0.69
English (3,672)	7,809	5.75
European (672)	725	0.53
Finnish (0)	9	0.01
French, ex. Basque (305)	1,980	1.46
French Canadian (30)	94	0.07
German (2,833)	9,158	6.74
Greek (32)	151	0.11
Hungarian (21)	82	0.06
Iranian (90)	109	0.08
Irish (2,321)	7,347	5.41
Italian (690)	2,050	1.51
Lithuanian (116)	171	0.13
Northern European (76)	76	0.06
Norwegian (246)	670	0.49
Polish (242)	839	0.62
Portuguese (14)	68	0.05
Romanian (143)	191	0.14
Russian (65)	339	0.25
Scandinavian (52)	52	0.04
Scotch-Irish (640)	1,337	0.98
Scottish (642)	1,372	1.01
Serbian (10)	21	0.02
Slavic (0)	16	0.01
Slovak (12)	27	0.02
Swedish (93)	375	0.28
Swiss (61)	134	0.10
Ukrainian (53)	53	0.04
Welsh (192)	545	0.40
West Indian, ex. Hispanic (145)	237	0.17
Belizean (13)	13	0.01
Dutch West Indian (9)	49	0.04
Jamaican (84)	128	0.09
West Indian (39)	47	0.03
Yugoslavian (0)	92	0.07

Hispanic Origin	Population	%
Hispanic or Latino (of any race)	44,133	31.56
Central American, ex. Mexican	2,210	1.58
Costa Rican	56	0.04
Guatemalan	415	0.30
Honduran	369	0.26
Nicaraguan	91	0.07
Panamanian	74	0.05
Salvadoran	1,197	0.86
Other Central American	8	0.01
Cuban	303	0.22
Dominican Republic	118	0.08
Mexican	37,430	26.77
Puerto Rican	615	0.44
South American	713	0.51
Argentinean	57	0.04
Bolivian	35	0.03
Chilean	39	0.03
Colombian	221	0.16
Ecuadorian	31	0.02
Paraguayan	2	<0.01
Peruvian	262	0.19
Uruguayan	19	0.01
Venezuelan	46	0.03
Other South American	1	<0.01
Other Hispanic or Latino	2,744	1.96

Race*	Population	%
African-American/Black (30,534)	32,028	22.91
Not Hispanic (30,019)	31,175	22.30
Hispanic (515)	853	0.61
American Indian/Alaska Native (1,181)	2,155	1.54
Not Hispanic (520)	1,149	0.82
Hispanic (661)	1,006	0.72
Alaska Athabascan *(Ala. Nat.)* (2)	4	<0.01
Aleut *(Alaska Native)* (4)	4	<0.01
Apache (32)	61	0.04
Arapaho (3)	3	<0.01
Blackfeet (4)	23	0.02
Canadian/French Am. Ind. (0)	1	<0.01
Central American Ind. (0)	7	0.01
Cherokee (97)	330	0.24
Cheyenne (0)	3	<0.01
Chickasaw (44)	58	0.04
Chippewa (2)	5	<0.01
Choctaw (153)	249	0.18
Colville (1)	1	<0.01
Comanche (12)	26	0.02
Cree (0)	1	<0.01
Creek (27)	34	0.02
Delaware (3)	4	<0.01
Hopi (0)	1	<0.01
Houma (0)	2	<0.01
Inupiat *(Alaska Native)* (1)	1	<0.01
Iroquois (7)	12	0.01
Kiowa (13)	16	0.01
Lumbee (1)	1	<0.01
Menominee (0)	1	<0.01
Mexican American Ind. (84)	121	0.09
Navajo (16)	24	0.02
Osage (0)	2	<0.01
Ottawa (0)	2	<0.01
Paiute (2)	6	<0.01
Potawatomi (7)	8	0.01
Pueblo (4)	7	0.01
Seminole (10)	17	0.01
Shoshone (0)	5	<0.01
Sioux (9)	21	0.02
South American Ind. (7)	20	0.01
Spanish American Ind. (7)	8	0.01
Tlingit-Haida *(Alaska Native)* (1)	1	<0.01
Tohono O'Odham (2)	2	<0.01
Ute (0)	1	<0.01
Yaqui (0)	1	<0.01
Asian (4,527)	5,307	3.80
Not Hispanic (4,430)	5,067	3.62
Hispanic (97)	240	0.17
Bangladeshi (29)	32	0.02
Burmese (8)	8	0.01
Cambodian (139)	149	0.11
Chinese, ex. Taiwanese (164)	221	0.16
Filipino (1,203)	1,382	0.99
Hmong (3)	3	<0.01
Indian (1,866)	2,052	1.47
Indonesian (4)	4	<0.01
Japanese (40)	114	0.08
Korean (113)	170	0.12
Laotian (46)	62	0.04
Malaysian (1)	3	<0.01
Nepalese (44)	54	0.04
Pakistani (90)	94	0.07
Sri Lankan (8)	8	0.01
Taiwanese (4)	7	0.01
Thai (26)	50	0.04
Vietnamese (615)	685	0.49
Hawaii Native/Pacific Islander (104)	250	0.18
Not Hispanic (77)	184	0.13
Hispanic (27)	66	0.05
Fijian (1)	5	<0.01
Guamanian/Chamorro (43)	57	0.04
Native Hawaiian (22)	67	0.05
Samoan (10)	22	0.02
Tongan (1)	6	<0.01
White (82,435)	86,049	61.54
Not Hispanic (58,215)	60,100	42.98
Hispanic (24,220)	25,949	18.56

Midland

Place Type: City
County: Midland
Population: 111,147†

Ancestry‡	Population	%
African, Sub-Saharan (269)	285	0.26
African (212)	228	0.21
Ethiopian (15)	15	0.01
Nigerian (42)	42	0.04
American (8,789)	8,789	8.17
Arab (38)	101	0.09
Lebanese (28)	91	0.08
Other Arab (10)	10	0.01
Armenian (14)	14	0.01
Australian (0)	17	0.02
Austrian (14)	86	0.08
Basque (0)	48	0.04
Belgian (14)	14	0.01
British (311)	484	0.45
Bulgarian (17)	17	0.02
Cajun (39)	39	0.04
Canadian (63)	73	0.07
Celtic (15)	43	0.04
Croatian (0)	13	0.01
Czech (91)	376	0.35
Czechoslovakian (0)	81	0.08
Danish (0)	111	0.10
Dutch (238)	1,467	1.36
Eastern European (16)	24	0.02
English (3,991)	9,467	8.80
European (847)	1,046	0.97
Finnish (31)	101	0.09
French, ex. Basque (355)	1,623	1.51
French Canadian (129)	210	0.20
German (3,738)	9,612	8.94
Greek (24)	73	0.07
Guyanese (23)	65	0.06
Hungarian (10)	30	0.03
Icelander (20)	50	0.05
Iranian (56)	56	0.05
Irish (2,984)	7,859	7.31
Israeli (62)	75	0.07
Italian (418)	1,217	1.13
Lithuanian (15)	28	0.03
Luxemburger (9)	9	0.01
Norwegian (164)	476	0.44
Polish (239)	828	0.77
Portuguese (0)	72	0.07
Romanian (0)	39	0.04
Russian (7)	120	0.11
Scandinavian (66)	95	0.09
Scotch-Irish (1,005)	2,197	2.04
Scottish (959)	2,194	2.04
Slovak (0)	17	0.02
Swedish (233)	750	0.70
Swiss (24)	132	0.12
Turkish (33)	33	0.03
Ukrainian (8)	21	0.02

*Notes: † The Census 2010 population figure is used to calculate the percentages in the Hispanic Origin and Race categories. Ancestry percentages are based on the 2006-2010 American Community Survey population (not shown); ‡ Numbers in parentheses indicate the number of people reporting a single ancestry; * Numbers in parentheses indicate the number of persons reporting this race alone, not in combination with any other race; Please refer to the Explanation of Data for more information.*

Ancestry	Population	%
Welsh (139)	547	0.51
West Indian, ex. Hispanic (84)	158	0.15
British West Indian (34)	34	0.03
Dutch West Indian (11)	40	0.04
Jamaican (0)	13	0.01
West Indian (39)	71	0.07
Yugoslavian (13)	13	0.01

Hispanic Origin	Population	%
Hispanic or Latino (of any race)	41,797	37.61
Central American, ex. Mexican	244	0.22
Costa Rican	8	0.01
Guatemalan	63	0.06
Honduran	20	0.02
Nicaraguan	12	0.01
Panamanian	22	0.02
Salvadoran	116	0.10
Other Central American	3	<0.01
Cuban	54	0.05
Dominican Republic	25	0.02
Mexican	36,996	33.29
Puerto Rican	257	0.23
South American	321	0.29
Argentinean	24	0.02
Bolivian	7	0.01
Chilean	30	0.03
Colombian	83	0.07
Ecuadorian	25	0.02
Paraguayan	1	<0.01
Peruvian	52	0.05
Venezuelan	96	0.09
Other South American	3	<0.01
Other Hispanic or Latino	3,900	3.51

Race*	Population	%
African-American/Black (8,793)	9,619	8.65
Not Hispanic (8,426)	8,930	8.03
Hispanic (367)	689	0.62
American Indian/Alaska Native (807)	1,389	1.25
Not Hispanic (421)	840	0.76
Hispanic (386)	549	0.49
Alaska Athabascan *(Ala. Nat.)* (2)	2	<0.01
Aleut *(Alaska Native)* (3)	4	<0.01
Apache (46)	73	0.07
Arapaho (1)	1	<0.01
Blackfeet (3)	16	0.01
Central American Ind. (0)	1	<0.01
Cherokee (105)	242	0.22
Chickasaw (16)	39	0.04
Chippewa (3)	3	<0.01
Choctaw (61)	119	0.11
Comanche (9)	23	0.02
Cree (0)	1	<0.01
Creek (6)	14	0.01
Delaware (5)	7	0.01
Hopi (2)	4	<0.01
Inupiat *(Alaska Native)* (0)	1	<0.01
Iroquois (0)	1	<0.01
Kiowa (2)	7	0.01
Lumbee (7)	7	0.01
Mexican American Ind. (61)	72	0.06
Navajo (37)	43	0.04
Osage (1)	9	0.01
Ottawa (2)	2	<0.01
Pima (0)	1	<0.01
Potawatomi (12)	17	0.02
Pueblo (2)	5	<0.01
Puget Sound Salish (1)	1	<0.01
Seminole (3)	3	<0.01
Sioux (13)	19	0.02
Spanish American Ind. (1)	5	<0.01
Tlingit-Haida *(Alaska Native)* (1)	1	<0.01
Tohono O'Odham (1)	1	<0.01
Ute (4)	4	<0.01
Yaqui (2)	2	<0.01
Asian (1,540)	1,869	1.68
Not Hispanic (1,474)	1,709	1.54
Hispanic (66)	160	0.14
Bangladeshi (6)	7	0.01
Burmese (125)	125	0.11
Cambodian (34)	47	0.04
Chinese, ex. Taiwanese (210)	273	0.25
Filipino (255)	358	0.32
Hmong (1)	1	<0.01
Indian (356)	399	0.36
Indonesian (12)	21	0.02
Japanese (27)	78	0.07
Korean (126)	146	0.13
Laotian (15)	19	0.02
Malaysian (5)	5	<0.01
Nepalese (10)	10	0.01
Pakistani (57)	61	0.05
Taiwanese (8)	11	0.01
Thai (28)	39	0.04
Vietnamese (203)	232	0.21
Hawaii Native/Pacific Islander (45)	108	0.10
Not Hispanic (39)	77	0.07
Hispanic (6)	31	0.03
Fijian (1)	1	<0.01
Guamanian/Chamorro (3)	9	0.01
Native Hawaiian (16)	39	0.04
Samoan (7)	17	0.02
Tongan (9)	9	0.01
White (83,967)	86,400	77.73
Not Hispanic (57,658)	58,672	52.79
Hispanic (26,309)	27,728	24.95

Midlothian

Place Type: City
County: Ellis
Population: 18,037†

Ancestry‡	Population	%
African, Sub-Saharan (9)	9	0.05
African (9)	9	0.05
American (1,539)	1,539	9.28
Arab (0)	32	0.19
Syrian (0)	32	0.19
Australian (0)	16	0.10
Brazilian (0)	7	0.04
British (22)	31	0.19
Cajun (11)	11	0.07
Canadian (71)	83	0.50
Croatian (0)	31	0.19
Czech (347)	532	3.21
Czechoslovakian (104)	133	0.80
Danish (0)	18	0.11
Dutch (51)	193	1.16
English (774)	2,271	13.69
European (154)	154	0.93
Finnish (44)	90	0.54
French, ex. Basque (28)	376	2.27
French Canadian (0)	5	0.03
German (832)	2,484	14.98
Iranian (0)	16	0.10
Irish (711)	2,095	12.63
Italian (92)	395	2.38
Maltese (11)	55	0.33
Norwegian (0)	45	0.27
Polish (53)	207	1.25
Portuguese (20)	27	0.16
Romanian (0)	24	0.14
Russian (6)	6	0.04
Scandinavian (40)	55	0.33
Scotch-Irish (156)	478	2.88
Scottish (260)	474	2.86
Swedish (55)	406	2.45
Swiss (10)	89	0.54
Ukrainian (15)	40	0.24
Welsh (0)	66	0.40
West Indian, ex. Hispanic (9)	92	0.55
Dutch West Indian (0)	71	0.43
Jamaican (9)	21	0.13
Yugoslavian (55)	55	0.33

Hispanic Origin	Population	%
Hispanic or Latino (of any race)	2,734	15.16
Central American, ex. Mexican	44	0.24
Costa Rican	4	0.02
Guatemalan	3	0.02
Honduran	14	0.08
Panamanian	5	0.03
Salvadoran	18	0.10
Cuban	8	0.04
Dominican Republic	4	0.02
Mexican	2,255	12.50
Puerto Rican	75	0.42
South American	32	0.18
Chilean	4	0.02
Colombian	3	0.02
Ecuadorian	5	0.03
Peruvian	10	0.06
Venezuelan	10	0.06
Other Hispanic or Latino	316	1.75

Race*	Population	%
African-American/Black (654)	736	4.08
Not Hispanic (616)	683	3.79
Hispanic (38)	53	0.29
American Indian/Alaska Native (74)	203	1.13
Not Hispanic (54)	161	0.89
Hispanic (20)	42	0.23
Apache (0)	8	0.04
Blackfeet (0)	5	0.03
Central American Ind. (1)	3	0.02
Cherokee (13)	38	0.21
Chickasaw (5)	9	0.05
Chippewa (5)	6	0.03
Choctaw (22)	32	0.18
Comanche (0)	6	0.03
Creek (1)	9	0.05
Delaware (0)	2	0.01
Iroquois (1)	1	0.01
Mexican American Ind. (4)	8	0.04
Ottawa (0)	1	0.01
Potawatomi (0)	1	0.01
Pueblo (1)	1	0.01
Sioux (1)	2	0.01
Spanish American Ind. (2)	2	0.01
Yaqui (0)	4	0.02
Asian (142)	221	1.23
Not Hispanic (136)	210	1.16
Hispanic (6)	11	0.06
Bangladeshi (8)	8	0.04
Cambodian (2)	2	0.01
Chinese, ex. Taiwanese (28)	38	0.21
Filipino (30)	53	0.29
Hmong (8)	8	0.04
Indian (25)	34	0.19
Japanese (7)	25	0.14
Korean (11)	16	0.09
Laotian (1)	4	0.02
Pakistani (2)	2	0.01
Sri Lankan (0)	2	0.01
Thai (4)	6	0.03
Vietnamese (4)	9	0.05
Hawaii Native/Pacific Islander (10)	32	0.18
Not Hispanic (10)	32	0.18
Guamanian/Chamorro (3)	11	0.06
Native Hawaiian (4)	10	0.06
Samoan (1)	1	0.01
White (15,965)	16,362	90.71
Not Hispanic (14,220)	14,452	80.12
Hispanic (1,745)	1,910	10.59

Mineral Wells

Place Type: City
County: Palo Pinto
Population: 16,788†

Ancestry‡	Population	%
African, Sub-Saharan (15)	23	0.13
African (15)	23	0.13
American (1,392)	1,392	8.08
Armenian (10)	10	0.06
Austrian (11)	17	0.10
British (48)	48	0.28
Canadian (10)	25	0.15

*Notes: † The Census 2010 population figure is used to calculate the percentages in the Hispanic Origin and Race categories. Ancestry percentages are based on the 2006-2010 American Community Survey population (not shown); ‡ Numbers in parentheses indicate the number of people reporting a single ancestry; * Numbers in parentheses indicate the number of persons reporting this race alone, not in combination with any other race; Please refer to the Explanation of Data for more information.*

Ancestry	Population	%
Danish (28)	76	0.44
Dutch (5)	192	1.11
English (482)	1,292	7.50
European (45)	67	0.39
Finnish (0)	27	0.16
French, ex. Basque (82)	378	2.19
French Canadian (21)	21	0.12
German (430)	1,519	8.82
Hungarian (79)	130	0.75
Irish (637)	1,538	8.93
Israeli (9)	9	0.05
Italian (34)	158	0.92
Norwegian (6)	6	0.03
Polish (36)	86	0.50
Portuguese (9)	9	0.05
Russian (10)	31	0.18
Scotch-Irish (134)	261	1.51
Scottish (94)	330	1.92
Swedish (19)	122	0.71
Swiss (7)	39	0.23
Welsh (0)	20	0.12
West Indian, ex. Hispanic (0)	39	0.23
Dutch West Indian (0)	39	0.23

Hispanic Origin	Population	%
Hispanic or Latino (of any race)	4,423	26.35
Central American, ex. Mexican	55	0.33
Guatemalan	11	0.07
Honduran	9	0.05
Panamanian	4	0.02
Salvadoran	31	0.18
Cuban	10	0.06
Dominican Republic	2	0.01
Mexican	3,457	20.59
Puerto Rican	34	0.20
South American	12	0.07
Colombian	1	0.01
Ecuadorian	3	0.02
Peruvian	4	0.02
Uruguayan	4	0.02
Other Hispanic or Latino	853	5.08

Race*	Population	%
African-American/Black (1,309)	1,413	8.42
Not Hispanic (1,292)	1,375	8.19
Hispanic (17)	38	0.23
American Indian/Alaska Native (117)	224	1.33
Not Hispanic (64)	145	0.86
Hispanic (53)	79	0.47
Apache (4)	12	0.07
Arapaho (4)	4	0.02
Blackfeet (0)	6	0.04
Cherokee (20)	65	0.39
Chickasaw (10)	19	0.11
Choctaw (8)	17	0.10
Comanche (1)	5	0.03
Creek (1)	3	0.02
Inupiat *(Alaska Native)* (0)	2	0.01
Mexican American Ind. (8)	9	0.05
Sioux (1)	3	0.02
Spanish American Ind. (1)	1	0.01
Yaqui (1)	4	0.02
Asian (91)	128	0.76
Not Hispanic (89)	117	0.70
Hispanic (2)	11	0.07
Cambodian (1)	1	0.01
Chinese, ex. Taiwanese (1)	1	0.01
Filipino (18)	32	0.19
Indian (37)	49	0.29
Japanese (9)	22	0.13
Korean (5)	6	0.04
Laotian (5)	5	0.03
Pakistani (0)	1	0.01
Thai (2)	2	0.01
Vietnamese (1)	2	0.01
Hawaii Native/Pacific Islander (5)	6	0.04
Not Hispanic (3)	4	0.02
Hispanic (2)	2	0.01
Tongan (2)	2	0.01
White (12,634)	12,956	77.17
Not Hispanic (10,712)	10,887	64.85
Hispanic (1,922)	2,069	12.32

Mission Bend

Place Type: CDP
County: Fort Bend
Population: 36,501†

Ancestry‡	Population	%
African, Sub-Saharan (2,328)	2,467	6.52
African (436)	449	1.19
Ghanaian (96)	96	0.25
Nigerian (1,777)	1,903	5.03
Sierra Leonean (19)	19	0.05
American (900)	900	2.38
Arab (111)	166	0.44
Arab (0)	55	0.15
Jordanian (12)	12	0.03
Lebanese (77)	77	0.20
Syrian (12)	12	0.03
Other Arab (10)	10	0.03
Armenian (57)	71	0.19
Austrian (12)	12	0.03
Brazilian (141)	179	0.47
British (0)	26	0.07
Celtic (11)	11	0.03
Czech (0)	57	0.15
Danish (0)	12	0.03
Dutch (29)	103	0.27
English (375)	847	2.24
European (100)	100	0.26
French, ex. Basque (25)	225	0.60
French Canadian (18)	30	0.08
German (573)	1,222	3.23
Greek (3)	3	0.01
Hungarian (10)	23	0.06
Iranian (12)	12	0.03
Irish (378)	836	2.21
Israeli (22)	22	0.06
Italian (200)	483	1.28
Norwegian (30)	61	0.16
Polish (96)	291	0.77
Portuguese (0)	94	0.25
Russian (0)	71	0.19
Scandinavian (0)	10	0.03
Scotch-Irish (50)	182	0.48
Scottish (85)	165	0.44
Swedish (14)	62	0.16
Swiss (0)	23	0.06
Welsh (11)	44	0.12
West Indian, ex. Hispanic (264)	264	0.70
Haitian (27)	27	0.07
Jamaican (217)	217	0.57
Trinidadian/Tobagonian (20)	20	0.05

Hispanic Origin	Population	%
Hispanic or Latino (of any race)	14,718	40.32
Central American, ex. Mexican	3,734	10.23
Costa Rican	42	0.12
Guatemalan	407	1.12
Honduran	405	1.11
Nicaraguan	181	0.50
Panamanian	76	0.21
Salvadoran	2,616	7.17
Other Central American	7	0.02
Cuban	406	1.11
Dominican Republic	74	0.20
Mexican	7,899	21.64
Puerto Rican	301	0.82
South American	1,243	3.41
Argentinean	115	0.32
Bolivian	42	0.12
Chilean	63	0.17
Colombian	661	1.81
Ecuadorian	99	0.27
Paraguayan	1	<0.01
Peruvian	149	0.41
Uruguayan	39	0.11
Venezuelan	71	0.19
Other South American	3	0.01
Other Hispanic or Latino	1,061	2.91

Race*	Population	%
African-American/Black (10,852)	11,267	30.87
Not Hispanic (10,581)	10,849	29.72
Hispanic (271)	418	1.15
American Indian/Alaska Native (167)	362	0.99
Not Hispanic (55)	166	0.45
Hispanic (112)	196	0.54
Alaska Athabascan *(Ala. Nat.)* (1)	1	<0.01
Apache (2)	4	0.01
Blackfeet (0)	1	<0.01
Canadian/French Am. Ind. (0)	1	<0.01
Central American Ind. (13)	14	0.04
Cherokee (9)	26	0.07
Cheyenne (1)	1	<0.01
Chickasaw (1)	1	<0.01
Chippewa (2)	2	0.01
Choctaw (5)	19	0.05
Comanche (0)	1	<0.01
Mexican American Ind. (17)	27	0.07
Osage (3)	7	0.02
Pueblo (2)	2	0.01
Puget Sound Salish (1)	4	0.01
Seminole (0)	1	<0.01
Sioux (1)	4	0.01
South American Ind. (1)	1	<0.01
Spanish American Ind. (0)	1	<0.01
Tohono O'Odham (1)	1	<0.01
Asian (5,568)	5,899	16.16
Not Hispanic (5,510)	5,776	15.82
Hispanic (58)	123	0.34
Bangladeshi (52)	63	0.17
Burmese (4)	4	0.01
Cambodian (31)	40	0.11
Chinese, ex. Taiwanese (554)	637	1.75
Filipino (880)	970	2.66
Indian (823)	898	2.46
Indonesian (21)	26	0.07
Japanese (12)	30	0.08
Korean (47)	68	0.19
Laotian (1)	1	<0.01
Malaysian (5)	5	0.01
Nepalese (8)	8	0.02
Pakistani (493)	538	1.47
Sri Lankan (1)	1	<0.01
Taiwanese (40)	40	0.11
Thai (25)	31	0.08
Vietnamese (2,407)	2,493	6.83
Hawaii Native/Pacific Islander (13)	78	0.21
Not Hispanic (11)	41	0.11
Hispanic (2)	37	0.10
Fijian (1)	1	<0.01
Guamanian/Chamorro (1)	1	<0.01
Native Hawaiian (1)	4	0.01
Samoan (6)	15	0.04
Tongan (0)	1	<0.01
White (13,165)	14,224	38.97
Not Hispanic (4,975)	5,358	14.68
Hispanic (8,190)	8,866	24.29

Mission

Place Type: City
County: Hidalgo
Population: 77,058†

Ancestry‡	Population	%
African, Sub-Saharan (97)	97	0.14
African (97)	97	0.14
American (1,157)	1,157	1.61
Arab (49)	103	0.14
Arab (0)	22	0.03
Egyptian (24)	56	0.08
Lebanese (11)	11	0.02
Other Arab (14)	14	0.02
Belgian (0)	130	0.18
British (29)	53	0.07
Canadian (16)	128	0.18

*Notes: † The Census 2010 population figure is used to calculate the percentages in the Hispanic Origin and Race categories. Ancestry percentages are based on the 2006-2010 American Community Survey population (not shown); ‡ Numbers in parentheses indicate the number of people reporting a single ancestry; * Numbers in parentheses indicate the number of persons reporting this race alone, not in combination with any other race; Please refer to the Explanation of Data for more information.*

Czech (11)	136	0.19
Czechoslovakian (49)	49	0.07
Danish (98)	244	0.34
Dutch (72)	389	0.54
English (468)	1,548	2.16
European (180)	180	0.25
Finnish (0)	96	0.13
French, ex. Basque (79)	292	0.41
French Canadian (66)	119	0.17
German (1,391)	3,042	4.24
Greek (12)	44	0.06
Guyanese (30)	30	0.04
Hungarian (68)	103	0.14
Irish (370)	2,222	3.10
Italian (120)	580	0.81
Norwegian (126)	381	0.53
Pennsylvania German (10)	10	0.01
Polish (90)	370	0.52
Portuguese (59)	148	0.21
Russian (8)	23	0.03
Scandinavian (44)	57	0.08
Scotch-Irish (179)	367	0.51
Scottish (78)	191	0.27
Serbian (11)	11	0.02
Slovak (0)	33	0.05
Swedish (178)	430	0.60
Swiss (40)	40	0.06
Turkish (0)	12	0.02
Ukrainian (56)	186	0.26
Welsh (21)	233	0.32

Hispanic Origin	Population	%
Hispanic or Latino (of any race)	65,812	85.41
Central American, ex. Mexican	209	0.27
Costa Rican	19	0.02
Guatemalan	33	0.04
Honduran	34	0.04
Nicaraguan	36	0.05
Panamanian	19	0.02
Salvadoran	68	0.09
Cuban	88	0.11
Dominican Republic	92	0.12
Mexican	61,703	80.07
Puerto Rican	254	0.33
South American	249	0.32
Argentinean	38	0.05
Bolivian	13	0.02
Chilean	19	0.02
Colombian	60	0.08
Ecuadorian	12	0.02
Paraguayan	4	0.01
Peruvian	47	0.06
Uruguayan	5	0.01
Venezuelan	51	0.07
Other Hispanic or Latino	3,217	4.17

Race*	Population	%
African-American/Black (521)	652	0.85
Not Hispanic (321)	365	0.47
Hispanic (200)	287	0.37
American Indian/Alaska Native (259)	350	0.45
Not Hispanic (71)	126	0.16
Hispanic (188)	224	0.29
Aleut *(Alaska Native)* (0)	1	<0.01
Apache (17)	27	0.04
Arapaho (0)	6	0.01
Canadian/French Am. Ind. (1)	1	<0.01
Cherokee (14)	18	0.02
Cheyenne (0)	1	<0.01
Chippewa (5)	6	0.01
Choctaw (8)	10	0.01
Comanche (1)	8	0.01
Creek (0)	2	<0.01
Iroquois (0)	2	<0.01
Kiowa (4)	5	0.01
Mexican American Ind. (28)	36	0.05
Navajo (5)	7	0.01
Osage (0)	3	<0.01
Pueblo (6)	6	0.01
Sioux (0)	1	<0.01
South American Ind. (1)	1	<0.01
Spanish American Ind. (3)	5	0.01
Asian (1,187)	1,356	1.76
Not Hispanic (1,135)	1,220	1.58
Hispanic (52)	136	0.18
Cambodian (0)	1	<0.01
Chinese, ex. Taiwanese (81)	118	0.15
Filipino (588)	661	0.86
Indian (159)	181	0.23
Indonesian (3)	5	0.01
Japanese (71)	96	0.12
Korean (156)	166	0.22
Laotian (6)	13	0.02
Malaysian (0)	3	<0.01
Pakistani (14)	17	0.02
Taiwanese (2)	3	<0.01
Thai (7)	8	0.01
Vietnamese (61)	68	0.09
Hawaii Native/Pacific Islander (16)	38	0.05
Not Hispanic (11)	18	0.02
Hispanic (5)	20	0.03
Guamanian/Chamorro (5)	7	0.01
Native Hawaiian (6)	17	0.02
White (68,291)	69,265	89.89
Not Hispanic (9,465)	9,634	12.50
Hispanic (58,826)	59,631	77.38

Missouri City

Place Type: City
County: Fort Bend
Population: 67,358†

Ancestry‡	Population	%
Afghan (11)	33	0.05
African, Sub-Saharan (2,495)	2,774	4.30
African (590)	856	1.33
Ethiopian (15)	15	0.02
Ghanaian (86)	99	0.15
Nigerian (1,795)	1,795	2.78
Other Sub-Saharan African (9)	9	0.01
American (1,766)	1,766	2.74
Arab (470)	512	0.79
Arab (52)	52	0.08
Egyptian (108)	118	0.18
Lebanese (167)	190	0.29
Palestinian (61)	61	0.09
Syrian (24)	24	0.04
Other Arab (58)	67	0.10
Austrian (0)	35	0.05
British (223)	248	0.38
Cajun (73)	99	0.15
Canadian (54)	54	0.08
Croatian (9)	28	0.04
Cypriot (12)	12	0.02
Czech (156)	365	0.57
Czechoslovakian (29)	135	0.21
Danish (38)	128	0.20
Dutch (25)	196	0.30
Eastern European (39)	39	0.06
English (1,121)	2,806	4.35
European (175)	206	0.32
Finnish (11)	49	0.08
French, ex. Basque (290)	1,213	1.88
French Canadian (59)	81	0.13
German (1,697)	4,394	6.81
Greek (0)	24	0.04
Guyanese (100)	100	0.15
Hungarian (18)	80	0.12
Iranian (168)	190	0.29
Irish (761)	2,558	3.96
Israeli (49)	49	0.08
Italian (371)	997	1.54
Lithuanian (35)	71	0.11
Maltese (10)	10	0.02
Norwegian (46)	178	0.28
Pennsylvania German (12)	12	0.02
Polish (107)	517	0.80
Portuguese (18)	66	0.10
Romanian (0)	13	0.02
Russian (58)	136	0.21
Scandinavian (0)	29	0.04
Scotch-Irish (116)	344	0.53
Scottish (254)	622	0.96
Slovak (0)	10	0.02
Swedish (41)	268	0.42
Swiss (19)	58	0.09
Turkish (110)	119	0.18
Ukrainian (175)	209	0.32
Welsh (45)	224	0.35
West Indian, ex. Hispanic (885)	1,063	1.65
Bahamian (10)	10	0.02
Barbadian (35)	35	0.05
Belizean (182)	182	0.28
British West Indian (12)	12	0.02
Dutch West Indian (9)	9	0.01
Haitian (73)	86	0.13
Jamaican (457)	517	0.80
Trinidadian/Tobagonian (13)	73	0.11
U.S. Virgin Islander (12)	34	0.05
West Indian (82)	105	0.16
Yugoslavian (0)	10	0.02

Hispanic Origin	Population	%
Hispanic or Latino (of any race)	10,306	15.30
Central American, ex. Mexican	1,604	2.38
Costa Rican	15	0.02
Guatemalan	140	0.21
Honduran	188	0.28
Nicaraguan	59	0.09
Panamanian	105	0.16
Salvadoran	1,084	1.61
Other Central American	13	0.02
Cuban	184	0.27
Dominican Republic	70	0.10
Mexican	6,658	9.88
Puerto Rican	289	0.43
South American	620	0.92
Argentinean	101	0.15
Bolivian	14	0.02
Chilean	18	0.03
Colombian	234	0.35
Ecuadorian	42	0.06
Paraguayan	1	<0.01
Peruvian	68	0.10
Uruguayan	9	0.01
Venezuelan	133	0.20
Other Hispanic or Latino	881	1.31

Race*	Population	%
African-American/Black (28,135)	28,963	43.00
Not Hispanic (27,754)	28,398	42.16
Hispanic (381)	565	0.84
American Indian/Alaska Native (278)	676	1.00
Not Hispanic (152)	465	0.69
Hispanic (126)	211	0.31
Apache (3)	5	0.01
Blackfeet (0)	2	<0.01
Canadian/French Am. Ind. (1)	1	<0.01
Central American Ind. (7)	8	0.01
Cherokee (12)	95	0.14
Chickasaw (2)	6	0.01
Choctaw (12)	31	0.05
Comanche (2)	6	0.01
Cree (0)	1	<0.01
Creek (13)	20	0.03
Houma (1)	10	0.01
Iroquois (0)	1	<0.01
Lumbee (1)	1	<0.01
Menominee (1)	2	<0.01
Mexican American Ind. (17)	25	0.04
Navajo (5)	7	0.01
Osage (1)	1	<0.01
Paiute (1)	1	<0.01
Pima (4)	4	0.01
Potawatomi (5)	5	0.01
Seminole (0)	7	0.01
Sioux (0)	3	<0.01
South American Ind. (0)	4	0.01
Spanish American Ind. (0)	2	<0.01

*Notes: † The Census 2010 population figure is used to calculate the percentages in the Hispanic Origin and Race categories. Ancestry percentages are based on the 2006-2010 American Community Survey population (not shown); ‡ Numbers in parentheses indicate the number of people reporting a single ancestry; * Numbers in parentheses indicate the number of persons reporting this race alone, not in combination with any other race; Please refer to the Explanation of Data for more information.*

Yup'ik *(Alaska Native)* (1)	1	<0.01
Asian (10,922)	11,701	17.37
Not Hispanic (10,859)	11,524	17.11
Hispanic (63)	177	0.26
Bangladeshi (14)	18	0.03
Burmese (19)	20	0.03
Cambodian (26)	29	0.04
Chinese, ex. Taiwanese (2,682)	2,898	4.30
Filipino (1,342)	1,554	2.31
Indian (4,485)	4,684	6.95
Indonesian (52)	66	0.10
Japanese (58)	117	0.17
Korean (93)	114	0.17
Laotian (2)	2	<0.01
Malaysian (17)	32	0.05
Nepalese (7)	8	0.01
Pakistani (470)	526	0.78
Sri Lankan (15)	15	0.02
Taiwanese (226)	262	0.39
Thai (79)	103	0.15
Vietnamese (1,054)	1,145	1.70
Hawaii Native/Pacific Islander (24)	110	0.16
Not Hispanic (20)	94	0.14
Hispanic (4)	16	0.02
Guamanian/Chamorro (13)	15	0.02
Native Hawaiian (3)	14	0.02
Samoan (1)	3	<0.01
White (22,611)	23,926	35.52
Not Hispanic (16,791)	17,636	26.18
Hispanic (5,820)	6,290	9.34

Mount Pleasant

Place Type: City
County: Titus
Population: 15,564†

Ancestry‡	Population	%
African, Sub-Saharan (668)	881	5.83
African (668)	881	5.83
American (854)	854	5.65
British (0)	11	0.07
Cajun (9)	17	0.11
Czech (0)	80	0.53
Czechoslovakian (0)	45	0.30
Dutch (37)	83	0.55
English (310)	669	4.43
European (70)	70	0.46
French, ex. Basque (41)	142	0.94
French Canadian (9)	9	0.06
German (88)	721	4.77
Irish (189)	892	5.90
Italian (41)	90	0.60
Northern European (7)	7	0.05
Norwegian (12)	31	0.21
Polish (50)	62	0.41
Romanian (5)	5	0.03
Russian (20)	41	0.27
Scotch-Irish (112)	117	0.77
Scottish (59)	134	0.89
Serbian (7)	33	0.22
Swedish (122)	122	0.81
Ukrainian (12)	12	0.08
Welsh (38)	60	0.40

Hispanic Origin	Population	%
Hispanic or Latino (of any race)	7,938	51.00
Central American, ex. Mexican	187	1.20
Costa Rican	12	0.08
Guatemalan	18	0.12
Honduran	74	0.48
Nicaraguan	5	0.03
Panamanian	1	0.01
Salvadoran	77	0.49
Cuban	20	0.13
Dominican Republic	4	0.03
Mexican	7,321	47.04
Puerto Rican	92	0.59
South American	28	0.18
Argentinean	3	0.02
Chilean	2	0.01
Colombian	21	0.13
Peruvian	1	0.01
Venezuelan	1	0.01
Other Hispanic or Latino	286	1.84

Race*	Population	%
African-American/Black (2,294)	2,386	15.33
Not Hispanic (2,230)	2,283	14.67
Hispanic (64)	103	0.66
American Indian/Alaska Native (188)	266	1.71
Not Hispanic (46)	77	0.49
Hispanic (142)	189	1.21
Blackfeet (0)	1	0.01
Central American Ind. (0)	2	0.01
Cherokee (8)	12	0.08
Choctaw (17)	32	0.21
Comanche (1)	4	0.03
Iroquois (0)	1	0.01
Mexican American Ind. (27)	33	0.21
Navajo (4)	4	0.03
Osage (3)	3	0.02
Pueblo (0)	3	0.02
Sioux (1)	2	0.01
Asian (170)	199	1.28
Not Hispanic (166)	176	1.13
Hispanic (4)	23	0.15
Cambodian (4)	4	0.03
Chinese, ex. Taiwanese (15)	17	0.11
Filipino (31)	37	0.24
Indian (53)	57	0.37
Japanese (3)	6	0.04
Korean (9)	9	0.06
Nepalese (9)	9	0.06
Pakistani (22)	22	0.14
Vietnamese (17)	19	0.12
Hawaii Native/Pacific Islander (11)	26	0.17
Not Hispanic (4)	6	0.04
Hispanic (7)	20	0.13
Native Hawaiian (10)	12	0.08
Samoan (1)	2	0.01
White (8,989)	9,354	60.10
Not Hispanic (5,086)	5,158	33.14
Hispanic (3,903)	4,196	26.96

Murphy

Place Type: City
County: Collin
Population: 17,708†

Ancestry‡	Population	%
African, Sub-Saharan (442)	442	2.90
African (151)	151	0.99
Ethiopian (8)	8	0.05
Kenyan (168)	168	1.10
Nigerian (115)	115	0.75
American (968)	968	6.34
Arab (203)	241	1.58
Arab (0)	22	0.14
Jordanian (59)	59	0.39
Lebanese (8)	24	0.16
Syrian (126)	126	0.83
Other Arab (10)	10	0.07
Brazilian (15)	15	0.10
British (29)	58	0.38
Canadian (32)	57	0.37
Croatian (14)	14	0.09
Czech (25)	94	0.62
Czechoslovakian (11)	24	0.16
Danish (49)	92	0.60
Dutch (85)	177	1.16
Eastern European (0)	11	0.07
English (296)	898	5.89
European (253)	279	1.83
French, ex. Basque (38)	330	2.16
German (710)	2,247	14.73
Greek (14)	52	0.34
Hungarian (12)	71	0.47
Irish (239)	1,286	8.43
Israeli (34)	34	0.22
Italian (85)	308	2.02
Latvian (23)	34	0.22
Lithuanian (13)	63	0.41
Macedonian (4)	18	0.12
Northern European (48)	48	0.31
Norwegian (0)	27	0.18
Polish (141)	324	2.12
Russian (12)	72	0.47
Scandinavian (6)	24	0.16
Scotch-Irish (89)	182	1.19
Scottish (279)	536	3.51
Serbian (0)	14	0.09
Slavic (12)	12	0.08
Slovak (8)	8	0.05
Swedish (38)	150	0.98
Swiss (34)	129	0.85
Turkish (18)	18	0.12
Ukrainian (0)	10	0.07
Welsh (11)	118	0.77

Hispanic Origin	Population	%
Hispanic or Latino (of any race)	1,384	7.82
Central American, ex. Mexican	65	0.37
Costa Rican	13	0.07
Guatemalan	9	0.05
Honduran	6	0.03
Nicaraguan	2	0.01
Panamanian	6	0.03
Salvadoran	29	0.16
Cuban	33	0.19
Dominican Republic	3	0.02
Mexican	1,006	5.68
Puerto Rican	76	0.43
South American	101	0.57
Argentinean	8	0.05
Bolivian	3	0.02
Chilean	1	0.01
Colombian	57	0.32
Ecuadorian	7	0.04
Peruvian	11	0.06
Uruguayan	2	0.01
Venezuelan	12	0.07
Other Hispanic or Latino	100	0.56

Race*	Population	%
African-American/Black (1,927)	2,048	11.57
Not Hispanic (1,900)	1,996	11.27
Hispanic (27)	52	0.29
American Indian/Alaska Native (89)	205	1.16
Not Hispanic (76)	171	0.97
Hispanic (13)	34	0.19
Apache (4)	4	0.02
Blackfeet (0)	2	0.01
Cherokee (28)	51	0.29
Chickasaw (5)	6	0.03
Chippewa (0)	1	0.01
Choctaw (3)	13	0.07
Cree (4)	4	0.02
Creek (1)	2	0.01
Delaware (1)	1	0.01
Hopi (0)	3	0.02
Houma (0)	4	0.02
Iroquois (0)	4	0.02
Kiowa (1)	1	0.01
Mexican American Ind. (2)	5	0.03
Osage (0)	1	0.01
Potawatomi (6)	6	0.03
Asian (4,145)	4,466	25.22
Not Hispanic (4,143)	4,430	25.02
Hispanic (2)	36	0.20
Bangladeshi (52)	55	0.31
Burmese (1)	2	0.01
Cambodian (18)	31	0.18
Chinese, ex. Taiwanese (296)	384	2.17
Filipino (128)	180	1.02
Indian (1,673)	1,757	9.92
Indonesian (6)	8	0.05
Japanese (29)	57	0.32
Korean (102)	122	0.69

*Notes: † The Census 2010 population figure is used to calculate the percentages in the Hispanic Origin and Race categories. Ancestry percentages are based on the 2006-2010 American Community Survey population (not shown); ‡ Numbers in parentheses indicate the number of people reporting a single ancestry; * Numbers in parentheses indicate the number of persons reporting this race alone, not in combination with any other race; Please refer to the Explanation of Data for more information.*

Laotian (40)	48	0.27
Malaysian (10)	12	0.07
Nepalese (7)	7	0.04
Pakistani (366)	390	2.20
Taiwanese (25)	28	0.16
Thai (31)	36	0.20
Vietnamese (1,239)	1,319	7.45
Hawaii Native/Pacific Islander (10)	36	0.20
Not Hispanic (9)	34	0.19
Hispanic (1)	2	0.01
Guamanian/Chamorro (4)	8	0.05
Native Hawaiian (4)	4	0.02
Samoan (1)	5	0.03
White (10,694)	11,101	62.69
Not Hispanic (9,716)	10,038	56.69
Hispanic (978)	1,063	6.00

Nacogdoches

Place Type: City
County: Nacogdoches
Population: 32,996†

Ancestry‡	Population	%
African, Sub-Saharan (481)	549	1.70
African (430)	430	1.33
Nigerian (51)	51	0.16
South African (0)	68	0.21
American (1,636)	1,636	5.07
Arab (60)	60	0.19
Arab (60)	60	0.19
Austrian (0)	12	0.04
Brazilian (10)	10	0.03
British (227)	282	0.87
Cajun (0)	9	0.03
Canadian (14)	29	0.09
Croatian (0)	18	0.06
Czech (109)	273	0.85
Czechoslovakian (0)	10	0.03
Danish (45)	220	0.68
Dutch (56)	306	0.95
English (1,617)	3,028	9.38
European (159)	179	0.55
Finnish (6)	12	0.04
French, ex. Basque (194)	1,012	3.13
French Canadian (40)	47	0.15
German (966)	2,933	9.08
Greek (0)	48	0.15
Hungarian (0)	22	0.07
Irish (785)	2,922	9.05
Italian (129)	485	1.50
Latvian (15)	15	0.05
Norwegian (35)	78	0.24
Pennsylvania German (0)	23	0.07
Polish (204)	475	1.47
Portuguese (0)	16	0.05
Russian (24)	180	0.56
Scotch-Irish (265)	665	2.06
Scottish (163)	457	1.42
Slovene (0)	8	0.02
Swedish (15)	55	0.17
Swiss (12)	123	0.38
Welsh (95)	274	0.85
West Indian, ex. Hispanic (42)	90	0.28
Dutch West Indian (42)	42	0.13
Jamaican (0)	48	0.15

Hispanic Origin	Population	%
Hispanic or Latino (of any race)	5,537	16.78
Central American, ex. Mexican	210	0.64
Costa Rican	5	0.02
Guatemalan	11	0.03
Honduran	30	0.09
Nicaraguan	9	0.03
Panamanian	4	0.01
Salvadoran	150	0.45
Other Central American	1	<0.01
Cuban	27	0.08
Dominican Republic	9	0.03
Mexican	4,742	14.37
Puerto Rican	79	0.24
South American	71	0.22
Argentinean	3	0.01
Bolivian	3	0.01
Chilean	4	0.01
Colombian	31	0.09
Ecuadorian	7	0.02
Peruvian	15	0.05
Uruguayan	2	0.01
Venezuelan	6	0.02
Other Hispanic or Latino	399	1.21

Race*	Population	%
African-American/Black (9,489)	9,821	29.76
Not Hispanic (9,371)	9,665	29.29
Hispanic (118)	156	0.47
American Indian/Alaska Native (167)	350	1.06
Not Hispanic (93)	246	0.75
Hispanic (74)	104	0.32
Apache (0)	7	0.02
Blackfeet (0)	4	0.01
Cherokee (15)	78	0.24
Chickasaw (0)	2	0.01
Chippewa (2)	5	0.02
Choctaw (8)	26	0.08
Comanche (1)	3	0.01
Creek (1)	2	0.01
Crow (0)	1	<0.01
Delaware (2)	2	0.01
Houma (1)	4	0.01
Iroquois (1)	4	0.01
Menominee (1)	1	<0.01
Mexican American Ind. (13)	20	0.06
Navajo (4)	5	0.02
Osage (1)	1	<0.01
Potawatomi (1)	1	<0.01
Pueblo (2)	2	0.01
Seminole (1)	1	<0.01
Sioux (1)	1	<0.01
Asian (597)	720	2.18
Not Hispanic (580)	690	2.09
Hispanic (17)	30	0.09
Burmese (7)	9	0.03
Cambodian (53)	56	0.17
Chinese, ex. Taiwanese (120)	146	0.44
Filipino (133)	169	0.51
Indian (90)	109	0.33
Indonesian (0)	3	0.01
Japanese (9)	30	0.09
Korean (24)	45	0.14
Laotian (2)	2	0.01
Malaysian (1)	1	<0.01
Nepalese (0)	1	<0.01
Pakistani (27)	30	0.09
Taiwanese (7)	8	0.02
Thai (4)	6	0.02
Vietnamese (95)	99	0.30
Hawaii Native/Pacific Islander (18)	44	0.13
Not Hispanic (9)	31	0.09
Hispanic (9)	13	0.04
Guamanian/Chamorro (4)	6	0.02
Native Hawaiian (10)	19	0.06
Samoan (0)	9	0.03
White (19,314)	19,947	60.45
Not Hispanic (16,885)	17,303	52.44
Hispanic (2,429)	2,644	8.01

Nederland

Place Type: City
County: Jefferson
Population: 17,547†

Ancestry‡	Population	%
African, Sub-Saharan (12)	12	0.07
African (12)	12	0.07
American (1,477)	1,477	8.50
Armenian (0)	18	0.10
British (95)	113	0.65
Cajun (377)	668	3.84
Czech (56)	230	1.32
Danish (0)	61	0.35
Dutch (63)	228	1.31
English (499)	1,555	8.94
European (61)	97	0.56
French, ex. Basque (1,210)	2,682	15.43
French Canadian (206)	329	1.89
German (702)	2,492	14.33
Greek (11)	11	0.06
Irish (585)	2,327	13.39
Italian (211)	749	4.31
Norwegian (12)	67	0.39
Polish (45)	77	0.44
Portuguese (9)	9	0.05
Russian (0)	27	0.16
Scandinavian (0)	26	0.15
Scotch-Irish (169)	359	2.06
Scottish (145)	285	1.64
Slavic (12)	12	0.07
Swedish (66)	135	0.78
Swiss (0)	10	0.06
Welsh (25)	101	0.58

Hispanic Origin	Population	%
Hispanic or Latino (of any race)	1,871	10.66
Central American, ex. Mexican	90	0.51
Guatemalan	6	0.03
Honduran	49	0.28
Nicaraguan	24	0.14
Panamanian	4	0.02
Salvadoran	3	0.02
Other Central American	4	0.02
Cuban	15	0.09
Dominican Republic	2	0.01
Mexican	1,469	8.37
Puerto Rican	53	0.30
South American	41	0.23
Bolivian	1	0.01
Colombian	20	0.11
Ecuadorian	5	0.03
Paraguayan	2	0.01
Peruvian	1	0.01
Uruguayan	2	0.01
Venezuelan	9	0.05
Other South American	1	0.01
Other Hispanic or Latino	201	1.15

Race*	Population	%
African-American/Black (703)	786	4.48
Not Hispanic (686)	749	4.27
Hispanic (17)	37	0.21
American Indian/Alaska Native (55)	118	0.67
Not Hispanic (46)	99	0.56
Hispanic (9)	19	0.11
Apache (4)	7	0.04
Blackfeet (0)	1	0.01
Cherokee (7)	22	0.13
Chickasaw (3)	3	0.02
Chippewa (2)	4	0.02
Choctaw (6)	12	0.07
Comanche (1)	1	0.01
Cree (1)	2	0.01
Creek (3)	4	0.02
Delaware (1)	1	0.01
Houma (0)	1	0.01
Mexican American Ind. (2)	2	0.01
Navajo (1)	1	0.01
Seminole (0)	1	0.01
Tlingit-Haida *(Alaska Native)* (0)	1	0.01
Asian (492)	569	3.24
Not Hispanic (487)	556	3.17
Hispanic (5)	13	0.07
Cambodian (0)	1	0.01
Chinese, ex. Taiwanese (12)	23	0.13
Filipino (43)	57	0.32
Indian (153)	171	0.97
Japanese (5)	15	0.09
Korean (3)	11	0.06
Pakistani (50)	55	0.31
Thai (0)	4	0.02

*Notes: † The Census 2010 population figure is used to calculate the percentages in the Hispanic Origin and Race categories. Ancestry percentages are based on the 2006-2010 American Community Survey population (not shown); ‡ Numbers in parentheses indicate the number of people reporting a single ancestry; * Numbers in parentheses indicate the number of persons reporting this race alone, not in combination with any other race; Please refer to the Explanation of Data for more information.*

Vietnamese (202)	224	1.28
Hawaii Native/Pacific Islander (3)	12	0.07
Not Hispanic (2)	5	0.03
Hispanic (1)	7	0.04
Guamanian/Chamorro (0)	1	0.01
Native Hawaiian (0)	8	0.05
Samoan (0)	1	0.01
White (15,406)	15,673	89.32
Not Hispanic (14,254)	14,407	82.11
Hispanic (1,152)	1,266	7.21

New Braunfels

Place Type: City
County: Comal
Population: 57,740†

Ancestry‡	Population	%
African, Sub-Saharan (64)	64	0.12
African (64)	64	0.12
American (2,898)	2,898	5.36
Arab (18)	111	0.21
Arab (18)	18	0.03
Lebanese (0)	60	0.11
Palestinian (0)	33	0.06
Armenian (8)	8	0.01
Austrian (0)	65	0.12
Belgian (12)	12	0.02
British (70)	132	0.24
Cajun (0)	10	0.02
Canadian (82)	96	0.18
Celtic (0)	95	0.18
Croatian (15)	27	0.05
Czech (246)	750	1.39
Czechoslovakian (10)	21	0.04
Danish (94)	359	0.66
Dutch (140)	506	0.94
English (1,754)	4,726	8.74
European (297)	357	0.66
Finnish (0)	23	0.04
French, ex. Basque (486)	1,937	3.58
French Canadian (51)	242	0.45
German (6,706)	13,502	24.97
Greek (0)	24	0.04
Hungarian (57)	169	0.31
Irish (1,670)	5,687	10.52
Italian (808)	1,763	3.26
Lithuanian (35)	47	0.09
Luxemburger (15)	15	0.03
Northern European (12)	40	0.07
Norwegian (71)	234	0.43
Polish (246)	645	1.19
Portuguese (9)	72	0.13
Romanian (24)	50	0.09
Russian (13)	64	0.12
Scandinavian (26)	26	0.05
Scotch-Irish (394)	1,008	1.86
Scottish (384)	1,418	2.62
Slavic (14)	14	0.03
Slovak (30)	48	0.09
Slovene (0)	19	0.04
Swedish (140)	502	0.93
Swiss (41)	181	0.33
Ukrainian (52)	52	0.10
Welsh (63)	431	0.80

Hispanic Origin	Population	%
Hispanic or Latino (of any race)	20,230	35.04
Central American, ex. Mexican	257	0.45
Costa Rican	15	0.03
Guatemalan	55	0.10
Honduran	37	0.06
Nicaraguan	24	0.04
Panamanian	27	0.05
Salvadoran	99	0.17
Cuban	81	0.14
Dominican Republic	18	0.03
Mexican	17,492	30.29
Puerto Rican	295	0.51
South American	120	0.21
Argentinean	15	0.03
Bolivian	2	<0.01
Chilean	2	<0.01
Colombian	37	0.06
Ecuadorian	12	0.02
Peruvian	35	0.06
Uruguayan	1	<0.01
Venezuelan	15	0.03
Other South American	1	<0.01
Other Hispanic or Latino	1,967	3.41

Race*	Population	%
African-American/Black (1,081)	1,366	2.37
Not Hispanic (990)	1,156	2.00
Hispanic (91)	210	0.36
American Indian/Alaska Native (385)	689	1.19
Not Hispanic (175)	372	0.64
Hispanic (210)	317	0.55
Alaska Athabascan *(Ala. Nat.)* (2)	2	<0.01
Aleut *(Alaska Native)* (1)	1	<0.01
Apache (10)	21	0.04
Blackfeet (0)	9	0.02
Canadian/French Am. Ind. (2)	2	<0.01
Cherokee (40)	100	0.17
Cheyenne (2)	2	<0.01
Chickasaw (23)	32	0.06
Chippewa (6)	7	0.01
Choctaw (21)	37	0.06
Comanche (2)	5	0.01
Creek (1)	9	0.02
Delaware (6)	7	0.01
Iroquois (3)	9	0.02
Kiowa (5)	5	0.01
Mexican American Ind. (28)	32	0.06
Navajo (18)	23	0.04
Osage (2)	7	0.01
Ottawa (9)	9	0.02
Paiute (0)	3	0.01
Pueblo (1)	2	<0.01
Seminole (1)	4	0.01
Sioux (1)	9	0.02
Spanish American Ind. (2)	3	0.01
Tlingit-Haida *(Alaska Native)* (2)	2	<0.01
Yaqui (3)	4	0.01
Asian (595)	852	1.48
Not Hispanic (570)	760	1.32
Hispanic (25)	92	0.16
Burmese (1)	2	<0.01
Cambodian (8)	11	0.02
Chinese, ex. Taiwanese (57)	93	0.16
Filipino (120)	190	0.33
Hmong (1)	2	<0.01
Indian (155)	176	0.30
Indonesian (2)	3	0.01
Japanese (39)	85	0.15
Korean (40)	79	0.14
Laotian (3)	3	0.01
Malaysian (3)	6	0.01
Nepalese (1)	1	<0.01
Pakistani (16)	17	0.03
Taiwanese (12)	12	0.02
Thai (10)	22	0.04
Vietnamese (107)	130	0.23
Hawaii Native/Pacific Islander (24)	92	0.16
Not Hispanic (21)	49	0.08
Hispanic (3)	43	0.07
Guamanian/Chamorro (10)	17	0.03
Native Hawaiian (6)	39	0.07
Samoan (5)	11	0.02
White (50,132)	51,299	88.84
Not Hispanic (35,132)	35,663	61.76
Hispanic (15,000)	15,636	27.08

New Territory

Place Type: CDP
County: Fort Bend
Population: 15,186†

Ancestry‡	Population	%
African, Sub-Saharan (179)	221	1.32
Ethiopian (73)	73	0.43
Nigerian (63)	105	0.62
South African (43)	43	0.26
American (563)	563	3.35
Arab (173)	185	1.10
Arab (46)	46	0.27
Palestinian (59)	59	0.35
Syrian (0)	12	0.07
Other Arab (68)	68	0.40
Australian (28)	28	0.17
Austrian (28)	55	0.33
British (13)	29	0.17
Cajun (21)	21	0.12
Canadian (12)	25	0.15
Czech (60)	93	0.55
Danish (43)	89	0.53
Dutch (73)	307	1.83
Eastern European (14)	14	0.08
English (284)	793	4.72
Estonian (0)	15	0.09
European (200)	200	1.19
French, ex. Basque (68)	329	1.96
German (624)	1,765	10.51
Greek (228)	405	2.41
Hungarian (0)	16	0.10
Iranian (13)	41	0.24
Irish (227)	1,148	6.83
Italian (168)	751	4.47
New Zealander (39)	39	0.23
Norwegian (0)	60	0.36
Polish (108)	242	1.44
Russian (0)	39	0.23
Scandinavian (0)	34	0.20
Scotch-Irish (119)	225	1.34
Scottish (58)	229	1.36
Serbian (16)	16	0.10
Slovak (0)	11	0.07
Slovene (0)	47	0.28
Swedish (14)	38	0.23
Swiss (0)	9	0.05
Turkish (13)	26	0.15
Ukrainian (0)	26	0.15
Welsh (29)	127	0.76
West Indian, ex. Hispanic (46)	46	0.27
Haitian (15)	15	0.09
Trinidadian/Tobagonian (31)	31	0.18
Yugoslavian (13)	13	0.08

Hispanic Origin	Population	%
Hispanic or Latino (of any race)	1,258	8.28
Central American, ex. Mexican	98	0.65
Costa Rican	3	0.02
Guatemalan	2	0.01
Honduran	15	0.10
Nicaraguan	18	0.12
Panamanian	3	0.02
Salvadoran	52	0.34
Other Central American	5	0.03
Cuban	48	0.32
Dominican Republic	20	0.13
Mexican	801	5.27
Puerto Rican	37	0.24
South American	174	1.15
Argentinean	22	0.14
Bolivian	9	0.06
Chilean	6	0.04
Colombian	65	0.43
Ecuadorian	21	0.14
Paraguayan	2	0.01
Peruvian	11	0.07
Uruguayan	2	0.01
Venezuelan	36	0.24
Other Hispanic or Latino	80	0.53

Race*	Population	%
African-American/Black (962)	1,050	6.91
Not Hispanic (948)	1,027	6.76
Hispanic (14)	23	0.15

SECTION TWO

*Notes: † The Census 2010 population figure is used to calculate the percentages in the Hispanic Origin and Race categories. Ancestry percentages are based on the 2006-2010 American Community Survey population (not shown); ‡ Numbers in parentheses indicate the number of people reporting a single ancestry; * Numbers in parentheses indicate the number of persons reporting this race alone, not in combination with any other race; Please refer to the Explanation of Data for more information.*

American Indian/Alaska Native (23)	86	0.57
Not Hispanic (15)	64	0.42
Hispanic (8)	22	0.14
Blackfeet (0)	2	0.01
Canadian/French Am. Ind. (0)	1	0.01
Cherokee (4)	7	0.05
Chickasaw (0)	5	0.03
Choctaw (0)	3	0.02
Creek (0)	1	0.01
Kiowa (0)	2	0.01
Osage (1)	2	0.01
Sioux (1)	1	0.01
Spanish American Ind. (4)	4	0.03
Asian (6,209)	6,627	43.64
Not Hispanic (6,188)	6,585	43.36
Hispanic (21)	42	0.28
Bangladeshi (26)	32	0.21
Burmese (3)	4	0.03
Chinese, ex. Taiwanese (972)	1,012	6.66
Filipino (386)	420	2.77
Indian (2,660)	2,829	18.63
Indonesian (32)	37	0.24
Japanese (20)	38	0.25
Korean (32)	47	0.31
Malaysian (6)	6	0.04
Nepalese (5)	6	0.04
Pakistani (1,414)	1,501	9.88
Sri Lankan (5)	5	0.03
Taiwanese (129)	131	0.86
Thai (17)	23	0.15
Vietnamese (312)	337	2.22
Hawaii Native/Pacific Islander (9)	35	0.23
Not Hispanic (9)	33	0.22
Hispanic (0)	2	0.01
Guamanian/Chamorro (1)	2	0.01
Marshallese (2)	2	0.01
Native Hawaiian (1)	5	0.03
Samoan (0)	1	0.01
White (7,204)	7,582	49.93
Not Hispanic (6,243)	6,558	43.18
Hispanic (961)	1,024	6.74

North Richland Hills

Place Type: City
County: Tarrant
Population: 63,343†

Ancestry‡	Population	%
Afghan (18)	25	0.04
African, Sub-Saharan (293)	322	0.52
African (125)	154	0.25
Kenyan (40)	40	0.06
Nigerian (74)	74	0.12
South African (10)	10	0.02
Other Sub-Saharan African (44)	44	0.07
Albanian (132)	132	0.21
American (9,156)	9,156	14.78
Arab (742)	840	1.36
Arab (438)	438	0.71
Egyptian (133)	133	0.21
Jordanian (20)	20	0.03
Lebanese (106)	204	0.33
Moroccan (36)	36	0.06
Syrian (9)	9	0.01
Armenian (0)	17	0.03
Australian (11)	11	0.02
Austrian (32)	44	0.07
Belgian (9)	41	0.07
Brazilian (10)	10	0.02
British (226)	264	0.43
Bulgarian (11)	11	0.02
Cajun (57)	67	0.11
Canadian (32)	214	0.35
Czech (212)	563	0.91
Czechoslovakian (0)	18	0.03
Danish (41)	173	0.28
Dutch (231)	1,009	1.63
English (2,491)	7,514	12.13
European (465)	553	0.89
Finnish (12)	12	0.02
French, ex. Basque (588)	1,605	2.59
French Canadian (191)	250	0.40
German (2,793)	9,645	15.57
Greek (136)	326	0.53
Hungarian (40)	124	0.20
Iranian (51)	51	0.08
Irish (2,219)	7,735	12.48
Italian (737)	1,652	2.67
Lithuanian (14)	120	0.19
Northern European (0)	11	0.02
Norwegian (101)	395	0.64
Pennsylvania German (0)	24	0.04
Polish (523)	1,336	2.16
Portuguese (7)	17	0.03
Russian (48)	377	0.61
Scandinavian (37)	120	0.19
Scotch-Irish (707)	1,710	2.76
Scottish (498)	1,465	2.36
Slavic (0)	5	0.01
Slovak (0)	50	0.08
Slovene (13)	13	0.02
Swedish (110)	646	1.04
Swiss (0)	154	0.25
Turkish (17)	17	0.03
Welsh (169)	473	0.76
West Indian, ex. Hispanic (19)	77	0.12
Belizean (8)	16	0.03
British West Indian (11)	11	0.02
Dutch West Indian (0)	13	0.02
West Indian (0)	37	0.06
Yugoslavian (33)	33	0.05

Hispanic Origin	Population	%
Hispanic or Latino (of any race)	9,906	15.64
Central American, ex. Mexican	492	0.78
Costa Rican	25	0.04
Guatemalan	60	0.09
Honduran	80	0.13
Nicaraguan	23	0.04
Panamanian	41	0.06
Salvadoran	261	0.41
Other Central American	2	<0.01
Cuban	111	0.18
Dominican Republic	30	0.05
Mexican	7,710	12.17
Puerto Rican	540	0.85
South American	260	0.41
Argentinean	42	0.07
Bolivian	12	0.02
Chilean	15	0.02
Colombian	61	0.10
Ecuadorian	33	0.05
Peruvian	68	0.11
Uruguayan	7	0.01
Venezuelan	19	0.03
Other South American	3	<0.01
Other Hispanic or Latino	763	1.20

Race*	Population	%
African-American/Black (3,031)	3,467	5.47
Not Hispanic (2,894)	3,230	5.10
Hispanic (137)	237	0.37
American Indian/Alaska Native (456)	928	1.47
Not Hispanic (339)	722	1.14
Hispanic (117)	206	0.33
Alaska Athabascan *(Ala. Nat.)* (3)	4	0.01
Aleut *(Alaska Native)* (4)	4	0.01
Apache (8)	17	0.03
Arapaho (1)	1	<0.01
Blackfeet (2)	15	0.02
Canadian/French Am. Ind. (1)	3	<0.01
Cherokee (67)	180	0.28
Chickasaw (24)	45	0.07
Chippewa (3)	4	0.01
Choctaw (64)	107	0.17
Colville (0)	2	<0.01
Comanche (6)	24	0.04
Cree (3)	4	0.01
Creek (10)	21	0.03
Crow (2)	2	<0.01
Houma (3)	4	0.01
Inupiat *(Alaska Native)* (0)	1	<0.01
Iroquois (6)	7	0.01
Kiowa (3)	11	0.02
Lumbee (3)	7	0.01
Mexican American Ind. (8)	14	0.02
Navajo (8)	11	0.02
Osage (5)	9	0.01
Ottawa (0)	1	<0.01
Paiute (0)	4	0.01
Potawatomi (1)	3	<0.01
Pueblo (2)	3	<0.01
Seminole (1)	10	0.02
Sioux (22)	29	0.05
South American Ind. (4)	4	0.01
Spanish American Ind. (1)	1	<0.01
Ute (1)	1	<0.01
Yaqui (0)	1	<0.01
Yup'ik *(Alaska Native)* (1)	2	<0.01
Asian (1,770)	2,199	3.47
Not Hispanic (1,750)	2,098	3.31
Hispanic (20)	101	0.16
Bangladeshi (9)	9	0.01
Burmese (29)	29	0.05
Cambodian (14)	19	0.03
Chinese, ex. Taiwanese (156)	240	0.38
Filipino (133)	256	0.40
Hmong (2)	4	0.01
Indian (311)	348	0.55
Indonesian (2)	4	0.01
Japanese (53)	124	0.20
Korean (142)	188	0.30
Laotian (156)	172	0.27
Nepalese (66)	66	0.10
Pakistani (83)	90	0.14
Sri Lankan (10)	10	0.02
Taiwanese (7)	14	0.02
Thai (62)	84	0.13
Vietnamese (460)	519	0.82
Hawaii Native/Pacific Islander (89)	189	0.30
Not Hispanic (78)	137	0.22
Hispanic (11)	52	0.08
Guamanian/Chamorro (16)	23	0.04
Marshallese (0)	1	<0.01
Native Hawaiian (8)	49	0.08
Samoan (12)	26	0.04
Tongan (31)	38	0.06
White (53,076)	54,571	86.15
Not Hispanic (47,290)	48,252	76.18
Hispanic (5,786)	6,319	9.98

Odessa

Place Type: City
County: Ector
Population: 99,940†

Ancestry‡	Population	%
African, Sub-Saharan (249)	509	0.52
African (181)	441	0.45
Nigerian (68)	68	0.07
Alsatian (21)	58	0.06
American (5,575)	5,575	5.71
Arab (99)	231	0.24
Arab (76)	105	0.11
Iraqi (9)	9	0.01
Jordanian (0)	12	0.01
Lebanese (0)	15	0.02
Palestinian (14)	90	0.09
Austrian (135)	246	0.25
Basque (0)	64	0.07
Belgian (11)	11	0.01
Brazilian (8)	23	0.02
British (125)	227	0.23
Cajun (18)	18	0.02
Canadian (69)	195	0.20
Celtic (49)	69	0.07
Czech (49)	98	0.10
Czechoslovakian (36)	66	0.07

*Notes: † The Census 2010 population figure is used to calculate the percentages in the Hispanic Origin and Race categories. Ancestry percentages are based on the 2006-2010 American Community Survey population (not shown); ‡ Numbers in parentheses indicate the number of people reporting a single ancestry; * Numbers in parentheses indicate the number of persons reporting this race alone, not in combination with any other race; Please refer to the Explanation of Data for more information.*

Danish (23)	50	0.05
Dutch (86)	704	0.72
English (2,506)	5,676	5.81
European (360)	375	0.38
French, ex. Basque (293)	1,724	1.77
French Canadian (68)	151	0.15
German (2,570)	7,665	7.85
Greek (26)	41	0.04
Guyanese (14)	14	0.01
Hungarian (16)	65	0.07
Iranian (21)	21	0.02
Irish (1,967)	6,020	6.16
Italian (251)	805	0.82
Norwegian (164)	555	0.57
Polish (110)	399	0.41
Portuguese (23)	38	0.04
Russian (9)	23	0.02
Scandinavian (28)	34	0.03
Scotch-Irish (654)	1,553	1.59
Scottish (399)	1,232	1.26
Slavic (0)	12	0.01
Swedish (497)	750	0.77
Swiss (0)	39	0.04
Ukrainian (32)	41	0.04
Welsh (117)	258	0.26
West Indian, ex. Hispanic (10)	210	0.22
Dutch West Indian (10)	189	0.19
Jamaican (0)	21	0.02

Hispanic Origin	Population	%
Hispanic or Latino (of any race)	50,601	50.63
Central American, ex. Mexican	120	0.12
Guatemalan	18	0.02
Honduran	32	0.03
Nicaraguan	10	0.01
Panamanian	10	0.01
Salvadoran	46	0.05
Other Central American	4	<0.01
Cuban	79	0.08
Dominican Republic	8	0.01
Mexican	46,042	46.07
Puerto Rican	178	0.18
South American	139	0.14
Argentinean	12	0.01
Bolivian	15	0.02
Chilean	2	<0.01
Colombian	37	0.04
Ecuadorian	1	<0.01
Peruvian	43	0.04
Venezuelan	28	0.03
Other South American	1	<0.01
Other Hispanic or Latino	4,035	4.04

Race*	Population	%
African-American/Black (5,736)	6,322	6.33
Not Hispanic (5,330)	5,708	5.71
Hispanic (406)	614	0.61
American Indian/Alaska Native (960)	1,517	1.52
Not Hispanic (445)	821	0.82
Hispanic (515)	696	0.70
Alaska Athabascan *(Ala. Nat.)* (1)	1	<0.01
Apache (62)	97	0.10
Blackfeet (2)	19	0.02
Canadian/French Am. Ind. (0)	2	<0.01
Cherokee (86)	232	0.23
Chickasaw (29)	51	0.05
Chippewa (8)	16	0.02
Choctaw (63)	111	0.11
Comanche (16)	43	0.04
Cree (0)	2	<0.01
Creek (12)	21	0.02
Crow (1)	2	<0.01
Delaware (3)	3	<0.01
Hopi (1)	1	<0.01
Iroquois (3)	5	0.01
Kiowa (4)	4	<0.01
Lumbee (0)	2	<0.01
Menominee (3)	3	<0.01
Mexican American Ind. (57)	83	0.08
Navajo (25)	35	0.04
Osage (11)	14	0.01
Paiute (3)	3	<0.01
Pima (1)	1	<0.01
Potawatomi (7)	13	0.01
Pueblo (4)	9	0.01
Seminole (1)	4	<0.01
Shoshone (2)	2	<0.01
Sioux (5)	12	0.01
Spanish American Ind. (1)	3	<0.01
Tlingit-Haida *(Alaska Native)* (0)	1	<0.01
Tohono O'Odham (5)	5	0.01
Yaqui (2)	5	0.01
Yuman (0)	4	<0.01
Asian (1,115)	1,348	1.35
Not Hispanic (1,056)	1,202	1.20
Hispanic (59)	146	0.15
Bangladeshi (5)	5	0.01
Burmese (6)	6	0.01
Cambodian (17)	18	0.02
Chinese, ex. Taiwanese (94)	117	0.12
Filipino (420)	492	0.49
Indian (281)	298	0.30
Indonesian (2)	2	<0.01
Japanese (22)	68	0.07
Korean (41)	80	0.08
Laotian (9)	9	0.01
Malaysian (3)	4	<0.01
Pakistani (29)	31	0.03
Sri Lankan (1)	1	<0.01
Taiwanese (3)	3	<0.01
Thai (20)	29	0.03
Vietnamese (149)	155	0.16
Hawaii Native/Pacific Islander (104)	165	0.17
Not Hispanic (92)	121	0.12
Hispanic (12)	44	0.04
Fijian (1)	1	<0.01
Guamanian/Chamorro (26)	44	0.04
Native Hawaiian (33)	64	0.06
Samoan (8)	13	0.01
White (75,320)	77,587	77.63
Not Hispanic (41,492)	42,316	42.34
Hispanic (33,828)	35,271	35.29

Orange

Place Type: City
County: Orange
Population: 18,595†

Ancestry‡	Population	%
African, Sub-Saharan (176)	176	0.93
African (75)	75	0.40
Kenyan (90)	90	0.48
Nigerian (11)	11	0.06
American (1,053)	1,053	5.57
Austrian (8)	43	0.23
British (32)	107	0.57
Cajun (208)	326	1.72
Czech (17)	85	0.45
Czechoslovakian (31)	31	0.16
Danish (0)	88	0.47
Dutch (16)	140	0.74
Eastern European (9)	9	0.05
English (657)	1,579	8.35
European (96)	96	0.51
French, ex. Basque (582)	1,629	8.61
French Canadian (548)	803	4.24
German (456)	1,749	9.24
Hungarian (0)	16	0.08
Irish (530)	1,765	9.33
Italian (129)	248	1.31
Lithuanian (22)	22	0.12
Norwegian (0)	35	0.18
Polish (32)	32	0.17
Portuguese (0)	46	0.24
Romanian (44)	44	0.23
Russian (7)	15	0.08
Scandinavian (31)	31	0.16
Scotch-Irish (138)	280	1.48
Scottish (43)	174	0.92
Slovak (14)	30	0.16
Swedish (15)	30	0.16
Swiss (0)	12	0.06
Ukrainian (0)	17	0.09
Welsh (0)	24	0.13
West Indian, ex. Hispanic (0)	20	0.11
Jamaican (0)	20	0.11
Yugoslavian (0)	15	0.08

Hispanic Origin	Population	%
Hispanic or Latino (of any race)	976	5.25
Central American, ex. Mexican	49	0.26
Costa Rican	1	0.01
Guatemalan	11	0.06
Honduran	14	0.08
Nicaraguan	13	0.07
Salvadoran	10	0.05
Cuban	5	0.03
Dominican Republic	1	0.01
Mexican	742	3.99
Puerto Rican	39	0.21
South American	7	0.04
Argentinean	1	0.01
Bolivian	1	0.01
Chilean	1	0.01
Ecuadorian	2	0.01
Peruvian	1	0.01
Venezuelan	1	0.01
Other Hispanic or Latino	133	0.72

Race*	Population	%
African-American/Black (6,169)	6,364	34.22
Not Hispanic (6,131)	6,317	33.97
Hispanic (38)	47	0.25
American Indian/Alaska Native (63)	153	0.82
Not Hispanic (56)	132	0.71
Hispanic (7)	21	0.11
Blackfeet (0)	1	0.01
Canadian/French Am. Ind. (0)	1	0.01
Cherokee (8)	34	0.18
Chickasaw (0)	1	0.01
Choctaw (5)	13	0.07
Creek (1)	4	0.02
Iroquois (0)	3	0.02
Mexican American Ind. (3)	6	0.03
Navajo (1)	1	0.01
Osage (0)	1	0.01
Paiute (2)	2	0.01
Potawatomi (1)	1	0.01
South American Ind. (0)	4	0.02
Asian (311)	361	1.94
Not Hispanic (309)	356	1.91
Hispanic (2)	5	0.03
Bangladeshi (7)	10	0.05
Cambodian (15)	15	0.08
Chinese, ex. Taiwanese (18)	27	0.15
Filipino (29)	32	0.17
Indian (66)	78	0.42
Indonesian (1)	1	0.01
Japanese (8)	14	0.08
Korean (13)	17	0.09
Laotian (3)	3	0.02
Malaysian (0)	1	0.01
Pakistani (11)	12	0.06
Taiwanese (1)	2	0.01
Vietnamese (115)	122	0.66
Hawaii Native/Pacific Islander (2)	9	0.05
Not Hispanic (2)	7	0.04
Hispanic (0)	2	0.01
Guamanian/Chamorro (1)	1	0.01
Native Hawaiian (0)	4	0.02
White (11,332)	11,656	62.68
Not Hispanic (10,817)	11,068	59.52
Hispanic (515)	588	3.16

Palestine

Place Type: City
County: Anderson
Population: 18,712†

*Notes: † The Census 2010 population figure is used to calculate the percentages in the Hispanic Origin and Race categories. Ancestry percentages are based on the 2006-2010 American Community Survey population (not shown); ‡ Numbers in parentheses indicate the number of people reporting a single ancestry; * Numbers in parentheses indicate the number of persons reporting this race alone, not in combination with any other race; Please refer to the Explanation of Data for more information.*

Ancestry‡	Population	%
African, Sub-Saharan (45)	45	0.24
African (45)	45	0.24
American (1,222)	1,222	6.55
Arab (51)	51	0.27
Lebanese (43)	43	0.23
Syrian (8)	8	0.04
Belgian (0)	11	0.06
British (20)	49	0.26
Czech (21)	39	0.21
Danish (0)	11	0.06
Dutch (50)	220	1.18
English (1,437)	2,194	11.76
European (14)	30	0.16
French, ex. Basque (58)	180	0.96
French Canadian (7)	18	0.10
German (838)	1,571	8.42
Greek (7)	58	0.31
Hungarian (11)	21	0.11
Irish (500)	1,588	8.51
Italian (72)	138	0.74
Norwegian (26)	84	0.45
Polish (17)	81	0.43
Scotch-Irish (136)	322	1.73
Scottish (44)	126	0.68
Swedish (10)	16	0.09
Swiss (0)	13	0.07
West Indian, ex. Hispanic (6)	30	0.16
Dutch West Indian (6)	30	0.16

Hispanic Origin	Population	%
Hispanic or Latino (of any race)	4,101	21.92
Central American, ex. Mexican	337	1.80
Guatemalan	105	0.56
Honduran	31	0.17
Nicaraguan	5	0.03
Panamanian	8	0.04
Salvadoran	186	0.99
Other Central American	2	0.01
Cuban	5	0.03
Dominican Republic	4	0.02
Mexican	3,460	18.49
Puerto Rican	34	0.18
South American	11	0.06
Argentinean	9	0.05
Colombian	1	0.01
Peruvian	1	0.01
Other Hispanic or Latino	250	1.34

Race*	Population	%
African-American/Black (4,357)	4,563	24.39
Not Hispanic (4,297)	4,453	23.80
Hispanic (60)	110	0.59
American Indian/Alaska Native (101)	205	1.10
Not Hispanic (64)	149	0.80
Hispanic (37)	56	0.30
Aleut *(Alaska Native)* (0)	1	0.01
Apache (3)	7	0.04
Blackfeet (1)	1	0.01
Cherokee (19)	38	0.20
Chickasaw (2)	3	0.02
Chippewa (3)	4	0.02
Choctaw (6)	22	0.12
Comanche (1)	3	0.02
Creek (1)	2	0.01
Mexican American Ind. (17)	21	0.11
Navajo (2)	4	0.02
Osage (2)	3	0.02
Shoshone (1)	1	0.01
Sioux (2)	3	0.02
Tohono O'Odham (1)	1	0.01
Asian (166)	225	1.20
Not Hispanic (162)	205	1.10
Hispanic (4)	20	0.11
Cambodian (20)	21	0.11
Chinese, ex. Taiwanese (9)	12	0.06
Filipino (64)	77	0.41
Indian (16)	39	0.21
Indonesian (4)	5	0.03
Japanese (8)	16	0.09
Korean (0)	5	0.03
Laotian (1)	3	0.02
Pakistani (2)	3	0.02
Thai (2)	2	0.01
Vietnamese (32)	33	0.18
Hawaii Native/Pacific Islander (12)	49	0.26
Not Hispanic (11)	19	0.10
Hispanic (1)	30	0.16
Guamanian/Chamorro (3)	8	0.04
Native Hawaiian (9)	13	0.07
White (11,625)	12,038	64.33
Not Hispanic (9,780)	10,020	53.55
Hispanic (1,845)	2,018	10.78

Pampa

Place Type: City
County: Gray
Population: 17,994†

Ancestry‡	Population	%
American (1,745)	1,745	9.75
Belgian (0)	13	0.07
Cajun (0)	12	0.07
Canadian (20)	20	0.11
Czech (20)	33	0.18
Czechoslovakian (13)	65	0.36
Danish (0)	73	0.41
Dutch (49)	171	0.96
English (879)	2,252	12.58
European (67)	67	0.37
Finnish (21)	29	0.16
French, ex. Basque (9)	297	1.66
German (746)	2,379	13.29
Greek (14)	24	0.13
Irish (571)	1,899	10.61
Italian (57)	195	1.09
Northern European (7)	7	0.04
Norwegian (30)	120	0.67
Polish (88)	154	0.86
Russian (0)	89	0.50
Scandinavian (9)	9	0.05
Scotch-Irish (150)	337	1.88
Scottish (208)	255	1.42
Serbian (0)	12	0.07
Swedish (0)	107	0.60
Swiss (0)	10	0.06
Turkish (148)	148	0.83
Ukrainian (10)	10	0.06
Welsh (10)	81	0.45
West Indian, ex. Hispanic (37)	105	0.59
Dutch West Indian (23)	91	0.51
West Indian (14)	14	0.08

Hispanic Origin	Population	%
Hispanic or Latino (of any race)	4,681	26.01
Central American, ex. Mexican	14	0.08
Guatemalan	1	0.01
Honduran	6	0.03
Nicaraguan	2	0.01
Panamanian	1	0.01
Salvadoran	4	0.02
Cuban	6	0.03
Mexican	4,227	23.49
Puerto Rican	19	0.11
South American	2	0.01
Argentinean	1	0.01
Chilean	1	0.01
Other Hispanic or Latino	413	2.30

Race*	Population	%
African-American/Black (595)	701	3.90
Not Hispanic (558)	645	3.58
Hispanic (37)	56	0.31
American Indian/Alaska Native (150)	322	1.79
Not Hispanic (119)	246	1.37
Hispanic (31)	76	0.42
Aleut *(Alaska Native)* (1)	1	0.01
Apache (6)	11	0.06
Blackfeet (2)	7	0.04
Cherokee (24)	88	0.49
Chickasaw (7)	17	0.09
Chippewa (2)	5	0.03
Choctaw (17)	46	0.26
Comanche (1)	5	0.03
Creek (4)	11	0.06
Mexican American Ind. (7)	16	0.09
Navajo (2)	3	0.02
Osage (1)	3	0.02
Paiute (0)	1	0.01
Potawatomi (5)	5	0.03
Sioux (6)	13	0.07
Spanish American Ind. (2)	3	0.02
Yup'ik *(Alaska Native)* (1)	1	0.01
Asian (77)	111	0.62
Not Hispanic (69)	100	0.56
Hispanic (8)	11	0.06
Chinese, ex. Taiwanese (8)	13	0.07
Filipino (15)	20	0.11
Indian (22)	30	0.17
Japanese (7)	15	0.08
Korean (8)	14	0.08
Laotian (1)	1	0.01
Taiwanese (1)	3	0.02
Thai (3)	3	0.02
Vietnamese (10)	10	0.06
Hawaii Native/Pacific Islander (0)	2	0.01
Not Hispanic (0)	2	0.01
Native Hawaiian (0)	2	0.01
Samoan (0)	2	0.01
White (14,558)	14,999	83.36
Not Hispanic (12,312)	12,547	69.73
Hispanic (2,246)	2,452	13.63

Paris

Place Type: City
County: Lamar
Population: 25,171†

Ancestry‡	Population	%
African, Sub-Saharan (502)	613	2.43
African (502)	613	2.43
American (2,563)	2,563	10.14
Arab (47)	55	0.22
Lebanese (42)	50	0.20
Other Arab (5)	5	0.02
Austrian (0)	78	0.31
British (0)	7	0.03
Canadian (0)	15	0.06
Czech (13)	42	0.17
Czechoslovakian (0)	12	0.05
Danish (20)	43	0.17
Dutch (104)	385	1.52
English (768)	1,717	6.79
European (175)	228	0.90
French, ex. Basque (56)	297	1.18
French Canadian (0)	12	0.05
German (957)	2,803	11.09
Hungarian (0)	19	0.08
Icelander (0)	7	0.03
Irish (1,000)	3,640	14.40
Italian (135)	245	0.97
Norwegian (8)	65	0.26
Pennsylvania German (0)	14	0.06
Polish (22)	230	0.91
Russian (8)	26	0.10
Scotch-Irish (175)	386	1.53
Scottish (44)	161	0.64
Slavic (0)	10	0.04
Swedish (22)	98	0.39
Swiss (0)	47	0.19
Ukrainian (0)	15	0.06
Welsh (27)	139	0.55
West Indian, ex. Hispanic (0)	161	0.64
Dutch West Indian (0)	161	0.64

Hispanic Origin	Population	%
Hispanic or Latino (of any race)	2,068	8.22
Central American, ex. Mexican	46	0.18

*Notes: † The Census 2010 population figure is used to calculate the percentages in the Hispanic Origin and Race categories. Ancestry percentages are based on the 2006-2010 American Community Survey population (not shown); ‡ Numbers in parentheses indicate the number of people reporting a single ancestry; * Numbers in parentheses indicate the number of persons reporting this race alone, not in combination with any other race; Please refer to the Explanation of Data for more information.*

Costa Rican	2	0.01
Guatemalan	17	0.07
Honduran	6	0.02
Nicaraguan	4	0.02
Panamanian	7	0.03
Salvadoran	10	0.04
Cuban	10	0.04
Dominican Republic	1	<0.01
Mexican	1,841	7.31
Puerto Rican	40	0.16
South American	12	0.05
Argentinean	3	0.01
Colombian	3	0.01
Ecuadorian	2	0.01
Peruvian	3	0.01
Venezuelan	1	<0.01
Other Hispanic or Latino	118	0.47

Race*	Population	%
African-American/Black (5,881)	6,251	24.83
Not Hispanic (5,813)	6,149	24.43
Hispanic (68)	102	0.41
American Indian/Alaska Native (374)	823	3.27
Not Hispanic (296)	700	2.78
Hispanic (78)	123	0.49
Alaska Athabascan *(Ala. Nat.)* (0)	1	<0.01
Apache (2)	14	0.06
Blackfeet (1)	11	0.04
Cherokee (47)	188	0.75
Cheyenne (1)	11	0.04
Chickasaw (11)	17	0.07
Chippewa (2)	6	0.02
Choctaw (147)	275	1.09
Comanche (3)	11	0.04
Creek (1)	3	0.01
Delaware (6)	6	0.02
Houma (1)	1	<0.01
Iroquois (3)	3	0.01
Mexican American Ind. (5)	11	0.04
Navajo (3)	7	0.03
Osage (0)	1	<0.01
Ottawa (2)	3	0.01
Potawatomi (1)	3	0.01
Pueblo (1)	1	<0.01
Seminole (1)	1	<0.01
Sioux (2)	13	0.05
South American Ind. (1)	4	0.02
Spanish American Ind. (1)	1	<0.01
Ute (1)	1	<0.01
Yaqui (0)	2	0.01
Asian (227)	284	1.13
Not Hispanic (222)	274	1.09
Hispanic (5)	10	0.04
Bangladeshi (3)	3	0.01
Cambodian (10)	16	0.06
Chinese, ex. Taiwanese (24)	29	0.12
Filipino (61)	86	0.34
Indian (51)	60	0.24
Japanese (7)	9	0.04
Korean (13)	17	0.07
Nepalese (1)	1	<0.01
Pakistani (7)	9	0.04
Sri Lankan (3)	3	0.01
Taiwanese (1)	2	0.01
Thai (4)	8	0.03
Vietnamese (28)	30	0.12
Hawaii Native/Pacific Islander (6)	26	0.10
Not Hispanic (1)	19	0.08
Hispanic (5)	7	0.03
Guamanian/Chamorro (4)	8	0.03
Native Hawaiian (1)	8	0.03
Samoan (0)	6	0.02
White (16,970)	17,695	70.30
Not Hispanic (16,059)	16,664	66.20
Hispanic (911)	1,031	4.10

Pasadena

Place Type: City
County: Harris
Population: 149,043†

Ancestry‡	Population	%
African, Sub-Saharan (126)	152	0.10
African (126)	152	0.10
American (6,440)	6,440	4.38
Arab (247)	464	0.32
Arab (197)	302	0.21
Jordanian (7)	45	0.03
Lebanese (8)	56	0.04
Palestinian (35)	44	0.03
Syrian (0)	9	0.01
Other Arab (0)	8	0.01
Australian (12)	12	0.01
Austrian (13)	48	0.03
Belgian (0)	28	0.02
Brazilian (15)	15	0.01
British (114)	241	0.16
Bulgarian (0)	8	0.01
Cajun (85)	187	0.13
Canadian (38)	46	0.03
Celtic (8)	8	0.01
Croatian (0)	6	<0.01
Czech (361)	1,283	0.87
Czechoslovakian (200)	288	0.20
Danish (24)	109	0.07
Dutch (195)	1,383	0.94
Eastern European (47)	47	0.03
English (2,574)	7,366	5.01
European (1,084)	1,200	0.82
Finnish (40)	78	0.05
French, ex. Basque (860)	2,955	2.01
French Canadian (311)	374	0.25
German (3,622)	10,652	7.24
Greek (38)	87	0.06
Hungarian (45)	136	0.09
Iranian (56)	56	0.04
Irish (1,942)	8,100	5.51
Italian (840)	2,205	1.50
Lithuanian (0)	7	<0.01
Luxemburger (0)	8	0.01
Northern European (40)	40	0.03
Norwegian (146)	395	0.27
Polish (391)	808	0.55
Portuguese (11)	108	0.07
Russian (69)	224	0.15
Scandinavian (68)	113	0.08
Scotch-Irish (920)	1,789	1.22
Scottish (757)	2,020	1.37
Serbian (5)	12	0.01
Slavic (0)	52	0.04
Slovak (25)	25	0.02
Slovene (0)	63	0.04
Swedish (38)	411	0.28
Swiss (37)	283	0.19
Ukrainian (38)	38	0.03
Welsh (72)	356	0.24
West Indian, ex. Hispanic (123)	123	0.08
Bahamian (10)	10	0.01
Trinidadian/Tobagonian (56)	56	0.04
U.S. Virgin Islander (57)	57	0.04
Yugoslavian (0)	14	0.01

Hispanic Origin	Population	%
Hispanic or Latino (of any race)	92,692	62.19
Central American, ex. Mexican	4,703	3.16
Costa Rican	60	0.04
Guatemalan	544	0.36
Honduran	1,335	0.90
Nicaraguan	175	0.12
Panamanian	53	0.04
Salvadoran	2,500	1.68
Other Central American	36	0.02
Cuban	398	0.27
Dominican Republic	103	0.07
Mexican	80,575	54.06
Puerto Rican	704	0.47
South American	711	0.48
Argentinean	48	0.03
Bolivian	23	0.02
Chilean	29	0.02
Colombian	326	0.22
Ecuadorian	49	0.03
Paraguayan	6	<0.01
Peruvian	116	0.08
Uruguayan	14	0.01
Venezuelan	95	0.06
Other South American	5	<0.01
Other Hispanic or Latino	5,498	3.69

Race*	Population	%
African-American/Black (3,485)	4,137	2.78
Not Hispanic (2,965)	3,306	2.22
Hispanic (520)	831	0.56
American Indian/Alaska Native (1,110)	1,768	1.19
Not Hispanic (312)	624	0.42
Hispanic (798)	1,144	0.77
Alaska Athabascan *(Ala. Nat.)* (1)	2	<0.01
Apache (15)	30	0.02
Blackfeet (6)	10	0.01
Central American Ind. (1)	5	<0.01
Cherokee (81)	200	0.13
Cheyenne (1)	4	<0.01
Chickasaw (11)	15	0.01
Chippewa (3)	11	0.01
Choctaw (43)	63	0.04
Comanche (8)	10	0.01
Cree (3)	3	<0.01
Creek (12)	21	0.01
Crow (0)	1	<0.01
Delaware (2)	4	<0.01
Inupiat *(Alaska Native)* (1)	1	<0.01
Iroquois (4)	5	<0.01
Kiowa (2)	2	<0.01
Mexican American Ind. (150)	236	0.16
Navajo (4)	9	0.01
Osage (8)	9	0.01
Ottawa (10)	10	0.01
Paiute (1)	1	<0.01
Pueblo (9)	9	0.01
Seminole (2)	8	0.01
Shoshone (0)	3	<0.01
Sioux (9)	16	0.01
South American Ind. (7)	10	0.01
Spanish American Ind. (11)	13	0.01
Asian (3,150)	3,718	2.49
Not Hispanic (3,074)	3,471	2.33
Hispanic (76)	247	0.17
Bangladeshi (8)	9	0.01
Burmese (6)	6	<0.01
Cambodian (84)	95	0.06
Chinese, ex. Taiwanese (337)	416	0.28
Filipino (271)	387	0.26
Hmong (3)	3	<0.01
Indian (1,013)	1,097	0.74
Indonesian (10)	18	0.01
Japanese (77)	139	0.09
Korean (162)	215	0.14
Laotian (5)	9	0.01
Malaysian (2)	6	<0.01
Nepalese (11)	11	0.01
Pakistani (112)	124	0.08
Sri Lankan (7)	8	0.01
Taiwanese (42)	46	0.03
Thai (17)	29	0.02
Vietnamese (880)	951	0.64
Hawaii Native/Pacific Islander (88)	197	0.13
Not Hispanic (68)	118	0.08
Hispanic (20)	79	0.05
Guamanian/Chamorro (21)	30	0.02
Marshallese (1)	2	<0.01
Native Hawaiian (28)	56	0.04
Samoan (22)	27	0.02
White (112,253)	116,045	77.86
Not Hispanic (48,734)	49,613	33.29
Hispanic (63,519)	66,432	44.57

*Notes: † The Census 2010 population figure is used to calculate the percentages in the Hispanic Origin and Race categories. Ancestry percentages are based on the 2006-2010 American Community Survey population (not shown); ‡ Numbers in parentheses indicate the number of people reporting a single ancestry; * Numbers in parentheses indicate the number of persons reporting this race alone, not in combination with any other race; Please refer to the Explanation of Data for more information.*

Pearland

Place Type: City
County: Brazoria
Population: 91,252†

Ancestry‡	Population	%
African, Sub-Saharan (999)	1,060	1.28
African (249)	265	0.32
Cape Verdean (0)	12	0.01
Ethiopian (14)	14	0.02
Nigerian (252)	252	0.30
Sierra Leonean (39)	39	0.05
Somalian (62)	95	0.11
Other Sub-Saharan African (383)	383	0.46
American (6,664)	6,664	8.05
Arab (437)	650	0.79
Arab (0)	72	0.09
Jordanian (10)	10	0.01
Lebanese (9)	31	0.04
Moroccan (0)	26	0.03
Palestinian (14)	14	0.02
Syrian (56)	77	0.09
Other Arab (348)	420	0.51
Armenian (0)	9	0.01
Australian (48)	48	0.06
Austrian (35)	175	0.21
Basque (0)	18	0.02
Belgian (50)	50	0.06
Brazilian (16)	70	0.08
British (189)	366	0.44
Cajun (63)	188	0.23
Canadian (51)	97	0.12
Czech (445)	1,010	1.22
Czechoslovakian (32)	42	0.05
Danish (33)	176	0.21
Dutch (403)	1,007	1.22
English (2,423)	6,768	8.18
European (828)	1,019	1.23
Finnish (82)	170	0.21
French, ex. Basque (634)	2,312	2.79
French Canadian (123)	345	0.42
German (3,627)	10,115	12.22
Greek (65)	193	0.23
Hungarian (46)	181	0.22
Iranian (33)	44	0.05
Irish (1,847)	6,525	7.89
Italian (1,132)	2,756	3.33
Northern European (55)	55	0.07
Norwegian (114)	300	0.36
Pennsylvania German (30)	49	0.06
Polish (412)	971	1.17
Portuguese (41)	62	0.07
Romanian (69)	80	0.10
Russian (83)	385	0.47
Scandinavian (9)	9	0.01
Scotch-Irish (692)	1,577	1.91
Scottish (313)	1,022	1.24
Serbian (14)	14	0.02
Slavic (0)	11	0.01
Slovak (22)	74	0.09
Swedish (323)	630	0.76
Swiss (26)	199	0.24
Turkish (14)	61	0.07
Ukrainian (13)	19	0.02
Welsh (106)	408	0.49
West Indian, ex. Hispanic (270)	352	0.43
Bahamian (42)	42	0.05
Bermudan (34)	34	0.04
British West Indian (36)	60	0.07
Jamaican (82)	82	0.10
Trinidadian/Tobagonian (51)	69	0.08
West Indian (25)	65	0.08
Yugoslavian (39)	63	0.08

Hispanic Origin	Population	%
Hispanic or Latino (of any race)	18,694	20.49
Central American, ex. Mexican	886	0.97
Costa Rican	25	0.03
Guatemalan	94	0.10
Honduran	140	0.15
Nicaraguan	45	0.05
Panamanian	58	0.06
Salvadoran	516	0.57
Other Central American	8	0.01
Cuban	207	0.23
Dominican Republic	67	0.07
Mexican	14,879	16.31
Puerto Rican	544	0.60
South American	694	0.76
Argentinean	73	0.08
Bolivian	28	0.03
Chilean	25	0.03
Colombian	292	0.32
Ecuadorian	58	0.06
Paraguayan	3	<0.01
Peruvian	87	0.10
Uruguayan	6	0.01
Venezuelan	116	0.13
Other South American	6	0.01
Other Hispanic or Latino	1,417	1.55

Race*	Population	%
African-American/Black (14,962)	15,805	17.32
Not Hispanic (14,709)	15,381	16.86
Hispanic (253)	424	0.46
American Indian/Alaska Native (427)	858	0.94
Not Hispanic (255)	610	0.67
Hispanic (172)	248	0.27
Alaska Athabascan *(Ala. Nat.)* (4)	4	<0.01
Aleut *(Alaska Native)* (1)	1	<0.01
Apache (2)	7	0.01
Blackfeet (1)	9	0.01
Canadian/French Am. Ind. (4)	4	<0.01
Central American Ind. (1)	1	<0.01
Cherokee (60)	151	0.17
Cheyenne (1)	1	<0.01
Chickasaw (8)	11	0.01
Chippewa (4)	6	0.01
Choctaw (27)	58	0.06
Comanche (0)	5	0.01
Creek (8)	18	0.02
Crow (1)	1	<0.01
Delaware (2)	6	0.01
Hopi (0)	3	<0.01
Houma (1)	2	<0.01
Iroquois (2)	2	<0.01
Kiowa (0)	3	<0.01
Lumbee (1)	1	<0.01
Menominee (0)	1	<0.01
Mexican American Ind. (27)	32	0.04
Navajo (1)	3	<0.01
Osage (2)	5	0.01
Ottawa (6)	13	0.01
Potawatomi (5)	6	0.01
Pueblo (4)	4	<0.01
Seminole (2)	6	0.01
Sioux (1)	7	0.01
South American Ind. (5)	6	0.01
Spanish American Ind. (0)	6	0.01
Ute (1)	1	<0.01
Yaqui (1)	1	<0.01
Yup'ik *(Alaska Native)* (0)	1	<0.01
Asian (11,302)	12,233	13.41
Not Hispanic (11,206)	12,033	13.19
Hispanic (96)	200	0.22
Bangladeshi (78)	78	0.09
Burmese (3)	3	<0.01
Cambodian (128)	143	0.16
Chinese, ex. Taiwanese (1,530)	1,719	1.88
Filipino (2,657)	2,925	3.21
Indian (2,752)	2,919	3.20
Indonesian (30)	46	0.05
Japanese (76)	162	0.18
Korean (247)	343	0.38
Laotian (9)	15	0.02
Malaysian (7)	9	0.01
Nepalese (23)	23	0.03
Pakistani (308)	332	0.36
Sri Lankan (49)	52	0.06
Taiwanese (55)	64	0.07
Thai (34)	60	0.07
Vietnamese (3,019)	3,244	3.55
Hawaii Native/Pacific Islander (37)	149	0.16
Not Hispanic (29)	118	0.13
Hispanic (8)	31	0.03
Fijian (1)	3	<0.01
Guamanian/Chamorro (7)	12	0.01
Marshallese (0)	1	<0.01
Native Hawaiian (16)	63	0.07
Samoan (0)	14	0.02
Tongan (1)	5	0.01
White (56,553)	58,542	64.15
Not Hispanic (44,522)	45,827	50.22
Hispanic (12,031)	12,715	13.93

Pearsall

Place Type: City
County: Frio
Population: 9,146†

Ancestry‡	Population	%
African, Sub-Saharan (0)	26	0.29
African (0)	26	0.29
Alsatian (18)	18	0.20
American (528)	528	5.96
Canadian (34)	34	0.38
Czech (41)	41	0.46
English (33)	259	2.92
French, ex. Basque (4)	4	0.05
German (98)	356	4.02
Greek (0)	9	0.10
Irish (0)	142	1.60
Scotch-Irish (0)	18	0.20
Scottish (18)	256	2.89

Hispanic Origin	Population	%
Hispanic or Latino (of any race)	7,784	85.11
Central American, ex. Mexican	497	5.43
Costa Rican	2	0.02
Guatemalan	5	0.05
Honduran	333	3.64
Nicaraguan	5	0.05
Panamanian	2	0.02
Salvadoran	150	1.64
Cuban	14	0.15
Dominican Republic	44	0.48
Mexican	6,328	69.19
Puerto Rican	15	0.16
South American	22	0.24
Argentinean	1	0.01
Bolivian	1	0.01
Colombian	17	0.19
Peruvian	3	0.03
Other Hispanic or Latino	864	9.45

Race*	Population	%
African-American/Black (120)	152	1.66
Not Hispanic (77)	87	0.95
Hispanic (43)	65	0.71
American Indian/Alaska Native (44)	70	0.77
Not Hispanic (18)	30	0.33
Hispanic (26)	40	0.44
Apache (0)	2	0.02
Cherokee (5)	17	0.19
Choctaw (4)	4	0.04
Hopi (0)	1	0.01
Mexican American Ind. (3)	9	0.10
Navajo (0)	1	0.01
Osage (0)	1	0.01
Asian (305)	323	3.53
Not Hispanic (300)	310	3.39
Hispanic (5)	13	0.14
Chinese, ex. Taiwanese (160)	161	1.76
Filipino (2)	4	0.04
Indian (121)	123	1.34
Japanese (0)	2	0.02
Korean (5)	5	0.05
Pakistani (11)	13	0.14

*Notes: † The Census 2010 population figure is used to calculate the percentages in the Hispanic Origin and Race categories. Ancestry percentages are based on the 2006-2010 American Community Survey population (not shown); ‡ Numbers in parentheses indicate the number of people reporting a single ancestry; * Numbers in parentheses indicate the number of persons reporting this race alone, not in combination with any other race; Please refer to the Explanation of Data for more information.*

Race*	Population	%
Vietnamese (4)	6	0.07
Hawaii Native/Pacific Islander (0)	6	0.07
Not Hispanic (0)	2	0.02
Hispanic (0)	4	0.04
Native Hawaiian (0)	2	0.02
White (7,219)	7,362	80.49
Not Hispanic (919)	946	10.34
Hispanic (6,300)	6,416	70.15

Pecan Grove

Place Type: CDP
County: Fort Bend
Population: 15,963†

Ancestry‡	Population	%
Albanian (0)	9	0.06
American (1,521)	1,521	9.61
Arab (18)	18	0.11
Lebanese (18)	18	0.11
Austrian (0)	21	0.13
Belgian (0)	44	0.28
British (15)	42	0.27
Cajun (0)	61	0.39
Croatian (0)	14	0.09
Czech (121)	645	4.08
Danish (23)	81	0.51
Dutch (229)	414	2.62
Eastern European (25)	25	0.16
English (746)	2,017	12.75
European (289)	318	2.01
French, ex. Basque (126)	830	5.25
French Canadian (43)	68	0.43
German (1,138)	3,409	21.55
Greek (38)	38	0.24
Hungarian (32)	129	0.82
Iranian (34)	34	0.21
Irish (444)	2,053	12.98
Italian (118)	584	3.69
Macedonian (45)	45	0.28
Norwegian (94)	239	1.51
Polish (100)	302	1.91
Portuguese (16)	58	0.37
Russian (41)	82	0.52
Scandinavian (14)	14	0.09
Scotch-Irish (134)	434	2.74
Scottish (120)	403	2.55
Slavic (46)	46	0.29
Slovak (24)	24	0.15
Slovene (20)	20	0.13
Swedish (65)	218	1.38
Swiss (0)	72	0.46
Ukrainian (0)	19	0.12
Welsh (20)	109	0.69

Hispanic Origin	Population	%
Hispanic or Latino (of any race)	2,253	14.11
Central American, ex. Mexican	132	0.83
Costa Rican	4	0.03
Guatemalan	17	0.11
Honduran	26	0.16
Nicaraguan	1	0.01
Panamanian	9	0.06
Salvadoran	72	0.45
Other Central American	3	0.02
Cuban	34	0.21
Dominican Republic	6	0.04
Mexican	1,615	10.12
Puerto Rican	72	0.45
South American	133	0.83
Argentinean	19	0.12
Chilean	4	0.03
Colombian	36	0.23
Ecuadorian	13	0.08
Paraguayan	1	0.01
Peruvian	16	0.10
Uruguayan	6	0.04
Venezuelan	36	0.23
Other South American	2	0.01
Other Hispanic or Latino	261	1.64

Race*	Population	%
African-American/Black (1,018)	1,089	6.82
Not Hispanic (997)	1,048	6.57
Hispanic (21)	41	0.26
American Indian/Alaska Native (50)	119	0.75
Not Hispanic (25)	69	0.43
Hispanic (25)	50	0.31
Apache (2)	4	0.03
Central American Ind. (1)	1	0.01
Cherokee (3)	24	0.15
Choctaw (4)	10	0.06
Creek (2)	2	0.01
Kiowa (0)	1	0.01
Mexican American Ind. (2)	2	0.01
Navajo (1)	1	0.01
Osage (5)	5	0.03
Potawatomi (0)	3	0.02
Seminole (0)	1	0.01
Sioux (2)	4	0.03
South American Ind. (1)	3	0.02
Asian (312)	428	2.68
Not Hispanic (311)	409	2.56
Hispanic (1)	19	0.12
Burmese (3)	3	0.02
Cambodian (4)	4	0.03
Chinese, ex. Taiwanese (48)	78	0.49
Filipino (72)	116	0.73
Indian (45)	50	0.31
Indonesian (5)	5	0.03
Japanese (10)	23	0.14
Korean (12)	15	0.09
Laotian (2)	2	0.01
Pakistani (14)	20	0.13
Taiwanese (2)	2	0.01
Thai (6)	11	0.07
Vietnamese (66)	78	0.49
Hawaii Native/Pacific Islander (1)	6	0.04
Not Hispanic (0)	4	0.03
Hispanic (1)	2	0.01
Guamanian/Chamorro (1)	1	0.01
White (13,752)	14,042	87.97
Not Hispanic (12,160)	12,331	77.25
Hispanic (1,592)	1,711	10.72

Pecos

Place Type: City
County: Reeves
Population: 8,780†

Ancestry‡	Population	%
African, Sub-Saharan (23)	23	0.27
African (14)	14	0.16
Liberian (9)	9	0.10
American (236)	236	2.75
Canadian (10)	10	0.12
Dutch (0)	27	0.31
English (124)	232	2.70
European (13)	13	0.15
French, ex. Basque (4)	4	0.05
German (12)	44	0.51
Irish (35)	43	0.50
Italian (0)	16	0.19
Portuguese (0)	7	0.08
Scotch-Irish (42)	101	1.18
Scottish (7)	41	0.48
Swedish (8)	8	0.09

Hispanic Origin	Population	%
Hispanic or Latino (of any race)	7,302	83.17
Central American, ex. Mexican	7	0.08
Guatemalan	3	0.03
Panamanian	2	0.02
Salvadoran	2	0.02
Cuban	21	0.24
Dominican Republic	2	0.02
Mexican	6,381	72.68
Puerto Rican	7	0.08
South American	4	0.05
Bolivian	2	0.02
Colombian	1	0.01
Ecuadorian	1	0.01
Other Hispanic or Latino	880	10.02

Race*	Population	%
African-American/Black (163)	184	2.10
Not Hispanic (147)	159	1.81
Hispanic (16)	25	0.28
American Indian/Alaska Native (39)	67	0.76
Not Hispanic (7)	15	0.17
Hispanic (32)	52	0.59
Apache (3)	4	0.05
Cherokee (2)	4	0.05
Chickasaw (1)	1	0.01
Choctaw (1)	4	0.05
Comanche (0)	1	0.01
Creek (1)	1	0.01
Mexican American Ind. (1)	3	0.03
Asian (88)	100	1.14
Not Hispanic (87)	88	1.00
Hispanic (1)	12	0.14
Bangladeshi (4)	4	0.05
Cambodian (1)	1	0.01
Chinese, ex. Taiwanese (4)	9	0.10
Filipino (58)	67	0.76
Indian (9)	9	0.10
Korean (7)	7	0.08
Hawaii Native/Pacific Islander (5)	14	0.16
Not Hispanic (1)	2	0.02
Hispanic (4)	12	0.14
Guamanian/Chamorro (4)	8	0.09
Native Hawaiian (1)	1	0.01
White (6,806)	6,957	79.24
Not Hispanic (1,211)	1,229	14.00
Hispanic (5,595)	5,728	65.24

Perryton

Place Type: City
County: Ochiltree
Population: 8,802†

Ancestry‡	Population	%
American (469)	469	5.31
British (13)	31	0.35
Danish (0)	7	0.08
Dutch (45)	112	1.27
English (272)	533	6.04
European (23)	23	0.26
French, ex. Basque (34)	107	1.21
French Canadian (7)	7	0.08
German (333)	837	9.48
Greek (12)	34	0.39
Irish (463)	939	10.64
Italian (74)	141	1.60
Norwegian (0)	22	0.25
Polish (97)	122	1.38
Portuguese (7)	42	0.48
Russian (47)	47	0.53
Scotch-Irish (112)	150	1.70
Scottish (71)	173	1.96
Swedish (6)	38	0.43
Swiss (0)	32	0.36
Ukrainian (17)	17	0.19
Welsh (0)	18	0.20

Hispanic Origin	Population	%
Hispanic or Latino (of any race)	4,558	51.78
Central American, ex. Mexican	25	0.28
Guatemalan	17	0.19
Honduran	3	0.03
Nicaraguan	2	0.02
Salvadoran	3	0.03
Cuban	2	0.02
Mexican	4,408	50.08
Puerto Rican	4	0.05
South American	6	0.07
Colombian	6	0.07
Other Hispanic or Latino	113	1.28

*Notes: † The Census 2010 population figure is used to calculate the percentages in the Hispanic Origin and Race categories. Ancestry percentages are based on the 2006-2010 American Community Survey population (not shown); ‡ Numbers in parentheses indicate the number of people reporting a single ancestry; * Numbers in parentheses indicate the number of persons reporting this race alone, not in combination with any other race; Please refer to the Explanation of Data for more information.*

Race*	Population	%
African-American/Black (35)	54	0.61
Not Hispanic (16)	25	0.28
Hispanic (19)	29	0.33
American Indian/Alaska Native (95)	151	1.72
Not Hispanic (63)	97	1.10
Hispanic (32)	54	0.61
Apache (2)	4	0.05
Blackfeet (0)	1	0.01
Cherokee (23)	35	0.40
Cheyenne (0)	1	0.01
Chickasaw (1)	3	0.03
Choctaw (12)	15	0.17
Comanche (1)	3	0.03
Creek (2)	2	0.02
Kiowa (1)	1	0.01
Mexican American Ind. (4)	4	0.05
Navajo (1)	7	0.08
Seminole (0)	7	0.08
Sioux (2)	4	0.05
Spanish American Ind. (1)	1	0.01
Asian (24)	33	0.37
Not Hispanic (21)	25	0.28
Hispanic (3)	8	0.09
Chinese, ex. Taiwanese (4)	4	0.05
Filipino (5)	9	0.10
Indian (2)	4	0.05
Japanese (10)	11	0.12
Malaysian (1)	1	0.01
Hawaii Native/Pacific Islander (4)	6	0.07
Not Hispanic (3)	4	0.05
Hispanic (1)	2	0.02
Guamanian/Chamorro (1)	2	0.02
Native Hawaiian (3)	4	0.05
White (7,454)	7,647	86.88
Not Hispanic (4,088)	4,140	47.03
Hispanic (3,366)	3,507	39.84

Pflugerville

Place Type: City
County: Travis
Population: 46,936†

Ancestry‡	Population	%
African, Sub-Saharan (544)	554	1.30
African (161)	171	0.40
Ethiopian (11)	11	0.03
Nigerian (372)	372	0.87
American (1,399)	1,399	3.27
Arab (168)	306	0.72
Arab (111)	129	0.30
Lebanese (28)	138	0.32
Moroccan (29)	39	0.09
Armenian (13)	13	0.03
Austrian (0)	33	0.08
Basque (0)	12	0.03
Belgian (58)	147	0.34
British (65)	181	0.42
Canadian (24)	64	0.15
Celtic (22)	22	0.05
Croatian (36)	72	0.17
Czech (207)	951	2.22
Czechoslovakian (26)	60	0.14
Danish (60)	217	0.51
Dutch (137)	455	1.06
English (877)	3,328	7.78
European (284)	311	0.73
Finnish (0)	24	0.06
French, ex. Basque (210)	1,250	2.92
French Canadian (90)	218	0.51
German (1,839)	4,993	11.67
Greek (0)	19	0.04
Hungarian (29)	29	0.07
Irish (1,029)	3,308	7.73
Italian (180)	1,012	2.37
Lithuanian (32)	45	0.11
Luxemburger (13)	13	0.03
Norwegian (272)	575	1.34
Polish (118)	687	1.61
Portuguese (17)	63	0.15
Romanian (33)	49	0.11
Russian (41)	213	0.50
Scandinavian (0)	5	0.01
Scotch-Irish (323)	648	1.52
Scottish (269)	847	1.98
Slovak (14)	14	0.03
Swedish (155)	610	1.43
Swiss (10)	95	0.22
Turkish (82)	112	0.26
Ukrainian (9)	133	0.31
Welsh (20)	68	0.16
West Indian, ex. Hispanic (0)	81	0.19
Jamaican (0)	81	0.19

Hispanic Origin	Population	%
Hispanic or Latino (of any race)	13,024	27.75
Central American, ex. Mexican	497	1.06
Costa Rican	12	0.03
Guatemalan	89	0.19
Honduran	100	0.21
Nicaraguan	60	0.13
Panamanian	52	0.11
Salvadoran	178	0.38
Other Central American	6	0.01
Cuban	255	0.54
Dominican Republic	22	0.05
Mexican	10,676	22.75
Puerto Rican	372	0.79
South American	253	0.54
Argentinean	33	0.07
Bolivian	10	0.02
Chilean	9	0.02
Colombian	53	0.11
Ecuadorian	36	0.08
Peruvian	56	0.12
Venezuelan	54	0.12
Other South American	2	<0.01
Other Hispanic or Latino	949	2.02

Race*	Population	%
African-American/Black (7,281)	7,921	16.88
Not Hispanic (7,028)	7,492	15.96
Hispanic (253)	429	0.91
American Indian/Alaska Native (289)	588	1.25
Not Hispanic (125)	314	0.67
Hispanic (164)	274	0.58
Apache (17)	30	0.06
Blackfeet (0)	4	0.01
Canadian/French Am. Ind. (2)	3	0.01
Central American Ind. (5)	5	0.01
Cherokee (26)	103	0.22
Cheyenne (0)	4	0.01
Chickasaw (3)	10	0.02
Chippewa (3)	8	0.02
Choctaw (8)	28	0.06
Comanche (2)	7	0.01
Cree (0)	1	<0.01
Creek (1)	3	0.01
Crow (0)	1	<0.01
Delaware (1)	2	<0.01
Houma (4)	4	0.01
Inupiat *(Alaska Native)* (0)	1	<0.01
Iroquois (4)	8	0.02
Mexican American Ind. (19)	35	0.07
Navajo (7)	9	0.02
Osage (5)	8	0.02
Ottawa (0)	3	0.01
Pueblo (0)	4	0.01
Seminole (1)	2	<0.01
Sioux (5)	6	0.01
South American Ind. (4)	4	0.01
Spanish American Ind. (0)	4	0.01
Ute (1)	1	<0.01
Asian (3,468)	3,991	8.50
Not Hispanic (3,407)	3,816	8.13
Hispanic (61)	175	0.37
Bangladeshi (28)	32	0.07
Burmese (5)	7	0.01
Cambodian (88)	104	0.22
Chinese, ex. Taiwanese (247)	323	0.69
Filipino (332)	476	1.01
Indian (554)	614	1.31
Indonesian (12)	12	0.03
Japanese (65)	164	0.35
Korean (246)	314	0.67
Laotian (9)	15	0.03
Malaysian (5)	11	0.02
Nepalese (17)	17	0.04
Pakistani (174)	194	0.41
Sri Lankan (5)	5	0.01
Taiwanese (19)	26	0.06
Thai (32)	49	0.10
Vietnamese (1,500)	1,580	3.37
Hawaii Native/Pacific Islander (64)	143	0.30
Not Hispanic (45)	95	0.20
Hispanic (19)	48	0.10
Fijian (1)	1	<0.01
Guamanian/Chamorro (13)	23	0.05
Native Hawaiian (17)	45	0.10
Samoan (12)	18	0.04
White (30,085)	31,543	67.20
Not Hispanic (22,257)	23,144	49.31
Hispanic (7,828)	8,399	17.89

Pharr

Place Type: City
County: Hidalgo
Population: 70,400†

Ancestry‡	Population	%
African, Sub-Saharan (0)	20	0.03
African (0)	20	0.03
American (437)	437	0.66
British (10)	15	0.02
Canadian (33)	33	0.05
Czech (0)	23	0.03
Danish (8)	8	0.01
Dutch (13)	115	0.17
English (345)	800	1.21
European (28)	37	0.06
Finnish (13)	17	0.03
French, ex. Basque (0)	195	0.29
French Canadian (8)	18	0.03
German (383)	980	1.48
Greek (0)	5	0.01
Hungarian (13)	13	0.02
Irish (141)	537	0.81
Italian (35)	136	0.21
Norwegian (27)	50	0.08
Polish (38)	75	0.11
Romanian (0)	4	0.01
Russian (8)	8	0.01
Scandinavian (30)	30	0.05
Scotch-Irish (138)	193	0.29
Scottish (55)	186	0.28
Swedish (45)	85	0.13
Swiss (0)	8	0.01
Ukrainian (22)	22	0.03
Welsh (0)	15	0.02

Hispanic Origin	Population	%
Hispanic or Latino (of any race)	65,496	93.03
Central American, ex. Mexican	225	0.32
Guatemalan	44	0.06
Honduran	76	0.11
Nicaraguan	23	0.03
Panamanian	11	0.02
Salvadoran	70	0.10
Other Central American	1	<0.01
Cuban	64	0.09
Dominican Republic	13	0.02
Mexican	61,340	87.13
Puerto Rican	117	0.17
South American	102	0.14
Argentinean	3	<0.01
Bolivian	2	<0.01
Chilean	4	0.01

*Notes: † The Census 2010 population figure is used to calculate the percentages in the Hispanic Origin and Race categories. Ancestry percentages are based on the 2006-2010 American Community Survey population (not shown); ‡ Numbers in parentheses indicate the number of people reporting a single ancestry; * Numbers in parentheses indicate the number of persons reporting this race alone, not in combination with any other race; Please refer to the Explanation of Data for more information.*

Colombian	49	0.07
Ecuadorian	2	<0.01
Peruvian	22	0.03
Uruguayan	3	<0.01
Venezuelan	17	0.02
Other Hispanic or Latino	3,635	5.16

Race*	Population	%
African-American/Black (401)	478	0.68
Not Hispanic (149)	161	0.23
Hispanic (252)	317	0.45
American Indian/Alaska Native (353)	484	0.69
Not Hispanic (42)	76	0.11
Hispanic (311)	408	0.58
Apache (15)	17	0.02
Central American Ind. (3)	5	0.01
Cherokee (14)	19	0.03
Chickasaw (0)	1	<0.01
Chippewa (0)	2	<0.01
Choctaw (4)	5	0.01
Comanche (0)	3	<0.01
Creek (4)	7	0.01
Delaware (3)	4	0.01
Mexican American Ind. (56)	67	0.10
Potawatomi (1)	1	<0.01
Seminole (0)	10	0.01
Sioux (0)	1	<0.01
Spanish American Ind. (6)	7	0.01
Asian (376)	476	0.68
Not Hispanic (347)	373	0.53
Hispanic (29)	103	0.15
Chinese, ex. Taiwanese (24)	30	0.04
Filipino (190)	217	0.31
Indian (60)	82	0.12
Japanese (11)	15	0.02
Korean (27)	33	0.05
Laotian (1)	1	<0.01
Pakistani (8)	8	0.01
Taiwanese (0)	1	<0.01
Thai (3)	7	0.01
Vietnamese (49)	53	0.08
Hawaii Native/Pacific Islander (0)	19	0.03
Not Hispanic (0)	2	<0.01
Hispanic (0)	17	0.02
Native Hawaiian (0)	5	0.01
Samoan (0)	1	<0.01
White (59,876)	60,926	86.54
Not Hispanic (4,256)	4,316	6.13
Hispanic (55,620)	56,610	80.41

Plainview

Place Type: City
County: Hale
Population: 22,194†

Ancestry‡	Population	%
African, Sub-Saharan (102)	138	0.63
African (102)	138	0.63
American (924)	924	4.20
Austrian (0)	10	0.05
British (60)	60	0.27
Czech (31)	41	0.19
Danish (20)	20	0.09
Dutch (27)	193	0.88
English (373)	1,007	4.57
European (73)	73	0.33
Finnish (0)	16	0.07
French, ex. Basque (83)	205	0.93
French Canadian (8)	8	0.04
German (1,056)	1,967	8.93
Iranian (14)	14	0.06
Irish (535)	1,383	6.28
Italian (67)	175	0.79
Lithuanian (9)	9	0.04
Macedonian (37)	37	0.17
Northern European (17)	17	0.08
Pennsylvania German (9)	9	0.04
Polish (44)	78	0.35
Portuguese (15)	61	0.28
Russian (0)	49	0.22
Scotch-Irish (190)	271	1.23
Scottish (60)	194	0.88
Swedish (7)	38	0.17
Swiss (0)	37	0.17
Ukrainian (24)	35	0.16
Welsh (0)	22	0.10
West Indian, ex. Hispanic (0)	16	0.07
Dutch West Indian (0)	16	0.07

Hispanic Origin	Population	%
Hispanic or Latino (of any race)	13,221	59.57
Central American, ex. Mexican	40	0.18
Guatemalan	12	0.05
Honduran	6	0.03
Nicaraguan	1	<0.01
Salvadoran	21	0.09
Cuban	25	0.11
Mexican	11,371	51.23
Puerto Rican	37	0.17
South American	3	0.01
Argentinean	1	<0.01
Colombian	2	0.01
Other Hispanic or Latino	1,745	7.86

Race*	Population	%
African-American/Black (1,152)	1,322	5.96
Not Hispanic (1,077)	1,164	5.24
Hispanic (75)	158	0.71
American Indian/Alaska Native (237)	353	1.59
Not Hispanic (65)	134	0.60
Hispanic (172)	219	0.99
Apache (11)	19	0.09
Cherokee (9)	41	0.18
Chickasaw (2)	10	0.05
Chippewa (1)	1	<0.01
Choctaw (15)	24	0.11
Comanche (1)	1	<0.01
Creek (1)	2	0.01
Crow (2)	3	0.01
Kiowa (1)	1	<0.01
Mexican American Ind. (23)	24	0.11
Navajo (18)	18	0.08
Osage (0)	1	<0.01
Ottawa (1)	4	0.02
Pueblo (1)	3	0.01
Shoshone (1)	1	<0.01
Sioux (8)	12	0.05
Yakama (1)	1	<0.01
Yaqui (1)	1	<0.01
Asian (108)	157	0.71
Not Hispanic (107)	137	0.62
Hispanic (1)	20	0.09
Bangladeshi (1)	1	<0.01
Chinese, ex. Taiwanese (32)	37	0.17
Filipino (15)	35	0.16
Indian (22)	32	0.14
Japanese (6)	16	0.07
Korean (5)	6	0.03
Sri Lankan (1)	1	<0.01
Taiwanese (1)	1	<0.01
Thai (1)	1	<0.01
Vietnamese (20)	20	0.09
Hawaii Native/Pacific Islander (20)	40	0.18
Not Hispanic (18)	25	0.11
Hispanic (2)	15	0.07
Fijian (6)	6	0.03
Guamanian/Chamorro (9)	9	0.04
Native Hawaiian (3)	10	0.05
Samoan (2)	4	0.02
White (15,212)	15,907	71.67
Not Hispanic (7,513)	7,658	34.50
Hispanic (7,699)	8,249	37.17

Plano

Place Type: City
County: Collin
Population: 259,841†

Ancestry‡	Population	%
Afghan (36)	54	0.02
African, Sub-Saharan (3,342)	3,587	1.40
African (671)	778	0.30
Cape Verdean (22)	22	0.01
Ethiopian (574)	574	0.22
Kenyan (417)	555	0.22
Nigerian (1,355)	1,355	0.53
South African (190)	190	0.07
Ugandan (48)	48	0.02
Zimbabwean (12)	12	<0.01
Other Sub-Saharan African (53)	53	0.02
Albanian (0)	15	0.01
American (17,867)	17,867	6.98
Arab (1,914)	2,465	0.96
Arab (194)	211	0.08
Egyptian (385)	385	0.15
Iraqi (114)	114	0.04
Jordanian (117)	133	0.05
Lebanese (707)	1,051	0.41
Moroccan (103)	222	0.09
Palestinian (9)	9	<0.01
Syrian (92)	92	0.04
Other Arab (193)	248	0.10
Armenian (144)	241	0.09
Assyrian/Chaldean/Syriac (8)	8	<0.01
Australian (117)	138	0.05
Austrian (152)	546	0.21
Belgian (25)	138	0.05
Brazilian (481)	515	0.20
British (659)	1,431	0.56
Bulgarian (275)	288	0.11
Cajun (61)	80	0.03
Canadian (613)	891	0.35
Celtic (18)	32	0.01
Croatian (88)	225	0.09
Czech (426)	1,343	0.52
Czechoslovakian (155)	239	0.09
Danish (221)	838	0.33
Dutch (643)	2,626	1.03
Eastern European (426)	520	0.20
English (9,057)	24,040	9.39
Estonian (15)	44	0.02
European (3,542)	4,179	1.63
Finnish (163)	413	0.16
French, ex. Basque (1,285)	6,844	2.67
French Canadian (451)	978	0.38
German (12,350)	35,329	13.80
Greek (545)	1,006	0.39
Guyanese (19)	47	0.02
Hungarian (438)	1,066	0.42
Iranian (3,197)	3,435	1.34
Irish (8,524)	26,087	10.19
Israeli (310)	420	0.16
Italian (3,428)	9,890	3.86
Latvian (0)	20	0.01
Lithuanian (44)	207	0.08
Luxemburger (32)	51	0.02
New Zealander (0)	8	<0.01
Northern European (155)	173	0.07
Norwegian (761)	2,160	0.84
Pennsylvania German (35)	88	0.03
Polish (1,407)	4,677	1.83
Portuguese (171)	499	0.19
Romanian (181)	292	0.11
Russian (1,708)	2,957	1.15
Scandinavian (119)	325	0.13
Scotch-Irish (2,217)	4,836	1.89
Scottish (2,000)	6,560	2.56
Serbian (8)	18	0.01
Slavic (10)	76	0.03
Slovak (125)	274	0.11
Slovene (47)	70	0.03
Swedish (856)	2,970	1.16
Swiss (90)	487	0.19
Turkish (405)	558	0.22
Ukrainian (173)	351	0.14
Welsh (401)	1,786	0.70
West Indian, ex. Hispanic (262)	392	0.15

SECTION TWO

*Notes: † The Census 2010 population figure is used to calculate the percentages in the Hispanic Origin and Race categories. Ancestry percentages are based on the 2006-2010 American Community Survey population (not shown); ‡ Numbers in parentheses indicate the number of people reporting a single ancestry; * Numbers in parentheses indicate the number of persons reporting this race alone, not in combination with any other race; Please refer to the Explanation of Data for more information.*

Dutch West Indian (7)	89	0.03
Jamaican (241)	276	0.11
West Indian (14)	27	0.01
Yugoslavian (212)	305	0.12

Hispanic Origin	Population	%
Hispanic or Latino (of any race)	38,174	14.69
Central American, ex. Mexican	3,833	1.48
Costa Rican	160	0.06
Guatemalan	1,097	0.42
Honduran	635	0.24
Nicaraguan	181	0.07
Panamanian	153	0.06
Salvadoran	1,544	0.59
Other Central American	63	0.02
Cuban	414	0.16
Dominican Republic	106	0.04
Mexican	27,465	10.57
Puerto Rican	1,217	0.47
South American	2,248	0.87
Argentinean	241	0.09
Bolivian	89	0.03
Chilean	151	0.06
Colombian	643	0.25
Ecuadorian	160	0.06
Paraguayan	24	0.01
Peruvian	573	0.22
Uruguayan	42	0.02
Venezuelan	289	0.11
Other South American	36	0.01
Other Hispanic or Latino	2,891	1.11

Race*	Population	%
African-American/Black (19,697)	21,580	8.31
Not Hispanic (19,199)	20,745	7.98
Hispanic (498)	835	0.32
American Indian/Alaska Native (1,138)	2,607	1.00
Not Hispanic (831)	1,994	0.77
Hispanic (307)	613	0.24
Alaska Athabascan *(Ala. Nat.)* (0)	2	<0.01
Aleut *(Alaska Native)* (3)	3	<0.01
Apache (29)	68	0.03
Blackfeet (1)	17	0.01
Canadian/French Am. Ind. (0)	6	<0.01
Central American Ind. (4)	10	<0.01
Cherokee (175)	523	0.20
Cheyenne (1)	1	<0.01
Chickasaw (42)	96	0.04
Chippewa (15)	24	0.01
Choctaw (172)	326	0.13
Comanche (8)	24	0.01
Cree (1)	2	<0.01
Creek (39)	81	0.03
Crow (1)	5	<0.01
Delaware (5)	10	<0.01
Hopi (0)	4	<0.01
Houma (1)	3	<0.01
Inupiat *(Alaska Native)* (1)	1	<0.01
Iroquois (9)	18	0.01
Kiowa (3)	14	0.01
Lumbee (0)	2	<0.01
Menominee (1)	8	<0.01
Mexican American Ind. (52)	96	0.04
Navajo (16)	34	0.01
Osage (7)	20	0.01
Ottawa (2)	2	<0.01
Pima (1)	3	<0.01
Potawatomi (22)	38	0.01
Pueblo (5)	9	<0.01
Puget Sound Salish (1)	1	<0.01
Seminole (1)	5	<0.01
Sioux (15)	47	0.02
South American Ind. (6)	22	0.01
Spanish American Ind. (2)	8	<0.01
Tohono O'Odham (3)	7	<0.01
Yaqui (0)	3	<0.01
Yup'ik *(Alaska Native)* (1)	1	<0.01
Asian (43,818)	47,565	18.31
Not Hispanic (43,659)	47,116	18.13
Hispanic (159)	449	0.17
Bangladeshi (539)	604	0.23
Bhutanese (5)	5	<0.01
Burmese (52)	60	0.02
Cambodian (153)	194	0.07
Chinese, ex. Taiwanese (12,065)	12,905	4.97
Filipino (1,647)	2,190	0.84
Hmong (5)	8	<0.01
Indian (16,939)	17,723	6.82
Indonesian (189)	224	0.09
Japanese (631)	1,005	0.39
Korean (3,223)	3,586	1.38
Laotian (90)	125	0.05
Malaysian (58)	82	0.03
Nepalese (151)	156	0.06
Pakistani (2,118)	2,314	0.89
Sri Lankan (158)	178	0.07
Taiwanese (1,386)	1,604	0.62
Thai (265)	347	0.13
Vietnamese (3,017)	3,333	1.28
Hawaii Native/Pacific Islander (149)	493	0.19
Not Hispanic (121)	401	0.15
Hispanic (28)	92	0.04
Fijian (7)	8	<0.01
Guamanian/Chamorro (67)	100	0.04
Marshallese (0)	1	<0.01
Native Hawaiian (42)	141	0.05
Samoan (14)	22	0.01
Tongan (1)	2	<0.01
White (173,865)	180,479	69.46
Not Hispanic (151,629)	156,421	60.20
Hispanic (22,236)	24,058	9.26

Pleasanton

Place Type: City
County: Atascosa
Population: 8,934†

Ancestry‡	Population	%
American (427)	427	4.82
Czech (84)	117	1.32
Dutch (178)	193	2.18
English (187)	1,008	11.37
European (47)	47	0.53
French, ex. Basque (21)	238	2.69
German (275)	839	9.47
Greek (0)	23	0.26
Irish (169)	1,018	11.49
Italian (12)	176	1.99
Norwegian (9)	9	0.10
Polish (214)	261	2.94
Russian (12)	41	0.46
Scotch-Irish (68)	164	1.85
Scottish (0)	14	0.16
Swedish (0)	26	0.29
Swiss (0)	13	0.15
Welsh (0)	14	0.16
West Indian, ex. Hispanic (0)	34	0.38
Dutch West Indian (0)	34	0.38

Hispanic Origin	Population	%
Hispanic or Latino (of any race)	5,029	56.29
Central American, ex. Mexican	6	0.07
Guatemalan	2	0.02
Honduran	1	0.01
Nicaraguan	1	0.01
Salvadoran	2	0.02
Cuban	5	0.06
Dominican Republic	1	0.01
Mexican	3,967	44.40
Puerto Rican	14	0.16
South American	14	0.16
Chilean	1	0.01
Colombian	7	0.08
Peruvian	1	0.01
Venezuelan	5	0.06
Other Hispanic or Latino	1,022	11.44

Race*	Population	%
African-American/Black (61)	75	0.84
Not Hispanic (56)	64	0.72
Hispanic (5)	11	0.12
American Indian/Alaska Native (56)	94	1.05
Not Hispanic (23)	48	0.54
Hispanic (33)	46	0.51
Apache (0)	2	0.02
Blackfeet (0)	1	0.01
Cherokee (1)	10	0.11
Cheyenne (0)	1	0.01
Chickasaw (0)	1	0.01
Choctaw (4)	5	0.06
Comanche (3)	3	0.03
Cree (0)	1	0.01
Creek (0)	1	0.01
Lumbee (2)	2	0.02
Mexican American Ind. (2)	2	0.02
Seminole (0)	1	0.01
Spanish American Ind. (1)	1	0.01
Asian (62)	82	0.92
Not Hispanic (49)	54	0.60
Hispanic (13)	28	0.31
Bangladeshi (1)	1	0.01
Cambodian (0)	10	0.11
Chinese, ex. Taiwanese (6)	18	0.20
Filipino (13)	17	0.19
Indian (7)	8	0.09
Japanese (6)	9	0.10
Korean (12)	21	0.24
Hawaii Native/Pacific Islander (7)	15	0.17
Not Hispanic (3)	10	0.11
Hispanic (4)	5	0.06
Native Hawaiian (0)	5	0.06
White (7,918)	8,072	90.35
Not Hispanic (3,721)	3,765	42.14
Hispanic (4,197)	4,307	48.21

Port Arthur

Place Type: City
County: Jefferson
Population: 53,818†

Ancestry‡	Population	%
African, Sub-Saharan (309)	509	0.95
African (309)	497	0.93
Other Sub-Saharan African (0)	12	0.02
American (1,217)	1,217	2.27
Arab (17)	35	0.07
Jordanian (7)	7	0.01
Lebanese (5)	14	0.03
Syrian (0)	9	0.02
Other Arab (5)	5	0.01
Austrian (0)	20	0.04
Belgian (0)	8	0.01
British (36)	41	0.08
Cajun (207)	343	0.64
Canadian (33)	33	0.06
Czech (11)	94	0.18
Czechoslovakian (10)	22	0.04
Danish (4)	43	0.08
Dutch (33)	225	0.42
English (606)	1,526	2.84
European (35)	35	0.07
French, ex. Basque (1,955)	3,225	6.01
French Canadian (515)	575	1.07
German (751)	2,451	4.57
Greek (9)	16	0.03
Iranian (15)	15	0.03
Irish (393)	1,797	3.35
Italian (254)	527	0.98
Norwegian (9)	20	0.04
Polish (28)	144	0.27
Portuguese (10)	10	0.02
Russian (0)	16	0.03
Scotch-Irish (151)	489	0.91
Scottish (59)	343	0.64
Serbian (0)	32	0.06
Swedish (22)	37	0.07
Swiss (0)	21	0.04
Welsh (19)	43	0.08

*Notes: † The Census 2010 population figure is used to calculate the percentages in the Hispanic Origin and Race categories. Ancestry percentages are based on the 2006-2010 American Community Survey population (not shown); ‡ Numbers in parentheses indicate the number of people reporting a single ancestry; * Numbers in parentheses indicate the number of persons reporting this race alone, not in combination with any other race; Please refer to the Explanation of Data for more information.*

West Indian, ex. Hispanic (11)	54	0.10
Dutch West Indian (7)	18	0.03
Jamaican (4)	4	0.01
West Indian (0)	24	0.04
Other West Indian (0)	8	0.01

Hispanic Origin	Population	%
Hispanic or Latino (of any race)	15,917	29.58
Central American, ex. Mexican	1,496	2.78
Costa Rican	5	0.01
Guatemalan	62	0.12
Honduran	362	0.67
Nicaraguan	822	1.53
Panamanian	8	0.01
Salvadoran	231	0.43
Other Central American	6	0.01
Cuban	61	0.11
Dominican Republic	33	0.06
Mexican	13,112	24.36
Puerto Rican	179	0.33
South American	116	0.22
Argentinean	4	0.01
Chilean	11	0.02
Colombian	28	0.05
Ecuadorian	6	0.01
Peruvian	37	0.07
Uruguayan	3	0.01
Venezuelan	26	0.05
Other South American	1	<0.01
Other Hispanic or Latino	920	1.71

Race*	Population	%
African-American/Black (21,921)	22,451	41.72
Not Hispanic (21,694)	22,056	40.98
Hispanic (227)	395	0.73
American Indian/Alaska Native (398)	657	1.22
Not Hispanic (166)	319	0.59
Hispanic (232)	338	0.63
Aleut *(Alaska Native)* (0)	1	<0.01
Apache (0)	2	<0.01
Blackfeet (2)	5	0.01
Central American Ind. (80)	90	0.17
Cherokee (18)	43	0.08
Chickasaw (2)	2	<0.01
Chippewa (2)	2	<0.01
Choctaw (16)	27	0.05
Comanche (0)	3	0.01
Cree (1)	1	<0.01
Creek (3)	4	0.01
Delaware (1)	1	<0.01
Mexican American Ind. (32)	52	0.10
Navajo (9)	9	0.02
Osage (2)	2	<0.01
Ottawa (4)	4	0.01
Paiute (4)	4	0.01
Pima (0)	2	<0.01
Potawatomi (2)	2	<0.01
Seminole (0)	3	0.01
Sioux (2)	2	<0.01
Spanish American Ind. (2)	6	0.01
Asian (3,180)	3,386	6.29
Not Hispanic (3,139)	3,297	6.13
Hispanic (41)	89	0.17
Bangladeshi (12)	12	0.02
Cambodian (10)	15	0.03
Chinese, ex. Taiwanese (61)	79	0.15
Filipino (89)	132	0.25
Indian (328)	383	0.71
Indonesian (1)	5	0.01
Japanese (12)	26	0.05
Korean (27)	37	0.07
Laotian (9)	11	0.02
Malaysian (1)	1	<0.01
Nepalese (2)	2	<0.01
Pakistani (120)	125	0.23
Sri Lankan (6)	6	0.01
Taiwanese (3)	4	0.01
Thai (11)	16	0.03
Vietnamese (2,402)	2,479	4.61
Hawaii Native/Pacific Islander (13)	62	0.12
Not Hispanic (13)	49	0.09
Hispanic (0)	13	0.02
Guamanian/Chamorro (2)	12	0.02
Marshallese (1)	1	<0.01
Native Hawaiian (3)	12	0.02
Samoan (2)	10	0.02
White (19,448)	20,394	37.89
Not Hispanic (12,294)	12,671	23.54
Hispanic (7,154)	7,723	14.35

Port Lavaca

Place Type: City
County: Calhoun
Population: 12,248†

Ancestry‡	Population	%
American (391)	391	3.22
Arab (33)	33	0.27
Egyptian (33)	33	0.27
Czech (99)	308	2.54
Dutch (57)	131	1.08
English (121)	707	5.82
European (10)	10	0.08
French, ex. Basque (24)	205	1.69
German (370)	1,343	11.06
Hungarian (9)	9	0.07
Irish (225)	1,034	8.51
Italian (12)	83	0.68
Luxemburger (0)	12	0.10
Norwegian (13)	59	0.49
Polish (57)	213	1.75
Portuguese (17)	17	0.14
Scotch-Irish (37)	190	1.56
Scottish (57)	231	1.90
Swedish (6)	25	0.21
Welsh (44)	71	0.58
West Indian, ex. Hispanic (0)	32	0.26
Dutch West Indian (0)	32	0.26

Hispanic Origin	Population	%
Hispanic or Latino (of any race)	6,933	56.61
Central American, ex. Mexican	41	0.33
Guatemalan	3	0.02
Honduran	15	0.12
Nicaraguan	1	0.01
Panamanian	2	0.02
Salvadoran	20	0.16
Cuban	10	0.08
Mexican	5,784	47.22
Puerto Rican	48	0.39
South American	13	0.11
Argentinean	1	0.01
Chilean	1	0.01
Colombian	7	0.06
Venezuelan	4	0.03
Other Hispanic or Latino	1,037	8.47

Race*	Population	%
African-American/Black (471)	530	4.33
Not Hispanic (439)	470	3.84
Hispanic (32)	60	0.49
American Indian/Alaska Native (63)	110	0.90
Not Hispanic (17)	53	0.43
Hispanic (46)	57	0.47
Aleut *(Alaska Native)* (0)	4	0.03
Apache (4)	4	0.03
Blackfeet (2)	5	0.04
Cherokee (3)	17	0.14
Chickasaw (1)	1	0.01
Choctaw (2)	3	0.02
Comanche (4)	4	0.03
Creek (0)	1	0.01
Houma (0)	1	0.01
Inupiat *(Alaska Native)* (2)	2	0.02
Mexican American Ind. (3)	3	0.02
Asian (748)	782	6.38
Not Hispanic (743)	766	6.25
Hispanic (5)	16	0.13
Burmese (241)	244	1.99
Cambodian (9)	9	0.07
Chinese, ex. Taiwanese (178)	188	1.53
Filipino (20)	22	0.18
Indian (23)	30	0.24
Japanese (3)	12	0.10
Korean (8)	10	0.08
Malaysian (2)	3	0.02
Taiwanese (197)	206	1.68
Thai (2)	2	0.02
Vietnamese (55)	58	0.47
Hawaii Native/Pacific Islander (6)	17	0.14
Not Hispanic (4)	12	0.10
Hispanic (2)	5	0.04
Guamanian/Chamorro (2)	3	0.02
Native Hawaiian (3)	4	0.03
Samoan (1)	1	0.01
White (9,381)	9,610	78.46
Not Hispanic (4,014)	4,090	33.39
Hispanic (5,367)	5,520	45.07

Port Neches

Place Type: City
County: Jefferson
Population: 13,040†

Ancestry‡	Population	%
American (749)	749	5.78
Arab (0)	57	0.44
Syrian (0)	57	0.44
Belgian (0)	15	0.12
British (31)	41	0.32
Cajun (321)	476	3.67
Croatian (11)	11	0.08
Czech (0)	26	0.20
Czechoslovakian (12)	12	0.09
Danish (31)	31	0.24
Dutch (55)	236	1.82
English (886)	1,926	14.85
European (10)	10	0.08
French, ex. Basque (1,040)	2,452	18.91
French Canadian (359)	561	4.33
German (563)	2,161	16.67
Greek (0)	14	0.11
Irish (272)	1,432	11.04
Italian (235)	598	4.61
Norwegian (32)	68	0.52
Polish (0)	109	0.84
Romanian (9)	9	0.07
Russian (54)	54	0.42
Scotch-Irish (187)	493	3.80
Scottish (132)	266	2.05
Swedish (0)	101	0.78
Ukrainian (0)	8	0.06
Welsh (11)	46	0.35

Hispanic Origin	Population	%
Hispanic or Latino (of any race)	1,296	9.94
Central American, ex. Mexican	48	0.37
Costa Rican	1	0.01
Guatemalan	2	0.02
Honduran	16	0.12
Nicaraguan	15	0.12
Salvadoran	12	0.09
Other Central American	2	0.02
Cuban	6	0.05
Dominican Republic	6	0.05
Mexican	1,087	8.34
Puerto Rican	29	0.22
South American	28	0.21
Argentinean	5	0.04
Chilean	3	0.02
Colombian	16	0.12
Peruvian	4	0.03
Other Hispanic or Latino	92	0.71

Race*	Population	%
African-American/Black (134)	189	1.45
Not Hispanic (124)	167	1.28
Hispanic (10)	22	0.17

*Notes: † The Census 2010 population figure is used to calculate the percentages in the Hispanic Origin and Race categories. Ancestry percentages are based on the 2006-2010 American Community Survey population (not shown); ‡ Numbers in parentheses indicate the number of people reporting a single ancestry; * Numbers in parentheses indicate the number of persons reporting this race alone, not in combination with any other race; Please refer to the Explanation of Data for more information.*

American Indian/Alaska Native (71)	121	0.93
Not Hispanic (37)	76	0.58
Hispanic (34)	45	0.35
Apache (2)	6	0.05
Central American Ind. (2)	2	0.02
Cherokee (7)	18	0.14
Chickasaw (0)	1	0.01
Choctaw (2)	3	0.02
Comanche (0)	1	0.01
Creek (2)	8	0.06
Hopi (0)	2	0.02
Mexican American Ind. (5)	5	0.04
Ottawa (1)	1	0.01
Potawatomi (4)	4	0.03
Sioux (4)	4	0.03
Yaqui (1)	4	0.03
Asian (309)	339	2.60
Not Hispanic (301)	329	2.52
Hispanic (8)	10	0.08
Cambodian (3)	3	0.02
Chinese, ex. Taiwanese (20)	26	0.20
Filipino (70)	77	0.59
Indian (74)	76	0.58
Japanese (3)	7	0.05
Korean (8)	18	0.14
Laotian (1)	1	0.01
Pakistani (16)	16	0.12
Thai (2)	5	0.04
Vietnamese (89)	94	0.72
Hawaii Native/Pacific Islander (14)	19	0.15
Not Hispanic (9)	12	0.09
Hispanic (5)	7	0.05
Guamanian/Chamorro (12)	13	0.10
Native Hawaiian (2)	5	0.04
White (11,859)	12,037	92.31
Not Hispanic (11,154)	11,257	86.33
Hispanic (705)	780	5.98

Portland

Place Type: City
County: San Patricio
Population: 15,099†

Ancestry‡	Population	%
American (867)	867	5.68
Arab (10)	10	0.07
Jordanian (10)	10	0.07
Australian (0)	12	0.08
Austrian (9)	34	0.22
British (8)	60	0.39
Cajun (8)	16	0.10
Canadian (56)	67	0.44
Czech (45)	179	1.17
Czechoslovakian (18)	44	0.29
Danish (58)	146	0.96
Dutch (80)	291	1.91
Eastern European (5)	5	0.03
English (378)	1,535	10.06
European (51)	77	0.50
Finnish (0)	26	0.17
French, ex. Basque (98)	778	5.10
French Canadian (0)	33	0.22
German (1,412)	3,229	21.16
Greek (31)	148	0.97
Irish (533)	2,000	13.11
Italian (72)	295	1.93
Norwegian (64)	207	1.36
Polish (21)	125	0.82
Portuguese (0)	42	0.28
Romanian (14)	14	0.09
Russian (12)	24	0.16
Scandinavian (9)	22	0.14
Scotch-Irish (305)	481	3.15
Scottish (95)	201	1.32
Swedish (64)	148	0.97
Swiss (9)	21	0.14
Turkish (0)	11	0.07
Ukrainian (14)	14	0.09
Welsh (5)	133	0.87
West Indian, ex. Hispanic (0)	27	0.18
Trinidadian/Tobagonian (0)	27	0.18

Hispanic Origin	Population	%
Hispanic or Latino (of any race)	5,326	35.27
Central American, ex. Mexican	28	0.19
Guatemalan	2	0.01
Honduran	12	0.08
Nicaraguan	6	0.04
Panamanian	5	0.03
Salvadoran	3	0.02
Cuban	36	0.24
Dominican Republic	5	0.03
Mexican	4,395	29.11
Puerto Rican	92	0.61
South American	48	0.32
Argentinean	2	0.01
Bolivian	2	0.01
Chilean	4	0.03
Colombian	11	0.07
Ecuadorian	3	0.02
Peruvian	21	0.14
Uruguayan	1	0.01
Venezuelan	4	0.03
Other Hispanic or Latino	722	4.78

Race*	Population	%
African-American/Black (238)	317	2.10
Not Hispanic (208)	271	1.79
Hispanic (30)	46	0.30
American Indian/Alaska Native (87)	192	1.27
Not Hispanic (57)	134	0.89
Hispanic (30)	58	0.38
Apache (0)	2	0.01
Blackfeet (0)	4	0.03
Canadian/French Am. Ind. (0)	1	0.01
Cherokee (11)	32	0.21
Chickasaw (3)	4	0.03
Chippewa (0)	1	0.01
Choctaw (3)	15	0.10
Crow (1)	1	0.01
Iroquois (1)	2	0.01
Lumbee (4)	4	0.03
Mexican American Ind. (4)	6	0.04
Navajo (4)	4	0.03
Osage (3)	3	0.02
Pima (0)	1	0.01
Potawatomi (2)	2	0.01
Pueblo (1)	1	0.01
Shoshone (0)	2	0.01
Sioux (4)	5	0.03
Asian (199)	299	1.98
Not Hispanic (189)	269	1.78
Hispanic (10)	30	0.20
Chinese, ex. Taiwanese (19)	29	0.19
Filipino (66)	103	0.68
Indian (52)	65	0.43
Indonesian (0)	2	0.01
Japanese (15)	35	0.23
Korean (8)	17	0.11
Pakistani (6)	6	0.04
Thai (5)	9	0.06
Vietnamese (16)	20	0.13
Hawaii Native/Pacific Islander (18)	36	0.24
Not Hispanic (14)	29	0.19
Hispanic (4)	7	0.05
Guamanian/Chamorro (10)	19	0.13
Native Hawaiian (1)	8	0.05
Samoan (2)	3	0.02
White (13,314)	13,627	90.25
Not Hispanic (9,079)	9,255	61.30
Hispanic (4,235)	4,372	28.96

Prosper

Place Type: Town
County: Collin
Population: 9,423†

Ancestry‡	Population	%
American (873)	873	10.68
Australian (21)	21	0.26
Austrian (0)	8	0.10
Belgian (10)	20	0.24
British (8)	15	0.18
Canadian (55)	55	0.67
Croatian (43)	43	0.53
Czech (52)	165	2.02
Czechoslovakian (22)	29	0.35
Danish (21)	21	0.26
Dutch (8)	154	1.88
English (324)	1,242	15.20
European (65)	65	0.80
Finnish (14)	25	0.31
French, ex. Basque (82)	305	3.73
German (500)	1,796	21.97
Greek (15)	26	0.32
Hungarian (14)	32	0.39
Irish (299)	1,085	13.28
Italian (75)	145	1.77
Lithuanian (11)	22	0.27
Norwegian (50)	97	1.19
Polish (68)	230	2.81
Portuguese (0)	10	0.12
Russian (0)	95	1.16
Scotch-Irish (21)	121	1.48
Scottish (81)	200	2.45
Serbian (8)	8	0.10
Swedish (45)	129	1.58
Welsh (10)	59	0.72
Yugoslavian (0)	18	0.22

Hispanic Origin	Population	%
Hispanic or Latino (of any race)	1,013	10.75
Central American, ex. Mexican	17	0.18
Costa Rican	2	0.02
Guatemalan	7	0.07
Honduran	1	0.01
Salvadoran	7	0.07
Cuban	22	0.23
Dominican Republic	1	0.01
Mexican	797	8.46
Puerto Rican	53	0.56
South American	67	0.71
Argentinean	1	0.01
Bolivian	2	0.02
Chilean	1	0.01
Colombian	20	0.21
Ecuadorian	11	0.12
Peruvian	14	0.15
Venezuelan	15	0.16
Other South American	3	0.03
Other Hispanic or Latino	56	0.59

Race*	Population	%
African-American/Black (496)	562	5.96
Not Hispanic (478)	535	5.68
Hispanic (18)	27	0.29
American Indian/Alaska Native (53)	131	1.39
Not Hispanic (44)	104	1.10
Hispanic (9)	27	0.29
Apache (0)	3	0.03
Blackfeet (1)	2	0.02
Cherokee (12)	32	0.34
Chickasaw (1)	1	0.01
Choctaw (4)	11	0.12
Creek (0)	3	0.03
Navajo (0)	2	0.02
Osage (0)	1	0.01
Potawatomi (6)	14	0.15
Sioux (7)	7	0.07
Yaqui (1)	3	0.03
Asian (179)	248	2.63
Not Hispanic (176)	240	2.55
Hispanic (3)	8	0.08
Burmese (0)	4	0.04
Cambodian (0)	2	0.02
Chinese, ex. Taiwanese (31)	39	0.41
Filipino (18)	38	0.40

*Notes: † The Census 2010 population figure is used to calculate the percentages in the Hispanic Origin and Race categories. Ancestry percentages are based on the 2006-2010 American Community Survey population (not shown); ‡ Numbers in parentheses indicate the number of people reporting a single ancestry; * Numbers in parentheses indicate the number of persons reporting this race alone, not in combination with any other race; Please refer to the Explanation of Data for more information.*

Indian (37)	46	0.49
Indonesian (2)	3	0.03
Japanese (8)	27	0.29
Korean (10)	20	0.21
Laotian (1)	3	0.03
Pakistani (6)	6	0.06
Thai (6)	6	0.06
Vietnamese (51)	62	0.66
Hawaii Native/Pacific Islander (2)	5	0.05
Not Hispanic (2)	5	0.05
Native Hawaiian (1)	2	0.02
Samoan (0)	1	0.01
Tongan (1)	1	0.01
White (8,204)	8,418	89.33
Not Hispanic (7,527)	7,686	81.57
Hispanic (677)	732	7.77

Raymondville

Place Type: City
County: Willacy
Population: 11,284†

Ancestry‡	Population	%
African, Sub-Saharan (37)	47	0.43
African (37)	47	0.43
American (259)	259	2.35
Belgian (0)	16	0.15
English (63)	200	1.81
French, ex. Basque (19)	51	0.46
German (107)	319	2.89
Greek (0)	9	0.08
Irish (26)	138	1.25
Italian (7)	44	0.40
Polish (9)	9	0.08
Scotch-Irish (10)	84	0.76
Scottish (10)	10	0.09
Welsh (0)	12	0.11

Hispanic Origin	Population	%
Hispanic or Latino (of any race)	9,801	86.86
Central American, ex. Mexican	929	8.23
Costa Rican	4	0.04
Guatemalan	247	2.19
Honduran	275	2.44
Nicaraguan	10	0.09
Salvadoran	393	3.48
Cuban	18	0.16
Dominican Republic	85	0.75
Mexican	7,105	62.97
Puerto Rican	6	0.05
South American	37	0.33
Argentinean	1	0.01
Colombian	6	0.05
Ecuadorian	19	0.17
Peruvian	6	0.05
Uruguayan	1	0.01
Venezuelan	4	0.04
Other Hispanic or Latino	1,621	14.37

Race*	Population	%
African-American/Black (395)	417	3.70
Not Hispanic (366)	375	3.32
Hispanic (29)	42	0.37
American Indian/Alaska Native (28)	61	0.54
Not Hispanic (6)	17	0.15
Hispanic (22)	44	0.39
Apache (8)	15	0.13
Blackfeet (0)	2	0.02
Cherokee (1)	2	0.02
Creek (0)	1	0.01
Inupiat *(Alaska Native)* (0)	1	0.01
Mexican American Ind. (6)	6	0.05
Osage (1)	1	0.01
Potawatomi (1)	1	0.01
Asian (124)	142	1.26
Not Hispanic (120)	127	1.13
Hispanic (4)	15	0.13
Bangladeshi (5)	5	0.04
Burmese (3)	3	0.03
Chinese, ex. Taiwanese (15)	15	0.13
Filipino (8)	14	0.12
Indian (74)	75	0.66
Japanese (1)	1	0.01
Sri Lankan (9)	9	0.08
Vietnamese (1)	1	0.01
Hawaii Native/Pacific Islander (6)	11	0.10
Not Hispanic (0)	4	0.04
Hispanic (6)	7	0.06
Samoan (6)	6	0.05
White (9,695)	9,856	87.34
Not Hispanic (964)	987	8.75
Hispanic (8,731)	8,869	78.60

Red Oak

Place Type: City
County: Ellis
Population: 10,769†

Ancestry‡	Population	%
African, Sub-Saharan (22)	22	0.22
Nigerian (22)	22	0.22
American (897)	897	9.03
Arab (39)	39	0.39
Arab (9)	9	0.09
Lebanese (30)	30	0.30
Australian (0)	102	1.03
British (93)	93	0.94
Canadian (11)	11	0.11
Czech (66)	66	0.66
Czechoslovakian (10)	34	0.34
Danish (0)	10	0.10
Dutch (46)	186	1.87
English (391)	990	9.97
European (0)	102	1.03
French, ex. Basque (21)	272	2.74
French Canadian (6)	47	0.47
German (311)	975	9.82
Hungarian (0)	27	0.27
Irish (399)	926	9.32
Israeli (11)	11	0.11
Italian (215)	482	4.85
Lithuanian (0)	6	0.06
Norwegian (18)	181	1.82
Polish (49)	134	1.35
Portuguese (0)	101	1.02
Russian (20)	20	0.20
Scandinavian (8)	8	0.08
Scotch-Irish (74)	251	2.53
Scottish (166)	342	3.44
Slovak (0)	7	0.07
Swedish (16)	44	0.44
West Indian, ex. Hispanic (17)	17	0.17
Dutch West Indian (17)	17	0.17

Hispanic Origin	Population	%
Hispanic or Latino (of any race)	2,219	20.61
Central American, ex. Mexican	66	0.61
Costa Rican	1	0.01
Guatemalan	11	0.10
Honduran	22	0.20
Nicaraguan	8	0.07
Panamanian	4	0.04
Salvadoran	20	0.19
Cuban	12	0.11
Dominican Republic	7	0.07
Mexican	1,898	17.62
Puerto Rican	29	0.27
South American	21	0.20
Argentinean	3	0.03
Chilean	2	0.02
Colombian	2	0.02
Ecuadorian	3	0.03
Peruvian	9	0.08
Venezuelan	2	0.02
Other Hispanic or Latino	186	1.73

Race*	Population	%
African-American/Black (1,822)	1,892	17.57
Not Hispanic (1,810)	1,859	17.26
Hispanic (12)	33	0.31
American Indian/Alaska Native (63)	151	1.40
Not Hispanic (44)	112	1.04
Hispanic (19)	39	0.36
Apache (0)	3	0.03
Blackfeet (1)	1	0.01
Central American Ind. (0)	3	0.03
Cherokee (7)	36	0.33
Chickasaw (4)	6	0.06
Chippewa (0)	2	0.02
Choctaw (3)	13	0.12
Creek (2)	2	0.02
Inupiat *(Alaska Native)* (1)	1	0.01
Iroquois (3)	4	0.04
Lumbee (0)	1	0.01
Mexican American Ind. (8)	8	0.07
Navajo (1)	3	0.03
Osage (1)	1	0.01
Pueblo (1)	1	0.01
Sioux (1)	5	0.05
South American Ind. (0)	3	0.03
Tlingit-Haida *(Alaska Native)* (4)	4	0.04
Asian (53)	92	0.85
Not Hispanic (51)	79	0.73
Hispanic (2)	13	0.12
Bangladeshi (2)	2	0.02
Chinese, ex. Taiwanese (7)	10	0.09
Filipino (12)	24	0.22
Indian (5)	10	0.09
Japanese (0)	10	0.09
Korean (5)	6	0.06
Laotian (1)	1	0.01
Pakistani (6)	9	0.08
Thai (3)	5	0.05
Vietnamese (10)	11	0.10
Hawaii Native/Pacific Islander (7)	10	0.09
Not Hispanic (5)	7	0.07
Hispanic (2)	3	0.03
Guamanian/Chamorro (5)	5	0.05
Native Hawaiian (0)	1	0.01
Samoan (0)	1	0.01
White (7,723)	7,964	73.95
Not Hispanic (6,468)	6,613	61.41
Hispanic (1,255)	1,351	12.55

Rendon

Place Type: CDP
County: Tarrant
Population: 12,552†

Ancestry‡	Population	%
American (1,233)	1,233	10.01
Arab (18)	18	0.15
Jordanian (18)	18	0.15
Austrian (0)	15	0.12
British (56)	81	0.66
Cajun (19)	57	0.46
Czech (11)	46	0.37
Danish (3)	22	0.18
Dutch (0)	73	0.59
English (1,066)	2,419	19.63
European (118)	118	0.96
French, ex. Basque (76)	388	3.15
French Canadian (15)	34	0.28
German (540)	1,794	14.56
Hungarian (0)	45	0.37
Irish (520)	1,761	14.29
Italian (13)	175	1.42
Norwegian (13)	159	1.29
Polish (11)	98	0.80
Russian (51)	51	0.41
Scandinavian (0)	9	0.07
Scotch-Irish (186)	382	3.10
Scottish (112)	235	1.91
Slavic (0)	16	0.13
Swedish (0)	144	1.17
Swiss (10)	29	0.24
Welsh (0)	28	0.23

*Notes: † The Census 2010 population figure is used to calculate the percentages in the Hispanic Origin and Race categories. Ancestry percentages are based on the 2006-2010 American Community Survey population (not shown); ‡ Numbers in parentheses indicate the number of people reporting a single ancestry; * Numbers in parentheses indicate the number of persons reporting this race alone, not in combination with any other race; Please refer to the Explanation of Data for more information.*

Hispanic Origin	Population	%
Hispanic or Latino (of any race)	1,799	14.33
Central American, ex. Mexican	31	0.25
Costa Rican	1	0.01
Guatemalan	4	0.03
Honduran	4	0.03
Nicaraguan	3	0.02
Panamanian	8	0.06
Salvadoran	11	0.09
Cuban	8	0.06
Mexican	1,575	12.55
Puerto Rican	42	0.33
South American	21	0.17
Chilean	1	0.01
Colombian	1	0.01
Ecuadorian	2	0.02
Peruvian	11	0.09
Venezuelan	6	0.05
Other Hispanic or Latino	122	0.97

Race*	Population	%
African-American/Black (735)	789	6.29
Not Hispanic (718)	759	6.05
Hispanic (17)	30	0.24
American Indian/Alaska Native (76)	170	1.35
Not Hispanic (61)	141	1.12
Hispanic (15)	29	0.23
Apache (1)	7	0.06
Blackfeet (0)	1	0.01
Cherokee (8)	40	0.32
Chickasaw (3)	10	0.08
Choctaw (25)	32	0.25
Comanche (3)	3	0.02
Cree (0)	2	0.02
Creek (4)	9	0.07
Crow (0)	1	0.01
Mexican American Ind. (4)	4	0.03
Navajo (1)	1	0.01
Seminole (0)	1	0.01
Sioux (6)	8	0.06
Asian (112)	142	1.13
Not Hispanic (110)	136	1.08
Hispanic (2)	6	0.05
Chinese, ex. Taiwanese (18)	22	0.18
Filipino (8)	19	0.15
Hmong (7)	7	0.06
Indian (13)	23	0.18
Japanese (5)	8	0.06
Korean (16)	21	0.17
Pakistani (2)	3	0.02
Sri Lankan (1)	2	0.02
Thai (6)	6	0.05
Vietnamese (21)	32	0.25
Hawaii Native/Pacific Islander (3)	4	0.03
Not Hispanic (3)	4	0.03
Guamanian/Chamorro (2)	3	0.02
Native Hawaiian (1)	1	0.01
White (10,704)	10,915	86.96
Not Hispanic (9,712)	9,845	78.43
Hispanic (992)	1,070	8.52

Richardson

Place Type: City
County: Dallas
Population: 99,223†

Ancestry‡	Population	%
African, Sub-Saharan (1,368)	1,583	1.62
African (263)	352	0.36
Ethiopian (590)	590	0.61
Kenyan (142)	142	0.15
Nigerian (130)	207	0.21
Senegalese (0)	12	0.01
Sierra Leonean (11)	11	0.01
South African (49)	49	0.05
Sudanese (183)	214	0.22
Other Sub-Saharan African (0)	6	0.01
American (10,636)	10,636	10.91
Arab (1,516)	1,710	1.75
Arab (178)	207	0.21
Egyptian (194)	204	0.21
Iraqi (75)	83	0.09
Jordanian (48)	48	0.05
Lebanese (113)	204	0.21
Moroccan (231)	231	0.24
Palestinian (191)	191	0.20
Syrian (430)	442	0.45
Other Arab (56)	100	0.10
Armenian (10)	32	0.03
Assyrian/Chaldean/Syriac (10)	10	0.01
Australian (74)	74	0.08
Austrian (66)	191	0.20
Basque (10)	10	0.01
Brazilian (3)	80	0.08
British (248)	494	0.51
Cajun (11)	28	0.03
Canadian (99)	200	0.21
Carpatho Rusyn (0)	6	0.01
Celtic (14)	25	0.03
Croatian (28)	97	0.10
Czech (211)	549	0.56
Czechoslovakian (10)	22	0.02
Danish (116)	410	0.42
Dutch (229)	1,214	1.25
Eastern European (10)	21	0.02
English (3,964)	10,324	10.59
European (1,068)	1,156	1.19
Finnish (43)	90	0.09
French, ex. Basque (534)	2,531	2.60
French Canadian (183)	332	0.34
German (4,373)	11,950	12.26
Greek (173)	267	0.27
Guyanese (27)	27	0.03
Hungarian (91)	270	0.28
Iranian (230)	230	0.24
Irish (2,102)	7,630	7.83
Israeli (12)	30	0.03
Italian (1,046)	2,786	2.86
Lithuanian (112)	248	0.25
Luxemburger (11)	11	0.01
Northern European (59)	59	0.06
Norwegian (244)	928	0.95
Pennsylvania German (0)	29	0.03
Polish (469)	1,217	1.25
Portuguese (46)	135	0.14
Romanian (110)	167	0.17
Russian (370)	692	0.71
Scandinavian (79)	148	0.15
Scotch-Irish (1,125)	2,409	2.47
Scottish (847)	2,425	2.49
Serbian (0)	11	0.01
Slovak (33)	89	0.09
Slovene (0)	18	0.02
Swedish (351)	1,140	1.17
Swiss (61)	429	0.44
Turkish (141)	141	0.14
Ukrainian (28)	76	0.08
Welsh (145)	882	0.90
West Indian, ex. Hispanic (165)	252	0.26
Belizean (72)	72	0.07
British West Indian (19)	19	0.02
Dutch West Indian (0)	23	0.02
Jamaican (19)	30	0.03
Trinidadian/Tobagonian (35)	44	0.05
West Indian (20)	64	0.07
Yugoslavian (0)	39	0.04

Hispanic Origin	Population	%
Hispanic or Latino (of any race)	15,849	15.97
Central American, ex. Mexican	1,575	1.59
Costa Rican	106	0.11
Guatemalan	349	0.35
Honduran	388	0.39
Nicaraguan	54	0.05
Panamanian	67	0.07
Salvadoran	588	0.59
Other Central American	23	0.02
Cuban	202	0.20
Dominican Republic	43	0.04
Mexican	11,789	11.88
Puerto Rican	339	0.34
South American	752	0.76
Argentinean	80	0.08
Bolivian	43	0.04
Chilean	51	0.05
Colombian	207	0.21
Ecuadorian	52	0.05
Paraguayan	6	0.01
Peruvian	242	0.24
Uruguayan	11	0.01
Venezuelan	58	0.06
Other South American	2	<0.01
Other Hispanic or Latino	1,149	1.16

Race*	Population	%
African-American/Black (8,507)	9,215	9.29
Not Hispanic (8,283)	8,815	8.88
Hispanic (224)	400	0.40
American Indian/Alaska Native (491)	1,114	1.12
Not Hispanic (318)	785	0.79
Hispanic (173)	329	0.33
Aleut *(Alaska Native)* (0)	1	<0.01
Apache (9)	21	0.02
Blackfeet (3)	22	0.02
Canadian/French Am. Ind. (2)	3	<0.01
Central American Ind. (1)	3	<0.01
Cherokee (78)	263	0.27
Cheyenne (1)	2	<0.01
Chickasaw (23)	43	0.04
Chippewa (4)	5	0.01
Choctaw (74)	132	0.13
Colville (1)	1	<0.01
Comanche (5)	8	0.01
Creek (12)	28	0.03
Delaware (1)	4	<0.01
Hopi (1)	1	<0.01
Iroquois (5)	8	0.01
Kiowa (1)	1	<0.01
Lumbee (3)	3	<0.01
Mexican American Ind. (17)	36	0.04
Navajo (7)	13	0.01
Osage (4)	10	0.01
Ottawa (7)	7	0.01
Potawatomi (7)	14	0.01
Pueblo (1)	7	0.01
Puget Sound Salish (0)	3	<0.01
Seminole (4)	5	0.01
Sioux (4)	9	0.01
South American Ind. (0)	10	0.01
Spanish American Ind. (0)	1	<0.01
Tlingit-Haida *(Alaska Native)* (1)	1	<0.01
Tohono O'Odham (4)	4	<0.01
Yup'ik *(Alaska Native)* (2)	2	<0.01
Asian (14,981)	16,237	16.36
Not Hispanic (14,929)	16,059	16.18
Hispanic (52)	178	0.18
Bangladeshi (287)	309	0.31
Burmese (9)	9	0.01
Cambodian (143)	159	0.16
Chinese, ex. Taiwanese (3,117)	3,426	3.45
Filipino (488)	665	0.67
Hmong (17)	18	0.02
Indian (4,362)	4,601	4.64
Indonesian (29)	37	0.04
Japanese (202)	350	0.35
Korean (1,024)	1,145	1.15
Laotian (93)	118	0.12
Malaysian (22)	35	0.04
Nepalese (48)	49	0.05
Pakistani (1,357)	1,465	1.48
Sri Lankan (44)	47	0.05
Taiwanese (368)	430	0.43
Thai (137)	167	0.17
Vietnamese (2,690)	2,861	2.88
Hawaii Native/Pacific Islander (53)	149	0.15
Not Hispanic (42)	128	0.13
Hispanic (11)	21	0.02
Fijian (0)	1	<0.01
Guamanian/Chamorro (11)	19	0.02

*Notes: † The Census 2010 population figure is used to calculate the percentages in the Hispanic Origin and Race categories. Ancestry percentages are based on the 2006-2010 American Community Survey population (not shown); ‡ Numbers in parentheses indicate the number of people reporting a single ancestry; * Numbers in parentheses indicate the number of persons reporting this race alone, not in combination with any other race; Please refer to the Explanation of Data for more information.*

Marshallese (1)	1	<0.01
Native Hawaiian (19)	53	0.05
Samoan (10)	15	0.02
White (66,613)	69,119	69.66
Not Hispanic (57,600)	59,296	59.76
Hispanic (9,013)	9,823	9.90

Richland Hills

Place Type: City
County: Tarrant
Population: 7,801†

Ancestry‡	Population	%
African, Sub-Saharan (13)	21	0.27
African (13)	13	0.17
South African (0)	8	0.10
Albanian (14)	14	0.18
American (1,246)	1,246	15.86
British (8)	18	0.23
Cajun (0)	17	0.22
Canadian (11)	11	0.14
Czech (57)	84	1.07
Danish (0)	25	0.32
Dutch (23)	320	4.07
English (349)	792	10.08
European (76)	76	0.97
French, ex. Basque (36)	124	1.58
French Canadian (12)	12	0.15
German (378)	1,112	14.15
Hungarian (8)	32	0.41
Irish (357)	1,205	15.34
Italian (35)	131	1.67
Latvian (0)	17	0.22
Norwegian (41)	88	1.12
Polish (9)	42	0.53
Portuguese (26)	26	0.33
Russian (11)	20	0.25
Scandinavian (10)	10	0.13
Scotch-Irish (146)	248	3.16
Scottish (44)	175	2.23
Swedish (25)	35	0.45
Swiss (0)	19	0.24
Welsh (0)	23	0.29

Hispanic Origin	Population	%
Hispanic or Latino (of any race)	1,491	19.11
Central American, ex. Mexican	79	1.01
Costa Rican	1	0.01
Guatemalan	22	0.28
Honduran	2	0.03
Nicaraguan	4	0.05
Panamanian	8	0.10
Salvadoran	42	0.54
Cuban	8	0.10
Mexican	1,254	16.07
Puerto Rican	57	0.73
South American	17	0.22
Argentinean	4	0.05
Colombian	2	0.03
Ecuadorian	1	0.01
Peruvian	4	0.05
Uruguayan	2	0.03
Venezuelan	4	0.05
Other Hispanic or Latino	76	0.97

Race*	Population	%
African-American/Black (195)	243	3.11
Not Hispanic (193)	232	2.97
Hispanic (2)	11	0.14
American Indian/Alaska Native (64)	146	1.87
Not Hispanic (61)	134	1.72
Hispanic (3)	12	0.15
Apache (2)	4	0.05
Blackfeet (1)	3	0.04
Cherokee (13)	45	0.58
Chickasaw (1)	2	0.03
Chippewa (2)	2	0.03
Choctaw (10)	19	0.24
Comanche (2)	10	0.13
Creek (0)	1	0.01
Crow (0)	3	0.04
Iroquois (0)	5	0.06
Kiowa (0)	1	0.01
Lumbee (1)	1	0.01
Mexican American Ind. (2)	2	0.03
Navajo (5)	5	0.06
Osage (4)	4	0.05
Potawatomi (0)	1	0.01
Puget Sound Salish (3)	3	0.04
Sioux (2)	2	0.03
Yuman (1)	2	0.03
Asian (104)	144	1.85
Not Hispanic (103)	137	1.76
Hispanic (1)	7	0.09
Cambodian (7)	8	0.10
Chinese, ex. Taiwanese (5)	9	0.12
Filipino (10)	22	0.28
Hmong (10)	15	0.19
Indian (11)	18	0.23
Indonesian (1)	1	0.01
Japanese (4)	11	0.14
Korean (0)	5	0.06
Laotian (9)	14	0.18
Pakistani (2)	2	0.03
Taiwanese (1)	3	0.04
Thai (3)	6	0.08
Vietnamese (22)	24	0.31
Hawaii Native/Pacific Islander (30)	47	0.60
Not Hispanic (28)	40	0.51
Hispanic (2)	7	0.09
Guamanian/Chamorro (3)	3	0.04
Native Hawaiian (5)	18	0.23
Samoan (1)	1	0.01
Tongan (12)	13	0.17
White (6,550)	6,797	87.13
Not Hispanic (5,779)	5,904	75.68
Hispanic (771)	893	11.45

Richmond

Place Type: City
County: Fort Bend
Population: 11,679†

Ancestry‡	Population	%
African, Sub-Saharan (43)	43	0.37
African (23)	23	0.20
Kenyan (11)	11	0.09
Nigerian (9)	9	0.08
American (341)	341	2.93
Arab (0)	9	0.08
Lebanese (0)	9	0.08
Austrian (0)	6	0.05
Czech (160)	311	2.67
Czechoslovakian (40)	40	0.34
Danish (11)	11	0.09
Dutch (0)	23	0.20
English (98)	249	2.14
European (23)	31	0.27
French, ex. Basque (24)	115	0.99
French Canadian (14)	45	0.39
German (258)	610	5.25
Irish (153)	438	3.77
Italian (35)	110	0.95
Northern European (8)	8	0.07
Norwegian (29)	111	0.95
Polish (51)	130	1.12
Romanian (0)	7	0.06
Russian (10)	26	0.22
Scotch-Irish (20)	87	0.75
Scottish (61)	135	1.16
Swedish (0)	7	0.06
Welsh (0)	7	0.06

Hispanic Origin	Population	%
Hispanic or Latino (of any race)	6,472	55.42
Central American, ex. Mexican	345	2.95
Guatemalan	13	0.11
Honduran	24	0.21
Nicaraguan	16	0.14
Salvadoran	291	2.49
Other Central American	1	0.01
Cuban	10	0.09
Dominican Republic	1	0.01
Mexican	5,646	48.34
Puerto Rican	36	0.31
South American	13	0.11
Colombian	2	0.02
Ecuadorian	2	0.02
Peruvian	3	0.03
Venezuelan	6	0.05
Other Hispanic or Latino	421	3.60

Race*	Population	%
African-American/Black (2,101)	2,188	18.73
Not Hispanic (2,023)	2,071	17.73
Hispanic (78)	117	1.00
American Indian/Alaska Native (102)	153	1.31
Not Hispanic (34)	67	0.57
Hispanic (68)	86	0.74
Alaska Athabascan *(Ala. Nat.)* (5)	5	0.04
Apache (2)	2	0.02
Cherokee (6)	15	0.13
Chickasaw (3)	7	0.06
Choctaw (4)	10	0.09
Creek (0)	2	0.02
Mexican American Ind. (12)	17	0.15
Potawatomi (2)	2	0.02
Asian (122)	137	1.17
Not Hispanic (121)	132	1.13
Hispanic (1)	5	0.04
Cambodian (5)	5	0.04
Chinese, ex. Taiwanese (16)	17	0.15
Filipino (13)	16	0.14
Indian (28)	32	0.27
Japanese (2)	2	0.02
Korean (0)	1	0.01
Pakistani (9)	11	0.09
Thai (2)	2	0.02
Vietnamese (27)	30	0.26
Hawaii Native/Pacific Islander (3)	13	0.11
Not Hispanic (1)	3	0.03
Hispanic (2)	10	0.09
Guamanian/Chamorro (1)	1	0.01
Native Hawaiian (2)	6	0.05
White (7,073)	7,301	62.51
Not Hispanic (2,951)	2,991	25.61
Hispanic (4,122)	4,310	36.90

Rio Grande City

Place Type: City
County: Starr
Population: 13,834†

Ancestry‡	Population	%
American (86)	86	0.63
Arab (0)	9	0.07
Lebanese (0)	9	0.07
Belgian (0)	25	0.18
Dutch (0)	31	0.23
English (55)	201	1.46
French, ex. Basque (0)	13	0.09
German (14)	81	0.59
Irish (15)	83	0.60
Italian (0)	23	0.17

Hispanic Origin	Population	%
Hispanic or Latino (of any race)	13,044	94.29
Central American, ex. Mexican	36	0.26
Costa Rican	1	0.01
Guatemalan	5	0.04
Honduran	18	0.13
Nicaraguan	4	0.03
Panamanian	2	0.01
Salvadoran	6	0.04
Cuban	2	0.01
Dominican Republic	11	0.08
Mexican	12,195	88.15

*Notes: † The Census 2010 population figure is used to calculate the percentages in the Hispanic Origin and Race categories. Ancestry percentages are based on the 2006-2010 American Community Survey population (not shown); ‡ Numbers in parentheses indicate the number of people reporting a single ancestry; * Numbers in parentheses indicate the number of persons reporting this race alone, not in combination with any other race; Please refer to the Explanation of Data for more information.*

Puerto Rican	17	0.12
South American	7	0.05
Colombian	7	0.05
Other Hispanic or Latino	776	5.61

Race*	Population	%
African-American/Black (28)	32	0.23
Not Hispanic (5)	5	0.04
Hispanic (23)	27	0.20
American Indian/Alaska Native (41)	58	0.42
Not Hispanic (7)	10	0.07
Hispanic (34)	48	0.35
Apache (3)	3	0.02
Cherokee (3)	3	0.02
Chickasaw (1)	1	0.01
Choctaw (2)	2	0.01
Creek (2)	2	0.01
Mexican American Ind. (3)	3	0.02
Asian (108)	125	0.90
Not Hispanic (105)	115	0.83
Hispanic (3)	10	0.07
Chinese, ex. Taiwanese (14)	14	0.10
Filipino (78)	84	0.61
Indian (4)	7	0.05
Japanese (0)	2	0.01
Korean (4)	4	0.03
Vietnamese (8)	12	0.09
Hawaii Native/Pacific Islander (0)	6	0.04
Not Hispanic (0)	1	0.01
Hispanic (0)	5	0.04
Fijian (0)	1	0.01
White (12,739)	12,879	93.10
Not Hispanic (653)	668	4.83
Hispanic (12,086)	12,211	88.27

Robinson

Place Type: City
County: McLennan
Population: 10,509†

Ancestry‡	Population	%
African, Sub-Saharan (14)	14	0.14
African (14)	14	0.14
American (893)	893	8.96
Arab (18)	26	0.26
Lebanese (18)	18	0.18
Syrian (0)	8	0.08
Armenian (0)	8	0.08
British (10)	10	0.10
Cajun (0)	43	0.43
Czech (113)	287	2.88
Czechoslovakian (108)	114	1.14
Danish (13)	59	0.59
Dutch (57)	124	1.24
English (553)	932	9.35
European (21)	61	0.61
French, ex. Basque (40)	235	2.36
French Canadian (101)	140	1.40
German (805)	2,080	20.87
Greek (19)	19	0.19
Irish (734)	1,687	16.93
Italian (12)	176	1.77
Lithuanian (0)	25	0.25
Norwegian (119)	183	1.84
Polish (67)	122	1.22
Russian (0)	10	0.10
Scotch-Irish (198)	275	2.76
Scottish (36)	190	1.91
Swedish (9)	95	0.95
Swiss (0)	38	0.38
Ukrainian (0)	10	0.10
Welsh (14)	79	0.79
West Indian, ex. Hispanic (0)	21	0.21
Dutch West Indian (0)	21	0.21

Hispanic Origin	Population	%
Hispanic or Latino (of any race)	1,475	14.04
Central American, ex. Mexican	14	0.13
Honduran	3	0.03
Nicaraguan	1	0.01
Panamanian	6	0.06
Salvadoran	4	0.04
Cuban	8	0.08
Mexican	1,281	12.19
Puerto Rican	38	0.36
South American	6	0.06
Argentinean	1	0.01
Colombian	3	0.03
Ecuadorian	1	0.01
Peruvian	1	0.01
Other Hispanic or Latino	128	1.22

Race*	Population	%
African-American/Black (397)	457	4.35
Not Hispanic (382)	433	4.12
Hispanic (15)	24	0.23
American Indian/Alaska Native (61)	124	1.18
Not Hispanic (42)	86	0.82
Hispanic (19)	38	0.36
Apache (3)	4	0.04
Blackfeet (0)	3	0.03
Cherokee (10)	18	0.17
Chickasaw (4)	4	0.04
Chippewa (0)	1	0.01
Choctaw (4)	12	0.11
Comanche (1)	1	0.01
Creek (0)	1	0.01
Iroquois (1)	1	0.01
Lumbee (0)	1	0.01
Mexican American Ind. (7)	8	0.08
Navajo (0)	1	0.01
Osage (0)	2	0.02
Potawatomi (2)	4	0.04
Seminole (1)	2	0.02
Asian (54)	99	0.94
Not Hispanic (54)	82	0.78
Hispanic (0)	17	0.16
Cambodian (3)	3	0.03
Chinese, ex. Taiwanese (3)	7	0.07
Filipino (10)	19	0.18
Indian (15)	20	0.19
Indonesian (0)	3	0.03
Japanese (7)	16	0.15
Korean (8)	13	0.12
Pakistani (5)	5	0.05
Vietnamese (2)	2	0.02
Hawaii Native/Pacific Islander (2)	8	0.08
Not Hispanic (2)	8	0.08
Guamanian/Chamorro (0)	3	0.03
White (9,249)	9,437	89.80
Not Hispanic (8,427)	8,551	81.37
Hispanic (822)	886	8.43

Robstown

Place Type: City
County: Nueces
Population: 11,487†

Ancestry‡	Population	%
American (102)	102	0.87
Arab (9)	20	0.17
Lebanese (9)	20	0.17
English (27)	53	0.45
French, ex. Basque (15)	24	0.21
German (88)	125	1.07
Irish (38)	238	2.04
Italian (12)	12	0.10
Swedish (0)	19	0.16

Hispanic Origin	Population	%
Hispanic or Latino (of any race)	10,752	93.60
Central American, ex. Mexican	49	0.43
Guatemalan	12	0.10
Honduran	25	0.22
Nicaraguan	1	0.01
Salvadoran	10	0.09
Other Central American	1	0.01
Cuban	3	0.03
Mexican	9,123	79.42
Puerto Rican	9	0.08
South American	2	0.02
Chilean	1	0.01
Ecuadorian	1	0.01
Other Hispanic or Latino	1,566	13.63

Race*	Population	%
African-American/Black (181)	214	1.86
Not Hispanic (131)	133	1.16
Hispanic (50)	81	0.71
American Indian/Alaska Native (44)	62	0.54
Not Hispanic (9)	13	0.11
Hispanic (35)	49	0.43
Apache (3)	3	0.03
Cherokee (2)	4	0.03
Creek (1)	1	0.01
Iroquois (1)	1	0.01
Mexican American Ind. (7)	12	0.10
Spanish American Ind. (0)	1	0.01
Asian (20)	31	0.27
Not Hispanic (14)	14	0.12
Hispanic (6)	17	0.15
Chinese, ex. Taiwanese (2)	2	0.02
Filipino (7)	8	0.07
Indian (6)	9	0.08
Korean (1)	2	0.02
Pakistani (1)	1	0.01
Thai (1)	1	0.01
Vietnamese (1)	2	0.02
Hawaii Native/Pacific Islander (3)	11	0.10
Not Hispanic (1)	1	0.01
Hispanic (2)	10	0.09
Guamanian/Chamorro (3)	3	0.03
Samoan (0)	1	0.01
White (9,696)	9,900	86.18
Not Hispanic (568)	573	4.99
Hispanic (9,128)	9,327	81.20

Rockport

Place Type: City
County: Aransas
Population: 8,766†

Ancestry‡	Population	%
American (460)	460	5.28
Austrian (11)	11	0.13
Belgian (9)	92	1.06
British (17)	17	0.20
Bulgarian (13)	13	0.15
Canadian (0)	15	0.17
Czech (26)	86	0.99
Danish (17)	48	0.55
Dutch (38)	170	1.95
English (587)	1,179	13.53
European (124)	124	1.42
French, ex. Basque (147)	452	5.19
French Canadian (0)	16	0.18
German (703)	1,925	22.08
Greek (0)	44	0.50
Hungarian (14)	14	0.16
Irish (584)	1,063	12.19
Italian (32)	121	1.39
New Zealander (9)	9	0.10
Norwegian (41)	87	1.00
Polish (30)	290	3.33
Portuguese (23)	23	0.26
Scotch-Irish (134)	284	3.26
Scottish (112)	276	3.17
Swedish (57)	78	0.89
Swiss (0)	12	0.14
Welsh (33)	76	0.87
West Indian, ex. Hispanic (17)	17	0.20
Dutch West Indian (17)	17	0.20

Hispanic Origin	Population	%
Hispanic or Latino (of any race)	1,826	20.83
Central American, ex. Mexican	14	0.16
Honduran	4	0.05

*Notes: † The Census 2010 population figure is used to calculate the percentages in the Hispanic Origin and Race categories. Ancestry percentages are based on the 2006-2010 American Community Survey population (not shown); ‡ Numbers in parentheses indicate the number of people reporting a single ancestry; * Numbers in parentheses indicate the number of persons reporting this race alone, not in combination with any other race; Please refer to the Explanation of Data for more information.*

Nicaraguan	5	0.06
Panamanian	1	0.01
Salvadoran	3	0.03
Other Central American	1	0.01
Cuban	5	0.06
Mexican	1,532	17.48
Puerto Rican	36	0.41
South American	3	0.03
Colombian	3	0.03
Other Hispanic or Latino	236	2.69

Race*	Population	%
African-American/Black (128)	162	1.85
Not Hispanic (112)	132	1.51
Hispanic (16)	30	0.34
American Indian/Alaska Native (57)	115	1.31
Not Hispanic (37)	82	0.94
Hispanic (20)	33	0.38
Apache (1)	3	0.03
Blackfeet (0)	2	0.02
Canadian/French Am. Ind. (1)	1	0.01
Cherokee (10)	26	0.30
Cheyenne (1)	1	0.01
Chickasaw (0)	3	0.03
Chippewa (0)	1	0.01
Choctaw (10)	15	0.17
Comanche (1)	1	0.01
Creek (1)	1	0.01
Crow (1)	1	0.01
Iroquois (1)	7	0.08
Lumbee (1)	1	0.01
Mexican American Ind. (4)	4	0.05
Potawatomi (0)	1	0.01
Sioux (2)	4	0.05
Ute (1)	1	0.01
Asian (213)	241	2.75
Not Hispanic (204)	224	2.56
Hispanic (9)	17	0.19
Cambodian (6)	6	0.07
Chinese, ex. Taiwanese (4)	14	0.16
Filipino (15)	17	0.19
Indian (16)	16	0.18
Japanese (7)	11	0.13
Korean (9)	17	0.19
Laotian (7)	12	0.14
Malaysian (0)	1	0.01
Thai (0)	1	0.01
Vietnamese (146)	149	1.70
Hawaii Native/Pacific Islander (5)	12	0.14
Not Hispanic (5)	9	0.10
Hispanic (0)	3	0.03
Native Hawaiian (4)	8	0.09
White (7,777)	7,927	90.43
Not Hispanic (6,489)	6,562	74.86
Hispanic (1,288)	1,365	15.57

Rockwall

Place Type: City
County: Rockwall
Population: 37,490†

Ancestry‡	Population	%
African, Sub-Saharan (342)	491	1.40
African (28)	152	0.43
Ethiopian (172)	172	0.49
Ghanaian (116)	116	0.33
Nigerian (0)	25	0.07
Other Sub-Saharan African (26)	26	0.07
American (4,239)	4,239	12.08
Arab (65)	176	0.50
Arab (0)	10	0.03
Egyptian (0)	9	0.03
Jordanian (56)	56	0.16
Lebanese (9)	91	0.26
Palestinian (0)	10	0.03
Austrian (51)	51	0.15
Basque (36)	36	0.10
Belgian (11)	75	0.21
British (70)	206	0.59
Cajun (0)	17	0.05
Canadian (11)	17	0.05
Croatian (20)	143	0.41
Czech (79)	279	0.80
Danish (47)	297	0.85
Dutch (207)	674	1.92
English (1,947)	4,397	12.53
European (324)	403	1.15
French, ex. Basque (227)	1,439	4.10
French Canadian (82)	170	0.48
German (1,989)	5,247	14.95
Greek (24)	131	0.37
Hungarian (92)	152	0.43
Irish (812)	3,019	8.60
Israeli (33)	33	0.09
Italian (303)	995	2.84
Lithuanian (0)	12	0.03
New Zealander (21)	21	0.06
Northern European (36)	36	0.10
Norwegian (22)	267	0.76
Polish (113)	475	1.35
Portuguese (13)	53	0.15
Romanian (42)	42	0.12
Russian (115)	189	0.54
Scandinavian (46)	58	0.17
Scotch-Irish (363)	760	2.17
Scottish (436)	888	2.53
Slavic (16)	46	0.13
Swedish (91)	449	1.28
Swiss (31)	174	0.50
Turkish (0)	35	0.10
Ukrainian (33)	92	0.26
Welsh (122)	348	0.99
Yugoslavian (0)	7	0.02

Hispanic Origin	Population	%
Hispanic or Latino (of any race)	6,214	16.58
Central American, ex. Mexican	392	1.05
Costa Rican	18	0.05
Guatemalan	68	0.18
Honduran	30	0.08
Nicaraguan	21	0.06
Panamanian	10	0.03
Salvadoran	239	0.64
Other Central American	6	0.02
Cuban	56	0.15
Dominican Republic	11	0.03
Mexican	4,990	13.31
Puerto Rican	193	0.51
South American	207	0.55
Argentinean	6	0.02
Bolivian	10	0.03
Chilean	7	0.02
Colombian	82	0.22
Ecuadorian	24	0.06
Paraguayan	2	0.01
Peruvian	25	0.07
Venezuelan	47	0.13
Other South American	4	0.01
Other Hispanic or Latino	365	0.97

Race*	Population	%
African-American/Black (2,215)	2,457	6.55
Not Hispanic (2,151)	2,327	6.21
Hispanic (64)	130	0.35
American Indian/Alaska Native (220)	469	1.25
Not Hispanic (156)	348	0.93
Hispanic (64)	121	0.32
Apache (2)	4	0.01
Arapaho (0)	1	<0.01
Blackfeet (5)	7	0.02
Central American Ind. (3)	3	0.01
Cherokee (44)	124	0.33
Cheyenne (2)	3	0.01
Chickasaw (10)	14	0.04
Chippewa (0)	5	0.01
Choctaw (49)	89	0.24
Comanche (2)	3	0.01
Cree (0)	1	<0.01
Creek (3)	11	0.03
Houma (0)	1	<0.01
Iroquois (0)	3	0.01
Lumbee (4)	6	0.02
Mexican American Ind. (7)	8	0.02
Navajo (2)	2	0.01
Osage (1)	4	0.01
Potawatomi (1)	1	<0.01
Seminole (0)	6	0.02
Shoshone (3)	4	0.01
Sioux (3)	5	0.01
South American Ind. (0)	3	0.01
Spanish American Ind. (0)	3	0.01
Yaqui (0)	1	<0.01
Asian (1,137)	1,381	3.68
Not Hispanic (1,096)	1,298	3.46
Hispanic (41)	83	0.22
Cambodian (52)	53	0.14
Chinese, ex. Taiwanese (97)	153	0.41
Filipino (210)	262	0.70
Hmong (1)	1	<0.01
Indian (243)	276	0.74
Indonesian (4)	10	0.03
Japanese (38)	57	0.15
Korean (110)	137	0.37
Laotian (28)	37	0.10
Malaysian (3)	3	0.01
Nepalese (6)	6	0.02
Pakistani (52)	53	0.14
Sri Lankan (3)	3	0.01
Taiwanese (9)	9	0.02
Thai (25)	32	0.09
Vietnamese (191)	218	0.58
Hawaii Native/Pacific Islander (25)	57	0.15
Not Hispanic (24)	48	0.13
Hispanic (1)	9	0.02
Guamanian/Chamorro (9)	13	0.03
Marshallese (3)	3	0.01
Native Hawaiian (4)	22	0.06
Samoan (1)	2	0.01
White (30,909)	31,650	84.42
Not Hispanic (27,264)	27,747	74.01
Hispanic (3,645)	3,903	10.41

Roma

Place Type: City
County: Starr
Population: 9,765†

Ancestry‡	Population	%
American (11)	11	0.11
English (0)	10	0.10
French, ex. Basque (0)	14	0.14
German (0)	26	0.26
Irish (20)	20	0.20
Portuguese (0)	14	0.14
Scottish (10)	10	0.10
Swedish (18)	18	0.18

Hispanic Origin	Population	%
Hispanic or Latino (of any race)	9,261	94.84
Dominican Republic	1	0.01
Mexican	8,870	90.83
Puerto Rican	5	0.05
South American	6	0.06
Peruvian	6	0.06
Other Hispanic or Latino	379	3.88

Race*	Population	%
African-American/Black (6)	8	0.08
Not Hispanic (2)	3	0.03
Hispanic (4)	5	0.05
American Indian/Alaska Native (5)	6	0.06
Hispanic (5)	6	0.06
Sioux (0)	1	0.01
Asian (3)	4	0.04
Not Hispanic (3)	3	0.03
Hispanic (0)	1	0.01
Filipino (2)	2	0.02
Indian (0)	1	0.01

*Notes: † The Census 2010 population figure is used to calculate the percentages in the Hispanic Origin and Race categories. Ancestry percentages are based on the 2006-2010 American Community Survey population (not shown); ‡ Numbers in parentheses indicate the number of people reporting a single ancestry; * Numbers in parentheses indicate the number of persons reporting this race alone, not in combination with any other race; Please refer to the Explanation of Data for more information.*

Japanese (1)	1	0.01
White (9,653)	9,669	99.02
Not Hispanic (498)	499	5.11
Hispanic (9,155)	9,170	93.91

Rosenberg

Place Type: City
County: Fort Bend
Population: 30,618†

Ancestry‡	Population	%
African, Sub-Saharan (30)	61	0.21
African (30)	61	0.21
American (940)	940	3.20
Arab (113)	121	0.41
Lebanese (113)	121	0.41
Austrian (0)	22	0.07
British (14)	14	0.05
Canadian (39)	104	0.35
Czech (325)	774	2.64
Czechoslovakian (121)	177	0.60
Dutch (0)	123	0.42
English (324)	1,005	3.42
European (24)	115	0.39
Finnish (0)	46	0.16
French, ex. Basque (28)	193	0.66
French Canadian (35)	49	0.17
German (1,163)	2,521	8.59
Greek (21)	58	0.20
Hungarian (9)	51	0.17
Irish (221)	915	3.12
Italian (99)	188	0.64
Norwegian (8)	63	0.21
Polish (152)	400	1.36
Portuguese (10)	19	0.06
Romanian (0)	16	0.05
Russian (0)	8	0.03
Scotch-Irish (126)	184	0.63
Scottish (33)	148	0.50
Swedish (41)	193	0.66
Swiss (20)	20	0.07
Ukrainian (26)	93	0.32
Welsh (13)	13	0.04
West Indian, ex. Hispanic (94)	94	0.32
British West Indian (22)	22	0.07
Jamaican (72)	72	0.25

Hispanic Origin	Population	%
Hispanic or Latino (of any race)	18,470	60.32
Central American, ex. Mexican	1,180	3.85
Costa Rican	4	0.01
Guatemalan	50	0.16
Honduran	109	0.36
Nicaraguan	31	0.10
Panamanian	6	0.02
Salvadoran	977	3.19
Other Central American	3	0.01
Cuban	23	0.08
Dominican Republic	8	0.03
Mexican	15,587	50.91
Puerto Rican	116	0.38
South American	105	0.34
Argentinean	9	0.03
Bolivian	7	0.02
Colombian	39	0.13
Ecuadorian	16	0.05
Peruvian	14	0.05
Uruguayan	3	0.01
Venezuelan	16	0.05
Other South American	1	<0.01
Other Hispanic or Latino	1,451	4.74

Race*	Population	%
African-American/Black (4,091)	4,337	14.16
Not Hispanic (3,887)	4,039	13.19
Hispanic (204)	298	0.97
American Indian/Alaska Native (173)	278	0.91
Not Hispanic (40)	101	0.33
Hispanic (133)	177	0.58
Apache (0)	4	0.01
Blackfeet (0)	3	0.01
Canadian/French Am. Ind. (2)	2	0.01
Cherokee (7)	21	0.07
Chickasaw (5)	5	0.02
Chippewa (0)	1	<0.01
Choctaw (5)	15	0.05
Creek (0)	3	0.01
Iroquois (0)	4	0.01
Mexican American Ind. (29)	33	0.11
Navajo (10)	10	0.03
Puget Sound Salish (2)	2	0.01
South American Ind. (1)	1	<0.01
Spanish American Ind. (3)	3	0.01
Asian (301)	393	1.28
Not Hispanic (292)	351	1.15
Hispanic (9)	42	0.14
Bangladeshi (15)	21	0.07
Cambodian (0)	3	0.01
Chinese, ex. Taiwanese (27)	42	0.14
Filipino (70)	115	0.38
Indian (64)	75	0.24
Indonesian (0)	2	0.01
Japanese (6)	11	0.04
Korean (8)	14	0.05
Laotian (1)	1	<0.01
Nepalese (1)	1	<0.01
Pakistani (30)	36	0.12
Vietnamese (50)	60	0.20
Hawaii Native/Pacific Islander (16)	47	0.15
Not Hispanic (13)	24	0.08
Hispanic (3)	23	0.08
Guamanian/Chamorro (1)	3	0.01
Native Hawaiian (9)	14	0.05
Samoan (0)	4	0.01
White (18,712)	19,498	63.68
Not Hispanic (7,608)	7,843	25.62
Hispanic (11,104)	11,655	38.07

Round Rock

Place Type: City
County: Williamson
Population: 99,887†

Ancestry‡	Population	%
African, Sub-Saharan (494)	641	0.69
African (400)	491	0.53
Ethiopian (50)	50	0.05
Nigerian (25)	63	0.07
Somalian (0)	18	0.02
South African (9)	9	0.01
Other Sub-Saharan African (10)	10	0.01
Albanian (27)	39	0.04
American (3,773)	3,773	4.05
Arab (385)	539	0.58
Egyptian (99)	99	0.11
Jordanian (28)	28	0.03
Lebanese (258)	381	0.41
Moroccan (0)	13	0.01
Syrian (0)	14	0.02
Other Arab (0)	4	<0.01
Armenian (13)	17	0.02
Australian (16)	16	0.02
Austrian (45)	146	0.16
Belgian (0)	191	0.21
Brazilian (91)	101	0.11
British (256)	655	0.70
Cajun (20)	33	0.04
Canadian (55)	153	0.16
Croatian (22)	36	0.04
Czech (254)	1,109	1.19
Czechoslovakian (26)	118	0.13
Danish (167)	453	0.49
Dutch (217)	1,144	1.23
Eastern European (47)	47	0.05
English (3,192)	9,246	9.93
European (1,106)	1,394	1.50
Finnish (0)	32	0.03
French, ex. Basque (701)	3,210	3.45
French Canadian (91)	166	0.18
German (5,500)	16,310	17.52
Greek (40)	242	0.26
Hungarian (60)	240	0.26
Iranian (213)	256	0.27
Irish (2,322)	9,446	10.15
Italian (848)	2,703	2.90
Lithuanian (0)	39	0.04
Macedonian (0)	20	0.02
Maltese (0)	19	0.02
Northern European (57)	57	0.06
Norwegian (147)	613	0.66
Polish (563)	1,886	2.03
Portuguese (21)	60	0.06
Romanian (88)	120	0.13
Russian (71)	516	0.55
Scandinavian (115)	374	0.40
Scotch-Irish (721)	1,606	1.73
Scottish (1,139)	2,724	2.93
Slavic (15)	26	0.03
Slovak (50)	188	0.20
Slovene (0)	32	0.03
Swedish (179)	1,248	1.34
Swiss (34)	323	0.35
Turkish (58)	58	0.06
Ukrainian (30)	30	0.03
Welsh (42)	516	0.55
West Indian, ex. Hispanic (109)	299	0.32
Barbadian (0)	46	0.05
Dutch West Indian (0)	15	0.02
Haitian (95)	165	0.18
Jamaican (14)	73	0.08
Yugoslavian (23)	64	0.07

Hispanic Origin	Population	%
Hispanic or Latino (of any race)	28,958	28.99
Central American, ex. Mexican	1,107	1.11
Costa Rican	43	0.04
Guatemalan	157	0.16
Honduran	242	0.24
Nicaraguan	96	0.10
Panamanian	119	0.12
Salvadoran	450	0.45
Cuban	313	0.31
Dominican Republic	95	0.10
Mexican	23,361	23.39
Puerto Rican	880	0.88
South American	652	0.65
Argentinean	62	0.06
Bolivian	40	0.04
Chilean	47	0.05
Colombian	241	0.24
Ecuadorian	53	0.05
Paraguayan	6	0.01
Peruvian	107	0.11
Uruguayan	8	0.01
Venezuelan	80	0.08
Other South American	8	0.01
Other Hispanic or Latino	2,550	2.55

Race*	Population	%
African-American/Black (9,744)	11,049	11.06
Not Hispanic (9,254)	10,192	10.20
Hispanic (490)	857	0.86
American Indian/Alaska Native (678)	1,441	1.44
Not Hispanic (288)	754	0.75
Hispanic (390)	687	0.69
Alaska Athabascan *(Ala. Nat.)* (2)	2	<0.01
Apache (24)	61	0.06
Blackfeet (4)	24	0.02
Canadian/French Am. Ind. (5)	6	0.01
Central American Ind. (5)	6	0.01
Cherokee (50)	209	0.21
Cheyenne (1)	3	<0.01
Chickasaw (9)	14	0.01
Chippewa (11)	14	0.01
Choctaw (19)	51	0.05
Comanche (4)	20	0.02
Cree (3)	5	0.01
Creek (5)	16	0.02

*Notes: † The Census 2010 population figure is used to calculate the percentages in the Hispanic Origin and Race categories. Ancestry percentages are based on the 2006-2010 American Community Survey population (not shown); ‡ Numbers in parentheses indicate the number of people reporting a single ancestry; * Numbers in parentheses indicate the number of persons reporting this race alone, not in combination with any other race; Please refer to the Explanation of Data for more information.*

Crow (3)	3	<0.01
Delaware (2)	3	<0.01
Hopi (1)	1	<0.01
Houma (1)	2	<0.01
Inupiat *(Alaska Native)* (0)	1	<0.01
Iroquois (3)	11	0.01
Kiowa (3)	4	<0.01
Lumbee (2)	2	<0.01
Menominee (1)	1	<0.01
Mexican American Ind. (56)	114	0.11
Navajo (14)	21	0.02
Osage (7)	16	0.02
Ottawa (1)	1	<0.01
Potawatomi (7)	11	0.01
Pueblo (4)	7	0.01
Seminole (1)	4	<0.01
Sioux (11)	20	0.02
South American Ind. (2)	7	0.01
Spanish American Ind. (0)	1	<0.01
Tohono O'Odham (1)	1	<0.01
Ute (1)	1	<0.01
Yakama (8)	8	0.01
Yaqui (7)	9	0.01
Asian (5,165)	6,247	6.25
Not Hispanic (5,056)	5,957	5.96
Hispanic (109)	290	0.29
Bangladeshi (36)	37	0.04
Burmese (2)	2	<0.01
Cambodian (54)	94	0.09
Chinese, ex. Taiwanese (615)	761	0.76
Filipino (530)	817	0.82
Hmong (7)	10	0.01
Indian (1,779)	1,918	1.92
Indonesian (19)	35	0.04
Japanese (123)	305	0.31
Korean (346)	516	0.52
Laotian (28)	38	0.04
Malaysian (4)	11	0.01
Nepalese (25)	29	0.03
Pakistani (304)	333	0.33
Sri Lankan (19)	25	0.03
Taiwanese (40)	48	0.05
Thai (55)	108	0.11
Vietnamese (1,001)	1,120	1.12
Hawaii Native/Pacific Islander (124)	315	0.32
Not Hispanic (105)	245	0.25
Hispanic (19)	70	0.07
Fijian (2)	5	0.01
Guamanian/Chamorro (31)	60	0.06
Marshallese (3)	6	0.01
Native Hawaiian (31)	106	0.11
Samoan (27)	37	0.04
Tongan (2)	4	<0.01
White (70,707)	73,921	74.00
Not Hispanic (53,924)	55,786	55.85
Hispanic (16,783)	18,135	18.16

Rowlett

Place Type: City
County: Dallas
Population: 56,199†

Ancestry‡	Population	%
African, Sub-Saharan (439)	453	0.84
African (381)	395	0.73
Nigerian (47)	47	0.09
South African (11)	11	0.02
Albanian (19)	19	0.04
American (3,455)	3,455	6.42
Arab (130)	290	0.54
Jordanian (0)	13	0.02
Lebanese (72)	153	0.28
Palestinian (58)	124	0.23
Armenian (0)	10	0.02
Australian (19)	19	0.04
Austrian (25)	70	0.13
Belgian (0)	14	0.03
Brazilian (20)	28	0.05
British (86)	156	0.29
Cajun (0)	16	0.03
Canadian (27)	122	0.23
Croatian (170)	254	0.47
Czech (134)	431	0.80
Czechoslovakian (49)	60	0.11
Danish (19)	156	0.29
Dutch (130)	478	0.89
English (2,032)	4,449	8.27
European (569)	631	1.17
Finnish (8)	56	0.10
French, ex. Basque (245)	1,129	2.10
French Canadian (111)	176	0.33
German (1,737)	6,082	11.31
Greek (0)	31	0.06
Hungarian (36)	36	0.07
Iranian (48)	48	0.09
Irish (1,237)	3,747	6.97
Italian (434)	1,257	2.34
Lithuanian (22)	40	0.07
Northern European (56)	56	0.10
Norwegian (36)	288	0.54
Polish (132)	443	0.82
Portuguese (0)	135	0.25
Romanian (34)	62	0.12
Russian (30)	65	0.12
Scandinavian (39)	80	0.15
Scotch-Irish (584)	932	1.73
Scottish (267)	814	1.51
Slavic (9)	57	0.11
Swedish (52)	265	0.49
Swiss (0)	9	0.02
Turkish (56)	56	0.10
Ukrainian (7)	59	0.11
Welsh (58)	234	0.44
West Indian, ex. Hispanic (174)	188	0.35
Jamaican (174)	174	0.32
West Indian (0)	14	0.03

Hispanic Origin	Population	%
Hispanic or Latino (of any race)	9,285	16.52
Central American, ex. Mexican	692	1.23
Costa Rican	73	0.13
Guatemalan	162	0.29
Honduran	117	0.21
Nicaraguan	48	0.09
Panamanian	13	0.02
Salvadoran	273	0.49
Other Central American	6	0.01
Cuban	110	0.20
Dominican Republic	38	0.07
Mexican	7,204	12.82
Puerto Rican	238	0.42
South American	411	0.73
Argentinean	37	0.07
Bolivian	26	0.05
Chilean	15	0.03
Colombian	160	0.28
Ecuadorian	26	0.05
Paraguayan	2	<0.01
Peruvian	69	0.12
Uruguayan	3	0.01
Venezuelan	57	0.10
Other South American	16	0.03
Other Hispanic or Latino	592	1.05

Race*	Population	%
African-American/Black (7,522)	7,955	14.16
Not Hispanic (7,397)	7,765	13.82
Hispanic (125)	190	0.34
American Indian/Alaska Native (328)	695	1.24
Not Hispanic (228)	535	0.95
Hispanic (100)	160	0.28
Aleut *(Alaska Native)* (1)	1	<0.01
Apache (9)	16	0.03
Blackfeet (1)	9	0.02
Canadian/French Am. Ind. (0)	1	<0.01
Cherokee (56)	145	0.26
Cheyenne (0)	1	<0.01
Chickasaw (10)	18	0.03
Chippewa (0)	1	<0.01
Choctaw (69)	115	0.20
Comanche (1)	3	0.01
Cree (1)	1	<0.01
Creek (12)	22	0.04
Delaware (1)	2	<0.01
Hopi (4)	4	0.01
Inupiat *(Alaska Native)* (0)	1	<0.01
Iroquois (2)	3	0.01
Kiowa (0)	4	0.01
Mexican American Ind. (20)	28	0.05
Navajo (2)	7	0.01
Osage (1)	1	<0.01
Ottawa (1)	1	<0.01
Potawatomi (1)	1	<0.01
Pueblo (5)	5	0.01
Seminole (0)	11	0.02
Shoshone (1)	1	<0.01
Sioux (2)	5	0.01
South American Ind. (1)	2	<0.01
Spanish American Ind. (1)	1	<0.01
Tlingit-Haida *(Alaska Native)* (4)	4	0.01
Tsimshian *(Alaska Native)* (1)	1	<0.01
Ute (3)	4	0.01
Asian (3,698)	4,136	7.36
Not Hispanic (3,649)	4,028	7.17
Hispanic (49)	108	0.19
Bangladeshi (24)	28	0.05
Cambodian (118)	134	0.24
Chinese, ex. Taiwanese (201)	262	0.47
Filipino (533)	649	1.15
Indian (1,026)	1,096	1.95
Indonesian (3)	7	0.01
Japanese (21)	47	0.08
Korean (103)	168	0.30
Laotian (65)	77	0.14
Malaysian (1)	9	0.02
Nepalese (6)	9	0.02
Pakistani (93)	106	0.19
Sri Lankan (3)	3	0.01
Taiwanese (8)	8	0.01
Thai (42)	72	0.13
Vietnamese (1,351)	1,424	2.53
Hawaii Native/Pacific Islander (16)	60	0.11
Not Hispanic (14)	51	0.09
Hispanic (2)	9	0.02
Fijian (2)	2	<0.01
Guamanian/Chamorro (4)	11	0.02
Marshallese (1)	1	<0.01
Native Hawaiian (2)	19	0.03
Samoan (3)	14	0.02
Tongan (0)	3	0.01
White (40,346)	41,645	74.10
Not Hispanic (34,556)	35,393	62.98
Hispanic (5,790)	6,252	11.12

Royse City

Place Type: City
County: Rockwall
Population: 9,349†

Ancestry‡	Population	%
African, Sub-Saharan (13)	13	0.16
Ethiopian (13)	13	0.16
American (1,145)	1,145	13.89
Arab (23)	28	0.34
Syrian (23)	28	0.34
British (9)	63	0.76
Czech (19)	31	0.38
Czechoslovakian (5)	5	0.06
Dutch (27)	121	1.47
English (319)	724	8.78
European (35)	91	1.10
French, ex. Basque (111)	277	3.36
French Canadian (39)	39	0.47
German (226)	798	9.68
Greek (0)	28	0.34
Irish (213)	918	11.14
Italian (145)	467	5.67
Norwegian (0)	50	0.61

*Notes: † The Census 2010 population figure is used to calculate the percentages in the Hispanic Origin and Race categories. Ancestry percentages are based on the 2006-2010 American Community Survey population (not shown); ‡ Numbers in parentheses indicate the number of people reporting a single ancestry; * Numbers in parentheses indicate the number of persons reporting this race alone, not in combination with any other race; Please refer to the Explanation of Data for more information.*

Polish (24)	88	1.07
Russian (10)	44	0.53
Scotch-Irish (40)	61	0.74
Scottish (94)	225	2.73
Swedish (17)	66	0.80
Swiss (0)	9	0.11
Welsh (23)	31	0.38
West Indian, ex. Hispanic (5)	5	0.06
Trinidadian/Tobagonian (5)	5	0.06

Hispanic Origin	Population	%
Hispanic or Latino (of any race)	1,753	18.75
Central American, ex. Mexican	80	0.86
Costa Rican	8	0.09
Guatemalan	13	0.14
Honduran	12	0.13
Panamanian	2	0.02
Salvadoran	45	0.48
Cuban	1	0.01
Dominican Republic	8	0.09
Mexican	1,435	15.35
Puerto Rican	57	0.61
South American	62	0.66
Argentinean	7	0.07
Bolivian	1	0.01
Chilean	6	0.06
Colombian	32	0.34
Ecuadorian	6	0.06
Peruvian	9	0.10
Venezuelan	1	0.01
Other Hispanic or Latino	110	1.18

Race*	Population	%
African-American/Black (780)	846	9.05
Not Hispanic (751)	810	8.66
Hispanic (29)	36	0.39
American Indian/Alaska Native (71)	142	1.52
Not Hispanic (52)	113	1.21
Hispanic (19)	29	0.31
Apache (0)	1	0.01
Cherokee (21)	55	0.59
Chickasaw (2)	4	0.04
Chippewa (0)	3	0.03
Choctaw (9)	20	0.21
Comanche (0)	5	0.05
Creek (8)	9	0.10
Lumbee (0)	1	0.01
Mexican American Ind. (1)	1	0.01
Potawatomi (1)	1	0.01
Spanish American Ind. (1)	1	0.01
Asian (105)	158	1.69
Not Hispanic (101)	150	1.60
Hispanic (4)	8	0.09
Chinese, ex. Taiwanese (4)	5	0.05
Filipino (30)	51	0.55
Indian (20)	22	0.24
Indonesian (1)	1	0.01
Japanese (11)	27	0.29
Korean (5)	10	0.11
Laotian (8)	8	0.09
Nepalese (0)	1	0.01
Pakistani (1)	1	0.01
Thai (2)	4	0.04
Vietnamese (18)	24	0.26
Hawaii Native/Pacific Islander (10)	26	0.28
Not Hispanic (10)	20	0.21
Hispanic (0)	6	0.06
Guamanian/Chamorro (2)	4	0.04
Native Hawaiian (4)	13	0.14
Samoan (4)	8	0.09
White (7,569)	7,785	83.27
Not Hispanic (6,512)	6,654	71.17
Hispanic (1,057)	1,131	12.10

Sachse

Place Type: City
County: Dallas
Population: 20,329†

Ancestry‡	Population	%
African, Sub-Saharan (371)	384	2.09
African (243)	243	1.32
Ethiopian (128)	128	0.70
South African (0)	13	0.07
American (793)	793	4.31
Arab (70)	70	0.38
Arab (12)	12	0.07
Other Arab (58)	58	0.32
Austrian (0)	13	0.07
Belgian (0)	13	0.07
British (16)	16	0.09
Carpatho Rusyn (0)	17	0.09
Croatian (248)	248	1.35
Czech (27)	66	0.36
Czechoslovakian (24)	24	0.13
Danish (0)	57	0.31
Dutch (83)	318	1.73
English (579)	1,588	8.63
European (159)	239	1.30
French, ex. Basque (23)	370	2.01
French Canadian (37)	89	0.48
German (987)	2,537	13.79
Hungarian (19)	60	0.33
Irish (528)	1,671	9.08
Italian (108)	412	2.24
Maltese (0)	14	0.08
Norwegian (11)	80	0.43
Polish (101)	215	1.17
Portuguese (0)	36	0.20
Russian (52)	103	0.56
Scandinavian (29)	54	0.29
Scotch-Irish (75)	354	1.92
Scottish (156)	347	1.89
Slovak (0)	17	0.09
Slovene (17)	17	0.09
Swedish (34)	120	0.65
Swiss (14)	27	0.15
Ukrainian (0)	15	0.08
Welsh (34)	141	0.77
West Indian, ex. Hispanic (0)	8	0.04
Dutch West Indian (0)	8	0.04
Yugoslavian (12)	12	0.07

Hispanic Origin	Population	%
Hispanic or Latino (of any race)	2,832	13.93
Central American, ex. Mexican	238	1.17
Costa Rican	21	0.10
Guatemalan	43	0.21
Honduran	29	0.14
Nicaraguan	15	0.07
Panamanian	12	0.06
Salvadoran	117	0.58
Other Central American	1	<0.01
Cuban	33	0.16
Dominican Republic	18	0.09
Mexican	2,078	10.22
Puerto Rican	97	0.48
South American	130	0.64
Argentinean	7	0.03
Bolivian	6	0.03
Chilean	8	0.04
Colombian	46	0.23
Ecuadorian	15	0.07
Paraguayan	2	0.01
Peruvian	32	0.16
Venezuelan	12	0.06
Other South American	2	0.01
Other Hispanic or Latino	238	1.17

Race*	Population	%
African-American/Black (1,808)	1,957	9.63
Not Hispanic (1,770)	1,881	9.25
Hispanic (38)	76	0.37
American Indian/Alaska Native (156)	306	1.51
Not Hispanic (106)	228	1.12
Hispanic (50)	78	0.38
Apache (2)	3	0.01
Blackfeet (0)	2	0.01
Canadian/French Am. Ind. (1)	1	<0.01
Cherokee (24)	63	0.31
Cheyenne (0)	1	<0.01
Chickasaw (7)	12	0.06
Choctaw (39)	66	0.32
Comanche (3)	4	0.02
Creek (4)	6	0.03
Inupiat *(Alaska Native)* (1)	1	<0.01
Mexican American Ind. (0)	2	0.01
Navajo (0)	2	0.01
Osage (1)	8	0.04
Sioux (5)	5	0.02
Asian (2,259)	2,445	12.03
Not Hispanic (2,240)	2,403	11.82
Hispanic (19)	42	0.21
Bangladeshi (12)	13	0.06
Burmese (6)	6	0.03
Cambodian (38)	47	0.23
Chinese, ex. Taiwanese (147)	190	0.93
Filipino (121)	167	0.82
Hmong (1)	1	<0.01
Indian (366)	383	1.88
Japanese (23)	47	0.23
Korean (97)	130	0.64
Laotian (43)	57	0.28
Pakistani (50)	53	0.26
Sri Lankan (1)	1	<0.01
Taiwanese (7)	7	0.03
Thai (13)	22	0.11
Vietnamese (1,269)	1,324	6.51
Hawaii Native/Pacific Islander (11)	45	0.22
Not Hispanic (11)	41	0.20
Hispanic (0)	4	0.02
Guamanian/Chamorro (5)	5	0.02
Marshallese (2)	2	0.01
Native Hawaiian (2)	19	0.09
Samoan (0)	5	0.02
White (14,609)	15,142	74.48
Not Hispanic (12,954)	13,289	65.37
Hispanic (1,655)	1,853	9.12

Saginaw

Place Type: City
County: Tarrant
Population: 19,806†

Ancestry‡	Population	%
African, Sub-Saharan (0)	11	0.06
South African (0)	11	0.06
American (2,565)	2,565	13.90
Australian (0)	11	0.06
Austrian (22)	52	0.28
Belgian (13)	27	0.15
British (9)	47	0.25
Czech (116)	138	0.75
Czechoslovakian (0)	12	0.07
Danish (10)	53	0.29
Dutch (258)	471	2.55
English (997)	1,500	8.13
Estonian (14)	14	0.08
European (60)	108	0.59
Finnish (38)	67	0.36
French, ex. Basque (49)	365	1.98
French Canadian (39)	52	0.28
German (1,011)	2,297	12.44
Greek (21)	109	0.59
Irish (806)	2,228	12.07
Italian (118)	403	2.18
Northern European (23)	23	0.12
Norwegian (76)	158	0.86
Polish (33)	170	0.92
Portuguese (12)	12	0.07
Russian (17)	28	0.15
Scotch-Irish (201)	312	1.69
Scottish (182)	302	1.64
Serbian (0)	15	0.08
Swedish (45)	99	0.54
Swiss (0)	14	0.08
Welsh (27)	147	0.80
West Indian, ex. Hispanic (50)	64	0.35

*Notes: † The Census 2010 population figure is used to calculate the percentages in the Hispanic Origin and Race categories. Ancestry percentages are based on the 2006-2010 American Community Survey population (not shown); ‡ Numbers in parentheses indicate the number of people reporting a single ancestry; * Numbers in parentheses indicate the number of persons reporting this race alone, not in combination with any other race; Please refer to the Explanation of Data for more information.*

Dutch West Indian (41)	55	0.30
West Indian (9)	9	0.05
Yugoslavian (0)	15	0.08

Hispanic Origin	Population	%
Hispanic or Latino (of any race)	4,668	23.57
Central American, ex. Mexican	108	0.55
Costa Rican	3	0.02
Guatemalan	17	0.09
Honduran	17	0.09
Nicaraguan	4	0.02
Panamanian	7	0.04
Salvadoran	60	0.30
Cuban	26	0.13
Dominican Republic	8	0.04
Mexican	3,993	20.16
Puerto Rican	160	0.81
South American	54	0.27
Argentinean	3	0.02
Chilean	7	0.04
Colombian	17	0.09
Ecuadorian	8	0.04
Peruvian	16	0.08
Venezuelan	3	0.02
Other Hispanic or Latino	319	1.61

Race*	Population	%
African-American/Black (847)	987	4.98
Not Hispanic (794)	903	4.56
Hispanic (53)	84	0.42
American Indian/Alaska Native (160)	303	1.53
Not Hispanic (112)	219	1.11
Hispanic (48)	84	0.42
Apache (1)	3	0.02
Blackfeet (0)	2	0.01
Canadian/French Am. Ind. (0)	1	0.01
Cherokee (24)	66	0.33
Chickasaw (4)	7	0.04
Choctaw (25)	38	0.19
Comanche (4)	11	0.06
Creek (5)	15	0.08
Delaware (0)	2	0.01
Houma (0)	3	0.02
Kiowa (6)	6	0.03
Lumbee (0)	2	0.01
Mexican American Ind. (4)	4	0.02
Navajo (3)	5	0.03
Osage (1)	1	0.01
Ottawa (1)	1	0.01
Potawatomi (5)	5	0.03
Pueblo (2)	3	0.02
Seminole (6)	6	0.03
Shoshone (0)	1	0.01
Sioux (2)	2	0.01
South American Ind. (0)	3	0.02
Tohono O'Odham (0)	3	0.02
Asian (365)	509	2.57
Not Hispanic (361)	492	2.48
Hispanic (4)	17	0.09
Cambodian (6)	6	0.03
Chinese, ex. Taiwanese (20)	33	0.17
Filipino (99)	148	0.75
Indian (25)	37	0.19
Japanese (18)	43	0.22
Korean (27)	52	0.26
Laotian (42)	50	0.25
Pakistani (15)	15	0.08
Sri Lankan (7)	9	0.05
Taiwanese (6)	7	0.04
Thai (10)	32	0.16
Vietnamese (74)	79	0.40
Hawaii Native/Pacific Islander (17)	54	0.27
Not Hispanic (14)	44	0.22
Hispanic (3)	10	0.05
Fijian (1)	1	0.01
Guamanian/Chamorro (2)	9	0.05
Native Hawaiian (6)	31	0.16
Samoan (2)	2	0.01
Tongan (5)	8	0.04
White (16,431)	16,961	85.64
Not Hispanic (13,498)	13,820	69.78
Hispanic (2,933)	3,141	15.86

San Angelo

Place Type: City
County: Tom Green
Population: 93,200†

Ancestry‡	Population	%
African, Sub-Saharan (127)	162	0.18
African (103)	138	0.15
Nigerian (24)	24	0.03
Albanian (195)	195	0.21
American (6,176)	6,176	6.76
Arab (322)	365	0.40
Arab (27)	46	0.05
Egyptian (13)	26	0.03
Lebanese (179)	190	0.21
Palestinian (103)	103	0.11
Armenian (12)	12	0.01
Australian (0)	21	0.02
Austrian (13)	51	0.06
Basque (0)	44	0.05
Belgian (14)	44	0.05
British (128)	268	0.29
Cajun (9)	25	0.03
Canadian (45)	57	0.06
Celtic (49)	49	0.05
Croatian (0)	7	0.01
Czech (451)	836	0.91
Czechoslovakian (90)	150	0.16
Danish (92)	161	0.18
Dutch (196)	1,106	1.21
English (2,777)	6,982	7.64
European (523)	571	0.62
Finnish (32)	136	0.15
French, ex. Basque (525)	1,902	2.08
French Canadian (197)	298	0.33
German (5,148)	11,680	12.78
Greek (81)	126	0.14
Hungarian (40)	92	0.10
Iranian (24)	38	0.04
Irish (3,000)	7,602	8.32
Italian (380)	1,286	1.41
Lithuanian (0)	13	0.01
Northern European (32)	32	0.04
Norwegian (151)	514	0.56
Pennsylvania German (8)	8	0.01
Polish (135)	647	0.71
Portuguese (0)	142	0.16
Romanian (8)	8	0.01
Russian (24)	74	0.08
Scandinavian (73)	86	0.09
Scotch-Irish (1,167)	2,185	2.39
Scottish (455)	1,487	1.63
Slavic (28)	28	0.03
Slovak (30)	69	0.08
Slovene (7)	7	0.01
Swedish (163)	457	0.50
Swiss (0)	115	0.13
Ukrainian (0)	46	0.05
Welsh (86)	373	0.41
West Indian, ex. Hispanic (100)	159	0.17
British West Indian (12)	12	0.01
Dutch West Indian (2)	53	0.06
Haitian (45)	53	0.06
Jamaican (20)	20	0.02
Trinidadian/Tobagonian (21)	21	0.02
Yugoslavian (0)	82	0.09

Hispanic Origin	Population	%
Hispanic or Latino (of any race)	35,862	38.48
Central American, ex. Mexican	159	0.17
Costa Rican	4	<0.01
Guatemalan	47	0.05
Honduran	32	0.03
Nicaraguan	11	0.01
Panamanian	39	0.04
Salvadoran	26	0.03
Cuban	55	0.06
Dominican Republic	43	0.05
Mexican	31,960	34.29
Puerto Rican	466	0.50
South American	119	0.13
Argentinean	11	0.01
Bolivian	4	<0.01
Chilean	9	0.01
Colombian	37	0.04
Ecuadorian	7	0.01
Paraguayan	3	<0.01
Peruvian	30	0.03
Venezuelan	18	0.02
Other Hispanic or Latino	3,060	3.28

Race*	Population	%
African-American/Black (4,313)	5,072	5.44
Not Hispanic (3,887)	4,379	4.70
Hispanic (426)	693	0.74
American Indian/Alaska Native (766)	1,314	1.41
Not Hispanic (350)	705	0.76
Hispanic (416)	609	0.65
Alaska Athabascan *(Ala. Nat.)* (1)	1	<0.01
Aleut *(Alaska Native)* (1)	1	<0.01
Apache (22)	48	0.05
Arapaho (1)	1	<0.01
Blackfeet (5)	19	0.02
Canadian/French Am. Ind. (1)	2	<0.01
Central American Ind. (4)	5	0.01
Cherokee (66)	183	0.20
Cheyenne (0)	5	0.01
Chickasaw (24)	30	0.03
Chippewa (4)	5	0.01
Choctaw (56)	92	0.10
Comanche (3)	14	0.02
Cree (0)	1	<0.01
Creek (10)	14	0.02
Crow (1)	2	<0.01
Delaware (1)	3	<0.01
Hopi (1)	10	0.01
Houma (5)	5	0.01
Inupiat *(Alaska Native)* (1)	2	<0.01
Iroquois (2)	7	0.01
Kiowa (2)	3	<0.01
Lumbee (4)	4	<0.01
Menominee (1)	3	<0.01
Mexican American Ind. (49)	73	0.08
Navajo (18)	27	0.03
Osage (2)	4	<0.01
Paiute (0)	3	<0.01
Pima (1)	8	0.01
Potawatomi (7)	13	0.01
Pueblo (7)	18	0.02
Puget Sound Salish (0)	1	<0.01
Seminole (10)	16	0.02
Shoshone (3)	3	<0.01
Sioux (11)	15	0.02
South American Ind. (0)	3	<0.01
Spanish American Ind. (1)	2	<0.01
Tlingit-Haida *(Alaska Native)* (1)	1	<0.01
Tohono O'Odham (4)	4	<0.01
Yakama (1)	1	<0.01
Yaqui (3)	3	<0.01
Asian (1,059)	1,625	1.74
Not Hispanic (989)	1,434	1.54
Hispanic (70)	191	0.20
Bangladeshi (3)	3	<0.01
Cambodian (4)	5	0.01
Chinese, ex. Taiwanese (101)	155	0.17
Filipino (291)	453	0.49
Hmong (3)	3	<0.01
Indian (127)	155	0.17
Indonesian (8)	10	0.01
Japanese (40)	120	0.13
Korean (153)	301	0.32
Laotian (46)	60	0.06
Nepalese (2)	2	<0.01
Pakistani (1)	4	<0.01
Taiwanese (1)	5	0.01
Thai (46)	78	0.08

*Notes: † The Census 2010 population figure is used to calculate the percentages in the Hispanic Origin and Race categories. Ancestry percentages are based on the 2006-2010 American Community Survey population (not shown); ‡ Numbers in parentheses indicate the number of people reporting a single ancestry; * Numbers in parentheses indicate the number of persons reporting this race alone, not in combination with any other race; Please refer to the Explanation of Data for more information.*

Vietnamese (192)	257	0.28
Hawaii Native/Pacific Islander (88)	213	0.23
Not Hispanic (70)	161	0.17
Hispanic (18)	52	0.06
Guamanian/Chamorro (33)	60	0.06
Marshallese (1)	3	<0.01
Native Hawaiian (34)	71	0.08
Samoan (5)	39	0.04
White (74,918)	77,369	83.01
Not Hispanic (50,663)	51,823	55.60
Hispanic (24,255)	25,546	27.41

San Antonio

Place Type: City
County: Medina
Population: 1,327,407†

Ancestry‡	Population	%
Afghan (0)	13	<0.01
African, Sub-Saharan (4,814)	6,311	0.49
African (3,443)	4,503	0.35
Cape Verdean (0)	136	0.01
Ethiopian (0)	21	<0.01
Kenyan (36)	36	<0.01
Nigerian (601)	830	0.06
Somalian (412)	412	0.03
South African (40)	65	0.01
Sudanese (0)	26	<0.01
Other Sub-Saharan African (282)	282	0.02
Albanian (101)	113	0.01
Alsatian (164)	662	0.05
American (49,486)	49,486	3.84
Arab (3,079)	4,433	0.34
Arab (439)	742	0.06
Egyptian (314)	432	0.03
Iraqi (136)	162	0.01
Jordanian (142)	173	0.01
Lebanese (897)	1,449	0.11
Moroccan (58)	68	0.01
Palestinian (311)	413	0.03
Syrian (130)	252	0.02
Other Arab (652)	742	0.06
Armenian (248)	323	0.03
Australian (99)	125	0.01
Austrian (184)	1,252	0.10
Basque (126)	230	0.02
Belgian (293)	1,182	0.09
Brazilian (98)	210	0.02
British (1,635)	3,160	0.24
Bulgarian (11)	48	<0.01
Cajun (255)	426	0.03
Canadian (562)	1,260	0.10
Celtic (101)	173	0.01
Croatian (257)	476	0.04
Czech (1,873)	6,245	0.48
Czechoslovakian (498)	1,035	0.08
Danish (507)	2,087	0.16
Dutch (1,171)	6,824	0.53
Eastern European (450)	586	0.05
English (19,745)	59,155	4.58
Estonian (33)	45	<0.01
European (5,035)	6,683	0.52
Finnish (128)	602	0.05
French, ex. Basque (4,433)	21,902	1.70
French Canadian (1,277)	2,643	0.20
German (39,403)	112,963	8.76
German Russian (0)	97	0.01
Greek (777)	1,914	0.15
Guyanese (95)	135	0.01
Hungarian (475)	1,998	0.15
Icelander (34)	95	0.01
Iranian (915)	1,074	0.08
Irish (17,604)	65,920	5.11
Israeli (159)	292	0.02
Italian (7,399)	24,332	1.89
Latvian (33)	78	0.01
Lithuanian (245)	920	0.07
Luxemburger (13)	66	0.01
Macedonian (17)	46	<0.01
Maltese (0)	26	<0.01
New Zealander (26)	80	0.01
Northern European (478)	518	0.04
Norwegian (1,715)	5,211	0.40
Pennsylvania German (42)	103	0.01
Polish (5,090)	15,204	1.18
Portuguese (339)	1,549	0.12
Romanian (503)	765	0.06
Russian (1,623)	3,645	0.28
Scandinavian (376)	1,106	0.09
Scotch-Irish (5,611)	14,143	1.10
Scottish (4,406)	14,856	1.15
Serbian (70)	201	0.02
Slavic (131)	184	0.01
Slovak (124)	647	0.05
Slovene (77)	239	0.02
Swedish (1,479)	6,093	0.47
Swiss (345)	1,111	0.09
Turkish (171)	340	0.03
Ukrainian (252)	774	0.06
Welsh (616)	3,900	0.30
West Indian, ex. Hispanic (1,596)	2,588	0.20
Bahamian (144)	162	0.01
Barbadian (71)	98	0.01
Belizean (50)	134	0.01
Bermudan (38)	68	0.01
Dutch West Indian (153)	400	0.03
Haitian (145)	239	0.02
Jamaican (655)	951	0.07
Trinidadian/Tobagonian (119)	192	0.01
U.S. Virgin Islander (14)	23	<0.01
West Indian (184)	298	0.02
Other West Indian (23)	23	<0.01
Yugoslavian (403)	705	0.05

Hispanic Origin	Population	%
Hispanic or Latino (of any race)	838,952	63.20
Central American, ex. Mexican	10,735	0.81
Costa Rican	364	0.03
Guatemalan	1,848	0.14
Honduran	2,776	0.21
Nicaraguan	1,059	0.08
Panamanian	1,602	0.12
Salvadoran	2,969	0.22
Other Central American	117	0.01
Cuban	2,468	0.19
Dominican Republic	735	0.06
Mexican	705,530	53.15
Puerto Rican	13,164	0.99
South American	5,698	0.43
Argentinean	488	0.04
Bolivian	284	0.02
Chilean	374	0.03
Colombian	2,139	0.16
Ecuadorian	471	0.04
Paraguayan	38	<0.01
Peruvian	1,258	0.09
Uruguayan	86	0.01
Venezuelan	505	0.04
Other South American	55	<0.01
Other Hispanic or Latino	100,622	7.58

Race*	Population	%
African-American/Black (91,280)	102,748	7.74
Not Hispanic (83,365)	89,802	6.77
Hispanic (7,915)	12,946	0.98
American Indian/Alaska Native (11,800)	20,137	1.52
Not Hispanic (2,771)	6,483	0.49
Hispanic (9,029)	13,654	1.03
Alaska Athabascan *(Ala. Nat.)* (5)	15	<0.01
Aleut *(Alaska Native)* (9)	16	<0.01
Apache (612)	1,050	0.08
Arapaho (3)	9	<0.01
Blackfeet (45)	210	0.02
Canadian/French Am. Ind. (24)	64	<0.01
Central American Ind. (35)	56	<0.01
Cherokee (635)	2,136	0.16
Cheyenne (18)	39	<0.01
Chickasaw (63)	145	0.01
Chippewa (91)	148	0.01
Choctaw (230)	514	0.04
Colville (3)	4	<0.01
Comanche (115)	200	0.02
Cree (2)	12	<0.01
Creek (47)	130	0.01
Crow (12)	20	<0.01
Delaware (14)	30	<0.01
Hopi (15)	23	<0.01
Houma (1)	3	<0.01
Inupiat *(Alaska Native)* (4)	15	<0.01
Iroquois (32)	85	0.01
Kiowa (19)	26	<0.01
Lumbee (13)	17	<0.01
Menominee (3)	4	<0.01
Mexican American Ind. (1,069)	1,546	0.12
Navajo (174)	278	0.02
Osage (27)	60	<0.01
Ottawa (9)	10	<0.01
Paiute (15)	20	<0.01
Pima (9)	12	<0.01
Potawatomi (26)	46	<0.01
Pueblo (61)	113	0.01
Puget Sound Salish (4)	7	<0.01
Seminole (24)	92	0.01
Shoshone (10)	16	<0.01
Sioux (100)	222	0.02
South American Ind. (43)	122	0.01
Spanish American Ind. (69)	117	0.01
Tlingit-Haida *(Alaska Native)* (7)	11	<0.01
Tohono O'Odham (13)	29	<0.01
Tsimshian *(Alaska Native)* (1)	2	<0.01
Ute (1)	6	<0.01
Yakama (1)	10	<0.01
Yaqui (40)	77	0.01
Yuman (9)	14	<0.01
Yup'ik *(Alaska Native)* (9)	11	<0.01
Asian (32,254)	42,623	3.21
Not Hispanic (30,596)	37,486	2.82
Hispanic (1,658)	5,137	0.39
Bangladeshi (141)	172	0.01
Bhutanese (153)	209	0.02
Burmese (503)	535	0.04
Cambodian (166)	228	0.02
Chinese, ex. Taiwanese (4,262)	5,707	0.43
Filipino (6,250)	9,328	0.70
Hmong (7)	10	<0.01
Indian (8,733)	9,716	0.73
Indonesian (106)	186	0.01
Japanese (1,405)	3,062	0.23
Korean (2,815)	4,337	0.33
Laotian (263)	389	0.03
Malaysian (34)	67	0.01
Nepalese (162)	213	0.02
Pakistani (1,057)	1,194	0.09
Sri Lankan (71)	86	0.01
Taiwanese (303)	385	0.03
Thai (645)	1,099	0.08
Vietnamese (3,655)	4,266	0.32
Hawaii Native/Pacific Islander (1,504)	3,453	0.26
Not Hispanic (1,097)	2,094	0.16
Hispanic (407)	1,359	0.10
Fijian (4)	8	<0.01
Guamanian/Chamorro (592)	968	0.07
Marshallese (0)	1	<0.01
Native Hawaiian (419)	1,076	0.08
Samoan (209)	365	0.03
Tongan (7)	20	<0.01
White (963,413)	1,001,202	75.43
Not Hispanic (353,106)	365,813	27.56
Hispanic (610,307)	635,389	47.87

San Benito

Place Type: City
County: Cameron
Population: 24,250†

Ancestry‡	Population	%
American (496)	496	2.04
Belgian (12)	12	0.05

*Notes: † The Census 2010 population figure is used to calculate the percentages in the Hispanic Origin and Race categories. Ancestry percentages are based on the 2006-2010 American Community Survey population (not shown); ‡ Numbers in parentheses indicate the number of people reporting a single ancestry; * Numbers in parentheses indicate the number of persons reporting this race alone, not in combination with any other race; Please refer to the Explanation of Data for more information.*

	Population	%
British (8)	8	0.03
Canadian (76)	85	0.35
Czech (0)	29	0.12
Danish (0)	35	0.14
Dutch (19)	83	0.34
English (130)	427	1.76
French, ex. Basque (10)	155	0.64
French Canadian (10)	45	0.19
German (166)	507	2.09
Hungarian (0)	12	0.05
Irish (114)	420	1.73
Italian (29)	90	0.37
Northern European (6)	6	0.02
Norwegian (96)	367	1.51
Polish (37)	63	0.26
Portuguese (0)	10	0.04
Scotch-Irish (52)	73	0.30
Scottish (0)	30	0.12
Slovene (0)	11	0.05
Swedish (11)	22	0.09

Hispanic Origin	Population	%
Hispanic or Latino (of any race)	21,995	90.70
Central American, ex. Mexican	97	0.40
Costa Rican	3	0.01
Guatemalan	18	0.07
Honduran	42	0.17
Nicaraguan	4	0.02
Salvadoran	30	0.12
Cuban	28	0.12
Dominican Republic	1	<0.01
Mexican	20,062	82.73
Puerto Rican	50	0.21
South American	14	0.06
Chilean	1	<0.01
Colombian	7	0.03
Peruvian	6	0.02
Other Hispanic or Latino	1,743	7.19

Race*	Population	%
African-American/Black (110)	149	0.61
Not Hispanic (38)	51	0.21
Hispanic (72)	98	0.40
American Indian/Alaska Native (83)	130	0.54
Not Hispanic (26)	41	0.17
Hispanic (57)	89	0.37
Alaska Athabascan *(Ala. Nat.)* (1)	1	<0.01
Apache (14)	19	0.08
Arapaho (0)	1	<0.01
Blackfeet (1)	1	<0.01
Central American Ind. (0)	2	0.01
Cherokee (4)	7	0.03
Chickasaw (1)	1	<0.01
Choctaw (1)	3	0.01
Creek (2)	2	0.01
Iroquois (0)	1	<0.01
Mexican American Ind. (3)	5	0.02
Navajo (3)	3	0.01
Osage (0)	1	<0.01
Spanish American Ind. (1)	3	0.01
Yaqui (0)	1	<0.01
Asian (67)	94	0.39
Not Hispanic (58)	69	0.28
Hispanic (9)	25	0.10
Chinese, ex. Taiwanese (10)	13	0.05
Filipino (18)	28	0.12
Indian (15)	23	0.09
Japanese (11)	12	0.05
Korean (5)	8	0.03
Thai (2)	2	0.01
Vietnamese (4)	8	0.03
Hawaii Native/Pacific Islander (2)	12	0.05
Not Hispanic (2)	2	0.01
Hispanic (0)	10	0.04
Guamanian/Chamorro (2)	3	0.01
Native Hawaiian (0)	1	<0.01
White (20,848)	21,222	87.51
Not Hispanic (2,082)	2,119	8.74
Hispanic (18,766)	19,103	78.78

San Elizario

Place Type: CDP
County: El Paso
Population: 13,603†

Ancestry‡	Population	%
American (115)	115	0.81
English (0)	12	0.08
French, ex. Basque (0)	11	0.08
German (0)	12	0.08
Irish (0)	44	0.31

Hispanic Origin	Population	%
Hispanic or Latino (of any race)	13,428	98.71
Central American, ex. Mexican	17	0.12
Guatemalan	4	0.03
Honduran	4	0.03
Salvadoran	9	0.07
Cuban	2	0.01
Mexican	12,785	93.99
Puerto Rican	13	0.10
South American	2	0.01
Peruvian	2	0.01
Other Hispanic or Latino	609	4.48

Race*	Population	%
African-American/Black (15)	30	0.22
Not Hispanic (6)	10	0.07
Hispanic (9)	20	0.15
American Indian/Alaska Native (73)	80	0.59
Not Hispanic (40)	41	0.30
Hispanic (33)	39	0.29
Apache (9)	10	0.07
Choctaw (1)	1	0.01
Creek (1)	2	0.01
Mexican American Ind. (2)	2	0.01
Pueblo (32)	36	0.26
Spanish American Ind. (1)	1	0.01
Asian (14)	25	0.18
Not Hispanic (6)	6	0.04
Hispanic (8)	19	0.14
Chinese, ex. Taiwanese (1)	1	0.01
Indian (8)	14	0.10
Japanese (1)	1	0.01
Korean (2)	6	0.04
Nepalese (2)	2	0.01
Vietnamese (0)	1	0.01
Hawaii Native/Pacific Islander (0)	1	0.01
Hispanic (0)	1	0.01
Samoan (0)	1	0.01
White (11,925)	12,020	88.36
Not Hispanic (116)	120	0.88
Hispanic (11,809)	11,900	87.48

San Juan

Place Type: City
County: Hidalgo
Population: 33,856†

Ancestry‡	Population	%
African, Sub-Saharan (11)	11	0.03
African (11)	11	0.03
American (316)	316	0.97
Dutch (6)	16	0.05
English (10)	299	0.92
French, ex. Basque (11)	86	0.26
French Canadian (25)	25	0.08
German (143)	397	1.22
Greek (15)	15	0.05
Irish (12)	284	0.87
Italian (17)	33	0.10
Norwegian (10)	21	0.06
Polish (20)	20	0.06
Scotch-Irish (15)	57	0.18
Scottish (0)	34	0.10
Swedish (0)	8	0.02

Hispanic Origin	Population	%
Hispanic or Latino (of any race)	32,734	96.69
Central American, ex. Mexican	83	0.25
Costa Rican	1	<0.01
Guatemalan	29	0.09
Honduran	30	0.09
Nicaraguan	5	0.01
Panamanian	1	<0.01
Salvadoran	17	0.05
Cuban	42	0.12
Dominican Republic	2	0.01
Mexican	31,279	92.39
Puerto Rican	38	0.11
South American	10	0.03
Bolivian	2	0.01
Colombian	4	0.01
Ecuadorian	1	<0.01
Peruvian	2	0.01
Venezuelan	1	<0.01
Other Hispanic or Latino	1,280	3.78

Race*	Population	%
African-American/Black (110)	145	0.43
Not Hispanic (32)	34	0.10
Hispanic (78)	111	0.33
American Indian/Alaska Native (80)	101	0.30
Not Hispanic (10)	15	0.04
Hispanic (70)	86	0.25
Apache (2)	2	0.01
Blackfeet (0)	1	<0.01
Cherokee (2)	3	0.01
Iroquois (0)	1	<0.01
Mexican American Ind. (15)	15	0.04
Navajo (7)	7	0.02
Spanish American Ind. (1)	3	0.01
Yaqui (1)	1	<0.01
Yup'ik *(Alaska Native)* (4)	4	0.01
Asian (62)	91	0.27
Not Hispanic (47)	50	0.15
Hispanic (15)	41	0.12
Chinese, ex. Taiwanese (10)	11	0.03
Filipino (31)	33	0.10
Indian (17)	22	0.06
Korean (1)	11	0.03
Vietnamese (3)	4	0.01
Hawaii Native/Pacific Islander (4)	15	0.04
Not Hispanic (0)	1	<0.01
Hispanic (4)	14	0.04
Guamanian/Chamorro (4)	7	0.02
Native Hawaiian (0)	3	0.01
Samoan (0)	4	0.01
White (30,211)	30,504	90.10
Not Hispanic (1,012)	1,020	3.01
Hispanic (29,199)	29,484	87.09

San Marcos

Place Type: City
County: Hays
Population: 44,894†

Ancestry‡	Population	%
African, Sub-Saharan (192)	246	0.57
African (132)	186	0.43
Nigerian (20)	20	0.05
Ugandan (15)	15	0.03
Other Sub-Saharan African (25)	25	0.06
Albanian (16)	16	0.04
Alsatian (0)	9	0.02
American (1,020)	1,020	2.36
Arab (16)	61	0.14
Lebanese (16)	45	0.10
Syrian (0)	16	0.04
Australian (29)	29	0.07
Austrian (23)	36	0.08
Belgian (17)	47	0.11
Brazilian (27)	27	0.06
British (78)	172	0.40
Cajun (11)	27	0.06
Canadian (0)	36	0.08

*Notes: † The Census 2010 population figure is used to calculate the percentages in the Hispanic Origin and Race categories. Ancestry percentages are based on the 2006-2010 American Community Survey population (not shown); ‡ Numbers in parentheses indicate the number of people reporting a single ancestry; * Numbers in parentheses indicate the number of persons reporting this race alone, not in combination with any other race; Please refer to the Explanation of Data for more information.*

Ancestry	Population	%
Celtic (11)	11	0.03
Czech (472)	823	1.90
Czechoslovakian (27)	55	0.13
Danish (0)	43	0.10
Dutch (94)	335	0.77
Eastern European (0)	45	0.10
English (1,186)	3,115	7.20
Estonian (0)	32	0.07
European (326)	356	0.82
Finnish (0)	55	0.13
French, ex. Basque (273)	1,123	2.59
French Canadian (76)	156	0.36
German (3,516)	7,307	16.88
Greek (47)	118	0.27
Hungarian (14)	101	0.23
Iranian (15)	29	0.07
Irish (1,130)	3,395	7.84
Italian (584)	1,431	3.31
Lithuanian (15)	15	0.03
Macedonian (15)	15	0.03
Northern European (42)	42	0.10
Norwegian (91)	246	0.57
Pennsylvania German (0)	17	0.04
Polish (249)	691	1.60
Portuguese (0)	76	0.18
Romanian (15)	36	0.08
Russian (125)	209	0.48
Scandinavian (4)	35	0.08
Scotch-Irish (598)	1,119	2.59
Scottish (205)	719	1.66
Slavic (10)	10	0.02
Slovene (0)	18	0.04
Swedish (127)	371	0.86
Swiss (11)	43	0.10
Ukrainian (26)	70	0.16
Welsh (16)	219	0.51
West Indian, ex. Hispanic (97)	171	0.40
Haitian (20)	20	0.05
Jamaican (10)	26	0.06
Trinidadian/Tobagonian (43)	101	0.23
West Indian (24)	24	0.06
Yugoslavian (17)	17	0.04

Hispanic Origin	Population	%
Hispanic or Latino (of any race)	16,967	37.79
Central American, ex. Mexican	214	0.48
Costa Rican	4	0.01
Guatemalan	47	0.10
Honduran	51	0.11
Nicaraguan	22	0.05
Panamanian	25	0.06
Salvadoran	64	0.14
Other Central American	1	<0.01
Cuban	81	0.18
Dominican Republic	15	0.03
Mexican	14,082	31.37
Puerto Rican	268	0.60
South American	210	0.47
Argentinean	12	0.03
Bolivian	16	0.04
Chilean	20	0.04
Colombian	72	0.16
Ecuadorian	24	0.05
Paraguayan	1	<0.01
Peruvian	27	0.06
Uruguayan	1	<0.01
Venezuelan	37	0.08
Other Hispanic or Latino	2,097	4.67

Race*	Population	%
African-American/Black (2,465)	2,881	6.42
Not Hispanic (2,244)	2,499	5.57
Hispanic (221)	382	0.85
American Indian/Alaska Native (383)	688	1.53
Not Hispanic (141)	348	0.78
Hispanic (242)	340	0.76
Apache (17)	26	0.06
Blackfeet (2)	14	0.03
Canadian/French Am. Ind. (1)	1	<0.01
Central American Ind. (2)	2	<0.01
Cherokee (35)	118	0.26
Cheyenne (0)	1	<0.01
Chickasaw (5)	17	0.04
Chippewa (2)	5	0.01
Choctaw (18)	34	0.08
Comanche (2)	6	0.01
Creek (1)	6	0.01
Crow (0)	1	<0.01
Delaware (0)	1	<0.01
Inupiat *(Alaska Native)* (4)	4	0.01
Iroquois (2)	4	0.01
Kiowa (1)	1	<0.01
Lumbee (5)	6	0.01
Mexican American Ind. (73)	86	0.19
Navajo (5)	7	0.02
Osage (2)	2	<0.01
Pima (4)	4	0.01
Potawatomi (3)	4	0.01
Pueblo (1)	1	<0.01
Puget Sound Salish (1)	1	<0.01
Shoshone (1)	1	<0.01
Sioux (4)	10	0.02
South American Ind. (2)	2	<0.01
Ute (1)	2	<0.01
Yaqui (1)	2	<0.01
Asian (697)	1,034	2.30
Not Hispanic (659)	904	2.01
Hispanic (38)	130	0.29
Bangladeshi (5)	6	0.01
Cambodian (10)	12	0.03
Chinese, ex. Taiwanese (127)	189	0.42
Filipino (90)	166	0.37
Hmong (0)	1	<0.01
Indian (154)	184	0.41
Indonesian (7)	18	0.04
Japanese (56)	120	0.27
Korean (72)	119	0.27
Laotian (9)	19	0.04
Malaysian (1)	2	<0.01
Nepalese (17)	18	0.04
Pakistani (22)	25	0.06
Sri Lankan (19)	19	0.04
Taiwanese (11)	14	0.03
Thai (8)	20	0.04
Vietnamese (58)	72	0.16
Hawaii Native/Pacific Islander (55)	107	0.24
Not Hispanic (35)	75	0.17
Hispanic (20)	32	0.07
Fijian (3)	3	0.01
Guamanian/Chamorro (21)	28	0.06
Marshallese (0)	1	<0.01
Native Hawaiian (16)	35	0.08
Samoan (6)	13	0.03
Tongan (0)	2	<0.01
White (35,221)	36,463	81.22
Not Hispanic (24,098)	24,724	55.07
Hispanic (11,123)	11,739	26.15

Santa Fe

Place Type: City
County: Galveston
Population: 12,222†

Ancestry‡	Population	%
American (949)	949	7.81
Arab (0)	36	0.30
Lebanese (0)	18	0.15
Syrian (0)	18	0.15
Armenian (70)	70	0.58
Austrian (0)	17	0.14
British (0)	23	0.19
Cajun (29)	29	0.24
Canadian (139)	139	1.14
Czech (31)	104	0.86
Czechoslovakian (0)	11	0.09
Dutch (58)	218	1.79
English (537)	1,321	10.87
European (180)	180	1.48
French, ex. Basque (238)	827	6.81
French Canadian (29)	49	0.40
German (772)	2,341	19.27
Greek (35)	35	0.29
Hungarian (0)	14	0.12
Irish (434)	1,908	15.71
Italian (316)	894	7.36
Northern European (8)	8	0.07
Norwegian (0)	93	0.77
Polish (41)	237	1.95
Portuguese (14)	41	0.34
Russian (23)	48	0.40
Scotch-Irish (60)	173	1.42
Scottish (35)	247	2.03
Serbian (0)	15	0.12
Swedish (169)	265	2.18
Welsh (0)	27	0.22
West Indian, ex. Hispanic (0)	8	0.07
Dutch West Indian (0)	8	0.07
Yugoslavian (6)	6	0.05

Hispanic Origin	Population	%
Hispanic or Latino (of any race)	1,412	11.55
Central American, ex. Mexican	14	0.11
Guatemalan	1	0.01
Honduran	5	0.04
Nicaraguan	1	0.01
Salvadoran	7	0.06
Cuban	24	0.20
Dominican Republic	1	0.01
Mexican	1,166	9.54
Puerto Rican	49	0.40
South American	17	0.14
Colombian	6	0.05
Ecuadorian	1	0.01
Peruvian	1	0.01
Venezuelan	9	0.07
Other Hispanic or Latino	141	1.15

Race*	Population	%
African-American/Black (46)	75	0.61
Not Hispanic (38)	62	0.51
Hispanic (8)	13	0.11
American Indian/Alaska Native (58)	110	0.90
Not Hispanic (42)	87	0.71
Hispanic (16)	23	0.19
Apache (1)	1	0.01
Cherokee (14)	27	0.22
Chickasaw (1)	1	0.01
Chippewa (1)	2	0.02
Choctaw (11)	20	0.16
Creek (2)	4	0.03
Delaware (0)	3	0.02
Inupiat *(Alaska Native)* (1)	1	0.01
Iroquois (2)	2	0.02
Mexican American Ind. (2)	3	0.02
Osage (0)	2	0.02
Potawatomi (3)	3	0.02
Seminole (4)	4	0.03
Sioux (1)	2	0.02
Asian (60)	84	0.69
Not Hispanic (60)	79	0.65
Hispanic (0)	5	0.04
Chinese, ex. Taiwanese (7)	8	0.07
Filipino (8)	18	0.15
Indian (11)	14	0.11
Japanese (1)	5	0.04
Korean (9)	12	0.10
Pakistani (3)	4	0.03
Thai (4)	6	0.05
Vietnamese (14)	16	0.13
Hawaii Native/Pacific Islander (11)	16	0.13
Not Hispanic (5)	9	0.07
Hispanic (6)	7	0.06
Native Hawaiian (5)	9	0.07
White (11,466)	11,642	95.25
Not Hispanic (10,560)	10,654	87.17
Hispanic (906)	988	8.08

*Notes: † The Census 2010 population figure is used to calculate the percentages in the Hispanic Origin and Race categories. Ancestry percentages are based on the 2006-2010 American Community Survey population (not shown); ‡ Numbers in parentheses indicate the number of people reporting a single ancestry; * Numbers in parentheses indicate the number of persons reporting this race alone, not in combination with any other race; Please refer to the Explanation of Data for more information.*

Schertz

Place Type: City
County: Guadalupe
Population: 31,465†

Ancestry‡	Population	%
African, Sub-Saharan (35)	112	0.39
African (28)	87	0.31
Ethiopian (7)	7	0.02
Nigerian (0)	18	0.06
American (1,331)	1,331	4.68
Arab (0)	108	0.38
Lebanese (0)	93	0.33
Syrian (0)	15	0.05
Austrian (37)	46	0.16
Basque (33)	33	0.12
Belgian (19)	91	0.32
British (12)	96	0.34
Cajun (0)	23	0.08
Canadian (34)	42	0.15
Croatian (10)	10	0.04
Czech (146)	293	1.03
Czechoslovakian (46)	46	0.16
Danish (22)	62	0.22
Dutch (31)	325	1.14
English (1,193)	3,235	11.38
European (317)	422	1.48
Finnish (0)	38	0.13
French, ex. Basque (260)	1,177	4.14
French Canadian (86)	302	1.06
German (2,385)	6,411	22.56
Greek (26)	26	0.09
Hungarian (79)	163	0.57
Irish (1,041)	3,492	12.29
Italian (551)	1,440	5.07
Lithuanian (0)	9	0.03
Luxemburger (11)	11	0.04
Norwegian (34)	180	0.63
Polish (302)	943	3.32
Portuguese (23)	86	0.30
Romanian (0)	13	0.05
Russian (39)	84	0.30
Scandinavian (21)	21	0.07
Scotch-Irish (175)	655	2.30
Scottish (258)	783	2.75
Serbian (0)	9	0.03
Slovak (18)	45	0.16
Slovene (15)	15	0.05
Swedish (35)	164	0.58
Swiss (11)	11	0.04
Ukrainian (29)	29	0.10
Welsh (86)	265	0.93
West Indian, ex. Hispanic (112)	131	0.46
Barbadian (0)	19	0.07
Bermudan (22)	22	0.08
Haitian (36)	36	0.13
Jamaican (54)	54	0.19
Yugoslavian (34)	79	0.28

Hispanic Origin	Population	%
Hispanic or Latino (of any race)	8,099	25.74
Central American, ex. Mexican	201	0.64
Costa Rican	9	0.03
Guatemalan	36	0.11
Honduran	11	0.03
Nicaraguan	17	0.05
Panamanian	89	0.28
Salvadoran	39	0.12
Cuban	54	0.17
Dominican Republic	16	0.05
Mexican	6,228	19.79
Puerto Rican	493	1.57
South American	102	0.32
Argentinean	9	0.03
Bolivian	17	0.05
Chilean	3	0.01
Colombian	45	0.14
Ecuadorian	3	0.01
Peruvian	15	0.05
Venezuelan	10	0.03
Other Hispanic or Latino	1,005	3.19

Race*	Population	%
African-American/Black (2,695)	3,130	9.95
Not Hispanic (2,583)	2,926	9.30
Hispanic (112)	204	0.65
American Indian/Alaska Native (226)	475	1.51
Not Hispanic (122)	299	0.95
Hispanic (104)	176	0.56
Alaska Athabascan *(Ala. Nat.)* (0)	1	<0.01
Aleut *(Alaska Native)* (0)	1	<0.01
Apache (9)	16	0.05
Blackfeet (1)	11	0.03
Central American Ind. (0)	2	0.01
Cherokee (35)	82	0.26
Chickasaw (10)	14	0.04
Chippewa (1)	11	0.03
Choctaw (14)	25	0.08
Cree (0)	1	<0.01
Creek (2)	7	0.02
Delaware (4)	4	0.01
Iroquois (1)	2	0.01
Lumbee (1)	7	0.02
Mexican American Ind. (15)	22	0.07
Navajo (5)	11	0.03
Osage (0)	4	0.01
Potawatomi (1)	1	<0.01
Pueblo (1)	3	0.01
Seminole (0)	4	0.01
Sioux (10)	11	0.03
South American Ind. (7)	8	0.03
Spanish American Ind. (2)	2	0.01
Tlingit-Haida *(Alaska Native)* (0)	5	0.02
Yaqui (0)	1	<0.01
Asian (738)	1,216	3.86
Not Hispanic (707)	1,093	3.47
Hispanic (31)	123	0.39
Bhutanese (1)	1	<0.01
Cambodian (12)	12	0.04
Chinese, ex. Taiwanese (54)	91	0.29
Filipino (238)	417	1.33
Indian (45)	65	0.21
Indonesian (2)	2	0.01
Japanese (65)	165	0.52
Korean (123)	212	0.67
Laotian (4)	6	0.02
Malaysian (1)	2	0.01
Nepalese (5)	5	0.02
Pakistani (7)	10	0.03
Sri Lankan (1)	1	<0.01
Taiwanese (1)	3	0.01
Thai (54)	93	0.30
Vietnamese (101)	139	0.44
Hawaii Native/Pacific Islander (58)	134	0.43
Not Hispanic (43)	105	0.33
Hispanic (15)	29	0.09
Guamanian/Chamorro (37)	65	0.21
Native Hawaiian (8)	34	0.11
Samoan (6)	11	0.03
White (24,809)	25,842	82.13
Not Hispanic (19,052)	19,744	62.75
Hispanic (5,757)	6,098	19.38

Seabrook

Place Type: City
County: Harris
Population: 11,952†

Ancestry‡	Population	%
American (452)	452	3.94
Arab (13)	13	0.11
Lebanese (13)	13	0.11
Australian (15)	15	0.13
Austrian (0)	11	0.10
Brazilian (0)	103	0.90
British (32)	249	2.17
Croatian (236)	236	2.06
Czech (91)	220	1.92
Czechoslovakian (9)	9	0.08
Danish (0)	13	0.11
Dutch (150)	205	1.79
Eastern European (27)	27	0.24
English (688)	1,546	13.49
European (138)	154	1.34
French, ex. Basque (199)	772	6.74
French Canadian (0)	65	0.57
German (1,026)	2,587	22.57
Greek (16)	16	0.14
Hungarian (8)	44	0.38
Iranian (57)	90	0.79
Irish (521)	1,450	12.65
Italian (104)	396	3.46
Norwegian (26)	172	1.50
Polish (77)	181	1.58
Portuguese (15)	100	0.87
Romanian (23)	23	0.20
Russian (42)	85	0.74
Scotch-Irish (103)	358	3.12
Scottish (43)	203	1.77
Slovak (16)	16	0.14
Swedish (27)	176	1.54
Ukrainian (0)	35	0.31
Welsh (32)	152	1.33
West Indian, ex. Hispanic (0)	30	0.26
Bahamian (0)	30	0.26

Hispanic Origin	Population	%
Hispanic or Latino (of any race)	1,701	14.23
Central American, ex. Mexican	124	1.04
Costa Rican	9	0.08
Guatemalan	10	0.08
Honduran	31	0.26
Nicaraguan	6	0.05
Panamanian	8	0.07
Salvadoran	60	0.50
Cuban	52	0.44
Dominican Republic	2	0.02
Mexican	1,188	9.94
Puerto Rican	73	0.61
South American	55	0.46
Argentinean	2	0.02
Bolivian	2	0.02
Chilean	8	0.07
Colombian	23	0.19
Ecuadorian	8	0.07
Paraguayan	3	0.03
Peruvian	6	0.05
Uruguayan	2	0.02
Venezuelan	1	0.01
Other Hispanic or Latino	207	1.73

Race*	Population	%
African-American/Black (486)	574	4.80
Not Hispanic (468)	528	4.42
Hispanic (18)	46	0.38
American Indian/Alaska Native (56)	148	1.24
Not Hispanic (44)	105	0.88
Hispanic (12)	43	0.36
Aleut *(Alaska Native)* (0)	1	0.01
Apache (1)	5	0.04
Blackfeet (0)	4	0.03
Central American Ind. (0)	1	0.01
Cherokee (10)	28	0.23
Cheyenne (0)	7	0.06
Chickasaw (2)	2	0.02
Choctaw (12)	15	0.13
Comanche (0)	1	0.01
Creek (3)	4	0.03
Iroquois (4)	4	0.03
Mexican American Ind. (1)	2	0.02
Navajo (1)	2	0.02
Seminole (1)	5	0.04
Sioux (1)	1	0.01
South American Ind. (0)	5	0.04
Spanish American Ind. (0)	1	0.01
Tlingit-Haida *(Alaska Native)* (1)	1	0.01
Yaqui (0)	1	0.01
Asian (530)	634	5.30

*Notes: † The Census 2010 population figure is used to calculate the percentages in the Hispanic Origin and Race categories. Ancestry percentages are based on the 2006-2010 American Community Survey population (not shown); ‡ Numbers in parentheses indicate the number of people reporting a single ancestry; * Numbers in parentheses indicate the number of persons reporting this race alone, not in combination with any other race; Please refer to the Explanation of Data for more information.*

Not Hispanic (517)	614	5.14
Hispanic (13)	20	0.17
Burmese (8)	8	0.07
Cambodian (2)	5	0.04
Chinese, ex. Taiwanese (57)	77	0.64
Filipino (91)	115	0.96
Hmong (1)	3	0.03
Indian (113)	130	1.09
Indonesian (4)	5	0.04
Japanese (18)	25	0.21
Korean (22)	37	0.31
Laotian (13)	17	0.14
Pakistani (36)	41	0.34
Taiwanese (4)	10	0.08
Thai (14)	17	0.14
Vietnamese (111)	118	0.99
Hawaii Native/Pacific Islander (4)	19	0.16
Not Hispanic (2)	12	0.10
Hispanic (2)	7	0.06
Guamanian/Chamorro (1)	2	0.02
Native Hawaiian (2)	6	0.05
Samoan (1)	1	0.01
White (10,157)	10,438	87.33
Not Hispanic (8,997)	9,189	76.88
Hispanic (1,160)	1,249	10.45

Seagoville

Place Type: City
County: Dallas
Population: 14,835†

Ancestry‡	Population	%
African, Sub-Saharan (94)	131	0.93
African (85)	122	0.87
Nigerian (9)	9	0.06
American (2,983)	2,983	21.24
British (23)	56	0.40
Czech (23)	36	0.26
Dutch (13)	148	1.05
English (311)	645	4.59
French, ex. Basque (154)	297	2.11
French Canadian (10)	10	0.07
German (519)	1,196	8.51
Irish (284)	850	6.05
Italian (82)	173	1.23
Lithuanian (0)	9	0.06
Norwegian (22)	47	0.33
Polish (34)	126	0.90
Russian (20)	29	0.21
Scandinavian (0)	10	0.07
Scotch-Irish (20)	67	0.48
Scottish (36)	54	0.38
Swedish (15)	74	0.53
Welsh (0)	29	0.21
West Indian, ex. Hispanic (9)	44	0.31
Dutch West Indian (0)	35	0.25
Haitian (9)	9	0.06

Hispanic Origin	Population	%
Hispanic or Latino (of any race)	4,845	32.66
Central American, ex. Mexican	189	1.27
Costa Rican	1	0.01
Guatemalan	28	0.19
Honduran	41	0.28
Nicaraguan	10	0.07
Panamanian	1	0.01
Salvadoran	108	0.73
Cuban	18	0.12
Dominican Republic	4	0.03
Mexican	4,288	28.90
Puerto Rican	54	0.36
South American	20	0.13
Argentinean	4	0.03
Chilean	1	0.01
Colombian	11	0.07
Ecuadorian	1	0.01
Peruvian	1	0.01
Venezuelan	2	0.01
Other Hispanic or Latino	272	1.83

Race*	Population	%
African-American/Black (2,488)	2,616	17.63
Not Hispanic (2,427)	2,528	17.04
Hispanic (61)	88	0.59
American Indian/Alaska Native (150)	263	1.77
Not Hispanic (95)	176	1.19
Hispanic (55)	87	0.59
Alaska Athabascan *(Ala. Nat.)* (0)	1	0.01
Apache (4)	7	0.05
Blackfeet (1)	6	0.04
Canadian/French Am. Ind. (0)	1	0.01
Cherokee (21)	44	0.30
Chickasaw (3)	11	0.07
Chippewa (1)	1	0.01
Choctaw (9)	18	0.12
Comanche (3)	4	0.03
Cree (0)	1	0.01
Creek (2)	4	0.03
Crow (4)	5	0.03
Houma (1)	1	0.01
Inupiat *(Alaska Native)* (2)	2	0.01
Iroquois (0)	2	0.01
Menominee (1)	1	0.01
Mexican American Ind. (10)	18	0.12
Navajo (9)	12	0.08
Pima (1)	1	0.01
Potawatomi (0)	1	0.01
Pueblo (4)	4	0.03
Sioux (7)	8	0.05
Tohono O'Odham (1)	1	0.01
Ute (1)	1	0.01
Yakama (2)	3	0.02
Yuman (0)	1	0.01
Asian (79)	141	0.95
Not Hispanic (76)	114	0.77
Hispanic (3)	27	0.18
Cambodian (2)	2	0.01
Chinese, ex. Taiwanese (16)	19	0.13
Filipino (18)	28	0.19
Indian (2)	10	0.07
Japanese (3)	15	0.10
Korean (7)	15	0.10
Laotian (5)	5	0.03
Taiwanese (1)	1	0.01
Thai (3)	4	0.03
Vietnamese (21)	24	0.16
Hawaii Native/Pacific Islander (6)	22	0.15
Not Hispanic (6)	17	0.11
Hispanic (0)	5	0.03
Guamanian/Chamorro (4)	12	0.08
Native Hawaiian (1)	5	0.03
Samoan (1)	2	0.01
White (9,962)	10,307	69.48
Not Hispanic (7,167)	7,343	49.50
Hispanic (2,795)	2,964	19.98

Seguin

Place Type: City
County: Guadalupe
Population: 25,175†

Ancestry‡	Population	%
African, Sub-Saharan (28)	28	0.11
African (10)	10	0.04
Sierra Leonean (18)	18	0.07
American (1,084)	1,084	4.37
Arab (34)	64	0.26
Lebanese (0)	11	0.04
Moroccan (34)	34	0.14
Syrian (0)	19	0.08
Austrian (0)	42	0.17
British (16)	16	0.06
Czech (82)	177	0.71
Czechoslovakian (20)	20	0.08
Danish (0)	10	0.04
Dutch (42)	88	0.36
English (512)	1,294	5.22
European (205)	236	0.95
Finnish (0)	36	0.15
French, ex. Basque (48)	539	2.17
French Canadian (11)	48	0.19
German (2,350)	3,953	15.95
Greek (0)	98	0.40
Hungarian (35)	35	0.14
Irish (365)	1,469	5.93
Italian (90)	294	1.19
Lithuanian (0)	105	0.42
Norwegian (84)	202	0.82
Polish (37)	221	0.89
Portuguese (0)	10	0.04
Russian (0)	14	0.06
Scandinavian (18)	18	0.07
Scotch-Irish (102)	323	1.30
Scottish (24)	265	1.07
Slovak (27)	47	0.19
Slovene (0)	14	0.06
Swedish (0)	46	0.19
Swiss (0)	47	0.19
Ukrainian (0)	47	0.19
Welsh (0)	77	0.31
West Indian, ex. Hispanic (25)	25	0.10
Bahamian (19)	19	0.08
Other West Indian (6)	6	0.02
Yugoslavian (23)	23	0.09

Hispanic Origin	Population	%
Hispanic or Latino (of any race)	13,938	55.36
Central American, ex. Mexican	106	0.42
Costa Rican	2	0.01
Guatemalan	21	0.08
Honduran	17	0.07
Panamanian	8	0.03
Salvadoran	58	0.23
Cuban	21	0.08
Mexican	12,263	48.71
Puerto Rican	34	0.14
South American	28	0.11
Argentinean	4	0.02
Bolivian	3	0.01
Chilean	4	0.02
Colombian	7	0.03
Ecuadorian	1	<0.01
Peruvian	7	0.03
Venezuelan	2	0.01
Other Hispanic or Latino	1,486	5.90

Race*	Population	%
African-American/Black (2,026)	2,222	8.83
Not Hispanic (1,839)	1,931	7.67
Hispanic (187)	291	1.16
American Indian/Alaska Native (138)	225	0.89
Not Hispanic (44)	96	0.38
Hispanic (94)	129	0.51
Apache (5)	9	0.04
Blackfeet (0)	2	0.01
Canadian/French Am. Ind. (0)	2	0.01
Central American Ind. (0)	1	<0.01
Cherokee (13)	26	0.10
Chickasaw (1)	1	<0.01
Chippewa (2)	3	0.01
Choctaw (8)	11	0.04
Inupiat *(Alaska Native)* (1)	1	<0.01
Iroquois (2)	2	0.01
Mexican American Ind. (4)	5	0.02
Navajo (1)	2	0.01
Ottawa (0)	1	<0.01
Sioux (6)	9	0.04
Spanish American Ind. (1)	1	<0.01
Asian (222)	269	1.07
Not Hispanic (202)	234	0.93
Hispanic (20)	35	0.14
Cambodian (9)	9	0.04
Chinese, ex. Taiwanese (43)	47	0.19
Filipino (15)	26	0.10
Indian (54)	61	0.24
Japanese (5)	12	0.05
Korean (14)	18	0.07
Pakistani (27)	30	0.12

*Notes: † The Census 2010 population figure is used to calculate the percentages in the Hispanic Origin and Race categories. Ancestry percentages are based on the 2006-2010 American Community Survey population (not shown); ‡ Numbers in parentheses indicate the number of people reporting a single ancestry; * Numbers in parentheses indicate the number of persons reporting this race alone, not in combination with any other race; Please refer to the Explanation of Data for more information.*

Sri Lankan (0)	1	<0.01
Thai (4)	4	0.02
Vietnamese (42)	42	0.17
Hawaii Native/Pacific Islander (10)	29	0.12
Not Hispanic (7)	12	0.05
Hispanic (3)	17	0.07
Guamanian/Chamorro (4)	5	0.02
Native Hawaiian (1)	5	0.02
Samoan (1)	6	0.02
White (19,114)	19,665	78.11
Not Hispanic (8,944)	9,087	36.10
Hispanic (10,170)	10,578	42.02

Sherman

Place Type: City
County: Grayson
Population: 38,521†

Ancestry‡	Population	%
African, Sub-Saharan (327)	422	1.11
African (304)	399	1.05
Kenyan (7)	7	0.02
Nigerian (16)	16	0.04
American (2,324)	2,324	6.12
Arab (92)	125	0.33
Arab (12)	45	0.12
Lebanese (80)	80	0.21
Austrian (17)	93	0.25
British (141)	261	0.69
Canadian (13)	69	0.18
Czech (271)	311	0.82
Danish (0)	35	0.09
Dutch (137)	728	1.92
English (1,457)	3,497	9.22
European (194)	194	0.51
French, ex. Basque (258)	1,078	2.84
French Canadian (0)	36	0.09
German (1,780)	4,548	11.99
Hungarian (14)	56	0.15
Iranian (15)	15	0.04
Irish (1,541)	4,670	12.31
Italian (408)	707	1.86
Lithuanian (13)	46	0.12
Northern European (21)	21	0.06
Norwegian (97)	247	0.65
Polish (136)	329	0.87
Romanian (35)	35	0.09
Russian (67)	206	0.54
Scandinavian (24)	50	0.13
Scotch-Irish (183)	669	1.76
Scottish (217)	599	1.58
Swedish (135)	346	0.91
Swiss (19)	106	0.28
Welsh (113)	326	0.86
West Indian, ex. Hispanic (0)	24	0.06
Dutch West Indian (0)	24	0.06
Yugoslavian (0)	19	0.05

Hispanic Origin	Population	%
Hispanic or Latino (of any race)	7,881	20.46
Central American, ex. Mexican	704	1.83
Costa Rican	4	0.01
Guatemalan	31	0.08
Honduran	21	0.05
Nicaraguan	8	0.02
Panamanian	15	0.04
Salvadoran	625	1.62
Cuban	23	0.06
Dominican Republic	8	0.02
Mexican	6,559	17.03
Puerto Rican	76	0.20
South American	52	0.13
Argentinean	4	0.01
Chilean	6	0.02
Colombian	9	0.02
Ecuadorian	4	0.01
Paraguayan	3	0.01
Peruvian	9	0.02
Uruguayan	5	0.01
Venezuelan	12	0.03
Other Hispanic or Latino	459	1.19

Race*	Population	%
African-American/Black (4,265)	4,754	12.34
Not Hispanic (4,176)	4,586	11.91
Hispanic (89)	168	0.44
American Indian/Alaska Native (536)	1,012	2.63
Not Hispanic (459)	880	2.28
Hispanic (77)	132	0.34
Apache (8)	16	0.04
Arapaho (0)	2	0.01
Blackfeet (1)	9	0.02
Canadian/French Am. Ind. (1)	1	<0.01
Cherokee (43)	134	0.35
Cheyenne (5)	10	0.03
Chickasaw (67)	111	0.29
Chippewa (0)	1	<0.01
Choctaw (169)	313	0.81
Comanche (1)	3	0.01
Cree (0)	1	<0.01
Creek (13)	29	0.08
Delaware (4)	4	0.01
Iroquois (1)	10	0.03
Kiowa (6)	6	0.02
Mexican American Ind. (13)	21	0.05
Navajo (2)	12	0.03
Osage (2)	3	0.01
Potawatomi (8)	12	0.03
Pueblo (3)	3	0.01
Seminole (5)	10	0.03
Sioux (6)	12	0.03
South American Ind. (0)	1	<0.01
Ute (1)	1	<0.01
Asian (648)	822	2.13
Not Hispanic (636)	777	2.02
Hispanic (12)	45	0.12
Bangladeshi (25)	27	0.07
Cambodian (5)	5	0.01
Chinese, ex. Taiwanese (61)	72	0.19
Filipino (76)	115	0.30
Indian (229)	259	0.67
Indonesian (2)	4	0.01
Japanese (18)	48	0.12
Korean (71)	99	0.26
Laotian (6)	7	0.02
Malaysian (0)	1	<0.01
Nepalese (37)	37	0.10
Pakistani (41)	45	0.12
Sri Lankan (1)	1	<0.01
Taiwanese (2)	4	0.01
Thai (3)	7	0.02
Vietnamese (55)	74	0.19
Hawaii Native/Pacific Islander (13)	45	0.12
Not Hispanic (12)	32	0.08
Hispanic (1)	13	0.03
Guamanian/Chamorro (8)	13	0.03
Native Hawaiian (3)	11	0.03
Samoan (1)	1	<0.01
White (27,599)	28,801	74.77
Not Hispanic (24,423)	25,235	65.51
Hispanic (3,176)	3,566	9.26

Sienna Plantation

Place Type: CDP
County: Fort Bend
Population: 13,721†

Ancestry‡	Population	%
African, Sub-Saharan (193)	193	1.55
African (47)	47	0.38
Nigerian (146)	146	1.18
American (498)	498	4.01
Arab (52)	177	1.42
Lebanese (10)	31	0.25
Syrian (42)	136	1.09
Other Arab (0)	10	0.08
Austrian (10)	29	0.23
Belgian (12)	26	0.21
Brazilian (12)	12	0.10
British (19)	29	0.23
Cajun (10)	35	0.28
Canadian (57)	57	0.46
Czech (47)	150	1.21
Czechoslovakian (9)	9	0.07
Danish (9)	106	0.85
Dutch (59)	154	1.24
English (311)	960	7.73
European (91)	118	0.95
French, ex. Basque (70)	415	3.34
French Canadian (57)	103	0.83
German (818)	2,260	18.19
Greek (0)	10	0.08
Irish (358)	898	7.23
Israeli (8)	23	0.19
Italian (211)	692	5.57
Lithuanian (0)	28	0.23
Norwegian (31)	135	1.09
Polish (92)	206	1.66
Portuguese (0)	11	0.09
Romanian (31)	31	0.25
Russian (15)	59	0.47
Scotch-Irish (81)	214	1.72
Scottish (162)	399	3.21
Slovene (0)	11	0.09
Swedish (50)	219	1.76
Turkish (33)	33	0.27
Ukrainian (10)	31	0.25
Welsh (24)	72	0.58
West Indian, ex. Hispanic (12)	23	0.19
Bahamian (0)	11	0.09
Barbadian (12)	12	0.10

Hispanic Origin	Population	%
Hispanic or Latino (of any race)	1,665	12.13
Central American, ex. Mexican	97	0.71
Costa Rican	1	0.01
Guatemalan	7	0.05
Honduran	18	0.13
Nicaraguan	23	0.17
Panamanian	13	0.09
Salvadoran	35	0.26
Cuban	44	0.32
Dominican Republic	4	0.03
Mexican	1,147	8.36
Puerto Rican	80	0.58
South American	157	1.14
Argentinean	17	0.12
Bolivian	3	0.02
Chilean	9	0.07
Colombian	49	0.36
Ecuadorian	7	0.05
Paraguayan	1	0.01
Peruvian	35	0.26
Uruguayan	3	0.02
Venezuelan	33	0.24
Other Hispanic or Latino	136	0.99

Race*	Population	%
African-American/Black (2,490)	2,604	18.98
Not Hispanic (2,456)	2,543	18.53
Hispanic (34)	61	0.44
American Indian/Alaska Native (52)	125	0.91
Not Hispanic (39)	84	0.61
Hispanic (13)	41	0.30
Blackfeet (0)	2	0.01
Cherokee (11)	22	0.16
Chickasaw (6)	6	0.04
Chippewa (0)	1	0.01
Choctaw (11)	16	0.12
Creek (3)	6	0.04
Delaware (1)	1	0.01
Iroquois (0)	3	0.02
Mexican American Ind. (1)	3	0.02
Navajo (0)	1	0.01
Sioux (3)	4	0.03
Spanish American Ind. (0)	2	0.01
Asian (1,512)	1,659	12.09
Not Hispanic (1,488)	1,621	11.81

*Notes: † The Census 2010 population figure is used to calculate the percentages in the Hispanic Origin and Race categories. Ancestry percentages are based on the 2006-2010 American Community Survey population (not shown); ‡ Numbers in parentheses indicate the number of people reporting a single ancestry; * Numbers in parentheses indicate the number of persons reporting this race alone, not in combination with any other race; Please refer to the Explanation of Data for more information.*

Hispanic (24)	38	0.28
Bangladeshi (9)	10	0.07
Cambodian (11)	13	0.09
Chinese, ex. Taiwanese (222)	254	1.85
Filipino (402)	439	3.20
Indian (565)	600	4.37
Indonesian (5)	5	0.04
Japanese (17)	27	0.20
Korean (16)	28	0.20
Malaysian (1)	2	0.01
Pakistani (66)	77	0.56
Sri Lankan (4)	4	0.03
Taiwanese (5)	11	0.08
Thai (10)	21	0.15
Vietnamese (127)	152	1.11
Hawaii Native/Pacific Islander (8)	15	0.11
Not Hispanic (8)	15	0.11
Guamanian/Chamorro (5)	5	0.04
Native Hawaiian (1)	6	0.04
Samoan (2)	3	0.02
White (8,931)	9,232	67.28
Not Hispanic (7,807)	8,008	58.36
Hispanic (1,124)	1,224	8.92

Snyder

Place Type: City
County: Scurry
Population: 11,202†

Ancestry‡	Population	%
African, Sub-Saharan (1)	3	0.03
African (1)	3	0.03
American (707)	707	6.46
Arab (0)	40	0.37
Lebanese (0)	40	0.37
Cajun (13)	13	0.12
Czech (9)	30	0.27
Danish (3)	21	0.19
Dutch (27)	193	1.76
English (402)	743	6.79
French, ex. Basque (55)	246	2.25
German (432)	1,062	9.70
Guyanese (6)	6	0.05
Iranian (15)	15	0.14
Irish (407)	979	8.94
Italian (11)	223	2.04
Lithuanian (0)	1	0.01
Norwegian (24)	31	0.28
Polish (40)	40	0.37
Portuguese (14)	31	0.28
Russian (0)	1	0.01
Scandinavian (13)	13	0.12
Scotch-Irish (75)	163	1.49
Scottish (55)	111	1.01
Swedish (0)	63	0.58
Welsh (12)	38	0.35

Hispanic Origin	Population	%
Hispanic or Latino (of any race)	4,641	41.43
Central American, ex. Mexican	22	0.20
Costa Rican	1	0.01
Guatemalan	4	0.04
Honduran	2	0.02
Panamanian	1	0.01
Salvadoran	14	0.12
Cuban	4	0.04
Mexican	3,756	33.53
Puerto Rican	8	0.07
South American	9	0.08
Bolivian	4	0.04
Chilean	2	0.02
Venezuelan	3	0.03
Other Hispanic or Latino	842	7.52

Race*	Population	%
African-American/Black (428)	516	4.61
Not Hispanic (402)	454	4.05
Hispanic (26)	62	0.55
American Indian/Alaska Native (79)	128	1.14
Not Hispanic (30)	59	0.53
Hispanic (49)	69	0.62
Alaska Athabascan *(Ala. Nat.)* (1)	1	0.01
Apache (0)	2	0.02
Blackfeet (0)	1	0.01
Canadian/French Am. Ind. (2)	2	0.02
Cherokee (6)	18	0.16
Chickasaw (6)	6	0.05
Choctaw (4)	6	0.05
Comanche (0)	1	0.01
Creek (2)	3	0.03
Lumbee (0)	3	0.03
Mexican American Ind. (7)	7	0.06
Navajo (2)	2	0.02
Potawatomi (1)	2	0.02
Sioux (1)	1	0.01
South American Ind. (0)	1	0.01
Tlingit-Haida *(Alaska Native)* (1)	1	0.01
Asian (51)	78	0.70
Not Hispanic (41)	50	0.45
Hispanic (10)	28	0.25
Cambodian (4)	8	0.07
Chinese, ex. Taiwanese (6)	14	0.12
Filipino (22)	34	0.30
Indian (1)	3	0.03
Japanese (0)	3	0.03
Korean (7)	9	0.08
Laotian (1)	1	0.01
Pakistani (1)	1	0.01
Vietnamese (3)	4	0.04
Hawaii Native/Pacific Islander (1)	5	0.04
Not Hispanic (1)	2	0.02
Hispanic (0)	3	0.03
Native Hawaiian (0)	2	0.02
Samoan (1)	2	0.02
White (8,855)	9,112	81.34
Not Hispanic (5,987)	6,082	54.29
Hispanic (2,868)	3,030	27.05

Socorro

Place Type: City
County: El Paso
Population: 32,013†

Ancestry‡	Population	%
American (791)	791	2.55
Arab (11)	11	0.04
Lebanese (11)	11	0.04
Dutch (14)	14	0.05
English (32)	83	0.27
French, ex. Basque (15)	175	0.56
German (44)	113	0.36
Irish (34)	278	0.90
Israeli (37)	37	0.12
Italian (14)	83	0.27
Russian (0)	39	0.13
Scotch-Irish (19)	54	0.17
Swedish (0)	26	0.08

Hispanic Origin	Population	%
Hispanic or Latino (of any race)	30,964	96.72
Central American, ex. Mexican	66	0.21
Costa Rican	3	0.01
Guatemalan	6	0.02
Honduran	14	0.04
Nicaraguan	6	0.02
Salvadoran	35	0.11
Other Central American	2	0.01
Cuban	10	0.03
Mexican	29,019	90.65
Puerto Rican	57	0.18
South American	15	0.05
Chilean	3	0.01
Colombian	6	0.02
Ecuadorian	4	0.01
Peruvian	2	0.01
Other Hispanic or Latino	1,797	5.61

Race*	Population	%
African-American/Black (78)	115	0.36
Not Hispanic (49)	61	0.19
Hispanic (29)	54	0.17
American Indian/Alaska Native (525)	619	1.93
Not Hispanic (265)	279	0.87
Hispanic (260)	340	1.06
Apache (15)	23	0.07
Blackfeet (3)	3	0.01
Cherokee (0)	8	0.02
Choctaw (5)	6	0.02
Colville (1)	3	0.01
Creek (2)	2	0.01
Iroquois (1)	1	<0.01
Mexican American Ind. (9)	13	0.04
Navajo (3)	4	0.01
Osage (0)	1	<0.01
Pueblo (318)	350	1.09
Sioux (1)	1	<0.01
Tohono O'Odham (1)	1	<0.01
Asian (37)	71	0.22
Not Hispanic (23)	31	0.10
Hispanic (14)	40	0.12
Chinese, ex. Taiwanese (4)	8	0.02
Filipino (12)	23	0.07
Indian (12)	16	0.05
Japanese (2)	5	0.02
Korean (4)	9	0.03
Pakistani (1)	1	<0.01
Thai (0)	1	<0.01
Vietnamese (0)	1	<0.01
Hawaii Native/Pacific Islander (3)	7	0.02
Not Hispanic (2)	2	0.01
Hispanic (1)	5	0.02
Native Hawaiian (3)	6	0.02
Samoan (0)	1	<0.01
White (30,184)	30,415	95.01
Not Hispanic (657)	695	2.17
Hispanic (29,527)	29,720	92.84

South Houston

Place Type: City
County: Harris
Population: 16,983†

Ancestry‡	Population	%
American (426)	426	2.55
Czech (30)	89	0.53
English (88)	342	2.05
European (32)	32	0.19
French, ex. Basque (0)	202	1.21
German (27)	321	1.92
Hungarian (11)	11	0.07
Irish (173)	390	2.34
Italian (56)	56	0.34
Russian (26)	55	0.33
Scotch-Irish (0)	19	0.11
Scottish (0)	113	0.68
Swedish (9)	39	0.23
West Indian, ex. Hispanic (0)	27	0.16
West Indian (0)	27	0.16

Hispanic Origin	Population	%
Hispanic or Latino (of any race)	14,954	88.05
Central American, ex. Mexican	901	5.31
Costa Rican	5	0.03
Guatemalan	86	0.51
Honduran	223	1.31
Nicaraguan	31	0.18
Panamanian	1	0.01
Salvadoran	545	3.21
Other Central American	10	0.06
Cuban	24	0.14
Dominican Republic	17	0.10
Mexican	13,193	77.68
Puerto Rican	53	0.31
South American	64	0.38
Chilean	12	0.07
Colombian	35	0.21

*Notes: † The Census 2010 population figure is used to calculate the percentages in the Hispanic Origin and Race categories. Ancestry percentages are based on the 2006-2010 American Community Survey population (not shown); ‡ Numbers in parentheses indicate the number of people reporting a single ancestry; * Numbers in parentheses indicate the number of persons reporting this race alone, not in combination with any other race; Please refer to the Explanation of Data for more information.*

Ecuadorian	3	0.02
Paraguayan	6	0.04
Peruvian	7	0.04
Venezuelan	1	0.01
Other Hispanic or Latino	702	4.13

Race*	Population	%
African-American/Black (262)	325	1.91
Not Hispanic (181)	198	1.17
Hispanic (81)	127	0.75
American Indian/Alaska Native (146)	218	1.28
Not Hispanic (22)	39	0.23
Hispanic (124)	179	1.05
Aleut *(Alaska Native)* (1)	1	0.01
Apache (11)	15	0.09
Blackfeet (1)	2	0.01
Central American Ind. (0)	1	0.01
Cherokee (8)	11	0.06
Choctaw (4)	9	0.05
Mexican American Ind. (12)	23	0.14
Sioux (1)	1	0.01
South American Ind. (4)	6	0.04
Spanish American Ind. (2)	3	0.02
Asian (95)	126	0.74
Not Hispanic (79)	89	0.52
Hispanic (16)	37	0.22
Cambodian (12)	12	0.07
Chinese, ex. Taiwanese (8)	13	0.08
Filipino (8)	10	0.06
Indian (16)	20	0.12
Japanese (1)	6	0.04
Korean (4)	8	0.05
Pakistani (1)	1	0.01
Thai (3)	3	0.02
Vietnamese (40)	42	0.25
Hawaii Native/Pacific Islander (3)	12	0.07
Hispanic (3)	12	0.07
Guamanian/Chamorro (3)	4	0.02
Native Hawaiian (0)	1	0.01
Samoan (0)	1	0.01
White (11,192)	11,731	69.07
Not Hispanic (1,682)	1,726	10.16
Hispanic (9,510)	10,005	58.91

Southlake

Place Type: City
County: Tarrant
Population: 26,575†

Ancestry‡	Population	%
African, Sub-Saharan (0)	16	0.06
African (0)	16	0.06
American (1,983)	1,983	7.76
Arab (197)	266	1.04
Arab (13)	34	0.13
Lebanese (126)	137	0.54
Palestinian (31)	31	0.12
Syrian (0)	37	0.14
Other Arab (27)	27	0.11
Armenian (35)	69	0.27
Australian (0)	28	0.11
Austrian (0)	45	0.18
Belgian (21)	129	0.50
Brazilian (47)	47	0.18
British (170)	284	1.11
Bulgarian (46)	46	0.18
Canadian (144)	233	0.91
Croatian (0)	61	0.24
Czech (102)	313	1.22
Czechoslovakian (0)	28	0.11
Danish (38)	308	1.20
Dutch (74)	376	1.47
Eastern European (36)	45	0.18
English (1,368)	4,415	17.27
European (515)	550	2.15
Finnish (54)	64	0.25
French, ex. Basque (175)	949	3.71
French Canadian (72)	150	0.59
German (1,467)	5,090	19.91
Greek (65)	174	0.68
Hungarian (0)	46	0.18
Iranian (27)	27	0.11
Irish (1,412)	4,386	17.15
Israeli (30)	30	0.12
Italian (393)	1,689	6.61
Lithuanian (0)	10	0.04
Maltese (16)	32	0.13
Northern European (119)	119	0.47
Norwegian (79)	261	1.02
Polish (330)	857	3.35
Portuguese (11)	25	0.10
Romanian (19)	50	0.20
Russian (68)	279	1.09
Scandinavian (20)	111	0.43
Scotch-Irish (301)	929	3.63
Scottish (349)	944	3.69
Serbian (10)	10	0.04
Slavic (12)	22	0.09
Slovak (22)	61	0.24
Swedish (163)	584	2.28
Swiss (35)	140	0.55
Turkish (25)	74	0.29
Ukrainian (70)	92	0.36
Welsh (59)	305	1.19
West Indian, ex. Hispanic (11)	55	0.22
Barbadian (11)	11	0.04
Dutch West Indian (0)	34	0.13
Jamaican (0)	10	0.04
Yugoslavian (17)	51	0.20

Hispanic Origin	Population	%
Hispanic or Latino (of any race)	1,458	5.49
Central American, ex. Mexican	78	0.29
Costa Rican	10	0.04
Guatemalan	16	0.06
Honduran	8	0.03
Nicaraguan	17	0.06
Panamanian	15	0.06
Salvadoran	12	0.05
Cuban	60	0.23
Dominican Republic	7	0.03
Mexican	894	3.36
Puerto Rican	100	0.38
South American	175	0.66
Argentinean	13	0.05
Bolivian	2	0.01
Chilean	15	0.06
Colombian	60	0.23
Ecuadorian	15	0.06
Peruvian	43	0.16
Uruguayan	1	<0.01
Venezuelan	26	0.10
Other Hispanic or Latino	144	0.54

Race*	Population	%
African-American/Black (548)	654	2.46
Not Hispanic (532)	628	2.36
Hispanic (16)	26	0.10
American Indian/Alaska Native (92)	221	0.83
Not Hispanic (80)	190	0.71
Hispanic (12)	31	0.12
Arapaho (0)	1	<0.01
Canadian/French Am. Ind. (1)	2	0.01
Central American Ind. (0)	1	<0.01
Cherokee (21)	66	0.25
Chickasaw (6)	23	0.09
Chippewa (3)	3	0.01
Choctaw (13)	26	0.10
Comanche (0)	1	<0.01
Creek (0)	7	0.03
Delaware (0)	1	<0.01
Inupiat *(Alaska Native)* (1)	1	<0.01
Iroquois (3)	3	0.01
Mexican American Ind. (1)	1	<0.01
Navajo (2)	2	0.01
Osage (2)	3	0.01
Potawatomi (7)	14	0.05
Pueblo (0)	3	0.01
Sioux (1)	1	<0.01
South American Ind. (0)	7	0.03
Yuman (0)	2	0.01
Asian (1,655)	1,957	7.36
Not Hispanic (1,648)	1,926	7.25
Hispanic (7)	31	0.12
Bangladeshi (4)	4	0.02
Cambodian (3)	3	0.01
Chinese, ex. Taiwanese (301)	377	1.42
Filipino (101)	151	0.57
Hmong (5)	5	0.02
Indian (588)	642	2.42
Indonesian (8)	12	0.05
Japanese (41)	88	0.33
Korean (169)	208	0.78
Laotian (5)	10	0.04
Malaysian (0)	2	0.01
Pakistani (162)	174	0.65
Sri Lankan (10)	12	0.05
Taiwanese (17)	19	0.07
Thai (22)	36	0.14
Vietnamese (130)	161	0.61
Hawaii Native/Pacific Islander (9)	19	0.07
Not Hispanic (8)	17	0.06
Hispanic (1)	2	0.01
Guamanian/Chamorro (1)	2	0.01
Native Hawaiian (6)	10	0.04
Samoan (2)	3	0.01
White (23,454)	23,981	90.24
Not Hispanic (22,324)	22,782	85.73
Hispanic (1,130)	1,199	4.51

Spring

Place Type: CDP
County: Harris
Population: 54,298†

Ancestry‡	Population	%
African, Sub-Saharan (613)	819	1.55
African (537)	689	1.30
Nigerian (44)	44	0.08
Senegalese (0)	54	0.10
South African (23)	23	0.04
Other Sub-Saharan African (9)	9	0.02
American (2,500)	2,500	4.72
Arab (130)	137	0.26
Arab (29)	36	0.07
Lebanese (13)	13	0.02
Moroccan (73)	73	0.14
Other Arab (15)	15	0.03
Australian (0)	10	0.02
Austrian (0)	46	0.09
Belgian (10)	10	0.02
British (38)	186	0.35
Cajun (34)	72	0.14
Canadian (140)	140	0.26
Croatian (0)	43	0.08
Czech (113)	550	1.04
Czechoslovakian (101)	114	0.22
Danish (0)	81	0.15
Dutch (76)	592	1.12
English (951)	3,638	6.87
European (421)	602	1.14
Finnish (13)	90	0.17
French, ex. Basque (529)	1,872	3.53
French Canadian (145)	297	0.56
German (2,625)	7,370	13.91
Greek (12)	108	0.20
Hungarian (32)	194	0.37
Irish (1,282)	4,216	7.96
Italian (392)	945	1.78
Latvian (0)	16	0.03
Lithuanian (0)	81	0.15
Luxemburger (0)	18	0.03
Norwegian (46)	147	0.28
Pennsylvania German (0)	36	0.07
Polish (419)	1,235	2.33
Portuguese (85)	158	0.30
Romanian (110)	150	0.28
Russian (12)	66	0.12

SECTION TWO

*Notes: † The Census 2010 population figure is used to calculate the percentages in the Hispanic Origin and Race categories. Ancestry percentages are based on the 2006-2010 American Community Survey population (not shown); ‡ Numbers in parentheses indicate the number of people reporting a single ancestry; * Numbers in parentheses indicate the number of persons reporting this race alone, not in combination with any other race; Please refer to the Explanation of Data for more information.*

	Population	%
Scandinavian (77)	90	0.17
Scotch-Irish (362)	925	1.75
Scottish (206)	755	1.43
Slavic (20)	44	0.08
Slovak (0)	12	0.02
Swedish (109)	378	0.71
Swiss (49)	165	0.31
Turkish (12)	12	0.02
Ukrainian (38)	38	0.07
Welsh (54)	277	0.52
West Indian, ex. Hispanic (216)	432	0.82
British West Indian (21)	21	0.04
Jamaican (62)	278	0.52
Trinidadian/Tobagonian (68)	68	0.13
West Indian (65)	65	0.12

Hispanic Origin	Population	%
Hispanic or Latino (of any race)	15,445	28.44
Central American, ex. Mexican	1,747	3.22
Costa Rican	36	0.07
Guatemalan	243	0.45
Honduran	346	0.64
Nicaraguan	159	0.29
Panamanian	36	0.07
Salvadoran	920	1.69
Other Central American	7	0.01
Cuban	153	0.28
Dominican Republic	99	0.18
Mexican	11,023	20.30
Puerto Rican	468	0.86
South American	708	1.30
Argentinean	123	0.23
Bolivian	21	0.04
Chilean	38	0.07
Colombian	267	0.49
Ecuadorian	64	0.12
Paraguayan	2	<0.01
Peruvian	82	0.15
Uruguayan	16	0.03
Venezuelan	93	0.17
Other South American	2	<0.01
Other Hispanic or Latino	1,247	2.30

Race*	Population	%
African-American/Black (10,580)	11,330	20.87
Not Hispanic (10,293)	10,847	19.98
Hispanic (287)	483	0.89
American Indian/Alaska Native (320)	620	1.14
Not Hispanic (157)	372	0.69
Hispanic (163)	248	0.46
Aleut *(Alaska Native)* (1)	1	<0.01
Apache (8)	12	0.02
Blackfeet (1)	13	0.02
Canadian/French Am. Ind. (0)	2	<0.01
Central American Ind. (0)	4	0.01
Cherokee (22)	88	0.16
Cheyenne (4)	4	0.01
Chickasaw (5)	9	0.02
Chippewa (2)	2	<0.01
Choctaw (8)	29	0.05
Comanche (0)	2	<0.01
Cree (1)	2	<0.01
Creek (7)	13	0.02
Delaware (1)	4	0.01
Houma (2)	2	<0.01
Inupiat *(Alaska Native)* (1)	1	<0.01
Iroquois (4)	5	0.01
Lumbee (1)	2	<0.01
Mexican American Ind. (19)	30	0.06
Navajo (5)	6	0.01
Osage (3)	3	0.01
Paiute (1)	1	<0.01
Potawatomi (4)	4	0.01
Pueblo (2)	3	0.01
Seminole (4)	8	0.01
Sioux (5)	9	0.02
South American Ind. (8)	12	0.02
Spanish American Ind. (3)	3	0.01
Yakama (2)	2	<0.01
Yaqui (1)	1	<0.01
Yup'ik *(Alaska Native)* (0)	1	<0.01
Asian (1,707)	2,031	3.74
Not Hispanic (1,671)	1,928	3.55
Hispanic (36)	103	0.19
Bangladeshi (0)	2	<0.01
Burmese (0)	1	<0.01
Cambodian (45)	53	0.10
Chinese, ex. Taiwanese (136)	180	0.33
Filipino (478)	579	1.07
Indian (262)	289	0.53
Indonesian (1)	6	0.01
Japanese (38)	96	0.18
Korean (56)	94	0.17
Laotian (32)	35	0.06
Malaysian (1)	4	0.01
Nepalese (19)	19	0.03
Pakistani (179)	193	0.36
Taiwanese (3)	3	0.01
Thai (29)	41	0.08
Vietnamese (372)	410	0.76
Hawaii Native/Pacific Islander (203)	307	0.57
Not Hispanic (178)	243	0.45
Hispanic (25)	64	0.12
Fijian (5)	6	0.01
Guamanian/Chamorro (84)	104	0.19
Native Hawaiian (37)	84	0.15
Samoan (8)	27	0.05
Tongan (35)	46	0.08
White (34,667)	36,139	66.56
Not Hispanic (25,477)	26,260	48.36
Hispanic (9,190)	9,879	18.19

Stafford

Place Type: City
County: Fort Bend
Population: 17,693†

Ancestry‡	Population	%
African, Sub-Saharan (553)	568	3.35
African (110)	125	0.74
Ethiopian (42)	42	0.25
Ghanaian (6)	6	0.04
Nigerian (395)	395	2.33
American (437)	437	2.58
Arab (145)	159	0.94
Arab (22)	22	0.13
Egyptian (45)	45	0.27
Jordanian (0)	7	0.04
Lebanese (7)	14	0.08
Syrian (71)	71	0.42
British (67)	89	0.53
Cajun (24)	24	0.14
Canadian (21)	21	0.12
Celtic (60)	60	0.35
Croatian (8)	8	0.05
Czech (14)	47	0.28
Czechoslovakian (33)	62	0.37
Danish (0)	29	0.17
Dutch (35)	90	0.53
English (158)	414	2.44
European (8)	24	0.14
French, ex. Basque (38)	341	2.01
French Canadian (8)	8	0.05
German (337)	1,149	6.78
German Russian (0)	13	0.08
Greek (13)	13	0.08
Hungarian (0)	26	0.15
Iranian (117)	117	0.69
Irish (187)	867	5.12
Italian (151)	367	2.17
Norwegian (25)	25	0.15
Polish (31)	83	0.49
Portuguese (0)	40	0.24
Romanian (19)	32	0.19
Russian (41)	58	0.34
Scandinavian (0)	23	0.14
Scotch-Irish (17)	134	0.79
Scottish (9)	72	0.43
Swedish (59)	97	0.57
Turkish (94)	94	0.55
Ukrainian (0)	13	0.08
Welsh (0)	82	0.48
West Indian, ex. Hispanic (67)	67	0.40
Bahamian (11)	11	0.06
Jamaican (30)	30	0.18
West Indian (26)	26	0.15

Hispanic Origin	Population	%
Hispanic or Latino (of any race)	4,590	25.94
Central American, ex. Mexican	338	1.91
Costa Rican	1	0.01
Guatemalan	12	0.07
Honduran	65	0.37
Nicaraguan	21	0.12
Panamanian	40	0.23
Salvadoran	198	1.12
Other Central American	1	0.01
Cuban	42	0.24
Dominican Republic	14	0.08
Mexican	3,411	19.28
Puerto Rican	143	0.81
South American	197	1.11
Argentinean	38	0.21
Bolivian	10	0.06
Chilean	2	0.01
Colombian	68	0.38
Ecuadorian	13	0.07
Peruvian	16	0.09
Uruguayan	10	0.06
Venezuelan	37	0.21
Other South American	3	0.02
Other Hispanic or Latino	445	2.52

Race*	Population	%
African-American/Black (4,856)	5,044	28.51
Not Hispanic (4,740)	4,857	27.45
Hispanic (116)	187	1.06
American Indian/Alaska Native (100)	187	1.06
Not Hispanic (42)	98	0.55
Hispanic (58)	89	0.50
Apache (1)	4	0.02
Blackfeet (0)	2	0.01
Central American Ind. (0)	3	0.02
Cherokee (6)	22	0.12
Chippewa (1)	2	0.01
Choctaw (3)	6	0.03
Comanche (0)	2	0.01
Creek (1)	3	0.02
Delaware (0)	1	0.01
Hopi (1)	5	0.03
Mexican American Ind. (6)	6	0.03
Osage (1)	1	0.01
Potawatomi (1)	2	0.01
Pueblo (0)	4	0.02
Sioux (1)	1	0.01
Asian (4,035)	4,254	24.04
Not Hispanic (4,000)	4,172	23.58
Hispanic (35)	82	0.46
Bangladeshi (10)	10	0.06
Cambodian (14)	18	0.10
Chinese, ex. Taiwanese (529)	583	3.30
Filipino (618)	677	3.83
Indian (1,445)	1,527	8.63
Indonesian (2)	2	0.01
Japanese (9)	14	0.08
Korean (11)	15	0.08
Laotian (4)	4	0.02
Malaysian (9)	10	0.06
Pakistani (453)	486	2.75
Sri Lankan (7)	7	0.04
Taiwanese (50)	55	0.31
Thai (13)	15	0.08
Vietnamese (728)	769	4.35
Hawaii Native/Pacific Islander (6)	25	0.14
Not Hispanic (6)	18	0.10
Hispanic (0)	7	0.04
Guamanian/Chamorro (5)	5	0.03
Native Hawaiian (1)	6	0.03
White (6,482)	6,889	38.94

*Notes: † The Census 2010 population figure is used to calculate the percentages in the Hispanic Origin and Race categories. Ancestry percentages are based on the 2006-2010 American Community Survey population (not shown); ‡ Numbers in parentheses indicate the number of people reporting a single ancestry; * Numbers in parentheses indicate the number of persons reporting this race alone, not in combination with any other race; Please refer to the Explanation of Data for more information.*

	Population	%
Not Hispanic (3,972)	4,168	23.56
Hispanic (2,510)	2,721	15.38

Stephenville

Place Type: City
County: Erath
Population: 17,123†

Ancestry‡	Population	%
African, Sub-Saharan (14)	14	0.08
Nigerian (14)	14	0.08
American (1,250)	1,250	7.38
Arab (0)	133	0.79
Lebanese (0)	133	0.79
Australian (15)	15	0.09
Austrian (24)	33	0.19
British (21)	37	0.22
Czech (327)	343	2.02
Czechoslovakian (0)	15	0.09
Danish (10)	10	0.06
Dutch (159)	302	1.78
Eastern European (5)	5	0.03
English (629)	1,550	9.15
European (175)	185	1.09
French, ex. Basque (96)	345	2.04
French Canadian (0)	9	0.05
German (1,113)	2,597	15.33
Greek (38)	38	0.22
Hungarian (0)	12	0.07
Irish (802)	2,056	12.14
Italian (81)	196	1.16
Norwegian (0)	73	0.43
Pennsylvania German (32)	32	0.19
Polish (9)	75	0.44
Portuguese (13)	42	0.25
Scandinavian (0)	60	0.35
Scotch-Irish (203)	390	2.30
Scottish (182)	458	2.70
Slovak (0)	12	0.07
Slovene (0)	13	0.08
Swedish (30)	153	0.90
Swiss (0)	40	0.24
Ukrainian (0)	12	0.07
Welsh (79)	106	0.63
West Indian, ex. Hispanic (0)	7	0.04
Dutch West Indian (0)	7	0.04

Hispanic Origin	Population	%
Hispanic or Latino (of any race)	2,690	15.71
Central American, ex. Mexican	21	0.12
Guatemalan	4	0.02
Honduran	6	0.04
Nicaraguan	1	0.01
Panamanian	1	0.01
Salvadoran	9	0.05
Cuban	11	0.06
Dominican Republic	3	0.02
Mexican	2,402	14.03
Puerto Rican	48	0.28
South American	21	0.12
Argentinean	7	0.04
Chilean	2	0.01
Colombian	7	0.04
Peruvian	3	0.02
Other South American	2	0.01
Other Hispanic or Latino	184	1.07

Race*	Population	%
African-American/Black (373)	423	2.47
Not Hispanic (363)	400	2.34
Hispanic (10)	23	0.13
American Indian/Alaska Native (85)	179	1.05
Not Hispanic (67)	143	0.84
Hispanic (18)	36	0.21
Apache (1)	4	0.02
Arapaho (1)	1	0.01
Blackfeet (1)	1	0.01
Canadian/French Am. Ind. (1)	1	0.01
Cherokee (14)	38	0.22
Chickasaw (0)	4	0.02
Choctaw (5)	14	0.08
Comanche (5)	14	0.08
Creek (4)	5	0.03
Crow (0)	2	0.01
Delaware (1)	1	0.01
Iroquois (1)	2	0.01
Kiowa (1)	1	0.01
Mexican American Ind. (4)	6	0.04
Osage (0)	2	0.01
Paiute (1)	1	0.01
Potawatomi (2)	2	0.01
Shoshone (1)	1	0.01
Sioux (0)	3	0.02
Yaqui (1)	1	0.01
Asian (203)	250	1.46
Not Hispanic (196)	236	1.38
Hispanic (7)	14	0.08
Bangladeshi (3)	3	0.02
Cambodian (4)	4	0.02
Chinese, ex. Taiwanese (38)	40	0.23
Filipino (19)	38	0.22
Indian (56)	58	0.34
Japanese (4)	8	0.05
Korean (16)	29	0.17
Nepalese (11)	11	0.06
Pakistani (18)	19	0.11
Taiwanese (0)	2	0.01
Thai (3)	3	0.02
Vietnamese (22)	23	0.13
Hawaii Native/Pacific Islander (11)	24	0.14
Not Hispanic (10)	20	0.12
Hispanic (1)	4	0.02
Guamanian/Chamorro (1)	2	0.01
Native Hawaiian (0)	8	0.05
Samoan (4)	5	0.03
Tongan (0)	2	0.01
White (14,932)	15,204	88.79
Not Hispanic (13,634)	13,778	80.46
Hispanic (1,298)	1,426	8.33

Sugar Land

Place Type: City
County: Fort Bend
Population: 78,817†

Ancestry‡	Population	%
Afghan (38)	38	0.05
African, Sub-Saharan (780)	869	1.14
African (376)	442	0.58
Ethiopian (15)	15	0.02
Nigerian (368)	368	0.48
South African (13)	13	0.02
Sudanese (8)	31	0.04
Albanian (0)	10	0.01
American (3,253)	3,253	4.28
Arab (1,585)	1,981	2.60
Arab (252)	428	0.56
Egyptian (88)	88	0.12
Jordanian (428)	451	0.59
Lebanese (302)	429	0.56
Moroccan (35)	35	0.05
Palestinian (204)	216	0.28
Syrian (18)	47	0.06
Other Arab (258)	287	0.38
Armenian (16)	16	0.02
Austrian (20)	101	0.13
Belgian (14)	64	0.08
Brazilian (26)	79	0.10
British (519)	812	1.07
Bulgarian (0)	12	0.02
Cajun (20)	20	0.03
Canadian (146)	319	0.42
Celtic (0)	11	0.01
Croatian (13)	13	0.02
Czech (372)	958	1.26
Czechoslovakian (74)	110	0.14
Danish (67)	233	0.31
Dutch (177)	648	0.85
Eastern European (92)	135	0.18
English (2,347)	6,343	8.34
European (783)	936	1.23
Finnish (9)	93	0.12
French, ex. Basque (540)	2,688	3.53
French Canadian (127)	204	0.27
German (3,017)	8,179	10.75
Greek (239)	311	0.41
Hungarian (55)	159	0.21
Icelander (0)	10	0.01
Iranian (223)	329	0.43
Irish (1,838)	5,065	6.66
Italian (903)	2,047	2.69
Latvian (0)	9	0.01
Lithuanian (5)	179	0.24
Luxemburger (0)	49	0.06
Northern European (66)	66	0.09
Norwegian (127)	404	0.53
Polish (241)	916	1.20
Portuguese (40)	129	0.17
Romanian (0)	34	0.04
Russian (167)	415	0.55
Scandinavian (122)	209	0.27
Scotch-Irish (346)	1,060	1.39
Scottish (352)	1,575	2.07
Slovak (21)	126	0.17
Slovene (13)	61	0.08
Swedish (135)	458	0.60
Swiss (43)	219	0.29
Turkish (80)	80	0.11
Ukrainian (29)	223	0.29
Welsh (78)	345	0.45
West Indian, ex. Hispanic (178)	251	0.33
British West Indian (19)	19	0.02
Dutch West Indian (0)	18	0.02
Jamaican (137)	154	0.20
Trinidadian/Tobagonian (10)	30	0.04
U.S. Virgin Islander (0)	18	0.02
West Indian (12)	12	0.02
Yugoslavian (28)	39	0.05

Hispanic Origin	Population	%
Hispanic or Latino (of any race)	8,324	10.56
Central American, ex. Mexican	582	0.74
Costa Rican	27	0.03
Guatemalan	94	0.12
Honduran	73	0.09
Nicaraguan	74	0.09
Panamanian	37	0.05
Salvadoran	276	0.35
Other Central American	1	<0.01
Cuban	376	0.48
Dominican Republic	38	0.05
Mexican	5,243	6.65
Puerto Rican	319	0.40
South American	1,080	1.37
Argentinean	157	0.20
Bolivian	67	0.09
Chilean	51	0.06
Colombian	366	0.46
Ecuadorian	111	0.14
Paraguayan	13	0.02
Peruvian	129	0.16
Uruguayan	13	0.02
Venezuelan	165	0.21
Other South American	8	0.01
Other Hispanic or Latino	686	0.87

Race*	Population	%
African-American/Black (5,853)	6,209	7.88
Not Hispanic (5,744)	6,029	7.65
Hispanic (109)	180	0.23
American Indian/Alaska Native (172)	521	0.66
Not Hispanic (135)	410	0.52
Hispanic (37)	111	0.14
Apache (1)	1	<0.01
Blackfeet (0)	3	<0.01
Central American Ind. (1)	2	<0.01
Cherokee (16)	76	0.10
Chickasaw (2)	5	0.01

*Notes: † The Census 2010 population figure is used to calculate the percentages in the Hispanic Origin and Race categories. Ancestry percentages are based on the 2006-2010 American Community Survey population (not shown); ‡ Numbers in parentheses indicate the number of people reporting a single ancestry; * Numbers in parentheses indicate the number of persons reporting this race alone, not in combination with any other race; Please refer to the Explanation of Data for more information.*

Choctaw (13)	24	0.03
Comanche (1)	5	0.01
Creek (3)	17	0.02
Delaware (3)	3	<0.01
Houma (2)	2	<0.01
Inupiat *(Alaska Native)* (0)	1	<0.01
Iroquois (1)	1	<0.01
Lumbee (2)	3	<0.01
Mexican American Ind. (5)	23	0.03
Navajo (1)	3	<0.01
Osage (1)	1	<0.01
Paiute (4)	4	0.01
Potawatomi (4)	5	0.01
Pueblo (0)	1	<0.01
Seminole (3)	3	<0.01
Sioux (3)	9	0.01
South American Ind. (0)	4	0.01
Yuman (0)	2	<0.01
Asian (27,796)	29,224	37.08
Not Hispanic (27,672)	28,966	36.75
Hispanic (124)	258	0.33
Bangladeshi (96)	99	0.13
Burmese (12)	15	0.02
Cambodian (34)	47	0.06
Chinese, ex. Taiwanese (7,748)	8,218	10.43
Filipino (1,614)	1,886	2.39
Indian (8,446)	8,856	11.24
Indonesian (160)	191	0.24
Japanese (134)	225	0.29
Korean (340)	395	0.50
Laotian (15)	19	0.02
Malaysian (55)	72	0.09
Nepalese (7)	7	0.01
Pakistani (3,312)	3,546	4.50
Sri Lankan (38)	40	0.05
Taiwanese (1,260)	1,394	1.77
Thai (87)	145	0.18
Vietnamese (3,536)	3,796	4.82
Hawaii Native/Pacific Islander (33)	130	0.16
Not Hispanic (26)	104	0.13
Hispanic (7)	26	0.03
Fijian (1)	4	0.01
Guamanian/Chamorro (4)	4	0.01
Native Hawaiian (15)	32	0.04
Samoan (6)	7	0.01
Tongan (2)	6	0.01
White (40,951)	42,570	54.01
Not Hispanic (35,014)	36,228	45.96
Hispanic (5,937)	6,342	8.05

Sulphur Springs

Place Type: City
County: Hopkins
Population: 15,449†

Ancestry‡	Population	%
African, Sub-Saharan (54)	54	0.35
African (54)	54	0.35
American (2,679)	2,679	17.47
British (0)	8	0.05
Czech (0)	12	0.08
Czechoslovakian (0)	9	0.06
Dutch (41)	296	1.93
English (728)	1,821	11.88
French, ex. Basque (19)	206	1.34
German (638)	2,003	13.06
Greek (7)	7	0.05
Irish (647)	1,681	10.96
Italian (34)	197	1.28
Norwegian (0)	143	0.93
Polish (10)	72	0.47
Russian (0)	13	0.08
Scotch-Irish (132)	204	1.33
Scottish (60)	273	1.78
Swedish (17)	21	0.14
Swiss (0)	44	0.29
Welsh (22)	36	0.23
West Indian, ex. Hispanic (8)	93	0.61
Dutch West Indian (8)	56	0.37
Jamaican (0)	37	0.24
Yugoslavian (0)	43	0.28

Hispanic Origin	Population	%
Hispanic or Latino (of any race)	2,460	15.92
Central American, ex. Mexican	111	0.72
Costa Rican	3	0.02
Guatemalan	9	0.06
Honduran	22	0.14
Panamanian	3	0.02
Salvadoran	74	0.48
Cuban	4	0.03
Dominican Republic	8	0.05
Mexican	2,208	14.29
Puerto Rican	20	0.13
South American	7	0.05
Argentinean	2	0.01
Colombian	1	0.01
Peruvian	4	0.03
Other Hispanic or Latino	102	0.66

Race*	Population	%
African-American/Black (1,962)	2,155	13.95
Not Hispanic (1,944)	2,118	13.71
Hispanic (18)	37	0.24
American Indian/Alaska Native (81)	197	1.28
Not Hispanic (57)	142	0.92
Hispanic (24)	55	0.36
Apache (1)	2	0.01
Blackfeet (1)	4	0.03
Cherokee (8)	38	0.25
Chickasaw (3)	12	0.08
Chippewa (2)	5	0.03
Choctaw (27)	44	0.28
Comanche (0)	5	0.03
Creek (8)	10	0.06
Kiowa (1)	1	0.01
Mexican American Ind. (1)	5	0.03
Potawatomi (3)	3	0.02
Spanish American Ind. (0)	1	0.01
Asian (81)	137	0.89
Not Hispanic (80)	130	0.84
Hispanic (1)	7	0.05
Cambodian (5)	5	0.03
Chinese, ex. Taiwanese (11)	18	0.12
Filipino (27)	36	0.23
Indian (4)	17	0.11
Indonesian (1)	1	0.01
Japanese (1)	11	0.07
Korean (3)	11	0.07
Pakistani (2)	6	0.04
Taiwanese (1)	1	0.01
Thai (3)	3	0.02
Vietnamese (20)	25	0.16
Hawaii Native/Pacific Islander (14)	36	0.23
Not Hispanic (5)	26	0.17
Hispanic (9)	10	0.06
Guamanian/Chamorro (9)	11	0.07
Native Hawaiian (0)	4	0.03
Samoan (2)	11	0.07
White (11,597)	11,997	77.66
Not Hispanic (10,574)	10,875	70.39
Hispanic (1,023)	1,122	7.26

Sweetwater

Place Type: City
County: Nolan
Population: 10,906†

Ancestry‡	Population	%
African, Sub-Saharan (0)	15	0.14
African (0)	15	0.14
American (1,150)	1,150	10.67
British (20)	56	0.52
Czech (3)	12	0.11
Danish (0)	11	0.10
Dutch (33)	178	1.65
English (254)	562	5.21
European (10)	10	0.09
French, ex. Basque (37)	243	2.25
German (245)	779	7.23
Irish (228)	787	7.30
Italian (14)	78	0.72
Norwegian (29)	39	0.36
Polish (9)	29	0.27
Romanian (23)	23	0.21
Russian (0)	6	0.06
Scandinavian (0)	23	0.21
Scotch-Irish (70)	155	1.44
Scottish (61)	156	1.45
Slovene (0)	11	0.10
Swedish (25)	88	0.82
Welsh (0)	14	0.13
West Indian, ex. Hispanic (0)	45	0.42
Dutch West Indian (0)	45	0.42
Yugoslavian (0)	19	0.18

Hispanic Origin	Population	%
Hispanic or Latino (of any race)	4,179	38.32
Central American, ex. Mexican	2	0.02
Costa Rican	1	0.01
Panamanian	1	0.01
Cuban	3	0.03
Dominican Republic	1	0.01
Mexican	3,710	34.02
Puerto Rican	5	0.05
South American	5	0.05
Argentinean	2	0.02
Colombian	2	0.02
Venezuelan	1	0.01
Other Hispanic or Latino	453	4.15

Race*	Population	%
African-American/Black (676)	778	7.13
Not Hispanic (629)	704	6.46
Hispanic (47)	74	0.68
American Indian/Alaska Native (56)	120	1.10
Not Hispanic (27)	64	0.59
Hispanic (29)	56	0.51
Apache (10)	11	0.10
Cherokee (8)	18	0.17
Chickasaw (0)	1	0.01
Chippewa (1)	1	0.01
Choctaw (7)	13	0.12
Comanche (2)	2	0.02
Creek (0)	1	0.01
Iroquois (1)	1	0.01
Mexican American Ind. (2)	4	0.04
Navajo (3)	3	0.03
Osage (1)	1	0.01
Pueblo (0)	1	0.01
Sioux (1)	1	0.01
Yaqui (0)	1	0.01
Asian (66)	82	0.75
Not Hispanic (57)	62	0.57
Hispanic (9)	20	0.18
Cambodian (4)	4	0.04
Chinese, ex. Taiwanese (7)	7	0.06
Filipino (9)	11	0.10
Indian (23)	26	0.24
Indonesian (4)	5	0.05
Japanese (2)	2	0.02
Korean (0)	2	0.02
Laotian (0)	1	0.01
Pakistani (3)	3	0.03
Thai (2)	3	0.03
Vietnamese (7)	7	0.06
Hawaii Native/Pacific Islander (0)	7	0.06
Not Hispanic (0)	3	0.03
Hispanic (0)	4	0.04
Guamanian/Chamorro (0)	1	0.01
Native Hawaiian (0)	2	0.02
Samoan (0)	1	0.01
White (8,920)	9,156	83.95
Not Hispanic (5,892)	5,998	55.00
Hispanic (3,028)	3,158	28.96

*Notes: † The Census 2010 population figure is used to calculate the percentages in the Hispanic Origin and Race categories. Ancestry percentages are based on the 2006-2010 American Community Survey population (not shown); ‡ Numbers in parentheses indicate the number of people reporting a single ancestry; * Numbers in parentheses indicate the number of persons reporting this race alone, not in combination with any other race; Please refer to the Explanation of Data for more information.*

Taylor

Place Type: City
County: Williamson
Population: 15,191†

Ancestry‡	Population	%
American (515)	515	3.45
Arab (12)	31	0.21
Lebanese (12)	25	0.17
Moroccan (0)	6	0.04
Australian (15)	15	0.10
Austrian (11)	11	0.07
British (76)	86	0.58
Canadian (12)	12	0.08
Celtic (21)	21	0.14
Czech (521)	1,189	7.96
Czechoslovakian (51)	66	0.44
Danish (5)	14	0.09
Dutch (28)	105	0.70
English (278)	666	4.46
European (95)	110	0.74
French, ex. Basque (19)	128	0.86
French Canadian (12)	12	0.08
German (1,184)	2,820	18.89
Hungarian (0)	4	0.03
Irish (297)	1,143	7.66
Italian (53)	123	0.82
Norwegian (38)	80	0.54
Polish (136)	202	1.35
Scotch-Irish (80)	223	1.49
Scottish (32)	99	0.66
Slovak (48)	48	0.32
Slovene (12)	12	0.08
Swedish (67)	300	2.01
Swiss (34)	41	0.27
Welsh (0)	46	0.31

Hispanic Origin	Population	%
Hispanic or Latino (of any race)	6,498	42.78
Central American, ex. Mexican	66	0.43
Costa Rican	4	0.03
Guatemalan	4	0.03
Honduran	26	0.17
Nicaraguan	2	0.01
Panamanian	4	0.03
Salvadoran	26	0.17
Cuban	16	0.11
Mexican	5,854	38.54
Puerto Rican	50	0.33
South American	17	0.11
Argentinean	1	0.01
Chilean	2	0.01
Colombian	3	0.02
Ecuadorian	3	0.02
Peruvian	7	0.05
Venezuelan	1	0.01
Other Hispanic or Latino	495	3.26

Race*	Population	%
African-American/Black (1,554)	1,707	11.24
Not Hispanic (1,434)	1,518	9.99
Hispanic (120)	189	1.24
American Indian/Alaska Native (185)	263	1.73
Not Hispanic (57)	104	0.68
Hispanic (128)	159	1.05
Apache (9)	10	0.07
Blackfeet (0)	2	0.01
Cherokee (15)	32	0.21
Chickasaw (4)	8	0.05
Chippewa (1)	2	0.01
Choctaw (12)	15	0.10
Comanche (2)	5	0.03
Cree (0)	1	0.01
Creek (0)	1	0.01
Inupiat *(Alaska Native)* (0)	1	0.01
Mexican American Ind. (2)	4	0.03
Navajo (2)	4	0.03
Seminole (5)	5	0.03
Shoshone (1)	1	0.01
Sioux (1)	2	0.01
South American Ind. (0)	1	0.01
Tlingit-Haida *(Alaska Native)* (1)	1	0.01
Yaqui (0)	2	0.01
Asian (102)	167	1.10
Not Hispanic (96)	137	0.90
Hispanic (6)	30	0.20
Cambodian (7)	7	0.05
Chinese, ex. Taiwanese (20)	31	0.20
Filipino (23)	51	0.34
Indian (23)	31	0.20
Japanese (3)	13	0.09
Korean (3)	6	0.04
Laotian (1)	3	0.02
Pakistani (4)	4	0.03
Taiwanese (0)	1	0.01
Thai (4)	5	0.03
Vietnamese (11)	11	0.07
Hawaii Native/Pacific Islander (12)	43	0.28
Not Hispanic (8)	26	0.17
Hispanic (4)	17	0.11
Fijian (3)	3	0.02
Guamanian/Chamorro (5)	9	0.06
Native Hawaiian (2)	18	0.12
Samoan (0)	1	0.01
White (10,885)	11,263	74.14
Not Hispanic (6,897)	7,041	46.35
Hispanic (3,988)	4,222	27.79

Temple

Place Type: City
County: Bell
Population: 66,102†

Ancestry‡	Population	%
African, Sub-Saharan (707)	835	1.31
African (707)	835	1.31
Albanian (10)	10	0.02
Alsatian (0)	9	0.01
American (3,512)	3,512	5.53
Arab (46)	107	0.17
Egyptian (22)	22	0.03
Lebanese (24)	74	0.12
Syrian (0)	11	0.02
Armenian (14)	26	0.04
Australian (15)	15	0.02
Austrian (11)	58	0.09
Belgian (8)	31	0.05
Brazilian (8)	8	0.01
British (91)	186	0.29
Canadian (12)	68	0.11
Czech (947)	1,468	2.31
Czechoslovakian (19)	67	0.11
Danish (13)	61	0.10
Dutch (167)	613	0.96
English (5,510)	8,354	13.15
European (364)	435	0.68
Finnish (34)	60	0.09
French, ex. Basque (474)	1,269	2.00
French Canadian (46)	95	0.15
German (5,274)	10,131	15.94
Greek (71)	134	0.21
Hungarian (10)	58	0.09
Irish (2,009)	5,172	8.14
Italian (595)	1,184	1.86
Latvian (31)	31	0.05
Lithuanian (0)	26	0.04
Luxemburger (0)	8	0.01
Northern European (8)	57	0.09
Norwegian (113)	258	0.41
Polish (238)	631	0.99
Portuguese (0)	160	0.25
Romanian (35)	48	0.08
Russian (9)	160	0.25
Scandinavian (46)	135	0.21
Scotch-Irish (848)	1,814	2.85
Scottish (566)	1,449	2.28
Serbian (0)	12	0.02
Slavic (14)	14	0.02
Slovak (0)	16	0.03
Slovene (19)	38	0.06
Swedish (131)	583	0.92
Swiss (40)	123	0.19
Ukrainian (52)	147	0.23
Welsh (25)	308	0.48
West Indian, ex. Hispanic (39)	104	0.16
Bermudan (17)	17	0.03
Dutch West Indian (0)	55	0.09
Haitian (14)	14	0.02
Trinidadian/Tobagonian (8)	18	0.03

Hispanic Origin	Population	%
Hispanic or Latino (of any race)	15,694	23.74
Central American, ex. Mexican	267	0.40
Costa Rican	16	0.02
Guatemalan	24	0.04
Honduran	53	0.08
Nicaraguan	11	0.02
Panamanian	63	0.10
Salvadoran	97	0.15
Other Central American	3	<0.01
Cuban	49	0.07
Dominican Republic	33	0.05
Mexican	13,179	19.94
Puerto Rican	795	1.20
South American	125	0.19
Argentinean	21	0.03
Bolivian	4	0.01
Chilean	7	0.01
Colombian	46	0.07
Ecuadorian	10	0.02
Peruvian	23	0.03
Venezuelan	12	0.02
Other South American	2	<0.01
Other Hispanic or Latino	1,246	1.88

Race*	Population	%
African-American/Black (11,190)	12,134	18.36
Not Hispanic (10,815)	11,503	17.40
Hispanic (375)	631	0.95
American Indian/Alaska Native (411)	812	1.23
Not Hispanic (226)	514	0.78
Hispanic (185)	298	0.45
Apache (13)	27	0.04
Blackfeet (6)	14	0.02
Canadian/French Am. Ind. (4)	6	0.01
Central American Ind. (1)	1	<0.01
Cherokee (41)	147	0.22
Cheyenne (0)	1	<0.01
Chickasaw (11)	19	0.03
Chippewa (11)	11	0.02
Choctaw (49)	70	0.11
Comanche (9)	18	0.03
Cree (0)	4	0.01
Creek (6)	13	0.02
Crow (0)	2	<0.01
Delaware (3)	5	0.01
Houma (4)	4	0.01
Iroquois (6)	11	0.02
Kiowa (4)	7	0.01
Mexican American Ind. (15)	23	0.03
Navajo (7)	17	0.03
Potawatomi (3)	7	0.01
Pueblo (0)	4	0.01
Puget Sound Salish (1)	1	<0.01
Seminole (3)	5	0.01
Sioux (7)	13	0.02
South American Ind. (4)	7	0.01
Spanish American Ind. (7)	12	0.02
Tlingit-Haida *(Alaska Native)* (1)	1	<0.01
Yaqui (0)	1	<0.01
Asian (1,373)	1,783	2.70
Not Hispanic (1,336)	1,658	2.51
Hispanic (37)	125	0.19
Bangladeshi (3)	3	<0.01
Burmese (3)	5	0.01
Cambodian (17)	23	0.03
Chinese, ex. Taiwanese (210)	265	0.40
Filipino (170)	282	0.43

*Notes: † The Census 2010 population figure is used to calculate the percentages in the Hispanic Origin and Race categories. Ancestry percentages are based on the 2006-2010 American Community Survey population (not shown); ‡ Numbers in parentheses indicate the number of people reporting a single ancestry; * Numbers in parentheses indicate the number of persons reporting this race alone, not in combination with any other race; Please refer to the Explanation of Data for more information.*

Indian (462)	498	0.75
Indonesian (6)	8	0.01
Japanese (48)	96	0.15
Korean (138)	235	0.36
Laotian (7)	13	0.02
Malaysian (2)	2	<0.01
Nepalese (29)	29	0.04
Pakistani (49)	58	0.09
Sri Lankan (4)	4	0.01
Taiwanese (33)	41	0.06
Thai (18)	40	0.06
Vietnamese (128)	156	0.24
Hawaii Native/Pacific Islander (90)	179	0.27
Not Hispanic (72)	127	0.19
Hispanic (18)	52	0.08
Guamanian/Chamorro (30)	48	0.07
Native Hawaiian (32)	72	0.11
Samoan (5)	10	0.02
Tongan (7)	7	0.01
White (45,043)	46,922	70.98
Not Hispanic (36,675)	37,746	57.10
Hispanic (8,368)	9,176	13.88

Terrell

Place Type: City
County: Kaufman
Population: 15,816†

Ancestry‡	Population	%
African, Sub-Saharan (118)	130	0.84
African (118)	130	0.84
American (600)	600	3.86
Arab (0)	8	0.05
Lebanese (0)	8	0.05
Austrian (0)	10	0.06
British (4)	4	0.03
Cajun (5)	5	0.03
Celtic (21)	21	0.14
Czech (16)	59	0.38
Danish (48)	67	0.43
Dutch (12)	184	1.18
English (569)	1,130	7.27
European (16)	24	0.15
French, ex. Basque (9)	210	1.35
German (485)	1,222	7.86
Irish (597)	1,420	9.14
Italian (13)	119	0.77
Lithuanian (0)	7	0.05
Norwegian (42)	42	0.27
Polish (0)	26	0.17
Portuguese (9)	9	0.06
Russian (29)	69	0.44
Scandinavian (11)	11	0.07
Scotch-Irish (129)	269	1.73
Scottish (60)	107	0.69
Slavic (14)	14	0.09
Swedish (19)	46	0.30
Swiss (9)	9	0.06
Welsh (0)	22	0.14
West Indian, ex. Hispanic (25)	25	0.16
Bahamian (13)	13	0.08
Jamaican (12)	12	0.08

Hispanic Origin	Population	%
Hispanic or Latino (of any race)	4,047	25.59
Central American, ex. Mexican	33	0.21
Guatemalan	8	0.05
Honduran	9	0.06
Panamanian	2	0.01
Salvadoran	14	0.09
Cuban	9	0.06
Dominican Republic	4	0.03
Mexican	3,689	23.32
Puerto Rican	41	0.26
South American	12	0.08
Argentinean	1	0.01
Chilean	3	0.02
Colombian	2	0.01
Peruvian	5	0.03
Venezuelan	1	0.01
Other Hispanic or Latino	259	1.64

Race*	Population	%
African-American/Black (4,337)	4,544	28.73
Not Hispanic (4,306)	4,464	28.22
Hispanic (31)	80	0.51
American Indian/Alaska Native (92)	159	1.01
Not Hispanic (44)	94	0.59
Hispanic (48)	65	0.41
Apache (4)	6	0.04
Canadian/French Am. Ind. (1)	1	0.01
Cherokee (11)	27	0.17
Chickasaw (2)	3	0.02
Chippewa (3)	3	0.02
Choctaw (7)	16	0.10
Comanche (0)	1	0.01
Creek (3)	3	0.02
Inupiat *(Alaska Native)* (1)	1	0.01
Iroquois (1)	1	0.01
Mexican American Ind. (12)	13	0.08
Osage (0)	1	0.01
Potawatomi (0)	1	0.01
Seminole (0)	1	0.01
Sioux (2)	3	0.02
Yup'ik *(Alaska Native)* (1)	1	0.01
Asian (82)	116	0.73
Not Hispanic (82)	106	0.67
Hispanic (0)	10	0.06
Cambodian (9)	21	0.13
Chinese, ex. Taiwanese (12)	16	0.10
Filipino (1)	9	0.06
Indian (18)	21	0.13
Japanese (0)	7	0.04
Korean (6)	12	0.08
Laotian (12)	16	0.10
Nepalese (1)	1	0.01
Sri Lankan (8)	8	0.05
Vietnamese (5)	14	0.09
Hawaii Native/Pacific Islander (1)	14	0.09
Not Hispanic (1)	12	0.08
Hispanic (0)	2	0.01
Guamanian/Chamorro (0)	1	0.01
Native Hawaiian (1)	7	0.04
Samoan (0)	1	0.01
White (9,008)	9,379	59.30
Not Hispanic (7,104)	7,306	46.19
Hispanic (1,904)	2,073	13.11

Texarkana

Place Type: City
County: Bowie
Population: 36,411†

Ancestry‡	Population	%
African, Sub-Saharan (1,640)	1,888	5.25
African (1,500)	1,748	4.86
Ghanaian (16)	16	0.04
Nigerian (124)	124	0.34
American (3,889)	3,889	10.82
Australian (6)	6	0.02
Belgian (36)	36	0.10
British (134)	205	0.57
Czech (14)	104	0.29
Czechoslovakian (14)	14	0.04
Danish (0)	60	0.17
Dutch (67)	349	0.97
English (1,243)	2,726	7.58
European (7)	33	0.09
Finnish (18)	18	0.05
French, ex. Basque (175)	518	1.44
French Canadian (12)	12	0.03
German (1,401)	3,760	10.46
Greek (12)	12	0.03
Hungarian (9)	9	0.03
Iranian (34)	34	0.09
Irish (1,244)	3,996	11.12
Italian (180)	526	1.46
Lithuanian (0)	25	0.07
Norwegian (11)	20	0.06
Polish (72)	206	0.57
Portuguese (11)	22	0.06
Romanian (5)	5	0.01
Russian (12)	43	0.12
Scandinavian (4)	4	0.01
Scotch-Irish (93)	262	0.73
Scottish (64)	276	0.77
Swedish (93)	246	0.68
Ukrainian (0)	9	0.03
Welsh (75)	248	0.69
West Indian, ex. Hispanic (10)	27	0.08
Dutch West Indian (0)	4	0.01
Haitian (10)	10	0.03
West Indian (0)	13	0.04
Yugoslavian (14)	40	0.11

Hispanic Origin	Population	%
Hispanic or Latino (of any race)	2,336	6.42
Central American, ex. Mexican	46	0.13
Guatemalan	9	0.02
Honduran	11	0.03
Nicaraguan	2	0.01
Panamanian	7	0.02
Salvadoran	17	0.05
Cuban	10	0.03
Dominican Republic	9	0.02
Mexican	1,930	5.30
Puerto Rican	65	0.18
South American	49	0.13
Argentinean	3	0.01
Colombian	13	0.04
Paraguayan	2	0.01
Peruvian	16	0.04
Venezuelan	13	0.04
Other South American	2	0.01
Other Hispanic or Latino	227	0.62

Race*	Population	%
African-American/Black (13,525)	13,980	38.39
Not Hispanic (13,438)	13,796	37.89
Hispanic (87)	184	0.51
American Indian/Alaska Native (182)	485	1.33
Not Hispanic (147)	388	1.07
Hispanic (35)	97	0.27
Alaska Athabascan *(Ala. Nat.)* (2)	2	0.01
Aleut *(Alaska Native)* (1)	1	<0.01
Apache (3)	5	0.01
Blackfeet (6)	13	0.04
Cherokee (26)	101	0.28
Chickasaw (6)	13	0.04
Choctaw (23)	61	0.17
Comanche (2)	3	0.01
Creek (5)	9	0.02
Iroquois (0)	2	0.01
Lumbee (0)	4	0.01
Menominee (1)	1	<0.01
Mexican American Ind. (6)	11	0.03
Navajo (8)	9	0.02
Osage (3)	3	0.01
Pueblo (2)	2	0.01
Seminole (1)	2	0.01
Sioux (1)	4	0.01
South American Ind. (1)	1	<0.01
Tohono O'Odham (2)	2	0.01
Ute (1)	3	0.01
Yuman (1)	1	<0.01
Asian (490)	583	1.60
Not Hispanic (484)	571	1.57
Hispanic (6)	12	0.03
Bangladeshi (7)	7	0.02
Cambodian (11)	11	0.03
Chinese, ex. Taiwanese (57)	72	0.20
Filipino (61)	88	0.24
Indian (83)	92	0.25
Indonesian (4)	5	0.01
Japanese (4)	27	0.07
Korean (105)	119	0.33
Nepalese (24)	24	0.07
Pakistani (13)	14	0.04

*Notes: † The Census 2010 population figure is used to calculate the percentages in the Hispanic Origin and Race categories. Ancestry percentages are based on the 2006-2010 American Community Survey population (not shown); ‡ Numbers in parentheses indicate the number of people reporting a single ancestry; * Numbers in parentheses indicate the number of persons reporting this race alone, not in combination with any other race; Please refer to the Explanation of Data for more information.*

	Population	%
Taiwanese (3)	3	0.01
Thai (4)	4	0.01
Vietnamese (93)	101	0.28
Hawaii Native/Pacific Islander (12)	35	0.10
Not Hispanic (9)	31	0.09
Hispanic (3)	4	0.01
Guamanian/Chamorro (5)	10	0.03
Native Hawaiian (3)	17	0.05
Samoan (0)	1	<0.01
White (20,163)	20,840	57.24
Not Hispanic (19,345)	19,886	54.62
Hispanic (818)	954	2.62

Texas City

Place Type: City
County: Galveston
Population: 45,099†

Ancestry‡	Population	%
African, Sub-Saharan (278)	278	0.62
African (278)	278	0.62
American (1,826)	1,826	4.07
Arab (24)	75	0.17
Arab (24)	63	0.14
Lebanese (0)	12	0.03
Austrian (8)	85	0.19
Brazilian (47)	47	0.10
British (49)	86	0.19
Cajun (56)	119	0.27
Canadian (8)	44	0.10
Croatian (11)	11	0.02
Czech (196)	559	1.25
Czechoslovakian (16)	56	0.12
Danish (31)	31	0.07
Dutch (79)	288	0.64
English (1,015)	2,426	5.41
European (327)	430	0.96
French, ex. Basque (174)	1,247	2.78
French Canadian (95)	210	0.47
German (1,566)	5,068	11.30
Greek (46)	115	0.26
Hungarian (0)	31	0.07
Iranian (15)	36	0.08
Irish (1,091)	3,805	8.48
Italian (318)	888	1.98
Norwegian (115)	356	0.79
Polish (98)	325	0.72
Russian (30)	89	0.20
Scandinavian (0)	32	0.07
Scotch-Irish (207)	573	1.28
Scottish (56)	357	0.80
Serbian (0)	14	0.03
Slovene (15)	15	0.03
Swedish (109)	314	0.70
Welsh (27)	158	0.35

Hispanic Origin	Population	%
Hispanic or Latino (of any race)	12,184	27.02
Central American, ex. Mexican	447	0.99
Costa Rican	8	0.02
Guatemalan	59	0.13
Honduran	122	0.27
Nicaraguan	9	0.02
Panamanian	22	0.05
Salvadoran	221	0.49
Other Central American	6	0.01
Cuban	43	0.10
Dominican Republic	10	0.02
Mexican	10,307	22.85
Puerto Rican	226	0.50
South American	36	0.08
Argentinean	2	<0.01
Chilean	2	<0.01
Colombian	2	<0.01
Ecuadorian	16	0.04
Paraguayan	1	<0.01
Peruvian	6	0.01
Venezuelan	7	0.02
Other Hispanic or Latino	1,115	2.47

Race*	Population	%
African-American/Black (13,397)	13,904	30.83
Not Hispanic (13,166)	13,499	29.93
Hispanic (231)	405	0.90
American Indian/Alaska Native (298)	545	1.21
Not Hispanic (156)	339	0.75
Hispanic (142)	206	0.46
Apache (5)	13	0.03
Arapaho (3)	3	0.01
Blackfeet (0)	9	0.02
Central American Ind. (0)	3	0.01
Cherokee (27)	104	0.23
Chickasaw (13)	17	0.04
Chippewa (8)	8	0.02
Choctaw (12)	41	0.09
Comanche (2)	4	0.01
Creek (1)	13	0.03
Delaware (3)	4	0.01
Houma (4)	4	0.01
Iroquois (0)	1	<0.01
Kiowa (0)	1	<0.01
Lumbee (2)	2	<0.01
Mexican American Ind. (28)	37	0.08
Navajo (1)	2	<0.01
Osage (0)	2	<0.01
Ottawa (4)	4	0.01
Pima (3)	3	0.01
Potawatomi (3)	6	0.01
Seminole (4)	10	0.02
Sioux (1)	1	<0.01
South American Ind. (0)	2	<0.01
Tlingit-Haida *(Alaska Native)* (1)	1	<0.01
Ute (1)	1	<0.01
Yakama (1)	1	<0.01
Yaqui (4)	4	0.01
Asian (468)	628	1.39
Not Hispanic (439)	560	1.24
Hispanic (29)	68	0.15
Cambodian (7)	8	0.02
Chinese, ex. Taiwanese (37)	53	0.12
Filipino (113)	182	0.40
Indian (123)	147	0.33
Indonesian (1)	1	<0.01
Japanese (8)	24	0.05
Korean (15)	27	0.06
Laotian (6)	9	0.02
Nepalese (5)	6	0.01
Pakistani (10)	12	0.03
Taiwanese (2)	3	0.01
Thai (0)	1	<0.01
Vietnamese (127)	134	0.30
Hawaii Native/Pacific Islander (25)	76	0.17
Not Hispanic (21)	57	0.13
Hispanic (4)	19	0.04
Fijian (4)	6	0.01
Guamanian/Chamorro (10)	12	0.03
Native Hawaiian (7)	33	0.07
Samoan (2)	10	0.02
White (25,277)	26,397	58.53
Not Hispanic (18,509)	18,989	42.11
Hispanic (6,768)	7,408	16.43

The Colony

Place Type: City
County: Denton
Population: 36,328†

Ancestry‡	Population	%
African, Sub-Saharan (338)	559	1.60
African (86)	159	0.45
Ghanaian (11)	11	0.03
Kenyan (88)	88	0.25
Nigerian (141)	289	0.83
South African (12)	12	0.03
American (1,538)	1,538	4.40
Arab (61)	61	0.17
Lebanese (18)	18	0.05
Other Arab (43)	43	0.12
Armenian (0)	13	0.04
Austrian (17)	73	0.21
Brazilian (0)	17	0.05
British (189)	193	0.55
Cajun (48)	48	0.14
Canadian (10)	10	0.03
Celtic (0)	12	0.03
Croatian (32)	96	0.27
Czech (14)	86	0.25
Czechoslovakian (63)	195	0.56
Danish (22)	245	0.70
Dutch (169)	423	1.21
English (823)	3,653	10.45
Estonian (25)	40	0.11
European (338)	835	2.39
Finnish (0)	25	0.07
French, ex. Basque (288)	1,316	3.77
French Canadian (109)	372	1.06
German (2,306)	6,121	17.52
Greek (29)	161	0.46
Hungarian (73)	295	0.84
Iranian (199)	240	0.69
Irish (1,192)	4,772	13.65
Israeli (136)	136	0.39
Italian (324)	996	2.85
Lithuanian (0)	43	0.12
Maltese (0)	10	0.03
New Zealander (8)	8	0.02
Northern European (15)	15	0.04
Norwegian (92)	334	0.96
Pennsylvania German (6)	26	0.07
Polish (186)	899	2.57
Portuguese (28)	45	0.13
Romanian (134)	134	0.38
Russian (111)	222	0.64
Scandinavian (12)	45	0.13
Scotch-Irish (448)	834	2.39
Scottish (420)	1,120	3.20
Slovak (16)	70	0.20
Swedish (84)	395	1.13
Swiss (27)	141	0.40
Turkish (46)	46	0.13
Ukrainian (0)	95	0.27
Welsh (113)	270	0.77
West Indian, ex. Hispanic (15)	195	0.56
Barbadian (0)	100	0.29
British West Indian (0)	70	0.20
Dutch West Indian (0)	10	0.03
Jamaican (15)	15	0.04
Yugoslavian (75)	127	0.36

Hispanic Origin	Population	%
Hispanic or Latino (of any race)	7,684	21.15
Central American, ex. Mexican	638	1.76
Costa Rican	4	0.01
Guatemalan	71	0.20
Honduran	137	0.38
Nicaraguan	27	0.07
Panamanian	22	0.06
Salvadoran	369	1.02
Other Central American	8	0.02
Cuban	107	0.29
Dominican Republic	17	0.05
Mexican	5,748	15.82
Puerto Rican	194	0.53
South American	349	0.96
Argentinean	56	0.15
Bolivian	8	0.02
Chilean	20	0.06
Colombian	102	0.28
Ecuadorian	18	0.05
Paraguayan	6	0.02
Peruvian	93	0.26
Uruguayan	8	0.02
Venezuelan	36	0.10
Other South American	2	0.01
Other Hispanic or Latino	631	1.74

Race*	Population	%
African-American/Black (2,960)	3,373	9.28

*Notes: † The Census 2010 population figure is used to calculate the percentages in the Hispanic Origin and Race categories. Ancestry percentages are based on the 2006-2010 American Community Survey population (not shown); ‡ Numbers in parentheses indicate the number of people reporting a single ancestry; * Numbers in parentheses indicate the number of persons reporting this race alone, not in combination with any other race; Please refer to the Explanation of Data for more information.*

Not Hispanic (2,874)	3,214	8.85
Hispanic (86)	159	0.44
American Indian/Alaska Native (291)	651	1.79
Not Hispanic (194)	465	1.28
Hispanic (97)	186	0.51
Apache (6)	15	0.04
Blackfeet (1)	3	0.01
Canadian/French Am. Ind. (0)	3	0.01
Cherokee (34)	119	0.33
Cheyenne (2)	2	0.01
Chickasaw (13)	17	0.05
Chippewa (2)	3	0.01
Choctaw (55)	113	0.31
Comanche (5)	14	0.04
Creek (6)	17	0.05
Delaware (1)	1	<0.01
Iroquois (2)	4	0.01
Kiowa (3)	3	0.01
Mexican American Ind. (13)	25	0.07
Navajo (4)	6	0.02
Osage (0)	9	0.02
Potawatomi (4)	4	0.01
Seminole (1)	1	<0.01
Sioux (5)	11	0.03
Spanish American Ind. (2)	3	0.01
Ute (3)	3	0.01
Yaqui (0)	1	<0.01
Yup'ik *(Alaska Native)* (1)	3	0.01
Asian (2,116)	2,474	6.81
Not Hispanic (2,070)	2,386	6.57
Hispanic (46)	88	0.24
Bangladeshi (16)	17	0.05
Burmese (3)	3	0.01
Cambodian (55)	58	0.16
Chinese, ex. Taiwanese (248)	295	0.81
Filipino (176)	276	0.76
Indian (585)	636	1.75
Indonesian (18)	23	0.06
Japanese (47)	99	0.27
Korean (277)	326	0.90
Laotian (16)	19	0.05
Malaysian (4)	7	0.02
Nepalese (16)	19	0.05
Pakistani (101)	113	0.31
Sri Lankan (11)	14	0.04
Taiwanese (17)	21	0.06
Thai (33)	54	0.15
Vietnamese (400)	432	1.19
Hawaii Native/Pacific Islander (32)	72	0.20
Not Hispanic (26)	62	0.17
Hispanic (6)	10	0.03
Guamanian/Chamorro (12)	22	0.06
Native Hawaiian (11)	32	0.09
Samoan (1)	3	0.01
Tongan (1)	2	0.01
White (27,389)	28,545	78.58
Not Hispanic (22,502)	23,295	64.12
Hispanic (4,887)	5,250	14.45

The Woodlands

Place Type: CDP
County: Montgomery
Population: 93,847†

Ancestry‡	Population	%
Afghan (27)	27	0.03
African, Sub-Saharan (292)	336	0.36
African (145)	167	0.18
South African (147)	169	0.18
Alsatian (0)	11	0.01
American (5,375)	5,375	5.84
Arab (305)	677	0.74
Arab (52)	67	0.07
Egyptian (38)	90	0.10
Iraqi (0)	48	0.05
Jordanian (49)	49	0.05
Lebanese (83)	255	0.28
Palestinian (68)	88	0.10
Syrian (10)	75	0.08
Other Arab (5)	5	0.01
Armenian (13)	13	0.01
Australian (285)	285	0.31
Austrian (169)	509	0.55
Basque (36)	59	0.06
Belgian (56)	127	0.14
Brazilian (150)	180	0.20
British (696)	1,088	1.18
Bulgarian (0)	16	0.02
Cajun (65)	218	0.24
Canadian (611)	826	0.90
Celtic (27)	36	0.04
Croatian (30)	104	0.11
Czech (377)	1,260	1.37
Czechoslovakian (67)	181	0.20
Danish (230)	633	0.69
Dutch (510)	1,740	1.89
Eastern European (111)	111	0.12
English (4,817)	13,370	14.52
European (1,827)	1,948	2.12
Finnish (106)	226	0.25
French, ex. Basque (960)	4,751	5.16
French Canadian (302)	782	0.85
German (5,001)	18,379	19.96
Greek (145)	384	0.42
Hungarian (71)	321	0.35
Iranian (141)	208	0.23
Irish (3,155)	11,815	12.83
Italian (2,319)	5,544	6.02
Latvian (13)	109	0.12
Lithuanian (69)	186	0.20
Macedonian (24)	24	0.03
Maltese (8)	8	0.01
Northern European (285)	311	0.34
Norwegian (423)	1,145	1.24
Pennsylvania German (10)	10	0.01
Polish (918)	2,951	3.21
Portuguese (21)	155	0.17
Romanian (71)	71	0.08
Russian (207)	746	0.81
Scandinavian (52)	176	0.19
Scotch-Irish (1,075)	2,600	2.82
Scottish (763)	3,208	3.48
Serbian (31)	45	0.05
Slavic (14)	70	0.08
Slovak (53)	207	0.22
Slovene (0)	14	0.02
Swedish (396)	1,841	2.00
Swiss (28)	458	0.50
Turkish (45)	45	0.05
Ukrainian (162)	383	0.42
Welsh (335)	994	1.08
West Indian, ex. Hispanic (283)	344	0.37
Bahamian (26)	49	0.05
Barbadian (58)	58	0.06
Jamaican (171)	181	0.20
Trinidadian/Tobagonian (28)	28	0.03
West Indian (0)	28	0.03
Yugoslavian (27)	62	0.07

Hispanic Origin	Population	%
Hispanic or Latino (of any race)	11,497	12.25
Central American, ex. Mexican	742	0.79
Costa Rican	60	0.06
Guatemalan	183	0.19
Honduran	139	0.15
Nicaraguan	77	0.08
Panamanian	51	0.05
Salvadoran	230	0.25
Other Central American	2	<0.01
Cuban	315	0.34
Dominican Republic	35	0.04
Mexican	6,919	7.37
Puerto Rican	501	0.53
South American	2,017	2.15
Argentinean	373	0.40
Bolivian	56	0.06
Chilean	62	0.07
Colombian	639	0.68
Ecuadorian	136	0.14
Paraguayan	3	<0.01
Peruvian	199	0.21
Uruguayan	27	0.03
Venezuelan	516	0.55
Other South American	6	0.01
Other Hispanic or Latino	968	1.03

Race*	Population	%
African-American/Black (2,268)	2,654	2.83
Not Hispanic (2,191)	2,525	2.69
Hispanic (77)	129	0.14
American Indian/Alaska Native (322)	783	0.83
Not Hispanic (253)	612	0.65
Hispanic (69)	171	0.18
Aleut *(Alaska Native)* (1)	4	<0.01
Apache (6)	6	0.01
Blackfeet (1)	10	0.01
Canadian/French Am. Ind. (0)	2	<0.01
Central American Ind. (0)	3	<0.01
Cherokee (66)	198	0.21
Chickasaw (17)	25	0.03
Chippewa (3)	4	<0.01
Choctaw (39)	90	0.10
Comanche (1)	8	0.01
Cree (0)	8	0.01
Creek (2)	10	0.01
Delaware (0)	3	<0.01
Houma (0)	3	<0.01
Iroquois (4)	13	0.01
Kiowa (0)	1	<0.01
Lumbee (3)	3	<0.01
Menominee (2)	2	<0.01
Mexican American Ind. (14)	26	0.03
Navajo (5)	6	0.01
Osage (4)	5	0.01
Ottawa (1)	2	<0.01
Potawatomi (4)	8	0.01
Puget Sound Salish (3)	3	<0.01
Seminole (0)	3	<0.01
Sioux (11)	15	0.02
South American Ind. (1)	15	0.02
Yakama (1)	1	<0.01
Yaqui (4)	5	0.01
Asian (4,625)	5,484	5.84
Not Hispanic (4,581)	5,331	5.68
Hispanic (44)	153	0.16
Bangladeshi (33)	40	0.04
Burmese (2)	3	<0.01
Cambodian (22)	29	0.03
Chinese, ex. Taiwanese (914)	1,066	1.14
Filipino (564)	752	0.80
Hmong (1)	1	<0.01
Indian (1,723)	1,880	2.00
Indonesian (42)	56	0.06
Japanese (148)	338	0.36
Korean (251)	354	0.38
Laotian (7)	11	0.01
Malaysian (48)	60	0.06
Nepalese (17)	17	0.02
Pakistani (270)	305	0.32
Sri Lankan (37)	42	0.04
Taiwanese (104)	108	0.12
Thai (54)	79	0.08
Vietnamese (228)	282	0.30
Hawaii Native/Pacific Islander (65)	159	0.17
Not Hispanic (54)	130	0.14
Hispanic (11)	29	0.03
Guamanian/Chamorro (29)	44	0.05
Native Hawaiian (15)	67	0.07
Samoan (3)	18	0.02
Tongan (0)	3	<0.01
White (82,947)	84,721	90.28
Not Hispanic (73,680)	74,960	79.87
Hispanic (9,267)	9,761	10.40

Timberwood Park

Place Type: CDP
County: Bexar
Population: 13,447†

*Notes: † The Census 2010 population figure is used to calculate the percentages in the Hispanic Origin and Race categories. Ancestry percentages are based on the 2006-2010 American Community Survey population (not shown); ‡ Numbers in parentheses indicate the number of people reporting a single ancestry; * Numbers in parentheses indicate the number of persons reporting this race alone, not in combination with any other race; Please refer to the Explanation of Data for more information.*

Ancestry‡	Population	%
African, Sub-Saharan (0)	9	0.08
African (0)	9	0.08
Alsatian (29)	29	0.25
American (672)	672	5.71
British (44)	88	0.75
Cajun (41)	41	0.35
Czech (10)	24	0.20
Czechoslovakian (7)	21	0.18
Danish (0)	95	0.81
Dutch (20)	128	1.09
Eastern European (8)	8	0.07
English (518)	1,406	11.95
European (117)	224	1.90
Finnish (0)	17	0.14
French, ex. Basque (67)	554	4.71
French Canadian (57)	57	0.48
German (801)	2,194	18.65
Greek (18)	35	0.30
Hungarian (0)	35	0.30
Iranian (6)	6	0.05
Irish (179)	1,037	8.81
Italian (219)	497	4.22
Lithuanian (0)	11	0.09
Norwegian (28)	71	0.60
Polish (121)	438	3.72
Russian (0)	37	0.31
Scandinavian (8)	8	0.07
Scotch-Irish (174)	246	2.09
Scottish (96)	331	2.81
Slovak (0)	12	0.10
Swedish (34)	78	0.66
Swiss (0)	81	0.69
Turkish (0)	15	0.13
Welsh (10)	36	0.31
West Indian, ex. Hispanic (12)	12	0.10
Barbadian (12)	12	0.10

Hispanic Origin	Population	%
Hispanic or Latino (of any race)	4,213	31.33
Central American, ex. Mexican	98	0.73
Costa Rican	15	0.11
Guatemalan	26	0.19
Honduran	16	0.12
Nicaraguan	6	0.04
Panamanian	14	0.10
Salvadoran	21	0.16
Cuban	46	0.34
Dominican Republic	7	0.05
Mexican	3,423	25.46
Puerto Rican	187	1.39
South American	123	0.91
Argentinean	9	0.07
Bolivian	6	0.04
Chilean	3	0.02
Colombian	52	0.39
Ecuadorian	6	0.04
Paraguayan	1	0.01
Peruvian	19	0.14
Uruguayan	6	0.04
Venezuelan	15	0.11
Other South American	6	0.04
Other Hispanic or Latino	329	2.45

Race*	Population	%
African-American/Black (657)	772	5.74
Not Hispanic (625)	691	5.14
Hispanic (32)	81	0.60
American Indian/Alaska Native (56)	167	1.24
Not Hispanic (40)	121	0.90
Hispanic (16)	46	0.34
Alaska Athabascan *(Ala. Nat.)* (1)	1	0.01
Apache (2)	3	0.02
Arapaho (0)	1	0.01
Blackfeet (1)	3	0.02
Cherokee (7)	29	0.22
Chickasaw (2)	3	0.02
Chippewa (3)	7	0.05
Choctaw (5)	22	0.16
Comanche (0)	5	0.04
Creek (1)	1	0.01
Iroquois (0)	3	0.02
Lumbee (2)	2	0.01
Mexican American Ind. (2)	2	0.01
Navajo (4)	4	0.03
Osage (0)	1	0.01
Seminole (0)	1	0.01
Sioux (2)	7	0.05
South American Ind. (2)	2	0.01
Asian (608)	811	6.03
Not Hispanic (588)	747	5.56
Hispanic (20)	64	0.48
Burmese (1)	1	0.01
Cambodian (0)	3	0.02
Chinese, ex. Taiwanese (74)	99	0.74
Filipino (114)	170	1.26
Indian (177)	203	1.51
Indonesian (4)	4	0.03
Japanese (24)	62	0.46
Korean (76)	103	0.77
Laotian (1)	1	0.01
Pakistani (64)	80	0.59
Taiwanese (1)	2	0.01
Thai (9)	24	0.18
Vietnamese (46)	54	0.40
Hawaii Native/Pacific Islander (17)	52	0.39
Not Hispanic (12)	44	0.33
Hispanic (5)	8	0.06
Guamanian/Chamorro (12)	22	0.16
Native Hawaiian (4)	9	0.07
Samoan (1)	5	0.04
White (10,730)	11,210	83.36
Not Hispanic (7,642)	7,924	58.93
Hispanic (3,088)	3,286	24.44

Tomball

Place Type: City
County: Harris
Population: 10,753†

Ancestry‡	Population	%
African, Sub-Saharan (0)	71	0.68
African (0)	71	0.68
American (960)	960	9.20
Czech (203)	228	2.18
Czechoslovakian (34)	76	0.73
Danish (38)	38	0.36
Dutch (25)	106	1.02
English (335)	1,386	13.28
Finnish (0)	14	0.13
French, ex. Basque (56)	396	3.79
French Canadian (13)	13	0.12
German (787)	2,102	20.14
Greek (0)	20	0.19
Irish (556)	1,403	13.45
Italian (122)	399	3.82
Norwegian (0)	61	0.58
Polish (21)	174	1.67
Portuguese (0)	32	0.31
Russian (0)	54	0.52
Scandinavian (21)	21	0.20
Scotch-Irish (45)	289	2.77
Scottish (26)	67	0.64
Swedish (116)	321	3.08
Ukrainian (0)	26	0.25
Welsh (0)	23	0.22

Hispanic Origin	Population	%
Hispanic or Latino (of any race)	1,830	17.02
Central American, ex. Mexican	143	1.33
Costa Rican	6	0.06
Guatemalan	30	0.28
Honduran	40	0.37
Nicaraguan	4	0.04
Panamanian	2	0.02
Salvadoran	60	0.56
Other Central American	1	0.01
Cuban	17	0.16
Dominican Republic	1	0.01
Mexican	1,394	12.96
Puerto Rican	51	0.47
South American	31	0.29
Argentinean	1	0.01
Chilean	7	0.07
Colombian	14	0.13
Ecuadorian	4	0.04
Uruguayan	1	0.01
Venezuelan	4	0.04
Other Hispanic or Latino	193	1.79

Race*	Population	%
African-American/Black (681)	749	6.97
Not Hispanic (661)	718	6.68
Hispanic (20)	31	0.29
American Indian/Alaska Native (84)	157	1.46
Not Hispanic (52)	121	1.13
Hispanic (32)	36	0.33
Aleut *(Alaska Native)* (2)	2	0.02
Blackfeet (0)	3	0.03
Canadian/French Am. Ind. (0)	1	0.01
Cherokee (11)	31	0.29
Chickasaw (5)	9	0.08
Choctaw (2)	9	0.08
Comanche (1)	1	0.01
Creek (2)	5	0.05
Kiowa (1)	1	0.01
Mexican American Ind. (3)	3	0.03
Navajo (1)	1	0.01
Potawatomi (0)	1	0.01
Seminole (0)	1	0.01
Sioux (2)	4	0.04
South American Ind. (4)	4	0.04
Spanish American Ind. (7)	7	0.07
Asian (120)	160	1.49
Not Hispanic (118)	148	1.38
Hispanic (2)	12	0.11
Bangladeshi (7)	7	0.07
Burmese (10)	10	0.09
Cambodian (3)	3	0.03
Chinese, ex. Taiwanese (1)	6	0.06
Filipino (31)	38	0.35
Indian (8)	8	0.07
Indonesian (1)	1	0.01
Japanese (7)	14	0.13
Korean (5)	12	0.11
Nepalese (6)	6	0.06
Pakistani (3)	3	0.03
Sri Lankan (3)	3	0.03
Thai (2)	6	0.06
Vietnamese (32)	45	0.42
Hawaii Native/Pacific Islander (7)	11	0.10
Not Hispanic (7)	11	0.10
Guamanian/Chamorro (0)	1	0.01
Native Hawaiian (0)	3	0.03
Samoan (4)	4	0.04
White (8,890)	9,130	84.91
Not Hispanic (7,908)	8,060	74.96
Hispanic (982)	1,070	9.95

Trophy Club

Place Type: Town
County: Denton
Population: 8,024†

Ancestry‡	Population	%
African, Sub-Saharan (16)	16	0.20
African (16)	16	0.20
American (316)	316	3.93
Australian (0)	191	2.38
Austrian (0)	44	0.55
British (29)	72	0.90
Celtic (15)	15	0.19
Croatian (0)	40	0.50
Czech (12)	55	0.68
Czechoslovakian (11)	22	0.27
Danish (0)	71	0.88
Dutch (85)	331	4.12
English (540)	1,573	19.56

*Notes: † The Census 2010 population figure is used to calculate the percentages in the Hispanic Origin and Race categories. Ancestry percentages are based on the 2006-2010 American Community Survey population (not shown); ‡ Numbers in parentheses indicate the number of people reporting a single ancestry; * Numbers in parentheses indicate the number of persons reporting this race alone, not in combination with any other race; Please refer to the Explanation of Data for more information.*

European (219)	253	3.15
Finnish (67)	90	1.12
French, ex. Basque (30)	172	2.14
French Canadian (55)	55	0.68
German (338)	1,536	19.10
Iranian (21)	21	0.26
Irish (530)	1,492	18.55
Italian (299)	604	7.51
New Zealander (0)	41	0.51
Norwegian (39)	178	2.21
Pennsylvania German (0)	21	0.26
Polish (111)	325	4.04
Russian (65)	65	0.81
Scotch-Irish (201)	227	2.82
Scottish (57)	161	2.00
Slovak (20)	33	0.41
Swedish (88)	273	3.39
Swiss (0)	17	0.21
Ukrainian (10)	58	0.72
Welsh (0)	43	0.53
West Indian, ex. Hispanic (0)	12	0.15
Dutch West Indian (0)	12	0.15

Hispanic Origin	Population	%
Hispanic or Latino (of any race)	510	6.36
Central American, ex. Mexican	35	0.44
Costa Rican	1	0.01
Guatemalan	6	0.07
Honduran	5	0.06
Nicaraguan	3	0.04
Panamanian	2	0.02
Salvadoran	18	0.22
Cuban	10	0.12
Dominican Republic	6	0.07
Mexican	308	3.84
Puerto Rican	49	0.61
South American	45	0.56
Argentinean	2	0.02
Chilean	5	0.06
Colombian	22	0.27
Ecuadorian	5	0.06
Peruvian	9	0.11
Venezuelan	2	0.02
Other Hispanic or Latino	57	0.71

Race*	Population	%
African-American/Black (151)	164	2.04
Not Hispanic (145)	158	1.97
Hispanic (6)	6	0.07
American Indian/Alaska Native (40)	70	0.87
Not Hispanic (26)	52	0.65
Hispanic (14)	18	0.22
Apache (1)	2	0.02
Cherokee (8)	21	0.26
Chickasaw (3)	3	0.04
Choctaw (5)	5	0.06
Creek (1)	1	0.01
Potawatomi (3)	3	0.04
Sioux (3)	4	0.05
South American Ind. (7)	7	0.09
Asian (283)	328	4.09
Not Hispanic (283)	321	4.00
Hispanic (0)	7	0.09
Bangladeshi (2)	2	0.02
Chinese, ex. Taiwanese (34)	49	0.61
Filipino (36)	48	0.60
Indian (142)	143	1.78
Indonesian (0)	1	0.01
Japanese (8)	17	0.21
Korean (9)	11	0.14
Malaysian (1)	3	0.04
Nepalese (2)	2	0.02
Pakistani (10)	10	0.12
Sri Lankan (1)	1	0.01
Taiwanese (5)	5	0.06
Thai (2)	2	0.02
Vietnamese (28)	28	0.35
Hawaii Native/Pacific Islander (2)	12	0.15
Not Hispanic (2)	12	0.15
Marshallese (1)	1	0.01
Native Hawaiian (1)	4	0.05
Samoan (0)	4	0.05
White (7,328)	7,437	92.68
Not Hispanic (6,962)	7,043	87.77
Hispanic (366)	394	4.91

Tyler

Place Type: City
County: Smith
Population: 96,900†

Ancestry‡	Population	%
African, Sub-Saharan (507)	551	0.58
African (357)	392	0.41
Cape Verdean (0)	9	0.01
Ethiopian (16)	16	0.02
Ghanaian (12)	12	0.01
Nigerian (111)	111	0.12
Other Sub-Saharan African (11)	11	0.01
American (5,974)	5,974	6.31
Arab (109)	233	0.25
Lebanese (97)	194	0.20
Other Arab (12)	39	0.04
Austrian (9)	43	0.05
Basque (0)	14	0.01
Belgian (10)	10	0.01
Brazilian (11)	29	0.03
British (216)	442	0.47
Cajun (28)	39	0.04
Canadian (108)	108	0.11
Croatian (0)	10	0.01
Czech (102)	342	0.36
Czechoslovakian (51)	59	0.06
Danish (22)	104	0.11
Dutch (108)	781	0.82
Eastern European (18)	18	0.02
English (4,587)	9,714	10.26
European (454)	476	0.50
Finnish (0)	31	0.03
French, ex. Basque (489)	2,053	2.17
French Canadian (85)	143	0.15
German (3,335)	8,487	8.96
Greek (87)	307	0.32
Hungarian (11)	29	0.03
Iranian (28)	28	0.03
Irish (2,932)	8,765	9.26
Italian (355)	1,243	1.31
Latvian (9)	24	0.03
Lithuanian (11)	49	0.05
Luxemburger (0)	27	0.03
Northern European (42)	42	0.04
Norwegian (145)	464	0.49
Pennsylvania German (0)	5	0.01
Polish (318)	873	0.92
Portuguese (0)	76	0.08
Romanian (26)	43	0.05
Russian (83)	143	0.15
Scandinavian (45)	127	0.13
Scotch-Irish (1,141)	1,950	2.06
Scottish (981)	2,371	2.50
Serbian (0)	14	0.01
Slavic (0)	13	0.01
Slovak (12)	19	0.02
Slovene (0)	20	0.02
Swedish (86)	350	0.37
Swiss (9)	59	0.06
Ukrainian (7)	120	0.13
Welsh (91)	372	0.39
West Indian, ex. Hispanic (91)	121	0.13
Bahamian (12)	42	0.04
Dutch West Indian (11)	11	0.01
Jamaican (46)	46	0.05
Trinidadian/Tobagonian (22)	22	0.02
Yugoslavian (13)	23	0.02

Hispanic Origin	Population	%
Hispanic or Latino (of any race)	20,511	21.17
Central American, ex. Mexican	666	0.69
Costa Rican	8	0.01
Guatemalan	98	0.10
Honduran	119	0.12
Nicaraguan	50	0.05
Panamanian	13	0.01
Salvadoran	376	0.39
Other Central American	2	<0.01
Cuban	49	0.05
Dominican Republic	21	0.02
Mexican	18,265	18.85
Puerto Rican	215	0.22
South American	192	0.20
Argentinean	16	0.02
Bolivian	4	<0.01
Chilean	4	<0.01
Colombian	54	0.06
Ecuadorian	24	0.02
Paraguayan	2	<0.01
Peruvian	42	0.04
Uruguayan	2	<0.01
Venezuelan	44	0.05
Other Hispanic or Latino	1,103	1.14

Race*	Population	%
African-American/Black (23,986)	24,754	25.55
Not Hispanic (23,742)	24,384	25.16
Hispanic (244)	370	0.38
American Indian/Alaska Native (493)	917	0.95
Not Hispanic (284)	631	0.65
Hispanic (209)	286	0.30
Alaska Athabascan *(Ala. Nat.)* (1)	1	<0.01
Aleut *(Alaska Native)* (0)	2	<0.01
Apache (9)	18	0.02
Blackfeet (5)	17	0.02
Cherokee (68)	178	0.18
Cheyenne (1)	1	<0.01
Chickasaw (2)	7	0.01
Chippewa (1)	2	<0.01
Choctaw (43)	78	0.08
Comanche (8)	9	0.01
Cree (1)	1	<0.01
Creek (6)	14	0.01
Crow (1)	4	<0.01
Delaware (1)	3	<0.01
Houma (3)	4	<0.01
Inupiat *(Alaska Native)* (2)	2	<0.01
Iroquois (5)	5	0.01
Kiowa (0)	2	<0.01
Lumbee (4)	5	0.01
Mexican American Ind. (68)	86	0.09
Navajo (14)	19	0.02
Osage (7)	10	0.01
Ottawa (1)	1	<0.01
Paiute (0)	2	<0.01
Pima (0)	1	<0.01
Potawatomi (10)	12	0.01
Seminole (4)	11	0.01
Sioux (8)	23	0.02
Spanish American Ind. (0)	2	<0.01
Tlingit-Haida *(Alaska Native)* (2)	2	<0.01
Yuman (1)	3	<0.01
Yup'ik *(Alaska Native)* (0)	1	<0.01
Asian (1,837)	2,149	2.22
Not Hispanic (1,807)	2,088	2.15
Hispanic (30)	61	0.06
Bangladeshi (10)	10	0.01
Burmese (5)	5	0.01
Cambodian (45)	63	0.07
Chinese, ex. Taiwanese (217)	281	0.29
Filipino (463)	545	0.56
Indian (369)	421	0.43
Indonesian (13)	15	0.02
Japanese (30)	85	0.09
Korean (104)	129	0.13
Laotian (1)	1	<0.01
Malaysian (2)	2	<0.01
Nepalese (30)	31	0.03
Pakistani (221)	246	0.25
Sri Lankan (0)	5	0.01
Taiwanese (9)	15	0.02
Thai (9)	10	0.01

*Notes: † The Census 2010 population figure is used to calculate the percentages in the Hispanic Origin and Race categories. Ancestry percentages are based on the 2006-2010 American Community Survey population (not shown); ‡ Numbers in parentheses indicate the number of people reporting a single ancestry; * Numbers in parentheses indicate the number of persons reporting this race alone, not in combination with any other race; Please refer to the Explanation of Data for more information.*

Vietnamese (198)	225	0.23
Hawaii Native/Pacific Islander (28)	82	0.08
Not Hispanic (18)	51	0.05
Hispanic (10)	31	0.03
Fijian (1)	1	<0.01
Guamanian/Chamorro (5)	8	0.01
Native Hawaiian (8)	25	0.03
Samoan (2)	16	0.02
White (58,632)	60,319	62.25
Not Hispanic (49,252)	50,248	51.86
Hispanic (9,380)	10,071	10.39

Universal City

Place Type: City
County: Bexar
Population: 18,530†

Ancestry‡	Population	%
African, Sub-Saharan (299)	347	1.96
African (299)	347	1.96
American (815)	815	4.60
Arab (40)	52	0.29
Lebanese (40)	52	0.29
Austrian (14)	45	0.25
Belgian (0)	15	0.08
British (0)	37	0.21
Cajun (148)	148	0.84
Canadian (10)	74	0.42
Czech (11)	120	0.68
Czechoslovakian (0)	9	0.05
Danish (16)	74	0.42
Dutch (15)	211	1.19
English (577)	1,670	9.43
European (154)	243	1.37
Finnish (0)	30	0.17
French, ex. Basque (68)	454	2.56
German (1,334)	3,686	20.82
Greek (0)	41	0.23
Hungarian (13)	46	0.26
Irish (348)	1,616	9.13
Italian (181)	582	3.29
Lithuanian (0)	53	0.30
Norwegian (85)	242	1.37
Polish (106)	367	2.07
Romanian (0)	33	0.19
Russian (0)	10	0.06
Scandinavian (14)	23	0.13
Scotch-Irish (161)	506	2.86
Scottish (121)	425	2.40
Slavic (7)	17	0.10
Slovak (0)	15	0.08
Swedish (8)	207	1.17
Swiss (0)	58	0.33
Turkish (21)	27	0.15
Welsh (13)	95	0.54
West Indian, ex. Hispanic (10)	56	0.32
Dutch West Indian (0)	46	0.26
West Indian (10)	10	0.06
Yugoslavian (0)	20	0.11

Hispanic Origin	Population	%
Hispanic or Latino (of any race)	5,980	32.27
Central American, ex. Mexican	151	0.81
Costa Rican	1	0.01
Guatemalan	32	0.17
Honduran	24	0.13
Nicaraguan	11	0.06
Panamanian	58	0.31
Salvadoran	25	0.13
Cuban	43	0.23
Dominican Republic	31	0.17
Mexican	4,610	24.88
Puerto Rican	333	1.80
South American	106	0.57
Argentinean	7	0.04
Bolivian	2	0.01
Chilean	3	0.02
Colombian	60	0.32
Ecuadorian	10	0.05
Peruvian	7	0.04
Uruguayan	1	0.01
Venezuelan	16	0.09
Other Hispanic or Latino	706	3.81

Race*	Population	%
African-American/Black (1,879)	2,158	11.65
Not Hispanic (1,731)	1,934	10.44
Hispanic (148)	224	1.21
American Indian/Alaska Native (135)	284	1.53
Not Hispanic (76)	167	0.90
Hispanic (59)	117	0.63
Alaska Athabascan *(Ala. Nat.)* (0)	1	0.01
Aleut *(Alaska Native)* (1)	2	0.01
Apache (11)	16	0.09
Blackfeet (2)	6	0.03
Cherokee (26)	80	0.43
Chickasaw (3)	4	0.02
Chippewa (4)	5	0.03
Choctaw (5)	12	0.06
Comanche (1)	2	0.01
Creek (5)	6	0.03
Delaware (3)	3	0.02
Hopi (1)	1	0.01
Iroquois (0)	2	0.01
Mexican American Ind. (4)	8	0.04
Navajo (1)	5	0.03
Pima (0)	1	0.01
Pueblo (6)	10	0.05
Seminole (2)	2	0.01
Sioux (8)	11	0.06
South American Ind. (1)	2	0.01
Spanish American Ind. (2)	2	0.01
Yaqui (1)	5	0.03
Asian (538)	758	4.09
Not Hispanic (505)	682	3.68
Hispanic (33)	76	0.41
Bangladeshi (1)	1	0.01
Burmese (4)	4	0.02
Cambodian (1)	1	0.01
Chinese, ex. Taiwanese (41)	65	0.35
Filipino (188)	284	1.53
Indian (27)	41	0.22
Indonesian (4)	7	0.04
Japanese (45)	89	0.48
Korean (68)	99	0.53
Laotian (4)	4	0.02
Pakistani (3)	4	0.02
Sri Lankan (1)	1	0.01
Taiwanese (0)	1	0.01
Thai (33)	48	0.26
Vietnamese (97)	107	0.58
Hawaii Native/Pacific Islander (53)	97	0.52
Not Hispanic (45)	76	0.41
Hispanic (8)	21	0.11
Guamanian/Chamorro (33)	43	0.23
Native Hawaiian (9)	32	0.17
Samoan (2)	7	0.04
White (13,970)	14,643	79.02
Not Hispanic (9,746)	10,104	54.53
Hispanic (4,224)	4,539	24.50

University Park

Place Type: City
County: Dallas
Population: 23,068†

Ancestry‡	Population	%
American (1,708)	1,708	7.44
Arab (103)	215	0.94
Arab (39)	58	0.25
Egyptian (11)	35	0.15
Lebanese (53)	81	0.35
Palestinian (0)	24	0.10
Other Arab (0)	17	0.07
Armenian (17)	17	0.07
Austrian (35)	117	0.51
Belgian (0)	15	0.07
British (202)	466	2.03
Cajun (5)	5	0.02
Canadian (19)	19	0.08
Czech (39)	182	0.79
Czechoslovakian (19)	19	0.08
Danish (0)	125	0.54
Dutch (41)	183	0.80
Eastern European (43)	43	0.19
English (2,030)	5,057	22.01
European (713)	827	3.60
French, ex. Basque (177)	1,422	6.19
German (1,408)	4,858	21.15
Greek (89)	110	0.48
Hungarian (63)	81	0.35
Iranian (0)	9	0.04
Irish (790)	3,128	13.62
Israeli (13)	13	0.06
Italian (295)	772	3.36
Latvian (0)	74	0.32
Lithuanian (0)	11	0.05
Maltese (13)	13	0.06
Northern European (37)	37	0.16
Norwegian (98)	370	1.61
Polish (109)	252	1.10
Romanian (0)	11	0.05
Russian (149)	257	1.12
Scandinavian (12)	167	0.73
Scotch-Irish (252)	720	3.13
Scottish (469)	1,611	7.01
Slovak (0)	16	0.07
Swedish (199)	525	2.29
Swiss (30)	268	1.17
Turkish (45)	45	0.20
Ukrainian (65)	102	0.44
Welsh (52)	158	0.69
West Indian, ex. Hispanic (16)	16	0.07
West Indian (16)	16	0.07
Yugoslavian (0)	13	0.06

Hispanic Origin	Population	%
Hispanic or Latino (of any race)	930	4.03
Central American, ex. Mexican	40	0.17
Costa Rican	1	<0.01
Guatemalan	4	0.02
Honduran	12	0.05
Nicaraguan	11	0.05
Panamanian	4	0.02
Salvadoran	8	0.03
Cuban	49	0.21
Mexican	600	2.60
Puerto Rican	28	0.12
South American	59	0.26
Argentinean	8	0.03
Bolivian	5	0.02
Chilean	3	0.01
Colombian	21	0.09
Ecuadorian	5	0.02
Peruvian	2	0.01
Uruguayan	3	0.01
Venezuelan	12	0.05
Other Hispanic or Latino	154	0.67

Race*	Population	%
African-American/Black (215)	273	1.18
Not Hispanic (210)	254	1.10
Hispanic (5)	19	0.08
American Indian/Alaska Native (54)	137	0.59
Not Hispanic (42)	110	0.48
Hispanic (12)	27	0.12
Apache (5)	5	0.02
Blackfeet (0)	5	0.02
Central American Ind. (1)	1	<0.01
Cherokee (12)	32	0.14
Cheyenne (1)	1	<0.01
Chickasaw (0)	9	0.04
Chippewa (1)	1	<0.01
Choctaw (13)	31	0.13
Comanche (1)	3	0.01
Creek (0)	4	0.02
Delaware (3)	6	0.03
Mexican American Ind. (1)	1	<0.01

*Notes: † The Census 2010 population figure is used to calculate the percentages in the Hispanic Origin and Race categories. Ancestry percentages are based on the 2006-2010 American Community Survey population (not shown); ‡ Numbers in parentheses indicate the number of people reporting a single ancestry; * Numbers in parentheses indicate the number of persons reporting this race alone, not in combination with any other race; Please refer to the Explanation of Data for more information.*

Navajo (0)	1	<0.01
Seminole (1)	1	<0.01
Spanish American Ind. (1)	1	<0.01
Asian (614)	777	3.37
Not Hispanic (611)	766	3.32
Hispanic (3)	11	0.05
Bangladeshi (2)	2	0.01
Cambodian (1)	1	<0.01
Chinese, ex. Taiwanese (226)	273	1.18
Filipino (11)	27	0.12
Indian (164)	196	0.85
Indonesian (2)	2	0.01
Japanese (16)	41	0.18
Korean (70)	94	0.41
Laotian (0)	1	<0.01
Nepalese (3)	3	0.01
Pakistani (13)	20	0.09
Sri Lankan (0)	5	0.02
Taiwanese (17)	20	0.09
Thai (2)	3	0.01
Vietnamese (58)	71	0.31
Hawaii Native/Pacific Islander (2)	12	0.05
Not Hispanic (1)	11	0.05
Hispanic (1)	1	<0.01
Guamanian/Chamorro (1)	2	0.01
Native Hawaiian (0)	5	0.02
Samoan (0)	1	<0.01
White (21,720)	22,025	95.48
Not Hispanic (20,991)	21,240	92.08
Hispanic (729)	785	3.40

Uvalde

Place Type: City
County: Uvalde
Population: 15,751†

Ancestry‡	Population	%
African, Sub-Saharan (15)	15	0.09
Other Sub-Saharan African (15)	15	0.09
American (514)	514	3.25
Armenian (0)	53	0.34
British (69)	69	0.44
Canadian (11)	11	0.07
Celtic (11)	11	0.07
Czech (0)	93	0.59
Czechoslovakian (11)	11	0.07
Danish (0)	4	0.03
Dutch (14)	90	0.57
English (257)	767	4.85
European (23)	23	0.15
French, ex. Basque (0)	132	0.83
German (225)	905	5.72
Greek (11)	11	0.07
Irish (197)	452	2.86
Italian (77)	235	1.49
Polish (0)	46	0.29
Scandinavian (19)	37	0.23
Scotch-Irish (123)	244	1.54
Scottish (74)	177	1.12
Swedish (0)	60	0.38
Welsh (0)	53	0.34
West Indian, ex. Hispanic (0)	30	0.19
Haitian (0)	30	0.19

Hispanic Origin	Population	%
Hispanic or Latino (of any race)	12,346	78.38
Central American, ex. Mexican	16	0.10
Guatemalan	3	0.02
Honduran	2	0.01
Panamanian	6	0.04
Salvadoran	5	0.03
Cuban	7	0.04
Dominican Republic	1	0.01
Mexican	10,532	66.87
Puerto Rican	52	0.33
South American	14	0.09
Chilean	4	0.03
Colombian	4	0.03
Ecuadorian	2	0.01
Venezuelan	4	0.03
Other Hispanic or Latino	1,724	10.95

Race*	Population	%
African-American/Black (129)	164	1.04
Not Hispanic (74)	92	0.58
Hispanic (55)	72	0.46
American Indian/Alaska Native (75)	125	0.79
Not Hispanic (35)	50	0.32
Hispanic (40)	75	0.48
Apache (3)	7	0.04
Blackfeet (1)	1	0.01
Cherokee (3)	8	0.05
Chickasaw (1)	2	0.01
Choctaw (9)	10	0.06
Comanche (0)	2	0.01
Mexican American Ind. (4)	5	0.03
Navajo (5)	5	0.03
Potawatomi (2)	2	0.01
Seminole (6)	6	0.04
Spanish American Ind. (1)	4	0.03
Ute (1)	1	0.01
Asian (104)	128	0.81
Not Hispanic (96)	111	0.70
Hispanic (8)	17	0.11
Chinese, ex. Taiwanese (13)	13	0.08
Filipino (58)	65	0.41
Indian (11)	14	0.09
Japanese (2)	6	0.04
Korean (3)	5	0.03
Vietnamese (12)	17	0.11
Hawaii Native/Pacific Islander (1)	14	0.09
Not Hispanic (1)	1	0.01
Hispanic (0)	13	0.08
White (12,280)	12,657	80.36
Not Hispanic (3,125)	3,179	20.18
Hispanic (9,155)	9,478	60.17

Vernon

Place Type: City
County: Wilbarger
Population: 11,002†

Ancestry‡	Population	%
American (2,045)	2,045	18.53
Arab (12)	71	0.64
Arab (0)	44	0.40
Lebanese (12)	27	0.24
Austrian (12)	55	0.50
British (3)	3	0.03
Canadian (18)	18	0.16
Czech (45)	67	0.61
Dutch (0)	6	0.05
English (349)	574	5.20
European (61)	61	0.55
French, ex. Basque (12)	84	0.76
German (598)	1,170	10.60
Greek (21)	21	0.19
Irish (392)	903	8.18
Italian (87)	170	1.54
Polish (10)	120	1.09
Russian (0)	14	0.13
Scotch-Irish (94)	252	2.28
Scottish (72)	112	1.01
Swedish (7)	21	0.19
Swiss (0)	37	0.34
West Indian, ex. Hispanic (0)	21	0.19
Dutch West Indian (0)	21	0.19

Hispanic Origin	Population	%
Hispanic or Latino (of any race)	3,128	28.43
Central American, ex. Mexican	52	0.47
Guatemalan	3	0.03
Honduran	6	0.05
Nicaraguan	1	0.01
Salvadoran	41	0.37
Other Central American	1	0.01
Cuban	4	0.04
Dominican Republic	1	0.01
Mexican	2,791	25.37
Puerto Rican	22	0.20
South American	1	0.01
Argentinean	1	0.01
Other Hispanic or Latino	257	2.34

Race*	Population	%
African-American/Black (1,034)	1,115	10.13
Not Hispanic (999)	1,067	9.70
Hispanic (35)	48	0.44
American Indian/Alaska Native (119)	189	1.72
Not Hispanic (96)	152	1.38
Hispanic (23)	37	0.34
Aleut *(Alaska Native)* (0)	1	0.01
Apache (3)	10	0.09
Arapaho (0)	1	0.01
Cherokee (7)	25	0.23
Chickasaw (1)	1	0.01
Choctaw (51)	68	0.62
Comanche (3)	3	0.03
Cree (0)	2	0.02
Creek (11)	13	0.12
Iroquois (0)	1	0.01
Mexican American Ind. (3)	6	0.05
Pueblo (1)	1	0.01
Seminole (1)	2	0.02
Sioux (2)	2	0.02
Ute (1)	3	0.03
Asian (92)	127	1.15
Not Hispanic (91)	114	1.04
Hispanic (1)	13	0.12
Cambodian (10)	10	0.09
Chinese, ex. Taiwanese (14)	15	0.14
Filipino (29)	38	0.35
Indian (11)	14	0.13
Japanese (4)	11	0.10
Korean (5)	8	0.07
Taiwanese (1)	1	0.01
Thai (0)	3	0.03
Vietnamese (17)	20	0.18
Hawaii Native/Pacific Islander (6)	19	0.17
Not Hispanic (6)	13	0.12
Hispanic (0)	6	0.05
Guamanian/Chamorro (1)	2	0.02
Native Hawaiian (5)	9	0.08
Samoan (0)	2	0.02
White (8,328)	8,585	78.03
Not Hispanic (6,534)	6,668	60.61
Hispanic (1,794)	1,917	17.42

Victoria

Place Type: City
County: Victoria
Population: 62,592†

Ancestry‡	Population	%
African, Sub-Saharan (127)	127	0.21
African (94)	94	0.15
Nigerian (33)	33	0.05
American (1,773)	1,773	2.86
Arab (147)	321	0.52
Arab (0)	80	0.13
Egyptian (8)	8	0.01
Lebanese (30)	70	0.11
Palestinian (99)	99	0.16
Syrian (10)	64	0.10
Armenian (0)	89	0.14
Australian (0)	9	0.01
Austrian (25)	59	0.10
Brazilian (0)	65	0.11
British (77)	106	0.17
Cajun (0)	42	0.07
Canadian (38)	71	0.11
Celtic (0)	14	0.02
Czech (1,155)	3,189	5.15
Czechoslovakian (58)	151	0.24
Danish (3)	52	0.08
Dutch (107)	488	0.79
Eastern European (10)	10	0.02

*Notes: † The Census 2010 population figure is used to calculate the percentages in the Hispanic Origin and Race categories. Ancestry percentages are based on the 2006-2010 American Community Survey population (not shown); ‡ Numbers in parentheses indicate the number of people reporting a single ancestry; * Numbers in parentheses indicate the number of persons reporting this race alone, not in combination with any other race; Please refer to the Explanation of Data for more information.*

Ancestry (continued)	Population	%
English (1,084)	3,782	6.11
European (153)	208	0.34
French, ex. Basque (161)	1,788	2.89
French Canadian (31)	226	0.37
German (3,931)	11,816	19.09
Greek (10)	93	0.15
Hungarian (12)	12	0.02
Iranian (119)	119	0.19
Irish (1,220)	5,885	9.51
Italian (412)	1,340	2.16
Lithuanian (0)	83	0.13
Northern European (22)	22	0.04
Norwegian (89)	211	0.34
Pennsylvania German (18)	49	0.08
Polish (124)	734	1.19
Portuguese (32)	236	0.38
Russian (8)	151	0.24
Scandinavian (39)	62	0.10
Scotch-Irish (351)	830	1.34
Scottish (149)	782	1.26
Slavic (71)	87	0.14
Swedish (90)	399	0.64
Swiss (0)	70	0.11
Turkish (0)	29	0.05
Welsh (19)	427	0.69
West Indian, ex. Hispanic (111)	162	0.26
Dutch West Indian (31)	82	0.13
Jamaican (80)	80	0.13
Yugoslavian (10)	44	0.07

Hispanic Origin	Population	%
Hispanic or Latino (of any race)	30,220	48.28
Central American, ex. Mexican	135	0.22
Costa Rican	10	0.02
Guatemalan	25	0.04
Honduran	33	0.05
Nicaraguan	17	0.03
Panamanian	9	0.01
Salvadoran	40	0.06
Other Central American	1	<0.01
Cuban	44	0.07
Dominican Republic	6	0.01
Mexican	25,500	40.74
Puerto Rican	215	0.34
South American	65	0.10
Argentinean	5	0.01
Bolivian	1	<0.01
Chilean	3	<0.01
Colombian	32	0.05
Ecuadorian	8	0.01
Peruvian	6	0.01
Uruguayan	1	<0.01
Venezuelan	8	0.01
Other South American	1	<0.01
Other Hispanic or Latino	4,255	6.80

Race*	Population	%
African-American/Black (4,849)	5,358	8.56
Not Hispanic (4,568)	4,880	7.80
Hispanic (281)	478	0.76
American Indian/Alaska Native (403)	671	1.07
Not Hispanic (136)	291	0.46
Hispanic (267)	380	0.61
Apache (8)	24	0.04
Blackfeet (0)	4	0.01
Central American Ind. (0)	1	<0.01
Cherokee (34)	110	0.18
Cheyenne (1)	1	<0.01
Chickasaw (10)	18	0.03
Chippewa (1)	1	<0.01
Choctaw (17)	39	0.06
Comanche (6)	19	0.03
Creek (0)	10	0.02
Iroquois (0)	1	<0.01
Mexican American Ind. (53)	64	0.10
Navajo (14)	22	0.04
Osage (5)	8	0.01
Paiute (0)	1	<0.01
Potawatomi (2)	2	<0.01
Seminole (0)	1	<0.01
Sioux (5)	6	0.01
South American Ind. (1)	1	<0.01
Tlingit-Haida *(Alaska Native)* (0)	3	<0.01
Asian (854)	1,058	1.69
Not Hispanic (821)	944	1.51
Hispanic (33)	114	0.18
Burmese (1)	1	<0.01
Cambodian (23)	24	0.04
Chinese, ex. Taiwanese (157)	177	0.28
Filipino (129)	199	0.32
Indian (175)	209	0.33
Indonesian (11)	14	0.02
Japanese (14)	40	0.06
Korean (30)	45	0.07
Laotian (7)	7	0.01
Malaysian (2)	3	<0.01
Nepalese (1)	1	<0.01
Pakistani (37)	42	0.07
Taiwanese (77)	86	0.14
Thai (6)	11	0.02
Vietnamese (164)	181	0.29
Hawaii Native/Pacific Islander (13)	81	0.13
Not Hispanic (7)	27	0.04
Hispanic (6)	54	0.09
Guamanian/Chamorro (4)	4	0.01
Marshallese (0)	4	0.01
Native Hawaiian (6)	25	0.04
Samoan (1)	3	<0.01
White (47,697)	49,120	78.48
Not Hispanic (26,178)	26,700	42.66
Hispanic (21,519)	22,420	35.82

Vidor

Place Type: City
County: Orange
Population: 10,579†

Ancestry‡	Population	%
American (936)	936	8.79
Austrian (0)	10	0.09
British (12)	28	0.26
Cajun (135)	212	1.99
Canadian (29)	41	0.38
Czech (15)	49	0.46
Danish (0)	23	0.22
Dutch (11)	102	0.96
English (630)	1,067	10.02
European (14)	14	0.13
French, ex. Basque (308)	925	8.68
French Canadian (606)	768	7.21
German (432)	1,280	12.02
Hungarian (0)	53	0.50
Irish (489)	1,281	12.03
Italian (161)	388	3.64
Norwegian (41)	97	0.91
Polish (21)	122	1.15
Scotch-Irish (145)	263	2.47
Scottish (94)	108	1.01
Slavic (0)	14	0.13
Slovak (0)	9	0.08
Swedish (10)	51	0.48
Ukrainian (0)	4	0.04
Welsh (0)	11	0.10

Hispanic Origin	Population	%
Hispanic or Latino (of any race)	540	5.10
Central American, ex. Mexican	11	0.10
Costa Rican	3	0.03
Guatemalan	4	0.04
Honduran	1	0.01
Nicaraguan	1	0.01
Salvadoran	2	0.02
Cuban	2	0.02
Mexican	446	4.22
Puerto Rican	7	0.07
South American	9	0.09
Argentinean	1	0.01
Colombian	4	0.04
Ecuadorian	1	0.01
Venezuelan	3	0.03
Other Hispanic or Latino	65	0.61

Race*	Population	%
African-American/Black (13)	28	0.26
Not Hispanic (13)	27	0.26
Hispanic (0)	1	0.01
American Indian/Alaska Native (56)	135	1.28
Not Hispanic (43)	114	1.08
Hispanic (13)	21	0.20
Apache (0)	1	0.01
Blackfeet (1)	6	0.06
Canadian/French Am. Ind. (0)	1	0.01
Cherokee (15)	42	0.40
Chippewa (0)	1	0.01
Choctaw (9)	20	0.19
Creek (2)	3	0.03
Crow (0)	2	0.02
Delaware (1)	1	0.01
Lumbee (0)	1	0.01
Mexican American Ind. (1)	3	0.03
Navajo (1)	5	0.05
Sioux (1)	1	0.01
South American Ind. (1)	1	0.01
Spanish American Ind. (1)	1	0.01
Tlingit-Haida *(Alaska Native)* (0)	2	0.02
Yaqui (0)	2	0.02
Asian (52)	72	0.68
Not Hispanic (51)	68	0.64
Hispanic (1)	4	0.04
Cambodian (13)	14	0.13
Chinese, ex. Taiwanese (6)	6	0.06
Filipino (13)	19	0.18
Indian (11)	12	0.11
Japanese (1)	5	0.05
Korean (2)	7	0.07
Pakistani (2)	2	0.02
Thai (2)	2	0.02
Vietnamese (2)	2	0.02
Hawaii Native/Pacific Islander (19)	24	0.23
Not Hispanic (19)	24	0.23
Guamanian/Chamorro (17)	17	0.16
Native Hawaiian (0)	2	0.02
Samoan (1)	3	0.03
White (10,128)	10,281	97.18
Not Hispanic (9,796)	9,902	93.60
Hispanic (332)	379	3.58

Waco

Place Type: City
County: McLennan
Population: 124,805†

Ancestry‡	Population	%
African, Sub-Saharan (593)	694	0.57
African (265)	333	0.27
Cape Verdean (13)	46	0.04
Ethiopian (81)	81	0.07
Kenyan (30)	30	0.02
Nigerian (174)	174	0.14
Zimbabwean (30)	30	0.02
Albanian (17)	17	0.01
American (6,915)	6,915	5.66
Arab (116)	345	0.28
Egyptian (24)	24	0.02
Jordanian (0)	126	0.10
Lebanese (30)	72	0.06
Palestinian (16)	16	0.01
Syrian (19)	51	0.04
Other Arab (27)	56	0.05
Armenian (20)	20	0.02
Australian (95)	95	0.08
Austrian (14)	78	0.06
Belgian (13)	13	0.01
Brazilian (28)	28	0.02
British (345)	475	0.39
Cajun (38)	98	0.08
Canadian (21)	36	0.03
Croatian (59)	74	0.06

*Notes: † The Census 2010 population figure is used to calculate the percentages in the Hispanic Origin and Race categories. Ancestry percentages are based on the 2006-2010 American Community Survey population (not shown); ‡ Numbers in parentheses indicate the number of people reporting a single ancestry; * Numbers in parentheses indicate the number of persons reporting this race alone, not in combination with any other race; Please refer to the Explanation of Data for more information.*

Czech (610)	1,243	1.02
Czechoslovakian (132)	220	0.18
Danish (108)	318	0.26
Dutch (340)	1,246	1.02
Eastern European (28)	28	0.02
English (3,351)	8,520	6.97
European (515)	599	0.49
Finnish (0)	77	0.06
French, ex. Basque (461)	2,212	1.81
French Canadian (82)	144	0.12
German (5,312)	14,867	12.16
Greek (90)	277	0.23
Hungarian (15)	132	0.11
Iranian (49)	49	0.04
Irish (3,084)	10,444	8.55
Italian (746)	1,819	1.49
Lithuanian (16)	59	0.05
Luxemburger (7)	7	0.01
Northern European (25)	57	0.05
Norwegian (313)	728	0.60
Polish (410)	1,337	1.09
Portuguese (12)	35	0.03
Russian (35)	268	0.22
Scandinavian (3)	9	0.01
Scotch-Irish (879)	2,220	1.82
Scottish (857)	1,991	1.63
Serbian (55)	55	0.05
Slavic (0)	9	0.01
Slovak (10)	38	0.03
Slovene (0)	38	0.03
Swedish (214)	782	0.64
Swiss (40)	217	0.18
Ukrainian (10)	40	0.03
Welsh (193)	538	0.44
West Indian, ex. Hispanic (56)	85	0.07
Bermudan (0)	29	0.02
British West Indian (14)	14	0.01
Dutch West Indian (5)	5	<0.01
Haitian (19)	19	0.02
West Indian (18)	18	0.01
Yugoslavian (0)	54	0.04

Hispanic Origin	Population	%
Hispanic or Latino (of any race)	36,947	29.60
Central American, ex. Mexican	487	0.39
Costa Rican	14	0.01
Guatemalan	80	0.06
Honduran	100	0.08
Nicaraguan	39	0.03
Panamanian	27	0.02
Salvadoran	225	0.18
Other Central American	2	<0.01
Cuban	114	0.09
Dominican Republic	22	0.02
Mexican	33,080	26.51
Puerto Rican	599	0.48
South American	236	0.19
Argentinean	21	0.02
Bolivian	13	0.01
Chilean	15	0.01
Colombian	95	0.08
Ecuadorian	26	0.02
Paraguayan	1	<0.01
Peruvian	22	0.02
Uruguayan	8	0.01
Venezuelan	34	0.03
Other South American	1	<0.01
Other Hispanic or Latino	2,409	1.93

Race*	Population	%
African-American/Black (26,856)	28,307	22.68
Not Hispanic (26,184)	27,229	21.82
Hispanic (672)	1,078	0.86
American Indian/Alaska Native (794)	1,398	1.12
Not Hispanic (310)	727	0.58
Hispanic (484)	671	0.54
Alaska Athabascan *(Ala. Nat.)* (2)	2	<0.01
Aleut *(Alaska Native)* (3)	3	<0.01
Apache (28)	47	0.04
Blackfeet (3)	19	0.02
Canadian/French Am. Ind. (2)	4	<0.01
Central American Ind. (2)	4	<0.01
Cherokee (74)	220	0.18
Cheyenne (1)	3	<0.01
Chickasaw (15)	24	0.02
Chippewa (3)	11	0.01
Choctaw (31)	70	0.06
Comanche (8)	15	0.01
Cree (0)	1	<0.01
Creek (4)	17	0.01
Delaware (1)	1	<0.01
Houma (1)	1	<0.01
Iroquois (0)	1	<0.01
Kiowa (1)	3	<0.01
Mexican American Ind. (77)	99	0.08
Navajo (23)	25	0.02
Osage (0)	3	<0.01
Paiute (1)	1	<0.01
Potawatomi (10)	12	0.01
Pueblo (7)	9	0.01
Puget Sound Salish (5)	6	<0.01
Seminole (6)	11	0.01
Shoshone (0)	1	<0.01
Sioux (8)	14	0.01
South American Ind. (3)	6	<0.01
Spanish American Ind. (3)	5	<0.01
Tlingit-Haida *(Alaska Native)* (1)	1	<0.01
Tsimshian *(Alaska Native)* (1)	1	<0.01
Yaqui (1)	3	<0.01
Yuman (0)	1	<0.01
Asian (2,206)	2,787	2.23
Not Hispanic (2,148)	2,626	2.10
Hispanic (58)	161	0.13
Bangladeshi (8)	12	0.01
Burmese (14)	14	0.01
Cambodian (25)	29	0.02
Chinese, ex. Taiwanese (414)	505	0.40
Filipino (210)	352	0.28
Hmong (1)	1	<0.01
Indian (496)	571	0.46
Indonesian (7)	8	0.01
Japanese (42)	135	0.11
Korean (337)	421	0.34
Laotian (9)	12	0.01
Malaysian (3)	3	<0.01
Nepalese (17)	20	0.02
Pakistani (123)	147	0.12
Sri Lankan (7)	8	0.01
Taiwanese (37)	40	0.03
Thai (22)	41	0.03
Vietnamese (305)	365	0.29
Hawaii Native/Pacific Islander (68)	171	0.14
Not Hispanic (49)	113	0.09
Hispanic (19)	58	0.05
Guamanian/Chamorro (18)	31	0.02
Marshallese (3)	3	<0.01
Native Hawaiian (23)	55	0.04
Samoan (6)	29	0.02
Tongan (1)	1	<0.01
White (73,916)	76,812	61.55
Not Hispanic (57,217)	58,753	47.08
Hispanic (16,699)	18,059	14.47

Watauga

Place Type: City
County: Tarrant
Population: 23,497†

Ancestry‡	Population	%
African, Sub-Saharan (149)	149	0.64
African (149)	149	0.64
Alsatian (9)	9	0.04
American (2,944)	2,944	12.69
Arab (162)	189	0.81
Egyptian (51)	51	0.22
Iraqi (98)	98	0.42
Lebanese (13)	40	0.17
Austrian (9)	97	0.42
British (52)	77	0.33
Bulgarian (0)	13	0.06
Cajun (13)	13	0.06
Czech (76)	181	0.78
Czechoslovakian (0)	27	0.12
Danish (117)	216	0.93
Dutch (164)	576	2.48
English (961)	2,060	8.88
European (26)	40	0.17
French, ex. Basque (131)	559	2.41
French Canadian (17)	131	0.56
German (1,135)	3,331	14.36
Greek (23)	23	0.10
Hungarian (33)	33	0.14
Irish (771)	2,479	10.69
Israeli (0)	12	0.05
Italian (254)	559	2.41
Lithuanian (16)	16	0.07
Northern European (10)	10	0.04
Norwegian (0)	19	0.08
Polish (90)	269	1.16
Portuguese (10)	60	0.26
Romanian (0)	12	0.05
Russian (33)	48	0.21
Scandinavian (0)	23	0.10
Scotch-Irish (274)	414	1.78
Scottish (196)	636	2.74
Slovak (0)	21	0.09
Swedish (22)	86	0.37
Swiss (8)	21	0.09
Welsh (61)	136	0.59
West Indian, ex. Hispanic (21)	50	0.22
Belizean (21)	21	0.09
Dutch West Indian (0)	29	0.13

Hispanic Origin	Population	%
Hispanic or Latino (of any race)	4,717	20.07
Central American, ex. Mexican	243	1.03
Costa Rican	6	0.03
Guatemalan	42	0.18
Honduran	39	0.17
Nicaraguan	6	0.03
Panamanian	17	0.07
Salvadoran	133	0.57
Cuban	39	0.17
Dominican Republic	21	0.09
Mexican	3,710	15.79
Puerto Rican	309	1.32
South American	109	0.46
Argentinean	16	0.07
Bolivian	1	<0.01
Chilean	12	0.05
Colombian	45	0.19
Ecuadorian	3	0.01
Peruvian	11	0.05
Uruguayan	6	0.03
Venezuelan	13	0.06
Other South American	2	0.01
Other Hispanic or Latino	286	1.22

Race*	Population	%
African-American/Black (1,387)	1,609	6.85
Not Hispanic (1,309)	1,487	6.33
Hispanic (78)	122	0.52
American Indian/Alaska Native (205)	365	1.55
Not Hispanic (144)	283	1.20
Hispanic (61)	82	0.35
Apache (5)	11	0.05
Blackfeet (1)	7	0.03
Cherokee (48)	102	0.43
Cheyenne (0)	1	<0.01
Chickasaw (2)	13	0.06
Chippewa (0)	1	<0.01
Choctaw (23)	33	0.14
Colville (1)	1	<0.01
Comanche (3)	10	0.04
Creek (11)	12	0.05
Delaware (0)	1	<0.01
Lumbee (1)	1	<0.01
Mexican American Ind. (12)	12	0.05
Navajo (2)	9	0.04

*Notes: † The Census 2010 population figure is used to calculate the percentages in the Hispanic Origin and Race categories. Ancestry percentages are based on the 2006-2010 American Community Survey population (not shown); ‡ Numbers in parentheses indicate the number of people reporting a single ancestry; * Numbers in parentheses indicate the number of persons reporting this race alone, not in combination with any other race; Please refer to the Explanation of Data for more information.*

Osage (3)	3	0.01
Ottawa (2)	2	0.01
Potawatomi (7)	9	0.04
Pueblo (4)	6	0.03
Seminole (1)	1	<0.01
Sioux (2)	3	0.01
Spanish American Ind. (2)	2	0.01
Asian (1,195)	1,381	5.88
Not Hispanic (1,169)	1,321	5.62
Hispanic (26)	60	0.26
Bangladeshi (1)	1	<0.01
Burmese (2)	2	0.01
Cambodian (5)	9	0.04
Chinese, ex. Taiwanese (34)	50	0.21
Filipino (80)	137	0.58
Hmong (16)	16	0.07
Indian (102)	123	0.52
Indonesian (2)	3	0.01
Japanese (7)	25	0.11
Korean (54)	63	0.27
Laotian (203)	220	0.94
Malaysian (1)	1	<0.01
Nepalese (11)	11	0.05
Pakistani (49)	59	0.25
Sri Lankan (14)	15	0.06
Taiwanese (2)	4	0.02
Thai (33)	52	0.22
Vietnamese (534)	566	2.41
Hawaii Native/Pacific Islander (59)	113	0.48
Not Hispanic (59)	104	0.44
Hispanic (0)	9	0.04
Guamanian/Chamorro (3)	5	0.02
Native Hawaiian (7)	25	0.11
Samoan (0)	4	0.02
Tongan (42)	51	0.22
White (18,639)	19,240	81.88
Not Hispanic (15,609)	16,012	68.14
Hispanic (3,030)	3,228	13.74

Waxahachie

Place Type: City
County: Ellis
Population: 29,621†

Ancestry‡	Population	%
African, Sub-Saharan (209)	407	1.44
African (190)	388	1.37
Nigerian (10)	10	0.04
Zimbabwean (9)	9	0.03
American (1,765)	1,765	6.24
Arab (61)	88	0.31
Jordanian (61)	61	0.22
Lebanese (0)	27	0.10
Australian (0)	14	0.05
British (0)	29	0.10
Cajun (16)	34	0.12
Canadian (0)	20	0.07
Czech (40)	193	0.68
Czechoslovakian (16)	16	0.06
Danish (7)	7	0.02
Dutch (29)	355	1.26
English (1,250)	2,726	9.64
European (193)	236	0.83
French, ex. Basque (312)	843	2.98
French Canadian (64)	101	0.36
German (1,273)	3,824	13.52
Greek (0)	22	0.08
Iranian (0)	17	0.06
Irish (1,187)	3,303	11.68
Italian (282)	590	2.09
Northern European (0)	49	0.17
Norwegian (41)	75	0.27
Polish (94)	264	0.93
Portuguese (13)	43	0.15
Russian (22)	45	0.16
Scotch-Irish (531)	755	2.67
Scottish (297)	633	2.24
Serbian (0)	32	0.11
Slovak (0)	24	0.08
Swedish (48)	282	1.00
Welsh (51)	285	1.01
West Indian, ex. Hispanic (0)	55	0.19
Barbadian (0)	40	0.14
Dutch West Indian (0)	4	0.01
West Indian (0)	11	0.04

Hispanic Origin	Population	%
Hispanic or Latino (of any race)	6,870	23.19
Central American, ex. Mexican	121	0.41
Costa Rican	1	<0.01
Guatemalan	27	0.09
Honduran	31	0.10
Nicaraguan	9	0.03
Panamanian	7	0.02
Salvadoran	46	0.16
Cuban	19	0.06
Dominican Republic	3	0.01
Mexican	5,998	20.25
Puerto Rican	100	0.34
South American	57	0.19
Argentinean	4	0.01
Colombian	25	0.08
Peruvian	19	0.06
Venezuelan	9	0.03
Other Hispanic or Latino	572	1.93

Race*	Population	%
African-American/Black (3,819)	4,007	13.53
Not Hispanic (3,717)	3,853	13.01
Hispanic (102)	154	0.52
American Indian/Alaska Native (175)	402	1.36
Not Hispanic (118)	293	0.99
Hispanic (57)	109	0.37
Apache (5)	12	0.04
Arapaho (0)	1	<0.01
Blackfeet (4)	6	0.02
Cherokee (26)	94	0.32
Cheyenne (1)	1	<0.01
Chickasaw (8)	13	0.04
Chippewa (0)	2	0.01
Choctaw (34)	54	0.18
Comanche (0)	6	0.02
Cree (0)	1	<0.01
Creek (1)	10	0.03
Crow (0)	4	0.01
Delaware (0)	5	0.02
Houma (0)	6	0.02
Iroquois (3)	6	0.02
Mexican American Ind. (11)	13	0.04
Navajo (5)	10	0.03
Osage (0)	1	<0.01
Paiute (0)	1	<0.01
Potawatomi (1)	2	0.01
Seminole (1)	1	<0.01
Sioux (1)	2	0.01
Yaqui (1)	1	<0.01
Asian (155)	226	0.76
Not Hispanic (137)	194	0.65
Hispanic (18)	32	0.11
Burmese (1)	1	<0.01
Cambodian (7)	7	0.02
Chinese, ex. Taiwanese (15)	20	0.07
Filipino (29)	69	0.23
Hmong (0)	1	<0.01
Indian (32)	36	0.12
Japanese (5)	9	0.03
Korean (20)	33	0.11
Laotian (2)	4	0.01
Nepalese (6)	7	0.02
Pakistani (5)	5	0.02
Thai (20)	22	0.07
Vietnamese (6)	7	0.02
Hawaii Native/Pacific Islander (25)	61	0.21
Not Hispanic (24)	51	0.17
Hispanic (1)	10	0.03
Guamanian/Chamorro (1)	4	0.01
Marshallese (1)	1	<0.01
Native Hawaiian (7)	22	0.07
Samoan (0)	6	0.02
White (22,381)	22,984	77.59
Not Hispanic (18,370)	18,689	63.09
Hispanic (4,011)	4,295	14.50

Weatherford

Place Type: City
County: Parker
Population: 25,250†

Ancestry‡	Population	%
African, Sub-Saharan (54)	71	0.29
African (54)	71	0.29
American (2,102)	2,102	8.68
Arab (167)	197	0.81
Arab (6)	21	0.09
Jordanian (6)	21	0.09
Lebanese (74)	74	0.31
Palestinian (68)	68	0.28
Syrian (13)	13	0.05
Armenian (7)	7	0.03
Austrian (0)	15	0.06
Belgian (10)	51	0.21
Brazilian (45)	45	0.19
British (12)	56	0.23
Cajun (12)	12	0.05
Canadian (0)	15	0.06
Celtic (62)	62	0.26
Czech (58)	166	0.69
Czechoslovakian (13)	58	0.24
Dutch (56)	548	2.26
English (1,361)	3,407	14.06
European (176)	224	0.92
Finnish (0)	11	0.05
French, ex. Basque (244)	856	3.53
French Canadian (56)	81	0.33
German (831)	3,751	15.48
Greek (6)	6	0.02
Hungarian (32)	90	0.37
Irish (1,094)	3,450	14.24
Italian (127)	477	1.97
Northern European (31)	31	0.13
Norwegian (39)	136	0.56
Pennsylvania German (11)	11	0.05
Polish (28)	323	1.33
Russian (0)	89	0.37
Scandinavian (0)	39	0.16
Scotch-Irish (253)	599	2.47
Scottish (382)	834	3.44
Slavic (0)	14	0.06
Slovene (0)	15	0.06
Swedish (89)	138	0.57
Swiss (10)	91	0.38
Ukrainian (0)	10	0.04
Welsh (14)	67	0.28
West Indian, ex. Hispanic (13)	25	0.10
Dutch West Indian (13)	25	0.10

Hispanic Origin	Population	%
Hispanic or Latino (of any race)	3,437	13.61
Central American, ex. Mexican	58	0.23
Costa Rican	4	0.02
Guatemalan	20	0.08
Honduran	6	0.02
Panamanian	7	0.03
Salvadoran	20	0.08
Other Central American	1	<0.01
Cuban	13	0.05
Mexican	3,046	12.06
Puerto Rican	40	0.16
South American	38	0.15
Argentinean	11	0.04
Bolivian	1	<0.01
Chilean	4	0.02
Colombian	11	0.04
Peruvian	3	0.01
Venezuelan	8	0.03
Other Hispanic or Latino	242	0.96

*Notes: † The Census 2010 population figure is used to calculate the percentages in the Hispanic Origin and Race categories. Ancestry percentages are based on the 2006-2010 American Community Survey population (not shown); ‡ Numbers in parentheses indicate the number of people reporting a single ancestry; * Numbers in parentheses indicate the number of persons reporting this race alone, not in combination with any other race; Please refer to the Explanation of Data for more information.*

Race*	Population	%
African-American/Black (605)	745	2.95
Not Hispanic (576)	705	2.79
Hispanic (29)	40	0.16
American Indian/Alaska Native (196)	418	1.66
Not Hispanic (150)	339	1.34
Hispanic (46)	79	0.31
Apache (7)	12	0.05
Arapaho (0)	1	<0.01
Blackfeet (1)	8	0.03
Canadian/French Am. Ind. (1)	1	<0.01
Cherokee (52)	118	0.47
Chickasaw (3)	8	0.03
Chippewa (7)	7	0.03
Choctaw (30)	53	0.21
Comanche (0)	2	0.01
Creek (2)	2	0.01
Delaware (4)	5	0.02
Hopi (0)	5	0.02
Iroquois (1)	6	0.02
Kiowa (0)	3	0.01
Mexican American Ind. (16)	23	0.09
Navajo (4)	11	0.04
Osage (2)	4	0.02
Pima (0)	1	<0.01
Potawatomi (5)	5	0.02
Seminole (0)	1	<0.01
Shoshone (1)	1	<0.01
Sioux (0)	13	0.05
Yaqui (1)	1	<0.01
Asian (225)	290	1.15
Not Hispanic (222)	274	1.09
Hispanic (3)	16	0.06
Cambodian (20)	28	0.11
Chinese, ex. Taiwanese (30)	36	0.14
Filipino (45)	59	0.23
Indian (38)	46	0.18
Indonesian (3)	3	0.01
Japanese (5)	17	0.07
Korean (16)	18	0.07
Laotian (0)	5	0.02
Nepalese (31)	31	0.12
Pakistani (4)	4	0.02
Thai (17)	23	0.09
Vietnamese (8)	10	0.04
Hawaii Native/Pacific Islander (14)	27	0.11
Not Hispanic (13)	24	0.10
Hispanic (1)	3	0.01
Native Hawaiian (2)	8	0.03
Samoan (1)	3	0.01
White (22,562)	23,063	91.34
Not Hispanic (20,494)	20,825	82.48
Hispanic (2,068)	2,238	8.86

Webster

Place Type: City
County: Harris
Population: 10,400†

Ancestry‡	Population	%
African, Sub-Saharan (45)	45	0.46
Kenyan (14)	14	0.14
Other Sub-Saharan African (31)	31	0.31
American (515)	515	5.22
Arab (98)	98	0.99
Egyptian (60)	60	0.61
Jordanian (32)	32	0.32
Lebanese (6)	6	0.06
British (45)	45	0.46
Cajun (0)	45	0.46
Canadian (3)	3	0.03
Czechoslovakian (0)	11	0.11
Danish (0)	33	0.33
Dutch (19)	52	0.53
English (168)	528	5.35
European (230)	230	2.33
Finnish (18)	18	0.18
French, ex. Basque (112)	231	2.34
French Canadian (48)	87	0.88
German (302)	886	8.98
Hungarian (6)	6	0.06
Iranian (262)	262	2.66
Irish (260)	1,076	10.91
Italian (71)	299	3.03
Norwegian (12)	105	1.06
Polish (150)	199	2.02
Portuguese (0)	41	0.42
Russian (4)	4	0.04
Scotch-Irish (0)	94	0.95
Scottish (59)	77	0.78
Slovene (0)	7	0.07
Swedish (0)	35	0.35
Turkish (38)	38	0.39
Welsh (0)	28	0.28
West Indian, ex. Hispanic (47)	47	0.48
Jamaican (34)	34	0.34
Trinidadian/Tobagonian (13)	13	0.13

Hispanic Origin	Population	%
Hispanic or Latino (of any race)	3,541	34.05
Central American, ex. Mexican	1,247	11.99
Costa Rican	4	0.04
Guatemalan	578	5.56
Honduran	146	1.40
Nicaraguan	8	0.08
Panamanian	9	0.09
Salvadoran	499	4.80
Other Central American	3	0.03
Cuban	46	0.44
Dominican Republic	5	0.05
Mexican	1,762	16.94
Puerto Rican	91	0.88
South American	66	0.63
Argentinean	5	0.05
Bolivian	5	0.05
Chilean	1	0.01
Colombian	20	0.19
Ecuadorian	2	0.02
Paraguayan	1	0.01
Peruvian	11	0.11
Uruguayan	1	0.01
Venezuelan	20	0.19
Other Hispanic or Latino	324	3.12

Race*	Population	%
African-American/Black (1,413)	1,553	14.93
Not Hispanic (1,366)	1,463	14.07
Hispanic (47)	90	0.87
American Indian/Alaska Native (74)	151	1.45
Not Hispanic (35)	81	0.78
Hispanic (39)	70	0.67
Apache (1)	1	0.01
Blackfeet (0)	5	0.05
Central American Ind. (0)	10	0.10
Cherokee (6)	18	0.17
Chickasaw (3)	3	0.03
Chippewa (0)	1	0.01
Choctaw (5)	9	0.09
Comanche (0)	1	0.01
Cree (0)	1	0.01
Delaware (0)	1	0.01
Iroquois (1)	1	0.01
Kiowa (0)	3	0.03
Mexican American Ind. (8)	12	0.12
Navajo (2)	2	0.02
Osage (1)	2	0.02
Ottawa (1)	2	0.02
Paiute (1)	1	0.01
Pueblo (3)	4	0.04
Shoshone (0)	2	0.02
Sioux (0)	1	0.01
South American Ind. (0)	1	0.01
Spanish American Ind. (2)	2	0.02
Asian (472)	545	5.24
Not Hispanic (466)	527	5.07
Hispanic (6)	18	0.17
Bangladeshi (8)	8	0.08
Burmese (6)	6	0.06
Cambodian (2)	2	0.02
Chinese, ex. Taiwanese (46)	59	0.57
Filipino (57)	71	0.68
Indian (150)	164	1.58
Indonesian (6)	9	0.09
Japanese (17)	23	0.22
Korean (18)	23	0.22
Malaysian (1)	1	0.01
Nepalese (10)	11	0.11
Pakistani (54)	61	0.59
Taiwanese (7)	7	0.07
Thai (9)	14	0.13
Vietnamese (57)	62	0.60
Hawaii Native/Pacific Islander (13)	32	0.31
Not Hispanic (6)	18	0.17
Hispanic (7)	14	0.13
Guamanian/Chamorro (7)	7	0.07
Native Hawaiian (3)	7	0.07
Samoan (1)	2	0.02
White (6,201)	6,526	62.75
Not Hispanic (4,762)	4,910	47.21
Hispanic (1,439)	1,616	15.54

Wells Branch

Place Type: CDP
County: Travis
Population: 12,120†

Ancestry‡	Population	%
African, Sub-Saharan (356)	378	3.27
African (31)	31	0.27
Cape Verdean (0)	22	0.19
Ethiopian (3)	3	0.03
Nigerian (86)	86	0.74
Senegalese (27)	27	0.23
Sudanese (100)	100	0.87
Other Sub-Saharan African (109)	109	0.94
American (483)	483	4.18
Arab (12)	12	0.10
Lebanese (12)	12	0.10
Brazilian (75)	75	0.65
British (50)	90	0.78
Croatian (0)	14	0.12
Czech (14)	87	0.75
Czechoslovakian (17)	25	0.22
Danish (0)	37	0.32
Dutch (0)	32	0.28
Eastern European (37)	37	0.32
English (262)	889	7.70
European (88)	100	0.87
Finnish (54)	63	0.55
French, ex. Basque (10)	203	1.76
French Canadian (75)	105	0.91
German (569)	1,530	13.25
Greek (44)	44	0.38
Hungarian (0)	21	0.18
Irish (269)	900	7.80
Italian (183)	282	2.44
Norwegian (13)	37	0.32
Polish (66)	228	1.97
Romanian (0)	8	0.07
Russian (19)	131	1.13
Scandinavian (9)	9	0.08
Scotch-Irish (78)	372	3.22
Scottish (167)	302	2.62
Swedish (46)	112	0.97
Welsh (16)	63	0.55
West Indian, ex. Hispanic (86)	145	1.26
Dutch West Indian (0)	27	0.23
Jamaican (86)	118	1.02

Hispanic Origin	Population	%
Hispanic or Latino (of any race)	3,475	28.67
Central American, ex. Mexican	150	1.24
Costa Rican	3	0.02
Guatemalan	41	0.34
Honduran	22	0.18
Nicaraguan	17	0.14
Panamanian	16	0.13

*Notes: † The Census 2010 population figure is used to calculate the percentages in the Hispanic Origin and Race categories. Ancestry percentages are based on the 2006-2010 American Community Survey population (not shown); ‡ Numbers in parentheses indicate the number of people reporting a single ancestry; * Numbers in parentheses indicate the number of persons reporting this race alone, not in combination with any other race; Please refer to the Explanation of Data for more information.*

Salvadoran	50	0.41
Other Central American	1	0.01
Cuban	65	0.54
Dominican Republic	3	0.02
Mexican	2,705	22.32
Puerto Rican	97	0.80
South American	100	0.83
Argentinean	10	0.08
Bolivian	3	0.02
Chilean	5	0.04
Colombian	29	0.24
Ecuadorian	6	0.05
Peruvian	21	0.17
Uruguayan	1	0.01
Venezuelan	23	0.19
Other South American	2	0.02
Other Hispanic or Latino	355	2.93

Race*	Population	%
African-American/Black (1,840)	2,041	16.84
Not Hispanic (1,776)	1,928	15.91
Hispanic (64)	113	0.93
American Indian/Alaska Native (101)	222	1.83
Not Hispanic (30)	107	0.88
Hispanic (71)	115	0.95
Apache (1)	2	0.02
Arapaho (1)	1	0.01
Blackfeet (1)	5	0.04
Central American Ind. (0)	1	0.01
Cherokee (12)	40	0.33
Chickasaw (0)	2	0.02
Choctaw (1)	8	0.07
Comanche (2)	4	0.03
Kiowa (3)	3	0.02
Mexican American Ind. (4)	7	0.06
Potawatomi (2)	3	0.02
Sioux (3)	8	0.07
South American Ind. (3)	9	0.07
Spanish American Ind. (1)	1	0.01
Asian (939)	1,109	9.15
Not Hispanic (915)	1,061	8.75
Hispanic (24)	48	0.40
Bangladeshi (7)	13	0.11
Cambodian (9)	16	0.13
Chinese, ex. Taiwanese (94)	108	0.89
Filipino (91)	130	1.07
Indian (318)	341	2.81
Indonesian (2)	2	0.02
Japanese (17)	42	0.35
Korean (67)	93	0.77
Laotian (3)	3	0.02
Malaysian (4)	5	0.04
Nepalese (100)	105	0.87
Pakistani (31)	32	0.26
Sri Lankan (0)	2	0.02
Taiwanese (10)	11	0.09
Thai (11)	25	0.21
Vietnamese (143)	154	1.27
Hawaii Native/Pacific Islander (23)	40	0.33
Not Hispanic (21)	34	0.28
Hispanic (2)	6	0.05
Fijian (0)	4	0.03
Guamanian/Chamorro (10)	15	0.12
Native Hawaiian (4)	5	0.04
Samoan (0)	4	0.03
Tongan (1)	3	0.02
White (7,470)	7,898	65.17
Not Hispanic (5,540)	5,814	47.97
Hispanic (1,930)	2,084	17.19

Weslaco

Place Type: City
County: Hidalgo
Population: 35,670†

Ancestry‡	Population	%
American (717)	717	2.08
Arab (0)	14	0.04
Lebanese (0)	14	0.04
Austrian (7)	14	0.04
Belgian (44)	55	0.16
British (9)	29	0.08
Canadian (71)	92	0.27
Croatian (27)	74	0.21
Danish (20)	138	0.40
Dutch (71)	247	0.72
English (390)	1,061	3.07
European (15)	15	0.04
French, ex. Basque (37)	416	1.20
French Canadian (29)	49	0.14
German (695)	1,897	5.49
Hungarian (16)	16	0.05
Irish (174)	607	1.76
Italian (130)	257	0.74
Norwegian (119)	235	0.68
Pennsylvania German (11)	11	0.03
Polish (50)	129	0.37
Portuguese (0)	65	0.19
Russian (53)	53	0.15
Scotch-Irish (23)	142	0.41
Scottish (32)	176	0.51
Swedish (96)	171	0.50
Swiss (0)	20	0.06
Ukrainian (13)	27	0.08
Welsh (44)	152	0.44
West Indian, ex. Hispanic (0)	20	0.06
Dutch West Indian (0)	20	0.06
Yugoslavian (0)	26	0.08

Hispanic Origin	Population	%
Hispanic or Latino (of any race)	30,312	84.98
Central American, ex. Mexican	79	0.22
Costa Rican	2	0.01
Guatemalan	15	0.04
Honduran	18	0.05
Nicaraguan	12	0.03
Panamanian	2	0.01
Salvadoran	30	0.08
Cuban	30	0.08
Dominican Republic	40	0.11
Mexican	27,801	77.94
Puerto Rican	91	0.26
South American	42	0.12
Argentinean	3	0.01
Chilean	1	<0.01
Colombian	16	0.04
Ecuadorian	3	0.01
Paraguayan	2	0.01
Peruvian	11	0.03
Venezuelan	6	0.02
Other Hispanic or Latino	2,229	6.25

Race*	Population	%
African-American/Black (195)	271	0.76
Not Hispanic (84)	112	0.31
Hispanic (111)	159	0.45
American Indian/Alaska Native (211)	285	0.80
Not Hispanic (32)	54	0.15
Hispanic (179)	231	0.65
Apache (9)	9	0.03
Blackfeet (0)	4	0.01
Cherokee (3)	8	0.02
Chickasaw (0)	6	0.02
Chippewa (9)	9	0.03
Choctaw (15)	20	0.06
Iroquois (0)	1	<0.01
Mexican American Ind. (29)	35	0.10
Navajo (1)	1	<0.01
Potawatomi (1)	1	<0.01
Seminole (2)	3	0.01
Sioux (2)	2	0.01
Tlingit-Haida *(Alaska Native)* (1)	1	<0.01
Asian (419)	462	1.30
Not Hispanic (402)	421	1.18
Hispanic (17)	41	0.11
Bangladeshi (9)	9	0.03
Chinese, ex. Taiwanese (39)	42	0.12
Filipino (194)	203	0.57
Indian (71)	84	0.24
Japanese (2)	5	0.01
Korean (20)	22	0.06
Pakistani (29)	29	0.08
Taiwanese (4)	4	0.01
Vietnamese (43)	44	0.12
Hawaii Native/Pacific Islander (5)	21	0.06
Not Hispanic (1)	8	0.02
Hispanic (4)	13	0.04
Guamanian/Chamorro (4)	4	0.01
Native Hawaiian (0)	4	0.01
Tongan (1)	1	<0.01
White (30,574)	31,096	87.18
Not Hispanic (4,750)	4,806	13.47
Hispanic (25,824)	26,290	73.70

West Livingston

Place Type: CDP
County: Polk
Population: 8,071†

Ancestry‡	Population	%
African, Sub-Saharan (39)	39	0.52
African (39)	39	0.52
American (710)	710	9.46
Arab (0)	10	0.13
Lebanese (0)	10	0.13
Armenian (9)	9	0.12
Austrian (0)	89	1.19
Celtic (0)	9	0.12
Czech (50)	224	2.98
Danish (0)	9	0.12
Dutch (0)	131	1.75
English (203)	596	7.94
European (9)	19	0.25
French, ex. Basque (149)	404	5.38
French Canadian (61)	61	0.81
German (328)	850	11.32
Irish (182)	806	10.74
Italian (129)	260	3.46
Norwegian (40)	100	1.33
Polish (10)	10	0.13
Portuguese (10)	10	0.13
Russian (0)	49	0.65
Scotch-Irish (20)	84	1.12
Scottish (16)	35	0.47
Serbian (0)	6	0.08
Welsh (0)	12	0.16
West Indian, ex. Hispanic (34)	34	0.45
Haitian (34)	34	0.45

Hispanic Origin	Population	%
Hispanic or Latino (of any race)	1,582	19.60
Central American, ex. Mexican	59	0.73
Guatemalan	12	0.15
Honduran	12	0.15
Nicaraguan	3	0.04
Panamanian	2	0.02
Salvadoran	28	0.35
Other Central American	2	0.02
Dominican Republic	1	0.01
Mexican	1,349	16.71
Puerto Rican	31	0.38
South American	2	0.02
Colombian	1	0.01
Ecuadorian	1	0.01
Other Hispanic or Latino	140	1.73

Race*	Population	%
African-American/Black (1,774)	1,811	22.44
Not Hispanic (1,763)	1,796	22.25
Hispanic (11)	15	0.19
American Indian/Alaska Native (44)	70	0.87
Not Hispanic (39)	62	0.77
Hispanic (5)	8	0.10
Apache (0)	3	0.04
Blackfeet (1)	4	0.05
Cherokee (6)	15	0.19
Chickasaw (1)	1	0.01
Choctaw (1)	2	0.02

*Notes: † The Census 2010 population figure is used to calculate the percentages in the Hispanic Origin and Race categories. Ancestry percentages are based on the 2006-2010 American Community Survey population (not shown); ‡ Numbers in parentheses indicate the number of people reporting a single ancestry; * Numbers in parentheses indicate the number of persons reporting this race alone, not in combination with any other race; Please refer to the Explanation of Data for more information.*

Comanche (0)	1	0.01
Mexican American Ind. (1)	2	0.02
Navajo (1)	4	0.05
Asian (24)	26	0.32
Not Hispanic (24)	25	0.31
Hispanic (0)	1	0.01
Chinese, ex. Taiwanese (1)	1	0.01
Filipino (4)	4	0.05
Indian (0)	1	0.01
Thai (1)	1	0.01
Vietnamese (4)	4	0.05
Hawaii Native/Pacific Islander (1)	7	0.09
Not Hispanic (1)	7	0.09
Guamanian/Chamorro (0)	2	0.02
Native Hawaiian (0)	1	0.01
White (5,143)	5,243	64.96
Not Hispanic (4,605)	4,651	57.63
Hispanic (538)	592	7.33

West Odessa

Place Type: CDP
County: Ector
Population: 22,707†

Ancestry‡	Population	%
African, Sub-Saharan (49)	49	0.23
African (49)	49	0.23
American (882)	882	4.10
British (13)	26	0.12
Canadian (11)	11	0.05
Czech (27)	92	0.43
Danish (40)	40	0.19
Dutch (58)	134	0.62
Eastern European (0)	12	0.06
English (412)	901	4.19
European (43)	43	0.20
Finnish (0)	42	0.20
French, ex. Basque (40)	312	1.45
French Canadian (28)	212	0.99
German (546)	1,639	7.62
Greek (111)	111	0.52
Irish (383)	1,217	5.66
Italian (13)	56	0.26
Norwegian (0)	73	0.34
Polish (100)	165	0.77
Portuguese (20)	20	0.09
Scandinavian (0)	17	0.08
Scotch-Irish (80)	224	1.04
Scottish (22)	65	0.30
Swedish (0)	34	0.16
Welsh (0)	35	0.16
West Indian, ex. Hispanic (13)	59	0.27
Dutch West Indian (13)	59	0.27
Yugoslavian (0)	7	0.03

Hispanic Origin	Population	%
Hispanic or Latino (of any race)	14,041	61.84
Central American, ex. Mexican	7	0.03
Guatemalan	1	<0.01
Honduran	1	<0.01
Panamanian	2	0.01
Salvadoran	3	0.01
Cuban	14	0.06
Dominican Republic	3	0.01
Mexican	12,976	57.15
Puerto Rican	20	0.09
South American	10	0.04
Chilean	1	<0.01
Ecuadorian	2	0.01
Paraguayan	1	<0.01
Peruvian	5	0.02
Venezuelan	1	<0.01
Other Hispanic or Latino	1,011	4.45

Race*	Population	%
African-American/Black (255)	322	1.42
Not Hispanic (162)	199	0.88
Hispanic (93)	123	0.54
American Indian/Alaska Native (255)	354	1.56
Not Hispanic (114)	191	0.84
Hispanic (141)	163	0.72
Alaska Athabascan *(Ala. Nat.)* (3)	4	0.02
Aleut *(Alaska Native)* (0)	1	<0.01
Apache (7)	14	0.06
Blackfeet (0)	4	0.02
Canadian/French Am. Ind. (6)	6	0.03
Cherokee (35)	56	0.25
Chickasaw (4)	7	0.03
Chippewa (1)	1	<0.01
Choctaw (12)	18	0.08
Comanche (3)	3	0.01
Creek (4)	9	0.04
Delaware (2)	2	0.01
Mexican American Ind. (30)	33	0.15
Navajo (11)	11	0.05
Ottawa (0)	1	<0.01
Potawatomi (2)	2	0.01
Pueblo (0)	1	<0.01
Seminole (1)	1	<0.01
Sioux (0)	2	0.01
Asian (37)	69	0.30
Not Hispanic (28)	42	0.18
Hispanic (9)	27	0.12
Chinese, ex. Taiwanese (5)	7	0.03
Filipino (16)	20	0.09
Indian (3)	6	0.03
Japanese (3)	6	0.03
Korean (10)	19	0.08
Hawaii Native/Pacific Islander (4)	18	0.08
Not Hispanic (3)	6	0.03
Hispanic (1)	12	0.05
Guamanian/Chamorro (1)	1	<0.01
Native Hawaiian (2)	5	0.02
Samoan (1)	1	<0.01
White (17,863)	18,344	80.79
Not Hispanic (8,216)	8,341	36.73
Hispanic (9,647)	10,003	44.05

West University Place

Place Type: City
County: Harris
Population: 14,787†

Ancestry‡	Population	%
American (657)	657	4.50
Arab (127)	244	1.67
Jordanian (4)	10	0.07
Lebanese (17)	69	0.47
Moroccan (62)	62	0.42
Syrian (0)	15	0.10
Other Arab (44)	88	0.60
Australian (15)	15	0.10
Austrian (15)	52	0.36
Belgian (15)	15	0.10
Brazilian (27)	41	0.28
British (185)	216	1.48
Cajun (0)	12	0.08
Canadian (15)	60	0.41
Croatian (42)	42	0.29
Czech (43)	129	0.88
Czechoslovakian (0)	24	0.16
Danish (0)	22	0.15
Dutch (55)	172	1.18
Eastern European (157)	157	1.07
English (816)	2,231	15.27
European (251)	283	1.94
Finnish (0)	70	0.48
French, ex. Basque (266)	782	5.35
French Canadian (14)	44	0.30
German (633)	2,321	15.88
Greek (46)	142	0.97
Hungarian (22)	43	0.29
Iranian (111)	111	0.76
Irish (540)	1,836	12.56
Israeli (0)	36	0.25
Italian (268)	957	6.55
Lithuanian (20)	109	0.75
New Zealander (12)	12	0.08
Northern European (112)	123	0.84
Norwegian (21)	87	0.60
Polish (37)	323	2.21
Portuguese (20)	55	0.38
Romanian (0)	39	0.27
Russian (141)	396	2.71
Scandinavian (16)	62	0.42
Scotch-Irish (150)	523	3.58
Scottish (260)	849	5.81
Slovak (15)	71	0.49
Swedish (97)	279	1.91
Swiss (14)	62	0.42
Ukrainian (9)	81	0.55
Welsh (0)	142	0.97
West Indian, ex. Hispanic (16)	111	0.76
British West Indian (0)	25	0.17
Dutch West Indian (0)	25	0.17
Trinidadian/Tobagonian (0)	45	0.31
West Indian (16)	16	0.11

Hispanic Origin	Population	%
Hispanic or Latino (of any race)	1,027	6.95
Central American, ex. Mexican	76	0.51
Costa Rican	5	0.03
Guatemalan	21	0.14
Honduran	12	0.08
Nicaraguan	12	0.08
Panamanian	2	0.01
Salvadoran	24	0.16
Cuban	90	0.61
Dominican Republic	2	0.01
Mexican	458	3.10
Puerto Rican	39	0.26
South American	239	1.62
Argentinean	47	0.32
Bolivian	3	0.02
Chilean	11	0.07
Colombian	72	0.49
Ecuadorian	22	0.15
Peruvian	28	0.19
Uruguayan	20	0.14
Venezuelan	36	0.24
Other Hispanic or Latino	123	0.83

Race*	Population	%
African-American/Black (119)	148	1.00
Not Hispanic (114)	138	0.93
Hispanic (5)	10	0.07
American Indian/Alaska Native (28)	60	0.41
Not Hispanic (27)	49	0.33
Hispanic (1)	11	0.07
Cherokee (6)	14	0.09
Chickasaw (3)	4	0.03
Choctaw (0)	4	0.03
Iroquois (0)	1	0.01
Mexican American Ind. (0)	4	0.03
Osage (2)	2	0.01
South American Ind. (0)	2	0.01
Asian (1,245)	1,476	9.98
Not Hispanic (1,225)	1,455	9.84
Hispanic (20)	21	0.14
Chinese, ex. Taiwanese (429)	517	3.50
Filipino (55)	72	0.49
Indian (368)	431	2.91
Indonesian (9)	9	0.06
Japanese (25)	46	0.31
Korean (77)	101	0.68
Pakistani (47)	52	0.35
Taiwanese (37)	48	0.32
Thai (9)	16	0.11
Vietnamese (127)	153	1.03
Hawaii Native/Pacific Islander (0)	9	0.06
Not Hispanic (0)	9	0.06
Guamanian/Chamorro (0)	1	0.01
Tongan (0)	3	0.02
White (12,935)	13,223	89.42
Not Hispanic (12,066)	12,319	83.31
Hispanic (869)	904	6.11

*Notes: † The Census 2010 population figure is used to calculate the percentages in the Hispanic Origin and Race categories. Ancestry percentages are based on the 2006-2010 American Community Survey population (not shown); ‡ Numbers in parentheses indicate the number of people reporting a single ancestry; * Numbers in parentheses indicate the number of persons reporting this race alone, not in combination with any other race; Please refer to the Explanation of Data for more information.*

Wharton

Place Type: City
County: Wharton
Population: 8,832†

Ancestry‡	Population	%
African, Sub-Saharan (44)	44	0.50
African (44)	44	0.50
American (157)	157	1.77
Arab (0)	3	0.03
Lebanese (0)	3	0.03
Austrian (0)	13	0.15
Czech (326)	671	7.58
Czechoslovakian (17)	19	0.21
Dutch (0)	11	0.12
English (189)	437	4.94
French, ex. Basque (0)	102	1.15
German (271)	671	7.58
Greek (14)	43	0.49
Irish (161)	968	10.94
Italian (49)	130	1.47
Lithuanian (11)	11	0.12
Polish (27)	99	1.12
Scotch-Irish (1)	28	0.32
Scottish (0)	64	0.72
Swedish (26)	32	0.36
Swiss (0)	3	0.03

Hispanic Origin	Population	%
Hispanic or Latino (of any race)	3,477	39.37
Central American, ex. Mexican	15	0.17
Guatemalan	9	0.10
Honduran	1	0.01
Nicaraguan	1	0.01
Salvadoran	4	0.05
Cuban	15	0.17
Dominican Republic	2	0.02
Mexican	2,942	33.31
Puerto Rican	29	0.33
South American	6	0.07
Argentinean	1	0.01
Bolivian	1	0.01
Colombian	1	0.01
Ecuadorian	2	0.02
Peruvian	1	0.01
Other Hispanic or Latino	468	5.30

Race*	Population	%
African-American/Black (2,415)	2,513	28.45
Not Hispanic (2,367)	2,430	27.51
Hispanic (48)	83	0.94
American Indian/Alaska Native (55)	86	0.97
Not Hispanic (18)	44	0.50
Hispanic (37)	42	0.48
Apache (4)	5	0.06
Blackfeet (0)	2	0.02
Cherokee (5)	17	0.19
Chickasaw (0)	2	0.02
Choctaw (2)	4	0.05
Comanche (0)	1	0.01
Delaware (1)	1	0.01
Navajo (1)	1	0.01
Sioux (3)	3	0.03
Asian (51)	65	0.74
Not Hispanic (48)	56	0.63
Hispanic (3)	9	0.10
Burmese (2)	2	0.02
Cambodian (3)	3	0.03
Chinese, ex. Taiwanese (12)	15	0.17
Filipino (8)	9	0.10
Indian (16)	17	0.19
Japanese (3)	5	0.06
Korean (0)	6	0.07
Pakistani (2)	4	0.05
Taiwanese (2)	2	0.02
Vietnamese (3)	3	0.03
Hawaii Native/Pacific Islander (1)	10	0.11
Not Hispanic (1)	9	0.10
Hispanic (0)	1	0.01
Guamanian/Chamorro (1)	6	0.07
Native Hawaiian (0)	1	0.01
Samoan (0)	1	0.01
White (4,690)	4,850	54.91
Not Hispanic (2,817)	2,897	32.80
Hispanic (1,873)	1,953	22.11

White Settlement

Place Type: City
County: Tarrant
Population: 16,116†

Ancestry‡	Population	%
African, Sub-Saharan (92)	124	0.78
African (46)	78	0.49
Nigerian (19)	19	0.12
Other Sub-Saharan African (27)	27	0.17
American (2,841)	2,841	17.88
Arab (11)	22	0.14
Arab (11)	22	0.14
Austrian (6)	6	0.04
Brazilian (5)	5	0.03
British (16)	74	0.47
Canadian (26)	40	0.25
Czech (22)	82	0.52
Danish (0)	43	0.27
Dutch (53)	153	0.96
English (520)	877	5.52
European (192)	192	1.21
Finnish (0)	14	0.09
French, ex. Basque (123)	272	1.71
French Canadian (0)	14	0.09
German (827)	1,851	11.65
Hungarian (12)	30	0.19
Irish (1,045)	1,829	11.51
Italian (109)	200	1.26
Norwegian (27)	46	0.29
Polish (106)	183	1.15
Portuguese (15)	15	0.09
Russian (0)	8	0.05
Scotch-Irish (147)	262	1.65
Scottish (124)	261	1.64
Swedish (9)	44	0.28
Welsh (14)	14	0.09
West Indian, ex. Hispanic (12)	12	0.08
Dutch West Indian (12)	12	0.08

Hispanic Origin	Population	%
Hispanic or Latino (of any race)	4,030	25.01
Central American, ex. Mexican	101	0.63
Guatemalan	19	0.12
Honduran	40	0.25
Nicaraguan	11	0.07
Panamanian	2	0.01
Salvadoran	27	0.17
Other Central American	2	0.01
Cuban	18	0.11
Dominican Republic	3	0.02
Mexican	3,515	21.81
Puerto Rican	64	0.40
South American	37	0.23
Argentinean	6	0.04
Chilean	1	0.01
Colombian	8	0.05
Ecuadorian	10	0.06
Peruvian	3	0.02
Venezuelan	8	0.05
Other South American	1	0.01
Other Hispanic or Latino	292	1.81

Race*	Population	%
African-American/Black (758)	897	5.57
Not Hispanic (725)	831	5.16
Hispanic (33)	66	0.41
American Indian/Alaska Native (140)	253	1.57
Not Hispanic (90)	165	1.02
Hispanic (50)	88	0.55
Apache (3)	12	0.07
Blackfeet (4)	4	0.02
Canadian/French Am. Ind. (0)	1	0.01
Central American Ind. (6)	7	0.04
Cherokee (26)	56	0.35
Chickasaw (3)	4	0.02
Chippewa (5)	5	0.03
Choctaw (21)	31	0.19
Comanche (2)	7	0.04
Cree (0)	3	0.02
Creek (4)	11	0.07
Iroquois (2)	2	0.01
Kiowa (2)	4	0.02
Mexican American Ind. (10)	10	0.06
Navajo (0)	6	0.04
Ottawa (2)	2	0.01
Potawatomi (1)	1	0.01
Pueblo (1)	1	0.01
Seminole (2)	3	0.02
Shoshone (0)	2	0.01
Sioux (6)	8	0.05
South American Ind. (1)	1	0.01
Asian (262)	347	2.15
Not Hispanic (250)	318	1.97
Hispanic (12)	29	0.18
Bangladeshi (5)	5	0.03
Cambodian (14)	18	0.11
Chinese, ex. Taiwanese (6)	12	0.07
Filipino (97)	140	0.87
Indian (15)	20	0.12
Japanese (15)	29	0.18
Korean (10)	19	0.12
Laotian (7)	8	0.05
Nepalese (19)	19	0.12
Pakistani (4)	8	0.05
Thai (28)	31	0.19
Vietnamese (29)	31	0.19
Hawaii Native/Pacific Islander (23)	48	0.30
Not Hispanic (23)	40	0.25
Hispanic (0)	8	0.05
Guamanian/Chamorro (20)	28	0.17
Native Hawaiian (1)	4	0.02
Samoan (1)	3	0.02
White (12,949)	13,404	83.17
Not Hispanic (10,721)	10,969	68.06
Hispanic (2,228)	2,435	15.11

Whitehouse

Place Type: City
County: Smith
Population: 7,660†

Ancestry‡	Population	%
American (592)	592	8.05
Arab (0)	22	0.30
Lebanese (0)	22	0.30
Basque (0)	14	0.19
Brazilian (39)	39	0.53
British (12)	12	0.16
Czech (0)	50	0.68
Czechoslovakian (14)	14	0.19
Danish (0)	11	0.15
Dutch (8)	302	4.11
English (477)	963	13.09
European (80)	91	1.24
French, ex. Basque (76)	382	5.19
French Canadian (19)	34	0.46
German (189)	896	12.18
Hungarian (7)	7	0.10
Irish (379)	1,162	15.80
Italian (63)	194	2.64
Norwegian (0)	45	0.61
Polish (0)	32	0.44
Scotch-Irish (90)	292	3.97
Scottish (170)	223	3.03
Swedish (0)	27	0.37
Ukrainian (0)	16	0.22
Welsh (8)	24	0.33
West Indian, ex. Hispanic (0)	79	1.07
Dutch West Indian (0)	79	1.07

SECTION TWO

*Notes: † The Census 2010 population figure is used to calculate the percentages in the Hispanic Origin and Race categories. Ancestry percentages are based on the 2006-2010 American Community Survey population (not shown); ‡ Numbers in parentheses indicate the number of people reporting a single ancestry; * Numbers in parentheses indicate the number of persons reporting this race alone, not in combination with any other race; Please refer to the Explanation of Data for more information.*

Hispanic Origin	Population	%
Hispanic or Latino (of any race)	542	7.08
Central American, ex. Mexican	11	0.14
Guatemalan	1	0.01
Honduran	4	0.05
Salvadoran	6	0.08
Cuban	11	0.14
Mexican	422	5.51
Puerto Rican	34	0.44
South American	23	0.30
Colombian	3	0.04
Ecuadorian	12	0.16
Paraguayan	4	0.05
Peruvian	4	0.05
Other Hispanic or Latino	41	0.54

Race*	Population	%
African-American/Black (327)	396	5.17
Not Hispanic (316)	377	4.92
Hispanic (11)	19	0.25
American Indian/Alaska Native (24)	70	0.91
Not Hispanic (19)	59	0.77
Hispanic (5)	11	0.14
Apache (0)	1	0.01
Blackfeet (0)	3	0.04
Cherokee (4)	24	0.31
Chickasaw (1)	2	0.03
Choctaw (0)	2	0.03
Creek (3)	3	0.04
Crow (1)	1	0.01
Iroquois (2)	2	0.03
Navajo (0)	2	0.03
Potawatomi (1)	1	0.01
Sioux (0)	2	0.03
Spanish American Ind. (0)	1	0.01
Yaqui (0)	1	0.01
Asian (125)	148	1.93
Not Hispanic (122)	142	1.85
Hispanic (3)	6	0.08
Cambodian (24)	32	0.42
Chinese, ex. Taiwanese (10)	14	0.18
Filipino (65)	74	0.97
Indian (5)	5	0.07
Indonesian (1)	1	0.01
Japanese (1)	3	0.04
Korean (2)	3	0.04
Malaysian (3)	3	0.04
Pakistani (4)	8	0.10
Vietnamese (1)	3	0.04
Hawaii Native/Pacific Islander (10)	13	0.17
Not Hispanic (9)	11	0.14
Hispanic (1)	2	0.03
Guamanian/Chamorro (8)	10	0.13
Samoan (2)	2	0.03
White (6,807)	6,959	90.85
Not Hispanic (6,534)	6,637	86.64
Hispanic (273)	322	4.20

Wichita Falls

Place Type: City
County: Wichita
Population: 104,553†

Ancestry‡	Population	%
Afghan (28)	28	0.03
African, Sub-Saharan (648)	699	0.67
African (541)	592	0.57
Ethiopian (10)	10	0.01
Liberian (8)	8	0.01
Nigerian (52)	52	0.05
South African (37)	37	0.04
American (16,094)	16,094	15.47
Arab (83)	167	0.16
Arab (0)	14	0.01
Egyptian (9)	9	0.01
Jordanian (0)	29	0.03
Lebanese (74)	115	0.11
Armenian (50)	69	0.07
Australian (0)	20	0.02
Austrian (95)	169	0.16
Belgian (8)	28	0.03
Brazilian (25)	38	0.04
British (251)	484	0.47
Canadian (75)	147	0.14
Croatian (20)	71	0.07
Czech (179)	674	0.65
Czechoslovakian (58)	93	0.09
Danish (120)	322	0.31
Dutch (308)	1,424	1.37
Eastern European (11)	11	0.01
English (3,181)	7,732	7.43
European (520)	571	0.55
Finnish (103)	164	0.16
French, ex. Basque (490)	2,446	2.35
French Canadian (135)	392	0.38
German (5,365)	13,798	13.26
Greek (117)	167	0.16
Hungarian (90)	137	0.13
Iranian (30)	30	0.03
Irish (2,882)	9,208	8.85
Israeli (10)	10	0.01
Italian (1,212)	2,236	2.15
Lithuanian (0)	40	0.04
Northern European (11)	25	0.02
Norwegian (328)	773	0.74
Pennsylvania German (10)	41	0.04
Polish (156)	789	0.76
Portuguese (117)	200	0.19
Romanian (0)	22	0.02
Russian (170)	326	0.31
Scandinavian (52)	75	0.07
Scotch-Irish (919)	1,831	1.76
Scottish (574)	1,671	1.61
Serbian (0)	13	0.01
Slavic (9)	9	0.01
Slovak (9)	23	0.02
Swedish (327)	738	0.71
Swiss (40)	113	0.11
Ukrainian (36)	36	0.03
Welsh (139)	686	0.66
West Indian, ex. Hispanic (189)	371	0.36
Barbadian (14)	14	0.01
British West Indian (60)	91	0.09
Dutch West Indian (53)	152	0.15
Jamaican (62)	114	0.11
Yugoslavian (24)	24	0.02

Hispanic Origin	Population	%
Hispanic or Latino (of any race)	19,771	18.91
Central American, ex. Mexican	256	0.24
Costa Rican	9	0.01
Guatemalan	40	0.04
Honduran	27	0.03
Nicaraguan	44	0.04
Panamanian	54	0.05
Salvadoran	82	0.08
Cuban	106	0.10
Dominican Republic	28	0.03
Mexican	16,429	15.71
Puerto Rican	666	0.64
South American	229	0.22
Argentinean	5	<0.01
Bolivian	2	<0.01
Chilean	17	0.02
Colombian	81	0.08
Ecuadorian	22	0.02
Peruvian	77	0.07
Uruguayan	2	<0.01
Venezuelan	16	0.02
Other South American	7	0.01
Other Hispanic or Latino	2,057	1.97

Race*	Population	%
African-American/Black (13,271)	14,549	13.92
Not Hispanic (12,812)	13,809	13.21
Hispanic (459)	740	0.71
American Indian/Alaska Native (1,043)	1,898	1.82
Not Hispanic (790)	1,440	1.38
Hispanic (253)	458	0.44
Alaska Athabascan *(Ala. Nat.)* (1)	3	<0.01
Aleut *(Alaska Native)* (1)	1	<0.01
Apache (25)	46	0.04
Arapaho (2)	2	<0.01
Blackfeet (3)	20	0.02
Canadian/French Am. Ind. (2)	2	<0.01
Central American Ind. (3)	6	0.01
Cherokee (138)	364	0.35
Cheyenne (3)	3	<0.01
Chickasaw (52)	83	0.08
Chippewa (28)	42	0.04
Choctaw (167)	283	0.27
Comanche (42)	68	0.07
Cree (0)	1	<0.01
Creek (36)	46	0.04
Delaware (4)	6	0.01
Hopi (1)	2	<0.01
Houma (1)	1	<0.01
Inupiat *(Alaska Native)* (2)	2	<0.01
Iroquois (1)	5	<0.01
Kiowa (24)	30	0.03
Lumbee (3)	3	<0.01
Mexican American Ind. (28)	46	0.04
Navajo (10)	17	0.02
Osage (4)	4	<0.01
Ottawa (0)	3	<0.01
Paiute (1)	2	<0.01
Pima (3)	3	<0.01
Potawatomi (7)	9	0.01
Pueblo (3)	5	<0.01
Puget Sound Salish (1)	1	<0.01
Seminole (7)	13	0.01
Shoshone (1)	2	<0.01
Sioux (12)	28	0.03
South American Ind. (0)	2	<0.01
Spanish American Ind. (6)	6	0.01
Tlingit-Haida *(Alaska Native)* (5)	6	0.01
Yakama (0)	2	<0.01
Yaqui (0)	1	<0.01
Yup'ik *(Alaska Native)* (0)	2	<0.01
Asian (2,472)	3,229	3.09
Not Hispanic (2,396)	3,021	2.89
Hispanic (76)	208	0.20
Bangladeshi (33)	44	0.04
Burmese (4)	6	0.01
Cambodian (65)	70	0.07
Chinese, ex. Taiwanese (136)	212	0.20
Filipino (476)	772	0.74
Hmong (4)	7	0.01
Indian (364)	429	0.41
Indonesian (3)	6	0.01
Japanese (117)	218	0.21
Korean (211)	337	0.32
Laotian (18)	19	0.02
Malaysian (2)	3	<0.01
Nepalese (3)	3	<0.01
Pakistani (71)	78	0.07
Sri Lankan (14)	14	0.01
Taiwanese (6)	15	0.01
Thai (54)	104	0.10
Vietnamese (798)	855	0.82
Hawaii Native/Pacific Islander (97)	251	0.24
Not Hispanic (82)	195	0.19
Hispanic (15)	56	0.05
Fijian (0)	1	<0.01
Guamanian/Chamorro (24)	69	0.07
Native Hawaiian (38)	96	0.09
Samoan (4)	16	0.02
Tongan (6)	7	0.01
White (76,565)	79,453	75.99
Not Hispanic (66,509)	68,378	65.40
Hispanic (10,056)	11,075	10.59

Woodway

Place Type: City
County: McLennan
Population: 8,452†

*Notes: † The Census 2010 population figure is used to calculate the percentages in the Hispanic Origin and Race categories. Ancestry percentages are based on the 2006-2010 American Community Survey population (not shown); ‡ Numbers in parentheses indicate the number of people reporting a single ancestry; * Numbers in parentheses indicate the number of persons reporting this race alone, not in combination with any other race; Please refer to the Explanation of Data for more information.*

Ancestry‡	Population	%
African, Sub-Saharan (22)	22	0.26
African (22)	22	0.26
Alsatian (18)	45	0.54
American (1,034)	1,034	12.35
Arab (0)	12	0.14
Moroccan (0)	12	0.14
Australian (0)	19	0.23
Austrian (0)	10	0.12
Belgian (11)	37	0.44
British (59)	69	0.82
Cajun (0)	11	0.13
Czech (201)	239	2.86
Czechoslovakian (21)	45	0.54
Danish (0)	18	0.22
Dutch (57)	194	2.32
English (466)	1,219	14.56
European (198)	198	2.37
Finnish (0)	11	0.13
French, ex. Basque (37)	194	2.32
French Canadian (0)	7	0.08
German (458)	1,226	14.65
Hungarian (0)	23	0.27
Irish (274)	844	10.08
Italian (110)	249	2.97
Northern European (13)	13	0.16
Norwegian (30)	120	1.43
Pennsylvania German (13)	13	0.16
Polish (34)	171	2.04
Portuguese (15)	46	0.55
Russian (16)	30	0.36
Scandinavian (0)	37	0.44
Scotch-Irish (199)	423	5.05
Scottish (92)	262	3.13
Swedish (10)	28	0.33
Swiss (25)	52	0.62
Welsh (8)	35	0.42
Yugoslavian (0)	32	0.38

Hispanic Origin	Population	%
Hispanic or Latino (of any race)	587	6.95
Central American, ex. Mexican	10	0.12
Guatemalan	3	0.04
Honduran	1	0.01
Panamanian	1	0.01
Salvadoran	5	0.06
Cuban	8	0.09
Mexican	489	5.79
Puerto Rican	19	0.22
South American	18	0.21
Argentinean	3	0.04
Bolivian	1	0.01
Chilean	2	0.02
Colombian	4	0.05
Peruvian	8	0.09
Other Hispanic or Latino	43	0.51

Race*	Population	%
African-American/Black (246)	272	3.22
Not Hispanic (232)	246	2.91
Hispanic (14)	26	0.31
American Indian/Alaska Native (40)	71	0.84
Not Hispanic (29)	55	0.65
Hispanic (11)	16	0.19
Apache (2)	3	0.04
Blackfeet (0)	1	0.01
Cherokee (7)	13	0.15
Cheyenne (0)	2	0.02
Chickasaw (1)	1	0.01
Choctaw (5)	7	0.08
Comanche (0)	2	0.02
Creek (0)	2	0.02
Paiute (1)	1	0.01
Potawatomi (1)	1	0.01
Puget Sound Salish (1)	4	0.05
Asian (183)	217	2.57
Not Hispanic (181)	214	2.53
Hispanic (2)	3	0.04
Cambodian (6)	6	0.07
Chinese, ex. Taiwanese (44)	50	0.59
Filipino (21)	32	0.38
Indian (41)	45	0.53
Indonesian (1)	2	0.02
Japanese (13)	20	0.24
Korean (21)	26	0.31
Pakistani (5)	5	0.06
Taiwanese (8)	8	0.09
Thai (1)	5	0.06
Vietnamese (13)	15	0.18
Hawaii Native/Pacific Islander (7)	12	0.14
Not Hispanic (7)	9	0.11
Hispanic (0)	3	0.04
Guamanian/Chamorro (2)	5	0.06
Native Hawaiian (1)	1	0.01
Samoan (4)	4	0.05
White (7,719)	7,828	92.62
Not Hispanic (7,331)	7,405	87.61
Hispanic (388)	423	5.00

Wylie

Place Type: City
County: Collin
Population: 41,427†

Ancestry‡	Population	%
African, Sub-Saharan (762)	875	2.36
African (176)	245	0.66
Ethiopian (308)	308	0.83
Ghanaian (0)	44	0.12
Nigerian (226)	226	0.61
Sierra Leonean (52)	52	0.14
American (2,084)	2,084	5.62
Arab (124)	132	0.36
Arab (45)	45	0.12
Lebanese (0)	8	0.02
Moroccan (19)	19	0.05
Other Arab (60)	60	0.16
Austrian (26)	26	0.07
Belgian (50)	50	0.13
Brazilian (40)	69	0.19
British (16)	91	0.25
Cajun (0)	35	0.09
Canadian (98)	122	0.33
Croatian (13)	13	0.04
Czech (58)	187	0.50
Czechoslovakian (36)	36	0.10
Danish (0)	22	0.06
Dutch (127)	604	1.63
English (839)	2,527	6.82
European (426)	499	1.35
French, ex. Basque (346)	1,244	3.35
French Canadian (69)	213	0.57
German (1,165)	4,013	10.82
Greek (41)	41	0.11
Hungarian (42)	74	0.20
Irish (879)	3,179	8.57
Italian (168)	974	2.63
Lithuanian (0)	14	0.04
Norwegian (118)	327	0.88
Pennsylvania German (0)	13	0.04
Polish (179)	538	1.45
Portuguese (0)	24	0.06
Russian (24)	71	0.19
Scandinavian (41)	55	0.15
Scotch-Irish (365)	590	1.59
Scottish (166)	613	1.65
Slovak (15)	48	0.13
Swedish (74)	299	0.81
Ukrainian (11)	55	0.15
Welsh (47)	173	0.47
West Indian, ex. Hispanic (47)	86	0.23
Belizean (24)	24	0.06
Dutch West Indian (0)	13	0.04
Jamaican (23)	23	0.06
West Indian (0)	26	0.07
Yugoslavian (0)	10	0.03

Hispanic Origin	Population	%
Hispanic or Latino (of any race)	7,420	17.91
Central American, ex. Mexican	563	1.36
Costa Rican	29	0.07
Guatemalan	131	0.32
Honduran	75	0.18
Nicaraguan	42	0.10
Panamanian	45	0.11
Salvadoran	233	0.56
Other Central American	8	0.02
Cuban	96	0.23
Dominican Republic	17	0.04
Mexican	5,672	13.69
Puerto Rican	264	0.64
South American	254	0.61
Argentinean	22	0.05
Bolivian	9	0.02
Chilean	1	<0.01
Colombian	67	0.16
Ecuadorian	21	0.05
Paraguayan	1	<0.01
Peruvian	82	0.20
Uruguayan	1	<0.01
Venezuelan	38	0.09
Other South American	12	0.03
Other Hispanic or Latino	554	1.34

Race*	Population	%
African-American/Black (5,141)	5,581	13.47
Not Hispanic (5,015)	5,372	12.97
Hispanic (126)	209	0.50
American Indian/Alaska Native (269)	556	1.34
Not Hispanic (200)	433	1.05
Hispanic (69)	123	0.30
Aleut *(Alaska Native)* (1)	1	<0.01
Apache (4)	7	0.02
Blackfeet (1)	4	0.01
Central American Ind. (2)	3	0.01
Cherokee (62)	153	0.37
Chickasaw (14)	23	0.06
Chippewa (1)	8	0.02
Choctaw (64)	101	0.24
Comanche (6)	7	0.02
Creek (8)	14	0.03
Delaware (1)	1	<0.01
Iroquois (2)	2	<0.01
Kiowa (3)	3	0.01
Mexican American Ind. (9)	20	0.05
Navajo (3)	3	0.01
Potawatomi (5)	5	0.01
Pueblo (1)	2	<0.01
Seminole (2)	6	0.01
Sioux (6)	9	0.02
South American Ind. (2)	3	0.01
Spanish American Ind. (1)	1	<0.01
Tlingit-Haida *(Alaska Native)* (0)	1	<0.01
Asian (2,300)	2,709	6.54
Not Hispanic (2,279)	2,628	6.34
Hispanic (21)	81	0.20
Bangladeshi (50)	55	0.13
Cambodian (35)	49	0.12
Chinese, ex. Taiwanese (166)	224	0.54
Filipino (232)	336	0.81
Hmong (17)	19	0.05
Indian (594)	646	1.56
Indonesian (15)	15	0.04
Japanese (31)	78	0.19
Korean (71)	123	0.30
Laotian (54)	63	0.15
Malaysian (1)	4	0.01
Nepalese (3)	3	0.01
Pakistani (207)	222	0.54
Sri Lankan (7)	7	0.02
Taiwanese (10)	17	0.04
Thai (8)	18	0.04
Vietnamese (701)	777	1.88
Hawaii Native/Pacific Islander (28)	111	0.27
Not Hispanic (18)	79	0.19
Hispanic (10)	32	0.08
Guamanian/Chamorro (17)	23	0.06
Native Hawaiian (2)	26	0.06
Samoan (3)	19	0.05

*Notes: † The Census 2010 population figure is used to calculate the percentages in the Hispanic Origin and Race categories. Ancestry percentages are based on the 2006-2010 American Community Survey population (not shown); ‡ Numbers in parentheses indicate the number of people reporting a single ancestry; * Numbers in parentheses indicate the number of persons reporting this race alone, not in combination with any other race; Please refer to the Explanation of Data for more information.*

White (29,483)	30,635	73.95
Not Hispanic (25,546)	26,301	63.49
Hispanic (3,937)	4,334	10.46

*Notes: † The Census 2010 population figure is used to calculate the percentages in the Hispanic Origin and Race categories. Ancestry percentages are based on the 2006-2010 American Community Survey population (not shown); ‡ Numbers in parentheses indicate the number of people reporting a single ancestry; * Numbers in parentheses indicate the number of persons reporting this race alone, not in combination with any other race; Please refer to the Explanation of Data for more information.*

UTAH

Place Type: State
Population: 2,763,885[†]

Ancestry[‡]	Population	%
Afghan (156)	158	0.01
African, Sub-Saharan (6,415)	8,735	0.33
African (2,645)	4,330	0.16
Cape Verdean (41)	50	<0.01
Ethiopian (165)	186	0.01
Ghanaian (150)	230	0.01
Kenyan (0)	66	<0.01
Liberian (81)	98	<0.01
Nigerian (295)	336	0.01
Sierra Leonean (55)	102	<0.01
Somalian (1,317)	1,348	0.05
South African (250)	453	0.02
Sudanese (694)	720	0.03
Ugandan (79)	79	<0.01
Zimbabwean (40)	51	<0.01
Other Sub-Saharan African (603)	686	0.03
Albanian (173)	466	0.02
Alsatian (0)	25	<0.01
American (171,689)	171,689	6.46
Arab (2,713)	4,815	0.18
Arab (405)	668	0.03
Egyptian (37)	162	0.01
Iraqi (334)	334	0.01
Jordanian (78)	137	0.01
Lebanese (636)	1,730	0.07
Moroccan (42)	75	<0.01
Palestinian (310)	357	0.01
Syrian (169)	446	0.02
Other Arab (702)	906	0.03
Armenian (1,324)	2,350	0.09
Assyrian/Chaldean/Syriac (9)	18	<0.01
Australian (801)	1,982	0.07
Austrian (1,742)	5,579	0.21
Basque (771)	1,598	0.06
Belgian (615)	1,514	0.06
Brazilian (2,806)	3,931	0.15
British (19,140)	37,360	1.41
Bulgarian (287)	395	0.01
Cajun (88)	125	<0.01
Canadian (4,243)	9,976	0.38
Celtic (221)	520	0.02
Croatian (974)	2,318	0.09
Czech (1,587)	6,122	0.23
Czechoslovakian (1,042)	1,853	0.07
Danish (41,165)	155,362	5.85
Dutch (18,099)	64,113	2.41
Eastern European (692)	864	0.03
English (307,055)	719,492	27.08
Estonian (74)	233	0.01
European (83,928)	93,786	3.53
Finnish (1,626)	5,409	0.20
French, ex. Basque (9,583)	57,011	2.15
French Canadian (2,712)	6,485	0.24
German (91,174)	323,162	12.16
German Russian (75)	103	<0.01
Greek (5,312)	13,047	0.49
Guyanese (0)	8	<0.01
Hungarian (1,178)	4,409	0.17
Icelander (1,264)	3,861	0.15
Iranian (1,141)	1,669	0.06
Irish (40,673)	164,050	6.17
Israeli (109)	245	0.01
Italian (24,472)	76,864	2.89
Latvian (138)	300	0.01
Lithuanian (489)	1,971	0.07
Luxemburger (52)	173	0.01
Macedonian (21)	33	<0.01
Maltese (63)	131	<0.01
New Zealander (212)	542	0.02
Northern European (4,339)	4,897	0.18
Norwegian (21,877)	65,960	2.48
Pennsylvania German (58)	225	0.01
Polish (6,842)	23,897	0.90
Portuguese (1,589)	4,433	0.17
Romanian (772)	1,673	0.06
Russian (3,980)	10,505	0.40
Scandinavian (14,492)	33,337	1.25
Scotch-Irish (11,981)	35,636	1.34
Scottish (30,497)	123,661	4.65
Serbian (492)	937	0.04
Slavic (211)	838	0.03
Slovak (654)	1,503	0.06
Slovene (344)	936	0.04
Soviet Union (0)	9	<0.01
Swedish (27,414)	108,734	4.09
Swiss (7,717)	33,898	1.28
Turkish (838)	956	0.04
Ukrainian (1,397)	3,140	0.12
Welsh (11,487)	58,155	2.19
West Indian, ex. Hispanic (893)	1,680	0.06
Bahamian (39)	72	<0.01
Barbadian (0)	33	<0.01
Belizean (68)	91	<0.01
Bermudan (0)	6	<0.01
British West Indian (6)	28	<0.01
Dutch West Indian (7)	61	<0.01
Haitian (250)	444	0.02
Jamaican (207)	433	0.02
Trinidadian/Tobagonian (123)	161	0.01
U.S. Virgin Islander (18)	18	<0.01
West Indian (175)	333	0.01
Yugoslavian (3,565)	5,589	0.21

Hispanic Origin	Population	%
Hispanic or Latino (of any race)	358,340	12.97
Central American, ex. Mexican	20,442	0.74
Costa Rican	775	0.03
Guatemalan	6,877	0.25
Honduran	2,087	0.08
Nicaraguan	1,043	0.04
Panamanian	531	0.02
Salvadoran	8,998	0.33
Other Central American	131	<0.01
Cuban	1,963	0.07
Dominican Republic	1,252	0.05
Mexican	258,905	9.37
Puerto Rican	7,182	0.26
South American	26,028	0.94
Argentinean	4,639	0.17
Bolivian	969	0.04
Chilean	3,364	0.12
Colombian	3,467	0.13
Ecuadorian	2,026	0.07
Paraguayan	158	0.01
Peruvian	7,514	0.27
Uruguayan	1,011	0.04
Venezuelan	2,698	0.10
Other South American	182	0.01
Other Hispanic or Latino	42,568	1.54

Race*	Population	%
African-American/Black (29,287)	43,209	1.56
Not Hispanic (25,951)	37,057	1.34
Hispanic (3,336)	6,152	0.22
American Indian/Alaska Native (32,927)	50,064	1.81
Not Hispanic (27,081)	39,575	1.43
Hispanic (5,846)	10,489	0.38
Alaska Athabascan *(Ala. Nat.)* (38)	64	<0.01
Aleut *(Alaska Native)* (36)	79	<0.01
Apache (342)	976	0.04
Arapaho (132)	199	0.01
Blackfeet (125)	489	0.02
Canadian/French Am. Ind. (29)	80	<0.01
Central American Ind. (60)	100	<0.01
Cherokee (747)	3,351	0.12
Cheyenne (89)	213	0.01
Chickasaw (66)	179	0.01
Chippewa (225)	486	0.02
Choctaw (245)	603	0.02
Colville (11)	16	<0.01
Comanche (51)	127	<0.01
Cree (48)	87	<0.01
Creek (98)	195	0.01
Crow (45)	109	<0.01
Delaware (16)	66	<0.01
Hopi (143)	327	0.01
Houma (6)	9	<0.01
Inupiat *(Alaska Native)* (46)	94	<0.01
Iroquois (150)	355	0.01
Kiowa (16)	53	<0.01
Lumbee (25)	61	<0.01
Menominee (7)	18	<0.01
Mexican American Ind. (1,038)	1,571	0.06
Navajo (14,542)	17,703	0.64
Osage (25)	95	<0.01
Ottawa (10)	29	<0.01
Paiute (768)	1,059	0.04
Pima (61)	100	<0.01
Potawatomi (86)	162	0.01
Pueblo (202)	463	0.02
Puget Sound Salish (31)	63	<0.01
Seminole (29)	120	<0.01
Shoshone (552)	960	0.03
Sioux (665)	1,384	0.05
South American Ind. (118)	340	0.01
Spanish American Ind. (103)	153	0.01
Tlingit-Haida *(Alaska Native)* (51)	88	<0.01
Tohono O'Odham (32)	46	<0.01
Tsimshian *(Alaska Native)* (7)	12	<0.01
Ute (2,994)	3,914	0.14
Yakama (6)	18	<0.01
Yaqui (57)	124	<0.01
Yuman (34)	53	<0.01
Yup'ik *(Alaska Native)* (27)	58	<0.01
Asian (55,285)	77,748	2.81
Not Hispanic (54,176)	74,064	2.68
Hispanic (1,109)	3,684	0.13
Bangladeshi (58)	68	<0.01
Bhutanese (246)	399	0.01
Burmese (1,037)	1,090	0.04
Cambodian (1,884)	2,328	0.08
Chinese, ex. Taiwanese (10,522)	15,597	0.56
Filipino (5,600)	10,657	0.39
Hmong (354)	426	0.02
Indian (6,212)	7,598	0.27
Indonesian (216)	472	0.02
Japanese (6,087)	12,782	0.46
Korean (5,379)	7,888	0.29
Laotian (2,463)	3,189	0.12
Malaysian (73)	128	<0.01
Nepalese (496)	693	0.03
Pakistani (871)	1,086	0.04
Sri Lankan (80)	102	<0.01
Taiwanese (616)	814	0.03
Thai (1,398)	2,276	0.08
Vietnamese (8,025)	9,338	0.34
Hawaii Native/Pacific Islander (24,554)	36,777	1.33
Not Hispanic (23,909)	34,819	1.26
Hispanic (645)	1,958	0.07
Fijian (161)	366	0.01
Guamanian/Chamorro (493)	880	0.03
Marshallese (729)	793	0.03
Native Hawaiian (1,911)	6,525	0.24
Samoan (8,246)	13,086	0.47
Tongan (9,395)	13,235	0.48
White (2,379,560)	2,447,583	88.56
Not Hispanic (2,221,719)	2,266,547	82.01
Hispanic (157,841)	181,036	6.55

*Notes: † The Census 2010 population figure is used to calculate the percentages in the Hispanic Origin and Race categories. Ancestry percentages are based on the 2006-2010 American Community Survey population (not shown); ‡ Numbers in parentheses indicate the number of people reporting a single ancestry; * Numbers in parentheses indicate the number of persons reporting this race alone, not in combination with any other race; Please refer to the Explanation of Data for more information.*

Alpine

Place Type: City
County: Utah
Population: 9,555†

Ancestry‡	Population	%
African, Sub-Saharan (14)	14	0.15
African (14)	14	0.15
Albanian (0)	16	0.18
American (182)	182	2.01
British (46)	177	1.95
Canadian (20)	20	0.22
Danish (176)	693	7.65
Dutch (93)	182	2.01
English (1,755)	3,898	43.02
European (293)	303	3.34
Finnish (0)	50	0.55
French, ex. Basque (40)	217	2.39
German (292)	1,160	12.80
Icelander (23)	55	0.61
Irish (91)	562	6.20
Israeli (10)	10	0.11
Italian (90)	228	2.52
Northern European (50)	50	0.55
Norwegian (0)	187	2.06
Polish (16)	87	0.96
Portuguese (39)	49	0.54
Romanian (0)	10	0.11
Scandinavian (350)	532	5.87
Scotch-Irish (23)	82	0.90
Scottish (148)	356	3.93
Swedish (108)	427	4.71
Swiss (80)	267	2.95
Welsh (35)	267	2.95

Hispanic Origin	Population	%
Hispanic or Latino (of any race)	232	2.43
Central American, ex. Mexican	11	0.12
Guatemalan	2	0.02
Panamanian	2	0.02
Salvadoran	7	0.07
Cuban	2	0.02
Mexican	135	1.41
Puerto Rican	8	0.08
South American	43	0.45
Argentinean	9	0.09
Chilean	10	0.10
Colombian	6	0.06
Peruvian	14	0.15
Uruguayan	4	0.04
Other Hispanic or Latino	33	0.35

Race*	Population	%
African-American/Black (57)	89	0.93
Not Hispanic (56)	82	0.86
Hispanic (1)	7	0.07
American Indian/Alaska Native (22)	57	0.60
Not Hispanic (20)	53	0.55
Hispanic (2)	4	0.04
Cherokee (7)	9	0.09
Chickasaw (1)	1	0.01
Choctaw (3)	3	0.03
Hopi (1)	1	0.01
Iroquois (0)	4	0.04
Navajo (5)	8	0.08
Pueblo (3)	11	0.12
Asian (87)	150	1.57
Not Hispanic (87)	147	1.54
Hispanic (0)	3	0.03
Cambodian (2)	2	0.02
Chinese, ex. Taiwanese (23)	34	0.36
Filipino (9)	24	0.25
Indian (17)	20	0.21
Indonesian (1)	5	0.05
Japanese (11)	40	0.42
Korean (19)	23	0.24
Nepalese (1)	4	0.04
Hawaii Native/Pacific Islander (13)	55	0.58
Not Hispanic (13)	53	0.55
Hispanic (0)	2	0.02
Guamanian/Chamorro (1)	1	0.01
Marshallese (2)	2	0.02
Native Hawaiian (2)	17	0.18
Samoan (6)	20	0.21
Tongan (0)	4	0.04
White (9,144)	9,307	97.40
Not Hispanic (8,995)	9,129	95.54
Hispanic (149)	178	1.86

American Fork

Place Type: City
County: Utah
Population: 26,263†

Ancestry‡	Population	%
African, Sub-Saharan (18)	18	0.07
South African (18)	18	0.07
American (1,840)	1,840	7.25
Arab (0)	10	0.04
Lebanese (0)	10	0.04
Austrian (9)	206	0.81
Basque (23)	41	0.16
Brazilian (9)	9	0.04
British (237)	409	1.61
Canadian (27)	149	0.59
Czech (10)	57	0.22
Czechoslovakian (0)	9	0.04
Danish (412)	1,842	7.26
Dutch (86)	376	1.48
English (4,317)	9,231	36.39
European (755)	900	3.55
Finnish (0)	93	0.37
French, ex. Basque (19)	625	2.46
French Canadian (15)	97	0.38
German (777)	3,044	12.00
Greek (32)	140	0.55
Hungarian (3)	25	0.10
Icelander (11)	11	0.04
Iranian (0)	22	0.09
Irish (196)	963	3.80
Italian (69)	324	1.28
Northern European (24)	24	0.09
Norwegian (149)	586	2.31
Polish (0)	33	0.13
Portuguese (27)	81	0.32
Russian (13)	13	0.05
Scandinavian (226)	458	1.81
Scotch-Irish (94)	285	1.12
Scottish (260)	1,206	4.75
Slovene (12)	12	0.05
Swedish (187)	935	3.69
Swiss (37)	414	1.63
Turkish (0)	5	0.02
Welsh (102)	526	2.07
Yugoslavian (12)	12	0.05

Hispanic Origin	Population	%
Hispanic or Latino (of any race)	1,941	7.39
Central American, ex. Mexican	117	0.45
Costa Rican	18	0.07
Guatemalan	48	0.18
Honduran	4	0.02
Nicaraguan	6	0.02
Panamanian	3	0.01
Salvadoran	37	0.14
Other Central American	1	<0.01
Cuban	10	0.04
Dominican Republic	4	0.02
Mexican	1,412	5.38
Puerto Rican	62	0.24
South American	181	0.69
Argentinean	53	0.20
Bolivian	14	0.05
Chilean	33	0.13
Colombian	10	0.04
Ecuadorian	29	0.11
Paraguayan	2	0.01
Peruvian	19	0.07
Uruguayan	10	0.04
Venezuelan	7	0.03
Other South American	4	0.02
Other Hispanic or Latino	155	0.59

Race*	Population	%
African-American/Black (95)	197	0.75
Not Hispanic (78)	153	0.58
Hispanic (17)	44	0.17
American Indian/Alaska Native (139)	260	0.99
Not Hispanic (106)	202	0.77
Hispanic (33)	58	0.22
Aleut *(Alaska Native)* (0)	7	0.03
Apache (2)	8	0.03
Arapaho (1)	1	<0.01
Blackfeet (1)	8	0.03
Cherokee (1)	28	0.11
Chickasaw (1)	1	<0.01
Choctaw (1)	1	<0.01
Colville (1)	1	<0.01
Creek (6)	6	0.02
Delaware (1)	1	<0.01
Hopi (0)	1	<0.01
Mexican American Ind. (4)	4	0.02
Navajo (35)	56	0.21
Paiute (1)	2	0.01
Potawatomi (1)	2	0.01
Pueblo (14)	14	0.05
Puget Sound Salish (5)	5	0.02
Seminole (1)	1	<0.01
Shoshone (2)	6	0.02
Sioux (5)	10	0.04
South American Ind. (3)	12	0.05
Ute (6)	11	0.04
Asian (225)	440	1.68
Not Hispanic (220)	390	1.48
Hispanic (5)	50	0.19
Cambodian (3)	3	0.01
Chinese, ex. Taiwanese (77)	160	0.61
Filipino (21)	62	0.24
Hmong (1)	4	0.02
Indian (20)	32	0.12
Indonesian (1)	3	0.01
Japanese (24)	91	0.35
Korean (14)	41	0.16
Laotian (5)	9	0.03
Malaysian (1)	2	0.01
Pakistani (1)	1	<0.01
Taiwanese (0)	4	0.02
Thai (1)	2	0.01
Vietnamese (42)	53	0.20
Hawaii Native/Pacific Islander (121)	325	1.24
Not Hispanic (119)	291	1.11
Hispanic (2)	34	0.13
Fijian (8)	8	0.03
Guamanian/Chamorro (0)	1	<0.01
Marshallese (7)	9	0.03
Native Hawaiian (16)	124	0.47
Samoan (40)	95	0.36
Tongan (40)	76	0.29
White (24,332)	24,893	94.78
Not Hispanic (23,333)	23,748	90.42
Hispanic (999)	1,145	4.36

Bluffdale

Place Type: City
County: Salt Lake
Population: 7,598†

Ancestry‡	Population	%
African, Sub-Saharan (16)	16	0.23
African (16)	16	0.23
American (481)	481	6.83
Arab (0)	9	0.13
Lebanese (0)	9	0.13
Brazilian (0)	31	0.44
British (73)	111	1.58
Czech (0)	74	1.05
Czechoslovakian (0)	24	0.34

*Notes: † The Census 2010 population figure is used to calculate the percentages in the Hispanic Origin and Race categories. Ancestry percentages are based on the 2006-2010 American Community Survey population (not shown); ‡ Numbers in parentheses indicate the number of people reporting a single ancestry; * Numbers in parentheses indicate the number of persons reporting this race alone, not in combination with any other race; Please refer to the Explanation of Data for more information.*

Danish (139)	646	9.17
Dutch (34)	213	3.02
English (788)	2,302	32.68
European (326)	335	4.76
Finnish (0)	33	0.47
French, ex. Basque (70)	133	1.89
French Canadian (49)	49	0.70
German (257)	1,003	14.24
Greek (22)	43	0.61
Hungarian (0)	10	0.14
Irish (41)	272	3.86
Italian (19)	242	3.44
Norwegian (106)	216	3.07
Polish (17)	88	1.25
Romanian (0)	10	0.14
Scandinavian (49)	104	1.48
Scotch-Irish (19)	113	1.60
Scottish (28)	328	4.66
Swedish (101)	283	4.02
Swiss (0)	94	1.33
Welsh (9)	206	2.92
Yugoslavian (14)	54	0.77

Hispanic Origin	Population	%
Hispanic or Latino (of any race)	334	4.40
Central American, ex. Mexican	13	0.17
Costa Rican	1	0.01
Guatemalan	1	0.01
Panamanian	6	0.08
Salvadoran	5	0.07
Cuban	8	0.11
Dominican Republic	2	0.03
Mexican	210	2.76
Puerto Rican	11	0.14
South American	33	0.43
Argentinean	2	0.03
Bolivian	1	0.01
Chilean	3	0.04
Colombian	7	0.09
Ecuadorian	3	0.04
Peruvian	12	0.16
Uruguayan	1	0.01
Venezuelan	4	0.05
Other Hispanic or Latino	57	0.75

Race*	Population	%
African-American/Black (32)	60	0.79
Not Hispanic (32)	56	0.74
Hispanic (0)	4	0.05
American Indian/Alaska Native (19)	41	0.54
Not Hispanic (19)	34	0.45
Hispanic (0)	7	0.09
Apache (0)	1	0.01
Blackfeet (1)	1	0.01
Canadian/French Am. Ind. (1)	3	0.04
Cherokee (0)	4	0.05
Choctaw (3)	3	0.04
Navajo (9)	11	0.14
Asian (27)	63	0.83
Not Hispanic (27)	62	0.82
Hispanic (0)	1	0.01
Chinese, ex. Taiwanese (10)	13	0.17
Filipino (6)	19	0.25
Indian (1)	1	0.01
Japanese (8)	13	0.17
Korean (0)	5	0.07
Laotian (0)	1	0.01
Thai (0)	8	0.11
Vietnamese (1)	2	0.03
Hawaii Native/Pacific Islander (22)	56	0.74
Not Hispanic (20)	45	0.59
Hispanic (2)	11	0.14
Guamanian/Chamorro (0)	1	0.01
Marshallese (1)	1	0.01
Native Hawaiian (0)	9	0.12
Samoan (7)	23	0.30
Tongan (6)	32	0.42
White (7,278)	7,404	97.45
Not Hispanic (7,056)	7,149	94.09
Hispanic (222)	255	3.36

Bountiful

Place Type: City
County: Davis
Population: 42,552†

Ancestry‡	Population	%
African, Sub-Saharan (11)	11	0.03
Nigerian (11)	11	0.03
American (2,320)	2,320	5.48
Arab (0)	10	0.02
Lebanese (0)	10	0.02
Armenian (11)	72	0.17
Australian (0)	9	0.02
Austrian (81)	154	0.36
Basque (7)	7	0.02
Belgian (85)	96	0.23
Brazilian (15)	96	0.23
British (555)	931	2.20
Canadian (197)	347	0.82
Celtic (9)	9	0.02
Croatian (10)	40	0.09
Czech (13)	62	0.15
Czechoslovakian (0)	21	0.05
Danish (750)	3,631	8.57
Dutch (295)	1,172	2.77
Eastern European (18)	18	0.04
English (7,017)	16,637	39.27
Estonian (9)	9	0.02
European (1,358)	1,451	3.43
Finnish (13)	79	0.19
French, ex. Basque (107)	786	1.86
French Canadian (11)	34	0.08
German (1,612)	6,178	14.58
Greek (89)	185	0.44
Hungarian (22)	28	0.07
Icelander (9)	29	0.07
Irish (388)	2,560	6.04
Italian (218)	1,179	2.78
Lithuanian (0)	21	0.05
Luxemburger (0)	18	0.04
Northern European (153)	153	0.36
Norwegian (309)	1,299	3.07
Polish (157)	494	1.17
Portuguese (42)	62	0.15
Romanian (0)	30	0.07
Russian (26)	147	0.35
Scandinavian (568)	1,031	2.43
Scotch-Irish (116)	574	1.35
Scottish (566)	2,410	5.69
Swedish (500)	2,084	4.92
Swiss (168)	773	1.82
Ukrainian (105)	176	0.42
Welsh (399)	1,258	2.97
Yugoslavian (0)	101	0.24

Hispanic Origin	Population	%
Hispanic or Latino (of any race)	2,068	4.86
Central American, ex. Mexican	171	0.40
Costa Rican	5	0.01
Guatemalan	66	0.16
Honduran	17	0.04
Nicaraguan	21	0.05
Panamanian	7	0.02
Salvadoran	54	0.13
Other Central American	1	<0.01
Cuban	20	0.05
Dominican Republic	17	0.04
Mexican	1,127	2.65
Puerto Rican	69	0.16
South American	359	0.84
Argentinean	55	0.13
Bolivian	12	0.03
Chilean	52	0.12
Colombian	37	0.09
Ecuadorian	41	0.10
Paraguayan	7	0.02
Peruvian	127	0.30
Uruguayan	1	<0.01
Venezuelan	26	0.06
Other South American	1	<0.01
Other Hispanic or Latino	305	0.72

Race*	Population	%
African-American/Black (232)	380	0.89
Not Hispanic (213)	339	0.80
Hispanic (19)	41	0.10
American Indian/Alaska Native (155)	285	0.67
Not Hispanic (122)	230	0.54
Hispanic (33)	55	0.13
Apache (4)	8	0.02
Arapaho (2)	2	<0.01
Blackfeet (1)	5	0.01
Canadian/French Am. Ind. (0)	1	<0.01
Central American Ind. (1)	1	<0.01
Cherokee (6)	35	0.08
Cheyenne (1)	1	<0.01
Chickasaw (1)	2	<0.01
Chippewa (0)	3	0.01
Choctaw (1)	2	<0.01
Colville (3)	3	0.01
Cree (2)	2	<0.01
Creek (1)	1	<0.01
Delaware (0)	4	0.01
Hopi (2)	3	0.01
Iroquois (0)	7	0.02
Kiowa (0)	1	<0.01
Mexican American Ind. (1)	2	<0.01
Navajo (68)	83	0.20
Osage (0)	4	0.01
Paiute (1)	1	<0.01
Pueblo (0)	7	0.02
Puget Sound Salish (0)	3	0.01
Seminole (0)	1	<0.01
Shoshone (5)	7	0.02
Sioux (5)	9	0.02
South American Ind. (0)	4	0.01
Spanish American Ind. (4)	4	0.01
Ute (2)	5	0.01
Asian (594)	875	2.06
Not Hispanic (588)	841	1.98
Hispanic (6)	34	0.08
Burmese (10)	10	0.02
Cambodian (3)	6	0.01
Chinese, ex. Taiwanese (150)	215	0.51
Filipino (46)	92	0.22
Indian (43)	70	0.16
Indonesian (2)	5	0.01
Japanese (134)	212	0.50
Korean (83)	124	0.29
Laotian (6)	6	0.01
Malaysian (2)	2	<0.01
Pakistani (1)	1	<0.01
Taiwanese (11)	11	0.03
Thai (33)	58	0.14
Vietnamese (47)	63	0.15
Hawaii Native/Pacific Islander (388)	548	1.29
Not Hispanic (380)	531	1.25
Hispanic (8)	17	0.04
Fijian (3)	9	0.02
Guamanian/Chamorro (1)	7	0.02
Marshallese (20)	20	0.05
Native Hawaiian (17)	74	0.17
Samoan (120)	206	0.48
Tongan (154)	211	0.50
White (39,629)	40,369	94.87
Not Hispanic (38,548)	39,090	91.86
Hispanic (1,081)	1,279	3.01

Brigham City

Place Type: City
County: Box Elder
Population: 17,899†

Ancestry‡	Population	%
African, Sub-Saharan (0)	33	0.19
South African (0)	15	0.09
Sudanese (0)	18	0.10
Albanian (10)	122	0.69

*Notes: † The Census 2010 population figure is used to calculate the percentages in the Hispanic Origin and Race categories. Ancestry percentages are based on the 2006-2010 American Community Survey population (not shown); ‡ Numbers in parentheses indicate the number of people reporting a single ancestry; * Numbers in parentheses indicate the number of persons reporting this race alone, not in combination with any other race; Please refer to the Explanation of Data for more information.*

Ancestry	Population	%
American (1,716)	1,716	9.73
Arab (0)	17	0.10
Egyptian (0)	17	0.10
Australian (0)	15	0.09
Brazilian (26)	138	0.78
British (259)	366	2.07
Canadian (29)	128	0.73
Celtic (13)	13	0.07
Danish (472)	1,901	10.78
Dutch (274)	553	3.14
English (1,722)	4,974	28.20
European (422)	525	2.98
Finnish (0)	41	0.23
French, ex. Basque (55)	588	3.33
French Canadian (76)	114	0.65
German (752)	2,259	12.81
Greek (12)	36	0.20
Hungarian (0)	37	0.21
Icelander (0)	85	0.48
Irish (203)	884	5.01
Italian (93)	318	1.80
Norwegian (107)	389	2.21
Polish (31)	104	0.59
Russian (0)	40	0.23
Scandinavian (87)	285	1.62
Scotch-Irish (71)	219	1.24
Scottish (172)	795	4.51
Swedish (158)	713	4.04
Swiss (53)	186	1.05
Ukrainian (26)	26	0.15
Welsh (36)	412	2.34

Hispanic Origin	Population	%
Hispanic or Latino (of any race)	1,928	10.77
Central American, ex. Mexican	51	0.28
Costa Rican	1	0.01
Guatemalan	15	0.08
Honduran	10	0.06
Nicaraguan	1	0.01
Panamanian	5	0.03
Salvadoran	19	0.11
Cuban	16	0.09
Dominican Republic	13	0.07
Mexican	1,537	8.59
Puerto Rican	16	0.09
South American	75	0.42
Argentinean	9	0.05
Chilean	29	0.16
Colombian	16	0.09
Peruvian	15	0.08
Uruguayan	3	0.02
Venezuelan	3	0.02
Other Hispanic or Latino	220	1.23

Race*	Population	%
African-American/Black (81)	154	0.86
Not Hispanic (63)	116	0.65
Hispanic (18)	38	0.21
American Indian/Alaska Native (261)	483	2.70
Not Hispanic (213)	377	2.11
Hispanic (48)	106	0.59
Apache (0)	9	0.05
Blackfeet (0)	4	0.02
Canadian/French Am. Ind. (0)	1	0.01
Cherokee (7)	40	0.22
Cheyenne (4)	4	0.02
Chippewa (3)	11	0.06
Choctaw (1)	9	0.05
Comanche (0)	1	0.01
Cree (5)	6	0.03
Creek (1)	2	0.01
Crow (3)	6	0.03
Delaware (1)	1	0.01
Hopi (10)	20	0.11
Inupiat *(Alaska Native)* (1)	1	0.01
Iroquois (1)	1	0.01
Lumbee (1)	1	0.01
Menominee (1)	1	0.01
Mexican American Ind. (2)	5	0.03
Navajo (88)	149	0.83
Osage (0)	1	0.01
Paiute (1)	9	0.05
Pueblo (3)	11	0.06
Puget Sound Salish (0)	3	0.02
Shoshone (23)	39	0.22
Sioux (16)	22	0.12
Spanish American Ind. (4)	4	0.02
Ute (9)	11	0.06
Yaqui (5)	5	0.03
Yuman (1)	1	0.01
Asian (111)	219	1.22
Not Hispanic (107)	193	1.08
Hispanic (4)	26	0.15
Chinese, ex. Taiwanese (16)	23	0.13
Filipino (37)	66	0.37
Indian (7)	12	0.07
Japanese (29)	76	0.42
Korean (13)	22	0.12
Laotian (1)	5	0.03
Vietnamese (6)	7	0.04
Hawaii Native/Pacific Islander (27)	49	0.27
Not Hispanic (24)	46	0.26
Hispanic (3)	3	0.02
Guamanian/Chamorro (1)	1	0.01
Marshallese (3)	3	0.02
Native Hawaiian (9)	18	0.10
Samoan (1)	2	0.01
Tongan (1)	8	0.04
White (15,980)	16,480	92.07
Not Hispanic (15,242)	15,538	86.81
Hispanic (738)	942	5.26

Cedar City

Place Type: City
County: Iron
Population: 28,857†

Ancestry‡	Population	%
American (1,197)	1,197	4.32
Arab (0)	18	0.06
Arab (0)	3	0.01
Lebanese (0)	15	0.05
Australian (23)	56	0.20
Austrian (32)	49	0.18
Basque (6)	9	0.03
Belgian (0)	63	0.23
Brazilian (21)	21	0.08
British (230)	263	0.95
Canadian (9)	47	0.17
Celtic (0)	3	0.01
Czech (0)	52	0.19
Czechoslovakian (0)	24	0.09
Danish (295)	1,485	5.36
Dutch (301)	823	2.97
Eastern European (0)	25	0.09
English (3,593)	8,751	31.57
European (799)	840	3.03
Finnish (0)	27	0.10
French, ex. Basque (123)	648	2.34
French Canadian (67)	99	0.36
German (1,294)	3,500	12.63
Greek (0)	155	0.56
Hungarian (20)	20	0.07
Iranian (0)	17	0.06
Irish (706)	2,038	7.35
Italian (254)	659	2.38
Lithuanian (14)	14	0.05
Luxemburger (0)	10	0.04
Northern European (38)	57	0.21
Norwegian (184)	794	2.86
Polish (141)	290	1.05
Portuguese (0)	29	0.10
Russian (37)	107	0.39
Scandinavian (92)	169	0.61
Scotch-Irish (176)	472	1.70
Scottish (854)	2,090	7.54
Slovene (20)	20	0.07
Swedish (520)	1,051	3.79
Swiss (124)	453	1.63
Ukrainian (0)	31	0.11
Welsh (175)	846	3.05
West Indian, ex. Hispanic (43)	49	0.18
Bahamian (26)	26	0.09
Belizean (0)	6	0.02
West Indian (17)	17	0.06

Hispanic Origin	Population	%
Hispanic or Latino (of any race)	2,283	7.91
Central American, ex. Mexican	87	0.30
Costa Rican	1	<0.01
Guatemalan	29	0.10
Honduran	8	0.03
Nicaraguan	6	0.02
Panamanian	2	0.01
Salvadoran	41	0.14
Cuban	31	0.11
Dominican Republic	7	0.02
Mexican	1,772	6.14
Puerto Rican	61	0.21
South American	75	0.26
Argentinean	10	0.03
Bolivian	4	0.01
Chilean	12	0.04
Colombian	20	0.07
Ecuadorian	5	0.02
Peruvian	19	0.07
Uruguayan	1	<0.01
Venezuelan	4	0.01
Other Hispanic or Latino	250	0.87

Race*	Population	%
African-American/Black (195)	324	1.12
Not Hispanic (178)	294	1.02
Hispanic (17)	30	0.10
American Indian/Alaska Native (766)	1,005	3.48
Not Hispanic (689)	877	3.04
Hispanic (77)	128	0.44
Aleut *(Alaska Native)* (1)	1	<0.01
Apache (4)	8	0.03
Blackfeet (0)	5	0.02
Canadian/French Am. Ind. (0)	4	0.01
Central American Ind. (1)	1	<0.01
Cherokee (3)	45	0.16
Chickasaw (0)	3	0.01
Chippewa (4)	5	0.02
Choctaw (7)	11	0.04
Comanche (2)	3	0.01
Cree (0)	4	0.01
Creek (2)	5	0.02
Delaware (0)	1	<0.01
Hopi (4)	6	0.02
Inupiat *(Alaska Native)* (4)	4	0.01
Lumbee (4)	4	0.01
Mexican American Ind. (9)	17	0.06
Navajo (274)	310	1.07
Paiute (211)	247	0.86
Pima (2)	2	0.01
Potawatomi (1)	1	<0.01
Pueblo (1)	1	<0.01
Seminole (0)	1	<0.01
Shoshone (5)	8	0.03
Sioux (9)	13	0.05
Tlingit-Haida *(Alaska Native)* (2)	2	0.01
Tohono O'Odham (1)	1	<0.01
Ute (8)	22	0.08
Yaqui (1)	1	<0.01
Yuman (2)	2	0.01
Yup'ik *(Alaska Native)* (2)	3	0.01
Asian (268)	471	1.63
Not Hispanic (258)	441	1.53
Hispanic (10)	30	0.10
Cambodian (6)	15	0.05
Chinese, ex. Taiwanese (49)	84	0.29
Filipino (27)	72	0.25
Hmong (4)	4	0.01
Indian (25)	37	0.13
Indonesian (1)	3	0.01
Japanese (52)	147	0.51
Korean (64)	77	0.27

*Notes: † The Census 2010 population figure is used to calculate the percentages in the Hispanic Origin and Race categories. Ancestry percentages are based on the 2006-2010 American Community Survey population (not shown); ‡ Numbers in parentheses indicate the number of people reporting a single ancestry; * Numbers in parentheses indicate the number of persons reporting this race alone, not in combination with any other race; Please refer to the Explanation of Data for more information.*

Laotian (3)	5	0.02
Malaysian (3)	3	0.01
Pakistani (1)	1	<0.01
Taiwanese (2)	2	0.01
Thai (7)	10	0.03
Vietnamese (13)	13	0.05
Hawaii Native/Pacific Islander (92)	221	0.77
Not Hispanic (91)	211	0.73
Hispanic (1)	10	0.03
Fijian (2)	2	0.01
Guamanian/Chamorro (6)	14	0.05
Native Hawaiian (27)	83	0.29
Samoan (21)	45	0.16
Tongan (23)	59	0.20
White (25,791)	26,514	91.88
Not Hispanic (24,794)	25,299	87.67
Hispanic (997)	1,215	4.21

Cedar Hills

Place Type: City
County: Utah
Population: 9,796†

Ancestry‡	Population	%
African, Sub-Saharan (7)	7	0.08
South African (7)	7	0.08
American (586)	586	6.84
Arab (5)	5	0.06
Lebanese (5)	5	0.06
Belgian (0)	4	0.05
British (175)	292	3.41
Canadian (0)	9	0.11
Croatian (20)	42	0.49
Czech (16)	16	0.19
Danish (62)	352	4.11
Dutch (27)	154	1.80
English (1,347)	2,762	32.24
European (687)	709	8.28
Finnish (40)	51	0.60
French, ex. Basque (26)	103	1.20
German (284)	1,067	12.45
Greek (0)	99	1.16
Irish (101)	703	8.21
Italian (23)	141	1.65
Northern European (16)	16	0.19
Norwegian (99)	253	2.95
Polish (19)	39	0.46
Portuguese (8)	37	0.43
Romanian (7)	7	0.08
Russian (16)	16	0.19
Scandinavian (57)	176	2.05
Scotch-Irish (41)	187	2.18
Scottish (78)	314	3.67
Swedish (41)	270	3.15
Swiss (15)	159	1.86
Welsh (45)	117	1.37

Hispanic Origin	Population	%
Hispanic or Latino (of any race)	411	4.20
Central American, ex. Mexican	27	0.28
Costa Rican	2	0.02
Guatemalan	16	0.16
Honduran	3	0.03
Panamanian	1	0.01
Salvadoran	4	0.04
Other Central American	1	0.01
Cuban	6	0.06
Dominican Republic	5	0.05
Mexican	226	2.31
Puerto Rican	14	0.14
South American	79	0.81
Argentinean	13	0.13
Bolivian	7	0.07
Chilean	11	0.11
Colombian	1	0.01
Ecuadorian	17	0.17
Peruvian	25	0.26
Venezuelan	5	0.05
Other Hispanic or Latino	54	0.55

Race*	Population	%
African-American/Black (41)	62	0.63
Not Hispanic (40)	58	0.59
Hispanic (1)	4	0.04
American Indian/Alaska Native (29)	64	0.65
Not Hispanic (28)	56	0.57
Hispanic (1)	8	0.08
Blackfeet (0)	1	0.01
Cherokee (4)	5	0.05
Choctaw (0)	10	0.10
Iroquois (1)	4	0.04
Mexican American Ind. (0)	2	0.02
Navajo (8)	17	0.17
Tlingit-Haida *(Alaska Native)* (1)	1	0.01
Yakama (0)	4	0.04
Asian (95)	199	2.03
Not Hispanic (95)	187	1.91
Hispanic (0)	12	0.12
Bangladeshi (0)	1	0.01
Chinese, ex. Taiwanese (39)	68	0.69
Filipino (1)	25	0.26
Indian (9)	12	0.12
Japanese (11)	59	0.60
Korean (13)	20	0.20
Laotian (7)	12	0.12
Pakistani (5)	5	0.05
Thai (2)	5	0.05
Vietnamese (5)	16	0.16
Hawaii Native/Pacific Islander (58)	98	1.00
Not Hispanic (53)	83	0.85
Hispanic (5)	15	0.15
Marshallese (2)	2	0.02
Native Hawaiian (21)	55	0.56
Samoan (27)	42	0.43
Tongan (3)	3	0.03
White (9,325)	9,481	96.78
Not Hispanic (9,023)	9,149	93.40
Hispanic (302)	332	3.39

Centerville

Place Type: City
County: Davis
Population: 15,335†

Ancestry‡	Population	%
African, Sub-Saharan (0)	8	0.05
African (0)	8	0.05
Albanian (10)	10	0.07
American (737)	737	4.84
Arab (9)	18	0.12
Syrian (9)	18	0.12
Armenian (0)	22	0.14
Austrian (10)	46	0.30
Basque (23)	23	0.15
Brazilian (0)	28	0.18
British (135)	371	2.44
Canadian (10)	47	0.31
Croatian (30)	50	0.33
Czech (0)	17	0.11
Danish (232)	1,342	8.82
Dutch (213)	673	4.42
English (2,796)	5,663	37.22
European (733)	783	5.15
Finnish (0)	15	0.10
French, ex. Basque (28)	171	1.12
French Canadian (0)	19	0.12
German (425)	1,820	11.96
Greek (0)	33	0.22
Hungarian (14)	107	0.70
Icelander (0)	24	0.16
Irish (115)	691	4.54
Italian (178)	498	3.27
Lithuanian (0)	14	0.09
Luxemburger (10)	10	0.07
Northern European (72)	89	0.58
Norwegian (71)	286	1.88
Polish (33)	144	0.95
Portuguese (0)	13	0.09
Romanian (11)	11	0.07
Russian (0)	28	0.18
Scandinavian (190)	328	2.16
Scotch-Irish (63)	230	1.51
Scottish (105)	643	4.23
Slovene (0)	12	0.08
Swedish (324)	1,114	7.32
Swiss (62)	506	3.33
Ukrainian (0)	8	0.05
Welsh (47)	626	4.11
Yugoslavian (0)	23	0.15

Hispanic Origin	Population	%
Hispanic or Latino (of any race)	573	3.74
Central American, ex. Mexican	33	0.22
Costa Rican	2	0.01
Guatemalan	15	0.10
Honduran	2	0.01
Nicaraguan	1	0.01
Panamanian	1	0.01
Salvadoran	12	0.08
Cuban	9	0.06
Dominican Republic	1	0.01
Mexican	300	1.96
Puerto Rican	22	0.14
South American	126	0.82
Argentinean	21	0.14
Chilean	17	0.11
Colombian	15	0.10
Ecuadorian	15	0.10
Paraguayan	3	0.02
Peruvian	46	0.30
Uruguayan	1	0.01
Venezuelan	8	0.05
Other Hispanic or Latino	82	0.53

Race*	Population	%
African-American/Black (59)	116	0.76
Not Hispanic (57)	109	0.71
Hispanic (2)	7	0.05
American Indian/Alaska Native (41)	80	0.52
Not Hispanic (34)	61	0.40
Hispanic (7)	19	0.12
Apache (0)	1	0.01
Blackfeet (1)	2	0.01
Cherokee (0)	3	0.02
Chippewa (1)	1	0.01
Choctaw (1)	1	0.01
Creek (1)	1	0.01
Crow (0)	2	0.01
Navajo (20)	24	0.16
Osage (3)	4	0.03
Paiute (1)	1	0.01
Potawatomi (2)	3	0.02
Pueblo (1)	2	0.01
Sioux (1)	6	0.04
Yaqui (0)	1	0.01
Asian (182)	308	2.01
Not Hispanic (178)	293	1.91
Hispanic (4)	15	0.10
Burmese (4)	4	0.03
Cambodian (0)	1	0.01
Chinese, ex. Taiwanese (29)	50	0.33
Filipino (12)	29	0.19
Indian (4)	10	0.07
Indonesian (2)	2	0.01
Japanese (64)	118	0.77
Korean (27)	56	0.37
Laotian (6)	12	0.08
Nepalese (1)	2	0.01
Taiwanese (3)	3	0.02
Thai (6)	19	0.12
Vietnamese (11)	18	0.12
Hawaii Native/Pacific Islander (28)	71	0.46
Not Hispanic (28)	70	0.46
Hispanic (0)	1	0.01
Fijian (1)	3	0.02
Guamanian/Chamorro (4)	4	0.03
Marshallese (2)	2	0.01
Native Hawaiian (5)	17	0.11

SECTION TWO

*Notes: † The Census 2010 population figure is used to calculate the percentages in the Hispanic Origin and Race categories. Ancestry percentages are based on the 2006-2010 American Community Survey population (not shown); ‡ Numbers in parentheses indicate the number of people reporting a single ancestry; * Numbers in parentheses indicate the number of persons reporting this race alone, not in combination with any other race; Please refer to the Explanation of Data for more information.*

Samoan (8)	21	0.14
Tongan (7)	9	0.06
White (14,583)	14,853	96.86
Not Hispanic (14,244)	14,448	94.22
Hispanic (339)	405	2.64

Clearfield

Place Type: City
County: Davis
Population: 30,112†

Ancestry‡	Population	%
African, Sub-Saharan (144)	209	0.71
African (100)	165	0.56
Somalian (44)	44	0.15
American (1,994)	1,994	6.76
Arab (7)	7	0.02
Syrian (7)	7	0.02
Australian (33)	33	0.11
Austrian (0)	28	0.09
Basque (11)	11	0.04
Belgian (0)	18	0.06
Brazilian (0)	7	0.02
British (200)	388	1.31
Cajun (41)	41	0.14
Canadian (63)	211	0.72
Czech (20)	49	0.17
Danish (110)	775	2.63
Dutch (267)	664	2.25
English (2,699)	6,741	22.84
European (698)	770	2.61
Finnish (23)	45	0.15
French, ex. Basque (89)	554	1.88
French Canadian (77)	103	0.35
German (1,261)	3,542	12.00
Greek (9)	132	0.45
Irish (487)	2,365	8.01
Israeli (39)	39	0.13
Italian (170)	923	3.13
Lithuanian (0)	11	0.04
Northern European (28)	60	0.20
Norwegian (245)	658	2.23
Pennsylvania German (0)	8	0.03
Polish (102)	333	1.13
Portuguese (17)	54	0.18
Russian (13)	36	0.12
Scandinavian (69)	94	0.32
Scotch-Irish (77)	275	0.93
Scottish (163)	1,032	3.50
Slovak (0)	27	0.09
Slovene (38)	38	0.13
Swedish (187)	797	2.70
Swiss (33)	172	0.58
Ukrainian (16)	16	0.05
Welsh (51)	549	1.86
West Indian, ex. Hispanic (12)	78	0.26
Bahamian (0)	33	0.11
Jamaican (0)	33	0.11
Trinidadian/Tobagonian (12)	12	0.04

Hispanic Origin	Population	%
Hispanic or Latino (of any race)	4,854	16.12
Central American, ex. Mexican	255	0.85
Costa Rican	6	0.02
Guatemalan	90	0.30
Honduran	39	0.13
Nicaraguan	14	0.05
Panamanian	18	0.06
Salvadoran	85	0.28
Other Central American	3	0.01
Cuban	31	0.10
Dominican Republic	22	0.07
Mexican	2,989	9.93
Puerto Rican	195	0.65
South American	307	1.02
Argentinean	71	0.24
Bolivian	5	0.02
Chilean	57	0.19
Colombian	21	0.07
Ecuadorian	24	0.08
Paraguayan	2	0.01
Peruvian	89	0.30
Uruguayan	28	0.09
Venezuelan	10	0.03
Other Hispanic or Latino	1,055	3.50

Race*	Population	%
African-American/Black (943)	1,309	4.35
Not Hispanic (887)	1,186	3.94
Hispanic (56)	123	0.41
American Indian/Alaska Native (231)	505	1.68
Not Hispanic (177)	392	1.30
Hispanic (54)	113	0.38
Aleut *(Alaska Native)* (0)	1	<0.01
Apache (3)	9	0.03
Blackfeet (1)	13	0.04
Cherokee (15)	65	0.22
Chickasaw (0)	3	0.01
Chippewa (3)	13	0.04
Choctaw (0)	5	0.02
Colville (1)	1	<0.01
Comanche (1)	4	0.01
Delaware (0)	1	<0.01
Hopi (1)	1	<0.01
Inupiat *(Alaska Native)* (1)	1	<0.01
Iroquois (1)	5	0.02
Kiowa (1)	1	<0.01
Mexican American Ind. (12)	26	0.09
Navajo (48)	81	0.27
Paiute (0)	1	<0.01
Pima (2)	2	0.01
Potawatomi (1)	2	0.01
Pueblo (2)	7	0.02
Puget Sound Salish (1)	8	0.03
Seminole (0)	1	<0.01
Shoshone (4)	12	0.04
Sioux (11)	37	0.12
South American Ind. (0)	1	<0.01
Spanish American Ind. (1)	1	<0.01
Tlingit-Haida *(Alaska Native)* (1)	3	0.01
Ute (3)	5	0.02
Yaqui (1)	3	0.01
Asian (775)	1,244	4.13
Not Hispanic (746)	1,146	3.81
Hispanic (29)	98	0.33
Cambodian (3)	3	0.01
Chinese, ex. Taiwanese (35)	74	0.25
Filipino (289)	502	1.67
Hmong (9)	14	0.05
Indian (39)	57	0.19
Indonesian (1)	1	<0.01
Japanese (99)	193	0.64
Korean (58)	102	0.34
Laotian (38)	53	0.18
Malaysian (0)	1	<0.01
Pakistani (5)	8	0.03
Sri Lankan (1)	1	<0.01
Taiwanese (3)	4	0.01
Thai (59)	132	0.44
Vietnamese (39)	54	0.18
Hawaii Native/Pacific Islander (209)	355	1.18
Not Hispanic (199)	318	1.06
Hispanic (10)	37	0.12
Guamanian/Chamorro (50)	70	0.23
Native Hawaiian (84)	151	0.50
Samoan (19)	56	0.19
Tongan (17)	31	0.10
White (24,559)	25,714	85.39
Not Hispanic (22,286)	23,094	76.69
Hispanic (2,273)	2,620	8.70

Clinton

Place Type: City
County: Davis
Population: 20,426†

Ancestry‡	Population	%
American (1,810)	1,810	9.51
Arab (53)	64	0.34
Jordanian (53)	53	0.28
Palestinian (0)	11	0.06
Australian (9)	21	0.11
Austrian (21)	29	0.15
Belgian (0)	10	0.05
British (46)	173	0.91
Cajun (6)	6	0.03
Canadian (17)	34	0.18
Czechoslovakian (50)	59	0.31
Danish (180)	723	3.80
Dutch (146)	497	2.61
English (2,301)	4,831	25.38
European (593)	714	3.75
Finnish (10)	10	0.05
French, ex. Basque (17)	515	2.71
French Canadian (18)	68	0.36
German (731)	2,681	14.09
Greek (34)	34	0.18
Hungarian (9)	143	0.75
Irish (156)	1,144	6.01
Italian (68)	375	1.97
Lithuanian (0)	93	0.49
Northern European (11)	11	0.06
Norwegian (44)	269	1.41
Polish (102)	166	0.87
Portuguese (75)	108	0.57
Romanian (0)	9	0.05
Russian (17)	40	0.21
Scandinavian (40)	91	0.48
Scotch-Irish (104)	331	1.74
Scottish (170)	956	5.02
Slavic (11)	21	0.11
Swedish (129)	512	2.69
Swiss (65)	270	1.42
Turkish (10)	10	0.05
Welsh (108)	249	1.31

Hispanic Origin	Population	%
Hispanic or Latino (of any race)	2,306	11.29
Central American, ex. Mexican	106	0.52
Costa Rican	6	0.03
Guatemalan	63	0.31
Honduran	1	<0.01
Nicaraguan	2	0.01
Panamanian	11	0.05
Salvadoran	20	0.10
Other Central American	3	0.01
Cuban	3	0.01
Dominican Republic	7	0.03
Mexican	1,636	8.01
Puerto Rican	80	0.39
South American	117	0.57
Argentinean	33	0.16
Bolivian	2	0.01
Chilean	21	0.10
Colombian	9	0.04
Ecuadorian	11	0.05
Peruvian	24	0.12
Uruguayan	6	0.03
Venezuelan	11	0.05
Other Hispanic or Latino	357	1.75

Race*	Population	%
African-American/Black (274)	411	2.01
Not Hispanic (245)	358	1.75
Hispanic (29)	53	0.26
American Indian/Alaska Native (95)	230	1.13
Not Hispanic (70)	174	0.85
Hispanic (25)	56	0.27
Alaska Athabascan *(Ala. Nat.)* (1)	1	<0.01
Apache (1)	2	0.01
Blackfeet (1)	6	0.03
Canadian/French Am. Ind. (1)	1	<0.01
Cherokee (9)	42	0.21
Cheyenne (0)	1	<0.01
Chippewa (3)	3	0.01
Choctaw (0)	7	0.03
Comanche (1)	1	<0.01
Creek (4)	4	0.02

*Notes: † The Census 2010 population figure is used to calculate the percentages in the Hispanic Origin and Race categories. Ancestry percentages are based on the 2006-2010 American Community Survey population (not shown); ‡ Numbers in parentheses indicate the number of people reporting a single ancestry; * Numbers in parentheses indicate the number of persons reporting this race alone, not in combination with any other race; Please refer to the Explanation of Data for more information.*

Delaware (0)	1	<0.01
Hopi (4)	4	0.02
Inupiat *(Alaska Native)* (0)	1	<0.01
Mexican American Ind. (6)	7	0.03
Navajo (22)	39	0.19
Paiute (1)	7	0.03
Potawatomi (1)	1	<0.01
Pueblo (0)	3	0.01
Puget Sound Salish (2)	2	0.01
Seminole (0)	1	<0.01
Shoshone (1)	4	0.02
Sioux (2)	9	0.04
South American Ind. (5)	5	0.02
Tlingit-Haida *(Alaska Native)* (0)	4	0.02
Ute (1)	5	0.02
Asian (470)	759	3.72
Not Hispanic (449)	698	3.42
Hispanic (21)	61	0.30
Cambodian (4)	5	0.02
Chinese, ex. Taiwanese (28)	47	0.23
Filipino (172)	276	1.35
Hmong (23)	23	0.11
Indian (2)	6	0.03
Indonesian (0)	2	0.01
Japanese (41)	109	0.53
Korean (45)	93	0.46
Laotian (17)	37	0.18
Pakistani (1)	1	<0.01
Taiwanese (5)	5	0.02
Thai (41)	71	0.35
Vietnamese (68)	77	0.38
Hawaii Native/Pacific Islander (90)	163	0.80
Not Hispanic (89)	159	0.78
Hispanic (1)	4	0.02
Guamanian/Chamorro (21)	30	0.15
Native Hawaiian (10)	50	0.24
Samoan (15)	37	0.18
Tongan (14)	15	0.07
White (18,028)	18,662	91.36
Not Hispanic (16,760)	17,220	84.30
Hispanic (1,268)	1,442	7.06

Cottonwood Heights

Place Type: City
County: Salt Lake
Population: 33,433[†]

Ancestry[‡]	Population	%
Afghan (17)	17	0.05
African, Sub-Saharan (26)	40	0.12
South African (0)	14	0.04
Ugandan (17)	17	0.05
Other Sub-Saharan African (9)	9	0.03
American (1,265)	1,265	3.77
Arab (63)	69	0.21
Arab (43)	43	0.13
Lebanese (12)	18	0.05
Palestinian (8)	8	0.02
Armenian (115)	179	0.53
Australian (0)	33	0.10
Austrian (12)	51	0.15
Basque (13)	13	0.04
Brazilian (15)	15	0.04
British (356)	731	2.18
Bulgarian (27)	40	0.12
Canadian (27)	132	0.39
Celtic (14)	21	0.06
Croatian (44)	90	0.27
Czech (28)	192	0.57
Czechoslovakian (24)	42	0.13
Danish (500)	1,868	5.57
Dutch (230)	779	2.32
Eastern European (12)	12	0.04
English (4,129)	10,398	31.00
European (645)	673	2.01
Finnish (101)	151	0.45
French, ex. Basque (61)	799	2.38
French Canadian (11)	84	0.25
German (1,365)	5,030	15.00
Greek (242)	363	1.08
Hungarian (53)	197	0.59
Icelander (0)	6	0.02
Iranian (143)	143	0.43
Irish (721)	2,847	8.49
Israeli (27)	27	0.08
Italian (551)	1,613	4.81
Lithuanian (25)	60	0.18
Northern European (86)	86	0.26
Norwegian (320)	1,623	4.84
Polish (129)	550	1.64
Portuguese (0)	38	0.11
Romanian (0)	14	0.04
Russian (91)	305	0.91
Scandinavian (409)	675	2.01
Scotch-Irish (139)	479	1.43
Scottish (457)	1,851	5.52
Slavic (0)	144	0.43
Slovak (23)	56	0.17
Swedish (199)	1,443	4.30
Swiss (86)	360	1.07
Ukrainian (0)	28	0.08
Welsh (345)	1,094	3.26
West Indian, ex. Hispanic (11)	11	0.03
Belizean (11)	11	0.03
Yugoslavian (169)	229	0.68

Hispanic Origin	Population	%
Hispanic or Latino (of any race)	1,719	5.14
Central American, ex. Mexican	99	0.30
Costa Rican	3	0.01
Guatemalan	46	0.14
Honduran	7	0.02
Nicaraguan	11	0.03
Panamanian	3	0.01
Salvadoran	21	0.06
Other Central American	8	0.02
Cuban	26	0.08
Dominican Republic	4	0.01
Mexican	919	2.75
Puerto Rican	61	0.18
South American	268	0.80
Argentinean	48	0.14
Bolivian	16	0.05
Chilean	33	0.10
Colombian	48	0.14
Ecuadorian	27	0.08
Paraguayan	1	<0.01
Peruvian	60	0.18
Uruguayan	13	0.04
Venezuelan	22	0.07
Other Hispanic or Latino	342	1.02

Race*	Population	%
African-American/Black (289)	467	1.40
Not Hispanic (267)	421	1.26
Hispanic (22)	46	0.14
American Indian/Alaska Native (131)	258	0.77
Not Hispanic (107)	201	0.60
Hispanic (24)	57	0.17
Alaska Athabascan *(Ala. Nat.)* (0)	3	0.01
Apache (0)	1	<0.01
Arapaho (0)	1	<0.01
Blackfeet (4)	6	0.02
Canadian/French Am. Ind. (1)	1	<0.01
Cherokee (8)	28	0.08
Chickasaw (4)	4	0.01
Chippewa (1)	5	0.01
Choctaw (3)	5	0.01
Comanche (2)	2	0.01
Creek (2)	2	0.01
Delaware (0)	1	<0.01
Hopi (0)	2	0.01
Iroquois (0)	3	0.01
Lumbee (5)	5	0.01
Menominee (0)	2	0.01
Mexican American Ind. (2)	3	0.01
Navajo (35)	44	0.13
Paiute (2)	6	0.02
Potawatomi (0)	1	<0.01
Pueblo (0)	1	<0.01
Seminole (1)	1	<0.01
Shoshone (1)	2	0.01
Sioux (2)	7	0.02
South American Ind. (4)	4	0.01
Ute (3)	6	0.02
Yaqui (0)	1	<0.01
Asian (1,085)	1,465	4.38
Not Hispanic (1,067)	1,401	4.19
Hispanic (18)	64	0.19
Burmese (1)	2	0.01
Cambodian (10)	11	0.03
Chinese, ex. Taiwanese (339)	406	1.21
Filipino (68)	140	0.42
Indian (149)	179	0.54
Indonesian (2)	17	0.05
Japanese (170)	299	0.89
Korean (162)	195	0.58
Laotian (7)	11	0.03
Nepalese (3)	3	0.01
Pakistani (23)	31	0.09
Sri Lankan (1)	1	<0.01
Taiwanese (39)	46	0.14
Thai (27)	31	0.09
Vietnamese (43)	62	0.19
Hawaii Native/Pacific Islander (108)	242	0.72
Not Hispanic (105)	220	0.66
Hispanic (3)	22	0.07
Guamanian/Chamorro (3)	15	0.04
Marshallese (3)	3	0.01
Native Hawaiian (20)	86	0.26
Samoan (24)	38	0.11
Tongan (34)	55	0.16
White (30,509)	31,275	93.55
Not Hispanic (29,476)	30,074	89.95
Hispanic (1,033)	1,201	3.59

Draper

Place Type: City
County: Salt Lake
Population: 42,274[†]

Ancestry[‡]	Population	%
African, Sub-Saharan (69)	117	0.30
African (26)	60	0.15
Cape Verdean (13)	13	0.03
South African (30)	44	0.11
American (2,015)	2,015	5.13
Arab (4)	4	0.01
Palestinian (4)	4	0.01
Armenian (6)	12	0.03
Austrian (0)	46	0.12
Basque (68)	68	0.17
Belgian (12)	20	0.05
Brazilian (74)	136	0.35
British (227)	506	1.29
Canadian (85)	119	0.30
Celtic (7)	7	0.02
Croatian (0)	14	0.04
Czech (14)	55	0.14
Czechoslovakian (0)	44	0.11
Danish (733)	2,854	7.27
Dutch (591)	1,184	3.02
English (4,171)	10,324	26.30
European (1,177)	1,462	3.72
Finnish (28)	55	0.14
French, ex. Basque (204)	1,032	2.63
French Canadian (24)	40	0.10
German (1,558)	5,164	13.16
Greek (115)	272	0.69
Hungarian (20)	71	0.18
Icelander (18)	18	0.05
Iranian (64)	75	0.19
Irish (741)	3,035	7.73
Italian (552)	1,438	3.66
Latvian (22)	22	0.06
Lithuanian (12)	21	0.05
Northern European (63)	63	0.16
Norwegian (451)	1,392	3.55

SECTION TWO

*Notes: † The Census 2010 population figure is used to calculate the percentages in the Hispanic Origin and Race categories. Ancestry percentages are based on the 2006-2010 American Community Survey population (not shown); ‡ Numbers in parentheses indicate the number of people reporting a single ancestry; * Numbers in parentheses indicate the number of persons reporting this race alone, not in combination with any other race; Please refer to the Explanation of Data for more information.*

Polish (306)	698	1.78
Portuguese (113)	126	0.32
Romanian (35)	35	0.09
Russian (53)	129	0.33
Scandinavian (82)	391	1.00
Scotch-Irish (304)	594	1.51
Scottish (489)	1,700	4.33
Slavic (2)	45	0.11
Slovak (0)	25	0.06
Slovene (34)	34	0.09
Swedish (628)	1,671	4.26
Swiss (78)	274	0.70
Ukrainian (153)	218	0.56
Welsh (232)	1,075	2.74
West Indian, ex. Hispanic (58)	99	0.25
Barbadian (0)	22	0.06
Haitian (0)	9	0.02
Jamaican (8)	18	0.05
Trinidadian/Tobagonian (12)	12	0.03
West Indian (38)	38	0.10
Yugoslavian (30)	69	0.18

Hispanic Origin	Population	%
Hispanic or Latino (of any race)	2,961	7.00
Central American, ex. Mexican	137	0.32
Costa Rican	18	0.04
Guatemalan	44	0.10
Honduran	13	0.03
Nicaraguan	12	0.03
Panamanian	7	0.02
Salvadoran	43	0.10
Cuban	53	0.13
Dominican Republic	9	0.02
Mexican	1,247	2.95
Puerto Rican	126	0.30
South American	376	0.89
Argentinean	78	0.18
Bolivian	16	0.04
Chilean	50	0.12
Colombian	84	0.20
Ecuadorian	24	0.06
Paraguayan	14	0.03
Peruvian	88	0.21
Uruguayan	2	<0.01
Venezuelan	18	0.04
Other South American	2	<0.01
Other Hispanic or Latino	1,013	2.40

Race*	Population	%
African-American/Black (594)	782	1.85
Not Hispanic (524)	680	1.61
Hispanic (70)	102	0.24
American Indian/Alaska Native (264)	442	1.05
Not Hispanic (193)	326	0.77
Hispanic (71)	116	0.27
Apache (4)	19	0.04
Canadian/French Am. Ind. (1)	1	<0.01
Cherokee (2)	26	0.06
Chickasaw (0)	3	0.01
Chippewa (2)	5	0.01
Choctaw (1)	11	0.03
Comanche (1)	1	<0.01
Crow (2)	2	<0.01
Delaware (0)	1	<0.01
Inupiat *(Alaska Native)* (0)	3	0.01
Iroquois (1)	6	0.01
Lumbee (0)	1	<0.01
Mexican American Ind. (6)	7	0.02
Navajo (30)	63	0.15
Paiute (6)	6	0.01
Potawatomi (0)	1	<0.01
Pueblo (2)	2	<0.01
Shoshone (2)	2	<0.01
Sioux (3)	11	0.03
Tlingit-Haida *(Alaska Native)* (1)	5	0.01
Ute (1)	12	0.03
Yuman (1)	1	<0.01
Asian (1,061)	1,586	3.75
Not Hispanic (1,048)	1,545	3.65
Hispanic (13)	41	0.10
Bangladeshi (3)	3	0.01
Cambodian (10)	13	0.03
Chinese, ex. Taiwanese (293)	432	1.02
Filipino (108)	186	0.44
Hmong (10)	10	0.02
Indian (161)	172	0.41
Indonesian (6)	9	0.02
Japanese (92)	231	0.55
Korean (115)	169	0.40
Laotian (27)	34	0.08
Nepalese (5)	5	0.01
Pakistani (26)	29	0.07
Taiwanese (14)	24	0.06
Thai (21)	32	0.08
Vietnamese (105)	134	0.32
Hawaii Native/Pacific Islander (186)	438	1.04
Not Hispanic (184)	419	0.99
Hispanic (2)	19	0.04
Guamanian/Chamorro (11)	22	0.05
Marshallese (2)	2	<0.01
Native Hawaiian (19)	90	0.21
Samoan (47)	107	0.25
Tongan (69)	94	0.22
White (38,233)	39,175	92.67
Not Hispanic (36,482)	37,184	87.96
Hispanic (1,751)	1,991	4.71

Eagle Mountain

Place Type: City
County: Utah
Population: 21,415†

Ancestry‡	Population	%
American (746)	746	4.17
Arab (0)	65	0.36
Lebanese (0)	65	0.36
Armenian (10)	10	0.06
Australian (19)	27	0.15
Austrian (0)	11	0.06
Brazilian (29)	29	0.16
British (49)	177	0.99
Bulgarian (6)	6	0.03
Canadian (25)	157	0.88
Celtic (0)	8	0.04
Czech (12)	96	0.54
Danish (451)	1,124	6.28
Dutch (34)	212	1.18
English (2,162)	4,852	27.12
European (1,385)	1,585	8.86
Finnish (12)	97	0.54
French, ex. Basque (36)	386	2.16
French Canadian (34)	63	0.35
German (504)	1,834	10.25
Greek (19)	77	0.43
Hungarian (0)	11	0.06
Irish (99)	413	2.31
Italian (259)	585	3.27
Lithuanian (0)	11	0.06
Northern European (144)	144	0.80
Norwegian (79)	330	1.84
Polish (48)	312	1.74
Portuguese (8)	21	0.12
Romanian (0)	12	0.07
Russian (24)	52	0.29
Scandinavian (24)	165	0.92
Scotch-Irish (39)	191	1.07
Scottish (238)	760	4.25
Swedish (254)	1,512	8.45
Swiss (20)	79	0.44
Ukrainian (1)	1	0.01
Welsh (112)	331	1.85
West Indian, ex. Hispanic (31)	31	0.17
West Indian (31)	31	0.17

Hispanic Origin	Population	%
Hispanic or Latino (of any race)	1,845	8.62
Central American, ex. Mexican	144	0.67
Costa Rican	11	0.05
Guatemalan	48	0.22
Honduran	4	0.02
Nicaraguan	8	0.04
Panamanian	3	0.01
Salvadoran	70	0.33
Cuban	15	0.07
Dominican Republic	28	0.13
Mexican	1,078	5.03
Puerto Rican	89	0.42
South American	319	1.49
Argentinean	89	0.42
Bolivian	4	0.02
Chilean	48	0.22
Colombian	39	0.18
Ecuadorian	20	0.09
Paraguayan	2	0.01
Peruvian	65	0.30
Uruguayan	13	0.06
Venezuelan	39	0.18
Other Hispanic or Latino	172	0.80

Race*	Population	%
African-American/Black (127)	247	1.15
Not Hispanic (114)	227	1.06
Hispanic (13)	20	0.09
American Indian/Alaska Native (105)	239	1.12
Not Hispanic (93)	201	0.94
Hispanic (12)	38	0.18
Aleut *(Alaska Native)* (1)	1	<0.01
Apache (1)	9	0.04
Arapaho (1)	1	<0.01
Blackfeet (0)	5	0.02
Central American Ind. (1)	2	0.01
Cherokee (7)	17	0.08
Cheyenne (7)	13	0.06
Chickasaw (1)	11	0.05
Choctaw (1)	7	0.03
Comanche (0)	4	0.02
Creek (0)	2	0.01
Inupiat *(Alaska Native)* (2)	3	0.01
Mexican American Ind. (1)	1	<0.01
Navajo (45)	70	0.33
Osage (2)	2	0.01
Paiute (2)	2	0.01
Potawatomi (3)	3	0.01
Pueblo (1)	7	0.03
Shoshone (0)	1	<0.01
Sioux (0)	1	<0.01
Ute (0)	1	<0.01
Yuman (0)	1	<0.01
Asian (125)	348	1.63
Not Hispanic (110)	306	1.43
Hispanic (15)	42	0.20
Cambodian (5)	7	0.03
Chinese, ex. Taiwanese (18)	84	0.39
Filipino (40)	116	0.54
Indian (7)	12	0.06
Indonesian (1)	5	0.02
Japanese (8)	75	0.35
Korean (14)	39	0.18
Laotian (6)	15	0.07
Pakistani (1)	4	0.02
Taiwanese (1)	3	0.01
Thai (2)	3	0.01
Vietnamese (5)	6	0.03
Hawaii Native/Pacific Islander (137)	293	1.37
Not Hispanic (135)	277	1.29
Hispanic (2)	16	0.07
Fijian (1)	3	0.01
Guamanian/Chamorro (1)	3	0.01
Native Hawaiian (20)	83	0.39
Samoan (43)	107	0.50
Tongan (44)	88	0.41
White (19,680)	20,287	94.73
Not Hispanic (18,583)	19,059	89.00
Hispanic (1,097)	1,228	5.73

*Notes: † The Census 2010 population figure is used to calculate the percentages in the Hispanic Origin and Race categories. Ancestry percentages are based on the 2006-2010 American Community Survey population (not shown); ‡ Numbers in parentheses indicate the number of people reporting a single ancestry; * Numbers in parentheses indicate the number of persons reporting this race alone, not in combination with any other race; Please refer to the Explanation of Data for more information.*

Farmington

Place Type: City
County: Davis
Population: 18,275†

Ancestry‡	Population	%
African, Sub-Saharan (0)	8	0.05
South African (0)	8	0.05
American (1,018)	1,018	5.92
Austrian (18)	58	0.34
Belgian (11)	11	0.06
Brazilian (40)	52	0.30
British (172)	421	2.45
Cajun (0)	9	0.05
Canadian (29)	73	0.42
Croatian (0)	18	0.10
Czech (0)	59	0.34
Czechoslovakian (0)	8	0.05
Danish (322)	1,406	8.18
Dutch (77)	521	3.03
Eastern European (9)	9	0.05
English (2,655)	6,447	37.51
European (851)	980	5.70
Finnish (0)	9	0.05
French, ex. Basque (40)	341	1.98
French Canadian (11)	21	0.12
German (655)	2,427	14.12
Greek (16)	92	0.54
Hungarian (9)	55	0.32
Icelander (54)	83	0.48
Irish (264)	929	5.40
Italian (208)	837	4.87
Northern European (59)	59	0.34
Norwegian (106)	766	4.46
Polish (61)	309	1.80
Portuguese (49)	60	0.35
Romanian (9)	9	0.05
Russian (62)	112	0.65
Scandinavian (105)	208	1.21
Scotch-Irish (131)	200	1.16
Scottish (160)	1,000	5.82
Swedish (95)	604	3.51
Swiss (11)	204	1.19
Welsh (60)	592	3.44
Yugoslavian (10)	10	0.06

Hispanic Origin	Population	%
Hispanic or Latino (of any race)	778	4.26
Central American, ex. Mexican	29	0.16
Guatemalan	13	0.07
Honduran	2	0.01
Panamanian	5	0.03
Salvadoran	9	0.05
Cuban	2	0.01
Mexican	573	3.14
Puerto Rican	16	0.09
South American	73	0.40
Argentinean	11	0.06
Bolivian	3	0.02
Chilean	8	0.04
Colombian	16	0.09
Ecuadorian	5	0.03
Peruvian	21	0.11
Uruguayan	4	0.02
Venezuelan	5	0.03
Other Hispanic or Latino	85	0.47

Race*	Population	%
African-American/Black (136)	197	1.08
Not Hispanic (132)	179	0.98
Hispanic (4)	18	0.10
American Indian/Alaska Native (63)	115	0.63
Not Hispanic (49)	91	0.50
Hispanic (14)	24	0.13
Cherokee (2)	21	0.11
Cheyenne (0)	1	0.01
Chippewa (1)	9	0.05
Creek (1)	1	0.01
Mexican American Ind. (1)	4	0.02
Navajo (11)	14	0.08
Paiute (2)	3	0.02
Sioux (1)	4	0.02
South American Ind. (0)	1	0.01
Ute (1)	3	0.02
Yaqui (1)	1	0.01
Asian (170)	276	1.51
Not Hispanic (166)	265	1.45
Hispanic (4)	11	0.06
Cambodian (5)	9	0.05
Chinese, ex. Taiwanese (39)	74	0.40
Filipino (20)	45	0.25
Indian (14)	20	0.11
Indonesian (3)	6	0.03
Japanese (37)	70	0.38
Korean (20)	35	0.19
Thai (2)	6	0.03
Vietnamese (20)	25	0.14
Hawaii Native/Pacific Islander (57)	117	0.64
Not Hispanic (57)	112	0.61
Hispanic (0)	5	0.03
Fijian (1)	7	0.04
Guamanian/Chamorro (2)	2	0.01
Native Hawaiian (3)	15	0.08
Samoan (11)	35	0.19
Tongan (16)	26	0.14
White (17,368)	17,647	96.56
Not Hispanic (16,860)	17,079	93.46
Hispanic (508)	568	3.11

Grantsville

Place Type: City
County: Tooele
Population: 8,893†

Ancestry‡	Population	%
American (570)	570	6.74
Basque (0)	31	0.37
British (186)	214	2.53
Canadian (0)	51	0.60
Czech (32)	48	0.57
Danish (45)	343	4.06
Dutch (148)	278	3.29
English (1,369)	2,755	32.57
European (268)	360	4.26
French, ex. Basque (27)	125	1.48
French Canadian (0)	132	1.56
German (214)	1,099	12.99
Greek (0)	31	0.37
Irish (173)	845	9.99
Italian (93)	213	2.52
Norwegian (28)	168	1.99
Polish (0)	14	0.17
Scandinavian (8)	34	0.40
Scotch-Irish (68)	105	1.24
Scottish (59)	207	2.45
Swedish (61)	364	4.30
Swiss (22)	65	0.77
Welsh (12)	123	1.45

Hispanic Origin	Population	%
Hispanic or Latino (of any race)	455	5.12
Central American, ex. Mexican	9	0.10
Guatemalan	5	0.06
Nicaraguan	1	0.01
Other Central American	3	0.03
Cuban	6	0.07
Dominican Republic	1	0.01
Mexican	304	3.42
Puerto Rican	1	0.01
South American	17	0.19
Colombian	9	0.10
Peruvian	6	0.07
Venezuelan	2	0.02
Other Hispanic or Latino	117	1.32

Race*	Population	%
African-American/Black (8)	29	0.33
Not Hispanic (7)	28	0.31
Hispanic (1)	1	0.01
American Indian/Alaska Native (65)	131	1.47
Not Hispanic (59)	115	1.29
Hispanic (6)	16	0.18
Apache (0)	2	0.02
Blackfeet (0)	1	0.01
Cherokee (3)	17	0.19
Chickasaw (3)	3	0.03
Chippewa (2)	8	0.09
Choctaw (0)	1	0.01
Comanche (1)	1	0.01
Cree (1)	1	0.01
Hopi (1)	3	0.03
Houma (1)	3	0.03
Iroquois (1)	1	0.01
Mexican American Ind. (0)	2	0.02
Navajo (12)	20	0.22
Paiute (2)	2	0.02
Pueblo (3)	3	0.03
Shoshone (12)	22	0.25
Sioux (3)	7	0.08
Ute (2)	5	0.06
Yakama (1)	1	0.01
Asian (13)	48	0.54
Not Hispanic (12)	46	0.52
Hispanic (1)	2	0.02
Chinese, ex. Taiwanese (5)	12	0.13
Filipino (2)	6	0.07
Indian (0)	2	0.02
Japanese (3)	19	0.21
Korean (3)	10	0.11
Hawaii Native/Pacific Islander (16)	29	0.33
Not Hispanic (16)	28	0.31
Hispanic (0)	1	0.01
Fijian (0)	3	0.03
Native Hawaiian (3)	7	0.08
Samoan (3)	6	0.07
Tongan (0)	7	0.08
White (8,457)	8,619	96.92
Not Hispanic (8,208)	8,332	93.69
Hispanic (249)	287	3.23

Heber

Place Type: City
County: Wasatch
Population: 11,362†

Ancestry‡	Population	%
American (556)	556	5.16
Austrian (132)	132	1.23
British (13)	13	0.12
Danish (85)	541	5.03
Dutch (32)	87	0.81
English (899)	2,232	20.73
European (405)	405	3.76
Finnish (24)	36	0.33
French, ex. Basque (21)	189	1.76
French Canadian (50)	95	0.88
German (215)	1,303	12.10
Greek (0)	36	0.33
Irish (184)	941	8.74
Italian (81)	223	2.07
Lithuanian (12)	12	0.11
Northern European (0)	41	0.38
Norwegian (157)	296	2.75
Polish (34)	79	0.73
Russian (50)	109	1.01
Scandinavian (96)	116	1.08
Scotch-Irish (99)	165	1.53
Scottish (300)	674	6.26
Swedish (79)	372	3.46
Swiss (37)	227	2.11
Turkish (8)	8	0.07
Welsh (0)	66	0.61

Hispanic Origin	Population	%
Hispanic or Latino (of any race)	2,092	18.41
Central American, ex. Mexican	59	0.52
Costa Rican	3	0.03

*Notes: † The Census 2010 population figure is used to calculate the percentages in the Hispanic Origin and Race categories. Ancestry percentages are based on the 2006-2010 American Community Survey population (not shown); ‡ Numbers in parentheses indicate the number of people reporting a single ancestry; * Numbers in parentheses indicate the number of persons reporting this race alone, not in combination with any other race; Please refer to the Explanation of Data for more information.*

Guatemalan	26	0.23
Honduran	8	0.07
Nicaraguan	2	0.02
Salvadoran	20	0.18
Cuban	3	0.03
Dominican Republic	6	0.05
Mexican	1,850	16.28
Puerto Rican	21	0.18
South American	26	0.23
Argentinean	11	0.10
Chilean	3	0.03
Colombian	7	0.06
Ecuadorian	1	0.01
Peruvian	4	0.04
Other Hispanic or Latino	127	1.12

Race*	Population	%
African-American/Black (47)	79	0.70
Not Hispanic (23)	37	0.33
Hispanic (24)	42	0.37
American Indian/Alaska Native (93)	146	1.28
Not Hispanic (26)	64	0.56
Hispanic (67)	82	0.72
Aleut *(Alaska Native)* (1)	1	0.01
Central American Ind. (1)	1	0.01
Cherokee (2)	11	0.10
Chippewa (1)	1	0.01
Choctaw (5)	8	0.07
Lumbee (0)	3	0.03
Mexican American Ind. (33)	33	0.29
Navajo (9)	15	0.13
Paiute (1)	1	0.01
Potawatomi (0)	1	0.01
Shoshone (1)	1	0.01
Sioux (2)	6	0.05
South American Ind. (2)	2	0.02
Ute (1)	3	0.03
Asian (121)	162	1.43
Not Hispanic (116)	153	1.35
Hispanic (5)	9	0.08
Chinese, ex. Taiwanese (13)	19	0.17
Filipino (57)	63	0.55
Indian (17)	19	0.17
Indonesian (2)	2	0.02
Japanese (12)	25	0.22
Korean (6)	15	0.13
Laotian (2)	2	0.02
Malaysian (1)	1	0.01
Vietnamese (5)	6	0.05
Hawaii Native/Pacific Islander (14)	33	0.29
Not Hispanic (9)	28	0.25
Hispanic (5)	5	0.04
Marshallese (2)	2	0.02
Native Hawaiian (1)	6	0.05
Samoan (5)	13	0.11
Tongan (0)	6	0.05
White (9,967)	10,139	89.24
Not Hispanic (8,984)	9,080	79.92
Hispanic (983)	1,059	9.32

Herriman

Place Type: City
County: Salt Lake
Population: 21,785†

Ancestry‡	Population	%
American (1,380)	1,380	7.53
Armenian (0)	9	0.05
Brazilian (22)	42	0.23
British (104)	241	1.31
Canadian (9)	41	0.22
Czech (26)	167	0.91
Czechoslovakian (6)	20	0.11
Danish (149)	652	3.56
Dutch (162)	509	2.78
Eastern European (0)	13	0.07
English (1,641)	5,134	28.01
European (547)	672	3.67
Finnish (0)	11	0.06
French, ex. Basque (36)	369	2.01
German (717)	2,350	12.82
Greek (9)	215	1.17
Hungarian (0)	23	0.13
Icelander (0)	14	0.08
Irish (337)	1,412	7.70
Italian (135)	641	3.50
Norwegian (263)	845	4.61
Polish (27)	62	0.34
Portuguese (0)	10	0.05
Russian (0)	9	0.05
Scandinavian (176)	322	1.76
Scotch-Irish (35)	187	1.02
Scottish (205)	908	4.95
Slovene (0)	9	0.05
Swedish (442)	1,238	6.75
Swiss (9)	109	0.59
Welsh (29)	586	3.20
West Indian, ex. Hispanic (12)	12	0.07
Jamaican (12)	12	0.07
Yugoslavian (10)	23	0.13

Hispanic Origin	Population	%
Hispanic or Latino (of any race)	1,358	6.23
Central American, ex. Mexican	139	0.64
Costa Rican	14	0.06
Guatemalan	39	0.18
Honduran	22	0.10
Nicaraguan	8	0.04
Panamanian	6	0.03
Salvadoran	50	0.23
Cuban	9	0.04
Dominican Republic	15	0.07
Mexican	791	3.63
Puerto Rican	35	0.16
South American	177	0.81
Argentinean	5	0.02
Bolivian	14	0.06
Chilean	15	0.07
Colombian	43	0.20
Ecuadorian	12	0.06
Peruvian	63	0.29
Uruguayan	5	0.02
Venezuelan	18	0.08
Other South American	2	0.01
Other Hispanic or Latino	192	0.88

Race*	Population	%
African-American/Black (121)	237	1.09
Not Hispanic (99)	196	0.90
Hispanic (22)	41	0.19
American Indian/Alaska Native (67)	152	0.70
Not Hispanic (47)	114	0.52
Hispanic (20)	38	0.17
Apache (0)	8	0.04
Blackfeet (0)	3	0.01
Cherokee (8)	22	0.10
Cheyenne (1)	3	0.01
Chippewa (1)	5	0.02
Choctaw (0)	1	<0.01
Comanche (1)	1	<0.01
Cree (0)	2	0.01
Mexican American Ind. (3)	5	0.02
Navajo (26)	39	0.18
Paiute (1)	3	0.01
Pima (1)	1	<0.01
Potawatomi (0)	6	0.03
Pueblo (0)	4	0.02
Shoshone (1)	1	<0.01
Sioux (2)	3	0.01
Ute (2)	3	0.01
Asian (279)	442	2.03
Not Hispanic (274)	410	1.88
Hispanic (5)	32	0.15
Burmese (1)	1	<0.01
Cambodian (10)	13	0.06
Chinese, ex. Taiwanese (49)	81	0.37
Filipino (24)	66	0.30
Indian (27)	32	0.15
Indonesian (0)	4	0.02
Japanese (18)	78	0.36
Korean (43)	74	0.34
Laotian (7)	11	0.05
Malaysian (10)	10	0.05
Pakistani (7)	7	0.03
Taiwanese (1)	4	0.02
Thai (5)	13	0.06
Vietnamese (55)	58	0.27
Hawaii Native/Pacific Islander (105)	199	0.91
Not Hispanic (102)	182	0.84
Hispanic (3)	17	0.08
Guamanian/Chamorro (0)	3	0.01
Marshallese (1)	1	<0.01
Native Hawaiian (12)	47	0.22
Samoan (47)	84	0.39
Tongan (24)	54	0.25
White (20,322)	20,787	95.42
Not Hispanic (19,519)	19,860	91.16
Hispanic (803)	927	4.26

Highland

Place Type: City
County: Utah
Population: 15,523†

Ancestry‡	Population	%
American (463)	463	3.29
Arab (7)	40	0.28
Arab (7)	40	0.28
Australian (0)	15	0.11
Austrian (0)	45	0.32
British (219)	364	2.59
Canadian (0)	20	0.14
Czech (13)	72	0.51
Danish (273)	1,220	8.66
Dutch (42)	451	3.20
English (1,876)	4,738	33.65
European (871)	871	6.19
Finnish (0)	33	0.23
French, ex. Basque (41)	184	1.31
French Canadian (0)	15	0.11
German (392)	2,133	15.15
Greek (8)	52	0.37
Icelander (0)	7	0.05
Iranian (52)	88	0.62
Irish (39)	430	3.05
Italian (88)	268	1.90
Northern European (46)	46	0.33
Norwegian (99)	289	2.05
Polish (0)	59	0.42
Romanian (11)	11	0.08
Russian (10)	10	0.07
Scandinavian (213)	282	2.00
Scotch-Irish (44)	255	1.81
Scottish (244)	770	5.47
Slovak (11)	11	0.08
Swedish (450)	1,012	7.19
Swiss (23)	461	3.27
Welsh (5)	91	0.65
West Indian, ex. Hispanic (18)	18	0.13
Haitian (18)	18	0.13

Hispanic Origin	Population	%
Hispanic or Latino (of any race)	431	2.78
Central American, ex. Mexican	38	0.24
Costa Rican	7	0.05
Guatemalan	13	0.08
Honduran	9	0.06
Salvadoran	9	0.06
Cuban	11	0.07
Dominican Republic	7	0.05
Mexican	213	1.37
Puerto Rican	21	0.14
South American	72	0.46
Argentinean	14	0.09
Bolivian	10	0.06
Chilean	13	0.08
Colombian	4	0.03
Ecuadorian	7	0.05

*Notes: † The Census 2010 population figure is used to calculate the percentages in the Hispanic Origin and Race categories. Ancestry percentages are based on the 2006-2010 American Community Survey population (not shown); ‡ Numbers in parentheses indicate the number of people reporting a single ancestry; * Numbers in parentheses indicate the number of persons reporting this race alone, not in combination with any other race; Please refer to the Explanation of Data for more information.*

Peruvian	16	0.10
Venezuelan	8	0.05
Other Hispanic or Latino	69	0.44

Race*	Population	%
African-American/Black (71)	110	0.71
Not Hispanic (70)	107	0.69
Hispanic (1)	3	0.02
American Indian/Alaska Native (32)	49	0.32
Not Hispanic (29)	42	0.27
Hispanic (3)	7	0.05
Apache (1)	1	0.01
Blackfeet (6)	6	0.04
Cherokee (1)	6	0.04
Cheyenne (1)	1	0.01
Chippewa (1)	2	0.01
Comanche (5)	5	0.03
Iroquois (4)	9	0.06
Mexican American Ind. (0)	1	0.01
Navajo (5)	6	0.04
Paiute (1)	1	0.01
Pima (2)	2	0.01
Puget Sound Salish (0)	1	0.01
Sioux (1)	1	0.01
Asian (109)	211	1.36
Not Hispanic (104)	205	1.32
Hispanic (5)	6	0.04
Cambodian (0)	1	0.01
Chinese, ex. Taiwanese (28)	69	0.44
Filipino (13)	25	0.16
Indian (6)	8	0.05
Japanese (30)	85	0.55
Korean (23)	34	0.22
Pakistani (3)	3	0.02
Taiwanese (1)	1	0.01
Thai (0)	1	0.01
Vietnamese (1)	2	0.01
Hawaii Native/Pacific Islander (116)	185	1.19
Not Hispanic (115)	184	1.19
Hispanic (1)	1	0.01
Fijian (9)	15	0.10
Guamanian/Chamorro (0)	1	0.01
Native Hawaiian (11)	42	0.27
Samoan (45)	87	0.56
Tongan (24)	58	0.37
White (14,884)	15,099	97.27
Not Hispanic (14,563)	14,755	95.05
Hispanic (321)	344	2.22

Holladay

Place Type: City
County: Salt Lake
Population: 26,472†

Ancestry‡	Population	%
African, Sub-Saharan (0)	11	0.04
South African (0)	11	0.04
Albanian (0)	28	0.11
American (942)	942	3.58
Arab (89)	118	0.45
Egyptian (0)	7	0.03
Lebanese (8)	30	0.11
Palestinian (16)	16	0.06
Other Arab (65)	65	0.25
Armenian (0)	20	0.08
Austrian (0)	28	0.11
British (269)	690	2.62
Canadian (76)	154	0.59
Celtic (0)	15	0.06
Croatian (0)	9	0.03
Czech (49)	90	0.34
Czechoslovakian (5)	11	0.04
Danish (454)	1,765	6.71
Dutch (118)	623	2.37
Eastern European (23)	23	0.09
English (3,440)	9,009	34.26
European (744)	872	3.32
French, ex. Basque (127)	546	2.08
French Canadian (0)	57	0.22
German (1,238)	3,909	14.86
Greek (236)	450	1.71
Guyanese (0)	8	0.03
Hungarian (86)	99	0.38
Iranian (61)	61	0.23
Irish (345)	2,263	8.60
Italian (506)	1,092	4.15
Lithuanian (33)	56	0.21
Luxemburger (0)	38	0.14
Northern European (152)	161	0.61
Norwegian (238)	810	3.08
Polish (91)	212	0.81
Portuguese (50)	71	0.27
Romanian (29)	29	0.11
Russian (10)	180	0.68
Scandinavian (122)	373	1.42
Scotch-Irish (138)	467	1.78
Scottish (451)	1,799	6.84
Slavic (13)	13	0.05
Slovak (0)	9	0.03
Slovene (0)	37	0.14
Swedish (206)	1,485	5.65
Swiss (85)	362	1.38
Ukrainian (21)	21	0.08
Welsh (61)	725	2.76
Yugoslavian (30)	66	0.25

Hispanic Origin	Population	%
Hispanic or Latino (of any race)	1,241	4.69
Central American, ex. Mexican	85	0.32
Costa Rican	2	0.01
Guatemalan	40	0.15
Honduran	10	0.04
Nicaraguan	6	0.02
Panamanian	5	0.02
Salvadoran	22	0.08
Cuban	18	0.07
Dominican Republic	23	0.09
Mexican	603	2.28
Puerto Rican	57	0.22
South American	262	0.99
Argentinean	21	0.08
Bolivian	17	0.06
Chilean	49	0.19
Colombian	33	0.12
Ecuadorian	16	0.06
Peruvian	79	0.30
Uruguayan	4	0.02
Venezuelan	43	0.16
Other Hispanic or Latino	193	0.73

Race*	Population	%
African-American/Black (227)	363	1.37
Not Hispanic (204)	319	1.21
Hispanic (23)	44	0.17
American Indian/Alaska Native (92)	195	0.74
Not Hispanic (82)	164	0.62
Hispanic (10)	31	0.12
Aleut *(Alaska Native)* (1)	1	<0.01
Apache (2)	8	0.03
Blackfeet (0)	4	0.02
Canadian/French Am. Ind. (0)	1	<0.01
Cherokee (3)	17	0.06
Cheyenne (2)	3	0.01
Chickasaw (0)	9	0.03
Choctaw (1)	6	0.02
Creek (0)	1	<0.01
Delaware (0)	2	0.01
Iroquois (0)	1	<0.01
Mexican American Ind. (1)	4	0.02
Navajo (34)	46	0.17
Paiute (0)	1	<0.01
Potawatomi (0)	1	<0.01
Shoshone (1)	1	<0.01
Sioux (4)	4	0.02
South American Ind. (1)	3	0.01
Ute (6)	13	0.05
Yaqui (0)	3	0.01
Asian (737)	968	3.66
Not Hispanic (729)	939	3.55
Hispanic (8)	29	0.11
Bhutanese (18)	19	0.07
Burmese (49)	50	0.19
Cambodian (10)	13	0.05
Chinese, ex. Taiwanese (162)	203	0.77
Filipino (24)	48	0.18
Indian (88)	114	0.43
Indonesian (3)	4	0.02
Japanese (137)	196	0.74
Korean (91)	117	0.44
Laotian (0)	4	0.02
Nepalese (8)	17	0.06
Pakistani (29)	29	0.11
Sri Lankan (1)	1	<0.01
Taiwanese (34)	35	0.13
Thai (14)	20	0.08
Vietnamese (30)	46	0.17
Hawaii Native/Pacific Islander (110)	177	0.67
Not Hispanic (106)	165	0.62
Hispanic (4)	12	0.05
Guamanian/Chamorro (3)	3	0.01
Marshallese (2)	2	0.01
Native Hawaiian (7)	24	0.09
Samoan (24)	36	0.14
Tongan (60)	89	0.34
White (24,294)	24,821	93.76
Not Hispanic (23,620)	24,039	90.81
Hispanic (674)	782	2.95

Hurricane

Place Type: City
County: Washington
Population: 13,748†

Ancestry‡	Population	%
African, Sub-Saharan (0)	19	0.14
Nigerian (0)	19	0.14
American (877)	877	6.63
Arab (47)	47	0.36
Syrian (47)	47	0.36
Brazilian (19)	19	0.14
British (109)	287	2.17
Canadian (119)	119	0.90
Czech (15)	55	0.42
Danish (73)	394	2.98
Dutch (46)	203	1.53
English (2,517)	4,323	32.67
European (220)	220	1.66
Finnish (9)	9	0.07
French, ex. Basque (67)	214	1.62
French Canadian (54)	121	0.91
German (913)	2,093	15.82
Greek (33)	65	0.49
Icelander (15)	47	0.36
Irish (214)	1,144	8.65
Italian (98)	289	2.18
Lithuanian (11)	11	0.08
Norwegian (177)	280	2.12
Polish (206)	369	2.79
Portuguese (65)	116	0.88
Russian (0)	22	0.17
Scandinavian (39)	69	0.52
Scotch-Irish (152)	282	2.13
Scottish (293)	547	4.13
Slovak (18)	32	0.24
Swedish (226)	810	6.12
Swiss (7)	45	0.34
Ukrainian (0)	26	0.20
Welsh (9)	138	1.04
Yugoslavian (0)	18	0.14

Hispanic Origin	Population	%
Hispanic or Latino (of any race)	986	7.17
Central American, ex. Mexican	61	0.44
Costa Rican	7	0.05
Guatemalan	8	0.06
Honduran	5	0.04
Nicaraguan	9	0.07
Panamanian	2	0.01

*Notes: † The Census 2010 population figure is used to calculate the percentages in the Hispanic Origin and Race categories. Ancestry percentages are based on the 2006-2010 American Community Survey population (not shown); ‡ Numbers in parentheses indicate the number of people reporting a single ancestry; * Numbers in parentheses indicate the number of persons reporting this race alone, not in combination with any other race; Please refer to the Explanation of Data for more information.*

Salvadoran	30	0.22
Cuban	8	0.06
Mexican	690	5.02
Puerto Rican	31	0.23
South American	41	0.30
Argentinean	11	0.08
Chilean	7	0.05
Colombian	4	0.03
Ecuadorian	3	0.02
Paraguayan	1	0.01
Peruvian	13	0.09
Venezuelan	2	0.01
Other Hispanic or Latino	155	1.13

Race*	Population	%
African-American/Black (72)	132	0.96
Not Hispanic (63)	114	0.83
Hispanic (9)	18	0.13
American Indian/Alaska Native (177)	275	2.00
Not Hispanic (132)	218	1.59
Hispanic (45)	57	0.41
Apache (3)	4	0.03
Blackfeet (3)	3	0.02
Canadian/French Am. Ind. (1)	1	0.01
Cherokee (9)	32	0.23
Chickasaw (0)	4	0.03
Choctaw (1)	4	0.03
Comanche (1)	1	0.01
Cree (0)	1	0.01
Inupiat *(Alaska Native)* (3)	3	0.02
Iroquois (1)	5	0.04
Mexican American Ind. (7)	11	0.08
Navajo (79)	104	0.76
Osage (0)	1	0.01
Paiute (2)	2	0.01
Potawatomi (0)	2	0.01
Seminole (0)	6	0.04
Shoshone (0)	1	0.01
Sioux (2)	4	0.03
South American Ind. (3)	8	0.06
Ute (2)	3	0.02
Asian (70)	141	1.03
Not Hispanic (68)	128	0.93
Hispanic (2)	13	0.09
Chinese, ex. Taiwanese (8)	22	0.16
Filipino (27)	67	0.49
Indian (6)	9	0.07
Indonesian (3)	4	0.03
Japanese (4)	16	0.12
Korean (4)	7	0.05
Pakistani (1)	1	0.01
Thai (3)	3	0.02
Vietnamese (5)	7	0.05
Hawaii Native/Pacific Islander (113)	188	1.37
Not Hispanic (105)	171	1.24
Hispanic (8)	17	0.12
Fijian (0)	7	0.05
Guamanian/Chamorro (3)	3	0.02
Marshallese (1)	1	0.01
Native Hawaiian (15)	43	0.31
Samoan (60)	95	0.69
Tongan (18)	37	0.27
White (12,555)	12,841	93.40
Not Hispanic (12,155)	12,371	89.98
Hispanic (400)	470	3.42

Hyrum

Place Type: City
County: Cache
Population: 7,609†

Ancestry‡	Population	%
American (480)	480	6.59
Basque (0)	11	0.15
British (53)	157	2.16
Czech (14)	14	0.19
Czechoslovakian (0)	11	0.15
Danish (107)	585	8.03
Dutch (11)	95	1.30
English (781)	1,939	26.62
European (223)	223	3.06
Finnish (0)	23	0.32
French, ex. Basque (0)	89	1.22
German (329)	1,176	16.14
Greek (0)	119	1.63
Irish (79)	474	6.51
Italian (79)	239	3.28
Norwegian (56)	159	2.18
Polish (6)	14	0.19
Russian (0)	66	0.91
Scandinavian (67)	99	1.36
Scotch-Irish (9)	144	1.98
Scottish (61)	317	4.35
Swedish (84)	401	5.51
Swiss (5)	95	1.30
Welsh (0)	175	2.40
West Indian, ex. Hispanic (0)	42	0.58
Haitian (0)	42	0.58

Hispanic Origin	Population	%
Hispanic or Latino (of any race)	1,332	17.51
Central American, ex. Mexican	143	1.88
Guatemalan	63	0.83
Honduran	3	0.04
Salvadoran	77	1.01
Cuban	1	0.01
Dominican Republic	8	0.11
Mexican	1,038	13.64
Puerto Rican	15	0.20
South American	38	0.50
Argentinean	3	0.04
Bolivian	4	0.05
Chilean	8	0.11
Peruvian	16	0.21
Venezuelan	7	0.09
Other Hispanic or Latino	89	1.17

Race*	Population	%
African-American/Black (24)	47	0.62
Not Hispanic (13)	28	0.37
Hispanic (11)	19	0.25
American Indian/Alaska Native (40)	107	1.41
Not Hispanic (32)	75	0.99
Hispanic (8)	32	0.42
Apache (0)	8	0.11
Cherokee (0)	10	0.13
Chippewa (7)	9	0.12
Creek (0)	2	0.03
Iroquois (1)	2	0.03
Mexican American Ind. (0)	6	0.08
Navajo (17)	23	0.30
Osage (0)	5	0.07
Pueblo (0)	1	0.01
Sioux (1)	1	0.01
South American Ind. (0)	1	0.01
Ute (1)	1	0.01
Yup'ik *(Alaska Native)* (2)	2	0.03
Asian (34)	59	0.78
Not Hispanic (34)	53	0.70
Hispanic (0)	6	0.08
Burmese (2)	2	0.03
Cambodian (2)	5	0.07
Chinese, ex. Taiwanese (4)	13	0.17
Filipino (7)	16	0.21
Indian (3)	6	0.08
Indonesian (1)	1	0.01
Japanese (2)	3	0.04
Korean (3)	5	0.07
Laotian (1)	2	0.03
Vietnamese (3)	3	0.04
Hawaii Native/Pacific Islander (61)	73	0.96
Not Hispanic (56)	66	0.87
Hispanic (5)	7	0.09
Guamanian/Chamorro (0)	1	0.01
Marshallese (5)	5	0.07
Native Hawaiian (3)	9	0.12
Samoan (19)	20	0.26
Tongan (26)	27	0.35
White (6,522)	6,652	87.42
Not Hispanic (6,065)	6,141	80.71
Hispanic (457)	511	6.72

Kaysville

Place Type: City
County: Davis
Population: 27,300†

Ancestry‡	Population	%
American (1,668)	1,668	6.40
Arab (7)	23	0.09
Palestinian (7)	23	0.09
Armenian (0)	18	0.07
Australian (12)	22	0.08
Austrian (10)	82	0.31
Belgian (0)	8	0.03
British (267)	608	2.33
Bulgarian (8)	17	0.07
Canadian (23)	93	0.36
Czech (11)	43	0.17
Danish (539)	1,856	7.12
Dutch (222)	882	3.39
Eastern European (23)	23	0.09
English (4,357)	9,929	38.11
European (1,588)	1,625	6.24
Finnish (16)	16	0.06
French, ex. Basque (214)	555	2.13
French Canadian (92)	101	0.39
German (835)	3,390	13.01
Greek (42)	189	0.73
Hungarian (0)	11	0.04
Irish (327)	1,929	7.40
Italian (133)	546	2.10
Lithuanian (9)	35	0.13
Northern European (65)	65	0.25
Norwegian (276)	889	3.41
Polish (22)	136	0.52
Portuguese (12)	12	0.05
Romanian (0)	25	0.10
Russian (0)	43	0.17
Scandinavian (208)	622	2.39
Scotch-Irish (67)	554	2.13
Scottish (167)	1,025	3.93
Slovak (0)	40	0.15
Slovene (0)	10	0.04
Swedish (329)	1,049	4.03
Swiss (181)	690	2.65
Welsh (135)	638	2.45
Yugoslavian (0)	12	0.05

Hispanic Origin	Population	%
Hispanic or Latino (of any race)	1,225	4.49
Central American, ex. Mexican	126	0.46
Guatemalan	64	0.23
Honduran	21	0.08
Nicaraguan	12	0.04
Panamanian	5	0.02
Salvadoran	24	0.09
Cuban	9	0.03
Dominican Republic	6	0.02
Mexican	745	2.73
Puerto Rican	35	0.13
South American	167	0.61
Argentinean	51	0.19
Bolivian	4	0.01
Chilean	8	0.03
Colombian	38	0.14
Ecuadorian	9	0.03
Paraguayan	1	<0.01
Peruvian	39	0.14
Uruguayan	8	0.03
Venezuelan	9	0.03
Other Hispanic or Latino	137	0.50

Race*	Population	%
African-American/Black (132)	218	0.80
Not Hispanic (119)	198	0.73
Hispanic (13)	20	0.07
American Indian/Alaska Native (88)	148	0.54

*Notes: † The Census 2010 population figure is used to calculate the percentages in the Hispanic Origin and Race categories. Ancestry percentages are based on the 2006-2010 American Community Survey population (not shown); ‡ Numbers in parentheses indicate the number of people reporting a single ancestry; * Numbers in parentheses indicate the number of persons reporting this race alone, not in combination with any other race; Please refer to the Explanation of Data for more information.*

Not Hispanic (70)	114	0.42
Hispanic (18)	34	0.12
Apache (0)	5	0.02
Arapaho (1)	1	<0.01
Blackfeet (0)	3	0.01
Central American Ind. (1)	1	<0.01
Cherokee (11)	21	0.08
Choctaw (6)	6	0.02
Comanche (0)	4	0.01
Lumbee (0)	1	<0.01
Mexican American Ind. (1)	6	0.02
Navajo (28)	38	0.14
Paiute (2)	2	0.01
Pueblo (2)	2	0.01
Shoshone (2)	2	0.01
Sioux (2)	4	0.01
Ute (2)	2	0.01
Asian (222)	409	1.50
Not Hispanic (221)	391	1.43
Hispanic (1)	18	0.07
Chinese, ex. Taiwanese (33)	61	0.22
Filipino (33)	83	0.30
Indian (21)	38	0.14
Indonesian (0)	4	0.01
Japanese (58)	105	0.38
Korean (35)	81	0.30
Laotian (6)	8	0.03
Malaysian (0)	1	<0.01
Pakistani (6)	11	0.04
Taiwanese (2)	6	0.02
Thai (4)	13	0.05
Vietnamese (10)	17	0.06
Hawaii Native/Pacific Islander (52)	117	0.43
Not Hispanic (51)	112	0.41
Hispanic (1)	5	0.02
Guamanian/Chamorro (4)	4	0.01
Marshallese (5)	5	0.02
Native Hawaiian (14)	44	0.16
Samoan (13)	44	0.16
Tongan (3)	6	0.02
White (25,995)	26,435	96.83
Not Hispanic (25,262)	25,577	93.69
Hispanic (733)	858	3.14

Kearns

Place Type: CDP
County: Salt Lake
Population: 35,731†

Ancestry‡	Population	%
Afghan (38)	38	0.11
African, Sub-Saharan (82)	82	0.24
African (27)	27	0.08
Sudanese (25)	25	0.07
Other Sub-Saharan African (30)	30	0.09
American (1,547)	1,547	4.45
Armenian (10)	22	0.06
Austrian (10)	10	0.03
Belgian (9)	9	0.03
Brazilian (35)	35	0.10
British (66)	220	0.63
Canadian (13)	42	0.12
Czech (0)	40	0.12
Czechoslovakian (0)	11	0.03
Danish (244)	1,449	4.17
Dutch (122)	651	1.87
English (2,801)	6,491	18.69
European (511)	563	1.62
Finnish (9)	71	0.20
French, ex. Basque (78)	566	1.63
French Canadian (191)	210	0.60
German (876)	2,977	8.57
Greek (24)	52	0.15
Hungarian (11)	40	0.12
Icelander (9)	49	0.14
Iranian (9)	27	0.08
Irish (716)	2,130	6.13
Italian (227)	676	1.95
Lithuanian (0)	7	0.02
Northern European (17)	17	0.05
Norwegian (174)	469	1.35
Pennsylvania German (0)	20	0.06
Polish (55)	152	0.44
Portuguese (21)	57	0.16
Romanian (0)	8	0.02
Russian (36)	183	0.53
Scandinavian (139)	264	0.76
Scotch-Irish (88)	202	0.58
Scottish (349)	1,254	3.61
Slovak (0)	18	0.05
Swedish (283)	770	2.22
Swiss (89)	213	0.61
Welsh (123)	800	2.30
West Indian, ex. Hispanic (126)	201	0.58
Haitian (55)	130	0.37
West Indian (71)	71	0.20
Yugoslavian (34)	34	0.10

Hispanic Origin	Population	%
Hispanic or Latino (of any race)	11,729	32.83
Central American, ex. Mexican	673	1.88
Costa Rican	4	0.01
Guatemalan	176	0.49
Honduran	52	0.15
Nicaraguan	37	0.10
Panamanian	5	0.01
Salvadoran	396	1.11
Other Central American	3	0.01
Cuban	26	0.07
Dominican Republic	27	0.08
Mexican	9,207	25.77
Puerto Rican	172	0.48
South American	527	1.47
Argentinean	47	0.13
Bolivian	14	0.04
Chilean	37	0.10
Colombian	37	0.10
Ecuadorian	49	0.14
Peruvian	204	0.57
Uruguayan	42	0.12
Venezuelan	88	0.25
Other South American	9	0.03
Other Hispanic or Latino	1,097	3.07

Race*	Population	%
African-American/Black (495)	733	2.05
Not Hispanic (405)	579	1.62
Hispanic (90)	154	0.43
American Indian/Alaska Native (513)	801	2.24
Not Hispanic (301)	463	1.30
Hispanic (212)	338	0.95
Apache (9)	29	0.08
Arapaho (6)	10	0.03
Blackfeet (4)	9	0.03
Canadian/French Am. Ind. (2)	2	0.01
Cherokee (9)	44	0.12
Cheyenne (4)	4	0.01
Chippewa (1)	3	0.01
Choctaw (2)	3	0.01
Colville (1)	1	<0.01
Creek (0)	1	<0.01
Hopi (5)	12	0.03
Iroquois (3)	10	0.03
Kiowa (0)	1	<0.01
Mexican American Ind. (29)	46	0.13
Navajo (178)	240	0.67
Paiute (4)	7	0.02
Pima (3)	3	0.01
Potawatomi (2)	6	0.02
Pueblo (1)	2	0.01
Shoshone (7)	18	0.05
Sioux (12)	21	0.06
South American Ind. (2)	14	0.04
Ute (13)	27	0.08
Yaqui (1)	2	0.01
Asian (742)	947	2.65
Not Hispanic (715)	882	2.47
Hispanic (27)	65	0.18
Cambodian (35)	45	0.13
Chinese, ex. Taiwanese (37)	67	0.19
Filipino (54)	97	0.27
Hmong (9)	9	0.03
Indian (24)	33	0.09
Indonesian (9)	12	0.03
Japanese (36)	83	0.23
Korean (18)	43	0.12
Laotian (152)	178	0.50
Malaysian (2)	3	0.01
Nepalese (6)	6	0.02
Pakistani (7)	7	0.02
Thai (21)	34	0.10
Vietnamese (281)	302	0.85
Hawaii Native/Pacific Islander (943)	1,111	3.11
Not Hispanic (922)	1,063	2.98
Hispanic (21)	48	0.13
Fijian (1)	1	<0.01
Guamanian/Chamorro (2)	3	0.01
Marshallese (11)	14	0.04
Native Hawaiian (38)	85	0.24
Samoan (426)	549	1.54
Tongan (344)	434	1.21
White (25,116)	26,197	73.32
Not Hispanic (20,976)	21,491	60.15
Hispanic (4,140)	4,706	13.17

Layton

Place Type: City
County: Davis
Population: 67,311†

Ancestry‡	Population	%
African, Sub-Saharan (50)	59	0.09
African (36)	36	0.05
Cape Verdean (14)	23	0.04
American (5,213)	5,213	7.94
Arab (74)	137	0.21
Arab (0)	37	0.06
Lebanese (74)	90	0.14
Syrian (0)	10	0.02
Australian (12)	71	0.11
Austrian (41)	139	0.21
Basque (10)	10	0.02
Belgian (0)	43	0.07
Brazilian (121)	121	0.18
British (429)	809	1.23
Bulgarian (9)	9	0.01
Canadian (71)	193	0.29
Croatian (15)	50	0.08
Czech (20)	76	0.12
Czechoslovakian (8)	24	0.04
Danish (917)	3,630	5.53
Dutch (480)	1,821	2.77
Eastern European (15)	15	0.02
English (7,528)	17,949	27.33
European (1,818)	1,927	2.93
Finnish (15)	58	0.09
French, ex. Basque (140)	2,064	3.14
French Canadian (52)	105	0.16
German (1,982)	7,486	11.40
Greek (79)	410	0.62
Hungarian (35)	58	0.09
Icelander (0)	11	0.02
Iranian (39)	39	0.06
Irish (1,109)	5,017	7.64
Italian (812)	2,712	4.13
Latvian (10)	41	0.06
Lithuanian (0)	22	0.03
New Zealander (0)	31	0.05
Northern European (51)	71	0.11
Norwegian (398)	1,582	2.41
Pennsylvania German (0)	12	0.02
Polish (435)	1,224	1.86
Portuguese (18)	105	0.16
Russian (117)	382	0.58
Scandinavian (393)	791	1.20
Scotch-Irish (352)	1,075	1.64
Scottish (1,009)	3,697	5.63
Serbian (25)	25	0.04

*Notes: † The Census 2010 population figure is used to calculate the percentages in the Hispanic Origin and Race categories. Ancestry percentages are based on the 2006-2010 American Community Survey population (not shown); ‡ Numbers in parentheses indicate the number of people reporting a single ancestry; * Numbers in parentheses indicate the number of persons reporting this race alone, not in combination with any other race; Please refer to the Explanation of Data for more information.*

Slavic (0)	9	0.01
Slovene (10)	22	0.03
Swedish (861)	2,239	3.41
Swiss (96)	726	1.11
Turkish (24)	24	0.04
Ukrainian (41)	64	0.10
Welsh (199)	1,288	1.96
West Indian, ex. Hispanic (103)	147	0.22
Belizean (38)	38	0.06
Bermudan (0)	6	0.01
Trinidadian/Tobagonian (65)	103	0.16
Yugoslavian (7)	38	0.06

Hispanic Origin	Population	%
Hispanic or Latino (of any race)	7,511	11.16
Central American, ex. Mexican	464	0.69
Costa Rican	18	0.03
Guatemalan	186	0.28
Honduran	33	0.05
Nicaraguan	20	0.03
Panamanian	22	0.03
Salvadoran	180	0.27
Other Central American	5	0.01
Cuban	28	0.04
Dominican Republic	19	0.03
Mexican	5,128	7.62
Puerto Rican	263	0.39
South American	588	0.87
Argentinean	144	0.21
Bolivian	16	0.02
Chilean	75	0.11
Colombian	61	0.09
Ecuadorian	49	0.07
Paraguayan	1	<0.01
Peruvian	181	0.27
Uruguayan	15	0.02
Venezuelan	46	0.07
Other Hispanic or Latino	1,021	1.52

Race*	Population	%
African-American/Black (1,143)	1,683	2.50
Not Hispanic (1,067)	1,499	2.23
Hispanic (76)	184	0.27
American Indian/Alaska Native (352)	770	1.14
Not Hispanic (251)	546	0.81
Hispanic (101)	224	0.33
Apache (17)	31	0.05
Blackfeet (0)	23	0.03
Canadian/French Am. Ind. (2)	4	0.01
Central American Ind. (1)	1	<0.01
Cherokee (27)	97	0.14
Cheyenne (3)	3	<0.01
Chickasaw (1)	2	<0.01
Chippewa (5)	10	0.01
Choctaw (5)	24	0.04
Comanche (0)	2	<0.01
Creek (1)	1	<0.01
Crow (0)	4	0.01
Delaware (1)	1	<0.01
Hopi (1)	2	<0.01
Houma (2)	2	<0.01
Inupiat *(Alaska Native)* (2)	5	0.01
Iroquois (3)	4	0.01
Kiowa (1)	1	<0.01
Mexican American Ind. (17)	29	0.04
Navajo (78)	138	0.21
Ottawa (0)	1	<0.01
Paiute (1)	2	<0.01
Pima (0)	1	<0.01
Potawatomi (2)	2	<0.01
Pueblo (12)	14	0.02
Puget Sound Salish (0)	3	<0.01
Seminole (3)	4	0.01
Shoshone (3)	7	0.01
Sioux (15)	43	0.06
South American Ind. (3)	11	0.02
Spanish American Ind. (3)	3	<0.01
Tlingit-Haida *(Alaska Native)* (2)	7	0.01
Ute (6)	25	0.04
Asian (1,408)	2,226	3.31
Not Hispanic (1,353)	2,077	3.09
Hispanic (55)	149	0.22
Bangladeshi (0)	5	0.01
Burmese (1)	1	<0.01
Cambodian (7)	14	0.02
Chinese, ex. Taiwanese (140)	258	0.38
Filipino (368)	657	0.98
Hmong (4)	8	0.01
Indian (78)	104	0.15
Indonesian (3)	12	0.02
Japanese (246)	447	0.66
Korean (190)	310	0.46
Laotian (58)	69	0.10
Pakistani (12)	19	0.03
Sri Lankan (1)	1	<0.01
Taiwanese (3)	7	0.01
Thai (113)	168	0.25
Vietnamese (109)	140	0.21
Hawaii Native/Pacific Islander (361)	595	0.88
Not Hispanic (342)	546	0.81
Hispanic (19)	49	0.07
Fijian (2)	4	0.01
Guamanian/Chamorro (36)	51	0.08
Marshallese (22)	23	0.03
Native Hawaiian (45)	123	0.18
Samoan (121)	203	0.30
Tongan (73)	101	0.15
White (58,787)	60,717	90.20
Not Hispanic (55,215)	56,567	84.04
Hispanic (3,572)	4,150	6.17

Lehi

Place Type: City
County: Utah
Population: 47,407†

Ancestry‡	Population	%
African, Sub-Saharan (54)	54	0.13
African (9)	9	0.02
Ethiopian (13)	13	0.03
South African (32)	32	0.08
American (2,938)	2,938	6.99
Arab (29)	36	0.09
Arab (10)	10	0.02
Lebanese (19)	26	0.06
Armenian (0)	9	0.02
Austrian (0)	11	0.03
Basque (26)	67	0.16
Brazilian (14)	59	0.14
British (221)	615	1.46
Canadian (48)	165	0.39
Croatian (10)	51	0.12
Czech (0)	19	0.05
Danish (627)	2,669	6.35
Dutch (168)	714	1.70
Eastern European (12)	24	0.06
English (4,968)	11,900	28.30
European (2,232)	2,389	5.68
Finnish (15)	164	0.39
French, ex. Basque (64)	501	1.19
French Canadian (13)	36	0.09
German (1,234)	5,466	13.00
Greek (56)	107	0.25
Hungarian (41)	107	0.25
Icelander (0)	29	0.07
Irish (314)	2,005	4.77
Italian (173)	993	2.36
Northern European (57)	132	0.31
Norwegian (324)	975	2.32
Polish (48)	224	0.53
Portuguese (0)	103	0.24
Russian (31)	135	0.32
Scandinavian (99)	281	0.67
Scotch-Irish (221)	616	1.47
Scottish (251)	2,502	5.95
Serbian (12)	12	0.03
Slovak (0)	25	0.06
Swedish (356)	1,849	4.40
Swiss (159)	453	1.08
Turkish (0)	7	0.02
Ukrainian (0)	34	0.08
Welsh (314)	1,270	3.02
West Indian, ex. Hispanic (0)	42	0.10
West Indian (0)	42	0.10
Yugoslavian (31)	105	0.25

Hispanic Origin	Population	%
Hispanic or Latino (of any race)	3,054	6.44
Central American, ex. Mexican	229	0.48
Costa Rican	19	0.04
Guatemalan	66	0.14
Honduran	27	0.06
Nicaraguan	20	0.04
Panamanian	10	0.02
Salvadoran	87	0.18
Cuban	22	0.05
Dominican Republic	16	0.03
Mexican	1,990	4.20
Puerto Rican	68	0.14
South American	489	1.03
Argentinean	77	0.16
Bolivian	21	0.04
Chilean	78	0.16
Colombian	77	0.16
Ecuadorian	39	0.08
Peruvian	115	0.24
Uruguayan	14	0.03
Venezuelan	62	0.13
Other South American	6	0.01
Other Hispanic or Latino	240	0.51

Race*	Population	%
African-American/Black (182)	364	0.77
Not Hispanic (176)	327	0.69
Hispanic (6)	37	0.08
American Indian/Alaska Native (208)	428	0.90
Not Hispanic (170)	353	0.74
Hispanic (38)	75	0.16
Alaska Athabascan *(Ala. Nat.)* (0)	1	<0.01
Aleut *(Alaska Native)* (0)	5	0.01
Apache (4)	13	0.03
Blackfeet (1)	3	0.01
Canadian/French Am. Ind. (3)	3	0.01
Central American Ind. (1)	6	0.01
Cherokee (7)	41	0.09
Chickasaw (1)	1	<0.01
Chippewa (5)	9	0.02
Choctaw (4)	8	0.02
Comanche (6)	11	0.02
Creek (1)	1	<0.01
Crow (0)	1	<0.01
Iroquois (5)	10	0.02
Kiowa (1)	1	<0.01
Lumbee (0)	1	<0.01
Mexican American Ind. (2)	5	0.01
Navajo (83)	122	0.26
Osage (0)	1	<0.01
Paiute (4)	6	0.01
Potawatomi (1)	1	<0.01
Pueblo (0)	6	0.01
Seminole (0)	5	0.01
Sioux (7)	16	0.03
South American Ind. (1)	8	0.02
Spanish American Ind. (0)	1	<0.01
Tohono O'Odham (0)	5	0.01
Ute (8)	13	0.03
Yaqui (1)	6	0.01
Yuman (0)	1	<0.01
Asian (645)	1,103	2.33
Not Hispanic (628)	1,035	2.18
Hispanic (17)	68	0.14
Cambodian (6)	12	0.03
Chinese, ex. Taiwanese (157)	297	0.63
Filipino (119)	204	0.43
Hmong (0)	4	0.01
Indian (31)	68	0.14
Japanese (58)	210	0.44
Korean (91)	155	0.33
Laotian (4)	12	0.03

*Notes: † The Census 2010 population figure is used to calculate the percentages in the Hispanic Origin and Race categories. Ancestry percentages are based on the 2006-2010 American Community Survey population (not shown); ‡ Numbers in parentheses indicate the number of people reporting a single ancestry; * Numbers in parentheses indicate the number of persons reporting this race alone, not in combination with any other race; Please refer to the Explanation of Data for more information.*

Nepalese (0)	1	<0.01
Pakistani (20)	20	0.04
Sri Lankan (2)	3	0.01
Taiwanese (0)	2	<0.01
Thai (12)	24	0.05
Vietnamese (104)	114	0.24
Hawaii Native/Pacific Islander (369)	637	1.34
Not Hispanic (367)	614	1.30
Hispanic (2)	23	0.05
Fijian (3)	20	0.04
Guamanian/Chamorro (0)	8	0.02
Marshallese (6)	6	0.01
Native Hawaiian (18)	141	0.30
Samoan (154)	281	0.59
Tongan (103)	189	0.40
White (43,924)	45,010	94.94
Not Hispanic (42,083)	42,932	90.56
Hispanic (1,841)	2,078	4.38

Lindon

Place Type: City
County: Utah
Population: 10,070†

Ancestry‡	Population	%
African, Sub-Saharan (20)	41	0.42
South African (20)	41	0.42
Albanian (0)	9	0.09
American (620)	620	6.39
Australian (0)	21	0.22
Belgian (0)	62	0.64
Brazilian (0)	10	0.10
British (92)	218	2.25
Czech (0)	6	0.06
Danish (199)	733	7.56
Dutch (36)	207	2.13
English (1,270)	3,217	33.17
European (497)	545	5.62
Finnish (12)	71	0.73
French, ex. Basque (13)	91	0.94
French Canadian (0)	21	0.22
German (152)	1,039	10.71
Greek (0)	51	0.53
Irish (12)	496	5.11
Italian (21)	245	2.53
Norwegian (90)	297	3.06
Polish (0)	11	0.11
Russian (0)	29	0.30
Scandinavian (71)	181	1.87
Scotch-Irish (10)	216	2.23
Scottish (89)	343	3.54
Swedish (132)	506	5.22
Swiss (11)	225	2.32
Welsh (63)	142	1.46

Hispanic Origin	Population	%
Hispanic or Latino (of any race)	720	7.15
Central American, ex. Mexican	45	0.45
Costa Rican	1	0.01
Guatemalan	8	0.08
Honduran	11	0.11
Panamanian	2	0.02
Salvadoran	23	0.23
Cuban	1	0.01
Dominican Republic	4	0.04
Mexican	451	4.48
Puerto Rican	3	0.03
South American	155	1.54
Argentinean	22	0.22
Bolivian	12	0.12
Chilean	24	0.24
Colombian	20	0.20
Ecuadorian	22	0.22
Paraguayan	1	0.01
Peruvian	44	0.44
Uruguayan	1	0.01
Venezuelan	9	0.09
Other Hispanic or Latino	61	0.61

Race*	Population	%
African-American/Black (50)	83	0.82
Not Hispanic (47)	76	0.75
Hispanic (3)	7	0.07
American Indian/Alaska Native (39)	86	0.85
Not Hispanic (28)	58	0.58
Hispanic (11)	28	0.28
Apache (0)	3	0.03
Arapaho (1)	2	0.02
Blackfeet (0)	1	0.01
Cherokee (1)	18	0.18
Cheyenne (0)	1	0.01
Chippewa (1)	1	0.01
Creek (0)	1	0.01
Iroquois (0)	3	0.03
Mexican American Ind. (3)	3	0.03
Navajo (10)	16	0.16
Paiute (0)	1	0.01
Shoshone (1)	2	0.02
Sioux (4)	6	0.06
South American Ind. (0)	3	0.03
Asian (135)	216	2.14
Not Hispanic (135)	214	2.13
Hispanic (0)	2	0.02
Chinese, ex. Taiwanese (31)	47	0.47
Filipino (14)	28	0.28
Indian (7)	7	0.07
Japanese (10)	43	0.43
Korean (32)	53	0.53
Laotian (6)	9	0.09
Taiwanese (4)	4	0.04
Thai (0)	1	0.01
Vietnamese (23)	23	0.23
Hawaii Native/Pacific Islander (42)	121	1.20
Not Hispanic (41)	103	1.02
Hispanic (1)	18	0.18
Fijian (0)	5	0.05
Guamanian/Chamorro (1)	4	0.04
Native Hawaiian (8)	39	0.39
Samoan (16)	50	0.50
Tongan (14)	36	0.36
White (9,241)	9,522	94.56
Not Hispanic (8,895)	9,085	90.22
Hispanic (346)	437	4.34

Logan

Place Type: City
County: Cache
Population: 48,174†

Ancestry‡	Population	%
African, Sub-Saharan (110)	238	0.51
African (16)	100	0.22
Ethiopian (14)	27	0.06
Sierra Leonean (0)	15	0.03
Sudanese (24)	24	0.05
Ugandan (17)	17	0.04
Other Sub-Saharan African (39)	55	0.12
American (2,562)	2,562	5.52
Arab (40)	80	0.17
Egyptian (0)	14	0.03
Lebanese (21)	34	0.07
Moroccan (19)	19	0.04
Palestinian (0)	13	0.03
Armenian (24)	163	0.35
Austrian (0)	61	0.13
Belgian (0)	26	0.06
Brazilian (15)	40	0.09
British (267)	463	1.00
Canadian (42)	116	0.25
Celtic (0)	14	0.03
Croatian (19)	19	0.04
Czech (21)	71	0.15
Czechoslovakian (12)	12	0.03
Danish (1,065)	3,533	7.61
Dutch (163)	800	1.72
English (4,546)	11,240	24.22
European (1,958)	2,062	4.44
Finnish (0)	47	0.10
French, ex. Basque (127)	870	1.87
French Canadian (95)	162	0.35
German (1,145)	4,623	9.96
Greek (73)	159	0.34
Hungarian (0)	16	0.03
Icelander (51)	147	0.32
Iranian (10)	10	0.02
Irish (890)	2,377	5.12
Italian (300)	1,113	2.40
Lithuanian (30)	30	0.06
Northern European (183)	193	0.42
Norwegian (229)	765	1.65
Polish (58)	282	0.61
Portuguese (15)	33	0.07
Russian (42)	86	0.19
Scandinavian (253)	596	1.28
Scotch-Irish (165)	627	1.35
Scottish (406)	2,311	4.98
Serbian (16)	16	0.03
Slovak (38)	46	0.10
Slovene (23)	56	0.12
Swedish (607)	1,903	4.10
Swiss (262)	909	1.96
Ukrainian (23)	35	0.08
Welsh (241)	1,042	2.25

Hispanic Origin	Population	%
Hispanic or Latino (of any race)	6,702	13.91
Central American, ex. Mexican	727	1.51
Costa Rican	5	0.01
Guatemalan	275	0.57
Honduran	34	0.07
Nicaraguan	13	0.03
Panamanian	15	0.03
Salvadoran	384	0.80
Other Central American	1	<0.01
Cuban	17	0.04
Dominican Republic	153	0.32
Mexican	4,825	10.02
Puerto Rican	97	0.20
South American	312	0.65
Argentinean	59	0.12
Bolivian	25	0.05
Chilean	42	0.09
Colombian	44	0.09
Ecuadorian	23	0.05
Peruvian	85	0.18
Uruguayan	6	0.01
Venezuelan	27	0.06
Other South American	1	<0.01
Other Hispanic or Latino	571	1.19

Race*	Population	%
African-American/Black (492)	661	1.37
Not Hispanic (427)	557	1.16
Hispanic (65)	104	0.22
American Indian/Alaska Native (463)	706	1.47
Not Hispanic (346)	516	1.07
Hispanic (117)	190	0.39
Apache (4)	8	0.02
Blackfeet (1)	4	0.01
Cherokee (4)	46	0.10
Cheyenne (0)	6	0.01
Chickasaw (1)	1	<0.01
Chippewa (3)	8	0.02
Choctaw (4)	11	0.02
Comanche (5)	5	0.01
Cree (0)	1	<0.01
Creek (3)	7	0.01
Crow (0)	1	<0.01
Hopi (4)	4	0.01
Mexican American Ind. (22)	23	0.05
Navajo (241)	305	0.63
Osage (1)	2	<0.01
Paiute (2)	5	0.01
Potawatomi (13)	13	0.03
Pueblo (0)	6	0.01
Seminole (0)	1	<0.01
Shoshone (6)	11	0.02

*Notes: † The Census 2010 population figure is used to calculate the percentages in the Hispanic Origin and Race categories. Ancestry percentages are based on the 2006-2010 American Community Survey population (not shown); ‡ Numbers in parentheses indicate the number of people reporting a single ancestry; * Numbers in parentheses indicate the number of persons reporting this race alone, not in combination with any other race; Please refer to the Explanation of Data for more information.*

Sioux (7)	18	0.04
South American Ind. (7)	10	0.02
Spanish American Ind. (1)	1	<0.01
Tlingit-Haida *(Alaska Native)* (2)	2	<0.01
Tsimshian *(Alaska Native)* (4)	4	0.01
Ute (7)	12	0.02
Yaqui (2)	2	<0.01
Yup'ik *(Alaska Native)* (1)	1	<0.01
Asian (1,592)	1,971	4.09
Not Hispanic (1,575)	1,933	4.01
Hispanic (17)	38	0.08
Burmese (127)	128	0.27
Cambodian (162)	197	0.41
Chinese, ex. Taiwanese (462)	548	1.14
Filipino (58)	111	0.23
Hmong (2)	2	<0.01
Indian (218)	246	0.51
Indonesian (4)	9	0.02
Japanese (87)	204	0.42
Korean (176)	213	0.44
Laotian (31)	37	0.08
Malaysian (2)	5	0.01
Nepalese (16)	16	0.03
Pakistani (6)	11	0.02
Sri Lankan (8)	9	0.02
Taiwanese (17)	27	0.06
Thai (23)	27	0.06
Vietnamese (121)	139	0.29
Hawaii Native/Pacific Islander (240)	390	0.81
Not Hispanic (222)	350	0.73
Hispanic (18)	40	0.08
Fijian (1)	2	<0.01
Guamanian/Chamorro (14)	21	0.04
Marshallese (30)	34	0.07
Native Hawaiian (39)	79	0.16
Samoan (65)	108	0.22
Tongan (59)	103	0.21
White (40,440)	41,442	86.03
Not Hispanic (38,125)	38,775	80.49
Hispanic (2,315)	2,667	5.54

Magna

Place Type: CDP
County: Salt Lake
Population: 26,505†

Ancestry‡	Population	%
African, Sub-Saharan (0)	74	0.28
African (0)	72	0.27
Somalian (0)	2	0.01
American (1,334)	1,334	4.96
Arab (9)	9	0.03
Moroccan (9)	9	0.03
Austrian (117)	131	0.49
Basque (28)	38	0.14
Brazilian (23)	69	0.26
British (46)	161	0.60
Canadian (24)	48	0.18
Croatian (12)	72	0.27
Czech (21)	88	0.33
Danish (480)	1,341	4.98
Dutch (169)	768	2.85
English (2,156)	5,797	21.55
European (172)	205	0.76
Finnish (0)	23	0.09
French, ex. Basque (30)	447	1.66
German (925)	2,858	10.62
Greek (73)	176	0.65
Icelander (63)	63	0.23
Irish (377)	1,499	5.57
Italian (295)	909	3.38
Lithuanian (13)	13	0.05
Northern European (0)	10	0.04
Norwegian (125)	365	1.36
Polish (69)	288	1.07
Portuguese (10)	33	0.12
Russian (59)	99	0.37
Scandinavian (108)	378	1.41
Scotch-Irish (153)	642	2.39
Scottish (215)	1,063	3.95
Swedish (175)	1,120	4.16
Swiss (43)	365	1.36
Welsh (25)	583	2.17

Hispanic Origin	Population	%
Hispanic or Latino (of any race)	6,188	23.35
Central American, ex. Mexican	279	1.05
Costa Rican	11	0.04
Guatemalan	95	0.36
Honduran	32	0.12
Nicaraguan	11	0.04
Panamanian	4	0.02
Salvadoran	126	0.48
Cuban	22	0.08
Dominican Republic	3	0.01
Mexican	4,662	17.59
Puerto Rican	98	0.37
South American	287	1.08
Argentinean	31	0.12
Bolivian	4	0.02
Chilean	51	0.19
Colombian	18	0.07
Ecuadorian	15	0.06
Peruvian	101	0.38
Uruguayan	15	0.06
Venezuelan	52	0.20
Other Hispanic or Latino	837	3.16

Race*	Population	%
African-American/Black (240)	373	1.41
Not Hispanic (202)	313	1.18
Hispanic (38)	60	0.23
American Indian/Alaska Native (262)	484	1.83
Not Hispanic (173)	325	1.23
Hispanic (89)	159	0.60
Apache (2)	11	0.04
Blackfeet (1)	2	0.01
Canadian/French Am. Ind. (0)	5	0.02
Central American Ind. (0)	2	0.01
Cherokee (4)	51	0.19
Cheyenne (0)	6	0.02
Chippewa (5)	10	0.04
Choctaw (3)	10	0.04
Cree (2)	2	0.01
Creek (1)	1	<0.01
Hopi (4)	4	0.02
Inupiat *(Alaska Native)* (0)	1	<0.01
Iroquois (3)	6	0.02
Menominee (1)	1	<0.01
Mexican American Ind. (10)	15	0.06
Navajo (82)	124	0.47
Paiute (3)	6	0.02
Pima (4)	4	0.02
Potawatomi (4)	4	0.02
Pueblo (4)	6	0.02
Puget Sound Salish (4)	4	0.02
Shoshone (6)	10	0.04
Sioux (7)	17	0.06
Spanish American Ind. (10)	12	0.05
Ute (9)	12	0.05
Yaqui (1)	1	<0.01
Yup'ik *(Alaska Native)* (0)	4	0.02
Asian (221)	414	1.56
Not Hispanic (218)	381	1.44
Hispanic (3)	33	0.12
Cambodian (30)	39	0.15
Chinese, ex. Taiwanese (24)	47	0.18
Filipino (32)	66	0.25
Indian (8)	15	0.06
Indonesian (1)	3	0.01
Japanese (24)	94	0.35
Korean (13)	39	0.15
Laotian (30)	44	0.17
Pakistani (1)	3	0.01
Sri Lankan (1)	2	0.01
Taiwanese (1)	3	0.01
Thai (5)	6	0.02
Vietnamese (34)	54	0.20
Hawaii Native/Pacific Islander (525)	712	2.69
Not Hispanic (520)	689	2.60
Hispanic (5)	23	0.09
Fijian (5)	8	0.03
Marshallese (36)	39	0.15
Native Hawaiian (21)	89	0.34
Samoan (194)	274	1.03
Tongan (212)	274	1.03
White (20,792)	21,646	81.67
Not Hispanic (18,632)	19,125	72.16
Hispanic (2,160)	2,521	9.51

Mapleton

Place Type: City
County: Utah
Population: 7,979†

Ancestry‡	Population	%
American (550)	550	7.29
Armenian (0)	14	0.19
Austrian (0)	28	0.37
Belgian (0)	12	0.16
British (50)	55	0.73
Canadian (18)	39	0.52
Czech (0)	16	0.21
Danish (264)	753	9.98
Dutch (45)	54	0.72
English (1,660)	3,438	45.58
European (387)	415	5.50
Finnish (29)	148	1.96
French, ex. Basque (3)	89	1.18
French Canadian (39)	39	0.52
German (296)	1,164	15.43
Greek (0)	9	0.12
Icelander (0)	80	1.06
Irish (0)	233	3.09
Italian (18)	18	0.24
Norwegian (46)	90	1.19
Scandinavian (17)	53	0.70
Scotch-Irish (0)	9	0.12
Scottish (95)	768	10.18
Slavic (9)	33	0.44
Swedish (39)	195	2.59
Swiss (17)	128	1.70
Welsh (94)	298	3.95

Hispanic Origin	Population	%
Hispanic or Latino (of any race)	279	3.50
Central American, ex. Mexican	32	0.40
Costa Rican	3	0.04
Guatemalan	11	0.14
Salvadoran	18	0.23
Cuban	2	0.03
Mexican	181	2.27
South American	26	0.33
Argentinean	1	0.01
Chilean	2	0.03
Colombian	1	0.01
Peruvian	13	0.16
Uruguayan	1	0.01
Venezuelan	8	0.10
Other Hispanic or Latino	38	0.48

Race*	Population	%
African-American/Black (22)	58	0.73
Not Hispanic (21)	56	0.70
Hispanic (1)	2	0.03
American Indian/Alaska Native (24)	66	0.83
Not Hispanic (21)	48	0.60
Hispanic (3)	18	0.23
Central American Ind. (0)	2	0.03
Cherokee (0)	6	0.08
Chippewa (0)	3	0.04
Lumbee (2)	8	0.10
Mexican American Ind. (1)	1	0.01
Navajo (19)	28	0.35
Paiute (0)	2	0.03
Pima (1)	1	0.01
Potawatomi (0)	1	0.01
Pueblo (0)	3	0.04

*Notes: † The Census 2010 population figure is used to calculate the percentages in the Hispanic Origin and Race categories. Ancestry percentages are based on the 2006-2010 American Community Survey population (not shown); ‡ Numbers in parentheses indicate the number of people reporting a single ancestry; * Numbers in parentheses indicate the number of persons reporting this race alone, not in combination with any other race; Please refer to the Explanation of Data for more information.*

Ute (0)	1	0.01
Asian (39)	96	1.20
Not Hispanic (39)	93	1.17
Hispanic (0)	3	0.04
Chinese, ex. Taiwanese (11)	24	0.30
Filipino (9)	18	0.23
Indian (2)	6	0.08
Indonesian (0)	1	0.01
Japanese (7)	29	0.36
Korean (5)	12	0.15
Thai (2)	7	0.09
Vietnamese (1)	3	0.04
Hawaii Native/Pacific Islander (32)	93	1.17
Not Hispanic (32)	87	1.09
Hispanic (0)	6	0.08
Guamanian/Chamorro (1)	2	0.03
Marshallese (2)	2	0.03
Native Hawaiian (1)	25	0.31
Samoan (4)	24	0.30
Tongan (20)	31	0.39
White (7,580)	7,773	97.42
Not Hispanic (7,424)	7,576	94.95
Hispanic (156)	197	2.47

Midvale

Place Type: City
County: Salt Lake
Population: 27,964†

Ancestry‡	Population	%
American (1,131)	1,131	4.10
Arab (7)	20	0.07
Lebanese (7)	20	0.07
Armenian (27)	57	0.21
Australian (21)	82	0.30
Austrian (5)	29	0.11
Basque (11)	35	0.13
Belgian (0)	11	0.04
Brazilian (20)	20	0.07
British (99)	273	0.99
Canadian (10)	79	0.29
Celtic (0)	23	0.08
Croatian (13)	13	0.05
Czech (26)	61	0.22
Czechoslovakian (0)	11	0.04
Danish (179)	833	3.02
Dutch (168)	491	1.78
Eastern European (0)	12	0.04
English (2,392)	5,575	20.19
European (289)	313	1.13
Finnish (0)	39	0.14
French, ex. Basque (193)	517	1.87
French Canadian (20)	20	0.07
German (910)	3,123	11.31
Greek (76)	157	0.57
Hungarian (9)	33	0.12
Icelander (0)	15	0.05
Irish (686)	2,110	7.64
Italian (214)	692	2.51
Lithuanian (12)	46	0.17
Maltese (39)	39	0.14
Northern European (50)	50	0.18
Norwegian (230)	507	1.84
Polish (0)	74	0.27
Portuguese (25)	92	0.33
Romanian (48)	59	0.21
Russian (180)	235	0.85
Scandinavian (158)	229	0.83
Scotch-Irish (28)	345	1.25
Scottish (126)	736	2.67
Slovak (0)	17	0.06
Swedish (263)	1,135	4.11
Swiss (114)	369	1.34
Ukrainian (0)	38	0.14
Welsh (107)	600	2.17
West Indian, ex. Hispanic (35)	35	0.13
Belizean (3)	3	0.01
Jamaican (32)	32	0.12
Yugoslavian (89)	104	0.38

Hispanic Origin	Population	%
Hispanic or Latino (of any race)	6,795	24.30
Central American, ex. Mexican	217	0.78
Costa Rican	10	0.04
Guatemalan	65	0.23
Honduran	35	0.13
Nicaraguan	10	0.04
Panamanian	7	0.03
Salvadoran	89	0.32
Other Central American	1	<0.01
Cuban	31	0.11
Dominican Republic	19	0.07
Mexican	5,342	19.10
Puerto Rican	132	0.47
South American	311	1.11
Argentinean	27	0.10
Bolivian	7	0.03
Chilean	29	0.10
Colombian	39	0.14
Ecuadorian	17	0.06
Paraguayan	1	<0.01
Peruvian	124	0.44
Uruguayan	14	0.05
Venezuelan	51	0.18
Other South American	2	0.01
Other Hispanic or Latino	743	2.66

Race*	Population	%
African-American/Black (513)	721	2.58
Not Hispanic (380)	513	1.83
Hispanic (133)	208	0.74
American Indian/Alaska Native (343)	555	1.98
Not Hispanic (233)	362	1.29
Hispanic (110)	193	0.69
Aleut *(Alaska Native)* (0)	1	<0.01
Apache (7)	24	0.09
Arapaho (6)	9	0.03
Central American Ind. (1)	5	0.02
Cherokee (8)	49	0.18
Cheyenne (2)	3	0.01
Chickasaw (0)	1	<0.01
Chippewa (1)	4	0.01
Choctaw (0)	5	0.02
Comanche (3)	3	0.01
Crow (1)	1	<0.01
Hopi (0)	1	<0.01
Inupiat *(Alaska Native)* (0)	1	<0.01
Iroquois (8)	8	0.03
Mexican American Ind. (39)	56	0.20
Navajo (128)	146	0.52
Osage (3)	3	0.01
Paiute (4)	5	0.02
Pima (1)	1	<0.01
Potawatomi (2)	2	0.01
Pueblo (11)	12	0.04
Seminole (0)	1	<0.01
Shoshone (18)	18	0.06
Sioux (5)	13	0.05
South American Ind. (10)	10	0.04
Spanish American Ind. (1)	1	<0.01
Tlingit-Haida *(Alaska Native)* (1)	1	<0.01
Ute (6)	8	0.03
Asian (670)	871	3.11
Not Hispanic (652)	831	2.97
Hispanic (18)	40	0.14
Burmese (9)	9	0.03
Cambodian (13)	17	0.06
Chinese, ex. Taiwanese (158)	217	0.78
Filipino (44)	83	0.30
Indian (133)	157	0.56
Indonesian (0)	3	0.01
Japanese (81)	125	0.45
Korean (47)	63	0.23
Laotian (32)	45	0.16
Malaysian (0)	4	0.01
Nepalese (14)	14	0.05
Pakistani (7)	10	0.04
Sri Lankan (4)	4	0.01
Taiwanese (1)	1	<0.01
Thai (12)	18	0.06
Vietnamese (64)	74	0.26
Hawaii Native/Pacific Islander (199)	316	1.13
Not Hispanic (199)	296	1.06
Hispanic (0)	20	0.07
Guamanian/Chamorro (1)	2	0.01
Native Hawaiian (15)	50	0.18
Samoan (77)	111	0.40
Tongan (74)	114	0.41
White (21,754)	22,615	80.87
Not Hispanic (19,106)	19,557	69.94
Hispanic (2,648)	3,058	10.94

Millcreek

Place Type: CDP
County: Salt Lake
Population: 62,139†

Ancestry‡	Population	%
African, Sub-Saharan (727)	861	1.41
African (279)	413	0.68
Somalian (342)	342	0.56
Sudanese (106)	106	0.17
Albanian (0)	8	0.01
American (2,188)	2,188	3.59
Arab (338)	399	0.65
Lebanese (67)	128	0.21
Other Arab (271)	271	0.44
Armenian (122)	160	0.26
Australian (11)	31	0.05
Austrian (59)	173	0.28
Basque (12)	84	0.14
Belgian (12)	12	0.02
Brazilian (45)	55	0.09
British (991)	1,516	2.49
Bulgarian (0)	6	0.01
Canadian (60)	212	0.35
Celtic (0)	4	0.01
Croatian (137)	161	0.26
Czech (33)	270	0.44
Czechoslovakian (10)	23	0.04
Danish (980)	3,590	5.89
Dutch (503)	1,614	2.65
Eastern European (48)	48	0.08
English (7,680)	18,283	29.97
European (2,063)	2,379	3.90
Finnish (39)	96	0.16
French, ex. Basque (161)	1,540	2.52
French Canadian (57)	107	0.18
German (2,791)	8,872	14.54
Greek (203)	407	0.67
Hungarian (53)	123	0.20
Icelander (0)	76	0.12
Iranian (44)	138	0.23
Irish (1,010)	3,702	6.07
Italian (542)	1,995	3.27
Lithuanian (29)	45	0.07
New Zealander (0)	9	0.01
Northern European (90)	145	0.24
Norwegian (581)	2,072	3.40
Pennsylvania German (0)	9	0.01
Polish (191)	619	1.01
Portuguese (7)	66	0.11
Romanian (14)	53	0.09
Russian (115)	433	0.71
Scandinavian (360)	1,133	1.86
Scotch-Irish (369)	879	1.44
Scottish (756)	3,225	5.29
Serbian (39)	58	0.10
Slavic (0)	18	0.03
Slovak (21)	70	0.11
Slovene (13)	17	0.03
Swedish (727)	2,399	3.93
Swiss (214)	737	1.21
Turkish (87)	118	0.19
Ukrainian (51)	152	0.25
Welsh (237)	1,423	2.33
Yugoslavian (228)	256	0.42

SECTION TWO

*Notes: † The Census 2010 population figure is used to calculate the percentages in the Hispanic Origin and Race categories. Ancestry percentages are based on the 2006-2010 American Community Survey population (not shown); ‡ Numbers in parentheses indicate the number of people reporting a single ancestry; * Numbers in parentheses indicate the number of persons reporting this race alone, not in combination with any other race; Please refer to the Explanation of Data for more information.*

Hispanic Origin	Population	%
Hispanic or Latino (of any race)	5,226	8.41
Central American, ex. Mexican	281	0.45
Costa Rican	10	0.02
Guatemalan	113	0.18
Honduran	37	0.06
Nicaraguan	13	0.02
Panamanian	11	0.02
Salvadoran	97	0.16
Cuban	76	0.12
Dominican Republic	24	0.04
Mexican	3,181	5.12
Puerto Rican	179	0.29
South American	738	1.19
Argentinean	106	0.17
Bolivian	34	0.05
Chilean	97	0.16
Colombian	95	0.15
Ecuadorian	42	0.07
Paraguayan	3	<0.01
Peruvian	226	0.36
Uruguayan	36	0.06
Venezuelan	93	0.15
Other South American	6	0.01
Other Hispanic or Latino	747	1.20

Race*	Population	%
African-American/Black (1,040)	1,458	2.35
Not Hispanic (972)	1,315	2.12
Hispanic (68)	143	0.23
American Indian/Alaska Native (503)	861	1.39
Not Hispanic (408)	675	1.09
Hispanic (95)	186	0.30
Apache (12)	19	0.03
Arapaho (2)	3	<0.01
Blackfeet (0)	4	0.01
Canadian/French Am. Ind. (0)	1	<0.01
Central American Ind. (0)	3	<0.01
Cherokee (12)	55	0.09
Chickasaw (2)	2	<0.01
Chippewa (4)	7	0.01
Choctaw (3)	15	0.02
Comanche (0)	2	<0.01
Cree (3)	3	<0.01
Creek (2)	6	0.01
Crow (3)	4	0.01
Delaware (4)	5	0.01
Hopi (1)	3	<0.01
Inupiat *(Alaska Native)* (1)	1	<0.01
Iroquois (3)	8	0.01
Lumbee (1)	2	<0.01
Mexican American Ind. (13)	26	0.04
Navajo (240)	332	0.53
Ottawa (0)	1	<0.01
Paiute (1)	5	0.01
Potawatomi (1)	9	0.01
Pueblo (3)	17	0.03
Seminole (1)	11	0.02
Shoshone (6)	13	0.02
Sioux (15)	26	0.04
South American Ind. (2)	4	0.01
Spanish American Ind. (4)	4	0.01
Tlingit-Haida *(Alaska Native)* (1)	1	<0.01
Tohono O'Odham (6)	7	0.01
Ute (14)	25	0.04
Yaqui (0)	2	<0.01
Yup'ik *(Alaska Native)* (1)	4	0.01
Asian (2,222)	2,864	4.61
Not Hispanic (2,196)	2,784	4.48
Hispanic (26)	80	0.13
Bangladeshi (1)	1	<0.01
Bhutanese (82)	139	0.22
Burmese (118)	123	0.20
Cambodian (4)	8	0.01
Chinese, ex. Taiwanese (633)	786	1.26
Filipino (95)	160	0.26
Hmong (1)	1	<0.01
Indian (332)	390	0.63
Indonesian (11)	20	0.03
Japanese (317)	500	0.80
Korean (275)	347	0.56
Laotian (2)	7	0.01
Malaysian (1)	1	<0.01
Nepalese (44)	96	0.15
Pakistani (24)	34	0.05
Sri Lankan (17)	17	0.03
Taiwanese (32)	43	0.07
Thai (32)	57	0.09
Vietnamese (64)	100	0.16
Hawaii Native/Pacific Islander (352)	570	0.92
Not Hispanic (334)	534	0.86
Hispanic (18)	36	0.06
Fijian (0)	2	<0.01
Guamanian/Chamorro (10)	17	0.03
Marshallese (6)	6	0.01
Native Hawaiian (33)	86	0.14
Samoan (107)	192	0.31
Tongan (143)	241	0.39
White (54,209)	55,861	89.90
Not Hispanic (51,590)	52,786	84.95
Hispanic (2,619)	3,075	4.95

Murray

Place Type: City
County: Salt Lake
Population: 46,746†

Ancestry‡	Population	%
Afghan (29)	29	0.06
African, Sub-Saharan (101)	178	0.38
African (35)	44	0.10
Ethiopian (14)	14	0.03
Ghanaian (0)	9	0.02
Liberian (0)	17	0.04
Sierra Leonean (39)	71	0.15
South African (13)	23	0.05
Albanian (17)	32	0.07
American (2,347)	2,347	5.07
Arab (8)	52	0.11
Lebanese (8)	31	0.07
Moroccan (0)	21	0.05
Armenian (192)	192	0.41
Austrian (10)	76	0.16
Basque (57)	57	0.12
Belgian (21)	44	0.10
Brazilian (70)	102	0.22
British (510)	713	1.54
Canadian (45)	113	0.24
Croatian (12)	53	0.11
Czech (28)	102	0.22
Czechoslovakian (0)	36	0.08
Danish (672)	2,847	6.15
Dutch (364)	1,672	3.61
Eastern European (27)	27	0.06
English (5,765)	13,181	28.49
European (1,157)	1,302	2.81
Finnish (12)	12	0.03
French, ex. Basque (186)	1,575	3.40
French Canadian (144)	251	0.54
German (1,674)	5,399	11.67
Greek (233)	354	0.77
Hungarian (11)	19	0.04
Icelander (108)	187	0.40
Iranian (122)	164	0.35
Irish (812)	3,059	6.61
Italian (595)	1,731	3.74
Lithuanian (6)	6	0.01
Northern European (98)	107	0.23
Norwegian (642)	1,644	3.55
Polish (211)	485	1.05
Portuguese (0)	83	0.18
Romanian (69)	69	0.15
Russian (109)	142	0.31
Scandinavian (161)	467	1.01
Scotch-Irish (290)	748	1.62
Scottish (556)	2,611	5.64
Slovene (0)	50	0.11
Swedish (622)	2,449	5.29
Swiss (59)	440	0.95
Ukrainian (52)	97	0.21
Welsh (223)	1,098	2.37
West Indian, ex. Hispanic (0)	33	0.07
Jamaican (0)	33	0.07
Yugoslavian (144)	191	0.41

Hispanic Origin	Population	%
Hispanic or Latino (of any race)	4,249	9.09
Central American, ex. Mexican	237	0.51
Costa Rican	14	0.03
Guatemalan	70	0.15
Honduran	42	0.09
Nicaraguan	8	0.02
Panamanian	8	0.02
Salvadoran	94	0.20
Other Central American	1	<0.01
Cuban	44	0.09
Dominican Republic	16	0.03
Mexican	2,715	5.81
Puerto Rican	153	0.33
South American	498	1.07
Argentinean	76	0.16
Bolivian	13	0.03
Chilean	71	0.15
Colombian	80	0.17
Ecuadorian	24	0.05
Paraguayan	3	0.01
Peruvian	145	0.31
Uruguayan	30	0.06
Venezuelan	42	0.09
Other South American	14	0.03
Other Hispanic or Latino	586	1.25

Race*	Population	%
African-American/Black (783)	1,093	2.34
Not Hispanic (710)	966	2.07
Hispanic (73)	127	0.27
American Indian/Alaska Native (386)	630	1.35
Not Hispanic (298)	483	1.03
Hispanic (88)	147	0.31
Alaska Athabascan *(Ala. Nat.)* (1)	1	<0.01
Apache (3)	12	0.03
Arapaho (1)	5	0.01
Blackfeet (2)	4	0.01
Canadian/French Am. Ind. (1)	1	<0.01
Central American Ind. (4)	4	0.01
Cherokee (12)	45	0.10
Cheyenne (1)	5	0.01
Chickasaw (1)	2	<0.01
Chippewa (5)	12	0.03
Choctaw (5)	7	0.01
Creek (1)	2	<0.01
Hopi (5)	10	0.02
Inupiat *(Alaska Native)* (2)	2	<0.01
Kiowa (1)	2	<0.01
Menominee (0)	4	0.01
Mexican American Ind. (22)	24	0.05
Navajo (168)	218	0.47
Potawatomi (1)	1	<0.01
Pueblo (2)	5	0.01
Seminole (0)	1	<0.01
Shoshone (12)	16	0.03
Sioux (14)	31	0.07
South American Ind. (2)	5	0.01
Spanish American Ind. (4)	6	0.01
Tlingit-Haida *(Alaska Native)* (1)	1	<0.01
Ute (17)	27	0.06
Yakama (1)	1	<0.01
Yuman (1)	2	<0.01
Asian (1,133)	1,569	3.36
Not Hispanic (1,120)	1,524	3.26
Hispanic (13)	45	0.10
Bangladeshi (4)	4	0.01
Bhutanese (3)	11	0.02
Burmese (23)	23	0.05
Cambodian (16)	26	0.06
Chinese, ex. Taiwanese (187)	295	0.63
Filipino (76)	172	0.37
Hmong (4)	4	0.01
Indian (220)	234	0.50

*Notes: † The Census 2010 population figure is used to calculate the percentages in the Hispanic Origin and Race categories. Ancestry percentages are based on the 2006-2010 American Community Survey population (not shown); ‡ Numbers in parentheses indicate the number of people reporting a single ancestry; * Numbers in parentheses indicate the number of persons reporting this race alone, not in combination with any other race; Please refer to the Explanation of Data for more information.*

	Population	%
Indonesian (1)	1	<0.01
Japanese (229)	376	0.80
Korean (102)	134	0.29
Laotian (25)	34	0.07
Malaysian (2)	4	0.01
Nepalese (14)	23	0.05
Pakistani (59)	66	0.14
Sri Lankan (1)	1	<0.01
Taiwanese (11)	14	0.03
Thai (25)	41	0.09
Vietnamese (81)	109	0.23
Hawaii Native/Pacific Islander (200)	385	0.82
Not Hispanic (182)	348	0.74
Hispanic (18)	37	0.08
Fijian (0)	4	0.01
Guamanian/Chamorro (9)	12	0.03
Marshallese (1)	1	<0.01
Native Hawaiian (22)	104	0.22
Samoan (94)	157	0.34
Tongan (40)	100	0.21
White (41,434)	42,602	91.14
Not Hispanic (39,171)	40,039	85.65
Hispanic (2,263)	2,563	5.48

North Logan

Place Type: City
County: Cache
Population: 8,269†

Ancestry‡	Population	%
American (343)	343	4.42
Belgian (0)	23	0.30
British (49)	209	2.69
Celtic (0)	12	0.15
Czechoslovakian (11)	11	0.14
Danish (124)	507	6.53
Dutch (13)	38	0.49
English (1,060)	2,744	35.34
European (436)	436	5.61
French, ex. Basque (37)	230	2.96
French Canadian (0)	22	0.28
German (293)	1,034	13.32
Hungarian (0)	4	0.05
Irish (6)	351	4.52
Italian (56)	224	2.88
Northern European (27)	27	0.35
Norwegian (111)	393	5.06
Polish (0)	17	0.22
Russian (16)	16	0.21
Scandinavian (52)	135	1.74
Scotch-Irish (25)	127	1.64
Scottish (121)	425	5.47
Swedish (84)	324	4.17
Swiss (53)	188	2.42
Ukrainian (0)	9	0.12
Welsh (79)	217	2.79

Hispanic Origin	Population	%
Hispanic or Latino (of any race)	520	6.29
Central American, ex. Mexican	62	0.75
Guatemalan	17	0.21
Honduran	17	0.21
Panamanian	7	0.08
Salvadoran	21	0.25
Cuban	1	0.01
Mexican	315	3.81
Puerto Rican	6	0.07
South American	70	0.85
Argentinean	13	0.16
Bolivian	1	0.01
Chilean	21	0.25
Colombian	20	0.24
Ecuadorian	4	0.05
Paraguayan	2	0.02
Peruvian	8	0.10
Venezuelan	1	0.01
Other Hispanic or Latino	66	0.80

Race*	Population	%
African-American/Black (28)	63	0.76
Not Hispanic (25)	55	0.67
Hispanic (3)	8	0.10
American Indian/Alaska Native (38)	63	0.76
Not Hispanic (31)	50	0.60
Hispanic (7)	13	0.16
Apache (0)	2	0.02
Cherokee (0)	4	0.05
Creek (1)	1	0.01
Mexican American Ind. (1)	5	0.06
Navajo (17)	22	0.27
South American Ind. (1)	1	0.01
Ute (1)	1	0.01
Asian (232)	278	3.36
Not Hispanic (232)	276	3.34
Hispanic (0)	2	0.02
Cambodian (15)	19	0.23
Chinese, ex. Taiwanese (60)	66	0.80
Filipino (8)	19	0.23
Indian (49)	55	0.67
Indonesian (6)	10	0.12
Japanese (9)	21	0.25
Korean (32)	35	0.42
Laotian (4)	9	0.11
Malaysian (2)	6	0.07
Pakistani (0)	2	0.02
Taiwanese (5)	5	0.06
Thai (7)	7	0.08
Vietnamese (26)	27	0.33
Hawaii Native/Pacific Islander (57)	89	1.08
Not Hispanic (57)	88	1.06
Hispanic (0)	1	0.01
Marshallese (29)	29	0.35
Native Hawaiian (5)	15	0.18
Samoan (9)	19	0.23
Tongan (13)	22	0.27
White (7,503)	7,657	92.60
Not Hispanic (7,288)	7,398	89.47
Hispanic (215)	259	3.13

North Ogden

Place Type: City
County: Weber
Population: 17,357†

Ancestry‡	Population	%
African, Sub-Saharan (9)	16	0.10
African (0)	7	0.04
Nigerian (9)	9	0.05
American (3,110)	3,110	18.54
Arab (33)	33	0.20
Other Arab (33)	33	0.20
Australian (9)	20	0.12
Austrian (25)	39	0.23
British (50)	119	0.71
Canadian (25)	25	0.15
Czech (28)	38	0.23
Czechoslovakian (11)	11	0.07
Danish (413)	915	5.45
Dutch (115)	602	3.59
English (2,501)	5,359	31.94
European (500)	547	3.26
Finnish (11)	47	0.28
French, ex. Basque (74)	477	2.84
French Canadian (17)	115	0.69
German (496)	1,887	11.25
Greek (19)	19	0.11
Icelander (0)	35	0.21
Irish (141)	788	4.70
Italian (96)	378	2.25
Latvian (0)	12	0.07
Maltese (0)	6	0.04
Northern European (59)	59	0.35
Norwegian (203)	507	3.02
Polish (31)	139	0.83
Portuguese (0)	42	0.25
Romanian (15)	30	0.18
Russian (8)	61	0.36
Scandinavian (85)	142	0.85
Scotch-Irish (21)	190	1.13
Scottish (161)	699	4.17
Swedish (72)	420	2.50
Swiss (45)	381	2.27
Welsh (131)	413	2.46
West Indian, ex. Hispanic (0)	7	0.04
Jamaican (0)	7	0.04

Hispanic Origin	Population	%
Hispanic or Latino (of any race)	945	5.44
Central American, ex. Mexican	43	0.25
Costa Rican	3	0.02
Guatemalan	4	0.02
Honduran	8	0.05
Nicaraguan	1	0.01
Panamanian	1	0.01
Salvadoran	25	0.14
Other Central American	1	0.01
Cuban	2	0.01
Dominican Republic	2	0.01
Mexican	618	3.56
Puerto Rican	28	0.16
South American	72	0.41
Argentinean	16	0.09
Chilean	15	0.09
Colombian	9	0.05
Ecuadorian	7	0.04
Peruvian	13	0.07
Venezuelan	12	0.07
Other Hispanic or Latino	180	1.04

Race*	Population	%
African-American/Black (82)	147	0.85
Not Hispanic (79)	134	0.77
Hispanic (3)	13	0.07
American Indian/Alaska Native (69)	156	0.90
Not Hispanic (55)	118	0.68
Hispanic (14)	38	0.22
Alaska Athabascan *(Ala. Nat.)* (0)	1	0.01
Apache (2)	12	0.07
Blackfeet (1)	5	0.03
Canadian/French Am. Ind. (1)	1	0.01
Cherokee (8)	20	0.12
Cheyenne (0)	3	0.02
Chippewa (2)	4	0.02
Choctaw (1)	1	0.01
Cree (0)	1	0.01
Delaware (0)	3	0.02
Hopi (0)	3	0.02
Mexican American Ind. (5)	6	0.03
Navajo (29)	44	0.25
Paiute (0)	1	0.01
Potawatomi (1)	1	0.01
Pueblo (1)	7	0.04
Sioux (1)	2	0.01
Ute (0)	2	0.01
Asian (161)	267	1.54
Not Hispanic (158)	251	1.45
Hispanic (3)	16	0.09
Cambodian (5)	6	0.03
Chinese, ex. Taiwanese (23)	41	0.24
Filipino (16)	37	0.21
Indian (10)	18	0.10
Indonesian (1)	2	0.01
Japanese (28)	80	0.46
Korean (13)	25	0.14
Laotian (14)	24	0.14
Pakistani (9)	9	0.05
Sri Lankan (0)	2	0.01
Taiwanese (1)	1	0.01
Thai (7)	11	0.06
Vietnamese (21)	24	0.14
Hawaii Native/Pacific Islander (34)	59	0.34
Not Hispanic (34)	52	0.30
Hispanic (0)	7	0.04
Guamanian/Chamorro (3)	3	0.02
Marshallese (13)	13	0.07
Native Hawaiian (6)	11	0.06

*Notes: † The Census 2010 population figure is used to calculate the percentages in the Hispanic Origin and Race categories. Ancestry percentages are based on the 2006-2010 American Community Survey population (not shown); ‡ Numbers in parentheses indicate the number of people reporting a single ancestry; * Numbers in parentheses indicate the number of persons reporting this race alone, not in combination with any other race; Please refer to the Explanation of Data for more information.*

Samoan (3)	10	0.06
Tongan (6)	16	0.09
White (16,365)	16,688	96.15
Not Hispanic (15,863)	16,077	92.63
Hispanic (502)	611	3.52

North Salt Lake

Place Type: City
County: Davis
Population: 16,322†

Ancestry‡	Population	%
American (632)	632	4.22
Arab (12)	46	0.31
Lebanese (0)	8	0.05
Palestinian (12)	12	0.08
Syrian (0)	26	0.17
Belgian (20)	38	0.25
Brazilian (11)	11	0.07
British (181)	296	1.98
Czech (0)	45	0.30
Czechoslovakian (245)	245	1.63
Danish (125)	816	5.45
Dutch (35)	151	1.01
English (2,379)	5,556	37.07
European (366)	377	2.52
Finnish (32)	44	0.29
French, ex. Basque (56)	255	1.70
German (700)	2,125	14.18
Greek (31)	156	1.04
Hungarian (10)	10	0.07
Iranian (0)	18	0.12
Irish (176)	744	4.96
Italian (113)	404	2.70
New Zealander (0)	16	0.11
Norwegian (229)	548	3.66
Polish (54)	230	1.53
Portuguese (7)	7	0.05
Russian (16)	87	0.58
Scandinavian (149)	335	2.24
Scotch-Irish (9)	51	0.34
Scottish (181)	806	5.38
Serbian (0)	10	0.07
Swedish (152)	741	4.94
Swiss (81)	208	1.39
Ukrainian (24)	46	0.31
Welsh (16)	195	1.30
Yugoslavian (20)	20	0.13

Hispanic Origin	Population	%
Hispanic or Latino (of any race)	1,876	11.49
Central American, ex. Mexican	165	1.01
Costa Rican	11	0.07
Guatemalan	83	0.51
Honduran	4	0.02
Nicaraguan	11	0.07
Panamanian	1	0.01
Salvadoran	53	0.32
Other Central American	2	0.01
Cuban	17	0.10
Dominican Republic	2	0.01
Mexican	1,081	6.62
Puerto Rican	52	0.32
South American	255	1.56
Argentinean	22	0.13
Bolivian	8	0.05
Chilean	43	0.26
Colombian	26	0.16
Ecuadorian	21	0.13
Peruvian	116	0.71
Uruguayan	3	0.02
Venezuelan	16	0.10
Other Hispanic or Latino	304	1.86

Race*	Population	%
African-American/Black (155)	260	1.59
Not Hispanic (128)	217	1.33
Hispanic (27)	43	0.26
American Indian/Alaska Native (93)	170	1.04
Not Hispanic (74)	131	0.80
Hispanic (19)	39	0.24
Apache (1)	4	0.02
Arapaho (3)	3	0.02
Blackfeet (0)	4	0.02
Cherokee (1)	13	0.08
Chickasaw (1)	1	0.01
Choctaw (0)	1	0.01
Creek (1)	3	0.02
Crow (0)	5	0.03
Hopi (2)	2	0.01
Mexican American Ind. (5)	7	0.04
Navajo (43)	55	0.34
Osage (1)	1	0.01
Ottawa (1)	1	0.01
Paiute (0)	2	0.01
Pueblo (1)	2	0.01
Puget Sound Salish (1)	3	0.02
Shoshone (0)	2	0.01
Sioux (3)	3	0.02
South American Ind. (1)	2	0.01
Ute (3)	6	0.04
Asian (460)	606	3.71
Not Hispanic (447)	580	3.55
Hispanic (13)	26	0.16
Cambodian (2)	2	0.01
Chinese, ex. Taiwanese (120)	168	1.03
Filipino (66)	91	0.56
Hmong (8)	8	0.05
Indian (34)	37	0.23
Indonesian (3)	5	0.03
Japanese (39)	87	0.53
Korean (62)	89	0.55
Laotian (6)	7	0.04
Malaysian (1)	3	0.02
Pakistani (15)	21	0.13
Taiwanese (4)	6	0.04
Thai (7)	10	0.06
Vietnamese (57)	77	0.47
Hawaii Native/Pacific Islander (273)	359	2.20
Not Hispanic (269)	342	2.10
Hispanic (4)	17	0.10
Fijian (0)	3	0.02
Guamanian/Chamorro (5)	8	0.05
Marshallese (23)	24	0.15
Native Hawaiian (6)	36	0.22
Samoan (114)	161	0.99
Tongan (97)	120	0.74
White (14,032)	14,436	88.45
Not Hispanic (13,173)	13,463	82.48
Hispanic (859)	973	5.96

Ogden

Place Type: City
County: Weber
Population: 82,825†

Ancestry‡	Population	%
African, Sub-Saharan (227)	345	0.43
African (227)	287	0.35
Kenyan (0)	34	0.04
South African (0)	24	0.03
Alsatian (0)	10	0.01
American (12,144)	12,144	14.98
Arab (233)	269	0.33
Egyptian (0)	10	0.01
Lebanese (29)	42	0.05
Palestinian (204)	204	0.25
Syrian (0)	13	0.02
Australian (22)	132	0.16
Austrian (46)	154	0.19
Basque (7)	7	0.01
Belgian (23)	50	0.06
British (356)	559	0.69
Bulgarian (53)	53	0.07
Canadian (197)	224	0.28
Celtic (0)	7	0.01
Croatian (8)	60	0.07
Czech (0)	55	0.07
Czechoslovakian (12)	37	0.05
Danish (795)	2,476	3.05
Dutch (770)	2,275	2.81
Eastern European (11)	11	0.01
English (5,027)	12,193	15.04
European (1,002)	1,150	1.42
Finnish (59)	82	0.10
French, ex. Basque (353)	1,767	2.18
French Canadian (88)	153	0.19
German (2,518)	7,404	9.13
Greek (119)	242	0.30
Hungarian (61)	159	0.20
Icelander (0)	8	0.01
Iranian (74)	93	0.11
Irish (891)	4,504	5.56
Israeli (0)	30	0.04
Italian (687)	1,880	2.32
Lithuanian (9)	66	0.08
Northern European (85)	85	0.10
Norwegian (400)	1,130	1.39
Polish (74)	343	0.42
Portuguese (24)	84	0.10
Romanian (64)	99	0.12
Russian (134)	414	0.51
Scandinavian (196)	446	0.55
Scotch-Irish (375)	1,327	1.64
Scottish (595)	2,285	2.82
Serbian (0)	21	0.03
Slovak (55)	55	0.07
Slovene (0)	20	0.02
Soviet Union (0)	9	0.01
Swedish (330)	1,776	2.19
Swiss (180)	359	0.44
Turkish (17)	17	0.02
Ukrainian (8)	75	0.09
Welsh (229)	1,358	1.68
West Indian, ex. Hispanic (0)	18	0.02
British West Indian (0)	18	0.02
Yugoslavian (0)	35	0.04

Hispanic Origin	Population	%
Hispanic or Latino (of any race)	24,940	30.11
Central American, ex. Mexican	894	1.08
Costa Rican	28	0.03
Guatemalan	179	0.22
Honduran	60	0.07
Nicaraguan	47	0.06
Panamanian	14	0.02
Salvadoran	557	0.67
Other Central American	9	0.01
Cuban	51	0.06
Dominican Republic	21	0.03
Mexican	20,118	24.29
Puerto Rican	310	0.37
South American	434	0.52
Argentinean	91	0.11
Bolivian	14	0.02
Chilean	51	0.06
Colombian	56	0.07
Ecuadorian	30	0.04
Paraguayan	16	0.02
Peruvian	81	0.10
Uruguayan	52	0.06
Venezuelan	34	0.04
Other South American	9	0.01
Other Hispanic or Latino	3,112	3.76

Race*	Population	%
African-American/Black (1,821)	2,528	3.05
Not Hispanic (1,553)	2,088	2.52
Hispanic (268)	440	0.53
American Indian/Alaska Native (1,156)	2,010	2.43
Not Hispanic (701)	1,282	1.55
Hispanic (455)	728	0.88
Alaska Athabascan *(Ala. Nat.)* (3)	4	<0.01
Aleut *(Alaska Native)* (1)	3	<0.01
Apache (15)	57	0.07
Arapaho (3)	4	<0.01
Blackfeet (9)	24	0.03
Canadian/French Am. Ind. (0)	1	<0.01

*Notes: † The Census 2010 population figure is used to calculate the percentages in the Hispanic Origin and Race categories. Ancestry percentages are based on the 2006-2010 American Community Survey population (not shown); ‡ Numbers in parentheses indicate the number of people reporting a single ancestry; * Numbers in parentheses indicate the number of persons reporting this race alone, not in combination with any other race; Please refer to the Explanation of Data for more information.*

Central American Ind. (3)	7	0.01
Cherokee (41)	171	0.21
Cheyenne (2)	8	0.01
Chickasaw (3)	4	<0.01
Chippewa (2)	14	0.02
Choctaw (9)	27	0.03
Colville (1)	1	<0.01
Comanche (5)	5	0.01
Cree (0)	2	<0.01
Creek (2)	5	0.01
Crow (5)	10	0.01
Delaware (2)	12	0.01
Hopi (8)	19	0.02
Inupiat *(Alaska Native)* (2)	5	0.01
Iroquois (4)	7	0.01
Kiowa (0)	1	<0.01
Menominee (1)	2	<0.01
Mexican American Ind. (41)	79	0.10
Navajo (268)	402	0.49
Osage (0)	1	<0.01
Ottawa (1)	1	<0.01
Paiute (4)	10	0.01
Pima (4)	4	<0.01
Potawatomi (0)	2	<0.01
Pueblo (11)	12	0.01
Puget Sound Salish (4)	4	<0.01
Seminole (0)	8	0.01
Shoshone (39)	70	0.08
Sioux (40)	71	0.09
South American Ind. (3)	21	0.03
Spanish American Ind. (5)	11	0.01
Tlingit-Haida *(Alaska Native)* (3)	5	0.01
Tsimshian *(Alaska Native)* (1)	1	<0.01
Ute (42)	77	0.09
Yakama (0)	1	<0.01
Yaqui (8)	28	0.03
Yuman (2)	5	0.01
Yup'ik *(Alaska Native)* (0)	1	<0.01
Asian (1,029)	1,768	2.13
Not Hispanic (966)	1,546	1.87
Hispanic (63)	222	0.27
Bangladeshi (2)	5	0.01
Cambodian (2)	12	0.01
Chinese, ex. Taiwanese (142)	250	0.30
Filipino (195)	414	0.50
Hmong (25)	27	0.03
Indian (74)	106	0.13
Indonesian (3)	17	0.02
Japanese (185)	359	0.43
Korean (61)	139	0.17
Laotian (46)	68	0.08
Nepalese (2)	2	<0.01
Pakistani (27)	27	0.03
Sri Lankan (3)	3	<0.01
Taiwanese (18)	19	0.02
Thai (38)	69	0.08
Vietnamese (137)	155	0.19
Hawaii Native/Pacific Islander (252)	525	0.63
Not Hispanic (241)	476	0.57
Hispanic (11)	49	0.06
Guamanian/Chamorro (16)	50	0.06
Marshallese (30)	35	0.04
Native Hawaiian (33)	123	0.15
Samoan (67)	140	0.17
Tongan (59)	103	0.12
White (62,318)	65,064	78.56
Not Hispanic (52,557)	54,120	65.34
Hispanic (9,761)	10,944	13.21

Orem

Place Type: City
County: Utah
Population: 88,328†

Ancestry‡	Population	%
African, Sub-Saharan (81)	94	0.11
African (55)	68	0.08
South African (26)	26	0.03
American (3,650)	3,650	4.20
Arab (263)	308	0.35
Arab (196)	212	0.24
Lebanese (6)	35	0.04
Moroccan (14)	14	0.02
Syrian (47)	47	0.05
Australian (8)	17	0.02
Austrian (33)	111	0.13
Basque (0)	30	0.03
Belgian (0)	22	0.03
Brazilian (224)	260	0.30
British (738)	1,439	1.66
Canadian (274)	594	0.68
Celtic (0)	13	0.01
Croatian (12)	106	0.12
Czech (104)	216	0.25
Czechoslovakian (253)	260	0.30
Danish (1,071)	5,572	6.42
Dutch (399)	1,423	1.64
English (9,876)	25,177	28.99
Estonian (21)	21	0.02
European (3,035)	3,386	3.90
Finnish (97)	146	0.17
French, ex. Basque (221)	1,760	2.03
French Canadian (34)	134	0.15
German (2,099)	9,943	11.45
Greek (24)	141	0.16
Hungarian (23)	100	0.12
Icelander (44)	132	0.15
Iranian (19)	52	0.06
Irish (797)	4,275	4.92
Israeli (0)	25	0.03
Italian (364)	1,494	1.72
Maltese (11)	24	0.03
Northern European (95)	104	0.12
Norwegian (538)	2,031	2.34
Polish (148)	488	0.56
Portuguese (29)	135	0.16
Romanian (9)	224	0.26
Russian (161)	396	0.46
Scandinavian (653)	1,689	1.94
Scotch-Irish (537)	1,285	1.48
Scottish (1,111)	5,672	6.53
Serbian (0)	14	0.02
Slavic (0)	18	0.02
Slovak (0)	8	0.01
Swedish (786)	3,563	4.10
Swiss (233)	1,084	1.25
Ukrainian (0)	26	0.03
Welsh (404)	2,447	2.82
West Indian, ex. Hispanic (22)	45	0.05
Belizean (0)	11	0.01
Haitian (22)	22	0.03
West Indian (0)	12	0.01
Yugoslavian (0)	14	0.02

Hispanic Origin	Population	%
Hispanic or Latino (of any race)	14,224	16.10
Central American, ex. Mexican	992	1.12
Costa Rican	52	0.06
Guatemalan	318	0.36
Honduran	83	0.09
Nicaraguan	54	0.06
Panamanian	34	0.04
Salvadoran	444	0.50
Other Central American	7	0.01
Cuban	56	0.06
Dominican Republic	91	0.10
Mexican	9,804	11.10
Puerto Rican	225	0.25
South American	2,121	2.40
Argentinean	623	0.71
Bolivian	83	0.09
Chilean	292	0.33
Colombian	135	0.15
Ecuadorian	223	0.25
Paraguayan	18	0.02
Peruvian	540	0.61
Uruguayan	73	0.08
Venezuelan	130	0.15
Other South American	4	<0.01
Other Hispanic or Latino	935	1.06

Race*	Population	%
African-American/Black (633)	1,035	1.17
Not Hispanic (524)	820	0.93
Hispanic (109)	215	0.24
American Indian/Alaska Native (766)	1,297	1.47
Not Hispanic (528)	923	1.04
Hispanic (238)	374	0.42
Alaska Athabascan *(Ala. Nat.)* (2)	5	0.01
Apache (9)	19	0.02
Arapaho (0)	1	<0.01
Blackfeet (4)	14	0.02
Canadian/French Am. Ind. (2)	6	0.01
Central American Ind. (6)	10	0.01
Cherokee (13)	82	0.09
Cheyenne (1)	2	<0.01
Chickasaw (4)	7	0.01
Chippewa (4)	7	0.01
Choctaw (10)	10	0.01
Comanche (1)	6	0.01
Cree (0)	1	<0.01
Creek (1)	2	<0.01
Delaware (0)	1	<0.01
Hopi (8)	19	0.02
Inupiat *(Alaska Native)* (0)	5	0.01
Iroquois (10)	16	0.02
Kiowa (1)	4	<0.01
Lumbee (0)	2	<0.01
Mexican American Ind. (69)	90	0.10
Navajo (303)	395	0.45
Osage (0)	4	<0.01
Ottawa (3)	5	0.01
Paiute (8)	9	0.01
Pima (1)	1	<0.01
Potawatomi (0)	5	0.01
Pueblo (8)	12	0.01
Puget Sound Salish (1)	2	<0.01
Seminole (0)	4	<0.01
Shoshone (3)	9	0.01
Sioux (20)	43	0.05
South American Ind. (13)	27	0.03
Spanish American Ind. (8)	9	0.01
Tlingit-Haida *(Alaska Native)* (8)	9	0.01
Tohono O'Odham (2)	3	<0.01
Ute (23)	36	0.04
Yaqui (4)	9	0.01
Yup'ik *(Alaska Native)* (1)	2	<0.01
Asian (1,713)	2,610	2.95
Not Hispanic (1,688)	2,495	2.82
Hispanic (25)	115	0.13
Bangladeshi (2)	2	<0.01
Burmese (1)	1	<0.01
Cambodian (13)	26	0.03
Chinese, ex. Taiwanese (364)	613	0.69
Filipino (148)	330	0.37
Hmong (10)	13	0.01
Indian (166)	203	0.23
Indonesian (11)	26	0.03
Japanese (285)	606	0.69
Korean (312)	435	0.49
Laotian (79)	107	0.12
Malaysian (1)	1	<0.01
Nepalese (13)	14	0.02
Pakistani (12)	14	0.02
Taiwanese (26)	35	0.04
Thai (73)	96	0.11
Vietnamese (60)	87	0.10
Hawaii Native/Pacific Islander (879)	1,666	1.89
Not Hispanic (856)	1,576	1.78
Hispanic (23)	90	0.10
Fijian (12)	38	0.04
Guamanian/Chamorro (3)	13	0.01
Marshallese (4)	6	0.01
Native Hawaiian (118)	521	0.59
Samoan (291)	595	0.67
Tongan (296)	509	0.58
White (74,616)	77,207	87.41
Not Hispanic (68,433)	70,194	79.47
Hispanic (6,183)	7,013	7.94

*Notes: † The Census 2010 population figure is used to calculate the percentages in the Hispanic Origin and Race categories. Ancestry percentages are based on the 2006-2010 American Community Survey population (not shown); ‡ Numbers in parentheses indicate the number of people reporting a single ancestry; * Numbers in parentheses indicate the number of persons reporting this race alone, not in combination with any other race; Please refer to the Explanation of Data for more information.*

Park City

Place Type: City
County: Summit
Population: 7,558†

Ancestry‡	Population	%
American (1,753)	1,753	23.21
Australian (0)	62	0.82
Austrian (16)	16	0.21
Brazilian (34)	34	0.45
British (183)	350	4.63
Czech (0)	23	0.30
Danish (0)	90	1.19
Dutch (29)	158	2.09
English (329)	1,134	15.01
European (143)	143	1.89
French, ex. Basque (0)	160	2.12
German (290)	927	12.27
Greek (22)	32	0.42
Hungarian (61)	115	1.52
Irish (171)	492	6.51
Italian (161)	459	6.08
Lithuanian (0)	51	0.68
Northern European (29)	29	0.38
Norwegian (57)	198	2.62
Polish (42)	58	0.77
Portuguese (12)	68	0.90
Russian (45)	137	1.81
Scotch-Irish (18)	98	1.30
Scottish (28)	119	1.58
Serbian (0)	22	0.29
Slovak (33)	33	0.44
Swedish (0)	301	3.99
Ukrainian (10)	10	0.13
Welsh (0)	206	2.73

Hispanic Origin	Population	%
Hispanic or Latino (of any race)	1,819	24.07
Central American, ex. Mexican	31	0.41
Guatemalan	8	0.11
Honduran	1	0.01
Nicaraguan	4	0.05
Panamanian	4	0.05
Salvadoran	14	0.19
Cuban	3	0.04
Dominican Republic	3	0.04
Mexican	1,542	20.40
Puerto Rican	9	0.12
South American	65	0.86
Argentinean	7	0.09
Bolivian	1	0.01
Chilean	10	0.13
Colombian	5	0.07
Paraguayan	2	0.03
Peruvian	34	0.45
Uruguayan	4	0.05
Other South American	2	0.03
Other Hispanic or Latino	166	2.20

Race*	Population	%
African-American/Black (49)	68	0.90
Not Hispanic (22)	36	0.48
Hispanic (27)	32	0.42
American Indian/Alaska Native (26)	53	0.70
Not Hispanic (19)	40	0.53
Hispanic (7)	13	0.17
Aleut *(Alaska Native)* (1)	1	0.01
Cherokee (0)	4	0.05
Chickasaw (1)	1	0.01
Choctaw (1)	1	0.01
Iroquois (0)	1	0.01
Menominee (0)	1	0.01
Mexican American Ind. (2)	7	0.09
Navajo (12)	14	0.19
Shoshone (1)	1	0.01
Sioux (0)	6	0.08
South American Ind. (1)	1	0.01
Yuman (2)	2	0.03
Asian (156)	194	2.57
Not Hispanic (150)	186	2.46
Hispanic (6)	8	0.11
Cambodian (2)	2	0.03
Chinese, ex. Taiwanese (18)	27	0.36
Filipino (79)	94	1.24
Indian (7)	10	0.13
Indonesian (5)	5	0.07
Japanese (17)	28	0.37
Korean (9)	9	0.12
Taiwanese (1)	2	0.03
Thai (1)	1	0.01
Vietnamese (8)	8	0.11
Hawaii Native/Pacific Islander (19)	27	0.36
Not Hispanic (13)	21	0.28
Hispanic (6)	6	0.08
Guamanian/Chamorro (1)	3	0.04
Native Hawaiian (11)	15	0.20
Samoan (4)	4	0.05
White (6,120)	6,285	83.16
Not Hispanic (5,429)	5,505	72.84
Hispanic (691)	780	10.32

Payson

Place Type: City
County: Utah
Population: 18,294†

Ancestry‡	Population	%
African, Sub-Saharan (9)	9	0.05
African (9)	9	0.05
American (1,233)	1,233	7.17
Australian (0)	9	0.05
Austrian (6)	287	1.67
Belgian (0)	7	0.04
Brazilian (39)	39	0.23
British (88)	286	1.66
Bulgarian (0)	8	0.05
Canadian (9)	9	0.05
Czech (7)	21	0.12
Czechoslovakian (0)	10	0.06
Danish (205)	843	4.90
Dutch (86)	367	2.14
English (1,887)	4,305	25.05
European (842)	899	5.23
Finnish (8)	30	0.17
French, ex. Basque (63)	384	2.23
French Canadian (7)	7	0.04
German (354)	1,713	9.97
Greek (33)	86	0.50
Icelander (50)	180	1.05
Iranian (12)	44	0.26
Irish (198)	810	4.71
Italian (115)	557	3.24
Northern European (45)	45	0.26
Norwegian (113)	299	1.74
Pennsylvania German (10)	10	0.06
Polish (14)	164	0.95
Portuguese (6)	6	0.03
Russian (29)	43	0.25
Scandinavian (117)	382	2.22
Scotch-Irish (49)	192	1.12
Scottish (158)	1,095	6.37
Swedish (195)	642	3.74
Swiss (195)	535	3.11
Turkish (79)	79	0.46
Ukrainian (13)	13	0.08
Welsh (36)	407	2.37
Yugoslavian (8)	8	0.05

Hispanic Origin	Population	%
Hispanic or Latino (of any race)	2,431	13.29
Central American, ex. Mexican	168	0.92
Costa Rican	3	0.02
Guatemalan	27	0.15
Honduran	28	0.15
Nicaraguan	2	0.01
Panamanian	4	0.02
Salvadoran	104	0.57
Cuban	2	0.01
Mexican	1,901	10.39
Puerto Rican	21	0.11
South American	164	0.90
Argentinean	75	0.41
Chilean	23	0.13
Colombian	14	0.08
Ecuadorian	17	0.09
Paraguayan	1	0.01
Peruvian	16	0.09
Uruguayan	7	0.04
Venezuelan	9	0.05
Other South American	2	0.01
Other Hispanic or Latino	175	0.96

Race*	Population	%
African-American/Black (48)	96	0.52
Not Hispanic (42)	75	0.41
Hispanic (6)	21	0.11
American Indian/Alaska Native (103)	218	1.19
Not Hispanic (82)	179	0.98
Hispanic (21)	39	0.21
Alaska Athabascan *(Ala. Nat.)* (2)	2	0.01
Apache (0)	2	0.01
Cherokee (9)	20	0.11
Cheyenne (0)	3	0.02
Chippewa (0)	5	0.03
Choctaw (1)	10	0.05
Iroquois (0)	1	0.01
Mexican American Ind. (12)	19	0.10
Navajo (24)	54	0.30
Paiute (0)	1	0.01
Seminole (0)	1	0.01
Sioux (10)	14	0.08
Tlingit-Haida *(Alaska Native)* (0)	2	0.01
Ute (1)	2	0.01
Yaqui (0)	1	0.01
Asian (67)	140	0.77
Not Hispanic (66)	120	0.66
Hispanic (1)	20	0.11
Burmese (1)	1	0.01
Cambodian (1)	5	0.03
Chinese, ex. Taiwanese (6)	13	0.07
Filipino (21)	39	0.21
Indian (14)	17	0.09
Japanese (6)	21	0.11
Korean (7)	24	0.13
Laotian (6)	6	0.03
Taiwanese (3)	3	0.02
Thai (2)	2	0.01
Hawaii Native/Pacific Islander (47)	103	0.56
Not Hispanic (44)	94	0.51
Hispanic (3)	9	0.05
Guamanian/Chamorro (1)	1	0.01
Marshallese (2)	2	0.01
Native Hawaiian (4)	15	0.08
Samoan (10)	47	0.26
Tongan (17)	32	0.17
White (16,532)	16,868	92.21
Not Hispanic (15,393)	15,607	85.31
Hispanic (1,139)	1,261	6.89

Pleasant Grove

Place Type: City
County: Utah
Population: 33,509†

Ancestry‡	Population	%
African, Sub-Saharan (10)	10	0.03
Liberian (10)	10	0.03
American (1,651)	1,651	5.25
Armenian (0)	84	0.27
Austrian (11)	78	0.25
Belgian (0)	12	0.04
Brazilian (34)	74	0.24
British (248)	371	1.18
Bulgarian (12)	12	0.04
Cajun (0)	15	0.05
Canadian (54)	235	0.75
Croatian (0)	11	0.03

*Notes: † The Census 2010 population figure is used to calculate the percentages in the Hispanic Origin and Race categories. Ancestry percentages are based on the 2006-2010 American Community Survey population (not shown); ‡ Numbers in parentheses indicate the number of people reporting a single ancestry; * Numbers in parentheses indicate the number of persons reporting this race alone, not in combination with any other race; Please refer to the Explanation of Data for more information.*

Czech (9)	60	0.19
Czechoslovakian (36)	36	0.11
Danish (572)	2,556	8.13
Dutch (213)	683	2.17
English (4,192)	9,869	31.37
European (1,515)	1,858	5.91
Finnish (0)	101	0.32
French, ex. Basque (25)	492	1.56
French Canadian (8)	40	0.13
German (826)	3,454	10.98
Greek (33)	214	0.68
Hungarian (14)	134	0.43
Icelander (17)	17	0.05
Iranian (9)	18	0.06
Irish (369)	1,844	5.86
Italian (209)	805	2.56
Lithuanian (0)	22	0.07
Norwegian (221)	525	1.67
Polish (14)	153	0.49
Portuguese (0)	108	0.34
Romanian (11)	25	0.08
Russian (51)	82	0.26
Scandinavian (83)	320	1.02
Scotch-Irish (120)	472	1.50
Scottish (353)	2,468	7.85
Slavic (0)	9	0.03
Slovene (0)	16	0.05
Swedish (343)	1,469	4.67
Swiss (113)	647	2.06
Ukrainian (44)	58	0.18
Welsh (110)	494	1.57
West Indian, ex. Hispanic (11)	30	0.10
Trinidadian/Tobagonian (11)	11	0.03
West Indian (0)	19	0.06

Hispanic Origin	Population	%
Hispanic or Latino (of any race)	2,577	7.69
Central American, ex. Mexican	162	0.48
Costa Rican	10	0.03
Guatemalan	59	0.18
Honduran	14	0.04
Nicaraguan	25	0.07
Panamanian	3	0.01
Salvadoran	49	0.15
Other Central American	2	0.01
Cuban	22	0.07
Dominican Republic	32	0.10
Mexican	1,593	4.75
Puerto Rican	49	0.15
South American	460	1.37
Argentinean	131	0.39
Bolivian	10	0.03
Chilean	76	0.23
Colombian	54	0.16
Ecuadorian	27	0.08
Paraguayan	1	<0.01
Peruvian	82	0.24
Uruguayan	22	0.07
Venezuelan	53	0.16
Other South American	4	0.01
Other Hispanic or Latino	259	0.77

Race*	Population	%
African-American/Black (178)	306	0.91
Not Hispanic (160)	255	0.76
Hispanic (18)	51	0.15
American Indian/Alaska Native (136)	332	0.99
Not Hispanic (106)	267	0.80
Hispanic (30)	65	0.19
Aleut *(Alaska Native)* (0)	1	<0.01
Apache (3)	13	0.04
Arapaho (0)	2	0.01
Blackfeet (1)	4	0.01
Central American Ind. (0)	1	<0.01
Cherokee (17)	39	0.12
Chickasaw (0)	1	<0.01
Chippewa (0)	2	0.01
Choctaw (2)	9	0.03
Cree (2)	2	0.01
Creek (0)	4	0.01
Hopi (2)	17	0.05
Iroquois (5)	14	0.04
Kiowa (1)	2	0.01
Lumbee (0)	3	0.01
Menominee (1)	1	<0.01
Mexican American Ind. (7)	9	0.03
Navajo (37)	61	0.18
Osage (0)	1	<0.01
Paiute (3)	6	0.02
Pima (7)	7	0.02
Potawatomi (0)	2	0.01
Shoshone (3)	3	0.01
Sioux (1)	6	0.02
South American Ind. (1)	8	0.02
Ute (5)	5	0.01
Yaqui (1)	1	<0.01
Asian (313)	586	1.75
Not Hispanic (308)	552	1.65
Hispanic (5)	34	0.10
Cambodian (8)	9	0.03
Chinese, ex. Taiwanese (92)	153	0.46
Filipino (15)	69	0.21
Hmong (5)	6	0.02
Indian (56)	80	0.24
Indonesian (1)	2	0.01
Japanese (28)	136	0.41
Korean (38)	64	0.19
Laotian (2)	4	0.01
Pakistani (12)	16	0.05
Taiwanese (1)	7	0.02
Thai (11)	21	0.06
Vietnamese (10)	18	0.05
Hawaii Native/Pacific Islander (187)	358	1.07
Not Hispanic (183)	340	1.01
Hispanic (4)	18	0.05
Fijian (1)	3	0.01
Guamanian/Chamorro (3)	11	0.03
Marshallese (21)	21	0.06
Native Hawaiian (13)	77	0.23
Samoan (62)	142	0.42
Tongan (58)	93	0.28
White (30,857)	31,680	94.54
Not Hispanic (29,541)	30,116	89.87
Hispanic (1,316)	1,564	4.67

Pleasant View

Place Type: City
County: Weber
Population: 7,979†

Ancestry‡	Population	%
American (1,222)	1,222	16.33
Belgian (5)	5	0.07
British (28)	60	0.80
Croatian (0)	36	0.48
Czech (0)	18	0.24
Czechoslovakian (0)	18	0.24
Danish (87)	491	6.56
Dutch (78)	184	2.46
English (674)	2,027	27.10
European (324)	339	4.53
French, ex. Basque (29)	190	2.54
French Canadian (5)	5	0.07
German (147)	1,181	15.79
Greek (11)	11	0.15
Icelander (0)	38	0.51
Irish (94)	441	5.89
Italian (46)	151	2.02
Northern European (49)	49	0.65
Norwegian (64)	476	6.36
Polish (0)	66	0.88
Scandinavian (27)	27	0.36
Scotch-Irish (21)	131	1.75
Scottish (47)	370	4.95
Swedish (21)	255	3.41
Swiss (16)	82	1.10
Welsh (3)	203	2.71
Yugoslavian (0)	17	0.23

Hispanic Origin	Population	%
Hispanic or Latino (of any race)	579	7.26
Central American, ex. Mexican	25	0.31
Costa Rican	2	0.03
Guatemalan	12	0.15
Honduran	5	0.06
Panamanian	1	0.01
Salvadoran	5	0.06
Cuban	3	0.04
Mexican	430	5.39
Puerto Rican	8	0.10
South American	23	0.29
Argentinean	3	0.04
Chilean	3	0.04
Colombian	11	0.14
Ecuadorian	5	0.06
Uruguayan	1	0.01
Other Hispanic or Latino	90	1.13

Race*	Population	%
African-American/Black (28)	59	0.74
Not Hispanic (25)	41	0.51
Hispanic (3)	18	0.23
American Indian/Alaska Native (19)	62	0.78
Not Hispanic (18)	58	0.73
Hispanic (1)	4	0.05
Arapaho (0)	3	0.04
Blackfeet (0)	10	0.13
Cherokee (0)	2	0.03
Chippewa (0)	1	0.01
Choctaw (3)	6	0.08
Navajo (7)	7	0.09
Osage (0)	5	0.06
Puget Sound Salish (0)	4	0.05
Seminole (0)	2	0.03
Asian (75)	122	1.53
Not Hispanic (70)	117	1.47
Hispanic (5)	5	0.06
Chinese, ex. Taiwanese (13)	18	0.23
Filipino (6)	10	0.13
Indian (11)	14	0.18
Japanese (25)	38	0.48
Korean (3)	15	0.19
Thai (3)	3	0.04
Vietnamese (3)	3	0.04
Hawaii Native/Pacific Islander (30)	44	0.55
Not Hispanic (29)	43	0.54
Hispanic (1)	1	0.01
Guamanian/Chamorro (2)	2	0.03
Marshallese (8)	9	0.11
Native Hawaiian (6)	14	0.18
Samoan (4)	4	0.05
Tongan (1)	6	0.08
White (7,425)	7,573	94.91
Not Hispanic (7,143)	7,255	90.93
Hispanic (282)	318	3.99

Price

Place Type: City
County: Carbon
Population: 8,715†

Ancestry‡	Population	%
American (215)	215	2.54
Armenian (0)	12	0.14
Austrian (87)	104	1.23
Belgian (8)	23	0.27
British (10)	10	0.12
Canadian (12)	18	0.21
Czech (0)	28	0.33
Czechoslovakian (13)	13	0.15
Danish (147)	554	6.54
Dutch (19)	215	2.54
English (755)	2,233	26.35
European (36)	36	0.42
Finnish (0)	47	0.55
French, ex. Basque (10)	172	2.03
German (364)	1,428	16.85
Greek (140)	252	2.97

SECTION TWO

*Notes: † The Census 2010 population figure is used to calculate the percentages in the Hispanic Origin and Race categories. Ancestry percentages are based on the 2006-2010 American Community Survey population (not shown); ‡ Numbers in parentheses indicate the number of people reporting a single ancestry; * Numbers in parentheses indicate the number of persons reporting this race alone, not in combination with any other race; Please refer to the Explanation of Data for more information.*

Hungarian (0)	55	0.65
Icelander (6)	27	0.32
Irish (126)	782	9.23
Italian (347)	728	8.59
Lithuanian (0)	83	0.98
Norwegian (46)	129	1.52
Pennsylvania German (0)	11	0.13
Polish (22)	74	0.87
Portuguese (0)	9	0.11
Romanian (0)	83	0.98
Scandinavian (0)	28	0.33
Scotch-Irish (14)	78	0.92
Scottish (51)	284	3.35
Serbian (9)	9	0.11
Slovak (0)	15	0.18
Slovene (0)	46	0.54
Swedish (63)	286	3.38
Swiss (16)	48	0.57
Welsh (30)	171	2.02
Yugoslavian (21)	40	0.47

Hispanic Origin	Population	%
Hispanic or Latino (of any race)	1,184	13.59
Central American, ex. Mexican	23	0.26
Guatemalan	18	0.21
Nicaraguan	1	0.01
Salvadoran	3	0.03
Other Central American	1	0.01
Cuban	3	0.03
Mexican	777	8.92
Puerto Rican	8	0.09
South American	22	0.25
Bolivian	6	0.07
Chilean	3	0.03
Colombian	1	0.01
Peruvian	11	0.13
Uruguayan	1	0.01
Other Hispanic or Latino	351	4.03

Race*	Population	%
African-American/Black (50)	91	1.04
Not Hispanic (48)	79	0.91
Hispanic (2)	12	0.14
American Indian/Alaska Native (123)	214	2.46
Not Hispanic (86)	141	1.62
Hispanic (37)	73	0.84
Apache (2)	11	0.13
Blackfeet (0)	2	0.02
Cherokee (5)	22	0.25
Chickasaw (0)	3	0.03
Chippewa (0)	2	0.02
Choctaw (3)	3	0.03
Comanche (1)	2	0.02
Hopi (1)	2	0.02
Mexican American Ind. (1)	3	0.03
Navajo (49)	79	0.91
Pima (1)	1	0.01
Pueblo (0)	1	0.01
Shoshone (1)	6	0.07
Sioux (3)	4	0.05
South American Ind. (0)	1	0.01
Spanish American Ind. (1)	1	0.01
Tlingit-Haida *(Alaska Native)* (0)	1	0.01
Tohono O'Odham (2)	2	0.02
Ute (11)	14	0.16
Asian (85)	112	1.29
Not Hispanic (85)	109	1.25
Hispanic (0)	3	0.03
Chinese, ex. Taiwanese (5)	6	0.07
Filipino (9)	14	0.16
Indian (2)	2	0.02
Japanese (8)	20	0.23
Korean (39)	44	0.50
Taiwanese (1)	1	0.01
Thai (3)	4	0.05
Vietnamese (3)	4	0.05
Hawaii Native/Pacific Islander (9)	19	0.22
Not Hispanic (9)	17	0.20
Hispanic (0)	2	0.02
Guamanian/Chamorro (3)	3	0.03
Native Hawaiian (3)	7	0.08
Samoan (3)	5	0.06
White (7,950)	8,128	93.26
Not Hispanic (7,182)	7,287	83.61
Hispanic (768)	841	9.65

Provo

Place Type: City
County: Utah
Population: 112,488†

Ancestry‡	Population	%
African, Sub-Saharan (256)	477	0.43
African (100)	272	0.25
Ethiopian (26)	26	0.02
Ghanaian (34)	48	0.04
Nigerian (11)	11	0.01
Sierra Leonean (16)	16	0.01
Somalian (0)	29	0.03
South African (0)	6	0.01
Ugandan (45)	45	0.04
Other Sub-Saharan African (24)	24	0.02
Albanian (65)	65	0.06
American (3,095)	3,095	2.81
Arab (56)	270	0.25
Arab (0)	75	0.07
Lebanese (0)	23	0.02
Syrian (46)	162	0.15
Other Arab (10)	10	0.01
Armenian (25)	25	0.02
Australian (55)	151	0.14
Austrian (60)	255	0.23
Basque (0)	74	0.07
Belgian (108)	122	0.11
Brazilian (403)	505	0.46
British (1,207)	2,706	2.46
Cajun (12)	12	0.01
Canadian (226)	509	0.46
Celtic (18)	18	0.02
Croatian (9)	86	0.08
Czech (80)	234	0.21
Czechoslovakian (0)	35	0.03
Danish (1,416)	6,933	6.29
Dutch (345)	1,481	1.34
Eastern European (27)	27	0.02
English (11,461)	30,420	27.60
Estonian (10)	10	0.01
European (6,087)	7,164	6.50
Finnish (47)	198	0.18
French, ex. Basque (545)	2,624	2.38
French Canadian (54)	303	0.27
German (2,931)	12,975	11.77
Greek (96)	387	0.35
Hungarian (67)	131	0.12
Icelander (65)	128	0.12
Iranian (38)	70	0.06
Irish (1,370)	6,146	5.58
Italian (777)	2,931	2.66
Lithuanian (31)	103	0.09
New Zealander (10)	163	0.15
Northern European (219)	246	0.22
Norwegian (855)	2,355	2.14
Polish (179)	881	0.80
Portuguese (69)	187	0.17
Romanian (26)	117	0.11
Russian (387)	683	0.62
Scandinavian (763)	1,775	1.61
Scotch-Irish (728)	1,959	1.78
Scottish (1,758)	6,448	5.85
Serbian (11)	47	0.04
Slavic (0)	13	0.01
Slovak (28)	61	0.06
Slovene (17)	17	0.02
Swedish (1,286)	5,073	4.60
Swiss (242)	1,574	1.43
Turkish (56)	56	0.05
Ukrainian (59)	151	0.14
Welsh (525)	3,138	2.85
West Indian, ex. Hispanic (40)	49	0.04
Bahamian (13)	13	0.01
Dutch West Indian (0)	9	0.01
Haitian (20)	20	0.02
West Indian (7)	7	0.01
Yugoslavian (13)	73	0.07

Hispanic Origin	Population	%
Hispanic or Latino (of any race)	17,091	15.19
Central American, ex. Mexican	1,282	1.14
Costa Rican	57	0.05
Guatemalan	390	0.35
Honduran	197	0.18
Nicaraguan	89	0.08
Panamanian	27	0.02
Salvadoran	519	0.46
Other Central American	3	<0.01
Cuban	117	0.10
Dominican Republic	161	0.14
Mexican	11,472	10.20
Puerto Rican	336	0.30
South American	2,374	2.11
Argentinean	635	0.56
Bolivian	105	0.09
Chilean	314	0.28
Colombian	194	0.17
Ecuadorian	224	0.20
Paraguayan	17	0.02
Peruvian	644	0.57
Uruguayan	53	0.05
Venezuelan	179	0.16
Other South American	9	0.01
Other Hispanic or Latino	1,349	1.20

Race*	Population	%
African-American/Black (808)	1,280	1.14
Not Hispanic (672)	1,007	0.90
Hispanic (136)	273	0.24
American Indian/Alaska Native (939)	1,680	1.49
Not Hispanic (719)	1,285	1.14
Hispanic (220)	395	0.35
Alaska Athabascan *(Ala. Nat.)* (2)	3	<0.01
Aleut *(Alaska Native)* (1)	1	<0.01
Apache (7)	21	0.02
Arapaho (15)	15	0.01
Blackfeet (8)	25	0.02
Canadian/French Am. Ind. (2)	3	<0.01
Central American Ind. (4)	8	0.01
Cherokee (25)	140	0.12
Cheyenne (1)	6	0.01
Chickasaw (0)	23	0.02
Chippewa (9)	22	0.02
Choctaw (11)	21	0.02
Comanche (4)	11	0.01
Cree (5)	11	0.01
Creek (3)	5	<0.01
Delaware (0)	1	<0.01
Hopi (1)	13	0.01
Inupiat *(Alaska Native)* (2)	5	<0.01
Iroquois (14)	43	0.04
Kiowa (1)	1	<0.01
Lumbee (4)	5	<0.01
Mexican American Ind. (25)	52	0.05
Navajo (341)	428	0.38
Osage (0)	5	<0.01
Paiute (5)	12	0.01
Pima (2)	3	<0.01
Potawatomi (2)	8	0.01
Pueblo (3)	8	0.01
Puget Sound Salish (0)	1	<0.01
Seminole (1)	3	<0.01
Shoshone (7)	23	0.02
Sioux (35)	60	0.05
South American Ind. (9)	30	0.03
Spanish American Ind. (1)	6	0.01
Tlingit-Haida *(Alaska Native)* (5)	6	0.01
Tohono O'Odham (2)	2	<0.01
Tsimshian *(Alaska Native)* (1)	1	<0.01
Ute (25)	42	0.04
Yaqui (11)	12	0.01
Yuman (1)	2	<0.01

*Notes: † The Census 2010 population figure is used to calculate the percentages in the Hispanic Origin and Race categories. Ancestry percentages are based on the 2006-2010 American Community Survey population (not shown); ‡ Numbers in parentheses indicate the number of people reporting a single ancestry; * Numbers in parentheses indicate the number of persons reporting this race alone, not in combination with any other race; Please refer to the Explanation of Data for more information.*

Yup'ik *(Alaska Native)* (2)	3	<0.01
Asian (2,772)	4,256	3.78
Not Hispanic (2,743)	4,088	3.63
Hispanic (29)	168	0.15
Burmese (2)	6	0.01
Cambodian (41)	64	0.06
Chinese, ex. Taiwanese (760)	1,316	1.17
Filipino (150)	492	0.44
Hmong (4)	4	<0.01
Indian (170)	232	0.21
Indonesian (9)	18	0.02
Japanese (352)	864	0.77
Korean (597)	747	0.66
Laotian (37)	43	0.04
Malaysian (0)	2	<0.01
Nepalese (133)	133	0.12
Pakistani (16)	16	0.01
Sri Lankan (1)	2	<0.01
Taiwanese (47)	65	0.06
Thai (23)	51	0.05
Vietnamese (99)	130	0.12
Hawaii Native/Pacific Islander (1,267)	2,258	2.01
Not Hispanic (1,229)	2,120	1.88
Hispanic (38)	138	0.12
Fijian (15)	24	0.02
Guamanian/Chamorro (7)	20	0.02
Marshallese (9)	9	0.01
Native Hawaiian (158)	685	0.61
Samoan (380)	705	0.63
Tongan (425)	680	0.60
White (95,393)	98,858	87.88
Not Hispanic (87,186)	89,596	79.65
Hispanic (8,207)	9,262	8.23

Richfield

Place Type: City
County: Sevier
Population: 7,551†

Ancestry‡	Population	%
American (573)	573	7.70
British (11)	76	1.02
Canadian (9)	61	0.82
Danish (583)	1,013	13.62
Dutch (7)	112	1.51
English (957)	2,214	29.77
European (107)	107	1.44
French, ex. Basque (0)	125	1.68
French Canadian (0)	5	0.07
German (234)	690	9.28
German Russian (10)	10	0.13
Greek (19)	26	0.35
Hungarian (12)	12	0.16
Irish (84)	226	3.04
Italian (0)	263	3.54
Norwegian (101)	223	3.00
Polish (0)	10	0.13
Portuguese (0)	56	0.75
Russian (15)	15	0.20
Scandinavian (118)	236	3.17
Scotch-Irish (22)	54	0.73
Scottish (54)	218	2.93
Swedish (20)	177	2.38
Swiss (0)	50	0.67
Welsh (0)	65	0.87

Hispanic Origin	Population	%
Hispanic or Latino (of any race)	310	4.11
Central American, ex. Mexican	7	0.09
Costa Rican	2	0.03
Honduran	3	0.04
Salvadoran	2	0.03
Cuban	4	0.05
Dominican Republic	1	0.01
Mexican	219	2.90
Puerto Rican	3	0.04
South American	9	0.12
Argentinean	1	0.01
Bolivian	1	0.01
Chilean	2	0.03
Colombian	1	0.01
Peruvian	4	0.05
Other Hispanic or Latino	67	0.89

Race*	Population	%
African-American/Black (22)	52	0.69
Not Hispanic (20)	44	0.58
Hispanic (2)	8	0.11
American Indian/Alaska Native (130)	188	2.49
Not Hispanic (118)	164	2.17
Hispanic (12)	24	0.32
Apache (2)	3	0.04
Cherokee (2)	11	0.15
Chippewa (1)	1	0.01
Choctaw (2)	3	0.04
Hopi (4)	5	0.07
Mexican American Ind. (5)	5	0.07
Navajo (56)	81	1.07
Paiute (17)	21	0.28
Shoshone (1)	1	0.01
Sioux (4)	6	0.08
South American Ind. (0)	1	0.01
Ute (4)	7	0.09
Yuman (3)	3	0.04
Asian (27)	49	0.65
Not Hispanic (26)	42	0.56
Hispanic (1)	7	0.09
Chinese, ex. Taiwanese (8)	17	0.23
Filipino (4)	20	0.26
Indian (5)	6	0.08
Japanese (1)	2	0.03
Korean (4)	10	0.13
Pakistani (1)	1	0.01
Thai (1)	1	0.01
Vietnamese (2)	2	0.03
Hawaii Native/Pacific Islander (9)	11	0.15
Not Hispanic (9)	11	0.15
Native Hawaiian (5)	6	0.08
Tongan (2)	2	0.03
White (7,129)	7,233	95.79
Not Hispanic (6,984)	7,064	93.55
Hispanic (145)	169	2.24

Riverdale

Place Type: City
County: Weber
Population: 8,426†

Ancestry‡	Population	%
American (1,303)	1,303	15.91
Arab (0)	12	0.15
Lebanese (0)	12	0.15
Austrian (0)	74	0.90
British (28)	69	0.84
Czech (11)	22	0.27
Danish (95)	273	3.33
Dutch (148)	378	4.62
English (617)	1,525	18.62
European (454)	526	6.42
French, ex. Basque (13)	224	2.74
French Canadian (10)	51	0.62
German (290)	872	10.65
Greek (17)	40	0.49
Hungarian (0)	10	0.12
Irish (207)	463	5.65
Italian (118)	458	5.59
Northern European (14)	14	0.17
Norwegian (64)	183	2.23
Polish (21)	46	0.56
Russian (8)	32	0.39
Scandinavian (17)	17	0.21
Scotch-Irish (70)	144	1.76
Scottish (283)	454	5.54
Swedish (70)	322	3.93
Swiss (10)	32	0.39
Welsh (22)	98	1.20

Hispanic Origin	Population	%
Hispanic or Latino (of any race)	1,079	12.81
Central American, ex. Mexican	49	0.58
Guatemalan	29	0.34
Honduran	2	0.02
Panamanian	3	0.04
Salvadoran	15	0.18
Mexican	846	10.04
Puerto Rican	12	0.14
South American	24	0.28
Argentinean	1	0.01
Chilean	9	0.11
Colombian	6	0.07
Peruvian	5	0.06
Uruguayan	1	0.01
Venezuelan	2	0.02
Other Hispanic or Latino	148	1.76

Race*	Population	%
African-American/Black (113)	173	2.05
Not Hispanic (103)	146	1.73
Hispanic (10)	27	0.32
American Indian/Alaska Native (64)	116	1.38
Not Hispanic (40)	78	0.93
Hispanic (24)	38	0.45
Apache (1)	3	0.04
Cherokee (2)	12	0.14
Cheyenne (0)	1	0.01
Comanche (1)	1	0.01
Creek (1)	5	0.06
Crow (3)	3	0.04
Inupiat *(Alaska Native)* (0)	1	0.01
Mexican American Ind. (5)	5	0.06
Navajo (19)	28	0.33
Paiute (0)	1	0.01
Pueblo (3)	3	0.04
Seminole (0)	2	0.02
Sioux (4)	6	0.07
Ute (1)	1	0.01
Asian (136)	195	2.31
Not Hispanic (127)	179	2.12
Hispanic (9)	16	0.19
Chinese, ex. Taiwanese (24)	40	0.47
Filipino (18)	32	0.38
Hmong (7)	12	0.14
Indian (11)	11	0.13
Japanese (29)	47	0.56
Korean (3)	8	0.09
Laotian (1)	1	0.01
Pakistani (1)	6	0.07
Thai (4)	6	0.07
Vietnamese (32)	33	0.39
Hawaii Native/Pacific Islander (38)	63	0.75
Not Hispanic (34)	57	0.68
Hispanic (4)	6	0.07
Guamanian/Chamorro (7)	8	0.09
Native Hawaiian (11)	29	0.34
Samoan (11)	25	0.30
Tongan (2)	6	0.07
White (7,390)	7,604	90.24
Not Hispanic (6,897)	7,029	83.42
Hispanic (493)	575	6.82

Riverton

Place Type: City
County: Salt Lake
Population: 38,753†

Ancestry‡	Population	%
African, Sub-Saharan (9)	38	0.11
African (9)	38	0.11
American (2,031)	2,031	5.64
Arab (15)	33	0.09
Lebanese (8)	26	0.07
Palestinian (7)	7	0.02
Australian (30)	30	0.08
Austrian (0)	27	0.08
Basque (13)	13	0.04
Belgian (9)	37	0.10

SECTION TWO

*Notes: † The Census 2010 population figure is used to calculate the percentages in the Hispanic Origin and Race categories. Ancestry percentages are based on the 2006-2010 American Community Survey population (not shown); ‡ Numbers in parentheses indicate the number of people reporting a single ancestry; * Numbers in parentheses indicate the number of persons reporting this race alone, not in combination with any other race; Please refer to the Explanation of Data for more information.*

British (436)	634	1.76
Canadian (11)	133	0.37
Croatian (0)	8	0.02
Czech (9)	29	0.08
Danish (621)	2,347	6.52
Dutch (287)	1,088	3.02
Eastern European (11)	26	0.07
English (5,115)	10,945	30.41
European (1,243)	1,453	4.04
Finnish (9)	107	0.30
French, ex. Basque (91)	725	2.01
French Canadian (0)	16	0.04
German (1,407)	4,970	13.81
Greek (66)	149	0.41
Hungarian (5)	130	0.36
Icelander (0)	21	0.06
Iranian (0)	12	0.03
Irish (722)	1,983	5.51
Italian (384)	1,291	3.59
Maltese (0)	28	0.08
Northern European (79)	79	0.22
Norwegian (321)	1,262	3.51
Polish (97)	352	0.98
Portuguese (0)	43	0.12
Romanian (0)	18	0.05
Russian (29)	135	0.38
Scandinavian (226)	729	2.03
Scotch-Irish (79)	338	0.94
Scottish (462)	1,751	4.87
Serbian (37)	64	0.18
Slavic (0)	9	0.03
Slovak (23)	91	0.25
Swedish (523)	1,592	4.42
Swiss (55)	473	1.31
Ukrainian (0)	73	0.20
Welsh (216)	730	2.03
West Indian, ex. Hispanic (0)	11	0.03
Haitian (0)	11	0.03
Yugoslavian (46)	115	0.32

Hispanic Origin	Population	%
Hispanic or Latino (of any race)	2,211	5.71
Central American, ex. Mexican	183	0.47
Costa Rican	3	0.01
Guatemalan	49	0.13
Honduran	22	0.06
Nicaraguan	3	0.01
Panamanian	1	<0.01
Salvadoran	105	0.27
Cuban	16	0.04
Dominican Republic	17	0.04
Mexican	1,294	3.34
Puerto Rican	95	0.25
South American	289	0.75
Argentinean	30	0.08
Bolivian	12	0.03
Chilean	27	0.07
Colombian	61	0.16
Ecuadorian	24	0.06
Peruvian	67	0.17
Uruguayan	7	0.02
Venezuelan	53	0.14
Other South American	8	0.02
Other Hispanic or Latino	317	0.82

Race*	Population	%
African-American/Black (169)	292	0.75
Not Hispanic (157)	262	0.68
Hispanic (12)	30	0.08
American Indian/Alaska Native (118)	270	0.70
Not Hispanic (95)	214	0.55
Hispanic (23)	56	0.14
Apache (5)	7	0.02
Arapaho (0)	1	<0.01
Canadian/French Am. Ind. (1)	1	<0.01
Central American Ind. (4)	4	0.01
Cherokee (7)	43	0.11
Chickasaw (0)	2	0.01
Chippewa (1)	5	0.01
Choctaw (6)	7	0.02
Comanche (0)	1	<0.01
Hopi (6)	6	0.02
Iroquois (1)	2	0.01
Kiowa (0)	3	0.01
Mexican American Ind. (7)	8	0.02
Navajo (19)	38	0.10
Osage (0)	1	<0.01
Paiute (1)	13	0.03
Pima (1)	1	<0.01
Potawatomi (4)	4	0.01
Pueblo (0)	2	0.01
Shoshone (6)	6	0.02
Sioux (0)	4	0.01
Spanish American Ind. (1)	1	<0.01
Ute (2)	9	0.02
Yaqui (4)	4	0.01
Yuman (1)	1	<0.01
Asian (510)	713	1.84
Not Hispanic (495)	673	1.74
Hispanic (15)	40	0.10
Cambodian (17)	21	0.05
Chinese, ex. Taiwanese (82)	128	0.33
Filipino (52)	95	0.25
Hmong (10)	10	0.03
Indian (71)	89	0.23
Indonesian (5)	5	0.01
Japanese (69)	144	0.37
Korean (31)	53	0.14
Laotian (22)	27	0.07
Malaysian (3)	3	0.01
Pakistani (7)	10	0.03
Taiwanese (4)	4	0.01
Thai (12)	15	0.04
Vietnamese (85)	104	0.27
Hawaii Native/Pacific Islander (262)	400	1.03
Not Hispanic (257)	385	0.99
Hispanic (5)	15	0.04
Fijian (11)	11	0.03
Guamanian/Chamorro (5)	8	0.02
Marshallese (2)	2	0.01
Native Hawaiian (18)	76	0.20
Samoan (54)	98	0.25
Tongan (126)	177	0.46
White (36,275)	36,921	95.27
Not Hispanic (35,016)	35,494	91.59
Hispanic (1,259)	1,427	3.68

Roy

Place Type: City
County: Weber
Population: 36,884†

Ancestry‡	Population	%
African, Sub-Saharan (19)	74	0.21
African (8)	13	0.04
Ghanaian (11)	45	0.13
South African (0)	16	0.04
American (6,424)	6,424	17.92
Arab (45)	45	0.13
Egyptian (11)	11	0.03
Lebanese (34)	34	0.09
Australian (8)	8	0.02
Austrian (0)	17	0.05
Basque (0)	41	0.11
Belgian (0)	28	0.08
British (212)	309	0.86
Canadian (35)	180	0.50
Celtic (0)	15	0.04
Croatian (51)	51	0.14
Czech (13)	67	0.19
Czechoslovakian (0)	12	0.03
Danish (280)	1,173	3.27
Dutch (269)	1,143	3.19
English (3,695)	8,101	22.60
European (557)	668	1.86
Finnish (0)	69	0.19
French, ex. Basque (169)	561	1.57
French Canadian (25)	142	0.40
German (1,180)	4,266	11.90
Greek (135)	216	0.60
Hungarian (0)	12	0.03
Irish (519)	1,972	5.50
Italian (409)	883	2.46
Lithuanian (0)	45	0.13
Northern European (51)	51	0.14
Norwegian (193)	831	2.32
Pennsylvania German (14)	54	0.15
Polish (113)	341	0.95
Portuguese (18)	18	0.05
Russian (6)	34	0.09
Scandinavian (222)	275	0.77
Scotch-Irish (232)	435	1.21
Scottish (343)	1,198	3.34
Slovene (14)	14	0.04
Swedish (258)	1,123	3.13
Swiss (154)	428	1.19
Ukrainian (0)	95	0.27
Welsh (131)	661	1.84
Yugoslavian (13)	13	0.04

Hispanic Origin	Population	%
Hispanic or Latino (of any race)	4,968	13.47
Central American, ex. Mexican	218	0.59
Costa Rican	8	0.02
Guatemalan	26	0.07
Honduran	14	0.04
Nicaraguan	13	0.04
Panamanian	8	0.02
Salvadoran	149	0.40
Cuban	12	0.03
Dominican Republic	18	0.05
Mexican	3,643	9.88
Puerto Rican	138	0.37
South American	172	0.47
Argentinean	26	0.07
Bolivian	1	<0.01
Chilean	39	0.11
Colombian	46	0.12
Ecuadorian	8	0.02
Paraguayan	5	0.01
Peruvian	31	0.08
Uruguayan	8	0.02
Venezuelan	8	0.02
Other Hispanic or Latino	767	2.08

Race*	Population	%
African-American/Black (406)	705	1.91
Not Hispanic (367)	615	1.67
Hispanic (39)	90	0.24
American Indian/Alaska Native (211)	485	1.31
Not Hispanic (152)	352	0.95
Hispanic (59)	133	0.36
Alaska Athabascan *(Ala. Nat.)* (0)	7	0.02
Apache (3)	16	0.04
Blackfeet (2)	6	0.02
Cherokee (13)	52	0.14
Chickasaw (1)	1	<0.01
Chippewa (10)	12	0.03
Choctaw (0)	8	0.02
Creek (2)	2	0.01
Crow (2)	2	0.01
Delaware (0)	2	0.01
Hopi (7)	9	0.02
Inupiat *(Alaska Native)* (0)	3	0.01
Iroquois (2)	2	0.01
Mexican American Ind. (8)	14	0.04
Navajo (44)	81	0.22
Ottawa (0)	1	<0.01
Paiute (3)	5	0.01
Pueblo (1)	4	0.01
Puget Sound Salish (2)	4	0.01
Seminole (0)	5	0.01
Shoshone (5)	11	0.03
Sioux (8)	23	0.06
South American Ind. (1)	1	<0.01
Spanish American Ind. (4)	5	0.01
Tohono O'Odham (1)	1	<0.01
Ute (5)	15	0.04
Yaqui (1)	1	<0.01

*Notes: † The Census 2010 population figure is used to calculate the percentages in the Hispanic Origin and Race categories. Ancestry percentages are based on the 2006-2010 American Community Survey population (not shown); ‡ Numbers in parentheses indicate the number of people reporting a single ancestry; * Numbers in parentheses indicate the number of persons reporting this race alone, not in combination with any other race; Please refer to the Explanation of Data for more information.*

Yuman (0)	1	<0.01
Yup'ik *(Alaska Native)* (0)	2	0.01
Asian (700)	1,118	3.03
Not Hispanic (670)	1,033	2.80
Hispanic (30)	85	0.23
Cambodian (9)	10	0.03
Chinese, ex. Taiwanese (67)	101	0.27
Filipino (151)	303	0.82
Hmong (31)	38	0.10
Indian (20)	37	0.10
Indonesian (3)	7	0.02
Japanese (135)	241	0.65
Korean (62)	106	0.29
Laotian (50)	62	0.17
Malaysian (1)	1	<0.01
Pakistani (4)	6	0.02
Sri Lankan (4)	4	0.01
Taiwanese (8)	11	0.03
Thai (39)	87	0.24
Vietnamese (83)	101	0.27
Hawaii Native/Pacific Islander (84)	186	0.50
Not Hispanic (74)	159	0.43
Hispanic (10)	27	0.07
Fijian (1)	3	0.01
Guamanian/Chamorro (20)	34	0.09
Marshallese (1)	1	<0.01
Native Hawaiian (33)	80	0.22
Samoan (20)	31	0.08
Tongan (4)	10	0.03
White (32,095)	33,249	90.14
Not Hispanic (29,812)	30,542	82.81
Hispanic (2,283)	2,707	7.34

Salt Lake City

Place Type: City
County: Salt Lake
Population: 186,440†

Ancestry‡	Population	%
Afghan (34)	34	0.02
African, Sub-Saharan (2,498)	2,993	1.62
African (707)	1,078	0.58
Cape Verdean (14)	14	0.01
Ethiopian (0)	8	<0.01
Ghanaian (0)	23	0.01
Liberian (41)	41	0.02
Nigerian (27)	37	0.02
Somalian (908)	908	0.49
South African (0)	17	0.01
Sudanese (458)	466	0.25
Other Sub-Saharan African (343)	401	0.22
Albanian (11)	30	0.02
Alsatian (0)	15	0.01
American (5,358)	5,358	2.90
Arab (656)	992	0.54
Arab (14)	53	0.03
Egyptian (5)	5	<0.01
Iraqi (211)	211	0.11
Jordanian (0)	13	0.01
Lebanese (107)	188	0.10
Moroccan (0)	8	<0.01
Palestinian (42)	42	0.02
Syrian (10)	70	0.04
Other Arab (267)	402	0.22
Armenian (236)	302	0.16
Australian (119)	211	0.11
Austrian (112)	383	0.21
Basque (21)	134	0.07
Belgian (31)	83	0.04
Brazilian (294)	412	0.22
British (1,593)	2,957	1.60
Bulgarian (0)	14	0.01
Cajun (0)	9	<0.01
Canadian (332)	689	0.37
Celtic (0)	73	0.04
Croatian (214)	340	0.18
Czech (229)	709	0.38
Czechoslovakian (46)	114	0.06
Danish (2,196)	8,002	4.34
Dutch (1,267)	3,648	1.98
Eastern European (246)	294	0.16
English (13,101)	37,181	20.15
European (4,850)	5,451	2.95
Finnish (155)	448	0.24
French, ex. Basque (685)	4,265	2.31
French Canadian (84)	479	0.26
German (5,926)	21,682	11.75
Greek (899)	1,542	0.84
Hungarian (139)	508	0.28
Icelander (6)	142	0.08
Iranian (308)	341	0.18
Irish (3,377)	12,501	6.78
Israeli (10)	78	0.04
Italian (2,304)	5,838	3.16
Latvian (10)	10	0.01
Lithuanian (81)	268	0.15
Luxemburger (11)	11	0.01
New Zealander (11)	50	0.03
Northern European (701)	743	0.40
Norwegian (1,697)	5,504	2.98
Pennsylvania German (5)	23	0.01
Polish (824)	2,497	1.35
Portuguese (184)	371	0.20
Romanian (9)	32	0.02
Russian (544)	1,310	0.71
Scandinavian (1,114)	2,060	1.12
Scotch-Irish (911)	2,584	1.40
Scottish (1,742)	7,160	3.88
Serbian (131)	206	0.11
Slavic (15)	110	0.06
Slovak (91)	179	0.10
Slovene (9)	82	0.04
Swedish (1,677)	7,051	3.82
Swiss (362)	1,861	1.01
Turkish (456)	480	0.26
Ukrainian (313)	473	0.26
Welsh (688)	3,831	2.08
West Indian, ex. Hispanic (27)	162	0.09
British West Indian (6)	6	<0.01
Jamaican (21)	71	0.04
West Indian (0)	85	0.05
Yugoslavian (983)	1,086	0.59

Hispanic Origin	Population	%
Hispanic or Latino (of any race)	41,637	22.33
Central American, ex. Mexican	2,209	1.18
Costa Rican	64	0.03
Guatemalan	1,029	0.55
Honduran	224	0.12
Nicaraguan	72	0.04
Panamanian	42	0.02
Salvadoran	758	0.41
Other Central American	20	0.01
Cuban	303	0.16
Dominican Republic	105	0.06
Mexican	32,094	17.21
Puerto Rican	655	0.35
South American	1,976	1.06
Argentinean	298	0.16
Bolivian	79	0.04
Chilean	240	0.13
Colombian	268	0.14
Ecuadorian	119	0.06
Paraguayan	17	0.01
Peruvian	651	0.35
Uruguayan	87	0.05
Venezuelan	190	0.10
Other South American	27	0.01
Other Hispanic or Latino	4,295	2.30

Race*	Population	%
African-American/Black (5,088)	6,460	3.46
Not Hispanic (4,613)	5,666	3.04
Hispanic (475)	794	0.43
American Indian/Alaska Native (2,316)	3,760	2.02
Not Hispanic (1,624)	2,529	1.36
Hispanic (692)	1,231	0.66
Alaska Athabascan *(Ala. Nat.)* (4)	4	<0.01
Apache (24)	77	0.04
Arapaho (18)	25	0.01
Blackfeet (5)	42	0.02
Canadian/French Am. Ind. (1)	7	<0.01
Central American Ind. (8)	10	0.01
Cherokee (43)	227	0.12
Cheyenne (22)	37	0.02
Chickasaw (8)	12	0.01
Chippewa (25)	38	0.02
Choctaw (15)	36	0.02
Comanche (0)	3	<0.01
Cree (4)	8	<0.01
Creek (3)	6	<0.01
Crow (2)	7	<0.01
Delaware (1)	1	<0.01
Hopi (10)	30	0.02
Houma (0)	1	<0.01
Inupiat *(Alaska Native)* (5)	9	<0.01
Iroquois (8)	31	0.02
Kiowa (2)	5	<0.01
Lumbee (2)	3	<0.01
Menominee (1)	1	<0.01
Mexican American Ind. (130)	197	0.11
Navajo (883)	1,137	0.61
Osage (2)	3	<0.01
Paiute (31)	47	0.03
Pima (9)	12	0.01
Potawatomi (6)	11	0.01
Pueblo (15)	43	0.02
Puget Sound Salish (1)	2	<0.01
Seminole (3)	15	0.01
Shoshone (41)	72	0.04
Sioux (57)	102	0.05
South American Ind. (7)	24	0.01
Spanish American Ind. (10)	15	0.01
Tlingit-Haida *(Alaska Native)* (5)	5	<0.01
Tohono O'Odham (3)	4	<0.01
Tsimshian *(Alaska Native)* (1)	1	<0.01
Ute (108)	188	0.10
Yaqui (2)	15	0.01
Yup'ik *(Alaska Native)* (1)	2	<0.01
Asian (8,247)	10,234	5.49
Not Hispanic (8,151)	9,903	5.31
Hispanic (96)	331	0.18
Bangladeshi (22)	23	0.01
Bhutanese (69)	92	0.05
Burmese (363)	385	0.21
Cambodian (92)	108	0.06
Chinese, ex. Taiwanese (1,870)	2,267	1.22
Filipino (469)	792	0.42
Hmong (15)	17	0.01
Indian (1,228)	1,417	0.76
Indonesian (29)	62	0.03
Japanese (784)	1,340	0.72
Korean (931)	1,133	0.61
Laotian (118)	157	0.08
Malaysian (17)	31	0.02
Nepalese (148)	196	0.11
Pakistani (141)	177	0.09
Sri Lankan (12)	21	0.01
Taiwanese (152)	177	0.09
Thai (161)	199	0.11
Vietnamese (1,226)	1,369	0.73
Hawaii Native/Pacific Islander (3,776)	4,660	2.50
Not Hispanic (3,706)	4,437	2.38
Hispanic (70)	223	0.12
Fijian (9)	16	0.01
Guamanian/Chamorro (17)	52	0.03
Marshallese (5)	5	<0.01
Native Hawaiian (144)	401	0.22
Samoan (727)	1,100	0.59
Tongan (2,413)	2,940	1.58
White (140,080)	145,969	78.29
Not Hispanic (122,325)	125,726	67.44
Hispanic (17,755)	20,243	10.86

*Notes: † The Census 2010 population figure is used to calculate the percentages in the Hispanic Origin and Race categories. Ancestry percentages are based on the 2006-2010 American Community Survey population (not shown); ‡ Numbers in parentheses indicate the number of people reporting a single ancestry; * Numbers in parentheses indicate the number of persons reporting this race alone, not in combination with any other race; Please refer to the Explanation of Data for more information.*

Sandy

Place Type: City
County: Salt Lake
Population: 87,461†

Ancestry‡	Population	%
Afghan (38)	38	0.04
African, Sub-Saharan (158)	222	0.25
African (70)	134	0.15
Ethiopian (14)	14	0.02
Nigerian (22)	22	0.03
South African (52)	52	0.06
American (5,429)	5,429	6.23
Arab (172)	236	0.27
Arab (26)	26	0.03
Iraqi (48)	48	0.06
Jordanian (25)	71	0.08
Lebanese (23)	41	0.05
Palestinian (10)	10	0.01
Other Arab (40)	40	0.05
Armenian (255)	384	0.44
Australian (86)	138	0.16
Austrian (142)	259	0.30
Basque (22)	69	0.08
Belgian (9)	113	0.13
Brazilian (92)	177	0.20
British (791)	1,810	2.08
Bulgarian (18)	49	0.06
Canadian (180)	272	0.31
Celtic (0)	9	0.01
Croatian (55)	132	0.15
Czech (55)	298	0.34
Czechoslovakian (0)	30	0.03
Danish (1,628)	5,910	6.78
Dutch (797)	2,624	3.01
Eastern European (80)	97	0.11
English (9,926)	24,864	28.52
European (2,911)	3,293	3.78
Finnish (11)	136	0.16
French, ex. Basque (377)	2,334	2.68
French Canadian (151)	230	0.26
German (3,829)	13,214	15.16
Greek (271)	839	0.96
Hungarian (42)	264	0.30
Icelander (0)	141	0.16
Iranian (34)	45	0.05
Irish (1,374)	6,287	7.21
Italian (816)	3,122	3.58
Latvian (16)	16	0.02
Lithuanian (33)	90	0.10
Macedonian (13)	25	0.03
New Zealander (0)	12	0.01
Northern European (208)	231	0.27
Norwegian (800)	2,363	2.71
Polish (270)	1,409	1.62
Portuguese (42)	123	0.14
Romanian (0)	35	0.04
Russian (353)	654	0.75
Scandinavian (496)	1,603	1.84
Scotch-Irish (245)	902	1.03
Scottish (1,101)	3,786	4.34
Serbian (27)	105	0.12
Slovak (2)	24	0.03
Slovene (10)	34	0.04
Swedish (1,022)	4,524	5.19
Swiss (166)	1,319	1.51
Ukrainian (32)	115	0.13
Welsh (266)	1,612	1.85
West Indian, ex. Hispanic (22)	22	0.03
Haitian (2)	2	<0.01
Jamaican (20)	20	0.02
Yugoslavian (130)	260	0.30

Hispanic Origin	Population	%
Hispanic or Latino (of any race)	6,447	7.37
Central American, ex. Mexican	313	0.36
Costa Rican	23	0.03
Guatemalan	96	0.11
Honduran	34	0.04
Nicaraguan	42	0.05
Panamanian	4	<0.01
Salvadoran	112	0.13
Other Central American	2	<0.01
Cuban	75	0.09
Dominican Republic	21	0.02
Mexican	4,099	4.69
Puerto Rican	193	0.22
South American	848	0.97
Argentinean	75	0.09
Bolivian	30	0.03
Chilean	125	0.14
Colombian	190	0.22
Ecuadorian	43	0.05
Peruvian	279	0.32
Uruguayan	42	0.05
Venezuelan	54	0.06
Other South American	10	0.01
Other Hispanic or Latino	898	1.03

Race*	Population	%
African-American/Black (635)	1,107	1.27
Not Hispanic (558)	971	1.11
Hispanic (77)	136	0.16
American Indian/Alaska Native (418)	822	0.94
Not Hispanic (335)	631	0.72
Hispanic (83)	191	0.22
Alaska Athabascan *(Ala. Nat.)* (4)	5	0.01
Aleut *(Alaska Native)* (1)	2	<0.01
Apache (8)	17	0.02
Blackfeet (6)	7	0.01
Canadian/French Am. Ind. (1)	2	<0.01
Cherokee (28)	94	0.11
Chickasaw (2)	2	<0.01
Chippewa (8)	16	0.02
Choctaw (1)	15	0.02
Colville (1)	1	<0.01
Comanche (0)	2	<0.01
Cree (4)	4	<0.01
Creek (3)	7	0.01
Crow (3)	5	0.01
Delaware (0)	1	<0.01
Hopi (0)	5	0.01
Iroquois (4)	5	0.01
Kiowa (1)	5	0.01
Mexican American Ind. (20)	27	0.03
Navajo (112)	154	0.18
Osage (1)	3	<0.01
Paiute (5)	8	0.01
Potawatomi (5)	9	0.01
Pueblo (10)	17	0.02
Seminole (3)	3	<0.01
Shoshone (7)	18	0.02
Sioux (15)	39	0.04
South American Ind. (4)	8	0.01
Spanish American Ind. (1)	2	<0.01
Tlingit-Haida *(Alaska Native)* (1)	3	<0.01
Tohono O'Odham (1)	1	<0.01
Ute (6)	17	0.02
Yaqui (0)	7	0.01
Asian (2,623)	3,386	3.87
Not Hispanic (2,599)	3,300	3.77
Hispanic (24)	86	0.10
Bangladeshi (15)	15	0.02
Burmese (11)	11	0.01
Cambodian (25)	31	0.04
Chinese, ex. Taiwanese (853)	1,039	1.19
Filipino (171)	308	0.35
Indian (458)	501	0.57
Indonesian (7)	9	0.01
Japanese (279)	555	0.63
Korean (332)	438	0.50
Laotian (88)	100	0.11
Malaysian (8)	11	0.01
Pakistani (54)	63	0.07
Sri Lankan (7)	11	0.01
Taiwanese (46)	48	0.05
Thai (31)	46	0.05
Vietnamese (112)	153	0.17
Hawaii Native/Pacific Islander (557)	929	1.06
Not Hispanic (541)	871	1.00
Hispanic (16)	58	0.07
Fijian (2)	8	0.01
Guamanian/Chamorro (12)	23	0.03
Marshallese (4)	7	0.01
Native Hawaiian (25)	141	0.16
Samoan (158)	301	0.34
Tongan (241)	404	0.46
White (78,714)	80,717	92.29
Not Hispanic (75,260)	76,733	87.73
Hispanic (3,454)	3,984	4.56

Santaquin

Place Type: City
County: Utah
Population: 9,128†

Ancestry‡	Population	%
American (465)	465	5.56
Arab (0)	41	0.49
Arab (0)	41	0.49
Austrian (22)	48	0.57
British (79)	130	1.55
Croatian (32)	80	0.96
Danish (134)	550	6.58
Dutch (36)	182	2.18
English (1,031)	2,268	27.11
Estonian (29)	177	2.12
European (231)	379	4.53
French, ex. Basque (90)	262	3.13
German (428)	1,159	13.86
Greek (16)	16	0.19
Icelander (10)	23	0.27
Irish (155)	572	6.84
Italian (13)	61	0.73
Norwegian (109)	109	1.30
Polish (0)	9	0.11
Portuguese (18)	18	0.22
Scandinavian (27)	127	1.52
Scotch-Irish (28)	79	0.94
Scottish (87)	161	1.92
Swedish (165)	616	7.36
Swiss (15)	78	0.93
Ukrainian (0)	6	0.07
Welsh (31)	208	2.49
West Indian, ex. Hispanic (0)	11	0.13
Barbadian (0)	11	0.13

Hispanic Origin	Population	%
Hispanic or Latino (of any race)	1,098	12.03
Central American, ex. Mexican	31	0.34
Guatemalan	5	0.05
Honduran	7	0.08
Salvadoran	18	0.20
Other Central American	1	0.01
Cuban	2	0.02
Mexican	927	10.16
Puerto Rican	17	0.19
South American	30	0.33
Argentinean	16	0.18
Chilean	6	0.07
Colombian	7	0.08
Ecuadorian	1	0.01
Other Hispanic or Latino	91	1.00

Race*	Population	%
African-American/Black (38)	58	0.64
Not Hispanic (32)	43	0.47
Hispanic (6)	15	0.16
American Indian/Alaska Native (72)	127	1.39
Not Hispanic (63)	104	1.14
Hispanic (9)	23	0.25
Apache (1)	4	0.04
Blackfeet (0)	4	0.04
Cherokee (5)	15	0.16
Cheyenne (0)	1	0.01
Chippewa (1)	1	0.01
Creek (0)	2	0.02
Delaware (1)	2	0.02

*Notes: † The Census 2010 population figure is used to calculate the percentages in the Hispanic Origin and Race categories. Ancestry percentages are based on the 2006-2010 American Community Survey population (not shown); ‡ Numbers in parentheses indicate the number of people reporting a single ancestry; * Numbers in parentheses indicate the number of persons reporting this race alone, not in combination with any other race; Please refer to the Explanation of Data for more information.*

Iroquois (1)	3	0.03
Mexican American Ind. (5)	7	0.08
Navajo (18)	34	0.37
Sioux (19)	19	0.21
Ute (10)	14	0.15
Yuman (0)	1	0.01
Asian (13)	27	0.30
Not Hispanic (13)	26	0.28
Hispanic (0)	1	0.01
Chinese, ex. Taiwanese (8)	11	0.12
Filipino (2)	6	0.07
Indian (1)	2	0.02
Japanese (0)	5	0.05
Korean (1)	1	0.01
Laotian (0)	2	0.02
Malaysian (0)	1	0.01
Thai (0)	2	0.02
Hawaii Native/Pacific Islander (10)	21	0.23
Not Hispanic (10)	21	0.23
Native Hawaiian (0)	1	0.01
Samoan (2)	12	0.13
Tongan (2)	2	0.02
White (8,155)	8,271	90.61
Not Hispanic (7,824)	7,895	86.49
Hispanic (331)	376	4.12

Saratoga Springs

Place Type: City
County: Utah
Population: 17,781†

Ancestry‡	Population	%
American (806)	806	5.48
Austrian (14)	18	0.12
Belgian (0)	7	0.05
British (70)	110	0.75
Canadian (42)	88	0.60
Celtic (78)	78	0.53
Croatian (15)	15	0.10
Czech (0)	176	1.20
Czechoslovakian (0)	40	0.27
Danish (172)	756	5.14
Dutch (40)	184	1.25
English (2,103)	3,816	25.97
European (1,245)	1,322	9.00
Finnish (0)	9	0.06
French, ex. Basque (47)	115	0.78
French Canadian (6)	6	0.04
German (669)	1,926	13.11
Greek (8)	44	0.30
Hungarian (0)	79	0.54
Icelander (7)	30	0.20
Iranian (3)	3	0.02
Irish (218)	594	4.04
Italian (94)	272	1.85
Lithuanian (0)	7	0.05
Northern European (27)	27	0.18
Norwegian (60)	272	1.85
Polish (38)	103	0.70
Portuguese (21)	111	0.76
Scandinavian (46)	227	1.54
Scotch-Irish (141)	225	1.53
Scottish (187)	485	3.30
Swedish (102)	570	3.88
Swiss (82)	223	1.52
Ukrainian (0)	3	0.02
Welsh (92)	223	1.52

Hispanic Origin	Population	%
Hispanic or Latino (of any race)	1,026	5.77
Central American, ex. Mexican	50	0.28
Costa Rican	1	0.01
Guatemalan	13	0.07
Honduran	4	0.02
Nicaraguan	2	0.01
Panamanian	7	0.04
Salvadoran	23	0.13
Cuban	10	0.06
Dominican Republic	9	0.05
Mexican	599	3.37
Puerto Rican	38	0.21
South American	217	1.22
Argentinean	26	0.15
Bolivian	1	0.01
Chilean	26	0.15
Colombian	49	0.28
Ecuadorian	24	0.13
Peruvian	66	0.37
Uruguayan	1	0.01
Venezuelan	24	0.13
Other Hispanic or Latino	103	0.58

Race*	Population	%
African-American/Black (94)	179	1.01
Not Hispanic (89)	161	0.91
Hispanic (5)	18	0.10
American Indian/Alaska Native (50)	91	0.51
Not Hispanic (43)	75	0.42
Hispanic (7)	16	0.09
Apache (1)	5	0.03
Canadian/French Am. Ind. (1)	1	0.01
Cherokee (3)	13	0.07
Chippewa (1)	1	0.01
Choctaw (3)	4	0.02
Creek (1)	1	0.01
Iroquois (0)	3	0.02
Mexican American Ind. (1)	1	0.01
Navajo (16)	23	0.13
Potawatomi (5)	5	0.03
Sioux (3)	3	0.02
South American Ind. (1)	3	0.02
Tlingit-Haida *(Alaska Native)* (1)	4	0.02
Ute (0)	1	0.01
Asian (163)	354	1.99
Not Hispanic (163)	335	1.88
Hispanic (0)	19	0.11
Burmese (2)	2	0.01
Cambodian (7)	11	0.06
Chinese, ex. Taiwanese (30)	90	0.51
Filipino (56)	108	0.61
Hmong (2)	4	0.02
Indian (12)	22	0.12
Japanese (9)	54	0.30
Korean (18)	45	0.25
Laotian (1)	7	0.04
Taiwanese (2)	3	0.02
Thai (5)	7	0.04
Vietnamese (11)	17	0.10
Hawaii Native/Pacific Islander (140)	296	1.66
Not Hispanic (140)	288	1.62
Hispanic (0)	8	0.04
Fijian (1)	8	0.04
Guamanian/Chamorro (1)	4	0.02
Marshallese (5)	5	0.03
Native Hawaiian (15)	74	0.42
Samoan (54)	95	0.53
Tongan (51)	101	0.57
White (16,501)	16,959	95.38
Not Hispanic (15,902)	16,266	91.48
Hispanic (599)	693	3.90

Smithfield

Place Type: City
County: Cache
Population: 9,495†

Ancestry‡	Population	%
African, Sub-Saharan (0)	13	0.15
African (0)	13	0.15
American (536)	536	5.98
Australian (19)	19	0.21
Austrian (0)	16	0.18
British (128)	250	2.79
Canadian (35)	35	0.39
Danish (173)	549	6.13
Dutch (30)	137	1.53
English (1,217)	2,622	29.27
European (326)	380	4.24
Finnish (0)	36	0.40
French, ex. Basque (30)	142	1.59
French Canadian (20)	42	0.47
German (354)	939	10.48
Greek (0)	22	0.25
Hungarian (0)	16	0.18
Icelander (10)	10	0.11
Irish (158)	450	5.02
Italian (22)	71	0.79
Northern European (11)	11	0.12
Norwegian (196)	290	3.24
Polish (11)	31	0.35
Russian (0)	10	0.11
Scandinavian (152)	377	4.21
Scotch-Irish (9)	42	0.47
Scottish (36)	246	2.75
Swedish (80)	350	3.91
Swiss (81)	153	1.71
Welsh (29)	87	0.97
West Indian, ex. Hispanic (5)	5	0.06
Haitian (5)	5	0.06

Hispanic Origin	Population	%
Hispanic or Latino (of any race)	571	6.01
Central American, ex. Mexican	49	0.52
Guatemalan	16	0.17
Honduran	5	0.05
Salvadoran	28	0.29
Cuban	7	0.07
Dominican Republic	3	0.03
Mexican	450	4.74
Puerto Rican	5	0.05
South American	19	0.20
Argentinean	1	0.01
Bolivian	3	0.03
Colombian	5	0.05
Ecuadorian	3	0.03
Paraguayan	1	0.01
Peruvian	5	0.05
Uruguayan	1	0.01
Other Hispanic or Latino	38	0.40

Race*	Population	%
African-American/Black (51)	80	0.84
Not Hispanic (49)	72	0.76
Hispanic (2)	8	0.08
American Indian/Alaska Native (15)	63	0.66
Not Hispanic (9)	51	0.54
Hispanic (6)	12	0.13
Apache (0)	10	0.11
Blackfeet (0)	1	0.01
Cherokee (1)	20	0.21
Chickasaw (1)	1	0.01
Chippewa (0)	6	0.06
Comanche (0)	2	0.02
Creek (0)	2	0.02
Lumbee (0)	1	0.01
Mexican American Ind. (1)	2	0.02
Navajo (4)	4	0.04
Shoshone (1)	3	0.03
Asian (40)	84	0.88
Not Hispanic (39)	78	0.82
Hispanic (1)	6	0.06
Cambodian (2)	4	0.04
Chinese, ex. Taiwanese (8)	18	0.19
Filipino (9)	21	0.22
Indian (1)	3	0.03
Japanese (4)	26	0.27
Korean (1)	3	0.03
Laotian (6)	6	0.06
Pakistani (0)	1	0.01
Taiwanese (1)	1	0.01
Vietnamese (6)	6	0.06
Hawaii Native/Pacific Islander (6)	32	0.34
Not Hispanic (5)	25	0.26
Hispanic (1)	7	0.07
Native Hawaiian (0)	5	0.05
Samoan (1)	2	0.02
Tongan (5)	21	0.22
White (8,919)	9,071	95.53

SECTION TWO

*Notes: † The Census 2010 population figure is used to calculate the percentages in the Hispanic Origin and Race categories. Ancestry percentages are based on the 2006-2010 American Community Survey population (not shown); ‡ Numbers in parentheses indicate the number of people reporting a single ancestry; * Numbers in parentheses indicate the number of persons reporting this race alone, not in combination with any other race; Please refer to the Explanation of Data for more information.*

Not Hispanic (8,707)	8,816	92.85
Hispanic (212)	255	2.69

South Jordan

Place Type: City
County: Salt Lake
Population: 50,418†

Ancestry‡	Population	%
African, Sub-Saharan (11)	32	0.07
South African (11)	21	0.05
Zimbabwean (0)	11	0.02
American (3,443)	3,443	7.43
Arab (21)	111	0.24
Iraqi (12)	12	0.03
Lebanese (9)	99	0.21
Armenian (86)	86	0.19
Australian (13)	13	0.03
Austrian (13)	84	0.18
Basque (94)	94	0.20
Belgian (11)	21	0.05
Brazilian (157)	157	0.34
British (558)	958	2.07
Bulgarian (45)	45	0.10
Canadian (69)	277	0.60
Croatian (36)	69	0.15
Czech (13)	96	0.21
Danish (532)	2,796	6.03
Dutch (348)	1,640	3.54
Eastern European (19)	19	0.04
English (6,201)	14,244	30.72
European (2,260)	2,477	5.34
Finnish (8)	83	0.18
French, ex. Basque (176)	954	2.06
French Canadian (11)	112	0.24
German (1,837)	6,272	13.53
Greek (54)	183	0.39
Hungarian (20)	81	0.17
Icelander (0)	89	0.19
Iranian (33)	33	0.07
Irish (417)	2,524	5.44
Israeli (12)	12	0.03
Italian (442)	1,357	2.93
Lithuanian (0)	13	0.03
Northern European (88)	99	0.21
Norwegian (337)	1,278	2.76
Polish (158)	708	1.53
Portuguese (21)	21	0.05
Romanian (79)	134	0.29
Russian (230)	310	0.67
Scandinavian (359)	659	1.42
Scotch-Irish (180)	482	1.04
Scottish (577)	2,084	4.49
Slavic (16)	37	0.08
Slovak (165)	183	0.39
Swedish (556)	2,344	5.06
Swiss (243)	831	1.79
Ukrainian (68)	126	0.27
Welsh (148)	1,336	2.88
Yugoslavian (68)	160	0.35

Hispanic Origin	Population	%
Hispanic or Latino (of any race)	3,008	5.97
Central American, ex. Mexican	233	0.46
Costa Rican	20	0.04
Guatemalan	64	0.13
Honduran	25	0.05
Nicaraguan	4	0.01
Panamanian	1	<0.01
Salvadoran	119	0.24
Cuban	32	0.06
Dominican Republic	3	0.01
Mexican	1,756	3.48
Puerto Rican	126	0.25
South American	388	0.77
Argentinean	35	0.07
Bolivian	20	0.04
Chilean	58	0.12
Colombian	107	0.21
Ecuadorian	21	0.04
Peruvian	67	0.13
Uruguayan	11	0.02
Venezuelan	66	0.13
Other South American	3	0.01
Other Hispanic or Latino	470	0.93

Race*	Population	%
African-American/Black (340)	569	1.13
Not Hispanic (316)	511	1.01
Hispanic (24)	58	0.12
American Indian/Alaska Native (104)	269	0.53
Not Hispanic (69)	171	0.34
Hispanic (35)	98	0.19
Apache (4)	13	0.03
Blackfeet (0)	4	0.01
Canadian/French Am. Ind. (0)	1	<0.01
Cherokee (4)	28	0.06
Cheyenne (2)	7	0.01
Chippewa (0)	2	<0.01
Choctaw (1)	1	<0.01
Hopi (0)	1	<0.01
Iroquois (1)	3	0.01
Kiowa (1)	1	<0.01
Mexican American Ind. (1)	2	<0.01
Navajo (19)	35	0.07
Osage (0)	3	0.01
Paiute (4)	4	0.01
Pima (0)	3	0.01
Potawatomi (1)	1	<0.01
Pueblo (5)	14	0.03
Shoshone (3)	6	0.01
Sioux (3)	7	0.01
South American Ind. (0)	2	<0.01
Tsimshian *(Alaska Native)* (0)	3	0.01
Ute (4)	8	0.02
Yaqui (1)	1	<0.01
Yup'ik *(Alaska Native)* (0)	1	<0.01
Asian (1,309)	1,776	3.52
Not Hispanic (1,295)	1,727	3.43
Hispanic (14)	49	0.10
Burmese (2)	4	0.01
Cambodian (47)	59	0.12
Chinese, ex. Taiwanese (202)	338	0.67
Filipino (110)	185	0.37
Hmong (1)	1	<0.01
Indian (283)	307	0.61
Indonesian (4)	6	0.01
Japanese (74)	251	0.50
Korean (105)	160	0.32
Laotian (56)	71	0.14
Malaysian (0)	4	0.01
Nepalese (9)	10	0.02
Pakistani (55)	59	0.12
Sri Lankan (0)	2	<0.01
Taiwanese (9)	10	0.02
Thai (15)	31	0.06
Vietnamese (259)	309	0.61
Hawaii Native/Pacific Islander (439)	677	1.34
Not Hispanic (424)	652	1.29
Hispanic (15)	25	0.05
Fijian (4)	10	0.02
Guamanian/Chamorro (1)	3	0.01
Marshallese (2)	2	<0.01
Native Hawaiian (32)	120	0.24
Samoan (119)	195	0.39
Tongan (239)	324	0.64
White (46,145)	47,270	93.76
Not Hispanic (44,387)	45,208	89.67
Hispanic (1,758)	2,062	4.09

South Ogden

Place Type: City
County: Weber
Population: 16,532†

Ancestry‡	Population	%
American (2,018)	2,018	12.64
Arab (0)	25	0.16
Lebanese (0)	25	0.16
Basque (12)	12	0.08
Belgian (16)	16	0.10
British (143)	180	1.13
Canadian (0)	29	0.18
Croatian (9)	18	0.11
Czech (11)	38	0.24
Danish (154)	575	3.60
Dutch (299)	652	4.08
English (2,057)	4,756	29.78
European (331)	379	2.37
Finnish (29)	58	0.36
French, ex. Basque (0)	538	3.37
French Canadian (46)	46	0.29
German (398)	1,566	9.81
Greek (17)	17	0.11
Hungarian (11)	32	0.20
Irish (182)	929	5.82
Italian (143)	606	3.79
Northern European (35)	35	0.22
Norwegian (178)	412	2.58
Polish (41)	207	1.30
Romanian (59)	59	0.37
Russian (0)	22	0.14
Scandinavian (84)	203	1.27
Scotch-Irish (98)	282	1.77
Scottish (320)	939	5.88
Swedish (150)	447	2.80
Swiss (22)	56	0.35
Ukrainian (0)	21	0.13
Welsh (80)	314	1.97
Yugoslavian (10)	10	0.06

Hispanic Origin	Population	%
Hispanic or Latino (of any race)	2,122	12.84
Central American, ex. Mexican	115	0.70
Costa Rican	2	0.01
Guatemalan	27	0.16
Honduran	10	0.06
Nicaraguan	1	0.01
Panamanian	3	0.02
Salvadoran	72	0.44
Cuban	9	0.05
Dominican Republic	2	0.01
Mexican	1,551	9.38
Puerto Rican	53	0.32
South American	74	0.45
Argentinean	13	0.08
Chilean	30	0.18
Colombian	11	0.07
Ecuadorian	1	0.01
Paraguayan	1	0.01
Peruvian	8	0.05
Uruguayan	2	0.01
Venezuelan	8	0.05
Other Hispanic or Latino	318	1.92

Race*	Population	%
African-American/Black (237)	386	2.33
Not Hispanic (209)	322	1.95
Hispanic (28)	64	0.39
American Indian/Alaska Native (93)	220	1.33
Not Hispanic (83)	176	1.06
Hispanic (10)	44	0.27
Apache (1)	3	0.02
Arapaho (0)	1	0.01
Blackfeet (2)	8	0.05
Canadian/French Am. Ind. (1)	2	0.01
Cherokee (1)	14	0.08
Cheyenne (1)	4	0.02
Chickasaw (6)	6	0.04
Chippewa (10)	12	0.07
Choctaw (1)	8	0.05
Colville (1)	1	0.01
Creek (1)	1	0.01
Crow (0)	1	0.01
Delaware (0)	3	0.02
Lumbee (0)	1	0.01
Mexican American Ind. (2)	4	0.02
Navajo (28)	41	0.25

*Notes: † The Census 2010 population figure is used to calculate the percentages in the Hispanic Origin and Race categories. Ancestry percentages are based on the 2006-2010 American Community Survey population (not shown); ‡ Numbers in parentheses indicate the number of people reporting a single ancestry; * Numbers in parentheses indicate the number of persons reporting this race alone, not in combination with any other race; Please refer to the Explanation of Data for more information.*

Ottawa (0)	2	0.01
Paiute (0)	3	0.02
Potawatomi (1)	2	0.01
Pueblo (1)	4	0.02
Shoshone (2)	3	0.02
Sioux (7)	11	0.07
South American Ind. (1)	6	0.04
Spanish American Ind. (0)	3	0.02
Tlingit-Haida *(Alaska Native)* (0)	3	0.02
Ute (1)	3	0.02
Asian (222)	391	2.37
Not Hispanic (217)	353	2.14
Hispanic (5)	38	0.23
Cambodian (2)	2	0.01
Chinese, ex. Taiwanese (49)	74	0.45
Filipino (14)	45	0.27
Hmong (4)	4	0.02
Indian (45)	49	0.30
Japanese (61)	123	0.74
Korean (17)	27	0.16
Laotian (5)	10	0.06
Nepalese (1)	2	0.01
Pakistani (1)	2	0.01
Taiwanese (3)	4	0.02
Thai (8)	15	0.09
Vietnamese (7)	14	0.08
Hawaii Native/Pacific Islander (54)	119	0.72
Not Hispanic (53)	115	0.70
Hispanic (1)	4	0.02
Fijian (0)	4	0.02
Guamanian/Chamorro (0)	5	0.03
Marshallese (16)	16	0.10
Native Hawaiian (7)	25	0.15
Samoan (11)	48	0.29
Tongan (3)	6	0.04
White (14,463)	14,939	90.36
Not Hispanic (13,463)	13,798	83.46
Hispanic (1,000)	1,141	6.90

South Salt Lake

Place Type: City
County: Salt Lake
Population: 23,617†

Ancestry‡	Population	%
African, Sub-Saharan (152)	221	0.95
African (86)	155	0.67
Sudanese (8)	8	0.03
Other Sub-Saharan African (58)	58	0.25
American (517)	517	2.23
Arab (63)	71	0.31
Iraqi (63)	63	0.27
Lebanese (0)	8	0.03
Australian (0)	17	0.07
Austrian (16)	70	0.30
Basque (9)	43	0.19
Belgian (8)	8	0.03
Brazilian (170)	183	0.79
British (59)	119	0.51
Bulgarian (28)	28	0.12
Canadian (25)	35	0.15
Czech (5)	27	0.12
Czechoslovakian (19)	19	0.08
Danish (177)	528	2.27
Dutch (23)	318	1.37
English (1,419)	3,703	15.94
European (345)	384	1.65
Finnish (0)	20	0.09
French, ex. Basque (69)	549	2.36
French Canadian (0)	15	0.06
German (1,252)	2,965	12.76
Greek (19)	59	0.25
Hungarian (17)	17	0.07
Icelander (0)	102	0.44
Iranian (26)	26	0.11
Irish (420)	1,260	5.42
Italian (101)	322	1.39
Lithuanian (12)	12	0.05
Northern European (8)	8	0.03
Norwegian (196)	428	1.84
Pennsylvania German (10)	10	0.04
Polish (69)	158	0.68
Portuguese (19)	59	0.25
Romanian (9)	19	0.08
Russian (0)	46	0.20
Scandinavian (83)	222	0.96
Scotch-Irish (134)	224	0.96
Scottish (89)	445	1.92
Slovak (14)	14	0.06
Swedish (86)	570	2.45
Swiss (43)	195	0.84
Turkish (62)	62	0.27
Ukrainian (14)	14	0.06
Welsh (112)	356	1.53
West Indian, ex. Hispanic (55)	65	0.28
Jamaican (55)	65	0.28
Yugoslavian (41)	41	0.18

Hispanic Origin	Population	%
Hispanic or Latino (of any race)	6,869	29.08
Central American, ex. Mexican	331	1.40
Costa Rican	19	0.08
Guatemalan	116	0.49
Honduran	67	0.28
Nicaraguan	20	0.08
Panamanian	7	0.03
Salvadoran	100	0.42
Other Central American	2	0.01
Cuban	34	0.14
Dominican Republic	16	0.07
Mexican	4,841	20.50
Puerto Rican	105	0.44
South American	443	1.88
Argentinean	92	0.39
Bolivian	15	0.06
Chilean	26	0.11
Colombian	40	0.17
Ecuadorian	12	0.05
Peruvian	178	0.75
Uruguayan	29	0.12
Venezuelan	47	0.20
Other South American	4	0.02
Other Hispanic or Latino	1,099	4.65

Race*	Population	%
African-American/Black (1,038)	1,233	5.22
Not Hispanic (962)	1,099	4.65
Hispanic (76)	134	0.57
American Indian/Alaska Native (625)	841	3.56
Not Hispanic (477)	634	2.68
Hispanic (148)	207	0.88
Alaska Athabascan *(Ala. Nat.)* (1)	2	0.01
Apache (8)	14	0.06
Arapaho (7)	7	0.03
Blackfeet (2)	7	0.03
Canadian/French Am. Ind. (0)	8	0.03
Central American Ind. (2)	4	0.02
Cherokee (11)	36	0.15
Cheyenne (0)	1	<0.01
Chickasaw (0)	1	<0.01
Chippewa (1)	1	<0.01
Choctaw (3)	7	0.03
Comanche (0)	3	0.01
Cree (1)	1	<0.01
Creek (0)	2	0.01
Delaware (0)	1	<0.01
Hopi (0)	2	0.01
Inupiat *(Alaska Native)* (0)	1	<0.01
Iroquois (2)	6	0.03
Mexican American Ind. (20)	35	0.15
Navajo (275)	321	1.36
Osage (0)	1	<0.01
Paiute (9)	12	0.05
Potawatomi (1)	1	<0.01
Pueblo (2)	3	0.01
Seminole (0)	1	<0.01
Shoshone (12)	22	0.09
Sioux (12)	25	0.11
South American Ind. (4)	7	0.03
Spanish American Ind. (1)	3	0.01
Tlingit-Haida *(Alaska Native)* (1)	1	<0.01
Ute (25)	31	0.13
Yakama (1)	1	<0.01
Yaqui (1)	1	<0.01
Yuman (1)	3	0.01
Asian (1,184)	1,445	6.12
Not Hispanic (1,168)	1,376	5.83
Hispanic (16)	69	0.29
Bhutanese (74)	138	0.58
Burmese (219)	228	0.97
Cambodian (11)	15	0.06
Chinese, ex. Taiwanese (175)	206	0.87
Filipino (60)	105	0.44
Indian (133)	169	0.72
Indonesian (7)	14	0.06
Japanese (66)	115	0.49
Korean (39)	55	0.23
Laotian (29)	35	0.15
Nepalese (59)	123	0.52
Pakistani (14)	18	0.08
Taiwanese (10)	12	0.05
Thai (52)	53	0.22
Vietnamese (99)	114	0.48
Hawaii Native/Pacific Islander (237)	344	1.46
Not Hispanic (223)	319	1.35
Hispanic (14)	25	0.11
Guamanian/Chamorro (0)	3	0.01
Marshallese (7)	7	0.03
Native Hawaiian (17)	62	0.26
Samoan (51)	79	0.33
Tongan (83)	132	0.56
White (16,420)	17,250	73.04
Not Hispanic (13,344)	13,801	58.44
Hispanic (3,076)	3,449	14.60

Spanish Fork

Place Type: City
County: Utah
Population: 34,691†

Ancestry‡	Population	%
African, Sub-Saharan (73)	73	0.23
Ghanaian (73)	73	0.23
Albanian (19)	53	0.17
American (2,081)	2,081	6.53
Armenian (17)	57	0.18
Australian (28)	84	0.26
Austrian (9)	9	0.03
Brazilian (10)	10	0.03
British (291)	669	2.10
Canadian (35)	103	0.32
Croatian (0)	9	0.03
Czech (6)	43	0.14
Czechoslovakian (0)	18	0.06
Danish (558)	2,293	7.20
Dutch (115)	947	2.97
English (4,312)	10,230	32.12
European (1,490)	1,690	5.31
Finnish (0)	101	0.32
French, ex. Basque (161)	641	2.01
French Canadian (26)	60	0.19
German (638)	3,292	10.34
Greek (0)	64	0.20
Hungarian (9)	16	0.05
Icelander (202)	544	1.71
Irish (348)	1,202	3.77
Italian (228)	732	2.30
Northern European (122)	138	0.43
Norwegian (175)	643	2.02
Polish (58)	105	0.33
Portuguese (0)	9	0.03
Romanian (0)	20	0.06
Russian (0)	10	0.03
Scandinavian (83)	440	1.38
Scotch-Irish (51)	222	0.70
Scottish (297)	1,754	5.51
Slovak (0)	79	0.25
Swedish (232)	1,311	4.12

SECTION TWO

*Notes: † The Census 2010 population figure is used to calculate the percentages in the Hispanic Origin and Race categories. Ancestry percentages are based on the 2006-2010 American Community Survey population (not shown); ‡ Numbers in parentheses indicate the number of people reporting a single ancestry; * Numbers in parentheses indicate the number of persons reporting this race alone, not in combination with any other race; Please refer to the Explanation of Data for more information.*

Swiss (24)	363	1.14
Ukrainian (16)	32	0.10
Welsh (145)	812	2.55

Hispanic Origin	Population	%
Hispanic or Latino (of any race)	3,678	10.60
Central American, ex. Mexican	344	0.99
Costa Rican	27	0.08
Guatemalan	115	0.33
Honduran	29	0.08
Nicaraguan	7	0.02
Panamanian	5	0.01
Salvadoran	161	0.46
Cuban	16	0.05
Dominican Republic	14	0.04
Mexican	2,359	6.80
Puerto Rican	100	0.29
South American	551	1.59
Argentinean	196	0.56
Bolivian	9	0.03
Chilean	58	0.17
Colombian	62	0.18
Ecuadorian	38	0.11
Paraguayan	1	<0.01
Peruvian	140	0.40
Uruguayan	18	0.05
Venezuelan	28	0.08
Other South American	1	<0.01
Other Hispanic or Latino	294	0.85

Race*	Population	%
African-American/Black (141)	264	0.76
Not Hispanic (108)	208	0.60
Hispanic (33)	56	0.16
American Indian/Alaska Native (189)	385	1.11
Not Hispanic (153)	300	0.86
Hispanic (36)	85	0.25
Alaska Athabascan *(Ala. Nat.)* (5)	5	0.01
Aleut *(Alaska Native)* (1)	8	0.02
Apache (6)	8	0.02
Arapaho (0)	1	<0.01
Blackfeet (4)	13	0.04
Canadian/French Am. Ind. (0)	1	<0.01
Central American Ind. (0)	2	0.01
Cherokee (7)	45	0.13
Cheyenne (0)	2	0.01
Chickasaw (0)	7	0.02
Chippewa (0)	3	0.01
Choctaw (1)	9	0.03
Comanche (1)	1	<0.01
Crow (0)	3	0.01
Inupiat *(Alaska Native)* (5)	5	0.01
Iroquois (4)	10	0.03
Lumbee (1)	7	0.02
Mexican American Ind. (6)	14	0.04
Navajo (75)	98	0.28
Osage (0)	1	<0.01
Paiute (1)	1	<0.01
Potawatomi (0)	1	<0.01
Shoshone (3)	3	0.01
Sioux (11)	32	0.09
South American Ind. (5)	5	0.01
Ute (11)	11	0.03
Asian (204)	400	1.15
Not Hispanic (194)	367	1.06
Hispanic (10)	33	0.10
Cambodian (2)	10	0.03
Chinese, ex. Taiwanese (59)	114	0.33
Filipino (27)	45	0.13
Indian (33)	45	0.13
Indonesian (0)	1	<0.01
Japanese (25)	90	0.26
Korean (16)	47	0.14
Laotian (6)	7	0.02
Malaysian (1)	1	<0.01
Taiwanese (3)	4	0.01
Thai (3)	5	0.01
Vietnamese (9)	22	0.06
Hawaii Native/Pacific Islander (241)	446	1.29
Not Hispanic (236)	426	1.23
Hispanic (5)	20	0.06
Fijian (0)	1	<0.01
Guamanian/Chamorro (0)	6	0.02
Marshallese (2)	2	0.01
Native Hawaiian (35)	114	0.33
Samoan (78)	140	0.40
Tongan (98)	165	0.48
White (31,538)	32,331	93.20
Not Hispanic (29,716)	30,247	87.19
Hispanic (1,822)	2,084	6.01

Springville

Place Type: City
County: Utah
Population: 29,466†

Ancestry‡	Population	%
African, Sub-Saharan (25)	37	0.13
African (8)	8	0.03
Ghanaian (17)	17	0.06
Nigerian (0)	12	0.04
American (1,409)	1,409	5.10
Arab (0)	13	0.05
Lebanese (0)	13	0.05
Armenian (32)	59	0.21
Basque (18)	18	0.07
Belgian (10)	10	0.04
Brazilian (13)	110	0.40
British (144)	316	1.14
Bulgarian (0)	6	0.02
Canadian (0)	37	0.13
Celtic (21)	21	0.08
Czech (0)	44	0.16
Czechoslovakian (12)	86	0.31
Danish (412)	1,620	5.86
Dutch (305)	1,073	3.88
Eastern European (10)	10	0.04
English (3,950)	9,347	33.83
European (1,402)	1,510	5.46
Finnish (43)	123	0.45
French, ex. Basque (59)	516	1.87
French Canadian (0)	54	0.20
German (628)	2,799	10.13
German Russian (19)	19	0.07
Greek (27)	101	0.37
Hungarian (11)	30	0.11
Icelander (85)	144	0.52
Irish (310)	1,167	4.22
Italian (324)	844	3.05
Lithuanian (0)	20	0.07
Norwegian (254)	702	2.54
Polish (47)	295	1.07
Romanian (89)	89	0.32
Russian (18)	113	0.41
Scandinavian (82)	441	1.60
Scotch-Irish (80)	449	1.62
Scottish (262)	2,073	7.50
Serbian (9)	17	0.06
Slavic (20)	31	0.11
Swedish (400)	1,721	6.23
Swiss (68)	483	1.75
Ukrainian (0)	90	0.33
Welsh (90)	742	2.69
West Indian, ex. Hispanic (8)	38	0.14
Haitian (8)	17	0.06
Jamaican (0)	21	0.08
Yugoslavian (52)	52	0.19

Hispanic Origin	Population	%
Hispanic or Latino (of any race)	3,482	11.82
Central American, ex. Mexican	218	0.74
Costa Rican	8	0.03
Guatemalan	79	0.27
Honduran	45	0.15
Nicaraguan	2	0.01
Panamanian	2	0.01
Salvadoran	82	0.28
Cuban	17	0.06
Dominican Republic	14	0.05
Mexican	2,437	8.27
Puerto Rican	59	0.20
South American	463	1.57
Argentinean	125	0.42
Bolivian	8	0.03
Chilean	79	0.27
Colombian	46	0.16
Ecuadorian	42	0.14
Paraguayan	1	<0.01
Peruvian	110	0.37
Uruguayan	14	0.05
Venezuelan	35	0.12
Other South American	3	0.01
Other Hispanic or Latino	274	0.93

Race*	Population	%
African-American/Black (129)	227	0.77
Not Hispanic (113)	192	0.65
Hispanic (16)	35	0.12
American Indian/Alaska Native (154)	321	1.09
Not Hispanic (132)	254	0.86
Hispanic (22)	67	0.23
Aleut *(Alaska Native)* (0)	1	<0.01
Apache (3)	7	0.02
Blackfeet (1)	3	0.01
Canadian/French Am. Ind. (2)	7	0.02
Central American Ind. (1)	1	<0.01
Cherokee (7)	30	0.10
Chippewa (1)	2	0.01
Choctaw (1)	4	0.01
Cree (1)	1	<0.01
Crow (1)	1	<0.01
Iroquois (5)	8	0.03
Mexican American Ind. (4)	7	0.02
Navajo (58)	89	0.30
Paiute (0)	4	0.01
Pueblo (1)	5	0.02
Seminole (0)	2	0.01
Sioux (11)	20	0.07
South American Ind. (1)	2	0.01
Ute (5)	6	0.02
Yaqui (1)	2	0.01
Yuman (0)	1	<0.01
Asian (179)	372	1.26
Not Hispanic (174)	341	1.16
Hispanic (5)	31	0.11
Cambodian (2)	5	0.02
Chinese, ex. Taiwanese (32)	90	0.31
Filipino (30)	89	0.30
Indian (21)	27	0.09
Japanese (40)	94	0.32
Korean (17)	38	0.13
Laotian (6)	10	0.03
Nepalese (2)	3	0.01
Taiwanese (3)	5	0.02
Thai (5)	10	0.03
Vietnamese (8)	15	0.05
Hawaii Native/Pacific Islander (170)	350	1.19
Not Hispanic (168)	332	1.13
Hispanic (2)	18	0.06
Fijian (1)	1	<0.01
Guamanian/Chamorro (3)	8	0.03
Marshallese (8)	8	0.03
Native Hawaiian (18)	93	0.32
Samoan (62)	99	0.34
Tongan (59)	105	0.36
White (26,617)	27,297	92.64
Not Hispanic (24,885)	25,351	86.03
Hispanic (1,732)	1,946	6.60

St. George

Place Type: City
County: Washington
Population: 72,897†

Ancestry‡	Population	%
African, Sub-Saharan (68)	68	0.10
African (20)	20	0.03
Nigerian (11)	11	0.02

*Notes: † The Census 2010 population figure is used to calculate the percentages in the Hispanic Origin and Race categories. Ancestry percentages are based on the 2006-2010 American Community Survey population (not shown); ‡ Numbers in parentheses indicate the number of people reporting a single ancestry; * Numbers in parentheses indicate the number of persons reporting this race alone, not in combination with any other race; Please refer to the Explanation of Data for more information.*

South African (37)	37	0.05
American (3,409)	3,409	4.79
Armenian (13)	54	0.08
Australian (41)	79	0.11
Austrian (22)	127	0.18
Brazilian (48)	48	0.07
British (408)	708	1.00
Canadian (129)	199	0.28
Celtic (0)	14	0.02
Croatian (9)	34	0.05
Czech (47)	187	0.26
Czechoslovakian (41)	41	0.06
Danish (1,522)	3,742	5.26
Dutch (431)	1,529	2.15
English (9,476)	20,786	29.22
European (1,819)	2,024	2.85
Finnish (59)	135	0.19
French, ex. Basque (138)	1,645	2.31
French Canadian (64)	151	0.21
German (3,204)	9,489	13.34
Greek (79)	258	0.36
Hungarian (61)	77	0.11
Icelander (40)	162	0.23
Irish (2,736)	6,966	9.79
Italian (460)	1,290	1.81
Lithuanian (23)	39	0.05
Luxemburger (10)	10	0.01
Norwegian (759)	2,343	3.29
Pennsylvania German (0)	15	0.02
Polish (251)	734	1.03
Portuguese (0)	235	0.33
Romanian (0)	9	0.01
Russian (101)	311	0.44
Scandinavian (264)	701	0.99
Scotch-Irish (530)	1,069	1.50
Scottish (920)	3,421	4.81
Slavic (0)	19	0.03
Slovak (8)	8	0.01
Swedish (710)	2,753	3.87
Swiss (505)	1,428	2.01
Ukrainian (21)	21	0.03
Welsh (445)	1,498	2.11
West Indian, ex. Hispanic (39)	113	0.16
Belizean (5)	11	0.02
Dutch West Indian (0)	20	0.03
Haitian (34)	82	0.12
Yugoslavian (21)	201	0.28

Hispanic Origin	Population	%
Hispanic or Latino (of any race)	9,302	12.76
Central American, ex. Mexican	1,058	1.45
Costa Rican	34	0.05
Guatemalan	417	0.57
Honduran	38	0.05
Nicaraguan	18	0.02
Panamanian	14	0.02
Salvadoran	536	0.74
Other Central American	1	<0.01
Cuban	46	0.06
Dominican Republic	17	0.02
Mexican	6,765	9.28
Puerto Rican	162	0.22
South American	320	0.44
Argentinean	52	0.07
Bolivian	9	0.01
Chilean	54	0.07
Colombian	39	0.05
Ecuadorian	41	0.06
Paraguayan	4	0.01
Peruvian	86	0.12
Uruguayan	16	0.02
Venezuelan	19	0.03
Other Hispanic or Latino	934	1.28

Race*	Population	%
African-American/Black (530)	882	1.21
Not Hispanic (406)	705	0.97
Hispanic (124)	177	0.24
American Indian/Alaska Native (1,124)	1,601	2.20
Not Hispanic (856)	1,208	1.66
Hispanic (268)	393	0.54
Aleut *(Alaska Native)* (1)	3	<0.01
Apache (2)	13	0.02
Blackfeet (1)	11	0.02
Canadian/French Am. Ind. (1)	1	<0.01
Central American Ind. (3)	4	0.01
Cherokee (17)	87	0.12
Cheyenne (7)	7	0.01
Chickasaw (3)	5	0.01
Chippewa (3)	7	0.01
Choctaw (5)	8	0.01
Comanche (2)	4	0.01
Cree (4)	4	0.01
Creek (2)	3	<0.01
Crow (2)	4	0.01
Hopi (3)	3	<0.01
Inupiat *(Alaska Native)* (1)	1	<0.01
Iroquois (10)	16	0.02
Lumbee (2)	3	<0.01
Mexican American Ind. (95)	124	0.17
Navajo (507)	642	0.88
Osage (6)	6	0.01
Paiute (119)	149	0.20
Pima (2)	10	0.01
Potawatomi (0)	2	<0.01
Pueblo (2)	12	0.02
Shoshone (4)	10	0.01
Sioux (4)	21	0.03
South American Ind. (1)	1	<0.01
Spanish American Ind. (10)	10	0.01
Tlingit-Haida *(Alaska Native)* (3)	3	<0.01
Ute (13)	19	0.03
Yakama (0)	2	<0.01
Yaqui (2)	2	<0.01
Yuman (1)	1	<0.01
Asian (582)	1,050	1.44
Not Hispanic (562)	991	1.36
Hispanic (20)	59	0.08
Burmese (8)	13	0.02
Cambodian (2)	2	<0.01
Chinese, ex. Taiwanese (125)	283	0.39
Filipino (140)	255	0.35
Indian (78)	115	0.16
Indonesian (2)	12	0.02
Japanese (80)	197	0.27
Korean (42)	80	0.11
Laotian (6)	9	0.01
Malaysian (0)	1	<0.01
Pakistani (6)	6	0.01
Taiwanese (6)	14	0.02
Thai (13)	37	0.05
Vietnamese (43)	61	0.08
Hawaii Native/Pacific Islander (741)	1,189	1.63
Not Hispanic (703)	1,123	1.54
Hispanic (38)	66	0.09
Fijian (5)	6	0.01
Guamanian/Chamorro (6)	18	0.02
Marshallese (2)	2	<0.01
Native Hawaiian (104)	327	0.45
Samoan (433)	658	0.90
Tongan (98)	165	0.23
White (63,565)	65,268	89.53
Not Hispanic (59,722)	60,898	83.54
Hispanic (3,843)	4,370	5.99

Summit Park

Place Type: CDP
County: Summit
Population: 7,775[†]

Ancestry‡	Population	%
American (857)	857	11.42
Arab (0)	13	0.17
Lebanese (0)	13	0.17
British (4)	72	0.96
Canadian (23)	48	0.64
Croatian (20)	20	0.27
Czech (18)	59	0.79
Danish (41)	180	2.40
Dutch (77)	123	1.64
English (561)	1,503	20.03
European (336)	336	4.48
Finnish (0)	37	0.49
French, ex. Basque (41)	337	4.49
French Canadian (15)	101	1.35
German (325)	1,476	19.67
Greek (0)	19	0.25
Irish (104)	633	8.44
Italian (138)	575	7.66
Latvian (15)	32	0.43
Northern European (133)	133	1.77
Norwegian (133)	281	3.74
Polish (48)	167	2.23
Portuguese (0)	10	0.13
Russian (30)	127	1.69
Scandinavian (0)	12	0.16
Scotch-Irish (157)	227	3.03
Scottish (233)	403	5.37
Serbian (0)	17	0.23
Slavic (0)	19	0.25
Slovak (0)	31	0.41
Slovene (0)	13	0.17
Swedish (81)	380	5.06
Swiss (15)	71	0.95
Ukrainian (15)	15	0.20
Welsh (33)	191	2.55
West Indian, ex. Hispanic (0)	11	0.15
Jamaican (0)	11	0.15
Yugoslavian (0)	23	0.31

Hispanic Origin	Population	%
Hispanic or Latino (of any race)	686	8.82
Central American, ex. Mexican	16	0.21
Guatemalan	10	0.13
Honduran	4	0.05
Panamanian	1	0.01
Salvadoran	1	0.01
Cuban	10	0.13
Dominican Republic	2	0.03
Mexican	536	6.89
Puerto Rican	21	0.27
South American	32	0.41
Argentinean	6	0.08
Chilean	7	0.09
Colombian	11	0.14
Peruvian	4	0.05
Uruguayan	4	0.05
Other Hispanic or Latino	69	0.89

Race*	Population	%
African-American/Black (39)	63	0.81
Not Hispanic (36)	59	0.76
Hispanic (3)	4	0.05
American Indian/Alaska Native (14)	27	0.35
Not Hispanic (10)	23	0.30
Hispanic (4)	4	0.05
Blackfeet (0)	1	0.01
Cherokee (3)	6	0.08
Chippewa (1)	1	0.01
Creek (3)	3	0.04
Crow (0)	1	0.01
Iroquois (0)	1	0.01
Mexican American Ind. (1)	1	0.01
Osage (0)	1	0.01
Asian (121)	174	2.24
Not Hispanic (121)	171	2.20
Hispanic (0)	3	0.04
Bangladeshi (2)	2	0.03
Cambodian (1)	1	0.01
Chinese, ex. Taiwanese (36)	46	0.59
Filipino (18)	25	0.32
Indian (7)	10	0.13
Indonesian (7)	10	0.13
Japanese (18)	40	0.51
Korean (16)	23	0.30
Taiwanese (3)	3	0.04
Thai (1)	3	0.04
Vietnamese (6)	9	0.12
Hawaii Native/Pacific Islander (1)	12	0.15

*Notes: † The Census 2010 population figure is used to calculate the percentages in the Hispanic Origin and Race categories. Ancestry percentages are based on the 2006-2010 American Community Survey population (not shown); ‡ Numbers in parentheses indicate the number of people reporting a single ancestry; * Numbers in parentheses indicate the number of persons reporting this race alone, not in combination with any other race; Please refer to the Explanation of Data for more information.*

Not Hispanic (0)	11	0.14
Hispanic (1)	1	0.01
Guamanian/Chamorro (1)	2	0.03
Native Hawaiian (0)	7	0.09
White (7,356)	7,459	95.94
Not Hispanic (6,832)	6,913	88.91
Hispanic (524)	546	7.02

Syracuse

Place Type: City
County: Davis
Population: 24,331†

Ancestry‡	Population	%
American (1,448)	1,448	6.68
Austrian (32)	42	0.19
Basque (0)	25	0.12
British (262)	406	1.87
Canadian (12)	27	0.12
Czech (18)	27	0.12
Czechoslovakian (0)	28	0.13
Danish (403)	1,223	5.64
Dutch (217)	554	2.55
English (2,852)	5,883	27.12
Estonian (0)	7	0.03
European (518)	547	2.52
Finnish (52)	62	0.29
French, ex. Basque (27)	328	1.51
French Canadian (38)	65	0.30
German (781)	3,106	14.32
Greek (21)	46	0.21
Irish (307)	1,125	5.19
Italian (251)	739	3.41
New Zealander (19)	44	0.20
Northern European (68)	68	0.31
Norwegian (182)	628	2.90
Polish (55)	194	0.89
Portuguese (21)	74	0.34
Russian (26)	36	0.17
Scandinavian (81)	236	1.09
Scotch-Irish (44)	135	0.62
Scottish (322)	1,320	6.09
Swedish (237)	746	3.44
Swiss (53)	332	1.53
Welsh (88)	365	1.68
West Indian, ex. Hispanic (23)	23	0.11
Trinidadian/Tobagonian (23)	23	0.11

Hispanic Origin	Population	%
Hispanic or Latino (of any race)	1,460	6.00
Central American, ex. Mexican	72	0.30
Guatemalan	23	0.09
Honduran	12	0.05
Nicaraguan	5	0.02
Panamanian	3	0.01
Salvadoran	26	0.11
Other Central American	3	0.01
Cuban	24	0.10
Dominican Republic	8	0.03
Mexican	905	3.72
Puerto Rican	78	0.32
South American	183	0.75
Argentinean	30	0.12
Bolivian	1	<0.01
Chilean	13	0.05
Colombian	31	0.13
Ecuadorian	22	0.09
Peruvian	65	0.27
Venezuelan	21	0.09
Other Hispanic or Latino	190	0.78

Race*	Population	%
African-American/Black (189)	296	1.22
Not Hispanic (182)	281	1.15
Hispanic (7)	15	0.06
American Indian/Alaska Native (68)	176	0.72
Not Hispanic (59)	142	0.58
Hispanic (9)	34	0.14
Apache (1)	1	<0.01
Blackfeet (1)	13	0.05
Cherokee (1)	29	0.12
Cheyenne (0)	1	<0.01
Choctaw (9)	14	0.06
Colville (0)	1	<0.01
Creek (6)	8	0.03
Houma (1)	1	<0.01
Iroquois (0)	4	0.02
Mexican American Ind. (6)	10	0.04
Navajo (12)	25	0.10
Paiute (5)	5	0.02
Pueblo (1)	1	<0.01
Seminole (0)	1	<0.01
Shoshone (0)	6	0.02
Sioux (1)	2	0.01
South American Ind. (0)	1	<0.01
Ute (8)	9	0.04
Yuman (1)	1	<0.01
Asian (452)	711	2.92
Not Hispanic (435)	676	2.78
Hispanic (17)	35	0.14
Cambodian (1)	4	0.02
Chinese, ex. Taiwanese (47)	86	0.35
Filipino (95)	179	0.74
Hmong (12)	28	0.12
Indian (10)	14	0.06
Japanese (87)	179	0.74
Korean (56)	84	0.35
Laotian (57)	76	0.31
Malaysian (4)	4	0.02
Pakistani (0)	3	0.01
Taiwanese (6)	10	0.04
Thai (17)	45	0.18
Vietnamese (21)	28	0.12
Hawaii Native/Pacific Islander (90)	158	0.65
Not Hispanic (84)	141	0.58
Hispanic (6)	17	0.07
Guamanian/Chamorro (11)	13	0.05
Marshallese (7)	7	0.03
Native Hawaiian (24)	52	0.21
Samoan (10)	32	0.13
Tongan (16)	18	0.07
White (22,443)	23,009	94.57
Not Hispanic (21,641)	22,051	90.63
Hispanic (802)	958	3.94

Taylorsville

Place Type: City
County: Salt Lake
Population: 58,652†

Ancestry‡	Population	%
African, Sub-Saharan (284)	347	0.59
African (178)	200	0.34
Ethiopian (28)	28	0.05
Kenyan (0)	32	0.05
Sudanese (73)	73	0.13
Other Sub-Saharan African (5)	14	0.02
American (3,077)	3,077	5.27
Arab (35)	66	0.11
Arab (24)	30	0.05
Lebanese (11)	11	0.02
Syrian (0)	25	0.04
Armenian (26)	35	0.06
Australian (10)	46	0.08
Austrian (16)	102	0.17
Basque (0)	22	0.04
Belgian (0)	10	0.02
Brazilian (151)	151	0.26
British (175)	446	0.76
Cajun (0)	4	0.01
Canadian (49)	214	0.37
Celtic (10)	10	0.02
Croatian (31)	76	0.13
Czech (66)	126	0.22
Czechoslovakian (0)	23	0.04
Danish (683)	2,806	4.81
Dutch (384)	1,226	2.10
English (5,598)	14,138	24.23
European (892)	1,043	1.79
Finnish (26)	50	0.09
French, ex. Basque (195)	1,225	2.10
French Canadian (55)	152	0.26
German (2,068)	6,895	11.82
Greek (181)	441	0.76
Hungarian (48)	62	0.11
Icelander (0)	17	0.03
Iranian (0)	8	0.01
Irish (594)	3,349	5.74
Italian (715)	1,707	2.93
Latvian (14)	14	0.02
Lithuanian (0)	50	0.09
Macedonian (8)	8	0.01
New Zealander (31)	31	0.05
Northern European (37)	37	0.06
Norwegian (637)	1,197	2.05
Pennsylvania German (0)	8	0.01
Polish (165)	473	0.81
Portuguese (18)	86	0.15
Romanian (0)	9	0.02
Russian (16)	64	0.11
Scandinavian (223)	413	0.71
Scotch-Irish (202)	537	0.92
Scottish (422)	2,388	4.09
Serbian (47)	47	0.08
Slavic (0)	21	0.04
Slovak (29)	29	0.05
Slovene (0)	12	0.02
Swedish (729)	1,991	3.41
Swiss (58)	478	0.82
Welsh (264)	902	1.55
West Indian, ex. Hispanic (18)	37	0.06
Dutch West Indian (0)	19	0.03
U.S. Virgin Islander (18)	18	0.03
Yugoslavian (100)	140	0.24

Hispanic Origin	Population	%
Hispanic or Latino (of any race)	10,931	18.64
Central American, ex. Mexican	638	1.09
Costa Rican	17	0.03
Guatemalan	183	0.31
Honduran	92	0.16
Nicaraguan	43	0.07
Panamanian	9	0.02
Salvadoran	290	0.49
Other Central American	4	0.01
Cuban	51	0.09
Dominican Republic	48	0.08
Mexican	7,647	13.04
Puerto Rican	232	0.40
South American	872	1.49
Argentinean	104	0.18
Bolivian	48	0.08
Chilean	83	0.14
Colombian	102	0.17
Ecuadorian	76	0.13
Paraguayan	5	0.01
Peruvian	220	0.38
Uruguayan	34	0.06
Venezuelan	194	0.33
Other South American	6	0.01
Other Hispanic or Latino	1,443	2.46

Race*	Population	%
African-American/Black (1,104)	1,559	2.66
Not Hispanic (988)	1,340	2.28
Hispanic (116)	219	0.37
American Indian/Alaska Native (564)	940	1.60
Not Hispanic (378)	609	1.04
Hispanic (186)	331	0.56
Alaska Athabascan *(Ala. Nat.)* (1)	1	<0.01
Aleut *(Alaska Native)* (1)	4	0.01
Apache (7)	20	0.03
Arapaho (2)	8	0.01
Blackfeet (2)	11	0.02
Canadian/French Am. Ind. (0)	1	<0.01
Central American Ind. (3)	4	0.01
Cherokee (9)	47	0.08
Cheyenne (1)	1	<0.01

*Notes: † The Census 2010 population figure is used to calculate the percentages in the Hispanic Origin and Race categories. Ancestry percentages are based on the 2006-2010 American Community Survey population (not shown); ‡ Numbers in parentheses indicate the number of people reporting a single ancestry; * Numbers in parentheses indicate the number of persons reporting this race alone, not in combination with any other race; Please refer to the Explanation of Data for more information.*

Chickasaw (0)	2	<0.01
Chippewa (2)	8	0.01
Choctaw (5)	11	0.02
Comanche (0)	3	0.01
Cree (2)	3	0.01
Creek (3)	5	0.01
Crow (0)	1	<0.01
Delaware (1)	2	<0.01
Iroquois (4)	7	0.01
Lumbee (1)	2	<0.01
Mexican American Ind. (33)	34	0.06
Navajo (222)	289	0.49
Paiute (2)	9	0.02
Pueblo (9)	23	0.04
Shoshone (4)	8	0.01
Sioux (15)	28	0.05
South American Ind. (2)	5	0.01
Spanish American Ind. (9)	12	0.02
Tlingit-Haida *(Alaska Native)* (2)	2	<0.01
Ute (23)	37	0.06
Yaqui (1)	2	<0.01
Yuman (0)	1	<0.01
Asian (2,285)	2,772	4.73
Not Hispanic (2,252)	2,665	4.54
Hispanic (33)	107	0.18
Bangladeshi (1)	1	<0.01
Burmese (16)	16	0.03
Cambodian (64)	79	0.13
Chinese, ex. Taiwanese (332)	477	0.81
Filipino (175)	277	0.47
Hmong (3)	3	0.01
Indian (408)	447	0.76
Indonesian (9)	12	0.02
Japanese (161)	323	0.55
Korean (77)	122	0.21
Laotian (141)	172	0.29
Nepalese (4)	4	0.01
Pakistani (99)	111	0.19
Taiwanese (7)	13	0.02
Thai (38)	55	0.09
Vietnamese (618)	692	1.18
Hawaii Native/Pacific Islander (1,285)	1,567	2.67
Not Hispanic (1,258)	1,512	2.58
Hispanic (27)	55	0.09
Fijian (13)	29	0.05
Guamanian/Chamorro (15)	19	0.03
Marshallese (28)	28	0.05
Native Hawaiian (48)	111	0.19
Samoan (614)	782	1.33
Tongan (412)	539	0.92
White (45,889)	47,625	81.20
Not Hispanic (41,540)	42,531	72.51
Hispanic (4,349)	5,094	8.69

Tooele

Place Type: City
County: Tooele
Population: 31,605†

Ancestry‡	Population	%
African, Sub-Saharan (12)	12	0.04
African (12)	12	0.04
American (1,658)	1,658	5.50
Arab (0)	27	0.09
Lebanese (0)	27	0.09
Australian (17)	37	0.12
Austrian (70)	132	0.44
Belgian (0)	36	0.12
Brazilian (9)	9	0.03
British (174)	478	1.58
Bulgarian (9)	9	0.03
Canadian (61)	101	0.33
Celtic (0)	19	0.06
Czech (0)	15	0.05
Czechoslovakian (14)	37	0.12
Danish (281)	1,648	5.46
Dutch (273)	847	2.81
English (2,546)	7,067	23.43
European (1,175)	1,228	4.07
Finnish (60)	102	0.34
French, ex. Basque (291)	733	2.43
French Canadian (33)	57	0.19
German (1,132)	4,517	14.97
Greek (10)	75	0.25
Hungarian (0)	125	0.41
Icelander (36)	44	0.15
Irish (520)	2,327	7.71
Italian (462)	1,185	3.93
Norwegian (144)	655	2.17
Polish (58)	463	1.53
Portuguese (14)	36	0.12
Russian (0)	8	0.03
Scandinavian (104)	417	1.38
Scotch-Irish (191)	475	1.57
Scottish (721)	1,759	5.83
Slovak (0)	28	0.09
Swedish (305)	878	2.91
Swiss (53)	390	1.29
Ukrainian (0)	22	0.07
Welsh (66)	484	1.60
Yugoslavian (0)	86	0.29

Hispanic Origin	Population	%
Hispanic or Latino (of any race)	4,080	12.91
Central American, ex. Mexican	160	0.51
Costa Rican	4	0.01
Guatemalan	54	0.17
Honduran	17	0.05
Nicaraguan	6	0.02
Panamanian	3	0.01
Salvadoran	72	0.23
Other Central American	4	0.01
Cuban	15	0.05
Dominican Republic	5	0.02
Mexican	2,531	8.01
Puerto Rican	131	0.41
South American	177	0.56
Argentinean	27	0.09
Bolivian	5	0.02
Chilean	37	0.12
Colombian	21	0.07
Ecuadorian	32	0.10
Paraguayan	4	0.01
Peruvian	32	0.10
Uruguayan	3	0.01
Venezuelan	15	0.05
Other South American	1	<0.01
Other Hispanic or Latino	1,061	3.36

Race*	Population	%
African-American/Black (260)	430	1.36
Not Hispanic (239)	373	1.18
Hispanic (21)	57	0.18
American Indian/Alaska Native (317)	615	1.95
Not Hispanic (253)	460	1.46
Hispanic (64)	155	0.49
Alaska Athabascan *(Ala. Nat.)* (0)	1	<0.01
Aleut *(Alaska Native)* (0)	5	0.02
Apache (7)	16	0.05
Blackfeet (9)	11	0.03
Canadian/French Am. Ind. (0)	1	<0.01
Cherokee (18)	74	0.23
Cheyenne (1)	1	<0.01
Chickasaw (0)	7	0.02
Chippewa (5)	7	0.02
Choctaw (9)	19	0.06
Comanche (0)	5	0.02
Cree (0)	3	0.01
Creek (1)	6	0.02
Crow (1)	1	<0.01
Hopi (0)	1	<0.01
Inupiat *(Alaska Native)* (2)	2	0.01
Iroquois (0)	1	<0.01
Lumbee (0)	1	<0.01
Mexican American Ind. (10)	19	0.06
Navajo (100)	162	0.51
Ottawa (1)	3	0.01
Paiute (1)	1	<0.01
Potawatomi (0)	4	0.01
Pueblo (7)	22	0.07
Seminole (2)	2	0.01
Shoshone (21)	34	0.11
Sioux (12)	21	0.07
South American Ind. (0)	5	0.02
Spanish American Ind. (1)	1	<0.01
Ute (9)	14	0.04
Yup'ik *(Alaska Native)* (2)	2	0.01
Asian (201)	383	1.21
Not Hispanic (191)	323	1.02
Hispanic (10)	60	0.19
Cambodian (5)	5	0.02
Chinese, ex. Taiwanese (33)	58	0.18
Filipino (77)	157	0.50
Hmong (1)	1	<0.01
Indian (12)	16	0.05
Indonesian (0)	1	<0.01
Japanese (24)	60	0.19
Korean (23)	53	0.17
Laotian (1)	5	0.02
Pakistani (1)	5	0.02
Taiwanese (0)	1	<0.01
Thai (4)	8	0.03
Vietnamese (9)	16	0.05
Hawaii Native/Pacific Islander (139)	237	0.75
Not Hispanic (136)	220	0.70
Hispanic (3)	17	0.05
Fijian (0)	2	0.01
Guamanian/Chamorro (23)	31	0.10
Native Hawaiian (6)	34	0.11
Samoan (22)	50	0.16
Tongan (63)	104	0.33
White (28,330)	29,191	92.36
Not Hispanic (26,172)	26,655	84.34
Hispanic (2,158)	2,536	8.02

Tremonton

Place Type: City
County: Box Elder
Population: 7,647†

Ancestry‡	Population	%
American (616)	616	8.53
Austrian (15)	15	0.21
British (62)	118	1.63
Danish (209)	665	9.21
Dutch (0)	90	1.25
English (1,015)	1,900	26.32
European (32)	32	0.44
French, ex. Basque (17)	62	0.86
German (336)	647	8.96
Greek (14)	14	0.19
Irish (72)	220	3.05
Italian (13)	24	0.33
Norwegian (73)	99	1.37
Scandinavian (0)	14	0.19
Scotch-Irish (46)	85	1.18
Scottish (33)	87	1.21
Swedish (14)	221	3.06
Swiss (31)	62	0.86
Welsh (43)	111	1.54

Hispanic Origin	Population	%
Hispanic or Latino (of any race)	896	11.72
Central American, ex. Mexican	20	0.26
Guatemalan	6	0.08
Honduran	4	0.05
Nicaraguan	1	0.01
Salvadoran	9	0.12
Cuban	4	0.05
Mexican	753	9.85
Puerto Rican	10	0.13
South American	29	0.38
Argentinean	2	0.03
Colombian	4	0.05
Peruvian	22	0.29
Uruguayan	1	0.01
Other Hispanic or Latino	80	1.05

*Notes: † The Census 2010 population figure is used to calculate the percentages in the Hispanic Origin and Race categories. Ancestry percentages are based on the 2006-2010 American Community Survey population (not shown); ‡ Numbers in parentheses indicate the number of people reporting a single ancestry; * Numbers in parentheses indicate the number of persons reporting this race alone, not in combination with any other race; Please refer to the Explanation of Data for more information.*

Race*	Population	%
African-American/Black (31)	50	0.65
Not Hispanic (24)	30	0.39
Hispanic (7)	20	0.26
American Indian/Alaska Native (44)	87	1.14
Not Hispanic (37)	68	0.89
Hispanic (7)	19	0.25
Apache (0)	4	0.05
Cherokee (0)	13	0.17
Chippewa (1)	1	0.01
Hopi (5)	5	0.07
Iroquois (0)	1	0.01
Kiowa (1)	1	0.01
Menominee (0)	1	0.01
Navajo (1)	1	0.01
Shoshone (4)	10	0.13
Sioux (3)	6	0.08
Ute (1)	5	0.07
Yup'ik *(Alaska Native)* (1)	1	0.01
Asian (109)	155	2.03
Not Hispanic (109)	153	2.00
Hispanic (0)	2	0.03
Cambodian (50)	57	0.75
Chinese, ex. Taiwanese (3)	4	0.05
Filipino (2)	7	0.09
Indian (14)	24	0.31
Indonesian (1)	1	0.01
Japanese (17)	39	0.51
Korean (3)	5	0.07
Laotian (3)	3	0.04
Thai (2)	5	0.07
Vietnamese (2)	2	0.03
Hawaii Native/Pacific Islander (15)	25	0.33
Not Hispanic (14)	18	0.24
Hispanic (1)	7	0.09
Marshallese (1)	1	0.01
Native Hawaiian (1)	6	0.08
Samoan (2)	3	0.04
Tongan (10)	10	0.13
White (6,898)	7,044	92.11
Not Hispanic (6,469)	6,557	85.75
Hispanic (429)	487	6.37

Vernal

Place Type: City
County: Uintah
Population: 9,089†

Ancestry‡	Population	%
American (574)	574	6.55
Arab (15)	15	0.17
Arab (15)	15	0.17
Belgian (0)	46	0.52
Brazilian (0)	23	0.26
British (15)	15	0.17
Canadian (77)	77	0.88
Czech (0)	38	0.43
Danish (57)	280	3.19
Dutch (0)	11	0.13
Eastern European (42)	42	0.48
English (887)	1,716	19.57
European (366)	425	4.85
Finnish (11)	25	0.29
French, ex. Basque (27)	139	1.59
German (713)	1,477	16.85
Greek (53)	53	0.60
Hungarian (0)	38	0.43
Icelander (18)	18	0.21
Irish (165)	491	5.60
Italian (39)	221	2.52
Norwegian (84)	203	2.32
Polish (31)	124	1.41
Portuguese (0)	10	0.11
Russian (0)	11	0.13
Scandinavian (34)	34	0.39
Scotch-Irish (14)	85	0.97
Scottish (105)	286	3.26
Serbian (14)	14	0.16
Swedish (96)	165	1.88
Swiss (10)	130	1.48
Welsh (17)	80	0.91
Yugoslavian (15)	42	0.48

Hispanic Origin	Population	%
Hispanic or Latino (of any race)	1,073	11.81
Central American, ex. Mexican	60	0.66
Guatemalan	21	0.23
Honduran	8	0.09
Nicaraguan	19	0.21
Panamanian	7	0.08
Salvadoran	5	0.06
Cuban	3	0.03
Dominican Republic	4	0.04
Mexican	833	9.16
Puerto Rican	15	0.17
South American	33	0.36
Argentinean	3	0.03
Chilean	1	0.01
Colombian	9	0.10
Ecuadorian	1	0.01
Peruvian	13	0.14
Venezuelan	6	0.07
Other Hispanic or Latino	125	1.38

Race*	Population	%
African-American/Black (46)	82	0.90
Not Hispanic (39)	72	0.79
Hispanic (7)	10	0.11
American Indian/Alaska Native (204)	293	3.22
Not Hispanic (174)	250	2.75
Hispanic (30)	43	0.47
Apache (5)	5	0.06
Arapaho (1)	1	0.01
Blackfeet (0)	2	0.02
Canadian/French Am. Ind. (2)	2	0.02
Cherokee (3)	12	0.13
Cheyenne (3)	3	0.03
Chippewa (2)	4	0.04
Choctaw (1)	1	0.01
Cree (0)	4	0.04
Iroquois (1)	1	0.01
Kiowa (0)	3	0.03
Mexican American Ind. (5)	5	0.06
Navajo (13)	25	0.28
Ottawa (1)	1	0.01
Potawatomi (2)	4	0.04
Pueblo (1)	2	0.02
Shoshone (7)	17	0.19
Sioux (10)	12	0.13
South American Ind. (0)	1	0.01
Ute (87)	111	1.22
Asian (63)	127	1.40
Not Hispanic (59)	110	1.21
Hispanic (4)	17	0.19
Cambodian (2)	5	0.06
Chinese, ex. Taiwanese (19)	26	0.29
Filipino (17)	35	0.39
Indian (5)	7	0.08
Indonesian (0)	1	0.01
Japanese (1)	26	0.29
Korean (5)	9	0.10
Laotian (0)	1	0.01
Sri Lankan (1)	1	0.01
Thai (2)	2	0.02
Vietnamese (10)	12	0.13
Hawaii Native/Pacific Islander (27)	46	0.51
Not Hispanic (25)	42	0.46
Hispanic (2)	4	0.04
Fijian (15)	15	0.17
Native Hawaiian (7)	15	0.17
Samoan (2)	5	0.06
Tongan (2)	4	0.04
White (8,148)	8,365	92.03
Not Hispanic (7,556)	7,697	84.68
Hispanic (592)	668	7.35

Washington Terrace

Place Type: City
County: Weber
Population: 9,067†

Ancestry‡	Population	%
American (2,144)	2,144	24.04
Australian (14)	29	0.33
Austrian (27)	27	0.30
Basque (8)	8	0.09
British (22)	65	0.73
Canadian (0)	10	0.11
Czech (0)	15	0.17
Danish (97)	451	5.06
Dutch (102)	353	3.96
Eastern European (12)	12	0.13
English (1,129)	2,242	25.14
European (185)	241	2.70
French, ex. Basque (58)	158	1.77
French Canadian (14)	39	0.44
German (126)	763	8.56
Greek (10)	10	0.11
Hungarian (0)	14	0.16
Irish (135)	530	5.94
Italian (71)	270	3.03
Northern European (9)	9	0.10
Norwegian (45)	88	0.99
Polish (9)	77	0.86
Portuguese (10)	18	0.20
Scandinavian (16)	24	0.27
Scotch-Irish (55)	129	1.45
Scottish (111)	436	4.89
Swedish (95)	386	4.33
Swiss (0)	42	0.47
Welsh (3)	65	0.73
West Indian, ex. Hispanic (55)	55	0.62
Haitian (55)	55	0.62
Yugoslavian (0)	48	0.54

Hispanic Origin	Population	%
Hispanic or Latino (of any race)	1,167	12.87
Central American, ex. Mexican	46	0.51
Guatemalan	7	0.08
Honduran	9	0.10
Salvadoran	29	0.32
Other Central American	1	0.01
Cuban	2	0.02
Mexican	805	8.88
Puerto Rican	22	0.24
South American	43	0.47
Argentinean	21	0.23
Chilean	4	0.04
Colombian	1	0.01
Ecuadorian	5	0.06
Paraguayan	1	0.01
Peruvian	6	0.07
Uruguayan	4	0.04
Venezuelan	1	0.01
Other Hispanic or Latino	249	2.75

Race*	Population	%
African-American/Black (187)	257	2.83
Not Hispanic (176)	233	2.57
Hispanic (11)	24	0.26
American Indian/Alaska Native (66)	142	1.57
Not Hispanic (51)	103	1.14
Hispanic (15)	39	0.43
Aleut *(Alaska Native)* (7)	9	0.10
Apache (3)	4	0.04
Blackfeet (0)	1	0.01
Cherokee (6)	17	0.19
Chippewa (0)	1	0.01
Choctaw (6)	11	0.12
Crow (1)	1	0.01
Iroquois (0)	1	0.01
Mexican American Ind. (0)	4	0.04
Navajo (15)	25	0.28
Pima (0)	2	0.02
Seminole (1)	1	0.01

*Notes: † The Census 2010 population figure is used to calculate the percentages in the Hispanic Origin and Race categories. Ancestry percentages are based on the 2006-2010 American Community Survey population (not shown); ‡ Numbers in parentheses indicate the number of people reporting a single ancestry; * Numbers in parentheses indicate the number of persons reporting this race alone, not in combination with any other race; Please refer to the Explanation of Data for more information.*

Shoshone (0)	2	0.02
Sioux (0)	2	0.02
South American Ind. (0)	1	0.01
Spanish American Ind. (1)	1	0.01
Ute (1)	4	0.04
Yuman (1)	1	0.01
Asian (116)	157	1.73
Not Hispanic (110)	146	1.61
Hispanic (6)	11	0.12
Chinese, ex. Taiwanese (18)	23	0.25
Filipino (20)	25	0.28
Hmong (15)	15	0.17
Indian (4)	8	0.09
Japanese (24)	39	0.43
Korean (4)	10	0.11
Laotian (3)	3	0.03
Malaysian (0)	1	0.01
Pakistani (6)	8	0.09
Taiwanese (10)	14	0.15
Thai (1)	2	0.02
Vietnamese (7)	7	0.08
Hawaii Native/Pacific Islander (31)	57	0.63
Not Hispanic (29)	54	0.60
Hispanic (2)	3	0.03
Guamanian/Chamorro (0)	1	0.01
Marshallese (1)	7	0.08
Native Hawaiian (12)	25	0.28
Samoan (5)	17	0.19
Tongan (5)	6	0.07
White (7,877)	8,089	89.21
Not Hispanic (7,354)	7,501	82.73
Hispanic (523)	588	6.49

Washington

Place Type: City
County: Washington
Population: 18,761†

Ancestry‡	Population	%
African, Sub-Saharan (0)	7	0.04
African (0)	7	0.04
American (1,099)	1,099	6.31
Austrian (0)	60	0.34
Belgian (0)	7	0.04
Brazilian (18)	18	0.10
British (49)	169	0.97
Czech (0)	11	0.06
Danish (155)	514	2.95
Dutch (41)	283	1.63
English (2,933)	5,555	31.91
European (286)	372	2.14
Finnish (14)	29	0.17
French, ex. Basque (149)	460	2.64
French Canadian (15)	37	0.21
German (878)	3,147	18.08
Greek (7)	20	0.11
Icelander (13)	13	0.07
Irish (560)	1,572	9.03
Italian (116)	624	3.58
Lithuanian (0)	9	0.05
Northern European (16)	16	0.09
Norwegian (207)	675	3.88
Pennsylvania German (0)	12	0.07
Polish (22)	48	0.28
Portuguese (0)	9	0.05
Romanian (9)	9	0.05
Russian (0)	29	0.17
Scandinavian (126)	506	2.91
Scotch-Irish (75)	252	1.45
Scottish (232)	1,020	5.86
Slavic (14)	14	0.08
Slovak (0)	32	0.18
Swedish (130)	864	4.96
Swiss (44)	123	0.71
Ukrainian (0)	11	0.06
Welsh (49)	368	2.11

Hispanic Origin	Population	%
Hispanic or Latino (of any race)	1,574	8.39
Central American, ex. Mexican	82	0.44
Costa Rican	10	0.05
Guatemalan	21	0.11
Honduran	7	0.04
Nicaraguan	2	0.01
Panamanian	3	0.02
Salvadoran	39	0.21
Cuban	14	0.07
Mexican	1,181	6.29
Puerto Rican	51	0.27
South American	54	0.29
Argentinean	14	0.07
Bolivian	3	0.02
Chilean	7	0.04
Colombian	6	0.03
Ecuadorian	6	0.03
Peruvian	11	0.06
Uruguayan	1	0.01
Venezuelan	4	0.02
Other South American	2	0.01
Other Hispanic or Latino	192	1.02

Race*	Population	%
African-American/Black (61)	120	0.64
Not Hispanic (58)	104	0.55
Hispanic (3)	16	0.09
American Indian/Alaska Native (185)	256	1.36
Not Hispanic (167)	225	1.20
Hispanic (18)	31	0.17
Apache (0)	1	0.01
Blackfeet (1)	1	0.01
Cherokee (6)	23	0.12
Chickasaw (0)	1	0.01
Chippewa (1)	1	0.01
Comanche (1)	1	0.01
Creek (1)	2	0.01
Crow (1)	1	0.01
Hopi (2)	3	0.02
Iroquois (6)	6	0.03
Mexican American Ind. (3)	4	0.02
Navajo (71)	87	0.46
Paiute (19)	24	0.13
Shoshone (1)	1	0.01
Sioux (3)	7	0.04
South American Ind. (0)	1	0.01
Spanish American Ind. (1)	1	0.01
Tlingit-Haida *(Alaska Native)* (1)	1	0.01
Ute (4)	7	0.04
Yakama (1)	2	0.01
Yuman (0)	3	0.02
Asian (168)	275	1.47
Not Hispanic (165)	262	1.40
Hispanic (3)	13	0.07
Cambodian (1)	4	0.02
Chinese, ex. Taiwanese (6)	23	0.12
Filipino (47)	77	0.41
Indian (37)	40	0.21
Indonesian (1)	2	0.01
Japanese (17)	43	0.23
Korean (20)	36	0.19
Laotian (3)	6	0.03
Malaysian (1)	1	0.01
Sri Lankan (3)	4	0.02
Thai (4)	11	0.06
Vietnamese (14)	15	0.08
Hawaii Native/Pacific Islander (127)	221	1.18
Not Hispanic (123)	201	1.07
Hispanic (4)	20	0.11
Guamanian/Chamorro (4)	5	0.03
Native Hawaiian (34)	88	0.47
Samoan (60)	105	0.56
Tongan (15)	22	0.12
White (17,010)	17,351	92.48
Not Hispanic (16,412)	16,636	88.67
Hispanic (598)	715	3.81

West Haven

Place Type: City
County: Weber
Population: 10,272†

Ancestry‡	Population	%
African, Sub-Saharan (15)	15	0.17
Nigerian (15)	15	0.17
American (1,852)	1,852	20.45
Belgian (0)	13	0.14
British (0)	8	0.09
Canadian (0)	25	0.28
Danish (103)	361	3.99
Dutch (85)	265	2.93
English (730)	1,777	19.62
European (207)	207	2.29
Finnish (43)	43	0.47
French, ex. Basque (79)	167	1.84
German (229)	959	10.59
Greek (11)	50	0.55
Irish (88)	436	4.81
Italian (41)	183	2.02
New Zealander (26)	50	0.55
Norwegian (15)	148	1.63
Polish (37)	67	0.74
Russian (17)	79	0.87
Scandinavian (15)	64	0.71
Scotch-Irish (0)	8	0.09
Scottish (129)	314	3.47
Swedish (53)	250	2.76
Swiss (0)	17	0.19
Ukrainian (20)	90	0.99
Welsh (21)	125	1.38

Hispanic Origin	Population	%
Hispanic or Latino (of any race)	916	8.92
Central American, ex. Mexican	33	0.32
Costa Rican	3	0.03
Guatemalan	4	0.04
Honduran	2	0.02
Nicaraguan	2	0.02
Panamanian	4	0.04
Salvadoran	18	0.18
Cuban	3	0.03
Dominican Republic	6	0.06
Mexican	684	6.66
Puerto Rican	15	0.15
South American	20	0.19
Argentinean	1	0.01
Bolivian	1	0.01
Chilean	1	0.01
Colombian	10	0.10
Ecuadorian	2	0.02
Peruvian	4	0.04
Venezuelan	1	0.01
Other Hispanic or Latino	155	1.51

Race*	Population	%
African-American/Black (101)	178	1.73
Not Hispanic (91)	147	1.43
Hispanic (10)	31	0.30
American Indian/Alaska Native (60)	122	1.19
Not Hispanic (49)	90	0.88
Hispanic (11)	32	0.31
Alaska Athabascan *(Ala. Nat.)* (1)	1	0.01
Apache (0)	2	0.02
Arapaho (0)	1	0.01
Blackfeet (1)	3	0.03
Cherokee (1)	12	0.12
Cheyenne (0)	1	0.01
Chickasaw (1)	1	0.01
Chippewa (0)	3	0.03
Choctaw (1)	1	0.01
Creek (0)	2	0.02
Hopi (0)	1	0.01
Navajo (15)	30	0.29
Pueblo (0)	2	0.02
Shoshone (5)	8	0.08
Sioux (2)	6	0.06

SECTION TWO

*Notes: † The Census 2010 population figure is used to calculate the percentages in the Hispanic Origin and Race categories. Ancestry percentages are based on the 2006-2010 American Community Survey population (not shown); ‡ Numbers in parentheses indicate the number of people reporting a single ancestry; * Numbers in parentheses indicate the number of persons reporting this race alone, not in combination with any other race; Please refer to the Explanation of Data for more information.*

Ute (0)	2	0.02
Asian (131)	258	2.51
Not Hispanic (131)	246	2.39
Hispanic (0)	12	0.12
Chinese, ex. Taiwanese (12)	19	0.18
Filipino (14)	41	0.40
Hmong (11)	11	0.11
Indian (16)	17	0.17
Indonesian (0)	7	0.07
Japanese (23)	65	0.63
Korean (12)	39	0.38
Laotian (9)	10	0.10
Thai (11)	17	0.17
Vietnamese (14)	14	0.14
Hawaii Native/Pacific Islander (14)	50	0.49
Not Hispanic (13)	46	0.45
Hispanic (1)	4	0.04
Guamanian/Chamorro (4)	13	0.13
Marshallese (1)	1	0.01
Native Hawaiian (3)	12	0.12
Samoan (3)	11	0.11
Tongan (1)	1	0.01
White (9,346)	9,625	93.70
Not Hispanic (8,855)	9,046	88.06
Hispanic (491)	579	5.64

West Jordan

Place Type: City
County: Salt Lake
Population: 103,712[†]

Ancestry[‡]	Population	%
African, Sub-Saharan (239)	282	0.29
African (10)	53	0.05
Nigerian (189)	189	0.19
Zimbabwean (40)	40	0.04
American (7,158)	7,158	7.26
Arab (73)	102	0.10
Lebanese (73)	102	0.10
Armenian (0)	9	0.01
Assyrian/Chaldean/Syriac (9)	18	0.02
Australian (26)	140	0.14
Austrian (46)	289	0.29
Basque (49)	165	0.17
Belgian (11)	18	0.02
Brazilian (264)	298	0.30
British (386)	752	0.76
Canadian (147)	377	0.38
Croatian (6)	46	0.05
Czech (194)	434	0.44
Czechoslovakian (45)	57	0.06
Danish (1,423)	5,433	5.51
Dutch (681)	2,863	2.90
English (10,429)	23,430	23.76
European (3,941)	4,258	4.32
Finnish (84)	365	0.37
French, ex. Basque (402)	2,151	2.18
French Canadian (124)	326	0.33
German (3,156)	11,671	11.83
Greek (34)	209	0.21
Icelander (27)	100	0.10
Irish (1,245)	5,375	5.45
Italian (1,131)	3,397	3.44
Lithuanian (5)	17	0.02
Luxemburger (0)	7	0.01
Maltese (0)	11	0.01
New Zealander (31)	31	0.03
Northern European (149)	149	0.15
Norwegian (814)	2,294	2.33
Polish (124)	604	0.61
Portuguese (152)	219	0.22
Romanian (0)	17	0.02
Russian (11)	142	0.14
Scandinavian (485)	870	0.88
Scotch-Irish (503)	1,021	1.04
Scottish (756)	3,464	3.51
Serbian (0)	11	0.01
Slavic (52)	55	0.06
Slovak (9)	16	0.02
Slovene (55)	101	0.10
Swedish (1,176)	4,599	4.66
Swiss (348)	1,159	1.18
Ukrainian (16)	59	0.06
Welsh (555)	1,797	1.82
West Indian, ex. Hispanic (31)	31	0.03
Haitian (31)	31	0.03
Yugoslavian (160)	335	0.34

Hispanic Origin	Population	%
Hispanic or Latino (of any race)	18,364	17.71
Central American, ex. Mexican	1,132	1.09
Costa Rican	28	0.03
Guatemalan	281	0.27
Honduran	140	0.13
Nicaraguan	71	0.07
Panamanian	52	0.05
Salvadoran	548	0.53
Other Central American	12	0.01
Cuban	75	0.07
Dominican Republic	52	0.05
Mexican	12,531	12.08
Puerto Rican	423	0.41
South American	1,868	1.80
Argentinean	206	0.20
Bolivian	71	0.07
Chilean	174	0.17
Colombian	353	0.34
Ecuadorian	120	0.12
Paraguayan	2	<0.01
Peruvian	480	0.46
Uruguayan	123	0.12
Venezuelan	330	0.32
Other South American	9	0.01
Other Hispanic or Latino	2,283	2.20

Race*	Population	%
African-American/Black (1,027)	1,650	1.59
Not Hispanic (855)	1,339	1.29
Hispanic (172)	311	0.30
American Indian/Alaska Native (712)	1,305	1.26
Not Hispanic (517)	896	0.86
Hispanic (195)	409	0.39
Alaska Athabascan *(Ala. Nat.)* (3)	4	<0.01
Aleut *(Alaska Native)* (3)	4	<0.01
Apache (24)	54	0.05
Arapaho (8)	9	0.01
Blackfeet (4)	11	0.01
Central American Ind. (0)	1	<0.01
Cherokee (15)	89	0.09
Cheyenne (1)	4	<0.01
Chippewa (4)	14	0.01
Choctaw (10)	21	0.02
Colville (0)	1	<0.01
Comanche (2)	2	<0.01
Cree (1)	3	<0.01
Creek (6)	16	0.02
Crow (6)	12	0.01
Delaware (0)	5	<0.01
Hopi (0)	2	<0.01
Inupiat *(Alaska Native)* (0)	2	<0.01
Iroquois (0)	6	0.01
Kiowa (0)	2	<0.01
Lumbee (0)	1	<0.01
Menominee (1)	1	<0.01
Mexican American Ind. (25)	56	0.05
Navajo (247)	365	0.35
Osage (1)	1	<0.01
Ottawa (1)	4	<0.01
Paiute (4)	6	0.01
Potawatomi (2)	4	<0.01
Pueblo (5)	8	0.01
Puget Sound Salish (0)	1	<0.01
Shoshone (8)	18	0.02
Sioux (9)	33	0.03
South American Ind. (4)	10	0.01
Spanish American Ind. (3)	4	<0.01
Tohono O'Odham (1)	1	<0.01
Ute (33)	62	0.06
Yuman (4)	5	<0.01
Yup'ik *(Alaska Native)* (1)	1	<0.01
Asian (2,788)	3,796	3.66
Not Hispanic (2,732)	3,606	3.48
Hispanic (56)	190	0.18
Burmese (2)	2	<0.01
Cambodian (134)	159	0.15
Chinese, ex. Taiwanese (390)	663	0.64
Filipino (289)	534	0.51
Hmong (6)	14	0.01
Indian (298)	360	0.35
Indonesian (19)	31	0.03
Japanese (170)	448	0.43
Korean (142)	225	0.22
Laotian (398)	496	0.48
Malaysian (5)	6	0.01
Nepalese (3)	6	0.01
Pakistani (44)	76	0.07
Sri Lankan (6)	6	0.01
Taiwanese (5)	6	0.01
Thai (50)	92	0.09
Vietnamese (622)	730	0.70
Hawaii Native/Pacific Islander (1,631)	2,268	2.19
Not Hispanic (1,588)	2,145	2.07
Hispanic (43)	123	0.12
Fijian (4)	16	0.02
Guamanian/Chamorro (11)	22	0.02
Marshallese (21)	26	0.03
Native Hawaiian (77)	253	0.24
Samoan (709)	1,079	1.04
Tongan (569)	818	0.79
White (85,500)	88,620	85.45
Not Hispanic (77,360)	79,302	76.46
Hispanic (8,140)	9,318	8.98

West Point

Place Type: City
County: Davis
Population: 9,511[†]

Ancestry[‡]	Population	%
American (823)	823	9.24
Austrian (0)	21	0.24
British (78)	190	2.13
Bulgarian (11)	23	0.26
Canadian (17)	17	0.19
Celtic (15)	15	0.17
Czech (0)	18	0.20
Danish (260)	606	6.80
Dutch (257)	354	3.97
English (1,128)	2,146	24.09
European (408)	427	4.79
Finnish (0)	10	0.11
French, ex. Basque (52)	194	2.18
German (275)	1,115	12.51
Greek (9)	9	0.10
Icelander (18)	18	0.20
Irish (118)	544	6.11
Italian (48)	325	3.65
Northern European (17)	56	0.63
Norwegian (112)	342	3.84
Polish (0)	71	0.80
Portuguese (102)	169	1.90
Russian (0)	52	0.58
Scandinavian (0)	11	0.12
Scotch-Irish (12)	83	0.93
Scottish (61)	492	5.52
Slavic (0)	87	0.98
Slovene (0)	36	0.40
Swedish (135)	394	4.42
Swiss (8)	50	0.56
Ukrainian (0)	35	0.39
Welsh (0)	74	0.83

Hispanic Origin	Population	%
Hispanic or Latino (of any race)	547	5.75
Central American, ex. Mexican	21	0.22
Costa Rican	1	0.01
Guatemalan	5	0.05
Honduran	1	0.01

*Notes: † The Census 2010 population figure is used to calculate the percentages in the Hispanic Origin and Race categories. Ancestry percentages are based on the 2006-2010 American Community Survey population (not shown); ‡ Numbers in parentheses indicate the number of people reporting a single ancestry; * Numbers in parentheses indicate the number of persons reporting this race alone, not in combination with any other race; Please refer to the Explanation of Data for more information.*

Panamanian	1	0.01
Salvadoran	13	0.14
Cuban	1	0.01
Mexican	377	3.96
Puerto Rican	11	0.12
South American	41	0.43
Argentinean	1	0.01
Chilean	5	0.05
Ecuadorian	5	0.05
Peruvian	28	0.29
Uruguayan	1	0.01
Venezuelan	1	0.01
Other Hispanic or Latino	96	1.01

Race*	Population	%
African-American/Black (70)	116	1.22
Not Hispanic (64)	100	1.05
Hispanic (6)	16	0.17
American Indian/Alaska Native (70)	110	1.16
Not Hispanic (47)	76	0.80
Hispanic (23)	34	0.36
Apache (3)	4	0.04
Arapaho (0)	1	0.01
Cherokee (6)	12	0.13
Chippewa (0)	2	0.02
Choctaw (3)	3	0.03
Creek (4)	4	0.04
Inupiat *(Alaska Native)* (1)	1	0.01
Mexican American Ind. (1)	2	0.02
Navajo (17)	25	0.26
Osage (0)	3	0.03
Pima (0)	1	0.01
Potawatomi (4)	4	0.04
Seminole (2)	2	0.02
Shoshone (5)	10	0.11
Sioux (1)	1	0.01
Spanish American Ind. (1)	1	0.01
Ute (0)	1	0.01
Asian (184)	300	3.15
Not Hispanic (176)	276	2.90
Hispanic (8)	24	0.25
Chinese, ex. Taiwanese (7)	28	0.29
Filipino (78)	121	1.27
Hmong (11)	11	0.12
Indian (0)	5	0.05
Japanese (51)	80	0.84
Korean (9)	23	0.24
Laotian (6)	9	0.09
Thai (5)	13	0.14
Vietnamese (3)	6	0.06
Hawaii Native/Pacific Islander (30)	59	0.62
Not Hispanic (28)	50	0.53
Hispanic (2)	9	0.09
Guamanian/Chamorro (4)	7	0.07
Native Hawaiian (0)	23	0.24
Samoan (4)	6	0.06
Tongan (9)	11	0.12
White (8,762)	8,970	94.31
Not Hispanic (8,471)	8,626	90.69
Hispanic (291)	344	3.62

West Valley City

Place Type: City
County: Salt Lake
Population: 129,480†

Ancestry‡	Population	%
African, Sub-Saharan (480)	686	0.55
African (322)	494	0.40
Ethiopian (35)	35	0.03
Liberian (30)	30	0.02
Somalian (23)	23	0.02
South African (0)	34	0.03
Other Sub-Saharan African (70)	70	0.06
American (5,358)	5,358	4.29
Arab (34)	65	0.05
Arab (9)	22	0.02
Egyptian (0)	10	0.01
Lebanese (17)	25	0.02
Other Arab (8)	8	0.01
Armenian (62)	141	0.11
Australian (0)	7	0.01
Austrian (61)	151	0.12
Basque (60)	60	0.05
Belgian (0)	23	0.02
Brazilian (135)	143	0.11
British (395)	754	0.60
Bulgarian (9)	9	0.01
Cajun (25)	25	0.02
Canadian (169)	320	0.26
Croatian (81)	108	0.09
Czech (22)	112	0.09
Czechoslovakian (84)	133	0.11
Danish (1,412)	4,543	3.63
Dutch (726)	2,412	1.93
English (8,589)	20,612	16.49
European (1,343)	1,805	1.44
Finnish (19)	58	0.05
French, ex. Basque (410)	2,026	1.62
French Canadian (106)	186	0.15
German (2,423)	10,165	8.13
German Russian (46)	74	0.06
Greek (157)	465	0.37
Hungarian (0)	78	0.06
Icelander (13)	23	0.02
Iranian (8)	34	0.03
Irish (1,194)	5,012	4.01
Italian (900)	3,024	2.42
Latvian (36)	108	0.09
Lithuanian (0)	21	0.02
Luxemburger (9)	9	0.01
New Zealander (34)	34	0.03
Northern European (86)	106	0.08
Norwegian (541)	1,535	1.23
Pennsylvania German (0)	10	0.01
Polish (159)	639	0.51
Portuguese (43)	166	0.13
Romanian (10)	10	0.01
Russian (83)	233	0.19
Scandinavian (298)	524	0.42
Scotch-Irish (294)	1,409	1.13
Scottish (1,192)	3,977	3.18
Serbian (106)	106	0.08
Slavic (17)	30	0.02
Slovene (15)	15	0.01
Swedish (797)	3,499	2.80
Swiss (270)	991	0.79
Turkish (0)	8	0.01
Ukrainian (0)	20	0.02
Welsh (325)	1,691	1.35
West Indian, ex. Hispanic (10)	10	0.01
Jamaican (10)	10	0.01
Yugoslavian (814)	861	0.69

Hispanic Origin	Population	%
Hispanic or Latino (of any race)	42,892	33.13
Central American, ex. Mexican	2,504	1.93
Costa Rican	65	0.05
Guatemalan	767	0.59
Honduran	261	0.20
Nicaraguan	131	0.10
Panamanian	30	0.02
Salvadoran	1,230	0.95
Other Central American	20	0.02
Cuban	128	0.10
Dominican Republic	48	0.04
Mexican	33,620	25.97
Puerto Rican	525	0.41
South American	2,126	1.64
Argentinean	204	0.16
Bolivian	78	0.06
Chilean	220	0.17
Colombian	305	0.24
Ecuadorian	196	0.15
Paraguayan	8	0.01
Peruvian	736	0.57
Uruguayan	38	0.03
Venezuelan	321	0.25
Other South American	20	0.02
Other Hispanic or Latino	3,941	3.04

Race*	Population	%
African-American/Black (2,533)	3,436	2.65
Not Hispanic (2,254)	2,955	2.28
Hispanic (279)	481	0.37
American Indian/Alaska Native (1,625)	2,560	1.98
Not Hispanic (1,137)	1,696	1.31
Hispanic (488)	864	0.67
Apache (31)	75	0.06
Arapaho (25)	36	0.03
Blackfeet (3)	16	0.01
Canadian/French Am. Ind. (1)	2	<0.01
Central American Ind. (8)	8	0.01
Cherokee (38)	122	0.09
Cheyenne (7)	17	0.01
Chickasaw (2)	3	<0.01
Chippewa (16)	19	0.01
Choctaw (10)	23	0.02
Colville (0)	1	<0.01
Comanche (1)	3	<0.01
Cree (5)	7	0.01
Creek (4)	6	<0.01
Crow (3)	4	<0.01
Hopi (7)	24	0.02
Inupiat *(Alaska Native)* (2)	5	<0.01
Iroquois (12)	18	0.01
Kiowa (1)	10	0.01
Mexican American Ind. (128)	193	0.15
Navajo (632)	818	0.63
Osage (0)	3	<0.01
Paiute (14)	23	0.02
Pima (2)	3	<0.01
Potawatomi (0)	1	<0.01
Pueblo (7)	17	0.01
Seminole (3)	13	0.01
Shoshone (35)	59	0.05
Sioux (41)	77	0.06
South American Ind. (3)	33	0.03
Spanish American Ind. (9)	11	0.01
Tlingit-Haida *(Alaska Native)* (2)	3	<0.01
Tohono O'Odham (5)	5	<0.01
Ute (55)	104	0.08
Yakama (1)	2	<0.01
Yaqui (7)	8	0.01
Yuman (4)	5	<0.01
Yup'ik *(Alaska Native)* (6)	16	0.01
Asian (6,441)	7,440	5.75
Not Hispanic (6,303)	7,140	5.51
Hispanic (138)	300	0.23
Bangladeshi (6)	6	<0.01
Burmese (43)	46	0.04
Cambodian (860)	971	0.75
Chinese, ex. Taiwanese (535)	848	0.65
Filipino (295)	485	0.37
Hmong (15)	20	0.02
Indian (343)	433	0.33
Indonesian (8)	21	0.02
Japanese (160)	345	0.27
Korean (132)	201	0.16
Laotian (657)	792	0.61
Nepalese (6)	8	0.01
Pakistani (89)	106	0.08
Sri Lankan (1)	1	<0.01
Taiwanese (15)	29	0.02
Thai (81)	158	0.12
Vietnamese (2,693)	2,927	2.26
Hawaii Native/Pacific Islander (4,714)	5,557	4.29
Not Hispanic (4,647)	5,385	4.16
Hispanic (67)	172	0.13
Fijian (12)	26	0.02
Guamanian/Chamorro (48)	63	0.05
Marshallese (214)	237	0.18
Native Hawaiian (142)	335	0.26
Samoan (1,875)	2,413	1.86
Tongan (1,893)	2,362	1.82
White (84,636)	88,972	68.71
Not Hispanic (69,498)	71,586	55.29
Hispanic (15,138)	17,386	13.43

*Notes: † The Census 2010 population figure is used to calculate the percentages in the Hispanic Origin and Race categories. Ancestry percentages are based on the 2006-2010 American Community Survey population (not shown); ‡ Numbers in parentheses indicate the number of people reporting a single ancestry; * Numbers in parentheses indicate the number of persons reporting this race alone, not in combination with any other race; Please refer to the Explanation of Data for more information.*

Woods Cross

Place Type: City
County: Davis
Population: 9,761†

Ancestry‡	Population	%
African, Sub-Saharan (32)	32	0.35
African (32)	32	0.35
American (416)	416	4.54
Arab (8)	23	0.25
Other Arab (8)	23	0.25
Armenian (7)	7	0.08
British (66)	141	1.54
Canadian (63)	134	1.46
Czech (12)	12	0.13
Danish (137)	335	3.65
Dutch (41)	220	2.40
English (1,544)	2,964	32.34
European (409)	527	5.75
Finnish (0)	21	0.23
French, ex. Basque (8)	130	1.42
French Canadian (14)	14	0.15
German (358)	1,230	13.42
Greek (16)	60	0.65
Hungarian (0)	12	0.13
Irish (232)	527	5.75
Italian (166)	255	2.78
Norwegian (66)	200	2.18
Polish (15)	41	0.45
Russian (0)	7	0.08
Scandinavian (45)	45	0.49
Scotch-Irish (73)	104	1.13
Scottish (241)	678	7.40
Swedish (128)	502	5.48
Swiss (8)	61	0.67
Ukrainian (23)	23	0.25
Welsh (39)	298	3.25
Yugoslavian (17)	17	0.19

Hispanic Origin	Population	%
Hispanic or Latino (of any race)	844	8.65
Central American, ex. Mexican	54	0.55
Costa Rican	1	0.01
Guatemalan	20	0.20
Honduran	5	0.05
Nicaraguan	10	0.10
Salvadoran	17	0.17
Other Central American	1	0.01
Cuban	3	0.03
Dominican Republic	3	0.03
Mexican	551	5.64
Puerto Rican	20	0.20
South American	109	1.12
Argentinean	8	0.08
Chilean	2	0.02
Colombian	15	0.15
Ecuadorian	9	0.09
Peruvian	68	0.70
Uruguayan	5	0.05
Venezuelan	2	0.02
Other Hispanic or Latino	104	1.07

Race*	Population	%
African-American/Black (104)	155	1.59
Not Hispanic (93)	140	1.43
Hispanic (11)	15	0.15
American Indian/Alaska Native (53)	113	1.16
Not Hispanic (44)	95	0.97
Hispanic (9)	18	0.18
Apache (0)	2	0.02
Cherokee (2)	20	0.20
Chickasaw (1)	1	0.01
Chippewa (1)	2	0.02
Hopi (0)	2	0.02
Navajo (18)	33	0.34
Osage (3)	3	0.03
Paiute (1)	1	0.01
Potawatomi (1)	1	0.01
Pueblo (0)	3	0.03
Seminole (1)	3	0.03
Shoshone (1)	5	0.05
Sioux (4)	7	0.07
Ute (3)	8	0.08
Yuman (1)	1	0.01
Asian (153)	252	2.58
Not Hispanic (150)	236	2.42
Hispanic (3)	16	0.16
Burmese (3)	3	0.03
Cambodian (5)	5	0.05
Chinese, ex. Taiwanese (30)	63	0.65
Filipino (24)	47	0.48
Hmong (4)	4	0.04
Indian (37)	42	0.43
Indonesian (0)	1	0.01
Japanese (7)	34	0.35
Korean (8)	16	0.16
Laotian (0)	3	0.03
Taiwanese (4)	6	0.06
Thai (2)	4	0.04
Vietnamese (16)	19	0.19
Hawaii Native/Pacific Islander (116)	173	1.77
Not Hispanic (116)	172	1.76
Hispanic (0)	1	0.01
Guamanian/Chamorro (1)	2	0.02
Marshallese (3)	4	0.04
Native Hawaiian (2)	29	0.30
Samoan (43)	68	0.70
Tongan (36)	59	0.60
White (8,684)	8,928	91.47
Not Hispanic (8,295)	8,482	86.90
Hispanic (389)	446	4.57

*Notes: † The Census 2010 population figure is used to calculate the percentages in the Hispanic Origin and Race categories. Ancestry percentages are based on the 2006-2010 American Community Survey population (not shown); ‡ Numbers in parentheses indicate the number of people reporting a single ancestry; * Numbers in parentheses indicate the number of persons reporting this race alone, not in combination with any other race; Please refer to the Explanation of Data for more information.*

VERMONT

Place Type: State
Population: 625,741[†]

Ancestry[‡]	Population	%
Afghan (10)	10	<0.01
African, Sub-Saharan (1,414)	1,770	0.28
African (589)	765	0.12
Cape Verdean (15)	49	0.01
Ethiopian (71)	155	0.02
Ghanaian (0)	6	<0.01
Kenyan (26)	26	<0.01
Liberian (4)	4	<0.01
Nigerian (29)	29	<0.01
Somalian (304)	304	0.05
South African (87)	122	0.02
Sudanese (35)	35	0.01
Ugandan (16)	16	<0.01
Other Sub-Saharan African (238)	259	0.04
Albanian (127)	228	0.04
Alsatian (5)	69	0.01
American (42,304)	42,304	6.78
Arab (941)	2,586	0.41
Arab (66)	98	0.02
Egyptian (50)	114	0.02
Iraqi (168)	194	0.03
Jordanian (0)	2	<0.01
Lebanese (464)	1,690	0.27
Moroccan (23)	37	0.01
Palestinian (7)	33	0.01
Syrian (90)	325	0.05
Other Arab (73)	93	0.01
Armenian (157)	672	0.11
Assyrian/Chaldean/Syriac (9)	12	<0.01
Australian (30)	146	0.02
Austrian (385)	2,219	0.36
Basque (22)	102	0.02
Belgian (106)	470	0.08
Brazilian (119)	270	0.04
British (2,526)	4,561	0.73
Bulgarian (36)	67	0.01
Cajun (7)	80	0.01
Canadian (3,711)	6,324	1.01
Carpatho Rusyn (13)	13	<0.01
Celtic (107)	192	0.03
Croatian (78)	267	0.04
Cypriot (20)	42	0.01
Czech (492)	2,529	0.41
Czechoslovakian (206)	665	0.11
Danish (523)	2,144	0.34
Dutch (2,034)	9,815	1.57
Eastern European (1,260)	1,400	0.22
English (38,625)	113,280	18.15
Estonian (3)	38	0.01
European (7,995)	8,825	1.41
Finnish (583)	1,907	0.31
French, ex. Basque (29,991)	96,627	15.48
French Canadian (31,374)	51,659	8.28
German (15,131)	64,779	10.38
German Russian (34)	34	0.01
Greek (939)	2,600	0.42
Guyanese (25)	38	0.01
Hungarian (540)	3,115	0.50
Icelander (28)	109	0.02
Iranian (121)	199	0.03
Irish (31,340)	111,761	17.90
Israeli (0)	70	0.01
Italian (14,033)	46,857	7.51
Latvian (104)	357	0.06
Lithuanian (720)	2,392	0.38
Luxemburger (13)	16	<0.01
Macedonian (15)	15	<0.01
Maltese (9)	23	<0.01
New Zealander (62)	79	0.01
Northern European (950)	1,055	0.17
Norwegian (1,505)	5,306	0.85
Pennsylvania German (252)	398	0.06
Polish (6,843)	24,566	3.94
Portuguese (858)	3,158	0.51
Romanian (234)	795	0.13
Russian (2,670)	8,473	1.36
Scandinavian (407)	1,216	0.19
Scotch-Irish (5,328)	16,765	2.69
Scottish (7,922)	30,724	4.92
Serbian (171)	304	0.05
Slavic (73)	209	0.03
Slovak (308)	1,037	0.17
Slovene (164)	329	0.05
Swedish (2,526)	11,399	1.83
Swiss (405)	2,092	0.34
Turkish (176)	295	0.05
Ukrainian (497)	1,750	0.28
Welsh (1,448)	7,758	1.24
West Indian, ex. Hispanic (359)	575	0.09
Barbadian (7)	7	<0.01
Belizean (18)	18	<0.01
Bermudan (0)	7	<0.01
British West Indian (6)	6	<0.01
Dutch West Indian (0)	14	<0.01
Haitian (91)	91	0.01
Jamaican (142)	290	0.05
Trinidadian/Tobagonian (20)	20	<0.01
West Indian (75)	118	0.02
Other West Indian (0)	4	<0.01
Yugoslavian (1,146)	1,354	0.22

Hispanic Origin	Population	%
Hispanic or Latino (of any race)	9,208	1.47
Central American, ex. Mexican	671	0.11
Costa Rican	73	0.01
Guatemalan	215	0.03
Honduran	109	0.02
Nicaraguan	66	0.01
Panamanian	91	0.01
Salvadoran	116	0.02
Other Central American	1	<0.01
Cuban	510	0.08
Dominican Republic	282	0.05
Mexican	2,534	0.40
Puerto Rican	2,261	0.36
South American	1,204	0.19
Argentinean	185	0.03
Bolivian	34	0.01
Chilean	127	0.02
Colombian	327	0.05
Ecuadorian	125	0.02
Paraguayan	34	0.01
Peruvian	242	0.04
Uruguayan	28	<0.01
Venezuelan	87	0.01
Other South American	15	<0.01
Other Hispanic or Latino	1,746	0.28

Race*	Population	%
African-American/Black (6,277)	9,343	1.49
Not Hispanic (5,943)	8,693	1.39
Hispanic (334)	650	0.10
American Indian/Alaska Native (2,207)	7,379	1.18
Not Hispanic (2,023)	6,897	1.10
Hispanic (184)	482	0.08
Alaska Athabascan *(Ala. Nat.)* (7)	8	<0.01
Aleut *(Alaska Native)* (2)	9	<0.01
Apache (29)	81	0.01
Arapaho (0)	1	<0.01
Blackfeet (62)	406	0.06
Canadian/French Am. Ind. (48)	144	0.02
Central American Ind. (10)	16	<0.01
Cherokee (121)	672	0.11
Cheyenne (4)	17	<0.01
Chickasaw (4)	13	<0.01
Chippewa (31)	77	0.01
Choctaw (19)	58	0.01
Comanche (5)	14	<0.01
Cree (10)	43	0.01
Creek (3)	13	<0.01
Crow (2)	23	<0.01
Delaware (2)	21	<0.01
Hopi (3)	6	<0.01
Houma (1)	2	<0.01
Inupiat *(Alaska Native)* (2)	12	<0.01
Iroquois (102)	524	0.08
Kiowa (1)	4	<0.01
Lumbee (6)	12	<0.01
Mexican American Ind. (52)	82	0.01
Navajo (20)	39	0.01
Osage (1)	13	<0.01
Ottawa (2)	7	<0.01
Paiute (1)	2	<0.01
Pima (2)	4	<0.01
Potawatomi (13)	27	<0.01
Pueblo (2)	6	<0.01
Puget Sound Salish (1)	1	<0.01
Seminole (0)	18	<0.01
Shoshone (5)	16	<0.01
Sioux (35)	125	0.02
South American Ind. (25)	56	0.01
Spanish American Ind. (7)	11	<0.01
Tlingit-Haida *(Alaska Native)* (0)	3	<0.01
Tsimshian *(Alaska Native)* (1)	1	<0.01
Ute (1)	2	<0.01
Yakama (3)	5	<0.01
Yaqui (1)	7	<0.01
Yuman (0)	1	<0.01
Yup'ik *(Alaska Native)* (4)	8	<0.01
Asian (7,947)	10,463	1.67
Not Hispanic (7,875)	10,278	1.64
Hispanic (72)	185	0.03
Bangladeshi (43)	47	0.01
Bhutanese (239)	276	0.04
Burmese (111)	126	0.02
Cambodian (81)	117	0.02
Chinese, ex. Taiwanese (2,207)	2,723	0.44
Filipino (558)	1,035	0.17
Hmong (0)	1	<0.01
Indian (1,359)	1,723	0.28
Indonesian (18)	39	0.01
Japanese (405)	842	0.13
Korean (889)	1,271	0.20
Laotian (95)	121	0.02
Malaysian (16)	28	<0.01
Nepalese (128)	159	0.03
Pakistani (124)	141	0.02
Sri Lankan (38)	43	0.01
Taiwanese (91)	117	0.02
Thai (183)	266	0.04
Vietnamese (1,019)	1,206	0.19
Hawaii Native/Pacific Islander (160)	465	0.07
Not Hispanic (140)	419	0.07
Hispanic (20)	46	0.01
Fijian (5)	8	<0.01
Guamanian/Chamorro (43)	81	0.01
Marshallese (8)	12	<0.01
Native Hawaiian (47)	158	0.03
Samoan (24)	50	0.01
Tongan (0)	1	<0.01
White (596,292)	606,588	96.94
Not Hispanic (590,223)	599,675	95.83
Hispanic (6,069)	6,913	1.10

*Notes: † The Census 2010 population figure is used to calculate the percentages in the Hispanic Origin and Race categories. Ancestry percentages are based on the 2006-2010 American Community Survey population (not shown); ‡ Numbers in parentheses indicate the number of people reporting a single ancestry; * Numbers in parentheses indicate the number of persons reporting this race alone, not in combination with any other race; Please refer to the Explanation of Data for more information.*

Barre

Place Type: City
County: Washington
Population: 9,052†

Ancestry‡	Population	%
American (366)	366	4.02
Arab (9)	37	0.41
Lebanese (9)	37	0.41
Armenian (24)	24	0.26
British (0)	21	0.23
Canadian (46)	90	0.99
Dutch (0)	19	0.21
English (502)	1,472	16.15
European (33)	78	0.86
Finnish (0)	14	0.15
French, ex. Basque (955)	2,042	22.41
French Canadian (656)	1,113	12.21
German (106)	526	5.77
Hungarian (8)	31	0.34
Irish (355)	1,466	16.09
Italian (122)	510	5.60
Norwegian (8)	8	0.09
Polish (91)	181	1.99
Russian (56)	93	1.02
Scandinavian (5)	5	0.05
Scotch-Irish (61)	105	1.15
Scottish (118)	587	6.44
Swedish (9)	128	1.40
Swiss (14)	49	0.54
Welsh (0)	86	0.94
West Indian, ex. Hispanic (23)	23	0.25
Haitian (23)	23	0.25
Yugoslavian (90)	90	0.99

Hispanic Origin	Population	%
Hispanic or Latino (of any race)	212	2.34
Central American, ex. Mexican	14	0.15
Guatemalan	2	0.02
Honduran	8	0.09
Nicaraguan	1	0.01
Panamanian	2	0.02
Salvadoran	1	0.01
Cuban	7	0.08
Dominican Republic	2	0.02
Mexican	48	0.53
Puerto Rican	64	0.71
South American	3	0.03
Ecuadorian	2	0.02
Peruvian	1	0.01
Other Hispanic or Latino	74	0.82

Race*	Population	%
African-American/Black (117)	195	2.15
Not Hispanic (108)	179	1.98
Hispanic (9)	16	0.18
American Indian/Alaska Native (20)	84	0.93
Not Hispanic (17)	80	0.88
Hispanic (3)	4	0.04
Apache (1)	4	0.04
Blackfeet (2)	5	0.06
Canadian/French Am. Ind. (2)	4	0.04
Cherokee (2)	12	0.13
Chippewa (3)	3	0.03
Choctaw (0)	1	0.01
Delaware (0)	1	0.01
Inupiat *(Alaska Native)* (0)	1	0.01
Iroquois (0)	9	0.10
Mexican American Ind. (1)	1	0.01
Sioux (0)	1	0.01
Asian (77)	109	1.20
Not Hispanic (77)	108	1.19
Hispanic (0)	1	0.01
Cambodian (1)	1	0.01
Chinese, ex. Taiwanese (22)	22	0.24
Filipino (9)	20	0.22
Indian (20)	27	0.30
Japanese (4)	9	0.10
Korean (3)	5	0.06
Sri Lankan (1)	1	0.01
Vietnamese (14)	15	0.17
Hawaii Native/Pacific Islander (1)	5	0.06
Not Hispanic (1)	4	0.04
Hispanic (0)	1	0.01
Guamanian/Chamorro (0)	1	0.01
Native Hawaiian (1)	2	0.02
White (8,622)	8,798	97.19
Not Hispanic (8,468)	8,627	95.30
Hispanic (154)	171	1.89

Barre

Place Type: Town
County: Washington
Population: 7,924†

Ancestry‡	Population	%
American (429)	429	5.44
Arab (0)	36	0.46
Lebanese (0)	14	0.18
Syrian (0)	22	0.28
Austrian (0)	32	0.41
British (20)	53	0.67
Canadian (79)	114	1.45
Croatian (7)	7	0.09
Danish (12)	43	0.55
Dutch (9)	25	0.32
Eastern European (16)	16	0.20
English (427)	1,561	19.81
European (0)	16	0.20
Finnish (10)	10	0.13
French, ex. Basque (281)	1,486	18.86
French Canadian (604)	1,030	13.07
German (27)	538	6.83
Hungarian (19)	28	0.36
Irish (266)	1,118	14.19
Italian (197)	778	9.87
Latvian (0)	17	0.22
Lithuanian (0)	17	0.22
Northern European (0)	8	0.10
Norwegian (6)	67	0.85
Pennsylvania German (8)	11	0.14
Polish (39)	186	2.36
Portuguese (12)	19	0.24
Scotch-Irish (134)	348	4.42
Scottish (198)	616	7.82
Slovak (0)	32	0.41
Swedish (32)	169	2.14
Swiss (0)	8	0.10
Ukrainian (0)	18	0.23
Welsh (58)	76	0.96

Hispanic Origin	Population	%
Hispanic or Latino (of any race)	117	1.48
Central American, ex. Mexican	4	0.05
Guatemalan	1	0.01
Honduran	3	0.04
Cuban	2	0.03
Dominican Republic	2	0.03
Mexican	16	0.20
Puerto Rican	25	0.32
South American	3	0.04
Argentinean	1	0.01
Colombian	2	0.03
Other Hispanic or Latino	65	0.82

Race*	Population	%
African-American/Black (31)	56	0.71
Not Hispanic (29)	54	0.68
Hispanic (2)	2	0.03
American Indian/Alaska Native (12)	66	0.83
Not Hispanic (12)	63	0.80
Hispanic (0)	3	0.04
Blackfeet (0)	3	0.04
Canadian/French Am. Ind. (1)	2	0.03
Cherokee (1)	4	0.05
Chippewa (1)	1	0.01
Choctaw (1)	1	0.01
Hopi (0)	1	0.01
Iroquois (1)	3	0.04
South American Ind. (0)	2	0.03
Asian (19)	41	0.52
Not Hispanic (19)	41	0.52
Chinese, ex. Taiwanese (4)	7	0.09
Filipino (6)	16	0.20
Indonesian (0)	1	0.01
Japanese (1)	2	0.03
Korean (7)	13	0.16
Thai (1)	1	0.01
Vietnamese (0)	1	0.01
Hawaii Native/Pacific Islander (0)	1	0.01
Not Hispanic (0)	1	0.01
Native Hawaiian (0)	1	0.01
White (7,757)	7,844	98.99
Not Hispanic (7,652)	7,736	97.63
Hispanic (105)	108	1.36

Bennington

Place Type: CDP
County: Bennington
Population: 9,074†

Ancestry‡	Population	%
American (603)	603	6.72
Arab (17)	66	0.74
Lebanese (17)	66	0.74
Austrian (0)	36	0.40
British (10)	37	0.41
Canadian (90)	128	1.43
Czech (0)	15	0.17
Danish (0)	16	0.18
Dutch (17)	183	2.04
Eastern European (22)	22	0.25
English (400)	1,193	13.30
European (78)	78	0.87
French, ex. Basque (188)	1,559	17.38
French Canadian (229)	497	5.54
German (201)	713	7.95
Greek (0)	32	0.36
Hungarian (0)	10	0.11
Irish (399)	1,472	16.41
Italian (273)	860	9.59
Lithuanian (17)	32	0.36
Norwegian (5)	74	0.83
Polish (83)	529	5.90
Russian (16)	25	0.28
Scandinavian (0)	14	0.16
Scotch-Irish (12)	46	0.51
Scottish (61)	204	2.27
Slovak (0)	30	0.33
Swedish (30)	152	1.69
Welsh (6)	35	0.39
Yugoslavian (14)	28	0.31

Hispanic Origin	Population	%
Hispanic or Latino (of any race)	154	1.70
Central American, ex. Mexican	8	0.09
Honduran	7	0.08
Salvadoran	1	0.01
Cuban	12	0.13
Dominican Republic	1	0.01
Mexican	36	0.40
Puerto Rican	56	0.62
South American	16	0.18
Argentinean	1	0.01
Bolivian	1	0.01
Colombian	4	0.04
Ecuadorian	3	0.03
Peruvian	4	0.04
Other South American	3	0.03
Other Hispanic or Latino	25	0.28

Race*	Population	%
African-American/Black (93)	141	1.55
Not Hispanic (88)	133	1.47
Hispanic (5)	8	0.09
American Indian/Alaska Native (41)	89	0.98
Not Hispanic (36)	79	0.87

*Notes: † The Census 2010 population figure is used to calculate the percentages in the Hispanic Origin and Race categories. Ancestry percentages are based on the 2006-2010 American Community Survey population (not shown); ‡ Numbers in parentheses indicate the number of people reporting a single ancestry; * Numbers in parentheses indicate the number of persons reporting this race alone, not in combination with any other race; Please refer to the Explanation of Data for more information.*

Hispanic (5)	10	0.11
Apache (0)	1	0.01
Blackfeet (0)	11	0.12
Canadian/French Am. Ind. (3)	3	0.03
Cherokee (4)	16	0.18
Chippewa (0)	1	0.01
Inupiat *(Alaska Native)* (0)	1	0.01
Iroquois (0)	5	0.06
Lumbee (1)	1	0.01
Mexican American Ind. (0)	1	0.01
Navajo (1)	1	0.01
Sioux (4)	5	0.06
South American Ind. (1)	1	0.01
Asian (53)	71	0.78
Not Hispanic (51)	69	0.76
Hispanic (2)	2	0.02
Chinese, ex. Taiwanese (12)	15	0.17
Filipino (9)	10	0.11
Indian (18)	20	0.22
Japanese (9)	15	0.17
Korean (1)	2	0.02
Thai (0)	4	0.04
Vietnamese (4)	4	0.04
Hawaii Native/Pacific Islander (6)	6	0.07
Not Hispanic (4)	4	0.04
Hispanic (2)	2	0.02
Guamanian/Chamorro (1)	1	0.01
Native Hawaiian (4)	4	0.04
Samoan (1)	1	0.01
White (8,727)	8,844	97.47
Not Hispanic (8,631)	8,732	96.23
Hispanic (96)	112	1.23

Bennington

Place Type: Town
County: Bennington
Population: 15,764†

Ancestry‡	Population	%
African, Sub-Saharan (5)	5	0.03
African (5)	5	0.03
American (1,095)	1,095	6.94
Arab (22)	89	0.56
Jordanian (0)	2	0.01
Lebanese (22)	87	0.55
Austrian (5)	59	0.37
Belgian (0)	2	0.01
British (83)	121	0.77
Canadian (123)	173	1.10
Czech (0)	65	0.41
Czechoslovakian (0)	6	0.04
Danish (4)	45	0.29
Dutch (30)	315	2.00
Eastern European (22)	22	0.14
English (676)	1,956	12.40
European (95)	95	0.60
Finnish (0)	16	0.10
French, ex. Basque (530)	2,442	15.48
French Canadian (432)	787	4.99
German (364)	1,514	9.60
Greek (12)	63	0.40
Hungarian (0)	26	0.16
Iranian (8)	15	0.10
Irish (631)	2,726	17.28
Italian (441)	1,601	10.15
Lithuanian (31)	81	0.51
Northern European (7)	7	0.04
Norwegian (35)	110	0.70
Pennsylvania German (0)	11	0.07
Polish (117)	762	4.83
Portuguese (0)	10	0.06
Romanian (0)	10	0.06
Russian (28)	102	0.65
Scandinavian (0)	14	0.09
Scotch-Irish (89)	231	1.46
Scottish (106)	386	2.45
Slovak (0)	31	0.20
Swedish (44)	179	1.13
Swiss (0)	3	0.02
Ukrainian (0)	15	0.10
Welsh (11)	87	0.55
Yugoslavian (14)	28	0.18

Hispanic Origin	Population	%
Hispanic or Latino (of any race)	274	1.74
Central American, ex. Mexican	18	0.11
Guatemalan	8	0.05
Honduran	8	0.05
Panamanian	1	0.01
Salvadoran	1	0.01
Cuban	19	0.12
Dominican Republic	5	0.03
Mexican	56	0.36
Puerto Rican	105	0.67
South American	33	0.21
Argentinean	1	0.01
Bolivian	1	0.01
Colombian	12	0.08
Ecuadorian	6	0.04
Peruvian	5	0.03
Venezuelan	5	0.03
Other South American	3	0.02
Other Hispanic or Latino	38	0.24

Race*	Population	%
African-American/Black (187)	263	1.67
Not Hispanic (173)	242	1.54
Hispanic (14)	21	0.13
American Indian/Alaska Native (52)	120	0.76
Not Hispanic (46)	108	0.69
Hispanic (6)	12	0.08
Apache (0)	1	0.01
Blackfeet (1)	13	0.08
Canadian/French Am. Ind. (3)	4	0.03
Central American Ind. (1)	1	0.01
Cherokee (6)	21	0.13
Chippewa (0)	1	0.01
Cree (0)	1	0.01
Inupiat *(Alaska Native)* (0)	1	0.01
Iroquois (0)	7	0.04
Lumbee (1)	1	0.01
Mexican American Ind. (0)	1	0.01
Navajo (1)	1	0.01
Sioux (4)	5	0.03
South American Ind. (1)	1	0.01
Asian (130)	171	1.08
Not Hispanic (127)	167	1.06
Hispanic (3)	4	0.03
Cambodian (2)	3	0.02
Chinese, ex. Taiwanese (39)	49	0.31
Filipino (14)	17	0.11
Hmong (0)	1	0.01
Indian (25)	29	0.18
Indonesian (1)	1	0.01
Japanese (15)	29	0.18
Korean (8)	11	0.07
Nepalese (1)	1	0.01
Pakistani (1)	1	0.01
Sri Lankan (1)	1	0.01
Thai (0)	4	0.03
Vietnamese (18)	18	0.11
Hawaii Native/Pacific Islander (13)	16	0.10
Not Hispanic (11)	14	0.09
Hispanic (2)	2	0.01
Guamanian/Chamorro (1)	1	0.01
Native Hawaiian (4)	7	0.04
Samoan (1)	1	0.01
White (15,113)	15,312	97.13
Not Hispanic (14,943)	15,118	95.90
Hispanic (170)	194	1.23

Brattleboro

Place Type: Town
County: Windham
Population: 12,046†

Ancestry‡	Population	%
African, Sub-Saharan (22)	37	0.31
African (0)	15	0.12
Other Sub-Saharan African (22)	22	0.18
American (683)	683	5.67
Arab (30)	76	0.63
Lebanese (30)	76	0.63
Austrian (8)	28	0.23
British (13)	62	0.51
Canadian (108)	161	1.34
Czech (51)	95	0.79
Danish (29)	79	0.66
Dutch (34)	190	1.58
Eastern European (24)	24	0.20
English (767)	2,706	22.47
European (210)	232	1.93
French, ex. Basque (441)	1,476	12.26
French Canadian (203)	496	4.12
German (336)	970	8.05
Greek (0)	13	0.11
Hungarian (21)	21	0.17
Irish (532)	2,262	18.78
Italian (303)	1,020	8.47
Lithuanian (17)	46	0.38
Maltese (0)	14	0.12
Northern European (38)	38	0.32
Norwegian (21)	90	0.75
Polish (297)	868	7.21
Portuguese (0)	153	1.27
Romanian (0)	54	0.45
Russian (44)	439	3.65
Scotch-Irish (97)	474	3.94
Scottish (178)	446	3.70
Swedish (93)	356	2.96
Swiss (19)	56	0.47
Ukrainian (9)	129	1.07
Welsh (11)	135	1.12
West Indian, ex. Hispanic (0)	22	0.18
Jamaican (0)	22	0.18
Yugoslavian (0)	14	0.12

Hispanic Origin	Population	%
Hispanic or Latino (of any race)	322	2.67
Central American, ex. Mexican	20	0.17
Guatemalan	8	0.07
Nicaraguan	3	0.02
Panamanian	2	0.02
Salvadoran	7	0.06
Cuban	9	0.07
Dominican Republic	5	0.04
Mexican	66	0.55
Puerto Rican	118	0.98
South American	57	0.47
Argentinean	10	0.08
Bolivian	5	0.04
Chilean	7	0.06
Colombian	16	0.13
Ecuadorian	2	0.02
Paraguayan	1	0.01
Peruvian	10	0.08
Uruguayan	2	0.02
Venezuelan	4	0.03
Other Hispanic or Latino	47	0.39

Race*	Population	%
African-American/Black (225)	374	3.10
Not Hispanic (202)	320	2.66
Hispanic (23)	54	0.45
American Indian/Alaska Native (37)	175	1.45
Not Hispanic (34)	152	1.26
Hispanic (3)	23	0.19
Blackfeet (0)	7	0.06
Canadian/French Am. Ind. (0)	4	0.03
Cherokee (4)	24	0.20
Cheyenne (1)	1	0.01
Choctaw (1)	5	0.04
Comanche (0)	1	0.01
Cree (0)	1	0.01
Crow (0)	2	0.02
Delaware (0)	1	0.01
Iroquois (5)	13	0.11
Mexican American Ind. (2)	3	0.02

*Notes: † The Census 2010 population figure is used to calculate the percentages in the Hispanic Origin and Race categories. Ancestry percentages are based on the 2006-2010 American Community Survey population (not shown); ‡ Numbers in parentheses indicate the number of people reporting a single ancestry; * Numbers in parentheses indicate the number of persons reporting this race alone, not in combination with any other race; Please refer to the Explanation of Data for more information.*

Sioux (1)	6	0.05
South American Ind. (0)	2	0.02
Asian (269)	323	2.68
Not Hispanic (268)	319	2.65
Hispanic (1)	4	0.03
Bangladeshi (3)	3	0.02
Burmese (1)	1	0.01
Cambodian (1)	5	0.04
Chinese, ex. Taiwanese (104)	115	0.95
Filipino (15)	22	0.18
Indian (34)	37	0.31
Indonesian (2)	2	0.02
Japanese (10)	22	0.18
Korean (30)	32	0.27
Laotian (11)	14	0.12
Nepalese (6)	6	0.05
Pakistani (7)	9	0.07
Taiwanese (12)	16	0.13
Thai (16)	21	0.17
Vietnamese (9)	13	0.11
Hawaii Native/Pacific Islander (5)	18	0.15
Not Hispanic (3)	14	0.12
Hispanic (2)	4	0.03
Guamanian/Chamorro (2)	4	0.03
Native Hawaiian (0)	5	0.04
Samoan (0)	1	0.01
White (11,090)	11,400	94.64
Not Hispanic (10,916)	11,173	92.75
Hispanic (174)	227	1.88

Burlington

Place Type: City
County: Chittenden
Population: 42,417†

Ancestry‡	Population	%
African, Sub-Saharan (390)	428	1.02
African (97)	109	0.26
Somalian (102)	102	0.24
South African (9)	16	0.04
Sudanese (14)	14	0.03
Other Sub-Saharan African (168)	187	0.45
Albanian (73)	73	0.17
Alsatian (0)	14	0.03
American (1,908)	1,908	4.55
Arab (32)	205	0.49
Arab (0)	14	0.03
Lebanese (20)	137	0.33
Moroccan (0)	14	0.03
Palestinian (0)	6	0.01
Syrian (12)	34	0.08
Armenian (38)	135	0.32
Australian (0)	15	0.04
Austrian (0)	212	0.51
Belgian (12)	37	0.09
Brazilian (42)	92	0.22
British (288)	507	1.21
Bulgarian (0)	14	0.03
Cajun (0)	52	0.12
Canadian (146)	327	0.78
Croatian (0)	95	0.23
Czech (13)	165	0.39
Czechoslovakian (21)	73	0.17
Danish (27)	123	0.29
Dutch (234)	718	1.71
Eastern European (208)	238	0.57
English (1,340)	5,300	12.64
Estonian (0)	27	0.06
European (833)	931	2.22
Finnish (5)	134	0.32
French, ex. Basque (1,658)	5,481	13.07
French Canadian (1,857)	3,131	7.47
German (1,108)	4,452	10.62
Greek (46)	210	0.50
Guyanese (14)	14	0.03
Hungarian (8)	241	0.57
Iranian (0)	3	0.01
Irish (2,675)	8,579	20.46
Israeli (0)	27	0.06
Italian (1,119)	4,148	9.89
Latvian (23)	28	0.07
Lithuanian (134)	275	0.66
New Zealander (0)	13	0.03
Northern European (34)	34	0.08
Norwegian (63)	293	0.70
Pennsylvania German (0)	14	0.03
Polish (454)	1,931	4.60
Portuguese (52)	220	0.52
Romanian (31)	133	0.32
Russian (362)	1,157	2.76
Scandinavian (30)	80	0.19
Scotch-Irish (338)	1,207	2.88
Scottish (445)	1,772	4.23
Serbian (13)	50	0.12
Slavic (0)	11	0.03
Slovak (19)	97	0.23
Slovene (9)	28	0.07
Swedish (192)	488	1.16
Swiss (33)	182	0.43
Turkish (20)	106	0.25
Ukrainian (13)	117	0.28
Welsh (57)	543	1.29
West Indian, ex. Hispanic (104)	168	0.40
Dutch West Indian (0)	14	0.03
Haitian (35)	35	0.08
Jamaican (39)	59	0.14
West Indian (30)	60	0.14
Yugoslavian (657)	707	1.69

Hispanic Origin	Population	%
Hispanic or Latino (of any race)	1,144	2.70
Central American, ex. Mexican	117	0.28
Costa Rican	17	0.04
Guatemalan	34	0.08
Honduran	19	0.04
Nicaraguan	15	0.04
Panamanian	20	0.05
Salvadoran	12	0.03
Cuban	78	0.18
Dominican Republic	76	0.18
Mexican	227	0.54
Puerto Rican	265	0.62
South American	197	0.46
Argentinean	26	0.06
Bolivian	2	<0.01
Chilean	15	0.04
Colombian	61	0.14
Ecuadorian	27	0.06
Paraguayan	5	0.01
Peruvian	36	0.08
Uruguayan	4	0.01
Venezuelan	20	0.05
Other South American	1	<0.01
Other Hispanic or Latino	184	0.43

Race*	Population	%
African-American/Black (1,653)	2,033	4.79
Not Hispanic (1,575)	1,897	4.47
Hispanic (78)	136	0.32
American Indian/Alaska Native (131)	483	1.14
Not Hispanic (111)	420	0.99
Hispanic (20)	63	0.15
Alaska Athabascan *(Ala. Nat.)* (3)	3	0.01
Aleut *(Alaska Native)* (1)	2	<0.01
Apache (3)	7	0.02
Blackfeet (5)	17	0.04
Canadian/French Am. Ind. (1)	4	0.01
Central American Ind. (1)	1	<0.01
Cherokee (4)	47	0.11
Chickasaw (2)	3	0.01
Chippewa (0)	3	0.01
Choctaw (2)	7	0.02
Cree (0)	3	0.01
Creek (0)	2	<0.01
Delaware (0)	3	0.01
Iroquois (11)	45	0.11
Lumbee (1)	1	<0.01
Mexican American Ind. (8)	14	0.03
Navajo (0)	1	<0.01
Ottawa (1)	1	<0.01
Paiute (0)	1	<0.01
Potawatomi (1)	1	<0.01
Shoshone (0)	1	<0.01
Sioux (4)	8	0.02
South American Ind. (6)	9	0.02
Yaqui (0)	1	<0.01
Yup'ik *(Alaska Native)* (2)	2	<0.01
Asian (1,510)	1,904	4.49
Not Hispanic (1,498)	1,879	4.43
Hispanic (12)	25	0.06
Bangladeshi (5)	5	0.01
Bhutanese (148)	175	0.41
Burmese (70)	76	0.18
Cambodian (8)	18	0.04
Chinese, ex. Taiwanese (257)	348	0.82
Filipino (66)	103	0.24
Indian (153)	216	0.51
Indonesian (1)	4	0.01
Japanese (43)	103	0.24
Korean (109)	173	0.41
Laotian (20)	24	0.06
Malaysian (3)	4	0.01
Nepalese (60)	79	0.19
Pakistani (7)	7	0.02
Sri Lankan (12)	12	0.03
Taiwanese (12)	20	0.05
Thai (26)	41	0.10
Vietnamese (401)	474	1.12
Hawaii Native/Pacific Islander (21)	59	0.14
Not Hispanic (20)	53	0.12
Hispanic (1)	6	0.01
Guamanian/Chamorro (2)	3	0.01
Native Hawaiian (4)	8	0.02
Samoan (6)	10	0.02
Tongan (0)	1	<0.01
White (37,727)	38,735	91.32
Not Hispanic (37,027)	37,932	89.43
Hispanic (700)	803	1.89

Colchester

Place Type: Town
County: Chittenden
Population: 17,067†

Ancestry‡	Population	%
African, Sub-Saharan (25)	25	0.15
African (6)	6	0.04
Ethiopian (7)	7	0.04
Nigerian (12)	12	0.07
American (971)	971	5.69
Arab (54)	155	0.91
Lebanese (53)	130	0.76
Syrian (0)	24	0.14
Other Arab (1)	1	0.01
Armenian (12)	18	0.11
Austrian (0)	13	0.08
Basque (0)	38	0.22
Belgian (0)	7	0.04
British (16)	33	0.19
Canadian (97)	254	1.49
Czech (27)	107	0.63
Czechoslovakian (12)	38	0.22
Danish (15)	56	0.33
Dutch (30)	197	1.15
Eastern European (20)	20	0.12
English (527)	2,325	13.62
European (73)	98	0.57
Finnish (19)	55	0.32
French, ex. Basque (1,306)	3,275	19.19
French Canadian (1,230)	1,974	11.57
German (338)	1,525	8.94
Greek (31)	124	0.73
Hungarian (0)	22	0.13
Iranian (12)	47	0.28
Irish (911)	3,683	21.58
Italian (335)	1,805	10.58
Lithuanian (9)	79	0.46
Northern European (9)	9	0.05

*Notes: † The Census 2010 population figure is used to calculate the percentages in the Hispanic Origin and Race categories. Ancestry percentages are based on the 2006-2010 American Community Survey population (not shown); ‡ Numbers in parentheses indicate the number of people reporting a single ancestry; * Numbers in parentheses indicate the number of persons reporting this race alone, not in combination with any other race; Please refer to the Explanation of Data for more information.*

Ancestry	Population	%
Norwegian (23)	115	0.67
Polish (157)	619	3.63
Portuguese (25)	43	0.25
Romanian (23)	36	0.21
Russian (55)	171	1.00
Scotch-Irish (158)	427	2.50
Scottish (128)	780	4.57
Serbian (57)	57	0.33
Slovak (66)	118	0.69
Swedish (33)	328	1.92
Swiss (16)	52	0.30
Turkish (27)	27	0.16
Ukrainian (0)	39	0.23
Welsh (23)	214	1.25

Hispanic Origin	Population	%
Hispanic or Latino (of any race)	270	1.58
Central American, ex. Mexican	18	0.11
Costa Rican	4	0.02
Guatemalan	2	0.01
Honduran	2	0.01
Nicaraguan	3	0.02
Panamanian	4	0.02
Salvadoran	3	0.02
Cuban	17	0.10
Dominican Republic	9	0.05
Mexican	89	0.52
Puerto Rican	45	0.26
South American	36	0.21
Argentinean	6	0.04
Chilean	2	0.01
Colombian	9	0.05
Ecuadorian	4	0.02
Paraguayan	2	0.01
Peruvian	7	0.04
Uruguayan	4	0.02
Venezuelan	2	0.01
Other Hispanic or Latino	56	0.33

Race*	Population	%
African-American/Black (210)	310	1.82
Not Hispanic (200)	294	1.72
Hispanic (10)	16	0.09
American Indian/Alaska Native (48)	123	0.72
Not Hispanic (42)	113	0.66
Hispanic (6)	10	0.06
Blackfeet (0)	5	0.03
Canadian/French Am. Ind. (2)	3	0.02
Cherokee (3)	6	0.04
Chippewa (0)	3	0.02
Iroquois (2)	9	0.05
Lumbee (1)	1	0.01
Mexican American Ind. (2)	2	0.01
Navajo (1)	1	0.01
Sioux (0)	4	0.02
South American Ind. (1)	2	0.01
Asian (359)	436	2.55
Not Hispanic (358)	433	2.54
Hispanic (1)	3	0.02
Bangladeshi (3)	3	0.02
Bhutanese (3)	3	0.02
Cambodian (6)	8	0.05
Chinese, ex. Taiwanese (132)	140	0.82
Filipino (17)	35	0.21
Indian (46)	55	0.32
Indonesian (1)	2	0.01
Japanese (16)	25	0.15
Korean (42)	59	0.35
Laotian (1)	2	0.01
Malaysian (0)	1	0.01
Nepalese (0)	1	0.01
Pakistani (11)	12	0.07
Sri Lankan (2)	2	0.01
Taiwanese (1)	1	0.01
Thai (5)	10	0.06
Vietnamese (63)	71	0.42
Hawaii Native/Pacific Islander (6)	19	0.11
Not Hispanic (5)	18	0.11
Hispanic (1)	1	0.01
Guamanian/Chamorro (1)	2	0.01
Marshallese (2)	2	0.01
Native Hawaiian (1)	2	0.01
Samoan (2)	3	0.02
White (16,148)	16,370	95.92
Not Hispanic (15,960)	16,165	94.71
Hispanic (188)	205	1.20

Essex Junction

Place Type: Village
County: Chittenden
Population: 9,271†

Ancestry‡	Population	%
African, Sub-Saharan (101)	111	1.21
African (89)	99	1.08
Ethiopian (12)	12	0.13
American (737)	737	8.05
Arab (13)	23	0.25
Lebanese (0)	10	0.11
Other Arab (13)	13	0.14
Armenian (0)	9	0.10
Austrian (0)	24	0.26
Belgian (0)	14	0.15
British (130)	184	2.01
Canadian (62)	77	0.84
Czech (8)	70	0.76
Czechoslovakian (14)	29	0.32
Danish (0)	46	0.50
Dutch (26)	184	2.01
Eastern European (21)	21	0.23
English (646)	1,547	16.90
European (184)	184	2.01
French, ex. Basque (192)	893	9.75
French Canadian (429)	811	8.86
German (199)	1,156	12.63
Greek (20)	62	0.68
Hungarian (15)	50	0.55
Iranian (30)	30	0.33
Irish (549)	1,565	17.09
Italian (213)	601	6.56
Lithuanian (0)	49	0.54
Northern European (25)	25	0.27
Norwegian (46)	76	0.83
Polish (21)	315	3.44
Portuguese (18)	28	0.31
Romanian (14)	14	0.15
Russian (0)	60	0.66
Scotch-Irish (128)	286	3.12
Scottish (64)	336	3.67
Slovak (15)	21	0.23
Swedish (8)	195	2.13
Swiss (0)	26	0.28
Welsh (60)	170	1.86
Yugoslavian (44)	60	0.66

Hispanic Origin	Population	%
Hispanic or Latino (of any race)	187	2.02
Central American, ex. Mexican	14	0.15
Costa Rican	1	0.01
Guatemalan	9	0.10
Honduran	2	0.02
Panamanian	1	0.01
Salvadoran	1	0.01
Cuban	7	0.08
Dominican Republic	16	0.17
Mexican	52	0.56
Puerto Rican	38	0.41
South American	19	0.20
Argentinean	5	0.05
Colombian	5	0.05
Ecuadorian	3	0.03
Peruvian	4	0.04
Venezuelan	2	0.02
Other Hispanic or Latino	41	0.44

Race*	Population	%
African-American/Black (155)	221	2.38
Not Hispanic (144)	206	2.22
Hispanic (11)	15	0.16
American Indian/Alaska Native (37)	73	0.79
Not Hispanic (33)	64	0.69
Hispanic (4)	9	0.10
Blackfeet (0)	1	0.01
Central American Ind. (1)	1	0.01
Cherokee (3)	3	0.03
Chippewa (4)	4	0.04
Cree (2)	3	0.03
Iroquois (2)	7	0.08
Kiowa (1)	1	0.01
Mexican American Ind. (2)	3	0.03
Navajo (1)	1	0.01
Pima (0)	2	0.02
Potawatomi (2)	2	0.02
Sioux (1)	4	0.04
Asian (362)	441	4.76
Not Hispanic (357)	434	4.68
Hispanic (5)	7	0.08
Bangladeshi (7)	7	0.08
Cambodian (2)	2	0.02
Chinese, ex. Taiwanese (89)	100	1.08
Filipino (18)	28	0.30
Indian (111)	132	1.42
Indonesian (0)	1	0.01
Japanese (13)	29	0.31
Korean (34)	42	0.45
Laotian (1)	4	0.04
Pakistani (6)	6	0.06
Sri Lankan (2)	2	0.02
Taiwanese (1)	1	0.01
Thai (4)	8	0.09
Vietnamese (61)	71	0.77
Hawaii Native/Pacific Islander (1)	5	0.05
Not Hispanic (1)	5	0.05
Marshallese (1)	3	0.03
White (8,486)	8,658	93.39
Not Hispanic (8,371)	8,526	91.96
Hispanic (115)	132	1.42

Essex

Place Type: Town
County: Chittenden
Population: 19,587†

Ancestry‡	Population	%
African, Sub-Saharan (216)	226	1.16
African (192)	202	1.04
Ethiopian (12)	12	0.06
Kenyan (12)	12	0.06
Albanian (5)	14	0.07
American (1,369)	1,369	7.05
Arab (18)	35	0.18
Arab (5)	5	0.03
Lebanese (0)	17	0.09
Other Arab (13)	13	0.07
Armenian (0)	9	0.05
Austrian (9)	45	0.23
Belgian (0)	14	0.07
British (236)	323	1.66
Canadian (105)	167	0.86
Croatian (12)	12	0.06
Czech (8)	94	0.48
Czechoslovakian (14)	29	0.15
Danish (8)	68	0.35
Dutch (65)	388	2.00
Eastern European (33)	33	0.17
English (1,380)	3,564	18.34
European (373)	414	2.13
Finnish (0)	20	0.10
French, ex. Basque (590)	2,188	11.26
French Canadian (1,032)	1,944	10.00
German (582)	2,404	12.37
Greek (20)	62	0.32
Hungarian (15)	75	0.39
Iranian (30)	30	0.15
Irish (929)	3,571	18.38
Italian (516)	1,607	8.27
Lithuanian (19)	154	0.79
Northern European (25)	25	0.13

*Notes: † The Census 2010 population figure is used to calculate the percentages in the Hispanic Origin and Race categories. Ancestry percentages are based on the 2006-2010 American Community Survey population (not shown); ‡ Numbers in parentheses indicate the number of people reporting a single ancestry; * Numbers in parentheses indicate the number of persons reporting this race alone, not in combination with any other race; Please refer to the Explanation of Data for more information.*

Norwegian (53)	151	0.78
Polish (210)	814	4.19
Portuguese (28)	50	0.26
Romanian (14)	14	0.07
Russian (25)	113	0.58
Scotch-Irish (189)	423	2.18
Scottish (181)	957	4.93
Slavic (0)	11	0.06
Slovak (47)	73	0.38
Slovene (38)	38	0.20
Swedish (18)	358	1.84
Swiss (15)	63	0.32
Ukrainian (0)	13	0.07
Welsh (81)	249	1.28
Yugoslavian (78)	103	0.53

Hispanic Origin	Population	%
Hispanic or Latino (of any race)	335	1.71
Central American, ex. Mexican	20	0.10
Costa Rican	1	0.01
Guatemalan	11	0.06
Honduran	2	0.01
Nicaraguan	1	0.01
Panamanian	1	0.01
Salvadoran	4	0.02
Cuban	12	0.06
Dominican Republic	22	0.11
Mexican	90	0.46
Puerto Rican	83	0.42
South American	38	0.19
Argentinean	9	0.05
Bolivian	2	0.01
Chilean	3	0.02
Colombian	9	0.05
Ecuadorian	4	0.02
Peruvian	7	0.04
Venezuelan	4	0.02
Other Hispanic or Latino	70	0.36

Race*	Population	%
African-American/Black (290)	400	2.04
Not Hispanic (277)	377	1.92
Hispanic (13)	23	0.12
American Indian/Alaska Native (52)	125	0.64
Not Hispanic (47)	110	0.56
Hispanic (5)	15	0.08
Blackfeet (0)	1	0.01
Central American Ind. (1)	2	0.01
Cherokee (3)	14	0.07
Chippewa (4)	6	0.03
Cree (2)	4	0.02
Delaware (0)	1	0.01
Iroquois (4)	12	0.06
Kiowa (1)	1	0.01
Mexican American Ind. (2)	3	0.02
Navajo (1)	1	0.01
Pima (0)	2	0.01
Potawatomi (2)	2	0.01
Sioux (1)	5	0.03
Yaqui (1)	1	0.01
Asian (631)	802	4.09
Not Hispanic (626)	793	4.05
Hispanic (5)	9	0.05
Bangladeshi (7)	7	0.04
Cambodian (11)	15	0.08
Chinese, ex. Taiwanese (167)	201	1.03
Filipino (27)	50	0.26
Indian (173)	209	1.07
Indonesian (1)	2	0.01
Japanese (28)	56	0.29
Korean (64)	82	0.42
Laotian (6)	11	0.06
Malaysian (0)	2	0.01
Pakistani (21)	21	0.11
Sri Lankan (2)	2	0.01
Taiwanese (3)	3	0.02
Thai (7)	12	0.06
Vietnamese (91)	107	0.55
Hawaii Native/Pacific Islander (2)	14	0.07
Not Hispanic (2)	14	0.07
Guamanian/Chamorro (1)	4	0.02
Marshallese (1)	3	0.02
Native Hawaiian (0)	1	0.01
White (18,174)	18,509	94.50
Not Hispanic (17,947)	18,256	93.20
Hispanic (227)	253	1.29

Hartford

Place Type: Town
County: Windsor
Population: 9,952†

Ancestry‡	Population	%
African, Sub-Saharan (65)	82	0.82
African (65)	82	0.82
American (305)	305	3.04
Australian (15)	15	0.15
Austrian (0)	8	0.08
British (33)	71	0.71
Canadian (65)	65	0.65
Czech (9)	48	0.48
Danish (0)	12	0.12
Dutch (0)	330	3.29
English (905)	2,465	24.58
European (43)	43	0.43
Finnish (11)	11	0.11
French, ex. Basque (576)	1,560	15.56
French Canadian (238)	565	5.63
German (284)	1,403	13.99
Greek (86)	86	0.86
Hungarian (19)	48	0.48
Irish (347)	1,701	16.96
Israeli (0)	6	0.06
Italian (203)	686	6.84
Lithuanian (0)	50	0.50
Norwegian (79)	123	1.23
Polish (157)	542	5.40
Portuguese (0)	29	0.29
Romanian (30)	54	0.54
Russian (68)	226	2.25
Scandinavian (28)	52	0.52
Scotch-Irish (97)	389	3.88
Scottish (197)	562	5.60
Serbian (68)	109	1.09
Slovak (0)	25	0.25
Swedish (58)	220	2.19
Swiss (15)	40	0.40
Welsh (0)	126	1.26
West Indian, ex. Hispanic (0)	21	0.21
Jamaican (0)	21	0.21

Hispanic Origin	Population	%
Hispanic or Latino (of any race)	116	1.17
Central American, ex. Mexican	13	0.13
Guatemalan	8	0.08
Honduran	3	0.03
Panamanian	1	0.01
Salvadoran	1	0.01
Cuban	4	0.04
Dominican Republic	6	0.06
Mexican	34	0.34
Puerto Rican	28	0.28
South American	13	0.13
Argentinean	1	0.01
Bolivian	1	0.01
Chilean	1	0.01
Colombian	4	0.04
Ecuadorian	1	0.01
Peruvian	3	0.03
Venezuelan	2	0.02
Other Hispanic or Latino	18	0.18

Race*	Population	%
African-American/Black (82)	128	1.29
Not Hispanic (77)	115	1.16
Hispanic (5)	13	0.13
American Indian/Alaska Native (30)	123	1.24
Not Hispanic (28)	105	1.06
Hispanic (2)	18	0.18
Apache (0)	1	0.01
Blackfeet (1)	8	0.08
Canadian/French Am. Ind. (0)	1	0.01
Cherokee (1)	6	0.06
Chippewa (1)	1	0.01
Choctaw (1)	2	0.02
Creek (0)	1	0.01
Iroquois (1)	7	0.07
Mexican American Ind. (1)	2	0.02
Navajo (0)	1	0.01
Seminole (0)	1	0.01
Sioux (1)	3	0.03
South American Ind. (0)	1	0.01
Asian (175)	222	2.23
Not Hispanic (175)	218	2.19
Hispanic (0)	4	0.04
Burmese (5)	5	0.05
Cambodian (3)	3	0.03
Chinese, ex. Taiwanese (44)	49	0.49
Filipino (13)	20	0.20
Indian (34)	43	0.43
Indonesian (1)	2	0.02
Japanese (16)	26	0.26
Korean (31)	40	0.40
Laotian (0)	1	0.01
Malaysian (2)	2	0.02
Pakistani (6)	8	0.08
Sri Lankan (0)	3	0.03
Thai (6)	8	0.08
Vietnamese (7)	8	0.08
Hawaii Native/Pacific Islander (3)	11	0.11
Not Hispanic (2)	9	0.09
Hispanic (1)	2	0.02
Guamanian/Chamorro (1)	1	0.01
Native Hawaiian (2)	6	0.06
Samoan (0)	3	0.03
White (9,448)	9,623	96.69
Not Hispanic (9,390)	9,538	95.84
Hispanic (58)	85	0.85

Middlebury

Place Type: Town
County: Addison
Population: 8,496†

Ancestry‡	Population	%
Afghan (6)	6	0.07
African, Sub-Saharan (59)	65	0.77
Ghanaian (0)	6	0.07
Kenyan (14)	14	0.17
South African (45)	45	0.53
American (357)	357	4.22
Arab (47)	58	0.68
Palestinian (7)	7	0.08
Syrian (9)	20	0.24
Other Arab (31)	31	0.37
Austrian (0)	66	0.78
Brazilian (0)	7	0.08
British (54)	100	1.18
Bulgarian (11)	11	0.13
Canadian (19)	47	0.56
Croatian (0)	3	0.04
Czech (29)	112	1.32
Danish (10)	44	0.52
Dutch (22)	113	1.33
Eastern European (9)	9	0.11
English (398)	1,668	19.70
European (145)	157	1.85
Finnish (0)	7	0.08
French, ex. Basque (472)	1,222	14.43
French Canadian (226)	328	3.87
German (174)	1,216	14.36
Greek (0)	39	0.46
Guyanese (8)	8	0.09
Hungarian (0)	44	0.52
Iranian (8)	8	0.09
Irish (577)	1,609	19.00
Italian (144)	475	5.61
Latvian (0)	7	0.08

*Notes: † The Census 2010 population figure is used to calculate the percentages in the Hispanic Origin and Race categories. Ancestry percentages are based on the 2006-2010 American Community Survey population (not shown); ‡ Numbers in parentheses indicate the number of people reporting a single ancestry; * Numbers in parentheses indicate the number of persons reporting this race alone, not in combination with any other race; Please refer to the Explanation of Data for more information.*

	Population	%
Lithuanian (14)	39	0.46
Northern European (0)	3	0.04
Norwegian (70)	138	1.63
Polish (142)	302	3.57
Portuguese (9)	19	0.22
Romanian (0)	12	0.14
Russian (33)	301	3.55
Scandinavian (0)	42	0.50
Scotch-Irish (67)	205	2.42
Scottish (77)	472	5.57
Slovak (0)	24	0.28
Swedish (0)	135	1.59
Swiss (0)	51	0.60
Turkish (10)	10	0.12
Ukrainian (11)	33	0.39
Welsh (5)	243	2.87
Yugoslavian (28)	28	0.33

Hispanic Origin	Population	%
Hispanic or Latino (of any race)	258	3.04
Central American, ex. Mexican	26	0.31
Costa Rican	3	0.04
Guatemalan	4	0.05
Honduran	2	0.02
Nicaraguan	2	0.02
Panamanian	3	0.04
Salvadoran	12	0.14
Cuban	15	0.18
Dominican Republic	22	0.26
Mexican	59	0.69
Puerto Rican	38	0.45
South American	64	0.75
Argentinean	11	0.13
Bolivian	7	0.08
Chilean	6	0.07
Colombian	12	0.14
Ecuadorian	6	0.07
Peruvian	11	0.13
Uruguayan	3	0.04
Venezuelan	4	0.05
Other South American	4	0.05
Other Hispanic or Latino	34	0.40

Race*	Population	%
African-American/Black (114)	178	2.10
Not Hispanic (106)	158	1.86
Hispanic (8)	20	0.24
American Indian/Alaska Native (15)	83	0.98
Not Hispanic (13)	75	0.88
Hispanic (2)	8	0.09
Apache (1)	4	0.05
Blackfeet (0)	7	0.08
Canadian/French Am. Ind. (1)	1	0.01
Central American Ind. (1)	1	0.01
Cherokee (1)	16	0.19
Chickasaw (0)	1	0.01
Chippewa (0)	1	0.01
Choctaw (0)	1	0.01
Delaware (0)	1	0.01
Iroquois (0)	3	0.04
Potawatomi (0)	2	0.02
Sioux (0)	1	0.01
South American Ind. (1)	3	0.04
Asian (367)	493	5.80
Not Hispanic (365)	486	5.72
Hispanic (2)	7	0.08
Bangladeshi (3)	3	0.04
Burmese (2)	5	0.06
Cambodian (1)	1	0.01
Chinese, ex. Taiwanese (154)	204	2.40
Filipino (12)	28	0.33
Indian (67)	80	0.94
Japanese (17)	44	0.52
Korean (58)	72	0.85
Malaysian (1)	4	0.05
Nepalese (0)	1	0.01
Pakistani (7)	9	0.11
Sri Lankan (1)	1	0.01
Taiwanese (8)	14	0.16
Thai (6)	9	0.11
Vietnamese (11)	17	0.20
Hawaii Native/Pacific Islander (1)	7	0.08
Not Hispanic (0)	5	0.06
Hispanic (1)	2	0.02
Guamanian/Chamorro (1)	2	0.02
Native Hawaiian (0)	3	0.04
White (7,676)	7,926	93.29
Not Hispanic (7,509)	7,736	91.05
Hispanic (167)	190	2.24

Milton

Place Type: Town
County: Chittenden
Population: 10,352†

Ancestry‡	Population	%
African, Sub-Saharan (23)	23	0.23
Other Sub-Saharan African (23)	23	0.23
American (1,630)	1,630	15.99
Arab (9)	14	0.14
Lebanese (9)	14	0.14
British (0)	24	0.24
Canadian (251)	294	2.88
Danish (0)	76	0.75
Dutch (43)	175	1.72
English (393)	1,033	10.14
European (57)	57	0.56
French, ex. Basque (724)	1,706	16.74
French Canadian (668)	1,063	10.43
German (162)	567	5.56
Greek (26)	76	0.75
Hungarian (0)	6	0.06
Irish (323)	1,454	14.27
Italian (264)	780	7.65
Lithuanian (31)	36	0.35
Northern European (29)	29	0.28
Norwegian (0)	56	0.55
Polish (136)	316	3.10
Portuguese (31)	31	0.30
Russian (0)	12	0.12
Scotch-Irish (0)	114	1.12
Scottish (116)	240	2.35
Slovak (0)	12	0.12
Swedish (77)	133	1.30
Welsh (0)	32	0.31
West Indian, ex. Hispanic (21)	21	0.21
Jamaican (21)	21	0.21

Hispanic Origin	Population	%
Hispanic or Latino (of any race)	68	0.66
Central American, ex. Mexican	4	0.04
Costa Rican	1	0.01
Guatemalan	3	0.03
Cuban	2	0.02
Mexican	22	0.21
Puerto Rican	17	0.16
South American	6	0.06
Colombian	1	0.01
Ecuadorian	2	0.02
Peruvian	1	0.01
Venezuelan	2	0.02
Other Hispanic or Latino	17	0.16

Race*	Population	%
African-American/Black (68)	119	1.15
Not Hispanic (68)	116	1.12
Hispanic (0)	3	0.03
American Indian/Alaska Native (33)	109	1.05
Not Hispanic (31)	105	1.01
Hispanic (2)	4	0.04
Apache (0)	1	0.01
Blackfeet (1)	7	0.07
Canadian/French Am. Ind. (1)	3	0.03
Cherokee (4)	6	0.06
Cree (0)	1	0.01
Iroquois (3)	8	0.08
Pima (2)	2	0.02
Sioux (0)	2	0.02
Spanish American Ind. (1)	1	0.01
Yup'ik *(Alaska Native)* (0)	1	0.01
Asian (57)	85	0.82
Not Hispanic (57)	85	0.82
Chinese, ex. Taiwanese (13)	14	0.14
Filipino (11)	18	0.17
Indian (10)	13	0.13
Japanese (1)	4	0.04
Korean (5)	12	0.12
Laotian (5)	5	0.05
Vietnamese (10)	14	0.14
Hawaii Native/Pacific Islander (2)	3	0.03
Not Hispanic (2)	3	0.03
Native Hawaiian (2)	2	0.02
Samoan (0)	1	0.01
White (10,029)	10,183	98.37
Not Hispanic (9,976)	10,123	97.79
Hispanic (53)	60	0.58

Montpelier

Place Type: City
County: Washington
Population: 7,855†

Ancestry‡	Population	%
American (315)	315	3.99
Arab (42)	42	0.53
Syrian (42)	42	0.53
Armenian (9)	9	0.11
Australian (0)	33	0.42
Austrian (0)	54	0.68
Belgian (0)	26	0.33
British (146)	169	2.14
Canadian (18)	27	0.34
Carpatho Rusyn (13)	13	0.16
Celtic (0)	4	0.05
Croatian (0)	10	0.13
Czech (9)	70	0.89
Danish (10)	19	0.24
Dutch (22)	71	0.90
Eastern European (21)	35	0.44
English (346)	1,376	17.41
European (289)	289	3.66
Finnish (0)	11	0.14
French, ex. Basque (185)	563	7.12
French Canadian (315)	520	6.58
German (204)	855	10.82
Hungarian (10)	40	0.51
Irish (355)	1,108	14.02
Italian (188)	633	8.01
Latvian (0)	23	0.29
Lithuanian (38)	71	0.90
Northern European (9)	9	0.11
Norwegian (8)	40	0.51
Pennsylvania German (62)	62	0.78
Polish (26)	159	2.01
Portuguese (12)	22	0.28
Russian (131)	267	3.38
Scandinavian (0)	11	0.14
Scotch-Irish (141)	333	4.21
Scottish (100)	547	6.92
Slovak (0)	13	0.16
Swedish (25)	107	1.35
Swiss (0)	12	0.15
Ukrainian (11)	11	0.14
Welsh (0)	77	0.97

Hispanic Origin	Population	%
Hispanic or Latino (of any race)	166	2.11
Central American, ex. Mexican	14	0.18
Costa Rican	1	0.01
Guatemalan	4	0.05
Honduran	3	0.04
Nicaraguan	3	0.04
Salvadoran	3	0.04
Cuban	9	0.11
Dominican Republic	6	0.08
Mexican	28	0.36
Puerto Rican	32	0.41
South American	24	0.31

SECTION TWO

*Notes: † The Census 2010 population figure is used to calculate the percentages in the Hispanic Origin and Race categories. Ancestry percentages are based on the 2006-2010 American Community Survey population (not shown); ‡ Numbers in parentheses indicate the number of people reporting a single ancestry; * Numbers in parentheses indicate the number of persons reporting this race alone, not in combination with any other race; Please refer to the Explanation of Data for more information.*

Argentinean	6	0.08
Colombian	12	0.15
Ecuadorian	2	0.03
Peruvian	2	0.03
Venezuelan	2	0.03
Other Hispanic or Latino	53	0.67

Race*	Population	%
African-American/Black (79)	129	1.64
Not Hispanic (74)	122	1.55
Hispanic (5)	7	0.09
American Indian/Alaska Native (23)	112	1.43
Not Hispanic (18)	102	1.30
Hispanic (5)	10	0.13
Apache (1)	1	0.01
Blackfeet (1)	6	0.08
Canadian/French Am. Ind. (0)	2	0.03
Central American Ind. (2)	2	0.03
Cherokee (2)	10	0.13
Chickasaw (0)	2	0.03
Choctaw (0)	1	0.01
Cree (1)	1	0.01
Iroquois (0)	6	0.08
Mexican American Ind. (0)	1	0.01
Navajo (0)	1	0.01
Sioux (3)	3	0.04
Asian (171)	225	2.86
Not Hispanic (168)	216	2.75
Hispanic (3)	9	0.11
Cambodian (3)	6	0.08
Chinese, ex. Taiwanese (53)	63	0.80
Filipino (7)	11	0.14
Indian (68)	73	0.93
Indonesian (0)	2	0.03
Japanese (3)	10	0.13
Korean (19)	33	0.42
Laotian (1)	1	0.01
Nepalese (1)	1	0.01
Pakistani (2)	2	0.03
Thai (6)	6	0.08
Vietnamese (5)	8	0.10
Hawaii Native/Pacific Islander (2)	6	0.08
Not Hispanic (2)	5	0.06
Hispanic (0)	1	0.01
Native Hawaiian (2)	4	0.05
White (7,362)	7,538	95.96
Not Hispanic (7,249)	7,410	94.33
Hispanic (113)	128	1.63

Rutland

Place Type: City
County: Rutland
Population: 16,495†

Ancestry‡	Population	%
African, Sub-Saharan (7)	7	0.04
African (7)	7	0.04
American (1,002)	1,002	5.99
Arab (0)	14	0.08
Lebanese (0)	14	0.08
Armenian (0)	24	0.14
Austrian (50)	98	0.59
Belgian (16)	45	0.27
British (32)	32	0.19
Canadian (38)	67	0.40
Czech (0)	16	0.10
Czechoslovakian (9)	74	0.44
Danish (16)	28	0.17
Dutch (42)	194	1.16
Eastern European (11)	11	0.07
English (550)	2,200	13.14
European (81)	81	0.48
Finnish (61)	162	0.97
French, ex. Basque (731)	3,096	18.50
French Canadian (340)	854	5.10
German (413)	1,708	10.20
Greek (23)	44	0.26
Guyanese (0)	10	0.06
Hungarian (14)	264	1.58
Icelander (0)	9	0.05
Iranian (18)	18	0.11
Irish (1,180)	4,139	24.73
Italian (773)	2,106	12.58
Latvian (0)	10	0.06
Lithuanian (0)	19	0.11
Norwegian (10)	39	0.23
Polish (449)	1,142	6.82
Portuguese (22)	108	0.65
Russian (11)	32	0.19
Scandinavian (34)	34	0.20
Scotch-Irish (48)	436	2.60
Scottish (44)	493	2.95
Swedish (113)	400	2.39
Swiss (0)	20	0.12
Ukrainian (8)	19	0.11
Welsh (61)	349	2.08
West Indian, ex. Hispanic (0)	10	0.06
Jamaican (0)	10	0.06

Hispanic Origin	Population	%
Hispanic or Latino (of any race)	250	1.52
Central American, ex. Mexican	18	0.11
Costa Rican	2	0.01
Guatemalan	7	0.04
Nicaraguan	2	0.01
Panamanian	1	0.01
Salvadoran	6	0.04
Cuban	6	0.04
Dominican Republic	9	0.05
Mexican	50	0.30
Puerto Rican	94	0.57
South American	38	0.23
Argentinean	2	0.01
Chilean	12	0.07
Colombian	10	0.06
Ecuadorian	2	0.01
Paraguayan	2	0.01
Peruvian	7	0.04
Venezuelan	2	0.01
Other South American	1	0.01
Other Hispanic or Latino	35	0.21

Race*	Population	%
African-American/Black (135)	256	1.55
Not Hispanic (128)	237	1.44
Hispanic (7)	19	0.12
American Indian/Alaska Native (52)	171	1.04
Not Hispanic (45)	161	0.98
Hispanic (7)	10	0.06
Blackfeet (4)	15	0.09
Canadian/French Am. Ind. (2)	7	0.04
Cherokee (6)	20	0.12
Cheyenne (0)	1	0.01
Chickasaw (1)	2	0.01
Chippewa (1)	1	0.01
Crow (0)	1	0.01
Inupiat *(Alaska Native)* (0)	1	0.01
Iroquois (2)	10	0.06
Mexican American Ind. (1)	1	0.01
Potawatomi (1)	1	0.01
Sioux (1)	6	0.04
South American Ind. (1)	2	0.01
Tlingit-Haida *(Alaska Native)* (0)	3	0.02
Asian (127)	173	1.05
Not Hispanic (127)	166	1.01
Hispanic (0)	7	0.04
Bangladeshi (1)	1	0.01
Cambodian (1)	1	0.01
Chinese, ex. Taiwanese (52)	59	0.36
Filipino (19)	36	0.22
Indian (11)	17	0.10
Japanese (14)	25	0.15
Korean (15)	23	0.14
Nepalese (3)	3	0.02
Thai (4)	4	0.02
Vietnamese (5)	6	0.04
Hawaii Native/Pacific Islander (4)	16	0.10
Not Hispanic (4)	14	0.08
Hispanic (0)	2	0.01
Guamanian/Chamorro (2)	3	0.02
Native Hawaiian (1)	8	0.05
Samoan (0)	5	0.03
White (15,822)	16,097	97.59
Not Hispanic (15,670)	15,918	96.50
Hispanic (152)	179	1.09

South Burlington

Place Type: City
County: Chittenden
Population: 17,904†

Ancestry‡	Population	%
African, Sub-Saharan (65)	77	0.44
African (46)	58	0.33
Somalian (4)	4	0.02
Other Sub-Saharan African (15)	15	0.09
Albanian (26)	26	0.15
American (818)	818	4.71
Arab (50)	88	0.51
Egyptian (21)	21	0.12
Lebanese (0)	26	0.15
Moroccan (4)	4	0.02
Syrian (11)	23	0.13
Other Arab (14)	14	0.08
Armenian (0)	36	0.21
Austrian (0)	37	0.21
British (58)	98	0.56
Bulgarian (0)	14	0.08
Canadian (91)	142	0.82
Celtic (36)	36	0.21
Croatian (24)	24	0.14
Czech (0)	39	0.22
Danish (27)	99	0.57
Dutch (137)	406	2.34
Eastern European (105)	105	0.60
English (703)	2,327	13.41
European (335)	335	1.93
Finnish (0)	53	0.31
French, ex. Basque (604)	2,315	13.34
French Canadian (1,376)	1,896	10.92
German (445)	1,823	10.50
Greek (31)	110	0.63
Hungarian (13)	98	0.56
Irish (1,078)	3,297	19.00
Italian (508)	1,596	9.20
Latvian (0)	58	0.33
Lithuanian (52)	73	0.42
Macedonian (15)	15	0.09
Northern European (13)	13	0.07
Norwegian (24)	221	1.27
Polish (201)	735	4.23
Portuguese (16)	95	0.55
Romanian (12)	23	0.13
Russian (77)	348	2.01
Scotch-Irish (61)	285	1.64
Scottish (199)	574	3.31
Slavic (14)	14	0.08
Slovak (12)	79	0.46
Slovene (17)	29	0.17
Swedish (89)	199	1.15
Swiss (25)	110	0.63
Ukrainian (56)	56	0.32
Welsh (9)	244	1.41
West Indian, ex. Hispanic (4)	19	0.11
Jamaican (0)	15	0.09
Trinidadian/Tobagonian (4)	4	0.02
Yugoslavian (82)	82	0.47

Hispanic Origin	Population	%
Hispanic or Latino (of any race)	336	1.88
Central American, ex. Mexican	33	0.18
Costa Rican	2	0.01
Guatemalan	9	0.05
Honduran	6	0.03
Nicaraguan	3	0.02
Panamanian	5	0.03
Salvadoran	8	0.04
Cuban	13	0.07

*Notes: † The Census 2010 population figure is used to calculate the percentages in the Hispanic Origin and Race categories. Ancestry percentages are based on the 2006-2010 American Community Survey population (not shown); ‡ Numbers in parentheses indicate the number of people reporting a single ancestry; * Numbers in parentheses indicate the number of persons reporting this race alone, not in combination with any other race; Please refer to the Explanation of Data for more information.*

Dominican Republic	7	0.04
Mexican	81	0.45
Puerto Rican	67	0.37
South American	63	0.35
Argentinean	4	0.02
Chilean	4	0.02
Colombian	22	0.12
Ecuadorian	4	0.02
Paraguayan	5	0.03
Peruvian	20	0.11
Uruguayan	1	0.01
Venezuelan	3	0.02
Other Hispanic or Latino	72	0.40

Race*	Population	%
African-American/Black (348)	462	2.58
Not Hispanic (337)	447	2.50
Hispanic (11)	15	0.08
American Indian/Alaska Native (35)	137	0.77
Not Hispanic (34)	125	0.70
Hispanic (1)	12	0.07
Aleut *(Alaska Native)* (0)	3	0.02
Blackfeet (0)	6	0.03
Canadian/French Am. Ind. (0)	1	0.01
Central American Ind. (0)	1	0.01
Cherokee (1)	16	0.09
Chippewa (0)	1	0.01
Choctaw (1)	1	0.01
Comanche (1)	2	0.01
Cree (1)	1	0.01
Hopi (1)	1	0.01
Iroquois (0)	3	0.02
Mexican American Ind. (1)	1	0.01
Ottawa (0)	1	0.01
Sioux (1)	1	0.01
Asian (969)	1,114	6.22
Not Hispanic (961)	1,100	6.14
Hispanic (8)	14	0.08
Bangladeshi (13)	16	0.09
Bhutanese (4)	9	0.05
Burmese (2)	2	0.01
Chinese, ex. Taiwanese (373)	423	2.36
Filipino (38)	54	0.30
Indian (269)	293	1.64
Indonesian (4)	4	0.02
Japanese (43)	57	0.32
Korean (53)	76	0.42
Laotian (2)	2	0.01
Nepalese (3)	3	0.02
Pakistani (23)	24	0.13
Sri Lankan (10)	10	0.06
Taiwanese (9)	9	0.05
Thai (18)	18	0.10
Vietnamese (76)	90	0.50
Hawaii Native/Pacific Islander (6)	19	0.11
Not Hispanic (6)	18	0.10
Hispanic (0)	1	0.01
Guamanian/Chamorro (0)	1	0.01
Native Hawaiian (4)	14	0.08
White (16,116)	16,463	91.95
Not Hispanic (15,876)	16,198	90.47
Hispanic (240)	265	1.48

Springfield

Place Type: Town
County: Windsor
Population: 9,373†

Ancestry‡	Population	%
African, Sub-Saharan (4)	4	0.04
African (4)	4	0.04
American (1,211)	1,211	12.97
Arab (25)	25	0.27
Arab (25)	25	0.27
Armenian (0)	29	0.31
Austrian (0)	52	0.56
British (25)	52	0.56
Canadian (68)	68	0.73
Danish (4)	11	0.12
Dutch (40)	144	1.54
English (581)	1,735	18.58
European (26)	26	0.28
Finnish (16)	58	0.62
French, ex. Basque (303)	1,211	12.97
French Canadian (248)	576	6.17
German (218)	843	9.03
Greek (0)	34	0.36
Hungarian (18)	56	0.60
Irish (380)	1,431	15.33
Italian (259)	576	6.17
Norwegian (42)	151	1.62
Polish (209)	547	5.86
Portuguese (58)	66	0.71
Romanian (0)	13	0.14
Russian (49)	117	1.25
Scandinavian (0)	9	0.10
Scotch-Irish (117)	309	3.31
Scottish (131)	410	4.39
Slovak (8)	8	0.09
Swedish (10)	171	1.83
Swiss (0)	25	0.27
Ukrainian (55)	55	0.59
Welsh (25)	42	0.45
Yugoslavian (0)	6	0.06

Hispanic Origin	Population	%
Hispanic or Latino (of any race)	149	1.59
Central American, ex. Mexican	6	0.06
Costa Rican	1	0.01
Guatemalan	1	0.01
Honduran	3	0.03
Panamanian	1	0.01
Cuban	7	0.07
Dominican Republic	3	0.03
Mexican	41	0.44
Puerto Rican	53	0.57
South American	13	0.14
Colombian	11	0.12
Other South American	2	0.02
Other Hispanic or Latino	26	0.28

Race*	Population	%
African-American/Black (75)	131	1.40
Not Hispanic (74)	125	1.33
Hispanic (1)	6	0.06
American Indian/Alaska Native (19)	125	1.33
Not Hispanic (17)	118	1.26
Hispanic (2)	7	0.07
Apache (1)	3	0.03
Blackfeet (1)	5	0.05
Canadian/French Am. Ind. (1)	4	0.04
Cherokee (1)	12	0.13
Chippewa (0)	2	0.02
Choctaw (0)	2	0.02
Comanche (0)	1	0.01
Creek (0)	2	0.02
Iroquois (0)	6	0.06
Navajo (3)	6	0.06
Pueblo (0)	1	0.01
Seminole (0)	3	0.03
Sioux (0)	1	0.01
Yaqui (0)	1	0.01
Asian (69)	92	0.98
Not Hispanic (68)	90	0.96
Hispanic (1)	2	0.02
Burmese (1)	1	0.01
Cambodian (7)	8	0.09
Chinese, ex. Taiwanese (27)	31	0.33
Filipino (6)	10	0.11
Indian (1)	2	0.02
Japanese (0)	11	0.12
Korean (1)	1	0.01
Laotian (13)	17	0.18
Thai (1)	2	0.02
Vietnamese (3)	4	0.04
Hawaii Native/Pacific Islander (1)	2	0.02
Not Hispanic (1)	2	0.02
Native Hawaiian (1)	1	0.01
White (8,989)	9,154	97.66
Not Hispanic (8,896)	9,046	96.51
Hispanic (93)	108	1.15

St. Johnsbury

Place Type: Town
County: Caledonia
Population: 7,603†

Ancestry‡	Population	%
African, Sub-Saharan (17)	17	0.22
Nigerian (17)	17	0.22
American (404)	404	5.28
Arab (0)	36	0.47
Iraqi (0)	10	0.13
Lebanese (0)	26	0.34
Australian (0)	9	0.12
Austrian (0)	32	0.42
British (11)	60	0.78
Canadian (7)	13	0.17
Celtic (7)	7	0.09
Czech (0)	13	0.17
Czechoslovakian (0)	29	0.38
Dutch (0)	73	0.95
English (602)	1,571	20.54
European (40)	40	0.52
Finnish (28)	28	0.37
French, ex. Basque (370)	1,254	16.39
French Canadian (660)	885	11.57
German (126)	735	9.61
Greek (6)	81	1.06
Hungarian (0)	57	0.75
Irish (420)	1,447	18.92
Italian (106)	534	6.98
Lithuanian (4)	4	0.05
Norwegian (14)	60	0.78
Polish (56)	137	1.79
Portuguese (0)	72	0.94
Romanian (0)	32	0.42
Russian (0)	41	0.54
Scotch-Irish (47)	122	1.59
Scottish (146)	532	6.95
Slavic (4)	4	0.05
Slovak (0)	28	0.37
Swedish (33)	196	2.56
Ukrainian (46)	81	1.06
Welsh (0)	42	0.55

Hispanic Origin	Population	%
Hispanic or Latino (of any race)	114	1.50
Central American, ex. Mexican	7	0.09
Costa Rican	1	0.01
Guatemalan	1	0.01
Honduran	4	0.05
Salvadoran	1	0.01
Cuban	9	0.12
Dominican Republic	8	0.11
Mexican	12	0.16
Puerto Rican	50	0.66
South American	5	0.07
Argentinean	4	0.05
Colombian	1	0.01
Other Hispanic or Latino	23	0.30

Race*	Population	%
African-American/Black (59)	94	1.24
Not Hispanic (54)	89	1.17
Hispanic (5)	5	0.07
American Indian/Alaska Native (51)	117	1.54
Not Hispanic (47)	112	1.47
Hispanic (4)	5	0.07
Alaska Athabascan *(Ala. Nat.)* (1)	1	0.01
Blackfeet (1)	5	0.07
Cherokee (1)	8	0.11
Crow (0)	1	0.01
Inupiat *(Alaska Native)* (0)	1	0.01
Iroquois (3)	9	0.12
Mexican American Ind. (1)	1	0.01
Navajo (1)	1	0.01
Sioux (1)	3	0.04

*Notes: † The Census 2010 population figure is used to calculate the percentages in the Hispanic Origin and Race categories. Ancestry percentages are based on the 2006-2010 American Community Survey population (not shown); ‡ Numbers in parentheses indicate the number of people reporting a single ancestry; * Numbers in parentheses indicate the number of persons reporting this race alone, not in combination with any other race; Please refer to the Explanation of Data for more information.*

Asian (89)	103	1.35
Not Hispanic (89)	103	1.35
Cambodian (1)	1	0.01
Chinese, ex. Taiwanese (28)	29	0.38
Filipino (7)	10	0.13
Indian (17)	18	0.24
Indonesian (1)	1	0.01
Japanese (4)	7	0.09
Korean (13)	20	0.26
Laotian (1)	3	0.04
Taiwanese (3)	3	0.04
Thai (4)	6	0.08
Vietnamese (8)	8	0.11
Hawaii Native/Pacific Islander (0)	1	0.01
Not Hispanic (0)	1	0.01
Native Hawaiian (0)	1	0.01
White (7,271)	7,371	96.95
Not Hispanic (7,187)	7,286	95.83
Hispanic (84)	85	1.12

Williston

Place Type: Town
County: Chittenden
Population: 8,698†

Ancestry‡	Population	%
African, Sub-Saharan (28)	28	0.33
African (28)	28	0.33
American (597)	597	7.03
Arab (17)	29	0.34
Lebanese (17)	29	0.34
Austrian (16)	42	0.49
British (47)	88	1.04
Canadian (30)	30	0.35
Czech (0)	55	0.65
Czechoslovakian (0)	14	0.16
Danish (29)	29	0.34
Dutch (30)	197	2.32
Eastern European (68)	68	0.80
English (538)	1,769	20.82
European (201)	201	2.37
Finnish (8)	23	0.27
French, ex. Basque (285)	1,066	12.55
French Canadian (502)	777	9.15
German (278)	1,217	14.32
German Russian (34)	34	0.40
Greek (69)	95	1.12
Hungarian (0)	39	0.46
Irish (697)	1,913	22.52
Italian (157)	630	7.42
Latvian (16)	32	0.38
Lithuanian (17)	33	0.39
Northern European (13)	13	0.15
Norwegian (14)	14	0.16
Pennsylvania German (0)	14	0.16
Polish (91)	270	3.18
Portuguese (0)	31	0.36
Romanian (0)	48	0.56
Russian (60)	145	1.71
Scandinavian (20)	20	0.24
Scotch-Irish (41)	195	2.30
Scottish (33)	234	2.75
Slovak (12)	12	0.14
Slovene (0)	17	0.20
Swedish (57)	112	1.32
Ukrainian (0)	16	0.19
Welsh (30)	134	1.58
Yugoslavian (15)	54	0.64

Hispanic Origin	Population	%
Hispanic or Latino (of any race)	127	1.46
Central American, ex. Mexican	11	0.13
Guatemalan	4	0.05
Honduran	1	0.01
Panamanian	6	0.07
Cuban	7	0.08
Dominican Republic	1	0.01
Mexican	31	0.36
Puerto Rican	23	0.26
South American	29	0.33
Argentinean	11	0.13
Chilean	5	0.06
Colombian	10	0.11
Peruvian	1	0.01
Uruguayan	2	0.02
Other Hispanic or Latino	25	0.29

Race*	Population	%
African-American/Black (87)	120	1.38
Not Hispanic (84)	115	1.32
Hispanic (3)	5	0.06
American Indian/Alaska Native (16)	34	0.39
Not Hispanic (16)	33	0.38
Hispanic (0)	1	0.01
Blackfeet (0)	2	0.02
Canadian/French Am. Ind. (2)	2	0.02
Central American Ind. (1)	2	0.02
Cherokee (2)	4	0.05
Paiute (1)	1	0.01
Sioux (0)	1	0.01
Asian (170)	210	2.41
Not Hispanic (170)	207	2.38
Hispanic (0)	3	0.03
Bangladeshi (3)	3	0.03
Cambodian (6)	7	0.08
Chinese, ex. Taiwanese (43)	50	0.57
Filipino (14)	15	0.17
Indian (42)	58	0.67
Japanese (7)	11	0.13
Korean (19)	23	0.26
Pakistani (2)	2	0.02
Taiwanese (2)	2	0.02
Thai (1)	2	0.02
Vietnamese (25)	29	0.33
Hawaii Native/Pacific Islander (0)	1	0.01
Not Hispanic (0)	1	0.01
White (8,314)	8,390	96.46
Not Hispanic (8,212)	8,274	95.13
Hispanic (102)	116	1.33

*Notes: † The Census 2010 population figure is used to calculate the percentages in the Hispanic Origin and Race categories. Ancestry percentages are based on the 2006-2010 American Community Survey population (not shown); ‡ Numbers in parentheses indicate the number of people reporting a single ancestry; * Numbers in parentheses indicate the number of persons reporting this race alone, not in combination with any other race; Please refer to the Explanation of Data for more information.*

VIRGINIA

Place Type: State
Population: 8,001,024[†]

Ancestry[‡]	Population	%
Afghan (10,032)	10,953	0.14
African, Sub-Saharan (139,196)	157,765	2.01
African (87,900)	101,824	1.30
Cape Verdean (654)	1,059	0.01
Ethiopian (18,119)	19,180	0.24
Ghanaian (8,784)	9,289	0.12
Kenyan (923)	1,135	0.01
Liberian (1,765)	2,087	0.03
Nigerian (4,895)	5,515	0.07
Senegalese (386)	551	0.01
Sierra Leonean (2,445)	2,475	0.03
Somalian (3,427)	3,460	0.04
South African (1,080)	1,420	0.02
Sudanese (3,212)	3,441	0.04
Ugandan (363)	416	0.01
Zimbabwean (141)	141	<0.01
Other Sub-Saharan African (5,102)	5,772	0.07
Albanian (2,026)	2,493	0.03
Alsatian (67)	258	<0.01
American (835,282)	835,282	10.65
Arab (35,664)	52,561	0.67
Arab (6,979)	9,329	0.12
Egyptian (5,552)	6,649	0.08
Iraqi (1,728)	1,958	0.02
Jordanian (1,180)	1,610	0.02
Lebanese (7,037)	14,509	0.19
Moroccan (4,122)	4,839	0.06
Palestinian (1,672)	2,371	0.03
Syrian (899)	2,769	0.04
Other Arab (6,495)	8,527	0.11
Armenian (2,834)	5,208	0.07
Assyrian/Chaldean/Syriac (244)	438	0.01
Australian (1,452)	2,692	0.03
Austrian (4,327)	16,342	0.21
Basque (121)	319	<0.01
Belgian (1,693)	5,213	0.07
Brazilian (3,842)	5,078	0.06
British (27,588)	51,637	0.66
Bulgarian (1,277)	1,989	0.03
Cajun (566)	1,295	0.02
Canadian (7,054)	14,555	0.19
Carpatho Rusyn (30)	112	<0.01
Celtic (1,037)	1,825	0.02
Croatian (2,055)	6,245	0.08
Cypriot (202)	246	<0.01
Czech (6,401)	24,760	0.32
Czechoslovakian (2,663)	5,977	0.08
Danish (5,158)	19,482	0.25
Dutch (18,864)	91,260	1.16
Eastern European (8,245)	9,708	0.12
English (393,788)	921,368	11.75
Estonian (473)	917	0.01
European (90,007)	101,514	1.29
Finnish (2,292)	7,593	0.10
French, ex. Basque (31,722)	166,835	2.13
French Canadian (13,399)	32,231	0.41
German (311,523)	1,011,507	12.90
German Russian (189)	457	0.01
Greek (17,282)	34,660	0.44
Guyanese (1,444)	2,032	0.03
Hungarian (8,537)	29,610	0.38
Icelander (637)	1,216	0.02
Iranian (16,652)	18,768	0.24
Irish (261,943)	845,204	10.78
Israeli (1,027)	1,494	0.02
Italian (108,536)	317,539	4.05
Latvian (717)	1,911	0.02
Lithuanian (4,159)	14,636	0.19
Luxemburger (147)	551	0.01
Macedonian (357)	676	0.01
Maltese (227)	510	0.01
New Zealander (465)	716	0.01
Northern European (6,328)	7,054	0.09
Norwegian (14,963)	50,733	0.65
Pennsylvania German (1,787)	3,235	0.04
Polish (45,588)	155,128	1.98
Portuguese (6,012)	15,036	0.19
Romanian (4,479)	8,442	0.11
Russian (21,683)	55,000	0.70
Scandinavian (4,356)	10,867	0.14
Scotch-Irish (93,242)	201,730	2.57
Scottish (62,608)	188,707	2.41
Serbian (1,370)	3,514	0.04
Slavic (1,337)	4,021	0.05
Slovak (4,574)	15,111	0.19
Slovene (825)	2,934	0.04
Soviet Union (38)	47	<0.01
Swedish (14,540)	60,352	0.77
Swiss (4,297)	20,872	0.27
Turkish (6,484)	8,040	0.10
Ukrainian (7,400)	18,941	0.24
Welsh (12,996)	58,256	0.74
West Indian, ex. Hispanic (23,444)	35,551	0.45
Bahamian (297)	534	0.01
Barbadian (605)	960	0.01
Belizean (715)	988	0.01
Bermudan (162)	233	<0.01
British West Indian (889)	1,335	0.02
Dutch West Indian (123)	310	<0.01
Haitian (4,096)	5,229	0.07
Jamaican (9,899)	15,574	0.20
Trinidadian/Tobagonian (2,867)	3,765	0.05
U.S. Virgin Islander (522)	682	0.01
West Indian (3,246)	5,880	0.07
Other West Indian (23)	61	<0.01
Yugoslavian (3,872)	5,936	0.08

Hispanic Origin	Population	%
Hispanic or Latino (of any race)	631,825	7.90
Central American, ex. Mexican	206,568	2.58
Costa Rican	2,630	0.03
Guatemalan	33,556	0.42
Honduran	30,583	0.38
Nicaraguan	7,388	0.09
Panamanian	7,180	0.09
Salvadoran	123,800	1.55
Other Central American	1,431	0.02
Cuban	15,229	0.19
Dominican Republic	10,504	0.13
Mexican	155,067	1.94
Puerto Rican	73,958	0.92
South American	101,480	1.27
Argentinean	6,263	0.08
Bolivian	31,333	0.39
Chilean	4,195	0.05
Colombian	15,797	0.20
Ecuadorian	6,902	0.09
Paraguayan	924	0.01
Peruvian	29,096	0.36
Uruguayan	1,594	0.02
Venezuelan	4,429	0.06
Other South American	947	0.01
Other Hispanic or Latino	69,019	0.86

Race*	Population	%
African-American/Black (1,551,399)	1,653,563	20.67
Not Hispanic (1,523,704)	1,611,361	20.14
Hispanic (27,695)	42,202	0.53
American Indian/Alaska Native (29,225)	80,924	1.01
Not Hispanic (20,679)	62,978	0.79
Hispanic (8,546)	17,946	0.22
Alaska Athabascan *(Ala. Nat.)* (45)	95	<0.01
Aleut *(Alaska Native)* (59)	99	<0.01
Apache (293)	860	0.01
Arapaho (26)	55	<0.01
Blackfeet (315)	2,209	0.03
Canadian/French Am. Ind. (116)	251	<0.01
Central American Ind. (401)	669	0.01
Cherokee (3,625)	17,433	0.22
Cheyenne (44)	145	<0.01
Chickasaw (154)	361	<0.01
Chippewa (440)	902	0.01
Choctaw (484)	1,386	0.02
Colville (13)	20	<0.01
Comanche (98)	275	<0.01
Cree (37)	131	<0.01
Creek (292)	715	0.01
Crow (44)	134	<0.01
Delaware (86)	301	<0.01
Hopi (25)	56	<0.01
Houma (19)	35	<0.01
Inupiat *(Alaska Native)* (91)	170	<0.01
Iroquois (560)	1,410	0.02
Kiowa (47)	81	<0.01
Lumbee (798)	1,302	0.02
Menominee (20)	39	<0.01
Mexican American Ind. (1,295)	1,979	0.02
Navajo (419)	753	0.01
Osage (69)	153	<0.01
Ottawa (53)	110	<0.01
Paiute (13)	34	<0.01
Pima (20)	40	<0.01
Potawatomi (130)	230	<0.01
Pueblo (135)	237	<0.01
Puget Sound Salish (22)	39	<0.01
Seminole (83)	439	0.01
Shoshone (26)	60	<0.01
Sioux (473)	1,356	0.02
South American Ind. (656)	1,526	0.02
Spanish American Ind. (272)	418	0.01
Tlingit-Haida *(Alaska Native)* (52)	107	<0.01
Tohono O'Odham (25)	61	<0.01
Tsimshian *(Alaska Native)* (3)	11	<0.01
Ute (18)	60	<0.01
Yakama (8)	16	<0.01
Yaqui (34)	83	<0.01
Yuman (16)	34	<0.01
Yup'ik *(Alaska Native)* (21)	36	<0.01
Asian (439,890)	522,199	6.53
Not Hispanic (436,298)	512,103	6.40
Hispanic (3,592)	10,096	0.13
Bangladeshi (5,848)	6,552	0.08
Bhutanese (442)	514	0.01
Burmese (1,463)	1,668	0.02
Cambodian (6,178)	7,306	0.09
Chinese, ex. Taiwanese (56,244)	68,707	0.86
Filipino (66,963)	90,493	1.13
Hmong (154)	188	<0.01
Indian (103,916)	114,471	1.43
Indonesian (1,745)	2,351	0.03
Japanese (9,471)	20,138	0.25
Korean (70,577)	82,006	1.02
Laotian (3,253)	3,980	0.05
Malaysian (557)	857	0.01
Nepalese (4,402)	4,770	0.06
Pakistani (24,464)	27,100	0.34
Sri Lankan (1,302)	1,529	0.02
Taiwanese (3,321)	4,130	0.05
Thai (6,729)	9,170	0.11
Vietnamese (53,529)	59,984	0.75
Hawaii Native/Pacific Islander (5,980)	15,422	0.19
Not Hispanic (5,061)	12,670	0.16
Hispanic (919)	2,752	0.03
Fijian (79)	136	<0.01
Guamanian/Chamorro (2,222)	3,592	0.04
Marshallese (39)	64	<0.01
Native Hawaiian (1,410)	4,699	0.06
Samoan (749)	1,569	0.02
Tongan (83)	138	<0.01
White (5,486,852)	5,681,937	71.02
Not Hispanic (5,186,450)	5,341,329	66.76
Hispanic (300,402)	340,608	4.26

*Notes: † The Census 2010 population figure is used to calculate the percentages in the Hispanic Origin and Race categories. Ancestry percentages are based on the 2006-2010 American Community Survey population (not shown); ‡ Numbers in parentheses indicate the number of people reporting a single ancestry; * Numbers in parentheses indicate the number of persons reporting this race alone, not in combination with any other race; Please refer to the Explanation of Data for more information.*

Abingdon

Place Type: Town
County: Washington
Population: 8,191†

Ancestry‡	Population	%
African, Sub-Saharan (0)	51	0.63
African (0)	51	0.63
American (904)	904	11.12
British (0)	27	0.33
Croatian (11)	11	0.14
Czechoslovakian (0)	19	0.23
Danish (33)	33	0.41
Dutch (18)	29	0.36
English (359)	721	8.87
European (149)	186	2.29
French, ex. Basque (31)	100	1.23
German (537)	1,132	13.93
Hungarian (11)	46	0.57
Irish (438)	972	11.96
Italian (30)	170	2.09
Northern European (11)	11	0.14
Norwegian (0)	5	0.06
Polish (199)	288	3.54
Romanian (0)	12	0.15
Russian (37)	37	0.46
Scandinavian (13)	13	0.16
Scotch-Irish (412)	647	7.96
Scottish (194)	395	4.86
Swedish (42)	143	1.76
Swiss (12)	40	0.49
Welsh (22)	75	0.92
Yugoslavian (0)	23	0.28

Hispanic Origin	Population	%
Hispanic or Latino (of any race)	209	2.55
Central American, ex. Mexican	6	0.07
Guatemalan	1	0.01
Honduran	2	0.02
Salvadoran	3	0.04
Cuban	8	0.10
Dominican Republic	3	0.04
Mexican	134	1.64
Puerto Rican	15	0.18
South American	5	0.06
Argentinean	2	0.02
Chilean	1	0.01
Colombian	2	0.02
Other Hispanic or Latino	38	0.46

Race*	Population	%
African-American/Black (257)	301	3.67
Not Hispanic (257)	301	3.67
American Indian/Alaska Native (15)	44	0.54
Not Hispanic (15)	43	0.52
Hispanic (0)	1	0.01
Alaska Athabascan *(Ala. Nat.)* (3)	3	0.04
Blackfeet (0)	1	0.01
Cherokee (4)	18	0.22
Cheyenne (1)	1	0.01
Delaware (1)	1	0.01
Iroquois (0)	1	0.01
Lumbee (1)	1	0.01
Asian (86)	104	1.27
Not Hispanic (86)	104	1.27
Chinese, ex. Taiwanese (19)	20	0.24
Filipino (10)	20	0.24
Indian (12)	14	0.17
Indonesian (1)	1	0.01
Japanese (2)	6	0.07
Korean (7)	10	0.12
Laotian (3)	3	0.04
Pakistani (19)	20	0.24
Vietnamese (9)	10	0.12
Hawaii Native/Pacific Islander (6)	11	0.13
Not Hispanic (0)	5	0.06
Hispanic (6)	6	0.07
Guamanian/Chamorro (0)	1	0.01
Native Hawaiian (0)	4	0.05
White (7,681)	7,755	94.68
Not Hispanic (7,540)	7,611	92.92
Hispanic (141)	144	1.76

Alexandria

Place Type: Independent City
County: Alexandria
Population: 139,966†

Ancestry‡	Population	%
Afghan (669)	701	0.52
African, Sub-Saharan (9,747)	10,686	8.00
African (2,741)	3,054	2.29
Cape Verdean (13)	42	0.03
Ethiopian (3,499)	3,617	2.71
Ghanaian (815)	923	0.69
Kenyan (16)	16	0.01
Liberian (17)	235	0.18
Nigerian (225)	272	0.20
Senegalese (48)	48	0.04
Sierra Leonean (833)	863	0.65
Somalian (560)	560	0.42
South African (45)	54	0.04
Sudanese (415)	450	0.34
Zimbabwean (31)	31	0.02
Other Sub-Saharan African (489)	521	0.39
Albanian (36)	36	0.03
Alsatian (9)	23	0.02
American (3,640)	3,640	2.72
Arab (1,372)	2,458	1.84
Arab (91)	194	0.15
Egyptian (338)	407	0.30
Iraqi (119)	119	0.09
Jordanian (56)	281	0.21
Lebanese (135)	366	0.27
Moroccan (328)	337	0.25
Palestinian (77)	122	0.09
Syrian (47)	379	0.28
Other Arab (181)	253	0.19
Armenian (148)	266	0.20
Assyrian/Chaldean/Syriac (0)	10	0.01
Australian (55)	101	0.08
Austrian (141)	689	0.52
Basque (6)	27	0.02
Belgian (22)	114	0.09
Brazilian (177)	274	0.21
British (762)	1,439	1.08
Bulgarian (44)	54	0.04
Cajun (35)	115	0.09
Canadian (150)	252	0.19
Carpatho Rusyn (14)	14	0.01
Celtic (74)	108	0.08
Croatian (52)	195	0.15
Cypriot (8)	8	0.01
Czech (139)	647	0.48
Czechoslovakian (17)	45	0.03
Danish (59)	463	0.35
Dutch (476)	1,734	1.30
Eastern European (440)	531	0.40
English (4,063)	14,500	10.85
Estonian (22)	54	0.04
European (1,913)	2,158	1.61
Finnish (76)	234	0.18
French, ex. Basque (454)	3,061	2.29
French Canadian (190)	810	0.61
German (4,553)	17,325	12.96
German Russian (14)	14	0.01
Greek (347)	673	0.50
Guyanese (82)	102	0.08
Hungarian (141)	577	0.43
Icelander (37)	46	0.03
Iranian (623)	658	0.49
Irish (4,331)	15,860	11.87
Israeli (19)	35	0.03
Italian (2,028)	6,580	4.92
Latvian (0)	46	0.03
Lithuanian (147)	570	0.43
Macedonian (9)	9	0.01
Northern European (634)	646	0.48
Norwegian (231)	1,182	0.88
Polish (901)	3,729	2.79
Portuguese (39)	271	0.20
Romanian (334)	369	0.28
Russian (612)	1,494	1.12
Scandinavian (81)	196	0.15
Scotch-Irish (1,540)	3,602	2.70
Scottish (885)	3,670	2.75
Serbian (88)	171	0.13
Slavic (19)	176	0.13
Slovak (78)	498	0.37
Slovene (26)	52	0.04
Swedish (256)	1,304	0.98
Swiss (89)	572	0.43
Turkish (248)	317	0.24
Ukrainian (209)	593	0.44
Welsh (227)	1,404	1.05
West Indian, ex. Hispanic (640)	835	0.62
Bahamian (13)	13	0.01
Belizean (53)	53	0.04
Bermudan (17)	17	0.01
British West Indian (38)	45	0.03
Dutch West Indian (33)	33	0.02
Haitian (61)	61	0.05
Jamaican (271)	376	0.28
Trinidadian/Tobagonian (69)	79	0.06
U.S. Virgin Islander (51)	60	0.04
West Indian (22)	86	0.06
Other West Indian (12)	12	0.01
Yugoslavian (18)	73	0.05

Hispanic Origin	Population	%
Hispanic or Latino (of any race)	22,524	16.09
Central American, ex. Mexican	10,963	7.83
Costa Rican	87	0.06
Guatemalan	1,587	1.13
Honduran	2,243	1.60
Nicaraguan	368	0.26
Panamanian	203	0.15
Salvadoran	6,436	4.60
Other Central American	39	0.03
Cuban	399	0.29
Dominican Republic	302	0.22
Mexican	2,352	1.68
Puerto Rican	1,603	1.15
South American	4,202	3.00
Argentinean	303	0.22
Bolivian	1,227	0.88
Chilean	274	0.20
Colombian	599	0.43
Ecuadorian	280	0.20
Paraguayan	39	0.03
Peruvian	1,174	0.84
Uruguayan	58	0.04
Venezuelan	229	0.16
Other South American	19	0.01
Other Hispanic or Latino	2,703	1.93

Race*	Population	%
African-American/Black (30,491)	32,378	23.13
Not Hispanic (29,778)	31,262	22.34
Hispanic (713)	1,116	0.80
American Indian/Alaska Native (589)	1,508	1.08
Not Hispanic (327)	958	0.68
Hispanic (262)	550	0.39
Alaska Athabascan *(Ala. Nat.)* (0)	1	<0.01
Aleut *(Alaska Native)* (1)	3	<0.01
Apache (1)	15	0.01
Blackfeet (6)	37	0.03
Canadian/French Am. Ind. (1)	5	<0.01
Central American Ind. (23)	32	0.02
Cherokee (47)	248	0.18
Cheyenne (1)	2	<0.01
Chickasaw (4)	7	0.01
Chippewa (8)	24	0.02
Choctaw (10)	29	0.02
Comanche (2)	4	<0.01
Cree (0)	3	<0.01
Creek (5)	12	0.01
Delaware (3)	5	<0.01

*Notes: † The Census 2010 population figure is used to calculate the percentages in the Hispanic Origin and Race categories. Ancestry percentages are based on the 2006-2010 American Community Survey population (not shown); ‡ Numbers in parentheses indicate the number of people reporting a single ancestry; * Numbers in parentheses indicate the number of persons reporting this race alone, not in combination with any other race; Please refer to the Explanation of Data for more information.*

Hopi (1)	1	<0.01
Houma (2)	2	<0.01
Iroquois (10)	24	0.02
Kiowa (2)	3	<0.01
Lumbee (13)	19	0.01
Menominee (0)	1	<0.01
Mexican American Ind. (39)	75	0.05
Navajo (18)	23	0.02
Osage (4)	8	0.01
Ottawa (2)	4	<0.01
Pima (1)	1	<0.01
Potawatomi (0)	8	0.01
Pueblo (11)	15	0.01
Puget Sound Salish (0)	1	<0.01
Seminole (0)	12	0.01
Shoshone (1)	1	<0.01
Sioux (7)	29	0.02
South American Ind. (16)	38	0.03
Spanish American Ind. (13)	15	0.01
Tlingit-Haida *(Alaska Native)* (1)	6	<0.01
Ute (1)	1	<0.01
Yaqui (0)	1	<0.01
Yuman (0)	2	<0.01
Asian (8,432)	10,441	7.46
Not Hispanic (8,351)	10,182	7.27
Hispanic (81)	259	0.19
Bangladeshi (305)	351	0.25
Burmese (25)	26	0.02
Cambodian (62)	87	0.06
Chinese, ex. Taiwanese (1,218)	1,505	1.08
Filipino (1,379)	1,780	1.27
Hmong (4)	4	<0.01
Indian (1,761)	2,098	1.50
Indonesian (77)	93	0.07
Japanese (280)	534	0.38
Korean (1,143)	1,365	0.98
Laotian (45)	60	0.04
Malaysian (7)	15	0.01
Nepalese (129)	148	0.11
Pakistani (587)	648	0.46
Sri Lankan (35)	41	0.03
Taiwanese (82)	110	0.08
Thai (234)	312	0.22
Vietnamese (485)	577	0.41
Hawaii Native/Pacific Islander (141)	363	0.26
Not Hispanic (109)	291	0.21
Hispanic (32)	72	0.05
Fijian (1)	4	<0.01
Guamanian/Chamorro (53)	83	0.06
Marshallese (0)	1	<0.01
Native Hawaiian (35)	93	0.07
Samoan (19)	37	0.03
Tongan (1)	1	<0.01
White (85,186)	89,445	63.90
Not Hispanic (74,878)	77,725	55.53
Hispanic (10,308)	11,720	8.37

Annandale

Place Type: CDP
County: Fairfax
Population: 41,008†

Ancestry‡	Population	%
Afghan (650)	650	1.69
African, Sub-Saharan (1,168)	1,222	3.18
African (450)	466	1.21
Ethiopian (579)	579	1.51
Ghanaian (31)	31	0.08
Sierra Leonean (9)	9	0.02
Sudanese (55)	55	0.14
Other Sub-Saharan African (44)	82	0.21
Albanian (0)	11	0.03
American (872)	872	2.27
Arab (688)	775	2.02
Arab (13)	13	0.03
Jordanian (0)	22	0.06
Lebanese (189)	254	0.66
Moroccan (121)	121	0.31
Palestinian (120)	120	0.31
Syrian (26)	26	0.07
Other Arab (219)	219	0.57
Armenian (19)	45	0.12
Austrian (51)	159	0.41
Belgian (0)	14	0.04
Brazilian (63)	87	0.23
British (55)	137	0.36
Bulgarian (0)	26	0.07
Canadian (45)	88	0.23
Celtic (0)	8	0.02
Croatian (23)	23	0.06
Czech (42)	155	0.40
Czechoslovakian (37)	37	0.10
Danish (43)	149	0.39
Dutch (60)	342	0.89
Eastern European (28)	38	0.10
English (817)	2,486	6.47
European (457)	556	1.45
French, ex. Basque (174)	782	2.03
French Canadian (14)	153	0.40
German (1,164)	3,624	9.43
Greek (201)	321	0.84
Hungarian (47)	153	0.40
Icelander (8)	8	0.02
Iranian (152)	182	0.47
Irish (878)	3,205	8.34
Italian (329)	1,219	3.17
Lithuanian (7)	17	0.04
New Zealander (34)	34	0.09
Northern European (15)	15	0.04
Norwegian (104)	296	0.77
Polish (172)	562	1.46
Portuguese (36)	95	0.25
Romanian (79)	91	0.24
Russian (149)	345	0.90
Scandinavian (15)	58	0.15
Scotch-Irish (146)	501	1.30
Scottish (231)	652	1.70
Slovak (23)	41	0.11
Swedish (28)	150	0.39
Swiss (18)	59	0.15
Turkish (0)	26	0.07
Ukrainian (47)	78	0.20
Welsh (52)	216	0.56
West Indian, ex. Hispanic (93)	105	0.27
Haitian (38)	38	0.10
Jamaican (35)	35	0.09
Trinidadian/Tobagonian (20)	32	0.08

Hispanic Origin	Population	%
Hispanic or Latino (of any race)	11,326	27.62
Central American, ex. Mexican	4,487	10.94
Costa Rican	22	0.05
Guatemalan	736	1.79
Honduran	611	1.49
Nicaraguan	262	0.64
Panamanian	40	0.10
Salvadoran	2,770	6.75
Other Central American	46	0.11
Cuban	123	0.30
Dominican Republic	107	0.26
Mexican	626	1.53
Puerto Rican	338	0.82
South American	4,473	10.91
Argentinean	313	0.76
Bolivian	2,740	6.68
Chilean	73	0.18
Colombian	196	0.48
Ecuadorian	118	0.29
Paraguayan	11	0.03
Peruvian	917	2.24
Uruguayan	24	0.06
Venezuelan	52	0.13
Other South American	29	0.07
Other Hispanic or Latino	1,172	2.86

Race*	Population	%
African-American/Black (3,533)	3,822	9.32
Not Hispanic (3,408)	3,639	8.87
Hispanic (125)	183	0.45
American Indian/Alaska Native (212)	414	1.01
Not Hispanic (80)	192	0.47
Hispanic (132)	222	0.54
Apache (3)	9	0.02
Blackfeet (2)	4	0.01
Central American Ind. (4)	7	0.02
Cherokee (9)	46	0.11
Chickasaw (0)	1	<0.01
Chippewa (3)	4	0.01
Comanche (0)	1	<0.01
Creek (0)	3	0.01
Delaware (5)	6	0.01
Iroquois (4)	9	0.02
Lumbee (0)	1	<0.01
Mexican American Ind. (18)	24	0.06
Navajo (9)	10	0.02
Osage (0)	1	<0.01
Potawatomi (1)	1	<0.01
Pueblo (2)	2	<0.01
Sioux (0)	1	<0.01
South American Ind. (29)	47	0.11
Spanish American Ind. (1)	1	<0.01
Asian (10,103)	10,890	26.56
Not Hispanic (10,050)	10,774	26.27
Hispanic (53)	116	0.28
Bangladeshi (73)	82	0.20
Burmese (15)	17	0.04
Cambodian (181)	218	0.53
Chinese, ex. Taiwanese (678)	834	2.03
Filipino (610)	728	1.78
Indian (807)	943	2.30
Indonesian (35)	45	0.11
Japanese (59)	102	0.25
Korean (3,256)	3,380	8.24
Laotian (32)	33	0.08
Malaysian (5)	8	0.02
Nepalese (90)	96	0.23
Pakistani (496)	571	1.39
Sri Lankan (10)	11	0.03
Taiwanese (16)	23	0.06
Thai (86)	105	0.26
Vietnamese (3,297)	3,467	8.45
Hawaii Native/Pacific Islander (53)	144	0.35
Not Hispanic (43)	95	0.23
Hispanic (10)	49	0.12
Guamanian/Chamorro (18)	24	0.06
Native Hawaiian (18)	36	0.09
Samoan (5)	5	0.01
White (20,670)	22,111	53.92
Not Hispanic (14,986)	15,855	38.66
Hispanic (5,684)	6,256	15.26

Arlington

Place Type: CDP
County: Arlington
Population: 207,627†

Ancestry‡	Population	%
Afghan (120)	160	0.08
African, Sub-Saharan (4,016)	4,902	2.48
African (1,468)	1,829	0.93
Cape Verdean (0)	11	0.01
Ethiopian (1,675)	1,974	1.00
Ghanaian (175)	175	0.09
Kenyan (141)	203	0.10
Nigerian (20)	47	0.02
Somalian (34)	34	0.02
South African (18)	29	0.01
Sudanese (292)	292	0.15
Ugandan (0)	13	0.01
Other Sub-Saharan African (193)	295	0.15
Albanian (222)	234	0.12
Alsatian (10)	40	0.02
American (5,396)	5,396	2.73
Arab (1,651)	2,931	1.48
Arab (406)	725	0.37
Egyptian (230)	299	0.15
Iraqi (190)	258	0.13
Jordanian (62)	128	0.06

*Notes: † The Census 2010 population figure is used to calculate the percentages in the Hispanic Origin and Race categories. Ancestry percentages are based on the 2006-2010 American Community Survey population (not shown); ‡ Numbers in parentheses indicate the number of people reporting a single ancestry; * Numbers in parentheses indicate the number of persons reporting this race alone, not in combination with any other race; Please refer to the Explanation of Data for more information.*

Lebanese (226)	672	0.34
Moroccan (139)	175	0.09
Palestinian (27)	77	0.04
Syrian (47)	119	0.06
Other Arab (324)	478	0.24
Armenian (84)	160	0.08
Assyrian/Chaldean/Syriac (0)	57	0.03
Australian (109)	150	0.08
Austrian (309)	1,139	0.58
Basque (10)	26	0.01
Belgian (60)	210	0.11
Brazilian (96)	222	0.11
British (1,124)	2,177	1.10
Bulgarian (85)	85	0.04
Cajun (13)	32	0.02
Canadian (160)	340	0.17
Celtic (43)	94	0.05
Croatian (189)	550	0.28
Czech (172)	1,076	0.54
Czechoslovakian (12)	103	0.05
Danish (277)	945	0.48
Dutch (442)	2,197	1.11
Eastern European (1,140)	1,323	0.67
English (5,528)	22,268	11.28
Estonian (7)	18	0.01
European (3,409)	3,919	1.98
Finnish (75)	357	0.18
French, ex. Basque (674)	4,199	2.13
French Canadian (446)	1,204	0.61
German (6,672)	26,481	13.41
German Russian (13)	13	0.01
Greek (791)	1,390	0.70
Guyanese (146)	146	0.07
Hungarian (299)	1,325	0.67
Icelander (70)	88	0.04
Iranian (657)	865	0.44
Irish (7,407)	26,567	13.45
Israeli (94)	110	0.06
Italian (3,409)	11,299	5.72
Latvian (51)	92	0.05
Lithuanian (166)	997	0.50
Luxemburger (9)	37	0.02
Macedonian (0)	10	0.01
Maltese (0)	8	<0.01
New Zealander (42)	68	0.03
Northern European (479)	592	0.30
Norwegian (599)	2,116	1.07
Pennsylvania German (48)	122	0.06
Polish (1,494)	6,664	3.37
Portuguese (325)	663	0.34
Romanian (64)	315	0.16
Russian (1,355)	4,145	2.10
Scandinavian (177)	364	0.18
Scotch-Irish (1,933)	5,275	2.67
Scottish (1,402)	5,607	2.84
Serbian (87)	301	0.15
Slavic (11)	112	0.06
Slovak (131)	628	0.32
Slovene (17)	184	0.09
Soviet Union (26)	26	0.01
Swedish (593)	2,581	1.31
Swiss (160)	787	0.40
Turkish (280)	355	0.18
Ukrainian (490)	1,375	0.70
Welsh (309)	1,767	0.89
West Indian, ex. Hispanic (462)	804	0.41
Bahamian (15)	26	0.01
Barbadian (14)	47	0.02
Bermudan (5)	5	<0.01
British West Indian (0)	43	0.02
Haitian (33)	33	0.02
Jamaican (277)	471	0.24
Trinidadian/Tobagonian (38)	38	0.02
West Indian (80)	141	0.07
Yugoslavian (111)	190	0.10

Hispanic Origin	Population	%
Hispanic or Latino (of any race)	31,382	15.11
Central American, ex. Mexican	12,171	5.86
Costa Rican	185	0.09
Guatemalan	3,017	1.45
Honduran	881	0.42
Nicaraguan	614	0.30
Panamanian	217	0.10
Salvadoran	7,088	3.41
Other Central American	169	0.08
Cuban	699	0.34
Dominican Republic	348	0.17
Mexican	3,590	1.73
Puerto Rican	1,664	0.80
South American	9,089	4.38
Argentinean	719	0.35
Bolivian	4,225	2.03
Chilean	302	0.15
Colombian	1,204	0.58
Ecuadorian	452	0.22
Paraguayan	113	0.05
Peruvian	1,531	0.74
Uruguayan	129	0.06
Venezuelan	279	0.13
Other South American	135	0.07
Other Hispanic or Latino	3,821	1.84

Race*	Population	%
African-American/Black (17,632)	19,465	9.37
Not Hispanic (17,088)	18,539	8.93
Hispanic (544)	926	0.45
American Indian/Alaska Native (971)	2,366	1.14
Not Hispanic (394)	1,192	0.57
Hispanic (577)	1,174	0.57
Alaska Athabascan *(Ala. Nat.)* (3)	5	<0.01
Aleut *(Alaska Native)* (1)	1	<0.01
Apache (2)	14	0.01
Arapaho (2)	3	<0.01
Blackfeet (4)	25	0.01
Canadian/French Am. Ind. (1)	9	<0.01
Central American Ind. (39)	61	0.03
Cherokee (73)	320	0.15
Cheyenne (2)	4	<0.01
Chickasaw (3)	9	<0.01
Chippewa (8)	15	0.01
Choctaw (18)	47	0.02
Comanche (1)	4	<0.01
Cree (0)	1	<0.01
Creek (12)	17	0.01
Crow (6)	8	<0.01
Delaware (0)	2	<0.01
Hopi (0)	1	<0.01
Houma (0)	1	<0.01
Inupiat *(Alaska Native)* (1)	8	<0.01
Iroquois (10)	35	0.02
Kiowa (1)	3	<0.01
Lumbee (6)	12	0.01
Menominee (1)	1	<0.01
Mexican American Ind. (96)	137	0.07
Navajo (16)	27	0.01
Osage (2)	7	<0.01
Paiute (3)	3	<0.01
Potawatomi (2)	5	<0.01
Pueblo (8)	16	0.01
Seminole (4)	12	0.01
Shoshone (0)	1	<0.01
Sioux (24)	45	0.02
South American Ind. (68)	156	0.08
Spanish American Ind. (15)	31	0.01
Tlingit-Haida *(Alaska Native)* (5)	9	<0.01
Tohono O'Odham (4)	4	<0.01
Ute (1)	2	<0.01
Yakama (0)	1	<0.01
Yaqui (0)	1	<0.01
Asian (19,931)	23,678	11.40
Not Hispanic (19,762)	23,197	11.17
Hispanic (169)	481	0.23
Bangladeshi (725)	802	0.39
Bhutanese (5)	5	<0.01
Burmese (38)	44	0.02
Cambodian (311)	362	0.17
Chinese, ex. Taiwanese (3,208)	4,053	1.95
Filipino (2,274)	2,998	1.44
Hmong (8)	8	<0.01
Indian (4,154)	4,813	2.32
Indonesian (180)	208	0.10
Japanese (969)	1,582	0.76
Korean (1,849)	2,270	1.09
Laotian (116)	139	0.07
Malaysian (58)	78	0.04
Nepalese (473)	506	0.24
Pakistani (959)	1,113	0.54
Sri Lankan (166)	185	0.09
Taiwanese (301)	352	0.17
Thai (550)	672	0.32
Vietnamese (1,462)	1,767	0.85
Hawaii Native/Pacific Islander (171)	491	0.24
Not Hispanic (133)	393	0.19
Hispanic (38)	98	0.05
Fijian (6)	8	<0.01
Guamanian/Chamorro (66)	99	0.05
Marshallese (1)	1	<0.01
Native Hawaiian (38)	138	0.07
Samoan (15)	39	0.02
Tongan (0)	6	<0.01
White (148,970)	155,517	74.90
Not Hispanic (132,961)	137,530	66.24
Hispanic (16,009)	17,987	8.66

Ashburn

Place Type: CDP
County: Loudoun
Population: 43,511†

Ancestry‡	Population	%
Afghan (256)	256	0.60
African, Sub-Saharan (603)	703	1.66
African (213)	297	0.70
Ethiopian (179)	179	0.42
Ghanaian (26)	26	0.06
Nigerian (90)	90	0.21
Somalian (0)	16	0.04
Other Sub-Saharan African (95)	95	0.22
Albanian (51)	51	0.12
American (1,921)	1,921	4.53
Arab (159)	454	1.07
Arab (59)	144	0.34
Egyptian (11)	30	0.07
Lebanese (55)	79	0.19
Syrian (0)	31	0.07
Other Arab (34)	170	0.40
Armenian (10)	10	0.02
Assyrian/Chaldean/Syriac (9)	9	0.02
Austrian (44)	196	0.46
Belgian (16)	16	0.04
British (230)	405	0.96
Canadian (49)	160	0.38
Celtic (11)	11	0.03
Croatian (10)	111	0.26
Czech (36)	211	0.50
Czechoslovakian (8)	8	0.02
Danish (15)	100	0.24
Dutch (144)	692	1.63
Eastern European (31)	74	0.17
English (1,377)	5,247	12.38
European (767)	791	1.87
Finnish (16)	156	0.37
French, ex. Basque (95)	877	2.07
French Canadian (69)	270	0.64
German (1,469)	7,658	18.07
Greek (208)	325	0.77
Guyanese (0)	11	0.03
Hungarian (95)	476	1.12
Iranian (661)	715	1.69
Irish (1,781)	6,301	14.87
Italian (1,152)	3,403	8.03
Lithuanian (66)	202	0.48
Macedonian (33)	40	0.09
Maltese (0)	5	0.01
Northern European (13)	39	0.09
Norwegian (357)	689	1.63
Pennsylvania German (6)	6	0.01
Polish (296)	1,504	3.55

*Notes: † The Census 2010 population figure is used to calculate the percentages in the Hispanic Origin and Race categories. Ancestry percentages are based on the 2006-2010 American Community Survey population (not shown); ‡ Numbers in parentheses indicate the number of people reporting a single ancestry; * Numbers in parentheses indicate the number of persons reporting this race alone, not in combination with any other race; Please refer to the Explanation of Data for more information.*

Portuguese (0)	104	0.25
Romanian (88)	109	0.26
Russian (342)	597	1.41
Scandinavian (54)	141	0.33
Scotch-Irish (304)	840	1.98
Scottish (279)	850	2.01
Serbian (14)	14	0.03
Slavic (0)	8	0.02
Slovak (15)	165	0.39
Slovene (13)	24	0.06
Swedish (46)	516	1.22
Swiss (44)	186	0.44
Turkish (193)	193	0.46
Ukrainian (36)	190	0.45
Welsh (80)	303	0.72
West Indian, ex. Hispanic (111)	160	0.38
Haitian (22)	52	0.12
Jamaican (69)	79	0.19
Trinidadian/Tobagonian (9)	9	0.02
West Indian (11)	20	0.05
Yugoslavian (0)	13	0.03

Hispanic Origin	Population	%
Hispanic or Latino (of any race)	4,245	9.76
Central American, ex. Mexican	904	2.08
Costa Rican	16	0.04
Guatemalan	121	0.28
Honduran	108	0.25
Nicaraguan	44	0.10
Panamanian	47	0.11
Salvadoran	560	1.29
Other Central American	8	0.02
Cuban	174	0.40
Dominican Republic	76	0.17
Mexican	635	1.46
Puerto Rican	440	1.01
South American	1,526	3.51
Argentinean	68	0.16
Bolivian	195	0.45
Chilean	38	0.09
Colombian	258	0.59
Ecuadorian	93	0.21
Paraguayan	6	0.01
Peruvian	751	1.73
Uruguayan	12	0.03
Venezuelan	96	0.22
Other South American	9	0.02
Other Hispanic or Latino	490	1.13

Race*	Population	%
African-American/Black (3,423)	3,924	9.02
Not Hispanic (3,302)	3,717	8.54
Hispanic (121)	207	0.48
American Indian/Alaska Native (120)	286	0.66
Not Hispanic (69)	211	0.48
Hispanic (51)	75	0.17
Blackfeet (0)	4	0.01
Canadian/French Am. Ind. (0)	1	<0.01
Cherokee (12)	60	0.14
Chippewa (1)	3	0.01
Choctaw (2)	16	0.04
Creek (1)	4	0.01
Inupiat *(Alaska Native)* (2)	2	<0.01
Iroquois (1)	2	<0.01
Lumbee (6)	13	0.03
Mexican American Ind. (2)	2	<0.01
Navajo (5)	6	0.01
Potawatomi (1)	1	<0.01
Sioux (2)	3	0.01
South American Ind. (7)	11	0.03
Spanish American Ind. (18)	18	0.04
Tlingit-Haida *(Alaska Native)* (0)	2	<0.01
Asian (6,530)	7,489	17.21
Not Hispanic (6,495)	7,387	16.98
Hispanic (35)	102	0.23
Bangladeshi (133)	141	0.32
Burmese (29)	31	0.07
Cambodian (47)	54	0.12
Chinese, ex. Taiwanese (645)	778	1.79
Filipino (483)	676	1.55
Indian (3,236)	3,376	7.76
Indonesian (9)	10	0.02
Japanese (76)	163	0.37
Korean (558)	689	1.58
Laotian (31)	36	0.08
Malaysian (6)	12	0.03
Nepalese (48)	51	0.12
Pakistani (601)	651	1.50
Sri Lankan (15)	24	0.06
Taiwanese (28)	45	0.10
Thai (35)	50	0.11
Vietnamese (376)	445	1.02
Hawaii Native/Pacific Islander (23)	92	0.21
Not Hispanic (16)	73	0.17
Hispanic (7)	19	0.04
Guamanian/Chamorro (8)	19	0.04
Native Hawaiian (8)	30	0.07
Tongan (0)	4	0.01
White (30,442)	31,867	73.24
Not Hispanic (27,881)	29,041	66.74
Hispanic (2,561)	2,826	6.49

Bailey's Crossroads

Place Type: CDP
County: Fairfax
Population: 23,643†

Ancestry‡	Population	%
Afghan (54)	54	0.26
African, Sub-Saharan (856)	885	4.24
African (250)	279	1.34
Ethiopian (429)	429	2.06
Nigerian (14)	14	0.07
Sudanese (107)	107	0.51
Other Sub-Saharan African (56)	56	0.27
American (484)	484	2.32
Arab (799)	829	3.98
Arab (344)	344	1.65
Jordanian (182)	182	0.87
Lebanese (112)	112	0.54
Moroccan (54)	63	0.30
Palestinian (29)	29	0.14
Syrian (0)	12	0.06
Other Arab (78)	87	0.42
Armenian (0)	10	0.05
Australian (0)	15	0.07
Austrian (0)	24	0.12
Belgian (0)	13	0.06
Brazilian (14)	14	0.07
British (65)	125	0.60
Canadian (0)	47	0.23
Carpatho Rusyn (0)	12	0.06
Croatian (0)	31	0.15
Czech (7)	64	0.31
Czechoslovakian (16)	16	0.08
Danish (0)	89	0.43
Dutch (12)	85	0.41
Eastern European (32)	32	0.15
English (380)	1,059	5.08
Estonian (29)	29	0.14
European (142)	150	0.72
Finnish (11)	29	0.14
French, ex. Basque (43)	254	1.22
French Canadian (41)	62	0.30
German (266)	1,082	5.19
Greek (79)	128	0.61
Hungarian (22)	50	0.24
Iranian (187)	196	0.94
Irish (312)	1,055	5.06
Italian (205)	395	1.89
Lithuanian (0)	51	0.24
Macedonian (103)	112	0.54
Norwegian (27)	155	0.74
Pennsylvania German (12)	12	0.06
Polish (126)	295	1.41
Portuguese (0)	10	0.05
Romanian (12)	12	0.06
Russian (104)	187	0.90
Scandinavian (8)	8	0.04
Scotch-Irish (34)	218	1.05
Scottish (46)	172	0.82
Serbian (0)	11	0.05
Slovak (15)	15	0.07
Slovene (10)	20	0.10
Swedish (11)	105	0.50
Swiss (12)	36	0.17
Ukrainian (0)	37	0.18
Welsh (14)	63	0.30
West Indian, ex. Hispanic (9)	9	0.04
Haitian (9)	9	0.04
Yugoslavian (11)	11	0.05

Hispanic Origin	Population	%
Hispanic or Latino (of any race)	9,336	39.49
Central American, ex. Mexican	5,312	22.47
Costa Rican	10	0.04
Guatemalan	1,754	7.42
Honduran	594	2.51
Nicaraguan	197	0.83
Panamanian	22	0.09
Salvadoran	2,730	11.55
Other Central American	5	0.02
Cuban	61	0.26
Dominican Republic	54	0.23
Mexican	1,018	4.31
Puerto Rican	167	0.71
South American	1,823	7.71
Argentinean	137	0.58
Bolivian	1,052	4.45
Chilean	55	0.23
Colombian	176	0.74
Ecuadorian	51	0.22
Paraguayan	15	0.06
Peruvian	284	1.20
Uruguayan	11	0.05
Venezuelan	32	0.14
Other South American	10	0.04
Other Hispanic or Latino	901	3.81

Race*	Population	%
African-American/Black (3,599)	3,852	16.29
Not Hispanic (3,475)	3,632	15.36
Hispanic (124)	220	0.93
American Indian/Alaska Native (241)	425	1.80
Not Hispanic (42)	109	0.46
Hispanic (199)	316	1.34
Alaska Athabascan *(Ala. Nat.)* (1)	1	<0.01
Apache (1)	1	<0.01
Blackfeet (0)	1	<0.01
Central American Ind. (24)	27	0.11
Cherokee (5)	14	0.06
Chickasaw (0)	2	0.01
Chippewa (2)	4	0.02
Choctaw (0)	5	0.02
Cree (0)	1	<0.01
Delaware (0)	1	<0.01
Hopi (1)	1	<0.01
Inupiat *(Alaska Native)* (1)	1	<0.01
Iroquois (1)	4	0.02
Mexican American Ind. (30)	44	0.19
Ottawa (1)	2	0.01
Potawatomi (0)	1	<0.01
Pueblo (1)	1	<0.01
Shoshone (0)	1	<0.01
South American Ind. (3)	8	0.03
Spanish American Ind. (36)	40	0.17
Asian (2,458)	2,772	11.72
Not Hispanic (2,445)	2,733	11.56
Hispanic (13)	39	0.16
Bangladeshi (98)	103	0.44
Burmese (19)	19	0.08
Cambodian (60)	73	0.31
Chinese, ex. Taiwanese (223)	271	1.15
Filipino (339)	394	1.67
Indian (418)	485	2.05
Indonesian (10)	11	0.05
Japanese (42)	54	0.23
Korean (180)	202	0.85
Laotian (19)	19	0.08

SECTION TWO

*Notes: † The Census 2010 population figure is used to calculate the percentages in the Hispanic Origin and Race categories. Ancestry percentages are based on the 2006-2010 American Community Survey population (not shown); ‡ Numbers in parentheses indicate the number of people reporting a single ancestry; * Numbers in parentheses indicate the number of persons reporting this race alone, not in combination with any other race; Please refer to the Explanation of Data for more information.*

Malaysian (3)	4	0.02
Nepalese (12)	12	0.05
Pakistani (317)	339	1.43
Sri Lankan (7)	9	0.04
Taiwanese (7)	7	0.03
Thai (51)	57	0.24
Vietnamese (528)	563	2.38
Hawaii Native/Pacific Islander (27)	61	0.26
Not Hispanic (24)	42	0.18
Hispanic (3)	19	0.08
Guamanian/Chamorro (4)	9	0.04
Native Hawaiian (1)	10	0.04
Samoan (1)	1	<0.01
White (12,109)	13,055	55.22
Not Hispanic (7,736)	8,135	34.41
Hispanic (4,373)	4,920	20.81

Blacksburg

Place Type: Town
County: Montgomery
Population: 42,620†

Ancestry‡	Population	%
Afghan (14)	14	0.03
African, Sub-Saharan (145)	145	0.34
African (107)	107	0.25
Ethiopian (12)	12	0.03
Kenyan (12)	12	0.03
Sudanese (14)	14	0.03
Albanian (188)	208	0.49
American (1,849)	1,849	4.39
Arab (252)	350	0.83
Arab (31)	43	0.10
Egyptian (154)	154	0.37
Jordanian (31)	31	0.07
Lebanese (23)	93	0.22
Palestinian (13)	13	0.03
Other Arab (0)	16	0.04
Armenian (13)	91	0.22
Australian (0)	12	0.03
Austrian (40)	111	0.26
Belgian (11)	70	0.17
Brazilian (89)	103	0.24
British (149)	373	0.88
Bulgarian (27)	27	0.06
Cajun (15)	28	0.07
Canadian (43)	68	0.16
Celtic (24)	24	0.06
Croatian (6)	72	0.17
Czech (33)	192	0.46
Czechoslovakian (0)	23	0.05
Danish (23)	139	0.33
Dutch (240)	701	1.66
Eastern European (33)	33	0.08
English (1,611)	5,025	11.92
European (760)	929	2.20
Finnish (13)	75	0.18
French, ex. Basque (193)	1,061	2.52
French Canadian (12)	131	0.31
German (2,382)	7,780	18.46
Greek (97)	249	0.59
Guyanese (14)	14	0.03
Hungarian (112)	305	0.72
Iranian (210)	223	0.53
Irish (1,818)	6,173	14.65
Italian (850)	2,601	6.17
Lithuanian (22)	87	0.21
Norwegian (105)	428	1.02
Polish (544)	1,589	3.77
Portuguese (41)	116	0.28
Romanian (98)	144	0.34
Russian (195)	498	1.18
Scandinavian (34)	87	0.21
Scotch-Irish (746)	1,474	3.50
Scottish (474)	1,461	3.47
Serbian (12)	28	0.07
Slavic (19)	32	0.08
Slovak (26)	39	0.09
Swedish (193)	674	1.60
Swiss (0)	122	0.29
Turkish (96)	129	0.31
Ukrainian (14)	132	0.31
Welsh (167)	632	1.50
West Indian, ex. Hispanic (66)	94	0.22
Belizean (25)	25	0.06
Jamaican (12)	27	0.06
Trinidadian/Tobagonian (21)	21	0.05
West Indian (8)	21	0.05
Yugoslavian (0)	8	0.02

Hispanic Origin	Population	%
Hispanic or Latino (of any race)	1,476	3.46
Central American, ex. Mexican	209	0.49
Costa Rican	26	0.06
Guatemalan	34	0.08
Honduran	39	0.09
Nicaraguan	18	0.04
Panamanian	32	0.08
Salvadoran	59	0.14
Other Central American	1	<0.01
Cuban	76	0.18
Dominican Republic	35	0.08
Mexican	375	0.88
Puerto Rican	192	0.45
South American	404	0.95
Argentinean	49	0.11
Bolivian	67	0.16
Chilean	42	0.10
Colombian	83	0.19
Ecuadorian	33	0.08
Paraguayan	10	0.02
Peruvian	83	0.19
Uruguayan	12	0.03
Venezuelan	24	0.06
Other South American	1	<0.01
Other Hispanic or Latino	185	0.43

Race*	Population	%
African-American/Black (1,818)	2,113	4.96
Not Hispanic (1,769)	2,036	4.78
Hispanic (49)	77	0.18
American Indian/Alaska Native (87)	278	0.65
Not Hispanic (72)	236	0.55
Hispanic (15)	42	0.10
Alaska Athabascan *(Ala. Nat.)* (0)	6	0.01
Apache (1)	1	<0.01
Blackfeet (1)	4	0.01
Canadian/French Am. Ind. (0)	2	<0.01
Cherokee (20)	70	0.16
Chickasaw (3)	4	0.01
Chippewa (4)	4	0.01
Choctaw (5)	11	0.03
Creek (0)	1	<0.01
Delaware (0)	1	<0.01
Iroquois (3)	10	0.02
Lumbee (1)	3	0.01
Menominee (0)	1	<0.01
Mexican American Ind. (8)	8	0.02
Navajo (2)	3	0.01
Osage (0)	2	<0.01
Ottawa (0)	1	<0.01
Pueblo (0)	1	<0.01
Shoshone (1)	1	<0.01
Sioux (1)	1	<0.01
South American Ind. (2)	5	0.01
Spanish American Ind. (0)	2	<0.01
Asian (4,518)	5,250	12.32
Not Hispanic (4,498)	5,205	12.21
Hispanic (20)	45	0.11
Bangladeshi (55)	57	0.13
Burmese (11)	15	0.04
Cambodian (16)	23	0.05
Chinese, ex. Taiwanese (1,394)	1,551	3.64
Filipino (199)	348	0.82
Indian (1,108)	1,192	2.80
Indonesian (30)	40	0.09
Japanese (81)	192	0.45
Korean (908)	1,024	2.40
Laotian (13)	14	0.03
Malaysian (15)	21	0.05
Nepalese (59)	64	0.15
Pakistani (94)	101	0.24
Sri Lankan (20)	27	0.06
Taiwanese (106)	121	0.28
Thai (58)	77	0.18
Vietnamese (212)	259	0.61
Hawaii Native/Pacific Islander (17)	83	0.19
Not Hispanic (12)	74	0.17
Hispanic (5)	9	0.02
Guamanian/Chamorro (3)	14	0.03
Native Hawaiian (7)	28	0.07
Samoan (3)	6	0.01
Tongan (0)	1	<0.01
White (34,588)	35,670	83.69
Not Hispanic (33,640)	34,621	81.23
Hispanic (948)	1,049	2.46

Bon Air

Place Type: CDP
County: Chesterfield
Population: 16,366†

Ancestry‡	Population	%
American (1,754)	1,754	11.06
Arab (205)	205	1.29
Egyptian (44)	44	0.28
Jordanian (39)	39	0.25
Lebanese (122)	122	0.77
Armenian (8)	8	0.05
Australian (10)	10	0.06
Austrian (11)	71	0.45
British (81)	134	0.84
Canadian (31)	42	0.26
Czech (22)	99	0.62
Czechoslovakian (14)	14	0.09
Danish (14)	40	0.25
Dutch (45)	355	2.24
Eastern European (13)	13	0.08
English (1,111)	2,749	17.33
European (251)	251	1.58
Finnish (0)	10	0.06
French, ex. Basque (94)	371	2.34
French Canadian (14)	24	0.15
German (1,000)	2,866	18.06
Greek (46)	85	0.54
Hungarian (0)	14	0.09
Icelander (0)	21	0.13
Iranian (12)	12	0.08
Irish (681)	2,295	14.47
Italian (189)	891	5.62
Latvian (0)	9	0.06
Lithuanian (0)	14	0.09
Northern European (10)	10	0.06
Norwegian (39)	134	0.84
Polish (78)	281	1.77
Portuguese (0)	42	0.26
Russian (16)	101	0.64
Scandinavian (0)	10	0.06
Scotch-Irish (304)	579	3.65
Scottish (274)	641	4.04
Slovak (0)	42	0.26
Slovene (11)	21	0.13
Swedish (95)	146	0.92
Swiss (7)	29	0.18
Ukrainian (10)	21	0.13
Welsh (136)	303	1.91
West Indian, ex. Hispanic (8)	23	0.14
Barbadian (0)	15	0.09
Jamaican (8)	8	0.05
Yugoslavian (44)	44	0.28

Hispanic Origin	Population	%
Hispanic or Latino (of any race)	897	5.48
Central American, ex. Mexican	207	1.26
Costa Rican	14	0.09
Guatemalan	62	0.38
Honduran	25	0.15
Nicaraguan	4	0.02

*Notes: † The Census 2010 population figure is used to calculate the percentages in the Hispanic Origin and Race categories. Ancestry percentages are based on the 2006-2010 American Community Survey population (not shown); ‡ Numbers in parentheses indicate the number of people reporting a single ancestry; * Numbers in parentheses indicate the number of persons reporting this race alone, not in combination with any other race; Please refer to the Explanation of Data for more information.*

Panamanian	7	0.04
Salvadoran	95	0.58
Cuban	31	0.19
Dominican Republic	22	0.13
Mexican	350	2.14
Puerto Rican	118	0.72
South American	87	0.53
Argentinean	2	0.01
Chilean	1	0.01
Colombian	44	0.27
Ecuadorian	12	0.07
Paraguayan	8	0.05
Peruvian	4	0.02
Uruguayan	3	0.02
Venezuelan	11	0.07
Other South American	2	0.01
Other Hispanic or Latino	82	0.50

Race*	Population	%
African-American/Black (1,665)	1,835	11.21
Not Hispanic (1,632)	1,774	10.84
Hispanic (33)	61	0.37
American Indian/Alaska Native (40)	141	0.86
Not Hispanic (25)	108	0.66
Hispanic (15)	33	0.20
Blackfeet (4)	8	0.05
Central American Ind. (0)	1	0.01
Cherokee (5)	33	0.20
Choctaw (0)	4	0.02
Creek (0)	1	0.01
Iroquois (0)	2	0.01
Mexican American Ind. (5)	8	0.05
Sioux (1)	9	0.05
South American Ind. (3)	5	0.03
Asian (606)	738	4.51
Not Hispanic (599)	718	4.39
Hispanic (7)	20	0.12
Bangladeshi (7)	7	0.04
Burmese (3)	3	0.02
Cambodian (81)	84	0.51
Chinese, ex. Taiwanese (103)	126	0.77
Filipino (28)	58	0.35
Indian (119)	131	0.80
Indonesian (4)	5	0.03
Japanese (14)	26	0.16
Korean (70)	80	0.49
Laotian (1)	2	0.01
Nepalese (1)	2	0.01
Pakistani (30)	32	0.20
Sri Lankan (1)	1	0.01
Taiwanese (5)	7	0.04
Thai (3)	11	0.07
Vietnamese (113)	130	0.79
Hawaii Native/Pacific Islander (3)	17	0.10
Not Hispanic (3)	9	0.05
Hispanic (0)	8	0.05
Guamanian/Chamorro (3)	5	0.03
Native Hawaiian (0)	2	0.01
Samoan (0)	2	0.01
White (13,393)	13,722	83.84
Not Hispanic (12,874)	13,143	80.31
Hispanic (519)	579	3.54

Brambleton

Place Type: CDP
County: Loudoun
Population: 9,845†

Ancestry‡	Population	%
African, Sub-Saharan (10)	29	0.34
African (0)	9	0.10
South African (10)	20	0.23
American (343)	343	3.99
Arab (18)	58	0.67
Arab (0)	16	0.19
Lebanese (0)	12	0.14
Moroccan (18)	18	0.21
Syrian (0)	12	0.14
Austrian (13)	26	0.30
British (41)	116	1.35
Czech (29)	52	0.61
Czechoslovakian (0)	10	0.12
Danish (0)	12	0.14
Dutch (49)	122	1.42
Eastern European (25)	25	0.29
English (329)	999	11.62
European (132)	132	1.54
Finnish (0)	13	0.15
French, ex. Basque (14)	148	1.72
French Canadian (0)	25	0.29
German (173)	807	9.39
Greek (32)	58	0.67
Iranian (52)	52	0.61
Irish (557)	1,095	12.74
Italian (94)	362	4.21
Northern European (15)	15	0.17
Norwegian (0)	41	0.48
Polish (106)	232	2.70
Romanian (28)	28	0.33
Russian (14)	66	0.77
Scandinavian (0)	29	0.34
Scotch-Irish (92)	131	1.52
Scottish (44)	206	2.40
Slovak (8)	8	0.09
Swedish (10)	55	0.64
Swiss (0)	14	0.16
Ukrainian (0)	96	1.12
Welsh (22)	101	1.18
West Indian, ex. Hispanic (26)	34	0.40
Bahamian (26)	26	0.30
Jamaican (0)	8	0.09
Yugoslavian (0)	7	0.08

Hispanic Origin	Population	%
Hispanic or Latino (of any race)	578	5.87
Central American, ex. Mexican	95	0.96
Costa Rican	5	0.05
Guatemalan	28	0.28
Honduran	3	0.03
Nicaraguan	13	0.13
Panamanian	1	0.01
Salvadoran	45	0.46
Cuban	19	0.19
Dominican Republic	16	0.16
Mexican	121	1.23
Puerto Rican	79	0.80
South American	189	1.92
Argentinean	10	0.10
Bolivian	34	0.35
Chilean	11	0.11
Colombian	47	0.48
Ecuadorian	4	0.04
Peruvian	57	0.58
Venezuelan	26	0.26
Other Hispanic or Latino	59	0.60

Race*	Population	%
African-American/Black (665)	795	8.08
Not Hispanic (647)	769	7.81
Hispanic (18)	26	0.26
American Indian/Alaska Native (20)	74	0.75
Not Hispanic (18)	62	0.63
Hispanic (2)	12	0.12
Blackfeet (1)	1	0.01
Cherokee (4)	18	0.18
Choctaw (0)	1	0.01
Iroquois (0)	1	0.01
Mexican American Ind. (2)	2	0.02
Pueblo (0)	1	0.01
Sioux (0)	2	0.02
South American Ind. (0)	1	0.01
Asian (2,547)	2,879	29.24
Not Hispanic (2,546)	2,866	29.11
Hispanic (1)	13	0.13
Bangladeshi (22)	22	0.22
Burmese (9)	12	0.12
Cambodian (20)	23	0.23
Chinese, ex. Taiwanese (207)	264	2.68
Filipino (140)	217	2.20
Hmong (8)	8	0.08
Indian (1,436)	1,482	15.05
Indonesian (0)	13	0.13
Japanese (6)	32	0.33
Korean (227)	290	2.95
Laotian (18)	32	0.33
Nepalese (4)	5	0.05
Pakistani (154)	161	1.64
Sri Lankan (6)	10	0.10
Taiwanese (8)	9	0.09
Thai (16)	28	0.28
Vietnamese (187)	239	2.43
Hawaii Native/Pacific Islander (7)	31	0.31
Not Hispanic (7)	27	0.27
Hispanic (0)	4	0.04
Guamanian/Chamorro (4)	4	0.04
Native Hawaiian (2)	15	0.15
White (5,966)	6,402	65.03
Not Hispanic (5,596)	5,990	60.84
Hispanic (370)	412	4.18

Brandermill

Place Type: CDP
County: Chesterfield
Population: 13,173†

Ancestry‡	Population	%
African, Sub-Saharan (56)	110	0.88
African (0)	54	0.43
Somalian (56)	56	0.45
American (1,023)	1,023	8.14
Arab (23)	79	0.63
Arab (11)	23	0.18
Palestinian (12)	12	0.10
Syrian (0)	44	0.35
Austrian (0)	29	0.23
British (70)	101	0.80
Canadian (45)	70	0.56
Carpatho Rusyn (9)	9	0.07
Czech (37)	192	1.53
Danish (0)	26	0.21
Dutch (93)	193	1.54
English (891)	2,354	18.73
European (64)	64	0.51
French, ex. Basque (100)	458	3.64
French Canadian (28)	48	0.38
German (750)	2,164	17.22
Greek (66)	125	0.99
Hungarian (11)	85	0.68
Irish (651)	1,981	15.76
Italian (164)	669	5.32
Latvian (0)	46	0.37
Lithuanian (0)	15	0.12
Northern European (0)	14	0.11
Norwegian (104)	190	1.51
Polish (117)	207	1.65
Portuguese (0)	22	0.18
Romanian (7)	7	0.06
Russian (30)	84	0.67
Scandinavian (40)	74	0.59
Scotch-Irish (274)	537	4.27
Scottish (144)	667	5.31
Slovak (0)	10	0.08
Swedish (39)	183	1.46
Swiss (44)	79	0.63
Ukrainian (15)	15	0.12
Welsh (68)	223	1.77
West Indian, ex. Hispanic (79)	133	1.06
Jamaican (59)	59	0.47
Trinidadian/Tobagonian (20)	66	0.53
West Indian (0)	8	0.06

Hispanic Origin	Population	%
Hispanic or Latino (of any race)	417	3.17
Central American, ex. Mexican	62	0.47
Costa Rican	9	0.07
Guatemalan	12	0.09
Honduran	9	0.07
Nicaraguan	4	0.03

*Notes: † The Census 2010 population figure is used to calculate the percentages in the Hispanic Origin and Race categories. Ancestry percentages are based on the 2006-2010 American Community Survey population (not shown); ‡ Numbers in parentheses indicate the number of people reporting a single ancestry; * Numbers in parentheses indicate the number of persons reporting this race alone, not in combination with any other race; Please refer to the Explanation of Data for more information.*

Panamanian	5	0.04
Salvadoran	23	0.17
Cuban	13	0.10
Dominican Republic	6	0.05
Mexican	104	0.79
Puerto Rican	105	0.80
South American	80	0.61
Argentinean	3	0.02
Bolivian	6	0.05
Chilean	1	0.01
Colombian	26	0.20
Ecuadorian	6	0.05
Paraguayan	9	0.07
Peruvian	19	0.14
Venezuelan	10	0.08
Other Hispanic or Latino	47	0.36

Race*	Population	%
African-American/Black (1,417)	1,537	11.67
Not Hispanic (1,402)	1,510	11.46
Hispanic (15)	27	0.20
American Indian/Alaska Native (35)	107	0.81
Not Hispanic (26)	93	0.71
Hispanic (9)	14	0.11
Apache (0)	5	0.04
Blackfeet (0)	2	0.02
Cherokee (8)	30	0.23
Chickasaw (0)	1	0.01
Chippewa (1)	5	0.04
Iroquois (1)	5	0.04
Lumbee (4)	4	0.03
Navajo (2)	2	0.02
Spanish American Ind. (5)	5	0.04
Asian (448)	571	4.33
Not Hispanic (448)	564	4.28
Hispanic (0)	7	0.05
Burmese (1)	1	0.01
Cambodian (9)	11	0.08
Chinese, ex. Taiwanese (54)	61	0.46
Filipino (40)	67	0.51
Indian (100)	115	0.87
Indonesian (2)	3	0.02
Japanese (49)	69	0.52
Korean (96)	112	0.85
Laotian (3)	4	0.03
Nepalese (4)	4	0.03
Pakistani (2)	10	0.08
Taiwanese (4)	4	0.03
Thai (5)	8	0.06
Vietnamese (58)	67	0.51
Hawaii Native/Pacific Islander (7)	18	0.14
Not Hispanic (7)	18	0.14
Native Hawaiian (0)	6	0.05
Samoan (3)	3	0.02
White (10,883)	11,132	84.51
Not Hispanic (10,607)	10,831	82.22
Hispanic (276)	301	2.28

Bristol

Place Type: Independent City
County: Bristol
Population: 17,835†

Ancestry‡	Population	%
African, Sub-Saharan (8)	27	0.15
African (8)	27	0.15
American (3,296)	3,296	18.62
British (29)	38	0.21
Czech (0)	8	0.05
Czechoslovakian (0)	7	0.04
Dutch (24)	272	1.54
English (998)	2,025	11.44
European (215)	215	1.21
Finnish (32)	45	0.25
French, ex. Basque (134)	334	1.89
French Canadian (44)	102	0.58
German (736)	2,402	13.57
Greek (19)	89	0.50
Hungarian (11)	25	0.14
Irish (704)	1,897	10.72
Italian (146)	434	2.45
Norwegian (71)	114	0.64
Polish (38)	90	0.51
Russian (0)	17	0.10
Scandinavian (0)	6	0.03
Scotch-Irish (354)	657	3.71
Scottish (301)	690	3.90
Swedish (11)	85	0.48
Swiss (0)	29	0.16
Ukrainian (8)	8	0.05
Welsh (0)	36	0.20

Hispanic Origin	Population	%
Hispanic or Latino (of any race)	221	1.24
Central American, ex. Mexican	10	0.06
Guatemalan	6	0.03
Honduran	2	0.01
Nicaraguan	1	0.01
Salvadoran	1	0.01
Cuban	6	0.03
Dominican Republic	2	0.01
Mexican	135	0.76
Puerto Rican	40	0.22
South American	7	0.04
Colombian	1	0.01
Ecuadorian	1	0.01
Peruvian	1	0.01
Uruguayan	2	0.01
Venezuelan	2	0.01
Other Hispanic or Latino	21	0.12

Race*	Population	%
African-American/Black (1,009)	1,233	6.91
Not Hispanic (1,000)	1,213	6.80
Hispanic (9)	20	0.11
American Indian/Alaska Native (52)	159	0.89
Not Hispanic (49)	151	0.85
Hispanic (3)	8	0.04
Apache (0)	1	0.01
Blackfeet (1)	3	0.02
Canadian/French Am. Ind. (1)	2	0.01
Cherokee (14)	64	0.36
Chippewa (1)	1	0.01
Choctaw (0)	3	0.02
Iroquois (3)	5	0.03
Lumbee (4)	4	0.02
Mexican American Ind. (1)	2	0.01
Sioux (2)	2	0.01
South American Ind. (1)	1	0.01
Asian (122)	159	0.89
Not Hispanic (121)	158	0.89
Hispanic (1)	1	0.01
Chinese, ex. Taiwanese (37)	39	0.22
Filipino (15)	28	0.16
Indian (24)	32	0.18
Japanese (2)	5	0.03
Korean (9)	13	0.07
Taiwanese (1)	2	0.01
Thai (4)	6	0.03
Vietnamese (27)	31	0.17
Hawaii Native/Pacific Islander (4)	10	0.06
Not Hispanic (4)	10	0.06
Guamanian/Chamorro (2)	3	0.02
Native Hawaiian (1)	4	0.02
White (16,214)	16,534	92.71
Not Hispanic (16,099)	16,400	91.95
Hispanic (115)	134	0.75

Broadlands

Place Type: CDP
County: Loudoun
Population: 12,313†

Ancestry‡	Population	%
African, Sub-Saharan (102)	129	1.21
African (65)	92	0.86
Liberian (37)	37	0.35
Albanian (122)	122	1.14
American (413)	413	3.86
Arab (0)	27	0.25
Lebanese (0)	27	0.25
Armenian (12)	12	0.11
Austrian (9)	28	0.26
British (53)	124	1.16
Canadian (0)	65	0.61
Croatian (11)	11	0.10
Czech (57)	187	1.75
Czechoslovakian (28)	96	0.90
Danish (0)	48	0.45
Dutch (66)	137	1.28
Eastern European (30)	30	0.28
English (476)	1,149	10.74
Estonian (12)	38	0.36
European (168)	212	1.98
Finnish (0)	27	0.25
French, ex. Basque (117)	399	3.73
French Canadian (13)	51	0.48
German (333)	1,466	13.70
Greek (37)	71	0.66
Guyanese (4)	4	0.04
Hungarian (13)	59	0.55
Iranian (173)	173	1.62
Irish (479)	1,647	15.39
Italian (258)	807	7.54
Lithuanian (0)	14	0.13
Northern European (34)	34	0.32
Norwegian (47)	90	0.84
Polish (211)	468	4.37
Portuguese (39)	52	0.49
Russian (205)	386	3.61
Scandinavian (15)	62	0.58
Scotch-Irish (43)	128	1.20
Scottish (46)	88	0.82
Slovak (0)	52	0.49
Swedish (0)	88	0.82
Swiss (18)	116	1.08
Turkish (12)	12	0.11
Ukrainian (49)	84	0.78
Welsh (16)	40	0.37
West Indian, ex. Hispanic (18)	18	0.17
Haitian (18)	18	0.17

Hispanic Origin	Population	%
Hispanic or Latino (of any race)	840	6.82
Central American, ex. Mexican	134	1.09
Costa Rican	6	0.05
Guatemalan	26	0.21
Honduran	14	0.11
Nicaraguan	9	0.07
Panamanian	9	0.07
Salvadoran	70	0.57
Cuban	47	0.38
Dominican Republic	10	0.08
Mexican	134	1.09
Puerto Rican	125	1.02
South American	280	2.27
Argentinean	7	0.06
Bolivian	39	0.32
Chilean	11	0.09
Colombian	50	0.41
Ecuadorian	30	0.24
Paraguayan	4	0.03
Peruvian	102	0.83
Uruguayan	6	0.05
Venezuelan	27	0.22
Other South American	4	0.03
Other Hispanic or Latino	110	0.89

Race*	Population	%
African-American/Black (696)	817	6.64
Not Hispanic (671)	767	6.23
Hispanic (25)	50	0.41
American Indian/Alaska Native (28)	94	0.76
Not Hispanic (21)	69	0.56
Hispanic (7)	25	0.20
Canadian/French Am. Ind. (1)	2	0.02
Cherokee (0)	5	0.04
Chippewa (0)	2	0.02

*Notes: † The Census 2010 population figure is used to calculate the percentages in the Hispanic Origin and Race categories. Ancestry percentages are based on the 2006-2010 American Community Survey population (not shown); ‡ Numbers in parentheses indicate the number of people reporting a single ancestry; * Numbers in parentheses indicate the number of persons reporting this race alone, not in combination with any other race; Please refer to the Explanation of Data for more information.*

Choctaw (1)	2	0.02
Cree (0)	1	0.01
Delaware (0)	3	0.02
Inupiat *(Alaska Native)* (2)	4	0.03
Iroquois (1)	4	0.03
Mexican American Ind. (0)	2	0.02
Navajo (3)	4	0.03
South American Ind. (0)	6	0.05
Ute (0)	4	0.03
Asian (2,095)	2,403	19.52
Not Hispanic (2,091)	2,382	19.35
Hispanic (4)	21	0.17
Bangladeshi (27)	27	0.22
Burmese (1)	4	0.03
Cambodian (12)	16	0.13
Chinese, ex. Taiwanese (210)	268	2.18
Filipino (148)	222	1.80
Indian (1,156)	1,196	9.71
Indonesian (3)	6	0.05
Japanese (23)	52	0.42
Korean (155)	221	1.79
Laotian (10)	12	0.10
Malaysian (1)	1	0.01
Nepalese (6)	6	0.05
Pakistani (147)	163	1.32
Sri Lankan (4)	4	0.03
Taiwanese (12)	15	0.12
Thai (11)	17	0.14
Vietnamese (115)	135	1.10
Hawaii Native/Pacific Islander (5)	19	0.15
Not Hispanic (5)	18	0.15
Hispanic (0)	1	0.01
Guamanian/Chamorro (4)	6	0.05
Native Hawaiian (1)	11	0.09
White (8,798)	9,233	74.99
Not Hispanic (8,220)	8,577	69.66
Hispanic (578)	656	5.33

Buckhall

Place Type: CDP
County: Prince William
Population: 16,293†

Ancestry‡	Population	%
Afghan (48)	48	0.31
African, Sub-Saharan (188)	210	1.37
African (167)	189	1.23
Ethiopian (21)	21	0.14
American (985)	985	6.42
Arab (80)	97	0.63
Arab (31)	31	0.20
Egyptian (30)	30	0.20
Lebanese (19)	36	0.23
Austrian (9)	32	0.21
Belgian (48)	48	0.31
Brazilian (23)	23	0.15
British (68)	130	0.85
Bulgarian (26)	26	0.17
Canadian (7)	15	0.10
Celtic (11)	11	0.07
Croatian (0)	52	0.34
Czech (0)	21	0.14
Danish (0)	35	0.23
Dutch (34)	287	1.87
English (557)	1,857	12.10
Estonian (19)	19	0.12
European (203)	211	1.37
French, ex. Basque (69)	461	3.00
French Canadian (21)	171	1.11
German (710)	3,320	21.63
Hungarian (8)	173	1.13
Iranian (21)	44	0.29
Irish (747)	2,574	16.77
Italian (286)	780	5.08
Northern European (8)	25	0.16
Norwegian (26)	113	0.74
Polish (237)	490	3.19
Portuguese (101)	153	1.00
Romanian (30)	30	0.20
Russian (33)	112	0.73
Scandinavian (6)	47	0.31
Scotch-Irish (116)	441	2.87
Scottish (138)	412	2.68
Slavic (38)	38	0.25
Slovak (14)	91	0.59
Swedish (101)	174	1.13
Swiss (12)	40	0.26
Ukrainian (41)	97	0.63
Welsh (0)	41	0.27

Hispanic Origin	Population	%
Hispanic or Latino (of any race)	1,665	10.22
Central American, ex. Mexican	561	3.44
Costa Rican	7	0.04
Guatemalan	113	0.69
Honduran	28	0.17
Nicaraguan	28	0.17
Panamanian	20	0.12
Salvadoran	365	2.24
Cuban	33	0.20
Dominican Republic	23	0.14
Mexican	470	2.88
Puerto Rican	152	0.93
South American	264	1.62
Argentinean	11	0.07
Bolivian	86	0.53
Chilean	1	0.01
Colombian	33	0.20
Ecuadorian	22	0.14
Peruvian	96	0.59
Uruguayan	8	0.05
Venezuelan	7	0.04
Other Hispanic or Latino	162	0.99

Race*	Population	%
African-American/Black (1,395)	1,581	9.70
Not Hispanic (1,355)	1,518	9.32
Hispanic (40)	63	0.39
American Indian/Alaska Native (101)	195	1.20
Not Hispanic (53)	126	0.77
Hispanic (48)	69	0.42
Apache (1)	1	0.01
Blackfeet (0)	1	0.01
Canadian/French Am. Ind. (0)	2	0.01
Central American Ind. (7)	11	0.07
Cherokee (9)	31	0.19
Cheyenne (0)	1	0.01
Chickasaw (0)	4	0.02
Chippewa (1)	1	0.01
Choctaw (0)	2	0.01
Comanche (1)	3	0.02
Creek (0)	2	0.01
Iroquois (3)	4	0.02
Mexican American Ind. (8)	8	0.05
Navajo (0)	1	0.01
Sioux (2)	7	0.04
South American Ind. (6)	6	0.04
Asian (1,166)	1,419	8.71
Not Hispanic (1,157)	1,392	8.54
Hispanic (9)	27	0.17
Bangladeshi (9)	9	0.06
Cambodian (34)	44	0.27
Chinese, ex. Taiwanese (130)	177	1.09
Filipino (203)	256	1.57
Indian (247)	296	1.82
Indonesian (3)	4	0.02
Japanese (22)	43	0.26
Korean (121)	159	0.98
Laotian (20)	25	0.15
Malaysian (1)	1	0.01
Nepalese (8)	8	0.05
Pakistani (114)	125	0.77
Taiwanese (5)	5	0.03
Thai (11)	15	0.09
Vietnamese (180)	202	1.24
Hawaii Native/Pacific Islander (12)	28	0.17
Not Hispanic (11)	24	0.15
Hispanic (1)	4	0.02
Guamanian/Chamorro (0)	2	0.01
Native Hawaiian (8)	14	0.09
Samoan (3)	3	0.02
White (12,570)	13,051	80.10
Not Hispanic (11,581)	11,970	73.47
Hispanic (989)	1,081	6.63

Bull Run

Place Type: CDP
County: Prince William
Population: 14,983†

Ancestry‡	Population	%
Afghan (12)	12	0.09
African, Sub-Saharan (693)	776	6.02
African (267)	350	2.72
Ethiopian (325)	325	2.52
Ghanaian (26)	26	0.20
Kenyan (28)	28	0.22
Nigerian (47)	47	0.36
American (538)	538	4.17
Arab (153)	164	1.27
Egyptian (136)	136	1.06
Jordanian (17)	17	0.13
Lebanese (0)	11	0.09
Armenian (16)	16	0.12
Austrian (0)	13	0.10
Belgian (0)	14	0.11
British (43)	75	0.58
Canadian (0)	40	0.31
Celtic (29)	29	0.22
Czech (24)	119	0.92
Danish (8)	8	0.06
Dutch (0)	44	0.34
English (82)	573	4.45
European (92)	101	0.78
Finnish (54)	54	0.42
French, ex. Basque (36)	217	1.68
French Canadian (57)	128	0.99
German (311)	1,188	9.22
Greek (0)	10	0.08
Hungarian (54)	68	0.53
Irish (101)	677	5.25
Italian (117)	406	3.15
Northern European (15)	15	0.12
Norwegian (10)	73	0.57
Pennsylvania German (0)	14	0.11
Polish (44)	147	1.14
Russian (137)	150	1.16
Scotch-Irish (95)	173	1.34
Scottish (8)	102	0.79
Serbian (0)	15	0.12
Slovak (15)	50	0.39
Slovene (18)	18	0.14
Swedish (0)	152	1.18
Turkish (71)	71	0.55
Ukrainian (50)	50	0.39
Welsh (11)	55	0.43
West Indian, ex. Hispanic (30)	30	0.23
Jamaican (11)	11	0.09
Trinidadian/Tobagonian (19)	19	0.15

Hispanic Origin	Population	%
Hispanic or Latino (of any race)	5,531	36.92
Central American, ex. Mexican	2,964	19.78
Costa Rican	16	0.11
Guatemalan	703	4.69
Honduran	249	1.66
Nicaraguan	64	0.43
Panamanian	26	0.17
Salvadoran	1,883	12.57
Other Central American	23	0.15
Cuban	25	0.17
Dominican Republic	77	0.51
Mexican	1,083	7.23
Puerto Rican	233	1.56
South American	528	3.52
Argentinean	26	0.17
Bolivian	115	0.77
Chilean	6	0.04

*Notes: † The Census 2010 population figure is used to calculate the percentages in the Hispanic Origin and Race categories. Ancestry percentages are based on the 2006-2010 American Community Survey population (not shown); ‡ Numbers in parentheses indicate the number of people reporting a single ancestry; * Numbers in parentheses indicate the number of persons reporting this race alone, not in combination with any other race; Please refer to the Explanation of Data for more information.*

Colombian	92	0.61
Ecuadorian	52	0.35
Peruvian	189	1.26
Uruguayan	8	0.05
Venezuelan	31	0.21
Other South American	9	0.06
Other Hispanic or Latino	621	4.14

Race*	Population	%
African-American/Black (3,006)	3,369	22.49
Not Hispanic (2,904)	3,180	21.22
Hispanic (102)	189	1.26
American Indian/Alaska Native (84)	217	1.45
Not Hispanic (31)	120	0.80
Hispanic (53)	97	0.65
Blackfeet (0)	5	0.03
Canadian/French Am. Ind. (1)	1	0.01
Central American Ind. (6)	6	0.04
Cherokee (4)	31	0.21
Chippewa (1)	2	0.01
Choctaw (2)	10	0.07
Comanche (0)	1	0.01
Delaware (1)	1	0.01
Inupiat *(Alaska Native)* (0)	3	0.02
Iroquois (2)	3	0.02
Lumbee (1)	3	0.02
Mexican American Ind. (1)	7	0.05
Ottawa (0)	1	0.01
Pueblo (0)	1	0.01
Seminole (0)	2	0.01
Sioux (1)	1	0.01
South American Ind. (0)	8	0.05
Spanish American Ind. (5)	5	0.03
Asian (1,079)	1,285	8.58
Not Hispanic (1,072)	1,260	8.41
Hispanic (7)	25	0.17
Bangladeshi (52)	60	0.40
Burmese (1)	1	0.01
Cambodian (30)	30	0.20
Chinese, ex. Taiwanese (55)	88	0.59
Filipino (106)	154	1.03
Hmong (1)	1	0.01
Indian (358)	404	2.70
Indonesian (2)	6	0.04
Japanese (13)	46	0.31
Korean (128)	154	1.03
Laotian (22)	23	0.15
Malaysian (1)	3	0.02
Nepalese (57)	63	0.42
Pakistani (92)	111	0.74
Sri Lankan (4)	4	0.03
Taiwanese (4)	5	0.03
Thai (17)	22	0.15
Vietnamese (74)	84	0.56
Hawaii Native/Pacific Islander (3)	58	0.39
Not Hispanic (3)	35	0.23
Hispanic (0)	23	0.15
Guamanian/Chamorro (0)	6	0.04
Native Hawaiian (3)	11	0.07
Samoan (0)	5	0.03
White (7,024)	7,697	51.37
Not Hispanic (4,916)	5,308	35.43
Hispanic (2,108)	2,389	15.94

Burke

Place Type: CDP
County: Fairfax
Population: 41,055†

Ancestry‡	Population	%
Afghan (190)	190	0.46
African, Sub-Saharan (985)	1,100	2.65
African (446)	522	1.26
Ethiopian (260)	299	0.72
Ghanaian (149)	149	0.36
Other Sub-Saharan African (130)	130	0.31
American (1,253)	1,253	3.02
Arab (533)	577	1.39
Arab (64)	64	0.15
Egyptian (112)	138	0.33
Iraqi (23)	23	0.06
Lebanese (62)	72	0.17
Moroccan (178)	186	0.45
Palestinian (25)	25	0.06
Syrian (23)	23	0.06
Other Arab (46)	46	0.11
Armenian (0)	25	0.06
Austrian (27)	167	0.40
Belgian (26)	40	0.10
Brazilian (45)	45	0.11
British (160)	523	1.26
Bulgarian (47)	47	0.11
Cajun (11)	11	0.03
Canadian (9)	9	0.02
Celtic (0)	28	0.07
Croatian (31)	52	0.13
Czech (41)	229	0.55
Czechoslovakian (16)	43	0.10
Danish (35)	169	0.41
Dutch (23)	351	0.85
Eastern European (226)	226	0.54
English (1,488)	5,145	12.41
European (980)	1,054	2.54
Finnish (31)	42	0.10
French, ex. Basque (101)	719	1.73
French Canadian (47)	196	0.47
German (1,654)	6,997	16.87
Greek (284)	446	1.08
Guyanese (12)	12	0.03
Hungarian (60)	109	0.26
Icelander (22)	44	0.11
Iranian (110)	110	0.27
Irish (1,233)	4,974	11.99
Israeli (60)	60	0.14
Italian (1,061)	2,891	6.97
Latvian (0)	36	0.09
Lithuanian (33)	120	0.29
Northern European (90)	90	0.22
Norwegian (107)	493	1.19
Polish (440)	1,347	3.25
Portuguese (0)	79	0.19
Romanian (0)	81	0.20
Russian (360)	702	1.69
Scandinavian (27)	143	0.34
Scotch-Irish (470)	1,280	3.09
Scottish (395)	1,177	2.84
Serbian (0)	49	0.12
Slavic (11)	11	0.03
Slovak (128)	219	0.53
Slovene (0)	1	<0.01
Swedish (107)	636	1.53
Swiss (13)	181	0.44
Turkish (119)	132	0.32
Ukrainian (35)	184	0.44
Welsh (94)	513	1.24
West Indian, ex. Hispanic (121)	121	0.29
Jamaican (106)	106	0.26
Trinidadian/Tobagonian (15)	15	0.04
Yugoslavian (0)	31	0.07

Hispanic Origin	Population	%
Hispanic or Latino (of any race)	5,175	12.61
Central American, ex. Mexican	1,340	3.26
Costa Rican	29	0.07
Guatemalan	223	0.54
Honduran	123	0.30
Nicaraguan	74	0.18
Panamanian	59	0.14
Salvadoran	823	2.00
Other Central American	9	0.02
Cuban	97	0.24
Dominican Republic	61	0.15
Mexican	461	1.12
Puerto Rican	401	0.98
South American	2,281	5.56
Argentinean	94	0.23
Bolivian	936	2.28
Chilean	121	0.29
Colombian	165	0.40
Ecuadorian	107	0.26
Paraguayan	9	0.02
Peruvian	774	1.89
Uruguayan	26	0.06
Venezuelan	38	0.09
Other South American	11	0.03
Other Hispanic or Latino	534	1.30

Race*	Population	%
African-American/Black (2,616)	2,955	7.20
Not Hispanic (2,522)	2,803	6.83
Hispanic (94)	152	0.37
American Indian/Alaska Native (112)	327	0.80
Not Hispanic (58)	195	0.47
Hispanic (54)	132	0.32
Apache (4)	9	0.02
Blackfeet (2)	14	0.03
Central American Ind. (1)	7	0.02
Cherokee (0)	51	0.12
Cheyenne (0)	2	<0.01
Chickasaw (0)	3	0.01
Choctaw (5)	15	0.04
Comanche (1)	3	0.01
Creek (3)	9	0.02
Iroquois (3)	5	0.01
Lumbee (5)	5	0.01
Mexican American Ind. (21)	25	0.06
Navajo (0)	4	0.01
Pueblo (1)	1	<0.01
Seminole (0)	1	<0.01
Sioux (5)	9	0.02
South American Ind. (8)	21	0.05
Spanish American Ind. (0)	1	<0.01
Asian (7,052)	7,926	19.31
Not Hispanic (7,018)	7,833	19.08
Hispanic (34)	93	0.23
Bangladeshi (86)	97	0.24
Burmese (32)	34	0.08
Cambodian (24)	38	0.09
Chinese, ex. Taiwanese (886)	1,064	2.59
Filipino (630)	769	1.87
Indian (958)	1,053	2.56
Indonesian (37)	39	0.09
Japanese (94)	187	0.46
Korean (2,337)	2,494	6.07
Laotian (46)	53	0.13
Malaysian (5)	7	0.02
Nepalese (26)	28	0.07
Pakistani (335)	375	0.91
Sri Lankan (9)	9	0.02
Taiwanese (37)	54	0.13
Thai (110)	133	0.32
Vietnamese (1,180)	1,284	3.13
Hawaii Native/Pacific Islander (20)	80	0.19
Not Hispanic (19)	65	0.16
Hispanic (1)	15	0.04
Guamanian/Chamorro (6)	8	0.02
Native Hawaiian (10)	46	0.11
Samoan (1)	1	<0.01
White (28,263)	29,684	72.30
Not Hispanic (24,953)	26,014	63.36
Hispanic (3,310)	3,670	8.94

Burke Centre

Place Type: CDP
County: Fairfax
Population: 17,326†

Ancestry‡	Population	%
Afghan (99)	99	0.58
African, Sub-Saharan (174)	198	1.17
African (61)	61	0.36
Ethiopian (7)	7	0.04
Somalian (106)	106	0.62
Other Sub-Saharan African (0)	24	0.14
American (537)	537	3.16
Arab (203)	380	2.24
Egyptian (66)	87	0.51
Lebanese (28)	150	0.88

*Notes: † The Census 2010 population figure is used to calculate the percentages in the Hispanic Origin and Race categories. Ancestry percentages are based on the 2006-2010 American Community Survey population (not shown); ‡ Numbers in parentheses indicate the number of people reporting a single ancestry; * Numbers in parentheses indicate the number of persons reporting this race alone, not in combination with any other race; Please refer to the Explanation of Data for more information.*

Syrian (0)	14	0.08
Other Arab (109)	129	0.76
Australian (0)	14	0.08
Austrian (64)	73	0.43
Basque (0)	28	0.16
Brazilian (0)	23	0.14
British (54)	88	0.52
Canadian (15)	15	0.09
Croatian (10)	10	0.06
Czech (7)	69	0.41
Czechoslovakian (0)	16	0.09
Danish (0)	39	0.23
Dutch (18)	97	0.57
Eastern European (92)	92	0.54
English (548)	2,240	13.20
European (405)	449	2.65
French, ex. Basque (109)	658	3.88
French Canadian (17)	155	0.91
German (717)	2,849	16.78
Greek (71)	77	0.45
Hungarian (9)	65	0.38
Iranian (36)	84	0.49
Irish (750)	2,609	15.37
Italian (297)	1,017	5.99
Lithuanian (13)	33	0.19
Northern European (93)	93	0.55
Norwegian (89)	290	1.71
Pennsylvania German (10)	22	0.13
Polish (133)	618	3.64
Portuguese (19)	30	0.18
Romanian (14)	28	0.16
Russian (71)	238	1.40
Scandinavian (0)	8	0.05
Scotch-Irish (202)	609	3.59
Scottish (156)	524	3.09
Serbian (0)	14	0.08
Slavic (0)	11	0.06
Slovak (23)	34	0.20
Swedish (49)	184	1.08
Swiss (0)	50	0.29
Turkish (14)	14	0.08
Ukrainian (0)	78	0.46
Welsh (45)	193	1.14
West Indian, ex. Hispanic (10)	10	0.06
Jamaican (10)	10	0.06

Hispanic Origin	Population	%
Hispanic or Latino (of any race)	2,214	12.78
Central American, ex. Mexican	502	2.90
Costa Rican	19	0.11
Guatemalan	83	0.48
Honduran	44	0.25
Nicaraguan	34	0.20
Panamanian	17	0.10
Salvadoran	303	1.75
Other Central American	2	0.01
Cuban	53	0.31
Dominican Republic	24	0.14
Mexican	224	1.29
Puerto Rican	156	0.90
South American	1,016	5.86
Argentinean	51	0.29
Bolivian	362	2.09
Chilean	19	0.11
Colombian	107	0.62
Ecuadorian	42	0.24
Paraguayan	10	0.06
Peruvian	390	2.25
Uruguayan	14	0.08
Venezuelan	10	0.06
Other South American	11	0.06
Other Hispanic or Latino	239	1.38

Race*	Population	%
African-American/Black (1,018)	1,186	6.85
Not Hispanic (993)	1,144	6.60
Hispanic (25)	42	0.24
American Indian/Alaska Native (45)	129	0.74
Not Hispanic (24)	100	0.58
Hispanic (21)	29	0.17
Blackfeet (0)	2	0.01
Central American Ind. (1)	1	0.01
Cherokee (6)	22	0.13
Chippewa (1)	4	0.02
Choctaw (0)	1	0.01
Comanche (0)	5	0.03
Creek (4)	4	0.02
Iroquois (0)	2	0.01
Lumbee (1)	1	0.01
Mexican American Ind. (1)	1	0.01
Osage (1)	2	0.01
Ottawa (0)	1	0.01
Yuman (1)	1	0.01
Asian (2,652)	3,087	17.82
Not Hispanic (2,631)	3,029	17.48
Hispanic (21)	58	0.33
Bangladeshi (7)	10	0.06
Burmese (0)	2	0.01
Cambodian (7)	12	0.07
Chinese, ex. Taiwanese (239)	296	1.71
Filipino (339)	405	2.34
Indian (362)	394	2.27
Indonesian (30)	32	0.18
Japanese (36)	132	0.76
Korean (1,109)	1,182	6.82
Laotian (20)	26	0.15
Malaysian (4)	4	0.02
Nepalese (11)	12	0.07
Pakistani (90)	102	0.59
Sri Lankan (6)	7	0.04
Taiwanese (35)	41	0.24
Thai (21)	33	0.19
Vietnamese (279)	307	1.77
Hawaii Native/Pacific Islander (16)	64	0.37
Not Hispanic (16)	53	0.31
Hispanic (0)	11	0.06
Fijian (2)	2	0.01
Guamanian/Chamorro (8)	19	0.11
Native Hawaiian (2)	16	0.09
Samoan (0)	1	0.01
White (12,163)	12,837	74.09
Not Hispanic (10,805)	11,326	65.37
Hispanic (1,358)	1,511	8.72

Cascades

Place Type: CDP
County: Loudoun
Population: 11,912†

Ancestry‡	Population	%
African, Sub-Saharan (222)	306	2.54
Cape Verdean (0)	20	0.17
Ghanaian (140)	164	1.36
Nigerian (21)	61	0.51
Somalian (42)	42	0.35
South African (19)	19	0.16
American (399)	399	3.31
Arab (7)	35	0.29
Egyptian (0)	28	0.23
Other Arab (7)	7	0.06
Austrian (50)	248	2.06
Belgian (10)	23	0.19
Brazilian (24)	24	0.20
British (77)	86	0.71
Canadian (4)	4	0.03
Czech (0)	70	0.58
Czechoslovakian (9)	28	0.23
Danish (13)	56	0.46
Dutch (56)	101	0.84
Eastern European (33)	33	0.27
English (384)	1,430	11.87
European (198)	198	1.64
French, ex. Basque (8)	236	1.96
French Canadian (28)	67	0.56
German (599)	2,253	18.70
Greek (39)	50	0.41
Hungarian (42)	114	0.95
Iranian (119)	134	1.11
Irish (381)	1,405	11.66
Italian (272)	861	7.14
Lithuanian (26)	102	0.85
Norwegian (57)	233	1.93
Polish (126)	424	3.52
Portuguese (11)	11	0.09
Romanian (22)	22	0.18
Russian (115)	192	1.59
Scotch-Irish (160)	374	3.10
Scottish (120)	364	3.02
Slavic (13)	65	0.54
Slovak (0)	15	0.12
Swedish (22)	220	1.83
Swiss (0)	40	0.33
Turkish (33)	33	0.27
Ukrainian (13)	71	0.59
Welsh (12)	57	0.47
West Indian, ex. Hispanic (0)	46	0.38
British West Indian (0)	11	0.09
Jamaican (0)	24	0.20
West Indian (0)	11	0.09
Yugoslavian (46)	72	0.60

Hispanic Origin	Population	%
Hispanic or Latino (of any race)	984	8.26
Central American, ex. Mexican	240	2.01
Costa Rican	7	0.06
Guatemalan	31	0.26
Honduran	32	0.27
Nicaraguan	26	0.22
Panamanian	12	0.10
Salvadoran	132	1.11
Cuban	40	0.34
Dominican Republic	22	0.18
Mexican	105	0.88
Puerto Rican	113	0.95
South American	352	2.96
Argentinean	14	0.12
Bolivian	62	0.52
Chilean	27	0.23
Colombian	71	0.60
Ecuadorian	31	0.26
Paraguayan	2	0.02
Peruvian	121	1.02
Uruguayan	3	0.03
Venezuelan	21	0.18
Other Hispanic or Latino	112	0.94

Race*	Population	%
African-American/Black (719)	873	7.33
Not Hispanic (686)	803	6.74
Hispanic (33)	70	0.59
American Indian/Alaska Native (27)	111	0.93
Not Hispanic (8)	68	0.57
Hispanic (19)	43	0.36
Blackfeet (1)	2	0.02
Canadian/French Am. Ind. (3)	3	0.03
Cherokee (1)	24	0.20
Choctaw (1)	1	0.01
Creek (0)	1	0.01
Hopi (0)	2	0.02
Houma (0)	1	0.01
Iroquois (0)	1	0.01
Lumbee (0)	1	0.01
South American Ind. (0)	5	0.04
Asian (1,652)	1,991	16.71
Not Hispanic (1,646)	1,970	16.54
Hispanic (6)	21	0.18
Bangladeshi (25)	28	0.24
Burmese (2)	2	0.02
Cambodian (13)	17	0.14
Chinese, ex. Taiwanese (238)	277	2.33
Filipino (212)	270	2.27
Indian (608)	665	5.58
Indonesian (0)	1	0.01
Japanese (20)	59	0.50
Korean (165)	198	1.66
Laotian (23)	27	0.23
Malaysian (4)	4	0.03
Nepalese (11)	11	0.09
Pakistani (90)	111	0.93

*Notes: † The Census 2010 population figure is used to calculate the percentages in the Hispanic Origin and Race categories. Ancestry percentages are based on the 2006-2010 American Community Survey population (not shown); ‡ Numbers in parentheses indicate the number of people reporting a single ancestry; * Numbers in parentheses indicate the number of persons reporting this race alone, not in combination with any other race; Please refer to the Explanation of Data for more information.*

Sri Lankan (5)	5	0.04
Taiwanese (27)	30	0.25
Thai (15)	21	0.18
Vietnamese (138)	170	1.43
Hawaii Native/Pacific Islander (17)	37	0.31
Not Hispanic (13)	31	0.26
Hispanic (4)	6	0.05
Guamanian/Chamorro (6)	10	0.08
Native Hawaiian (10)	15	0.13
Samoan (1)	1	0.01
White (8,653)	9,132	76.66
Not Hispanic (8,085)	8,479	71.18
Hispanic (568)	653	5.48

Cave Spring

Place Type: CDP
County: Roanoke
Population: 24,922†

Ancestry‡	Population	%
African, Sub-Saharan (120)	120	0.47
Ghanaian (48)	48	0.19
South African (72)	72	0.28
American (2,811)	2,811	11.01
Arab (103)	117	0.46
Lebanese (96)	110	0.43
Other Arab (7)	7	0.03
Armenian (0)	14	0.05
Austrian (10)	56	0.22
Belgian (0)	12	0.05
Brazilian (19)	19	0.07
British (37)	104	0.41
Canadian (0)	13	0.05
Croatian (137)	137	0.54
Czech (50)	136	0.53
Czechoslovakian (0)	16	0.06
Danish (0)	14	0.05
Dutch (53)	461	1.81
Eastern European (26)	26	0.10
English (2,228)	5,248	20.55
European (517)	552	2.16
Finnish (0)	37	0.14
French, ex. Basque (145)	500	1.96
French Canadian (20)	57	0.22
German (1,356)	4,616	18.07
Greek (17)	34	0.13
Guyanese (32)	32	0.13
Hungarian (66)	184	0.72
Iranian (12)	12	0.05
Irish (1,246)	3,796	14.86
Italian (611)	1,074	4.21
Lithuanian (12)	78	0.31
Northern European (30)	30	0.12
Norwegian (101)	254	0.99
Pennsylvania German (0)	9	0.04
Polish (394)	737	2.89
Portuguese (15)	15	0.06
Russian (90)	156	0.61
Scandinavian (13)	13	0.05
Scotch-Irish (544)	1,188	4.65
Scottish (359)	1,296	5.07
Slovak (44)	44	0.17
Slovene (0)	15	0.06
Swedish (29)	124	0.49
Swiss (5)	48	0.19
Turkish (20)	20	0.08
Ukrainian (27)	41	0.16
Welsh (33)	239	0.94
West Indian, ex. Hispanic (7)	7	0.03
Trinidadian/Tobagonian (7)	7	0.03
Yugoslavian (76)	81	0.32

Hispanic Origin	Population	%
Hispanic or Latino (of any race)	693	2.78
Central American, ex. Mexican	99	0.40
Costa Rican	2	0.01
Guatemalan	18	0.07
Honduran	66	0.26
Nicaraguan	6	0.02
Panamanian	3	0.01
Salvadoran	2	0.01
Other Central American	2	0.01
Cuban	51	0.20
Dominican Republic	13	0.05
Mexican	240	0.96
Puerto Rican	75	0.30
South American	127	0.51
Argentinean	12	0.05
Bolivian	9	0.04
Chilean	9	0.04
Colombian	64	0.26
Ecuadorian	7	0.03
Peruvian	8	0.03
Uruguayan	1	<0.01
Venezuelan	16	0.06
Other South American	1	<0.01
Other Hispanic or Latino	88	0.35

Race*	Population	%
African-American/Black (1,063)	1,251	5.02
Not Hispanic (1,044)	1,221	4.90
Hispanic (19)	30	0.12
American Indian/Alaska Native (46)	160	0.64
Not Hispanic (36)	133	0.53
Hispanic (10)	27	0.11
Blackfeet (0)	4	0.02
Canadian/French Am. Ind. (3)	3	0.01
Cherokee (6)	50	0.20
Cheyenne (0)	2	0.01
Chippewa (10)	13	0.05
Choctaw (0)	4	0.02
Creek (0)	5	0.02
Crow (0)	1	<0.01
Iroquois (2)	3	0.01
Mexican American Ind. (6)	16	0.06
Sioux (0)	3	0.01
South American Ind. (4)	6	0.02
Asian (1,070)	1,233	4.95
Not Hispanic (1,066)	1,220	4.90
Hispanic (4)	13	0.05
Bangladeshi (1)	1	<0.01
Burmese (7)	7	0.03
Cambodian (5)	10	0.04
Chinese, ex. Taiwanese (149)	178	0.71
Filipino (91)	126	0.51
Indian (484)	523	2.10
Indonesian (2)	2	0.01
Japanese (36)	58	0.23
Korean (79)	98	0.39
Laotian (5)	5	0.02
Pakistani (49)	50	0.20
Sri Lankan (3)	3	0.01
Taiwanese (9)	12	0.05
Thai (13)	19	0.08
Vietnamese (64)	76	0.30
Hawaii Native/Pacific Islander (7)	26	0.10
Not Hispanic (7)	26	0.10
Guamanian/Chamorro (1)	1	<0.01
Native Hawaiian (0)	7	0.03
Samoan (2)	13	0.05
White (22,083)	22,484	90.22
Not Hispanic (21,641)	21,992	88.24
Hispanic (442)	492	1.97

Centreville

Place Type: CDP
County: Fairfax
Population: 71,135†

Ancestry‡	Population	%
Afghan (387)	387	0.53
African, Sub-Saharan (1,663)	1,854	2.56
African (901)	1,092	1.51
Ethiopian (90)	90	0.12
Ghanaian (81)	81	0.11
Nigerian (14)	14	0.02
Somalian (144)	144	0.20
South African (21)	21	0.03
Sudanese (225)	225	0.31
Other Sub-Saharan African (187)	187	0.26
Albanian (108)	120	0.17
American (2,765)	2,765	3.82
Arab (1,041)	1,328	1.83
Arab (304)	388	0.54
Egyptian (59)	59	0.08
Iraqi (188)	201	0.28
Jordanian (20)	36	0.05
Lebanese (124)	176	0.24
Moroccan (95)	143	0.20
Palestinian (33)	42	0.06
Syrian (0)	13	0.02
Other Arab (218)	270	0.37
Armenian (123)	147	0.20
Australian (11)	39	0.05
Austrian (77)	129	0.18
Belgian (51)	69	0.10
Brazilian (96)	106	0.15
British (128)	275	0.38
Bulgarian (0)	18	0.02
Cajun (0)	40	0.06
Canadian (93)	183	0.25
Croatian (31)	89	0.12
Czech (112)	364	0.50
Czechoslovakian (23)	47	0.06
Danish (27)	216	0.30
Dutch (187)	829	1.14
Eastern European (75)	90	0.12
English (1,568)	6,130	8.47
Estonian (15)	30	0.04
European (1,662)	1,780	2.46
Finnish (21)	65	0.09
French, ex. Basque (192)	1,405	1.94
French Canadian (174)	367	0.51
German (1,875)	8,316	11.49
Greek (332)	548	0.76
Hungarian (112)	330	0.46
Icelander (17)	17	0.02
Iranian (372)	425	0.59
Irish (2,482)	8,533	11.78
Italian (1,237)	4,291	5.93
Latvian (57)	75	0.10
Lithuanian (66)	222	0.31
Maltese (0)	15	0.02
Northern European (132)	132	0.18
Norwegian (65)	246	0.34
Pennsylvania German (19)	19	0.03
Polish (458)	1,693	2.34
Portuguese (20)	60	0.08
Romanian (55)	145	0.20
Russian (132)	690	0.95
Scandinavian (12)	67	0.09
Scotch-Irish (457)	1,314	1.81
Scottish (482)	1,715	2.37
Serbian (70)	115	0.16
Slavic (0)	40	0.06
Slovak (57)	267	0.37
Slovene (11)	11	0.02
Swedish (63)	454	0.63
Swiss (0)	196	0.27
Turkish (30)	30	0.04
Ukrainian (49)	222	0.31
Welsh (30)	411	0.57
West Indian, ex. Hispanic (254)	277	0.38
Haitian (119)	119	0.16
Jamaican (89)	112	0.15
West Indian (46)	46	0.06
Yugoslavian (132)	182	0.25

Hispanic Origin	Population	%
Hispanic or Latino (of any race)	9,498	13.35
Central American, ex. Mexican	3,312	4.66
Costa Rican	22	0.03
Guatemalan	1,120	1.57
Honduran	230	0.32
Nicaraguan	145	0.20
Panamanian	64	0.09
Salvadoran	1,714	2.41
Other Central American	17	0.02

*Notes: † The Census 2010 population figure is used to calculate the percentages in the Hispanic Origin and Race categories. Ancestry percentages are based on the 2006-2010 American Community Survey population (not shown); ‡ Numbers in parentheses indicate the number of people reporting a single ancestry; * Numbers in parentheses indicate the number of persons reporting this race alone, not in combination with any other race; Please refer to the Explanation of Data for more information.*

Cuban	197	0.28
Dominican Republic	127	0.18
Mexican	954	1.34
Puerto Rican	608	0.85
South American	3,253	4.57
Argentinean	94	0.13
Bolivian	818	1.15
Chilean	114	0.16
Colombian	416	0.58
Ecuadorian	198	0.28
Paraguayan	14	0.02
Peruvian	1,406	1.98
Uruguayan	26	0.04
Venezuelan	117	0.16
Other South American	50	0.07
Other Hispanic or Latino	1,047	1.47

Race*	Population	%
African-American/Black (5,334)	6,232	8.76
Not Hispanic (5,114)	5,856	8.23
Hispanic (220)	376	0.53
American Indian/Alaska Native (206)	558	0.78
Not Hispanic (111)	368	0.52
Hispanic (95)	190	0.27
Apache (3)	7	0.01
Blackfeet (2)	10	0.01
Canadian/French Am. Ind. (0)	2	<0.01
Central American Ind. (1)	15	0.02
Cherokee (21)	88	0.12
Cheyenne (0)	1	<0.01
Chickasaw (1)	1	<0.01
Chippewa (7)	7	0.01
Choctaw (2)	8	0.01
Comanche (0)	3	<0.01
Creek (2)	6	0.01
Inupiat *(Alaska Native)* (5)	5	0.01
Iroquois (10)	19	0.03
Lumbee (0)	1	<0.01
Mexican American Ind. (11)	27	0.04
Navajo (1)	1	<0.01
Osage (2)	3	<0.01
Ottawa (3)	3	<0.01
Paiute (1)	1	<0.01
Potawatomi (0)	1	<0.01
Pueblo (2)	3	<0.01
Puget Sound Salish (3)	3	<0.01
Seminole (1)	12	0.02
Sioux (1)	7	0.01
South American Ind. (17)	27	0.04
Spanish American Ind. (5)	5	0.01
Tohono O'Odham (2)	2	<0.01
Asian (18,264)	19,925	28.01
Not Hispanic (18,217)	19,744	27.76
Hispanic (47)	181	0.25
Bangladeshi (115)	129	0.18
Burmese (24)	34	0.05
Cambodian (101)	122	0.17
Chinese, ex. Taiwanese (1,780)	2,041	2.87
Filipino (1,126)	1,423	2.00
Hmong (10)	10	0.01
Indian (4,014)	4,251	5.98
Indonesian (64)	79	0.11
Japanese (134)	281	0.40
Korean (7,415)	7,747	10.89
Laotian (43)	54	0.08
Malaysian (5)	11	0.02
Nepalese (123)	131	0.18
Pakistani (798)	852	1.20
Sri Lankan (23)	27	0.04
Taiwanese (94)	117	0.16
Thai (178)	221	0.31
Vietnamese (1,782)	1,966	2.76
Hawaii Native/Pacific Islander (82)	206	0.29
Not Hispanic (78)	181	0.25
Hispanic (4)	25	0.04
Fijian (2)	2	<0.01
Guamanian/Chamorro (36)	54	0.08
Native Hawaiian (18)	42	0.06
Samoan (10)	19	0.03
White (40,565)	43,174	60.69
Not Hispanic (35,573)	37,568	52.81
Hispanic (4,992)	5,606	7.88

Chantilly

Place Type: CDP
County: Fairfax
Population: 23,039†

Ancestry‡	Population	%
Afghan (125)	139	0.63
African, Sub-Saharan (851)	851	3.85
African (562)	562	2.54
Somalian (182)	182	0.82
Other Sub-Saharan African (107)	107	0.48
Albanian (108)	108	0.49
American (753)	753	3.40
Arab (435)	466	2.11
Arab (61)	61	0.28
Egyptian (84)	115	0.52
Jordanian (16)	16	0.07
Lebanese (184)	184	0.83
Syrian (16)	16	0.07
Other Arab (74)	74	0.33
Australian (0)	12	0.05
Austrian (0)	11	0.05
British (88)	146	0.66
Canadian (14)	14	0.06
Croatian (0)	14	0.06
Czech (68)	118	0.53
Czechoslovakian (0)	20	0.09
Danish (7)	24	0.11
Dutch (29)	169	0.76
Eastern European (21)	21	0.09
English (316)	1,613	7.29
European (484)	497	2.25
Finnish (11)	11	0.05
French, ex. Basque (17)	307	1.39
French Canadian (20)	51	0.23
German (691)	2,600	11.75
Greek (52)	155	0.70
Hungarian (11)	51	0.23
Iranian (228)	274	1.24
Irish (652)	1,925	8.70
Italian (381)	1,306	5.90
Latvian (0)	11	0.05
Lithuanian (32)	65	0.29
Norwegian (56)	149	0.67
Polish (140)	663	3.00
Portuguese (51)	68	0.31
Romanian (32)	32	0.14
Russian (145)	244	1.10
Scandinavian (13)	27	0.12
Scotch-Irish (242)	461	2.08
Scottish (85)	318	1.44
Slavic (14)	93	0.42
Slovak (0)	119	0.54
Swedish (49)	212	0.96
Swiss (0)	70	0.32
Turkish (196)	196	0.89
Ukrainian (23)	116	0.52
Welsh (15)	111	0.50
West Indian, ex. Hispanic (177)	177	0.80
Barbadian (23)	23	0.10
Jamaican (43)	43	0.19
West Indian (111)	111	0.50

Hispanic Origin	Population	%
Hispanic or Latino (of any race)	3,661	15.89
Central American, ex. Mexican	1,450	6.29
Costa Rican	12	0.05
Guatemalan	424	1.84
Honduran	100	0.43
Nicaraguan	46	0.20
Panamanian	21	0.09
Salvadoran	840	3.65
Other Central American	7	0.03
Cuban	65	0.28
Dominican Republic	50	0.22
Mexican	456	1.98
Puerto Rican	162	0.70
South American	1,092	4.74
Argentinean	25	0.11
Bolivian	396	1.72
Chilean	65	0.28
Colombian	82	0.36
Ecuadorian	70	0.30
Paraguayan	11	0.05
Peruvian	408	1.77
Uruguayan	6	0.03
Venezuelan	19	0.08
Other South American	10	0.04
Other Hispanic or Latino	386	1.68

Race*	Population	%
African-American/Black (1,506)	1,689	7.33
Not Hispanic (1,432)	1,590	6.90
Hispanic (74)	99	0.43
American Indian/Alaska Native (58)	160	0.69
Not Hispanic (31)	98	0.43
Hispanic (27)	62	0.27
Alaska Athabascan *(Ala. Nat.)* (1)	2	0.01
Aleut *(Alaska Native)* (0)	4	0.02
Blackfeet (1)	5	0.02
Central American Ind. (1)	1	<0.01
Cherokee (2)	23	0.10
Chickasaw (4)	4	0.02
Choctaw (0)	5	0.02
Comanche (0)	2	0.01
Cree (2)	2	0.01
Delaware (0)	2	0.01
Hopi (0)	1	<0.01
Iroquois (2)	4	0.02
Mexican American Ind. (1)	2	0.01
Osage (2)	2	0.01
Potawatomi (0)	1	<0.01
Sioux (1)	1	<0.01
South American Ind. (4)	7	0.03
Ute (0)	1	<0.01
Asian (5,814)	6,366	27.63
Not Hispanic (5,787)	6,307	27.38
Hispanic (27)	59	0.26
Bangladeshi (60)	75	0.33
Burmese (5)	6	0.03
Cambodian (39)	46	0.20
Chinese, ex. Taiwanese (774)	883	3.83
Filipino (413)	505	2.19
Hmong (2)	3	0.01
Indian (1,431)	1,520	6.60
Indonesian (1)	2	0.01
Japanese (43)	102	0.44
Korean (1,051)	1,132	4.91
Laotian (49)	56	0.24
Malaysian (2)	7	0.03
Nepalese (161)	174	0.76
Pakistani (334)	364	1.58
Sri Lankan (10)	10	0.04
Taiwanese (66)	80	0.35
Thai (68)	81	0.35
Vietnamese (1,091)	1,158	5.03
Hawaii Native/Pacific Islander (15)	65	0.28
Not Hispanic (12)	53	0.23
Hispanic (3)	12	0.05
Guamanian/Chamorro (5)	13	0.06
Marshallese (2)	2	0.01
Native Hawaiian (6)	20	0.09
Samoan (0)	1	<0.01
White (13,261)	14,142	61.38
Not Hispanic (11,283)	11,968	51.95
Hispanic (1,978)	2,174	9.44

Charlottesville

Place Type: Independent City
County: Charlottesville
Population: 43,475†

Ancestry‡	Population	%
Afghan (18)	18	0.04
African, Sub-Saharan (831)	1,131	2.68

*Notes: † The Census 2010 population figure is used to calculate the percentages in the Hispanic Origin and Race categories. Ancestry percentages are based on the 2006-2010 American Community Survey population (not shown); ‡ Numbers in parentheses indicate the number of people reporting a single ancestry; * Numbers in parentheses indicate the number of persons reporting this race alone, not in combination with any other race; Please refer to the Explanation of Data for more information.*

African (387)	564	1.33
Ghanaian (48)	48	0.11
Liberian (36)	36	0.09
Nigerian (20)	135	0.32
Somalian (310)	310	0.73
South African (18)	26	0.06
Sudanese (12)	12	0.03
Albanian (34)	34	0.08
American (3,502)	3,502	8.29
Arab (304)	468	1.11
Arab (10)	48	0.11
Egyptian (81)	92	0.22
Iraqi (42)	42	0.10
Lebanese (118)	195	0.46
Moroccan (0)	19	0.04
Palestinian (11)	11	0.03
Syrian (30)	30	0.07
Other Arab (12)	31	0.07
Armenian (0)	22	0.05
Australian (0)	8	0.02
Austrian (17)	121	0.29
Belgian (72)	175	0.41
Brazilian (63)	63	0.15
British (289)	536	1.27
Canadian (9)	16	0.04
Croatian (7)	32	0.08
Czech (72)	132	0.31
Czechoslovakian (0)	15	0.04
Danish (21)	95	0.22
Dutch (188)	560	1.32
Eastern European (46)	46	0.11
English (1,974)	5,539	13.10
European (547)	641	1.52
Finnish (19)	49	0.12
French, ex. Basque (267)	1,168	2.76
French Canadian (69)	234	0.55
German (1,355)	5,795	13.71
Greek (148)	351	0.83
Guyanese (10)	22	0.05
Hungarian (13)	128	0.30
Icelander (0)	25	0.06
Iranian (221)	234	0.55
Irish (1,332)	4,111	9.73
Israeli (22)	35	0.08
Italian (885)	2,133	5.05
Latvian (9)	21	0.05
Lithuanian (48)	112	0.26
Northern European (70)	70	0.17
Norwegian (114)	405	0.96
Polish (214)	924	2.19
Portuguese (12)	44	0.10
Romanian (24)	52	0.12
Russian (123)	480	1.14
Scandinavian (11)	201	0.48
Scotch-Irish (580)	1,306	3.09
Scottish (218)	1,258	2.98
Serbian (23)	23	0.05
Slavic (13)	13	0.03
Slovak (26)	47	0.11
Slovene (19)	43	0.10
Swedish (87)	407	0.96
Swiss (46)	140	0.33
Turkish (261)	285	0.67
Ukrainian (45)	203	0.48
Welsh (110)	471	1.11
West Indian, ex. Hispanic (129)	175	0.41
Barbadian (0)	10	0.02
Belizean (21)	21	0.05
Bermudan (10)	10	0.02
Haitian (26)	26	0.06
Jamaican (62)	98	0.23
Trinidadian/Tobagonian (10)	10	0.02

Hispanic Origin	Population	%
Hispanic or Latino (of any race)	2,223	5.11
Central American, ex. Mexican	385	0.89
Costa Rican	20	0.05
Guatemalan	60	0.14
Honduran	74	0.17
Nicaraguan	27	0.06
Panamanian	34	0.08
Salvadoran	164	0.38
Other Central American	6	0.01
Cuban	119	0.27
Dominican Republic	25	0.06
Mexican	954	2.19
Puerto Rican	200	0.46
South American	321	0.74
Argentinean	49	0.11
Bolivian	31	0.07
Chilean	28	0.06
Colombian	98	0.23
Ecuadorian	26	0.06
Paraguayan	9	0.02
Peruvian	58	0.13
Uruguayan	4	0.01
Venezuelan	17	0.04
Other South American	1	<0.01
Other Hispanic or Latino	219	0.50

Race*	Population	%
African-American/Black (8,437)	9,010	20.72
Not Hispanic (8,344)	8,877	20.42
Hispanic (93)	133	0.31
American Indian/Alaska Native (116)	379	0.87
Not Hispanic (65)	288	0.66
Hispanic (51)	91	0.21
Aleut *(Alaska Native)* (0)	1	<0.01
Apache (0)	3	0.01
Blackfeet (0)	10	0.02
Canadian/French Am. Ind. (0)	4	0.01
Central American Ind. (4)	4	0.01
Cherokee (15)	78	0.18
Chickasaw (1)	8	0.02
Chippewa (1)	1	<0.01
Choctaw (4)	13	0.03
Cree (1)	2	<0.01
Crow (0)	1	<0.01
Delaware (0)	1	<0.01
Inupiat *(Alaska Native)* (3)	4	0.01
Iroquois (1)	8	0.02
Lumbee (2)	2	<0.01
Mexican American Ind. (24)	32	0.07
Navajo (1)	1	<0.01
Potawatomi (0)	2	<0.01
Seminole (1)	1	<0.01
Sioux (2)	6	0.01
South American Ind. (5)	12	0.03
Tohono O'Odham (1)	3	0.01
Asian (2,771)	3,330	7.66
Not Hispanic (2,758)	3,302	7.60
Hispanic (13)	28	0.06
Bangladeshi (13)	16	0.04
Bhutanese (50)	59	0.14
Burmese (171)	183	0.42
Cambodian (6)	7	0.02
Chinese, ex. Taiwanese (826)	968	2.23
Filipino (167)	247	0.57
Indian (506)	576	1.32
Indonesian (5)	8	0.02
Japanese (73)	160	0.37
Korean (403)	482	1.11
Laotian (11)	11	0.03
Malaysian (15)	16	0.04
Nepalese (43)	52	0.12
Pakistani (64)	74	0.17
Sri Lankan (14)	15	0.03
Taiwanese (55)	65	0.15
Thai (47)	60	0.14
Vietnamese (143)	180	0.41
Hawaii Native/Pacific Islander (17)	55	0.13
Not Hispanic (13)	49	0.11
Hispanic (4)	6	0.01
Fijian (1)	2	<0.01
Guamanian/Chamorro (3)	8	0.02
Native Hawaiian (8)	21	0.05
Samoan (1)	4	0.01
White (30,031)	31,197	71.76
Not Hispanic (28,827)	29,856	68.67
Hispanic (1,204)	1,341	3.08

Cherry Hill

Place Type: CDP
County: Prince William
Population: 16,000†

Ancestry‡	Population	%
Afghan (44)	44	0.28
African, Sub-Saharan (1,198)	1,331	8.58
African (574)	707	4.56
Ethiopian (95)	95	0.61
Ghanaian (332)	332	2.14
Liberian (10)	10	0.06
Sierra Leonean (147)	147	0.95
Other Sub-Saharan African (40)	40	0.26
American (380)	380	2.45
Arab (97)	247	1.59
Jordanian (97)	97	0.63
Lebanese (0)	49	0.32
Other Arab (0)	101	0.65
British (36)	52	0.34
Canadian (0)	20	0.13
Czech (0)	12	0.08
Danish (24)	47	0.30
Dutch (10)	81	0.52
English (129)	571	3.68
European (53)	135	0.87
Finnish (15)	15	0.10
French, ex. Basque (19)	131	0.84
French Canadian (0)	19	0.12
German (190)	1,013	6.53
Guyanese (0)	148	0.95
Irish (272)	953	6.14
Italian (52)	286	1.84
Lithuanian (0)	48	0.31
Norwegian (10)	62	0.40
Pennsylvania German (0)	80	0.52
Polish (0)	167	1.08
Portuguese (6)	29	0.19
Romanian (13)	23	0.15
Russian (10)	42	0.27
Scotch-Irish (138)	268	1.73
Scottish (27)	112	0.72
Slovak (12)	12	0.08
Swedish (0)	59	0.38
Swiss (0)	8	0.05
Ukrainian (51)	62	0.40
Welsh (0)	26	0.17
West Indian, ex. Hispanic (103)	434	2.80
Jamaican (70)	218	1.41
Trinidadian/Tobagonian (33)	33	0.21
West Indian (0)	183	1.18

Hispanic Origin	Population	%
Hispanic or Latino (of any race)	2,603	16.27
Central American, ex. Mexican	1,095	6.84
Costa Rican	6	0.04
Guatemalan	100	0.63
Honduran	123	0.77
Nicaraguan	68	0.43
Panamanian	58	0.36
Salvadoran	740	4.63
Cuban	35	0.22
Dominican Republic	68	0.43
Mexican	299	1.87
Puerto Rican	462	2.89
South American	337	2.11
Argentinean	28	0.18
Bolivian	49	0.31
Chilean	2	0.01
Colombian	57	0.36
Ecuadorian	22	0.14
Peruvian	171	1.07
Uruguayan	4	0.03
Venezuelan	2	0.01
Other South American	2	0.01
Other Hispanic or Latino	307	1.92

Race*	Population	%
African-American/Black (7,792)	8,318	51.99

*Notes: † The Census 2010 population figure is used to calculate the percentages in the Hispanic Origin and Race categories. Ancestry percentages are based on the 2006-2010 American Community Survey population (not shown); ‡ Numbers in parentheses indicate the number of people reporting a single ancestry; * Numbers in parentheses indicate the number of persons reporting this race alone, not in combination with any other race; Please refer to the Explanation of Data for more information.*

Not Hispanic (7,541)	7,961	49.76
Hispanic (251)	357	2.23
American Indian/Alaska Native (66)	235	1.47
Not Hispanic (32)	152	0.95
Hispanic (34)	83	0.52
Blackfeet (0)	11	0.07
Cherokee (10)	49	0.31
Chippewa (3)	3	0.02
Choctaw (0)	1	0.01
Creek (0)	1	0.01
Delaware (0)	2	0.01
Iroquois (2)	5	0.03
Mexican American Ind. (4)	12	0.08
Osage (0)	1	0.01
Seminole (0)	3	0.02
Sioux (0)	1	0.01
South American Ind. (1)	14	0.09
Spanish American Ind. (2)	2	0.01
Tohono O'Odham (0)	3	0.02
Yaqui (2)	2	0.01
Asian (1,303)	1,618	10.11
Not Hispanic (1,296)	1,576	9.85
Hispanic (7)	42	0.26
Bangladeshi (63)	70	0.44
Burmese (10)	10	0.06
Cambodian (20)	21	0.13
Chinese, ex. Taiwanese (79)	94	0.59
Filipino (259)	367	2.29
Hmong (1)	1	0.01
Indian (271)	308	1.93
Indonesian (9)	14	0.09
Japanese (10)	53	0.33
Korean (87)	139	0.87
Laotian (5)	8	0.05
Malaysian (0)	1	0.01
Nepalese (9)	11	0.07
Pakistani (278)	289	1.81
Taiwanese (1)	2	0.01
Thai (16)	25	0.16
Vietnamese (118)	125	0.78
Hawaii Native/Pacific Islander (28)	95	0.59
Not Hispanic (26)	71	0.44
Hispanic (2)	24	0.15
Fijian (1)	1	0.01
Guamanian/Chamorro (16)	19	0.12
Native Hawaiian (2)	24	0.15
Samoan (1)	5	0.03
Tongan (1)	3	0.02
White (4,823)	5,543	34.64
Not Hispanic (3,796)	4,306	26.91
Hispanic (1,027)	1,237	7.73

Chesapeake

Place Type: Independent City
County: Chesapeake
Population: 222,209†

Ancestry‡	Population	%
African, Sub-Saharan (4,914)	6,008	2.74
African (4,661)	5,745	2.62
Cape Verdean (77)	87	0.04
Ethiopian (98)	98	0.04
Ghanaian (17)	17	0.01
Nigerian (44)	44	0.02
Ugandan (17)	17	0.01
Albanian (55)	75	0.03
American (30,037)	30,037	13.70
Arab (347)	725	0.33
Arab (89)	89	0.04
Egyptian (14)	26	0.01
Lebanese (166)	448	0.20
Moroccan (38)	38	0.02
Syrian (23)	63	0.03
Other Arab (17)	61	0.03
Armenian (36)	71	0.03
Australian (7)	7	<0.01
Austrian (57)	221	0.10
Belgian (135)	266	0.12
Brazilian (67)	77	0.04
British (475)	983	0.45
Bulgarian (25)	48	0.02
Canadian (289)	459	0.21
Celtic (13)	13	0.01
Croatian (30)	97	0.04
Czech (83)	553	0.25
Czechoslovakian (71)	150	0.07
Danish (181)	412	0.19
Dutch (397)	1,807	0.82
Eastern European (233)	260	0.12
English (9,383)	23,701	10.81
European (2,142)	2,336	1.07
Finnish (49)	156	0.07
French, ex. Basque (706)	4,892	2.23
French Canadian (424)	1,011	0.46
German (7,230)	24,649	11.24
Greek (348)	955	0.44
Guyanese (114)	114	0.05
Hungarian (246)	667	0.30
Iranian (23)	30	0.01
Irish (6,875)	23,626	10.77
Israeli (90)	117	0.05
Italian (3,967)	9,760	4.45
Latvian (0)	40	0.02
Lithuanian (145)	356	0.16
Luxemburger (0)	13	0.01
Maltese (0)	19	0.01
Northern European (190)	190	0.09
Norwegian (359)	1,192	0.54
Pennsylvania German (82)	113	0.05
Polish (1,307)	4,283	1.95
Portuguese (146)	306	0.14
Romanian (0)	36	0.02
Russian (405)	1,048	0.48
Scandinavian (84)	164	0.07
Scotch-Irish (2,174)	4,910	2.24
Scottish (1,695)	4,830	2.20
Serbian (8)	39	0.02
Slavic (105)	200	0.09
Slovak (64)	221	0.10
Slovene (45)	109	0.05
Swedish (280)	1,429	0.65
Swiss (73)	342	0.16
Turkish (65)	65	0.03
Ukrainian (195)	340	0.16
Welsh (373)	1,492	0.68
West Indian, ex. Hispanic (934)	1,340	0.61
Bahamian (10)	38	0.02
Barbadian (61)	74	0.03
Belizean (61)	61	0.03
Bermudan (32)	32	0.01
British West Indian (10)	10	<0.01
Haitian (154)	178	0.08
Jamaican (219)	292	0.13
Trinidadian/Tobagonian (50)	50	0.02
West Indian (337)	605	0.28
Yugoslavian (24)	40	0.02

Hispanic Origin	Population	%
Hispanic or Latino (of any race)	9,706	4.37
Central American, ex. Mexican	998	0.45
Costa Rican	40	0.02
Guatemalan	255	0.11
Honduran	191	0.09
Nicaraguan	45	0.02
Panamanian	267	0.12
Salvadoran	192	0.09
Other Central American	8	<0.01
Cuban	408	0.18
Dominican Republic	286	0.13
Mexican	3,579	1.61
Puerto Rican	2,739	1.23
South American	710	0.32
Argentinean	46	0.02
Bolivian	27	0.01
Chilean	55	0.02
Colombian	266	0.12
Ecuadorian	103	0.05
Paraguayan	4	<0.01
Peruvian	137	0.06
Uruguayan	27	0.01
Venezuelan	35	0.02
Other South American	10	<0.01
Other Hispanic or Latino	986	0.44

Race*	Population	%
African-American/Black (66,237)	69,511	31.28
Not Hispanic (65,204)	67,958	30.58
Hispanic (1,033)	1,553	0.70
American Indian/Alaska Native (871)	2,543	1.14
Not Hispanic (720)	2,156	0.97
Hispanic (151)	387	0.17
Alaska Athabascan *(Ala. Nat.)* (1)	2	<0.01
Aleut *(Alaska Native)* (5)	9	<0.01
Apache (10)	41	0.02
Arapaho (0)	1	<0.01
Blackfeet (21)	84	0.04
Canadian/French Am. Ind. (3)	11	<0.01
Central American Ind. (12)	26	0.01
Cherokee (129)	585	0.26
Cheyenne (1)	2	<0.01
Chickasaw (12)	20	0.01
Chippewa (23)	41	0.02
Choctaw (18)	53	0.02
Comanche (3)	10	<0.01
Cree (0)	10	<0.01
Creek (12)	33	0.01
Crow (4)	11	<0.01
Delaware (3)	8	<0.01
Hopi (1)	3	<0.01
Inupiat *(Alaska Native)* (3)	5	<0.01
Iroquois (7)	39	0.02
Kiowa (11)	15	0.01
Lumbee (47)	99	0.04
Menominee (4)	6	<0.01
Mexican American Ind. (25)	38	0.02
Navajo (16)	26	0.01
Osage (1)	7	<0.01
Ottawa (1)	1	<0.01
Pima (0)	1	<0.01
Potawatomi (1)	5	<0.01
Pueblo (4)	6	<0.01
Puget Sound Salish (0)	1	<0.01
Seminole (9)	23	0.01
Shoshone (1)	3	<0.01
Sioux (15)	40	0.02
South American Ind. (3)	26	0.01
Spanish American Ind. (0)	2	<0.01
Tlingit-Haida *(Alaska Native)* (6)	8	<0.01
Ute (2)	2	<0.01
Yuman (0)	1	<0.01
Asian (6,383)	8,937	4.02
Not Hispanic (6,289)	8,626	3.88
Hispanic (94)	311	0.14
Bangladeshi (9)	15	0.01
Burmese (9)	12	0.01
Cambodian (7)	13	0.01
Chinese, ex. Taiwanese (631)	825	0.37
Filipino (3,165)	4,583	2.06
Hmong (3)	3	<0.01
Indian (820)	986	0.44
Indonesian (6)	13	0.01
Japanese (233)	648	0.29
Korean (546)	803	0.36
Laotian (8)	11	<0.01
Malaysian (1)	10	<0.01
Nepalese (24)	29	0.01
Pakistani (112)	120	0.05
Sri Lankan (10)	14	0.01
Taiwanese (17)	31	0.01
Thai (73)	141	0.06
Vietnamese (506)	616	0.28
Hawaii Native/Pacific Islander (169)	494	0.22
Not Hispanic (147)	423	0.19
Hispanic (22)	71	0.03
Fijian (1)	1	<0.01
Guamanian/Chamorro (80)	146	0.07
Marshallese (1)	1	<0.01
Native Hawaiian (38)	172	0.08
Samoan (9)	41	0.02

*Notes: † The Census 2010 population figure is used to calculate the percentages in the Hispanic Origin and Race categories. Ancestry percentages are based on the 2006-2010 American Community Survey population (not shown); ‡ Numbers in parentheses indicate the number of people reporting a single ancestry; * Numbers in parentheses indicate the number of persons reporting this race alone, not in combination with any other race; Please refer to the Explanation of Data for more information.*

Tongan (2)	2	<0.01
White (139,012)	144,601	65.07
Not Hispanic (134,251)	138,994	62.55
Hispanic (4,761)	5,607	2.52

Chester

Place Type: CDP
County: Chesterfield
Population: 20,987†

Ancestry‡	Population	%
African, Sub-Saharan (62)	91	0.46
African (62)	69	0.35
Cape Verdean (0)	22	0.11
American (2,868)	2,868	14.40
Arab (53)	53	0.27
Egyptian (31)	31	0.16
Lebanese (22)	22	0.11
Armenian (7)	7	0.04
Belgian (0)	11	0.06
Brazilian (30)	30	0.15
British (43)	82	0.41
Canadian (9)	27	0.14
Czech (27)	69	0.35
Czechoslovakian (13)	13	0.07
Danish (0)	18	0.09
Dutch (42)	312	1.57
English (2,999)	4,378	21.98
Estonian (0)	21	0.11
European (276)	300	1.51
Finnish (0)	15	0.08
French, ex. Basque (46)	274	1.38
French Canadian (7)	49	0.25
German (1,025)	2,533	12.72
Hungarian (0)	44	0.22
Irish (482)	1,669	8.38
Italian (422)	752	3.78
Lithuanian (0)	64	0.32
Northern European (0)	13	0.07
Norwegian (44)	136	0.68
Pennsylvania German (0)	11	0.06
Polish (79)	180	0.90
Portuguese (10)	10	0.05
Romanian (0)	16	0.08
Russian (59)	117	0.59
Scotch-Irish (101)	457	2.29
Scottish (254)	572	2.87
Slovak (42)	42	0.21
Slovene (18)	18	0.09
Swedish (34)	143	0.72
Swiss (34)	70	0.35
Welsh (67)	126	0.63
West Indian, ex. Hispanic (12)	12	0.06
Haitian (12)	12	0.06
Yugoslavian (12)	25	0.13

Hispanic Origin	Population	%
Hispanic or Latino (of any race)	1,761	8.39
Central American, ex. Mexican	366	1.74
Costa Rican	5	0.02
Guatemalan	101	0.48
Honduran	40	0.19
Nicaraguan	5	0.02
Panamanian	40	0.19
Salvadoran	175	0.83
Cuban	44	0.21
Dominican Republic	22	0.10
Mexican	731	3.48
Puerto Rican	307	1.46
South American	101	0.48
Argentinean	9	0.04
Colombian	47	0.22
Ecuadorian	17	0.08
Paraguayan	9	0.04
Peruvian	6	0.03
Uruguayan	2	0.01
Venezuelan	6	0.03
Other South American	5	0.02
Other Hispanic or Latino	190	0.91

Race*	Population	%
African-American/Black (4,095)	4,396	20.95
Not Hispanic (4,010)	4,268	20.34
Hispanic (85)	128	0.61
American Indian/Alaska Native (104)	236	1.12
Not Hispanic (73)	180	0.86
Hispanic (31)	56	0.27
Alaska Athabascan *(Ala. Nat.)* (1)	4	0.02
Apache (5)	7	0.03
Blackfeet (0)	2	0.01
Cherokee (19)	55	0.26
Cheyenne (1)	1	<0.01
Chippewa (0)	1	<0.01
Choctaw (0)	7	0.03
Creek (1)	2	0.01
Crow (0)	1	<0.01
Iroquois (0)	2	0.01
Lumbee (5)	10	0.05
Mexican American Ind. (3)	3	0.01
Ottawa (1)	1	<0.01
Seminole (1)	2	0.01
Sioux (0)	1	<0.01
Asian (472)	626	2.98
Not Hispanic (465)	613	2.92
Hispanic (7)	13	0.06
Bangladeshi (8)	8	0.04
Cambodian (21)	24	0.11
Chinese, ex. Taiwanese (51)	66	0.31
Filipino (83)	106	0.51
Indian (130)	152	0.72
Indonesian (1)	1	<0.01
Japanese (18)	51	0.24
Korean (95)	127	0.61
Laotian (1)	3	0.01
Pakistani (5)	6	0.03
Sri Lankan (3)	3	0.01
Taiwanese (5)	5	0.02
Thai (6)	12	0.06
Vietnamese (29)	39	0.19
Hawaii Native/Pacific Islander (13)	33	0.16
Not Hispanic (9)	24	0.11
Hispanic (4)	9	0.04
Guamanian/Chamorro (5)	12	0.06
Native Hawaiian (1)	12	0.06
Samoan (4)	8	0.04
Tongan (1)	1	<0.01
White (14,906)	15,362	73.20
Not Hispanic (14,182)	14,562	69.39
Hispanic (724)	800	3.81

Christiansburg

Place Type: Town
County: Montgomery
Population: 21,041†

Ancestry‡	Population	%
African, Sub-Saharan (47)	74	0.36
African (38)	65	0.32
South African (9)	9	0.04
American (2,835)	2,835	13.97
Arab (106)	170	0.84
Arab (45)	45	0.22
Egyptian (31)	63	0.31
Other Arab (30)	62	0.31
Austrian (0)	11	0.05
British (91)	164	0.81
Canadian (0)	9	0.04
Celtic (0)	19	0.09
Czech (0)	22	0.11
Danish (0)	12	0.06
Dutch (46)	277	1.37
English (1,454)	2,951	14.55
European (181)	199	0.98
Finnish (0)	69	0.34
French, ex. Basque (172)	534	2.63
French Canadian (9)	19	0.09
German (1,191)	3,332	16.42
Greek (241)	241	1.19
Hungarian (12)	118	0.58
Iranian (0)	11	0.05
Irish (763)	2,480	12.22
Italian (342)	734	3.62
Northern European (53)	53	0.26
Norwegian (10)	60	0.30
Polish (107)	240	1.18
Portuguese (0)	30	0.15
Romanian (85)	85	0.42
Russian (47)	127	0.63
Scandinavian (17)	17	0.08
Scotch-Irish (280)	709	3.49
Scottish (214)	814	4.01
Swedish (110)	127	0.63
Swiss (30)	30	0.15
Turkish (16)	16	0.08
Ukrainian (0)	17	0.08
Welsh (35)	215	1.06
West Indian, ex. Hispanic (0)	33	0.16
Jamaican (0)	33	0.16

Hispanic Origin	Population	%
Hispanic or Latino (of any race)	461	2.19
Central American, ex. Mexican	54	0.26
Costa Rican	7	0.03
Guatemalan	14	0.07
Honduran	6	0.03
Nicaraguan	1	<0.01
Panamanian	10	0.05
Salvadoran	16	0.08
Cuban	24	0.11
Dominican Republic	5	0.02
Mexican	199	0.95
Puerto Rican	93	0.44
South American	45	0.21
Argentinean	5	0.02
Bolivian	2	0.01
Chilean	2	0.01
Colombian	14	0.07
Ecuadorian	1	<0.01
Paraguayan	4	0.02
Peruvian	17	0.08
Other Hispanic or Latino	41	0.19

Race*	Population	%
African-American/Black (1,295)	1,526	7.25
Not Hispanic (1,270)	1,489	7.08
Hispanic (25)	37	0.18
American Indian/Alaska Native (53)	176	0.84
Not Hispanic (35)	145	0.69
Hispanic (18)	31	0.15
Apache (4)	10	0.05
Blackfeet (2)	6	0.03
Cherokee (6)	59	0.28
Choctaw (0)	7	0.03
Colville (1)	1	<0.01
Creek (0)	1	<0.01
Iroquois (2)	2	0.01
Lumbee (1)	1	<0.01
Mexican American Ind. (2)	2	0.01
Shoshone (4)	4	0.02
Sioux (0)	1	<0.01
Yaqui (0)	1	<0.01
Asian (302)	379	1.80
Not Hispanic (300)	373	1.77
Hispanic (2)	6	0.03
Bangladeshi (2)	2	0.01
Chinese, ex. Taiwanese (59)	65	0.31
Filipino (35)	53	0.25
Indian (102)	115	0.55
Japanese (5)	17	0.08
Korean (43)	63	0.30
Pakistani (3)	3	0.01
Taiwanese (2)	2	0.01
Thai (9)	11	0.05
Vietnamese (30)	33	0.16
Hawaii Native/Pacific Islander (9)	26	0.12
Not Hispanic (5)	18	0.09
Hispanic (4)	8	0.04
Fijian (0)	1	<0.01

*Notes: † The Census 2010 population figure is used to calculate the percentages in the Hispanic Origin and Race categories. Ancestry percentages are based on the 2006-2010 American Community Survey population (not shown); ‡ Numbers in parentheses indicate the number of people reporting a single ancestry; * Numbers in parentheses indicate the number of persons reporting this race alone, not in combination with any other race; Please refer to the Explanation of Data for more information.*

Guamanian/Chamorro (7)	9	0.04
Native Hawaiian (2)	10	0.05
White (18,831)	19,210	91.30
Not Hispanic (18,579)	18,927	89.95
Hispanic (252)	283	1.34

Colonial Heights

Place Type: Independent City
County: Colonial Heights
Population: 17,411†

Ancestry‡	Population	%
African, Sub-Saharan (117)	289	1.65
African (29)	133	0.76
Ethiopian (14)	14	0.08
Nigerian (74)	74	0.42
South African (0)	68	0.39
American (2,227)	2,227	12.75
Arab (35)	35	0.20
Lebanese (10)	10	0.06
Palestinian (25)	25	0.14
Australian (0)	13	0.07
Belgian (17)	40	0.23
British (65)	117	0.67
Bulgarian (7)	53	0.30
Croatian (0)	9	0.05
Czech (49)	165	0.94
Czechoslovakian (36)	45	0.26
Danish (10)	22	0.13
Dutch (52)	210	1.20
English (2,771)	3,948	22.60
European (114)	125	0.72
French, ex. Basque (103)	385	2.20
French Canadian (53)	66	0.38
German (949)	2,085	11.93
German Russian (0)	12	0.07
Greek (20)	27	0.15
Hungarian (0)	17	0.10
Irish (815)	2,067	11.83
Italian (312)	494	2.83
Norwegian (19)	41	0.23
Pennsylvania German (0)	8	0.05
Polish (138)	276	1.58
Portuguese (114)	163	0.93
Romanian (0)	17	0.10
Russian (22)	22	0.13
Scotch-Irish (405)	657	3.76
Scottish (221)	502	2.87
Slavic (0)	15	0.09
Slovak (0)	10	0.06
Swedish (0)	74	0.42
Swiss (25)	35	0.20
Ukrainian (0)	32	0.18
Welsh (108)	189	1.08
West Indian, ex. Hispanic (0)	30	0.17
Jamaican (0)	30	0.17

Hispanic Origin	Population	%
Hispanic or Latino (of any race)	674	3.87
Central American, ex. Mexican	130	0.75
Costa Rican	3	0.02
Guatemalan	10	0.06
Honduran	47	0.27
Nicaraguan	1	0.01
Panamanian	12	0.07
Salvadoran	57	0.33
Cuban	15	0.09
Dominican Republic	29	0.17
Mexican	209	1.20
Puerto Rican	196	1.13
South American	36	0.21
Argentinean	1	0.01
Bolivian	2	0.01
Colombian	24	0.14
Ecuadorian	3	0.02
Peruvian	3	0.02
Uruguayan	1	0.01
Other South American	2	0.01
Other Hispanic or Latino	59	0.34

Race*	Population	%
African-American/Black (1,783)	1,974	11.34
Not Hispanic (1,732)	1,904	10.94
Hispanic (51)	70	0.40
American Indian/Alaska Native (68)	141	0.81
Not Hispanic (63)	134	0.77
Hispanic (5)	7	0.04
Alaska Athabascan *(Ala. Nat.)* (1)	1	0.01
Blackfeet (4)	8	0.05
Cherokee (5)	15	0.09
Chickasaw (0)	1	0.01
Chippewa (3)	3	0.02
Choctaw (1)	2	0.01
Comanche (1)	1	0.01
Creek (1)	7	0.04
Crow (1)	1	0.01
Iroquois (1)	2	0.01
Lumbee (7)	10	0.06
Mexican American Ind. (2)	2	0.01
Navajo (0)	1	0.01
Potawatomi (1)	1	0.01
Seminole (0)	5	0.03
Sioux (2)	2	0.01
Asian (578)	710	4.08
Not Hispanic (570)	687	3.95
Hispanic (8)	23	0.13
Bangladeshi (4)	4	0.02
Burmese (3)	3	0.02
Cambodian (2)	6	0.03
Chinese, ex. Taiwanese (122)	128	0.74
Filipino (49)	76	0.44
Indian (139)	145	0.83
Indonesian (2)	2	0.01
Japanese (17)	50	0.29
Korean (136)	179	1.03
Pakistani (16)	20	0.11
Thai (5)	11	0.06
Vietnamese (62)	68	0.39
Hawaii Native/Pacific Islander (8)	35	0.20
Not Hispanic (8)	25	0.14
Hispanic (0)	10	0.06
Fijian (1)	1	0.01
Guamanian/Chamorro (3)	10	0.06
Native Hawaiian (2)	7	0.04
Samoan (2)	3	0.02
White (14,326)	14,658	84.19
Not Hispanic (14,020)	14,313	82.21
Hispanic (306)	345	1.98

Countryside

Place Type: CDP
County: Loudoun
Population: 10,072†

Ancestry‡	Population	%
Afghan (15)	15	0.16
African, Sub-Saharan (170)	231	2.42
African (121)	182	1.90
Liberian (24)	24	0.25
Other Sub-Saharan African (25)	25	0.26
American (356)	356	3.72
Arab (58)	58	0.61
Palestinian (58)	58	0.61
Austrian (17)	65	0.68
Belgian (0)	47	0.49
British (42)	103	1.08
Canadian (0)	16	0.17
Croatian (22)	22	0.23
Czech (0)	111	1.16
Danish (59)	125	1.31
Dutch (43)	224	2.34
Eastern European (40)	40	0.42
English (345)	1,526	15.96
European (212)	220	2.30
Finnish (0)	23	0.24
French, ex. Basque (42)	165	1.73
French Canadian (10)	26	0.27
German (433)	1,626	17.00
Hungarian (45)	59	0.62
Iranian (140)	140	1.46
Irish (269)	1,384	14.47
Italian (261)	564	5.90
Lithuanian (0)	22	0.23
Luxemburger (0)	12	0.13
New Zealander (23)	23	0.24
Northern European (11)	11	0.12
Norwegian (37)	121	1.27
Polish (49)	311	3.25
Romanian (0)	25	0.26
Russian (8)	32	0.33
Scotch-Irish (135)	180	1.88
Scottish (45)	199	2.08
Swedish (69)	185	1.93
Swiss (0)	68	0.71
Ukrainian (0)	8	0.08
Welsh (0)	175	1.83
West Indian, ex. Hispanic (0)	18	0.19
U.S. Virgin Islander (0)	18	0.19

Hispanic Origin	Population	%
Hispanic or Latino (of any race)	1,505	14.94
Central American, ex. Mexican	470	4.67
Costa Rican	2	0.02
Guatemalan	64	0.64
Honduran	36	0.36
Nicaraguan	7	0.07
Panamanian	25	0.25
Salvadoran	334	3.32
Other Central American	2	0.02
Cuban	19	0.19
Dominican Republic	22	0.22
Mexican	172	1.71
Puerto Rican	117	1.16
South American	519	5.15
Argentinean	24	0.24
Bolivian	119	1.18
Chilean	14	0.14
Colombian	51	0.51
Ecuadorian	28	0.28
Peruvian	273	2.71
Uruguayan	2	0.02
Venezuelan	8	0.08
Other Hispanic or Latino	186	1.85

Race*	Population	%
African-American/Black (697)	812	8.06
Not Hispanic (675)	771	7.65
Hispanic (22)	41	0.41
American Indian/Alaska Native (25)	89	0.88
Not Hispanic (5)	45	0.45
Hispanic (20)	44	0.44
Apache (2)	2	0.02
Blackfeet (0)	3	0.03
Central American Ind. (0)	1	0.01
Cherokee (4)	19	0.19
Chippewa (0)	1	0.01
Choctaw (0)	1	0.01
Delaware (0)	2	0.02
Mexican American Ind. (7)	8	0.08
Ottawa (0)	2	0.02
Seminole (0)	1	0.01
Sioux (0)	3	0.03
South American Ind. (0)	2	0.02
Asian (1,041)	1,228	12.19
Not Hispanic (1,036)	1,206	11.97
Hispanic (5)	22	0.22
Bangladeshi (30)	30	0.30
Burmese (12)	12	0.12
Cambodian (20)	23	0.23
Chinese, ex. Taiwanese (75)	87	0.86
Filipino (153)	196	1.95
Indian (388)	407	4.04
Indonesian (4)	4	0.04
Japanese (17)	52	0.52
Korean (54)	73	0.72
Laotian (15)	21	0.21
Malaysian (1)	1	0.01
Nepalese (13)	15	0.15

*Notes: † The Census 2010 population figure is used to calculate the percentages in the Hispanic Origin and Race categories. Ancestry percentages are based on the 2006-2010 American Community Survey population (not shown); ‡ Numbers in parentheses indicate the number of people reporting a single ancestry; * Numbers in parentheses indicate the number of persons reporting this race alone, not in combination with any other race; Please refer to the Explanation of Data for more information.*

Pakistani (106)	112	1.11
Taiwanese (3)	5	0.05
Thai (17)	22	0.22
Vietnamese (105)	116	1.15
Hawaii Native/Pacific Islander (7)	31	0.31
Not Hispanic (6)	28	0.28
Hispanic (1)	3	0.03
Fijian (0)	2	0.02
Guamanian/Chamorro (0)	4	0.04
Native Hawaiian (4)	13	0.13
Samoan (0)	4	0.04
Tongan (0)	1	0.01
White (7,353)	7,716	76.61
Not Hispanic (6,529)	6,792	67.43
Hispanic (824)	924	9.17

Culpeper

Place Type: Town
County: Culpeper
Population: 16,379†

Ancestry‡	Population	%
African, Sub-Saharan (210)	233	1.49
African (163)	186	1.19
Ethiopian (28)	28	0.18
South African (19)	19	0.12
Albanian (140)	140	0.90
American (1,275)	1,275	8.17
Arab (23)	79	0.51
Palestinian (23)	51	0.33
Other Arab (0)	28	0.18
Armenian (0)	15	0.10
Austrian (0)	14	0.09
Belgian (0)	22	0.14
British (16)	74	0.47
Croatian (41)	41	0.26
Czech (0)	8	0.05
Danish (8)	70	0.45
Dutch (0)	58	0.37
English (893)	1,718	11.01
European (24)	24	0.15
French, ex. Basque (32)	290	1.86
French Canadian (10)	10	0.06
German (574)	2,021	12.95
Greek (114)	156	1.00
Hungarian (23)	37	0.24
Irish (365)	1,599	10.25
Italian (181)	373	2.39
Norwegian (46)	108	0.69
Polish (124)	171	1.10
Portuguese (0)	12	0.08
Russian (0)	12	0.08
Scotch-Irish (47)	195	1.25
Scottish (130)	236	1.51
Slavic (0)	16	0.10
Slovak (0)	22	0.14
Swedish (10)	107	0.69
Swiss (0)	66	0.42
Ukrainian (0)	38	0.24
Welsh (14)	40	0.26
West Indian, ex. Hispanic (0)	77	0.49
Jamaican (0)	30	0.19
West Indian (0)	28	0.18
Other West Indian (0)	19	0.12

Hispanic Origin	Population	%
Hispanic or Latino (of any race)	2,788	17.02
Central American, ex. Mexican	816	4.98
Costa Rican	4	0.02
Guatemalan	166	1.01
Honduran	171	1.04
Nicaraguan	18	0.11
Panamanian	10	0.06
Salvadoran	447	2.73
Cuban	25	0.15
Dominican Republic	29	0.18
Mexican	1,255	7.66
Puerto Rican	200	1.22
South American	172	1.05
Argentinean	7	0.04
Bolivian	22	0.13
Chilean	12	0.07
Colombian	26	0.16
Ecuadorian	7	0.04
Peruvian	81	0.49
Uruguayan	8	0.05
Venezuelan	8	0.05
Other South American	1	0.01
Other Hispanic or Latino	291	1.78

Race*	Population	%
African-American/Black (3,594)	4,020	24.54
Not Hispanic (3,482)	3,862	23.58
Hispanic (112)	158	0.96
American Indian/Alaska Native (92)	178	1.09
Not Hispanic (46)	118	0.72
Hispanic (46)	60	0.37
Apache (1)	1	0.01
Blackfeet (0)	5	0.03
Central American Ind. (3)	3	0.02
Cherokee (9)	45	0.27
Chippewa (1)	3	0.02
Choctaw (1)	1	0.01
Creek (1)	1	0.01
Houma (0)	1	0.01
Iroquois (2)	2	0.01
Lumbee (1)	1	0.01
Mexican American Ind. (4)	10	0.06
Potawatomi (0)	1	0.01
Pueblo (1)	1	0.01
Puget Sound Salish (1)	1	0.01
Sioux (1)	1	0.01
South American Ind. (2)	2	0.01
Tsimshian *(Alaska Native)* (0)	1	0.01
Asian (341)	437	2.67
Not Hispanic (330)	405	2.47
Hispanic (11)	32	0.20
Bangladeshi (8)	8	0.05
Bhutanese (1)	1	0.01
Cambodian (2)	2	0.01
Chinese, ex. Taiwanese (22)	27	0.16
Filipino (73)	101	0.62
Indian (113)	131	0.80
Indonesian (1)	1	0.01
Japanese (3)	11	0.07
Korean (24)	36	0.22
Malaysian (1)	1	0.01
Nepalese (6)	6	0.04
Pakistani (27)	28	0.17
Sri Lankan (5)	5	0.03
Thai (7)	9	0.05
Vietnamese (44)	53	0.32
Hawaii Native/Pacific Islander (17)	39	0.24
Not Hispanic (5)	21	0.13
Hispanic (12)	18	0.11
Guamanian/Chamorro (14)	22	0.13
Native Hawaiian (0)	6	0.04
Samoan (0)	5	0.03
White (10,070)	10,658	65.07
Not Hispanic (9,191)	9,637	58.84
Hispanic (879)	1,021	6.23

Dale City

Place Type: CDP
County: Prince William
Population: 65,969†

Ancestry‡	Population	%
Afghan (74)	107	0.17
African, Sub-Saharan (3,786)	4,147	6.52
African (1,627)	1,780	2.80
Ethiopian (298)	383	0.60
Ghanaian (574)	608	0.96
Liberian (0)	8	0.01
Nigerian (168)	168	0.26
Sierra Leonean (150)	150	0.24
Somalian (148)	148	0.23
Sudanese (37)	37	0.06
Ugandan (193)	193	0.30
Other Sub-Saharan African (591)	672	1.06
American (2,584)	2,584	4.06
Arab (452)	494	0.78
Arab (75)	75	0.12
Egyptian (16)	16	0.03
Lebanese (35)	77	0.12
Moroccan (224)	224	0.35
Palestinian (102)	102	0.16
Australian (0)	32	0.05
Austrian (88)	196	0.31
Belgian (22)	22	0.03
Brazilian (64)	64	0.10
British (50)	243	0.38
Bulgarian (27)	27	0.04
Canadian (92)	103	0.16
Croatian (37)	162	0.25
Czech (41)	135	0.21
Czechoslovakian (16)	16	0.03
Danish (12)	220	0.35
Dutch (205)	571	0.90
English (624)	3,700	5.82
European (453)	527	0.83
Finnish (21)	89	0.14
French, ex. Basque (108)	1,047	1.65
French Canadian (144)	233	0.37
German (1,391)	6,284	9.88
Greek (22)	112	0.18
Hungarian (38)	174	0.27
Iranian (43)	76	0.12
Irish (1,331)	4,890	7.69
Italian (578)	1,687	2.65
Lithuanian (41)	115	0.18
Northern European (12)	12	0.02
Norwegian (179)	332	0.52
Pennsylvania German (9)	33	0.05
Polish (383)	1,226	1.93
Portuguese (73)	181	0.28
Romanian (6)	15	0.02
Russian (68)	270	0.42
Scandinavian (45)	164	0.26
Scotch-Irish (322)	642	1.01
Scottish (208)	946	1.49
Slavic (8)	18	0.03
Slovak (66)	77	0.12
Slovene (0)	12	0.02
Swedish (68)	340	0.53
Swiss (22)	107	0.17
Turkish (41)	41	0.06
Ukrainian (85)	202	0.32
Welsh (197)	370	0.58
West Indian, ex. Hispanic (487)	754	1.19
Bahamian (22)	91	0.14
Barbadian (21)	36	0.06
Belizean (227)	227	0.36
British West Indian (0)	23	0.04
Haitian (15)	19	0.03
Jamaican (151)	202	0.32
Trinidadian/Tobagonian (51)	84	0.13
U.S. Virgin Islander (0)	29	0.05
West Indian (0)	43	0.07
Yugoslavian (98)	118	0.19

Hispanic Origin	Population	%
Hispanic or Latino (of any race)	17,648	26.75
Central American, ex. Mexican	9,389	14.23
Costa Rican	26	0.04
Guatemalan	833	1.26
Honduran	925	1.40
Nicaraguan	282	0.43
Panamanian	185	0.28
Salvadoran	7,036	10.67
Other Central American	102	0.15
Cuban	110	0.17
Dominican Republic	229	0.35
Mexican	2,373	3.60
Puerto Rican	1,504	2.28
South American	2,142	3.25
Argentinean	97	0.15
Bolivian	656	0.99

*Notes: † The Census 2010 population figure is used to calculate the percentages in the Hispanic Origin and Race categories. Ancestry percentages are based on the 2006-2010 American Community Survey population (not shown); ‡ Numbers in parentheses indicate the number of people reporting a single ancestry; * Numbers in parentheses indicate the number of persons reporting this race alone, not in combination with any other race; Please refer to the Explanation of Data for more information.*

Chilean	88	0.13
Colombian	246	0.37
Ecuadorian	124	0.19
Paraguayan	15	0.02
Peruvian	766	1.16
Uruguayan	54	0.08
Venezuelan	59	0.09
Other South American	37	0.06
Other Hispanic or Latino	1,901	2.88

Race*	Population	%
African-American/Black (18,883)	20,540	31.14
Not Hispanic (18,229)	19,575	29.67
Hispanic (654)	965	1.46
American Indian/Alaska Native (471)	1,335	2.02
Not Hispanic (186)	618	0.94
Hispanic (285)	717	1.09
Apache (2)	5	0.01
Blackfeet (1)	24	0.04
Canadian/French Am. Ind. (4)	4	0.01
Central American Ind. (21)	26	0.04
Cherokee (10)	128	0.19
Chippewa (6)	11	0.02
Choctaw (11)	19	0.03
Comanche (1)	2	<0.01
Creek (2)	6	0.01
Crow (0)	1	<0.01
Hopi (1)	1	<0.01
Iroquois (8)	15	0.02
Kiowa (4)	4	0.01
Lumbee (8)	13	0.02
Mexican American Ind. (22)	51	0.08
Navajo (3)	5	0.01
Potawatomi (4)	4	0.01
Pueblo (3)	3	<0.01
Seminole (0)	3	<0.01
Sioux (10)	14	0.02
South American Ind. (14)	46	0.07
Spanish American Ind. (11)	26	0.04
Tlingit-Haida *(Alaska Native)* (0)	1	<0.01
Tohono O'Odham (0)	1	<0.01
Ute (3)	3	<0.01
Yuman (0)	1	<0.01
Yup'ik *(Alaska Native)* (1)	1	<0.01
Asian (5,005)	6,144	9.31
Not Hispanic (4,920)	5,932	8.99
Hispanic (85)	212	0.32
Bangladeshi (105)	121	0.18
Bhutanese (12)	24	0.04
Burmese (15)	17	0.03
Cambodian (138)	150	0.23
Chinese, ex. Taiwanese (270)	385	0.58
Filipino (976)	1,299	1.97
Hmong (1)	1	<0.01
Indian (824)	974	1.48
Indonesian (15)	20	0.03
Japanese (82)	217	0.33
Korean (446)	590	0.89
Laotian (157)	187	0.28
Malaysian (4)	4	0.01
Nepalese (38)	55	0.08
Pakistani (939)	1,013	1.54
Sri Lankan (6)	7	0.01
Taiwanese (5)	10	0.02
Thai (69)	113	0.17
Vietnamese (564)	671	1.02
Hawaii Native/Pacific Islander (111)	253	0.38
Not Hispanic (103)	218	0.33
Hispanic (8)	35	0.05
Guamanian/Chamorro (46)	75	0.11
Native Hawaiian (24)	80	0.12
Samoan (30)	39	0.06
White (29,976)	33,035	50.08
Not Hispanic (22,258)	24,222	36.72
Hispanic (7,718)	8,813	13.36

Danville

Place Type: Independent City
County: Danville
Population: 43,055†

Ancestry‡	Population	%
African, Sub-Saharan (362)	398	0.91
African (219)	255	0.58
Ghanaian (37)	37	0.08
Liberian (34)	34	0.08
Sierra Leonean (72)	72	0.16
Albanian (12)	12	0.03
American (4,110)	4,110	9.39
Arab (73)	73	0.17
Moroccan (73)	73	0.17
Austrian (16)	16	0.04
Belgian (13)	21	0.05
British (124)	162	0.37
Canadian (52)	64	0.15
Celtic (0)	7	0.02
Czech (16)	16	0.04
Danish (8)	63	0.14
Dutch (53)	259	0.59
English (2,458)	3,939	9.00
Estonian (4)	13	0.03
European (308)	463	1.06
Finnish (11)	17	0.04
French, ex. Basque (109)	359	0.82
French Canadian (8)	26	0.06
German (798)	2,338	5.34
Greek (45)	66	0.15
Hungarian (73)	73	0.17
Irish (1,275)	2,896	6.61
Italian (189)	461	1.05
Lithuanian (0)	64	0.15
Norwegian (35)	83	0.19
Polish (80)	224	0.51
Portuguese (18)	18	0.04
Romanian (7)	7	0.02
Russian (9)	50	0.11
Scotch-Irish (559)	957	2.19
Scottish (305)	722	1.65
Slovene (0)	9	0.02
Swedish (17)	66	0.15
Swiss (5)	34	0.08
Welsh (57)	88	0.20
West Indian, ex. Hispanic (80)	167	0.38
British West Indian (15)	27	0.06
Haitian (14)	26	0.06
Jamaican (22)	85	0.19
West Indian (29)	29	0.07
Yugoslavian (0)	4	0.01

Hispanic Origin	Population	%
Hispanic or Latino (of any race)	1,245	2.89
Central American, ex. Mexican	75	0.17
Costa Rican	1	<0.01
Guatemalan	7	0.02
Honduran	14	0.03
Nicaraguan	5	0.01
Panamanian	2	<0.01
Salvadoran	46	0.11
Cuban	23	0.05
Dominican Republic	17	0.04
Mexican	814	1.89
Puerto Rican	107	0.25
South American	114	0.26
Argentinean	2	<0.01
Bolivian	4	0.01
Chilean	3	0.01
Colombian	27	0.06
Ecuadorian	12	0.03
Peruvian	3	0.01
Uruguayan	55	0.13
Venezuelan	8	0.02
Other Hispanic or Latino	95	0.22

Race*	Population	%
African-American/Black (20,795)	21,143	49.11
Not Hispanic (20,725)	21,047	48.88
Hispanic (70)	96	0.22
American Indian/Alaska Native (75)	266	0.62
Not Hispanic (66)	233	0.54
Hispanic (9)	33	0.08
Apache (0)	3	0.01
Blackfeet (0)	6	0.01
Cherokee (14)	77	0.18
Chippewa (1)	1	<0.01
Choctaw (2)	8	0.02
Comanche (0)	1	<0.01
Creek (0)	2	<0.01
Crow (0)	1	<0.01
Delaware (0)	6	0.01
Iroquois (1)	2	<0.01
Kiowa (1)	4	0.01
Lumbee (1)	4	0.01
Mexican American Ind. (4)	5	0.01
Navajo (0)	3	0.01
Seminole (0)	3	0.01
Sioux (0)	7	0.02
Spanish American Ind. (1)	1	<0.01
Asian (403)	492	1.14
Not Hispanic (394)	477	1.11
Hispanic (9)	15	0.03
Burmese (0)	1	<0.01
Chinese, ex. Taiwanese (71)	86	0.20
Filipino (69)	103	0.24
Indian (115)	129	0.30
Indonesian (0)	1	<0.01
Japanese (9)	12	0.03
Korean (9)	17	0.04
Malaysian (1)	1	<0.01
Nepalese (3)	3	0.01
Pakistani (48)	52	0.12
Taiwanese (3)	3	0.01
Thai (3)	3	0.01
Vietnamese (65)	70	0.16
Hawaii Native/Pacific Islander (11)	34	0.08
Not Hispanic (11)	30	0.07
Hispanic (0)	4	0.01
Guamanian/Chamorro (0)	3	0.01
Native Hawaiian (5)	14	0.03
Samoan (1)	3	0.01
White (20,531)	21,010	48.80
Not Hispanic (20,107)	20,514	47.65
Hispanic (424)	496	1.15

Dranesville

Place Type: CDP
County: Fairfax
Population: 11,921†

Ancestry‡	Population	%
Afghan (153)	153	1.22
American (450)	450	3.58
Arab (56)	133	1.06
Arab (14)	14	0.11
Egyptian (14)	14	0.11
Lebanese (0)	32	0.25
Moroccan (0)	31	0.25
Syrian (0)	14	0.11
Other Arab (28)	28	0.22
Armenian (0)	13	0.10
Austrian (16)	97	0.77
British (130)	244	1.94
Canadian (49)	49	0.39
Czechoslovakian (14)	14	0.11
Danish (13)	35	0.28
Dutch (14)	100	0.80
Eastern European (58)	58	0.46
English (654)	1,506	12.00
European (521)	541	4.31
Finnish (72)	101	0.80
French, ex. Basque (64)	469	3.74
French Canadian (95)	152	1.21
German (536)	2,056	16.38
Greek (51)	110	0.88
Hungarian (29)	73	0.58

*Notes: † The Census 2010 population figure is used to calculate the percentages in the Hispanic Origin and Race categories. Ancestry percentages are based on the 2006-2010 American Community Survey population (not shown); ‡ Numbers in parentheses indicate the number of people reporting a single ancestry; * Numbers in parentheses indicate the number of persons reporting this race alone, not in combination with any other race; Please refer to the Explanation of Data for more information.*

SECTION TWO

Iranian (44)	44	0.35
Irish (272)	1,571	12.51
Italian (362)	1,049	8.36
Lithuanian (0)	15	0.12
Luxemburger (0)	39	0.31
Macedonian (0)	12	0.10
Norwegian (13)	91	0.72
Polish (141)	481	3.83
Romanian (18)	94	0.75
Russian (145)	374	2.98
Scandinavian (15)	74	0.59
Scotch-Irish (88)	229	1.82
Scottish (29)	291	2.32
Serbian (0)	12	0.10
Slavic (0)	45	0.36
Slovak (14)	126	1.00
Slovene (13)	39	0.31
Swedish (16)	132	1.05
Swiss (0)	33	0.26
Ukrainian (0)	33	0.26
Welsh (45)	133	1.06
West Indian, ex. Hispanic (168)	168	1.34
Barbadian (67)	67	0.53
Trinidadian/Tobagonian (101)	101	0.80

Hispanic Origin	Population	%
Hispanic or Latino (of any race)	848	7.11
Central American, ex. Mexican	293	2.46
Costa Rican	9	0.08
Guatemalan	34	0.29
Honduran	19	0.16
Nicaraguan	27	0.23
Panamanian	4	0.03
Salvadoran	200	1.68
Cuban	23	0.19
Dominican Republic	24	0.20
Mexican	84	0.70
Puerto Rican	84	0.70
South American	226	1.90
Argentinean	14	0.12
Bolivian	48	0.40
Chilean	10	0.08
Colombian	46	0.39
Ecuadorian	30	0.25
Peruvian	63	0.53
Uruguayan	2	0.02
Venezuelan	12	0.10
Other South American	1	0.01
Other Hispanic or Latino	114	0.96

Race*	Population	%
African-American/Black (504)	601	5.04
Not Hispanic (492)	579	4.86
Hispanic (12)	22	0.18
American Indian/Alaska Native (27)	91	0.76
Not Hispanic (13)	62	0.52
Hispanic (14)	29	0.24
Apache (1)	1	0.01
Blackfeet (0)	5	0.04
Central American Ind. (2)	3	0.03
Cherokee (4)	17	0.14
Choctaw (1)	3	0.03
Comanche (1)	1	0.01
Creek (0)	2	0.02
Mexican American Ind. (1)	5	0.04
Navajo (0)	3	0.03
Puget Sound Salish (0)	1	0.01
Sioux (1)	3	0.03
South American Ind. (0)	2	0.02
Ute (0)	3	0.03
Asian (1,555)	1,830	15.35
Not Hispanic (1,554)	1,811	15.19
Hispanic (1)	19	0.16
Bangladeshi (30)	32	0.27
Cambodian (41)	42	0.35
Chinese, ex. Taiwanese (293)	368	3.09
Filipino (112)	145	1.22
Indian (509)	557	4.67
Indonesian (13)	17	0.14
Japanese (7)	34	0.29
Korean (113)	139	1.17
Laotian (6)	12	0.10
Malaysian (2)	7	0.06
Nepalese (1)	1	0.01
Pakistani (127)	144	1.21
Sri Lankan (5)	11	0.09
Taiwanese (18)	21	0.18
Thai (22)	34	0.29
Vietnamese (183)	214	1.80
Hawaii Native/Pacific Islander (8)	27	0.23
Not Hispanic (8)	23	0.19
Hispanic (0)	4	0.03
Fijian (1)	4	0.03
Guamanian/Chamorro (5)	7	0.06
Native Hawaiian (2)	9	0.08
White (9,087)	9,470	79.44
Not Hispanic (8,597)	8,928	74.89
Hispanic (490)	542	4.55

Dumbarton

Place Type: CDP
County: Henrico
Population: 7,879†

Ancestry‡	Population	%
African, Sub-Saharan (132)	132	1.97
African (62)	62	0.93
Ethiopian (59)	59	0.88
Ugandan (11)	11	0.16
American (517)	517	7.73
Arab (86)	86	1.29
Egyptian (67)	67	1.00
Lebanese (8)	8	0.12
Moroccan (11)	11	0.16
British (0)	28	0.42
Canadian (0)	14	0.21
Celtic (15)	15	0.22
Danish (0)	27	0.40
Dutch (0)	80	1.20
English (236)	567	8.48
European (12)	24	0.36
French, ex. Basque (20)	72	1.08
German (212)	678	10.14
Greek (0)	11	0.16
Hungarian (0)	15	0.22
Irish (181)	590	8.82
Italian (31)	110	1.65
Lithuanian (0)	11	0.16
Norwegian (39)	78	1.17
Pennsylvania German (0)	15	0.22
Polish (21)	61	0.91
Romanian (21)	21	0.31
Russian (23)	23	0.34
Scotch-Irish (32)	81	1.21
Scottish (10)	82	1.23
Swedish (0)	15	0.22
Swiss (0)	27	0.40
Ukrainian (26)	26	0.39
Welsh (10)	73	1.09

Hispanic Origin	Population	%
Hispanic or Latino (of any race)	1,468	18.63
Central American, ex. Mexican	508	6.45
Costa Rican	15	0.19
Guatemalan	122	1.55
Honduran	98	1.24
Nicaraguan	7	0.09
Panamanian	3	0.04
Salvadoran	259	3.29
Other Central American	4	0.05
Cuban	24	0.30
Dominican Republic	12	0.15
Mexican	568	7.21
Puerto Rican	107	1.36
South American	96	1.22
Argentinean	5	0.06
Bolivian	7	0.09
Chilean	3	0.04
Colombian	21	0.27
Ecuadorian	4	0.05
Paraguayan	2	0.03
Peruvian	15	0.19
Uruguayan	3	0.04
Venezuelan	32	0.41
Other South American	4	0.05
Other Hispanic or Latino	153	1.94

Race*	Population	%
African-American/Black (2,567)	2,711	34.41
Not Hispanic (2,485)	2,600	33.00
Hispanic (82)	111	1.41
American Indian/Alaska Native (27)	93	1.18
Not Hispanic (22)	72	0.91
Hispanic (5)	21	0.27
Blackfeet (1)	2	0.03
Cherokee (2)	25	0.32
Chickasaw (0)	1	0.01
Chippewa (1)	2	0.03
Iroquois (1)	1	0.01
Lumbee (2)	4	0.05
Mexican American Ind. (4)	10	0.13
Pima (1)	1	0.01
Sioux (1)	1	0.01
South American Ind. (0)	2	0.03
Asian (477)	535	6.79
Not Hispanic (472)	526	6.68
Hispanic (5)	9	0.11
Bangladeshi (35)	35	0.44
Cambodian (47)	53	0.67
Chinese, ex. Taiwanese (30)	42	0.53
Filipino (35)	49	0.62
Indian (84)	90	1.14
Japanese (1)	7	0.09
Korean (20)	21	0.27
Malaysian (5)	5	0.06
Nepalese (5)	5	0.06
Pakistani (9)	11	0.14
Sri Lankan (2)	2	0.03
Taiwanese (0)	1	0.01
Thai (2)	6	0.08
Vietnamese (162)	177	2.25
Hawaii Native/Pacific Islander (7)	17	0.22
Not Hispanic (7)	17	0.22
Guamanian/Chamorro (1)	2	0.03
Native Hawaiian (5)	12	0.15
Samoan (0)	2	0.03
White (3,724)	3,946	50.08
Not Hispanic (3,202)	3,356	42.59
Hispanic (522)	590	7.49

Dunn Loring

Place Type: CDP
County: Fairfax
Population: 8,803†

Ancestry‡	Population	%
Afghan (33)	33	0.36
African, Sub-Saharan (65)	82	0.89
African (49)	49	0.53
Other Sub-Saharan African (16)	33	0.36
American (308)	308	3.33
Arab (305)	322	3.48
Lebanese (17)	34	0.37
Moroccan (55)	55	0.59
Palestinian (40)	40	0.43
Other Arab (193)	193	2.09
Armenian (9)	9	0.10
Austrian (0)	13	0.14
Belgian (0)	10	0.11
Brazilian (4)	4	0.04
British (31)	54	0.58
Canadian (10)	22	0.24
Celtic (11)	31	0.34
Croatian (0)	28	0.30
Czech (13)	13	0.14
Danish (27)	47	0.51
Dutch (47)	154	1.67
English (383)	1,242	13.43

*Notes: † The Census 2010 population figure is used to calculate the percentages in the Hispanic Origin and Race categories. Ancestry percentages are based on the 2006-2010 American Community Survey population (not shown); ‡ Numbers in parentheses indicate the number of people reporting a single ancestry; * Numbers in parentheses indicate the number of persons reporting this race alone, not in combination with any other race; Please refer to the Explanation of Data for more information.*

European (217)	217	2.35
Finnish (0)	10	0.11
French, ex. Basque (18)	141	1.52
French Canadian (22)	71	0.77
German (471)	1,285	13.89
Greek (9)	26	0.28
Hungarian (17)	27	0.29
Icelander (0)	16	0.17
Iranian (139)	139	1.50
Irish (310)	886	9.58
Italian (170)	349	3.77
Latvian (0)	11	0.12
Lithuanian (0)	80	0.86
Norwegian (40)	75	0.81
Polish (35)	224	2.42
Portuguese (87)	87	0.94
Romanian (9)	9	0.10
Russian (28)	95	1.03
Scandinavian (12)	53	0.57
Scotch-Irish (54)	254	2.75
Scottish (125)	444	4.80
Serbian (0)	34	0.37
Slavic (10)	10	0.11
Slovak (39)	115	1.24
Swedish (50)	115	1.24
Swiss (11)	29	0.31
Turkish (18)	18	0.19
Ukrainian (38)	78	0.84
Welsh (16)	103	1.11
West Indian, ex. Hispanic (19)	39	0.42
Haitian (19)	19	0.21
West Indian (0)	20	0.22
Yugoslavian (9)	9	0.10

Hispanic Origin	Population	%
Hispanic or Latino (of any race)	540	6.13
Central American, ex. Mexican	73	0.83
Costa Rican	1	0.01
Guatemalan	6	0.07
Honduran	21	0.24
Nicaraguan	10	0.11
Panamanian	1	0.01
Salvadoran	34	0.39
Cuban	32	0.36
Dominican Republic	10	0.11
Mexican	84	0.95
Puerto Rican	33	0.37
South American	240	2.73
Argentinean	14	0.16
Bolivian	75	0.85
Chilean	3	0.03
Colombian	49	0.56
Ecuadorian	21	0.24
Paraguayan	2	0.02
Peruvian	65	0.74
Uruguayan	1	0.01
Venezuelan	10	0.11
Other Hispanic or Latino	68	0.77

Race*	Population	%
African-American/Black (279)	324	3.68
Not Hispanic (272)	304	3.45
Hispanic (7)	20	0.23
American Indian/Alaska Native (17)	37	0.42
Not Hispanic (10)	22	0.25
Hispanic (7)	15	0.17
Cherokee (0)	5	0.06
Creek (0)	1	0.01
Iroquois (2)	2	0.02
Navajo (2)	2	0.02
Sioux (4)	4	0.05
South American Ind. (4)	6	0.07
Asian (1,741)	1,995	22.66
Not Hispanic (1,739)	1,981	22.50
Hispanic (2)	14	0.16
Bangladeshi (10)	11	0.12
Burmese (8)	8	0.09
Cambodian (3)	4	0.05
Chinese, ex. Taiwanese (358)	394	4.48
Filipino (130)	165	1.87
Indian (348)	380	4.32
Indonesian (9)	9	0.10
Japanese (54)	79	0.90
Korean (325)	369	4.19
Laotian (6)	12	0.14
Malaysian (18)	19	0.22
Pakistani (70)	70	0.80
Sri Lankan (12)	15	0.17
Taiwanese (29)	30	0.34
Thai (38)	45	0.51
Vietnamese (282)	317	3.60
Hawaii Native/Pacific Islander (6)	12	0.14
Not Hispanic (6)	11	0.12
Hispanic (0)	1	0.01
Guamanian/Chamorro (0)	1	0.01
Native Hawaiian (4)	5	0.06
White (6,358)	6,644	75.47
Not Hispanic (5,949)	6,205	70.49
Hispanic (409)	439	4.99

East Highland Park

Place Type: CDP
County: Henrico
Population: 14,796†

Ancestry‡	Population	%
African, Sub-Saharan (171)	182	1.30
African (123)	134	0.95
Nigerian (35)	35	0.25
Other Sub-Saharan African (13)	13	0.09
American (526)	526	3.75
British (68)	68	0.48
Dutch (0)	15	0.11
English (169)	347	2.47
European (79)	79	0.56
Finnish (0)	14	0.10
French, ex. Basque (6)	52	0.37
French Canadian (0)	14	0.10
German (105)	297	2.12
Guyanese (15)	15	0.11
Hungarian (0)	13	0.09
Irish (68)	262	1.87
Italian (18)	31	0.22
Pennsylvania German (14)	14	0.10
Polish (34)	48	0.34
Portuguese (0)	13	0.09
Scotch-Irish (28)	37	0.26
Scottish (14)	58	0.41
Swedish (0)	30	0.21
Welsh (0)	33	0.24
West Indian, ex. Hispanic (46)	82	0.58
Haitian (11)	23	0.16
Jamaican (15)	39	0.28
Trinidadian/Tobagonian (20)	20	0.14

Hispanic Origin	Population	%
Hispanic or Latino (of any race)	351	2.37
Central American, ex. Mexican	40	0.27
Guatemalan	5	0.03
Honduran	6	0.04
Nicaraguan	1	0.01
Panamanian	10	0.07
Salvadoran	18	0.12
Cuban	11	0.07
Dominican Republic	33	0.22
Mexican	89	0.60
Puerto Rican	129	0.87
South American	13	0.09
Bolivian	1	0.01
Colombian	3	0.02
Ecuadorian	2	0.01
Peruvian	2	0.01
Venezuelan	5	0.03
Other Hispanic or Latino	36	0.24

Race*	Population	%
African-American/Black (12,584)	12,869	86.98
Not Hispanic (12,459)	12,710	85.90
Hispanic (125)	159	1.07
American Indian/Alaska Native (55)	206	1.39
Not Hispanic (50)	191	1.29
Hispanic (5)	15	0.10
Apache (0)	1	0.01
Blackfeet (0)	2	0.01
Cherokee (8)	37	0.25
Iroquois (1)	2	0.01
Lumbee (1)	5	0.03
Seminole (0)	4	0.03
Sioux (1)	7	0.05
South American Ind. (2)	4	0.03
Asian (106)	128	0.87
Not Hispanic (104)	122	0.82
Hispanic (2)	6	0.04
Bangladeshi (3)	3	0.02
Burmese (1)	1	0.01
Cambodian (21)	22	0.15
Chinese, ex. Taiwanese (11)	25	0.17
Filipino (15)	27	0.18
Indian (12)	14	0.09
Indonesian (5)	5	0.03
Japanese (0)	2	0.01
Korean (5)	5	0.03
Laotian (8)	8	0.05
Nepalese (4)	4	0.03
Pakistani (11)	11	0.07
Vietnamese (4)	10	0.07
Hawaii Native/Pacific Islander (5)	20	0.14
Not Hispanic (5)	19	0.13
Hispanic (0)	1	0.01
Guamanian/Chamorro (5)	13	0.09
Native Hawaiian (0)	1	0.01
Samoan (0)	3	0.02
White (1,605)	1,797	12.15
Not Hispanic (1,522)	1,682	11.37
Hispanic (83)	115	0.78

Fair Lakes

Place Type: CDP
County: Fairfax
Population: 7,942†

Ancestry‡	Population	%
African, Sub-Saharan (80)	91	1.14
African (72)	83	1.04
Ghanaian (8)	8	0.10
American (200)	200	2.51
Arab (158)	285	3.58
Egyptian (83)	101	1.27
Lebanese (62)	168	2.11
Syrian (13)	16	0.20
Austrian (26)	44	0.55
Brazilian (23)	35	0.44
British (15)	28	0.35
Canadian (0)	16	0.20
Czech (5)	12	0.15
Danish (0)	12	0.15
Dutch (0)	53	0.67
Eastern European (36)	36	0.45
English (260)	651	8.18
European (155)	169	2.12
Finnish (0)	6	0.08
French, ex. Basque (0)	57	0.72
French Canadian (0)	14	0.18
German (232)	910	11.43
Greek (18)	51	0.64
Hungarian (0)	28	0.35
Iranian (268)	268	3.37
Irish (189)	716	8.99
Italian (70)	317	3.98
Lithuanian (0)	12	0.15
Norwegian (81)	105	1.32
Polish (34)	164	2.06
Portuguese (15)	57	0.72
Romanian (0)	29	0.36
Russian (0)	56	0.70
Scandinavian (0)	28	0.35
Scotch-Irish (64)	83	1.04
Scottish (3)	127	1.60

*Notes: † The Census 2010 population figure is used to calculate the percentages in the Hispanic Origin and Race categories. Ancestry percentages are based on the 2006-2010 American Community Survey population (not shown); ‡ Numbers in parentheses indicate the number of people reporting a single ancestry; * Numbers in parentheses indicate the number of persons reporting this race alone, not in combination with any other race; Please refer to the Explanation of Data for more information.*

Swedish (0)	10	0.13
Swiss (0)	29	0.36
Ukrainian (21)	68	0.85
Welsh (0)	36	0.45

Hispanic Origin	Population	%
Hispanic or Latino (of any race)	606	7.63
Central American, ex. Mexican	114	1.44
Costa Rican	8	0.10
Guatemalan	24	0.30
Honduran	8	0.10
Nicaraguan	10	0.13
Panamanian	6	0.08
Salvadoran	58	0.73
Cuban	34	0.43
Dominican Republic	18	0.23
Mexican	66	0.83
Puerto Rican	62	0.78
South American	253	3.19
Argentinean	11	0.14
Bolivian	58	0.73
Chilean	2	0.03
Colombian	65	0.82
Ecuadorian	20	0.25
Peruvian	73	0.92
Uruguayan	4	0.05
Venezuelan	20	0.25
Other Hispanic or Latino	59	0.74

Race*	Population	%
African-American/Black (690)	781	9.83
Not Hispanic (670)	751	9.46
Hispanic (20)	30	0.38
American Indian/Alaska Native (12)	61	0.77
Not Hispanic (10)	55	0.69
Hispanic (2)	6	0.08
Cherokee (0)	9	0.11
Chickasaw (0)	1	0.01
Choctaw (2)	6	0.08
Cree (0)	1	0.01
Inupiat *(Alaska Native)* (0)	1	0.01
Lumbee (1)	1	0.01
Potawatomi (1)	1	0.01
Sioux (1)	1	0.01
South American Ind. (0)	4	0.05
Ute (0)	1	0.01
Asian (2,632)	2,836	35.71
Not Hispanic (2,616)	2,811	35.39
Hispanic (16)	25	0.31
Bangladeshi (11)	11	0.14
Burmese (12)	12	0.15
Cambodian (21)	21	0.26
Chinese, ex. Taiwanese (294)	337	4.24
Filipino (136)	162	2.04
Hmong (1)	1	0.01
Indian (723)	740	9.32
Indonesian (4)	11	0.14
Japanese (15)	26	0.33
Korean (819)	864	10.88
Laotian (5)	9	0.11
Nepalese (28)	29	0.37
Pakistani (98)	108	1.36
Sri Lankan (5)	5	0.06
Taiwanese (28)	30	0.38
Thai (19)	23	0.29
Vietnamese (338)	369	4.65
Hawaii Native/Pacific Islander (2)	18	0.23
Not Hispanic (2)	18	0.23
Guamanian/Chamorro (0)	1	0.01
Native Hawaiian (1)	2	0.03
White (4,117)	4,396	55.35
Not Hispanic (3,740)	3,984	50.16
Hispanic (377)	412	5.19

Fair Oaks

Place Type: CDP
County: Fairfax
Population: 30,223†

Ancestry‡	Population	%
Afghan (182)	182	0.66
African, Sub-Saharan (685)	758	2.75
African (337)	366	1.33
Ethiopian (29)	44	0.16
Liberian (82)	82	0.30
Nigerian (25)	25	0.09
South African (0)	15	0.05
Sudanese (134)	134	0.49
Ugandan (12)	12	0.04
Other Sub-Saharan African (66)	80	0.29
Albanian (13)	13	0.05
American (907)	907	3.29
Arab (703)	738	2.68
Arab (290)	290	1.05
Egyptian (77)	77	0.28
Iraqi (163)	163	0.59
Lebanese (27)	54	0.20
Moroccan (37)	37	0.13
Other Arab (109)	117	0.42
Armenian (22)	51	0.19
Austrian (10)	102	0.37
Basque (0)	24	0.09
Belgian (0)	34	0.12
Brazilian (39)	39	0.14
British (51)	127	0.46
Bulgarian (17)	37	0.13
Canadian (44)	54	0.20
Croatian (13)	32	0.12
Czech (224)	349	1.27
Czechoslovakian (0)	30	0.11
Danish (0)	150	0.54
Dutch (136)	265	0.96
Eastern European (112)	143	0.52
English (665)	2,498	9.07
European (294)	332	1.21
Finnish (17)	44	0.16
French, ex. Basque (78)	573	2.08
French Canadian (21)	67	0.24
German (1,003)	3,481	12.64
Greek (72)	149	0.54
Guyanese (0)	14	0.05
Hungarian (56)	173	0.63
Icelander (13)	13	0.05
Iranian (100)	100	0.36
Irish (669)	2,992	10.86
Israeli (68)	68	0.25
Italian (345)	1,586	5.76
Lithuanian (7)	30	0.11
Norwegian (84)	282	1.02
Polish (249)	921	3.34
Portuguese (84)	143	0.52
Romanian (36)	64	0.23
Russian (111)	375	1.36
Scandinavian (61)	110	0.40
Scotch-Irish (294)	636	2.31
Scottish (232)	708	2.57
Serbian (0)	18	0.07
Slavic (0)	13	0.05
Slovak (18)	70	0.25
Swedish (80)	312	1.13
Swiss (12)	12	0.04
Turkish (430)	444	1.61
Ukrainian (91)	210	0.76
Welsh (0)	146	0.53
West Indian, ex. Hispanic (130)	199	0.72
Bahamian (27)	27	0.10
Jamaican (103)	161	0.58
West Indian (0)	11	0.04
Yugoslavian (0)	12	0.04

Hispanic Origin	Population	%
Hispanic or Latino (of any race)	2,799	9.26
Central American, ex. Mexican	723	2.39
Costa Rican	24	0.08
Guatemalan	279	0.92
Honduran	61	0.20
Nicaraguan	40	0.13
Panamanian	38	0.13
Salvadoran	270	0.89
Other Central American	11	0.04
Cuban	94	0.31
Dominican Republic	64	0.21
Mexican	375	1.24
Puerto Rican	299	0.99
South American	942	3.12
Argentinean	47	0.16
Bolivian	203	0.67
Chilean	57	0.19
Colombian	205	0.68
Ecuadorian	90	0.30
Paraguayan	10	0.03
Peruvian	234	0.77
Uruguayan	10	0.03
Venezuelan	73	0.24
Other South American	13	0.04
Other Hispanic or Latino	302	1.00

Race*	Population	%
African-American/Black (2,673)	3,002	9.93
Not Hispanic (2,583)	2,836	9.38
Hispanic (90)	166	0.55
American Indian/Alaska Native (62)	190	0.63
Not Hispanic (34)	124	0.41
Hispanic (28)	66	0.22
Alaska Athabascan *(Ala. Nat.)* (1)	1	<0.01
Aleut *(Alaska Native)* (0)	1	<0.01
Apache (1)	3	0.01
Blackfeet (0)	3	0.01
Central American Ind. (0)	1	<0.01
Cherokee (7)	35	0.12
Cheyenne (0)	1	<0.01
Chippewa (1)	6	0.02
Choctaw (1)	2	0.01
Comanche (0)	1	<0.01
Creek (1)	6	0.02
Crow (0)	1	<0.01
Iroquois (1)	4	0.01
Mexican American Ind. (3)	7	0.02
Navajo (0)	3	0.01
Osage (0)	1	<0.01
Potawatomi (3)	3	0.01
Seminole (0)	1	<0.01
Sioux (2)	4	0.01
South American Ind. (0)	3	0.01
Spanish American Ind. (0)	1	<0.01
Asian (7,815)	8,625	28.54
Not Hispanic (7,784)	8,557	28.31
Hispanic (31)	68	0.22
Bangladeshi (27)	29	0.10
Bhutanese (1)	1	<0.01
Burmese (12)	17	0.06
Cambodian (25)	39	0.13
Chinese, ex. Taiwanese (969)	1,134	3.75
Filipino (482)	647	2.14
Hmong (5)	5	0.02
Indian (1,825)	1,893	6.26
Indonesian (20)	30	0.10
Japanese (76)	169	0.56
Korean (2,924)	3,075	10.17
Laotian (17)	28	0.09
Malaysian (3)	8	0.03
Nepalese (59)	65	0.22
Pakistani (235)	260	0.86
Sri Lankan (10)	10	0.03
Taiwanese (61)	74	0.24
Thai (65)	95	0.31
Vietnamese (682)	785	2.60
Hawaii Native/Pacific Islander (42)	75	0.25
Not Hispanic (41)	69	0.23
Hispanic (1)	6	0.02
Guamanian/Chamorro (27)	32	0.11
Native Hawaiian (6)	15	0.05
Samoan (0)	1	<0.01
Tongan (3)	3	0.01
White (17,464)	18,552	61.38
Not Hispanic (15,799)	16,708	55.28
Hispanic (1,665)	1,844	6.10

*Notes: † The Census 2010 population figure is used to calculate the percentages in the Hispanic Origin and Race categories. Ancestry percentages are based on the 2006-2010 American Community Survey population (not shown); ‡ Numbers in parentheses indicate the number of people reporting a single ancestry; * Numbers in parentheses indicate the number of persons reporting this race alone, not in combination with any other race; Please refer to the Explanation of Data for more information.*

Fairfax Station

Place Type: CDP
County: Fairfax
Population: 12,030†

Ancestry‡	Population	%
Afghan (66)	80	0.68
African, Sub-Saharan (184)	205	1.75
African (0)	21	0.18
Cape Verdean (17)	17	0.15
Ghanaian (40)	40	0.34
Nigerian (78)	78	0.67
Sierra Leonean (23)	23	0.20
Other Sub-Saharan African (26)	26	0.22
American (584)	584	4.99
Arab (197)	233	1.99
Arab (112)	112	0.96
Egyptian (48)	48	0.41
Lebanese (17)	53	0.45
Other Arab (20)	20	0.17
Australian (8)	8	0.07
Austrian (13)	87	0.74
Belgian (0)	41	0.35
British (94)	122	1.04
Canadian (38)	38	0.32
Croatian (0)	33	0.28
Czech (13)	48	0.41
Danish (0)	71	0.61
Dutch (25)	181	1.55
Eastern European (13)	13	0.11
English (517)	1,918	16.38
European (292)	366	3.13
French, ex. Basque (69)	442	3.78
French Canadian (9)	9	0.08
German (492)	2,030	17.34
Greek (31)	31	0.26
Hungarian (0)	31	0.26
Iranian (93)	93	0.79
Irish (561)	1,909	16.31
Italian (437)	1,080	9.22
Northern European (29)	29	0.25
Norwegian (58)	356	3.04
Pennsylvania German (7)	7	0.06
Polish (171)	341	2.91
Romanian (31)	31	0.26
Russian (175)	214	1.83
Scandinavian (17)	17	0.15
Scotch-Irish (134)	397	3.39
Scottish (82)	372	3.18
Slavic (0)	14	0.12
Slovak (13)	13	0.11
Slovene (0)	12	0.10
Swedish (40)	222	1.90
Swiss (0)	23	0.20
Turkish (25)	25	0.21
Ukrainian (12)	25	0.21
Welsh (0)	73	0.62
West Indian, ex. Hispanic (24)	24	0.20
Trinidadian/Tobagonian (8)	8	0.07
West Indian (16)	16	0.14
Yugoslavian (0)	44	0.38

Hispanic Origin	Population	%
Hispanic or Latino (of any race)	869	7.22
Central American, ex. Mexican	138	1.15
Costa Rican	2	0.02
Guatemalan	19	0.16
Honduran	11	0.09
Nicaraguan	16	0.13
Panamanian	8	0.07
Salvadoran	82	0.68
Cuban	36	0.30
Dominican Republic	8	0.07
Mexican	128	1.06
Puerto Rican	97	0.81
South American	358	2.98
Argentinean	17	0.14
Bolivian	80	0.67
Chilean	16	0.13
Colombian	47	0.39
Ecuadorian	21	0.17
Paraguayan	3	0.02
Peruvian	150	1.25
Uruguayan	10	0.08
Venezuelan	14	0.12
Other Hispanic or Latino	104	0.86

Race*	Population	%
African-American/Black (472)	568	4.72
Not Hispanic (460)	548	4.56
Hispanic (12)	20	0.17
American Indian/Alaska Native (15)	65	0.54
Not Hispanic (11)	45	0.37
Hispanic (4)	20	0.17
Central American Ind. (0)	1	0.01
Cherokee (3)	17	0.14
Chippewa (1)	1	0.01
Choctaw (4)	5	0.04
Creek (0)	2	0.02
Iroquois (0)	1	0.01
Mexican American Ind. (1)	1	0.01
Navajo (0)	1	0.01
South American Ind. (0)	7	0.06
Asian (1,462)	1,664	13.83
Not Hispanic (1,457)	1,646	13.68
Hispanic (5)	18	0.15
Bangladeshi (16)	21	0.17
Burmese (3)	3	0.02
Chinese, ex. Taiwanese (186)	216	1.80
Filipino (117)	160	1.33
Indian (213)	232	1.93
Indonesian (4)	5	0.04
Japanese (27)	59	0.49
Korean (544)	582	4.84
Laotian (2)	2	0.02
Malaysian (0)	1	0.01
Nepalese (19)	20	0.17
Pakistani (64)	78	0.65
Taiwanese (10)	16	0.13
Thai (23)	23	0.19
Vietnamese (195)	214	1.78
Hawaii Native/Pacific Islander (5)	17	0.14
Not Hispanic (5)	17	0.14
Guamanian/Chamorro (4)	6	0.05
Native Hawaiian (1)	6	0.05
White (9,487)	9,834	81.75
Not Hispanic (8,883)	9,165	76.18
Hispanic (604)	669	5.56

Fairfax

Place Type: Independent City
County: Fairfax
Population: 22,565†

Ancestry‡	Population	%
Afghan (77)	77	0.35
African, Sub-Saharan (279)	300	1.36
African (49)	70	0.32
Ethiopian (69)	69	0.31
Nigerian (39)	39	0.18
Zimbabwean (62)	62	0.28
Other Sub-Saharan African (60)	60	0.27
American (669)	669	3.03
Arab (137)	159	0.72
Arab (70)	70	0.32
Lebanese (9)	26	0.12
Syrian (0)	5	0.02
Other Arab (58)	58	0.26
Assyrian/Chaldean/Syriac (55)	55	0.25
Australian (19)	19	0.09
Austrian (26)	93	0.42
Belgian (6)	6	0.03
Brazilian (11)	60	0.27
British (158)	218	0.99
Bulgarian (17)	17	0.08
Cajun (16)	27	0.12
Canadian (49)	107	0.49
Croatian (0)	70	0.32
Cypriot (6)	6	0.03
Czech (41)	135	0.61
Czechoslovakian (6)	29	0.13
Danish (30)	61	0.28
Dutch (104)	349	1.58
Eastern European (41)	41	0.19
English (772)	2,994	13.57
Estonian (18)	18	0.08
European (457)	513	2.33
Finnish (59)	76	0.34
French, ex. Basque (42)	566	2.57
French Canadian (9)	31	0.14
German (951)	3,687	16.72
Greek (96)	170	0.77
Hungarian (43)	88	0.40
Iranian (10)	10	0.05
Irish (801)	3,000	13.60
Italian (396)	1,218	5.52
Lithuanian (24)	31	0.14
Northern European (64)	71	0.32
Norwegian (61)	238	1.08
Pennsylvania German (0)	10	0.05
Polish (193)	506	2.29
Portuguese (100)	176	0.80
Romanian (15)	15	0.07
Russian (82)	281	1.27
Scandinavian (0)	20	0.09
Scotch-Irish (229)	731	3.31
Scottish (143)	576	2.61
Slovak (0)	104	0.47
Swedish (19)	207	0.94
Swiss (0)	43	0.19
Turkish (18)	18	0.08
Ukrainian (53)	115	0.52
Welsh (55)	362	1.64
West Indian, ex. Hispanic (15)	15	0.07
Jamaican (15)	15	0.07
Yugoslavian (14)	14	0.06

Hispanic Origin	Population	%
Hispanic or Latino (of any race)	3,556	15.76
Central American, ex. Mexican	1,440	6.38
Costa Rican	22	0.10
Guatemalan	247	1.09
Honduran	119	0.53
Nicaraguan	95	0.42
Panamanian	10	0.04
Salvadoran	939	4.16
Other Central American	8	0.04
Cuban	60	0.27
Dominican Republic	41	0.18
Mexican	348	1.54
Puerto Rican	164	0.73
South American	1,064	4.72
Argentinean	66	0.29
Bolivian	414	1.83
Chilean	55	0.24
Colombian	97	0.43
Ecuadorian	57	0.25
Paraguayan	7	0.03
Peruvian	311	1.38
Uruguayan	7	0.03
Venezuelan	43	0.19
Other South American	7	0.03
Other Hispanic or Latino	439	1.95

Race*	Population	%
African-American/Black (1,071)	1,278	5.66
Not Hispanic (1,030)	1,186	5.26
Hispanic (41)	92	0.41
American Indian/Alaska Native (111)	257	1.14
Not Hispanic (62)	143	0.63
Hispanic (49)	114	0.51
Alaska Athabascan *(Ala. Nat.)* (1)	2	0.01
Apache (0)	1	<0.01
Blackfeet (1)	3	0.01
Central American Ind. (2)	2	0.01
Cherokee (6)	35	0.16
Chippewa (1)	2	0.01
Choctaw (2)	11	0.05

SECTION TWO

*Notes: † The Census 2010 population figure is used to calculate the percentages in the Hispanic Origin and Race categories. Ancestry percentages are based on the 2006-2010 American Community Survey population (not shown); ‡ Numbers in parentheses indicate the number of people reporting a single ancestry; * Numbers in parentheses indicate the number of persons reporting this race alone, not in combination with any other race; Please refer to the Explanation of Data for more information.*

Creek (1)	2	0.01
Delaware (1)	2	0.01
Inupiat *(Alaska Native)* (0)	3	0.01
Iroquois (5)	8	0.04
Mexican American Ind. (7)	10	0.04
Navajo (2)	2	0.01
Pima (0)	1	<0.01
Potawatomi (3)	3	0.01
Pueblo (3)	3	0.01
Sioux (1)	1	<0.01
South American Ind. (2)	14	0.06
Spanish American Ind. (1)	1	<0.01
Tlingit-Haida *(Alaska Native)* (2)	2	0.01
Asian (3,432)	3,874	17.17
Not Hispanic (3,403)	3,800	16.84
Hispanic (29)	74	0.33
Bangladeshi (33)	37	0.16
Burmese (23)	25	0.11
Cambodian (54)	60	0.27
Chinese, ex. Taiwanese (470)	552	2.45
Filipino (321)	414	1.83
Indian (615)	696	3.08
Indonesian (43)	44	0.19
Japanese (50)	86	0.38
Korean (764)	828	3.67
Laotian (18)	23	0.10
Malaysian (11)	12	0.05
Nepalese (101)	127	0.56
Pakistani (175)	181	0.80
Sri Lankan (5)	8	0.04
Taiwanese (26)	27	0.12
Thai (29)	36	0.16
Vietnamese (544)	596	2.64
Hawaii Native/Pacific Islander (14)	51	0.23
Not Hispanic (11)	46	0.20
Hispanic (3)	5	0.02
Guamanian/Chamorro (1)	6	0.03
Native Hawaiian (4)	9	0.04
Samoan (0)	2	0.01
Tongan (1)	1	<0.01
White (15,706)	16,499	73.12
Not Hispanic (13,849)	14,378	63.72
Hispanic (1,857)	2,121	9.40

Falls Church

Place Type: Independent City
County: Falls Church
Population: 12,332†

Ancestry‡	Population	%
Afghan (12)	12	0.10
African, Sub-Saharan (245)	245	2.14
African (39)	39	0.34
Ethiopian (81)	81	0.71
Ghanaian (36)	36	0.31
Nigerian (77)	77	0.67
Other Sub-Saharan African (12)	12	0.10
American (537)	537	4.68
Arab (145)	210	1.83
Arab (9)	9	0.08
Egyptian (43)	43	0.38
Lebanese (7)	43	0.38
Syrian (0)	24	0.21
Other Arab (86)	91	0.79
Armenian (0)	12	0.10
Austrian (16)	33	0.29
Belgian (11)	21	0.18
Brazilian (27)	73	0.64
British (160)	220	1.92
Bulgarian (19)	19	0.17
Canadian (19)	27	0.24
Celtic (12)	12	0.10
Croatian (0)	20	0.17
Czech (9)	77	0.67
Danish (34)	61	0.53
Dutch (38)	223	1.95
Eastern European (43)	43	0.38
English (349)	1,707	14.89
European (414)	500	4.36
Finnish (11)	52	0.45
French, ex. Basque (82)	249	2.17
French Canadian (11)	34	0.30
German (302)	1,935	16.88
Greek (20)	148	1.29
Hungarian (17)	43	0.38
Icelander (0)	10	0.09
Irish (382)	1,633	14.24
Italian (118)	649	5.66
Lithuanian (0)	9	0.08
Norwegian (61)	132	1.15
Polish (99)	402	3.51
Portuguese (0)	8	0.07
Russian (143)	317	2.76
Scandinavian (0)	71	0.62
Scotch-Irish (166)	418	3.65
Scottish (153)	546	4.76
Slavic (9)	19	0.17
Slovak (15)	74	0.65
Swedish (21)	166	1.45
Swiss (0)	102	0.89
Ukrainian (15)	74	0.65
Welsh (45)	218	1.90
Yugoslavian (0)	29	0.25

Hispanic Origin	Population	%
Hispanic or Latino (of any race)	1,109	8.99
Central American, ex. Mexican	295	2.39
Costa Rican	15	0.12
Guatemalan	44	0.36
Honduran	42	0.34
Nicaraguan	11	0.09
Panamanian	5	0.04
Salvadoran	178	1.44
Cuban	56	0.45
Dominican Republic	24	0.19
Mexican	173	1.40
Puerto Rican	74	0.60
South American	381	3.09
Argentinean	28	0.23
Bolivian	139	1.13
Chilean	18	0.15
Colombian	51	0.41
Ecuadorian	18	0.15
Paraguayan	15	0.12
Peruvian	77	0.62
Uruguayan	6	0.05
Venezuelan	24	0.19
Other South American	5	0.04
Other Hispanic or Latino	106	0.86

Race*	Population	%
African-American/Black (532)	639	5.18
Not Hispanic (523)	616	5.00
Hispanic (9)	23	0.19
American Indian/Alaska Native (33)	119	0.96
Not Hispanic (23)	87	0.71
Hispanic (10)	32	0.26
Blackfeet (1)	1	0.01
Central American Ind. (0)	4	0.03
Cherokee (7)	17	0.14
Choctaw (1)	9	0.07
Comanche (3)	3	0.02
Cree (0)	1	0.01
Crow (0)	3	0.02
Delaware (0)	1	0.01
Inupiat *(Alaska Native)* (1)	1	0.01
Iroquois (1)	3	0.02
Lumbee (1)	1	0.01
Mexican American Ind. (3)	3	0.02
Navajo (1)	1	0.01
Osage (0)	2	0.02
Pueblo (3)	3	0.02
Puget Sound Salish (1)	1	0.01
Seminole (0)	1	0.01
Sioux (1)	2	0.02
South American Ind. (1)	6	0.05
Asian (1,162)	1,482	12.02
Not Hispanic (1,150)	1,443	11.70
Hispanic (12)	39	0.32
Bangladeshi (16)	17	0.14
Burmese (4)	5	0.04
Cambodian (11)	11	0.09
Chinese, ex. Taiwanese (171)	254	2.06
Filipino (170)	227	1.84
Hmong (2)	2	0.02
Indian (232)	279	2.26
Indonesian (4)	9	0.07
Japanese (41)	94	0.76
Korean (160)	223	1.81
Laotian (1)	1	0.01
Malaysian (1)	1	0.01
Nepalese (16)	18	0.15
Pakistani (44)	53	0.43
Sri Lankan (9)	9	0.07
Taiwanese (5)	5	0.04
Thai (34)	48	0.39
Vietnamese (166)	188	1.52
Hawaii Native/Pacific Islander (4)	14	0.11
Not Hispanic (4)	14	0.11
Fijian (1)	2	0.02
Guamanian/Chamorro (2)	3	0.02
Native Hawaiian (1)	5	0.04
White (9,853)	10,311	83.61
Not Hispanic (9,093)	9,482	76.89
Hispanic (760)	829	6.72

Farmville

Place Type: Town
County: Prince Edward
Population: 8,216†

Ancestry‡	Population	%
African, Sub-Saharan (22)	36	0.43
African (22)	36	0.43
American (722)	722	8.58
Arab (12)	12	0.14
Lebanese (12)	12	0.14
Austrian (0)	18	0.21
Belgian (0)	13	0.15
British (50)	118	1.40
Czech (0)	50	0.59
Danish (0)	72	0.86
Dutch (15)	90	1.07
English (481)	1,339	15.91
European (171)	194	2.30
French, ex. Basque (23)	91	1.08
French Canadian (27)	55	0.65
German (274)	1,002	11.90
Greek (33)	45	0.53
Irish (217)	899	10.68
Italian (131)	527	6.26
Norwegian (0)	44	0.52
Polish (0)	62	0.74
Portuguese (0)	85	1.01
Romanian (10)	10	0.12
Russian (15)	54	0.64
Scotch-Irish (111)	318	3.78
Scottish (10)	181	2.15
Slovak (14)	14	0.17
Swedish (7)	89	1.06
Swiss (0)	9	0.11
Ukrainian (12)	12	0.14
Welsh (0)	100	1.19

Hispanic Origin	Population	%
Hispanic or Latino (of any race)	192	2.34
Central American, ex. Mexican	25	0.30
Costa Rican	3	0.04
Guatemalan	5	0.06
Honduran	6	0.07
Panamanian	5	0.06
Salvadoran	6	0.07
Cuban	10	0.12
Dominican Republic	7	0.09
Mexican	53	0.65
Puerto Rican	33	0.40
South American	27	0.33
Argentinean	6	0.07

*Notes: † The Census 2010 population figure is used to calculate the percentages in the Hispanic Origin and Race categories. Ancestry percentages are based on the 2006-2010 American Community Survey population (not shown); ‡ Numbers in parentheses indicate the number of people reporting a single ancestry; * Numbers in parentheses indicate the number of persons reporting this race alone, not in combination with any other race; Please refer to the Explanation of Data for more information.*

Bolivian	8	0.10
Colombian	5	0.06
Ecuadorian	6	0.07
Venezuelan	2	0.02
Other Hispanic or Latino	37	0.45

Race*	Population	%
African-American/Black (1,958)	2,049	24.94
Not Hispanic (1,927)	2,014	24.51
Hispanic (31)	35	0.43
American Indian/Alaska Native (29)	49	0.60
Not Hispanic (29)	47	0.57
Hispanic (0)	2	0.02
Blackfeet (4)	4	0.05
Cherokee (1)	8	0.10
Iroquois (0)	1	0.01
Lumbee (1)	1	0.01
Mexican American Ind. (0)	2	0.02
Asian (101)	117	1.42
Not Hispanic (101)	117	1.42
Cambodian (1)	1	0.01
Chinese, ex. Taiwanese (28)	33	0.40
Filipino (13)	16	0.19
Indian (32)	34	0.41
Indonesian (0)	2	0.02
Japanese (0)	3	0.04
Korean (5)	7	0.09
Pakistani (6)	6	0.07
Thai (2)	2	0.02
Vietnamese (10)	13	0.16
Hawaii Native/Pacific Islander (10)	14	0.17
Not Hispanic (9)	13	0.16
Hispanic (1)	1	0.01
Guamanian/Chamorro (3)	3	0.04
Native Hawaiian (4)	6	0.07
Samoan (3)	3	0.04
White (5,941)	6,051	73.65
Not Hispanic (5,844)	5,938	72.27
Hispanic (97)	113	1.38

Floris

Place Type: CDP
County: Fairfax
Population: 8,375†

Ancestry‡	Population	%
Albanian (0)	26	0.32
American (335)	335	4.11
Arab (29)	103	1.27
Egyptian (16)	35	0.43
Lebanese (0)	32	0.39
Syrian (0)	23	0.28
Other Arab (13)	13	0.16
Assyrian/Chaldean/Syriac (15)	15	0.18
Austrian (10)	45	0.55
British (15)	15	0.18
Celtic (0)	21	0.26
Czech (0)	63	0.77
Czechoslovakian (21)	55	0.68
Danish (34)	85	1.04
Dutch (0)	68	0.84
Eastern European (37)	37	0.45
English (238)	860	10.56
European (126)	138	1.70
Finnish (0)	23	0.28
French, ex. Basque (52)	208	2.55
French Canadian (38)	38	0.47
German (212)	826	10.15
Greek (37)	153	1.88
Hungarian (12)	72	0.88
Iranian (87)	113	1.39
Irish (237)	869	10.67
Italian (65)	426	5.23
Lithuanian (0)	92	1.13
Norwegian (24)	51	0.63
Polish (155)	346	4.25
Romanian (27)	47	0.58
Russian (27)	65	0.80
Scandinavian (0)	14	0.17
Scotch-Irish (38)	79	0.97
Scottish (77)	228	2.80
Serbian (10)	10	0.12
Slovak (0)	34	0.42
Slovene (0)	37	0.45
Swedish (16)	78	0.96
Swiss (19)	71	0.87
Turkish (25)	25	0.31
Ukrainian (34)	34	0.42
Welsh (17)	21	0.26

Hispanic Origin	Population	%
Hispanic or Latino (of any race)	311	3.71
Central American, ex. Mexican	59	0.70
Costa Rican	1	0.01
Guatemalan	5	0.06
Honduran	2	0.02
Nicaraguan	1	0.01
Panamanian	2	0.02
Salvadoran	46	0.55
Other Central American	2	0.02
Cuban	22	0.26
Dominican Republic	7	0.08
Mexican	53	0.63
Puerto Rican	47	0.56
South American	83	0.99
Argentinean	5	0.06
Bolivian	18	0.21
Chilean	1	0.01
Colombian	24	0.29
Ecuadorian	7	0.08
Peruvian	22	0.26
Venezuelan	6	0.07
Other Hispanic or Latino	40	0.48

Race*	Population	%
African-American/Black (294)	334	3.99
Not Hispanic (291)	326	3.89
Hispanic (3)	8	0.10
American Indian/Alaska Native (18)	48	0.57
Not Hispanic (17)	40	0.48
Hispanic (1)	8	0.10
Blackfeet (0)	1	0.01
Central American Ind. (1)	2	0.02
Cherokee (0)	8	0.10
Choctaw (3)	3	0.04
Iroquois (1)	1	0.01
Lumbee (4)	4	0.05
Mexican American Ind. (1)	1	0.01
Navajo (4)	4	0.05
Pima (0)	2	0.02
South American Ind. (0)	1	0.01
Asian (2,785)	3,027	36.14
Not Hispanic (2,782)	3,013	35.98
Hispanic (3)	14	0.17
Bangladeshi (35)	41	0.49
Burmese (4)	4	0.05
Cambodian (13)	15	0.18
Chinese, ex. Taiwanese (835)	909	10.85
Filipino (53)	76	0.91
Indian (1,246)	1,285	15.34
Indonesian (8)	10	0.12
Japanese (41)	82	0.98
Korean (193)	225	2.69
Laotian (10)	11	0.13
Malaysian (1)	3	0.04
Nepalese (10)	11	0.13
Pakistani (85)	88	1.05
Sri Lankan (0)	4	0.05
Taiwanese (64)	75	0.90
Thai (15)	29	0.35
Vietnamese (101)	114	1.36
Hawaii Native/Pacific Islander (6)	27	0.32
Not Hispanic (5)	26	0.31
Hispanic (1)	1	0.01
Guamanian/Chamorro (2)	8	0.10
Native Hawaiian (0)	5	0.06
Samoan (2)	2	0.02
White (4,883)	5,135	61.31
Not Hispanic (4,667)	4,897	58.47
Hispanic (216)	238	2.84

Forest

Place Type: CDP
County: Bedford
Population: 9,106†

Ancestry‡	Population	%
American (1,146)	1,146	12.57
Arab (0)	14	0.15
Lebanese (0)	14	0.15
Austrian (14)	14	0.15
British (140)	140	1.54
Canadian (10)	10	0.11
Croatian (21)	21	0.23
Czech (0)	17	0.19
Dutch (95)	141	1.55
Eastern European (11)	11	0.12
English (831)	1,598	17.53
European (108)	185	2.03
French, ex. Basque (28)	272	2.98
French Canadian (56)	215	2.36
German (489)	1,200	13.16
Greek (14)	14	0.15
Hungarian (0)	65	0.71
Irish (325)	940	10.31
Italian (160)	447	4.90
Lithuanian (0)	12	0.13
Norwegian (8)	17	0.19
Polish (58)	103	1.13
Romanian (0)	12	0.13
Russian (26)	39	0.43
Scotch-Irish (227)	335	3.67
Scottish (93)	306	3.36
Slavic (0)	9	0.10
Slovak (0)	23	0.25
Swedish (0)	95	1.04
Swiss (13)	41	0.45
Ukrainian (16)	35	0.38
Welsh (39)	195	2.14

Hispanic Origin	Population	%
Hispanic or Latino (of any race)	265	2.91
Central American, ex. Mexican	32	0.35
Guatemalan	5	0.05
Honduran	13	0.14
Nicaraguan	2	0.02
Salvadoran	12	0.13
Cuban	8	0.09
Dominican Republic	6	0.07
Mexican	126	1.38
Puerto Rican	47	0.52
South American	15	0.16
Argentinean	1	0.01
Chilean	8	0.09
Colombian	3	0.03
Ecuadorian	1	0.01
Peruvian	1	0.01
Uruguayan	1	0.01
Other Hispanic or Latino	31	0.34

Race*	Population	%
African-American/Black (652)	703	7.72
Not Hispanic (644)	694	7.62
Hispanic (8)	9	0.10
American Indian/Alaska Native (10)	25	0.27
Not Hispanic (9)	24	0.26
Hispanic (1)	1	0.01
Apache (2)	2	0.02
Cherokee (0)	8	0.09
Creek (2)	2	0.02
Crow (0)	1	0.01
Iroquois (1)	1	0.01
Lumbee (0)	1	0.01
Asian (277)	301	3.31
Not Hispanic (274)	298	3.27
Hispanic (3)	3	0.03
Chinese, ex. Taiwanese (68)	70	0.77
Filipino (24)	30	0.33

SECTION TWO

*Notes: † The Census 2010 population figure is used to calculate the percentages in the Hispanic Origin and Race categories. Ancestry percentages are based on the 2006-2010 American Community Survey population (not shown); ‡ Numbers in parentheses indicate the number of people reporting a single ancestry; * Numbers in parentheses indicate the number of persons reporting this race alone, not in combination with any other race; Please refer to the Explanation of Data for more information.*

Indian (37)	41	0.45
Japanese (2)	5	0.05
Korean (93)	98	1.08
Nepalese (1)	1	0.01
Pakistani (7)	7	0.08
Taiwanese (6)	6	0.07
Vietnamese (37)	39	0.43
Hawaii Native/Pacific Islander (2)	4	0.04
Not Hispanic (2)	4	0.04
Native Hawaiian (1)	1	0.01
Samoan (1)	2	0.02
White (7,996)	8,073	88.66
Not Hispanic (7,818)	7,886	86.60
Hispanic (178)	187	2.05

Fort Hunt

Place Type: CDP
County: Fairfax
Population: 16,045†

Ancestry‡	Population	%
Afghan (52)	52	0.33
African, Sub-Saharan (0)	19	0.12
African (0)	9	0.06
Other Sub-Saharan African (0)	10	0.06
American (1,015)	1,015	6.37
Arab (33)	55	0.34
Arab (10)	10	0.06
Egyptian (13)	13	0.08
Lebanese (10)	23	0.14
Syrian (0)	9	0.06
Armenian (37)	37	0.23
Australian (20)	20	0.13
Austrian (59)	157	0.98
Belgian (0)	7	0.04
Brazilian (51)	51	0.32
British (198)	297	1.86
Bulgarian (0)	27	0.17
Canadian (54)	104	0.65
Croatian (12)	37	0.23
Cypriot (11)	11	0.07
Czech (18)	219	1.37
Czechoslovakian (17)	50	0.31
Danish (22)	50	0.31
Dutch (49)	276	1.73
Eastern European (66)	111	0.70
English (906)	3,045	19.10
European (412)	421	2.64
Finnish (0)	26	0.16
French, ex. Basque (32)	265	1.66
French Canadian (39)	134	0.84
German (980)	3,579	22.45
Greek (22)	164	1.03
Hungarian (97)	237	1.49
Irish (1,055)	3,334	20.91
Italian (433)	1,277	8.01
Lithuanian (18)	149	0.93
Luxemburger (0)	15	0.09
Northern European (57)	70	0.44
Norwegian (95)	299	1.88
Pennsylvania German (0)	15	0.09
Polish (149)	677	4.25
Romanian (10)	10	0.06
Russian (185)	296	1.86
Scandinavian (23)	38	0.24
Scotch-Irish (245)	704	4.42
Scottish (163)	686	4.30
Serbian (0)	7	0.04
Slavic (10)	10	0.06
Slovak (82)	234	1.47
Swedish (44)	328	2.06
Swiss (11)	159	1.00
Ukrainian (49)	101	0.63
Welsh (46)	197	1.24
Yugoslavian (30)	42	0.26

Hispanic Origin	Population	%
Hispanic or Latino (of any race)	698	4.35
Central American, ex. Mexican	74	0.46
Costa Rican	6	0.04
Guatemalan	18	0.11
Honduran	11	0.07
Nicaraguan	6	0.04
Panamanian	10	0.06
Salvadoran	23	0.14
Cuban	48	0.30
Dominican Republic	11	0.07
Mexican	191	1.19
Puerto Rican	89	0.55
South American	175	1.09
Argentinean	26	0.16
Bolivian	25	0.16
Chilean	7	0.04
Colombian	42	0.26
Ecuadorian	16	0.10
Paraguayan	3	0.02
Peruvian	33	0.21
Uruguayan	7	0.04
Venezuelan	16	0.10
Other Hispanic or Latino	110	0.69

Race*	Population	%
African-American/Black (368)	457	2.85
Not Hispanic (359)	439	2.74
Hispanic (9)	18	0.11
American Indian/Alaska Native (28)	100	0.62
Not Hispanic (22)	79	0.49
Hispanic (6)	21	0.13
Blackfeet (0)	3	0.02
Canadian/French Am. Ind. (2)	2	0.01
Cherokee (3)	19	0.12
Chickasaw (0)	4	0.02
Choctaw (2)	5	0.03
Creek (1)	1	0.01
Delaware (0)	2	0.01
Iroquois (1)	8	0.05
Kiowa (1)	1	0.01
Lumbee (1)	1	0.01
Mexican American Ind. (3)	7	0.04
Navajo (1)	3	0.02
Potawatomi (0)	4	0.02
Seminole (1)	2	0.01
Sioux (1)	1	0.01
South American Ind. (1)	3	0.02
Yaqui (1)	1	0.01
Asian (449)	642	4.00
Not Hispanic (437)	623	3.88
Hispanic (12)	19	0.12
Cambodian (0)	2	0.01
Chinese, ex. Taiwanese (96)	125	0.78
Filipino (69)	93	0.58
Indian (85)	104	0.65
Indonesian (2)	3	0.02
Japanese (36)	81	0.50
Korean (97)	146	0.91
Laotian (1)	1	0.01
Malaysian (2)	2	0.01
Pakistani (17)	19	0.12
Sri Lankan (4)	7	0.04
Taiwanese (2)	2	0.01
Thai (8)	19	0.12
Vietnamese (11)	23	0.14
Hawaii Native/Pacific Islander (9)	26	0.16
Not Hispanic (9)	25	0.16
Hispanic (0)	1	0.01
Guamanian/Chamorro (0)	2	0.01
Native Hawaiian (5)	14	0.09
Samoan (1)	3	0.02
White (14,698)	15,053	93.82
Not Hispanic (14,184)	14,486	90.28
Hispanic (514)	567	3.53

Franconia

Place Type: CDP
County: Fairfax
Population: 18,245†

Ancestry‡	Population	%
Afghan (402)	410	2.22
African, Sub-Saharan (926)	926	5.02
African (85)	85	0.46
Ethiopian (700)	700	3.79
Sudanese (141)	141	0.76
American (756)	756	4.10
Arab (481)	608	3.30
Arab (191)	247	1.34
Egyptian (67)	67	0.36
Jordanian (77)	77	0.42
Lebanese (15)	86	0.47
Moroccan (131)	131	0.71
Armenian (0)	14	0.08
Australian (0)	13	0.07
Austrian (17)	17	0.09
Belgian (0)	39	0.21
British (45)	126	0.68
Canadian (0)	17	0.09
Celtic (0)	8	0.04
Croatian (0)	27	0.15
Czech (17)	85	0.46
Czechoslovakian (0)	11	0.06
Danish (0)	96	0.52
Dutch (48)	349	1.89
Eastern European (85)	85	0.46
English (346)	1,453	7.87
Estonian (0)	14	0.08
European (198)	198	1.07
French, ex. Basque (66)	373	2.02
French Canadian (18)	18	0.10
German (650)	2,393	12.97
Greek (99)	259	1.40
Hungarian (0)	46	0.25
Icelander (12)	12	0.07
Iranian (14)	29	0.16
Irish (473)	2,060	11.16
Italian (283)	1,048	5.68
Lithuanian (49)	66	0.36
Northern European (113)	113	0.61
Norwegian (16)	159	0.86
Polish (114)	414	2.24
Portuguese (10)	55	0.30
Romanian (0)	8	0.04
Russian (118)	166	0.90
Scotch-Irish (108)	274	1.49
Scottish (184)	419	2.27
Slavic (0)	11	0.06
Slovak (71)	154	0.83
Swedish (0)	127	0.69
Swiss (0)	48	0.26
Ukrainian (29)	107	0.58
Welsh (34)	218	1.18
West Indian, ex. Hispanic (64)	88	0.48
Haitian (17)	28	0.15
Jamaican (36)	49	0.27
Trinidadian/Tobagonian (11)	11	0.06

Hispanic Origin	Population	%
Hispanic or Latino (of any race)	2,200	12.06
Central American, ex. Mexican	620	3.40
Costa Rican	11	0.06
Guatemalan	63	0.35
Honduran	86	0.47
Nicaraguan	24	0.13
Panamanian	22	0.12
Salvadoran	412	2.26
Other Central American	2	0.01
Cuban	47	0.26
Dominican Republic	35	0.19
Mexican	355	1.95
Puerto Rican	270	1.48
South American	666	3.65
Argentinean	48	0.26
Bolivian	189	1.04
Chilean	25	0.14
Colombian	98	0.54
Ecuadorian	48	0.26
Paraguayan	10	0.05
Peruvian	196	1.07

*Notes: † The Census 2010 population figure is used to calculate the percentages in the Hispanic Origin and Race categories. Ancestry percentages are based on the 2006-2010 American Community Survey population (not shown); ‡ Numbers in parentheses indicate the number of people reporting a single ancestry; * Numbers in parentheses indicate the number of persons reporting this race alone, not in combination with any other race; Please refer to the Explanation of Data for more information.*

Uruguayan	3	0.02
Venezuelan	46	0.25
Other South American	3	0.02
Other Hispanic or Latino	207	1.13

Race*	Population	%
African-American/Black (3,393)	3,653	20.02
Not Hispanic (3,309)	3,522	19.30
Hispanic (84)	131	0.72
American Indian/Alaska Native (69)	183	1.00
Not Hispanic (37)	123	0.67
Hispanic (32)	60	0.33
Cherokee (5)	31	0.17
Chickasaw (0)	1	0.01
Chippewa (0)	3	0.02
Comanche (0)	1	0.01
Creek (0)	2	0.01
Hopi (0)	1	0.01
Iroquois (2)	8	0.04
Kiowa (0)	1	0.01
Mexican American Ind. (6)	8	0.04
Navajo (3)	3	0.02
Paiute (1)	4	0.02
Pueblo (0)	4	0.02
Sioux (3)	9	0.05
South American Ind. (2)	9	0.05
Spanish American Ind. (0)	6	0.03
Asian (2,635)	3,081	16.89
Not Hispanic (2,619)	3,041	16.67
Hispanic (16)	40	0.22
Bangladeshi (71)	82	0.45
Burmese (29)	31	0.17
Cambodian (14)	14	0.08
Chinese, ex. Taiwanese (352)	425	2.33
Filipino (398)	516	2.83
Indian (503)	568	3.11
Indonesian (21)	23	0.13
Japanese (30)	101	0.55
Korean (263)	327	1.79
Laotian (21)	21	0.12
Malaysian (4)	12	0.07
Nepalese (6)	6	0.03
Pakistani (261)	282	1.55
Sri Lankan (5)	5	0.03
Taiwanese (9)	10	0.05
Thai (98)	111	0.61
Vietnamese (408)	433	2.37
Hawaii Native/Pacific Islander (23)	59	0.32
Not Hispanic (21)	48	0.26
Hispanic (2)	11	0.06
Guamanian/Chamorro (10)	17	0.09
Native Hawaiian (2)	10	0.05
Samoan (9)	17	0.09
Tongan (0)	3	0.02
White (10,739)	11,431	62.65
Not Hispanic (9,362)	9,916	54.35
Hispanic (1,377)	1,515	8.30

Franklin Farm

Place Type: CDP
County: Fairfax
Population: 19,288†

Ancestry‡	Population	%
Afghan (47)	196	1.00
African, Sub-Saharan (244)	255	1.31
African (59)	70	0.36
Ghanaian (34)	34	0.17
Nigerian (151)	151	0.77
American (608)	608	3.11
Arab (155)	198	1.01
Egyptian (104)	104	0.53
Lebanese (12)	55	0.28
Other Arab (39)	39	0.20
Austrian (37)	126	0.65
British (114)	270	1.38
Celtic (15)	15	0.08
Croatian (0)	9	0.05
Czech (36)	88	0.45
Danish (25)	74	0.38
Dutch (37)	286	1.46
Eastern European (128)	128	0.66
English (770)	2,913	14.91
European (489)	524	2.68
Finnish (0)	12	0.06
French, ex. Basque (106)	808	4.14
French Canadian (36)	148	0.76
German (685)	3,248	16.63
Greek (37)	107	0.55
Hungarian (32)	175	0.90
Iranian (322)	322	1.65
Irish (527)	2,621	13.42
Italian (543)	1,364	6.98
Latvian (0)	14	0.07
Lithuanian (0)	48	0.25
Maltese (0)	13	0.07
Norwegian (80)	223	1.14
Polish (324)	1,105	5.66
Portuguese (42)	127	0.65
Romanian (30)	55	0.28
Russian (60)	443	2.27
Scandinavian (103)	175	0.90
Scotch-Irish (149)	401	2.05
Scottish (118)	603	3.09
Slovak (36)	135	0.69
Swedish (22)	115	0.59
Swiss (9)	23	0.12
Turkish (99)	162	0.83
Ukrainian (67)	136	0.70
Welsh (28)	208	1.06

Hispanic Origin	Population	%
Hispanic or Latino (of any race)	1,005	5.21
Central American, ex. Mexican	212	1.10
Costa Rican	18	0.09
Guatemalan	34	0.18
Honduran	11	0.06
Nicaraguan	15	0.08
Panamanian	10	0.05
Salvadoran	124	0.64
Cuban	65	0.34
Dominican Republic	14	0.07
Mexican	147	0.76
Puerto Rican	82	0.43
South American	357	1.85
Argentinean	19	0.10
Bolivian	71	0.37
Chilean	12	0.06
Colombian	71	0.37
Ecuadorian	37	0.19
Paraguayan	3	0.02
Peruvian	115	0.60
Venezuelan	20	0.10
Other South American	9	0.05
Other Hispanic or Latino	128	0.66

Race*	Population	%
African-American/Black (634)	775	4.02
Not Hispanic (620)	743	3.85
Hispanic (14)	32	0.17
American Indian/Alaska Native (38)	97	0.50
Not Hispanic (31)	80	0.41
Hispanic (7)	17	0.09
Apache (1)	3	0.02
Blackfeet (0)	4	0.02
Canadian/French Am. Ind. (0)	1	0.01
Central American Ind. (1)	3	0.02
Cherokee (3)	23	0.12
Chickasaw (4)	4	0.02
Choctaw (1)	4	0.02
Iroquois (3)	6	0.03
Mexican American Ind. (2)	4	0.02
Potawatomi (3)	3	0.02
Sioux (2)	6	0.03
South American Ind. (0)	2	0.01
Asian (2,996)	3,379	17.52
Not Hispanic (2,986)	3,346	17.35
Hispanic (10)	33	0.17
Bangladeshi (19)	19	0.10
Burmese (13)	13	0.07
Cambodian (39)	39	0.20
Chinese, ex. Taiwanese (834)	906	4.70
Filipino (195)	270	1.40
Indian (924)	1,003	5.20
Indonesian (1)	6	0.03
Japanese (112)	191	0.99
Korean (334)	377	1.95
Laotian (8)	10	0.05
Malaysian (3)	8	0.04
Nepalese (25)	27	0.14
Pakistani (81)	108	0.56
Sri Lankan (9)	12	0.06
Taiwanese (63)	70	0.36
Thai (16)	22	0.11
Vietnamese (227)	249	1.29
Hawaii Native/Pacific Islander (7)	34	0.18
Not Hispanic (7)	31	0.16
Hispanic (0)	3	0.02
Guamanian/Chamorro (1)	2	0.01
Native Hawaiian (4)	17	0.09
Samoan (0)	3	0.02
White (14,766)	15,278	79.21
Not Hispanic (14,087)	14,522	75.29
Hispanic (679)	756	3.92

Franklin

Place Type: Independent City
County: Franklin
Population: 8,582†

Ancestry‡	Population	%
African, Sub-Saharan (1,406)	1,406	16.45
African (1,406)	1,406	16.45
American (1,422)	1,422	16.63
Australian (0)	28	0.33
British (22)	31	0.36
Danish (7)	20	0.23
Dutch (0)	11	0.13
English (537)	898	10.50
French, ex. Basque (20)	140	1.64
French Canadian (15)	54	0.63
German (119)	413	4.83
Hungarian (16)	43	0.50
Irish (105)	358	4.19
Italian (83)	110	1.29
Lithuanian (24)	24	0.28
Norwegian (8)	36	0.42
Polish (17)	144	1.68
Portuguese (0)	17	0.20
Russian (12)	45	0.53
Scotch-Irish (38)	118	1.38
Scottish (102)	160	1.87
Serbian (0)	8	0.09
Swedish (0)	4	0.05
Swiss (0)	10	0.12
Welsh (8)	32	0.37
West Indian, ex. Hispanic (261)	261	3.05
Jamaican (257)	257	3.01
West Indian (4)	4	0.05

Hispanic Origin	Population	%
Hispanic or Latino (of any race)	141	1.64
Central American, ex. Mexican	16	0.19
Honduran	3	0.03
Nicaraguan	2	0.02
Salvadoran	11	0.13
Cuban	4	0.05
Dominican Republic	4	0.05
Mexican	63	0.73
Puerto Rican	24	0.28
South American	7	0.08
Bolivian	7	0.08
Other Hispanic or Latino	23	0.27

Race*	Population	%
African-American/Black (4,884)	5,004	58.31
Not Hispanic (4,867)	4,977	57.99
Hispanic (17)	27	0.31

*Notes: † The Census 2010 population figure is used to calculate the percentages in the Hispanic Origin and Race categories. Ancestry percentages are based on the 2006-2010 American Community Survey population (not shown); ‡ Numbers in parentheses indicate the number of people reporting a single ancestry; * Numbers in parentheses indicate the number of persons reporting this race alone, not in combination with any other race; Please refer to the Explanation of Data for more information.*

American Indian/Alaska Native (28)	88	1.03
Not Hispanic (27)	82	0.96
Hispanic (1)	6	0.07
Cherokee (8)	19	0.22
Chickasaw (2)	3	0.03
Iroquois (1)	9	0.10
Lumbee (4)	9	0.10
Navajo (1)	3	0.03
Asian (64)	95	1.11
Not Hispanic (63)	90	1.05
Hispanic (1)	5	0.06
Cambodian (1)	1	0.01
Chinese, ex. Taiwanese (16)	18	0.21
Filipino (12)	24	0.28
Indian (4)	13	0.15
Japanese (2)	6	0.07
Korean (9)	14	0.16
Vietnamese (19)	21	0.24
Hawaii Native/Pacific Islander (2)	10	0.12
Not Hispanic (2)	7	0.08
Hispanic (0)	3	0.03
Guamanian/Chamorro (0)	2	0.02
Native Hawaiian (1)	2	0.02
Samoan (0)	1	0.01
White (3,380)	3,500	40.78
Not Hispanic (3,333)	3,439	40.07
Hispanic (47)	61	0.71

Fredericksburg

Place Type: Independent City
County: Fredericksburg
Population: 24,286†

Ancestry‡	Population	%
Afghan (72)	93	0.40
African, Sub-Saharan (121)	168	0.72
African (83)	114	0.49
Cape Verdean (0)	16	0.07
Ghanaian (13)	13	0.06
Kenyan (15)	15	0.06
Sierra Leonean (10)	10	0.04
American (2,586)	2,586	11.06
Arab (53)	98	0.42
Egyptian (0)	12	0.05
Lebanese (53)	72	0.31
Palestinian (0)	14	0.06
Armenian (8)	8	0.03
Australian (12)	12	0.05
Austrian (49)	49	0.21
Belgian (0)	25	0.11
Brazilian (0)	14	0.06
British (78)	174	0.74
Canadian (71)	88	0.38
Celtic (13)	13	0.06
Croatian (15)	49	0.21
Czech (0)	55	0.24
Danish (13)	59	0.25
Dutch (0)	92	0.39
Eastern European (0)	37	0.16
English (1,280)	2,749	11.76
European (268)	268	1.15
Finnish (0)	13	0.06
French, ex. Basque (79)	408	1.75
French Canadian (22)	85	0.36
German (638)	2,373	10.15
Greek (30)	48	0.21
Hungarian (21)	35	0.15
Iranian (6)	6	0.03
Irish (868)	2,501	10.70
Israeli (0)	37	0.16
Italian (650)	1,324	5.66
Lithuanian (16)	16	0.07
Northern European (0)	16	0.07
Norwegian (30)	86	0.37
Polish (157)	455	1.95
Portuguese (0)	25	0.11
Romanian (24)	52	0.22
Russian (0)	65	0.28
Scandinavian (0)	26	0.11
Scotch-Irish (152)	424	1.81
Scottish (102)	575	2.46
Slovak (20)	40	0.17
Swedish (62)	123	0.53
Swiss (0)	66	0.28
Ukrainian (11)	54	0.23
Welsh (8)	131	0.56
West Indian, ex. Hispanic (153)	184	0.79
Haitian (90)	90	0.39
Jamaican (0)	31	0.13
Trinidadian/Tobagonian (47)	47	0.20
West Indian (16)	16	0.07

Hispanic Origin	Population	%
Hispanic or Latino (of any race)	2,607	10.73
Central American, ex. Mexican	766	3.15
Costa Rican	7	0.03
Guatemalan	158	0.65
Honduran	125	0.51
Nicaraguan	23	0.09
Panamanian	19	0.08
Salvadoran	425	1.75
Other Central American	9	0.04
Cuban	43	0.18
Dominican Republic	48	0.20
Mexican	940	3.87
Puerto Rican	326	1.34
South American	196	0.81
Argentinean	1	<0.01
Bolivian	13	0.05
Chilean	12	0.05
Colombian	32	0.13
Ecuadorian	27	0.11
Peruvian	64	0.26
Uruguayan	16	0.07
Venezuelan	23	0.09
Other South American	8	0.03
Other Hispanic or Latino	288	1.19

Race*	Population	%
African-American/Black (5,498)	6,051	24.92
Not Hispanic (5,367)	5,818	23.96
Hispanic (131)	233	0.96
American Indian/Alaska Native (100)	310	1.28
Not Hispanic (58)	240	0.99
Hispanic (42)	70	0.29
Apache (0)	2	0.01
Blackfeet (5)	18	0.07
Canadian/French Am. Ind. (1)	1	<0.01
Central American Ind. (0)	2	0.01
Cherokee (12)	57	0.23
Chickasaw (0)	1	<0.01
Chippewa (3)	6	0.02
Choctaw (0)	4	0.02
Cree (0)	1	<0.01
Creek (0)	3	0.01
Delaware (3)	3	0.01
Iroquois (1)	4	0.02
Lumbee (0)	5	0.02
Mexican American Ind. (5)	7	0.03
Navajo (1)	2	0.01
Pueblo (1)	8	0.03
Seminole (0)	6	0.02
Shoshone (0)	1	<0.01
Sioux (1)	3	0.01
South American Ind. (1)	3	0.01
Spanish American Ind. (4)	4	0.02
Yup'ik *(Alaska Native)* (0)	2	0.01
Asian (689)	967	3.98
Not Hispanic (670)	927	3.82
Hispanic (19)	40	0.16
Bangladeshi (3)	3	0.01
Bhutanese (35)	41	0.17
Cambodian (1)	2	0.01
Chinese, ex. Taiwanese (112)	150	0.62
Filipino (80)	157	0.65
Indian (120)	153	0.63
Indonesian (4)	11	0.05
Japanese (24)	57	0.23
Korean (89)	123	0.51
Laotian (12)	13	0.05
Malaysian (0)	2	0.01
Nepalese (20)	25	0.10
Pakistani (32)	37	0.15
Sri Lankan (2)	2	0.01
Taiwanese (2)	4	0.02
Thai (14)	25	0.10
Vietnamese (107)	112	0.46
Hawaii Native/Pacific Islander (17)	50	0.21
Not Hispanic (16)	40	0.16
Hispanic (1)	10	0.04
Guamanian/Chamorro (5)	10	0.04
Native Hawaiian (7)	16	0.07
Samoan (1)	5	0.02
White (15,596)	16,373	67.42
Not Hispanic (14,760)	15,376	63.31
Hispanic (836)	997	4.11

Front Royal

Place Type: Town
County: Warren
Population: 14,440†

Ancestry‡	Population	%
African, Sub-Saharan (109)	109	0.75
African (109)	109	0.75
American (1,898)	1,898	13.08
Austrian (16)	47	0.32
British (48)	129	0.89
Bulgarian (45)	103	0.71
Czech (0)	24	0.17
Danish (0)	34	0.23
Dutch (0)	146	1.01
English (848)	2,054	14.16
European (228)	260	1.79
Finnish (0)	13	0.09
French, ex. Basque (8)	356	2.45
French Canadian (21)	104	0.72
German (639)	2,323	16.01
Hungarian (0)	11	0.08
Iranian (42)	42	0.29
Irish (555)	1,587	10.94
Italian (434)	738	5.09
Lithuanian (17)	31	0.21
Norwegian (0)	50	0.34
Polish (79)	128	0.88
Portuguese (0)	21	0.14
Scotch-Irish (234)	502	3.46
Scottish (273)	484	3.34
Serbian (0)	12	0.08
Slavic (0)	11	0.08
Swedish (50)	108	0.74
Swiss (0)	15	0.10
Ukrainian (41)	41	0.28
Welsh (35)	82	0.57
West Indian, ex. Hispanic (0)	77	0.53
Jamaican (0)	77	0.53
Yugoslavian (0)	34	0.23

Hispanic Origin	Population	%
Hispanic or Latino (of any race)	666	4.61
Central American, ex. Mexican	168	1.16
Costa Rican	5	0.03
Guatemalan	7	0.05
Honduran	16	0.11
Nicaraguan	5	0.03
Panamanian	5	0.03
Salvadoran	127	0.88
Other Central American	3	0.02
Cuban	13	0.09
Dominican Republic	7	0.05
Mexican	255	1.77
Puerto Rican	95	0.66
South American	61	0.42
Argentinean	11	0.08
Chilean	3	0.02
Colombian	9	0.06
Peruvian	28	0.19
Uruguayan	2	0.01

*Notes: † The Census 2010 population figure is used to calculate the percentages in the Hispanic Origin and Race categories. Ancestry percentages are based on the 2006-2010 American Community Survey population (not shown); ‡ Numbers in parentheses indicate the number of people reporting a single ancestry; * Numbers in parentheses indicate the number of persons reporting this race alone, not in combination with any other race; Please refer to the Explanation of Data for more information.*

Venezuelan	8	0.06
Other Hispanic or Latino	67	0.46

Race*	Population	%
African-American/Black (1,292)	1,551	10.74
Not Hispanic (1,270)	1,506	10.43
Hispanic (22)	45	0.31
American Indian/Alaska Native (35)	135	0.93
Not Hispanic (32)	128	0.89
Hispanic (3)	7	0.05
Apache (1)	1	0.01
Blackfeet (0)	7	0.05
Cherokee (4)	40	0.28
Cheyenne (3)	3	0.02
Chippewa (0)	1	0.01
Cree (0)	2	0.01
Creek (0)	3	0.02
Iroquois (0)	2	0.01
Lumbee (3)	3	0.02
Navajo (1)	1	0.01
Osage (2)	2	0.01
Potawatomi (0)	2	0.01
Seminole (0)	2	0.01
Sioux (0)	6	0.04
Tlingit-Haida *(Alaska Native)* (2)	3	0.02
Asian (204)	256	1.77
Not Hispanic (202)	253	1.75
Hispanic (2)	3	0.02
Chinese, ex. Taiwanese (35)	41	0.28
Filipino (52)	72	0.50
Indian (28)	39	0.27
Indonesian (0)	2	0.01
Japanese (5)	8	0.06
Korean (29)	33	0.23
Pakistani (7)	7	0.05
Taiwanese (1)	1	0.01
Thai (3)	4	0.03
Vietnamese (33)	42	0.29
Hawaii Native/Pacific Islander (7)	24	0.17
Not Hispanic (4)	13	0.09
Hispanic (3)	11	0.08
Guamanian/Chamorro (2)	6	0.04
Native Hawaiian (4)	9	0.06
Samoan (0)	4	0.03
White (12,295)	12,652	87.62
Not Hispanic (11,897)	12,222	84.64
Hispanic (398)	430	2.98

Gainesville

Place Type: CDP
County: Prince William
Population: 11,481†

Ancestry‡	Population	%
Afghan (353)	353	3.27
African, Sub-Saharan (79)	97	0.90
African (79)	97	0.90
American (931)	931	8.63
Arab (130)	161	1.49
Arab (0)	18	0.17
Jordanian (56)	56	0.52
Lebanese (14)	14	0.13
Syrian (0)	13	0.12
Other Arab (60)	60	0.56
Belgian (0)	13	0.12
Brazilian (13)	13	0.12
British (88)	88	0.82
Canadian (0)	15	0.14
Czech (0)	39	0.36
Danish (0)	86	0.80
Dutch (60)	101	0.94
English (311)	784	7.26
Estonian (0)	15	0.14
European (47)	55	0.51
French, ex. Basque (119)	317	2.94
French Canadian (36)	52	0.48
German (554)	1,413	13.09
Greek (40)	40	0.37
Hungarian (0)	89	0.82
Icelander (0)	47	0.44
Iranian (99)	99	0.92
Irish (264)	923	8.55
Israeli (13)	13	0.12
Italian (157)	408	3.78
Lithuanian (10)	50	0.46
Norwegian (0)	126	1.17
Polish (14)	230	2.13
Portuguese (14)	27	0.25
Romanian (0)	25	0.23
Russian (60)	187	1.73
Scotch-Irish (42)	172	1.59
Scottish (41)	244	2.26
Slovene (0)	26	0.24
Swedish (0)	59	0.55
Swiss (27)	27	0.25
Ukrainian (5)	16	0.15
Welsh (39)	56	0.52
West Indian, ex. Hispanic (28)	28	0.26
West Indian (28)	28	0.26

Hispanic Origin	Population	%
Hispanic or Latino (of any race)	1,175	10.23
Central American, ex. Mexican	328	2.86
Costa Rican	8	0.07
Guatemalan	76	0.66
Honduran	48	0.42
Nicaraguan	10	0.09
Panamanian	9	0.08
Salvadoran	171	1.49
Other Central American	6	0.05
Cuban	27	0.24
Dominican Republic	17	0.15
Mexican	167	1.45
Puerto Rican	150	1.31
South American	337	2.94
Argentinean	18	0.16
Bolivian	73	0.64
Chilean	13	0.11
Colombian	73	0.64
Ecuadorian	15	0.13
Paraguayan	4	0.03
Peruvian	98	0.85
Uruguayan	3	0.03
Venezuelan	25	0.22
Other South American	15	0.13
Other Hispanic or Latino	149	1.30

Race*	Population	%
African-American/Black (1,346)	1,517	13.21
Not Hispanic (1,316)	1,470	12.80
Hispanic (30)	47	0.41
American Indian/Alaska Native (34)	91	0.79
Not Hispanic (22)	63	0.55
Hispanic (12)	28	0.24
Central American Ind. (0)	2	0.02
Cherokee (8)	18	0.16
Chickasaw (0)	3	0.03
Chippewa (0)	1	0.01
Comanche (5)	5	0.04
Creek (1)	5	0.04
Pueblo (0)	4	0.03
Sioux (1)	1	0.01
Yaqui (1)	1	0.01
Asian (1,782)	2,042	17.79
Not Hispanic (1,776)	2,030	17.68
Hispanic (6)	12	0.10
Bangladeshi (7)	7	0.06
Burmese (1)	3	0.03
Cambodian (24)	27	0.24
Chinese, ex. Taiwanese (205)	239	2.08
Filipino (174)	222	1.93
Indian (379)	408	3.55
Indonesian (1)	1	0.01
Japanese (24)	40	0.35
Korean (515)	564	4.91
Laotian (18)	18	0.16
Malaysian (1)	1	0.01
Nepalese (19)	20	0.17
Pakistani (123)	136	1.18
Sri Lankan (4)	6	0.05
Taiwanese (13)	15	0.13
Thai (14)	24	0.21
Vietnamese (187)	215	1.87
Hawaii Native/Pacific Islander (7)	21	0.18
Not Hispanic (4)	14	0.12
Hispanic (3)	7	0.06
Guamanian/Chamorro (2)	3	0.03
Native Hawaiian (1)	5	0.04
Samoan (1)	1	0.01
White (7,455)	7,905	68.85
Not Hispanic (6,760)	7,131	62.11
Hispanic (695)	774	6.74

George Mason

Place Type: CDP
County: Fairfax
Population: 9,496†

Ancestry‡	Population	%
Afghan (28)	28	0.32
African, Sub-Saharan (96)	124	1.40
African (53)	67	0.75
Nigerian (0)	14	0.16
Sierra Leonean (15)	15	0.17
Other Sub-Saharan African (28)	28	0.32
American (191)	191	2.15
Arab (108)	134	1.51
Arab (44)	44	0.50
Lebanese (34)	47	0.53
Moroccan (0)	13	0.15
Palestinian (30)	30	0.34
Austrian (13)	13	0.15
Belgian (13)	13	0.15
British (20)	109	1.23
Bulgarian (27)	27	0.30
Canadian (0)	14	0.16
Czech (14)	71	0.80
Czechoslovakian (0)	14	0.16
Danish (30)	45	0.51
Dutch (44)	69	0.78
Eastern European (0)	19	0.21
English (323)	844	9.51
European (118)	131	1.48
Finnish (0)	15	0.17
French, ex. Basque (29)	93	1.05
French Canadian (0)	31	0.35
German (304)	1,036	11.67
Greek (74)	119	1.34
Hungarian (0)	42	0.47
Icelander (13)	13	0.15
Iranian (46)	46	0.52
Irish (397)	1,129	12.72
Italian (196)	624	7.03
Latvian (17)	17	0.19
Lithuanian (18)	18	0.20
Luxemburger (0)	15	0.17
Northern European (31)	31	0.35
Norwegian (47)	91	1.03
Polish (59)	283	3.19
Portuguese (0)	17	0.19
Romanian (38)	38	0.43
Russian (38)	124	1.40
Scandinavian (8)	8	0.09
Scotch-Irish (74)	257	2.90
Scottish (84)	309	3.48
Slovak (0)	33	0.37
Swedish (18)	99	1.12
Swiss (0)	23	0.26
Turkish (26)	26	0.29
Welsh (14)	57	0.64
West Indian, ex. Hispanic (201)	244	2.75
Barbadian (13)	28	0.32
Haitian (14)	14	0.16
Jamaican (14)	42	0.47
West Indian (160)	160	1.80

Hispanic Origin	Population	%
Hispanic or Latino (of any race)	921	9.70

*Notes: † The Census 2010 population figure is used to calculate the percentages in the Hispanic Origin and Race categories. Ancestry percentages are based on the 2006-2010 American Community Survey population (not shown); ‡ Numbers in parentheses indicate the number of people reporting a single ancestry; * Numbers in parentheses indicate the number of persons reporting this race alone, not in combination with any other race; Please refer to the Explanation of Data for more information.*

Central American, ex. Mexican	263	2.77
Costa Rican	11	0.12
Guatemalan	27	0.28
Honduran	17	0.18
Nicaraguan	15	0.16
Panamanian	9	0.09
Salvadoran	183	1.93
Other Central American	1	0.01
Cuban	43	0.45
Dominican Republic	16	0.17
Mexican	157	1.65
Puerto Rican	105	1.11
South American	244	2.57
Argentinean	32	0.34
Bolivian	81	0.85
Chilean	21	0.22
Colombian	38	0.40
Ecuadorian	10	0.11
Peruvian	54	0.57
Uruguayan	1	0.01
Venezuelan	7	0.07
Other Hispanic or Latino	93	0.98

Race*	Population	%
African-American/Black (893)	1,034	10.89
Not Hispanic (863)	982	10.34
Hispanic (30)	52	0.55
American Indian/Alaska Native (39)	97	1.02
Not Hispanic (14)	59	0.62
Hispanic (25)	38	0.40
Apache (2)	2	0.02
Blackfeet (0)	3	0.03
Central American Ind. (1)	5	0.05
Cherokee (1)	12	0.13
Chickasaw (0)	1	0.01
Choctaw (3)	4	0.04
Creek (0)	2	0.02
Delaware (0)	2	0.02
Iroquois (3)	3	0.03
Lumbee (0)	1	0.01
Mexican American Ind. (1)	3	0.03
Navajo (2)	5	0.05
Osage (0)	1	0.01
South American Ind. (9)	11	0.12
Yuman (1)	1	0.01
Asian (1,417)	1,666	17.54
Not Hispanic (1,401)	1,625	17.11
Hispanic (16)	41	0.43
Bangladeshi (6)	6	0.06
Burmese (1)	2	0.02
Cambodian (6)	7	0.07
Chinese, ex. Taiwanese (337)	401	4.22
Filipino (125)	168	1.77
Hmong (1)	1	0.01
Indian (188)	209	2.20
Indonesian (2)	5	0.05
Japanese (21)	46	0.48
Korean (336)	378	3.98
Laotian (1)	8	0.08
Malaysian (3)	5	0.05
Nepalese (6)	6	0.06
Pakistani (61)	67	0.71
Sri Lankan (9)	9	0.09
Taiwanese (22)	23	0.24
Thai (27)	40	0.42
Vietnamese (199)	212	2.23
Hawaii Native/Pacific Islander (7)	24	0.25
Not Hispanic (7)	23	0.24
Hispanic (0)	1	0.01
Guamanian/Chamorro (4)	6	0.06
Native Hawaiian (2)	8	0.08
Samoan (1)	3	0.03
White (6,374)	6,745	71.03
Not Hispanic (5,911)	6,220	65.50
Hispanic (463)	525	5.53

Glen Allen

Place Type: CDP
County: Henrico
Population: 14,774†

Ancestry‡	Population	%
African, Sub-Saharan (83)	83	0.53
African (65)	65	0.42
Other Sub-Saharan African (18)	18	0.12
American (1,952)	1,952	12.53
Arab (29)	243	1.56
Egyptian (16)	16	0.10
Lebanese (13)	227	1.46
Austrian (0)	16	0.10
Brazilian (84)	84	0.54
British (187)	202	1.30
Canadian (0)	27	0.17
Czech (0)	42	0.27
Danish (0)	13	0.08
Dutch (49)	186	1.19
English (1,198)	1,976	12.68
European (84)	92	0.59
Finnish (17)	17	0.11
French, ex. Basque (68)	182	1.17
French Canadian (38)	53	0.34
German (392)	1,619	10.39
Greek (27)	56	0.36
Hungarian (0)	16	0.10
Irish (472)	1,643	10.55
Italian (250)	628	4.03
Norwegian (14)	41	0.26
Pennsylvania German (26)	26	0.17
Polish (27)	89	0.57
Portuguese (19)	93	0.60
Scotch-Irish (251)	478	3.07
Scottish (177)	324	2.08
Slavic (11)	33	0.21
Swedish (30)	83	0.53
Swiss (16)	32	0.21
Turkish (17)	30	0.19
Ukrainian (17)	17	0.11
Welsh (84)	164	1.05
West Indian, ex. Hispanic (45)	45	0.29
Jamaican (45)	45	0.29
Yugoslavian (170)	183	1.17

Hispanic Origin	Population	%
Hispanic or Latino (of any race)	574	3.89
Central American, ex. Mexican	113	0.76
Costa Rican	8	0.05
Guatemalan	14	0.09
Honduran	9	0.06
Nicaraguan	6	0.04
Panamanian	7	0.05
Salvadoran	69	0.47
Cuban	17	0.12
Dominican Republic	13	0.09
Mexican	159	1.08
Puerto Rican	120	0.81
South American	94	0.64
Argentinean	11	0.07
Bolivian	8	0.05
Chilean	2	0.01
Colombian	28	0.19
Ecuadorian	1	0.01
Paraguayan	1	0.01
Peruvian	31	0.21
Uruguayan	3	0.02
Venezuelan	9	0.06
Other Hispanic or Latino	58	0.39

Race*	Population	%
African-American/Black (3,781)	3,979	26.93
Not Hispanic (3,714)	3,888	26.32
Hispanic (67)	91	0.62
American Indian/Alaska Native (36)	124	0.84
Not Hispanic (31)	113	0.76
Hispanic (5)	11	0.07
Blackfeet (0)	2	0.01
Cherokee (4)	8	0.05
Chippewa (1)	2	0.01
Choctaw (0)	1	0.01
Creek (1)	2	0.01
Lumbee (0)	1	0.01
Pueblo (0)	1	0.01
Sioux (2)	5	0.03
Spanish American Ind. (0)	1	0.01
Asian (925)	1,030	6.97
Not Hispanic (923)	1,021	6.91
Hispanic (2)	9	0.06
Bangladeshi (8)	8	0.05
Burmese (5)	5	0.03
Cambodian (47)	57	0.39
Chinese, ex. Taiwanese (116)	134	0.91
Filipino (117)	142	0.96
Indian (236)	264	1.79
Japanese (13)	25	0.17
Korean (33)	42	0.28
Laotian (15)	18	0.12
Nepalese (5)	5	0.03
Pakistani (46)	52	0.35
Taiwanese (1)	7	0.05
Thai (3)	12	0.08
Vietnamese (223)	241	1.63
Hawaii Native/Pacific Islander (11)	27	0.18
Not Hispanic (9)	20	0.14
Hispanic (2)	7	0.05
Fijian (4)	4	0.03
Guamanian/Chamorro (2)	5	0.03
Native Hawaiian (5)	5	0.03
White (9,431)	9,712	65.74
Not Hispanic (9,185)	9,425	63.79
Hispanic (246)	287	1.94

Gloucester Point

Place Type: CDP
County: Gloucester
Population: 9,402†

Ancestry‡	Population	%
Alsatian (0)	10	0.10
American (1,097)	1,097	10.54
Arab (10)	10	0.10
Arab (10)	10	0.10
Belgian (35)	103	0.99
British (26)	35	0.34
Croatian (0)	24	0.23
Dutch (78)	428	4.11
English (1,301)	2,792	26.83
European (87)	87	0.84
French, ex. Basque (6)	464	4.46
French Canadian (12)	67	0.64
German (334)	1,224	11.76
Greek (0)	3	0.03
Hungarian (0)	28	0.27
Irish (408)	1,647	15.83
Italian (50)	572	5.50
Lithuanian (6)	6	0.06
Macedonian (6)	15	0.14
Norwegian (0)	8	0.08
Polish (44)	112	1.08
Portuguese (14)	50	0.48
Russian (0)	52	0.50
Scotch-Irish (359)	582	5.59
Scottish (38)	171	1.64
Slovak (0)	9	0.09
Swedish (55)	96	0.92
Swiss (0)	43	0.41
Turkish (11)	11	0.11
Ukrainian (0)	143	1.37
Welsh (46)	94	0.90
West Indian, ex. Hispanic (0)	16	0.15
West Indian (0)	16	0.15

Hispanic Origin	Population	%
Hispanic or Latino (of any race)	230	2.45
Central American, ex. Mexican	33	0.35
Costa Rican	2	0.02

*Notes: † The Census 2010 population figure is used to calculate the percentages in the Hispanic Origin and Race categories. Ancestry percentages are based on the 2006-2010 American Community Survey population (not shown); ‡ Numbers in parentheses indicate the number of people reporting a single ancestry; * Numbers in parentheses indicate the number of persons reporting this race alone, not in combination with any other race; Please refer to the Explanation of Data for more information.*

Guatemalan	6	0.06
Honduran	8	0.09
Panamanian	9	0.10
Salvadoran	5	0.05
Other Central American	3	0.03
Cuban	15	0.16
Dominican Republic	6	0.06
Mexican	53	0.56
Puerto Rican	82	0.87
South American	15	0.16
Chilean	8	0.09
Ecuadorian	1	0.01
Peruvian	3	0.03
Uruguayan	2	0.02
Venezuelan	1	0.01
Other Hispanic or Latino	26	0.28

Race*	Population	%
African-American/Black (708)	812	8.64
Not Hispanic (699)	792	8.42
Hispanic (9)	20	0.21
American Indian/Alaska Native (22)	108	1.15
Not Hispanic (22)	99	1.05
Hispanic (0)	9	0.10
Apache (0)	1	0.01
Blackfeet (1)	3	0.03
Cherokee (4)	43	0.46
Cheyenne (0)	1	0.01
Chickasaw (2)	2	0.02
Chippewa (5)	7	0.07
Delaware (0)	1	0.01
Iroquois (1)	6	0.06
Kiowa (0)	1	0.01
Lumbee (0)	1	0.01
Sioux (1)	1	0.01
Asian (83)	142	1.51
Not Hispanic (81)	135	1.44
Hispanic (2)	7	0.07
Cambodian (5)	5	0.05
Chinese, ex. Taiwanese (25)	27	0.29
Filipino (12)	19	0.20
Indian (8)	19	0.20
Japanese (8)	28	0.30
Korean (10)	25	0.27
Laotian (0)	4	0.04
Pakistani (1)	1	0.01
Taiwanese (2)	3	0.03
Thai (2)	9	0.10
Vietnamese (6)	6	0.06
Hawaii Native/Pacific Islander (3)	11	0.12
Not Hispanic (3)	6	0.06
Hispanic (0)	5	0.05
Guamanian/Chamorro (2)	4	0.04
Native Hawaiian (0)	5	0.05
White (8,287)	8,496	90.36
Not Hispanic (8,161)	8,334	88.64
Hispanic (126)	162	1.72

Great Falls

Place Type: CDP
County: Fairfax
Population: 15,427†

Ancestry‡	Population	%
Afghan (38)	38	0.24
African, Sub-Saharan (81)	81	0.51
African (81)	81	0.51
American (555)	555	3.49
Arab (305)	336	2.11
Arab (36)	36	0.23
Egyptian (120)	120	0.75
Jordanian (14)	14	0.09
Lebanese (57)	80	0.50
Syrian (15)	15	0.09
Other Arab (63)	71	0.45
Armenian (9)	9	0.06
Austrian (0)	44	0.28
British (125)	177	1.11
Bulgarian (0)	50	0.31
Canadian (0)	85	0.53
Czech (22)	70	0.44
Danish (10)	82	0.51
Dutch (28)	306	1.92
Eastern European (17)	17	0.11
English (652)	2,462	15.46
European (439)	482	3.03
Finnish (10)	28	0.18
French, ex. Basque (42)	363	2.28
French Canadian (25)	86	0.54
German (510)	2,413	15.15
Greek (105)	200	1.26
Hungarian (44)	197	1.24
Iranian (782)	800	5.02
Irish (631)	2,777	17.44
Israeli (13)	13	0.08
Italian (608)	1,477	9.27
Lithuanian (28)	107	0.67
Northern European (40)	40	0.25
Norwegian (33)	572	3.59
Polish (120)	607	3.81
Portuguese (0)	13	0.08
Romanian (33)	44	0.28
Russian (67)	273	1.71
Scandinavian (24)	24	0.15
Scotch-Irish (201)	315	1.98
Scottish (144)	685	4.30
Slovak (0)	37	0.23
Swedish (19)	74	0.46
Swiss (35)	182	1.14
Turkish (20)	20	0.13
Ukrainian (14)	55	0.35
Welsh (12)	80	0.50
West Indian, ex. Hispanic (15)	15	0.09
Haitian (15)	15	0.09
Yugoslavian (0)	28	0.18

Hispanic Origin	Population	%
Hispanic or Latino (of any race)	603	3.91
Central American, ex. Mexican	50	0.32
Costa Rican	2	0.01
Guatemalan	6	0.04
Honduran	11	0.07
Nicaraguan	1	0.01
Panamanian	1	0.01
Salvadoran	29	0.19
Cuban	66	0.43
Dominican Republic	3	0.02
Mexican	89	0.58
Puerto Rican	77	0.50
South American	217	1.41
Argentinean	36	0.23
Bolivian	35	0.23
Chilean	23	0.15
Colombian	44	0.29
Ecuadorian	12	0.08
Paraguayan	2	0.01
Peruvian	33	0.21
Uruguayan	3	0.02
Venezuelan	28	0.18
Other South American	1	0.01
Other Hispanic or Latino	101	0.65

Race*	Population	%
African-American/Black (280)	337	2.18
Not Hispanic (268)	317	2.05
Hispanic (12)	20	0.13
American Indian/Alaska Native (17)	53	0.34
Not Hispanic (10)	42	0.27
Hispanic (7)	11	0.07
Alaska Athabascan *(Ala. Nat.)* (0)	2	0.01
Apache (4)	4	0.03
Canadian/French Am. Ind. (1)	2	0.01
Central American Ind. (0)	4	0.03
Cherokee (5)	16	0.10
Cheyenne (0)	1	0.01
Chickasaw (0)	3	0.02
Comanche (1)	1	0.01
Mexican American Ind. (1)	2	0.01
Sioux (1)	1	0.01
South American Ind. (1)	1	0.01
Asian (2,085)	2,503	16.22
Not Hispanic (2,082)	2,478	16.06
Hispanic (3)	25	0.16
Bangladeshi (15)	15	0.10
Bhutanese (1)	1	0.01
Burmese (7)	11	0.07
Cambodian (8)	10	0.06
Chinese, ex. Taiwanese (620)	677	4.39
Filipino (67)	106	0.69
Indian (591)	656	4.25
Indonesian (2)	3	0.02
Japanese (55)	115	0.75
Korean (365)	420	2.72
Laotian (1)	2	0.01
Malaysian (5)	6	0.04
Nepalese (1)	1	0.01
Pakistani (114)	122	0.79
Sri Lankan (0)	5	0.03
Taiwanese (35)	41	0.27
Thai (10)	12	0.08
Vietnamese (109)	132	0.86
Hawaii Native/Pacific Islander (3)	21	0.14
Not Hispanic (3)	21	0.14
Guamanian/Chamorro (1)	2	0.01
Native Hawaiian (2)	4	0.03
White (12,424)	12,903	83.64
Not Hispanic (11,939)	12,372	80.20
Hispanic (485)	531	3.44

Greenbriar

Place Type: CDP
County: Fairfax
Population: 8,166†

Ancestry‡	Population	%
African, Sub-Saharan (94)	94	1.23
African (94)	94	1.23
American (554)	554	7.22
Arab (95)	127	1.66
Lebanese (0)	32	0.42
Moroccan (68)	68	0.89
Other Arab (27)	27	0.35
Austrian (52)	96	1.25
Belgian (0)	13	0.17
Brazilian (118)	118	1.54
British (100)	153	1.99
Canadian (0)	12	0.16
Croatian (0)	10	0.13
Czech (0)	37	0.48
Danish (0)	12	0.16
Dutch (17)	175	2.28
Eastern European (11)	36	0.47
English (149)	1,032	13.45
European (474)	568	7.40
French, ex. Basque (24)	271	3.53
French Canadian (11)	64	0.83
German (372)	1,411	18.39
Greek (43)	83	1.08
Hungarian (20)	75	0.98
Iranian (74)	104	1.36
Irish (286)	1,250	16.29
Italian (193)	544	7.09
Lithuanian (43)	111	1.45
Northern European (10)	10	0.13
Norwegian (0)	131	1.71
Polish (33)	223	2.91
Portuguese (33)	33	0.43
Russian (56)	149	1.94
Scotch-Irish (64)	216	2.82
Scottish (35)	215	2.80
Slovak (31)	40	0.52
Slovene (0)	12	0.16
Swedish (15)	62	0.81
Turkish (0)	37	0.48
Welsh (0)	64	0.83
West Indian, ex. Hispanic (0)	13	0.17
Bermudan (0)	13	0.17
Yugoslavian (0)	12	0.16

SECTION TWO

*Notes: † The Census 2010 population figure is used to calculate the percentages in the Hispanic Origin and Race categories. Ancestry percentages are based on the 2006-2010 American Community Survey population (not shown); ‡ Numbers in parentheses indicate the number of people reporting a single ancestry; * Numbers in parentheses indicate the number of persons reporting this race alone, not in combination with any other race; Please refer to the Explanation of Data for more information.*

Hispanic Origin	Population	%
Hispanic or Latino (of any race)	1,043	12.77
Central American, ex. Mexican	488	5.98
Costa Rican	1	0.01
Guatemalan	226	2.77
Honduran	49	0.60
Nicaraguan	14	0.17
Panamanian	7	0.09
Salvadoran	188	2.30
Other Central American	3	0.04
Cuban	11	0.13
Dominican Republic	19	0.23
Mexican	111	1.36
Puerto Rican	58	0.71
South American	271	3.32
Argentinean	13	0.16
Bolivian	90	1.10
Chilean	3	0.04
Colombian	43	0.53
Ecuadorian	13	0.16
Peruvian	82	1.00
Uruguayan	5	0.06
Venezuelan	7	0.09
Other South American	15	0.18
Other Hispanic or Latino	85	1.04

Race*	Population	%
African-American/Black (440)	517	6.33
Not Hispanic (424)	481	5.89
Hispanic (16)	36	0.44
American Indian/Alaska Native (19)	75	0.92
Not Hispanic (10)	53	0.65
Hispanic (9)	22	0.27
Apache (1)	1	0.01
Blackfeet (0)	4	0.05
Central American Ind. (0)	1	0.01
Cherokee (5)	16	0.20
Choctaw (1)	2	0.02
Creek (0)	1	0.01
Iroquois (0)	3	0.04
Mexican American Ind. (2)	2	0.02
Seminole (0)	4	0.05
South American Ind. (0)	4	0.05
Spanish American Ind. (7)	12	0.15
Asian (1,450)	1,615	19.78
Not Hispanic (1,448)	1,604	19.64
Hispanic (2)	11	0.13
Bangladeshi (17)	22	0.27
Burmese (2)	2	0.02
Cambodian (10)	10	0.12
Chinese, ex. Taiwanese (138)	174	2.13
Filipino (84)	109	1.33
Indian (500)	524	6.42
Indonesian (1)	2	0.02
Japanese (15)	27	0.33
Korean (297)	326	3.99
Laotian (7)	9	0.11
Malaysian (1)	2	0.02
Nepalese (27)	29	0.36
Pakistani (44)	47	0.58
Sri Lankan (13)	13	0.16
Taiwanese (12)	16	0.20
Thai (13)	13	0.16
Vietnamese (199)	218	2.67
Hawaii Native/Pacific Islander (7)	15	0.18
Not Hispanic (7)	14	0.17
Hispanic (0)	1	0.01
Guamanian/Chamorro (2)	5	0.06
Native Hawaiian (1)	2	0.02
Samoan (4)	4	0.05
White (5,556)	5,838	71.49
Not Hispanic (4,992)	5,193	63.59
Hispanic (564)	645	7.90

Groveton

Place Type: CDP
County: Fairfax
Population: 14,598†

Ancestry‡	Population	%
Afghan (119)	119	0.87
African, Sub-Saharan (429)	453	3.32
African (96)	96	0.70
Ethiopian (80)	80	0.59
Ghanaian (239)	239	1.75
Nigerian (14)	38	0.28
American (628)	628	4.61
Arab (39)	66	0.48
Jordanian (11)	11	0.08
Lebanese (0)	27	0.20
Moroccan (13)	13	0.10
Syrian (15)	15	0.11
Austrian (0)	27	0.20
Belgian (0)	19	0.14
Brazilian (10)	21	0.15
British (39)	87	0.64
Croatian (0)	8	0.06
Czech (10)	81	0.59
Czechoslovakian (19)	19	0.14
Danish (18)	40	0.29
Dutch (0)	194	1.42
Eastern European (20)	20	0.15
English (378)	1,037	7.61
European (100)	114	0.84
Finnish (0)	17	0.12
French, ex. Basque (41)	301	2.21
French Canadian (0)	95	0.70
German (448)	1,542	11.31
Greek (18)	120	0.88
Hungarian (31)	69	0.51
Irish (216)	1,197	8.78
Italian (134)	447	3.28
Lithuanian (20)	39	0.29
Norwegian (10)	16	0.12
Pennsylvania German (0)	9	0.07
Polish (76)	369	2.71
Russian (102)	211	1.55
Scandinavian (0)	10	0.07
Scotch-Irish (75)	277	2.03
Scottish (31)	267	1.96
Slovak (9)	43	0.32
Swedish (10)	72	0.53
Swiss (17)	30	0.22
Turkish (25)	36	0.26
Ukrainian (12)	58	0.43
Welsh (12)	86	0.63
West Indian, ex. Hispanic (70)	126	0.92
Barbadian (10)	10	0.07
British West Indian (22)	46	0.34
Haitian (10)	10	0.07
Jamaican (14)	46	0.34
U.S. Virgin Islander (14)	14	0.10
Yugoslavian (10)	10	0.07

Hispanic Origin	Population	%
Hispanic or Latino (of any race)	4,123	28.24
Central American, ex. Mexican	2,609	17.87
Costa Rican	6	0.04
Guatemalan	131	0.90
Honduran	511	3.50
Nicaraguan	52	0.36
Panamanian	23	0.16
Salvadoran	1,870	12.81
Other Central American	16	0.11
Cuban	34	0.23
Dominican Republic	29	0.20
Mexican	385	2.64
Puerto Rican	181	1.24
South American	379	2.60
Argentinean	18	0.12
Bolivian	137	0.94
Chilean	7	0.05
Colombian	59	0.40
Ecuadorian	19	0.13
Paraguayan	3	0.02
Peruvian	119	0.82
Uruguayan	1	0.01
Venezuelan	16	0.11
Other Hispanic or Latino	506	3.47

Race*	Population	%
African-American/Black (3,330)	3,549	24.31
Not Hispanic (3,218)	3,384	23.18
Hispanic (112)	165	1.13
American Indian/Alaska Native (76)	202	1.38
Not Hispanic (33)	105	0.72
Hispanic (43)	97	0.66
Apache (1)	1	0.01
Cherokee (5)	21	0.14
Cheyenne (0)	3	0.02
Chippewa (1)	8	0.05
Choctaw (1)	2	0.01
Iroquois (3)	5	0.03
Mexican American Ind. (10)	11	0.08
Ottawa (0)	1	0.01
Seminole (2)	2	0.01
Sioux (1)	2	0.01
South American Ind. (4)	14	0.10
Spanish American Ind. (4)	11	0.08
Tlingit-Haida *(Alaska Native)* (0)	2	0.01
Ute (0)	2	0.01
Asian (1,171)	1,340	9.18
Not Hispanic (1,159)	1,311	8.98
Hispanic (12)	29	0.20
Bangladeshi (16)	30	0.21
Cambodian (30)	35	0.24
Chinese, ex. Taiwanese (116)	135	0.92
Filipino (207)	242	1.66
Indian (175)	230	1.58
Indonesian (2)	3	0.02
Japanese (38)	65	0.45
Korean (83)	104	0.71
Laotian (12)	15	0.10
Nepalese (8)	8	0.05
Pakistani (258)	276	1.89
Taiwanese (4)	5	0.03
Thai (24)	30	0.21
Vietnamese (94)	105	0.72
Hawaii Native/Pacific Islander (7)	38	0.26
Not Hispanic (7)	29	0.20
Hispanic (0)	9	0.06
Guamanian/Chamorro (3)	4	0.03
Native Hawaiian (3)	15	0.10
Samoan (1)	5	0.03
Tongan (0)	4	0.03
White (7,369)	7,901	54.12
Not Hispanic (5,687)	5,959	40.82
Hispanic (1,682)	1,942	13.30

Hampton

Place Type: Independent City
County: Hampton
Population: 137,436†

Ancestry‡	Population	%
Afghan (91)	91	0.07
African, Sub-Saharan (1,297)	1,581	1.14
African (754)	1,001	0.72
Cape Verdean (24)	32	0.02
Ethiopian (19)	19	0.01
Ghanaian (35)	35	0.03
Kenyan (26)	26	0.02
Nigerian (220)	249	0.18
Somalian (71)	71	0.05
South African (47)	47	0.03
Other Sub-Saharan African (101)	101	0.07
American (11,117)	11,117	8.00
Arab (532)	630	0.45
Arab (349)	369	0.27
Egyptian (60)	79	0.06
Lebanese (71)	102	0.07
Moroccan (41)	41	0.03
Syrian (0)	11	0.01
Other Arab (11)	28	0.02
Armenian (0)	15	0.01
Australian (11)	34	0.02
Austrian (89)	183	0.13
Basque (0)	22	0.02

*Notes: † The Census 2010 population figure is used to calculate the percentages in the Hispanic Origin and Race categories. Ancestry percentages are based on the 2006-2010 American Community Survey population (not shown); ‡ Numbers in parentheses indicate the number of people reporting a single ancestry; * Numbers in parentheses indicate the number of persons reporting this race alone, not in combination with any other race; Please refer to the Explanation of Data for more information.*

Belgian (10)	10	0.01
British (298)	735	0.53
Bulgarian (0)	24	0.02
Cajun (0)	16	0.01
Canadian (71)	230	0.17
Celtic (0)	31	0.02
Croatian (24)	39	0.03
Cypriot (31)	31	0.02
Czech (37)	150	0.11
Czechoslovakian (30)	99	0.07
Danish (58)	169	0.12
Dutch (226)	868	0.62
English (5,991)	11,579	8.33
European (906)	1,050	0.76
Finnish (25)	88	0.06
French, ex. Basque (397)	1,874	1.35
French Canadian (93)	300	0.22
German (4,723)	11,524	8.29
Greek (86)	245	0.18
Guyanese (37)	46	0.03
Hungarian (82)	349	0.25
Icelander (0)	30	0.02
Iranian (177)	177	0.13
Irish (3,192)	9,024	6.49
Italian (1,209)	3,745	2.69
Lithuanian (10)	41	0.03
Northern European (115)	115	0.08
Norwegian (209)	718	0.52
Pennsylvania German (0)	9	0.01
Polish (679)	2,033	1.46
Portuguese (116)	228	0.16
Romanian (21)	34	0.02
Russian (130)	382	0.27
Scandinavian (148)	218	0.16
Scotch-Irish (972)	2,249	1.62
Scottish (897)	2,398	1.72
Serbian (20)	20	0.01
Slavic (0)	10	0.01
Slovak (42)	116	0.08
Slovene (16)	16	0.01
Swedish (192)	654	0.47
Swiss (14)	146	0.11
Ukrainian (65)	203	0.15
Welsh (112)	747	0.54
West Indian, ex. Hispanic (1,278)	1,688	1.21
Barbadian (72)	72	0.05
Belizean (9)	57	0.04
British West Indian (44)	44	0.03
Dutch West Indian (15)	28	0.02
Haitian (187)	280	0.20
Jamaican (679)	873	0.63
Trinidadian/Tobagonian (50)	77	0.06
U.S. Virgin Islander (109)	118	0.08
West Indian (113)	139	0.10
Yugoslavian (8)	17	0.01

Hispanic Origin	Population	%
Hispanic or Latino (of any race)	6,241	4.54
Central American, ex. Mexican	661	0.48
Costa Rican	26	0.02
Guatemalan	33	0.02
Honduran	143	0.10
Nicaraguan	27	0.02
Panamanian	319	0.23
Salvadoran	111	0.08
Other Central American	2	<0.01
Cuban	256	0.19
Dominican Republic	251	0.18
Mexican	1,868	1.36
Puerto Rican	2,339	1.70
South American	286	0.21
Argentinean	17	0.01
Bolivian	7	0.01
Chilean	9	0.01
Colombian	125	0.09
Ecuadorian	56	0.04
Paraguayan	7	0.01
Peruvian	44	0.03
Uruguayan	3	<0.01
Venezuelan	18	0.01
Other Hispanic or Latino	580	0.42

Race*	Population	%
African-American/Black (68,104)	71,569	52.07
Not Hispanic (66,878)	69,775	50.77
Hispanic (1,226)	1,794	1.31
American Indian/Alaska Native (594)	2,170	1.58
Not Hispanic (498)	1,892	1.38
Hispanic (96)	278	0.20
Alaska Athabascan *(Ala. Nat.)* (5)	9	0.01
Aleut *(Alaska Native)* (2)	4	<0.01
Apache (16)	26	0.02
Arapaho (2)	4	<0.01
Blackfeet (11)	105	0.08
Canadian/French Am. Ind. (1)	4	<0.01
Central American Ind. (1)	3	<0.01
Cherokee (92)	541	0.39
Cheyenne (0)	3	<0.01
Chickasaw (2)	10	0.01
Chippewa (8)	16	0.01
Choctaw (5)	28	0.02
Comanche (1)	3	<0.01
Cree (0)	1	<0.01
Creek (5)	16	0.01
Crow (1)	2	<0.01
Delaware (2)	10	0.01
Inupiat *(Alaska Native)* (1)	6	<0.01
Iroquois (4)	26	0.02
Lumbee (20)	53	0.04
Mexican American Ind. (7)	13	0.01
Navajo (10)	21	0.02
Osage (4)	6	<0.01
Ottawa (1)	3	<0.01
Pima (1)	2	<0.01
Potawatomi (1)	2	<0.01
Pueblo (1)	3	<0.01
Puget Sound Salish (1)	1	<0.01
Seminole (5)	19	0.01
Sioux (7)	37	0.03
South American Ind. (5)	12	0.01
Spanish American Ind. (1)	2	<0.01
Tlingit-Haida *(Alaska Native)* (1)	2	<0.01
Tohono O'Odham (0)	1	<0.01
Yakama (0)	1	<0.01
Yaqui (2)	2	<0.01
Yup'ik *(Alaska Native)* (0)	3	<0.01
Asian (2,992)	4,352	3.17
Not Hispanic (2,950)	4,199	3.06
Hispanic (42)	153	0.11
Bangladeshi (11)	11	0.01
Bhutanese (26)	26	0.02
Burmese (16)	21	0.02
Cambodian (110)	122	0.09
Chinese, ex. Taiwanese (294)	437	0.32
Filipino (710)	1,267	0.92
Hmong (8)	8	0.01
Indian (243)	332	0.24
Indonesian (2)	4	<0.01
Japanese (138)	369	0.27
Korean (294)	496	0.36
Laotian (26)	40	0.03
Malaysian (4)	4	<0.01
Nepalese (13)	13	0.01
Pakistani (30)	31	0.02
Sri Lankan (3)	3	<0.01
Taiwanese (3)	13	0.01
Thai (98)	184	0.13
Vietnamese (810)	888	0.65
Hawaii Native/Pacific Islander (154)	407	0.30
Not Hispanic (132)	337	0.25
Hispanic (22)	70	0.05
Guamanian/Chamorro (35)	59	0.04
Native Hawaiian (52)	132	0.10
Samoan (33)	76	0.06
Tongan (0)	2	<0.01
White (58,642)	62,254	45.30
Not Hispanic (56,283)	59,275	43.13
Hispanic (2,359)	2,979	2.17

Harrisonburg

Place Type: Independent City
County: Harrisonburg
Population: 48,914†

Ancestry‡	Population	%
Afghan (60)	60	0.13
African, Sub-Saharan (517)	569	1.20
African (161)	187	0.39
Ethiopian (117)	117	0.25
Kenyan (0)	26	0.05
Nigerian (24)	24	0.05
Sudanese (168)	168	0.35
Other Sub-Saharan African (47)	47	0.10
Albanian (0)	13	0.03
American (14,504)	14,504	30.60
Arab (262)	361	0.76
Arab (131)	131	0.28
Jordanian (13)	13	0.03
Lebanese (46)	108	0.23
Moroccan (61)	74	0.16
Syrian (0)	13	0.03
Other Arab (11)	22	0.05
Armenian (17)	30	0.06
Australian (10)	10	0.02
Austrian (7)	94	0.20
Belgian (0)	64	0.14
Brazilian (4)	18	0.04
British (68)	187	0.39
Canadian (117)	220	0.46
Celtic (0)	27	0.06
Croatian (15)	36	0.08
Cypriot (24)	24	0.05
Czech (0)	52	0.11
Czechoslovakian (14)	14	0.03
Danish (0)	17	0.04
Dutch (68)	268	0.57
Eastern European (15)	15	0.03
English (974)	2,685	5.66
Estonian (16)	16	0.03
European (498)	535	1.13
Finnish (34)	60	0.13
French, ex. Basque (130)	657	1.39
French Canadian (149)	335	0.71
German (2,031)	6,413	13.53
Greek (41)	84	0.18
Hungarian (23)	116	0.24
Icelander (0)	12	0.03
Iranian (72)	72	0.15
Irish (887)	3,088	6.51
Italian (382)	1,542	3.25
Lithuanian (15)	68	0.14
Northern European (70)	101	0.21
Norwegian (45)	315	0.66
Pennsylvania German (76)	76	0.16
Polish (185)	710	1.50
Portuguese (21)	74	0.16
Romanian (23)	74	0.16
Russian (119)	419	0.88
Scandinavian (12)	12	0.03
Scotch-Irish (290)	905	1.91
Scottish (300)	806	1.70
Serbian (31)	31	0.07
Slovak (50)	95	0.20
Swedish (117)	471	0.99
Swiss (118)	999	2.11
Turkish (58)	66	0.14
Ukrainian (106)	106	0.22
Welsh (95)	289	0.61
West Indian, ex. Hispanic (25)	38	0.08
Haitian (25)	25	0.05
Jamaican (0)	13	0.03
Yugoslavian (115)	136	0.29

Hispanic Origin	Population	%
Hispanic or Latino (of any race)	7,665	15.67
Central American, ex. Mexican	2,317	4.74
Costa Rican	12	0.02
Guatemalan	228	0.47

*Notes: † The Census 2010 population figure is used to calculate the percentages in the Hispanic Origin and Race categories. Ancestry percentages are based on the 2006-2010 American Community Survey population (not shown); ‡ Numbers in parentheses indicate the number of people reporting a single ancestry; * Numbers in parentheses indicate the number of persons reporting this race alone, not in combination with any other race; Please refer to the Explanation of Data for more information.*

Honduran	978	2.00
Nicaraguan	41	0.08
Panamanian	9	0.02
Salvadoran	1,039	2.12
Other Central American	10	0.02
Cuban	340	0.70
Dominican Republic	257	0.53
Mexican	2,836	5.80
Puerto Rican	910	1.86
South American	304	0.62
Argentinean	28	0.06
Bolivian	23	0.05
Chilean	18	0.04
Colombian	74	0.15
Ecuadorian	33	0.07
Paraguayan	5	0.01
Peruvian	42	0.09
Uruguayan	56	0.11
Venezuelan	24	0.05
Other South American	1	<0.01
Other Hispanic or Latino	701	1.43

Race*	Population	%
African-American/Black (3,112)	3,680	7.52
Not Hispanic (2,911)	3,360	6.87
Hispanic (201)	320	0.65
American Indian/Alaska Native (127)	337	0.69
Not Hispanic (67)	205	0.42
Hispanic (60)	132	0.27
Apache (1)	6	0.01
Blackfeet (1)	15	0.03
Canadian/French Am. Ind. (2)	3	0.01
Central American Ind. (2)	3	0.01
Cherokee (11)	65	0.13
Chickasaw (0)	1	<0.01
Chippewa (1)	3	0.01
Choctaw (2)	3	0.01
Comanche (0)	1	<0.01
Cree (1)	1	<0.01
Inupiat *(Alaska Native)* (1)	3	0.01
Iroquois (1)	5	0.01
Lumbee (3)	4	0.01
Mexican American Ind. (7)	16	0.03
Navajo (0)	5	0.01
Pueblo (0)	1	<0.01
Sioux (2)	5	0.01
South American Ind. (7)	10	0.02
Asian (1,718)	2,206	4.51
Not Hispanic (1,705)	2,160	4.42
Hispanic (13)	46	0.09
Bangladeshi (3)	3	0.01
Burmese (7)	7	0.01
Cambodian (5)	14	0.03
Chinese, ex. Taiwanese (261)	333	0.68
Filipino (80)	157	0.32
Indian (235)	280	0.57
Indonesian (1)	2	<0.01
Japanese (46)	108	0.22
Korean (262)	318	0.65
Laotian (107)	119	0.24
Malaysian (0)	3	0.01
Nepalese (27)	27	0.06
Pakistani (103)	110	0.22
Sri Lankan (0)	1	<0.01
Taiwanese (15)	20	0.04
Thai (25)	38	0.08
Vietnamese (154)	203	0.42
Hawaii Native/Pacific Islander (62)	116	0.24
Not Hispanic (54)	93	0.19
Hispanic (8)	23	0.05
Fijian (1)	2	<0.01
Guamanian/Chamorro (11)	19	0.04
Marshallese (1)	1	<0.01
Native Hawaiian (37)	49	0.10
Samoan (1)	3	0.01
Tongan (1)	5	0.01
White (38,371)	39,682	81.13
Not Hispanic (35,391)	36,332	74.28
Hispanic (2,980)	3,350	6.85

Herndon

Place Type: Town
County: Fairfax
Population: 23,292†

Ancestry‡	Population	%
Afghan (55)	55	0.24
African, Sub-Saharan (986)	1,204	5.30
African (330)	330	1.45
Ethiopian (597)	597	2.63
Senegalese (21)	86	0.38
South African (0)	28	0.12
Other Sub-Saharan African (38)	163	0.72
American (926)	926	4.07
Arab (63)	102	0.45
Arab (17)	17	0.07
Egyptian (36)	36	0.16
Lebanese (0)	39	0.17
Palestinian (10)	10	0.04
Armenian (50)	50	0.22
Australian (23)	23	0.10
Austrian (21)	113	0.50
Brazilian (64)	64	0.28
British (28)	92	0.40
Cajun (16)	16	0.07
Canadian (121)	121	0.53
Celtic (0)	24	0.11
Croatian (13)	13	0.06
Czech (0)	84	0.37
Danish (37)	129	0.57
Dutch (45)	195	0.86
English (493)	1,645	7.24
European (177)	177	0.78
Finnish (0)	9	0.04
French, ex. Basque (179)	560	2.46
French Canadian (30)	61	0.27
German (627)	2,093	9.21
Greek (79)	140	0.62
Hungarian (10)	53	0.23
Iranian (60)	60	0.26
Irish (632)	2,069	9.10
Italian (363)	868	3.82
Lithuanian (16)	28	0.12
Northern European (23)	23	0.10
Norwegian (0)	155	0.68
Polish (291)	657	2.89
Portuguese (63)	63	0.28
Russian (53)	76	0.33
Scotch-Irish (96)	449	1.98
Scottish (104)	446	1.96
Serbian (0)	14	0.06
Slavic (10)	10	0.04
Swedish (0)	129	0.57
Swiss (0)	7	0.03
Turkish (115)	115	0.51
Ukrainian (19)	70	0.31
Welsh (33)	211	0.93
West Indian, ex. Hispanic (15)	15	0.07
Jamaican (15)	15	0.07

Hispanic Origin	Population	%
Hispanic or Latino (of any race)	7,826	33.60
Central American, ex. Mexican	5,149	22.11
Costa Rican	5	0.02
Guatemalan	225	0.97
Honduran	1,159	4.98
Nicaraguan	83	0.36
Panamanian	17	0.07
Salvadoran	3,603	15.47
Other Central American	57	0.24
Cuban	49	0.21
Dominican Republic	25	0.11
Mexican	592	2.54
Puerto Rican	176	0.76
South American	927	3.98
Argentinean	42	0.18
Bolivian	268	1.15
Chilean	21	0.09
Colombian	93	0.40
Ecuadorian	39	0.17
Paraguayan	8	0.03
Peruvian	443	1.90
Uruguayan	1	<0.01
Venezuelan	11	0.05
Other South American	1	<0.01
Other Hispanic or Latino	908	3.90

Race*	Population	%
African-American/Black (2,223)	2,448	10.51
Not Hispanic (2,141)	2,303	9.89
Hispanic (82)	145	0.62
American Indian/Alaska Native (154)	333	1.43
Not Hispanic (50)	129	0.55
Hispanic (104)	204	0.88
Blackfeet (0)	5	0.02
Central American Ind. (6)	8	0.03
Cherokee (8)	34	0.15
Chickasaw (1)	1	<0.01
Choctaw (6)	6	0.03
Creek (3)	3	0.01
Inupiat *(Alaska Native)* (1)	1	<0.01
Iroquois (1)	3	0.01
Lumbee (3)	4	0.02
Mexican American Ind. (8)	20	0.09
Navajo (0)	3	0.01
Osage (1)	1	<0.01
Seminole (1)	2	0.01
Sioux (2)	2	0.01
South American Ind. (4)	25	0.11
Spanish American Ind. (0)	5	0.02
Ute (0)	2	0.01
Asian (4,170)	4,646	19.95
Not Hispanic (4,159)	4,608	19.78
Hispanic (11)	38	0.16
Bangladeshi (115)	128	0.55
Burmese (10)	10	0.04
Cambodian (67)	85	0.36
Chinese, ex. Taiwanese (344)	394	1.69
Filipino (289)	349	1.50
Indian (1,977)	2,082	8.94
Indonesian (26)	30	0.13
Japanese (30)	74	0.32
Korean (159)	186	0.80
Laotian (9)	15	0.06
Malaysian (28)	36	0.15
Nepalese (87)	92	0.39
Pakistani (410)	460	1.97
Sri Lankan (20)	20	0.09
Taiwanese (14)	20	0.09
Thai (45)	57	0.24
Vietnamese (380)	414	1.78
Hawaii Native/Pacific Islander (5)	30	0.13
Not Hispanic (3)	22	0.09
Hispanic (2)	8	0.03
Guamanian/Chamorro (3)	5	0.02
Native Hawaiian (2)	7	0.03
White (11,810)	12,862	55.22
Not Hispanic (8,429)	8,979	38.55
Hispanic (3,381)	3,883	16.67

Highland Springs

Place Type: CDP
County: Henrico
Population: 15,711†

Ancestry‡	Population	%
African, Sub-Saharan (205)	205	1.26
African (164)	164	1.00
Other Sub-Saharan African (41)	41	0.25
American (746)	746	4.57
Austrian (0)	31	0.19
British (86)	152	0.93
Canadian (15)	28	0.17
Czech (0)	28	0.17
Dutch (10)	93	0.57
English (488)	1,029	6.30
European (60)	118	0.72
French, ex. Basque (15)	88	0.54

*Notes: † The Census 2010 population figure is used to calculate the percentages in the Hispanic Origin and Race categories. Ancestry percentages are based on the 2006-2010 American Community Survey population (not shown); ‡ Numbers in parentheses indicate the number of people reporting a single ancestry; * Numbers in parentheses indicate the number of persons reporting this race alone, not in combination with any other race; Please refer to the Explanation of Data for more information.*

German (347)	1,388	8.50
Greek (43)	75	0.46
Irish (235)	1,216	7.45
Israeli (22)	22	0.13
Italian (140)	223	1.37
Polish (27)	76	0.47
Portuguese (0)	33	0.20
Scotch-Irish (34)	99	0.61
Scottish (9)	48	0.29
Swedish (0)	60	0.37
Swiss (0)	43	0.26
Welsh (16)	40	0.24
West Indian, ex. Hispanic (72)	219	1.34
Bahamian (19)	57	0.35
Barbadian (0)	30	0.18
Haitian (15)	83	0.51
Jamaican (25)	25	0.15
Trinidadian/Tobagonian (13)	13	0.08
West Indian (0)	11	0.07

Hispanic Origin	Population	%
Hispanic or Latino (of any race)	334	2.13
Central American, ex. Mexican	42	0.27
Guatemalan	7	0.04
Honduran	6	0.04
Nicaraguan	1	0.01
Panamanian	9	0.06
Salvadoran	19	0.12
Cuban	16	0.10
Dominican Republic	9	0.06
Mexican	114	0.73
Puerto Rican	119	0.76
South American	13	0.08
Bolivian	1	0.01
Chilean	2	0.01
Colombian	4	0.03
Peruvian	3	0.02
Venezuelan	3	0.02
Other Hispanic or Latino	21	0.13

Race*	Population	%
African-American/Black (10,388)	10,659	67.84
Not Hispanic (10,303)	10,549	67.14
Hispanic (85)	110	0.70
American Indian/Alaska Native (73)	198	1.26
Not Hispanic (66)	180	1.15
Hispanic (7)	18	0.11
Apache (0)	1	0.01
Blackfeet (1)	5	0.03
Cherokee (6)	42	0.27
Choctaw (0)	5	0.03
Crow (0)	1	0.01
Lumbee (6)	6	0.04
Seminole (0)	1	0.01
Shoshone (0)	1	0.01
Sioux (1)	10	0.06
South American Ind. (2)	2	0.01
Asian (77)	122	0.78
Not Hispanic (76)	121	0.77
Hispanic (1)	1	0.01
Cambodian (3)	3	0.02
Chinese, ex. Taiwanese (11)	18	0.11
Filipino (18)	27	0.17
Indian (18)	27	0.17
Japanese (4)	13	0.08
Korean (0)	7	0.04
Laotian (12)	12	0.08
Pakistani (1)	1	0.01
Thai (1)	1	0.01
Vietnamese (4)	7	0.04
Hawaii Native/Pacific Islander (8)	15	0.10
Not Hispanic (7)	10	0.06
Hispanic (1)	5	0.03
Guamanian/Chamorro (4)	5	0.03
Native Hawaiian (1)	2	0.01
White (4,659)	4,922	31.33
Not Hispanic (4,580)	4,830	30.74
Hispanic (79)	92	0.59

Hollins

Place Type: CDP
County: Roanoke
Population: 14,673†

Ancestry‡	Population	%
African, Sub-Saharan (27)	39	0.26
African (27)	39	0.26
Albanian (56)	56	0.38
American (2,574)	2,574	17.25
Arab (46)	46	0.31
Arab (46)	46	0.31
British (32)	44	0.29
Canadian (12)	37	0.25
Celtic (8)	8	0.05
Czech (0)	12	0.08
Czechoslovakian (0)	15	0.10
Danish (24)	24	0.16
Dutch (54)	240	1.61
English (1,071)	1,936	12.97
European (67)	92	0.62
Finnish (13)	13	0.09
French, ex. Basque (81)	462	3.10
French Canadian (38)	129	0.86
German (764)	2,164	14.50
Greek (0)	29	0.19
Hungarian (28)	54	0.36
Irish (634)	1,879	12.59
Italian (308)	1,032	6.92
Lithuanian (0)	15	0.10
Luxemburger (0)	15	0.10
Norwegian (48)	131	0.88
Polish (49)	111	0.74
Portuguese (0)	28	0.19
Scandinavian (0)	11	0.07
Scotch-Irish (263)	440	2.95
Scottish (85)	241	1.61
Slavic (13)	13	0.09
Slovak (11)	11	0.07
Swedish (24)	55	0.37
Swiss (0)	15	0.10
Turkish (19)	19	0.13
Ukrainian (0)	36	0.24
Welsh (136)	277	1.86
West Indian, ex. Hispanic (71)	71	0.48
Jamaican (71)	71	0.48
Yugoslavian (53)	63	0.42

Hispanic Origin	Population	%
Hispanic or Latino (of any race)	427	2.91
Central American, ex. Mexican	34	0.23
Costa Rican	1	0.01
Guatemalan	12	0.08
Honduran	15	0.10
Panamanian	2	0.01
Salvadoran	4	0.03
Cuban	64	0.44
Dominican Republic	7	0.05
Mexican	178	1.21
Puerto Rican	74	0.50
South American	20	0.14
Chilean	3	0.02
Colombian	12	0.08
Ecuadorian	4	0.03
Venezuelan	1	0.01
Other Hispanic or Latino	50	0.34

Race*	Population	%
African-American/Black (1,282)	1,408	9.60
Not Hispanic (1,263)	1,379	9.40
Hispanic (19)	29	0.20
American Indian/Alaska Native (14)	58	0.40
Not Hispanic (13)	55	0.37
Hispanic (1)	3	0.02
Canadian/French Am. Ind. (1)	1	0.01
Cherokee (1)	15	0.10
Chippewa (0)	1	0.01
Choctaw (0)	1	0.01
Crow (0)	3	0.02
Delaware (2)	2	0.01
Iroquois (1)	1	0.01
Lumbee (0)	1	0.01
Mexican American Ind. (1)	1	0.01
Sioux (1)	1	0.01
Asian (475)	537	3.66
Not Hispanic (469)	520	3.54
Hispanic (6)	17	0.12
Burmese (3)	3	0.02
Cambodian (8)	9	0.06
Chinese, ex. Taiwanese (62)	78	0.53
Filipino (11)	32	0.22
Indian (51)	61	0.42
Japanese (3)	16	0.11
Korean (25)	31	0.21
Laotian (1)	2	0.01
Malaysian (1)	1	0.01
Nepalese (5)	5	0.03
Pakistani (10)	10	0.07
Taiwanese (4)	8	0.05
Thai (6)	6	0.04
Vietnamese (251)	268	1.83
Hawaii Native/Pacific Islander (5)	36	0.25
Not Hispanic (4)	35	0.24
Hispanic (1)	1	0.01
Fijian (1)	4	0.03
Guamanian/Chamorro (3)	3	0.02
Native Hawaiian (1)	10	0.07
White (12,549)	12,768	87.02
Not Hispanic (12,271)	12,460	84.92
Hispanic (278)	308	2.10

Hollymead

Place Type: CDP
County: Albemarle
Population: 7,690†

Ancestry‡	Population	%
African, Sub-Saharan (74)	74	0.92
Ethiopian (74)	74	0.92
American (645)	645	8.04
Arab (126)	126	1.57
Egyptian (14)	14	0.17
Lebanese (33)	33	0.41
Other Arab (79)	79	0.98
Australian (33)	33	0.41
Austrian (0)	34	0.42
British (9)	21	0.26
Canadian (0)	30	0.37
Czech (0)	49	0.61
Danish (0)	16	0.20
Dutch (32)	119	1.48
Eastern European (27)	27	0.34
English (256)	1,162	14.48
European (199)	268	3.34
Finnish (0)	45	0.56
French, ex. Basque (0)	176	2.19
French Canadian (23)	53	0.66
German (418)	1,576	19.64
Greek (16)	105	1.31
Hungarian (0)	52	0.65
Irish (303)	1,038	12.93
Italian (213)	787	9.81
Norwegian (78)	114	1.42
Polish (47)	255	3.18
Portuguese (21)	82	1.02
Russian (36)	222	2.77
Scotch-Irish (150)	490	6.11
Scottish (71)	325	4.05
Slovak (0)	35	0.44
Slovene (0)	35	0.44
Swedish (12)	73	0.91
Swiss (10)	25	0.31
Welsh (34)	192	2.39
Yugoslavian (69)	69	0.86

Hispanic Origin	Population	%
Hispanic or Latino (of any race)	224	2.91
Central American, ex. Mexican	24	0.31

SECTION TWO

*Notes: † The Census 2010 population figure is used to calculate the percentages in the Hispanic Origin and Race categories. Ancestry percentages are based on the 2006-2010 American Community Survey population (not shown); ‡ Numbers in parentheses indicate the number of people reporting a single ancestry; * Numbers in parentheses indicate the number of persons reporting this race alone, not in combination with any other race; Please refer to the Explanation of Data for more information.*

Costa Rican	3	0.04
Guatemalan	7	0.09
Honduran	1	0.01
Nicaraguan	2	0.03
Panamanian	2	0.03
Salvadoran	9	0.12
Cuban	6	0.08
Dominican Republic	3	0.04
Mexican	102	1.33
Puerto Rican	45	0.59
South American	28	0.36
Argentinean	5	0.07
Colombian	12	0.16
Ecuadorian	3	0.04
Peruvian	4	0.05
Uruguayan	1	0.01
Venezuelan	3	0.04
Other Hispanic or Latino	16	0.21

Race*	Population	%
African-American/Black (406)	484	6.29
Not Hispanic (401)	471	6.12
Hispanic (5)	13	0.17
American Indian/Alaska Native (13)	58	0.75
Not Hispanic (9)	46	0.60
Hispanic (4)	12	0.16
Alaska Athabascan *(Ala. Nat.)* (0)	3	0.04
Apache (0)	1	0.01
Blackfeet (0)	4	0.05
Cherokee (0)	8	0.10
Chickasaw (0)	2	0.03
Choctaw (0)	1	0.01
Comanche (1)	1	0.01
Delaware (0)	3	0.04
Mexican American Ind. (1)	1	0.01
Pueblo (1)	1	0.01
Seminole (0)	3	0.04
Asian (611)	694	9.02
Not Hispanic (610)	683	8.88
Hispanic (1)	11	0.14
Cambodian (4)	4	0.05
Chinese, ex. Taiwanese (227)	249	3.24
Filipino (29)	46	0.60
Hmong (1)	4	0.05
Indian (121)	131	1.70
Indonesian (7)	9	0.12
Japanese (15)	34	0.44
Korean (101)	113	1.47
Malaysian (1)	1	0.01
Nepalese (9)	9	0.12
Pakistani (11)	16	0.21
Sri Lankan (4)	4	0.05
Taiwanese (22)	25	0.33
Thai (8)	8	0.10
Vietnamese (30)	30	0.39
Hawaii Native/Pacific Islander (2)	11	0.14
Not Hispanic (2)	8	0.10
Hispanic (0)	3	0.04
Guamanian/Chamorro (0)	3	0.04
Native Hawaiian (1)	7	0.09
White (6,376)	6,552	85.20
Not Hispanic (6,258)	6,411	83.37
Hispanic (118)	141	1.83

Hopewell

Place Type: Independent City
County: Hopewell
Population: 22,591†

Ancestry‡	Population	%
African, Sub-Saharan (27)	49	0.22
African (27)	49	0.22
American (2,170)	2,170	9.64
Arab (63)	63	0.28
Arab (32)	32	0.14
Palestinian (31)	31	0.14
Armenian (20)	22	0.10
British (16)	33	0.15
Canadian (0)	13	0.06
Croatian (5)	5	0.02
Czech (59)	76	0.34
Czechoslovakian (0)	18	0.08
Danish (0)	10	0.04
Dutch (43)	107	0.48
English (2,791)	3,554	15.79
European (73)	73	0.32
French, ex. Basque (42)	249	1.11
French Canadian (55)	66	0.29
German (814)	1,594	7.08
Greek (60)	60	0.27
Hungarian (0)	91	0.40
Irish (1,179)	1,956	8.69
Italian (247)	410	1.82
Norwegian (29)	77	0.34
Polish (123)	174	0.77
Portuguese (10)	25	0.11
Russian (13)	16	0.07
Scotch-Irish (148)	157	0.70
Scottish (179)	352	1.56
Slavic (0)	14	0.06
Slovak (17)	17	0.08
Swedish (19)	45	0.20
Swiss (0)	67	0.30
Welsh (36)	110	0.49
West Indian, ex. Hispanic (10)	39	0.17
Jamaican (10)	39	0.17

Hispanic Origin	Population	%
Hispanic or Latino (of any race)	1,480	6.55
Central American, ex. Mexican	188	0.83
Guatemalan	9	0.04
Honduran	76	0.34
Nicaraguan	2	0.01
Panamanian	52	0.23
Salvadoran	49	0.22
Cuban	12	0.05
Dominican Republic	18	0.08
Mexican	550	2.43
Puerto Rican	565	2.50
South American	51	0.23
Argentinean	4	0.02
Bolivian	4	0.02
Chilean	2	0.01
Colombian	14	0.06
Ecuadorian	12	0.05
Peruvian	10	0.04
Venezuelan	3	0.01
Other South American	2	0.01
Other Hispanic or Latino	96	0.42

Race*	Population	%
African-American/Black (8,367)	8,832	39.10
Not Hispanic (8,216)	8,611	38.12
Hispanic (151)	221	0.98
American Indian/Alaska Native (87)	234	1.04
Not Hispanic (78)	209	0.93
Hispanic (9)	25	0.11
Apache (0)	2	0.01
Blackfeet (1)	5	0.02
Canadian/French Am. Ind. (1)	1	<0.01
Central American Ind. (0)	2	0.01
Cherokee (13)	60	0.27
Choctaw (4)	6	0.03
Comanche (0)	1	<0.01
Creek (4)	5	0.02
Inupiat *(Alaska Native)* (1)	1	<0.01
Iroquois (1)	5	0.02
Mexican American Ind. (0)	1	<0.01
Navajo (0)	2	0.01
Osage (0)	1	<0.01
Pima (1)	1	<0.01
Sioux (0)	2	0.01
South American Ind. (0)	1	<0.01
Tlingit-Haida *(Alaska Native)* (1)	1	<0.01
Asian (181)	314	1.39
Not Hispanic (174)	298	1.32
Hispanic (7)	16	0.07
Cambodian (0)	1	<0.01
Chinese, ex. Taiwanese (18)	28	0.12
Filipino (50)	78	0.35
Indian (12)	20	0.09
Japanese (12)	27	0.12
Korean (49)	91	0.40
Pakistani (2)	7	0.03
Thai (14)	25	0.11
Vietnamese (12)	18	0.08
Hawaii Native/Pacific Islander (24)	62	0.27
Not Hispanic (23)	46	0.20
Hispanic (1)	16	0.07
Guamanian/Chamorro (12)	18	0.08
Native Hawaiian (5)	24	0.11
Samoan (4)	5	0.02
Tongan (2)	2	0.01
White (12,515)	13,107	58.02
Not Hispanic (12,005)	12,516	55.40
Hispanic (510)	591	2.62

Huntington

Place Type: CDP
County: Fairfax
Population: 11,267†

Ancestry‡	Population	%
African, Sub-Saharan (416)	425	4.10
African (44)	44	0.42
Ethiopian (79)	88	0.85
Ghanaian (256)	256	2.47
Nigerian (28)	28	0.27
Other Sub-Saharan African (9)	9	0.09
American (342)	342	3.30
Arab (103)	229	2.21
Moroccan (103)	166	1.60
Other Arab (0)	63	0.61
Armenian (11)	11	0.11
Austrian (0)	59	0.57
Brazilian (134)	134	1.29
British (79)	168	1.62
Bulgarian (0)	14	0.14
Canadian (10)	35	0.34
Croatian (11)	23	0.22
Czech (0)	53	0.51
Danish (0)	10	0.10
Dutch (51)	167	1.61
Eastern European (48)	48	0.46
English (365)	1,285	12.40
Estonian (21)	21	0.20
European (190)	210	2.03
French, ex. Basque (56)	195	1.88
French Canadian (20)	40	0.39
German (274)	1,114	10.75
Hungarian (26)	36	0.35
Iranian (32)	32	0.31
Irish (324)	1,215	11.73
Italian (182)	345	3.33
Lithuanian (36)	64	0.62
Northern European (14)	14	0.14
Norwegian (0)	76	0.73
Polish (60)	212	2.05
Romanian (24)	24	0.23
Russian (84)	208	2.01
Scotch-Irish (98)	366	3.53
Scottish (106)	276	2.66
Slovak (10)	22	0.21
Swedish (19)	40	0.39
Swiss (0)	67	0.65
Turkish (57)	57	0.55
Ukrainian (33)	33	0.32
Welsh (40)	76	0.73
West Indian, ex. Hispanic (98)	110	1.06
Bahamian (13)	25	0.24
Haitian (62)	62	0.60
Jamaican (23)	23	0.22

Hispanic Origin	Population	%
Hispanic or Latino (of any race)	2,445	21.70
Central American, ex. Mexican	1,453	12.90
Costa Rican	5	0.04
Guatemalan	105	0.93

*Notes: † The Census 2010 population figure is used to calculate the percentages in the Hispanic Origin and Race categories. Ancestry percentages are based on the 2006-2010 American Community Survey population (not shown); ‡ Numbers in parentheses indicate the number of people reporting a single ancestry; * Numbers in parentheses indicate the number of persons reporting this race alone, not in combination with any other race; Please refer to the Explanation of Data for more information.*

Honduran	280	2.49
Nicaraguan	54	0.48
Panamanian	19	0.17
Salvadoran	958	8.50
Other Central American	32	0.28
Cuban	22	0.20
Dominican Republic	16	0.14
Mexican	203	1.80
Puerto Rican	150	1.33
South American	296	2.63
Argentinean	19	0.17
Bolivian	80	0.71
Chilean	12	0.11
Colombian	45	0.40
Ecuadorian	10	0.09
Paraguayan	4	0.04
Peruvian	83	0.74
Uruguayan	12	0.11
Venezuelan	24	0.21
Other South American	7	0.06
Other Hispanic or Latino	305	2.71

Race*	Population	%
African-American/Black (1,521)	1,689	14.99
Not Hispanic (1,485)	1,612	14.31
Hispanic (36)	77	0.68
American Indian/Alaska Native (46)	144	1.28
Not Hispanic (30)	91	0.81
Hispanic (16)	53	0.47
Apache (0)	1	0.01
Blackfeet (0)	5	0.04
Central American Ind. (5)	6	0.05
Cherokee (2)	22	0.20
Chippewa (0)	1	0.01
Choctaw (1)	3	0.03
Delaware (0)	2	0.02
Inupiat *(Alaska Native)* (2)	2	0.02
Iroquois (4)	7	0.06
Lumbee (0)	1	0.01
Mexican American Ind. (1)	3	0.03
Navajo (1)	2	0.02
Osage (0)	1	0.01
Ottawa (1)	3	0.03
Pueblo (1)	2	0.02
South American Ind. (5)	11	0.10
Spanish American Ind. (0)	1	0.01
Asian (1,066)	1,245	11.05
Not Hispanic (1,064)	1,232	10.93
Hispanic (2)	13	0.12
Bangladeshi (22)	24	0.21
Burmese (1)	1	0.01
Cambodian (16)	18	0.16
Chinese, ex. Taiwanese (161)	190	1.69
Filipino (174)	206	1.83
Indian (181)	204	1.81
Indonesian (15)	17	0.15
Japanese (40)	61	0.54
Korean (136)	159	1.41
Laotian (11)	12	0.11
Malaysian (0)	1	0.01
Nepalese (10)	10	0.09
Pakistani (153)	172	1.53
Taiwanese (9)	10	0.09
Thai (39)	43	0.38
Vietnamese (58)	64	0.57
Hawaii Native/Pacific Islander (7)	21	0.19
Not Hispanic (7)	16	0.14
Hispanic (0)	5	0.04
Fijian (1)	2	0.02
Native Hawaiian (3)	7	0.06
Tongan (1)	3	0.03
White (7,021)	7,404	65.71
Not Hispanic (5,896)	6,149	54.58
Hispanic (1,125)	1,255	11.14

Hybla Valley

Place Type: CDP
County: Fairfax
Population: 15,801†

Ancestry‡	Population	%
Afghan (66)	66	0.45
African, Sub-Saharan (1,136)	1,203	8.23
African (128)	128	0.88
Ethiopian (296)	296	2.03
Ghanaian (271)	271	1.85
Liberian (231)	231	1.58
Nigerian (0)	28	0.19
Senegalese (54)	54	0.37
Sierra Leonean (25)	25	0.17
Sudanese (131)	131	0.90
Other Sub-Saharan African (0)	39	0.27
American (656)	656	4.49
Arab (36)	36	0.25
Moroccan (36)	36	0.25
Austrian (6)	20	0.14
Belgian (16)	16	0.11
British (23)	33	0.23
Czech (0)	40	0.27
Danish (15)	65	0.44
Dutch (21)	71	0.49
English (341)	890	6.09
European (22)	22	0.15
French, ex. Basque (14)	148	1.01
French Canadian (17)	17	0.12
German (285)	1,210	8.28
Greek (63)	73	0.50
Guyanese (35)	35	0.24
Hungarian (0)	39	0.27
Iranian (12)	37	0.25
Irish (175)	599	4.10
Italian (161)	482	3.30
Norwegian (21)	126	0.86
Polish (47)	309	2.11
Portuguese (0)	54	0.37
Romanian (37)	37	0.25
Russian (13)	247	1.69
Scandinavian (15)	15	0.10
Scotch-Irish (61)	160	1.09
Scottish (44)	323	2.21
Swedish (0)	13	0.09
Swiss (0)	2	0.01
Ukrainian (37)	43	0.29
Welsh (14)	72	0.49

Hispanic Origin	Population	%
Hispanic or Latino (of any race)	4,922	31.15
Central American, ex. Mexican	2,101	13.30
Costa Rican	1	0.01
Guatemalan	182	1.15
Honduran	331	2.09
Nicaraguan	44	0.28
Panamanian	36	0.23
Salvadoran	1,494	9.46
Other Central American	13	0.08
Cuban	18	0.11
Dominican Republic	35	0.22
Mexican	1,681	10.64
Puerto Rican	241	1.53
South American	410	2.59
Argentinean	34	0.22
Bolivian	107	0.68
Chilean	27	0.17
Colombian	50	0.32
Ecuadorian	21	0.13
Paraguayan	5	0.03
Peruvian	149	0.94
Uruguayan	4	0.03
Venezuelan	13	0.08
Other Hispanic or Latino	436	2.76

Race*	Population	%
African-American/Black (5,028)	5,314	33.63
Not Hispanic (4,924)	5,145	32.56
Hispanic (104)	169	1.07
American Indian/Alaska Native (82)	174	1.10
Not Hispanic (45)	96	0.61
Hispanic (37)	78	0.49
Apache (1)	4	0.03
Arapaho (2)	2	0.01
Blackfeet (0)	2	0.01
Central American Ind. (1)	1	0.01
Cherokee (5)	12	0.08
Chippewa (2)	2	0.01
Choctaw (1)	1	0.01
Creek (0)	1	0.01
Crow (0)	2	0.01
Iroquois (0)	2	0.01
Lumbee (2)	2	0.01
Mexican American Ind. (6)	12	0.08
Navajo (0)	1	0.01
Pima (1)	1	0.01
Potawatomi (1)	1	0.01
Puget Sound Salish (1)	1	0.01
Seminole (2)	3	0.02
Sioux (1)	1	0.01
South American Ind. (3)	3	0.02
Spanish American Ind. (0)	2	0.01
Asian (1,412)	1,624	10.28
Not Hispanic (1,403)	1,591	10.07
Hispanic (9)	33	0.21
Bangladeshi (75)	78	0.49
Burmese (5)	5	0.03
Cambodian (24)	26	0.16
Chinese, ex. Taiwanese (85)	103	0.65
Filipino (182)	229	1.45
Hmong (0)	1	0.01
Indian (190)	241	1.53
Indonesian (3)	5	0.03
Japanese (24)	45	0.28
Korean (141)	158	1.00
Laotian (29)	30	0.19
Malaysian (0)	2	0.01
Nepalese (24)	27	0.17
Pakistani (309)	345	2.18
Sri Lankan (5)	5	0.03
Taiwanese (1)	1	0.01
Thai (82)	99	0.63
Vietnamese (118)	125	0.79
Hawaii Native/Pacific Islander (20)	53	0.34
Not Hispanic (16)	37	0.23
Hispanic (4)	16	0.10
Guamanian/Chamorro (11)	12	0.08
Native Hawaiian (2)	12	0.08
Samoan (1)	1	0.01
White (6,115)	6,641	42.03
Not Hispanic (4,048)	4,362	27.61
Hispanic (2,067)	2,279	14.42

Idylwood

Place Type: CDP
County: Fairfax
Population: 17,288†

Ancestry‡	Population	%
Afghan (70)	70	0.45
African, Sub-Saharan (88)	88	0.56
African (23)	23	0.15
Ethiopian (65)	65	0.41
Albanian (0)	16	0.10
American (511)	511	3.26
Arab (282)	336	2.14
Arab (50)	50	0.32
Egyptian (14)	14	0.09
Iraqi (47)	47	0.30
Lebanese (0)	54	0.34
Syrian (12)	12	0.08
Other Arab (159)	159	1.01
Austrian (0)	67	0.43
Belgian (0)	33	0.21
British (76)	332	2.12
Bulgarian (0)	7	0.04
Canadian (26)	26	0.17
Croatian (24)	24	0.15
Czech (0)	50	0.32
Czechoslovakian (19)	54	0.34
Danish (0)	51	0.33
Dutch (37)	198	1.26
Eastern European (24)	24	0.15

SECTION TWO

*Notes: † The Census 2010 population figure is used to calculate the percentages in the Hispanic Origin and Race categories. Ancestry percentages are based on the 2006-2010 American Community Survey population (not shown); ‡ Numbers in parentheses indicate the number of people reporting a single ancestry; * Numbers in parentheses indicate the number of persons reporting this race alone, not in combination with any other race; Please refer to the Explanation of Data for more information.*

Ancestry	Population	%
English (171)	1,421	9.06
Estonian (27)	27	0.17
European (177)	194	1.24
Finnish (0)	13	0.08
French, ex. Basque (22)	604	3.85
French Canadian (59)	148	0.94
German (387)	1,888	12.04
Greek (0)	66	0.42
Hungarian (72)	112	0.71
Iranian (317)	331	2.11
Irish (417)	1,679	10.71
Italian (252)	983	6.27
Lithuanian (42)	76	0.48
Macedonian (0)	16	0.10
Northern European (12)	12	0.08
Norwegian (14)	92	0.59
Polish (29)	338	2.16
Russian (197)	352	2.25
Scandinavian (36)	67	0.43
Scotch-Irish (70)	292	1.86
Scottish (41)	296	1.89
Slovak (20)	60	0.38
Slovene (17)	31	0.20
Swedish (7)	98	0.63
Swiss (10)	40	0.26
Turkish (80)	80	0.51
Ukrainian (39)	86	0.55
Welsh (13)	66	0.42
West Indian, ex. Hispanic (46)	84	0.54
Jamaican (46)	84	0.54
Yugoslavian (20)	20	0.13

Hispanic Origin	Population	%
Hispanic or Latino (of any race)	3,472	20.08
Central American, ex. Mexican	1,507	8.72
Costa Rican	23	0.13
Guatemalan	194	1.12
Honduran	107	0.62
Nicaraguan	40	0.23
Panamanian	16	0.09
Salvadoran	1,111	6.43
Other Central American	16	0.09
Cuban	43	0.25
Dominican Republic	21	0.12
Mexican	449	2.60
Puerto Rican	93	0.54
South American	929	5.37
Argentinean	46	0.27
Bolivian	362	2.09
Chilean	30	0.17
Colombian	103	0.60
Ecuadorian	41	0.24
Paraguayan	16	0.09
Peruvian	277	1.60
Uruguayan	8	0.05
Venezuelan	37	0.21
Other South American	9	0.05
Other Hispanic or Latino	430	2.49

Race*	Population	%
African-American/Black (976)	1,085	6.28
Not Hispanic (950)	1,030	5.96
Hispanic (26)	55	0.32
American Indian/Alaska Native (65)	157	0.91
Not Hispanic (29)	82	0.47
Hispanic (36)	75	0.43
Apache (0)	2	0.01
Blackfeet (0)	5	0.03
Central American Ind. (1)	1	0.01
Cherokee (2)	10	0.06
Creek (1)	1	0.01
Delaware (0)	1	0.01
Iroquois (1)	1	0.01
Mexican American Ind. (18)	19	0.11
Navajo (1)	1	0.01
Pueblo (2)	2	0.01
Sioux (0)	4	0.02
South American Ind. (2)	8	0.05
Spanish American Ind. (0)	1	0.01
Asian (3,697)	4,082	23.61
Not Hispanic (3,660)	4,019	23.25
Hispanic (37)	63	0.36
Bangladeshi (22)	40	0.23
Burmese (17)	21	0.12
Cambodian (15)	21	0.12
Chinese, ex. Taiwanese (518)	594	3.44
Filipino (325)	393	2.27
Indian (1,343)	1,445	8.36
Indonesian (35)	40	0.23
Japanese (49)	67	0.39
Korean (306)	330	1.91
Laotian (7)	8	0.05
Malaysian (6)	6	0.03
Nepalese (211)	214	1.24
Pakistani (116)	135	0.78
Sri Lankan (20)	20	0.12
Taiwanese (32)	37	0.21
Thai (52)	55	0.32
Vietnamese (454)	493	2.85
Hawaii Native/Pacific Islander (8)	29	0.17
Not Hispanic (8)	20	0.12
Hispanic (0)	9	0.05
Guamanian/Chamorro (1)	1	0.01
Native Hawaiian (1)	4	0.02
Samoan (0)	2	0.01
White (10,262)	10,765	62.27
Not Hispanic (8,632)	8,979	51.94
Hispanic (1,630)	1,786	10.33

Innsbrook

Place Type: CDP
County: Henrico
Population: 7,753†

Ancestry‡	Population	%
African, Sub-Saharan (159)	159	2.17
South African (159)	159	2.17
American (564)	564	7.71
Arab (106)	152	2.08
Arab (12)	36	0.49
Egyptian (82)	104	1.42
Lebanese (12)	12	0.16
Austrian (0)	16	0.22
Belgian (0)	13	0.18
Brazilian (0)	32	0.44
British (9)	51	0.70
Canadian (10)	22	0.30
Danish (0)	54	0.74
Dutch (0)	25	0.34
English (331)	810	11.07
European (33)	33	0.45
French, ex. Basque (10)	343	4.69
French Canadian (41)	93	1.27
German (225)	1,014	13.85
Greek (25)	77	1.05
Hungarian (14)	14	0.19
Irish (226)	1,112	15.19
Italian (102)	245	3.35
Lithuanian (36)	36	0.49
Norwegian (10)	10	0.14
Polish (135)	350	4.78
Russian (10)	24	0.33
Scandinavian (25)	52	0.71
Scotch-Irish (75)	128	1.75
Scottish (28)	127	1.74
Slovak (0)	12	0.16
Slovene (0)	12	0.16
Swedish (12)	95	1.30
Swiss (0)	12	0.16
Welsh (0)	70	0.96
Yugoslavian (102)	102	1.39

Hispanic Origin	Population	%
Hispanic or Latino (of any race)	298	3.84
Central American, ex. Mexican	49	0.63
Costa Rican	1	0.01
Guatemalan	14	0.18
Honduran	2	0.03
Nicaraguan	4	0.05
Panamanian	12	0.15
Salvadoran	15	0.19
Other Central American	1	0.01
Cuban	17	0.22
Dominican Republic	9	0.12
Mexican	71	0.92
Puerto Rican	46	0.59
South American	69	0.89
Argentinean	5	0.06
Chilean	2	0.03
Colombian	38	0.49
Ecuadorian	9	0.12
Peruvian	7	0.09
Venezuelan	8	0.10
Other Hispanic or Latino	37	0.48

Race*	Population	%
African-American/Black (880)	944	12.18
Not Hispanic (848)	911	11.75
Hispanic (32)	33	0.43
American Indian/Alaska Native (23)	66	0.85
Not Hispanic (21)	59	0.76
Hispanic (2)	7	0.09
Blackfeet (0)	1	0.01
Central American Ind. (0)	1	0.01
Cherokee (6)	9	0.12
Chippewa (1)	1	0.01
Creek (0)	3	0.04
Asian (1,713)	1,815	23.41
Not Hispanic (1,711)	1,812	23.37
Hispanic (2)	3	0.04
Bangladeshi (26)	32	0.41
Cambodian (14)	15	0.19
Chinese, ex. Taiwanese (219)	247	3.19
Filipino (72)	85	1.10
Indian (1,040)	1,063	13.71
Indonesian (4)	4	0.05
Japanese (8)	14	0.18
Korean (53)	62	0.80
Laotian (5)	5	0.06
Pakistani (51)	61	0.79
Sri Lankan (15)	16	0.21
Taiwanese (3)	3	0.04
Thai (5)	7	0.09
Vietnamese (164)	173	2.23
Hawaii Native/Pacific Islander (3)	5	0.06
Not Hispanic (2)	4	0.05
Hispanic (1)	1	0.01
Guamanian/Chamorro (1)	1	0.01
Native Hawaiian (1)	3	0.04
White (4,850)	5,006	64.57
Not Hispanic (4,687)	4,834	62.35
Hispanic (163)	172	2.22

Kings Park West

Place Type: CDP
County: Fairfax
Population: 13,390†

Ancestry‡	Population	%
African, Sub-Saharan (273)	282	1.96
African (158)	167	1.16
Ethiopian (115)	115	0.80
Albanian (24)	24	0.17
American (491)	491	3.41
Arab (21)	84	0.58
Arab (0)	10	0.07
Egyptian (0)	25	0.17
Iraqi (0)	18	0.13
Jordanian (7)	7	0.05
Moroccan (0)	10	0.07
Other Arab (14)	14	0.10
Armenian (27)	36	0.25
Austrian (15)	59	0.41
Basque (16)	16	0.11
Brazilian (12)	12	0.08
British (131)	160	1.11
Canadian (10)	10	0.07
Celtic (14)	14	0.10

*Notes: † The Census 2010 population figure is used to calculate the percentages in the Hispanic Origin and Race categories. Ancestry percentages are based on the 2006-2010 American Community Survey population (not shown); ‡ Numbers in parentheses indicate the number of people reporting a single ancestry; * Numbers in parentheses indicate the number of persons reporting this race alone, not in combination with any other race; Please refer to the Explanation of Data for more information.*

Croatian (14)	14	0.10
Czech (0)	31	0.22
Czechoslovakian (17)	31	0.22
Danish (0)	40	0.28
Dutch (0)	21	0.15
Eastern European (71)	71	0.49
English (449)	1,688	11.74
Estonian (22)	22	0.15
European (396)	520	3.62
Finnish (0)	22	0.15
French, ex. Basque (28)	275	1.91
French Canadian (6)	6	0.04
German (514)	2,474	17.20
Greek (72)	72	0.50
Hungarian (7)	22	0.15
Iranian (0)	25	0.17
Irish (683)	1,945	13.52
Israeli (35)	87	0.60
Italian (262)	468	3.25
Lithuanian (36)	43	0.30
Norwegian (78)	304	2.11
Pennsylvania German (0)	16	0.11
Polish (108)	467	3.25
Portuguese (0)	18	0.13
Romanian (32)	32	0.22
Russian (118)	215	1.49
Scandinavian (190)	236	1.64
Scotch-Irish (146)	335	2.33
Scottish (63)	303	2.11
Slavic (35)	78	0.54
Slovak (38)	136	0.95
Slovene (11)	11	0.08
Swedish (49)	263	1.83
Swiss (0)	37	0.26
Turkish (84)	84	0.58
Ukrainian (13)	24	0.17
Welsh (36)	136	0.95

Hispanic Origin	Population	%
Hispanic or Latino (of any race)	1,345	10.04
Central American, ex. Mexican	296	2.21
Costa Rican	6	0.04
Guatemalan	39	0.29
Honduran	23	0.17
Nicaraguan	28	0.21
Panamanian	10	0.07
Salvadoran	189	1.41
Other Central American	1	0.01
Cuban	46	0.34
Dominican Republic	7	0.05
Mexican	154	1.15
Puerto Rican	96	0.72
South American	613	4.58
Argentinean	31	0.23
Bolivian	275	2.05
Chilean	29	0.22
Colombian	60	0.45
Ecuadorian	24	0.18
Paraguayan	1	0.01
Peruvian	156	1.17
Uruguayan	11	0.08
Venezuelan	25	0.19
Other South American	1	0.01
Other Hispanic or Latino	133	0.99

Race*	Population	%
African-American/Black (688)	809	6.04
Not Hispanic (675)	787	5.88
Hispanic (13)	22	0.16
American Indian/Alaska Native (24)	88	0.66
Not Hispanic (15)	66	0.49
Hispanic (9)	22	0.16
Aleut *(Alaska Native)* (1)	1	0.01
Apache (0)	3	0.02
Canadian/French Am. Ind. (1)	2	0.01
Cherokee (1)	22	0.16
Chickasaw (1)	6	0.04
Choctaw (0)	4	0.03
Comanche (0)	1	0.01
Iroquois (1)	1	0.01
Lumbee (2)	6	0.04
Mexican American Ind. (1)	1	0.01
Pima (1)	2	0.01
Potawatomi (0)	1	0.01
Sioux (1)	4	0.03
South American Ind. (1)	8	0.06
Spanish American Ind. (1)	1	0.01
Tlingit-Haida *(Alaska Native)* (0)	1	0.01
Asian (2,278)	2,563	19.14
Not Hispanic (2,275)	2,543	18.99
Hispanic (3)	20	0.15
Bangladeshi (16)	20	0.15
Burmese (2)	5	0.04
Cambodian (9)	9	0.07
Chinese, ex. Taiwanese (324)	387	2.89
Filipino (166)	222	1.66
Indian (240)	270	2.02
Indonesian (1)	1	0.01
Japanese (41)	84	0.63
Korean (804)	851	6.36
Malaysian (1)	1	0.01
Nepalese (10)	10	0.07
Pakistani (71)	90	0.67
Sri Lankan (11)	11	0.08
Taiwanese (35)	36	0.27
Thai (37)	48	0.36
Vietnamese (437)	468	3.50
Hawaii Native/Pacific Islander (21)	41	0.31
Not Hispanic (21)	37	0.28
Hispanic (0)	4	0.03
Guamanian/Chamorro (15)	21	0.16
Marshallese (1)	3	0.02
Native Hawaiian (2)	7	0.05
Samoan (1)	1	0.01
White (9,462)	9,978	74.52
Not Hispanic (8,591)	8,979	67.06
Hispanic (871)	999	7.46

Kingstowne

Place Type: CDP
County: Fairfax
Population: 15,556†

Ancestry‡	Population	%
Afghan (229)	229	1.58
African, Sub-Saharan (475)	511	3.52
African (13)	49	0.34
Ethiopian (357)	357	2.46
Somalian (76)	76	0.52
Sudanese (29)	29	0.20
Albanian (0)	16	0.11
American (617)	617	4.25
Arab (347)	526	3.62
Arab (37)	37	0.25
Iraqi (17)	50	0.34
Jordanian (12)	12	0.08
Lebanese (29)	125	0.86
Moroccan (145)	162	1.12
Other Arab (107)	140	0.96
Austrian (0)	62	0.43
Belgian (11)	25	0.17
Brazilian (61)	61	0.42
British (0)	34	0.23
Cajun (17)	17	0.12
Canadian (0)	13	0.09
Croatian (0)	33	0.23
Czech (16)	45	0.31
Czechoslovakian (23)	37	0.25
Danish (9)	81	0.56
Dutch (0)	259	1.78
Eastern European (15)	28	0.19
English (426)	1,545	10.65
European (155)	169	1.16
Finnish (0)	7	0.05
French, ex. Basque (38)	428	2.95
French Canadian (48)	64	0.44
German (496)	2,268	15.63
Greek (21)	72	0.50
Hungarian (51)	88	0.61
Iranian (9)	9	0.06
Irish (575)	1,854	12.77
Italian (261)	719	4.95
Lithuanian (0)	19	0.13
Luxemburger (0)	7	0.05
Northern European (24)	24	0.17
Norwegian (95)	284	1.96
Pennsylvania German (0)	14	0.10
Polish (90)	519	3.58
Portuguese (24)	38	0.26
Romanian (20)	20	0.14
Russian (30)	128	0.88
Scandinavian (16)	65	0.45
Scotch-Irish (58)	166	1.14
Scottish (51)	328	2.26
Slavic (0)	11	0.08
Slovak (41)	41	0.28
Slovene (0)	64	0.44
Swedish (9)	90	0.62
Swiss (0)	152	1.05
Turkish (66)	66	0.45
Ukrainian (21)	21	0.14
Welsh (0)	120	0.83
West Indian, ex. Hispanic (114)	114	0.79
Trinidadian/Tobagonian (11)	11	0.08
West Indian (103)	103	0.71
Yugoslavian (0)	10	0.07

Hispanic Origin	Population	%
Hispanic or Latino (of any race)	1,395	8.97
Central American, ex. Mexican	276	1.77
Costa Rican	4	0.03
Guatemalan	35	0.22
Honduran	34	0.22
Nicaraguan	23	0.15
Panamanian	52	0.33
Salvadoran	128	0.82
Cuban	43	0.28
Dominican Republic	19	0.12
Mexican	284	1.83
Puerto Rican	209	1.34
South American	416	2.67
Argentinean	37	0.24
Bolivian	101	0.65
Chilean	24	0.15
Colombian	63	0.40
Ecuadorian	31	0.20
Paraguayan	4	0.03
Peruvian	110	0.71
Venezuelan	44	0.28
Other South American	2	0.01
Other Hispanic or Latino	148	0.95

Race*	Population	%
African-American/Black (2,631)	2,870	18.45
Not Hispanic (2,563)	2,753	17.70
Hispanic (68)	117	0.75
American Indian/Alaska Native (45)	135	0.87
Not Hispanic (40)	101	0.65
Hispanic (5)	34	0.22
Apache (1)	5	0.03
Blackfeet (0)	3	0.02
Cherokee (10)	22	0.14
Chippewa (0)	2	0.01
Choctaw (0)	1	0.01
Cree (0)	1	0.01
Iroquois (2)	2	0.01
Lumbee (0)	1	0.01
Navajo (1)	1	0.01
Pueblo (2)	2	0.01
Sioux (3)	5	0.03
South American Ind. (0)	3	0.02
Spanish American Ind. (0)	6	0.04
Asian (2,019)	2,451	15.76
Not Hispanic (2,007)	2,406	15.47
Hispanic (12)	45	0.29
Bangladeshi (56)	69	0.44
Burmese (11)	11	0.07
Cambodian (18)	23	0.15
Chinese, ex. Taiwanese (302)	399	2.56

*Notes: † The Census 2010 population figure is used to calculate the percentages in the Hispanic Origin and Race categories. Ancestry percentages are based on the 2006-2010 American Community Survey population (not shown); ‡ Numbers in parentheses indicate the number of people reporting a single ancestry; * Numbers in parentheses indicate the number of persons reporting this race alone, not in combination with any other race; Please refer to the Explanation of Data for more information.*

Filipino (347)	436	2.80
Indian (308)	354	2.28
Indonesian (3)	3	0.02
Japanese (44)	117	0.75
Korean (332)	387	2.49
Laotian (12)	13	0.08
Malaysian (1)	2	0.01
Nepalese (5)	6	0.04
Pakistani (158)	174	1.12
Sri Lankan (6)	6	0.04
Taiwanese (16)	27	0.17
Thai (41)	51	0.33
Vietnamese (241)	268	1.72
Hawaii Native/Pacific Islander (7)	26	0.17
Not Hispanic (7)	22	0.14
Hispanic (0)	4	0.03
Guamanian/Chamorro (4)	8	0.05
Native Hawaiian (2)	10	0.06
Samoan (0)	3	0.02
White (9,770)	10,408	66.91
Not Hispanic (8,887)	9,398	60.41
Hispanic (883)	1,010	6.49

Lake Barcroft

Place Type: CDP
County: Fairfax
Population: 9,558†

Ancestry‡	Population	%
Afghan (21)	21	0.23
African, Sub-Saharan (383)	383	4.23
African (110)	110	1.21
Ethiopian (33)	33	0.36
Sudanese (229)	229	2.53
Zimbabwean (11)	11	0.12
American (136)	136	1.50
Arab (456)	575	6.35
Arab (173)	186	2.05
Egyptian (130)	183	2.02
Syrian (11)	11	0.12
Other Arab (142)	195	2.15
Austrian (9)	23	0.25
Belgian (10)	10	0.11
Brazilian (35)	35	0.39
British (27)	56	0.62
Canadian (24)	24	0.26
Croatian (33)	33	0.36
Czech (10)	95	1.05
Danish (51)	115	1.27
Dutch (8)	87	0.96
Eastern European (34)	34	0.38
English (347)	870	9.60
Estonian (47)	47	0.52
European (244)	244	2.69
Finnish (0)	21	0.23
French, ex. Basque (132)	217	2.39
French Canadian (26)	46	0.51
German (475)	1,487	16.41
Greek (15)	33	0.36
Hungarian (112)	137	1.51
Iranian (66)	66	0.73
Irish (341)	875	9.66
Italian (140)	275	3.03
Latvian (0)	10	0.11
Lithuanian (14)	42	0.46
Northern European (19)	19	0.21
Norwegian (0)	26	0.29
Pennsylvania German (11)	11	0.12
Polish (193)	397	4.38
Portuguese (16)	25	0.28
Romanian (0)	46	0.51
Russian (39)	203	2.24
Scandinavian (0)	19	0.21
Scotch-Irish (161)	383	4.23
Scottish (27)	230	2.54
Serbian (32)	32	0.35
Slovak (42)	74	0.82
Swedish (0)	153	1.69
Swiss (12)	91	1.00
Turkish (64)	74	0.82
Ukrainian (33)	40	0.44
Welsh (0)	62	0.68
West Indian, ex. Hispanic (26)	26	0.29
Jamaican (26)	26	0.29

Hispanic Origin	Population	%
Hispanic or Latino (of any race)	1,797	18.80
Central American, ex. Mexican	537	5.62
Costa Rican	7	0.07
Guatemalan	112	1.17
Honduran	39	0.41
Nicaraguan	45	0.47
Panamanian	9	0.09
Salvadoran	322	3.37
Other Central American	3	0.03
Cuban	86	0.90
Dominican Republic	21	0.22
Mexican	156	1.63
Puerto Rican	68	0.71
South American	737	7.71
Argentinean	45	0.47
Bolivian	472	4.94
Chilean	20	0.21
Colombian	42	0.44
Ecuadorian	15	0.16
Paraguayan	2	0.02
Peruvian	101	1.06
Uruguayan	12	0.13
Venezuelan	16	0.17
Other South American	12	0.13
Other Hispanic or Latino	192	2.01

Race*	Population	%
African-American/Black (496)	571	5.97
Not Hispanic (474)	537	5.62
Hispanic (22)	34	0.36
American Indian/Alaska Native (24)	93	0.97
Not Hispanic (10)	35	0.37
Hispanic (14)	58	0.61
Blackfeet (1)	1	0.01
Central American Ind. (1)	5	0.05
Cherokee (2)	9	0.09
Choctaw (0)	2	0.02
Iroquois (0)	3	0.03
Lumbee (1)	1	0.01
Mexican American Ind. (3)	4	0.04
Navajo (3)	3	0.03
Pueblo (2)	2	0.02
South American Ind. (1)	2	0.02
Asian (1,100)	1,319	13.80
Not Hispanic (1,087)	1,298	13.58
Hispanic (13)	21	0.22
Bangladeshi (5)	5	0.05
Burmese (6)	9	0.09
Cambodian (26)	32	0.33
Chinese, ex. Taiwanese (122)	144	1.51
Filipino (110)	142	1.49
Hmong (1)	1	0.01
Indian (161)	194	2.03
Indonesian (10)	16	0.17
Japanese (28)	48	0.50
Korean (38)	60	0.63
Malaysian (7)	11	0.12
Nepalese (21)	21	0.22
Pakistani (138)	155	1.62
Sri Lankan (6)	13	0.14
Taiwanese (2)	2	0.02
Thai (37)	53	0.55
Vietnamese (327)	344	3.60
Hawaii Native/Pacific Islander (3)	18	0.19
Not Hispanic (3)	17	0.18
Hispanic (0)	1	0.01
Tongan (0)	1	0.01
White (6,944)	7,311	76.49
Not Hispanic (5,831)	6,086	63.67
Hispanic (1,113)	1,225	12.82

Lake Monticello

Place Type: CDP
County: Fluvanna
Population: 9,920†

Ancestry‡	Population	%
American (1,584)	1,584	14.90
Australian (0)	16	0.15
Austrian (0)	36	0.34
British (0)	137	1.29
Canadian (13)	13	0.12
Croatian (0)	37	0.35
Czech (13)	45	0.42
Czechoslovakian (0)	13	0.12
Danish (0)	57	0.54
Dutch (45)	174	1.64
English (837)	2,440	22.95
European (117)	117	1.10
Finnish (31)	64	0.60
French, ex. Basque (0)	106	1.00
French Canadian (50)	113	1.06
German (688)	2,332	21.93
Greek (62)	85	0.80
Hungarian (13)	48	0.45
Irish (300)	1,613	15.17
Italian (198)	588	5.53
Lithuanian (14)	140	1.32
Northern European (12)	12	0.11
Norwegian (81)	124	1.17
Polish (115)	302	2.84
Portuguese (14)	14	0.13
Russian (0)	159	1.50
Scotch-Irish (129)	274	2.58
Scottish (98)	427	4.02
Slavic (19)	19	0.18
Slovak (14)	90	0.85
Swedish (66)	171	1.61
Swiss (0)	20	0.19
Welsh (18)	119	1.12
Yugoslavian (0)	16	0.15

Hispanic Origin	Population	%
Hispanic or Latino (of any race)	317	3.20
Central American, ex. Mexican	16	0.16
Guatemalan	3	0.03
Honduran	6	0.06
Panamanian	5	0.05
Salvadoran	2	0.02
Cuban	15	0.15
Dominican Republic	7	0.07
Mexican	106	1.07
Puerto Rican	111	1.12
South American	23	0.23
Bolivian	6	0.06
Chilean	2	0.02
Colombian	5	0.05
Ecuadorian	2	0.02
Peruvian	5	0.05
Uruguayan	1	0.01
Venezuelan	2	0.02
Other Hispanic or Latino	39	0.39

Race*	Population	%
African-American/Black (635)	780	7.86
Not Hispanic (626)	758	7.64
Hispanic (9)	22	0.22
American Indian/Alaska Native (18)	73	0.74
Not Hispanic (16)	68	0.69
Hispanic (2)	5	0.05
Apache (1)	4	0.04
Blackfeet (0)	1	0.01
Canadian/French Am. Ind. (0)	1	0.01
Cherokee (5)	24	0.24
Chippewa (0)	2	0.02
Choctaw (0)	3	0.03
Lumbee (0)	1	0.01
Mexican American Ind. (1)	1	0.01
Navajo (0)	1	0.01
Potawatomi (1)	1	0.01

*Notes: † The Census 2010 population figure is used to calculate the percentages in the Hispanic Origin and Race categories. Ancestry percentages are based on the 2006-2010 American Community Survey population (not shown); ‡ Numbers in parentheses indicate the number of people reporting a single ancestry; * Numbers in parentheses indicate the number of persons reporting this race alone, not in combination with any other race; Please refer to the Explanation of Data for more information.*

Sioux (1)	1	0.01
Asian (86)	140	1.41
Not Hispanic (75)	122	1.23
Hispanic (11)	18	0.18
Chinese, ex. Taiwanese (13)	23	0.23
Filipino (32)	51	0.51
Indian (20)	27	0.27
Indonesian (2)	2	0.02
Japanese (4)	13	0.13
Korean (4)	15	0.15
Malaysian (1)	1	0.01
Pakistani (2)	2	0.02
Thai (1)	1	0.01
Vietnamese (5)	6	0.06
Hawaii Native/Pacific Islander (6)	12	0.12
Not Hispanic (6)	12	0.12
Guamanian/Chamorro (1)	1	0.01
Native Hawaiian (1)	2	0.02
Samoan (2)	2	0.02
Tongan (2)	2	0.02
White (8,861)	9,090	91.63
Not Hispanic (8,649)	8,857	89.28
Hispanic (212)	233	2.35

Lake Ridge

Place Type: CDP
County: Prince William
Population: 41,058†

Ancestry‡	Population	%
Afghan (199)	199	0.50
African, Sub-Saharan (1,185)	1,220	3.09
African (319)	332	0.84
Ethiopian (339)	339	0.86
Ghanaian (246)	246	0.62
Nigerian (44)	44	0.11
Other Sub-Saharan African (237)	259	0.66
American (1,710)	1,710	4.34
Arab (112)	153	0.39
Egyptian (34)	34	0.09
Lebanese (32)	32	0.08
Syrian (46)	46	0.12
Other Arab (0)	41	0.10
Australian (16)	16	0.04
Austrian (25)	104	0.26
Brazilian (8)	8	0.02
British (75)	219	0.56
Bulgarian (16)	16	0.04
Canadian (42)	136	0.34
Celtic (0)	66	0.17
Croatian (52)	52	0.13
Czech (0)	187	0.47
Czechoslovakian (0)	90	0.23
Danish (54)	158	0.40
Dutch (2)	254	0.64
Eastern European (121)	121	0.31
English (1,378)	4,193	10.64
European (556)	649	1.65
French, ex. Basque (77)	923	2.34
French Canadian (73)	177	0.45
German (1,567)	5,923	15.02
Greek (71)	165	0.42
Guyanese (0)	36	0.09
Hungarian (0)	125	0.32
Iranian (23)	23	0.06
Irish (1,269)	4,744	12.03
Italian (731)	2,743	6.96
Lithuanian (30)	99	0.25
Northern European (20)	20	0.05
Norwegian (11)	123	0.31
Pennsylvania German (11)	11	0.03
Polish (311)	972	2.47
Portuguese (0)	33	0.08
Romanian (0)	66	0.17
Russian (80)	322	0.82
Scandinavian (40)	40	0.10
Scotch-Irish (170)	790	2.00
Scottish (169)	817	2.07
Serbian (82)	93	0.24
Slavic (15)	15	0.04
Slovak (20)	85	0.22
Slovene (0)	12	0.03
Swedish (182)	645	1.64
Swiss (7)	131	0.33
Turkish (14)	21	0.05
Ukrainian (64)	155	0.39
Welsh (73)	469	1.19
West Indian, ex. Hispanic (160)	192	0.49
British West Indian (8)	8	0.02
Haitian (81)	81	0.21
Jamaican (71)	85	0.22
West Indian (0)	18	0.05
Yugoslavian (0)	25	0.06

Hispanic Origin	Population	%
Hispanic or Latino (of any race)	6,311	15.37
Central American, ex. Mexican	2,217	5.40
Costa Rican	29	0.07
Guatemalan	223	0.54
Honduran	238	0.58
Nicaraguan	144	0.35
Panamanian	114	0.28
Salvadoran	1,463	3.56
Other Central American	6	0.01
Cuban	99	0.24
Dominican Republic	119	0.29
Mexican	912	2.22
Puerto Rican	769	1.87
South American	1,543	3.76
Argentinean	53	0.13
Bolivian	375	0.91
Chilean	82	0.20
Colombian	180	0.44
Ecuadorian	91	0.22
Paraguayan	11	0.03
Peruvian	642	1.56
Uruguayan	24	0.06
Venezuelan	72	0.18
Other South American	13	0.03
Other Hispanic or Latino	652	1.59

Race*	Population	%
African-American/Black (8,283)	9,181	22.36
Not Hispanic (8,036)	8,773	21.37
Hispanic (247)	408	0.99
American Indian/Alaska Native (242)	630	1.53
Not Hispanic (87)	368	0.90
Hispanic (155)	262	0.64
Apache (0)	4	0.01
Blackfeet (0)	25	0.06
Central American Ind. (12)	13	0.03
Cherokee (19)	127	0.31
Chickasaw (0)	1	<0.01
Chippewa (4)	9	0.02
Choctaw (0)	8	0.02
Comanche (4)	4	0.01
Cree (3)	3	0.01
Creek (0)	1	<0.01
Crow (4)	5	0.01
Delaware (2)	2	<0.01
Inupiat *(Alaska Native)* (0)	1	<0.01
Iroquois (4)	10	0.02
Lumbee (1)	4	0.01
Mexican American Ind. (4)	4	0.01
Navajo (0)	4	0.01
Pima (2)	2	<0.01
Potawatomi (0)	3	0.01
Seminole (0)	1	<0.01
Shoshone (3)	5	0.01
Sioux (8)	11	0.03
South American Ind. (5)	16	0.04
Spanish American Ind. (6)	6	0.01
Asian (2,737)	3,505	8.54
Not Hispanic (2,711)	3,389	8.25
Hispanic (26)	116	0.28
Bangladeshi (100)	109	0.27
Burmese (4)	5	0.01
Cambodian (43)	44	0.11
Chinese, ex. Taiwanese (217)	316	0.77
Filipino (527)	698	1.70
Hmong (1)	1	<0.01
Indian (438)	506	1.23
Indonesian (22)	36	0.09
Japanese (86)	230	0.56
Korean (377)	530	1.29
Laotian (36)	42	0.10
Malaysian (7)	7	0.02
Nepalese (31)	31	0.08
Pakistani (369)	409	1.00
Sri Lankan (1)	3	0.01
Taiwanese (6)	12	0.03
Thai (37)	64	0.16
Vietnamese (268)	323	0.79
Hawaii Native/Pacific Islander (49)	155	0.38
Not Hispanic (41)	124	0.30
Hispanic (8)	31	0.08
Guamanian/Chamorro (16)	38	0.09
Native Hawaiian (17)	49	0.12
Samoan (9)	19	0.05
Tongan (0)	1	<0.01
White (25,481)	27,207	66.26
Not Hispanic (22,209)	23,517	57.28
Hispanic (3,272)	3,690	8.99

Lakeside

Place Type: CDP
County: Henrico
Population: 11,849†

Ancestry‡	Population	%
Afghan (72)	72	0.60
African, Sub-Saharan (633)	666	5.55
African (514)	547	4.56
Kenyan (119)	119	0.99
American (1,311)	1,311	10.92
Arab (0)	25	0.21
Lebanese (0)	14	0.12
Other Arab (0)	11	0.09
Armenian (0)	15	0.12
Austrian (33)	41	0.34
Belgian (0)	11	0.09
British (104)	153	1.27
Canadian (162)	175	1.46
Czech (0)	15	0.12
Czechoslovakian (11)	11	0.09
Danish (0)	20	0.17
Dutch (11)	109	0.91
English (792)	1,766	14.72
European (179)	228	1.90
French, ex. Basque (28)	300	2.50
French Canadian (24)	40	0.33
German (582)	1,479	12.32
Greek (38)	54	0.45
Hungarian (29)	58	0.48
Iranian (0)	11	0.09
Irish (476)	1,313	10.94
Italian (86)	211	1.76
Lithuanian (0)	8	0.07
Luxemburger (0)	12	0.10
Norwegian (30)	67	0.56
Polish (20)	198	1.65
Portuguese (0)	11	0.09
Romanian (0)	14	0.12
Russian (0)	33	0.27
Scotch-Irish (259)	524	4.37
Scottish (28)	250	2.08
Slavic (0)	12	0.10
Slovak (0)	12	0.10
Swedish (16)	49	0.41
Swiss (0)	11	0.09
Welsh (20)	157	1.31
West Indian, ex. Hispanic (32)	32	0.27
Jamaican (32)	32	0.27
Yugoslavian (106)	106	0.88

Hispanic Origin	Population	%
Hispanic or Latino (of any race)	902	7.61
Central American, ex. Mexican	242	2.04

*Notes: † The Census 2010 population figure is used to calculate the percentages in the Hispanic Origin and Race categories. Ancestry percentages are based on the 2006-2010 American Community Survey population (not shown); ‡ Numbers in parentheses indicate the number of people reporting a single ancestry; * Numbers in parentheses indicate the number of persons reporting this race alone, not in combination with any other race; Please refer to the Explanation of Data for more information.*

Hispanic Origin (cont.)	Population	%
Costa Rican	6	0.05
Guatemalan	26	0.22
Honduran	37	0.31
Nicaraguan	8	0.07
Panamanian	3	0.03
Salvadoran	158	1.33
Other Central American	4	0.03
Cuban	32	0.27
Dominican Republic	5	0.04
Mexican	357	3.01
Puerto Rican	86	0.73
South American	62	0.52
Argentinean	2	0.02
Bolivian	9	0.08
Chilean	1	0.01
Colombian	7	0.06
Ecuadorian	14	0.12
Peruvian	10	0.08
Uruguayan	9	0.08
Venezuelan	9	0.08
Other South American	1	0.01
Other Hispanic or Latino	118	1.00

Race*	Population	%
African-American/Black (1,978)	2,103	17.75
Not Hispanic (1,937)	2,051	17.31
Hispanic (41)	52	0.44
American Indian/Alaska Native (49)	136	1.15
Not Hispanic (35)	118	1.00
Hispanic (14)	18	0.15
Apache (1)	1	0.01
Blackfeet (1)	3	0.03
Cherokee (8)	34	0.29
Choctaw (2)	2	0.02
Lumbee (0)	1	0.01
Mexican American Ind. (2)	2	0.02
Ottawa (0)	1	0.01
Sioux (0)	1	0.01
South American Ind. (0)	1	0.01
Spanish American Ind. (0)	1	0.01
Asian (310)	360	3.04
Not Hispanic (299)	347	2.93
Hispanic (11)	13	0.11
Bangladeshi (7)	16	0.14
Cambodian (36)	40	0.34
Chinese, ex. Taiwanese (55)	67	0.57
Filipino (34)	42	0.35
Indian (27)	43	0.36
Indonesian (2)	3	0.03
Japanese (0)	7	0.06
Korean (11)	22	0.19
Laotian (4)	4	0.03
Nepalese (3)	3	0.03
Taiwanese (1)	1	0.01
Thai (14)	16	0.14
Vietnamese (80)	93	0.78
Hawaii Native/Pacific Islander (2)	11	0.09
Not Hispanic (2)	9	0.08
Hispanic (0)	2	0.02
Native Hawaiian (0)	2	0.02
Samoan (1)	1	0.01
White (8,815)	9,075	76.59
Not Hispanic (8,403)	8,621	72.76
Hispanic (412)	454	3.83

Lansdowne

Place Type: CDP
County: Loudoun
Population: 11,253†

Ancestry‡	Population	%
Afghan (84)	84	0.86
African, Sub-Saharan (141)	141	1.44
African (36)	36	0.37
Nigerian (53)	53	0.54
Senegalese (7)	7	0.07
Other Sub-Saharan African (45)	45	0.46
American (274)	274	2.79
Arab (204)	224	2.28
Arab (101)	101	1.03
Lebanese (10)	10	0.10
Moroccan (10)	30	0.31
Other Arab (83)	83	0.84
Assyrian/Chaldean/Syriac (76)	76	0.77
Austrian (0)	50	0.51
British (24)	70	0.71
Cajun (0)	16	0.16
Canadian (27)	27	0.27
Czech (9)	25	0.25
Danish (0)	12	0.12
Dutch (39)	133	1.35
English (503)	1,341	13.65
Estonian (12)	12	0.12
European (247)	266	2.71
French, ex. Basque (39)	282	2.87
French Canadian (10)	98	1.00
German (388)	1,444	14.70
Greek (9)	154	1.57
Hungarian (33)	81	0.82
Iranian (211)	254	2.59
Irish (459)	1,335	13.59
Italian (179)	704	7.17
Lithuanian (0)	27	0.27
Norwegian (41)	177	1.80
Polish (69)	397	4.04
Portuguese (39)	52	0.53
Russian (0)	170	1.73
Scandinavian (12)	12	0.12
Scotch-Irish (33)	234	2.38
Scottish (104)	501	5.10
Serbian (0)	37	0.38
Slovak (10)	21	0.21
Swedish (0)	26	0.26
Swiss (0)	13	0.13
Ukrainian (0)	15	0.15
Welsh (29)	97	0.99
West Indian, ex. Hispanic (17)	31	0.32
Jamaican (17)	31	0.32
Yugoslavian (0)	14	0.14

Hispanic Origin	Population	%
Hispanic or Latino (of any race)	811	7.21
Central American, ex. Mexican	144	1.28
Costa Rican	2	0.02
Guatemalan	29	0.26
Honduran	12	0.11
Nicaraguan	12	0.11
Panamanian	8	0.07
Salvadoran	79	0.70
Other Central American	2	0.02
Cuban	36	0.32
Dominican Republic	11	0.10
Mexican	133	1.18
Puerto Rican	86	0.76
South American	296	2.63
Argentinean	27	0.24
Bolivian	32	0.28
Chilean	2	0.02
Colombian	38	0.34
Ecuadorian	18	0.16
Paraguayan	1	0.01
Peruvian	155	1.38
Uruguayan	5	0.04
Venezuelan	17	0.15
Other South American	1	0.01
Other Hispanic or Latino	105	0.93

Race*	Population	%
African-American/Black (1,051)	1,185	10.53
Not Hispanic (1,024)	1,144	10.17
Hispanic (27)	41	0.36
American Indian/Alaska Native (29)	80	0.71
Not Hispanic (14)	48	0.43
Hispanic (15)	32	0.28
Canadian/French Am. Ind. (1)	2	0.02
Central American Ind. (7)	7	0.06
Cherokee (3)	10	0.09
Choctaw (0)	3	0.03
South American Ind. (1)	7	0.06
Asian (1,774)	2,077	18.46
Not Hispanic (1,762)	2,050	18.22
Hispanic (12)	27	0.24
Bangladeshi (30)	30	0.27
Burmese (2)	2	0.02
Cambodian (11)	17	0.15
Chinese, ex. Taiwanese (191)	247	2.19
Filipino (212)	254	2.26
Indian (588)	628	5.58
Indonesian (1)	9	0.08
Japanese (29)	55	0.49
Korean (276)	321	2.85
Laotian (3)	16	0.14
Pakistani (131)	140	1.24
Sri Lankan (7)	8	0.07
Taiwanese (10)	21	0.19
Thai (23)	31	0.28
Vietnamese (162)	192	1.71
Hawaii Native/Pacific Islander (3)	20	0.18
Not Hispanic (2)	13	0.12
Hispanic (1)	7	0.06
Guamanian/Chamorro (0)	2	0.02
Native Hawaiian (2)	5	0.04
Samoan (1)	2	0.02
White (7,699)	8,104	72.02
Not Hispanic (7,184)	7,547	67.07
Hispanic (515)	557	4.95

Laurel

Place Type: CDP
County: Henrico
Population: 16,713†

Ancestry‡	Population	%
African, Sub-Saharan (229)	229	1.42
African (52)	52	0.32
Nigerian (23)	23	0.14
Sudanese (88)	88	0.55
Zimbabwean (23)	23	0.14
Other Sub-Saharan African (43)	43	0.27
Albanian (10)	10	0.06
American (1,039)	1,039	6.45
Arab (336)	390	2.42
Egyptian (303)	303	1.88
Lebanese (9)	55	0.34
Other Arab (24)	32	0.20
Armenian (0)	9	0.06
Australian (0)	23	0.14
Austrian (0)	9	0.06
Brazilian (19)	19	0.12
British (44)	73	0.45
Celtic (11)	11	0.07
Czech (12)	25	0.16
Czechoslovakian (37)	37	0.23
Danish (24)	24	0.15
Dutch (40)	175	1.09
English (663)	1,646	10.22
European (54)	68	0.42
French, ex. Basque (43)	271	1.68
French Canadian (19)	57	0.35
German (286)	1,534	9.53
Greek (8)	8	0.05
Guyanese (13)	13	0.08
Hungarian (39)	89	0.55
Iranian (8)	8	0.05
Irish (470)	1,597	9.92
Italian (405)	840	5.22
Lithuanian (0)	60	0.37
Norwegian (22)	62	0.39
Polish (57)	276	1.71
Portuguese (19)	27	0.17
Romanian (7)	7	0.04
Russian (22)	40	0.25
Scotch-Irish (144)	312	1.94
Scottish (85)	289	1.79
Serbian (0)	9	0.06
Slovak (12)	85	0.53
Swedish (29)	96	0.60
Ukrainian (56)	56	0.35

*Notes: † The Census 2010 population figure is used to calculate the percentages in the Hispanic Origin and Race categories. Ancestry percentages are based on the 2006-2010 American Community Survey population (not shown); ‡ Numbers in parentheses indicate the number of people reporting a single ancestry; * Numbers in parentheses indicate the number of persons reporting this race alone, not in combination with any other race; Please refer to the Explanation of Data for more information.*

Welsh (0)	103	0.64
West Indian, ex. Hispanic (121)	165	1.02
Dutch West Indian (0)	19	0.12
Jamaican (9)	26	0.16
Trinidadian/Tobagonian (11)	11	0.07
West Indian (101)	109	0.68
Yugoslavian (105)	105	0.65

Hispanic Origin	Population	%
Hispanic or Latino (of any race)	1,846	11.05
Central American, ex. Mexican	513	3.07
Costa Rican	39	0.23
Guatemalan	158	0.95
Honduran	75	0.45
Nicaraguan	5	0.03
Panamanian	18	0.11
Salvadoran	213	1.27
Other Central American	5	0.03
Cuban	33	0.20
Dominican Republic	35	0.21
Mexican	770	4.61
Puerto Rican	194	1.16
South American	108	0.65
Argentinean	4	0.02
Bolivian	3	0.02
Colombian	28	0.17
Ecuadorian	6	0.04
Paraguayan	4	0.02
Peruvian	33	0.20
Uruguayan	7	0.04
Venezuelan	22	0.13
Other South American	1	0.01
Other Hispanic or Latino	193	1.15

Race*	Population	%
African-American/Black (5,076)	5,356	32.05
Not Hispanic (4,989)	5,232	31.30
Hispanic (87)	124	0.74
American Indian/Alaska Native (68)	160	0.96
Not Hispanic (53)	130	0.78
Hispanic (15)	30	0.18
Apache (1)	1	0.01
Blackfeet (0)	5	0.03
Central American Ind. (5)	9	0.05
Cherokee (4)	30	0.18
Chippewa (1)	1	0.01
Choctaw (0)	3	0.02
Comanche (0)	1	0.01
Iroquois (0)	1	0.01
Lumbee (3)	7	0.04
Mexican American Ind. (2)	2	0.01
Osage (4)	4	0.02
Sioux (2)	5	0.03
Spanish American Ind. (0)	1	0.01
Asian (1,043)	1,130	6.76
Not Hispanic (1,031)	1,104	6.61
Hispanic (12)	26	0.16
Bangladeshi (3)	3	0.02
Burmese (5)	5	0.03
Cambodian (33)	39	0.23
Chinese, ex. Taiwanese (152)	179	1.07
Filipino (104)	115	0.69
Hmong (1)	1	0.01
Indian (244)	258	1.54
Japanese (5)	12	0.07
Korean (29)	43	0.26
Laotian (1)	1	0.01
Malaysian (5)	5	0.03
Nepalese (11)	11	0.07
Pakistani (42)	46	0.28
Sri Lankan (3)	3	0.02
Taiwanese (1)	1	0.01
Thai (17)	21	0.13
Vietnamese (337)	367	2.20
Hawaii Native/Pacific Islander (14)	24	0.14
Not Hispanic (9)	15	0.09
Hispanic (5)	9	0.05
Guamanian/Chamorro (1)	1	0.01
Native Hawaiian (7)	9	0.05
Samoan (1)	1	0.01
White (9,169)	9,523	56.98
Not Hispanic (8,373)	8,629	51.63
Hispanic (796)	894	5.35

Leesburg

Place Type: Town
County: Loudoun
Population: 42,616†

Ancestry‡	Population	%
Afghan (20)	20	0.05
African, Sub-Saharan (371)	402	0.99
African (136)	167	0.41
Liberian (126)	126	0.31
Somalian (97)	97	0.24
South African (12)	12	0.03
American (2,597)	2,597	6.38
Arab (344)	510	1.25
Arab (36)	36	0.09
Egyptian (19)	19	0.05
Lebanese (8)	36	0.09
Palestinian (42)	82	0.20
Syrian (92)	135	0.33
Other Arab (147)	202	0.50
Armenian (29)	64	0.16
Australian (0)	19	0.05
Austrian (0)	155	0.38
Belgian (17)	33	0.08
Brazilian (55)	55	0.14
British (208)	461	1.13
Canadian (76)	132	0.32
Celtic (11)	11	0.03
Croatian (0)	15	0.04
Czech (15)	63	0.15
Czechoslovakian (52)	103	0.25
Danish (46)	140	0.34
Dutch (191)	810	1.99
English (1,726)	4,627	11.36
European (703)	782	1.92
Finnish (0)	20	0.05
French, ex. Basque (394)	1,462	3.59
French Canadian (59)	181	0.44
German (1,718)	6,957	17.09
Greek (21)	131	0.32
Hungarian (109)	203	0.50
Icelander (0)	13	0.03
Iranian (219)	219	0.54
Irish (1,416)	5,608	13.77
Italian (952)	3,047	7.48
Lithuanian (11)	79	0.19
Macedonian (8)	8	0.02
New Zealander (40)	40	0.10
Northern European (0)	7	0.02
Norwegian (194)	431	1.06
Pennsylvania German (9)	28	0.07
Polish (225)	1,310	3.22
Portuguese (9)	82	0.20
Russian (194)	310	0.76
Scandinavian (69)	247	0.61
Scotch-Irish (311)	775	1.90
Scottish (338)	1,020	2.51
Serbian (49)	59	0.14
Slavic (0)	13	0.03
Slovak (12)	119	0.29
Slovene (0)	96	0.24
Swedish (85)	523	1.28
Swiss (14)	85	0.21
Turkish (0)	21	0.05
Ukrainian (118)	200	0.49
Welsh (38)	352	0.86
West Indian, ex. Hispanic (212)	309	0.76
Dutch West Indian (0)	9	0.02
Jamaican (48)	85	0.21
Trinidadian/Tobagonian (164)	164	0.40
West Indian (0)	51	0.13
Yugoslavian (115)	115	0.28

Hispanic Origin	Population	%
Hispanic or Latino (of any race)	7,431	17.44
Central American, ex. Mexican	3,419	8.02
Costa Rican	29	0.07
Guatemalan	411	0.96
Honduran	334	0.78
Nicaraguan	100	0.23
Panamanian	28	0.07
Salvadoran	2,500	5.87
Other Central American	17	0.04
Cuban	95	0.22
Dominican Republic	41	0.10
Mexican	1,158	2.72
Puerto Rican	531	1.25
South American	1,407	3.30
Argentinean	36	0.08
Bolivian	238	0.56
Chilean	37	0.09
Colombian	184	0.43
Ecuadorian	99	0.23
Paraguayan	4	0.01
Peruvian	736	1.73
Uruguayan	5	0.01
Venezuelan	50	0.12
Other South American	18	0.04
Other Hispanic or Latino	780	1.83

Race*	Population	%
African-American/Black (4,063)	4,713	11.06
Not Hispanic (3,921)	4,465	10.48
Hispanic (142)	248	0.58
American Indian/Alaska Native (162)	457	1.07
Not Hispanic (78)	280	0.66
Hispanic (84)	177	0.42
Alaska Athabascan *(Ala. Nat.)* (1)	1	<0.01
Aleut *(Alaska Native)* (1)	1	<0.01
Apache (3)	4	0.01
Blackfeet (1)	3	0.01
Canadian/French Am. Ind. (3)	3	0.01
Central American Ind. (2)	6	0.01
Cherokee (14)	57	0.13
Chickasaw (0)	5	0.01
Chippewa (1)	9	0.02
Choctaw (3)	5	0.01
Creek (5)	8	0.02
Crow (4)	4	0.01
Delaware (2)	3	0.01
Houma (1)	3	0.01
Iroquois (5)	6	0.01
Lumbee (2)	4	0.01
Mexican American Ind. (1)	4	0.01
Ottawa (0)	5	0.01
Potawatomi (1)	1	<0.01
Pueblo (1)	1	<0.01
Seminole (0)	1	<0.01
Sioux (1)	14	0.03
South American Ind. (13)	20	0.05
Spanish American Ind. (0)	2	<0.01
Yaqui (0)	2	<0.01
Asian (3,025)	3,740	8.78
Not Hispanic (2,982)	3,627	8.51
Hispanic (43)	113	0.27
Bangladeshi (52)	60	0.14
Burmese (1)	3	0.01
Cambodian (59)	84	0.20
Chinese, ex. Taiwanese (315)	437	1.03
Filipino (419)	592	1.39
Hmong (3)	3	0.01
Indian (990)	1,073	2.52
Indonesian (20)	21	0.05
Japanese (44)	128	0.30
Korean (229)	318	0.75
Laotian (23)	37	0.09
Malaysian (2)	5	0.01
Nepalese (63)	63	0.15
Pakistani (387)	403	0.95
Sri Lankan (6)	6	0.01
Taiwanese (7)	15	0.04
Thai (54)	68	0.16
Vietnamese (193)	248	0.58
Hawaii Native/Pacific Islander (19)	80	0.19
Not Hispanic (15)	57	0.13

*Notes: † The Census 2010 population figure is used to calculate the percentages in the Hispanic Origin and Race categories. Ancestry percentages are based on the 2006-2010 American Community Survey population (not shown); ‡ Numbers in parentheses indicate the number of people reporting a single ancestry; * Numbers in parentheses indicate the number of persons reporting this race alone, not in combination with any other race; Please refer to the Explanation of Data for more information.*

Hispanic (4)	23	0.05
Guamanian/Chamorro (3)	5	0.01
Native Hawaiian (6)	33	0.08
Samoan (3)	6	0.01
Tongan (1)	1	<0.01
White (30,313)	31,867	74.78
Not Hispanic (26,829)	27,939	65.56
Hispanic (3,484)	3,928	9.22

Lincolnia

Place Type: CDP
County: Fairfax
Population: 22,855†

Ancestry‡	Population	%
African, Sub-Saharan (2,691)	3,016	14.61
African (958)	1,078	5.22
Cape Verdean (13)	13	0.06
Ethiopian (903)	1,026	4.97
Ghanaian (242)	242	1.17
Liberian (29)	29	0.14
Sierra Leonean (144)	144	0.70
Somalian (32)	32	0.15
Sudanese (153)	235	1.14
Other Sub-Saharan African (217)	217	1.05
American (595)	595	2.88
Arab (489)	500	2.42
Arab (40)	51	0.25
Egyptian (15)	15	0.07
Lebanese (148)	148	0.72
Moroccan (264)	264	1.28
Other Arab (22)	22	0.11
Armenian (0)	43	0.21
Austrian (0)	17	0.08
British (37)	114	0.55
Cajun (0)	14	0.07
Canadian (31)	42	0.20
Carpatho Rusyn (0)	13	0.06
Czech (10)	119	0.58
Czechoslovakian (5)	20	0.10
Danish (0)	44	0.21
Dutch (0)	126	0.61
Eastern European (18)	18	0.09
English (313)	1,580	7.65
Estonian (0)	23	0.11
European (137)	153	0.74
French, ex. Basque (71)	352	1.70
French Canadian (5)	64	0.31
German (606)	2,110	10.22
Greek (85)	122	0.59
Hungarian (23)	130	0.63
Iranian (21)	21	0.10
Irish (371)	1,690	8.19
Italian (304)	762	3.69
Lithuanian (0)	8	0.04
Norwegian (27)	148	0.72
Polish (102)	288	1.39
Portuguese (54)	68	0.33
Romanian (0)	14	0.07
Russian (52)	136	0.66
Scandinavian (46)	46	0.22
Scotch-Irish (73)	226	1.09
Scottish (149)	452	2.19
Slovak (0)	82	0.40
Slovene (5)	5	0.02
Swedish (28)	133	0.64
Swiss (12)	38	0.18
Turkish (16)	74	0.36
Ukrainian (47)	68	0.33
Welsh (0)	163	0.79
West Indian, ex. Hispanic (25)	34	0.16
British West Indian (9)	9	0.04
Haitian (8)	8	0.04
Trinidadian/Tobagonian (8)	8	0.04
West Indian (0)	9	0.04

Hispanic Origin	Population	%
Hispanic or Latino (of any race)	6,014	26.31
Central American, ex. Mexican	2,615	11.44
Costa Rican	19	0.08
Guatemalan	517	2.26
Honduran	371	1.62
Nicaraguan	138	0.60
Panamanian	15	0.07
Salvadoran	1,538	6.73
Other Central American	17	0.07
Cuban	58	0.25
Dominican Republic	64	0.28
Mexican	516	2.26
Puerto Rican	143	0.63
South American	1,754	7.67
Argentinean	62	0.27
Bolivian	1,003	4.39
Chilean	84	0.37
Colombian	111	0.49
Ecuadorian	40	0.18
Paraguayan	7	0.03
Peruvian	376	1.65
Uruguayan	15	0.07
Venezuelan	48	0.21
Other South American	8	0.04
Other Hispanic or Latino	864	3.78

Race*	Population	%
African-American/Black (4,761)	5,003	21.89
Not Hispanic (4,679)	4,880	21.35
Hispanic (82)	123	0.54
American Indian/Alaska Native (109)	256	1.12
Not Hispanic (42)	118	0.52
Hispanic (67)	138	0.60
Aleut *(Alaska Native)* (0)	2	0.01
Blackfeet (0)	6	0.03
Central American Ind. (9)	24	0.11
Cherokee (7)	20	0.09
Cheyenne (0)	1	<0.01
Choctaw (0)	2	0.01
Hopi (0)	1	<0.01
Houma (1)	1	<0.01
Inupiat *(Alaska Native)* (1)	1	<0.01
Iroquois (1)	5	0.02
Mexican American Ind. (11)	19	0.08
Navajo (3)	4	0.02
Osage (1)	1	<0.01
Ottawa (1)	1	<0.01
Pueblo (0)	1	<0.01
Seminole (1)	1	<0.01
Sioux (1)	3	0.01
South American Ind. (7)	9	0.04
Spanish American Ind. (1)	1	<0.01
Asian (3,492)	3,882	16.99
Not Hispanic (3,469)	3,829	16.75
Hispanic (23)	53	0.23
Bangladeshi (158)	176	0.77
Bhutanese (6)	6	0.03
Cambodian (62)	80	0.35
Chinese, ex. Taiwanese (270)	331	1.45
Filipino (281)	322	1.41
Indian (486)	542	2.37
Indonesian (27)	34	0.15
Japanese (42)	67	0.29
Korean (495)	532	2.33
Laotian (49)	51	0.22
Malaysian (2)	2	0.01
Nepalese (28)	29	0.13
Pakistani (562)	593	2.59
Sri Lankan (1)	2	0.01
Taiwanese (10)	15	0.07
Thai (101)	113	0.49
Vietnamese (735)	786	3.44
Hawaii Native/Pacific Islander (14)	56	0.25
Not Hispanic (10)	44	0.19
Hispanic (4)	12	0.05
Guamanian/Chamorro (8)	8	0.04
Native Hawaiian (4)	10	0.04
Samoan (2)	2	0.01
White (10,872)	11,628	50.88
Not Hispanic (7,979)	8,435	36.91
Hispanic (2,893)	3,193	13.97

Linton Hall

Place Type: CDP
County: Prince William
Population: 35,725†

Ancestry‡	Population	%
African, Sub-Saharan (738)	798	2.39
African (357)	417	1.25
Ethiopian (46)	46	0.14
Ghanaian (240)	240	0.72
Nigerian (12)	12	0.04
Somalian (21)	21	0.06
Sudanese (59)	59	0.18
Other Sub-Saharan African (3)	3	0.01
American (1,974)	1,974	5.90
Arab (188)	382	1.14
Arab (51)	132	0.39
Egyptian (38)	38	0.11
Jordanian (0)	13	0.04
Lebanese (51)	122	0.36
Palestinian (23)	36	0.11
Other Arab (25)	41	0.12
Armenian (13)	22	0.07
Austrian (26)	124	0.37
Brazilian (0)	9	0.03
British (164)	353	1.06
Canadian (20)	55	0.16
Croatian (11)	35	0.10
Czech (19)	191	0.57
Czechoslovakian (9)	9	0.03
Danish (32)	50	0.15
Dutch (0)	339	1.01
Eastern European (10)	10	0.03
English (725)	3,197	9.56
European (510)	552	1.65
Finnish (14)	50	0.15
French, ex. Basque (175)	994	2.97
French Canadian (63)	276	0.82
German (1,019)	5,234	15.64
German Russian (0)	11	0.03
Greek (117)	291	0.87
Guyanese (15)	15	0.04
Hungarian (35)	127	0.38
Iranian (196)	196	0.59
Irish (1,091)	4,949	14.79
Italian (575)	2,087	6.24
Lithuanian (11)	62	0.19
Northern European (44)	44	0.13
Norwegian (60)	177	0.53
Polish (253)	1,236	3.69
Portuguese (44)	53	0.16
Romanian (23)	46	0.14
Russian (73)	360	1.08
Scandinavian (0)	11	0.03
Scotch-Irish (310)	672	2.01
Scottish (200)	760	2.27
Slovak (12)	59	0.18
Swedish (97)	492	1.47
Turkish (51)	62	0.19
Ukrainian (56)	66	0.20
Welsh (16)	135	0.40
West Indian, ex. Hispanic (73)	171	0.51
Jamaican (24)	24	0.07
West Indian (49)	147	0.44
Yugoslavian (44)	44	0.13

Hispanic Origin	Population	%
Hispanic or Latino (of any race)	4,456	12.47
Central American, ex. Mexican	1,563	4.38
Costa Rican	40	0.11
Guatemalan	234	0.66
Honduran	97	0.27
Nicaraguan	106	0.30
Panamanian	80	0.22
Salvadoran	993	2.78
Other Central American	13	0.04
Cuban	88	0.25
Dominican Republic	91	0.25
Mexican	696	1.95

*Notes: † The Census 2010 population figure is used to calculate the percentages in the Hispanic Origin and Race categories. Ancestry percentages are based on the 2006-2010 American Community Survey population (not shown); ‡ Numbers in parentheses indicate the number of people reporting a single ancestry; * Numbers in parentheses indicate the number of persons reporting this race alone, not in combination with any other race; Please refer to the Explanation of Data for more information.*

Puerto Rican	490	1.37
South American	1,133	3.17
Argentinean	33	0.09
Bolivian	289	0.81
Chilean	30	0.08
Colombian	150	0.42
Ecuadorian	99	0.28
Paraguayan	5	0.01
Peruvian	430	1.20
Uruguayan	14	0.04
Venezuelan	71	0.20
Other South American	12	0.03
Other Hispanic or Latino	395	1.11

Race*	Population	%
African-American/Black (4,273)	4,932	13.81
Not Hispanic (4,136)	4,691	13.13
Hispanic (137)	241	0.67
American Indian/Alaska Native (147)	436	1.22
Not Hispanic (69)	238	0.67
Hispanic (78)	198	0.55
Apache (0)	4	0.01
Arapaho (0)	3	0.01
Blackfeet (0)	19	0.05
Central American Ind. (4)	5	0.01
Cherokee (9)	73	0.20
Chickasaw (2)	7	0.02
Chippewa (3)	4	0.01
Choctaw (4)	8	0.02
Comanche (0)	3	0.01
Cree (0)	1	<0.01
Creek (0)	1	<0.01
Iroquois (0)	10	0.03
Kiowa (0)	4	0.01
Lumbee (6)	10	0.03
Mexican American Ind. (5)	15	0.04
Navajo (0)	1	<0.01
Osage (0)	3	0.01
Pueblo (6)	7	0.02
Sioux (2)	4	0.01
South American Ind. (3)	11	0.03
Ute (0)	2	0.01
Yaqui (0)	4	0.01
Asian (3,935)	4,834	13.53
Not Hispanic (3,913)	4,731	13.24
Hispanic (22)	103	0.29
Bangladeshi (85)	88	0.25
Burmese (2)	2	0.01
Cambodian (70)	92	0.26
Chinese, ex. Taiwanese (365)	504	1.41
Filipino (534)	773	2.16
Hmong (4)	4	0.01
Indian (1,026)	1,156	3.24
Indonesian (27)	31	0.09
Japanese (51)	184	0.52
Korean (668)	799	2.24
Laotian (85)	110	0.31
Malaysian (2)	2	0.01
Nepalese (34)	39	0.11
Pakistani (291)	338	0.95
Sri Lankan (14)	18	0.05
Taiwanese (18)	23	0.06
Thai (43)	73	0.20
Vietnamese (431)	518	1.45
Hawaii Native/Pacific Islander (39)	125	0.35
Not Hispanic (16)	85	0.24
Hispanic (23)	40	0.11
Guamanian/Chamorro (27)	35	0.10
Native Hawaiian (6)	44	0.12
Samoan (0)	4	0.01
White (24,279)	25,851	72.36
Not Hispanic (21,661)	22,890	64.07
Hispanic (2,618)	2,961	8.29

Long Branch

Place Type: CDP
County: Fairfax
Population: 7,593†

Ancestry‡	Population	%
Afghan (0)	30	0.38
Alsatian (0)	12	0.15
American (376)	376	4.73
Arab (0)	139	1.75
Lebanese (0)	139	1.75
Armenian (42)	53	0.67
Austrian (0)	49	0.62
Belgian (11)	28	0.35
British (0)	49	0.62
Croatian (0)	128	1.61
Czech (0)	11	0.14
Danish (0)	42	0.53
Dutch (0)	54	0.68
English (320)	1,115	14.04
European (102)	109	1.37
French, ex. Basque (22)	277	3.49
French Canadian (14)	63	0.79
German (408)	1,494	18.81
Greek (0)	12	0.15
Guyanese (12)	12	0.15
Hungarian (30)	56	0.71
Iranian (49)	49	0.62
Irish (366)	986	12.41
Italian (104)	642	8.08
Latvian (0)	13	0.16
Lithuanian (0)	50	0.63
Northern European (13)	29	0.37
Norwegian (19)	178	2.24
Pennsylvania German (0)	14	0.18
Polish (75)	219	2.76
Portuguese (35)	35	0.44
Romanian (11)	36	0.45
Russian (123)	160	2.01
Scandinavian (26)	50	0.63
Scotch-Irish (66)	328	4.13
Scottish (47)	185	2.33
Serbian (47)	47	0.59
Slavic (0)	12	0.15
Slovak (14)	56	0.71
Swedish (12)	169	2.13
Swiss (52)	103	1.30
Ukrainian (0)	25	0.31
Welsh (0)	62	0.78

Hispanic Origin	Population	%
Hispanic or Latino (of any race)	555	7.31
Central American, ex. Mexican	127	1.67
Costa Rican	4	0.05
Guatemalan	45	0.59
Honduran	6	0.08
Nicaraguan	4	0.05
Panamanian	4	0.05
Salvadoran	64	0.84
Cuban	21	0.28
Dominican Republic	5	0.07
Mexican	78	1.03
Puerto Rican	31	0.41
South American	207	2.73
Argentinean	11	0.14
Bolivian	81	1.07
Chilean	4	0.05
Colombian	27	0.36
Ecuadorian	9	0.12
Paraguayan	4	0.05
Peruvian	57	0.75
Uruguayan	6	0.08
Venezuelan	3	0.04
Other South American	5	0.07
Other Hispanic or Latino	86	1.13

Race*	Population	%
African-American/Black (192)	229	3.02
Not Hispanic (187)	219	2.88
Hispanic (5)	10	0.13
American Indian/Alaska Native (21)	44	0.58
Not Hispanic (16)	32	0.42
Hispanic (5)	12	0.16
Apache (1)	1	0.01
Canadian/French Am. Ind. (3)	3	0.04
Cherokee (0)	6	0.08
Chippewa (1)	1	0.01
Choctaw (4)	9	0.12
Comanche (0)	2	0.03
Iroquois (1)	1	0.01
Mexican American Ind. (2)	6	0.08
Navajo (3)	3	0.04
South American Ind. (1)	1	0.01
Asian (1,654)	1,764	23.23
Not Hispanic (1,646)	1,746	22.99
Hispanic (8)	18	0.24
Bangladeshi (12)	12	0.16
Burmese (1)	2	0.03
Cambodian (7)	11	0.14
Chinese, ex. Taiwanese (282)	337	4.44
Filipino (62)	71	0.94
Indian (115)	137	1.80
Indonesian (14)	14	0.18
Japanese (15)	24	0.32
Korean (685)	704	9.27
Laotian (5)	5	0.07
Malaysian (1)	1	0.01
Nepalese (4)	4	0.05
Pakistani (24)	25	0.33
Sri Lankan (1)	4	0.05
Taiwanese (23)	32	0.42
Thai (7)	15	0.20
Vietnamese (361)	380	5.00
Hawaii Native/Pacific Islander (3)	14	0.18
Not Hispanic (3)	13	0.17
Hispanic (0)	1	0.01
Guamanian/Chamorro (0)	2	0.03
Native Hawaiian (3)	3	0.04
Samoan (0)	3	0.04
White (5,392)	5,551	73.11
Not Hispanic (5,014)	5,140	67.69
Hispanic (378)	411	5.41

Lorton

Place Type: CDP
County: Fairfax
Population: 18,610†

Ancestry‡	Population	%
Afghan (48)	85	0.44
African, Sub-Saharan (1,840)	1,879	9.75
African (517)	541	2.81
Ethiopian (598)	613	3.18
Ghanaian (238)	238	1.24
Liberian (38)	38	0.20
Sierra Leonean (46)	46	0.24
Somalian (280)	280	1.45
Other Sub-Saharan African (123)	123	0.64
American (435)	435	2.26
Arab (154)	154	0.80
Egyptian (89)	89	0.46
Lebanese (65)	65	0.34
Austrian (0)	33	0.17
British (0)	71	0.37
Bulgarian (20)	20	0.10
Cajun (37)	37	0.19
Croatian (0)	28	0.15
Czech (0)	70	0.36
Danish (21)	56	0.29
Dutch (50)	253	1.31
Eastern European (10)	10	0.05
English (408)	1,043	5.41
Estonian (27)	27	0.14
European (106)	190	0.99
Finnish (0)	6	0.03
French, ex. Basque (45)	242	1.26
French Canadian (51)	75	0.39
German (383)	1,268	6.58
Greek (9)	35	0.18
Hungarian (37)	70	0.36
Iranian (12)	12	0.06
Irish (259)	804	4.17
Italian (170)	498	2.59
Lithuanian (25)	25	0.13

*Notes: † The Census 2010 population figure is used to calculate the percentages in the Hispanic Origin and Race categories. Ancestry percentages are based on the 2006-2010 American Community Survey population (not shown); ‡ Numbers in parentheses indicate the number of people reporting a single ancestry; * Numbers in parentheses indicate the number of persons reporting this race alone, not in combination with any other race; Please refer to the Explanation of Data for more information.*

Ancestry	Population	%
Norwegian (0)	34	0.18
Polish (13)	210	1.09
Portuguese (45)	90	0.47
Russian (46)	75	0.39
Scotch-Irish (82)	137	0.71
Scottish (112)	333	1.73
Slavic (33)	70	0.36
Slovak (27)	27	0.14
Slovene (0)	16	0.08
Swedish (18)	33	0.17
Swiss (12)	12	0.06
Turkish (13)	13	0.07
Ukrainian (0)	110	0.57
Welsh (0)	32	0.17
West Indian, ex. Hispanic (114)	194	1.01
Jamaican (103)	183	0.95
Trinidadian/Tobagonian (11)	11	0.06

Hispanic Origin	Population	%
Hispanic or Latino (of any race)	3,116	16.74
Central American, ex. Mexican	1,347	7.24
Costa Rican	13	0.07
Guatemalan	113	0.61
Honduran	188	1.01
Nicaraguan	70	0.38
Panamanian	46	0.25
Salvadoran	912	4.90
Other Central American	5	0.03
Cuban	61	0.33
Dominican Republic	46	0.25
Mexican	329	1.77
Puerto Rican	262	1.41
South American	684	3.68
Argentinean	24	0.13
Bolivian	263	1.41
Chilean	26	0.14
Colombian	65	0.35
Ecuadorian	32	0.17
Paraguayan	3	0.02
Peruvian	242	1.30
Venezuelan	18	0.10
Other South American	11	0.06
Other Hispanic or Latino	387	2.08

Race*	Population	%
African-American/Black (5,571)	5,905	31.73
Not Hispanic (5,414)	5,683	30.54
Hispanic (157)	222	1.19
American Indian/Alaska Native (58)	164	0.88
Not Hispanic (32)	117	0.63
Hispanic (26)	47	0.25
Apache (1)	1	0.01
Blackfeet (0)	2	0.01
Central American Ind. (1)	1	0.01
Cherokee (2)	19	0.10
Chickasaw (1)	2	0.01
Chippewa (0)	3	0.02
Choctaw (3)	9	0.05
Cree (0)	1	0.01
Creek (1)	2	0.01
Iroquois (3)	5	0.03
Mexican American Ind. (1)	1	0.01
Pueblo (0)	2	0.01
Seminole (1)	2	0.01
Sioux (1)	5	0.03
South American Ind. (2)	3	0.02
Asian (3,386)	3,864	20.76
Not Hispanic (3,353)	3,806	20.45
Hispanic (33)	58	0.31
Bangladeshi (75)	87	0.47
Cambodian (15)	18	0.10
Chinese, ex. Taiwanese (188)	258	1.39
Filipino (505)	589	3.16
Indian (520)	591	3.18
Indonesian (10)	13	0.07
Japanese (29)	76	0.41
Korean (627)	705	3.79
Laotian (33)	40	0.21
Malaysian (1)	5	0.03
Nepalese (78)	80	0.43
Pakistani (561)	594	3.19
Sri Lankan (3)	3	0.02
Taiwanese (5)	8	0.04
Thai (53)	77	0.41
Vietnamese (508)	562	3.02
Hawaii Native/Pacific Islander (37)	91	0.49
Not Hispanic (33)	75	0.40
Hispanic (4)	16	0.09
Fijian (0)	2	0.01
Guamanian/Chamorro (9)	22	0.12
Native Hawaiian (9)	32	0.17
Samoan (6)	13	0.07
White (7,256)	8,003	43.00
Not Hispanic (5,864)	6,433	34.57
Hispanic (1,392)	1,570	8.44

Lowes Island

Place Type: CDP
County: Loudoun
Population: 10,756†

Ancestry‡	Population	%
African, Sub-Saharan (187)	241	2.12
African (22)	48	0.42
Nigerian (132)	160	1.40
Other Sub-Saharan African (33)	33	0.29
American (353)	353	3.10
Arab (181)	242	2.12
Iraqi (17)	17	0.15
Lebanese (31)	45	0.40
Other Arab (133)	180	1.58
Armenian (78)	78	0.68
Austrian (0)	31	0.27
Belgian (0)	10	0.09
British (58)	108	0.95
Bulgarian (0)	35	0.31
Canadian (87)	93	0.82
Czech (0)	56	0.49
Czechoslovakian (19)	19	0.17
Danish (0)	9	0.08
Dutch (41)	90	0.79
Eastern European (89)	122	1.07
English (347)	1,111	9.75
European (373)	373	3.27
Finnish (10)	10	0.09
French, ex. Basque (13)	168	1.47
French Canadian (13)	25	0.22
German (623)	1,969	17.29
Greek (32)	126	1.11
Hungarian (38)	145	1.27
Iranian (345)	360	3.16
Irish (467)	1,480	12.99
Israeli (0)	27	0.24
Italian (436)	1,298	11.40
Lithuanian (0)	12	0.11
Northern European (26)	66	0.58
Norwegian (0)	34	0.30
Polish (195)	588	5.16
Romanian (0)	64	0.56
Russian (62)	310	2.72
Scandinavian (0)	40	0.35
Scotch-Irish (90)	257	2.26
Scottish (0)	133	1.17
Slavic (0)	35	0.31
Slovak (0)	13	0.11
Slovene (0)	8	0.07
Swedish (16)	151	1.33
Swiss (0)	55	0.48
Ukrainian (25)	25	0.22
Welsh (0)	118	1.04
West Indian, ex. Hispanic (16)	16	0.14
Haitian (16)	16	0.14
Yugoslavian (9)	9	0.08

Hispanic Origin	Population	%
Hispanic or Latino (of any race)	680	6.32
Central American, ex. Mexican	146	1.36
Costa Rican	3	0.03
Guatemalan	21	0.20
Honduran	25	0.23
Nicaraguan	11	0.10
Panamanian	9	0.08
Salvadoran	77	0.72
Cuban	29	0.27
Dominican Republic	10	0.09
Mexican	138	1.28
Puerto Rican	52	0.48
South American	254	2.36
Argentinean	9	0.08
Bolivian	42	0.39
Chilean	33	0.31
Colombian	43	0.40
Ecuadorian	18	0.17
Paraguayan	1	0.01
Peruvian	88	0.82
Uruguayan	5	0.05
Venezuelan	15	0.14
Other Hispanic or Latino	51	0.47

Race*	Population	%
African-American/Black (497)	580	5.39
Not Hispanic (487)	565	5.25
Hispanic (10)	15	0.14
American Indian/Alaska Native (31)	75	0.70
Not Hispanic (17)	55	0.51
Hispanic (14)	20	0.19
Blackfeet (0)	2	0.02
Cherokee (1)	14	0.13
Chickasaw (4)	4	0.04
Chippewa (0)	1	0.01
Inupiat *(Alaska Native)* (2)	2	0.02
Lumbee (0)	4	0.04
Mexican American Ind. (3)	6	0.06
Osage (1)	1	0.01
Potawatomi (1)	1	0.01
Sioux (0)	1	0.01
South American Ind. (11)	11	0.10
Asian (1,585)	1,892	17.59
Not Hispanic (1,580)	1,880	17.48
Hispanic (5)	12	0.11
Bangladeshi (38)	41	0.38
Burmese (1)	1	0.01
Cambodian (8)	9	0.08
Chinese, ex. Taiwanese (286)	330	3.07
Filipino (93)	129	1.20
Indian (575)	615	5.72
Indonesian (16)	16	0.15
Japanese (24)	45	0.42
Korean (217)	252	2.34
Laotian (9)	17	0.16
Malaysian (2)	2	0.02
Nepalese (6)	6	0.06
Pakistani (87)	97	0.90
Sri Lankan (7)	8	0.07
Taiwanese (17)	19	0.18
Thai (14)	29	0.27
Vietnamese (130)	164	1.52
Hawaii Native/Pacific Islander (6)	22	0.20
Not Hispanic (6)	22	0.20
Fijian (0)	1	0.01
Guamanian/Chamorro (5)	13	0.12
Samoan (1)	1	0.01
White (8,072)	8,488	78.91
Not Hispanic (7,559)	7,931	73.74
Hispanic (513)	557	5.18

Lynchburg

Place Type: Independent City
County: Lynchburg
Population: 75,568†

Ancestry‡	Population	%
African, Sub-Saharan (378)	441	0.60
African (283)	320	0.43
Ethiopian (41)	41	0.06
Kenyan (44)	44	0.06
Nigerian (0)	15	0.02
South African (0)	11	0.01

*Notes: † The Census 2010 population figure is used to calculate the percentages in the Hispanic Origin and Race categories. Ancestry percentages are based on the 2006-2010 American Community Survey population (not shown); ‡ Numbers in parentheses indicate the number of people reporting a single ancestry; * Numbers in parentheses indicate the number of persons reporting this race alone, not in combination with any other race; Please refer to the Explanation of Data for more information.*

Ancestry (continued)	Population	%
Other Sub-Saharan African (10)	10	0.01
American (6,756)	6,756	9.16
Arab (12)	186	0.25
Egyptian (12)	72	0.10
Lebanese (0)	85	0.12
Palestinian (0)	29	0.04
Armenian (28)	28	0.04
Australian (0)	8	0.01
Austrian (22)	117	0.16
Belgian (8)	27	0.04
Brazilian (13)	28	0.04
British (230)	538	0.73
Bulgarian (26)	26	0.04
Cajun (0)	14	0.02
Canadian (129)	187	0.25
Croatian (0)	27	0.04
Czech (36)	245	0.33
Czechoslovakian (24)	42	0.06
Danish (89)	182	0.25
Dutch (177)	911	1.24
Eastern European (11)	11	0.01
English (4,421)	10,448	14.17
Estonian (44)	60	0.08
European (1,087)	1,281	1.74
Finnish (48)	62	0.08
French, ex. Basque (338)	1,740	2.36
French Canadian (64)	253	0.34
German (2,844)	10,118	13.72
Greek (56)	358	0.49
Hungarian (68)	294	0.40
Iranian (72)	99	0.13
Irish (2,523)	7,852	10.65
Italian (467)	2,183	2.96
Latvian (25)	25	0.03
Lithuanian (28)	120	0.16
Macedonian (0)	70	0.09
Northern European (58)	66	0.09
Norwegian (203)	636	0.86
Polish (108)	846	1.15
Portuguese (46)	86	0.12
Russian (194)	319	0.43
Scandinavian (14)	14	0.02
Scotch-Irish (996)	2,370	3.21
Scottish (712)	2,107	2.86
Slavic (0)	24	0.03
Slovak (61)	119	0.16
Slovene (0)	55	0.07
Swedish (127)	786	1.07
Swiss (52)	146	0.20
Ukrainian (84)	213	0.29
Welsh (84)	580	0.79
West Indian, ex. Hispanic (189)	336	0.46
Bahamian (9)	9	0.01
Barbadian (0)	15	0.02
Bermudan (3)	3	<0.01
Haitian (25)	40	0.05
Jamaican (57)	148	0.20
Trinidadian/Tobagonian (0)	14	0.02
West Indian (95)	107	0.15
Yugoslavian (0)	81	0.11

Hispanic Origin	Population	%
Hispanic or Latino (of any race)	2,300	3.04
Central American, ex. Mexican	289	0.38
Costa Rican	3	<0.01
Guatemalan	71	0.09
Honduran	84	0.11
Nicaraguan	11	0.01
Panamanian	7	0.01
Salvadoran	112	0.15
Other Central American	1	<0.01
Cuban	90	0.12
Dominican Republic	35	0.05
Mexican	836	1.11
Puerto Rican	396	0.52
South American	203	0.27
Argentinean	28	0.04
Bolivian	5	0.01
Chilean	23	0.03
Colombian	47	0.06
Ecuadorian	17	0.02
Paraguayan	6	0.01
Peruvian	43	0.06
Uruguayan	4	0.01
Venezuelan	28	0.04
Other South American	2	<0.01
Other Hispanic or Latino	451	0.60

Race*	Population	%
African-American/Black (22,140)	23,229	30.74
Not Hispanic (21,984)	23,014	30.45
Hispanic (156)	215	0.28
American Indian/Alaska Native (237)	714	0.94
Not Hispanic (200)	635	0.84
Hispanic (37)	79	0.10
Apache (0)	4	0.01
Blackfeet (2)	12	0.02
Canadian/French Am. Ind. (0)	1	<0.01
Central American Ind. (1)	1	<0.01
Cherokee (22)	193	0.26
Chickasaw (1)	8	0.01
Chippewa (3)	5	0.01
Choctaw (3)	14	0.02
Cree (0)	2	<0.01
Creek (0)	1	<0.01
Crow (0)	1	<0.01
Delaware (4)	5	0.01
Inupiat *(Alaska Native)* (0)	1	<0.01
Iroquois (6)	20	0.03
Lumbee (5)	5	0.01
Menominee (0)	1	<0.01
Mexican American Ind. (2)	5	0.01
Navajo (4)	7	0.01
Ottawa (2)	2	<0.01
Paiute (0)	1	<0.01
Potawatomi (3)	3	<0.01
Seminole (2)	2	<0.01
Sioux (3)	8	0.01
South American Ind. (1)	1	<0.01
Yup'ik *(Alaska Native)* (1)	3	<0.01
Asian (1,868)	2,145	2.84
Not Hispanic (1,852)	2,104	2.78
Hispanic (16)	41	0.05
Bangladeshi (22)	22	0.03
Burmese (10)	10	0.01
Cambodian (2)	2	<0.01
Chinese, ex. Taiwanese (229)	275	0.36
Filipino (152)	224	0.30
Hmong (1)	1	<0.01
Indian (391)	431	0.57
Indonesian (4)	7	0.01
Japanese (29)	58	0.08
Korean (577)	618	0.82
Laotian (1)	1	<0.01
Malaysian (7)	8	0.01
Nepalese (14)	19	0.03
Pakistani (48)	61	0.08
Sri Lankan (5)	6	0.01
Taiwanese (13)	17	0.02
Thai (18)	33	0.04
Vietnamese (80)	93	0.12
Hawaii Native/Pacific Islander (37)	88	0.12
Not Hispanic (27)	68	0.09
Hispanic (10)	20	0.03
Fijian (1)	1	<0.01
Guamanian/Chamorro (10)	13	0.02
Native Hawaiian (3)	20	0.03
Samoan (7)	13	0.02
Tongan (1)	1	<0.01
White (48,674)	50,079	66.27
Not Hispanic (47,574)	48,812	64.59
Hispanic (1,100)	1,267	1.68

Madison Heights

Place Type: CDP
County: Amherst
Population: 11,285†

Ancestry‡	Population	%
African, Sub-Saharan (8)	88	0.80
African (8)	8	0.07
Ghanaian (0)	32	0.29
Nigerian (0)	48	0.43
American (1,856)	1,856	16.82
Austrian (0)	17	0.15
Belgian (8)	8	0.07
British (28)	28	0.25
Czech (0)	12	0.11
Dutch (85)	177	1.60
English (364)	794	7.19
European (131)	131	1.19
French, ex. Basque (66)	301	2.73
French Canadian (15)	36	0.33
German (261)	816	7.39
Greek (7)	31	0.28
Hungarian (13)	13	0.12
Irish (410)	1,138	10.31
Italian (106)	256	2.32
Polish (54)	198	1.79
Russian (0)	62	0.56
Scotch-Irish (112)	266	2.41
Scottish (121)	356	3.23
Slovak (0)	8	0.07
Swedish (17)	37	0.34
Swiss (11)	16	0.14
Ukrainian (0)	9	0.08
Welsh (31)	66	0.60

Hispanic Origin	Population	%
Hispanic or Latino (of any race)	176	1.56
Central American, ex. Mexican	12	0.11
Costa Rican	4	0.04
Honduran	8	0.07
Cuban	5	0.04
Mexican	103	0.91
Puerto Rican	18	0.16
South American	11	0.10
Argentinean	9	0.08
Bolivian	2	0.02
Other Hispanic or Latino	27	0.24

Race*	Population	%
African-American/Black (2,453)	2,628	23.29
Not Hispanic (2,437)	2,608	23.11
Hispanic (16)	20	0.18
American Indian/Alaska Native (99)	193	1.71
Not Hispanic (99)	190	1.68
Hispanic (0)	3	0.03
Apache (1)	1	0.01
Blackfeet (1)	4	0.04
Cherokee (16)	46	0.41
Choctaw (1)	1	0.01
Iroquois (0)	1	0.01
Menominee (3)	4	0.04
Potawatomi (2)	2	0.02
Sioux (0)	4	0.04
Asian (79)	110	0.97
Not Hispanic (78)	107	0.95
Hispanic (1)	3	0.03
Bangladeshi (0)	2	0.02
Chinese, ex. Taiwanese (12)	16	0.14
Filipino (12)	18	0.16
Indian (25)	29	0.26
Indonesian (0)	3	0.03
Japanese (4)	10	0.09
Korean (3)	9	0.08
Laotian (1)	3	0.03
Taiwanese (1)	1	0.01
Vietnamese (15)	15	0.13
Hawaii Native/Pacific Islander (5)	11	0.10
Not Hispanic (5)	11	0.10
Fijian (4)	4	0.04
Guamanian/Chamorro (1)	1	0.01
Native Hawaiian (0)	2	0.02
Samoan (0)	3	0.03
White (8,314)	8,538	75.66
Not Hispanic (8,225)	8,439	74.78
Hispanic (89)	99	0.88

*Notes: † The Census 2010 population figure is used to calculate the percentages in the Hispanic Origin and Race categories. Ancestry percentages are based on the 2006-2010 American Community Survey population (not shown); ‡ Numbers in parentheses indicate the number of people reporting a single ancestry; * Numbers in parentheses indicate the number of persons reporting this race alone, not in combination with any other race; Please refer to the Explanation of Data for more information.*

Manassas Park

Place Type: Independent City
County: Manassas Park
Population: 14,273†

Ancestry‡	Population	%
Afghan (159)	159	1.21
African, Sub-Saharan (236)	290	2.20
African (112)	166	1.26
Ethiopian (40)	40	0.30
Ghanaian (84)	84	0.64
American (783)	783	5.93
Arab (124)	144	1.09
Arab (107)	127	0.96
Moroccan (17)	17	0.13
Armenian (23)	23	0.17
British (44)	44	0.33
Czech (0)	12	0.09
Czechoslovakian (10)	10	0.08
Danish (0)	21	0.16
Dutch (21)	190	1.44
English (280)	689	5.22
European (131)	200	1.52
French, ex. Basque (0)	62	0.47
German (149)	1,255	9.51
Greek (31)	64	0.49
Hungarian (16)	16	0.12
Irish (301)	960	7.28
Italian (47)	310	2.35
Lithuanian (0)	34	0.26
Northern European (14)	14	0.11
Norwegian (22)	146	1.11
Polish (25)	128	0.97
Portuguese (17)	27	0.20
Romanian (42)	42	0.32
Russian (0)	11	0.08
Scandinavian (11)	30	0.23
Scotch-Irish (77)	160	1.21
Scottish (8)	153	1.16
Slavic (0)	20	0.15
Slovak (9)	33	0.25
Swedish (9)	73	0.55
Swiss (45)	112	0.85
Turkish (16)	16	0.12
Ukrainian (0)	20	0.15
West Indian, ex. Hispanic (36)	36	0.27
Jamaican (36)	36	0.27

Hispanic Origin	Population	%
Hispanic or Latino (of any race)	4,645	32.54
Central American, ex. Mexican	2,459	17.23
Costa Rican	5	0.04
Guatemalan	428	3.00
Honduran	198	1.39
Nicaraguan	56	0.39
Panamanian	22	0.15
Salvadoran	1,724	12.08
Other Central American	26	0.18
Cuban	41	0.29
Dominican Republic	55	0.39
Mexican	947	6.63
Puerto Rican	161	1.13
South American	481	3.37
Argentinean	14	0.10
Bolivian	180	1.26
Chilean	10	0.07
Colombian	51	0.36
Ecuadorian	39	0.27
Peruvian	168	1.18
Uruguayan	6	0.04
Venezuelan	13	0.09
Other Hispanic or Latino	501	3.51

Race*	Population	%
African-American/Black (1,852)	2,115	14.82
Not Hispanic (1,784)	1,984	13.90
Hispanic (68)	131	0.92
American Indian/Alaska Native (56)	152	1.06
Not Hispanic (31)	93	0.65
Hispanic (25)	59	0.41
Apache (1)	1	0.01
Arapaho (1)	1	0.01
Blackfeet (0)	1	0.01
Central American Ind. (3)	3	0.02
Cherokee (6)	23	0.16
Chickasaw (1)	1	0.01
Chippewa (0)	1	0.01
Choctaw (1)	5	0.04
Comanche (0)	2	0.01
Creek (4)	4	0.03
Iroquois (2)	5	0.04
Lumbee (6)	8	0.06
Mexican American Ind. (2)	7	0.05
Seminole (0)	1	0.01
Sioux (0)	2	0.01
South American Ind. (9)	15	0.11
Spanish American Ind. (0)	1	0.01
Yaqui (1)	1	0.01
Asian (1,281)	1,498	10.50
Not Hispanic (1,261)	1,453	10.18
Hispanic (20)	45	0.32
Bangladeshi (20)	21	0.15
Burmese (3)	3	0.02
Cambodian (62)	64	0.45
Chinese, ex. Taiwanese (137)	166	1.16
Filipino (246)	296	2.07
Indian (243)	263	1.84
Indonesian (3)	3	0.02
Japanese (8)	28	0.20
Korean (135)	168	1.18
Laotian (22)	30	0.21
Nepalese (14)	14	0.10
Pakistani (101)	109	0.76
Sri Lankan (4)	4	0.03
Taiwanese (5)	6	0.04
Thai (22)	22	0.15
Vietnamese (209)	238	1.67
Hawaii Native/Pacific Islander (20)	38	0.27
Not Hispanic (17)	29	0.20
Hispanic (3)	9	0.06
Guamanian/Chamorro (17)	26	0.18
Native Hawaiian (1)	5	0.04
Samoan (1)	1	0.01
White (7,985)	8,641	60.54
Not Hispanic (6,070)	6,430	45.05
Hispanic (1,915)	2,211	15.49

Manassas

Place Type: Independent City
County: Manassas
Population: 37,821†

Ancestry‡	Population	%
Afghan (0)	35	0.10
African, Sub-Saharan (463)	533	1.48
African (314)	372	1.03
Nigerian (149)	149	0.41
South African (0)	12	0.03
American (2,399)	2,399	6.65
Arab (221)	363	1.01
Arab (197)	197	0.55
Lebanese (24)	138	0.38
Moroccan (0)	10	0.03
Syrian (0)	8	0.02
Other Arab (0)	10	0.03
Armenian (11)	20	0.06
Australian (61)	61	0.17
Austrian (10)	95	0.26
Brazilian (42)	42	0.12
British (21)	66	0.18
Cajun (0)	22	0.06
Canadian (107)	178	0.49
Croatian (15)	15	0.04
Czech (43)	67	0.19
Czechoslovakian (44)	88	0.24
Danish (8)	113	0.31
Dutch (93)	330	0.91
Eastern European (51)	51	0.14
English (1,070)	3,105	8.61
European (332)	497	1.38
Finnish (15)	41	0.11
French, ex. Basque (46)	479	1.33
French Canadian (103)	271	0.75
German (1,032)	4,744	13.15
Greek (15)	78	0.22
Hungarian (0)	28	0.08
Iranian (11)	11	0.03
Irish (1,041)	4,410	12.23
Italian (606)	1,270	3.52
Lithuanian (0)	78	0.22
Luxemburger (13)	13	0.04
New Zealander (0)	18	0.05
Northern European (0)	9	0.02
Norwegian (58)	205	0.57
Pennsylvania German (14)	14	0.04
Polish (234)	873	2.42
Portuguese (70)	104	0.29
Romanian (66)	66	0.18
Russian (79)	153	0.42
Scandinavian (16)	76	0.21
Scotch-Irish (291)	696	1.93
Scottish (258)	692	1.92
Serbian (16)	16	0.04
Slavic (10)	10	0.03
Slovak (30)	43	0.12
Slovene (0)	7	0.02
Swedish (43)	193	0.54
Swiss (0)	134	0.37
Turkish (131)	131	0.36
Ukrainian (91)	150	0.42
Welsh (51)	222	0.62
West Indian, ex. Hispanic (97)	159	0.44
Haitian (35)	35	0.10
Jamaican (0)	14	0.04
Trinidadian/Tobagonian (46)	56	0.16
U.S. Virgin Islander (16)	16	0.04
West Indian (0)	38	0.11

Hispanic Origin	Population	%
Hispanic or Latino (of any race)	11,876	31.40
Central American, ex. Mexican	5,529	14.62
Costa Rican	20	0.05
Guatemalan	708	1.87
Honduran	657	1.74
Nicaraguan	177	0.47
Panamanian	71	0.19
Salvadoran	3,870	10.23
Other Central American	26	0.07
Cuban	64	0.17
Dominican Republic	101	0.27
Mexican	3,754	9.93
Puerto Rican	417	1.10
South American	924	2.44
Argentinean	54	0.14
Bolivian	233	0.62
Chilean	14	0.04
Colombian	122	0.32
Ecuadorian	68	0.18
Paraguayan	6	0.02
Peruvian	369	0.98
Uruguayan	28	0.07
Venezuelan	26	0.07
Other South American	4	0.01
Other Hispanic or Latino	1,087	2.87

Race*	Population	%
African-American/Black (5,188)	5,947	15.72
Not Hispanic (4,905)	5,490	14.52
Hispanic (283)	457	1.21
American Indian/Alaska Native (229)	505	1.34
Not Hispanic (99)	270	0.71
Hispanic (130)	235	0.62
Apache (2)	3	0.01
Blackfeet (0)	8	0.02
Canadian/French Am. Ind. (1)	2	0.01
Central American Ind. (1)	3	0.01
Cherokee (12)	62	0.16
Cheyenne (0)	2	0.01

*Notes: † The Census 2010 population figure is used to calculate the percentages in the Hispanic Origin and Race categories. Ancestry percentages are based on the 2006-2010 American Community Survey population (not shown); ‡ Numbers in parentheses indicate the number of people reporting a single ancestry; * Numbers in parentheses indicate the number of persons reporting this race alone, not in combination with any other race; Please refer to the Explanation of Data for more information.*

Chippewa (6)	7	0.02
Choctaw (3)	5	0.01
Cree (0)	1	<0.01
Creek (0)	2	0.01
Crow (0)	3	0.01
Delaware (0)	4	0.01
Hopi (0)	1	<0.01
Iroquois (2)	8	0.02
Lumbee (3)	5	0.01
Mexican American Ind. (24)	37	0.10
Navajo (2)	3	0.01
Osage (0)	1	<0.01
Potawatomi (0)	4	0.01
Pueblo (5)	8	0.02
Seminole (0)	7	0.02
Sioux (3)	5	0.01
South American Ind. (2)	12	0.03
Spanish American Ind. (11)	11	0.03
Yaqui (1)	1	<0.01
Yuman (1)	1	<0.01
Asian (1,884)	2,236	5.91
Not Hispanic (1,861)	2,159	5.71
Hispanic (23)	77	0.20
Bangladeshi (7)	15	0.04
Burmese (8)	9	0.02
Cambodian (83)	103	0.27
Chinese, ex. Taiwanese (161)	204	0.54
Filipino (400)	516	1.36
Indian (352)	413	1.09
Indonesian (12)	20	0.05
Japanese (34)	85	0.22
Korean (127)	171	0.45
Laotian (97)	102	0.27
Malaysian (0)	1	<0.01
Nepalese (29)	29	0.08
Pakistani (131)	132	0.35
Sri Lankan (5)	8	0.02
Taiwanese (5)	5	0.01
Thai (21)	31	0.08
Vietnamese (323)	346	0.91
Hawaii Native/Pacific Islander (52)	97	0.26
Not Hispanic (41)	81	0.21
Hispanic (11)	16	0.04
Guamanian/Chamorro (31)	49	0.13
Native Hawaiian (4)	20	0.05
Samoan (1)	9	0.02
White (23,336)	24,693	65.29
Not Hispanic (17,994)	18,779	49.65
Hispanic (5,342)	5,914	15.64

Manchester

Place Type: CDP
County: Chesterfield
Population: 10,804†

Ancestry‡	Population	%
African, Sub-Saharan (84)	116	1.05
African (38)	70	0.63
Nigerian (46)	46	0.42
American (742)	742	6.70
Arab (71)	185	1.67
Arab (11)	34	0.31
Egyptian (33)	71	0.64
Lebanese (0)	22	0.20
Syrian (0)	15	0.14
Other Arab (27)	43	0.39
Australian (12)	26	0.23
British (58)	58	0.52
Croatian (11)	11	0.10
Czech (10)	52	0.47
Dutch (61)	103	0.93
English (687)	1,291	11.66
European (22)	38	0.34
French, ex. Basque (60)	282	2.55
German (363)	1,103	9.96
Greek (36)	59	0.53
Hungarian (25)	25	0.23
Irish (331)	1,199	10.83
Italian (171)	548	4.95
Lithuanian (13)	48	0.43
Norwegian (12)	12	0.11
Polish (52)	88	0.79
Russian (0)	62	0.56
Scandinavian (16)	44	0.40
Scotch-Irish (143)	260	2.35
Scottish (13)	109	0.98
Slovak (0)	43	0.39
Swedish (7)	36	0.33
Ukrainian (24)	76	0.69
Welsh (16)	102	0.92
West Indian, ex. Hispanic (78)	186	1.68
Jamaican (11)	11	0.10
Trinidadian/Tobagonian (21)	21	0.19
West Indian (46)	154	1.39

Hispanic Origin	Population	%
Hispanic or Latino (of any race)	1,436	13.29
Central American, ex. Mexican	556	5.15
Costa Rican	9	0.08
Guatemalan	198	1.83
Honduran	76	0.70
Nicaraguan	18	0.17
Panamanian	10	0.09
Salvadoran	235	2.18
Other Central American	10	0.09
Cuban	20	0.19
Dominican Republic	44	0.41
Mexican	458	4.24
Puerto Rican	117	1.08
South American	78	0.72
Argentinean	2	0.02
Bolivian	1	0.01
Chilean	1	0.01
Colombian	45	0.42
Ecuadorian	12	0.11
Peruvian	13	0.12
Venezuelan	1	0.01
Other South American	3	0.03
Other Hispanic or Latino	163	1.51

Race*	Population	%
African-American/Black (3,438)	3,609	33.40
Not Hispanic (3,386)	3,530	32.67
Hispanic (52)	79	0.73
American Indian/Alaska Native (69)	160	1.48
Not Hispanic (21)	85	0.79
Hispanic (48)	75	0.69
Aleut *(Alaska Native)* (1)	1	0.01
Blackfeet (0)	3	0.03
Canadian/French Am. Ind. (1)	1	0.01
Central American Ind. (2)	2	0.02
Cherokee (2)	27	0.25
Chippewa (0)	3	0.03
Choctaw (1)	2	0.02
Iroquois (0)	1	0.01
Lumbee (1)	5	0.05
Mexican American Ind. (25)	30	0.28
Navajo (0)	3	0.03
Sioux (1)	2	0.02
South American Ind. (3)	3	0.03
Spanish American Ind. (1)	1	0.01
Asian (317)	382	3.54
Not Hispanic (313)	375	3.47
Hispanic (4)	7	0.06
Cambodian (30)	35	0.32
Chinese, ex. Taiwanese (32)	39	0.36
Filipino (24)	45	0.42
Indian (77)	82	0.76
Indonesian (1)	1	0.01
Japanese (3)	3	0.03
Korean (71)	88	0.81
Nepalese (3)	3	0.03
Pakistani (22)	22	0.20
Taiwanese (1)	2	0.02
Thai (3)	5	0.05
Vietnamese (41)	50	0.46
Hawaii Native/Pacific Islander (13)	35	0.32
Not Hispanic (7)	27	0.25
Hispanic (6)	8	0.07
Guamanian/Chamorro (11)	11	0.10
Native Hawaiian (2)	14	0.13
Samoan (0)	1	0.01
White (5,919)	6,184	57.24
Not Hispanic (5,390)	5,552	51.39
Hispanic (529)	632	5.85

Martinsville

Place Type: Independent City
County: Martinsville
Population: 13,821†

Ancestry‡	Population	%
African, Sub-Saharan (181)	181	1.29
African (149)	149	1.06
Ethiopian (32)	32	0.23
American (1,408)	1,408	10.04
Arab (31)	31	0.22
Lebanese (31)	31	0.22
Armenian (53)	53	0.38
British (19)	51	0.36
Canadian (8)	8	0.06
Czech (0)	34	0.24
Czechoslovakian (18)	18	0.13
Danish (0)	9	0.06
Dutch (7)	75	0.53
Eastern European (15)	15	0.11
English (841)	1,447	10.31
European (36)	36	0.26
French, ex. Basque (59)	191	1.36
German (254)	931	6.64
Greek (10)	10	0.07
Hungarian (9)	9	0.06
Iranian (42)	42	0.30
Irish (307)	1,024	7.30
Italian (77)	219	1.56
Lithuanian (0)	8	0.06
Norwegian (38)	74	0.53
Polish (21)	97	0.69
Portuguese (0)	27	0.19
Russian (9)	27	0.19
Scotch-Irish (146)	324	2.31
Scottish (142)	208	1.48
Swiss (0)	9	0.06
Welsh (14)	70	0.50
West Indian, ex. Hispanic (36)	77	0.55
Barbadian (5)	5	0.04
Jamaican (0)	33	0.24
West Indian (31)	39	0.28
Yugoslavian (42)	42	0.30

Hispanic Origin	Population	%
Hispanic or Latino (of any race)	552	3.99
Central American, ex. Mexican	60	0.43
Guatemalan	3	0.02
Honduran	4	0.03
Nicaraguan	6	0.04
Salvadoran	47	0.34
Dominican Republic	12	0.09
Mexican	380	2.75
Puerto Rican	41	0.30
South American	19	0.14
Colombian	7	0.05
Ecuadorian	2	0.01
Peruvian	3	0.02
Venezuelan	7	0.05
Other Hispanic or Latino	40	0.29

Race*	Population	%
African-American/Black (6,213)	6,403	46.33
Not Hispanic (6,191)	6,367	46.07
Hispanic (22)	36	0.26
American Indian/Alaska Native (27)	72	0.52
Not Hispanic (18)	61	0.44
Hispanic (9)	11	0.08
Blackfeet (0)	6	0.04
Cherokee (1)	13	0.09
Inupiat *(Alaska Native)* (0)	2	0.01
Asian (129)	153	1.11

SECTION TWO

*Notes: † The Census 2010 population figure is used to calculate the percentages in the Hispanic Origin and Race categories. Ancestry percentages are based on the 2006-2010 American Community Survey population (not shown); ‡ Numbers in parentheses indicate the number of people reporting a single ancestry; * Numbers in parentheses indicate the number of persons reporting this race alone, not in combination with any other race; Please refer to the Explanation of Data for more information.*

Not Hispanic (127)	146	1.06
Hispanic (2)	7	0.05
Chinese, ex. Taiwanese (21)	24	0.17
Filipino (13)	21	0.15
Indian (33)	34	0.25
Japanese (9)	10	0.07
Korean (2)	7	0.05
Pakistani (9)	9	0.07
Vietnamese (33)	35	0.25
Hawaii Native/Pacific Islander (1)	10	0.07
Not Hispanic (0)	9	0.07
Hispanic (1)	1	0.01
Native Hawaiian (0)	1	0.01
Samoan (1)	3	0.02
Tongan (0)	1	0.01
White (6,903)	7,134	51.62
Not Hispanic (6,707)	6,896	49.90
Hispanic (196)	238	1.72

Marumsco

Place Type: CDP
County: Prince William
Population: 35,036†

Ancestry‡	Population	%
Afghan (26)	26	0.08
African, Sub-Saharan (694)	835	2.58
African (189)	208	0.64
Cape Verdean (76)	76	0.23
Ethiopian (28)	28	0.09
Ghanaian (224)	346	1.07
Liberian (17)	17	0.05
Somalian (160)	160	0.49
American (1,346)	1,346	4.15
Arab (43)	188	0.58
Arab (23)	45	0.14
Lebanese (0)	26	0.08
Syrian (0)	8	0.02
Other Arab (20)	109	0.34
Armenian (43)	43	0.13
Australian (0)	19	0.06
Austrian (3)	14	0.04
Brazilian (50)	79	0.24
British (0)	18	0.06
Canadian (0)	26	0.08
Czech (0)	8	0.02
Czechoslovakian (0)	13	0.04
Danish (10)	50	0.15
Dutch (10)	197	0.61
Eastern European (14)	14	0.04
English (387)	1,301	4.01
European (119)	119	0.37
Finnish (14)	31	0.10
French, ex. Basque (14)	238	0.73
French Canadian (36)	103	0.32
German (785)	2,529	7.80
Greek (0)	66	0.20
Hungarian (0)	6	0.02
Iranian (63)	80	0.25
Irish (527)	1,588	4.90
Italian (193)	635	1.96
Lithuanian (16)	28	0.09
Norwegian (68)	93	0.29
Polish (176)	450	1.39
Portuguese (218)	218	0.67
Romanian (10)	10	0.03
Russian (83)	139	0.43
Scandinavian (8)	8	0.02
Scotch-Irish (114)	282	0.87
Scottish (153)	243	0.75
Slovak (9)	19	0.06
Swedish (0)	51	0.16
Swiss (0)	40	0.12
Ukrainian (0)	23	0.07
Welsh (44)	138	0.43
West Indian, ex. Hispanic (151)	176	0.54
Haitian (46)	46	0.14
Trinidadian/Tobagonian (18)	18	0.06
West Indian (87)	112	0.35

Hispanic Origin	Population	%
Hispanic or Latino (of any race)	14,372	41.02
Central American, ex. Mexican	8,223	23.47
Costa Rican	17	0.05
Guatemalan	594	1.70
Honduran	973	2.78
Nicaraguan	255	0.73
Panamanian	72	0.21
Salvadoran	6,261	17.87
Other Central American	51	0.15
Cuban	73	0.21
Dominican Republic	137	0.39
Mexican	2,729	7.79
Puerto Rican	669	1.91
South American	1,194	3.41
Argentinean	60	0.17
Bolivian	327	0.93
Chilean	30	0.09
Colombian	111	0.32
Ecuadorian	80	0.23
Paraguayan	5	0.01
Peruvian	509	1.45
Uruguayan	22	0.06
Venezuelan	45	0.13
Other South American	5	0.01
Other Hispanic or Latino	1,347	3.84

Race*	Population	%
African-American/Black (7,833)	8,709	24.86
Not Hispanic (7,474)	8,155	23.28
Hispanic (359)	554	1.58
American Indian/Alaska Native (316)	740	2.11
Not Hispanic (87)	333	0.95
Hispanic (229)	407	1.16
Apache (1)	1	<0.01
Blackfeet (0)	9	0.03
Canadian/French Am. Ind. (0)	5	0.01
Central American Ind. (10)	14	0.04
Cherokee (4)	49	0.14
Cheyenne (4)	5	0.01
Chickasaw (1)	5	0.01
Chippewa (3)	6	0.02
Choctaw (1)	4	0.01
Colville (0)	1	<0.01
Delaware (1)	1	<0.01
Houma (0)	1	<0.01
Inupiat *(Alaska Native)* (2)	4	0.01
Iroquois (3)	11	0.03
Kiowa (0)	1	<0.01
Lumbee (6)	6	0.02
Mexican American Ind. (15)	32	0.09
Navajo (1)	2	0.01
Pima (1)	1	<0.01
Potawatomi (1)	1	<0.01
Pueblo (1)	3	0.01
Seminole (1)	1	<0.01
Sioux (7)	12	0.03
South American Ind. (6)	13	0.04
Spanish American Ind. (9)	12	0.03
Asian (2,381)	2,812	8.03
Not Hispanic (2,346)	2,720	7.76
Hispanic (35)	92	0.26
Bangladeshi (162)	171	0.49
Burmese (4)	4	0.01
Cambodian (30)	38	0.11
Chinese, ex. Taiwanese (116)	156	0.45
Filipino (397)	501	1.43
Indian (399)	442	1.26
Indonesian (8)	11	0.03
Japanese (29)	100	0.29
Korean (220)	286	0.82
Laotian (158)	173	0.49
Nepalese (105)	108	0.31
Pakistani (343)	368	1.05
Taiwanese (1)	2	0.01
Thai (82)	104	0.30
Vietnamese (220)	249	0.71
Hawaii Native/Pacific Islander (44)	114	0.33
Not Hispanic (35)	73	0.21
Hispanic (9)	41	0.12
Guamanian/Chamorro (26)	32	0.09
Marshallese (0)	1	<0.01
Native Hawaiian (7)	30	0.09
Samoan (2)	11	0.03
White (15,086)	16,749	47.81
Not Hispanic (9,510)	10,333	29.49
Hispanic (5,576)	6,416	18.31

McLean

Place Type: CDP
County: Fairfax
Population: 48,115†

Ancestry‡	Population	%
African, Sub-Saharan (213)	239	0.52
African (36)	36	0.08
Cape Verdean (12)	23	0.05
Ethiopian (18)	18	0.04
Ghanaian (126)	126	0.27
South African (21)	36	0.08
American (1,549)	1,549	3.36
Arab (955)	1,172	2.54
Arab (230)	230	0.50
Egyptian (106)	118	0.26
Iraqi (47)	87	0.19
Jordanian (29)	29	0.06
Lebanese (440)	504	1.09
Moroccan (13)	13	0.03
Palestinian (26)	51	0.11
Syrian (0)	32	0.07
Other Arab (64)	108	0.23
Armenian (94)	135	0.29
Australian (55)	55	0.12
Austrian (0)	176	0.38
Basque (17)	17	0.04
Belgian (22)	145	0.31
Brazilian (18)	38	0.08
British (496)	941	2.04
Bulgarian (0)	30	0.07
Canadian (35)	192	0.42
Celtic (21)	21	0.05
Croatian (81)	89	0.19
Czech (56)	180	0.39
Czechoslovakian (14)	14	0.03
Danish (88)	268	0.58
Dutch (221)	896	1.94
Eastern European (397)	439	0.95
English (2,316)	7,324	15.88
European (853)	1,044	2.26
Finnish (31)	82	0.18
French, ex. Basque (374)	1,611	3.49
French Canadian (90)	196	0.42
German (1,836)	7,063	15.31
Greek (365)	578	1.25
Hungarian (118)	385	0.83
Iranian (464)	497	1.08
Irish (2,383)	6,927	15.02
Italian (995)	3,239	7.02
Latvian (0)	42	0.09
Lithuanian (45)	163	0.35
Luxemburger (11)	19	0.04
Macedonian (19)	27	0.06
New Zealander (0)	32	0.07
Northern European (68)	104	0.23
Norwegian (132)	411	0.89
Polish (516)	1,773	3.84
Portuguese (43)	74	0.16
Romanian (44)	137	0.30
Russian (626)	1,388	3.01
Scandinavian (41)	117	0.25
Scotch-Irish (647)	1,583	3.43
Scottish (627)	1,937	4.20
Serbian (35)	35	0.08
Slavic (36)	94	0.20
Slovak (39)	162	0.35
Slovene (24)	64	0.14
Swedish (194)	630	1.37
Swiss (39)	305	0.66
Turkish (127)	176	0.38

*Notes: † The Census 2010 population figure is used to calculate the percentages in the Hispanic Origin and Race categories. Ancestry percentages are based on the 2006-2010 American Community Survey population (not shown); ‡ Numbers in parentheses indicate the number of people reporting a single ancestry; * Numbers in parentheses indicate the number of persons reporting this race alone, not in combination with any other race; Please refer to the Explanation of Data for more information.*

Ukrainian (71)	272	0.59
Welsh (52)	337	0.73
West Indian, ex. Hispanic (13)	24	0.05
Trinidadian/Tobagonian (13)	24	0.05

Hispanic Origin	Population	%
Hispanic or Latino (of any race)	2,335	4.85
Central American, ex. Mexican	264	0.55
Costa Rican	17	0.04
Guatemalan	71	0.15
Honduran	14	0.03
Nicaraguan	53	0.11
Panamanian	28	0.06
Salvadoran	81	0.17
Cuban	162	0.34
Dominican Republic	54	0.11
Mexican	375	0.78
Puerto Rican	174	0.36
South American	1,008	2.09
Argentinean	171	0.36
Bolivian	167	0.35
Chilean	96	0.20
Colombian	191	0.40
Ecuadorian	82	0.17
Paraguayan	11	0.02
Peruvian	213	0.44
Uruguayan	25	0.05
Venezuelan	48	0.10
Other South American	4	0.01
Other Hispanic or Latino	298	0.62

Race*	Population	%
African-American/Black (875)	1,100	2.29
Not Hispanic (851)	1,037	2.16
Hispanic (24)	63	0.13
American Indian/Alaska Native (66)	230	0.48
Not Hispanic (48)	185	0.38
Hispanic (18)	45	0.09
Alaska Athabascan *(Ala. Nat.)* (1)	1	<0.01
Aleut *(Alaska Native)* (3)	3	0.01
Apache (4)	4	0.01
Arapaho (0)	1	<0.01
Blackfeet (1)	2	<0.01
Canadian/French Am. Ind. (1)	1	<0.01
Central American Ind. (2)	2	<0.01
Cherokee (10)	51	0.11
Cheyenne (0)	1	<0.01
Chickasaw (3)	8	0.02
Chippewa (2)	8	0.02
Choctaw (2)	6	0.01
Comanche (1)	1	<0.01
Creek (2)	3	0.01
Mexican American Ind. (5)	12	0.02
Osage (2)	2	<0.01
Sioux (3)	8	0.02
South American Ind. (2)	4	0.01
Yaqui (0)	1	<0.01
Yuman (1)	1	<0.01
Yup'ik *(Alaska Native)* (1)	1	<0.01
Asian (7,186)	8,239	17.12
Not Hispanic (7,156)	8,151	16.94
Hispanic (30)	88	0.18
Bangladeshi (40)	44	0.09
Bhutanese (1)	1	<0.01
Burmese (25)	26	0.05
Cambodian (33)	37	0.08
Chinese, ex. Taiwanese (1,746)	2,013	4.18
Filipino (424)	556	1.16
Indian (1,365)	1,539	3.20
Indonesian (46)	64	0.13
Japanese (369)	506	1.05
Korean (1,890)	2,057	4.28
Laotian (2)	3	0.01
Malaysian (23)	29	0.06
Nepalese (30)	34	0.07
Pakistani (243)	270	0.56
Sri Lankan (38)	40	0.08
Taiwanese (224)	263	0.55
Thai (80)	105	0.22
Vietnamese (402)	477	0.99
Hawaii Native/Pacific Islander (14)	61	0.13
Not Hispanic (14)	57	0.12
Hispanic (0)	4	0.01
Guamanian/Chamorro (3)	6	0.01
Native Hawaiian (7)	19	0.04
Samoan (1)	1	<0.01
Tongan (0)	1	<0.01
White (38,159)	39,470	82.03
Not Hispanic (36,273)	37,443	77.82
Hispanic (1,886)	2,027	4.21

McNair

Place Type: CDP
County: Fairfax
Population: 17,513†

Ancestry‡	Population	%
Afghan (6)	6	0.04
African, Sub-Saharan (758)	871	5.73
African (437)	531	3.49
Cape Verdean (13)	25	0.16
Ethiopian (177)	177	1.16
Ghanaian (97)	97	0.64
Sudanese (0)	7	0.05
Ugandan (11)	11	0.07
Other Sub-Saharan African (23)	23	0.15
American (170)	170	1.12
Arab (238)	245	1.61
Arab (72)	79	0.52
Jordanian (130)	130	0.85
Palestinian (36)	36	0.24
Austrian (0)	29	0.19
Belgian (6)	54	0.35
British (85)	169	1.11
Canadian (0)	10	0.07
Croatian (0)	17	0.11
Czech (9)	49	0.32
Danish (0)	45	0.30
Dutch (0)	20	0.13
English (279)	809	5.32
European (185)	201	1.32
Finnish (10)	10	0.07
French, ex. Basque (0)	248	1.63
French Canadian (10)	30	0.20
German (357)	1,156	7.60
Greek (16)	26	0.17
Hungarian (0)	10	0.07
Iranian (88)	88	0.58
Irish (290)	945	6.21
Italian (185)	406	2.67
Lithuanian (32)	32	0.21
Norwegian (52)	93	0.61
Pennsylvania German (0)	15	0.10
Polish (50)	262	1.72
Portuguese (10)	67	0.44
Romanian (108)	108	0.71
Russian (91)	91	0.60
Scandinavian (5)	5	0.03
Scotch-Irish (93)	240	1.58
Scottish (61)	148	0.97
Serbian (0)	74	0.49
Slovene (0)	8	0.05
Swedish (15)	93	0.61
Swiss (86)	90	0.59
Turkish (26)	65	0.43
Welsh (18)	68	0.45

Hispanic Origin	Population	%
Hispanic or Latino (of any race)	1,792	10.23
Central American, ex. Mexican	707	4.04
Costa Rican	5	0.03
Guatemalan	81	0.46
Honduran	154	0.88
Nicaraguan	31	0.18
Panamanian	17	0.10
Salvadoran	399	2.28
Other Central American	20	0.11
Cuban	33	0.19
Dominican Republic	50	0.29
Mexican	193	1.10
Puerto Rican	194	1.11
South American	466	2.66
Argentinean	18	0.10
Bolivian	73	0.42
Chilean	7	0.04
Colombian	92	0.53
Ecuadorian	33	0.19
Paraguayan	1	0.01
Peruvian	214	1.22
Uruguayan	2	0.01
Venezuelan	19	0.11
Other South American	7	0.04
Other Hispanic or Latino	149	0.85

Race*	Population	%
African-American/Black (2,607)	2,827	16.14
Not Hispanic (2,543)	2,728	15.58
Hispanic (64)	99	0.57
American Indian/Alaska Native (49)	138	0.79
Not Hispanic (45)	111	0.63
Hispanic (4)	27	0.15
Blackfeet (0)	1	0.01
Cherokee (4)	11	0.06
Chickasaw (0)	1	0.01
Choctaw (2)	3	0.02
Iroquois (2)	4	0.02
Lumbee (1)	1	0.01
Navajo (1)	2	0.01
Paiute (0)	1	0.01
Seminole (0)	1	0.01
Sioux (0)	1	0.01
South American Ind. (0)	2	0.01
Asian (7,089)	7,460	42.60
Not Hispanic (7,077)	7,433	42.44
Hispanic (12)	27	0.15
Bangladeshi (45)	51	0.29
Burmese (1)	1	0.01
Cambodian (15)	18	0.10
Chinese, ex. Taiwanese (587)	640	3.65
Filipino (190)	222	1.27
Indian (5,019)	5,125	29.26
Indonesian (21)	23	0.13
Japanese (58)	96	0.55
Korean (353)	398	2.27
Laotian (14)	28	0.16
Malaysian (6)	11	0.06
Nepalese (53)	54	0.31
Pakistani (270)	290	1.66
Sri Lankan (24)	27	0.15
Taiwanese (28)	36	0.21
Thai (45)	57	0.33
Vietnamese (219)	239	1.36
Hawaii Native/Pacific Islander (5)	41	0.23
Not Hispanic (4)	26	0.15
Hispanic (1)	15	0.09
Fijian (1)	1	0.01
Guamanian/Chamorro (2)	3	0.02
Native Hawaiian (0)	4	0.02
Samoan (1)	1	0.01
Tongan (0)	2	0.01
White (6,362)	6,851	39.12
Not Hispanic (5,457)	5,825	33.26
Hispanic (905)	1,026	5.86

Meadowbrook

Place Type: CDP
County: Chesterfield
Population: 18,312†

Ancestry‡	Population	%
African, Sub-Saharan (186)	249	1.29
African (33)	72	0.37
Ethiopian (12)	36	0.19
Nigerian (129)	129	0.67
Other Sub-Saharan African (12)	12	0.06
American (2,198)	2,198	11.39
Arab (34)	34	0.18
Lebanese (34)	34	0.18

*Notes: † The Census 2010 population figure is used to calculate the percentages in the Hispanic Origin and Race categories. Ancestry percentages are based on the 2006-2010 American Community Survey population (not shown); ‡ Numbers in parentheses indicate the number of people reporting a single ancestry; * Numbers in parentheses indicate the number of persons reporting this race alone, not in combination with any other race; Please refer to the Explanation of Data for more information.*

Basque (0)	14	0.07
Brazilian (14)	14	0.07
British (11)	71	0.37
Canadian (0)	14	0.07
Czech (20)	33	0.17
Danish (4)	4	0.02
Dutch (53)	188	0.97
English (745)	1,485	7.70
European (126)	126	0.65
French, ex. Basque (72)	190	0.98
French Canadian (18)	18	0.09
German (269)	1,108	5.74
Hungarian (0)	27	0.14
Irish (276)	933	4.84
Italian (109)	298	1.54
Lithuanian (0)	11	0.06
Norwegian (0)	22	0.11
Polish (36)	124	0.64
Portuguese (53)	53	0.27
Romanian (0)	14	0.07
Russian (0)	13	0.07
Scandinavian (39)	39	0.20
Scotch-Irish (209)	430	2.23
Scottish (87)	184	0.95
Swedish (12)	50	0.26
Swiss (0)	9	0.05
Welsh (0)	84	0.44
West Indian, ex. Hispanic (181)	216	1.12
British West Indian (122)	122	0.63
Jamaican (59)	94	0.49

Hispanic Origin	Population	%
Hispanic or Latino (of any race)	2,813	15.36
Central American, ex. Mexican	1,440	7.86
Costa Rican	32	0.17
Guatemalan	354	1.93
Honduran	61	0.33
Nicaraguan	18	0.10
Panamanian	12	0.07
Salvadoran	951	5.19
Other Central American	12	0.07
Cuban	18	0.10
Dominican Republic	87	0.48
Mexican	470	2.57
Puerto Rican	241	1.32
South American	146	0.80
Argentinean	2	0.01
Bolivian	30	0.16
Colombian	85	0.46
Ecuadorian	2	0.01
Peruvian	22	0.12
Uruguayan	4	0.02
Venezuelan	1	0.01
Other Hispanic or Latino	411	2.24

Race*	Population	%
African-American/Black (7,895)	8,229	44.94
Not Hispanic (7,755)	8,040	43.91
Hispanic (140)	189	1.03
American Indian/Alaska Native (131)	268	1.46
Not Hispanic (73)	176	0.96
Hispanic (58)	92	0.50
Apache (1)	1	0.01
Blackfeet (4)	12	0.07
Central American Ind. (4)	8	0.04
Cherokee (7)	47	0.26
Chickasaw (1)	1	0.01
Choctaw (1)	1	0.01
Iroquois (3)	4	0.02
Lumbee (7)	10	0.05
Mexican American Ind. (14)	22	0.12
Seminole (0)	5	0.03
Sioux (0)	2	0.01
South American Ind. (3)	6	0.03
Spanish American Ind. (0)	4	0.02
Tohono O'Odham (6)	6	0.03
Asian (764)	867	4.73
Not Hispanic (763)	849	4.64
Hispanic (1)	18	0.10
Cambodian (175)	193	1.05
Chinese, ex. Taiwanese (31)	37	0.20
Filipino (35)	58	0.32
Hmong (1)	1	0.01
Indian (261)	282	1.54
Japanese (12)	22	0.12
Korean (35)	51	0.28
Pakistani (3)	3	0.02
Sri Lankan (1)	1	0.01
Thai (4)	11	0.06
Vietnamese (178)	199	1.09
Hawaii Native/Pacific Islander (26)	33	0.18
Not Hispanic (12)	19	0.10
Hispanic (14)	14	0.08
Guamanian/Chamorro (21)	23	0.13
Native Hawaiian (1)	1	0.01
White (7,154)	7,527	41.10
Not Hispanic (6,507)	6,761	36.92
Hispanic (647)	766	4.18

Mechanicsville

Place Type: CDP
County: Hanover
Population: 36,348†

Ancestry‡	Population	%
African, Sub-Saharan (83)	112	0.31
African (83)	112	0.31
American (6,090)	6,090	17.09
Arab (68)	206	0.58
Egyptian (32)	32	0.09
Iraqi (14)	28	0.08
Lebanese (22)	126	0.35
Syrian (0)	20	0.06
Armenian (12)	35	0.10
Austrian (0)	97	0.27
Belgian (0)	9	0.03
Brazilian (21)	21	0.06
British (119)	153	0.43
Canadian (8)	48	0.13
Carpatho Rusyn (0)	20	0.06
Celtic (25)	45	0.13
Czech (57)	300	0.84
Czechoslovakian (44)	86	0.24
Danish (29)	44	0.12
Dutch (97)	451	1.27
Eastern European (0)	16	0.04
English (2,396)	5,808	16.30
European (582)	642	1.80
Finnish (0)	11	0.03
French, ex. Basque (229)	1,108	3.11
French Canadian (93)	203	0.57
German (1,285)	4,625	12.98
Greek (38)	60	0.17
Hungarian (21)	252	0.71
Irish (1,184)	4,335	12.17
Italian (616)	1,428	4.01
Latvian (0)	8	0.02
Lithuanian (0)	87	0.24
Northern European (15)	15	0.04
Norwegian (48)	149	0.42
Pennsylvania German (9)	9	0.03
Polish (290)	807	2.27
Portuguese (17)	93	0.26
Romanian (0)	20	0.06
Russian (23)	106	0.30
Scandinavian (0)	14	0.04
Scotch-Irish (762)	1,520	4.27
Scottish (361)	998	2.80
Serbian (0)	57	0.16
Slavic (11)	11	0.03
Slovak (69)	132	0.37
Swedish (8)	84	0.24
Swiss (15)	90	0.25
Ukrainian (0)	11	0.03
Welsh (44)	309	0.87

Hispanic Origin	Population	%
Hispanic or Latino (of any race)	839	2.31
Central American, ex. Mexican	121	0.33
Costa Rican	5	0.01
Guatemalan	12	0.03
Honduran	15	0.04
Nicaraguan	1	<0.01
Panamanian	7	0.02
Salvadoran	80	0.22
Other Central American	1	<0.01
Cuban	35	0.10
Dominican Republic	25	0.07
Mexican	245	0.67
Puerto Rican	176	0.48
South American	131	0.36
Argentinean	5	0.01
Bolivian	6	0.02
Chilean	3	0.01
Colombian	41	0.11
Ecuadorian	14	0.04
Paraguayan	2	0.01
Peruvian	27	0.07
Uruguayan	23	0.06
Venezuelan	10	0.03
Other Hispanic or Latino	106	0.29

Race*	Population	%
African-American/Black (3,086)	3,321	9.14
Not Hispanic (3,035)	3,254	8.95
Hispanic (51)	67	0.18
American Indian/Alaska Native (167)	329	0.91
Not Hispanic (143)	293	0.81
Hispanic (24)	36	0.10
Apache (1)	4	0.01
Blackfeet (2)	5	0.01
Central American Ind. (3)	3	0.01
Cherokee (19)	73	0.20
Chippewa (1)	7	0.02
Choctaw (0)	1	<0.01
Iroquois (6)	6	0.02
Lumbee (9)	10	0.03
Menominee (1)	1	<0.01
Mexican American Ind. (1)	1	<0.01
Osage (4)	4	0.01
Seminole (0)	2	0.01
Sioux (1)	2	0.01
South American Ind. (2)	2	0.01
Yuman (0)	1	<0.01
Asian (643)	818	2.25
Not Hispanic (639)	802	2.21
Hispanic (4)	16	0.04
Bangladeshi (5)	5	0.01
Burmese (1)	1	<0.01
Cambodian (29)	29	0.08
Chinese, ex. Taiwanese (90)	102	0.28
Filipino (147)	209	0.57
Indian (127)	147	0.40
Indonesian (1)	1	<0.01
Japanese (21)	48	0.13
Korean (63)	84	0.23
Laotian (7)	11	0.03
Malaysian (4)	4	0.01
Pakistani (12)	18	0.05
Taiwanese (6)	6	0.02
Thai (13)	17	0.05
Vietnamese (91)	106	0.29
Hawaii Native/Pacific Islander (18)	33	0.09
Not Hispanic (14)	28	0.08
Hispanic (4)	5	0.01
Guamanian/Chamorro (3)	9	0.02
Native Hawaiian (1)	4	0.01
Samoan (1)	3	0.01
White (31,623)	32,112	88.35
Not Hispanic (31,137)	31,581	86.89
Hispanic (486)	531	1.46

Merrifield

Place Type: CDP
County: Fairfax
Population: 15,212†

*Notes: † The Census 2010 population figure is used to calculate the percentages in the Hispanic Origin and Race categories. Ancestry percentages are based on the 2006-2010 American Community Survey population (not shown); ‡ Numbers in parentheses indicate the number of people reporting a single ancestry; * Numbers in parentheses indicate the number of persons reporting this race alone, not in combination with any other race; Please refer to the Explanation of Data for more information.*

Ancestry‡	Population	%
Afghan (8)	8	0.06
African, Sub-Saharan (85)	142	1.00
African (35)	66	0.46
Nigerian (0)	13	0.09
Other Sub-Saharan African (50)	63	0.44
Albanian (47)	47	0.33
American (354)	354	2.48
Arab (133)	241	1.69
Egyptian (14)	28	0.20
Jordanian (14)	28	0.20
Lebanese (54)	119	0.83
Moroccan (49)	64	0.45
Other Arab (2)	2	0.01
Armenian (41)	41	0.29
Austrian (0)	26	0.18
Belgian (8)	23	0.16
Brazilian (15)	15	0.11
British (0)	18	0.13
Bulgarian (0)	10	0.07
Cajun (0)	26	0.18
Czech (33)	43	0.30
Danish (15)	30	0.21
Dutch (0)	83	0.58
Eastern European (84)	84	0.59
English (125)	783	5.49
European (269)	269	1.89
French, ex. Basque (27)	123	0.86
French Canadian (24)	35	0.25
German (450)	1,450	10.17
Greek (12)	12	0.08
Hungarian (20)	47	0.33
Iranian (83)	91	0.64
Irish (293)	1,162	8.15
Israeli (15)	15	0.11
Italian (128)	634	4.44
Latvian (7)	7	0.05
Lithuanian (18)	18	0.13
Maltese (0)	32	0.22
Norwegian (0)	98	0.69
Polish (102)	351	2.46
Romanian (79)	102	0.72
Russian (45)	185	1.30
Scandinavian (18)	49	0.34
Scotch-Irish (91)	286	2.01
Scottish (61)	297	2.08
Serbian (14)	53	0.37
Slovak (0)	11	0.08
Swedish (0)	50	0.35
Swiss (6)	22	0.15
Ukrainian (14)	22	0.15
Welsh (34)	75	0.53
West Indian, ex. Hispanic (21)	36	0.25
Haitian (0)	15	0.11
West Indian (21)	21	0.15

Hispanic Origin	Population	%
Hispanic or Latino (of any race)	2,298	15.11
Central American, ex. Mexican	838	5.51
Costa Rican	15	0.10
Guatemalan	104	0.68
Honduran	116	0.76
Nicaraguan	39	0.26
Panamanian	23	0.15
Salvadoran	536	3.52
Other Central American	5	0.03
Cuban	48	0.32
Dominican Republic	43	0.28
Mexican	158	1.04
Puerto Rican	115	0.76
South American	838	5.51
Argentinean	43	0.28
Bolivian	310	2.04
Chilean	13	0.09
Colombian	82	0.54
Ecuadorian	29	0.19
Paraguayan	9	0.06
Peruvian	304	2.00
Uruguayan	10	0.07
Venezuelan	30	0.20
Other South American	8	0.05
Other Hispanic or Latino	258	1.70

Race*	Population	%
African-American/Black (913)	1,020	6.71
Not Hispanic (849)	937	6.16
Hispanic (64)	83	0.55
American Indian/Alaska Native (71)	128	0.84
Not Hispanic (37)	74	0.49
Hispanic (34)	54	0.35
Apache (1)	2	0.01
Blackfeet (1)	5	0.03
Canadian/French Am. Ind. (0)	2	0.01
Cherokee (5)	11	0.07
Choctaw (4)	7	0.05
Creek (0)	1	0.01
Iroquois (2)	2	0.01
Lumbee (3)	3	0.02
Mexican American Ind. (2)	5	0.03
Navajo (1)	1	0.01
Pueblo (1)	2	0.01
Seminole (0)	1	0.01
Sioux (2)	2	0.01
South American Ind. (4)	6	0.04
Asian (5,366)	5,718	37.59
Not Hispanic (5,351)	5,695	37.44
Hispanic (15)	23	0.15
Bangladeshi (21)	24	0.16
Burmese (12)	18	0.12
Cambodian (29)	32	0.21
Chinese, ex. Taiwanese (828)	911	5.99
Filipino (278)	329	2.16
Indian (1,789)	1,851	12.17
Indonesian (44)	47	0.31
Japanese (77)	114	0.75
Korean (959)	1,011	6.65
Laotian (13)	13	0.09
Malaysian (38)	42	0.28
Nepalese (140)	142	0.93
Pakistani (146)	168	1.10
Sri Lankan (14)	14	0.09
Taiwanese (61)	68	0.45
Thai (46)	54	0.35
Vietnamese (670)	706	4.64
Hawaii Native/Pacific Islander (10)	34	0.22
Not Hispanic (7)	30	0.20
Hispanic (3)	4	0.03
Fijian (3)	3	0.02
Guamanian/Chamorro (1)	3	0.02
Native Hawaiian (4)	8	0.05
Samoan (0)	4	0.03
White (7,549)	8,047	52.90
Not Hispanic (6,156)	6,544	43.02
Hispanic (1,393)	1,503	9.88

Montclair

Place Type: CDP
County: Prince William
Population: 19,570†

Ancestry‡	Population	%
Afghan (0)	50	0.26
African, Sub-Saharan (370)	435	2.25
African (370)	435	2.25
Albanian (20)	20	0.10
American (1,002)	1,002	5.18
Arab (85)	162	0.84
Arab (15)	64	0.33
Egyptian (70)	70	0.36
Lebanese (0)	28	0.14
Armenian (33)	33	0.17
Austrian (10)	27	0.14
British (103)	279	1.44
Cajun (14)	14	0.07
Celtic (15)	15	0.08
Croatian (0)	36	0.19
Czech (0)	51	0.26
Czechoslovakian (11)	11	0.06
Danish (34)	80	0.41
Dutch (29)	57	0.29
Eastern European (32)	32	0.17
English (669)	2,182	11.27
European (536)	598	3.09
Finnish (17)	43	0.22
French, ex. Basque (146)	702	3.63
French Canadian (20)	309	1.60
German (928)	3,274	16.91
Greek (24)	56	0.29
Icelander (0)	16	0.08
Irish (738)	2,506	12.94
Italian (278)	1,260	6.51
Lithuanian (9)	40	0.21
Maltese (0)	10	0.05
Norwegian (38)	191	0.99
Polish (287)	693	3.58
Portuguese (0)	10	0.05
Romanian (0)	10	0.05
Russian (0)	195	1.01
Scandinavian (38)	199	1.03
Scotch-Irish (228)	508	2.62
Scottish (90)	466	2.41
Slovak (10)	30	0.15
Slovene (0)	10	0.05
Swedish (32)	149	0.77
Swiss (10)	143	0.74
Turkish (12)	12	0.06
Ukrainian (33)	81	0.42
Welsh (11)	178	0.92
West Indian, ex. Hispanic (59)	308	1.59
British West Indian (0)	87	0.45
Jamaican (59)	93	0.48
Trinidadian/Tobagonian (0)	31	0.16
West Indian (0)	97	0.50

Hispanic Origin	Population	%
Hispanic or Latino (of any race)	1,939	9.91
Central American, ex. Mexican	535	2.73
Costa Rican	4	0.02
Guatemalan	67	0.34
Honduran	21	0.11
Nicaraguan	25	0.13
Panamanian	65	0.33
Salvadoran	351	1.79
Other Central American	2	0.01
Cuban	50	0.26
Dominican Republic	44	0.22
Mexican	357	1.82
Puerto Rican	420	2.15
South American	326	1.67
Argentinean	20	0.10
Bolivian	68	0.35
Chilean	12	0.06
Colombian	73	0.37
Ecuadorian	27	0.14
Paraguayan	1	0.01
Peruvian	81	0.41
Uruguayan	20	0.10
Venezuelan	24	0.12
Other Hispanic or Latino	207	1.06

Race*	Population	%
African-American/Black (3,595)	3,954	20.20
Not Hispanic (3,462)	3,763	19.23
Hispanic (133)	191	0.98
American Indian/Alaska Native (123)	285	1.46
Not Hispanic (82)	200	1.02
Hispanic (41)	85	0.43
Aleut *(Alaska Native)* (0)	1	0.01
Blackfeet (4)	10	0.05
Central American Ind. (3)	4	0.02
Cherokee (16)	65	0.33
Chickasaw (0)	1	0.01
Chippewa (2)	5	0.03
Choctaw (5)	5	0.03
Creek (2)	4	0.02
Delaware (0)	1	0.01
Inupiat *(Alaska Native)* (1)	1	0.01
Iroquois (5)	5	0.03
Kiowa (1)	1	0.01

*Notes: † The Census 2010 population figure is used to calculate the percentages in the Hispanic Origin and Race categories. Ancestry percentages are based on the 2006-2010 American Community Survey population (not shown); ‡ Numbers in parentheses indicate the number of people reporting a single ancestry; * Numbers in parentheses indicate the number of persons reporting this race alone, not in combination with any other race; Please refer to the Explanation of Data for more information.*

Lumbee (4)	16	0.08
Mexican American Ind. (4)	6	0.03
Navajo (2)	5	0.03
Paiute (1)	1	0.01
Potawatomi (1)	1	0.01
Pueblo (2)	3	0.02
Sioux (2)	2	0.01
South American Ind. (3)	4	0.02
Tlingit-Haida *(Alaska Native)* (0)	2	0.01
Tohono O'Odham (0)	2	0.01
Asian (1,067)	1,494	7.63
Not Hispanic (1,054)	1,447	7.39
Hispanic (13)	47	0.24
Bangladeshi (14)	17	0.09
Burmese (6)	7	0.04
Cambodian (10)	10	0.05
Chinese, ex. Taiwanese (98)	154	0.79
Filipino (246)	376	1.92
Indian (154)	201	1.03
Indonesian (0)	4	0.02
Japanese (36)	99	0.51
Korean (169)	243	1.24
Laotian (0)	5	0.03
Nepalese (10)	10	0.05
Pakistani (130)	154	0.79
Taiwanese (4)	4	0.02
Thai (12)	35	0.18
Vietnamese (140)	155	0.79
Hawaii Native/Pacific Islander (47)	92	0.47
Not Hispanic (43)	79	0.40
Hispanic (4)	13	0.07
Guamanian/Chamorro (14)	29	0.15
Native Hawaiian (19)	36	0.18
Samoan (10)	10	0.05
White (13,285)	14,069	71.89
Not Hispanic (12,232)	12,848	65.65
Hispanic (1,053)	1,221	6.24

Montrose

Place Type: CDP
County: Henrico
Population: 7,993†

Ancestry‡	Population	%
African, Sub-Saharan (74)	81	1.13
African (74)	74	1.03
Ethiopian (0)	7	0.10
American (565)	565	7.87
British (13)	13	0.18
Dutch (0)	27	0.38
English (84)	209	2.91
French, ex. Basque (0)	30	0.42
French Canadian (0)	11	0.15
German (125)	387	5.39
Hungarian (0)	6	0.08
Irish (159)	553	7.70
Italian (128)	340	4.73
Polish (19)	51	0.71
Scandinavian (11)	22	0.31
Scotch-Irish (54)	105	1.46
Scottish (0)	53	0.74
Slovak (0)	8	0.11
Swedish (11)	40	0.56
Welsh (0)	18	0.25
West Indian, ex. Hispanic (0)	114	1.59
Jamaican (0)	114	1.59

Hispanic Origin	Population	%
Hispanic or Latino (of any race)	206	2.58
Central American, ex. Mexican	29	0.36
Costa Rican	4	0.05
Guatemalan	4	0.05
Honduran	5	0.06
Nicaraguan	3	0.04
Panamanian	4	0.05
Salvadoran	9	0.11
Cuban	6	0.08
Dominican Republic	2	0.03
Mexican	71	0.89
Puerto Rican	67	0.84
South American	10	0.13
Bolivian	4	0.05
Colombian	1	0.01
Ecuadorian	3	0.04
Peruvian	2	0.03
Other Hispanic or Latino	21	0.26

Race*	Population	%
African-American/Black (5,329)	5,480	68.56
Not Hispanic (5,270)	5,410	67.68
Hispanic (59)	70	0.88
American Indian/Alaska Native (31)	124	1.55
Not Hispanic (29)	117	1.46
Hispanic (2)	7	0.09
Blackfeet (1)	4	0.05
Cherokee (1)	25	0.31
Chickasaw (1)	1	0.01
Choctaw (0)	2	0.03
Creek (1)	1	0.01
Osage (1)	1	0.01
Asian (82)	121	1.51
Not Hispanic (82)	116	1.45
Hispanic (0)	5	0.06
Cambodian (2)	5	0.06
Chinese, ex. Taiwanese (18)	19	0.24
Filipino (12)	26	0.33
Indian (21)	28	0.35
Indonesian (0)	3	0.04
Japanese (9)	9	0.11
Korean (5)	11	0.14
Sri Lankan (3)	3	0.04
Thai (0)	1	0.01
Vietnamese (9)	9	0.11
Hawaii Native/Pacific Islander (2)	7	0.09
Not Hispanic (2)	7	0.09
Guamanian/Chamorro (0)	1	0.01
Native Hawaiian (2)	2	0.03
White (2,266)	2,432	30.43
Not Hispanic (2,198)	2,348	29.38
Hispanic (68)	84	1.05

Mount Vernon

Place Type: CDP
County: Fairfax
Population: 12,416†

Ancestry‡	Population	%
African, Sub-Saharan (311)	311	2.65
African (48)	48	0.41
Ghanaian (254)	254	2.16
Sierra Leonean (9)	9	0.08
Albanian (0)	33	0.28
American (854)	854	7.27
Arab (27)	46	0.39
Lebanese (27)	46	0.39
Armenian (0)	46	0.39
Australian (0)	12	0.10
Austrian (9)	41	0.35
Belgian (9)	37	0.31
British (50)	85	0.72
Bulgarian (0)	11	0.09
Canadian (8)	28	0.24
Croatian (22)	60	0.51
Czech (31)	107	0.91
Czechoslovakian (10)	10	0.09
Danish (0)	42	0.36
Dutch (97)	209	1.78
Eastern European (18)	18	0.15
English (504)	1,508	12.83
European (254)	275	2.34
Finnish (8)	23	0.20
French, ex. Basque (15)	302	2.57
French Canadian (0)	12	0.10
German (373)	1,983	16.87
Greek (56)	108	0.92
Hungarian (24)	89	0.76
Irish (524)	1,891	16.09
Italian (203)	617	5.25
Latvian (0)	15	0.13
Lithuanian (0)	18	0.15
Northern European (9)	9	0.08
Norwegian (65)	228	1.94
Polish (77)	442	3.76
Portuguese (8)	27	0.23
Romanian (0)	37	0.31
Russian (31)	122	1.04
Scandinavian (0)	8	0.07
Scotch-Irish (48)	340	2.89
Scottish (113)	401	3.41
Slavic (0)	56	0.48
Slovak (17)	63	0.54
Swedish (56)	147	1.25
Swiss (0)	97	0.83
Ukrainian (95)	95	0.81
Welsh (28)	193	1.64
West Indian, ex. Hispanic (10)	10	0.09
British West Indian (10)	10	0.09

Hispanic Origin	Population	%
Hispanic or Latino (of any race)	1,670	13.45
Central American, ex. Mexican	611	4.92
Costa Rican	8	0.06
Guatemalan	86	0.69
Honduran	83	0.67
Nicaraguan	21	0.17
Panamanian	15	0.12
Salvadoran	392	3.16
Other Central American	6	0.05
Cuban	44	0.35
Dominican Republic	13	0.10
Mexican	473	3.81
Puerto Rican	122	0.98
South American	222	1.79
Argentinean	18	0.14
Bolivian	45	0.36
Chilean	13	0.10
Colombian	45	0.36
Ecuadorian	4	0.03
Paraguayan	2	0.02
Peruvian	82	0.66
Uruguayan	4	0.03
Venezuelan	9	0.07
Other Hispanic or Latino	185	1.49

Race*	Population	%
African-American/Black (1,588)	1,730	13.93
Not Hispanic (1,539)	1,664	13.40
Hispanic (49)	66	0.53
American Indian/Alaska Native (54)	125	1.01
Not Hispanic (38)	104	0.84
Hispanic (16)	21	0.17
Blackfeet (0)	2	0.02
Central American Ind. (3)	5	0.04
Cherokee (2)	22	0.18
Chickasaw (1)	2	0.02
Chippewa (1)	1	0.01
Choctaw (1)	1	0.01
Hopi (1)	1	0.01
Iroquois (3)	8	0.06
Lumbee (5)	8	0.06
Mexican American Ind. (2)	3	0.02
Osage (0)	1	0.01
Shoshone (3)	3	0.02
Sioux (1)	2	0.02
Asian (828)	984	7.93
Not Hispanic (818)	962	7.75
Hispanic (10)	22	0.18
Bangladeshi (31)	31	0.25
Burmese (2)	2	0.02
Cambodian (6)	7	0.06
Chinese, ex. Taiwanese (73)	111	0.89
Filipino (131)	185	1.49
Indian (125)	140	1.13
Indonesian (2)	2	0.02
Japanese (26)	46	0.37
Korean (65)	89	0.72
Laotian (4)	4	0.03
Malaysian (0)	1	0.01

*Notes: † The Census 2010 population figure is used to calculate the percentages in the Hispanic Origin and Race categories. Ancestry percentages are based on the 2006-2010 American Community Survey population (not shown); ‡ Numbers in parentheses indicate the number of people reporting a single ancestry; * Numbers in parentheses indicate the number of persons reporting this race alone, not in combination with any other race; Please refer to the Explanation of Data for more information.*

Nepalese (10)	10	0.08
Pakistani (170)	184	1.48
Sri Lankan (3)	3	0.02
Taiwanese (1)	1	0.01
Thai (14)	18	0.14
Vietnamese (73)	91	0.73
Hawaii Native/Pacific Islander (8)	20	0.16
Not Hispanic (7)	18	0.14
Hispanic (1)	2	0.02
Guamanian/Chamorro (5)	6	0.05
Native Hawaiian (3)	5	0.04
Samoan (0)	1	0.01
White (8,881)	9,216	74.23
Not Hispanic (8,016)	8,280	66.69
Hispanic (865)	936	7.54

Neabsco

Place Type: CDP
County: Prince William
Population: 12,068†

Ancestry‡	Population	%
Afghan (20)	20	0.21
African, Sub-Saharan (753)	768	8.15
African (442)	442	4.69
Ethiopian (228)	243	2.58
Ghanaian (50)	50	0.53
Liberian (12)	12	0.13
Sierra Leonean (11)	11	0.12
Other Sub-Saharan African (10)	10	0.11
American (276)	276	2.93
Arab (10)	10	0.11
Other Arab (10)	10	0.11
Belgian (12)	12	0.13
British (14)	25	0.27
Czech (0)	45	0.48
Czechoslovakian (17)	17	0.18
Danish (0)	60	0.64
Dutch (19)	50	0.53
English (365)	1,070	11.35
European (8)	40	0.42
French, ex. Basque (5)	98	1.04
French Canadian (0)	21	0.22
German (284)	712	7.55
Greek (28)	28	0.30
Hungarian (0)	28	0.30
Iranian (104)	104	1.10
Irish (188)	692	7.34
Italian (122)	242	2.57
Northern European (15)	15	0.16
Norwegian (25)	39	0.41
Polish (71)	311	3.30
Russian (18)	33	0.35
Scandinavian (14)	41	0.44
Scotch-Irish (65)	316	3.35
Scottish (72)	184	1.95
Slavic (8)	8	0.08
Slovene (0)	18	0.19
Swedish (0)	159	1.69
Turkish (12)	12	0.13
Ukrainian (16)	16	0.17
Welsh (0)	86	0.91
West Indian, ex. Hispanic (96)	231	2.45
Jamaican (61)	196	2.08
U.S. Virgin Islander (35)	35	0.37

Hispanic Origin	Population	%
Hispanic or Latino (of any race)	1,778	14.73
Central American, ex. Mexican	667	5.53
Costa Rican	14	0.12
Guatemalan	76	0.63
Honduran	76	0.63
Nicaraguan	33	0.27
Panamanian	37	0.31
Salvadoran	431	3.57
Cuban	25	0.21
Dominican Republic	29	0.24
Mexican	283	2.35
Puerto Rican	346	2.87
South American	259	2.15
Argentinean	12	0.10
Bolivian	51	0.42
Chilean	11	0.09
Colombian	32	0.27
Ecuadorian	21	0.17
Peruvian	115	0.95
Uruguayan	4	0.03
Venezuelan	10	0.08
Other South American	3	0.02
Other Hispanic or Latino	169	1.40

Race*	Population	%
African-American/Black (4,620)	4,938	40.92
Not Hispanic (4,509)	4,767	39.50
Hispanic (111)	171	1.42
American Indian/Alaska Native (52)	135	1.12
Not Hispanic (20)	82	0.68
Hispanic (32)	53	0.44
Apache (0)	1	0.01
Blackfeet (0)	1	0.01
Cherokee (1)	7	0.06
Cheyenne (1)	1	0.01
Choctaw (0)	1	0.01
Comanche (0)	1	0.01
Creek (0)	2	0.02
Iroquois (1)	6	0.05
Mexican American Ind. (5)	5	0.04
South American Ind. (0)	4	0.03
Asian (1,252)	1,593	13.20
Not Hispanic (1,230)	1,543	12.79
Hispanic (22)	50	0.41
Bangladeshi (60)	61	0.51
Burmese (6)	6	0.05
Cambodian (16)	21	0.17
Chinese, ex. Taiwanese (99)	132	1.09
Filipino (251)	324	2.68
Indian (229)	261	2.16
Indonesian (6)	6	0.05
Japanese (25)	55	0.46
Korean (121)	182	1.51
Laotian (15)	19	0.16
Malaysian (1)	3	0.02
Nepalese (13)	21	0.17
Pakistani (187)	203	1.68
Sri Lankan (1)	1	0.01
Taiwanese (4)	4	0.03
Thai (20)	33	0.27
Vietnamese (133)	152	1.26
Hawaii Native/Pacific Islander (18)	37	0.31
Not Hispanic (18)	32	0.27
Hispanic (0)	5	0.04
Guamanian/Chamorro (13)	14	0.12
Native Hawaiian (0)	11	0.09
Samoan (2)	3	0.02
White (4,693)	5,289	43.83
Not Hispanic (3,927)	4,390	36.38
Hispanic (766)	899	7.45

New Baltimore

Place Type: CDP
County: Fauquier
Population: 8,119†

Ancestry‡	Population	%
Afghan (3)	3	0.04
American (768)	768	9.78
Arab (99)	199	2.53
Arab (88)	88	1.12
Lebanese (11)	111	1.41
British (0)	25	0.32
Czech (11)	45	0.57
Danish (0)	22	0.28
Dutch (28)	133	1.69
English (372)	1,397	17.79
European (198)	220	2.80
French, ex. Basque (19)	258	3.28
French Canadian (20)	20	0.25
German (424)	1,927	24.54
Hungarian (24)	48	0.61
Iranian (1)	1	0.01
Irish (376)	1,133	14.43
Italian (202)	527	6.71
Latvian (24)	24	0.31
Norwegian (8)	40	0.51
Polish (78)	239	3.04
Portuguese (52)	63	0.80
Russian (0)	9	0.11
Scandinavian (36)	82	1.04
Scotch-Irish (159)	427	5.44
Scottish (44)	231	2.94
Slovak (27)	39	0.50
Slovene (9)	9	0.11
Swedish (14)	254	3.23
Swiss (11)	71	0.90
Ukrainian (0)	20	0.25
Welsh (10)	56	0.71

Hispanic Origin	Population	%
Hispanic or Latino (of any race)	402	4.95
Central American, ex. Mexican	72	0.89
Guatemalan	18	0.22
Honduran	3	0.04
Nicaraguan	4	0.05
Panamanian	17	0.21
Salvadoran	30	0.37
Cuban	41	0.50
Dominican Republic	11	0.14
Mexican	91	1.12
Puerto Rican	60	0.74
South American	70	0.86
Argentinean	8	0.10
Bolivian	17	0.21
Chilean	1	0.01
Colombian	17	0.21
Ecuadorian	2	0.02
Peruvian	18	0.22
Venezuelan	7	0.09
Other Hispanic or Latino	57	0.70

Race*	Population	%
African-American/Black (349)	415	5.11
Not Hispanic (323)	373	4.59
Hispanic (26)	42	0.52
American Indian/Alaska Native (15)	47	0.58
Not Hispanic (14)	43	0.53
Hispanic (1)	4	0.05
Blackfeet (0)	3	0.04
Cherokee (5)	13	0.16
Chickasaw (0)	3	0.04
Chippewa (1)	1	0.01
Choctaw (2)	2	0.02
Comanche (1)	2	0.02
Delaware (1)	1	0.01
Iroquois (1)	1	0.01
Lumbee (2)	2	0.02
Navajo (0)	2	0.02
Ottawa (1)	1	0.01
South American Ind. (0)	1	0.01
Asian (158)	231	2.85
Not Hispanic (156)	225	2.77
Hispanic (2)	6	0.07
Chinese, ex. Taiwanese (10)	33	0.41
Filipino (22)	42	0.52
Indian (26)	33	0.41
Indonesian (0)	1	0.01
Japanese (11)	15	0.18
Korean (35)	51	0.63
Nepalese (1)	1	0.01
Pakistani (13)	13	0.16
Sri Lankan (4)	4	0.05
Taiwanese (0)	5	0.06
Thai (1)	1	0.01
Vietnamese (25)	35	0.43
Hawaii Native/Pacific Islander (3)	19	0.23
Not Hispanic (3)	17	0.21
Hispanic (0)	2	0.02
Guamanian/Chamorro (3)	8	0.10
Native Hawaiian (0)	8	0.10

SECTION TWO

*Notes: † The Census 2010 population figure is used to calculate the percentages in the Hispanic Origin and Race categories. Ancestry percentages are based on the 2006-2010 American Community Survey population (not shown); ‡ Numbers in parentheses indicate the number of people reporting a single ancestry; * Numbers in parentheses indicate the number of persons reporting this race alone, not in combination with any other race; Please refer to the Explanation of Data for more information.*

Samoan (0)	1	0.01
White (7,327)	7,488	92.23
Not Hispanic (7,070)	7,196	88.63
Hispanic (257)	292	3.60

Newington

Place Type: CDP
County: Fairfax
Population: 12,943†

Ancestry‡	Population	%
Afghan (52)	61	0.46
African, Sub-Saharan (739)	905	6.85
African (218)	218	1.65
Ethiopian (210)	246	1.86
Ghanaian (231)	261	1.98
Senegalese (67)	167	1.26
Sudanese (13)	13	0.10
American (435)	435	3.29
Arab (25)	38	0.29
Arab (13)	13	0.10
Jordanian (12)	12	0.09
Lebanese (0)	13	0.10
Australian (0)	13	0.10
Austrian (0)	30	0.23
Belgian (0)	11	0.08
Brazilian (56)	56	0.42
British (68)	168	1.27
Canadian (9)	9	0.07
Croatian (0)	14	0.11
Czech (13)	51	0.39
Danish (81)	91	0.69
Dutch (15)	132	1.00
English (232)	1,130	8.55
European (134)	161	1.22
French, ex. Basque (114)	456	3.45
French Canadian (0)	77	0.58
German (742)	1,995	15.10
Greek (103)	210	1.59
Guyanese (0)	11	0.08
Hungarian (31)	139	1.05
Iranian (53)	53	0.40
Irish (257)	1,264	9.57
Italian (141)	695	5.26
Lithuanian (9)	26	0.20
Northern European (18)	18	0.14
Norwegian (12)	52	0.39
Polish (49)	349	2.64
Romanian (16)	16	0.12
Russian (25)	152	1.15
Scandinavian (20)	20	0.15
Scotch-Irish (163)	251	1.90
Scottish (93)	433	3.28
Serbian (0)	17	0.13
Slovak (0)	48	0.36
Swedish (30)	172	1.30
Swiss (10)	41	0.31
Welsh (0)	115	0.87
West Indian, ex. Hispanic (11)	11	0.08
Haitian (11)	11	0.08

Hispanic Origin	Population	%
Hispanic or Latino (of any race)	1,833	14.16
Central American, ex. Mexican	602	4.65
Costa Rican	9	0.07
Guatemalan	83	0.64
Honduran	66	0.51
Nicaraguan	35	0.27
Panamanian	30	0.23
Salvadoran	379	2.93
Cuban	37	0.29
Dominican Republic	21	0.16
Mexican	206	1.59
Puerto Rican	143	1.10
South American	671	5.18
Argentinean	28	0.22
Bolivian	260	2.01
Chilean	16	0.12
Colombian	84	0.65
Ecuadorian	20	0.15
Paraguayan	2	0.02
Peruvian	221	1.71
Uruguayan	12	0.09
Venezuelan	23	0.18
Other South American	5	0.04
Other Hispanic or Latino	153	1.18

Race*	Population	%
African-American/Black (1,996)	2,203	17.02
Not Hispanic (1,959)	2,130	16.46
Hispanic (37)	73	0.56
American Indian/Alaska Native (40)	108	0.83
Not Hispanic (28)	76	0.59
Hispanic (12)	32	0.25
Blackfeet (0)	2	0.02
Central American Ind. (1)	1	0.01
Cherokee (2)	22	0.17
Chippewa (1)	4	0.03
Creek (1)	2	0.02
Iroquois (9)	9	0.07
Mexican American Ind. (4)	4	0.03
Navajo (0)	1	0.01
Osage (0)	1	0.01
Potawatomi (0)	1	0.01
Sioux (0)	3	0.02
South American Ind. (0)	2	0.02
Asian (1,870)	2,255	17.42
Not Hispanic (1,856)	2,231	17.24
Hispanic (14)	24	0.19
Bangladeshi (28)	30	0.23
Burmese (9)	10	0.08
Cambodian (17)	20	0.15
Chinese, ex. Taiwanese (133)	181	1.40
Filipino (250)	305	2.36
Indian (347)	398	3.08
Indonesian (5)	9	0.07
Japanese (22)	50	0.39
Korean (291)	350	2.70
Laotian (30)	32	0.25
Nepalese (10)	10	0.08
Pakistani (308)	327	2.53
Sri Lankan (7)	8	0.06
Taiwanese (6)	6	0.05
Thai (46)	56	0.43
Vietnamese (286)	313	2.42
Hawaii Native/Pacific Islander (14)	67	0.52
Not Hispanic (11)	42	0.32
Hispanic (3)	25	0.19
Guamanian/Chamorro (8)	10	0.08
Native Hawaiian (4)	19	0.15
Samoan (1)	5	0.04
White (7,600)	8,220	63.51
Not Hispanic (6,623)	7,122	55.03
Hispanic (977)	1,098	8.48

Newington Forest

Place Type: CDP
County: Fairfax
Population: 12,442†

Ancestry‡	Population	%
Afghan (73)	73	0.56
African, Sub-Saharan (175)	184	1.40
African (34)	43	0.33
Ethiopian (47)	47	0.36
Sierra Leonean (8)	8	0.06
Somalian (86)	86	0.66
American (588)	588	4.48
Arab (90)	90	0.69
Arab (14)	14	0.11
Lebanese (43)	43	0.33
Palestinian (33)	33	0.25
Austrian (0)	71	0.54
British (19)	72	0.55
Bulgarian (16)	16	0.12
Canadian (11)	110	0.84
Czech (13)	24	0.18
Danish (0)	14	0.11
Dutch (44)	147	1.12
Eastern European (15)	15	0.11
English (369)	1,375	10.48
European (193)	228	1.74
Finnish (0)	30	0.23
French, ex. Basque (22)	225	1.72
French Canadian (31)	40	0.31
German (429)	1,862	14.20
Greek (44)	98	0.75
Hungarian (54)	109	0.83
Iranian (78)	78	0.59
Irish (447)	1,848	14.09
Italian (193)	569	4.34
Lithuanian (0)	15	0.11
Northern European (69)	69	0.53
Norwegian (38)	96	0.73
Polish (173)	370	2.82
Portuguese (64)	64	0.49
Romanian (0)	14	0.11
Russian (31)	94	0.72
Scandinavian (0)	11	0.08
Scotch-Irish (145)	320	2.44
Scottish (133)	396	3.02
Slovak (13)	98	0.75
Swedish (9)	100	0.76
Swiss (0)	96	0.73
Welsh (34)	71	0.54
West Indian, ex. Hispanic (8)	19	0.14
Haitian (8)	8	0.06
West Indian (0)	11	0.08

Hispanic Origin	Population	%
Hispanic or Latino (of any race)	1,652	13.28
Central American, ex. Mexican	478	3.84
Costa Rican	11	0.09
Guatemalan	73	0.59
Honduran	79	0.63
Nicaraguan	30	0.24
Panamanian	20	0.16
Salvadoran	264	2.12
Other Central American	1	0.01
Cuban	35	0.28
Dominican Republic	35	0.28
Mexican	181	1.45
Puerto Rican	132	1.06
South American	610	4.90
Argentinean	30	0.24
Bolivian	235	1.89
Chilean	32	0.26
Colombian	40	0.32
Ecuadorian	27	0.22
Paraguayan	10	0.08
Peruvian	198	1.59
Uruguayan	12	0.10
Venezuelan	24	0.19
Other South American	2	0.02
Other Hispanic or Latino	181	1.45

Race*	Population	%
African-American/Black (1,399)	1,561	12.55
Not Hispanic (1,363)	1,493	12.00
Hispanic (36)	68	0.55
American Indian/Alaska Native (49)	136	1.09
Not Hispanic (33)	97	0.78
Hispanic (16)	39	0.31
Apache (1)	5	0.04
Cherokee (8)	21	0.17
Chippewa (0)	2	0.02
Choctaw (5)	7	0.06
Comanche (0)	2	0.02
Cree (1)	1	0.01
Creek (0)	2	0.02
Houma (1)	1	0.01
Inupiat *(Alaska Native)* (1)	2	0.02
Iroquois (0)	2	0.02
Mexican American Ind. (1)	2	0.02
South American Ind. (2)	7	0.06
Tohono O'Odham (0)	3	0.02
Asian (1,821)	2,182	17.54
Not Hispanic (1,807)	2,152	17.30

*Notes: † The Census 2010 population figure is used to calculate the percentages in the Hispanic Origin and Race categories. Ancestry percentages are based on the 2006-2010 American Community Survey population (not shown); ‡ Numbers in parentheses indicate the number of people reporting a single ancestry; * Numbers in parentheses indicate the number of persons reporting this race alone, not in combination with any other race; Please refer to the Explanation of Data for more information.*

Hispanic (14)	30	0.24
Bangladeshi (30)	32	0.26
Burmese (3)	3	0.02
Cambodian (17)	19	0.15
Chinese, ex. Taiwanese (146)	198	1.59
Filipino (302)	362	2.91
Indian (269)	315	2.53
Indonesian (5)	5	0.04
Japanese (17)	57	0.46
Korean (254)	296	2.38
Laotian (22)	27	0.22
Malaysian (0)	1	0.01
Nepalese (22)	24	0.19
Pakistani (245)	274	2.20
Taiwanese (6)	8	0.06
Thai (46)	54	0.43
Vietnamese (330)	353	2.84
Hawaii Native/Pacific Islander (18)	42	0.34
Not Hispanic (14)	36	0.29
Hispanic (4)	6	0.05
Guamanian/Chamorro (9)	13	0.10
Native Hawaiian (7)	17	0.14
Samoan (1)	3	0.02
White (8,018)	8,605	69.16
Not Hispanic (7,037)	7,488	60.18
Hispanic (981)	1,117	8.98

Newport News

Place Type: Independent City
County: Newport News
Population: 180,719†

Ancestry‡	Population	%
Afghan (30)	30	0.02
African, Sub-Saharan (2,122)	2,685	1.48
African (1,487)	1,871	1.03
Cape Verdean (13)	53	0.03
Ethiopian (105)	208	0.11
Ghanaian (74)	74	0.04
Kenyan (78)	78	0.04
Liberian (19)	19	0.01
Nigerian (23)	23	0.01
Somalian (15)	15	0.01
Sudanese (172)	208	0.11
Other Sub-Saharan African (136)	136	0.07
Alsatian (0)	13	0.01
American (8,706)	8,706	4.79
Arab (358)	460	0.25
Arab (40)	40	0.02
Egyptian (73)	97	0.05
Lebanese (120)	198	0.11
Moroccan (125)	125	0.07
Armenian (53)	91	0.05
Assyrian/Chaldean/Syriac (5)	5	<0.01
Australian (18)	81	0.04
Austrian (249)	354	0.19
Belgian (37)	84	0.05
British (684)	961	0.53
Cajun (18)	18	0.01
Canadian (276)	574	0.32
Celtic (16)	46	0.03
Croatian (0)	10	0.01
Czech (153)	550	0.30
Czechoslovakian (55)	101	0.06
Danish (84)	260	0.14
Dutch (299)	1,675	0.92
Eastern European (57)	57	0.03
English (6,183)	15,413	8.48
European (1,431)	1,594	0.88
Finnish (49)	223	0.12
French, ex. Basque (476)	2,791	1.54
French Canadian (311)	809	0.44
German (5,740)	19,574	10.77
German Russian (0)	27	0.01
Greek (358)	619	0.34
Guyanese (69)	77	0.04
Hungarian (47)	351	0.19
Icelander (10)	56	0.03
Iranian (32)	40	0.02
Irish (4,314)	14,391	7.91
Israeli (11)	11	0.01
Italian (2,281)	6,379	3.51
Lithuanian (66)	355	0.20
Maltese (9)	9	<0.01
Northern European (67)	67	0.04
Norwegian (167)	972	0.53
Pennsylvania German (136)	189	0.10
Polish (848)	2,621	1.44
Portuguese (179)	716	0.39
Romanian (61)	68	0.04
Russian (540)	1,050	0.58
Scandinavian (54)	246	0.14
Scotch-Irish (1,369)	3,100	1.70
Scottish (1,424)	3,422	1.88
Serbian (29)	71	0.04
Slavic (31)	39	0.02
Slovak (110)	207	0.11
Slovene (10)	69	0.04
Swedish (312)	1,289	0.71
Swiss (67)	331	0.18
Turkish (68)	105	0.06
Ukrainian (141)	507	0.28
Welsh (281)	1,112	0.61
West Indian, ex. Hispanic (1,016)	1,678	0.92
Bahamian (35)	35	0.02
Barbadian (53)	93	0.05
Belizean (168)	261	0.14
British West Indian (66)	91	0.05
Haitian (150)	170	0.09
Jamaican (275)	636	0.35
Trinidadian/Tobagonian (107)	107	0.06
West Indian (157)	280	0.15
Other West Indian (5)	5	<0.01
Yugoslavian (150)	176	0.10

Hispanic Origin	Population	%
Hispanic or Latino (of any race)	13,590	7.52
Central American, ex. Mexican	1,714	0.95
Costa Rican	51	0.03
Guatemalan	337	0.19
Honduran	379	0.21
Nicaraguan	59	0.03
Panamanian	615	0.34
Salvadoran	264	0.15
Other Central American	9	<0.01
Cuban	772	0.43
Dominican Republic	422	0.23
Mexican	4,473	2.48
Puerto Rican	4,544	2.51
South American	607	0.34
Argentinean	35	0.02
Bolivian	22	0.01
Chilean	31	0.02
Colombian	225	0.12
Ecuadorian	112	0.06
Paraguayan	6	<0.01
Peruvian	115	0.06
Uruguayan	7	<0.01
Venezuelan	49	0.03
Other South American	5	<0.01
Other Hispanic or Latino	1,058	0.59

Race*	Population	%
African-American/Black (73,514)	78,376	43.37
Not Hispanic (71,727)	75,788	41.94
Hispanic (1,787)	2,588	1.43
American Indian/Alaska Native (851)	2,802	1.55
Not Hispanic (682)	2,327	1.29
Hispanic (169)	475	0.26
Alaska Athabascan *(Ala. Nat.)* (3)	5	<0.01
Apache (5)	32	0.02
Arapaho (0)	1	<0.01
Blackfeet (9)	113	0.06
Canadian/French Am. Ind. (3)	13	0.01
Central American Ind. (4)	6	<0.01
Cherokee (134)	620	0.34
Cheyenne (0)	6	<0.01
Chickasaw (2)	3	<0.01
Chippewa (13)	24	0.01
Choctaw (10)	47	0.03
Comanche (2)	3	<0.01
Cree (2)	6	<0.01
Creek (10)	21	0.01
Crow (0)	6	<0.01
Delaware (0)	7	<0.01
Hopi (2)	4	<0.01
Houma (5)	5	<0.01
Inupiat *(Alaska Native)* (7)	7	<0.01
Iroquois (11)	28	0.02
Kiowa (2)	2	<0.01
Lumbee (27)	45	0.02
Mexican American Ind. (11)	13	0.01
Navajo (16)	29	0.02
Osage (1)	1	<0.01
Ottawa (7)	9	<0.01
Potawatomi (6)	10	0.01
Pueblo (2)	2	<0.01
Seminole (2)	18	0.01
Shoshone (1)	4	<0.01
Sioux (16)	36	0.02
South American Ind. (21)	44	0.02
Spanish American Ind. (0)	6	<0.01
Tlingit-Haida *(Alaska Native)* (2)	5	<0.01
Tohono O'Odham (0)	5	<0.01
Tsimshian *(Alaska Native)* (1)	1	<0.01
Ute (3)	5	<0.01
Yaqui (0)	5	<0.01
Yuman (0)	3	<0.01
Asian (4,956)	7,207	3.99
Not Hispanic (4,858)	6,871	3.80
Hispanic (98)	336	0.19
Bangladeshi (33)	36	0.02
Bhutanese (43)	50	0.03
Burmese (52)	55	0.03
Cambodian (181)	232	0.13
Chinese, ex. Taiwanese (372)	616	0.34
Filipino (1,386)	2,194	1.21
Hmong (6)	9	<0.01
Indian (419)	569	0.31
Indonesian (5)	13	0.01
Japanese (241)	614	0.34
Korean (1,121)	1,608	0.89
Laotian (55)	71	0.04
Malaysian (0)	4	<0.01
Nepalese (20)	32	0.02
Pakistani (52)	56	0.03
Sri Lankan (22)	26	0.01
Taiwanese (31)	41	0.02
Thai (129)	248	0.14
Vietnamese (541)	672	0.37
Hawaii Native/Pacific Islander (315)	682	0.38
Not Hispanic (284)	566	0.31
Hispanic (31)	116	0.06
Fijian (6)	14	0.01
Guamanian/Chamorro (84)	146	0.08
Marshallese (1)	16	0.01
Native Hawaiian (88)	235	0.13
Samoan (51)	94	0.05
Tongan (2)	8	<0.01
White (88,518)	94,315	52.19
Not Hispanic (83,153)	87,892	48.63
Hispanic (5,365)	6,423	3.55

Norfolk

Place Type: Independent City
County: Norfolk
Population: 242,803†

Ancestry‡	Population	%
African, Sub-Saharan (6,412)	7,047	2.91
African (5,245)	5,828	2.41
Cape Verdean (127)	127	0.05
Ethiopian (183)	208	0.09
Ghanaian (309)	309	0.13
Kenyan (12)	12	<0.01
Liberian (38)	46	0.02
Nigerian (293)	306	0.13
Senegalese (50)	50	0.02

*Notes: † The Census 2010 population figure is used to calculate the percentages in the Hispanic Origin and Race categories. Ancestry percentages are based on the 2006-2010 American Community Survey population (not shown); ‡ Numbers in parentheses indicate the number of people reporting a single ancestry; * Numbers in parentheses indicate the number of persons reporting this race alone, not in combination with any other race; Please refer to the Explanation of Data for more information.*

South African (0)	6	<0.01
Sudanese (20)	20	0.01
Other Sub-Saharan African (135)	135	0.06
Albanian (28)	37	0.02
Alsatian (0)	18	0.01
American (25,600)	25,600	10.57
Arab (722)	930	0.38
Arab (70)	105	0.04
Egyptian (29)	29	0.01
Iraqi (270)	270	0.11
Lebanese (166)	275	0.11
Moroccan (38)	46	0.02
Palestinian (13)	13	0.01
Syrian (19)	67	0.03
Other Arab (117)	125	0.05
Armenian (129)	182	0.08
Australian (54)	73	0.03
Austrian (124)	425	0.18
Belgian (28)	185	0.08
Brazilian (51)	62	0.03
British (480)	1,031	0.43
Bulgarian (39)	39	0.02
Cajun (16)	16	0.01
Canadian (240)	522	0.22
Celtic (10)	10	<0.01
Croatian (45)	63	0.03
Cypriot (7)	22	0.01
Czech (154)	439	0.18
Czechoslovakian (50)	138	0.06
Danish (171)	653	0.27
Dutch (297)	1,875	0.77
Eastern European (155)	209	0.09
English (6,686)	17,520	7.24
Estonian (0)	11	<0.01
European (1,579)	1,731	0.71
Finnish (113)	239	0.10
French, ex. Basque (991)	5,155	2.13
French Canadian (418)	743	0.31
German (6,348)	21,168	8.74
German Russian (0)	20	0.01
Greek (664)	1,328	0.55
Guyanese (53)	53	0.02
Hungarian (205)	928	0.38
Icelander (145)	145	0.06
Iranian (270)	292	0.12
Irish (5,394)	18,649	7.70
Israeli (35)	63	0.03
Italian (2,874)	7,671	3.17
Latvian (16)	24	0.01
Lithuanian (141)	401	0.17
Luxemburger (0)	12	<0.01
Maltese (11)	11	<0.01
New Zealander (0)	26	0.01
Northern European (100)	100	0.04
Norwegian (522)	1,317	0.54
Pennsylvania German (46)	106	0.04
Polish (1,421)	3,837	1.58
Portuguese (213)	458	0.19
Romanian (199)	276	0.11
Russian (589)	1,240	0.51
Scandinavian (138)	274	0.11
Scotch-Irish (1,712)	3,980	1.64
Scottish (1,389)	3,912	1.62
Serbian (18)	201	0.08
Slavic (22)	116	0.05
Slovak (88)	545	0.23
Slovene (0)	19	0.01
Swedish (303)	1,308	0.54
Swiss (10)	140	0.06
Turkish (53)	96	0.04
Ukrainian (245)	343	0.14
Welsh (314)	1,390	0.57
West Indian, ex. Hispanic (2,085)	2,941	1.21
Bahamian (18)	18	0.01
Barbadian (44)	44	0.02
Bermudan (21)	21	0.01
British West Indian (113)	136	0.06
Haitian (239)	534	0.22
Jamaican (835)	1,082	0.45
Trinidadian/Tobagonian (342)	459	0.19
U.S. Virgin Islander (56)	56	0.02
West Indian (417)	591	0.24
Yugoslavian (0)	51	0.02

Hispanic Origin	Population	%
Hispanic or Latino (of any race)	16,144	6.65
Central American, ex. Mexican	2,278	0.94
Costa Rican	42	0.02
Guatemalan	211	0.09
Honduran	856	0.35
Nicaraguan	141	0.06
Panamanian	330	0.14
Salvadoran	676	0.28
Other Central American	22	0.01
Cuban	623	0.26
Dominican Republic	795	0.33
Mexican	5,432	2.24
Puerto Rican	4,387	1.81
South American	1,047	0.43
Argentinean	74	0.03
Bolivian	48	0.02
Chilean	67	0.03
Colombian	310	0.13
Ecuadorian	195	0.08
Paraguayan	17	0.01
Peruvian	249	0.10
Uruguayan	16	0.01
Venezuelan	58	0.02
Other South American	13	0.01
Other Hispanic or Latino	1,582	0.65

Race*	Population	%
African-American/Black (104,672)	109,734	45.19
Not Hispanic (102,452)	106,646	43.92
Hispanic (2,220)	3,088	1.27
American Indian/Alaska Native (1,200)	3,594	1.48
Not Hispanic (935)	2,967	1.22
Hispanic (265)	627	0.26
Alaska Athabascan *(Ala. Nat.)* (2)	3	<0.01
Aleut *(Alaska Native)* (4)	9	<0.01
Apache (15)	51	0.02
Arapaho (2)	11	<0.01
Blackfeet (13)	137	0.06
Canadian/French Am. Ind. (4)	10	<0.01
Central American Ind. (8)	17	0.01
Cherokee (140)	818	0.34
Cheyenne (2)	6	<0.01
Chickasaw (9)	15	0.01
Chippewa (23)	65	0.03
Choctaw (28)	78	0.03
Colville (1)	4	<0.01
Comanche (7)	13	0.01
Cree (4)	6	<0.01
Creek (7)	27	0.01
Crow (2)	7	<0.01
Delaware (5)	8	<0.01
Hopi (2)	2	<0.01
Houma (0)	5	<0.01
Inupiat *(Alaska Native)* (6)	8	<0.01
Iroquois (34)	57	0.02
Kiowa (1)	1	<0.01
Lumbee (47)	69	0.03
Menominee (2)	2	<0.01
Mexican American Ind. (24)	48	0.02
Navajo (43)	55	0.02
Osage (1)	4	<0.01
Ottawa (2)	8	<0.01
Paiute (0)	1	<0.01
Potawatomi (3)	8	<0.01
Pueblo (3)	9	<0.01
Seminole (6)	20	0.01
Shoshone (0)	2	<0.01
Sioux (38)	69	0.03
South American Ind. (17)	41	0.02
Spanish American Ind. (2)	4	<0.01
Tlingit-Haida *(Alaska Native)* (3)	5	<0.01
Ute (0)	3	<0.01
Yakama (1)	1	<0.01
Yaqui (0)	5	<0.01
Yuman (0)	2	<0.01
Yup'ik *(Alaska Native)* (1)	2	<0.01
Asian (7,999)	10,738	4.42
Not Hispanic (7,861)	10,320	4.25
Hispanic (138)	418	0.17
Bangladeshi (28)	29	0.01
Burmese (7)	9	<0.01
Cambodian (21)	28	0.01
Chinese, ex. Taiwanese (865)	1,163	0.48
Filipino (4,716)	6,326	2.61
Hmong (20)	21	0.01
Indian (765)	963	0.40
Indonesian (33)	45	0.02
Japanese (176)	488	0.20
Korean (352)	580	0.24
Laotian (28)	32	0.01
Malaysian (8)	16	0.01
Nepalese (57)	62	0.03
Pakistani (86)	104	0.04
Sri Lankan (40)	48	0.02
Taiwanese (29)	42	0.02
Thai (98)	150	0.06
Vietnamese (418)	528	0.22
Hawaii Native/Pacific Islander (396)	911	0.38
Not Hispanic (359)	788	0.32
Hispanic (37)	123	0.05
Fijian (2)	9	<0.01
Guamanian/Chamorro (114)	187	0.08
Native Hawaiian (56)	241	0.10
Samoan (93)	152	0.06
Tongan (21)	25	0.01
White (114,304)	121,016	49.84
Not Hispanic (107,463)	113,086	46.58
Hispanic (6,841)	7,930	3.27

Oakton

Place Type: CDP
County: Fairfax
Population: 34,166†

Ancestry‡	Population	%
Afghan (97)	97	0.29
African, Sub-Saharan (613)	641	1.91
African (98)	121	0.36
Cape Verdean (12)	12	0.04
Ethiopian (331)	331	0.99
Kenyan (57)	57	0.17
Nigerian (53)	53	0.16
Somalian (35)	35	0.10
South African (0)	5	0.01
Sudanese (27)	27	0.08
American (668)	668	1.99
Arab (542)	670	2.00
Arab (33)	50	0.15
Egyptian (56)	56	0.17
Iraqi (17)	17	0.05
Lebanese (45)	83	0.25
Moroccan (229)	276	0.82
Palestinian (18)	35	0.10
Syrian (11)	20	0.06
Other Arab (133)	133	0.40
Armenian (20)	32	0.10
Australian (15)	15	0.04
Austrian (0)	95	0.28
Belgian (0)	18	0.05
British (252)	480	1.43
Bulgarian (0)	24	0.07
Canadian (30)	91	0.27
Carpatho Rusyn (0)	12	0.04
Croatian (22)	38	0.11
Cypriot (14)	14	0.04
Czech (61)	80	0.24
Czechoslovakian (0)	15	0.04
Danish (41)	122	0.36
Dutch (54)	318	0.95
Eastern European (186)	186	0.55
English (1,297)	4,188	12.49
European (865)	894	2.67
Finnish (21)	21	0.06
French, ex. Basque (99)	740	2.21

*Notes: † The Census 2010 population figure is used to calculate the percentages in the Hispanic Origin and Race categories. Ancestry percentages are based on the 2006-2010 American Community Survey population (not shown); ‡ Numbers in parentheses indicate the number of people reporting a single ancestry; * Numbers in parentheses indicate the number of persons reporting this race alone, not in combination with any other race; Please refer to the Explanation of Data for more information.*

French Canadian (49)	190	0.57
German (1,188)	4,767	14.22
Greek (146)	237	0.71
Hungarian (144)	400	1.19
Iranian (381)	421	1.26
Irish (1,346)	4,334	12.93
Italian (744)	2,102	6.27
Latvian (12)	24	0.07
Lithuanian (39)	259	0.77
Luxemburger (0)	14	0.04
Northern European (34)	34	0.10
Norwegian (95)	413	1.23
Pennsylvania German (35)	35	0.10
Polish (308)	1,015	3.03
Portuguese (0)	6	0.02
Romanian (10)	58	0.17
Russian (303)	609	1.82
Scandinavian (24)	71	0.21
Scotch-Irish (342)	747	2.23
Scottish (293)	1,040	3.10
Serbian (0)	16	0.05
Slavic (16)	37	0.11
Slovak (39)	61	0.18
Slovene (0)	12	0.04
Swedish (45)	386	1.15
Swiss (112)	264	0.79
Turkish (210)	223	0.67
Ukrainian (97)	278	0.83
Welsh (62)	229	0.68
West Indian, ex. Hispanic (19)	30	0.09
British West Indian (11)	11	0.03
Jamaican (8)	19	0.06

Hispanic Origin	Population	%
Hispanic or Latino (of any race)	4,022	11.77
Central American, ex. Mexican	1,328	3.89
Costa Rican	30	0.09
Guatemalan	201	0.59
Honduran	250	0.73
Nicaraguan	64	0.19
Panamanian	29	0.08
Salvadoran	745	2.18
Other Central American	9	0.03
Cuban	134	0.39
Dominican Republic	63	0.18
Mexican	451	1.32
Puerto Rican	211	0.62
South American	1,289	3.77
Argentinean	69	0.20
Bolivian	338	0.99
Chilean	67	0.20
Colombian	186	0.54
Ecuadorian	106	0.31
Paraguayan	22	0.06
Peruvian	406	1.19
Uruguayan	18	0.05
Venezuelan	71	0.21
Other South American	6	0.02
Other Hispanic or Latino	546	1.60

Race*	Population	%
African-American/Black (1,711)	1,967	5.76
Not Hispanic (1,640)	1,858	5.44
Hispanic (71)	109	0.32
American Indian/Alaska Native (105)	283	0.83
Not Hispanic (72)	187	0.55
Hispanic (33)	96	0.28
Alaska Athabascan *(Ala. Nat.)* (0)	3	0.01
Apache (0)	2	0.01
Blackfeet (1)	5	0.01
Canadian/French Am. Ind. (1)	9	0.03
Central American Ind. (4)	10	0.03
Cherokee (14)	39	0.11
Cheyenne (1)	2	0.01
Chickasaw (0)	2	0.01
Chippewa (3)	3	0.01
Choctaw (4)	8	0.02
Comanche (0)	2	0.01
Creek (1)	3	0.01
Iroquois (1)	5	0.01
Lumbee (4)	6	0.02
Mexican American Ind. (9)	16	0.05
Navajo (7)	11	0.03
Ottawa (1)	4	0.01
Sioux (1)	3	0.01
South American Ind. (5)	17	0.05
Yuman (0)	1	<0.01
Asian (6,805)	7,665	22.43
Not Hispanic (6,769)	7,586	22.20
Hispanic (36)	79	0.23
Bangladeshi (54)	54	0.16
Burmese (32)	33	0.10
Cambodian (29)	44	0.13
Chinese, ex. Taiwanese (1,315)	1,475	4.32
Filipino (414)	523	1.53
Indian (1,472)	1,553	4.55
Indonesian (45)	51	0.15
Japanese (165)	271	0.79
Korean (1,932)	2,043	5.98
Laotian (9)	11	0.03
Malaysian (15)	18	0.05
Nepalese (150)	155	0.45
Pakistani (218)	234	0.68
Sri Lankan (30)	30	0.09
Taiwanese (88)	101	0.30
Thai (113)	127	0.37
Vietnamese (575)	626	1.83
Hawaii Native/Pacific Islander (10)	78	0.23
Not Hispanic (10)	57	0.17
Hispanic (0)	21	0.06
Guamanian/Chamorro (2)	12	0.04
Native Hawaiian (5)	19	0.06
Samoan (0)	2	0.01
Tongan (3)	3	0.01
White (22,642)	23,898	69.95
Not Hispanic (20,411)	21,399	62.63
Hispanic (2,231)	2,499	7.31

Petersburg

Place Type: Independent City
County: Petersburg
Population: 32,420†

Ancestry‡	Population	%
African, Sub-Saharan (414)	423	1.31
African (388)	397	1.23
Ethiopian (26)	26	0.08
American (724)	724	2.24
Arab (9)	9	0.03
Moroccan (9)	9	0.03
Austrian (26)	40	0.12
British (24)	42	0.13
Canadian (8)	8	0.02
Czech (28)	89	0.28
Czechoslovakian (11)	36	0.11
Dutch (0)	58	0.18
English (1,374)	1,822	5.64
Estonian (0)	6	0.02
European (46)	46	0.14
Finnish (0)	13	0.04
French, ex. Basque (106)	262	0.81
French Canadian (9)	21	0.07
German (198)	664	2.06
Greek (15)	15	0.05
Guyanese (6)	6	0.02
Hungarian (0)	37	0.11
Irish (163)	627	1.94
Italian (46)	278	0.86
Latvian (7)	7	0.02
Norwegian (22)	42	0.13
Polish (16)	63	0.20
Portuguese (0)	24	0.07
Russian (14)	27	0.08
Scandinavian (0)	9	0.03
Scotch-Irish (34)	150	0.46
Scottish (102)	235	0.73
Soviet Union (12)	12	0.04
Swedish (0)	27	0.08
Swiss (0)	11	0.03
Ukrainian (0)	11	0.03
Welsh (0)	34	0.11
West Indian, ex. Hispanic (204)	214	0.66
British West Indian (38)	38	0.12
Jamaican (29)	39	0.12
Trinidadian/Tobagonian (137)	137	0.42

Hispanic Origin	Population	%
Hispanic or Latino (of any race)	1,216	3.75
Central American, ex. Mexican	142	0.44
Costa Rican	1	<0.01
Guatemalan	27	0.08
Honduran	42	0.13
Panamanian	33	0.10
Salvadoran	39	0.12
Cuban	29	0.09
Dominican Republic	30	0.09
Mexican	617	1.90
Puerto Rican	249	0.77
South American	20	0.06
Colombian	8	0.02
Ecuadorian	1	<0.01
Peruvian	6	0.02
Venezuelan	2	0.01
Other South American	3	0.01
Other Hispanic or Latino	129	0.40

Race*	Population	%
African-American/Black (25,646)	26,106	80.52
Not Hispanic (25,419)	25,827	79.66
Hispanic (227)	279	0.86
American Indian/Alaska Native (97)	267	0.82
Not Hispanic (87)	246	0.76
Hispanic (10)	21	0.06
Apache (1)	2	0.01
Blackfeet (1)	12	0.04
Canadian/French Am. Ind. (1)	1	<0.01
Central American Ind. (1)	2	0.01
Cherokee (10)	62	0.19
Cheyenne (0)	2	0.01
Chickasaw (1)	1	<0.01
Chippewa (1)	1	<0.01
Choctaw (1)	1	<0.01
Cree (1)	1	<0.01
Creek (5)	5	0.02
Iroquois (0)	3	0.01
Lumbee (3)	3	0.01
Mexican American Ind. (1)	1	<0.01
Navajo (9)	9	0.03
Ottawa (1)	1	<0.01
Sioux (0)	2	0.01
South American Ind. (0)	3	0.01
Asian (267)	366	1.13
Not Hispanic (263)	340	1.05
Hispanic (4)	26	0.08
Burmese (1)	1	<0.01
Cambodian (3)	3	0.01
Chinese, ex. Taiwanese (16)	31	0.10
Filipino (112)	130	0.40
Indian (22)	37	0.11
Japanese (21)	33	0.10
Korean (44)	81	0.25
Laotian (2)	2	0.01
Pakistani (3)	3	0.01
Taiwanese (1)	1	<0.01
Thai (6)	11	0.03
Vietnamese (23)	24	0.07
Hawaii Native/Pacific Islander (19)	50	0.15
Not Hispanic (12)	40	0.12
Hispanic (7)	10	0.03
Guamanian/Chamorro (4)	5	0.02
Native Hawaiian (2)	10	0.03
Samoan (9)	17	0.05
White (5,217)	5,606	17.29
Not Hispanic (4,902)	5,244	16.18
Hispanic (315)	362	1.12

*Notes: † The Census 2010 population figure is used to calculate the percentages in the Hispanic Origin and Race categories. Ancestry percentages are based on the 2006-2010 American Community Survey population (not shown); ‡ Numbers in parentheses indicate the number of people reporting a single ancestry; * Numbers in parentheses indicate the number of persons reporting this race alone, not in combination with any other race; Please refer to the Explanation of Data for more information.*

Poquoson

Place Type: Independent City
County: Poquoson
Population: 12,150†

Ancestry‡	Population	%
African, Sub-Saharan (0)	16	0.13
African (0)	16	0.13
American (1,447)	1,447	11.96
Arab (74)	130	1.07
Arab (6)	48	0.40
Egyptian (52)	52	0.43
Palestinian (0)	14	0.12
Other Arab (16)	16	0.13
Austrian (0)	42	0.35
Belgian (0)	39	0.32
British (0)	44	0.36
Canadian (46)	46	0.38
Croatian (0)	13	0.11
Czech (10)	25	0.21
Danish (0)	20	0.17
Dutch (50)	172	1.42
English (1,208)	2,413	19.94
European (178)	207	1.71
French, ex. Basque (35)	350	2.89
French Canadian (44)	68	0.56
German (697)	2,264	18.71
Greek (56)	130	1.07
Hungarian (0)	7	0.06
Irish (648)	1,834	15.16
Italian (177)	513	4.24
Northern European (19)	46	0.38
Norwegian (137)	168	1.39
Pennsylvania German (10)	23	0.19
Polish (191)	350	2.89
Portuguese (20)	20	0.17
Romanian (0)	32	0.26
Russian (30)	122	1.01
Scandinavian (0)	16	0.13
Scotch-Irish (208)	341	2.82
Scottish (166)	419	3.46
Slavic (10)	10	0.08
Slovak (0)	9	0.07
Swedish (52)	199	1.64
Swiss (0)	8	0.07
Ukrainian (30)	38	0.31
Welsh (17)	52	0.43
Yugoslavian (0)	18	0.15

Hispanic Origin	Population	%
Hispanic or Latino (of any race)	221	1.82
Central American, ex. Mexican	15	0.12
Guatemalan	2	0.02
Nicaraguan	6	0.05
Panamanian	3	0.02
Salvadoran	4	0.03
Cuban	10	0.08
Dominican Republic	2	0.02
Mexican	83	0.68
Puerto Rican	54	0.44
South American	21	0.17
Bolivian	1	0.01
Chilean	6	0.05
Colombian	8	0.07
Ecuadorian	2	0.02
Peruvian	2	0.02
Venezuelan	2	0.02
Other Hispanic or Latino	36	0.30

Race*	Population	%
African-American/Black (78)	109	0.90
Not Hispanic (78)	106	0.87
Hispanic (0)	3	0.02
American Indian/Alaska Native (38)	89	0.73
Not Hispanic (34)	80	0.66
Hispanic (4)	9	0.07
Blackfeet (0)	2	0.02
Cherokee (5)	29	0.24
Cheyenne (0)	1	0.01
Chickasaw (1)	1	0.01
Chippewa (6)	6	0.05
Choctaw (2)	5	0.04
Iroquois (0)	1	0.01
Mexican American Ind. (2)	2	0.02
Ottawa (0)	3	0.02
Potawatomi (1)	1	0.01
Pueblo (0)	1	0.01
Puget Sound Salish (1)	1	0.01
Seminole (0)	1	0.01
Sioux (2)	5	0.04
South American Ind. (1)	1	0.01
Asian (260)	335	2.76
Not Hispanic (259)	329	2.71
Hispanic (1)	6	0.05
Cambodian (1)	3	0.02
Chinese, ex. Taiwanese (59)	71	0.58
Filipino (36)	59	0.49
Indian (39)	46	0.38
Japanese (16)	37	0.30
Korean (71)	92	0.76
Laotian (2)	3	0.02
Pakistani (6)	6	0.05
Taiwanese (4)	4	0.03
Thai (5)	8	0.07
Vietnamese (11)	15	0.12
Hawaii Native/Pacific Islander (3)	14	0.12
Not Hispanic (3)	10	0.08
Hispanic (0)	4	0.03
Guamanian/Chamorro (0)	1	0.01
Native Hawaiian (3)	8	0.07
Samoan (0)	1	0.01
White (11,557)	11,717	96.44
Not Hispanic (11,398)	11,538	94.96
Hispanic (159)	179	1.47

Portsmouth

Place Type: Independent City
County: Portsmouth
Population: 95,535†

Ancestry‡	Population	%
Afghan (44)	44	0.05
African, Sub-Saharan (997)	1,173	1.21
African (773)	949	0.98
Ethiopian (63)	63	0.07
Ghanaian (66)	66	0.07
Liberian (14)	14	0.01
Nigerian (44)	44	0.05
Other Sub-Saharan African (37)	37	0.04
American (9,562)	9,562	9.88
Arab (44)	90	0.09
Jordanian (44)	44	0.05
Lebanese (0)	46	0.05
Australian (17)	17	0.02
Austrian (13)	110	0.11
Belgian (9)	17	0.02
British (119)	312	0.32
Bulgarian (6)	6	0.01
Cajun (16)	54	0.06
Canadian (10)	133	0.14
Celtic (11)	11	0.01
Croatian (0)	29	0.03
Czech (15)	154	0.16
Czechoslovakian (18)	18	0.02
Danish (100)	174	0.18
Dutch (124)	726	0.75
Eastern European (18)	38	0.04
English (3,123)	7,031	7.26
European (432)	491	0.51
Finnish (0)	70	0.07
French, ex. Basque (233)	1,390	1.44
French Canadian (155)	333	0.34
German (2,005)	7,191	7.43
German Russian (0)	27	0.03
Greek (96)	192	0.20
Guyanese (0)	6	0.01
Hungarian (18)	127	0.13
Iranian (36)	80	0.08
Irish (2,089)	7,238	7.48
Israeli (11)	11	0.01
Italian (938)	2,382	2.46
Lithuanian (0)	11	0.01
Northern European (18)	18	0.02
Norwegian (68)	354	0.37
Pennsylvania German (8)	22	0.02
Polish (282)	911	0.94
Portuguese (11)	30	0.03
Romanian (108)	117	0.12
Russian (45)	222	0.23
Scandinavian (3)	19	0.02
Scotch-Irish (709)	1,638	1.69
Scottish (360)	1,150	1.19
Slavic (9)	15	0.02
Slovak (13)	64	0.07
Swedish (48)	345	0.36
Swiss (43)	138	0.14
Turkish (0)	4	<0.01
Ukrainian (24)	56	0.06
Welsh (83)	553	0.57
West Indian, ex. Hispanic (365)	489	0.51
Bahamian (11)	11	0.01
Barbadian (10)	23	0.02
British West Indian (8)	8	0.01
Haitian (22)	22	0.02
Jamaican (290)	334	0.35
Trinidadian/Tobagonian (0)	58	0.06
West Indian (18)	27	0.03
Other West Indian (6)	6	0.01
Yugoslavian (18)	18	0.02

Hispanic Origin	Population	%
Hispanic or Latino (of any race)	2,919	3.06
Central American, ex. Mexican	377	0.39
Costa Rican	7	0.01
Guatemalan	52	0.05
Honduran	72	0.08
Nicaraguan	12	0.01
Panamanian	93	0.10
Salvadoran	138	0.14
Other Central American	3	<0.01
Cuban	127	0.13
Dominican Republic	123	0.13
Mexican	1,016	1.06
Puerto Rican	832	0.87
South American	134	0.14
Argentinean	17	0.02
Bolivian	4	<0.01
Chilean	7	0.01
Colombian	47	0.05
Ecuadorian	20	0.02
Paraguayan	1	<0.01
Peruvian	26	0.03
Uruguayan	2	<0.01
Venezuelan	8	0.01
Other South American	2	<0.01
Other Hispanic or Latino	310	0.32

Race*	Population	%
African-American/Black (50,878)	52,499	54.95
Not Hispanic (50,327)	51,758	54.18
Hispanic (551)	741	0.78
American Indian/Alaska Native (421)	1,241	1.30
Not Hispanic (379)	1,124	1.18
Hispanic (42)	117	0.12
Alaska Athabascan *(Ala. Nat.)* (1)	1	<0.01
Aleut *(Alaska Native)* (1)	5	0.01
Apache (11)	18	0.02
Arapaho (0)	1	<0.01
Blackfeet (10)	48	0.05
Canadian/French Am. Ind. (1)	1	<0.01
Central American Ind. (2)	7	0.01
Cherokee (75)	330	0.35
Chickasaw (1)	1	<0.01
Chippewa (6)	11	0.01
Choctaw (2)	14	0.01
Colville (0)	1	<0.01
Comanche (1)	3	<0.01
Creek (1)	10	0.01

*Notes: † The Census 2010 population figure is used to calculate the percentages in the Hispanic Origin and Race categories. Ancestry percentages are based on the 2006-2010 American Community Survey population (not shown); ‡ Numbers in parentheses indicate the number of people reporting a single ancestry; * Numbers in parentheses indicate the number of persons reporting this race alone, not in combination with any other race; Please refer to the Explanation of Data for more information.*

Crow (0)	1	<0.01
Delaware (0)	1	<0.01
Inupiat *(Alaska Native)* (0)	2	<0.01
Iroquois (6)	16	0.02
Kiowa (1)	4	<0.01
Lumbee (14)	20	0.02
Mexican American Ind. (3)	3	<0.01
Navajo (10)	22	0.02
Ottawa (1)	1	<0.01
Paiute (0)	6	0.01
Potawatomi (5)	5	0.01
Pueblo (6)	7	0.01
Seminole (5)	20	0.02
Sioux (7)	24	0.03
South American Ind. (1)	5	0.01
Spanish American Ind. (1)	1	<0.01
Tlingit-Haida *(Alaska Native)* (1)	2	<0.01
Ute (0)	2	<0.01
Asian (1,019)	1,595	1.67
Not Hispanic (994)	1,514	1.58
Hispanic (25)	81	0.08
Bangladeshi (8)	8	0.01
Burmese (1)	2	<0.01
Cambodian (8)	20	0.02
Chinese, ex. Taiwanese (120)	191	0.20
Filipino (521)	826	0.86
Hmong (2)	2	<0.01
Indian (84)	131	0.14
Indonesian (2)	3	<0.01
Japanese (40)	98	0.10
Korean (54)	106	0.11
Laotian (1)	8	0.01
Malaysian (0)	1	<0.01
Nepalese (2)	2	<0.01
Pakistani (9)	18	0.02
Sri Lankan (5)	5	0.01
Taiwanese (8)	8	0.01
Thai (18)	27	0.03
Vietnamese (92)	127	0.13
Hawaii Native/Pacific Islander (112)	245	0.26
Not Hispanic (104)	213	0.22
Hispanic (8)	32	0.03
Fijian (2)	2	<0.01
Guamanian/Chamorro (39)	85	0.09
Native Hawaiian (24)	66	0.07
Samoan (19)	28	0.03
White (39,701)	41,586	43.53
Not Hispanic (38,526)	40,202	42.08
Hispanic (1,175)	1,384	1.45

Pulaski

Place Type: Town
County: Pulaski
Population: 9,086†

Ancestry‡	Population	%
American (1,298)	1,298	14.14
Arab (11)	27	0.29
Egyptian (11)	27	0.29
British (18)	18	0.20
Canadian (7)	7	0.08
Czechoslovakian (7)	7	0.08
Dutch (0)	91	0.99
English (695)	999	10.88
European (126)	126	1.37
French, ex. Basque (35)	70	0.76
French Canadian (0)	46	0.50
German (421)	1,169	12.73
Hungarian (0)	18	0.20
Irish (463)	1,235	13.45
Italian (69)	202	2.20
Polish (0)	29	0.32
Russian (10)	10	0.11
Scotch-Irish (111)	132	1.44
Scottish (32)	169	1.84
Slovak (0)	20	0.22
Swedish (0)	182	1.98
Swiss (14)	27	0.29
Ukrainian (0)	18	0.20
Welsh (20)	20	0.22
West Indian, ex. Hispanic (15)	15	0.16
British West Indian (15)	15	0.16

Hispanic Origin	Population	%
Hispanic or Latino (of any race)	172	1.89
Central American, ex. Mexican	19	0.21
Guatemalan	15	0.17
Honduran	2	0.02
Salvadoran	2	0.02
Cuban	3	0.03
Dominican Republic	4	0.04
Mexican	103	1.13
Puerto Rican	15	0.17
South American	8	0.09
Bolivian	1	0.01
Ecuadorian	1	0.01
Peruvian	6	0.07
Other Hispanic or Latino	20	0.22

Race*	Population	%
African-American/Black (708)	820	9.02
Not Hispanic (700)	804	8.85
Hispanic (8)	16	0.18
American Indian/Alaska Native (24)	75	0.83
Not Hispanic (24)	64	0.70
Hispanic (0)	11	0.12
Arapaho (1)	1	0.01
Cherokee (4)	22	0.24
Iroquois (1)	1	0.01
Lumbee (1)	1	0.01
Navajo (6)	6	0.07
Seminole (1)	1	0.01
Asian (53)	79	0.87
Not Hispanic (53)	74	0.81
Hispanic (0)	5	0.06
Cambodian (1)	1	0.01
Chinese, ex. Taiwanese (17)	24	0.26
Filipino (2)	7	0.08
Indian (17)	21	0.23
Japanese (6)	11	0.12
Korean (3)	5	0.06
Laotian (1)	1	0.01
Thai (1)	3	0.03
Vietnamese (5)	9	0.10
Hawaii Native/Pacific Islander (1)	3	0.03
Not Hispanic (1)	2	0.02
Hispanic (0)	1	0.01
Guamanian/Chamorro (0)	1	0.01
Native Hawaiian (1)	1	0.01
White (8,086)	8,270	91.02
Not Hispanic (7,967)	8,126	89.43
Hispanic (119)	144	1.58

Purcellville

Place Type: Town
County: Loudoun
Population: 7,727†

Ancestry‡	Population	%
African, Sub-Saharan (75)	95	1.34
African (66)	66	0.93
South African (9)	29	0.41
American (359)	359	5.05
Arab (22)	71	1.00
Arab (22)	71	1.00
Austrian (0)	13	0.18
British (41)	60	0.84
Canadian (0)	11	0.15
Czech (31)	31	0.44
Danish (0)	46	0.65
Dutch (86)	146	2.06
English (508)	1,414	19.91
European (59)	74	1.04
Finnish (0)	53	0.75
French, ex. Basque (8)	396	5.58
French Canadian (9)	31	0.44
German (638)	1,655	23.30
Hungarian (16)	27	0.38
Irish (160)	1,042	14.67
Italian (518)	855	12.04
Norwegian (25)	154	2.17
Polish (122)	455	6.41
Portuguese (0)	25	0.35
Romanian (6)	21	0.30
Russian (21)	21	0.30
Scotch-Irish (66)	153	2.15
Scottish (84)	264	3.72
Slovak (13)	38	0.54
Swedish (32)	221	3.11
Ukrainian (0)	21	0.30
Welsh (7)	183	2.58

Hispanic Origin	Population	%
Hispanic or Latino (of any race)	513	6.64
Central American, ex. Mexican	178	2.30
Guatemalan	15	0.19
Honduran	6	0.08
Nicaraguan	5	0.06
Panamanian	2	0.03
Salvadoran	144	1.86
Other Central American	6	0.08
Cuban	28	0.36
Dominican Republic	2	0.03
Mexican	96	1.24
Puerto Rican	52	0.67
South American	113	1.46
Argentinean	2	0.03
Bolivian	18	0.23
Colombian	25	0.32
Ecuadorian	7	0.09
Peruvian	59	0.76
Uruguayan	1	0.01
Venezuelan	1	0.01
Other Hispanic or Latino	44	0.57

Race*	Population	%
African-American/Black (404)	520	6.73
Not Hispanic (388)	485	6.28
Hispanic (16)	35	0.45
American Indian/Alaska Native (12)	70	0.91
Not Hispanic (7)	51	0.66
Hispanic (5)	19	0.25
Aleut *(Alaska Native)* (2)	2	0.03
Apache (1)	2	0.03
Blackfeet (0)	4	0.05
Central American Ind. (1)	1	0.01
Cherokee (3)	21	0.27
Chickasaw (0)	1	0.01
Iroquois (0)	1	0.01
Mexican American Ind. (1)	2	0.03
Navajo (1)	1	0.01
Seminole (0)	4	0.05
Sioux (0)	2	0.03
Asian (250)	346	4.48
Not Hispanic (248)	337	4.36
Hispanic (2)	9	0.12
Cambodian (8)	8	0.10
Chinese, ex. Taiwanese (59)	84	1.09
Filipino (45)	70	0.91
Indian (56)	65	0.84
Japanese (12)	33	0.43
Korean (28)	32	0.41
Laotian (3)	5	0.06
Pakistani (4)	4	0.05
Sri Lankan (0)	2	0.03
Taiwanese (0)	1	0.01
Thai (8)	10	0.13
Vietnamese (22)	28	0.36
Hawaii Native/Pacific Islander (2)	9	0.12
Not Hispanic (2)	9	0.12
Guamanian/Chamorro (2)	2	0.03
Native Hawaiian (0)	7	0.09
White (6,648)	6,878	89.01
Not Hispanic (6,342)	6,542	84.66
Hispanic (306)	336	4.35

SECTION TWO

*Notes: † The Census 2010 population figure is used to calculate the percentages in the Hispanic Origin and Race categories. Ancestry percentages are based on the 2006-2010 American Community Survey population (not shown); ‡ Numbers in parentheses indicate the number of people reporting a single ancestry; * Numbers in parentheses indicate the number of persons reporting this race alone, not in combination with any other race; Please refer to the Explanation of Data for more information.*

Radford

Place Type: Independent City
County: Radford
Population: 16,408†

Ancestry‡	Population	%
African, Sub-Saharan (166)	181	1.11
African (31)	31	0.19
Ethiopian (135)	135	0.83
South African (0)	15	0.09
Albanian (16)	16	0.10
American (1,631)	1,631	10.00
Arab (27)	27	0.17
Jordanian (14)	14	0.09
Palestinian (13)	13	0.08
Australian (12)	12	0.07
Belgian (0)	27	0.17
British (35)	111	0.68
Canadian (14)	14	0.09
Czech (15)	32	0.20
Czechoslovakian (0)	29	0.18
Danish (0)	47	0.29
Dutch (14)	161	0.99
Eastern European (44)	59	0.36
English (803)	1,738	10.65
European (116)	132	0.81
French, ex. Basque (118)	475	2.91
French Canadian (18)	69	0.42
German (1,392)	3,510	21.51
Greek (57)	168	1.03
Hungarian (13)	68	0.42
Irish (956)	2,651	16.25
Italian (194)	912	5.59
Lithuanian (25)	37	0.23
Norwegian (58)	128	0.78
Polish (93)	373	2.29
Portuguese (0)	12	0.07
Romanian (0)	12	0.07
Russian (117)	196	1.20
Scotch-Irish (351)	561	3.44
Scottish (180)	567	3.47
Serbian (0)	13	0.08
Slovak (0)	32	0.20
Swedish (15)	70	0.43
Swiss (20)	51	0.31
Turkish (98)	98	0.60
Ukrainian (0)	31	0.19
Welsh (71)	197	1.21
West Indian, ex. Hispanic (13)	13	0.08
Jamaican (13)	13	0.08
Yugoslavian (14)	14	0.09

Hispanic Origin	Population	%
Hispanic or Latino (of any race)	385	2.35
Central American, ex. Mexican	60	0.37
Guatemalan	12	0.07
Honduran	19	0.12
Nicaraguan	2	0.01
Panamanian	3	0.02
Salvadoran	24	0.15
Cuban	29	0.18
Dominican Republic	5	0.03
Mexican	133	0.81
Puerto Rican	59	0.36
South American	60	0.37
Argentinean	3	0.02
Bolivian	16	0.10
Chilean	1	0.01
Colombian	12	0.07
Ecuadorian	4	0.02
Peruvian	15	0.09
Uruguayan	1	0.01
Venezuelan	8	0.05
Other Hispanic or Latino	39	0.24

Race*	Population	%
African-American/Black (1,279)	1,531	9.33
Not Hispanic (1,262)	1,508	9.19
Hispanic (17)	23	0.14
American Indian/Alaska Native (33)	119	0.73
Not Hispanic (30)	114	0.69
Hispanic (3)	5	0.03
Apache (1)	2	0.01
Blackfeet (1)	2	0.01
Cherokee (7)	45	0.27
Chippewa (0)	1	0.01
Choctaw (4)	5	0.03
Creek (1)	2	0.01
Delaware (0)	1	0.01
Iroquois (1)	3	0.02
Lumbee (3)	3	0.02
Ottawa (1)	1	0.01
Potawatomi (0)	1	0.01
Puget Sound Salish (1)	1	0.01
Seminole (0)	1	0.01
South American Ind. (1)	1	0.01
Tlingit-Haida *(Alaska Native)* (0)	2	0.01
Yakama (0)	4	0.02
Asian (256)	346	2.11
Not Hispanic (251)	341	2.08
Hispanic (5)	5	0.03
Cambodian (1)	1	0.01
Chinese, ex. Taiwanese (57)	65	0.40
Filipino (37)	54	0.33
Indian (62)	66	0.40
Indonesian (1)	2	0.01
Japanese (9)	22	0.13
Korean (37)	62	0.38
Laotian (2)	2	0.01
Nepalese (1)	1	0.01
Pakistani (6)	6	0.04
Taiwanese (4)	5	0.03
Thai (1)	9	0.05
Vietnamese (14)	23	0.14
Hawaii Native/Pacific Islander (5)	22	0.13
Not Hispanic (5)	22	0.13
Fijian (0)	1	0.01
Guamanian/Chamorro (1)	2	0.01
Native Hawaiian (2)	9	0.05
Samoan (1)	5	0.03
White (14,273)	14,639	89.22
Not Hispanic (14,075)	14,415	87.85
Hispanic (198)	224	1.37

Reston

Place Type: CDP
County: Fairfax
Population: 58,404†

Ancestry‡	Population	%
Afghan (142)	142	0.27
African, Sub-Saharan (2,842)	3,009	5.65
African (693)	770	1.45
Ethiopian (49)	65	0.12
Ghanaian (191)	205	0.38
Kenyan (16)	30	0.06
Liberian (790)	836	1.57
Nigerian (15)	15	0.03
Sierra Leonean (330)	330	0.62
Somalian (103)	103	0.19
South African (11)	11	0.02
Sudanese (525)	525	0.99
Ugandan (14)	14	0.03
Other Sub-Saharan African (105)	105	0.20
American (1,578)	1,578	2.96
Arab (795)	1,061	1.99
Arab (65)	65	0.12
Egyptian (307)	374	0.70
Iraqi (50)	50	0.09
Jordanian (33)	33	0.06
Lebanese (58)	181	0.34
Moroccan (25)	25	0.05
Palestinian (134)	151	0.28
Syrian (14)	32	0.06
Other Arab (109)	150	0.28
Armenian (62)	104	0.20
Assyrian/Chaldean/Syriac (25)	25	0.05
Austrian (134)	403	0.76
Belgian (13)	117	0.22
Brazilian (39)	70	0.13
British (200)	496	0.93
Bulgarian (6)	16	0.03
Canadian (110)	227	0.43
Croatian (31)	156	0.29
Czech (26)	279	0.52
Czechoslovakian (124)	243	0.46
Danish (24)	243	0.46
Dutch (313)	761	1.43
Eastern European (279)	295	0.55
English (2,005)	6,626	12.44
Estonian (0)	10	0.02
European (1,072)	1,235	2.32
Finnish (27)	222	0.42
French, ex. Basque (486)	1,613	3.03
French Canadian (197)	409	0.77
German (2,041)	7,817	14.68
Greek (51)	142	0.27
Guyanese (11)	11	0.02
Hungarian (72)	356	0.67
Iranian (646)	727	1.37
Irish (2,284)	7,570	14.21
Italian (806)	2,370	4.45
Latvian (18)	18	0.03
Lithuanian (46)	314	0.59
Northern European (176)	176	0.33
Norwegian (240)	528	0.99
Pennsylvania German (21)	21	0.04
Polish (505)	1,853	3.48
Portuguese (72)	132	0.25
Romanian (214)	334	0.63
Russian (625)	1,421	2.67
Scandinavian (20)	63	0.12
Scotch-Irish (386)	1,193	2.24
Scottish (598)	1,602	3.01
Serbian (86)	134	0.25
Slavic (21)	88	0.17
Slovak (35)	241	0.45
Slovene (14)	113	0.21
Swedish (251)	615	1.15
Swiss (63)	323	0.61
Turkish (138)	138	0.26
Ukrainian (91)	286	0.54
Welsh (59)	499	0.94
West Indian, ex. Hispanic (221)	235	0.44
Haitian (50)	50	0.09
Jamaican (63)	77	0.14
Trinidadian/Tobagonian (11)	11	0.02
West Indian (97)	97	0.18
Yugoslavian (16)	122	0.23

Hispanic Origin	Population	%
Hispanic or Latino (of any race)	7,479	12.81
Central American, ex. Mexican	3,225	5.52
Costa Rican	41	0.07
Guatemalan	290	0.50
Honduran	478	0.82
Nicaraguan	131	0.22
Panamanian	47	0.08
Salvadoran	2,194	3.76
Other Central American	44	0.08
Cuban	168	0.29
Dominican Republic	104	0.18
Mexican	983	1.68
Puerto Rican	591	1.01
South American	1,615	2.77
Argentinean	128	0.22
Bolivian	387	0.66
Chilean	83	0.14
Colombian	264	0.45
Ecuadorian	93	0.16
Paraguayan	30	0.05
Peruvian	484	0.83
Uruguayan	25	0.04
Venezuelan	84	0.14
Other South American	37	0.06
Other Hispanic or Latino	793	1.36

*Notes: † The Census 2010 population figure is used to calculate the percentages in the Hispanic Origin and Race categories. Ancestry percentages are based on the 2006-2010 American Community Survey population (not shown); ‡ Numbers in parentheses indicate the number of people reporting a single ancestry; * Numbers in parentheses indicate the number of persons reporting this race alone, not in combination with any other race; Please refer to the Explanation of Data for more information.*

Race*	Population	%
African-American/Black (5,654)	6,367	10.90
Not Hispanic (5,467)	6,081	10.41
Hispanic (187)	286	0.49
American Indian/Alaska Native (183)	543	0.93
Not Hispanic (99)	376	0.64
Hispanic (84)	167	0.29
Aleut *(Alaska Native)* (1)	1	<0.01
Apache (1)	3	0.01
Blackfeet (1)	10	0.02
Central American Ind. (8)	13	0.02
Cherokee (12)	82	0.14
Chickasaw (4)	4	0.01
Chippewa (6)	15	0.03
Choctaw (3)	13	0.02
Comanche (0)	1	<0.01
Cree (1)	1	<0.01
Creek (0)	5	0.01
Delaware (0)	2	<0.01
Inupiat *(Alaska Native)* (1)	1	<0.01
Iroquois (7)	18	0.03
Lumbee (3)	3	0.01
Mexican American Ind. (12)	16	0.03
Navajo (2)	5	0.01
Potawatomi (2)	2	<0.01
Pueblo (1)	1	<0.01
Puget Sound Salish (0)	1	<0.01
Seminole (0)	1	<0.01
Shoshone (0)	3	0.01
Sioux (1)	11	0.02
South American Ind. (9)	29	0.05
Spanish American Ind. (2)	2	<0.01
Tohono O'Odham (0)	3	0.01
Tsimshian *(Alaska Native)* (1)	1	<0.01
Yup'ik *(Alaska Native)* (0)	1	<0.01
Asian (6,382)	7,548	12.92
Not Hispanic (6,328)	7,435	12.73
Hispanic (54)	113	0.19
Bangladeshi (53)	66	0.11
Bhutanese (3)	3	0.01
Burmese (35)	43	0.07
Cambodian (29)	43	0.07
Chinese, ex. Taiwanese (975)	1,169	2.00
Filipino (561)	741	1.27
Hmong (0)	1	<0.01
Indian (2,465)	2,657	4.55
Indonesian (24)	34	0.06
Japanese (169)	332	0.57
Korean (684)	818	1.40
Laotian (57)	73	0.12
Malaysian (11)	20	0.03
Nepalese (38)	44	0.08
Pakistani (372)	434	0.74
Sri Lankan (13)	18	0.03
Taiwanese (71)	83	0.14
Thai (69)	93	0.16
Vietnamese (473)	575	0.98
Hawaii Native/Pacific Islander (26)	88	0.15
Not Hispanic (22)	78	0.13
Hispanic (4)	10	0.02
Guamanian/Chamorro (9)	16	0.03
Native Hawaiian (5)	26	0.04
Samoan (2)	9	0.02
Tongan (2)	5	0.01
White (40,959)	43,048	73.71
Not Hispanic (36,952)	38,593	66.08
Hispanic (4,007)	4,455	7.63

Richmond

Place Type: Independent City
County: Richmond
Population: 204,214†

Ancestry‡	Population	%
Afghan (72)	99	0.05
African, Sub-Saharan (2,757)	3,477	1.72
African (1,438)	2,048	1.01
Cape Verdean (33)	46	0.02
Ethiopian (707)	728	0.36
Ghanaian (235)	281	0.14
Liberian (22)	22	0.01
Nigerian (24)	36	0.02
Somalian (62)	62	0.03
South African (83)	101	0.05
Sudanese (16)	16	0.01
Ugandan (82)	82	0.04
Zimbabwean (14)	14	0.01
Other Sub-Saharan African (41)	41	0.02
Albanian (9)	17	0.01
American (7,748)	7,748	3.84
Arab (734)	1,199	0.59
Arab (51)	69	0.03
Egyptian (99)	99	0.05
Iraqi (13)	25	0.01
Jordanian (0)	10	<0.01
Lebanese (219)	526	0.26
Moroccan (167)	180	0.09
Palestinian (0)	23	0.01
Syrian (0)	31	0.02
Other Arab (185)	236	0.12
Armenian (71)	113	0.06
Australian (0)	27	0.01
Austrian (132)	367	0.18
Basque (0)	9	<0.01
Belgian (13)	30	0.01
Brazilian (90)	123	0.06
British (888)	1,398	0.69
Bulgarian (14)	14	0.01
Cajun (39)	54	0.03
Canadian (64)	282	0.14
Celtic (0)	7	<0.01
Croatian (33)	80	0.04
Cypriot (0)	21	0.01
Czech (84)	359	0.18
Czechoslovakian (0)	30	0.01
Danish (105)	374	0.19
Dutch (366)	1,217	0.60
Eastern European (113)	121	0.06
English (7,268)	17,923	8.88
Estonian (26)	26	0.01
European (2,114)	2,494	1.24
Finnish (48)	133	0.07
French, ex. Basque (509)	3,218	1.59
French Canadian (244)	530	0.26
German (4,133)	15,322	7.59
German Russian (16)	16	0.01
Greek (242)	441	0.22
Guyanese (14)	14	0.01
Hungarian (135)	598	0.30
Icelander (8)	8	<0.01
Iranian (199)	251	0.12
Irish (4,276)	13,244	6.56
Israeli (0)	31	0.02
Italian (2,046)	6,021	2.98
Latvian (17)	42	0.02
Lithuanian (145)	334	0.17
Luxemburger (7)	7	<0.01
Macedonian (8)	8	<0.01
New Zealander (34)	47	0.02
Northern European (176)	176	0.09
Norwegian (178)	808	0.40
Pennsylvania German (0)	32	0.02
Polish (783)	3,121	1.55
Portuguese (78)	214	0.11
Romanian (53)	156	0.08
Russian (378)	1,322	0.66
Scandinavian (23)	124	0.06
Scotch-Irish (2,248)	4,401	2.18
Scottish (1,627)	4,564	2.26
Serbian (0)	44	0.02
Slavic (0)	32	0.02
Slovak (82)	359	0.18
Slovene (9)	16	0.01
Soviet Union (0)	9	<0.01
Swedish (394)	1,105	0.55
Swiss (54)	498	0.25
Turkish (276)	314	0.16
Ukrainian (57)	277	0.14
Welsh (337)	1,390	0.69
West Indian, ex. Hispanic (779)	1,257	0.62
Bahamian (0)	15	0.01
Belizean (12)	12	0.01
British West Indian (46)	46	0.02
Haitian (247)	295	0.15
Jamaican (189)	521	0.26
Trinidadian/Tobagonian (143)	182	0.09
U.S. Virgin Islander (66)	66	0.03
West Indian (76)	120	0.06
Yugoslavian (69)	86	0.04

Hispanic Origin	Population	%
Hispanic or Latino (of any race)	12,803	6.27
Central American, ex. Mexican	4,382	2.15
Costa Rican	90	0.04
Guatemalan	1,936	0.95
Honduran	640	0.31
Nicaraguan	56	0.03
Panamanian	98	0.05
Salvadoran	1,551	0.76
Other Central American	11	0.01
Cuban	347	0.17
Dominican Republic	420	0.21
Mexican	4,161	2.04
Puerto Rican	1,486	0.73
South American	767	0.38
Argentinean	72	0.04
Bolivian	112	0.05
Chilean	50	0.02
Colombian	179	0.09
Ecuadorian	71	0.03
Paraguayan	14	0.01
Peruvian	170	0.08
Uruguayan	20	0.01
Venezuelan	70	0.03
Other South American	9	<0.01
Other Hispanic or Latino	1,240	0.61

Race*	Population	%
African-American/Black (103,342)	106,068	51.94
Not Hispanic (102,264)	104,588	51.21
Hispanic (1,078)	1,480	0.72
American Indian/Alaska Native (705)	2,007	0.98
Not Hispanic (514)	1,657	0.81
Hispanic (191)	350	0.17
Apache (5)	10	<0.01
Arapaho (1)	2	<0.01
Blackfeet (10)	85	0.04
Canadian/French Am. Ind. (0)	3	<0.01
Central American Ind. (13)	15	0.01
Cherokee (69)	427	0.21
Cheyenne (0)	5	<0.01
Chickasaw (5)	7	<0.01
Chippewa (5)	19	0.01
Choctaw (8)	25	0.01
Comanche (0)	3	<0.01
Cree (0)	2	<0.01
Creek (4)	14	0.01
Crow (1)	1	<0.01
Houma (1)	1	<0.01
Iroquois (7)	21	0.01
Lumbee (16)	28	0.01
Mexican American Ind. (52)	61	0.03
Navajo (5)	10	<0.01
Osage (2)	5	<0.01
Ottawa (0)	1	<0.01
Potawatomi (2)	3	<0.01
Seminole (6)	10	<0.01
Shoshone (0)	1	<0.01
Sioux (7)	29	0.01
South American Ind. (6)	10	<0.01
Spanish American Ind. (6)	6	<0.01
Tlingit-Haida *(Alaska Native)* (1)	1	<0.01
Ute (0)	1	<0.01
Yaqui (2)	2	<0.01
Asian (4,750)	6,071	2.97
Not Hispanic (4,679)	5,903	2.89
Hispanic (71)	168	0.08
Bangladeshi (40)	43	0.02

*Notes: † The Census 2010 population figure is used to calculate the percentages in the Hispanic Origin and Race categories. Ancestry percentages are based on the 2006-2010 American Community Survey population (not shown); ‡ Numbers in parentheses indicate the number of people reporting a single ancestry; * Numbers in parentheses indicate the number of persons reporting this race alone, not in combination with any other race; Please refer to the Explanation of Data for more information.*

Bhutanese (9)	9	<0.01
Burmese (14)	17	0.01
Cambodian (167)	187	0.09
Chinese, ex. Taiwanese (780)	1,013	0.50
Filipino (535)	850	0.42
Hmong (1)	1	<0.01
Indian (1,169)	1,343	0.66
Indonesian (18)	32	0.02
Japanese (105)	277	0.14
Korean (831)	1,064	0.52
Laotian (25)	31	0.02
Malaysian (3)	6	<0.01
Nepalese (56)	58	0.03
Pakistani (150)	182	0.09
Sri Lankan (13)	22	0.01
Taiwanese (59)	71	0.03
Thai (78)	105	0.05
Vietnamese (473)	564	0.28
Hawaii Native/Pacific Islander (158)	345	0.17
Not Hispanic (93)	235	0.12
Hispanic (65)	110	0.05
Fijian (1)	2	<0.01
Guamanian/Chamorro (103)	126	0.06
Native Hawaiian (32)	79	0.04
Samoan (10)	23	0.01
Tongan (1)	1	<0.01
White (83,288)	86,658	42.43
Not Hispanic (79,813)	82,555	40.43
Hispanic (3,475)	4,103	2.01

Roanoke

Place Type: Independent City
County: Roanoke
Population: 97,032†

Ancestry‡	Population	%
African, Sub-Saharan (990)	1,077	1.12
African (892)	949	0.99
Ethiopian (40)	40	0.04
Sierra Leonean (13)	13	0.01
Somalian (45)	45	0.05
South African (0)	9	0.01
Other Sub-Saharan African (0)	21	0.02
Albanian (7)	7	0.01
American (11,233)	11,233	11.73
Arab (352)	465	0.49
Arab (110)	159	0.17
Egyptian (9)	18	0.02
Iraqi (30)	30	0.03
Lebanese (164)	219	0.23
Moroccan (39)	39	0.04
Armenian (11)	145	0.15
Australian (61)	61	0.06
Austrian (11)	11	0.01
Belgian (0)	17	0.02
Brazilian (62)	62	0.06
British (184)	338	0.35
Cajun (0)	24	0.03
Canadian (22)	69	0.07
Celtic (43)	73	0.08
Croatian (16)	16	0.02
Czech (34)	104	0.11
Czechoslovakian (15)	23	0.02
Danish (19)	52	0.05
Dutch (97)	1,132	1.18
Eastern European (34)	45	0.05
English (6,136)	11,748	12.26
European (687)	719	0.75
Finnish (0)	17	0.02
French, ex. Basque (439)	1,890	1.97
French Canadian (167)	234	0.24
German (3,558)	11,470	11.97
Greek (196)	316	0.33
Guyanese (15)	15	0.02
Hungarian (47)	222	0.23
Iranian (62)	62	0.06
Irish (3,472)	8,565	8.94
Israeli (0)	9	0.01
Italian (815)	2,083	2.17
Lithuanian (56)	82	0.09
Northern European (35)	35	0.04
Norwegian (134)	489	0.51
Polish (395)	939	0.98
Portuguese (23)	103	0.11
Romanian (111)	111	0.12
Russian (23)	196	0.20
Scandinavian (13)	68	0.07
Scotch-Irish (1,715)	3,985	4.16
Scottish (756)	1,714	1.79
Slavic (104)	132	0.14
Slovak (30)	97	0.10
Swedish (85)	401	0.42
Swiss (3)	73	0.08
Turkish (44)	65	0.07
Ukrainian (58)	100	0.10
Welsh (214)	513	0.54
West Indian, ex. Hispanic (881)	1,006	1.05
Haitian (725)	725	0.76
Jamaican (156)	239	0.25
West Indian (0)	42	0.04
Yugoslavian (232)	232	0.24

Hispanic Origin	Population	%
Hispanic or Latino (of any race)	5,345	5.51
Central American, ex. Mexican	1,333	1.37
Costa Rican	22	0.02
Guatemalan	139	0.14
Honduran	936	0.96
Nicaraguan	28	0.03
Panamanian	29	0.03
Salvadoran	166	0.17
Other Central American	13	0.01
Cuban	352	0.36
Dominican Republic	77	0.08
Mexican	2,273	2.34
Puerto Rican	601	0.62
South American	200	0.21
Argentinean	9	0.01
Bolivian	9	0.01
Chilean	8	0.01
Colombian	83	0.09
Ecuadorian	34	0.04
Paraguayan	2	<0.01
Peruvian	33	0.03
Venezuelan	21	0.02
Other South American	1	<0.01
Other Hispanic or Latino	509	0.52

Race*	Population	%
African-American/Black (27,612)	29,465	30.37
Not Hispanic (27,256)	28,925	29.81
Hispanic (356)	540	0.56
American Indian/Alaska Native (279)	881	0.91
Not Hispanic (198)	720	0.74
Hispanic (81)	161	0.17
Alaska Athabascan *(Ala. Nat.)* (1)	2	<0.01
Apache (4)	12	0.01
Blackfeet (12)	37	0.04
Central American Ind. (7)	7	0.01
Cherokee (27)	230	0.24
Cheyenne (0)	3	<0.01
Chickasaw (0)	3	<0.01
Chippewa (1)	1	<0.01
Choctaw (5)	10	0.01
Comanche (2)	7	0.01
Cree (1)	1	<0.01
Crow (0)	6	0.01
Delaware (1)	3	<0.01
Inupiat *(Alaska Native)* (5)	7	0.01
Iroquois (9)	17	0.02
Lumbee (9)	12	0.01
Mexican American Ind. (15)	17	0.02
Navajo (2)	5	0.01
Osage (1)	1	<0.01
Pueblo (2)	3	<0.01
Seminole (0)	1	<0.01
Shoshone (0)	2	<0.01
Sioux (3)	17	0.02
South American Ind. (2)	8	0.01
Spanish American Ind. (0)	1	<0.01
Tlingit-Haida *(Alaska Native)* (3)	3	<0.01
Tohono O'Odham (1)	2	<0.01
Yuman (1)	1	<0.01
Asian (1,704)	2,119	2.18
Not Hispanic (1,676)	2,044	2.11
Hispanic (28)	75	0.08
Bangladeshi (1)	2	<0.01
Bhutanese (120)	132	0.14
Burmese (75)	82	0.08
Cambodian (68)	73	0.08
Chinese, ex. Taiwanese (114)	154	0.16
Filipino (175)	260	0.27
Indian (274)	345	0.36
Indonesian (3)	4	<0.01
Japanese (46)	94	0.10
Korean (77)	133	0.14
Laotian (28)	34	0.04
Malaysian (2)	4	<0.01
Nepalese (48)	56	0.06
Pakistani (16)	18	0.02
Sri Lankan (5)	7	0.01
Taiwanese (6)	10	0.01
Thai (18)	24	0.02
Vietnamese (522)	569	0.59
Hawaii Native/Pacific Islander (53)	122	0.13
Not Hispanic (36)	89	0.09
Hispanic (17)	33	0.03
Fijian (1)	1	<0.01
Guamanian/Chamorro (16)	21	0.02
Native Hawaiian (8)	39	0.04
Samoan (5)	14	0.01
White (62,343)	64,678	66.66
Not Hispanic (60,042)	62,022	63.92
Hispanic (2,301)	2,656	2.74

Rockwood

Place Type: CDP
County: Chesterfield
Population: 8,431†

Ancestry‡	Population	%
African, Sub-Saharan (20)	20	0.26
African (6)	6	0.08
South African (14)	14	0.18
American (783)	783	9.99
Arab (80)	111	1.42
Arab (24)	24	0.31
Lebanese (43)	43	0.55
Palestinian (13)	13	0.17
Syrian (0)	31	0.40
Austrian (8)	19	0.24
Belgian (10)	10	0.13
British (84)	164	2.09
Canadian (4)	14	0.18
Croatian (32)	32	0.41
Czech (0)	21	0.27
Czechoslovakian (0)	6	0.08
Danish (0)	19	0.24
Dutch (0)	47	0.60
Eastern European (0)	29	0.37
English (476)	1,084	13.83
European (69)	104	1.33
French, ex. Basque (75)	442	5.64
French Canadian (11)	32	0.41
German (250)	917	11.70
Hungarian (10)	10	0.13
Iranian (12)	12	0.15
Irish (238)	815	10.40
Italian (199)	487	6.21
Lithuanian (11)	52	0.66
Polish (43)	237	3.02
Portuguese (0)	16	0.20
Russian (0)	23	0.29
Scotch-Irish (187)	346	4.41
Scottish (117)	443	5.65
Slovak (0)	6	0.08
Swedish (33)	110	1.40
Swiss (44)	44	0.56

*Notes: † The Census 2010 population figure is used to calculate the percentages in the Hispanic Origin and Race categories. Ancestry percentages are based on the 2006-2010 American Community Survey population (not shown); ‡ Numbers in parentheses indicate the number of people reporting a single ancestry; * Numbers in parentheses indicate the number of persons reporting this race alone, not in combination with any other race; Please refer to the Explanation of Data for more information.*

Ancestry	Population	%
Welsh (29)	79	1.01

Hispanic Origin	Population	%
Hispanic or Latino (of any race)	462	5.48
Central American, ex. Mexican	147	1.74
Costa Rican	2	0.02
Guatemalan	44	0.52
Honduran	15	0.18
Nicaraguan	3	0.04
Panamanian	1	0.01
Salvadoran	82	0.97
Cuban	8	0.09
Dominican Republic	8	0.09
Mexican	97	1.15
Puerto Rican	91	1.08
South American	62	0.74
Argentinean	9	0.11
Bolivian	1	0.01
Chilean	1	0.01
Colombian	16	0.19
Ecuadorian	19	0.23
Paraguayan	5	0.06
Peruvian	6	0.07
Venezuelan	5	0.06
Other Hispanic or Latino	49	0.58

Race*	Population	%
African-American/Black (1,760)	1,901	22.55
Not Hispanic (1,726)	1,854	21.99
Hispanic (34)	47	0.56
American Indian/Alaska Native (21)	99	1.17
Not Hispanic (15)	83	0.98
Hispanic (6)	16	0.19
Blackfeet (0)	1	0.01
Cherokee (5)	35	0.42
Creek (0)	2	0.02
Delaware (0)	1	0.01
Iroquois (1)	1	0.01
Lumbee (1)	1	0.01
Mexican American Ind. (6)	7	0.08
Sioux (0)	5	0.06
Asian (349)	408	4.84
Not Hispanic (340)	399	4.73
Hispanic (9)	9	0.11
Bangladeshi (4)	4	0.05
Cambodian (28)	30	0.36
Chinese, ex. Taiwanese (43)	51	0.60
Filipino (24)	36	0.43
Indian (99)	114	1.35
Japanese (10)	12	0.14
Korean (35)	53	0.63
Laotian (3)	3	0.04
Pakistani (30)	30	0.36
Sri Lankan (3)	3	0.04
Taiwanese (4)	4	0.05
Thai (2)	2	0.02
Vietnamese (60)	66	0.78
Hawaii Native/Pacific Islander (1)	10	0.12
Not Hispanic (1)	9	0.11
Hispanic (0)	1	0.01
Guamanian/Chamorro (1)	2	0.02
Samoan (0)	3	0.04
White (5,839)	6,032	71.55
Not Hispanic (5,649)	5,823	69.07
Hispanic (190)	209	2.48

Rose Hill

Place Type: CDP
County: Fairfax
Population: 20,226†

Ancestry‡	Population	%
Afghan (77)	77	0.39
African, Sub-Saharan (882)	928	4.69
African (299)	345	1.75
Ethiopian (235)	235	1.19
Liberian (39)	39	0.20
Other Sub-Saharan African (309)	309	1.56
Albanian (0)	29	0.15
American (762)	762	3.85
Arab (464)	524	2.65
Arab (197)	197	1.00
Egyptian (41)	41	0.21
Moroccan (0)	30	0.15
Other Arab (226)	256	1.30
Armenian (47)	47	0.24
Australian (33)	33	0.17
Austrian (52)	175	0.89
British (42)	156	0.79
Bulgarian (3)	9	0.05
Croatian (25)	47	0.24
Czech (37)	104	0.53
Danish (0)	22	0.11
Dutch (22)	211	1.07
English (804)	2,392	12.10
European (318)	430	2.18
Finnish (0)	10	0.05
French, ex. Basque (137)	497	2.51
French Canadian (3)	54	0.27
German (460)	2,446	12.37
Greek (159)	183	0.93
Hungarian (73)	157	0.79
Iranian (6)	6	0.03
Irish (664)	2,215	11.21
Italian (233)	843	4.26
Lithuanian (0)	44	0.22
Norwegian (38)	308	1.56
Pennsylvania German (9)	41	0.21
Polish (164)	433	2.19
Portuguese (90)	145	0.73
Romanian (0)	46	0.23
Russian (50)	136	0.69
Scandinavian (12)	12	0.06
Scotch-Irish (207)	651	3.29
Scottish (110)	731	3.70
Slavic (0)	14	0.07
Slovak (8)	27	0.14
Swedish (65)	248	1.25
Swiss (0)	18	0.09
Turkish (25)	101	0.51
Ukrainian (8)	8	0.04
Welsh (41)	233	1.18
West Indian, ex. Hispanic (0)	12	0.06
Jamaican (0)	12	0.06
Yugoslavian (0)	20	0.10

Hispanic Origin	Population	%
Hispanic or Latino (of any race)	4,220	20.86
Central American, ex. Mexican	2,271	11.23
Costa Rican	11	0.05
Guatemalan	185	0.91
Honduran	331	1.64
Nicaraguan	64	0.32
Panamanian	31	0.15
Salvadoran	1,639	8.10
Other Central American	10	0.05
Cuban	47	0.23
Dominican Republic	36	0.18
Mexican	519	2.57
Puerto Rican	183	0.90
South American	731	3.61
Argentinean	25	0.12
Bolivian	341	1.69
Chilean	41	0.20
Colombian	54	0.27
Ecuadorian	35	0.17
Paraguayan	1	<0.01
Peruvian	205	1.01
Uruguayan	12	0.06
Venezuelan	16	0.08
Other South American	1	<0.01
Other Hispanic or Latino	433	2.14

Race*	Population	%
African-American/Black (2,225)	2,465	12.19
Not Hispanic (2,161)	2,355	11.64
Hispanic (64)	110	0.54
American Indian/Alaska Native (82)	207	1.02
Not Hispanic (43)	126	0.62
Hispanic (39)	81	0.40
Apache (0)	2	0.01
Blackfeet (0)	2	0.01
Cherokee (3)	36	0.18
Cheyenne (0)	1	<0.01
Chickasaw (1)	1	<0.01
Chippewa (0)	1	<0.01
Choctaw (1)	5	0.02
Cree (0)	2	0.01
Creek (3)	5	0.02
Delaware (2)	3	0.01
Iroquois (1)	3	0.01
Kiowa (2)	2	0.01
Lumbee (2)	2	0.01
Mexican American Ind. (6)	10	0.05
Navajo (2)	3	0.01
Seminole (0)	3	0.01
Sioux (2)	5	0.02
South American Ind. (5)	17	0.08
Spanish American Ind. (3)	3	0.01
Asian (1,989)	2,281	11.28
Not Hispanic (1,977)	2,235	11.05
Hispanic (12)	46	0.23
Bangladeshi (28)	30	0.15
Burmese (5)	5	0.02
Cambodian (51)	54	0.27
Chinese, ex. Taiwanese (198)	242	1.20
Filipino (297)	367	1.81
Indian (294)	360	1.78
Indonesian (7)	12	0.06
Japanese (34)	63	0.31
Korean (175)	218	1.08
Laotian (18)	21	0.10
Malaysian (0)	1	<0.01
Nepalese (11)	11	0.05
Pakistani (350)	389	1.92
Sri Lankan (2)	2	0.01
Taiwanese (11)	14	0.07
Thai (105)	116	0.57
Vietnamese (284)	300	1.48
Hawaii Native/Pacific Islander (19)	62	0.31
Not Hispanic (18)	48	0.24
Hispanic (1)	14	0.07
Fijian (1)	1	<0.01
Guamanian/Chamorro (4)	9	0.04
Native Hawaiian (7)	23	0.11
Samoan (2)	7	0.03
White (13,358)	14,006	69.25
Not Hispanic (11,238)	11,662	57.66
Hispanic (2,120)	2,344	11.59

Salem

Place Type: Independent City
County: Salem
Population: 24,802†

Ancestry‡	Population	%
African, Sub-Saharan (31)	68	0.28
African (17)	43	0.17
Nigerian (14)	25	0.10
American (3,300)	3,300	13.39
Arab (54)	102	0.41
Arab (32)	32	0.13
Lebanese (22)	52	0.21
Other Arab (0)	18	0.07
Armenian (0)	11	0.04
British (145)	265	1.08
Canadian (12)	12	0.05
Croatian (27)	27	0.11
Czech (0)	12	0.05
Danish (0)	55	0.22
Dutch (75)	332	1.35
Eastern European (11)	11	0.04
English (1,699)	3,825	15.52
European (422)	422	1.71
Finnish (0)	24	0.10
French, ex. Basque (118)	593	2.41
French Canadian (112)	112	0.45
German (1,572)	4,254	17.26

*Notes: † The Census 2010 population figure is used to calculate the percentages in the Hispanic Origin and Race categories. Ancestry percentages are based on the 2006-2010 American Community Survey population (not shown); ‡ Numbers in parentheses indicate the number of people reporting a single ancestry; * Numbers in parentheses indicate the number of persons reporting this race alone, not in combination with any other race; Please refer to the Explanation of Data for more information.*

SECTION TWO

Ancestry	Population	%
Greek (25)	54	0.22
Guyanese (0)	26	0.11
Hungarian (12)	26	0.11
Irish (1,149)	3,326	13.50
Italian (257)	731	2.97
Lithuanian (0)	3	0.01
Norwegian (60)	120	0.49
Polish (82)	258	1.05
Portuguese (0)	14	0.06
Russian (0)	40	0.16
Scandinavian (17)	29	0.12
Scotch-Irish (326)	849	3.45
Scottish (311)	701	2.84
Slavic (17)	17	0.07
Slovak (0)	29	0.12
Slovene (11)	11	0.04
Swedish (77)	135	0.55
Swiss (18)	64	0.26
Ukrainian (0)	57	0.23
Welsh (61)	307	1.25
West Indian, ex. Hispanic (6)	6	0.02
Jamaican (6)	6	0.02
Yugoslavian (36)	36	0.15

Hispanic Origin	Population	%
Hispanic or Latino (of any race)	601	2.42
Central American, ex. Mexican	62	0.25
Costa Rican	5	0.02
Guatemalan	6	0.02
Honduran	37	0.15
Nicaraguan	2	0.01
Panamanian	9	0.04
Salvadoran	3	0.01
Cuban	41	0.17
Dominican Republic	4	0.02
Mexican	304	1.23
Puerto Rican	76	0.31
South American	44	0.18
Argentinean	4	0.02
Chilean	2	0.01
Colombian	19	0.08
Ecuadorian	8	0.03
Peruvian	6	0.02
Venezuelan	4	0.02
Other South American	1	<0.01
Other Hispanic or Latino	70	0.28

Race*	Population	%
African-American/Black (1,763)	1,978	7.98
Not Hispanic (1,732)	1,932	7.79
Hispanic (31)	46	0.19
American Indian/Alaska Native (62)	145	0.58
Not Hispanic (55)	135	0.54
Hispanic (7)	10	0.04
Apache (0)	1	<0.01
Blackfeet (0)	2	0.01
Canadian/French Am. Ind. (0)	1	<0.01
Central American Ind. (1)	1	<0.01
Cherokee (18)	54	0.22
Cheyenne (2)	2	0.01
Chickasaw (0)	1	<0.01
Chippewa (0)	2	0.01
Choctaw (1)	1	<0.01
Comanche (0)	2	0.01
Creek (1)	1	<0.01
Iroquois (1)	2	0.01
Lumbee (4)	4	0.02
Menominee (0)	1	<0.01
Mexican American Ind. (4)	4	0.02
Navajo (1)	1	<0.01
Seminole (0)	1	<0.01
Asian (402)	461	1.86
Not Hispanic (398)	452	1.82
Hispanic (4)	9	0.04
Bangladeshi (13)	13	0.05
Burmese (1)	1	<0.01
Chinese, ex. Taiwanese (28)	38	0.15
Filipino (49)	73	0.29
Hmong (1)	1	<0.01
Indian (150)	158	0.64
Japanese (10)	22	0.09
Korean (32)	38	0.15
Laotian (3)	3	0.01
Nepalese (3)	3	0.01
Pakistani (5)	5	0.02
Sri Lankan (1)	1	<0.01
Taiwanese (3)	3	0.01
Thai (3)	3	0.01
Vietnamese (46)	47	0.19
Hawaii Native/Pacific Islander (6)	13	0.05
Not Hispanic (6)	13	0.05
Native Hawaiian (2)	6	0.02
Samoan (3)	3	0.01
White (21,872)	22,219	89.59
Not Hispanic (21,653)	21,961	88.55
Hispanic (219)	258	1.04

Sandston

Place Type: CDP
County: Henrico
Population: 7,571†

Ancestry‡	Population	%
American (811)	811	10.57
Belgian (0)	8	0.10
British (13)	44	0.57
Canadian (0)	27	0.35
Croatian (0)	10	0.13
Czechoslovakian (14)	14	0.18
Danish (13)	13	0.17
Dutch (9)	36	0.47
English (301)	690	8.99
European (56)	56	0.73
French, ex. Basque (12)	96	1.25
French Canadian (0)	26	0.34
German (319)	858	11.18
Greek (43)	64	0.83
Irish (288)	1,116	14.54
Italian (68)	232	3.02
Northern European (12)	12	0.16
Norwegian (10)	18	0.23
Polish (34)	64	0.83
Russian (0)	23	0.30
Scandinavian (0)	30	0.39
Scotch-Irish (80)	164	2.14
Scottish (20)	79	1.03
Swedish (8)	128	1.67
Ukrainian (8)	8	0.10
Welsh (7)	33	0.43
West Indian, ex. Hispanic (9)	41	0.53
Jamaican (9)	41	0.53

Hispanic Origin	Population	%
Hispanic or Latino (of any race)	359	4.74
Central American, ex. Mexican	52	0.69
Guatemalan	17	0.22
Honduran	11	0.15
Panamanian	3	0.04
Salvadoran	21	0.28
Cuban	3	0.04
Dominican Republic	3	0.04
Mexican	156	2.06
Puerto Rican	86	1.14
South American	15	0.20
Colombian	13	0.17
Peruvian	1	0.01
Uruguayan	1	0.01
Other Hispanic or Latino	44	0.58

Race*	Population	%
African-American/Black (2,493)	2,604	34.39
Not Hispanic (2,456)	2,557	33.77
Hispanic (37)	47	0.62
American Indian/Alaska Native (67)	102	1.35
Not Hispanic (57)	90	1.19
Hispanic (10)	12	0.16
Cherokee (8)	18	0.24
Choctaw (1)	1	0.01
Delaware (0)	1	0.01
Lumbee (0)	2	0.03
Menominee (0)	1	0.01
Mexican American Ind. (1)	2	0.03
Sioux (0)	1	0.01
Yaqui (1)	1	0.01
Asian (98)	117	1.55
Not Hispanic (95)	110	1.45
Hispanic (3)	7	0.09
Cambodian (2)	2	0.03
Chinese, ex. Taiwanese (33)	33	0.44
Filipino (18)	25	0.33
Indian (19)	21	0.28
Japanese (2)	2	0.03
Korean (2)	3	0.04
Thai (1)	6	0.08
Vietnamese (19)	20	0.26
Hawaii Native/Pacific Islander (4)	6	0.08
Not Hispanic (2)	4	0.05
Hispanic (2)	2	0.03
Guamanian/Chamorro (2)	2	0.03
Native Hawaiian (1)	2	0.03
White (4,587)	4,740	62.61
Not Hispanic (4,459)	4,580	60.49
Hispanic (128)	160	2.11

Seven Corners

Place Type: CDP
County: Fairfax
Population: 9,255†

Ancestry‡	Population	%
Afghan (51)	87	1.04
African, Sub-Saharan (331)	458	5.50
African (183)	248	2.98
Ethiopian (48)	48	0.58
Kenyan (0)	62	0.74
Nigerian (24)	24	0.29
Somalian (55)	55	0.66
Sudanese (21)	21	0.25
Alsatian (0)	6	0.07
American (345)	345	4.14
Arab (178)	280	3.36
Arab (29)	29	0.35
Egyptian (71)	71	0.85
Moroccan (43)	94	1.13
Other Arab (35)	86	1.03
Brazilian (13)	13	0.16
British (63)	74	0.89
Croatian (0)	12	0.14
Czech (0)	12	0.14
Dutch (21)	34	0.41
English (72)	371	4.45
European (61)	81	0.97
French, ex. Basque (19)	143	1.72
French Canadian (0)	31	0.37
German (86)	429	5.15
Greek (32)	32	0.38
Hungarian (0)	27	0.32
Iranian (33)	33	0.40
Irish (50)	367	4.40
Italian (23)	152	1.82
Lithuanian (7)	17	0.20
Norwegian (11)	49	0.59
Polish (61)	187	2.24
Portuguese (20)	20	0.24
Russian (19)	57	0.68
Scotch-Irish (101)	101	1.21
Scottish (12)	47	0.56
Slavic (0)	11	0.13
Slovak (0)	12	0.14
Swedish (0)	5	0.06
Swiss (37)	59	0.71
Turkish (55)	55	0.66
Ukrainian (33)	43	0.52
West Indian, ex. Hispanic (35)	35	0.42
West Indian (35)	35	0.42
Yugoslavian (0)	43	0.52

*Notes: † The Census 2010 population figure is used to calculate the percentages in the Hispanic Origin and Race categories. Ancestry percentages are based on the 2006-2010 American Community Survey population (not shown); ‡ Numbers in parentheses indicate the number of people reporting a single ancestry; * Numbers in parentheses indicate the number of persons reporting this race alone, not in combination with any other race; Please refer to the Explanation of Data for more information.*

Hispanic Origin	Population	%
Hispanic or Latino (of any race)	4,096	44.26
Central American, ex. Mexican	2,230	24.10
Costa Rican	6	0.06
Guatemalan	462	4.99
Honduran	438	4.73
Nicaraguan	44	0.48
Panamanian	17	0.18
Salvadoran	1,255	13.56
Other Central American	8	0.09
Cuban	28	0.30
Dominican Republic	22	0.24
Mexican	387	4.18
Puerto Rican	54	0.58
South American	962	10.39
Argentinean	44	0.48
Bolivian	601	6.49
Chilean	19	0.21
Colombian	65	0.70
Ecuadorian	32	0.35
Paraguayan	8	0.09
Peruvian	179	1.93
Uruguayan	1	0.01
Venezuelan	9	0.10
Other South American	4	0.04
Other Hispanic or Latino	413	4.46

Race*	Population	%
African-American/Black (664)	797	8.61
Not Hispanic (605)	706	7.63
Hispanic (59)	91	0.98
American Indian/Alaska Native (85)	165	1.78
Not Hispanic (23)	60	0.65
Hispanic (62)	105	1.13
Canadian/French Am. Ind. (0)	1	0.01
Central American Ind. (5)	6	0.06
Cherokee (6)	12	0.13
Chippewa (1)	1	0.01
Choctaw (0)	2	0.02
Hopi (0)	2	0.02
Mexican American Ind. (2)	4	0.04
Navajo (1)	1	0.01
Sioux (0)	6	0.06
South American Ind. (14)	22	0.24
Spanish American Ind. (4)	7	0.08
Asian (1,842)	2,026	21.89
Not Hispanic (1,822)	1,985	21.45
Hispanic (20)	41	0.44
Bangladeshi (23)	26	0.28
Burmese (7)	7	0.08
Cambodian (30)	37	0.40
Chinese, ex. Taiwanese (133)	160	1.73
Filipino (182)	207	2.24
Indian (162)	220	2.38
Indonesian (12)	14	0.15
Japanese (9)	19	0.21
Korean (114)	121	1.31
Laotian (4)	4	0.04
Malaysian (7)	7	0.08
Nepalese (80)	80	0.86
Pakistani (117)	136	1.47
Sri Lankan (9)	9	0.10
Taiwanese (2)	7	0.08
Thai (22)	29	0.31
Vietnamese (818)	877	9.48
Hawaii Native/Pacific Islander (12)	37	0.40
Not Hispanic (8)	24	0.26
Hispanic (4)	13	0.14
Guamanian/Chamorro (4)	7	0.08
Native Hawaiian (0)	5	0.05
Samoan (4)	5	0.05
White (4,109)	4,558	49.25
Not Hispanic (2,371)	2,578	27.86
Hispanic (1,738)	1,980	21.39

Short Pump

Place Type: CDP
County: Henrico
Population: 24,729†

Ancestry‡	Population	%
African, Sub-Saharan (0)	7	0.03
Ethiopian (0)	7	0.03
American (1,438)	1,438	5.98
Arab (343)	459	1.91
Arab (36)	36	0.15
Egyptian (38)	38	0.16
Iraqi (232)	232	0.97
Lebanese (37)	153	0.64
Armenian (150)	162	0.67
Austrian (47)	101	0.42
British (91)	235	0.98
Canadian (10)	22	0.09
Celtic (36)	36	0.15
Czech (39)	149	0.62
Czechoslovakian (12)	12	0.05
Danish (11)	11	0.05
Dutch (77)	262	1.09
Eastern European (8)	8	0.03
English (1,367)	3,726	15.50
European (425)	566	2.35
Finnish (0)	15	0.06
French, ex. Basque (92)	735	3.06
French Canadian (24)	152	0.63
German (966)	4,693	19.53
Greek (253)	610	2.54
Hungarian (0)	305	1.27
Iranian (233)	233	0.97
Irish (1,166)	4,374	18.20
Israeli (86)	86	0.36
Italian (320)	1,301	5.41
Lithuanian (0)	9	0.04
Northern European (76)	76	0.32
Norwegian (76)	175	0.73
Pennsylvania German (0)	11	0.05
Polish (99)	551	2.29
Portuguese (15)	38	0.16
Romanian (37)	115	0.48
Russian (201)	379	1.58
Scandinavian (19)	52	0.22
Scotch-Irish (288)	575	2.39
Scottish (497)	1,088	4.53
Serbian (0)	12	0.05
Slavic (0)	24	0.10
Slovak (13)	99	0.41
Slovene (0)	15	0.06
Swedish (35)	244	1.02
Swiss (0)	31	0.13
Turkish (49)	49	0.20
Ukrainian (18)	62	0.26
Welsh (62)	160	0.67
West Indian, ex. Hispanic (36)	47	0.20
Haitian (22)	22	0.09
Jamaican (14)	14	0.06
West Indian (0)	11	0.05

Hispanic Origin	Population	%
Hispanic or Latino (of any race)	784	3.17
Central American, ex. Mexican	101	0.41
Costa Rican	13	0.05
Guatemalan	27	0.11
Honduran	15	0.06
Nicaraguan	5	0.02
Panamanian	18	0.07
Salvadoran	23	0.09
Cuban	61	0.25
Dominican Republic	20	0.08
Mexican	205	0.83
Puerto Rican	171	0.69
South American	142	0.57
Argentinean	16	0.06
Bolivian	8	0.03
Chilean	7	0.03
Colombian	38	0.15
Ecuadorian	16	0.06
Peruvian	17	0.07
Uruguayan	1	<0.01
Venezuelan	37	0.15
Other South American	2	0.01
Other Hispanic or Latino	84	0.34

Race*	Population	%
African-American/Black (1,411)	1,622	6.56
Not Hispanic (1,383)	1,574	6.36
Hispanic (28)	48	0.19
American Indian/Alaska Native (33)	138	0.56
Not Hispanic (29)	123	0.50
Hispanic (4)	15	0.06
Blackfeet (0)	2	0.01
Cherokee (2)	39	0.16
Choctaw (0)	8	0.03
Creek (1)	1	<0.01
Iroquois (1)	1	<0.01
Navajo (3)	3	0.01
Shoshone (0)	1	<0.01
Spanish American Ind. (0)	1	<0.01
Asian (3,939)	4,282	17.32
Not Hispanic (3,929)	4,262	17.23
Hispanic (10)	20	0.08
Bangladeshi (49)	52	0.21
Burmese (3)	3	0.01
Cambodian (3)	9	0.04
Chinese, ex. Taiwanese (667)	731	2.96
Filipino (91)	140	0.57
Hmong (1)	2	0.01
Indian (2,326)	2,409	9.74
Indonesian (7)	9	0.04
Japanese (57)	72	0.29
Korean (310)	361	1.46
Laotian (3)	4	0.02
Malaysian (1)	6	0.02
Nepalese (6)	7	0.03
Pakistani (148)	161	0.65
Sri Lankan (8)	9	0.04
Taiwanese (12)	18	0.07
Thai (24)	30	0.12
Vietnamese (116)	153	0.62
Hawaii Native/Pacific Islander (3)	28	0.11
Not Hispanic (3)	21	0.08
Hispanic (0)	7	0.03
Guamanian/Chamorro (2)	4	0.02
Native Hawaiian (1)	15	0.06
White (18,551)	19,052	77.04
Not Hispanic (17,993)	18,453	74.62
Hispanic (558)	599	2.42

Smithfield

Place Type: Town
County: Isle of Wight
Population: 8,089†

Ancestry‡	Population	%
African, Sub-Saharan (215)	215	2.73
African (215)	215	2.73
Alsatian (0)	14	0.18
American (1,356)	1,356	17.23
Austrian (0)	26	0.33
British (22)	36	0.46
Canadian (13)	13	0.17
Celtic (0)	25	0.32
Czech (13)	13	0.17
Danish (25)	54	0.69
Dutch (16)	148	1.88
English (603)	1,112	14.13
European (61)	61	0.78
French, ex. Basque (51)	183	2.33
French Canadian (46)	46	0.58
German (176)	881	11.20
Greek (13)	29	0.37
Hungarian (7)	49	0.62
Irish (179)	821	10.43
Italian (87)	130	1.65
Norwegian (30)	42	0.53

*Notes: † The Census 2010 population figure is used to calculate the percentages in the Hispanic Origin and Race categories. Ancestry percentages are based on the 2006-2010 American Community Survey population (not shown); ‡ Numbers in parentheses indicate the number of people reporting a single ancestry; * Numbers in parentheses indicate the number of persons reporting this race alone, not in combination with any other race; Please refer to the Explanation of Data for more information.*

Pennsylvania German (6)	6	0.08
Polish (24)	125	1.59
Portuguese (12)	26	0.33
Scotch-Irish (65)	172	2.19
Scottish (60)	264	3.35
Slovak (0)	24	0.30
Swedish (0)	12	0.15
Swiss (25)	54	0.69
Ukrainian (32)	32	0.41
Welsh (0)	20	0.25
West Indian, ex. Hispanic (7)	7	0.09
Barbadian (7)	7	0.09

Hispanic Origin	Population	%
Hispanic or Latino (of any race)	175	2.16
Central American, ex. Mexican	14	0.17
Honduran	1	0.01
Nicaraguan	2	0.02
Panamanian	10	0.12
Salvadoran	1	0.01
Cuban	7	0.09
Dominican Republic	4	0.05
Mexican	89	1.10
Puerto Rican	34	0.42
South American	11	0.14
Argentinean	1	0.01
Chilean	4	0.05
Colombian	5	0.06
Ecuadorian	1	0.01
Other Hispanic or Latino	16	0.20

Race*	Population	%
African-American/Black (2,322)	2,419	29.90
Not Hispanic (2,305)	2,388	29.52
Hispanic (17)	31	0.38
American Indian/Alaska Native (30)	98	1.21
Not Hispanic (26)	87	1.08
Hispanic (4)	11	0.14
Blackfeet (0)	4	0.05
Cherokee (14)	28	0.35
Chickasaw (0)	1	0.01
Chippewa (1)	2	0.02
Choctaw (1)	6	0.07
Comanche (0)	3	0.04
Cree (1)	3	0.04
Creek (0)	5	0.06
Kiowa (0)	3	0.04
Lumbee (0)	6	0.07
Mexican American Ind. (2)	2	0.02
Sioux (0)	1	0.01
Tlingit-Haida *(Alaska Native)* (1)	3	0.04
Asian (73)	125	1.55
Not Hispanic (72)	112	1.38
Hispanic (1)	13	0.16
Cambodian (16)	16	0.20
Chinese, ex. Taiwanese (10)	13	0.16
Filipino (18)	41	0.51
Indian (6)	6	0.07
Japanese (4)	16	0.20
Korean (12)	27	0.33
Malaysian (0)	1	0.01
Pakistani (1)	1	0.01
Vietnamese (5)	5	0.06
Hawaii Native/Pacific Islander (8)	14	0.17
Not Hispanic (7)	9	0.11
Hispanic (1)	5	0.06
Guamanian/Chamorro (2)	2	0.02
Native Hawaiian (1)	2	0.02
White (5,439)	5,600	69.23
Not Hispanic (5,344)	5,483	67.78
Hispanic (95)	117	1.45

South Boston

Place Type: Town
County: Halifax
Population: 8,142†

Ancestry‡	Population	%
African, Sub-Saharan (137)	137	1.67
African (137)	137	1.67
American (1,252)	1,252	15.26
British (12)	30	0.37
Canadian (27)	27	0.33
Czech (0)	43	0.52
Dutch (0)	65	0.79
English (479)	698	8.51
European (71)	100	1.22
French, ex. Basque (34)	142	1.73
German (166)	467	5.69
Greek (87)	87	1.06
Hungarian (13)	45	0.55
Irish (149)	299	3.65
Italian (60)	70	0.85
Polish (52)	52	0.63
Russian (0)	23	0.28
Scotch-Irish (68)	128	1.56
Scottish (20)	54	0.66
Slovene (0)	18	0.22
Swedish (0)	52	0.63
Swiss (0)	16	0.20
Ukrainian (12)	28	0.34
Welsh (0)	51	0.62
West Indian, ex. Hispanic (14)	14	0.17
Bermudan (14)	14	0.17

Hispanic Origin	Population	%
Hispanic or Latino (of any race)	185	2.27
Central American, ex. Mexican	13	0.16
Costa Rican	6	0.07
Guatemalan	2	0.02
Honduran	1	0.01
Salvadoran	4	0.05
Dominican Republic	1	0.01
Mexican	109	1.34
Puerto Rican	26	0.32
South American	11	0.14
Colombian	2	0.02
Ecuadorian	7	0.09
Uruguayan	2	0.02
Other Hispanic or Latino	25	0.31

Race*	Population	%
African-American/Black (4,087)	4,161	51.11
Not Hispanic (4,070)	4,141	50.86
Hispanic (17)	20	0.25
American Indian/Alaska Native (20)	54	0.66
Not Hispanic (20)	54	0.66
Cherokee (3)	14	0.17
Cree (1)	1	0.01
Creek (1)	1	0.01
Lumbee (1)	1	0.01
Navajo (1)	2	0.02
Asian (45)	50	0.61
Not Hispanic (45)	50	0.61
Chinese, ex. Taiwanese (17)	17	0.21
Filipino (6)	8	0.10
Indian (4)	5	0.06
Japanese (3)	4	0.05
Korean (0)	1	0.01
Pakistani (1)	1	0.01
Sri Lankan (1)	1	0.01
Thai (3)	3	0.04
Vietnamese (10)	10	0.12
Hawaii Native/Pacific Islander (0)	2	0.02
Not Hispanic (0)	2	0.02
Native Hawaiian (0)	1	0.01
White (3,763)	3,845	47.22
Not Hispanic (3,712)	3,791	46.56
Hispanic (51)	54	0.66

South Riding

Place Type: CDP
County: Loudoun
Population: 24,256†

Ancestry‡	Population	%
Afghan (282)	437	1.90
African, Sub-Saharan (358)	358	1.56
African (257)	257	1.12
Ethiopian (86)	86	0.37
Other Sub-Saharan African (15)	15	0.07
American (689)	689	3.00
Arab (225)	344	1.50
Arab (17)	74	0.32
Egyptian (56)	56	0.24
Lebanese (98)	160	0.70
Moroccan (54)	54	0.23
Armenian (19)	83	0.36
Austrian (41)	130	0.57
Brazilian (36)	36	0.16
British (172)	565	2.46
Canadian (66)	141	0.61
Croatian (9)	87	0.38
Czech (27)	54	0.23
Czechoslovakian (13)	39	0.17
Danish (0)	123	0.54
Dutch (0)	87	0.38
Eastern European (49)	49	0.21
English (316)	1,802	7.84
European (415)	452	1.97
Finnish (19)	77	0.34
French, ex. Basque (38)	752	3.27
French Canadian (60)	94	0.41
German (584)	2,678	11.65
Greek (35)	92	0.40
Hungarian (26)	77	0.34
Iranian (205)	281	1.22
Irish (341)	2,582	11.23
Israeli (0)	55	0.24
Italian (433)	1,530	6.66
Lithuanian (28)	266	1.16
Luxemburger (15)	15	0.07
Macedonian (0)	17	0.07
Northern European (0)	20	0.09
Norwegian (30)	168	0.73
Polish (228)	810	3.52
Russian (21)	113	0.49
Scandinavian (0)	82	0.36
Scotch-Irish (126)	410	1.78
Scottish (190)	604	2.63
Serbian (16)	71	0.31
Slavic (0)	156	0.68
Slovak (20)	46	0.20
Swedish (11)	131	0.57
Swiss (0)	46	0.20
Turkish (41)	41	0.18
Ukrainian (12)	122	0.53
Welsh (0)	155	0.67

Hispanic Origin	Population	%
Hispanic or Latino (of any race)	1,806	7.45
Central American, ex. Mexican	416	1.72
Costa Rican	10	0.04
Guatemalan	85	0.35
Honduran	16	0.07
Nicaraguan	33	0.14
Panamanian	26	0.11
Salvadoran	241	0.99
Other Central American	5	0.02
Cuban	72	0.30
Dominican Republic	35	0.14
Mexican	292	1.20
Puerto Rican	256	1.06
South American	511	2.11
Argentinean	20	0.08
Bolivian	116	0.48
Chilean	25	0.10
Colombian	97	0.40
Ecuadorian	48	0.20
Paraguayan	3	0.01
Peruvian	163	0.67
Uruguayan	2	0.01
Venezuelan	22	0.09
Other South American	15	0.06
Other Hispanic or Latino	224	0.92

Race*	Population	%
African-American/Black (1,564)	1,805	7.44

*Notes: † The Census 2010 population figure is used to calculate the percentages in the Hispanic Origin and Race categories. Ancestry percentages are based on the 2006-2010 American Community Survey population (not shown); ‡ Numbers in parentheses indicate the number of people reporting a single ancestry; * Numbers in parentheses indicate the number of persons reporting this race alone, not in combination with any other race; Please refer to the Explanation of Data for more information.*

Not Hispanic (1,506)	1,701	7.01
Hispanic (58)	104	0.43
American Indian/Alaska Native (52)	154	0.63
Not Hispanic (39)	117	0.48
Hispanic (13)	37	0.15
Apache (0)	1	<0.01
Blackfeet (2)	13	0.05
Canadian/French Am. Ind. (0)	1	<0.01
Central American Ind. (0)	1	<0.01
Cherokee (5)	24	0.10
Chippewa (0)	1	<0.01
Choctaw (1)	3	0.01
Iroquois (4)	6	0.02
Lumbee (0)	1	<0.01
Mexican American Ind. (1)	1	<0.01
Navajo (2)	9	0.04
Potawatomi (1)	1	<0.01
Pueblo (1)	1	<0.01
Sioux (0)	4	0.02
South American Ind. (4)	7	0.03
Tohono O'Odham (1)	3	0.01
Yakama (1)	1	<0.01
Asian (7,019)	7,661	31.58
Not Hispanic (6,995)	7,607	31.36
Hispanic (24)	54	0.22
Bangladeshi (92)	96	0.40
Burmese (7)	7	0.03
Cambodian (68)	76	0.31
Chinese, ex. Taiwanese (682)	818	3.37
Filipino (435)	586	2.42
Indian (2,862)	2,982	12.29
Indonesian (20)	21	0.09
Japanese (43)	108	0.45
Korean (1,193)	1,302	5.37
Laotian (13)	18	0.07
Malaysian (2)	2	0.01
Nepalese (81)	89	0.37
Pakistani (319)	335	1.38
Sri Lankan (23)	28	0.12
Taiwanese (29)	32	0.13
Thai (47)	61	0.25
Vietnamese (928)	1,012	4.17
Hawaii Native/Pacific Islander (14)	47	0.19
Not Hispanic (10)	39	0.16
Hispanic (4)	8	0.03
Guamanian/Chamorro (6)	12	0.05
Marshallese (1)	1	<0.01
Native Hawaiian (2)	9	0.04
Samoan (5)	11	0.05
White (14,120)	14,949	61.63
Not Hispanic (13,019)	13,725	56.58
Hispanic (1,101)	1,224	5.05

Springfield

Place Type: CDP
County: Fairfax
Population: 30,484†

Ancestry‡	Population	%
Afghan (189)	189	0.62
African, Sub-Saharan (753)	770	2.52
African (189)	189	0.62
Ethiopian (487)	487	1.59
Nigerian (59)	59	0.19
Somalian (18)	35	0.11
Albanian (0)	9	0.03
Alsatian (13)	13	0.04
American (778)	778	2.55
Arab (251)	371	1.21
Arab (48)	48	0.16
Egyptian (38)	62	0.20
Jordanian (0)	16	0.05
Lebanese (35)	49	0.16
Moroccan (11)	11	0.04
Palestinian (30)	46	0.15
Other Arab (89)	139	0.46
Austrian (0)	15	0.05
Belgian (0)	34	0.11
Brazilian (7)	7	0.02
British (73)	165	0.54
Canadian (16)	29	0.09
Croatian (0)	5	0.02
Czech (14)	14	0.05
Danish (100)	125	0.41
Dutch (43)	174	0.57
English (1,022)	2,282	7.47
European (71)	71	0.23
French, ex. Basque (60)	518	1.70
French Canadian (44)	56	0.18
German (746)	2,637	8.63
Greek (85)	270	0.88
Hungarian (6)	274	0.90
Iranian (46)	83	0.27
Irish (544)	1,757	5.75
Israeli (0)	16	0.05
Italian (252)	627	2.05
Latvian (28)	41	0.13
Lithuanian (12)	29	0.09
Luxemburger (0)	13	0.04
Norwegian (41)	240	0.79
Pennsylvania German (12)	30	0.10
Polish (215)	618	2.02
Portuguese (13)	27	0.09
Romanian (0)	26	0.09
Russian (45)	167	0.55
Scandinavian (14)	14	0.05
Scotch-Irish (143)	363	1.19
Scottish (90)	401	1.31
Serbian (11)	31	0.10
Slovak (54)	177	0.58
Swedish (122)	262	0.86
Swiss (0)	127	0.42
Turkish (147)	147	0.48
Ukrainian (12)	24	0.08
Welsh (41)	213	0.70
West Indian, ex. Hispanic (0)	50	0.16
Haitian (0)	50	0.16

Hispanic Origin	Population	%
Hispanic or Latino (of any race)	7,766	25.48
Central American, ex. Mexican	4,125	13.53
Costa Rican	21	0.07
Guatemalan	240	0.79
Honduran	1,759	5.77
Nicaraguan	90	0.30
Panamanian	15	0.05
Salvadoran	1,961	6.43
Other Central American	39	0.13
Cuban	56	0.18
Dominican Republic	45	0.15
Mexican	485	1.59
Puerto Rican	233	0.76
South American	1,868	6.13
Argentinean	121	0.40
Bolivian	855	2.80
Chilean	53	0.17
Colombian	110	0.36
Ecuadorian	86	0.28
Paraguayan	2	0.01
Peruvian	573	1.88
Uruguayan	10	0.03
Venezuelan	33	0.11
Other South American	25	0.08
Other Hispanic or Latino	954	3.13

Race*	Population	%
African-American/Black (2,739)	3,006	9.86
Not Hispanic (2,659)	2,868	9.41
Hispanic (80)	138	0.45
American Indian/Alaska Native (211)	473	1.55
Not Hispanic (38)	155	0.51
Hispanic (173)	318	1.04
Arapaho (1)	1	<0.01
Blackfeet (1)	1	<0.01
Canadian/French Am. Ind. (5)	5	0.02
Central American Ind. (4)	7	0.02
Cherokee (2)	29	0.10
Chippewa (1)	3	0.01
Choctaw (2)	3	0.01
Comanche (0)	4	0.01
Creek (1)	6	0.02
Delaware (1)	1	<0.01
Iroquois (1)	3	0.01
Lumbee (1)	1	<0.01
Mexican American Ind. (2)	2	0.01
Navajo (0)	1	<0.01
Seminole (1)	1	<0.01
Shoshone (1)	2	0.01
South American Ind. (16)	23	0.08
Spanish American Ind. (1)	1	<0.01
Yaqui (3)	3	0.01
Asian (7,415)	8,056	26.43
Not Hispanic (7,382)	7,974	26.16
Hispanic (33)	82	0.27
Bangladeshi (215)	240	0.79
Bhutanese (9)	9	0.03
Burmese (15)	15	0.05
Cambodian (149)	156	0.51
Chinese, ex. Taiwanese (507)	587	1.93
Filipino (802)	946	3.10
Hmong (1)	1	<0.01
Indian (889)	1,030	3.38
Indonesian (32)	32	0.10
Japanese (48)	97	0.32
Korean (644)	706	2.32
Laotian (220)	228	0.75
Malaysian (6)	12	0.04
Nepalese (54)	62	0.20
Pakistani (836)	926	3.04
Sri Lankan (10)	10	0.03
Taiwanese (6)	9	0.03
Thai (298)	323	1.06
Vietnamese (2,311)	2,420	7.94
Hawaii Native/Pacific Islander (26)	73	0.24
Not Hispanic (20)	56	0.18
Hispanic (6)	17	0.06
Guamanian/Chamorro (12)	18	0.06
Marshallese (0)	2	0.01
Native Hawaiian (3)	10	0.03
Samoan (0)	2	0.01
White (14,846)	15,965	52.37
Not Hispanic (11,659)	12,351	40.52
Hispanic (3,187)	3,614	11.86

Staunton

Place Type: Independent City
County: Staunton
Population: 23,746†

Ancestry‡	Population	%
African, Sub-Saharan (38)	52	0.22
African (38)	38	0.16
Nigerian (0)	14	0.06
Alsatian (4)	4	0.02
American (4,752)	4,752	19.96
Arab (0)	41	0.17
Syrian (0)	41	0.17
Australian (0)	10	0.04
Austrian (20)	34	0.14
British (73)	217	0.91
Bulgarian (0)	8	0.03
Czech (0)	49	0.21
Czechoslovakian (32)	36	0.15
Danish (43)	63	0.26
Dutch (95)	442	1.86
English (1,142)	2,813	11.82
European (58)	72	0.30
Finnish (0)	10	0.04
French, ex. Basque (144)	429	1.80
French Canadian (35)	64	0.27
German (1,260)	3,725	15.65
Greek (85)	96	0.40
Hungarian (0)	14	0.06
Iranian (14)	14	0.06
Irish (820)	2,067	8.68
Italian (230)	879	3.69
Latvian (8)	8	0.03
Lithuanian (0)	29	0.12

*Notes: † The Census 2010 population figure is used to calculate the percentages in the Hispanic Origin and Race categories. Ancestry percentages are based on the 2006-2010 American Community Survey population (not shown); ‡ Numbers in parentheses indicate the number of people reporting a single ancestry; * Numbers in parentheses indicate the number of persons reporting this race alone, not in combination with any other race; Please refer to the Explanation of Data for more information.*

Northern European (21)	21	0.09
Norwegian (9)	80	0.34
Pennsylvania German (51)	51	0.21
Polish (131)	240	1.01
Portuguese (0)	65	0.27
Romanian (21)	21	0.09
Russian (38)	111	0.47
Scandinavian (0)	13	0.05
Scotch-Irish (809)	1,505	6.32
Scottish (306)	857	3.60
Swedish (94)	386	1.62
Swiss (30)	138	0.58
Ukrainian (0)	25	0.11
Welsh (63)	177	0.74
West Indian, ex. Hispanic (14)	14	0.06
Haitian (14)	14	0.06
Yugoslavian (15)	23	0.10

Hispanic Origin	Population	%
Hispanic or Latino (of any race)	513	2.16
Central American, ex. Mexican	43	0.18
Costa Rican	2	0.01
Guatemalan	14	0.06
Honduran	8	0.03
Nicaraguan	2	0.01
Panamanian	7	0.03
Salvadoran	10	0.04
Cuban	40	0.17
Dominican Republic	12	0.05
Mexican	180	0.76
Puerto Rican	84	0.35
South American	87	0.37
Argentinean	7	0.03
Bolivian	2	0.01
Chilean	2	0.01
Colombian	15	0.06
Ecuadorian	4	0.02
Peruvian	22	0.09
Uruguayan	31	0.13
Venezuelan	4	0.02
Other Hispanic or Latino	67	0.28

Race*	Population	%
African-American/Black (2,885)	3,274	13.79
Not Hispanic (2,859)	3,230	13.60
Hispanic (26)	44	0.19
American Indian/Alaska Native (48)	164	0.69
Not Hispanic (41)	149	0.63
Hispanic (7)	15	0.06
Apache (0)	3	0.01
Arapaho (1)	1	<0.01
Blackfeet (1)	9	0.04
Cherokee (10)	35	0.15
Chickasaw (0)	1	<0.01
Chippewa (1)	1	<0.01
Choctaw (0)	2	0.01
Creek (1)	3	0.01
Delaware (1)	1	<0.01
Iroquois (1)	7	0.03
Lumbee (7)	7	0.03
Mexican American Ind. (2)	2	0.01
Navajo (1)	2	0.01
Osage (2)	2	0.01
Seminole (0)	1	<0.01
Sioux (0)	3	0.01
South American Ind. (2)	2	0.01
Yakama (0)	1	<0.01
Yaqui (0)	4	0.02
Asian (185)	262	1.10
Not Hispanic (182)	257	1.08
Hispanic (3)	5	0.02
Bangladeshi (1)	1	<0.01
Chinese, ex. Taiwanese (37)	47	0.20
Filipino (17)	36	0.15
Indian (39)	43	0.18
Indonesian (0)	4	0.02
Japanese (11)	21	0.09
Korean (15)	25	0.11
Pakistani (3)	4	0.02
Thai (7)	8	0.03
Vietnamese (17)	19	0.08
Hawaii Native/Pacific Islander (7)	21	0.09
Not Hispanic (3)	17	0.07
Hispanic (4)	4	0.02
Guamanian/Chamorro (4)	7	0.03
Native Hawaiian (2)	6	0.03
Samoan (0)	1	<0.01
White (19,874)	20,387	85.85
Not Hispanic (19,584)	20,048	84.43
Hispanic (290)	339	1.43

Sterling

Place Type: CDP
County: Loudoun
Population: 27,822†

Ancestry‡	Population	%
Afghan (38)	38	0.15
African, Sub-Saharan (197)	288	1.13
African (71)	81	0.32
Ethiopian (10)	10	0.04
Ghanaian (22)	22	0.09
Liberian (36)	48	0.19
Sudanese (58)	127	0.50
Albanian (38)	48	0.19
American (1,013)	1,013	3.97
Arab (209)	338	1.32
Arab (61)	117	0.46
Egyptian (39)	39	0.15
Iraqi (52)	63	0.25
Palestinian (32)	73	0.29
Other Arab (25)	46	0.18
Armenian (75)	129	0.51
Austrian (10)	36	0.14
Brazilian (0)	21	0.08
British (43)	100	0.39
Bulgarian (16)	16	0.06
Cajun (0)	9	0.04
Canadian (0)	31	0.12
Croatian (0)	28	0.11
Czech (18)	101	0.40
Danish (8)	8	0.03
Dutch (57)	321	1.26
English (726)	2,509	9.83
European (316)	316	1.24
Finnish (0)	24	0.09
French, ex. Basque (34)	399	1.56
French Canadian (39)	48	0.19
German (940)	3,059	11.99
Greek (62)	105	0.41
Guyanese (63)	63	0.25
Hungarian (57)	109	0.43
Iranian (145)	186	0.73
Irish (633)	2,462	9.65
Italian (252)	1,040	4.08
Lithuanian (35)	136	0.53
Norwegian (59)	190	0.74
Polish (116)	737	2.89
Portuguese (85)	123	0.48
Romanian (0)	20	0.08
Russian (16)	181	0.71
Scandinavian (14)	36	0.14
Scotch-Irish (90)	427	1.67
Scottish (247)	557	2.18
Serbian (12)	12	0.05
Slovak (10)	28	0.11
Swedish (14)	388	1.52
Swiss (19)	19	0.07
Turkish (33)	33	0.13
Ukrainian (6)	32	0.13
Welsh (20)	280	1.10
West Indian, ex. Hispanic (24)	24	0.09
Jamaican (15)	15	0.06
West Indian (9)	9	0.04
Yugoslavian (0)	12	0.05

Hispanic Origin	Population	%
Hispanic or Latino (of any race)	9,230	33.18
Central American, ex. Mexican	5,227	18.79
Costa Rican	23	0.08
Guatemalan	384	1.38
Honduran	779	2.80
Nicaraguan	110	0.40
Panamanian	13	0.05
Salvadoran	3,903	14.03
Other Central American	15	0.05
Cuban	55	0.20
Dominican Republic	54	0.19
Mexican	803	2.89
Puerto Rican	285	1.02
South American	1,597	5.74
Argentinean	48	0.17
Bolivian	483	1.74
Chilean	50	0.18
Colombian	138	0.50
Ecuadorian	126	0.45
Paraguayan	7	0.03
Peruvian	694	2.49
Uruguayan	11	0.04
Venezuelan	26	0.09
Other South American	14	0.05
Other Hispanic or Latino	1,209	4.35

Race*	Population	%
African-American/Black (2,258)	2,604	9.36
Not Hispanic (2,149)	2,435	8.75
Hispanic (109)	169	0.61
American Indian/Alaska Native (131)	301	1.08
Not Hispanic (46)	166	0.60
Hispanic (85)	135	0.49
Alaska Athabascan *(Ala. Nat.)* (0)	1	<0.01
Apache (6)	7	0.03
Blackfeet (0)	4	0.01
Canadian/French Am. Ind. (0)	1	<0.01
Central American Ind. (0)	1	<0.01
Cherokee (11)	50	0.18
Cheyenne (0)	1	<0.01
Choctaw (5)	8	0.03
Comanche (0)	2	0.01
Cree (0)	1	<0.01
Delaware (0)	1	<0.01
Hopi (1)	1	<0.01
Iroquois (2)	4	0.01
Mexican American Ind. (7)	10	0.04
Navajo (1)	4	0.01
Pueblo (1)	1	<0.01
Seminole (0)	1	<0.01
Sioux (3)	11	0.04
South American Ind. (10)	15	0.05
Spanish American Ind. (6)	6	0.02
Tohono O'Odham (2)	2	0.01
Asian (3,925)	4,391	15.78
Not Hispanic (3,897)	4,320	15.53
Hispanic (28)	71	0.26
Bangladeshi (86)	96	0.35
Burmese (28)	33	0.12
Cambodian (181)	197	0.71
Chinese, ex. Taiwanese (247)	298	1.07
Filipino (485)	566	2.03
Hmong (3)	3	0.01
Indian (962)	1,093	3.93
Indonesian (8)	10	0.04
Japanese (39)	67	0.24
Korean (126)	154	0.55
Laotian (176)	188	0.68
Malaysian (2)	2	0.01
Nepalese (21)	23	0.08
Pakistani (403)	468	1.68
Sri Lankan (25)	25	0.09
Taiwanese (15)	17	0.06
Thai (120)	139	0.50
Vietnamese (808)	863	3.10
Hawaii Native/Pacific Islander (23)	60	0.22
Not Hispanic (17)	38	0.14
Hispanic (6)	22	0.08
Fijian (1)	1	<0.01
Guamanian/Chamorro (3)	3	0.01
Native Hawaiian (7)	11	0.04
Samoan (3)	7	0.03

*Notes: † The Census 2010 population figure is used to calculate the percentages in the Hispanic Origin and Race categories. Ancestry percentages are based on the 2006-2010 American Community Survey population (not shown); ‡ Numbers in parentheses indicate the number of people reporting a single ancestry; * Numbers in parentheses indicate the number of persons reporting this race alone, not in combination with any other race; Please refer to the Explanation of Data for more information.*

White (15,147)	16,302	58.59
Not Hispanic (11,631)	12,252	44.04
Hispanic (3,516)	4,050	14.56

Stuarts Draft

Place Type: CDP
County: Augusta
Population: 9,235†

Ancestry‡	Population	%
American (1,554)	1,554	20.61
Basque (11)	11	0.15
British (26)	43	0.57
Canadian (0)	12	0.16
Danish (36)	115	1.53
Dutch (44)	123	1.63
English (705)	1,021	13.54
European (87)	105	1.39
French, ex. Basque (37)	87	1.15
French Canadian (11)	24	0.32
German (639)	1,662	22.04
Irish (292)	843	11.18
Italian (141)	332	4.40
Polish (10)	50	0.66
Russian (0)	66	0.88
Scotch-Irish (179)	319	4.23
Scottish (146)	155	2.06
Slavic (0)	31	0.41
Slovak (19)	39	0.52
Swedish (12)	12	0.16
Swiss (0)	13	0.17
Welsh (42)	67	0.89

Hispanic Origin	Population	%
Hispanic or Latino (of any race)	158	1.71
Central American, ex. Mexican	11	0.12
Costa Rican	1	0.01
Honduran	1	0.01
Panamanian	2	0.02
Salvadoran	7	0.08
Cuban	6	0.06
Dominican Republic	2	0.02
Mexican	84	0.91
Puerto Rican	35	0.38
South American	7	0.08
Argentinean	3	0.03
Colombian	1	0.01
Peruvian	2	0.02
Venezuelan	1	0.01
Other Hispanic or Latino	13	0.14

Race*	Population	%
African-American/Black (347)	420	4.55
Not Hispanic (335)	407	4.41
Hispanic (12)	13	0.14
American Indian/Alaska Native (14)	45	0.49
Not Hispanic (14)	41	0.44
Hispanic (0)	4	0.04
Cherokee (2)	14	0.15
Cheyenne (0)	1	0.01
Chickasaw (1)	1	0.01
Chippewa (0)	1	0.01
Choctaw (1)	4	0.04
Creek (1)	1	0.01
Mexican American Ind. (0)	1	0.01
Asian (46)	69	0.75
Not Hispanic (45)	67	0.73
Hispanic (1)	2	0.02
Chinese, ex. Taiwanese (17)	21	0.23
Filipino (9)	17	0.18
Indian (3)	4	0.04
Japanese (2)	5	0.05
Korean (7)	10	0.11
Laotian (0)	1	0.01
Nepalese (1)	1	0.01
Pakistani (3)	3	0.03
Vietnamese (1)	1	0.01
Hawaii Native/Pacific Islander (0)	6	0.06
Not Hispanic (0)	6	0.06
Samoan (0)	1	0.01
White (8,657)	8,792	95.20
Not Hispanic (8,556)	8,678	93.97
Hispanic (101)	114	1.23

Sudley

Place Type: CDP
County: Prince William
Population: 16,203†

Ancestry‡	Population	%
Afghan (28)	28	0.18
African, Sub-Saharan (497)	563	3.68
African (435)	501	3.28
Ethiopian (37)	37	0.24
Sierra Leonean (25)	25	0.16
American (437)	437	2.86
Arab (0)	49	0.32
Lebanese (0)	25	0.16
Syrian (0)	24	0.16
British (60)	119	0.78
Bulgarian (11)	11	0.07
Czech (0)	53	0.35
Czechoslovakian (24)	24	0.16
Danish (0)	73	0.48
Dutch (0)	82	0.54
Eastern European (10)	10	0.07
English (465)	1,338	8.75
European (281)	291	1.90
French, ex. Basque (65)	129	0.84
French Canadian (27)	77	0.50
German (167)	1,397	9.14
Greek (0)	27	0.18
Guyanese (31)	45	0.29
Hungarian (0)	35	0.23
Irish (290)	1,099	7.19
Italian (140)	314	2.05
Lithuanian (0)	77	0.50
Norwegian (0)	49	0.32
Pennsylvania German (21)	21	0.14
Polish (90)	286	1.87
Russian (30)	75	0.49
Scotch-Irish (129)	189	1.24
Scottish (25)	90	0.59
Serbian (17)	25	0.16
Slavic (0)	10	0.07
Slovak (0)	36	0.24
Swedish (58)	149	0.97
Swiss (10)	22	0.14
Ukrainian (0)	10	0.07
Welsh (16)	118	0.77
West Indian, ex. Hispanic (97)	164	1.07
Haitian (79)	95	0.62
Trinidadian/Tobagonian (18)	69	0.45
Yugoslavian (12)	12	0.08

Hispanic Origin	Population	%
Hispanic or Latino (of any race)	6,115	37.74
Central American, ex. Mexican	3,551	21.92
Costa Rican	21	0.13
Guatemalan	543	3.35
Honduran	243	1.50
Nicaraguan	78	0.48
Panamanian	9	0.06
Salvadoran	2,651	16.36
Other Central American	6	0.04
Cuban	36	0.22
Dominican Republic	59	0.36
Mexican	1,120	6.91
Puerto Rican	204	1.26
South American	477	2.94
Argentinean	40	0.25
Bolivian	132	0.81
Chilean	11	0.07
Colombian	59	0.36
Ecuadorian	33	0.20
Peruvian	180	1.11
Uruguayan	7	0.04
Venezuelan	11	0.07
Other South American	4	0.02
Other Hispanic or Latino	668	4.12

Race*	Population	%
African-American/Black (2,500)	2,833	17.48
Not Hispanic (2,417)	2,681	16.55
Hispanic (83)	152	0.94
American Indian/Alaska Native (147)	279	1.72
Not Hispanic (51)	132	0.81
Hispanic (96)	147	0.91
Alaska Athabascan *(Ala. Nat.)* (0)	1	0.01
Aleut *(Alaska Native)* (4)	4	0.02
Apache (1)	7	0.04
Blackfeet (8)	10	0.06
Canadian/French Am. Ind. (0)	2	0.01
Central American Ind. (2)	2	0.01
Cherokee (8)	33	0.20
Chickasaw (0)	3	0.02
Cree (0)	3	0.02
Creek (0)	1	0.01
Delaware (0)	2	0.01
Hopi (0)	3	0.02
Iroquois (0)	1	0.01
Lumbee (10)	10	0.06
Mexican American Ind. (20)	20	0.12
Osage (0)	1	0.01
Sioux (0)	1	0.01
South American Ind. (4)	5	0.03
Spanish American Ind. (1)	1	0.01
Tlingit-Haida *(Alaska Native)* (1)	1	0.01
Asian (993)	1,177	7.26
Not Hispanic (983)	1,151	7.10
Hispanic (10)	26	0.16
Bangladeshi (22)	22	0.14
Bhutanese (2)	2	0.01
Cambodian (25)	26	0.16
Chinese, ex. Taiwanese (92)	107	0.66
Filipino (137)	184	1.14
Indian (176)	212	1.31
Indonesian (3)	3	0.02
Japanese (9)	16	0.10
Korean (78)	99	0.61
Laotian (19)	22	0.14
Nepalese (68)	76	0.47
Pakistani (127)	155	0.96
Taiwanese (11)	11	0.07
Thai (14)	21	0.13
Vietnamese (150)	172	1.06
Hawaii Native/Pacific Islander (40)	55	0.34
Not Hispanic (12)	24	0.15
Hispanic (28)	31	0.19
Guamanian/Chamorro (35)	35	0.22
Native Hawaiian (4)	8	0.05
White (8,213)	8,947	55.22
Not Hispanic (6,080)	6,505	40.15
Hispanic (2,133)	2,442	15.07

Suffolk

Place Type: Independent City
County: Suffolk
Population: 84,585†

Ancestry‡	Population	%
African, Sub-Saharan (1,080)	1,182	1.43
African (1,032)	1,072	1.30
Nigerian (35)	97	0.12
Somalian (6)	6	0.01
South African (7)	7	0.01
American (12,434)	12,434	15.06
Arab (80)	230	0.28
Lebanese (80)	219	0.27
Moroccan (0)	11	0.01
Armenian (0)	45	0.05
Australian (0)	41	0.05
Austrian (0)	149	0.18
Basque (0)	3	<0.01
Belgian (0)	30	0.04
British (173)	302	0.37
Canadian (131)	192	0.23

*Notes: † The Census 2010 population figure is used to calculate the percentages in the Hispanic Origin and Race categories. Ancestry percentages are based on the 2006-2010 American Community Survey population (not shown); ‡ Numbers in parentheses indicate the number of people reporting a single ancestry; * Numbers in parentheses indicate the number of persons reporting this race alone, not in combination with any other race; Please refer to the Explanation of Data for more information.*

Croatian (0)	27	0.03
Czech (13)	100	0.12
Czechoslovakian (16)	28	0.03
Danish (100)	280	0.34
Dutch (158)	701	0.85
Eastern European (11)	11	0.01
English (3,879)	7,950	9.63
European (634)	725	0.88
Finnish (16)	16	0.02
French, ex. Basque (284)	1,510	1.83
French Canadian (232)	438	0.53
German (2,392)	7,867	9.53
Greek (8)	120	0.15
Guyanese (12)	12	0.01
Hungarian (31)	200	0.24
Icelander (7)	7	0.01
Irish (2,041)	6,482	7.85
Italian (774)	2,427	2.94
Latvian (28)	82	0.10
Lithuanian (44)	106	0.13
New Zealander (17)	17	0.02
Northern European (10)	10	0.01
Norwegian (208)	497	0.60
Polish (214)	1,075	1.30
Portuguese (74)	177	0.21
Romanian (0)	45	0.05
Russian (160)	255	0.31
Scandinavian (31)	65	0.08
Scotch-Irish (976)	1,657	2.01
Scottish (477)	1,459	1.77
Slovak (0)	13	0.02
Swedish (96)	405	0.49
Swiss (91)	171	0.21
Ukrainian (15)	53	0.06
Welsh (95)	260	0.31
West Indian, ex. Hispanic (213)	463	0.56
Bermudan (0)	5	0.01
British West Indian (16)	16	0.02
Haitian (54)	99	0.12
Jamaican (101)	246	0.30
Trinidadian/Tobagonian (24)	24	0.03
West Indian (18)	60	0.07
Other West Indian (0)	13	0.02
Yugoslavian (21)	21	0.03

Hispanic Origin	Population	%
Hispanic or Latino (of any race)	2,415	2.86
Central American, ex. Mexican	250	0.30
Costa Rican	8	0.01
Guatemalan	74	0.09
Honduran	39	0.05
Nicaraguan	19	0.02
Panamanian	65	0.08
Salvadoran	39	0.05
Other Central American	6	0.01
Cuban	110	0.13
Dominican Republic	66	0.08
Mexican	800	0.95
Puerto Rican	806	0.95
South American	140	0.17
Argentinean	2	<0.01
Bolivian	3	<0.01
Chilean	11	0.01
Colombian	43	0.05
Ecuadorian	34	0.04
Peruvian	28	0.03
Uruguayan	1	<0.01
Venezuelan	18	0.02
Other Hispanic or Latino	243	0.29

Race*	Population	%
African-American/Black (36,120)	37,278	44.07
Not Hispanic (35,771)	36,790	43.49
Hispanic (349)	488	0.58
American Indian/Alaska Native (268)	780	0.92
Not Hispanic (232)	718	0.85
Hispanic (36)	62	0.07
Aleut *(Alaska Native)* (2)	3	<0.01
Apache (2)	2	<0.01
Arapaho (0)	1	<0.01
Blackfeet (5)	38	0.04
Central American Ind. (1)	1	<0.01
Cherokee (42)	182	0.22
Cheyenne (0)	4	<0.01
Chickasaw (3)	5	0.01
Chippewa (8)	21	0.02
Choctaw (5)	19	0.02
Creek (5)	8	0.01
Houma (0)	2	<0.01
Iroquois (4)	14	0.02
Kiowa (1)	1	<0.01
Lumbee (6)	18	0.02
Mexican American Ind. (1)	2	<0.01
Navajo (6)	9	0.01
Osage (0)	2	<0.01
Ottawa (3)	3	<0.01
Potawatomi (3)	5	0.01
Seminole (0)	3	<0.01
Sioux (11)	25	0.03
Spanish American Ind. (1)	1	<0.01
Asian (1,350)	1,931	2.28
Not Hispanic (1,324)	1,849	2.19
Hispanic (26)	82	0.10
Bangladeshi (16)	21	0.02
Burmese (4)	5	0.01
Cambodian (4)	4	<0.01
Chinese, ex. Taiwanese (165)	261	0.31
Filipino (471)	756	0.89
Indian (224)	259	0.31
Indonesian (0)	2	<0.01
Japanese (47)	147	0.17
Korean (170)	260	0.31
Laotian (1)	1	<0.01
Pakistani (28)	29	0.03
Sri Lankan (5)	6	0.01
Taiwanese (3)	7	0.01
Thai (12)	27	0.03
Vietnamese (148)	165	0.20
Hawaii Native/Pacific Islander (54)	124	0.15
Not Hispanic (50)	109	0.13
Hispanic (4)	15	0.02
Guamanian/Chamorro (21)	35	0.04
Native Hawaiian (8)	33	0.04
Samoan (12)	17	0.02
White (44,197)	45,726	54.06
Not Hispanic (43,034)	44,354	52.44
Hispanic (1,163)	1,372	1.62

Sugarland Run

Place Type: CDP
County: Loudoun
Population: 11,799†

Ancestry‡	Population	%
Afghan (19)	19	0.17
African, Sub-Saharan (367)	429	3.93
African (265)	327	2.99
Ghanaian (102)	102	0.93
American (562)	562	5.15
Arab (110)	185	1.69
Lebanese (39)	114	1.04
Other Arab (71)	71	0.65
Austrian (0)	50	0.46
Belgian (0)	32	0.29
British (19)	136	1.25
Canadian (12)	45	0.41
Croatian (0)	11	0.10
Czech (7)	34	0.31
Danish (0)	43	0.39
Dutch (24)	126	1.15
Eastern European (10)	10	0.09
English (145)	676	6.19
European (82)	89	0.82
French, ex. Basque (94)	254	2.33
French Canadian (47)	71	0.65
German (237)	930	8.52
Greek (13)	67	0.61
Hungarian (94)	105	0.96
Icelander (8)	8	0.07
Iranian (238)	265	2.43
Irish (194)	863	7.90
Italian (278)	557	5.10
Lithuanian (8)	8	0.07
Norwegian (0)	70	0.64
Pennsylvania German (14)	14	0.13
Polish (49)	180	1.65
Portuguese (0)	10	0.09
Russian (42)	73	0.67
Scandinavian (20)	20	0.18
Scotch-Irish (80)	224	2.05
Scottish (36)	153	1.40
Serbian (0)	8	0.07
Slovak (0)	20	0.18
Swedish (0)	59	0.54
Ukrainian (0)	33	0.30
Welsh (20)	91	0.83
West Indian, ex. Hispanic (10)	42	0.38
Trinidadian/Tobagonian (10)	42	0.38

Hispanic Origin	Population	%
Hispanic or Latino (of any race)	3,397	28.79
Central American, ex. Mexican	1,818	15.41
Costa Rican	10	0.08
Guatemalan	129	1.09
Honduran	253	2.14
Nicaraguan	50	0.42
Panamanian	12	0.10
Salvadoran	1,364	11.56
Cuban	43	0.36
Dominican Republic	11	0.09
Mexican	344	2.92
Puerto Rican	131	1.11
South American	641	5.43
Argentinean	12	0.10
Bolivian	212	1.80
Chilean	8	0.07
Colombian	59	0.50
Ecuadorian	38	0.32
Paraguayan	6	0.05
Peruvian	277	2.35
Venezuelan	24	0.20
Other South American	5	0.04
Other Hispanic or Latino	409	3.47

Race*	Population	%
African-American/Black (990)	1,175	9.96
Not Hispanic (951)	1,103	9.35
Hispanic (39)	72	0.61
American Indian/Alaska Native (50)	116	0.98
Not Hispanic (23)	65	0.55
Hispanic (27)	51	0.43
Blackfeet (2)	4	0.03
Cherokee (5)	23	0.19
Choctaw (2)	5	0.04
Iroquois (1)	1	0.01
Mexican American Ind. (2)	3	0.03
Seminole (0)	1	0.01
Sioux (1)	6	0.05
South American Ind. (2)	2	0.02
Tlingit-Haida *(Alaska Native)* (0)	1	0.01
Asian (1,742)	1,942	16.46
Not Hispanic (1,737)	1,924	16.31
Hispanic (5)	18	0.15
Bangladeshi (86)	86	0.73
Cambodian (25)	27	0.23
Chinese, ex. Taiwanese (178)	206	1.75
Filipino (168)	218	1.85
Hmong (6)	9	0.08
Indian (536)	567	4.81
Indonesian (8)	14	0.12
Japanese (13)	25	0.21
Korean (80)	98	0.83
Laotian (33)	42	0.36
Nepalese (11)	11	0.09
Pakistani (155)	168	1.42
Sri Lankan (0)	1	0.01
Taiwanese (6)	6	0.05
Thai (47)	51	0.43
Vietnamese (330)	343	2.91

*Notes: † The Census 2010 population figure is used to calculate the percentages in the Hispanic Origin and Race categories. Ancestry percentages are based on the 2006-2010 American Community Survey population (not shown); ‡ Numbers in parentheses indicate the number of people reporting a single ancestry; * Numbers in parentheses indicate the number of persons reporting this race alone, not in combination with any other race; Please refer to the Explanation of Data for more information.*

Hawaii Native/Pacific Islander (6)	22	0.19
Not Hispanic (3)	9	0.08
Hispanic (3)	13	0.11
Guamanian/Chamorro (5)	6	0.05
Native Hawaiian (1)	12	0.10
White (6,545)	7,034	59.62
Not Hispanic (5,315)	5,599	47.45
Hispanic (1,230)	1,435	12.16

Timberlake

Place Type: CDP
County: Campbell
Population: 12,183†

Ancestry‡	Population	%
African, Sub-Saharan (21)	21	0.15
Other Sub-Saharan African (21)	21	0.15
American (2,895)	2,895	20.58
British (0)	31	0.22
Cajun (0)	11	0.08
Canadian (32)	71	0.50
Czechoslovakian (15)	25	0.18
Danish (0)	4	0.03
Dutch (13)	209	1.49
English (1,264)	2,121	15.08
European (307)	390	2.77
Finnish (31)	31	0.22
French, ex. Basque (41)	399	2.84
French Canadian (35)	35	0.25
German (647)	2,311	16.43
Greek (0)	53	0.38
Hungarian (42)	70	0.50
Irish (667)	1,924	13.68
Italian (350)	862	6.13
Lithuanian (0)	91	0.65
Northern European (15)	15	0.11
Norwegian (0)	11	0.08
Polish (0)	132	0.94
Russian (8)	8	0.06
Scandinavian (25)	25	0.18
Scotch-Irish (256)	442	3.14
Scottish (103)	546	3.88
Swedish (63)	63	0.45
Swiss (11)	26	0.18
Ukrainian (0)	37	0.26
Welsh (0)	9	0.06
West Indian, ex. Hispanic (20)	34	0.24
Bahamian (20)	20	0.14
Belizean (0)	14	0.10

Hispanic Origin	Population	%
Hispanic or Latino (of any race)	358	2.94
Central American, ex. Mexican	49	0.40
Guatemalan	4	0.03
Honduran	21	0.17
Panamanian	6	0.05
Salvadoran	18	0.15
Cuban	13	0.11
Dominican Republic	2	0.02
Mexican	200	1.64
Puerto Rican	46	0.38
South American	23	0.19
Argentinean	3	0.02
Chilean	1	0.01
Colombian	11	0.09
Ecuadorian	6	0.05
Paraguayan	1	0.01
Venezuelan	1	0.01
Other Hispanic or Latino	25	0.21

Race*	Population	%
African-American/Black (980)	1,090	8.95
Not Hispanic (977)	1,086	8.91
Hispanic (3)	4	0.03
American Indian/Alaska Native (21)	97	0.80
Not Hispanic (21)	94	0.77
Hispanic (0)	3	0.02
Apache (0)	4	0.03
Blackfeet (0)	8	0.07
Cherokee (3)	30	0.25
Choctaw (2)	3	0.02
Crow (0)	1	0.01
Delaware (0)	1	0.01
Navajo (1)	2	0.02
Seminole (0)	1	0.01
Sioux (2)	3	0.02
Asian (303)	353	2.90
Not Hispanic (302)	347	2.85
Hispanic (1)	6	0.05
Chinese, ex. Taiwanese (52)	54	0.44
Filipino (18)	35	0.29
Indian (44)	57	0.47
Japanese (5)	10	0.08
Korean (139)	147	1.21
Nepalese (3)	3	0.02
Pakistani (1)	1	0.01
Taiwanese (3)	3	0.02
Thai (2)	2	0.02
Vietnamese (24)	29	0.24
Hawaii Native/Pacific Islander (1)	6	0.05
Not Hispanic (1)	6	0.05
Guamanian/Chamorro (1)	2	0.02
Native Hawaiian (0)	4	0.03
White (10,469)	10,666	87.55
Not Hispanic (10,305)	10,483	86.05
Hispanic (164)	183	1.50

Triangle

Place Type: CDP
County: Prince William
Population: 8,188†

Ancestry‡	Population	%
Afghan (77)	77	1.00
African, Sub-Saharan (479)	557	7.24
African (147)	225	2.92
Ethiopian (125)	125	1.62
Ghanaian (55)	55	0.71
Nigerian (13)	13	0.17
Senegalese (139)	139	1.81
American (375)	375	4.87
British (12)	36	0.47
Czech (13)	13	0.17
Czechoslovakian (0)	18	0.23
Dutch (0)	62	0.81
Eastern European (53)	149	1.94
English (164)	335	4.35
European (51)	68	0.88
French, ex. Basque (43)	183	2.38
French Canadian (10)	19	0.25
German (134)	444	5.77
German Russian (0)	13	0.17
Greek (82)	203	2.64
Irish (202)	560	7.28
Italian (78)	242	3.15
Northern European (111)	111	1.44
Norwegian (0)	46	0.60
Pennsylvania German (6)	6	0.08
Polish (47)	74	0.96
Portuguese (0)	5	0.06
Russian (0)	13	0.17
Scandinavian (0)	19	0.25
Scotch-Irish (0)	85	1.10
Scottish (61)	119	1.55
Slavic (0)	9	0.12
Slovak (12)	25	0.32
Swiss (0)	13	0.17
Turkish (19)	43	0.56
Welsh (0)	26	0.34
West Indian, ex. Hispanic (277)	277	3.60
Haitian (178)	178	2.31
Jamaican (99)	99	1.29

Hispanic Origin	Population	%
Hispanic or Latino (of any race)	1,508	18.42
Central American, ex. Mexican	531	6.49
Costa Rican	8	0.10
Guatemalan	51	0.62
Honduran	57	0.70
Nicaraguan	16	0.20
Panamanian	21	0.26
Salvadoran	372	4.54
Other Central American	6	0.07
Cuban	26	0.32
Dominican Republic	36	0.44
Mexican	358	4.37
Puerto Rican	222	2.71
South American	112	1.37
Argentinean	6	0.07
Bolivian	22	0.27
Chilean	1	0.01
Colombian	17	0.21
Ecuadorian	14	0.17
Paraguayan	2	0.02
Peruvian	50	0.61
Other Hispanic or Latino	223	2.72

Race*	Population	%
African-American/Black (3,039)	3,329	40.66
Not Hispanic (2,962)	3,217	39.29
Hispanic (77)	112	1.37
American Indian/Alaska Native (45)	179	2.19
Not Hispanic (18)	127	1.55
Hispanic (27)	52	0.64
Apache (1)	1	0.01
Blackfeet (0)	4	0.05
Central American Ind. (2)	5	0.06
Cherokee (1)	38	0.46
Hopi (0)	1	0.01
Inupiat *(Alaska Native)* (0)	3	0.04
Iroquois (0)	5	0.06
Mexican American Ind. (3)	7	0.09
Potawatomi (5)	5	0.06
Pueblo (2)	2	0.02
Sioux (0)	4	0.05
Asian (444)	592	7.23
Not Hispanic (438)	578	7.06
Hispanic (6)	14	0.17
Bangladeshi (4)	7	0.09
Cambodian (23)	26	0.32
Chinese, ex. Taiwanese (41)	67	0.82
Filipino (97)	144	1.76
Indian (51)	64	0.78
Indonesian (0)	3	0.04
Japanese (10)	26	0.32
Korean (47)	76	0.93
Laotian (4)	8	0.10
Nepalese (3)	3	0.04
Pakistani (76)	81	0.99
Taiwanese (2)	2	0.02
Thai (5)	15	0.18
Vietnamese (56)	69	0.84
Hawaii Native/Pacific Islander (13)	34	0.42
Not Hispanic (9)	28	0.34
Hispanic (4)	6	0.07
Guamanian/Chamorro (8)	11	0.13
Native Hawaiian (0)	11	0.13
Samoan (4)	5	0.06
White (3,378)	3,774	46.09
Not Hispanic (2,836)	3,145	38.41
Hispanic (542)	629	7.68

Tuckahoe

Place Type: CDP
County: Henrico
Population: 44,990†

Ancestry‡	Population	%
African, Sub-Saharan (281)	281	0.62
African (20)	20	0.04
Ethiopian (53)	53	0.12
Kenyan (150)	150	0.33
Sudanese (13)	13	0.03
Other Sub-Saharan African (45)	45	0.10
Albanian (82)	82	0.18
American (4,567)	4,567	10.11
Arab (405)	568	1.26

SECTION TWO

*Notes: † The Census 2010 population figure is used to calculate the percentages in the Hispanic Origin and Race categories. Ancestry percentages are based on the 2006-2010 American Community Survey population (not shown); ‡ Numbers in parentheses indicate the number of people reporting a single ancestry; * Numbers in parentheses indicate the number of persons reporting this race alone, not in combination with any other race; Please refer to the Explanation of Data for more information.*

Egyptian (159)	159	0.35
Lebanese (224)	387	0.86
Palestinian (22)	22	0.05
Armenian (77)	77	0.17
Australian (15)	29	0.06
Austrian (47)	87	0.19
Brazilian (130)	203	0.45
British (345)	449	0.99
Bulgarian (113)	113	0.25
Cajun (10)	40	0.09
Canadian (12)	60	0.13
Croatian (0)	51	0.11
Cypriot (0)	8	0.02
Czech (35)	111	0.25
Czechoslovakian (12)	67	0.15
Danish (82)	152	0.34
Dutch (201)	726	1.61
Eastern European (211)	245	0.54
English (4,901)	10,349	22.91
Estonian (0)	13	0.03
European (937)	989	2.19
Finnish (48)	65	0.14
French, ex. Basque (156)	1,567	3.47
French Canadian (33)	164	0.36
German (1,815)	5,986	13.25
Greek (277)	414	0.92
Hungarian (221)	350	0.77
Iranian (45)	45	0.10
Irish (1,585)	4,939	10.93
Israeli (23)	35	0.08
Italian (709)	1,724	3.82
Latvian (0)	9	0.02
Lithuanian (187)	255	0.56
Maltese (24)	24	0.05
Northern European (14)	14	0.03
Norwegian (109)	345	0.76
Pennsylvania German (11)	11	0.02
Polish (170)	712	1.58
Portuguese (35)	67	0.15
Romanian (75)	137	0.30
Russian (240)	525	1.16
Scandinavian (0)	12	0.03
Scotch-Irish (860)	1,835	4.06
Scottish (640)	2,009	4.45
Serbian (12)	26	0.06
Slavic (6)	49	0.11
Slovak (16)	68	0.15
Swedish (76)	348	0.77
Swiss (25)	200	0.44
Turkish (169)	183	0.41
Ukrainian (107)	159	0.35
Welsh (142)	573	1.27
West Indian, ex. Hispanic (188)	266	0.59
Barbadian (12)	12	0.03
Belizean (43)	104	0.23
Haitian (108)	125	0.28
Jamaican (25)	25	0.06
Yugoslavian (498)	498	1.10

Hispanic Origin	Population	%
Hispanic or Latino (of any race)	2,640	5.87
Central American, ex. Mexican	453	1.01
Costa Rican	33	0.07
Guatemalan	72	0.16
Honduran	150	0.33
Nicaraguan	4	0.01
Panamanian	15	0.03
Salvadoran	176	0.39
Other Central American	3	0.01
Cuban	147	0.33
Dominican Republic	28	0.06
Mexican	1,067	2.37
Puerto Rican	331	0.74
South American	363	0.81
Argentinean	35	0.08
Bolivian	17	0.04
Chilean	12	0.03
Colombian	113	0.25
Ecuadorian	58	0.13
Paraguayan	12	0.03
Peruvian	41	0.09
Uruguayan	4	0.01
Venezuelan	69	0.15
Other South American	2	<0.01
Other Hispanic or Latino	251	0.56

Race*	Population	%
African-American/Black (4,355)	4,730	10.51
Not Hispanic (4,250)	4,561	10.14
Hispanic (105)	169	0.38
American Indian/Alaska Native (93)	274	0.61
Not Hispanic (75)	232	0.52
Hispanic (18)	42	0.09
Blackfeet (1)	8	0.02
Cherokee (9)	66	0.15
Chickasaw (3)	7	0.02
Chippewa (1)	3	0.01
Choctaw (2)	5	0.01
Crow (0)	1	<0.01
Delaware (1)	1	<0.01
Hopi (1)	1	<0.01
Iroquois (3)	4	0.01
Lumbee (1)	5	0.01
Mexican American Ind. (5)	7	0.02
Navajo (0)	2	<0.01
Pueblo (1)	1	<0.01
Puget Sound Salish (1)	1	<0.01
Seminole (0)	1	<0.01
Sioux (1)	7	0.02
South American Ind. (0)	1	<0.01
Asian (1,845)	2,155	4.79
Not Hispanic (1,822)	2,116	4.70
Hispanic (23)	39	0.09
Bangladeshi (26)	40	0.09
Bhutanese (66)	77	0.17
Burmese (2)	2	<0.01
Cambodian (97)	110	0.24
Chinese, ex. Taiwanese (383)	449	1.00
Filipino (150)	196	0.44
Hmong (2)	2	<0.01
Indian (439)	507	1.13
Indonesian (8)	16	0.04
Japanese (36)	65	0.14
Korean (181)	225	0.50
Laotian (3)	5	0.01
Malaysian (1)	1	<0.01
Nepalese (42)	47	0.10
Pakistani (53)	60	0.13
Sri Lankan (23)	24	0.05
Taiwanese (3)	5	0.01
Thai (9)	14	0.03
Vietnamese (215)	249	0.55
Hawaii Native/Pacific Islander (16)	47	0.10
Not Hispanic (13)	41	0.09
Hispanic (3)	6	0.01
Guamanian/Chamorro (3)	3	0.01
Native Hawaiian (2)	9	0.02
Samoan (3)	7	0.02
White (36,832)	37,534	83.43
Not Hispanic (35,358)	35,929	79.86
Hispanic (1,474)	1,605	3.57

Tysons Corner

Place Type: CDP
County: Fairfax
Population: 19,627†

Ancestry‡	Population	%
Afghan (19)	19	0.11
African, Sub-Saharan (63)	84	0.49
African (30)	51	0.30
Kenyan (19)	19	0.11
Other Sub-Saharan African (14)	14	0.08
American (437)	437	2.56
Arab (806)	983	5.75
Arab (62)	81	0.47
Egyptian (73)	73	0.43
Iraqi (77)	77	0.45
Lebanese (137)	226	1.32
Moroccan (95)	95	0.56
Palestinian (12)	12	0.07
Syrian (64)	81	0.47
Other Arab (286)	338	1.98
Armenian (55)	85	0.50
Australian (8)	8	0.05
Austrian (64)	118	0.69
Belgian (0)	13	0.08
Brazilian (11)	24	0.14
British (132)	207	1.21
Canadian (35)	48	0.28
Croatian (15)	26	0.15
Czech (28)	41	0.24
Czechoslovakian (16)	16	0.09
Danish (33)	43	0.25
Dutch (0)	162	0.95
Eastern European (127)	127	0.74
English (468)	1,939	11.35
Estonian (13)	13	0.08
European (337)	363	2.12
French, ex. Basque (166)	509	2.98
French Canadian (30)	56	0.33
German (274)	1,913	11.20
Greek (442)	494	2.89
Hungarian (73)	160	0.94
Iranian (337)	337	1.97
Irish (443)	1,623	9.50
Israeli (16)	16	0.09
Italian (297)	845	4.95
Lithuanian (0)	13	0.08
Northern European (13)	13	0.08
Norwegian (14)	63	0.37
Polish (72)	456	2.67
Portuguese (40)	58	0.34
Russian (107)	231	1.35
Scandinavian (0)	13	0.08
Scotch-Irish (68)	286	1.67
Scottish (55)	425	2.49
Serbian (16)	16	0.09
Slavic (0)	30	0.18
Slovak (0)	48	0.28
Slovene (9)	9	0.05
Swedish (17)	97	0.57
Swiss (33)	111	0.65
Turkish (127)	127	0.74
Ukrainian (62)	125	0.73
Welsh (12)	184	1.08
West Indian, ex. Hispanic (0)	49	0.29
Jamaican (0)	49	0.29
Yugoslavian (65)	65	0.38

Hispanic Origin	Population	%
Hispanic or Latino (of any race)	1,589	8.10
Central American, ex. Mexican	322	1.64
Costa Rican	16	0.08
Guatemalan	50	0.25
Honduran	14	0.07
Nicaraguan	32	0.16
Panamanian	30	0.15
Salvadoran	174	0.89
Other Central American	6	0.03
Cuban	48	0.24
Dominican Republic	24	0.12
Mexican	229	1.17
Puerto Rican	127	0.65
South American	711	3.62
Argentinean	48	0.24
Bolivian	181	0.92
Chilean	29	0.15
Colombian	182	0.93
Ecuadorian	34	0.17
Paraguayan	8	0.04
Peruvian	177	0.90
Uruguayan	16	0.08
Venezuelan	22	0.11
Other South American	14	0.07
Other Hispanic or Latino	128	0.65

Race*	Population	%
African-American/Black (953)	1,106	5.64

*Notes: † The Census 2010 population figure is used to calculate the percentages in the Hispanic Origin and Race categories. Ancestry percentages are based on the 2006-2010 American Community Survey population (not shown); ‡ Numbers in parentheses indicate the number of people reporting a single ancestry; * Numbers in parentheses indicate the number of persons reporting this race alone, not in combination with any other race; Please refer to the Explanation of Data for more information.*

Not Hispanic (923)	1,058	5.39
Hispanic (30)	48	0.24
American Indian/Alaska Native (32)	82	0.42
Not Hispanic (26)	65	0.33
Hispanic (6)	17	0.09
Alaska Athabascan *(Ala. Nat.)* (0)	1	0.01
Aleut *(Alaska Native)* (0)	1	0.01
Apache (1)	1	0.01
Blackfeet (0)	1	0.01
Central American Ind. (0)	1	0.01
Cherokee (0)	13	0.07
Chippewa (1)	1	0.01
Iroquois (4)	4	0.02
Navajo (2)	3	0.02
Osage (1)	1	0.01
Potawatomi (0)	1	0.01
Pueblo (2)	2	0.01
South American Ind. (3)	4	0.02
Yup'ik *(Alaska Native)* (2)	2	0.01
Asian (5,399)	6,054	30.85
Not Hispanic (5,382)	6,013	30.64
Hispanic (17)	41	0.21
Bangladeshi (21)	31	0.16
Burmese (20)	22	0.11
Cambodian (18)	20	0.10
Chinese, ex. Taiwanese (956)	1,044	5.32
Filipino (264)	326	1.66
Indian (1,753)	1,835	9.35
Indonesian (39)	44	0.22
Japanese (125)	161	0.82
Korean (1,437)	1,513	7.71
Laotian (2)	2	0.01
Malaysian (56)	56	0.29
Nepalese (25)	25	0.13
Pakistani (132)	161	0.82
Sri Lankan (13)	20	0.10
Taiwanese (91)	101	0.51
Thai (67)	75	0.38
Vietnamese (185)	217	1.11
Hawaii Native/Pacific Islander (22)	45	0.23
Not Hispanic (20)	40	0.20
Hispanic (2)	5	0.03
Fijian (1)	1	0.01
Guamanian/Chamorro (3)	4	0.02
Native Hawaiian (1)	4	0.02
Samoan (4)	9	0.05
White (11,954)	12,716	64.79
Not Hispanic (10,816)	11,508	58.63
Hispanic (1,138)	1,208	6.15

University of Virginia

Place Type: CDP
County: Albemarle
Population: 7,704†

Ancestry‡	Population	%
African, Sub-Saharan (65)	89	1.27
African (16)	40	0.57
Ethiopian (25)	25	0.36
Nigerian (12)	12	0.17
Sierra Leonean (12)	12	0.17
American (58)	58	0.83
Arab (44)	55	0.79
Arab (0)	11	0.16
Iraqi (13)	13	0.19
Jordanian (17)	17	0.24
Lebanese (14)	14	0.20
Armenian (19)	19	0.27
Austrian (0)	24	0.34
British (40)	129	1.84
Croatian (15)	40	0.57
Czech (0)	75	1.07
Danish (0)	28	0.40
Dutch (9)	35	0.50
Eastern European (13)	13	0.19
English (293)	1,062	15.18
European (60)	73	1.04
Finnish (0)	16	0.23
French, ex. Basque (39)	208	2.97
German (191)	1,128	16.13
Greek (16)	45	0.64
Hungarian (30)	70	1.00
Iranian (56)	56	0.80
Irish (90)	839	12.00
Israeli (10)	10	0.14
Italian (110)	489	6.99
Latvian (0)	15	0.21
Lithuanian (0)	24	0.34
Norwegian (13)	101	1.44
Pennsylvania German (0)	11	0.16
Polish (45)	250	3.57
Portuguese (0)	9	0.13
Romanian (10)	89	1.27
Russian (41)	163	2.33
Scandinavian (0)	30	0.43
Scotch-Irish (56)	133	1.90
Scottish (62)	305	4.36
Serbian (24)	37	0.53
Slavic (13)	13	0.19
Slovak (0)	13	0.19
Slovene (14)	14	0.20
Swedish (0)	74	1.06
Swiss (0)	14	0.20
Turkish (37)	37	0.53
Ukrainian (14)	52	0.74
Welsh (58)	113	1.62
West Indian, ex. Hispanic (15)	83	1.19
Barbadian (15)	15	0.21
Bermudan (0)	13	0.19
Jamaican (0)	43	0.61
West Indian (0)	12	0.17

Hispanic Origin	Population	%
Hispanic or Latino (of any race)	425	5.52
Central American, ex. Mexican	79	1.03
Costa Rican	3	0.04
Guatemalan	20	0.26
Honduran	10	0.13
Nicaraguan	4	0.05
Panamanian	11	0.14
Salvadoran	28	0.36
Other Central American	3	0.04
Cuban	37	0.48
Dominican Republic	9	0.12
Mexican	81	1.05
Puerto Rican	45	0.58
South American	114	1.48
Argentinean	14	0.18
Bolivian	6	0.08
Chilean	14	0.18
Colombian	36	0.47
Ecuadorian	9	0.12
Paraguayan	1	0.01
Peruvian	20	0.26
Uruguayan	2	0.03
Venezuelan	12	0.16
Other Hispanic or Latino	60	0.78

Race*	Population	%
African-American/Black (594)	694	9.01
Not Hispanic (572)	656	8.52
Hispanic (22)	38	0.49
American Indian/Alaska Native (11)	57	0.74
Not Hispanic (9)	45	0.58
Hispanic (2)	12	0.16
Blackfeet (0)	2	0.03
Cherokee (3)	16	0.21
Chickasaw (0)	1	0.01
Choctaw (0)	2	0.03
Creek (0)	1	0.01
Iroquois (0)	1	0.01
Lumbee (0)	1	0.01
South American Ind. (2)	2	0.03
Asian (1,633)	1,830	23.75
Not Hispanic (1,624)	1,815	23.56
Hispanic (9)	15	0.19
Bangladeshi (14)	15	0.19
Burmese (6)	6	0.08
Cambodian (4)	7	0.09
Chinese, ex. Taiwanese (604)	663	8.61
Filipino (46)	75	0.97
Indian (355)	384	4.98
Indonesian (0)	1	0.01
Japanese (56)	86	1.12
Korean (309)	349	4.53
Laotian (2)	3	0.04
Malaysian (1)	2	0.03
Nepalese (11)	15	0.19
Pakistani (39)	43	0.56
Sri Lankan (3)	3	0.04
Taiwanese (36)	42	0.55
Thai (13)	19	0.25
Vietnamese (66)	78	1.01
Hawaii Native/Pacific Islander (1)	20	0.26
Not Hispanic (1)	14	0.18
Hispanic (0)	6	0.08
Guamanian/Chamorro (1)	3	0.04
Native Hawaiian (0)	7	0.09
Samoan (0)	1	0.01
White (5,074)	5,340	69.31
Not Hispanic (4,791)	5,028	65.26
Hispanic (283)	312	4.05

Vienna

Place Type: Town
County: Fairfax
Population: 15,687†

Ancestry‡	Population	%
African, Sub-Saharan (237)	247	1.61
African (217)	227	1.48
Ethiopian (20)	20	0.13
Alsatian (0)	6	0.04
American (663)	663	4.31
Arab (115)	135	0.88
Egyptian (25)	25	0.16
Syrian (6)	6	0.04
Other Arab (84)	104	0.68
Armenian (56)	56	0.36
Austrian (0)	58	0.38
Brazilian (0)	53	0.34
British (138)	200	1.30
Bulgarian (14)	28	0.18
Cajun (0)	32	0.21
Canadian (11)	69	0.45
Celtic (13)	13	0.08
Croatian (18)	28	0.18
Czech (10)	100	0.65
Czechoslovakian (15)	52	0.34
Danish (23)	114	0.74
Dutch (105)	341	2.22
Eastern European (25)	62	0.40
English (461)	1,897	12.33
Estonian (11)	11	0.07
European (113)	277	1.80
Finnish (32)	41	0.27
French, ex. Basque (73)	329	2.14
French Canadian (46)	103	0.67
German (481)	2,155	14.01
Greek (76)	88	0.57
Hungarian (57)	104	0.68
Iranian (314)	452	2.94
Irish (634)	2,228	14.48
Italian (293)	1,147	7.45
Latvian (0)	11	0.07
Lithuanian (13)	32	0.21
Macedonian (79)	79	0.51
Northern European (85)	85	0.55
Norwegian (48)	163	1.06
Polish (190)	493	3.20
Portuguese (0)	39	0.25
Romanian (45)	56	0.36
Russian (63)	240	1.56
Scandinavian (29)	29	0.19
Scotch-Irish (185)	594	3.86
Scottish (67)	303	1.97
Serbian (18)	43	0.28
Slavic (0)	12	0.08

*Notes: † The Census 2010 population figure is used to calculate the percentages in the Hispanic Origin and Race categories. Ancestry percentages are based on the 2006-2010 American Community Survey population (not shown); ‡ Numbers in parentheses indicate the number of people reporting a single ancestry; * Numbers in parentheses indicate the number of persons reporting this race alone, not in combination with any other race; Please refer to the Explanation of Data for more information.*

Ancestry	Population	%
Slovak (43)	132	0.86
Slovene (10)	135	0.88
Swedish (0)	106	0.69
Swiss (44)	148	0.96
Ukrainian (85)	208	1.35
Welsh (9)	86	0.56
West Indian, ex. Hispanic (9)	9	0.06
Jamaican (9)	9	0.06

Hispanic Origin	Population	%
Hispanic or Latino (of any race)	1,887	12.03
Central American, ex. Mexican	926	5.90
Costa Rican	14	0.09
Guatemalan	36	0.23
Honduran	253	1.61
Nicaraguan	38	0.24
Panamanian	22	0.14
Salvadoran	563	3.59
Cuban	27	0.17
Dominican Republic	16	0.10
Mexican	154	0.98
Puerto Rican	72	0.46
South American	497	3.17
Argentinean	25	0.16
Bolivian	156	0.99
Chilean	22	0.14
Colombian	68	0.43
Ecuadorian	34	0.22
Paraguayan	2	0.01
Peruvian	144	0.92
Uruguayan	8	0.05
Venezuelan	30	0.19
Other South American	8	0.05
Other Hispanic or Latino	195	1.24

Race*	Population	%
African-American/Black (495)	575	3.67
Not Hispanic (464)	532	3.39
Hispanic (31)	43	0.27
American Indian/Alaska Native (48)	121	0.77
Not Hispanic (18)	78	0.50
Hispanic (30)	43	0.27
Blackfeet (0)	1	0.01
Central American Ind. (0)	1	0.01
Cherokee (1)	19	0.12
Chippewa (0)	1	0.01
Choctaw (4)	6	0.04
Delaware (1)	1	0.01
Iroquois (0)	3	0.02
Lumbee (1)	1	0.01
Navajo (0)	1	0.01
Potawatomi (1)	1	0.01
Pueblo (0)	2	0.01
Sioux (0)	2	0.01
South American Ind. (0)	2	0.01
Asian (1,891)	2,243	14.30
Not Hispanic (1,886)	2,218	14.14
Hispanic (5)	25	0.16
Bangladeshi (24)	24	0.15
Burmese (5)	5	0.03
Cambodian (11)	13	0.08
Chinese, ex. Taiwanese (354)	435	2.77
Filipino (131)	197	1.26
Indian (393)	432	2.75
Indonesian (3)	7	0.04
Japanese (71)	118	0.75
Korean (384)	447	2.85
Laotian (16)	18	0.11
Malaysian (6)	6	0.04
Nepalese (30)	30	0.19
Pakistani (106)	119	0.76
Sri Lankan (13)	13	0.08
Taiwanese (14)	16	0.10
Thai (66)	71	0.45
Vietnamese (202)	225	1.43
Hawaii Native/Pacific Islander (7)	26	0.17
Not Hispanic (7)	22	0.14
Hispanic (0)	4	0.03
Guamanian/Chamorro (1)	2	0.01
Marshallese (4)	4	0.03
Native Hawaiian (1)	12	0.08
White (11,844)	12,370	78.86
Not Hispanic (10,942)	11,353	72.37
Hispanic (902)	1,017	6.48

Vinton

Place Type: Town
County: Roanoke
Population: 8,098†

Ancestry‡	Population	%
Afghan (110)	110	1.36
Albanian (9)	9	0.11
American (1,566)	1,566	19.40
Arab (22)	22	0.27
Lebanese (22)	22	0.27
Austrian (0)	8	0.10
British (39)	39	0.48
Dutch (25)	91	1.13
Eastern European (21)	21	0.26
English (721)	1,170	14.49
European (2)	2	0.02
French, ex. Basque (33)	279	3.46
French Canadian (8)	32	0.40
German (648)	1,200	14.86
Irish (281)	765	9.47
Italian (97)	108	1.34
Norwegian (11)	33	0.41
Polish (59)	59	0.73
Russian (33)	33	0.41
Scotch-Irish (275)	430	5.33
Scottish (195)	352	4.36
Swedish (0)	62	0.77
Welsh (31)	43	0.53
West Indian, ex. Hispanic (46)	46	0.57
Jamaican (46)	46	0.57
Yugoslavian (18)	18	0.22

Hispanic Origin	Population	%
Hispanic or Latino (of any race)	230	2.84
Central American, ex. Mexican	36	0.44
Guatemalan	1	0.01
Honduran	31	0.38
Salvadoran	4	0.05
Cuban	23	0.28
Dominican Republic	2	0.02
Mexican	126	1.56
Puerto Rican	16	0.20
South American	3	0.04
Colombian	1	0.01
Peruvian	2	0.02
Other Hispanic or Latino	24	0.30

Race*	Population	%
African-American/Black (452)	566	6.99
Not Hispanic (439)	547	6.75
Hispanic (13)	19	0.23
American Indian/Alaska Native (9)	39	0.48
Not Hispanic (8)	32	0.40
Hispanic (1)	7	0.09
Blackfeet (1)	3	0.04
Cherokee (1)	10	0.12
Iroquois (0)	1	0.01
Sioux (0)	1	0.01
Asian (78)	94	1.16
Not Hispanic (78)	94	1.16
Cambodian (4)	4	0.05
Chinese, ex. Taiwanese (7)	7	0.09
Filipino (16)	24	0.30
Indian (24)	27	0.33
Japanese (6)	10	0.12
Korean (2)	2	0.02
Pakistani (1)	1	0.01
Vietnamese (11)	11	0.14
Hawaii Native/Pacific Islander (4)	7	0.09
Not Hispanic (4)	7	0.09
Samoan (3)	5	0.06
White (7,285)	7,441	91.89
Not Hispanic (7,187)	7,329	90.50
Hispanic (98)	112	1.38

Virginia Beach

Place Type: Independent City
County: Virginia Beach
Population: 437,994†

Ancestry‡	Population	%
Afghan (67)	67	0.02
African, Sub-Saharan (17,842)	21,562	4.95
African (16,560)	20,099	4.61
Cape Verdean (173)	229	0.05
Ethiopian (354)	354	0.08
Ghanaian (20)	27	0.01
Nigerian (550)	610	0.14
Somalian (60)	60	0.01
South African (48)	73	0.02
Sudanese (44)	44	0.01
Other Sub-Saharan African (33)	66	0.02
Albanian (9)	20	<0.01
American (47,698)	47,698	10.94
Arab (1,226)	1,861	0.43
Arab (168)	273	0.06
Egyptian (76)	76	0.02
Jordanian (112)	125	0.03
Lebanese (375)	647	0.15
Moroccan (219)	242	0.06
Palestinian (78)	177	0.04
Syrian (51)	113	0.03
Other Arab (147)	208	0.05
Armenian (16)	61	0.01
Assyrian/Chaldean/Syriac (16)	61	0.01
Australian (71)	312	0.07
Austrian (177)	636	0.15
Basque (31)	31	0.01
Belgian (110)	473	0.11
Brazilian (195)	306	0.07
British (1,595)	2,913	0.67
Bulgarian (68)	68	0.02
Cajun (19)	59	0.01
Canadian (730)	1,216	0.28
Celtic (147)	170	0.04
Croatian (79)	264	0.06
Cypriot (38)	38	0.01
Czech (423)	1,563	0.36
Czechoslovakian (266)	631	0.14
Danish (262)	1,106	0.25
Dutch (1,361)	6,989	1.60
Eastern European (473)	493	0.11
English (17,579)	47,398	10.87
Estonian (13)	54	0.01
European (4,135)	4,603	1.06
Finnish (146)	654	0.15
French, ex. Basque (2,082)	12,038	2.76
French Canadian (1,765)	3,266	0.75
German (16,507)	59,578	13.66
Greek (1,778)	3,185	0.73
Guyanese (149)	207	0.05
Hungarian (603)	1,964	0.45
Icelander (82)	110	0.03
Iranian (507)	555	0.13
Irish (14,548)	54,157	12.42
Israeli (114)	120	0.03
Italian (9,884)	29,188	6.69
Latvian (79)	239	0.05
Lithuanian (393)	1,067	0.24
Luxemburger (0)	15	<0.01
Maltese (122)	139	0.03
New Zealander (13)	26	0.01
Northern European (201)	201	0.05
Norwegian (915)	3,228	0.74
Pennsylvania German (164)	228	0.05
Polish (3,100)	11,914	2.73
Portuguese (421)	1,425	0.33
Romanian (255)	580	0.13
Russian (1,619)	3,863	0.89
Scandinavian (416)	961	0.22
Scotch-Irish (4,672)	10,850	2.49
Scottish (3,900)	11,456	2.63

*Notes: † The Census 2010 population figure is used to calculate the percentages in the Hispanic Origin and Race categories. Ancestry percentages are based on the 2006-2010 American Community Survey population (not shown); ‡ Numbers in parentheses indicate the number of people reporting a single ancestry; * Numbers in parentheses indicate the number of persons reporting this race alone, not in combination with any other race; Please refer to the Explanation of Data for more information.*

Serbian (117)	254	0.06
Slavic (79)	148	0.03
Slovak (245)	774	0.18
Slovene (112)	218	0.05
Swedish (1,110)	4,008	0.92
Swiss (352)	1,090	0.25
Turkish (274)	407	0.09
Ukrainian (591)	1,201	0.28
Welsh (793)	3,937	0.90
West Indian, ex. Hispanic (2,566)	4,166	0.96
Barbadian (108)	198	0.05
Belizean (15)	15	<0.01
Bermudan (0)	24	0.01
British West Indian (128)	302	0.07
Haitian (152)	222	0.05
Jamaican (1,106)	1,895	0.43
Trinidadian/Tobagonian (614)	809	0.19
U.S. Virgin Islander (76)	76	0.02
West Indian (367)	625	0.14
Yugoslavian (52)	337	0.08

Hispanic Origin	Population	%
Hispanic or Latino (of any race)	28,987	6.62
Central American, ex. Mexican	2,755	0.63
Costa Rican	131	0.03
Guatemalan	425	0.10
Honduran	555	0.13
Nicaraguan	185	0.04
Panamanian	702	0.16
Salvadoran	741	0.17
Other Central American	16	<0.01
Cuban	1,040	0.24
Dominican Republic	1,135	0.26
Mexican	8,528	1.95
Puerto Rican	9,461	2.16
South American	2,517	0.57
Argentinean	127	0.03
Bolivian	74	0.02
Chilean	151	0.03
Colombian	929	0.21
Ecuadorian	414	0.09
Paraguayan	19	<0.01
Peruvian	609	0.14
Uruguayan	25	0.01
Venezuelan	143	0.03
Other South American	26	0.01
Other Hispanic or Latino	3,551	0.81

Race*	Population	%
African-American/Black (85,935)	94,211	21.51
Not Hispanic (83,210)	90,128	20.58
Hispanic (2,725)	4,083	0.93
American Indian/Alaska Native (1,685)	5,331	1.22
Not Hispanic (1,349)	4,456	1.02
Hispanic (336)	875	0.20
Alaska Athabascan *(Ala. Nat.)* (1)	1	<0.01
Aleut *(Alaska Native)* (1)	4	<0.01
Apache (21)	60	0.01
Arapaho (0)	1	<0.01
Blackfeet (31)	211	0.05
Canadian/French Am. Ind. (8)	16	<0.01
Central American Ind. (13)	19	<0.01
Cherokee (219)	1,222	0.28
Cheyenne (5)	9	<0.01
Chickasaw (8)	24	0.01
Chippewa (41)	79	0.02
Choctaw (40)	121	0.03
Colville (4)	4	<0.01
Comanche (6)	20	<0.01
Cree (0)	3	<0.01
Creek (25)	64	0.01
Crow (4)	10	<0.01
Delaware (9)	26	0.01
Hopi (8)	12	<0.01
Houma (3)	3	<0.01
Inupiat *(Alaska Native)* (4)	11	<0.01
Iroquois (46)	112	0.03
Kiowa (4)	9	<0.01
Lumbee (88)	120	0.03
Menominee (1)	1	<0.01
Mexican American Ind. (81)	111	0.03
Navajo (58)	107	0.02
Osage (1)	3	<0.01
Ottawa (6)	10	<0.01
Paiute (1)	3	<0.01
Pima (3)	8	<0.01
Potawatomi (14)	20	<0.01
Pueblo (13)	22	0.01
Puget Sound Salish (5)	9	<0.01
Seminole (3)	34	0.01
Shoshone (3)	4	<0.01
Sioux (37)	96	0.02
South American Ind. (39)	76	0.02
Spanish American Ind. (4)	5	<0.01
Tlingit-Haida *(Alaska Native)* (10)	19	<0.01
Tohono O'Odham (2)	4	<0.01
Ute (0)	14	<0.01
Yaqui (4)	13	<0.01
Yuman (5)	5	<0.01
Yup'ik *(Alaska Native)* (1)	1	<0.01
Asian (26,769)	33,906	7.74
Not Hispanic (26,312)	32,681	7.46
Hispanic (457)	1,225	0.28
Bangladeshi (68)	79	0.02
Burmese (38)	48	0.01
Cambodian (107)	139	0.03
Chinese, ex. Taiwanese (2,156)	2,842	0.65
Filipino (17,481)	22,092	5.04
Hmong (18)	25	0.01
Indian (1,862)	2,274	0.52
Indonesian (40)	74	0.02
Japanese (721)	1,609	0.37
Korean (1,215)	1,802	0.41
Laotian (49)	69	0.02
Malaysian (14)	47	0.01
Nepalese (32)	32	0.01
Pakistani (147)	180	0.04
Sri Lankan (29)	38	0.01
Taiwanese (82)	113	0.03
Thai (204)	353	0.08
Vietnamese (1,784)	2,097	0.48
Hawaii Native/Pacific Islander (657)	1,579	0.36
Not Hispanic (602)	1,375	0.31
Hispanic (55)	204	0.05
Fijian (5)	7	<0.01
Guamanian/Chamorro (271)	453	0.10
Marshallese (2)	2	<0.01
Native Hawaiian (147)	466	0.11
Samoan (106)	193	0.04
Tongan (8)	8	<0.01
White (296,670)	311,177	71.05
Not Hispanic (282,470)	294,477	67.23
Hispanic (14,200)	16,700	3.81

Wakefield

Place Type: CDP
County: Fairfax
Population: 11,275†

Ancestry‡	Population	%
Afghan (32)	32	0.28
African, Sub-Saharan (39)	39	0.34
Somalian (39)	39	0.34
American (535)	535	4.63
Arab (31)	101	0.87
Lebanese (23)	70	0.61
Palestinian (8)	8	0.07
Other Arab (0)	23	0.20
Austrian (70)	124	1.07
British (43)	135	1.17
Cajun (10)	10	0.09
Canadian (0)	34	0.29
Croatian (0)	11	0.10
Czech (11)	121	1.05
Danish (24)	59	0.51
Dutch (16)	122	1.06
Eastern European (61)	61	0.53
English (521)	1,519	13.15
European (366)	366	3.17
French, ex. Basque (47)	221	1.91
French Canadian (55)	151	1.31
German (607)	1,996	17.28
Greek (123)	136	1.18
Hungarian (32)	50	0.43
Irish (540)	1,691	14.64
Israeli (0)	10	0.09
Italian (226)	776	6.72
Lithuanian (0)	11	0.10
New Zealander (16)	16	0.14
Northern European (32)	60	0.52
Norwegian (17)	67	0.58
Polish (165)	373	3.23
Portuguese (0)	35	0.30
Romanian (41)	41	0.35
Russian (73)	202	1.75
Scandinavian (8)	24	0.21
Scotch-Irish (214)	477	4.13
Scottish (166)	372	3.22
Slavic (0)	34	0.29
Slovak (17)	28	0.24
Swedish (68)	208	1.80
Swiss (8)	89	0.77
Ukrainian (0)	19	0.16
Welsh (10)	80	0.69

Hispanic Origin	Population	%
Hispanic or Latino (of any race)	821	7.28
Central American, ex. Mexican	158	1.40
Costa Rican	2	0.02
Guatemalan	18	0.16
Honduran	13	0.12
Nicaraguan	9	0.08
Panamanian	9	0.08
Salvadoran	102	0.90
Other Central American	5	0.04
Cuban	55	0.49
Dominican Republic	5	0.04
Mexican	122	1.08
Puerto Rican	62	0.55
South American	323	2.86
Argentinean	21	0.19
Bolivian	148	1.31
Chilean	30	0.27
Colombian	28	0.25
Ecuadorian	20	0.18
Paraguayan	1	0.01
Peruvian	48	0.43
Uruguayan	3	0.03
Venezuelan	24	0.21
Other Hispanic or Latino	96	0.85

Race*	Population	%
African-American/Black (250)	306	2.71
Not Hispanic (247)	297	2.63
Hispanic (3)	9	0.08
American Indian/Alaska Native (20)	62	0.55
Not Hispanic (13)	44	0.39
Hispanic (7)	18	0.16
Cherokee (6)	18	0.16
Chippewa (1)	1	0.01
Choctaw (0)	5	0.04
Colville (1)	1	0.01
Delaware (0)	2	0.02
Iroquois (1)	3	0.03
Mexican American Ind. (1)	2	0.02
Sioux (1)	1	0.01
South American Ind. (1)	2	0.02
Spanish American Ind. (0)	2	0.02
Asian (1,870)	2,062	18.29
Not Hispanic (1,861)	2,024	17.95
Hispanic (9)	38	0.34
Burmese (6)	7	0.06
Cambodian (23)	25	0.22
Chinese, ex. Taiwanese (280)	341	3.02
Filipino (118)	169	1.50
Indian (125)	144	1.28
Indonesian (5)	11	0.10
Japanese (31)	56	0.50
Korean (590)	621	5.51

*Notes: † The Census 2010 population figure is used to calculate the percentages in the Hispanic Origin and Race categories. Ancestry percentages are based on the 2006-2010 American Community Survey population (not shown); ‡ Numbers in parentheses indicate the number of people reporting a single ancestry; * Numbers in parentheses indicate the number of persons reporting this race alone, not in combination with any other race; Please refer to the Explanation of Data for more information.*

Laotian (3)	4	0.04
Nepalese (5)	5	0.04
Pakistani (36)	40	0.35
Sri Lankan (2)	2	0.02
Taiwanese (10)	15	0.13
Thai (15)	21	0.19
Vietnamese (582)	600	5.32
Hawaii Native/Pacific Islander (7)	31	0.27
Not Hispanic (7)	29	0.26
Hispanic (0)	2	0.02
Native Hawaiian (2)	16	0.14
Samoan (1)	1	0.01
White (8,698)	8,968	79.54
Not Hispanic (8,064)	8,275	73.39
Hispanic (634)	693	6.15

Warrenton

Place Type: Town
County: Fauquier
Population: 9,611[†]

Ancestry[‡]	Population	%
African, Sub-Saharan (52)	153	1.65
African (52)	153	1.65
Albanian (56)	56	0.61
American (959)	959	10.37
Arab (0)	12	0.13
Lebanese (0)	12	0.13
Australian (27)	75	0.81
Austrian (0)	25	0.27
British (18)	32	0.35
Canadian (32)	32	0.35
Croatian (0)	76	0.82
Czech (0)	25	0.27
Danish (60)	60	0.65
Dutch (8)	94	1.02
English (474)	1,220	13.20
European (189)	189	2.04
Finnish (8)	8	0.09
French, ex. Basque (28)	113	1.22
French Canadian (30)	138	1.49
German (485)	1,378	14.91
Hungarian (0)	10	0.11
Iranian (0)	12	0.13
Irish (261)	1,183	12.80
Italian (99)	483	5.22
Norwegian (32)	186	2.01
Polish (32)	213	2.30
Portuguese (38)	176	1.90
Scotch-Irish (119)	420	4.54
Scottish (111)	297	3.21
Slovak (10)	54	0.58
Swedish (0)	60	0.65
Swiss (0)	30	0.32
Ukrainian (0)	12	0.13
Welsh (45)	132	1.43
West Indian, ex. Hispanic (0)	34	0.37
Jamaican (0)	34	0.37

Hispanic Origin	Population	%
Hispanic or Latino (of any race)	709	7.38
Central American, ex. Mexican	141	1.47
Costa Rican	1	0.01
Guatemalan	40	0.42
Honduran	6	0.06
Nicaraguan	4	0.04
Panamanian	1	0.01
Salvadoran	85	0.88
Other Central American	4	0.04
Cuban	31	0.32
Mexican	278	2.89
Puerto Rican	87	0.91
South American	82	0.85
Argentinean	5	0.05
Bolivian	10	0.10
Chilean	7	0.07
Colombian	17	0.18
Paraguayan	1	0.01
Peruvian	30	0.31
Uruguayan	5	0.05
Venezuelan	6	0.06
Other South American	1	0.01
Other Hispanic or Latino	90	0.94

Race*	Population	%
African-American/Black (1,303)	1,459	15.18
Not Hispanic (1,282)	1,428	14.86
Hispanic (21)	31	0.32
American Indian/Alaska Native (25)	95	0.99
Not Hispanic (23)	83	0.86
Hispanic (2)	12	0.12
Blackfeet (1)	7	0.07
Canadian/French Am. Ind. (2)	2	0.02
Cherokee (9)	35	0.36
Cheyenne (0)	2	0.02
Chippewa (0)	2	0.02
Creek (0)	2	0.02
Iroquois (0)	1	0.01
Lumbee (1)	1	0.01
Sioux (3)	3	0.03
Yaqui (1)	2	0.02
Asian (222)	268	2.79
Not Hispanic (221)	263	2.74
Hispanic (1)	5	0.05
Bangladeshi (18)	18	0.19
Burmese (4)	4	0.04
Cambodian (2)	2	0.02
Chinese, ex. Taiwanese (31)	40	0.42
Filipino (33)	45	0.47
Indian (64)	72	0.75
Japanese (9)	22	0.23
Korean (9)	16	0.17
Pakistani (4)	7	0.07
Taiwanese (1)	3	0.03
Thai (4)	7	0.07
Vietnamese (26)	27	0.28
Hawaii Native/Pacific Islander (11)	22	0.23
Not Hispanic (7)	15	0.16
Hispanic (4)	7	0.07
Guamanian/Chamorro (3)	8	0.08
Native Hawaiian (3)	6	0.06
White (7,509)	7,752	80.66
Not Hispanic (7,126)	7,323	76.19
Hispanic (383)	429	4.46

Waynesboro

Place Type: Independent City
County: Waynesboro
Population: 21,006[†]

Ancestry[‡]	Population	%
Afghan (10)	10	0.05
African, Sub-Saharan (65)	65	0.31
African (65)	65	0.31
American (3,166)	3,166	15.16
Australian (16)	16	0.08
British (27)	116	0.56
Canadian (0)	11	0.05
Czech (0)	7	0.03
Czechoslovakian (0)	11	0.05
Danish (0)	30	0.14
Dutch (53)	291	1.39
English (1,635)	3,139	15.03
European (115)	130	0.62
French, ex. Basque (87)	532	2.55
French Canadian (6)	61	0.29
German (1,061)	3,369	16.13
German Russian (26)	26	0.12
Greek (0)	19	0.09
Hungarian (33)	80	0.38
Irish (677)	2,628	12.58
Italian (106)	479	2.29
Luxemburger (10)	10	0.05
Northern European (34)	34	0.16
Norwegian (11)	107	0.51
Pennsylvania German (13)	18	0.09
Polish (36)	266	1.27
Romanian (19)	34	0.16
Russian (44)	107	0.51
Scandinavian (14)	69	0.33
Scotch-Irish (517)	903	4.32
Scottish (78)	608	2.91
Slavic (20)	20	0.10
Swedish (115)	205	0.98
Swiss (0)	63	0.30
Welsh (33)	371	1.78
West Indian, ex. Hispanic (90)	90	0.43
Haitian (90)	90	0.43

Hispanic Origin	Population	%
Hispanic or Latino (of any race)	1,337	6.36
Central American, ex. Mexican	98	0.47
Costa Rican	3	0.01
Guatemalan	25	0.12
Honduran	3	0.01
Nicaraguan	6	0.03
Panamanian	6	0.03
Salvadoran	55	0.26
Cuban	35	0.17
Dominican Republic	18	0.09
Mexican	947	4.51
Puerto Rican	101	0.48
South American	67	0.32
Argentinean	27	0.13
Chilean	2	0.01
Colombian	14	0.07
Ecuadorian	6	0.03
Peruvian	10	0.05
Uruguayan	4	0.02
Venezuelan	4	0.02
Other Hispanic or Latino	71	0.34

Race*	Population	%
African-American/Black (2,229)	2,671	12.72
Not Hispanic (2,176)	2,571	12.24
Hispanic (53)	100	0.48
American Indian/Alaska Native (58)	212	1.01
Not Hispanic (50)	181	0.86
Hispanic (8)	31	0.15
Apache (0)	5	0.02
Arapaho (1)	3	0.01
Blackfeet (2)	5	0.02
Cherokee (13)	58	0.28
Chickasaw (0)	1	<0.01
Choctaw (5)	5	0.02
Creek (0)	1	<0.01
Iroquois (5)	8	0.04
Paiute (1)	1	<0.01
Pueblo (1)	1	<0.01
Sioux (0)	4	0.02
South American Ind. (1)	4	0.02
Ute (0)	1	<0.01
Asian (154)	236	1.12
Not Hispanic (154)	227	1.08
Hispanic (0)	9	0.04
Cambodian (1)	1	<0.01
Chinese, ex. Taiwanese (16)	31	0.15
Filipino (16)	37	0.18
Indian (46)	51	0.24
Indonesian (2)	2	0.01
Japanese (7)	15	0.07
Korean (13)	27	0.13
Laotian (1)	1	<0.01
Pakistani (4)	4	0.02
Thai (5)	7	0.03
Vietnamese (39)	43	0.20
Hawaii Native/Pacific Islander (5)	25	0.12
Not Hispanic (5)	21	0.10
Hispanic (0)	4	0.02
Guamanian/Chamorro (0)	6	0.03
Native Hawaiian (2)	3	0.01
Samoan (0)	1	<0.01
Tongan (2)	2	0.01
White (17,274)	17,894	85.19
Not Hispanic (16,704)	17,214	81.95
Hispanic (570)	680	3.24

*Notes: † The Census 2010 population figure is used to calculate the percentages in the Hispanic Origin and Race categories. Ancestry percentages are based on the 2006-2010 American Community Survey population (not shown); ‡ Numbers in parentheses indicate the number of people reporting a single ancestry; * Numbers in parentheses indicate the number of persons reporting this race alone, not in combination with any other race; Please refer to the Explanation of Data for more information.*

West Falls Church

Place Type: CDP
County: Fairfax
Population: 29,207†

Ancestry‡	Population	%
Afghan (101)	101	0.37
African, Sub-Saharan (163)	163	0.59
African (163)	163	0.59
Albanian (61)	89	0.32
American (970)	970	3.51
Arab (142)	175	0.63
Arab (19)	28	0.10
Egyptian (84)	84	0.30
Jordanian (1)	1	<0.01
Lebanese (20)	31	0.11
Moroccan (18)	18	0.07
Syrian (0)	13	0.05
Armenian (0)	34	0.12
Australian (42)	42	0.15
Austrian (41)	142	0.51
Belgian (0)	12	0.04
British (85)	254	0.92
Canadian (0)	73	0.26
Czech (32)	42	0.15
Czechoslovakian (15)	26	0.09
Danish (59)	277	1.00
Dutch (36)	270	0.98
Eastern European (44)	44	0.16
English (956)	2,872	10.40
Estonian (0)	12	0.04
European (427)	507	1.84
Finnish (0)	13	0.05
French, ex. Basque (31)	327	1.18
French Canadian (27)	59	0.21
German (467)	2,614	9.47
Greek (40)	84	0.30
Hungarian (0)	61	0.22
Iranian (66)	75	0.27
Irish (700)	2,555	9.25
Israeli (0)	60	0.22
Italian (317)	821	2.97
Lithuanian (0)	17	0.06
Macedonian (11)	11	0.04
Northern European (88)	88	0.32
Norwegian (28)	281	1.02
Pennsylvania German (9)	17	0.06
Polish (96)	580	2.10
Portuguese (21)	63	0.23
Russian (178)	367	1.33
Scandinavian (8)	55	0.20
Scotch-Irish (153)	455	1.65
Scottish (108)	481	1.74
Slovak (36)	62	0.22
Swedish (23)	109	0.39
Swiss (12)	85	0.31
Ukrainian (70)	90	0.33
Welsh (21)	188	0.68
West Indian, ex. Hispanic (0)	29	0.11
Bermudan (0)	16	0.06
Jamaican (0)	13	0.05

Hispanic Origin	Population	%
Hispanic or Latino (of any race)	9,679	33.14
Central American, ex. Mexican	4,274	14.63
Costa Rican	26	0.09
Guatemalan	845	2.89
Honduran	441	1.51
Nicaraguan	180	0.62
Panamanian	16	0.05
Salvadoran	2,748	9.41
Other Central American	18	0.06
Cuban	83	0.28
Dominican Republic	45	0.15
Mexican	693	2.37
Puerto Rican	161	0.55
South American	3,296	11.28
Argentinean	198	0.68
Bolivian	2,226	7.62
Chilean	72	0.25
Colombian	130	0.45
Ecuadorian	96	0.33
Paraguayan	13	0.04
Peruvian	480	1.64
Uruguayan	19	0.07
Venezuelan	50	0.17
Other South American	12	0.04
Other Hispanic or Latino	1,127	3.86

Race*	Population	%
African-American/Black (1,415)	1,618	5.54
Not Hispanic (1,317)	1,476	5.05
Hispanic (98)	142	0.49
American Indian/Alaska Native (146)	345	1.18
Not Hispanic (41)	126	0.43
Hispanic (105)	219	0.75
Apache (1)	5	0.02
Blackfeet (0)	5	0.02
Canadian/French Am. Ind. (4)	5	0.02
Central American Ind. (7)	24	0.08
Cherokee (6)	29	0.10
Cheyenne (1)	1	<0.01
Chickasaw (0)	1	<0.01
Chippewa (3)	4	0.01
Choctaw (1)	2	0.01
Colville (1)	1	<0.01
Iroquois (1)	6	0.02
Lumbee (1)	4	0.01
Mexican American Ind. (10)	18	0.06
Navajo (1)	1	<0.01
Osage (0)	1	<0.01
Ottawa (0)	2	0.01
Seminole (1)	1	<0.01
Sioux (2)	2	0.01
South American Ind. (2)	13	0.04
Spanish American Ind. (2)	4	0.01
Asian (5,554)	6,046	20.70
Not Hispanic (5,521)	5,943	20.35
Hispanic (33)	103	0.35
Bangladeshi (51)	53	0.18
Burmese (31)	32	0.11
Cambodian (111)	130	0.45
Chinese, ex. Taiwanese (433)	540	1.85
Filipino (638)	730	2.50
Indian (909)	1,000	3.42
Indonesian (28)	39	0.13
Japanese (51)	103	0.35
Korean (170)	197	0.67
Laotian (69)	72	0.25
Malaysian (7)	9	0.03
Nepalese (159)	166	0.57
Pakistani (177)	201	0.69
Sri Lankan (55)	55	0.19
Taiwanese (20)	24	0.08
Thai (74)	83	0.28
Vietnamese (2,389)	2,499	8.56
Hawaii Native/Pacific Islander (8)	48	0.16
Not Hispanic (4)	37	0.13
Hispanic (4)	11	0.04
Guamanian/Chamorro (0)	5	0.02
Marshallese (1)	1	<0.01
Native Hawaiian (1)	10	0.03
Samoan (4)	9	0.03
White (16,156)	17,249	59.06
Not Hispanic (11,918)	12,480	42.73
Hispanic (4,238)	4,769	16.33

West Springfield

Place Type: CDP
County: Fairfax
Population: 22,460†

Ancestry‡	Population	%
Afghan (181)	181	0.81
African, Sub-Saharan (591)	637	2.86
African (157)	193	0.87
Ethiopian (303)	303	1.36
Ghanaian (55)	55	0.25
Kenyan (13)	23	0.10
Nigerian (19)	19	0.09
Somalian (44)	44	0.20
Albanian (18)	18	0.08
American (705)	705	3.17
Arab (45)	199	0.89
Arab (0)	41	0.18
Egyptian (10)	10	0.04
Lebanese (35)	95	0.43
Palestinian (0)	41	0.18
Syrian (0)	12	0.05
Austrian (15)	69	0.31
Belgian (0)	15	0.07
British (131)	296	1.33
Canadian (17)	17	0.08
Croatian (0)	24	0.11
Czech (100)	252	1.13
Czechoslovakian (39)	47	0.21
Danish (0)	68	0.31
Dutch (76)	422	1.89
Eastern European (36)	36	0.16
English (874)	2,780	12.48
European (85)	193	0.87
Finnish (33)	75	0.34
French, ex. Basque (92)	412	1.85
French Canadian (60)	110	0.49
German (862)	3,181	14.28
Greek (37)	125	0.56
Hungarian (72)	230	1.03
Iranian (33)	33	0.15
Irish (955)	3,008	13.51
Italian (372)	1,505	6.76
Latvian (10)	19	0.09
Lithuanian (10)	98	0.44
Northern European (58)	58	0.26
Norwegian (26)	101	0.45
Polish (197)	726	3.26
Portuguese (0)	45	0.20
Romanian (24)	61	0.27
Russian (111)	348	1.56
Scandinavian (9)	49	0.22
Scotch-Irish (260)	551	2.47
Scottish (199)	758	3.40
Serbian (11)	26	0.12
Slavic (21)	21	0.09
Slovak (0)	95	0.43
Slovene (0)	88	0.40
Swedish (56)	177	0.79
Swiss (0)	54	0.24
Turkish (10)	10	0.04
Ukrainian (35)	79	0.35
Welsh (36)	331	1.49
West Indian, ex. Hispanic (24)	52	0.23
Barbadian (9)	9	0.04
Jamaican (8)	24	0.11
Trinidadian/Tobagonian (7)	7	0.03
West Indian (0)	12	0.05

Hispanic Origin	Population	%
Hispanic or Latino (of any race)	2,967	13.21
Central American, ex. Mexican	758	3.37
Costa Rican	8	0.04
Guatemalan	85	0.38
Honduran	116	0.52
Nicaraguan	48	0.21
Panamanian	50	0.22
Salvadoran	446	1.99
Other Central American	5	0.02
Cuban	76	0.34
Dominican Republic	39	0.17
Mexican	257	1.14
Puerto Rican	265	1.18
South American	1,190	5.30
Argentinean	64	0.28
Bolivian	372	1.66
Chilean	44	0.20
Colombian	139	0.62
Ecuadorian	79	0.35
Paraguayan	5	0.02
Peruvian	410	1.83

*Notes: † The Census 2010 population figure is used to calculate the percentages in the Hispanic Origin and Race categories. Ancestry percentages are based on the 2006-2010 American Community Survey population (not shown); ‡ Numbers in parentheses indicate the number of people reporting a single ancestry; * Numbers in parentheses indicate the number of persons reporting this race alone, not in combination with any other race; Please refer to the Explanation of Data for more information.*

Uruguayan	23	0.10
Venezuelan	44	0.20
Other South American	10	0.04
Other Hispanic or Latino	382	1.70

Race*	Population	%
African-American/Black (1,746)	2,001	8.91
Not Hispanic (1,690)	1,893	8.43
Hispanic (56)	108	0.48
American Indian/Alaska Native (72)	227	1.01
Not Hispanic (36)	137	0.61
Hispanic (36)	90	0.40
Apache (1)	3	0.01
Blackfeet (0)	4	0.02
Central American Ind. (4)	4	0.02
Cherokee (4)	36	0.16
Chippewa (4)	7	0.03
Choctaw (2)	10	0.04
Comanche (2)	2	0.01
Creek (0)	4	0.02
Delaware (1)	1	<0.01
Iroquois (5)	8	0.04
Lumbee (1)	2	0.01
Mexican American Ind. (1)	5	0.02
Navajo (2)	6	0.03
Osage (2)	2	0.01
Pueblo (1)	2	0.01
Seminole (0)	3	0.01
South American Ind. (7)	19	0.08
Yaqui (1)	2	0.01
Asian (3,511)	4,024	17.92
Not Hispanic (3,486)	3,948	17.58
Hispanic (25)	76	0.34
Bangladeshi (44)	44	0.20
Burmese (1)	2	0.01
Cambodian (26)	27	0.12
Chinese, ex. Taiwanese (269)	361	1.61
Filipino (422)	494	2.20
Indian (464)	532	2.37
Indonesian (21)	21	0.09
Japanese (40)	111	0.49
Korean (1,139)	1,202	5.35
Laotian (11)	17	0.08
Malaysian (1)	1	<0.01
Nepalese (20)	21	0.09
Pakistani (272)	304	1.35
Sri Lankan (5)	5	0.02
Taiwanese (24)	28	0.12
Thai (98)	120	0.53
Vietnamese (520)	580	2.58
Hawaii Native/Pacific Islander (34)	51	0.23
Not Hispanic (32)	47	0.21
Hispanic (2)	4	0.02
Fijian (2)	2	0.01
Guamanian/Chamorro (10)	13	0.06
Native Hawaiian (8)	14	0.06
Samoan (9)	9	0.04
White (15,292)	16,082	71.60
Not Hispanic (13,499)	14,110	62.82
Hispanic (1,793)	1,972	8.78

Williamsburg

Place Type: Independent City
County: Williamsburg
Population: 14,068†

Ancestry‡	Population	%
African, Sub-Saharan (81)	90	0.67
African (53)	62	0.46
Ghanaian (28)	28	0.21
Albanian (0)	16	0.12
American (426)	426	3.17
Arab (12)	63	0.47
Egyptian (12)	26	0.19
Lebanese (0)	28	0.21
Moroccan (0)	9	0.07
Armenian (10)	10	0.07
Austrian (0)	36	0.27
Belgian (7)	7	0.05
British (26)	124	0.92
Canadian (9)	59	0.44
Croatian (14)	14	0.10
Cypriot (13)	13	0.10
Czech (12)	79	0.59
Czechoslovakian (0)	34	0.25
Danish (23)	82	0.61
Dutch (33)	125	0.93
Eastern European (38)	38	0.28
English (661)	2,299	17.13
European (227)	253	1.89
Finnish (12)	20	0.15
French, ex. Basque (176)	594	4.43
French Canadian (50)	76	0.57
German (591)	2,758	20.55
Greek (45)	124	0.92
Hungarian (0)	70	0.52
Irish (450)	1,970	14.68
Italian (205)	1,156	8.61
Lithuanian (13)	75	0.56
Luxemburger (0)	11	0.08
New Zealander (0)	13	0.10
Northern European (36)	36	0.27
Norwegian (27)	85	0.63
Polish (85)	444	3.31
Portuguese (24)	24	0.18
Romanian (0)	40	0.30
Russian (102)	344	2.56
Scandinavian (0)	57	0.42
Scotch-Irish (153)	522	3.89
Scottish (133)	529	3.94
Serbian (10)	25	0.19
Slavic (0)	13	0.10
Slovak (13)	82	0.61
Slovene (7)	15	0.11
Swedish (43)	219	1.63
Swiss (0)	7	0.05
Ukrainian (26)	50	0.37
Welsh (35)	231	1.72
West Indian, ex. Hispanic (103)	117	0.87
Haitian (9)	9	0.07
Jamaican (94)	108	0.80
Yugoslavian (14)	14	0.10

Hispanic Origin	Population	%
Hispanic or Latino (of any race)	941	6.69
Central American, ex. Mexican	240	1.71
Costa Rican	3	0.02
Guatemalan	32	0.23
Honduran	25	0.18
Nicaraguan	4	0.03
Panamanian	9	0.06
Salvadoran	162	1.15
Other Central American	5	0.04
Cuban	60	0.43
Dominican Republic	17	0.12
Mexican	231	1.64
Puerto Rican	160	1.14
South American	133	0.95
Argentinean	14	0.10
Bolivian	14	0.10
Chilean	4	0.03
Colombian	40	0.28
Ecuadorian	17	0.12
Paraguayan	5	0.04
Peruvian	27	0.19
Uruguayan	7	0.05
Venezuelan	5	0.04
Other Hispanic or Latino	100	0.71

Race*	Population	%
African-American/Black (1,968)	2,176	15.47
Not Hispanic (1,918)	2,103	14.95
Hispanic (50)	73	0.52
American Indian/Alaska Native (38)	111	0.79
Not Hispanic (35)	98	0.70
Hispanic (3)	13	0.09
Apache (2)	3	0.02
Blackfeet (0)	1	0.01
Cherokee (12)	36	0.26
Cheyenne (0)	1	0.01
Chickasaw (0)	1	0.01
Chippewa (0)	2	0.01
Choctaw (0)	1	0.01
Creek (0)	1	0.01
Crow (2)	2	0.01
Iroquois (3)	5	0.04
Mexican American Ind. (0)	2	0.01
Navajo (0)	1	0.01
Potawatomi (1)	1	0.01
Pueblo (4)	4	0.03
Seminole (0)	1	0.01
Sioux (1)	1	0.01
Spanish American Ind. (0)	1	0.01
Asian (808)	1,004	7.14
Not Hispanic (802)	985	7.00
Hispanic (6)	19	0.14
Bangladeshi (6)	6	0.04
Burmese (1)	1	0.01
Cambodian (1)	2	0.01
Chinese, ex. Taiwanese (231)	279	1.98
Filipino (55)	99	0.70
Indian (178)	208	1.48
Indonesian (3)	6	0.04
Japanese (25)	50	0.36
Korean (174)	203	1.44
Laotian (1)	2	0.01
Malaysian (0)	1	0.01
Nepalese (3)	4	0.03
Pakistani (22)	27	0.19
Sri Lankan (2)	2	0.01
Taiwanese (14)	17	0.12
Thai (18)	23	0.16
Vietnamese (49)	59	0.42
Hawaii Native/Pacific Islander (5)	20	0.14
Not Hispanic (4)	18	0.13
Hispanic (1)	2	0.01
Fijian (1)	1	0.01
Native Hawaiian (4)	14	0.10
White (10,407)	10,845	77.09
Not Hispanic (9,952)	10,308	73.27
Hispanic (455)	537	3.82

Winchester

Place Type: Independent City
County: Winchester
Population: 26,203†

Ancestry‡	Population	%
African, Sub-Saharan (115)	115	0.44
African (5)	5	0.02
Ghanaian (24)	24	0.09
Somalian (86)	86	0.33
American (2,597)	2,597	10.01
Arab (58)	58	0.22
Egyptian (12)	12	0.05
Syrian (20)	20	0.08
Other Arab (26)	26	0.10
Austrian (0)	48	0.18
Belgian (0)	10	0.04
British (29)	29	0.11
Bulgarian (148)	148	0.57
Canadian (13)	13	0.05
Czech (15)	15	0.06
Dutch (210)	415	1.60
English (1,095)	3,019	11.63
European (269)	269	1.04
Finnish (0)	40	0.15
French, ex. Basque (107)	466	1.80
French Canadian (14)	72	0.28
German (1,829)	4,943	19.05
Greek (45)	71	0.27
Hungarian (21)	76	0.29
Iranian (7)	16	0.06
Irish (826)	2,677	10.31
Italian (362)	1,121	4.32
Latvian (0)	17	0.07
Lithuanian (11)	11	0.04
Northern European (16)	16	0.06

*Notes: † The Census 2010 population figure is used to calculate the percentages in the Hispanic Origin and Race categories. Ancestry percentages are based on the 2006-2010 American Community Survey population (not shown); ‡ Numbers in parentheses indicate the number of people reporting a single ancestry; * Numbers in parentheses indicate the number of persons reporting this race alone, not in combination with any other race; Please refer to the Explanation of Data for more information.*

Norwegian (57)	182	0.70
Pennsylvania German (14)	14	0.05
Polish (210)	524	2.02
Romanian (0)	8	0.03
Russian (40)	81	0.31
Scandinavian (0)	36	0.14
Scotch-Irish (391)	954	3.68
Scottish (172)	646	2.49
Slovak (0)	51	0.20
Swedish (13)	116	0.45
Swiss (0)	78	0.30
Turkish (0)	4	0.02
Ukrainian (0)	12	0.05
Welsh (47)	209	0.81
West Indian, ex. Hispanic (942)	942	3.63
Jamaican (934)	934	3.60
Trinidadian/Tobagonian (8)	8	0.03

Hispanic Origin	Population	%
Hispanic or Latino (of any race)	4,041	15.42
Central American, ex. Mexican	1,028	3.92
Costa Rican	6	0.02
Guatemalan	146	0.56
Honduran	117	0.45
Nicaraguan	13	0.05
Panamanian	15	0.06
Salvadoran	722	2.76
Other Central American	9	0.03
Cuban	33	0.13
Dominican Republic	11	0.04
Mexican	2,253	8.60
Puerto Rican	235	0.90
South American	94	0.36
Argentinean	14	0.05
Bolivian	19	0.07
Chilean	4	0.02
Colombian	14	0.05
Ecuadorian	4	0.02
Paraguayan	1	<0.01
Peruvian	19	0.07
Uruguayan	2	0.01
Venezuelan	17	0.06
Other Hispanic or Latino	387	1.48

Race*	Population	%
African-American/Black (2,864)	3,313	12.64
Not Hispanic (2,783)	3,194	12.19
Hispanic (81)	119	0.45
American Indian/Alaska Native (93)	222	0.85
Not Hispanic (37)	134	0.51
Hispanic (56)	88	0.34
Apache (0)	3	0.01
Blackfeet (2)	7	0.03
Canadian/French Am. Ind. (1)	1	<0.01
Cherokee (9)	38	0.15
Cheyenne (0)	1	<0.01
Chippewa (1)	1	<0.01
Choctaw (1)	1	<0.01
Delaware (1)	2	0.01
Inupiat *(Alaska Native)* (0)	1	<0.01
Iroquois (1)	8	0.03
Mexican American Ind. (15)	22	0.08
Navajo (1)	1	<0.01
Osage (1)	1	<0.01
Sioux (1)	5	0.02
South American Ind. (2)	4	0.02
Spanish American Ind. (4)	4	0.02
Asian (611)	750	2.86
Not Hispanic (599)	723	2.76
Hispanic (12)	27	0.10
Bangladeshi (9)	9	0.03
Burmese (4)	4	0.02
Cambodian (2)	2	0.01
Chinese, ex. Taiwanese (98)	111	0.42
Filipino (100)	137	0.52
Hmong (2)	2	0.01
Indian (123)	134	0.51
Indonesian (1)	2	0.01
Japanese (19)	43	0.16
Korean (62)	97	0.37
Laotian (4)	4	0.02
Malaysian (0)	1	<0.01
Nepalese (1)	4	0.02
Pakistani (33)	35	0.13
Sri Lankan (6)	7	0.03
Taiwanese (9)	10	0.04
Thai (9)	12	0.05
Vietnamese (98)	105	0.40
Hawaii Native/Pacific Islander (4)	32	0.12
Not Hispanic (3)	18	0.07
Hispanic (1)	14	0.05
Guamanian/Chamorro (1)	1	<0.01
Native Hawaiian (3)	9	0.03
White (19,532)	20,243	77.25
Not Hispanic (18,085)	18,638	71.13
Hispanic (1,447)	1,605	6.13

Wolf Trap

Place Type: CDP
County: Fairfax
Population: 16,131†

Ancestry‡	Population	%
Afghan (152)	152	0.91
African, Sub-Saharan (25)	54	0.32
African (25)	25	0.15
South African (0)	29	0.17
American (783)	783	4.69
Arab (412)	511	3.06
Arab (149)	149	0.89
Iraqi (21)	21	0.13
Lebanese (88)	155	0.93
Moroccan (0)	10	0.06
Palestinian (13)	13	0.08
Syrian (6)	28	0.17
Other Arab (135)	135	0.81
Armenian (54)	65	0.39
Australian (24)	33	0.20
Austrian (31)	91	0.55
British (100)	229	1.37
Canadian (0)	35	0.21
Celtic (25)	50	0.30
Croatian (0)	10	0.06
Czech (25)	67	0.40
Danish (22)	83	0.50
Dutch (45)	190	1.14
Eastern European (73)	73	0.44
English (711)	2,428	14.56
Estonian (0)	11	0.07
European (461)	474	2.84
French, ex. Basque (93)	550	3.30
French Canadian (38)	191	1.15
German (707)	2,967	17.79
Greek (181)	256	1.53
Hungarian (38)	87	0.52
Iranian (806)	853	5.11
Irish (963)	2,923	17.52
Israeli (15)	15	0.09
Italian (589)	1,471	8.82
Lithuanian (18)	69	0.41
New Zealander (0)	11	0.07
Northern European (17)	17	0.10
Norwegian (35)	107	0.64
Polish (225)	846	5.07
Portuguese (11)	18	0.11
Romanian (0)	26	0.16
Russian (137)	488	2.93
Scandinavian (13)	69	0.41
Scotch-Irish (214)	453	2.72
Scottish (123)	532	3.19
Slavic (16)	16	0.10
Slovak (60)	133	0.80
Slovene (16)	58	0.35
Swedish (61)	403	2.42
Swiss (0)	87	0.52
Ukrainian (31)	183	1.10
Welsh (35)	174	1.04
West Indian, ex. Hispanic (104)	122	0.73
Dutch West Indian (0)	11	0.07
Haitian (7)	7	0.04
Jamaican (32)	39	0.23
West Indian (65)	65	0.39
Yugoslavian (10)	19	0.11

Hispanic Origin	Population	%
Hispanic or Latino (of any race)	655	4.06
Central American, ex. Mexican	70	0.43
Costa Rican	4	0.02
Guatemalan	16	0.10
Honduran	2	0.01
Nicaraguan	11	0.07
Panamanian	6	0.04
Salvadoran	31	0.19
Cuban	43	0.27
Dominican Republic	11	0.07
Mexican	116	0.72
Puerto Rican	63	0.39
South American	239	1.48
Argentinean	28	0.17
Bolivian	38	0.24
Chilean	10	0.06
Colombian	48	0.30
Ecuadorian	14	0.09
Paraguayan	6	0.04
Peruvian	49	0.30
Uruguayan	4	0.02
Venezuelan	42	0.26
Other Hispanic or Latino	113	0.70

Race*	Population	%
African-American/Black (264)	322	2.00
Not Hispanic (261)	306	1.90
Hispanic (3)	16	0.10
American Indian/Alaska Native (25)	69	0.43
Not Hispanic (18)	54	0.33
Hispanic (7)	15	0.09
Blackfeet (1)	1	0.01
Cherokee (2)	13	0.08
Choctaw (3)	3	0.02
Creek (1)	2	0.01
Inupiat *(Alaska Native)* (0)	1	0.01
Iroquois (0)	5	0.03
Mexican American Ind. (1)	1	0.01
Navajo (1)	1	0.01
Osage (2)	2	0.01
Potawatomi (0)	1	0.01
Asian (2,054)	2,415	14.97
Not Hispanic (2,047)	2,392	14.83
Hispanic (7)	23	0.14
Bangladeshi (2)	3	0.02
Cambodian (15)	18	0.11
Chinese, ex. Taiwanese (558)	641	3.97
Filipino (77)	131	0.81
Indian (580)	647	4.01
Indonesian (1)	2	0.01
Japanese (46)	74	0.46
Korean (336)	384	2.38
Laotian (8)	10	0.06
Malaysian (2)	2	0.01
Nepalese (15)	15	0.09
Pakistani (93)	107	0.66
Sri Lankan (9)	9	0.06
Taiwanese (62)	66	0.41
Thai (30)	32	0.20
Vietnamese (151)	185	1.15
Hawaii Native/Pacific Islander (6)	16	0.10
Not Hispanic (5)	14	0.09
Hispanic (1)	2	0.01
Guamanian/Chamorro (4)	5	0.03
Native Hawaiian (0)	1	0.01
White (13,222)	13,672	84.76
Not Hispanic (12,684)	13,090	81.15
Hispanic (538)	582	3.61

Woodburn

Place Type: CDP
County: Fairfax
Population: 8,480†

SECTION TWO

*Notes: † The Census 2010 population figure is used to calculate the percentages in the Hispanic Origin and Race categories. Ancestry percentages are based on the 2006-2010 American Community Survey population (not shown); ‡ Numbers in parentheses indicate the number of people reporting a single ancestry; * Numbers in parentheses indicate the number of persons reporting this race alone, not in combination with any other race; Please refer to the Explanation of Data for more information.*

Ancestry‡	Population	%
African, Sub-Saharan (338)	367	4.21
African (201)	230	2.64
Ethiopian (24)	24	0.28
Kenyan (113)	113	1.30
American (482)	482	5.54
Arab (126)	277	3.18
Arab (0)	66	0.76
Iraqi (33)	33	0.38
Lebanese (77)	77	0.88
Moroccan (5)	7	0.08
Syrian (0)	83	0.95
Other Arab (11)	11	0.13
Armenian (0)	11	0.13
Belgian (7)	7	0.08
British (64)	222	2.55
Croatian (30)	40	0.46
Czech (16)	16	0.18
Danish (0)	11	0.13
Dutch (16)	93	1.07
Eastern European (49)	66	0.76
English (209)	898	10.31
Estonian (0)	26	0.30
European (236)	270	3.10
French, ex. Basque (60)	297	3.41
French Canadian (15)	28	0.32
German (312)	1,170	13.44
Greek (0)	37	0.42
Hungarian (28)	44	0.51
Iranian (30)	30	0.34
Irish (277)	781	8.97
Israeli (23)	23	0.26
Italian (129)	407	4.67
Latvian (18)	18	0.21
Lithuanian (0)	14	0.16
Maltese (0)	14	0.16
Norwegian (0)	80	0.92
Polish (42)	73	0.84
Romanian (0)	11	0.13
Russian (73)	154	1.77
Scandinavian (0)	34	0.39
Scotch-Irish (93)	232	2.66
Scottish (28)	122	1.40
Slavic (0)	8	0.09
Swedish (0)	57	0.65
Swiss (14)	90	1.03
Ukrainian (0)	9	0.10
Welsh (26)	37	0.42
Yugoslavian (0)	10	0.11

Hispanic Origin	Population	%
Hispanic or Latino (of any race)	1,376	16.23
Central American, ex. Mexican	436	5.14
Costa Rican	12	0.14
Guatemalan	48	0.57
Honduran	31	0.37
Nicaraguan	35	0.41
Panamanian	11	0.13
Salvadoran	295	3.48
Other Central American	4	0.05
Cuban	29	0.34
Dominican Republic	47	0.55
Mexican	94	1.11
Puerto Rican	62	0.73
South American	490	5.78
Argentinean	32	0.38
Bolivian	230	2.71
Chilean	36	0.42
Colombian	37	0.44
Ecuadorian	13	0.15
Paraguayan	2	0.02
Peruvian	122	1.44
Uruguayan	4	0.05
Venezuelan	14	0.17
Other Hispanic or Latino	218	2.57

Race*	Population	%
African-American/Black (540)	637	7.51
Not Hispanic (510)	575	6.78
Hispanic (30)	62	0.73
American Indian/Alaska Native (65)	108	1.27
Not Hispanic (16)	40	0.47
Hispanic (49)	68	0.80
Blackfeet (0)	2	0.02
Cherokee (3)	6	0.07
Iroquois (1)	1	0.01
South American Ind. (3)	8	0.09
Asian (1,617)	1,814	21.39
Not Hispanic (1,608)	1,796	21.18
Hispanic (9)	18	0.21
Bangladeshi (41)	42	0.50
Burmese (4)	4	0.05
Cambodian (15)	15	0.18
Chinese, ex. Taiwanese (178)	217	2.56
Filipino (192)	227	2.68
Hmong (1)	2	0.02
Indian (333)	361	4.26
Indonesian (9)	12	0.14
Japanese (16)	28	0.33
Korean (246)	264	3.11
Laotian (1)	3	0.04
Nepalese (32)	33	0.39
Pakistani (57)	60	0.71
Sri Lankan (18)	25	0.29
Taiwanese (11)	12	0.14
Thai (19)	22	0.26
Vietnamese (394)	420	4.95
Hawaii Native/Pacific Islander (5)	14	0.17
Not Hispanic (5)	9	0.11
Hispanic (0)	5	0.06
Fijian (1)	1	0.01
Guamanian/Chamorro (0)	1	0.01
Native Hawaiian (1)	2	0.02
Samoan (2)	2	0.02
White (5,431)	5,760	67.92
Not Hispanic (4,689)	4,915	57.96
Hispanic (742)	845	9.96

Woodlawn

Place Type: CDP
County: Fairfax
Population: 20,804†

Ancestry‡	Population	%
Afghan (20)	20	0.10
African, Sub-Saharan (1,884)	1,961	10.02
African (446)	475	2.43
Ethiopian (142)	142	0.73
Ghanaian (694)	742	3.79
Liberian (28)	28	0.14
Nigerian (204)	204	1.04
Sierra Leonean (116)	116	0.59
Other Sub-Saharan African (254)	254	1.30
American (856)	856	4.37
Arab (12)	12	0.06
Arab (12)	12	0.06
Austrian (47)	47	0.24
British (0)	35	0.18
Bulgarian (44)	44	0.22
Czech (58)	129	0.66
Danish (0)	21	0.11
Dutch (44)	69	0.35
English (136)	582	2.97
European (79)	94	0.48
Finnish (37)	37	0.19
French, ex. Basque (12)	124	0.63
German (286)	702	3.59
Greek (66)	66	0.34
Hungarian (0)	10	0.05
Iranian (49)	49	0.25
Irish (293)	775	3.96
Italian (231)	429	2.19
Lithuanian (14)	14	0.07
Northern European (14)	14	0.07
Norwegian (0)	20	0.10
Polish (18)	108	0.55
Russian (29)	50	0.26
Scotch-Irish (13)	68	0.35
Scottish (92)	166	0.85
Slovak (40)	82	0.42
Swedish (39)	60	0.31
Swiss (0)	33	0.17
Ukrainian (18)	36	0.18
Welsh (8)	8	0.04
West Indian, ex. Hispanic (198)	198	1.01
Jamaican (171)	171	0.87
West Indian (27)	27	0.14
Yugoslavian (18)	18	0.09

Hispanic Origin	Population	%
Hispanic or Latino (of any race)	7,590	36.48
Central American, ex. Mexican	5,190	24.95
Costa Rican	14	0.07
Guatemalan	312	1.50
Honduran	925	4.45
Nicaraguan	145	0.70
Panamanian	43	0.21
Salvadoran	3,728	17.92
Other Central American	23	0.11
Cuban	26	0.12
Dominican Republic	88	0.42
Mexican	607	2.92
Puerto Rican	207	1.00
South American	549	2.64
Argentinean	30	0.14
Bolivian	204	0.98
Chilean	22	0.11
Colombian	64	0.31
Ecuadorian	40	0.19
Peruvian	176	0.85
Uruguayan	4	0.02
Venezuelan	8	0.04
Other South American	1	<0.01
Other Hispanic or Latino	923	4.44

Race*	Population	%
African-American/Black (6,997)	7,381	35.48
Not Hispanic (6,799)	7,113	34.19
Hispanic (198)	268	1.29
American Indian/Alaska Native (168)	446	2.14
Not Hispanic (42)	151	0.73
Hispanic (126)	295	1.42
Aleut *(Alaska Native)* (0)	1	<0.01
Apache (1)	5	0.02
Blackfeet (2)	12	0.06
Canadian/French Am. Ind. (0)	2	0.01
Central American Ind. (18)	21	0.10
Cherokee (3)	38	0.18
Chippewa (2)	3	0.01
Choctaw (0)	1	<0.01
Colville (2)	2	0.01
Creek (1)	1	<0.01
Iroquois (0)	5	0.02
Mexican American Ind. (22)	30	0.14
Navajo (2)	2	0.01
Ottawa (2)	2	0.01
Sioux (0)	1	<0.01
South American Ind. (4)	9	0.04
Spanish American Ind. (2)	6	0.03
Asian (1,675)	1,930	9.28
Not Hispanic (1,664)	1,886	9.07
Hispanic (11)	44	0.21
Bangladeshi (83)	109	0.52
Burmese (5)	5	0.02
Cambodian (7)	12	0.06
Chinese, ex. Taiwanese (77)	90	0.43
Filipino (274)	340	1.63
Hmong (1)	3	0.01
Indian (255)	349	1.68
Indonesian (10)	10	0.05
Japanese (24)	55	0.26
Korean (98)	132	0.63
Laotian (26)	27	0.13
Nepalese (12)	12	0.06
Pakistani (365)	401	1.93
Sri Lankan (9)	10	0.05
Taiwanese (2)	2	0.01
Thai (61)	65	0.31
Vietnamese (225)	253	1.22

*Notes: † The Census 2010 population figure is used to calculate the percentages in the Hispanic Origin and Race categories. Ancestry percentages are based on the 2006-2010 American Community Survey population (not shown); ‡ Numbers in parentheses indicate the number of people reporting a single ancestry; * Numbers in parentheses indicate the number of persons reporting this race alone, not in combination with any other race; Please refer to the Explanation of Data for more information.*

Hawaii Native/Pacific Islander (27)	74	0.36
Not Hispanic (19)	46	0.22
Hispanic (8)	28	0.13
Guamanian/Chamorro (8)	9	0.04
Native Hawaiian (4)	14	0.07
Samoan (8)	16	0.08
White (6,984)	7,844	37.70
Not Hispanic (4,101)	4,499	21.63
Hispanic (2,883)	3,345	16.08

Wyndham

Place Type: CDP
County: Henrico
Population: 9,785†

Ancestry‡	Population	%
African, Sub-Saharan (29)	52	0.56
African (0)	23	0.25
Ethiopian (29)	29	0.31
American (1,009)	1,009	10.80
Arab (72)	72	0.77
Lebanese (72)	72	0.77
Austrian (0)	11	0.12
British (28)	28	0.30
Canadian (15)	15	0.16
Croatian (14)	14	0.15
Danish (11)	36	0.39
Dutch (21)	44	0.47
Eastern European (15)	15	0.16
English (695)	1,984	21.23
European (131)	131	1.40
French, ex. Basque (59)	310	3.32
French Canadian (0)	14	0.15
German (323)	1,351	14.46
Greek (14)	14	0.15
Hungarian (0)	35	0.37
Irish (565)	1,515	16.21
Italian (251)	934	9.99
Norwegian (23)	77	0.82
Polish (47)	503	5.38
Portuguese (32)	45	0.48
Romanian (27)	92	0.98
Russian (26)	124	1.33
Scandinavian (18)	18	0.19
Scotch-Irish (93)	444	4.75
Scottish (53)	301	3.22
Serbian (14)	30	0.32
Swedish (16)	16	0.17
Swiss (16)	45	0.48
Turkish (67)	67	0.72
Ukrainian (13)	13	0.14
Welsh (61)	72	0.77
West Indian, ex. Hispanic (19)	19	0.20
Bahamian (19)	19	0.20
Yugoslavian (32)	95	1.02

Hispanic Origin	Population	%
Hispanic or Latino (of any race)	178	1.82
Central American, ex. Mexican	9	0.09
Costa Rican	3	0.03
Guatemalan	2	0.02
Honduran	3	0.03
Salvadoran	1	0.01
Cuban	33	0.34
Dominican Republic	6	0.06
Mexican	52	0.53
Puerto Rican	12	0.12
South American	45	0.46
Argentinean	6	0.06
Bolivian	2	0.02
Colombian	10	0.10
Ecuadorian	12	0.12
Peruvian	9	0.09
Venezuelan	6	0.06
Other Hispanic or Latino	21	0.21

Race*	Population	%
African-American/Black (293)	327	3.34
Not Hispanic (290)	323	3.30
Hispanic (3)	4	0.04
American Indian/Alaska Native (15)	40	0.41
Not Hispanic (11)	31	0.32
Hispanic (4)	9	0.09
Cherokee (4)	19	0.19
Choctaw (1)	1	0.01
Mexican American Ind. (1)	1	0.01
South American Ind. (2)	2	0.02
Asian (1,381)	1,491	15.24
Not Hispanic (1,379)	1,483	15.16
Hispanic (2)	8	0.08
Bangladeshi (5)	8	0.08
Burmese (6)	6	0.06
Cambodian (1)	1	0.01
Chinese, ex. Taiwanese (331)	367	3.75
Filipino (44)	60	0.61
Indian (676)	737	7.53
Indonesian (4)	4	0.04
Japanese (25)	36	0.37
Korean (111)	134	1.37
Nepalese (9)	10	0.10
Pakistani (55)	68	0.69
Sri Lankan (2)	2	0.02
Thai (1)	3	0.03
Vietnamese (65)	77	0.79
Hawaii Native/Pacific Islander (0)	1	0.01
Not Hispanic (0)	1	0.01
White (7,921)	8,050	82.27
Not Hispanic (7,777)	7,892	80.65
Hispanic (144)	158	1.61

Wytheville

Place Type: Town
County: Wythe
Population: 8,211†

Ancestry‡	Population	%
American (1,362)	1,362	16.69
Croatian (24)	24	0.29
Danish (0)	10	0.12
Dutch (19)	106	1.30
English (472)	1,129	13.83
European (55)	55	0.67
Finnish (0)	8	0.10
French, ex. Basque (34)	57	0.70
German (589)	1,481	18.14
Hungarian (0)	9	0.11
Irish (224)	798	9.78
Italian (43)	249	3.05
Polish (0)	12	0.15
Scotch-Irish (76)	241	2.95
Scottish (52)	60	0.74
Slovak (12)	12	0.15
Swedish (0)	45	0.55
Welsh (17)	17	0.21

Hispanic Origin	Population	%
Hispanic or Latino (of any race)	115	1.40
Central American, ex. Mexican	2	0.02
Guatemalan	2	0.02
Cuban	15	0.18
Mexican	56	0.68
Puerto Rican	23	0.28
South American	4	0.05
Bolivian	1	0.01
Chilean	1	0.01
Colombian	2	0.02
Other Hispanic or Latino	15	0.18

Race*	Population	%
African-American/Black (606)	709	8.63
Not Hispanic (598)	695	8.46
Hispanic (8)	14	0.17
American Indian/Alaska Native (5)	42	0.51
Not Hispanic (5)	39	0.47
Hispanic (0)	3	0.04
Apache (1)	1	0.01
Blackfeet (0)	6	0.07
Cherokee (2)	15	0.18
Asian (78)	93	1.13
Not Hispanic (76)	91	1.11
Hispanic (2)	2	0.02
Chinese, ex. Taiwanese (8)	15	0.18
Filipino (12)	18	0.22
Indian (32)	34	0.41
Japanese (7)	7	0.09
Korean (1)	3	0.04
Taiwanese (6)	6	0.07
Vietnamese (9)	9	0.11
Hawaii Native/Pacific Islander (2)	8	0.10
Not Hispanic (1)	7	0.09
Hispanic (1)	1	0.01
Guamanian/Chamorro (1)	1	0.01
Native Hawaiian (1)	7	0.09
White (7,331)	7,476	91.05
Not Hispanic (7,271)	7,401	90.14
Hispanic (60)	75	0.91

Yorkshire

Place Type: CDP
County: Prince William
Population: 7,541†

Ancestry‡	Population	%
American (362)	362	5.32
Arab (218)	218	3.21
Arab (65)	65	0.96
Moroccan (25)	25	0.37
Other Arab (128)	128	1.88
British (23)	34	0.50
Croatian (0)	5	0.07
Czech (0)	15	0.22
Dutch (35)	45	0.66
English (110)	419	6.16
French, ex. Basque (36)	127	1.87
French Canadian (22)	22	0.32
German (282)	694	10.21
Greek (14)	27	0.40
Hungarian (10)	10	0.15
Iranian (0)	44	0.65
Irish (137)	539	7.93
Italian (29)	154	2.26
Northern European (0)	14	0.21
Norwegian (0)	77	1.13
Polish (10)	164	2.41
Portuguese (58)	58	0.85
Russian (20)	20	0.29
Scotch-Irish (43)	88	1.29
Scottish (48)	103	1.51
Welsh (0)	59	0.87
West Indian, ex. Hispanic (62)	62	0.91
Jamaican (15)	15	0.22
U.S. Virgin Islander (47)	47	0.69

Hispanic Origin	Population	%
Hispanic or Latino (of any race)	2,940	38.99
Central American, ex. Mexican	1,645	21.81
Costa Rican	7	0.09
Guatemalan	251	3.33
Honduran	107	1.42
Nicaraguan	30	0.40
Panamanian	7	0.09
Salvadoran	1,229	16.30
Other Central American	14	0.19
Cuban	8	0.11
Dominican Republic	26	0.34
Mexican	615	8.16
Puerto Rican	72	0.95
South American	248	3.29
Argentinean	9	0.12
Bolivian	75	0.99
Chilean	9	0.12
Colombian	20	0.27
Ecuadorian	9	0.12
Peruvian	110	1.46
Uruguayan	8	0.11
Venezuelan	7	0.09
Other South American	1	0.01

*Notes: † The Census 2010 population figure is used to calculate the percentages in the Hispanic Origin and Race categories. Ancestry percentages are based on the 2006-2010 American Community Survey population (not shown); ‡ Numbers in parentheses indicate the number of people reporting a single ancestry; * Numbers in parentheses indicate the number of persons reporting this race alone, not in combination with any other race; Please refer to the Explanation of Data for more information.*

Other Hispanic or Latino	326	4.32

Race*	Population	%
African-American/Black (745)	920	12.20
Not Hispanic (704)	852	11.30
Hispanic (41)	68	0.90
American Indian/Alaska Native (41)	114	1.51
Not Hispanic (14)	53	0.70
Hispanic (27)	61	0.81
Blackfeet (0)	5	0.07
Central American Ind. (1)	1	0.01
Cherokee (7)	30	0.40
Cheyenne (1)	1	0.01
Chippewa (1)	3	0.04
Choctaw (0)	1	0.01
Iroquois (0)	1	0.01
Mexican American Ind. (1)	2	0.03
Seminole (0)	1	0.01
Spanish American Ind. (1)	2	0.03
Asian (579)	687	9.11
Not Hispanic (571)	675	8.95
Hispanic (8)	12	0.16
Bangladeshi (17)	17	0.23
Burmese (0)	1	0.01
Cambodian (8)	9	0.12
Chinese, ex. Taiwanese (42)	58	0.77
Filipino (74)	92	1.22
Indian (109)	133	1.76
Indonesian (5)	5	0.07
Japanese (2)	8	0.11
Korean (91)	103	1.37
Laotian (12)	13	0.17
Nepalese (29)	37	0.49
Pakistani (56)	62	0.82
Sri Lankan (8)	8	0.11
Taiwanese (0)	1	0.01
Thai (12)	14	0.19
Vietnamese (83)	104	1.38
Hawaii Native/Pacific Islander (5)	11	0.15
Not Hispanic (1)	1	0.01
Hispanic (4)	10	0.13
Native Hawaiian (5)	5	0.07
White (4,363)	4,730	62.72
Not Hispanic (3,036)	3,253	43.14
Hispanic (1,327)	1,477	19.59

*Notes: † The Census 2010 population figure is used to calculate the percentages in the Hispanic Origin and Race categories. Ancestry percentages are based on the 2006-2010 American Community Survey population (not shown); ‡ Numbers in parentheses indicate the number of people reporting a single ancestry; * Numbers in parentheses indicate the number of persons reporting this race alone, not in combination with any other race; Please refer to the Explanation of Data for more information.*

WASHINGTON

Place Type: State
Population: 6,724,540[†]

Ancestry[‡]	Population	%
Afghan (605)	693	0.01
African, Sub-Saharan (47,544)	56,489	0.86
African (17,228)	23,144	0.35
Cape Verdean (72)	217	<0.01
Ethiopian (12,287)	13,093	0.20
Ghanaian (444)	550	0.01
Kenyan (1,767)	1,905	0.03
Liberian (225)	246	<0.01
Nigerian (2,394)	2,896	0.04
Senegalese (55)	55	<0.01
Sierra Leonean (116)	135	<0.01
Somalian (9,219)	9,543	0.15
South African (790)	1,247	0.02
Sudanese (318)	350	0.01
Ugandan (141)	194	<0.01
Zimbabwean (129)	158	<0.01
Other Sub-Saharan African (2,359)	2,756	0.04
Albanian (567)	867	0.01
Alsatian (46)	138	<0.01
American (268,313)	268,313	4.09
Arab (11,480)	20,528	0.31
Arab (1,989)	2,993	0.05
Egyptian (2,437)	3,083	0.05
Iraqi (487)	920	0.01
Jordanian (513)	702	0.01
Lebanese (2,463)	6,412	0.10
Moroccan (379)	614	0.01
Palestinian (620)	1,132	0.02
Syrian (597)	1,864	0.03
Other Arab (1,995)	2,808	0.04
Armenian (3,427)	5,924	0.09
Assyrian/Chaldean/Syriac (116)	227	<0.01
Australian (1,702)	4,271	0.07
Austrian (5,054)	20,651	0.31
Basque (1,172)	2,847	0.04
Belgian (2,590)	9,226	0.14
Brazilian (1,843)	2,999	0.05
British (22,159)	44,417	0.68
Bulgarian (1,906)	3,286	0.05
Cajun (411)	956	0.01
Canadian (15,615)	31,516	0.48
Carpatho Rusyn (39)	79	<0.01
Celtic (1,415)	2,693	0.04
Croatian (5,068)	13,268	0.20
Cypriot (60)	75	<0.01
Czech (9,171)	31,684	0.48
Czechoslovakian (3,582)	8,284	0.13
Danish (18,566)	75,185	1.15
Dutch (43,189)	161,947	2.47
Eastern European (6,149)	7,317	0.11
English (206,876)	794,895	12.11
Estonian (645)	1,536	0.02
European (121,391)	138,348	2.11
Finnish (16,289)	48,045	0.73
French, ex. Basque (36,200)	248,969	3.79
French Canadian (19,559)	54,989	0.84
German (376,818)	1,331,078	20.29
German Russian (243)	576	0.01
Greek (10,588)	25,865	0.39
Guyanese (140)	236	<0.01
Hungarian (6,983)	23,840	0.36
Icelander (2,377)	6,800	0.10
Iranian (7,816)	8,943	0.14
Irish (188,738)	806,898	12.30
Israeli (933)	1,596	0.02
Italian (73,449)	238,187	3.63
Latvian (1,929)	3,380	0.05
Lithuanian (3,562)	10,573	0.16
Luxemburger (335)	1,417	0.02
Macedonian (96)	258	<0.01
Maltese (315)	663	0.01
New Zealander (454)	927	0.01
Northern European (17,961)	19,819	0.30
Norwegian (135,566)	396,418	6.04
Pennsylvania German (1,557)	3,453	0.05
Polish (34,526)	125,635	1.91
Portuguese (6,656)	22,051	0.34
Romanian (11,188)	15,804	0.24
Russian (40,274)	86,098	1.31
Scandinavian (26,309)	51,902	0.79
Scotch-Irish (51,799)	162,034	2.47
Scottish (54,353)	212,424	3.24
Serbian (1,016)	2,232	0.03
Slavic (1,397)	3,287	0.05
Slovak (2,175)	6,718	0.10
Slovene (787)	2,254	0.03
Soviet Union (168)	168	<0.01
Swedish (58,792)	244,773	3.73
Swiss (9,425)	37,409	0.57
Turkish (2,900)	5,149	0.08
Ukrainian (33,716)	47,100	0.72
Welsh (11,786)	70,800	1.08
West Indian, ex. Hispanic (5,375)	9,017	0.14
Bahamian (32)	117	<0.01
Barbadian (196)	321	<0.01
Belizean (237)	367	0.01
Bermudan (39)	103	<0.01
British West Indian (148)	215	<0.01
Dutch West Indian (108)	324	<0.01
Haitian (1,155)	1,652	0.03
Jamaican (2,273)	3,920	0.06
Trinidadian/Tobagonian (320)	567	0.01
U.S. Virgin Islander (103)	139	<0.01
West Indian (743)	1,238	0.02
Other West Indian (21)	54	<0.01
Yugoslavian (6,200)	12,619	0.19

Hispanic Origin	Population	%
Hispanic or Latino (of any race)	755,790	11.24
Central American, ex. Mexican	33,661	0.50
Costa Rican	1,563	0.02
Guatemalan	9,520	0.14
Honduran	4,381	0.07
Nicaraguan	2,313	0.03
Panamanian	2,939	0.04
Salvadoran	12,637	0.19
Other Central American	308	<0.01
Cuban	6,744	0.10
Dominican Republic	1,819	0.03
Mexican	601,768	8.95
Puerto Rican	25,838	0.38
South American	20,742	0.31
Argentinean	2,376	0.04
Bolivian	782	0.01
Chilean	2,625	0.04
Colombian	5,560	0.08
Ecuadorian	1,855	0.03
Paraguayan	165	<0.01
Peruvian	5,276	0.08
Uruguayan	301	<0.01
Venezuelan	1,556	0.02
Other South American	246	<0.01
Other Hispanic or Latino	65,218	0.97

Race*	Population	%
African-American/Black (240,042)	325,004	4.83
Not Hispanic (229,603)	302,894	4.50
Hispanic (10,439)	22,110	0.33
American Indian/Alaska Native (103,869)	198,998	2.96
Not Hispanic (88,735)	168,849	2.51
Hispanic (15,134)	30,149	0.45
Alaska Athabascan *(Ala. Nat.)* (644)	1,222	0.02
Aleut *(Alaska Native)* (1,411)	2,870	0.04
Apache (757)	2,234	0.03
Arapaho (192)	326	<0.01
Blackfeet (2,020)	6,573	0.10
Canadian/French Am. Ind. (1,001)	2,079	0.03
Central American Ind. (223)	386	0.01
Cherokee (4,482)	20,257	0.30
Cheyenne (312)	764	0.01
Chickasaw (315)	945	0.01
Chippewa (3,035)	6,519	0.10
Choctaw (1,196)	3,886	0.06
Colville (6,954)	8,645	0.13
Comanche (134)	488	0.01
Cree (219)	736	0.01
Creek (355)	1,008	0.01
Crow (229)	484	0.01
Delaware (133)	383	0.01
Hopi (97)	260	<0.01
Houma (19)	34	<0.01
Inupiat *(Alaska Native)* (685)	1,365	0.02
Iroquois (498)	1,542	0.02
Kiowa (90)	203	<0.01
Lumbee (165)	293	<0.01
Menominee (35)	95	<0.01
Mexican American Ind. (3,521)	5,060	0.08
Navajo (1,319)	2,372	0.04
Osage (133)	518	0.01
Ottawa (99)	191	<0.01
Paiute (184)	363	0.01
Pima (82)	175	<0.01
Potawatomi (367)	801	0.01
Pueblo (300)	592	0.01
Puget Sound Salish (12,422)	16,964	0.25
Seminole (123)	596	0.01
Shoshone (218)	499	0.01
Sioux (2,497)	5,702	0.08
South American Ind. (181)	489	0.01
Spanish American Ind. (183)	257	<0.01
Tlingit-Haida *(Alaska Native)* (3,019)	5,733	0.09
Tohono O'Odham (58)	113	<0.01
Tsimshian *(Alaska Native)* (451)	956	0.01
Ute (56)	182	<0.01
Yakama (7,325)	8,974	0.13
Yaqui (162)	387	0.01
Yuman (54)	106	<0.01
Yup'ik *(Alaska Native)* (301)	584	0.01
Asian (481,067)	604,251	8.99
Not Hispanic (475,634)	587,411	8.74
Hispanic (5,433)	16,840	0.25
Bangladeshi (590)	666	0.01
Bhutanese (846)	977	0.01
Burmese (1,857)	2,058	0.03
Cambodian (19,101)	22,934	0.34
Chinese, ex. Taiwanese (86,977)	113,144	1.68
Filipino (91,367)	137,083	2.04
Hmong (2,186)	2,404	0.04
Indian (61,124)	68,978	1.03
Indonesian (2,686)	4,081	0.06
Japanese (35,008)	67,597	1.01
Korean (62,374)	80,049	1.19
Laotian (9,333)	11,568	0.17
Malaysian (431)	798	0.01
Nepalese (939)	1,158	0.02
Pakistani (3,908)	4,594	0.07
Sri Lankan (680)	861	0.01
Taiwanese (6,832)	8,130	0.12
Thai (6,154)	9,699	0.14
Vietnamese (66,575)	75,843	1.13
Hawaii Native/Pacific Islander (40,475)	70,322	1.05
Not Hispanic (38,783)	64,689	0.96
Hispanic (1,692)	5,633	0.08
Fijian (2,016)	2,639	0.04
Guamanian/Chamorro (9,746)	14,829	0.22
Marshallese (1,964)	2,207	0.03
Native Hawaiian (5,861)	19,863	0.30
Samoan (13,110)	18,351	0.27
Tongan (1,268)	1,934	0.03
White (5,196,362)	5,471,864	81.37
Not Hispanic (4,876,804)	5,097,076	75.80
Hispanic (319,558)	374,788	5.57

*Notes: † The Census 2010 population figure is used to calculate the percentages in the Hispanic Origin and Race categories. Ancestry percentages are based on the 2006-2010 American Community Survey population (not shown); ‡ Numbers in parentheses indicate the number of people reporting a single ancestry; * Numbers in parentheses indicate the number of persons reporting this race alone, not in combination with any other race; Please refer to the Explanation of Data for more information.*

Aberdeen

Place Type: City
County: Grays Harbor
Population: 16,896†

Ancestry‡	Population	%
American (872)	872	5.17
Arab (0)	25	0.15
Lebanese (0)	25	0.15
Austrian (9)	21	0.12
Brazilian (14)	14	0.08
British (57)	123	0.73
Bulgarian (0)	32	0.19
Canadian (17)	107	0.63
Croatian (81)	250	1.48
Czech (27)	45	0.27
Czechoslovakian (0)	9	0.05
Danish (30)	133	0.79
Dutch (118)	398	2.36
English (528)	1,590	9.42
European (104)	116	0.69
Finnish (91)	185	1.10
French, ex. Basque (79)	677	4.01
French Canadian (33)	61	0.36
German (614)	2,719	16.11
Greek (0)	28	0.17
Hungarian (0)	10	0.06
Irish (721)	2,098	12.43
Israeli (0)	82	0.49
Italian (229)	475	2.81
Lithuanian (12)	12	0.07
Northern European (12)	12	0.07
Norwegian (328)	1,123	6.65
Polish (133)	363	2.15
Russian (12)	125	0.74
Scandinavian (7)	50	0.30
Scotch-Irish (88)	330	1.95
Scottish (65)	318	1.88
Slovak (0)	22	0.13
Slovene (0)	33	0.20
Swedish (182)	652	3.86
Swiss (0)	38	0.23
Ukrainian (14)	17	0.10
Welsh (15)	156	0.92
Yugoslavian (0)	101	0.60

Hispanic Origin	Population	%
Hispanic or Latino (of any race)	2,678	15.85
Central American, ex. Mexican	278	1.65
Guatemalan	47	0.28
Honduran	3	0.02
Nicaraguan	1	0.01
Panamanian	3	0.02
Salvadoran	224	1.33
Cuban	11	0.07
Dominican Republic	1	0.01
Mexican	2,166	12.82
Puerto Rican	31	0.18
South American	10	0.06
Bolivian	1	0.01
Chilean	4	0.02
Colombian	1	0.01
Peruvian	2	0.01
Venezuelan	1	0.01
Other South American	1	0.01
Other Hispanic or Latino	181	1.07

Race*	Population	%
African-American/Black (135)	257	1.52
Not Hispanic (118)	223	1.32
Hispanic (17)	34	0.20
American Indian/Alaska Native (617)	1,010	5.98
Not Hispanic (515)	864	5.11
Hispanic (102)	146	0.86
Alaska Athabascan *(Ala. Nat.)* (2)	3	0.02
Aleut *(Alaska Native)* (4)	8	0.05
Apache (4)	11	0.07
Blackfeet (6)	16	0.09
Canadian/French Am. Ind. (5)	15	0.09
Cherokee (31)	106	0.63
Cheyenne (1)	1	0.01
Chickasaw (0)	1	0.01
Chippewa (17)	22	0.13
Choctaw (9)	20	0.12
Colville (14)	20	0.12
Creek (0)	3	0.02
Crow (2)	2	0.01
Inupiat *(Alaska Native)* (2)	2	0.01
Iroquois (0)	1	0.01
Lumbee (0)	1	0.01
Menominee (2)	2	0.01
Mexican American Ind. (12)	22	0.13
Navajo (6)	9	0.05
Osage (0)	1	0.01
Ottawa (1)	1	0.01
Pima (2)	2	0.01
Potawatomi (1)	1	0.01
Pueblo (1)	5	0.03
Puget Sound Salish (39)	50	0.30
Seminole (2)	5	0.03
Shoshone (2)	2	0.01
Sioux (6)	11	0.07
Tlingit-Haida *(Alaska Native)* (11)	18	0.11
Tsimshian *(Alaska Native)* (0)	1	0.01
Yakama (7)	8	0.05
Yup'ik *(Alaska Native)* (1)	2	0.01
Asian (319)	517	3.06
Not Hispanic (302)	467	2.76
Hispanic (17)	50	0.30
Cambodian (80)	103	0.61
Chinese, ex. Taiwanese (29)	52	0.31
Filipino (86)	182	1.08
Indian (29)	44	0.26
Indonesian (0)	1	0.01
Japanese (10)	30	0.18
Korean (32)	36	0.21
Laotian (2)	11	0.07
Pakistani (9)	9	0.05
Taiwanese (1)	4	0.02
Thai (7)	20	0.12
Vietnamese (7)	13	0.08
Hawaii Native/Pacific Islander (49)	105	0.62
Not Hispanic (45)	91	0.54
Hispanic (4)	14	0.08
Guamanian/Chamorro (9)	20	0.12
Native Hawaiian (15)	40	0.24
Samoan (10)	18	0.11
Tongan (3)	5	0.03
White (13,584)	14,348	84.92
Not Hispanic (12,610)	13,182	78.02
Hispanic (974)	1,166	6.90

Alderwood Manor

Place Type: CDP
County: Snohomish
Population: 8,442†

Ancestry‡	Population	%
African, Sub-Saharan (12)	83	1.05
African (0)	40	0.51
Nigerian (12)	43	0.54
American (101)	101	1.28
Armenian (0)	31	0.39
Austrian (0)	23	0.29
Belgian (0)	20	0.25
Canadian (97)	109	1.38
Croatian (0)	47	0.60
Czech (0)	30	0.38
Danish (27)	121	1.53
Dutch (42)	156	1.98
Eastern European (10)	59	0.75
English (116)	665	8.42
European (187)	187	2.37
Finnish (0)	58	0.73
French, ex. Basque (19)	192	2.43
French Canadian (13)	13	0.16
German (399)	1,774	22.46
German Russian (19)	19	0.24
Greek (56)	74	0.94
Icelander (0)	23	0.29
Irish (164)	1,156	14.64
Italian (90)	440	5.57
Northern European (36)	36	0.46
Norwegian (265)	564	7.14
Polish (0)	89	1.13
Portuguese (37)	37	0.47
Romanian (69)	132	1.67
Russian (0)	54	0.68
Scandinavian (7)	17	0.22
Scotch-Irish (37)	192	2.43
Scottish (22)	125	1.58
Slavic (0)	10	0.13
Swedish (69)	289	3.66
Swiss (36)	36	0.46
Ukrainian (135)	194	2.46
Welsh (121)	225	2.85

Hispanic Origin	Population	%
Hispanic or Latino (of any race)	575	6.81
Central American, ex. Mexican	27	0.32
Costa Rican	3	0.04
Guatemalan	5	0.06
Honduran	1	0.01
Nicaraguan	7	0.08
Panamanian	8	0.09
Salvadoran	2	0.02
Other Central American	1	0.01
Cuban	9	0.11
Dominican Republic	1	0.01
Mexican	414	4.90
Puerto Rican	24	0.28
South American	47	0.56
Argentinean	2	0.02
Chilean	6	0.07
Colombian	8	0.09
Ecuadorian	2	0.02
Peruvian	29	0.34
Other Hispanic or Latino	53	0.63

Race*	Population	%
African-American/Black (348)	469	5.56
Not Hispanic (342)	452	5.35
Hispanic (6)	17	0.20
American Indian/Alaska Native (68)	162	1.92
Not Hispanic (57)	141	1.67
Hispanic (11)	21	0.25
Alaska Athabascan *(Ala. Nat.)* (1)	1	0.01
Aleut *(Alaska Native)* (3)	8	0.09
Blackfeet (1)	9	0.11
Cherokee (0)	21	0.25
Chickasaw (0)	2	0.02
Chippewa (1)	5	0.06
Choctaw (0)	5	0.06
Colville (2)	2	0.02
Cree (0)	2	0.02
Creek (1)	1	0.01
Hopi (1)	1	0.01
Mexican American Ind. (1)	6	0.07
Navajo (0)	1	0.01
Potawatomi (1)	1	0.01
Pueblo (0)	1	0.01
Puget Sound Salish (3)	3	0.04
Seminole (0)	1	0.01
Shoshone (0)	1	0.01
Sioux (3)	4	0.05
Tlingit-Haida *(Alaska Native)* (12)	15	0.18
Yakama (2)	3	0.04
Yup'ik *(Alaska Native)* (1)	3	0.04
Asian (1,493)	1,723	20.41
Not Hispanic (1,475)	1,682	19.92
Hispanic (18)	41	0.49
Bangladeshi (1)	3	0.04
Burmese (14)	14	0.17
Cambodian (44)	47	0.56
Chinese, ex. Taiwanese (205)	257	3.04
Filipino (250)	362	4.29
Hmong (6)	6	0.07
Indian (172)	190	2.25

*Notes: † The Census 2010 population figure is used to calculate the percentages in the Hispanic Origin and Race categories. Ancestry percentages are based on the 2006-2010 American Community Survey population (not shown); ‡ Numbers in parentheses indicate the number of people reporting a single ancestry; * Numbers in parentheses indicate the number of persons reporting this race alone, not in combination with any other race; Please refer to the Explanation of Data for more information.*

Indonesian (2)	4	0.05
Japanese (63)	109	1.29
Korean (235)	263	3.12
Laotian (20)	21	0.25
Malaysian (1)	1	0.01
Nepalese (5)	6	0.07
Pakistani (48)	49	0.58
Sri Lankan (2)	2	0.02
Taiwanese (10)	11	0.13
Thai (17)	23	0.27
Vietnamese (327)	358	4.24
Hawaii Native/Pacific Islander (60)	119	1.41
Not Hispanic (60)	117	1.39
Hispanic (0)	2	0.02
Fijian (24)	31	0.37
Guamanian/Chamorro (4)	13	0.15
Marshallese (4)	4	0.05
Native Hawaiian (10)	32	0.38
Samoan (10)	14	0.17
Tongan (1)	2	0.02
White (5,796)	6,175	73.15
Not Hispanic (5,543)	5,868	69.51
Hispanic (253)	307	3.64

Anacortes

Place Type: City
County: Skagit
Population: 15,778†

Ancestry‡	Population	%
African, Sub-Saharan (37)	37	0.24
African (33)	33	0.21
South African (4)	4	0.03
Alsatian (3)	3	0.02
American (662)	662	4.23
Arab (27)	53	0.34
Jordanian (0)	3	0.02
Lebanese (27)	43	0.27
Other Arab (0)	7	0.04
Armenian (3)	9	0.06
Australian (11)	11	0.07
Austrian (9)	57	0.36
Basque (2)	8	0.05
Belgian (6)	18	0.11
Brazilian (0)	12	0.08
British (116)	189	1.21
Canadian (105)	170	1.09
Celtic (3)	6	0.04
Croatian (65)	122	0.78
Cypriot (0)	3	0.02
Czech (43)	77	0.49
Czechoslovakian (0)	10	0.06
Danish (47)	159	1.01
Dutch (184)	565	3.61
Eastern European (11)	11	0.07
English (687)	2,636	16.82
Estonian (5)	8	0.05
European (318)	385	2.46
Finnish (36)	103	0.66
French, ex. Basque (117)	677	4.32
French Canadian (42)	123	0.79
German (807)	3,131	19.98
Greek (16)	58	0.37
Hungarian (33)	60	0.38
Icelander (13)	16	0.10
Iranian (7)	7	0.04
Irish (558)	2,087	13.32
Italian (191)	574	3.66
Latvian (7)	13	0.08
Lithuanian (9)	36	0.23
New Zealander (9)	12	0.08
Northern European (133)	145	0.93
Norwegian (650)	1,351	8.62
Pennsylvania German (4)	10	0.06
Polish (168)	390	2.49
Portuguese (36)	92	0.59
Romanian (0)	8	0.05
Russian (29)	114	0.73
Scandinavian (49)	125	0.80
Scotch-Irish (249)	539	3.44
Scottish (192)	630	4.02
Serbian (0)	6	0.04
Slavic (21)	35	0.22
Slovak (3)	18	0.11
Slovene (3)	9	0.06
Swedish (224)	777	4.96
Swiss (17)	120	0.77
Turkish (19)	24	0.15
Ukrainian (12)	61	0.39
Welsh (65)	210	1.34
Yugoslavian (7)	7	0.04

Hispanic Origin	Population	%
Hispanic or Latino (of any race)	794	5.03
Central American, ex. Mexican	16	0.10
Guatemalan	8	0.05
Honduran	1	0.01
Nicaraguan	4	0.03
Panamanian	1	0.01
Salvadoran	1	0.01
Other Central American	1	0.01
Cuban	17	0.11
Mexican	585	3.71
Puerto Rican	46	0.29
South American	19	0.12
Argentinean	3	0.02
Bolivian	1	0.01
Colombian	4	0.03
Ecuadorian	4	0.03
Peruvian	2	0.01
Uruguayan	1	0.01
Venezuelan	4	0.03
Other Hispanic or Latino	111	0.70

Race*	Population	%
African-American/Black (104)	179	1.13
Not Hispanic (97)	166	1.05
Hispanic (7)	13	0.08
American Indian/Alaska Native (154)	379	2.40
Not Hispanic (129)	323	2.05
Hispanic (25)	56	0.35
Alaska Athabascan *(Ala. Nat.)* (1)	2	0.01
Aleut *(Alaska Native)* (9)	22	0.14
Apache (2)	6	0.04
Blackfeet (12)	17	0.11
Canadian/French Am. Ind. (1)	1	0.01
Cherokee (7)	43	0.27
Cheyenne (0)	2	0.01
Chickasaw (1)	2	0.01
Chippewa (1)	6	0.04
Choctaw (4)	12	0.08
Colville (0)	2	0.01
Comanche (0)	2	0.01
Cree (0)	6	0.04
Creek (4)	6	0.04
Crow (0)	1	0.01
Delaware (0)	1	0.01
Inupiat *(Alaska Native)* (0)	1	0.01
Iroquois (1)	2	0.01
Mexican American Ind. (9)	11	0.07
Navajo (1)	5	0.03
Osage (0)	1	0.01
Potawatomi (0)	1	0.01
Puget Sound Salish (27)	57	0.36
Seminole (1)	2	0.01
Shoshone (0)	1	0.01
Sioux (5)	14	0.09
South American Ind. (0)	1	0.01
Spanish American Ind. (1)	1	0.01
Tlingit-Haida *(Alaska Native)* (17)	30	0.19
Yakama (1)	8	0.05
Yup'ik *(Alaska Native)* (1)	1	0.01
Asian (305)	488	3.09
Not Hispanic (302)	467	2.96
Hispanic (3)	21	0.13
Bhutanese (0)	1	0.01
Burmese (1)	1	0.01
Cambodian (1)	4	0.03
Chinese, ex. Taiwanese (49)	85	0.54
Filipino (79)	159	1.01
Indian (17)	28	0.18
Indonesian (0)	3	0.02
Japanese (48)	101	0.64
Korean (41)	51	0.32
Laotian (1)	1	0.01
Malaysian (0)	5	0.03
Pakistani (1)	3	0.02
Taiwanese (8)	8	0.05
Thai (18)	19	0.12
Vietnamese (18)	23	0.15
Hawaii Native/Pacific Islander (17)	54	0.34
Not Hispanic (17)	51	0.32
Hispanic (0)	3	0.02
Fijian (0)	1	0.01
Guamanian/Chamorro (1)	2	0.01
Native Hawaiian (12)	37	0.23
Samoan (0)	5	0.03
White (14,433)	14,917	94.54
Not Hispanic (13,993)	14,399	91.26
Hispanic (440)	518	3.28

Arlington

Place Type: City
County: Snohomish
Population: 17,926†

Ancestry‡	Population	%
African, Sub-Saharan (0)	42	0.25
African (0)	42	0.25
American (698)	698	4.13
Austrian (15)	28	0.17
Belgian (11)	11	0.07
British (46)	89	0.53
Cajun (16)	16	0.09
Canadian (87)	126	0.74
Croatian (0)	12	0.07
Czech (33)	135	0.80
Czechoslovakian (10)	48	0.28
Danish (29)	155	0.92
Dutch (186)	541	3.20
English (633)	2,059	12.17
European (229)	441	2.61
Finnish (20)	55	0.33
French, ex. Basque (85)	527	3.12
French Canadian (25)	229	1.35
German (885)	3,350	19.81
Greek (34)	55	0.33
Hungarian (9)	34	0.20
Icelander (0)	9	0.05
Irish (722)	2,123	12.55
Italian (169)	494	2.92
Northern European (13)	13	0.08
Norwegian (586)	1,520	8.99
Pennsylvania German (15)	15	0.09
Polish (16)	176	1.04
Portuguese (0)	138	0.82
Romanian (13)	13	0.08
Russian (106)	186	1.10
Scandinavian (113)	139	0.82
Scotch-Irish (92)	413	2.44
Scottish (108)	646	3.82
Slavic (43)	55	0.33
Slovak (13)	27	0.16
Swedish (196)	806	4.77
Swiss (0)	53	0.31
Ukrainian (217)	231	1.37
Welsh (22)	78	0.46
Yugoslavian (0)	14	0.08

Hispanic Origin	Population	%
Hispanic or Latino (of any race)	1,700	9.48
Central American, ex. Mexican	41	0.23
Costa Rican	2	0.01
Guatemalan	14	0.08
Honduran	2	0.01
Nicaraguan	3	0.02
Panamanian	7	0.04
Salvadoran	13	0.07

*Notes: † The Census 2010 population figure is used to calculate the percentages in the Hispanic Origin and Race categories. Ancestry percentages are based on the 2006-2010 American Community Survey population (not shown); ‡ Numbers in parentheses indicate the number of people reporting a single ancestry; * Numbers in parentheses indicate the number of persons reporting this race alone, not in combination with any other race; Please refer to the Explanation of Data for more information.*

Cuban	13	0.07
Dominican Republic	8	0.04
Mexican	1,402	7.82
Puerto Rican	55	0.31
South American	52	0.29
Argentinean	7	0.04
Bolivian	6	0.03
Chilean	3	0.02
Colombian	12	0.07
Ecuadorian	6	0.03
Peruvian	18	0.10
Other Hispanic or Latino	129	0.72

Race*	Population	%
African-American/Black (212)	405	2.26
Not Hispanic (197)	375	2.09
Hispanic (15)	30	0.17
American Indian/Alaska Native (255)	479	2.67
Not Hispanic (223)	415	2.32
Hispanic (32)	64	0.36
Alaska Athabascan *(Ala. Nat.)* (2)	2	0.01
Aleut *(Alaska Native)* (4)	13	0.07
Apache (0)	4	0.02
Blackfeet (5)	15	0.08
Canadian/French Am. Ind. (1)	3	0.02
Cherokee (13)	64	0.36
Chippewa (10)	17	0.09
Choctaw (3)	6	0.03
Colville (2)	5	0.03
Comanche (3)	4	0.02
Cree (2)	2	0.01
Creek (0)	2	0.01
Hopi (0)	4	0.02
Inupiat *(Alaska Native)* (3)	10	0.06
Iroquois (2)	8	0.04
Mexican American Ind. (5)	6	0.03
Navajo (1)	10	0.06
Osage (1)	3	0.02
Potawatomi (1)	1	0.01
Pueblo (3)	5	0.03
Puget Sound Salish (87)	115	0.64
Seminole (0)	2	0.01
Shoshone (0)	1	0.01
Sioux (2)	4	0.02
South American Ind. (0)	4	0.02
Tlingit-Haida *(Alaska Native)* (9)	13	0.07
Yakama (1)	1	0.01
Yaqui (0)	1	0.01
Yup'ik *(Alaska Native)* (1)	1	0.01
Asian (584)	904	5.04
Not Hispanic (576)	858	4.79
Hispanic (8)	46	0.26
Cambodian (10)	17	0.09
Chinese, ex. Taiwanese (38)	72	0.40
Filipino (319)	479	2.67
Indian (29)	37	0.21
Indonesian (1)	2	0.01
Japanese (32)	126	0.70
Korean (50)	89	0.50
Laotian (11)	11	0.06
Nepalese (1)	2	0.01
Pakistani (3)	4	0.02
Taiwanese (3)	3	0.02
Thai (16)	22	0.12
Vietnamese (54)	64	0.36
Hawaii Native/Pacific Islander (60)	134	0.75
Not Hispanic (58)	122	0.68
Hispanic (2)	12	0.07
Fijian (1)	2	0.01
Guamanian/Chamorro (18)	32	0.18
Native Hawaiian (28)	70	0.39
Samoan (3)	5	0.03
Tongan (3)	3	0.02
White (15,352)	16,040	89.48
Not Hispanic (14,539)	15,086	84.16
Hispanic (813)	954	5.32

Artondale

Place Type: CDP
County: Pierce
Population: 12,653†

Ancestry‡	Population	%
American (565)	565	4.98
Arab (0)	45	0.40
Lebanese (0)	45	0.40
Armenian (12)	12	0.11
Austrian (4)	33	0.29
Belgian (0)	30	0.26
Brazilian (18)	54	0.48
British (25)	68	0.60
Cajun (9)	9	0.08
Canadian (41)	97	0.85
Croatian (7)	34	0.30
Czech (0)	93	0.82
Czechoslovakian (10)	31	0.27
Danish (50)	84	0.74
Dutch (100)	250	2.20
English (386)	1,739	15.32
European (259)	297	2.62
Finnish (0)	79	0.70
French, ex. Basque (81)	538	4.74
French Canadian (24)	118	1.04
German (748)	2,662	23.45
Greek (37)	105	0.92
Hungarian (11)	37	0.33
Icelander (0)	18	0.16
Irish (616)	1,770	15.59
Italian (179)	616	5.43
Latvian (12)	12	0.11
Northern European (19)	36	0.32
Norwegian (450)	1,269	11.18
Pennsylvania German (0)	21	0.18
Polish (65)	306	2.70
Romanian (18)	28	0.25
Russian (18)	78	0.69
Scandinavian (58)	172	1.52
Scotch-Irish (117)	341	3.00
Scottish (84)	370	3.26
Slavic (6)	6	0.05
Slovak (7)	28	0.25
Swedish (194)	699	6.16
Swiss (13)	97	0.85
Ukrainian (21)	31	0.27
Welsh (30)	170	1.50
West Indian, ex. Hispanic (10)	58	0.51
Bahamian (0)	11	0.10
Haitian (0)	37	0.33
Jamaican (10)	10	0.09
Yugoslavian (0)	83	0.73

Hispanic Origin	Population	%
Hispanic or Latino (of any race)	587	4.64
Central American, ex. Mexican	27	0.21
Costa Rican	7	0.06
Guatemalan	8	0.06
Honduran	4	0.03
Panamanian	4	0.03
Salvadoran	4	0.03
Cuban	8	0.06
Dominican Republic	1	0.01
Mexican	356	2.81
Puerto Rican	36	0.28
South American	46	0.36
Argentinean	5	0.04
Chilean	8	0.06
Colombian	11	0.09
Ecuadorian	4	0.03
Peruvian	14	0.11
Venezuelan	4	0.03
Other Hispanic or Latino	113	0.89

Race*	Population	%
African-American/Black (74)	174	1.38
Not Hispanic (71)	161	1.27
Hispanic (3)	13	0.10
American Indian/Alaska Native (87)	231	1.83
Not Hispanic (73)	198	1.56
Hispanic (14)	33	0.26
Aleut *(Alaska Native)* (1)	4	0.03
Apache (0)	6	0.05
Blackfeet (4)	11	0.09
Canadian/French Am. Ind. (1)	2	0.02
Cherokee (7)	29	0.23
Chickasaw (0)	6	0.05
Chippewa (0)	4	0.03
Choctaw (3)	12	0.09
Colville (4)	4	0.03
Cree (0)	1	0.01
Creek (6)	7	0.06
Delaware (0)	1	0.01
Hopi (3)	4	0.03
Iroquois (1)	10	0.08
Navajo (0)	2	0.02
Osage (2)	9	0.07
Paiute (1)	2	0.02
Pueblo (0)	3	0.02
Puget Sound Salish (10)	20	0.16
Sioux (2)	9	0.07
Tlingit-Haida *(Alaska Native)* (1)	7	0.06
Tsimshian *(Alaska Native)* (1)	1	0.01
Yakama (0)	5	0.04
Yaqui (1)	4	0.03
Asian (273)	482	3.81
Not Hispanic (253)	437	3.45
Hispanic (20)	45	0.36
Chinese, ex. Taiwanese (64)	106	0.84
Filipino (46)	102	0.81
Indian (16)	26	0.21
Indonesian (2)	2	0.02
Japanese (53)	143	1.13
Korean (46)	76	0.60
Pakistani (5)	6	0.05
Taiwanese (2)	2	0.02
Thai (6)	15	0.12
Vietnamese (11)	18	0.14
Hawaii Native/Pacific Islander (47)	96	0.76
Not Hispanic (47)	91	0.72
Hispanic (0)	5	0.04
Guamanian/Chamorro (26)	39	0.31
Native Hawaiian (16)	42	0.33
Samoan (0)	7	0.06
Tongan (3)	5	0.04
White (11,567)	12,001	94.85
Not Hispanic (11,223)	11,587	91.58
Hispanic (344)	414	3.27

Auburn

Place Type: City
County: King
Population: 70,180†

Ancestry‡	Population	%
African, Sub-Saharan (784)	905	1.35
African (327)	436	0.65
Ethiopian (31)	31	0.05
Kenyan (40)	40	0.06
Nigerian (131)	143	0.21
Somalian (234)	234	0.35
Other Sub-Saharan African (21)	21	0.03
American (1,832)	1,832	2.73
Arab (24)	131	0.20
Lebanese (24)	110	0.16
Other Arab (0)	21	0.03
Armenian (0)	9	0.01
Australian (0)	77	0.11
Austrian (29)	127	0.19
Basque (26)	41	0.06
Belgian (0)	36	0.05
British (161)	523	0.78
Cajun (13)	13	0.02
Canadian (124)	237	0.35
Celtic (11)	11	0.02
Croatian (49)	88	0.13
Czech (178)	369	0.55

*Notes: † The Census 2010 population figure is used to calculate the percentages in the Hispanic Origin and Race categories. Ancestry percentages are based on the 2006-2010 American Community Survey population (not shown); ‡ Numbers in parentheses indicate the number of people reporting a single ancestry; * Numbers in parentheses indicate the number of persons reporting this race alone, not in combination with any other race; Please refer to the Explanation of Data for more information.*

Czechoslovakian (0)	28	0.04
Danish (138)	509	0.76
Dutch (308)	1,397	2.09
Eastern European (9)	9	0.01
English (1,974)	7,269	10.85
European (1,152)	1,243	1.86
Finnish (105)	331	0.49
French, ex. Basque (327)	2,172	3.24
French Canadian (240)	563	0.84
German (3,054)	11,211	16.74
Greek (39)	78	0.12
Hungarian (30)	107	0.16
Icelander (13)	31	0.05
Iranian (27)	27	0.04
Irish (1,614)	7,264	10.84
Italian (669)	2,376	3.55
Lithuanian (22)	42	0.06
Luxemburger (0)	23	0.03
Northern European (178)	178	0.27
Norwegian (1,432)	3,770	5.63
Polish (451)	1,283	1.92
Portuguese (65)	132	0.20
Romanian (95)	140	0.21
Russian (866)	1,506	2.25
Scandinavian (122)	228	0.34
Scotch-Irish (398)	1,388	2.07
Scottish (381)	1,713	2.56
Slovak (0)	19	0.03
Swedish (445)	2,025	3.02
Swiss (137)	308	0.46
Turkish (40)	49	0.07
Ukrainian (2,208)	2,463	3.68
Welsh (39)	627	0.94
West Indian, ex. Hispanic (38)	197	0.29
Barbadian (11)	11	0.02
Dutch West Indian (0)	3	<0.01
Haitian (0)	27	0.04
Jamaican (18)	122	0.18
West Indian (9)	34	0.05
Yugoslavian (33)	66	0.10

Hispanic Origin	Population	%
Hispanic or Latino (of any race)	9,032	12.87
Central American, ex. Mexican	350	0.50
Costa Rican	7	0.01
Guatemalan	105	0.15
Honduran	44	0.06
Nicaraguan	11	0.02
Panamanian	26	0.04
Salvadoran	157	0.22
Cuban	75	0.11
Dominican Republic	25	0.04
Mexican	7,311	10.42
Puerto Rican	278	0.40
South American	223	0.32
Argentinean	16	0.02
Bolivian	11	0.02
Chilean	15	0.02
Colombian	71	0.10
Ecuadorian	11	0.02
Peruvian	75	0.11
Uruguayan	7	0.01
Venezuelan	17	0.02
Other Hispanic or Latino	770	1.10

Race*	Population	%
African-American/Black (3,469)	4,718	6.72
Not Hispanic (3,338)	4,405	6.28
Hispanic (131)	313	0.45
American Indian/Alaska Native (1,608)	2,684	3.82
Not Hispanic (1,413)	2,310	3.29
Hispanic (195)	374	0.53
Alaska Athabascan *(Ala. Nat.)* (19)	22	0.03
Aleut *(Alaska Native)* (25)	44	0.06
Apache (5)	25	0.04
Arapaho (7)	9	0.01
Blackfeet (42)	104	0.15
Canadian/French Am. Ind. (15)	21	0.03
Cherokee (42)	195	0.28
Cheyenne (4)	16	0.02
Chickasaw (1)	10	0.01
Chippewa (49)	89	0.13
Choctaw (14)	33	0.05
Colville (26)	39	0.06
Comanche (1)	6	0.01
Cree (2)	3	<0.01
Creek (4)	13	0.02
Crow (7)	10	0.01
Delaware (1)	1	<0.01
Inupiat *(Alaska Native)* (12)	18	0.03
Iroquois (8)	12	0.02
Lumbee (2)	2	<0.01
Mexican American Ind. (41)	51	0.07
Navajo (12)	27	0.04
Osage (3)	9	0.01
Ottawa (5)	8	0.01
Paiute (1)	4	0.01
Pima (0)	1	<0.01
Potawatomi (5)	17	0.02
Pueblo (8)	9	0.01
Puget Sound Salish (657)	772	1.10
Seminole (0)	5	0.01
Shoshone (5)	10	0.01
Sioux (39)	80	0.11
South American Ind. (7)	10	0.01
Tlingit-Haida *(Alaska Native)* (64)	102	0.15
Tsimshian *(Alaska Native)* (24)	30	0.04
Ute (1)	1	<0.01
Yakama (47)	59	0.08
Yaqui (1)	2	<0.01
Yuman (1)	1	<0.01
Yup'ik *(Alaska Native)* (14)	25	0.04
Asian (6,251)	7,659	10.91
Not Hispanic (6,178)	7,476	10.65
Hispanic (73)	183	0.26
Bangladeshi (3)	4	0.01
Burmese (7)	7	0.01
Cambodian (217)	269	0.38
Chinese, ex. Taiwanese (666)	921	1.31
Filipino (1,485)	2,142	3.05
Hmong (42)	42	0.06
Indian (881)	994	1.42
Indonesian (77)	99	0.14
Japanese (342)	650	0.93
Korean (1,025)	1,206	1.72
Laotian (165)	195	0.28
Malaysian (6)	7	0.01
Nepalese (15)	16	0.02
Pakistani (22)	26	0.04
Sri Lankan (1)	2	<0.01
Taiwanese (41)	50	0.07
Thai (67)	93	0.13
Vietnamese (918)	1,009	1.44
Hawaii Native/Pacific Islander (1,150)	1,620	2.31
Not Hispanic (1,137)	1,564	2.23
Hispanic (13)	56	0.08
Fijian (66)	76	0.11
Guamanian/Chamorro (84)	130	0.19
Marshallese (364)	399	0.57
Native Hawaiian (91)	301	0.43
Samoan (369)	471	0.67
Tongan (24)	32	0.05
White (49,452)	52,654	75.03
Not Hispanic (45,954)	48,511	69.12
Hispanic (3,498)	4,143	5.90

Bainbridge Island

Place Type: City
County: Kitsap
Population: 23,025†

Ancestry‡	Population	%
African, Sub-Saharan (24)	94	0.42
African (0)	70	0.31
Other Sub-Saharan African (24)	24	0.11
American (694)	694	3.09
Arab (30)	138	0.61
Iraqi (14)	62	0.28
Lebanese (0)	29	0.13
Palestinian (16)	33	0.15
Syrian (0)	14	0.06
Armenian (0)	11	0.05
Australian (30)	86	0.38
Austrian (24)	93	0.41
Belgian (0)	49	0.22
Brazilian (12)	12	0.05
British (333)	417	1.85
Cajun (0)	24	0.11
Canadian (132)	235	1.05
Celtic (0)	10	0.04
Croatian (14)	84	0.37
Czech (16)	218	0.97
Czechoslovakian (20)	64	0.28
Danish (113)	528	2.35
Dutch (88)	408	1.81
Eastern European (147)	147	0.65
English (1,075)	4,074	18.12
European (728)	911	4.05
Finnish (101)	264	1.17
French, ex. Basque (134)	965	4.29
French Canadian (98)	156	0.69
German (1,232)	5,195	23.10
Greek (26)	74	0.33
Hungarian (69)	182	0.81
Icelander (0)	15	0.07
Iranian (0)	9	0.04
Irish (1,122)	3,829	17.03
Israeli (34)	34	0.15
Italian (299)	889	3.95
Latvian (0)	13	0.06
Lithuanian (43)	105	0.47
Northern European (126)	126	0.56
Norwegian (422)	1,637	7.28
Pennsylvania German (13)	13	0.06
Polish (171)	524	2.33
Portuguese (61)	129	0.57
Romanian (58)	58	0.26
Russian (130)	374	1.66
Scandinavian (165)	218	0.97
Scotch-Irish (281)	838	3.73
Scottish (309)	1,421	6.32
Slavic (16)	29	0.13
Slovak (0)	62	0.28
Slovene (8)	8	0.04
Swedish (230)	992	4.41
Swiss (50)	276	1.23
Turkish (14)	27	0.12
Ukrainian (54)	117	0.52
Welsh (34)	295	1.31
West Indian, ex. Hispanic (17)	63	0.28
Jamaican (0)	9	0.04
Trinidadian/Tobagonian (17)	54	0.24
Yugoslavian (0)	106	0.47

Hispanic Origin	Population	%
Hispanic or Latino (of any race)	887	3.85
Central American, ex. Mexican	72	0.31
Costa Rican	10	0.04
Guatemalan	30	0.13
Honduran	1	<0.01
Nicaraguan	9	0.04
Panamanian	5	0.02
Salvadoran	15	0.07
Other Central American	2	0.01
Cuban	34	0.15
Dominican Republic	4	0.02
Mexican	497	2.16
Puerto Rican	54	0.23
South American	110	0.48
Argentinean	22	0.10
Bolivian	11	0.05
Chilean	16	0.07
Colombian	24	0.10
Ecuadorian	1	<0.01
Peruvian	25	0.11
Venezuelan	10	0.04
Other South American	1	<0.01
Other Hispanic or Latino	116	0.50

*Notes: † The Census 2010 population figure is used to calculate the percentages in the Hispanic Origin and Race categories. Ancestry percentages are based on the 2006-2010 American Community Survey population (not shown); ‡ Numbers in parentheses indicate the number of people reporting a single ancestry; * Numbers in parentheses indicate the number of persons reporting this race alone, not in combination with any other race; Please refer to the Explanation of Data for more information.*

Race*	Population	%
African-American/Black (100)	236	1.02
Not Hispanic (93)	209	0.91
Hispanic (7)	27	0.12
American Indian/Alaska Native (111)	417	1.81
Not Hispanic (89)	355	1.54
Hispanic (22)	62	0.27
Alaska Athabascan *(Ala. Nat.)* (2)	10	0.04
Aleut *(Alaska Native)* (4)	12	0.05
Apache (1)	6	0.03
Arapaho (3)	3	0.01
Blackfeet (2)	12	0.05
Canadian/French Am. Ind. (6)	21	0.09
Cherokee (2)	39	0.17
Chippewa (4)	6	0.03
Choctaw (1)	11	0.05
Colville (0)	1	<0.01
Comanche (0)	6	0.03
Cree (0)	2	0.01
Creek (0)	3	0.01
Inupiat *(Alaska Native)* (1)	3	0.01
Iroquois (2)	4	0.02
Kiowa (1)	2	0.01
Mexican American Ind. (9)	14	0.06
Navajo (4)	6	0.03
Osage (1)	1	<0.01
Paiute (0)	1	<0.01
Potawatomi (2)	2	0.01
Puget Sound Salish (10)	55	0.24
Shoshone (0)	1	<0.01
Sioux (2)	14	0.06
South American Ind. (0)	1	<0.01
Tlingit-Haida *(Alaska Native)* (6)	19	0.08
Tsimshian *(Alaska Native)* (0)	5	0.02
Yakama (0)	1	<0.01
Yaqui (0)	2	0.01
Yuman (6)	6	0.03
Yup'ik *(Alaska Native)* (4)	6	0.03
Asian (742)	1,263	5.49
Not Hispanic (735)	1,223	5.31
Hispanic (7)	40	0.17
Bangladeshi (0)	1	<0.01
Cambodian (1)	1	<0.01
Chinese, ex. Taiwanese (150)	258	1.12
Filipino (115)	308	1.34
Indian (38)	59	0.26
Indonesian (4)	11	0.05
Japanese (220)	386	1.68
Korean (109)	155	0.67
Laotian (3)	3	0.01
Malaysian (0)	1	<0.01
Nepalese (1)	2	0.01
Taiwanese (6)	6	0.03
Thai (20)	34	0.15
Vietnamese (38)	44	0.19
Hawaii Native/Pacific Islander (42)	118	0.51
Not Hispanic (42)	111	0.48
Hispanic (0)	7	0.03
Guamanian/Chamorro (7)	26	0.11
Native Hawaiian (15)	52	0.23
Samoan (8)	13	0.06
White (20,963)	21,763	94.52
Not Hispanic (20,370)	21,061	91.47
Hispanic (593)	702	3.05

Battle Ground

Place Type: City
County: Clark
Population: 17,571†

Ancestry‡	Population	%
African, Sub-Saharan (18)	18	0.11
Ethiopian (11)	11	0.07
Other Sub-Saharan African (7)	7	0.04
American (609)	609	3.73
Arab (0)	40	0.24
Syrian (0)	40	0.24
Austrian (0)	22	0.13
British (67)	67	0.41
Bulgarian (0)	17	0.10
Canadian (5)	38	0.23
Croatian (0)	8	0.05
Czech (11)	98	0.60
Danish (54)	162	0.99
Dutch (41)	375	2.30
English (570)	1,827	11.18
European (156)	188	1.15
Finnish (384)	701	4.29
French, ex. Basque (46)	398	2.44
French Canadian (30)	208	1.27
German (1,310)	4,136	25.32
Greek (30)	90	0.55
Irish (480)	2,232	13.66
Italian (253)	1,031	6.31
Lithuanian (5)	5	0.03
New Zealander (13)	13	0.08
Northern European (32)	32	0.20
Norwegian (205)	708	4.33
Pennsylvania German (0)	15	0.09
Polish (96)	383	2.34
Portuguese (73)	172	1.05
Romanian (14)	14	0.09
Russian (572)	705	4.32
Scandinavian (59)	267	1.63
Scotch-Irish (83)	342	2.09
Scottish (42)	411	2.52
Serbian (19)	19	0.12
Slavic (0)	17	0.10
Swedish (81)	479	2.93
Swiss (0)	50	0.31
Ukrainian (440)	561	3.43
Welsh (29)	118	0.72
West Indian, ex. Hispanic (40)	40	0.24
Jamaican (40)	40	0.24
Yugoslavian (30)	57	0.35

Hispanic Origin	Population	%
Hispanic or Latino (of any race)	1,150	6.54
Central American, ex. Mexican	83	0.47
Costa Rican	12	0.07
Guatemalan	7	0.04
Honduran	15	0.09
Nicaraguan	4	0.02
Panamanian	11	0.06
Salvadoran	34	0.19
Cuban	11	0.06
Dominican Republic	1	0.01
Mexican	851	4.84
Puerto Rican	36	0.20
South American	45	0.26
Argentinean	7	0.04
Chilean	15	0.09
Colombian	14	0.08
Ecuadorian	2	0.01
Peruvian	6	0.03
Venezuelan	1	0.01
Other Hispanic or Latino	123	0.70

Race*	Population	%
African-American/Black (138)	269	1.53
Not Hispanic (134)	254	1.45
Hispanic (4)	15	0.09
American Indian/Alaska Native (146)	343	1.95
Not Hispanic (131)	305	1.74
Hispanic (15)	38	0.22
Aleut *(Alaska Native)* (0)	1	0.01
Apache (1)	2	0.01
Blackfeet (1)	8	0.05
Canadian/French Am. Ind. (0)	1	0.01
Central American Ind. (0)	2	0.01
Cherokee (13)	59	0.34
Chippewa (8)	21	0.12
Choctaw (4)	5	0.03
Cree (1)	4	0.02
Creek (1)	3	0.02
Hopi (1)	4	0.02
Inupiat *(Alaska Native)* (2)	3	0.02
Iroquois (0)	1	0.01
Kiowa (0)	1	0.01
Mexican American Ind. (8)	12	0.07
Navajo (2)	3	0.02
Osage (0)	1	0.01
Ottawa (0)	1	0.01
Pima (1)	1	0.01
Puget Sound Salish (4)	6	0.03
Seminole (3)	3	0.02
Sioux (4)	9	0.05
South American Ind. (1)	1	0.01
Tlingit-Haida *(Alaska Native)* (3)	6	0.03
Yakama (2)	3	0.02
Yaqui (1)	1	0.01
Yup'ik *(Alaska Native)* (1)	1	0.01
Asian (330)	547	3.11
Not Hispanic (322)	526	2.99
Hispanic (8)	21	0.12
Cambodian (34)	43	0.24
Chinese, ex. Taiwanese (25)	56	0.32
Filipino (90)	161	0.92
Hmong (6)	9	0.05
Indian (23)	35	0.20
Indonesian (1)	2	0.01
Japanese (42)	106	0.60
Korean (28)	48	0.27
Laotian (2)	7	0.04
Pakistani (2)	2	0.01
Taiwanese (6)	9	0.05
Thai (11)	23	0.13
Vietnamese (45)	52	0.30
Hawaii Native/Pacific Islander (60)	125	0.71
Not Hispanic (56)	118	0.67
Hispanic (4)	7	0.04
Fijian (6)	6	0.03
Guamanian/Chamorro (17)	26	0.15
Native Hawaiian (22)	46	0.26
Samoan (0)	9	0.05
Tongan (2)	6	0.03
White (15,904)	16,480	93.79
Not Hispanic (15,239)	15,720	89.47
Hispanic (665)	760	4.33

Bellevue

Place Type: City
County: King
Population: 122,363†

Ancestry‡	Population	%
Afghan (14)	14	0.01
African, Sub-Saharan (779)	1,002	0.84
African (339)	412	0.34
Ethiopian (123)	138	0.12
Kenyan (44)	44	0.04
Nigerian (32)	32	0.03
Somalian (38)	50	0.04
South African (13)	65	0.05
Ugandan (0)	42	0.04
Other Sub-Saharan African (190)	219	0.18
Albanian (118)	118	0.10
Alsatian (15)	15	0.01
American (2,886)	2,886	2.42
Arab (360)	503	0.42
Arab (53)	65	0.05
Egyptian (83)	98	0.08
Lebanese (82)	139	0.12
Moroccan (0)	18	0.02
Palestinian (34)	40	0.03
Syrian (44)	72	0.06
Other Arab (64)	71	0.06
Armenian (612)	737	0.62
Australian (96)	165	0.14
Austrian (145)	535	0.45
Basque (14)	37	0.03
Belgian (73)	133	0.11
Brazilian (192)	222	0.19
British (706)	1,238	1.04
Bulgarian (242)	304	0.25
Canadian (320)	608	0.51
Celtic (32)	77	0.06

*Notes: † The Census 2010 population figure is used to calculate the percentages in the Hispanic Origin and Race categories. Ancestry percentages are based on the 2006-2010 American Community Survey population (not shown); ‡ Numbers in parentheses indicate the number of people reporting a single ancestry; * Numbers in parentheses indicate the number of persons reporting this race alone, not in combination with any other race; Please refer to the Explanation of Data for more information.*

Croatian (172)	358	0.30
Czech (93)	607	0.51
Czechoslovakian (39)	118	0.10
Danish (249)	1,239	1.04
Dutch (526)	1,866	1.56
Eastern European (336)	371	0.31
English (3,344)	13,278	11.12
Estonian (18)	36	0.03
European (2,564)	3,016	2.52
Finnish (81)	394	0.33
French, ex. Basque (948)	3,938	3.30
French Canadian (201)	432	0.36
German (4,230)	16,688	13.97
Greek (332)	485	0.41
Hungarian (304)	845	0.71
Icelander (19)	73	0.06
Iranian (1,139)	1,139	0.95
Irish (2,342)	10,504	8.79
Israeli (133)	151	0.13
Italian (1,610)	4,173	3.49
Latvian (93)	93	0.08
Lithuanian (82)	192	0.16
Luxemburger (0)	14	0.01
New Zealander (31)	45	0.04
Northern European (537)	594	0.50
Norwegian (1,990)	4,786	4.01
Pennsylvania German (36)	53	0.04
Polish (837)	2,750	2.30
Portuguese (48)	193	0.16
Romanian (1,096)	1,262	1.06
Russian (1,461)	2,825	2.36
Scandinavian (446)	790	0.66
Scotch-Irish (814)	2,817	2.36
Scottish (854)	3,541	2.96
Serbian (0)	51	0.04
Slavic (59)	59	0.05
Slovak (102)	169	0.14
Slovene (0)	13	0.01
Swedish (924)	3,603	3.02
Swiss (225)	818	0.68
Turkish (89)	246	0.21
Ukrainian (300)	474	0.40
Welsh (118)	766	0.64
West Indian, ex. Hispanic (52)	52	0.04
Jamaican (7)	7	0.01
Trinidadian/Tobagonian (45)	45	0.04
Yugoslavian (91)	199	0.17

Hispanic Origin	Population	%
Hispanic or Latino (of any race)	8,545	6.98
Central American, ex. Mexican	738	0.60
Costa Rican	37	0.03
Guatemalan	195	0.16
Honduran	146	0.12
Nicaraguan	72	0.06
Panamanian	28	0.02
Salvadoran	250	0.20
Other Central American	10	0.01
Cuban	147	0.12
Dominican Republic	45	0.04
Mexican	5,728	4.68
Puerto Rican	269	0.22
South American	753	0.62
Argentinean	75	0.06
Bolivian	36	0.03
Chilean	64	0.05
Colombian	209	0.17
Ecuadorian	61	0.05
Paraguayan	9	0.01
Peruvian	192	0.16
Uruguayan	14	0.01
Venezuelan	85	0.07
Other South American	8	0.01
Other Hispanic or Latino	865	0.71

Race*	Population	%
African-American/Black (2,815)	3,698	3.02
Not Hispanic (2,700)	3,470	2.84
Hispanic (115)	228	0.19
American Indian/Alaska Native (452)	1,187	0.97
Not Hispanic (349)	958	0.78
Hispanic (103)	229	0.19
Alaska Athabascan *(Ala. Nat.)* (3)	6	<0.01
Aleut *(Alaska Native)* (11)	18	0.01
Apache (5)	14	0.01
Arapaho (1)	3	<0.01
Blackfeet (2)	44	0.04
Canadian/French Am. Ind. (7)	15	0.01
Central American Ind. (8)	8	0.01
Cherokee (26)	146	0.12
Cheyenne (0)	4	<0.01
Chickasaw (2)	8	0.01
Chippewa (19)	41	0.03
Choctaw (5)	16	0.01
Colville (9)	12	0.01
Comanche (3)	5	<0.01
Cree (0)	8	0.01
Creek (6)	15	0.01
Crow (0)	8	0.01
Delaware (1)	2	<0.01
Hopi (1)	3	<0.01
Inupiat *(Alaska Native)* (5)	17	0.01
Iroquois (8)	15	0.01
Lumbee (0)	1	<0.01
Mexican American Ind. (51)	61	0.05
Navajo (14)	18	0.01
Osage (1)	2	<0.01
Ottawa (0)	1	<0.01
Paiute (5)	7	0.01
Potawatomi (1)	6	<0.01
Pueblo (3)	12	0.01
Puget Sound Salish (9)	25	0.02
Seminole (0)	7	0.01
Shoshone (3)	4	<0.01
Sioux (13)	35	0.03
South American Ind. (5)	14	0.01
Tlingit-Haida *(Alaska Native)* (23)	54	0.04
Tsimshian *(Alaska Native)* (5)	13	0.01
Ute (0)	3	<0.01
Yakama (1)	5	<0.01
Yaqui (1)	8	0.01
Yuman (0)	2	<0.01
Yup'ik *(Alaska Native)* (6)	7	0.01
Asian (33,743)	36,899	30.16
Not Hispanic (33,659)	36,656	29.96
Hispanic (84)	243	0.20
Bangladeshi (47)	56	0.05
Burmese (46)	57	0.05
Cambodian (294)	374	0.31
Chinese, ex. Taiwanese (10,402)	11,725	9.58
Filipino (1,429)	2,023	1.65
Hmong (42)	48	0.04
Indian (8,963)	9,343	7.64
Indonesian (135)	176	0.14
Japanese (2,687)	3,765	3.08
Korean (4,479)	4,912	4.01
Laotian (155)	181	0.15
Malaysian (29)	52	0.04
Nepalese (51)	53	0.04
Pakistani (472)	523	0.43
Sri Lankan (42)	51	0.04
Taiwanese (1,235)	1,374	1.12
Thai (379)	480	0.39
Vietnamese (1,734)	2,013	1.65
Hawaii Native/Pacific Islander (229)	575	0.47
Not Hispanic (219)	535	0.44
Hispanic (10)	40	0.03
Fijian (23)	34	0.03
Guamanian/Chamorro (50)	92	0.08
Native Hawaiian (56)	233	0.19
Samoan (39)	80	0.07
Tongan (8)	14	0.01
White (76,547)	80,793	66.03
Not Hispanic (72,397)	76,060	62.16
Hispanic (4,150)	4,733	3.87

Bellingham

Place Type: City
County: Whatcom
Population: 80,885†

Ancestry‡	Population	%
African, Sub-Saharan (391)	423	0.54
African (198)	230	0.29
Ethiopian (128)	128	0.16
South African (15)	15	0.02
Other Sub-Saharan African (50)	50	0.06
American (3,369)	3,369	4.27
Arab (101)	189	0.24
Egyptian (26)	38	0.05
Lebanese (45)	94	0.12
Palestinian (0)	12	0.02
Syrian (13)	28	0.04
Other Arab (17)	17	0.02
Armenian (0)	108	0.14
Australian (25)	73	0.09
Austrian (45)	275	0.35
Basque (0)	122	0.15
Belgian (17)	84	0.11
Brazilian (0)	14	0.02
British (477)	829	1.05
Bulgarian (0)	30	0.04
Canadian (482)	799	1.01
Celtic (26)	45	0.06
Croatian (154)	538	0.68
Czech (84)	481	0.61
Czechoslovakian (24)	83	0.11
Danish (285)	1,165	1.47
Dutch (1,031)	3,095	3.92
Eastern European (75)	100	0.13
English (2,655)	10,399	13.17
Estonian (21)	21	0.03
European (1,991)	2,191	2.77
Finnish (164)	751	0.95
French, ex. Basque (329)	2,632	3.33
French Canadian (341)	750	0.95
German (4,391)	17,161	21.73
Greek (62)	298	0.38
Hungarian (121)	501	0.63
Icelander (72)	204	0.26
Iranian (333)	333	0.42
Irish (3,334)	12,286	15.55
Israeli (28)	28	0.04
Italian (1,006)	3,593	4.55
Lithuanian (30)	118	0.15
New Zealander (0)	14	0.02
Northern European (293)	330	0.42
Norwegian (1,947)	6,023	7.63
Polish (669)	1,818	2.30
Portuguese (101)	313	0.40
Romanian (46)	60	0.08
Russian (319)	1,076	1.36
Scandinavian (548)	792	1.00
Scotch-Irish (693)	2,678	3.39
Scottish (1,060)	3,739	4.73
Serbian (0)	11	0.01
Slavic (0)	77	0.10
Slovak (13)	41	0.05
Slovene (0)	19	0.02
Swedish (831)	3,705	4.69
Swiss (94)	555	0.70
Turkish (35)	143	0.18
Ukrainian (358)	571	0.72
Welsh (103)	658	0.83
West Indian, ex. Hispanic (55)	105	0.13
Jamaican (19)	19	0.02
Trinidadian/Tobagonian (36)	36	0.05
West Indian (0)	39	0.05
Other West Indian (0)	11	0.01
Yugoslavian (75)	262	0.33

Hispanic Origin	Population	%
Hispanic or Latino (of any race)	5,665	7.00
Central American, ex. Mexican	422	0.52
Costa Rican	20	0.02

*Notes: † The Census 2010 population figure is used to calculate the percentages in the Hispanic Origin and Race categories. Ancestry percentages are based on the 2006-2010 American Community Survey population (not shown); ‡ Numbers in parentheses indicate the number of people reporting a single ancestry; * Numbers in parentheses indicate the number of persons reporting this race alone, not in combination with any other race; Please refer to the Explanation of Data for more information.*

Guatemalan	153	0.19
Honduran	41	0.05
Nicaraguan	27	0.03
Panamanian	12	0.01
Salvadoran	162	0.20
Other Central American	7	0.01
Cuban	94	0.12
Dominican Republic	6	0.01
Mexican	4,067	5.03
Puerto Rican	244	0.30
South American	218	0.27
Argentinean	21	0.03
Bolivian	11	0.01
Chilean	31	0.04
Colombian	66	0.08
Ecuadorian	17	0.02
Paraguayan	1	<0.01
Peruvian	50	0.06
Uruguayan	2	<0.01
Venezuelan	18	0.02
Other South American	1	<0.01
Other Hispanic or Latino	614	0.76

Race*	Population	%
African-American/Black (1,068)	1,865	2.31
Not Hispanic (1,015)	1,716	2.12
Hispanic (53)	149	0.18
American Indian/Alaska Native (1,088)	2,145	2.65
Not Hispanic (964)	1,874	2.32
Hispanic (124)	271	0.34
Alaska Athabascan *(Ala. Nat.)* (8)	15	0.02
Aleut *(Alaska Native)* (38)	69	0.09
Apache (7)	16	0.02
Arapaho (1)	5	0.01
Blackfeet (17)	54	0.07
Canadian/French Am. Ind. (25)	52	0.06
Central American Ind. (6)	8	0.01
Cherokee (33)	204	0.25
Cheyenne (3)	9	0.01
Chickasaw (1)	8	0.01
Chippewa (32)	53	0.07
Choctaw (6)	35	0.04
Colville (12)	17	0.02
Comanche (0)	1	<0.01
Cree (3)	12	0.01
Creek (3)	9	0.01
Crow (4)	7	0.01
Delaware (0)	4	<0.01
Hopi (1)	1	<0.01
Inupiat *(Alaska Native)* (14)	29	0.04
Iroquois (7)	22	0.03
Lumbee (2)	2	<0.01
Mexican American Ind. (27)	35	0.04
Navajo (11)	22	0.03
Osage (2)	9	0.01
Ottawa (0)	5	0.01
Potawatomi (8)	16	0.02
Pueblo (1)	6	0.01
Puget Sound Salish (90)	149	0.18
Seminole (1)	3	<0.01
Shoshone (1)	6	0.01
Sioux (24)	57	0.07
South American Ind. (4)	5	0.01
Tlingit-Haida *(Alaska Native)* (71)	111	0.14
Tohono O'Odham (3)	4	<0.01
Tsimshian *(Alaska Native)* (9)	17	0.02
Ute (0)	1	<0.01
Yakama (4)	8	0.01
Yaqui (1)	3	<0.01
Yuman (1)	5	0.01
Yup'ik *(Alaska Native)* (7)	8	0.01
Asian (4,135)	5,683	7.03
Not Hispanic (4,086)	5,512	6.81
Hispanic (49)	171	0.21
Bangladeshi (5)	7	0.01
Bhutanese (1)	1	<0.01
Burmese (2)	7	0.01
Cambodian (98)	142	0.18
Chinese, ex. Taiwanese (692)	1,002	1.24
Filipino (618)	1,061	1.31
Hmong (9)	14	0.02
Indian (874)	991	1.23
Indonesian (11)	26	0.03
Japanese (332)	779	0.96
Korean (486)	645	0.80
Laotian (16)	20	0.02
Malaysian (5)	8	0.01
Nepalese (2)	5	0.01
Pakistani (45)	64	0.08
Sri Lankan (3)	9	0.01
Taiwanese (63)	79	0.10
Thai (71)	118	0.15
Vietnamese (647)	747	0.92
Hawaii Native/Pacific Islander (214)	487	0.60
Not Hispanic (201)	433	0.54
Hispanic (13)	54	0.07
Fijian (58)	82	0.10
Guamanian/Chamorro (38)	84	0.10
Marshallese (1)	1	<0.01
Native Hawaiian (42)	169	0.21
Samoan (30)	70	0.09
Tongan (1)	10	0.01
White (68,652)	71,790	88.76
Not Hispanic (65,907)	68,522	84.72
Hispanic (2,745)	3,268	4.04

Birch Bay

Place Type: CDP
County: Whatcom
Population: 8,413†

Ancestry‡	Population	%
African, Sub-Saharan (11)	11	0.14
South African (11)	11	0.14
American (332)	332	4.21
Belgian (0)	20	0.25
British (10)	10	0.13
Canadian (90)	102	1.29
Celtic (0)	20	0.25
Croatian (13)	67	0.85
Czech (14)	26	0.33
Danish (97)	164	2.08
Dutch (208)	516	6.55
Eastern European (41)	41	0.52
English (183)	909	11.53
European (385)	385	4.89
Finnish (13)	67	0.85
French, ex. Basque (18)	219	2.78
French Canadian (28)	156	1.98
German (365)	1,258	15.96
Greek (14)	14	0.18
Guyanese (19)	19	0.24
Hungarian (45)	96	1.22
Icelander (91)	140	1.78
Irish (312)	954	12.11
Italian (102)	246	3.12
Lithuanian (13)	13	0.16
Luxemburger (0)	11	0.14
Northern European (15)	15	0.19
Norwegian (211)	521	6.61
Pennsylvania German (0)	20	0.25
Polish (37)	104	1.32
Portuguese (9)	36	0.46
Russian (13)	54	0.69
Scandinavian (13)	121	1.54
Scotch-Irish (70)	181	2.30
Scottish (97)	246	3.12
Slovene (17)	17	0.22
Swedish (97)	264	3.35
Swiss (0)	22	0.28
Ukrainian (0)	16	0.20
Welsh (0)	38	0.48

Hispanic Origin	Population	%
Hispanic or Latino (of any race)	521	6.19
Central American, ex. Mexican	28	0.33
Costa Rican	3	0.04
Guatemalan	9	0.11
Panamanian	4	0.05
Salvadoran	12	0.14
Cuban	9	0.11
Dominican Republic	5	0.06
Mexican	368	4.37
Puerto Rican	23	0.27
South American	24	0.29
Argentinean	1	0.01
Colombian	6	0.07
Ecuadorian	3	0.04
Peruvian	8	0.10
Venezuelan	6	0.07
Other Hispanic or Latino	64	0.76

Race*	Population	%
African-American/Black (80)	142	1.69
Not Hispanic (77)	133	1.58
Hispanic (3)	9	0.11
American Indian/Alaska Native (102)	266	3.16
Not Hispanic (91)	241	2.86
Hispanic (11)	25	0.30
Aleut *(Alaska Native)* (9)	14	0.17
Apache (0)	1	0.01
Blackfeet (1)	7	0.08
Canadian/French Am. Ind. (7)	8	0.10
Central American Ind. (1)	2	0.02
Cherokee (4)	34	0.40
Chickasaw (0)	3	0.04
Chippewa (4)	12	0.14
Choctaw (0)	5	0.06
Colville (0)	1	0.01
Comanche (0)	1	0.01
Cree (1)	5	0.06
Creek (1)	1	0.01
Inupiat *(Alaska Native)* (1)	2	0.02
Iroquois (0)	8	0.10
Mexican American Ind. (1)	4	0.05
Navajo (2)	2	0.02
Osage (1)	1	0.01
Paiute (0)	1	0.01
Potawatomi (0)	1	0.01
Pueblo (0)	2	0.02
Puget Sound Salish (5)	15	0.18
Sioux (7)	11	0.13
South American Ind. (0)	1	0.01
Tlingit-Haida *(Alaska Native)* (3)	6	0.07
Tsimshian *(Alaska Native)* (1)	1	0.01
Yakama (1)	2	0.02
Yup'ik *(Alaska Native)* (0)	2	0.02
Asian (271)	368	4.37
Not Hispanic (270)	348	4.14
Hispanic (1)	20	0.24
Cambodian (9)	11	0.13
Chinese, ex. Taiwanese (40)	55	0.65
Filipino (85)	135	1.60
Indian (56)	67	0.80
Indonesian (2)	3	0.04
Japanese (20)	39	0.46
Korean (28)	35	0.42
Laotian (1)	3	0.04
Sri Lankan (2)	2	0.02
Taiwanese (1)	1	0.01
Thai (4)	5	0.06
Vietnamese (13)	18	0.21
Hawaii Native/Pacific Islander (29)	49	0.58
Not Hispanic (28)	45	0.53
Hispanic (1)	4	0.05
Fijian (11)	14	0.17
Guamanian/Chamorro (2)	2	0.02
Marshallese (1)	4	0.05
Native Hawaiian (2)	11	0.13
Samoan (1)	2	0.02
White (7,455)	7,759	92.23
Not Hispanic (7,139)	7,399	87.95
Hispanic (316)	360	4.28

Bonney Lake

Place Type: City
County: Pierce
Population: 17,374†

*Notes: † The Census 2010 population figure is used to calculate the percentages in the Hispanic Origin and Race categories. Ancestry percentages are based on the 2006-2010 American Community Survey population (not shown); ‡ Numbers in parentheses indicate the number of people reporting a single ancestry; * Numbers in parentheses indicate the number of persons reporting this race alone, not in combination with any other race; Please refer to the Explanation of Data for more information.*

Ancestry‡	Population	%
American (631)	631	3.85
Arab (0)	24	0.15
Lebanese (0)	24	0.15
Armenian (0)	6	0.04
Australian (0)	13	0.08
Austrian (0)	78	0.48
British (77)	130	0.79
Canadian (17)	60	0.37
Croatian (37)	83	0.51
Czech (18)	57	0.35
Czechoslovakian (18)	18	0.11
Danish (22)	75	0.46
Dutch (211)	646	3.94
English (403)	2,170	13.23
European (254)	348	2.12
Finnish (19)	115	0.70
French, ex. Basque (208)	666	4.06
French Canadian (95)	245	1.49
German (1,182)	4,087	24.91
Greek (0)	51	0.31
Hungarian (9)	55	0.34
Icelander (0)	42	0.26
Irish (581)	2,536	15.46
Italian (277)	1,001	6.10
Luxemburger (0)	11	0.07
Northern European (45)	45	0.27
Norwegian (524)	1,615	9.84
Polish (55)	625	3.81
Portuguese (0)	10	0.06
Romanian (8)	47	0.29
Russian (29)	137	0.83
Scandinavian (87)	118	0.72
Scotch-Irish (68)	542	3.30
Scottish (138)	532	3.24
Slovak (0)	45	0.27
Slovene (14)	14	0.09
Swedish (61)	494	3.01
Swiss (52)	98	0.60
Ukrainian (8)	81	0.49
Welsh (41)	317	1.93
Yugoslavian (39)	78	0.48

Hispanic Origin	Population	%
Hispanic or Latino (of any race)	1,063	6.12
Central American, ex. Mexican	57	0.33
Costa Rican	16	0.09
Guatemalan	13	0.07
Honduran	1	0.01
Nicaraguan	6	0.03
Panamanian	4	0.02
Salvadoran	17	0.10
Cuban	12	0.07
Dominican Republic	3	0.02
Mexican	737	4.24
Puerto Rican	94	0.54
South American	33	0.19
Bolivian	3	0.02
Chilean	6	0.03
Colombian	3	0.02
Peruvian	16	0.09
Venezuelan	5	0.03
Other Hispanic or Latino	127	0.73

Race*	Population	%
African-American/Black (223)	421	2.42
Not Hispanic (206)	370	2.13
Hispanic (17)	51	0.29
American Indian/Alaska Native (175)	412	2.37
Not Hispanic (150)	346	1.99
Hispanic (25)	66	0.38
Alaska Athabascan *(Ala. Nat.)* (1)	1	0.01
Aleut *(Alaska Native)* (4)	7	0.04
Apache (4)	6	0.03
Blackfeet (8)	20	0.12
Canadian/French Am. Ind. (3)	3	0.02
Cherokee (11)	47	0.27
Chickasaw (0)	2	0.01
Chippewa (7)	17	0.10
Choctaw (9)	19	0.11
Colville (3)	6	0.03
Comanche (3)	6	0.03
Cree (1)	1	0.01
Creek (1)	1	0.01
Crow (1)	1	0.01
Delaware (0)	4	0.02
Inupiat *(Alaska Native)* (3)	5	0.03
Iroquois (0)	4	0.02
Kiowa (0)	6	0.03
Mexican American Ind. (1)	7	0.04
Navajo (4)	8	0.05
Potawatomi (4)	4	0.02
Puget Sound Salish (18)	36	0.21
Shoshone (1)	1	0.01
Sioux (2)	13	0.07
Spanish American Ind. (1)	1	0.01
Tlingit-Haida *(Alaska Native)* (14)	23	0.13
Tsimshian *(Alaska Native)* (0)	1	0.01
Yakama (3)	14	0.08
Yup'ik *(Alaska Native)* (1)	4	0.02
Asian (417)	767	4.41
Not Hispanic (402)	724	4.17
Hispanic (15)	43	0.25
Burmese (0)	5	0.03
Cambodian (27)	36	0.21
Chinese, ex. Taiwanese (51)	100	0.58
Filipino (128)	268	1.54
Indian (38)	51	0.29
Indonesian (0)	5	0.03
Japanese (34)	125	0.72
Korean (57)	121	0.70
Laotian (6)	9	0.05
Taiwanese (1)	2	0.01
Thai (17)	27	0.16
Vietnamese (33)	50	0.29
Hawaii Native/Pacific Islander (43)	115	0.66
Not Hispanic (40)	100	0.58
Hispanic (3)	15	0.09
Fijian (2)	4	0.02
Guamanian/Chamorro (9)	17	0.10
Marshallese (0)	1	0.01
Native Hawaiian (15)	48	0.28
Samoan (11)	26	0.15
Tongan (3)	3	0.02
White (15,427)	16,152	92.97
Not Hispanic (14,848)	15,444	88.89
Hispanic (579)	708	4.08

Bothell East

Place Type: CDP
County: Snohomish
Population: 8,018†

Ancestry‡	Population	%
African, Sub-Saharan (36)	36	0.53
African (36)	36	0.53
American (210)	210	3.09
Austrian (8)	56	0.83
British (36)	79	1.16
Czech (0)	22	0.32
Danish (64)	125	1.84
Dutch (62)	197	2.90
Eastern European (9)	9	0.13
English (53)	489	7.20
European (232)	275	4.05
Finnish (0)	28	0.41
French, ex. Basque (23)	145	2.14
French Canadian (14)	31	0.46
German (240)	758	11.17
Greek (19)	56	0.83
Hungarian (0)	9	0.13
Iranian (86)	86	1.27
Irish (100)	696	10.25
Italian (79)	463	6.82
Latvian (25)	76	1.12
Northern European (16)	29	0.43
Norwegian (247)	573	8.44
Polish (62)	187	2.76
Portuguese (0)	51	0.75
Romanian (33)	33	0.49
Russian (54)	142	2.09
Scandinavian (21)	39	0.57
Scotch-Irish (22)	156	2.30
Scottish (120)	184	2.71
Swedish (75)	529	7.79
Swiss (38)	51	0.75
Ukrainian (13)	13	0.19
Yugoslavian (82)	133	1.96

Hispanic Origin	Population	%
Hispanic or Latino (of any race)	459	5.72
Central American, ex. Mexican	18	0.22
Guatemalan	5	0.06
Honduran	2	0.02
Nicaraguan	2	0.02
Panamanian	1	0.01
Salvadoran	8	0.10
Cuban	2	0.02
Dominican Republic	1	0.01
Mexican	328	4.09
Puerto Rican	25	0.31
South American	24	0.30
Colombian	8	0.10
Ecuadorian	4	0.05
Paraguayan	1	0.01
Peruvian	5	0.06
Uruguayan	1	0.01
Other South American	5	0.06
Other Hispanic or Latino	61	0.76

Race*	Population	%
African-American/Black (166)	230	2.87
Not Hispanic (154)	210	2.62
Hispanic (12)	20	0.25
American Indian/Alaska Native (46)	101	1.26
Not Hispanic (36)	79	0.99
Hispanic (10)	22	0.27
Aleut *(Alaska Native)* (1)	2	0.02
Apache (1)	4	0.05
Blackfeet (0)	1	0.01
Canadian/French Am. Ind. (0)	1	0.01
Cherokee (4)	16	0.20
Chippewa (3)	3	0.04
Choctaw (3)	6	0.07
Colville (1)	1	0.01
Cree (0)	2	0.02
Mexican American Ind. (3)	6	0.07
Navajo (11)	11	0.14
Pueblo (3)	3	0.04
Puget Sound Salish (2)	3	0.04
Sioux (3)	5	0.06
Tlingit-Haida *(Alaska Native)* (4)	9	0.11
Tsimshian *(Alaska Native)* (0)	1	0.01
Yakama (1)	1	0.01
Asian (2,229)	2,443	30.47
Not Hispanic (2,220)	2,417	30.14
Hispanic (9)	26	0.32
Bangladeshi (2)	2	0.02
Burmese (3)	3	0.04
Cambodian (57)	60	0.75
Chinese, ex. Taiwanese (342)	395	4.93
Filipino (135)	203	2.53
Hmong (3)	5	0.06
Indian (927)	950	11.85
Indonesian (7)	7	0.09
Japanese (47)	102	1.27
Korean (368)	395	4.93
Laotian (13)	19	0.24
Malaysian (1)	1	0.01
Nepalese (5)	5	0.06
Pakistani (19)	19	0.24
Sri Lankan (6)	9	0.11
Taiwanese (17)	20	0.25
Thai (11)	17	0.21
Vietnamese (221)	237	2.96
Hawaii Native/Pacific Islander (20)	58	0.72
Not Hispanic (17)	54	0.67
Hispanic (3)	4	0.05
Fijian (12)	13	0.16

*Notes: † The Census 2010 population figure is used to calculate the percentages in the Hispanic Origin and Race categories. Ancestry percentages are based on the 2006-2010 American Community Survey population (not shown); ‡ Numbers in parentheses indicate the number of people reporting a single ancestry; * Numbers in parentheses indicate the number of persons reporting this race alone, not in combination with any other race; Please refer to the Explanation of Data for more information.*

Guamanian/Chamorro (5)	8	0.10
Native Hawaiian (2)	22	0.27
Samoan (1)	5	0.06
White (5,057)	5,363	66.89
Not Hispanic (4,830)	5,079	63.34
Hispanic (227)	284	3.54

Bothell West

Place Type: CDP
County: Snohomish
Population: 16,607†

Ancestry‡	Population	%
African, Sub-Saharan (54)	211	1.35
African (22)	22	0.14
Nigerian (18)	175	1.12
Ugandan (14)	14	0.09
American (326)	326	2.09
Arab (10)	58	0.37
Egyptian (10)	10	0.06
Lebanese (0)	35	0.22
Syrian (0)	13	0.08
Armenian (0)	5	0.03
Australian (12)	12	0.08
Austrian (0)	15	0.10
Belgian (28)	68	0.44
British (11)	75	0.48
Canadian (36)	89	0.57
Celtic (0)	24	0.15
Croatian (0)	16	0.10
Czech (25)	78	0.50
Czechoslovakian (25)	25	0.16
Danish (121)	492	3.15
Dutch (52)	238	1.52
English (760)	2,837	18.18
Estonian (0)	36	0.23
European (163)	180	1.15
Finnish (32)	72	0.46
French, ex. Basque (66)	585	3.75
French Canadian (32)	132	0.85
German (846)	3,129	20.05
Greek (14)	51	0.33
Hungarian (29)	69	0.44
Icelander (0)	9	0.06
Iranian (11)	11	0.07
Irish (178)	1,839	11.78
Italian (322)	898	5.75
Lithuanian (19)	19	0.12
Luxemburger (30)	84	0.54
Maltese (10)	10	0.06
Northern European (71)	90	0.58
Norwegian (393)	1,743	11.17
Polish (68)	377	2.42
Portuguese (0)	54	0.35
Romanian (121)	121	0.78
Russian (149)	203	1.30
Scandinavian (151)	168	1.08
Scotch-Irish (443)	877	5.62
Scottish (102)	560	3.59
Serbian (0)	16	0.10
Slavic (17)	35	0.22
Swedish (192)	588	3.77
Swiss (0)	86	0.55
Ukrainian (9)	18	0.12
Welsh (39)	117	0.75
West Indian, ex. Hispanic (0)	36	0.23
Jamaican (0)	36	0.23
Yugoslavian (9)	9	0.06

Hispanic Origin	Population	%
Hispanic or Latino (of any race)	1,201	7.23
Central American, ex. Mexican	66	0.40
Costa Rican	6	0.04
Guatemalan	16	0.10
Honduran	11	0.07
Nicaraguan	9	0.05
Panamanian	6	0.04
Salvadoran	18	0.11
Cuban	17	0.10
Dominican Republic	2	0.01
Mexican	884	5.32
Puerto Rican	42	0.25
South American	93	0.56
Argentinean	8	0.05
Bolivian	2	0.01
Chilean	7	0.04
Colombian	24	0.14
Ecuadorian	11	0.07
Peruvian	31	0.19
Uruguayan	1	0.01
Venezuelan	9	0.05
Other Hispanic or Latino	97	0.58

Race*	Population	%
African-American/Black (337)	500	3.01
Not Hispanic (326)	462	2.78
Hispanic (11)	38	0.23
American Indian/Alaska Native (123)	249	1.50
Not Hispanic (102)	221	1.33
Hispanic (21)	28	0.17
Alaska Athabascan *(Ala. Nat.)* (1)	2	0.01
Aleut *(Alaska Native)* (3)	3	0.02
Apache (1)	3	0.02
Blackfeet (0)	9	0.05
Cherokee (5)	18	0.11
Cheyenne (0)	1	0.01
Chippewa (2)	8	0.05
Choctaw (1)	6	0.04
Colville (5)	5	0.03
Comanche (3)	3	0.02
Creek (1)	1	0.01
Crow (0)	1	0.01
Hopi (1)	1	0.01
Houma (0)	1	0.01
Inupiat *(Alaska Native)* (1)	3	0.02
Mexican American Ind. (4)	5	0.03
Navajo (3)	6	0.04
Potawatomi (0)	1	0.01
Pueblo (1)	5	0.03
Puget Sound Salish (12)	26	0.16
Seminole (3)	4	0.02
Sioux (5)	10	0.06
Tlingit-Haida *(Alaska Native)* (15)	30	0.18
Tsimshian *(Alaska Native)* (1)	5	0.03
Yakama (1)	2	0.01
Yaqui (1)	1	0.01
Asian (2,111)	2,524	15.20
Not Hispanic (2,102)	2,498	15.04
Hispanic (9)	26	0.16
Bangladeshi (5)	5	0.03
Burmese (1)	1	0.01
Cambodian (138)	163	0.98
Chinese, ex. Taiwanese (383)	496	2.99
Filipino (355)	514	3.10
Hmong (4)	4	0.02
Indian (339)	365	2.20
Indonesian (4)	8	0.05
Japanese (113)	225	1.35
Korean (258)	324	1.95
Laotian (13)	19	0.11
Malaysian (4)	5	0.03
Nepalese (1)	3	0.02
Pakistani (43)	51	0.31
Sri Lankan (0)	3	0.02
Taiwanese (19)	28	0.17
Thai (24)	31	0.19
Vietnamese (288)	341	2.05
Hawaii Native/Pacific Islander (46)	133	0.80
Not Hispanic (45)	129	0.78
Hispanic (1)	4	0.02
Fijian (6)	6	0.04
Guamanian/Chamorro (7)	21	0.13
Native Hawaiian (14)	58	0.35
Samoan (11)	20	0.12
Tongan (1)	2	0.01
White (12,799)	13,496	81.27
Not Hispanic (12,163)	12,760	76.84
Hispanic (636)	736	4.43

Bothell

Place Type: City
County: King
Population: 33,505†

Ancestry‡	Population	%
African, Sub-Saharan (95)	140	0.43
Cape Verdean (14)	26	0.08
Ethiopian (0)	33	0.10
South African (81)	81	0.25
American (860)	860	2.63
Arab (26)	40	0.12
Jordanian (18)	18	0.06
Lebanese (8)	8	0.02
Other Arab (0)	14	0.04
Armenian (29)	47	0.14
Australian (9)	25	0.08
Austrian (27)	93	0.28
Belgian (33)	44	0.13
Brazilian (30)	73	0.22
British (84)	193	0.59
Cajun (0)	12	0.04
Canadian (60)	153	0.47
Croatian (12)	58	0.18
Czech (40)	168	0.51
Czechoslovakian (0)	30	0.09
Danish (43)	546	1.67
Dutch (97)	1,042	3.19
Eastern European (34)	52	0.16
English (1,034)	5,142	15.74
European (479)	524	1.60
Finnish (0)	82	0.25
French, ex. Basque (193)	2,000	6.12
French Canadian (142)	276	0.85
German (1,666)	7,122	21.81
Greek (81)	178	0.55
Hungarian (12)	153	0.47
Icelander (0)	64	0.20
Iranian (119)	119	0.36
Irish (988)	4,449	13.62
Italian (447)	1,606	4.92
Latvian (20)	20	0.06
Lithuanian (31)	64	0.20
New Zealander (26)	26	0.08
Northern European (37)	52	0.16
Norwegian (722)	2,329	7.13
Pennsylvania German (10)	10	0.03
Polish (274)	792	2.43
Portuguese (26)	130	0.40
Romanian (174)	270	0.83
Russian (41)	236	0.72
Scandinavian (132)	375	1.15
Scotch-Irish (147)	992	3.04
Scottish (394)	1,412	4.32
Serbian (13)	13	0.04
Slavic (0)	11	0.03
Slovak (6)	115	0.35
Slovene (19)	19	0.06
Swedish (405)	1,415	4.33
Swiss (21)	89	0.27
Turkish (17)	27	0.08
Ukrainian (101)	246	0.75
Welsh (95)	658	2.01
West Indian, ex. Hispanic (28)	72	0.22
West Indian (28)	72	0.22
Yugoslavian (31)	50	0.15

Hispanic Origin	Population	%
Hispanic or Latino (of any race)	2,911	8.69
Central American, ex. Mexican	141	0.42
Costa Rican	14	0.04
Guatemalan	32	0.10
Honduran	14	0.04
Nicaraguan	19	0.06
Panamanian	10	0.03
Salvadoran	52	0.16
Cuban	46	0.14
Dominican Republic	5	0.01
Mexican	2,199	6.56

*Notes: † The Census 2010 population figure is used to calculate the percentages in the Hispanic Origin and Race categories. Ancestry percentages are based on the 2006-2010 American Community Survey population (not shown); ‡ Numbers in parentheses indicate the number of people reporting a single ancestry; * Numbers in parentheses indicate the number of persons reporting this race alone, not in combination with any other race; Please refer to the Explanation of Data for more information.*

Puerto Rican	89	0.27
South American	179	0.53
Argentinean	21	0.06
Bolivian	2	0.01
Chilean	20	0.06
Colombian	59	0.18
Ecuadorian	14	0.04
Peruvian	45	0.13
Uruguayan	1	<0.01
Venezuelan	15	0.04
Other South American	2	0.01
Other Hispanic or Latino	252	0.75

Race*	Population	%
African-American/Black (521)	849	2.53
Not Hispanic (486)	773	2.31
Hispanic (35)	76	0.23
American Indian/Alaska Native (191)	538	1.61
Not Hispanic (141)	436	1.30
Hispanic (50)	102	0.30
Alaska Athabascan *(Ala. Nat.)* (6)	8	0.02
Aleut *(Alaska Native)* (2)	2	0.01
Apache (1)	8	0.02
Arapaho (0)	1	<0.01
Blackfeet (1)	11	0.03
Canadian/French Am. Ind. (2)	9	0.03
Cherokee (9)	61	0.18
Chickasaw (0)	2	0.01
Chippewa (6)	15	0.04
Choctaw (3)	7	0.02
Colville (6)	7	0.02
Comanche (0)	1	<0.01
Cree (0)	1	<0.01
Creek (0)	5	0.01
Delaware (0)	3	0.01
Inupiat *(Alaska Native)* (6)	7	0.02
Iroquois (1)	6	0.02
Lumbee (0)	1	<0.01
Mexican American Ind. (24)	24	0.07
Navajo (3)	4	0.01
Osage (0)	2	0.01
Potawatomi (3)	3	0.01
Puget Sound Salish (9)	19	0.06
Seminole (0)	5	0.01
Shoshone (1)	2	0.01
Sioux (8)	29	0.09
South American Ind. (0)	1	<0.01
Tlingit-Haida *(Alaska Native)* (20)	46	0.14
Tsimshian *(Alaska Native)* (4)	7	0.02
Ute (0)	3	0.01
Yakama (0)	1	<0.01
Yuman (0)	1	<0.01
Yup'ik *(Alaska Native)* (1)	1	<0.01
Asian (3,407)	4,171	12.45
Not Hispanic (3,376)	4,072	12.15
Hispanic (31)	99	0.30
Bangladeshi (1)	1	<0.01
Burmese (2)	4	0.01
Cambodian (65)	82	0.24
Chinese, ex. Taiwanese (640)	865	2.58
Filipino (348)	579	1.73
Hmong (7)	9	0.03
Indian (1,074)	1,138	3.40
Indonesian (12)	24	0.07
Japanese (237)	489	1.46
Korean (450)	530	1.58
Laotian (21)	30	0.09
Malaysian (1)	8	0.02
Nepalese (1)	1	<0.01
Pakistani (43)	54	0.16
Sri Lankan (6)	11	0.03
Taiwanese (44)	57	0.17
Thai (32)	59	0.18
Vietnamese (267)	328	0.98
Hawaii Native/Pacific Islander (59)	173	0.52
Not Hispanic (56)	155	0.46
Hispanic (3)	18	0.05
Fijian (4)	8	0.02
Guamanian/Chamorro (16)	22	0.07
Marshallese (0)	1	<0.01
Native Hawaiian (13)	77	0.23
Samoan (13)	24	0.07
Tongan (8)	8	0.02
White (26,699)	28,048	83.71
Not Hispanic (25,235)	26,346	78.63
Hispanic (1,464)	1,702	5.08

Bremerton

Place Type: City
County: Kitsap
Population: 37,729†

Ancestry‡	Population	%
African, Sub-Saharan (185)	271	0.72
African (104)	190	0.50
Nigerian (20)	20	0.05
Other Sub-Saharan African (61)	61	0.16
American (1,354)	1,354	3.59
Arab (9)	52	0.14
Lebanese (0)	34	0.09
Other Arab (9)	18	0.05
Austrian (74)	133	0.35
Belgian (34)	102	0.27
Brazilian (7)	24	0.06
British (72)	207	0.55
Cajun (0)	10	0.03
Canadian (144)	197	0.52
Celtic (12)	12	0.03
Croatian (12)	38	0.10
Czech (58)	189	0.50
Danish (82)	326	0.86
Dutch (120)	966	2.56
English (1,193)	4,635	12.30
Estonian (0)	10	0.03
European (673)	759	2.01
Finnish (0)	104	0.28
French, ex. Basque (223)	1,007	2.67
French Canadian (132)	323	0.86
German (1,976)	8,044	21.34
German Russian (0)	31	0.08
Greek (19)	68	0.18
Hungarian (40)	126	0.33
Irish (827)	4,542	12.05
Italian (365)	1,560	4.14
Latvian (16)	28	0.07
Lithuanian (0)	51	0.14
Northern European (65)	65	0.17
Norwegian (974)	2,347	6.23
Pennsylvania German (0)	10	0.03
Polish (50)	660	1.75
Portuguese (93)	291	0.77
Romanian (50)	50	0.13
Russian (79)	118	0.31
Scandinavian (137)	257	0.68
Scotch-Irish (296)	1,306	3.47
Scottish (293)	1,328	3.52
Serbian (11)	11	0.03
Slavic (0)	12	0.03
Slovak (8)	8	0.02
Swedish (287)	1,145	3.04
Swiss (9)	127	0.34
Ukrainian (46)	61	0.16
Welsh (101)	307	0.81
West Indian, ex. Hispanic (81)	178	0.47
Belizean (58)	155	0.41
Haitian (23)	23	0.06
Yugoslavian (109)	109	0.29

Hispanic Origin	Population	%
Hispanic or Latino (of any race)	3,612	9.57
Central American, ex. Mexican	407	1.08
Costa Rican	10	0.03
Guatemalan	317	0.84
Honduran	10	0.03
Nicaraguan	15	0.04
Panamanian	13	0.03
Salvadoran	36	0.10
Other Central American	6	0.02
Cuban	67	0.18
Dominican Republic	22	0.06
Mexican	2,136	5.66
Puerto Rican	392	1.04
South American	91	0.24
Argentinean	4	0.01
Bolivian	3	0.01
Chilean	10	0.03
Colombian	36	0.10
Ecuadorian	3	0.01
Paraguayan	2	0.01
Peruvian	11	0.03
Venezuelan	22	0.06
Other Hispanic or Latino	497	1.32

Race*	Population	%
African-American/Black (2,514)	3,570	9.46
Not Hispanic (2,387)	3,291	8.72
Hispanic (127)	279	0.74
American Indian/Alaska Native (772)	1,624	4.30
Not Hispanic (600)	1,307	3.46
Hispanic (172)	317	0.84
Alaska Athabascan *(Ala. Nat.)* (6)	10	0.03
Aleut *(Alaska Native)* (11)	24	0.06
Apache (11)	23	0.06
Arapaho (3)	4	0.01
Blackfeet (19)	86	0.23
Canadian/French Am. Ind. (12)	22	0.06
Central American Ind. (21)	30	0.08
Cherokee (57)	239	0.63
Cheyenne (5)	8	0.02
Chickasaw (1)	5	0.01
Chippewa (23)	60	0.16
Choctaw (6)	29	0.08
Colville (4)	5	0.01
Comanche (0)	9	0.02
Cree (0)	4	0.01
Creek (3)	5	0.01
Crow (4)	4	0.01
Delaware (8)	9	0.02
Hopi (5)	5	0.01
Houma (1)	2	0.01
Inupiat *(Alaska Native)* (10)	13	0.03
Iroquois (1)	6	0.02
Kiowa (4)	5	0.01
Lumbee (2)	3	0.01
Menominee (0)	1	<0.01
Mexican American Ind. (62)	72	0.19
Navajo (34)	52	0.14
Osage (1)	2	0.01
Ottawa (0)	7	0.02
Paiute (0)	1	<0.01
Pima (3)	6	0.02
Potawatomi (5)	7	0.02
Pueblo (1)	6	0.02
Puget Sound Salish (54)	81	0.21
Seminole (2)	8	0.02
Shoshone (1)	3	0.01
Sioux (41)	74	0.20
South American Ind. (1)	2	0.01
Spanish American Ind. (2)	3	0.01
Tlingit-Haida *(Alaska Native)* (15)	42	0.11
Tohono O'Odham (0)	4	0.01
Tsimshian *(Alaska Native)* (1)	2	0.01
Ute (0)	1	<0.01
Yakama (3)	11	0.03
Yaqui (6)	7	0.02
Yup'ik *(Alaska Native)* (1)	3	0.01
Asian (2,087)	3,092	8.20
Not Hispanic (2,029)	2,927	7.76
Hispanic (58)	165	0.44
Bangladeshi (1)	1	<0.01
Burmese (1)	1	<0.01
Cambodian (5)	9	0.02
Chinese, ex. Taiwanese (136)	227	0.60
Filipino (1,473)	2,118	5.61
Hmong (2)	4	0.01
Indian (52)	94	0.25
Indonesian (9)	16	0.04
Japanese (104)	309	0.82
Korean (91)	172	0.46

*Notes: † The Census 2010 population figure is used to calculate the percentages in the Hispanic Origin and Race categories. Ancestry percentages are based on the 2006-2010 American Community Survey population (not shown); ‡ Numbers in parentheses indicate the number of people reporting a single ancestry; * Numbers in parentheses indicate the number of persons reporting this race alone, not in combination with any other race; Please refer to the Explanation of Data for more information.*

Laotian (14)	16	0.04
Malaysian (3)	4	0.01
Pakistani (1)	1	<0.01
Taiwanese (11)	13	0.03
Thai (17)	26	0.07
Vietnamese (113)	133	0.35
Hawaii Native/Pacific Islander (484)	825	2.19
Not Hispanic (462)	753	2.00
Hispanic (22)	72	0.19
Fijian (7)	7	0.02
Guamanian/Chamorro (283)	417	1.11
Marshallese (3)	3	0.01
Native Hawaiian (61)	164	0.43
Samoan (79)	156	0.41
Tongan (4)	5	0.01
White (27,922)	30,436	80.67
Not Hispanic (26,236)	28,293	74.99
Hispanic (1,686)	2,143	5.68

Bryn Mawr-Skyway

Place Type: CDP
County: King
Population: 15,645†

Ancestry‡	Population	%
African, Sub-Saharan (478)	492	3.44
African (154)	161	1.12
Ethiopian (227)	227	1.59
Kenyan (59)	59	0.41
Nigerian (6)	13	0.09
Somalian (32)	32	0.22
American (399)	399	2.79
Austrian (9)	39	0.27
Belgian (0)	22	0.15
British (66)	74	0.52
Croatian (17)	17	0.12
Czech (0)	43	0.30
Danish (0)	88	0.61
Dutch (29)	91	0.64
Eastern European (28)	28	0.20
English (218)	822	5.74
European (10)	17	0.12
Finnish (0)	55	0.38
French, ex. Basque (23)	227	1.59
French Canadian (25)	69	0.48
German (308)	1,305	9.11
Greek (22)	22	0.15
Hungarian (28)	46	0.32
Irish (75)	750	5.24
Italian (262)	486	3.39
Lithuanian (10)	20	0.14
Norwegian (72)	298	2.08
Polish (10)	92	0.64
Russian (0)	11	0.08
Scandinavian (69)	69	0.48
Scotch-Irish (66)	204	1.42
Scottish (51)	157	1.10
Serbian (20)	20	0.14
Slavic (0)	11	0.08
Slovak (9)	9	0.06
Swedish (64)	408	2.85
Swiss (18)	64	0.45
Welsh (42)	128	0.89
West Indian, ex. Hispanic (48)	70	0.49
Jamaican (48)	60	0.42
West Indian (0)	10	0.07
Yugoslavian (11)	11	0.08

Hispanic Origin	Population	%
Hispanic or Latino (of any race)	1,208	7.72
Central American, ex. Mexican	103	0.66
Costa Rican	7	0.04
Guatemalan	19	0.12
Honduran	17	0.11
Nicaraguan	5	0.03
Panamanian	7	0.04
Salvadoran	48	0.31
Cuban	13	0.08
Dominican Republic	6	0.04
Mexican	811	5.18
Puerto Rican	72	0.46
South American	29	0.19
Argentinean	7	0.04
Chilean	8	0.05
Colombian	6	0.04
Ecuadorian	1	0.01
Peruvian	6	0.04
Uruguayan	1	0.01
Other Hispanic or Latino	174	1.11

Race*	Population	%
African-American/Black (4,913)	5,551	35.48
Not Hispanic (4,797)	5,348	34.18
Hispanic (116)	203	1.30
American Indian/Alaska Native (132)	422	2.70
Not Hispanic (96)	338	2.16
Hispanic (36)	84	0.54
Aleut *(Alaska Native)* (0)	3	0.02
Apache (1)	6	0.04
Blackfeet (8)	44	0.28
Canadian/French Am. Ind. (4)	17	0.11
Cherokee (5)	37	0.24
Cheyenne (1)	1	0.01
Chippewa (3)	10	0.06
Choctaw (0)	3	0.02
Colville (1)	4	0.03
Cree (2)	9	0.06
Inupiat *(Alaska Native)* (1)	3	0.02
Iroquois (3)	5	0.03
Lumbee (1)	1	0.01
Mexican American Ind. (16)	23	0.15
Navajo (2)	7	0.04
Pueblo (1)	2	0.01
Puget Sound Salish (6)	12	0.08
Seminole (0)	1	0.01
Shoshone (0)	2	0.01
Sioux (1)	11	0.07
South American Ind. (0)	3	0.02
Tlingit-Haida *(Alaska Native)* (7)	24	0.15
Tsimshian *(Alaska Native)* (2)	4	0.03
Ute (0)	2	0.01
Yakama (2)	5	0.03
Yaqui (1)	1	0.01
Yup'ik *(Alaska Native)* (1)	5	0.03
Asian (4,239)	4,711	30.11
Not Hispanic (4,176)	4,602	29.42
Hispanic (63)	109	0.70
Burmese (1)	1	0.01
Cambodian (88)	118	0.75
Chinese, ex. Taiwanese (699)	849	5.43
Filipino (1,120)	1,372	8.77
Hmong (41)	41	0.26
Indian (44)	95	0.61
Indonesian (8)	10	0.06
Japanese (310)	431	2.75
Korean (38)	67	0.43
Laotian (452)	515	3.29
Pakistani (1)	5	0.03
Taiwanese (4)	5	0.03
Thai (24)	48	0.31
Vietnamese (1,201)	1,321	8.44
Hawaii Native/Pacific Islander (132)	263	1.68
Not Hispanic (122)	237	1.51
Hispanic (10)	26	0.17
Fijian (6)	19	0.12
Guamanian/Chamorro (7)	15	0.10
Native Hawaiian (15)	55	0.35
Samoan (75)	115	0.74
Tongan (16)	29	0.19
White (4,638)	5,403	34.53
Not Hispanic (4,240)	4,921	31.45
Hispanic (398)	482	3.08

Burien

Place Type: City
County: King
Population: 33,313†

Ancestry‡	Population	%
African, Sub-Saharan (873)	955	2.92
African (79)	134	0.41
Ethiopian (616)	643	1.96
Nigerian (158)	158	0.48
Somalian (20)	20	0.06
American (1,467)	1,467	4.48
Arab (11)	39	0.12
Arab (0)	12	0.04
Lebanese (0)	16	0.05
Palestinian (11)	11	0.03
Australian (0)	8	0.02
Austrian (12)	192	0.59
Belgian (38)	96	0.29
British (47)	165	0.50
Bulgarian (0)	15	0.05
Canadian (52)	136	0.42
Croatian (41)	94	0.29
Czech (95)	175	0.53
Czechoslovakian (8)	25	0.08
Danish (140)	554	1.69
Dutch (119)	666	2.03
English (999)	3,649	11.14
European (510)	655	2.00
Finnish (49)	120	0.37
French, ex. Basque (90)	1,115	3.41
French Canadian (75)	242	0.74
German (1,299)	5,678	17.34
Greek (12)	153	0.47
Hungarian (23)	206	0.63
Icelander (49)	129	0.39
Iranian (291)	291	0.89
Irish (686)	3,355	10.25
Italian (434)	1,459	4.46
Latvian (42)	92	0.28
Northern European (30)	30	0.09
Norwegian (584)	2,386	7.29
Pennsylvania German (10)	37	0.11
Polish (170)	416	1.27
Portuguese (81)	189	0.58
Romanian (23)	23	0.07
Russian (90)	214	0.65
Scandinavian (29)	212	0.65
Scotch-Irish (280)	938	2.86
Scottish (232)	905	2.76
Serbian (7)	15	0.05
Slovak (0)	11	0.03
Swedish (375)	1,283	3.92
Swiss (14)	34	0.10
Turkish (0)	20	0.06
Ukrainian (63)	113	0.35
Welsh (12)	225	0.69
Yugoslavian (147)	238	0.73

Hispanic Origin	Population	%
Hispanic or Latino (of any race)	6,902	20.72
Central American, ex. Mexican	823	2.47
Costa Rican	11	0.03
Guatemalan	164	0.49
Honduran	269	0.81
Nicaraguan	41	0.12
Panamanian	24	0.07
Salvadoran	305	0.92
Other Central American	9	0.03
Cuban	52	0.16
Dominican Republic	16	0.05
Mexican	5,136	15.42
Puerto Rican	132	0.40
South American	240	0.72
Argentinean	21	0.06
Bolivian	2	0.01
Chilean	56	0.17
Colombian	47	0.14
Ecuadorian	15	0.05
Peruvian	92	0.28
Uruguayan	2	0.01
Venezuelan	5	0.02
Other Hispanic or Latino	503	1.51

*Notes: † The Census 2010 population figure is used to calculate the percentages in the Hispanic Origin and Race categories. Ancestry percentages are based on the 2006-2010 American Community Survey population (not shown); ‡ Numbers in parentheses indicate the number of people reporting a single ancestry; * Numbers in parentheses indicate the number of persons reporting this race alone, not in combination with any other race; Please refer to the Explanation of Data for more information.*

Race*	Population	%
African-American/Black (1,960)	2,557	7.68
Not Hispanic (1,845)	2,296	6.89
Hispanic (115)	261	0.78
American Indian/Alaska Native (513)	1,106	3.32
Not Hispanic (291)	723	2.17
Hispanic (222)	383	1.15
Alaska Athabascan *(Ala. Nat.)* (3)	5	0.02
Aleut *(Alaska Native)* (6)	9	0.03
Apache (10)	19	0.06
Arapaho (0)	2	0.01
Blackfeet (21)	62	0.19
Canadian/French Am. Ind. (17)	36	0.11
Central American Ind. (10)	19	0.06
Cherokee (17)	98	0.29
Cheyenne (2)	6	0.02
Chickasaw (0)	1	<0.01
Chippewa (13)	30	0.09
Choctaw (1)	13	0.04
Colville (2)	3	0.01
Comanche (0)	4	0.01
Cree (1)	4	0.01
Creek (0)	3	0.01
Crow (0)	1	<0.01
Delaware (1)	3	0.01
Inupiat *(Alaska Native)* (1)	5	0.02
Iroquois (1)	13	0.04
Lumbee (3)	4	0.01
Mexican American Ind. (73)	102	0.31
Navajo (8)	15	0.05
Osage (0)	4	0.01
Potawatomi (3)	4	0.01
Pueblo (1)	6	0.02
Puget Sound Salish (12)	29	0.09
Seminole (0)	7	0.02
Sioux (24)	44	0.13
South American Ind. (5)	6	0.02
Spanish American Ind. (2)	4	0.01
Tlingit-Haida *(Alaska Native)* (25)	53	0.16
Tohono O'Odham (2)	2	0.01
Tsimshian *(Alaska Native)* (10)	19	0.06
Yakama (8)	20	0.06
Yaqui (1)	6	0.02
Yup'ik *(Alaska Native)* (3)	7	0.02
Asian (3,304)	4,017	12.06
Not Hispanic (3,275)	3,902	11.71
Hispanic (29)	115	0.35
Bhutanese (26)	35	0.11
Burmese (50)	58	0.17
Cambodian (372)	413	1.24
Chinese, ex. Taiwanese (222)	362	1.09
Filipino (580)	895	2.69
Hmong (30)	30	0.09
Indian (298)	336	1.01
Indonesian (7)	14	0.04
Japanese (138)	288	0.86
Korean (137)	195	0.59
Laotian (60)	75	0.23
Nepalese (14)	21	0.06
Pakistani (24)	31	0.09
Sri Lankan (1)	4	0.01
Taiwanese (14)	15	0.05
Thai (27)	46	0.14
Vietnamese (1,139)	1,220	3.66
Hawaii Native/Pacific Islander (591)	836	2.51
Not Hispanic (585)	776	2.33
Hispanic (6)	60	0.18
Fijian (34)	39	0.12
Guamanian/Chamorro (61)	91	0.27
Marshallese (0)	1	<0.01
Native Hawaiian (47)	132	0.40
Samoan (299)	384	1.15
Tongan (45)	71	0.21
White (21,158)	22,783	68.39
Not Hispanic (18,979)	20,118	60.39
Hispanic (2,179)	2,665	8.00

Burlington

Place Type: City
County: Skagit
Population: 8,388†

Ancestry‡	Population	%
American (141)	141	1.73
Armenian (21)	21	0.26
Austrian (0)	9	0.11
Belgian (0)	22	0.27
British (0)	11	0.13
Canadian (7)	38	0.47
Croatian (0)	15	0.18
Czech (0)	8	0.10
Czechoslovakian (0)	13	0.16
Danish (20)	238	2.91
Dutch (33)	215	2.63
English (249)	1,039	12.72
European (14)	29	0.35
Finnish (10)	49	0.60
French, ex. Basque (29)	151	1.85
French Canadian (30)	30	0.37
German (366)	1,224	14.98
Irish (212)	687	8.41
Italian (132)	285	3.49
Luxemburger (0)	6	0.07
Northern European (9)	9	0.11
Norwegian (223)	699	8.55
Pennsylvania German (16)	16	0.20
Polish (5)	63	0.77
Portuguese (11)	11	0.13
Russian (29)	63	0.77
Scandinavian (9)	40	0.49
Scotch-Irish (47)	98	1.20
Scottish (104)	225	2.75
Swedish (112)	510	6.24
Swiss (9)	18	0.22
Ukrainian (0)	24	0.29
Welsh (50)	198	2.42

Hispanic Origin	Population	%
Hispanic or Latino (of any race)	2,631	31.37
Central American, ex. Mexican	31	0.37
Costa Rican	5	0.06
Guatemalan	8	0.10
Honduran	3	0.04
Panamanian	4	0.05
Salvadoran	11	0.13
Cuban	9	0.11
Dominican Republic	1	0.01
Mexican	2,384	28.42
Puerto Rican	24	0.29
South American	23	0.27
Argentinean	6	0.07
Colombian	5	0.06
Ecuadorian	2	0.02
Peruvian	9	0.11
Other South American	1	0.01
Other Hispanic or Latino	159	1.90

Race*	Population	%
African-American/Black (104)	168	2.00
Not Hispanic (79)	127	1.51
Hispanic (25)	41	0.49
American Indian/Alaska Native (155)	244	2.91
Not Hispanic (97)	158	1.88
Hispanic (58)	86	1.03
Alaska Athabascan *(Ala. Nat.)* (1)	1	0.01
Aleut *(Alaska Native)* (8)	10	0.12
Apache (0)	7	0.08
Blackfeet (3)	4	0.05
Canadian/French Am. Ind. (3)	4	0.05
Cherokee (4)	12	0.14
Chippewa (6)	7	0.08
Choctaw (1)	1	0.01
Colville (0)	1	0.01
Creek (0)	1	0.01
Inupiat *(Alaska Native)* (2)	2	0.02
Mexican American Ind. (53)	59	0.70
Navajo (1)	3	0.04
Potawatomi (1)	1	0.01
Puget Sound Salish (26)	44	0.52
Seminole (0)	7	0.08
Sioux (2)	3	0.04
Tlingit-Haida *(Alaska Native)* (5)	8	0.10
Ute (1)	3	0.04
Asian (249)	320	3.81
Not Hispanic (242)	292	3.48
Hispanic (7)	28	0.33
Cambodian (1)	3	0.04
Chinese, ex. Taiwanese (25)	34	0.41
Filipino (86)	131	1.56
Indian (53)	54	0.64
Indonesian (2)	2	0.02
Japanese (20)	30	0.36
Korean (29)	29	0.35
Laotian (4)	5	0.06
Malaysian (1)	1	0.01
Taiwanese (0)	1	0.01
Thai (2)	4	0.05
Vietnamese (18)	19	0.23
Hawaii Native/Pacific Islander (28)	50	0.60
Not Hispanic (15)	20	0.24
Hispanic (13)	30	0.36
Guamanian/Chamorro (8)	11	0.13
Native Hawaiian (10)	19	0.23
Samoan (0)	6	0.07
Tongan (0)	5	0.06
White (6,051)	6,297	75.07
Not Hispanic (5,162)	5,304	63.23
Hispanic (889)	993	11.84

Camas

Place Type: City
County: Clark
Population: 19,355†

Ancestry‡	Population	%
African, Sub-Saharan (47)	47	0.26
South African (47)	47	0.26
Albanian (0)	37	0.20
American (817)	817	4.45
Arab (17)	39	0.21
Moroccan (13)	26	0.14
Syrian (0)	9	0.05
Other Arab (4)	4	0.02
Armenian (10)	10	0.05
Australian (0)	37	0.20
Austrian (21)	88	0.48
British (59)	140	0.76
Bulgarian (7)	7	0.04
Canadian (56)	333	1.81
Croatian (39)	73	0.40
Danish (53)	383	2.09
Dutch (122)	515	2.81
English (503)	2,535	13.82
European (319)	344	1.87
Finnish (72)	168	0.92
French, ex. Basque (55)	867	4.73
French Canadian (245)	398	2.17
German (960)	4,183	22.80
Greek (10)	94	0.51
Hungarian (17)	34	0.19
Iranian (116)	116	0.63
Irish (776)	2,783	15.17
Italian (258)	913	4.98
Lithuanian (0)	8	0.04
Norwegian (290)	1,427	7.78
Polish (104)	580	3.16
Portuguese (58)	67	0.37
Romanian (114)	213	1.16
Russian (145)	420	2.29
Scandinavian (32)	123	0.67
Scotch-Irish (50)	195	1.06
Scottish (164)	1,005	5.48
Serbian (12)	25	0.14
Slovak (10)	18	0.10
Swedish (175)	795	4.33

*Notes: † The Census 2010 population figure is used to calculate the percentages in the Hispanic Origin and Race categories. Ancestry percentages are based on the 2006-2010 American Community Survey population (not shown); ‡ Numbers in parentheses indicate the number of people reporting a single ancestry; * Numbers in parentheses indicate the number of persons reporting this race alone, not in combination with any other race; Please refer to the Explanation of Data for more information.*

Swiss (0)	97	0.53
Turkish (37)	110	0.60
Ukrainian (116)	130	0.71
Welsh (78)	233	1.27
Yugoslavian (0)	19	0.10

Hispanic Origin	Population	%
Hispanic or Latino (of any race)	790	4.08
Central American, ex. Mexican	44	0.23
Guatemalan	6	0.03
Honduran	3	0.02
Nicaraguan	18	0.09
Panamanian	5	0.03
Salvadoran	9	0.05
Other Central American	3	0.02
Cuban	13	0.07
Dominican Republic	7	0.04
Mexican	510	2.63
Puerto Rican	39	0.20
South American	56	0.29
Argentinean	4	0.02
Chilean	8	0.04
Colombian	11	0.06
Ecuadorian	10	0.05
Peruvian	14	0.07
Uruguayan	6	0.03
Venezuelan	3	0.02
Other Hispanic or Latino	121	0.63

Race*	Population	%
African-American/Black (198)	311	1.61
Not Hispanic (195)	302	1.56
Hispanic (3)	9	0.05
American Indian/Alaska Native (123)	292	1.51
Not Hispanic (104)	250	1.29
Hispanic (19)	42	0.22
Alaska Athabascan *(Ala. Nat.)* (1)	2	0.01
Aleut *(Alaska Native)* (0)	1	0.01
Apache (4)	11	0.06
Arapaho (0)	1	0.01
Blackfeet (0)	6	0.03
Canadian/French Am. Ind. (1)	2	0.01
Cherokee (12)	46	0.24
Cheyenne (0)	3	0.02
Chickasaw (3)	3	0.02
Chippewa (6)	11	0.06
Choctaw (7)	12	0.06
Colville (1)	2	0.01
Comanche (0)	1	0.01
Creek (0)	4	0.02
Crow (5)	5	0.03
Hopi (1)	1	0.01
Inupiat *(Alaska Native)* (3)	3	0.02
Iroquois (0)	1	0.01
Mexican American Ind. (4)	10	0.05
Navajo (0)	3	0.02
Osage (2)	3	0.02
Paiute (1)	3	0.02
Pima (0)	3	0.02
Pueblo (0)	4	0.02
Puget Sound Salish (2)	3	0.02
Seminole (0)	1	0.01
Sioux (2)	5	0.03
South American Ind. (1)	2	0.01
Tlingit-Haida *(Alaska Native)* (4)	4	0.02
Yakama (1)	5	0.03
Asian (1,160)	1,538	7.95
Not Hispanic (1,152)	1,501	7.76
Hispanic (8)	37	0.19
Cambodian (14)	15	0.08
Chinese, ex. Taiwanese (325)	409	2.11
Filipino (121)	223	1.15
Indian (126)	157	0.81
Indonesian (3)	19	0.10
Japanese (128)	245	1.27
Korean (118)	169	0.87
Laotian (18)	38	0.20
Nepalese (4)	4	0.02
Pakistani (17)	22	0.11
Sri Lankan (2)	2	0.01
Taiwanese (80)	85	0.44
Thai (21)	37	0.19
Vietnamese (121)	151	0.78
Hawaii Native/Pacific Islander (43)	126	0.65
Not Hispanic (38)	115	0.59
Hispanic (5)	11	0.06
Fijian (2)	5	0.03
Guamanian/Chamorro (6)	16	0.08
Native Hawaiian (15)	60	0.31
Samoan (7)	11	0.06
White (16,910)	17,552	90.68
Not Hispanic (16,429)	16,986	87.76
Hispanic (481)	566	2.92

Centralia

Place Type: City
County: Lewis
Population: 16,336†

Ancestry‡	Population	%
African, Sub-Saharan (0)	9	0.06
Nigerian (0)	9	0.06
American (1,419)	1,419	8.78
Arab (17)	17	0.11
Lebanese (17)	17	0.11
Austrian (14)	61	0.38
Basque (0)	15	0.09
Belgian (22)	32	0.20
British (16)	23	0.14
Canadian (0)	12	0.07
Croatian (0)	20	0.12
Czech (0)	52	0.32
Danish (34)	227	1.40
Dutch (91)	271	1.68
Eastern European (7)	7	0.04
English (377)	1,391	8.60
European (169)	169	1.05
Finnish (150)	222	1.37
French, ex. Basque (133)	717	4.43
French Canadian (19)	76	0.47
German (1,015)	3,309	20.47
Greek (0)	50	0.31
Hungarian (0)	54	0.33
Irish (882)	2,742	16.96
Italian (85)	232	1.43
New Zealander (17)	25	0.15
Northern European (16)	16	0.10
Norwegian (320)	955	5.91
Pennsylvania German (0)	13	0.08
Polish (43)	144	0.89
Portuguese (26)	71	0.44
Russian (84)	98	0.61
Scandinavian (62)	146	0.90
Scotch-Irish (379)	623	3.85
Scottish (105)	526	3.25
Slavic (0)	7	0.04
Slovak (6)	14	0.09
Swedish (155)	455	2.81
Swiss (23)	175	1.08
Ukrainian (35)	47	0.29
Welsh (35)	158	0.98

Hispanic Origin	Population	%
Hispanic or Latino (of any race)	2,634	16.12
Central American, ex. Mexican	204	1.25
Costa Rican	4	0.02
Guatemalan	21	0.13
Honduran	45	0.28
Panamanian	4	0.02
Salvadoran	124	0.76
Other Central American	6	0.04
Cuban	7	0.04
Dominican Republic	4	0.02
Mexican	2,190	13.41
Puerto Rican	44	0.27
South American	20	0.12
Argentinean	5	0.03
Bolivian	2	0.01
Colombian	6	0.04
Ecuadorian	4	0.02
Peruvian	3	0.02
Other Hispanic or Latino	165	1.01

Race*	Population	%
African-American/Black (106)	220	1.35
Not Hispanic (89)	183	1.12
Hispanic (17)	37	0.23
American Indian/Alaska Native (234)	491	3.01
Not Hispanic (209)	437	2.68
Hispanic (25)	54	0.33
Alaska Athabascan *(Ala. Nat.)* (2)	3	0.02
Aleut *(Alaska Native)* (5)	11	0.07
Apache (0)	10	0.06
Blackfeet (7)	17	0.10
Canadian/French Am. Ind. (2)	3	0.02
Cherokee (18)	70	0.43
Cheyenne (0)	2	0.01
Chickasaw (0)	1	0.01
Choctaw (2)	2	0.01
Colville (4)	6	0.04
Cree (0)	1	0.01
Creek (2)	2	0.01
Delaware (0)	2	0.01
Hopi (0)	1	0.01
Inupiat *(Alaska Native)* (2)	5	0.03
Iroquois (2)	3	0.02
Mexican American Ind. (3)	15	0.09
Navajo (3)	9	0.06
Osage (1)	1	0.01
Potawatomi (0)	1	0.01
Pueblo (1)	1	0.01
Puget Sound Salish (12)	29	0.18
Seminole (0)	3	0.02
Shoshone (1)	1	0.01
Sioux (7)	13	0.08
Spanish American Ind. (0)	1	0.01
Tlingit-Haida *(Alaska Native)* (11)	14	0.09
Tsimshian *(Alaska Native)* (1)	6	0.04
Yakama (1)	2	0.01
Yaqui (1)	1	0.01
Yup'ik *(Alaska Native)* (1)	1	0.01
Asian (163)	303	1.85
Not Hispanic (155)	281	1.72
Hispanic (8)	22	0.13
Burmese (2)	2	0.01
Cambodian (1)	1	0.01
Chinese, ex. Taiwanese (24)	45	0.28
Filipino (39)	80	0.49
Hmong (1)	1	0.01
Indian (11)	14	0.09
Indonesian (0)	2	0.01
Japanese (11)	30	0.18
Korean (31)	70	0.43
Laotian (10)	14	0.09
Thai (16)	21	0.13
Vietnamese (6)	16	0.10
Hawaii Native/Pacific Islander (50)	98	0.60
Not Hispanic (43)	78	0.48
Hispanic (7)	20	0.12
Guamanian/Chamorro (23)	32	0.20
Marshallese (1)	1	0.01
Native Hawaiian (7)	31	0.19
Samoan (11)	20	0.12
Tongan (5)	7	0.04
White (13,901)	14,540	89.01
Not Hispanic (12,729)	13,177	80.66
Hispanic (1,172)	1,363	8.34

Cheney

Place Type: City
County: Spokane
Population: 10,590†

Ancestry‡	Population	%
African, Sub-Saharan (30)	52	0.51
African (13)	35	0.34
Ethiopian (17)	17	0.17
American (266)	266	2.59

*Notes: † The Census 2010 population figure is used to calculate the percentages in the Hispanic Origin and Race categories. Ancestry percentages are based on the 2006-2010 American Community Survey population (not shown); ‡ Numbers in parentheses indicate the number of people reporting a single ancestry; * Numbers in parentheses indicate the number of persons reporting this race alone, not in combination with any other race; Please refer to the Explanation of Data for more information.*

Ancestry	Population	%
Austrian (0)	10	0.10
Basque (0)	23	0.22
Belgian (28)	42	0.41
British (39)	50	0.49
Canadian (8)	21	0.20
Czech (26)	64	0.62
Czechoslovakian (11)	11	0.11
Danish (0)	92	0.89
Dutch (18)	188	1.83
English (336)	1,584	15.40
European (368)	397	3.86
Finnish (0)	19	0.18
French, ex. Basque (13)	453	4.41
French Canadian (56)	89	0.87
German (909)	2,800	27.23
Hungarian (21)	52	0.51
Icelander (0)	10	0.10
Iranian (44)	44	0.43
Irish (480)	1,447	14.07
Israeli (32)	54	0.53
Italian (242)	759	7.38
Lithuanian (11)	11	0.11
Norwegian (295)	799	7.77
Polish (12)	175	1.70
Romanian (0)	34	0.33
Russian (0)	20	0.19
Scandinavian (8)	8	0.08
Scotch-Irish (51)	415	4.04
Scottish (75)	453	4.41
Swedish (72)	191	1.86
Swiss (10)	152	1.48
Ukrainian (0)	35	0.34
Welsh (10)	185	1.80
West Indian, ex. Hispanic (14)	58	0.56
Haitian (14)	14	0.14
Jamaican (0)	44	0.43

Hispanic Origin	Population	%
Hispanic or Latino (of any race)	990	9.35
Central American, ex. Mexican	35	0.33
Costa Rican	2	0.02
Guatemalan	10	0.09
Honduran	1	0.01
Nicaraguan	5	0.05
Panamanian	5	0.05
Salvadoran	12	0.11
Cuban	2	0.02
Mexican	773	7.30
Puerto Rican	40	0.38
South American	29	0.27
Argentinean	3	0.03
Bolivian	2	0.02
Colombian	10	0.09
Ecuadorian	2	0.02
Peruvian	1	0.01
Uruguayan	11	0.10
Other Hispanic or Latino	111	1.05

Race*	Population	%
African-American/Black (423)	586	5.53
Not Hispanic (397)	541	5.11
Hispanic (26)	45	0.42
American Indian/Alaska Native (137)	295	2.79
Not Hispanic (118)	246	2.32
Hispanic (19)	49	0.46
Aleut *(Alaska Native)* (1)	5	0.05
Apache (0)	1	0.01
Blackfeet (5)	13	0.12
Canadian/French Am. Ind. (1)	3	0.03
Central American Ind. (0)	1	0.01
Cherokee (5)	28	0.26
Cheyenne (2)	2	0.02
Chickasaw (1)	1	0.01
Chippewa (4)	11	0.10
Choctaw (3)	5	0.05
Colville (30)	38	0.36
Cree (5)	7	0.07
Creek (0)	1	0.01
Crow (1)	2	0.02
Delaware (1)	3	0.03
Hopi (1)	1	0.01
Iroquois (1)	2	0.02
Kiowa (0)	1	0.01
Mexican American Ind. (1)	2	0.02
Navajo (1)	2	0.02
Osage (0)	1	0.01
Ottawa (2)	2	0.02
Paiute (2)	2	0.02
Potawatomi (1)	1	0.01
Puget Sound Salish (2)	6	0.06
Seminole (1)	1	0.01
Sioux (3)	7	0.07
Tlingit-Haida *(Alaska Native)* (6)	9	0.08
Tsimshian *(Alaska Native)* (1)	1	0.01
Yakama (4)	11	0.10
Yaqui (1)	1	0.01
Asian (424)	612	5.78
Not Hispanic (416)	588	5.55
Hispanic (8)	24	0.23
Bangladeshi (3)	3	0.03
Cambodian (6)	8	0.08
Chinese, ex. Taiwanese (111)	146	1.38
Filipino (73)	139	1.31
Indian (46)	51	0.48
Indonesian (0)	2	0.02
Japanese (66)	124	1.17
Korean (63)	98	0.93
Laotian (1)	1	0.01
Malaysian (2)	4	0.04
Taiwanese (10)	10	0.09
Thai (7)	14	0.13
Vietnamese (17)	19	0.18
Hawaii Native/Pacific Islander (45)	100	0.94
Not Hispanic (40)	87	0.82
Hispanic (5)	13	0.12
Guamanian/Chamorro (3)	7	0.07
Marshallese (0)	1	0.01
Native Hawaiian (13)	48	0.45
Samoan (19)	31	0.29
Tongan (1)	2	0.02
White (8,653)	9,097	85.90
Not Hispanic (8,199)	8,582	81.04
Hispanic (454)	515	4.86

College Place

Place Type: City
County: Walla Walla
Population: 8,765†

Ancestry‡	Population	%
African, Sub-Saharan (0)	22	0.26
African (0)	11	0.13
South African (0)	11	0.13
American (606)	606	7.13
Armenian (6)	6	0.07
Australian (0)	10	0.12
Austrian (0)	39	0.46
British (10)	25	0.29
Canadian (39)	39	0.46
Croatian (0)	8	0.09
Czech (4)	9	0.11
Czechoslovakian (0)	11	0.13
Danish (37)	203	2.39
Dutch (56)	155	1.82
English (394)	1,346	15.83
Estonian (0)	14	0.16
European (87)	187	2.20
Finnish (67)	67	0.79
French, ex. Basque (19)	430	5.06
French Canadian (0)	24	0.28
German (638)	2,024	23.81
Hungarian (0)	24	0.28
Irish (266)	966	11.36
Italian (125)	310	3.65
Macedonian (0)	9	0.11
Norwegian (142)	587	6.90
Pennsylvania German (0)	9	0.11
Polish (26)	40	0.47
Portuguese (0)	20	0.24
Romanian (24)	48	0.56
Russian (0)	185	2.18
Scandinavian (10)	19	0.22
Scotch-Irish (26)	147	1.73
Scottish (16)	414	4.87
Slavic (0)	9	0.11
Slovak (13)	13	0.15
Swedish (41)	453	5.33
Swiss (2)	118	1.39
Ukrainian (40)	105	1.24
Welsh (44)	122	1.43
West Indian, ex. Hispanic (17)	19	0.22
British West Indian (1)	1	0.01
Haitian (0)	2	0.02
Jamaican (16)	16	0.19
Yugoslavian (55)	55	0.65

Hispanic Origin	Population	%
Hispanic or Latino (of any race)	1,618	18.46
Central American, ex. Mexican	81	0.92
Costa Rican	8	0.09
Guatemalan	15	0.17
Honduran	2	0.02
Nicaraguan	9	0.10
Panamanian	4	0.05
Salvadoran	43	0.49
Cuban	15	0.17
Dominican Republic	8	0.09
Mexican	1,320	15.06
Puerto Rican	46	0.52
South American	76	0.87
Argentinean	14	0.16
Bolivian	6	0.07
Chilean	22	0.25
Colombian	12	0.14
Ecuadorian	8	0.09
Peruvian	13	0.15
Venezuelan	1	0.01
Other Hispanic or Latino	72	0.82

Race*	Population	%
African-American/Black (136)	178	2.03
Not Hispanic (128)	164	1.87
Hispanic (8)	14	0.16
American Indian/Alaska Native (59)	128	1.46
Not Hispanic (51)	114	1.30
Hispanic (8)	14	0.16
Aleut *(Alaska Native)* (0)	2	0.02
Apache (2)	2	0.02
Blackfeet (1)	2	0.02
Central American Ind. (1)	1	0.01
Cherokee (4)	22	0.25
Chippewa (2)	2	0.02
Choctaw (2)	7	0.08
Colville (0)	4	0.05
Comanche (1)	1	0.01
Cree (1)	1	0.01
Inupiat *(Alaska Native)* (1)	1	0.01
Iroquois (1)	10	0.11
Mexican American Ind. (1)	3	0.03
Navajo (0)	8	0.09
Potawatomi (0)	1	0.01
Puget Sound Salish (1)	1	0.01
Sioux (5)	11	0.13
Tlingit-Haida *(Alaska Native)* (7)	7	0.08
Yakama (0)	3	0.03
Asian (166)	260	2.97
Not Hispanic (154)	240	2.74
Hispanic (12)	20	0.23
Chinese, ex. Taiwanese (22)	44	0.50
Filipino (48)	80	0.91
Hmong (2)	2	0.02
Indian (18)	25	0.29
Indonesian (1)	2	0.02
Japanese (25)	56	0.64
Korean (25)	39	0.44
Laotian (4)	6	0.07
Nepalese (1)	1	0.01
Sri Lankan (2)	2	0.02
Taiwanese (0)	1	0.01

SECTION TWO

*Notes: † The Census 2010 population figure is used to calculate the percentages in the Hispanic Origin and Race categories. Ancestry percentages are based on the 2006-2010 American Community Survey population (not shown); ‡ Numbers in parentheses indicate the number of people reporting a single ancestry; * Numbers in parentheses indicate the number of persons reporting this race alone, not in combination with any other race; Please refer to the Explanation of Data for more information.*

Thai (5)	7	0.08
Vietnamese (2)	4	0.05
Hawaii Native/Pacific Islander (23)	52	0.59
Not Hispanic (22)	36	0.41
Hispanic (1)	16	0.18
Fijian (1)	1	0.01
Guamanian/Chamorro (3)	12	0.14
Native Hawaiian (9)	19	0.22
Samoan (8)	9	0.10
Tongan (0)	1	0.01
White (7,510)	7,761	88.55
Not Hispanic (6,606)	6,777	77.32
Hispanic (904)	984	11.23

Cottage Lake

Place Type: CDP
County: King
Population: 22,494†

Ancestry‡	Population	%
African, Sub-Saharan (11)	21	0.09
South African (11)	21	0.09
American (1,001)	1,001	4.50
Arab (33)	92	0.41
Lebanese (12)	29	0.13
Moroccan (0)	8	0.04
Syrian (9)	43	0.19
Other Arab (12)	12	0.05
Armenian (80)	177	0.80
Australian (21)	47	0.21
Austrian (8)	163	0.73
Belgian (0)	46	0.21
Brazilian (12)	12	0.05
British (282)	398	1.79
Canadian (87)	131	0.59
Celtic (21)	21	0.09
Croatian (0)	28	0.13
Czech (8)	46	0.21
Czechoslovakian (22)	22	0.10
Danish (195)	628	2.82
Dutch (152)	644	2.90
Eastern European (32)	32	0.14
English (911)	4,047	18.20
European (597)	699	3.14
Finnish (101)	239	1.08
French, ex. Basque (73)	835	3.76
French Canadian (12)	160	0.72
German (949)	5,005	22.51
Greek (41)	143	0.64
Hungarian (72)	373	1.68
Icelander (12)	35	0.16
Iranian (31)	41	0.18
Irish (527)	2,821	12.69
Israeli (37)	37	0.17
Italian (365)	1,155	5.20
Latvian (18)	18	0.08
Lithuanian (0)	80	0.36
Northern European (92)	102	0.46
Norwegian (572)	1,838	8.27
Pennsylvania German (10)	19	0.09
Polish (178)	823	3.70
Portuguese (0)	26	0.12
Romanian (12)	25	0.11
Russian (179)	361	1.62
Scandinavian (222)	347	1.56
Scotch-Irish (119)	411	1.85
Scottish (242)	915	4.12
Serbian (0)	10	0.04
Slavic (19)	34	0.15
Slovak (0)	11	0.05
Swedish (339)	1,355	6.09
Swiss (40)	288	1.30
Turkish (18)	18	0.08
Ukrainian (14)	14	0.06
Welsh (33)	257	1.16
West Indian, ex. Hispanic (70)	70	0.31
Jamaican (70)	70	0.31

Hispanic Origin	Population	%
Hispanic or Latino (of any race)	800	3.56
Central American, ex. Mexican	73	0.32
Costa Rican	1	<0.01
Guatemalan	34	0.15
Honduran	5	0.02
Nicaraguan	14	0.06
Panamanian	3	0.01
Salvadoran	16	0.07
Cuban	27	0.12
Dominican Republic	2	0.01
Mexican	453	2.01
Puerto Rican	38	0.17
South American	101	0.45
Argentinean	15	0.07
Bolivian	1	<0.01
Chilean	20	0.09
Colombian	35	0.16
Ecuadorian	9	0.04
Paraguayan	2	0.01
Peruvian	12	0.05
Uruguayan	2	0.01
Venezuelan	4	0.02
Other South American	1	<0.01
Other Hispanic or Latino	106	0.47

Race*	Population	%
African-American/Black (158)	263	1.17
Not Hispanic (156)	254	1.13
Hispanic (2)	9	0.04
American Indian/Alaska Native (85)	259	1.15
Not Hispanic (77)	225	1.00
Hispanic (8)	34	0.15
Alaska Athabascan *(Ala. Nat.)* (1)	4	0.02
Aleut *(Alaska Native)* (0)	3	0.01
Apache (2)	2	0.01
Blackfeet (1)	8	0.04
Cherokee (6)	43	0.19
Chippewa (4)	6	0.03
Choctaw (7)	11	0.05
Comanche (1)	1	<0.01
Cree (0)	5	0.02
Creek (0)	2	0.01
Hopi (1)	4	0.02
Inupiat *(Alaska Native)* (0)	1	<0.01
Iroquois (0)	3	0.01
Lumbee (0)	1	<0.01
Mexican American Ind. (3)	3	0.01
Osage (0)	4	0.02
Pueblo (1)	1	<0.01
Puget Sound Salish (9)	14	0.06
Sioux (2)	5	0.02
South American Ind. (1)	3	0.01
Spanish American Ind. (0)	3	0.01
Tlingit-Haida *(Alaska Native)* (4)	10	0.04
Tsimshian *(Alaska Native)* (0)	4	0.02
Ute (0)	2	0.01
Yup'ik *(Alaska Native)* (1)	2	0.01
Asian (1,184)	1,675	7.45
Not Hispanic (1,172)	1,633	7.26
Hispanic (12)	42	0.19
Bangladeshi (5)	5	0.02
Burmese (5)	5	0.02
Cambodian (16)	25	0.11
Chinese, ex. Taiwanese (293)	420	1.87
Filipino (83)	202	0.90
Hmong (10)	15	0.07
Indian (180)	216	0.96
Indonesian (4)	6	0.03
Japanese (201)	372	1.65
Korean (159)	236	1.05
Laotian (5)	5	0.02
Nepalese (0)	1	<0.01
Pakistani (20)	23	0.10
Sri Lankan (7)	7	0.03
Taiwanese (41)	49	0.22
Thai (31)	43	0.19
Vietnamese (53)	74	0.33
Hawaii Native/Pacific Islander (32)	73	0.32
Not Hispanic (31)	68	0.30
Hispanic (1)	5	0.02
Guamanian/Chamorro (5)	7	0.03
Native Hawaiian (20)	45	0.20
Samoan (0)	5	0.02
White (20,031)	20,794	92.44
Not Hispanic (19,515)	20,181	89.72
Hispanic (516)	613	2.73

Covington

Place Type: City
County: King
Population: 17,575†

Ancestry‡	Population	%
African, Sub-Saharan (25)	37	0.22
African (11)	11	0.07
Nigerian (14)	14	0.08
Other Sub-Saharan African (0)	12	0.07
Albanian (20)	20	0.12
American (577)	577	3.43
Arab (32)	43	0.26
Egyptian (0)	11	0.07
Other Arab (32)	32	0.19
Australian (0)	14	0.08
Austrian (0)	40	0.24
Basque (0)	8	0.05
British (0)	9	0.05
Canadian (11)	24	0.14
Czech (39)	102	0.61
Czechoslovakian (0)	14	0.08
Danish (28)	193	1.15
Dutch (125)	317	1.89
English (842)	3,024	17.99
European (413)	433	2.58
Finnish (9)	52	0.31
French, ex. Basque (59)	525	3.12
French Canadian (70)	202	1.20
German (1,289)	3,927	23.36
Greek (13)	13	0.08
Hungarian (0)	48	0.29
Icelander (7)	21	0.12
Irish (623)	2,312	13.75
Italian (152)	617	3.67
Lithuanian (93)	93	0.55
Norwegian (278)	823	4.89
Polish (31)	306	1.82
Portuguese (9)	74	0.44
Russian (40)	81	0.48
Scandinavian (106)	133	0.79
Scotch-Irish (66)	480	2.85
Scottish (129)	724	4.31
Slovak (0)	19	0.11
Slovene (0)	8	0.05
Swedish (142)	460	2.74
Swiss (23)	86	0.51
Turkish (0)	42	0.25
Ukrainian (244)	291	1.73
Welsh (28)	112	0.67
West Indian, ex. Hispanic (0)	15	0.09
Jamaican (0)	15	0.09
Yugoslavian (0)	23	0.14

Hispanic Origin	Population	%
Hispanic or Latino (of any race)	1,634	9.30
Central American, ex. Mexican	90	0.51
Costa Rican	5	0.03
Guatemalan	28	0.16
Honduran	6	0.03
Nicaraguan	10	0.06
Panamanian	7	0.04
Salvadoran	34	0.19
Cuban	17	0.10
Dominican Republic	3	0.02
Mexican	1,199	6.82
Puerto Rican	85	0.48
South American	70	0.40
Argentinean	7	0.04
Chilean	7	0.04
Colombian	22	0.13

*Notes: † The Census 2010 population figure is used to calculate the percentages in the Hispanic Origin and Race categories. Ancestry percentages are based on the 2006-2010 American Community Survey population (not shown); ‡ Numbers in parentheses indicate the number of people reporting a single ancestry; * Numbers in parentheses indicate the number of persons reporting this race alone, not in combination with any other race; Please refer to the Explanation of Data for more information.*

Ecuadorian	9	0.05
Peruvian	21	0.12
Venezuelan	4	0.02
Other Hispanic or Latino	170	0.97

Race*	Population	%
African-American/Black (741)	1,033	5.88
Not Hispanic (714)	967	5.50
Hispanic (27)	66	0.38
American Indian/Alaska Native (145)	429	2.44
Not Hispanic (118)	358	2.04
Hispanic (27)	71	0.40
Alaska Athabascan *(Ala. Nat.)* (1)	3	0.02
Aleut *(Alaska Native)* (1)	5	0.03
Apache (3)	10	0.06
Blackfeet (8)	24	0.14
Canadian/French Am. Ind. (3)	10	0.06
Cherokee (13)	41	0.23
Cheyenne (1)	6	0.03
Chickasaw (0)	2	0.01
Chippewa (4)	12	0.07
Choctaw (1)	4	0.02
Colville (5)	6	0.03
Cree (1)	3	0.02
Creek (0)	3	0.02
Crow (0)	3	0.02
Delaware (0)	1	0.01
Inupiat *(Alaska Native)* (0)	2	0.01
Iroquois (0)	7	0.04
Mexican American Ind. (7)	11	0.06
Navajo (0)	2	0.01
Ottawa (0)	1	0.01
Pima (2)	3	0.02
Potawatomi (1)	1	0.01
Puget Sound Salish (8)	15	0.09
Sioux (3)	17	0.10
South American Ind. (0)	3	0.02
Tlingit-Haida *(Alaska Native)* (10)	26	0.15
Tsimshian *(Alaska Native)* (3)	6	0.03
Yakama (2)	4	0.02
Yaqui (0)	1	0.01
Yup'ik *(Alaska Native)* (3)	3	0.02
Asian (1,491)	1,938	11.03
Not Hispanic (1,469)	1,880	10.70
Hispanic (22)	58	0.33
Bangladeshi (1)	2	0.01
Burmese (10)	10	0.06
Cambodian (48)	58	0.33
Chinese, ex. Taiwanese (154)	232	1.32
Filipino (467)	650	3.70
Hmong (8)	13	0.07
Indian (257)	283	1.61
Indonesian (4)	10	0.06
Japanese (101)	218	1.24
Korean (153)	208	1.18
Laotian (37)	49	0.28
Nepalese (7)	7	0.04
Pakistani (10)	19	0.11
Sri Lankan (0)	1	0.01
Taiwanese (6)	10	0.06
Thai (20)	32	0.18
Vietnamese (133)	174	0.99
Hawaii Native/Pacific Islander (100)	192	1.09
Not Hispanic (98)	176	1.00
Hispanic (2)	16	0.09
Fijian (9)	10	0.06
Guamanian/Chamorro (5)	17	0.10
Native Hawaiian (15)	52	0.30
Samoan (43)	60	0.34
Tongan (1)	9	0.05
White (13,378)	14,297	81.35
Not Hispanic (12,680)	13,426	76.39
Hispanic (698)	871	4.96

Des Moines

Place Type: City
County: King
Population: 29,673†

Ancestry‡	Population	%
African, Sub-Saharan (1,639)	1,689	5.74
African (373)	386	1.31
Ethiopian (603)	603	2.05
Somalian (535)	535	1.82
South African (0)	37	0.13
Other Sub-Saharan African (128)	128	0.44
American (976)	976	3.32
Arab (91)	91	0.31
Lebanese (16)	16	0.05
Other Arab (75)	75	0.26
Armenian (44)	130	0.44
Austrian (25)	165	0.56
Belgian (18)	18	0.06
Brazilian (0)	18	0.06
British (86)	188	0.64
Cajun (27)	80	0.27
Canadian (37)	125	0.43
Croatian (0)	29	0.10
Czech (44)	205	0.70
Danish (31)	262	0.89
Dutch (35)	445	1.51
English (989)	3,670	12.48
European (276)	282	0.96
Finnish (13)	63	0.21
French, ex. Basque (122)	815	2.77
French Canadian (28)	189	0.64
German (1,377)	4,911	16.70
Greek (8)	60	0.20
Hungarian (24)	112	0.38
Icelander (0)	11	0.04
Irish (876)	2,727	9.28
Italian (211)	649	2.21
Latvian (0)	14	0.05
Lithuanian (31)	80	0.27
Luxemburger (37)	37	0.13
Maltese (7)	7	0.02
Northern European (234)	234	0.80
Norwegian (652)	2,098	7.14
Polish (32)	264	0.90
Portuguese (33)	89	0.30
Russian (70)	211	0.72
Scandinavian (50)	202	0.69
Scotch-Irish (274)	715	2.43
Scottish (212)	794	2.70
Serbian (0)	10	0.03
Slavic (0)	9	0.03
Slovak (73)	139	0.47
Slovene (0)	30	0.10
Swedish (247)	984	3.35
Swiss (34)	93	0.32
Ukrainian (11)	38	0.13
Welsh (17)	199	0.68
West Indian, ex. Hispanic (189)	189	0.64
Haitian (144)	144	0.49
Jamaican (45)	45	0.15
Yugoslavian (47)	123	0.42

Hispanic Origin	Population	%
Hispanic or Latino (of any race)	4,500	15.17
Central American, ex. Mexican	398	1.34
Costa Rican	9	0.03
Guatemalan	122	0.41
Honduran	56	0.19
Nicaraguan	23	0.08
Panamanian	23	0.08
Salvadoran	157	0.53
Other Central American	8	0.03
Cuban	38	0.13
Dominican Republic	13	0.04
Mexican	3,445	11.61
Puerto Rican	128	0.43
South American	111	0.37
Argentinean	6	0.02
Bolivian	1	<0.01
Chilean	21	0.07
Colombian	21	0.07
Ecuadorian	13	0.04
Paraguayan	2	0.01
Peruvian	35	0.12
Venezuelan	12	0.04
Other Hispanic or Latino	367	1.24

Race*	Population	%
African-American/Black (2,695)	3,233	10.90
Not Hispanic (2,605)	3,070	10.35
Hispanic (90)	163	0.55
American Indian/Alaska Native (317)	733	2.47
Not Hispanic (257)	589	1.98
Hispanic (60)	144	0.49
Alaska Athabascan *(Ala. Nat.)* (6)	6	0.02
Aleut *(Alaska Native)* (8)	19	0.06
Apache (1)	11	0.04
Arapaho (0)	2	0.01
Blackfeet (9)	39	0.13
Canadian/French Am. Ind. (8)	18	0.06
Central American Ind. (12)	12	0.04
Cherokee (14)	90	0.30
Cheyenne (0)	1	<0.01
Chickasaw (1)	4	0.01
Chippewa (22)	28	0.09
Choctaw (7)	17	0.06
Colville (1)	6	0.02
Cree (0)	5	0.02
Creek (0)	1	<0.01
Crow (0)	3	0.01
Delaware (0)	3	0.01
Inupiat *(Alaska Native)* (5)	6	0.02
Iroquois (1)	11	0.04
Mexican American Ind. (7)	9	0.03
Navajo (5)	10	0.03
Osage (0)	2	0.01
Ottawa (1)	1	<0.01
Paiute (0)	5	0.02
Potawatomi (3)	4	0.01
Pueblo (0)	3	0.01
Puget Sound Salish (40)	50	0.17
Shoshone (0)	1	<0.01
Sioux (10)	32	0.11
South American Ind. (0)	3	0.01
Spanish American Ind. (0)	1	<0.01
Tlingit-Haida *(Alaska Native)* (13)	37	0.12
Tohono O'Odham (1)	1	<0.01
Tsimshian *(Alaska Native)* (6)	9	0.03
Yakama (2)	5	0.02
Yup'ik *(Alaska Native)* (3)	3	0.01
Asian (3,163)	3,814	12.85
Not Hispanic (3,106)	3,688	12.43
Hispanic (57)	126	0.42
Burmese (6)	9	0.03
Cambodian (226)	265	0.89
Chinese, ex. Taiwanese (224)	339	1.14
Filipino (1,031)	1,334	4.50
Hmong (45)	48	0.16
Indian (269)	327	1.10
Indonesian (4)	8	0.03
Japanese (172)	330	1.11
Korean (233)	287	0.97
Laotian (134)	176	0.59
Malaysian (3)	3	0.01
Nepalese (7)	8	0.03
Pakistani (9)	18	0.06
Sri Lankan (2)	3	0.01
Taiwanese (4)	4	0.01
Thai (38)	81	0.27
Vietnamese (613)	690	2.33
Hawaii Native/Pacific Islander (715)	925	3.12
Not Hispanic (699)	874	2.95
Hispanic (16)	51	0.17
Fijian (22)	26	0.09
Guamanian/Chamorro (38)	64	0.22
Marshallese (22)	25	0.08
Native Hawaiian (33)	83	0.28
Samoan (427)	496	1.67
Tongan (42)	51	0.17
White (18,857)	20,213	68.12
Not Hispanic (17,212)	18,278	61.60
Hispanic (1,645)	1,935	6.52

*Notes: † The Census 2010 population figure is used to calculate the percentages in the Hispanic Origin and Race categories. Ancestry percentages are based on the 2006-2010 American Community Survey population (not shown); ‡ Numbers in parentheses indicate the number of people reporting a single ancestry; * Numbers in parentheses indicate the number of persons reporting this race alone, not in combination with any other race; Please refer to the Explanation of Data for more information.*

DuPont

Place Type: City
County: Pierce
Population: 8,199†

Ancestry‡	Population	%
African, Sub-Saharan (39)	39	0.55
African (39)	39	0.55
American (274)	274	3.84
Arab (0)	32	0.45
Lebanese (0)	32	0.45
Australian (0)	12	0.17
Austrian (0)	60	0.84
British (30)	35	0.49
Canadian (0)	32	0.45
Czech (16)	24	0.34
Dutch (0)	48	0.67
Eastern European (30)	30	0.42
English (321)	888	12.44
European (349)	385	5.39
French, ex. Basque (30)	164	2.30
French Canadian (10)	19	0.27
German (435)	1,598	22.38
German Russian (10)	10	0.14
Greek (18)	84	1.18
Hungarian (38)	56	0.78
Irish (333)	1,218	17.06
Italian (139)	408	5.71
Lithuanian (6)	6	0.08
Norwegian (49)	193	2.70
Polish (7)	62	0.87
Portuguese (0)	11	0.15
Russian (46)	87	1.22
Scandinavian (32)	87	1.22
Scotch-Irish (88)	171	2.39
Scottish (61)	167	2.34
Swedish (43)	242	3.39
Swiss (0)	3	0.04
Ukrainian (0)	4	0.06
Welsh (0)	31	0.43
West Indian, ex. Hispanic (28)	61	0.85
Jamaican (12)	12	0.17
West Indian (16)	49	0.69
Yugoslavian (0)	13	0.18

Hispanic Origin	Population	%
Hispanic or Latino (of any race)	792	9.66
Central American, ex. Mexican	76	0.93
Costa Rican	1	0.01
Guatemalan	14	0.17
Honduran	14	0.17
Nicaraguan	2	0.02
Panamanian	35	0.43
Salvadoran	9	0.11
Other Central American	1	0.01
Cuban	6	0.07
Dominican Republic	8	0.10
Mexican	413	5.04
Puerto Rican	169	2.06
South American	42	0.51
Bolivian	6	0.07
Colombian	15	0.18
Ecuadorian	3	0.04
Peruvian	13	0.16
Venezuelan	5	0.06
Other Hispanic or Latino	78	0.95

Race*	Population	%
African-American/Black (664)	932	11.37
Not Hispanic (624)	845	10.31
Hispanic (40)	87	1.06
American Indian/Alaska Native (42)	145	1.77
Not Hispanic (39)	121	1.48
Hispanic (3)	24	0.29
Apache (0)	8	0.10
Blackfeet (1)	1	0.01
Canadian/French Am. Ind. (1)	1	0.01
Cherokee (2)	22	0.27
Chippewa (0)	1	0.01
Choctaw (6)	8	0.10
Creek (1)	2	0.02
Hopi (0)	5	0.06
Houma (0)	2	0.02
Mexican American Ind. (2)	13	0.16
Navajo (2)	7	0.09
Paiute (0)	1	0.01
Potawatomi (2)	2	0.02
Pueblo (1)	2	0.02
Puget Sound Salish (1)	2	0.02
Seminole (0)	3	0.04
Sioux (2)	7	0.09
Yakama (1)	1	0.01
Asian (833)	1,225	14.94
Not Hispanic (817)	1,168	14.25
Hispanic (16)	57	0.70
Cambodian (4)	4	0.05
Chinese, ex. Taiwanese (54)	101	1.23
Filipino (395)	558	6.81
Indian (17)	23	0.28
Indonesian (1)	4	0.05
Japanese (35)	111	1.35
Korean (249)	361	4.40
Laotian (5)	10	0.12
Malaysian (0)	1	0.01
Pakistani (5)	8	0.10
Taiwanese (5)	6	0.07
Thai (12)	21	0.26
Vietnamese (23)	46	0.56
Hawaii Native/Pacific Islander (90)	166	2.02
Not Hispanic (84)	152	1.85
Hispanic (6)	14	0.17
Fijian (0)	2	0.02
Guamanian/Chamorro (30)	49	0.60
Marshallese (1)	1	0.01
Native Hawaiian (18)	55	0.67
Samoan (30)	36	0.44
White (5,631)	6,246	76.18
Not Hispanic (5,229)	5,725	69.83
Hispanic (402)	521	6.35

East Hill-Meridian

Place Type: CDP
County: King
Population: 29,878†

Ancestry‡	Population	%
African, Sub-Saharan (595)	692	2.39
African (171)	268	0.93
Ethiopian (163)	163	0.56
Kenyan (21)	21	0.07
Nigerian (124)	124	0.43
Somalian (116)	116	0.40
American (970)	970	3.36
Arab (127)	178	0.62
Arab (0)	9	0.03
Iraqi (0)	32	0.11
Lebanese (0)	10	0.03
Other Arab (127)	127	0.44
Armenian (11)	11	0.04
Austrian (0)	10	0.03
Basque (31)	31	0.11
Belgian (30)	30	0.10
British (98)	227	0.79
Bulgarian (42)	42	0.15
Canadian (27)	43	0.15
Carpatho Rusyn (12)	12	0.04
Celtic (15)	15	0.05
Croatian (0)	77	0.27
Czech (36)	153	0.53
Czechoslovakian (44)	93	0.32
Danish (155)	408	1.41
Dutch (110)	500	1.73
Eastern European (14)	14	0.05
English (514)	2,516	8.70
Estonian (0)	41	0.14
European (158)	218	0.75
Finnish (82)	190	0.66
French, ex. Basque (99)	1,151	3.98
French Canadian (62)	187	0.65
German (1,439)	4,861	16.82
Greek (33)	87	0.30
Hungarian (12)	22	0.08
Irish (436)	2,237	7.74
Italian (242)	775	2.68
Latvian (33)	96	0.33
Lithuanian (14)	14	0.05
Northern European (49)	49	0.17
Norwegian (392)	1,195	4.13
Polish (29)	300	1.04
Portuguese (0)	8	0.03
Romanian (414)	455	1.57
Russian (287)	400	1.38
Scandinavian (87)	178	0.62
Scotch-Irish (149)	371	1.28
Scottish (201)	877	3.03
Slavic (21)	21	0.07
Slovene (0)	47	0.16
Swedish (156)	772	2.67
Swiss (0)	66	0.23
Ukrainian (627)	647	2.24
Welsh (58)	301	1.04
West Indian, ex. Hispanic (30)	90	0.31
Barbadian (30)	90	0.31
Yugoslavian (20)	73	0.25

Hispanic Origin	Population	%
Hispanic or Latino (of any race)	2,692	9.01
Central American, ex. Mexican	218	0.73
Costa Rican	1	<0.01
Guatemalan	68	0.23
Honduran	40	0.13
Nicaraguan	13	0.04
Panamanian	9	0.03
Salvadoran	80	0.27
Other Central American	7	0.02
Cuban	30	0.10
Dominican Republic	18	0.06
Mexican	2,007	6.72
Puerto Rican	72	0.24
South American	114	0.38
Argentinean	11	0.04
Bolivian	10	0.03
Chilean	23	0.08
Colombian	33	0.11
Ecuadorian	13	0.04
Peruvian	13	0.04
Venezuelan	9	0.03
Other South American	2	0.01
Other Hispanic or Latino	233	0.78

Race*	Population	%
African-American/Black (2,337)	2,868	9.60
Not Hispanic (2,292)	2,755	9.22
Hispanic (45)	113	0.38
American Indian/Alaska Native (170)	516	1.73
Not Hispanic (125)	420	1.41
Hispanic (45)	96	0.32
Alaska Athabascan *(Ala. Nat.)* (1)	4	0.01
Aleut *(Alaska Native)* (5)	11	0.04
Apache (2)	6	0.02
Arapaho (6)	9	0.03
Blackfeet (10)	25	0.08
Canadian/French Am. Ind. (6)	7	0.02
Central American Ind. (1)	7	0.02
Cherokee (9)	60	0.20
Chickasaw (0)	3	0.01
Chippewa (6)	20	0.07
Choctaw (0)	1	<0.01
Colville (8)	9	0.03
Cree (0)	1	<0.01
Creek (0)	1	<0.01
Crow (0)	5	0.02
Inupiat *(Alaska Native)* (2)	9	0.03
Iroquois (5)	14	0.05
Lumbee (0)	1	<0.01
Mexican American Ind. (14)	18	0.06
Navajo (1)	2	0.01
Paiute (0)	1	<0.01

*Notes: † The Census 2010 population figure is used to calculate the percentages in the Hispanic Origin and Race categories. Ancestry percentages are based on the 2006-2010 American Community Survey population (not shown); ‡ Numbers in parentheses indicate the number of people reporting a single ancestry; * Numbers in parentheses indicate the number of persons reporting this race alone, not in combination with any other race; Please refer to the Explanation of Data for more information.*

Pima (0)	1	<0.01
Potawatomi (4)	4	0.01
Puget Sound Salish (10)	28	0.09
Seminole (0)	1	<0.01
Sioux (2)	8	0.03
South American Ind. (0)	2	0.01
Tlingit-Haida *(Alaska Native)* (11)	34	0.11
Tsimshian *(Alaska Native)* (2)	5	0.02
Yaqui (0)	2	0.01
Asian (7,030)	7,920	26.51
Not Hispanic (6,984)	7,797	26.10
Hispanic (46)	123	0.41
Bangladeshi (9)	10	0.03
Bhutanese (34)	36	0.12
Burmese (26)	28	0.09
Cambodian (428)	476	1.59
Chinese, ex. Taiwanese (772)	981	3.28
Filipino (1,595)	1,977	6.62
Hmong (57)	60	0.20
Indian (1,623)	1,727	5.78
Indonesian (17)	24	0.08
Japanese (247)	462	1.55
Korean (239)	313	1.05
Laotian (366)	419	1.40
Malaysian (0)	2	0.01
Nepalese (10)	12	0.04
Pakistani (60)	68	0.23
Taiwanese (13)	16	0.05
Thai (23)	43	0.14
Vietnamese (1,246)	1,395	4.67
Hawaii Native/Pacific Islander (404)	619	2.07
Not Hispanic (398)	604	2.02
Hispanic (6)	15	0.05
Fijian (87)	96	0.32
Guamanian/Chamorro (23)	34	0.11
Native Hawaiian (42)	137	0.46
Samoan (164)	215	0.72
Tongan (47)	48	0.16
White (17,017)	18,287	61.21
Not Hispanic (15,944)	16,997	56.89
Hispanic (1,073)	1,290	4.32

East Renton Highlands

Place Type: CDP
County: King
Population: 11,140†

Ancestry‡	Population	%
African, Sub-Saharan (10)	50	0.45
African (0)	40	0.36
Kenyan (10)	10	0.09
American (476)	476	4.31
Armenian (16)	32	0.29
Austrian (39)	39	0.35
Belgian (0)	13	0.12
Brazilian (32)	32	0.29
British (24)	66	0.60
Canadian (51)	51	0.46
Croatian (12)	103	0.93
Czech (0)	20	0.18
Danish (0)	132	1.20
Dutch (77)	283	2.56
Eastern European (50)	50	0.45
English (453)	2,017	18.27
Estonian (16)	32	0.29
European (282)	315	2.85
Finnish (34)	216	1.96
French, ex. Basque (54)	436	3.95
French Canadian (10)	65	0.59
German (638)	2,863	25.94
Greek (0)	69	0.63
Hungarian (0)	13	0.12
Irish (413)	1,522	13.79
Italian (46)	272	2.46
Latvian (19)	19	0.17
Lithuanian (0)	7	0.06
Northern European (0)	12	0.11
Norwegian (218)	703	6.37
Polish (29)	284	2.57
Portuguese (23)	50	0.45
Romanian (80)	96	0.87
Russian (141)	192	1.74
Scandinavian (83)	198	1.79
Scotch-Irish (185)	339	3.07
Scottish (135)	527	4.77
Swedish (137)	583	5.28
Swiss (21)	90	0.82
Ukrainian (0)	10	0.09
Welsh (0)	216	1.96
West Indian, ex. Hispanic (0)	12	0.11
Jamaican (0)	12	0.11
Yugoslavian (12)	34	0.31

Hispanic Origin	Population	%
Hispanic or Latino (of any race)	719	6.45
Central American, ex. Mexican	31	0.28
Guatemalan	17	0.15
Honduran	2	0.02
Nicaraguan	3	0.03
Panamanian	4	0.04
Salvadoran	5	0.04
Cuban	12	0.11
Mexican	547	4.91
Puerto Rican	30	0.27
South American	34	0.31
Argentinean	3	0.03
Chilean	1	0.01
Colombian	5	0.04
Ecuadorian	9	0.08
Peruvian	14	0.13
Venezuelan	2	0.02
Other Hispanic or Latino	65	0.58

Race*	Population	%
African-American/Black (158)	263	2.36
Not Hispanic (155)	251	2.25
Hispanic (3)	12	0.11
American Indian/Alaska Native (80)	196	1.76
Not Hispanic (73)	176	1.58
Hispanic (7)	20	0.18
Alaska Athabascan *(Ala. Nat.)* (0)	2	0.02
Aleut *(Alaska Native)* (7)	15	0.13
Apache (2)	2	0.02
Blackfeet (2)	20	0.18
Canadian/French Am. Ind. (2)	7	0.06
Cherokee (2)	12	0.11
Chippewa (7)	15	0.13
Choctaw (0)	4	0.04
Colville (2)	4	0.04
Lumbee (2)	2	0.02
Osage (1)	1	0.01
Potawatomi (0)	2	0.02
Puget Sound Salish (11)	13	0.12
Seminole (0)	3	0.03
Shoshone (4)	4	0.04
Sioux (1)	6	0.05
Tlingit-Haida *(Alaska Native)* (5)	7	0.06
Yakama (0)	1	0.01
Asian (518)	709	6.36
Not Hispanic (517)	698	6.27
Hispanic (1)	11	0.10
Cambodian (7)	12	0.11
Chinese, ex. Taiwanese (93)	143	1.28
Filipino (72)	141	1.27
Indian (28)	36	0.32
Indonesian (2)	3	0.03
Japanese (98)	177	1.59
Korean (40)	59	0.53
Laotian (15)	19	0.17
Pakistani (6)	6	0.05
Taiwanese (1)	3	0.03
Thai (5)	10	0.09
Vietnamese (119)	133	1.19
Hawaii Native/Pacific Islander (37)	73	0.66
Not Hispanic (37)	70	0.63
Hispanic (0)	3	0.03
Fijian (6)	6	0.05
Guamanian/Chamorro (8)	8	0.07
Native Hawaiian (11)	28	0.25
Samoan (3)	15	0.13
Tongan (3)	4	0.04
White (9,618)	10,022	89.96
Not Hispanic (9,259)	9,601	86.18
Hispanic (359)	421	3.78

East Wenatchee

Place Type: City
County: Douglas
Population: 13,190†

Ancestry‡	Population	%
American (800)	800	6.23
Arab (29)	34	0.26
Lebanese (29)	29	0.23
Syrian (0)	5	0.04
Armenian (11)	11	0.09
Austrian (0)	7	0.05
Belgian (9)	9	0.07
British (9)	36	0.28
Bulgarian (0)	7	0.05
Canadian (18)	30	0.23
Carpatho Rusyn (0)	7	0.05
Celtic (0)	17	0.13
Croatian (7)	7	0.05
Czech (0)	74	0.58
Czechoslovakian (0)	10	0.08
Danish (24)	158	1.23
Dutch (90)	351	2.73
English (287)	1,280	9.97
European (109)	109	0.85
Finnish (8)	15	0.12
French, ex. Basque (55)	546	4.25
French Canadian (37)	81	0.63
German (616)	2,270	17.67
Hungarian (40)	50	0.39
Icelander (0)	33	0.26
Irish (377)	1,225	9.54
Israeli (0)	26	0.20
Italian (68)	441	3.43
Norwegian (325)	862	6.71
Polish (61)	156	1.21
Portuguese (15)	15	0.12
Romanian (19)	19	0.15
Russian (8)	34	0.26
Scandinavian (41)	67	0.52
Scotch-Irish (58)	314	2.44
Scottish (175)	437	3.40
Slovak (4)	11	0.09
Swedish (154)	383	2.98
Swiss (26)	75	0.58
Ukrainian (10)	49	0.38
Welsh (20)	110	0.86

Hispanic Origin	Population	%
Hispanic or Latino (of any race)	3,092	23.44
Central American, ex. Mexican	93	0.71
Guatemalan	29	0.22
Honduran	8	0.06
Panamanian	5	0.04
Salvadoran	51	0.39
Cuban	5	0.04
Dominican Republic	2	0.02
Mexican	2,815	21.34
Puerto Rican	9	0.07
South American	18	0.14
Colombian	7	0.05
Ecuadorian	4	0.03
Peruvian	4	0.03
Venezuelan	3	0.02
Other Hispanic or Latino	150	1.14

Race*	Population	%
African-American/Black (33)	103	0.78
Not Hispanic (24)	77	0.58
Hispanic (9)	26	0.20
American Indian/Alaska Native (159)	285	2.16
Not Hispanic (121)	215	1.63
Hispanic (38)	70	0.53

*Notes: † The Census 2010 population figure is used to calculate the percentages in the Hispanic Origin and Race categories. Ancestry percentages are based on the 2006-2010 American Community Survey population (not shown); ‡ Numbers in parentheses indicate the number of people reporting a single ancestry; * Numbers in parentheses indicate the number of persons reporting this race alone, not in combination with any other race; Please refer to the Explanation of Data for more information.*

Aleut *(Alaska Native)* (1)	2	0.02
Apache (2)	2	0.02
Blackfeet (1)	4	0.03
Canadian/French Am. Ind. (12)	13	0.10
Cherokee (12)	34	0.26
Cheyenne (2)	2	0.02
Chickasaw (0)	3	0.02
Chippewa (6)	13	0.10
Choctaw (2)	5	0.04
Colville (22)	30	0.23
Cree (2)	3	0.02
Hopi (1)	1	0.01
Inupiat *(Alaska Native)* (2)	3	0.02
Iroquois (0)	2	0.02
Mexican American Ind. (11)	25	0.19
Navajo (1)	3	0.02
Paiute (0)	1	0.01
Potawatomi (0)	2	0.02
Puget Sound Salish (3)	9	0.07
Sioux (4)	8	0.06
Tlingit-Haida *(Alaska Native)* (7)	10	0.08
Tsimshian *(Alaska Native)* (2)	2	0.02
Yakama (2)	2	0.02
Asian (125)	229	1.74
Not Hispanic (118)	202	1.53
Hispanic (7)	27	0.20
Cambodian (5)	8	0.06
Chinese, ex. Taiwanese (29)	38	0.29
Filipino (32)	65	0.49
Indian (12)	16	0.12
Indonesian (1)	1	0.01
Japanese (10)	29	0.22
Korean (10)	15	0.11
Laotian (8)	8	0.06
Thai (2)	11	0.08
Vietnamese (11)	21	0.16
Hawaii Native/Pacific Islander (16)	46	0.35
Not Hispanic (15)	40	0.30
Hispanic (1)	6	0.05
Fijian (1)	4	0.03
Guamanian/Chamorro (6)	13	0.10
Native Hawaiian (3)	17	0.13
Samoan (2)	12	0.09
White (10,562)	10,976	83.21
Not Hispanic (9,560)	9,797	74.28
Hispanic (1,002)	1,179	8.94

Eastmont

Place Type: CDP
County: Snohomish
Population: 20,101†

Ancestry‡	Population	%
African, Sub-Saharan (10)	10	0.05
Nigerian (10)	10	0.05
American (787)	787	4.07
Arab (43)	68	0.35
Arab (43)	43	0.22
Lebanese (0)	25	0.13
Armenian (91)	91	0.47
Austrian (8)	38	0.20
Belgian (23)	36	0.19
Brazilian (5)	5	0.03
British (107)	133	0.69
Canadian (70)	190	0.98
Croatian (10)	27	0.14
Czech (52)	133	0.69
Czechoslovakian (11)	40	0.21
Danish (42)	206	1.06
Dutch (76)	446	2.30
English (517)	2,488	12.85
European (444)	500	2.58
Finnish (64)	162	0.84
French, ex. Basque (117)	720	3.72
French Canadian (14)	66	0.34
German (1,206)	5,226	27.00
Greek (14)	21	0.11
Hungarian (12)	53	0.27
Iranian (79)	79	0.41
Irish (554)	2,616	13.52
Italian (210)	559	2.89
Lithuanian (8)	45	0.23
Luxemburger (13)	13	0.07
Northern European (40)	70	0.36
Norwegian (513)	1,973	10.19
Pennsylvania German (26)	91	0.47
Polish (195)	392	2.03
Portuguese (12)	53	0.27
Romanian (17)	17	0.09
Russian (111)	368	1.90
Scandinavian (61)	93	0.48
Scotch-Irish (168)	671	3.47
Scottish (193)	595	3.07
Serbian (0)	10	0.05
Slavic (13)	13	0.07
Slovak (0)	33	0.17
Slovene (14)	24	0.12
Swedish (165)	763	3.94
Swiss (23)	154	0.80
Ukrainian (386)	449	2.32
Welsh (9)	124	0.64
West Indian, ex. Hispanic (0)	10	0.05
Jamaican (0)	10	0.05
Yugoslavian (14)	28	0.14

Hispanic Origin	Population	%
Hispanic or Latino (of any race)	1,258	6.26
Central American, ex. Mexican	96	0.48
Costa Rican	13	0.06
Guatemalan	26	0.13
Honduran	16	0.08
Nicaraguan	13	0.06
Panamanian	8	0.04
Salvadoran	20	0.10
Cuban	16	0.08
Dominican Republic	7	0.03
Mexican	886	4.41
Puerto Rican	48	0.24
South American	72	0.36
Argentinean	10	0.05
Bolivian	1	<0.01
Chilean	12	0.06
Colombian	14	0.07
Ecuadorian	6	0.03
Peruvian	21	0.10
Uruguayan	1	<0.01
Venezuelan	5	0.02
Other South American	2	0.01
Other Hispanic or Latino	133	0.66

Race*	Population	%
African-American/Black (441)	722	3.59
Not Hispanic (421)	686	3.41
Hispanic (20)	36	0.18
American Indian/Alaska Native (118)	342	1.70
Not Hispanic (108)	296	1.47
Hispanic (10)	46	0.23
Alaska Athabascan *(Ala. Nat.)* (2)	2	0.01
Aleut *(Alaska Native)* (1)	7	0.03
Apache (1)	6	0.03
Arapaho (0)	1	<0.01
Blackfeet (5)	19	0.09
Canadian/French Am. Ind. (2)	5	0.02
Central American Ind. (0)	1	<0.01
Cherokee (2)	31	0.15
Cheyenne (1)	3	0.01
Chickasaw (2)	3	0.01
Chippewa (8)	17	0.08
Choctaw (1)	11	0.05
Colville (2)	2	0.01
Comanche (0)	1	<0.01
Cree (1)	5	0.02
Creek (1)	3	0.01
Inupiat *(Alaska Native)* (0)	1	<0.01
Iroquois (3)	3	0.01
Menominee (0)	1	<0.01
Mexican American Ind. (3)	9	0.04
Navajo (1)	4	0.02
Puget Sound Salish (14)	22	0.11
Sioux (3)	7	0.03
Tlingit-Haida *(Alaska Native)* (5)	17	0.08
Yakama (1)	1	<0.01
Yup'ik *(Alaska Native)* (1)	1	<0.01
Asian (2,087)	2,546	12.67
Not Hispanic (2,065)	2,490	12.39
Hispanic (22)	56	0.28
Cambodian (251)	262	1.30
Chinese, ex. Taiwanese (228)	305	1.52
Filipino (416)	609	3.03
Hmong (20)	20	0.10
Indian (212)	235	1.17
Indonesian (16)	24	0.12
Japanese (127)	230	1.14
Korean (217)	277	1.38
Laotian (50)	54	0.27
Malaysian (3)	5	0.02
Nepalese (1)	3	0.01
Pakistani (31)	31	0.15
Sri Lankan (8)	8	0.04
Taiwanese (2)	5	0.02
Thai (21)	31	0.15
Vietnamese (401)	443	2.20
Hawaii Native/Pacific Islander (36)	107	0.53
Not Hispanic (34)	98	0.49
Hispanic (2)	9	0.04
Fijian (4)	8	0.04
Guamanian/Chamorro (15)	24	0.12
Marshallese (1)	7	0.03
Native Hawaiian (6)	31	0.15
Samoan (3)	5	0.02
White (16,039)	16,910	84.13
Not Hispanic (15,379)	16,105	80.12
Hispanic (660)	805	4.00

Edgewood

Place Type: City
County: Pierce
Population: 9,387†

Ancestry‡	Population	%
American (457)	457	4.88
Austrian (0)	28	0.30
Basque (10)	10	0.11
British (88)	211	2.25
Canadian (11)	30	0.32
Croatian (29)	33	0.35
Czech (8)	29	0.31
Danish (0)	139	1.48
Dutch (3)	191	2.04
English (271)	1,488	15.88
European (197)	291	3.11
Finnish (77)	117	1.25
French, ex. Basque (4)	282	3.01
French Canadian (0)	15	0.16
German (739)	2,625	28.02
Greek (24)	41	0.44
Hungarian (0)	4	0.04
Irish (238)	1,307	13.95
Italian (373)	663	7.08
Norwegian (226)	878	9.37
Polish (31)	96	1.02
Russian (47)	69	0.74
Scandinavian (16)	179	1.91
Scotch-Irish (57)	308	3.29
Scottish (79)	349	3.73
Serbian (0)	7	0.07
Slovak (14)	24	0.26
Slovene (7)	7	0.07
Swedish (141)	560	5.98
Swiss (46)	141	1.50
Ukrainian (57)	102	1.09
Welsh (22)	77	0.82
Yugoslavian (15)	39	0.42

Hispanic Origin	Population	%
Hispanic or Latino (of any race)	412	4.39
Central American, ex. Mexican	27	0.29
Guatemalan	8	0.09

*Notes: † The Census 2010 population figure is used to calculate the percentages in the Hispanic Origin and Race categories. Ancestry percentages are based on the 2006-2010 American Community Survey population (not shown); ‡ Numbers in parentheses indicate the number of people reporting a single ancestry; * Numbers in parentheses indicate the number of persons reporting this race alone, not in combination with any other race; Please refer to the Explanation of Data for more information.*

Honduran	11	0.12
Nicaraguan	3	0.03
Salvadoran	4	0.04
Other Central American	1	0.01
Cuban	3	0.03
Dominican Republic	1	0.01
Mexican	297	3.16
Puerto Rican	21	0.22
South American	17	0.18
Argentinean	2	0.02
Bolivian	3	0.03
Chilean	1	0.01
Colombian	7	0.07
Ecuadorian	1	0.01
Paraguayan	2	0.02
Peruvian	1	0.01
Other Hispanic or Latino	46	0.49

Race*	Population	%
African-American/Black (98)	152	1.62
Not Hispanic (90)	142	1.51
Hispanic (8)	10	0.11
American Indian/Alaska Native (88)	199	2.12
Not Hispanic (78)	179	1.91
Hispanic (10)	20	0.21
Aleut *(Alaska Native)* (1)	4	0.04
Apache (2)	2	0.02
Blackfeet (0)	5	0.05
Canadian/French Am. Ind. (1)	2	0.02
Central American Ind. (0)	1	0.01
Cherokee (5)	18	0.19
Chippewa (5)	9	0.10
Choctaw (2)	5	0.05
Colville (2)	3	0.03
Cree (0)	2	0.02
Crow (0)	2	0.02
Inupiat *(Alaska Native)* (3)	3	0.03
Iroquois (1)	5	0.05
Lumbee (1)	1	0.01
Mexican American Ind. (0)	1	0.01
Navajo (5)	5	0.05
Puget Sound Salish (21)	29	0.31
Seminole (0)	2	0.02
Shoshone (0)	1	0.01
Sioux (0)	2	0.02
Tlingit-Haida *(Alaska Native)* (4)	12	0.13
Ute (0)	3	0.03
Yakama (4)	7	0.07
Asian (232)	369	3.93
Not Hispanic (227)	355	3.78
Hispanic (5)	14	0.15
Bangladeshi (0)	1	0.01
Cambodian (14)	21	0.22
Chinese, ex. Taiwanese (29)	50	0.53
Filipino (35)	77	0.82
Hmong (4)	4	0.04
Indian (2)	4	0.04
Indonesian (1)	3	0.03
Japanese (64)	118	1.26
Korean (46)	68	0.72
Laotian (1)	4	0.04
Pakistani (1)	1	0.01
Sri Lankan (1)	1	0.01
Taiwanese (3)	3	0.03
Thai (6)	14	0.15
Vietnamese (14)	18	0.19
Hawaii Native/Pacific Islander (28)	63	0.67
Not Hispanic (25)	58	0.62
Hispanic (3)	5	0.05
Guamanian/Chamorro (6)	11	0.12
Marshallese (7)	7	0.07
Native Hawaiian (7)	28	0.30
Samoan (7)	7	0.07
White (8,486)	8,790	93.64
Not Hispanic (8,269)	8,535	90.92
Hispanic (217)	255	2.72

Edmonds

Place Type: City
County: Snohomish
Population: 39,709†

Ancestry‡	Population	%
African, Sub-Saharan (396)	517	1.30
African (91)	179	0.45
Ethiopian (237)	237	0.60
South African (0)	33	0.08
Other Sub-Saharan African (68)	68	0.17
American (1,394)	1,394	3.51
Arab (158)	210	0.53
Arab (15)	30	0.08
Egyptian (124)	161	0.41
Lebanese (7)	7	0.02
Other Arab (12)	12	0.03
Armenian (42)	68	0.17
Australian (0)	17	0.04
Austrian (11)	167	0.42
Basque (0)	10	0.03
Belgian (0)	44	0.11
Brazilian (14)	35	0.09
British (175)	261	0.66
Canadian (80)	233	0.59
Croatian (15)	38	0.10
Czech (56)	150	0.38
Czechoslovakian (9)	25	0.06
Danish (156)	545	1.37
Dutch (314)	984	2.48
Eastern European (58)	58	0.15
English (1,514)	5,717	14.41
Estonian (27)	69	0.17
European (682)	743	1.87
Finnish (77)	277	0.70
French, ex. Basque (168)	1,686	4.25
French Canadian (91)	256	0.65
German (2,215)	8,956	22.57
Greek (85)	213	0.54
Hungarian (107)	175	0.44
Icelander (72)	100	0.25
Iranian (6)	6	0.02
Irish (1,886)	6,851	17.26
Israeli (49)	49	0.12
Italian (397)	1,100	2.77
Latvian (25)	25	0.06
Lithuanian (42)	42	0.11
Luxemburger (9)	29	0.07
Northern European (312)	381	0.96
Norwegian (1,111)	4,133	10.42
Polish (278)	800	2.02
Portuguese (38)	133	0.34
Romanian (0)	41	0.10
Russian (149)	616	1.55
Scandinavian (351)	525	1.32
Scotch-Irish (501)	1,446	3.64
Scottish (381)	1,715	4.32
Serbian (13)	29	0.07
Slovak (0)	14	0.04
Slovene (44)	60	0.15
Swedish (595)	2,872	7.24
Swiss (46)	265	0.67
Turkish (76)	90	0.23
Ukrainian (35)	105	0.26
Welsh (58)	615	1.55
West Indian, ex. Hispanic (50)	78	0.20
Jamaican (36)	36	0.09
West Indian (14)	42	0.11
Yugoslavian (29)	72	0.18

Hispanic Origin	Population	%
Hispanic or Latino (of any race)	2,121	5.34
Central American, ex. Mexican	149	0.38
Costa Rican	8	0.02
Guatemalan	27	0.07
Honduran	22	0.06
Nicaraguan	21	0.05
Panamanian	11	0.03
Salvadoran	60	0.15
Cuban	43	0.11
Dominican Republic	10	0.03
Mexican	1,296	3.26
Puerto Rican	107	0.27
South American	240	0.60
Argentinean	14	0.04
Bolivian	13	0.03
Chilean	37	0.09
Colombian	53	0.13
Ecuadorian	17	0.04
Paraguayan	3	0.01
Peruvian	84	0.21
Uruguayan	4	0.01
Venezuelan	11	0.03
Other South American	4	0.01
Other Hispanic or Latino	276	0.70

Race*	Population	%
African-American/Black (1,045)	1,390	3.50
Not Hispanic (1,027)	1,342	3.38
Hispanic (18)	48	0.12
American Indian/Alaska Native (290)	725	1.83
Not Hispanic (244)	617	1.55
Hispanic (46)	108	0.27
Alaska Athabascan *(Ala. Nat.)* (8)	18	0.05
Aleut *(Alaska Native)* (24)	40	0.10
Apache (4)	10	0.03
Arapaho (0)	1	<0.01
Blackfeet (7)	28	0.07
Canadian/French Am. Ind. (6)	11	0.03
Cherokee (13)	82	0.21
Cheyenne (1)	8	0.02
Chickasaw (1)	6	0.02
Chippewa (1)	23	0.06
Choctaw (5)	11	0.03
Colville (3)	3	0.01
Comanche (0)	2	0.01
Cree (0)	5	0.01
Creek (0)	1	<0.01
Delaware (2)	10	0.03
Hopi (0)	1	<0.01
Inupiat *(Alaska Native)* (6)	11	0.03
Iroquois (1)	15	0.04
Mexican American Ind. (6)	12	0.03
Navajo (3)	5	0.01
Osage (1)	1	<0.01
Paiute (0)	1	<0.01
Potawatomi (4)	5	0.01
Pueblo (2)	3	0.01
Puget Sound Salish (12)	22	0.06
Seminole (0)	1	<0.01
Shoshone (1)	1	<0.01
Sioux (12)	40	0.10
South American Ind. (1)	5	0.01
Spanish American Ind. (1)	1	<0.01
Tlingit-Haida *(Alaska Native)* (43)	75	0.19
Tsimshian *(Alaska Native)* (7)	12	0.03
Ute (1)	3	0.01
Yakama (2)	5	0.01
Yaqui (0)	4	0.01
Yuman (1)	1	<0.01
Yup'ik *(Alaska Native)* (1)	1	<0.01
Asian (2,800)	3,620	9.12
Not Hispanic (2,764)	3,529	8.89
Hispanic (36)	91	0.23
Bhutanese (1)	1	<0.01
Burmese (3)	3	0.01
Cambodian (23)	37	0.09
Chinese, ex. Taiwanese (496)	686	1.73
Filipino (503)	749	1.89
Indian (166)	215	0.54
Indonesian (19)	37	0.09
Japanese (286)	536	1.35
Korean (747)	875	2.20
Laotian (8)	14	0.04
Malaysian (1)	4	0.01
Pakistani (57)	62	0.16
Sri Lankan (10)	15	0.04
Taiwanese (43)	51	0.13
Thai (48)	53	0.13

*Notes: † The Census 2010 population figure is used to calculate the percentages in the Hispanic Origin and Race categories. Ancestry percentages are based on the 2006-2010 American Community Survey population (not shown); ‡ Numbers in parentheses indicate the number of people reporting a single ancestry; * Numbers in parentheses indicate the number of persons reporting this race alone, not in combination with any other race; Please refer to the Explanation of Data for more information.*

Vietnamese (275)	313	0.79
Hawaii Native/Pacific Islander (134)	308	0.78
Not Hispanic (134)	288	0.73
Hispanic (0)	20	0.05
Fijian (24)	31	0.08
Guamanian/Chamorro (13)	28	0.07
Native Hawaiian (30)	121	0.30
Samoan (12)	27	0.07
Tongan (9)	10	0.03
White (33,114)	34,581	87.09
Not Hispanic (31,949)	33,216	83.65
Hispanic (1,165)	1,365	3.44

Elk Plain

Place Type: CDP
County: Pierce
Population: 14,205†

Ancestry‡	Population	%
African, Sub-Saharan (46)	53	0.37
African (37)	37	0.26
Sierra Leonean (9)	16	0.11
American (801)	801	5.61
Arab (37)	143	1.00
Arab (37)	71	0.50
Iraqi (0)	62	0.43
Syrian (0)	10	0.07
Austrian (0)	39	0.27
Belgian (8)	8	0.06
Brazilian (0)	10	0.07
Canadian (10)	22	0.15
Croatian (9)	9	0.06
Czech (0)	22	0.15
Danish (14)	67	0.47
Dutch (58)	173	1.21
English (364)	1,206	8.45
Estonian (0)	9	0.06
European (207)	231	1.62
Finnish (17)	69	0.48
French, ex. Basque (48)	297	2.08
French Canadian (50)	168	1.18
German (937)	2,432	17.05
Hungarian (0)	13	0.09
Irish (458)	1,582	11.09
Italian (316)	723	5.07
Lithuanian (30)	54	0.38
Norwegian (222)	994	6.97
Polish (62)	217	1.52
Portuguese (0)	25	0.18
Romanian (0)	6	0.04
Russian (23)	130	0.91
Scandinavian (0)	48	0.34
Scotch-Irish (136)	277	1.94
Scottish (181)	452	3.17
Slavic (0)	10	0.07
Swedish (100)	728	5.10
Swiss (57)	168	1.18
Ukrainian (0)	18	0.13
Welsh (29)	94	0.66
West Indian, ex. Hispanic (20)	39	0.27
Haitian (6)	12	0.08
Jamaican (14)	27	0.19
Yugoslavian (19)	19	0.13

Hispanic Origin	Population	%
Hispanic or Latino (of any race)	986	6.94
Central American, ex. Mexican	39	0.27
Costa Rican	1	0.01
Honduran	3	0.02
Nicaraguan	2	0.01
Panamanian	26	0.18
Salvadoran	7	0.05
Cuban	15	0.11
Dominican Republic	3	0.02
Mexican	638	4.49
Puerto Rican	141	0.99
South American	23	0.16
Argentinean	3	0.02
Bolivian	5	0.04
Chilean	3	0.02
Colombian	6	0.04
Ecuadorian	4	0.03
Peruvian	1	0.01
Venezuelan	1	0.01
Other Hispanic or Latino	127	0.89

Race*	Population	%
African-American/Black (654)	997	7.02
Not Hispanic (628)	924	6.50
Hispanic (26)	73	0.51
American Indian/Alaska Native (177)	458	3.22
Not Hispanic (157)	390	2.75
Hispanic (20)	68	0.48
Alaska Athabascan *(Ala. Nat.)* (0)	4	0.03
Aleut *(Alaska Native)* (4)	6	0.04
Apache (0)	1	0.01
Blackfeet (5)	18	0.13
Canadian/French Am. Ind. (0)	1	0.01
Cherokee (14)	66	0.46
Cheyenne (0)	1	0.01
Chickasaw (1)	2	0.01
Chippewa (18)	34	0.24
Choctaw (2)	20	0.14
Colville (1)	5	0.04
Crow (1)	1	0.01
Inupiat *(Alaska Native)* (1)	1	0.01
Lumbee (0)	1	0.01
Mexican American Ind. (2)	7	0.05
Navajo (0)	1	0.01
Ottawa (0)	2	0.01
Potawatomi (0)	2	0.01
Puget Sound Salish (34)	50	0.35
Shoshone (1)	2	0.01
Sioux (4)	6	0.04
South American Ind. (0)	2	0.01
Spanish American Ind. (1)	1	0.01
Tlingit-Haida *(Alaska Native)* (3)	11	0.08
Ute (1)	6	0.04
Yaqui (5)	5	0.04
Yup'ik *(Alaska Native)* (0)	4	0.03
Asian (509)	939	6.61
Not Hispanic (484)	862	6.07
Hispanic (25)	77	0.54
Burmese (1)	1	0.01
Cambodian (22)	28	0.20
Chinese, ex. Taiwanese (8)	53	0.37
Filipino (229)	423	2.98
Hmong (1)	1	0.01
Indian (4)	6	0.04
Indonesian (4)	4	0.03
Japanese (53)	143	1.01
Korean (133)	232	1.63
Laotian (3)	7	0.05
Malaysian (2)	2	0.01
Taiwanese (0)	1	0.01
Thai (19)	44	0.31
Vietnamese (2)	8	0.06
Hawaii Native/Pacific Islander (336)	527	3.71
Not Hispanic (324)	490	3.45
Hispanic (12)	37	0.26
Fijian (1)	1	0.01
Guamanian/Chamorro (205)	270	1.90
Marshallese (7)	11	0.08
Native Hawaiian (39)	122	0.86
Samoan (67)	106	0.75
White (11,175)	12,101	85.19
Not Hispanic (10,722)	11,501	80.96
Hispanic (453)	600	4.22

Ellensburg

Place Type: City
County: Kittitas
Population: 18,174†

Ancestry‡	Population	%
African, Sub-Saharan (0)	56	0.31
African (0)	56	0.31
American (494)	494	2.77
Arab (12)	30	0.17
Lebanese (0)	18	0.10
Other Arab (12)	12	0.07
Armenian (0)	56	0.31
Austrian (0)	40	0.22
Basque (32)	49	0.27
Belgian (11)	64	0.36
Brazilian (53)	53	0.30
British (23)	53	0.30
Canadian (0)	44	0.25
Croatian (49)	89	0.50
Czech (64)	281	1.57
Danish (16)	195	1.09
Dutch (106)	493	2.76
English (235)	1,663	9.32
European (348)	359	2.01
Finnish (16)	125	0.70
French, ex. Basque (50)	604	3.38
French Canadian (74)	123	0.69
German (1,296)	4,256	23.85
Greek (0)	108	0.61
Hungarian (45)	106	0.59
Icelander (18)	38	0.21
Iranian (13)	20	0.11
Irish (833)	2,741	15.36
Israeli (0)	11	0.06
Italian (492)	875	4.90
Lithuanian (43)	43	0.24
Northern European (97)	97	0.54
Norwegian (592)	1,704	9.55
Pennsylvania German (0)	10	0.06
Polish (59)	327	1.83
Portuguese (0)	32	0.18
Romanian (0)	33	0.18
Russian (2)	148	0.83
Scandinavian (45)	72	0.40
Scotch-Irish (152)	477	2.67
Scottish (123)	686	3.84
Slovak (19)	19	0.11
Slovene (0)	8	0.04
Swedish (247)	858	4.81
Swiss (100)	328	1.84
Turkish (0)	43	0.24
Ukrainian (44)	77	0.43
Welsh (60)	297	1.66
West Indian, ex. Hispanic (0)	61	0.34
Jamaican (0)	61	0.34
Yugoslavian (25)	50	0.28

Hispanic Origin	Population	%
Hispanic or Latino (of any race)	1,764	9.71
Central American, ex. Mexican	51	0.28
Costa Rican	4	0.02
Guatemalan	9	0.05
Honduran	1	0.01
Panamanian	9	0.05
Salvadoran	28	0.15
Cuban	10	0.06
Dominican Republic	5	0.03
Mexican	1,494	8.22
Puerto Rican	41	0.23
South American	31	0.17
Argentinean	1	0.01
Bolivian	1	0.01
Chilean	5	0.03
Colombian	6	0.03
Ecuadorian	3	0.02
Paraguayan	1	0.01
Peruvian	10	0.06
Venezuelan	4	0.02
Other Hispanic or Latino	132	0.73

Race*	Population	%
African-American/Black (275)	413	2.27
Not Hispanic (256)	368	2.02
Hispanic (19)	45	0.25
American Indian/Alaska Native (189)	385	2.12
Not Hispanic (170)	339	1.87
Hispanic (19)	46	0.25
Alaska Athabascan *(Ala. Nat.)* (2)	4	0.02

*Notes: † The Census 2010 population figure is used to calculate the percentages in the Hispanic Origin and Race categories. Ancestry percentages are based on the 2006-2010 American Community Survey population (not shown); ‡ Numbers in parentheses indicate the number of people reporting a single ancestry; * Numbers in parentheses indicate the number of persons reporting this race alone, not in combination with any other race; Please refer to the Explanation of Data for more information.*

Aleut *(Alaska Native)* (8)	14	0.08
Arapaho (0)	1	0.01
Blackfeet (7)	10	0.06
Canadian/French Am. Ind. (5)	6	0.03
Cherokee (9)	40	0.22
Chickasaw (0)	1	0.01
Chippewa (6)	15	0.08
Choctaw (1)	5	0.03
Colville (5)	11	0.06
Cree (0)	1	0.01
Creek (1)	2	0.01
Hopi (1)	4	0.02
Inupiat *(Alaska Native)* (7)	8	0.04
Iroquois (1)	1	0.01
Lumbee (3)	3	0.02
Mexican American Ind. (0)	6	0.03
Navajo (2)	4	0.02
Paiute (4)	4	0.02
Pueblo (2)	2	0.01
Puget Sound Salish (12)	17	0.09
Shoshone (0)	2	0.01
Sioux (5)	10	0.06
Tlingit-Haida *(Alaska Native)* (9)	13	0.07
Yakama (16)	22	0.12
Yaqui (1)	1	0.01
Yup'ik *(Alaska Native)* (2)	3	0.02
Asian (587)	863	4.75
Not Hispanic (575)	824	4.53
Hispanic (12)	39	0.21
Cambodian (20)	26	0.14
Chinese, ex. Taiwanese (128)	177	0.97
Filipino (81)	154	0.85
Hmong (1)	1	0.01
Indian (31)	44	0.24
Indonesian (1)	5	0.03
Japanese (109)	203	1.12
Korean (91)	134	0.74
Laotian (1)	4	0.02
Malaysian (0)	3	0.02
Nepalese (1)	3	0.02
Pakistani (6)	8	0.04
Sri Lankan (1)	2	0.01
Taiwanese (20)	20	0.11
Thai (9)	22	0.12
Vietnamese (53)	60	0.33
Hawaii Native/Pacific Islander (28)	89	0.49
Not Hispanic (28)	77	0.42
Hispanic (0)	12	0.07
Fijian (1)	5	0.03
Guamanian/Chamorro (7)	14	0.08
Native Hawaiian (8)	26	0.14
Samoan (8)	20	0.11
Tongan (1)	3	0.02
White (15,583)	16,217	89.23
Not Hispanic (14,833)	15,335	84.38
Hispanic (750)	882	4.85

Enumclaw

Place Type: City
County: King
Population: 10,669†

Ancestry‡	Population	%
American (727)	727	6.82
Arab (41)	80	0.75
Syrian (41)	80	0.75
Austrian (13)	69	0.65
Basque (0)	22	0.21
Belgian (0)	11	0.10
British (32)	52	0.49
Canadian (12)	91	0.85
Croatian (10)	61	0.57
Czech (0)	12	0.11
Czechoslovakian (10)	10	0.09
Danish (53)	263	2.47
Dutch (109)	386	3.62
English (336)	1,029	9.65
European (276)	289	2.71
Finnish (33)	90	0.84
French, ex. Basque (47)	284	2.66
French Canadian (67)	140	1.31
German (937)	2,593	24.33
Greek (12)	12	0.11
Hungarian (0)	67	0.63
Icelander (18)	33	0.31
Irish (329)	1,708	16.02
Italian (131)	421	3.95
Lithuanian (22)	33	0.31
Northern European (75)	81	0.76
Norwegian (315)	757	7.10
Polish (145)	400	3.75
Portuguese (0)	32	0.30
Romanian (12)	12	0.11
Russian (19)	100	0.94
Scandinavian (96)	96	0.90
Scotch-Irish (152)	498	4.67
Scottish (27)	215	2.02
Swedish (199)	794	7.45
Swiss (8)	56	0.53
Ukrainian (0)	15	0.14
Welsh (9)	83	0.78
Yugoslavian (13)	13	0.12

Hispanic Origin	Population	%
Hispanic or Latino (of any race)	703	6.59
Central American, ex. Mexican	20	0.19
Costa Rican	1	0.01
Honduran	6	0.06
Nicaraguan	4	0.04
Panamanian	2	0.02
Salvadoran	7	0.07
Cuban	10	0.09
Dominican Republic	8	0.07
Mexican	547	5.13
Puerto Rican	32	0.30
South American	13	0.12
Argentinean	6	0.06
Colombian	2	0.02
Peruvian	5	0.05
Other Hispanic or Latino	73	0.68

Race*	Population	%
African-American/Black (52)	123	1.15
Not Hispanic (39)	101	0.95
Hispanic (13)	22	0.21
American Indian/Alaska Native (105)	215	2.02
Not Hispanic (101)	196	1.84
Hispanic (4)	19	0.18
Alaska Athabascan *(Ala. Nat.)* (2)	2	0.02
Aleut *(Alaska Native)* (0)	4	0.04
Apache (0)	1	0.01
Blackfeet (1)	2	0.02
Canadian/French Am. Ind. (1)	4	0.04
Cherokee (9)	20	0.19
Chippewa (6)	11	0.10
Choctaw (2)	6	0.06
Colville (0)	2	0.02
Comanche (4)	10	0.09
Delaware (0)	1	0.01
Hopi (0)	1	0.01
Inupiat *(Alaska Native)* (1)	2	0.02
Iroquois (0)	4	0.04
Mexican American Ind. (1)	4	0.04
Navajo (4)	6	0.06
Ottawa (2)	2	0.02
Pima (1)	1	0.01
Potawatomi (0)	6	0.06
Pueblo (5)	7	0.07
Puget Sound Salish (21)	25	0.23
Sioux (3)	8	0.07
South American Ind. (1)	1	0.01
Tlingit-Haida *(Alaska Native)* (2)	5	0.05
Yakama (4)	5	0.05
Asian (99)	176	1.65
Not Hispanic (97)	170	1.59
Hispanic (2)	6	0.06
Chinese, ex. Taiwanese (20)	38	0.36
Filipino (22)	45	0.42
Indian (10)	10	0.09
Indonesian (1)	1	0.01
Japanese (22)	46	0.43
Korean (11)	17	0.16
Laotian (1)	2	0.02
Nepalese (1)	1	0.01
Thai (2)	2	0.02
Vietnamese (6)	8	0.07
Hawaii Native/Pacific Islander (16)	60	0.56
Not Hispanic (15)	50	0.47
Hispanic (1)	10	0.09
Fijian (4)	4	0.04
Guamanian/Chamorro (0)	6	0.06
Native Hawaiian (4)	20	0.19
Samoan (7)	23	0.22
Tongan (1)	1	0.01
White (9,793)	10,067	94.36
Not Hispanic (9,467)	9,697	90.89
Hispanic (326)	370	3.47

Ephrata

Place Type: City
County: Grant
Population: 7,664†

Ancestry‡	Population	%
African, Sub-Saharan (17)	17	0.23
Ethiopian (17)	17	0.23
American (437)	437	5.90
British (30)	103	1.39
Canadian (17)	32	0.43
Danish (17)	88	1.19
Dutch (86)	477	6.44
English (219)	768	10.37
European (142)	142	1.92
Finnish (8)	8	0.11
French, ex. Basque (15)	172	2.32
French Canadian (72)	85	1.15
German (565)	1,721	23.23
Greek (61)	147	1.98
Hungarian (45)	45	0.61
Icelander (147)	147	1.98
Irish (118)	633	8.55
Italian (15)	68	0.92
Northern European (61)	61	0.82
Norwegian (138)	291	3.93
Pennsylvania German (17)	17	0.23
Polish (0)	119	1.61
Portuguese (16)	16	0.22
Russian (10)	10	0.14
Scandinavian (15)	15	0.20
Scotch-Irish (80)	142	1.92
Scottish (91)	329	4.44
Swedish (58)	191	2.58
Ukrainian (49)	49	0.66
Welsh (16)	117	1.58

Hispanic Origin	Population	%
Hispanic or Latino (of any race)	1,277	16.66
Central American, ex. Mexican	68	0.89
Guatemalan	16	0.21
Honduran	2	0.03
Nicaraguan	2	0.03
Panamanian	2	0.03
Salvadoran	46	0.60
Cuban	4	0.05
Mexican	1,063	13.87
Puerto Rican	13	0.17
South American	15	0.20
Bolivian	1	0.01
Colombian	2	0.03
Ecuadorian	1	0.01
Peruvian	7	0.09
Venezuelan	4	0.05
Other Hispanic or Latino	114	1.49

Race*	Population	%
African-American/Black (63)	105	1.37
Not Hispanic (58)	91	1.19
Hispanic (5)	14	0.18

SECTION TWO

*Notes: † The Census 2010 population figure is used to calculate the percentages in the Hispanic Origin and Race categories. Ancestry percentages are based on the 2006-2010 American Community Survey population (not shown); ‡ Numbers in parentheses indicate the number of people reporting a single ancestry; * Numbers in parentheses indicate the number of persons reporting this race alone, not in combination with any other race; Please refer to the Explanation of Data for more information.*

American Indian/Alaska Native (87)	177	2.31
Not Hispanic (68)	140	1.83
Hispanic (19)	37	0.48
Alaska Athabascan *(Ala. Nat.)* (1)	6	0.08
Blackfeet (2)	2	0.03
Canadian/French Am. Ind. (1)	5	0.07
Cherokee (6)	27	0.35
Chippewa (8)	8	0.10
Choctaw (4)	7	0.09
Colville (6)	8	0.10
Comanche (0)	1	0.01
Creek (1)	1	0.01
Mexican American Ind. (5)	7	0.09
Navajo (3)	7	0.09
Pueblo (0)	2	0.03
Puget Sound Salish (1)	1	0.01
Sioux (1)	3	0.04
Yaqui (1)	1	0.01
Asian (97)	142	1.85
Not Hispanic (97)	140	1.83
Hispanic (0)	2	0.03
Chinese, ex. Taiwanese (7)	15	0.20
Filipino (20)	41	0.53
Indian (17)	18	0.23
Japanese (6)	13	0.17
Korean (10)	14	0.18
Taiwanese (4)	4	0.05
Thai (3)	5	0.07
Vietnamese (29)	39	0.51
Hawaii Native/Pacific Islander (8)	20	0.26
Not Hispanic (8)	20	0.26
Native Hawaiian (3)	8	0.10
Samoan (4)	8	0.10
White (6,447)	6,666	86.98
Not Hispanic (6,002)	6,145	80.18
Hispanic (445)	521	6.80

Everett

Place Type: City
County: Snohomish
Population: 103,019†

Ancestry‡	Population	%
Afghan (0)	28	0.03
African, Sub-Saharan (1,505)	1,530	1.50
African (161)	182	0.18
Ethiopian (131)	131	0.13
Kenyan (82)	86	0.08
Liberian (4)	4	<0.01
Nigerian (181)	181	0.18
Somalian (787)	787	0.77
Sudanese (15)	15	0.01
Other Sub-Saharan African (144)	144	0.14
Albanian (0)	81	0.08
American (3,273)	3,273	3.22
Arab (162)	313	0.31
Egyptian (54)	54	0.05
Iraqi (83)	83	0.08
Lebanese (0)	122	0.12
Syrian (0)	29	0.03
Other Arab (25)	25	0.02
Armenian (32)	65	0.06
Australian (0)	10	0.01
Austrian (120)	260	0.26
Basque (0)	15	0.01
Belgian (45)	99	0.10
Brazilian (37)	92	0.09
British (380)	667	0.66
Canadian (309)	397	0.39
Celtic (26)	26	0.03
Croatian (18)	138	0.14
Czech (28)	250	0.25
Czechoslovakian (16)	41	0.04
Danish (124)	964	0.95
Dutch (719)	3,363	3.31
Eastern European (29)	63	0.06
English (1,677)	10,254	10.09
Estonian (21)	21	0.02
European (1,641)	1,783	1.75
Finnish (116)	526	0.52
French, ex. Basque (530)	3,420	3.36
French Canadian (315)	921	0.91
German (4,454)	17,997	17.70
German Russian (11)	11	0.01
Greek (117)	587	0.58
Guyanese (24)	24	0.02
Hungarian (42)	234	0.23
Icelander (91)	180	0.18
Iranian (11)	11	0.01
Irish (2,398)	11,217	11.03
Israeli (0)	24	0.02
Italian (1,004)	3,418	3.36
Lithuanian (12)	52	0.05
Maltese (0)	16	0.02
Northern European (79)	87	0.09
Norwegian (2,831)	7,415	7.29
Pennsylvania German (0)	68	0.07
Polish (324)	1,604	1.58
Portuguese (64)	210	0.21
Romanian (280)	299	0.29
Russian (580)	1,015	1.00
Scandinavian (268)	657	0.65
Scotch-Irish (620)	2,371	2.33
Scottish (924)	2,974	2.93
Serbian (19)	48	0.05
Slavic (96)	115	0.11
Slovak (0)	55	0.05
Swedish (834)	3,941	3.88
Swiss (16)	456	0.45
Turkish (0)	59	0.06
Ukrainian (1,627)	2,019	1.99
Welsh (96)	838	0.82
West Indian, ex. Hispanic (121)	170	0.17
Belizean (27)	27	0.03
Haitian (56)	56	0.06
Jamaican (38)	55	0.05
Trinidadian/Tobagonian (0)	25	0.02
Other West Indian (0)	7	0.01
Yugoslavian (211)	276	0.27

Hispanic Origin	Population	%
Hispanic or Latino (of any race)	14,595	14.17
Central American, ex. Mexican	643	0.62
Costa Rican	18	0.02
Guatemalan	131	0.13
Honduran	99	0.10
Nicaraguan	89	0.09
Panamanian	42	0.04
Salvadoran	258	0.25
Other Central American	6	0.01
Cuban	86	0.08
Dominican Republic	51	0.05
Mexican	11,676	11.33
Puerto Rican	459	0.45
South American	410	0.40
Argentinean	38	0.04
Bolivian	18	0.02
Chilean	39	0.04
Colombian	123	0.12
Ecuadorian	52	0.05
Paraguayan	1	<0.01
Peruvian	108	0.10
Uruguayan	4	<0.01
Venezuelan	23	0.02
Other South American	4	<0.01
Other Hispanic or Latino	1,270	1.23

Race*	Population	%
African-American/Black (4,198)	5,934	5.76
Not Hispanic (3,921)	5,384	5.23
Hispanic (277)	550	0.53
American Indian/Alaska Native (1,408)	2,963	2.88
Not Hispanic (1,129)	2,358	2.29
Hispanic (279)	605	0.59
Alaska Athabascan *(Ala. Nat.)* (20)	25	0.02
Aleut *(Alaska Native)* (31)	60	0.06
Apache (12)	26	0.03
Arapaho (1)	1	<0.01
Blackfeet (12)	77	0.07
Canadian/French Am. Ind. (19)	33	0.03
Central American Ind. (7)	7	0.01
Cherokee (56)	299	0.29
Cheyenne (2)	7	0.01
Chickasaw (2)	6	0.01
Chippewa (61)	125	0.12
Choctaw (12)	58	0.06
Colville (25)	32	0.03
Comanche (7)	9	0.01
Cree (3)	11	0.01
Creek (8)	21	0.02
Crow (4)	5	<0.01
Hopi (2)	3	<0.01
Inupiat *(Alaska Native)* (25)	39	0.04
Iroquois (3)	18	0.02
Kiowa (2)	7	0.01
Lumbee (1)	1	<0.01
Mexican American Ind. (39)	61	0.06
Navajo (35)	52	0.05
Osage (0)	5	<0.01
Ottawa (2)	3	<0.01
Paiute (3)	3	<0.01
Pima (0)	6	0.01
Potawatomi (7)	11	0.01
Pueblo (5)	13	0.01
Puget Sound Salish (185)	286	0.28
Seminole (3)	6	0.01
Shoshone (5)	10	0.01
Sioux (50)	132	0.13
South American Ind. (3)	9	0.01
Spanish American Ind. (5)	6	0.01
Tlingit-Haida *(Alaska Native)* (89)	148	0.14
Tohono O'Odham (0)	1	<0.01
Tsimshian *(Alaska Native)* (10)	26	0.03
Ute (1)	3	<0.01
Yakama (19)	45	0.04
Yaqui (2)	9	0.01
Yup'ik *(Alaska Native)* (6)	10	0.01
Asian (8,056)	9,969	9.68
Not Hispanic (7,949)	9,639	9.36
Hispanic (107)	330	0.32
Bangladeshi (10)	10	0.01
Bhutanese (82)	106	0.10
Burmese (25)	36	0.03
Cambodian (575)	709	0.69
Chinese, ex. Taiwanese (572)	896	0.87
Filipino (1,920)	2,686	2.61
Hmong (62)	69	0.07
Indian (744)	932	0.90
Indonesian (220)	291	0.28
Japanese (276)	654	0.63
Korean (665)	879	0.85
Laotian (256)	326	0.32
Malaysian (7)	12	0.01
Nepalese (35)	55	0.05
Pakistani (54)	70	0.07
Sri Lankan (12)	14	0.01
Taiwanese (24)	32	0.03
Thai (90)	139	0.13
Vietnamese (1,962)	2,140	2.08
Hawaii Native/Pacific Islander (735)	1,238	1.20
Not Hispanic (712)	1,122	1.09
Hispanic (23)	116	0.11
Fijian (98)	119	0.12
Guamanian/Chamorro (96)	155	0.15
Marshallese (226)	246	0.24
Native Hawaiian (102)	324	0.31
Samoan (51)	107	0.10
Tongan (16)	26	0.03
White (76,844)	81,591	79.20
Not Hispanic (70,489)	74,066	71.90
Hispanic (6,355)	7,525	7.30

Fairwood

Place Type: CDP
County: King
Population: 19,102†

*Notes: † The Census 2010 population figure is used to calculate the percentages in the Hispanic Origin and Race categories. Ancestry percentages are based on the 2006-2010 American Community Survey population (not shown); ‡ Numbers in parentheses indicate the number of people reporting a single ancestry; * Numbers in parentheses indicate the number of persons reporting this race alone, not in combination with any other race; Please refer to the Explanation of Data for more information.*

Ancestry‡	Population	%
African, Sub-Saharan (9)	41	0.21
African (9)	41	0.21
Albanian (0)	8	0.04
American (679)	679	3.52
Arab (34)	67	0.35
Arab (14)	35	0.18
Syrian (0)	5	0.03
Other Arab (20)	27	0.14
Armenian (7)	7	0.04
Australian (0)	9	0.05
Austrian (0)	22	0.11
Belgian (30)	123	0.64
British (132)	194	1.01
Bulgarian (13)	13	0.07
Canadian (14)	163	0.85
Croatian (0)	18	0.09
Czech (34)	59	0.31
Czechoslovakian (80)	80	0.41
Danish (37)	272	1.41
Dutch (113)	329	1.71
English (280)	2,113	10.96
European (108)	108	0.56
Finnish (16)	127	0.66
French, ex. Basque (103)	946	4.91
French Canadian (38)	158	0.82
German (1,096)	3,539	18.35
Greek (54)	86	0.45
Hungarian (0)	38	0.20
Icelander (15)	44	0.23
Irish (421)	2,102	10.90
Italian (208)	666	3.45
Lithuanian (0)	15	0.08
Northern European (92)	92	0.48
Norwegian (270)	1,098	5.69
Polish (101)	388	2.01
Portuguese (24)	88	0.46
Romanian (100)	100	0.52
Russian (288)	396	2.05
Scandinavian (171)	239	1.24
Scotch-Irish (153)	423	2.19
Scottish (128)	517	2.68
Slovak (30)	44	0.23
Slovene (15)	25	0.13
Swedish (141)	648	3.36
Swiss (12)	137	0.71
Turkish (27)	37	0.19
Ukrainian (15)	78	0.40
Welsh (32)	192	1.00
West Indian, ex. Hispanic (23)	23	0.12
British West Indian (12)	12	0.06
Jamaican (11)	11	0.06
Yugoslavian (0)	7	0.04

Hispanic Origin	Population	%
Hispanic or Latino (of any race)	1,240	6.49
Central American, ex. Mexican	96	0.50
Costa Rican	3	0.02
Guatemalan	34	0.18
Honduran	7	0.04
Nicaraguan	11	0.06
Panamanian	7	0.04
Salvadoran	29	0.15
Other Central American	5	0.03
Cuban	31	0.16
Dominican Republic	4	0.02
Mexican	773	4.05
Puerto Rican	94	0.49
South American	106	0.55
Argentinean	13	0.07
Chilean	9	0.05
Colombian	34	0.18
Ecuadorian	16	0.08
Paraguayan	1	0.01
Peruvian	27	0.14
Venezuelan	6	0.03
Other Hispanic or Latino	136	0.71

Race*	Population	%
African-American/Black (1,413)	1,821	9.53
Not Hispanic (1,391)	1,766	9.25
Hispanic (22)	55	0.29
American Indian/Alaska Native (88)	310	1.62
Not Hispanic (79)	277	1.45
Hispanic (9)	33	0.17
Aleut *(Alaska Native)* (1)	4	0.02
Apache (1)	2	0.01
Blackfeet (2)	12	0.06
Canadian/French Am. Ind. (1)	3	0.02
Cherokee (1)	34	0.18
Cheyenne (0)	1	0.01
Chickasaw (1)	4	0.02
Chippewa (6)	22	0.12
Choctaw (0)	6	0.03
Cree (1)	2	0.01
Inupiat *(Alaska Native)* (0)	2	0.01
Lumbee (1)	2	0.01
Mexican American Ind. (2)	3	0.02
Navajo (0)	5	0.03
Osage (2)	5	0.03
Pueblo (0)	5	0.03
Puget Sound Salish (4)	5	0.03
Seminole (0)	1	0.01
Shoshone (1)	1	0.01
Sioux (3)	7	0.04
Spanish American Ind. (0)	2	0.01
Tlingit-Haida *(Alaska Native)* (4)	27	0.14
Tsimshian *(Alaska Native)* (0)	4	0.02
Yakama (3)	5	0.03
Asian (3,365)	4,009	20.99
Not Hispanic (3,345)	3,935	20.60
Hispanic (20)	74	0.39
Bangladeshi (10)	10	0.05
Burmese (3)	3	0.02
Cambodian (74)	97	0.51
Chinese, ex. Taiwanese (709)	884	4.63
Filipino (869)	1,200	6.28
Hmong (2)	5	0.03
Indian (378)	439	2.30
Indonesian (2)	5	0.03
Japanese (294)	485	2.54
Korean (265)	308	1.61
Laotian (76)	103	0.54
Malaysian (3)	6	0.03
Nepalese (9)	9	0.05
Pakistani (33)	35	0.18
Taiwanese (41)	49	0.26
Thai (29)	45	0.24
Vietnamese (397)	467	2.44
Hawaii Native/Pacific Islander (107)	263	1.38
Not Hispanic (103)	249	1.30
Hispanic (4)	14	0.07
Fijian (12)	15	0.08
Guamanian/Chamorro (11)	29	0.15
Native Hawaiian (16)	102	0.53
Samoan (33)	48	0.25
Tongan (9)	14	0.07
White (12,471)	13,459	70.46
Not Hispanic (11,862)	12,741	66.70
Hispanic (609)	718	3.76

Fairwood

Place Type: CDP
County: Spokane
Population: 7,905†

Ancestry‡	Population	%
American (391)	391	5.27
British (148)	232	3.13
Canadian (31)	61	0.82
Croatian (55)	55	0.74
Czech (30)	225	3.03
Czechoslovakian (14)	14	0.19
Danish (0)	98	1.32
Dutch (28)	265	3.57
English (398)	1,267	17.08
European (192)	192	2.59
Finnish (0)	145	1.95
French, ex. Basque (13)	317	4.27
German (469)	2,227	30.02
Greek (0)	49	0.66
Hungarian (12)	36	0.49
Iranian (12)	12	0.16
Irish (196)	1,116	15.04
Italian (116)	456	6.15
Lithuanian (0)	29	0.39
Norwegian (223)	515	6.94
Polish (0)	158	2.13
Russian (0)	30	0.40
Scandinavian (11)	11	0.15
Scotch-Irish (17)	310	4.18
Scottish (133)	220	2.97
Slovak (0)	15	0.20
Swedish (19)	144	1.94
Swiss (0)	44	0.59
Ukrainian (16)	26	0.35
Welsh (0)	69	0.93
West Indian, ex. Hispanic (39)	39	0.53
Barbadian (20)	20	0.27
Haitian (19)	19	0.26

Hispanic Origin	Population	%
Hispanic or Latino (of any race)	255	3.23
Central American, ex. Mexican	7	0.09
Costa Rican	2	0.03
Guatemalan	1	0.01
Panamanian	2	0.03
Salvadoran	2	0.03
Cuban	3	0.04
Dominican Republic	1	0.01
Mexican	178	2.25
Puerto Rican	10	0.13
South American	18	0.23
Chilean	6	0.08
Colombian	6	0.08
Ecuadorian	3	0.04
Peruvian	3	0.04
Other Hispanic or Latino	38	0.48

Race*	Population	%
African-American/Black (79)	159	2.01
Not Hispanic (76)	155	1.96
Hispanic (3)	4	0.05
American Indian/Alaska Native (111)	200	2.53
Not Hispanic (103)	183	2.31
Hispanic (8)	17	0.22
Arapaho (0)	3	0.04
Blackfeet (4)	5	0.06
Cherokee (4)	16	0.20
Chickasaw (1)	2	0.03
Chippewa (7)	21	0.27
Choctaw (1)	1	0.01
Colville (30)	37	0.47
Creek (1)	1	0.01
Iroquois (0)	4	0.05
Kiowa (3)	3	0.04
Navajo (0)	2	0.03
Potawatomi (0)	3	0.04
Shoshone (0)	3	0.04
Sioux (3)	10	0.13
Tlingit-Haida *(Alaska Native)* (1)	1	0.01
Yaqui (0)	2	0.03
Yup'ik *(Alaska Native)* (1)	1	0.01
Asian (158)	232	2.93
Not Hispanic (158)	228	2.88
Hispanic (0)	4	0.05
Chinese, ex. Taiwanese (24)	37	0.47
Filipino (17)	37	0.47
Hmong (5)	5	0.06
Indian (16)	21	0.27
Indonesian (4)	4	0.05
Japanese (20)	46	0.58
Korean (39)	60	0.76
Malaysian (0)	2	0.03
Pakistani (4)	4	0.05
Sri Lankan (1)	1	0.01
Thai (2)	2	0.03
Vietnamese (19)	21	0.27
Hawaii Native/Pacific Islander (20)	50	0.63

*Notes: † The Census 2010 population figure is used to calculate the percentages in the Hispanic Origin and Race categories. Ancestry percentages are based on the 2006-2010 American Community Survey population (not shown); ‡ Numbers in parentheses indicate the number of people reporting a single ancestry; * Numbers in parentheses indicate the number of persons reporting this race alone, not in combination with any other race; Please refer to the Explanation of Data for more information.*

Not Hispanic (16)	42	0.53
Hispanic (4)	8	0.10
Guamanian/Chamorro (4)	7	0.09
Native Hawaiian (8)	33	0.42
Samoan (7)	7	0.09
White (7,215)	7,463	94.41
Not Hispanic (7,066)	7,272	91.99
Hispanic (149)	191	2.42

Federal Way

Place Type: City
County: King
Population: 89,306†

Ancestry‡	Population	%
African, Sub-Saharan (1,645)	2,154	2.45
African (755)	923	1.05
Ethiopian (370)	485	0.55
Kenyan (221)	221	0.25
Nigerian (0)	158	0.18
Sierra Leonean (80)	80	0.09
Somalian (28)	57	0.06
South African (36)	36	0.04
Sudanese (48)	48	0.05
Ugandan (50)	50	0.06
Other Sub-Saharan African (57)	96	0.11
Alsatian (0)	14	0.02
American (2,080)	2,080	2.37
Arab (144)	194	0.22
Arab (10)	10	0.01
Egyptian (78)	78	0.09
Iraqi (0)	21	0.02
Jordanian (30)	30	0.03
Lebanese (17)	27	0.03
Syrian (9)	9	0.01
Other Arab (0)	19	0.02
Armenian (47)	87	0.10
Australian (0)	27	0.03
Austrian (43)	187	0.21
Basque (0)	23	0.03
Belgian (35)	94	0.11
British (234)	406	0.46
Bulgarian (11)	22	0.03
Canadian (230)	431	0.49
Croatian (151)	273	0.31
Czech (164)	369	0.42
Czechoslovakian (56)	86	0.10
Danish (65)	465	0.53
Dutch (314)	1,397	1.59
Eastern European (89)	116	0.13
English (2,038)	7,552	8.60
Estonian (0)	6	0.01
European (1,159)	1,344	1.53
Finnish (120)	427	0.49
French, ex. Basque (379)	2,631	3.00
French Canadian (132)	355	0.40
German (4,552)	14,173	16.14
Greek (64)	288	0.33
Hungarian (40)	185	0.21
Icelander (0)	32	0.04
Iranian (14)	14	0.02
Irish (2,219)	8,138	9.27
Israeli (9)	9	0.01
Italian (721)	2,506	2.85
Latvian (0)	31	0.04
Lithuanian (11)	25	0.03
Northern European (210)	210	0.24
Norwegian (1,508)	4,011	4.57
Pennsylvania German (10)	23	0.03
Polish (723)	1,561	1.78
Portuguese (44)	370	0.42
Romanian (233)	245	0.28
Russian (733)	1,162	1.32
Scandinavian (211)	440	0.50
Scotch-Irish (415)	1,425	1.62
Scottish (611)	2,384	2.72
Slavic (0)	29	0.03
Slovak (23)	23	0.03
Slovene (15)	57	0.06
Swedish (582)	2,036	2.32
Swiss (93)	424	0.48
Ukrainian (1,548)	1,665	1.90
Welsh (128)	654	0.74
West Indian, ex. Hispanic (235)	321	0.37
Haitian (150)	180	0.21
Jamaican (54)	110	0.13
Trinidadian/Tobagonian (31)	31	0.04
Yugoslavian (36)	223	0.25

Hispanic Origin	Population	%
Hispanic or Latino (of any race)	14,476	16.21
Central American, ex. Mexican	1,064	1.19
Costa Rican	24	0.03
Guatemalan	244	0.27
Honduran	173	0.19
Nicaraguan	82	0.09
Panamanian	64	0.07
Salvadoran	469	0.53
Other Central American	8	0.01
Cuban	101	0.11
Dominican Republic	28	0.03
Mexican	11,242	12.59
Puerto Rican	504	0.56
South American	356	0.40
Argentinean	35	0.04
Bolivian	11	0.01
Chilean	22	0.02
Colombian	103	0.12
Ecuadorian	35	0.04
Paraguayan	5	0.01
Peruvian	117	0.13
Uruguayan	2	<0.01
Venezuelan	15	0.02
Other South American	11	0.01
Other Hispanic or Latino	1,181	1.32

Race*	Population	%
African-American/Black (8,703)	11,041	12.36
Not Hispanic (8,406)	10,385	11.63
Hispanic (297)	656	0.73
American Indian/Alaska Native (836)	2,210	2.47
Not Hispanic (625)	1,785	2.00
Hispanic (211)	425	0.48
Alaska Athabascan *(Ala. Nat.)* (8)	19	0.02
Aleut *(Alaska Native)* (18)	32	0.04
Apache (5)	29	0.03
Arapaho (0)	4	<0.01
Blackfeet (38)	124	0.14
Canadian/French Am. Ind. (13)	38	0.04
Central American Ind. (7)	9	0.01
Cherokee (49)	265	0.30
Cheyenne (0)	3	<0.01
Chickasaw (0)	9	0.01
Chippewa (30)	70	0.08
Choctaw (4)	37	0.04
Colville (17)	22	0.02
Comanche (0)	16	0.02
Cree (1)	6	0.01
Creek (4)	19	0.02
Crow (5)	12	0.01
Delaware (1)	1	<0.01
Hopi (0)	1	<0.01
Inupiat *(Alaska Native)* (8)	25	0.03
Iroquois (6)	31	0.03
Lumbee (0)	4	<0.01
Mexican American Ind. (57)	80	0.09
Navajo (27)	46	0.05
Osage (2)	4	<0.01
Ottawa (2)	2	<0.01
Paiute (2)	2	<0.01
Pueblo (2)	4	<0.01
Puget Sound Salish (60)	115	0.13
Seminole (1)	5	0.01
Shoshone (1)	4	<0.01
Sioux (20)	47	0.05
South American Ind. (3)	6	0.01
Spanish American Ind. (19)	19	0.02
Tlingit-Haida *(Alaska Native)* (35)	97	0.11
Tohono O'Odham (0)	1	<0.01
Tsimshian *(Alaska Native)* (4)	18	0.02
Yakama (8)	20	0.02
Yaqui (3)	12	0.01
Yuman (3)	3	<0.01
Yup'ik *(Alaska Native)* (4)	10	0.01
Asian (12,642)	14,994	16.79
Not Hispanic (12,521)	14,651	16.41
Hispanic (121)	343	0.38
Bangladeshi (8)	8	0.01
Burmese (24)	25	0.03
Cambodian (404)	491	0.55
Chinese, ex. Taiwanese (1,031)	1,411	1.58
Filipino (2,474)	3,552	3.98
Hmong (61)	73	0.08
Indian (822)	987	1.11
Indonesian (24)	45	0.05
Japanese (491)	981	1.10
Korean (4,850)	5,303	5.94
Laotian (181)	215	0.24
Malaysian (1)	4	<0.01
Nepalese (9)	9	0.01
Pakistani (91)	105	0.12
Sri Lankan (37)	44	0.05
Taiwanese (101)	120	0.13
Thai (111)	182	0.20
Vietnamese (1,433)	1,607	1.80
Hawaii Native/Pacific Islander (2,399)	3,204	3.59
Not Hispanic (2,331)	3,035	3.40
Hispanic (68)	169	0.19
Fijian (89)	127	0.14
Guamanian/Chamorro (290)	419	0.47
Marshallese (162)	188	0.21
Native Hawaiian (193)	520	0.58
Samoan (1,205)	1,459	1.63
Tongan (110)	155	0.17
White (51,346)	56,139	62.86
Not Hispanic (46,102)	49,885	55.86
Hispanic (5,244)	6,254	7.00

Ferndale

Place Type: City
County: Whatcom
Population: 11,415†

Ancestry‡	Population	%
African, Sub-Saharan (28)	28	0.25
African (28)	28	0.25
American (235)	235	2.14
Arab (33)	61	0.55
Egyptian (33)	33	0.30
Syrian (0)	28	0.25
Austrian (14)	14	0.13
Belgian (16)	16	0.15
British (69)	127	1.16
Canadian (84)	109	0.99
Celtic (9)	18	0.16
Czech (20)	34	0.31
Czechoslovakian (0)	15	0.14
Danish (59)	150	1.36
Dutch (189)	724	6.59
English (309)	1,183	10.76
European (165)	227	2.06
Finnish (69)	130	1.18
French, ex. Basque (40)	230	2.09
French Canadian (28)	87	0.79
German (628)	1,792	16.30
Greek (32)	56	0.51
Icelander (14)	32	0.29
Irish (116)	842	7.66
Italian (106)	350	3.18
Northern European (35)	54	0.49
Norwegian (235)	807	7.34
Polish (21)	147	1.34
Portuguese (0)	27	0.25
Russian (633)	691	6.29
Scandinavian (311)	433	3.94
Scotch-Irish (89)	389	3.54
Scottish (116)	533	4.85
Slovak (0)	37	0.34

*Notes: † The Census 2010 population figure is used to calculate the percentages in the Hispanic Origin and Race categories. Ancestry percentages are based on the 2006-2010 American Community Survey population (not shown); ‡ Numbers in parentheses indicate the number of people reporting a single ancestry; * Numbers in parentheses indicate the number of persons reporting this race alone, not in combination with any other race; Please refer to the Explanation of Data for more information.*

Swedish (70)	322	2.93
Swiss (79)	131	1.19
Ukrainian (234)	234	2.13
Welsh (25)	195	1.77

Hispanic Origin	Population	%
Hispanic or Latino (of any race)	1,374	12.04
Central American, ex. Mexican	97	0.85
Costa Rican	13	0.11
Guatemalan	34	0.30
Honduran	7	0.06
Nicaraguan	6	0.05
Panamanian	1	0.01
Salvadoran	36	0.32
Cuban	1	0.01
Dominican Republic	2	0.02
Mexican	1,065	9.33
Puerto Rican	31	0.27
South American	9	0.08
Argentinean	1	0.01
Chilean	3	0.03
Colombian	3	0.03
Peruvian	1	0.01
Venezuelan	1	0.01
Other Hispanic or Latino	169	1.48

Race*	Population	%
African-American/Black (117)	231	2.02
Not Hispanic (104)	198	1.73
Hispanic (13)	33	0.29
American Indian/Alaska Native (292)	470	4.12
Not Hispanic (239)	377	3.30
Hispanic (53)	93	0.81
Alaska Athabascan *(Ala. Nat.)* (3)	4	0.04
Aleut *(Alaska Native)* (10)	13	0.11
Apache (3)	11	0.10
Blackfeet (5)	14	0.12
Canadian/French Am. Ind. (8)	10	0.09
Central American Ind. (0)	5	0.04
Cherokee (5)	23	0.20
Cheyenne (0)	3	0.03
Chickasaw (0)	1	0.01
Chippewa (3)	4	0.04
Choctaw (4)	5	0.04
Comanche (0)	1	0.01
Cree (1)	1	0.01
Creek (3)	6	0.05
Inupiat *(Alaska Native)* (3)	4	0.04
Iroquois (5)	6	0.05
Mexican American Ind. (13)	14	0.12
Navajo (3)	3	0.03
Paiute (2)	2	0.02
Potawatomi (1)	1	0.01
Puget Sound Salish (30)	42	0.37
Sioux (2)	6	0.05
Spanish American Ind. (1)	1	0.01
Tlingit-Haida *(Alaska Native)* (11)	19	0.17
Yakama (1)	2	0.02
Yuman (0)	1	0.01
Yup'ik *(Alaska Native)* (5)	7	0.06
Asian (416)	587	5.14
Not Hispanic (401)	557	4.88
Hispanic (15)	30	0.26
Burmese (1)	1	0.01
Cambodian (26)	35	0.31
Chinese, ex. Taiwanese (39)	68	0.60
Filipino (68)	122	1.07
Hmong (1)	1	0.01
Indian (172)	190	1.66
Japanese (11)	45	0.39
Korean (22)	51	0.45
Laotian (1)	3	0.03
Pakistani (2)	3	0.03
Taiwanese (2)	2	0.02
Thai (9)	15	0.13
Vietnamese (45)	54	0.47
Hawaii Native/Pacific Islander (26)	61	0.53
Not Hispanic (26)	59	0.52
Hispanic (0)	2	0.02
Fijian (11)	15	0.13
Guamanian/Chamorro (7)	8	0.07
Native Hawaiian (4)	16	0.14
Samoan (1)	8	0.07
Tongan (2)	2	0.02
White (9,490)	9,927	86.96
Not Hispanic (8,879)	9,226	80.82
Hispanic (611)	701	6.14

Fife

Place Type: City
County: Pierce
Population: 9,173†

Ancestry‡	Population	%
African, Sub-Saharan (318)	337	4.00
African (271)	290	3.44
Ethiopian (27)	27	0.32
Kenyan (20)	20	0.24
American (148)	148	1.75
Austrian (0)	6	0.07
British (3)	3	0.04
Canadian (4)	30	0.36
Croatian (8)	38	0.45
Czech (4)	21	0.25
Czechoslovakian (0)	7	0.08
Danish (0)	26	0.31
Dutch (43)	95	1.13
Eastern European (4)	4	0.05
English (93)	450	5.34
European (40)	46	0.55
Finnish (0)	7	0.08
French, ex. Basque (35)	293	3.47
French Canadian (43)	86	1.02
German (349)	1,383	16.40
Greek (8)	8	0.09
Guyanese (10)	10	0.12
Hungarian (26)	75	0.89
Iranian (6)	6	0.07
Irish (336)	906	10.74
Italian (87)	278	3.30
Lithuanian (0)	4	0.05
Norwegian (46)	377	4.47
Polish (37)	143	1.70
Portuguese (4)	4	0.05
Romanian (4)	4	0.05
Russian (30)	85	1.01
Scandinavian (24)	128	1.52
Scotch-Irish (43)	100	1.19
Scottish (18)	112	1.33
Slovene (3)	7	0.08
Swedish (64)	191	2.26
Swiss (6)	16	0.19
Ukrainian (90)	113	1.34
Welsh (15)	38	0.45
West Indian, ex. Hispanic (0)	6	0.07
Dutch West Indian (0)	6	0.07

Hispanic Origin	Population	%
Hispanic or Latino (of any race)	1,595	17.39
Central American, ex. Mexican	95	1.04
Guatemalan	15	0.16
Honduran	7	0.08
Nicaraguan	1	0.01
Panamanian	11	0.12
Salvadoran	60	0.65
Other Central American	1	0.01
Cuban	4	0.04
Dominican Republic	4	0.04
Mexican	1,301	14.18
Puerto Rican	85	0.93
South American	33	0.36
Argentinean	4	0.04
Chilean	1	0.01
Colombian	12	0.13
Peruvian	16	0.17
Other Hispanic or Latino	73	0.80

Race*	Population	%
African-American/Black (749)	949	10.35
Not Hispanic (726)	898	9.79
Hispanic (23)	51	0.56
American Indian/Alaska Native (275)	442	4.82
Not Hispanic (221)	356	3.88
Hispanic (54)	86	0.94
Aleut *(Alaska Native)* (1)	8	0.09
Arapaho (2)	2	0.02
Blackfeet (5)	14	0.15
Canadian/French Am. Ind. (1)	2	0.02
Central American Ind. (1)	1	0.01
Cherokee (10)	42	0.46
Cheyenne (0)	3	0.03
Chickasaw (0)	1	0.01
Chippewa (6)	6	0.07
Choctaw (1)	3	0.03
Colville (12)	15	0.16
Creek (0)	1	0.01
Inupiat *(Alaska Native)* (2)	3	0.03
Mexican American Ind. (29)	46	0.50
Navajo (5)	7	0.08
Osage (0)	5	0.05
Puget Sound Salish (95)	111	1.21
Sioux (5)	11	0.12
South American Ind. (1)	1	0.01
Tlingit-Haida *(Alaska Native)* (7)	12	0.13
Tsimshian *(Alaska Native)* (0)	2	0.02
Yakama (4)	4	0.04
Yaqui (1)	1	0.01
Asian (1,425)	1,767	19.26
Not Hispanic (1,400)	1,709	18.63
Hispanic (25)	58	0.63
Bangladeshi (3)	3	0.03
Cambodian (129)	158	1.72
Chinese, ex. Taiwanese (39)	78	0.85
Filipino (361)	529	5.77
Indian (87)	109	1.19
Indonesian (0)	2	0.02
Japanese (38)	102	1.11
Korean (467)	537	5.85
Laotian (17)	22	0.24
Pakistani (13)	14	0.15
Taiwanese (2)	3	0.03
Thai (37)	46	0.50
Vietnamese (156)	183	1.99
Hawaii Native/Pacific Islander (252)	377	4.11
Not Hispanic (248)	366	3.99
Hispanic (4)	11	0.12
Fijian (8)	10	0.11
Guamanian/Chamorro (40)	85	0.93
Marshallese (21)	27	0.29
Native Hawaiian (13)	58	0.63
Samoan (146)	173	1.89
White (5,061)	5,631	61.39
Not Hispanic (4,406)	4,856	52.94
Hispanic (655)	775	8.45

Five Corners

Place Type: CDP
County: Clark
Population: 18,159†

Ancestry‡	Population	%
African, Sub-Saharan (57)	57	0.33
African (18)	18	0.10
Ghanaian (39)	39	0.22
American (636)	636	3.65
Arab (0)	52	0.30
Iraqi (0)	21	0.12
Lebanese (0)	31	0.18
Assyrian/Chaldean/Syriac (0)	21	0.12
Austrian (0)	28	0.16
Belgian (9)	57	0.33
British (0)	153	0.88
Cajun (23)	23	0.13
Canadian (33)	43	0.25
Croatian (0)	10	0.06
Czech (34)	120	0.69
Czechoslovakian (0)	27	0.15
Danish (46)	195	1.12

SECTION TWO

*Notes: † The Census 2010 population figure is used to calculate the percentages in the Hispanic Origin and Race categories. Ancestry percentages are based on the 2006-2010 American Community Survey population (not shown); ‡ Numbers in parentheses indicate the number of people reporting a single ancestry; * Numbers in parentheses indicate the number of persons reporting this race alone, not in combination with any other race; Please refer to the Explanation of Data for more information.*

Ancestry (cont.)	Population	%
Dutch (82)	477	2.74
English (341)	1,780	10.21
European (266)	266	1.53
Finnish (42)	128	0.73
French, ex. Basque (168)	781	4.48
French Canadian (77)	127	0.73
German (976)	3,632	20.83
German Russian (0)	28	0.16
Greek (0)	45	0.26
Hungarian (0)	23	0.13
Icelander (30)	30	0.17
Irish (413)	2,057	11.80
Italian (95)	376	2.16
Lithuanian (61)	67	0.38
Northern European (44)	44	0.25
Norwegian (261)	681	3.91
Polish (29)	203	1.16
Portuguese (53)	97	0.56
Romanian (0)	58	0.33
Russian (913)	1,468	8.42
Scandinavian (74)	145	0.83
Scotch-Irish (118)	505	2.90
Scottish (94)	628	3.60
Slavic (0)	33	0.19
Slovak (13)	13	0.07
Swedish (63)	308	1.77
Swiss (17)	148	0.85
Ukrainian (1,069)	1,598	9.16
Welsh (28)	87	0.50
West Indian, ex. Hispanic (20)	48	0.28
Haitian (20)	20	0.11
West Indian (0)	28	0.16

Hispanic Origin	Population	%
Hispanic or Latino (of any race)	1,413	7.78
Central American, ex. Mexican	40	0.22
Costa Rican	1	0.01
Guatemalan	8	0.04
Honduran	6	0.03
Nicaraguan	7	0.04
Panamanian	2	0.01
Salvadoran	16	0.09
Cuban	17	0.09
Dominican Republic	1	0.01
Mexican	1,111	6.12
Puerto Rican	42	0.23
South American	46	0.25
Argentinean	5	0.03
Chilean	1	0.01
Colombian	18	0.10
Ecuadorian	4	0.02
Peruvian	7	0.04
Uruguayan	4	0.02
Venezuelan	7	0.04
Other Hispanic or Latino	156	0.86

Race*	Population	%
African-American/Black (354)	561	3.09
Not Hispanic (335)	502	2.76
Hispanic (19)	59	0.32
American Indian/Alaska Native (146)	428	2.36
Not Hispanic (133)	363	2.00
Hispanic (13)	65	0.36
Alaska Athabascan *(Ala. Nat.)* (0)	1	0.01
Aleut *(Alaska Native)* (2)	3	0.02
Apache (1)	2	0.01
Blackfeet (2)	12	0.07
Canadian/French Am. Ind. (4)	4	0.02
Central American Ind. (0)	2	0.01
Cherokee (13)	66	0.36
Chickasaw (3)	6	0.03
Chippewa (8)	20	0.11
Choctaw (3)	4	0.02
Comanche (0)	4	0.02
Cree (0)	1	0.01
Creek (0)	1	0.01
Crow (0)	4	0.02
Delaware (0)	1	0.01
Iroquois (2)	2	0.01
Lumbee (0)	2	0.01
Mexican American Ind. (2)	10	0.06
Navajo (2)	8	0.04
Osage (0)	1	0.01
Potawatomi (1)	1	0.01
Pueblo (1)	3	0.02
Puget Sound Salish (2)	4	0.02
Seminole (1)	4	0.02
Shoshone (0)	1	0.01
Sioux (5)	15	0.08
Tlingit-Haida *(Alaska Native)* (5)	18	0.10
Tsimshian *(Alaska Native)* (4)	4	0.02
Yakama (1)	2	0.01
Yaqui (0)	1	0.01
Yup'ik *(Alaska Native)* (1)	1	0.01
Asian (902)	1,198	6.60
Not Hispanic (883)	1,159	6.38
Hispanic (19)	39	0.21
Burmese (1)	1	0.01
Cambodian (104)	119	0.66
Chinese, ex. Taiwanese (61)	100	0.55
Filipino (172)	307	1.69
Hmong (9)	10	0.06
Indian (112)	140	0.77
Indonesian (4)	8	0.04
Japanese (32)	96	0.53
Korean (37)	71	0.39
Laotian (53)	61	0.34
Pakistani (3)	4	0.02
Taiwanese (1)	4	0.02
Thai (15)	25	0.14
Vietnamese (258)	274	1.51
Hawaii Native/Pacific Islander (152)	251	1.38
Not Hispanic (144)	227	1.25
Hispanic (8)	24	0.13
Fijian (12)	17	0.09
Guamanian/Chamorro (56)	69	0.38
Marshallese (0)	1	0.01
Native Hawaiian (29)	77	0.42
Samoan (19)	38	0.21
Tongan (0)	1	0.01
White (15,260)	16,051	88.39
Not Hispanic (14,553)	15,178	83.58
Hispanic (707)	873	4.81

Fort Lewis

Place Type: CDP
County: Pierce
Population: 11,046†

Ancestry‡	Population	%
American (252)	252	1.84
Armenian (48)	244	1.78
Austrian (38)	86	0.63
Brazilian (0)	2	0.01
Czech (10)	23	0.17
Danish (0)	14	0.10
Dutch (20)	206	1.50
English (483)	1,111	8.12
Estonian (0)	35	0.26
European (341)	381	2.78
Finnish (11)	23	0.17
French, ex. Basque (52)	262	1.91
French Canadian (0)	18	0.13
German (943)	2,699	19.72
Greek (50)	79	0.58
Hungarian (22)	26	0.19
Irish (375)	2,040	14.90
Italian (396)	713	5.21
Lithuanian (0)	74	0.54
Norwegian (51)	348	2.54
Polish (100)	336	2.45
Portuguese (15)	56	0.41
Russian (100)	158	1.15
Scandinavian (25)	25	0.18
Scotch-Irish (19)	177	1.29
Scottish (61)	379	2.77
Swedish (15)	16	0.12
Swiss (0)	28	0.20
Welsh (118)	180	1.31
West Indian, ex. Hispanic (75)	116	0.85
Barbadian (9)	9	0.07
Jamaican (60)	101	0.74
Trinidadian/Tobagonian (2)	2	0.01
West Indian (4)	4	0.03

Hispanic Origin	Population	%
Hispanic or Latino (of any race)	1,800	16.30
Central American, ex. Mexican	77	0.70
Costa Rican	2	0.02
Guatemalan	11	0.10
Honduran	11	0.10
Nicaraguan	7	0.06
Panamanian	23	0.21
Salvadoran	21	0.19
Other Central American	2	0.02
Cuban	41	0.37
Dominican Republic	48	0.43
Mexican	993	8.99
Puerto Rican	456	4.13
South American	58	0.53
Argentinean	2	0.02
Bolivian	3	0.03
Colombian	25	0.23
Ecuadorian	8	0.07
Peruvian	9	0.08
Venezuelan	11	0.10
Other Hispanic or Latino	127	1.15

Race*	Population	%
African-American/Black (1,253)	1,647	14.91
Not Hispanic (1,122)	1,442	13.05
Hispanic (131)	205	1.86
American Indian/Alaska Native (170)	492	4.45
Not Hispanic (138)	393	3.56
Hispanic (32)	99	0.90
Alaska Athabascan *(Ala. Nat.)* (0)	1	0.01
Aleut *(Alaska Native)* (2)	2	0.02
Apache (5)	19	0.17
Arapaho (0)	3	0.03
Blackfeet (9)	27	0.24
Central American Ind. (0)	1	0.01
Cherokee (16)	101	0.91
Cheyenne (0)	2	0.02
Chickasaw (0)	2	0.02
Chippewa (0)	12	0.11
Choctaw (9)	19	0.17
Comanche (0)	5	0.05
Cree (0)	2	0.02
Creek (1)	4	0.04
Delaware (1)	1	0.01
Hopi (6)	7	0.06
Iroquois (1)	2	0.02
Lumbee (0)	4	0.04
Mexican American Ind. (2)	7	0.06
Navajo (15)	25	0.23
Osage (1)	1	0.01
Pima (1)	1	0.01
Pueblo (2)	2	0.02
Puget Sound Salish (6)	12	0.11
Seminole (0)	1	0.01
Shoshone (0)	1	0.01
Sioux (4)	18	0.16
Tlingit-Haida *(Alaska Native)* (0)	1	0.01
Ute (1)	1	0.01
Yaqui (0)	4	0.04
Asian (336)	659	5.97
Not Hispanic (323)	589	5.33
Hispanic (13)	70	0.63
Burmese (2)	2	0.02
Cambodian (8)	11	0.10
Chinese, ex. Taiwanese (16)	35	0.32
Filipino (151)	313	2.83
Indian (23)	26	0.24
Indonesian (0)	1	0.01
Japanese (16)	81	0.73
Korean (81)	150	1.36
Laotian (3)	9	0.08
Malaysian (2)	2	0.02
Nepalese (5)	5	0.05

*Notes: † The Census 2010 population figure is used to calculate the percentages in the Hispanic Origin and Race categories. Ancestry percentages are based on the 2006-2010 American Community Survey population (not shown); ‡ Numbers in parentheses indicate the number of people reporting a single ancestry; * Numbers in parentheses indicate the number of persons reporting this race alone, not in combination with any other race; Please refer to the Explanation of Data for more information.*

Pakistani (0)	3	0.03
Sri Lankan (1)	2	0.02
Taiwanese (1)	1	0.01
Thai (5)	23	0.21
Vietnamese (8)	11	0.10
Hawaii Native/Pacific Islander (258)	359	3.25
Not Hispanic (238)	322	2.92
Hispanic (20)	37	0.33
Guamanian/Chamorro (47)	70	0.63
Marshallese (11)	11	0.10
Native Hawaiian (17)	86	0.78
Samoan (69)	93	0.84
Tongan (0)	8	0.07
White (7,538)	8,459	76.58
Not Hispanic (6,635)	7,316	66.23
Hispanic (903)	1,143	10.35

Frederickson

Place Type: CDP
County: Pierce
Population: 18,719†

Ancestry‡	Population	%
African, Sub-Saharan (70)	70	0.40
African (54)	54	0.31
Other Sub-Saharan African (16)	16	0.09
American (576)	576	3.25
Arab (28)	53	0.30
Arab (28)	28	0.16
Lebanese (0)	25	0.14
Austrian (20)	37	0.21
Basque (0)	49	0.28
Belgian (38)	47	0.27
British (60)	89	0.50
Canadian (11)	56	0.32
Croatian (0)	22	0.12
Czech (10)	64	0.36
Czechoslovakian (31)	79	0.45
Danish (0)	44	0.25
Dutch (152)	601	3.39
English (396)	1,365	7.71
European (318)	318	1.80
Finnish (23)	72	0.41
French, ex. Basque (135)	650	3.67
French Canadian (53)	183	1.03
German (944)	3,843	21.71
Greek (0)	13	0.07
Hungarian (25)	46	0.26
Icelander (6)	6	0.03
Irish (355)	2,038	11.51
Italian (239)	716	4.04
Lithuanian (0)	3	0.02
Luxemburger (8)	8	0.05
Norwegian (250)	736	4.16
Pennsylvania German (0)	16	0.09
Polish (17)	231	1.30
Portuguese (17)	38	0.21
Russian (50)	106	0.60
Scandinavian (119)	184	1.04
Scotch-Irish (66)	316	1.78
Scottish (186)	518	2.93
Slovak (0)	10	0.06
Swedish (143)	779	4.40
Swiss (6)	44	0.25
Ukrainian (0)	40	0.23
Welsh (8)	117	0.66
West Indian, ex. Hispanic (6)	13	0.07
Bahamian (0)	7	0.04
British West Indian (6)	6	0.03
Yugoslavian (0)	44	0.25

Hispanic Origin	Population	%
Hispanic or Latino (of any race)	1,673	8.94
Central American, ex. Mexican	106	0.57
Costa Rican	17	0.09
Guatemalan	10	0.05
Honduran	12	0.06
Nicaraguan	8	0.04
Panamanian	36	0.19
Salvadoran	23	0.12
Cuban	16	0.09
Dominican Republic	16	0.09
Mexican	1,128	6.03
Puerto Rican	194	1.04
South American	37	0.20
Chilean	5	0.03
Colombian	3	0.02
Ecuadorian	7	0.04
Peruvian	13	0.07
Venezuelan	9	0.05
Other Hispanic or Latino	176	0.94

Race*	Population	%
African-American/Black (1,361)	1,892	10.11
Not Hispanic (1,284)	1,747	9.33
Hispanic (77)	145	0.77
American Indian/Alaska Native (211)	527	2.82
Not Hispanic (166)	427	2.28
Hispanic (45)	100	0.53
Aleut *(Alaska Native)* (4)	6	0.03
Apache (2)	3	0.02
Blackfeet (6)	33	0.18
Canadian/French Am. Ind. (1)	5	0.03
Cherokee (10)	58	0.31
Cheyenne (6)	6	0.03
Chickasaw (3)	4	0.02
Chippewa (7)	27	0.14
Choctaw (1)	4	0.02
Colville (3)	8	0.04
Cree (0)	3	0.02
Creek (1)	2	0.01
Hopi (2)	2	0.01
Inupiat *(Alaska Native)* (3)	8	0.04
Iroquois (0)	3	0.02
Kiowa (2)	2	0.01
Lumbee (1)	2	0.01
Mexican American Ind. (11)	17	0.09
Navajo (2)	7	0.04
Ottawa (1)	2	0.01
Pima (0)	3	0.02
Potawatomi (0)	3	0.02
Pueblo (0)	1	0.01
Puget Sound Salish (34)	57	0.30
Seminole (0)	1	0.01
Sioux (8)	11	0.06
Spanish American Ind. (1)	1	0.01
Tlingit-Haida *(Alaska Native)* (1)	6	0.03
Tsimshian *(Alaska Native)* (3)	6	0.03
Yakama (2)	12	0.06
Yuman (1)	3	0.02
Yup'ik *(Alaska Native)* (1)	2	0.01
Asian (1,046)	1,784	9.53
Not Hispanic (1,013)	1,661	8.87
Hispanic (33)	123	0.66
Cambodian (128)	195	1.04
Chinese, ex. Taiwanese (57)	140	0.75
Filipino (381)	692	3.70
Hmong (5)	8	0.04
Indian (34)	55	0.29
Indonesian (0)	3	0.02
Japanese (69)	198	1.06
Korean (212)	405	2.16
Laotian (12)	14	0.07
Malaysian (0)	2	0.01
Nepalese (5)	5	0.03
Taiwanese (3)	6	0.03
Thai (21)	60	0.32
Vietnamese (54)	90	0.48
Hawaii Native/Pacific Islander (420)	650	3.47
Not Hispanic (409)	602	3.22
Hispanic (11)	48	0.26
Fijian (4)	7	0.04
Guamanian/Chamorro (193)	253	1.35
Marshallese (1)	8	0.04
Native Hawaiian (29)	148	0.79
Samoan (161)	220	1.18
Tongan (0)	3	0.02
White (13,633)	14,898	79.59
Not Hispanic (12,903)	13,942	74.48
Hispanic (730)	956	5.11

Graham

Place Type: CDP
County: Pierce
Population: 23,491†

Ancestry‡	Population	%
African, Sub-Saharan (51)	174	0.80
African (19)	142	0.65
Kenyan (32)	32	0.15
American (1,300)	1,300	5.99
Austrian (10)	38	0.18
Belgian (21)	58	0.27
British (34)	95	0.44
Cajun (18)	18	0.08
Canadian (197)	208	0.96
Croatian (0)	8	0.04
Czech (20)	88	0.41
Czechoslovakian (8)	8	0.04
Danish (86)	189	0.87
Dutch (37)	377	1.74
Eastern European (8)	8	0.04
English (657)	2,646	12.19
European (474)	638	2.94
Finnish (0)	38	0.18
French, ex. Basque (124)	906	4.17
French Canadian (95)	230	1.06
German (1,619)	5,027	23.15
Greek (0)	16	0.07
Hungarian (0)	118	0.54
Icelander (0)	15	0.07
Irish (806)	3,103	14.29
Italian (337)	979	4.51
Lithuanian (0)	19	0.09
Northern European (28)	40	0.18
Norwegian (655)	1,421	6.54
Pennsylvania German (23)	23	0.11
Polish (90)	353	1.63
Portuguese (21)	140	0.64
Romanian (0)	22	0.10
Russian (175)	268	1.23
Scandinavian (33)	77	0.35
Scotch-Irish (282)	646	2.98
Scottish (104)	476	2.19
Slavic (0)	9	0.04
Slovak (9)	20	0.09
Swedish (247)	755	3.48
Swiss (218)	280	1.29
Turkish (0)	136	0.63
Ukrainian (46)	56	0.26
Welsh (50)	227	1.05
West Indian, ex. Hispanic (22)	22	0.10
Jamaican (22)	22	0.10

Hispanic Origin	Population	%
Hispanic or Latino (of any race)	1,477	6.29
Central American, ex. Mexican	78	0.33
Costa Rican	2	0.01
Guatemalan	10	0.04
Honduran	14	0.06
Nicaraguan	2	0.01
Panamanian	21	0.09
Salvadoran	29	0.12
Cuban	11	0.05
Dominican Republic	12	0.05
Mexican	953	4.06
Puerto Rican	161	0.69
South American	43	0.18
Argentinean	5	0.02
Bolivian	2	0.01
Colombian	12	0.05
Ecuadorian	6	0.03
Peruvian	18	0.08
Other Hispanic or Latino	219	0.93

Race*	Population	%
African-American/Black (942)	1,353	5.76
Not Hispanic (899)	1,259	5.36

*Notes: † The Census 2010 population figure is used to calculate the percentages in the Hispanic Origin and Race categories. Ancestry percentages are based on the 2006-2010 American Community Survey population (not shown); ‡ Numbers in parentheses indicate the number of people reporting a single ancestry; * Numbers in parentheses indicate the number of persons reporting this race alone, not in combination with any other race; Please refer to the Explanation of Data for more information.*

Hispanic (43)	94	0.40
American Indian/Alaska Native (280)	687	2.92
Not Hispanic (245)	611	2.60
Hispanic (35)	76	0.32
Alaska Athabascan *(Ala. Nat.)* (2)	13	0.06
Aleut *(Alaska Native)* (6)	10	0.04
Apache (3)	4	0.02
Blackfeet (14)	60	0.26
Canadian/French Am. Ind. (3)	12	0.05
Central American Ind. (0)	1	<0.01
Cherokee (28)	114	0.49
Chickasaw (0)	4	0.02
Chippewa (20)	40	0.17
Choctaw (6)	12	0.05
Colville (1)	1	<0.01
Comanche (0)	5	0.02
Cree (0)	6	0.03
Creek (0)	2	0.01
Crow (0)	1	<0.01
Delaware (2)	4	0.02
Hopi (1)	3	0.01
Houma (0)	2	0.01
Inupiat *(Alaska Native)* (4)	5	0.02
Iroquois (0)	1	<0.01
Lumbee (5)	5	0.02
Navajo (3)	8	0.03
Osage (0)	5	0.02
Ottawa (1)	1	<0.01
Potawatomi (2)	4	0.02
Pueblo (1)	4	0.02
Puget Sound Salish (36)	46	0.20
Seminole (1)	4	0.02
Shoshone (1)	1	<0.01
Sioux (5)	15	0.06
Spanish American Ind. (1)	1	<0.01
Tlingit-Haida *(Alaska Native)* (13)	29	0.12
Tohono O'Odham (1)	1	<0.01
Tsimshian *(Alaska Native)* (0)	4	0.02
Ute (0)	1	<0.01
Yakama (2)	6	0.03
Yaqui (1)	1	<0.01
Asian (668)	1,323	5.63
Not Hispanic (650)	1,245	5.30
Hispanic (18)	78	0.33
Cambodian (60)	73	0.31
Chinese, ex. Taiwanese (35)	118	0.50
Filipino (274)	526	2.24
Hmong (3)	3	0.01
Indian (37)	54	0.23
Indonesian (3)	16	0.07
Japanese (75)	239	1.02
Korean (111)	248	1.06
Laotian (11)	14	0.06
Malaysian (1)	1	<0.01
Taiwanese (2)	5	0.02
Thai (12)	27	0.11
Vietnamese (19)	36	0.15
Hawaii Native/Pacific Islander (281)	464	1.98
Not Hispanic (275)	447	1.90
Hispanic (6)	17	0.07
Fijian (0)	3	0.01
Guamanian/Chamorro (93)	161	0.69
Native Hawaiian (40)	136	0.58
Samoan (113)	154	0.66
Tongan (1)	1	<0.01
White (19,399)	20,734	88.26
Not Hispanic (18,674)	19,778	84.19
Hispanic (725)	956	4.07

Grandview

Place Type: City
County: Yakima
Population: 10,862†

Ancestry‡	Population	%
American (179)	179	1.72
Austrian (0)	11	0.11
Croatian (0)	25	0.24
Czechoslovakian (40)	183	1.76
Dutch (32)	59	0.57
Eastern European (0)	11	0.11
English (136)	344	3.31
European (14)	14	0.13
French, ex. Basque (17)	307	2.95
German (281)	1,113	10.71
Hungarian (0)	18	0.17
Irish (107)	334	3.21
Italian (0)	14	0.13
Norwegian (10)	55	0.53
Polish (46)	46	0.44
Russian (0)	60	0.58
Scotch-Irish (0)	52	0.50
Scottish (14)	14	0.13
Swedish (15)	25	0.24
Swiss (0)	55	0.53
Welsh (0)	16	0.15

Hispanic Origin	Population	%
Hispanic or Latino (of any race)	8,655	79.68
Central American, ex. Mexican	51	0.47
Guatemalan	14	0.13
Honduran	10	0.09
Nicaraguan	7	0.06
Panamanian	3	0.03
Salvadoran	17	0.16
Cuban	3	0.03
Mexican	8,172	75.23
Puerto Rican	10	0.09
South American	6	0.06
Argentinean	1	0.01
Colombian	1	0.01
Peruvian	4	0.04
Other Hispanic or Latino	413	3.80

Race*	Population	%
African-American/Black (93)	135	1.24
Not Hispanic (29)	46	0.42
Hispanic (64)	89	0.82
American Indian/Alaska Native (63)	135	1.24
Not Hispanic (24)	66	0.61
Hispanic (39)	69	0.64
Alaska Athabascan *(Ala. Nat.)* (1)	5	0.05
Aleut *(Alaska Native)* (1)	6	0.06
Blackfeet (5)	6	0.06
Central American Ind. (1)	4	0.04
Cherokee (0)	4	0.04
Chickasaw (1)	1	0.01
Chippewa (0)	2	0.02
Choctaw (0)	3	0.03
Inupiat *(Alaska Native)* (2)	2	0.02
Iroquois (0)	1	0.01
Mexican American Ind. (4)	5	0.05
Navajo (2)	3	0.03
Puget Sound Salish (1)	4	0.04
Seminole (0)	2	0.02
Sioux (1)	2	0.02
Spanish American Ind. (1)	1	0.01
Tlingit-Haida *(Alaska Native)* (0)	4	0.04
Ute (0)	2	0.02
Yakama (12)	14	0.13
Asian (51)	90	0.83
Not Hispanic (47)	59	0.54
Hispanic (4)	31	0.29
Chinese, ex. Taiwanese (6)	14	0.13
Filipino (14)	22	0.20
Indian (3)	5	0.05
Japanese (6)	10	0.09
Korean (12)	17	0.16
Vietnamese (9)	11	0.10
Hawaii Native/Pacific Islander (6)	9	0.08
Not Hispanic (2)	2	0.02
Hispanic (4)	7	0.06
Guamanian/Chamorro (1)	2	0.02
White (5,995)	6,381	58.75
Not Hispanic (2,011)	2,081	19.16
Hispanic (3,984)	4,300	39.59

Hazel Dell

Place Type: CDP
County: Clark
Population: 19,435†

Ancestry‡	Population	%
African, Sub-Saharan (187)	207	1.07
Somalian (176)	176	0.91
South African (11)	31	0.16
American (681)	681	3.53
Arab (43)	150	0.78
Palestinian (43)	142	0.74
Syrian (0)	8	0.04
Austrian (0)	25	0.13
Basque (23)	23	0.12
Belgian (0)	43	0.22
Brazilian (0)	13	0.07
British (73)	287	1.49
Bulgarian (18)	18	0.09
Czech (26)	140	0.73
Danish (105)	331	1.72
Dutch (147)	521	2.70
English (504)	2,027	10.51
European (179)	205	1.06
Finnish (23)	61	0.32
French, ex. Basque (44)	868	4.50
French Canadian (97)	324	1.68
German (1,097)	4,517	23.42
Greek (31)	90	0.47
Hungarian (74)	106	0.55
Iranian (0)	42	0.22
Irish (642)	2,438	12.64
Italian (211)	609	3.16
Latvian (15)	15	0.08
Maltese (0)	9	0.05
Northern European (17)	17	0.09
Norwegian (413)	1,107	5.74
Pennsylvania German (0)	16	0.08
Polish (89)	387	2.01
Portuguese (11)	42	0.22
Romanian (21)	21	0.11
Russian (340)	561	2.91
Scandinavian (70)	286	1.48
Scotch-Irish (225)	409	2.12
Scottish (117)	629	3.26
Swedish (166)	634	3.29
Swiss (40)	217	1.13
Ukrainian (34)	124	0.64
Welsh (6)	201	1.04

Hispanic Origin	Population	%
Hispanic or Latino (of any race)	2,143	11.03
Central American, ex. Mexican	65	0.33
Costa Rican	4	0.02
Guatemalan	13	0.07
Honduran	5	0.03
Nicaraguan	5	0.03
Panamanian	4	0.02
Salvadoran	34	0.17
Cuban	25	0.13
Dominican Republic	3	0.02
Mexican	1,783	9.17
Puerto Rican	53	0.27
South American	45	0.23
Argentinean	7	0.04
Bolivian	2	0.01
Chilean	9	0.05
Colombian	12	0.06
Ecuadorian	2	0.01
Paraguayan	2	0.01
Peruvian	7	0.04
Venezuelan	1	0.01
Other South American	3	0.02
Other Hispanic or Latino	169	0.87

Race*	Population	%
African-American/Black (518)	795	4.09
Not Hispanic (486)	746	3.84
Hispanic (32)	49	0.25

*Notes: † The Census 2010 population figure is used to calculate the percentages in the Hispanic Origin and Race categories. Ancestry percentages are based on the 2006-2010 American Community Survey population (not shown); ‡ Numbers in parentheses indicate the number of people reporting a single ancestry; * Numbers in parentheses indicate the number of persons reporting this race alone, not in combination with any other race; Please refer to the Explanation of Data for more information.*

American Indian/Alaska Native (156)	431	2.22
Not Hispanic (134)	387	1.99
Hispanic (22)	44	0.23
Alaska Athabascan *(Ala. Nat.)* (1)	1	0.01
Aleut *(Alaska Native)* (3)	8	0.04
Apache (3)	18	0.09
Blackfeet (9)	22	0.11
Canadian/French Am. Ind. (1)	3	0.02
Cherokee (8)	54	0.28
Cheyenne (2)	8	0.04
Chickasaw (0)	1	0.01
Chippewa (6)	14	0.07
Choctaw (4)	9	0.05
Colville (1)	3	0.02
Comanche (0)	3	0.02
Cree (0)	1	0.01
Delaware (0)	2	0.01
Hopi (1)	1	0.01
Inupiat *(Alaska Native)* (1)	1	0.01
Iroquois (3)	9	0.05
Mexican American Ind. (2)	7	0.04
Navajo (3)	3	0.02
Osage (0)	2	0.01
Ottawa (0)	1	0.01
Paiute (1)	1	0.01
Potawatomi (3)	3	0.02
Pueblo (3)	5	0.03
Puget Sound Salish (1)	2	0.01
Seminole (1)	3	0.02
Sioux (4)	25	0.13
South American Ind. (0)	1	0.01
Tlingit-Haida *(Alaska Native)* (1)	3	0.02
Tsimshian *(Alaska Native)* (0)	1	0.01
Yakama (2)	4	0.02
Yuman (0)	1	0.01
Asian (720)	930	4.79
Not Hispanic (715)	905	4.66
Hispanic (5)	25	0.13
Bangladeshi (5)	5	0.03
Cambodian (34)	42	0.22
Chinese, ex. Taiwanese (69)	122	0.63
Filipino (98)	164	0.84
Hmong (32)	32	0.16
Indian (65)	83	0.43
Indonesian (1)	6	0.03
Japanese (54)	102	0.52
Korean (86)	105	0.54
Laotian (27)	29	0.15
Malaysian (1)	4	0.02
Pakistani (0)	1	0.01
Sri Lankan (1)	6	0.03
Taiwanese (3)	3	0.02
Thai (9)	14	0.07
Vietnamese (200)	230	1.18
Hawaii Native/Pacific Islander (131)	230	1.18
Not Hispanic (122)	210	1.08
Hispanic (9)	20	0.10
Fijian (12)	13	0.07
Guamanian/Chamorro (18)	29	0.15
Marshallese (1)	1	0.01
Native Hawaiian (23)	63	0.32
Samoan (34)	47	0.24
Tongan (11)	14	0.07
White (15,945)	16,729	86.08
Not Hispanic (15,112)	15,753	81.05
Hispanic (833)	976	5.02

Hoquiam

Place Type: City
County: Grays Harbor
Population: 8,726†

Ancestry‡	Population	%
African, Sub-Saharan (28)	28	0.32
African (28)	28	0.32
American (470)	470	5.33
Austrian (0)	13	0.15
Basque (0)	14	0.16
British (9)	21	0.24
Canadian (20)	24	0.27
Croatian (19)	52	0.59
Czech (0)	9	0.10
Danish (21)	45	0.51
Dutch (0)	301	3.42
English (271)	1,024	11.62
European (101)	110	1.25
Finnish (74)	202	2.29
French, ex. Basque (93)	295	3.35
French Canadian (73)	153	1.74
German (527)	2,022	22.95
Icelander (0)	9	0.10
Irish (229)	1,671	18.96
Israeli (0)	32	0.36
Italian (43)	301	3.42
Luxemburger (0)	21	0.24
New Zealander (0)	33	0.37
Norwegian (179)	645	7.32
Pennsylvania German (0)	34	0.39
Polish (84)	259	2.94
Portuguese (12)	61	0.69
Romanian (11)	22	0.25
Russian (0)	34	0.39
Scandinavian (0)	87	0.99
Scotch-Irish (167)	297	3.37
Scottish (84)	257	2.92
Swedish (75)	574	6.51
Swiss (0)	17	0.19
Ukrainian (67)	76	0.86
Welsh (13)	64	0.73
Yugoslavian (9)	9	0.10

Hispanic Origin	Population	%
Hispanic or Latino (of any race)	831	9.52
Central American, ex. Mexican	62	0.71
Costa Rican	3	0.03
Guatemalan	17	0.19
Honduran	3	0.03
Panamanian	1	0.01
Salvadoran	38	0.44
Cuban	6	0.07
Mexican	691	7.92
Puerto Rican	11	0.13
South American	13	0.15
Chilean	4	0.05
Colombian	5	0.06
Peruvian	3	0.03
Venezuelan	1	0.01
Other Hispanic or Latino	48	0.55

Race*	Population	%
African-American/Black (74)	118	1.35
Not Hispanic (61)	101	1.16
Hispanic (13)	17	0.19
American Indian/Alaska Native (342)	568	6.51
Not Hispanic (309)	508	5.82
Hispanic (33)	60	0.69
Alaska Athabascan *(Ala. Nat.)* (6)	8	0.09
Aleut *(Alaska Native)* (3)	8	0.09
Apache (2)	11	0.13
Blackfeet (2)	5	0.06
Canadian/French Am. Ind. (0)	5	0.06
Cherokee (5)	33	0.38
Chickasaw (0)	2	0.02
Chippewa (0)	5	0.06
Choctaw (2)	7	0.08
Colville (12)	12	0.14
Comanche (0)	1	0.01
Creek (0)	2	0.02
Crow (1)	1	0.01
Hopi (1)	1	0.01
Inupiat *(Alaska Native)* (2)	4	0.05
Iroquois (3)	3	0.03
Mexican American Ind. (5)	5	0.06
Ottawa (3)	3	0.03
Puget Sound Salish (13)	22	0.25
Shoshone (0)	1	0.01
Sioux (6)	7	0.08
Tlingit-Haida *(Alaska Native)* (1)	4	0.05
Tsimshian *(Alaska Native)* (4)	6	0.07
Yakama (5)	6	0.07
Asian (98)	171	1.96
Not Hispanic (92)	165	1.89
Hispanic (6)	6	0.07
Cambodian (6)	6	0.07
Chinese, ex. Taiwanese (9)	23	0.26
Filipino (22)	55	0.63
Indian (5)	7	0.08
Japanese (4)	17	0.19
Korean (29)	35	0.40
Laotian (10)	12	0.14
Thai (2)	6	0.07
Vietnamese (9)	10	0.11
Hawaii Native/Pacific Islander (15)	42	0.48
Not Hispanic (15)	42	0.48
Guamanian/Chamorro (7)	7	0.08
Native Hawaiian (4)	23	0.26
Samoan (2)	2	0.02
White (7,460)	7,802	89.41
Not Hispanic (7,108)	7,394	84.74
Hispanic (352)	408	4.68

Inglewood-Finn Hill

Place Type: CDP
County: King
Population: 22,707†

Ancestry‡	Population	%
Afghan (37)	74	0.32
African, Sub-Saharan (70)	167	0.72
African (62)	132	0.57
Kenyan (0)	12	0.05
Nigerian (8)	23	0.10
Albanian (0)	14	0.06
American (625)	625	2.70
Arab (47)	56	0.24
Lebanese (24)	33	0.14
Other Arab (23)	23	0.10
Armenian (0)	17	0.07
Assyrian/Chaldean/Syriac (16)	16	0.07
Australian (24)	46	0.20
Austrian (10)	10	0.04
Basque (12)	12	0.05
Belgian (13)	26	0.11
Brazilian (71)	71	0.31
British (113)	256	1.11
Canadian (74)	86	0.37
Celtic (0)	8	0.03
Croatian (19)	35	0.15
Czech (32)	78	0.34
Czechoslovakian (39)	83	0.36
Danish (9)	340	1.47
Dutch (116)	519	2.24
Eastern European (29)	29	0.13
English (980)	3,254	14.07
European (495)	643	2.78
Finnish (33)	69	0.30
French, ex. Basque (259)	1,101	4.76
French Canadian (89)	187	0.81
German (946)	4,147	17.93
Greek (66)	149	0.64
Hungarian (11)	69	0.30
Icelander (36)	76	0.33
Iranian (86)	134	0.58
Irish (770)	3,165	13.68
Italian (463)	1,215	5.25
Lithuanian (14)	21	0.09
Northern European (120)	120	0.52
Norwegian (476)	1,788	7.73
Pennsylvania German (0)	11	0.05
Polish (152)	932	4.03
Portuguese (8)	64	0.28
Romanian (98)	126	0.54
Russian (293)	493	2.13
Scandinavian (103)	205	0.89
Scotch-Irish (93)	433	1.87
Scottish (236)	1,208	5.22
Serbian (0)	33	0.14
Slovak (0)	9	0.04

SECTION TWO

*Notes: † The Census 2010 population figure is used to calculate the percentages in the Hispanic Origin and Race categories. Ancestry percentages are based on the 2006-2010 American Community Survey population (not shown); ‡ Numbers in parentheses indicate the number of people reporting a single ancestry; * Numbers in parentheses indicate the number of persons reporting this race alone, not in combination with any other race; Please refer to the Explanation of Data for more information.*

Slovene (0)	37	0.16
Swedish (421)	1,577	6.82
Swiss (0)	82	0.35
Turkish (12)	53	0.23
Ukrainian (110)	132	0.57
Welsh (33)	399	1.72
West Indian, ex. Hispanic (10)	28	0.12
Jamaican (10)	28	0.12
Yugoslavian (47)	83	0.36

Hispanic Origin	Population	%
Hispanic or Latino (of any race)	1,455	6.41
Central American, ex. Mexican	101	0.44
Costa Rican	13	0.06
Guatemalan	20	0.09
Honduran	14	0.06
Nicaraguan	6	0.03
Panamanian	11	0.05
Salvadoran	36	0.16
Other Central American	1	<0.01
Cuban	26	0.11
Dominican Republic	6	0.03
Mexican	950	4.18
Puerto Rican	64	0.28
South American	157	0.69
Argentinean	17	0.07
Bolivian	6	0.03
Chilean	16	0.07
Colombian	42	0.18
Ecuadorian	11	0.05
Peruvian	55	0.24
Uruguayan	1	<0.01
Venezuelan	8	0.04
Other South American	1	<0.01
Other Hispanic or Latino	151	0.66

Race*	Population	%
African-American/Black (378)	605	2.66
Not Hispanic (363)	556	2.45
Hispanic (15)	49	0.22
American Indian/Alaska Native (104)	290	1.28
Not Hispanic (75)	239	1.05
Hispanic (29)	51	0.22
Alaska Athabascan *(Ala. Nat.)* (0)	4	0.02
Aleut *(Alaska Native)* (3)	6	0.03
Apache (0)	5	0.02
Blackfeet (3)	5	0.02
Canadian/French Am. Ind. (1)	3	0.01
Central American Ind. (0)	1	<0.01
Cherokee (5)	34	0.15
Cheyenne (1)	1	<0.01
Chickasaw (1)	1	<0.01
Chippewa (8)	14	0.06
Choctaw (1)	6	0.03
Colville (1)	3	0.01
Comanche (1)	3	0.01
Cree (0)	2	0.01
Creek (4)	4	0.02
Delaware (1)	2	0.01
Hopi (0)	1	<0.01
Inupiat *(Alaska Native)* (2)	2	0.01
Lumbee (0)	1	<0.01
Mexican American Ind. (10)	10	0.04
Navajo (1)	1	<0.01
Osage (0)	1	<0.01
Potawatomi (0)	3	0.01
Pueblo (2)	2	0.01
Puget Sound Salish (6)	10	0.04
Seminole (0)	3	0.01
Shoshone (1)	5	0.02
Sioux (1)	4	0.02
South American Ind. (1)	2	0.01
Tlingit-Haida *(Alaska Native)* (6)	8	0.04
Tsimshian *(Alaska Native)* (6)	10	0.04
Ute (0)	3	0.01
Yaqui (0)	1	<0.01
Asian (1,994)	2,565	11.30
Not Hispanic (1,974)	2,505	11.03
Hispanic (20)	60	0.26
Bangladeshi (11)	11	0.05
Burmese (7)	12	0.05
Cambodian (47)	62	0.27
Chinese, ex. Taiwanese (453)	611	2.69
Filipino (276)	434	1.91
Indian (295)	333	1.47
Indonesian (14)	24	0.11
Japanese (224)	387	1.70
Korean (167)	237	1.04
Laotian (53)	61	0.27
Malaysian (2)	7	0.03
Nepalese (4)	4	0.02
Pakistani (46)	47	0.21
Sri Lankan (9)	12	0.05
Taiwanese (47)	61	0.27
Thai (22)	35	0.15
Vietnamese (228)	267	1.18
Hawaii Native/Pacific Islander (45)	142	0.63
Not Hispanic (43)	130	0.57
Hispanic (2)	12	0.05
Fijian (3)	3	0.01
Guamanian/Chamorro (15)	22	0.10
Native Hawaiian (15)	68	0.30
Samoan (3)	11	0.05
Tongan (2)	2	0.01
White (18,635)	19,563	86.15
Not Hispanic (17,874)	18,650	82.13
Hispanic (761)	913	4.02

Issaquah

Place Type: City
County: King
Population: 30,434†

Ancestry‡	Population	%
African, Sub-Saharan (74)	90	0.32
African (0)	8	0.03
South African (74)	82	0.29
American (653)	653	2.35
Arab (291)	368	1.32
Arab (14)	14	0.05
Egyptian (141)	141	0.51
Lebanese (136)	180	0.65
Syrian (0)	33	0.12
Armenian (23)	41	0.15
Australian (41)	65	0.23
Austrian (0)	104	0.37
Basque (25)	75	0.27
Belgian (16)	188	0.68
Brazilian (0)	16	0.06
British (163)	323	1.16
Bulgarian (46)	46	0.17
Canadian (39)	116	0.42
Celtic (11)	23	0.08
Croatian (0)	26	0.09
Czech (40)	253	0.91
Czechoslovakian (0)	8	0.03
Danish (87)	236	0.85
Dutch (151)	579	2.08
Eastern European (29)	29	0.10
English (1,034)	3,750	13.47
Estonian (23)	73	0.26
European (300)	453	1.63
Finnish (77)	138	0.50
French, ex. Basque (144)	780	2.80
French Canadian (68)	295	1.06
German (1,037)	5,024	18.05
Greek (0)	89	0.32
Hungarian (36)	158	0.57
Icelander (0)	91	0.33
Iranian (213)	237	0.85
Irish (1,216)	4,150	14.91
Italian (468)	1,375	4.94
Lithuanian (27)	27	0.10
Northern European (66)	92	0.33
Norwegian (477)	1,422	5.11
Pennsylvania German (0)	12	0.04
Polish (158)	626	2.25
Portuguese (13)	65	0.23
Romanian (45)	103	0.37
Russian (542)	912	3.28
Scandinavian (96)	162	0.58
Scotch-Irish (287)	732	2.63
Scottish (150)	730	2.62
Slavic (0)	11	0.04
Slovak (0)	11	0.04
Slovene (0)	11	0.04
Swedish (350)	1,208	4.34
Swiss (18)	167	0.60
Ukrainian (28)	122	0.44
Welsh (12)	304	1.09
West Indian, ex. Hispanic (0)	65	0.23
Jamaican (0)	65	0.23
Yugoslavian (40)	53	0.19

Hispanic Origin	Population	%
Hispanic or Latino (of any race)	1,764	5.80
Central American, ex. Mexican	104	0.34
Costa Rican	15	0.05
Guatemalan	18	0.06
Honduran	14	0.05
Nicaraguan	14	0.05
Panamanian	19	0.06
Salvadoran	23	0.08
Other Central American	1	<0.01
Cuban	49	0.16
Dominican Republic	12	0.04
Mexican	1,127	3.70
Puerto Rican	102	0.34
South American	143	0.47
Argentinean	19	0.06
Bolivian	4	0.01
Chilean	10	0.03
Colombian	42	0.14
Ecuadorian	10	0.03
Peruvian	45	0.15
Uruguayan	2	0.01
Venezuelan	11	0.04
Other Hispanic or Latino	227	0.75

Race*	Population	%
African-American/Black (422)	625	2.05
Not Hispanic (405)	590	1.94
Hispanic (17)	35	0.12
American Indian/Alaska Native (115)	359	1.18
Not Hispanic (95)	296	0.97
Hispanic (20)	63	0.21
Alaska Athabascan *(Ala. Nat.)* (1)	8	0.03
Aleut *(Alaska Native)* (3)	6	0.02
Apache (0)	7	0.02
Arapaho (0)	1	<0.01
Blackfeet (3)	9	0.03
Canadian/French Am. Ind. (5)	6	0.02
Cherokee (3)	59	0.19
Chickasaw (3)	3	0.01
Chippewa (9)	23	0.08
Choctaw (1)	2	0.01
Colville (0)	4	0.01
Creek (0)	3	0.01
Delaware (1)	1	<0.01
Inupiat *(Alaska Native)* (2)	9	0.03
Iroquois (1)	1	<0.01
Kiowa (0)	1	<0.01
Lumbee (1)	1	<0.01
Mexican American Ind. (3)	9	0.03
Navajo (4)	7	0.02
Potawatomi (0)	2	0.01
Puget Sound Salish (1)	8	0.03
Seminole (3)	3	0.01
Sioux (1)	8	0.03
South American Ind. (0)	1	<0.01
Tlingit-Haida *(Alaska Native)* (12)	20	0.07
Tsimshian *(Alaska Native)* (0)	1	<0.01
Yakama (0)	1	<0.01
Asian (5,322)	6,083	19.99
Not Hispanic (5,307)	6,027	19.80
Hispanic (15)	56	0.18
Bangladeshi (15)	15	0.05
Burmese (16)	16	0.05
Cambodian (18)	25	0.08

*Notes: † The Census 2010 population figure is used to calculate the percentages in the Hispanic Origin and Race categories. Ancestry percentages are based on the 2006-2010 American Community Survey population (not shown); ‡ Numbers in parentheses indicate the number of people reporting a single ancestry; * Numbers in parentheses indicate the number of persons reporting this race alone, not in combination with any other race; Please refer to the Explanation of Data for more information.*

Chinese, ex. Taiwanese (1,579)	1,839	6.04
Filipino (333)	498	1.64
Hmong (1)	2	0.01
Indian (1,498)	1,548	5.09
Indonesian (43)	47	0.15
Japanese (333)	581	1.91
Korean (883)	1,005	3.30
Laotian (14)	24	0.08
Malaysian (9)	20	0.07
Nepalese (9)	9	0.03
Pakistani (74)	78	0.26
Sri Lankan (1)	1	<0.01
Taiwanese (145)	174	0.57
Thai (52)	81	0.27
Vietnamese (138)	190	0.62
Hawaii Native/Pacific Islander (36)	151	0.50
Not Hispanic (36)	136	0.45
Hispanic (0)	15	0.05
Fijian (3)	5	0.02
Guamanian/Chamorro (15)	26	0.09
Native Hawaiian (10)	78	0.26
Samoan (2)	20	0.07
White (22,736)	23,877	78.46
Not Hispanic (21,701)	22,684	74.54
Hispanic (1,035)	1,193	3.92

Kelso

Place Type: City
County: Cowlitz
Population: 11,925†

Ancestry‡	Population	%
American (643)	643	5.37
Austrian (0)	68	0.57
Brazilian (8)	8	0.07
British (22)	48	0.40
Canadian (10)	39	0.33
Czech (0)	39	0.33
Czechoslovakian (40)	40	0.33
Danish (8)	126	1.05
Dutch (10)	105	0.88
English (139)	972	8.12
European (150)	150	1.25
Finnish (45)	120	1.00
French, ex. Basque (73)	419	3.50
French Canadian (134)	189	1.58
German (1,014)	2,986	24.93
Greek (0)	21	0.18
Hungarian (0)	29	0.24
Icelander (0)	13	0.11
Irish (524)	1,635	13.65
Italian (117)	411	3.43
Northern European (58)	58	0.48
Norwegian (242)	550	4.59
Polish (38)	319	2.66
Romanian (69)	69	0.58
Russian (0)	44	0.37
Scandinavian (55)	105	0.88
Scotch-Irish (60)	274	2.29
Scottish (170)	343	2.86
Slavic (9)	9	0.08
Swedish (206)	473	3.95
Swiss (31)	132	1.10
Ukrainian (0)	11	0.09
Welsh (52)	320	2.67
West Indian, ex. Hispanic (0)	49	0.41
Jamaican (0)	49	0.41
Yugoslavian (0)	10	0.08

Hispanic Origin	Population	%
Hispanic or Latino (of any race)	1,346	11.29
Central American, ex. Mexican	47	0.39
Guatemalan	7	0.06
Honduran	5	0.04
Nicaraguan	3	0.03
Panamanian	2	0.02
Salvadoran	30	0.25
Cuban	10	0.08
Mexican	1,152	9.66
Puerto Rican	39	0.33
Other Hispanic or Latino	98	0.82

Race*	Population	%
African-American/Black (97)	190	1.59
Not Hispanic (78)	157	1.32
Hispanic (19)	33	0.28
American Indian/Alaska Native (251)	549	4.60
Not Hispanic (196)	461	3.87
Hispanic (55)	88	0.74
Aleut *(Alaska Native)* (2)	8	0.07
Apache (7)	15	0.13
Blackfeet (7)	25	0.21
Canadian/French Am. Ind. (0)	2	0.02
Cherokee (23)	114	0.96
Chickasaw (0)	2	0.02
Chippewa (12)	35	0.29
Choctaw (4)	11	0.09
Colville (3)	4	0.03
Comanche (0)	1	0.01
Creek (3)	5	0.04
Hopi (0)	1	0.01
Iroquois (2)	2	0.02
Lumbee (8)	11	0.09
Mexican American Ind. (21)	23	0.19
Navajo (10)	11	0.09
Puget Sound Salish (8)	10	0.08
Sioux (11)	30	0.25
Tlingit-Haida *(Alaska Native)* (4)	5	0.04
Yakama (4)	9	0.08
Yup'ik *(Alaska Native)* (4)	4	0.03
Asian (189)	292	2.45
Not Hispanic (189)	284	2.38
Hispanic (0)	8	0.07
Cambodian (30)	34	0.29
Chinese, ex. Taiwanese (49)	59	0.49
Filipino (32)	67	0.56
Indian (15)	23	0.19
Japanese (8)	38	0.32
Korean (17)	24	0.20
Laotian (1)	2	0.02
Malaysian (0)	1	0.01
Pakistani (2)	2	0.02
Taiwanese (1)	3	0.03
Thai (3)	5	0.04
Vietnamese (21)	28	0.23
Hawaii Native/Pacific Islander (15)	61	0.51
Not Hispanic (13)	51	0.43
Hispanic (2)	10	0.08
Guamanian/Chamorro (4)	14	0.12
Marshallese (1)	1	0.01
Native Hawaiian (6)	34	0.29
Samoan (0)	6	0.05
White (10,161)	10,729	89.97
Not Hispanic (9,664)	10,069	84.44
Hispanic (497)	660	5.53

Kenmore

Place Type: City
County: King
Population: 20,460†

Ancestry‡	Population	%
African, Sub-Saharan (520)	520	2.61
Ethiopian (335)	335	1.68
Kenyan (148)	148	0.74
Other Sub-Saharan African (37)	37	0.19
American (464)	464	2.33
Arab (47)	126	0.63
Arab (0)	32	0.16
Egyptian (7)	17	0.09
Lebanese (26)	53	0.27
Syrian (0)	10	0.05
Other Arab (14)	14	0.07
Armenian (157)	233	1.17
Australian (9)	9	0.05
Austrian (0)	44	0.22
Basque (0)	8	0.04
Belgian (34)	60	0.30
Brazilian (0)	10	0.05
British (115)	207	1.04
Bulgarian (32)	32	0.16
Cajun (0)	10	0.05
Canadian (61)	102	0.51
Croatian (8)	8	0.04
Czech (43)	150	0.75
Czechoslovakian (25)	47	0.24
Danish (54)	285	1.43
Dutch (76)	288	1.44
Eastern European (32)	32	0.16
English (513)	2,587	12.97
European (493)	561	2.81
Finnish (10)	232	1.16
French, ex. Basque (143)	771	3.87
French Canadian (20)	111	0.56
German (1,080)	4,413	22.12
Greek (51)	87	0.44
Hungarian (25)	98	0.49
Icelander (15)	130	0.65
Iranian (183)	183	0.92
Irish (601)	2,336	11.71
Italian (157)	550	2.76
Latvian (49)	49	0.25
Lithuanian (21)	36	0.18
New Zealander (0)	22	0.11
Northern European (39)	49	0.25
Norwegian (423)	1,275	6.39
Pennsylvania German (0)	15	0.08
Polish (69)	307	1.54
Romanian (38)	66	0.33
Russian (175)	260	1.30
Scandinavian (50)	138	0.69
Scotch-Irish (166)	408	2.05
Scottish (111)	605	3.03
Serbian (0)	10	0.05
Slovak (0)	21	0.11
Swedish (102)	1,129	5.66
Swiss (0)	99	0.50
Turkish (36)	36	0.18
Ukrainian (55)	84	0.42
Welsh (24)	261	1.31
West Indian, ex. Hispanic (94)	105	0.53
Belizean (94)	94	0.47
West Indian (0)	11	0.06
Yugoslavian (0)	24	0.12

Hispanic Origin	Population	%
Hispanic or Latino (of any race)	1,439	7.03
Central American, ex. Mexican	76	0.37
Costa Rican	5	0.02
Guatemalan	9	0.04
Honduran	23	0.11
Nicaraguan	3	0.01
Panamanian	15	0.07
Salvadoran	21	0.10
Cuban	23	0.11
Dominican Republic	3	0.01
Mexican	1,065	5.21
Puerto Rican	45	0.22
South American	98	0.48
Argentinean	8	0.04
Bolivian	6	0.03
Chilean	15	0.07
Colombian	28	0.14
Ecuadorian	12	0.06
Peruvian	20	0.10
Venezuelan	8	0.04
Other South American	1	<0.01
Other Hispanic or Latino	129	0.63

Race*	Population	%
African-American/Black (337)	566	2.77
Not Hispanic (325)	524	2.56
Hispanic (12)	42	0.21
American Indian/Alaska Native (111)	290	1.42
Not Hispanic (75)	230	1.12
Hispanic (36)	60	0.29
Alaska Athabascan *(Ala. Nat.)* (2)	2	0.01
Aleut *(Alaska Native)* (6)	16	0.08

*Notes: † The Census 2010 population figure is used to calculate the percentages in the Hispanic Origin and Race categories. Ancestry percentages are based on the 2006-2010 American Community Survey population (not shown); ‡ Numbers in parentheses indicate the number of people reporting a single ancestry; * Numbers in parentheses indicate the number of persons reporting this race alone, not in combination with any other race; Please refer to the Explanation of Data for more information.*

Apache (1)	3	0.01
Blackfeet (1)	4	0.02
Canadian/French Am. Ind. (0)	10	0.05
Central American Ind. (1)	2	0.01
Cherokee (7)	36	0.18
Chippewa (2)	9	0.04
Choctaw (1)	6	0.03
Colville (1)	3	0.01
Comanche (0)	1	<0.01
Delaware (0)	2	0.01
Inupiat *(Alaska Native)* (1)	1	<0.01
Iroquois (0)	2	0.01
Menominee (1)	2	0.01
Mexican American Ind. (17)	22	0.11
Navajo (1)	1	<0.01
Osage (0)	2	0.01
Paiute (0)	1	<0.01
Pima (0)	1	<0.01
Pueblo (1)	1	<0.01
Puget Sound Salish (2)	3	0.01
Sioux (7)	13	0.06
South American Ind. (1)	2	0.01
Tlingit-Haida *(Alaska Native)* (7)	21	0.10
Tsimshian *(Alaska Native)* (0)	4	0.02
Yakama (1)	1	<0.01
Yaqui (2)	2	0.01
Yup'ik *(Alaska Native)* (2)	2	0.01
Asian (2,157)	2,635	12.88
Not Hispanic (2,138)	2,596	12.69
Hispanic (19)	39	0.19
Bangladeshi (2)	2	0.01
Burmese (3)	3	0.01
Cambodian (20)	25	0.12
Chinese, ex. Taiwanese (644)	771	3.77
Filipino (389)	536	2.62
Hmong (1)	1	<0.01
Indian (221)	254	1.24
Indonesian (25)	28	0.14
Japanese (182)	307	1.50
Korean (235)	289	1.41
Laotian (7)	7	0.03
Malaysian (3)	7	0.03
Nepalese (5)	5	0.02
Pakistani (28)	34	0.17
Sri Lankan (4)	7	0.03
Taiwanese (65)	75	0.37
Thai (34)	49	0.24
Vietnamese (182)	223	1.09
Hawaii Native/Pacific Islander (59)	128	0.63
Not Hispanic (56)	118	0.58
Hispanic (3)	10	0.05
Fijian (6)	6	0.03
Guamanian/Chamorro (6)	13	0.06
Native Hawaiian (15)	46	0.22
Samoan (7)	16	0.08
Tongan (6)	11	0.05
White (16,351)	17,198	84.06
Not Hispanic (15,586)	16,301	79.67
Hispanic (765)	897	4.38

Kennewick

Place Type: City
County: Benton
Population: 73,917†

Ancestry‡	Population	%
African, Sub-Saharan (80)	127	0.18
African (69)	104	0.15
Sierra Leonean (11)	11	0.02
South African (0)	12	0.02
American (5,447)	5,447	7.74
Arab (65)	236	0.34
Arab (0)	73	0.10
Egyptian (11)	11	0.02
Iraqi (54)	54	0.08
Lebanese (0)	25	0.04
Other Arab (0)	73	0.10
Armenian (36)	55	0.08
Austrian (9)	262	0.37
Brazilian (0)	21	0.03
British (106)	283	0.40
Bulgarian (0)	93	0.13
Cajun (15)	25	0.04
Canadian (58)	147	0.21
Croatian (24)	110	0.16
Cypriot (46)	46	0.07
Czech (81)	262	0.37
Czechoslovakian (22)	96	0.14
Danish (100)	557	0.79
Dutch (304)	1,502	2.14
Eastern European (18)	18	0.03
English (2,618)	8,726	12.41
European (763)	863	1.23
Finnish (138)	267	0.38
French, ex. Basque (706)	2,769	3.94
French Canadian (256)	512	0.73
German (4,149)	15,172	21.57
Greek (106)	216	0.31
Hungarian (90)	229	0.33
Icelander (0)	9	0.01
Irish (2,151)	9,285	13.20
Italian (746)	1,855	2.64
Latvian (0)	11	0.02
Lithuanian (52)	67	0.10
Northern European (65)	77	0.11
Norwegian (717)	2,785	3.96
Pennsylvania German (9)	42	0.06
Polish (135)	970	1.38
Portuguese (44)	112	0.16
Romanian (8)	19	0.03
Russian (112)	504	0.72
Scandinavian (176)	333	0.47
Scotch-Irish (344)	1,395	1.98
Scottish (362)	1,169	1.66
Serbian (11)	17	0.02
Slavic (36)	36	0.05
Slovak (0)	33	0.05
Slovene (0)	17	0.02
Swedish (396)	2,019	2.87
Swiss (37)	160	0.23
Ukrainian (228)	429	0.61
Welsh (141)	830	1.18
West Indian, ex. Hispanic (29)	60	0.09
Belizean (29)	29	0.04
Jamaican (0)	31	0.04
Yugoslavian (221)	227	0.32

Hispanic Origin	Population	%
Hispanic or Latino (of any race)	17,909	24.23
Central American, ex. Mexican	416	0.56
Costa Rican	20	0.03
Guatemalan	81	0.11
Honduran	33	0.04
Nicaraguan	17	0.02
Panamanian	3	<0.01
Salvadoran	259	0.35
Other Central American	3	<0.01
Cuban	125	0.17
Dominican Republic	9	0.01
Mexican	15,887	21.49
Puerto Rican	160	0.22
South American	140	0.19
Argentinean	28	0.04
Bolivian	10	0.01
Chilean	24	0.03
Colombian	31	0.04
Ecuadorian	11	0.01
Peruvian	27	0.04
Uruguayan	1	<0.01
Venezuelan	8	0.01
Other Hispanic or Latino	1,172	1.59

Race*	Population	%
African-American/Black (1,262)	1,940	2.62
Not Hispanic (1,144)	1,643	2.22
Hispanic (118)	297	0.40
American Indian/Alaska Native (627)	1,307	1.77
Not Hispanic (477)	1,018	1.38
Hispanic (150)	289	0.39
Alaska Athabascan *(Ala. Nat.)* (2)	12	0.02
Aleut *(Alaska Native)* (5)	13	0.02
Apache (0)	11	0.01
Arapaho (1)	2	<0.01
Blackfeet (7)	26	0.04
Canadian/French Am. Ind. (9)	15	0.02
Cherokee (63)	190	0.26
Cheyenne (3)	11	0.01
Chickasaw (3)	12	0.02
Chippewa (15)	31	0.04
Choctaw (20)	39	0.05
Colville (21)	26	0.04
Comanche (0)	2	<0.01
Cree (2)	6	0.01
Creek (6)	11	0.01
Crow (1)	2	<0.01
Delaware (1)	7	0.01
Hopi (0)	1	<0.01
Inupiat *(Alaska Native)* (3)	5	0.01
Iroquois (8)	16	0.02
Kiowa (0)	3	<0.01
Lumbee (1)	1	<0.01
Mexican American Ind. (33)	58	0.08
Navajo (13)	15	0.02
Osage (1)	7	0.01
Ottawa (0)	2	<0.01
Paiute (1)	5	0.01
Pima (4)	7	0.01
Potawatomi (1)	4	0.01
Pueblo (1)	1	<0.01
Puget Sound Salish (16)	24	0.03
Seminole (4)	8	0.01
Shoshone (0)	1	<0.01
Sioux (14)	37	0.05
South American Ind. (1)	7	0.01
Tlingit-Haida *(Alaska Native)* (14)	21	0.03
Tohono O'Odham (3)	4	0.01
Tsimshian *(Alaska Native)* (5)	8	0.01
Ute (1)	1	<0.01
Yakama (14)	23	0.03
Yaqui (4)	4	0.01
Yup'ik *(Alaska Native)* (2)	3	<0.01
Asian (1,743)	2,406	3.26
Not Hispanic (1,705)	2,273	3.08
Hispanic (38)	133	0.18
Bangladeshi (2)	2	<0.01
Bhutanese (6)	6	0.01
Burmese (151)	157	0.21
Cambodian (42)	51	0.07
Chinese, ex. Taiwanese (184)	284	0.38
Filipino (385)	629	0.85
Hmong (2)	2	<0.01
Indian (172)	212	0.29
Indonesian (3)	4	0.01
Japanese (105)	248	0.34
Korean (132)	226	0.31
Laotian (148)	197	0.27
Malaysian (1)	1	<0.01
Pakistani (13)	15	0.02
Sri Lankan (3)	3	<0.01
Taiwanese (11)	11	0.01
Thai (37)	53	0.07
Vietnamese (263)	295	0.40
Hawaii Native/Pacific Islander (148)	308	0.42
Not Hispanic (123)	256	0.35
Hispanic (25)	52	0.07
Fijian (1)	1	<0.01
Guamanian/Chamorro (19)	30	0.04
Marshallese (9)	9	0.01
Native Hawaiian (57)	164	0.22
Samoan (25)	38	0.05
Tongan (21)	23	0.03
White (58,053)	60,995	82.52
Not Hispanic (50,835)	52,372	70.85
Hispanic (7,218)	8,623	11.67

*Notes: † The Census 2010 population figure is used to calculate the percentages in the Hispanic Origin and Race categories. Ancestry percentages are based on the 2006-2010 American Community Survey population (not shown); ‡ Numbers in parentheses indicate the number of people reporting a single ancestry; * Numbers in parentheses indicate the number of persons reporting this race alone, not in combination with any other race; Please refer to the Explanation of Data for more information.*

Kent

Place Type: City
County: King
Population: 92,411†

Ancestry‡	Population	%
Afghan (269)	269	0.30
African, Sub-Saharan (3,028)	3,346	3.74
African (1,240)	1,431	1.60
Ethiopian (95)	106	0.12
Ghanaian (0)	24	0.03
Kenyan (171)	210	0.23
Liberian (100)	100	0.11
Sierra Leonean (3)	3	<0.01
Somalian (1,051)	1,051	1.18
Sudanese (10)	10	0.01
Other Sub-Saharan African (358)	411	0.46
Alsatian (8)	8	0.01
American (2,193)	2,193	2.45
Arab (828)	924	1.03
Arab (215)	215	0.24
Egyptian (120)	120	0.13
Iraqi (0)	29	0.03
Lebanese (98)	98	0.11
Moroccan (26)	38	0.04
Syrian (0)	26	0.03
Other Arab (369)	398	0.44
Armenian (56)	163	0.18
Austrian (27)	170	0.19
Belgian (40)	157	0.18
Brazilian (0)	33	0.04
British (148)	295	0.33
Bulgarian (23)	60	0.07
Canadian (199)	247	0.28
Carpatho Rusyn (13)	13	0.01
Celtic (0)	8	0.01
Croatian (55)	81	0.09
Czech (7)	199	0.22
Czechoslovakian (13)	24	0.03
Danish (159)	710	0.79
Dutch (154)	1,043	1.17
Eastern European (22)	22	0.02
English (2,041)	6,947	7.77
European (1,167)	1,230	1.38
Finnish (142)	403	0.45
French, ex. Basque (196)	2,342	2.62
French Canadian (152)	359	0.40
German (3,545)	12,452	13.92
German Russian (3)	3	<0.01
Greek (81)	184	0.21
Guyanese (0)	13	0.01
Hungarian (158)	345	0.39
Icelander (0)	9	0.01
Irish (1,619)	7,778	8.70
Italian (701)	2,334	2.61
Latvian (12)	25	0.03
Lithuanian (56)	106	0.12
Northern European (94)	94	0.11
Norwegian (1,428)	3,872	4.33
Polish (372)	1,234	1.38
Portuguese (79)	191	0.21
Romanian (106)	131	0.15
Russian (1,197)	1,899	2.12
Scandinavian (154)	411	0.46
Scotch-Irish (417)	1,476	1.65
Scottish (473)	1,627	1.82
Slovak (0)	59	0.07
Swedish (542)	2,722	3.04
Swiss (204)	522	0.58
Turkish (304)	445	0.50
Ukrainian (2,046)	2,259	2.53
Welsh (166)	722	0.81
West Indian, ex. Hispanic (21)	31	0.03
Haitian (0)	10	0.01
Jamaican (14)	14	0.02
West Indian (7)	7	0.01
Yugoslavian (21)	124	0.14

Hispanic Origin	Population	%
Hispanic or Latino (of any race)	15,386	16.65
Central American, ex. Mexican	1,092	1.18
Costa Rican	31	0.03
Guatemalan	245	0.27
Honduran	206	0.22
Nicaraguan	61	0.07
Panamanian	51	0.06
Salvadoran	483	0.52
Other Central American	15	0.02
Cuban	146	0.16
Dominican Republic	38	0.04
Mexican	12,055	13.04
Puerto Rican	424	0.46
South American	470	0.51
Argentinean	37	0.04
Bolivian	33	0.04
Chilean	51	0.06
Colombian	120	0.13
Ecuadorian	50	0.05
Paraguayan	2	<0.01
Peruvian	127	0.14
Uruguayan	8	0.01
Venezuelan	38	0.04
Other South American	4	<0.01
Other Hispanic or Latino	1,161	1.26

Race*	Population	%
African-American/Black (10,434)	12,648	13.69
Not Hispanic (10,088)	11,970	12.95
Hispanic (346)	678	0.73
American Indian/Alaska Native (913)	2,441	2.64
Not Hispanic (677)	1,684	1.82
Hispanic (236)	757	0.82
Alaska Athabascan *(Ala. Nat.)* (12)	25	0.03
Aleut *(Alaska Native)* (11)	23	0.02
Apache (11)	34	0.04
Arapaho (11)	11	0.01
Blackfeet (22)	109	0.12
Canadian/French Am. Ind. (16)	48	0.05
Central American Ind. (0)	2	<0.01
Cherokee (39)	266	0.29
Cheyenne (1)	19	0.02
Chickasaw (0)	5	0.01
Chippewa (27)	59	0.06
Choctaw (9)	32	0.03
Colville (13)	21	0.02
Comanche (0)	6	0.01
Cree (8)	16	0.02
Creek (1)	13	0.01
Crow (6)	9	0.01
Delaware (0)	1	<0.01
Hopi (1)	5	0.01
Inupiat *(Alaska Native)* (4)	9	0.01
Iroquois (3)	17	0.02
Kiowa (2)	3	<0.01
Lumbee (1)	2	<0.01
Mexican American Ind. (60)	91	0.10
Navajo (9)	26	0.03
Osage (1)	5	0.01
Ottawa (4)	6	0.01
Paiute (2)	2	<0.01
Pima (0)	4	<0.01
Potawatomi (6)	10	0.01
Pueblo (11)	13	0.01
Puget Sound Salish (34)	77	0.08
Seminole (0)	2	<0.01
Shoshone (2)	6	0.01
Sioux (40)	76	0.08
South American Ind. (5)	6	0.01
Spanish American Ind. (0)	1	<0.01
Tlingit-Haida *(Alaska Native)* (36)	95	0.10
Tsimshian *(Alaska Native)* (12)	20	0.02
Ute (0)	2	<0.01
Yakama (17)	33	0.04
Yaqui (2)	3	<0.01
Yuman (5)	10	0.01
Yup'ik *(Alaska Native)* (4)	5	0.01
Asian (14,008)	16,382	17.73
Not Hispanic (13,841)	15,982	17.29
Hispanic (167)	400	0.43
Bangladeshi (32)	32	0.03
Bhutanese (111)	143	0.15
Burmese (364)	384	0.42
Cambodian (795)	1,003	1.09
Chinese, ex. Taiwanese (1,081)	1,636	1.77
Filipino (3,396)	4,431	4.79
Hmong (58)	67	0.07
Indian (2,900)	3,182	3.44
Indonesian (31)	55	0.06
Japanese (552)	1,038	1.12
Korean (660)	860	0.93
Laotian (507)	604	0.65
Malaysian (5)	6	0.01
Nepalese (65)	93	0.10
Pakistani (117)	135	0.15
Sri Lankan (15)	15	0.02
Taiwanese (64)	76	0.08
Thai (119)	195	0.21
Vietnamese (2,348)	2,634	2.85
Hawaii Native/Pacific Islander (1,773)	2,536	2.74
Not Hispanic (1,731)	2,408	2.61
Hispanic (42)	128	0.14
Fijian (150)	201	0.22
Guamanian/Chamorro (189)	264	0.29
Marshallese (33)	39	0.04
Native Hawaiian (130)	417	0.45
Samoan (843)	1,079	1.17
Tongan (92)	122	0.13
White (51,331)	56,265	60.89
Not Hispanic (45,969)	49,550	53.62
Hispanic (5,362)	6,715	7.27

Kingsgate

Place Type: CDP
County: King
Population: 13,065†

Ancestry‡	Population	%
African, Sub-Saharan (78)	90	0.66
African (6)	18	0.13
Ethiopian (72)	72	0.53
American (237)	237	1.74
Arab (29)	39	0.29
Lebanese (0)	10	0.07
Other Arab (29)	29	0.21
Australian (12)	12	0.09
Austrian (45)	144	1.05
Basque (0)	16	0.12
British (63)	97	0.71
Bulgarian (24)	24	0.18
Canadian (22)	45	0.33
Croatian (25)	25	0.18
Czech (123)	170	1.25
Czechoslovakian (0)	8	0.06
Danish (120)	340	2.49
Dutch (74)	132	0.97
Eastern European (76)	102	0.75
English (412)	1,694	12.41
European (322)	387	2.84
Finnish (69)	185	1.36
French, ex. Basque (53)	451	3.30
French Canadian (38)	73	0.53
German (741)	2,233	16.36
Hungarian (10)	33	0.24
Icelander (0)	17	0.12
Iranian (208)	208	1.52
Irish (321)	1,229	9.00
Italian (197)	400	2.93
Latvian (9)	64	0.47
Lithuanian (43)	54	0.40
Northern European (8)	8	0.06
Norwegian (264)	986	7.22
Pennsylvania German (0)	14	0.10
Polish (74)	193	1.41
Portuguese (0)	10	0.07
Romanian (137)	137	1.00
Russian (99)	380	2.78
Scandinavian (18)	103	0.75

*Notes: † The Census 2010 population figure is used to calculate the percentages in the Hispanic Origin and Race categories. Ancestry percentages are based on the 2006-2010 American Community Survey population (not shown); ‡ Numbers in parentheses indicate the number of people reporting a single ancestry; * Numbers in parentheses indicate the number of persons reporting this race alone, not in combination with any other race; Please refer to the Explanation of Data for more information.*

SECTION TWO

Scotch-Irish (32)	177	1.30
Scottish (54)	371	2.72
Slavic (21)	21	0.15
Swedish (106)	568	4.16
Swiss (17)	27	0.20
Ukrainian (24)	150	1.10
Welsh (0)	53	0.39
West Indian, ex. Hispanic (0)	11	0.08
Jamaican (0)	11	0.08
Yugoslavian (0)	44	0.32

Hispanic Origin	Population	%
Hispanic or Latino (of any race)	1,232	9.43
Central American, ex. Mexican	85	0.65
Costa Rican	4	0.03
Guatemalan	25	0.19
Honduran	23	0.18
Nicaraguan	1	0.01
Panamanian	3	0.02
Salvadoran	29	0.22
Cuban	16	0.12
Dominican Republic	5	0.04
Mexican	854	6.54
Puerto Rican	20	0.15
South American	101	0.77
Argentinean	12	0.09
Chilean	2	0.02
Colombian	32	0.24
Ecuadorian	10	0.08
Peruvian	36	0.28
Uruguayan	5	0.04
Venezuelan	1	0.01
Other South American	3	0.02
Other Hispanic or Latino	151	1.16

Race*	Population	%
African-American/Black (232)	342	2.62
Not Hispanic (225)	320	2.45
Hispanic (7)	22	0.17
American Indian/Alaska Native (52)	162	1.24
Not Hispanic (47)	142	1.09
Hispanic (5)	20	0.15
Alaska Athabascan *(Ala. Nat.)* (0)	6	0.05
Aleut *(Alaska Native)* (2)	6	0.05
Apache (0)	5	0.04
Blackfeet (1)	5	0.04
Central American Ind. (0)	1	0.01
Cherokee (4)	18	0.14
Chippewa (5)	6	0.05
Choctaw (2)	6	0.05
Colville (2)	2	0.02
Creek (0)	2	0.02
Delaware (0)	1	0.01
Inupiat *(Alaska Native)* (1)	1	0.01
Iroquois (2)	3	0.02
Mexican American Ind. (0)	1	0.01
Navajo (5)	8	0.06
Pueblo (0)	3	0.02
Puget Sound Salish (2)	6	0.05
Seminole (0)	2	0.02
Sioux (4)	6	0.05
Tlingit-Haida *(Alaska Native)* (2)	5	0.04
Tsimshian *(Alaska Native)* (3)	3	0.02
Yakama (1)	1	0.01
Asian (2,110)	2,403	18.39
Not Hispanic (2,094)	2,374	18.17
Hispanic (16)	29	0.22
Burmese (5)	5	0.04
Cambodian (162)	183	1.40
Chinese, ex. Taiwanese (395)	493	3.77
Filipino (220)	303	2.32
Hmong (176)	193	1.48
Indian (333)	358	2.74
Indonesian (10)	17	0.13
Japanese (130)	217	1.66
Korean (150)	173	1.32
Laotian (77)	86	0.66
Malaysian (2)	7	0.05
Nepalese (4)	4	0.03
Pakistani (51)	59	0.45
Sri Lankan (5)	5	0.04
Taiwanese (26)	35	0.27
Thai (53)	66	0.51
Vietnamese (166)	197	1.51
Hawaii Native/Pacific Islander (43)	96	0.73
Not Hispanic (37)	90	0.69
Hispanic (6)	6	0.05
Fijian (3)	3	0.02
Guamanian/Chamorro (6)	11	0.08
Native Hawaiian (10)	31	0.24
Samoan (4)	5	0.04
White (9,547)	10,021	76.70
Not Hispanic (8,922)	9,320	71.34
Hispanic (625)	701	5.37

Kirkland

Place Type: City
County: King
Population: 48,787†

Ancestry‡	Population	%
African, Sub-Saharan (138)	216	0.45
African (16)	31	0.07
Kenyan (0)	49	0.10
South African (15)	29	0.06
Zimbabwean (95)	95	0.20
Other Sub-Saharan African (12)	12	0.03
Albanian (161)	161	0.34
American (1,078)	1,078	2.26
Arab (68)	112	0.23
Arab (0)	26	0.05
Egyptian (68)	68	0.14
Lebanese (0)	18	0.04
Armenian (169)	200	0.42
Australian (62)	62	0.13
Austrian (128)	277	0.58
Basque (0)	29	0.06
Belgian (23)	112	0.23
Brazilian (37)	45	0.09
British (248)	534	1.12
Bulgarian (23)	23	0.05
Cajun (31)	31	0.07
Canadian (238)	346	0.73
Celtic (11)	21	0.04
Croatian (78)	193	0.40
Czech (109)	510	1.07
Czechoslovakian (13)	77	0.16
Danish (116)	537	1.13
Dutch (329)	1,086	2.28
Eastern European (139)	176	0.37
English (1,734)	7,009	14.70
European (978)	1,062	2.23
Finnish (86)	247	0.52
French, ex. Basque (370)	2,191	4.60
French Canadian (220)	487	1.02
German (2,054)	9,215	19.33
Greek (75)	142	0.30
Hungarian (74)	202	0.42
Icelander (51)	106	0.22
Iranian (410)	410	0.86
Irish (1,434)	6,698	14.05
Italian (719)	2,144	4.50
Latvian (12)	38	0.08
Lithuanian (27)	145	0.30
Luxemburger (0)	10	0.02
Northern European (97)	97	0.20
Norwegian (1,017)	3,534	7.41
Pennsylvania German (30)	30	0.06
Polish (236)	1,318	2.76
Portuguese (60)	256	0.54
Romanian (156)	212	0.44
Russian (359)	1,043	2.19
Scandinavian (168)	360	0.76
Scotch-Irish (318)	1,249	2.62
Scottish (544)	2,223	4.66
Serbian (66)	88	0.18
Slavic (0)	12	0.03
Slovak (27)	146	0.31
Slovene (19)	28	0.06
Soviet Union (104)	104	0.22
Swedish (561)	2,182	4.58
Swiss (19)	321	0.67
Turkish (40)	59	0.12
Ukrainian (90)	248	0.52
Welsh (172)	916	1.92
West Indian, ex. Hispanic (0)	11	0.02
Haitian (0)	11	0.02
Yugoslavian (84)	104	0.22

Hispanic Origin	Population	%
Hispanic or Latino (of any race)	3,085	6.32
Central American, ex. Mexican	236	0.48
Costa Rican	26	0.05
Guatemalan	50	0.10
Honduran	52	0.11
Nicaraguan	20	0.04
Panamanian	18	0.04
Salvadoran	67	0.14
Other Central American	3	0.01
Cuban	42	0.09
Dominican Republic	7	0.01
Mexican	1,995	4.09
Puerto Rican	125	0.26
South American	308	0.63
Argentinean	47	0.10
Bolivian	6	0.01
Chilean	30	0.06
Colombian	82	0.17
Ecuadorian	15	0.03
Paraguayan	1	<0.01
Peruvian	81	0.17
Uruguayan	8	0.02
Venezuelan	35	0.07
Other South American	3	0.01
Other Hispanic or Latino	372	0.76

Race*	Population	%
African-American/Black (855)	1,321	2.71
Not Hispanic (805)	1,229	2.52
Hispanic (50)	92	0.19
American Indian/Alaska Native (202)	605	1.24
Not Hispanic (148)	484	0.99
Hispanic (54)	121	0.25
Alaska Athabascan *(Ala. Nat.)* (8)	16	0.03
Aleut *(Alaska Native)* (5)	10	0.02
Apache (1)	7	0.01
Arapaho (0)	3	0.01
Blackfeet (4)	12	0.02
Canadian/French Am. Ind. (4)	6	0.01
Cherokee (15)	86	0.18
Cheyenne (1)	1	<0.01
Chickasaw (3)	5	0.01
Chippewa (5)	19	0.04
Choctaw (3)	8	0.02
Colville (0)	4	0.01
Comanche (0)	2	<0.01
Cree (0)	1	<0.01
Creek (0)	4	0.01
Inupiat *(Alaska Native)* (1)	3	0.01
Iroquois (1)	5	0.01
Kiowa (1)	2	<0.01
Mexican American Ind. (13)	20	0.04
Navajo (4)	18	0.04
Osage (0)	2	<0.01
Potawatomi (1)	4	0.01
Pueblo (1)	2	<0.01
Puget Sound Salish (3)	8	0.02
Seminole (0)	6	0.01
Sioux (7)	19	0.04
South American Ind. (2)	6	0.01
Spanish American Ind. (4)	4	0.01
Tlingit-Haida *(Alaska Native)* (4)	21	0.04
Tsimshian *(Alaska Native)* (0)	2	<0.01
Ute (0)	1	<0.01
Yakama (1)	6	0.01
Yaqui (0)	1	<0.01
Yuman (0)	1	<0.01
Yup'ik *(Alaska Native)* (1)	5	0.01
Asian (5,490)	6,761	13.86

*Notes: † The Census 2010 population figure is used to calculate the percentages in the Hispanic Origin and Race categories. Ancestry percentages are based on the 2006-2010 American Community Survey population (not shown); ‡ Numbers in parentheses indicate the number of people reporting a single ancestry; * Numbers in parentheses indicate the number of persons reporting this race alone, not in combination with any other race; Please refer to the Explanation of Data for more information.*

	Population	%
Not Hispanic (5,465)	6,664	13.66
Hispanic (25)	97	0.20
Bangladeshi (10)	10	0.02
Bhutanese (1)	1	<0.01
Burmese (7)	11	0.02
Cambodian (82)	105	0.22
Chinese, ex. Taiwanese (1,264)	1,614	3.31
Filipino (503)	815	1.67
Hmong (11)	13	0.03
Indian (1,269)	1,381	2.83
Indonesian (41)	61	0.13
Japanese (663)	1,056	2.16
Korean (619)	772	1.58
Laotian (51)	66	0.14
Malaysian (7)	10	0.02
Nepalese (12)	13	0.03
Pakistani (89)	96	0.20
Sri Lankan (19)	20	0.04
Taiwanese (97)	125	0.26
Thai (65)	97	0.20
Vietnamese (420)	496	1.02
Hawaii Native/Pacific Islander (134)	308	0.63
Not Hispanic (123)	287	0.59
Hispanic (11)	21	0.04
Fijian (17)	20	0.04
Guamanian/Chamorro (27)	46	0.09
Marshallese (6)	6	0.01
Native Hawaiian (42)	130	0.27
Samoan (29)	49	0.10
Tongan (1)	2	<0.01
White (38,692)	40,643	83.31
Not Hispanic (37,024)	38,738	79.40
Hispanic (1,668)	1,905	3.90

Klahanie

Place Type: CDP
County: King
Population: 10,674†

Ancestry‡	Population	%
African, Sub-Saharan (0)	120	1.06
African (0)	120	1.06
American (318)	318	2.82
Arab (41)	84	0.75
Lebanese (41)	84	0.75
Australian (15)	30	0.27
Austrian (32)	61	0.54
Brazilian (13)	13	0.12
British (13)	48	0.43
Canadian (0)	11	0.10
Croatian (50)	135	1.20
Czech (19)	70	0.62
Danish (13)	81	0.72
Dutch (124)	244	2.16
Eastern European (32)	32	0.28
English (202)	1,274	11.30
European (262)	324	2.87
Finnish (0)	69	0.61
French, ex. Basque (43)	376	3.34
French Canadian (10)	46	0.41
German (300)	1,411	12.52
Greek (31)	31	0.27
Hungarian (12)	68	0.60
Iranian (24)	24	0.21
Irish (308)	1,692	15.01
Italian (159)	429	3.81
New Zealander (22)	32	0.28
Northern European (10)	10	0.09
Norwegian (162)	363	3.22
Pennsylvania German (16)	16	0.14
Polish (45)	384	3.41
Portuguese (52)	75	0.67
Romanian (58)	71	0.63
Russian (14)	88	0.78
Scandinavian (0)	16	0.14
Scotch-Irish (109)	335	2.97
Scottish (55)	495	4.39
Slovene (0)	10	0.09
Swedish (104)	360	3.19
Swiss (0)	77	0.68
Ukrainian (56)	56	0.50
Welsh (65)	151	1.34
Yugoslavian (0)	9	0.08

Hispanic Origin	Population	%
Hispanic or Latino (of any race)	550	5.15
Central American, ex. Mexican	19	0.18
Costa Rican	3	0.03
Guatemalan	4	0.04
Panamanian	9	0.08
Salvadoran	3	0.03
Cuban	9	0.08
Dominican Republic	2	0.02
Mexican	322	3.02
Puerto Rican	28	0.26
South American	81	0.76
Argentinean	6	0.06
Bolivian	4	0.04
Chilean	4	0.04
Colombian	24	0.22
Ecuadorian	15	0.14
Peruvian	17	0.16
Venezuelan	9	0.08
Other South American	2	0.02
Other Hispanic or Latino	89	0.83

Race*	Population	%
African-American/Black (136)	228	2.14
Not Hispanic (133)	215	2.01
Hispanic (3)	13	0.12
American Indian/Alaska Native (26)	72	0.67
Not Hispanic (17)	54	0.51
Hispanic (9)	18	0.17
Alaska Athabascan *(Ala. Nat.)* (0)	2	0.02
Blackfeet (0)	2	0.02
Canadian/French Am. Ind. (0)	1	0.01
Cherokee (2)	6	0.06
Chippewa (0)	2	0.02
Choctaw (3)	3	0.03
Colville (0)	2	0.02
Comanche (0)	1	0.01
Creek (1)	1	0.01
Mexican American Ind. (1)	1	0.01
Navajo (6)	8	0.07
Potawatomi (0)	1	0.01
Shoshone (0)	2	0.02
Sioux (1)	1	0.01
South American Ind. (4)	4	0.04
Spanish American Ind. (0)	2	0.02
Asian (2,553)	2,863	26.82
Not Hispanic (2,547)	2,843	26.63
Hispanic (6)	20	0.19
Bangladeshi (8)	8	0.07
Burmese (5)	5	0.05
Cambodian (7)	14	0.13
Chinese, ex. Taiwanese (901)	1,046	9.80
Filipino (91)	181	1.70
Hmong (11)	14	0.13
Indian (711)	730	6.84
Indonesian (13)	14	0.13
Japanese (251)	393	3.68
Korean (235)	264	2.47
Laotian (0)	2	0.02
Malaysian (7)	7	0.07
Nepalese (8)	8	0.07
Pakistani (31)	31	0.29
Taiwanese (76)	91	0.85
Thai (19)	36	0.34
Vietnamese (66)	84	0.79
Hawaii Native/Pacific Islander (12)	55	0.52
Not Hispanic (12)	54	0.51
Hispanic (0)	1	0.01
Fijian (1)	1	0.01
Guamanian/Chamorro (2)	16	0.15
Marshallese (2)	2	0.02
Native Hawaiian (1)	19	0.18
Samoan (6)	9	0.08
Tongan (0)	2	0.02
White (7,352)	7,757	72.67
Not Hispanic (7,002)	7,355	68.91
Hispanic (350)	402	3.77

Lacey

Place Type: City
County: Thurston
Population: 42,393†

Ancestry‡	Population	%
African, Sub-Saharan (12)	45	0.11
African (0)	33	0.08
Other Sub-Saharan African (12)	12	0.03
American (1,831)	1,831	4.54
Arab (11)	39	0.10
Lebanese (11)	21	0.05
Syrian (0)	18	0.04
Armenian (12)	12	0.03
Austrian (18)	99	0.25
Belgian (16)	75	0.19
Brazilian (21)	21	0.05
British (134)	306	0.76
Cajun (26)	26	0.06
Canadian (195)	246	0.61
Celtic (0)	12	0.03
Croatian (41)	90	0.22
Czech (57)	124	0.31
Czechoslovakian (100)	100	0.25
Danish (133)	578	1.43
Dutch (124)	920	2.28
Eastern European (30)	30	0.07
English (1,719)	4,878	12.09
European (743)	888	2.20
Finnish (64)	172	0.43
French, ex. Basque (191)	1,622	4.02
French Canadian (42)	227	0.56
German (2,950)	7,909	19.61
Greek (0)	62	0.15
Hungarian (43)	169	0.42
Icelander (0)	8	0.02
Irish (1,418)	4,997	12.39
Italian (551)	1,311	3.25
Lithuanian (17)	79	0.20
Northern European (143)	143	0.35
Norwegian (709)	1,850	4.59
Polish (453)	897	2.22
Portuguese (40)	56	0.14
Romanian (37)	81	0.20
Russian (26)	317	0.79
Scandinavian (66)	156	0.39
Scotch-Irish (353)	964	2.39
Scottish (354)	1,131	2.80
Slovak (19)	37	0.09
Slovene (17)	17	0.04
Swedish (316)	1,271	3.15
Swiss (66)	336	0.83
Ukrainian (0)	24	0.06
Welsh (75)	600	1.49
West Indian, ex. Hispanic (88)	245	0.61
Belizean (0)	21	0.05
Jamaican (79)	193	0.48
West Indian (9)	31	0.08
Yugoslavian (0)	25	0.06

Hispanic Origin	Population	%
Hispanic or Latino (of any race)	3,886	9.17
Central American, ex. Mexican	299	0.71
Costa Rican	6	0.01
Guatemalan	39	0.09
Honduran	19	0.04
Nicaraguan	17	0.04
Panamanian	91	0.21
Salvadoran	124	0.29
Other Central American	3	0.01
Cuban	49	0.12
Dominican Republic	37	0.09
Mexican	2,454	5.79
Puerto Rican	558	1.32
South American	112	0.26
Argentinean	7	0.02

*Notes: † The Census 2010 population figure is used to calculate the percentages in the Hispanic Origin and Race categories. Ancestry percentages are based on the 2006-2010 American Community Survey population (not shown); ‡ Numbers in parentheses indicate the number of people reporting a single ancestry; * Numbers in parentheses indicate the number of persons reporting this race alone, not in combination with any other race; Please refer to the Explanation of Data for more information.*

Bolivian	1	<0.01
Chilean	9	0.02
Colombian	38	0.09
Ecuadorian	14	0.03
Peruvian	23	0.05
Uruguayan	1	<0.01
Venezuelan	15	0.04
Other South American	4	0.01
Other Hispanic or Latino	377	0.89

Race*	Population	%
African-American/Black (2,302)	3,286	7.75
Not Hispanic (2,179)	3,001	7.08
Hispanic (123)	285	0.67
American Indian/Alaska Native (490)	1,143	2.70
Not Hispanic (389)	897	2.12
Hispanic (101)	246	0.58
Alaska Athabascan *(Ala. Nat.)* (2)	7	0.02
Aleut *(Alaska Native)* (6)	14	0.03
Apache (8)	20	0.05
Arapaho (3)	3	0.01
Blackfeet (7)	24	0.06
Canadian/French Am. Ind. (1)	8	0.02
Central American Ind. (3)	3	0.01
Cherokee (26)	139	0.33
Cheyenne (1)	9	0.02
Chickasaw (1)	4	0.01
Chippewa (12)	32	0.08
Choctaw (8)	32	0.08
Colville (14)	16	0.04
Comanche (0)	2	<0.01
Cree (0)	2	<0.01
Creek (7)	11	0.03
Crow (1)	2	<0.01
Delaware (1)	2	<0.01
Hopi (3)	3	0.01
Inupiat *(Alaska Native)* (1)	5	0.01
Iroquois (5)	9	0.02
Lumbee (1)	6	0.01
Menominee (3)	4	0.01
Mexican American Ind. (7)	21	0.05
Navajo (15)	27	0.06
Osage (1)	5	0.01
Ottawa (1)	1	<0.01
Paiute (1)	3	0.01
Potawatomi (4)	10	0.02
Pueblo (4)	8	0.02
Puget Sound Salish (61)	88	0.21
Seminole (0)	3	0.01
Shoshone (0)	1	<0.01
Sioux (12)	32	0.08
South American Ind. (9)	10	0.02
Tlingit-Haida *(Alaska Native)* (18)	27	0.06
Tohono O'Odham (0)	1	<0.01
Tsimshian *(Alaska Native)* (1)	3	0.01
Ute (1)	1	<0.01
Yakama (7)	10	0.02
Yaqui (1)	8	0.02
Yup'ik *(Alaska Native)* (1)	4	0.01
Asian (3,376)	4,704	11.10
Not Hispanic (3,326)	4,509	10.64
Hispanic (50)	195	0.46
Bangladeshi (14)	15	0.04
Burmese (2)	2	<0.01
Cambodian (266)	327	0.77
Chinese, ex. Taiwanese (207)	386	0.91
Filipino (852)	1,375	3.24
Hmong (4)	10	0.02
Indian (152)	205	0.48
Indonesian (4)	8	0.02
Japanese (181)	466	1.10
Korean (781)	1,160	2.74
Laotian (24)	46	0.11
Malaysian (1)	9	0.02
Nepalese (4)	4	0.01
Pakistani (17)	21	0.05
Sri Lankan (6)	6	0.01
Taiwanese (13)	16	0.04
Thai (49)	102	0.24
Vietnamese (633)	701	1.65
Hawaii Native/Pacific Islander (722)	1,133	2.67
Not Hispanic (701)	1,054	2.49
Hispanic (21)	79	0.19
Fijian (3)	4	0.01
Guamanian/Chamorro (377)	515	1.21
Marshallese (15)	19	0.04
Native Hawaiian (79)	279	0.66
Samoan (175)	229	0.54
Tongan (3)	5	0.01
White (31,446)	33,949	80.08
Not Hispanic (29,489)	31,512	74.33
Hispanic (1,957)	2,437	5.75

Lake Forest Park

Place Type: City
County: King
Population: 12,598†

Ancestry‡	Population	%
African, Sub-Saharan (26)	38	0.30
African (0)	12	0.10
Somalian (14)	14	0.11
Other Sub-Saharan African (12)	12	0.10
American (292)	292	2.32
Arab (75)	83	0.66
Egyptian (17)	17	0.14
Lebanese (8)	16	0.13
Other Arab (50)	50	0.40
Armenian (9)	9	0.07
Austrian (13)	56	0.44
Basque (0)	13	0.10
Brazilian (11)	33	0.26
British (38)	132	1.05
Bulgarian (9)	19	0.15
Canadian (37)	79	0.63
Croatian (129)	139	1.10
Czech (29)	204	1.62
Czechoslovakian (9)	18	0.14
Danish (40)	168	1.33
Dutch (39)	230	1.83
Eastern European (19)	19	0.15
English (501)	2,247	17.85
Estonian (0)	14	0.11
European (327)	442	3.51
Finnish (53)	168	1.33
French, ex. Basque (48)	511	4.06
French Canadian (49)	127	1.01
German (666)	2,661	21.14
Greek (40)	81	0.64
Hungarian (23)	32	0.25
Icelander (12)	73	0.58
Iranian (55)	55	0.44
Irish (414)	1,905	15.14
Italian (91)	475	3.77
Lithuanian (0)	30	0.24
Northern European (101)	112	0.89
Norwegian (387)	1,078	8.57
Polish (54)	341	2.71
Portuguese (32)	43	0.34
Romanian (68)	68	0.54
Russian (112)	143	1.14
Scandinavian (128)	199	1.58
Scotch-Irish (154)	420	3.34
Scottish (78)	492	3.91
Serbian (0)	10	0.08
Slavic (14)	14	0.11
Slovene (10)	20	0.16
Swedish (289)	743	5.90
Swiss (81)	190	1.51
Ukrainian (119)	153	1.22
Welsh (37)	173	1.37
Yugoslavian (12)	55	0.44

Hispanic Origin	Population	%
Hispanic or Latino (of any race)	455	3.61
Central American, ex. Mexican	43	0.34
Costa Rican	3	0.02
Guatemalan	5	0.04
Honduran	1	0.01
Nicaraguan	14	0.11
Panamanian	3	0.02
Salvadoran	17	0.13
Cuban	11	0.09
Dominican Republic	11	0.09
Mexican	227	1.80
Puerto Rican	29	0.23
South American	78	0.62
Argentinean	16	0.13
Chilean	14	0.11
Colombian	12	0.10
Ecuadorian	8	0.06
Peruvian	27	0.21
Venezuelan	1	0.01
Other Hispanic or Latino	56	0.44

Race*	Population	%
African-American/Black (229)	338	2.68
Not Hispanic (221)	321	2.55
Hispanic (8)	17	0.13
American Indian/Alaska Native (77)	194	1.54
Not Hispanic (61)	173	1.37
Hispanic (16)	21	0.17
Alaska Athabascan *(Ala. Nat.)* (6)	7	0.06
Aleut *(Alaska Native)* (2)	7	0.06
Apache (1)	2	0.02
Arapaho (0)	1	0.01
Blackfeet (2)	3	0.02
Canadian/French Am. Ind. (0)	5	0.04
Cherokee (5)	28	0.22
Chickasaw (1)	1	0.01
Chippewa (4)	6	0.05
Choctaw (2)	6	0.05
Colville (2)	2	0.02
Comanche (1)	1	0.01
Creek (0)	4	0.03
Mexican American Ind. (4)	6	0.05
Osage (0)	1	0.01
Potawatomi (1)	2	0.02
Puget Sound Salish (6)	11	0.09
Sioux (0)	2	0.02
Tlingit-Haida *(Alaska Native)* (12)	19	0.15
Yup'ik *(Alaska Native)* (1)	1	0.01
Asian (1,105)	1,477	11.72
Not Hispanic (1,097)	1,445	11.47
Hispanic (8)	32	0.25
Burmese (3)	3	0.02
Cambodian (29)	29	0.23
Chinese, ex. Taiwanese (295)	373	2.96
Filipino (184)	308	2.44
Indian (119)	146	1.16
Indonesian (10)	21	0.17
Japanese (136)	248	1.97
Korean (159)	194	1.54
Laotian (8)	15	0.12
Malaysian (1)	1	0.01
Pakistani (19)	25	0.20
Sri Lankan (1)	4	0.03
Taiwanese (20)	23	0.18
Thai (12)	19	0.15
Vietnamese (70)	90	0.71
Hawaii Native/Pacific Islander (23)	67	0.53
Not Hispanic (23)	63	0.50
Hispanic (0)	4	0.03
Fijian (2)	3	0.02
Guamanian/Chamorro (3)	6	0.05
Marshallese (1)	3	0.02
Native Hawaiian (9)	32	0.25
Samoan (5)	11	0.09
White (10,456)	10,996	87.28
Not Hispanic (10,178)	10,667	84.67
Hispanic (278)	329	2.61

Lake Morton-Berrydale

Place Type: CDP
County: King
Population: 10,160†

*Notes: † The Census 2010 population figure is used to calculate the percentages in the Hispanic Origin and Race categories. Ancestry percentages are based on the 2006-2010 American Community Survey population (not shown); ‡ Numbers in parentheses indicate the number of people reporting a single ancestry; * Numbers in parentheses indicate the number of persons reporting this race alone, not in combination with any other race; Please refer to the Explanation of Data for more information.*

Ancestry‡	Population	%
African, Sub-Saharan (39)	39	0.40
African (39)	39	0.40
American (388)	388	4.00
Armenian (11)	11	0.11
Austrian (25)	80	0.83
Basque (10)	10	0.10
Belgian (0)	12	0.12
British (36)	77	0.79
Canadian (6)	19	0.20
Celtic (9)	9	0.09
Croatian (0)	34	0.35
Czech (8)	23	0.24
Czechoslovakian (0)	109	1.12
Danish (90)	298	3.08
Dutch (60)	281	2.90
Eastern European (0)	12	0.12
English (232)	1,362	14.05
European (206)	206	2.13
Finnish (12)	31	0.32
French, ex. Basque (93)	400	4.13
French Canadian (33)	43	0.44
German (916)	2,634	27.18
Hungarian (22)	63	0.65
Irish (437)	1,397	14.42
Israeli (0)	5	0.05
Italian (99)	372	3.84
Lithuanian (8)	8	0.08
Maltese (134)	164	1.69
Northern European (50)	50	0.52
Norwegian (267)	717	7.40
Polish (113)	303	3.13
Romanian (0)	18	0.19
Russian (12)	66	0.68
Scandinavian (11)	117	1.21
Scotch-Irish (45)	190	1.96
Scottish (37)	260	2.68
Slovak (12)	24	0.25
Swedish (129)	347	3.58
Swiss (21)	78	0.80
Ukrainian (0)	22	0.23
Welsh (42)	120	1.24
Yugoslavian (0)	11	0.11

Hispanic Origin	Population	%
Hispanic or Latino (of any race)	566	5.57
Central American, ex. Mexican	9	0.09
Costa Rican	2	0.02
Guatemalan	3	0.03
Honduran	1	0.01
Salvadoran	3	0.03
Cuban	3	0.03
Mexican	404	3.98
Puerto Rican	48	0.47
South American	21	0.21
Argentinean	9	0.09
Chilean	2	0.02
Colombian	3	0.03
Peruvian	7	0.07
Other Hispanic or Latino	81	0.80

Race*	Population	%
African-American/Black (166)	232	2.28
Not Hispanic (160)	221	2.18
Hispanic (6)	11	0.11
American Indian/Alaska Native (96)	223	2.19
Not Hispanic (88)	201	1.98
Hispanic (8)	22	0.22
Alaska Athabascan *(Ala. Nat.)* (1)	1	0.01
Aleut *(Alaska Native)* (1)	5	0.05
Apache (1)	1	0.01
Blackfeet (2)	5	0.05
Canadian/French Am. Ind. (1)	5	0.05
Cherokee (8)	33	0.32
Cheyenne (0)	2	0.02
Chickasaw (1)	1	0.01
Chippewa (8)	15	0.15
Choctaw (0)	2	0.02
Colville (1)	1	0.01
Creek (1)	1	0.01
Crow (0)	3	0.03
Delaware (1)	1	0.01
Iroquois (0)	2	0.02
Kiowa (1)	1	0.01
Mexican American Ind. (1)	1	0.01
Navajo (1)	3	0.03
Ottawa (3)	3	0.03
Puget Sound Salish (10)	18	0.18
Seminole (3)	3	0.03
Sioux (4)	10	0.10
Tlingit-Haida *(Alaska Native)* (2)	4	0.04
Tsimshian *(Alaska Native)* (1)	1	0.01
Asian (303)	493	4.85
Not Hispanic (292)	463	4.56
Hispanic (11)	30	0.30
Bangladeshi (4)	4	0.04
Cambodian (8)	12	0.12
Chinese, ex. Taiwanese (32)	69	0.68
Filipino (120)	205	2.02
Hmong (2)	2	0.02
Indian (22)	30	0.30
Indonesian (4)	4	0.04
Japanese (30)	91	0.90
Korean (30)	52	0.51
Laotian (11)	17	0.17
Pakistani (2)	2	0.02
Thai (3)	9	0.09
Vietnamese (17)	26	0.26
Hawaii Native/Pacific Islander (29)	78	0.77
Not Hispanic (23)	67	0.66
Hispanic (6)	11	0.11
Guamanian/Chamorro (5)	11	0.11
Native Hawaiian (13)	37	0.36
Samoan (3)	13	0.13
White (8,934)	9,301	91.55
Not Hispanic (8,673)	8,985	88.44
Hispanic (261)	316	3.11

Lake Stevens

Place Type: City
County: Snohomish
Population: 28,069†

Ancestry‡	Population	%
African, Sub-Saharan (84)	102	0.38
African (62)	62	0.23
Nigerian (13)	13	0.05
Other Sub-Saharan African (9)	27	0.10
American (1,249)	1,249	4.64
Arab (31)	79	0.29
Lebanese (10)	17	0.06
Palestinian (7)	7	0.03
Syrian (14)	40	0.15
Other Arab (0)	15	0.06
Armenian (0)	22	0.08
Austrian (32)	80	0.30
Belgian (0)	132	0.49
British (24)	64	0.24
Bulgarian (40)	40	0.15
Cajun (48)	48	0.18
Canadian (18)	104	0.39
Croatian (0)	12	0.04
Czech (36)	181	0.67
Czechoslovakian (11)	11	0.04
Danish (130)	474	1.76
Dutch (300)	707	2.63
Eastern European (9)	27	0.10
English (659)	2,901	10.78
European (526)	548	2.04
Finnish (43)	116	0.43
French, ex. Basque (142)	1,211	4.50
French Canadian (117)	204	0.76
German (1,445)	5,058	18.80
German Russian (0)	11	0.04
Greek (70)	127	0.47
Hungarian (52)	155	0.58
Icelander (8)	25	0.09
Iranian (0)	48	0.18
Irish (686)	3,245	12.06
Italian (284)	1,316	4.89
Lithuanian (10)	63	0.23
Maltese (7)	7	0.03
Northern European (156)	156	0.58
Norwegian (828)	2,488	9.25
Pennsylvania German (9)	23	0.09
Polish (160)	607	2.26
Portuguese (78)	184	0.68
Russian (19)	176	0.65
Scandinavian (217)	299	1.11
Scotch-Irish (299)	705	2.62
Scottish (224)	941	3.50
Serbian (10)	10	0.04
Slovak (0)	28	0.10
Slovene (12)	12	0.04
Swedish (223)	1,326	4.93
Swiss (36)	169	0.63
Ukrainian (83)	141	0.52
Welsh (72)	331	1.23
West Indian, ex. Hispanic (13)	13	0.05
British West Indian (13)	13	0.05
Yugoslavian (0)	29	0.11

Hispanic Origin	Population	%
Hispanic or Latino (of any race)	2,424	8.64
Central American, ex. Mexican	86	0.31
Costa Rican	6	0.02
Guatemalan	22	0.08
Honduran	13	0.05
Nicaraguan	10	0.04
Panamanian	13	0.05
Salvadoran	17	0.06
Other Central American	5	0.02
Cuban	20	0.07
Dominican Republic	7	0.02
Mexican	1,859	6.62
Puerto Rican	120	0.43
South American	107	0.38
Argentinean	15	0.05
Bolivian	3	0.01
Chilean	14	0.05
Colombian	30	0.11
Ecuadorian	1	<0.01
Peruvian	28	0.10
Uruguayan	1	<0.01
Venezuelan	15	0.05
Other Hispanic or Latino	225	0.80

Race*	Population	%
African-American/Black (482)	822	2.93
Not Hispanic (440)	732	2.61
Hispanic (42)	90	0.32
American Indian/Alaska Native (254)	677	2.41
Not Hispanic (195)	548	1.95
Hispanic (59)	129	0.46
Alaska Athabascan *(Ala. Nat.)* (0)	12	0.04
Aleut *(Alaska Native)* (12)	33	0.12
Apache (0)	8	0.03
Blackfeet (1)	18	0.06
Canadian/French Am. Ind. (3)	11	0.04
Cherokee (7)	57	0.20
Chickasaw (1)	1	<0.01
Chippewa (6)	25	0.09
Choctaw (3)	12	0.04
Colville (4)	8	0.03
Cree (0)	4	0.01
Creek (1)	4	0.01
Crow (0)	1	<0.01
Delaware (3)	3	0.01
Inupiat *(Alaska Native)* (3)	5	0.02
Iroquois (1)	1	<0.01
Lumbee (1)	1	<0.01
Mexican American Ind. (22)	35	0.12
Navajo (5)	7	0.02
Potawatomi (3)	8	0.03
Pueblo (3)	3	0.01
Puget Sound Salish (42)	74	0.26
Shoshone (2)	3	0.01
Sioux (11)	31	0.11
South American Ind. (0)	11	0.04

*Notes: † The Census 2010 population figure is used to calculate the percentages in the Hispanic Origin and Race categories. Ancestry percentages are based on the 2006-2010 American Community Survey population (not shown); ‡ Numbers in parentheses indicate the number of people reporting a single ancestry; * Numbers in parentheses indicate the number of persons reporting this race alone, not in combination with any other race; Please refer to the Explanation of Data for more information.*

Spanish American Ind. (0)	1	<0.01
Tlingit-Haida *(Alaska Native)* (15)	35	0.12
Tsimshian *(Alaska Native)* (0)	2	0.01
Ute (0)	1	<0.01
Yakama (0)	1	<0.01
Yuman (0)	1	<0.01
Yup'ik *(Alaska Native)* (0)	1	<0.01
Asian (1,012)	1,584	5.64
Not Hispanic (980)	1,473	5.25
Hispanic (32)	111	0.40
Bangladeshi (3)	3	0.01
Burmese (4)	9	0.03
Cambodian (52)	67	0.24
Chinese, ex. Taiwanese (104)	218	0.78
Filipino (317)	554	1.97
Hmong (48)	49	0.17
Indian (59)	78	0.28
Indonesian (15)	27	0.10
Japanese (85)	233	0.83
Korean (79)	140	0.50
Laotian (70)	85	0.30
Malaysian (2)	2	0.01
Pakistani (12)	13	0.05
Taiwanese (7)	12	0.04
Thai (13)	33	0.12
Vietnamese (77)	122	0.43
Hawaii Native/Pacific Islander (121)	313	1.12
Not Hispanic (119)	289	1.03
Hispanic (2)	24	0.09
Fijian (12)	12	0.04
Guamanian/Chamorro (37)	73	0.26
Native Hawaiian (47)	149	0.53
Samoan (11)	41	0.15
Tongan (2)	8	0.03
White (23,882)	25,186	89.73
Not Hispanic (22,714)	23,765	84.67
Hispanic (1,168)	1,421	5.06

Lake Stickney

Place Type: CDP
County: Snohomish
Population: 7,777†

Ancestry‡	Population	%
African, Sub-Saharan (115)	115	1.56
African (40)	40	0.54
Nigerian (66)	66	0.90
Other Sub-Saharan African (9)	9	0.12
American (270)	270	3.67
Arab (0)	32	0.43
Arab (0)	32	0.43
Armenian (12)	12	0.16
Austrian (9)	18	0.24
British (13)	13	0.18
Bulgarian (24)	24	0.33
Czech (0)	7	0.10
Danish (46)	111	1.51
Dutch (9)	103	1.40
English (196)	642	8.72
European (66)	82	1.11
Finnish (0)	16	0.22
French, ex. Basque (12)	227	3.08
French Canadian (0)	43	0.58
German (156)	1,116	15.16
Greek (0)	61	0.83
Hungarian (56)	63	0.86
Iranian (76)	76	1.03
Irish (119)	489	6.64
Italian (8)	234	3.18
Norwegian (91)	297	4.03
Polish (48)	88	1.20
Portuguese (15)	15	0.20
Romanian (155)	155	2.11
Russian (319)	319	4.33
Scandinavian (15)	67	0.91
Scotch-Irish (88)	251	3.41
Scottish (7)	127	1.72
Slovak (0)	125	1.70
Swedish (45)	188	2.55
Ukrainian (79)	79	1.07
Welsh (0)	45	0.61

Hispanic Origin	Population	%
Hispanic or Latino (of any race)	1,032	13.27
Central American, ex. Mexican	69	0.89
Costa Rican	1	0.01
Guatemalan	9	0.12
Honduran	11	0.14
Nicaraguan	4	0.05
Panamanian	3	0.04
Salvadoran	41	0.53
Cuban	3	0.04
Dominican Republic	2	0.03
Mexican	825	10.61
Puerto Rican	29	0.37
South American	41	0.53
Argentinean	4	0.05
Chilean	3	0.04
Colombian	7	0.09
Peruvian	23	0.30
Venezuelan	2	0.03
Other South American	2	0.03
Other Hispanic or Latino	63	0.81

Race*	Population	%
African-American/Black (417)	519	6.67
Not Hispanic (404)	489	6.29
Hispanic (13)	30	0.39
American Indian/Alaska Native (84)	172	2.21
Not Hispanic (75)	144	1.85
Hispanic (9)	28	0.36
Alaska Athabascan *(Ala. Nat.)* (1)	2	0.03
Aleut *(Alaska Native)* (2)	3	0.04
Apache (0)	1	0.01
Blackfeet (0)	1	0.01
Canadian/French Am. Ind. (1)	1	0.01
Central American Ind. (0)	5	0.06
Cherokee (8)	27	0.35
Cheyenne (1)	1	0.01
Chickasaw (0)	1	0.01
Chippewa (1)	10	0.13
Choctaw (0)	4	0.05
Colville (0)	1	0.01
Delaware (2)	2	0.03
Inupiat *(Alaska Native)* (0)	1	0.01
Mexican American Ind. (0)	1	0.01
Navajo (1)	5	0.06
Pueblo (1)	1	0.01
Puget Sound Salish (13)	17	0.22
Sioux (2)	3	0.04
South American Ind. (0)	4	0.05
Tlingit-Haida *(Alaska Native)* (22)	25	0.32
Yakama (7)	7	0.09
Asian (1,826)	2,018	25.95
Not Hispanic (1,802)	1,975	25.40
Hispanic (24)	43	0.55
Bangladeshi (19)	19	0.24
Burmese (1)	1	0.01
Cambodian (95)	105	1.35
Chinese, ex. Taiwanese (181)	226	2.91
Filipino (375)	464	5.97
Hmong (5)	5	0.06
Indian (132)	151	1.94
Indonesian (46)	46	0.59
Japanese (31)	62	0.80
Korean (422)	463	5.95
Laotian (28)	32	0.41
Nepalese (7)	7	0.09
Pakistani (13)	13	0.17
Sri Lankan (1)	1	0.01
Taiwanese (11)	13	0.17
Thai (20)	20	0.26
Vietnamese (363)	385	4.95
Hawaii Native/Pacific Islander (78)	140	1.80
Not Hispanic (78)	131	1.68
Hispanic (0)	9	0.12
Fijian (26)	27	0.35
Guamanian/Chamorro (5)	13	0.17
Marshallese (15)	15	0.19
Native Hawaiian (10)	44	0.57
Samoan (8)	13	0.17
Tongan (7)	9	0.12
White (4,592)	4,936	63.47
Not Hispanic (4,057)	4,333	55.72
Hispanic (535)	603	7.75

Lake Tapps

Place Type: CDP
County: Pierce
Population: 11,859†

Ancestry‡	Population	%
African, Sub-Saharan (0)	21	0.19
African (0)	21	0.19
American (365)	365	3.24
Austrian (9)	9	0.08
Belgian (8)	15	0.13
British (44)	76	0.67
Canadian (0)	71	0.63
Czech (0)	44	0.39
Czechoslovakian (31)	60	0.53
Danish (24)	118	1.05
Dutch (72)	238	2.11
Eastern European (12)	12	0.11
English (535)	1,689	14.98
European (296)	314	2.79
Finnish (21)	86	0.76
French, ex. Basque (74)	596	5.29
French Canadian (11)	75	0.67
German (899)	3,268	28.99
Greek (8)	52	0.46
Icelander (0)	25	0.22
Irish (324)	1,616	14.33
Italian (75)	578	5.13
Luxemburger (0)	10	0.09
Northern European (15)	15	0.13
Norwegian (246)	778	6.90
Pennsylvania German (0)	13	0.12
Polish (68)	188	1.67
Portuguese (0)	55	0.49
Russian (15)	232	2.06
Scandinavian (128)	166	1.47
Scotch-Irish (180)	496	4.40
Scottish (130)	467	4.14
Slavic (7)	16	0.14
Swedish (140)	525	4.66
Swiss (46)	80	0.71
Turkish (0)	11	0.10
Ukrainian (26)	83	0.74
Welsh (26)	55	0.49
Yugoslavian (0)	78	0.69

Hispanic Origin	Population	%
Hispanic or Latino (of any race)	534	4.50
Central American, ex. Mexican	28	0.24
Costa Rican	3	0.03
Guatemalan	5	0.04
Nicaraguan	2	0.02
Panamanian	6	0.05
Salvadoran	12	0.10
Cuban	12	0.10
Dominican Republic	1	0.01
Mexican	335	2.82
Puerto Rican	44	0.37
South American	23	0.19
Argentinean	2	0.02
Colombian	9	0.08
Ecuadorian	6	0.05
Peruvian	6	0.05
Other Hispanic or Latino	91	0.77

Race*	Population	%
African-American/Black (80)	160	1.35
Not Hispanic (70)	144	1.21
Hispanic (10)	16	0.13
American Indian/Alaska Native (73)	212	1.79
Not Hispanic (65)	187	1.58
Hispanic (8)	25	0.21

*Notes: † The Census 2010 population figure is used to calculate the percentages in the Hispanic Origin and Race categories. Ancestry percentages are based on the 2006-2010 American Community Survey population (not shown); ‡ Numbers in parentheses indicate the number of people reporting a single ancestry; * Numbers in parentheses indicate the number of persons reporting this race alone, not in combination with any other race; Please refer to the Explanation of Data for more information.*

Race* (continued)	Population	%
Aleut *(Alaska Native)* (1)	3	0.03
Blackfeet (3)	9	0.08
Canadian/French Am. Ind. (2)	5	0.04
Cherokee (9)	41	0.35
Chickasaw (0)	4	0.03
Chippewa (5)	9	0.08
Choctaw (4)	10	0.08
Colville (2)	3	0.03
Cree (3)	3	0.03
Creek (0)	1	0.01
Inupiat *(Alaska Native)* (2)	2	0.02
Iroquois (0)	3	0.03
Kiowa (1)	1	0.01
Mexican American Ind. (1)	3	0.03
Navajo (4)	4	0.03
Paiute (1)	3	0.03
Potawatomi (1)	3	0.03
Pueblo (0)	1	0.01
Puget Sound Salish (11)	18	0.15
Sioux (3)	9	0.08
Tlingit-Haida *(Alaska Native)* (5)	16	0.13
Asian (251)	400	3.37
Not Hispanic (239)	371	3.13
Hispanic (12)	29	0.24
Cambodian (2)	5	0.04
Chinese, ex. Taiwanese (31)	51	0.43
Filipino (71)	136	1.15
Indian (12)	24	0.20
Indonesian (1)	3	0.03
Japanese (28)	66	0.56
Korean (59)	70	0.59
Laotian (1)	3	0.03
Sri Lankan (2)	4	0.03
Taiwanese (0)	2	0.02
Thai (7)	18	0.15
Vietnamese (27)	30	0.25
Hawaii Native/Pacific Islander (28)	66	0.56
Not Hispanic (28)	62	0.52
Hispanic (0)	4	0.03
Fijian (4)	4	0.03
Guamanian/Chamorro (8)	15	0.13
Native Hawaiian (13)	42	0.35
Samoan (3)	4	0.03
White (10,911)	11,283	95.14
Not Hispanic (10,574)	10,889	91.82
Hispanic (337)	394	3.32

Lakeland North

Place Type: CDP
County: King
Population: 12,942†

Ancestry‡	Population	%
African, Sub-Saharan (42)	42	0.34
African (42)	42	0.34
American (428)	428	3.51
Austrian (0)	12	0.10
Basque (25)	25	0.21
Brazilian (28)	68	0.56
British (0)	68	0.56
Canadian (8)	39	0.32
Croatian (0)	17	0.14
Czech (0)	10	0.08
Danish (44)	135	1.11
Dutch (38)	202	1.66
English (286)	1,117	9.16
European (345)	417	3.42
Finnish (21)	88	0.72
French, ex. Basque (111)	535	4.39
French Canadian (0)	15	0.12
German (501)	2,172	17.81
Greek (0)	76	0.62
Hungarian (14)	49	0.40
Irish (328)	1,554	12.75
Israeli (9)	9	0.07
Italian (85)	399	3.27
Norwegian (223)	724	5.94
Polish (43)	133	1.09
Portuguese (18)	29	0.24
Romanian (56)	56	0.46
Russian (295)	347	2.85
Scandinavian (36)	66	0.54
Scotch-Irish (18)	220	1.80
Scottish (73)	248	2.03
Swedish (167)	414	3.40
Swiss (30)	56	0.46
Ukrainian (464)	464	3.81
Welsh (0)	144	1.18
West Indian, ex. Hispanic (15)	15	0.12
Belizean (15)	15	0.12

Hispanic Origin	Population	%
Hispanic or Latino (of any race)	1,439	11.12
Central American, ex. Mexican	123	0.95
Costa Rican	4	0.03
Guatemalan	36	0.28
Honduran	7	0.05
Panamanian	14	0.11
Salvadoran	61	0.47
Other Central American	1	0.01
Cuban	13	0.10
Dominican Republic	1	0.01
Mexican	1,105	8.54
Puerto Rican	35	0.27
South American	43	0.33
Argentinean	3	0.02
Bolivian	2	0.02
Chilean	3	0.02
Colombian	8	0.06
Ecuadorian	13	0.10
Peruvian	11	0.08
Uruguayan	2	0.02
Venezuelan	1	0.01
Other Hispanic or Latino	119	0.92

Race*	Population	%
African-American/Black (734)	988	7.63
Not Hispanic (714)	924	7.14
Hispanic (20)	64	0.49
American Indian/Alaska Native (98)	281	2.17
Not Hispanic (69)	221	1.71
Hispanic (29)	60	0.46
Alaska Athabascan *(Ala. Nat.)* (3)	5	0.04
Aleut *(Alaska Native)* (2)	4	0.03
Apache (0)	5	0.04
Blackfeet (5)	14	0.11
Canadian/French Am. Ind. (0)	2	0.02
Central American Ind. (1)	3	0.02
Cherokee (2)	30	0.23
Cheyenne (0)	2	0.02
Chippewa (12)	18	0.14
Choctaw (1)	3	0.02
Cree (1)	1	0.01
Delaware (1)	1	0.01
Inupiat *(Alaska Native)* (0)	1	0.01
Iroquois (1)	2	0.02
Menominee (0)	1	0.01
Mexican American Ind. (13)	13	0.10
Navajo (1)	1	0.01
Osage (0)	2	0.02
Paiute (1)	1	0.01
Puget Sound Salish (9)	16	0.12
Seminole (0)	1	0.01
Shoshone (1)	2	0.02
Sioux (6)	11	0.08
Tlingit-Haida *(Alaska Native)* (2)	13	0.10
Tsimshian *(Alaska Native)* (0)	4	0.03
Yup'ik *(Alaska Native)* (0)	1	0.01
Asian (1,675)	1,978	15.28
Not Hispanic (1,657)	1,924	14.87
Hispanic (18)	54	0.42
Burmese (2)	2	0.02
Cambodian (79)	92	0.71
Chinese, ex. Taiwanese (125)	175	1.35
Filipino (357)	500	3.86
Hmong (10)	10	0.08
Indian (245)	257	1.99
Indonesian (2)	3	0.02
Japanese (70)	142	1.10
Korean (447)	493	3.81
Laotian (32)	40	0.31
Pakistani (14)	14	0.11
Taiwanese (1)	3	0.02
Thai (25)	39	0.30
Vietnamese (207)	238	1.84
Hawaii Native/Pacific Islander (185)	282	2.18
Not Hispanic (182)	265	2.05
Hispanic (3)	17	0.13
Fijian (21)	22	0.17
Guamanian/Chamorro (26)	43	0.33
Marshallese (0)	1	0.01
Native Hawaiian (12)	46	0.36
Samoan (85)	136	1.05
Tongan (16)	17	0.13
White (8,835)	9,439	72.93
Not Hispanic (8,285)	8,760	67.69
Hispanic (550)	679	5.25

Lakeland South

Place Type: CDP
County: King
Population: 11,574†

Ancestry‡	Population	%
African, Sub-Saharan (12)	12	0.11
African (12)	12	0.11
American (607)	607	5.41
Arab (6)	6	0.05
Lebanese (6)	6	0.05
Armenian (14)	14	0.12
Austrian (0)	12	0.11
British (24)	24	0.21
Canadian (67)	100	0.89
Czech (12)	72	0.64
Czechoslovakian (63)	103	0.92
Danish (96)	131	1.17
Dutch (31)	177	1.58
English (423)	1,622	14.46
European (87)	87	0.78
Finnish (0)	14	0.12
French, ex. Basque (80)	475	4.23
French Canadian (33)	146	1.30
German (658)	2,467	21.99
Greek (12)	21	0.19
Hungarian (52)	52	0.46
Irish (462)	1,387	12.36
Italian (96)	200	1.78
Norwegian (213)	798	7.11
Polish (46)	184	1.64
Portuguese (0)	6	0.05
Romanian (42)	42	0.37
Russian (287)	396	3.53
Scandinavian (0)	21	0.19
Scotch-Irish (60)	304	2.71
Scottish (37)	313	2.79
Serbian (0)	11	0.10
Swedish (81)	432	3.85
Swiss (0)	42	0.37
Ukrainian (198)	198	1.76
Welsh (6)	90	0.80
West Indian, ex. Hispanic (12)	12	0.11
Haitian (12)	12	0.11
Yugoslavian (0)	44	0.39

Hispanic Origin	Population	%
Hispanic or Latino (of any race)	799	6.90
Central American, ex. Mexican	61	0.53
Costa Rican	3	0.03
Guatemalan	21	0.18
Honduran	3	0.03
Nicaraguan	4	0.03
Panamanian	5	0.04
Salvadoran	25	0.22
Cuban	5	0.04
Dominican Republic	6	0.05
Mexican	584	5.05
Puerto Rican	48	0.41
South American	27	0.23

*Notes: † The Census 2010 population figure is used to calculate the percentages in the Hispanic Origin and Race categories. Ancestry percentages are based on the 2006-2010 American Community Survey population (not shown); ‡ Numbers in parentheses indicate the number of people reporting a single ancestry; * Numbers in parentheses indicate the number of persons reporting this race alone, not in combination with any other race; Please refer to the Explanation of Data for more information.*

Argentinean	5	0.04
Bolivian	3	0.03
Chilean	2	0.02
Colombian	5	0.04
Ecuadorian	1	0.01
Peruvian	9	0.08
Venezuelan	2	0.02
Other Hispanic or Latino	68	0.59

Race*	Population	%
African-American/Black (489)	677	5.85
Not Hispanic (465)	616	5.32
Hispanic (24)	61	0.53
American Indian/Alaska Native (120)	264	2.28
Not Hispanic (112)	239	2.06
Hispanic (8)	25	0.22
Alaska Athabascan *(Ala. Nat.)* (2)	2	0.02
Aleut *(Alaska Native)* (5)	9	0.08
Apache (0)	5	0.04
Arapaho (2)	2	0.02
Blackfeet (11)	16	0.14
Cherokee (7)	33	0.29
Cheyenne (0)	3	0.03
Chippewa (2)	3	0.03
Choctaw (0)	2	0.02
Colville (1)	3	0.03
Cree (1)	4	0.03
Crow (1)	2	0.02
Inupiat *(Alaska Native)* (1)	1	0.01
Kiowa (1)	1	0.01
Mexican American Ind. (2)	2	0.02
Navajo (4)	15	0.13
Potawatomi (1)	1	0.01
Puget Sound Salish (12)	21	0.18
Seminole (2)	5	0.04
Sioux (4)	5	0.04
South American Ind. (0)	3	0.03
Tlingit-Haida *(Alaska Native)* (8)	16	0.14
Tsimshian *(Alaska Native)* (2)	6	0.05
Yakama (0)	1	0.01
Yup'ik *(Alaska Native)* (1)	1	0.01
Asian (1,088)	1,317	11.38
Not Hispanic (1,076)	1,286	11.11
Hispanic (12)	31	0.27
Cambodian (39)	48	0.41
Chinese, ex. Taiwanese (59)	104	0.90
Filipino (212)	299	2.58
Indian (91)	109	0.94
Indonesian (0)	3	0.03
Japanese (54)	96	0.83
Korean (462)	507	4.38
Laotian (12)	19	0.16
Malaysian (1)	1	0.01
Sri Lankan (13)	13	0.11
Taiwanese (0)	1	0.01
Thai (18)	20	0.17
Vietnamese (86)	109	0.94
Hawaii Native/Pacific Islander (130)	200	1.73
Not Hispanic (130)	184	1.59
Hispanic (0)	16	0.14
Fijian (14)	14	0.12
Guamanian/Chamorro (19)	25	0.22
Marshallese (1)	1	0.01
Native Hawaiian (11)	38	0.33
Samoan (61)	97	0.84
Tongan (2)	3	0.03
White (8,875)	9,391	81.14
Not Hispanic (8,509)	8,934	77.19
Hispanic (366)	457	3.95

Lakewood

Place Type: City
County: Pierce
Population: 58,163†

Ancestry‡	Population	%
African, Sub-Saharan (487)	582	0.99
African (300)	368	0.63
Ethiopian (47)	63	0.11
Kenyan (73)	73	0.12
South African (0)	11	0.02
Other Sub-Saharan African (67)	67	0.11
American (3,232)	3,232	5.51
Arab (50)	85	0.14
Arab (29)	29	0.05
Egyptian (14)	14	0.02
Lebanese (7)	42	0.07
Austrian (0)	88	0.15
Belgian (0)	22	0.04
British (40)	124	0.21
Cajun (11)	11	0.02
Canadian (46)	143	0.24
Croatian (31)	50	0.09
Czech (50)	177	0.30
Czechoslovakian (16)	42	0.07
Danish (60)	329	0.56
Dutch (135)	614	1.05
Eastern European (23)	23	0.04
English (1,359)	4,561	7.77
Estonian (11)	11	0.02
European (1,012)	1,084	1.85
Finnish (38)	114	0.19
French, ex. Basque (268)	1,930	3.29
French Canadian (99)	276	0.47
German (3,432)	10,557	17.98
German Russian (18)	51	0.09
Greek (19)	142	0.24
Guyanese (15)	15	0.03
Hungarian (73)	224	0.38
Iranian (36)	36	0.06
Irish (1,391)	5,665	9.65
Italian (629)	2,199	3.75
Latvian (8)	19	0.03
Lithuanian (11)	45	0.08
Luxemburger (0)	20	0.03
Northern European (95)	117	0.20
Norwegian (789)	2,051	3.49
Pennsylvania German (0)	21	0.04
Polish (276)	1,106	1.88
Portuguese (82)	321	0.55
Romanian (0)	7	0.01
Russian (219)	444	0.76
Scandinavian (60)	195	0.33
Scotch-Irish (357)	1,255	2.14
Scottish (376)	1,228	2.09
Slavic (35)	35	0.06
Slovak (78)	78	0.13
Slovene (12)	24	0.04
Swedish (116)	1,091	1.86
Swiss (50)	143	0.24
Turkish (0)	10	0.02
Ukrainian (138)	194	0.33
Welsh (33)	460	0.78
West Indian, ex. Hispanic (200)	351	0.60
Haitian (52)	63	0.11
Jamaican (133)	273	0.47
Trinidadian/Tobagonian (15)	15	0.03
Yugoslavian (36)	66	0.11

Hispanic Origin	Population	%
Hispanic or Latino (of any race)	8,877	15.26
Central American, ex. Mexican	504	0.87
Costa Rican	20	0.03
Guatemalan	94	0.16
Honduran	50	0.09
Nicaraguan	36	0.06
Panamanian	169	0.29
Salvadoran	134	0.23
Other Central American	1	<0.01
Cuban	80	0.14
Dominican Republic	51	0.09
Mexican	6,318	10.86
Puerto Rican	935	1.61
South American	176	0.30
Argentinean	11	0.02
Bolivian	12	0.02
Chilean	8	0.01
Colombian	68	0.12
Ecuadorian	26	0.04
Peruvian	39	0.07
Venezuelan	8	0.01
Other South American	4	0.01
Other Hispanic or Latino	813	1.40

Race*	Population	%
African-American/Black (6,849)	9,125	15.69
Not Hispanic (6,468)	8,424	14.48
Hispanic (381)	701	1.21
American Indian/Alaska Native (760)	1,978	3.40
Not Hispanic (607)	1,589	2.73
Hispanic (153)	389	0.67
Alaska Athabascan *(Ala. Nat.)* (8)	12	0.02
Aleut *(Alaska Native)* (12)	17	0.03
Apache (18)	46	0.08
Arapaho (4)	7	0.01
Blackfeet (13)	81	0.14
Canadian/French Am. Ind. (4)	7	0.01
Central American Ind. (1)	2	<0.01
Cherokee (43)	270	0.46
Cheyenne (2)	6	0.01
Chickasaw (1)	13	0.02
Chippewa (26)	56	0.10
Choctaw (9)	46	0.08
Colville (2)	8	0.01
Comanche (0)	4	0.01
Creek (2)	9	0.02
Crow (0)	1	<0.01
Delaware (1)	2	<0.01
Hopi (1)	2	<0.01
Inupiat *(Alaska Native)* (8)	18	0.03
Iroquois (0)	10	0.02
Kiowa (0)	1	<0.01
Mexican American Ind. (31)	55	0.09
Navajo (22)	35	0.06
Osage (0)	7	0.01
Paiute (0)	2	<0.01
Pima (2)	4	0.01
Potawatomi (1)	2	<0.01
Pueblo (8)	17	0.03
Puget Sound Salish (65)	104	0.18
Seminole (2)	14	0.02
Shoshone (2)	12	0.02
Sioux (27)	63	0.11
South American Ind. (0)	5	0.01
Tlingit-Haida *(Alaska Native)* (25)	47	0.08
Tohono O'Odham (0)	5	0.01
Tsimshian *(Alaska Native)* (5)	10	0.02
Ute (0)	2	<0.01
Yakama (28)	32	0.06
Yaqui (2)	2	<0.01
Yuman (1)	2	<0.01
Yup'ik *(Alaska Native)* (5)	8	0.01
Asian (5,206)	7,204	12.39
Not Hispanic (5,116)	6,900	11.86
Hispanic (90)	304	0.52
Burmese (7)	8	0.01
Cambodian (139)	176	0.30
Chinese, ex. Taiwanese (210)	435	0.75
Filipino (1,718)	2,473	4.25
Hmong (9)	10	0.02
Indian (109)	171	0.29
Indonesian (6)	16	0.03
Japanese (454)	965	1.66
Korean (1,844)	2,412	4.15
Laotian (19)	31	0.05
Malaysian (1)	7	0.01
Pakistani (12)	15	0.03
Sri Lankan (0)	1	<0.01
Taiwanese (29)	33	0.06
Thai (82)	160	0.28
Vietnamese (366)	471	0.81
Hawaii Native/Pacific Islander (1,506)	2,155	3.71
Not Hispanic (1,445)	2,006	3.45
Hispanic (61)	149	0.26
Fijian (4)	6	0.01
Guamanian/Chamorro (399)	559	0.96
Marshallese (21)	34	0.06
Native Hawaiian (163)	473	0.81
Samoan (684)	826	1.42

*Notes: † The Census 2010 population figure is used to calculate the percentages in the Hispanic Origin and Race categories. Ancestry percentages are based on the 2006-2010 American Community Survey population (not shown); ‡ Numbers in parentheses indicate the number of people reporting a single ancestry; * Numbers in parentheses indicate the number of persons reporting this race alone, not in combination with any other race; Please refer to the Explanation of Data for more information.*

Tongan (6)	18	0.03
White (34,506)	38,625	66.41
Not Hispanic (31,438)	34,778	59.79
Hispanic (3,068)	3,847	6.61

Liberty Lake

Place Type: City
County: Spokane
Population: 7,591†

Ancestry‡	Population	%
American (292)	292	4.27
Arab (43)	146	2.14
Arab (21)	44	0.64
Egyptian (0)	25	0.37
Lebanese (0)	55	0.80
Syrian (22)	22	0.32
Austrian (0)	24	0.35
Belgian (0)	8	0.12
Canadian (26)	108	1.58
Czech (0)	9	0.13
Danish (12)	46	0.67
Dutch (19)	413	6.04
English (269)	978	14.31
Estonian (0)	10	0.15
European (276)	276	4.04
Finnish (123)	179	2.62
French, ex. Basque (37)	223	3.26
French Canadian (67)	119	1.74
German (507)	1,944	28.44
Greek (0)	44	0.64
Hungarian (0)	18	0.26
Irish (210)	1,097	16.05
Italian (134)	459	6.72
Norwegian (130)	604	8.84
Pennsylvania German (0)	19	0.28
Polish (25)	143	2.09
Portuguese (12)	20	0.29
Russian (73)	104	1.52
Scandinavian (13)	63	0.92
Scotch-Irish (53)	141	2.06
Scottish (38)	315	4.61
Slavic (28)	28	0.41
Slovak (0)	46	0.67
Swedish (16)	296	4.33
Swiss (0)	41	0.60
Ukrainian (9)	40	0.59
Welsh (0)	65	0.95

Hispanic Origin	Population	%
Hispanic or Latino (of any race)	228	3.00
Central American, ex. Mexican	9	0.12
Guatemalan	3	0.04
Honduran	1	0.01
Panamanian	1	0.01
Salvadoran	4	0.05
Cuban	2	0.03
Dominican Republic	1	0.01
Mexican	149	1.96
Puerto Rican	8	0.11
South American	10	0.13
Chilean	2	0.03
Colombian	4	0.05
Ecuadorian	1	0.01
Paraguayan	1	0.01
Other South American	2	0.03
Other Hispanic or Latino	49	0.65

Race*	Population	%
African-American/Black (51)	105	1.38
Not Hispanic (50)	99	1.30
Hispanic (1)	6	0.08
American Indian/Alaska Native (39)	110	1.45
Not Hispanic (36)	100	1.32
Hispanic (3)	10	0.13
Alaska Athabascan *(Ala. Nat.)* (4)	4	0.05
Aleut *(Alaska Native)* (1)	4	0.05
Apache (2)	2	0.03
Blackfeet (1)	4	0.05
Central American Ind. (0)	4	0.05
Cherokee (1)	9	0.12
Chippewa (3)	8	0.11
Choctaw (0)	1	0.01
Colville (8)	10	0.13
Cree (0)	2	0.03
Creek (3)	3	0.04
Delaware (0)	1	0.01
Iroquois (2)	4	0.05
Kiowa (0)	4	0.05
Potawatomi (0)	2	0.03
Puget Sound Salish (0)	2	0.03
Seminole (1)	2	0.03
Sioux (0)	7	0.09
South American Ind. (0)	4	0.05
Tlingit-Haida *(Alaska Native)* (1)	4	0.05
Yaqui (1)	1	0.01
Asian (269)	358	4.72
Not Hispanic (267)	346	4.56
Hispanic (2)	12	0.16
Chinese, ex. Taiwanese (81)	98	1.29
Filipino (21)	56	0.74
Hmong (1)	1	0.01
Indian (66)	73	0.96
Japanese (18)	38	0.50
Korean (38)	53	0.70
Pakistani (1)	1	0.01
Taiwanese (3)	3	0.04
Thai (1)	4	0.05
Vietnamese (30)	33	0.43
Hawaii Native/Pacific Islander (16)	32	0.42
Not Hispanic (16)	31	0.41
Hispanic (0)	1	0.01
Guamanian/Chamorro (2)	3	0.04
Native Hawaiian (9)	24	0.32
Samoan (4)	4	0.05
White (6,930)	7,152	94.22
Not Hispanic (6,788)	6,986	92.03
Hispanic (142)	166	2.19

Longview

Place Type: City
County: Cowlitz
Population: 36,648†

Ancestry‡	Population	%
African, Sub-Saharan (0)	7	0.02
African (0)	7	0.02
American (1,713)	1,713	4.68
Arab (83)	83	0.23
Arab (83)	83	0.23
Australian (0)	10	0.03
Austrian (7)	37	0.10
Belgian (41)	140	0.38
British (49)	181	0.49
Canadian (8)	62	0.17
Croatian (0)	12	0.03
Czech (67)	120	0.33
Czechoslovakian (0)	33	0.09
Danish (69)	372	1.02
Dutch (193)	901	2.46
English (1,316)	4,181	11.42
European (841)	868	2.37
Finnish (541)	1,211	3.31
French, ex. Basque (236)	1,529	4.18
French Canadian (185)	713	1.95
German (2,179)	8,531	23.31
Greek (19)	93	0.25
Hungarian (27)	151	0.41
Icelander (0)	38	0.10
Iranian (35)	40	0.11
Irish (1,356)	5,513	15.06
Italian (427)	1,406	3.84
Lithuanian (0)	9	0.02
Northern European (26)	26	0.07
Norwegian (796)	2,359	6.44
Pennsylvania German (30)	53	0.14
Polish (102)	425	1.16
Portuguese (68)	284	0.78
Romanian (0)	9	0.02
Russian (96)	138	0.38
Scandinavian (128)	325	0.89
Scotch-Irish (330)	1,186	3.24
Scottish (269)	771	2.11
Swedish (322)	1,426	3.90
Swiss (24)	113	0.31
Ukrainian (71)	95	0.26
Welsh (75)	412	1.13
West Indian, ex. Hispanic (0)	9	0.02
West Indian (0)	9	0.02

Hispanic Origin	Population	%
Hispanic or Latino (of any race)	3,571	9.74
Central American, ex. Mexican	97	0.26
Costa Rican	1	<0.01
Guatemalan	33	0.09
Honduran	22	0.06
Nicaraguan	1	<0.01
Panamanian	10	0.03
Salvadoran	29	0.08
Other Central American	1	<0.01
Cuban	18	0.05
Dominican Republic	9	0.02
Mexican	2,915	7.95
Puerto Rican	67	0.18
South American	43	0.12
Argentinean	13	0.04
Chilean	1	<0.01
Colombian	9	0.02
Ecuadorian	4	0.01
Paraguayan	1	<0.01
Peruvian	14	0.04
Other South American	1	<0.01
Other Hispanic or Latino	422	1.15

Race*	Population	%
African-American/Black (333)	620	1.69
Not Hispanic (307)	563	1.54
Hispanic (26)	57	0.16
American Indian/Alaska Native (629)	1,360	3.71
Not Hispanic (550)	1,180	3.22
Hispanic (79)	180	0.49
Alaska Athabascan *(Ala. Nat.)* (11)	11	0.03
Aleut *(Alaska Native)* (6)	13	0.04
Apache (1)	18	0.05
Arapaho (1)	1	<0.01
Blackfeet (12)	67	0.18
Canadian/French Am. Ind. (3)	6	0.02
Cherokee (75)	262	0.71
Cheyenne (1)	9	0.02
Chickasaw (7)	9	0.02
Chippewa (31)	86	0.23
Choctaw (11)	39	0.11
Colville (7)	12	0.03
Comanche (1)	3	0.01
Cree (3)	11	0.03
Creek (5)	15	0.04
Crow (0)	1	<0.01
Delaware (2)	7	0.02
Hopi (0)	1	<0.01
Inupiat *(Alaska Native)* (12)	13	0.04
Iroquois (4)	8	0.02
Lumbee (15)	22	0.06
Menominee (1)	1	<0.01
Mexican American Ind. (15)	30	0.08
Navajo (1)	7	0.02
Ottawa (1)	1	<0.01
Paiute (2)	2	0.01
Pima (0)	1	<0.01
Potawatomi (0)	2	0.01
Puget Sound Salish (17)	20	0.05
Seminole (1)	5	0.01
Shoshone (1)	2	0.01
Sioux (15)	47	0.13
Tlingit-Haida *(Alaska Native)* (16)	25	0.07
Tohono O'Odham (2)	2	0.01
Tsimshian *(Alaska Native)* (6)	6	0.02
Yakama (11)	15	0.04
Yaqui (0)	1	<0.01

*Notes: † The Census 2010 population figure is used to calculate the percentages in the Hispanic Origin and Race categories. Ancestry percentages are based on the 2006-2010 American Community Survey population (not shown); ‡ Numbers in parentheses indicate the number of people reporting a single ancestry; * Numbers in parentheses indicate the number of persons reporting this race alone, not in combination with any other race; Please refer to the Explanation of Data for more information.*

Yuman (1)	5	0.01
Yup'ik *(Alaska Native)* (2)	2	0.01
Asian (791)	1,066	2.91
Not Hispanic (778)	1,029	2.81
Hispanic (13)	37	0.10
Burmese (0)	1	<0.01
Cambodian (120)	150	0.41
Chinese, ex. Taiwanese (142)	194	0.53
Filipino (115)	195	0.53
Hmong (0)	1	<0.01
Indian (48)	66	0.18
Indonesian (5)	6	0.02
Japanese (55)	123	0.34
Korean (55)	97	0.26
Laotian (7)	13	0.04
Malaysian (1)	1	<0.01
Nepalese (3)	3	0.01
Pakistani (9)	9	0.02
Sri Lankan (1)	1	<0.01
Taiwanese (4)	4	0.01
Thai (19)	30	0.08
Vietnamese (171)	199	0.54
Hawaii Native/Pacific Islander (115)	231	0.63
Not Hispanic (103)	205	0.56
Hispanic (12)	26	0.07
Fijian (2)	2	0.01
Guamanian/Chamorro (11)	25	0.07
Marshallese (1)	1	<0.01
Native Hawaiian (44)	106	0.29
Samoan (4)	24	0.07
Tongan (5)	9	0.02
White (31,500)	32,948	89.90
Not Hispanic (30,167)	31,260	85.30
Hispanic (1,333)	1,688	4.61

Lynden

Place Type: City
County: Whatcom
Population: 11,951†

Ancestry‡	Population	%
African, Sub-Saharan (7)	7	0.06
African (7)	7	0.06
American (758)	758	6.55
Arab (6)	6	0.05
Other Arab (6)	6	0.05
Austrian (9)	9	0.08
Basque (7)	7	0.06
Belgian (0)	19	0.16
British (48)	86	0.74
Bulgarian (0)	11	0.09
Canadian (147)	235	2.03
Czech (18)	56	0.48
Danish (11)	96	0.83
Dutch (2,573)	3,829	33.07
English (227)	1,063	9.18
European (284)	284	2.45
Finnish (0)	41	0.35
French, ex. Basque (0)	181	1.56
French Canadian (0)	7	0.06
German (433)	2,108	18.20
Greek (9)	20	0.17
Hungarian (0)	21	0.18
Icelander (7)	30	0.26
Irish (211)	870	7.51
Italian (37)	227	1.96
Northern European (24)	24	0.21
Norwegian (153)	553	4.78
Polish (26)	126	1.09
Portuguese (7)	41	0.35
Romanian (0)	7	0.06
Russian (31)	123	1.06
Scandinavian (10)	17	0.15
Scotch-Irish (59)	222	1.92
Scottish (61)	353	3.05
Swedish (78)	408	3.52
Swiss (9)	40	0.35
Ukrainian (0)	97	0.84
Welsh (47)	107	0.92

Hispanic Origin	Population	%
Hispanic or Latino (of any race)	1,036	8.67
Central American, ex. Mexican	64	0.54
Costa Rican	1	0.01
Guatemalan	35	0.29
Honduran	7	0.06
Nicaraguan	1	0.01
Panamanian	5	0.04
Salvadoran	15	0.13
Cuban	4	0.03
Dominican Republic	2	0.02
Mexican	837	7.00
Puerto Rican	17	0.14
South American	22	0.18
Argentinean	5	0.04
Colombian	8	0.07
Paraguayan	3	0.03
Peruvian	6	0.05
Other Hispanic or Latino	90	0.75

Race*	Population	%
African-American/Black (79)	123	1.03
Not Hispanic (77)	119	1.00
Hispanic (2)	4	0.03
American Indian/Alaska Native (105)	182	1.52
Not Hispanic (71)	135	1.13
Hispanic (34)	47	0.39
Aleut *(Alaska Native)* (4)	11	0.09
Blackfeet (1)	4	0.03
Canadian/French Am. Ind. (3)	3	0.03
Cherokee (8)	16	0.13
Cheyenne (2)	3	0.03
Chippewa (1)	4	0.03
Choctaw (2)	4	0.03
Colville (1)	1	0.01
Cree (0)	1	0.01
Creek (1)	1	0.01
Inupiat *(Alaska Native)* (3)	3	0.03
Mexican American Ind. (17)	24	0.20
Navajo (0)	1	0.01
Puget Sound Salish (9)	9	0.08
Sioux (3)	4	0.03
Tlingit-Haida *(Alaska Native)* (4)	5	0.04
Tohono O'Odham (0)	2	0.02
Yakama (1)	1	0.01
Yaqui (0)	1	0.01
Yup'ik *(Alaska Native)* (3)	7	0.06
Asian (301)	375	3.14
Not Hispanic (298)	366	3.06
Hispanic (3)	9	0.08
Cambodian (9)	9	0.08
Chinese, ex. Taiwanese (33)	40	0.33
Filipino (56)	79	0.66
Indian (154)	158	1.32
Japanese (16)	44	0.37
Korean (20)	30	0.25
Pakistani (1)	1	0.01
Sri Lankan (1)	4	0.03
Thai (3)	7	0.06
Vietnamese (5)	8	0.07
Hawaii Native/Pacific Islander (18)	43	0.36
Not Hispanic (15)	33	0.28
Hispanic (3)	10	0.08
Guamanian/Chamorro (2)	3	0.03
Native Hawaiian (9)	25	0.21
Samoan (2)	3	0.03
Tongan (2)	2	0.02
White (10,719)	10,952	91.64
Not Hispanic (10,264)	10,434	87.31
Hispanic (455)	518	4.33

Lynnwood

Place Type: City
County: Snohomish
Population: 35,836†

Ancestry‡	Population	%
African, Sub-Saharan (1,011)	1,039	2.92
African (198)	226	0.64
Ethiopian (794)	794	2.23
Other Sub-Saharan African (19)	19	0.05
American (1,241)	1,241	3.49
Arab (351)	578	1.63
Egyptian (276)	438	1.23
Iraqi (60)	125	0.35
Lebanese (15)	15	0.04
Armenian (15)	15	0.04
Australian (0)	30	0.08
Austrian (36)	77	0.22
Belgian (0)	22	0.06
Brazilian (13)	13	0.04
British (84)	143	0.40
Bulgarian (103)	103	0.29
Canadian (33)	108	0.30
Croatian (31)	46	0.13
Czech (0)	95	0.27
Czechoslovakian (58)	268	0.75
Danish (48)	275	0.77
Dutch (79)	458	1.29
Eastern European (12)	12	0.03
English (706)	3,052	8.59
Estonian (0)	19	0.05
European (320)	414	1.17
Finnish (87)	191	0.54
French, ex. Basque (84)	906	2.55
French Canadian (56)	283	0.80
German (1,404)	5,763	16.22
Greek (82)	182	0.51
Hungarian (72)	108	0.30
Icelander (0)	30	0.08
Iranian (190)	196	0.55
Irish (524)	3,536	9.95
Israeli (0)	21	0.06
Italian (138)	828	2.33
Latvian (10)	10	0.03
Lithuanian (0)	32	0.09
Macedonian (0)	17	0.05
Northern European (74)	74	0.21
Norwegian (674)	2,232	6.28
Pennsylvania German (22)	22	0.06
Polish (188)	600	1.69
Portuguese (19)	39	0.11
Romanian (168)	168	0.47
Russian (141)	404	1.14
Scandinavian (254)	429	1.21
Scotch-Irish (193)	626	1.76
Scottish (166)	1,179	3.32
Serbian (19)	30	0.08
Slavic (0)	14	0.04
Slovak (0)	14	0.04
Slovene (0)	28	0.08
Swedish (199)	1,333	3.75
Swiss (11)	124	0.35
Ukrainian (280)	290	0.82
Welsh (7)	257	0.72
West Indian, ex. Hispanic (76)	85	0.24
Haitian (40)	40	0.11
Jamaican (36)	45	0.13
Yugoslavian (25)	61	0.17

Hispanic Origin	Population	%
Hispanic or Latino (of any race)	4,750	13.25
Central American, ex. Mexican	329	0.92
Costa Rican	27	0.08
Guatemalan	31	0.09
Honduran	91	0.25
Nicaraguan	23	0.06
Panamanian	14	0.04
Salvadoran	142	0.40
Other Central American	1	<0.01
Cuban	25	0.07
Dominican Republic	8	0.02
Mexican	3,451	9.63
Puerto Rican	145	0.40
South American	273	0.76
Argentinean	15	0.04
Bolivian	9	0.03
Chilean	43	0.12
Colombian	47	0.13

*Notes: † The Census 2010 population figure is used to calculate the percentages in the Hispanic Origin and Race categories. Ancestry percentages are based on the 2006-2010 American Community Survey population (not shown); ‡ Numbers in parentheses indicate the number of people reporting a single ancestry; * Numbers in parentheses indicate the number of persons reporting this race alone, not in combination with any other race; Please refer to the Explanation of Data for more information.*

Ecuadorian	9	0.03
Paraguayan	1	<0.01
Peruvian	126	0.35
Uruguayan	7	0.02
Venezuelan	9	0.03
Other South American	7	0.02
Other Hispanic or Latino	519	1.45

Race*	Population	%
African-American/Black (1,976)	2,506	6.99
Not Hispanic (1,895)	2,334	6.51
Hispanic (81)	172	0.48
American Indian/Alaska Native (404)	833	2.32
Not Hispanic (320)	658	1.84
Hispanic (84)	175	0.49
Alaska Athabascan *(Ala. Nat.)* (9)	18	0.05
Aleut *(Alaska Native)* (11)	31	0.09
Apache (2)	9	0.03
Arapaho (1)	2	0.01
Blackfeet (9)	36	0.10
Canadian/French Am. Ind. (14)	19	0.05
Central American Ind. (1)	1	<0.01
Cherokee (19)	69	0.19
Cheyenne (0)	4	0.01
Chickasaw (2)	2	0.01
Chippewa (11)	34	0.09
Choctaw (3)	13	0.04
Colville (12)	22	0.06
Comanche (1)	2	0.01
Cree (0)	1	<0.01
Creek (0)	2	0.01
Crow (2)	2	0.01
Delaware (1)	1	<0.01
Inupiat *(Alaska Native)* (9)	18	0.05
Iroquois (0)	1	<0.01
Mexican American Ind. (23)	38	0.11
Navajo (10)	21	0.06
Osage (4)	7	0.02
Ottawa (0)	1	<0.01
Paiute (0)	3	0.01
Pueblo (3)	6	0.02
Puget Sound Salish (19)	27	0.08
Seminole (2)	2	0.01
Shoshone (1)	1	<0.01
Sioux (15)	23	0.06
South American Ind. (3)	3	0.01
Spanish American Ind. (2)	2	0.01
Tlingit-Haida *(Alaska Native)* (18)	38	0.11
Tsimshian *(Alaska Native)* (2)	7	0.02
Yakama (3)	8	0.02
Yup'ik *(Alaska Native)* (1)	1	<0.01
Asian (6,185)	7,039	19.64
Not Hispanic (6,163)	6,950	19.39
Hispanic (22)	89	0.25
Bangladeshi (6)	6	0.02
Burmese (4)	4	0.01
Cambodian (203)	232	0.65
Chinese, ex. Taiwanese (919)	1,136	3.17
Filipino (1,163)	1,501	4.19
Hmong (7)	10	0.03
Indian (416)	472	1.32
Indonesian (69)	94	0.26
Japanese (233)	405	1.13
Korean (1,293)	1,412	3.94
Laotian (56)	75	0.21
Malaysian (2)	7	0.02
Nepalese (31)	33	0.09
Pakistani (105)	118	0.33
Sri Lankan (15)	17	0.05
Taiwanese (65)	76	0.21
Thai (72)	98	0.27
Vietnamese (1,256)	1,337	3.73
Hawaii Native/Pacific Islander (192)	403	1.12
Not Hispanic (182)	371	1.04
Hispanic (10)	32	0.09
Fijian (39)	51	0.14
Guamanian/Chamorro (13)	40	0.11
Marshallese (13)	20	0.06
Native Hawaiian (50)	158	0.44
Samoan (23)	57	0.16
Tongan (7)	15	0.04
White (22,875)	24,423	68.15
Not Hispanic (20,991)	22,252	62.09
Hispanic (1,884)	2,171	6.06

Maltby

Place Type: CDP
County: Snohomish
Population: 10,830†

Ancestry‡	Population	%
American (528)	528	4.53
Arab (0)	223	1.91
Lebanese (0)	223	1.91
Armenian (7)	19	0.16
Australian (0)	13	0.11
Austrian (14)	60	0.51
British (104)	130	1.11
Canadian (0)	40	0.34
Croatian (41)	61	0.52
Czech (44)	130	1.11
Danish (48)	149	1.28
Dutch (59)	222	1.90
Eastern European (36)	36	0.31
English (450)	1,595	13.67
European (247)	295	2.53
Finnish (23)	52	0.45
French, ex. Basque (81)	649	5.56
French Canadian (44)	129	1.11
German (815)	3,111	26.67
Greek (0)	13	0.11
Hungarian (13)	110	0.94
Irish (130)	1,543	13.23
Italian (151)	926	7.94
Lithuanian (0)	19	0.16
Maltese (13)	51	0.44
Norwegian (612)	1,190	10.20
Polish (94)	329	2.82
Portuguese (12)	39	0.33
Romanian (14)	56	0.48
Russian (24)	131	1.12
Scandinavian (40)	60	0.51
Scotch-Irish (101)	394	3.38
Scottish (70)	334	2.86
Swedish (149)	685	5.87
Swiss (20)	122	1.05
Ukrainian (38)	81	0.69
Welsh (109)	539	4.62
Yugoslavian (11)	24	0.21

Hispanic Origin	Population	%
Hispanic or Latino (of any race)	379	3.50
Central American, ex. Mexican	18	0.17
Costa Rican	7	0.06
Nicaraguan	2	0.02
Panamanian	5	0.05
Salvadoran	4	0.04
Cuban	2	0.02
Dominican Republic	1	0.01
Mexican	247	2.28
Puerto Rican	23	0.21
South American	21	0.19
Argentinean	6	0.06
Chilean	5	0.05
Colombian	1	0.01
Ecuadorian	1	0.01
Peruvian	6	0.06
Venezuelan	2	0.02
Other Hispanic or Latino	67	0.62

Race*	Population	%
African-American/Black (43)	93	0.86
Not Hispanic (35)	82	0.76
Hispanic (8)	11	0.10
American Indian/Alaska Native (64)	146	1.35
Not Hispanic (51)	123	1.14
Hispanic (13)	23	0.21
Alaska Athabascan *(Ala. Nat.)* (1)	1	0.01
Aleut *(Alaska Native)* (0)	4	0.04
Apache (2)	3	0.03
Blackfeet (0)	2	0.02
Canadian/French Am. Ind. (1)	2	0.02
Central American Ind. (1)	1	0.01
Cherokee (3)	16	0.15
Chickasaw (1)	4	0.04
Chippewa (2)	5	0.05
Choctaw (2)	10	0.09
Colville (4)	4	0.04
Delaware (1)	1	0.01
Iroquois (0)	5	0.05
Kiowa (0)	1	0.01
Mexican American Ind. (6)	6	0.06
Osage (3)	5	0.05
Potawatomi (2)	2	0.02
Puget Sound Salish (9)	9	0.08
Seminole (0)	4	0.04
Sioux (1)	3	0.03
Tlingit-Haida *(Alaska Native)* (1)	5	0.05
Tsimshian *(Alaska Native)* (0)	1	0.01
Yakama (2)	2	0.02
Yup'ik *(Alaska Native)* (1)	2	0.02
Asian (387)	514	4.75
Not Hispanic (386)	508	4.69
Hispanic (1)	6	0.06
Cambodian (27)	38	0.35
Chinese, ex. Taiwanese (49)	70	0.65
Filipino (44)	65	0.60
Hmong (18)	18	0.17
Indian (13)	24	0.22
Indonesian (2)	8	0.07
Japanese (67)	108	1.00
Korean (38)	65	0.60
Laotian (13)	22	0.20
Pakistani (11)	11	0.10
Sri Lankan (4)	4	0.04
Taiwanese (5)	5	0.05
Thai (3)	10	0.09
Vietnamese (59)	66	0.61
Hawaii Native/Pacific Islander (16)	47	0.43
Not Hispanic (12)	40	0.37
Hispanic (4)	7	0.06
Guamanian/Chamorro (3)	4	0.04
Native Hawaiian (5)	18	0.17
Samoan (5)	15	0.14
Tongan (2)	3	0.03
White (9,921)	10,191	94.10
Not Hispanic (9,696)	9,931	91.70
Hispanic (225)	260	2.40

Maple Valley

Place Type: City
County: King
Population: 22,684†

Ancestry‡	Population	%
African, Sub-Saharan (0)	52	0.25
African (0)	52	0.25
American (1,166)	1,166	5.56
Arab (0)	53	0.25
Arab (0)	11	0.05
Lebanese (0)	42	0.20
Armenian (8)	8	0.04
Australian (26)	48	0.23
Austrian (0)	74	0.35
Belgian (11)	17	0.08
British (88)	143	0.68
Canadian (18)	88	0.42
Croatian (11)	21	0.10
Czech (21)	87	0.41
Danish (178)	568	2.71
Dutch (158)	404	1.93
English (683)	2,757	13.14
European (549)	549	2.62
Finnish (13)	50	0.24
French, ex. Basque (86)	822	3.92
French Canadian (90)	225	1.07
German (1,427)	4,283	20.42
Greek (22)	134	0.64

*Notes: † The Census 2010 population figure is used to calculate the percentages in the Hispanic Origin and Race categories. Ancestry percentages are based on the 2006-2010 American Community Survey population (not shown); ‡ Numbers in parentheses indicate the number of people reporting a single ancestry; * Numbers in parentheses indicate the number of persons reporting this race alone, not in combination with any other race; Please refer to the Explanation of Data for more information.*

Ancestry	Population	%
Hungarian (0)	71	0.34
Icelander (0)	29	0.14
Iranian (14)	14	0.07
Irish (879)	2,933	13.98
Italian (252)	1,011	4.82
Lithuanian (0)	12	0.06
Norwegian (666)	1,763	8.41
Polish (119)	551	2.63
Portuguese (0)	39	0.19
Romanian (11)	23	0.11
Russian (92)	301	1.44
Scandinavian (145)	299	1.43
Scotch-Irish (176)	470	2.24
Scottish (177)	525	2.50
Slavic (0)	6	0.03
Swedish (263)	974	4.64
Swiss (11)	62	0.30
Ukrainian (91)	129	0.62
Welsh (111)	228	1.09
Yugoslavian (17)	55	0.26

Hispanic Origin	Population	%
Hispanic or Latino (of any race)	1,293	5.70
Central American, ex. Mexican	52	0.23
Costa Rican	4	0.02
Guatemalan	23	0.10
Honduran	2	0.01
Nicaraguan	7	0.03
Panamanian	5	0.02
Salvadoran	11	0.05
Cuban	17	0.07
Dominican Republic	7	0.03
Mexican	882	3.89
Puerto Rican	78	0.34
South American	92	0.41
Argentinean	13	0.06
Bolivian	11	0.05
Chilean	10	0.04
Colombian	24	0.11
Ecuadorian	11	0.05
Paraguayan	6	0.03
Peruvian	13	0.06
Venezuelan	2	0.01
Other South American	2	0.01
Other Hispanic or Latino	165	0.73

Race*	Population	%
African-American/Black (471)	754	3.32
Not Hispanic (453)	709	3.13
Hispanic (18)	45	0.20
American Indian/Alaska Native (111)	366	1.61
Not Hispanic (105)	325	1.43
Hispanic (6)	41	0.18
Alaska Athabascan *(Ala. Nat.)* (1)	4	0.02
Aleut *(Alaska Native)* (1)	8	0.04
Apache (3)	4	0.02
Blackfeet (0)	7	0.03
Cherokee (4)	52	0.23
Chickasaw (1)	1	<0.01
Chippewa (9)	27	0.12
Choctaw (5)	11	0.05
Colville (2)	7	0.03
Cree (0)	2	0.01
Creek (1)	2	0.01
Crow (0)	3	0.01
Houma (3)	3	0.01
Inupiat *(Alaska Native)* (0)	4	0.02
Iroquois (4)	7	0.03
Lumbee (1)	3	0.01
Mexican American Ind. (1)	3	0.01
Navajo (6)	16	0.07
Osage (0)	2	0.01
Paiute (1)	1	<0.01
Pima (1)	1	<0.01
Potawatomi (0)	3	0.01
Puget Sound Salish (19)	28	0.12
Seminole (0)	1	<0.01
Sioux (6)	12	0.05
Tlingit-Haida *(Alaska Native)* (4)	20	0.09
Yakama (0)	1	<0.01
Yaqui (0)	1	<0.01
Asian (1,013)	1,628	7.18
Not Hispanic (995)	1,550	6.83
Hispanic (18)	78	0.34
Burmese (1)	3	0.01
Cambodian (21)	32	0.14
Chinese, ex. Taiwanese (120)	263	1.16
Filipino (308)	580	2.56
Hmong (20)	23	0.10
Indian (142)	169	0.75
Indonesian (6)	8	0.04
Japanese (89)	255	1.12
Korean (140)	194	0.86
Laotian (38)	51	0.22
Pakistani (18)	18	0.08
Taiwanese (0)	7	0.03
Thai (13)	29	0.13
Vietnamese (56)	74	0.33
Hawaii Native/Pacific Islander (91)	207	0.91
Not Hispanic (90)	204	0.90
Hispanic (1)	3	0.01
Fijian (3)	8	0.04
Guamanian/Chamorro (17)	21	0.09
Native Hawaiian (33)	109	0.48
Samoan (27)	44	0.19
Tongan (1)	3	0.01
White (19,465)	20,504	90.39
Not Hispanic (18,745)	19,631	86.54
Hispanic (720)	873	3.85

Martha Lake

Place Type: CDP
County: Snohomish
Population: 15,473†

Ancestry‡	Population	%
African, Sub-Saharan (159)	159	1.02
African (26)	26	0.17
South African (10)	10	0.06
Other Sub-Saharan African (123)	123	0.79
American (377)	377	2.41
Arab (93)	93	0.59
Lebanese (56)	56	0.36
Palestinian (25)	25	0.16
Syrian (12)	12	0.08
Australian (0)	36	0.23
Belgian (27)	27	0.17
British (12)	79	0.51
Bulgarian (34)	34	0.22
Czech (31)	65	0.42
Czechoslovakian (28)	28	0.18
Danish (68)	238	1.52
Dutch (71)	370	2.37
Eastern European (8)	8	0.05
English (443)	2,043	13.07
European (625)	714	4.57
Finnish (19)	19	0.12
French, ex. Basque (128)	676	4.32
French Canadian (62)	165	1.06
German (668)	3,286	21.02
Greek (31)	31	0.20
Hungarian (0)	45	0.29
Icelander (0)	17	0.11
Irish (305)	1,624	10.39
Italian (11)	390	2.49
Northern European (26)	26	0.17
Norwegian (153)	592	3.79
Pennsylvania German (0)	27	0.17
Polish (4)	254	1.62
Romanian (85)	85	0.54
Russian (216)	314	2.01
Scandinavian (84)	138	0.88
Scotch-Irish (96)	456	2.92
Scottish (179)	592	3.79
Swedish (133)	828	5.30
Swiss (75)	122	0.78
Turkish (174)	174	1.11
Ukrainian (0)	7	0.04
Welsh (0)	130	0.83
West Indian, ex. Hispanic (0)	98	0.63
Haitian (0)	77	0.49
Jamaican (0)	21	0.13
Yugoslavian (11)	11	0.07

Hispanic Origin	Population	%
Hispanic or Latino (of any race)	1,335	8.63
Central American, ex. Mexican	98	0.63
Costa Rican	8	0.05
Guatemalan	25	0.16
Honduran	4	0.03
Nicaraguan	18	0.12
Panamanian	6	0.04
Salvadoran	37	0.24
Cuban	16	0.10
Dominican Republic	2	0.01
Mexican	904	5.84
Puerto Rican	92	0.59
South American	113	0.73
Argentinean	9	0.06
Bolivian	11	0.07
Chilean	15	0.10
Colombian	38	0.25
Ecuadorian	12	0.08
Peruvian	21	0.14
Uruguayan	2	0.01
Venezuelan	5	0.03
Other Hispanic or Latino	110	0.71

Race*	Population	%
African-American/Black (464)	662	4.28
Not Hispanic (450)	627	4.05
Hispanic (14)	35	0.23
American Indian/Alaska Native (131)	273	1.76
Not Hispanic (103)	218	1.41
Hispanic (28)	55	0.36
Alaska Athabascan *(Ala. Nat.)* (1)	1	0.01
Aleut *(Alaska Native)* (6)	9	0.06
Apache (1)	1	0.01
Blackfeet (2)	6	0.04
Canadian/French Am. Ind. (0)	2	0.01
Cherokee (8)	33	0.21
Chickasaw (3)	3	0.02
Chippewa (12)	15	0.10
Choctaw (2)	5	0.03
Colville (1)	4	0.03
Crow (1)	1	0.01
Inupiat *(Alaska Native)* (0)	2	0.01
Iroquois (2)	3	0.02
Mexican American Ind. (3)	15	0.10
Navajo (0)	1	0.01
Paiute (1)	4	0.03
Potawatomi (0)	3	0.02
Puget Sound Salish (6)	8	0.05
Seminole (0)	1	0.01
Sioux (9)	11	0.07
Tlingit-Haida *(Alaska Native)* (11)	37	0.24
Tsimshian *(Alaska Native)* (1)	2	0.01
Yakama (2)	3	0.02
Yaqui (1)	1	0.01
Yup'ik *(Alaska Native)* (3)	4	0.03
Asian (2,387)	2,811	18.17
Not Hispanic (2,375)	2,756	17.81
Hispanic (12)	55	0.36
Bangladeshi (9)	9	0.06
Burmese (6)	7	0.05
Cambodian (201)	224	1.45
Chinese, ex. Taiwanese (286)	396	2.56
Filipino (381)	565	3.65
Indian (277)	298	1.93
Indonesian (28)	40	0.26
Japanese (105)	214	1.38
Korean (304)	368	2.38
Laotian (51)	52	0.34
Malaysian (6)	7	0.05
Nepalese (9)	9	0.06
Pakistani (19)	26	0.17
Sri Lankan (3)	5	0.03
Taiwanese (3)	19	0.12
Thai (31)	40	0.26

*Notes: † The Census 2010 population figure is used to calculate the percentages in the Hispanic Origin and Race categories. Ancestry percentages are based on the 2006-2010 American Community Survey population (not shown); ‡ Numbers in parentheses indicate the number of people reporting a single ancestry; * Numbers in parentheses indicate the number of persons reporting this race alone, not in combination with any other race; Please refer to the Explanation of Data for more information.*

Vietnamese (541)	578	3.74
Hawaii Native/Pacific Islander (63)	148	0.96
Not Hispanic (63)	140	0.90
Hispanic (0)	8	0.05
Fijian (4)	4	0.03
Guamanian/Chamorro (20)	32	0.21
Marshallese (7)	9	0.06
Native Hawaiian (9)	42	0.27
Samoan (1)	8	0.05
Tongan (5)	15	0.10
White (11,204)	11,842	76.53
Not Hispanic (10,497)	11,032	71.30
Hispanic (707)	810	5.23

Marysville

Place Type: City
County: Snohomish
Population: 60,020†

Ancestry‡	Population	%
African, Sub-Saharan (13)	83	0.14
African (13)	27	0.05
Ethiopian (0)	56	0.10
American (2,327)	2,327	4.02
Arab (96)	170	0.29
Lebanese (17)	35	0.06
Palestinian (8)	64	0.11
Other Arab (71)	71	0.12
Armenian (23)	23	0.04
Assyrian/Chaldean/Syriac (0)	7	0.01
Australian (109)	130	0.22
Austrian (15)	129	0.22
Basque (14)	14	0.02
British (114)	319	0.55
Canadian (206)	417	0.72
Celtic (9)	17	0.03
Croatian (0)	11	0.02
Czech (32)	136	0.24
Czechoslovakian (0)	30	0.05
Danish (198)	494	0.85
Dutch (476)	1,391	2.40
Eastern European (23)	23	0.04
English (2,052)	6,895	11.92
European (707)	903	1.56
Finnish (84)	367	0.63
French, ex. Basque (338)	1,904	3.29
French Canadian (252)	639	1.10
German (3,534)	11,937	20.63
German Russian (0)	12	0.02
Greek (87)	250	0.43
Hungarian (87)	156	0.27
Icelander (14)	68	0.12
Iranian (40)	80	0.14
Irish (1,515)	7,504	12.97
Italian (562)	1,887	3.26
Latvian (14)	29	0.05
Lithuanian (35)	35	0.06
Northern European (32)	32	0.06
Norwegian (2,136)	5,047	8.72
Pennsylvania German (0)	22	0.04
Polish (178)	760	1.31
Portuguese (171)	283	0.49
Romanian (21)	53	0.09
Russian (149)	533	0.92
Scandinavian (295)	614	1.06
Scotch-Irish (332)	1,256	2.17
Scottish (490)	1,954	3.38
Serbian (29)	42	0.07
Slavic (0)	42	0.07
Slovak (0)	83	0.14
Swedish (669)	2,227	3.85
Swiss (110)	266	0.46
Turkish (0)	29	0.05
Ukrainian (311)	387	0.67
Welsh (76)	433	0.75
West Indian, ex. Hispanic (24)	78	0.13
Jamaican (0)	13	0.02
West Indian (24)	65	0.11
Yugoslavian (43)	61	0.11

Hispanic Origin	Population	%
Hispanic or Latino (of any race)	6,178	10.29
Central American, ex. Mexican	221	0.37
Costa Rican	17	0.03
Guatemalan	52	0.09
Honduran	23	0.04
Nicaraguan	36	0.06
Panamanian	23	0.04
Salvadoran	68	0.11
Other Central American	2	<0.01
Cuban	40	0.07
Dominican Republic	19	0.03
Mexican	4,932	8.22
Puerto Rican	255	0.42
South American	174	0.29
Argentinean	14	0.02
Bolivian	3	<0.01
Chilean	21	0.03
Colombian	53	0.09
Ecuadorian	24	0.04
Paraguayan	2	<0.01
Peruvian	44	0.07
Uruguayan	3	<0.01
Venezuelan	10	0.02
Other Hispanic or Latino	537	0.89

Race*	Population	%
African-American/Black (1,114)	1,846	3.08
Not Hispanic (1,034)	1,678	2.80
Hispanic (80)	168	0.28
American Indian/Alaska Native (1,169)	2,188	3.65
Not Hispanic (1,030)	1,887	3.14
Hispanic (139)	301	0.50
Alaska Athabascan *(Ala. Nat.)* (10)	13	0.02
Aleut *(Alaska Native)* (23)	57	0.09
Apache (15)	29	0.05
Arapaho (5)	5	0.01
Blackfeet (14)	84	0.14
Canadian/French Am. Ind. (18)	22	0.04
Cherokee (30)	170	0.28
Cheyenne (2)	10	0.02
Chickasaw (7)	13	0.02
Chippewa (44)	100	0.17
Choctaw (17)	45	0.07
Colville (12)	18	0.03
Comanche (1)	7	0.01
Cree (5)	9	0.01
Creek (2)	7	0.01
Delaware (2)	3	<0.01
Hopi (2)	6	0.01
Inupiat *(Alaska Native)* (10)	15	0.02
Iroquois (5)	16	0.03
Kiowa (1)	3	<0.01
Lumbee (3)	3	<0.01
Menominee (1)	3	<0.01
Mexican American Ind. (20)	33	0.05
Navajo (14)	27	0.04
Osage (0)	5	0.01
Ottawa (3)	3	<0.01
Paiute (1)	5	0.01
Potawatomi (3)	12	0.02
Pueblo (3)	6	0.01
Puget Sound Salish (412)	568	0.95
Seminole (5)	13	0.02
Shoshone (0)	1	<0.01
Sioux (34)	56	0.09
South American Ind. (1)	1	<0.01
Spanish American Ind. (4)	4	0.01
Tlingit-Haida *(Alaska Native)* (49)	98	0.16
Tsimshian *(Alaska Native)* (10)	16	0.03
Ute (0)	1	<0.01
Yakama (16)	21	0.03
Yaqui (2)	2	<0.01
Yuman (0)	3	<0.01
Yup'ik *(Alaska Native)* (1)	2	<0.01
Asian (3,382)	4,773	7.95
Not Hispanic (3,312)	4,567	7.61
Hispanic (70)	206	0.34
Cambodian (107)	144	0.24
Chinese, ex. Taiwanese (162)	328	0.55
Filipino (1,641)	2,289	3.81
Hmong (22)	25	0.04
Indian (477)	548	0.91
Indonesian (32)	70	0.12
Japanese (158)	451	0.75
Korean (163)	313	0.52
Laotian (97)	129	0.21
Malaysian (1)	6	0.01
Nepalese (3)	3	<0.01
Pakistani (5)	6	0.01
Sri Lankan (5)	12	0.02
Taiwanese (5)	8	0.01
Thai (50)	99	0.16
Vietnamese (342)	396	0.66
Hawaii Native/Pacific Islander (372)	695	1.16
Not Hispanic (356)	635	1.06
Hispanic (16)	60	0.10
Fijian (33)	40	0.07
Guamanian/Chamorro (101)	158	0.26
Marshallese (34)	39	0.06
Native Hawaiian (82)	244	0.41
Samoan (45)	83	0.14
Tongan (7)	9	0.01
White (48,029)	50,940	84.87
Not Hispanic (45,396)	47,733	79.53
Hispanic (2,633)	3,207	5.34

Mercer Island

Place Type: City
County: King
Population: 22,699†

Ancestry‡	Population	%
African, Sub-Saharan (41)	112	0.50
African (0)	26	0.12
South African (41)	86	0.38
American (740)	740	3.31
Arab (145)	155	0.69
Egyptian (94)	94	0.42
Iraqi (9)	9	0.04
Lebanese (33)	43	0.19
Other Arab (9)	9	0.04
Armenian (33)	55	0.25
Australian (8)	8	0.04
Austrian (44)	200	0.89
Belgian (96)	115	0.51
Brazilian (16)	16	0.07
British (197)	230	1.03
Bulgarian (0)	9	0.04
Canadian (58)	165	0.74
Celtic (14)	14	0.06
Croatian (30)	66	0.29
Czech (24)	98	0.44
Czechoslovakian (19)	19	0.08
Danish (48)	256	1.14
Dutch (91)	467	2.09
Eastern European (150)	150	0.67
English (885)	3,262	14.58
Estonian (36)	60	0.27
European (586)	665	2.97
Finnish (7)	58	0.26
French, ex. Basque (90)	641	2.86
French Canadian (80)	161	0.72
German (1,028)	3,985	17.81
Greek (91)	130	0.58
Hungarian (57)	154	0.69
Icelander (0)	41	0.18
Iranian (73)	73	0.33
Irish (854)	2,955	13.21
Italian (336)	860	3.84
Latvian (18)	40	0.18
Lithuanian (44)	160	0.72
Northern European (114)	123	0.55
Norwegian (501)	1,154	5.16
Polish (200)	632	2.82
Portuguese (30)	86	0.38
Romanian (142)	226	1.01
Russian (432)	907	4.05
Scandinavian (87)	153	0.68

*Notes: † The Census 2010 population figure is used to calculate the percentages in the Hispanic Origin and Race categories. Ancestry percentages are based on the 2006-2010 American Community Survey population (not shown); ‡ Numbers in parentheses indicate the number of people reporting a single ancestry; * Numbers in parentheses indicate the number of persons reporting this race alone, not in combination with any other race; Please refer to the Explanation of Data for more information.*

Scotch-Irish (150)	429	1.92
Scottish (240)	715	3.20
Slovak (0)	8	0.04
Slovene (48)	102	0.46
Swedish (416)	1,050	4.69
Swiss (39)	127	0.57
Turkish (0)	85	0.38
Ukrainian (16)	120	0.54
Welsh (40)	355	1.59
West Indian, ex. Hispanic (0)	14	0.06
West Indian (0)	14	0.06
Yugoslavian (21)	49	0.22

Hispanic Origin	Population	%
Hispanic or Latino (of any race)	634	2.79
Central American, ex. Mexican	41	0.18
Costa Rican	5	0.02
Guatemalan	12	0.05
Nicaraguan	8	0.04
Panamanian	5	0.02
Salvadoran	11	0.05
Cuban	9	0.04
Dominican Republic	1	<0.01
Mexican	301	1.33
Puerto Rican	34	0.15
South American	108	0.48
Argentinean	18	0.08
Bolivian	2	0.01
Chilean	10	0.04
Colombian	31	0.14
Ecuadorian	6	0.03
Peruvian	20	0.09
Uruguayan	8	0.04
Venezuelan	13	0.06
Other Hispanic or Latino	140	0.62

Race*	Population	%
African-American/Black (286)	407	1.79
Not Hispanic (282)	389	1.71
Hispanic (4)	18	0.08
American Indian/Alaska Native (51)	169	0.74
Not Hispanic (40)	136	0.60
Hispanic (11)	33	0.15
Alaska Athabascan *(Ala. Nat.)* (2)	2	0.01
Aleut *(Alaska Native)* (1)	1	<0.01
Arapaho (1)	2	0.01
Blackfeet (0)	1	<0.01
Central American Ind. (1)	1	<0.01
Cherokee (7)	23	0.10
Chippewa (1)	2	0.01
Choctaw (0)	2	0.01
Cree (0)	1	<0.01
Creek (2)	6	0.03
Crow (0)	1	<0.01
Hopi (0)	1	<0.01
Iroquois (0)	6	0.03
Mexican American Ind. (7)	10	0.04
Navajo (0)	1	<0.01
Paiute (0)	4	0.02
Potawatomi (0)	1	<0.01
Pueblo (1)	1	<0.01
Puget Sound Salish (2)	4	0.02
Seminole (0)	3	0.01
Sioux (1)	2	0.01
Tlingit-Haida *(Alaska Native)* (3)	6	0.03
Tsimshian *(Alaska Native)* (0)	2	0.01
Yakama (1)	2	0.01
Asian (3,615)	4,279	18.85
Not Hispanic (3,598)	4,229	18.63
Hispanic (17)	50	0.22
Burmese (2)	2	0.01
Cambodian (6)	13	0.06
Chinese, ex. Taiwanese (1,500)	1,777	7.83
Filipino (120)	244	1.07
Indian (392)	445	1.96
Indonesian (1)	2	0.01
Japanese (511)	772	3.40
Korean (600)	745	3.28
Laotian (3)	4	0.02
Malaysian (0)	3	0.01
Nepalese (8)	8	0.04
Pakistani (15)	18	0.08
Taiwanese (144)	176	0.78
Thai (19)	36	0.16
Vietnamese (112)	171	0.75
Hawaii Native/Pacific Islander (26)	84	0.37
Not Hispanic (25)	83	0.37
Hispanic (1)	1	<0.01
Fijian (4)	6	0.03
Guamanian/Chamorro (11)	16	0.07
Native Hawaiian (4)	33	0.15
Samoan (2)	7	0.03
Tongan (2)	3	0.01
White (17,677)	18,494	81.47
Not Hispanic (17,255)	18,006	79.33
Hispanic (422)	488	2.15

Midland

Place Type: CDP
County: Pierce
Population: 8,962†

Ancestry‡	Population	%
African, Sub-Saharan (51)	51	0.53
African (51)	51	0.53
American (414)	414	4.31
Belgian (0)	10	0.10
Canadian (14)	35	0.36
Czechoslovakian (0)	48	0.50
Danish (22)	60	0.62
Dutch (14)	106	1.10
English (166)	898	9.34
European (53)	59	0.61
Finnish (23)	54	0.56
French, ex. Basque (13)	439	4.57
French Canadian (10)	34	0.35
German (609)	2,106	21.91
German Russian (0)	25	0.26
Greek (14)	70	0.73
Hungarian (0)	30	0.31
Irish (164)	1,258	13.09
Italian (139)	338	3.52
Norwegian (98)	652	6.78
Pennsylvania German (11)	11	0.11
Polish (20)	65	0.68
Portuguese (8)	35	0.36
Romanian (192)	192	2.00
Russian (41)	83	0.86
Scandinavian (0)	22	0.23
Scotch-Irish (40)	243	2.53
Scottish (96)	266	2.77
Slovak (11)	11	0.11
Swedish (10)	124	1.29
Swiss (0)	22	0.23
Welsh (9)	32	0.33
West Indian, ex. Hispanic (0)	8	0.08
Dutch West Indian (0)	8	0.08

Hispanic Origin	Population	%
Hispanic or Latino (of any race)	1,577	17.60
Central American, ex. Mexican	57	0.64
Costa Rican	1	0.01
Guatemalan	17	0.19
Honduran	11	0.12
Panamanian	14	0.16
Salvadoran	14	0.16
Cuban	6	0.07
Dominican Republic	6	0.07
Mexican	1,321	14.74
Puerto Rican	67	0.75
South American	7	0.08
Argentinean	1	0.01
Bolivian	1	0.01
Colombian	4	0.04
Peruvian	1	0.01
Other Hispanic or Latino	113	1.26

Race*	Population	%
African-American/Black (807)	1,120	12.50
Not Hispanic (755)	1,036	11.56
Hispanic (52)	84	0.94
American Indian/Alaska Native (230)	432	4.82
Not Hispanic (193)	358	3.99
Hispanic (37)	74	0.83
Alaska Athabascan *(Ala. Nat.)* (0)	2	0.02
Aleut *(Alaska Native)* (2)	8	0.09
Blackfeet (7)	11	0.12
Canadian/French Am. Ind. (7)	9	0.10
Cherokee (8)	24	0.27
Cheyenne (8)	11	0.12
Chippewa (13)	25	0.28
Choctaw (15)	29	0.32
Colville (1)	3	0.03
Comanche (1)	1	0.01
Creek (0)	3	0.03
Inupiat *(Alaska Native)* (0)	4	0.04
Iroquois (2)	3	0.03
Mexican American Ind. (2)	4	0.04
Navajo (3)	9	0.10
Osage (0)	3	0.03
Potawatomi (1)	2	0.02
Puget Sound Salish (59)	82	0.91
Seminole (0)	2	0.02
Sioux (3)	10	0.11
Spanish American Ind. (1)	1	0.01
Tlingit-Haida *(Alaska Native)* (9)	14	0.16
Tsimshian *(Alaska Native)* (1)	1	0.01
Yakama (4)	6	0.07
Yup'ik *(Alaska Native)* (2)	2	0.02
Asian (944)	1,142	12.74
Not Hispanic (934)	1,118	12.47
Hispanic (10)	24	0.27
Cambodian (404)	446	4.98
Chinese, ex. Taiwanese (7)	30	0.33
Filipino (74)	139	1.55
Indian (11)	38	0.42
Indonesian (1)	2	0.02
Japanese (21)	70	0.78
Korean (150)	195	2.18
Laotian (35)	39	0.44
Thai (6)	12	0.13
Vietnamese (186)	201	2.24
Hawaii Native/Pacific Islander (267)	344	3.84
Not Hispanic (254)	308	3.44
Hispanic (13)	36	0.40
Fijian (0)	1	0.01
Guamanian/Chamorro (40)	50	0.56
Native Hawaiian (24)	58	0.65
Samoan (189)	220	2.45
Tongan (1)	4	0.04
White (5,053)	5,606	62.55
Not Hispanic (4,696)	5,149	57.45
Hispanic (357)	457	5.10

Mill Creek East

Place Type: CDP
County: Snohomish
Population: 15,709†

Ancestry‡	Population	%
African, Sub-Saharan (22)	28	0.20
Ethiopian (22)	28	0.20
American (381)	381	2.71
Armenian (0)	10	0.07
Austrian (0)	48	0.34
British (7)	80	0.57
Canadian (38)	57	0.41
Celtic (9)	9	0.06
Czech (9)	18	0.13
Czechoslovakian (12)	33	0.23
Danish (93)	163	1.16
Dutch (36)	217	1.54
English (814)	1,815	12.91
European (194)	204	1.45
Finnish (10)	56	0.40
French, ex. Basque (65)	605	4.30
French Canadian (19)	84	0.60
German (776)	2,872	20.43

*Notes: † The Census 2010 population figure is used to calculate the percentages in the Hispanic Origin and Race categories. Ancestry percentages are based on the 2006-2010 American Community Survey population (not shown); ‡ Numbers in parentheses indicate the number of people reporting a single ancestry; * Numbers in parentheses indicate the number of persons reporting this race alone, not in combination with any other race; Please refer to the Explanation of Data for more information.*

Ancestry	Population	%
Greek (0)	136	0.97
Hungarian (0)	50	0.36
Iranian (52)	52	0.37
Irish (340)	1,501	10.68
Italian (146)	749	5.33
Northern European (33)	33	0.23
Norwegian (247)	937	6.67
Pennsylvania German (10)	46	0.33
Polish (106)	330	2.35
Portuguese (0)	129	0.92
Romanian (70)	80	0.57
Russian (43)	147	1.05
Scandinavian (0)	40	0.28
Scotch-Irish (124)	293	2.08
Scottish (47)	358	2.55
Serbian (0)	13	0.09
Slovak (0)	30	0.21
Swedish (59)	517	3.68
Swiss (50)	122	0.87
Turkish (26)	102	0.73
Ukrainian (82)	82	0.58
Welsh (42)	144	1.02

Hispanic Origin	Population	%
Hispanic or Latino (of any race)	1,162	7.40
Central American, ex. Mexican	84	0.53
Costa Rican	9	0.06
Guatemalan	15	0.10
Honduran	6	0.04
Nicaraguan	6	0.04
Panamanian	10	0.06
Salvadoran	35	0.22
Other Central American	3	0.02
Cuban	20	0.13
Dominican Republic	14	0.09
Mexican	776	4.94
Puerto Rican	70	0.45
South American	94	0.60
Argentinean	8	0.05
Chilean	4	0.03
Colombian	18	0.11
Ecuadorian	13	0.08
Peruvian	22	0.14
Uruguayan	6	0.04
Venezuelan	20	0.13
Other South American	3	0.02
Other Hispanic or Latino	104	0.66

Race*	Population	%
African-American/Black (282)	432	2.75
Not Hispanic (258)	393	2.50
Hispanic (24)	39	0.25
American Indian/Alaska Native (107)	220	1.40
Not Hispanic (79)	181	1.15
Hispanic (28)	39	0.25
Alaska Athabascan *(Ala. Nat.)* (0)	1	0.01
Aleut *(Alaska Native)* (3)	3	0.02
Blackfeet (3)	4	0.03
Canadian/French Am. Ind. (2)	3	0.02
Cherokee (6)	27	0.17
Cheyenne (2)	4	0.03
Chippewa (0)	2	0.01
Choctaw (2)	8	0.05
Colville (2)	5	0.03
Comanche (1)	2	0.01
Creek (0)	1	0.01
Delaware (1)	1	0.01
Inupiat *(Alaska Native)* (0)	3	0.02
Iroquois (5)	6	0.04
Kiowa (6)	6	0.04
Mexican American Ind. (5)	5	0.03
Navajo (2)	2	0.01
Paiute (0)	4	0.03
Pueblo (4)	6	0.04
Puget Sound Salish (8)	12	0.08
Shoshone (2)	3	0.02
Sioux (4)	5	0.03
South American Ind. (1)	1	0.01
Tlingit-Haida *(Alaska Native)* (6)	6	0.04
Tsimshian *(Alaska Native)* (1)	1	0.01
Ute (1)	1	0.01
Yakama (1)	1	0.01
Asian (3,112)	3,504	22.31
Not Hispanic (3,097)	3,470	22.09
Hispanic (15)	34	0.22
Bangladeshi (5)	5	0.03
Burmese (1)	1	0.01
Cambodian (112)	124	0.79
Chinese, ex. Taiwanese (538)	641	4.08
Filipino (364)	503	3.20
Indian (671)	702	4.47
Indonesian (31)	35	0.22
Japanese (97)	219	1.39
Korean (712)	787	5.01
Laotian (28)	34	0.22
Malaysian (1)	1	0.01
Nepalese (4)	4	0.03
Pakistani (32)	35	0.22
Sri Lankan (9)	9	0.06
Taiwanese (45)	50	0.32
Thai (31)	39	0.25
Vietnamese (318)	356	2.27
Hawaii Native/Pacific Islander (50)	120	0.76
Not Hispanic (45)	107	0.68
Hispanic (5)	13	0.08
Fijian (4)	8	0.05
Guamanian/Chamorro (16)	27	0.17
Native Hawaiian (13)	33	0.21
Samoan (3)	10	0.06
Tongan (4)	5	0.03
White (11,028)	11,597	73.82
Not Hispanic (10,438)	10,937	69.62
Hispanic (590)	660	4.20

Mill Creek

Place Type: City
County: Snohomish
Population: 18,244†

Ancestry‡	Population	%
African, Sub-Saharan (102)	102	0.58
Ethiopian (88)	88	0.50
Nigerian (14)	14	0.08
American (430)	430	2.46
Arab (69)	110	0.63
Lebanese (21)	62	0.35
Moroccan (48)	48	0.27
Austrian (5)	24	0.14
Belgian (16)	16	0.09
Brazilian (36)	45	0.26
British (84)	140	0.80
Canadian (43)	119	0.68
Croatian (11)	76	0.43
Czech (22)	54	0.31
Czechoslovakian (0)	18	0.10
Danish (69)	302	1.73
Dutch (31)	314	1.80
Eastern European (22)	22	0.13
English (585)	1,894	10.83
European (189)	204	1.17
Finnish (29)	113	0.65
French, ex. Basque (204)	926	5.30
French Canadian (10)	62	0.35
German (1,015)	3,397	19.43
Greek (62)	294	1.68
Hungarian (11)	138	0.79
Icelander (28)	69	0.39
Iranian (41)	41	0.23
Irish (494)	2,551	14.59
Italian (240)	795	4.55
Northern European (23)	39	0.22
Norwegian (478)	1,251	7.15
Polish (46)	268	1.53
Portuguese (20)	31	0.18
Russian (62)	202	1.16
Scandinavian (112)	136	0.78
Scotch-Irish (230)	623	3.56
Scottish (216)	637	3.64
Slovak (0)	15	0.09
Swedish (135)	687	3.93
Swiss (19)	187	1.07
Ukrainian (202)	214	1.22
Welsh (11)	159	0.91
West Indian, ex. Hispanic (15)	15	0.09
Jamaican (15)	15	0.09
Yugoslavian (0)	24	0.14

Hispanic Origin	Population	%
Hispanic or Latino (of any race)	1,026	5.62
Central American, ex. Mexican	68	0.37
Costa Rican	11	0.06
Guatemalan	12	0.07
Honduran	5	0.03
Nicaraguan	13	0.07
Panamanian	5	0.03
Salvadoran	22	0.12
Cuban	16	0.09
Dominican Republic	2	0.01
Mexican	669	3.67
Puerto Rican	52	0.29
South American	79	0.43
Argentinean	10	0.05
Chilean	8	0.04
Colombian	23	0.13
Ecuadorian	12	0.07
Peruvian	17	0.09
Venezuelan	8	0.04
Other South American	1	0.01
Other Hispanic or Latino	140	0.77

Race*	Population	%
African-American/Black (396)	591	3.24
Not Hispanic (384)	564	3.09
Hispanic (12)	27	0.15
American Indian/Alaska Native (92)	217	1.19
Not Hispanic (78)	190	1.04
Hispanic (14)	27	0.15
Alaska Athabascan *(Ala. Nat.)* (1)	4	0.02
Aleut *(Alaska Native)* (3)	9	0.05
Blackfeet (6)	12	0.07
Cherokee (4)	22	0.12
Chickasaw (1)	3	0.02
Chippewa (7)	12	0.07
Choctaw (0)	3	0.02
Colville (0)	1	0.01
Cree (0)	1	0.01
Creek (0)	1	0.01
Crow (1)	1	0.01
Hopi (3)	5	0.03
Inupiat *(Alaska Native)* (5)	5	0.03
Iroquois (2)	4	0.02
Mexican American Ind. (0)	1	0.01
Navajo (2)	2	0.01
Osage (1)	1	0.01
Potawatomi (0)	1	0.01
Puget Sound Salish (8)	11	0.06
Seminole (1)	1	0.01
Sioux (7)	9	0.05
Tlingit-Haida *(Alaska Native)* (5)	17	0.09
Tsimshian *(Alaska Native)* (1)	2	0.01
Yakama (2)	3	0.02
Asian (3,046)	3,508	19.23
Not Hispanic (3,033)	3,468	19.01
Hispanic (13)	40	0.22
Bangladeshi (3)	3	0.02
Cambodian (90)	99	0.54
Chinese, ex. Taiwanese (454)	587	3.22
Filipino (356)	490	2.69
Hmong (10)	11	0.06
Indian (271)	308	1.69
Indonesian (23)	34	0.19
Japanese (209)	338	1.85
Korean (1,108)	1,183	6.48
Laotian (16)	18	0.10
Malaysian (4)	8	0.04
Pakistani (61)	80	0.44
Sri Lankan (4)	4	0.02
Taiwanese (67)	76	0.42
Thai (12)	14	0.08

*Notes: † The Census 2010 population figure is used to calculate the percentages in the Hispanic Origin and Race categories. Ancestry percentages are based on the 2006-2010 American Community Survey population (not shown); ‡ Numbers in parentheses indicate the number of people reporting a single ancestry; * Numbers in parentheses indicate the number of persons reporting this race alone, not in combination with any other race; Please refer to the Explanation of Data for more information.*

Vietnamese (245)	286	1.57
Hawaii Native/Pacific Islander (81)	149	0.82
Not Hispanic (78)	140	0.77
Hispanic (3)	9	0.05
Fijian (7)	9	0.05
Guamanian/Chamorro (18)	24	0.13
Native Hawaiian (30)	73	0.40
Samoan (16)	19	0.10
White (13,537)	14,256	78.14
Not Hispanic (12,922)	13,546	74.25
Hispanic (615)	710	3.89

Minnehaha

Place Type: CDP
County: Clark
Population: 9,771†

Ancestry‡	Population	%
American (590)	590	6.12
Arab (0)	17	0.18
Lebanese (0)	17	0.18
Armenian (0)	17	0.18
Australian (19)	19	0.20
Belgian (0)	60	0.62
British (38)	53	0.55
Cajun (0)	10	0.10
Canadian (14)	14	0.15
Danish (17)	54	0.56
Dutch (13)	87	0.90
Eastern European (11)	11	0.11
English (249)	1,189	12.33
European (36)	36	0.37
Finnish (18)	95	0.99
French, ex. Basque (10)	373	3.87
French Canadian (60)	150	1.56
German (701)	1,964	20.37
Greek (12)	12	0.12
Hungarian (0)	24	0.25
Irish (286)	1,185	12.29
Italian (76)	313	3.25
Latvian (0)	8	0.08
Lithuanian (22)	22	0.23
Norwegian (110)	535	5.55
Pennsylvania German (15)	15	0.16
Polish (107)	171	1.77
Portuguese (0)	37	0.38
Romanian (44)	59	0.61
Russian (369)	590	6.12
Scandinavian (45)	61	0.63
Scotch-Irish (37)	212	2.20
Scottish (25)	178	1.85
Slovene (0)	49	0.51
Swedish (141)	423	4.39
Ukrainian (209)	209	2.17
Welsh (18)	134	1.39
West Indian, ex. Hispanic (0)	21	0.22
Haitian (0)	21	0.22
Yugoslavian (28)	28	0.29

Hispanic Origin	Population	%
Hispanic or Latino (of any race)	772	7.90
Central American, ex. Mexican	14	0.14
Guatemalan	11	0.11
Honduran	1	0.01
Panamanian	1	0.01
Salvadoran	1	0.01
Cuban	23	0.24
Dominican Republic	3	0.03
Mexican	618	6.32
Puerto Rican	16	0.16
South American	22	0.23
Argentinean	8	0.08
Colombian	9	0.09
Ecuadorian	2	0.02
Paraguayan	1	0.01
Peruvian	2	0.02
Other Hispanic or Latino	76	0.78

Race*	Population	%
African-American/Black (284)	409	4.19
Not Hispanic (274)	380	3.89
Hispanic (10)	29	0.30
American Indian/Alaska Native (72)	186	1.90
Not Hispanic (48)	130	1.33
Hispanic (24)	56	0.57
Apache (2)	4	0.04
Blackfeet (0)	5	0.05
Canadian/French Am. Ind. (1)	1	0.01
Cherokee (7)	23	0.24
Chippewa (1)	2	0.02
Choctaw (1)	7	0.07
Comanche (1)	7	0.07
Cree (0)	1	0.01
Creek (1)	6	0.06
Iroquois (0)	1	0.01
Mexican American Ind. (5)	7	0.07
Navajo (2)	3	0.03
Osage (0)	2	0.02
Paiute (1)	1	0.01
Pima (0)	4	0.04
Puget Sound Salish (1)	1	0.01
Sioux (6)	9	0.09
Tlingit-Haida *(Alaska Native)* (1)	1	0.01
Tsimshian *(Alaska Native)* (2)	4	0.04
Ute (2)	2	0.02
Yakama (3)	3	0.03
Asian (491)	608	6.22
Not Hispanic (482)	586	6.00
Hispanic (9)	22	0.23
Cambodian (23)	31	0.32
Chinese, ex. Taiwanese (43)	71	0.73
Filipino (96)	137	1.40
Hmong (1)	1	0.01
Indian (27)	31	0.32
Indonesian (0)	1	0.01
Japanese (24)	50	0.51
Korean (49)	68	0.70
Laotian (18)	23	0.24
Malaysian (1)	1	0.01
Pakistani (1)	1	0.01
Taiwanese (6)	6	0.06
Thai (9)	14	0.14
Vietnamese (152)	155	1.59
Hawaii Native/Pacific Islander (54)	84	0.86
Not Hispanic (52)	80	0.82
Hispanic (2)	4	0.04
Fijian (4)	5	0.05
Guamanian/Chamorro (7)	8	0.08
Native Hawaiian (16)	31	0.32
Samoan (20)	25	0.26
White (8,189)	8,525	87.25
Not Hispanic (7,855)	8,110	83.00
Hispanic (334)	415	4.25

Monroe

Place Type: City
County: Snohomish
Population: 17,304†

Ancestry‡	Population	%
African, Sub-Saharan (79)	112	0.67
African (68)	101	0.60
Somalian (11)	11	0.07
Albanian (0)	10	0.06
American (550)	550	3.29
Arab (9)	40	0.24
Egyptian (9)	9	0.05
Palestinian (0)	31	0.19
Armenian (10)	19	0.11
Austrian (13)	69	0.41
Basque (26)	26	0.16
Belgian (11)	11	0.07
Brazilian (0)	17	0.10
British (32)	41	0.25
Cajun (10)	15	0.09
Canadian (18)	60	0.36
Czech (0)	34	0.20
Danish (54)	379	2.27
Dutch (158)	755	4.52
English (380)	1,533	9.18
European (299)	323	1.93
Finnish (17)	47	0.28
French, ex. Basque (92)	676	4.05
French Canadian (57)	106	0.63
German (950)	3,774	22.61
Greek (30)	84	0.50
Hungarian (11)	48	0.29
Irish (538)	2,360	14.14
Italian (135)	534	3.20
Luxemburger (11)	24	0.14
New Zealander (0)	37	0.22
Norwegian (337)	1,418	8.49
Polish (108)	334	2.00
Portuguese (0)	34	0.20
Romanian (12)	12	0.07
Russian (25)	133	0.80
Scandinavian (86)	115	0.69
Scotch-Irish (72)	226	1.35
Scottish (106)	440	2.64
Slavic (0)	10	0.06
Slovak (0)	23	0.14
Swedish (180)	1,199	7.18
Swiss (9)	44	0.26
Turkish (7)	7	0.04
Ukrainian (63)	63	0.38
Welsh (44)	202	1.21
West Indian, ex. Hispanic (0)	38	0.23
Jamaican (0)	20	0.12
West Indian (0)	18	0.11

Hispanic Origin	Population	%
Hispanic or Latino (of any race)	2,962	17.12
Central American, ex. Mexican	65	0.38
Costa Rican	5	0.03
Guatemalan	6	0.03
Honduran	8	0.05
Nicaraguan	7	0.04
Panamanian	6	0.03
Salvadoran	32	0.18
Other Central American	1	0.01
Cuban	15	0.09
Mexican	2,564	14.82
Puerto Rican	49	0.28
South American	52	0.30
Argentinean	11	0.06
Chilean	9	0.05
Colombian	20	0.12
Ecuadorian	4	0.02
Peruvian	3	0.02
Venezuelan	5	0.03
Other Hispanic or Latino	217	1.25

Race*	Population	%
African-American/Black (611)	700	4.05
Not Hispanic (595)	674	3.90
Hispanic (16)	26	0.15
American Indian/Alaska Native (239)	436	2.52
Not Hispanic (211)	373	2.16
Hispanic (28)	63	0.36
Alaska Athabascan *(Ala. Nat.)* (3)	3	0.02
Aleut *(Alaska Native)* (3)	11	0.06
Apache (7)	15	0.09
Blackfeet (3)	10	0.06
Cherokee (12)	46	0.27
Chickasaw (1)	1	0.01
Chippewa (9)	16	0.09
Choctaw (6)	23	0.13
Colville (0)	2	0.01
Comanche (0)	4	0.02
Cree (5)	6	0.03
Creek (1)	1	0.01
Delaware (0)	1	0.01
Inupiat *(Alaska Native)* (2)	2	0.01
Iroquois (3)	7	0.04
Mexican American Ind. (6)	12	0.07
Navajo (3)	9	0.05

*Notes: † The Census 2010 population figure is used to calculate the percentages in the Hispanic Origin and Race categories. Ancestry percentages are based on the 2006-2010 American Community Survey population (not shown); ‡ Numbers in parentheses indicate the number of people reporting a single ancestry; * Numbers in parentheses indicate the number of persons reporting this race alone, not in combination with any other race; Please refer to the Explanation of Data for more information.*

Pueblo (4)	4	0.02
Puget Sound Salish (6)	14	0.08
Sioux (6)	12	0.07
South American Ind. (0)	1	0.01
Spanish American Ind. (0)	1	0.01
Tlingit-Haida *(Alaska Native)* (5)	15	0.09
Tsimshian *(Alaska Native)* (0)	1	0.01
Yakama (0)	4	0.02
Yup'ik *(Alaska Native)* (1)	1	0.01
Asian (479)	739	4.27
Not Hispanic (477)	722	4.17
Hispanic (2)	17	0.10
Cambodian (28)	29	0.17
Chinese, ex. Taiwanese (47)	87	0.50
Filipino (105)	205	1.18
Hmong (37)	38	0.22
Indian (46)	58	0.34
Indonesian (5)	5	0.03
Japanese (28)	81	0.47
Korean (36)	64	0.37
Laotian (24)	27	0.16
Malaysian (1)	2	0.01
Pakistani (4)	4	0.02
Taiwanese (10)	11	0.06
Thai (18)	24	0.14
Vietnamese (60)	78	0.45
Hawaii Native/Pacific Islander (67)	191	1.10
Not Hispanic (63)	174	1.01
Hispanic (4)	17	0.10
Fijian (0)	2	0.01
Guamanian/Chamorro (8)	14	0.08
Marshallese (3)	3	0.02
Native Hawaiian (9)	41	0.24
Samoan (6)	23	0.13
Tongan (1)	2	0.01
White (13,598)	14,174	81.91
Not Hispanic (12,454)	12,887	74.47
Hispanic (1,144)	1,287	7.44

Moses Lake

Place Type: City
County: Grant
Population: 20,366†

Ancestry‡	Population	%
American (646)	646	3.37
Arab (0)	7	0.04
Lebanese (0)	7	0.04
Australian (11)	11	0.06
Basque (14)	14	0.07
Belgian (0)	10	0.05
British (22)	74	0.39
Canadian (51)	81	0.42
Croatian (0)	73	0.38
Czech (49)	92	0.48
Danish (78)	219	1.14
Dutch (190)	336	1.75
English (808)	1,847	9.64
European (258)	269	1.40
Finnish (33)	56	0.29
French, ex. Basque (169)	486	2.54
French Canadian (30)	132	0.69
German (929)	2,981	15.57
Greek (32)	85	0.44
Hungarian (7)	14	0.07
Irish (329)	1,638	8.55
Italian (162)	470	2.45
Northern European (26)	26	0.14
Norwegian (511)	1,107	5.78
Pennsylvania German (22)	34	0.18
Polish (57)	171	0.89
Portuguese (0)	79	0.41
Romanian (0)	14	0.07
Russian (24)	145	0.76
Scandinavian (81)	121	0.63
Scotch-Irish (67)	263	1.37
Scottish (131)	395	2.06
Swedish (201)	635	3.32
Swiss (0)	83	0.43
Ukrainian (259)	259	1.35
Welsh (30)	187	0.98

Hispanic Origin	Population	%
Hispanic or Latino (of any race)	6,123	30.06
Central American, ex. Mexican	126	0.62
Guatemalan	32	0.16
Honduran	25	0.12
Nicaraguan	5	0.02
Panamanian	3	0.01
Salvadoran	61	0.30
Cuban	17	0.08
Dominican Republic	2	0.01
Mexican	5,327	26.16
Puerto Rican	56	0.27
South American	39	0.19
Argentinean	12	0.06
Bolivian	1	<0.01
Chilean	1	<0.01
Colombian	10	0.05
Ecuadorian	2	0.01
Paraguayan	3	0.01
Peruvian	3	0.01
Uruguayan	2	0.01
Venezuelan	5	0.02
Other Hispanic or Latino	556	2.73

Race*	Population	%
African-American/Black (334)	502	2.46
Not Hispanic (283)	394	1.93
Hispanic (51)	108	0.53
American Indian/Alaska Native (213)	490	2.41
Not Hispanic (135)	329	1.62
Hispanic (78)	161	0.79
Alaska Athabascan *(Ala. Nat.)* (0)	5	0.02
Apache (2)	8	0.04
Blackfeet (3)	21	0.10
Canadian/French Am. Ind. (2)	2	0.01
Cherokee (16)	48	0.24
Cheyenne (2)	2	0.01
Chickasaw (1)	3	0.01
Chippewa (7)	21	0.10
Choctaw (1)	3	0.01
Colville (11)	28	0.14
Comanche (0)	1	<0.01
Cree (1)	2	0.01
Creek (1)	2	0.01
Crow (1)	1	<0.01
Hopi (0)	1	<0.01
Inupiat *(Alaska Native)* (0)	1	<0.01
Iroquois (3)	5	0.02
Mexican American Ind. (18)	27	0.13
Navajo (2)	3	0.01
Osage (0)	4	0.02
Ottawa (1)	1	<0.01
Paiute (4)	5	0.02
Pima (1)	1	<0.01
Potawatomi (1)	1	<0.01
Puget Sound Salish (2)	7	0.03
Shoshone (2)	2	0.01
Sioux (11)	32	0.16
South American Ind. (0)	1	<0.01
Spanish American Ind. (1)	2	0.01
Tlingit-Haida *(Alaska Native)* (3)	15	0.07
Yakama (3)	4	0.02
Yaqui (0)	4	0.02
Asian (298)	438	2.15
Not Hispanic (286)	396	1.94
Hispanic (12)	42	0.21
Cambodian (7)	9	0.04
Chinese, ex. Taiwanese (28)	41	0.20
Filipino (40)	110	0.54
Indian (62)	71	0.35
Indonesian (1)	3	0.01
Japanese (73)	102	0.50
Korean (26)	45	0.22
Laotian (2)	7	0.03
Malaysian (1)	1	<0.01
Pakistani (0)	1	<0.01
Taiwanese (3)	4	0.02
Thai (13)	17	0.08
Vietnamese (32)	35	0.17
Hawaii Native/Pacific Islander (28)	51	0.25
Not Hispanic (24)	42	0.21
Hispanic (4)	9	0.04
Guamanian/Chamorro (9)	11	0.05
Native Hawaiian (14)	22	0.11
Samoan (2)	7	0.03
White (15,550)	16,388	80.47
Not Hispanic (13,063)	13,459	66.09
Hispanic (2,487)	2,929	14.38

Mount Vernon

Place Type: City
County: Skagit
Population: 31,743†

Ancestry‡	Population	%
African, Sub-Saharan (0)	17	0.05
African (0)	17	0.05
American (1,097)	1,097	3.53
Arab (11)	26	0.08
Arab (11)	11	0.04
Lebanese (0)	15	0.05
Austrian (25)	36	0.12
Basque (9)	9	0.03
Belgian (0)	16	0.05
British (75)	144	0.46
Cajun (0)	10	0.03
Canadian (47)	155	0.50
Celtic (28)	72	0.23
Croatian (15)	40	0.13
Czech (13)	56	0.18
Czechoslovakian (12)	39	0.13
Danish (62)	199	0.64
Dutch (443)	1,076	3.47
Eastern European (11)	11	0.04
English (1,035)	3,197	10.30
European (199)	256	0.82
Finnish (112)	234	0.75
French, ex. Basque (118)	1,033	3.33
French Canadian (38)	179	0.58
German (1,205)	3,573	11.51
Hungarian (0)	65	0.21
Icelander (84)	155	0.50
Iranian (78)	78	0.25
Irish (653)	2,560	8.25
Italian (237)	735	2.37
Lithuanian (0)	8	0.03
Northern European (138)	138	0.44
Norwegian (937)	1,938	6.24
Pennsylvania German (9)	45	0.14
Polish (53)	229	0.74
Portuguese (33)	98	0.32
Romanian (78)	88	0.28
Russian (447)	680	2.19
Scandinavian (122)	175	0.56
Scotch-Irish (167)	542	1.75
Scottish (273)	692	2.23
Slovak (0)	13	0.04
Swedish (330)	924	2.98
Swiss (8)	113	0.36
Ukrainian (149)	317	1.02
Welsh (88)	250	0.81
West Indian, ex. Hispanic (19)	19	0.06
Jamaican (19)	19	0.06
Yugoslavian (67)	80	0.26

Hispanic Origin	Population	%
Hispanic or Latino (of any race)	10,686	33.66
Central American, ex. Mexican	137	0.43
Costa Rican	9	0.03
Guatemalan	61	0.19
Honduran	8	0.03
Nicaraguan	3	0.01
Panamanian	2	0.01
Salvadoran	53	0.17
Other Central American	1	<0.01
Cuban	29	0.09

*Notes: † The Census 2010 population figure is used to calculate the percentages in the Hispanic Origin and Race categories. Ancestry percentages are based on the 2006-2010 American Community Survey population (not shown); ‡ Numbers in parentheses indicate the number of people reporting a single ancestry; * Numbers in parentheses indicate the number of persons reporting this race alone, not in combination with any other race; Please refer to the Explanation of Data for more information.*

Hispanic Origin (continued)	Population	%
Dominican Republic	11	0.03
Mexican	9,651	30.40
Puerto Rican	107	0.34
South American	83	0.26
Argentinean	4	0.01
Bolivian	1	<0.01
Chilean	10	0.03
Colombian	13	0.04
Ecuadorian	6	0.02
Paraguayan	1	<0.01
Peruvian	45	0.14
Venezuelan	3	0.01
Other Hispanic or Latino	668	2.10

Race*	Population	%
African-American/Black (323)	570	1.80
Not Hispanic (251)	426	1.34
Hispanic (72)	144	0.45
American Indian/Alaska Native (513)	908	2.86
Not Hispanic (287)	556	1.75
Hispanic (226)	352	1.11
Alaska Athabascan *(Ala. Nat.)* (1)	9	0.03
Aleut *(Alaska Native)* (3)	11	0.03
Apache (3)	8	0.03
Arapaho (1)	2	0.01
Blackfeet (12)	31	0.10
Canadian/French Am. Ind. (1)	4	0.01
Central American Ind. (3)	3	0.01
Cherokee (15)	85	0.27
Cheyenne (2)	5	0.02
Chickasaw (2)	3	0.01
Chippewa (13)	26	0.08
Choctaw (0)	12	0.04
Colville (2)	2	0.01
Cree (0)	1	<0.01
Creek (1)	1	<0.01
Inupiat *(Alaska Native)* (6)	12	0.04
Iroquois (0)	1	<0.01
Lumbee (0)	2	0.01
Menominee (1)	3	0.01
Mexican American Ind. (98)	142	0.45
Navajo (2)	5	0.02
Paiute (3)	3	0.01
Potawatomi (0)	1	<0.01
Puget Sound Salish (75)	99	0.31
Seminole (2)	7	0.02
Shoshone (2)	3	0.01
Sioux (8)	24	0.08
South American Ind. (1)	1	<0.01
Spanish American Ind. (0)	1	<0.01
Tlingit-Haida *(Alaska Native)* (35)	52	0.16
Tohono O'Odham (6)	6	0.02
Tsimshian *(Alaska Native)* (1)	4	0.01
Ute (3)	4	0.01
Yakama (4)	4	0.01
Yaqui (3)	3	0.01
Yuman (1)	1	<0.01
Yup'ik *(Alaska Native)* (9)	9	0.03
Asian (846)	1,144	3.60
Not Hispanic (814)	1,061	3.34
Hispanic (32)	83	0.26
Burmese (0)	1	<0.01
Cambodian (1)	6	0.02
Chinese, ex. Taiwanese (143)	179	0.56
Filipino (303)	446	1.41
Hmong (0)	1	<0.01
Indian (108)	122	0.38
Indonesian (6)	9	0.03
Japanese (72)	125	0.39
Korean (99)	117	0.37
Laotian (1)	3	0.01
Malaysian (7)	8	0.03
Pakistani (8)	9	0.03
Taiwanese (5)	8	0.03
Thai (20)	28	0.09
Vietnamese (51)	58	0.18
Hawaii Native/Pacific Islander (68)	148	0.47
Not Hispanic (63)	121	0.38
Hispanic (5)	27	0.09
Fijian (3)	4	0.01
Guamanian/Chamorro (13)	28	0.09
Marshallese (16)	16	0.05
Native Hawaiian (16)	52	0.16
Samoan (12)	23	0.07
White (23,120)	24,256	76.41
Not Hispanic (18,935)	19,559	61.62
Hispanic (4,185)	4,697	14.80

Mount Vista

Place Type: CDP
County: Clark
Population: 7,850†

Ancestry‡	Population	%
African, Sub-Saharan (11)	11	0.15
African (11)	11	0.15
American (250)	250	3.47
Arab (13)	40	0.56
Egyptian (13)	40	0.56
Austrian (0)	13	0.18
Belgian (0)	40	0.56
British (14)	33	0.46
Canadian (14)	30	0.42
Czech (13)	26	0.36
Danish (30)	172	2.39
Dutch (0)	65	0.90
Eastern European (0)	20	0.28
English (325)	929	12.90
European (175)	255	3.54
Finnish (0)	53	0.74
French, ex. Basque (25)	325	4.51
French Canadian (13)	60	0.83
German (743)	2,159	29.98
Hungarian (0)	17	0.24
Irish (426)	1,037	14.40
Italian (16)	151	2.10
Lithuanian (17)	36	0.50
Northern European (32)	32	0.44
Norwegian (101)	407	5.65
Polish (39)	47	0.65
Russian (45)	61	0.85
Scandinavian (12)	12	0.17
Scotch-Irish (72)	217	3.01
Scottish (125)	344	4.78
Slovak (0)	16	0.22
Swedish (32)	274	3.81
Swiss (0)	85	1.18
Ukrainian (0)	9	0.12
Welsh (12)	38	0.53
West Indian, ex. Hispanic (23)	23	0.32
Jamaican (23)	23	0.32
Yugoslavian (12)	12	0.17

Hispanic Origin	Population	%
Hispanic or Latino (of any race)	395	5.03
Central American, ex. Mexican	16	0.20
Guatemalan	2	0.03
Panamanian	1	0.01
Salvadoran	13	0.17
Cuban	8	0.10
Dominican Republic	8	0.10
Mexican	276	3.52
Puerto Rican	13	0.17
South American	32	0.41
Argentinean	7	0.09
Bolivian	4	0.05
Chilean	5	0.06
Colombian	7	0.09
Paraguayan	1	0.01
Venezuelan	8	0.10
Other Hispanic or Latino	42	0.54

Race*	Population	%
African-American/Black (150)	219	2.79
Not Hispanic (143)	199	2.54
Hispanic (7)	20	0.25
American Indian/Alaska Native (66)	155	1.97
Not Hispanic (62)	146	1.86
Hispanic (4)	9	0.11
Alaska Athabascan *(Ala. Nat.)* (1)	2	0.03
Aleut *(Alaska Native)* (3)	7	0.09
Apache (0)	3	0.04
Blackfeet (3)	9	0.11
Canadian/French Am. Ind. (1)	2	0.03
Cherokee (8)	20	0.25
Cheyenne (5)	5	0.06
Chickasaw (3)	3	0.04
Chippewa (3)	5	0.06
Choctaw (2)	3	0.04
Colville (1)	1	0.01
Delaware (1)	1	0.01
Iroquois (0)	1	0.01
Mexican American Ind. (2)	2	0.03
Osage (1)	1	0.01
Paiute (0)	2	0.03
Pima (1)	1	0.01
Potawatomi (0)	5	0.06
Sioux (4)	4	0.05
Tohono O'Odham (0)	2	0.03
Tsimshian *(Alaska Native)* (1)	1	0.01
Asian (307)	436	5.55
Not Hispanic (305)	422	5.38
Hispanic (2)	14	0.18
Cambodian (17)	19	0.24
Chinese, ex. Taiwanese (65)	91	1.16
Filipino (45)	80	1.02
Indian (38)	51	0.65
Indonesian (2)	2	0.03
Japanese (33)	61	0.78
Korean (50)	71	0.90
Laotian (6)	9	0.11
Pakistani (4)	20	0.25
Taiwanese (4)	4	0.05
Thai (4)	7	0.09
Vietnamese (29)	33	0.42
Hawaii Native/Pacific Islander (21)	51	0.65
Not Hispanic (21)	50	0.64
Hispanic (0)	1	0.01
Fijian (1)	1	0.01
Guamanian/Chamorro (3)	5	0.06
Native Hawaiian (3)	13	0.17
Samoan (5)	12	0.15
Tongan (1)	1	0.01
White (6,893)	7,152	91.11
Not Hispanic (6,656)	6,888	87.75
Hispanic (237)	264	3.36

Mountlake Terrace

Place Type: City
County: Snohomish
Population: 19,909†

Ancestry‡	Population	%
African, Sub-Saharan (492)	492	2.46
African (128)	128	0.64
Ethiopian (153)	153	0.77
Somalian (211)	211	1.06
American (536)	536	2.68
Arab (45)	82	0.41
Egyptian (13)	26	0.13
Jordanian (10)	10	0.05
Lebanese (0)	24	0.12
Other Arab (22)	22	0.11
Austrian (0)	110	0.55
Belgian (0)	24	0.12
British (50)	162	0.81
Bulgarian (27)	27	0.14
Canadian (98)	128	0.64
Celtic (8)	8	0.04
Croatian (0)	11	0.06
Czech (8)	63	0.32
Czechoslovakian (0)	13	0.07
Danish (73)	484	2.42
Dutch (53)	319	1.60
English (402)	2,280	11.40
European (540)	667	3.34
Finnish (23)	91	0.46
French, ex. Basque (37)	684	3.42

*Notes: † The Census 2010 population figure is used to calculate the percentages in the Hispanic Origin and Race categories. Ancestry percentages are based on the 2006-2010 American Community Survey population (not shown); ‡ Numbers in parentheses indicate the number of people reporting a single ancestry; * Numbers in parentheses indicate the number of persons reporting this race alone, not in combination with any other race; Please refer to the Explanation of Data for more information.*

Ancestry (continued)	Population	%
French Canadian (11)	85	0.43
German (816)	3,843	19.22
Greek (18)	38	0.19
Hungarian (39)	39	0.20
Icelander (0)	20	0.10
Iranian (34)	43	0.22
Irish (801)	2,885	14.43
Italian (143)	583	2.92
Latvian (40)	40	0.20
Lithuanian (0)	19	0.10
Northern European (130)	130	0.65
Norwegian (558)	1,563	7.82
Pennsylvania German (0)	13	0.07
Polish (57)	373	1.87
Portuguese (0)	33	0.17
Romanian (66)	66	0.33
Russian (60)	365	1.83
Scandinavian (46)	57	0.29
Scotch-Irish (47)	348	1.74
Scottish (248)	775	3.88
Slavic (0)	51	0.26
Swedish (118)	690	3.45
Swiss (0)	93	0.47
Ukrainian (23)	23	0.12
Welsh (25)	172	0.86
West Indian, ex. Hispanic (44)	44	0.22
Jamaican (5)	5	0.03
West Indian (39)	39	0.20
Yugoslavian (0)	19	0.10

Hispanic Origin	Population	%
Hispanic or Latino (of any race)	2,100	10.55
Central American, ex. Mexican	259	1.30
Costa Rican	10	0.05
Guatemalan	39	0.20
Honduran	30	0.15
Nicaraguan	41	0.21
Panamanian	5	0.03
Salvadoran	134	0.67
Cuban	10	0.05
Dominican Republic	2	0.01
Mexican	1,377	6.92
Puerto Rican	70	0.35
South American	190	0.95
Argentinean	16	0.08
Bolivian	8	0.04
Chilean	18	0.09
Colombian	39	0.20
Ecuadorian	23	0.12
Peruvian	70	0.35
Uruguayan	3	0.02
Venezuelan	12	0.06
Other South American	1	0.01
Other Hispanic or Latino	192	0.96

Race*	Population	%
African-American/Black (853)	1,186	5.96
Not Hispanic (830)	1,117	5.61
Hispanic (23)	69	0.35
American Indian/Alaska Native (212)	529	2.66
Not Hispanic (188)	458	2.30
Hispanic (24)	71	0.36
Alaska Athabascan *(Ala. Nat.)* (5)	6	0.03
Aleut *(Alaska Native)* (8)	12	0.06
Apache (3)	9	0.05
Arapaho (2)	2	0.01
Blackfeet (10)	29	0.15
Canadian/French Am. Ind. (4)	8	0.04
Central American Ind. (3)	3	0.02
Cherokee (8)	61	0.31
Chickasaw (0)	1	0.01
Chippewa (3)	23	0.12
Choctaw (0)	12	0.06
Colville (6)	12	0.06
Cree (1)	1	0.01
Delaware (1)	1	0.01
Hopi (0)	3	0.02
Inupiat *(Alaska Native)* (3)	5	0.03
Iroquois (0)	2	0.01
Lumbee (1)	1	0.01
Mexican American Ind. (3)	7	0.04
Navajo (5)	14	0.07
Pima (1)	1	0.01
Pueblo (0)	1	0.01
Puget Sound Salish (14)	20	0.10
Seminole (0)	1	0.01
Sioux (11)	31	0.16
South American Ind. (0)	1	0.01
Tlingit-Haida *(Alaska Native)* (30)	56	0.28
Tsimshian *(Alaska Native)* (3)	5	0.03
Yakama (3)	4	0.02
Yup'ik *(Alaska Native)* (1)	1	0.01
Asian (2,221)	2,763	13.88
Not Hispanic (2,193)	2,680	13.46
Hispanic (28)	83	0.42
Bangladeshi (5)	5	0.03
Burmese (2)	7	0.04
Cambodian (78)	91	0.46
Chinese, ex. Taiwanese (287)	371	1.86
Filipino (650)	858	4.31
Hmong (21)	23	0.12
Indian (153)	222	1.12
Indonesian (34)	51	0.26
Japanese (130)	267	1.34
Korean (314)	374	1.88
Laotian (25)	40	0.20
Malaysian (1)	1	0.01
Nepalese (7)	7	0.04
Pakistani (66)	81	0.41
Sri Lankan (5)	5	0.03
Taiwanese (18)	19	0.10
Thai (49)	59	0.30
Vietnamese (248)	287	1.44
Hawaii Native/Pacific Islander (159)	310	1.56
Not Hispanic (154)	289	1.45
Hispanic (5)	21	0.11
Fijian (68)	77	0.39
Guamanian/Chamorro (11)	19	0.10
Marshallese (4)	6	0.03
Native Hawaiian (30)	101	0.51
Samoan (24)	35	0.18
Tongan (9)	9	0.05
White (14,280)	15,351	77.11
Not Hispanic (13,390)	14,285	71.75
Hispanic (890)	1,066	5.35

Mukilteo

Place Type: City
County: Snohomish
Population: 20,254†

Ancestry‡	Population	%
African, Sub-Saharan (35)	53	0.27
African (35)	35	0.18
South African (0)	18	0.09
American (567)	567	2.86
Arab (356)	499	2.51
Egyptian (107)	128	0.64
Jordanian (153)	153	0.77
Lebanese (56)	161	0.81
Syrian (0)	7	0.04
Other Arab (40)	50	0.25
Australian (0)	24	0.12
Austrian (14)	45	0.23
British (66)	150	0.76
Canadian (210)	265	1.34
Celtic (10)	21	0.11
Croatian (0)	21	0.11
Czech (47)	160	0.81
Czechoslovakian (48)	58	0.29
Danish (193)	572	2.88
Dutch (179)	494	2.49
Eastern European (0)	12	0.06
English (810)	2,974	14.98
Estonian (6)	40	0.20
European (647)	696	3.51
Finnish (0)	93	0.47
French, ex. Basque (127)	624	3.14
French Canadian (67)	141	0.71
German (850)	3,135	15.80
Greek (27)	108	0.54
Hungarian (38)	85	0.43
Icelander (12)	78	0.39
Iranian (58)	58	0.29
Irish (626)	2,625	13.23
Italian (167)	744	3.75
Latvian (27)	27	0.14
Lithuanian (0)	17	0.09
Northern European (50)	50	0.25
Norwegian (433)	1,309	6.60
Polish (56)	375	1.89
Portuguese (11)	34	0.17
Romanian (27)	27	0.14
Russian (31)	94	0.47
Scandinavian (316)	427	2.15
Scotch-Irish (160)	407	2.05
Scottish (288)	875	4.41
Serbian (19)	19	0.10
Slavic (9)	9	0.05
Swedish (134)	840	4.23
Swiss (10)	171	0.86
Ukrainian (84)	132	0.67
Welsh (37)	286	1.44
West Indian, ex. Hispanic (81)	114	0.57
Haitian (15)	37	0.19
Jamaican (42)	42	0.21
West Indian (24)	35	0.18
Yugoslavian (0)	12	0.06

Hispanic Origin	Population	%
Hispanic or Latino (of any race)	882	4.35
Central American, ex. Mexican	45	0.22
Costa Rican	10	0.05
Guatemalan	13	0.06
Honduran	1	<0.01
Nicaraguan	7	0.03
Panamanian	8	0.04
Salvadoran	6	0.03
Cuban	12	0.06
Dominican Republic	6	0.03
Mexican	501	2.47
Puerto Rican	88	0.43
South American	102	0.50
Argentinean	8	0.04
Chilean	5	0.02
Colombian	46	0.23
Ecuadorian	13	0.06
Peruvian	22	0.11
Uruguayan	1	<0.01
Venezuelan	6	0.03
Other South American	1	<0.01
Other Hispanic or Latino	128	0.63

Race*	Population	%
African-American/Black (346)	539	2.66
Not Hispanic (331)	496	2.45
Hispanic (15)	43	0.21
American Indian/Alaska Native (115)	283	1.40
Not Hispanic (103)	243	1.20
Hispanic (12)	40	0.20
Alaska Athabascan *(Ala. Nat.)* (2)	4	0.02
Aleut *(Alaska Native)* (2)	6	0.03
Apache (6)	7	0.03
Blackfeet (2)	13	0.06
Canadian/French Am. Ind. (6)	13	0.06
Cherokee (5)	31	0.15
Cheyenne (2)	5	0.02
Chickasaw (0)	1	<0.01
Chippewa (2)	3	0.01
Choctaw (3)	8	0.04
Colville (2)	2	0.01
Comanche (0)	3	0.01
Cree (2)	2	0.01
Creek (1)	1	<0.01
Delaware (2)	2	0.01
Hopi (1)	3	0.01
Inupiat *(Alaska Native)* (4)	6	0.03
Mexican American Ind. (1)	5	0.02
Navajo (3)	7	0.03

*Notes: † The Census 2010 population figure is used to calculate the percentages in the Hispanic Origin and Race categories. Ancestry percentages are based on the 2006-2010 American Community Survey population (not shown); ‡ Numbers in parentheses indicate the number of people reporting a single ancestry; * Numbers in parentheses indicate the number of persons reporting this race alone, not in combination with any other race; Please refer to the Explanation of Data for more information.*

Paiute (1)	1	<0.01
Potawatomi (2)	3	0.01
Pueblo (0)	1	<0.01
Puget Sound Salish (3)	5	0.02
Shoshone (1)	5	0.02
Sioux (1)	11	0.05
South American Ind. (2)	2	0.01
Spanish American Ind. (0)	2	0.01
Tlingit-Haida *(Alaska Native)* (9)	17	0.08
Tsimshian *(Alaska Native)* (3)	4	0.02
Yakama (1)	1	<0.01
Yup'ik *(Alaska Native)* (1)	1	<0.01
Asian (3,457)	3,988	19.69
Not Hispanic (3,435)	3,937	19.44
Hispanic (22)	51	0.25
Bangladeshi (5)	5	0.02
Cambodian (31)	33	0.16
Chinese, ex. Taiwanese (411)	506	2.50
Filipino (319)	470	2.32
Hmong (5)	5	0.02
Indian (386)	431	2.13
Indonesian (47)	62	0.31
Japanese (195)	327	1.61
Korean (1,596)	1,698	8.38
Laotian (7)	15	0.07
Malaysian (4)	4	0.02
Nepalese (8)	8	0.04
Pakistani (32)	35	0.17
Sri Lankan (4)	8	0.04
Taiwanese (48)	53	0.26
Thai (31)	41	0.20
Vietnamese (252)	289	1.43
Hawaii Native/Pacific Islander (34)	111	0.55
Not Hispanic (34)	111	0.55
Fijian (2)	5	0.02
Guamanian/Chamorro (6)	16	0.08
Native Hawaiian (12)	46	0.23
Samoan (4)	9	0.04
Tongan (0)	1	<0.01
White (15,172)	15,942	78.71
Not Hispanic (14,650)	15,321	75.64
Hispanic (522)	621	3.07

Newcastle

Place Type: City
County: King
Population: 10,380[†]

Ancestry[‡]	Population	%
American (109)	109	1.10
Arab (161)	170	1.72
Arab (152)	152	1.54
Lebanese (9)	18	0.18
Austrian (55)	90	0.91
Basque (0)	24	0.24
Belgian (0)	24	0.24
British (38)	101	1.02
Canadian (28)	112	1.13
Croatian (12)	44	0.45
Czech (0)	53	0.54
Danish (0)	133	1.35
Dutch (28)	134	1.36
Eastern European (40)	60	0.61
English (275)	1,436	14.55
Estonian (0)	14	0.14
European (236)	292	2.96
Finnish (0)	27	0.27
French, ex. Basque (29)	318	3.22
German (468)	1,878	19.03
Greek (8)	62	0.63
Hungarian (12)	92	0.93
Icelander (0)	36	0.36
Irish (179)	822	8.33
Italian (184)	393	3.98
Latvian (12)	12	0.12
Lithuanian (57)	118	1.20
Northern European (33)	58	0.59
Norwegian (149)	376	3.81
Polish (11)	203	2.06
Russian (107)	168	1.70
Scandinavian (21)	74	0.75
Scotch-Irish (115)	341	3.46
Scottish (55)	251	2.54
Slovak (49)	59	0.60
Swedish (101)	465	4.71
Swiss (26)	121	1.23
Turkish (0)	13	0.13
Ukrainian (0)	12	0.12
Welsh (0)	91	0.92
Yugoslavian (0)	25	0.25

Hispanic Origin	Population	%
Hispanic or Latino (of any race)	440	4.24
Central American, ex. Mexican	23	0.22
Guatemalan	6	0.06
Honduran	8	0.08
Nicaraguan	2	0.02
Panamanian	5	0.05
Salvadoran	2	0.02
Cuban	17	0.16
Dominican Republic	5	0.05
Mexican	259	2.50
Puerto Rican	32	0.31
South American	43	0.41
Argentinean	6	0.06
Bolivian	3	0.03
Chilean	3	0.03
Colombian	14	0.13
Paraguayan	1	0.01
Peruvian	9	0.09
Venezuelan	7	0.07
Other Hispanic or Latino	61	0.59

Race*	Population	%
African-American/Black (270)	408	3.93
Not Hispanic (259)	388	3.74
Hispanic (11)	20	0.19
American Indian/Alaska Native (38)	117	1.13
Not Hispanic (34)	109	1.05
Hispanic (4)	8	0.08
Blackfeet (1)	3	0.03
Canadian/French Am. Ind. (0)	2	0.02
Cherokee (6)	14	0.13
Chippewa (1)	4	0.04
Choctaw (0)	5	0.05
Colville (1)	3	0.03
Inupiat *(Alaska Native)* (1)	1	0.01
Iroquois (1)	5	0.05
Menominee (1)	1	0.01
Mexican American Ind. (2)	2	0.02
Navajo (1)	1	0.01
Puget Sound Salish (2)	4	0.04
Sioux (1)	5	0.05
Tlingit-Haida *(Alaska Native)* (3)	6	0.06
Tsimshian *(Alaska Native)* (1)	2	0.02
Ute (0)	1	0.01
Yup'ik *(Alaska Native)* (1)	1	0.01
Asian (2,561)	2,909	28.03
Not Hispanic (2,549)	2,879	27.74
Hispanic (12)	30	0.29
Cambodian (16)	21	0.20
Chinese, ex. Taiwanese (824)	1,036	9.98
Filipino (131)	236	2.27
Indian (297)	312	3.01
Indonesian (15)	21	0.20
Japanese (300)	459	4.42
Korean (416)	468	4.51
Laotian (10)	17	0.16
Pakistani (10)	10	0.10
Taiwanese (76)	90	0.87
Thai (24)	35	0.34
Vietnamese (286)	336	3.24
Hawaii Native/Pacific Islander (34)	79	0.76
Not Hispanic (32)	73	0.70
Hispanic (2)	6	0.06
Fijian (7)	7	0.07
Guamanian/Chamorro (7)	8	0.08
Native Hawaiian (4)	36	0.35
Samoan (1)	2	0.02
Tongan (1)	4	0.04
White (6,784)	7,263	69.97
Not Hispanic (6,551)	6,995	67.39
Hispanic (233)	268	2.58

North Lynnwood

Place Type: CDP
County: Snohomish
Population: 16,574[†]

Ancestry[‡]	Population	%
African, Sub-Saharan (288)	308	1.94
African (128)	148	0.93
Ethiopian (44)	44	0.28
Nigerian (65)	65	0.41
Other Sub-Saharan African (51)	51	0.32
American (174)	174	1.10
Arab (98)	102	0.64
Arab (0)	4	0.03
Egyptian (44)	44	0.28
Iraqi (54)	54	0.34
Armenian (0)	38	0.24
Austrian (81)	94	0.59
British (52)	96	0.60
Bulgarian (144)	144	0.91
Canadian (30)	94	0.59
Croatian (0)	51	0.32
Czech (8)	34	0.21
Czechoslovakian (0)	20	0.13
Danish (28)	141	0.89
Dutch (144)	302	1.90
English (359)	1,365	8.59
European (172)	223	1.40
Finnish (17)	70	0.44
French, ex. Basque (129)	421	2.65
French Canadian (42)	203	1.28
German (431)	2,646	16.66
Hungarian (16)	40	0.25
Icelander (10)	29	0.18
Iranian (18)	57	0.36
Irish (412)	2,278	14.34
Italian (168)	557	3.51
Lithuanian (9)	9	0.06
New Zealander (10)	10	0.06
Northern European (19)	19	0.12
Norwegian (309)	837	5.27
Polish (137)	365	2.30
Portuguese (8)	21	0.13
Romanian (58)	86	0.54
Russian (59)	178	1.12
Scandinavian (68)	225	1.42
Scotch-Irish (205)	381	2.40
Scottish (110)	251	1.58
Slovak (0)	10	0.06
Swedish (127)	449	2.83
Swiss (13)	44	0.28
Ukrainian (29)	39	0.25
Welsh (13)	237	1.49

Hispanic Origin	Population	%
Hispanic or Latino (of any race)	1,793	10.82
Central American, ex. Mexican	123	0.74
Costa Rican	15	0.09
Guatemalan	15	0.09
Honduran	11	0.07
Nicaraguan	13	0.08
Panamanian	7	0.04
Salvadoran	62	0.37
Cuban	14	0.08
Dominican Republic	8	0.05
Mexican	1,318	7.95
Puerto Rican	69	0.42
South American	95	0.57
Argentinean	10	0.06
Bolivian	3	0.02
Chilean	7	0.04
Colombian	17	0.10
Ecuadorian	6	0.04
Peruvian	38	0.23

*Notes: † The Census 2010 population figure is used to calculate the percentages in the Hispanic Origin and Race categories. Ancestry percentages are based on the 2006-2010 American Community Survey population (not shown); ‡ Numbers in parentheses indicate the number of people reporting a single ancestry; * Numbers in parentheses indicate the number of persons reporting this race alone, not in combination with any other race; Please refer to the Explanation of Data for more information.*

Uruguayan	6	0.04
Venezuelan	7	0.04
Other South American	1	0.01
Other Hispanic or Latino	166	1.00

Race*	Population	%
African-American/Black (1,105)	1,431	8.63
Not Hispanic (1,081)	1,373	8.28
Hispanic (24)	58	0.35
American Indian/Alaska Native (142)	414	2.50
Not Hispanic (111)	340	2.05
Hispanic (31)	74	0.45
Alaska Athabascan *(Ala. Nat.)* (1)	4	0.02
Aleut *(Alaska Native)* (3)	9	0.05
Apache (1)	3	0.02
Blackfeet (2)	15	0.09
Canadian/French Am. Ind. (1)	7	0.04
Cherokee (8)	49	0.30
Chippewa (2)	13	0.08
Choctaw (6)	14	0.08
Colville (3)	8	0.05
Creek (0)	3	0.02
Hopi (1)	2	0.01
Inupiat *(Alaska Native)* (2)	6	0.04
Iroquois (1)	2	0.01
Kiowa (0)	1	0.01
Mexican American Ind. (4)	6	0.04
Navajo (3)	4	0.02
Pima (1)	1	0.01
Potawatomi (0)	2	0.01
Puget Sound Salish (14)	18	0.11
Seminole (2)	3	0.02
Sioux (3)	15	0.09
South American Ind. (0)	1	0.01
Tlingit-Haida *(Alaska Native)* (8)	17	0.10
Tsimshian *(Alaska Native)* (1)	1	0.01
Yakama (7)	10	0.06
Yuman (0)	1	0.01
Asian (3,385)	3,818	23.04
Not Hispanic (3,355)	3,755	22.66
Hispanic (30)	63	0.38
Bangladeshi (10)	14	0.08
Burmese (1)	1	0.01
Cambodian (104)	132	0.80
Chinese, ex. Taiwanese (408)	539	3.25
Filipino (620)	818	4.94
Hmong (8)	8	0.05
Indian (171)	199	1.20
Indonesian (72)	79	0.48
Japanese (100)	195	1.18
Korean (938)	1,021	6.16
Laotian (23)	32	0.19
Malaysian (3)	8	0.05
Nepalese (17)	17	0.10
Pakistani (44)	51	0.31
Sri Lankan (3)	3	0.02
Taiwanese (25)	27	0.16
Thai (42)	63	0.38
Vietnamese (606)	648	3.91
Hawaii Native/Pacific Islander (161)	262	1.58
Not Hispanic (156)	244	1.47
Hispanic (5)	18	0.11
Fijian (37)	40	0.24
Guamanian/Chamorro (28)	43	0.26
Marshallese (31)	37	0.22
Native Hawaiian (21)	73	0.44
Samoan (18)	29	0.17
White (10,016)	10,881	65.65
Not Hispanic (9,221)	9,945	60.00
Hispanic (795)	936	5.65

Oak Harbor

Place Type: City
County: Island
Population: 22,075†

Ancestry‡	Population	%
African, Sub-Saharan (153)	166	0.75
African (72)	85	0.39
Ethiopian (17)	17	0.08
Other Sub-Saharan African (64)	64	0.29
American (845)	845	3.84
Arab (0)	26	0.12
Lebanese (0)	26	0.12
Australian (37)	47	0.21
Austrian (0)	81	0.37
Belgian (0)	31	0.14
British (0)	29	0.13
Bulgarian (107)	118	0.54
Canadian (14)	48	0.22
Croatian (10)	19	0.09
Czech (26)	195	0.89
Czechoslovakian (31)	36	0.16
Danish (50)	201	0.91
Dutch (396)	1,007	4.57
Eastern European (27)	27	0.12
English (683)	2,152	9.77
European (416)	486	2.21
Finnish (0)	80	0.36
French, ex. Basque (222)	1,156	5.25
French Canadian (33)	192	0.87
German (1,265)	4,611	20.94
Greek (0)	31	0.14
Hungarian (45)	126	0.57
Iranian (13)	29	0.13
Irish (584)	2,993	13.59
Italian (204)	705	3.20
Latvian (14)	14	0.06
Lithuanian (44)	146	0.66
Northern European (61)	61	0.28
Norwegian (285)	713	3.24
Polish (71)	369	1.68
Portuguese (34)	117	0.53
Romanian (0)	36	0.16
Russian (14)	80	0.36
Scandinavian (109)	200	0.91
Scotch-Irish (84)	487	2.21
Scottish (150)	675	3.07
Slavic (13)	13	0.06
Swedish (91)	443	2.01
Swiss (18)	71	0.32
Ukrainian (25)	35	0.16
Welsh (53)	200	0.91
West Indian, ex. Hispanic (8)	34	0.15
Jamaican (8)	34	0.15

Hispanic Origin	Population	%
Hispanic or Latino (of any race)	2,055	9.31
Central American, ex. Mexican	74	0.34
Costa Rican	8	0.04
Guatemalan	7	0.03
Honduran	11	0.05
Nicaraguan	13	0.06
Panamanian	13	0.06
Salvadoran	22	0.10
Cuban	34	0.15
Dominican Republic	28	0.13
Mexican	1,313	5.95
Puerto Rican	224	1.01
South American	78	0.35
Argentinean	2	0.01
Bolivian	1	<0.01
Chilean	3	0.01
Colombian	34	0.15
Ecuadorian	15	0.07
Paraguayan	2	0.01
Peruvian	16	0.07
Venezuelan	5	0.02
Other Hispanic or Latino	304	1.38

Race*	Population	%
African-American/Black (1,071)	1,631	7.39
Not Hispanic (1,021)	1,495	6.77
Hispanic (50)	136	0.62
American Indian/Alaska Native (195)	577	2.61
Not Hispanic (157)	461	2.09
Hispanic (38)	116	0.53
Alaska Athabascan *(Ala. Nat.)* (3)	5	0.02
Aleut *(Alaska Native)* (4)	11	0.05
Apache (4)	9	0.04
Blackfeet (2)	19	0.09
Canadian/French Am. Ind. (3)	6	0.03
Cherokee (12)	79	0.36
Cheyenne (1)	6	0.03
Chickasaw (1)	1	<0.01
Chippewa (7)	18	0.08
Choctaw (0)	13	0.06
Comanche (4)	4	0.02
Cree (7)	7	0.03
Creek (0)	2	0.01
Crow (1)	1	<0.01
Iroquois (6)	13	0.06
Mexican American Ind. (3)	4	0.02
Navajo (12)	20	0.09
Osage (1)	1	<0.01
Paiute (1)	3	0.01
Potawatomi (3)	6	0.03
Pueblo (3)	7	0.03
Puget Sound Salish (6)	13	0.06
Seminole (0)	6	0.03
Shoshone (0)	3	0.01
Sioux (13)	33	0.15
South American Ind. (1)	2	0.01
Tlingit-Haida *(Alaska Native)* (3)	10	0.05
Tohono O'Odham (2)	4	0.02
Yakama (1)	2	0.01
Yaqui (8)	8	0.04
Yup'ik *(Alaska Native)* (0)	5	0.02
Asian (2,254)	3,118	14.12
Not Hispanic (2,205)	2,979	13.49
Hispanic (49)	139	0.63
Burmese (5)	5	0.02
Cambodian (2)	3	0.01
Chinese, ex. Taiwanese (87)	165	0.75
Filipino (1,749)	2,285	10.35
Hmong (5)	7	0.03
Indian (14)	36	0.16
Indonesian (1)	4	0.02
Japanese (194)	416	1.88
Korean (69)	138	0.63
Laotian (9)	12	0.05
Pakistani (0)	1	<0.01
Taiwanese (2)	2	0.01
Thai (33)	61	0.28
Vietnamese (41)	54	0.24
Hawaii Native/Pacific Islander (221)	421	1.91
Not Hispanic (208)	380	1.72
Hispanic (13)	41	0.19
Fijian (2)	5	0.02
Guamanian/Chamorro (99)	145	0.66
Marshallese (2)	6	0.03
Native Hawaiian (51)	141	0.64
Samoan (26)	45	0.20
Tongan (0)	4	0.02
White (16,023)	17,462	79.10
Not Hispanic (14,975)	16,190	73.34
Hispanic (1,048)	1,272	5.76

Olympia

Place Type: City
County: Thurston
Population: 46,478†

Ancestry‡	Population	%
African, Sub-Saharan (247)	255	0.56
African (193)	201	0.44
Nigerian (38)	38	0.08
Other Sub-Saharan African (16)	16	0.04
American (1,748)	1,748	3.82
Arab (48)	104	0.23
Egyptian (26)	26	0.06
Iraqi (0)	21	0.05
Lebanese (15)	31	0.07
Palestinian (7)	7	0.02
Syrian (0)	19	0.04
Armenian (12)	12	0.03
Australian (0)	13	0.03
Austrian (14)	282	0.62

SECTION TWO

*Notes: † The Census 2010 population figure is used to calculate the percentages in the Hispanic Origin and Race categories. Ancestry percentages are based on the 2006-2010 American Community Survey population (not shown); ‡ Numbers in parentheses indicate the number of people reporting a single ancestry; * Numbers in parentheses indicate the number of persons reporting this race alone, not in combination with any other race; Please refer to the Explanation of Data for more information.*

Basque (11)	11	0.02
Belgian (32)	67	0.15
British (231)	441	0.96
Bulgarian (15)	47	0.10
Cajun (10)	10	0.02
Canadian (92)	246	0.54
Celtic (10)	26	0.06
Croatian (39)	87	0.19
Czech (39)	205	0.45
Czechoslovakian (53)	76	0.17
Danish (114)	329	0.72
Dutch (273)	1,243	2.72
Eastern European (62)	62	0.14
English (1,527)	6,725	14.71
European (2,032)	2,239	4.90
Finnish (79)	305	0.67
French, ex. Basque (304)	2,145	4.69
French Canadian (95)	279	0.61
German (2,233)	8,390	18.36
Greek (110)	269	0.59
Hungarian (37)	144	0.32
Icelander (18)	41	0.09
Irish (1,616)	6,552	14.33
Italian (516)	1,704	3.73
Lithuanian (30)	72	0.16
Northern European (149)	166	0.36
Norwegian (715)	2,116	4.63
Pennsylvania German (0)	12	0.03
Polish (259)	953	2.08
Portuguese (54)	218	0.48
Romanian (39)	77	0.17
Russian (81)	511	1.12
Scandinavian (247)	583	1.28
Scotch-Irish (387)	1,465	3.21
Scottish (413)	1,760	3.85
Slovak (0)	54	0.12
Slovene (0)	24	0.05
Swedish (346)	1,987	4.35
Swiss (49)	248	0.54
Ukrainian (81)	224	0.49
Welsh (167)	737	1.61
West Indian, ex. Hispanic (15)	90	0.20
Bermudan (15)	79	0.17
Haitian (0)	11	0.02
Yugoslavian (0)	47	0.10

Hispanic Origin	Population	%
Hispanic or Latino (of any race)	2,919	6.28
Central American, ex. Mexican	207	0.45
Costa Rican	17	0.04
Guatemalan	59	0.13
Honduran	31	0.07
Nicaraguan	5	0.01
Panamanian	28	0.06
Salvadoran	66	0.14
Other Central American	1	<0.01
Cuban	75	0.16
Dominican Republic	15	0.03
Mexican	1,857	4.00
Puerto Rican	242	0.52
South American	181	0.39
Argentinean	17	0.04
Chilean	22	0.05
Colombian	56	0.12
Ecuadorian	27	0.06
Paraguayan	1	<0.01
Peruvian	44	0.09
Uruguayan	1	<0.01
Venezuelan	12	0.03
Other South American	1	<0.01
Other Hispanic or Latino	342	0.74

Race*	Population	%
African-American/Black (931)	1,602	3.45
Not Hispanic (895)	1,478	3.18
Hispanic (36)	124	0.27
American Indian/Alaska Native (498)	1,258	2.71
Not Hispanic (403)	1,046	2.25
Hispanic (95)	212	0.46
Alaska Athabascan *(Ala. Nat.)* (4)	11	0.02
Aleut *(Alaska Native)* (8)	18	0.04
Apache (12)	40	0.09
Arapaho (1)	1	<0.01
Blackfeet (11)	41	0.09
Canadian/French Am. Ind. (3)	15	0.03
Central American Ind. (1)	2	<0.01
Cherokee (23)	141	0.30
Cheyenne (3)	7	0.02
Chickasaw (0)	2	<0.01
Chippewa (12)	40	0.09
Choctaw (5)	18	0.04
Colville (16)	21	0.05
Comanche (1)	4	0.01
Cree (0)	1	<0.01
Creek (1)	6	0.01
Crow (1)	3	0.01
Delaware (1)	1	<0.01
Houma (0)	1	<0.01
Inupiat *(Alaska Native)* (4)	11	0.02
Iroquois (1)	9	0.02
Lumbee (5)	6	0.01
Menominee (0)	1	<0.01
Mexican American Ind. (20)	28	0.06
Navajo (8)	14	0.03
Osage (0)	4	0.01
Ottawa (1)	4	0.01
Paiute (0)	1	<0.01
Pima (7)	9	0.02
Potawatomi (2)	5	0.01
Pueblo (1)	4	0.01
Puget Sound Salish (48)	79	0.17
Seminole (1)	5	0.01
Shoshone (0)	1	<0.01
Sioux (26)	60	0.13
South American Ind. (7)	12	0.03
Spanish American Ind. (3)	4	0.01
Tlingit-Haida *(Alaska Native)* (10)	13	0.03
Tsimshian *(Alaska Native)* (1)	2	<0.01
Yakama (8)	17	0.04
Yaqui (4)	7	0.02
Yuman (0)	1	<0.01
Yup'ik *(Alaska Native)* (0)	2	<0.01
Asian (2,799)	3,643	7.84
Not Hispanic (2,763)	3,520	7.57
Hispanic (36)	123	0.26
Bangladeshi (5)	5	0.01
Bhutanese (4)	4	0.01
Cambodian (62)	84	0.18
Chinese, ex. Taiwanese (394)	553	1.19
Filipino (359)	624	1.34
Indian (277)	324	0.70
Indonesian (4)	16	0.03
Japanese (176)	404	0.87
Korean (348)	475	1.02
Laotian (26)	39	0.08
Malaysian (1)	7	0.02
Nepalese (11)	12	0.03
Pakistani (5)	12	0.03
Sri Lankan (3)	5	0.01
Taiwanese (21)	31	0.07
Thai (27)	51	0.11
Vietnamese (968)	1,045	2.25
Hawaii Native/Pacific Islander (180)	387	0.83
Not Hispanic (172)	353	0.76
Hispanic (8)	34	0.07
Fijian (0)	1	<0.01
Guamanian/Chamorro (48)	83	0.18
Marshallese (5)	5	0.01
Native Hawaiian (64)	184	0.40
Samoan (51)	67	0.14
Tongan (1)	4	0.01
White (38,895)	41,044	88.31
Not Hispanic (37,328)	39,114	84.16
Hispanic (1,567)	1,930	4.15

Orchards

Place Type: CDP
County: Clark
Population: 19,556†

Ancestry‡	Population	%
African, Sub-Saharan (0)	26	0.13
African (0)	26	0.13
American (927)	927	4.58
Arab (10)	10	0.05
Lebanese (10)	10	0.05
Austrian (11)	58	0.29
Belgian (34)	399	1.97
Brazilian (0)	35	0.17
British (63)	226	1.12
Canadian (74)	156	0.77
Celtic (0)	11	0.05
Czech (13)	25	0.12
Czechoslovakian (42)	42	0.21
Danish (30)	96	0.47
Dutch (114)	406	2.00
English (601)	2,154	10.63
European (351)	396	1.96
Finnish (77)	214	1.06
French, ex. Basque (29)	935	4.62
French Canadian (54)	115	0.57
German (1,086)	4,087	20.18
Greek (11)	30	0.15
Hungarian (54)	91	0.45
Iranian (115)	115	0.57
Irish (249)	2,393	11.81
Italian (218)	680	3.36
Lithuanian (11)	75	0.37
Northern European (10)	10	0.05
Norwegian (152)	845	4.17
Polish (56)	549	2.71
Portuguese (16)	113	0.56
Romanian (98)	98	0.48
Russian (1,106)	1,348	6.66
Scandinavian (37)	64	0.32
Scotch-Irish (145)	490	2.42
Scottish (131)	765	3.78
Swedish (125)	538	2.66
Swiss (9)	71	0.35
Turkish (256)	256	1.26
Ukrainian (355)	502	2.48
Welsh (46)	305	1.51
Yugoslavian (83)	83	0.41

Hispanic Origin	Population	%
Hispanic or Latino (of any race)	1,841	9.41
Central American, ex. Mexican	63	0.32
Costa Rican	2	0.01
Guatemalan	21	0.11
Honduran	6	0.03
Nicaraguan	5	0.03
Panamanian	4	0.02
Salvadoran	25	0.13
Cuban	22	0.11
Dominican Republic	12	0.06
Mexican	1,502	7.68
Puerto Rican	33	0.17
South American	44	0.22
Argentinean	3	0.02
Chilean	16	0.08
Colombian	14	0.07
Ecuadorian	5	0.03
Peruvian	5	0.03
Other South American	1	0.01
Other Hispanic or Latino	165	0.84

Race*	Population	%
African-American/Black (405)	672	3.44
Not Hispanic (375)	603	3.08
Hispanic (30)	69	0.35
American Indian/Alaska Native (175)	478	2.44
Not Hispanic (147)	412	2.11
Hispanic (28)	66	0.34
Alaska Athabascan *(Ala. Nat.)* (5)	5	0.03

*Notes: † The Census 2010 population figure is used to calculate the percentages in the Hispanic Origin and Race categories. Ancestry percentages are based on the 2006-2010 American Community Survey population (not shown); ‡ Numbers in parentheses indicate the number of people reporting a single ancestry; * Numbers in parentheses indicate the number of persons reporting this race alone, not in combination with any other race; Please refer to the Explanation of Data for more information.*

Aleut *(Alaska Native)* (2)	8	0.04
Apache (2)	5	0.03
Blackfeet (3)	25	0.13
Cherokee (9)	58	0.30
Cheyenne (0)	1	0.01
Chickasaw (4)	8	0.04
Chippewa (7)	24	0.12
Choctaw (2)	9	0.05
Colville (4)	4	0.02
Creek (3)	5	0.03
Delaware (0)	1	0.01
Hopi (0)	3	0.02
Iroquois (3)	8	0.04
Mexican American Ind. (9)	19	0.10
Navajo (1)	13	0.07
Osage (2)	5	0.03
Ottawa (1)	3	0.02
Paiute (1)	1	0.01
Pima (0)	1	0.01
Potawatomi (0)	1	0.01
Pueblo (1)	1	0.01
Puget Sound Salish (6)	10	0.05
Seminole (0)	4	0.02
Shoshone (2)	2	0.01
Sioux (11)	27	0.14
South American Ind. (1)	6	0.03
Tlingit-Haida *(Alaska Native)* (4)	5	0.03
Tsimshian *(Alaska Native)* (0)	2	0.01
Yakama (2)	9	0.05
Yup'ik *(Alaska Native)* (1)	1	0.01
Asian (967)	1,271	6.50
Not Hispanic (954)	1,242	6.35
Hispanic (13)	29	0.15
Cambodian (130)	152	0.78
Chinese, ex. Taiwanese (76)	121	0.62
Filipino (217)	334	1.71
Hmong (2)	2	0.01
Indian (52)	73	0.37
Indonesian (3)	8	0.04
Japanese (50)	126	0.64
Korean (52)	77	0.39
Laotian (66)	89	0.46
Pakistani (0)	1	0.01
Taiwanese (6)	11	0.06
Thai (11)	31	0.16
Vietnamese (232)	260	1.33
Hawaii Native/Pacific Islander (175)	299	1.53
Not Hispanic (167)	280	1.43
Hispanic (8)	19	0.10
Fijian (5)	12	0.06
Guamanian/Chamorro (70)	86	0.44
Native Hawaiian (18)	87	0.44
Samoan (34)	52	0.27
Tongan (11)	12	0.06
White (16,106)	16,967	86.76
Not Hispanic (15,243)	15,957	81.60
Hispanic (863)	1,010	5.16

Parkland

Place Type: CDP
County: Pierce
Population: 35,803†

Ancestry‡	Population	%
African, Sub-Saharan (509)	663	1.87
African (146)	300	0.85
Ethiopian (41)	41	0.12
Kenyan (11)	11	0.03
Nigerian (253)	253	0.71
Somalian (58)	58	0.16
American (1,042)	1,042	2.94
Arab (0)	146	0.41
Lebanese (0)	94	0.27
Syrian (0)	52	0.15
Armenian (0)	31	0.09
Australian (0)	15	0.04
Austrian (10)	89	0.25
British (46)	138	0.39
Bulgarian (8)	8	0.02
Cajun (0)	25	0.07
Canadian (32)	58	0.16
Celtic (26)	26	0.07
Croatian (16)	24	0.07
Czech (57)	118	0.33
Czechoslovakian (0)	89	0.25
Danish (31)	248	0.70
Dutch (42)	338	0.95
Eastern European (0)	48	0.14
English (537)	2,356	6.65
Estonian (0)	12	0.03
European (145)	186	0.53
Finnish (26)	122	0.34
French, ex. Basque (146)	1,085	3.06
French Canadian (27)	186	0.53
German (2,204)	6,084	17.18
Greek (12)	103	0.29
Hungarian (13)	36	0.10
Iranian (0)	6	0.02
Irish (1,005)	4,338	12.25
Italian (336)	984	2.78
Latvian (0)	12	0.03
Northern European (56)	56	0.16
Norwegian (888)	1,911	5.40
Polish (81)	433	1.22
Portuguese (53)	64	0.18
Romanian (299)	323	0.91
Russian (113)	201	0.57
Scandinavian (66)	131	0.37
Scotch-Irish (63)	478	1.35
Scottish (233)	791	2.23
Slavic (0)	23	0.06
Slovak (0)	32	0.09
Slovene (11)	11	0.03
Swedish (400)	949	2.68
Swiss (12)	185	0.52
Turkish (0)	25	0.07
Ukrainian (327)	366	1.03
Welsh (52)	235	0.66
West Indian, ex. Hispanic (270)	304	0.86
Jamaican (211)	245	0.69
Trinidadian/Tobagonian (39)	39	0.11
West Indian (20)	20	0.06
Yugoslavian (7)	7	0.02

Hispanic Origin	Population	%
Hispanic or Latino (of any race)	4,626	12.92
Central American, ex. Mexican	199	0.56
Costa Rican	2	0.01
Guatemalan	55	0.15
Honduran	21	0.06
Nicaraguan	7	0.02
Panamanian	64	0.18
Salvadoran	46	0.13
Other Central American	4	0.01
Cuban	52	0.15
Dominican Republic	21	0.06
Mexican	3,449	9.63
Puerto Rican	523	1.46
South American	67	0.19
Argentinean	8	0.02
Bolivian	4	0.01
Chilean	11	0.03
Colombian	16	0.04
Ecuadorian	4	0.01
Peruvian	17	0.05
Venezuelan	6	0.02
Other South American	1	<0.01
Other Hispanic or Latino	315	0.88

Race*	Population	%
African-American/Black (4,144)	5,517	15.41
Not Hispanic (3,971)	5,160	14.41
Hispanic (173)	357	1.00
American Indian/Alaska Native (496)	1,174	3.28
Not Hispanic (398)	997	2.78
Hispanic (98)	177	0.49
Alaska Athabascan *(Ala. Nat.)* (9)	14	0.04
Aleut *(Alaska Native)* (16)	23	0.06
Apache (6)	12	0.03
Arapaho (1)	1	<0.01
Blackfeet (23)	70	0.20
Canadian/French Am. Ind. (4)	9	0.03
Central American Ind. (0)	6	0.02
Cherokee (36)	154	0.43
Cheyenne (1)	6	0.02
Chickasaw (0)	1	<0.01
Chippewa (24)	56	0.16
Choctaw (13)	31	0.09
Colville (1)	5	0.01
Crow (0)	2	0.01
Delaware (0)	3	0.01
Hopi (0)	1	<0.01
Inupiat *(Alaska Native)* (5)	14	0.04
Iroquois (1)	7	0.02
Kiowa (1)	1	<0.01
Menominee (0)	3	0.01
Mexican American Ind. (19)	24	0.07
Navajo (9)	11	0.03
Osage (1)	1	<0.01
Paiute (3)	3	0.01
Pueblo (4)	4	0.01
Puget Sound Salish (79)	98	0.27
Seminole (0)	1	<0.01
Shoshone (0)	2	0.01
Sioux (18)	46	0.13
Spanish American Ind. (1)	1	<0.01
Tlingit-Haida *(Alaska Native)* (20)	40	0.11
Tsimshian *(Alaska Native)* (3)	8	0.02
Yakama (2)	6	0.02
Yaqui (0)	1	<0.01
Yup'ik *(Alaska Native)* (3)	7	0.02
Asian (2,969)	4,192	11.71
Not Hispanic (2,920)	4,006	11.19
Hispanic (49)	186	0.52
Cambodian (299)	358	1.00
Chinese, ex. Taiwanese (171)	342	0.96
Filipino (654)	1,063	2.97
Hmong (1)	2	0.01
Indian (42)	72	0.20
Indonesian (5)	12	0.03
Japanese (215)	501	1.40
Korean (1,151)	1,524	4.26
Laotian (12)	38	0.11
Malaysian (0)	1	<0.01
Taiwanese (15)	23	0.06
Thai (55)	95	0.27
Vietnamese (233)	277	0.77
Hawaii Native/Pacific Islander (1,304)	1,774	4.95
Not Hispanic (1,261)	1,671	4.67
Hispanic (43)	103	0.29
Fijian (10)	13	0.04
Guamanian/Chamorro (562)	708	1.98
Marshallese (12)	12	0.03
Native Hawaiian (77)	241	0.67
Samoan (539)	708	1.98
Tongan (4)	7	0.02
White (21,549)	24,108	67.34
Not Hispanic (19,976)	22,085	61.68
Hispanic (1,573)	2,023	5.65

Pasco

Place Type: City
County: Franklin
Population: 59,781†

Ancestry‡	Population	%
African, Sub-Saharan (37)	85	0.16
African (37)	85	0.16
American (1,596)	1,596	2.95
Arab (8)	216	0.40
Arab (8)	19	0.04
Iraqi (0)	64	0.12
Syrian (0)	50	0.09
Other Arab (0)	83	0.15
Armenian (39)	39	0.07
Austrian (61)	92	0.17
Belgian (6)	30	0.06
Brazilian (11)	70	0.13

*Notes: † The Census 2010 population figure is used to calculate the percentages in the Hispanic Origin and Race categories. Ancestry percentages are based on the 2006-2010 American Community Survey population (not shown); ‡ Numbers in parentheses indicate the number of people reporting a single ancestry; * Numbers in parentheses indicate the number of persons reporting this race alone, not in combination with any other race; Please refer to the Explanation of Data for more information.*

British (74)	98	0.18
Bulgarian (9)	36	0.07
Cajun (17)	35	0.06
Canadian (42)	107	0.20
Croatian (0)	33	0.06
Czech (11)	19	0.04
Danish (91)	284	0.52
Dutch (312)	827	1.53
English (873)	2,852	5.27
European (302)	364	0.67
Finnish (109)	231	0.43
French, ex. Basque (104)	845	1.56
French Canadian (85)	263	0.49
German (1,544)	5,703	10.54
Greek (0)	139	0.26
Hungarian (19)	60	0.11
Icelander (7)	7	0.01
Irish (662)	3,062	5.66
Italian (157)	751	1.39
Lithuanian (0)	9	0.02
Luxemburger (0)	6	0.01
Northern European (10)	10	0.02
Norwegian (573)	1,613	2.98
Polish (158)	402	0.74
Portuguese (10)	82	0.15
Romanian (97)	168	0.31
Russian (171)	351	0.65
Scandinavian (54)	97	0.18
Scotch-Irish (270)	752	1.39
Scottish (449)	921	1.70
Serbian (38)	38	0.07
Swedish (122)	748	1.38
Swiss (32)	80	0.15
Ukrainian (354)	437	0.81
Welsh (46)	300	0.55
West Indian, ex. Hispanic (12)	12	0.02
Jamaican (12)	12	0.02
Yugoslavian (170)	203	0.38

Hispanic Origin	Population	%
Hispanic or Latino (of any race)	33,314	55.73
Central American, ex. Mexican	637	1.07
Costa Rican	6	0.01
Guatemalan	139	0.23
Honduran	57	0.10
Nicaraguan	28	0.05
Panamanian	3	0.01
Salvadoran	398	0.67
Other Central American	6	0.01
Cuban	73	0.12
Dominican Republic	29	0.05
Mexican	30,104	50.36
Puerto Rican	167	0.28
South American	111	0.19
Argentinean	5	0.01
Bolivian	6	0.01
Chilean	7	0.01
Colombian	43	0.07
Ecuadorian	8	0.01
Peruvian	36	0.06
Uruguayan	1	<0.01
Venezuelan	5	0.01
Other Hispanic or Latino	2,193	3.67

Race*	Population	%
African-American/Black (1,120)	1,571	2.63
Not Hispanic (1,012)	1,300	2.17
Hispanic (108)	271	0.45
American Indian/Alaska Native (328)	699	1.17
Not Hispanic (208)	458	0.77
Hispanic (120)	241	0.40
Alaska Athabascan *(Ala. Nat.)* (1)	8	0.01
Aleut *(Alaska Native)* (2)	3	0.01
Apache (4)	21	0.04
Arapaho (2)	2	<0.01
Blackfeet (7)	15	0.03
Canadian/French Am. Ind. (1)	1	<0.01
Central American Ind. (2)	3	0.01
Cherokee (14)	78	0.13
Chickasaw (1)	13	0.02
Chippewa (16)	39	0.07
Choctaw (12)	27	0.05
Colville (8)	21	0.04
Cree (1)	1	<0.01
Creek (4)	7	0.01
Crow (5)	7	0.01
Delaware (0)	3	0.01
Inupiat *(Alaska Native)* (7)	11	0.02
Iroquois (3)	14	0.02
Mexican American Ind. (57)	73	0.12
Navajo (4)	11	0.02
Osage (0)	1	<0.01
Pima (0)	7	0.01
Potawatomi (5)	5	0.01
Pueblo (0)	1	<0.01
Puget Sound Salish (5)	10	0.02
Seminole (1)	1	<0.01
Shoshone (1)	4	0.01
Sioux (8)	21	0.04
South American Ind. (1)	3	0.01
Spanish American Ind. (3)	3	0.01
Tlingit-Haida *(Alaska Native)* (3)	4	0.01
Tohono O'Odham (2)	4	0.01
Yakama (5)	10	0.02
Yup'ik *(Alaska Native)* (0)	1	<0.01
Asian (1,155)	1,548	2.59
Not Hispanic (1,114)	1,411	2.36
Hispanic (41)	137	0.23
Burmese (1)	1	<0.01
Cambodian (17)	20	0.03
Chinese, ex. Taiwanese (76)	137	0.23
Filipino (194)	347	0.58
Hmong (2)	5	0.01
Indian (76)	85	0.14
Indonesian (2)	7	0.01
Japanese (60)	140	0.23
Korean (81)	117	0.20
Laotian (204)	242	0.40
Pakistani (9)	12	0.02
Taiwanese (8)	10	0.02
Thai (5)	18	0.03
Vietnamese (362)	399	0.67
Hawaii Native/Pacific Islander (74)	200	0.33
Not Hispanic (62)	145	0.24
Hispanic (12)	55	0.09
Guamanian/Chamorro (18)	30	0.05
Native Hawaiian (34)	93	0.16
Samoan (9)	30	0.05
Tongan (1)	1	<0.01
White (33,349)	35,109	58.73
Not Hispanic (23,150)	23,955	40.07
Hispanic (10,199)	11,154	18.66

Picnic Point

Place Type: CDP
County: Snohomish
Population: 8,809†

Ancestry‡	Population	%
African, Sub-Saharan (47)	95	1.12
African (0)	48	0.56
Ethiopian (47)	47	0.55
American (406)	406	4.77
Arab (83)	83	0.98
Egyptian (83)	83	0.98
Austrian (40)	100	1.18
Brazilian (10)	10	0.12
British (26)	80	0.94
Canadian (13)	42	0.49
Czech (0)	28	0.33
Czechoslovakian (0)	13	0.15
Danish (0)	65	0.76
Dutch (26)	154	1.81
English (213)	878	10.32
European (339)	339	3.98
Finnish (9)	34	0.40
French, ex. Basque (45)	270	3.17
French Canadian (4)	23	0.27
German (410)	1,417	16.65
Greek (17)	29	0.34
Hungarian (20)	20	0.24
Iranian (24)	51	0.60
Irish (122)	1,002	11.78
Italian (33)	111	1.30
Northern European (10)	10	0.12
Norwegian (300)	747	8.78
Polish (67)	121	1.42
Portuguese (0)	10	0.12
Romanian (25)	25	0.29
Russian (87)	247	2.90
Scandinavian (4)	63	0.74
Scotch-Irish (98)	304	3.57
Scottish (50)	283	3.33
Swedish (175)	432	5.08
Swiss (0)	32	0.38
Ukrainian (294)	306	3.60
Welsh (25)	141	1.66
West Indian, ex. Hispanic (0)	48	0.56
West Indian (0)	48	0.56
Yugoslavian (0)	10	0.12

Hispanic Origin	Population	%
Hispanic or Latino (of any race)	504	5.72
Central American, ex. Mexican	39	0.44
Guatemalan	19	0.22
Honduran	3	0.03
Nicaraguan	1	0.01
Panamanian	2	0.02
Salvadoran	14	0.16
Cuban	11	0.12
Mexican	322	3.66
Puerto Rican	25	0.28
South American	30	0.34
Argentinean	3	0.03
Chilean	4	0.05
Colombian	3	0.03
Ecuadorian	1	0.01
Peruvian	18	0.20
Venezuelan	1	0.01
Other Hispanic or Latino	77	0.87

Race*	Population	%
African-American/Black (218)	322	3.66
Not Hispanic (205)	301	3.42
Hispanic (13)	21	0.24
American Indian/Alaska Native (84)	192	2.18
Not Hispanic (76)	174	1.98
Hispanic (8)	18	0.20
Alaska Athabascan *(Ala. Nat.)* (3)	7	0.08
Aleut *(Alaska Native)* (3)	5	0.06
Apache (2)	3	0.03
Blackfeet (1)	7	0.08
Canadian/French Am. Ind. (0)	4	0.05
Cherokee (8)	26	0.30
Chippewa (4)	8	0.09
Choctaw (4)	6	0.07
Colville (3)	4	0.05
Cree (0)	1	0.01
Creek (1)	1	0.01
Crow (0)	3	0.03
Inupiat *(Alaska Native)* (7)	7	0.08
Iroquois (0)	1	0.01
Mexican American Ind. (1)	1	0.01
Navajo (0)	1	0.01
Pima (0)	1	0.01
Potawatomi (0)	3	0.03
Puget Sound Salish (6)	10	0.11
Sioux (6)	10	0.11
South American Ind. (1)	2	0.02
Tlingit-Haida *(Alaska Native)* (6)	13	0.15
Ute (0)	2	0.02
Asian (1,178)	1,411	16.02
Not Hispanic (1,175)	1,393	15.81
Hispanic (3)	18	0.20
Burmese (1)	1	0.01
Cambodian (60)	71	0.81
Chinese, ex. Taiwanese (124)	188	2.13
Filipino (141)	227	2.58
Indian (72)	79	0.90

*Notes: † The Census 2010 population figure is used to calculate the percentages in the Hispanic Origin and Race categories. Ancestry percentages are based on the 2006-2010 American Community Survey population (not shown); ‡ Numbers in parentheses indicate the number of people reporting a single ancestry; * Numbers in parentheses indicate the number of persons reporting this race alone, not in combination with any other race; Please refer to the Explanation of Data for more information.*

Indonesian (7)	8	0.09
Japanese (70)	116	1.32
Korean (425)	469	5.32
Laotian (11)	12	0.14
Malaysian (2)	2	0.02
Nepalese (1)	1	0.01
Pakistani (14)	14	0.16
Sri Lankan (1)	4	0.05
Taiwanese (15)	16	0.18
Thai (12)	15	0.17
Vietnamese (177)	207	2.35
Hawaii Native/Pacific Islander (30)	90	1.02
Not Hispanic (27)	79	0.90
Hispanic (3)	11	0.12
Fijian (0)	3	0.03
Guamanian/Chamorro (2)	7	0.08
Marshallese (5)	5	0.06
Native Hawaiian (17)	53	0.60
Samoan (0)	5	0.06
Tongan (1)	8	0.09
White (6,686)	7,099	80.59
Not Hispanic (6,417)	6,773	76.89
Hispanic (269)	326	3.70

Port Angeles

Place Type: City
County: Clallam
Population: 19,038†

Ancestry‡	Population	%
African, Sub-Saharan (75)	75	0.39
African (75)	75	0.39
Albanian (13)	13	0.07
American (1,016)	1,016	5.33
Arab (0)	10	0.05
Syrian (0)	10	0.05
Armenian (10)	10	0.05
Australian (0)	19	0.10
Austrian (0)	63	0.33
Basque (13)	13	0.07
British (190)	242	1.27
Canadian (88)	177	0.93
Celtic (23)	32	0.17
Croatian (0)	19	0.10
Czech (53)	201	1.05
Czechoslovakian (34)	34	0.18
Danish (49)	223	1.17
Dutch (152)	336	1.76
Eastern European (36)	36	0.19
English (990)	2,966	15.55
European (222)	250	1.31
Finnish (132)	338	1.77
French, ex. Basque (243)	995	5.22
French Canadian (60)	103	0.54
German (1,118)	4,010	21.02
Greek (10)	10	0.05
Hungarian (0)	45	0.24
Icelander (11)	11	0.06
Iranian (15)	29	0.15
Irish (613)	2,782	14.59
Italian (224)	809	4.24
Latvian (24)	24	0.13
Lithuanian (14)	46	0.24
Northern European (54)	54	0.28
Norwegian (578)	1,451	7.61
Polish (116)	372	1.95
Portuguese (13)	57	0.30
Romanian (0)	44	0.23
Russian (60)	135	0.71
Scandinavian (87)	176	0.92
Scotch-Irish (207)	731	3.83
Scottish (159)	760	3.98
Slovak (9)	17	0.09
Slovene (0)	9	0.05
Swedish (264)	850	4.46
Swiss (0)	93	0.49
Ukrainian (3)	92	0.48
Welsh (25)	188	0.99
Yugoslavian (0)	5	0.03

Hispanic Origin	Population	%
Hispanic or Latino (of any race)	767	4.03
Central American, ex. Mexican	53	0.28
Costa Rican	3	0.02
Guatemalan	9	0.05
Honduran	13	0.07
Nicaraguan	9	0.05
Panamanian	3	0.02
Salvadoran	11	0.06
Other Central American	5	0.03
Cuban	6	0.03
Mexican	518	2.72
Puerto Rican	60	0.32
South American	26	0.14
Argentinean	6	0.03
Bolivian	3	0.02
Chilean	1	0.01
Colombian	3	0.02
Ecuadorian	10	0.05
Peruvian	2	0.01
Other South American	1	0.01
Other Hispanic or Latino	104	0.55

Race*	Population	%
African-American/Black (158)	300	1.58
Not Hispanic (153)	277	1.45
Hispanic (5)	23	0.12
American Indian/Alaska Native (610)	1,096	5.76
Not Hispanic (578)	1,022	5.37
Hispanic (32)	74	0.39
Alaska Athabascan *(Ala. Nat.)* (4)	11	0.06
Aleut *(Alaska Native)* (15)	28	0.15
Apache (3)	9	0.05
Blackfeet (1)	12	0.06
Canadian/French Am. Ind. (7)	18	0.09
Cherokee (23)	97	0.51
Cheyenne (0)	3	0.02
Chickasaw (1)	4	0.02
Chippewa (17)	31	0.16
Choctaw (1)	3	0.02
Colville (3)	3	0.02
Comanche (0)	1	0.01
Cree (0)	4	0.02
Creek (3)	8	0.04
Crow (1)	2	0.01
Delaware (2)	2	0.01
Houma (0)	2	0.01
Inupiat *(Alaska Native)* (0)	5	0.03
Iroquois (1)	9	0.05
Kiowa (1)	1	0.01
Mexican American Ind. (5)	7	0.04
Navajo (9)	10	0.05
Osage (0)	1	0.01
Ottawa (0)	3	0.02
Paiute (1)	1	0.01
Potawatomi (0)	3	0.02
Puget Sound Salish (19)	32	0.17
Seminole (0)	6	0.03
Sioux (15)	22	0.12
South American Ind. (0)	1	0.01
Tlingit-Haida *(Alaska Native)* (36)	61	0.32
Tsimshian *(Alaska Native)* (3)	8	0.04
Yakama (4)	4	0.02
Yuman (1)	5	0.03
Yup'ik *(Alaska Native)* (1)	1	0.01
Asian (334)	513	2.69
Not Hispanic (329)	492	2.58
Hispanic (5)	21	0.11
Bangladeshi (1)	3	0.02
Burmese (1)	1	0.01
Cambodian (0)	1	0.01
Chinese, ex. Taiwanese (111)	136	0.71
Filipino (92)	172	0.90
Indian (39)	43	0.23
Indonesian (1)	2	0.01
Japanese (31)	82	0.43
Korean (37)	47	0.25
Malaysian (3)	3	0.02
Taiwanese (1)	2	0.01
Thai (4)	9	0.05
Vietnamese (9)	16	0.08
Hawaii Native/Pacific Islander (34)	96	0.50
Not Hispanic (30)	84	0.44
Hispanic (4)	12	0.06
Guamanian/Chamorro (12)	20	0.11
Native Hawaiian (9)	54	0.28
Samoan (1)	7	0.04
Tongan (5)	5	0.03
White (16,917)	17,669	92.81
Not Hispanic (16,456)	17,116	89.90
Hispanic (461)	553	2.90

Port Orchard

Place Type: City
County: Kitsap
Population: 11,144†

Ancestry‡	Population	%
African, Sub-Saharan (23)	23	0.21
African (23)	23	0.21
American (647)	647	6.03
Armenian (14)	27	0.25
Australian (0)	9	0.08
Austrian (0)	68	0.63
Belgian (13)	61	0.57
British (47)	61	0.57
Canadian (16)	16	0.15
Croatian (0)	13	0.12
Czech (0)	32	0.30
Danish (25)	145	1.35
Dutch (137)	183	1.70
Eastern European (35)	35	0.33
English (228)	1,529	14.24
European (71)	109	1.02
Finnish (11)	11	0.10
French, ex. Basque (61)	656	6.11
French Canadian (40)	144	1.34
German (530)	2,388	22.25
Greek (0)	98	0.91
Irish (250)	1,217	11.34
Italian (186)	564	5.25
Lithuanian (0)	29	0.27
Northern European (18)	42	0.39
Norwegian (269)	565	5.26
Pennsylvania German (11)	11	0.10
Polish (61)	304	2.83
Portuguese (17)	56	0.52
Russian (0)	82	0.76
Scandinavian (115)	159	1.48
Scotch-Irish (73)	240	2.24
Scottish (137)	516	4.81
Swedish (186)	525	4.89
Swiss (0)	38	0.35
Turkish (0)	19	0.18
Ukrainian (0)	41	0.38
Welsh (0)	124	1.16
West Indian, ex. Hispanic (21)	21	0.20
West Indian (21)	21	0.20
Yugoslavian (0)	33	0.31

Hispanic Origin	Population	%
Hispanic or Latino (of any race)	730	6.55
Central American, ex. Mexican	20	0.18
Costa Rican	1	0.01
Guatemalan	3	0.03
Honduran	5	0.04
Panamanian	7	0.06
Salvadoran	4	0.04
Cuban	7	0.06
Mexican	447	4.01
Puerto Rican	112	1.01
South American	14	0.13
Argentinean	1	0.01
Bolivian	1	0.01
Chilean	4	0.04
Colombian	5	0.04
Ecuadorian	1	0.01
Peruvian	1	0.01
Venezuelan	1	0.01

SECTION TWO

*Notes: † The Census 2010 population figure is used to calculate the percentages in the Hispanic Origin and Race categories. Ancestry percentages are based on the 2006-2010 American Community Survey population (not shown); ‡ Numbers in parentheses indicate the number of people reporting a single ancestry; * Numbers in parentheses indicate the number of persons reporting this race alone, not in combination with any other race; Please refer to the Explanation of Data for more information.*

Other Hispanic or Latino	130	1.17

Race*	Population	%
African-American/Black (375)	566	5.08
Not Hispanic (349)	509	4.57
Hispanic (26)	57	0.51
American Indian/Alaska Native (146)	350	3.14
Not Hispanic (123)	303	2.72
Hispanic (23)	47	0.42
Alaska Athabascan *(Ala. Nat.)* (1)	1	0.01
Aleut *(Alaska Native)* (3)	3	0.03
Apache (2)	4	0.04
Blackfeet (8)	19	0.17
Canadian/French Am. Ind. (4)	8	0.07
Cherokee (6)	49	0.44
Chickasaw (1)	2	0.02
Chippewa (5)	8	0.07
Choctaw (1)	4	0.04
Comanche (4)	7	0.06
Cree (0)	1	0.01
Creek (0)	1	0.01
Crow (1)	1	0.01
Inupiat *(Alaska Native)* (0)	1	0.01
Navajo (1)	1	0.01
Osage (1)	1	0.01
Potawatomi (1)	8	0.07
Pueblo (3)	3	0.03
Puget Sound Salish (13)	24	0.22
Sioux (6)	15	0.13
Tlingit-Haida *(Alaska Native)* (2)	9	0.08
Tsimshian *(Alaska Native)* (3)	3	0.03
Yakama (0)	2	0.02
Asian (644)	978	8.78
Not Hispanic (634)	935	8.39
Hispanic (10)	43	0.39
Burmese (1)	1	0.01
Cambodian (1)	7	0.06
Chinese, ex. Taiwanese (38)	78	0.70
Filipino (416)	622	5.58
Indian (18)	24	0.22
Indonesian (3)	4	0.04
Japanese (45)	107	0.96
Korean (80)	116	1.04
Laotian (1)	2	0.02
Malaysian (0)	1	0.01
Thai (14)	19	0.17
Vietnamese (12)	21	0.19
Hawaii Native/Pacific Islander (153)	255	2.29
Not Hispanic (138)	226	2.03
Hispanic (15)	29	0.26
Fijian (1)	2	0.02
Guamanian/Chamorro (101)	155	1.39
Marshallese (0)	1	0.01
Native Hawaiian (13)	53	0.48
Samoan (13)	19	0.17
Tongan (1)	1	0.01
White (9,001)	9,632	86.43
Not Hispanic (8,548)	9,087	81.54
Hispanic (453)	545	4.89

Port Townsend

Place Type: City
County: Jefferson
Population: 9,113†

Ancestry‡	Population	%
American (312)	312	3.44
Austrian (17)	57	0.63
Belgian (0)	39	0.43
British (96)	137	1.51
Canadian (44)	83	0.91
Czech (0)	97	1.07
Danish (31)	116	1.28
Dutch (65)	269	2.96
Eastern European (40)	45	0.50
English (446)	1,879	20.71
European (280)	338	3.72
Finnish (20)	77	0.85
French, ex. Basque (92)	631	6.95
French Canadian (0)	112	1.23
German (400)	1,926	21.23
Greek (25)	33	0.36
Hungarian (14)	112	1.23
Irish (216)	1,510	16.64
Italian (35)	283	3.12
Latvian (8)	60	0.66
Lithuanian (0)	18	0.20
Northern European (42)	42	0.46
Norwegian (216)	838	9.24
Polish (128)	253	2.79
Portuguese (0)	25	0.28
Russian (74)	109	1.20
Scandinavian (12)	25	0.28
Scotch-Irish (148)	501	5.52
Scottish (148)	539	5.94
Slavic (13)	13	0.14
Swedish (66)	423	4.66
Swiss (32)	72	0.79
Ukrainian (0)	82	0.90
Welsh (12)	98	1.08

Hispanic Origin	Population	%
Hispanic or Latino (of any race)	305	3.35
Central American, ex. Mexican	13	0.14
Guatemalan	4	0.04
Honduran	2	0.02
Nicaraguan	3	0.03
Panamanian	1	0.01
Salvadoran	3	0.03
Cuban	8	0.09
Dominican Republic	4	0.04
Mexican	203	2.23
Puerto Rican	16	0.18
South American	8	0.09
Argentinean	2	0.02
Chilean	2	0.02
Colombian	1	0.01
Paraguayan	1	0.01
Peruvian	2	0.02
Other Hispanic or Latino	53	0.58

Race*	Population	%
African-American/Black (46)	86	0.94
Not Hispanic (43)	77	0.84
Hispanic (3)	9	0.10
American Indian/Alaska Native (97)	246	2.70
Not Hispanic (85)	223	2.45
Hispanic (12)	23	0.25
Alaska Athabascan *(Ala. Nat.)* (4)	6	0.07
Aleut *(Alaska Native)* (4)	4	0.04
Apache (1)	2	0.02
Blackfeet (1)	8	0.09
Canadian/French Am. Ind. (4)	6	0.07
Cherokee (7)	27	0.30
Chickasaw (0)	1	0.01
Chippewa (0)	9	0.10
Choctaw (0)	6	0.07
Colville (0)	1	0.01
Comanche (1)	1	0.01
Cree (2)	2	0.02
Creek (2)	5	0.05
Inupiat *(Alaska Native)* (0)	1	0.01
Iroquois (1)	3	0.03
Mexican American Ind. (1)	1	0.01
Navajo (3)	4	0.04
Potawatomi (1)	2	0.02
Puget Sound Salish (11)	15	0.16
Sioux (1)	10	0.11
South American Ind. (3)	4	0.04
Tlingit-Haida *(Alaska Native)* (8)	9	0.10
Tsimshian *(Alaska Native)* (1)	1	0.01
Yakama (0)	1	0.01
Yaqui (0)	1	0.01
Asian (156)	234	2.57
Not Hispanic (155)	227	2.49
Hispanic (1)	7	0.08
Cambodian (0)	1	0.01
Chinese, ex. Taiwanese (32)	43	0.47
Filipino (35)	57	0.63
Indian (8)	13	0.14
Indonesian (1)	4	0.04
Japanese (40)	69	0.76
Korean (18)	27	0.30
Laotian (1)	1	0.01
Malaysian (1)	2	0.02
Pakistani (0)	4	0.04
Thai (5)	6	0.07
Vietnamese (11)	15	0.16
Hawaii Native/Pacific Islander (27)	49	0.54
Not Hispanic (27)	49	0.54
Guamanian/Chamorro (2)	3	0.03
Native Hawaiian (1)	11	0.12
Samoan (16)	24	0.26
White (8,424)	8,697	95.44
Not Hispanic (8,224)	8,462	92.86
Hispanic (200)	235	2.58

Poulsbo

Place Type: City
County: Kitsap
Population: 9,200†

Ancestry‡	Population	%
American (595)	595	6.77
Arab (15)	15	0.17
Lebanese (15)	15	0.17
Armenian (9)	9	0.10
Austrian (0)	12	0.14
Belgian (10)	24	0.27
Brazilian (0)	15	0.17
British (52)	93	1.06
Canadian (8)	17	0.19
Croatian (0)	14	0.16
Czech (4)	4	0.05
Danish (50)	119	1.35
Dutch (24)	109	1.24
English (291)	1,107	12.59
European (263)	406	4.62
Finnish (26)	152	1.73
French, ex. Basque (63)	435	4.95
French Canadian (7)	7	0.08
German (436)	1,768	20.10
Greek (0)	24	0.27
Hungarian (23)	153	1.74
Iranian (10)	10	0.11
Irish (254)	1,163	13.22
Italian (92)	439	4.99
Lithuanian (14)	14	0.16
Northern European (43)	43	0.49
Norwegian (459)	1,091	12.40
Polish (61)	148	1.68
Portuguese (0)	50	0.57
Russian (41)	112	1.27
Scandinavian (4)	40	0.45
Scotch-Irish (0)	189	2.15
Scottish (158)	403	4.58
Swedish (85)	437	4.97
Swiss (10)	78	0.89
Ukrainian (14)	21	0.24
Welsh (0)	46	0.52
Yugoslavian (8)	8	0.09

Hispanic Origin	Population	%
Hispanic or Latino (of any race)	844	9.17
Central American, ex. Mexican	22	0.24
Costa Rican	3	0.03
Guatemalan	6	0.07
Honduran	1	0.01
Nicaraguan	1	0.01
Panamanian	2	0.02
Salvadoran	9	0.10
Cuban	12	0.13
Dominican Republic	4	0.04
Mexican	646	7.02
Puerto Rican	50	0.54
South American	41	0.45
Argentinean	4	0.04
Chilean	9	0.10

*Notes: † The Census 2010 population figure is used to calculate the percentages in the Hispanic Origin and Race categories. Ancestry percentages are based on the 2006-2010 American Community Survey population (not shown); ‡ Numbers in parentheses indicate the number of people reporting a single ancestry; * Numbers in parentheses indicate the number of persons reporting this race alone, not in combination with any other race; Please refer to the Explanation of Data for more information.*

Colombian	17	0.18
Paraguayan	2	0.02
Peruvian	1	0.01
Uruguayan	3	0.03
Venezuelan	5	0.05
Other Hispanic or Latino	69	0.75

Race*	Population	%
African-American/Black (103)	209	2.27
Not Hispanic (99)	187	2.03
Hispanic (4)	22	0.24
American Indian/Alaska Native (87)	230	2.50
Not Hispanic (80)	201	2.18
Hispanic (7)	29	0.32
Alaska Athabascan *(Ala. Nat.)* (1)	1	0.01
Aleut *(Alaska Native)* (1)	4	0.04
Apache (2)	6	0.07
Blackfeet (1)	6	0.07
Canadian/French Am. Ind. (0)	4	0.04
Cherokee (3)	35	0.38
Chickasaw (0)	1	0.01
Chippewa (1)	6	0.07
Choctaw (3)	11	0.12
Colville (5)	5	0.05
Creek (2)	4	0.04
Crow (0)	3	0.03
Delaware (0)	2	0.02
Inupiat *(Alaska Native)* (1)	3	0.03
Iroquois (0)	2	0.02
Lumbee (1)	1	0.01
Mexican American Ind. (3)	3	0.03
Navajo (3)	4	0.04
Paiute (0)	1	0.01
Potawatomi (2)	2	0.02
Pueblo (1)	1	0.01
Puget Sound Salish (12)	32	0.35
Seminole (0)	1	0.01
Sioux (0)	2	0.02
South American Ind. (1)	2	0.02
Tlingit-Haida *(Alaska Native)* (12)	15	0.16
Tsimshian *(Alaska Native)* (1)	4	0.04
Asian (527)	772	8.39
Not Hispanic (512)	736	8.00
Hispanic (15)	36	0.39
Cambodian (1)	1	0.01
Chinese, ex. Taiwanese (46)	78	0.85
Filipino (267)	394	4.28
Indian (22)	28	0.30
Indonesian (0)	3	0.03
Japanese (55)	124	1.35
Korean (43)	71	0.77
Laotian (4)	11	0.12
Nepalese (1)	3	0.03
Taiwanese (8)	8	0.09
Thai (11)	23	0.25
Vietnamese (50)	61	0.66
Hawaii Native/Pacific Islander (25)	64	0.70
Not Hispanic (25)	59	0.64
Hispanic (0)	5	0.05
Fijian (0)	2	0.02
Guamanian/Chamorro (7)	18	0.20
Native Hawaiian (8)	28	0.30
Samoan (7)	8	0.09
White (7,631)	8,081	87.84
Not Hispanic (7,203)	7,584	82.43
Hispanic (428)	497	5.40

Prairie Ridge

Place Type: CDP
County: Pierce
Population: 11,464†

Ancestry‡	Population	%
African, Sub-Saharan (14)	14	0.12
African (14)	14	0.12
American (696)	696	5.99
Austrian (0)	8	0.07
British (18)	47	0.40
Canadian (21)	43	0.37
Croatian (0)	31	0.27
Czech (6)	70	0.60
Czechoslovakian (0)	35	0.30
Danish (0)	141	1.21
Dutch (72)	233	2.01
English (323)	1,355	11.67
European (127)	318	2.74
Finnish (25)	71	0.61
French, ex. Basque (11)	377	3.25
French Canadian (58)	213	1.83
German (659)	2,622	22.58
Greek (0)	45	0.39
Hungarian (22)	71	0.61
Irish (441)	1,592	13.71
Italian (227)	623	5.37
Lithuanian (15)	15	0.13
Macedonian (13)	13	0.11
Norwegian (258)	794	6.84
Pennsylvania German (9)	21	0.18
Polish (44)	345	2.97
Portuguese (10)	173	1.49
Romanian (28)	28	0.24
Russian (30)	132	1.14
Scotch-Irish (61)	197	1.70
Scottish (86)	351	3.02
Slovak (11)	52	0.45
Swedish (146)	547	4.71
Swiss (0)	36	0.31
Ukrainian (23)	23	0.20
Welsh (21)	31	0.27
Yugoslavian (10)	10	0.09

Hispanic Origin	Population	%
Hispanic or Latino (of any race)	687	5.99
Central American, ex. Mexican	22	0.19
Costa Rican	2	0.02
Guatemalan	2	0.02
Honduran	3	0.03
Nicaraguan	6	0.05
Panamanian	2	0.02
Salvadoran	4	0.03
Other Central American	3	0.03
Cuban	16	0.14
Mexican	494	4.31
Puerto Rican	29	0.25
South American	8	0.07
Argentinean	1	0.01
Colombian	2	0.02
Ecuadorian	4	0.03
Peruvian	1	0.01
Other Hispanic or Latino	118	1.03

Race*	Population	%
African-American/Black (112)	207	1.81
Not Hispanic (107)	198	1.73
Hispanic (5)	9	0.08
American Indian/Alaska Native (177)	378	3.30
Not Hispanic (153)	337	2.94
Hispanic (24)	41	0.36
Aleut *(Alaska Native)* (1)	6	0.05
Blackfeet (1)	10	0.09
Canadian/French Am. Ind. (2)	3	0.03
Cherokee (25)	65	0.57
Cheyenne (2)	2	0.02
Chippewa (13)	21	0.18
Choctaw (6)	14	0.12
Colville (1)	7	0.06
Comanche (1)	4	0.03
Cree (1)	1	0.01
Creek (1)	3	0.03
Inupiat *(Alaska Native)* (1)	4	0.03
Iroquois (2)	5	0.04
Lumbee (1)	1	0.01
Menominee (1)	1	0.01
Mexican American Ind. (9)	14	0.12
Navajo (0)	2	0.02
Osage (0)	1	0.01
Paiute (0)	1	0.01
Potawatomi (0)	4	0.03
Pueblo (1)	5	0.04
Puget Sound Salish (18)	28	0.24
Seminole (1)	1	0.01
Shoshone (0)	1	0.01
Sioux (6)	16	0.14
Tlingit-Haida *(Alaska Native)* (11)	23	0.20
Yakama (0)	3	0.03
Yup'ik *(Alaska Native)* (4)	5	0.04
Asian (177)	330	2.88
Not Hispanic (166)	306	2.67
Hispanic (11)	24	0.21
Burmese (3)	3	0.03
Cambodian (4)	10	0.09
Chinese, ex. Taiwanese (11)	34	0.30
Filipino (77)	144	1.26
Indian (7)	12	0.10
Indonesian (1)	4	0.03
Japanese (20)	70	0.61
Korean (28)	40	0.35
Laotian (1)	1	0.01
Thai (4)	4	0.03
Vietnamese (8)	18	0.16
Hawaii Native/Pacific Islander (33)	83	0.72
Not Hispanic (30)	75	0.65
Hispanic (3)	8	0.07
Fijian (1)	1	0.01
Guamanian/Chamorro (15)	21	0.18
Native Hawaiian (4)	36	0.31
Samoan (4)	8	0.07
White (10,270)	10,706	93.39
Not Hispanic (9,904)	10,287	89.73
Hispanic (366)	419	3.65

Pullman

Place Type: City
County: Whitman
Population: 29,799†

Ancestry‡	Population	%
African, Sub-Saharan (513)	591	2.06
African (144)	152	0.53
Ethiopian (146)	146	0.51
Ghanaian (0)	35	0.12
Kenyan (120)	120	0.42
Nigerian (74)	74	0.26
Other Sub-Saharan African (29)	64	0.22
American (735)	735	2.56
Arab (178)	221	0.77
Arab (64)	102	0.36
Lebanese (18)	23	0.08
Palestinian (70)	70	0.24
Other Arab (26)	26	0.09
Armenian (12)	12	0.04
Australian (32)	32	0.11
Austrian (0)	100	0.35
Belgian (23)	37	0.13
Brazilian (14)	14	0.05
British (135)	247	0.86
Bulgarian (12)	12	0.04
Canadian (83)	166	0.58
Carpatho Rusyn (0)	4	0.01
Celtic (10)	10	0.03
Croatian (9)	54	0.19
Czech (78)	199	0.69
Czechoslovakian (21)	21	0.07
Danish (96)	388	1.35
Dutch (250)	656	2.29
Eastern European (18)	18	0.06
English (803)	3,594	12.54
European (774)	919	3.21
Finnish (96)	179	0.62
French, ex. Basque (97)	1,161	4.05
French Canadian (56)	86	0.30
German (2,407)	7,634	26.64
Greek (58)	80	0.28
Hungarian (9)	157	0.55
Iranian (18)	35	0.12
Irish (568)	3,322	11.59
Israeli (0)	21	0.07
Italian (473)	1,474	5.14

SECTION TWO

*Notes: † The Census 2010 population figure is used to calculate the percentages in the Hispanic Origin and Race categories. Ancestry percentages are based on the 2006-2010 American Community Survey population (not shown); ‡ Numbers in parentheses indicate the number of people reporting a single ancestry; * Numbers in parentheses indicate the number of persons reporting this race alone, not in combination with any other race; Please refer to the Explanation of Data for more information.*

Latvian (15)	15	0.05
Lithuanian (35)	116	0.40
New Zealander (0)	4	0.01
Northern European (129)	139	0.49
Norwegian (622)	2,130	7.43
Pennsylvania German (11)	11	0.04
Polish (230)	669	2.33
Portuguese (43)	164	0.57
Romanian (7)	11	0.04
Russian (167)	387	1.35
Scandinavian (147)	247	0.86
Scotch-Irish (129)	564	1.97
Scottish (141)	889	3.10
Serbian (21)	21	0.07
Slavic (66)	66	0.23
Slovak (11)	21	0.07
Swedish (245)	1,069	3.73
Swiss (0)	152	0.53
Ukrainian (28)	132	0.46
Welsh (30)	345	1.20
West Indian, ex. Hispanic (8)	18	0.06
Haitian (8)	8	0.03
Jamaican (0)	10	0.03
Yugoslavian (79)	99	0.35

Hispanic Origin	Population	%
Hispanic or Latino (of any race)	1,620	5.44
Central American, ex. Mexican	71	0.24
Costa Rican	10	0.03
Guatemalan	11	0.04
Honduran	10	0.03
Nicaraguan	13	0.04
Panamanian	13	0.04
Salvadoran	14	0.05
Cuban	30	0.10
Dominican Republic	3	0.01
Mexican	1,111	3.73
Puerto Rican	89	0.30
South American	158	0.53
Argentinean	43	0.14
Bolivian	5	0.02
Chilean	26	0.09
Colombian	37	0.12
Ecuadorian	8	0.03
Paraguayan	2	0.01
Peruvian	23	0.08
Uruguayan	2	0.01
Venezuelan	12	0.04
Other Hispanic or Latino	158	0.53

Race*	Population	%
African-American/Black (686)	967	3.25
Not Hispanic (662)	907	3.04
Hispanic (24)	60	0.20
American Indian/Alaska Native (196)	525	1.76
Not Hispanic (178)	453	1.52
Hispanic (18)	72	0.24
Alaska Athabascan *(Ala. Nat.)* (0)	5	0.02
Aleut *(Alaska Native)* (1)	5	0.02
Apache (5)	14	0.05
Blackfeet (4)	11	0.04
Canadian/French Am. Ind. (1)	6	0.02
Central American Ind. (0)	5	0.02
Cherokee (11)	75	0.25
Cheyenne (1)	1	<0.01
Chickasaw (1)	2	0.01
Chippewa (7)	19	0.06
Choctaw (3)	7	0.02
Colville (12)	18	0.06
Cree (1)	3	0.01
Creek (2)	5	0.02
Crow (1)	2	0.01
Delaware (2)	2	0.01
Inupiat *(Alaska Native)* (5)	5	0.02
Iroquois (0)	7	0.02
Mexican American Ind. (1)	3	0.01
Navajo (12)	16	0.05
Osage (0)	2	0.01
Ottawa (0)	1	<0.01
Potawatomi (1)	1	<0.01
Puget Sound Salish (2)	8	0.03
Seminole (0)	3	0.01
Shoshone (1)	1	<0.01
Sioux (6)	11	0.04
Spanish American Ind. (1)	1	<0.01
Tlingit-Haida *(Alaska Native)* (4)	8	0.03
Tohono O'Odham (0)	1	<0.01
Tsimshian *(Alaska Native)* (0)	1	<0.01
Yakama (3)	11	0.04
Yaqui (1)	4	0.01
Yup'ik *(Alaska Native)* (2)	3	0.01
Asian (3,348)	4,056	13.61
Not Hispanic (3,328)	4,000	13.42
Hispanic (20)	56	0.19
Bangladeshi (27)	27	0.09
Burmese (3)	3	0.01
Cambodian (20)	27	0.09
Chinese, ex. Taiwanese (1,316)	1,506	5.05
Filipino (250)	475	1.59
Hmong (11)	13	0.04
Indian (463)	503	1.69
Indonesian (5)	10	0.03
Japanese (257)	501	1.68
Korean (483)	588	1.97
Laotian (16)	20	0.07
Malaysian (15)	17	0.06
Nepalese (27)	30	0.10
Pakistani (11)	17	0.06
Sri Lankan (30)	32	0.11
Taiwanese (59)	66	0.22
Thai (26)	43	0.14
Vietnamese (197)	226	0.76
Hawaii Native/Pacific Islander (87)	209	0.70
Not Hispanic (85)	196	0.66
Hispanic (2)	13	0.04
Fijian (2)	3	0.01
Guamanian/Chamorro (13)	21	0.07
Native Hawaiian (32)	111	0.37
Samoan (22)	36	0.12
Tongan (5)	7	0.02
White (23,619)	24,836	83.35
Not Hispanic (22,745)	23,812	79.91
Hispanic (874)	1,024	3.44

Puyallup

Place Type: City
County: Pierce
Population: 37,022†

Ancestry‡	Population	%
African, Sub-Saharan (77)	112	0.31
African (77)	105	0.29
South African (0)	7	0.02
American (1,658)	1,658	4.52
Arab (84)	99	0.27
Lebanese (0)	15	0.04
Palestinian (84)	84	0.23
Armenian (12)	28	0.08
Australian (0)	68	0.19
Austrian (0)	119	0.32
Belgian (110)	185	0.50
British (77)	151	0.41
Canadian (79)	178	0.48
Celtic (0)	51	0.14
Croatian (50)	216	0.59
Czech (26)	194	0.53
Czechoslovakian (37)	55	0.15
Danish (169)	558	1.52
Dutch (176)	529	1.44
English (933)	4,229	11.52
European (640)	773	2.11
Finnish (79)	225	0.61
French, ex. Basque (183)	1,513	4.12
French Canadian (173)	318	0.87
German (2,592)	8,877	24.19
German Russian (12)	12	0.03
Greek (33)	255	0.69
Hungarian (21)	28	0.08
Icelander (26)	89	0.24
Iranian (10)	10	0.03
Irish (1,071)	5,058	13.78
Italian (706)	1,814	4.94
Latvian (53)	53	0.14
Lithuanian (22)	64	0.17
Luxemburger (7)	7	0.02
Norwegian (914)	2,494	6.80
Pennsylvania German (17)	41	0.11
Polish (221)	784	2.14
Portuguese (18)	102	0.28
Romanian (0)	12	0.03
Russian (79)	384	1.05
Scandinavian (159)	285	0.78
Scotch-Irish (234)	794	2.16
Scottish (333)	1,228	3.35
Slavic (13)	43	0.12
Slovak (13)	34	0.09
Slovene (0)	13	0.04
Swedish (407)	1,592	4.34
Swiss (127)	402	1.10
Ukrainian (130)	149	0.41
Welsh (81)	394	1.07
West Indian, ex. Hispanic (112)	112	0.31
Jamaican (112)	112	0.31
Yugoslavian (47)	55	0.15

Hispanic Origin	Population	%
Hispanic or Latino (of any race)	2,539	6.86
Central American, ex. Mexican	132	0.36
Costa Rican	12	0.03
Guatemalan	32	0.09
Honduran	16	0.04
Nicaraguan	13	0.04
Panamanian	25	0.07
Salvadoran	32	0.09
Other Central American	2	0.01
Cuban	57	0.15
Dominican Republic	6	0.02
Mexican	1,789	4.83
Puerto Rican	191	0.52
South American	71	0.19
Argentinean	9	0.02
Bolivian	2	0.01
Chilean	2	0.01
Colombian	18	0.05
Ecuadorian	10	0.03
Peruvian	27	0.07
Venezuelan	2	0.01
Other South American	1	<0.01
Other Hispanic or Latino	293	0.79

Race*	Population	%
African-American/Black (781)	1,352	3.65
Not Hispanic (752)	1,240	3.35
Hispanic (29)	112	0.30
American Indian/Alaska Native (511)	1,099	2.97
Not Hispanic (445)	940	2.54
Hispanic (66)	159	0.43
Alaska Athabascan *(Ala. Nat.)* (3)	4	0.01
Aleut *(Alaska Native)* (5)	36	0.10
Apache (7)	23	0.06
Blackfeet (9)	29	0.08
Canadian/French Am. Ind. (6)	9	0.02
Cherokee (32)	107	0.29
Cheyenne (0)	2	0.01
Chickasaw (4)	7	0.02
Chippewa (15)	61	0.16
Choctaw (8)	24	0.06
Colville (8)	11	0.03
Cree (1)	1	<0.01
Creek (3)	9	0.02
Crow (0)	1	<0.01
Delaware (1)	5	0.01
Inupiat *(Alaska Native)* (7)	12	0.03
Iroquois (3)	4	0.01
Kiowa (1)	3	0.01
Lumbee (1)	1	<0.01
Menominee (0)	1	<0.01
Mexican American Ind. (7)	7	0.02
Navajo (3)	18	0.05

*Notes: † The Census 2010 population figure is used to calculate the percentages in the Hispanic Origin and Race categories. Ancestry percentages are based on the 2006-2010 American Community Survey population (not shown); ‡ Numbers in parentheses indicate the number of people reporting a single ancestry; * Numbers in parentheses indicate the number of persons reporting this race alone, not in combination with any other race; Please refer to the Explanation of Data for more information.*

Osage (0)	6	0.02
Ottawa (2)	2	0.01
Paiute (2)	3	0.01
Pima (1)	5	0.01
Potawatomi (2)	5	0.01
Pueblo (1)	3	0.01
Puget Sound Salish (99)	144	0.39
Seminole (0)	3	0.01
Shoshone (2)	2	0.01
Sioux (23)	47	0.13
South American Ind. (0)	3	0.01
Spanish American Ind. (7)	9	0.02
Tlingit-Haida *(Alaska Native)* (25)	45	0.12
Tohono O'Odham (0)	4	0.01
Tsimshian *(Alaska Native)* (3)	6	0.02
Yakama (8)	11	0.03
Asian (1,396)	2,222	6.00
Not Hispanic (1,377)	2,141	5.78
Hispanic (19)	81	0.22
Bangladeshi (3)	3	0.01
Burmese (1)	1	<0.01
Cambodian (89)	111	0.30
Chinese, ex. Taiwanese (95)	237	0.64
Filipino (290)	610	1.65
Hmong (6)	6	0.02
Indian (220)	254	0.69
Indonesian (3)	7	0.02
Japanese (118)	338	0.91
Korean (270)	431	1.16
Laotian (26)	33	0.09
Malaysian (1)	2	0.01
Pakistani (10)	16	0.04
Sri Lankan (3)	5	0.01
Taiwanese (13)	15	0.04
Thai (26)	57	0.15
Vietnamese (130)	162	0.44
Hawaii Native/Pacific Islander (259)	495	1.34
Not Hispanic (240)	439	1.19
Hispanic (19)	56	0.15
Fijian (2)	2	0.01
Guamanian/Chamorro (100)	136	0.37
Marshallese (5)	5	0.01
Native Hawaiian (41)	186	0.50
Samoan (71)	104	0.28
Tongan (2)	8	0.02
White (31,245)	33,099	89.40
Not Hispanic (29,970)	31,485	85.04
Hispanic (1,275)	1,614	4.36

Redmond

Place Type: City
County: King
Population: 54,144†

Ancestry‡	Population	%
African, Sub-Saharan (59)	92	0.18
African (35)	35	0.07
Ethiopian (11)	44	0.08
Ghanaian (13)	13	0.02
Albanian (0)	14	0.03
Alsatian (9)	9	0.02
American (1,103)	1,103	2.12
Arab (340)	434	0.83
Arab (52)	69	0.13
Egyptian (124)	124	0.24
Jordanian (29)	46	0.09
Lebanese (93)	133	0.26
Moroccan (0)	10	0.02
Palestinian (14)	14	0.03
Other Arab (28)	38	0.07
Armenian (100)	100	0.19
Australian (26)	66	0.13
Austrian (32)	81	0.16
Basque (20)	37	0.07
Belgian (113)	139	0.27
Brazilian (141)	221	0.42
British (367)	644	1.24
Bulgarian (62)	74	0.14
Canadian (281)	472	0.91
Croatian (17)	45	0.09
Czech (78)	220	0.42
Czechoslovakian (37)	62	0.12
Danish (151)	690	1.32
Dutch (163)	731	1.40
Eastern European (70)	70	0.13
English (1,235)	6,739	12.93
European (959)	1,110	2.13
Finnish (24)	84	0.16
French, ex. Basque (103)	1,451	2.78
French Canadian (112)	316	0.61
German (2,306)	9,066	17.39
Greek (53)	256	0.49
Guyanese (22)	22	0.04
Hungarian (99)	223	0.43
Icelander (35)	61	0.12
Iranian (170)	200	0.38
Irish (1,297)	5,226	10.03
Israeli (100)	100	0.19
Italian (668)	1,987	3.81
Latvian (51)	106	0.20
Lithuanian (23)	175	0.34
Luxemburger (40)	40	0.08
Northern European (178)	178	0.34
Norwegian (668)	1,901	3.65
Pennsylvania German (14)	14	0.03
Polish (407)	1,541	2.96
Portuguese (86)	176	0.34
Romanian (259)	378	0.73
Russian (936)	1,451	2.78
Scandinavian (168)	280	0.54
Scotch-Irish (263)	1,364	2.62
Scottish (372)	1,796	3.45
Serbian (137)	137	0.26
Slavic (13)	35	0.07
Slovak (38)	61	0.12
Slovene (30)	30	0.06
Swedish (456)	1,576	3.02
Swiss (32)	134	0.26
Turkish (187)	187	0.36
Ukrainian (129)	294	0.56
Welsh (66)	392	0.75
West Indian, ex. Hispanic (18)	18	0.03
Trinidadian/Tobagonian (18)	18	0.03
Yugoslavian (33)	72	0.14

Hispanic Origin	Population	%
Hispanic or Latino (of any race)	4,214	7.78
Central American, ex. Mexican	249	0.46
Costa Rican	14	0.03
Guatemalan	84	0.16
Honduran	38	0.07
Nicaraguan	21	0.04
Panamanian	20	0.04
Salvadoran	72	0.13
Cuban	55	0.10
Dominican Republic	33	0.06
Mexican	2,862	5.29
Puerto Rican	163	0.30
South American	441	0.81
Argentinean	82	0.15
Bolivian	8	0.01
Chilean	54	0.10
Colombian	142	0.26
Ecuadorian	21	0.04
Paraguayan	2	<0.01
Peruvian	67	0.12
Uruguayan	9	0.02
Venezuelan	54	0.10
Other South American	2	<0.01
Other Hispanic or Latino	411	0.76

Race*	Population	%
African-American/Black (924)	1,306	2.41
Not Hispanic (876)	1,201	2.22
Hispanic (48)	105	0.19
American Indian/Alaska Native (200)	586	1.08
Not Hispanic (140)	445	0.82
Hispanic (60)	141	0.26
Alaska Athabascan *(Ala. Nat.)* (0)	2	<0.01
Aleut *(Alaska Native)* (5)	13	0.02
Apache (4)	11	0.02
Blackfeet (3)	24	0.04
Canadian/French Am. Ind. (10)	20	0.04
Central American Ind. (1)	2	<0.01
Cherokee (15)	74	0.14
Cheyenne (0)	2	<0.01
Chickasaw (0)	4	0.01
Chippewa (8)	21	0.04
Choctaw (4)	8	0.01
Colville (0)	2	<0.01
Comanche (0)	1	<0.01
Cree (1)	8	0.01
Creek (0)	4	0.01
Delaware (0)	4	0.01
Hopi (5)	7	0.01
Inupiat *(Alaska Native)* (1)	5	0.01
Iroquois (3)	7	0.01
Lumbee (3)	6	0.01
Menominee (0)	1	<0.01
Mexican American Ind. (12)	22	0.04
Navajo (4)	7	0.01
Ottawa (6)	8	0.01
Puget Sound Salish (4)	10	0.02
Shoshone (0)	1	<0.01
Sioux (7)	17	0.03
South American Ind. (3)	20	0.04
Tlingit-Haida *(Alaska Native)* (12)	23	0.04
Tsimshian *(Alaska Native)* (2)	2	<0.01
Yakama (2)	2	<0.01
Yaqui (0)	2	<0.01
Yup'ik *(Alaska Native)* (1)	2	<0.01
Asian (13,733)	15,037	27.77
Not Hispanic (13,702)	14,931	27.58
Hispanic (31)	106	0.20
Bangladeshi (45)	45	0.08
Burmese (39)	42	0.08
Cambodian (108)	147	0.27
Chinese, ex. Taiwanese (3,439)	3,886	7.18
Filipino (481)	722	1.33
Hmong (17)	20	0.04
Indian (6,281)	6,433	11.88
Indonesian (70)	88	0.16
Japanese (876)	1,284	2.37
Korean (636)	788	1.46
Laotian (41)	60	0.11
Malaysian (14)	24	0.04
Nepalese (51)	53	0.10
Pakistani (304)	328	0.61
Sri Lankan (26)	30	0.06
Taiwanese (397)	439	0.81
Thai (119)	148	0.27
Vietnamese (427)	519	0.96
Hawaii Native/Pacific Islander (82)	205	0.38
Not Hispanic (81)	187	0.35
Hispanic (1)	18	0.03
Fijian (2)	3	0.01
Guamanian/Chamorro (14)	27	0.05
Marshallese (5)	5	0.01
Native Hawaiian (25)	86	0.16
Samoan (13)	23	0.04
Tongan (8)	9	0.02
White (35,296)	37,221	68.74
Not Hispanic (33,049)	34,639	63.98
Hispanic (2,247)	2,582	4.77

Renton

Place Type: City
County: King
Population: 90,927†

Ancestry‡	Population	%
Afghan (8)	8	0.01
African, Sub-Saharan (2,042)	2,226	2.58
African (1,094)	1,195	1.38
Ethiopian (237)	266	0.31
Ghanaian (12)	12	0.01
Kenyan (78)	78	0.09
Somalian (582)	582	0.67

*Notes: † The Census 2010 population figure is used to calculate the percentages in the Hispanic Origin and Race categories. Ancestry percentages are based on the 2006-2010 American Community Survey population (not shown); ‡ Numbers in parentheses indicate the number of people reporting a single ancestry; * Numbers in parentheses indicate the number of persons reporting this race alone, not in combination with any other race; Please refer to the Explanation of Data for more information.*

South African (0)	7	0.01
Sudanese (24)	56	0.06
Other Sub-Saharan African (15)	30	0.03
Albanian (13)	13	0.02
American (1,924)	1,924	2.23
Arab (214)	294	0.34
Egyptian (68)	68	0.08
Lebanese (27)	107	0.12
Other Arab (119)	119	0.14
Armenian (116)	116	0.13
Australian (39)	70	0.08
Austrian (31)	266	0.31
Basque (0)	8	0.01
Belgian (0)	29	0.03
Brazilian (29)	29	0.03
British (183)	458	0.53
Bulgarian (56)	68	0.08
Canadian (114)	248	0.29
Celtic (16)	16	0.02
Croatian (31)	126	0.15
Cypriot (14)	14	0.02
Czech (66)	226	0.26
Czechoslovakian (197)	219	0.25
Danish (167)	606	0.70
Dutch (314)	1,585	1.84
Eastern European (22)	22	0.03
English (1,631)	6,914	8.00
Estonian (18)	18	0.02
European (897)	1,037	1.20
Finnish (116)	416	0.48
French, ex. Basque (251)	2,684	3.11
French Canadian (133)	307	0.36
German (3,650)	13,325	15.43
Greek (115)	264	0.31
Hungarian (0)	136	0.16
Iranian (159)	166	0.19
Irish (1,698)	7,600	8.80
Italian (767)	2,462	2.85
Latvian (44)	44	0.05
Lithuanian (0)	55	0.06
Luxemburger (0)	9	0.01
Northern European (182)	206	0.24
Norwegian (1,362)	3,952	4.58
Pennsylvania German (13)	27	0.03
Polish (510)	1,480	1.71
Portuguese (109)	289	0.33
Romanian (31)	57	0.07
Russian (1,029)	1,449	1.68
Scandinavian (142)	214	0.25
Scotch-Irish (379)	1,367	1.58
Scottish (418)	1,402	1.62
Slavic (0)	38	0.04
Slovak (36)	59	0.07
Swedish (445)	2,189	2.53
Swiss (96)	425	0.49
Turkish (93)	231	0.27
Ukrainian (751)	936	1.08
Welsh (155)	629	0.73
West Indian, ex. Hispanic (97)	131	0.15
Haitian (0)	16	0.02
Jamaican (97)	97	0.11
Trinidadian/Tobagonian (0)	18	0.02
Yugoslavian (134)	204	0.24

Hispanic Origin	Population	%
Hispanic or Latino (of any race)	11,947	13.14
Central American, ex. Mexican	1,092	1.20
Costa Rican	31	0.03
Guatemalan	363	0.40
Honduran	133	0.15
Nicaraguan	58	0.06
Panamanian	49	0.05
Salvadoran	437	0.48
Other Central American	21	0.02
Cuban	110	0.12
Dominican Republic	31	0.03
Mexican	8,982	9.88
Puerto Rican	392	0.43
South American	370	0.41
Argentinean	28	0.03
Bolivian	15	0.02
Chilean	51	0.06
Colombian	125	0.14
Ecuadorian	28	0.03
Peruvian	88	0.10
Uruguayan	2	<0.01
Venezuelan	33	0.04
Other Hispanic or Latino	970	1.07

Race*	Population	%
African-American/Black (9,670)	11,700	12.87
Not Hispanic (9,435)	11,218	12.34
Hispanic (235)	482	0.53
American Indian/Alaska Native (600)	1,755	1.93
Not Hispanic (423)	1,400	1.54
Hispanic (177)	355	0.39
Alaska Athabascan *(Ala. Nat.)* (9)	13	0.01
Aleut *(Alaska Native)* (21)	44	0.05
Apache (8)	33	0.04
Blackfeet (16)	61	0.07
Canadian/French Am. Ind. (11)	44	0.05
Central American Ind. (3)	3	<0.01
Cherokee (28)	197	0.22
Cheyenne (2)	3	<0.01
Chickasaw (2)	12	0.01
Chippewa (22)	52	0.06
Choctaw (3)	42	0.05
Colville (5)	10	0.01
Comanche (0)	1	<0.01
Cree (4)	6	0.01
Creek (2)	3	<0.01
Crow (3)	10	0.01
Delaware (3)	5	0.01
Hopi (1)	1	<0.01
Inupiat *(Alaska Native)* (4)	7	0.01
Iroquois (3)	11	0.01
Kiowa (4)	7	0.01
Lumbee (1)	1	<0.01
Menominee (3)	3	<0.01
Mexican American Ind. (72)	94	0.10
Navajo (1)	5	0.01
Osage (0)	2	<0.01
Ottawa (1)	1	<0.01
Potawatomi (2)	6	0.01
Pueblo (1)	3	<0.01
Puget Sound Salish (32)	58	0.06
Seminole (0)	1	<0.01
Shoshone (3)	7	0.01
Sioux (28)	69	0.08
South American Ind. (0)	5	0.01
Spanish American Ind. (0)	1	<0.01
Tlingit-Haida *(Alaska Native)* (33)	95	0.10
Tohono O'Odham (1)	2	<0.01
Tsimshian *(Alaska Native)* (11)	15	0.02
Yakama (8)	13	0.01
Yaqui (3)	6	0.01
Yup'ik *(Alaska Native)* (3)	7	0.01
Asian (19,298)	21,646	23.81
Not Hispanic (19,148)	21,275	23.40
Hispanic (150)	371	0.41
Bangladeshi (14)	20	0.02
Burmese (30)	48	0.05
Cambodian (668)	837	0.92
Chinese, ex. Taiwanese (3,533)	4,414	4.85
Filipino (4,171)	5,295	5.82
Hmong (78)	88	0.10
Indian (1,761)	1,954	2.15
Indonesian (48)	66	0.07
Japanese (880)	1,450	1.59
Korean (734)	1,018	1.12
Laotian (655)	798	0.88
Malaysian (13)	21	0.02
Nepalese (35)	42	0.05
Pakistani (83)	107	0.12
Sri Lankan (9)	12	0.01
Taiwanese (146)	164	0.18
Thai (128)	228	0.25
Vietnamese (5,236)	5,753	6.33
Hawaii Native/Pacific Islander (686)	1,211	1.33
Not Hispanic (635)	1,091	1.20
Hispanic (51)	120	0.13
Fijian (107)	133	0.15
Guamanian/Chamorro (100)	174	0.19
Native Hawaiian (67)	276	0.30
Samoan (286)	389	0.43
Tongan (39)	56	0.06
White (49,684)	54,010	59.40
Not Hispanic (44,937)	48,414	53.24
Hispanic (4,747)	5,596	6.15

Richland

Place Type: City
County: Benton
Population: 48,058†

Ancestry‡	Population	%
African, Sub-Saharan (71)	85	0.19
African (48)	62	0.14
Ethiopian (23)	23	0.05
Albanian (27)	27	0.06
American (3,639)	3,639	7.95
Arab (153)	300	0.66
Arab (0)	104	0.23
Egyptian (28)	28	0.06
Lebanese (17)	17	0.04
Other Arab (108)	151	0.33
Armenian (17)	17	0.04
Australian (0)	43	0.09
Austrian (28)	43	0.09
Belgian (0)	22	0.05
British (191)	471	1.03
Canadian (55)	83	0.18
Celtic (0)	25	0.05
Croatian (20)	31	0.07
Czech (58)	319	0.70
Czechoslovakian (55)	75	0.16
Danish (179)	675	1.47
Dutch (237)	936	2.04
Eastern European (78)	87	0.19
English (2,352)	7,157	15.63
Estonian (69)	69	0.15
European (1,089)	1,188	2.60
Finnish (94)	358	0.78
French, ex. Basque (365)	2,053	4.48
French Canadian (188)	399	0.87
German (3,108)	10,713	23.40
Greek (84)	148	0.32
Hungarian (32)	171	0.37
Icelander (9)	26	0.06
Iranian (12)	12	0.03
Irish (1,146)	5,580	12.19
Israeli (10)	10	0.02
Italian (590)	1,793	3.92
Lithuanian (0)	40	0.09
Northern European (156)	156	0.34
Norwegian (713)	1,868	4.08
Pennsylvania German (20)	28	0.06
Polish (387)	1,370	2.99
Portuguese (84)	125	0.27
Romanian (125)	211	0.46
Russian (144)	749	1.64
Scandinavian (86)	283	0.62
Scotch-Irish (334)	790	1.73
Scottish (585)	1,921	4.20
Slavic (0)	4	0.01
Slovak (22)	88	0.19
Slovene (0)	11	0.02
Swedish (314)	1,594	3.48
Swiss (6)	186	0.41
Ukrainian (244)	388	0.85
Welsh (59)	849	1.85
West Indian, ex. Hispanic (0)	15	0.03
Jamaican (0)	15	0.03
Yugoslavian (19)	57	0.12

Hispanic Origin	Population	%
Hispanic or Latino (of any race)	3,728	7.76
Central American, ex. Mexican	117	0.24
Costa Rican	8	0.02

*Notes: † The Census 2010 population figure is used to calculate the percentages in the Hispanic Origin and Race categories. Ancestry percentages are based on the 2006-2010 American Community Survey population (not shown); ‡ Numbers in parentheses indicate the number of people reporting a single ancestry; * Numbers in parentheses indicate the number of persons reporting this race alone, not in combination with any other race; Please refer to the Explanation of Data for more information.*

Guatemalan	26	0.05
Honduran	10	0.02
Nicaraguan	19	0.04
Panamanian	17	0.04
Salvadoran	37	0.08
Cuban	32	0.07
Dominican Republic	8	0.02
Mexican	2,792	5.81
Puerto Rican	90	0.19
South American	186	0.39
Argentinean	13	0.03
Bolivian	16	0.03
Chilean	31	0.06
Colombian	52	0.11
Ecuadorian	27	0.06
Paraguayan	1	<0.01
Peruvian	32	0.07
Uruguayan	2	<0.01
Venezuelan	12	0.02
Other Hispanic or Latino	503	1.05

Race*	Population	%
African-American/Black (672)	1,024	2.13
Not Hispanic (640)	919	1.91
Hispanic (32)	105	0.22
American Indian/Alaska Native (391)	832	1.73
Not Hispanic (337)	706	1.47
Hispanic (54)	126	0.26
Alaska Athabascan *(Ala. Nat.)* (3)	5	0.01
Aleut *(Alaska Native)* (7)	12	0.02
Apache (3)	8	0.02
Blackfeet (11)	24	0.05
Canadian/French Am. Ind. (8)	12	0.02
Cherokee (58)	150	0.31
Cheyenne (3)	9	0.02
Chickasaw (5)	14	0.03
Chippewa (13)	22	0.05
Choctaw (12)	31	0.06
Colville (3)	14	0.03
Comanche (0)	1	<0.01
Cree (0)	7	0.01
Creek (6)	14	0.03
Crow (0)	3	0.01
Delaware (2)	4	0.01
Inupiat *(Alaska Native)* (3)	8	0.02
Iroquois (6)	10	0.02
Lumbee (0)	1	<0.01
Mexican American Ind. (8)	14	0.03
Navajo (5)	13	0.03
Osage (0)	5	0.01
Ottawa (1)	1	<0.01
Paiute (0)	1	<0.01
Potawatomi (7)	7	0.01
Pueblo (4)	9	0.02
Puget Sound Salish (11)	19	0.04
Seminole (1)	2	<0.01
Shoshone (7)	8	0.02
Sioux (13)	29	0.06
South American Ind. (1)	2	<0.01
Spanish American Ind. (0)	2	<0.01
Tlingit-Haida *(Alaska Native)* (10)	15	0.03
Ute (0)	1	<0.01
Yakama (13)	25	0.05
Yaqui (1)	2	<0.01
Yuman (1)	1	<0.01
Asian (2,273)	2,792	5.81
Not Hispanic (2,255)	2,712	5.64
Hispanic (18)	80	0.17
Bangladeshi (28)	30	0.06
Burmese (1)	1	<0.01
Cambodian (5)	15	0.03
Chinese, ex. Taiwanese (708)	793	1.65
Filipino (223)	385	0.80
Hmong (1)	1	<0.01
Indian (401)	443	0.92
Indonesian (9)	10	0.02
Japanese (103)	201	0.42
Korean (238)	303	0.63
Laotian (52)	64	0.13
Malaysian (1)	1	<0.01
Nepalese (2)	4	0.01
Pakistani (35)	41	0.09
Sri Lankan (17)	17	0.04
Taiwanese (47)	56	0.12
Thai (41)	65	0.14
Vietnamese (273)	327	0.68
Hawaii Native/Pacific Islander (52)	132	0.27
Not Hispanic (50)	118	0.25
Hispanic (2)	14	0.03
Guamanian/Chamorro (9)	18	0.04
Native Hawaiian (21)	74	0.15
Samoan (3)	13	0.03
Tongan (1)	1	<0.01
White (41,834)	43,271	90.04
Not Hispanic (39,886)	40,917	85.14
Hispanic (1,948)	2,354	4.90

Salmon Creek

Place Type: CDP
County: Clark
Population: 19,686†

Ancestry‡	Population	%
African, Sub-Saharan (89)	106	0.53
African (40)	57	0.28
Ethiopian (49)	49	0.24
American (872)	872	4.35
Armenian (0)	41	0.20
Australian (11)	44	0.22
Austrian (0)	78	0.39
Belgian (41)	65	0.32
Brazilian (0)	14	0.07
British (177)	263	1.31
Canadian (26)	81	0.40
Croatian (20)	20	0.10
Czech (10)	59	0.29
Czechoslovakian (0)	23	0.11
Danish (40)	271	1.35
Dutch (103)	648	3.23
English (972)	2,743	13.69
European (460)	526	2.63
Finnish (27)	272	1.36
French, ex. Basque (35)	795	3.97
French Canadian (54)	169	0.84
German (1,391)	5,187	25.89
German Russian (0)	12	0.06
Greek (44)	44	0.22
Hungarian (0)	40	0.20
Icelander (9)	71	0.35
Iranian (42)	42	0.21
Irish (464)	2,541	12.68
Italian (293)	687	3.43
Lithuanian (7)	58	0.29
New Zealander (0)	22	0.11
Northern European (39)	39	0.19
Norwegian (243)	1,356	6.77
Polish (15)	329	1.64
Portuguese (10)	136	0.68
Romanian (84)	93	0.46
Russian (63)	158	0.79
Scandinavian (12)	195	0.97
Scotch-Irish (149)	624	3.11
Scottish (183)	956	4.77
Slavic (9)	15	0.07
Swedish (200)	831	4.15
Swiss (0)	46	0.23
Ukrainian (66)	77	0.38
Welsh (20)	148	0.74
West Indian, ex. Hispanic (15)	15	0.07
Jamaican (15)	15	0.07

Hispanic Origin	Population	%
Hispanic or Latino (of any race)	1,289	6.55
Central American, ex. Mexican	92	0.47
Costa Rican	5	0.03
Guatemalan	34	0.17
Honduran	16	0.08
Nicaraguan	1	0.01
Panamanian	6	0.03
Salvadoran	28	0.14
Other Central American	2	0.01
Cuban	27	0.14
Dominican Republic	2	0.01
Mexican	932	4.73
Puerto Rican	61	0.31
South American	32	0.16
Argentinean	1	0.01
Bolivian	2	0.01
Chilean	2	0.01
Colombian	12	0.06
Ecuadorian	6	0.03
Peruvian	7	0.04
Uruguayan	1	0.01
Venezuelan	1	0.01
Other Hispanic or Latino	143	0.73

Race*	Population	%
African-American/Black (305)	490	2.49
Not Hispanic (291)	452	2.30
Hispanic (14)	38	0.19
American Indian/Alaska Native (138)	326	1.66
Not Hispanic (109)	283	1.44
Hispanic (29)	43	0.22
Alaska Athabascan *(Ala. Nat.)* (0)	4	0.02
Aleut *(Alaska Native)* (4)	6	0.03
Apache (2)	10	0.05
Blackfeet (3)	15	0.08
Cherokee (8)	51	0.26
Chickasaw (0)	2	0.01
Chippewa (13)	22	0.11
Choctaw (4)	9	0.05
Colville (2)	4	0.02
Cree (0)	1	0.01
Creek (3)	3	0.02
Crow (0)	1	0.01
Hopi (0)	1	0.01
Inupiat *(Alaska Native)* (1)	5	0.03
Iroquois (1)	9	0.05
Menominee (0)	3	0.02
Mexican American Ind. (3)	3	0.02
Navajo (2)	4	0.02
Paiute (0)	1	0.01
Potawatomi (0)	5	0.03
Pueblo (0)	1	0.01
Puget Sound Salish (11)	12	0.06
Sioux (3)	9	0.05
South American Ind. (1)	1	0.01
Tlingit-Haida *(Alaska Native)* (11)	13	0.07
Tsimshian *(Alaska Native)* (3)	3	0.02
Yakama (0)	5	0.03
Yup'ik *(Alaska Native)* (1)	4	0.02
Asian (783)	1,123	5.70
Not Hispanic (765)	1,082	5.50
Hispanic (18)	41	0.21
Burmese (1)	1	0.01
Cambodian (21)	34	0.17
Chinese, ex. Taiwanese (175)	277	1.41
Filipino (134)	232	1.18
Hmong (12)	12	0.06
Indian (68)	94	0.48
Indonesian (4)	6	0.03
Japanese (65)	180	0.91
Korean (111)	145	0.74
Laotian (27)	28	0.14
Malaysian (1)	1	0.01
Nepalese (1)	1	0.01
Pakistani (7)	9	0.05
Sri Lankan (1)	2	0.01
Taiwanese (9)	10	0.05
Thai (19)	23	0.12
Vietnamese (92)	115	0.58
Hawaii Native/Pacific Islander (114)	200	1.02
Not Hispanic (107)	190	0.97
Hispanic (7)	10	0.05
Fijian (1)	2	0.01
Guamanian/Chamorro (14)	22	0.11
Marshallese (2)	2	0.01
Native Hawaiian (18)	89	0.45
Samoan (8)	15	0.08

*Notes: † The Census 2010 population figure is used to calculate the percentages in the Hispanic Origin and Race categories. Ancestry percentages are based on the 2006-2010 American Community Survey population (not shown); ‡ Numbers in parentheses indicate the number of people reporting a single ancestry; * Numbers in parentheses indicate the number of persons reporting this race alone, not in combination with any other race; Please refer to the Explanation of Data for more information.*

Tongan (10)	10	0.05
White (17,087)	17,840	90.62
Not Hispanic (16,460)	17,059	86.66
Hispanic (627)	781	3.97

Sammamish

Place Type: City
County: King
Population: 45,780†

Ancestry‡	Population	%
Afghan (35)	35	0.08
African, Sub-Saharan (203)	258	0.60
African (77)	122	0.28
Nigerian (60)	60	0.14
South African (66)	76	0.18
American (1,090)	1,090	2.51
Arab (147)	202	0.47
Arab (0)	28	0.06
Egyptian (46)	46	0.11
Lebanese (27)	42	0.10
Palestinian (5)	17	0.04
Syrian (8)	8	0.02
Other Arab (61)	61	0.14
Armenian (42)	52	0.12
Australian (25)	61	0.14
Austrian (10)	122	0.28
Basque (21)	49	0.11
Belgian (10)	63	0.15
Brazilian (216)	216	0.50
British (297)	588	1.36
Bulgarian (58)	58	0.13
Canadian (397)	662	1.53
Celtic (20)	20	0.05
Croatian (40)	192	0.44
Czech (123)	415	0.96
Czechoslovakian (68)	156	0.36
Danish (224)	582	1.34
Dutch (316)	973	2.24
Eastern European (95)	109	0.25
English (1,232)	5,451	12.58
Estonian (15)	15	0.03
European (1,474)	1,651	3.81
Finnish (86)	371	0.86
French, ex. Basque (144)	1,354	3.12
French Canadian (179)	382	0.88
German (2,117)	8,407	19.40
Greek (182)	280	0.65
Hungarian (63)	387	0.89
Icelander (24)	24	0.06
Iranian (284)	298	0.69
Irish (1,468)	5,441	12.55
Israeli (38)	38	0.09
Italian (576)	1,684	3.89
Latvian (55)	76	0.18
Lithuanian (138)	255	0.59
Maltese (4)	4	0.01
New Zealander (42)	129	0.30
Northern European (23)	80	0.18
Norwegian (472)	2,088	4.82
Pennsylvania German (16)	16	0.04
Polish (419)	1,357	3.13
Portuguese (42)	215	0.50
Romanian (388)	441	1.02
Russian (459)	891	2.06
Scandinavian (115)	157	0.36
Scotch-Irish (251)	814	1.88
Scottish (398)	1,655	3.82
Serbian (0)	50	0.12
Slovak (26)	130	0.30
Slovene (0)	27	0.06
Swedish (366)	1,763	4.07
Swiss (144)	412	0.95
Turkish (27)	144	0.33
Ukrainian (61)	195	0.45
Welsh (67)	578	1.33
West Indian, ex. Hispanic (14)	28	0.06
Jamaican (14)	28	0.06
Yugoslavian (0)	32	0.07

Hispanic Origin	Population	%
Hispanic or Latino (of any race)	1,804	3.94
Central American, ex. Mexican	62	0.14
Costa Rican	21	0.05
Guatemalan	11	0.02
Honduran	7	0.02
Nicaraguan	5	0.01
Panamanian	9	0.02
Salvadoran	9	0.02
Cuban	53	0.12
Dominican Republic	7	0.02
Mexican	969	2.12
Puerto Rican	112	0.24
South American	370	0.81
Argentinean	74	0.16
Bolivian	12	0.03
Chilean	51	0.11
Colombian	123	0.27
Ecuadorian	17	0.04
Paraguayan	1	<0.01
Peruvian	48	0.10
Uruguayan	5	0.01
Venezuelan	38	0.08
Other South American	1	<0.01
Other Hispanic or Latino	231	0.50

Race*	Population	%
African-American/Black (439)	724	1.58
Not Hispanic (427)	679	1.48
Hispanic (12)	45	0.10
American Indian/Alaska Native (126)	368	0.80
Not Hispanic (106)	317	0.69
Hispanic (20)	51	0.11
Alaska Athabascan *(Ala. Nat.)* (2)	5	0.01
Aleut *(Alaska Native)* (0)	5	0.01
Apache (1)	2	<0.01
Blackfeet (1)	9	0.02
Canadian/French Am. Ind. (0)	1	<0.01
Cherokee (17)	62	0.14
Chickasaw (3)	11	0.02
Chippewa (6)	8	0.02
Choctaw (3)	14	0.03
Colville (1)	1	<0.01
Comanche (0)	1	<0.01
Cree (0)	1	<0.01
Delaware (1)	2	<0.01
Hopi (0)	1	<0.01
Inupiat *(Alaska Native)* (3)	9	0.02
Iroquois (4)	4	0.01
Kiowa (1)	3	0.01
Lumbee (2)	2	<0.01
Mexican American Ind. (3)	5	0.01
Osage (1)	5	0.01
Puget Sound Salish (11)	26	0.06
Shoshone (0)	1	<0.01
Sioux (2)	3	0.01
South American Ind. (0)	2	<0.01
Spanish American Ind. (1)	1	<0.01
Tlingit-Haida *(Alaska Native)* (4)	23	0.05
Tsimshian *(Alaska Native)* (7)	9	0.02
Ute (3)	3	0.01
Yakama (1)	2	<0.01
Yup'ik *(Alaska Native)* (3)	5	0.01
Asian (8,852)	10,036	21.92
Not Hispanic (8,841)	9,967	21.77
Hispanic (11)	69	0.15
Bangladeshi (18)	21	0.05
Burmese (5)	5	0.01
Cambodian (8)	18	0.04
Chinese, ex. Taiwanese (3,166)	3,574	7.81
Filipino (321)	557	1.22
Hmong (1)	4	0.01
Indian (3,237)	3,337	7.29
Indonesian (47)	62	0.14
Japanese (426)	858	1.87
Korean (769)	945	2.06
Laotian (16)	20	0.04
Malaysian (18)	22	0.05
Nepalese (2)	6	0.01
Pakistani (79)	89	0.19
Sri Lankan (12)	14	0.03
Taiwanese (215)	245	0.54
Thai (50)	76	0.17
Vietnamese (208)	267	0.58
Hawaii Native/Pacific Islander (47)	171	0.37
Not Hispanic (46)	161	0.35
Hispanic (1)	10	0.02
Fijian (1)	4	0.01
Guamanian/Chamorro (15)	40	0.09
Native Hawaiian (12)	77	0.17
Samoan (3)	14	0.03
Tongan (2)	3	0.01
White (34,207)	35,786	78.17
Not Hispanic (32,909)	34,343	75.02
Hispanic (1,298)	1,443	3.15

SeaTac

Place Type: City
County: King
Population: 26,909†

Ancestry‡	Population	%
Afghan (45)	45	0.17
African, Sub-Saharan (2,106)	2,295	8.68
African (677)	732	2.77
Ethiopian (511)	547	2.07
Ghanaian (37)	37	0.14
Kenyan (13)	13	0.05
Somalian (776)	823	3.11
South African (0)	15	0.06
Sudanese (92)	92	0.35
Other Sub-Saharan African (0)	36	0.14
American (528)	528	2.00
Arab (54)	113	0.43
Arab (17)	17	0.06
Iraqi (14)	14	0.05
Lebanese (23)	82	0.31
Austrian (8)	62	0.23
Belgian (11)	21	0.08
British (63)	82	0.31
Canadian (0)	66	0.25
Celtic (13)	13	0.05
Croatian (19)	75	0.28
Czech (27)	87	0.33
Czechoslovakian (51)	62	0.23
Danish (27)	99	0.37
Dutch (167)	529	2.00
Eastern European (0)	12	0.05
English (526)	2,009	7.60
European (234)	271	1.03
Finnish (40)	94	0.36
French, ex. Basque (89)	676	2.56
French Canadian (10)	100	0.38
German (679)	2,698	10.21
Greek (97)	179	0.68
Hungarian (39)	39	0.15
Icelander (13)	13	0.05
Irish (503)	2,039	7.71
Italian (311)	737	2.79
Lithuanian (0)	20	0.08
Northern European (40)	40	0.15
Norwegian (456)	1,297	4.91
Pennsylvania German (12)	24	0.09
Polish (228)	377	1.43
Portuguese (0)	39	0.15
Romanian (56)	56	0.21
Russian (28)	167	0.63
Scandinavian (11)	51	0.19
Scotch-Irish (66)	451	1.71
Scottish (138)	293	1.11
Serbian (11)	11	0.04
Slovak (0)	9	0.03
Swedish (62)	614	2.32
Swiss (11)	43	0.16
Turkish (147)	147	0.56
Ukrainian (68)	78	0.30
Welsh (56)	212	0.80
West Indian, ex. Hispanic (41)	51	0.19
Jamaican (41)	51	0.19

*Notes: † The Census 2010 population figure is used to calculate the percentages in the Hispanic Origin and Race categories. Ancestry percentages are based on the 2006-2010 American Community Survey population (not shown); ‡ Numbers in parentheses indicate the number of people reporting a single ancestry; * Numbers in parentheses indicate the number of persons reporting this race alone, not in combination with any other race; Please refer to the Explanation of Data for more information.*

Yugoslavian (167)	178	0.67

Hispanic Origin	Population	%
Hispanic or Latino (of any race)	5,474	20.34
Central American, ex. Mexican	620	2.30
Costa Rican	10	0.04
Guatemalan	144	0.54
Honduran	164	0.61
Nicaraguan	14	0.05
Panamanian	10	0.04
Salvadoran	278	1.03
Cuban	29	0.11
Dominican Republic	18	0.07
Mexican	4,172	15.50
Puerto Rican	77	0.29
South American	102	0.38
Argentinean	2	0.01
Chilean	17	0.06
Colombian	33	0.12
Ecuadorian	29	0.11
Peruvian	16	0.06
Uruguayan	3	0.01
Venezuelan	2	0.01
Other Hispanic or Latino	456	1.69

Race*	Population	%
African-American/Black (4,532)	5,038	18.72
Not Hispanic (4,455)	4,890	18.17
Hispanic (77)	148	0.55
American Indian/Alaska Native (399)	847	3.15
Not Hispanic (299)	652	2.42
Hispanic (100)	195	0.72
Alaska Athabascan *(Ala. Nat.)* (2)	10	0.04
Aleut *(Alaska Native)* (5)	10	0.04
Apache (7)	10	0.04
Arapaho (1)	1	<0.01
Blackfeet (20)	50	0.19
Canadian/French Am. Ind. (18)	20	0.07
Central American Ind. (6)	8	0.03
Cherokee (11)	69	0.26
Cheyenne (1)	3	0.01
Chippewa (12)	24	0.09
Choctaw (6)	27	0.10
Colville (12)	18	0.07
Comanche (0)	6	0.02
Cree (0)	2	0.01
Creek (0)	1	<0.01
Crow (0)	1	<0.01
Inupiat *(Alaska Native)* (5)	10	0.04
Iroquois (2)	4	0.01
Lumbee (1)	1	<0.01
Mexican American Ind. (26)	39	0.14
Navajo (6)	15	0.06
Osage (0)	2	0.01
Paiute (1)	1	<0.01
Potawatomi (1)	2	0.01
Pueblo (0)	2	0.01
Puget Sound Salish (18)	33	0.12
Seminole (0)	4	0.01
Shoshone (1)	2	0.01
Sioux (12)	38	0.14
South American Ind. (1)	1	<0.01
Spanish American Ind. (4)	5	0.02
Tlingit-Haida *(Alaska Native)* (23)	41	0.15
Tohono O'Odham (1)	3	0.01
Tsimshian *(Alaska Native)* (4)	6	0.02
Ute (0)	2	0.01
Yakama (1)	3	0.01
Yaqui (1)	1	<0.01
Yuman (1)	1	<0.01
Yup'ik *(Alaska Native)* (6)	10	0.04
Asian (3,910)	4,553	16.92
Not Hispanic (3,874)	4,450	16.54
Hispanic (36)	103	0.38
Bangladeshi (28)	28	0.10
Bhutanese (63)	72	0.27
Burmese (13)	13	0.05
Cambodian (418)	467	1.74
Chinese, ex. Taiwanese (153)	259	0.96
Filipino (873)	1,140	4.24
Hmong (55)	64	0.24
Indian (796)	890	3.31
Indonesian (2)	6	0.02
Japanese (110)	223	0.83
Korean (82)	123	0.46
Laotian (155)	183	0.68
Nepalese (9)	21	0.08
Pakistani (27)	29	0.11
Sri Lankan (4)	5	0.02
Taiwanese (7)	9	0.03
Thai (89)	120	0.45
Vietnamese (862)	932	3.46
Hawaii Native/Pacific Islander (958)	1,157	4.30
Not Hispanic (946)	1,115	4.14
Hispanic (12)	42	0.16
Fijian (44)	48	0.18
Guamanian/Chamorro (32)	54	0.20
Marshallese (7)	7	0.03
Native Hawaiian (21)	91	0.34
Samoan (581)	693	2.58
Tongan (76)	95	0.35
White (12,362)	13,649	50.72
Not Hispanic (10,619)	11,551	42.93
Hispanic (1,743)	2,098	7.80

Seattle

Place Type: City
County: King
Population: 608,660†

Ancestry‡	Population	%
Afghan (43)	56	0.01
African, Sub-Saharan (13,091)	14,788	2.48
African (3,452)	4,331	0.73
Cape Verdean (37)	93	0.02
Ethiopian (4,033)	4,391	0.74
Ghanaian (96)	96	0.02
Kenyan (513)	513	0.09
Liberian (47)	47	0.01
Nigerian (480)	523	0.09
Senegalese (55)	55	0.01
Somalian (3,654)	3,872	0.65
South African (190)	281	0.05
Sudanese (48)	48	0.01
Ugandan (21)	21	<0.01
Zimbabwean (22)	22	<0.01
Other Sub-Saharan African (443)	495	0.08
Albanian (49)	84	0.01
Alsatian (0)	24	<0.01
American (15,466)	15,466	2.60
Arab (1,377)	2,600	0.44
Arab (164)	184	0.03
Egyptian (86)	188	0.03
Iraqi (29)	39	0.01
Jordanian (53)	66	0.01
Lebanese (529)	1,156	0.19
Moroccan (81)	143	0.02
Palestinian (122)	162	0.03
Syrian (44)	157	0.03
Other Arab (269)	505	0.08
Armenian (261)	634	0.11
Assyrian/Chaldean/Syriac (21)	21	<0.01
Australian (388)	631	0.11
Austrian (460)	2,639	0.44
Basque (180)	441	0.07
Belgian (170)	909	0.15
Brazilian (312)	394	0.07
British (3,406)	6,970	1.17
Bulgarian (217)	506	0.09
Cajun (27)	54	0.01
Canadian (1,746)	3,240	0.54
Carpatho Rusyn (11)	11	<0.01
Celtic (192)	321	0.05
Croatian (646)	1,828	0.31
Czech (1,270)	3,837	0.64
Czechoslovakian (206)	629	0.11
Danish (1,675)	6,649	1.12
Dutch (2,774)	11,744	1.97
Eastern European (2,257)	2,615	0.44
English (15,114)	68,827	11.56
Estonian (84)	213	0.04
European (18,134)	20,109	3.38
Finnish (821)	3,089	0.52
French, ex. Basque (2,672)	18,860	3.17
French Canadian (1,505)	4,894	0.82
German (22,265)	97,270	16.34
German Russian (10)	20	<0.01
Greek (2,263)	4,462	0.75
Guyanese (0)	20	<0.01
Hungarian (991)	3,531	0.59
Icelander (293)	893	0.15
Iranian (934)	1,225	0.21
Irish (17,965)	71,012	11.93
Israeli (219)	466	0.08
Italian (7,914)	25,949	4.36
Latvian (405)	624	0.10
Lithuanian (726)	2,126	0.36
Luxemburger (53)	166	0.03
Macedonian (29)	102	0.02
Maltese (12)	19	<0.01
New Zealander (118)	197	0.03
Northern European (4,175)	4,576	0.77
Norwegian (10,311)	30,449	5.12
Pennsylvania German (96)	127	0.02
Polish (4,158)	14,995	2.52
Portuguese (576)	1,823	0.31
Romanian (783)	1,402	0.24
Russian (3,270)	9,615	1.62
Scandinavian (2,132)	4,424	0.74
Scotch-Irish (4,566)	14,973	2.52
Scottish (5,598)	22,301	3.75
Serbian (132)	386	0.06
Slavic (227)	444	0.07
Slovak (382)	1,056	0.18
Slovene (151)	536	0.09
Soviet Union (64)	64	0.01
Swedish (5,118)	21,937	3.69
Swiss (853)	3,689	0.62
Turkish (331)	736	0.12
Ukrainian (812)	2,427	0.41
Welsh (1,106)	7,475	1.26
West Indian, ex. Hispanic (899)	1,223	0.21
Barbadian (37)	79	0.01
Belizean (6)	18	<0.01
British West Indian (72)	107	0.02
Dutch West Indian (0)	36	0.01
Haitian (290)	305	0.05
Jamaican (166)	269	0.05
Trinidadian/Tobagonian (9)	34	0.01
West Indian (319)	366	0.06
Other West Indian (0)	9	<0.01
Yugoslavian (497)	919	0.15

Hispanic Origin	Population	%
Hispanic or Latino (of any race)	40,329	6.63
Central American, ex. Mexican	3,740	0.61
Costa Rican	166	0.03
Guatemalan	1,056	0.17
Honduran	633	0.10
Nicaraguan	299	0.05
Panamanian	231	0.04
Salvadoran	1,322	0.22
Other Central American	33	0.01
Cuban	1,068	0.18
Dominican Republic	200	0.03
Mexican	24,800	4.07
Puerto Rican	2,127	0.35
South American	3,346	0.55
Argentinean	505	0.08
Bolivian	150	0.02
Chilean	438	0.07
Colombian	784	0.13
Ecuadorian	309	0.05
Paraguayan	31	0.01
Peruvian	774	0.13
Uruguayan	51	0.01
Venezuelan	267	0.04
Other South American	37	0.01
Other Hispanic or Latino	5,048	0.83

*Notes: † The Census 2010 population figure is used to calculate the percentages in the Hispanic Origin and Race categories. Ancestry percentages are based on the 2006-2010 American Community Survey population (not shown); ‡ Numbers in parentheses indicate the number of people reporting a single ancestry; * Numbers in parentheses indicate the number of persons reporting this race alone, not in combination with any other race; Please refer to the Explanation of Data for more information.*

Race*	Population	%
African-American/Black (48,316)	57,716	9.48
Not Hispanic (47,113)	55,325	9.09
Hispanic (1,203)	2,391	0.39
American Indian/Alaska Native (4,809)	12,549	2.06
Not Hispanic (3,881)	10,346	1.70
Hispanic (928)	2,203	0.36
Alaska Athabascan *(Ala. Nat.)* (53)	90	0.01
Aleut *(Alaska Native)* (125)	224	0.04
Apache (54)	151	0.02
Arapaho (14)	22	<0.01
Blackfeet (123)	567	0.09
Canadian/French Am. Ind. (100)	198	0.03
Central American Ind. (25)	64	0.01
Cherokee (182)	1,364	0.22
Cheyenne (20)	43	0.01
Chickasaw (16)	70	0.01
Chippewa (178)	399	0.07
Choctaw (46)	287	0.05
Colville (80)	129	0.02
Comanche (10)	40	0.01
Cree (20)	61	0.01
Creek (16)	78	0.01
Crow (15)	38	0.01
Delaware (6)	37	0.01
Hopi (7)	20	<0.01
Houma (0)	1	<0.01
Inupiat *(Alaska Native)* (57)	112	0.02
Iroquois (21)	110	0.02
Kiowa (5)	22	<0.01
Lumbee (5)	20	<0.01
Menominee (2)	9	<0.01
Mexican American Ind. (236)	372	0.06
Navajo (114)	208	0.03
Osage (4)	33	0.01
Ottawa (3)	10	<0.01
Paiute (11)	24	<0.01
Pima (12)	14	<0.01
Potawatomi (16)	54	0.01
Pueblo (26)	64	0.01
Puget Sound Salish (209)	394	0.06
Seminole (3)	63	0.01
Shoshone (22)	41	0.01
Sioux (190)	462	0.08
South American Ind. (27)	103	0.02
Spanish American Ind. (19)	30	<0.01
Tlingit-Haida *(Alaska Native)* (384)	729	0.12
Tohono O'Odham (3)	10	<0.01
Tsimshian *(Alaska Native)* (33)	108	0.02
Ute (5)	20	<0.01
Yakama (66)	111	0.02
Yaqui (18)	53	0.01
Yuman (2)	5	<0.01
Yup'ik *(Alaska Native)* (24)	41	0.01
Asian (84,215)	100,727	16.55
Not Hispanic (83,537)	98,921	16.25
Hispanic (678)	1,806	0.30
Bangladeshi (65)	86	0.01
Bhutanese (83)	94	0.02
Burmese (149)	182	0.03
Cambodian (1,841)	2,185	0.36
Chinese, ex. Taiwanese (23,391)	28,837	4.74
Filipino (15,757)	21,003	3.45
Hmong (112)	123	0.02
Indian (4,770)	5,988	0.98
Indonesian (585)	832	0.14
Japanese (7,829)	13,064	2.15
Korean (6,635)	8,682	1.43
Laotian (1,809)	2,085	0.34
Malaysian (105)	178	0.03
Nepalese (196)	245	0.04
Pakistani (336)	427	0.07
Sri Lankan (102)	133	0.02
Taiwanese (1,627)	1,940	0.32
Thai (1,100)	1,479	0.24
Vietnamese (13,252)	14,987	2.46
Hawaii Native/Pacific Islander (2,351)	4,754	0.78
Not Hispanic (2,246)	4,368	0.72
Hispanic (105)	386	0.06
Fijian (154)	219	0.04
Guamanian/Chamorro (356)	612	0.10
Marshallese (9)	12	<0.01
Native Hawaiian (368)	1,414	0.23
Samoan (961)	1,352	0.22
Tongan (146)	215	0.04
White (422,870)	449,536	73.86
Not Hispanic (403,578)	426,420	70.06
Hispanic (19,292)	23,116	3.80

Sedro-Woolley

Place Type: City
County: Skagit
Population: 10,540†

Ancestry‡	Population	%
American (414)	414	4.01
Arab (0)	8	0.08
Lebanese (0)	8	0.08
Austrian (30)	30	0.29
British (0)	13	0.13
Canadian (36)	91	0.88
Czech (37)	118	1.14
Danish (27)	135	1.31
Dutch (80)	243	2.35
English (307)	1,283	12.43
European (107)	287	2.78
Finnish (0)	16	0.16
French, ex. Basque (233)	517	5.01
French Canadian (17)	109	1.06
German (677)	2,056	19.92
Icelander (10)	24	0.23
Irish (346)	1,337	12.96
Italian (193)	387	3.75
Northern European (59)	59	0.57
Norwegian (344)	988	9.57
Polish (75)	265	2.57
Portuguese (0)	17	0.16
Russian (17)	30	0.29
Scandinavian (16)	128	1.24
Scotch-Irish (156)	204	1.98
Scottish (112)	329	3.19
Slovene (12)	12	0.12
Swedish (83)	536	5.19
Swiss (0)	28	0.27
Welsh (23)	90	0.87
Yugoslavian (0)	28	0.27

Hispanic Origin	Population	%
Hispanic or Latino (of any race)	1,474	13.98
Central American, ex. Mexican	32	0.30
Guatemalan	7	0.07
Honduran	1	0.01
Panamanian	1	0.01
Salvadoran	23	0.22
Cuban	2	0.02
Dominican Republic	1	0.01
Mexican	1,280	12.14
Puerto Rican	28	0.27
South American	18	0.17
Bolivian	2	0.02
Chilean	1	0.01
Colombian	5	0.05
Ecuadorian	1	0.01
Peruvian	9	0.09
Other Hispanic or Latino	113	1.07

Race*	Population	%
African-American/Black (34)	102	0.97
Not Hispanic (34)	92	0.87
Hispanic (0)	10	0.09
American Indian/Alaska Native (205)	373	3.54
Not Hispanic (158)	288	2.73
Hispanic (47)	85	0.81
Alaska Athabascan *(Ala. Nat.)* (3)	5	0.05
Aleut *(Alaska Native)* (7)	11	0.10
Apache (1)	7	0.07
Blackfeet (2)	2	0.02
Canadian/French Am. Ind. (1)	3	0.03
Cherokee (9)	37	0.35
Cheyenne (1)	5	0.05
Chippewa (2)	5	0.05
Choctaw (2)	7	0.07
Colville (4)	5	0.05
Comanche (0)	6	0.06
Cree (0)	4	0.04
Creek (5)	5	0.05
Crow (1)	3	0.03
Hopi (0)	4	0.04
Inupiat *(Alaska Native)* (1)	2	0.02
Mexican American Ind. (8)	15	0.14
Navajo (4)	7	0.07
Paiute (0)	2	0.02
Potawatomi (1)	1	0.01
Puget Sound Salish (51)	69	0.65
Seminole (0)	3	0.03
Sioux (1)	6	0.06
Tlingit-Haida *(Alaska Native)* (4)	16	0.15
Tsimshian *(Alaska Native)* (1)	4	0.04
Yakama (2)	2	0.02
Yup'ik *(Alaska Native)* (1)	2	0.02
Asian (150)	237	2.25
Not Hispanic (147)	225	2.13
Hispanic (3)	12	0.11
Chinese, ex. Taiwanese (20)	29	0.28
Filipino (76)	106	1.01
Indian (9)	15	0.14
Indonesian (2)	7	0.07
Japanese (11)	36	0.34
Korean (22)	30	0.28
Sri Lankan (1)	1	0.01
Thai (6)	8	0.08
Vietnamese (0)	4	0.04
Hawaii Native/Pacific Islander (5)	24	0.23
Not Hispanic (5)	24	0.23
Guamanian/Chamorro (1)	4	0.04
Native Hawaiian (0)	8	0.08
Tongan (3)	4	0.04
White (9,080)	9,403	89.21
Not Hispanic (8,475)	8,690	82.45
Hispanic (605)	713	6.76

Shelton

Place Type: City
County: Mason
Population: 9,834†

Ancestry‡	Population	%
American (759)	759	7.83
Arab (29)	54	0.56
Arab (16)	16	0.16
Lebanese (13)	38	0.39
Austrian (0)	70	0.72
Belgian (10)	10	0.10
British (17)	20	0.21
Canadian (8)	47	0.48
Celtic (22)	22	0.23
Croatian (8)	8	0.08
Czech (0)	10	0.10
Danish (8)	113	1.17
Dutch (58)	135	1.39
English (416)	1,245	12.84
European (158)	179	1.85
Finnish (25)	35	0.36
French, ex. Basque (13)	189	1.95
French Canadian (40)	142	1.46
German (463)	1,496	15.42
Greek (8)	37	0.38
Irish (253)	1,054	10.87
Italian (43)	87	0.90
Norwegian (158)	616	6.35
Polish (34)	209	2.15
Portuguese (0)	46	0.47
Russian (36)	63	0.65
Scandinavian (8)	8	0.08
Scotch-Irish (95)	220	2.27
Scottish (119)	258	2.66
Slovak (0)	9	0.09

*Notes: † The Census 2010 population figure is used to calculate the percentages in the Hispanic Origin and Race categories. Ancestry percentages are based on the 2006-2010 American Community Survey population (not shown); ‡ Numbers in parentheses indicate the number of people reporting a single ancestry; * Numbers in parentheses indicate the number of persons reporting this race alone, not in combination with any other race; Please refer to the Explanation of Data for more information.*

Swedish (32)	262	2.70
Swiss (0)	18	0.19
Welsh (0)	78	0.80

Hispanic Origin	Population	%
Hispanic or Latino (of any race)	1,893	19.25
Central American, ex. Mexican	477	4.85
Guatemalan	454	4.62
Honduran	5	0.05
Salvadoran	18	0.18
Cuban	4	0.04
Mexican	1,193	12.13
Puerto Rican	36	0.37
South American	15	0.15
Argentinean	2	0.02
Chilean	7	0.07
Colombian	6	0.06
Other Hispanic or Latino	168	1.71

Race*	Population	%
African-American/Black (82)	157	1.60
Not Hispanic (60)	113	1.15
Hispanic (22)	44	0.45
American Indian/Alaska Native (359)	599	6.09
Not Hispanic (231)	447	4.55
Hispanic (128)	152	1.55
Alaska Athabascan *(Ala. Nat.)* (2)	2	0.02
Aleut *(Alaska Native)* (6)	13	0.13
Apache (1)	6	0.06
Arapaho (1)	1	0.01
Blackfeet (12)	24	0.24
Canadian/French Am. Ind. (1)	2	0.02
Central American Ind. (16)	17	0.17
Cherokee (13)	56	0.57
Chickasaw (2)	3	0.03
Chippewa (4)	19	0.19
Choctaw (7)	10	0.10
Colville (11)	13	0.13
Creek (0)	2	0.02
Inupiat *(Alaska Native)* (4)	6	0.06
Iroquois (1)	1	0.01
Mexican American Ind. (74)	75	0.76
Navajo (1)	1	0.01
Osage (0)	2	0.02
Pima (0)	1	0.01
Potawatomi (0)	2	0.02
Puget Sound Salish (77)	130	1.32
Sioux (4)	6	0.06
Tlingit-Haida *(Alaska Native)* (8)	14	0.14
Yakama (1)	1	0.01
Yaqui (0)	1	0.01
Asian (105)	181	1.84
Not Hispanic (91)	161	1.64
Hispanic (14)	20	0.20
Cambodian (5)	6	0.06
Chinese, ex. Taiwanese (34)	45	0.46
Filipino (21)	57	0.58
Indian (8)	14	0.14
Japanese (11)	37	0.38
Korean (15)	26	0.26
Malaysian (1)	2	0.02
Thai (2)	4	0.04
Vietnamese (0)	3	0.03
Hawaii Native/Pacific Islander (78)	123	1.25
Not Hispanic (75)	113	1.15
Hispanic (3)	10	0.10
Guamanian/Chamorro (11)	19	0.19
Native Hawaiian (9)	27	0.27
Samoan (58)	72	0.73
White (7,763)	8,205	83.44
Not Hispanic (7,117)	7,448	75.74
Hispanic (646)	757	7.70

Shoreline

Place Type: City
County: King
Population: 53,007†

Ancestry‡	Population	%
African, Sub-Saharan (1,693)	1,808	3.44
African (323)	373	0.71
Ethiopian (1,085)	1,085	2.07
Ghanaian (16)	48	0.09
Nigerian (63)	63	0.12
Somalian (176)	176	0.34
South African (13)	13	0.02
Other Sub-Saharan African (17)	50	0.10
Albanian (105)	105	0.20
American (1,549)	1,549	2.95
Arab (85)	219	0.42
Arab (31)	63	0.12
Egyptian (44)	44	0.08
Jordanian (0)	36	0.07
Lebanese (0)	30	0.06
Palestinian (10)	10	0.02
Other Arab (0)	36	0.07
Armenian (61)	110	0.21
Australian (62)	62	0.12
Austrian (97)	230	0.44
Basque (0)	55	0.10
Belgian (18)	128	0.24
Brazilian (0)	71	0.14
British (118)	394	0.75
Bulgarian (38)	38	0.07
Canadian (66)	146	0.28
Celtic (9)	22	0.04
Croatian (33)	77	0.15
Czech (112)	466	0.89
Czechoslovakian (0)	25	0.05
Danish (62)	452	0.86
Dutch (203)	1,000	1.90
Eastern European (86)	98	0.19
English (1,622)	7,227	13.76
European (1,107)	1,257	2.39
Finnish (60)	385	0.73
French, ex. Basque (258)	1,762	3.35
French Canadian (180)	580	1.10
German (2,057)	8,471	16.13
German Russian (10)	10	0.02
Greek (446)	774	1.47
Hungarian (78)	193	0.37
Icelander (32)	40	0.08
Iranian (146)	146	0.28
Irish (1,315)	6,386	12.16
Israeli (13)	13	0.02
Italian (465)	1,416	2.70
Latvian (51)	104	0.20
Lithuanian (19)	116	0.22
Luxemburger (0)	188	0.36
Northern European (305)	435	0.83
Norwegian (1,148)	3,651	6.95
Pennsylvania German (22)	38	0.07
Polish (182)	737	1.40
Portuguese (90)	170	0.32
Romanian (40)	50	0.10
Russian (323)	506	0.96
Scandinavian (214)	452	0.86
Scotch-Irish (378)	1,144	2.18
Scottish (438)	1,757	3.34
Slavic (76)	104	0.20
Slovak (59)	92	0.18
Slovene (16)	16	0.03
Swedish (556)	2,616	4.98
Swiss (10)	227	0.43
Turkish (0)	13	0.02
Ukrainian (192)	337	0.64
Welsh (114)	680	1.29
West Indian, ex. Hispanic (18)	18	0.03
Bermudan (18)	18	0.03
Yugoslavian (161)	186	0.35

Hispanic Origin	Population	%
Hispanic or Latino (of any race)	3,493	6.59
Central American, ex. Mexican	372	0.70
Costa Rican	13	0.02
Guatemalan	58	0.11
Honduran	48	0.09
Nicaraguan	31	0.06
Panamanian	21	0.04
Salvadoran	196	0.37
Other Central American	5	0.01
Cuban	72	0.14
Dominican Republic	4	0.01
Mexican	2,124	4.01
Puerto Rican	166	0.31
South American	345	0.65
Argentinean	32	0.06
Bolivian	9	0.02
Chilean	68	0.13
Colombian	33	0.06
Ecuadorian	34	0.06
Peruvian	152	0.29
Uruguayan	2	<0.01
Venezuelan	14	0.03
Other South American	1	<0.01
Other Hispanic or Latino	410	0.77

Race*	Population	%
African-American/Black (2,652)	3,324	6.27
Not Hispanic (2,579)	3,163	5.97
Hispanic (73)	161	0.30
American Indian/Alaska Native (442)	1,147	2.16
Not Hispanic (376)	993	1.87
Hispanic (66)	154	0.29
Alaska Athabascan *(Ala. Nat.)* (1)	3	0.01
Aleut *(Alaska Native)* (20)	45	0.08
Apache (2)	11	0.02
Arapaho (0)	1	<0.01
Blackfeet (14)	44	0.08
Canadian/French Am. Ind. (2)	15	0.03
Central American Ind. (0)	2	<0.01
Cherokee (20)	131	0.25
Cheyenne (4)	10	0.02
Chickasaw (0)	6	0.01
Chippewa (18)	47	0.09
Choctaw (3)	28	0.05
Colville (8)	9	0.02
Comanche (4)	13	0.02
Cree (2)	5	0.01
Creek (0)	6	0.01
Crow (1)	2	<0.01
Delaware (0)	2	<0.01
Hopi (2)	3	0.01
Inupiat *(Alaska Native)* (3)	13	0.02
Iroquois (2)	13	0.02
Kiowa (1)	1	<0.01
Lumbee (1)	2	<0.01
Mexican American Ind. (9)	18	0.03
Navajo (12)	14	0.03
Osage (4)	7	0.01
Ottawa (3)	3	0.01
Paiute (0)	1	<0.01
Pima (1)	1	<0.01
Potawatomi (2)	4	0.01
Pueblo (9)	11	0.02
Puget Sound Salish (13)	29	0.05
Seminole (1)	6	0.01
Shoshone (0)	6	0.01
Sioux (19)	53	0.10
South American Ind. (6)	8	0.02
Spanish American Ind. (7)	7	0.01
Tlingit-Haida *(Alaska Native)* (44)	74	0.14
Tohono O'Odham (1)	1	<0.01
Tsimshian *(Alaska Native)* (19)	22	0.04
Ute (0)	2	<0.01
Yakama (2)	10	0.02
Yup'ik *(Alaska Native)* (4)	8	0.02
Asian (8,051)	9,418	17.77
Not Hispanic (7,995)	9,276	17.50
Hispanic (56)	142	0.27
Bhutanese (5)	5	0.01
Burmese (23)	25	0.05
Cambodian (114)	136	0.26
Chinese, ex. Taiwanese (2,023)	2,440	4.60
Filipino (1,791)	2,267	4.28
Hmong (14)	14	0.03
Indian (455)	555	1.05
Indonesian (70)	88	0.17

*Notes: † The Census 2010 population figure is used to calculate the percentages in the Hispanic Origin and Race categories. Ancestry percentages are based on the 2006-2010 American Community Survey population (not shown); ‡ Numbers in parentheses indicate the number of people reporting a single ancestry; * Numbers in parentheses indicate the number of persons reporting this race alone, not in combination with any other race; Please refer to the Explanation of Data for more information.*

Race (continued)	Population	%
Japanese (527)	976	1.84
Korean (1,232)	1,377	2.60
Laotian (42)	65	0.12
Malaysian (11)	18	0.03
Nepalese (48)	52	0.10
Pakistani (122)	134	0.25
Sri Lankan (7)	11	0.02
Taiwanese (190)	216	0.41
Thai (137)	190	0.36
Vietnamese (828)	980	1.85
Hawaii Native/Pacific Islander (172)	424	0.80
Not Hispanic (171)	402	0.76
Hispanic (1)	22	0.04
Fijian (45)	63	0.12
Guamanian/Chamorro (19)	45	0.08
Marshallese (1)	2	<0.01
Native Hawaiian (34)	178	0.34
Samoan (30)	51	0.10
Tongan (2)	3	0.01
White (37,849)	40,215	75.87
Not Hispanic (36,014)	38,035	71.75
Hispanic (1,835)	2,180	4.11

Silver Firs

Place Type: CDP
County: Snohomish
Population: 20,891†

Ancestry‡	Population	%
African, Sub-Saharan (11)	11	0.05
Ethiopian (11)	11	0.05
American (769)	769	3.54
Arab (86)	127	0.59
Arab (8)	8	0.04
Egyptian (8)	16	0.07
Lebanese (39)	39	0.18
Palestinian (8)	16	0.07
Syrian (0)	25	0.12
Other Arab (23)	23	0.11
Australian (0)	17	0.08
Austrian (26)	144	0.66
Belgian (13)	27	0.12
Brazilian (15)	15	0.07
British (149)	184	0.85
Bulgarian (38)	38	0.18
Canadian (61)	207	0.95
Croatian (0)	16	0.07
Czech (33)	198	0.91
Czechoslovakian (14)	14	0.06
Danish (135)	370	1.70
Dutch (81)	661	3.05
English (634)	2,919	13.45
European (423)	451	2.08
Finnish (27)	152	0.70
French, ex. Basque (52)	857	3.95
French Canadian (63)	151	0.70
German (943)	4,337	19.98
Greek (0)	51	0.23
Hungarian (16)	164	0.76
Icelander (24)	46	0.21
Iranian (177)	177	0.82
Irish (474)	2,548	11.74
Italian (182)	609	2.81
Latvian (0)	37	0.17
Lithuanian (0)	118	0.54
Northern European (15)	15	0.07
Norwegian (543)	1,676	7.72
Pennsylvania German (23)	23	0.11
Polish (181)	428	1.97
Portuguese (35)	66	0.30
Romanian (12)	37	0.17
Russian (207)	303	1.40
Scandinavian (73)	143	0.66
Scotch-Irish (304)	570	2.63
Scottish (146)	897	4.13
Serbian (0)	13	0.06
Slovak (0)	46	0.21
Slovene (0)	9	0.04
Swedish (169)	971	4.47
Swiss (12)	75	0.35
Ukrainian (327)	411	1.89
Welsh (25)	308	1.42
West Indian, ex. Hispanic (35)	54	0.25
Barbadian (19)	38	0.18
West Indian (16)	16	0.07

Hispanic Origin	Population	%
Hispanic or Latino (of any race)	1,285	6.15
Central American, ex. Mexican	107	0.51
Costa Rican	24	0.11
Guatemalan	26	0.12
Honduran	4	0.02
Nicaraguan	24	0.11
Panamanian	14	0.07
Salvadoran	14	0.07
Other Central American	1	<0.01
Cuban	22	0.11
Dominican Republic	6	0.03
Mexican	813	3.89
Puerto Rican	50	0.24
South American	127	0.61
Argentinean	10	0.05
Bolivian	8	0.04
Chilean	1	<0.01
Colombian	39	0.19
Ecuadorian	9	0.04
Peruvian	37	0.18
Venezuelan	18	0.09
Other South American	5	0.02
Other Hispanic or Latino	160	0.77

Race*	Population	%
African-American/Black (349)	563	2.69
Not Hispanic (329)	529	2.53
Hispanic (20)	34	0.16
American Indian/Alaska Native (105)	240	1.15
Not Hispanic (87)	205	0.98
Hispanic (18)	35	0.17
Alaska Athabascan *(Ala. Nat.)* (1)	4	0.02
Aleut *(Alaska Native)* (11)	11	0.05
Apache (0)	1	<0.01
Blackfeet (5)	15	0.07
Canadian/French Am. Ind. (0)	2	0.01
Cherokee (2)	27	0.13
Chickasaw (0)	5	0.02
Chippewa (3)	7	0.03
Choctaw (2)	9	0.04
Colville (2)	5	0.02
Creek (1)	1	<0.01
Crow (0)	1	<0.01
Delaware (0)	4	0.02
Hopi (1)	1	<0.01
Kiowa (0)	1	<0.01
Lumbee (0)	3	0.01
Navajo (1)	2	0.01
Osage (0)	4	0.02
Potawatomi (2)	2	0.01
Puget Sound Salish (17)	17	0.08
Seminole (1)	1	<0.01
Sioux (2)	9	0.04
South American Ind. (0)	1	<0.01
Tlingit-Haida *(Alaska Native)* (9)	15	0.07
Tsimshian *(Alaska Native)* (1)	1	<0.01
Yakama (1)	1	<0.01
Asian (2,803)	3,432	16.43
Not Hispanic (2,780)	3,358	16.07
Hispanic (23)	74	0.35
Bangladeshi (10)	11	0.05
Burmese (6)	7	0.03
Cambodian (166)	186	0.89
Chinese, ex. Taiwanese (351)	500	2.39
Filipino (589)	812	3.89
Hmong (1)	1	<0.01
Indian (359)	392	1.88
Indonesian (26)	48	0.23
Japanese (108)	294	1.41
Korean (489)	576	2.76
Laotian (51)	56	0.27
Malaysian (13)	15	0.07
Pakistani (50)	56	0.27
Sri Lankan (9)	9	0.04
Taiwanese (11)	20	0.10
Thai (22)	39	0.19
Vietnamese (388)	469	2.24
Hawaii Native/Pacific Islander (41)	136	0.65
Not Hispanic (38)	126	0.60
Hispanic (3)	10	0.05
Fijian (8)	9	0.04
Guamanian/Chamorro (6)	16	0.08
Native Hawaiian (17)	56	0.27
Samoan (3)	13	0.06
Tongan (1)	1	<0.01
White (16,214)	17,120	81.95
Not Hispanic (15,449)	16,237	77.72
Hispanic (765)	883	4.23

Silverdale

Place Type: CDP
County: Kitsap
Population: 19,204†

Ancestry‡	Population	%
African, Sub-Saharan (147)	169	0.90
African (113)	113	0.60
Kenyan (34)	34	0.18
South African (0)	22	0.12
American (614)	614	3.26
Arab (0)	9	0.05
Lebanese (0)	9	0.05
Australian (0)	8	0.04
Austrian (7)	30	0.16
Belgian (0)	13	0.07
British (34)	130	0.69
Croatian (51)	98	0.52
Czech (70)	131	0.70
Danish (63)	165	0.88
Dutch (132)	669	3.55
Eastern European (0)	17	0.09
English (574)	2,475	13.14
European (594)	594	3.15
Finnish (39)	147	0.78
French, ex. Basque (97)	1,077	5.72
French Canadian (71)	248	1.32
German (891)	3,848	20.43
Greek (26)	66	0.35
Hungarian (34)	51	0.27
Icelander (13)	13	0.07
Irish (570)	2,901	15.40
Italian (243)	712	3.78
Northern European (7)	7	0.04
Norwegian (495)	1,262	6.70
Polish (161)	565	3.00
Portuguese (45)	65	0.35
Romanian (0)	9	0.05
Russian (67)	167	0.89
Scandinavian (60)	81	0.43
Scotch-Irish (145)	376	2.00
Scottish (111)	482	2.56
Serbian (40)	126	0.67
Slavic (13)	13	0.07
Swedish (86)	613	3.25
Swiss (0)	21	0.11
Ukrainian (12)	22	0.12
Welsh (62)	182	0.97
West Indian, ex. Hispanic (25)	84	0.45
Jamaican (25)	25	0.13
Trinidadian/Tobagonian (0)	59	0.31
Yugoslavian (0)	19	0.10

Hispanic Origin	Population	%
Hispanic or Latino (of any race)	1,204	6.27
Central American, ex. Mexican	70	0.36
Costa Rican	3	0.02
Guatemalan	19	0.10
Honduran	9	0.05
Nicaraguan	11	0.06
Panamanian	10	0.05
Salvadoran	15	0.08

*Notes: † The Census 2010 population figure is used to calculate the percentages in the Hispanic Origin and Race categories. Ancestry percentages are based on the 2006-2010 American Community Survey population (not shown); ‡ Numbers in parentheses indicate the number of people reporting a single ancestry; * Numbers in parentheses indicate the number of persons reporting this race alone, not in combination with any other race; Please refer to the Explanation of Data for more information.*

Other Central American	3	0.02
Cuban	26	0.14
Dominican Republic	11	0.06
Mexican	717	3.73
Puerto Rican	136	0.71
South American	56	0.29
Argentinean	6	0.03
Bolivian	2	0.01
Chilean	7	0.04
Colombian	19	0.10
Ecuadorian	9	0.05
Peruvian	9	0.05
Venezuelan	4	0.02
Other Hispanic or Latino	188	0.98

Race*	Population	%
African-American/Black (623)	893	4.65
Not Hispanic (601)	833	4.34
Hispanic (22)	60	0.31
American Indian/Alaska Native (185)	509	2.65
Not Hispanic (160)	441	2.30
Hispanic (25)	68	0.35
Alaska Athabascan *(Ala. Nat.)* (0)	2	0.01
Aleut *(Alaska Native)* (3)	4	0.02
Apache (3)	8	0.04
Blackfeet (1)	13	0.07
Canadian/French Am. Ind. (1)	2	0.01
Cherokee (18)	76	0.40
Chickasaw (2)	4	0.02
Chippewa (2)	5	0.03
Choctaw (1)	9	0.05
Colville (7)	12	0.06
Comanche (2)	6	0.03
Cree (1)	4	0.02
Creek (4)	9	0.05
Crow (0)	1	0.01
Delaware (1)	1	0.01
Inupiat *(Alaska Native)* (2)	3	0.02
Iroquois (0)	6	0.03
Kiowa (2)	2	0.01
Lumbee (0)	4	0.02
Menominee (0)	1	0.01
Mexican American Ind. (7)	11	0.06
Navajo (8)	14	0.07
Osage (0)	5	0.03
Pima (1)	3	0.02
Potawatomi (1)	1	0.01
Pueblo (1)	1	0.01
Puget Sound Salish (19)	26	0.14
Seminole (0)	2	0.01
Sioux (13)	24	0.12
South American Ind. (0)	2	0.01
Tlingit-Haida *(Alaska Native)* (8)	9	0.05
Tohono O'Odham (0)	1	0.01
Tsimshian *(Alaska Native)* (0)	5	0.03
Ute (1)	1	0.01
Yakama (1)	1	0.01
Asian (2,109)	2,836	14.77
Not Hispanic (2,067)	2,728	14.21
Hispanic (42)	108	0.56
Cambodian (0)	4	0.02
Chinese, ex. Taiwanese (132)	228	1.19
Filipino (1,493)	1,948	10.14
Hmong (1)	3	0.02
Indian (34)	46	0.24
Indonesian (2)	8	0.04
Japanese (141)	316	1.65
Korean (143)	198	1.03
Laotian (6)	6	0.03
Malaysian (0)	5	0.03
Taiwanese (6)	12	0.06
Thai (16)	34	0.18
Vietnamese (73)	107	0.56
Hawaii Native/Pacific Islander (178)	378	1.97
Not Hispanic (164)	330	1.72
Hispanic (14)	48	0.25
Fijian (2)	2	0.01
Guamanian/Chamorro (80)	140	0.73
Marshallese (4)	6	0.03
Native Hawaiian (41)	141	0.73
Samoan (30)	56	0.29
Tongan (0)	1	0.01
White (14,554)	15,705	81.78
Not Hispanic (13,893)	14,880	77.48
Hispanic (661)	825	4.30

Snohomish

Place Type: City
County: Snohomish
Population: 9,098†

Ancestry‡	Population	%
American (536)	536	5.92
Austrian (12)	12	0.13
Brazilian (2)	2	0.02
British (138)	175	1.93
Canadian (0)	18	0.20
Czech (0)	24	0.27
Danish (90)	237	2.62
Dutch (135)	297	3.28
Eastern European (0)	12	0.13
English (404)	1,383	15.29
European (17)	38	0.42
Finnish (12)	56	0.62
French, ex. Basque (69)	316	3.49
French Canadian (64)	142	1.57
German (425)	1,843	20.37
Greek (108)	118	1.30
Hungarian (0)	26	0.29
Irish (157)	1,164	12.87
Italian (50)	213	2.35
Luxemburger (0)	12	0.13
Norwegian (156)	644	7.12
Polish (0)	77	0.85
Portuguese (0)	35	0.39
Russian (0)	24	0.27
Scandinavian (61)	190	2.10
Scotch-Irish (74)	209	2.31
Scottish (78)	310	3.43
Serbian (0)	12	0.13
Swedish (80)	368	4.07
Swiss (30)	165	1.82
Ukrainian (13)	74	0.82
Welsh (10)	112	1.24

Hispanic Origin	Population	%
Hispanic or Latino (of any race)	724	7.96
Central American, ex. Mexican	2	0.02
Costa Rican	1	0.01
Guatemalan	1	0.01
Cuban	3	0.03
Mexican	570	6.27
Puerto Rican	31	0.34
South American	18	0.20
Argentinean	2	0.02
Bolivian	4	0.04
Chilean	4	0.04
Colombian	2	0.02
Ecuadorian	4	0.04
Peruvian	1	0.01
Venezuelan	1	0.01
Other Hispanic or Latino	100	1.10

Race*	Population	%
African-American/Black (44)	104	1.14
Not Hispanic (40)	90	0.99
Hispanic (4)	14	0.15
American Indian/Alaska Native (102)	230	2.53
Not Hispanic (83)	188	2.07
Hispanic (19)	42	0.46
Alaska Athabascan *(Ala. Nat.)* (2)	2	0.02
Aleut *(Alaska Native)* (7)	13	0.14
Apache (2)	4	0.04
Blackfeet (0)	10	0.11
Canadian/French Am. Ind. (1)	4	0.04
Cherokee (3)	19	0.21
Cheyenne (0)	1	0.01
Chippewa (3)	4	0.04
Choctaw (3)	5	0.05
Colville (1)	1	0.01
Cree (0)	2	0.02
Creek (0)	2	0.02
Hopi (0)	1	0.01
Inupiat *(Alaska Native)* (3)	3	0.03
Iroquois (0)	3	0.03
Lumbee (0)	4	0.04
Mexican American Ind. (1)	2	0.02
Navajo (1)	2	0.02
Paiute (1)	1	0.01
Potawatomi (0)	1	0.01
Puget Sound Salish (13)	22	0.24
Shoshone (4)	4	0.04
Sioux (2)	6	0.07
South American Ind. (0)	3	0.03
Tlingit-Haida *(Alaska Native)* (1)	3	0.03
Asian (195)	296	3.25
Not Hispanic (193)	279	3.07
Hispanic (2)	17	0.19
Burmese (3)	3	0.03
Cambodian (5)	5	0.05
Chinese, ex. Taiwanese (29)	49	0.54
Filipino (61)	106	1.17
Hmong (24)	25	0.27
Indian (19)	24	0.26
Indonesian (1)	1	0.01
Japanese (17)	41	0.45
Korean (10)	16	0.18
Laotian (3)	9	0.10
Taiwanese (0)	1	0.01
Thai (2)	9	0.10
Vietnamese (15)	20	0.22
Hawaii Native/Pacific Islander (23)	56	0.62
Not Hispanic (16)	44	0.48
Hispanic (7)	12	0.13
Guamanian/Chamorro (10)	16	0.18
Native Hawaiian (9)	27	0.30
Samoan (3)	7	0.08
White (8,093)	8,395	92.27
Not Hispanic (7,770)	8,007	88.01
Hispanic (323)	388	4.26

Snoqualmie

Place Type: City
County: King
Population: 10,670†

Ancestry‡	Population	%
American (262)	262	2.89
Arab (7)	100	1.10
Lebanese (7)	73	0.81
Syrian (0)	12	0.13
Other Arab (0)	15	0.17
Australian (33)	33	0.36
Austrian (9)	21	0.23
Belgian (0)	8	0.09
British (36)	90	0.99
Canadian (29)	43	0.47
Croatian (0)	12	0.13
Czech (16)	50	0.55
Danish (13)	211	2.33
Dutch (62)	180	1.99
Eastern European (14)	14	0.15
English (91)	676	7.46
European (211)	290	3.20
Finnish (0)	75	0.83
French, ex. Basque (164)	381	4.21
French Canadian (29)	105	1.16
German (389)	2,054	22.68
Greek (0)	25	0.28
Hungarian (0)	19	0.21
Iranian (9)	9	0.10
Irish (218)	1,324	14.62
Israeli (19)	19	0.21
Italian (109)	640	7.07
Lithuanian (0)	35	0.39
Northern European (85)	85	0.94
Norwegian (140)	659	7.28
Polish (99)	461	5.09

*Notes: † The Census 2010 population figure is used to calculate the percentages in the Hispanic Origin and Race categories. Ancestry percentages are based on the 2006-2010 American Community Survey population (not shown); ‡ Numbers in parentheses indicate the number of people reporting a single ancestry; * Numbers in parentheses indicate the number of persons reporting this race alone, not in combination with any other race; Please refer to the Explanation of Data for more information.*

Portuguese (11)	11	0.12
Romanian (31)	45	0.50
Russian (0)	10	0.11
Scandinavian (50)	81	0.89
Scotch-Irish (31)	195	2.15
Scottish (201)	446	4.92
Serbian (0)	22	0.24
Slovak (39)	61	0.67
Swedish (123)	538	5.94
Swiss (36)	121	1.34
Ukrainian (21)	55	0.61
Welsh (104)	229	2.53
West Indian, ex. Hispanic (39)	39	0.43
Trinidadian/Tobagonian (39)	39	0.43
Yugoslavian (0)	7	0.08

Hispanic Origin	Population	%
Hispanic or Latino (of any race)	566	5.30
Central American, ex. Mexican	35	0.33
Costa Rican	4	0.04
Guatemalan	14	0.13
Honduran	4	0.04
Panamanian	4	0.04
Salvadoran	9	0.08
Cuban	25	0.23
Dominican Republic	4	0.04
Mexican	336	3.15
Puerto Rican	35	0.33
South American	60	0.56
Argentinean	5	0.05
Bolivian	1	0.01
Chilean	8	0.07
Colombian	26	0.24
Ecuadorian	4	0.04
Peruvian	5	0.05
Venezuelan	9	0.08
Other South American	2	0.02
Other Hispanic or Latino	71	0.67

Race*	Population	%
African-American/Black (81)	174	1.63
Not Hispanic (80)	158	1.48
Hispanic (1)	16	0.15
American Indian/Alaska Native (92)	183	1.72
Not Hispanic (85)	168	1.57
Hispanic (7)	15	0.14
Aleut *(Alaska Native)* (4)	8	0.07
Apache (2)	2	0.02
Blackfeet (0)	3	0.03
Cherokee (5)	23	0.22
Chickasaw (0)	2	0.02
Chippewa (1)	1	0.01
Choctaw (2)	8	0.07
Colville (3)	4	0.04
Creek (0)	1	0.01
Iroquois (1)	2	0.02
Mexican American Ind. (1)	1	0.01
Navajo (1)	1	0.01
Osage (2)	3	0.03
Ottawa (0)	1	0.01
Potawatomi (0)	1	0.01
Puget Sound Salish (15)	20	0.19
Sioux (1)	4	0.04
Tlingit-Haida *(Alaska Native)* (1)	2	0.02
Tsimshian *(Alaska Native)* (0)	1	0.01
Yakama (1)	2	0.02
Yup'ik *(Alaska Native)* (2)	2	0.02
Asian (987)	1,241	11.63
Not Hispanic (971)	1,211	11.35
Hispanic (16)	30	0.28
Bangladeshi (4)	8	0.07
Cambodian (2)	4	0.04
Chinese, ex. Taiwanese (186)	243	2.28
Filipino (119)	213	2.00
Hmong (20)	20	0.19
Indian (360)	374	3.51
Indonesian (6)	8	0.07
Japanese (52)	117	1.10
Korean (96)	128	1.20
Laotian (3)	4	0.04
Malaysian (2)	3	0.03
Pakistani (49)	49	0.46
Taiwanese (11)	13	0.12
Thai (11)	21	0.20
Vietnamese (30)	52	0.49
Hawaii Native/Pacific Islander (8)	35	0.33
Not Hispanic (8)	34	0.32
Hispanic (0)	1	0.01
Fijian (1)	1	0.01
Guamanian/Chamorro (1)	9	0.08
Native Hawaiian (1)	13	0.12
Samoan (0)	5	0.05
White (8,887)	9,329	87.43
Not Hispanic (8,535)	8,924	83.64
Hispanic (352)	405	3.80

South Hill

Place Type: CDP
County: Pierce
Population: 52,431†

Ancestry‡	Population	%
African, Sub-Saharan (96)	130	0.25
African (96)	130	0.25
American (1,880)	1,880	3.58
Arab (268)	482	0.92
Arab (0)	14	0.03
Egyptian (52)	52	0.10
Lebanese (0)	135	0.26
Syrian (216)	257	0.49
Other Arab (0)	24	0.05
Australian (7)	7	0.01
Austrian (19)	176	0.34
Belgian (10)	66	0.13
British (45)	162	0.31
Bulgarian (0)	68	0.13
Canadian (85)	134	0.26
Celtic (12)	12	0.02
Croatian (45)	89	0.17
Czech (107)	220	0.42
Czechoslovakian (68)	130	0.25
Danish (145)	738	1.41
Dutch (210)	1,182	2.25
Eastern European (36)	36	0.07
English (1,635)	6,343	12.09
European (1,152)	1,304	2.48
Finnish (95)	304	0.58
French, ex. Basque (329)	2,084	3.97
French Canadian (137)	418	0.80
German (3,346)	12,093	23.04
German Russian (15)	15	0.03
Greek (23)	80	0.15
Hungarian (42)	121	0.23
Icelander (15)	15	0.03
Irish (1,323)	7,361	14.03
Israeli (0)	79	0.15
Italian (696)	2,547	4.85
Latvian (37)	37	0.07
Lithuanian (36)	36	0.07
New Zealander (0)	16	0.03
Northern European (29)	29	0.06
Norwegian (1,242)	3,747	7.14
Pennsylvania German (10)	24	0.05
Polish (375)	1,478	2.82
Portuguese (23)	150	0.29
Romanian (11)	21	0.04
Russian (52)	493	0.94
Scandinavian (78)	218	0.42
Scotch-Irish (294)	882	1.68
Scottish (451)	1,657	3.16
Slavic (0)	15	0.03
Slovak (0)	34	0.06
Slovene (11)	11	0.02
Swedish (286)	2,013	3.84
Swiss (156)	331	0.63
Ukrainian (100)	253	0.48
Welsh (25)	352	0.67
West Indian, ex. Hispanic (27)	32	0.06
Jamaican (27)	32	0.06
Yugoslavian (0)	115	0.22

Hispanic Origin	Population	%
Hispanic or Latino (of any race)	4,442	8.47
Central American, ex. Mexican	199	0.38
Costa Rican	17	0.03
Guatemalan	40	0.08
Honduran	17	0.03
Nicaraguan	13	0.02
Panamanian	55	0.10
Salvadoran	57	0.11
Cuban	67	0.13
Dominican Republic	30	0.06
Mexican	3,002	5.73
Puerto Rican	429	0.82
South American	181	0.35
Argentinean	14	0.03
Bolivian	6	0.01
Chilean	19	0.04
Colombian	46	0.09
Ecuadorian	27	0.05
Peruvian	48	0.09
Uruguayan	4	0.01
Venezuelan	16	0.03
Other South American	1	<0.01
Other Hispanic or Latino	534	1.02

Race*	Population	%
African-American/Black (2,269)	3,302	6.30
Not Hispanic (2,161)	3,073	5.86
Hispanic (108)	229	0.44
American Indian/Alaska Native (516)	1,300	2.48
Not Hispanic (434)	1,080	2.06
Hispanic (82)	220	0.42
Alaska Athabascan *(Ala. Nat.)* (3)	3	0.01
Aleut *(Alaska Native)* (14)	29	0.06
Apache (6)	24	0.05
Arapaho (1)	1	<0.01
Blackfeet (10)	30	0.06
Canadian/French Am. Ind. (2)	16	0.03
Central American Ind. (1)	1	<0.01
Cherokee (37)	204	0.39
Cheyenne (5)	7	0.01
Chickasaw (3)	8	0.02
Chippewa (20)	48	0.09
Choctaw (9)	49	0.09
Colville (3)	6	0.01
Comanche (0)	1	<0.01
Cree (1)	1	<0.01
Creek (0)	2	<0.01
Crow (3)	3	0.01
Delaware (2)	5	0.01
Inupiat *(Alaska Native)* (6)	8	0.02
Iroquois (0)	6	0.01
Lumbee (4)	5	0.01
Menominee (3)	3	0.01
Mexican American Ind. (10)	23	0.04
Navajo (9)	20	0.04
Osage (1)	6	0.01
Ottawa (2)	3	0.01
Paiute (4)	4	0.01
Pima (3)	4	0.01
Potawatomi (7)	8	0.02
Pueblo (2)	7	0.01
Puget Sound Salish (101)	152	0.29
Seminole (0)	4	0.01
Shoshone (0)	4	0.01
Sioux (28)	53	0.10
South American Ind. (1)	2	<0.01
Spanish American Ind. (0)	1	<0.01
Tlingit-Haida *(Alaska Native)* (14)	39	0.07
Tsimshian *(Alaska Native)* (0)	1	<0.01
Yakama (5)	8	0.02
Yaqui (2)	2	<0.01
Yup'ik *(Alaska Native)* (2)	2	<0.01
Asian (3,120)	4,728	9.02
Not Hispanic (3,046)	4,486	8.56
Hispanic (74)	242	0.46
Bangladeshi (6)	6	0.01
Burmese (3)	3	0.01

*Notes: † The Census 2010 population figure is used to calculate the percentages in the Hispanic Origin and Race categories. Ancestry percentages are based on the 2006-2010 American Community Survey population (not shown); ‡ Numbers in parentheses indicate the number of people reporting a single ancestry; * Numbers in parentheses indicate the number of persons reporting this race alone, not in combination with any other race; Please refer to the Explanation of Data for more information.*

Cambodian (177)	219	0.42
Chinese, ex. Taiwanese (228)	425	0.81
Filipino (769)	1,406	2.68
Hmong (1)	2	<0.01
Indian (389)	445	0.85
Indonesian (10)	12	0.02
Japanese (213)	641	1.22
Korean (812)	1,205	2.30
Laotian (38)	69	0.13
Pakistani (5)	9	0.02
Sri Lankan (1)	4	0.01
Taiwanese (27)	43	0.08
Thai (46)	100	0.19
Vietnamese (223)	285	0.54
Hawaii Native/Pacific Islander (552)	956	1.82
Not Hispanic (539)	883	1.68
Hispanic (13)	73	0.14
Fijian (10)	15	0.03
Guamanian/Chamorro (176)	293	0.56
Marshallese (8)	11	0.02
Native Hawaiian (67)	261	0.50
Samoan (216)	322	0.61
Tongan (15)	22	0.04
White (40,980)	43,947	83.82
Not Hispanic (38,895)	41,400	78.96
Hispanic (2,085)	2,547	4.86

Spanaway

Place Type: CDP
County: Pierce
Population: 27,227†

Ancestry‡	Population	%
African, Sub-Saharan (69)	69	0.25
African (51)	51	0.18
Ethiopian (18)	18	0.06
American (1,412)	1,412	5.03
Austrian (0)	33	0.12
British (16)	64	0.23
Bulgarian (14)	14	0.05
Canadian (18)	38	0.14
Celtic (31)	31	0.11
Croatian (0)	9	0.03
Czech (11)	133	0.47
Czechoslovakian (56)	56	0.20
Danish (7)	200	0.71
Dutch (29)	430	1.53
English (606)	2,937	10.47
European (167)	186	0.66
Finnish (15)	136	0.48
French, ex. Basque (98)	1,203	4.29
French Canadian (60)	174	0.62
German (1,453)	4,932	17.58
Greek (23)	40	0.14
Hungarian (0)	43	0.15
Icelander (0)	9	0.03
Iranian (20)	20	0.07
Irish (690)	3,967	14.14
Italian (270)	1,101	3.92
Latvian (0)	11	0.04
Lithuanian (0)	10	0.04
Maltese (29)	56	0.20
New Zealander (20)	20	0.07
Northern European (62)	62	0.22
Norwegian (346)	1,376	4.90
Polish (120)	600	2.14
Portuguese (15)	51	0.18
Romanian (23)	73	0.26
Russian (97)	294	1.05
Scandinavian (56)	74	0.26
Scotch-Irish (153)	446	1.59
Scottish (201)	564	2.01
Serbian (0)	33	0.12
Slavic (0)	10	0.04
Slovak (0)	10	0.04
Slovene (0)	9	0.03
Swedish (45)	452	1.61
Swiss (9)	72	0.26
Ukrainian (79)	144	0.51
Welsh (31)	240	0.86
West Indian, ex. Hispanic (37)	72	0.26
Haitian (0)	12	0.04
Jamaican (37)	60	0.21
Yugoslavian (9)	25	0.09

Hispanic Origin	Population	%
Hispanic or Latino (of any race)	2,899	10.65
Central American, ex. Mexican	126	0.46
Costa Rican	3	0.01
Guatemalan	23	0.08
Honduran	14	0.05
Nicaraguan	11	0.04
Panamanian	50	0.18
Salvadoran	24	0.09
Other Central American	1	<0.01
Cuban	33	0.12
Dominican Republic	21	0.08
Mexican	1,950	7.16
Puerto Rican	375	1.38
South American	83	0.30
Argentinean	17	0.06
Bolivian	2	0.01
Chilean	18	0.07
Colombian	21	0.08
Ecuadorian	7	0.03
Peruvian	12	0.04
Venezuelan	4	0.01
Other South American	2	0.01
Other Hispanic or Latino	311	1.14

Race*	Population	%
African-American/Black (2,927)	4,015	14.75
Not Hispanic (2,822)	3,792	13.93
Hispanic (105)	223	0.82
American Indian/Alaska Native (306)	869	3.19
Not Hispanic (266)	738	2.71
Hispanic (40)	131	0.48
Alaska Athabascan *(Ala. Nat.)* (6)	7	0.03
Aleut *(Alaska Native)* (7)	11	0.04
Apache (3)	13	0.05
Blackfeet (3)	26	0.10
Canadian/French Am. Ind. (1)	3	0.01
Cherokee (26)	138	0.51
Cheyenne (3)	3	0.01
Chickasaw (0)	3	0.01
Chippewa (20)	38	0.14
Choctaw (0)	26	0.10
Colville (2)	12	0.04
Comanche (1)	2	0.01
Cree (0)	7	0.03
Creek (3)	6	0.02
Delaware (1)	8	0.03
Houma (2)	2	0.01
Inupiat *(Alaska Native)* (0)	8	0.03
Iroquois (3)	15	0.06
Kiowa (0)	1	<0.01
Lumbee (1)	1	<0.01
Mexican American Ind. (7)	10	0.04
Navajo (1)	6	0.02
Osage (0)	6	0.02
Paiute (0)	1	<0.01
Potawatomi (2)	5	0.02
Puget Sound Salish (29)	54	0.20
Shoshone (3)	4	0.01
Sioux (10)	32	0.12
South American Ind. (1)	2	0.01
Spanish American Ind. (1)	2	0.01
Tlingit-Haida *(Alaska Native)* (13)	17	0.06
Tsimshian *(Alaska Native)* (0)	1	<0.01
Ute (0)	2	0.01
Yakama (1)	2	0.01
Yup'ik *(Alaska Native)* (1)	2	0.01
Asian (1,791)	2,861	10.51
Not Hispanic (1,736)	2,658	9.76
Hispanic (55)	203	0.75
Burmese (1)	1	<0.01
Cambodian (131)	147	0.54
Chinese, ex. Taiwanese (41)	164	0.60
Filipino (732)	1,213	4.46
Indian (24)	44	0.16
Indonesian (3)	6	0.02
Japanese (115)	369	1.36
Korean (486)	794	2.92
Laotian (8)	20	0.07
Malaysian (0)	1	<0.01
Sri Lankan (0)	2	0.01
Taiwanese (6)	11	0.04
Thai (49)	82	0.30
Vietnamese (106)	144	0.53
Hawaii Native/Pacific Islander (1,038)	1,418	5.21
Not Hispanic (1,016)	1,331	4.89
Hispanic (22)	87	0.32
Fijian (6)	6	0.02
Guamanian/Chamorro (574)	730	2.68
Marshallese (1)	2	0.01
Native Hawaiian (65)	230	0.84
Samoan (298)	382	1.40
Tongan (1)	9	0.03
White (17,351)	19,504	71.63
Not Hispanic (16,325)	18,107	66.50
Hispanic (1,026)	1,397	5.13

Spokane Valley

Place Type: City
County: Spokane
Population: 89,755†

Ancestry‡	Population	%
African, Sub-Saharan (190)	297	0.34
African (0)	89	0.10
Ethiopian (136)	154	0.17
Liberian (54)	54	0.06
American (4,202)	4,202	4.77
Arab (99)	375	0.43
Jordanian (22)	114	0.13
Lebanese (37)	82	0.09
Moroccan (17)	17	0.02
Palestinian (23)	115	0.13
Syrian (0)	47	0.05
Armenian (9)	28	0.03
Australian (10)	31	0.04
Austrian (27)	240	0.27
Basque (14)	140	0.16
Belgian (33)	100	0.11
Brazilian (0)	16	0.02
British (91)	436	0.49
Canadian (231)	362	0.41
Celtic (0)	2	<0.01
Croatian (98)	193	0.22
Czech (171)	495	0.56
Czechoslovakian (60)	97	0.11
Danish (321)	1,223	1.39
Dutch (421)	2,574	2.92
English (3,199)	11,506	13.06
European (1,620)	1,883	2.14
Finnish (91)	327	0.37
French, ex. Basque (732)	4,308	4.89
French Canadian (412)	930	1.06
German (7,408)	24,029	27.27
Greek (117)	242	0.27
Hungarian (36)	164	0.19
Icelander (0)	11	0.01
Iranian (40)	40	0.05
Irish (3,171)	13,266	15.06
Italian (1,414)	4,558	5.17
Lithuanian (13)	38	0.04
Luxemburger (0)	10	0.01
Northern European (91)	94	0.11
Norwegian (1,950)	6,078	6.90
Pennsylvania German (16)	73	0.08
Polish (329)	1,541	1.75
Portuguese (137)	261	0.30
Romanian (39)	48	0.05
Russian (1,193)	1,828	2.07
Scandinavian (174)	391	0.44
Scotch-Irish (714)	2,210	2.51
Scottish (842)	2,945	3.34
Slavic (0)	60	0.07

SECTION TWO

*Notes: † The Census 2010 population figure is used to calculate the percentages in the Hispanic Origin and Race categories. Ancestry percentages are based on the 2006-2010 American Community Survey population (not shown); ‡ Numbers in parentheses indicate the number of people reporting a single ancestry; * Numbers in parentheses indicate the number of persons reporting this race alone, not in combination with any other race; Please refer to the Explanation of Data for more information.*

Slovak (9)	9	0.01
Swedish (794)	3,481	3.95
Swiss (68)	386	0.44
Ukrainian (596)	770	0.87
Welsh (196)	843	0.96
West Indian, ex. Hispanic (0)	40	0.05
Jamaican (0)	40	0.05
Yugoslavian (49)	114	0.13

Hispanic Origin	Population	%
Hispanic or Latino (of any race)	4,130	4.60
Central American, ex. Mexican	133	0.15
Costa Rican	8	0.01
Guatemalan	54	0.06
Honduran	20	0.02
Nicaraguan	7	0.01
Panamanian	14	0.02
Salvadoran	30	0.03
Cuban	55	0.06
Dominican Republic	1	<0.01
Mexican	3,013	3.36
Puerto Rican	230	0.26
South American	100	0.11
Argentinean	13	0.01
Chilean	2	<0.01
Colombian	50	0.06
Ecuadorian	16	0.02
Peruvian	3	<0.01
Uruguayan	3	<0.01
Venezuelan	7	0.01
Other South American	6	0.01
Other Hispanic or Latino	598	0.67

Race*	Population	%
African-American/Black (1,031)	1,913	2.13
Not Hispanic (982)	1,786	1.99
Hispanic (49)	127	0.14
American Indian/Alaska Native (1,081)	2,217	2.47
Not Hispanic (952)	1,946	2.17
Hispanic (129)	271	0.30
Alaska Athabascan *(Ala. Nat.)* (9)	18	0.02
Aleut *(Alaska Native)* (10)	15	0.02
Apache (8)	23	0.03
Arapaho (2)	3	<0.01
Blackfeet (41)	114	0.13
Canadian/French Am. Ind. (8)	16	0.02
Cherokee (35)	202	0.23
Cheyenne (13)	20	0.02
Chickasaw (11)	20	0.02
Chippewa (99)	184	0.21
Choctaw (9)	34	0.04
Colville (101)	140	0.16
Comanche (3)	4	<0.01
Cree (2)	24	0.03
Creek (4)	13	0.01
Crow (2)	9	0.01
Inupiat *(Alaska Native)* (8)	13	0.01
Iroquois (6)	16	0.02
Kiowa (2)	2	<0.01
Lumbee (4)	6	0.01
Mexican American Ind. (12)	25	0.03
Navajo (7)	19	0.02
Osage (1)	2	<0.01
Ottawa (2)	2	<0.01
Paiute (1)	3	<0.01
Pima (1)	1	<0.01
Potawatomi (0)	5	0.01
Puget Sound Salish (35)	45	0.05
Seminole (0)	4	<0.01
Shoshone (2)	6	0.01
Sioux (62)	101	0.11
South American Ind. (2)	3	<0.01
Spanish American Ind. (3)	3	<0.01
Tlingit-Haida *(Alaska Native)* (13)	28	0.03
Tohono O'Odham (1)	1	<0.01
Tsimshian *(Alaska Native)* (2)	2	<0.01
Ute (0)	3	<0.01
Yakama (14)	19	0.02
Yaqui (1)	5	0.01
Yup'ik *(Alaska Native)* (5)	13	0.01
Asian (1,552)	2,371	2.64
Not Hispanic (1,528)	2,239	2.49
Hispanic (24)	132	0.15
Burmese (41)	43	0.05
Cambodian (13)	21	0.02
Chinese, ex. Taiwanese (186)	307	0.34
Filipino (219)	517	0.58
Hmong (103)	107	0.12
Indian (126)	160	0.18
Indonesian (5)	13	0.01
Japanese (156)	353	0.39
Korean (131)	234	0.26
Laotian (17)	29	0.03
Malaysian (2)	2	<0.01
Nepalese (6)	6	0.01
Pakistani (7)	12	0.01
Sri Lankan (2)	3	<0.01
Taiwanese (10)	17	0.02
Thai (36)	72	0.08
Vietnamese (420)	493	0.55
Hawaii Native/Pacific Islander (238)	390	0.43
Not Hispanic (230)	359	0.40
Hispanic (8)	31	0.03
Fijian (2)	5	0.01
Guamanian/Chamorro (59)	83	0.09
Marshallese (32)	32	0.04
Native Hawaiian (56)	130	0.14
Samoan (46)	64	0.07
White (81,614)	84,343	93.97
Not Hispanic (79,467)	81,716	91.04
Hispanic (2,147)	2,627	2.93

Spokane

Place Type: City
County: Spokane
Population: 208,916[†]

Ancestry[‡]	Population	%
Afghan (65)	65	0.03
African, Sub-Saharan (581)	797	0.39
African (407)	559	0.27
Cape Verdean (0)	19	0.01
Ethiopian (48)	48	0.02
Ghanaian (28)	28	0.01
Kenyan (19)	19	0.01
Liberian (13)	13	0.01
Nigerian (58)	83	0.04
Somalian (0)	9	<0.01
Ugandan (0)	11	0.01
Other Sub-Saharan African (8)	8	<0.01
American (8,496)	8,496	4.11
Arab (667)	1,085	0.53
Arab (209)	209	0.10
Egyptian (265)	327	0.16
Iraqi (0)	48	0.02
Lebanese (33)	126	0.06
Moroccan (56)	108	0.05
Syrian (52)	177	0.09
Other Arab (52)	90	0.04
Armenian (105)	136	0.07
Assyrian/Chaldean/Syriac (0)	48	0.02
Australian (128)	321	0.16
Austrian (181)	720	0.35
Basque (56)	136	0.07
Belgian (102)	254	0.12
Brazilian (93)	126	0.06
British (470)	1,092	0.53
Bulgarian (36)	152	0.07
Cajun (25)	64	0.03
Canadian (336)	730	0.35
Carpatho Rusyn (0)	15	0.01
Celtic (14)	93	0.05
Croatian (249)	455	0.22
Czech (323)	1,105	0.54
Czechoslovakian (127)	236	0.11
Danish (601)	2,307	1.12
Dutch (933)	4,231	2.05
Eastern European (160)	160	0.08
English (6,394)	26,107	12.64
Estonian (37)	76	0.04
European (3,640)	4,189	2.03
Finnish (354)	1,221	0.59
French, ex. Basque (1,489)	8,862	4.29
French Canadian (787)	2,559	1.24
German (15,104)	52,196	25.27
German Russian (0)	14	0.01
Greek (290)	924	0.45
Guyanese (0)	16	0.01
Hungarian (243)	776	0.38
Icelander (25)	64	0.03
Iranian (66)	100	0.05
Irish (7,840)	33,567	16.25
Italian (3,151)	10,336	5.00
Latvian (7)	68	0.03
Lithuanian (58)	244	0.12
Luxemburger (0)	28	0.01
New Zealander (14)	30	0.01
Northern European (459)	488	0.24
Norwegian (4,995)	14,582	7.06
Pennsylvania German (85)	101	0.05
Polish (1,181)	3,809	1.84
Portuguese (291)	723	0.35
Romanian (215)	375	0.18
Russian (1,560)	2,911	1.41
Scandinavian (717)	1,455	0.70
Scotch-Irish (1,968)	5,621	2.72
Scottish (2,476)	7,802	3.78
Serbian (24)	55	0.03
Slavic (35)	84	0.04
Slovak (55)	154	0.07
Slovene (8)	8	<0.01
Swedish (1,778)	7,476	3.62
Swiss (130)	1,057	0.51
Turkish (14)	30	0.01
Ukrainian (1,018)	1,433	0.69
Welsh (350)	2,279	1.10
West Indian, ex. Hispanic (56)	97	0.05
Bermudan (6)	6	<0.01
Dutch West Indian (9)	9	<0.01
Haitian (0)	41	0.02
Jamaican (26)	26	0.01
Trinidadian/Tobagonian (15)	15	0.01
Yugoslavian (338)	627	0.30

Hispanic Origin	Population	%
Hispanic or Latino (of any race)	10,467	5.01
Central American, ex. Mexican	464	0.22
Costa Rican	23	0.01
Guatemalan	119	0.06
Honduran	37	0.02
Nicaraguan	21	0.01
Panamanian	67	0.03
Salvadoran	196	0.09
Other Central American	1	<0.01
Cuban	333	0.16
Dominican Republic	34	0.02
Mexican	7,006	3.35
Puerto Rican	651	0.31
South American	348	0.17
Argentinean	54	0.03
Bolivian	14	0.01
Chilean	36	0.02
Colombian	116	0.06
Ecuadorian	33	0.02
Paraguayan	2	<0.01
Peruvian	50	0.02
Uruguayan	5	<0.01
Venezuelan	30	0.01
Other South American	8	<0.01
Other Hispanic or Latino	1,631	0.78

Race*	Population	%
African-American/Black (4,843)	8,109	3.88
Not Hispanic (4,643)	7,565	3.62
Hispanic (200)	544	0.26
American Indian/Alaska Native (4,149)	7,880	3.77
Not Hispanic (3,663)	6,894	3.30
Hispanic (486)	986	0.47
Alaska Athabascan *(Ala. Nat.)* (19)	31	0.01

*Notes: † The Census 2010 population figure is used to calculate the percentages in the Hispanic Origin and Race categories. Ancestry percentages are based on the 2006-2010 American Community Survey population (not shown); ‡ Numbers in parentheses indicate the number of people reporting a single ancestry; * Numbers in parentheses indicate the number of persons reporting this race alone, not in combination with any other race; Please refer to the Explanation of Data for more information.*

Aleut *(Alaska Native)* (25)	38	0.02
Apache (30)	91	0.04
Arapaho (6)	19	0.01
Blackfeet (223)	441	0.21
Canadian/French Am. Ind. (18)	49	0.02
Central American Ind. (2)	9	<0.01
Cherokee (157)	637	0.30
Cheyenne (36)	76	0.04
Chickasaw (3)	22	0.01
Chippewa (279)	523	0.25
Choctaw (55)	156	0.07
Colville (429)	599	0.29
Comanche (12)	20	0.01
Cree (24)	51	0.02
Creek (3)	27	0.01
Crow (16)	28	0.01
Delaware (5)	12	0.01
Hopi (1)	4	<0.01
Inupiat *(Alaska Native)* (18)	34	0.02
Iroquois (16)	49	0.02
Kiowa (5)	5	<0.01
Lumbee (9)	13	0.01
Menominee (1)	3	<0.01
Mexican American Ind. (39)	67	0.03
Navajo (45)	78	0.04
Osage (7)	27	0.01
Ottawa (6)	7	<0.01
Paiute (14)	30	0.01
Pima (1)	1	<0.01
Potawatomi (11)	25	0.01
Pueblo (9)	12	0.01
Puget Sound Salish (93)	136	0.07
Seminole (5)	18	0.01
Shoshone (9)	35	0.02
Sioux (150)	293	0.14
South American Ind. (0)	7	<0.01
Spanish American Ind. (4)	5	<0.01
Tlingit-Haida *(Alaska Native)* (52)	95	0.05
Tohono O'Odham (4)	9	<0.01
Tsimshian *(Alaska Native)* (5)	7	<0.01
Ute (5)	9	<0.01
Yakama (70)	91	0.04
Yaqui (14)	18	0.01
Yuman (2)	4	<0.01
Yup'ik *(Alaska Native)* (9)	28	0.01
Asian (5,358)	8,005	3.83
Not Hispanic (5,266)	7,682	3.68
Hispanic (92)	323	0.15
Bangladeshi (5)	5	<0.01
Bhutanese (173)	198	0.09
Burmese (336)	343	0.16
Cambodian (43)	60	0.03
Chinese, ex. Taiwanese (637)	991	0.47
Filipino (791)	1,610	0.77
Hmong (224)	238	0.11
Indian (337)	474	0.23
Indonesian (11)	38	0.02
Japanese (577)	1,308	0.63
Korean (546)	899	0.43
Laotian (105)	156	0.07
Malaysian (1)	6	<0.01
Nepalese (49)	75	0.04
Pakistani (36)	57	0.03
Sri Lankan (2)	6	<0.01
Taiwanese (46)	61	0.03
Thai (106)	206	0.10
Vietnamese (1,093)	1,228	0.59
Hawaii Native/Pacific Islander (1,210)	1,907	0.91
Not Hispanic (1,152)	1,744	0.83
Hispanic (58)	163	0.08
Fijian (2)	7	<0.01
Guamanian/Chamorro (184)	287	0.14
Marshallese (581)	606	0.29
Native Hawaiian (179)	524	0.25
Samoan (57)	117	0.06
Tongan (16)	29	0.01
White (181,039)	189,684	90.79
Not Hispanic (175,482)	182,799	87.50
Hispanic (5,557)	6,885	3.30

Summit

Place Type: CDP
County: Pierce
Population: 7,985†

Ancestry‡	Population	%
American (303)	303	3.82
Arab (11)	41	0.52
Lebanese (11)	41	0.52
Australian (0)	33	0.42
Belgian (10)	23	0.29
Bulgarian (20)	20	0.25
Canadian (46)	55	0.69
Czech (16)	23	0.29
Czechoslovakian (15)	67	0.84
Danish (0)	76	0.96
Dutch (58)	145	1.83
English (227)	1,168	14.73
European (253)	272	3.43
Finnish (40)	55	0.69
French, ex. Basque (45)	363	4.58
French Canadian (10)	45	0.57
German (421)	1,392	17.55
Greek (0)	9	0.11
Hungarian (0)	15	0.19
Irish (392)	1,169	14.74
Italian (84)	390	4.92
Lithuanian (0)	12	0.15
Norwegian (185)	617	7.78
Polish (55)	222	2.80
Portuguese (11)	11	0.14
Russian (0)	13	0.16
Scandinavian (36)	100	1.26
Scotch-Irish (0)	83	1.05
Scottish (93)	439	5.53
Slovak (37)	37	0.47
Swedish (104)	393	4.95
Swiss (29)	81	1.02
Welsh (0)	45	0.57
Yugoslavian (20)	59	0.74

Hispanic Origin	Population	%
Hispanic or Latino (of any race)	447	5.60
Central American, ex. Mexican	33	0.41
Costa Rican	1	0.01
Guatemalan	5	0.06
Honduran	7	0.09
Nicaraguan	5	0.06
Panamanian	9	0.11
Salvadoran	6	0.08
Cuban	2	0.03
Dominican Republic	1	0.01
Mexican	319	3.99
Puerto Rican	37	0.46
South American	9	0.11
Argentinean	1	0.01
Chilean	2	0.03
Colombian	6	0.08
Other Hispanic or Latino	46	0.58

Race*	Population	%
African-American/Black (222)	306	3.83
Not Hispanic (206)	281	3.52
Hispanic (16)	25	0.31
American Indian/Alaska Native (126)	261	3.27
Not Hispanic (113)	235	2.94
Hispanic (13)	26	0.33
Alaska Athabascan *(Ala. Nat.)* (4)	4	0.05
Apache (2)	2	0.03
Blackfeet (2)	12	0.15
Canadian/French Am. Ind. (1)	2	0.03
Cherokee (10)	34	0.43
Chippewa (4)	10	0.13
Choctaw (7)	8	0.10
Colville (2)	3	0.04
Creek (2)	2	0.03
Hopi (0)	1	0.01
Inupiat *(Alaska Native)* (0)	2	0.03
Iroquois (3)	4	0.05
Kiowa (1)	5	0.06
Mexican American Ind. (2)	2	0.03
Navajo (2)	2	0.03
Potawatomi (1)	1	0.01
Puget Sound Salish (34)	60	0.75
Sioux (3)	9	0.11
Spanish American Ind. (1)	1	0.01
Tlingit-Haida *(Alaska Native)* (8)	9	0.11
Yakama (1)	4	0.05
Asian (286)	426	5.34
Not Hispanic (279)	403	5.05
Hispanic (7)	23	0.29
Cambodian (59)	69	0.86
Chinese, ex. Taiwanese (14)	42	0.53
Filipino (54)	113	1.42
Indian (9)	16	0.20
Indonesian (0)	1	0.01
Japanese (24)	63	0.79
Korean (72)	95	1.19
Laotian (2)	6	0.08
Thai (9)	14	0.18
Vietnamese (21)	26	0.33
Hawaii Native/Pacific Islander (38)	83	1.04
Not Hispanic (37)	73	0.91
Hispanic (1)	10	0.13
Guamanian/Chamorro (9)	17	0.21
Native Hawaiian (5)	37	0.46
Samoan (21)	27	0.34
White (6,776)	7,140	89.42
Not Hispanic (6,585)	6,865	85.97
Hispanic (191)	275	3.44

Sumner

Place Type: City
County: Pierce
Population: 9,451†

Ancestry‡	Population	%
American (303)	303	3.25
Austrian (0)	14	0.15
Basque (15)	15	0.16
Belgian (10)	10	0.11
Brazilian (15)	15	0.16
British (37)	55	0.59
Canadian (0)	8	0.09
Croatian (0)	58	0.62
Czech (11)	32	0.34
Czechoslovakian (8)	8	0.09
Danish (23)	63	0.68
Dutch (0)	249	2.67
English (351)	1,357	14.55
European (100)	155	1.66
Finnish (32)	84	0.90
French, ex. Basque (172)	876	9.39
French Canadian (0)	63	0.68
German (424)	1,781	19.10
Greek (0)	20	0.21
Hungarian (0)	8	0.09
Icelander (0)	12	0.13
Irish (394)	1,707	18.31
Israeli (9)	9	0.10
Italian (137)	526	5.64
Luxemburger (0)	10	0.11
Norwegian (72)	325	3.49
Pennsylvania German (17)	43	0.46
Polish (26)	118	1.27
Portuguese (21)	99	1.06
Russian (10)	10	0.11
Scandinavian (31)	103	1.10
Scotch-Irish (59)	228	2.45
Scottish (36)	230	2.47
Slovene (0)	30	0.32
Swedish (195)	608	6.52
Swiss (21)	37	0.40
Welsh (17)	171	1.83
West Indian, ex. Hispanic (0)	24	0.26
Bahamian (0)	24	0.26
Yugoslavian (43)	43	0.46

*Notes: † The Census 2010 population figure is used to calculate the percentages in the Hispanic Origin and Race categories. Ancestry percentages are based on the 2006-2010 American Community Survey population (not shown); ‡ Numbers in parentheses indicate the number of people reporting a single ancestry; * Numbers in parentheses indicate the number of persons reporting this race alone, not in combination with any other race; Please refer to the Explanation of Data for more information.*

Hispanic Origin	Population	%
Hispanic or Latino (of any race)	955	10.10
Central American, ex. Mexican	26	0.28
Costa Rican	1	0.01
Guatemalan	1	0.01
Nicaraguan	4	0.04
Panamanian	4	0.04
Salvadoran	13	0.14
Other Central American	3	0.03
Cuban	5	0.05
Dominican Republic	1	0.01
Mexican	790	8.36
Puerto Rican	36	0.38
South American	15	0.16
Bolivian	1	0.01
Colombian	3	0.03
Ecuadorian	4	0.04
Peruvian	6	0.06
Other South American	1	0.01
Other Hispanic or Latino	82	0.87

Race*	Population	%
African-American/Black (111)	215	2.27
Not Hispanic (107)	197	2.08
Hispanic (4)	18	0.19
American Indian/Alaska Native (98)	230	2.43
Not Hispanic (85)	198	2.10
Hispanic (13)	32	0.34
Alaska Athabascan *(Ala. Nat.)* (1)	1	0.01
Aleut *(Alaska Native)* (3)	7	0.07
Arapaho (1)	1	0.01
Blackfeet (3)	11	0.12
Canadian/French Am. Ind. (2)	2	0.02
Cherokee (13)	50	0.53
Chickasaw (1)	2	0.02
Chippewa (3)	7	0.07
Choctaw (2)	2	0.02
Colville (5)	6	0.06
Cree (1)	1	0.01
Hopi (0)	1	0.01
Inupiat *(Alaska Native)* (5)	8	0.08
Iroquois (3)	7	0.07
Lumbee (0)	1	0.01
Mexican American Ind. (5)	10	0.11
Navajo (1)	6	0.06
Puget Sound Salish (10)	17	0.18
Sioux (5)	12	0.13
Tlingit-Haida *(Alaska Native)* (5)	9	0.10
Tsimshian *(Alaska Native)* (4)	4	0.04
Asian (226)	364	3.85
Not Hispanic (212)	343	3.63
Hispanic (14)	21	0.22
Cambodian (13)	19	0.20
Chinese, ex. Taiwanese (16)	34	0.36
Filipino (90)	152	1.61
Hmong (2)	2	0.02
Indian (14)	23	0.24
Indonesian (0)	4	0.04
Japanese (17)	47	0.50
Korean (30)	46	0.49
Laotian (3)	7	0.07
Pakistani (4)	4	0.04
Taiwanese (1)	1	0.01
Thai (5)	7	0.07
Vietnamese (16)	22	0.23
Hawaii Native/Pacific Islander (40)	87	0.92
Not Hispanic (39)	78	0.83
Hispanic (1)	9	0.10
Guamanian/Chamorro (3)	13	0.14
Native Hawaiian (6)	20	0.21
Samoan (27)	44	0.47
White (8,252)	8,622	91.23
Not Hispanic (7,727)	8,022	84.88
Hispanic (525)	600	6.35

Sunnyside

Place Type: City
County: Yakima
Population: 15,858†

Ancestry‡	Population	%
American (285)	285	1.86
Australian (0)	11	0.07
British (13)	44	0.29
Czech (0)	11	0.07
Czechoslovakian (14)	14	0.09
Danish (25)	47	0.31
Dutch (83)	394	2.57
English (243)	647	4.21
European (16)	31	0.20
French, ex. Basque (8)	142	0.93
French Canadian (12)	12	0.08
German (324)	925	6.03
Irish (65)	305	1.99
Italian (13)	94	0.61
Northern European (11)	11	0.07
Norwegian (73)	230	1.50
Polish (13)	24	0.16
Scandinavian (0)	10	0.07
Scotch-Irish (34)	60	0.39
Scottish (0)	124	0.81
Swedish (56)	145	0.94
Welsh (0)	7	0.05

Hispanic Origin	Population	%
Hispanic or Latino (of any race)	13,043	82.25
Central American, ex. Mexican	67	0.42
Costa Rican	2	0.01
Guatemalan	16	0.10
Honduran	10	0.06
Nicaraguan	2	0.01
Salvadoran	37	0.23
Cuban	12	0.08
Mexican	12,296	77.54
Puerto Rican	31	0.20
South American	32	0.20
Argentinean	7	0.04
Chilean	2	0.01
Colombian	1	0.01
Ecuadorian	5	0.03
Peruvian	17	0.11
Other Hispanic or Latino	605	3.82

Race*	Population	%
African-American/Black (48)	80	0.50
Not Hispanic (26)	50	0.32
Hispanic (22)	30	0.19
American Indian/Alaska Native (149)	218	1.37
Not Hispanic (81)	122	0.77
Hispanic (68)	96	0.61
Blackfeet (0)	1	0.01
Canadian/French Am. Ind. (0)	1	0.01
Central American Ind. (1)	1	0.01
Cherokee (6)	21	0.13
Chickasaw (0)	2	0.01
Chippewa (7)	7	0.04
Choctaw (2)	2	0.01
Colville (2)	3	0.02
Cree (0)	1	0.01
Creek (0)	1	0.01
Iroquois (4)	4	0.03
Mexican American Ind. (14)	19	0.12
Potawatomi (0)	1	0.01
Pueblo (4)	5	0.03
Puget Sound Salish (1)	1	0.01
Seminole (0)	1	0.01
Sioux (5)	5	0.03
South American Ind. (1)	1	0.01
Spanish American Ind. (3)	3	0.02
Ute (0)	1	0.01
Yakama (19)	28	0.18
Asian (113)	157	0.99
Not Hispanic (104)	120	0.76
Hispanic (9)	37	0.23
Cambodian (1)	1	0.01
Chinese, ex. Taiwanese (25)	28	0.18
Filipino (24)	57	0.36
Indian (11)	13	0.08
Indonesian (1)	2	0.01
Japanese (4)	9	0.06
Korean (18)	19	0.12
Taiwanese (1)	1	0.01
Vietnamese (12)	13	0.08
Hawaii Native/Pacific Islander (5)	19	0.12
Not Hispanic (5)	7	0.04
Hispanic (0)	12	0.08
Guamanian/Chamorro (1)	1	0.01
Native Hawaiian (4)	4	0.03
Samoan (0)	5	0.03
White (6,880)	7,212	45.48
Not Hispanic (2,494)	2,569	16.20
Hispanic (4,386)	4,643	29.28

Tacoma

Place Type: City
County: Pierce
Population: 198,397†

Ancestry‡	Population	%
African, Sub-Saharan (1,967)	2,852	1.43
African (1,544)	2,387	1.20
Cape Verdean (8)	8	<0.01
Ethiopian (102)	116	0.06
Ghanaian (51)	51	0.03
Kenyan (58)	74	0.04
Nigerian (108)	108	0.05
Sierra Leonean (13)	25	0.01
Somalian (37)	37	0.02
Sudanese (26)	26	0.01
Ugandan (8)	8	<0.01
Zimbabwean (12)	12	0.01
Albanian (10)	10	0.01
American (7,800)	7,800	3.92
Arab (230)	297	0.15
Arab (14)	18	0.01
Egyptian (0)	14	0.01
Iraqi (56)	56	0.03
Lebanese (62)	99	0.05
Moroccan (41)	41	0.02
Syrian (21)	21	0.01
Other Arab (36)	48	0.02
Armenian (48)	84	0.04
Australian (25)	148	0.07
Austrian (102)	490	0.25
Basque (8)	18	0.01
Belgian (60)	240	0.12
Brazilian (14)	26	0.01
British (459)	1,001	0.50
Bulgarian (18)	51	0.03
Cajun (3)	26	0.01
Canadian (290)	558	0.28
Celtic (33)	74	0.04
Croatian (319)	628	0.32
Czech (229)	920	0.46
Czechoslovakian (152)	328	0.16
Danish (301)	1,617	0.81
Dutch (437)	3,136	1.58
Eastern European (90)	295	0.15
English (4,130)	17,591	8.85
Estonian (30)	55	0.03
European (2,914)	3,412	1.72
Finnish (417)	1,082	0.54
French, ex. Basque (604)	6,584	3.31
French Canadian (451)	1,495	0.75
German (8,988)	33,501	16.85
German Russian (36)	56	0.03
Greek (360)	671	0.34
Hungarian (49)	364	0.18
Icelander (30)	91	0.05
Iranian (26)	51	0.03
Irish (5,261)	23,291	11.71
Italian (2,539)	7,752	3.90
Latvian (44)	65	0.03

*Notes: † The Census 2010 population figure is used to calculate the percentages in the Hispanic Origin and Race categories. Ancestry percentages are based on the 2006-2010 American Community Survey population (not shown); ‡ Numbers in parentheses indicate the number of people reporting a single ancestry; * Numbers in parentheses indicate the number of persons reporting this race alone, not in combination with any other race; Please refer to the Explanation of Data for more information.*

Ancestry	Population	%
Lithuanian (103)	166	0.08
Luxemburger (0)	26	0.01
Macedonian (0)	2	<0.01
New Zealander (26)	26	0.01
Northern European (456)	477	0.24
Norwegian (3,508)	11,116	5.59
Pennsylvania German (98)	168	0.08
Polish (1,095)	3,943	1.98
Portuguese (157)	643	0.32
Romanian (449)	538	0.27
Russian (1,423)	2,468	1.24
Scandinavian (819)	1,465	0.74
Scotch-Irish (1,487)	4,764	2.40
Scottish (1,100)	4,962	2.50
Serbian (33)	86	0.04
Slavic (71)	193	0.10
Slovak (53)	328	0.16
Slovene (24)	82	0.04
Swedish (1,546)	6,871	3.46
Swiss (216)	915	0.46
Turkish (49)	76	0.04
Ukrainian (1,851)	2,166	1.09
Welsh (379)	1,803	0.91
West Indian, ex. Hispanic (224)	401	0.20
Barbadian (42)	46	0.02
British West Indian (9)	9	<0.01
Haitian (0)	20	0.01
Jamaican (31)	129	0.06
U.S. Virgin Islander (103)	139	0.07
West Indian (39)	52	0.03
Other West Indian (0)	6	<0.01
Yugoslavian (137)	402	0.20

Hispanic Origin	Population	%
Hispanic or Latino (of any race)	22,390	11.29
Central American, ex. Mexican	1,322	0.67
Costa Rican	38	0.02
Guatemalan	246	0.12
Honduran	134	0.07
Nicaraguan	62	0.03
Panamanian	263	0.13
Salvadoran	565	0.28
Other Central American	14	0.01
Cuban	319	0.16
Dominican Republic	101	0.05
Mexican	16,145	8.14
Puerto Rican	1,964	0.99
South American	585	0.29
Argentinean	30	0.02
Bolivian	14	0.01
Chilean	58	0.03
Colombian	168	0.08
Ecuadorian	39	0.02
Paraguayan	8	<0.01
Peruvian	224	0.11
Uruguayan	2	<0.01
Venezuelan	26	0.01
Other South American	16	0.01
Other Hispanic or Latino	1,954	0.98

Race*	Population	%
African-American/Black (22,210)	29,842	15.04
Not Hispanic (21,222)	27,877	14.05
Hispanic (988)	1,965	0.99
American Indian/Alaska Native (3,648)	7,863	3.96
Not Hispanic (2,988)	6,404	3.23
Hispanic (660)	1,459	0.74
Alaska Athabascan *(Ala. Nat.)* (34)	74	0.04
Aleut *(Alaska Native)* (35)	88	0.04
Apache (24)	92	0.05
Arapaho (15)	18	0.01
Blackfeet (122)	378	0.19
Canadian/French Am. Ind. (49)	104	0.05
Central American Ind. (3)	8	<0.01
Cherokee (132)	765	0.39
Cheyenne (28)	60	0.03
Chickasaw (8)	18	0.01
Chippewa (146)	306	0.15
Choctaw (41)	154	0.08
Colville (82)	112	0.06
Comanche (7)	17	0.01
Cree (1)	13	0.01
Creek (11)	28	0.01
Crow (8)	12	0.01
Delaware (5)	14	0.01
Hopi (6)	18	0.01
Houma (1)	3	<0.01
Inupiat *(Alaska Native)* (25)	69	0.03
Iroquois (22)	56	0.03
Kiowa (3)	7	<0.01
Lumbee (6)	14	0.01
Menominee (1)	2	<0.01
Mexican American Ind. (120)	206	0.10
Navajo (65)	97	0.05
Osage (13)	19	0.01
Ottawa (4)	10	0.01
Paiute (8)	12	0.01
Pima (0)	1	<0.01
Potawatomi (18)	30	0.02
Pueblo (23)	28	0.01
Puget Sound Salish (713)	1,014	0.51
Seminole (9)	30	0.02
Shoshone (3)	11	0.01
Sioux (102)	240	0.12
South American Ind. (5)	17	0.01
Spanish American Ind. (1)	2	<0.01
Tlingit-Haida *(Alaska Native)* (101)	201	0.10
Tohono O'Odham (0)	1	<0.01
Tsimshian *(Alaska Native)* (10)	24	0.01
Ute (1)	5	<0.01
Yakama (88)	138	0.07
Yaqui (2)	17	0.01
Yup'ik *(Alaska Native)* (9)	23	0.01
Asian (16,274)	21,903	11.04
Not Hispanic (16,013)	21,087	10.63
Hispanic (261)	816	0.41
Bangladeshi (0)	1	<0.01
Bhutanese (1)	8	<0.01
Burmese (3)	11	0.01
Cambodian (3,078)	3,562	1.80
Chinese, ex. Taiwanese (806)	1,568	0.79
Filipino (2,604)	4,507	2.27
Hmong (7)	9	<0.01
Indian (479)	731	0.37
Indonesian (29)	67	0.03
Japanese (828)	2,242	1.13
Korean (2,642)	3,880	1.96
Laotian (332)	430	0.22
Malaysian (10)	18	0.01
Nepalese (2)	9	<0.01
Pakistani (62)	71	0.04
Sri Lankan (12)	13	0.01
Taiwanese (59)	84	0.04
Thai (191)	391	0.20
Vietnamese (4,196)	4,651	2.34
Hawaii Native/Pacific Islander (2,455)	4,002	2.02
Not Hispanic (2,358)	3,665	1.85
Hispanic (97)	337	0.17
Fijian (29)	44	0.02
Guamanian/Chamorro (465)	726	0.37
Marshallese (7)	17	0.01
Native Hawaiian (265)	990	0.50
Samoan (1,383)	1,784	0.90
Tongan (53)	94	0.05
White (128,670)	142,044	71.60
Not Hispanic (119,981)	131,049	66.05
Hispanic (8,689)	10,995	5.54

Toppenish

Place Type: City
County: Yakima
Population: 8,949[†]

Ancestry[‡]	Population	%
British (0)	11	0.12
Canadian (0)	20	0.23
Danish (19)	29	0.33
Dutch (0)	8	0.09
English (48)	220	2.49
European (11)	11	0.12
French, ex. Basque (14)	57	0.65
German (94)	337	3.82
Irish (12)	65	0.74
Maltese (31)	31	0.35
Norwegian (0)	8	0.09
Russian (11)	11	0.12
Scotch-Irish (0)	42	0.48
Scottish (0)	50	0.57
Swedish (0)	32	0.36
Swiss (0)	18	0.20
Welsh (24)	24	0.27

Hispanic Origin	Population	%
Hispanic or Latino (of any race)	7,388	82.56
Central American, ex. Mexican	20	0.22
Guatemalan	8	0.09
Nicaraguan	2	0.02
Salvadoran	10	0.11
Cuban	2	0.02
Mexican	6,994	78.15
Puerto Rican	9	0.10
South American	3	0.03
Colombian	2	0.02
Ecuadorian	1	0.01
Other Hispanic or Latino	360	4.02

Race*	Population	%
African-American/Black (61)	93	1.04
Not Hispanic (18)	27	0.30
Hispanic (43)	66	0.74
American Indian/Alaska Native (720)	859	9.60
Not Hispanic (627)	704	7.87
Hispanic (93)	155	1.73
Aleut *(Alaska Native)* (0)	2	0.02
Apache (5)	5	0.06
Arapaho (7)	7	0.08
Blackfeet (6)	8	0.09
Canadian/French Am. Ind. (1)	4	0.04
Cherokee (0)	2	0.02
Chickasaw (0)	1	0.01
Chippewa (4)	5	0.06
Choctaw (0)	1	0.01
Colville (16)	19	0.21
Cree (2)	3	0.03
Creek (1)	2	0.02
Crow (10)	13	0.15
Delaware (0)	1	0.01
Iroquois (0)	2	0.02
Kiowa (2)	2	0.02
Menominee (1)	1	0.01
Mexican American Ind. (22)	27	0.30
Navajo (5)	7	0.08
Paiute (0)	1	0.01
Pima (0)	3	0.03
Pueblo (3)	3	0.03
Puget Sound Salish (12)	14	0.16
Seminole (1)	1	0.01
Sioux (4)	9	0.10
Tsimshian *(Alaska Native)* (1)	1	0.01
Ute (1)	1	0.01
Yakama (427)	492	5.50
Asian (28)	76	0.85
Not Hispanic (13)	33	0.37
Hispanic (15)	43	0.48
Chinese, ex. Taiwanese (3)	8	0.09
Filipino (17)	45	0.50
Indian (1)	6	0.07
Japanese (1)	3	0.03
Korean (1)	1	0.01
Thai (1)	1	0.01
Vietnamese (2)	2	0.02
Hawaii Native/Pacific Islander (6)	30	0.34
Not Hispanic (0)	5	0.06
Hispanic (6)	25	0.28
Guamanian/Chamorro (0)	1	0.01
Native Hawaiian (0)	14	0.16
Samoan (6)	6	0.07
White (3,029)	3,347	37.40
Not Hispanic (785)	859	9.60

SECTION TWO

*Notes: † The Census 2010 population figure is used to calculate the percentages in the Hispanic Origin and Race categories. Ancestry percentages are based on the 2006-2010 American Community Survey population (not shown); ‡ Numbers in parentheses indicate the number of people reporting a single ancestry; * Numbers in parentheses indicate the number of persons reporting this race alone, not in combination with any other race; Please refer to the Explanation of Data for more information.*

Hispanic (2,244)	2,488	27.80

Tukwila

Place Type: City
County: King
Population: 19,107†

Ancestry‡	Population	%
Afghan (86)	86	0.46
African, Sub-Saharan (1,169)	1,197	6.45
African (574)	584	3.15
Ethiopian (158)	158	0.85
Nigerian (0)	18	0.10
Somalian (407)	407	2.19
Ugandan (30)	30	0.16
American (350)	350	1.89
Arab (0)	12	0.06
Arab (0)	12	0.06
Armenian (9)	9	0.05
Brazilian (21)	31	0.17
British (76)	87	0.47
Canadian (0)	65	0.35
Croatian (33)	68	0.37
Czech (15)	54	0.29
Czechoslovakian (0)	12	0.06
Danish (23)	42	0.23
Dutch (27)	222	1.20
English (347)	726	3.91
European (31)	86	0.46
Finnish (59)	70	0.38
French, ex. Basque (47)	346	1.86
French Canadian (27)	121	0.65
German (1,050)	2,029	10.93
Greek (0)	9	0.05
Iranian (43)	43	0.23
Irish (325)	966	5.20
Italian (112)	318	1.71
Latvian (29)	42	0.23
Maltese (0)	17	0.09
Northern European (4)	4	0.02
Norwegian (293)	650	3.50
Polish (98)	162	0.87
Romanian (7)	7	0.04
Russian (245)	272	1.46
Scandinavian (83)	95	0.51
Scotch-Irish (76)	171	0.92
Scottish (76)	207	1.11
Swedish (114)	277	1.49
Swiss (0)	34	0.18
Turkish (451)	460	2.48
Ukrainian (52)	79	0.43
Welsh (5)	57	0.31
West Indian, ex. Hispanic (0)	9	0.05
Jamaican (0)	9	0.05
Yugoslavian (503)	513	2.76

Hispanic Origin	Population	%
Hispanic or Latino (of any race)	3,349	17.53
Central American, ex. Mexican	339	1.77
Costa Rican	3	0.02
Guatemalan	62	0.32
Honduran	62	0.32
Nicaraguan	24	0.13
Panamanian	8	0.04
Salvadoran	173	0.91
Other Central American	7	0.04
Cuban	20	0.10
Dominican Republic	1	0.01
Mexican	2,513	13.15
Puerto Rican	74	0.39
South American	49	0.26
Argentinean	1	0.01
Bolivian	1	0.01
Chilean	12	0.06
Colombian	11	0.06
Paraguayan	2	0.01
Peruvian	18	0.09
Venezuelan	4	0.02
Other Hispanic or Latino	353	1.85

Race*	Population	%
African-American/Black (3,418)	3,857	20.19
Not Hispanic (3,350)	3,728	19.51
Hispanic (68)	129	0.68
American Indian/Alaska Native (214)	537	2.81
Not Hispanic (143)	399	2.09
Hispanic (71)	138	0.72
Alaska Athabascan *(Ala. Nat.)* (0)	1	0.01
Aleut *(Alaska Native)* (3)	16	0.08
Apache (0)	5	0.03
Blackfeet (5)	31	0.16
Canadian/French Am. Ind. (2)	18	0.09
Central American Ind. (3)	4	0.02
Cherokee (16)	47	0.25
Cheyenne (0)	2	0.01
Chickasaw (0)	6	0.03
Chippewa (1)	8	0.04
Choctaw (3)	12	0.06
Colville (6)	8	0.04
Cree (1)	1	0.01
Hopi (0)	2	0.01
Inupiat *(Alaska Native)* (1)	1	0.01
Iroquois (0)	5	0.03
Kiowa (0)	8	0.04
Lumbee (2)	2	0.01
Mexican American Ind. (28)	41	0.21
Navajo (2)	6	0.03
Osage (0)	2	0.01
Pueblo (0)	1	0.01
Puget Sound Salish (8)	18	0.09
Shoshone (2)	2	0.01
Sioux (4)	9	0.05
South American Ind. (0)	1	0.01
Spanish American Ind. (2)	3	0.02
Tlingit-Haida *(Alaska Native)* (11)	15	0.08
Tsimshian *(Alaska Native)* (2)	4	0.02
Yaqui (2)	6	0.03
Yup'ik *(Alaska Native)* (1)	2	0.01
Asian (3,638)	4,079	21.35
Not Hispanic (3,615)	4,016	21.02
Hispanic (23)	63	0.33
Bangladeshi (12)	12	0.06
Bhutanese (210)	221	1.16
Burmese (266)	269	1.41
Cambodian (289)	333	1.74
Chinese, ex. Taiwanese (239)	324	1.70
Filipino (591)	789	4.13
Hmong (28)	28	0.15
Indian (276)	315	1.65
Indonesian (22)	25	0.13
Japanese (118)	191	1.00
Korean (83)	115	0.60
Laotian (180)	205	1.07
Malaysian (2)	3	0.02
Nepalese (19)	28	0.15
Pakistani (6)	7	0.04
Sri Lankan (1)	2	0.01
Taiwanese (3)	4	0.02
Thai (49)	59	0.31
Vietnamese (1,059)	1,152	6.03
Hawaii Native/Pacific Islander (527)	674	3.53
Not Hispanic (521)	653	3.42
Hispanic (6)	21	0.11
Fijian (33)	37	0.19
Guamanian/Chamorro (53)	83	0.43
Native Hawaiian (28)	84	0.44
Samoan (273)	333	1.74
Tongan (39)	49	0.26
White (8,393)	9,226	48.29
Not Hispanic (7,186)	7,836	41.01
Hispanic (1,207)	1,390	7.27

Tumwater

Place Type: City
County: Thurston
Population: 17,371†

Ancestry‡	Population	%
African, Sub-Saharan (12)	12	0.07
African (12)	12	0.07
American (559)	559	3.32
Arab (0)	11	0.07
Syrian (0)	11	0.07
Armenian (12)	12	0.07
Austrian (59)	59	0.35
Basque (0)	10	0.06
Belgian (11)	11	0.07
British (26)	78	0.46
Canadian (78)	90	0.53
Celtic (11)	24	0.14
Croatian (41)	74	0.44
Czech (20)	145	0.86
Czechoslovakian (10)	10	0.06
Danish (55)	221	1.31
Dutch (34)	253	1.50
Eastern European (12)	12	0.07
English (825)	2,349	13.95
European (273)	404	2.40
Finnish (68)	282	1.68
French, ex. Basque (224)	1,088	6.46
French Canadian (48)	186	1.10
German (720)	3,747	22.26
Greek (24)	70	0.42
Hungarian (26)	42	0.25
Icelander (0)	15	0.09
Iranian (9)	18	0.11
Irish (633)	2,619	15.56
Italian (253)	897	5.33
Latvian (14)	14	0.08
Maltese (0)	7	0.04
Northern European (25)	25	0.15
Norwegian (480)	1,248	7.41
Pennsylvania German (0)	27	0.16
Polish (68)	159	0.94
Portuguese (140)	198	1.18
Romanian (14)	26	0.15
Russian (14)	94	0.56
Scandinavian (98)	172	1.02
Scotch-Irish (156)	540	3.21
Scottish (236)	522	3.10
Slovak (16)	47	0.28
Swedish (107)	478	2.84
Swiss (31)	88	0.52
Ukrainian (41)	41	0.24
Welsh (27)	101	0.60
West Indian, ex. Hispanic (16)	26	0.15
Belizean (8)	8	0.05
British West Indian (8)	8	0.05
Trinidadian/Tobagonian (0)	10	0.06
Yugoslavian (0)	40	0.24

Hispanic Origin	Population	%
Hispanic or Latino (of any race)	1,069	6.15
Central American, ex. Mexican	37	0.21
Costa Rican	2	0.01
Guatemalan	11	0.06
Honduran	4	0.02
Nicaraguan	1	0.01
Panamanian	10	0.06
Salvadoran	9	0.05
Cuban	31	0.18
Dominican Republic	7	0.04
Mexican	665	3.83
Puerto Rican	91	0.52
South American	60	0.35
Argentinean	3	0.02
Bolivian	1	0.01
Chilean	2	0.01
Colombian	14	0.08
Ecuadorian	20	0.12
Peruvian	15	0.09
Venezuelan	4	0.02
Other South American	1	0.01
Other Hispanic or Latino	178	1.02

Race*	Population	%
African-American/Black (301)	535	3.08

*Notes: † The Census 2010 population figure is used to calculate the percentages in the Hispanic Origin and Race categories. Ancestry percentages are based on the 2006-2010 American Community Survey population (not shown); ‡ Numbers in parentheses indicate the number of people reporting a single ancestry; * Numbers in parentheses indicate the number of persons reporting this race alone, not in combination with any other race; Please refer to the Explanation of Data for more information.*

Not Hispanic (283)	485	2.79
Hispanic (18)	50	0.29
American Indian/Alaska Native (201)	514	2.96
Not Hispanic (178)	443	2.55
Hispanic (23)	71	0.41
Alaska Athabascan *(Ala. Nat.)* (0)	2	0.01
Aleut *(Alaska Native)* (3)	5	0.03
Apache (3)	17	0.10
Blackfeet (10)	17	0.10
Canadian/French Am. Ind. (0)	3	0.02
Cherokee (21)	78	0.45
Cheyenne (0)	1	0.01
Chickasaw (3)	5	0.03
Chippewa (11)	14	0.08
Choctaw (0)	8	0.05
Colville (3)	6	0.03
Comanche (0)	1	0.01
Cree (0)	2	0.01
Creek (5)	6	0.03
Crow (0)	2	0.01
Inupiat *(Alaska Native)* (0)	1	0.01
Iroquois (1)	11	0.06
Menominee (0)	2	0.01
Mexican American Ind. (1)	2	0.01
Navajo (6)	11	0.06
Osage (1)	2	0.01
Ottawa (0)	3	0.02
Potawatomi (0)	8	0.05
Pueblo (3)	3	0.02
Puget Sound Salish (13)	35	0.20
Seminole (0)	1	0.01
Shoshone (1)	2	0.01
Sioux (4)	12	0.07
Spanish American Ind. (0)	2	0.01
Tlingit-Haida *(Alaska Native)* (7)	10	0.06
Tsimshian *(Alaska Native)* (1)	2	0.01
Ute (1)	1	0.01
Yakama (0)	3	0.02
Yaqui (0)	1	0.01
Yup'ik *(Alaska Native)* (0)	6	0.03
Asian (841)	1,133	6.52
Not Hispanic (819)	1,084	6.24
Hispanic (22)	49	0.28
Bhutanese (6)	6	0.03
Burmese (0)	1	0.01
Cambodian (19)	32	0.18
Chinese, ex. Taiwanese (94)	159	0.92
Filipino (113)	189	1.09
Indian (186)	203	1.17
Indonesian (2)	7	0.04
Japanese (42)	128	0.74
Korean (107)	169	0.97
Laotian (4)	8	0.05
Sri Lankan (5)	5	0.03
Taiwanese (9)	10	0.06
Thai (11)	16	0.09
Vietnamese (206)	229	1.32
Hawaii Native/Pacific Islander (90)	197	1.13
Not Hispanic (89)	183	1.05
Hispanic (1)	14	0.08
Guamanian/Chamorro (38)	71	0.41
Native Hawaiian (16)	74	0.43
Samoan (22)	42	0.24
Tongan (1)	4	0.02
White (14,769)	15,580	89.69
Not Hispanic (14,195)	14,850	85.49
Hispanic (574)	730	4.20

Union Hill-Novelty Hill

Place Type: CDP
County: King
Population: 18,805†

Ancestry‡	Population	%
African, Sub-Saharan (32)	61	0.33
African (21)	50	0.27
South African (11)	11	0.06
Albanian (0)	96	0.52
American (728)	728	3.97
Arab (154)	213	1.16
Arab (28)	28	0.15
Egyptian (12)	37	0.20
Lebanese (114)	131	0.71
Palestinian (0)	17	0.09
Armenian (9)	9	0.05
Austrian (17)	33	0.18
Basque (0)	13	0.07
Belgian (0)	8	0.04
Brazilian (7)	7	0.04
British (267)	334	1.82
Bulgarian (110)	110	0.60
Canadian (55)	88	0.48
Croatian (8)	8	0.04
Czech (79)	154	0.84
Czechoslovakian (0)	8	0.04
Danish (110)	238	1.30
Dutch (64)	226	1.23
Eastern European (68)	68	0.37
English (617)	2,856	15.56
Estonian (0)	9	0.05
European (786)	931	5.07
Finnish (27)	138	0.75
French, ex. Basque (88)	732	3.99
French Canadian (84)	204	1.11
German (872)	3,613	19.69
Greek (91)	136	0.74
Hungarian (12)	127	0.69
Icelander (0)	22	0.12
Iranian (76)	110	0.60
Irish (652)	2,091	11.39
Italian (163)	571	3.11
Lithuanian (0)	58	0.32
Northern European (48)	72	0.39
Norwegian (392)	840	4.58
Polish (153)	538	2.93
Portuguese (0)	62	0.34
Romanian (46)	114	0.62
Russian (100)	289	1.57
Scandinavian (105)	153	0.83
Scotch-Irish (143)	461	2.51
Scottish (108)	779	4.24
Serbian (85)	85	0.46
Slavic (30)	65	0.35
Slovak (107)	166	0.90
Slovene (0)	17	0.09
Swedish (137)	672	3.66
Swiss (30)	205	1.12
Turkish (65)	65	0.35
Ukrainian (66)	216	1.18
Welsh (62)	233	1.27
West Indian, ex. Hispanic (0)	12	0.07
Jamaican (0)	12	0.07
Yugoslavian (0)	44	0.24

Hispanic Origin	Population	%
Hispanic or Latino (of any race)	718	3.82
Central American, ex. Mexican	52	0.28
Costa Rican	5	0.03
Guatemalan	15	0.08
Honduran	12	0.06
Nicaraguan	3	0.02
Panamanian	4	0.02
Salvadoran	13	0.07
Cuban	8	0.04
Dominican Republic	3	0.02
Mexican	432	2.30
Puerto Rican	27	0.14
South American	122	0.65
Argentinean	19	0.10
Bolivian	6	0.03
Chilean	12	0.06
Colombian	21	0.11
Ecuadorian	12	0.06
Peruvian	20	0.11
Uruguayan	9	0.05
Venezuelan	23	0.12
Other Hispanic or Latino	74	0.39

Race*	Population	%
African-American/Black (143)	244	1.30
Not Hispanic (143)	239	1.27
Hispanic (0)	5	0.03
American Indian/Alaska Native (39)	145	0.77
Not Hispanic (28)	126	0.67
Hispanic (11)	19	0.10
Apache (0)	2	0.01
Arapaho (2)	2	0.01
Blackfeet (0)	5	0.03
Canadian/French Am. Ind. (0)	2	0.01
Cherokee (2)	28	0.15
Chippewa (1)	4	0.02
Choctaw (3)	11	0.06
Creek (0)	5	0.03
Crow (0)	2	0.01
Inupiat *(Alaska Native)* (1)	1	0.01
Mexican American Ind. (5)	8	0.04
Puget Sound Salish (1)	11	0.06
South American Ind. (0)	1	0.01
Spanish American Ind. (0)	1	0.01
Tlingit-Haida *(Alaska Native)* (1)	2	0.01
Tsimshian *(Alaska Native)* (1)	1	0.01
Yakama (0)	2	0.01
Yup'ik *(Alaska Native)* (0)	4	0.02
Asian (2,801)	3,230	17.18
Not Hispanic (2,792)	3,196	17.00
Hispanic (9)	34	0.18
Bangladeshi (0)	1	0.01
Burmese (2)	2	0.01
Cambodian (2)	5	0.03
Chinese, ex. Taiwanese (743)	882	4.69
Filipino (106)	183	0.97
Indian (1,268)	1,318	7.01
Indonesian (18)	30	0.16
Japanese (147)	292	1.55
Korean (210)	297	1.58
Laotian (9)	9	0.05
Malaysian (5)	10	0.05
Nepalese (11)	11	0.06
Pakistani (48)	49	0.26
Sri Lankan (3)	3	0.02
Taiwanese (39)	44	0.23
Thai (34)	39	0.21
Vietnamese (39)	57	0.30
Hawaii Native/Pacific Islander (10)	54	0.29
Not Hispanic (10)	50	0.27
Hispanic (0)	4	0.02
Guamanian/Chamorro (3)	4	0.02
Native Hawaiian (5)	35	0.19
Samoan (1)	4	0.02
Tongan (1)	1	0.01
White (14,956)	15,547	82.67
Not Hispanic (14,460)	15,000	79.77
Hispanic (496)	547	2.91

University Place

Place Type: City
County: Pierce
Population: 31,144†

Ancestry‡	Population	%
African, Sub-Saharan (88)	144	0.46
African (63)	113	0.36
Ethiopian (25)	25	0.08
Kenyan (0)	6	0.02
American (1,869)	1,869	6.01
Arab (67)	124	0.40
Egyptian (35)	35	0.11
Lebanese (32)	74	0.24
Syrian (0)	15	0.05
Armenian (0)	9	0.03
Austrian (93)	173	0.56
Belgian (0)	8	0.03
Brazilian (0)	32	0.10
British (31)	227	0.73
Cajun (0)	53	0.17
Canadian (69)	222	0.71

*Notes: † The Census 2010 population figure is used to calculate the percentages in the Hispanic Origin and Race categories. Ancestry percentages are based on the 2006-2010 American Community Survey population (not shown); ‡ Numbers in parentheses indicate the number of people reporting a single ancestry; * Numbers in parentheses indicate the number of persons reporting this race alone, not in combination with any other race; Please refer to the Explanation of Data for more information.*

Celtic (0)	50	0.16
Croatian (97)	131	0.42
Czech (12)	122	0.39
Czechoslovakian (8)	8	0.03
Danish (79)	453	1.46
Dutch (142)	498	1.60
English (841)	3,657	11.77
European (320)	510	1.64
Finnish (25)	164	0.53
French, ex. Basque (67)	1,166	3.75
French Canadian (12)	183	0.59
German (1,760)	5,848	18.81
German Russian (0)	11	0.04
Greek (17)	59	0.19
Hungarian (13)	38	0.12
Iranian (39)	39	0.13
Irish (879)	3,477	11.19
Italian (419)	1,409	4.53
Latvian (7)	14	0.05
Lithuanian (0)	29	0.09
Luxemburger (0)	14	0.05
Northern European (125)	125	0.40
Norwegian (557)	1,919	6.17
Pennsylvania German (11)	11	0.04
Polish (202)	801	2.58
Portuguese (0)	59	0.19
Romanian (15)	31	0.10
Russian (455)	595	1.91
Scandinavian (70)	219	0.70
Scotch-Irish (338)	924	2.97
Scottish (213)	775	2.49
Slovak (17)	35	0.11
Slovene (13)	13	0.04
Swedish (147)	1,229	3.95
Swiss (16)	179	0.58
Turkish (10)	46	0.15
Ukrainian (193)	258	0.83
Welsh (50)	294	0.95
West Indian, ex. Hispanic (47)	70	0.23
Jamaican (47)	70	0.23
Yugoslavian (12)	144	0.46

Hispanic Origin	Population	%
Hispanic or Latino (of any race)	2,077	6.67
Central American, ex. Mexican	141	0.45
Costa Rican	17	0.05
Guatemalan	27	0.09
Honduran	13	0.04
Nicaraguan	15	0.05
Panamanian	36	0.12
Salvadoran	33	0.11
Cuban	49	0.16
Dominican Republic	15	0.05
Mexican	1,193	3.83
Puerto Rican	317	1.02
South American	98	0.31
Argentinean	9	0.03
Bolivian	3	0.01
Chilean	15	0.05
Colombian	29	0.09
Ecuadorian	7	0.02
Peruvian	29	0.09
Uruguayan	2	0.01
Venezuelan	4	0.01
Other Hispanic or Latino	264	0.85

Race*	Population	%
African-American/Black (2,641)	3,764	12.09
Not Hispanic (2,508)	3,474	11.15
Hispanic (133)	290	0.93
American Indian/Alaska Native (235)	780	2.50
Not Hispanic (208)	654	2.10
Hispanic (27)	126	0.40
Alaska Athabascan *(Ala. Nat.)* (0)	1	<0.01
Aleut *(Alaska Native)* (5)	9	0.03
Apache (0)	3	0.01
Arapaho (1)	1	<0.01
Blackfeet (6)	36	0.12
Canadian/French Am. Ind. (1)	4	0.01
Central American Ind. (0)	1	<0.01
Cherokee (17)	129	0.41
Cheyenne (3)	6	0.02
Chickasaw (0)	7	0.02
Chippewa (6)	20	0.06
Choctaw (8)	39	0.13
Colville (4)	7	0.02
Comanche (0)	2	0.01
Cree (0)	1	<0.01
Creek (1)	9	0.03
Crow (0)	3	0.01
Delaware (3)	7	0.02
Hopi (2)	4	0.01
Inupiat *(Alaska Native)* (3)	8	0.03
Iroquois (1)	16	0.05
Mexican American Ind. (1)	2	0.01
Navajo (8)	13	0.04
Osage (7)	8	0.03
Ottawa (1)	1	<0.01
Paiute (1)	4	0.01
Pima (0)	4	0.01
Potawatomi (1)	2	0.01
Pueblo (2)	5	0.02
Puget Sound Salish (24)	60	0.19
Seminole (0)	10	0.03
Sioux (11)	33	0.11
South American Ind. (1)	1	<0.01
Tlingit-Haida *(Alaska Native)* (15)	24	0.08
Tohono O'Odham (5)	5	0.02
Tsimshian *(Alaska Native)* (0)	3	0.01
Yakama (1)	2	0.01
Yaqui (1)	4	0.01
Asian (2,792)	3,963	12.72
Not Hispanic (2,755)	3,789	12.17
Hispanic (37)	174	0.56
Bangladeshi (2)	3	0.01
Bhutanese (1)	1	<0.01
Burmese (5)	6	0.02
Cambodian (57)	90	0.29
Chinese, ex. Taiwanese (262)	424	1.36
Filipino (511)	877	2.82
Indian (110)	154	0.49
Indonesian (1)	8	0.03
Japanese (153)	512	1.64
Korean (1,175)	1,469	4.72
Laotian (10)	15	0.05
Malaysian (0)	1	<0.01
Pakistani (19)	19	0.06
Taiwanese (19)	28	0.09
Thai (30)	49	0.16
Vietnamese (348)	413	1.33
Hawaii Native/Pacific Islander (258)	520	1.67
Not Hispanic (248)	480	1.54
Hispanic (10)	40	0.13
Fijian (8)	16	0.05
Guamanian/Chamorro (61)	120	0.39
Marshallese (13)	17	0.05
Native Hawaiian (33)	186	0.60
Samoan (55)	94	0.30
Tongan (11)	13	0.04
White (22,120)	24,293	78.00
Not Hispanic (21,150)	22,995	73.83
Hispanic (970)	1,298	4.17

Vancouver

Place Type: City
County: Clark
Population: 161,791†

Ancestry‡	Population	%
African, Sub-Saharan (792)	1,092	0.68
African (242)	542	0.34
Ethiopian (369)	369	0.23
Ghanaian (144)	144	0.09
Nigerian (37)	37	0.02
Alsatian (0)	14	0.01
American (5,756)	5,756	3.59
Arab (126)	248	0.15
Arab (43)	75	0.05
Egyptian (27)	62	0.04
Iraqi (0)	12	0.01
Lebanese (39)	69	0.04
Palestinian (17)	17	0.01
Other Arab (0)	13	0.01
Armenian (127)	193	0.12
Assyrian/Chaldean/Syriac (0)	22	0.01
Australian (23)	106	0.07
Austrian (156)	410	0.26
Basque (0)	51	0.03
Belgian (0)	183	0.11
Brazilian (16)	69	0.04
British (386)	1,110	0.69
Bulgarian (34)	34	0.02
Canadian (278)	656	0.41
Celtic (105)	183	0.11
Croatian (12)	138	0.09
Czech (242)	942	0.59
Czechoslovakian (16)	179	0.11
Danish (446)	1,881	1.17
Dutch (611)	3,903	2.44
Eastern European (39)	39	0.02
English (5,041)	19,703	12.30
European (2,417)	2,603	1.62
Finnish (761)	1,892	1.18
French, ex. Basque (1,108)	8,494	5.30
French Canadian (502)	1,554	0.97
German (9,811)	36,923	23.05
German Russian (0)	37	0.02
Greek (363)	714	0.45
Hungarian (96)	543	0.34
Icelander (24)	64	0.04
Iranian (227)	334	0.21
Irish (4,265)	20,712	12.93
Israeli (70)	70	0.04
Italian (1,734)	6,261	3.91
Latvian (47)	101	0.06
Lithuanian (151)	359	0.22
Luxemburger (0)	38	0.02
Macedonian (0)	16	0.01
New Zealander (18)	18	0.01
Northern European (313)	344	0.21
Norwegian (2,424)	7,639	4.77
Pennsylvania German (36)	60	0.04
Polish (561)	2,583	1.61
Portuguese (174)	643	0.40
Romanian (803)	895	0.56
Russian (2,222)	3,529	2.20
Scandinavian (597)	1,246	0.78
Scotch-Irish (1,542)	4,328	2.70
Scottish (968)	5,534	3.45
Serbian (10)	22	0.01
Slavic (4)	32	0.02
Slovak (63)	193	0.12
Slovene (20)	40	0.02
Swedish (963)	5,301	3.31
Swiss (163)	903	0.56
Turkish (68)	68	0.04
Ukrainian (2,516)	3,056	1.91
Welsh (311)	1,965	1.23
West Indian, ex. Hispanic (65)	179	0.11
Dutch West Indian (9)	12	0.01
Haitian (31)	83	0.05
Jamaican (17)	45	0.03
Trinidadian/Tobagonian (8)	39	0.02
Yugoslavian (441)	544	0.34

Hispanic Origin	Population	%
Hispanic or Latino (of any race)	16,756	10.36
Central American, ex. Mexican	698	0.43
Costa Rican	37	0.02
Guatemalan	240	0.15
Honduran	104	0.06
Nicaraguan	58	0.04
Panamanian	63	0.04
Salvadoran	189	0.12
Other Central American	7	<0.01
Cuban	193	0.12
Dominican Republic	22	0.01
Mexican	13,240	8.18
Puerto Rican	553	0.34

*Notes: † The Census 2010 population figure is used to calculate the percentages in the Hispanic Origin and Race categories. Ancestry percentages are based on the 2006-2010 American Community Survey population (not shown); ‡ Numbers in parentheses indicate the number of people reporting a single ancestry; * Numbers in parentheses indicate the number of persons reporting this race alone, not in combination with any other race; Please refer to the Explanation of Data for more information.*

South American	465	0.29
Argentinean	51	0.03
Bolivian	14	0.01
Chilean	94	0.06
Colombian	94	0.06
Ecuadorian	29	0.02
Paraguayan	11	0.01
Peruvian	138	0.09
Uruguayan	13	0.01
Venezuelan	18	0.01
Other South American	3	<0.01
Other Hispanic or Latino	1,585	0.98

Race*	Population	%
African-American/Black (4,763)	7,174	4.43
Not Hispanic (4,525)	6,609	4.08
Hispanic (238)	565	0.35
American Indian/Alaska Native (1,629)	4,013	2.48
Not Hispanic (1,252)	3,236	2.00
Hispanic (377)	777	0.48
Alaska Athabascan *(Ala. Nat.)* (11)	21	0.01
Aleut *(Alaska Native)* (25)	52	0.03
Apache (23)	73	0.05
Arapaho (2)	5	<0.01
Blackfeet (24)	137	0.08
Canadian/French Am. Ind. (3)	20	0.01
Central American Ind. (5)	6	<0.01
Cherokee (115)	598	0.37
Cheyenne (8)	25	0.02
Chickasaw (16)	27	0.02
Chippewa (59)	153	0.09
Choctaw (39)	106	0.07
Colville (26)	34	0.02
Comanche (2)	13	0.01
Cree (2)	11	0.01
Creek (13)	27	0.02
Crow (2)	4	<0.01
Delaware (2)	14	0.01
Hopi (2)	5	<0.01
Houma (1)	1	<0.01
Inupiat *(Alaska Native)* (16)	30	0.02
Iroquois (10)	29	0.02
Kiowa (0)	6	<0.01
Lumbee (3)	8	<0.01
Menominee (4)	9	0.01
Mexican American Ind. (108)	157	0.10
Navajo (32)	67	0.04
Osage (3)	12	0.01
Ottawa (4)	8	<0.01
Paiute (5)	13	0.01
Pima (8)	12	0.01
Potawatomi (4)	23	0.01
Pueblo (13)	23	0.01
Puget Sound Salish (14)	26	0.02
Seminole (2)	18	0.01
Shoshone (11)	24	0.01
Sioux (65)	148	0.09
South American Ind. (4)	17	0.01
Spanish American Ind. (4)	5	<0.01
Tlingit-Haida *(Alaska Native)* (42)	88	0.05
Tohono O'Odham (1)	1	<0.01
Tsimshian *(Alaska Native)* (9)	21	0.01
Ute (1)	3	<0.01
Yakama (31)	55	0.03
Yaqui (7)	15	0.01
Yuman (0)	2	<0.01
Yup'ik *(Alaska Native)* (8)	13	0.01
Asian (8,146)	10,657	6.59
Not Hispanic (8,039)	10,298	6.37
Hispanic (107)	359	0.22
Bangladeshi (14)	15	0.01
Bhutanese (1)	1	<0.01
Burmese (10)	10	0.01
Cambodian (433)	538	0.33
Chinese, ex. Taiwanese (1,488)	1,990	1.23
Filipino (1,388)	2,262	1.40
Hmong (30)	37	0.02
Indian (725)	908	0.56
Indonesian (27)	55	0.03
Japanese (594)	1,149	0.71
Korean (840)	1,190	0.74
Laotian (246)	315	0.19
Malaysian (7)	16	0.01
Nepalese (15)	15	0.01
Pakistani (39)	45	0.03
Sri Lankan (68)	74	0.05
Taiwanese (208)	239	0.15
Thai (97)	167	0.10
Vietnamese (1,543)	1,719	1.06
Hawaii Native/Pacific Islander (1,589)	2,411	1.49
Not Hispanic (1,527)	2,237	1.38
Hispanic (62)	174	0.11
Fijian (86)	115	0.07
Guamanian/Chamorro (501)	685	0.42
Marshallese (4)	5	<0.01
Native Hawaiian (239)	584	0.36
Samoan (240)	361	0.22
Tongan (31)	63	0.04
White (130,960)	137,927	85.25
Not Hispanic (123,347)	128,851	79.64
Hispanic (7,613)	9,076	5.61

Vashon

Place Type: CDP
County: King
Population: 10,624†

Ancestry‡	Population	%
Alsatian (0)	14	0.14
American (298)	298	3.00
Arab (0)	12	0.12
Lebanese (0)	12	0.12
Armenian (12)	46	0.46
Australian (0)	70	0.71
Austrian (0)	43	0.43
Basque (16)	28	0.28
Belgian (6)	22	0.22
British (12)	86	0.87
Cajun (0)	26	0.26
Canadian (19)	43	0.43
Czech (51)	51	0.51
Danish (8)	83	0.84
Dutch (25)	183	1.84
Eastern European (24)	24	0.24
English (502)	2,025	20.40
European (354)	434	4.37
Finnish (0)	151	1.52
French, ex. Basque (83)	614	6.19
German (320)	1,873	18.87
German Russian (25)	25	0.25
Greek (16)	42	0.42
Icelander (15)	15	0.15
Irish (226)	1,363	13.73
Italian (188)	322	3.24
Lithuanian (10)	33	0.33
Maltese (9)	9	0.09
Northern European (283)	305	3.07
Norwegian (388)	1,098	11.06
Polish (21)	153	1.54
Portuguese (0)	91	0.92
Romanian (0)	9	0.09
Russian (27)	154	1.55
Scandinavian (65)	193	1.94
Scotch-Irish (107)	270	2.72
Scottish (197)	874	8.80
Slavic (0)	9	0.09
Slovak (0)	10	0.10
Swedish (164)	858	8.64
Swiss (7)	7	0.07
Ukrainian (11)	51	0.51
Welsh (23)	197	1.98
Yugoslavian (13)	13	0.13

Hispanic Origin	Population	%
Hispanic or Latino (of any race)	434	4.09
Central American, ex. Mexican	57	0.54
Guatemalan	25	0.24
Honduran	23	0.22
Nicaraguan	4	0.04
Panamanian	1	0.01
Salvadoran	4	0.04
Cuban	6	0.06
Dominican Republic	2	0.02
Mexican	277	2.61
Puerto Rican	15	0.14
South American	19	0.18
Argentinean	6	0.06
Bolivian	1	0.01
Chilean	5	0.05
Colombian	3	0.03
Ecuadorian	1	0.01
Peruvian	1	0.01
Other South American	2	0.02
Other Hispanic or Latino	58	0.55

Race*	Population	%
African-American/Black (90)	166	1.56
Not Hispanic (81)	143	1.35
Hispanic (9)	23	0.22
American Indian/Alaska Native (61)	220	2.07
Not Hispanic (48)	187	1.76
Hispanic (13)	33	0.31
Alaska Athabascan *(Ala. Nat.)* (4)	4	0.04
Aleut *(Alaska Native)* (2)	8	0.08
Apache (1)	1	0.01
Arapaho (0)	1	0.01
Blackfeet (0)	6	0.06
Canadian/French Am. Ind. (0)	1	0.01
Central American Ind. (1)	1	0.01
Cherokee (5)	31	0.29
Cheyenne (4)	4	0.04
Chickasaw (0)	1	0.01
Chippewa (0)	8	0.08
Choctaw (4)	12	0.11
Cree (0)	1	0.01
Crow (0)	1	0.01
Delaware (0)	1	0.01
Inupiat *(Alaska Native)* (1)	4	0.04
Iroquois (0)	3	0.03
Mexican American Ind. (3)	7	0.07
Navajo (0)	2	0.02
Paiute (2)	2	0.02
Potawatomi (0)	3	0.03
Puget Sound Salish (0)	7	0.07
Shoshone (0)	1	0.01
Sioux (2)	9	0.08
Tlingit-Haida *(Alaska Native)* (8)	17	0.16
Tsimshian *(Alaska Native)* (0)	1	0.01
Yakama (2)	3	0.03
Asian (175)	296	2.79
Not Hispanic (172)	283	2.66
Hispanic (3)	13	0.12
Cambodian (5)	5	0.05
Chinese, ex. Taiwanese (45)	75	0.71
Filipino (26)	54	0.51
Indian (10)	24	0.23
Indonesian (2)	4	0.04
Japanese (42)	63	0.59
Korean (18)	33	0.31
Laotian (2)	2	0.02
Nepalese (3)	9	0.08
Taiwanese (1)	1	0.01
Thai (4)	8	0.08
Vietnamese (7)	13	0.12
Hawaii Native/Pacific Islander (5)	27	0.25
Not Hispanic (5)	25	0.24
Hispanic (0)	2	0.02
Fijian (0)	1	0.01
Guamanian/Chamorro (2)	5	0.05
Native Hawaiian (1)	10	0.09
Samoan (0)	7	0.07
White (9,808)	10,141	95.45
Not Hispanic (9,556)	9,841	92.63
Hispanic (252)	300	2.82

*Notes: † The Census 2010 population figure is used to calculate the percentages in the Hispanic Origin and Race categories. Ancestry percentages are based on the 2006-2010 American Community Survey population (not shown); ‡ Numbers in parentheses indicate the number of people reporting a single ancestry; * Numbers in parentheses indicate the number of persons reporting this race alone, not in combination with any other race; Please refer to the Explanation of Data for more information.*

Walla Walla

Place Type: City
County: Walla Walla
Population: 31,731†

Ancestry‡	Population	%
African, Sub-Saharan (68)	111	0.36
African (43)	78	0.25
Ethiopian (12)	20	0.06
Other Sub-Saharan African (13)	13	0.04
Alsatian (0)	7	0.02
American (2,203)	2,203	7.07
Arab (9)	9	0.03
Lebanese (9)	9	0.03
Armenian (8)	15	0.05
Australian (0)	7	0.02
Austrian (56)	83	0.27
Basque (37)	48	0.15
British (42)	129	0.41
Canadian (9)	49	0.16
Croatian (9)	9	0.03
Czech (19)	97	0.31
Danish (64)	229	0.73
Dutch (127)	793	2.54
English (1,104)	3,697	11.86
European (317)	431	1.38
Finnish (37)	104	0.33
French, ex. Basque (149)	1,249	4.01
French Canadian (124)	310	0.99
German (2,234)	6,604	21.18
German Russian (11)	35	0.11
Greek (23)	39	0.13
Hungarian (14)	14	0.04
Icelander (16)	39	0.13
Iranian (79)	113	0.36
Irish (1,022)	4,245	13.62
Italian (460)	1,224	3.93
Northern European (33)	60	0.19
Norwegian (433)	1,184	3.80
Pennsylvania German (14)	23	0.07
Polish (178)	620	1.99
Portuguese (29)	88	0.28
Romanian (18)	29	0.09
Russian (14)	226	0.72
Scandinavian (70)	247	0.79
Scotch-Irish (233)	680	2.18
Scottish (286)	946	3.03
Serbian (21)	21	0.07
Slavic (10)	28	0.09
Swedish (269)	1,077	3.45
Swiss (69)	201	0.64
Ukrainian (9)	74	0.24
Welsh (45)	256	0.82
West Indian, ex. Hispanic (27)	36	0.12
Jamaican (16)	25	0.08
Trinidadian/Tobagonian (11)	11	0.04
Yugoslavian (0)	7	0.02

Hispanic Origin	Population	%
Hispanic or Latino (of any race)	6,970	21.97
Central American, ex. Mexican	150	0.47
Costa Rican	7	0.02
Guatemalan	37	0.12
Honduran	3	0.01
Nicaraguan	5	0.02
Panamanian	7	0.02
Salvadoran	91	0.29
Cuban	18	0.06
Dominican Republic	4	0.01
Mexican	6,300	19.85
Puerto Rican	51	0.16
South American	72	0.23
Argentinean	4	0.01
Bolivian	1	<0.01
Chilean	17	0.05
Colombian	17	0.05
Ecuadorian	3	0.01
Paraguayan	1	<0.01
Peruvian	26	0.08
Uruguayan	1	<0.01
Venezuelan	2	0.01
Other Hispanic or Latino	375	1.18

Race*	Population	%
African-American/Black (852)	1,075	3.39
Not Hispanic (795)	975	3.07
Hispanic (57)	100	0.32
American Indian/Alaska Native (407)	768	2.42
Not Hispanic (291)	588	1.85
Hispanic (116)	180	0.57
Alaska Athabascan *(Ala. Nat.)* (0)	1	<0.01
Aleut *(Alaska Native)* (8)	9	0.03
Apache (3)	4	0.01
Arapaho (1)	3	0.01
Blackfeet (10)	24	0.08
Canadian/French Am. Ind. (1)	2	0.01
Cherokee (19)	90	0.28
Cheyenne (2)	2	0.01
Chickasaw (0)	7	0.02
Chippewa (6)	13	0.04
Choctaw (2)	8	0.03
Colville (2)	4	0.01
Cree (1)	3	0.01
Creek (0)	7	0.02
Crow (0)	1	<0.01
Delaware (0)	2	0.01
Inupiat *(Alaska Native)* (3)	10	0.03
Iroquois (2)	9	0.03
Mexican American Ind. (22)	37	0.12
Navajo (9)	16	0.05
Osage (0)	1	<0.01
Paiute (1)	4	0.01
Potawatomi (0)	1	<0.01
Puget Sound Salish (2)	6	0.02
Seminole (1)	1	<0.01
Shoshone (1)	2	0.01
Sioux (4)	11	0.03
South American Ind. (4)	4	0.01
Spanish American Ind. (6)	7	0.02
Tlingit-Haida *(Alaska Native)* (4)	10	0.03
Tsimshian *(Alaska Native)* (1)	2	0.01
Yakama (5)	7	0.02
Yup'ik *(Alaska Native)* (3)	4	0.01
Asian (454)	747	2.35
Not Hispanic (444)	708	2.23
Hispanic (10)	39	0.12
Burmese (3)	4	0.01
Cambodian (2)	3	0.01
Chinese, ex. Taiwanese (110)	155	0.49
Filipino (58)	125	0.39
Indian (55)	69	0.22
Indonesian (4)	9	0.03
Japanese (60)	150	0.47
Korean (46)	76	0.24
Laotian (29)	38	0.12
Malaysian (2)	2	0.01
Pakistani (4)	4	0.01
Sri Lankan (2)	3	0.01
Taiwanese (2)	3	0.01
Thai (11)	22	0.07
Vietnamese (31)	44	0.14
Hawaii Native/Pacific Islander (107)	216	0.68
Not Hispanic (106)	210	0.66
Hispanic (1)	6	0.02
Guamanian/Chamorro (11)	21	0.07
Native Hawaiian (8)	34	0.11
Samoan (30)	47	0.15
White (25,894)	26,932	84.88
Not Hispanic (22,329)	23,023	72.56
Hispanic (3,565)	3,909	12.32

Waller

Place Type: CDP
County: Pierce
Population: 7,922†

Ancestry‡	Population	%
African, Sub-Saharan (18)	29	0.40
African (0)	11	0.15
Somalian (18)	18	0.25
American (292)	292	4.00
Arab (4)	6	0.08
Arab (4)	4	0.05
Syrian (0)	2	0.03
Australian (0)	17	0.23
Austrian (3)	20	0.27
Belgian (0)	6	0.08
British (5)	38	0.52
Bulgarian (4)	4	0.05
Canadian (10)	21	0.29
Croatian (4)	18	0.25
Czech (15)	48	0.66
Czechoslovakian (2)	13	0.18
Danish (25)	103	1.41
Dutch (42)	166	2.27
English (287)	1,066	14.60
European (103)	174	2.38
Finnish (7)	32	0.44
French, ex. Basque (32)	250	3.42
French Canadian (74)	111	1.52
German (626)	1,962	26.87
Greek (0)	12	0.16
Hungarian (16)	26	0.36
Icelander (0)	3	0.04
Irish (184)	1,064	14.57
Italian (131)	310	4.25
Latvian (3)	14	0.19
Luxemburger (3)	3	0.04
Northern European (29)	29	0.40
Norwegian (298)	895	12.26
Polish (53)	166	2.27
Portuguese (3)	42	0.58
Romanian (0)	13	0.18
Russian (20)	93	1.27
Scandinavian (107)	152	2.08
Scotch-Irish (91)	194	2.66
Scottish (51)	194	2.66
Slavic (4)	4	0.05
Slovak (0)	6	0.08
Swedish (77)	277	3.79
Swiss (17)	29	0.40
Ukrainian (17)	26	0.36
Welsh (0)	140	1.92
Yugoslavian (14)	14	0.19

Hispanic Origin	Population	%
Hispanic or Latino (of any race)	392	4.95
Central American, ex. Mexican	17	0.21
Costa Rican	4	0.05
Guatemalan	3	0.04
Salvadoran	10	0.13
Cuban	5	0.06
Mexican	282	3.56
Puerto Rican	34	0.43
South American	5	0.06
Argentinean	2	0.03
Colombian	2	0.03
Other South American	1	0.01
Other Hispanic or Latino	49	0.62

Race*	Population	%
African-American/Black (172)	279	3.52
Not Hispanic (163)	260	3.28
Hispanic (9)	19	0.24
American Indian/Alaska Native (200)	338	4.27
Not Hispanic (165)	290	3.66
Hispanic (35)	48	0.61
Alaska Athabascan *(Ala. Nat.)* (1)	2	0.03
Aleut *(Alaska Native)* (0)	3	0.04
Blackfeet (3)	5	0.06
Canadian/French Am. Ind. (4)	9	0.11
Cherokee (12)	31	0.39
Chippewa (8)	20	0.25
Choctaw (1)	3	0.04
Colville (0)	1	0.01
Cree (1)	1	0.01
Delaware (1)	1	0.01
Inupiat *(Alaska Native)* (4)	5	0.06

*Notes: † The Census 2010 population figure is used to calculate the percentages in the Hispanic Origin and Race categories. Ancestry percentages are based on the 2006-2010 American Community Survey population (not shown); ‡ Numbers in parentheses indicate the number of people reporting a single ancestry; * Numbers in parentheses indicate the number of persons reporting this race alone, not in combination with any other race; Please refer to the Explanation of Data for more information.*

Iroquois (2)	2	0.03
Mexican American Ind. (5)	6	0.08
Navajo (2)	6	0.08
Osage (1)	1	0.01
Potawatomi (1)	1	0.01
Puget Sound Salish (85)	111	1.40
Sioux (9)	22	0.28
South American Ind. (1)	2	0.03
Tlingit-Haida *(Alaska Native)* (1)	5	0.06
Tohono O'Odham (1)	1	0.01
Yakama (5)	5	0.06
Yup'ik *(Alaska Native)* (1)	2	0.03
Asian (282)	399	5.04
Not Hispanic (273)	378	4.77
Hispanic (9)	21	0.27
Cambodian (52)	55	0.69
Chinese, ex. Taiwanese (15)	23	0.29
Filipino (30)	81	1.02
Indian (12)	13	0.16
Indonesian (0)	1	0.01
Japanese (21)	48	0.61
Korean (91)	118	1.49
Laotian (1)	3	0.04
Thai (9)	11	0.14
Vietnamese (39)	45	0.57
Hawaii Native/Pacific Islander (11)	37	0.47
Not Hispanic (10)	32	0.40
Hispanic (1)	5	0.06
Guamanian/Chamorro (3)	10	0.13
Native Hawaiian (6)	23	0.29
Samoan (0)	1	0.01
White (6,785)	7,118	89.85
Not Hispanic (6,611)	6,886	86.92
Hispanic (174)	232	2.93

Walnut Grove

Place Type: CDP
County: Clark
Population: 9,790†

Ancestry‡	Population	%
American (220)	220	2.50
Assyrian/Chaldean/Syriac (6)	6	0.07
Austrian (0)	54	0.61
Belgian (12)	26	0.29
British (9)	18	0.20
Canadian (0)	12	0.14
Croatian (11)	11	0.12
Czech (0)	30	0.34
Danish (42)	117	1.33
Dutch (19)	214	2.43
English (149)	1,094	12.41
European (97)	149	1.69
Finnish (20)	20	0.23
French, ex. Basque (15)	400	4.54
French Canadian (34)	150	1.70
German (304)	2,108	23.92
Greek (36)	199	2.26
Hungarian (13)	63	0.71
Iranian (24)	52	0.59
Irish (134)	1,290	14.64
Italian (75)	369	4.19
Norwegian (279)	673	7.64
Polish (0)	143	1.62
Portuguese (0)	41	0.47
Romanian (56)	56	0.64
Russian (344)	386	4.38
Scandinavian (95)	122	1.38
Scotch-Irish (88)	294	3.34
Scottish (41)	148	1.68
Slovak (0)	7	0.08
Slovene (0)	10	0.11
Swedish (63)	305	3.46
Swiss (10)	63	0.71
Ukrainian (509)	509	5.77
Welsh (0)	142	1.61
Yugoslavian (57)	57	0.65

Hispanic Origin	Population	%
Hispanic or Latino (of any race)	628	6.41
Central American, ex. Mexican	33	0.34
Costa Rican	5	0.05
Guatemalan	10	0.10
Honduran	3	0.03
Nicaraguan	1	0.01
Panamanian	7	0.07
Salvadoran	7	0.07
Cuban	11	0.11
Mexican	479	4.89
Puerto Rican	23	0.23
South American	18	0.18
Argentinean	1	0.01
Colombian	1	0.01
Ecuadorian	3	0.03
Paraguayan	6	0.06
Peruvian	7	0.07
Other Hispanic or Latino	64	0.65

Race*	Population	%
African-American/Black (219)	328	3.35
Not Hispanic (215)	314	3.21
Hispanic (4)	14	0.14
American Indian/Alaska Native (66)	169	1.73
Not Hispanic (57)	149	1.52
Hispanic (9)	20	0.20
Aleut *(Alaska Native)* (1)	2	0.02
Apache (0)	4	0.04
Blackfeet (0)	11	0.11
Canadian/French Am. Ind. (3)	4	0.04
Central American Ind. (2)	2	0.02
Cherokee (7)	34	0.35
Chickasaw (3)	3	0.03
Chippewa (3)	9	0.09
Choctaw (0)	3	0.03
Colville (1)	1	0.01
Cree (0)	1	0.01
Inupiat *(Alaska Native)* (1)	1	0.01
Iroquois (1)	3	0.03
Mexican American Ind. (3)	7	0.07
Navajo (1)	4	0.04
Potawatomi (2)	2	0.02
Sioux (1)	8	0.08
Tlingit-Haida *(Alaska Native)* (3)	5	0.05
Asian (445)	592	6.05
Not Hispanic (443)	571	5.83
Hispanic (2)	21	0.21
Bhutanese (5)	5	0.05
Cambodian (37)	41	0.42
Chinese, ex. Taiwanese (62)	91	0.93
Filipino (99)	153	1.56
Hmong (2)	2	0.02
Indian (52)	68	0.69
Indonesian (1)	2	0.02
Japanese (31)	57	0.58
Korean (27)	44	0.45
Laotian (22)	26	0.27
Pakistani (0)	1	0.01
Taiwanese (4)	4	0.04
Thai (8)	10	0.10
Vietnamese (80)	95	0.97
Hawaii Native/Pacific Islander (71)	134	1.37
Not Hispanic (67)	116	1.18
Hispanic (4)	18	0.18
Fijian (11)	19	0.19
Guamanian/Chamorro (26)	31	0.32
Marshallese (2)	5	0.05
Native Hawaiian (14)	44	0.45
Samoan (4)	7	0.07
White (8,353)	8,717	89.04
Not Hispanic (8,049)	8,351	85.30
Hispanic (304)	366	3.74

Washougal

Place Type: City
County: Clark
Population: 14,095†

Ancestry‡	Population	%
American (868)	868	6.56
Arab (14)	14	0.11
Arab (14)	14	0.11
Australian (0)	11	0.08
Belgian (55)	65	0.49
British (58)	126	0.95
Bulgarian (0)	12	0.09
Canadian (48)	125	0.95
Czech (18)	78	0.59
Danish (123)	349	2.64
Dutch (77)	588	4.45
Eastern European (19)	19	0.14
English (546)	1,947	14.72
European (183)	187	1.41
Finnish (53)	101	0.76
French, ex. Basque (22)	346	2.62
French Canadian (8)	36	0.27
German (924)	3,788	28.65
Hungarian (0)	62	0.47
Icelander (0)	46	0.35
Irish (504)	2,080	15.73
Israeli (75)	115	0.87
Italian (148)	539	4.08
Lithuanian (20)	64	0.48
Northern European (0)	58	0.44
Norwegian (408)	913	6.90
Pennsylvania German (17)	17	0.13
Polish (33)	216	1.63
Portuguese (0)	103	0.78
Russian (37)	64	0.48
Scandinavian (22)	65	0.49
Scotch-Irish (481)	679	5.13
Scottish (90)	418	3.16
Slovene (18)	18	0.14
Swedish (111)	518	3.92
Swiss (10)	65	0.49
Turkish (0)	12	0.09
Ukrainian (72)	81	0.61
Welsh (28)	221	1.67
Yugoslavian (9)	25	0.19

Hispanic Origin	Population	%
Hispanic or Latino (of any race)	753	5.34
Central American, ex. Mexican	42	0.30
Costa Rican	4	0.03
Guatemalan	10	0.07
Nicaraguan	11	0.08
Panamanian	3	0.02
Salvadoran	12	0.09
Other Central American	2	0.01
Cuban	9	0.06
Dominican Republic	1	0.01
Mexican	560	3.97
Puerto Rican	33	0.23
South American	25	0.18
Argentinean	3	0.02
Chilean	6	0.04
Colombian	5	0.04
Ecuadorian	1	0.01
Peruvian	5	0.04
Venezuelan	4	0.03
Other South American	1	0.01
Other Hispanic or Latino	83	0.59

Race*	Population	%
African-American/Black (91)	196	1.39
Not Hispanic (85)	187	1.33
Hispanic (6)	9	0.06
American Indian/Alaska Native (140)	356	2.53
Not Hispanic (120)	310	2.20
Hispanic (20)	46	0.33
Aleut *(Alaska Native)* (0)	6	0.04
Apache (4)	8	0.06
Blackfeet (3)	24	0.17
Cherokee (17)	88	0.62
Cheyenne (3)	5	0.04
Chickasaw (1)	1	0.01
Chippewa (4)	17	0.12
Choctaw (6)	10	0.07

*Notes: † The Census 2010 population figure is used to calculate the percentages in the Hispanic Origin and Race categories. Ancestry percentages are based on the 2006-2010 American Community Survey population (not shown); ‡ Numbers in parentheses indicate the number of people reporting a single ancestry; * Numbers in parentheses indicate the number of persons reporting this race alone, not in combination with any other race; Please refer to the Explanation of Data for more information.*

Colville (2)	6	0.04
Comanche (0)	1	0.01
Hopi (0)	2	0.01
Inupiat *(Alaska Native)* (0)	5	0.04
Iroquois (4)	8	0.06
Kiowa (2)	2	0.01
Mexican American Ind. (4)	4	0.03
Navajo (1)	2	0.01
Osage (0)	4	0.03
Paiute (1)	1	0.01
Potawatomi (1)	1	0.01
Puget Sound Salish (6)	7	0.05
Sioux (0)	6	0.04
Spanish American Ind. (5)	5	0.04
Tlingit-Haida *(Alaska Native)* (7)	11	0.08
Yakama (0)	2	0.01
Yaqui (0)	1	0.01
Yup'ik *(Alaska Native)* (0)	5	0.04
Asian (336)	515	3.65
Not Hispanic (332)	491	3.48
Hispanic (4)	24	0.17
Burmese (2)	2	0.01
Cambodian (2)	4	0.03
Chinese, ex. Taiwanese (57)	77	0.55
Filipino (59)	114	0.81
Hmong (10)	12	0.09
Indian (26)	33	0.23
Indonesian (0)	4	0.03
Japanese (36)	97	0.69
Korean (60)	97	0.69
Laotian (1)	2	0.01
Pakistani (1)	3	0.02
Taiwanese (1)	1	0.01
Thai (10)	11	0.08
Vietnamese (47)	71	0.50
Hawaii Native/Pacific Islander (22)	67	0.48
Not Hispanic (21)	60	0.43
Hispanic (1)	7	0.05
Fijian (3)	4	0.03
Guamanian/Chamorro (7)	13	0.09
Marshallese (2)	2	0.01
Native Hawaiian (5)	34	0.24
Samoan (4)	8	0.06
White (12,729)	13,240	93.93
Not Hispanic (12,327)	12,756	90.50
Hispanic (402)	484	3.43

Wenatchee

Place Type: City
County: Chelan
Population: 31,925†

Ancestry‡	Population	%
African, Sub-Saharan (0)	70	0.22
Ethiopian (0)	31	0.10
Liberian (0)	21	0.07
Other Sub-Saharan African (0)	18	0.06
American (4,115)	4,115	13.20
Arab (14)	17	0.05
Arab (14)	17	0.05
Australian (0)	10	0.03
Austrian (91)	106	0.34
British (36)	50	0.16
Cajun (0)	70	0.22
Canadian (43)	83	0.27
Celtic (0)	14	0.04
Croatian (13)	111	0.36
Czech (73)	100	0.32
Czechoslovakian (0)	11	0.04
Danish (17)	141	0.45
Dutch (94)	459	1.47
Eastern European (12)	12	0.04
English (1,067)	3,122	10.02
European (290)	333	1.07
Finnish (80)	145	0.47
French, ex. Basque (198)	1,101	3.53
French Canadian (90)	196	0.63
German (2,696)	5,727	18.37
Greek (34)	34	0.11
Hungarian (80)	120	0.38
Irish (641)	2,566	8.23
Italian (175)	569	1.83
Lithuanian (0)	32	0.10
Northern European (94)	94	0.30
Norwegian (601)	1,337	4.29
Pennsylvania German (0)	34	0.11
Polish (144)	411	1.32
Portuguese (14)	167	0.54
Romanian (41)	51	0.16
Russian (5)	70	0.22
Scandinavian (108)	170	0.55
Scotch-Irish (139)	588	1.89
Scottish (266)	789	2.53
Slavic (8)	8	0.03
Swedish (172)	749	2.40
Swiss (51)	127	0.41
Ukrainian (136)	153	0.49
Welsh (21)	156	0.50
Yugoslavian (57)	57	0.18

Hispanic Origin	Population	%
Hispanic or Latino (of any race)	9,388	29.41
Central American, ex. Mexican	307	0.96
Costa Rican	1	<0.01
Guatemalan	71	0.22
Honduran	25	0.08
Nicaraguan	14	0.04
Panamanian	15	0.05
Salvadoran	178	0.56
Other Central American	3	0.01
Cuban	8	0.03
Dominican Republic	1	<0.01
Mexican	8,567	26.83
Puerto Rican	71	0.22
South American	46	0.14
Argentinean	4	0.01
Bolivian	3	0.01
Chilean	6	0.02
Colombian	7	0.02
Ecuadorian	7	0.02
Paraguayan	3	0.01
Peruvian	10	0.03
Uruguayan	2	0.01
Venezuelan	2	0.01
Other South American	2	0.01
Other Hispanic or Latino	388	1.22

Race*	Population	%
African-American/Black (142)	264	0.83
Not Hispanic (109)	215	0.67
Hispanic (33)	49	0.15
American Indian/Alaska Native (368)	692	2.17
Not Hispanic (263)	524	1.64
Hispanic (105)	168	0.53
Aleut *(Alaska Native)* (4)	5	0.02
Apache (7)	10	0.03
Arapaho (0)	1	<0.01
Blackfeet (6)	20	0.06
Canadian/French Am. Ind. (7)	12	0.04
Cherokee (29)	71	0.22
Cheyenne (0)	1	<0.01
Chickasaw (0)	3	0.01
Chippewa (14)	22	0.07
Choctaw (6)	21	0.07
Colville (53)	76	0.24
Comanche (0)	3	0.01
Cree (2)	6	0.02
Creek (2)	5	0.02
Inupiat *(Alaska Native)* (5)	6	0.02
Iroquois (1)	2	0.01
Mexican American Ind. (37)	48	0.15
Navajo (5)	13	0.04
Ottawa (0)	3	0.01
Paiute (2)	2	0.01
Potawatomi (1)	1	<0.01
Pueblo (0)	1	<0.01
Puget Sound Salish (6)	16	0.05
Seminole (0)	2	0.01
Sioux (7)	14	0.04
Spanish American Ind. (1)	1	<0.01
Tlingit-Haida *(Alaska Native)* (4)	7	0.02
Tsimshian *(Alaska Native)* (2)	2	0.01
Yakama (2)	2	0.01
Yup'ik *(Alaska Native)* (2)	2	0.01
Asian (350)	526	1.65
Not Hispanic (337)	493	1.54
Hispanic (13)	33	0.10
Cambodian (13)	19	0.06
Chinese, ex. Taiwanese (56)	74	0.23
Filipino (50)	122	0.38
Indian (32)	39	0.12
Indonesian (2)	3	0.01
Japanese (57)	102	0.32
Korean (35)	56	0.18
Laotian (9)	9	0.03
Pakistani (3)	5	0.02
Thai (11)	17	0.05
Vietnamese (59)	67	0.21
Hawaii Native/Pacific Islander (51)	115	0.36
Not Hispanic (43)	102	0.32
Hispanic (8)	13	0.04
Guamanian/Chamorro (20)	28	0.09
Native Hawaiian (12)	48	0.15
Samoan (10)	15	0.05
White (24,490)	25,415	79.61
Not Hispanic (21,198)	21,720	68.03
Hispanic (3,292)	3,695	11.57

West Richland

Place Type: City
County: Benton
Population: 11,811†

Ancestry‡	Population	%
African, Sub-Saharan (0)	12	0.11
Kenyan (0)	12	0.11
American (1,034)	1,034	9.37
Arab (0)	23	0.21
Lebanese (0)	23	0.21
Austrian (30)	46	0.42
Belgian (0)	10	0.09
British (8)	8	0.07
Canadian (0)	27	0.24
Czech (11)	32	0.29
Danish (72)	199	1.80
Dutch (34)	142	1.29
English (503)	1,463	13.26
European (288)	301	2.73
Finnish (23)	73	0.66
French, ex. Basque (37)	323	2.93
French Canadian (44)	100	0.91
German (869)	2,988	27.07
Greek (61)	61	0.55
Hungarian (0)	8	0.07
Irish (216)	1,276	11.56
Italian (178)	547	4.96
Lithuanian (0)	15	0.14
Northern European (15)	23	0.21
Norwegian (308)	858	7.77
Polish (56)	236	2.14
Portuguese (0)	20	0.18
Romanian (47)	47	0.43
Russian (68)	87	0.79
Scandinavian (13)	13	0.12
Scotch-Irish (45)	126	1.14
Scottish (58)	349	3.16
Slovak (12)	38	0.34
Swedish (147)	452	4.10
Swiss (0)	40	0.36
Ukrainian (12)	24	0.22
Welsh (14)	75	0.68

Hispanic Origin	Population	%
Hispanic or Latino (of any race)	844	7.15
Central American, ex. Mexican	14	0.12
Costa Rican	2	0.02
Guatemalan	2	0.02
Honduran	1	0.01

*Notes: † The Census 2010 population figure is used to calculate the percentages in the Hispanic Origin and Race categories. Ancestry percentages are based on the 2006-2010 American Community Survey population (not shown); ‡ Numbers in parentheses indicate the number of people reporting a single ancestry; * Numbers in parentheses indicate the number of persons reporting this race alone, not in combination with any other race; Please refer to the Explanation of Data for more information.*

Panamanian	2	0.02
Salvadoran	7	0.06
Cuban	9	0.08
Dominican Republic	2	0.02
Mexican	651	5.51
Puerto Rican	29	0.25
South American	33	0.28
Argentinean	2	0.02
Chilean	7	0.06
Colombian	4	0.03
Ecuadorian	10	0.08
Peruvian	9	0.08
Venezuelan	1	0.01
Other Hispanic or Latino	106	0.90

Race*	Population	%
African-American/Black (95)	179	1.52
Not Hispanic (93)	170	1.44
Hispanic (2)	9	0.08
American Indian/Alaska Native (136)	254	2.15
Not Hispanic (128)	227	1.92
Hispanic (8)	27	0.23
Alaska Athabascan *(Ala. Nat.)* (4)	5	0.04
Aleut *(Alaska Native)* (2)	2	0.02
Apache (0)	1	0.01
Blackfeet (3)	6	0.05
Canadian/French Am. Ind. (8)	8	0.07
Cherokee (28)	59	0.50
Cheyenne (0)	1	0.01
Chickasaw (4)	4	0.03
Chippewa (5)	8	0.07
Choctaw (4)	5	0.04
Colville (1)	2	0.02
Comanche (0)	1	0.01
Creek (4)	5	0.04
Iroquois (6)	8	0.07
Mexican American Ind. (0)	1	0.01
Navajo (2)	15	0.13
Paiute (5)	5	0.04
Potawatomi (1)	5	0.04
Puget Sound Salish (0)	1	0.01
Seminole (0)	1	0.01
Sioux (2)	7	0.06
Tlingit-Haida *(Alaska Native)* (2)	8	0.07
Yakama (3)	3	0.03
Asian (224)	361	3.06
Not Hispanic (224)	350	2.96
Hispanic (0)	11	0.09
Cambodian (11)	13	0.11
Chinese, ex. Taiwanese (30)	37	0.31
Filipino (43)	78	0.66
Indian (31)	41	0.35
Japanese (13)	61	0.52
Korean (24)	34	0.29
Laotian (34)	41	0.35
Malaysian (0)	1	0.01
Nepalese (1)	1	0.01
Pakistani (1)	1	0.01
Taiwanese (0)	1	0.01
Thai (11)	24	0.20
Vietnamese (17)	19	0.16
Hawaii Native/Pacific Islander (23)	44	0.37
Not Hispanic (20)	38	0.32
Hispanic (3)	6	0.05
Guamanian/Chamorro (4)	8	0.07
Native Hawaiian (3)	14	0.12
Samoan (5)	7	0.06
White (10,671)	11,031	93.40
Not Hispanic (10,209)	10,482	88.75
Hispanic (462)	549	4.65

White Center

Place Type: CDP
County: King
Population: 13,495†

Ancestry‡	Population	%
African, Sub-Saharan (291)	291	2.30
African (25)	25	0.20
Ethiopian (8)	8	0.06
Somalian (186)	186	1.47
Other Sub-Saharan African (72)	72	0.57
American (497)	497	3.93
Arab (83)	83	0.66
Iraqi (83)	83	0.66
Armenian (12)	12	0.09
Austrian (15)	60	0.47
British (17)	89	0.70
Canadian (14)	23	0.18
Croatian (32)	32	0.25
Czech (0)	43	0.34
Danish (33)	145	1.15
Dutch (13)	151	1.19
English (144)	740	5.85
European (32)	41	0.32
Finnish (18)	75	0.59
French, ex. Basque (21)	421	3.33
French Canadian (0)	8	0.06
German (390)	1,182	9.34
Greek (12)	48	0.38
Hungarian (11)	26	0.21
Irish (207)	806	6.37
Italian (86)	441	3.48
Norwegian (96)	472	3.73
Polish (35)	78	0.62
Portuguese (0)	21	0.17
Romanian (0)	9	0.07
Russian (19)	112	0.88
Scandinavian (64)	144	1.14
Scotch-Irish (43)	103	0.81
Scottish (97)	234	1.85
Swedish (59)	243	1.92
Swiss (0)	20	0.16
Turkish (0)	28	0.22
Ukrainian (28)	28	0.22
Welsh (9)	62	0.49
Yugoslavian (37)	37	0.29

Hispanic Origin	Population	%
Hispanic or Latino (of any race)	2,906	21.53
Central American, ex. Mexican	323	2.39
Costa Rican	4	0.03
Guatemalan	87	0.64
Honduran	41	0.30
Nicaraguan	12	0.09
Panamanian	1	0.01
Salvadoran	178	1.32
Cuban	16	0.12
Dominican Republic	17	0.13
Mexican	2,207	16.35
Puerto Rican	84	0.62
South American	76	0.56
Argentinean	4	0.03
Bolivian	1	0.01
Chilean	31	0.23
Colombian	11	0.08
Ecuadorian	4	0.03
Peruvian	23	0.17
Uruguayan	1	0.01
Other South American	1	0.01
Other Hispanic or Latino	183	1.36

Race*	Population	%
African-American/Black (1,220)	1,487	11.02
Not Hispanic (1,159)	1,363	10.10
Hispanic (61)	124	0.92
American Indian/Alaska Native (221)	426	3.16
Not Hispanic (186)	345	2.56
Hispanic (35)	81	0.60
Alaska Athabascan *(Ala. Nat.)* (0)	1	0.01
Aleut *(Alaska Native)* (3)	8	0.06
Apache (0)	1	0.01
Arapaho (0)	2	0.01
Blackfeet (26)	38	0.28
Canadian/French Am. Ind. (4)	9	0.07
Central American Ind. (0)	3	0.02
Cherokee (18)	54	0.40
Cheyenne (0)	1	0.01
Chickasaw (1)	2	0.01
Chippewa (10)	13	0.10
Choctaw (0)	6	0.04
Colville (1)	9	0.07
Cree (2)	4	0.03
Creek (1)	1	0.01
Inupiat *(Alaska Native)* (3)	3	0.02
Iroquois (2)	2	0.01
Mexican American Ind. (11)	14	0.10
Navajo (6)	8	0.06
Paiute (0)	2	0.01
Potawatomi (0)	1	0.01
Puget Sound Salish (17)	26	0.19
Sioux (1)	14	0.10
Spanish American Ind. (2)	3	0.02
Tlingit-Haida *(Alaska Native)* (12)	22	0.16
Tsimshian *(Alaska Native)* (1)	2	0.01
Ute (0)	1	0.01
Yakama (3)	3	0.02
Asian (3,091)	3,374	25.00
Not Hispanic (3,065)	3,326	24.65
Hispanic (26)	48	0.36
Burmese (0)	3	0.02
Cambodian (583)	642	4.76
Chinese, ex. Taiwanese (140)	211	1.56
Filipino (368)	452	3.35
Hmong (6)	6	0.04
Indian (69)	105	0.78
Indonesian (5)	12	0.09
Japanese (46)	86	0.64
Korean (72)	92	0.68
Laotian (70)	76	0.56
Malaysian (0)	4	0.03
Nepalese (1)	1	0.01
Taiwanese (4)	4	0.03
Thai (30)	37	0.27
Vietnamese (1,568)	1,679	12.44
Hawaii Native/Pacific Islander (226)	346	2.56
Not Hispanic (224)	335	2.48
Hispanic (2)	11	0.08
Fijian (14)	15	0.11
Guamanian/Chamorro (2)	8	0.06
Native Hawaiian (2)	31	0.23
Samoan (162)	212	1.57
Tongan (24)	30	0.22
White (6,337)	7,055	52.28
Not Hispanic (5,341)	5,826	43.17
Hispanic (996)	1,229	9.11

Woodinville

Place Type: City
County: King
Population: 10,938†

Ancestry‡	Population	%
American (304)	304	2.85
Armenian (15)	15	0.14
Belgian (23)	32	0.30
British (58)	97	0.91
Bulgarian (19)	19	0.18
Canadian (75)	111	1.04
Czech (0)	29	0.27
Czechoslovakian (14)	14	0.13
Danish (0)	87	0.82
Dutch (149)	453	4.25
Eastern European (69)	69	0.65
English (282)	1,356	12.73
Estonian (16)	16	0.15
European (295)	406	3.81
Finnish (59)	143	1.34
French, ex. Basque (49)	535	5.02
French Canadian (24)	158	1.48
German (745)	2,568	24.11
Greek (12)	63	0.59
Hungarian (0)	26	0.24
Irish (332)	1,391	13.06
Italian (206)	412	3.87
Latvian (0)	13	0.12
Lithuanian (13)	58	0.54
Northern European (11)	11	0.10

SECTION TWO

*Notes: † The Census 2010 population figure is used to calculate the percentages in the Hispanic Origin and Race categories. Ancestry percentages are based on the 2006-2010 American Community Survey population (not shown); ‡ Numbers in parentheses indicate the number of people reporting a single ancestry; * Numbers in parentheses indicate the number of persons reporting this race alone, not in combination with any other race; Please refer to the Explanation of Data for more information.*

Norwegian (249)	684	6.42
Polish (41)	250	2.35
Portuguese (8)	24	0.23
Romanian (14)	27	0.25
Russian (33)	82	0.77
Scandinavian (34)	76	0.71
Scotch-Irish (120)	275	2.58
Scottish (133)	471	4.42
Slovak (0)	22	0.21
Swedish (90)	458	4.30
Swiss (34)	81	0.76
Welsh (6)	75	0.70
West Indian, ex. Hispanic (32)	47	0.44
West Indian (11)	26	0.24
Other West Indian (21)	21	0.20

Hispanic Origin	Population	%
Hispanic or Latino (of any race)	801	7.32
Central American, ex. Mexican	37	0.34
Costa Rican	4	0.04
Guatemalan	12	0.11
Honduran	5	0.05
Salvadoran	16	0.15
Cuban	3	0.03
Dominican Republic	2	0.02
Mexican	568	5.19
Puerto Rican	31	0.28
South American	61	0.56
Argentinean	12	0.11
Chilean	2	0.02
Colombian	12	0.11
Ecuadorian	3	0.03
Peruvian	25	0.23
Uruguayan	1	0.01
Venezuelan	3	0.03
Other South American	3	0.03
Other Hispanic or Latino	99	0.91

Race*	Population	%
African-American/Black (158)	257	2.35
Not Hispanic (151)	237	2.17
Hispanic (7)	20	0.18
American Indian/Alaska Native (48)	152	1.39
Not Hispanic (39)	132	1.21
Hispanic (9)	20	0.18
Alaska Athabascan *(Ala. Nat.)* (0)	1	0.01
Aleut *(Alaska Native)* (2)	4	0.04
Apache (1)	6	0.05
Blackfeet (1)	9	0.08
Canadian/French Am. Ind. (1)	3	0.03
Central American Ind. (3)	3	0.03
Cherokee (1)	28	0.26
Cheyenne (0)	3	0.03
Chippewa (1)	1	0.01
Choctaw (0)	2	0.02
Colville (1)	2	0.02
Comanche (0)	1	0.01
Cree (0)	1	0.01
Delaware (1)	1	0.01
Inupiat *(Alaska Native)* (0)	1	0.01
Iroquois (0)	2	0.02
Puget Sound Salish (1)	3	0.03
Sioux (4)	5	0.05
Spanish American Ind. (1)	1	0.01
Tlingit-Haida *(Alaska Native)* (2)	8	0.07
Yakama (2)	2	0.02
Asian (1,230)	1,459	13.34
Not Hispanic (1,217)	1,426	13.04
Hispanic (13)	33	0.30
Burmese (12)	12	0.11
Cambodian (41)	55	0.50
Chinese, ex. Taiwanese (267)	365	3.34
Filipino (155)	229	2.09
Hmong (6)	7	0.06
Indian (261)	287	2.62
Indonesian (12)	13	0.12
Japanese (106)	205	1.87
Korean (115)	145	1.33
Laotian (10)	10	0.09
Malaysian (0)	2	0.02
Nepalese (3)	3	0.03
Pakistani (40)	44	0.40
Sri Lankan (9)	10	0.09
Taiwanese (33)	42	0.38
Thai (11)	11	0.10
Vietnamese (74)	96	0.88
Hawaii Native/Pacific Islander (19)	52	0.48
Not Hispanic (19)	50	0.46
Hispanic (0)	2	0.02
Fijian (1)	1	0.01
Guamanian/Chamorro (0)	1	0.01
Native Hawaiian (3)	24	0.22
Samoan (5)	5	0.05
White (8,769)	9,172	83.85
Not Hispanic (8,308)	8,657	79.15
Hispanic (461)	515	4.71

Yakima

Place Type: City
County: Yakima
Population: 91,067†

Ancestry‡	Population	%
African, Sub-Saharan (135)	205	0.23
African (110)	180	0.20
Other Sub-Saharan African (25)	25	0.03
Alsatian (11)	27	0.03
American (3,483)	3,483	3.93
Arab (184)	184	0.21
Arab (174)	174	0.20
Lebanese (10)	10	0.01
Armenian (43)	84	0.09
Australian (39)	39	0.04
Austrian (14)	81	0.09
Basque (14)	24	0.03
Belgian (0)	11	0.01
Brazilian (0)	16	0.02
British (64)	129	0.15
Bulgarian (13)	63	0.07
Canadian (85)	273	0.31
Croatian (0)	47	0.05
Czech (75)	274	0.31
Czechoslovakian (39)	96	0.11
Danish (104)	614	0.69
Dutch (341)	1,907	2.15
English (2,431)	8,445	9.53
European (680)	863	0.97
Finnish (87)	187	0.21
French, ex. Basque (894)	3,606	4.07
French Canadian (194)	482	0.54
German (5,569)	14,958	16.88
German Russian (0)	25	0.03
Greek (45)	237	0.27
Hungarian (65)	142	0.16
Icelander (0)	30	0.03
Irish (2,046)	7,822	8.83
Italian (481)	1,539	1.74
Luxemburger (0)	85	0.10
Northern European (126)	156	0.18
Norwegian (1,038)	3,271	3.69
Polish (374)	859	0.97
Portuguese (58)	261	0.29
Romanian (70)	116	0.13
Russian (57)	589	0.66
Scandinavian (161)	253	0.29
Scotch-Irish (498)	1,472	1.66
Scottish (469)	2,062	2.33
Slavic (21)	21	0.02
Slovak (9)	24	0.03
Swedish (676)	2,075	2.34
Swiss (21)	164	0.19
Turkish (0)	8	0.01
Ukrainian (68)	148	0.17
Welsh (60)	355	0.40
Yugoslavian (37)	80	0.09

Hispanic Origin	Population	%
Hispanic or Latino (of any race)	37,587	41.27
Central American, ex. Mexican	338	0.37
Costa Rican	15	0.02
Guatemalan	72	0.08
Honduran	42	0.05
Nicaraguan	28	0.03
Panamanian	17	0.02
Salvadoran	162	0.18
Other Central American	2	<0.01
Cuban	48	0.05
Dominican Republic	23	0.03
Mexican	34,697	38.10
Puerto Rican	232	0.25
South American	149	0.16
Argentinean	9	0.01
Bolivian	12	0.01
Chilean	12	0.01
Colombian	39	0.04
Ecuadorian	7	0.01
Paraguayan	1	<0.01
Peruvian	47	0.05
Uruguayan	2	<0.01
Venezuelan	16	0.02
Other South American	4	<0.01
Other Hispanic or Latino	2,100	2.31

Race*	Population	%
African-American/Black (1,556)	2,373	2.61
Not Hispanic (1,311)	1,860	2.04
Hispanic (245)	513	0.56
American Indian/Alaska Native (1,838)	3,152	3.46
Not Hispanic (1,311)	2,228	2.45
Hispanic (527)	924	1.01
Alaska Athabascan *(Ala. Nat.)* (9)	12	0.01
Aleut *(Alaska Native)* (7)	11	0.01
Apache (11)	30	0.03
Arapaho (10)	13	0.01
Blackfeet (64)	167	0.18
Canadian/French Am. Ind. (3)	10	0.01
Cherokee (49)	238	0.26
Cheyenne (2)	7	0.01
Chickasaw (12)	32	0.04
Chippewa (45)	88	0.10
Choctaw (21)	58	0.06
Colville (62)	103	0.11
Comanche (1)	4	<0.01
Cree (0)	4	<0.01
Creek (9)	20	0.02
Crow (2)	7	0.01
Delaware (0)	2	<0.01
Hopi (5)	8	0.01
Inupiat *(Alaska Native)* (3)	7	0.01
Iroquois (5)	11	0.01
Lumbee (0)	1	<0.01
Mexican American Ind. (80)	118	0.13
Navajo (17)	33	0.04
Osage (0)	8	0.01
Ottawa (1)	3	<0.01
Paiute (8)	8	0.01
Pima (6)	6	0.01
Potawatomi (11)	16	0.02
Pueblo (4)	6	0.01
Puget Sound Salish (44)	82	0.09
Seminole (3)	8	0.01
Shoshone (1)	1	<0.01
Sioux (48)	87	0.10
South American Ind. (1)	3	<0.01
Spanish American Ind. (6)	9	0.01
Tlingit-Haida *(Alaska Native)* (26)	47	0.05
Tohono O'Odham (0)	1	<0.01
Tsimshian *(Alaska Native)* (6)	10	0.01
Ute (1)	4	<0.01
Yakama (457)	657	0.72
Yaqui (5)	18	0.02
Yuman (6)	6	0.01
Yup'ik *(Alaska Native)* (2)	4	<0.01
Asian (1,347)	2,058	2.26
Not Hispanic (1,286)	1,787	1.96
Hispanic (61)	271	0.30
Bangladeshi (2)	2	<0.01
Bhutanese (1)	1	<0.01
Cambodian (10)	19	0.02

*Notes: † The Census 2010 population figure is used to calculate the percentages in the Hispanic Origin and Race categories. Ancestry percentages are based on the 2006-2010 American Community Survey population (not shown); ‡ Numbers in parentheses indicate the number of people reporting a single ancestry; * Numbers in parentheses indicate the number of persons reporting this race alone, not in combination with any other race; Please refer to the Explanation of Data for more information.*

Category	Number	Percent
Chinese, ex. Taiwanese (227)	327	0.36
Filipino (302)	627	0.69
Hmong (1)	1	<0.01
Indian (229)	275	0.30
Indonesian (0)	1	<0.01
Japanese (108)	234	0.26
Korean (223)	311	0.34
Laotian (14)	17	0.02
Malaysian (0)	1	<0.01
Nepalese (2)	2	<0.01
Pakistani (47)	55	0.06
Taiwanese (17)	24	0.03
Thai (15)	33	0.04
Vietnamese (97)	110	0.12
Hawaii Native/Pacific Islander (83)	261	0.29
Not Hispanic (46)	144	0.16
Hispanic (37)	117	0.13
Guamanian/Chamorro (29)	39	0.04
Marshallese (2)	2	<0.01
Native Hawaiian (15)	86	0.09
Samoan (15)	56	0.06
Tongan (6)	11	0.01
White (61,065)	64,616	70.95
Not Hispanic (47,523)	49,267	54.10
Hispanic (13,542)	15,349	16.85

*Notes: † The Census 2010 population figure is used to calculate the percentages in the Hispanic Origin and Race categories. Ancestry percentages are based on the 2006-2010 American Community Survey population (not shown); ‡ Numbers in parentheses indicate the number of people reporting a single ancestry; * Numbers in parentheses indicate the number of persons reporting this race alone, not in combination with any other race; Please refer to the Explanation of Data for more information.*

WEST VIRGINIA

Place Type: State
Population: 1,852,994†

Ancestry‡	Population	%
Afghan (12)	12	<0.01
African, Sub-Saharan (3,296)	4,094	0.22
African (2,383)	3,004	0.16
Cape Verdean (26)	43	<0.01
Ethiopian (297)	306	0.02
Ghanaian (47)	47	<0.01
Kenyan (182)	214	0.01
Liberian (28)	28	<0.01
Nigerian (171)	262	0.01
South African (32)	36	<0.01
Ugandan (50)	50	<0.01
Other Sub-Saharan African (80)	104	0.01
Albanian (35)	35	<0.01
Alsatian (16)	18	<0.01
American (246,632)	246,632	13.40
Arab (3,353)	6,081	0.33
Arab (484)	517	0.03
Egyptian (141)	408	0.02
Iraqi (99)	99	0.01
Jordanian (29)	44	<0.01
Lebanese (1,362)	3,189	0.17
Moroccan (102)	111	0.01
Palestinian (25)	44	<0.01
Syrian (595)	1,035	0.06
Other Arab (516)	634	0.03
Armenian (52)	196	0.01
Assyrian/Chaldean/Syriac (24)	24	<0.01
Australian (70)	174	0.01
Austrian (557)	2,133	0.12
Basque (49)	67	<0.01
Belgian (486)	1,311	0.07
Brazilian (237)	237	0.01
British (2,959)	5,294	0.29
Bulgarian (136)	188	0.01
Cajun (96)	171	0.01
Canadian (564)	1,179	0.06
Carpatho Rusyn (9)	35	<0.01
Celtic (119)	238	0.01
Croatian (978)	2,396	0.13
Cypriot (21)	21	<0.01
Czech (1,129)	3,834	0.21
Czechoslovakian (789)	1,634	0.09
Danish (458)	1,451	0.08
Dutch (6,594)	46,046	2.50
Eastern European (445)	536	0.03
English (110,194)	225,960	12.28
Estonian (26)	40	<0.01
European (10,045)	11,343	0.62
Finnish (264)	796	0.04
French, ex. Basque (6,913)	31,698	1.72
French Canadian (1,536)	3,272	0.18
German (130,824)	364,092	19.78
German Russian (34)	64	<0.01
Greek (2,153)	5,595	0.30
Guyanese (22)	46	<0.01
Hungarian (3,558)	9,727	0.53
Icelander (13)	66	<0.01
Iranian (202)	288	0.02
Irish (90,447)	278,642	15.14
Israeli (55)	110	0.01
Italian (37,681)	85,791	4.66
Latvian (63)	96	0.01
Lithuanian (688)	1,960	0.11
Luxemburger (2)	13	<0.01
Macedonian (47)	47	<0.01
Maltese (9)	32	<0.01
New Zealander (10)	10	<0.01
Northern European (416)	451	0.02
Norwegian (1,249)	4,093	0.22
Pennsylvania German (678)	1,048	0.06
Polish (11,098)	34,920	1.90
Portuguese (400)	1,161	0.06
Romanian (263)	829	0.05
Russian (2,124)	6,836	0.37
Scandinavian (456)	1,064	0.06
Scotch-Irish (24,930)	52,433	2.85
Scottish (15,171)	39,458	2.14
Serbian (526)	1,507	0.08
Slavic (293)	1,048	0.06
Slovak (1,476)	4,579	0.25
Slovene (219)	432	0.02
Swedish (1,772)	7,471	0.41
Swiss (987)	3,806	0.21
Turkish (358)	585	0.03
Ukrainian (612)	1,952	0.11
Welsh (4,037)	14,347	0.78
West Indian, ex. Hispanic (1,210)	2,079	0.11
Bahamian (26)	26	<0.01
Belizean (11)	11	<0.01
Bermudan (14)	28	<0.01
British West Indian (39)	39	<0.01
Dutch West Indian (218)	689	0.04
Haitian (11)	21	<0.01
Jamaican (723)	963	0.05
Trinidadian/Tobagonian (42)	63	<0.01
U.S. Virgin Islander (35)	35	<0.01
West Indian (91)	204	0.01
Yugoslavian (491)	1,103	0.06

Hispanic Origin	Population	%
Hispanic or Latino (of any race)	22,268	1.20
Central American, ex. Mexican	2,081	0.11
Costa Rican	68	<0.01
Guatemalan	347	0.02
Honduran	333	0.02
Nicaraguan	162	0.01
Panamanian	261	0.01
Salvadoran	893	0.05
Other Central American	17	<0.01
Cuban	764	0.04
Dominican Republic	363	0.02
Mexican	9,704	0.52
Puerto Rican	3,701	0.20
South American	1,700	0.09
Argentinean	165	0.01
Bolivian	139	0.01
Chilean	110	0.01
Colombian	483	0.03
Ecuadorian	155	0.01
Paraguayan	16	<0.01
Peruvian	444	0.02
Uruguayan	26	<0.01
Venezuelan	142	0.01
Other South American	20	<0.01
Other Hispanic or Latino	3,955	0.21

Race*	Population	%
African-American/Black (63,124)	76,945	4.15
Not Hispanic (62,122)	75,277	4.06
Hispanic (1,002)	1,668	0.09
American Indian/Alaska Native (3,787)	13,314	0.72
Not Hispanic (3,493)	12,539	0.68
Hispanic (294)	775	0.04
Alaska Athabascan *(Ala. Nat.)* (1)	7	<0.01
Aleut *(Alaska Native)* (5)	6	<0.01
Apache (45)	157	0.01
Arapaho (1)	12	<0.01
Blackfeet (120)	636	0.03
Canadian/French Am. Ind. (13)	35	<0.01
Central American Ind. (10)	15	<0.01
Cherokee (1,085)	4,600	0.25
Cheyenne (9)	34	<0.01
Chickasaw (25)	44	<0.01
Chippewa (65)	119	0.01
Choctaw (42)	120	0.01
Colville (0)	1	<0.01
Comanche (7)	32	<0.01
Cree (9)	23	<0.01
Creek (22)	54	<0.01
Crow (8)	31	<0.01
Delaware (50)	123	0.01
Hopi (0)	12	<0.01
Houma (2)	2	<0.01
Inupiat *(Alaska Native)* (24)	34	<0.01
Iroquois (92)	267	0.01
Kiowa (2)	2	<0.01
Lumbee (52)	76	<0.01
Menominee (0)	4	<0.01
Mexican American Ind. (86)	140	0.01
Navajo (53)	111	0.01
Osage (2)	7	<0.01
Ottawa (2)	9	<0.01
Paiute (8)	10	<0.01
Pima (9)	15	<0.01
Potawatomi (13)	36	<0.01
Pueblo (6)	18	<0.01
Puget Sound Salish (1)	5	<0.01
Seminole (7)	44	<0.01
Shoshone (10)	29	<0.01
Sioux (84)	262	0.01
South American Ind. (20)	48	<0.01
Spanish American Ind. (9)	9	<0.01
Tlingit-Haida *(Alaska Native)* (19)	29	<0.01
Tohono O'Odham (0)	2	<0.01
Yakama (2)	3	<0.01
Yaqui (3)	13	<0.01
Yuman (2)	2	<0.01
Yup'ik *(Alaska Native)* (5)	11	<0.01
Asian (12,406)	16,465	0.89
Not Hispanic (12,285)	16,096	0.87
Hispanic (121)	369	0.02
Bangladeshi (73)	82	<0.01
Burmese (105)	109	0.01
Cambodian (46)	65	<0.01
Chinese, ex. Taiwanese (2,581)	3,044	0.16
Filipino (1,939)	3,059	0.17
Hmong (5)	5	<0.01
Indian (3,304)	3,969	0.21
Indonesian (55)	83	<0.01
Japanese (586)	1,159	0.06
Korean (1,039)	1,571	0.08
Laotian (48)	72	<0.01
Malaysian (41)	63	<0.01
Nepalese (186)	195	0.01
Pakistani (508)	602	0.03
Sri Lankan (64)	69	<0.01
Taiwanese (131)	171	0.01
Thai (261)	389	0.02
Vietnamese (901)	1,104	0.06
Hawaii Native/Pacific Islander (428)	1,254	0.07
Not Hispanic (387)	1,102	0.06
Hispanic (41)	152	0.01
Fijian (1)	2	<0.01
Guamanian/Chamorro (80)	194	0.01
Marshallese (1)	1	<0.01
Native Hawaiian (141)	442	0.02
Samoan (51)	142	0.01
Tongan (10)	17	<0.01
White (1,739,988)	1,765,642	95.29
Not Hispanic (1,726,256)	1,750,043	94.44
Hispanic (13,732)	15,599	0.84

*Notes: † The Census 2010 population figure is used to calculate the percentages in the Hispanic Origin and Race categories. Ancestry percentages are based on the 2006-2010 American Community Survey population (not shown); ‡ Numbers in parentheses indicate the number of people reporting a single ancestry; * Numbers in parentheses indicate the number of persons reporting this race alone, not in combination with any other race; Please refer to the Explanation of Data for more information.*

Beckley

Place Type: City
County: Raleigh
Population: 17,614†

Ancestry‡	Population	%
African, Sub-Saharan (99)	99	0.57
African (45)	45	0.26
Ethiopian (30)	30	0.17
Nigerian (11)	11	0.06
Other Sub-Saharan African (13)	13	0.07
American (3,981)	3,981	22.74
Arab (89)	89	0.51
Egyptian (40)	40	0.23
Lebanese (14)	14	0.08
Syrian (35)	35	0.20
Austrian (0)	20	0.11
British (12)	12	0.07
Canadian (0)	35	0.20
Czech (0)	39	0.22
Czechoslovakian (0)	2	0.01
Dutch (26)	296	1.69
Eastern European (10)	10	0.06
English (974)	1,715	9.80
European (87)	87	0.50
French, ex. Basque (35)	150	0.86
French Canadian (19)	50	0.29
German (254)	1,626	9.29
Greek (0)	11	0.06
Hungarian (23)	58	0.33
Irish (516)	1,657	9.47
Italian (352)	791	4.52
Lithuanian (14)	40	0.23
Norwegian (0)	18	0.10
Polish (101)	303	1.73
Portuguese (0)	10	0.06
Russian (31)	42	0.24
Scandinavian (0)	17	0.10
Scotch-Irish (258)	455	2.60
Scottish (112)	340	1.94
Slavic (10)	10	0.06
Slovak (13)	13	0.07
Swedish (4)	16	0.09
Swiss (47)	85	0.49
Welsh (29)	96	0.55

Hispanic Origin	Population	%
Hispanic or Latino (of any race)	265	1.50
Central American, ex. Mexican	12	0.07
Guatemalan	1	0.01
Honduran	2	0.01
Panamanian	8	0.05
Salvadoran	1	0.01
Cuban	13	0.07
Dominican Republic	9	0.05
Mexican	111	0.63
Puerto Rican	53	0.30
South American	14	0.08
Argentinean	2	0.01
Bolivian	1	0.01
Colombian	8	0.05
Peruvian	2	0.01
Other South American	1	0.01
Other Hispanic or Latino	53	0.30

Race*	Population	%
African-American/Black (3,735)	4,104	23.30
Not Hispanic (3,704)	4,046	22.97
Hispanic (31)	58	0.33
American Indian/Alaska Native (56)	216	1.23
Not Hispanic (54)	195	1.11
Hispanic (2)	21	0.12
Blackfeet (1)	6	0.03
Cherokee (15)	70	0.40
Chippewa (1)	1	0.01
Delaware (1)	1	0.01
Mexican American Ind. (0)	3	0.02
Paiute (1)	1	0.01
Pueblo (2)	2	0.01
Seminole (0)	1	0.01
Sioux (3)	3	0.02
Asian (431)	523	2.97
Not Hispanic (428)	514	2.92
Hispanic (3)	9	0.05
Bangladeshi (7)	7	0.04
Chinese, ex. Taiwanese (24)	28	0.16
Filipino (53)	74	0.42
Indian (160)	191	1.08
Japanese (6)	14	0.08
Korean (13)	21	0.12
Nepalese (104)	109	0.62
Pakistani (16)	30	0.17
Sri Lankan (7)	7	0.04
Taiwanese (1)	1	0.01
Thai (2)	4	0.02
Vietnamese (10)	12	0.07
Hawaii Native/Pacific Islander (1)	23	0.13
Not Hispanic (1)	15	0.09
Hispanic (0)	8	0.05
Guamanian/Chamorro (1)	1	0.01
Native Hawaiian (0)	8	0.05
Samoan (0)	2	0.01
Tongan (0)	1	0.01
White (12,743)	13,229	75.11
Not Hispanic (12,635)	13,078	74.25
Hispanic (108)	151	0.86

Bluefield

Place Type: City
County: Mercer
Population: 10,447†

Ancestry‡	Population	%
African, Sub-Saharan (48)	48	0.46
African (48)	48	0.46
American (782)	782	7.42
British (0)	103	0.98
Czech (0)	18	0.17
Czechoslovakian (9)	34	0.32
Dutch (12)	204	1.94
English (509)	1,177	11.17
European (28)	28	0.27
French, ex. Basque (65)	132	1.25
German (268)	1,289	12.23
Greek (0)	72	0.68
Hungarian (39)	100	0.95
Irish (565)	1,429	13.56
Italian (304)	451	4.28
Norwegian (35)	35	0.33
Polish (60)	206	1.95
Portuguese (0)	14	0.13
Romanian (6)	6	0.06
Russian (12)	12	0.11
Scotch-Irish (286)	488	4.63
Scottish (98)	273	2.59
Slovak (12)	28	0.27
Swedish (0)	58	0.55
Welsh (0)	10	0.09

Hispanic Origin	Population	%
Hispanic or Latino (of any race)	96	0.92
Central American, ex. Mexican	7	0.07
Honduran	4	0.04
Nicaraguan	2	0.02
Panamanian	1	0.01
Cuban	4	0.04
Dominican Republic	2	0.02
Mexican	34	0.33
Puerto Rican	27	0.26
South American	4	0.04
Venezuelan	4	0.04
Other Hispanic or Latino	18	0.17

Race*	Population	%
African-American/Black (2,404)	2,596	24.85
Not Hispanic (2,374)	2,556	24.47
Hispanic (30)	40	0.38
American Indian/Alaska Native (28)	77	0.74
Not Hispanic (27)	69	0.66
Hispanic (1)	8	0.08
Blackfeet (0)	3	0.03
Cherokee (9)	20	0.19
Comanche (0)	1	0.01
Creek (2)	2	0.02
Inupiat *(Alaska Native)* (1)	1	0.01
Navajo (0)	1	0.01
Asian (51)	62	0.59
Not Hispanic (49)	58	0.56
Hispanic (2)	4	0.04
Chinese, ex. Taiwanese (9)	9	0.09
Filipino (7)	10	0.10
Indian (20)	21	0.20
Japanese (2)	3	0.03
Korean (1)	3	0.03
Nepalese (1)	1	0.01
Pakistani (1)	1	0.01
Thai (1)	1	0.01
Vietnamese (7)	8	0.08
Hawaii Native/Pacific Islander (0)	4	0.04
Not Hispanic (0)	3	0.03
Hispanic (0)	1	0.01
Native Hawaiian (0)	3	0.03
White (7,703)	7,931	75.92
Not Hispanic (7,667)	7,883	75.46
Hispanic (36)	48	0.46

Bridgeport

Place Type: City
County: Harrison
Population: 8,149†

Ancestry‡	Population	%
American (882)	882	11.06
Arab (37)	85	1.07
Lebanese (37)	85	1.07
Belgian (40)	103	1.29
British (0)	10	0.13
Canadian (13)	37	0.46
Czech (14)	14	0.18
Danish (0)	46	0.58
Dutch (12)	191	2.39
Eastern European (14)	14	0.18
English (370)	1,158	14.51
European (0)	37	0.46
French, ex. Basque (92)	268	3.36
German (305)	1,636	20.51
Greek (16)	52	0.65
Hungarian (0)	146	1.83
Irish (498)	1,247	15.63
Italian (692)	1,158	14.51
Lithuanian (13)	13	0.16
Norwegian (13)	27	0.34
Polish (28)	125	1.57
Romanian (0)	23	0.29
Russian (43)	84	1.05
Scotch-Irish (166)	445	5.58
Scottish (129)	340	4.26
Serbian (0)	36	0.45
Slavic (30)	70	0.88
Slovak (16)	144	1.80
Swedish (0)	9	0.11
Swiss (0)	32	0.40
Welsh (0)	135	1.69
West Indian, ex. Hispanic (11)	11	0.14
Jamaican (11)	11	0.14
Yugoslavian (12)	12	0.15

Hispanic Origin	Population	%
Hispanic or Latino (of any race)	135	1.66
Central American, ex. Mexican	4	0.05
Costa Rican	3	0.04
Guatemalan	1	0.01
Mexican	49	0.60
Puerto Rican	19	0.23
South American	7	0.09
Chilean	3	0.04
Colombian	1	0.01

*Notes: † The Census 2010 population figure is used to calculate the percentages in the Hispanic Origin and Race categories. Ancestry percentages are based on the 2006-2010 American Community Survey population (not shown); ‡ Numbers in parentheses indicate the number of people reporting a single ancestry; * Numbers in parentheses indicate the number of persons reporting this race alone, not in combination with any other race; Please refer to the Explanation of Data for more information.*

Peruvian	1	0.01
Venezuelan	2	0.02
Other Hispanic or Latino	56	0.69

Race*	Population	%
African-American/Black (91)	125	1.53
Not Hispanic (91)	124	1.52
Hispanic (0)	1	0.01
American Indian/Alaska Native (17)	44	0.54
Not Hispanic (17)	42	0.52
Hispanic (0)	2	0.02
Cherokee (4)	14	0.17
Chippewa (1)	1	0.01
Delaware (4)	4	0.05
Asian (152)	186	2.28
Not Hispanic (149)	183	2.25
Hispanic (3)	3	0.04
Chinese, ex. Taiwanese (28)	31	0.38
Filipino (25)	32	0.39
Indian (39)	46	0.56
Indonesian (1)	2	0.02
Japanese (2)	3	0.04
Korean (6)	15	0.18
Pakistani (19)	19	0.23
Taiwanese (1)	1	0.01
Thai (0)	1	0.01
Vietnamese (24)	27	0.33
Hawaii Native/Pacific Islander (0)	5	0.06
Not Hispanic (0)	4	0.05
Hispanic (0)	1	0.01
White (7,784)	7,869	96.56
Not Hispanic (7,667)	7,750	95.10
Hispanic (117)	119	1.46

Charleston

Place Type: City
County: Kanawha
Population: 51,400†

Ancestry‡	Population	%
African, Sub-Saharan (286)	338	0.66
African (231)	283	0.55
Ethiopian (13)	13	0.03
Nigerian (42)	42	0.08
American (5,334)	5,334	10.37
Arab (639)	1,027	2.00
Arab (62)	71	0.14
Egyptian (6)	68	0.13
Lebanese (321)	618	1.20
Palestinian (9)	9	0.02
Syrian (231)	251	0.49
Other Arab (10)	10	0.02
Austrian (11)	40	0.08
Belgian (23)	68	0.13
British (115)	265	0.52
Bulgarian (21)	21	0.04
Canadian (12)	12	0.02
Croatian (43)	149	0.29
Czech (32)	48	0.09
Danish (19)	52	0.10
Dutch (123)	1,168	2.27
Eastern European (11)	11	0.02
English (3,257)	7,289	14.17
European (356)	356	0.69
French, ex. Basque (199)	1,230	2.39
French Canadian (31)	195	0.38
German (2,013)	7,511	14.60
Greek (27)	119	0.23
Hungarian (207)	262	0.51
Iranian (83)	83	0.16
Irish (2,392)	6,884	13.38
Italian (1,026)	2,426	4.72
Latvian (10)	10	0.02
Lithuanian (72)	159	0.31
Luxemburger (0)	9	0.02
Norwegian (54)	300	0.58
Pennsylvania German (30)	30	0.06
Polish (122)	783	1.52
Portuguese (18)	36	0.07
Romanian (0)	84	0.16
Russian (96)	429	0.83
Scandinavian (30)	64	0.12
Scotch-Irish (1,056)	2,220	4.32
Scottish (384)	1,326	2.58
Serbian (12)	12	0.02
Slovene (8)	13	0.03
Swedish (59)	307	0.60
Swiss (0)	60	0.12
Ukrainian (0)	59	0.11
Welsh (250)	745	1.45
West Indian, ex. Hispanic (84)	171	0.33
Bahamian (26)	26	0.05
Dutch West Indian (0)	16	0.03
Jamaican (45)	54	0.10
U.S. Virgin Islander (13)	13	0.03
West Indian (0)	62	0.12
Yugoslavian (20)	31	0.06

Hispanic Origin	Population	%
Hispanic or Latino (of any race)	694	1.35
Central American, ex. Mexican	48	0.09
Guatemalan	20	0.04
Honduran	6	0.01
Nicaraguan	7	0.01
Panamanian	11	0.02
Salvadoran	4	0.01
Cuban	56	0.11
Dominican Republic	21	0.04
Mexican	211	0.41
Puerto Rican	144	0.28
South American	75	0.15
Argentinean	19	0.04
Bolivian	1	<0.01
Chilean	2	<0.01
Colombian	22	0.04
Ecuadorian	4	0.01
Paraguayan	2	<0.01
Peruvian	10	0.02
Venezuelan	15	0.03
Other Hispanic or Latino	139	0.27

Race*	Population	%
African-American/Black (7,965)	9,113	17.73
Not Hispanic (7,867)	8,959	17.43
Hispanic (98)	154	0.30
American Indian/Alaska Native (122)	520	1.01
Not Hispanic (116)	483	0.94
Hispanic (6)	37	0.07
Apache (2)	8	0.02
Arapaho (0)	7	0.01
Blackfeet (1)	37	0.07
Cherokee (31)	169	0.33
Cheyenne (0)	1	<0.01
Chippewa (3)	3	0.01
Choctaw (1)	1	<0.01
Comanche (0)	1	<0.01
Cree (2)	3	0.01
Creek (1)	2	<0.01
Delaware (0)	1	<0.01
Inupiat *(Alaska Native)* (1)	1	<0.01
Iroquois (4)	8	0.02
Lumbee (1)	1	<0.01
Mexican American Ind. (2)	6	0.01
Navajo (3)	7	0.01
Paiute (1)	3	0.01
Potawatomi (1)	1	<0.01
Seminole (0)	1	<0.01
Sioux (3)	7	0.01
South American Ind. (1)	7	0.01
Tlingit-Haida *(Alaska Native)* (1)	1	<0.01
Asian (1,181)	1,433	2.79
Not Hispanic (1,178)	1,419	2.76
Hispanic (3)	14	0.03
Bangladeshi (13)	13	0.03
Burmese (4)	4	0.01
Chinese, ex. Taiwanese (153)	185	0.36
Filipino (153)	213	0.41
Indian (473)	515	1.00
Indonesian (2)	3	0.01
Japanese (45)	64	0.12
Korean (56)	83	0.16
Laotian (5)	9	0.02
Malaysian (1)	1	<0.01
Nepalese (2)	2	<0.01
Pakistani (88)	94	0.18
Sri Lankan (10)	10	0.02
Taiwanese (9)	9	0.02
Thai (16)	20	0.04
Vietnamese (102)	118	0.23
Hawaii Native/Pacific Islander (19)	48	0.09
Not Hispanic (17)	41	0.08
Hispanic (2)	7	0.01
Guamanian/Chamorro (3)	10	0.02
Native Hawaiian (2)	11	0.02
Samoan (1)	2	<0.01
White (40,291)	41,784	81.29
Not Hispanic (39,900)	41,318	80.39
Hispanic (391)	466	0.91

Cheat Lake

Place Type: CDP
County: Monongalia
Population: 7,988†

Ancestry‡	Population	%
American (484)	484	6.34
Arab (69)	113	1.48
Lebanese (69)	97	1.27
Syrian (0)	16	0.21
Austrian (38)	47	0.62
British (62)	62	0.81
Croatian (27)	82	1.07
Czech (32)	86	1.13
Dutch (0)	131	1.72
English (456)	1,023	13.39
European (266)	335	4.39
Finnish (0)	17	0.22
French, ex. Basque (92)	159	2.08
French Canadian (0)	9	0.12
German (539)	1,744	22.83
Greek (111)	145	1.90
Hungarian (14)	76	1.00
Irish (385)	1,185	15.51
Italian (395)	1,046	13.69
Lithuanian (0)	9	0.12
Northern European (12)	12	0.16
Norwegian (47)	88	1.15
Pennsylvania German (0)	14	0.18
Polish (101)	303	3.97
Portuguese (0)	23	0.30
Romanian (8)	8	0.10
Russian (24)	104	1.36
Scotch-Irish (49)	131	1.72
Scottish (80)	298	3.90
Serbian (0)	49	0.64
Slavic (45)	102	1.34
Slovak (46)	153	2.00
Slovene (0)	12	0.16
Swiss (0)	8	0.10
Ukrainian (14)	14	0.18
Welsh (10)	54	0.71
West Indian, ex. Hispanic (19)	79	1.03
Jamaican (19)	79	1.03

Hispanic Origin	Population	%
Hispanic or Latino (of any race)	127	1.59
Central American, ex. Mexican	7	0.09
Guatemalan	3	0.04
Panamanian	3	0.04
Salvadoran	1	0.01
Cuban	2	0.03
Dominican Republic	3	0.04
Mexican	53	0.66
Puerto Rican	7	0.09
South American	36	0.45
Argentinean	5	0.06
Bolivian	5	0.06
Chilean	4	0.05

*Notes: † The Census 2010 population figure is used to calculate the percentages in the Hispanic Origin and Race categories. Ancestry percentages are based on the 2006-2010 American Community Survey population (not shown); ‡ Numbers in parentheses indicate the number of people reporting a single ancestry; * Numbers in parentheses indicate the number of persons reporting this race alone, not in combination with any other race; Please refer to the Explanation of Data for more information.*

Colombian	11	0.14
Ecuadorian	4	0.05
Peruvian	3	0.04
Uruguayan	1	0.01
Venezuelan	3	0.04
Other Hispanic or Latino	19	0.24

Race*	Population	%
African-American/Black (128)	157	1.97
Not Hispanic (127)	154	1.93
Hispanic (1)	3	0.04
American Indian/Alaska Native (7)	18	0.23
Not Hispanic (7)	17	0.21
Hispanic (0)	1	0.01
Cherokee (6)	10	0.13
Iroquois (0)	2	0.03
Osage (0)	2	0.03
Sioux (1)	1	0.01
Asian (194)	221	2.77
Not Hispanic (194)	219	2.74
Hispanic (0)	2	0.03
Chinese, ex. Taiwanese (36)	38	0.48
Filipino (13)	16	0.20
Indian (85)	88	1.10
Japanese (3)	6	0.08
Korean (14)	16	0.20
Pakistani (8)	13	0.16
Taiwanese (16)	17	0.21
Vietnamese (17)	19	0.24
Hawaii Native/Pacific Islander (5)	7	0.09
Not Hispanic (5)	6	0.08
Hispanic (0)	1	0.01
Native Hawaiian (5)	6	0.08
White (7,566)	7,630	95.52
Not Hispanic (7,465)	7,524	94.19
Hispanic (101)	106	1.33

Clarksburg

Place Type: City
County: Harrison
Population: 16,578†

Ancestry‡	Population	%
African, Sub-Saharan (19)	19	0.11
Ethiopian (19)	19	0.11
American (3,094)	3,094	18.70
Arab (0)	43	0.26
Lebanese (0)	35	0.21
Syrian (0)	8	0.05
Armenian (0)	40	0.24
Austrian (10)	71	0.43
Belgian (36)	45	0.27
British (48)	69	0.42
Czech (43)	74	0.45
Czechoslovakian (8)	16	0.10
Dutch (57)	654	3.95
English (770)	1,772	10.71
European (49)	73	0.44
French, ex. Basque (45)	282	1.70
French Canadian (13)	13	0.08
German (833)	3,406	20.59
Greek (11)	46	0.28
Hungarian (20)	97	0.59
Irish (1,015)	3,644	22.03
Italian (967)	1,979	11.96
Lithuanian (0)	63	0.38
Northern European (10)	10	0.06
Norwegian (9)	9	0.05
Pennsylvania German (9)	9	0.05
Polish (16)	171	1.03
Russian (16)	16	0.10
Scandinavian (4)	45	0.27
Scotch-Irish (341)	611	3.69
Scottish (88)	201	1.22
Slavic (17)	17	0.10
Slovak (40)	70	0.42
Swedish (67)	165	1.00
Swiss (0)	33	0.20
Turkish (9)	9	0.05
Welsh (24)	95	0.57
Yugoslavian (10)	39	0.24

Hispanic Origin	Population	%
Hispanic or Latino (of any race)	269	1.62
Central American, ex. Mexican	8	0.05
Guatemalan	2	0.01
Nicaraguan	1	0.01
Panamanian	2	0.01
Salvadoran	3	0.02
Cuban	4	0.02
Dominican Republic	3	0.02
Mexican	99	0.60
Puerto Rican	48	0.29
South American	2	0.01
Colombian	1	0.01
Paraguayan	1	0.01
Other Hispanic or Latino	105	0.63

Race*	Population	%
African-American/Black (646)	882	5.32
Not Hispanic (643)	874	5.27
Hispanic (3)	8	0.05
American Indian/Alaska Native (40)	147	0.89
Not Hispanic (40)	142	0.86
Hispanic (0)	5	0.03
Alaska Athabascan *(Ala. Nat.)* (0)	1	0.01
Apache (0)	3	0.02
Blackfeet (0)	7	0.04
Canadian/French Am. Ind. (1)	1	0.01
Cherokee (12)	52	0.31
Chippewa (1)	1	0.01
Creek (0)	3	0.02
Delaware (0)	1	0.01
Hopi (0)	1	0.01
Iroquois (1)	1	0.01
Sioux (3)	4	0.02
Asian (44)	89	0.54
Not Hispanic (43)	86	0.52
Hispanic (1)	3	0.02
Chinese, ex. Taiwanese (9)	9	0.05
Filipino (6)	15	0.09
Indian (7)	23	0.14
Indonesian (0)	3	0.02
Japanese (2)	9	0.05
Korean (6)	8	0.05
Malaysian (0)	1	0.01
Pakistani (1)	2	0.01
Thai (2)	6	0.04
Vietnamese (7)	7	0.04
Hawaii Native/Pacific Islander (4)	17	0.10
Not Hispanic (4)	15	0.09
Hispanic (0)	2	0.01
Native Hawaiian (4)	8	0.05
Samoan (0)	3	0.02
White (15,398)	15,786	95.22
Not Hispanic (15,202)	15,560	93.86
Hispanic (196)	226	1.36

Cross Lanes

Place Type: CDP
County: Kanawha
Population: 9,995†

Ancestry‡	Population	%
African, Sub-Saharan (0)	18	0.20
African (0)	18	0.20
American (1,478)	1,478	16.03
Arab (14)	14	0.15
Lebanese (14)	14	0.15
Australian (0)	40	0.43
British (15)	26	0.28
Bulgarian (28)	28	0.30
Croatian (0)	16	0.17
Czech (21)	21	0.23
Danish (0)	12	0.13
Dutch (58)	243	2.64
English (528)	1,168	12.67
European (12)	12	0.13
French, ex. Basque (64)	247	2.68
German (549)	1,526	16.55
Greek (0)	32	0.35
Hungarian (13)	33	0.36
Irish (411)	1,202	13.04
Italian (81)	223	2.42
Northern European (37)	37	0.40
Polish (29)	68	0.74
Russian (18)	51	0.55
Scotch-Irish (147)	300	3.25
Scottish (132)	234	2.54
Serbian (0)	22	0.24
Slovak (8)	32	0.35
Swedish (17)	35	0.38
Welsh (28)	61	0.66

Hispanic Origin	Population	%
Hispanic or Latino (of any race)	113	1.13
Central American, ex. Mexican	11	0.11
Costa Rican	1	0.01
Guatemalan	4	0.04
Honduran	1	0.01
Salvadoran	5	0.05
Cuban	1	0.01
Dominican Republic	1	0.01
Mexican	49	0.49
Puerto Rican	28	0.28
South American	10	0.10
Colombian	4	0.04
Ecuadorian	2	0.02
Peruvian	4	0.04
Other Hispanic or Latino	13	0.13

Race*	Population	%
African-American/Black (467)	554	5.54
Not Hispanic (460)	547	5.47
Hispanic (7)	7	0.07
American Indian/Alaska Native (17)	61	0.61
Not Hispanic (13)	50	0.50
Hispanic (4)	11	0.11
Blackfeet (1)	2	0.02
Cherokee (5)	20	0.20
Chippewa (1)	1	0.01
Mexican American Ind. (0)	1	0.01
Seminole (0)	2	0.02
Sioux (1)	1	0.01
South American Ind. (1)	1	0.01
Spanish American Ind. (1)	1	0.01
Tlingit-Haida *(Alaska Native)* (1)	1	0.01
Asian (122)	153	1.53
Not Hispanic (120)	151	1.51
Hispanic (2)	2	0.02
Chinese, ex. Taiwanese (24)	25	0.25
Filipino (24)	32	0.32
Indian (30)	33	0.33
Japanese (2)	8	0.08
Korean (5)	9	0.09
Laotian (3)	3	0.03
Pakistani (12)	12	0.12
Sri Lankan (2)	2	0.02
Thai (2)	9	0.09
Vietnamese (17)	21	0.21
Hawaii Native/Pacific Islander (2)	9	0.09
Not Hispanic (2)	9	0.09
Fijian (1)	1	0.01
Native Hawaiian (0)	2	0.02
White (9,176)	9,333	93.38
Not Hispanic (9,110)	9,258	92.63
Hispanic (66)	75	0.75

Dunbar

Place Type: City
County: Kanawha
Population: 7,907†

Ancestry‡	Population	%
African, Sub-Saharan (8)	8	0.10
Ethiopian (8)	8	0.10
American (777)	777	9.88

*Notes: † The Census 2010 population figure is used to calculate the percentages in the Hispanic Origin and Race categories. Ancestry percentages are based on the 2006-2010 American Community Survey population (not shown); ‡ Numbers in parentheses indicate the number of people reporting a single ancestry; * Numbers in parentheses indicate the number of persons reporting this race alone, not in combination with any other race; Please refer to the Explanation of Data for more information.*

Arab (31)	31	0.39
Lebanese (31)	31	0.39
Belgian (36)	64	0.81
British (12)	75	0.95
Canadian (42)	42	0.53
Croatian (0)	11	0.14
Dutch (5)	39	0.50
English (467)	1,026	13.04
European (96)	96	1.22
Finnish (0)	5	0.06
French, ex. Basque (7)	152	1.93
German (449)	1,398	17.77
German Russian (34)	34	0.43
Hungarian (0)	24	0.31
Irish (506)	1,381	17.56
Italian (170)	372	4.73
Lithuanian (0)	7	0.09
Norwegian (8)	14	0.18
Polish (43)	69	0.88
Romanian (11)	11	0.14
Scandinavian (13)	13	0.17
Scotch-Irish (161)	281	3.57
Scottish (149)	279	3.55
Slavic (9)	9	0.11
Slovak (0)	5	0.06
Slovene (10)	10	0.13
Swedish (0)	46	0.58
Welsh (46)	68	0.86

Hispanic Origin	Population	%
Hispanic or Latino (of any race)	79	1.00
Central American, ex. Mexican	8	0.10
Guatemalan	4	0.05
Honduran	3	0.04
Panamanian	1	0.01
Cuban	1	0.01
Dominican Republic	6	0.08
Mexican	35	0.44
Puerto Rican	17	0.21
South American	2	0.03
Peruvian	2	0.03
Other Hispanic or Latino	10	0.13

Race*	Population	%
African-American/Black (966)	1,107	14.00
Not Hispanic (955)	1,090	13.79
Hispanic (11)	17	0.21
American Indian/Alaska Native (17)	86	1.09
Not Hispanic (16)	83	1.05
Hispanic (1)	3	0.04
Blackfeet (0)	4	0.05
Cherokee (6)	31	0.39
Chippewa (1)	3	0.04
Creek (0)	1	0.01
Crow (0)	2	0.03
Delaware (0)	1	0.01
Mexican American Ind. (0)	1	0.01
Paiute (1)	1	0.01
Asian (138)	173	2.19
Not Hispanic (136)	171	2.16
Hispanic (2)	2	0.03
Bangladeshi (2)	2	0.03
Cambodian (1)	1	0.01
Chinese, ex. Taiwanese (6)	6	0.08
Filipino (15)	22	0.28
Indian (71)	74	0.94
Japanese (3)	14	0.18
Korean (10)	19	0.24
Laotian (4)	4	0.05
Pakistani (12)	12	0.15
Thai (6)	6	0.08
Vietnamese (6)	8	0.10
Hawaii Native/Pacific Islander (2)	4	0.05
Not Hispanic (2)	4	0.05
Native Hawaiian (1)	2	0.03
Samoan (1)	2	0.03
White (6,539)	6,722	85.01
Not Hispanic (6,498)	6,673	84.39
Hispanic (41)	49	0.62

Fairmont

Place Type: City
County: Marion
Population: 18,704†

Ancestry‡	Population	%
African, Sub-Saharan (0)	22	0.12
African (0)	22	0.12
American (1,928)	1,928	10.22
Arab (28)	36	0.19
Egyptian (28)	28	0.15
Lebanese (0)	8	0.04
Austrian (30)	55	0.29
Belgian (21)	41	0.22
British (62)	62	0.33
Croatian (32)	66	0.35
Czech (50)	61	0.32
Czechoslovakian (12)	24	0.13
Danish (0)	32	0.17
Dutch (30)	506	2.68
Eastern European (0)	17	0.09
English (849)	2,391	12.67
European (16)	16	0.08
French, ex. Basque (54)	420	2.23
French Canadian (0)	26	0.14
German (1,152)	4,344	23.03
Greek (41)	66	0.35
Hungarian (51)	232	1.23
Irish (899)	3,244	17.20
Italian (1,504)	2,742	14.53
Macedonian (21)	21	0.11
Northern European (15)	15	0.08
Norwegian (26)	33	0.17
Pennsylvania German (10)	10	0.05
Polish (263)	798	4.23
Russian (10)	78	0.41
Scandinavian (0)	13	0.07
Scotch-Irish (319)	714	3.78
Scottish (21)	274	1.45
Serbian (0)	7	0.04
Slavic (0)	39	0.21
Slovak (32)	75	0.40
Swedish (23)	171	0.91
Swiss (10)	58	0.31
Turkish (5)	5	0.03
Ukrainian (14)	21	0.11
Welsh (17)	159	0.84
Yugoslavian (9)	18	0.10

Hispanic Origin	Population	%
Hispanic or Latino (of any race)	257	1.37
Central American, ex. Mexican	17	0.09
Costa Rican	3	0.02
Guatemalan	1	0.01
Honduran	4	0.02
Salvadoran	9	0.05
Cuban	11	0.06
Mexican	100	0.53
Puerto Rican	46	0.25
South American	15	0.08
Argentinean	2	0.01
Colombian	2	0.01
Ecuadorian	2	0.01
Peruvian	2	0.01
Venezuelan	7	0.04
Other Hispanic or Latino	68	0.36

Race*	Population	%
African-American/Black (1,411)	1,700	9.09
Not Hispanic (1,394)	1,669	8.92
Hispanic (17)	31	0.17
American Indian/Alaska Native (39)	153	0.82
Not Hispanic (36)	143	0.76
Hispanic (3)	10	0.05
Blackfeet (2)	10	0.05
Cherokee (8)	49	0.26
Choctaw (0)	1	0.01
Creek (0)	3	0.02
Crow (0)	2	0.01
Delaware (1)	2	0.01
Mexican American Ind. (1)	1	0.01
Navajo (0)	3	0.02
Potawatomi (0)	3	0.02
Sioux (3)	4	0.02
Tlingit-Haida *(Alaska Native)* (2)	2	0.01
Yaqui (0)	1	0.01
Asian (113)	167	0.89
Not Hispanic (113)	166	0.89
Hispanic (0)	1	0.01
Chinese, ex. Taiwanese (24)	31	0.17
Filipino (16)	24	0.13
Indian (26)	32	0.17
Japanese (11)	22	0.12
Korean (8)	16	0.09
Laotian (1)	1	0.01
Malaysian (3)	4	0.02
Nepalese (3)	3	0.02
Pakistani (6)	7	0.04
Taiwanese (1)	2	0.01
Thai (0)	1	0.01
Vietnamese (5)	7	0.04
Hawaii Native/Pacific Islander (3)	11	0.06
Not Hispanic (2)	8	0.04
Hispanic (1)	3	0.02
Guamanian/Chamorro (1)	1	0.01
Native Hawaiian (1)	5	0.03
White (16,637)	17,035	91.08
Not Hispanic (16,476)	16,850	90.09
Hispanic (161)	185	0.99

Huntington

Place Type: City
County: Cabell
Population: 49,138†

Ancestry‡	Population	%
African, Sub-Saharan (210)	210	0.43
African (105)	105	0.21
Ethiopian (88)	88	0.18
Kenyan (17)	17	0.03
American (4,502)	4,502	9.15
Arab (205)	270	0.55
Arab (64)	64	0.13
Lebanese (121)	186	0.38
Other Arab (20)	20	0.04
Armenian (0)	8	0.02
Austrian (0)	15	0.03
Belgian (0)	36	0.07
British (196)	319	0.65
Celtic (5)	23	0.05
Croatian (0)	21	0.04
Czech (18)	64	0.13
Danish (0)	31	0.06
Dutch (151)	803	1.63
Eastern European (25)	25	0.05
English (4,590)	7,577	15.39
European (215)	239	0.49
Finnish (87)	87	0.18
French, ex. Basque (145)	600	1.22
French Canadian (13)	89	0.18
German (2,424)	7,529	15.29
Greek (79)	169	0.34
Hungarian (84)	178	0.36
Iranian (0)	4	0.01
Irish (3,530)	8,274	16.81
Israeli (0)	4	0.01
Italian (893)	1,995	4.05
Latvian (0)	4	0.01
Lithuanian (0)	17	0.03
Northern European (6)	6	0.01
Norwegian (36)	130	0.26
Polish (244)	487	0.99
Portuguese (0)	5	0.01
Romanian (0)	9	0.02
Russian (51)	151	0.31
Scotch-Irish (910)	1,733	3.52
Scottish (534)	1,216	2.47
Serbian (10)	28	0.06

*Notes: † The Census 2010 population figure is used to calculate the percentages in the Hispanic Origin and Race categories. Ancestry percentages are based on the 2006-2010 American Community Survey population (not shown); ‡ Numbers in parentheses indicate the number of people reporting a single ancestry; * Numbers in parentheses indicate the number of persons reporting this race alone, not in combination with any other race; Please refer to the Explanation of Data for more information.*

SECTION TWO

Slavic (0)	23	0.05
Slovak (20)	29	0.06
Swedish (83)	168	0.34
Swiss (0)	77	0.16
Turkish (184)	184	0.37
Ukrainian (12)	97	0.20
Welsh (108)	374	0.76
West Indian, ex. Hispanic (0)	13	0.03
Dutch West Indian (0)	13	0.03
Yugoslavian (14)	25	0.05

Hispanic Origin	Population	%
Hispanic or Latino (of any race)	685	1.39
Central American, ex. Mexican	33	0.07
Costa Rican	1	<0.01
Guatemalan	9	0.02
Honduran	1	<0.01
Nicaraguan	1	<0.01
Panamanian	11	0.02
Salvadoran	7	0.01
Other Central American	3	0.01
Cuban	45	0.09
Dominican Republic	11	0.02
Mexican	338	0.69
Puerto Rican	76	0.15
South American	67	0.14
Argentinean	4	0.01
Bolivian	7	0.01
Chilean	5	0.01
Colombian	21	0.04
Ecuadorian	7	0.01
Peruvian	8	0.02
Uruguayan	2	<0.01
Venezuelan	13	0.03
Other Hispanic or Latino	115	0.23

Race*	Population	%
African-American/Black (4,202)	5,099	10.38
Not Hispanic (4,155)	5,014	10.20
Hispanic (47)	85	0.17
American Indian/Alaska Native (147)	501	1.02
Not Hispanic (142)	479	0.97
Hispanic (5)	22	0.04
Apache (0)	1	<0.01
Blackfeet (1)	20	0.04
Cherokee (58)	201	0.41
Cheyenne (0)	1	<0.01
Chickasaw (1)	1	<0.01
Chippewa (2)	2	<0.01
Choctaw (8)	11	0.02
Cree (0)	6	0.01
Creek (1)	1	<0.01
Iroquois (2)	6	0.01
Mexican American Ind. (1)	5	0.01
Navajo (0)	2	<0.01
Pima (5)	5	0.01
Pueblo (0)	1	<0.01
Seminole (1)	4	0.01
Sioux (6)	12	0.02
South American Ind. (1)	1	<0.01
Yaqui (0)	3	0.01
Yuman (1)	1	<0.01
Asian (532)	693	1.41
Not Hispanic (527)	683	1.39
Hispanic (5)	10	0.02
Bangladeshi (1)	1	<0.01
Cambodian (2)	2	<0.01
Chinese, ex. Taiwanese (147)	169	0.34
Filipino (47)	93	0.19
Indian (90)	114	0.23
Indonesian (3)	5	0.01
Japanese (32)	55	0.11
Korean (44)	72	0.15
Malaysian (0)	2	<0.01
Nepalese (5)	5	0.01
Pakistani (11)	13	0.03
Sri Lankan (1)	1	<0.01
Taiwanese (3)	3	0.01
Thai (5)	8	0.02
Vietnamese (121)	129	0.26
Hawaii Native/Pacific Islander (20)	57	0.12
Not Hispanic (17)	52	0.11
Hispanic (3)	5	0.01
Guamanian/Chamorro (1)	2	<0.01
Native Hawaiian (10)	29	0.06
Samoan (2)	6	0.01
Tongan (3)	4	0.01
White (42,723)	43,972	89.49
Not Hispanic (42,287)	43,474	88.47
Hispanic (436)	498	1.01

Martinsburg

Place Type: City
County: Berkeley
Population: 17,227†

Ancestry‡	Population	%
African, Sub-Saharan (90)	166	0.97
African (90)	166	0.97
American (1,623)	1,623	9.47
British (0)	34	0.20
Canadian (20)	20	0.12
Croatian (0)	24	0.14
Czech (0)	50	0.29
Czechoslovakian (0)	11	0.06
Dutch (49)	266	1.55
English (891)	1,932	11.28
European (101)	101	0.59
Finnish (0)	25	0.15
French, ex. Basque (192)	467	2.73
French Canadian (23)	85	0.50
German (1,126)	4,140	24.16
Guyanese (8)	8	0.05
Hungarian (25)	56	0.33
Iranian (13)	13	0.08
Irish (876)	2,840	16.58
Italian (337)	686	4.00
Lithuanian (0)	13	0.08
Norwegian (18)	95	0.55
Pennsylvania German (15)	15	0.09
Polish (146)	294	1.72
Portuguese (63)	89	0.52
Romanian (0)	13	0.08
Russian (33)	50	0.29
Scotch-Irish (142)	306	1.79
Scottish (157)	426	2.49
Swedish (23)	49	0.29
Swiss (0)	35	0.20
Ukrainian (0)	23	0.13
Welsh (0)	89	0.52
West Indian, ex. Hispanic (304)	348	2.03
Jamaican (232)	276	1.61
Trinidadian/Tobagonian (10)	10	0.06
West Indian (62)	62	0.36
Yugoslavian (13)	37	0.22

Hispanic Origin	Population	%
Hispanic or Latino (of any race)	1,069	6.21
Central American, ex. Mexican	133	0.77
Guatemalan	15	0.09
Honduran	22	0.13
Nicaraguan	6	0.03
Panamanian	12	0.07
Salvadoran	78	0.45
Cuban	18	0.10
Dominican Republic	22	0.13
Mexican	600	3.48
Puerto Rican	181	1.05
South American	44	0.26
Argentinean	1	0.01
Bolivian	3	0.02
Chilean	4	0.02
Colombian	6	0.03
Ecuadorian	15	0.09
Peruvian	7	0.04
Uruguayan	2	0.01
Venezuelan	6	0.03
Other Hispanic or Latino	71	0.41

Race*	Population	%
African-American/Black (2,570)	2,991	17.36
Not Hispanic (2,485)	2,869	16.65
Hispanic (85)	122	0.71
American Indian/Alaska Native (61)	191	1.11
Not Hispanic (45)	168	0.98
Hispanic (16)	23	0.13
Apache (1)	7	0.04
Blackfeet (1)	13	0.08
Cherokee (6)	47	0.27
Chippewa (0)	1	0.01
Creek (0)	1	0.01
Crow (0)	1	0.01
Iroquois (0)	1	0.01
Lumbee (6)	7	0.04
Mexican American Ind. (7)	7	0.04
Navajo (1)	8	0.05
Sioux (4)	9	0.05
South American Ind. (1)	1	0.01
Asian (204)	299	1.74
Not Hispanic (201)	289	1.68
Hispanic (3)	10	0.06
Bangladeshi (6)	6	0.03
Burmese (11)	11	0.06
Cambodian (5)	9	0.05
Chinese, ex. Taiwanese (44)	68	0.39
Filipino (25)	48	0.28
Indian (25)	31	0.18
Indonesian (1)	4	0.02
Japanese (8)	23	0.13
Korean (28)	52	0.30
Laotian (4)	4	0.02
Malaysian (0)	1	0.01
Pakistani (8)	10	0.06
Thai (5)	8	0.05
Vietnamese (20)	23	0.13
Hawaii Native/Pacific Islander (10)	26	0.15
Not Hispanic (5)	18	0.10
Hispanic (5)	8	0.05
Guamanian/Chamorro (1)	2	0.01
Native Hawaiian (2)	10	0.06
Samoan (1)	2	0.01
White (13,343)	13,935	80.89
Not Hispanic (12,842)	13,372	77.62
Hispanic (501)	563	3.27

Morgantown

Place Type: City
County: Monongalia
Population: 29,660†

Ancestry‡	Population	%
African, Sub-Saharan (85)	202	0.69
African (30)	38	0.13
Kenyan (0)	24	0.08
Nigerian (39)	124	0.43
South African (16)	16	0.06
American (1,366)	1,366	4.70
Arab (122)	471	1.62
Arab (34)	34	0.12
Egyptian (9)	148	0.51
Lebanese (14)	110	0.38
Moroccan (13)	13	0.04
Palestinian (8)	8	0.03
Syrian (0)	104	0.36
Other Arab (44)	54	0.19
Armenian (0)	5	0.02
Assyrian/Chaldean/Syriac (10)	10	0.03
Austrian (10)	133	0.46
Belgian (69)	142	0.49
Brazilian (14)	14	0.05
British (134)	241	0.83
Canadian (55)	93	0.32
Celtic (0)	3	0.01
Croatian (10)	64	0.22
Czech (39)	136	0.47
Czechoslovakian (28)	110	0.38
Danish (0)	67	0.23

*Notes: † The Census 2010 population figure is used to calculate the percentages in the Hispanic Origin and Race categories. Ancestry percentages are based on the 2006-2010 American Community Survey population (not shown); ‡ Numbers in parentheses indicate the number of people reporting a single ancestry; * Numbers in parentheses indicate the number of persons reporting this race alone, not in combination with any other race; Please refer to the Explanation of Data for more information.*

Dutch (59)	531	1.83
English (1,221)	3,979	13.68
European (328)	350	1.20
French, ex. Basque (109)	796	2.74
French Canadian (30)	91	0.31
German (1,813)	7,275	25.02
Greek (116)	161	0.55
Guyanese (14)	32	0.11
Hungarian (69)	363	1.25
Iranian (8)	8	0.03
Irish (1,448)	5,962	20.50
Israeli (0)	15	0.05
Italian (1,287)	4,295	14.77
Lithuanian (31)	144	0.50
Northern European (21)	21	0.07
Norwegian (25)	252	0.87
Pennsylvania German (0)	10	0.03
Polish (329)	1,550	5.33
Portuguese (0)	49	0.17
Romanian (0)	7	0.02
Russian (130)	380	1.31
Scandinavian (15)	15	0.05
Scotch-Irish (339)	1,171	4.03
Scottish (258)	1,009	3.47
Serbian (18)	87	0.30
Slavic (0)	21	0.07
Slovak (137)	422	1.45
Slovene (0)	39	0.13
Swedish (15)	317	1.09
Swiss (0)	36	0.12
Turkish (14)	43	0.15
Ukrainian (37)	94	0.32
Welsh (74)	593	2.04
West Indian, ex. Hispanic (55)	70	0.24
Haitian (11)	11	0.04
Jamaican (23)	38	0.13
Trinidadian/Tobagonian (21)	21	0.07
Yugoslavian (33)	49	0.17

Hispanic Origin	Population	%
Hispanic or Latino (of any race)	765	2.58
Central American, ex. Mexican	43	0.14
Costa Rican	3	0.01
Guatemalan	4	0.01
Honduran	2	0.01
Nicaraguan	18	0.06
Panamanian	3	0.01
Salvadoran	12	0.04
Other Central American	1	<0.01
Cuban	24	0.08
Dominican Republic	19	0.06
Mexican	252	0.85
Puerto Rican	127	0.43
South American	181	0.61
Argentinean	19	0.06
Bolivian	12	0.04
Chilean	13	0.04
Colombian	60	0.20
Ecuadorian	24	0.08
Paraguayan	2	0.01
Peruvian	24	0.08
Uruguayan	3	0.01
Venezuelan	22	0.07
Other South American	2	0.01
Other Hispanic or Latino	119	0.40

Race*	Population	%
African-American/Black (1,205)	1,498	5.05
Not Hispanic (1,177)	1,452	4.90
Hispanic (28)	46	0.16
American Indian/Alaska Native (39)	163	0.55
Not Hispanic (32)	142	0.48
Hispanic (7)	21	0.07
Blackfeet (1)	6	0.02
Cherokee (6)	49	0.17
Chickasaw (0)	4	0.01
Chippewa (1)	2	0.01
Choctaw (0)	2	0.01
Delaware (0)	2	0.01
Iroquois (1)	8	0.03
Mexican American Ind. (5)	12	0.04
Sioux (1)	7	0.02
Asian (1,021)	1,207	4.07
Not Hispanic (1,011)	1,189	4.01
Hispanic (10)	18	0.06
Bangladeshi (8)	8	0.03
Burmese (3)	3	0.01
Cambodian (3)	3	0.01
Chinese, ex. Taiwanese (317)	339	1.14
Filipino (63)	108	0.36
Indian (311)	339	1.14
Indonesian (6)	6	0.02
Japanese (50)	80	0.27
Korean (84)	108	0.36
Laotian (1)	1	<0.01
Malaysian (10)	14	0.05
Nepalese (8)	9	0.03
Pakistani (41)	42	0.14
Sri Lankan (4)	5	0.02
Taiwanese (24)	29	0.10
Thai (17)	17	0.06
Vietnamese (35)	43	0.14
Hawaii Native/Pacific Islander (26)	40	0.13
Not Hispanic (23)	36	0.12
Hispanic (3)	4	0.01
Fijian (0)	1	<0.01
Guamanian/Chamorro (3)	5	0.02
Native Hawaiian (11)	13	0.04
Samoan (5)	8	0.03
Tongan (0)	1	<0.01
White (26,597)	27,157	91.56
Not Hispanic (26,083)	26,574	89.60
Hispanic (514)	583	1.97

Moundsville

Place Type: City
County: Marshall
Population: 9,318†

Ancestry‡	Population	%
American (1,129)	1,129	12.01
Arab (0)	22	0.23
Lebanese (0)	22	0.23
Austrian (11)	11	0.12
Croatian (42)	69	0.73
Czech (11)	23	0.24
Danish (0)	9	0.10
Dutch (0)	227	2.41
English (519)	1,129	12.01
European (31)	31	0.33
French, ex. Basque (13)	152	1.62
German (861)	2,333	24.81
Greek (49)	49	0.52
Hungarian (0)	17	0.18
Irish (410)	1,465	15.58
Italian (191)	555	5.90
Lithuanian (0)	47	0.50
Polish (160)	532	5.66
Portuguese (16)	16	0.17
Russian (21)	66	0.70
Scandinavian (0)	9	0.10
Scotch-Irish (165)	233	2.48
Scottish (9)	117	1.24
Serbian (11)	54	0.57
Swiss (29)	66	0.70
Ukrainian (19)	31	0.33
Welsh (64)	117	1.24
Yugoslavian (9)	26	0.28

Hispanic Origin	Population	%
Hispanic or Latino (of any race)	105	1.13
Central American, ex. Mexican	1	0.01
Honduran	1	0.01
Cuban	3	0.03
Mexican	48	0.52
Puerto Rican	11	0.12
Other Hispanic or Latino	42	0.45

Race*	Population	%
African-American/Black (79)	98	1.05
Not Hispanic (78)	92	0.99
Hispanic (1)	6	0.06
American Indian/Alaska Native (15)	54	0.58
Not Hispanic (15)	50	0.54
Hispanic (0)	4	0.04
Apache (1)	2	0.02
Blackfeet (0)	2	0.02
Cherokee (3)	14	0.15
Choctaw (1)	1	0.01
Comanche (0)	1	0.01
Delaware (1)	1	0.01
Iroquois (2)	3	0.03
Sioux (1)	5	0.05
Asian (35)	47	0.50
Not Hispanic (35)	46	0.49
Hispanic (0)	1	0.01
Chinese, ex. Taiwanese (7)	9	0.10
Filipino (11)	18	0.19
Indian (4)	5	0.05
Japanese (2)	3	0.03
Korean (4)	5	0.05
Vietnamese (4)	4	0.04
Hawaii Native/Pacific Islander (0)	4	0.04
Not Hispanic (0)	3	0.03
Hispanic (0)	1	0.01
Guamanian/Chamorro (0)	2	0.02
Native Hawaiian (0)	2	0.02
White (9,086)	9,166	98.37
Not Hispanic (9,015)	9,081	97.46
Hispanic (71)	85	0.91

Oak Hill

Place Type: City
County: Fayette
Population: 7,730†

Ancestry‡	Population	%
American (989)	989	12.91
Arab (7)	16	0.21
Palestinian (7)	16	0.21
British (10)	10	0.13
Cajun (50)	50	0.65
Czech (12)	106	1.38
Danish (46)	46	0.60
Dutch (91)	156	2.04
English (652)	1,229	16.05
Finnish (0)	4	0.05
French, ex. Basque (0)	34	0.44
French Canadian (15)	15	0.20
German (225)	1,577	20.59
Hungarian (45)	255	3.33
Irish (517)	1,270	16.58
Italian (265)	388	5.07
Lithuanian (36)	36	0.47
Polish (16)	51	0.67
Russian (0)	31	0.40
Scotch-Irish (78)	98	1.28
Scottish (45)	131	1.71
Swedish (6)	12	0.16
Swiss (0)	16	0.21
Ukrainian (0)	6	0.08
Welsh (67)	139	1.81

Hispanic Origin	Population	%
Hispanic or Latino (of any race)	94	1.22
Central American, ex. Mexican	1	0.01
Panamanian	1	0.01
Cuban	4	0.05
Dominican Republic	1	0.01
Mexican	55	0.71
Puerto Rican	14	0.18
South American	4	0.05
Colombian	3	0.04
Peruvian	1	0.01
Other Hispanic or Latino	15	0.19

*Notes: † The Census 2010 population figure is used to calculate the percentages in the Hispanic Origin and Race categories. Ancestry percentages are based on the 2006-2010 American Community Survey population (not shown); ‡ Numbers in parentheses indicate the number of people reporting a single ancestry; * Numbers in parentheses indicate the number of persons reporting this race alone, not in combination with any other race; Please refer to the Explanation of Data for more information.*

Race*	Population	%
African-American/Black (334)	398	5.15
Not Hispanic (332)	391	5.06
Hispanic (2)	7	0.09
American Indian/Alaska Native (21)	52	0.67
Not Hispanic (21)	50	0.65
Hispanic (0)	2	0.03
Blackfeet (3)	3	0.04
Cherokee (3)	12	0.16
Chippewa (3)	3	0.04
Iroquois (0)	1	0.01
Sioux (0)	1	0.01
Asian (19)	28	0.36
Not Hispanic (19)	27	0.35
Hispanic (0)	1	0.01
Chinese, ex. Taiwanese (4)	4	0.05
Filipino (6)	11	0.14
Indian (4)	6	0.08
Japanese (3)	3	0.04
Korean (0)	2	0.03
Hawaii Native/Pacific Islander (1)	18	0.23
Not Hispanic (1)	17	0.22
Hispanic (0)	1	0.01
Guamanian/Chamorro (1)	14	0.18
Native Hawaiian (0)	3	0.04
Samoan (0)	1	0.01
White (7,209)	7,333	94.86
Not Hispanic (7,152)	7,262	93.95
Hispanic (57)	71	0.92

Parkersburg

Place Type: City
County: Wood
Population: 31,492†

Ancestry‡	Population	%
African, Sub-Saharan (11)	11	0.03
Other Sub-Saharan African (11)	11	0.03
American (6,009)	6,009	18.93
Arab (39)	61	0.19
Lebanese (6)	15	0.05
Syrian (33)	46	0.14
Austrian (10)	10	0.03
Belgian (0)	9	0.03
British (96)	178	0.56
Canadian (10)	10	0.03
Czech (0)	10	0.03
Czechoslovakian (0)	3	0.01
Danish (0)	12	0.04
Dutch (153)	967	3.05
English (1,828)	4,202	13.24
European (151)	158	0.50
Finnish (0)	17	0.05
French, ex. Basque (204)	672	2.12
French Canadian (0)	19	0.06
German (2,305)	7,033	22.16
Greek (60)	100	0.32
Hungarian (60)	97	0.31
Irish (1,582)	4,359	13.73
Italian (220)	948	2.99
Maltese (0)	8	0.03
Northern European (19)	19	0.06
Norwegian (36)	44	0.14
Polish (52)	364	1.15
Portuguese (0)	48	0.15
Russian (0)	47	0.15
Scotch-Irish (312)	831	2.62
Scottish (252)	777	2.45
Serbian (14)	14	0.04
Slovak (9)	17	0.05
Swedish (41)	117	0.37
Swiss (19)	108	0.34
Ukrainian (0)	10	0.03
Welsh (60)	159	0.50

Hispanic Origin	Population	%
Hispanic or Latino (of any race)	368	1.17
Central American, ex. Mexican	33	0.10
Guatemalan	1	<0.01
Honduran	9	0.03
Nicaraguan	5	0.02
Panamanian	11	0.03
Salvadoran	7	0.02
Cuban	7	0.02
Dominican Republic	3	0.01
Mexican	156	0.50
Puerto Rican	76	0.24
South American	10	0.03
Argentinean	1	<0.01
Chilean	1	<0.01
Colombian	2	0.01
Ecuadorian	1	<0.01
Peruvian	5	0.02
Other Hispanic or Latino	83	0.26

Race*	Population	%
African-American/Black (624)	986	3.13
Not Hispanic (614)	959	3.05
Hispanic (10)	27	0.09
American Indian/Alaska Native (89)	308	0.98
Not Hispanic (87)	290	0.92
Hispanic (2)	18	0.06
Aleut *(Alaska Native)* (1)	1	<0.01
Apache (3)	4	0.01
Blackfeet (1)	12	0.04
Cherokee (30)	108	0.34
Cheyenne (0)	1	<0.01
Chippewa (2)	3	0.01
Comanche (1)	2	0.01
Cree (0)	1	<0.01
Crow (1)	1	<0.01
Delaware (0)	4	0.01
Inupiat *(Alaska Native)* (0)	4	0.01
Iroquois (1)	1	<0.01
Mexican American Ind. (1)	1	<0.01
Navajo (1)	4	0.01
Shoshone (0)	2	0.01
Sioux (2)	7	0.02
Yaqui (0)	1	<0.01
Yup'ik *(Alaska Native)* (0)	1	<0.01
Asian (138)	223	0.71
Not Hispanic (137)	217	0.69
Hispanic (1)	6	0.02
Chinese, ex. Taiwanese (25)	39	0.12
Filipino (27)	49	0.16
Indian (16)	27	0.09
Japanese (13)	31	0.10
Korean (11)	22	0.07
Malaysian (0)	1	<0.01
Pakistani (0)	1	<0.01
Sri Lankan (2)	2	0.01
Taiwanese (1)	1	<0.01
Thai (3)	8	0.03
Vietnamese (26)	32	0.10
Hawaii Native/Pacific Islander (18)	44	0.14
Not Hispanic (17)	39	0.12
Hispanic (1)	5	0.02
Guamanian/Chamorro (0)	2	0.01
Native Hawaiian (12)	17	0.05
Samoan (1)	1	<0.01
White (29,879)	30,507	96.87
Not Hispanic (29,642)	30,218	95.95
Hispanic (237)	289	0.92

South Charleston

Place Type: City
County: Kanawha
Population: 13,450†

Ancestry‡	Population	%
African, Sub-Saharan (47)	47	0.35
African (25)	25	0.19
Ghanaian (9)	9	0.07
Nigerian (13)	13	0.10
American (1,814)	1,814	13.55
Arab (27)	64	0.48
Lebanese (27)	64	0.48
Belgian (0)	34	0.25
British (103)	116	0.87
Canadian (0)	8	0.06
Celtic (0)	8	0.06
Czechoslovakian (9)	9	0.07
Danish (26)	50	0.37
Dutch (94)	299	2.23
Eastern European (12)	12	0.09
English (809)	1,688	12.61
European (134)	157	1.17
French, ex. Basque (45)	311	2.32
French Canadian (0)	15	0.11
German (805)	2,334	17.43
Greek (12)	42	0.31
Hungarian (20)	55	0.41
Iranian (6)	18	0.13
Irish (757)	1,890	14.12
Italian (241)	478	3.57
Latvian (8)	8	0.06
Norwegian (22)	141	1.05
Polish (53)	78	0.58
Russian (0)	69	0.52
Scotch-Irish (391)	613	4.58
Scottish (98)	295	2.20
Slovak (0)	9	0.07
Swedish (9)	34	0.25
Swiss (0)	39	0.29
Welsh (16)	69	0.52

Hispanic Origin	Population	%
Hispanic or Latino (of any race)	140	1.04
Central American, ex. Mexican	18	0.13
Costa Rican	2	0.01
Guatemalan	8	0.06
Nicaraguan	1	0.01
Panamanian	6	0.04
Salvadoran	1	0.01
Cuban	10	0.07
Dominican Republic	2	0.01
Mexican	61	0.45
Puerto Rican	25	0.19
South American	4	0.03
Colombian	1	0.01
Ecuadorian	1	0.01
Peruvian	2	0.01
Other Hispanic or Latino	20	0.15

Race*	Population	%
African-American/Black (1,134)	1,438	10.69
Not Hispanic (1,127)	1,416	10.53
Hispanic (7)	22	0.16
American Indian/Alaska Native (34)	105	0.78
Not Hispanic (28)	99	0.74
Hispanic (6)	6	0.04
Blackfeet (2)	6	0.04
Canadian/French Am. Ind. (0)	1	0.01
Central American Ind. (2)	2	0.01
Cherokee (6)	23	0.17
Creek (1)	4	0.03
Delaware (1)	1	0.01
Mexican American Ind. (3)	3	0.02
Navajo (1)	1	0.01
Sioux (0)	1	0.01
Asian (143)	203	1.51
Not Hispanic (135)	187	1.39
Hispanic (8)	16	0.12
Burmese (1)	1	0.01
Chinese, ex. Taiwanese (16)	18	0.13
Filipino (46)	66	0.49
Indian (36)	44	0.33
Japanese (5)	10	0.07
Korean (15)	20	0.15
Laotian (1)	2	0.01
Pakistani (1)	8	0.06
Thai (5)	8	0.06
Vietnamese (14)	17	0.13
Hawaii Native/Pacific Islander (2)	6	0.04
Not Hispanic (2)	5	0.04
Hispanic (0)	1	0.01
Guamanian/Chamorro (0)	1	0.01
Native Hawaiian (0)	3	0.02

*Notes: † The Census 2010 population figure is used to calculate the percentages in the Hispanic Origin and Race categories. Ancestry percentages are based on the 2006-2010 American Community Survey population (not shown); ‡ Numbers in parentheses indicate the number of people reporting a single ancestry; * Numbers in parentheses indicate the number of persons reporting this race alone, not in combination with any other race; Please refer to the Explanation of Data for more information.*

White (11,689)	12,078	89.80
Not Hispanic (11,620)	11,989	89.14
Hispanic (69)	89	0.66

St. Albans

Place Type: City
County: Kanawha
Population: 11,044†

Ancestry‡	Population	%
American (1,278)	1,278	11.54
Arab (9)	9	0.08
Lebanese (9)	9	0.08
Belgian (12)	12	0.11
British (6)	6	0.05
Bulgarian (0)	12	0.11
Czech (0)	12	0.11
Czechoslovakian (11)	77	0.70
Danish (0)	10	0.09
Dutch (10)	123	1.11
English (867)	1,869	16.88
European (23)	23	0.21
French, ex. Basque (17)	94	0.85
German (561)	1,956	17.67
Hungarian (33)	46	0.42
Irish (448)	1,412	12.75
Italian (55)	140	1.26
Latvian (10)	10	0.09
Lithuanian (9)	9	0.08
Northern European (50)	50	0.45
Norwegian (0)	18	0.16
Pennsylvania German (11)	11	0.10
Polish (58)	200	1.81
Romanian (0)	19	0.17
Scandinavian (10)	10	0.09
Scotch-Irish (225)	573	5.18
Scottish (86)	235	2.12
Slovak (16)	50	0.45
Swedish (106)	145	1.31
Swiss (0)	28	0.25
Turkish (75)	114	1.03
Welsh (71)	90	0.81

Hispanic Origin	Population	%
Hispanic or Latino (of any race)	90	0.81
Central American, ex. Mexican	4	0.04
Honduran	1	0.01
Nicaraguan	2	0.02
Salvadoran	1	0.01
Cuban	1	0.01
Dominican Republic	1	0.01
Mexican	44	0.40
Puerto Rican	17	0.15
South American	8	0.07
Bolivian	1	0.01
Colombian	2	0.02
Ecuadorian	2	0.02
Venezuelan	3	0.03
Other Hispanic or Latino	15	0.14

Race*	Population	%
African-American/Black (377)	493	4.46
Not Hispanic (374)	484	4.38
Hispanic (3)	9	0.08
American Indian/Alaska Native (32)	85	0.77
Not Hispanic (32)	79	0.72
Hispanic (0)	6	0.05
Apache (0)	1	0.01
Blackfeet (0)	6	0.05
Cherokee (20)	28	0.25
Inupiat *(Alaska Native)* (3)	3	0.03
Iroquois (2)	3	0.03
Navajo (2)	5	0.05
Seminole (0)	1	0.01
Sioux (1)	2	0.02
Asian (52)	73	0.66
Not Hispanic (52)	73	0.66
Chinese, ex. Taiwanese (12)	12	0.11
Filipino (10)	23	0.21
Indian (8)	10	0.09
Japanese (3)	5	0.05
Korean (4)	5	0.05
Laotian (1)	1	0.01
Malaysian (1)	2	0.02
Thai (0)	1	0.01
Vietnamese (11)	12	0.11
Hawaii Native/Pacific Islander (0)	6	0.05
Not Hispanic (0)	6	0.05
Native Hawaiian (0)	3	0.03
Samoan (0)	1	0.01
White (10,376)	10,552	95.55
Not Hispanic (10,322)	10,490	94.98
Hispanic (54)	62	0.56

Teays Valley

Place Type: CDP
County: Putnam
Population: 13,175†

Ancestry‡	Population	%
American (1,701)	1,701	12.45
Arab (181)	181	1.33
Arab (74)	74	0.54
Syrian (107)	107	0.78
Austrian (0)	110	0.81
Belgian (12)	12	0.09
British (0)	29	0.21
Bulgarian (15)	15	0.11
Canadian (30)	40	0.29
Czechoslovakian (0)	17	0.12
Dutch (29)	160	1.17
English (711)	1,802	13.19
European (84)	84	0.61
Finnish (14)	14	0.10
French, ex. Basque (44)	282	2.06
German (666)	2,212	16.19
Greek (38)	80	0.59
Hungarian (32)	50	0.37
Irish (686)	1,823	13.35
Italian (182)	402	2.94
Norwegian (0)	34	0.25
Polish (90)	154	1.13
Portuguese (12)	42	0.31
Russian (0)	20	0.15
Scotch-Irish (345)	625	4.58
Scottish (181)	439	3.21
Serbian (18)	18	0.13
Slovak (0)	54	0.40
Slovene (19)	19	0.14
Swedish (0)	17	0.12
Swiss (18)	64	0.47
Turkish (22)	22	0.16
Ukrainian (0)	15	0.11
Welsh (0)	77	0.56

Hispanic Origin	Population	%
Hispanic or Latino (of any race)	126	0.96
Central American, ex. Mexican	7	0.05
Guatemalan	4	0.03
Honduran	2	0.02
Salvadoran	1	0.01
Cuban	6	0.05
Dominican Republic	1	0.01
Mexican	68	0.52
Puerto Rican	13	0.10
South American	8	0.06
Argentinean	1	0.01
Colombian	6	0.05
Peruvian	1	0.01
Other Hispanic or Latino	23	0.17

Race*	Population	%
African-American/Black (207)	267	2.03
Not Hispanic (203)	263	2.00
Hispanic (4)	4	0.03
American Indian/Alaska Native (16)	55	0.42
Not Hispanic (13)	46	0.35
Hispanic (3)	9	0.07
Arapaho (0)	1	0.01
Blackfeet (3)	6	0.05
Cherokee (1)	9	0.07
Chippewa (1)	1	0.01
Choctaw (1)	2	0.02
Iroquois (0)	1	0.01
Osage (0)	1	0.01
Sioux (1)	1	0.01
South American Ind. (0)	1	0.01
Spanish American Ind. (1)	1	0.01
Asian (208)	249	1.89
Not Hispanic (208)	248	1.88
Hispanic (0)	1	0.01
Chinese, ex. Taiwanese (47)	52	0.39
Filipino (19)	27	0.20
Indian (43)	51	0.39
Japanese (32)	40	0.30
Korean (21)	27	0.20
Laotian (5)	6	0.05
Pakistani (8)	8	0.06
Thai (13)	17	0.13
Vietnamese (19)	21	0.16
Hawaii Native/Pacific Islander (7)	10	0.08
Not Hispanic (7)	10	0.08
Native Hawaiian (1)	4	0.03
White (12,558)	12,700	96.39
Not Hispanic (12,476)	12,608	95.70
Hispanic (82)	92	0.70

Vienna

Place Type: City
County: Wood
Population: 10,749†

Ancestry‡	Population	%
African, Sub-Saharan (0)	48	0.45
African (0)	48	0.45
American (1,673)	1,673	15.60
Arab (10)	10	0.09
Lebanese (10)	10	0.09
Austrian (11)	32	0.30
Belgian (0)	12	0.11
British (0)	55	0.51
Czech (10)	49	0.46
Czechoslovakian (11)	11	0.10
Danish (0)	12	0.11
Dutch (0)	223	2.08
English (666)	1,510	14.08
European (191)	235	2.19
Finnish (18)	36	0.34
French, ex. Basque (154)	446	4.16
French Canadian (28)	28	0.26
German (616)	2,456	22.90
Greek (57)	57	0.53
Hungarian (20)	44	0.41
Irish (549)	1,535	14.31
Italian (79)	225	2.10
Polish (78)	119	1.11
Portuguese (0)	10	0.09
Russian (49)	60	0.56
Scotch-Irish (155)	307	2.86
Scottish (34)	211	1.97
Serbian (0)	32	0.30
Slovak (12)	96	0.90
Swedish (0)	23	0.21
Swiss (12)	121	1.13
Welsh (59)	69	0.64
Yugoslavian (0)	31	0.29

Hispanic Origin	Population	%
Hispanic or Latino (of any race)	83	0.77
Central American, ex. Mexican	7	0.07
Honduran	3	0.03
Panamanian	4	0.04
Cuban	6	0.06
Dominican Republic	4	0.04
Mexican	35	0.33
Puerto Rican	11	0.10
South American	9	0.08

*Notes: † The Census 2010 population figure is used to calculate the percentages in the Hispanic Origin and Race categories. Ancestry percentages are based on the 2006-2010 American Community Survey population (not shown); ‡ Numbers in parentheses indicate the number of people reporting a single ancestry; * Numbers in parentheses indicate the number of persons reporting this race alone, not in combination with any other race; Please refer to the Explanation of Data for more information.*

Bolivian	3	0.03
Colombian	5	0.05
Other South American	1	0.01
Other Hispanic or Latino	11	0.10

Race*	Population	%
African-American/Black (119)	185	1.72
Not Hispanic (116)	178	1.66
Hispanic (3)	7	0.07
American Indian/Alaska Native (21)	46	0.43
Not Hispanic (21)	44	0.41
Hispanic (0)	2	0.02
Aleut *(Alaska Native)* (0)	1	0.01
Apache (0)	1	0.01
Blackfeet (0)	4	0.04
Cherokee (7)	13	0.12
Chickasaw (4)	4	0.04
South American Ind. (0)	1	0.01
Yakama (1)	1	0.01
Asian (155)	177	1.65
Not Hispanic (155)	176	1.64
Hispanic (0)	1	0.01
Chinese, ex. Taiwanese (36)	37	0.34
Filipino (15)	27	0.25
Indian (50)	51	0.47
Indonesian (7)	7	0.07
Japanese (8)	11	0.10
Korean (9)	14	0.13
Pakistani (3)	3	0.03
Thai (1)	1	0.01
Vietnamese (21)	21	0.20
Hawaii Native/Pacific Islander (3)	7	0.07
Not Hispanic (3)	5	0.05
Hispanic (0)	2	0.02
Native Hawaiian (0)	3	0.03
Samoan (3)	3	0.03
White (10,310)	10,413	96.87
Not Hispanic (10,253)	10,348	96.27
Hispanic (57)	65	0.60

Weirton

Place Type: City
County: Hancock
Population: 19,746†

Ancestry‡	Population	%
African, Sub-Saharan (20)	20	0.10
African (20)	20	0.10
Albanian (16)	16	0.08
American (849)	849	4.30
Arab (29)	104	0.53
Lebanese (29)	68	0.34
Syrian (0)	36	0.18
Austrian (4)	31	0.16
Belgian (12)	31	0.16
Bulgarian (9)	9	0.05
Croatian (145)	255	1.29
Czech (31)	126	0.64
Czechoslovakian (55)	66	0.33
Dutch (30)	319	1.61
Eastern European (0)	28	0.14
English (466)	1,981	10.03
European (38)	66	0.33
Finnish (12)	75	0.38
French, ex. Basque (30)	251	1.27
French Canadian (10)	10	0.05
German (867)	3,926	19.88
Greek (186)	486	2.46
Hungarian (81)	294	1.49
Irish (1,204)	3,650	18.48
Italian (2,349)	4,435	22.45
Lithuanian (26)	56	0.28
New Zealander (10)	10	0.05
Norwegian (35)	47	0.24
Polish (502)	1,850	9.37
Portuguese (0)	23	0.12
Romanian (7)	7	0.04
Russian (112)	351	1.78
Scotch-Irish (287)	762	3.86
Scottish (182)	427	2.16
Serbian (152)	324	1.64
Slavic (10)	42	0.21
Slovak (188)	443	2.24
Slovene (5)	44	0.22
Swedish (15)	116	0.59
Swiss (0)	57	0.29
Turkish (0)	40	0.20
Ukrainian (42)	64	0.32
Welsh (17)	255	1.29
Yugoslavian (23)	23	0.12

Hispanic Origin	Population	%
Hispanic or Latino (of any race)	197	1.00
Central American, ex. Mexican	11	0.06
Guatemalan	2	0.01
Nicaraguan	9	0.05
Cuban	7	0.04
Dominican Republic	4	0.02
Mexican	69	0.35
Puerto Rican	36	0.18
South American	5	0.03
Chilean	1	0.01
Paraguayan	1	0.01
Peruvian	1	0.01
Other South American	2	0.01
Other Hispanic or Latino	65	0.33

Race*	Population	%
African-American/Black (770)	975	4.94
Not Hispanic (765)	962	4.87
Hispanic (5)	13	0.07
American Indian/Alaska Native (20)	92	0.47
Not Hispanic (18)	83	0.42
Hispanic (2)	9	0.05
Apache (2)	2	0.01
Blackfeet (0)	1	0.01
Cherokee (1)	28	0.14
Chickasaw (0)	1	0.01
Choctaw (0)	1	0.01
Iroquois (0)	1	0.01
Lumbee (1)	1	0.01
Mexican American Ind. (2)	2	0.01
Potawatomi (1)	1	0.01
Sioux (0)	1	0.01
Asian (100)	142	0.72
Not Hispanic (98)	137	0.69
Hispanic (2)	5	0.03
Chinese, ex. Taiwanese (30)	34	0.17
Filipino (19)	38	0.19
Indian (36)	43	0.22
Japanese (4)	9	0.05
Korean (2)	6	0.03
Thai (2)	2	0.01
Vietnamese (4)	5	0.03
Hawaii Native/Pacific Islander (7)	15	0.08
Not Hispanic (7)	14	0.07
Hispanic (0)	1	0.01
Native Hawaiian (3)	4	0.02
Samoan (3)	7	0.04
White (18,500)	18,801	95.21
Not Hispanic (18,356)	18,634	94.37
Hispanic (144)	167	0.85

Wheeling

Place Type: City
County: Ohio
Population: 28,486†

Ancestry‡	Population	%
African, Sub-Saharan (15)	15	0.05
African (15)	15	0.05
American (1,716)	1,716	5.95
Arab (131)	400	1.39
Lebanese (131)	360	1.25
Syrian (0)	40	0.14
Austrian (10)	73	0.25
Belgian (6)	59	0.20
British (53)	68	0.24
Canadian (0)	33	0.11
Croatian (139)	347	1.20
Czech (20)	70	0.24
Czechoslovakian (41)	57	0.20
Danish (12)	54	0.19
Dutch (9)	430	1.49
English (1,170)	4,374	15.16
Estonian (7)	7	0.02
European (232)	307	1.06
Finnish (0)	27	0.09
French, ex. Basque (106)	642	2.22
French Canadian (0)	19	0.07
German (2,884)	9,072	31.43
Greek (142)	601	2.08
Hungarian (72)	226	0.78
Iranian (24)	24	0.08
Irish (1,431)	5,541	19.20
Italian (1,009)	2,132	7.39
Lithuanian (55)	140	0.49
Macedonian (12)	12	0.04
Northern European (5)	5	0.02
Norwegian (29)	38	0.13
Pennsylvania German (12)	12	0.04
Polish (615)	2,220	7.69
Romanian (0)	38	0.13
Russian (42)	188	0.65
Scandinavian (0)	10	0.03
Scotch-Irish (263)	727	2.52
Scottish (124)	535	1.85
Serbian (0)	19	0.07
Slavic (0)	23	0.08
Slovak (68)	207	0.72
Slovene (0)	23	0.08
Swedish (52)	212	0.73
Swiss (20)	157	0.54
Ukrainian (38)	166	0.58
Welsh (51)	277	0.96
Yugoslavian (18)	38	0.13

Hispanic Origin	Population	%
Hispanic or Latino (of any race)	248	0.87
Central American, ex. Mexican	13	0.05
Costa Rican	1	<0.01
Guatemalan	5	0.02
Honduran	2	0.01
Nicaraguan	2	0.01
Salvadoran	2	0.01
Other Central American	1	<0.01
Cuban	13	0.05
Dominican Republic	7	0.02
Mexican	106	0.37
Puerto Rican	40	0.14
South American	19	0.07
Argentinean	6	0.02
Bolivian	2	0.01
Chilean	5	0.02
Colombian	3	0.01
Peruvian	3	0.01
Other Hispanic or Latino	50	0.18

Race*	Population	%
African-American/Black (1,463)	1,929	6.77
Not Hispanic (1,442)	1,900	6.67
Hispanic (21)	29	0.10
American Indian/Alaska Native (46)	203	0.71
Not Hispanic (43)	191	0.67
Hispanic (3)	12	0.04
Apache (0)	4	0.01
Arapaho (1)	1	<0.01
Blackfeet (1)	13	0.05
Canadian/French Am. Ind. (0)	1	<0.01
Cherokee (10)	70	0.25
Inupiat *(Alaska Native)* (1)	1	<0.01
Iroquois (0)	4	0.01
Kiowa (1)	1	<0.01
Mexican American Ind. (0)	1	<0.01
Navajo (0)	1	<0.01
Potawatomi (1)	1	<0.01
Seminole (0)	5	0.02
Shoshone (6)	7	0.02

*Notes: † The Census 2010 population figure is used to calculate the percentages in the Hispanic Origin and Race categories. Ancestry percentages are based on the 2006-2010 American Community Survey population (not shown); ‡ Numbers in parentheses indicate the number of people reporting a single ancestry; * Numbers in parentheses indicate the number of persons reporting this race alone, not in combination with any other race; Please refer to the Explanation of Data for more information.*

Sioux (0)	4	0.01
South American Ind. (0)	2	0.01
Tlingit-Haida *(Alaska Native)* (1)	1	<0.01
Asian (266)	339	1.19
Not Hispanic (261)	334	1.17
Hispanic (5)	5	0.02
Burmese (3)	3	0.01
Chinese, ex. Taiwanese (63)	76	0.27
Filipino (71)	98	0.34
Indian (51)	62	0.22
Indonesian (1)	1	<0.01
Japanese (3)	17	0.06
Korean (19)	22	0.08
Malaysian (1)	1	<0.01
Pakistani (19)	19	0.07
Sri Lankan (1)	1	<0.01
Taiwanese (4)	4	0.01
Thai (4)	5	0.02
Vietnamese (15)	17	0.06
Hawaii Native/Pacific Islander (4)	26	0.09
Not Hispanic (1)	23	0.08
Hispanic (3)	3	0.01
Guamanian/Chamorro (4)	5	0.02
Native Hawaiian (0)	13	0.05
Samoan (0)	3	0.01
White (25,966)	26,603	93.39
Not Hispanic (25,800)	26,414	92.73
Hispanic (166)	189	0.66

*Notes: † The Census 2010 population figure is used to calculate the percentages in the Hispanic Origin and Race categories. Ancestry percentages are based on the 2006-2010 American Community Survey population (not shown); ‡ Numbers in parentheses indicate the number of people reporting a single ancestry; * Numbers in parentheses indicate the number of persons reporting this race alone, not in combination with any other race; Please refer to the Explanation of Data for more information.*

WISCONSIN

Place Type: State
Population: 5,686,986†

Ancestry‡	Population	%
Afghan (78)	78	<0.01
African, Sub-Saharan (20,509)	25,325	0.45
African (15,964)	19,892	0.35
Cape Verdean (22)	24	<0.01
Ethiopian (443)	597	0.01
Ghanaian (112)	153	<0.01
Kenyan (85)	258	<0.01
Liberian (402)	414	0.01
Nigerian (1,613)	1,812	0.03
Senegalese (0)	18	<0.01
Sierra Leonean (24)	29	<0.01
Somalian (693)	701	0.01
South African (507)	666	0.01
Sudanese (182)	182	<0.01
Ugandan (62)	62	<0.01
Zimbabwean (40)	55	<0.01
Other Sub-Saharan African (360)	462	0.01
Albanian (2,557)	2,903	0.05
Alsatian (35)	235	<0.01
American (168,101)	168,101	2.98
Arab (5,765)	10,677	0.19
Arab (1,049)	1,749	0.03
Egyptian (530)	900	0.02
Iraqi (122)	185	<0.01
Jordanian (422)	642	0.01
Lebanese (1,048)	3,016	0.05
Moroccan (251)	412	0.01
Palestinian (1,006)	1,297	0.02
Syrian (255)	950	0.02
Other Arab (1,082)	1,526	0.03
Armenian (1,449)	3,438	0.06
Assyrian/Chaldean/Syriac (38)	97	<0.01
Australian (551)	1,470	0.03
Austrian (5,770)	27,068	0.48
Basque (124)	235	<0.01
Belgian (15,796)	57,524	1.02
Brazilian (492)	1,014	0.02
British (4,745)	13,311	0.24
Bulgarian (626)	1,113	0.02
Cajun (52)	246	<0.01
Canadian (2,513)	6,962	0.12
Carpatho Rusyn (18)	48	<0.01
Celtic (197)	451	0.01
Croatian (4,566)	15,775	0.28
Cypriot (31)	81	<0.01
Czech (24,003)	100,716	1.79
Czechoslovakian (3,605)	9,277	0.16
Danish (13,440)	68,154	1.21
Dutch (39,270)	153,363	2.72
Eastern European (2,473)	2,877	0.05
English (78,909)	371,912	6.60
Estonian (263)	560	0.01
European (38,225)	42,467	0.75
Finnish (12,390)	40,565	0.72
French, ex. Basque (23,610)	214,749	3.81
French Canadian (17,612)	61,687	1.09
German (1,035,082)	2,500,074	44.34
German Russian (338)	679	0.01
Greek (6,387)	19,155	0.34
Guyanese (36)	41	<0.01
Hungarian (5,908)	26,169	0.46
Icelander (248)	927	0.02
Iranian (880)	1,534	0.03
Irish (118,174)	660,884	11.72
Israeli (292)	495	0.01
Italian (56,312)	201,496	3.57
Latvian (1,372)	2,810	0.05
Lithuanian (4,631)	14,584	0.26
Luxemburger (1,913)	6,313	0.11
Macedonian (234)	554	0.01
Maltese (11)	61	<0.01
New Zealander (112)	164	<0.01
Northern European (3,887)	4,302	0.08
Norwegian (143,059)	466,309	8.27
Pennsylvania German (5,694)	7,015	0.12
Polish (156,360)	538,214	9.55
Portuguese (857)	2,905	0.05
Romanian (2,117)	5,184	0.09
Russian (12,064)	41,891	0.74
Scandinavian (10,582)	20,652	0.37
Scotch-Irish (12,191)	48,166	0.85
Scottish (12,248)	64,470	1.14
Serbian (4,623)	8,548	0.15
Slavic (840)	3,684	0.07
Slovak (4,537)	14,101	0.25
Slovene (3,269)	9,199	0.16
Soviet Union (4)	12	<0.01
Swedish (31,306)	158,306	2.81
Swiss (12,161)	60,339	1.07
Turkish (994)	1,395	0.02
Ukrainian (4,379)	9,752	0.17
Welsh (3,886)	28,171	0.50
West Indian, ex. Hispanic (2,769)	4,801	0.09
Bahamian (45)	70	<0.01
Barbadian (37)	136	<0.01
Belizean (241)	293	0.01
Bermudan (5)	5	<0.01
British West Indian (93)	158	<0.01
Dutch West Indian (16)	172	<0.01
Haitian (377)	613	0.01
Jamaican (1,702)	2,747	0.05
Trinidadian/Tobagonian (25)	45	<0.01
U.S. Virgin Islander (17)	51	<0.01
West Indian (211)	511	0.01
Yugoslavian (2,765)	6,408	0.11

Hispanic Origin	Population	%
Hispanic or Latino (of any race)	336,056	5.91
Central American, ex. Mexican	10,616	0.19
Costa Rican	779	0.01
Guatemalan	3,037	0.05
Honduran	2,402	0.04
Nicaraguan	1,624	0.03
Panamanian	822	0.01
Salvadoran	1,867	0.03
Other Central American	85	<0.01
Cuban	3,696	0.06
Dominican Republic	1,786	0.03
Mexican	244,248	4.29
Puerto Rican	46,323	0.81
South American	9,675	0.17
Argentinean	1,065	0.02
Bolivian	430	0.01
Chilean	815	0.01
Colombian	2,941	0.05
Ecuadorian	886	0.02
Paraguayan	176	<0.01
Peruvian	2,029	0.04
Uruguayan	338	0.01
Venezuelan	868	0.02
Other South American	127	<0.01
Other Hispanic or Latino	19,712	0.35

Race*	Population	%
African-American/Black (359,148)	403,527	7.10
Not Hispanic (350,898)	388,920	6.84
Hispanic (8,250)	14,607	0.26
American Indian/Alaska Native (54,526)	86,228	1.52
Not Hispanic (48,511)	75,495	1.33
Hispanic (6,015)	10,733	0.19
Alaska Athabascan *(Ala. Nat.)* (50)	93	<0.01
Aleut *(Alaska Native)* (32)	73	<0.01
Apache (202)	593	0.01
Arapaho (17)	35	<0.01
Blackfeet (149)	942	0.02
Canadian/French Am. Ind. (123)	255	<0.01
Central American Ind. (50)	80	<0.01
Cherokee (824)	4,226	0.07
Cheyenne (39)	98	<0.01
Chickasaw (63)	127	<0.01
Chippewa (14,137)	19,326	0.34
Choctaw (124)	548	0.01
Colville (7)	17	<0.01
Comanche (84)	148	<0.01
Cree (25)	105	<0.01
Creek (70)	209	<0.01
Crow (20)	67	<0.01
Delaware (22)	61	<0.01
Hopi (19)	58	<0.01
Houma (9)	14	<0.01
Inupiat *(Alaska Native)* (63)	129	<0.01
Iroquois (4,247)	6,677	0.12
Kiowa (21)	58	<0.01
Lumbee (63)	98	<0.01
Menominee (6,938)	8,388	0.15
Mexican American Ind. (1,024)	1,559	0.03
Navajo (198)	411	0.01
Osage (35)	70	<0.01
Ottawa (319)	543	0.01
Paiute (22)	40	<0.01
Pima (46)	71	<0.01
Potawatomi (1,377)	1,874	0.03
Pueblo (39)	85	<0.01
Puget Sound Salish (15)	28	<0.01
Seminole (33)	130	<0.01
Shoshone (13)	44	<0.01
Sioux (768)	1,615	0.03
South American Ind. (196)	406	0.01
Spanish American Ind. (61)	93	<0.01
Tlingit-Haida *(Alaska Native)* (42)	86	<0.01
Tohono O'Odham (11)	18	<0.01
Tsimshian *(Alaska Native)* (3)	13	<0.01
Ute (18)	33	<0.01
Yakama (5)	9	<0.01
Yaqui (26)	74	<0.01
Yuman (8)	10	<0.01
Yup'ik *(Alaska Native)* (24)	35	<0.01
Asian (129,234)	151,513	2.66
Not Hispanic (128,052)	148,605	2.61
Hispanic (1,182)	2,908	0.05
Bangladeshi (246)	283	<0.01
Bhutanese (2)	2	<0.01
Burmese (1,119)	1,197	0.02
Cambodian (975)	1,294	0.02
Chinese, ex. Taiwanese (16,684)	20,056	0.35
Filipino (7,930)	13,158	0.23
Hmong (47,127)	49,240	0.87
Indian (22,899)	25,998	0.46
Indonesian (368)	629	0.01
Japanese (2,729)	5,967	0.10
Korean (7,919)	10,949	0.19
Laotian (3,721)	4,562	0.08
Malaysian (248)	338	0.01
Nepalese (464)	500	0.01
Pakistani (2,593)	2,984	0.05
Sri Lankan (273)	307	0.01
Taiwanese (839)	1,036	0.02
Thai (1,328)	2,050	0.04
Vietnamese (4,877)	6,191	0.11
Hawaii Native/Pacific Islander (1,827)	5,117	0.09
Not Hispanic (1,565)	4,187	0.07
Hispanic (262)	930	0.02
Fijian (23)	43	<0.01
Guamanian/Chamorro (387)	716	0.01
Marshallese (22)	25	<0.01
Native Hawaiian (547)	1,638	0.03
Samoan (184)	458	0.01
Tongan (19)	55	<0.01
White (4,902,067)	4,995,836	87.85
Not Hispanic (4,738,411)	4,811,054	84.60
Hispanic (163,656)	184,782	3.25

*Notes: † The Census 2010 population figure is used to calculate the percentages in the Hispanic Origin and Race categories. Ancestry percentages are based on the 2006-2010 American Community Survey population (not shown); ‡ Numbers in parentheses indicate the number of people reporting a single ancestry; * Numbers in parentheses indicate the number of persons reporting this race alone, not in combination with any other race; Please refer to the Explanation of Data for more information.*

Allouez

Place Type: Village
County: Brown
Population: 13,975†

Ancestry‡	Population	%
African, Sub-Saharan (91)	91	0.64
African (91)	91	0.64
American (669)	669	4.70
Arab (7)	20	0.14
Lebanese (0)	13	0.09
Moroccan (7)	7	0.05
Australian (36)	94	0.66
Austrian (0)	84	0.59
Belgian (398)	1,032	7.24
Brazilian (0)	8	0.06
British (28)	69	0.48
Canadian (59)	64	0.45
Croatian (11)	39	0.27
Czech (67)	443	3.11
Czechoslovakian (36)	65	0.46
Danish (10)	193	1.35
Dutch (81)	729	5.12
Eastern European (13)	13	0.09
English (93)	853	5.99
European (181)	191	1.34
Finnish (52)	81	0.57
French, ex. Basque (32)	881	6.18
French Canadian (108)	215	1.51
German (1,844)	5,886	41.32
Greek (43)	61	0.43
Hungarian (21)	70	0.49
Irish (282)	1,970	13.83
Italian (110)	272	1.91
Lithuanian (41)	53	0.37
Luxemburger (0)	11	0.08
Northern European (77)	86	0.60
Norwegian (123)	610	4.28
Polish (302)	1,232	8.65
Romanian (0)	26	0.18
Russian (64)	77	0.54
Scandinavian (11)	96	0.67
Scotch-Irish (0)	64	0.45
Scottish (9)	105	0.74
Serbian (0)	26	0.18
Slovak (36)	59	0.41
Swedish (37)	356	2.50
Swiss (0)	51	0.36
Welsh (7)	61	0.43
West Indian, ex. Hispanic (9)	9	0.06
Jamaican (9)	9	0.06
Yugoslavian (46)	81	0.57

Hispanic Origin	Population	%
Hispanic or Latino (of any race)	383	2.74
Central American, ex. Mexican	27	0.19
Guatemalan	6	0.04
Honduran	6	0.04
Salvadoran	15	0.11
Cuban	11	0.08
Mexican	273	1.95
Puerto Rican	25	0.18
South American	17	0.12
Bolivian	3	0.02
Chilean	1	0.01
Colombian	6	0.04
Paraguayan	5	0.04
Peruvian	2	0.01
Other Hispanic or Latino	30	0.21

Race*	Population	%
African-American/Black (703)	775	5.55
Not Hispanic (695)	756	5.41
Hispanic (8)	19	0.14
American Indian/Alaska Native (137)	209	1.50
Not Hispanic (130)	191	1.37
Hispanic (7)	18	0.13
Apache (0)	1	0.01
Cherokee (1)	2	0.01
Chippewa (14)	21	0.15
Iroquois (33)	55	0.39
Menominee (7)	20	0.14
Mexican American Ind. (2)	3	0.02
Osage (1)	1	0.01
Potawatomi (0)	1	0.01
South American Ind. (1)	3	0.02
Asian (249)	298	2.13
Not Hispanic (248)	297	2.13
Hispanic (1)	1	0.01
Bangladeshi (1)	2	0.01
Cambodian (0)	2	0.01
Chinese, ex. Taiwanese (18)	22	0.16
Filipino (29)	44	0.31
Hmong (103)	107	0.77
Indian (21)	25	0.18
Indonesian (2)	2	0.01
Japanese (6)	11	0.08
Korean (9)	20	0.14
Laotian (18)	21	0.15
Malaysian (0)	1	0.01
Thai (4)	4	0.03
Vietnamese (6)	6	0.04
Hawaii Native/Pacific Islander (7)	14	0.10
Not Hispanic (7)	12	0.09
Hispanic (0)	2	0.01
Guamanian/Chamorro (2)	4	0.03
Marshallese (1)	1	0.01
Samoan (4)	6	0.04
White (12,534)	12,738	91.15
Not Hispanic (12,340)	12,501	89.45
Hispanic (194)	237	1.70

Antigo

Place Type: City
County: Langlade
Population: 8,234†

Ancestry‡	Population	%
American (273)	273	3.28
Austrian (43)	62	0.75
Belgian (0)	14	0.17
British (17)	51	0.61
Canadian (0)	20	0.24
Czech (254)	661	7.95
Czechoslovakian (14)	52	0.63
Danish (0)	74	0.89
Dutch (0)	87	1.05
English (214)	715	8.60
European (0)	24	0.29
Finnish (22)	22	0.26
French, ex. Basque (8)	298	3.59
French Canadian (8)	177	2.13
German (1,927)	4,099	49.31
Hungarian (0)	66	0.79
Irish (194)	1,206	14.51
Italian (33)	148	1.78
Northern European (107)	107	1.29
Norwegian (20)	272	3.27
Polish (309)	915	11.01
Scandinavian (40)	40	0.48
Scotch-Irish (44)	62	0.75
Scottish (32)	134	1.61
Swedish (119)	166	2.00
Swiss (0)	20	0.24
Welsh (24)	24	0.29

Hispanic Origin	Population	%
Hispanic or Latino (of any race)	226	2.74
Central American, ex. Mexican	1	0.01
Guatemalan	1	0.01
Cuban	4	0.05
Dominican Republic	1	0.01
Mexican	182	2.21
Puerto Rican	20	0.24
South American	2	0.02
Colombian	1	0.01
Ecuadorian	1	0.01
Other Hispanic or Latino	16	0.19

Race*	Population	%
African-American/Black (45)	95	1.15
Not Hispanic (43)	90	1.09
Hispanic (2)	5	0.06
American Indian/Alaska Native (117)	167	2.03
Not Hispanic (104)	148	1.80
Hispanic (13)	19	0.23
Blackfeet (0)	2	0.02
Cherokee (6)	8	0.10
Chippewa (21)	28	0.34
Creek (2)	6	0.07
Iroquois (20)	27	0.33
Menominee (3)	8	0.10
Mexican American Ind. (0)	5	0.06
Navajo (1)	1	0.01
Ottawa (2)	2	0.02
Potawatomi (8)	14	0.17
Sioux (3)	5	0.06
Asian (34)	49	0.60
Not Hispanic (34)	49	0.60
Chinese, ex. Taiwanese (8)	9	0.11
Filipino (4)	7	0.09
Hmong (1)	3	0.04
Indian (1)	1	0.01
Japanese (4)	11	0.13
Korean (5)	8	0.10
Thai (1)	2	0.02
Vietnamese (5)	5	0.06
Hawaii Native/Pacific Islander (0)	3	0.04
Not Hispanic (0)	3	0.04
Native Hawaiian (0)	3	0.04
White (7,831)	7,966	96.75
Not Hispanic (7,720)	7,826	95.04
Hispanic (111)	140	1.70

Appleton

Place Type: City
County: Calumet
Population: 11,088†

Ancestry‡	Population	%
American (658)	658	5.89
Austrian (0)	66	0.59
Belgian (0)	17	0.15
British (14)	55	0.49
Czech (0)	76	0.68
Danish (0)	198	1.77
Dutch (259)	869	7.78
English (160)	615	5.50
European (66)	66	0.59
Finnish (32)	103	0.92
French, ex. Basque (53)	589	5.27
French Canadian (36)	149	1.33
German (2,415)	6,090	54.51
Greek (15)	15	0.13
Hungarian (0)	29	0.26
Irish (310)	1,051	9.41
Italian (44)	361	3.23
Lithuanian (0)	11	0.10
Luxemburger (21)	21	0.19
Norwegian (254)	724	6.48
Polish (199)	1,022	9.15
Russian (18)	69	0.62
Scandinavian (21)	56	0.50
Scotch-Irish (18)	132	1.18
Scottish (19)	112	1.00
Swedish (24)	273	2.44
Swiss (0)	24	0.21
Ukrainian (16)	16	0.14
Welsh (0)	71	0.64

Hispanic Origin	Population	%
Hispanic or Latino (of any race)	719	6.48
Central American, ex. Mexican	30	0.27
Costa Rican	1	0.01
Guatemalan	5	0.05
Honduran	5	0.05
Nicaraguan	1	0.01
Panamanian	1	0.01

*Notes: † The Census 2010 population figure is used to calculate the percentages in the Hispanic Origin and Race categories. Ancestry percentages are based on the 2006-2010 American Community Survey population (not shown); ‡ Numbers in parentheses indicate the number of people reporting a single ancestry; * Numbers in parentheses indicate the number of persons reporting this race alone, not in combination with any other race; Please refer to the Explanation of Data for more information.*

Salvadoran	17	0.15
Cuban	2	0.02
Dominican Republic	1	0.01
Mexican	579	5.22
Puerto Rican	36	0.32
South American	16	0.14
Colombian	11	0.10
Ecuadorian	2	0.02
Peruvian	1	0.01
Venezuelan	2	0.02
Other Hispanic or Latino	55	0.50

Race*	Population	%
African-American/Black (135)	231	2.08
Not Hispanic (128)	217	1.96
Hispanic (7)	14	0.13
American Indian/Alaska Native (56)	114	1.03
Not Hispanic (50)	97	0.87
Hispanic (6)	17	0.15
Blackfeet (0)	1	0.01
Cherokee (0)	1	0.01
Chippewa (13)	20	0.18
Choctaw (0)	1	0.01
Cree (1)	2	0.02
Iroquois (16)	19	0.17
Menominee (5)	12	0.11
Potawatomi (2)	4	0.04
Sioux (0)	2	0.02
Ute (0)	2	0.02
Asian (704)	759	6.85
Not Hispanic (703)	758	6.84
Hispanic (1)	1	0.01
Chinese, ex. Taiwanese (36)	42	0.38
Filipino (29)	47	0.42
Hmong (527)	553	4.99
Indian (20)	30	0.27
Japanese (1)	6	0.05
Korean (15)	22	0.20
Laotian (5)	7	0.06
Malaysian (1)	3	0.03
Sri Lankan (1)	1	0.01
Taiwanese (3)	3	0.03
Thai (0)	1	0.01
Vietnamese (12)	19	0.17
Hawaii Native/Pacific Islander (3)	7	0.06
Not Hispanic (2)	6	0.05
Hispanic (1)	1	0.01
Guamanian/Chamorro (1)	1	0.01
Native Hawaiian (1)	2	0.02
White (9,638)	9,858	88.91
Not Hispanic (9,298)	9,474	85.44
Hispanic (340)	384	3.46

Appleton

Place Type: City
County: Outagamie
Population: 60,045†

Ancestry‡	Population	%
African, Sub-Saharan (51)	90	0.15
African (15)	41	0.07
Ethiopian (36)	36	0.06
South African (0)	13	0.02
Albanian (0)	16	0.03
American (1,895)	1,895	3.16
Arab (47)	70	0.12
Syrian (47)	70	0.12
Armenian (0)	11	0.02
Australian (0)	10	0.02
Austrian (28)	174	0.29
Basque (9)	9	0.01
Belgian (205)	799	1.33
British (26)	118	0.20
Bulgarian (0)	8	0.01
Canadian (0)	77	0.13
Croatian (35)	112	0.19
Cypriot (0)	11	0.02
Czech (179)	981	1.63
Czechoslovakian (35)	96	0.16
Danish (113)	605	1.01
Dutch (1,191)	4,342	7.24
Eastern European (13)	23	0.04
English (584)	3,826	6.38
European (532)	550	0.92
Finnish (184)	564	0.94
French, ex. Basque (329)	2,951	4.92
French Canadian (202)	939	1.56
German (12,433)	29,980	49.97
Greek (26)	166	0.28
Hungarian (61)	242	0.40
Iranian (0)	8	0.01
Irish (1,389)	8,548	14.25
Israeli (0)	5	0.01
Italian (462)	1,887	3.14
Latvian (59)	150	0.25
Lithuanian (24)	114	0.19
Luxemburger (0)	10	0.02
Northern European (50)	74	0.12
Norwegian (758)	3,129	5.21
Pennsylvania German (0)	10	0.02
Polish (785)	3,843	6.40
Portuguese (0)	13	0.02
Romanian (5)	54	0.09
Russian (55)	337	0.56
Scandinavian (38)	271	0.45
Scotch-Irish (60)	519	0.86
Scottish (179)	721	1.20
Serbian (20)	65	0.11
Slavic (30)	50	0.08
Slovak (54)	149	0.25
Slovene (7)	16	0.03
Swedish (381)	1,826	3.04
Swiss (13)	275	0.46
Ukrainian (30)	90	0.15
Welsh (0)	282	0.47
West Indian, ex. Hispanic (24)	24	0.04
Bahamian (24)	24	0.04
Yugoslavian (215)	243	0.40

Hispanic Origin	Population	%
Hispanic or Latino (of any race)	2,675	4.45
Central American, ex. Mexican	93	0.15
Costa Rican	4	0.01
Guatemalan	25	0.04
Honduran	30	0.05
Nicaraguan	11	0.02
Panamanian	5	0.01
Salvadoran	18	0.03
Cuban	34	0.06
Dominican Republic	26	0.04
Mexican	2,063	3.44
Puerto Rican	162	0.27
South American	107	0.18
Argentinean	9	0.01
Bolivian	4	0.01
Chilean	17	0.03
Colombian	37	0.06
Ecuadorian	6	0.01
Paraguayan	1	<0.01
Peruvian	16	0.03
Venezuelan	17	0.03
Other Hispanic or Latino	190	0.32

Race*	Population	%
African-American/Black (992)	1,458	2.43
Not Hispanic (965)	1,395	2.32
Hispanic (27)	63	0.10
American Indian/Alaska Native (418)	724	1.21
Not Hispanic (371)	627	1.04
Hispanic (47)	97	0.16
Blackfeet (4)	15	0.02
Cherokee (4)	45	0.07
Chippewa (35)	60	0.10
Choctaw (1)	2	<0.01
Colville (0)	3	<0.01
Comanche (5)	5	0.01
Creek (2)	6	0.01
Crow (1)	1	<0.01
Delaware (0)	1	<0.01
Iroquois (86)	129	0.21
Menominee (59)	77	0.13
Mexican American Ind. (11)	11	0.02
Navajo (4)	6	0.01
Osage (0)	1	<0.01
Ottawa (7)	7	0.01
Paiute (0)	2	<0.01
Pima (1)	1	<0.01
Potawatomi (10)	17	0.03
Puget Sound Salish (1)	1	<0.01
Seminole (0)	1	<0.01
Sioux (0)	7	0.01
South American Ind. (0)	6	0.01
Asian (3,473)	3,824	6.37
Not Hispanic (3,459)	3,778	6.29
Hispanic (14)	46	0.08
Bangladeshi (7)	7	0.01
Burmese (1)	5	0.01
Cambodian (2)	5	0.01
Chinese, ex. Taiwanese (246)	301	0.50
Filipino (94)	161	0.27
Hmong (2,428)	2,521	4.20
Indian (256)	297	0.49
Indonesian (3)	5	0.01
Japanese (43)	99	0.16
Korean (89)	151	0.25
Laotian (29)	34	0.06
Nepalese (3)	3	<0.01
Pakistani (27)	29	0.05
Sri Lankan (2)	3	<0.01
Taiwanese (15)	18	0.03
Thai (16)	22	0.04
Vietnamese (63)	73	0.12
Hawaii Native/Pacific Islander (22)	58	0.10
Not Hispanic (17)	46	0.08
Hispanic (5)	12	0.02
Guamanian/Chamorro (5)	8	0.01
Marshallese (2)	2	<0.01
Native Hawaiian (2)	13	0.02
Samoan (4)	8	0.01
White (52,851)	53,912	89.79
Not Hispanic (51,560)	52,451	87.35
Hispanic (1,291)	1,461	2.43

Appleton

Place Type: City
County: Outagamie
Population: 72,623†

Ancestry‡	Population	%
African, Sub-Saharan (51)	90	0.12
African (15)	41	0.06
Ethiopian (36)	36	0.05
South African (0)	13	0.02
Albanian (0)	16	0.02
American (2,566)	2,566	3.53
Arab (47)	70	0.10
Syrian (47)	70	0.10
Armenian (0)	11	0.02
Australian (0)	10	0.01
Austrian (28)	263	0.36
Basque (9)	9	0.01
Belgian (205)	816	1.12
British (40)	173	0.24
Bulgarian (0)	8	0.01
Canadian (0)	77	0.11
Croatian (35)	112	0.15
Cypriot (0)	11	0.02
Czech (179)	1,057	1.46
Czechoslovakian (35)	96	0.13
Danish (113)	803	1.11
Dutch (1,468)	5,229	7.20
Eastern European (13)	23	0.03
English (775)	4,563	6.28
Estonian (24)	24	0.03
European (598)	616	0.85
Finnish (216)	667	0.92
French, ex. Basque (382)	3,558	4.90
French Canadian (238)	1,097	1.51

*Notes: † The Census 2010 population figure is used to calculate the percentages in the Hispanic Origin and Race categories. Ancestry percentages are based on the 2006-2010 American Community Survey population (not shown); ‡ Numbers in parentheses indicate the number of people reporting a single ancestry; * Numbers in parentheses indicate the number of persons reporting this race alone, not in combination with any other race; Please refer to the Explanation of Data for more information.*

SECTION TWO

German (15,280)	36,784	50.65
Greek (41)	181	0.25
Hungarian (61)	271	0.37
Iranian (0)	8	0.01
Irish (1,724)	9,774	13.46
Israeli (0)	5	0.01
Italian (506)	2,265	3.12
Latvian (59)	150	0.21
Lithuanian (24)	125	0.17
Luxemburger (21)	31	0.04
Northern European (50)	74	0.10
Norwegian (1,012)	3,880	5.34
Pennsylvania German (0)	10	0.01
Polish (998)	4,965	6.84
Portuguese (0)	13	0.02
Romanian (5)	54	0.07
Russian (73)	406	0.56
Scandinavian (59)	327	0.45
Scotch-Irish (78)	651	0.90
Scottish (198)	858	1.18
Serbian (20)	65	0.09
Slavic (30)	50	0.07
Slovak (54)	149	0.21
Slovene (7)	16	0.02
Swedish (423)	2,117	2.92
Swiss (13)	322	0.44
Ukrainian (46)	106	0.15
Welsh (0)	353	0.49
West Indian, ex. Hispanic (24)	35	0.05
Bahamian (24)	24	0.03
Jamaican (0)	11	0.02
Yugoslavian (215)	243	0.33

Hispanic Origin	Population	%
Hispanic or Latino (of any race)	3,643	5.02
Central American, ex. Mexican	130	0.18
Costa Rican	5	0.01
Guatemalan	30	0.04
Honduran	35	0.05
Nicaraguan	13	0.02
Panamanian	7	0.01
Salvadoran	40	0.06
Cuban	41	0.06
Dominican Republic	30	0.04
Mexican	2,844	3.92
Puerto Rican	207	0.29
South American	129	0.18
Argentinean	9	0.01
Bolivian	4	0.01
Chilean	17	0.02
Colombian	54	0.07
Ecuadorian	8	0.01
Paraguayan	1	<0.01
Peruvian	17	0.02
Venezuelan	19	0.03
Other Hispanic or Latino	262	0.36

Race*	Population	%
African-American/Black (1,216)	1,807	2.49
Not Hispanic (1,178)	1,721	2.37
Hispanic (38)	86	0.12
American Indian/Alaska Native (489)	870	1.20
Not Hispanic (434)	753	1.04
Hispanic (55)	117	0.16
Blackfeet (4)	16	0.02
Canadian/French Am. Ind. (0)	1	<0.01
Cherokee (6)	51	0.07
Chippewa (48)	81	0.11
Choctaw (1)	3	<0.01
Colville (0)	3	<0.01
Comanche (5)	5	0.01
Cree (1)	2	<0.01
Creek (2)	6	0.01
Crow (1)	1	<0.01
Delaware (0)	1	<0.01
Iroquois (102)	150	0.21
Menominee (64)	89	0.12
Mexican American Ind. (11)	11	0.02
Navajo (4)	6	0.01
Osage (0)	1	<0.01
Ottawa (10)	10	0.01
Paiute (0)	2	<0.01
Pima (1)	1	<0.01
Potawatomi (13)	26	0.04
Puget Sound Salish (1)	1	<0.01
Seminole (0)	1	<0.01
Sioux (0)	9	0.01
South American Ind. (0)	6	0.01
Ute (0)	2	<0.01
Asian (4,279)	4,693	6.46
Not Hispanic (4,264)	4,646	6.40
Hispanic (15)	47	0.06
Bangladeshi (7)	7	0.01
Burmese (1)	5	0.01
Cambodian (2)	5	0.01
Chinese, ex. Taiwanese (282)	343	0.47
Filipino (123)	210	0.29
Hmong (3,035)	3,156	4.35
Indian (279)	331	0.46
Indonesian (3)	5	0.01
Japanese (45)	106	0.15
Korean (105)	176	0.24
Laotian (34)	41	0.06
Malaysian (1)	3	<0.01
Nepalese (3)	3	<0.01
Pakistani (27)	29	0.04
Sri Lankan (3)	4	0.01
Taiwanese (18)	21	0.03
Thai (16)	23	0.03
Vietnamese (86)	104	0.14
Hawaii Native/Pacific Islander (25)	65	0.09
Not Hispanic (19)	52	0.07
Hispanic (6)	13	0.02
Guamanian/Chamorro (6)	9	0.01
Marshallese (2)	2	<0.01
Native Hawaiian (3)	15	0.02
Samoan (4)	8	0.01
White (63,553)	64,894	89.36
Not Hispanic (61,856)	62,960	86.69
Hispanic (1,697)	1,934	2.66

Ashland

Place Type: City
County: Ashland
Population: 8,216†

Ancestry‡	Population	%
American (599)	599	7.23
Austrian (0)	23	0.28
Belgian (0)	25	0.30
Brazilian (7)	7	0.08
British (0)	63	0.76
Canadian (31)	39	0.47
Croatian (76)	193	2.33
Czech (28)	108	1.30
Czechoslovakian (18)	35	0.42
Danish (0)	39	0.47
Dutch (15)	189	2.28
English (124)	519	6.27
European (64)	64	0.77
Finnish (204)	449	5.42
French, ex. Basque (60)	422	5.09
French Canadian (75)	308	3.72
German (924)	2,542	30.69
Greek (9)	25	0.30
Hungarian (0)	11	0.13
Irish (139)	1,027	12.40
Italian (68)	246	2.97
Lithuanian (0)	14	0.17
New Zealander (0)	14	0.17
Norwegian (263)	794	9.59
Polish (129)	771	9.31
Russian (0)	21	0.25
Scandinavian (55)	77	0.93
Scotch-Irish (6)	106	1.28
Scottish (10)	40	0.48
Slavic (0)	8	0.10
Slovak (83)	103	1.24
Swedish (183)	678	8.19
Swiss (5)	15	0.18
Turkish (38)	38	0.46
Ukrainian (13)	40	0.48
Welsh (17)	70	0.85

Hispanic Origin	Population	%
Hispanic or Latino (of any race)	176	2.14
Cuban	1	0.01
Mexican	113	1.38
Puerto Rican	28	0.34
South American	6	0.07
Argentinean	1	0.01
Chilean	2	0.02
Paraguayan	1	0.01
Peruvian	2	0.02
Other Hispanic or Latino	28	0.34

Race*	Population	%
African-American/Black (37)	63	0.77
Not Hispanic (37)	62	0.75
Hispanic (0)	1	0.01
American Indian/Alaska Native (615)	898	10.93
Not Hispanic (592)	866	10.54
Hispanic (23)	32	0.39
Aleut *(Alaska Native)* (0)	1	0.01
Cherokee (0)	4	0.05
Chippewa (501)	688	8.37
Creek (1)	2	0.02
Inupiat *(Alaska Native)* (0)	2	0.02
Iroquois (1)	5	0.06
Menominee (4)	7	0.09
Mexican American Ind. (6)	6	0.07
Navajo (1)	2	0.02
Potawatomi (0)	4	0.05
Puget Sound Salish (0)	1	0.01
Shoshone (0)	1	0.01
Sioux (6)	8	0.10
Spanish American Ind. (1)	1	0.01
Yup'ik *(Alaska Native)* (0)	1	0.01
Asian (38)	67	0.82
Not Hispanic (37)	66	0.80
Hispanic (1)	1	0.01
Chinese, ex. Taiwanese (10)	12	0.15
Filipino (8)	10	0.12
Indian (3)	3	0.04
Indonesian (0)	1	0.01
Japanese (4)	11	0.13
Korean (3)	14	0.17
Thai (1)	1	0.01
Vietnamese (4)	7	0.09
Hawaii Native/Pacific Islander (3)	7	0.09
Not Hispanic (3)	7	0.09
Guamanian/Chamorro (1)	1	0.01
Native Hawaiian (1)	1	0.01
White (7,149)	7,454	90.73
Not Hispanic (7,054)	7,342	89.36
Hispanic (95)	112	1.36

Ashwaubenon

Place Type: Village
County: Brown
Population: 16,963†

Ancestry‡	Population	%
African, Sub-Saharan (14)	14	0.08
African (14)	14	0.08
American (424)	424	2.48
Australian (21)	33	0.19
Austrian (0)	72	0.42
Belgian (338)	1,666	9.74
British (20)	20	0.12
Canadian (18)	119	0.70
Croatian (30)	46	0.27
Czech (220)	613	3.58
Danish (83)	310	1.81
Dutch (296)	1,105	6.46
English (246)	1,176	6.87
Estonian (0)	10	0.06
European (134)	165	0.96

*Notes: † The Census 2010 population figure is used to calculate the percentages in the Hispanic Origin and Race categories. Ancestry percentages are based on the 2006-2010 American Community Survey population (not shown); ‡ Numbers in parentheses indicate the number of people reporting a single ancestry; * Numbers in parentheses indicate the number of persons reporting this race alone, not in combination with any other race; Please refer to the Explanation of Data for more information.*

Finnish (55)	129	0.75
French, ex. Basque (249)	1,147	6.70
French Canadian (144)	412	2.41
German (2,134)	7,393	43.21
Hungarian (12)	39	0.23
Irish (359)	1,942	11.35
Italian (75)	440	2.57
Lithuanian (32)	69	0.40
Luxemburger (0)	11	0.06
Northern European (38)	38	0.22
Norwegian (369)	937	5.48
Pennsylvania German (5)	5	0.03
Polish (459)	1,838	10.74
Russian (28)	116	0.68
Scandinavian (22)	41	0.24
Scotch-Irish (23)	127	0.74
Scottish (32)	140	0.82
Slovak (0)	32	0.19
Swedish (58)	676	3.95
Swiss (0)	56	0.33
Ukrainian (0)	9	0.05
Welsh (17)	57	0.33

Hispanic Origin	Population	%
Hispanic or Latino (of any race)	471	2.78
Central American, ex. Mexican	38	0.22
Guatemalan	4	0.02
Honduran	20	0.12
Panamanian	8	0.05
Salvadoran	6	0.04
Cuban	9	0.05
Dominican Republic	3	0.02
Mexican	309	1.82
Puerto Rican	69	0.41
South American	16	0.09
Argentinean	2	0.01
Bolivian	3	0.02
Colombian	8	0.05
Peruvian	3	0.02
Other Hispanic or Latino	27	0.16

Race*	Population	%
African-American/Black (204)	328	1.93
Not Hispanic (203)	322	1.90
Hispanic (1)	6	0.04
American Indian/Alaska Native (363)	512	3.02
Not Hispanic (338)	461	2.72
Hispanic (25)	51	0.30
Apache (1)	1	0.01
Blackfeet (0)	5	0.03
Cherokee (3)	6	0.04
Chickasaw (3)	3	0.02
Chippewa (40)	58	0.34
Choctaw (5)	6	0.04
Creek (1)	3	0.02
Iroquois (117)	155	0.91
Menominee (30)	48	0.28
Mexican American Ind. (0)	2	0.01
Navajo (0)	2	0.01
Osage (1)	2	0.01
Potawatomi (6)	6	0.04
Pueblo (1)	1	0.01
Seminole (1)	1	0.01
Sioux (5)	7	0.04
Asian (534)	601	3.54
Not Hispanic (530)	596	3.51
Hispanic (4)	5	0.03
Chinese, ex. Taiwanese (29)	34	0.20
Filipino (24)	38	0.22
Hmong (152)	160	0.94
Indian (233)	244	1.44
Indonesian (4)	4	0.02
Japanese (4)	7	0.04
Korean (16)	29	0.17
Laotian (6)	11	0.06
Nepalese (1)	1	0.01
Pakistani (9)	9	0.05
Thai (2)	4	0.02
Vietnamese (44)	44	0.26
Hawaii Native/Pacific Islander (4)	13	0.08
Not Hispanic (4)	13	0.08
Samoan (3)	8	0.05
White (15,366)	15,676	92.41
Not Hispanic (15,117)	15,383	90.69
Hispanic (249)	293	1.73

Baraboo

Place Type: City
County: Sauk
Population: 12,048†

Ancestry‡	Population	%
Albanian (43)	57	0.48
American (476)	476	4.01
Arab (0)	15	0.13
Jordanian (0)	15	0.13
Austrian (18)	61	0.51
Belgian (21)	45	0.38
British (7)	49	0.41
Bulgarian (30)	30	0.25
Canadian (20)	20	0.17
Croatian (0)	10	0.08
Czech (87)	283	2.39
Danish (11)	36	0.30
Dutch (33)	192	1.62
English (346)	1,419	11.96
European (114)	114	0.96
Finnish (0)	40	0.34
French, ex. Basque (34)	366	3.09
French Canadian (84)	180	1.52
German (2,659)	5,892	49.68
Greek (14)	14	0.12
Hungarian (10)	36	0.30
Irish (354)	1,718	14.48
Italian (121)	256	2.16
Lithuanian (40)	59	0.50
Macedonian (0)	14	0.12
Norwegian (195)	706	5.95
Pennsylvania German (16)	16	0.13
Polish (280)	770	6.49
Portuguese (0)	17	0.14
Scotch-Irish (16)	85	0.72
Scottish (38)	127	1.07
Swedish (33)	292	2.46
Swiss (14)	92	0.78
Ukrainian (8)	8	0.07
Welsh (17)	38	0.32

Hispanic Origin	Population	%
Hispanic or Latino (of any race)	446	3.70
Central American, ex. Mexican	16	0.13
Costa Rican	1	0.01
Guatemalan	4	0.03
Honduran	4	0.03
Panamanian	4	0.03
Salvadoran	3	0.02
Cuban	5	0.04
Dominican Republic	5	0.04
Mexican	332	2.76
Puerto Rican	27	0.22
South American	29	0.24
Argentinean	7	0.06
Chilean	2	0.02
Colombian	3	0.02
Ecuadorian	6	0.05
Peruvian	3	0.02
Uruguayan	8	0.07
Other Hispanic or Latino	32	0.27

Race*	Population	%
African-American/Black (162)	252	2.09
Not Hispanic (159)	232	1.93
Hispanic (3)	20	0.17
American Indian/Alaska Native (119)	210	1.74
Not Hispanic (98)	173	1.44
Hispanic (21)	37	0.31
Apache (1)	3	0.02
Blackfeet (0)	1	0.01
Cherokee (4)	10	0.08
Chippewa (14)	24	0.20
Choctaw (0)	1	0.01
Iroquois (0)	2	0.02
Menominee (2)	4	0.03
Mexican American Ind. (2)	2	0.02
Navajo (2)	2	0.02
Ottawa (0)	1	0.01
Potawatomi (0)	1	0.01
Seminole (0)	4	0.03
Sioux (1)	2	0.02
Spanish American Ind. (0)	1	0.01
Asian (65)	98	0.81
Not Hispanic (64)	85	0.71
Hispanic (1)	13	0.11
Cambodian (0)	2	0.02
Chinese, ex. Taiwanese (20)	22	0.18
Filipino (9)	15	0.12
Hmong (2)	2	0.02
Indian (14)	16	0.13
Japanese (2)	9	0.07
Korean (7)	9	0.07
Pakistani (0)	2	0.02
Thai (1)	3	0.02
Vietnamese (8)	8	0.07
Hawaii Native/Pacific Islander (8)	24	0.20
Not Hispanic (8)	11	0.09
Hispanic (0)	13	0.11
Fijian (0)	1	0.01
Guamanian/Chamorro (2)	2	0.02
Native Hawaiian (6)	9	0.07
Samoan (0)	4	0.03
Tongan (0)	1	0.01
White (11,323)	11,507	95.51
Not Hispanic (11,115)	11,260	93.46
Hispanic (208)	247	2.05

Beaver Dam

Place Type: City
County: Dodge
Population: 16,214†

Ancestry‡	Population	%
African, Sub-Saharan (71)	71	0.44
South African (58)	58	0.36
Zimbabwean (13)	13	0.08
American (379)	379	2.35
Arab (16)	16	0.10
Lebanese (16)	16	0.10
Austrian (42)	116	0.72
Belgian (12)	40	0.25
British (33)	82	0.51
Croatian (0)	33	0.20
Czech (0)	146	0.90
Czechoslovakian (0)	59	0.37
Danish (31)	122	0.76
Dutch (147)	542	3.36
English (396)	1,134	7.03
European (28)	28	0.17
Finnish (0)	81	0.50
French, ex. Basque (35)	550	3.41
French Canadian (60)	172	1.07
German (4,466)	8,808	54.60
Greek (0)	85	0.53
Hungarian (9)	104	0.64
Irish (291)	1,575	9.76
Italian (134)	595	3.69
Lithuanian (0)	21	0.13
Luxemburger (0)	9	0.06
Norwegian (293)	1,116	6.92
Polish (334)	1,548	9.60
Russian (10)	82	0.51
Scandinavian (0)	48	0.30
Scotch-Irish (40)	191	1.18
Scottish (24)	195	1.21
Slovak (9)	38	0.24
Swedish (30)	249	1.54
Swiss (24)	238	1.48
Ukrainian (0)	33	0.20
Welsh (33)	133	0.82

*Notes: † The Census 2010 population figure is used to calculate the percentages in the Hispanic Origin and Race categories. Ancestry percentages are based on the 2006-2010 American Community Survey population (not shown); ‡ Numbers in parentheses indicate the number of people reporting a single ancestry; * Numbers in parentheses indicate the number of persons reporting this race alone, not in combination with any other race; Please refer to the Explanation of Data for more information.*

Yugoslavian (0)	11	0.07

Hispanic Origin	Population	%
Hispanic or Latino (of any race)	1,210	7.46
Central American, ex. Mexican	16	0.10
Guatemalan	2	0.01
Honduran	2	0.01
Nicaraguan	2	0.01
Panamanian	1	0.01
Salvadoran	9	0.06
Cuban	6	0.04
Dominican Republic	2	0.01
Mexican	1,086	6.70
Puerto Rican	44	0.27
South American	10	0.06
Bolivian	1	0.01
Chilean	2	0.01
Colombian	1	0.01
Ecuadorian	1	0.01
Peruvian	5	0.03
Other Hispanic or Latino	46	0.28

Race*	Population	%
African-American/Black (133)	226	1.39
Not Hispanic (125)	218	1.34
Hispanic (8)	8	0.05
American Indian/Alaska Native (51)	115	0.71
Not Hispanic (50)	110	0.68
Hispanic (1)	5	0.03
Apache (1)	1	0.01
Blackfeet (0)	8	0.05
Cherokee (2)	7	0.04
Chippewa (14)	18	0.11
Iroquois (1)	4	0.02
Menominee (2)	4	0.02
Navajo (3)	3	0.02
Ottawa (6)	6	0.04
Potawatomi (2)	2	0.01
Sioux (0)	2	0.01
Asian (160)	184	1.13
Not Hispanic (153)	172	1.06
Hispanic (7)	12	0.07
Chinese, ex. Taiwanese (28)	35	0.22
Filipino (28)	35	0.22
Hmong (0)	1	0.01
Indian (27)	31	0.19
Japanese (4)	6	0.04
Korean (48)	53	0.33
Laotian (6)	13	0.08
Malaysian (1)	1	0.01
Pakistani (2)	2	0.01
Vietnamese (6)	12	0.07
Hawaii Native/Pacific Islander (1)	2	0.01
Hispanic (1)	2	0.01
Guamanian/Chamorro (1)	2	0.01
White (15,074)	15,315	94.46
Not Hispanic (14,502)	14,658	90.40
Hispanic (572)	657	4.05

Bellevue

Place Type: Village
County: Brown
Population: 14,570†

Ancestry‡	Population	%
African, Sub-Saharan (0)	15	0.11
African (0)	15	0.11
American (492)	492	3.50
Arab (9)	9	0.06
Lebanese (9)	9	0.06
Armenian (0)	14	0.10
Australian (0)	12	0.09
Basque (0)	16	0.11
Belgian (618)	1,555	11.07
Croatian (9)	23	0.16
Czech (33)	203	1.44
Danish (22)	150	1.07
Dutch (229)	965	6.87
English (142)	665	4.73
European (42)	75	0.53
Finnish (33)	199	1.42
French, ex. Basque (75)	691	4.92
French Canadian (36)	372	2.65
German (1,606)	5,053	35.96
German Russian (11)	11	0.08
Greek (0)	14	0.10
Irish (232)	1,261	8.97
Italian (77)	210	1.49
Lithuanian (0)	26	0.19
Norwegian (82)	427	3.04
Polish (441)	2,071	14.74
Portuguese (0)	9	0.06
Russian (15)	22	0.16
Scandinavian (12)	28	0.20
Scotch-Irish (37)	84	0.60
Scottish (28)	71	0.51
Slovene (0)	21	0.15
Swedish (137)	582	4.14
Swiss (0)	96	0.68
Welsh (0)	7	0.05

Hispanic Origin	Population	%
Hispanic or Latino (of any race)	1,359	9.33
Central American, ex. Mexican	77	0.53
Guatemalan	8	0.05
Honduran	19	0.13
Nicaraguan	26	0.18
Salvadoran	24	0.16
Cuban	6	0.04
Dominican Republic	9	0.06
Mexican	1,105	7.58
Puerto Rican	47	0.32
South American	13	0.09
Colombian	6	0.04
Ecuadorian	2	0.01
Peruvian	5	0.03
Other Hispanic or Latino	102	0.70

Race*	Population	%
African-American/Black (149)	249	1.71
Not Hispanic (129)	224	1.54
Hispanic (20)	25	0.17
American Indian/Alaska Native (126)	224	1.54
Not Hispanic (78)	154	1.06
Hispanic (48)	70	0.48
Alaska Athabascan *(Ala. Nat.)* (1)	1	0.01
Cherokee (0)	8	0.05
Chippewa (5)	11	0.08
Iroquois (33)	53	0.36
Menominee (16)	30	0.21
Potawatomi (2)	3	0.02
Pueblo (0)	1	0.01
Sioux (0)	2	0.01
South American Ind. (0)	1	0.01
Tlingit-Haida *(Alaska Native)* (0)	1	0.01
Asian (565)	609	4.18
Not Hispanic (564)	608	4.17
Hispanic (1)	1	0.01
Cambodian (0)	3	0.02
Chinese, ex. Taiwanese (26)	37	0.25
Filipino (16)	27	0.19
Hmong (396)	403	2.77
Indian (22)	31	0.21
Indonesian (1)	1	0.01
Japanese (3)	7	0.05
Korean (13)	19	0.13
Laotian (17)	22	0.15
Thai (4)	4	0.03
Vietnamese (27)	36	0.25
Hawaii Native/Pacific Islander (1)	3	0.02
Not Hispanic (1)	3	0.02
Native Hawaiian (0)	2	0.01
White (12,748)	13,002	89.24
Not Hispanic (12,241)	12,419	85.24
Hispanic (507)	583	4.00

Beloit

Place Type: City
County: Rock
Population: 36,966†

Ancestry‡	Population	%
African, Sub-Saharan (1,274)	1,593	4.30
African (1,274)	1,578	4.26
Nigerian (0)	15	0.04
American (1,458)	1,458	3.94
Armenian (0)	12	0.03
Austrian (0)	13	0.04
Belgian (13)	32	0.09
British (19)	229	0.62
Bulgarian (13)	13	0.04
Canadian (22)	32	0.09
Celtic (0)	18	0.05
Croatian (0)	14	0.04
Czech (191)	414	1.12
Czechoslovakian (70)	102	0.28
Danish (37)	370	1.00
Dutch (50)	602	1.63
Eastern European (24)	24	0.06
English (644)	3,242	8.76
European (216)	229	0.62
Finnish (0)	44	0.12
French, ex. Basque (41)	947	2.56
French Canadian (106)	303	0.82
German (3,025)	9,619	25.98
Greek (47)	96	0.26
Hungarian (19)	64	0.17
Icelander (13)	29	0.08
Irish (1,003)	4,844	13.08
Israeli (0)	13	0.04
Italian (411)	1,247	3.37
Latvian (16)	16	0.04
Lithuanian (20)	100	0.27
Northern European (28)	28	0.08
Norwegian (1,261)	3,526	9.52
Pennsylvania German (53)	64	0.17
Polish (422)	1,534	4.14
Russian (94)	388	1.05
Scandinavian (37)	63	0.17
Scotch-Irish (69)	301	0.81
Scottish (37)	250	0.68
Slovak (8)	17	0.05
Slovene (21)	21	0.06
Swedish (281)	1,171	3.16
Swiss (107)	308	0.83
Welsh (11)	113	0.31
West Indian, ex. Hispanic (11)	11	0.03
Jamaican (11)	11	0.03
Yugoslavian (0)	12	0.03

Hispanic Origin	Population	%
Hispanic or Latino (of any race)	6,332	17.13
Central American, ex. Mexican	99	0.27
Costa Rican	9	0.02
Guatemalan	20	0.05
Honduran	34	0.09
Nicaraguan	12	0.03
Panamanian	5	0.01
Salvadoran	19	0.05
Cuban	36	0.10
Dominican Republic	103	0.28
Mexican	5,522	14.94
Puerto Rican	190	0.51
South American	73	0.20
Argentinean	2	0.01
Bolivian	2	0.01
Chilean	2	0.01
Colombian	21	0.06
Ecuadorian	3	0.01
Paraguayan	3	0.01
Peruvian	31	0.08
Venezuelan	9	0.02
Other Hispanic or Latino	309	0.84

*Notes: † The Census 2010 population figure is used to calculate the percentages in the Hispanic Origin and Race categories. Ancestry percentages are based on the 2006-2010 American Community Survey population (not shown); ‡ Numbers in parentheses indicate the number of people reporting a single ancestry; * Numbers in parentheses indicate the number of persons reporting this race alone, not in combination with any other race; Please refer to the Explanation of Data for more information.*

Race*	Population	%
African-American/Black (5,572)	6,482	17.54
Not Hispanic (5,440)	6,237	16.87
Hispanic (132)	245	0.66
American Indian/Alaska Native (158)	486	1.31
Not Hispanic (114)	381	1.03
Hispanic (44)	105	0.28
Aleut *(Alaska Native)* (0)	1	<0.01
Apache (2)	14	0.04
Blackfeet (2)	13	0.04
Cherokee (7)	97	0.26
Cheyenne (0)	6	0.02
Chickasaw (0)	2	0.01
Chippewa (8)	21	0.06
Choctaw (1)	5	0.01
Comanche (0)	4	0.01
Inupiat *(Alaska Native)* (0)	1	<0.01
Iroquois (6)	15	0.04
Menominee (16)	26	0.07
Mexican American Ind. (13)	16	0.04
Navajo (0)	2	0.01
Ottawa (0)	1	<0.01
Pima (0)	1	<0.01
Potawatomi (0)	3	0.01
Pueblo (0)	1	<0.01
Puget Sound Salish (0)	2	0.01
Shoshone (1)	4	0.01
Sioux (3)	21	0.06
South American Ind. (0)	2	0.01
Spanish American Ind. (0)	1	<0.01
Tlingit-Haida *(Alaska Native)* (1)	2	0.01
Ute (1)	4	0.01
Asian (415)	600	1.62
Not Hispanic (409)	580	1.57
Hispanic (6)	20	0.05
Burmese (2)	2	0.01
Cambodian (10)	14	0.04
Chinese, ex. Taiwanese (94)	135	0.37
Filipino (49)	102	0.28
Indian (72)	95	0.26
Indonesian (10)	13	0.04
Japanese (17)	38	0.10
Korean (34)	51	0.14
Laotian (5)	8	0.02
Malaysian (4)	5	0.01
Nepalese (2)	3	0.01
Pakistani (7)	8	0.02
Thai (8)	21	0.06
Vietnamese (81)	99	0.27
Hawaii Native/Pacific Islander (10)	55	0.15
Not Hispanic (9)	35	0.09
Hispanic (1)	20	0.05
Guamanian/Chamorro (4)	5	0.01
Native Hawaiian (2)	24	0.06
Samoan (0)	1	<0.01
White (25,485)	26,952	72.91
Not Hispanic (23,485)	24,527	66.35
Hispanic (2,000)	2,425	6.56

Beloit

Place Type: Town
County: Rock
Population: 7,662†

Ancestry‡	Population	%
African, Sub-Saharan (46)	99	1.30
African (46)	99	1.30
American (285)	285	3.76
Arab (59)	59	0.78
Palestinian (59)	59	0.78
British (22)	22	0.29
Czech (37)	93	1.23
Danish (40)	240	3.16
Dutch (26)	204	2.69
English (151)	780	10.28
European (138)	138	1.82
French, ex. Basque (0)	218	2.87
French Canadian (14)	29	0.38
German (796)	3,099	40.84
Greek (11)	11	0.14
Hungarian (11)	35	0.46
Irish (228)	1,390	18.32
Italian (142)	355	4.68
Lithuanian (10)	40	0.53
Norwegian (288)	896	11.81
Polish (143)	488	6.43
Portuguese (0)	16	0.21
Russian (0)	45	0.59
Scandinavian (11)	33	0.43
Scotch-Irish (31)	109	1.44
Scottish (36)	155	2.04
Serbian (10)	20	0.26
Swedish (52)	341	4.49
Swiss (41)	276	3.64
Welsh (21)	101	1.33

Hispanic Origin	Population	%
Hispanic or Latino (of any race)	511	6.67
Central American, ex. Mexican	7	0.09
Guatemalan	1	0.01
Honduran	4	0.05
Nicaraguan	2	0.03
Cuban	4	0.05
Dominican Republic	4	0.05
Mexican	430	5.61
Puerto Rican	22	0.29
South American	3	0.04
Colombian	2	0.03
Peruvian	1	0.01
Other Hispanic or Latino	41	0.54

Race*	Population	%
African-American/Black (427)	526	6.87
Not Hispanic (415)	507	6.62
Hispanic (12)	19	0.25
American Indian/Alaska Native (21)	58	0.76
Not Hispanic (20)	53	0.69
Hispanic (1)	5	0.07
Apache (0)	4	0.05
Cherokee (0)	12	0.16
Chippewa (4)	5	0.07
Iroquois (2)	8	0.10
Navajo (0)	1	0.01
Potawatomi (1)	1	0.01
Sioux (1)	1	0.01
Tlingit-Haida *(Alaska Native)* (1)	2	0.03
Asian (73)	106	1.38
Not Hispanic (66)	96	1.25
Hispanic (7)	10	0.13
Chinese, ex. Taiwanese (9)	9	0.12
Filipino (9)	12	0.16
Indian (12)	12	0.16
Japanese (5)	18	0.23
Korean (6)	19	0.25
Laotian (0)	1	0.01
Pakistani (0)	1	0.01
Vietnamese (30)	30	0.39
Hawaii Native/Pacific Islander (2)	5	0.07
Not Hispanic (2)	5	0.07
Native Hawaiian (2)	5	0.07
White (6,689)	6,859	89.52
Not Hispanic (6,488)	6,627	86.49
Hispanic (201)	232	3.03

Brookfield

Place Type: City
County: Waukesha
Population: 37,920†

Ancestry‡	Population	%
African, Sub-Saharan (16)	34	0.09
Kenyan (4)	4	0.01
Nigerian (12)	30	0.08
Alsatian (14)	14	0.04
American (842)	842	2.20
Arab (48)	56	0.15
Arab (22)	22	0.06
Lebanese (17)	25	0.07
Moroccan (9)	9	0.02
Armenian (43)	130	0.34
Australian (15)	43	0.11
Austrian (137)	449	1.18
Belgian (38)	154	0.40
Brazilian (16)	16	0.04
British (94)	173	0.45
Canadian (10)	42	0.11
Croatian (34)	264	0.69
Czech (137)	611	1.60
Czechoslovakian (43)	68	0.18
Danish (39)	247	0.65
Dutch (185)	758	1.98
English (556)	3,295	8.63
European (521)	541	1.42
Finnish (42)	288	0.75
French, ex. Basque (131)	1,063	2.78
French Canadian (54)	245	0.64
German (7,618)	18,690	48.93
Greek (481)	821	2.15
Hungarian (99)	441	1.15
Icelander (0)	8	0.02
Iranian (21)	21	0.05
Irish (1,146)	5,562	14.56
Italian (800)	2,657	6.96
Latvian (54)	82	0.21
Lithuanian (0)	69	0.18
Luxemburger (0)	35	0.09
Northern European (41)	41	0.11
Norwegian (477)	1,869	4.89
Polish (1,357)	4,731	12.39
Romanian (41)	89	0.23
Russian (150)	419	1.10
Scandinavian (20)	50	0.13
Scotch-Irish (137)	658	1.72
Scottish (160)	866	2.27
Serbian (11)	39	0.10
Slavic (0)	34	0.09
Slovak (75)	205	0.54
Slovene (36)	198	0.52
Soviet Union (0)	8	0.02
Swedish (188)	900	2.36
Swiss (32)	460	1.20
Ukrainian (38)	209	0.55
Welsh (41)	258	0.68
Yugoslavian (46)	65	0.17

Hispanic Origin	Population	%
Hispanic or Latino (of any race)	853	2.25
Central American, ex. Mexican	69	0.18
Costa Rican	2	0.01
Guatemalan	32	0.08
Nicaraguan	11	0.03
Panamanian	2	0.01
Salvadoran	19	0.05
Other Central American	3	0.01
Cuban	22	0.06
Dominican Republic	10	0.03
Mexican	478	1.26
Puerto Rican	122	0.32
South American	75	0.20
Argentinean	15	0.04
Bolivian	4	0.01
Chilean	5	0.01
Colombian	17	0.04
Ecuadorian	4	0.01
Paraguayan	1	<0.01
Peruvian	16	0.04
Uruguayan	5	0.01
Venezuelan	8	0.02
Other Hispanic or Latino	77	0.20

Race*	Population	%
African-American/Black (460)	596	1.57
Not Hispanic (456)	574	1.51
Hispanic (4)	22	0.06
American Indian/Alaska Native (64)	135	0.36
Not Hispanic (51)	107	0.28
Hispanic (13)	28	0.07

*Notes: † The Census 2010 population figure is used to calculate the percentages in the Hispanic Origin and Race categories. Ancestry percentages are based on the 2006-2010 American Community Survey population (not shown); ‡ Numbers in parentheses indicate the number of people reporting a single ancestry; * Numbers in parentheses indicate the number of persons reporting this race alone, not in combination with any other race; Please refer to the Explanation of Data for more information.*

Alaska Athabascan *(Ala. Nat.)* (2)	2	0.01
Blackfeet (0)	6	0.02
Cherokee (0)	9	0.02
Chickasaw (0)	1	<0.01
Chippewa (12)	27	0.07
Iroquois (2)	2	0.01
Lumbee (0)	3	0.01
Menominee (8)	9	0.02
Mexican American Ind. (8)	10	0.03
Navajo (0)	1	<0.01
Ottawa (1)	1	<0.01
Seminole (0)	2	0.01
Sioux (0)	1	<0.01
South American Ind. (1)	1	<0.01
Asian (2,538)	2,829	7.46
Not Hispanic (2,531)	2,809	7.41
Hispanic (7)	20	0.05
Bangladeshi (20)	24	0.06
Burmese (1)	1	<0.01
Chinese, ex. Taiwanese (576)	686	1.81
Filipino (134)	205	0.54
Hmong (44)	48	0.13
Indian (1,148)	1,210	3.19
Indonesian (1)	2	0.01
Japanese (58)	85	0.22
Korean (195)	232	0.61
Laotian (10)	10	0.03
Malaysian (0)	3	0.01
Nepalese (6)	8	0.02
Pakistani (151)	164	0.43
Sri Lankan (19)	19	0.05
Taiwanese (19)	25	0.07
Thai (5)	9	0.02
Vietnamese (66)	91	0.24
Hawaii Native/Pacific Islander (16)	40	0.11
Not Hispanic (16)	35	0.09
Hispanic (0)	5	0.01
Guamanian/Chamorro (4)	6	0.02
Native Hawaiian (5)	10	0.03
Samoan (1)	10	0.03
Tongan (0)	2	0.01
White (34,114)	34,609	91.27
Not Hispanic (33,522)	33,936	89.49
Hispanic (592)	673	1.77

Brown Deer

Place Type: Village
County: Milwaukee
Population: 11,999†

Ancestry‡	Population	%
African, Sub-Saharan (121)	165	1.39
African (25)	69	0.58
Ghanaian (18)	18	0.15
Liberian (44)	44	0.37
Nigerian (21)	21	0.18
Ugandan (13)	13	0.11
American (411)	411	3.46
Armenian (176)	184	1.55
Austrian (20)	108	0.91
Belgian (23)	62	0.52
British (22)	48	0.40
Croatian (13)	47	0.40
Czech (0)	30	0.25
Czechoslovakian (29)	48	0.40
Danish (10)	38	0.32
Dutch (79)	293	2.47
Eastern European (19)	19	0.16
English (66)	396	3.34
European (91)	91	0.77
Finnish (42)	60	0.51
French, ex. Basque (47)	210	1.77
French Canadian (0)	23	0.19
German (1,696)	3,766	31.74
Greek (48)	125	1.05
Hungarian (35)	58	0.49
Irish (95)	886	7.47
Italian (61)	487	4.10
Luxemburger (0)	12	0.10
Northern European (38)	38	0.32
Norwegian (44)	409	3.45
Pennsylvania German (0)	9	0.08
Polish (245)	991	8.35
Russian (163)	323	2.72
Scandinavian (0)	41	0.35
Scotch-Irish (0)	9	0.08
Scottish (31)	106	0.89
Slavic (0)	31	0.26
Slovak (11)	33	0.28
Slovene (15)	15	0.13
Swedish (33)	251	2.12
Swiss (15)	24	0.20
Ukrainian (45)	45	0.38
Welsh (16)	44	0.37
Yugoslavian (12)	12	0.10

Hispanic Origin	Population	%
Hispanic or Latino (of any race)	471	3.93
Central American, ex. Mexican	18	0.15
Costa Rican	3	0.03
Guatemalan	2	0.02
Honduran	2	0.02
Nicaraguan	3	0.03
Panamanian	5	0.04
Salvadoran	3	0.03
Cuban	7	0.06
Dominican Republic	2	0.02
Mexican	238	1.98
Puerto Rican	122	1.02
South American	42	0.35
Argentinean	11	0.09
Colombian	2	0.02
Ecuadorian	9	0.08
Paraguayan	3	0.03
Peruvian	12	0.10
Venezuelan	5	0.04
Other Hispanic or Latino	42	0.35

Race*	Population	%
African-American/Black (3,431)	3,695	30.79
Not Hispanic (3,387)	3,612	30.10
Hispanic (44)	83	0.69
American Indian/Alaska Native (42)	124	1.03
Not Hispanic (42)	117	0.98
Hispanic (0)	7	0.06
Apache (0)	1	0.01
Blackfeet (0)	2	0.02
Cherokee (1)	10	0.08
Chippewa (2)	3	0.03
Choctaw (0)	4	0.03
Creek (0)	2	0.02
Iroquois (4)	11	0.09
Menominee (1)	1	0.01
Potawatomi (0)	1	0.01
Sioux (1)	2	0.02
Tlingit-Haida *(Alaska Native)* (2)	2	0.02
Asian (584)	665	5.54
Not Hispanic (582)	658	5.48
Hispanic (2)	7	0.06
Cambodian (2)	2	0.02
Chinese, ex. Taiwanese (64)	86	0.72
Filipino (43)	69	0.58
Hmong (278)	289	2.41
Indian (71)	80	0.67
Indonesian (2)	2	0.02
Japanese (13)	33	0.28
Korean (15)	21	0.18
Laotian (3)	9	0.08
Malaysian (1)	1	0.01
Nepalese (3)	3	0.03
Pakistani (10)	17	0.14
Sri Lankan (4)	5	0.04
Taiwanese (2)	5	0.04
Thai (4)	5	0.04
Vietnamese (18)	18	0.15
Hawaii Native/Pacific Islander (7)	24	0.20
Not Hispanic (5)	22	0.18
Hispanic (2)	2	0.02
Guamanian/Chamorro (5)	7	0.06
Native Hawaiian (2)	4	0.03
White (7,430)	7,747	64.56
Not Hispanic (7,170)	7,442	62.02
Hispanic (260)	305	2.54

Burlington

Place Type: City
County: Racine
Population: 10,464†

Ancestry‡	Population	%
American (473)	473	4.55
Austrian (0)	13	0.13
Belgian (0)	38	0.37
Croatian (0)	17	0.16
Czech (68)	154	1.48
Danish (50)	274	2.64
Dutch (27)	84	0.81
English (67)	697	6.70
European (80)	80	0.77
Finnish (27)	27	0.26
French, ex. Basque (190)	574	5.52
French Canadian (0)	76	0.73
German (1,785)	4,687	45.08
Hungarian (7)	41	0.39
Irish (378)	1,280	12.31
Italian (478)	1,045	10.05
Lithuanian (29)	39	0.38
Norwegian (190)	581	5.59
Polish (224)	852	8.19
Russian (55)	55	0.53
Scotch-Irish (20)	113	1.09
Scottish (53)	106	1.02
Serbian (10)	26	0.25
Slovak (11)	11	0.11
Slovene (22)	22	0.21
Swedish (49)	204	1.96
Swiss (0)	30	0.29
Welsh (0)	102	0.98

Hispanic Origin	Population	%
Hispanic or Latino (of any race)	898	8.58
Central American, ex. Mexican	19	0.18
Guatemalan	16	0.15
Honduran	1	0.01
Nicaraguan	2	0.02
Cuban	6	0.06
Mexican	783	7.48
Puerto Rican	21	0.20
South American	8	0.08
Chilean	1	0.01
Ecuadorian	4	0.04
Peruvian	3	0.03
Other Hispanic or Latino	61	0.58

Race*	Population	%
African-American/Black (90)	144	1.38
Not Hispanic (87)	137	1.31
Hispanic (3)	7	0.07
American Indian/Alaska Native (38)	71	0.68
Not Hispanic (22)	47	0.45
Hispanic (16)	24	0.23
Apache (0)	1	0.01
Blackfeet (1)	2	0.02
Canadian/French Am. Ind. (1)	2	0.02
Cherokee (0)	3	0.03
Chickasaw (1)	1	0.01
Chippewa (4)	8	0.08
Mexican American Ind. (5)	6	0.06
Potawatomi (1)	1	0.01
Sioux (0)	3	0.03
Yaqui (0)	4	0.04
Asian (118)	148	1.41
Not Hispanic (115)	140	1.34
Hispanic (3)	8	0.08
Burmese (31)	32	0.31
Chinese, ex. Taiwanese (12)	15	0.14
Filipino (19)	32	0.31
Indian (10)	12	0.11

*Notes: † The Census 2010 population figure is used to calculate the percentages in the Hispanic Origin and Race categories. Ancestry percentages are based on the 2006-2010 American Community Survey population (not shown); ‡ Numbers in parentheses indicate the number of people reporting a single ancestry; * Numbers in parentheses indicate the number of persons reporting this race alone, not in combination with any other race; Please refer to the Explanation of Data for more information.*

Indonesian (0)	2	0.02
Japanese (1)	4	0.04
Korean (14)	16	0.15
Laotian (9)	11	0.11
Taiwanese (1)	1	0.01
Vietnamese (11)	17	0.16
Hawaii Native/Pacific Islander (0)	6	0.06
Not Hispanic (0)	3	0.03
Hispanic (0)	3	0.03
Native Hawaiian (0)	1	0.01
White (9,707)	9,847	94.10
Not Hispanic (9,239)	9,327	89.13
Hispanic (468)	520	4.97

Caledonia

Place Type: Village
County: Racine
Population: 24,705†

Ancestry‡	Population	%
African, Sub-Saharan (66)	85	0.35
African (38)	40	0.16
Ghanaian (0)	14	0.06
Nigerian (4)	7	0.03
South African (8)	8	0.03
Other Sub-Saharan African (16)	16	0.07
Albanian (42)	42	0.17
American (505)	505	2.06
Arab (34)	82	0.33
Lebanese (34)	82	0.33
Armenian (29)	65	0.26
Austrian (29)	75	0.31
Belgian (20)	91	0.37
British (7)	52	0.21
Bulgarian (0)	11	0.04
Croatian (15)	135	0.55
Czech (221)	1,011	4.12
Czechoslovakian (21)	42	0.17
Danish (441)	1,378	5.62
Dutch (231)	719	2.93
English (280)	1,642	6.69
European (103)	103	0.42
Finnish (47)	151	0.62
French, ex. Basque (62)	921	3.75
French Canadian (208)	439	1.79
German (3,705)	11,339	46.21
Greek (10)	26	0.11
Hungarian (62)	222	0.90
Irish (460)	2,702	11.01
Italian (377)	1,365	5.56
Lithuanian (45)	96	0.39
Northern European (9)	23	0.09
Norwegian (233)	1,338	5.45
Pennsylvania German (0)	26	0.11
Polish (667)	2,758	11.24
Russian (7)	132	0.54
Scandinavian (52)	79	0.32
Scotch-Irish (23)	314	1.28
Scottish (62)	345	1.41
Serbian (12)	28	0.11
Slavic (11)	34	0.14
Slovak (22)	234	0.95
Slovene (0)	40	0.16
Swedish (48)	459	1.87
Swiss (9)	295	1.20
Ukrainian (9)	30	0.12
Welsh (0)	53	0.22
West Indian, ex. Hispanic (57)	57	0.23
Haitian (20)	20	0.08
Jamaican (37)	37	0.15
Yugoslavian (27)	48	0.20

Hispanic Origin	Population	%
Hispanic or Latino (of any race)	1,303	5.27
Central American, ex. Mexican	42	0.17
Costa Rican	12	0.05
Guatemalan	6	0.02
Honduran	4	0.02
Nicaraguan	9	0.04
Panamanian	4	0.02
Salvadoran	7	0.03
Cuban	10	0.04
Dominican Republic	5	0.02
Mexican	968	3.92
Puerto Rican	157	0.64
South American	44	0.18
Argentinean	15	0.06
Bolivian	2	0.01
Chilean	1	<0.01
Colombian	18	0.07
Peruvian	2	0.01
Venezuelan	6	0.02
Other Hispanic or Latino	77	0.31

Race*	Population	%
African-American/Black (688)	865	3.50
Not Hispanic (667)	812	3.29
Hispanic (21)	53	0.21
American Indian/Alaska Native (91)	219	0.89
Not Hispanic (87)	191	0.77
Hispanic (4)	28	0.11
Blackfeet (0)	1	<0.01
Cherokee (3)	25	0.10
Chippewa (36)	68	0.28
Cree (0)	1	<0.01
Creek (0)	1	<0.01
Iroquois (8)	21	0.09
Lumbee (1)	2	0.01
Menominee (3)	9	0.04
Ottawa (3)	8	0.03
Potawatomi (5)	6	0.02
Pueblo (0)	3	0.01
Puget Sound Salish (2)	2	0.01
Sioux (0)	7	0.03
South American Ind. (0)	1	<0.01
Asian (456)	565	2.29
Not Hispanic (453)	550	2.23
Hispanic (3)	15	0.06
Bangladeshi (1)	1	<0.01
Chinese, ex. Taiwanese (70)	85	0.34
Filipino (34)	60	0.24
Hmong (38)	38	0.15
Indian (174)	183	0.74
Indonesian (1)	2	0.01
Japanese (15)	41	0.17
Korean (52)	63	0.26
Laotian (12)	15	0.06
Malaysian (2)	2	0.01
Pakistani (19)	22	0.09
Taiwanese (0)	1	<0.01
Thai (2)	2	0.01
Vietnamese (24)	42	0.17
Hawaii Native/Pacific Islander (4)	14	0.06
Not Hispanic (4)	13	0.05
Hispanic (0)	1	<0.01
Guamanian/Chamorro (2)	3	0.01
Native Hawaiian (2)	8	0.03
White (22,656)	23,061	93.35
Not Hispanic (21,839)	22,145	89.64
Hispanic (817)	916	3.71

Cedarburg

Place Type: City
County: Ozaukee
Population: 11,412†

Ancestry‡	Population	%
American (199)	199	1.75
Arab (40)	73	0.64
Lebanese (40)	40	0.35
Palestinian (0)	19	0.17
Syrian (0)	14	0.12
Australian (0)	11	0.10
Austrian (0)	67	0.59
Belgian (0)	142	1.25
British (54)	69	0.61
Croatian (0)	44	0.39
Czech (49)	180	1.58
Danish (0)	123	1.08
Dutch (28)	372	3.27
English (158)	1,135	9.97
European (40)	40	0.35
Finnish (45)	59	0.52
French, ex. Basque (13)	495	4.35
French Canadian (28)	94	0.83
German (2,852)	6,639	58.33
Greek (12)	109	0.96
Hungarian (182)	241	2.12
Icelander (0)	12	0.11
Iranian (20)	20	0.18
Irish (249)	1,784	15.67
Italian (107)	647	5.68
Luxemburger (13)	69	0.61
Norwegian (147)	611	5.37
Pennsylvania German (0)	12	0.11
Polish (257)	1,277	11.22
Russian (33)	81	0.71
Scandinavian (19)	19	0.17
Scotch-Irish (30)	96	0.84
Scottish (19)	318	2.79
Slovak (17)	152	1.34
Slovene (38)	38	0.33
Swedish (23)	576	5.06
Swiss (46)	68	0.60
Welsh (52)	63	0.55
West Indian, ex. Hispanic (10)	10	0.09
Jamaican (10)	10	0.09

Hispanic Origin	Population	%
Hispanic or Latino (of any race)	197	1.73
Central American, ex. Mexican	9	0.08
Costa Rican	2	0.02
Guatemalan	1	0.01
Honduran	1	0.01
Nicaraguan	2	0.02
Panamanian	2	0.02
Salvadoran	1	0.01
Cuban	3	0.03
Dominican Republic	2	0.02
Mexican	136	1.19
Puerto Rican	19	0.17
South American	14	0.12
Argentinean	2	0.02
Colombian	7	0.06
Ecuadorian	4	0.04
Venezuelan	1	0.01
Other Hispanic or Latino	14	0.12

Race*	Population	%
African-American/Black (87)	109	0.96
Not Hispanic (83)	103	0.90
Hispanic (4)	6	0.05
American Indian/Alaska Native (13)	34	0.30
Not Hispanic (11)	30	0.26
Hispanic (2)	4	0.04
Cherokee (0)	5	0.04
Chippewa (0)	1	0.01
Colville (1)	1	0.01
Iroquois (1)	6	0.05
Menominee (2)	2	0.02
Mexican American Ind. (1)	1	0.01
Ottawa (1)	1	0.01
Potawatomi (0)	1	0.01
Tohono O'Odham (0)	2	0.02
Asian (170)	236	2.07
Not Hispanic (169)	229	2.01
Hispanic (1)	7	0.06
Cambodian (1)	1	0.01
Chinese, ex. Taiwanese (47)	70	0.61
Filipino (12)	20	0.18
Hmong (20)	26	0.23
Indian (44)	47	0.41
Indonesian (0)	2	0.02
Japanese (7)	22	0.19
Korean (19)	27	0.24
Nepalese (1)	2	0.02
Pakistani (0)	1	0.01
Thai (2)	2	0.02

*Notes: † The Census 2010 population figure is used to calculate the percentages in the Hispanic Origin and Race categories. Ancestry percentages are based on the 2006-2010 American Community Survey population (not shown); ‡ Numbers in parentheses indicate the number of people reporting a single ancestry; * Numbers in parentheses indicate the number of persons reporting this race alone, not in combination with any other race; Please refer to the Explanation of Data for more information.*

	Population	%
Vietnamese (3)	5	0.04
Hawaii Native/Pacific Islander (3)	11	0.10
Not Hispanic (3)	11	0.10
Guamanian/Chamorro (1)	1	0.01
Native Hawaiian (0)	8	0.07
White (10,989)	11,098	97.25
Not Hispanic (10,848)	10,946	95.92
Hispanic (141)	152	1.33

Chippewa Falls

Place Type: City
County: Chippewa
Population: 13,661†

Ancestry‡	Population	%
American (435)	435	3.19
Arab (0)	42	0.31
Lebanese (0)	42	0.31
Austrian (7)	35	0.26
Belgian (0)	24	0.18
British (16)	16	0.12
Czech (112)	286	2.10
Czechoslovakian (15)	35	0.26
Danish (26)	137	1.00
Dutch (60)	274	2.01
English (198)	817	5.99
European (67)	96	0.70
Finnish (57)	78	0.57
French, ex. Basque (132)	1,354	9.93
French Canadian (55)	100	0.73
German (2,237)	5,857	42.94
Hungarian (12)	112	0.82
Irish (145)	2,208	16.19
Italian (24)	333	2.44
Lithuanian (10)	10	0.07
Norwegian (909)	2,412	17.68
Polish (251)	1,100	8.06
Russian (20)	60	0.44
Scandinavian (111)	159	1.17
Scotch-Irish (77)	291	2.13
Scottish (12)	87	0.64
Slovak (0)	10	0.07
Slovene (0)	15	0.11
Swedish (115)	381	2.79
Swiss (0)	37	0.27
Ukrainian (0)	60	0.44
Welsh (0)	122	0.89
West Indian, ex. Hispanic (0)	79	0.58
Dutch West Indian (0)	79	0.58
Yugoslavian (0)	12	0.09

Hispanic Origin	Population	%
Hispanic or Latino (of any race)	221	1.62
Central American, ex. Mexican	15	0.11
Guatemalan	5	0.04
Nicaraguan	7	0.05
Panamanian	2	0.01
Salvadoran	1	0.01
Cuban	7	0.05
Mexican	128	0.94
Puerto Rican	18	0.13
South American	6	0.04
Argentinean	2	0.01
Colombian	2	0.01
Ecuadorian	1	0.01
Peruvian	1	0.01
Other Hispanic or Latino	47	0.34

Race*	Population	%
African-American/Black (228)	295	2.16
Not Hispanic (224)	284	2.08
Hispanic (4)	11	0.08
American Indian/Alaska Native (96)	183	1.34
Not Hispanic (91)	165	1.21
Hispanic (5)	18	0.13
Apache (0)	3	0.02
Blackfeet (1)	1	0.01
Canadian/French Am. Ind. (2)	5	0.04
Cherokee (4)	16	0.12
Chippewa (20)	46	0.34
Choctaw (0)	2	0.01
Creek (0)	1	0.01
Crow (0)	1	0.01
Inupiat *(Alaska Native)* (1)	1	0.01
Iroquois (1)	5	0.04
Lumbee (3)	3	0.02
Menominee (5)	7	0.05
Mexican American Ind. (1)	4	0.03
Navajo (0)	1	0.01
Potawatomi (1)	1	0.01
Seminole (0)	3	0.02
Sioux (2)	4	0.03
Spanish American Ind. (1)	1	0.01
Asian (127)	159	1.16
Not Hispanic (125)	153	1.12
Hispanic (2)	6	0.04
Chinese, ex. Taiwanese (24)	33	0.24
Filipino (24)	35	0.26
Hmong (39)	41	0.30
Indian (15)	16	0.12
Japanese (5)	14	0.10
Korean (6)	9	0.07
Thai (5)	5	0.04
Vietnamese (4)	6	0.04
Hawaii Native/Pacific Islander (4)	11	0.08
Not Hispanic (3)	9	0.07
Hispanic (1)	2	0.01
Guamanian/Chamorro (1)	1	0.01
Native Hawaiian (2)	7	0.05
White (12,986)	13,170	96.41
Not Hispanic (12,835)	12,986	95.06
Hispanic (151)	184	1.35

Cudahy

Place Type: City
County: Milwaukee
Population: 18,267†

Ancestry‡	Population	%
Albanian (153)	153	0.84
American (416)	416	2.29
Arab (11)	54	0.30
Arab (11)	54	0.30
Armenian (63)	98	0.54
Austrian (28)	108	0.60
Belgian (0)	18	0.10
Brazilian (6)	18	0.10
British (0)	48	0.26
Canadian (29)	41	0.23
Croatian (45)	132	0.73
Czech (40)	284	1.57
Czechoslovakian (0)	42	0.23
Danish (44)	110	0.61
Dutch (53)	319	1.76
Eastern European (12)	12	0.07
English (152)	758	4.18
European (43)	86	0.47
Finnish (24)	54	0.30
French, ex. Basque (39)	699	3.86
French Canadian (125)	320	1.77
German (2,477)	6,994	38.58
Greek (24)	63	0.35
Hungarian (90)	296	1.63
Iranian (7)	7	0.04
Irish (590)	2,129	11.74
Italian (276)	883	4.87
Latvian (0)	5	0.03
Lithuanian (0)	47	0.26
Luxemburger (0)	9	0.05
Northern European (12)	12	0.07
Norwegian (46)	417	2.30
Polish (1,844)	5,166	28.50
Romanian (80)	80	0.44
Russian (0)	183	1.01
Scandinavian (11)	23	0.13
Scotch-Irish (0)	32	0.18
Scottish (6)	99	0.55
Serbian (154)	180	0.99
Slavic (11)	32	0.18
Slovak (213)	312	1.72
Slovene (0)	18	0.10
Swedish (55)	352	1.94
Swiss (29)	72	0.40
Ukrainian (22)	22	0.12
Welsh (9)	55	0.30
West Indian, ex. Hispanic (0)	22	0.12
Jamaican (0)	22	0.12
Yugoslavian (0)	12	0.07

Hispanic Origin	Population	%
Hispanic or Latino (of any race)	1,769	9.68
Central American, ex. Mexican	37	0.20
Costa Rican	4	0.02
Guatemalan	12	0.07
Honduran	5	0.03
Nicaraguan	8	0.04
Panamanian	1	0.01
Salvadoran	7	0.04
Cuban	10	0.05
Dominican Republic	3	0.02
Mexican	1,010	5.53
Puerto Rican	571	3.13
South American	58	0.32
Argentinean	3	0.02
Bolivian	1	0.01
Chilean	2	0.01
Colombian	5	0.03
Ecuadorian	6	0.03
Peruvian	37	0.20
Other South American	4	0.02
Other Hispanic or Latino	80	0.44

Race*	Population	%
African-American/Black (486)	672	3.68
Not Hispanic (439)	590	3.23
Hispanic (47)	82	0.45
American Indian/Alaska Native (161)	286	1.57
Not Hispanic (136)	244	1.34
Hispanic (25)	42	0.23
Alaska Athabascan *(Ala. Nat.)* (0)	1	0.01
Apache (5)	7	0.04
Blackfeet (0)	4	0.02
Canadian/French Am. Ind. (0)	2	0.01
Cherokee (4)	18	0.10
Chippewa (48)	69	0.38
Choctaw (1)	4	0.02
Comanche (1)	2	0.01
Cree (0)	1	0.01
Iroquois (23)	36	0.20
Menominee (6)	18	0.10
Mexican American Ind. (1)	2	0.01
Navajo (1)	1	0.01
Ottawa (3)	5	0.03
Potawatomi (1)	3	0.02
Seminole (0)	1	0.01
Sioux (0)	5	0.03
Asian (253)	332	1.82
Not Hispanic (245)	316	1.73
Hispanic (8)	16	0.09
Burmese (6)	6	0.03
Cambodian (0)	3	0.02
Chinese, ex. Taiwanese (23)	32	0.18
Filipino (86)	112	0.61
Hmong (15)	16	0.09
Indian (51)	55	0.30
Indonesian (0)	5	0.03
Japanese (3)	6	0.03
Korean (10)	18	0.10
Laotian (15)	21	0.11
Pakistani (0)	4	0.02
Thai (7)	10	0.05
Vietnamese (15)	17	0.09
Hawaii Native/Pacific Islander (6)	24	0.13
Not Hispanic (6)	21	0.11
Hispanic (0)	3	0.02
Guamanian/Chamorro (2)	2	0.01
Native Hawaiian (3)	9	0.05
Samoan (1)	3	0.02

*Notes: † The Census 2010 population figure is used to calculate the percentages in the Hispanic Origin and Race categories. Ancestry percentages are based on the 2006-2010 American Community Survey population (not shown); ‡ Numbers in parentheses indicate the number of people reporting a single ancestry; * Numbers in parentheses indicate the number of persons reporting this race alone, not in combination with any other race; Please refer to the Explanation of Data for more information.*

White (16,219)	16,663	91.22
Not Hispanic (15,356)	15,643	85.64
Hispanic (863)	1,020	5.58

De Pere

Place Type: City
County: Brown
Population: 23,800†

Ancestry‡	Population	%
African, Sub-Saharan (56)	56	0.24
Ghanaian (56)	56	0.24
American (703)	703	3.03
Arab (119)	119	0.51
Other Arab (119)	119	0.51
Austrian (21)	98	0.42
Belgian (481)	1,847	7.95
British (10)	10	0.04
Bulgarian (6)	6	0.03
Canadian (16)	37	0.16
Croatian (0)	25	0.11
Czech (173)	458	1.97
Czechoslovakian (6)	30	0.13
Danish (54)	411	1.77
Dutch (566)	1,863	8.02
Eastern European (17)	17	0.07
English (145)	875	3.77
European (330)	340	1.46
Finnish (33)	229	0.99
French, ex. Basque (110)	1,192	5.13
French Canadian (127)	429	1.85
German (3,525)	9,957	42.87
Greek (0)	34	0.15
Hungarian (10)	31	0.13
Irish (457)	2,808	12.09
Italian (171)	815	3.51
Lithuanian (33)	103	0.44
Norwegian (192)	1,175	5.06
Polish (637)	2,285	9.84
Romanian (54)	69	0.30
Russian (70)	95	0.41
Scandinavian (13)	34	0.15
Scotch-Irish (37)	244	1.05
Scottish (154)	347	1.49
Slovak (0)	113	0.49
Swedish (85)	773	3.33
Swiss (12)	112	0.48
Turkish (35)	70	0.30
Ukrainian (104)	115	0.50
Welsh (15)	173	0.74
Yugoslavian (13)	13	0.06

Hispanic Origin	Population	%
Hispanic or Latino (of any race)	511	2.15
Central American, ex. Mexican	33	0.14
Guatemalan	7	0.03
Honduran	10	0.04
Nicaraguan	4	0.02
Panamanian	3	0.01
Salvadoran	9	0.04
Cuban	21	0.09
Dominican Republic	6	0.03
Mexican	333	1.40
Puerto Rican	57	0.24
South American	28	0.12
Argentinean	1	<0.01
Bolivian	1	<0.01
Chilean	1	<0.01
Colombian	15	0.06
Ecuadorian	6	0.03
Peruvian	2	0.01
Venezuelan	2	0.01
Other Hispanic or Latino	33	0.14

Race*	Population	%
African-American/Black (212)	355	1.49
Not Hispanic (201)	335	1.41
Hispanic (11)	20	0.08
American Indian/Alaska Native (281)	440	1.85
Not Hispanic (258)	405	1.70
Hispanic (23)	35	0.15
Aleut *(Alaska Native)* (1)	1	<0.01
Apache (1)	1	<0.01
Arapaho (0)	1	<0.01
Blackfeet (0)	2	0.01
Canadian/French Am. Ind. (3)	3	0.01
Cherokee (2)	7	0.03
Cheyenne (0)	1	<0.01
Chippewa (26)	47	0.20
Creek (0)	1	<0.01
Iroquois (89)	151	0.63
Menominee (32)	37	0.16
Mexican American Ind. (3)	4	0.02
Ottawa (3)	3	0.01
Pima (5)	7	0.03
Potawatomi (2)	5	0.02
Pueblo (3)	3	0.01
Sioux (5)	5	0.02
Asian (350)	454	1.91
Not Hispanic (347)	448	1.88
Hispanic (3)	6	0.03
Cambodian (1)	1	<0.01
Chinese, ex. Taiwanese (69)	78	0.33
Filipino (11)	37	0.16
Hmong (76)	83	0.35
Indian (82)	93	0.39
Japanese (18)	33	0.14
Korean (24)	36	0.15
Laotian (7)	12	0.05
Malaysian (1)	1	<0.01
Pakistani (2)	3	0.01
Taiwanese (4)	5	0.02
Thai (6)	13	0.05
Vietnamese (30)	40	0.17
Hawaii Native/Pacific Islander (6)	35	0.15
Not Hispanic (5)	33	0.14
Hispanic (1)	2	0.01
Guamanian/Chamorro (1)	3	0.01
Native Hawaiian (2)	17	0.07
Samoan (2)	6	0.03
White (22,366)	22,772	95.68
Not Hispanic (22,082)	22,447	94.32
Hispanic (284)	325	1.37

DeForest

Place Type: Village
County: Dane
Population: 8,936†

Ancestry‡	Population	%
American (266)	266	3.07
Arab (15)	15	0.17
Lebanese (15)	15	0.17
Armenian (0)	17	0.20
Austrian (0)	32	0.37
Belgian (0)	68	0.78
British (0)	83	0.96
Cypriot (0)	18	0.21
Czech (13)	168	1.94
Czechoslovakian (11)	41	0.47
Danish (12)	113	1.30
Dutch (14)	94	1.08
English (282)	1,045	12.05
European (13)	26	0.30
Finnish (13)	25	0.29
French, ex. Basque (25)	245	2.83
French Canadian (32)	70	0.81
German (1,674)	4,827	55.68
Greek (0)	50	0.58
Hungarian (0)	9	0.10
Irish (255)	1,140	13.15
Italian (115)	261	3.01
Maltese (0)	15	0.17
Norwegian (236)	1,555	17.94
Polish (112)	757	8.73
Russian (0)	89	1.03
Scotch-Irish (0)	86	0.99
Scottish (34)	145	1.67
Swedish (58)	186	2.15
Swiss (23)	107	1.23
Welsh (0)	9	0.10
Yugoslavian (13)	13	0.15

Hispanic Origin	Population	%
Hispanic or Latino (of any race)	325	3.64
Central American, ex. Mexican	18	0.20
Costa Rican	3	0.03
Guatemalan	2	0.02
Honduran	2	0.02
Nicaraguan	6	0.07
Panamanian	4	0.04
Salvadoran	1	0.01
Cuban	6	0.07
Mexican	240	2.69
Puerto Rican	18	0.20
South American	20	0.22
Argentinean	1	0.01
Bolivian	4	0.04
Colombian	4	0.04
Ecuadorian	1	0.01
Peruvian	1	0.01
Uruguayan	6	0.07
Venezuelan	3	0.03
Other Hispanic or Latino	23	0.26

Race*	Population	%
African-American/Black (184)	253	2.83
Not Hispanic (175)	240	2.69
Hispanic (9)	13	0.15
American Indian/Alaska Native (28)	41	0.46
Not Hispanic (25)	37	0.41
Hispanic (3)	4	0.04
Cherokee (1)	2	0.02
Chippewa (6)	8	0.09
Houma (1)	1	0.01
Inupiat *(Alaska Native)* (2)	4	0.04
Menominee (1)	1	0.01
Navajo (1)	1	0.01
Osage (0)	1	0.01
Sioux (0)	2	0.02
South American Ind. (1)	1	0.01
Asian (134)	181	2.03
Not Hispanic (133)	177	1.98
Hispanic (1)	4	0.04
Cambodian (0)	4	0.04
Chinese, ex. Taiwanese (16)	24	0.27
Filipino (22)	37	0.41
Hmong (50)	54	0.60
Indian (6)	6	0.07
Japanese (7)	20	0.22
Korean (8)	15	0.17
Laotian (4)	5	0.06
Sri Lankan (3)	3	0.03
Thai (3)	11	0.12
Vietnamese (6)	9	0.10
Hawaii Native/Pacific Islander (3)	10	0.11
Not Hispanic (3)	10	0.11
Guamanian/Chamorro (0)	1	0.01
Native Hawaiian (3)	5	0.06
White (8,334)	8,473	94.82
Not Hispanic (8,144)	8,263	92.47
Hispanic (190)	210	2.35

Delafield

Place Type: Town
County: Waukesha
Population: 8,400†

Ancestry‡	Population	%
American (125)	125	1.50
Arab (10)	19	0.23
Arab (0)	9	0.11
Palestinian (10)	10	0.12
Austrian (0)	12	0.14
Belgian (36)	45	0.54
Bulgarian (0)	39	0.47
Canadian (0)	7	0.08

*Notes: † The Census 2010 population figure is used to calculate the percentages in the Hispanic Origin and Race categories. Ancestry percentages are based on the 2006-2010 American Community Survey population (not shown); ‡ Numbers in parentheses indicate the number of people reporting a single ancestry; * Numbers in parentheses indicate the number of persons reporting this race alone, not in combination with any other race; Please refer to the Explanation of Data for more information.*

SECTION TWO

Ancestry (continued)	Population	%
Croatian (29)	157	1.89
Czech (51)	159	1.91
Czechoslovakian (0)	10	0.12
Danish (0)	82	0.99
Dutch (23)	192	2.31
Eastern European (16)	16	0.19
English (123)	509	6.11
European (99)	112	1.35
Finnish (9)	62	0.74
French, ex. Basque (32)	186	2.23
French Canadian (22)	89	1.07
German (2,077)	4,675	56.16
Greek (12)	12	0.14
Hungarian (31)	50	0.60
Irish (274)	1,195	14.36
Italian (196)	565	6.79
Latvian (18)	18	0.22
Luxemburger (0)	12	0.14
Norwegian (83)	511	6.14
Pennsylvania German (11)	11	0.13
Polish (281)	1,018	12.23
Portuguese (13)	13	0.16
Romanian (22)	33	0.40
Russian (13)	116	1.39
Scandinavian (0)	20	0.24
Scotch-Irish (10)	45	0.54
Scottish (0)	60	0.72
Slovak (11)	24	0.29
Swedish (93)	299	3.59
Swiss (0)	26	0.31
Ukrainian (0)	9	0.11
Welsh (0)	96	1.15
Yugoslavian (0)	9	0.11

Hispanic Origin	Population	%
Hispanic or Latino (of any race)	200	2.38
Central American, ex. Mexican	12	0.14
Guatemalan	7	0.08
Honduran	2	0.02
Panamanian	2	0.02
Salvadoran	1	0.01
Cuban	11	0.13
Dominican Republic	1	0.01
Mexican	102	1.21
Puerto Rican	40	0.48
South American	26	0.31
Argentinean	5	0.06
Chilean	3	0.04
Colombian	8	0.10
Ecuadorian	5	0.06
Paraguayan	2	0.02
Venezuelan	3	0.04
Other Hispanic or Latino	8	0.10

Race*	Population	%
African-American/Black (241)	263	3.13
Not Hispanic (234)	255	3.04
Hispanic (7)	8	0.10
American Indian/Alaska Native (26)	42	0.50
Not Hispanic (19)	30	0.36
Hispanic (7)	12	0.14
Cherokee (1)	2	0.02
Chippewa (5)	5	0.06
Menominee (3)	3	0.04
Mexican American Ind. (2)	3	0.04
Potawatomi (0)	3	0.04
Asian (133)	174	2.07
Not Hispanic (133)	174	2.07
Cambodian (2)	2	0.02
Chinese, ex. Taiwanese (38)	40	0.48
Filipino (20)	28	0.33
Indian (41)	48	0.57
Japanese (6)	14	0.17
Korean (8)	23	0.27
Pakistani (3)	3	0.04
Taiwanese (1)	1	0.01
Thai (1)	1	0.01
Vietnamese (8)	13	0.15
Hawaii Native/Pacific Islander (0)	5	0.06
Not Hispanic (0)	5	0.06
Native Hawaiian (0)	3	0.04
White (7,902)	7,982	95.02
Not Hispanic (7,742)	7,812	93.00
Hispanic (160)	170	2.02

Delavan

Place Type: City
County: Walworth
Population: 8,463†

Ancestry‡	Population	%
American (272)	272	3.18
Arab (0)	50	0.59
Palestinian (0)	25	0.29
Other Arab (0)	25	0.29
Armenian (13)	39	0.46
Belgian (15)	15	0.18
British (0)	20	0.23
Croatian (0)	40	0.47
Czech (14)	30	0.35
Czechoslovakian (10)	10	0.12
Danish (0)	88	1.03
Dutch (161)	544	6.37
English (81)	590	6.91
European (49)	49	0.57
Finnish (7)	65	0.76
French, ex. Basque (0)	530	6.20
French Canadian (0)	94	1.10
German (843)	2,997	35.09
Greek (0)	51	0.60
Hungarian (0)	49	0.57
Irish (171)	1,310	15.34
Italian (53)	286	3.35
Latvian (0)	10	0.12
Lithuanian (18)	18	0.21
Norwegian (133)	311	3.64
Polish (102)	597	6.99
Russian (0)	34	0.40
Scandinavian (39)	39	0.46
Scotch-Irish (114)	178	2.08
Scottish (17)	111	1.30
Swedish (41)	335	3.92
Swiss (0)	99	1.16
Ukrainian (0)	10	0.12
Welsh (0)	68	0.80
Yugoslavian (24)	53	0.62

Hispanic Origin	Population	%
Hispanic or Latino (of any race)	2,492	29.45
Central American, ex. Mexican	16	0.19
Costa Rican	2	0.02
Guatemalan	7	0.08
Honduran	6	0.07
Panamanian	1	0.01
Cuban	9	0.11
Mexican	2,256	26.66
Puerto Rican	57	0.67
South American	9	0.11
Peruvian	7	0.08
Venezuelan	2	0.02
Other Hispanic or Latino	145	1.71

Race*	Population	%
African-American/Black (144)	196	2.32
Not Hispanic (107)	140	1.65
Hispanic (37)	56	0.66
American Indian/Alaska Native (60)	103	1.22
Not Hispanic (11)	42	0.50
Hispanic (49)	61	0.72
Apache (0)	5	0.06
Canadian/French Am. Ind. (0)	1	0.01
Cherokee (0)	4	0.05
Chippewa (3)	9	0.11
Choctaw (0)	1	0.01
Iroquois (2)	4	0.05
Menominee (3)	3	0.04
Mexican American Ind. (12)	14	0.17
Sioux (2)	3	0.04
Tohono O'Odham (0)	1	0.01
Asian (82)	114	1.35
Not Hispanic (75)	102	1.21
Hispanic (7)	12	0.14
Chinese, ex. Taiwanese (24)	30	0.35
Filipino (13)	20	0.24
Hmong (1)	4	0.05
Indian (21)	22	0.26
Japanese (0)	7	0.08
Korean (8)	16	0.19
Pakistani (1)	1	0.01
Thai (0)	1	0.01
Vietnamese (7)	11	0.13
Hawaii Native/Pacific Islander (2)	7	0.08
Not Hispanic (2)	2	0.02
Hispanic (0)	5	0.06
Native Hawaiian (1)	1	0.01
Samoan (1)	1	0.01
White (6,874)	7,074	83.59
Not Hispanic (5,684)	5,767	68.14
Hispanic (1,190)	1,307	15.44

Eau Claire

Place Type: City
County: Eau Claire
Population: 63,902†

Ancestry‡	Population	%
African, Sub-Saharan (21)	41	0.07
African (9)	29	0.05
Somalian (12)	12	0.02
Albanian (16)	16	0.03
American (2,188)	2,188	3.47
Arab (49)	80	0.13
Lebanese (37)	37	0.06
Other Arab (12)	43	0.07
Australian (40)	59	0.09
Austrian (105)	353	0.56
Belgian (16)	122	0.19
Brazilian (16)	27	0.04
British (62)	185	0.29
Bulgarian (13)	13	0.02
Canadian (77)	99	0.16
Croatian (17)	48	0.08
Czech (340)	1,266	2.01
Czechoslovakian (56)	127	0.20
Danish (239)	766	1.22
Dutch (251)	942	1.49
Eastern European (1)	1	<0.01
English (914)	4,131	6.56
European (573)	573	0.91
Finnish (63)	215	0.34
French, ex. Basque (343)	2,370	3.76
French Canadian (107)	662	1.05
German (9,802)	27,764	44.06
Greek (30)	274	0.43
Hungarian (12)	206	0.33
Icelander (0)	39	0.06
Iranian (41)	59	0.09
Irish (1,088)	7,285	11.56
Italian (463)	1,860	2.95
Latvian (25)	37	0.06
Lithuanian (20)	53	0.08
Luxemburger (31)	58	0.09
Northern European (47)	63	0.10
Norwegian (4,475)	12,789	20.30
Pennsylvania German (24)	38	0.06
Polish (871)	3,876	6.15
Portuguese (17)	30	0.05
Romanian (0)	81	0.13
Russian (147)	406	0.64
Scandinavian (203)	419	0.66
Scotch-Irish (261)	615	0.98
Scottish (106)	864	1.37
Serbian (14)	20	0.03
Slavic (0)	36	0.06
Slovak (18)	96	0.15
Slovene (21)	129	0.20
Swedish (443)	2,181	3.46
Swiss (51)	450	0.71

*Notes: † The Census 2010 population figure is used to calculate the percentages in the Hispanic Origin and Race categories. Ancestry percentages are based on the 2006-2010 American Community Survey population (not shown); ‡ Numbers in parentheses indicate the number of people reporting a single ancestry; * Numbers in parentheses indicate the number of persons reporting this race alone, not in combination with any other race; Please refer to the Explanation of Data for more information.*

Ukrainian (122)	167	0.27
Welsh (20)	356	0.56
West Indian, ex. Hispanic (21)	32	0.05
Haitian (21)	32	0.05
Yugoslavian (47)	166	0.26

Hispanic Origin	Population	%
Hispanic or Latino (of any race)	1,232	1.93
Central American, ex. Mexican	72	0.11
Costa Rican	9	0.01
Guatemalan	22	0.03
Honduran	4	0.01
Nicaraguan	22	0.03
Panamanian	14	0.02
Salvadoran	1	<0.01
Cuban	41	0.06
Dominican Republic	10	0.02
Mexican	739	1.16
Puerto Rican	141	0.22
South American	79	0.12
Argentinean	5	0.01
Bolivian	2	<0.01
Chilean	3	<0.01
Colombian	24	0.04
Ecuadorian	6	0.01
Paraguayan	1	<0.01
Peruvian	25	0.04
Uruguayan	1	<0.01
Venezuelan	12	0.02
Other Hispanic or Latino	150	0.23

Race*	Population	%
African-American/Black (730)	1,166	1.82
Not Hispanic (701)	1,099	1.72
Hispanic (29)	67	0.10
American Indian/Alaska Native (343)	692	1.08
Not Hispanic (323)	639	1.00
Hispanic (20)	53	0.08
Alaska Athabascan *(Ala. Nat.)* (1)	4	0.01
Aleut *(Alaska Native)* (1)	1	<0.01
Apache (2)	9	0.01
Blackfeet (0)	7	0.01
Canadian/French Am. Ind. (0)	2	<0.01
Cherokee (1)	37	0.06
Chippewa (106)	182	0.28
Choctaw (0)	14	0.02
Cree (1)	1	<0.01
Hopi (0)	1	<0.01
Inupiat *(Alaska Native)* (4)	4	0.01
Iroquois (7)	17	0.03
Lumbee (1)	5	0.01
Menominee (9)	11	0.02
Mexican American Ind. (4)	10	0.02
Navajo (6)	8	0.01
Osage (2)	4	0.01
Ottawa (0)	8	0.01
Paiute (0)	4	0.01
Potawatomi (7)	11	0.02
Sioux (10)	19	0.03
Ute (0)	2	<0.01
Yaqui (0)	3	<0.01
Yup'ik *(Alaska Native)* (1)	1	<0.01
Asian (2,770)	3,094	4.84
Not Hispanic (2,751)	3,063	4.79
Hispanic (19)	31	0.05
Bangladeshi (1)	1	<0.01
Cambodian (4)	5	0.01
Chinese, ex. Taiwanese (189)	220	0.34
Filipino (109)	177	0.28
Hmong (1,895)	1,987	3.11
Indian (142)	186	0.29
Indonesian (4)	4	0.01
Japanese (34)	67	0.10
Korean (166)	214	0.33
Laotian (9)	12	0.02
Malaysian (4)	6	0.01
Nepalese (2)	2	<0.01
Pakistani (12)	16	0.03
Taiwanese (3)	7	0.01
Thai (20)	29	0.05
Vietnamese (49)	80	0.13
Hawaii Native/Pacific Islander (29)	81	0.13
Not Hispanic (28)	75	0.12
Hispanic (1)	6	0.01
Guamanian/Chamorro (2)	2	<0.01
Native Hawaiian (6)	28	0.04
Samoan (2)	9	0.01
White (58,574)	59,588	93.25
Not Hispanic (57,865)	58,754	91.94
Hispanic (709)	834	1.31

Eau Claire

Place Type: City
County: Eau Claire
Population: 65,883†

Ancestry‡	Population	%
African, Sub-Saharan (21)	41	0.06
African (9)	29	0.04
Somalian (12)	12	0.02
Albanian (16)	16	0.02
American (2,241)	2,241	3.44
Arab (49)	80	0.12
Lebanese (37)	37	0.06
Other Arab (12)	43	0.07
Australian (40)	59	0.09
Austrian (105)	353	0.54
Belgian (16)	122	0.19
Brazilian (16)	27	0.04
British (62)	185	0.28
Bulgarian (13)	13	0.02
Canadian (77)	99	0.15
Croatian (17)	48	0.07
Czech (365)	1,307	2.01
Czechoslovakian (86)	157	0.24
Danish (239)	766	1.18
Dutch (260)	969	1.49
Eastern European (1)	1	<0.01
English (928)	4,260	6.54
European (621)	621	0.95
Finnish (63)	215	0.33
French, ex. Basque (355)	2,482	3.81
French Canadian (107)	673	1.03
German (9,988)	28,452	43.68
Greek (30)	282	0.43
Hungarian (12)	206	0.32
Icelander (0)	39	0.06
Iranian (41)	59	0.09
Irish (1,114)	7,494	11.51
Italian (472)	1,914	2.94
Latvian (25)	37	0.06
Lithuanian (31)	64	0.10
Luxemburger (31)	58	0.09
Northern European (47)	63	0.10
Norwegian (4,668)	13,218	20.29
Pennsylvania German (24)	38	0.06
Polish (926)	4,058	6.23
Portuguese (17)	30	0.05
Romanian (0)	81	0.12
Russian (147)	406	0.62
Scandinavian (203)	429	0.66
Scotch-Irish (261)	636	0.98
Scottish (106)	876	1.34
Serbian (14)	20	0.03
Slavic (0)	36	0.06
Slovak (18)	96	0.15
Slovene (21)	129	0.20
Swedish (443)	2,202	3.38
Swiss (62)	461	0.71
Ukrainian (122)	167	0.26
Welsh (20)	356	0.55
West Indian, ex. Hispanic (21)	32	0.05
Haitian (21)	32	0.05
Yugoslavian (47)	166	0.25

Hispanic Origin	Population	%
Hispanic or Latino (of any race)	1,268	1.92
Central American, ex. Mexican	72	0.11
Costa Rican	9	0.01
Guatemalan	22	0.03
Honduran	4	0.01
Nicaraguan	22	0.03
Panamanian	14	0.02
Salvadoran	1	<0.01
Cuban	44	0.07
Dominican Republic	10	0.02
Mexican	764	1.16
Puerto Rican	141	0.21
South American	85	0.13
Argentinean	5	0.01
Bolivian	2	<0.01
Chilean	3	<0.01
Colombian	25	0.04
Ecuadorian	6	0.01
Paraguayan	3	<0.01
Peruvian	26	0.04
Uruguayan	1	<0.01
Venezuelan	14	0.02
Other Hispanic or Latino	152	0.23

Race*	Population	%
African-American/Black (752)	1,211	1.84
Not Hispanic (723)	1,144	1.74
Hispanic (29)	67	0.10
American Indian/Alaska Native (347)	705	1.07
Not Hispanic (327)	651	0.99
Hispanic (20)	54	0.08
Alaska Athabascan *(Ala. Nat.)* (1)	4	0.01
Aleut *(Alaska Native)* (1)	1	<0.01
Apache (2)	9	0.01
Blackfeet (0)	7	0.01
Canadian/French Am. Ind. (0)	2	<0.01
Cherokee (1)	37	0.06
Chippewa (108)	185	0.28
Choctaw (0)	14	0.02
Cree (1)	1	<0.01
Hopi (0)	1	<0.01
Inupiat *(Alaska Native)* (4)	4	0.01
Iroquois (7)	17	0.03
Lumbee (1)	5	0.01
Menominee (9)	11	0.02
Mexican American Ind. (4)	10	0.02
Navajo (6)	8	0.01
Osage (2)	4	0.01
Ottawa (0)	8	0.01
Paiute (0)	4	0.01
Potawatomi (7)	11	0.02
Sioux (10)	19	0.03
Tlingit-Haida *(Alaska Native)* (1)	1	<0.01
Ute (0)	2	<0.01
Yaqui (0)	3	<0.01
Yup'ik *(Alaska Native)* (1)	1	<0.01
Asian (3,014)	3,355	5.09
Not Hispanic (2,995)	3,324	5.05
Hispanic (19)	31	0.05
Bangladeshi (1)	1	<0.01
Cambodian (4)	5	0.01
Chinese, ex. Taiwanese (189)	220	0.33
Filipino (113)	186	0.28
Hmong (2,113)	2,213	3.36
Indian (145)	189	0.29
Indonesian (4)	4	0.01
Japanese (37)	74	0.11
Korean (167)	215	0.33
Laotian (9)	12	0.02
Malaysian (4)	6	0.01
Nepalese (2)	2	<0.01
Pakistani (12)	16	0.02
Taiwanese (3)	7	0.01
Thai (20)	29	0.04
Vietnamese (49)	80	0.12
Hawaii Native/Pacific Islander (29)	84	0.13
Not Hispanic (28)	78	0.12
Hispanic (1)	6	0.01
Guamanian/Chamorro (2)	2	<0.01
Native Hawaiian (6)	31	0.05
Samoan (2)	9	0.01
White (60,226)	61,277	93.01
Not Hispanic (59,499)	60,425	91.72

SECTION TWO

*Notes: † The Census 2010 population figure is used to calculate the percentages in the Hispanic Origin and Race categories. Ancestry percentages are based on the 2006-2010 American Community Survey population (not shown); ‡ Numbers in parentheses indicate the number of people reporting a single ancestry; * Numbers in parentheses indicate the number of persons reporting this race alone, not in combination with any other race; Please refer to the Explanation of Data for more information.*

Hispanic (727)	852	1.29

Elkhorn

Place Type: City
County: Walworth
Population: 10,084†

Ancestry‡	Population	%
American (257)	257	2.65
Austrian (0)	28	0.29
Belgian (0)	44	0.45
British (12)	12	0.12
Canadian (12)	55	0.57
Croatian (0)	10	0.10
Czech (22)	89	0.92
Czechoslovakian (12)	12	0.12
Danish (18)	101	1.04
Dutch (156)	342	3.53
English (197)	1,049	10.82
European (72)	85	0.88
Finnish (19)	111	1.15
French, ex. Basque (33)	307	3.17
French Canadian (53)	76	0.78
German (1,171)	3,811	39.32
Greek (0)	39	0.40
Hungarian (0)	59	0.61
Irish (365)	1,455	15.01
Italian (75)	458	4.73
Lithuanian (12)	26	0.27
Norwegian (215)	641	6.61
Pennsylvania German (0)	10	0.10
Polish (102)	1,065	10.99
Russian (7)	111	1.15
Scandinavian (44)	44	0.45
Scotch-Irish (62)	172	1.77
Scottish (48)	153	1.58
Slovak (20)	20	0.21
Swedish (64)	323	3.33
Swiss (0)	106	1.09
Welsh (0)	116	1.20
Yugoslavian (0)	12	0.12

Hispanic Origin	Population	%
Hispanic or Latino (of any race)	1,108	10.99
Central American, ex. Mexican	16	0.16
Guatemalan	3	0.03
Honduran	6	0.06
Nicaraguan	1	0.01
Salvadoran	6	0.06
Cuban	10	0.10
Mexican	962	9.54
Puerto Rican	58	0.58
South American	23	0.23
Argentinean	1	0.01
Ecuadorian	5	0.05
Peruvian	12	0.12
Venezuelan	5	0.05
Other Hispanic or Latino	39	0.39

Race*	Population	%
African-American/Black (120)	168	1.67
Not Hispanic (111)	152	1.51
Hispanic (9)	16	0.16
American Indian/Alaska Native (23)	72	0.71
Not Hispanic (19)	51	0.51
Hispanic (4)	21	0.21
Apache (1)	1	0.01
Cherokee (3)	8	0.08
Chippewa (8)	11	0.11
Choctaw (0)	1	0.01
Creek (1)	3	0.03
Iroquois (0)	3	0.03
Menominee (2)	3	0.03
Mexican American Ind. (0)	4	0.04
Navajo (0)	2	0.02
Potawatomi (1)	2	0.02
Sioux (2)	4	0.04
Asian (68)	109	1.08
Not Hispanic (62)	102	1.01
Hispanic (6)	7	0.07
Cambodian (4)	4	0.04
Chinese, ex. Taiwanese (15)	17	0.17
Filipino (8)	19	0.19
Hmong (3)	3	0.03
Indian (4)	13	0.13
Japanese (4)	12	0.12
Korean (10)	13	0.13
Pakistani (4)	4	0.04
Thai (5)	8	0.08
Vietnamese (11)	14	0.14
Hawaii Native/Pacific Islander (2)	6	0.06
Not Hispanic (1)	5	0.05
Hispanic (1)	1	0.01
Guamanian/Chamorro (0)	2	0.02
Native Hawaiian (2)	3	0.03
White (9,220)	9,367	92.89
Not Hispanic (8,669)	8,768	86.95
Hispanic (551)	599	5.94

Fitchburg

Place Type: City
County: Dane
Population: 25,260†

Ancestry‡	Population	%
African, Sub-Saharan (573)	1,004	4.10
African (573)	1,004	4.10
Albanian (92)	92	0.38
American (536)	536	2.19
Arab (6)	64	0.26
Arab (0)	58	0.24
Moroccan (6)	6	0.02
Armenian (0)	30	0.12
Australian (0)	16	0.07
Austrian (9)	33	0.13
Belgian (15)	73	0.30
British (23)	178	0.73
Bulgarian (67)	67	0.27
Canadian (12)	12	0.05
Croatian (9)	17	0.07
Czech (96)	274	1.12
Czechoslovakian (0)	14	0.06
Danish (49)	128	0.52
Dutch (68)	398	1.63
English (361)	2,037	8.33
European (252)	266	1.09
Finnish (13)	118	0.48
French, ex. Basque (85)	605	2.47
French Canadian (28)	146	0.60
German (2,683)	8,043	32.87
Greek (0)	116	0.47
Hungarian (85)	112	0.46
Icelander (0)	39	0.16
Irish (732)	3,924	16.04
Italian (252)	856	3.50
Lithuanian (0)	24	0.10
Luxemburger (0)	17	0.07
Northern European (11)	11	0.04
Norwegian (664)	2,670	10.91
Pennsylvania German (29)	29	0.12
Polish (328)	1,153	4.71
Portuguese (0)	11	0.04
Romanian (0)	42	0.17
Russian (143)	289	1.18
Scandinavian (23)	39	0.16
Scotch-Irish (142)	308	1.26
Scottish (103)	378	1.55
Slavic (9)	9	0.04
Swedish (77)	467	1.91
Swiss (88)	554	2.26
Turkish (110)	110	0.45
Ukrainian (25)	25	0.10
Welsh (24)	299	1.22
West Indian, ex. Hispanic (0)	9	0.04
West Indian (0)	9	0.04
Yugoslavian (0)	13	0.05

Hispanic Origin	Population	%
Hispanic or Latino (of any race)	4,341	17.19
Central American, ex. Mexican	170	0.67
Costa Rican	5	0.02
Guatemalan	24	0.10
Honduran	80	0.32
Nicaraguan	32	0.13
Panamanian	15	0.06
Salvadoran	10	0.04
Other Central American	4	0.02
Cuban	42	0.17
Dominican Republic	27	0.11
Mexican	3,508	13.89
Puerto Rican	193	0.76
South American	248	0.98
Argentinean	59	0.23
Bolivian	16	0.06
Chilean	11	0.04
Colombian	67	0.27
Ecuadorian	10	0.04
Paraguayan	2	0.01
Peruvian	45	0.18
Uruguayan	22	0.09
Venezuelan	14	0.06
Other South American	2	0.01
Other Hispanic or Latino	153	0.61

Race*	Population	%
African-American/Black (2,633)	3,093	12.24
Not Hispanic (2,557)	2,930	11.60
Hispanic (76)	163	0.65
American Indian/Alaska Native (103)	270	1.07
Not Hispanic (63)	180	0.71
Hispanic (40)	90	0.36
Blackfeet (0)	7	0.03
Canadian/French Am. Ind. (0)	5	0.02
Central American Ind. (1)	1	<0.01
Cherokee (1)	39	0.15
Chippewa (7)	24	0.10
Choctaw (0)	5	0.02
Creek (0)	1	<0.01
Iroquois (5)	6	0.02
Menominee (5)	6	0.02
Mexican American Ind. (9)	12	0.05
Navajo (0)	3	0.01
Potawatomi (1)	1	<0.01
Shoshone (0)	1	<0.01
Sioux (2)	3	0.01
South American Ind. (1)	1	<0.01
Spanish American Ind. (0)	2	0.01
Yup'ik *(Alaska Native)* (1)	1	<0.01
Asian (1,233)	1,409	5.58
Not Hispanic (1,217)	1,381	5.47
Hispanic (16)	28	0.11
Bangladeshi (1)	1	<0.01
Burmese (2)	2	0.01
Cambodian (32)	48	0.19
Chinese, ex. Taiwanese (221)	256	1.01
Filipino (74)	114	0.45
Hmong (237)	249	0.99
Indian (251)	289	1.14
Indonesian (3)	4	0.02
Japanese (34)	55	0.22
Korean (64)	89	0.35
Laotian (70)	83	0.33
Malaysian (0)	5	0.02
Nepalese (14)	14	0.06
Pakistani (44)	51	0.20
Sri Lankan (5)	7	0.03
Taiwanese (15)	20	0.08
Thai (16)	36	0.14
Vietnamese (66)	74	0.29
Hawaii Native/Pacific Islander (10)	28	0.11
Not Hispanic (8)	22	0.09
Hispanic (2)	6	0.02
Fijian (4)	4	0.02
Guamanian/Chamorro (1)	1	<0.01
Native Hawaiian (3)	10	0.04
White (18,230)	18,954	75.04
Not Hispanic (16,455)	16,989	67.26

*Notes: † The Census 2010 population figure is used to calculate the percentages in the Hispanic Origin and Race categories. Ancestry percentages are based on the 2006-2010 American Community Survey population (not shown); ‡ Numbers in parentheses indicate the number of people reporting a single ancestry; * Numbers in parentheses indicate the number of persons reporting this race alone, not in combination with any other race; Please refer to the Explanation of Data for more information.*

Hispanic (1,775)	1,965	7.78

Fond du Lac

Place Type: City
County: Fond du Lac
Population: 43,021†

Ancestry‡	Population	%
African, Sub-Saharan (12)	12	0.03
African (12)	12	0.03
American (1,270)	1,270	2.96
Arab (67)	198	0.46
Arab (0)	10	0.02
Lebanese (67)	143	0.33
Syrian (0)	45	0.10
Armenian (10)	71	0.17
Australian (0)	14	0.03
Austrian (40)	91	0.21
Belgian (60)	159	0.37
British (24)	33	0.08
Bulgarian (9)	9	0.02
Canadian (28)	60	0.14
Croatian (19)	28	0.07
Czech (48)	469	1.09
Czechoslovakian (0)	43	0.10
Danish (17)	184	0.43
Dutch (222)	1,195	2.79
Eastern European (10)	10	0.02
English (538)	2,518	5.87
European (144)	201	0.47
Finnish (129)	247	0.58
French, ex. Basque (157)	1,839	4.29
French Canadian (63)	564	1.31
German (11,836)	24,411	56.90
Greek (233)	514	1.20
Hungarian (26)	98	0.23
Irish (888)	5,813	13.55
Italian (313)	1,255	2.93
Lithuanian (75)	164	0.38
Luxemburger (10)	59	0.14
Northern European (16)	16	0.04
Norwegian (531)	2,163	5.04
Pennsylvania German (0)	13	0.03
Polish (521)	2,702	6.30
Portuguese (31)	56	0.13
Romanian (11)	27	0.06
Russian (95)	329	0.77
Scandinavian (26)	149	0.35
Scotch-Irish (108)	333	0.78
Scottish (38)	289	0.67
Slavic (0)	20	0.05
Slovak (26)	55	0.13
Swedish (203)	867	2.02
Swiss (51)	239	0.56
Turkish (7)	7	0.02
Ukrainian (0)	7	0.02
Welsh (22)	133	0.31
West Indian, ex. Hispanic (13)	13	0.03
Jamaican (13)	13	0.03
Yugoslavian (50)	50	0.12

Hispanic Origin	Population	%
Hispanic or Latino (of any race)	2,742	6.37
Central American, ex. Mexican	128	0.30
Costa Rican	1	<0.01
Guatemalan	42	0.10
Honduran	57	0.13
Nicaraguan	7	0.02
Salvadoran	21	0.05
Cuban	35	0.08
Dominican Republic	7	0.02
Mexican	2,131	4.95
Puerto Rican	183	0.43
South American	33	0.08
Argentinean	2	<0.01
Chilean	3	0.01
Colombian	10	0.02
Ecuadorian	5	0.01
Paraguayan	2	<0.01
Peruvian	6	0.01
Venezuelan	4	0.01
Other South American	1	<0.01
Other Hispanic or Latino	225	0.52

Race*	Population	%
African-American/Black (1,096)	1,464	3.40
Not Hispanic (1,040)	1,377	3.20
Hispanic (56)	87	0.20
American Indian/Alaska Native (293)	513	1.19
Not Hispanic (263)	450	1.05
Hispanic (30)	63	0.15
Aleut *(Alaska Native)* (1)	1	<0.01
Apache (0)	1	<0.01
Blackfeet (3)	10	0.02
Cherokee (9)	28	0.07
Chickasaw (1)	1	<0.01
Chippewa (36)	67	0.16
Choctaw (1)	3	0.01
Iroquois (9)	25	0.06
Lumbee (3)	3	0.01
Menominee (14)	26	0.06
Mexican American Ind. (10)	11	0.03
Ottawa (1)	5	0.01
Potawatomi (10)	11	0.03
Sioux (8)	8	0.02
Yaqui (1)	1	<0.01
Asian (755)	893	2.08
Not Hispanic (743)	869	2.02
Hispanic (12)	24	0.06
Burmese (1)	6	0.01
Chinese, ex. Taiwanese (63)	74	0.17
Filipino (42)	88	0.20
Hmong (407)	419	0.97
Indian (98)	113	0.26
Indonesian (0)	1	<0.01
Japanese (24)	46	0.11
Korean (34)	53	0.12
Laotian (3)	3	0.01
Nepalese (1)	1	<0.01
Pakistani (10)	11	0.03
Taiwanese (6)	6	0.01
Thai (8)	17	0.04
Vietnamese (28)	30	0.07
Hawaii Native/Pacific Islander (5)	31	0.07
Not Hispanic (5)	28	0.07
Hispanic (0)	3	0.01
Guamanian/Chamorro (0)	2	<0.01
Native Hawaiian (1)	10	0.02
Samoan (1)	2	<0.01
White (38,967)	39,756	92.41
Not Hispanic (37,584)	38,191	88.77
Hispanic (1,383)	1,565	3.64

Fort Atkinson

Place Type: City
County: Jefferson
Population: 12,368†

Ancestry‡	Population	%
African, Sub-Saharan (18)	18	0.15
African (18)	18	0.15
Albanian (71)	71	0.58
American (376)	376	3.06
Armenian (12)	12	0.10
Australian (18)	18	0.15
Austrian (21)	40	0.33
British (0)	35	0.28
Canadian (0)	27	0.22
Czech (19)	121	0.98
Danish (68)	162	1.32
Dutch (43)	247	2.01
English (124)	1,141	9.27
Estonian (9)	9	0.07
European (111)	121	0.98
French, ex. Basque (99)	472	3.84
French Canadian (13)	118	0.96
German (2,588)	6,253	50.83
Hungarian (0)	30	0.24
Iranian (0)	9	0.07
Irish (189)	1,395	11.34
Italian (55)	410	3.33
Lithuanian (6)	59	0.48
Norwegian (324)	1,015	8.25
Polish (97)	753	6.12
Romanian (38)	38	0.31
Russian (27)	27	0.22
Scandinavian (27)	35	0.28
Scotch-Irish (31)	236	1.92
Scottish (44)	119	0.97
Serbian (0)	17	0.14
Slavic (0)	16	0.13
Slovene (0)	16	0.13
Swedish (74)	279	2.27
Swiss (24)	148	1.20
Ukrainian (11)	11	0.09
Welsh (14)	93	0.76

Hispanic Origin	Population	%
Hispanic or Latino (of any race)	1,128	9.12
Central American, ex. Mexican	14	0.11
Guatemalan	3	0.02
Honduran	3	0.02
Panamanian	2	0.02
Salvadoran	6	0.05
Cuban	8	0.06
Dominican Republic	16	0.13
Mexican	976	7.89
Puerto Rican	24	0.19
South American	14	0.11
Colombian	1	0.01
Ecuadorian	2	0.02
Paraguayan	2	0.02
Peruvian	5	0.04
Uruguayan	3	0.02
Venezuelan	1	0.01
Other Hispanic or Latino	76	0.61

Race*	Population	%
African-American/Black (77)	129	1.04
Not Hispanic (67)	110	0.89
Hispanic (10)	19	0.15
American Indian/Alaska Native (40)	92	0.74
Not Hispanic (30)	72	0.58
Hispanic (10)	20	0.16
Aleut *(Alaska Native)* (0)	1	0.01
Blackfeet (0)	8	0.06
Cherokee (1)	12	0.10
Chippewa (4)	12	0.10
Iroquois (2)	3	0.02
Menominee (0)	1	0.01
Mexican American Ind. (5)	7	0.06
Ottawa (15)	21	0.17
Potawatomi (3)	4	0.03
Asian (88)	121	0.98
Not Hispanic (88)	119	0.96
Hispanic (0)	2	0.02
Chinese, ex. Taiwanese (27)	29	0.23
Filipino (22)	37	0.30
Hmong (10)	10	0.08
Indian (11)	18	0.15
Indonesian (1)	3	0.02
Japanese (1)	2	0.02
Korean (7)	8	0.06
Laotian (3)	5	0.04
Pakistani (3)	3	0.02
Thai (1)	1	0.01
Vietnamese (2)	3	0.02
Hawaii Native/Pacific Islander (2)	10	0.08
Not Hispanic (2)	9	0.07
Hispanic (0)	1	0.01
Guamanian/Chamorro (0)	2	0.02
Native Hawaiian (0)	3	0.02
Samoan (2)	6	0.05
White (11,439)	11,606	93.84
Not Hispanic (10,925)	11,032	89.20
Hispanic (514)	574	4.64

*Notes: † The Census 2010 population figure is used to calculate the percentages in the Hispanic Origin and Race categories. Ancestry percentages are based on the 2006-2010 American Community Survey population (not shown); ‡ Numbers in parentheses indicate the number of people reporting a single ancestry; * Numbers in parentheses indicate the number of persons reporting this race alone, not in combination with any other race; Please refer to the Explanation of Data for more information.*

Franklin

Place Type: City
County: Milwaukee
Population: 35,451†

Ancestry‡	Population	%
African, Sub-Saharan (9)	29	0.09
African (9)	29	0.09
Albanian (23)	23	0.07
American (694)	694	2.04
Arab (198)	213	0.63
Arab (35)	41	0.12
Egyptian (10)	19	0.06
Palestinian (81)	81	0.24
Other Arab (72)	72	0.21
Armenian (12)	99	0.29
Austrian (15)	151	0.44
Belgian (36)	125	0.37
Brazilian (0)	3	0.01
British (9)	41	0.12
Bulgarian (0)	15	0.04
Canadian (0)	40	0.12
Croatian (124)	437	1.28
Czech (109)	409	1.20
Czechoslovakian (22)	22	0.06
Danish (45)	185	0.54
Dutch (120)	541	1.59
Eastern European (12)	12	0.04
English (202)	1,653	4.85
European (363)	379	1.11
Finnish (81)	201	0.59
French, ex. Basque (100)	1,510	4.43
French Canadian (37)	388	1.14
German (5,000)	14,541	42.69
Greek (121)	319	0.94
Hungarian (63)	174	0.51
Irish (503)	3,776	11.09
Italian (739)	2,380	6.99
Latvian (11)	11	0.03
Lithuanian (42)	108	0.32
Luxemburger (39)	50	0.15
Northern European (8)	8	0.02
Norwegian (295)	1,217	3.57
Pennsylvania German (8)	8	0.02
Polish (2,378)	7,698	22.60
Portuguese (0)	14	0.04
Romanian (0)	90	0.26
Russian (57)	195	0.57
Scandinavian (8)	52	0.15
Scotch-Irish (60)	211	0.62
Scottish (70)	352	1.03
Serbian (296)	526	1.54
Slavic (9)	9	0.03
Slovak (35)	126	0.37
Slovene (73)	176	0.52
Swedish (122)	666	1.96
Swiss (78)	165	0.48
Turkish (16)	19	0.06
Ukrainian (71)	133	0.39
Welsh (82)	149	0.44
West Indian, ex. Hispanic (28)	28	0.08
Jamaican (28)	28	0.08
Yugoslavian (99)	99	0.29

Hispanic Origin	Population	%
Hispanic or Latino (of any race)	1,592	4.49
Central American, ex. Mexican	65	0.18
Costa Rican	4	0.01
Guatemalan	22	0.06
Honduran	3	0.01
Nicaraguan	12	0.03
Panamanian	10	0.03
Salvadoran	14	0.04
Cuban	30	0.08
Dominican Republic	6	0.02
Mexican	910	2.57
Puerto Rican	369	1.04
South American	80	0.23
Argentinean	3	0.01
Bolivian	5	0.01
Chilean	10	0.03
Colombian	26	0.07
Peruvian	29	0.08
Venezuelan	7	0.02
Other Hispanic or Latino	132	0.37

Race*	Population	%
African-American/Black (1,734)	1,907	5.38
Not Hispanic (1,698)	1,837	5.18
Hispanic (36)	70	0.20
American Indian/Alaska Native (126)	245	0.69
Not Hispanic (108)	210	0.59
Hispanic (18)	35	0.10
Apache (1)	3	0.01
Cherokee (1)	23	0.06
Chickasaw (3)	3	0.01
Chippewa (19)	28	0.08
Choctaw (0)	1	<0.01
Creek (0)	1	<0.01
Inupiat *(Alaska Native)* (0)	1	<0.01
Iroquois (17)	20	0.06
Menominee (12)	23	0.06
Mexican American Ind. (1)	5	0.01
Ottawa (1)	1	<0.01
Potawatomi (8)	9	0.03
Sioux (1)	6	0.02
South American Ind. (0)	1	<0.01
Spanish American Ind. (0)	1	<0.01
Asian (1,910)	2,151	6.07
Not Hispanic (1,892)	2,121	5.98
Hispanic (18)	30	0.08
Bangladeshi (2)	2	0.01
Cambodian (3)	3	0.01
Chinese, ex. Taiwanese (161)	201	0.57
Filipino (130)	203	0.57
Hmong (75)	75	0.21
Indian (834)	891	2.51
Indonesian (5)	7	0.02
Japanese (25)	39	0.11
Korean (131)	173	0.49
Laotian (64)	72	0.20
Malaysian (1)	1	<0.01
Nepalese (3)	3	0.01
Pakistani (195)	200	0.56
Taiwanese (9)	12	0.03
Thai (23)	37	0.10
Vietnamese (185)	198	0.56
Hawaii Native/Pacific Islander (8)	32	0.09
Not Hispanic (7)	31	0.09
Hispanic (1)	1	<0.01
Guamanian/Chamorro (1)	1	<0.01
Native Hawaiian (2)	13	0.04
Samoan (2)	2	0.01
White (30,866)	31,339	88.40
Not Hispanic (29,691)	30,069	84.82
Hispanic (1,175)	1,270	3.58

Germantown

Place Type: Village
County: Washington
Population: 19,749†

Ancestry‡	Population	%
African, Sub-Saharan (34)	34	0.17
African (12)	12	0.06
South African (11)	11	0.06
Other Sub-Saharan African (11)	11	0.06
American (663)	663	3.38
Arab (31)	31	0.16
Moroccan (31)	31	0.16
Austrian (10)	70	0.36
Belgian (39)	102	0.52
British (0)	35	0.18
Canadian (26)	66	0.34
Croatian (0)	36	0.18
Czech (50)	175	0.89
Czechoslovakian (0)	14	0.07
Danish (34)	175	0.89
Dutch (88)	409	2.09
English (106)	1,545	7.88
European (209)	231	1.18
Finnish (0)	103	0.53
French, ex. Basque (32)	797	4.06
French Canadian (67)	189	0.96
German (4,939)	11,784	60.09
Greek (12)	49	0.25
Hungarian (9)	84	0.43
Irish (313)	2,881	14.69
Italian (360)	1,356	6.92
Latvian (0)	120	0.61
Lithuanian (0)	12	0.06
Norwegian (139)	1,028	5.24
Pennsylvania German (0)	14	0.07
Polish (337)	2,100	10.71
Romanian (13)	24	0.12
Russian (10)	209	1.07
Scandinavian (44)	76	0.39
Scotch-Irish (41)	94	0.48
Scottish (23)	127	0.65
Serbian (13)	13	0.07
Slovak (25)	97	0.49
Slovene (27)	61	0.31
Swedish (46)	390	1.99
Swiss (54)	276	1.41
Ukrainian (45)	69	0.35
Welsh (11)	37	0.19
Yugoslavian (0)	135	0.69

Hispanic Origin	Population	%
Hispanic or Latino (of any race)	400	2.03
Central American, ex. Mexican	25	0.13
Costa Rican	1	0.01
Guatemalan	16	0.08
Honduran	6	0.03
Panamanian	1	0.01
Salvadoran	1	0.01
Cuban	3	0.02
Dominican Republic	8	0.04
Mexican	257	1.30
Puerto Rican	67	0.34
South American	13	0.07
Argentinean	3	0.02
Colombian	2	0.01
Ecuadorian	2	0.01
Peruvian	6	0.03
Other Hispanic or Latino	27	0.14

Race*	Population	%
African-American/Black (430)	564	2.86
Not Hispanic (421)	548	2.77
Hispanic (9)	16	0.08
American Indian/Alaska Native (46)	108	0.55
Not Hispanic (40)	101	0.51
Hispanic (6)	7	0.04
Aleut *(Alaska Native)* (1)	3	0.02
Blackfeet (0)	2	0.01
Canadian/French Am. Ind. (5)	5	0.03
Cherokee (1)	13	0.07
Chippewa (10)	17	0.09
Choctaw (0)	3	0.02
Cree (0)	1	0.01
Creek (0)	2	0.01
Iroquois (3)	8	0.04
Menominee (3)	5	0.03
Mexican American Ind. (1)	2	0.01
Potawatomi (0)	1	0.01
Pueblo (1)	1	0.01
Puget Sound Salish (0)	1	0.01
Sioux (3)	5	0.03
Asian (618)	703	3.56
Not Hispanic (615)	695	3.52
Hispanic (3)	8	0.04
Cambodian (1)	1	0.01
Chinese, ex. Taiwanese (114)	126	0.64
Filipino (40)	73	0.37
Hmong (60)	61	0.31
Indian (284)	295	1.49
Indonesian (1)	2	0.01

*Notes: † The Census 2010 population figure is used to calculate the percentages in the Hispanic Origin and Race categories. Ancestry percentages are based on the 2006-2010 American Community Survey population (not shown); ‡ Numbers in parentheses indicate the number of people reporting a single ancestry; * Numbers in parentheses indicate the number of persons reporting this race alone, not in combination with any other race; Please refer to the Explanation of Data for more information.*

Japanese (6)	12	0.06
Korean (23)	36	0.18
Laotian (0)	1	0.01
Nepalese (7)	7	0.04
Pakistani (4)	4	0.02
Taiwanese (2)	2	0.01
Thai (3)	4	0.02
Vietnamese (56)	59	0.30
Hawaii Native/Pacific Islander (0)	11	0.06
Not Hispanic (0)	11	0.06
Guamanian/Chamorro (0)	4	0.02
Native Hawaiian (0)	3	0.02
White (18,290)	18,532	93.84
Not Hispanic (18,015)	18,235	92.33
Hispanic (275)	297	1.50

Glendale

Place Type: City
County: Milwaukee
Population: 12,872†

Ancestry‡	Population	%
African, Sub-Saharan (63)	91	0.71
African (49)	62	0.48
Nigerian (14)	14	0.11
Zimbabwean (0)	15	0.12
American (509)	509	3.98
Arab (71)	71	0.56
Lebanese (34)	34	0.27
Other Arab (37)	37	0.29
Armenian (12)	12	0.09
Austrian (31)	115	0.90
Belgian (13)	13	0.10
British (0)	8	0.06
Croatian (15)	90	0.70
Czech (43)	151	1.18
Czechoslovakian (14)	14	0.11
Danish (0)	47	0.37
Dutch (0)	76	0.59
Eastern European (34)	34	0.27
English (207)	1,044	8.16
European (65)	65	0.51
Finnish (0)	40	0.31
French, ex. Basque (64)	521	4.07
French Canadian (0)	41	0.32
German (1,937)	4,680	36.59
Greek (0)	73	0.57
Hungarian (46)	104	0.81
Irish (375)	1,943	15.19
Israeli (0)	17	0.13
Italian (270)	560	4.38
Latvian (87)	87	0.68
Lithuanian (18)	30	0.23
Norwegian (58)	475	3.71
Pennsylvania German (0)	32	0.25
Polish (384)	1,323	10.34
Romanian (42)	89	0.70
Russian (362)	657	5.14
Scandinavian (0)	16	0.13
Scotch-Irish (3)	70	0.55
Scottish (0)	257	2.01
Slavic (0)	11	0.09
Slovak (0)	93	0.73
Slovene (65)	131	1.02
Swedish (54)	194	1.52
Swiss (19)	66	0.52
Turkish (53)	53	0.41
Ukrainian (47)	71	0.56
Welsh (41)	104	0.81
Yugoslavian (14)	14	0.11

Hispanic Origin	Population	%
Hispanic or Latino (of any race)	465	3.61
Central American, ex. Mexican	28	0.22
Costa Rican	5	0.04
Guatemalan	9	0.07
Honduran	1	0.01
Nicaraguan	3	0.02
Panamanian	6	0.05
Salvadoran	4	0.03
Cuban	12	0.09
Dominican Republic	1	0.01
Mexican	212	1.65
Puerto Rican	102	0.79
South American	72	0.56
Argentinean	12	0.09
Bolivian	1	0.01
Colombian	28	0.22
Ecuadorian	3	0.02
Paraguayan	1	0.01
Peruvian	18	0.14
Venezuelan	5	0.04
Other South American	4	0.03
Other Hispanic or Latino	38	0.30

Race*	Population	%
African-American/Black (1,813)	1,981	15.39
Not Hispanic (1,774)	1,928	14.98
Hispanic (39)	53	0.41
American Indian/Alaska Native (32)	91	0.71
Not Hispanic (26)	75	0.58
Hispanic (6)	16	0.12
Apache (0)	1	0.01
Blackfeet (0)	1	0.01
Canadian/French Am. Ind. (1)	1	0.01
Cherokee (1)	5	0.04
Chickasaw (0)	2	0.02
Chippewa (3)	17	0.13
Choctaw (0)	5	0.04
Inupiat *(Alaska Native)* (1)	2	0.02
Iroquois (1)	5	0.04
Menominee (4)	4	0.03
Mexican American Ind. (1)	3	0.02
Navajo (1)	1	0.01
Ottawa (1)	1	0.01
Potawatomi (1)	1	0.01
Seminole (0)	3	0.02
Sioux (0)	3	0.02
South American Ind. (1)	3	0.02
Asian (409)	493	3.83
Not Hispanic (405)	487	3.78
Hispanic (4)	6	0.05
Bangladeshi (5)	5	0.04
Burmese (8)	8	0.06
Chinese, ex. Taiwanese (81)	91	0.71
Filipino (37)	64	0.50
Hmong (11)	12	0.09
Indian (115)	141	1.10
Indonesian (14)	14	0.11
Japanese (21)	24	0.19
Korean (32)	51	0.40
Laotian (3)	6	0.05
Pakistani (15)	21	0.16
Taiwanese (6)	6	0.05
Thai (4)	9	0.07
Vietnamese (38)	43	0.33
Hawaii Native/Pacific Islander (10)	18	0.14
Not Hispanic (9)	17	0.13
Hispanic (1)	1	0.01
Guamanian/Chamorro (5)	5	0.04
Native Hawaiian (0)	1	0.01
Samoan (2)	2	0.02
Tongan (1)	4	0.03
White (10,221)	10,495	81.53
Not Hispanic (9,908)	10,156	78.90
Hispanic (313)	339	2.63

Grafton

Place Type: Village
County: Ozaukee
Population: 11,459†

Ancestry‡	Population	%
African, Sub-Saharan (0)	28	0.25
African (0)	14	0.12
South African (0)	14	0.12
Albanian (12)	12	0.11
American (240)	240	2.12
Armenian (12)	45	0.40
Australian (12)	24	0.21
Austrian (0)	94	0.83
Belgian (75)	206	1.82
British (0)	31	0.27
Canadian (10)	25	0.22
Croatian (0)	96	0.85
Czech (25)	187	1.65
Czechoslovakian (0)	45	0.40
Danish (11)	101	0.89
Dutch (0)	146	1.29
Eastern European (0)	15	0.13
English (92)	816	7.20
European (44)	64	0.56
Finnish (15)	127	1.12
French, ex. Basque (32)	429	3.78
French Canadian (45)	73	0.64
German (2,603)	5,887	51.92
Greek (16)	47	0.41
Hungarian (33)	85	0.75
Irish (214)	1,489	13.13
Italian (261)	968	8.54
Lithuanian (58)	84	0.74
Luxemburger (17)	40	0.35
Norwegian (152)	542	4.78
Pennsylvania German (11)	11	0.10
Polish (308)	1,425	12.57
Russian (178)	337	2.97
Scandinavian (15)	27	0.24
Scotch-Irish (30)	152	1.34
Scottish (13)	115	1.01
Slovak (22)	69	0.61
Slovene (10)	26	0.23
Swedish (48)	253	2.23
Swiss (25)	123	1.08
Ukrainian (45)	45	0.40
Welsh (0)	59	0.52

Hispanic Origin	Population	%
Hispanic or Latino (of any race)	266	2.32
Central American, ex. Mexican	7	0.06
Costa Rican	1	0.01
Guatemalan	2	0.02
Honduran	4	0.03
Cuban	9	0.08
Dominican Republic	1	0.01
Mexican	171	1.49
Puerto Rican	35	0.31
South American	15	0.13
Argentinean	3	0.03
Colombian	8	0.07
Ecuadorian	4	0.03
Other Hispanic or Latino	28	0.24

Race*	Population	%
African-American/Black (86)	129	1.13
Not Hispanic (81)	115	1.00
Hispanic (5)	14	0.12
American Indian/Alaska Native (38)	60	0.52
Not Hispanic (35)	51	0.45
Hispanic (3)	9	0.08
Aleut *(Alaska Native)* (0)	2	0.02
Canadian/French Am. Ind. (1)	1	0.01
Cherokee (1)	3	0.03
Chippewa (9)	13	0.11
Choctaw (0)	1	0.01
Delaware (1)	1	0.01
Iroquois (7)	9	0.08
Ottawa (3)	3	0.03
Potawatomi (0)	3	0.03
Asian (197)	254	2.22
Not Hispanic (195)	247	2.16
Hispanic (2)	7	0.06
Bangladeshi (8)	8	0.07
Chinese, ex. Taiwanese (37)	42	0.37
Filipino (7)	27	0.24
Hmong (14)	14	0.12
Indian (71)	76	0.66
Indonesian (1)	1	0.01
Japanese (5)	11	0.10

*Notes: † The Census 2010 population figure is used to calculate the percentages in the Hispanic Origin and Race categories. Ancestry percentages are based on the 2006-2010 American Community Survey population (not shown); ‡ Numbers in parentheses indicate the number of people reporting a single ancestry; * Numbers in parentheses indicate the number of persons reporting this race alone, not in combination with any other race; Please refer to the Explanation of Data for more information.*

Korean (10)	18	0.16
Laotian (0)	1	0.01
Pakistani (4)	7	0.06
Taiwanese (7)	7	0.06
Thai (3)	3	0.03
Vietnamese (18)	22	0.19
Hawaii Native/Pacific Islander (1)	7	0.06
Not Hispanic (1)	3	0.03
Hispanic (0)	4	0.03
Guamanian/Chamorro (0)	1	0.01
Native Hawaiian (0)	1	0.01
White (10,946)	11,058	96.50
Not Hispanic (10,772)	10,869	94.85
Hispanic (174)	189	1.65

Grand Chute

Place Type: Town
County: Outagamie
Population: 20,919†

Ancestry‡	Population	%
African, Sub-Saharan (0)	25	0.12
African (0)	25	0.12
American (421)	421	2.05
Arab (10)	10	0.05
Palestinian (10)	10	0.05
Armenian (0)	22	0.11
Austrian (11)	16	0.08
Belgian (80)	178	0.87
Brazilian (15)	45	0.22
British (17)	83	0.40
Canadian (0)	8	0.04
Croatian (0)	14	0.07
Czech (19)	202	0.99
Danish (52)	229	1.12
Dutch (349)	1,494	7.29
English (188)	1,375	6.71
European (197)	197	0.96
Finnish (284)	440	2.15
French, ex. Basque (154)	788	3.84
French Canadian (22)	230	1.12
German (5,256)	11,164	54.46
Greek (44)	57	0.28
Hungarian (58)	117	0.57
Irish (621)	3,043	14.85
Italian (190)	646	3.15
Latvian (0)	13	0.06
Luxemburger (0)	9	0.04
Northern European (33)	33	0.16
Norwegian (301)	841	4.10
Pennsylvania German (12)	12	0.06
Polish (294)	1,475	7.20
Romanian (50)	50	0.24
Russian (18)	78	0.38
Scandinavian (60)	66	0.32
Scotch-Irish (0)	56	0.27
Scottish (50)	314	1.53
Serbian (16)	16	0.08
Slovak (0)	23	0.11
Slovene (0)	15	0.07
Swedish (101)	534	2.61
Swiss (0)	40	0.20
Ukrainian (0)	39	0.19
Welsh (34)	138	0.67
Yugoslavian (12)	12	0.06

Hispanic Origin	Population	%
Hispanic or Latino (of any race)	1,019	4.87
Central American, ex. Mexican	64	0.31
Costa Rican	6	0.03
Guatemalan	20	0.10
Honduran	16	0.08
Nicaraguan	12	0.06
Panamanian	3	0.01
Salvadoran	6	0.03
Other Central American	1	<0.01
Cuban	30	0.14
Dominican Republic	5	0.02
Mexican	773	3.70
Puerto Rican	67	0.32
South American	30	0.14
Argentinean	10	0.05
Chilean	1	<0.01
Colombian	12	0.06
Paraguayan	3	0.01
Peruvian	4	0.02
Other Hispanic or Latino	50	0.24

Race*	Population	%
African-American/Black (296)	426	2.04
Not Hispanic (282)	396	1.89
Hispanic (14)	30	0.14
American Indian/Alaska Native (92)	198	0.95
Not Hispanic (87)	172	0.82
Hispanic (5)	26	0.12
Apache (1)	3	0.01
Blackfeet (0)	6	0.03
Cherokee (0)	13	0.06
Cheyenne (0)	1	<0.01
Chippewa (9)	20	0.10
Choctaw (1)	2	0.01
Creek (2)	2	0.01
Delaware (0)	1	<0.01
Inupiat *(Alaska Native)* (1)	1	<0.01
Iroquois (18)	30	0.14
Menominee (9)	15	0.07
Mexican American Ind. (0)	4	0.02
Ottawa (0)	2	0.01
Paiute (0)	2	0.01
Pima (1)	1	<0.01
Potawatomi (2)	12	0.06
Sioux (2)	4	0.02
Asian (948)	1,018	4.87
Not Hispanic (945)	1,012	4.84
Hispanic (3)	6	0.03
Chinese, ex. Taiwanese (83)	90	0.43
Filipino (29)	43	0.21
Hmong (331)	338	1.62
Indian (300)	312	1.49
Indonesian (2)	3	0.01
Japanese (9)	18	0.09
Korean (40)	62	0.30
Laotian (8)	13	0.06
Malaysian (2)	2	0.01
Nepalese (4)	4	0.02
Pakistani (20)	20	0.10
Taiwanese (5)	7	0.03
Thai (9)	11	0.05
Vietnamese (70)	74	0.35
Hawaii Native/Pacific Islander (22)	40	0.19
Not Hispanic (20)	27	0.13
Hispanic (2)	13	0.06
Guamanian/Chamorro (8)	9	0.04
Native Hawaiian (3)	11	0.05
Samoan (2)	2	0.01
White (18,690)	19,009	90.87
Not Hispanic (18,288)	18,536	88.61
Hispanic (402)	473	2.26

Grand Rapids

Place Type: Town
County: Wood
Population: 7,646†

Ancestry‡	Population	%
American (212)	212	2.77
Armenian (0)	28	0.37
Austrian (0)	12	0.16
Belgian (13)	25	0.33
Czech (0)	120	1.57
Danish (11)	41	0.54
Dutch (35)	272	3.56
Eastern European (13)	13	0.17
English (326)	757	9.90
European (103)	135	1.77
Finnish (0)	82	1.07
French, ex. Basque (63)	494	6.46
French Canadian (61)	100	1.31
German (1,543)	4,025	52.63
Greek (0)	7	0.09
Hungarian (0)	37	0.48
Irish (200)	1,014	13.26
Italian (29)	79	1.03
Latvian (20)	20	0.26
Lithuanian (11)	49	0.64
Norwegian (226)	740	9.68
Polish (273)	1,230	16.08
Russian (0)	33	0.43
Scandinavian (0)	28	0.37
Scotch-Irish (21)	87	1.14
Scottish (0)	39	0.51
Serbian (0)	15	0.20
Swedish (21)	329	4.30
Swiss (10)	220	2.88
Turkish (0)	28	0.37
Welsh (23)	48	0.63

Hispanic Origin	Population	%
Hispanic or Latino (of any race)	100	1.31
Central American, ex. Mexican	1	0.01
Guatemalan	1	0.01
Cuban	3	0.04
Mexican	73	0.95
Puerto Rican	8	0.10
South American	3	0.04
Chilean	2	0.03
Paraguayan	1	0.01
Other Hispanic or Latino	12	0.16

Race*	Population	%
African-American/Black (27)	49	0.64
Not Hispanic (26)	44	0.58
Hispanic (1)	5	0.07
American Indian/Alaska Native (43)	62	0.81
Not Hispanic (36)	53	0.69
Hispanic (7)	9	0.12
Cherokee (2)	4	0.05
Chippewa (4)	5	0.07
Iroquois (0)	5	0.07
Kiowa (1)	1	0.01
Menominee (1)	1	0.01
Navajo (1)	1	0.01
Potawatomi (2)	2	0.03
Shoshone (0)	1	0.01
Asian (73)	90	1.18
Not Hispanic (72)	89	1.16
Hispanic (1)	1	0.01
Chinese, ex. Taiwanese (15)	17	0.22
Filipino (14)	22	0.29
Hmong (13)	13	0.17
Indian (16)	16	0.21
Japanese (0)	2	0.03
Korean (13)	17	0.22
Thai (1)	1	0.01
Vietnamese (1)	1	0.01
Hawaii Native/Pacific Islander (1)	3	0.04
Not Hispanic (1)	1	0.01
Hispanic (0)	2	0.03
Guamanian/Chamorro (0)	2	0.03
Native Hawaiian (1)	1	0.01
White (7,394)	7,459	97.55
Not Hispanic (7,357)	7,409	96.90
Hispanic (37)	50	0.65

Green Bay

Place Type: City
County: Brown
Population: 104,057†

Ancestry‡	Population	%
African, Sub-Saharan (139)	209	0.20
African (84)	117	0.11
Nigerian (55)	92	0.09
American (2,866)	2,866	2.76
Arab (50)	228	0.22
Egyptian (0)	16	0.02
Lebanese (50)	197	0.19

*Notes: † The Census 2010 population figure is used to calculate the percentages in the Hispanic Origin and Race categories. Ancestry percentages are based on the 2006-2010 American Community Survey population (not shown); ‡ Numbers in parentheses indicate the number of people reporting a single ancestry; * Numbers in parentheses indicate the number of persons reporting this race alone, not in combination with any other race; Please refer to the Explanation of Data for more information.*

Ancestry (continued)	Population	%
Syrian (0)	15	0.01
Australian (0)	5	<0.01
Austrian (58)	276	0.27
Belgian (2,896)	9,328	8.97
Brazilian (8)	8	0.01
British (94)	214	0.21
Bulgarian (34)	34	0.03
Canadian (51)	166	0.16
Croatian (54)	160	0.15
Czech (553)	2,282	2.20
Czechoslovakian (34)	131	0.13
Danish (176)	1,267	1.22
Dutch (562)	4,002	3.85
Eastern European (70)	76	0.07
English (845)	3,946	3.80
European (909)	1,204	1.16
Finnish (253)	846	0.81
French, ex. Basque (755)	5,835	5.61
French Canadian (1,005)	3,037	2.92
German (12,357)	35,077	33.74
German Russian (0)	13	0.01
Greek (43)	78	0.08
Hungarian (69)	256	0.25
Iranian (10)	10	0.01
Irish (1,512)	10,065	9.68
Italian (736)	2,941	2.83
Lithuanian (22)	101	0.10
Luxemburger (30)	84	0.08
Maltese (0)	15	0.01
Northern European (30)	30	0.03
Norwegian (1,077)	3,611	3.47
Pennsylvania German (0)	34	0.03
Polish (3,047)	10,763	10.35
Portuguese (19)	53	0.05
Romanian (0)	25	0.02
Russian (144)	561	0.54
Scandinavian (114)	236	0.23
Scotch-Irish (291)	790	0.76
Scottish (95)	651	0.63
Serbian (0)	13	0.01
Slavic (8)	113	0.11
Slovak (26)	47	0.05
Slovene (18)	68	0.07
Swedish (332)	2,552	2.45
Swiss (50)	197	0.19
Ukrainian (0)	14	0.01
Welsh (10)	250	0.24
West Indian, ex. Hispanic (54)	141	0.14
Belizean (17)	17	0.02
Dutch West Indian (0)	9	0.01
Haitian (13)	18	0.02
Jamaican (24)	97	0.09
Yugoslavian (11)	43	0.04

Hispanic Origin	Population	%
Hispanic or Latino (of any race)	13,896	13.35
Central American, ex. Mexican	751	0.72
Costa Rican	9	0.01
Guatemalan	100	0.10
Honduran	428	0.41
Nicaraguan	62	0.06
Panamanian	28	0.03
Salvadoran	112	0.11
Other Central American	12	0.01
Cuban	76	0.07
Dominican Republic	47	0.05
Mexican	11,115	10.68
Puerto Rican	982	0.94
South American	173	0.17
Argentinean	12	0.01
Bolivian	2	<0.01
Chilean	14	0.01
Colombian	47	0.05
Ecuadorian	10	0.01
Paraguayan	1	<0.01
Peruvian	72	0.07
Uruguayan	4	<0.01
Venezuelan	9	0.01
Other South American	2	<0.01
Other Hispanic or Latino	752	0.72

Race*	Population	%
African-American/Black (3,691)	4,952	4.76
Not Hispanic (3,544)	4,621	4.44
Hispanic (147)	331	0.32
American Indian/Alaska Native (4,241)	5,599	5.38
Not Hispanic (3,710)	4,837	4.65
Hispanic (531)	762	0.73
Alaska Athabascan *(Ala. Nat.)* (1)	5	<0.01
Aleut *(Alaska Native)* (0)	1	<0.01
Apache (1)	6	0.01
Arapaho (0)	1	<0.01
Blackfeet (2)	13	0.01
Canadian/French Am. Ind. (3)	4	<0.01
Cherokee (20)	59	0.06
Cheyenne (1)	9	0.01
Chippewa (263)	388	0.37
Choctaw (7)	11	0.01
Comanche (1)	2	<0.01
Cree (1)	2	<0.01
Creek (0)	1	<0.01
Crow (1)	2	<0.01
Delaware (0)	1	<0.01
Hopi (1)	2	<0.01
Inupiat *(Alaska Native)* (0)	1	<0.01
Iroquois (1,043)	1,426	1.37
Menominee (593)	757	0.73
Mexican American Ind. (21)	36	0.03
Navajo (11)	14	0.01
Osage (6)	12	0.01
Ottawa (13)	23	0.02
Paiute (1)	1	<0.01
Pima (1)	1	<0.01
Potawatomi (54)	85	0.08
Pueblo (6)	8	0.01
Seminole (1)	1	<0.01
Shoshone (1)	1	<0.01
Sioux (41)	90	0.09
South American Ind. (11)	16	0.02
Spanish American Ind. (10)	10	0.01
Tohono O'Odham (3)	3	<0.01
Asian (4,210)	4,673	4.49
Not Hispanic (4,159)	4,566	4.39
Hispanic (51)	107	0.10
Cambodian (17)	30	0.03
Chinese, ex. Taiwanese (142)	185	0.18
Filipino (93)	186	0.18
Hmong (2,876)	3,020	2.90
Indian (232)	325	0.31
Indonesian (1)	4	<0.01
Japanese (33)	116	0.11
Korean (78)	135	0.13
Laotian (268)	315	0.30
Malaysian (0)	1	<0.01
Nepalese (3)	3	<0.01
Pakistani (6)	7	0.01
Sri Lankan (3)	3	<0.01
Taiwanese (1)	3	<0.01
Thai (12)	22	0.02
Vietnamese (73)	103	0.10
Hawaii Native/Pacific Islander (63)	159	0.15
Not Hispanic (49)	110	0.11
Hispanic (14)	49	0.05
Guamanian/Chamorro (14)	20	0.02
Native Hawaiian (12)	26	0.02
Samoan (13)	30	0.03
Tongan (1)	2	<0.01
White (81,075)	83,902	80.63
Not Hispanic (76,249)	78,358	75.30
Hispanic (4,826)	5,544	5.33

Greendale

Place Type: Village
County: Milwaukee
Population: 14,046†

Ancestry‡	Population	%
African, Sub-Saharan (84)	117	0.84
African (65)	98	0.70
Sudanese (19)	19	0.14
American (235)	235	1.68
Arab (0)	9	0.06
Syrian (0)	9	0.06
Austrian (35)	128	0.92
Belgian (0)	45	0.32
British (12)	27	0.19
Bulgarian (9)	9	0.06
Croatian (27)	53	0.38
Czech (87)	419	3.00
Czechoslovakian (0)	32	0.23
Danish (49)	162	1.16
Dutch (15)	85	0.61
English (191)	1,209	8.65
European (51)	64	0.46
Finnish (17)	47	0.34
French, ex. Basque (21)	638	4.56
French Canadian (40)	139	0.99
German (2,398)	6,642	47.51
Greek (0)	26	0.19
Hungarian (0)	71	0.51
Iranian (6)	6	0.04
Irish (314)	2,143	15.33
Italian (230)	811	5.80
Lithuanian (12)	20	0.14
Luxemburger (22)	42	0.30
Northern European (0)	28	0.20
Norwegian (166)	684	4.89
Polish (1,113)	3,243	23.20
Romanian (23)	23	0.16
Russian (26)	81	0.58
Scandinavian (22)	32	0.23
Scotch-Irish (12)	100	0.72
Scottish (15)	103	0.74
Serbian (52)	127	0.91
Slavic (0)	27	0.19
Slovak (48)	48	0.34
Slovene (12)	111	0.79
Swedish (16)	262	1.87
Swiss (0)	100	0.72
Ukrainian (28)	28	0.20
Welsh (13)	166	1.19
Yugoslavian (23)	23	0.16

Hispanic Origin	Population	%
Hispanic or Latino (of any race)	667	4.75
Central American, ex. Mexican	29	0.21
Costa Rican	5	0.04
Guatemalan	10	0.07
Honduran	6	0.04
Nicaraguan	1	0.01
Panamanian	1	0.01
Salvadoran	6	0.04
Cuban	10	0.07
Dominican Republic	3	0.02
Mexican	415	2.95
Puerto Rican	155	1.10
South American	24	0.17
Bolivian	1	0.01
Chilean	2	0.01
Colombian	13	0.09
Ecuadorian	2	0.01
Peruvian	2	0.01
Venezuelan	4	0.03
Other Hispanic or Latino	31	0.22

Race*	Population	%
African-American/Black (170)	244	1.74
Not Hispanic (143)	207	1.47
Hispanic (27)	37	0.26
American Indian/Alaska Native (59)	113	0.80
Not Hispanic (45)	88	0.63
Hispanic (14)	25	0.18
Apache (0)	1	0.01
Arapaho (2)	2	0.01
Cherokee (0)	4	0.03
Chippewa (18)	19	0.14
Iroquois (4)	13	0.09
Menominee (4)	11	0.08
Mexican American Ind. (1)	4	0.03

*Notes: † The Census 2010 population figure is used to calculate the percentages in the Hispanic Origin and Race categories. Ancestry percentages are based on the 2006-2010 American Community Survey population (not shown); ‡ Numbers in parentheses indicate the number of people reporting a single ancestry; * Numbers in parentheses indicate the number of persons reporting this race alone, not in combination with any other race; Please refer to the Explanation of Data for more information.*

Navajo (4)	4	0.03
Sioux (3)	3	0.02
Asian (434)	520	3.70
Not Hispanic (430)	509	3.62
Hispanic (4)	11	0.08
Bangladeshi (4)	4	0.03
Chinese, ex. Taiwanese (31)	40	0.28
Filipino (73)	90	0.64
Hmong (24)	25	0.18
Indian (145)	157	1.12
Indonesian (0)	4	0.03
Japanese (12)	27	0.19
Korean (29)	38	0.27
Laotian (6)	7	0.05
Malaysian (1)	2	0.01
Pakistani (34)	38	0.27
Taiwanese (9)	9	0.06
Thai (3)	6	0.04
Vietnamese (47)	49	0.35
Hawaii Native/Pacific Islander (2)	10	0.07
Not Hispanic (2)	9	0.06
Hispanic (0)	1	0.01
Native Hawaiian (1)	2	0.01
Samoan (1)	3	0.02
White (13,037)	13,239	94.25
Not Hispanic (12,574)	12,739	90.69
Hispanic (463)	500	3.56

Greenfield

Place Type: City
County: Milwaukee
Population: 36,720†

Ancestry‡	Population	%
African, Sub-Saharan (44)	44	0.12
African (34)	34	0.09
South African (10)	10	0.03
American (756)	756	2.09
Arab (285)	323	0.89
Arab (102)	119	0.33
Egyptian (29)	29	0.08
Jordanian (25)	25	0.07
Lebanese (9)	13	0.04
Palestinian (120)	120	0.33
Syrian (0)	17	0.05
Armenian (18)	18	0.05
Australian (9)	9	0.02
Austrian (54)	268	0.74
Belgian (29)	207	0.57
Brazilian (9)	9	0.02
British (0)	24	0.07
Cajun (0)	42	0.12
Canadian (0)	11	0.03
Croatian (106)	217	0.60
Czech (191)	570	1.57
Czechoslovakian (10)	171	0.47
Danish (71)	356	0.98
Dutch (106)	620	1.71
English (358)	1,798	4.96
European (85)	85	0.23
Finnish (82)	243	0.67
French, ex. Basque (197)	1,241	3.43
French Canadian (125)	296	0.82
German (5,270)	16,051	44.32
Greek (145)	252	0.70
Hungarian (51)	240	0.66
Icelander (0)	67	0.19
Iranian (27)	27	0.07
Irish (747)	3,935	10.87
Italian (616)	2,330	6.43
Latvian (13)	31	0.09
Lithuanian (8)	38	0.10
Luxemburger (0)	23	0.06
New Zealander (0)	9	0.02
Norwegian (451)	1,770	4.89
Polish (3,355)	8,647	23.88
Portuguese (0)	59	0.16
Romanian (14)	26	0.07
Russian (36)	314	0.87
Scandinavian (0)	44	0.12
Scotch-Irish (33)	246	0.68
Scottish (117)	422	1.17
Serbian (412)	737	2.04
Slavic (20)	61	0.17
Slovak (48)	145	0.40
Slovene (104)	398	1.10
Swedish (78)	605	1.67
Swiss (28)	181	0.50
Turkish (40)	69	0.19
Ukrainian (32)	96	0.27
Welsh (21)	135	0.37
Yugoslavian (29)	51	0.14

Hispanic Origin	Population	%
Hispanic or Latino (of any race)	3,087	8.41
Central American, ex. Mexican	81	0.22
Costa Rican	27	0.07
Guatemalan	9	0.02
Honduran	10	0.03
Nicaraguan	20	0.05
Panamanian	1	<0.01
Salvadoran	14	0.04
Cuban	38	0.10
Dominican Republic	21	0.06
Mexican	1,953	5.32
Puerto Rican	772	2.10
South American	116	0.32
Argentinean	6	0.02
Bolivian	13	0.04
Chilean	11	0.03
Colombian	44	0.12
Ecuadorian	9	0.02
Paraguayan	1	<0.01
Peruvian	29	0.08
Venezuelan	3	0.01
Other Hispanic or Latino	106	0.29

Race*	Population	%
African-American/Black (857)	1,136	3.09
Not Hispanic (808)	1,039	2.83
Hispanic (49)	97	0.26
American Indian/Alaska Native (249)	457	1.24
Not Hispanic (228)	390	1.06
Hispanic (21)	67	0.18
Alaska Athabascan *(Ala. Nat.)* (3)	3	0.01
Apache (0)	7	0.02
Blackfeet (2)	9	0.02
Canadian/French Am. Ind. (0)	1	<0.01
Central American Ind. (1)	1	<0.01
Cherokee (4)	17	0.05
Chippewa (55)	95	0.26
Choctaw (0)	1	<0.01
Cree (0)	1	<0.01
Iroquois (41)	71	0.19
Lumbee (2)	2	0.01
Menominee (16)	22	0.06
Mexican American Ind. (1)	8	0.02
Navajo (0)	1	<0.01
Ottawa (1)	1	<0.01
Potawatomi (13)	15	0.04
Sioux (5)	6	0.02
South American Ind. (0)	2	0.01
Spanish American Ind. (1)	1	<0.01
Asian (1,425)	1,652	4.50
Not Hispanic (1,411)	1,619	4.41
Hispanic (14)	33	0.09
Bangladeshi (4)	4	0.01
Burmese (5)	5	0.01
Cambodian (6)	10	0.03
Chinese, ex. Taiwanese (123)	156	0.42
Filipino (149)	206	0.56
Hmong (144)	155	0.42
Indian (566)	596	1.62
Indonesian (7)	15	0.04
Japanese (18)	39	0.11
Korean (57)	83	0.23
Laotian (52)	68	0.19
Malaysian (6)	6	0.02
Nepalese (0)	1	<0.01
Pakistani (85)	97	0.26
Sri Lankan (2)	2	0.01
Taiwanese (0)	4	0.01
Thai (7)	16	0.04
Vietnamese (144)	152	0.41
Hawaii Native/Pacific Islander (14)	53	0.14
Not Hispanic (6)	30	0.08
Hispanic (8)	23	0.06
Guamanian/Chamorro (4)	5	0.01
Native Hawaiian (4)	17	0.05
Samoan (2)	2	0.01
White (32,525)	33,261	90.58
Not Hispanic (30,590)	31,094	84.68
Hispanic (1,935)	2,167	5.90

Greenville

Place Type: Town
County: Outagamie
Population: 10,309†

Ancestry‡	Population	%
American (341)	341	3.51
Austrian (0)	57	0.59
Belgian (16)	136	1.40
British (0)	85	0.88
Canadian (23)	37	0.38
Croatian (0)	16	0.16
Czech (37)	146	1.50
Danish (26)	118	1.21
Dutch (104)	489	5.04
English (46)	393	4.05
European (12)	12	0.12
Finnish (19)	91	0.94
French, ex. Basque (34)	622	6.40
French Canadian (10)	100	1.03
German (3,028)	5,639	58.06
Hungarian (9)	29	0.30
Irish (95)	640	6.59
Italian (32)	305	3.14
Latvian (12)	12	0.12
Lithuanian (0)	20	0.21
Northern European (21)	54	0.56
Norwegian (173)	536	5.52
Polish (171)	767	7.90
Russian (0)	23	0.24
Scandinavian (0)	9	0.09
Scotch-Irish (0)	24	0.25
Scottish (70)	114	1.17
Swedish (23)	210	2.16
Swiss (0)	83	0.85
Welsh (0)	30	0.31

Hispanic Origin	Population	%
Hispanic or Latino (of any race)	367	3.56
Central American, ex. Mexican	6	0.06
Guatemalan	3	0.03
Honduran	1	0.01
Nicaraguan	1	0.01
Panamanian	1	0.01
Cuban	1	0.01
Dominican Republic	1	0.01
Mexican	313	3.04
Puerto Rican	3	0.03
South American	9	0.09
Argentinean	1	0.01
Chilean	2	0.02
Colombian	4	0.04
Uruguayan	1	0.01
Venezuelan	1	0.01
Other Hispanic or Latino	34	0.33

Race*	Population	%
African-American/Black (33)	64	0.62
Not Hispanic (32)	59	0.57
Hispanic (1)	5	0.05
American Indian/Alaska Native (40)	58	0.56
Not Hispanic (33)	44	0.43
Hispanic (7)	14	0.14
Apache (2)	2	0.02

*Notes: † The Census 2010 population figure is used to calculate the percentages in the Hispanic Origin and Race categories. Ancestry percentages are based on the 2006-2010 American Community Survey population (not shown); ‡ Numbers in parentheses indicate the number of people reporting a single ancestry; * Numbers in parentheses indicate the number of persons reporting this race alone, not in combination with any other race; Please refer to the Explanation of Data for more information.*

	Population	%
Cherokee (3)	7	0.07
Chippewa (1)	1	0.01
Iroquois (2)	4	0.04
Menominee (2)	2	0.02
Mexican American Ind. (5)	6	0.06
Paiute (1)	1	0.01
Potawatomi (2)	2	0.02
Sioux (1)	3	0.03
Asian (97)	120	1.16
Not Hispanic (97)	120	1.16
Chinese, ex. Taiwanese (15)	19	0.18
Filipino (5)	7	0.07
Hmong (59)	61	0.59
Indian (6)	8	0.08
Japanese (3)	6	0.06
Korean (7)	8	0.08
Pakistani (1)	1	0.01
Vietnamese (1)	1	0.01
Hawaii Native/Pacific Islander (2)	6	0.06
Not Hispanic (1)	4	0.04
Hispanic (1)	2	0.02
Guamanian/Chamorro (2)	3	0.03
Native Hawaiian (0)	1	0.01
White (9,884)	9,946	96.48
Not Hispanic (9,716)	9,763	94.70
Hispanic (168)	183	1.78

Hales Corners

Place Type: Village
County: Milwaukee
Population: 7,692†

Ancestry‡	Population	%
American (286)	286	3.74
Arab (0)	52	0.68
Arab (0)	52	0.68
Armenian (14)	14	0.18
Australian (6)	6	0.08
Austrian (26)	80	1.05
Belgian (0)	17	0.22
Canadian (0)	19	0.25
Croatian (37)	63	0.82
Czech (50)	205	2.68
Czechoslovakian (0)	20	0.26
Danish (0)	7	0.09
Dutch (49)	148	1.94
English (25)	444	5.81
European (278)	278	3.64
Finnish (33)	182	2.38
French, ex. Basque (31)	207	2.71
French Canadian (0)	6	0.08
German (1,165)	3,672	48.02
Greek (8)	8	0.10
Hungarian (19)	99	1.29
Irish (110)	830	10.85
Italian (119)	558	7.30
Lithuanian (22)	22	0.29
Norwegian (44)	237	3.10
Polish (804)	2,052	26.83
Romanian (0)	35	0.46
Russian (8)	44	0.58
Scotch-Irish (0)	39	0.51
Scottish (32)	73	0.95
Slavic (6)	6	0.08
Swedish (42)	328	4.29
Swiss (0)	24	0.31
Ukrainian (13)	46	0.60
Welsh (0)	46	0.60
Yugoslavian (0)	24	0.31

Hispanic Origin	Population	%
Hispanic or Latino (of any race)	333	4.33
Central American, ex. Mexican	9	0.12
Guatemalan	1	0.01
Nicaraguan	3	0.04
Salvadoran	5	0.07
Cuban	4	0.05
Dominican Republic	2	0.03
Mexican	200	2.60
Puerto Rican	69	0.90
South American	11	0.14
Argentinean	2	0.03
Chilean	1	0.01
Colombian	3	0.04
Peruvian	5	0.07
Other Hispanic or Latino	38	0.49

Race*	Population	%
African-American/Black (75)	115	1.50
Not Hispanic (68)	104	1.35
Hispanic (7)	11	0.14
American Indian/Alaska Native (37)	49	0.64
Not Hispanic (33)	45	0.59
Hispanic (4)	4	0.05
Cherokee (1)	1	0.01
Chippewa (5)	8	0.10
Creek (1)	1	0.01
Iroquois (3)	5	0.07
Menominee (1)	1	0.01
Mexican American Ind. (2)	2	0.03
Potawatomi (1)	1	0.01
Sioux (1)	2	0.03
Asian (134)	158	2.05
Not Hispanic (134)	151	1.96
Hispanic (0)	7	0.09
Chinese, ex. Taiwanese (22)	24	0.31
Filipino (6)	19	0.25
Hmong (8)	8	0.10
Indian (68)	68	0.88
Japanese (5)	5	0.07
Korean (16)	20	0.26
Vietnamese (3)	6	0.08
Hawaii Native/Pacific Islander (1)	4	0.05
Not Hispanic (1)	4	0.05
Native Hawaiian (0)	1	0.01
Samoan (0)	1	0.01
White (7,284)	7,373	95.85
Not Hispanic (7,048)	7,118	92.54
Hispanic (236)	255	3.32

Harrison

Place Type: Town
County: Calumet
Population: 10,839†

Ancestry‡	Population	%
American (308)	308	3.08
Arab (9)	9	0.09
Lebanese (9)	9	0.09
Austrian (22)	29	0.29
Belgian (9)	203	2.03
British (0)	14	0.14
Czech (0)	115	1.15
Czechoslovakian (0)	9	0.09
Danish (0)	21	0.21
Dutch (262)	1,247	12.47
English (167)	692	6.92
European (136)	163	1.63
Finnish (31)	173	1.73
French, ex. Basque (41)	395	3.95
French Canadian (48)	184	1.84
German (2,804)	5,692	56.93
Hungarian (11)	47	0.47
Icelander (0)	30	0.30
Iranian (0)	4	0.04
Irish (236)	1,135	11.35
Italian (32)	197	1.97
Lithuanian (0)	39	0.39
Luxemburger (0)	8	0.08
Norwegian (206)	454	4.54
Polish (105)	862	8.62
Russian (9)	9	0.09
Scotch-Irish (0)	27	0.27
Scottish (12)	35	0.35
Serbian (0)	32	0.32
Slavic (0)	10	0.10
Slovak (0)	21	0.21
Swedish (45)	362	3.62
Swiss (38)	57	0.57
Ukrainian (0)	32	0.32
Welsh (9)	17	0.17

Hispanic Origin	Population	%
Hispanic or Latino (of any race)	233	2.15
Central American, ex. Mexican	19	0.18
Guatemalan	10	0.09
Honduran	4	0.04
Nicaraguan	2	0.02
Panamanian	2	0.02
Salvadoran	1	0.01
Cuban	1	0.01
Dominican Republic	2	0.02
Mexican	172	1.59
Puerto Rican	18	0.17
South American	7	0.06
Chilean	2	0.02
Colombian	2	0.02
Ecuadorian	2	0.02
Venezuelan	1	0.01
Other Hispanic or Latino	14	0.13

Race*	Population	%
African-American/Black (32)	63	0.58
Not Hispanic (31)	59	0.54
Hispanic (1)	4	0.04
American Indian/Alaska Native (27)	55	0.51
Not Hispanic (24)	48	0.44
Hispanic (3)	7	0.06
Apache (0)	1	0.01
Cherokee (0)	4	0.04
Chippewa (2)	2	0.02
Iroquois (9)	14	0.13
Menominee (2)	3	0.03
Mexican American Ind. (2)	3	0.03
Ottawa (1)	1	0.01
Potawatomi (1)	3	0.03
Ute (0)	1	0.01
Yaqui (0)	2	0.02
Yup'ik *(Alaska Native)* (1)	1	0.01
Asian (169)	195	1.80
Not Hispanic (167)	193	1.78
Hispanic (2)	2	0.02
Cambodian (1)	1	0.01
Chinese, ex. Taiwanese (31)	38	0.35
Filipino (7)	16	0.15
Hmong (80)	84	0.77
Indian (9)	10	0.09
Japanese (1)	2	0.02
Korean (14)	18	0.17
Laotian (7)	7	0.06
Pakistani (6)	6	0.06
Thai (1)	1	0.01
Vietnamese (2)	8	0.07
Hawaii Native/Pacific Islander (1)	4	0.04
Not Hispanic (1)	3	0.03
Hispanic (0)	1	0.01
Native Hawaiian (1)	3	0.03
White (10,428)	10,523	97.08
Not Hispanic (10,305)	10,382	95.78
Hispanic (123)	141	1.30

Hartford

Place Type: City
County: Washington
Population: 14,223†

Ancestry‡	Population	%
Albanian (106)	106	0.77
American (602)	602	4.38
Austrian (0)	41	0.30
Belgian (0)	102	0.74
British (11)	11	0.08
Canadian (0)	53	0.39
Croatian (0)	24	0.17
Czech (8)	85	0.62
Czechoslovakian (0)	15	0.11
Danish (24)	173	1.26

*Notes: † The Census 2010 population figure is used to calculate the percentages in the Hispanic Origin and Race categories. Ancestry percentages are based on the 2006-2010 American Community Survey population (not shown); ‡ Numbers in parentheses indicate the number of people reporting a single ancestry; * Numbers in parentheses indicate the number of persons reporting this race alone, not in combination with any other race; Please refer to the Explanation of Data for more information.*

Ancestry	Population	%
Dutch (57)	264	1.92
English (256)	842	6.12
European (32)	32	0.23
Finnish (75)	111	0.81
French, ex. Basque (60)	539	3.92
French Canadian (18)	59	0.43
German (3,243)	7,426	54.02
Hungarian (41)	116	0.84
Irish (236)	1,950	14.18
Italian (45)	506	3.68
Macedonian (0)	29	0.21
Northern European (11)	11	0.08
Norwegian (129)	858	6.24
Polish (477)	1,766	12.85
Romanian (66)	66	0.48
Russian (35)	82	0.60
Scotch-Irish (20)	77	0.56
Scottish (55)	198	1.44
Serbian (13)	13	0.09
Slovak (15)	35	0.25
Swedish (17)	492	3.58
Swiss (9)	232	1.69
Welsh (7)	15	0.11
Yugoslavian (0)	7	0.05

Hispanic Origin	Population	%
Hispanic or Latino (of any race)	686	4.82
Central American, ex. Mexican	13	0.09
Costa Rican	6	0.04
Guatemalan	1	0.01
Honduran	5	0.04
Panamanian	1	0.01
Cuban	3	0.02
Dominican Republic	3	0.02
Mexican	550	3.87
Puerto Rican	83	0.58
South American	14	0.10
Argentinean	1	0.01
Chilean	3	0.02
Colombian	7	0.05
Peruvian	3	0.02
Other Hispanic or Latino	20	0.14

Race*	Population	%
African-American/Black (122)	185	1.30
Not Hispanic (111)	171	1.20
Hispanic (11)	14	0.10
American Indian/Alaska Native (67)	105	0.74
Not Hispanic (50)	85	0.60
Hispanic (17)	20	0.14
Apache (0)	1	0.01
Blackfeet (0)	3	0.02
Cherokee (1)	6	0.04
Chippewa (13)	20	0.14
Delaware (1)	1	0.01
Inupiat *(Alaska Native)* (2)	2	0.01
Iroquois (12)	13	0.09
Menominee (1)	2	0.01
Navajo (0)	1	0.01
Sioux (1)	1	0.01
Spanish American Ind. (6)	6	0.04
Asian (117)	171	1.20
Not Hispanic (111)	162	1.14
Hispanic (6)	9	0.06
Burmese (2)	2	0.01
Chinese, ex. Taiwanese (20)	35	0.25
Filipino (9)	14	0.10
Hmong (5)	5	0.04
Indian (20)	27	0.19
Japanese (3)	14	0.10
Korean (14)	28	0.20
Laotian (10)	15	0.11
Pakistani (6)	7	0.05
Sri Lankan (1)	1	0.01
Taiwanese (1)	1	0.01
Thai (11)	11	0.08
Vietnamese (9)	16	0.11
Hawaii Native/Pacific Islander (4)	10	0.07
Not Hispanic (4)	10	0.07
Guamanian/Chamorro (2)	7	0.05
Samoan (0)	1	0.01
White (13,475)	13,647	95.95
Not Hispanic (13,112)	13,252	93.17
Hispanic (363)	395	2.78

Hartland

Place Type: Village
County: Waukesha
Population: 9,110†

Ancestry‡	Population	%
American (253)	253	2.83
Arab (29)	39	0.44
Arab (29)	29	0.32
Lebanese (0)	10	0.11
Austrian (65)	184	2.06
Belgian (8)	43	0.48
British (10)	10	0.11
Canadian (6)	6	0.07
Czech (37)	98	1.10
Czechoslovakian (12)	12	0.13
Danish (33)	117	1.31
Dutch (31)	116	1.30
English (164)	835	9.35
Estonian (23)	23	0.26
European (78)	78	0.87
Finnish (0)	58	0.65
French, ex. Basque (34)	284	3.18
French Canadian (9)	109	1.22
German (1,712)	4,337	48.58
Greek (9)	163	1.83
Hungarian (11)	54	0.60
Irish (435)	1,402	15.70
Italian (107)	656	7.35
Latvian (14)	14	0.16
Lithuanian (10)	10	0.11
Northern European (19)	19	0.21
Norwegian (116)	513	5.75
Polish (211)	1,198	13.42
Portuguese (0)	4	0.04
Russian (0)	119	1.33
Scandinavian (3)	3	0.03
Scotch-Irish (13)	77	0.86
Scottish (0)	38	0.43
Serbian (0)	12	0.13
Slovene (34)	78	0.87
Swedish (160)	322	3.61
Swiss (0)	55	0.62
Welsh (0)	62	0.69

Hispanic Origin	Population	%
Hispanic or Latino (of any race)	262	2.88
Central American, ex. Mexican	16	0.18
Guatemalan	8	0.09
Honduran	3	0.03
Panamanian	4	0.04
Salvadoran	1	0.01
Cuban	9	0.10
Mexican	156	1.71
Puerto Rican	49	0.54
South American	17	0.19
Argentinean	1	0.01
Bolivian	1	0.01
Colombian	3	0.03
Ecuadorian	1	0.01
Peruvian	9	0.10
Venezuelan	2	0.02
Other Hispanic or Latino	15	0.16

Race*	Population	%
African-American/Black (77)	121	1.33
Not Hispanic (75)	110	1.21
Hispanic (2)	11	0.12
American Indian/Alaska Native (29)	61	0.67
Not Hispanic (28)	55	0.60
Hispanic (1)	6	0.07
Apache (0)	3	0.03
Blackfeet (1)	1	0.01
Cherokee (1)	6	0.07
Chippewa (12)	15	0.16
Iroquois (4)	6	0.07
Asian (156)	207	2.27
Not Hispanic (156)	206	2.26
Hispanic (0)	1	0.01
Cambodian (1)	1	0.01
Chinese, ex. Taiwanese (40)	45	0.49
Filipino (10)	24	0.26
Indian (69)	74	0.81
Japanese (2)	10	0.11
Korean (18)	31	0.34
Laotian (3)	4	0.04
Malaysian (0)	1	0.01
Pakistani (5)	5	0.05
Sri Lankan (1)	1	0.01
Thai (1)	1	0.01
Vietnamese (4)	6	0.07
Hawaii Native/Pacific Islander (6)	8	0.09
Not Hispanic (6)	8	0.09
Native Hawaiian (0)	1	0.01
White (8,664)	8,789	96.48
Not Hispanic (8,471)	8,579	94.17
Hispanic (193)	210	2.31

Holmen

Place Type: Village
County: La Crosse
Population: 9,005†

Ancestry‡	Population	%
American (127)	127	1.50
Arab (10)	10	0.12
Syrian (10)	10	0.12
Austrian (0)	60	0.71
Belgian (10)	38	0.45
British (56)	56	0.66
Czech (0)	141	1.67
Danish (22)	49	0.58
Dutch (0)	132	1.56
English (205)	675	7.98
European (21)	21	0.25
Finnish (0)	31	0.37
French, ex. Basque (149)	347	4.10
French Canadian (11)	11	0.13
German (1,308)	3,610	42.70
Greek (0)	37	0.44
Irish (286)	1,122	13.27
Italian (5)	163	1.93
Luxemburger (0)	6	0.07
Norwegian (845)	2,069	24.47
Polish (79)	417	4.93
Russian (0)	49	0.58
Scandinavian (82)	89	1.05
Scotch-Irish (0)	205	2.42
Scottish (12)	87	1.03
Slovene (0)	7	0.08
Swedish (10)	74	0.88
Swiss (9)	37	0.44
Ukrainian (0)	49	0.58
Welsh (0)	35	0.41
Yugoslavian (12)	12	0.14

Hispanic Origin	Population	%
Hispanic or Latino (of any race)	96	1.07
Central American, ex. Mexican	5	0.06
Guatemalan	1	0.01
Honduran	2	0.02
Nicaraguan	1	0.01
Panamanian	1	0.01
Cuban	2	0.02
Dominican Republic	5	0.06
Mexican	47	0.52
Puerto Rican	19	0.21
South American	4	0.04
Colombian	1	0.01
Ecuadorian	1	0.01
Peruvian	1	0.01
Venezuelan	1	0.01
Other Hispanic or Latino	14	0.16

*Notes: † The Census 2010 population figure is used to calculate the percentages in the Hispanic Origin and Race categories. Ancestry percentages are based on the 2006-2010 American Community Survey population (not shown); ‡ Numbers in parentheses indicate the number of people reporting a single ancestry; * Numbers in parentheses indicate the number of persons reporting this race alone, not in combination with any other race; Please refer to the Explanation of Data for more information.*

Race*	Population	%
African-American/Black (58)	112	1.24
Not Hispanic (51)	105	1.17
Hispanic (7)	7	0.08
American Indian/Alaska Native (17)	48	0.53
Not Hispanic (15)	39	0.43
Hispanic (2)	9	0.10
Aleut *(Alaska Native)* (1)	1	0.01
Blackfeet (1)	1	0.01
Cherokee (0)	4	0.04
Chippewa (0)	2	0.02
Comanche (1)	1	0.01
Inupiat *(Alaska Native)* (1)	1	0.01
Iroquois (1)	1	0.01
Navajo (0)	4	0.04
Sioux (1)	4	0.04
Asian (631)	671	7.45
Not Hispanic (631)	669	7.43
Hispanic (0)	2	0.02
Cambodian (3)	3	0.03
Chinese, ex. Taiwanese (12)	16	0.18
Filipino (15)	24	0.27
Hmong (528)	538	5.97
Indian (19)	22	0.24
Japanese (1)	6	0.07
Korean (8)	17	0.19
Laotian (5)	5	0.06
Taiwanese (8)	8	0.09
Thai (0)	5	0.06
Vietnamese (3)	6	0.07
Hawaii Native/Pacific Islander (4)	11	0.12
Not Hispanic (4)	11	0.12
Native Hawaiian (4)	10	0.11
White (8,140)	8,267	91.80
Not Hispanic (8,082)	8,198	91.04
Hispanic (58)	69	0.77

Howard

Place Type: Village
County: Brown
Population: 17,399†

Ancestry‡	Population	%
American (463)	463	2.77
Arab (15)	26	0.16
Lebanese (15)	15	0.09
Syrian (0)	11	0.07
Armenian (13)	13	0.08
Austrian (0)	37	0.22
Belgian (295)	1,379	8.24
British (0)	23	0.14
Canadian (9)	25	0.15
Czech (152)	487	2.91
Czechoslovakian (14)	55	0.33
Danish (26)	187	1.12
Dutch (243)	1,128	6.74
English (26)	591	3.53
European (163)	201	1.20
Finnish (134)	250	1.49
French, ex. Basque (168)	1,672	9.99
French Canadian (155)	518	3.10
German (2,664)	7,185	42.93
Greek (20)	75	0.45
Hungarian (14)	27	0.16
Irish (284)	1,715	10.25
Italian (123)	576	3.44
Lithuanian (12)	44	0.26
Norwegian (274)	800	4.78
Pennsylvania German (15)	15	0.09
Polish (705)	2,275	13.59
Portuguese (0)	16	0.10
Romanian (0)	15	0.09
Russian (40)	75	0.45
Scandinavian (61)	61	0.36
Scotch-Irish (129)	269	1.61
Scottish (18)	166	0.99
Slovak (0)	10	0.06
Swedish (89)	248	1.48
Swiss (0)	79	0.47
Ukrainian (36)	144	0.86
Welsh (0)	45	0.27
West Indian, ex. Hispanic (0)	14	0.08
Haitian (0)	14	0.08
Yugoslavian (15)	15	0.09

Hispanic Origin	Population	%
Hispanic or Latino (of any race)	410	2.36
Central American, ex. Mexican	31	0.18
Costa Rican	1	0.01
Guatemalan	7	0.04
Honduran	7	0.04
Nicaraguan	1	0.01
Panamanian	4	0.02
Salvadoran	11	0.06
Cuban	5	0.03
Dominican Republic	5	0.03
Mexican	245	1.41
Puerto Rican	81	0.47
South American	17	0.10
Argentinean	1	0.01
Bolivian	2	0.01
Chilean	4	0.02
Colombian	4	0.02
Ecuadorian	3	0.02
Paraguayan	1	0.01
Peruvian	2	0.01
Other Hispanic or Latino	26	0.15

Race*	Population	%
African-American/Black (261)	373	2.14
Not Hispanic (253)	352	2.02
Hispanic (8)	21	0.12
American Indian/Alaska Native (205)	318	1.83
Not Hispanic (189)	292	1.68
Hispanic (16)	26	0.15
Apache (1)	2	0.01
Blackfeet (1)	1	0.01
Cherokee (7)	18	0.10
Chippewa (24)	32	0.18
Choctaw (0)	5	0.03
Crow (1)	1	0.01
Iroquois (58)	102	0.59
Menominee (24)	34	0.20
Mexican American Ind. (1)	1	0.01
Ottawa (4)	4	0.02
Potawatomi (1)	3	0.02
Sioux (5)	5	0.03
Spanish American Ind. (0)	2	0.01
Asian (229)	269	1.55
Not Hispanic (228)	267	1.53
Hispanic (1)	2	0.01
Chinese, ex. Taiwanese (14)	22	0.13
Filipino (14)	21	0.12
Hmong (119)	133	0.76
Indian (27)	33	0.19
Japanese (3)	8	0.05
Korean (11)	20	0.11
Laotian (0)	2	0.01
Vietnamese (4)	6	0.03
Hawaii Native/Pacific Islander (4)	12	0.07
Not Hispanic (4)	11	0.06
Hispanic (0)	1	0.01
Guamanian/Chamorro (0)	2	0.01
Native Hawaiian (4)	9	0.05
White (16,316)	16,582	95.30
Not Hispanic (16,070)	16,300	93.68
Hispanic (246)	282	1.62

Hudson

Place Type: City
County: St. Croix
Population: 12,719†

Ancestry‡	Population	%
African, Sub-Saharan (14)	142	1.15
African (14)	142	1.15
American (310)	310	2.51
Arab (0)	67	0.54
Arab (0)	23	0.19
Jordanian (0)	44	0.36
Assyrian/Chaldean/Syriac (0)	12	0.10
Austrian (0)	32	0.26
Belgian (132)	166	1.35
Canadian (18)	18	0.15
Croatian (0)	18	0.15
Czech (12)	123	1.00
Danish (72)	206	1.67
Dutch (50)	192	1.56
Eastern European (14)	14	0.11
English (121)	1,229	9.97
European (126)	126	1.02
Finnish (0)	144	1.17
French, ex. Basque (34)	587	4.76
French Canadian (15)	147	1.19
German (1,800)	5,298	42.96
Greek (0)	16	0.13
Hungarian (11)	31	0.25
Icelander (0)	12	0.10
Irish (183)	1,547	12.54
Italian (165)	467	3.79
Latvian (0)	11	0.09
Lithuanian (8)	8	0.06
New Zealander (14)	14	0.11
Northern European (16)	16	0.13
Norwegian (591)	2,239	18.15
Pennsylvania German (21)	21	0.17
Polish (120)	727	5.89
Russian (0)	66	0.54
Scandinavian (196)	246	1.99
Scotch-Irish (106)	179	1.45
Scottish (33)	161	1.31
Serbian (0)	11	0.09
Swedish (252)	1,096	8.89
Swiss (20)	123	1.00
Ukrainian (12)	24	0.19
Welsh (7)	155	1.26
Yugoslavian (0)	17	0.14

Hispanic Origin	Population	%
Hispanic or Latino (of any race)	347	2.73
Central American, ex. Mexican	17	0.13
Costa Rican	5	0.04
Guatemalan	8	0.06
Panamanian	2	0.02
Salvadoran	2	0.02
Cuban	10	0.08
Dominican Republic	1	0.01
Mexican	228	1.79
Puerto Rican	25	0.20
South American	38	0.30
Argentinean	4	0.03
Chilean	1	0.01
Colombian	15	0.12
Ecuadorian	4	0.03
Peruvian	12	0.09
Venezuelan	2	0.02
Other Hispanic or Latino	28	0.22

Race*	Population	%
African-American/Black (119)	203	1.60
Not Hispanic (116)	191	1.50
Hispanic (3)	12	0.09
American Indian/Alaska Native (43)	110	0.86
Not Hispanic (35)	94	0.74
Hispanic (8)	16	0.13
Apache (0)	2	0.02
Blackfeet (0)	3	0.02
Cherokee (1)	4	0.03
Chippewa (10)	16	0.13
Choctaw (0)	1	0.01
Comanche (0)	2	0.02
Cree (0)	3	0.02
Crow (0)	1	0.01
Delaware (0)	1	0.01
Iroquois (4)	4	0.03
Mexican American Ind. (2)	4	0.03
Potawatomi (0)	1	0.01

SECTION TWO

*Notes: † The Census 2010 population figure is used to calculate the percentages in the Hispanic Origin and Race categories. Ancestry percentages are based on the 2006-2010 American Community Survey population (not shown); ‡ Numbers in parentheses indicate the number of people reporting a single ancestry; * Numbers in parentheses indicate the number of persons reporting this race alone, not in combination with any other race; Please refer to the Explanation of Data for more information.*

Pueblo (0)	1	0.01
Sioux (0)	7	0.06
South American Ind. (6)	6	0.05
Yakama (0)	1	0.01
Asian (175)	249	1.96
Not Hispanic (174)	248	1.95
Hispanic (1)	1	0.01
Chinese, ex. Taiwanese (24)	25	0.20
Filipino (15)	34	0.27
Hmong (46)	48	0.38
Indian (25)	35	0.28
Indonesian (1)	1	0.01
Japanese (9)	16	0.13
Korean (30)	52	0.41
Laotian (5)	5	0.04
Nepalese (2)	2	0.02
Thai (0)	3	0.02
Vietnamese (15)	20	0.16
Hawaii Native/Pacific Islander (4)	12	0.09
Not Hispanic (4)	11	0.09
Hispanic (0)	1	0.01
Guamanian/Chamorro (1)	1	0.01
Samoan (0)	3	0.02
Tongan (0)	2	0.02
White (12,057)	12,283	96.57
Not Hispanic (11,833)	12,027	94.56
Hispanic (224)	256	2.01

Hudson

Place Type: Town
County: St. Croix
Population: 8,461†

Ancestry‡	Population	%
American (235)	235	2.85
Austrian (0)	69	0.84
Belgian (0)	10	0.12
British (15)	23	0.28
Croatian (9)	38	0.46
Czech (31)	174	2.11
Czechoslovakian (0)	11	0.13
Danish (34)	211	2.56
Dutch (56)	207	2.51
Eastern European (0)	12	0.15
English (54)	557	6.75
European (28)	28	0.34
Finnish (13)	112	1.36
French, ex. Basque (28)	332	4.03
French Canadian (48)	128	1.55
German (1,562)	4,511	54.70
Greek (10)	21	0.25
Hungarian (36)	110	1.33
Iranian (16)	33	0.40
Irish (152)	1,143	13.86
Italian (16)	288	3.49
Lithuanian (17)	17	0.21
Northern European (61)	78	0.95
Norwegian (245)	1,136	13.77
Pennsylvania German (0)	18	0.22
Polish (88)	438	5.31
Russian (13)	54	0.65
Scandinavian (26)	69	0.84
Scotch-Irish (0)	35	0.42
Scottish (0)	115	1.39
Slovak (23)	66	0.80
Swedish (200)	872	10.57
Swiss (0)	35	0.42
Ukrainian (24)	24	0.29
Welsh (0)	20	0.24

Hispanic Origin	Population	%
Hispanic or Latino (of any race)	126	1.49
Central American, ex. Mexican	12	0.14
Costa Rican	2	0.02
Guatemalan	10	0.12
Cuban	1	0.01
Mexican	64	0.76
Puerto Rican	10	0.12
South American	14	0.17
Chilean	2	0.02
Colombian	9	0.11
Ecuadorian	2	0.02
Peruvian	1	0.01
Other Hispanic or Latino	25	0.30

Race*	Population	%
African-American/Black (34)	49	0.58
Not Hispanic (34)	48	0.57
Hispanic (0)	1	0.01
American Indian/Alaska Native (29)	73	0.86
Not Hispanic (22)	64	0.76
Hispanic (7)	9	0.11
Cherokee (1)	9	0.11
Chippewa (6)	21	0.25
Iroquois (3)	4	0.05
Lumbee (4)	4	0.05
Mexican American Ind. (6)	8	0.09
Sioux (1)	2	0.02
Asian (169)	208	2.46
Not Hispanic (168)	207	2.45
Hispanic (1)	1	0.01
Cambodian (5)	5	0.06
Chinese, ex. Taiwanese (12)	16	0.19
Filipino (10)	13	0.15
Hmong (96)	97	1.15
Indian (5)	11	0.13
Japanese (6)	10	0.12
Korean (20)	32	0.38
Laotian (6)	8	0.09
Nepalese (2)	2	0.02
Vietnamese (5)	9	0.11
Hawaii Native/Pacific Islander (1)	10	0.12
Not Hispanic (1)	10	0.12
Native Hawaiian (1)	3	0.04
White (8,096)	8,203	96.95
Not Hispanic (8,001)	8,103	95.77
Hispanic (95)	100	1.18

Janesville

Place Type: City
County: Rock
Population: 63,575†

Ancestry‡	Population	%
African, Sub-Saharan (876)	968	1.53
African (876)	946	1.49
Nigerian (0)	22	0.03
Alsatian (0)	8	0.01
American (2,959)	2,959	4.66
Arab (59)	127	0.20
Egyptian (0)	8	0.01
Lebanese (59)	119	0.19
Austrian (54)	237	0.37
Basque (41)	41	0.06
Belgian (16)	234	0.37
Brazilian (6)	6	0.01
British (62)	141	0.22
Canadian (9)	48	0.08
Croatian (15)	84	0.13
Czech (209)	696	1.10
Czechoslovakian (35)	36	0.06
Danish (173)	775	1.22
Dutch (367)	1,395	2.20
Eastern European (38)	45	0.07
English (1,739)	7,785	12.27
European (717)	785	1.24
Finnish (127)	316	0.50
French, ex. Basque (357)	2,558	4.03
French Canadian (131)	276	0.44
German (9,861)	26,507	41.78
Greek (30)	98	0.15
Hungarian (31)	173	0.27
Irish (2,140)	10,577	16.67
Italian (579)	2,057	3.24
Latvian (59)	59	0.09
Lithuanian (63)	166	0.26
Luxemburger (12)	36	0.06
Northern European (25)	25	0.04
Norwegian (2,490)	8,447	13.31
Pennsylvania German (0)	8	0.01
Polish (622)	2,769	4.36
Portuguese (8)	146	0.23
Romanian (32)	68	0.11
Russian (140)	315	0.50
Scandinavian (113)	193	0.30
Scotch-Irish (124)	674	1.06
Scottish (204)	992	1.56
Slavic (0)	25	0.04
Slovak (0)	40	0.06
Slovene (10)	64	0.10
Swedish (216)	1,515	2.39
Swiss (116)	957	1.51
Ukrainian (48)	67	0.11
Welsh (47)	522	0.82
West Indian, ex. Hispanic (18)	18	0.03
Haitian (18)	18	0.03

Hispanic Origin	Population	%
Hispanic or Latino (of any race)	3,421	5.38
Central American, ex. Mexican	96	0.15
Costa Rican	6	0.01
Guatemalan	21	0.03
Honduran	31	0.05
Nicaraguan	5	0.01
Panamanian	8	0.01
Salvadoran	25	0.04
Cuban	30	0.05
Dominican Republic	14	0.02
Mexican	2,851	4.48
Puerto Rican	179	0.28
South American	79	0.12
Argentinean	12	0.02
Chilean	2	<0.01
Colombian	19	0.03
Ecuadorian	8	0.01
Peruvian	10	0.02
Uruguayan	19	0.03
Venezuelan	6	0.01
Other South American	3	<0.01
Other Hispanic or Latino	172	0.27

Race*	Population	%
African-American/Black (1,633)	2,307	3.63
Not Hispanic (1,574)	2,189	3.44
Hispanic (59)	118	0.19
American Indian/Alaska Native (187)	454	0.71
Not Hispanic (149)	367	0.58
Hispanic (38)	87	0.14
Apache (4)	7	0.01
Blackfeet (4)	12	0.02
Canadian/French Am. Ind. (0)	7	0.01
Cherokee (16)	57	0.09
Chickasaw (0)	1	<0.01
Chippewa (27)	40	0.06
Choctaw (0)	4	0.01
Colville (1)	1	<0.01
Comanche (2)	4	0.01
Creek (2)	4	0.01
Crow (0)	1	<0.01
Iroquois (15)	25	0.04
Lumbee (0)	2	<0.01
Menominee (8)	13	0.02
Mexican American Ind. (20)	23	0.04
Navajo (2)	3	<0.01
Ottawa (6)	13	0.02
Pima (1)	1	<0.01
Potawatomi (5)	5	0.01
Sioux (3)	15	0.02
South American Ind. (0)	1	<0.01
Tohono O'Odham (3)	3	<0.01
Asian (857)	1,108	1.74
Not Hispanic (846)	1,078	1.70
Hispanic (11)	30	0.05
Bangladeshi (5)	5	0.01
Cambodian (249)	293	0.46
Chinese, ex. Taiwanese (130)	163	0.26
Filipino (82)	151	0.24
Hmong (14)	16	0.03

*Notes: † The Census 2010 population figure is used to calculate the percentages in the Hispanic Origin and Race categories. Ancestry percentages are based on the 2006-2010 American Community Survey population (not shown); ‡ Numbers in parentheses indicate the number of people reporting a single ancestry; * Numbers in parentheses indicate the number of persons reporting this race alone, not in combination with any other race; Please refer to the Explanation of Data for more information.*

Indian (90)	114	0.18
Japanese (12)	43	0.07
Korean (64)	110	0.17
Laotian (50)	66	0.10
Malaysian (1)	1	<0.01
Nepalese (1)	1	<0.01
Pakistani (11)	13	0.02
Sri Lankan (1)	1	<0.01
Taiwanese (5)	6	0.01
Thai (15)	27	0.04
Vietnamese (60)	71	0.11
Hawaii Native/Pacific Islander (22)	68	0.11
Not Hispanic (21)	63	0.10
Hispanic (1)	5	0.01
Guamanian/Chamorro (4)	5	0.01
Marshallese (1)	1	<0.01
Native Hawaiian (8)	15	0.02
Samoan (3)	19	0.03
Tongan (1)	1	<0.01
White (58,299)	59,563	93.69
Not Hispanic (56,465)	57,481	90.41
Hispanic (1,834)	2,082	3.27

Jefferson

Place Type: City
County: Jefferson
Population: 7,973[†]

Ancestry[‡]	Population	%
American (335)	335	4.23
Arab (11)	11	0.14
Jordanian (11)	11	0.14
Austrian (0)	18	0.23
Belgian (0)	8	0.10
British (0)	10	0.13
Canadian (21)	21	0.27
Czech (7)	38	0.48
Czechoslovakian (0)	10	0.13
Danish (11)	50	0.63
Dutch (8)	143	1.81
Eastern European (10)	10	0.13
English (102)	548	6.93
European (41)	41	0.52
Finnish (0)	15	0.19
French, ex. Basque (10)	146	1.85
French Canadian (9)	9	0.11
German (2,363)	4,330	54.72
Greek (0)	28	0.35
Hungarian (0)	34	0.43
Irish (52)	558	7.05
Italian (14)	91	1.15
Lithuanian (0)	29	0.37
Norwegian (211)	812	10.26
Polish (74)	278	3.51
Romanian (14)	14	0.18
Russian (14)	32	0.40
Scotch-Irish (13)	35	0.44
Scottish (6)	54	0.68
Swedish (19)	60	0.76
Swiss (9)	38	0.48
Ukrainian (0)	24	0.30
Welsh (0)	31	0.39

Hispanic Origin	Population	%
Hispanic or Latino (of any race)	937	11.75
Central American, ex. Mexican	16	0.20
Guatemalan	13	0.16
Nicaraguan	3	0.04
Cuban	5	0.06
Dominican Republic	1	0.01
Mexican	810	10.16
Puerto Rican	47	0.59
South American	3	0.04
Chilean	2	0.03
Peruvian	1	0.01
Other Hispanic or Latino	55	0.69

Race*	Population	%
African-American/Black (57)	95	1.19
Not Hispanic (41)	73	0.92
Hispanic (16)	22	0.28
American Indian/Alaska Native (34)	67	0.84
Not Hispanic (31)	57	0.71
Hispanic (3)	10	0.13
Alaska Athabascan *(Ala. Nat.)* (1)	1	0.01
Apache (2)	2	0.03
Cherokee (1)	5	0.06
Chippewa (5)	10	0.13
Creek (1)	1	0.01
Crow (0)	2	0.03
Iroquois (1)	1	0.01
Menominee (1)	3	0.04
Mexican American Ind. (1)	2	0.03
Ottawa (3)	5	0.06
Paiute (0)	1	0.01
Pueblo (0)	1	0.01
Asian (57)	80	1.00
Not Hispanic (49)	68	0.85
Hispanic (8)	12	0.15
Chinese, ex. Taiwanese (10)	11	0.14
Filipino (3)	10	0.13
Hmong (13)	14	0.18
Indian (16)	20	0.25
Japanese (3)	9	0.11
Korean (1)	5	0.06
Vietnamese (4)	6	0.08
Hawaii Native/Pacific Islander (5)	6	0.08
Not Hispanic (5)	6	0.08
Native Hawaiian (0)	4	0.05
Samoan (0)	5	0.06
White (7,272)	7,383	92.60
Not Hispanic (6,833)	6,905	86.60
Hispanic (439)	478	6.00

Kaukauna

Place Type: City
County: Outagamie
Population: 15,462[†]

Ancestry[‡]	Population	%
Albanian (14)	14	0.09
American (664)	664	4.40
Austrian (0)	22	0.15
Belgian (76)	351	2.33
British (16)	28	0.19
Czech (69)	97	0.64
Czechoslovakian (0)	16	0.11
Danish (37)	174	1.15
Dutch (779)	2,534	16.81
English (153)	605	4.01
European (33)	33	0.22
Finnish (8)	66	0.44
French, ex. Basque (106)	798	5.29
French Canadian (113)	354	2.35
German (3,308)	8,603	57.07
Greek (17)	47	0.31
Hungarian (0)	19	0.13
Irish (293)	2,010	13.33
Italian (142)	295	1.96
Lithuanian (0)	20	0.13
Norwegian (154)	637	4.23
Polish (168)	822	5.45
Romanian (9)	34	0.23
Russian (0)	22	0.15
Scotch-Irish (25)	54	0.36
Scottish (0)	33	0.22
Swedish (42)	342	2.27
Swiss (9)	69	0.46
Ukrainian (24)	37	0.25
Welsh (0)	6	0.04
Yugoslavian (0)	31	0.21

Hispanic Origin	Population	%
Hispanic or Latino (of any race)	407	2.63
Central American, ex. Mexican	15	0.10
Guatemalan	7	0.05
Honduran	7	0.05
Salvadoran	1	0.01
Cuban	1	0.01
Mexican	313	2.02
Puerto Rican	33	0.21
South American	19	0.12
Chilean	1	0.01
Colombian	6	0.04
Ecuadorian	2	0.01
Peruvian	2	0.01
Venezuelan	8	0.05
Other Hispanic or Latino	26	0.17

Race*	Population	%
African-American/Black (111)	199	1.29
Not Hispanic (110)	195	1.26
Hispanic (1)	4	0.03
American Indian/Alaska Native (127)	236	1.53
Not Hispanic (120)	217	1.40
Hispanic (7)	19	0.12
Cherokee (2)	5	0.03
Chippewa (16)	26	0.17
Iroquois (33)	64	0.41
Menominee (18)	31	0.20
Mexican American Ind. (0)	1	0.01
Navajo (1)	1	0.01
Potawatomi (2)	4	0.03
Pueblo (3)	3	0.02
Puget Sound Salish (1)	1	0.01
Sioux (2)	2	0.01
Asian (207)	239	1.55
Not Hispanic (206)	237	1.53
Hispanic (1)	2	0.01
Cambodian (1)	1	0.01
Chinese, ex. Taiwanese (8)	9	0.06
Filipino (2)	9	0.06
Hmong (156)	162	1.05
Indian (15)	19	0.12
Japanese (4)	11	0.07
Korean (9)	15	0.10
Laotian (6)	6	0.04
Vietnamese (2)	2	0.01
Hawaii Native/Pacific Islander (6)	15	0.10
Not Hispanic (6)	14	0.09
Hispanic (0)	1	0.01
Guamanian/Chamorro (0)	2	0.01
Native Hawaiian (3)	7	0.05
White (14,610)	14,852	96.05
Not Hispanic (14,401)	14,606	94.46
Hispanic (209)	246	1.59

Kenosha

Place Type: City
County: Kenosha
Population: 99,218[†]

Ancestry[‡]	Population	%
African, Sub-Saharan (556)	713	0.73
African (471)	628	0.64
Liberian (44)	44	0.04
Nigerian (41)	41	0.04
Albanian (97)	149	0.15
American (2,375)	2,375	2.42
Arab (96)	149	0.15
Arab (35)	52	0.05
Egyptian (11)	21	0.02
Lebanese (0)	11	0.01
Moroccan (7)	7	0.01
Palestinian (27)	27	0.03
Syrian (16)	31	0.03
Armenian (13)	71	0.07
Assyrian/Chaldean/Syriac (0)	19	0.02
Austrian (49)	233	0.24
Belgian (10)	301	0.31
Brazilian (11)	43	0.04
British (85)	290	0.30
Bulgarian (0)	45	0.05
Cajun (0)	19	0.02
Canadian (78)	153	0.16
Croatian (54)	308	0.31
Czech (160)	849	0.86

*Notes: † The Census 2010 population figure is used to calculate the percentages in the Hispanic Origin and Race categories. Ancestry percentages are based on the 2006-2010 American Community Survey population (not shown); ‡ Numbers in parentheses indicate the number of people reporting a single ancestry; * Numbers in parentheses indicate the number of persons reporting this race alone, not in combination with any other race; Please refer to the Explanation of Data for more information.*

Czechoslovakian (47)	108	0.11
Danish (325)	1,951	1.98
Dutch (372)	1,747	1.78
Eastern European (22)	22	0.02
English (1,299)	6,275	6.38
Estonian (13)	13	0.01
European (617)	711	0.72
Finnish (369)	719	0.73
French, ex. Basque (326)	3,063	3.12
French Canadian (115)	845	0.86
German (8,035)	28,280	28.77
Greek (196)	456	0.46
Hungarian (76)	687	0.70
Iranian (21)	21	0.02
Irish (1,800)	11,701	11.90
Israeli (0)	15	0.02
Italian (3,924)	10,786	10.97
Lithuanian (248)	885	0.90
Luxemburger (13)	64	0.07
Macedonian (30)	30	0.03
Northern European (16)	23	0.02
Norwegian (639)	2,895	2.95
Pennsylvania German (0)	31	0.03
Polish (2,103)	8,503	8.65
Portuguese (0)	17	0.02
Romanian (27)	110	0.11
Russian (162)	675	0.69
Scandinavian (158)	269	0.27
Scotch-Irish (241)	945	0.96
Scottish (114)	1,309	1.33
Serbian (237)	409	0.42
Slavic (0)	92	0.09
Slovak (207)	568	0.58
Slovene (50)	148	0.15
Swedish (406)	2,719	2.77
Swiss (47)	234	0.24
Turkish (7)	7	0.01
Ukrainian (52)	217	0.22
Welsh (107)	471	0.48
West Indian, ex. Hispanic (194)	234	0.24
Barbadian (0)	8	0.01
Belizean (141)	150	0.15
Haitian (0)	10	0.01
Jamaican (41)	54	0.05
West Indian (12)	12	0.01
Yugoslavian (72)	180	0.18

Hispanic Origin	Population	%
Hispanic or Latino (of any race)	16,130	16.26
Central American, ex. Mexican	562	0.57
Costa Rican	15	0.02
Guatemalan	208	0.21
Honduran	149	0.15
Nicaraguan	89	0.09
Panamanian	19	0.02
Salvadoran	82	0.08
Cuban	131	0.13
Dominican Republic	66	0.07
Mexican	12,363	12.46
Puerto Rican	1,698	1.71
South American	210	0.21
Argentinean	34	0.03
Bolivian	1	<0.01
Chilean	19	0.02
Colombian	69	0.07
Ecuadorian	31	0.03
Paraguayan	7	0.01
Peruvian	27	0.03
Uruguayan	3	<0.01
Venezuelan	15	0.02
Other South American	4	<0.01
Other Hispanic or Latino	1,100	1.11

Race*	Population	%
African-American/Black (9,876)	11,826	11.92
Not Hispanic (9,540)	11,106	11.19
Hispanic (336)	720	0.73
American Indian/Alaska Native (578)	1,353	1.36
Not Hispanic (332)	910	0.92
Hispanic (246)	443	0.45
Apache (9)	33	0.03
Arapaho (0)	1	<0.01
Blackfeet (3)	52	0.05
Canadian/French Am. Ind. (1)	4	<0.01
Cherokee (27)	191	0.19
Chickasaw (1)	5	0.01
Chippewa (103)	180	0.18
Choctaw (2)	29	0.03
Cree (2)	3	<0.01
Creek (1)	5	0.01
Hopi (0)	3	<0.01
Houma (0)	1	<0.01
Iroquois (18)	43	0.04
Lumbee (5)	8	0.01
Menominee (37)	52	0.05
Mexican American Ind. (121)	146	0.15
Navajo (5)	9	0.01
Ottawa (0)	3	<0.01
Potawatomi (12)	16	0.02
Seminole (0)	1	<0.01
Shoshone (0)	2	<0.01
Sioux (17)	37	0.04
South American Ind. (0)	6	0.01
Tlingit-Haida *(Alaska Native)* (1)	2	<0.01
Yaqui (1)	3	<0.01
Yup'ik *(Alaska Native)* (2)	2	<0.01
Asian (1,671)	2,324	2.34
Not Hispanic (1,637)	2,211	2.23
Hispanic (34)	113	0.11
Burmese (4)	4	<0.01
Cambodian (11)	17	0.02
Chinese, ex. Taiwanese (209)	296	0.30
Filipino (396)	634	0.64
Hmong (40)	43	0.04
Indian (477)	577	0.58
Indonesian (4)	5	0.01
Japanese (58)	166	0.17
Korean (161)	248	0.25
Laotian (1)	3	<0.01
Malaysian (3)	3	<0.01
Nepalese (4)	4	<0.01
Pakistani (114)	142	0.14
Sri Lankan (4)	4	<0.01
Taiwanese (4)	17	0.02
Thai (15)	36	0.04
Vietnamese (80)	108	0.11
Hawaii Native/Pacific Islander (61)	176	0.18
Not Hispanic (48)	118	0.12
Hispanic (13)	58	0.06
Fijian (1)	3	<0.01
Guamanian/Chamorro (28)	43	0.04
Native Hawaiian (17)	51	0.05
Samoan (4)	13	0.01
White (76,519)	79,810	80.44
Not Hispanic (68,967)	71,174	71.73
Hispanic (7,552)	8,636	8.70

La Crosse

Place Type: City
County: La Crosse
Population: 51,320†

Ancestry‡	Population	%
African, Sub-Saharan (63)	116	0.23
African (48)	89	0.17
Ethiopian (12)	12	0.02
Liberian (0)	12	0.02
Other Sub-Saharan African (3)	3	0.01
Albanian (0)	19	0.04
American (1,226)	1,226	2.39
Arab (284)	427	0.83
Arab (12)	12	0.02
Egyptian (11)	11	0.02
Lebanese (75)	124	0.24
Palestinian (23)	23	0.04
Syrian (24)	118	0.23
Other Arab (139)	139	0.27
Armenian (12)	25	0.05
Australian (30)	68	0.13
Austrian (40)	253	0.49
Belgian (20)	133	0.26
British (54)	151	0.29
Bulgarian (24)	24	0.05
Cajun (0)	8	0.02
Canadian (13)	67	0.13
Carpatho Rusyn (8)	8	0.02
Croatian (102)	102	0.20
Czech (227)	1,156	2.26
Czechoslovakian (22)	67	0.13
Danish (80)	360	0.70
Dutch (205)	1,019	1.99
Eastern European (21)	21	0.04
English (509)	3,275	6.39
Estonian (9)	9	0.02
European (373)	387	0.76
Finnish (95)	400	0.78
French, ex. Basque (184)	1,534	2.99
French Canadian (136)	441	0.86
German (8,955)	23,911	46.67
Greek (9)	42	0.08
Hungarian (0)	51	0.10
Icelander (0)	10	0.02
Irish (1,531)	7,987	15.59
Italian (410)	1,778	3.47
Lithuanian (0)	51	0.10
Luxemburger (17)	61	0.12
Maltese (0)	7	0.01
Northern European (29)	29	0.06
Norwegian (3,443)	9,468	18.48
Pennsylvania German (0)	23	0.04
Polish (885)	3,362	6.56
Portuguese (22)	22	0.04
Russian (41)	139	0.27
Scandinavian (65)	159	0.31
Scotch-Irish (152)	384	0.75
Scottish (118)	644	1.26
Serbian (0)	23	0.04
Slavic (0)	23	0.04
Slovak (22)	41	0.08
Slovene (16)	49	0.10
Swedish (393)	1,355	2.64
Swiss (71)	439	0.86
Turkish (0)	26	0.05
Ukrainian (54)	79	0.15
Welsh (0)	396	0.77
West Indian, ex. Hispanic (13)	51	0.10
Barbadian (13)	13	0.03
Jamaican (0)	38	0.07
Yugoslavian (0)	21	0.04

Hispanic Origin	Population	%
Hispanic or Latino (of any race)	1,012	1.97
Central American, ex. Mexican	45	0.09
Costa Rican	3	0.01
Guatemalan	19	0.04
Honduran	6	0.01
Nicaraguan	5	0.01
Panamanian	1	<0.01
Salvadoran	11	0.02
Cuban	67	0.13
Dominican Republic	22	0.04
Mexican	581	1.13
Puerto Rican	128	0.25
South American	64	0.12
Argentinean	7	0.01
Bolivian	1	<0.01
Chilean	3	0.01
Colombian	18	0.04
Ecuadorian	13	0.03
Paraguayan	1	<0.01
Peruvian	15	0.03
Uruguayan	3	0.01
Venezuelan	3	0.01
Other Hispanic or Latino	105	0.20

Race*	Population	%
African-American/Black (1,155)	1,660	3.23
Not Hispanic (1,114)	1,574	3.07
Hispanic (41)	86	0.17

*Notes: † The Census 2010 population figure is used to calculate the percentages in the Hispanic Origin and Race categories. Ancestry percentages are based on the 2006-2010 American Community Survey population (not shown); ‡ Numbers in parentheses indicate the number of people reporting a single ancestry; * Numbers in parentheses indicate the number of persons reporting this race alone, not in combination with any other race; Please refer to the Explanation of Data for more information.*

American Indian/Alaska Native (286)	598	1.17
Not Hispanic (253)	536	1.04
Hispanic (33)	62	0.12
Aleut *(Alaska Native)* (1)	2	<0.01
Apache (0)	2	<0.01
Arapaho (1)	1	<0.01
Blackfeet (0)	15	0.03
Canadian/French Am. Ind. (0)	1	<0.01
Cherokee (9)	49	0.10
Chippewa (51)	86	0.17
Choctaw (0)	3	0.01
Comanche (2)	2	<0.01
Cree (0)	1	<0.01
Creek (2)	2	<0.01
Crow (0)	2	<0.01
Delaware (0)	1	<0.01
Inupiat *(Alaska Native)* (1)	3	0.01
Iroquois (8)	16	0.03
Lumbee (1)	3	0.01
Menominee (5)	12	0.02
Mexican American Ind. (8)	12	0.02
Navajo (2)	3	0.01
Pima (3)	3	0.01
Potawatomi (4)	8	0.02
Seminole (1)	2	<0.01
Shoshone (0)	2	<0.01
Sioux (14)	26	0.05
Spanish American Ind. (1)	1	<0.01
Yaqui (0)	3	0.01
Yup'ik *(Alaska Native)* (1)	1	<0.01
Asian (2,490)	2,802	5.46
Not Hispanic (2,482)	2,778	5.41
Hispanic (8)	24	0.05
Bangladeshi (8)	11	0.02
Cambodian (6)	8	0.02
Chinese, ex. Taiwanese (233)	277	0.54
Filipino (49)	102	0.20
Hmong (1,475)	1,563	3.05
Indian (176)	232	0.45
Indonesian (3)	7	0.01
Japanese (46)	83	0.16
Korean (98)	130	0.25
Laotian (34)	38	0.07
Nepalese (4)	4	0.01
Pakistani (27)	30	0.06
Taiwanese (15)	17	0.03
Thai (9)	21	0.04
Vietnamese (83)	112	0.22
Hawaii Native/Pacific Islander (12)	47	0.09
Not Hispanic (12)	40	0.08
Hispanic (0)	7	0.01
Fijian (0)	1	<0.01
Guamanian/Chamorro (3)	5	0.01
Native Hawaiian (4)	14	0.03
Samoan (1)	6	0.01
White (46,072)	47,091	91.76
Not Hispanic (45,423)	46,338	90.29
Hispanic (649)	753	1.47

Lake Geneva

Place Type: City
County: Walworth
Population: 7,651†

Ancestry‡	Population	%
American (167)	167	2.17
Australian (0)	9	0.12
Austrian (0)	19	0.25
Belgian (13)	28	0.36
British (12)	12	0.16
Czech (15)	137	1.78
Czechoslovakian (0)	13	0.17
Danish (10)	75	0.98
Dutch (0)	246	3.20
Eastern European (0)	23	0.30
English (46)	838	10.90
European (37)	37	0.48
Finnish (13)	25	0.33
French, ex. Basque (13)	234	3.04
French Canadian (52)	65	0.85
German (760)	2,276	29.62
Greek (106)	190	2.47
Hungarian (13)	57	0.74
Irish (150)	865	11.26
Italian (190)	476	6.19
Latvian (0)	45	0.59
Lithuanian (11)	73	0.95
Norwegian (60)	322	4.19
Polish (196)	591	7.69
Scandinavian (14)	64	0.83
Scotch-Irish (15)	128	1.67
Scottish (72)	186	2.42
Serbian (0)	23	0.30
Slovak (0)	15	0.20
Swedish (91)	254	3.31
Swiss (0)	12	0.16
Ukrainian (9)	9	0.12
Welsh (0)	10	0.13

Hispanic Origin	Population	%
Hispanic or Latino (of any race)	1,323	17.29
Central American, ex. Mexican	41	0.54
Costa Rican	1	0.01
Guatemalan	2	0.03
Honduran	1	0.01
Nicaraguan	2	0.03
Salvadoran	35	0.46
Cuban	8	0.10
Dominican Republic	3	0.04
Mexican	1,127	14.73
Puerto Rican	35	0.46
South American	23	0.30
Argentinean	1	0.01
Bolivian	1	0.01
Colombian	1	0.01
Ecuadorian	3	0.04
Peruvian	17	0.22
Other Hispanic or Latino	86	1.12

Race*	Population	%
African-American/Black (45)	92	1.20
Not Hispanic (44)	74	0.97
Hispanic (1)	18	0.24
American Indian/Alaska Native (15)	42	0.55
Not Hispanic (14)	28	0.37
Hispanic (1)	14	0.18
Aleut *(Alaska Native)* (2)	2	0.03
Blackfeet (1)	1	0.01
Cherokee (1)	4	0.05
Chippewa (4)	5	0.07
Choctaw (0)	1	0.01
Menominee (0)	1	0.01
Mexican American Ind. (0)	3	0.04
Sioux (4)	4	0.05
South American Ind. (0)	9	0.12
Asian (111)	132	1.73
Not Hispanic (111)	130	1.70
Hispanic (0)	2	0.03
Burmese (6)	6	0.08
Cambodian (1)	1	0.01
Chinese, ex. Taiwanese (25)	26	0.34
Filipino (10)	26	0.34
Hmong (1)	1	0.01
Indian (30)	30	0.39
Japanese (14)	15	0.20
Korean (1)	2	0.03
Nepalese (1)	1	0.01
Pakistani (6)	6	0.08
Taiwanese (5)	5	0.07
Thai (1)	1	0.01
Vietnamese (9)	10	0.13
Hawaii Native/Pacific Islander (1)	8	0.10
Not Hispanic (1)	8	0.10
Fijian (1)	1	0.01
Guamanian/Chamorro (0)	1	0.01
Native Hawaiian (0)	1	0.01
White (6,704)	6,823	89.18
Not Hispanic (6,091)	6,155	80.45
Hispanic (613)	668	8.73

Lisbon

Place Type: Town
County: Waukesha
Population: 10,157†

Ancestry‡	Population	%
African, Sub-Saharan (14)	30	0.30
African (14)	14	0.14
South African (0)	16	0.16
Albanian (0)	3	0.03
American (314)	314	3.13
Austrian (14)	51	0.51
Belgian (7)	17	0.17
British (0)	2	0.02
Canadian (0)	6	0.06
Croatian (13)	115	1.14
Czech (6)	381	3.79
Czechoslovakian (0)	61	0.61
Danish (19)	144	1.43
Dutch (21)	107	1.07
English (111)	726	7.23
European (90)	116	1.15
Finnish (14)	140	1.39
French, ex. Basque (42)	540	5.38
French Canadian (22)	94	0.94
German (2,235)	5,808	57.83
Greek (8)	35	0.35
Hungarian (8)	192	1.91
Irish (255)	1,444	14.38
Italian (167)	785	7.82
Norwegian (58)	517	5.15
Polish (252)	1,422	14.16
Romanian (13)	82	0.82
Russian (21)	55	0.55
Scandinavian (0)	8	0.08
Scotch-Irish (33)	44	0.44
Scottish (77)	146	1.45
Slovak (31)	42	0.42
Slovene (13)	13	0.13
Swedish (42)	400	3.98
Swiss (21)	115	1.14
Ukrainian (36)	118	1.17
Welsh (0)	25	0.25
West Indian, ex. Hispanic (0)	4	0.04
Belizean (0)	4	0.04
Yugoslavian (0)	20	0.20

Hispanic Origin	Population	%
Hispanic or Latino (of any race)	142	1.40
Central American, ex. Mexican	9	0.09
Guatemalan	6	0.06
Nicaraguan	1	0.01
Panamanian	2	0.02
Cuban	4	0.04
Mexican	88	0.87
Puerto Rican	12	0.12
South American	7	0.07
Colombian	3	0.03
Peruvian	4	0.04
Other Hispanic or Latino	22	0.22

Race*	Population	%
African-American/Black (35)	54	0.53
Not Hispanic (35)	54	0.53
American Indian/Alaska Native (36)	67	0.66
Not Hispanic (30)	56	0.55
Hispanic (6)	11	0.11
Canadian/French Am. Ind. (0)	1	0.01
Cherokee (1)	1	0.01
Chippewa (6)	6	0.06
Choctaw (1)	4	0.04
Iroquois (9)	18	0.18
Menominee (1)	1	0.01
Mexican American Ind. (3)	10	0.10
Ottawa (1)	1	0.01
Potawatomi (2)	2	0.02
Sioux (0)	1	0.01
Asian (69)	100	0.98
Not Hispanic (69)	99	0.97

*Notes: † The Census 2010 population figure is used to calculate the percentages in the Hispanic Origin and Race categories. Ancestry percentages are based on the 2006-2010 American Community Survey population (not shown); ‡ Numbers in parentheses indicate the number of people reporting a single ancestry; * Numbers in parentheses indicate the number of persons reporting this race alone, not in combination with any other race; Please refer to the Explanation of Data for more information.*

Hispanic (0)	1	0.01
Chinese, ex. Taiwanese (15)	22	0.22
Filipino (9)	20	0.20
Hmong (0)	1	0.01
Indian (5)	12	0.12
Japanese (1)	1	0.01
Korean (19)	24	0.24
Malaysian (0)	1	0.01
Pakistani (5)	5	0.05
Taiwanese (2)	3	0.03
Thai (3)	3	0.03
Vietnamese (7)	9	0.09
Hawaii Native/Pacific Islander (9)	11	0.11
Not Hispanic (9)	11	0.11
Guamanian/Chamorro (5)	7	0.07
Samoan (4)	4	0.04
White (9,909)	9,995	98.41
Not Hispanic (9,796)	9,871	97.18
Hispanic (113)	124	1.22

Little Chute

Place Type: Village
County: Outagamie
Population: 10,449†

Ancestry‡	Population	%
Albanian (7)	7	0.07
American (445)	445	4.24
Austrian (8)	20	0.19
Belgian (17)	217	2.07
British (12)	36	0.34
Croatian (36)	110	1.05
Czech (10)	52	0.50
Danish (8)	85	0.81
Dutch (1,020)	2,988	28.48
English (52)	237	2.26
European (128)	128	1.22
Finnish (13)	13	0.12
French, ex. Basque (55)	466	4.44
French Canadian (109)	249	2.37
German (2,119)	5,195	49.51
Hungarian (0)	35	0.33
Irish (295)	1,244	11.86
Italian (108)	305	2.91
Luxemburger (37)	37	0.35
Norwegian (110)	472	4.50
Polish (145)	562	5.36
Russian (0)	24	0.23
Scandinavian (0)	24	0.23
Scotch-Irish (14)	107	1.02
Swedish (0)	98	0.93
Swiss (0)	62	0.59
Welsh (11)	71	0.68
Yugoslavian (0)	12	0.11

Hispanic Origin	Population	%
Hispanic or Latino (of any race)	327	3.13
Central American, ex. Mexican	14	0.13
Guatemalan	9	0.09
Honduran	3	0.03
Nicaraguan	1	0.01
Salvadoran	1	0.01
Cuban	6	0.06
Dominican Republic	6	0.06
Mexican	265	2.54
Puerto Rican	8	0.08
South American	2	0.02
Bolivian	2	0.02
Other Hispanic or Latino	26	0.25

Race*	Population	%
African-American/Black (78)	132	1.26
Not Hispanic (76)	128	1.22
Hispanic (2)	4	0.04
American Indian/Alaska Native (73)	108	1.03
Not Hispanic (64)	97	0.93
Hispanic (9)	11	0.11
Central American Ind. (0)	1	0.01
Cherokee (0)	1	0.01
Chippewa (14)	17	0.16
Iroquois (21)	27	0.26
Menominee (7)	13	0.12
Ottawa (1)	1	0.01
Potawatomi (1)	1	0.01
Sioux (1)	1	0.01
Asian (89)	112	1.07
Not Hispanic (87)	109	1.04
Hispanic (2)	3	0.03
Chinese, ex. Taiwanese (6)	8	0.08
Filipino (1)	2	0.02
Hmong (58)	73	0.70
Indian (9)	9	0.09
Japanese (2)	6	0.06
Korean (6)	7	0.07
Taiwanese (0)	1	0.01
Thai (1)	3	0.03
Vietnamese (4)	6	0.06
Hawaii Native/Pacific Islander (4)	13	0.12
Not Hispanic (3)	12	0.11
Hispanic (1)	1	0.01
Guamanian/Chamorro (1)	2	0.02
Native Hawaiian (0)	3	0.03
Tongan (1)	4	0.04
White (9,909)	10,028	95.97
Not Hispanic (9,785)	9,872	94.48
Hispanic (124)	156	1.49

Madison

Place Type: City
County: Dane
Population: 233,209†

Ancestry‡	Population	%
Afghan (71)	71	0.03
African, Sub-Saharan (4,384)	4,972	2.17
African (3,120)	3,419	1.49
Cape Verdean (14)	14	0.01
Ethiopian (92)	115	0.05
Kenyan (0)	144	0.06
Liberian (209)	209	0.09
Nigerian (571)	571	0.25
Sierra Leonean (9)	9	<0.01
Somalian (103)	111	0.05
South African (22)	69	0.03
Sudanese (53)	53	0.02
Other Sub-Saharan African (191)	258	0.11
Albanian (382)	404	0.18
Alsatian (0)	66	0.03
American (4,593)	4,593	2.00
Arab (430)	1,062	0.46
Arab (98)	118	0.05
Egyptian (86)	142	0.06
Iraqi (10)	32	0.01
Jordanian (13)	13	0.01
Lebanese (29)	273	0.12
Moroccan (38)	68	0.03
Palestinian (43)	70	0.03
Syrian (23)	46	0.02
Other Arab (90)	300	0.13
Armenian (155)	264	0.12
Australian (58)	86	0.04
Austrian (180)	1,082	0.47
Basque (11)	21	0.01
Belgian (100)	759	0.33
Brazilian (145)	198	0.09
British (441)	1,387	0.61
Bulgarian (0)	37	0.02
Cajun (13)	13	0.01
Canadian (116)	358	0.16
Celtic (36)	69	0.03
Croatian (114)	415	0.18
Cypriot (27)	27	0.01
Czech (484)	2,835	1.24
Czechoslovakian (167)	445	0.19
Danish (540)	3,128	1.36
Dutch (984)	4,872	2.13
Eastern European (480)	564	0.25
English (3,537)	20,405	8.90
Estonian (62)	95	0.04
European (2,732)	3,091	1.35
Finnish (314)	947	0.41
French, ex. Basque (692)	6,955	3.03
French Canadian (327)	1,203	0.52
German (25,369)	81,466	35.54
Greek (259)	919	0.40
Hungarian (289)	1,275	0.56
Icelander (33)	92	0.04
Iranian (164)	406	0.18
Irish (5,793)	31,932	13.93
Israeli (49)	103	0.04
Italian (2,335)	9,422	4.11
Latvian (25)	149	0.06
Lithuanian (189)	545	0.24
Luxemburger (0)	57	0.02
Macedonian (58)	126	0.05
New Zealander (7)	7	<0.01
Northern European (683)	737	0.32
Norwegian (6,219)	22,465	9.80
Pennsylvania German (28)	72	0.03
Polish (2,564)	12,532	5.47
Portuguese (110)	192	0.08
Romanian (178)	490	0.21
Russian (1,087)	3,045	1.33
Scandinavian (569)	1,128	0.49
Scotch-Irish (782)	3,171	1.38
Scottish (537)	4,523	1.97
Serbian (25)	124	0.05
Slavic (83)	194	0.08
Slovak (47)	319	0.14
Slovene (40)	243	0.11
Swedish (1,147)	6,536	2.85
Swiss (736)	3,652	1.59
Turkish (163)	163	0.07
Ukrainian (220)	636	0.28
Welsh (362)	2,470	1.08
West Indian, ex. Hispanic (223)	475	0.21
Dutch West Indian (16)	63	0.03
Haitian (20)	73	0.03
Jamaican (176)	316	0.14
West Indian (11)	23	0.01
Yugoslavian (26)	166	0.07

Hispanic Origin	Population	%
Hispanic or Latino (of any race)	15,948	6.84
Central American, ex. Mexican	980	0.42
Costa Rican	70	0.03
Guatemalan	167	0.07
Honduran	350	0.15
Nicaraguan	179	0.08
Panamanian	47	0.02
Salvadoran	163	0.07
Other Central American	4	<0.01
Cuban	299	0.13
Dominican Republic	155	0.07
Mexican	10,558	4.53
Puerto Rican	1,165	0.50
South American	1,740	0.75
Argentinean	219	0.09
Bolivian	100	0.04
Chilean	167	0.07
Colombian	512	0.22
Ecuadorian	184	0.08
Paraguayan	30	0.01
Peruvian	295	0.13
Uruguayan	70	0.03
Venezuelan	156	0.07
Other South American	7	<0.01
Other Hispanic or Latino	1,051	0.45

Race*	Population	%
African-American/Black (16,926)	20,490	8.79
Not Hispanic (16,507)	19,659	8.43
Hispanic (419)	831	0.36
American Indian/Alaska Native (1,001)	2,419	1.04
Not Hispanic (763)	1,917	0.82
Hispanic (238)	502	0.22
Alaska Athabascan *(Ala. Nat.)* (7)	9	<0.01
Aleut *(Alaska Native)* (0)	1	<0.01

*Notes: † The Census 2010 population figure is used to calculate the percentages in the Hispanic Origin and Race categories. Ancestry percentages are based on the 2006-2010 American Community Survey population (not shown); ‡ Numbers in parentheses indicate the number of people reporting a single ancestry; * Numbers in parentheses indicate the number of persons reporting this race alone, not in combination with any other race; Please refer to the Explanation of Data for more information.*

Apache (14)	30	0.01
Arapaho (0)	1	<0.01
Blackfeet (6)	52	0.02
Canadian/French Am. Ind. (0)	5	<0.01
Central American Ind. (2)	6	<0.01
Cherokee (41)	281	0.12
Cheyenne (2)	3	<0.01
Chickasaw (4)	8	<0.01
Chippewa (130)	270	0.12
Choctaw (17)	42	0.02
Colville (5)	5	<0.01
Comanche (4)	7	<0.01
Cree (2)	6	<0.01
Creek (7)	22	0.01
Crow (3)	9	<0.01
Delaware (1)	4	<0.01
Hopi (1)	1	<0.01
Houma (0)	1	<0.01
Inupiat *(Alaska Native)* (5)	11	<0.01
Iroquois (47)	95	0.04
Lumbee (2)	7	<0.01
Menominee (41)	62	0.03
Mexican American Ind. (61)	86	0.04
Navajo (16)	31	0.01
Osage (0)	1	<0.01
Ottawa (4)	7	<0.01
Pima (2)	3	<0.01
Potawatomi (12)	22	0.01
Pueblo (2)	7	<0.01
Seminole (1)	7	<0.01
Shoshone (0)	1	<0.01
Sioux (46)	96	0.04
South American Ind. (21)	52	0.02
Tlingit-Haida *(Alaska Native)* (2)	6	<0.01
Yaqui (2)	8	<0.01
Yup'ik *(Alaska Native)* (1)	3	<0.01
Asian (17,211)	19,548	8.38
Not Hispanic (17,126)	19,326	8.29
Hispanic (85)	222	0.10
Bangladeshi (31)	35	0.02
Bhutanese (1)	1	<0.01
Burmese (23)	33	0.01
Cambodian (326)	390	0.17
Chinese, ex. Taiwanese (4,779)	5,402	2.32
Filipino (613)	960	0.41
Hmong (2,637)	2,728	1.17
Indian (3,539)	3,851	1.65
Indonesian (115)	145	0.06
Japanese (467)	912	0.39
Korean (1,962)	2,261	0.97
Laotian (275)	350	0.15
Malaysian (131)	162	0.07
Nepalese (143)	151	0.06
Pakistani (239)	262	0.11
Sri Lankan (55)	60	0.03
Taiwanese (392)	426	0.18
Thai (219)	298	0.13
Vietnamese (587)	729	0.31
Hawaii Native/Pacific Islander (81)	279	0.12
Not Hispanic (67)	243	0.10
Hispanic (14)	36	0.02
Guamanian/Chamorro (16)	33	0.01
Marshallese (1)	1	<0.01
Native Hawaiian (35)	100	0.04
Samoan (7)	27	0.01
White (184,030)	190,519	81.69
Not Hispanic (176,463)	181,869	77.99
Hispanic (7,567)	8,650	3.71

Manitowoc

Place Type: City
County: Manitowoc
Population: 33,736†

Ancestry‡	Population	%
African, Sub-Saharan (0)	54	0.16
African (0)	54	0.16
Albanian (45)	45	0.13
American (1,059)	1,059	3.13
Arab (0)	49	0.15
Egyptian (0)	37	0.11
Lebanese (0)	12	0.04
Austrian (10)	64	0.19
Belgian (56)	194	0.57
British (15)	48	0.14
Canadian (0)	8	0.02
Croatian (0)	16	0.05
Czech (619)	2,632	7.79
Czechoslovakian (0)	64	0.19
Danish (10)	165	0.49
Dutch (156)	668	1.98
Eastern European (44)	55	0.16
English (432)	1,465	4.34
European (182)	182	0.54
Finnish (73)	296	0.88
French, ex. Basque (259)	2,230	6.60
French Canadian (209)	772	2.28
German (7,896)	17,143	50.73
Greek (23)	53	0.16
Hungarian (0)	57	0.17
Irish (882)	3,538	10.47
Italian (189)	899	2.66
Latvian (0)	10	0.03
Luxemburger (11)	23	0.07
Northern European (30)	30	0.09
Norwegian (445)	1,240	3.67
Polish (1,122)	3,867	11.44
Portuguese (52)	75	0.22
Romanian (11)	11	0.03
Russian (103)	321	0.95
Scandinavian (18)	18	0.05
Scotch-Irish (45)	216	0.64
Scottish (47)	286	0.85
Slovak (52)	96	0.28
Swedish (109)	502	1.49
Swiss (30)	80	0.24
Ukrainian (18)	31	0.09
Welsh (22)	79	0.23
Yugoslavian (0)	8	0.02

Hispanic Origin	Population	%
Hispanic or Latino (of any race)	1,695	5.02
Central American, ex. Mexican	29	0.09
Guatemalan	8	0.02
Honduran	16	0.05
Nicaraguan	2	0.01
Panamanian	3	0.01
Cuban	16	0.05
Dominican Republic	1	<0.01
Mexican	1,339	3.97
Puerto Rican	89	0.26
South American	33	0.10
Argentinean	2	0.01
Chilean	1	<0.01
Colombian	14	0.04
Ecuadorian	6	0.02
Peruvian	5	0.01
Uruguayan	1	<0.01
Venezuelan	4	0.01
Other Hispanic or Latino	188	0.56

Race*	Population	%
African-American/Black (329)	513	1.52
Not Hispanic (303)	466	1.38
Hispanic (26)	47	0.14
American Indian/Alaska Native (206)	403	1.19
Not Hispanic (179)	334	0.99
Hispanic (27)	69	0.20
Alaska Athabascan *(Ala. Nat.)* (0)	3	0.01
Apache (4)	4	0.01
Blackfeet (8)	12	0.04
Canadian/French Am. Ind. (0)	1	<0.01
Cherokee (3)	15	0.04
Chippewa (32)	67	0.20
Choctaw (0)	1	<0.01
Inupiat *(Alaska Native)* (0)	2	0.01
Iroquois (42)	73	0.22
Menominee (21)	30	0.09
Mexican American Ind. (2)	7	0.02
Navajo (1)	2	0.01
Ottawa (2)	5	0.01
Pima (4)	4	0.01
Potawatomi (7)	10	0.03
Spanish American Ind. (1)	1	<0.01
Tohono O'Odham (1)	1	<0.01
Yuman (1)	1	<0.01
Asian (1,545)	1,714	5.08
Not Hispanic (1,526)	1,683	4.99
Hispanic (19)	31	0.09
Cambodian (3)	4	0.01
Chinese, ex. Taiwanese (29)	36	0.11
Filipino (27)	48	0.14
Hmong (1,204)	1,278	3.79
Indian (69)	96	0.28
Japanese (12)	33	0.10
Korean (18)	35	0.10
Laotian (46)	63	0.19
Nepalese (0)	1	<0.01
Pakistani (7)	9	0.03
Sri Lankan (1)	1	<0.01
Taiwanese (3)	5	0.01
Thai (4)	13	0.04
Vietnamese (39)	58	0.17
Hawaii Native/Pacific Islander (3)	29	0.09
Not Hispanic (3)	26	0.08
Hispanic (0)	3	0.01
Guamanian/Chamorro (0)	10	0.03
Native Hawaiian (2)	9	0.03
Samoan (0)	2	0.01
White (30,325)	30,890	91.56
Not Hispanic (29,555)	29,972	88.84
Hispanic (770)	918	2.72

Marinette

Place Type: City
County: Marinette
Population: 10,968†

Ancestry‡	Population	%
American (474)	474	4.27
Australian (0)	14	0.13
Austrian (0)	36	0.32
Belgian (18)	189	1.70
British (0)	18	0.16
Canadian (0)	38	0.34
Croatian (10)	21	0.19
Czech (28)	195	1.76
Czechoslovakian (0)	10	0.09
Danish (58)	188	1.69
Dutch (40)	123	1.11
English (247)	541	4.88
Finnish (42)	153	1.38
French, ex. Basque (79)	813	7.33
French Canadian (221)	784	7.07
German (1,626)	4,444	40.05
Greek (0)	10	0.09
Hungarian (10)	50	0.45
Iranian (0)	29	0.26
Irish (141)	1,142	10.29
Italian (80)	281	2.53
Lithuanian (0)	8	0.07
Luxemburger (0)	37	0.33
Norwegian (114)	544	4.90
Polish (431)	1,365	12.30
Russian (15)	46	0.41
Scandinavian (29)	42	0.38
Scotch-Irish (9)	107	0.96
Scottish (15)	217	1.96
Slavic (0)	14	0.13
Swedish (196)	942	8.49
Swiss (0)	12	0.11
Welsh (0)	9	0.08

Hispanic Origin	Population	%
Hispanic or Latino (of any race)	149	1.36
Central American, ex. Mexican	6	0.05
Costa Rican	2	0.02
Guatemalan	3	0.03

SECTION TWO

*Notes: † The Census 2010 population figure is used to calculate the percentages in the Hispanic Origin and Race categories. Ancestry percentages are based on the 2006-2010 American Community Survey population (not shown); ‡ Numbers in parentheses indicate the number of people reporting a single ancestry; * Numbers in parentheses indicate the number of persons reporting this race alone, not in combination with any other race; Please refer to the Explanation of Data for more information.*

Panamanian	1	0.01
Cuban	7	0.06
Mexican	86	0.78
Puerto Rican	11	0.10
South American	11	0.10
Bolivian	1	0.01
Colombian	2	0.02
Peruvian	4	0.04
Venezuelan	3	0.03
Other South American	1	0.01
Other Hispanic or Latino	28	0.26

Race*	Population	%
African-American/Black (32)	79	0.72
Not Hispanic (32)	74	0.67
Hispanic (0)	5	0.05
American Indian/Alaska Native (64)	110	1.00
Not Hispanic (61)	101	0.92
Hispanic (3)	9	0.08
Cherokee (3)	5	0.05
Chippewa (19)	27	0.25
Comanche (0)	1	0.01
Cree (0)	1	0.01
Creek (5)	5	0.05
Iroquois (3)	8	0.07
Menominee (1)	2	0.02
Mexican American Ind. (1)	1	0.01
Navajo (1)	1	0.01
Ottawa (2)	3	0.03
Potawatomi (7)	9	0.08
Sioux (3)	3	0.03
Tsimshian *(Alaska Native)* (1)	1	0.01
Asian (60)	93	0.85
Not Hispanic (60)	92	0.84
Hispanic (0)	1	0.01
Chinese, ex. Taiwanese (10)	10	0.09
Filipino (8)	18	0.16
Indian (18)	19	0.17
Indonesian (0)	1	0.01
Japanese (3)	11	0.10
Korean (10)	15	0.14
Malaysian (1)	1	0.01
Taiwanese (2)	4	0.04
Thai (3)	8	0.07
Vietnamese (3)	3	0.03
Hawaii Native/Pacific Islander (0)	3	0.03
Not Hispanic (0)	3	0.03
Samoan (0)	1	0.01
White (10,633)	10,759	98.09
Not Hispanic (10,548)	10,657	97.16
Hispanic (85)	102	0.93

Marshfield

Place Type: City
County: Wood
Population: 18,218†

Ancestry‡	Population	%
American (789)	789	4.34
Arab (36)	36	0.20
Egyptian (32)	32	0.18
Other Arab (4)	4	0.02
Armenian (29)	29	0.16
Austrian (14)	98	0.54
Belgian (42)	68	0.37
British (0)	42	0.23
Canadian (0)	7	0.04
Croatian (9)	9	0.05
Czech (76)	305	1.68
Czechoslovakian (0)	10	0.06
Danish (26)	149	0.82
Dutch (50)	305	1.68
Eastern European (16)	16	0.09
English (161)	802	4.41
Estonian (11)	11	0.06
European (90)	137	0.75
Finnish (48)	74	0.41
French, ex. Basque (167)	980	5.39
French Canadian (39)	149	0.82
German (5,563)	10,323	56.78
German Russian (0)	11	0.06
Guyanese (11)	11	0.06
Hungarian (31)	63	0.35
Irish (224)	1,649	9.07
Italian (70)	265	1.46
Lithuanian (0)	22	0.12
Luxemburger (0)	9	0.05
Norwegian (429)	1,402	7.71
Pennsylvania German (8)	8	0.04
Polish (308)	1,239	6.82
Russian (31)	51	0.28
Scandinavian (169)	254	1.40
Scotch-Irish (54)	135	0.74
Scottish (26)	231	1.27
Slovak (16)	43	0.24
Slovene (0)	14	0.08
Swedish (121)	626	3.44
Swiss (15)	198	1.09
Ukrainian (45)	68	0.37
Welsh (8)	71	0.39
Yugoslavian (0)	48	0.26

Hispanic Origin	Population	%
Hispanic or Latino (of any race)	448	2.46
Central American, ex. Mexican	15	0.08
Guatemalan	8	0.04
Honduran	2	0.01
Nicaraguan	3	0.02
Panamanian	1	0.01
Salvadoran	1	0.01
Cuban	13	0.07
Dominican Republic	3	0.02
Mexican	308	1.69
Puerto Rican	35	0.19
South American	29	0.16
Argentinean	1	0.01
Chilean	2	0.01
Colombian	8	0.04
Ecuadorian	7	0.04
Paraguayan	2	0.01
Peruvian	4	0.02
Venezuelan	5	0.03
Other Hispanic or Latino	45	0.25

Race*	Population	%
African-American/Black (127)	202	1.11
Not Hispanic (124)	197	1.08
Hispanic (3)	5	0.03
American Indian/Alaska Native (34)	81	0.44
Not Hispanic (33)	71	0.39
Hispanic (1)	10	0.05
Alaska Athabascan *(Ala. Nat.)* (0)	2	0.01
Apache (0)	1	0.01
Blackfeet (3)	7	0.04
Cherokee (1)	3	0.02
Chippewa (4)	5	0.03
Cree (1)	1	0.01
Iroquois (2)	2	0.01
Kiowa (0)	1	0.01
Menominee (3)	5	0.03
Mexican American Ind. (1)	5	0.03
Navajo (0)	1	0.01
Potawatomi (2)	3	0.02
Pueblo (1)	1	0.01
Seminole (0)	2	0.01
Sioux (0)	1	0.01
Tlingit-Haida *(Alaska Native)* (0)	1	0.01
Asian (387)	449	2.46
Not Hispanic (386)	448	2.46
Hispanic (1)	1	0.01
Chinese, ex. Taiwanese (45)	49	0.27
Filipino (48)	75	0.41
Hmong (30)	30	0.16
Indian (138)	145	0.80
Japanese (6)	7	0.04
Korean (40)	49	0.27
Laotian (3)	7	0.04
Nepalese (4)	4	0.02
Pakistani (28)	31	0.17
Sri Lankan (5)	5	0.03
Thai (3)	3	0.02
Vietnamese (20)	26	0.14
Hawaii Native/Pacific Islander (1)	3	0.02
Not Hispanic (1)	3	0.02
Guamanian/Chamorro (0)	1	0.01
White (17,301)	17,503	96.08
Not Hispanic (17,048)	17,212	94.48
Hispanic (253)	291	1.60

Marshfield

Place Type: City
County: Wood
Population: 19,118†

Ancestry‡	Population	%
American (806)	806	4.31
Arab (36)	36	0.19
Egyptian (32)	32	0.17
Other Arab (4)	4	0.02
Armenian (29)	29	0.15
Austrian (14)	98	0.52
Belgian (42)	68	0.36
British (0)	42	0.22
Canadian (0)	7	0.04
Croatian (9)	9	0.05
Czech (76)	305	1.63
Czechoslovakian (0)	10	0.05
Danish (26)	149	0.80
Dutch (50)	305	1.63
Eastern European (16)	16	0.09
English (161)	829	4.43
Estonian (11)	11	0.06
European (90)	137	0.73
Finnish (60)	92	0.49
French, ex. Basque (167)	1,003	5.36
French Canadian (46)	164	0.88
German (5,785)	10,606	56.65
German Russian (0)	11	0.06
Guyanese (11)	11	0.06
Hungarian (31)	63	0.34
Irish (235)	1,680	8.97
Italian (130)	325	1.74
Lithuanian (0)	22	0.12
Luxemburger (0)	9	0.05
Norwegian (465)	1,441	7.70
Pennsylvania German (8)	8	0.04
Polish (322)	1,275	6.81
Russian (43)	63	0.34
Scandinavian (169)	254	1.36
Scotch-Irish (54)	135	0.72
Scottish (26)	231	1.23
Slovak (16)	43	0.23
Slovene (0)	14	0.07
Swedish (121)	646	3.45
Swiss (15)	198	1.06
Ukrainian (45)	68	0.36
Welsh (8)	71	0.38
Yugoslavian (0)	48	0.26

Hispanic Origin	Population	%
Hispanic or Latino (of any race)	452	2.36
Central American, ex. Mexican	15	0.08
Guatemalan	8	0.04
Honduran	2	0.01
Nicaraguan	3	0.02
Panamanian	1	0.01
Salvadoran	1	0.01
Cuban	13	0.07
Dominican Republic	3	0.02
Mexican	312	1.63
Puerto Rican	35	0.18
South American	29	0.15
Argentinean	1	0.01
Chilean	2	0.01
Colombian	8	0.04
Ecuadorian	7	0.04
Paraguayan	2	0.01
Peruvian	4	0.02

*Notes: † The Census 2010 population figure is used to calculate the percentages in the Hispanic Origin and Race categories. Ancestry percentages are based on the 2006-2010 American Community Survey population (not shown); ‡ Numbers in parentheses indicate the number of people reporting a single ancestry; * Numbers in parentheses indicate the number of persons reporting this race alone, not in combination with any other race; Please refer to the Explanation of Data for more information.*

Venezuelan	5	0.03
Other Hispanic or Latino	45	0.24

Race*	Population	%
African-American/Black (131)	208	1.09
Not Hispanic (128)	203	1.06
Hispanic (3)	5	0.03
American Indian/Alaska Native (39)	88	0.46
Not Hispanic (38)	78	0.41
Hispanic (1)	10	0.05
Alaska Athabascan *(Ala. Nat.)* (0)	2	0.01
Apache (0)	1	0.01
Blackfeet (3)	7	0.04
Cherokee (1)	4	0.02
Chippewa (4)	5	0.03
Cree (1)	1	0.01
Iroquois (2)	2	0.01
Kiowa (0)	1	0.01
Menominee (3)	5	0.03
Mexican American Ind. (1)	5	0.03
Navajo (0)	1	0.01
Potawatomi (3)	4	0.02
Pueblo (1)	1	0.01
Seminole (0)	2	0.01
Sioux (0)	1	0.01
Tlingit-Haida *(Alaska Native)* (0)	1	0.01
Asian (437)	509	2.66
Not Hispanic (436)	508	2.66
Hispanic (1)	1	0.01
Bangladeshi (3)	4	0.02
Chinese, ex. Taiwanese (50)	54	0.28
Filipino (55)	85	0.44
Hmong (30)	31	0.16
Indian (161)	169	0.88
Japanese (6)	7	0.04
Korean (49)	59	0.31
Laotian (3)	7	0.04
Nepalese (4)	4	0.02
Pakistani (28)	31	0.16
Sri Lankan (5)	5	0.03
Thai (3)	3	0.02
Vietnamese (21)	32	0.17
Hawaii Native/Pacific Islander (1)	3	0.02
Not Hispanic (1)	3	0.02
Guamanian/Chamorro (0)	1	0.01
White (18,127)	18,342	95.94
Not Hispanic (17,870)	18,047	94.40
Hispanic (257)	295	1.54

McFarland

Place Type: Village
County: Dane
Population: 7,808†

Ancestry‡	Population	%
American (375)	375	4.95
Arab (0)	22	0.29
Lebanese (0)	22	0.29
Austrian (0)	14	0.18
Belgian (0)	16	0.21
British (9)	9	0.12
Canadian (0)	7	0.09
Croatian (14)	14	0.18
Czech (42)	247	3.26
Danish (0)	144	1.90
Dutch (47)	178	2.35
English (132)	1,039	13.72
European (40)	68	0.90
Finnish (0)	22	0.29
French, ex. Basque (17)	314	4.15
French Canadian (0)	12	0.16
German (1,036)	3,109	41.05
Hungarian (14)	135	1.78
Irish (271)	1,331	17.57
Italian (59)	506	6.68
Lithuanian (42)	42	0.55
Luxemburger (10)	46	0.61
Norwegian (457)	1,191	15.72
Polish (74)	330	4.36
Romanian (0)	19	0.25
Russian (15)	22	0.29
Scandinavian (11)	11	0.15
Scotch-Irish (13)	66	0.87
Scottish (48)	162	2.14
Slovene (7)	25	0.33
Swedish (23)	243	3.21
Swiss (0)	266	3.51
Welsh (0)	37	0.49

Hispanic Origin	Population	%
Hispanic or Latino (of any race)	176	2.25
Central American, ex. Mexican	27	0.35
Costa Rican	1	0.01
Guatemalan	3	0.04
Nicaraguan	21	0.27
Salvadoran	2	0.03
Cuban	3	0.04
Dominican Republic	2	0.03
Mexican	101	1.29
Puerto Rican	21	0.27
South American	7	0.09
Bolivian	1	0.01
Colombian	3	0.04
Peruvian	3	0.04
Other Hispanic or Latino	15	0.19

Race*	Population	%
African-American/Black (94)	160	2.05
Not Hispanic (91)	155	1.99
Hispanic (3)	5	0.06
American Indian/Alaska Native (33)	53	0.68
Not Hispanic (28)	48	0.61
Hispanic (5)	5	0.06
Cherokee (1)	3	0.04
Chippewa (6)	7	0.09
Comanche (2)	2	0.03
Inupiat *(Alaska Native)* (2)	2	0.03
Menominee (3)	4	0.05
Mexican American Ind. (4)	4	0.05
Asian (132)	168	2.15
Not Hispanic (130)	166	2.13
Hispanic (2)	2	0.03
Cambodian (6)	6	0.08
Chinese, ex. Taiwanese (24)	28	0.36
Filipino (8)	11	0.14
Hmong (20)	20	0.26
Indian (32)	40	0.51
Indonesian (0)	1	0.01
Japanese (8)	23	0.29
Korean (16)	21	0.27
Laotian (4)	4	0.05
Taiwanese (5)	5	0.06
Thai (0)	2	0.03
Vietnamese (6)	6	0.08
Hawaii Native/Pacific Islander (5)	5	0.06
Not Hispanic (5)	5	0.06
Native Hawaiian (5)	5	0.06
White (7,373)	7,483	95.84
Not Hispanic (7,267)	7,369	94.38
Hispanic (106)	114	1.46

Menasha

Place Type: City
County: Winnebago
Population: 15,144†

Ancestry‡	Population	%
African, Sub-Saharan (15)	15	0.10
Cape Verdean (6)	6	0.04
Ethiopian (9)	9	0.06
American (463)	463	3.05
Arab (0)	104	0.68
Lebanese (0)	52	0.34
Syrian (0)	52	0.34
Austrian (11)	122	0.80
Belgian (46)	149	0.98
British (11)	11	0.07
Canadian (0)	17	0.11
Croatian (0)	24	0.16
Czech (46)	238	1.57
Danish (20)	123	0.81
Dutch (142)	872	5.74
English (217)	983	6.47
European (120)	120	0.79
Finnish (12)	74	0.49
French, ex. Basque (266)	916	6.03
French Canadian (93)	245	1.61
German (3,471)	7,864	51.76
Greek (0)	47	0.31
Hungarian (0)	17	0.11
Icelander (15)	15	0.10
Irish (206)	1,469	9.67
Italian (210)	420	2.76
Latvian (5)	5	0.03
Lithuanian (0)	12	0.08
Luxemburger (10)	28	0.18
Norwegian (109)	783	5.15
Polish (604)	1,911	12.58
Romanian (0)	7	0.05
Russian (0)	73	0.48
Scandinavian (12)	82	0.54
Scotch-Irish (0)	19	0.13
Scottish (10)	168	1.11
Slovak (11)	24	0.16
Swedish (117)	389	2.56
Swiss (14)	75	0.49
Ukrainian (11)	23	0.15
Welsh (12)	71	0.47
Yugoslavian (0)	16	0.11

Hispanic Origin	Population	%
Hispanic or Latino (of any race)	1,116	7.37
Central American, ex. Mexican	24	0.16
Guatemalan	19	0.13
Honduran	2	0.01
Panamanian	1	0.01
Salvadoran	2	0.01
Cuban	8	0.05
Dominican Republic	2	0.01
Mexican	928	6.13
Puerto Rican	67	0.44
South American	21	0.14
Chilean	3	0.02
Colombian	3	0.02
Ecuadorian	9	0.06
Peruvian	2	0.01
Other South American	4	0.03
Other Hispanic or Latino	66	0.44

Race*	Population	%
African-American/Black (192)	341	2.25
Not Hispanic (178)	317	2.09
Hispanic (14)	24	0.16
American Indian/Alaska Native (121)	222	1.47
Not Hispanic (101)	178	1.18
Hispanic (20)	44	0.29
Apache (0)	3	0.02
Central American Ind. (1)	1	0.01
Cherokee (2)	11	0.07
Chippewa (18)	30	0.20
Creek (0)	2	0.01
Hopi (0)	2	0.01
Iroquois (20)	28	0.18
Menominee (7)	15	0.10
Mexican American Ind. (1)	2	0.01
Navajo (0)	1	0.01
Paiute (2)	2	0.01
Potawatomi (9)	16	0.11
Sioux (1)	1	0.01
South American Ind. (12)	12	0.08
Asian (312)	362	2.39
Not Hispanic (312)	356	2.35
Hispanic (0)	6	0.04
Burmese (1)	1	0.01
Cambodian (2)	4	0.03
Chinese, ex. Taiwanese (12)	17	0.11
Filipino (14)	28	0.18
Hmong (217)	231	1.53

SECTION TWO

*Notes: † The Census 2010 population figure is used to calculate the percentages in the Hispanic Origin and Race categories. Ancestry percentages are based on the 2006-2010 American Community Survey population (not shown); ‡ Numbers in parentheses indicate the number of people reporting a single ancestry; * Numbers in parentheses indicate the number of persons reporting this race alone, not in combination with any other race; Please refer to the Explanation of Data for more information.*

Indian (36)	37	0.24
Japanese (4)	9	0.06
Korean (9)	15	0.10
Laotian (7)	8	0.05
Vietnamese (4)	5	0.03
Hawaii Native/Pacific Islander (10)	15	0.10
Not Hispanic (6)	11	0.07
Hispanic (4)	4	0.03
Guamanian/Chamorro (4)	4	0.03
Native Hawaiian (4)	6	0.04
Samoan (0)	2	0.01
White (13,700)	14,006	92.49
Not Hispanic (13,189)	13,414	88.58
Hispanic (511)	592	3.91

Menasha

Place Type: City
County: Winnebago
Population: 17,353†

Ancestry‡	Population	%
African, Sub-Saharan (15)	15	0.09
Cape Verdean (6)	6	0.04
Ethiopian (9)	9	0.05
American (531)	531	3.12
Arab (0)	104	0.61
Lebanese (0)	52	0.31
Syrian (0)	52	0.31
Austrian (11)	122	0.72
Belgian (46)	149	0.87
British (11)	16	0.09
Canadian (34)	51	0.30
Croatian (0)	24	0.14
Czech (46)	250	1.47
Danish (49)	152	0.89
Dutch (161)	970	5.69
English (233)	1,115	6.55
European (120)	120	0.70
Finnish (12)	74	0.43
French, ex. Basque (266)	964	5.66
French Canadian (99)	258	1.51
German (3,977)	8,713	51.15
Greek (0)	47	0.28
Hungarian (0)	17	0.10
Icelander (32)	32	0.19
Irish (299)	1,737	10.20
Italian (227)	478	2.81
Latvian (5)	5	0.03
Lithuanian (0)	17	0.10
Luxemburger (10)	28	0.16
Norwegian (136)	822	4.83
Polish (624)	2,052	12.05
Romanian (0)	7	0.04
Russian (0)	116	0.68
Scandinavian (12)	82	0.48
Scotch-Irish (0)	31	0.18
Scottish (15)	173	1.02
Slovak (11)	24	0.14
Swedish (117)	403	2.37
Swiss (14)	75	0.44
Ukrainian (11)	23	0.14
Welsh (12)	77	0.45
Yugoslavian (0)	16	0.09

Hispanic Origin	Population	%
Hispanic or Latino (of any race)	1,204	6.94
Central American, ex. Mexican	31	0.18
Guatemalan	20	0.12
Honduran	8	0.05
Panamanian	1	0.01
Salvadoran	2	0.01
Cuban	8	0.05
Dominican Republic	2	0.01
Mexican	985	5.68
Puerto Rican	76	0.44
South American	36	0.21
Chilean	4	0.02
Colombian	11	0.06
Ecuadorian	9	0.05
Peruvian	8	0.05
Other South American	4	0.02
Other Hispanic or Latino	66	0.38

Race*	Population	%
African-American/Black (211)	367	2.11
Not Hispanic (195)	339	1.95
Hispanic (16)	28	0.16
American Indian/Alaska Native (125)	231	1.33
Not Hispanic (105)	187	1.08
Hispanic (20)	44	0.25
Apache (0)	3	0.02
Central American Ind. (1)	1	0.01
Cherokee (2)	11	0.06
Chippewa (18)	30	0.17
Creek (0)	2	0.01
Hopi (0)	2	0.01
Iroquois (20)	30	0.17
Menominee (7)	15	0.09
Mexican American Ind. (1)	2	0.01
Navajo (0)	1	0.01
Paiute (2)	2	0.01
Potawatomi (9)	16	0.09
Sioux (1)	1	0.01
South American Ind. (12)	12	0.07
Asian (382)	443	2.55
Not Hispanic (382)	436	2.51
Hispanic (0)	7	0.04
Burmese (1)	1	0.01
Cambodian (4)	7	0.04
Chinese, ex. Taiwanese (19)	24	0.14
Filipino (20)	38	0.22
Hmong (251)	265	1.53
Indian (55)	58	0.33
Japanese (4)	10	0.06
Korean (11)	19	0.11
Laotian (7)	8	0.05
Vietnamese (4)	5	0.03
Hawaii Native/Pacific Islander (10)	15	0.09
Not Hispanic (6)	11	0.06
Hispanic (4)	4	0.02
Guamanian/Chamorro (4)	4	0.02
Native Hawaiian (4)	6	0.03
Samoan (0)	2	0.01
White (15,751)	16,082	92.68
Not Hispanic (15,195)	15,440	88.98
Hispanic (556)	642	3.70

Menasha

Place Type: Town
County: Winnebago
Population: 18,498†

Ancestry‡	Population	%
American (607)	607	3.37
Arab (33)	33	0.18
Arab (16)	16	0.09
Moroccan (17)	17	0.09
Austrian (64)	96	0.53
Belgian (38)	118	0.65
Brazilian (5)	21	0.12
British (49)	66	0.37
Celtic (0)	15	0.08
Czech (98)	262	1.45
Czechoslovakian (22)	46	0.26
Danish (13)	257	1.43
Dutch (369)	1,348	7.48
English (233)	1,081	6.00
European (165)	165	0.92
Finnish (14)	109	0.60
French, ex. Basque (41)	1,009	5.60
French Canadian (41)	124	0.69
German (4,915)	10,106	56.05
Greek (0)	26	0.14
Hungarian (14)	48	0.27
Irish (432)	1,811	10.04
Italian (174)	360	2.00
Latvian (19)	19	0.11
Lithuanian (0)	21	0.12
Norwegian (85)	657	3.64
Polish (424)	1,666	9.24
Romanian (0)	15	0.08
Russian (22)	76	0.42
Scandinavian (0)	41	0.23
Scotch-Irish (42)	189	1.05
Scottish (34)	198	1.10
Serbian (0)	13	0.07
Slovak (7)	47	0.26
Swedish (49)	320	1.77
Swiss (0)	87	0.48
Ukrainian (12)	12	0.07
Welsh (37)	117	0.65
Yugoslavian (16)	16	0.09

Hispanic Origin	Population	%
Hispanic or Latino (of any race)	1,131	6.11
Central American, ex. Mexican	42	0.23
Costa Rican	3	0.02
Guatemalan	7	0.04
Honduran	20	0.11
Nicaraguan	6	0.03
Salvadoran	6	0.03
Cuban	12	0.06
Dominican Republic	3	0.02
Mexican	956	5.17
Puerto Rican	61	0.33
South American	18	0.10
Bolivian	1	0.01
Chilean	3	0.02
Ecuadorian	4	0.02
Peruvian	2	0.01
Venezuelan	6	0.03
Other South American	2	0.01
Other Hispanic or Latino	39	0.21

Race*	Population	%
African-American/Black (206)	305	1.65
Not Hispanic (182)	270	1.46
Hispanic (24)	35	0.19
American Indian/Alaska Native (108)	169	0.91
Not Hispanic (95)	145	0.78
Hispanic (13)	24	0.13
Alaska Athabascan *(Ala. Nat.)* (1)	1	0.01
Aleut *(Alaska Native)* (1)	3	0.02
Apache (1)	1	0.01
Blackfeet (0)	1	0.01
Canadian/French Am. Ind. (0)	1	0.01
Cherokee (3)	6	0.03
Chippewa (16)	27	0.15
Comanche (1)	7	0.04
Crow (0)	1	0.01
Iroquois (22)	24	0.13
Kiowa (1)	5	0.03
Menominee (16)	22	0.12
Mexican American Ind. (2)	2	0.01
Ottawa (0)	1	0.01
Potawatomi (8)	8	0.04
Sioux (1)	1	0.01
South American Ind. (0)	1	0.01
Asian (531)	613	3.31
Not Hispanic (529)	606	3.28
Hispanic (2)	7	0.04
Bangladeshi (4)	4	0.02
Chinese, ex. Taiwanese (12)	12	0.06
Filipino (18)	51	0.28
Hmong (274)	293	1.58
Indian (127)	134	0.72
Indonesian (1)	1	0.01
Japanese (7)	20	0.11
Korean (13)	22	0.12
Laotian (8)	8	0.04
Nepalese (16)	16	0.09
Pakistani (2)	4	0.02
Sri Lankan (2)	2	0.01
Thai (8)	8	0.04
Vietnamese (8)	13	0.07
Hawaii Native/Pacific Islander (1)	5	0.03
Not Hispanic (1)	3	0.02
Hispanic (0)	2	0.01

*Notes: † The Census 2010 population figure is used to calculate the percentages in the Hispanic Origin and Race categories. Ancestry percentages are based on the 2006-2010 American Community Survey population (not shown); ‡ Numbers in parentheses indicate the number of people reporting a single ancestry; * Numbers in parentheses indicate the number of persons reporting this race alone, not in combination with any other race; Please refer to the Explanation of Data for more information.*

Guamanian/Chamorro (0)	2	0.01
Native Hawaiian (0)	3	0.02
White (16,747)	17,029	92.06
Not Hispanic (16,337)	16,542	89.43
Hispanic (410)	487	2.63

Menomonee Falls

Place Type: Village
County: Waukesha
Population: 35,626†

Ancestry‡	Population	%
African, Sub-Saharan (51)	51	0.14
African (51)	51	0.14
American (1,095)	1,095	3.11
Arab (10)	31	0.09
Egyptian (10)	10	0.03
Lebanese (0)	21	0.06
Armenian (0)	21	0.06
Austrian (63)	354	1.01
Belgian (21)	229	0.65
British (134)	162	0.46
Canadian (0)	23	0.07
Croatian (31)	195	0.55
Czech (68)	434	1.23
Czechoslovakian (68)	176	0.50
Danish (72)	324	0.92
Dutch (125)	647	1.84
Eastern European (22)	33	0.09
English (269)	1,996	5.67
European (160)	198	0.56
Finnish (84)	282	0.80
French, ex. Basque (134)	1,231	3.50
French Canadian (8)	144	0.41
German (8,185)	18,977	53.88
Greek (162)	324	0.92
Hungarian (48)	319	0.91
Irish (952)	4,796	13.62
Italian (448)	2,039	5.79
Lithuanian (8)	40	0.11
Luxemburger (0)	11	0.03
Maltese (8)	8	0.02
Northern European (17)	17	0.05
Norwegian (514)	1,572	4.46
Polish (1,232)	4,937	14.02
Romanian (26)	26	0.07
Russian (55)	282	0.80
Scandinavian (35)	129	0.37
Scotch-Irish (55)	179	0.51
Scottish (86)	466	1.32
Serbian (19)	42	0.12
Slavic (0)	16	0.05
Slovak (97)	199	0.57
Slovene (49)	97	0.28
Swedish (133)	780	2.21
Swiss (17)	147	0.42
Turkish (16)	16	0.05
Ukrainian (31)	44	0.12
Welsh (25)	213	0.60
Yugoslavian (50)	87	0.25

Hispanic Origin	Population	%
Hispanic or Latino (of any race)	697	1.96
Central American, ex. Mexican	39	0.11
Guatemalan	22	0.06
Honduran	2	0.01
Nicaraguan	7	0.02
Panamanian	2	0.01
Salvadoran	6	0.02
Cuban	6	0.02
Dominican Republic	5	0.01
Mexican	391	1.10
Puerto Rican	139	0.39
South American	58	0.16
Argentinean	3	0.01
Bolivian	2	0.01
Chilean	4	0.01
Colombian	15	0.04
Ecuadorian	6	0.02
Paraguayan	1	<0.01
Peruvian	18	0.05
Venezuelan	9	0.03
Other Hispanic or Latino	59	0.17

Race*	Population	%
African-American/Black (1,062)	1,250	3.51
Not Hispanic (1,043)	1,217	3.42
Hispanic (19)	33	0.09
American Indian/Alaska Native (76)	193	0.54
Not Hispanic (63)	156	0.44
Hispanic (13)	37	0.10
Arapaho (0)	1	<0.01
Blackfeet (2)	6	0.02
Central American Ind. (1)	1	<0.01
Cherokee (1)	15	0.04
Chippewa (19)	35	0.10
Choctaw (0)	2	0.01
Inupiat *(Alaska Native)* (0)	1	<0.01
Iroquois (14)	20	0.06
Menominee (5)	18	0.05
Mexican American Ind. (4)	6	0.02
Ottawa (5)	6	0.02
Puget Sound Salish (0)	1	<0.01
Seminole (0)	1	<0.01
Shoshone (0)	3	0.01
Sioux (0)	4	0.01
South American Ind. (0)	4	0.01
Spanish American Ind. (1)	1	<0.01
Tlingit-Haida *(Alaska Native)* (1)	1	<0.01
Asian (1,250)	1,414	3.97
Not Hispanic (1,243)	1,400	3.93
Hispanic (7)	14	0.04
Bangladeshi (2)	2	0.01
Burmese (9)	9	0.03
Cambodian (3)	3	0.01
Chinese, ex. Taiwanese (172)	201	0.56
Filipino (70)	96	0.27
Hmong (118)	126	0.35
Indian (589)	638	1.79
Indonesian (1)	4	0.01
Japanese (21)	42	0.12
Korean (77)	92	0.26
Laotian (13)	18	0.05
Malaysian (1)	1	<0.01
Pakistani (20)	25	0.07
Sri Lankan (5)	5	0.01
Taiwanese (7)	10	0.03
Thai (13)	14	0.04
Vietnamese (98)	106	0.30
Hawaii Native/Pacific Islander (4)	12	0.03
Not Hispanic (4)	12	0.03
Fijian (1)	1	<0.01
Guamanian/Chamorro (0)	3	0.01
Marshallese (1)	1	<0.01
Native Hawaiian (2)	3	0.01
Samoan (0)	1	<0.01
White (32,626)	33,058	92.79
Not Hispanic (32,140)	32,511	91.26
Hispanic (486)	547	1.54

Menomonie

Place Type: City
County: Dunn
Population: 16,264†

Ancestry‡	Population	%
American (498)	498	3.10
Arab (0)	11	0.07
Lebanese (0)	11	0.07
Austrian (0)	197	1.23
Basque (0)	12	0.07
Belgian (26)	186	1.16
British (0)	45	0.28
Canadian (0)	14	0.09
Czech (31)	181	1.13
Czechoslovakian (54)	54	0.34
Danish (87)	210	1.31
Dutch (94)	139	0.87
Eastern European (14)	32	0.20
English (244)	982	6.11
European (86)	99	0.62
Finnish (38)	103	0.64
French, ex. Basque (44)	624	3.89
French Canadian (50)	148	0.92
German (3,144)	7,542	46.96
Greek (13)	107	0.67
Hungarian (12)	37	0.23
Irish (278)	1,937	12.06
Italian (109)	471	2.93
Latvian (0)	14	0.09
Luxemburger (0)	10	0.06
Norwegian (892)	2,607	16.23
Polish (227)	804	5.01
Romanian (0)	8	0.05
Russian (42)	129	0.80
Scandinavian (111)	135	0.84
Scotch-Irish (47)	100	0.62
Scottish (55)	134	0.83
Serbian (0)	11	0.07
Slovak (0)	40	0.25
Slovene (0)	44	0.27
Swedish (64)	688	4.28
Swiss (25)	160	1.00
Welsh (0)	18	0.11
Yugoslavian (0)	9	0.06

Hispanic Origin	Population	%
Hispanic or Latino (of any race)	276	1.70
Central American, ex. Mexican	18	0.11
Costa Rican	2	0.01
Guatemalan	8	0.05
Honduran	2	0.01
Panamanian	5	0.03
Salvadoran	1	0.01
Cuban	6	0.04
Mexican	170	1.05
Puerto Rican	20	0.12
South American	20	0.12
Bolivian	2	0.01
Chilean	2	0.01
Colombian	8	0.05
Ecuadorian	2	0.01
Peruvian	2	0.01
Venezuelan	4	0.02
Other Hispanic or Latino	42	0.26

Race*	Population	%
African-American/Black (137)	241	1.48
Not Hispanic (134)	230	1.41
Hispanic (3)	11	0.07
American Indian/Alaska Native (82)	172	1.06
Not Hispanic (72)	158	0.97
Hispanic (10)	14	0.09
Apache (1)	1	0.01
Cherokee (3)	14	0.09
Cheyenne (0)	2	0.01
Chippewa (21)	37	0.23
Choctaw (0)	2	0.01
Comanche (1)	2	0.01
Iroquois (7)	11	0.07
Menominee (0)	4	0.02
Mexican American Ind. (1)	1	0.01
Ottawa (1)	4	0.02
Sioux (2)	12	0.07
Asian (684)	793	4.88
Not Hispanic (683)	788	4.85
Hispanic (1)	5	0.03
Cambodian (0)	1	0.01
Chinese, ex. Taiwanese (33)	52	0.32
Filipino (12)	33	0.20
Hmong (431)	450	2.77
Indian (71)	89	0.55
Japanese (7)	23	0.14
Korean (33)	49	0.30
Laotian (15)	17	0.10
Malaysian (2)	2	0.01
Nepalese (23)	23	0.14
Sri Lankan (1)	1	0.01

*Notes: † The Census 2010 population figure is used to calculate the percentages in the Hispanic Origin and Race categories. Ancestry percentages are based on the 2006-2010 American Community Survey population (not shown); ‡ Numbers in parentheses indicate the number of people reporting a single ancestry; * Numbers in parentheses indicate the number of persons reporting this race alone, not in combination with any other race; Please refer to the Explanation of Data for more information.*

Taiwanese (4)	5	0.03
Thai (4)	9	0.06
Vietnamese (4)	9	0.06
Hawaii Native/Pacific Islander (8)	32	0.20
Not Hispanic (8)	31	0.19
Hispanic (0)	1	0.01
Native Hawaiian (6)	12	0.07
Samoan (1)	2	0.01
White (14,943)	15,219	93.57
Not Hispanic (14,812)	15,052	92.55
Hispanic (131)	167	1.03

Mequon

Place Type: City
County: Ozaukee
Population: 23,132†

Ancestry‡	Population	%
African, Sub-Saharan (188)	199	0.86
African (16)	27	0.12
Ethiopian (46)	46	0.20
Nigerian (36)	36	0.16
South African (90)	90	0.39
American (732)	732	3.17
Arab (63)	135	0.58
Egyptian (52)	111	0.48
Lebanese (11)	24	0.10
Armenian (74)	137	0.59
Austrian (71)	166	0.72
Belgian (26)	78	0.34
British (143)	238	1.03
Bulgarian (12)	12	0.05
Cajun (0)	14	0.06
Canadian (0)	12	0.05
Carpatho Rusyn (0)	6	0.03
Celtic (12)	12	0.05
Croatian (34)	127	0.55
Czech (97)	327	1.42
Czechoslovakian (20)	35	0.15
Danish (43)	376	1.63
Dutch (170)	457	1.98
Eastern European (117)	117	0.51
English (407)	1,895	8.20
European (227)	227	0.98
Finnish (9)	48	0.21
French, ex. Basque (100)	695	3.01
French Canadian (20)	120	0.52
German (4,287)	9,633	41.71
Greek (39)	96	0.42
Hungarian (42)	94	0.41
Iranian (35)	65	0.28
Irish (642)	3,585	15.52
Italian (349)	1,057	4.58
Lithuanian (25)	51	0.22
Luxemburger (0)	17	0.07
New Zealander (0)	10	0.04
Norwegian (125)	945	4.09
Pennsylvania German (12)	12	0.05
Polish (558)	2,246	9.72
Portuguese (10)	19	0.08
Romanian (28)	51	0.22
Russian (907)	1,151	4.98
Scandinavian (49)	121	0.52
Scotch-Irish (105)	284	1.23
Scottish (70)	439	1.90
Serbian (0)	76	0.33
Slovak (0)	75	0.32
Slovene (8)	132	0.57
Swedish (136)	569	2.46
Swiss (96)	244	1.06
Ukrainian (61)	97	0.42
Welsh (0)	132	0.57
West Indian, ex. Hispanic (0)	9	0.04
Jamaican (0)	9	0.04
Yugoslavian (7)	7	0.03

Hispanic Origin	Population	%
Hispanic or Latino (of any race)	467	2.02
Central American, ex. Mexican	38	0.16
Costa Rican	3	0.01
Guatemalan	21	0.09
Honduran	1	<0.01
Nicaraguan	6	0.03
Panamanian	5	0.02
Salvadoran	2	0.01
Cuban	29	0.13
Dominican Republic	1	<0.01
Mexican	185	0.80
Puerto Rican	57	0.25
South American	98	0.42
Argentinean	8	0.03
Bolivian	2	0.01
Chilean	8	0.03
Colombian	45	0.19
Ecuadorian	1	<0.01
Peruvian	18	0.08
Uruguayan	1	<0.01
Venezuelan	9	0.04
Other South American	6	0.03
Other Hispanic or Latino	59	0.26

Race*	Population	%
African-American/Black (641)	740	3.20
Not Hispanic (630)	714	3.09
Hispanic (11)	26	0.11
American Indian/Alaska Native (31)	98	0.42
Not Hispanic (23)	89	0.38
Hispanic (8)	9	0.04
Arapaho (0)	1	<0.01
Blackfeet (0)	1	<0.01
Central American Ind. (3)	3	0.01
Cherokee (3)	10	0.04
Chippewa (3)	14	0.06
Choctaw (0)	9	0.04
Iroquois (5)	11	0.05
Menominee (1)	1	<0.01
Mexican American Ind. (0)	1	<0.01
Osage (0)	1	<0.01
Potawatomi (0)	1	<0.01
Seminole (2)	2	0.01
Shoshone (1)	2	0.01
Sioux (1)	6	0.03
Asian (824)	969	4.19
Not Hispanic (823)	963	4.16
Hispanic (1)	6	0.03
Bangladeshi (0)	1	<0.01
Chinese, ex. Taiwanese (197)	227	0.98
Filipino (29)	50	0.22
Hmong (18)	20	0.09
Indian (296)	324	1.40
Indonesian (4)	5	0.02
Japanese (18)	38	0.16
Korean (83)	107	0.46
Laotian (1)	4	0.02
Pakistani (82)	97	0.42
Sri Lankan (0)	3	0.01
Taiwanese (12)	12	0.05
Thai (10)	12	0.05
Vietnamese (37)	46	0.20
Hawaii Native/Pacific Islander (7)	17	0.07
Not Hispanic (7)	14	0.06
Hispanic (0)	3	0.01
Guamanian/Chamorro (1)	1	<0.01
Native Hawaiian (1)	5	0.02
Samoan (2)	7	0.03
White (21,272)	21,539	93.11
Not Hispanic (20,905)	21,151	91.44
Hispanic (367)	388	1.68

Merrill

Place Type: City
County: Lincoln
Population: 9,661†

Ancestry‡	Population	%
American (404)	404	4.12
Arab (0)	36	0.37
Lebanese (0)	36	0.37
Austrian (0)	70	0.71
Belgian (0)	25	0.26
British (0)	13	0.13
Canadian (0)	26	0.27
Czech (57)	187	1.91
Danish (11)	76	0.78
Dutch (7)	77	0.79
English (121)	593	6.05
Finnish (0)	66	0.67
French, ex. Basque (0)	394	4.02
French Canadian (98)	162	1.65
German (3,389)	6,302	64.31
Greek (12)	12	0.12
Hungarian (0)	97	0.99
Irish (148)	862	8.80
Italian (60)	145	1.48
Latvian (0)	11	0.11
Luxemburger (0)	11	0.11
Norwegian (126)	546	5.57
Polish (253)	1,080	11.02
Russian (21)	74	0.76
Scandinavian (0)	117	1.19
Scotch-Irish (0)	92	0.94
Scottish (0)	56	0.57
Swedish (45)	277	2.83
Swiss (32)	185	1.89
Ukrainian (0)	7	0.07
Welsh (0)	20	0.20
West Indian, ex. Hispanic (26)	26	0.27
Jamaican (26)	26	0.27

Hispanic Origin	Population	%
Hispanic or Latino (of any race)	196	2.03
Central American, ex. Mexican	12	0.12
Guatemalan	3	0.03
Nicaraguan	9	0.09
Mexican	145	1.50
Puerto Rican	21	0.22
South American	3	0.03
Peruvian	3	0.03
Other Hispanic or Latino	15	0.16

Race*	Population	%
African-American/Black (52)	96	0.99
Not Hispanic (50)	94	0.97
Hispanic (2)	2	0.02
American Indian/Alaska Native (40)	89	0.92
Not Hispanic (32)	80	0.83
Hispanic (8)	9	0.09
Apache (1)	2	0.02
Blackfeet (0)	2	0.02
Canadian/French Am. Ind. (0)	1	0.01
Cherokee (2)	6	0.06
Chickasaw (0)	1	0.01
Chippewa (11)	25	0.26
Choctaw (0)	3	0.03
Creek (1)	1	0.01
Delaware (0)	1	0.01
Inupiat *(Alaska Native)* (0)	1	0.01
Iroquois (3)	7	0.07
Menominee (1)	1	0.01
Potawatomi (0)	2	0.02
Seminole (1)	2	0.02
Sioux (1)	1	0.01
Tlingit-Haida *(Alaska Native)* (0)	1	0.01
Asian (58)	75	0.78
Not Hispanic (58)	75	0.78
Chinese, ex. Taiwanese (10)	13	0.13
Filipino (17)	20	0.21
Hmong (8)	8	0.08
Indian (4)	9	0.09
Japanese (2)	4	0.04
Korean (5)	5	0.05
Laotian (2)	2	0.02
Pakistani (1)	1	0.01
Taiwanese (0)	2	0.02
Thai (2)	5	0.05
Vietnamese (3)	4	0.04
Hawaii Native/Pacific Islander (3)	7	0.07
Not Hispanic (3)	7	0.07

*Notes: † The Census 2010 population figure is used to calculate the percentages in the Hispanic Origin and Race categories. Ancestry percentages are based on the 2006-2010 American Community Survey population (not shown); ‡ Numbers in parentheses indicate the number of people reporting a single ancestry; * Numbers in parentheses indicate the number of persons reporting this race alone, not in combination with any other race; Please refer to the Explanation of Data for more information.*

Guamanian/Chamorro (0)	2	0.02
Native Hawaiian (2)	2	0.02
White (9,306)	9,423	97.54
Not Hispanic (9,217)	9,316	96.43
Hispanic (89)	107	1.11

Merton

Place Type: Town
County: Waukesha
Population: 8,338†

Ancestry‡	Population	%
American (197)	197	2.37
Arab (4)	8	0.10
Arab (4)	8	0.10
Armenian (0)	13	0.16
Austrian (12)	73	0.88
Belgian (0)	18	0.22
Brazilian (16)	43	0.52
British (0)	40	0.48
Canadian (12)	21	0.25
Croatian (16)	55	0.66
Czech (12)	100	1.20
Czechoslovakian (8)	8	0.10
Danish (35)	138	1.66
Dutch (6)	118	1.42
Eastern European (32)	32	0.38
English (126)	634	7.63
Estonian (0)	10	0.12
European (104)	108	1.30
Finnish (6)	18	0.22
French, ex. Basque (22)	236	2.84
French Canadian (15)	75	0.90
German (1,883)	4,821	57.99
Greek (11)	104	1.25
Hungarian (16)	40	0.48
Irish (205)	1,276	15.35
Italian (79)	334	4.02
Lithuanian (6)	19	0.23
Luxemburger (0)	8	0.10
Northern European (7)	7	0.08
Norwegian (106)	451	5.43
Polish (274)	1,234	14.84
Portuguese (7)	12	0.14
Romanian (0)	11	0.13
Russian (10)	67	0.81
Scandinavian (17)	94	1.13
Scotch-Irish (19)	79	0.95
Scottish (5)	77	0.93
Serbian (0)	7	0.08
Slavic (0)	4	0.05
Slovak (17)	68	0.82
Slovene (0)	12	0.14
Soviet Union (4)	4	0.05
Swedish (50)	202	2.43
Swiss (7)	83	1.00
Welsh (8)	37	0.45
Yugoslavian (0)	34	0.41

Hispanic Origin	Population	%
Hispanic or Latino (of any race)	104	1.25
Central American, ex. Mexican	7	0.08
Costa Rican	1	0.01
Guatemalan	3	0.04
Salvadoran	3	0.04
Cuban	10	0.12
Dominican Republic	1	0.01
Mexican	54	0.65
Puerto Rican	12	0.14
South American	7	0.08
Argentinean	1	0.01
Bolivian	1	0.01
Ecuadorian	4	0.05
Peruvian	1	0.01
Other Hispanic or Latino	13	0.16

Race*	Population	%
African-American/Black (21)	34	0.41
Not Hispanic (19)	32	0.38
Hispanic (2)	2	0.02
American Indian/Alaska Native (15)	28	0.34
Not Hispanic (15)	28	0.34
Blackfeet (0)	1	0.01
Cherokee (1)	1	0.01
Chippewa (3)	5	0.06
Creek (0)	3	0.04
Inupiat *(Alaska Native)* (1)	1	0.01
Mexican American Ind. (0)	1	0.01
Navajo (1)	1	0.01
Asian (90)	114	1.37
Not Hispanic (90)	114	1.37
Chinese, ex. Taiwanese (24)	27	0.32
Filipino (8)	11	0.13
Hmong (10)	10	0.12
Indian (16)	16	0.19
Japanese (5)	12	0.14
Korean (16)	22	0.26
Laotian (1)	3	0.04
Thai (1)	3	0.04
Vietnamese (7)	8	0.10
Hawaii Native/Pacific Islander (1)	3	0.04
Not Hispanic (1)	3	0.04
Guamanian/Chamorro (1)	2	0.02
Native Hawaiian (0)	1	0.01
White (8,130)	8,190	98.22
Not Hispanic (8,052)	8,101	97.16
Hispanic (78)	89	1.07

Middleton

Place Type: City
County: Dane
Population: 17,442†

Ancestry‡	Population	%
African, Sub-Saharan (179)	188	1.10
African (85)	85	0.50
South African (59)	68	0.40
Other Sub-Saharan African (35)	35	0.20
American (244)	244	1.42
Arab (64)	77	0.45
Arab (64)	64	0.37
Other Arab (0)	13	0.08
Armenian (0)	19	0.11
Australian (0)	15	0.09
Austrian (0)	134	0.78
Basque (0)	8	0.05
Belgian (17)	93	0.54
British (45)	100	0.58
Cajun (0)	10	0.06
Canadian (25)	33	0.19
Croatian (0)	17	0.10
Czech (46)	361	2.10
Czechoslovakian (0)	27	0.16
Danish (16)	254	1.48
Dutch (82)	241	1.40
Eastern European (20)	20	0.12
English (506)	2,411	14.05
European (225)	347	2.02
Finnish (19)	34	0.20
French, ex. Basque (10)	459	2.67
French Canadian (42)	127	0.74
German (2,545)	7,600	44.28
Greek (26)	54	0.31
Iranian (27)	65	0.38
Irish (536)	2,855	16.63
Italian (119)	426	2.48
Lithuanian (13)	51	0.30
New Zealander (12)	25	0.15
Northern European (44)	44	0.26
Norwegian (454)	1,806	10.52
Polish (268)	1,056	6.15
Portuguese (0)	37	0.22
Russian (111)	223	1.30
Scandinavian (39)	47	0.27
Scotch-Irish (65)	290	1.69
Scottish (39)	397	2.31
Serbian (13)	25	0.15
Slovak (0)	25	0.15
Swedish (74)	385	2.24
Swiss (115)	390	2.27
Turkish (0)	10	0.06
Ukrainian (0)	35	0.20
Welsh (0)	79	0.46
Yugoslavian (0)	30	0.17

Hispanic Origin	Population	%
Hispanic or Latino (of any race)	984	5.64
Central American, ex. Mexican	59	0.34
Costa Rican	8	0.05
Guatemalan	16	0.09
Honduran	10	0.06
Nicaraguan	14	0.08
Panamanian	7	0.04
Salvadoran	4	0.02
Cuban	26	0.15
Dominican Republic	7	0.04
Mexican	562	3.22
Puerto Rican	80	0.46
South American	160	0.92
Argentinean	15	0.09
Bolivian	41	0.24
Chilean	18	0.10
Colombian	35	0.20
Ecuadorian	1	0.01
Paraguayan	1	0.01
Peruvian	23	0.13
Uruguayan	6	0.03
Venezuelan	20	0.11
Other Hispanic or Latino	90	0.52

Race*	Population	%
African-American/Black (606)	824	4.72
Not Hispanic (582)	784	4.49
Hispanic (24)	40	0.23
American Indian/Alaska Native (58)	126	0.72
Not Hispanic (41)	102	0.58
Hispanic (17)	24	0.14
Blackfeet (0)	3	0.02
Cherokee (1)	5	0.03
Cheyenne (5)	5	0.03
Chippewa (4)	9	0.05
Choctaw (0)	4	0.02
Comanche (3)	3	0.02
Delaware (0)	3	0.02
Iroquois (2)	6	0.03
Menominee (2)	5	0.03
Mexican American Ind. (9)	12	0.07
Ottawa (1)	2	0.01
Sioux (1)	4	0.02
South American Ind. (0)	3	0.02
Yup'ik *(Alaska Native)* (1)	1	0.01
Asian (734)	881	5.05
Not Hispanic (730)	870	4.99
Hispanic (4)	11	0.06
Cambodian (8)	9	0.05
Chinese, ex. Taiwanese (241)	279	1.60
Filipino (55)	84	0.48
Hmong (28)	28	0.16
Indian (176)	197	1.13
Indonesian (8)	8	0.05
Japanese (27)	48	0.28
Korean (123)	138	0.79
Laotian (5)	6	0.03
Malaysian (1)	3	0.02
Nepalese (7)	7	0.04
Pakistani (7)	8	0.05
Sri Lankan (1)	1	0.01
Taiwanese (15)	19	0.11
Thai (6)	10	0.06
Vietnamese (11)	17	0.10
Hawaii Native/Pacific Islander (8)	12	0.07
Not Hispanic (7)	11	0.06
Hispanic (1)	1	0.01
Fijian (0)	1	0.01
Guamanian/Chamorro (1)	2	0.01
Native Hawaiian (3)	3	0.02
White (15,191)	15,606	89.47
Not Hispanic (14,694)	15,052	86.30

*Notes: † The Census 2010 population figure is used to calculate the percentages in the Hispanic Origin and Race categories. Ancestry percentages are based on the 2006-2010 American Community Survey population (not shown); ‡ Numbers in parentheses indicate the number of people reporting a single ancestry; * Numbers in parentheses indicate the number of persons reporting this race alone, not in combination with any other race; Please refer to the Explanation of Data for more information.*

SECTION TWO

Hispanic (497)	554	3.18

Milwaukee

Place Type: City
County: Milwaukee
Population: 594,833†

Ancestry‡	Population	%
African, Sub-Saharan (6,417)	7,187	1.22
African (5,096)	5,691	0.97
Ethiopian (38)	104	0.02
Ghanaian (19)	19	<0.01
Kenyan (35)	44	0.01
Liberian (70)	70	0.01
Nigerian (550)	599	0.10
Senegalese (0)	18	<0.01
Sierra Leonean (15)	15	<0.01
Somalian (381)	381	0.06
South African (103)	128	0.02
Sudanese (19)	19	<0.01
Ugandan (33)	33	0.01
Zimbabwean (19)	19	<0.01
Other Sub-Saharan African (39)	47	0.01
Albanian (105)	109	0.02
Alsatian (12)	30	0.01
American (5,809)	5,809	0.99
Arab (1,555)	2,196	0.37
Arab (326)	396	0.07
Egyptian (14)	14	<0.01
Iraqi (97)	135	0.02
Jordanian (166)	327	0.06
Lebanese (80)	192	0.03
Moroccan (52)	144	0.02
Palestinian (385)	507	0.09
Syrian (9)	24	<0.01
Other Arab (426)	457	0.08
Armenian (134)	191	0.03
Assyrian/Chaldean/Syriac (13)	28	<0.01
Australian (100)	159	0.03
Austrian (409)	1,985	0.34
Basque (16)	28	<0.01
Belgian (276)	1,121	0.19
Brazilian (56)	73	0.01
British (235)	719	0.12
Bulgarian (8)	70	0.01
Cajun (0)	33	0.01
Canadian (151)	407	0.07
Celtic (13)	30	0.01
Croatian (475)	1,587	0.27
Czech (943)	3,843	0.65
Czechoslovakian (171)	411	0.07
Danish (238)	1,843	0.31
Dutch (966)	4,173	0.71
Eastern European (250)	302	0.05
English (3,342)	15,507	2.63
Estonian (22)	54	0.01
European (2,512)	2,989	0.51
Finnish (502)	1,685	0.29
French, ex. Basque (1,097)	10,118	1.72
French Canadian (519)	2,607	0.44
German (41,743)	116,547	19.76
German Russian (310)	376	0.06
Greek (684)	1,571	0.27
Hungarian (563)	2,141	0.36
Iranian (139)	177	0.03
Irish (8,135)	37,577	6.37
Israeli (36)	42	0.01
Italian (5,525)	16,628	2.82
Latvian (216)	413	0.07
Lithuanian (244)	643	0.11
Luxemburger (27)	219	0.04
Macedonian (19)	127	0.02
Northern European (225)	225	0.04
Norwegian (2,950)	12,450	2.11
Pennsylvania German (32)	61	0.01
Polish (16,887)	47,271	8.02
Portuguese (68)	341	0.06
Romanian (116)	273	0.05
Russian (960)	3,017	0.51
Scandinavian (251)	660	0.11
Scotch-Irish (603)	2,581	0.44
Scottish (554)	2,988	0.51
Serbian (1,418)	2,035	0.35
Slavic (112)	281	0.05
Slovak (383)	1,159	0.20
Slovene (348)	851	0.14
Swedish (1,046)	5,711	0.97
Swiss (167)	1,595	0.27
Turkish (133)	209	0.04
Ukrainian (423)	830	0.14
Welsh (213)	1,285	0.22
West Indian, ex. Hispanic (1,114)	1,812	0.31
Bahamian (13)	13	<0.01
Barbadian (24)	46	0.01
Belizean (0)	39	0.01
British West Indian (14)	23	<0.01
Haitian (188)	196	0.03
Jamaican (801)	1,209	0.21
Trinidadian/Tobagonian (18)	32	0.01
U.S. Virgin Islander (8)	42	0.01
West Indian (48)	212	0.04
Yugoslavian (497)	674	0.11

Hispanic Origin	Population	%
Hispanic or Latino (of any race)	103,007	17.32
Central American, ex. Mexican	1,962	0.33
Costa Rican	210	0.04
Guatemalan	432	0.07
Honduran	282	0.05
Nicaraguan	397	0.07
Panamanian	150	0.03
Salvadoran	473	0.08
Other Central American	18	<0.01
Cuban	866	0.15
Dominican Republic	720	0.12
Mexican	69,680	11.71
Puerto Rican	24,672	4.15
South American	1,299	0.22
Argentinean	85	0.01
Bolivian	59	0.01
Chilean	115	0.02
Colombian	440	0.07
Ecuadorian	112	0.02
Paraguayan	20	<0.01
Peruvian	307	0.05
Uruguayan	12	<0.01
Venezuelan	137	0.02
Other South American	12	<0.01
Other Hispanic or Latino	3,808	0.64

Race*	Population	%
African-American/Black (237,769)	250,003	42.03
Not Hispanic (233,325)	243,059	40.86
Hispanic (4,444)	6,944	1.17
American Indian/Alaska Native (4,695)	9,678	1.63
Not Hispanic (3,408)	7,226	1.21
Hispanic (1,287)	2,452	0.41
Alaska Athabascan *(Ala. Nat.)* (1)	5	<0.01
Apache (35)	91	0.02
Arapaho (0)	1	<0.01
Blackfeet (24)	213	0.04
Canadian/French Am. Ind. (17)	29	<0.01
Central American Ind. (17)	25	<0.01
Cherokee (91)	738	0.12
Cheyenne (9)	13	<0.01
Chickasaw (11)	26	<0.01
Chippewa (818)	1,301	0.22
Choctaw (12)	111	0.02
Comanche (4)	11	<0.01
Cree (5)	25	<0.01
Creek (8)	31	0.01
Crow (3)	11	<0.01
Delaware (2)	12	<0.01
Hopi (1)	5	<0.01
Houma (1)	1	<0.01
Inupiat *(Alaska Native)* (4)	12	<0.01
Iroquois (562)	938	0.16
Kiowa (2)	6	<0.01
Lumbee (5)	6	<0.01
Menominee (344)	504	0.08
Mexican American Ind. (169)	291	0.05
Navajo (20)	48	0.01
Osage (5)	6	<0.01
Ottawa (20)	40	0.01
Paiute (0)	1	<0.01
Pima (6)	13	<0.01
Potawatomi (111)	161	0.03
Pueblo (0)	6	<0.01
Puget Sound Salish (0)	1	<0.01
Seminole (1)	19	<0.01
Shoshone (1)	1	<0.01
Sioux (71)	166	0.03
South American Ind. (75)	141	0.02
Spanish American Ind. (13)	26	<0.01
Tlingit-Haida *(Alaska Native)* (2)	6	<0.01
Tohono O'Odham (2)	2	<0.01
Ute (4)	5	<0.01
Yaqui (4)	6	<0.01
Yuman (2)	2	<0.01
Yup'ik *(Alaska Native)* (0)	1	<0.01
Asian (20,851)	23,685	3.98
Not Hispanic (20,553)	22,970	3.86
Hispanic (298)	715	0.12
Bangladeshi (16)	16	<0.01
Burmese (837)	882	0.15
Cambodian (52)	83	0.01
Chinese, ex. Taiwanese (1,250)	1,666	0.28
Filipino (895)	1,473	0.25
Hmong (9,862)	10,245	1.72
Indian (2,510)	3,037	0.51
Indonesian (26)	69	0.01
Japanese (227)	529	0.09
Korean (537)	771	0.13
Laotian (1,526)	1,749	0.29
Malaysian (42)	46	0.01
Nepalese (19)	24	<0.01
Pakistani (542)	629	0.11
Sri Lankan (31)	37	0.01
Taiwanese (49)	64	0.01
Thai (162)	252	0.04
Vietnamese (811)	1,025	0.17
Hawaii Native/Pacific Islander (241)	786	0.13
Not Hispanic (195)	565	0.09
Hispanic (46)	221	0.04
Fijian (2)	11	<0.01
Guamanian/Chamorro (45)	103	0.02
Marshallese (7)	7	<0.01
Native Hawaiian (74)	199	0.03
Samoan (37)	66	0.01
Tongan (4)	8	<0.01
White (266,339)	282,615	47.51
Not Hispanic (220,219)	231,019	38.84
Hispanic (46,120)	51,596	8.67

Monona

Place Type: City
County: Dane
Population: 7,533†

Ancestry‡	Population	%
African, Sub-Saharan (0)	11	0.14
Ghanaian (0)	11	0.14
American (304)	304	4.00
Austrian (0)	66	0.87
Basque (0)	10	0.13
Belgian (11)	11	0.14
British (76)	87	1.15
Bulgarian (10)	10	0.13
Canadian (30)	63	0.83
Czech (10)	215	2.83
Czechoslovakian (11)	11	0.14
Danish (23)	147	1.93
Dutch (46)	119	1.57
Eastern European (12)	24	0.32
English (104)	958	12.61
European (112)	121	1.59
Finnish (0)	18	0.24
French, ex. Basque (50)	294	3.87

*Notes: † The Census 2010 population figure is used to calculate the percentages in the Hispanic Origin and Race categories. Ancestry percentages are based on the 2006-2010 American Community Survey population (not shown); ‡ Numbers in parentheses indicate the number of people reporting a single ancestry; * Numbers in parentheses indicate the number of persons reporting this race alone, not in combination with any other race; Please refer to the Explanation of Data for more information.*

Ancestry	Population	%
French Canadian (20)	52	0.68
German (1,129)	3,444	45.33
Greek (0)	13	0.17
Hungarian (12)	57	0.75
Irish (294)	1,345	17.70
Italian (114)	422	5.55
Macedonian (11)	32	0.42
Norwegian (381)	1,186	15.61
Polish (103)	337	4.44
Russian (19)	86	1.13
Scandinavian (12)	12	0.16
Scotch-Irish (33)	161	2.12
Scottish (0)	171	2.25
Serbian (0)	13	0.17
Slavic (0)	38	0.50
Slovak (0)	13	0.17
Slovene (0)	9	0.12
Swedish (54)	218	2.87
Swiss (19)	185	2.43
Welsh (14)	69	0.91

Hispanic Origin	Population	%
Hispanic or Latino (of any race)	232	3.08
Central American, ex. Mexican	11	0.15
Guatemalan	3	0.04
Honduran	3	0.04
Nicaraguan	1	0.01
Panamanian	2	0.03
Salvadoran	1	0.01
Other Central American	1	0.01
Cuban	9	0.12
Dominican Republic	2	0.03
Mexican	136	1.81
Puerto Rican	24	0.32
South American	31	0.41
Argentinean	1	0.01
Bolivian	5	0.07
Colombian	3	0.04
Ecuadorian	3	0.04
Paraguayan	1	0.01
Peruvian	10	0.13
Venezuelan	1	0.01
Other South American	7	0.09
Other Hispanic or Latino	19	0.25

Race*	Population	%
African-American/Black (210)	268	3.56
Not Hispanic (202)	255	3.39
Hispanic (8)	13	0.17
American Indian/Alaska Native (39)	84	1.12
Not Hispanic (31)	69	0.92
Hispanic (8)	15	0.20
Alaska Athabascan *(Ala. Nat.)* (1)	1	0.01
Blackfeet (0)	1	0.01
Cherokee (1)	11	0.15
Chickasaw (2)	2	0.03
Chippewa (7)	9	0.12
Cree (0)	1	0.01
Iroquois (0)	1	0.01
Menominee (1)	1	0.01
Mexican American Ind. (3)	3	0.04
Navajo (1)	1	0.01
South American Ind. (3)	4	0.05
Asian (102)	134	1.78
Not Hispanic (100)	132	1.75
Hispanic (2)	2	0.03
Chinese, ex. Taiwanese (23)	30	0.40
Filipino (9)	13	0.17
Hmong (11)	11	0.15
Indian (8)	9	0.12
Indonesian (1)	4	0.05
Japanese (13)	24	0.32
Korean (6)	13	0.17
Laotian (7)	7	0.09
Nepalese (3)	3	0.04
Sri Lankan (1)	1	0.01
Taiwanese (2)	3	0.04
Thai (2)	4	0.05
Vietnamese (8)	10	0.13
Hawaii Native/Pacific Islander (2)	6	0.08
Not Hispanic (2)	6	0.08
Native Hawaiian (1)	2	0.03
Samoan (1)	1	0.01
White (6,970)	7,091	94.13
Not Hispanic (6,842)	6,947	92.22
Hispanic (128)	144	1.91

Monroe

Place Type: City
County: Green
Population: 10,827†

Ancestry‡	Population	%
African, Sub-Saharan (16)	16	0.15
African (16)	16	0.15
Albanian (0)	24	0.22
American (393)	393	3.62
Austrian (9)	26	0.24
Belgian (0)	11	0.10
Canadian (11)	22	0.20
Czech (30)	111	1.02
Danish (0)	29	0.27
Dutch (51)	191	1.76
English (256)	847	7.79
European (13)	58	0.53
Finnish (25)	34	0.31
French, ex. Basque (21)	404	3.72
French Canadian (0)	42	0.39
German (1,668)	4,256	39.17
Greek (0)	10	0.09
Hungarian (0)	7	0.06
Irish (428)	1,172	10.79
Italian (22)	97	0.89
Norwegian (638)	1,523	14.02
Pennsylvania German (48)	96	0.88
Polish (65)	172	1.58
Romanian (7)	7	0.06
Russian (27)	27	0.25
Scandinavian (0)	33	0.30
Scotch-Irish (21)	107	0.98
Scottish (0)	31	0.29
Slovak (0)	10	0.09
Swedish (17)	236	2.17
Swiss (903)	2,626	24.17
Welsh (12)	30	0.28
Yugoslavian (8)	8	0.07

Hispanic Origin	Population	%
Hispanic or Latino (of any race)	526	4.86
Central American, ex. Mexican	15	0.14
Guatemalan	8	0.07
Honduran	3	0.03
Salvadoran	4	0.04
Cuban	12	0.11
Mexican	439	4.05
Puerto Rican	11	0.10
South American	3	0.03
Peruvian	1	0.01
Venezuelan	1	0.01
Other South American	1	0.01
Other Hispanic or Latino	46	0.42

Race*	Population	%
African-American/Black (62)	118	1.09
Not Hispanic (59)	114	1.05
Hispanic (3)	4	0.04
American Indian/Alaska Native (19)	41	0.38
Not Hispanic (17)	38	0.35
Hispanic (2)	3	0.03
Apache (0)	3	0.03
Cherokee (2)	4	0.04
Chippewa (5)	5	0.05
Iroquois (0)	1	0.01
Potawatomi (1)	1	0.01
Sioux (0)	1	0.01
Asian (76)	97	0.90
Not Hispanic (75)	95	0.88
Hispanic (1)	2	0.02
Chinese, ex. Taiwanese (4)	6	0.06
Filipino (23)	31	0.29
Indian (13)	21	0.19
Japanese (5)	7	0.06
Korean (7)	8	0.07
Sri Lankan (4)	4	0.04
Thai (1)	1	0.01
Vietnamese (15)	16	0.15
Hawaii Native/Pacific Islander (3)	7	0.06
Not Hispanic (3)	5	0.05
Hispanic (0)	2	0.02
Guamanian/Chamorro (0)	3	0.03
Native Hawaiian (3)	4	0.04
Samoan (0)	1	0.01
White (10,261)	10,380	95.87
Not Hispanic (10,049)	10,145	93.70
Hispanic (212)	235	2.17

Mount Pleasant

Place Type: Village
County: Racine
Population: 26,197†

Ancestry‡	Population	%
African, Sub-Saharan (115)	115	0.45
African (115)	115	0.45
American (769)	769	2.99
Armenian (42)	153	0.60
Australian (0)	11	0.04
Austrian (14)	75	0.29
Belgian (11)	141	0.55
British (20)	127	0.49
Canadian (16)	70	0.27
Celtic (18)	18	0.07
Croatian (37)	37	0.14
Czech (179)	667	2.60
Czechoslovakian (37)	174	0.68
Danish (464)	1,671	6.50
Dutch (135)	509	1.98
Eastern European (9)	9	0.04
English (585)	2,009	7.82
European (318)	325	1.26
Finnish (10)	127	0.49
French, ex. Basque (94)	942	3.67
French Canadian (203)	383	1.49
German (3,191)	9,794	38.11
Greek (45)	87	0.34
Hungarian (146)	535	2.08
Irish (412)	2,837	11.04
Israeli (0)	14	0.05
Italian (619)	1,669	6.49
Latvian (0)	15	0.06
Lithuanian (26)	339	1.32
Luxemburger (0)	24	0.09
Northern European (16)	16	0.06
Norwegian (435)	1,661	6.46
Polish (720)	2,111	8.21
Portuguese (0)	10	0.04
Romanian (28)	28	0.11
Russian (46)	367	1.43
Scandinavian (45)	68	0.26
Scotch-Irish (73)	314	1.22
Scottish (93)	340	1.32
Serbian (128)	171	0.67
Slavic (0)	43	0.17
Slovak (42)	85	0.33
Slovene (0)	22	0.09
Swedish (115)	673	2.62
Swiss (0)	92	0.36
Ukrainian (10)	31	0.12
Welsh (19)	157	0.61
West Indian, ex. Hispanic (8)	8	0.03
Jamaican (8)	8	0.03
Yugoslavian (26)	26	0.10

Hispanic Origin	Population	%
Hispanic or Latino (of any race)	2,181	8.33
Central American, ex. Mexican	45	0.17
Costa Rican	5	0.02
Guatemalan	18	0.07

*Notes: † The Census 2010 population figure is used to calculate the percentages in the Hispanic Origin and Race categories. Ancestry percentages are based on the 2006-2010 American Community Survey population (not shown); ‡ Numbers in parentheses indicate the number of people reporting a single ancestry; * Numbers in parentheses indicate the number of persons reporting this race alone, not in combination with any other race; Please refer to the Explanation of Data for more information.*

Honduran	10	0.04
Nicaraguan	1	<0.01
Panamanian	4	0.02
Salvadoran	3	0.01
Other Central American	4	0.02
Cuban	9	0.03
Dominican Republic	2	0.01
Mexican	1,787	6.82
Puerto Rican	144	0.55
South American	60	0.23
Argentinean	16	0.06
Chilean	1	<0.01
Colombian	13	0.05
Ecuadorian	2	0.01
Peruvian	4	0.02
Venezuelan	24	0.09
Other Hispanic or Latino	134	0.51

Race*	Population	%
African-American/Black (1,752)	2,023	7.72
Not Hispanic (1,701)	1,922	7.34
Hispanic (51)	101	0.39
American Indian/Alaska Native (58)	179	0.68
Not Hispanic (48)	156	0.60
Hispanic (10)	23	0.09
Apache (0)	3	0.01
Blackfeet (0)	2	0.01
Central American Ind. (1)	4	0.02
Cherokee (0)	17	0.06
Chippewa (17)	22	0.08
Choctaw (0)	3	0.01
Comanche (0)	1	<0.01
Delaware (0)	3	0.01
Inupiat *(Alaska Native)* (1)	1	<0.01
Iroquois (3)	4	0.02
Menominee (5)	10	0.04
Mexican American Ind. (3)	3	0.01
Ottawa (3)	4	0.02
Seminole (0)	1	<0.01
Shoshone (0)	1	<0.01
Sioux (2)	6	0.02
Asian (561)	660	2.52
Not Hispanic (559)	648	2.47
Hispanic (2)	12	0.05
Chinese, ex. Taiwanese (63)	76	0.29
Filipino (54)	70	0.27
Hmong (6)	6	0.02
Indian (278)	294	1.12
Indonesian (2)	7	0.03
Japanese (15)	23	0.09
Korean (30)	48	0.18
Laotian (12)	14	0.05
Pakistani (22)	28	0.11
Sri Lankan (5)	5	0.02
Taiwanese (4)	4	0.02
Thai (8)	14	0.05
Vietnamese (50)	59	0.23
Hawaii Native/Pacific Islander (4)	14	0.05
Not Hispanic (2)	9	0.03
Hispanic (2)	5	0.02
Guamanian/Chamorro (0)	1	<0.01
Native Hawaiian (2)	3	0.01
Samoan (1)	4	0.02
White (22,523)	23,005	87.82
Not Hispanic (21,302)	21,654	82.66
Hispanic (1,221)	1,351	5.16

Mukwonago

Place Type: Town
County: Waukesha
Population: 7,959†

Ancestry‡	Population	%
American (245)	245	3.14
Austrian (9)	98	1.26
Belgian (0)	18	0.23
Croatian (0)	103	1.32
Czech (43)	137	1.76
Danish (11)	161	2.06
Dutch (25)	118	1.51
English (115)	815	10.45
European (99)	99	1.27
Finnish (0)	46	0.59
French, ex. Basque (0)	344	4.41
French Canadian (9)	104	1.33
German (1,354)	4,406	56.49
Greek (18)	209	2.68
Hungarian (8)	133	1.71
Irish (190)	1,287	16.50
Italian (106)	723	9.27
Latvian (18)	18	0.23
Lithuanian (0)	21	0.27
Norwegian (39)	477	6.12
Polish (480)	1,323	16.96
Russian (0)	14	0.18
Scandinavian (10)	10	0.13
Scotch-Irish (0)	37	0.47
Scottish (10)	87	1.12
Serbian (25)	25	0.32
Slavic (0)	9	0.12
Slovak (0)	53	0.68
Slovene (18)	18	0.23
Swedish (0)	185	2.37
Swiss (0)	42	0.54
Ukrainian (0)	24	0.31
Welsh (43)	102	1.31
Yugoslavian (0)	63	0.81

Hispanic Origin	Population	%
Hispanic or Latino (of any race)	206	2.59
Central American, ex. Mexican	8	0.10
Guatemalan	2	0.03
Honduran	3	0.04
Panamanian	3	0.04
Cuban	1	0.01
Dominican Republic	2	0.03
Mexican	125	1.57
Puerto Rican	38	0.48
South American	11	0.14
Argentinean	2	0.03
Colombian	6	0.08
Ecuadorian	3	0.04
Other Hispanic or Latino	21	0.26

Race*	Population	%
African-American/Black (28)	47	0.59
Not Hispanic (27)	40	0.50
Hispanic (1)	7	0.09
American Indian/Alaska Native (22)	61	0.77
Not Hispanic (17)	47	0.59
Hispanic (5)	14	0.18
Cherokee (2)	4	0.05
Chickasaw (0)	2	0.03
Chippewa (4)	13	0.16
Choctaw (1)	1	0.01
Iroquois (0)	4	0.05
Menominee (3)	7	0.09
Ottawa (1)	1	0.01
Asian (50)	87	1.09
Not Hispanic (50)	85	1.07
Hispanic (0)	2	0.03
Chinese, ex. Taiwanese (14)	17	0.21
Filipino (13)	24	0.30
Hmong (0)	1	0.01
Indian (4)	7	0.09
Indonesian (2)	4	0.05
Japanese (2)	5	0.06
Korean (4)	9	0.11
Thai (3)	6	0.08
Vietnamese (0)	3	0.04
White (7,727)	7,827	98.34
Not Hispanic (7,572)	7,649	96.11
Hispanic (155)	178	2.24

Muskego

Place Type: City
County: Waukesha
Population: 24,135†

Ancestry‡	Population	%
American (716)	716	3.02
Arab (13)	24	0.10
Arab (0)	11	0.05
Lebanese (13)	13	0.05
Armenian (0)	17	0.07
Austrian (43)	284	1.20
Belgian (11)	33	0.14
British (7)	46	0.19
Croatian (11)	282	1.19
Czech (66)	270	1.14
Czechoslovakian (10)	19	0.08
Danish (61)	504	2.12
Dutch (70)	308	1.30
Eastern European (14)	14	0.06
English (236)	1,514	6.38
European (179)	207	0.87
Finnish (51)	246	1.04
French, ex. Basque (110)	833	3.51
French Canadian (27)	186	0.78
German (4,054)	12,615	53.17
Greek (87)	258	1.09
Hungarian (18)	199	0.84
Irish (555)	3,539	14.92
Italian (560)	1,654	6.97
Lithuanian (0)	73	0.31
Luxemburger (10)	48	0.20
Northern European (15)	15	0.06
Norwegian (283)	1,359	5.73
Pennsylvania German (8)	23	0.10
Polish (1,622)	5,534	23.32
Romanian (38)	77	0.32
Russian (101)	226	0.95
Scandinavian (32)	59	0.25
Scotch-Irish (55)	202	0.85
Scottish (40)	180	0.76
Serbian (101)	108	0.46
Slavic (0)	18	0.08
Slovak (32)	89	0.38
Slovene (30)	212	0.89
Swedish (91)	544	2.29
Swiss (0)	185	0.78
Welsh (12)	164	0.69
Yugoslavian (13)	38	0.16

Hispanic Origin	Population	%
Hispanic or Latino (of any race)	545	2.26
Central American, ex. Mexican	17	0.07
Costa Rican	5	0.02
Guatemalan	5	0.02
Honduran	1	<0.01
Nicaraguan	1	<0.01
Panamanian	1	<0.01
Salvadoran	4	0.02
Cuban	12	0.05
Dominican Republic	1	<0.01
Mexican	341	1.41
Puerto Rican	114	0.47
South American	21	0.09
Argentinean	5	0.02
Bolivian	1	<0.01
Chilean	4	0.02
Colombian	4	0.02
Peruvian	4	0.02
Venezuelan	3	0.01
Other Hispanic or Latino	39	0.16

Race*	Population	%
African-American/Black (67)	121	0.50
Not Hispanic (61)	101	0.42
Hispanic (6)	20	0.08
American Indian/Alaska Native (39)	111	0.46
Not Hispanic (36)	99	0.41
Hispanic (3)	12	0.05
Blackfeet (1)	1	<0.01
Cherokee (5)	14	0.06
Chippewa (7)	25	0.10
Inupiat *(Alaska Native)* (1)	1	<0.01
Iroquois (8)	15	0.06
Lumbee (0)	1	<0.01

*Notes: † The Census 2010 population figure is used to calculate the percentages in the Hispanic Origin and Race categories. Ancestry percentages are based on the 2006-2010 American Community Survey population (not shown); ‡ Numbers in parentheses indicate the number of people reporting a single ancestry; * Numbers in parentheses indicate the number of persons reporting this race alone, not in combination with any other race; Please refer to the Explanation of Data for more information.*

Menominee (2)	3	0.01
Mexican American Ind. (0)	1	<0.01
Navajo (0)	5	0.02
Ottawa (1)	2	0.01
Potawatomi (1)	1	<0.01
Sioux (0)	1	<0.01
Asian (215)	315	1.31
Not Hispanic (212)	311	1.29
Hispanic (3)	4	0.02
Chinese, ex. Taiwanese (47)	64	0.27
Filipino (25)	44	0.18
Hmong (3)	3	0.01
Indian (33)	40	0.17
Indonesian (0)	1	<0.01
Japanese (20)	38	0.16
Korean (20)	32	0.13
Laotian (7)	10	0.04
Malaysian (0)	1	<0.01
Pakistani (27)	32	0.13
Taiwanese (0)	1	<0.01
Thai (1)	5	0.02
Vietnamese (17)	34	0.14
Hawaii Native/Pacific Islander (9)	18	0.07
Not Hispanic (9)	18	0.07
Guamanian/Chamorro (3)	5	0.02
Native Hawaiian (1)	5	0.02
Samoan (1)	1	<0.01
White (23,453)	23,695	98.18
Not Hispanic (23,061)	23,256	96.36
Hispanic (392)	439	1.82

Neenah

Place Type: City
County: Winnebago
Population: 25,501†

Ancestry‡	Population	%
African, Sub-Saharan (0)	3	0.01
African (0)	3	0.01
American (1,211)	1,211	4.78
Australian (11)	11	0.04
Austrian (23)	156	0.62
Belgian (68)	234	0.92
British (28)	43	0.17
Bulgarian (0)	11	0.04
Canadian (41)	116	0.46
Croatian (9)	31	0.12
Czech (90)	348	1.37
Czechoslovakian (29)	41	0.16
Danish (90)	314	1.24
Dutch (144)	825	3.26
Eastern European (20)	20	0.08
English (314)	1,851	7.31
Estonian (27)	37	0.15
European (191)	266	1.05
Finnish (88)	207	0.82
French, ex. Basque (110)	1,068	4.22
French Canadian (56)	306	1.21
German (6,866)	13,932	55.01
Greek (46)	72	0.28
Hungarian (12)	67	0.26
Irish (652)	3,083	12.17
Italian (214)	680	2.68
Lithuanian (46)	46	0.18
Norwegian (331)	1,347	5.32
Polish (598)	2,218	8.76
Romanian (0)	9	0.04
Russian (34)	145	0.57
Scandinavian (42)	59	0.23
Scotch-Irish (154)	241	0.95
Scottish (145)	501	1.98
Slovak (20)	72	0.28
Slovene (0)	9	0.04
Swedish (91)	614	2.42
Swiss (0)	160	0.63
Ukrainian (9)	39	0.15
Welsh (0)	164	0.65
West Indian, ex. Hispanic (19)	19	0.08
British West Indian (19)	19	0.08
Yugoslavian (108)	108	0.43

Hispanic Origin	Population	%
Hispanic or Latino (of any race)	967	3.79
Central American, ex. Mexican	38	0.15
Costa Rican	6	0.02
Guatemalan	19	0.07
Nicaraguan	9	0.04
Panamanian	3	0.01
Salvadoran	1	<0.01
Cuban	11	0.04
Dominican Republic	15	0.06
Mexican	702	2.75
Puerto Rican	82	0.32
South American	22	0.09
Argentinean	2	0.01
Chilean	7	0.03
Colombian	11	0.04
Venezuelan	2	0.01
Other Hispanic or Latino	97	0.38

Race*	Population	%
African-American/Black (323)	496	1.95
Not Hispanic (302)	462	1.81
Hispanic (21)	34	0.13
American Indian/Alaska Native (183)	304	1.19
Not Hispanic (160)	278	1.09
Hispanic (23)	26	0.10
Aleut *(Alaska Native)* (1)	1	<0.01
Blackfeet (3)	6	0.02
Canadian/French Am. Ind. (2)	2	0.01
Cherokee (3)	14	0.05
Chippewa (16)	33	0.13
Iroquois (22)	39	0.15
Lumbee (0)	1	<0.01
Menominee (21)	24	0.09
Mexican American Ind. (11)	13	0.05
Navajo (0)	1	<0.01
Ottawa (2)	3	0.01
Potawatomi (22)	33	0.13
Pueblo (0)	4	0.02
Sioux (2)	4	0.02
Asian (367)	455	1.78
Not Hispanic (358)	433	1.70
Hispanic (9)	22	0.09
Burmese (7)	7	0.03
Chinese, ex. Taiwanese (43)	50	0.20
Filipino (28)	50	0.20
Hmong (89)	95	0.37
Indian (66)	78	0.31
Indonesian (1)	1	<0.01
Japanese (12)	38	0.15
Korean (26)	38	0.15
Laotian (15)	19	0.07
Pakistani (11)	11	0.04
Sri Lankan (1)	1	<0.01
Taiwanese (2)	2	0.01
Thai (13)	15	0.06
Vietnamese (21)	30	0.12
Hawaii Native/Pacific Islander (9)	14	0.05
Not Hispanic (8)	13	0.05
Hispanic (1)	1	<0.01
Native Hawaiian (3)	6	0.02
Samoan (0)	1	<0.01
White (23,899)	24,269	95.17
Not Hispanic (23,371)	23,684	92.87
Hispanic (528)	585	2.29

New Berlin

Place Type: City
County: Waukesha
Population: 39,584†

Ancestry‡	Population	%
African, Sub-Saharan (0)	5	0.01
African (0)	5	0.01
American (977)	977	2.47
Arab (129)	210	0.53
Arab (0)	56	0.14
Egyptian (111)	111	0.28
Lebanese (18)	36	0.09
Syrian (0)	7	0.02
Armenian (9)	72	0.18
Austrian (99)	351	0.89
Basque (10)	10	0.03
Belgian (67)	267	0.68
British (55)	168	0.43
Bulgarian (29)	29	0.07
Canadian (0)	43	0.11
Croatian (80)	452	1.14
Czech (56)	396	1.00
Czechoslovakian (23)	68	0.17
Danish (48)	397	1.00
Dutch (149)	671	1.70
Eastern European (13)	13	0.03
English (581)	2,535	6.41
Estonian (0)	8	0.02
European (396)	453	1.15
Finnish (37)	226	0.57
French, ex. Basque (101)	1,510	3.82
French Canadian (17)	115	0.29
German (6,196)	19,800	50.10
Greek (291)	345	0.87
Hungarian (150)	527	1.33
Icelander (0)	10	0.03
Irish (759)	5,668	14.34
Italian (598)	2,214	5.60
Latvian (0)	9	0.02
Lithuanian (34)	137	0.35
Luxemburger (18)	18	0.05
Northern European (61)	81	0.20
Norwegian (520)	2,321	5.87
Pennsylvania German (0)	6	0.02
Polish (2,294)	8,398	21.25
Portuguese (10)	35	0.09
Romanian (14)	126	0.32
Russian (43)	351	0.89
Scandinavian (0)	43	0.11
Scotch-Irish (108)	360	0.91
Scottish (54)	561	1.42
Serbian (234)	275	0.70
Slavic (0)	100	0.25
Slovak (95)	345	0.87
Slovene (55)	166	0.42
Swedish (121)	1,087	2.75
Swiss (20)	274	0.69
Ukrainian (0)	39	0.10
Welsh (34)	230	0.58
West Indian, ex. Hispanic (4)	4	0.01
British West Indian (4)	4	0.01
Yugoslavian (34)	67	0.17

Hispanic Origin	Population	%
Hispanic or Latino (of any race)	1,036	2.62
Central American, ex. Mexican	47	0.12
Guatemalan	25	0.06
Honduran	5	0.01
Nicaraguan	11	0.03
Panamanian	5	0.01
Salvadoran	1	<0.01
Cuban	24	0.06
Dominican Republic	4	0.01
Mexican	635	1.60
Puerto Rican	181	0.46
South American	61	0.15
Argentinean	6	0.02
Chilean	5	0.01
Colombian	30	0.08
Ecuadorian	4	0.01
Paraguayan	1	<0.01
Peruvian	12	0.03
Venezuelan	3	0.01
Other Hispanic or Latino	84	0.21

Race*	Population	%
African-American/Black (290)	413	1.04
Not Hispanic (287)	396	1.00
Hispanic (3)	17	0.04
American Indian/Alaska Native (118)	238	0.60

*Notes: † The Census 2010 population figure is used to calculate the percentages in the Hispanic Origin and Race categories. Ancestry percentages are based on the 2006-2010 American Community Survey population (not shown); ‡ Numbers in parentheses indicate the number of people reporting a single ancestry; * Numbers in parentheses indicate the number of persons reporting this race alone, not in combination with any other race; Please refer to the Explanation of Data for more information.*

Not Hispanic (101)	186	0.47
Hispanic (17)	52	0.13
Apache (2)	3	0.01
Blackfeet (0)	3	0.01
Central American Ind. (0)	2	0.01
Cherokee (10)	29	0.07
Chippewa (42)	59	0.15
Choctaw (0)	2	0.01
Creek (0)	4	0.01
Iroquois (21)	28	0.07
Menominee (8)	8	0.02
Mexican American Ind. (2)	11	0.03
Navajo (0)	4	0.01
Ottawa (1)	3	0.01
Potawatomi (1)	6	0.02
Seminole (2)	3	0.01
Sioux (0)	1	<0.01
South American Ind. (0)	7	0.02
Asian (1,492)	1,668	4.21
Not Hispanic (1,492)	1,663	4.20
Hispanic (0)	5	0.01
Bangladeshi (6)	6	0.02
Burmese (1)	1	<0.01
Cambodian (1)	1	<0.01
Chinese, ex. Taiwanese (372)	422	1.07
Filipino (103)	152	0.38
Hmong (18)	20	0.05
Indian (576)	615	1.55
Indonesian (3)	6	0.02
Japanese (40)	69	0.17
Korean (109)	126	0.32
Laotian (8)	11	0.03
Nepalese (24)	24	0.06
Pakistani (68)	76	0.19
Sri Lankan (2)	7	0.02
Taiwanese (6)	8	0.02
Thai (15)	20	0.05
Vietnamese (81)	96	0.24
Hawaii Native/Pacific Islander (10)	23	0.06
Not Hispanic (10)	22	0.06
Hispanic (0)	1	<0.01
Guamanian/Chamorro (1)	2	0.01
Native Hawaiian (3)	13	0.03
White (36,987)	37,412	94.51
Not Hispanic (36,292)	36,616	92.50
Hispanic (695)	796	2.01

New Richmond

Place Type: City
County: St. Croix
Population: 8,375†

Ancestry‡	Population	%
African, Sub-Saharan (0)	1	0.01
African (0)	1	0.01
American (287)	287	3.48
Austrian (19)	37	0.45
Belgian (0)	13	0.16
British (22)	34	0.41
Czech (10)	66	0.80
Danish (7)	74	0.90
Dutch (18)	160	1.94
English (60)	443	5.37
European (55)	55	0.67
Finnish (67)	111	1.34
French, ex. Basque (73)	443	5.37
French Canadian (17)	44	0.53
German (1,352)	3,825	46.34
Irish (247)	1,130	13.69
Italian (16)	72	0.87
Northern European (19)	19	0.23
Norwegian (425)	1,353	16.39
Polish (118)	304	3.68
Russian (51)	65	0.79
Scandinavian (65)	122	1.48
Scotch-Irish (23)	164	1.99
Scottish (11)	38	0.46
Slavic (11)	43	0.52
Swedish (86)	548	6.64
Swiss (0)	26	0.31
Welsh (0)	63	0.76
Yugoslavian (9)	27	0.33

Hispanic Origin	Population	%
Hispanic or Latino (of any race)	174	2.08
Central American, ex. Mexican	4	0.05
Guatemalan	2	0.02
Panamanian	1	0.01
Salvadoran	1	0.01
Cuban	3	0.04
Mexican	124	1.48
Puerto Rican	22	0.26
South American	7	0.08
Argentinean	1	0.01
Colombian	5	0.06
Peruvian	1	0.01
Other Hispanic or Latino	14	0.17

Race*	Population	%
African-American/Black (108)	169	2.02
Not Hispanic (106)	166	1.98
Hispanic (2)	3	0.04
American Indian/Alaska Native (52)	108	1.29
Not Hispanic (44)	94	1.12
Hispanic (8)	14	0.17
Aleut *(Alaska Native)* (0)	4	0.05
Apache (1)	1	0.01
Blackfeet (1)	1	0.01
Canadian/French Am. Ind. (0)	1	0.01
Chippewa (17)	22	0.26
Comanche (0)	3	0.04
Creek (5)	5	0.06
Iroquois (5)	6	0.07
Seminole (0)	1	0.01
Sioux (6)	9	0.11
Tlingit-Haida *(Alaska Native)* (1)	1	0.01
Asian (60)	92	1.10
Not Hispanic (60)	92	1.10
Chinese, ex. Taiwanese (7)	11	0.13
Filipino (6)	18	0.21
Hmong (18)	18	0.21
Indian (6)	12	0.14
Japanese (3)	5	0.06
Korean (10)	17	0.20
Laotian (0)	2	0.02
Nepalese (2)	2	0.02
Taiwanese (1)	1	0.01
Thai (1)	1	0.01
Vietnamese (3)	6	0.07
Hawaii Native/Pacific Islander (1)	6	0.07
Not Hispanic (1)	4	0.05
Hispanic (0)	2	0.02
Native Hawaiian (0)	1	0.01
White (7,994)	8,120	96.96
Not Hispanic (7,870)	7,984	95.33
Hispanic (124)	136	1.62

Norway

Place Type: Town
County: Racine
Population: 7,948†

Ancestry‡	Population	%
Albanian (15)	15	0.19
American (139)	139	1.76
Arab (0)	13	0.16
Lebanese (0)	13	0.16
Armenian (11)	11	0.14
Assyrian/Chaldean/Syriac (11)	11	0.14
Austrian (3)	60	0.76
Belgian (9)	24	0.30
British (5)	52	0.66
Bulgarian (10)	10	0.13
Croatian (0)	71	0.90
Czech (53)	161	2.04
Danish (20)	119	1.50
Dutch (71)	195	2.47
English (81)	327	4.13
European (65)	70	0.89
Finnish (3)	6	0.08
French, ex. Basque (10)	387	4.89
French Canadian (39)	158	2.00
German (1,435)	4,235	53.55
Greek (0)	37	0.47
Hungarian (0)	42	0.53
Irish (118)	750	9.48
Italian (152)	525	6.64
Lithuanian (17)	31	0.39
Luxemburger (5)	5	0.06
Norwegian (193)	683	8.64
Polish (576)	1,912	24.17
Portuguese (0)	18	0.23
Russian (13)	79	1.00
Scandinavian (0)	85	1.07
Scotch-Irish (0)	7	0.09
Scottish (10)	108	1.37
Serbian (2)	63	0.80
Slovak (0)	2	0.03
Swedish (24)	143	1.81
Swiss (0)	102	1.29
Ukrainian (5)	29	0.37
Welsh (0)	2	0.03
Yugoslavian (0)	36	0.46

Hispanic Origin	Population	%
Hispanic or Latino (of any race)	200	2.52
Central American, ex. Mexican	5	0.06
Guatemalan	3	0.04
Honduran	1	0.01
Nicaraguan	1	0.01
Cuban	2	0.03
Mexican	153	1.93
Puerto Rican	24	0.30
South American	5	0.06
Argentinean	1	0.01
Chilean	1	0.01
Colombian	1	0.01
Peruvian	2	0.03
Other Hispanic or Latino	11	0.14

Race*	Population	%
African-American/Black (27)	46	0.58
Not Hispanic (25)	44	0.55
Hispanic (2)	2	0.03
American Indian/Alaska Native (29)	73	0.92
Not Hispanic (19)	60	0.75
Hispanic (10)	13	0.16
Aleut *(Alaska Native)* (1)	1	0.01
Blackfeet (0)	1	0.01
Cherokee (0)	11	0.14
Chippewa (6)	8	0.10
Comanche (0)	1	0.01
Creek (1)	1	0.01
Iroquois (7)	13	0.16
Menominee (2)	3	0.04
Mexican American Ind. (3)	4	0.05
Navajo (0)	3	0.04
Ottawa (0)	1	0.01
Potawatomi (4)	4	0.05
Asian (35)	66	0.83
Not Hispanic (35)	66	0.83
Chinese, ex. Taiwanese (15)	21	0.26
Filipino (5)	16	0.20
Hmong (2)	2	0.03
Indian (8)	11	0.14
Japanese (0)	9	0.11
Korean (3)	3	0.04
Laotian (1)	2	0.03
Hawaii Native/Pacific Islander (4)	6	0.08
Not Hispanic (4)	6	0.08
Guamanian/Chamorro (2)	3	0.04
Native Hawaiian (2)	3	0.04
White (7,705)	7,802	98.16
Not Hispanic (7,580)	7,659	96.36
Hispanic (125)	143	1.80

*Notes: † The Census 2010 population figure is used to calculate the percentages in the Hispanic Origin and Race categories. Ancestry percentages are based on the 2006-2010 American Community Survey population (not shown); ‡ Numbers in parentheses indicate the number of people reporting a single ancestry; * Numbers in parentheses indicate the number of persons reporting this race alone, not in combination with any other race; Please refer to the Explanation of Data for more information.*

Oak Creek

Place Type: City
County: Milwaukee
Population: 34,451†

Ancestry‡	Population	%
African, Sub-Saharan (230)	318	0.96
African (154)	226	0.68
Ghanaian (0)	16	0.05
Nigerian (76)	76	0.23
Albanian (114)	158	0.48
American (642)	642	1.94
Arab (319)	375	1.13
Arab (55)	55	0.17
Egyptian (11)	11	0.03
Jordanian (68)	68	0.21
Lebanese (13)	21	0.06
Moroccan (32)	32	0.10
Palestinian (83)	123	0.37
Other Arab (57)	65	0.20
Armenian (29)	72	0.22
Australian (0)	13	0.04
Austrian (20)	72	0.22
Belgian (0)	69	0.21
Brazilian (10)	26	0.08
British (12)	19	0.06
Canadian (0)	73	0.22
Croatian (63)	181	0.55
Czech (0)	358	1.08
Czechoslovakian (0)	20	0.06
Danish (76)	348	1.05
Dutch (23)	292	0.88
English (662)	1,897	5.74
European (232)	232	0.70
Finnish (59)	283	0.86
French, ex. Basque (134)	1,532	4.63
French Canadian (57)	247	0.75
German (4,137)	13,746	41.57
Greek (73)	315	0.95
Guyanese (25)	25	0.08
Hungarian (8)	202	0.61
Irish (487)	3,687	11.15
Israeli (37)	75	0.23
Italian (714)	2,262	6.84
Lithuanian (0)	158	0.48
Northern European (11)	11	0.03
Norwegian (287)	1,476	4.46
Pennsylvania German (0)	37	0.11
Polish (3,015)	8,339	25.22
Romanian (19)	19	0.06
Russian (59)	274	0.83
Scandinavian (80)	165	0.50
Scotch-Irish (102)	271	0.82
Scottish (44)	203	0.61
Serbian (29)	127	0.38
Slovak (41)	286	0.86
Slovene (247)	277	0.84
Swedish (97)	535	1.62
Swiss (0)	80	0.24
Ukrainian (11)	37	0.11
Welsh (0)	57	0.17
Yugoslavian (0)	12	0.04

Hispanic Origin	Population	%
Hispanic or Latino (of any race)	2,582	7.49
Central American, ex. Mexican	103	0.30
Costa Rican	12	0.03
Guatemalan	31	0.09
Honduran	7	0.02
Nicaraguan	19	0.06
Panamanian	13	0.04
Salvadoran	16	0.05
Other Central American	5	0.01
Cuban	22	0.06
Dominican Republic	23	0.07
Mexican	1,566	4.55
Puerto Rican	630	1.83
South American	90	0.26
Argentinean	7	0.02
Bolivian	2	0.01
Chilean	11	0.03
Colombian	33	0.10
Ecuadorian	9	0.03
Peruvian	24	0.07
Venezuelan	2	0.01
Other South American	2	0.01
Other Hispanic or Latino	148	0.43

Race*	Population	%
African-American/Black (958)	1,211	3.52
Not Hispanic (904)	1,128	3.27
Hispanic (54)	83	0.24
American Indian/Alaska Native (247)	411	1.19
Not Hispanic (215)	362	1.05
Hispanic (32)	49	0.14
Apache (4)	5	0.01
Arapaho (0)	1	<0.01
Blackfeet (2)	6	0.02
Canadian/French Am. Ind. (1)	2	0.01
Cherokee (2)	18	0.05
Chickasaw (0)	1	<0.01
Chippewa (55)	83	0.24
Choctaw (2)	2	0.01
Creek (0)	2	0.01
Delaware (0)	1	<0.01
Iroquois (29)	39	0.11
Lumbee (2)	2	0.01
Menominee (10)	15	0.04
Mexican American Ind. (2)	7	0.02
Navajo (4)	4	0.01
Ottawa (2)	9	0.03
Potawatomi (0)	3	0.01
Seminole (0)	1	<0.01
Sioux (3)	5	0.01
Ute (1)	1	<0.01
Asian (1,553)	1,808	5.25
Not Hispanic (1,546)	1,781	5.17
Hispanic (7)	27	0.08
Bangladeshi (2)	2	0.01
Burmese (4)	4	0.01
Cambodian (5)	5	0.01
Chinese, ex. Taiwanese (119)	149	0.43
Filipino (118)	167	0.48
Hmong (130)	134	0.39
Indian (757)	800	2.32
Indonesian (2)	8	0.02
Japanese (20)	54	0.16
Korean (78)	117	0.34
Laotian (51)	59	0.17
Malaysian (0)	4	0.01
Pakistani (71)	79	0.23
Sri Lankan (4)	5	0.01
Taiwanese (7)	9	0.03
Thai (6)	11	0.03
Vietnamese (133)	148	0.43
Hawaii Native/Pacific Islander (17)	37	0.11
Not Hispanic (14)	25	0.07
Hispanic (3)	12	0.03
Guamanian/Chamorro (3)	4	0.01
Native Hawaiian (4)	11	0.03
White (30,222)	30,888	89.66
Not Hispanic (28,587)	29,112	84.50
Hispanic (1,635)	1,776	5.16

Oconomowoc

Place Type: City
County: Waukesha
Population: 15,759†

Ancestry‡	Population	%
American (247)	247	1.62
Arab (14)	45	0.29
Lebanese (14)	45	0.29
Australian (0)	17	0.11
Austrian (0)	67	0.44
Belgian (0)	32	0.21
British (16)	16	0.10
Celtic (15)	15	0.10
Croatian (0)	59	0.39
Czech (10)	117	0.77
Czechoslovakian (15)	40	0.26
Danish (0)	229	1.50
Dutch (20)	263	1.72
Eastern European (0)	8	0.05
English (318)	1,255	8.22
European (70)	87	0.57
Finnish (16)	25	0.16
French, ex. Basque (80)	624	4.09
French Canadian (43)	91	0.60
German (3,505)	8,673	56.82
Greek (67)	99	0.65
Hungarian (30)	206	1.35
Irish (360)	2,302	15.08
Italian (186)	903	5.92
Lithuanian (0)	28	0.18
New Zealander (14)	14	0.09
Norwegian (353)	1,190	7.80
Pennsylvania German (13)	13	0.09
Polish (439)	1,715	11.23
Portuguese (0)	17	0.11
Romanian (0)	27	0.18
Russian (0)	166	1.09
Scandinavian (24)	124	0.81
Scotch-Irish (43)	267	1.75
Scottish (161)	398	2.61
Serbian (21)	45	0.29
Slovak (0)	10	0.07
Slovene (80)	90	0.59
Swedish (39)	370	2.42
Swiss (10)	104	0.68
Welsh (16)	79	0.52
West Indian, ex. Hispanic (8)	8	0.05
West Indian (8)	8	0.05
Yugoslavian (0)	34	0.22

Hispanic Origin	Population	%
Hispanic or Latino (of any race)	559	3.55
Central American, ex. Mexican	21	0.13
Costa Rican	1	0.01
Guatemalan	13	0.08
Nicaraguan	6	0.04
Salvadoran	1	0.01
Cuban	17	0.11
Dominican Republic	6	0.04
Mexican	402	2.55
Puerto Rican	54	0.34
South American	39	0.25
Argentinean	7	0.04
Bolivian	1	0.01
Chilean	3	0.02
Colombian	14	0.09
Ecuadorian	5	0.03
Peruvian	5	0.03
Venezuelan	4	0.03
Other Hispanic or Latino	20	0.13

Race*	Population	%
African-American/Black (71)	133	0.84
Not Hispanic (62)	119	0.76
Hispanic (9)	14	0.09
American Indian/Alaska Native (35)	84	0.53
Not Hispanic (30)	74	0.47
Hispanic (5)	10	0.06
Apache (1)	2	0.01
Blackfeet (0)	2	0.01
Central American Ind. (2)	2	0.01
Cherokee (2)	6	0.04
Chippewa (10)	21	0.13
Comanche (1)	3	0.02
Iroquois (4)	7	0.04
Menominee (8)	8	0.05
Potawatomi (1)	2	0.01
Sioux (0)	3	0.02
Asian (160)	226	1.43
Not Hispanic (157)	220	1.40
Hispanic (3)	6	0.04
Cambodian (1)	1	0.01
Chinese, ex. Taiwanese (38)	41	0.26

SECTION TWO

*Notes: † The Census 2010 population figure is used to calculate the percentages in the Hispanic Origin and Race categories. Ancestry percentages are based on the 2006-2010 American Community Survey population (not shown); ‡ Numbers in parentheses indicate the number of people reporting a single ancestry; * Numbers in parentheses indicate the number of persons reporting this race alone, not in combination with any other race; Please refer to the Explanation of Data for more information.*

Filipino (29)	59	0.37
Hmong (16)	16	0.10
Indian (22)	31	0.20
Indonesian (1)	1	0.01
Japanese (10)	13	0.08
Korean (12)	28	0.18
Laotian (4)	4	0.03
Pakistani (6)	6	0.04
Taiwanese (2)	2	0.01
Thai (0)	1	0.01
Vietnamese (17)	17	0.11
Hawaii Native/Pacific Islander (2)	8	0.05
Not Hispanic (2)	8	0.05
Guamanian/Chamorro (0)	1	0.01
Native Hawaiian (0)	4	0.03
White (15,130)	15,315	97.18
Not Hispanic (14,778)	14,936	94.78
Hispanic (352)	379	2.40

Oconomowoc

Place Type: Town
County: Waukesha
Population: 8,408†

Ancestry‡	Population	%
African, Sub-Saharan (12)	12	0.14
South African (12)	12	0.14
Albanian (12)	23	0.28
American (259)	259	3.13
Armenian (0)	39	0.47
Austrian (32)	63	0.76
Belgian (0)	66	0.80
British (40)	75	0.91
Canadian (16)	16	0.19
Croatian (18)	18	0.22
Czech (64)	177	2.14
Danish (43)	214	2.59
Dutch (37)	144	1.74
English (109)	584	7.05
European (122)	122	1.47
Finnish (0)	32	0.39
French, ex. Basque (0)	252	3.04
French Canadian (50)	86	1.04
German (1,929)	4,415	53.33
Greek (10)	10	0.12
Hungarian (0)	76	0.92
Irish (269)	1,119	13.52
Italian (101)	581	7.02
Latvian (28)	45	0.54
Lithuanian (34)	34	0.41
Norwegian (163)	727	8.78
Polish (275)	906	10.94
Russian (18)	104	1.26
Scandinavian (0)	16	0.19
Scotch-Irish (26)	58	0.70
Scottish (41)	99	1.20
Slavic (0)	40	0.48
Slovak (0)	11	0.13
Slovene (0)	15	0.18
Swedish (27)	234	2.83
Swiss (0)	84	1.01
Ukrainian (44)	60	0.72
Welsh (5)	57	0.69
Yugoslavian (8)	8	0.10

Hispanic Origin	Population	%
Hispanic or Latino (of any race)	124	1.47
Central American, ex. Mexican	16	0.19
Guatemalan	7	0.08
Honduran	4	0.05
Nicaraguan	3	0.04
Salvadoran	2	0.02
Cuban	6	0.07
Mexican	62	0.74
Puerto Rican	9	0.11
South American	28	0.33
Argentinean	4	0.05
Chilean	7	0.08
Colombian	13	0.15
Peruvian	1	0.01
Venezuelan	3	0.04
Other Hispanic or Latino	3	0.04

Race*	Population	%
African-American/Black (46)	70	0.83
Not Hispanic (45)	69	0.82
Hispanic (1)	1	0.01
American Indian/Alaska Native (10)	33	0.39
Not Hispanic (8)	26	0.31
Hispanic (2)	7	0.08
Central American Ind. (0)	1	0.01
Cherokee (0)	7	0.08
Chippewa (4)	4	0.05
Iroquois (1)	2	0.02
Menominee (0)	1	0.01
Mexican American Ind. (1)	1	0.01
Potawatomi (0)	3	0.04
Tlingit-Haida *(Alaska Native)* (1)	2	0.02
Asian (47)	71	0.84
Not Hispanic (47)	67	0.80
Hispanic (0)	4	0.05
Chinese, ex. Taiwanese (12)	16	0.19
Filipino (7)	15	0.18
Indian (4)	11	0.13
Indonesian (0)	1	0.01
Japanese (6)	8	0.10
Korean (15)	18	0.21
Thai (0)	1	0.01
Vietnamese (1)	6	0.07
Hawaii Native/Pacific Islander (5)	8	0.10
Not Hispanic (3)	6	0.07
Hispanic (2)	2	0.02
Guamanian/Chamorro (2)	2	0.02
Native Hawaiian (2)	4	0.05
White (8,197)	8,273	98.39
Not Hispanic (8,101)	8,168	97.15
Hispanic (96)	105	1.25

Onalaska

Place Type: City
County: La Crosse
Population: 17,736†

Ancestry‡	Population	%
African, Sub-Saharan (8)	8	0.05
African (8)	8	0.05
American (568)	568	3.31
Arab (0)	50	0.29
Lebanese (0)	50	0.29
Australian (0)	13	0.08
Austrian (0)	24	0.14
Belgian (0)	97	0.57
British (8)	22	0.13
Canadian (61)	61	0.36
Croatian (0)	10	0.06
Czech (39)	242	1.41
Czechoslovakian (15)	31	0.18
Danish (16)	184	1.07
Dutch (30)	330	1.93
English (423)	1,476	8.61
European (257)	308	1.80
Finnish (0)	112	0.65
French, ex. Basque (24)	594	3.47
French Canadian (30)	92	0.54
German (2,717)	7,495	43.74
Greek (28)	59	0.34
Hungarian (58)	168	0.98
Irish (294)	2,101	12.26
Italian (127)	460	2.68
Lithuanian (28)	44	0.26
Northern European (17)	17	0.10
Norwegian (1,066)	3,897	22.74
Polish (226)	1,103	6.44
Romanian (0)	10	0.06
Russian (0)	58	0.34
Scandinavian (31)	69	0.40
Scotch-Irish (12)	116	0.68
Scottish (11)	102	0.60
Slovak (8)	19	0.11
Slovene (18)	28	0.16
Swedish (146)	673	3.93
Swiss (9)	144	0.84
Welsh (0)	100	0.58
West Indian, ex. Hispanic (28)	28	0.16
Jamaican (28)	28	0.16
Yugoslavian (13)	13	0.08

Hispanic Origin	Population	%
Hispanic or Latino (of any race)	276	1.56
Central American, ex. Mexican	25	0.14
Guatemalan	14	0.08
Honduran	1	0.01
Panamanian	8	0.05
Salvadoran	2	0.01
Cuban	7	0.04
Dominican Republic	5	0.03
Mexican	152	0.86
Puerto Rican	30	0.17
South American	12	0.07
Chilean	2	0.01
Colombian	4	0.02
Peruvian	4	0.02
Venezuelan	2	0.01
Other Hispanic or Latino	45	0.25

Race*	Population	%
African-American/Black (200)	325	1.83
Not Hispanic (196)	314	1.77
Hispanic (4)	11	0.06
American Indian/Alaska Native (58)	133	0.75
Not Hispanic (54)	126	0.71
Hispanic (4)	7	0.04
Alaska Athabascan *(Ala. Nat.)* (0)	2	0.01
Apache (0)	4	0.02
Blackfeet (0)	4	0.02
Cherokee (2)	15	0.08
Chippewa (3)	11	0.06
Choctaw (1)	2	0.01
Comanche (1)	1	0.01
Cree (0)	1	0.01
Creek (0)	2	0.01
Iroquois (2)	2	0.01
Lumbee (2)	2	0.01
Menominee (0)	4	0.02
Mexican American Ind. (2)	2	0.01
Navajo (1)	2	0.01
Ottawa (1)	1	0.01
Potawatomi (1)	2	0.01
Puget Sound Salish (1)	1	0.01
Sioux (6)	9	0.05
Asian (1,007)	1,096	6.18
Not Hispanic (1,002)	1,085	6.12
Hispanic (5)	11	0.06
Bangladeshi (5)	5	0.03
Cambodian (1)	3	0.02
Chinese, ex. Taiwanese (93)	101	0.57
Filipino (26)	44	0.25
Hmong (658)	674	3.80
Indian (78)	90	0.51
Indonesian (4)	5	0.03
Japanese (13)	22	0.12
Korean (31)	53	0.30
Laotian (3)	3	0.02
Malaysian (1)	1	0.01
Pakistani (7)	9	0.05
Taiwanese (8)	9	0.05
Thai (4)	11	0.06
Vietnamese (17)	21	0.12
Hawaii Native/Pacific Islander (2)	11	0.06
Not Hispanic (2)	10	0.06
Hispanic (0)	1	0.01
Guamanian/Chamorro (1)	1	0.01
Native Hawaiian (0)	5	0.03
White (16,084)	16,371	92.30
Not Hispanic (15,921)	16,173	91.19
Hispanic (163)	198	1.12

*Notes: † The Census 2010 population figure is used to calculate the percentages in the Hispanic Origin and Race categories. Ancestry percentages are based on the 2006-2010 American Community Survey population (not shown); ‡ Numbers in parentheses indicate the number of people reporting a single ancestry; * Numbers in parentheses indicate the number of persons reporting this race alone, not in combination with any other race; Please refer to the Explanation of Data for more information.*

Oregon

Place Type: Village
County: Dane
Population: 9,231†

Ancestry‡	Population	%
American (220)	220	2.46
Austrian (0)	15	0.17
Belgian (0)	103	1.15
British (50)	69	0.77
Canadian (13)	13	0.15
Czech (0)	67	0.75
Czechoslovakian (23)	50	0.56
Danish (64)	229	2.56
Dutch (38)	159	1.78
Eastern European (34)	34	0.38
English (134)	923	10.32
European (90)	90	1.01
Finnish (12)	31	0.35
French, ex. Basque (28)	397	4.44
French Canadian (6)	23	0.26
German (1,530)	4,010	44.84
Greek (0)	20	0.22
Hungarian (5)	44	0.49
Irish (284)	1,398	15.63
Italian (155)	449	5.02
Latvian (0)	31	0.35
Lithuanian (0)	12	0.13
Luxemburger (13)	38	0.42
Norwegian (457)	1,454	16.26
Polish (145)	321	3.59
Russian (0)	67	0.75
Scandinavian (13)	13	0.15
Scotch-Irish (59)	83	0.93
Scottish (55)	173	1.93
Slavic (0)	19	0.21
Swedish (125)	331	3.70
Swiss (98)	221	2.47
Welsh (0)	50	0.56

Hispanic Origin	Population	%
Hispanic or Latino (of any race)	204	2.21
Central American, ex. Mexican	12	0.13
Guatemalan	5	0.05
Nicaraguan	5	0.05
Panamanian	1	0.01
Salvadoran	1	0.01
Cuban	9	0.10
Mexican	120	1.30
Puerto Rican	6	0.06
South American	41	0.44
Bolivian	11	0.12
Chilean	2	0.02
Colombian	12	0.13
Ecuadorian	1	0.01
Paraguayan	1	0.01
Peruvian	3	0.03
Uruguayan	5	0.05
Venezuelan	6	0.06
Other Hispanic or Latino	16	0.17

Race*	Population	%
African-American/Black (108)	173	1.87
Not Hispanic (106)	169	1.83
Hispanic (2)	4	0.04
American Indian/Alaska Native (15)	39	0.42
Not Hispanic (14)	36	0.39
Hispanic (1)	3	0.03
Blackfeet (0)	1	0.01
Cherokee (1)	7	0.08
Chippewa (3)	8	0.09
Choctaw (0)	1	0.01
Comanche (3)	3	0.03
Menominee (0)	1	0.01
Mexican American Ind. (1)	1	0.01
Ottawa (1)	1	0.01
Sioux (1)	3	0.03
Tlingit-Haida *(Alaska Native)* (2)	2	0.02
Asian (72)	111	1.20
Not Hispanic (72)	111	1.20
Bangladeshi (1)	1	0.01
Cambodian (2)	5	0.05
Chinese, ex. Taiwanese (21)	29	0.31
Filipino (6)	12	0.13
Hmong (0)	2	0.02
Indian (14)	21	0.23
Japanese (4)	13	0.14
Korean (15)	15	0.16
Pakistani (2)	2	0.02
Sri Lankan (1)	1	0.01
Taiwanese (1)	3	0.03
Vietnamese (3)	3	0.03
Hawaii Native/Pacific Islander (14)	21	0.23
Not Hispanic (13)	20	0.22
Hispanic (1)	1	0.01
Guamanian/Chamorro (6)	6	0.06
Native Hawaiian (5)	8	0.09
White (8,806)	8,942	96.87
Not Hispanic (8,683)	8,799	95.32
Hispanic (123)	143	1.55

Oshkosh

Place Type: City
County: Winnebago
Population: 66,083†

Ancestry‡	Population	%
African, Sub-Saharan (134)	188	0.29
African (29)	83	0.13
Ghanaian (9)	9	0.01
Nigerian (8)	8	0.01
Sudanese (88)	88	0.13
American (1,694)	1,694	2.59
Arab (23)	64	0.10
Arab (0)	9	0.01
Lebanese (0)	32	0.05
Other Arab (23)	23	0.04
Austrian (144)	410	0.63
Belgian (38)	305	0.47
British (46)	117	0.18
Canadian (0)	100	0.15
Celtic (7)	7	0.01
Croatian (12)	144	0.22
Czech (141)	572	0.87
Czechoslovakian (40)	63	0.10
Danish (128)	631	0.96
Dutch (233)	1,141	1.74
Eastern European (11)	11	0.02
English (1,017)	3,821	5.83
European (285)	297	0.45
Finnish (102)	515	0.79
French, ex. Basque (439)	2,502	3.82
French Canadian (166)	606	0.93
German (20,531)	35,453	54.12
Greek (23)	94	0.14
Hungarian (71)	190	0.29
Iranian (19)	33	0.05
Irish (1,723)	6,930	10.58
Italian (557)	1,983	3.03
Latvian (0)	11	0.02
Lithuanian (17)	48	0.07
Luxemburger (9)	21	0.03
Northern European (138)	138	0.21
Norwegian (929)	3,074	4.69
Pennsylvania German (10)	19	0.03
Polish (1,333)	5,337	8.15
Romanian (6)	21	0.03
Russian (185)	644	0.98
Scandinavian (128)	177	0.27
Scotch-Irish (92)	513	0.78
Scottish (192)	611	0.93
Slavic (24)	24	0.04
Slovak (22)	44	0.07
Slovene (0)	25	0.04
Swedish (193)	951	1.45
Swiss (77)	458	0.70
Ukrainian (12)	96	0.15
Welsh (63)	630	0.96
West Indian, ex. Hispanic (17)	17	0.03
Haitian (7)	7	0.01
Jamaican (10)	10	0.02
Yugoslavian (11)	55	0.08

Hispanic Origin	Population	%
Hispanic or Latino (of any race)	1,770	2.68
Central American, ex. Mexican	57	0.09
Costa Rican	4	0.01
Guatemalan	13	0.02
Honduran	16	0.02
Nicaraguan	1	<0.01
Panamanian	10	0.02
Salvadoran	13	0.02
Cuban	32	0.05
Dominican Republic	2	<0.01
Mexican	1,182	1.79
Puerto Rican	223	0.34
South American	70	0.11
Argentinean	11	0.02
Chilean	10	0.02
Colombian	18	0.03
Ecuadorian	2	<0.01
Peruvian	17	0.03
Uruguayan	5	0.01
Venezuelan	6	0.01
Other South American	1	<0.01
Other Hispanic or Latino	204	0.31

Race*	Population	%
African-American/Black (2,051)	2,497	3.78
Not Hispanic (1,997)	2,398	3.63
Hispanic (54)	99	0.15
American Indian/Alaska Native (510)	823	1.25
Not Hispanic (479)	750	1.13
Hispanic (31)	73	0.11
Aleut *(Alaska Native)* (3)	10	0.02
Apache (3)	13	0.02
Arapaho (1)	2	<0.01
Blackfeet (0)	6	0.01
Canadian/French Am. Ind. (6)	10	0.02
Cherokee (4)	32	0.05
Chickasaw (1)	1	<0.01
Chippewa (40)	62	0.09
Comanche (3)	4	0.01
Cree (0)	1	<0.01
Crow (0)	1	<0.01
Delaware (0)	1	<0.01
Iroquois (56)	91	0.14
Kiowa (1)	4	0.01
Menominee (51)	79	0.12
Mexican American Ind. (9)	23	0.03
Navajo (2)	4	0.01
Ottawa (8)	8	0.01
Paiute (0)	1	<0.01
Potawatomi (13)	17	0.03
Sioux (1)	5	0.01
South American Ind. (0)	4	0.01
Yuman (0)	1	<0.01
Asian (2,113)	2,394	3.62
Not Hispanic (2,097)	2,351	3.56
Hispanic (16)	43	0.07
Bangladeshi (11)	12	0.02
Burmese (4)	5	0.01
Cambodian (1)	3	<0.01
Chinese, ex. Taiwanese (86)	115	0.17
Filipino (73)	145	0.22
Hmong (1,420)	1,469	2.22
Indian (183)	210	0.32
Indonesian (1)	2	<0.01
Japanese (19)	53	0.08
Korean (47)	85	0.13
Laotian (14)	15	0.02
Nepalese (6)	6	0.01
Pakistani (38)	44	0.07
Sri Lankan (7)	7	0.01
Taiwanese (9)	9	0.01
Thai (5)	9	0.01
Vietnamese (26)	32	0.05
Hawaii Native/Pacific Islander (30)	85	0.13

*Notes: † The Census 2010 population figure is used to calculate the percentages in the Hispanic Origin and Race categories. Ancestry percentages are based on the 2006-2010 American Community Survey population (not shown); ‡ Numbers in parentheses indicate the number of people reporting a single ancestry; * Numbers in parentheses indicate the number of persons reporting this race alone, not in combination with any other race; Please refer to the Explanation of Data for more information.*

Not Hispanic (29)	68	0.10
Hispanic (1)	17	0.03
Fijian (3)	3	<0.01
Guamanian/Chamorro (4)	14	0.02
Native Hawaiian (6)	18	0.03
Samoan (0)	5	0.01
White (59,812)	60,797	92.00
Not Hispanic (58,774)	59,575	90.15
Hispanic (1,038)	1,222	1.85

Pewaukee

Place Type: City
County: Waukesha
Population: 13,195†

Ancestry‡	Population	%
African, Sub-Saharan (60)	97	0.75
African (49)	49	0.38
Ethiopian (11)	48	0.37
American (350)	350	2.70
Arab (0)	16	0.12
Lebanese (0)	16	0.12
Armenian (0)	17	0.13
Austrian (60)	155	1.20
Belgian (22)	146	1.13
British (12)	40	0.31
Bulgarian (8)	8	0.06
Croatian (9)	37	0.29
Czech (116)	272	2.10
Czechoslovakian (42)	108	0.83
Danish (0)	320	2.47
Dutch (42)	253	1.95
English (149)	978	7.54
European (186)	186	1.43
Finnish (13)	13	0.10
French, ex. Basque (68)	507	3.91
French Canadian (47)	74	0.57
German (3,055)	7,372	56.87
Greek (0)	37	0.29
Hungarian (67)	199	1.54
Irish (197)	1,738	13.41
Israeli (11)	11	0.08
Italian (435)	875	6.75
Latvian (13)	13	0.10
Lithuanian (25)	37	0.29
Luxemburger (12)	47	0.36
Northern European (22)	50	0.39
Norwegian (52)	379	2.92
Polish (530)	1,702	13.13
Portuguese (0)	15	0.12
Russian (25)	100	0.77
Scandinavian (0)	36	0.28
Scotch-Irish (14)	100	0.77
Scottish (14)	156	1.20
Serbian (0)	9	0.07
Slovak (19)	76	0.59
Slovene (18)	29	0.22
Swedish (40)	254	1.96
Swiss (61)	237	1.83
Turkish (43)	43	0.33
Ukrainian (8)	39	0.30
Welsh (0)	82	0.63
West Indian, ex. Hispanic (11)	11	0.08
Jamaican (11)	11	0.08
Yugoslavian (0)	11	0.08

Hispanic Origin	Population	%
Hispanic or Latino (of any race)	281	2.13
Central American, ex. Mexican	27	0.20
Costa Rican	4	0.03
Guatemalan	7	0.05
Honduran	2	0.02
Nicaraguan	5	0.04
Panamanian	1	0.01
Salvadoran	8	0.06
Cuban	7	0.05
Dominican Republic	2	0.02
Mexican	165	1.25
Puerto Rican	41	0.31
South American	13	0.10
Argentinean	1	0.01
Chilean	6	0.05
Ecuadorian	4	0.03
Peruvian	2	0.02
Other Hispanic or Latino	26	0.20

Race*	Population	%
African-American/Black (144)	184	1.39
Not Hispanic (136)	174	1.32
Hispanic (8)	10	0.08
American Indian/Alaska Native (35)	65	0.49
Not Hispanic (32)	60	0.45
Hispanic (3)	5	0.04
Cherokee (2)	4	0.03
Chippewa (8)	13	0.10
Creek (0)	2	0.02
Iroquois (1)	4	0.03
Menominee (6)	6	0.05
Mexican American Ind. (1)	1	0.01
Ottawa (4)	4	0.03
Potawatomi (2)	2	0.02
Sioux (1)	1	0.01
Asian (344)	444	3.36
Not Hispanic (338)	438	3.32
Hispanic (6)	6	0.05
Burmese (3)	3	0.02
Cambodian (1)	1	0.01
Chinese, ex. Taiwanese (81)	101	0.77
Filipino (30)	48	0.36
Hmong (3)	3	0.02
Indian (132)	141	1.07
Indonesian (3)	4	0.03
Japanese (7)	20	0.15
Korean (41)	58	0.44
Laotian (5)	5	0.04
Pakistani (20)	23	0.17
Sri Lankan (1)	1	0.01
Taiwanese (2)	2	0.02
Thai (3)	4	0.03
Vietnamese (6)	10	0.08
Hawaii Native/Pacific Islander (3)	14	0.11
Not Hispanic (2)	10	0.08
Hispanic (1)	4	0.03
Guamanian/Chamorro (1)	1	0.01
Native Hawaiian (0)	1	0.01
Samoan (1)	4	0.03
White (12,438)	12,590	95.41
Not Hispanic (12,247)	12,385	93.86
Hispanic (191)	205	1.55

Pewaukee

Place Type: Village
County: Waukesha
Population: 8,166†

Ancestry‡	Population	%
American (183)	183	2.25
Arab (0)	11	0.14
Palestinian (0)	11	0.14
Austrian (0)	69	0.85
Belgian (0)	18	0.22
Canadian (0)	25	0.31
Croatian (5)	35	0.43
Czech (19)	137	1.68
Czechoslovakian (4)	17	0.21
Danish (12)	92	1.13
Dutch (23)	174	2.14
Eastern European (12)	12	0.15
English (102)	480	5.89
European (34)	34	0.42
French, ex. Basque (11)	302	3.71
French Canadian (16)	24	0.29
German (1,808)	4,348	53.40
Hungarian (46)	119	1.46
Irish (278)	1,406	17.27
Italian (267)	831	10.21
Lithuanian (16)	16	0.20
Luxemburger (28)	28	0.34
Norwegian (134)	420	5.16
Polish (279)	967	11.88
Russian (0)	29	0.36
Scotch-Irish (0)	26	0.32
Scottish (0)	67	0.82
Serbian (9)	9	0.11
Slavic (0)	15	0.18
Slovak (0)	52	0.64
Slovene (9)	54	0.66
Swedish (58)	81	0.99
Swiss (11)	59	0.72
Welsh (11)	61	0.75
Yugoslavian (53)	53	0.65

Hispanic Origin	Population	%
Hispanic or Latino (of any race)	286	3.50
Central American, ex. Mexican	22	0.27
Costa Rican	1	0.01
Guatemalan	10	0.12
Honduran	6	0.07
Nicaraguan	2	0.02
Panamanian	1	0.01
Salvadoran	2	0.02
Cuban	9	0.11
Mexican	209	2.56
Puerto Rican	27	0.33
South American	5	0.06
Bolivian	3	0.04
Colombian	1	0.01
Venezuelan	1	0.01
Other Hispanic or Latino	14	0.17

Race*	Population	%
African-American/Black (93)	120	1.47
Not Hispanic (88)	113	1.38
Hispanic (5)	7	0.09
American Indian/Alaska Native (17)	52	0.64
Not Hispanic (13)	44	0.54
Hispanic (4)	8	0.10
Cherokee (0)	6	0.07
Chippewa (7)	8	0.10
Creek (0)	1	0.01
Iroquois (5)	6	0.07
Menominee (0)	1	0.01
Mexican American Ind. (3)	6	0.07
Pima (1)	1	0.01
Potawatomi (0)	1	0.01
Asian (316)	350	4.29
Not Hispanic (315)	348	4.26
Hispanic (1)	2	0.02
Chinese, ex. Taiwanese (50)	53	0.65
Filipino (29)	33	0.40
Hmong (9)	9	0.11
Indian (169)	179	2.19
Japanese (4)	11	0.13
Korean (13)	19	0.23
Laotian (9)	12	0.15
Malaysian (1)	1	0.01
Nepalese (1)	1	0.01
Pakistani (5)	7	0.09
Sri Lankan (1)	1	0.01
Taiwanese (1)	1	0.01
Thai (3)	3	0.04
Vietnamese (12)	12	0.15
Hawaii Native/Pacific Islander (6)	7	0.09
Not Hispanic (6)	7	0.09
Guamanian/Chamorro (1)	1	0.01
Native Hawaiian (3)	3	0.04
White (7,545)	7,638	93.53
Not Hispanic (7,363)	7,442	91.13
Hispanic (182)	196	2.40

Platteville

Place Type: City
County: Grant
Population: 11,224†

Ancestry‡	Population	%
African, Sub-Saharan (15)	42	0.38

*Notes: † The Census 2010 population figure is used to calculate the percentages in the Hispanic Origin and Race categories. Ancestry percentages are based on the 2006-2010 American Community Survey population (not shown); ‡ Numbers in parentheses indicate the number of people reporting a single ancestry; * Numbers in parentheses indicate the number of persons reporting this race alone, not in combination with any other race; Please refer to the Explanation of Data for more information.*

Ancestry	Population	%
African (15)	42	0.38
American (370)	370	3.38
Armenian (0)	6	0.05
Austrian (11)	11	0.10
Belgian (15)	58	0.53
British (0)	13	0.12
Canadian (7)	14	0.13
Czech (54)	212	1.94
Czechoslovakian (0)	25	0.23
Danish (13)	65	0.59
Dutch (72)	244	2.23
English (315)	1,328	12.13
European (118)	118	1.08
Finnish (43)	43	0.39
French, ex. Basque (9)	168	1.53
French Canadian (0)	13	0.12
German (2,732)	5,734	52.36
Greek (11)	22	0.20
Hungarian (0)	13	0.12
Iranian (12)	12	0.11
Irish (460)	1,979	18.07
Italian (84)	330	3.01
Lithuanian (13)	13	0.12
Luxemburger (0)	6	0.05
Norwegian (292)	924	8.44
Polish (106)	489	4.47
Romanian (0)	34	0.31
Russian (11)	59	0.54
Scandinavian (59)	112	1.02
Scotch-Irish (13)	148	1.35
Scottish (26)	311	2.84
Serbian (15)	15	0.14
Slavic (12)	25	0.23
Swedish (70)	221	2.02
Swiss (63)	219	2.00
West Indian, ex. Hispanic (0)	18	0.16
British West Indian (0)	18	0.16
Yugoslavian (0)	36	0.33

Hispanic Origin	Population	%
Hispanic or Latino (of any race)	179	1.59
Central American, ex. Mexican	11	0.10
Costa Rican	3	0.03
Guatemalan	4	0.04
Honduran	1	0.01
Salvadoran	3	0.03
Cuban	5	0.04
Dominican Republic	5	0.04
Mexican	111	0.99
Puerto Rican	15	0.13
South American	21	0.19
Argentinean	3	0.03
Bolivian	2	0.02
Chilean	1	0.01
Colombian	2	0.02
Ecuadorian	2	0.02
Paraguayan	2	0.02
Peruvian	4	0.04
Venezuelan	2	0.02
Other South American	3	0.03
Other Hispanic or Latino	11	0.10

Race*	Population	%
African-American/Black (233)	285	2.54
Not Hispanic (227)	278	2.48
Hispanic (6)	7	0.06
American Indian/Alaska Native (25)	45	0.40
Not Hispanic (21)	39	0.35
Hispanic (4)	6	0.05
Cherokee (1)	4	0.04
Chickasaw (4)	6	0.05
Chippewa (2)	5	0.04
Choctaw (0)	3	0.03
Cree (0)	1	0.01
Iroquois (3)	4	0.04
Potawatomi (0)	1	0.01
Pueblo (1)	1	0.01
Sioux (1)	3	0.03
South American Ind. (2)	2	0.02
Asian (188)	218	1.94
Not Hispanic (187)	215	1.92
Hispanic (1)	3	0.03
Bangladeshi (9)	9	0.08
Chinese, ex. Taiwanese (75)	77	0.69
Filipino (8)	17	0.15
Hmong (46)	54	0.48
Indian (18)	19	0.17
Indonesian (3)	5	0.04
Japanese (5)	8	0.07
Korean (8)	11	0.10
Laotian (1)	1	0.01
Sri Lankan (2)	2	0.02
Taiwanese (1)	3	0.03
Thai (1)	3	0.03
Vietnamese (6)	7	0.06
Hawaii Native/Pacific Islander (0)	7	0.06
Not Hispanic (0)	7	0.06
Guamanian/Chamorro (0)	3	0.03
Native Hawaiian (0)	2	0.02
White (10,634)	10,729	95.59
Not Hispanic (10,510)	10,596	94.40
Hispanic (124)	133	1.18

Pleasant Prairie

Place Type: Village
County: Kenosha
Population: 19,719†

Ancestry‡	Population	%
African, Sub-Saharan (40)	40	0.21
Ethiopian (18)	18	0.09
Nigerian (22)	22	0.12
Albanian (6)	26	0.14
American (584)	584	3.05
Arab (0)	10	0.05
Lebanese (0)	10	0.05
Armenian (12)	32	0.17
Austrian (10)	25	0.13
Belgian (12)	63	0.33
Bulgarian (8)	8	0.04
Croatian (31)	86	0.45
Czech (34)	184	0.96
Czechoslovakian (52)	63	0.33
Danish (66)	371	1.94
Dutch (38)	320	1.67
English (364)	1,681	8.79
European (32)	32	0.17
Finnish (118)	217	1.13
French, ex. Basque (164)	885	4.63
French Canadian (43)	239	1.25
German (2,757)	7,260	37.96
Greek (7)	90	0.47
Hungarian (17)	48	0.25
Iranian (13)	49	0.26
Irish (428)	2,501	13.08
Italian (728)	2,250	11.77
Lithuanian (78)	205	1.07
Luxemburger (9)	9	0.05
Norwegian (190)	723	3.78
Polish (494)	1,782	9.32
Portuguese (17)	17	0.09
Russian (44)	192	1.00
Scandinavian (11)	85	0.44
Scotch-Irish (25)	68	0.36
Scottish (83)	332	1.74
Serbian (125)	161	0.84
Slavic (0)	9	0.05
Slovak (27)	104	0.54
Slovene (52)	137	0.72
Swedish (98)	576	3.01
Swiss (11)	28	0.15
Turkish (0)	12	0.06
Ukrainian (62)	62	0.32
Welsh (0)	68	0.36
Yugoslavian (26)	50	0.26

Hispanic Origin	Population	%
Hispanic or Latino (of any race)	1,332	6.75
Central American, ex. Mexican	57	0.29
Costa Rican	1	0.01
Guatemalan	7	0.04
Honduran	10	0.05
Nicaraguan	10	0.05
Panamanian	3	0.02
Salvadoran	22	0.11
Other Central American	4	0.02
Cuban	17	0.09
Dominican Republic	2	0.01
Mexican	942	4.78
Puerto Rican	190	0.96
South American	47	0.24
Argentinean	8	0.04
Bolivian	4	0.02
Chilean	10	0.05
Colombian	7	0.04
Ecuadorian	6	0.03
Paraguayan	1	0.01
Peruvian	5	0.03
Uruguayan	5	0.03
Venezuelan	1	0.01
Other Hispanic or Latino	77	0.39

Race*	Population	%
African-American/Black (488)	622	3.15
Not Hispanic (459)	575	2.92
Hispanic (29)	47	0.24
American Indian/Alaska Native (75)	160	0.81
Not Hispanic (52)	127	0.64
Hispanic (23)	33	0.17
Apache (4)	4	0.02
Blackfeet (1)	2	0.01
Canadian/French Am. Ind. (0)	2	0.01
Cherokee (16)	35	0.18
Chippewa (12)	21	0.11
Iroquois (4)	4	0.02
Menominee (3)	5	0.03
Mexican American Ind. (7)	7	0.04
Navajo (0)	1	0.01
Potawatomi (3)	4	0.02
Seminole (1)	2	0.01
Sioux (1)	4	0.02
South American Ind. (0)	1	0.01
Asian (333)	446	2.26
Not Hispanic (329)	433	2.20
Hispanic (4)	13	0.07
Bangladeshi (7)	7	0.04
Cambodian (1)	2	0.01
Chinese, ex. Taiwanese (44)	59	0.30
Filipino (79)	120	0.61
Hmong (2)	13	0.07
Indian (86)	97	0.49
Indonesian (0)	3	0.02
Japanese (18)	33	0.17
Korean (49)	64	0.32
Laotian (1)	3	0.02
Pakistani (5)	5	0.03
Sri Lankan (2)	2	0.01
Thai (4)	6	0.03
Vietnamese (12)	22	0.11
Hawaii Native/Pacific Islander (12)	28	0.14
Not Hispanic (7)	19	0.10
Hispanic (5)	9	0.05
Guamanian/Chamorro (6)	7	0.04
Native Hawaiian (3)	8	0.04
Samoan (2)	3	0.02
White (17,964)	18,307	92.84
Not Hispanic (17,246)	17,505	88.77
Hispanic (718)	802	4.07

Plover

Place Type: Village
County: Portage
Population: 12,123†

Ancestry‡	Population	%
African, Sub-Saharan (0)	8	0.07
African (0)	8	0.07
American (371)	371	3.14

*Notes: † The Census 2010 population figure is used to calculate the percentages in the Hispanic Origin and Race categories. Ancestry percentages are based on the 2006-2010 American Community Survey population (not shown); ‡ Numbers in parentheses indicate the number of people reporting a single ancestry; * Numbers in parentheses indicate the number of persons reporting this race alone, not in combination with any other race; Please refer to the Explanation of Data for more information.*

Ancestry	Population	%
Austrian (16)	16	0.14
Belgian (0)	40	0.34
British (0)	55	0.46
Bulgarian (7)	7	0.06
Canadian (0)	13	0.11
Celtic (0)	15	0.13
Croatian (47)	47	0.40
Czech (22)	253	2.14
Danish (14)	52	0.44
Dutch (58)	288	2.43
English (216)	834	7.05
European (110)	110	0.93
Finnish (30)	144	1.22
French, ex. Basque (41)	454	3.84
French Canadian (41)	75	0.63
German (1,789)	5,664	47.88
Greek (0)	14	0.12
Hungarian (0)	44	0.37
Irish (243)	1,616	13.66
Italian (70)	363	3.07
Lithuanian (27)	27	0.23
Norwegian (268)	960	8.11
Polish (1,239)	2,954	24.97
Russian (73)	140	1.18
Scandinavian (36)	120	1.01
Scotch-Irish (49)	151	1.28
Scottish (0)	87	0.74
Slavic (0)	9	0.08
Slovak (0)	12	0.10
Slovene (15)	15	0.13
Swedish (85)	362	3.06
Ukrainian (0)	15	0.13
Welsh (11)	36	0.30

Hispanic Origin	Population	%
Hispanic or Latino (of any race)	393	3.24
Central American, ex. Mexican	15	0.12
Guatemalan	7	0.06
Honduran	2	0.02
Nicaraguan	6	0.05
Cuban	5	0.04
Dominican Republic	1	0.01
Mexican	301	2.48
Puerto Rican	11	0.09
South American	9	0.07
Bolivian	1	0.01
Colombian	8	0.07
Other Hispanic or Latino	51	0.42

Race*	Population	%
African-American/Black (65)	124	1.02
Not Hispanic (56)	113	0.93
Hispanic (9)	11	0.09
American Indian/Alaska Native (48)	99	0.82
Not Hispanic (32)	80	0.66
Hispanic (16)	19	0.16
Alaska Athabascan *(Ala. Nat.)* (0)	1	0.01
Cherokee (0)	6	0.05
Chickasaw (1)	1	0.01
Chippewa (7)	16	0.13
Choctaw (1)	4	0.03
Comanche (0)	1	0.01
Iroquois (4)	5	0.04
Menominee (6)	9	0.07
Potawatomi (0)	1	0.01
Puget Sound Salish (1)	1	0.01
Sioux (3)	4	0.03
South American Ind. (4)	4	0.03
Asian (456)	504	4.16
Not Hispanic (454)	497	4.10
Hispanic (2)	7	0.06
Chinese, ex. Taiwanese (29)	32	0.26
Filipino (10)	15	0.12
Hmong (336)	343	2.83
Indian (20)	26	0.21
Indonesian (0)	3	0.02
Japanese (5)	12	0.10
Korean (12)	21	0.17
Laotian (4)	4	0.03
Nepalese (2)	2	0.02
Pakistani (2)	2	0.02
Sri Lankan (1)	1	0.01
Taiwanese (4)	4	0.03
Thai (3)	9	0.07
Vietnamese (5)	6	0.05
Hawaii Native/Pacific Islander (3)	7	0.06
Not Hispanic (2)	6	0.05
Hispanic (1)	1	0.01
Marshallese (1)	1	0.01
Native Hawaiian (1)	1	0.01
Samoan (1)	1	0.01
White (11,247)	11,417	94.18
Not Hispanic (11,046)	11,173	92.16
Hispanic (201)	244	2.01

Plymouth

Place Type: City
County: Sheboygan
Population: 8,445†

Ancestry‡	Population	%
Albanian (122)	122	1.46
American (293)	293	3.50
Austrian (0)	34	0.41
Belgian (0)	129	1.54
British (0)	52	0.62
Canadian (7)	63	0.75
Czech (0)	72	0.86
Czechoslovakian (0)	28	0.33
Danish (32)	118	1.41
Dutch (56)	392	4.68
Eastern European (5)	5	0.06
English (53)	418	4.99
European (23)	23	0.27
Finnish (0)	30	0.36
French, ex. Basque (43)	308	3.68
French Canadian (16)	35	0.42
German (2,923)	5,139	61.38
Greek (44)	53	0.63
Irish (81)	808	9.65
Italian (41)	126	1.51
Luxemburger (52)	78	0.93
Norwegian (28)	279	3.33
Polish (110)	460	5.49
Romanian (17)	17	0.20
Russian (0)	47	0.56
Scandinavian (32)	98	1.17
Scotch-Irish (27)	106	1.27
Scottish (74)	140	1.67
Slavic (0)	20	0.24
Slovene (0)	9	0.11
Swedish (58)	455	5.43
Swiss (0)	70	0.84
Ukrainian (0)	278	3.32

Hispanic Origin	Population	%
Hispanic or Latino (of any race)	205	2.43
Central American, ex. Mexican	9	0.11
Costa Rican	2	0.02
Guatemalan	2	0.02
Honduran	4	0.05
Panamanian	1	0.01
Cuban	2	0.02
Dominican Republic	1	0.01
Mexican	147	1.74
Puerto Rican	23	0.27
South American	4	0.05
Argentinean	1	0.01
Venezuelan	3	0.04
Other Hispanic or Latino	19	0.22

Race*	Population	%
African-American/Black (32)	50	0.59
Not Hispanic (31)	47	0.56
Hispanic (1)	3	0.04
American Indian/Alaska Native (35)	73	0.86
Not Hispanic (33)	61	0.72
Hispanic (2)	12	0.14
Apache (0)	2	0.02
Blackfeet (1)	1	0.01
Cherokee (5)	5	0.06
Chickasaw (0)	2	0.02
Chippewa (2)	4	0.05
Iroquois (3)	4	0.05
Menominee (3)	3	0.04
Navajo (1)	1	0.01
Ottawa (1)	2	0.02
Pueblo (1)	1	0.01
Sioux (0)	6	0.07
Asian (63)	110	1.30
Not Hispanic (61)	107	1.27
Hispanic (2)	3	0.04
Chinese, ex. Taiwanese (19)	29	0.34
Filipino (11)	46	0.54
Hmong (11)	16	0.19
Indian (4)	4	0.05
Indonesian (2)	5	0.06
Japanese (1)	1	0.01
Korean (7)	9	0.11
Pakistani (1)	1	0.01
Taiwanese (1)	1	0.01
Vietnamese (0)	3	0.04
Hawaii Native/Pacific Islander (0)	2	0.02
Not Hispanic (0)	1	0.01
Hispanic (0)	1	0.01
Guamanian/Chamorro (0)	1	0.01
Native Hawaiian (0)	1	0.01
White (8,125)	8,233	97.49
Not Hispanic (8,027)	8,111	96.04
Hispanic (98)	122	1.44

Port Washington

Place Type: City
County: Ozaukee
Population: 11,250†

Ancestry‡	Population	%
African, Sub-Saharan (14)	14	0.13
Ethiopian (14)	14	0.13
American (434)	434	3.89
Arab (0)	54	0.48
Arab (0)	17	0.15
Lebanese (0)	37	0.33
Austrian (9)	32	0.29
Belgian (17)	78	0.70
British (0)	8	0.07
Croatian (11)	88	0.79
Czech (14)	179	1.61
Danish (29)	123	1.10
Dutch (48)	355	3.18
Eastern European (11)	11	0.10
English (187)	612	5.49
European (141)	178	1.60
Finnish (23)	90	0.81
French, ex. Basque (24)	507	4.55
French Canadian (28)	150	1.35
German (2,599)	6,230	55.89
Hungarian (24)	170	1.53
Iranian (9)	9	0.08
Irish (249)	1,358	12.18
Italian (107)	786	7.05
Latvian (0)	10	0.09
Lithuanian (12)	85	0.76
Luxemburger (153)	361	3.24
Maltese (0)	6	0.05
Norwegian (154)	543	4.87
Polish (329)	1,181	10.60
Portuguese (0)	10	0.09
Russian (38)	75	0.67
Scandinavian (38)	76	0.68
Scotch-Irish (9)	69	0.62
Scottish (27)	87	0.78
Serbian (0)	6	0.05
Slavic (0)	14	0.13
Slovak (0)	9	0.08
Slovene (10)	16	0.14
Swedish (22)	311	2.79
Swiss (0)	70	0.63

*Notes: † The Census 2010 population figure is used to calculate the percentages in the Hispanic Origin and Race categories. Ancestry percentages are based on the 2006-2010 American Community Survey population (not shown); ‡ Numbers in parentheses indicate the number of people reporting a single ancestry; * Numbers in parentheses indicate the number of persons reporting this race alone, not in combination with any other race; Please refer to the Explanation of Data for more information.*

Ukrainian (30)	49	0.44
Welsh (0)	39	0.35
Yugoslavian (0)	33	0.30

Hispanic Origin	Population	%
Hispanic or Latino (of any race)	347	3.08
Central American, ex. Mexican	18	0.16
Guatemalan	5	0.04
Honduran	2	0.02
Nicaraguan	3	0.03
Salvadoran	8	0.07
Cuban	2	0.02
Dominican Republic	3	0.03
Mexican	219	1.95
Puerto Rican	63	0.56
South American	12	0.11
Colombian	4	0.04
Venezuelan	8	0.07
Other Hispanic or Latino	30	0.27

Race*	Population	%
African-American/Black (181)	242	2.15
Not Hispanic (177)	234	2.08
Hispanic (4)	8	0.07
American Indian/Alaska Native (46)	115	1.02
Not Hispanic (44)	108	0.96
Hispanic (2)	7	0.06
Alaska Athabascan *(Ala. Nat.)* (1)	1	0.01
Apache (0)	1	0.01
Cherokee (0)	4	0.04
Chickasaw (0)	2	0.02
Chippewa (10)	24	0.21
Creek (1)	1	0.01
Iroquois (7)	13	0.12
Mexican American Ind. (0)	1	0.01
Navajo (0)	1	0.01
Puget Sound Salish (0)	1	0.01
Sioux (5)	6	0.05
Yup'ik *(Alaska Native)* (0)	1	0.01
Asian (84)	114	1.01
Not Hispanic (84)	114	1.01
Chinese, ex. Taiwanese (26)	30	0.27
Filipino (11)	23	0.20
Hmong (9)	9	0.08
Indian (17)	19	0.17
Indonesian (1)	1	0.01
Japanese (1)	7	0.06
Korean (14)	20	0.18
Laotian (0)	1	0.01
Taiwanese (1)	1	0.01
Vietnamese (3)	3	0.03
Hawaii Native/Pacific Islander (2)	9	0.08
Not Hispanic (2)	9	0.08
Native Hawaiian (1)	4	0.04
White (10,690)	10,841	96.36
Not Hispanic (10,446)	10,580	94.04
Hispanic (244)	261	2.32

Portage

Place Type: City
County: Columbia
Population: 10,324†

Ancestry‡	Population	%
African, Sub-Saharan (33)	62	0.60
African (33)	54	0.53
Nigerian (0)	8	0.08
Albanian (8)	8	0.08
American (258)	258	2.52
Arab (37)	49	0.48
Arab (0)	12	0.12
Egyptian (37)	37	0.36
Austrian (12)	68	0.66
British (0)	13	0.13
Croatian (0)	32	0.31
Czech (20)	56	0.55
Danish (0)	173	1.69
Dutch (52)	212	2.07
English (265)	703	6.86
European (19)	28	0.27
Finnish (0)	5	0.05
French, ex. Basque (46)	360	3.51
French Canadian (34)	74	0.72
German (2,283)	4,916	47.94
Greek (0)	49	0.48
Hungarian (25)	34	0.33
Irish (572)	2,092	20.40
Israeli (8)	17	0.17
Italian (37)	106	1.03
Latvian (13)	13	0.13
Lithuanian (122)	179	1.75
Northern European (14)	14	0.14
Norwegian (247)	860	8.39
Polish (193)	658	6.42
Portuguese (0)	6	0.06
Romanian (9)	9	0.09
Russian (0)	80	0.78
Scandinavian (12)	12	0.12
Scotch-Irish (34)	142	1.38
Scottish (33)	72	0.70
Slovak (0)	10	0.10
Swedish (31)	119	1.16
Swiss (9)	149	1.45
Welsh (26)	101	0.98
West Indian, ex. Hispanic (0)	17	0.17
West Indian (0)	17	0.17

Hispanic Origin	Population	%
Hispanic or Latino (of any race)	414	4.01
Central American, ex. Mexican	5	0.05
Guatemalan	1	0.01
Honduran	3	0.03
Nicaraguan	1	0.01
Dominican Republic	2	0.02
Mexican	293	2.84
Puerto Rican	31	0.30
South American	1	0.01
Argentinean	1	0.01
Other Hispanic or Latino	82	0.79

Race*	Population	%
African-American/Black (517)	572	5.54
Not Hispanic (504)	556	5.39
Hispanic (13)	16	0.15
American Indian/Alaska Native (98)	168	1.63
Not Hispanic (83)	144	1.39
Hispanic (15)	24	0.23
Apache (2)	2	0.02
Blackfeet (4)	4	0.04
Cherokee (3)	12	0.12
Chippewa (16)	20	0.19
Choctaw (2)	7	0.07
Cree (0)	1	0.01
Crow (1)	1	0.01
Iroquois (2)	8	0.08
Menominee (3)	7	0.07
Mexican American Ind. (2)	5	0.05
Potawatomi (2)	2	0.02
Sioux (1)	2	0.02
Asian (79)	108	1.05
Not Hispanic (79)	108	1.05
Chinese, ex. Taiwanese (17)	19	0.18
Filipino (21)	31	0.30
Hmong (5)	5	0.05
Indian (14)	14	0.14
Japanese (1)	6	0.06
Korean (8)	13	0.13
Taiwanese (0)	3	0.03
Vietnamese (9)	12	0.12
Hawaii Native/Pacific Islander (4)	13	0.13
Not Hispanic (0)	9	0.09
Hispanic (4)	4	0.04
Native Hawaiian (4)	9	0.09
White (9,386)	9,546	92.46
Not Hispanic (9,099)	9,239	89.49
Hispanic (287)	307	2.97

Racine

Place Type: City
County: Racine
Population: 78,860†

Ancestry‡	Population	%
African, Sub-Saharan (1,483)	1,772	2.22
African (1,462)	1,751	2.20
Nigerian (21)	21	0.03
Albanian (14)	29	0.04
American (1,062)	1,062	1.33
Arab (118)	158	0.20
Arab (13)	53	0.07
Moroccan (14)	14	0.02
Palestinian (91)	91	0.11
Armenian (216)	447	0.56
Australian (0)	17	0.02
Austrian (0)	209	0.26
Belgian (69)	192	0.24
Brazilian (7)	37	0.05
British (22)	77	0.10
Bulgarian (14)	14	0.02
Canadian (0)	171	0.21
Celtic (46)	46	0.06
Croatian (14)	68	0.09
Czech (208)	1,306	1.64
Czechoslovakian (30)	159	0.20
Danish (872)	3,974	4.99
Dutch (374)	1,327	1.67
English (657)	3,514	4.41
Estonian (0)	65	0.08
European (491)	491	0.62
Finnish (59)	402	0.50
French, ex. Basque (283)	2,200	2.76
French Canadian (125)	546	0.69
German (5,825)	19,326	24.26
German Russian (0)	51	0.06
Greek (82)	221	0.28
Hungarian (95)	662	0.83
Iranian (0)	23	0.03
Irish (778)	5,763	7.23
Italian (1,209)	3,380	4.24
Latvian (31)	38	0.05
Lithuanian (106)	338	0.42
Luxemburger (0)	23	0.03
Northern European (61)	61	0.08
Norwegian (832)	2,689	3.38
Pennsylvania German (16)	44	0.06
Polish (1,181)	4,756	5.97
Portuguese (10)	97	0.12
Romanian (0)	90	0.11
Russian (30)	532	0.67
Scandinavian (178)	220	0.28
Scotch-Irish (122)	527	0.66
Scottish (89)	772	0.97
Serbian (135)	200	0.25
Slavic (20)	66	0.08
Slovak (97)	165	0.21
Slovene (9)	26	0.03
Swedish (295)	1,237	1.55
Swiss (22)	183	0.23
Turkish (0)	14	0.02
Ukrainian (130)	142	0.18
Welsh (69)	244	0.31
West Indian, ex. Hispanic (56)	82	0.10
Belizean (56)	56	0.07
Haitian (0)	13	0.02
Jamaican (0)	13	0.02
Yugoslavian (34)	102	0.13

Hispanic Origin	Population	%
Hispanic or Latino (of any race)	16,309	20.68
Central American, ex. Mexican	213	0.27
Costa Rican	6	0.01
Guatemalan	78	0.10
Honduran	56	0.07
Nicaraguan	9	0.01
Panamanian	9	0.01
Salvadoran	48	0.06

SECTION TWO

*Notes: † The Census 2010 population figure is used to calculate the percentages in the Hispanic Origin and Race categories. Ancestry percentages are based on the 2006-2010 American Community Survey population (not shown); ‡ Numbers in parentheses indicate the number of people reporting a single ancestry; * Numbers in parentheses indicate the number of persons reporting this race alone, not in combination with any other race; Please refer to the Explanation of Data for more information.*

Other Central American	7	0.01
Cuban	64	0.08
Dominican Republic	21	0.03
Mexican	13,731	17.41
Puerto Rican	1,224	1.55
South American	87	0.11
Argentinean	17	0.02
Bolivian	5	0.01
Chilean	11	0.01
Colombian	32	0.04
Ecuadorian	4	0.01
Paraguayan	1	<0.01
Peruvian	11	0.01
Uruguayan	1	<0.01
Venezuelan	4	0.01
Other South American	1	<0.01
Other Hispanic or Latino	969	1.23

Race*	Population	%
African-American/Black (17,799)	19,808	25.12
Not Hispanic (17,341)	18,921	23.99
Hispanic (458)	887	1.12
American Indian/Alaska Native (381)	914	1.16
Not Hispanic (279)	667	0.85
Hispanic (102)	247	0.31
Apache (6)	16	0.02
Blackfeet (3)	22	0.03
Canadian/French Am. Ind. (0)	2	<0.01
Cherokee (24)	106	0.13
Cheyenne (3)	3	<0.01
Chickasaw (0)	1	<0.01
Chippewa (69)	159	0.20
Choctaw (3)	10	0.01
Comanche (1)	3	<0.01
Cree (0)	2	<0.01
Crow (0)	1	<0.01
Inupiat *(Alaska Native)* (1)	1	<0.01
Iroquois (14)	27	0.03
Kiowa (0)	5	0.01
Lumbee (2)	4	0.01
Menominee (6)	10	0.01
Mexican American Ind. (25)	40	0.05
Navajo (1)	4	0.01
Ottawa (13)	32	0.04
Pima (3)	3	<0.01
Potawatomi (7)	13	0.02
Puget Sound Salish (3)	4	0.01
Shoshone (1)	1	<0.01
Sioux (4)	9	0.01
South American Ind. (0)	4	0.01
Asian (603)	806	1.02
Not Hispanic (578)	752	0.95
Hispanic (25)	54	0.07
Burmese (11)	11	0.01
Cambodian (3)	3	<0.01
Chinese, ex. Taiwanese (90)	111	0.14
Filipino (69)	144	0.18
Hmong (38)	38	0.05
Indian (170)	190	0.24
Indonesian (7)	12	0.02
Japanese (23)	40	0.05
Korean (60)	88	0.11
Laotian (15)	20	0.03
Pakistani (16)	19	0.02
Sri Lankan (6)	6	0.01
Taiwanese (3)	5	0.01
Thai (19)	23	0.03
Vietnamese (40)	50	0.06
Hawaii Native/Pacific Islander (27)	101	0.13
Not Hispanic (17)	51	0.06
Hispanic (10)	50	0.06
Guamanian/Chamorro (2)	5	0.01
Native Hawaiian (8)	33	0.04
Samoan (6)	12	0.02
White (48,712)	51,518	65.33
Not Hispanic (42,189)	44,062	55.87
Hispanic (6,523)	7,456	9.45

Reedsburg

Place Type: City
County: Sauk
Population: 9,200†

Ancestry‡	Population	%
American (327)	327	3.64
Arab (12)	12	0.13
Iraqi (12)	12	0.13
Belgian (25)	57	0.63
Brazilian (0)	12	0.13
Canadian (15)	42	0.47
Croatian (8)	8	0.09
Czech (53)	208	2.32
Czechoslovakian (7)	17	0.19
Danish (0)	102	1.14
Dutch (16)	56	0.62
English (292)	920	10.24
European (21)	21	0.23
Finnish (44)	44	0.49
French, ex. Basque (0)	364	4.05
French Canadian (16)	26	0.29
German (2,045)	4,427	49.29
Irish (107)	1,405	15.64
Italian (67)	199	2.22
Lithuanian (9)	80	0.89
Norwegian (221)	720	8.02
Polish (167)	507	5.64
Portuguese (0)	20	0.22
Romanian (0)	5	0.06
Scotch-Irish (0)	54	0.60
Scottish (0)	50	0.56
Swedish (0)	321	3.57
Swiss (0)	67	0.75
Turkish (0)	13	0.14
Welsh (0)	83	0.92

Hispanic Origin	Population	%
Hispanic or Latino (of any race)	393	4.27
Central American, ex. Mexican	14	0.15
Guatemalan	3	0.03
Honduran	5	0.05
Panamanian	6	0.07
Cuban	8	0.09
Mexican	321	3.49
Puerto Rican	24	0.26
South American	15	0.16
Argentinean	1	0.01
Chilean	1	0.01
Colombian	4	0.04
Ecuadorian	1	0.01
Peruvian	8	0.09
Other Hispanic or Latino	11	0.12

Race*	Population	%
African-American/Black (52)	89	0.97
Not Hispanic (45)	78	0.85
Hispanic (7)	11	0.12
American Indian/Alaska Native (96)	129	1.40
Not Hispanic (78)	109	1.18
Hispanic (18)	20	0.22
Cherokee (0)	2	0.02
Chippewa (14)	16	0.17
Choctaw (0)	1	0.01
Crow (1)	1	0.01
Iroquois (5)	5	0.05
Mexican American Ind. (4)	4	0.04
Ottawa (0)	1	0.01
Tlingit-Haida *(Alaska Native)* (0)	1	0.01
Ute (3)	3	0.03
Asian (39)	56	0.61
Not Hispanic (38)	55	0.60
Hispanic (1)	1	0.01
Chinese, ex. Taiwanese (14)	19	0.21
Filipino (5)	6	0.07
Indian (7)	12	0.13
Japanese (1)	2	0.02
Korean (6)	8	0.09
Malaysian (0)	1	0.01
Thai (4)	4	0.04
Vietnamese (1)	8	0.09
Hawaii Native/Pacific Islander (0)	2	0.02
Not Hispanic (0)	2	0.02
Native Hawaiian (0)	1	0.01
White (8,766)	8,863	96.34
Not Hispanic (8,566)	8,643	93.95
Hispanic (200)	220	2.39

Rhinelander

Place Type: City
County: Oneida
Population: 7,798†

Ancestry‡	Population	%
African, Sub-Saharan (36)	36	0.46
African (36)	36	0.46
American (437)	437	5.54
Austrian (6)	17	0.22
Brazilian (16)	16	0.20
British (44)	44	0.56
Croatian (14)	29	0.37
Czech (37)	147	1.86
Danish (69)	171	2.17
Dutch (19)	151	1.91
English (79)	519	6.57
European (81)	81	1.03
Finnish (64)	115	1.46
French, ex. Basque (70)	424	5.37
French Canadian (24)	222	2.81
German (1,427)	3,336	42.26
Greek (27)	29	0.37
Hungarian (0)	54	0.68
Irish (213)	935	11.84
Italian (143)	262	3.32
Lithuanian (31)	73	0.92
Northern European (24)	24	0.30
Norwegian (157)	646	8.18
Polish (183)	787	9.97
Portuguese (27)	27	0.34
Russian (0)	49	0.62
Scandinavian (29)	43	0.54
Scotch-Irish (32)	121	1.53
Scottish (24)	60	0.76
Serbian (0)	8	0.10
Slovak (0)	28	0.35
Swedish (40)	326	4.13
Swiss (26)	66	0.84
Welsh (11)	66	0.84

Hispanic Origin	Population	%
Hispanic or Latino (of any race)	104	1.33
Central American, ex. Mexican	3	0.04
Costa Rican	1	0.01
Honduran	1	0.01
Salvadoran	1	0.01
Cuban	3	0.04
Dominican Republic	2	0.03
Mexican	71	0.91
Puerto Rican	11	0.14
South American	3	0.04
Venezuelan	3	0.04
Other Hispanic or Latino	11	0.14

Race*	Population	%
African-American/Black (80)	107	1.37
Not Hispanic (79)	104	1.33
Hispanic (1)	3	0.04
American Indian/Alaska Native (92)	170	2.18
Not Hispanic (85)	158	2.03
Hispanic (7)	12	0.15
Canadian/French Am. Ind. (5)	5	0.06
Cherokee (0)	4	0.05
Chippewa (29)	42	0.54
Choctaw (1)	1	0.01
Cree (1)	2	0.03
Iroquois (10)	16	0.21
Menominee (7)	13	0.17
Ottawa (0)	3	0.04

*Notes: † The Census 2010 population figure is used to calculate the percentages in the Hispanic Origin and Race categories. Ancestry percentages are based on the 2006-2010 American Community Survey population (not shown); ‡ Numbers in parentheses indicate the number of people reporting a single ancestry; * Numbers in parentheses indicate the number of persons reporting this race alone, not in combination with any other race; Please refer to the Explanation of Data for more information.*

Potawatomi (22)	27	0.35
Sioux (0)	5	0.06
Tlingit-Haida *(Alaska Native)* (0)	2	0.03
Yaqui (1)	1	0.01
Asian (58)	70	0.90
Not Hispanic (58)	69	0.88
Hispanic (0)	1	0.01
Bangladeshi (3)	3	0.04
Cambodian (1)	1	0.01
Chinese, ex. Taiwanese (11)	14	0.18
Filipino (5)	6	0.08
Hmong (9)	9	0.12
Indian (12)	14	0.18
Indonesian (1)	1	0.01
Japanese (2)	4	0.05
Korean (5)	7	0.09
Pakistani (1)	1	0.01
Thai (1)	1	0.01
Vietnamese (7)	9	0.12
Hawaii Native/Pacific Islander (1)	3	0.04
Not Hispanic (1)	3	0.04
Guamanian/Chamorro (1)	3	0.04
White (7,427)	7,548	96.79
Not Hispanic (7,360)	7,470	95.79
Hispanic (67)	78	1.00

Rice Lake

Place Type: City
County: Barron
Population: 8,438†

Ancestry‡	Population	%
African, Sub-Saharan (0)	45	0.53
African (0)	45	0.53
American (594)	594	7.03
Austrian (0)	40	0.47
Brazilian (0)	9	0.11
British (0)	27	0.32
Croatian (0)	9	0.11
Czech (91)	311	3.68
Czechoslovakian (15)	29	0.34
Danish (16)	157	1.86
Dutch (34)	160	1.89
English (246)	792	9.37
European (138)	138	1.63
Finnish (11)	154	1.82
French, ex. Basque (45)	568	6.72
French Canadian (40)	177	2.09
German (1,225)	3,383	40.02
Greek (0)	35	0.41
Irish (137)	973	11.51
Italian (57)	169	2.00
New Zealander (10)	10	0.12
Norwegian (440)	1,612	19.07
Pennsylvania German (16)	16	0.19
Polish (210)	795	9.40
Scandinavian (49)	112	1.32
Scotch-Irish (20)	78	0.92
Scottish (18)	146	1.73
Serbian (0)	8	0.09
Slovak (0)	8	0.09
Slovene (9)	42	0.50
Swedish (86)	519	6.14
Swiss (8)	92	1.09
Welsh (11)	41	0.49

Hispanic Origin	Population	%
Hispanic or Latino (of any race)	203	2.41
Central American, ex. Mexican	2	0.02
Guatemalan	2	0.02
Dominican Republic	2	0.02
Mexican	163	1.93
Puerto Rican	9	0.11
South American	9	0.11
Colombian	9	0.11
Other Hispanic or Latino	18	0.21

Race*	Population	%
African-American/Black (26)	69	0.82
Not Hispanic (26)	61	0.72
Hispanic (0)	8	0.09
American Indian/Alaska Native (72)	105	1.24
Not Hispanic (62)	91	1.08
Hispanic (10)	14	0.17
Alaska Athabascan *(Ala. Nat.)* (0)	2	0.02
Apache (0)	2	0.02
Canadian/French Am. Ind. (0)	3	0.04
Central American Ind. (1)	1	0.01
Cherokee (4)	4	0.05
Chickasaw (1)	1	0.01
Chippewa (38)	46	0.55
Choctaw (1)	1	0.01
Inupiat *(Alaska Native)* (1)	1	0.01
Iroquois (1)	1	0.01
Menominee (1)	2	0.02
Mexican American Ind. (1)	1	0.01
Ottawa (1)	1	0.01
Seminole (0)	2	0.02
Sioux (4)	7	0.08
Asian (67)	94	1.11
Not Hispanic (67)	94	1.11
Chinese, ex. Taiwanese (10)	11	0.13
Filipino (10)	18	0.21
Indian (18)	18	0.21
Japanese (2)	6	0.07
Korean (13)	25	0.30
Pakistani (5)	5	0.06
Thai (4)	6	0.07
Vietnamese (5)	5	0.06
Hawaii Native/Pacific Islander (1)	3	0.04
Not Hispanic (1)	3	0.04
Native Hawaiian (1)	1	0.01
White (8,118)	8,219	97.40
Not Hispanic (7,984)	8,070	95.64
Hispanic (134)	149	1.77

Richfield

Place Type: Village
County: Washington
Population: 11,300†

Ancestry‡	Population	%
African, Sub-Saharan (0)	16	0.14
African (0)	8	0.07
Ethiopian (0)	8	0.07
American (332)	332	2.96
Austrian (0)	27	0.24
Belgian (14)	51	0.45
British (12)	28	0.25
Canadian (0)	66	0.59
Croatian (0)	25	0.22
Czech (14)	162	1.44
Czechoslovakian (15)	50	0.45
Danish (24)	96	0.86
Dutch (63)	296	2.64
English (101)	619	5.51
European (117)	117	1.04
Finnish (31)	95	0.85
French, ex. Basque (9)	458	4.08
French Canadian (0)	15	0.13
German (3,759)	7,127	63.49
Hungarian (10)	146	1.30
Icelander (7)	7	0.06
Irish (142)	1,203	10.72
Italian (64)	411	3.66
Latvian (30)	47	0.42
Lithuanian (72)	81	0.72
Luxemburger (0)	75	0.67
Norwegian (188)	556	4.95
Polish (399)	1,697	15.12
Russian (13)	55	0.49
Scandinavian (55)	117	1.04
Scotch-Irish (0)	7	0.06
Scottish (14)	99	0.88
Serbian (0)	6	0.05
Slavic (0)	13	0.12
Slovak (7)	89	0.79
Slovene (22)	22	0.20
Swedish (14)	144	1.28
Swiss (0)	135	1.20
Ukrainian (16)	57	0.51
Welsh (7)	51	0.45
West Indian, ex. Hispanic (62)	62	0.55
Jamaican (62)	62	0.55
Yugoslavian (0)	21	0.19

Hispanic Origin	Population	%
Hispanic or Latino (of any race)	162	1.43
Central American, ex. Mexican	18	0.16
Guatemalan	7	0.06
Honduran	6	0.05
Panamanian	5	0.04
Cuban	7	0.06
Mexican	77	0.68
Puerto Rican	16	0.14
South American	19	0.17
Chilean	4	0.04
Colombian	8	0.07
Ecuadorian	4	0.04
Peruvian	3	0.03
Other Hispanic or Latino	25	0.22

Race*	Population	%
African-American/Black (92)	105	0.93
Not Hispanic (91)	103	0.91
Hispanic (1)	2	0.02
American Indian/Alaska Native (29)	54	0.48
Not Hispanic (26)	48	0.42
Hispanic (3)	6	0.05
Blackfeet (0)	7	0.06
Cherokee (0)	10	0.09
Chickasaw (0)	1	0.01
Chippewa (1)	2	0.02
Choctaw (1)	1	0.01
Creek (1)	1	0.01
Menominee (10)	11	0.10
Sioux (1)	2	0.02
South American Ind. (1)	1	0.01
Asian (126)	148	1.31
Not Hispanic (126)	147	1.30
Hispanic (0)	1	0.01
Chinese, ex. Taiwanese (23)	26	0.23
Filipino (12)	17	0.15
Hmong (22)	22	0.19
Indian (35)	37	0.33
Japanese (3)	4	0.04
Korean (16)	25	0.22
Pakistani (2)	2	0.02
Thai (2)	2	0.02
Vietnamese (3)	3	0.03
Hawaii Native/Pacific Islander (3)	3	0.03
Not Hispanic (3)	3	0.03
Native Hawaiian (1)	1	0.01
White (10,945)	11,004	97.38
Not Hispanic (10,834)	10,885	96.33
Hispanic (111)	119	1.05

Ripon

Place Type: City
County: Fond du Lac
Population: 7,733†

Ancestry‡	Population	%
American (255)	255	3.32
Austrian (0)	17	0.22
Belgian (0)	56	0.73
British (46)	46	0.60
Canadian (9)	20	0.26
Czech (48)	156	2.03
Danish (9)	20	0.26
Dutch (67)	240	3.12
English (189)	697	9.07
European (41)	41	0.53
Finnish (0)	111	1.44
French, ex. Basque (17)	301	3.92
French Canadian (41)	53	0.69
German (1,535)	3,920	51.00

*Notes: † The Census 2010 population figure is used to calculate the percentages in the Hispanic Origin and Race categories. Ancestry percentages are based on the 2006-2010 American Community Survey population (not shown); ‡ Numbers in parentheses indicate the number of people reporting a single ancestry; * Numbers in parentheses indicate the number of persons reporting this race alone, not in combination with any other race; Please refer to the Explanation of Data for more information.*

Hungarian (0)	43	0.56
Iranian (0)	14	0.18
Irish (140)	698	9.08
Italian (40)	278	3.62
Lithuanian (0)	9	0.12
Norwegian (48)	207	2.69
Polish (185)	738	9.60
Russian (14)	53	0.69
Scandinavian (0)	15	0.20
Scotch-Irish (0)	44	0.57
Scottish (58)	117	1.52
Slavic (11)	11	0.14
Slovak (0)	31	0.40
Swedish (0)	49	0.64
Swiss (16)	44	0.57
Welsh (0)	15	0.20
West Indian, ex. Hispanic (0)	13	0.17
West Indian (0)	13	0.17
Yugoslavian (6)	6	0.08

Hispanic Origin	Population	%
Hispanic or Latino (of any race)	388	5.02
Central American, ex. Mexican	17	0.22
Costa Rican	1	0.01
Guatemalan	3	0.04
Honduran	8	0.10
Salvadoran	5	0.06
Cuban	1	0.01
Dominican Republic	2	0.03
Mexican	333	4.31
Puerto Rican	13	0.17
South American	4	0.05
Ecuadorian	2	0.03
Paraguayan	1	0.01
Peruvian	1	0.01
Other Hispanic or Latino	18	0.23

Race*	Population	%
African-American/Black (51)	73	0.94
Not Hispanic (47)	65	0.84
Hispanic (4)	8	0.10
American Indian/Alaska Native (24)	43	0.56
Not Hispanic (17)	33	0.43
Hispanic (7)	10	0.13
Arapaho (1)	1	0.01
Cherokee (0)	1	0.01
Chippewa (5)	10	0.13
Creek (1)	1	0.01
Iroquois (1)	1	0.01
Menominee (1)	4	0.05
Ottawa (1)	1	0.01
Sioux (2)	2	0.03
Asian (60)	72	0.93
Not Hispanic (60)	72	0.93
Burmese (5)	5	0.06
Chinese, ex. Taiwanese (9)	11	0.14
Filipino (12)	16	0.21
Hmong (1)	1	0.01
Indian (10)	11	0.14
Indonesian (0)	1	0.01
Japanese (5)	12	0.16
Korean (10)	12	0.16
Nepalese (2)	2	0.03
Pakistani (0)	1	0.01
Thai (1)	1	0.01
Hawaii Native/Pacific Islander (2)	11	0.14
Not Hispanic (2)	11	0.14
Fijian (1)	1	0.01
Guamanian/Chamorro (1)	2	0.03
Native Hawaiian (0)	5	0.06
White (7,327)	7,392	95.59
Not Hispanic (7,162)	7,212	93.26
Hispanic (165)	180	2.33

River Falls

Place Type: City
County: Pierce
Population: 11,851†

Ancestry‡	Population	%
African, Sub-Saharan (14)	14	0.12
African (14)	14	0.12
American (138)	138	1.19
Austrian (24)	76	0.65
Belgian (0)	28	0.24
British (10)	40	0.34
Bulgarian (38)	93	0.80
Canadian (0)	19	0.16
Czech (58)	370	3.18
Czechoslovakian (0)	47	0.40
Danish (8)	158	1.36
Dutch (38)	270	2.32
English (270)	866	7.45
European (152)	166	1.43
Finnish (32)	94	0.81
French, ex. Basque (0)	457	3.93
French Canadian (40)	95	0.82
German (1,965)	5,762	49.57
Greek (0)	126	1.08
Hungarian (0)	15	0.13
Irish (402)	1,942	16.71
Italian (98)	376	3.23
Lithuanian (0)	12	0.10
Northern European (0)	40	0.34
Norwegian (559)	1,804	15.52
Polish (94)	775	6.67
Russian (0)	88	0.76
Scandinavian (53)	242	2.08
Scotch-Irish (0)	81	0.70
Scottish (6)	86	0.74
Slavic (11)	11	0.09
Slovene (33)	40	0.34
Swedish (107)	753	6.48
Swiss (31)	146	1.26
Ukrainian (31)	64	0.55
Welsh (19)	118	1.02
Yugoslavian (0)	14	0.12

Hispanic Origin	Population	%
Hispanic or Latino (of any race)	218	1.84
Central American, ex. Mexican	19	0.16
Costa Rican	4	0.03
Guatemalan	8	0.07
Honduran	1	0.01
Nicaraguan	3	0.03
Panamanian	1	0.01
Salvadoran	2	0.02
Cuban	6	0.05
Dominican Republic	1	0.01
Mexican	133	1.12
Puerto Rican	29	0.24
South American	15	0.13
Argentinean	2	0.02
Colombian	6	0.05
Paraguayan	2	0.02
Peruvian	4	0.03
Venezuelan	1	0.01
Other Hispanic or Latino	15	0.13

Race*	Population	%
African-American/Black (147)	224	1.89
Not Hispanic (145)	218	1.84
Hispanic (2)	6	0.05
American Indian/Alaska Native (53)	102	0.86
Not Hispanic (49)	88	0.74
Hispanic (4)	14	0.12
Blackfeet (0)	1	0.01
Cherokee (4)	8	0.07
Chippewa (26)	36	0.30
Cree (0)	1	0.01
Crow (0)	1	0.01
Inupiat *(Alaska Native)* (0)	1	0.01
Iroquois (1)	1	0.01
Mexican American Ind. (3)	3	0.03
Navajo (0)	1	0.01
Osage (0)	1	0.01
Ottawa (0)	1	0.01
Seminole (0)	3	0.03
Sioux (1)	3	0.03
South American Ind. (0)	1	0.01
Yaqui (0)	1	0.01
Asian (188)	264	2.23
Not Hispanic (188)	262	2.21
Hispanic (0)	2	0.02
Cambodian (1)	1	0.01
Chinese, ex. Taiwanese (38)	41	0.35
Filipino (7)	24	0.20
Hmong (56)	58	0.49
Indian (17)	20	0.17
Indonesian (1)	2	0.02
Japanese (18)	34	0.29
Korean (35)	63	0.53
Laotian (3)	3	0.03
Nepalese (1)	3	0.03
Taiwanese (3)	6	0.05
Thai (1)	4	0.03
Vietnamese (3)	6	0.05
Hawaii Native/Pacific Islander (3)	14	0.12
Not Hispanic (3)	14	0.12
Native Hawaiian (1)	2	0.02
Samoan (0)	3	0.03
Tongan (1)	7	0.06
White (11,181)	11,386	96.08
Not Hispanic (11,055)	11,234	94.79
Hispanic (126)	152	1.28

River Falls

Place Type: City
County: Pierce
Population: 15,000†

Ancestry‡	Population	%
African, Sub-Saharan (14)	14	0.10
African (14)	14	0.10
American (260)	260	1.77
Australian (0)	13	0.09
Austrian (24)	105	0.71
Belgian (0)	28	0.19
British (49)	89	0.61
Bulgarian (38)	93	0.63
Canadian (0)	19	0.13
Czech (94)	549	3.74
Czechoslovakian (0)	47	0.32
Danish (13)	207	1.41
Dutch (58)	347	2.36
English (320)	1,202	8.18
European (179)	193	1.31
Finnish (32)	94	0.64
French, ex. Basque (0)	522	3.55
French Canadian (40)	95	0.65
German (2,470)	7,210	49.06
Greek (14)	158	1.08
Hungarian (0)	31	0.21
Irish (488)	2,254	15.34
Italian (106)	402	2.74
Lithuanian (0)	12	0.08
Northern European (0)	40	0.27
Norwegian (866)	2,664	18.13
Polish (111)	861	5.86
Romanian (0)	16	0.11
Russian (8)	96	0.65
Scandinavian (65)	254	1.73
Scotch-Irish (0)	91	0.62
Scottish (6)	149	1.01
Slavic (11)	11	0.07
Slovak (0)	11	0.07
Slovene (33)	40	0.27
Swedish (200)	1,069	7.27
Swiss (31)	159	1.08
Ukrainian (31)	64	0.44
Welsh (19)	118	0.80
Yugoslavian (0)	14	0.10

Hispanic Origin	Population	%
Hispanic or Latino (of any race)	270	1.80
Central American, ex. Mexican	25	0.17
Costa Rican	8	0.05
Guatemalan	10	0.07

*Notes: † The Census 2010 population figure is used to calculate the percentages in the Hispanic Origin and Race categories. Ancestry percentages are based on the 2006-2010 American Community Survey population (not shown); ‡ Numbers in parentheses indicate the number of people reporting a single ancestry; * Numbers in parentheses indicate the number of persons reporting this race alone, not in combination with any other race; Please refer to the Explanation of Data for more information.*

Hispanic Origin	Population	%
Honduran	1	0.01
Nicaraguan	3	0.02
Panamanian	1	0.01
Salvadoran	2	0.01
Cuban	6	0.04
Dominican Republic	5	0.03
Mexican	167	1.11
Puerto Rican	30	0.20
South American	18	0.12
Argentinean	2	0.01
Chilean	1	0.01
Colombian	8	0.05
Paraguayan	2	0.01
Peruvian	4	0.03
Venezuelan	1	0.01
Other Hispanic or Latino	19	0.13

Race*	Population	%
African-American/Black (177)	266	1.77
Not Hispanic (175)	258	1.72
Hispanic (2)	8	0.05
American Indian/Alaska Native (63)	116	0.77
Not Hispanic (58)	100	0.67
Hispanic (5)	16	0.11
Blackfeet (0)	1	0.01
Cherokee (5)	10	0.07
Chippewa (27)	38	0.25
Cree (0)	1	0.01
Crow (0)	1	0.01
Inupiat *(Alaska Native)* (0)	1	0.01
Iroquois (2)	2	0.01
Mexican American Ind. (4)	4	0.03
Navajo (0)	1	0.01
Osage (0)	1	0.01
Ottawa (0)	1	0.01
Seminole (0)	3	0.02
Sioux (1)	3	0.02
South American Ind. (0)	1	0.01
Yaqui (0)	1	0.01
Asian (218)	304	2.03
Not Hispanic (218)	302	2.01
Hispanic (0)	2	0.01
Cambodian (1)	1	0.01
Chinese, ex. Taiwanese (40)	44	0.29
Filipino (8)	27	0.18
Hmong (67)	69	0.46
Indian (17)	22	0.15
Indonesian (1)	2	0.01
Japanese (21)	37	0.25
Korean (39)	68	0.45
Laotian (3)	3	0.02
Nepalese (1)	3	0.02
Taiwanese (3)	6	0.04
Thai (1)	4	0.03
Vietnamese (11)	14	0.09
Hawaii Native/Pacific Islander (3)	15	0.10
Not Hispanic (3)	15	0.10
Native Hawaiian (1)	3	0.02
Samoan (0)	3	0.02
Tongan (1)	7	0.05
White (14,219)	14,454	96.36
Not Hispanic (14,057)	14,261	95.07
Hispanic (162)	193	1.29

Salem

Place Type: Town
County: Kenosha
Population: 12,067†

Ancestry‡	Population	%
American (435)	435	3.70
Armenian (0)	4	0.03
Australian (11)	11	0.09
Austrian (0)	58	0.49
Belgian (0)	28	0.24
British (16)	62	0.53
Canadian (51)	51	0.43
Croatian (15)	15	0.13
Czech (139)	311	2.65
Czechoslovakian (0)	31	0.26
Danish (38)	310	2.64
Dutch (46)	312	2.66
English (310)	1,151	9.80
European (63)	79	0.67
Finnish (46)	99	0.84
French, ex. Basque (14)	357	3.04
French Canadian (33)	153	1.30
German (1,477)	4,949	42.14
Greek (25)	25	0.21
Hungarian (3)	76	0.65
Irish (512)	2,086	17.76
Italian (332)	931	7.93
Lithuanian (14)	49	0.42
Luxemburger (14)	14	0.12
Norwegian (257)	680	5.79
Polish (551)	1,381	11.76
Russian (0)	126	1.07
Scandinavian (24)	41	0.35
Scotch-Irish (32)	119	1.01
Scottish (17)	164	1.40
Serbian (5)	33	0.28
Slovak (18)	71	0.60
Swedish (12)	527	4.49
Swiss (8)	16	0.14
Ukrainian (22)	30	0.26
Welsh (0)	26	0.22

Hispanic Origin	Population	%
Hispanic or Latino (of any race)	542	4.49
Central American, ex. Mexican	17	0.14
Guatemalan	7	0.06
Honduran	2	0.02
Panamanian	5	0.04
Salvadoran	3	0.02
Cuban	2	0.02
Mexican	392	3.25
Puerto Rican	68	0.56
South American	27	0.22
Argentinean	4	0.03
Chilean	5	0.04
Colombian	2	0.02
Ecuadorian	2	0.02
Peruvian	5	0.04
Venezuelan	9	0.07
Other Hispanic or Latino	36	0.30

Race*	Population	%
African-American/Black (70)	110	0.91
Not Hispanic (67)	100	0.83
Hispanic (3)	10	0.08
American Indian/Alaska Native (54)	92	0.76
Not Hispanic (53)	86	0.71
Hispanic (1)	6	0.05
Apache (0)	1	0.01
Blackfeet (5)	5	0.04
Canadian/French Am. Ind. (0)	1	0.01
Cherokee (0)	7	0.06
Chippewa (7)	8	0.07
Choctaw (0)	1	0.01
Comanche (0)	1	0.01
Creek (0)	1	0.01
Iroquois (6)	6	0.05
Menominee (5)	7	0.06
Potawatomi (4)	5	0.04
Sioux (1)	1	0.01
Asian (63)	93	0.77
Not Hispanic (61)	86	0.71
Hispanic (2)	7	0.06
Chinese, ex. Taiwanese (14)	20	0.17
Filipino (19)	35	0.29
Hmong (1)	1	0.01
Indian (16)	18	0.15
Indonesian (0)	1	0.01
Japanese (2)	6	0.05
Korean (6)	11	0.09
Thai (1)	1	0.01
Vietnamese (2)	2	0.02
Hawaii Native/Pacific Islander (3)	5	0.04
Not Hispanic (2)	4	0.03
Hispanic (1)	1	0.01
Guamanian/Chamorro (1)	1	0.01
Native Hawaiian (1)	2	0.02
Samoan (1)	1	0.01
White (11,567)	11,693	96.90
Not Hispanic (11,246)	11,334	93.93
Hispanic (321)	359	2.98

Shawano

Place Type: City
County: Shawano
Population: 9,305†

Ancestry‡	Population	%
African, Sub-Saharan (45)	45	0.49
African (45)	45	0.49
American (429)	429	4.65
Arab (10)	10	0.11
Jordanian (10)	10	0.11
Australian (0)	10	0.11
Austrian (11)	44	0.48
Belgian (27)	95	1.03
Czech (37)	240	2.60
Danish (14)	126	1.37
Dutch (19)	82	0.89
English (117)	399	4.33
European (52)	52	0.56
Finnish (11)	30	0.33
French, ex. Basque (32)	436	4.73
French Canadian (199)	343	3.72
German (2,363)	4,155	45.08
Greek (0)	63	0.68
Hungarian (0)	60	0.65
Irish (188)	782	8.49
Italian (79)	159	1.73
Lithuanian (9)	9	0.10
Norwegian (77)	410	4.45
Polish (362)	600	6.51
Scandinavian (20)	20	0.22
Scotch-Irish (23)	85	0.92
Scottish (33)	91	0.99
Slovak (0)	12	0.13
Swedish (49)	147	1.60
Swiss (17)	55	0.60
Welsh (0)	20	0.22

Hispanic Origin	Population	%
Hispanic or Latino (of any race)	286	3.07
Central American, ex. Mexican	7	0.08
Nicaraguan	2	0.02
Salvadoran	5	0.05
Cuban	4	0.04
Mexican	212	2.28
Puerto Rican	39	0.42
South American	12	0.13
Argentinean	7	0.08
Bolivian	3	0.03
Paraguayan	1	0.01
Peruvian	1	0.01
Other Hispanic or Latino	12	0.13

Race*	Population	%
African-American/Black (66)	95	1.02
Not Hispanic (64)	91	0.98
Hispanic (2)	4	0.04
American Indian/Alaska Native (1,146)	1,376	14.79
Not Hispanic (1,080)	1,291	13.87
Hispanic (66)	85	0.91
Apache (0)	1	0.01
Arapaho (4)	4	0.04
Blackfeet (0)	1	0.01
Cherokee (1)	4	0.04
Chickasaw (0)	1	0.01
Chippewa (77)	95	1.02
Comanche (1)	1	0.01
Crow (3)	3	0.03
Iroquois (50)	80	0.86
Menominee (715)	826	8.88
Mexican American Ind. (4)	4	0.04

SECTION TWO

*Notes: † The Census 2010 population figure is used to calculate the percentages in the Hispanic Origin and Race categories. Ancestry percentages are based on the 2006-2010 American Community Survey population (not shown); ‡ Numbers in parentheses indicate the number of people reporting a single ancestry; * Numbers in parentheses indicate the number of persons reporting this race alone, not in combination with any other race; Please refer to the Explanation of Data for more information.*

Navajo (3)	3	0.03
Ottawa (4)	4	0.04
Pima (4)	4	0.04
Potawatomi (12)	18	0.19
Sioux (11)	11	0.12
Asian (39)	57	0.61
Not Hispanic (39)	57	0.61
Chinese, ex. Taiwanese (16)	16	0.17
Filipino (4)	11	0.12
Hmong (2)	2	0.02
Indian (6)	9	0.10
Japanese (2)	4	0.04
Korean (4)	7	0.08
Pakistani (1)	1	0.01
Thai (1)	3	0.03
Vietnamese (1)	1	0.01
Hawaii Native/Pacific Islander (6)	9	0.10
Not Hispanic (5)	8	0.09
Hispanic (1)	1	0.01
Native Hawaiian (1)	1	0.01
White (7,671)	7,911	85.02
Not Hispanic (7,581)	7,805	83.88
Hispanic (90)	106	1.14

Sheboygan Falls

Place Type: City
County: Sheboygan
Population: 7,775†

Ancestry‡	Population	%
Albanian (0)	22	0.29
American (279)	279	3.67
Austrian (12)	83	1.09
Belgian (0)	9	0.12
Canadian (9)	9	0.12
Croatian (12)	26	0.34
Czech (12)	51	0.67
Danish (0)	164	2.16
Dutch (217)	659	8.66
English (157)	547	7.19
European (25)	25	0.33
Finnish (28)	70	0.92
French, ex. Basque (65)	321	4.22
French Canadian (0)	20	0.26
German (2,600)	4,792	62.99
Hungarian (20)	31	0.41
Irish (130)	846	11.12
Italian (34)	167	2.20
Lithuanian (66)	93	1.22
Luxemburger (0)	24	0.32
Northern European (22)	38	0.50
Norwegian (45)	200	2.63
Polish (60)	336	4.42
Romanian (0)	43	0.57
Russian (8)	90	1.18
Scotch-Irish (9)	66	0.87
Scottish (0)	16	0.21
Slavic (42)	56	0.74
Slovak (0)	10	0.13
Slovene (60)	76	1.00
Swedish (29)	152	2.00
Swiss (0)	47	0.62
Welsh (13)	13	0.17

Hispanic Origin	Population	%
Hispanic or Latino (of any race)	197	2.53
Central American, ex. Mexican	6	0.08
Costa Rican	3	0.04
Honduran	2	0.03
Salvadoran	1	0.01
Cuban	5	0.06
Dominican Republic	6	0.08
Mexican	146	1.88
Puerto Rican	16	0.21
South American	2	0.03
Colombian	2	0.03
Other Hispanic or Latino	16	0.21

Race*	Population	%
African-American/Black (43)	78	1.00
Not Hispanic (39)	63	0.81
Hispanic (4)	15	0.19
American Indian/Alaska Native (23)	42	0.54
Not Hispanic (22)	36	0.46
Hispanic (1)	6	0.08
Alaska Athabascan *(Ala. Nat.)* (1)	1	0.01
Aleut *(Alaska Native)* (1)	1	0.01
Cherokee (5)	6	0.08
Chippewa (6)	8	0.10
Iroquois (5)	6	0.08
Menominee (0)	2	0.03
Pima (1)	1	0.01
Asian (69)	88	1.13
Not Hispanic (68)	82	1.05
Hispanic (1)	6	0.08
Chinese, ex. Taiwanese (8)	13	0.17
Filipino (9)	11	0.14
Hmong (24)	29	0.37
Indian (7)	8	0.10
Korean (2)	6	0.08
Laotian (9)	9	0.12
Thai (1)	1	0.01
Vietnamese (5)	5	0.06
White (7,475)	7,570	97.36
Not Hispanic (7,393)	7,444	95.74
Hispanic (82)	126	1.62

Sheboygan

Place Type: City
County: Sheboygan
Population: 49,288†

Ancestry‡	Population	%
American (1,690)	1,690	3.40
Arab (30)	45	0.09
Arab (10)	10	0.02
Jordanian (10)	10	0.02
Lebanese (0)	15	0.03
Palestinian (10)	10	0.02
Austrian (32)	219	0.44
Belgian (61)	290	0.58
British (10)	57	0.11
Canadian (80)	101	0.20
Croatian (29)	162	0.33
Czech (106)	544	1.09
Czechoslovakian (0)	8	0.02
Danish (22)	187	0.38
Dutch (852)	2,853	5.74
English (385)	2,122	4.27
European (151)	240	0.48
Finnish (57)	230	0.46
French, ex. Basque (239)	1,631	3.28
French Canadian (118)	587	1.18
German (12,813)	25,594	51.46
Greek (106)	346	0.70
Hungarian (9)	153	0.31
Iranian (33)	33	0.07
Irish (574)	4,160	8.36
Italian (162)	1,225	2.46
Lithuanian (159)	486	0.98
Luxemburger (28)	208	0.42
Norwegian (389)	1,629	3.28
Pennsylvania German (0)	14	0.03
Polish (383)	1,850	3.72
Portuguese (0)	38	0.08
Russian (124)	1,820	3.66
Scandinavian (0)	12	0.02
Scotch-Irish (49)	187	0.38
Scottish (81)	362	0.73
Slavic (32)	76	0.15
Slovak (78)	139	0.28
Slovene (229)	462	0.93
Swedish (211)	724	1.46
Swiss (28)	84	0.17
Turkish (37)	48	0.10
Ukrainian (70)	118	0.24
Welsh (19)	213	0.43
West Indian, ex. Hispanic (57)	86	0.17
Jamaican (57)	57	0.11
West Indian (0)	29	0.06
Yugoslavian (67)	116	0.23

Hispanic Origin	Population	%
Hispanic or Latino (of any race)	4,866	9.87
Central American, ex. Mexican	144	0.29
Costa Rican	8	0.02
Guatemalan	43	0.09
Honduran	15	0.03
Nicaraguan	9	0.02
Panamanian	29	0.06
Salvadoran	39	0.08
Other Central American	1	<0.01
Cuban	38	0.08
Dominican Republic	5	0.01
Mexican	4,111	8.34
Puerto Rican	220	0.45
South American	72	0.15
Bolivian	2	<0.01
Chilean	1	<0.01
Colombian	25	0.05
Ecuadorian	4	0.01
Paraguayan	1	<0.01
Peruvian	12	0.02
Uruguayan	11	0.02
Venezuelan	16	0.03
Other Hispanic or Latino	276	0.56

Race*	Population	%
African-American/Black (885)	1,352	2.74
Not Hispanic (832)	1,250	2.54
Hispanic (53)	102	0.21
American Indian/Alaska Native (242)	534	1.08
Not Hispanic (209)	449	0.91
Hispanic (33)	85	0.17
Apache (2)	6	0.01
Blackfeet (2)	8	0.02
Canadian/French Am. Ind. (0)	3	0.01
Central American Ind. (1)	1	<0.01
Cherokee (8)	28	0.06
Chippewa (51)	92	0.19
Choctaw (0)	3	0.01
Creek (0)	1	<0.01
Crow (1)	3	0.01
Inupiat *(Alaska Native)* (0)	3	0.01
Iroquois (12)	22	0.04
Kiowa (0)	6	0.01
Menominee (37)	52	0.11
Mexican American Ind. (7)	13	0.03
Navajo (1)	7	0.01
Ottawa (0)	1	<0.01
Pima (2)	5	0.01
Potawatomi (6)	12	0.02
Sioux (3)	6	0.01
South American Ind. (3)	3	0.01
Spanish American Ind. (1)	1	<0.01
Yaqui (0)	1	<0.01
Asian (4,439)	4,690	9.52
Not Hispanic (4,412)	4,638	9.41
Hispanic (27)	52	0.11
Burmese (32)	32	0.06
Cambodian (23)	34	0.07
Chinese, ex. Taiwanese (69)	103	0.21
Filipino (116)	165	0.33
Hmong (3,618)	3,716	7.54
Indian (88)	116	0.24
Indonesian (3)	4	0.01
Japanese (15)	53	0.11
Korean (43)	70	0.14
Laotian (109)	144	0.29
Malaysian (1)	1	<0.01
Pakistani (17)	17	0.03
Taiwanese (1)	4	0.01
Thai (51)	64	0.13
Vietnamese (44)	67	0.14
Hawaii Native/Pacific Islander (12)	42	0.09
Not Hispanic (6)	28	0.06

*Notes: † The Census 2010 population figure is used to calculate the percentages in the Hispanic Origin and Race categories. Ancestry percentages are based on the 2006-2010 American Community Survey population (not shown); ‡ Numbers in parentheses indicate the number of people reporting a single ancestry; * Numbers in parentheses indicate the number of persons reporting this race alone, not in combination with any other race; Please refer to the Explanation of Data for more information.*

	Population	%
Hispanic (6)	14	0.03
Guamanian/Chamorro (2)	3	0.01
Native Hawaiian (4)	7	0.01
Samoan (1)	3	0.01
White (40,685)	41,823	84.85
Not Hispanic (38,108)	38,853	78.83
Hispanic (2,577)	2,970	6.03

Shorewood

Place Type: Village
County: Milwaukee
Population: 13,162†

Ancestry‡	Population	%
African, Sub-Saharan (12)	12	0.09
Liberian (12)	12	0.09
American (138)	138	1.05
Arab (10)	52	0.40
Lebanese (0)	8	0.06
Moroccan (0)	13	0.10
Palestinian (0)	8	0.06
Syrian (10)	10	0.08
Other Arab (0)	13	0.10
Armenian (28)	41	0.31
Austrian (8)	90	0.68
Belgian (16)	16	0.12
British (9)	60	0.46
Bulgarian (26)	26	0.20
Canadian (0)	11	0.08
Croatian (9)	17	0.13
Czech (117)	237	1.80
Czechoslovakian (13)	13	0.10
Danish (22)	170	1.29
Dutch (96)	401	3.05
Eastern European (37)	68	0.52
English (135)	1,016	7.73
Estonian (0)	11	0.08
European (202)	202	1.54
Finnish (0)	57	0.43
French, ex. Basque (42)	442	3.36
French Canadian (7)	111	0.84
German (1,637)	5,034	38.30
Greek (64)	91	0.69
Hungarian (0)	94	0.72
Iranian (0)	13	0.10
Irish (646)	2,493	18.97
Italian (211)	1,053	8.01
Latvian (7)	73	0.56
Lithuanian (0)	78	0.59
Luxemburger (26)	26	0.20
Northern European (17)	17	0.13
Norwegian (145)	601	4.57
Polish (282)	1,112	8.46
Portuguese (0)	12	0.09
Romanian (96)	125	0.95
Russian (543)	943	7.17
Scandinavian (9)	33	0.25
Scotch-Irish (45)	132	1.00
Scottish (61)	239	1.82
Serbian (0)	7	0.05
Slavic (0)	11	0.08
Slovak (9)	30	0.23
Slovene (0)	27	0.21
Swedish (37)	496	3.77
Swiss (15)	138	1.05
Turkish (5)	30	0.23
Ukrainian (36)	98	0.75
Welsh (21)	114	0.87
West Indian, ex. Hispanic (25)	25	0.19
West Indian (25)	25	0.19
Yugoslavian (6)	56	0.43

Hispanic Origin	Population	%
Hispanic or Latino (of any race)	447	3.40
Central American, ex. Mexican	28	0.21
Costa Rican	1	0.01
Guatemalan	15	0.11
Honduran	1	0.01
Nicaraguan	3	0.02
Panamanian	3	0.02
Salvadoran	4	0.03
Other Central American	1	0.01
Cuban	21	0.16
Dominican Republic	3	0.02
Mexican	193	1.47
Puerto Rican	78	0.59
South American	74	0.56
Argentinean	6	0.05
Bolivian	6	0.05
Chilean	7	0.05
Colombian	13	0.10
Ecuadorian	3	0.02
Paraguayan	5	0.04
Peruvian	23	0.17
Uruguayan	1	0.01
Venezuelan	10	0.08
Other Hispanic or Latino	50	0.38

Race*	Population	%
African-American/Black (384)	486	3.69
Not Hispanic (382)	468	3.56
Hispanic (2)	18	0.14
American Indian/Alaska Native (31)	96	0.73
Not Hispanic (24)	80	0.61
Hispanic (7)	16	0.12
Blackfeet (0)	3	0.02
Central American Ind. (1)	1	0.01
Cherokee (1)	15	0.11
Chippewa (3)	8	0.06
Iroquois (2)	5	0.04
Menominee (1)	4	0.03
Mexican American Ind. (5)	5	0.04
Navajo (0)	1	0.01
Seminole (0)	2	0.02
Shoshone (0)	1	0.01
Sioux (0)	2	0.02
South American Ind. (0)	1	0.01
Asian (740)	884	6.72
Not Hispanic (734)	873	6.63
Hispanic (6)	11	0.08
Bangladeshi (18)	18	0.14
Chinese, ex. Taiwanese (208)	246	1.87
Filipino (32)	51	0.39
Hmong (50)	50	0.38
Indian (162)	187	1.42
Indonesian (2)	2	0.02
Japanese (20)	45	0.34
Korean (96)	107	0.81
Laotian (6)	7	0.05
Malaysian (11)	12	0.09
Nepalese (54)	56	0.43
Pakistani (17)	22	0.17
Sri Lankan (5)	5	0.04
Taiwanese (9)	9	0.07
Thai (10)	14	0.11
Vietnamese (15)	19	0.14
Hawaii Native/Pacific Islander (2)	12	0.09
Not Hispanic (2)	12	0.09
Guamanian/Chamorro (0)	4	0.03
Native Hawaiian (0)	2	0.02
White (11,601)	11,887	90.31
Not Hispanic (11,299)	11,546	87.72
Hispanic (302)	341	2.59

Somers

Place Type: Town
County: Kenosha
Population: 9,597†

Ancestry‡	Population	%
American (232)	232	2.45
Armenian (0)	17	0.18
Australian (0)	36	0.38
Austrian (0)	38	0.40
Belgian (15)	58	0.61
Croatian (0)	68	0.72
Czech (46)	165	1.74
Czechoslovakian (0)	35	0.37
Danish (29)	111	1.17
Dutch (76)	277	2.92
English (247)	770	8.12
European (53)	53	0.56
Finnish (14)	76	0.80
French, ex. Basque (16)	257	2.71
French Canadian (0)	24	0.25
German (1,439)	3,582	37.78
Greek (22)	41	0.43
Hungarian (0)	179	1.89
Irish (266)	1,135	11.97
Israeli (20)	20	0.21
Italian (447)	1,377	14.52
Lithuanian (58)	98	1.03
Norwegian (111)	537	5.66
Polish (187)	806	8.50
Russian (58)	86	0.91
Scandinavian (20)	77	0.81
Scotch-Irish (0)	70	0.74
Scottish (44)	126	1.33
Serbian (0)	17	0.18
Slovak (11)	39	0.41
Slovene (0)	32	0.34
Swedish (44)	244	2.57
Swiss (10)	90	0.95
Welsh (0)	24	0.25

Hispanic Origin	Population	%
Hispanic or Latino (of any race)	614	6.40
Central American, ex. Mexican	11	0.11
Costa Rican	1	0.01
Guatemalan	6	0.06
Honduran	2	0.02
Nicaraguan	1	0.01
Salvadoran	1	0.01
Cuban	9	0.09
Dominican Republic	4	0.04
Mexican	444	4.63
Puerto Rican	73	0.76
South American	30	0.31
Argentinean	2	0.02
Colombian	9	0.09
Ecuadorian	8	0.08
Peruvian	10	0.10
Other South American	1	0.01
Other Hispanic or Latino	43	0.45

Race*	Population	%
African-American/Black (474)	553	5.76
Not Hispanic (458)	524	5.46
Hispanic (16)	29	0.30
American Indian/Alaska Native (38)	85	0.89
Not Hispanic (18)	60	0.63
Hispanic (20)	25	0.26
Apache (2)	3	0.03
Blackfeet (2)	2	0.02
Central American Ind. (1)	1	0.01
Cherokee (0)	8	0.08
Chippewa (5)	17	0.18
Comanche (3)	3	0.03
Creek (0)	1	0.01
Iroquois (1)	1	0.01
Menominee (1)	5	0.05
Ottawa (0)	2	0.02
South American Ind. (1)	1	0.01
Asian (196)	253	2.64
Not Hispanic (188)	239	2.49
Hispanic (8)	14	0.15
Chinese, ex. Taiwanese (23)	31	0.32
Filipino (26)	37	0.39
Hmong (19)	20	0.21
Indian (61)	76	0.79
Japanese (14)	21	0.22
Korean (24)	28	0.29
Nepalese (2)	3	0.03
Pakistani (11)	12	0.13
Sri Lankan (2)	2	0.02
Thai (4)	7	0.07
Vietnamese (8)	14	0.15
Hawaii Native/Pacific Islander (4)	15	0.16

SECTION TWO

*Notes: † The Census 2010 population figure is used to calculate the percentages in the Hispanic Origin and Race categories. Ancestry percentages are based on the 2006-2010 American Community Survey population (not shown); ‡ Numbers in parentheses indicate the number of people reporting a single ancestry; * Numbers in parentheses indicate the number of persons reporting this race alone, not in combination with any other race; Please refer to the Explanation of Data for more information.*

Not Hispanic (2)	10	0.10
Hispanic (2)	5	0.05
Fijian (1)	1	0.01
Guamanian/Chamorro (1)	1	0.01
Native Hawaiian (1)	7	0.07
Samoan (1)	1	0.01
White (8,452)	8,658	90.22
Not Hispanic (8,135)	8,286	86.34
Hispanic (317)	372	3.88

South Milwaukee

Place Type: City
County: Milwaukee
Population: 21,156†

Ancestry‡	Population	%
Albanian (419)	419	2.00
American (570)	570	2.72
Arab (38)	65	0.31
Arab (0)	18	0.09
Lebanese (0)	9	0.04
Palestinian (38)	38	0.18
Armenian (0)	50	0.24
Australian (0)	57	0.27
Austrian (5)	93	0.44
Belgian (25)	33	0.16
Brazilian (0)	9	0.04
British (0)	24	0.11
Canadian (0)	10	0.05
Croatian (20)	128	0.61
Czech (36)	328	1.56
Czechoslovakian (20)	43	0.21
Danish (37)	128	0.61
Dutch (43)	354	1.69
English (110)	960	4.58
European (128)	128	0.61
Finnish (57)	300	1.43
French, ex. Basque (186)	1,210	5.77
French Canadian (129)	201	0.96
German (2,359)	9,451	45.07
Greek (39)	116	0.55
Hungarian (67)	146	0.70
Icelander (0)	10	0.05
Irish (339)	2,718	12.96
Italian (188)	868	4.14
Latvian (18)	18	0.09
Lithuanian (20)	60	0.29
Macedonian (33)	33	0.16
Norwegian (277)	1,281	6.11
Polish (1,832)	5,374	25.63
Portuguese (0)	43	0.21
Romanian (48)	71	0.34
Russian (0)	172	0.82
Scandinavian (0)	24	0.11
Scotch-Irish (11)	177	0.84
Scottish (23)	159	0.76
Serbian (138)	199	0.95
Slavic (18)	35	0.17
Slovak (101)	250	1.19
Slovene (10)	61	0.29
Swedish (29)	585	2.79
Swiss (0)	113	0.54
Ukrainian (39)	39	0.19
Welsh (11)	74	0.35
West Indian, ex. Hispanic (8)	8	0.04
U.S. Virgin Islander (8)	8	0.04
Yugoslavian (10)	10	0.05

Hispanic Origin	Population	%
Hispanic or Latino (of any race)	1,699	8.03
Central American, ex. Mexican	37	0.17
Costa Rican	4	0.02
Guatemalan	10	0.05
Nicaraguan	13	0.06
Panamanian	4	0.02
Salvadoran	2	0.01
Other Central American	4	0.02
Cuban	25	0.12
Dominican Republic	11	0.05
Mexican	1,016	4.80
Puerto Rican	466	2.20
South American	52	0.25
Argentinean	11	0.05
Chilean	6	0.03
Colombian	4	0.02
Ecuadorian	2	0.01
Peruvian	29	0.14
Other Hispanic or Latino	92	0.43

Race*	Population	%
African-American/Black (432)	583	2.76
Not Hispanic (391)	520	2.46
Hispanic (41)	63	0.30
American Indian/Alaska Native (174)	345	1.63
Not Hispanic (150)	284	1.34
Hispanic (24)	61	0.29
Alaska Athabascan *(Ala. Nat.)* (0)	1	<0.01
Apache (4)	6	0.03
Blackfeet (4)	5	0.02
Canadian/French Am. Ind. (0)	1	<0.01
Cherokee (9)	26	0.12
Chippewa (38)	71	0.34
Hopi (0)	1	<0.01
Iroquois (23)	37	0.17
Menominee (18)	25	0.12
Mexican American Ind. (8)	10	0.05
Navajo (0)	1	<0.01
Ottawa (3)	3	0.01
Pima (2)	2	0.01
Potawatomi (1)	1	<0.01
Sioux (10)	13	0.06
Yaqui (1)	3	0.01
Asian (233)	299	1.41
Not Hispanic (226)	286	1.35
Hispanic (7)	13	0.06
Chinese, ex. Taiwanese (30)	34	0.16
Filipino (49)	68	0.32
Hmong (14)	15	0.07
Indian (59)	64	0.30
Japanese (15)	27	0.13
Korean (16)	33	0.16
Laotian (6)	10	0.05
Nepalese (2)	2	0.01
Pakistani (13)	14	0.07
Thai (2)	2	0.01
Vietnamese (16)	16	0.08
Hawaii Native/Pacific Islander (2)	9	0.04
Not Hispanic (1)	7	0.03
Hispanic (1)	2	0.01
Guamanian/Chamorro (0)	1	<0.01
Native Hawaiian (1)	4	0.02
White (19,389)	19,842	93.79
Not Hispanic (18,357)	18,663	88.22
Hispanic (1,032)	1,179	5.57

Sparta

Place Type: City
County: Monroe
Population: 9,522†

Ancestry‡	Population	%
African, Sub-Saharan (39)	39	0.42
African (39)	39	0.42
American (388)	388	4.13
Austrian (40)	62	0.66
Belgian (12)	12	0.13
British (0)	30	0.32
Canadian (0)	25	0.27
Czech (60)	137	1.46
Danish (45)	151	1.61
Dutch (86)	223	2.37
English (146)	719	7.66
European (28)	28	0.30
Finnish (0)	40	0.43
French, ex. Basque (97)	416	4.43
French Canadian (21)	70	0.75
German (1,552)	3,294	35.07
Greek (0)	13	0.14
Hungarian (0)	10	0.11
Irish (262)	1,180	12.56
Italian (16)	173	1.84
Lithuanian (16)	45	0.48
Norwegian (877)	1,958	20.85
Pennsylvania German (0)	11	0.12
Polish (349)	549	5.85
Russian (24)	60	0.64
Scandinavian (37)	37	0.39
Scotch-Irish (64)	158	1.68
Scottish (0)	214	2.28
Slovene (0)	3	0.03
Swedish (16)	130	1.38
Swiss (0)	8	0.09
Welsh (0)	58	0.62

Hispanic Origin	Population	%
Hispanic or Latino (of any race)	643	6.75
Central American, ex. Mexican	17	0.18
Guatemalan	10	0.11
Honduran	2	0.02
Panamanian	5	0.05
Cuban	17	0.18
Mexican	519	5.45
Puerto Rican	51	0.54
South American	4	0.04
Colombian	1	0.01
Peruvian	3	0.03
Other Hispanic or Latino	35	0.37

Race*	Population	%
African-American/Black (144)	209	2.19
Not Hispanic (124)	182	1.91
Hispanic (20)	27	0.28
American Indian/Alaska Native (61)	89	0.93
Not Hispanic (51)	77	0.81
Hispanic (10)	12	0.13
Apache (0)	5	0.05
Cherokee (6)	12	0.13
Chippewa (13)	13	0.14
Iroquois (0)	1	0.01
Lumbee (1)	1	0.01
Menominee (1)	1	0.01
Ottawa (0)	1	0.01
Potawatomi (3)	3	0.03
Asian (44)	75	0.79
Not Hispanic (44)	73	0.77
Hispanic (0)	2	0.02
Chinese, ex. Taiwanese (10)	11	0.12
Filipino (13)	21	0.22
Indian (3)	6	0.06
Indonesian (0)	1	0.01
Japanese (5)	11	0.12
Korean (11)	21	0.22
Thai (1)	1	0.01
Hawaii Native/Pacific Islander (8)	12	0.13
Not Hispanic (8)	10	0.11
Hispanic (0)	2	0.02
Guamanian/Chamorro (2)	2	0.02
Native Hawaiian (1)	2	0.02
Samoan (0)	1	0.01
Tongan (5)	5	0.05
White (8,781)	8,925	93.73
Not Hispanic (8,534)	8,642	90.76
Hispanic (247)	283	2.97

St. Francis

Place Type: City
County: Milwaukee
Population: 9,365†

Ancestry‡	Population	%
African, Sub-Saharan (56)	101	1.10
African (56)	101	1.10
Albanian (32)	32	0.35
American (31)	31	0.34
Arab (24)	46	0.50
Lebanese (10)	10	0.11
Other Arab (14)	36	0.39

*Notes: † The Census 2010 population figure is used to calculate the percentages in the Hispanic Origin and Race categories. Ancestry percentages are based on the 2006-2010 American Community Survey population (not shown); ‡ Numbers in parentheses indicate the number of people reporting a single ancestry; * Numbers in parentheses indicate the number of persons reporting this race alone, not in combination with any other race; Please refer to the Explanation of Data for more information.*

Ancestry (continued)	Population	%
Austrian (22)	73	0.80
Basque (0)	10	0.11
Belgian (0)	14	0.15
British (12)	12	0.13
Croatian (14)	25	0.27
Czech (35)	154	1.68
Czechoslovakian (13)	27	0.29
Danish (11)	30	0.33
Dutch (0)	52	0.57
English (55)	337	3.68
European (38)	38	0.41
Finnish (12)	177	1.93
French, ex. Basque (0)	650	7.09
French Canadian (10)	122	1.33
German (1,388)	4,320	47.13
Greek (18)	28	0.31
Hungarian (46)	126	1.37
Irish (197)	996	10.87
Italian (160)	531	5.79
Luxemburger (9)	20	0.22
Norwegian (96)	351	3.83
Pennsylvania German (0)	9	0.10
Polish (890)	2,053	22.40
Russian (9)	63	0.69
Scotch-Irish (21)	67	0.73
Scottish (34)	152	1.66
Serbian (36)	46	0.50
Slavic (0)	24	0.26
Slovak (21)	34	0.37
Slovene (10)	14	0.15
Swedish (26)	134	1.46
Swiss (27)	99	1.08
Turkish (19)	41	0.45
Ukrainian (27)	40	0.44
Welsh (0)	38	0.41
West Indian, ex. Hispanic (27)	27	0.29
Belizean (27)	27	0.29
Yugoslavian (0)	16	0.17

Hispanic Origin	Population	%
Hispanic or Latino (of any race)	884	9.44
Central American, ex. Mexican	22	0.23
Guatemalan	4	0.04
Honduran	6	0.06
Nicaraguan	10	0.11
Panamanian	1	0.01
Salvadoran	1	0.01
Cuban	7	0.07
Dominican Republic	10	0.11
Mexican	534	5.70
Puerto Rican	248	2.65
South American	29	0.31
Argentinean	2	0.02
Chilean	2	0.02
Colombian	16	0.17
Peruvian	8	0.09
Venezuelan	1	0.01
Other Hispanic or Latino	34	0.36

Race*	Population	%
African-American/Black (253)	330	3.52
Not Hispanic (239)	307	3.28
Hispanic (14)	23	0.25
American Indian/Alaska Native (90)	154	1.64
Not Hispanic (72)	120	1.28
Hispanic (18)	34	0.36
Apache (1)	3	0.03
Blackfeet (0)	2	0.02
Canadian/French Am. Ind. (0)	2	0.02
Cherokee (2)	4	0.04
Chippewa (20)	34	0.36
Iroquois (8)	20	0.21
Menominee (5)	7	0.07
Mexican American Ind. (0)	2	0.02
Ottawa (2)	3	0.03
Potawatomi (1)	1	0.01
Sioux (3)	6	0.06
South American Ind. (4)	4	0.04
Asian (200)	246	2.63
Not Hispanic (193)	232	2.48
Hispanic (7)	14	0.15
Bangladeshi (2)	2	0.02
Chinese, ex. Taiwanese (28)	35	0.37
Filipino (32)	41	0.44
Hmong (5)	5	0.05
Indian (60)	69	0.74
Indonesian (1)	1	0.01
Japanese (14)	21	0.22
Korean (12)	14	0.15
Laotian (8)	14	0.15
Pakistani (11)	16	0.17
Taiwanese (2)	2	0.02
Thai (3)	5	0.05
Vietnamese (6)	10	0.11
Hawaii Native/Pacific Islander (1)	3	0.03
Not Hispanic (0)	2	0.02
Hispanic (1)	1	0.01
Guamanian/Chamorro (0)	1	0.01
White (8,320)	8,539	91.18
Not Hispanic (7,825)	7,964	85.04
Hispanic (495)	575	6.14

Stevens Point

Place Type: City
County: Portage
Population: 26,717†

Ancestry‡	Population	%
African, Sub-Saharan (41)	69	0.26
African (0)	28	0.11
Other Sub-Saharan African (41)	41	0.15
American (610)	610	2.30
Arab (12)	12	0.05
Egyptian (12)	12	0.05
Armenian (8)	8	0.03
Austrian (0)	126	0.48
Belgian (0)	60	0.23
British (28)	123	0.46
Canadian (0)	26	0.10
Celtic (0)	4	0.02
Croatian (15)	38	0.14
Czech (93)	453	1.71
Czechoslovakian (0)	33	0.12
Danish (17)	272	1.03
Dutch (102)	475	1.79
Eastern European (10)	10	0.04
English (310)	1,643	6.20
European (174)	215	0.81
Finnish (41)	130	0.49
French, ex. Basque (42)	873	3.30
French Canadian (72)	230	0.87
German (3,320)	11,693	44.15
Greek (0)	32	0.12
Hungarian (8)	284	1.07
Irish (487)	3,315	12.52
Italian (211)	993	3.75
Latvian (38)	49	0.19
Lithuanian (0)	18	0.07
Luxemburger (0)	9	0.03
Macedonian (10)	10	0.04
Northern European (7)	7	0.03
Norwegian (520)	2,181	8.24
Pennsylvania German (0)	21	0.08
Polish (3,315)	7,335	27.70
Portuguese (7)	41	0.15
Romanian (0)	18	0.07
Russian (43)	180	0.68
Scandinavian (27)	96	0.36
Scotch-Irish (66)	270	1.02
Scottish (61)	430	1.62
Slavic (0)	15	0.06
Slovak (0)	33	0.12
Swedish (69)	583	2.20
Swiss (3)	154	0.58
Ukrainian (15)	62	0.23
Welsh (40)	78	0.29
West Indian, ex. Hispanic (14)	14	0.05
British West Indian (14)	14	0.05
Yugoslavian (25)	42	0.16

Hispanic Origin	Population	%
Hispanic or Latino (of any race)	696	2.61
Central American, ex. Mexican	22	0.08
Costa Rican	6	0.02
Guatemalan	8	0.03
Nicaraguan	1	<0.01
Salvadoran	7	0.03
Cuban	17	0.06
Dominican Republic	4	0.01
Mexican	488	1.83
Puerto Rican	50	0.19
South American	41	0.15
Argentinean	3	0.01
Chilean	2	0.01
Colombian	20	0.07
Ecuadorian	2	0.01
Paraguayan	1	<0.01
Peruvian	8	0.03
Venezuelan	4	0.01
Other South American	1	<0.01
Other Hispanic or Latino	74	0.28

Race*	Population	%
African-American/Black (246)	408	1.53
Not Hispanic (237)	377	1.41
Hispanic (9)	31	0.12
American Indian/Alaska Native (116)	229	0.86
Not Hispanic (102)	202	0.76
Hispanic (14)	27	0.10
Aleut *(Alaska Native)* (0)	1	<0.01
Apache (0)	3	0.01
Blackfeet (1)	3	0.01
Canadian/French Am. Ind. (3)	4	0.01
Cherokee (0)	14	0.05
Cheyenne (0)	1	<0.01
Chippewa (29)	47	0.18
Choctaw (1)	3	0.01
Creek (0)	7	0.03
Crow (0)	1	<0.01
Iroquois (7)	18	0.07
Menominee (10)	13	0.05
Mexican American Ind. (0)	1	<0.01
Potawatomi (3)	4	0.01
Pueblo (0)	1	<0.01
Sioux (4)	8	0.03
South American Ind. (0)	1	<0.01
Asian (1,252)	1,371	5.13
Not Hispanic (1,241)	1,353	5.06
Hispanic (11)	18	0.07
Burmese (1)	1	<0.01
Cambodian (3)	6	0.02
Chinese, ex. Taiwanese (201)	220	0.82
Filipino (26)	43	0.16
Hmong (734)	757	2.83
Indian (120)	134	0.50
Indonesian (2)	6	0.02
Japanese (28)	46	0.17
Korean (50)	66	0.25
Laotian (1)	2	0.01
Malaysian (1)	3	0.01
Pakistani (2)	3	0.01
Sri Lankan (2)	2	0.01
Taiwanese (5)	5	0.02
Thai (14)	18	0.07
Vietnamese (15)	18	0.07
Hawaii Native/Pacific Islander (9)	28	0.10
Not Hispanic (9)	27	0.10
Hispanic (0)	1	<0.01
Guamanian/Chamorro (1)	2	0.01
Native Hawaiian (4)	10	0.04
Samoan (0)	3	0.01
White (24,499)	24,865	93.07
Not Hispanic (24,075)	24,386	91.28
Hispanic (424)	479	1.79

*Notes: † The Census 2010 population figure is used to calculate the percentages in the Hispanic Origin and Race categories. Ancestry percentages are based on the 2006-2010 American Community Survey population (not shown); ‡ Numbers in parentheses indicate the number of people reporting a single ancestry; * Numbers in parentheses indicate the number of persons reporting this race alone, not in combination with any other race; Please refer to the Explanation of Data for more information.*

Stoughton

Place Type: City
County: Dane
Population: 12,611†

Ancestry‡	Population	%
African, Sub-Saharan (0)	209	1.66
African (0)	209	1.66
Albanian (108)	108	0.86
American (361)	361	2.87
Australian (8)	8	0.06
Austrian (0)	49	0.39
British (0)	36	0.29
Canadian (0)	35	0.28
Croatian (0)	17	0.13
Czech (0)	76	0.60
Czechoslovakian (21)	34	0.27
Danish (86)	121	0.96
Dutch (27)	349	2.77
English (194)	1,394	11.06
European (81)	81	0.64
Finnish (0)	61	0.48
French, ex. Basque (6)	306	2.43
French Canadian (55)	176	1.40
German (1,369)	5,225	41.47
Greek (0)	28	0.22
Hungarian (0)	69	0.55
Irish (401)	1,658	13.16
Italian (11)	126	1.00
Latvian (13)	13	0.10
Norwegian (1,634)	3,477	27.60
Pennsylvania German (46)	46	0.37
Polish (136)	639	5.07
Russian (0)	63	0.50
Scandinavian (12)	56	0.44
Scotch-Irish (40)	142	1.13
Scottish (56)	131	1.04
Slovene (14)	23	0.18
Swedish (48)	359	2.85
Swiss (61)	214	1.70
Welsh (0)	48	0.38

Hispanic Origin	Population	%
Hispanic or Latino (of any race)	230	1.82
Central American, ex. Mexican	13	0.10
Costa Rican	1	0.01
Guatemalan	5	0.04
Honduran	1	0.01
Panamanian	6	0.05
Cuban	4	0.03
Mexican	137	1.09
Puerto Rican	22	0.17
South American	36	0.29
Argentinean	3	0.02
Chilean	5	0.04
Colombian	9	0.07
Peruvian	12	0.10
Uruguayan	7	0.06
Other Hispanic or Latino	18	0.14

Race*	Population	%
African-American/Black (178)	278	2.20
Not Hispanic (178)	278	2.20
American Indian/Alaska Native (31)	72	0.57
Not Hispanic (26)	66	0.52
Hispanic (5)	6	0.05
Arapaho (1)	1	0.01
Canadian/French Am. Ind. (0)	2	0.02
Cherokee (0)	9	0.07
Chippewa (5)	8	0.06
Choctaw (0)	2	0.02
Cree (0)	3	0.02
Creek (1)	4	0.03
Iroquois (3)	5	0.04
Menominee (1)	1	0.01
Mexican American Ind. (3)	4	0.03
Navajo (0)	3	0.02
Pueblo (1)	2	0.02
Sioux (2)	2	0.02
Asian (169)	206	1.63
Not Hispanic (169)	197	1.56
Hispanic (0)	9	0.07
Cambodian (32)	38	0.30
Chinese, ex. Taiwanese (22)	25	0.20
Filipino (9)	12	0.10
Hmong (8)	8	0.06
Indian (48)	51	0.40
Indonesian (1)	1	0.01
Japanese (7)	22	0.17
Korean (19)	26	0.21
Pakistani (2)	2	0.02
Taiwanese (1)	1	0.01
Vietnamese (11)	11	0.09
Hawaii Native/Pacific Islander (6)	10	0.08
Not Hispanic (6)	10	0.08
Guamanian/Chamorro (2)	2	0.02
Native Hawaiian (4)	7	0.06
White (11,990)	12,174	96.53
Not Hispanic (11,827)	11,994	95.11
Hispanic (163)	180	1.43

Sturgeon Bay

Place Type: City
County: Door
Population: 9,144†

Ancestry‡	Population	%
American (601)	601	6.53
Austrian (0)	23	0.25
Belgian (364)	1,335	14.51
British (12)	34	0.37
Canadian (11)	69	0.75
Croatian (0)	13	0.14
Czech (47)	230	2.50
Czechoslovakian (0)	12	0.13
Danish (0)	229	2.49
Dutch (81)	159	1.73
English (39)	501	5.45
European (104)	104	1.13
Finnish (32)	100	1.09
French, ex. Basque (28)	471	5.12
French Canadian (31)	207	2.25
German (1,321)	4,333	47.11
Greek (0)	1	0.01
Hungarian (0)	48	0.52
Icelander (29)	49	0.53
Irish (285)	1,103	11.99
Italian (170)	280	3.04
Northern European (14)	14	0.15
Norwegian (225)	967	10.51
Polish (144)	588	6.39
Russian (0)	69	0.75
Scandinavian (0)	9	0.10
Scotch-Irish (0)	22	0.24
Scottish (27)	150	1.63
Slovak (10)	35	0.38
Slovene (47)	47	0.51
Swedish (66)	370	4.02
Swiss (0)	26	0.28
Welsh (0)	52	0.57
West Indian, ex. Hispanic (30)	30	0.33
U.S. Virgin Islander (1)	1	0.01
West Indian (29)	29	0.32
Yugoslavian (11)	35	0.38

Hispanic Origin	Population	%
Hispanic or Latino (of any race)	251	2.74
Central American, ex. Mexican	17	0.19
Guatemalan	2	0.02
Honduran	4	0.04
Nicaraguan	9	0.10
Salvadoran	2	0.02
Cuban	7	0.08
Mexican	175	1.91
Puerto Rican	18	0.20
South American	9	0.10
Chilean	1	0.01
Colombian	3	0.03
Peruvian	3	0.03
Venezuelan	2	0.02
Other Hispanic or Latino	25	0.27

Race*	Population	%
African-American/Black (92)	137	1.50
Not Hispanic (88)	128	1.40
Hispanic (4)	9	0.10
American Indian/Alaska Native (79)	135	1.48
Not Hispanic (70)	116	1.27
Hispanic (9)	19	0.21
Apache (0)	3	0.03
Canadian/French Am. Ind. (1)	1	0.01
Cherokee (0)	5	0.05
Chippewa (19)	25	0.27
Comanche (1)	1	0.01
Hopi (3)	3	0.03
Iroquois (28)	44	0.48
Menominee (2)	6	0.07
Mexican American Ind. (2)	2	0.02
Navajo (0)	3	0.03
Potawatomi (4)	6	0.07
Sioux (1)	1	0.01
Asian (54)	69	0.75
Not Hispanic (54)	69	0.75
Chinese, ex. Taiwanese (8)	9	0.10
Filipino (18)	27	0.30
Indian (8)	8	0.09
Japanese (3)	3	0.03
Korean (6)	6	0.07
Nepalese (1)	1	0.01
Thai (3)	3	0.03
Vietnamese (5)	5	0.05
Hawaii Native/Pacific Islander (2)	4	0.04
Not Hispanic (2)	4	0.04
Native Hawaiian (1)	1	0.01
White (8,697)	8,818	96.43
Not Hispanic (8,578)	8,670	94.82
Hispanic (119)	148	1.62

Suamico

Place Type: Village
County: Brown
Population: 11,346†

Ancestry‡	Population	%
American (408)	408	3.75
Arab (0)	48	0.44
Syrian (0)	48	0.44
Austrian (0)	28	0.26
Belgian (433)	1,268	11.67
Canadian (38)	63	0.58
Croatian (13)	13	0.12
Czech (28)	306	2.82
Czechoslovakian (0)	12	0.11
Danish (13)	153	1.41
Dutch (104)	706	6.50
English (90)	440	4.05
European (35)	35	0.32
Finnish (16)	172	1.58
French, ex. Basque (99)	823	7.57
French Canadian (89)	429	3.95
German (2,127)	5,468	50.32
Icelander (0)	37	0.34
Irish (102)	1,008	9.28
Israeli (0)	16	0.15
Italian (38)	303	2.79
Lithuanian (0)	48	0.44
Norwegian (137)	647	5.95
Polish (382)	1,452	13.36
Romanian (24)	24	0.22
Russian (27)	54	0.50
Scotch-Irish (0)	76	0.70
Scottish (24)	66	0.61
Slavic (0)	11	0.10
Slovak (69)	110	1.01
Swedish (70)	261	2.40
Swiss (12)	42	0.39
West Indian, ex. Hispanic (8)	8	0.07

*Notes: † The Census 2010 population figure is used to calculate the percentages in the Hispanic Origin and Race categories. Ancestry percentages are based on the 2006-2010 American Community Survey population (not shown); ‡ Numbers in parentheses indicate the number of people reporting a single ancestry; * Numbers in parentheses indicate the number of persons reporting this race alone, not in combination with any other race; Please refer to the Explanation of Data for more information.*

West Indian (8)	8	0.07

Hispanic Origin	Population	%
Hispanic or Latino (of any race)	112	0.99
Central American, ex. Mexican	18	0.16
Guatemalan	8	0.07
Panamanian	7	0.06
Salvadoran	3	0.03
Cuban	1	0.01
Mexican	65	0.57
Puerto Rican	11	0.10
South American	7	0.06
Chilean	1	0.01
Colombian	2	0.02
Ecuadorian	1	0.01
Paraguayan	2	0.02
Peruvian	1	0.01
Other Hispanic or Latino	10	0.09

Race*	Population	%
African-American/Black (30)	69	0.61
Not Hispanic (27)	60	0.53
Hispanic (3)	9	0.08
American Indian/Alaska Native (80)	117	1.03
Not Hispanic (63)	94	0.83
Hispanic (17)	23	0.20
Canadian/French Am. Ind. (0)	1	0.01
Cherokee (2)	3	0.03
Chippewa (20)	25	0.22
Iroquois (21)	27	0.24
Menominee (8)	11	0.10
Ottawa (1)	1	0.01
Sioux (0)	1	0.01
Yaqui (2)	2	0.02
Asian (71)	91	0.80
Not Hispanic (69)	89	0.78
Hispanic (2)	2	0.02
Chinese, ex. Taiwanese (18)	22	0.19
Filipino (4)	17	0.15
Hmong (26)	27	0.24
Indian (6)	6	0.05
Japanese (2)	3	0.03
Korean (7)	8	0.07
Thai (1)	1	0.01
Vietnamese (4)	4	0.04
Hawaii Native/Pacific Islander (4)	9	0.08
Not Hispanic (4)	7	0.06
Hispanic (0)	2	0.02
Guamanian/Chamorro (1)	2	0.02
Native Hawaiian (1)	2	0.02
Samoan (2)	2	0.02
White (11,047)	11,130	98.10
Not Hispanic (10,992)	11,064	97.51
Hispanic (55)	66	0.58

Sun Prairie

Place Type: City
County: Dane
Population: 29,364†

Ancestry‡	Population	%
African, Sub-Saharan (312)	312	1.12
African (312)	312	1.12
Alsatian (0)	6	0.02
American (984)	984	3.54
Arab (17)	36	0.13
Egyptian (0)	19	0.07
Jordanian (9)	9	0.03
Lebanese (8)	8	0.03
Austrian (9)	18	0.06
Belgian (16)	206	0.74
British (0)	21	0.08
Canadian (14)	14	0.05
Croatian (31)	92	0.33
Czech (82)	355	1.28
Czechoslovakian (0)	73	0.26
Danish (151)	455	1.64
Dutch (81)	740	2.66
English (390)	2,080	7.48
European (254)	296	1.06
Finnish (80)	204	0.73
French, ex. Basque (72)	1,093	3.93
French Canadian (160)	269	0.97
German (4,942)	12,422	44.67
Greek (10)	119	0.43
Hungarian (15)	91	0.33
Irish (634)	3,825	13.76
Italian (307)	1,112	4.00
Lithuanian (0)	47	0.17
Northern European (70)	70	0.25
Norwegian (899)	3,481	12.52
Pennsylvania German (25)	42	0.15
Polish (387)	1,641	5.90
Portuguese (7)	7	0.03
Russian (12)	138	0.50
Scandinavian (41)	81	0.29
Scotch-Irish (77)	417	1.50
Scottish (155)	518	1.86
Serbian (0)	12	0.04
Slavic (0)	17	0.06
Slovak (12)	22	0.08
Slovene (10)	66	0.24
Swedish (99)	733	2.64
Swiss (79)	406	1.46
Turkish (32)	32	0.12
Ukrainian (23)	23	0.08
Welsh (31)	241	0.87

Hispanic Origin	Population	%
Hispanic or Latino (of any race)	1,253	4.27
Central American, ex. Mexican	87	0.30
Costa Rican	5	0.02
Guatemalan	23	0.08
Honduran	12	0.04
Nicaraguan	27	0.09
Panamanian	5	0.02
Salvadoran	15	0.05
Cuban	21	0.07
Dominican Republic	2	0.01
Mexican	861	2.93
Puerto Rican	72	0.25
South American	108	0.37
Argentinean	18	0.06
Colombian	21	0.07
Ecuadorian	9	0.03
Paraguayan	1	<0.01
Peruvian	47	0.16
Venezuelan	12	0.04
Other Hispanic or Latino	102	0.35

Race*	Population	%
African-American/Black (1,804)	2,297	7.82
Not Hispanic (1,785)	2,243	7.64
Hispanic (19)	54	0.18
American Indian/Alaska Native (91)	271	0.92
Not Hispanic (72)	218	0.74
Hispanic (19)	53	0.18
Alaska Athabascan *(Ala. Nat.)* (0)	3	0.01
Apache (0)	2	0.01
Blackfeet (0)	9	0.03
Cherokee (8)	41	0.14
Chippewa (23)	47	0.16
Choctaw (0)	9	0.03
Creek (0)	1	<0.01
Hopi (2)	2	0.01
Inupiat *(Alaska Native)* (0)	2	0.01
Iroquois (6)	9	0.03
Lumbee (1)	3	0.01
Menominee (3)	3	0.01
Mexican American Ind. (6)	16	0.05
Ottawa (1)	1	<0.01
Paiute (3)	3	0.01
Potawatomi (0)	3	0.01
Sioux (4)	7	0.02
South American Ind. (0)	3	0.01
Tlingit-Haida *(Alaska Native)* (0)	3	0.01
Ute (1)	2	0.01
Asian (1,077)	1,301	4.43
Not Hispanic (1,074)	1,280	4.36
Hispanic (3)	21	0.07
Bangladeshi (2)	2	0.01
Cambodian (13)	23	0.08
Chinese, ex. Taiwanese (147)	183	0.62
Filipino (34)	67	0.23
Hmong (410)	434	1.48
Indian (261)	282	0.96
Indonesian (8)	12	0.04
Japanese (12)	35	0.12
Korean (63)	110	0.37
Laotian (15)	19	0.06
Malaysian (0)	1	<0.01
Nepalese (5)	5	0.02
Pakistani (10)	15	0.05
Sri Lankan (0)	3	0.01
Taiwanese (6)	9	0.03
Thai (2)	12	0.04
Vietnamese (29)	36	0.12
Hawaii Native/Pacific Islander (13)	35	0.12
Not Hispanic (13)	33	0.11
Hispanic (0)	2	0.01
Fijian (0)	1	<0.01
Guamanian/Chamorro (3)	5	0.02
Native Hawaiian (4)	9	0.03
Samoan (5)	6	0.02
Tongan (0)	3	0.01
White (25,089)	25,879	88.13
Not Hispanic (24,362)	25,049	85.31
Hispanic (727)	830	2.83

Superior

Place Type: City
County: Douglas
Population: 27,244†

Ancestry‡	Population	%
African, Sub-Saharan (13)	13	0.05
Ugandan (13)	13	0.05
American (651)	651	2.39
Arab (0)	28	0.10
Syrian (0)	28	0.10
Austrian (0)	44	0.16
Belgian (85)	322	1.18
British (42)	102	0.38
Canadian (28)	89	0.33
Croatian (0)	37	0.14
Czech (37)	202	0.74
Czechoslovakian (0)	34	0.13
Danish (58)	476	1.75
Dutch (7)	366	1.35
English (462)	1,909	7.02
European (220)	262	0.96
Finnish (716)	1,885	6.93
French, ex. Basque (215)	1,525	5.61
French Canadian (172)	723	2.66
German (1,992)	7,878	28.97
Greek (27)	172	0.63
Hungarian (0)	42	0.15
Icelander (9)	9	0.03
Irish (539)	3,505	12.89
Italian (340)	864	3.18
Latvian (0)	14	0.05
Lithuanian (39)	71	0.26
Luxemburger (26)	26	0.10
Norwegian (1,218)	4,344	15.97
Polish (670)	2,127	7.82
Romanian (0)	11	0.04
Russian (14)	104	0.38
Scandinavian (244)	350	1.29
Scotch-Irish (72)	544	2.00
Scottish (28)	251	0.92
Serbian (11)	36	0.13
Slavic (13)	49	0.18
Slovak (56)	135	0.50
Swedish (976)	3,428	12.61
Swiss (0)	158	0.58
Ukrainian (9)	55	0.20
Welsh (0)	166	0.61
West Indian, ex. Hispanic (19)	34	0.13

*Notes: † The Census 2010 population figure is used to calculate the percentages in the Hispanic Origin and Race categories. Ancestry percentages are based on the 2006-2010 American Community Survey population (not shown); ‡ Numbers in parentheses indicate the number of people reporting a single ancestry; * Numbers in parentheses indicate the number of persons reporting this race alone, not in combination with any other race; Please refer to the Explanation of Data for more information.*

Dutch West Indian (0)	15	0.06
Haitian (19)	19	0.07
Yugoslavian (11)	60	0.22

Hispanic Origin	Population	%
Hispanic or Latino (of any race)	382	1.40
Central American, ex. Mexican	33	0.12
Costa Rican	4	0.01
Guatemalan	14	0.05
Honduran	5	0.02
Panamanian	6	0.02
Salvadoran	4	0.01
Cuban	6	0.02
Dominican Republic	2	0.01
Mexican	217	0.80
Puerto Rican	53	0.19
South American	24	0.09
Argentinean	2	0.01
Bolivian	2	0.01
Colombian	4	0.01
Ecuadorian	2	0.01
Peruvian	6	0.02
Venezuelan	8	0.03
Other Hispanic or Latino	47	0.17

Race*	Population	%
African-American/Black (391)	680	2.50
Not Hispanic (380)	653	2.40
Hispanic (11)	27	0.10
American Indian/Alaska Native (702)	1,203	4.42
Not Hispanic (673)	1,152	4.23
Hispanic (29)	51	0.19
Alaska Athabascan *(Ala. Nat.)* (1)	1	<0.01
Arapaho (1)	1	<0.01
Blackfeet (0)	1	<0.01
Canadian/French Am. Ind. (7)	10	0.04
Cherokee (4)	21	0.08
Cheyenne (0)	1	<0.01
Chippewa (395)	586	2.15
Choctaw (3)	5	0.02
Cree (0)	1	<0.01
Creek (1)	1	<0.01
Delaware (1)	1	<0.01
Houma (0)	2	0.01
Inupiat *(Alaska Native)* (0)	1	<0.01
Iroquois (8)	12	0.04
Mexican American Ind. (4)	4	0.01
Navajo (1)	2	0.01
Potawatomi (1)	1	<0.01
Seminole (2)	4	0.01
Sioux (6)	16	0.06
South American Ind. (1)	3	0.01
Tlingit-Haida *(Alaska Native)* (1)	1	<0.01
Yaqui (1)	1	<0.01
Asian (316)	410	1.50
Not Hispanic (312)	403	1.48
Hispanic (4)	7	0.03
Cambodian (4)	4	0.01
Chinese, ex. Taiwanese (85)	95	0.35
Filipino (30)	64	0.23
Hmong (42)	46	0.17
Indian (35)	41	0.15
Indonesian (5)	5	0.02
Japanese (10)	19	0.07
Korean (39)	66	0.24
Laotian (1)	6	0.02
Malaysian (1)	2	0.01
Nepalese (17)	17	0.06
Sri Lankan (7)	7	0.03
Taiwanese (1)	1	<0.01
Thai (4)	5	0.02
Vietnamese (29)	31	0.11
Hawaii Native/Pacific Islander (7)	23	0.08
Not Hispanic (6)	21	0.08
Hispanic (1)	2	0.01
Guamanian/Chamorro (0)	1	<0.01
Native Hawaiian (3)	8	0.03
Samoan (2)	2	0.01
White (24,928)	25,738	94.47
Not Hispanic (24,696)	25,453	93.43
Hispanic (232)	285	1.05

Sussex

Place Type: Village
County: Waukesha
Population: 10,518†

Ancestry‡	Population	%
African, Sub-Saharan (81)	81	0.79
Nigerian (81)	81	0.79
American (342)	342	3.33
Austrian (10)	63	0.61
Belgian (0)	20	0.19
British (12)	50	0.49
Croatian (6)	41	0.40
Czech (60)	216	2.10
Czechoslovakian (11)	21	0.20
Danish (26)	155	1.51
Dutch (33)	158	1.54
English (112)	777	7.57
European (73)	73	0.71
Finnish (0)	30	0.29
French, ex. Basque (8)	394	3.84
French Canadian (21)	58	0.57
German (2,456)	6,496	63.30
Greek (23)	50	0.49
Hungarian (8)	55	0.54
Irish (116)	1,477	14.39
Italian (90)	438	4.27
Lithuanian (0)	27	0.26
Luxemburger (0)	10	0.10
Northern European (11)	11	0.11
Norwegian (92)	524	5.11
Polish (339)	1,523	14.84
Portuguese (0)	14	0.14
Romanian (0)	5	0.05
Russian (35)	100	0.97
Scandinavian (0)	54	0.53
Scotch-Irish (11)	50	0.49
Scottish (18)	195	1.90
Serbian (11)	11	0.11
Slavic (0)	15	0.15
Slovak (0)	34	0.33
Slovene (11)	31	0.30
Swedish (56)	267	2.60
Swiss (8)	99	0.96
Ukrainian (9)	9	0.09
Welsh (20)	104	1.01
Yugoslavian (8)	20	0.19

Hispanic Origin	Population	%
Hispanic or Latino (of any race)	249	2.37
Central American, ex. Mexican	21	0.20
Costa Rican	1	0.01
Guatemalan	15	0.14
Panamanian	3	0.03
Salvadoran	2	0.02
Dominican Republic	6	0.06
Mexican	158	1.50
Puerto Rican	31	0.29
South American	15	0.14
Argentinean	1	0.01
Bolivian	1	0.01
Colombian	12	0.11
Ecuadorian	1	0.01
Other Hispanic or Latino	18	0.17

Race*	Population	%
African-American/Black (84)	134	1.27
Not Hispanic (81)	127	1.21
Hispanic (3)	7	0.07
American Indian/Alaska Native (35)	48	0.46
Not Hispanic (26)	39	0.37
Hispanic (9)	9	0.09
Central American Ind. (1)	1	0.01
Chippewa (8)	8	0.08
Iroquois (4)	7	0.07
Menominee (1)	2	0.02
Mexican American Ind. (3)	3	0.03
Asian (224)	268	2.55
Not Hispanic (222)	264	2.51
Hispanic (2)	4	0.04
Burmese (1)	2	0.02
Chinese, ex. Taiwanese (32)	36	0.34
Filipino (23)	39	0.37
Indian (81)	92	0.87
Indonesian (1)	1	0.01
Japanese (28)	35	0.33
Korean (14)	17	0.16
Laotian (14)	19	0.18
Pakistani (5)	5	0.05
Thai (4)	7	0.07
Vietnamese (7)	8	0.08
Hawaii Native/Pacific Islander (0)	1	0.01
Not Hispanic (0)	1	0.01
Native Hawaiian (0)	1	0.01
White (10,013)	10,118	96.20
Not Hispanic (9,838)	9,935	94.46
Hispanic (175)	183	1.74

Tomah

Place Type: City
County: Monroe
Population: 9,093†

Ancestry‡	Population	%
African, Sub-Saharan (4)	12	0.13
African (4)	12	0.13
American (188)	188	2.09
Austrian (25)	173	1.93
Belgian (0)	22	0.25
British (0)	12	0.13
Czech (0)	93	1.04
Danish (22)	113	1.26
Dutch (26)	296	3.30
English (385)	968	10.79
European (57)	57	0.64
Finnish (27)	27	0.30
French, ex. Basque (7)	331	3.69
French Canadian (18)	109	1.21
German (1,920)	4,268	47.55
Hungarian (12)	12	0.13
Irish (345)	1,163	12.96
Italian (124)	228	2.54
Lithuanian (0)	23	0.26
Norwegian (389)	1,023	11.40
Polish (173)	529	5.89
Portuguese (0)	16	0.18
Russian (47)	78	0.87
Scandinavian (64)	81	0.90
Scotch-Irish (52)	98	1.09
Scottish (29)	70	0.78
Slovak (6)	6	0.07
Swedish (11)	192	2.14
Swiss (10)	54	0.60
Ukrainian (12)	40	0.45
Welsh (0)	18	0.20
West Indian, ex. Hispanic (33)	48	0.53
Haitian (0)	15	0.17
Jamaican (33)	33	0.37

Hispanic Origin	Population	%
Hispanic or Latino (of any race)	366	4.03
Central American, ex. Mexican	19	0.21
Guatemalan	2	0.02
Nicaraguan	3	0.03
Panamanian	10	0.11
Salvadoran	4	0.04
Cuban	9	0.10
Mexican	223	2.45
Puerto Rican	81	0.89
South American	10	0.11
Bolivian	1	0.01
Colombian	5	0.05
Peruvian	1	0.01
Other South American	3	0.03
Other Hispanic or Latino	24	0.26

*Notes: † The Census 2010 population figure is used to calculate the percentages in the Hispanic Origin and Race categories. Ancestry percentages are based on the 2006-2010 American Community Survey population (not shown); ‡ Numbers in parentheses indicate the number of people reporting a single ancestry; * Numbers in parentheses indicate the number of persons reporting this race alone, not in combination with any other race; Please refer to the Explanation of Data for more information.*

Race*	Population	%
African-American/Black (238)	301	3.31
Not Hispanic (227)	282	3.10
Hispanic (11)	19	0.21
American Indian/Alaska Native (158)	242	2.66
Not Hispanic (141)	210	2.31
Hispanic (17)	32	0.35
Blackfeet (1)	2	0.02
Canadian/French Am. Ind. (4)	4	0.04
Cherokee (5)	21	0.23
Chickasaw (0)	1	0.01
Chippewa (13)	19	0.21
Choctaw (1)	1	0.01
Creek (2)	2	0.02
Iroquois (2)	3	0.03
Lumbee (1)	1	0.01
Menominee (4)	5	0.05
Sioux (8)	9	0.10
South American Ind. (0)	3	0.03
Asian (110)	152	1.67
Not Hispanic (105)	142	1.56
Hispanic (5)	10	0.11
Chinese, ex. Taiwanese (8)	8	0.09
Filipino (29)	37	0.41
Hmong (0)	7	0.08
Indian (32)	33	0.36
Japanese (7)	11	0.12
Korean (24)	35	0.38
Pakistani (3)	3	0.03
Thai (1)	4	0.04
Vietnamese (4)	5	0.05
Hawaii Native/Pacific Islander (25)	35	0.38
Not Hispanic (25)	32	0.35
Hispanic (0)	3	0.03
Guamanian/Chamorro (6)	7	0.08
Native Hawaiian (1)	4	0.04
Samoan (7)	13	0.14
Tongan (0)	2	0.02
White (8,262)	8,436	92.77
Not Hispanic (8,077)	8,212	90.31
Hispanic (185)	224	2.46

Two Rivers

Place Type: City
County: Manitowoc
Population: 11,712†

Ancestry‡	Population	%
Alsatian (0)	7	0.06
American (527)	527	4.44
Austrian (9)	9	0.08
Belgian (111)	208	1.75
British (45)	45	0.38
Czech (291)	1,321	11.13
Czechoslovakian (22)	22	0.19
Danish (14)	115	0.97
Dutch (12)	96	0.81
English (136)	572	4.82
European (45)	45	0.38
Finnish (8)	21	0.18
French, ex. Basque (325)	1,097	9.24
French Canadian (135)	309	2.60
German (2,400)	5,661	47.68
Greek (0)	16	0.13
Hungarian (28)	38	0.32
Irish (215)	1,071	9.02
Italian (57)	102	0.86
Lithuanian (0)	11	0.09
Luxemburger (0)	9	0.08
Norwegian (87)	463	3.90
Polish (408)	1,511	12.73
Portuguese (12)	26	0.22
Romanian (6)	6	0.05
Russian (48)	68	0.57
Scandinavian (38)	71	0.60
Scotch-Irish (26)	125	1.05
Scottish (26)	97	0.82
Swedish (40)	190	1.60
Swiss (14)	27	0.23
Ukrainian (0)	38	0.32
Welsh (24)	51	0.43

Hispanic Origin	Population	%
Hispanic or Latino (of any race)	224	1.91
Central American, ex. Mexican	9	0.08
Guatemalan	1	0.01
Honduran	1	0.01
Panamanian	5	0.04
Salvadoran	2	0.02
Cuban	2	0.02
Dominican Republic	2	0.02
Mexican	147	1.26
Puerto Rican	29	0.25
South American	13	0.11
Bolivian	1	0.01
Chilean	10	0.09
Peruvian	2	0.02
Other Hispanic or Latino	22	0.19

Race*	Population	%
African-American/Black (60)	85	0.73
Not Hispanic (59)	83	0.71
Hispanic (1)	2	0.02
American Indian/Alaska Native (92)	150	1.28
Not Hispanic (83)	134	1.14
Hispanic (9)	16	0.14
Apache (1)	4	0.03
Canadian/French Am. Ind. (0)	1	0.01
Cherokee (0)	3	0.03
Chickasaw (0)	2	0.02
Chippewa (15)	22	0.19
Creek (1)	1	0.01
Iroquois (12)	16	0.14
Menominee (22)	23	0.20
Mexican American Ind. (2)	5	0.04
Navajo (1)	1	0.01
Ottawa (0)	1	0.01
Potawatomi (1)	3	0.03
Asian (277)	309	2.64
Not Hispanic (276)	306	2.61
Hispanic (1)	3	0.03
Chinese, ex. Taiwanese (8)	8	0.07
Filipino (7)	17	0.15
Hmong (195)	212	1.81
Indian (18)	29	0.25
Japanese (1)	3	0.03
Korean (7)	7	0.06
Laotian (22)	22	0.19
Thai (0)	2	0.02
Vietnamese (2)	3	0.03
Hawaii Native/Pacific Islander (0)	8	0.07
Not Hispanic (0)	2	0.02
Hispanic (0)	6	0.05
Native Hawaiian (0)	2	0.02
White (11,070)	11,196	95.59
Not Hispanic (10,952)	11,054	94.38
Hispanic (118)	142	1.21

Vernon

Place Type: Town
County: Waukesha
Population: 7,601†

Ancestry‡	Population	%
American (266)	266	3.51
Austrian (10)	82	1.08
Belgian (0)	13	0.17
British (12)	24	0.32
Croatian (0)	56	0.74
Czech (36)	81	1.07
Danish (3)	58	0.76
Dutch (9)	84	1.11
English (101)	422	5.57
European (132)	132	1.74
Finnish (9)	51	0.67
French, ex. Basque (20)	135	1.78
French Canadian (19)	101	1.33
German (1,673)	4,290	56.57
Greek (45)	187	2.47
Hungarian (22)	120	1.58
Irish (124)	1,003	13.23
Italian (57)	303	4.00
Lithuanian (12)	29	0.38
Norwegian (61)	321	4.23
Polish (392)	1,593	21.01
Portuguese (0)	9	0.12
Romanian (0)	12	0.16
Russian (0)	54	0.71
Scotch-Irish (0)	54	0.71
Scottish (34)	88	1.16
Serbian (20)	57	0.75
Slavic (0)	7	0.09
Slovak (41)	50	0.66
Slovene (21)	46	0.61
Swedish (19)	210	2.77
Swiss (0)	33	0.44
Ukrainian (9)	9	0.12
Welsh (11)	11	0.15
Yugoslavian (0)	10	0.13

Hispanic Origin	Population	%
Hispanic or Latino (of any race)	153	2.01
Central American, ex. Mexican	6	0.08
Guatemalan	1	0.01
Honduran	1	0.01
Panamanian	4	0.05
Cuban	5	0.07
Mexican	95	1.25
Puerto Rican	32	0.42
South American	6	0.08
Argentinean	1	0.01
Chilean	1	0.01
Colombian	3	0.04
Peruvian	1	0.01
Other Hispanic or Latino	9	0.12

Race*	Population	%
African-American/Black (53)	66	0.87
Not Hispanic (53)	66	0.87
American Indian/Alaska Native (16)	46	0.61
Not Hispanic (15)	43	0.57
Hispanic (1)	3	0.04
Apache (0)	2	0.03
Cherokee (0)	2	0.03
Chippewa (4)	8	0.11
Hopi (0)	1	0.01
Iroquois (2)	6	0.08
Potawatomi (4)	5	0.07
Sioux (0)	2	0.03
Asian (52)	77	1.01
Not Hispanic (52)	77	1.01
Chinese, ex. Taiwanese (16)	22	0.29
Filipino (5)	8	0.11
Indian (10)	10	0.13
Indonesian (0)	2	0.03
Japanese (5)	21	0.28
Korean (2)	5	0.07
Laotian (5)	5	0.07
Thai (1)	1	0.01
Vietnamese (7)	7	0.09
White (7,388)	7,456	98.09
Not Hispanic (7,261)	7,327	96.40
Hispanic (127)	129	1.70

Verona

Place Type: City
County: Dane
Population: 10,619†

Ancestry‡	Population	%
African, Sub-Saharan (11)	51	0.51
African (11)	51	0.51
American (345)	345	3.44
Arab (21)	21	0.21
Arab (21)	21	0.21
Austrian (13)	13	0.13

*Notes: † The Census 2010 population figure is used to calculate the percentages in the Hispanic Origin and Race categories. Ancestry percentages are based on the 2006-2010 American Community Survey population (not shown); ‡ Numbers in parentheses indicate the number of people reporting a single ancestry; * Numbers in parentheses indicate the number of persons reporting this race alone, not in combination with any other race; Please refer to the Explanation of Data for more information.*

Ancestry	Population	%
Belgian (0)	100	1.00
British (8)	41	0.41
Canadian (0)	20	0.20
Croatian (8)	8	0.08
Czech (21)	225	2.24
Czechoslovakian (0)	15	0.15
Danish (20)	55	0.55
Dutch (88)	282	2.81
Eastern European (13)	13	0.13
English (166)	1,224	12.20
European (165)	215	2.14
Finnish (0)	31	0.31
French, ex. Basque (13)	317	3.16
French Canadian (9)	84	0.84
German (1,395)	4,552	45.37
Greek (0)	58	0.58
Hungarian (11)	73	0.73
Irish (203)	1,635	16.30
Italian (107)	386	3.85
Lithuanian (36)	95	0.95
Norwegian (271)	1,141	11.37
Polish (79)	447	4.46
Portuguese (9)	23	0.23
Russian (0)	81	0.81
Scandinavian (70)	72	0.72
Scotch-Irish (18)	114	1.14
Scottish (50)	290	2.89
Slovak (0)	14	0.14
Swedish (121)	351	3.50
Swiss (88)	587	5.85
Ukrainian (13)	13	0.13
Welsh (0)	74	0.74

Hispanic Origin	Population	%
Hispanic or Latino (of any race)	258	2.43
Central American, ex. Mexican	16	0.15
Costa Rican	1	0.01
Guatemalan	9	0.08
Honduran	1	0.01
Nicaraguan	5	0.05
Cuban	11	0.10
Mexican	150	1.41
Puerto Rican	19	0.18
South American	47	0.44
Argentinean	1	0.01
Bolivian	11	0.10
Chilean	3	0.03
Colombian	11	0.10
Ecuadorian	6	0.06
Paraguayan	1	0.01
Peruvian	8	0.08
Uruguayan	1	0.01
Venezuelan	5	0.05
Other Hispanic or Latino	15	0.14

Race*	Population	%
African-American/Black (138)	246	2.32
Not Hispanic (134)	238	2.24
Hispanic (4)	8	0.08
American Indian/Alaska Native (28)	58	0.55
Not Hispanic (17)	46	0.43
Hispanic (11)	12	0.11
Apache (0)	1	0.01
Blackfeet (0)	1	0.01
Cherokee (1)	2	0.02
Chippewa (1)	2	0.02
Inupiat *(Alaska Native)* (0)	1	0.01
Iroquois (0)	1	0.01
Mexican American Ind. (2)	2	0.02
Potawatomi (1)	1	0.01
Sioux (5)	5	0.05
South American Ind. (6)	6	0.06
Ute (1)	1	0.01
Yakama (0)	1	0.01
Asian (268)	333	3.14
Not Hispanic (266)	330	3.11
Hispanic (2)	3	0.03
Cambodian (3)	5	0.05
Chinese, ex. Taiwanese (72)	94	0.89
Filipino (23)	35	0.33
Hmong (8)	8	0.08
Indian (100)	107	1.01
Indonesian (4)	5	0.05
Japanese (9)	23	0.22
Korean (7)	10	0.09
Nepalese (2)	2	0.02
Pakistani (14)	14	0.13
Sri Lankan (5)	6	0.06
Taiwanese (1)	1	0.01
Thai (3)	3	0.03
Vietnamese (9)	10	0.09
Hawaii Native/Pacific Islander (3)	11	0.10
Not Hispanic (3)	11	0.10
Native Hawaiian (0)	3	0.03
White (9,906)	10,095	95.07
Not Hispanic (9,744)	9,925	93.46
Hispanic (162)	170	1.60

Watertown

Place Type: City
County: Dodge
Population: 8,459†

Ancestry‡	Population	%
Albanian (11)	11	0.13
American (250)	250	2.96
Austrian (15)	165	1.95
Belgian (0)	43	0.51
Czech (23)	101	1.20
Czechoslovakian (0)	25	0.30
Danish (12)	44	0.52
Dutch (114)	152	1.80
English (157)	585	6.93
European (48)	140	1.66
French, ex. Basque (24)	289	3.42
French Canadian (0)	11	0.13
German (3,399)	5,575	66.05
Hungarian (11)	108	1.28
Irish (169)	1,027	12.17
Italian (86)	187	2.22
Norwegian (129)	600	7.11
Polish (85)	405	4.80
Russian (0)	17	0.20
Scotch-Irish (27)	54	0.64
Scottish (6)	63	0.75
Slovak (0)	10	0.12
Slovene (0)	13	0.15
Swedish (69)	215	2.55
Swiss (20)	41	0.49
Welsh (0)	46	0.55
Yugoslavian (0)	15	0.18

Hispanic Origin	Population	%
Hispanic or Latino (of any race)	447	5.28
Central American, ex. Mexican	3	0.04
Guatemalan	1	0.01
Honduran	2	0.02
Cuban	1	0.01
Mexican	397	4.69
Puerto Rican	26	0.31
South American	4	0.05
Argentinean	1	0.01
Bolivian	2	0.02
Peruvian	1	0.01
Other Hispanic or Latino	16	0.19

Race*	Population	%
African-American/Black (24)	41	0.48
Not Hispanic (24)	41	0.48
American Indian/Alaska Native (22)	46	0.54
Not Hispanic (21)	44	0.52
Hispanic (1)	2	0.02
Chippewa (3)	10	0.12
Iroquois (1)	2	0.02
Menominee (1)	3	0.04
Ottawa (2)	3	0.04
Sioux (1)	1	0.01
Asian (56)	94	1.11
Not Hispanic (55)	92	1.09
Hispanic (1)	2	0.02
Chinese, ex. Taiwanese (11)	15	0.18
Filipino (13)	31	0.37
Hmong (12)	14	0.17
Indian (5)	7	0.08
Japanese (1)	7	0.08
Korean (4)	4	0.05
Laotian (0)	2	0.02
Pakistani (0)	3	0.04
Thai (0)	4	0.05
Vietnamese (7)	7	0.08
Hawaii Native/Pacific Islander (5)	8	0.09
Not Hispanic (5)	8	0.09
Guamanian/Chamorro (5)	5	0.06
Native Hawaiian (0)	2	0.02
White (8,114)	8,212	97.08
Not Hispanic (7,829)	7,905	93.45
Hispanic (285)	307	3.63

Watertown

Place Type: City
County: Jefferson
Population: 15,402†

Ancestry‡	Population	%
American (561)	561	3.70
Arab (0)	6	0.04
Egyptian (0)	6	0.04
Armenian (0)	13	0.09
Austrian (0)	98	0.65
Belgian (13)	33	0.22
British (34)	34	0.22
Canadian (16)	16	0.11
Czech (31)	190	1.25
Czechoslovakian (12)	12	0.08
Danish (7)	73	0.48
Dutch (47)	352	2.32
English (419)	1,264	8.34
European (75)	75	0.49
Finnish (9)	31	0.20
French, ex. Basque (52)	783	5.16
French Canadian (12)	58	0.38
German (4,398)	8,352	55.09
Greek (17)	42	0.28
Hungarian (0)	48	0.32
Irish (127)	1,494	9.85
Italian (70)	523	3.45
Norwegian (181)	971	6.41
Pennsylvania German (0)	11	0.07
Polish (146)	981	6.47
Romanian (68)	68	0.45
Russian (0)	9	0.06
Scandinavian (59)	87	0.57
Scotch-Irish (39)	122	0.80
Scottish (25)	107	0.71
Slavic (0)	23	0.15
Slovak (0)	29	0.19
Swedish (50)	271	1.79
Swiss (27)	121	0.80
Ukrainian (0)	18	0.12
Welsh (0)	35	0.23
West Indian, ex. Hispanic (24)	30	0.20
Haitian (24)	24	0.16
Jamaican (0)	6	0.04

Hispanic Origin	Population	%
Hispanic or Latino (of any race)	1,284	8.34
Central American, ex. Mexican	20	0.13
Guatemalan	5	0.03
Honduran	2	0.01
Nicaraguan	8	0.05
Panamanian	3	0.02
Salvadoran	2	0.01
Cuban	9	0.06
Dominican Republic	1	0.01
Mexican	1,133	7.36
Puerto Rican	37	0.24
South American	16	0.10
Chilean	2	0.01

*Notes: † The Census 2010 population figure is used to calculate the percentages in the Hispanic Origin and Race categories. Ancestry percentages are based on the 2006-2010 American Community Survey population (not shown); ‡ Numbers in parentheses indicate the number of people reporting a single ancestry; * Numbers in parentheses indicate the number of persons reporting this race alone, not in combination with any other race; Please refer to the Explanation of Data for more information.*

Colombian	6	0.04
Ecuadorian	3	0.02
Peruvian	1	0.01
Venezuelan	4	0.03
Other Hispanic or Latino	68	0.44

Race*	Population	%
African-American/Black (172)	264	1.71
Not Hispanic (159)	250	1.62
Hispanic (13)	14	0.09
American Indian/Alaska Native (47)	111	0.72
Not Hispanic (34)	96	0.62
Hispanic (13)	15	0.10
Apache (0)	4	0.03
Blackfeet (0)	3	0.02
Cherokee (0)	6	0.04
Chippewa (12)	20	0.13
Choctaw (2)	5	0.03
Iroquois (3)	4	0.03
Menominee (1)	1	0.01
Mexican American Ind. (2)	2	0.01
Navajo (1)	1	0.01
Ottawa (0)	1	0.01
Potawatomi (4)	4	0.03
Spanish American Ind. (1)	3	0.02
Asian (131)	174	1.13
Not Hispanic (131)	171	1.11
Hispanic (0)	3	0.02
Chinese, ex. Taiwanese (30)	36	0.23
Filipino (16)	31	0.20
Hmong (7)	17	0.11
Indian (28)	35	0.23
Japanese (3)	9	0.06
Korean (22)	25	0.16
Malaysian (2)	2	0.01
Nepalese (1)	1	0.01
Pakistani (0)	2	0.01
Taiwanese (0)	2	0.01
Thai (2)	5	0.03
Vietnamese (8)	9	0.06
Hawaii Native/Pacific Islander (5)	9	0.06
Not Hispanic (2)	6	0.04
Hispanic (3)	3	0.02
Guamanian/Chamorro (2)	5	0.03
Native Hawaiian (3)	3	0.02
White (14,313)	14,534	94.36
Not Hispanic (13,595)	13,771	89.41
Hispanic (718)	763	4.95

Watertown

Place Type: City
County: Jefferson
Population: 23,861†

Ancestry‡	Population	%
Albanian (11)	11	0.05
American (811)	811	3.44
Arab (0)	6	0.03
Egyptian (0)	6	0.03
Armenian (0)	13	0.06
Austrian (15)	263	1.11
Belgian (13)	76	0.32
British (34)	34	0.14
Canadian (16)	16	0.07
Czech (54)	291	1.23
Czechoslovakian (12)	37	0.16
Danish (19)	117	0.50
Dutch (161)	504	2.14
English (576)	1,849	7.83
European (123)	215	0.91
Finnish (9)	31	0.13
French, ex. Basque (76)	1,072	4.54
French Canadian (12)	69	0.29
German (7,797)	13,927	59.01
Greek (17)	42	0.18
Hungarian (11)	156	0.66
Irish (296)	2,521	10.68
Italian (156)	710	3.01
Norwegian (310)	1,571	6.66
Pennsylvania German (0)	11	0.05
Polish (231)	1,386	5.87
Romanian (68)	68	0.29
Russian (0)	26	0.11
Scandinavian (59)	87	0.37
Scotch-Irish (66)	176	0.75
Scottish (31)	170	0.72
Slavic (0)	23	0.10
Slovak (0)	39	0.17
Slovene (0)	13	0.06
Swedish (119)	486	2.06
Swiss (47)	162	0.69
Ukrainian (0)	18	0.08
Welsh (0)	81	0.34
West Indian, ex. Hispanic (24)	30	0.13
Haitian (24)	24	0.10
Jamaican (0)	6	0.03
Yugoslavian (0)	15	0.06

Hispanic Origin	Population	%
Hispanic or Latino (of any race)	1,731	7.25
Central American, ex. Mexican	23	0.10
Guatemalan	6	0.03
Honduran	4	0.02
Nicaraguan	8	0.03
Panamanian	3	0.01
Salvadoran	2	0.01
Cuban	10	0.04
Dominican Republic	1	<0.01
Mexican	1,530	6.41
Puerto Rican	63	0.26
South American	20	0.08
Argentinean	1	<0.01
Bolivian	2	0.01
Chilean	2	0.01
Colombian	6	0.03
Ecuadorian	3	0.01
Peruvian	2	0.01
Venezuelan	4	0.02
Other Hispanic or Latino	84	0.35

Race*	Population	%
African-American/Black (196)	305	1.28
Not Hispanic (183)	291	1.22
Hispanic (13)	14	0.06
American Indian/Alaska Native (69)	157	0.66
Not Hispanic (55)	140	0.59
Hispanic (14)	17	0.07
Apache (0)	4	0.02
Blackfeet (0)	3	0.01
Cherokee (0)	6	0.03
Chippewa (15)	30	0.13
Choctaw (2)	5	0.02
Iroquois (4)	6	0.03
Menominee (2)	4	0.02
Mexican American Ind. (2)	2	0.01
Navajo (1)	1	<0.01
Ottawa (2)	4	0.02
Potawatomi (4)	4	0.02
Sioux (1)	1	<0.01
Spanish American Ind. (1)	3	0.01
Asian (187)	268	1.12
Not Hispanic (186)	263	1.10
Hispanic (1)	5	0.02
Chinese, ex. Taiwanese (41)	51	0.21
Filipino (29)	62	0.26
Hmong (19)	31	0.13
Indian (33)	42	0.18
Japanese (4)	16	0.07
Korean (26)	29	0.12
Laotian (0)	2	0.01
Malaysian (2)	2	0.01
Nepalese (1)	1	<0.01
Pakistani (0)	5	0.02
Taiwanese (0)	2	0.01
Thai (2)	9	0.04
Vietnamese (15)	16	0.07
Hawaii Native/Pacific Islander (10)	17	0.07
Not Hispanic (7)	14	0.06
Hispanic (3)	3	0.01
Guamanian/Chamorro (7)	10	0.04
Native Hawaiian (3)	5	0.02
White (22,427)	22,746	95.33
Not Hispanic (21,424)	21,676	90.84
Hispanic (1,003)	1,070	4.48

Waukesha

Place Type: City
County: Waukesha
Population: 70,718†

Ancestry‡	Population	%
African, Sub-Saharan (138)	167	0.24
African (92)	111	0.16
Nigerian (18)	21	0.03
South African (28)	28	0.04
Other Sub-Saharan African (0)	7	0.01
Albanian (9)	9	0.01
American (1,314)	1,314	1.88
Arab (89)	283	0.40
Arab (20)	37	0.05
Egyptian (45)	58	0.08
Lebanese (12)	76	0.11
Moroccan (0)	17	0.02
Palestinian (12)	35	0.05
Syrian (0)	45	0.06
Other Arab (0)	15	0.02
Australian (0)	12	0.02
Austrian (40)	296	0.42
Belgian (26)	305	0.44
Brazilian (0)	32	0.05
British (72)	194	0.28
Canadian (30)	63	0.09
Carpatho Rusyn (0)	8	0.01
Croatian (90)	315	0.45
Czech (117)	1,105	1.58
Czechoslovakian (21)	62	0.09
Danish (93)	579	0.83
Dutch (307)	1,367	1.95
Eastern European (36)	51	0.07
English (937)	5,286	7.56
European (431)	449	0.64
Finnish (112)	603	0.86
French, ex. Basque (223)	2,604	3.72
French Canadian (126)	803	1.15
German (12,018)	32,644	46.67
German Russian (0)	27	0.04
Greek (83)	515	0.74
Hungarian (106)	539	0.77
Irish (1,406)	9,292	13.28
Italian (1,106)	3,920	5.60
Latvian (18)	63	0.09
Lithuanian (30)	161	0.23
Luxemburger (9)	56	0.08
Northern European (17)	17	0.02
Norwegian (817)	3,623	5.18
Polish (1,629)	7,678	10.98
Portuguese (0)	21	0.03
Romanian (75)	115	0.16
Russian (103)	259	0.37
Scandinavian (80)	209	0.30
Scotch-Irish (246)	601	0.86
Scottish (205)	1,289	1.84
Serbian (11)	153	0.22
Slavic (11)	86	0.12
Slovak (32)	203	0.29
Slovene (44)	120	0.17
Swedish (224)	1,519	2.17
Swiss (109)	761	1.09
Turkish (17)	17	0.02
Ukrainian (47)	123	0.18
Welsh (100)	498	0.71
Yugoslavian (124)	147	0.21

Hispanic Origin	Population	%
Hispanic or Latino (of any race)	8,529	12.06
Central American, ex. Mexican	191	0.27
Costa Rican	16	0.02
Guatemalan	51	0.07

*Notes: † The Census 2010 population figure is used to calculate the percentages in the Hispanic Origin and Race categories. Ancestry percentages are based on the 2006-2010 American Community Survey population (not shown); ‡ Numbers in parentheses indicate the number of people reporting a single ancestry; * Numbers in parentheses indicate the number of persons reporting this race alone, not in combination with any other race; Please refer to the Explanation of Data for more information.*

Honduran	29	0.04
Nicaraguan	53	0.07
Panamanian	17	0.02
Salvadoran	25	0.04
Cuban	51	0.07
Dominican Republic	19	0.03
Mexican	6,758	9.56
Puerto Rican	976	1.38
South American	226	0.32
Argentinean	44	0.06
Bolivian	8	0.01
Chilean	20	0.03
Colombian	43	0.06
Ecuadorian	20	0.03
Paraguayan	5	0.01
Peruvian	46	0.07
Uruguayan	3	<0.01
Venezuelan	31	0.04
Other South American	6	0.01
Other Hispanic or Latino	308	0.44

Race*	Population	%
African-American/Black (1,660)	2,270	3.21
Not Hispanic (1,570)	2,091	2.96
Hispanic (90)	179	0.25
American Indian/Alaska Native (275)	543	0.77
Not Hispanic (189)	404	0.57
Hispanic (86)	139	0.20
Aleut *(Alaska Native)* (1)	1	<0.01
Apache (3)	10	0.01
Arapaho (0)	1	<0.01
Blackfeet (0)	13	0.02
Canadian/French Am. Ind. (2)	2	<0.01
Cherokee (13)	53	0.07
Cheyenne (0)	1	<0.01
Chickasaw (5)	7	0.01
Chippewa (50)	75	0.11
Choctaw (1)	6	0.01
Comanche (1)	2	<0.01
Cree (0)	1	<0.01
Houma (2)	2	<0.01
Iroquois (24)	38	0.05
Kiowa (0)	1	<0.01
Menominee (5)	9	0.01
Mexican American Ind. (21)	31	0.04
Navajo (1)	5	0.01
Ottawa (0)	1	<0.01
Pima (1)	4	0.01
Potawatomi (2)	8	0.01
Seminole (0)	1	<0.01
Sioux (4)	16	0.02
South American Ind. (0)	1	<0.01
Spanish American Ind. (2)	3	<0.01
Tlingit-Haida *(Alaska Native)* (0)	1	<0.01
Yaqui (1)	4	0.01
Yup'ik *(Alaska Native)* (0)	1	<0.01
Asian (2,495)	2,835	4.01
Not Hispanic (2,483)	2,805	3.97
Hispanic (12)	30	0.04
Bangladeshi (11)	16	0.02
Burmese (61)	62	0.09
Chinese, ex. Taiwanese (310)	363	0.51
Filipino (119)	183	0.26
Hmong (44)	53	0.07
Indian (1,331)	1,369	1.94
Indonesian (5)	16	0.02
Japanese (42)	91	0.13
Korean (100)	150	0.21
Laotian (130)	160	0.23
Malaysian (3)	4	0.01
Nepalese (11)	11	0.02
Pakistani (76)	84	0.12
Sri Lankan (15)	15	0.02
Taiwanese (18)	24	0.03
Thai (27)	41	0.06
Vietnamese (99)	128	0.18
Hawaii Native/Pacific Islander (30)	81	0.11
Not Hispanic (19)	55	0.08
Hispanic (11)	26	0.04
Guamanian/Chamorro (9)	20	0.03
Native Hawaiian (10)	25	0.04
Samoan (0)	5	0.01
White (62,301)	63,662	90.02
Not Hispanic (56,868)	57,817	81.76
Hispanic (5,433)	5,845	8.27

Waukesha

Place Type: Town
County: Waukesha
Population: 9,133[†]

Ancestry[‡]	Population	%
African, Sub-Saharan (15)	15	0.17
African (15)	15	0.17
American (253)	253	2.79
Armenian (0)	34	0.38
Austrian (14)	70	0.77
Belgian (81)	95	1.05
Canadian (34)	34	0.38
Croatian (14)	25	0.28
Czech (28)	82	0.90
Czechoslovakian (13)	23	0.25
Danish (0)	16	0.18
Dutch (0)	131	1.45
English (133)	883	9.75
European (149)	149	1.64
Finnish (10)	136	1.50
French, ex. Basque (36)	466	5.14
French Canadian (17)	66	0.73
German (1,803)	5,189	57.27
Greek (0)	12	0.13
Hungarian (31)	125	1.38
Iranian (0)	16	0.18
Irish (399)	1,884	20.79
Italian (131)	486	5.36
Northern European (29)	29	0.32
Norwegian (135)	720	7.95
Polish (158)	1,135	12.53
Russian (31)	116	1.28
Scandinavian (8)	59	0.65
Scotch-Irish (10)	33	0.36
Scottish (19)	129	1.42
Slovak (29)	61	0.67
Slovene (0)	44	0.49
Swedish (55)	227	2.51
Swiss (33)	33	0.36
Welsh (0)	14	0.15
Yugoslavian (31)	31	0.34

Hispanic Origin	Population	%
Hispanic or Latino (of any race)	338	3.70
Central American, ex. Mexican	20	0.22
Guatemalan	3	0.03
Nicaraguan	9	0.10
Panamanian	5	0.05
Salvadoran	3	0.03
Cuban	8	0.09
Mexican	260	2.85
Puerto Rican	28	0.31
South American	9	0.10
Chilean	2	0.02
Colombian	6	0.07
Peruvian	1	0.01
Other Hispanic or Latino	13	0.14

Race*	Population	%
African-American/Black (45)	74	0.81
Not Hispanic (42)	68	0.74
Hispanic (3)	6	0.07
American Indian/Alaska Native (27)	54	0.59
Not Hispanic (23)	47	0.51
Hispanic (4)	7	0.08
Apache (0)	2	0.02
Cherokee (0)	1	0.01
Chippewa (6)	9	0.10
Choctaw (0)	1	0.01
Iroquois (6)	7	0.08
Menominee (0)	4	0.04
Navajo (4)	4	0.04
Osage (1)	5	0.05
Sioux (1)	1	0.01
Asian (157)	184	2.01
Not Hispanic (157)	184	2.01
Chinese, ex. Taiwanese (46)	54	0.59
Filipino (3)	7	0.08
Indian (40)	45	0.49
Indonesian (3)	4	0.04
Japanese (3)	3	0.03
Korean (3)	5	0.05
Laotian (31)	33	0.36
Malaysian (1)	1	0.01
Pakistani (1)	2	0.02
Thai (1)	2	0.02
Vietnamese (25)	25	0.27
Hawaii Native/Pacific Islander (2)	7	0.08
Not Hispanic (2)	6	0.07
Hispanic (0)	1	0.01
Samoan (0)	4	0.04
White (8,742)	8,824	96.62
Not Hispanic (8,499)	8,563	93.76
Hispanic (243)	261	2.86

Waunakee

Place Type: Village
County: Dane
Population: 12,097[†]

Ancestry[‡]	Population	%
African, Sub-Saharan (80)	80	0.69
African (14)	14	0.12
Kenyan (23)	23	0.20
South African (43)	43	0.37
Albanian (22)	34	0.29
American (315)	315	2.73
Armenian (9)	9	0.08
Australian (15)	15	0.13
Austrian (0)	20	0.17
Belgian (53)	119	1.03
Canadian (36)	36	0.31
Croatian (16)	40	0.35
Czech (36)	343	2.97
Czechoslovakian (0)	23	0.20
Danish (42)	164	1.42
Dutch (50)	248	2.15
Eastern European (22)	22	0.19
English (92)	705	6.10
European (58)	67	0.58
Finnish (0)	50	0.43
French, ex. Basque (84)	508	4.40
French Canadian (8)	12	0.10
German (2,575)	6,722	58.16
Greek (0)	118	1.02
Hungarian (10)	95	0.82
Irish (208)	1,971	17.05
Italian (91)	402	3.48
Lithuanian (10)	39	0.34
Luxemburger (0)	19	0.16
Norwegian (285)	1,561	13.51
Polish (74)	702	6.07
Portuguese (0)	14	0.12
Romanian (0)	11	0.10
Russian (27)	27	0.23
Scandinavian (5)	42	0.36
Scotch-Irish (19)	169	1.46
Scottish (5)	114	0.99
Slavic (0)	9	0.08
Slovak (0)	15	0.13
Swedish (48)	273	2.36
Swiss (24)	241	2.09
Ukrainian (13)	58	0.50
Welsh (7)	72	0.62
Yugoslavian (0)	29	0.25

Hispanic Origin	Population	%
Hispanic or Latino (of any race)	269	2.22
Central American, ex. Mexican	26	0.21
Costa Rican	2	0.02
Guatemalan	17	0.14

*Notes: † The Census 2010 population figure is used to calculate the percentages in the Hispanic Origin and Race categories. Ancestry percentages are based on the 2006-2010 American Community Survey population (not shown); ‡ Numbers in parentheses indicate the number of people reporting a single ancestry; * Numbers in parentheses indicate the number of persons reporting this race alone, not in combination with any other race; Please refer to the Explanation of Data for more information.*

Nicaraguan	7	0.06
Cuban	11	0.09
Dominican Republic	5	0.04
Mexican	162	1.34
Puerto Rican	28	0.23
South American	20	0.17
Argentinean	2	0.02
Colombian	13	0.11
Ecuadorian	1	0.01
Peruvian	3	0.02
Uruguayan	1	0.01
Other Hispanic or Latino	17	0.14

Race*	Population	%
African-American/Black (125)	199	1.65
Not Hispanic (117)	181	1.50
Hispanic (8)	18	0.15
American Indian/Alaska Native (28)	55	0.45
Not Hispanic (23)	37	0.31
Hispanic (5)	18	0.15
Apache (0)	2	0.02
Cherokee (1)	5	0.04
Chippewa (9)	9	0.07
Menominee (0)	3	0.02
Mexican American Ind. (2)	8	0.07
South American Ind. (0)	3	0.02
Asian (142)	196	1.62
Not Hispanic (142)	195	1.61
Hispanic (0)	1	0.01
Burmese (1)	3	0.02
Cambodian (0)	5	0.04
Chinese, ex. Taiwanese (57)	70	0.58
Filipino (8)	26	0.21
Hmong (1)	2	0.02
Indian (35)	46	0.38
Japanese (5)	16	0.13
Korean (12)	15	0.12
Laotian (5)	5	0.04
Taiwanese (5)	5	0.04
Thai (1)	2	0.02
Vietnamese (1)	4	0.03
Hawaii Native/Pacific Islander (2)	5	0.04
Not Hispanic (1)	4	0.03
Hispanic (1)	1	0.01
Guamanian/Chamorro (1)	1	0.01
Marshallese (1)	1	0.01
White (11,592)	11,742	97.07
Not Hispanic (11,412)	11,538	95.38
Hispanic (180)	204	1.69

Waupun

Place Type: City
County: Dodge
Population: 7,864†

Ancestry‡	Population	%
African, Sub-Saharan (42)	60	0.76
African (34)	40	0.50
Zimbabwean (8)	8	0.10
Other Sub-Saharan African (0)	12	0.15
American (138)	138	1.74
Arab (0)	13	0.16
Lebanese (0)	13	0.16
Austrian (16)	31	0.39
Belgian (0)	10	0.13
Canadian (0)	14	0.18
Croatian (0)	9	0.11
Czech (31)	54	0.68
Czechoslovakian (10)	10	0.13
Danish (8)	25	0.31
Dutch (683)	1,343	16.90
English (16)	201	2.53
French, ex. Basque (11)	134	1.69
French Canadian (0)	10	0.13
German (1,371)	2,939	36.99
Greek (6)	6	0.08
Hungarian (0)	7	0.09
Irish (149)	736	9.26
Italian (22)	156	1.96
Latvian (0)	6	0.08
Lithuanian (0)	9	0.11
Norwegian (56)	269	3.39
Polish (43)	316	3.98
Portuguese (9)	9	0.11
Russian (0)	11	0.14
Scandinavian (20)	42	0.53
Scotch-Irish (0)	30	0.38
Scottish (9)	50	0.63
Swedish (9)	65	0.82
Swiss (0)	14	0.18
Welsh (0)	25	0.31
West Indian, ex. Hispanic (0)	9	0.11
Haitian (0)	9	0.11

Hispanic Origin	Population	%
Hispanic or Latino (of any race)	134	1.70
Central American, ex. Mexican	2	0.03
Guatemalan	2	0.03
Cuban	5	0.06
Mexican	94	1.20
Puerto Rican	7	0.09
South American	2	0.03
Other South American	2	0.03
Other Hispanic or Latino	24	0.31

Race*	Population	%
African-American/Black (1,378)	1,402	17.83
Not Hispanic (1,377)	1,401	17.82
Hispanic (1)	1	0.01
American Indian/Alaska Native (124)	137	1.74
Not Hispanic (124)	133	1.69
Hispanic (0)	4	0.05
Cherokee (0)	4	0.05
Chippewa (2)	5	0.06
Iroquois (1)	1	0.01
Menominee (2)	2	0.03
Navajo (1)	1	0.01
Asian (12)	30	0.38
Not Hispanic (12)	30	0.38
Chinese, ex. Taiwanese (1)	4	0.05
Filipino (3)	7	0.09
Indian (7)	7	0.09
Japanese (0)	1	0.01
Korean (1)	4	0.05
Taiwanese (0)	1	0.01
Hawaii Native/Pacific Islander (19)	27	0.34
Not Hispanic (19)	27	0.34
White (6,234)	6,283	79.90
Not Hispanic (6,148)	6,187	78.67
Hispanic (86)	96	1.22

Waupun

Place Type: City
County: Dodge
Population: 11,340†

Ancestry‡	Population	%
African, Sub-Saharan (42)	60	0.53
African (34)	40	0.35
Zimbabwean (8)	8	0.07
Other Sub-Saharan African (0)	12	0.11
American (396)	396	3.48
Arab (9)	22	0.19
Lebanese (0)	13	0.11
Other Arab (9)	9	0.08
Austrian (16)	41	0.36
Belgian (0)	10	0.09
British (14)	22	0.19
Canadian (0)	14	0.12
Croatian (0)	9	0.08
Czech (31)	54	0.47
Czechoslovakian (10)	10	0.09
Danish (38)	64	0.56
Dutch (1,230)	2,184	19.19
English (102)	480	4.22
European (19)	19	0.17
Finnish (31)	40	0.35
French, ex. Basque (21)	215	1.89
French Canadian (0)	22	0.19
German (2,245)	4,592	40.35
Greek (6)	6	0.05
Hungarian (0)	7	0.06
Irish (192)	1,019	8.95
Italian (56)	207	1.82
Latvian (0)	6	0.05
Lithuanian (0)	9	0.08
Norwegian (111)	418	3.67
Polish (64)	433	3.80
Portuguese (9)	9	0.08
Russian (0)	22	0.19
Scandinavian (28)	50	0.44
Scotch-Irish (0)	40	0.35
Scottish (9)	60	0.53
Swedish (29)	113	0.99
Swiss (9)	23	0.20
Welsh (10)	101	0.89
West Indian, ex. Hispanic (0)	9	0.08
Haitian (0)	9	0.08

Hispanic Origin	Population	%
Hispanic or Latino (of any race)	217	1.91
Central American, ex. Mexican	5	0.04
Guatemalan	2	0.02
Honduran	1	0.01
Panamanian	1	0.01
Salvadoran	1	0.01
Cuban	13	0.11
Mexican	152	1.34
Puerto Rican	15	0.13
South American	5	0.04
Chilean	1	0.01
Colombian	1	0.01
Paraguayan	1	0.01
Other South American	2	0.02
Other Hispanic or Latino	27	0.24

Race*	Population	%
African-American/Black (1,384)	1,420	12.52
Not Hispanic (1,382)	1,418	12.50
Hispanic (2)	2	0.02
American Indian/Alaska Native (133)	165	1.46
Not Hispanic (133)	155	1.37
Hispanic (0)	10	0.09
Blackfeet (1)	1	0.01
Cherokee (0)	4	0.04
Chippewa (5)	14	0.12
Iroquois (1)	1	0.01
Menominee (2)	2	0.02
Navajo (1)	1	0.01
Asian (36)	60	0.53
Not Hispanic (36)	57	0.50
Hispanic (0)	3	0.03
Chinese, ex. Taiwanese (6)	9	0.08
Filipino (7)	14	0.12
Hmong (4)	4	0.04
Indian (10)	10	0.09
Japanese (0)	1	0.01
Korean (5)	9	0.08
Taiwanese (4)	5	0.04
Hawaii Native/Pacific Islander (19)	30	0.26
Not Hispanic (19)	30	0.26
Native Hawaiian (0)	3	0.03
White (9,609)	9,693	85.48
Not Hispanic (9,472)	9,538	84.11
Hispanic (137)	155	1.37

Wausau

Place Type: City
County: Marathon
Population: 39,106†

Ancestry‡	Population	%
African, Sub-Saharan (53)	76	0.19
African (42)	65	0.17
Somalian (11)	11	0.03
American (997)	997	2.55
Arab (117)	141	0.36

*Notes: † The Census 2010 population figure is used to calculate the percentages in the Hispanic Origin and Race categories. Ancestry percentages are based on the 2006-2010 American Community Survey population (not shown); ‡ Numbers in parentheses indicate the number of people reporting a single ancestry; * Numbers in parentheses indicate the number of persons reporting this race alone, not in combination with any other race; Please refer to the Explanation of Data for more information.*

Egyptian (53)	53	0.14
Lebanese (54)	78	0.20
Other Arab (10)	10	0.03
Australian (9)	18	0.05
Austrian (33)	145	0.37
Belgian (41)	320	0.82
Brazilian (0)	45	0.12
British (23)	67	0.17
Bulgarian (0)	6	0.02
Canadian (10)	10	0.03
Croatian (0)	43	0.11
Czech (56)	428	1.10
Czechoslovakian (29)	69	0.18
Danish (131)	562	1.44
Dutch (132)	724	1.85
Eastern European (39)	39	0.10
English (358)	2,173	5.57
European (273)	320	0.82
Finnish (132)	462	1.18
French, ex. Basque (142)	1,680	4.30
French Canadian (82)	459	1.18
German (8,855)	18,828	48.23
Greek (0)	20	0.05
Hungarian (0)	75	0.19
Iranian (6)	18	0.05
Irish (642)	2,967	7.60
Italian (216)	1,006	2.58
Lithuanian (21)	84	0.22
Norwegian (668)	2,074	5.31
Pennsylvania German (0)	13	0.03
Polish (1,442)	5,316	13.62
Romanian (20)	78	0.20
Russian (81)	320	0.82
Scandinavian (35)	111	0.28
Scotch-Irish (74)	177	0.45
Scottish (263)	537	1.38
Serbian (7)	27	0.07
Slavic (8)	23	0.06
Slovak (0)	54	0.14
Slovene (13)	27	0.07
Swedish (223)	1,284	3.29
Swiss (82)	273	0.70
Ukrainian (0)	12	0.03
Welsh (0)	74	0.19
West Indian, ex. Hispanic (41)	76	0.19
British West Indian (33)	68	0.17
Jamaican (8)	8	0.02
Yugoslavian (11)	18	0.05

Hispanic Origin	Population	%
Hispanic or Latino (of any race)	1,149	2.94
Central American, ex. Mexican	91	0.23
Costa Rican	4	0.01
Guatemalan	26	0.07
Honduran	19	0.05
Nicaraguan	22	0.06
Panamanian	13	0.03
Salvadoran	6	0.02
Other Central American	1	<0.01
Cuban	15	0.04
Dominican Republic	11	0.03
Mexican	774	1.98
Puerto Rican	81	0.21
South American	54	0.14
Argentinean	4	0.01
Bolivian	2	0.01
Chilean	13	0.03
Colombian	7	0.02
Ecuadorian	8	0.02
Paraguayan	1	<0.01
Peruvian	11	0.03
Venezuelan	1	<0.01
Other South American	7	0.02
Other Hispanic or Latino	123	0.31

Race*	Population	%
African-American/Black (533)	860	2.20
Not Hispanic (519)	804	2.06
Hispanic (14)	56	0.14
American Indian/Alaska Native (304)	570	1.46
Not Hispanic (277)	503	1.29
Hispanic (27)	67	0.17
Apache (2)	5	0.01
Blackfeet (1)	6	0.02
Canadian/French Am. Ind. (0)	1	<0.01
Cherokee (5)	24	0.06
Chippewa (52)	87	0.22
Comanche (2)	2	0.01
Crow (1)	1	<0.01
Hopi (1)	2	0.01
Inupiat *(Alaska Native)* (1)	1	<0.01
Iroquois (17)	30	0.08
Menominee (43)	51	0.13
Mexican American Ind. (0)	11	0.03
Navajo (3)	6	0.02
Ottawa (1)	2	0.01
Potawatomi (32)	42	0.11
Seminole (0)	1	<0.01
Sioux (9)	16	0.04
South American Ind. (4)	5	0.01
Asian (4,325)	4,664	11.93
Not Hispanic (4,301)	4,632	11.84
Hispanic (24)	32	0.08
Bangladeshi (6)	6	0.02
Cambodian (12)	22	0.06
Chinese, ex. Taiwanese (93)	112	0.29
Filipino (41)	85	0.22
Hmong (3,569)	3,783	9.67
Indian (97)	150	0.38
Japanese (8)	16	0.04
Korean (38)	62	0.16
Laotian (125)	188	0.48
Malaysian (4)	4	0.01
Sri Lankan (6)	6	0.02
Taiwanese (8)	11	0.03
Thai (16)	31	0.08
Vietnamese (11)	22	0.06
Hawaii Native/Pacific Islander (8)	51	0.13
Not Hispanic (8)	47	0.12
Hispanic (0)	4	0.01
Fijian (1)	1	<0.01
Guamanian/Chamorro (1)	4	0.01
Native Hawaiian (3)	11	0.03
Samoan (1)	2	0.01
White (32,717)	33,464	85.57
Not Hispanic (32,066)	32,709	83.64
Hispanic (651)	755	1.93

Wauwatosa

Place Type: City
County: Milwaukee
Population: 46,396†

Ancestry‡	Population	%
Afghan (7)	7	0.02
African, Sub-Saharan (47)	47	0.10
African (33)	33	0.07
South African (14)	14	0.03
Albanian (16)	16	0.03
Alsatian (0)	10	0.02
American (886)	886	1.92
Arab (54)	130	0.28
Arab (0)	38	0.08
Egyptian (0)	8	0.02
Lebanese (54)	54	0.12
Syrian (0)	30	0.06
Armenian (8)	8	0.02
Australian (0)	23	0.05
Austrian (88)	684	1.48
Belgian (25)	86	0.19
Brazilian (9)	41	0.09
British (49)	114	0.25
Canadian (24)	32	0.07
Celtic (0)	12	0.03
Croatian (64)	282	0.61
Czech (149)	747	1.62
Czechoslovakian (33)	48	0.10
Danish (94)	480	1.04
Dutch (245)	1,138	2.46
Eastern European (31)	44	0.10
English (525)	2,888	6.25
Estonian (0)	9	0.02
European (462)	497	1.08
Finnish (49)	264	0.57
French, ex. Basque (189)	1,701	3.68
French Canadian (66)	416	0.90
German (8,130)	22,644	49.04
German Russian (0)	20	0.04
Greek (409)	730	1.58
Hungarian (42)	381	0.83
Icelander (0)	46	0.10
Iranian (13)	13	0.03
Irish (1,707)	8,570	18.56
Israeli (10)	10	0.02
Italian (832)	3,039	6.58
Latvian (30)	38	0.08
Lithuanian (0)	133	0.29
Luxemburger (33)	73	0.16
Norwegian (488)	2,202	4.77
Pennsylvania German (3)	17	0.04
Polish (1,079)	5,336	11.56
Portuguese (10)	59	0.13
Romanian (28)	50	0.11
Russian (246)	600	1.30
Scandinavian (60)	145	0.31
Scotch-Irish (191)	504	1.09
Scottish (81)	524	1.13
Serbian (45)	147	0.32
Slavic (0)	96	0.21
Slovak (124)	300	0.65
Slovene (58)	138	0.30
Swedish (272)	1,314	2.85
Swiss (43)	468	1.01
Turkish (33)	44	0.10
Ukrainian (43)	145	0.31
Welsh (56)	279	0.60
West Indian, ex. Hispanic (0)	28	0.06
Jamaican (0)	28	0.06
Yugoslavian (38)	118	0.26

Hispanic Origin	Population	%
Hispanic or Latino (of any race)	1,450	3.13
Central American, ex. Mexican	94	0.20
Costa Rican	6	0.01
Guatemalan	48	0.10
Honduran	8	0.02
Nicaraguan	10	0.02
Panamanian	10	0.02
Salvadoran	11	0.02
Other Central American	1	<0.01
Cuban	47	0.10
Dominican Republic	7	0.02
Mexican	753	1.62
Puerto Rican	298	0.64
South American	128	0.28
Argentinean	10	0.02
Chilean	19	0.04
Colombian	31	0.07
Ecuadorian	20	0.04
Paraguayan	7	0.02
Peruvian	23	0.05
Uruguayan	2	<0.01
Venezuelan	11	0.02
Other South American	5	0.01
Other Hispanic or Latino	123	0.27

Race*	Population	%
African-American/Black (2,070)	2,583	5.57
Not Hispanic (2,026)	2,492	5.37
Hispanic (44)	91	0.20
American Indian/Alaska Native (139)	320	0.69
Not Hispanic (120)	262	0.56
Hispanic (19)	58	0.13
Apache (0)	4	0.01
Blackfeet (0)	1	<0.01
Canadian/French Am. Ind. (1)	1	<0.01
Central American Ind. (1)	3	0.01
Cherokee (1)	11	0.02
Cheyenne (0)	1	<0.01

*Notes: † The Census 2010 population figure is used to calculate the percentages in the Hispanic Origin and Race categories. Ancestry percentages are based on the 2006-2010 American Community Survey population (not shown); ‡ Numbers in parentheses indicate the number of people reporting a single ancestry; * Numbers in parentheses indicate the number of persons reporting this race alone, not in combination with any other race; Please refer to the Explanation of Data for more information.*

Chippewa (39)	63	0.14
Choctaw (0)	1	<0.01
Comanche (1)	1	<0.01
Creek (0)	2	<0.01
Inupiat *(Alaska Native)* (2)	2	<0.01
Iroquois (12)	25	0.05
Kiowa (0)	1	<0.01
Menominee (3)	16	0.03
Mexican American Ind. (3)	7	0.02
Osage (0)	1	<0.01
Ottawa (1)	2	<0.01
Pima (1)	1	<0.01
Potawatomi (4)	9	0.02
Sioux (0)	3	0.01
South American Ind. (1)	2	<0.01
Ute (1)	1	<0.01
Asian (1,289)	1,620	3.49
Not Hispanic (1,273)	1,589	3.42
Hispanic (16)	31	0.07
Bangladeshi (0)	3	0.01
Burmese (15)	15	0.03
Cambodian (2)	2	<0.01
Chinese, ex. Taiwanese (377)	436	0.94
Filipino (108)	177	0.38
Hmong (90)	98	0.21
Indian (365)	422	0.91
Indonesian (8)	11	0.02
Japanese (75)	122	0.26
Korean (87)	130	0.28
Laotian (7)	14	0.03
Nepalese (3)	3	0.01
Pakistani (28)	38	0.08
Sri Lankan (4)	6	0.01
Taiwanese (12)	15	0.03
Thai (18)	31	0.07
Vietnamese (47)	65	0.14
Hawaii Native/Pacific Islander (28)	57	0.12
Not Hispanic (27)	50	0.11
Hispanic (1)	7	0.02
Fijian (2)	2	<0.01
Guamanian/Chamorro (4)	10	0.02
Native Hawaiian (1)	19	0.04
Samoan (4)	4	0.01
White (41,574)	42,485	91.57
Not Hispanic (40,585)	41,387	89.20
Hispanic (989)	1,098	2.37

West Allis

Place Type: City
County: Milwaukee
Population: 60,411†

Ancestry‡	Population	%
African, Sub-Saharan (71)	154	0.26
African (71)	154	0.26
Albanian (0)	28	0.05
American (1,353)	1,353	2.25
Arab (22)	56	0.09
Arab (0)	10	0.02
Lebanese (12)	25	0.04
Palestinian (10)	10	0.02
Syrian (0)	11	0.02
Armenian (63)	82	0.14
Australian (0)	24	0.04
Austrian (32)	576	0.96
Belgian (72)	208	0.35
British (33)	139	0.23
Bulgarian (33)	85	0.14
Canadian (9)	9	0.01
Croatian (330)	731	1.22
Czech (202)	1,066	1.78
Czechoslovakian (80)	134	0.22
Danish (67)	393	0.65
Dutch (59)	715	1.19
Eastern European (11)	11	0.02
English (493)	2,737	4.56
Estonian (8)	8	0.01
European (614)	691	1.15
Finnish (20)	312	0.52
French, ex. Basque (320)	2,473	4.12
French Canadian (125)	443	0.74
German (8,757)	26,168	43.61
German Russian (0)	25	0.04
Greek (61)	223	0.37
Hungarian (134)	540	0.90
Icelander (0)	12	0.02
Iranian (10)	10	0.02
Irish (1,193)	7,894	13.15
Italian (890)	3,553	5.92
Latvian (94)	94	0.16
Lithuanian (44)	187	0.31
Luxemburger (11)	25	0.04
Macedonian (0)	10	0.02
Northern European (15)	15	0.02
Norwegian (548)	3,242	5.40
Polish (3,256)	11,608	19.34
Portuguese (0)	84	0.14
Romanian (34)	61	0.10
Russian (87)	393	0.65
Scandinavian (41)	172	0.29
Scotch-Irish (141)	545	0.91
Scottish (138)	624	1.04
Serbian (124)	279	0.46
Slavic (18)	57	0.09
Slovak (72)	312	0.52
Slovene (118)	388	0.65
Swedish (256)	1,768	2.95
Swiss (42)	254	0.42
Ukrainian (308)	312	0.52
Welsh (39)	404	0.67
West Indian, ex. Hispanic (75)	75	0.12
Jamaican (75)	75	0.12
Yugoslavian (10)	51	0.08

Hispanic Origin	Population	%
Hispanic or Latino (of any race)	5,770	9.55
Central American, ex. Mexican	106	0.18
Costa Rican	19	0.03
Guatemalan	17	0.03
Honduran	9	0.01
Nicaraguan	16	0.03
Panamanian	15	0.02
Salvadoran	29	0.05
Other Central American	1	<0.01
Cuban	56	0.09
Dominican Republic	33	0.05
Mexican	3,800	6.29
Puerto Rican	1,462	2.42
South American	108	0.18
Argentinean	8	0.01
Chilean	9	0.01
Colombian	52	0.09
Ecuadorian	9	0.01
Paraguayan	3	<0.01
Peruvian	23	0.04
Uruguayan	1	<0.01
Venezuelan	3	<0.01
Other Hispanic or Latino	205	0.34

Race*	Population	%
African-American/Black (2,199)	2,965	4.91
Not Hispanic (2,110)	2,730	4.52
Hispanic (89)	235	0.39
American Indian/Alaska Native (648)	1,154	1.91
Not Hispanic (541)	927	1.53
Hispanic (107)	227	0.38
Alaska Athabascan *(Ala. Nat.)* (4)	4	0.01
Apache (9)	14	0.02
Arapaho (1)	2	<0.01
Blackfeet (0)	16	0.03
Canadian/French Am. Ind. (0)	1	<0.01
Central American Ind. (1)	1	<0.01
Cherokee (8)	49	0.08
Cheyenne (2)	2	<0.01
Chickasaw (0)	1	<0.01
Chippewa (157)	244	0.40
Choctaw (0)	10	0.02
Comanche (4)	4	0.01
Creek (1)	1	<0.01
Crow (0)	1	<0.01
Houma (0)	1	<0.01
Iroquois (84)	127	0.21
Lumbee (0)	1	<0.01
Menominee (45)	83	0.14
Mexican American Ind. (11)	16	0.03
Navajo (0)	2	<0.01
Osage (3)	3	<0.01
Ottawa (4)	14	0.02
Pima (3)	3	<0.01
Potawatomi (20)	29	0.05
Pueblo (2)	2	<0.01
Puget Sound Salish (1)	1	<0.01
Seminole (1)	3	<0.01
Sioux (18)	30	0.05
South American Ind. (0)	5	0.01
Spanish American Ind. (0)	1	<0.01
Tlingit-Haida *(Alaska Native)* (1)	2	<0.01
Yup'ik *(Alaska Native)* (1)	1	<0.01
Asian (1,231)	1,522	2.52
Not Hispanic (1,214)	1,466	2.43
Hispanic (17)	56	0.09
Burmese (14)	14	0.02
Cambodian (1)	2	<0.01
Chinese, ex. Taiwanese (162)	198	0.33
Filipino (98)	157	0.26
Hmong (175)	185	0.31
Indian (431)	467	0.77
Indonesian (1)	6	0.01
Japanese (19)	84	0.14
Korean (62)	105	0.17
Laotian (68)	82	0.14
Malaysian (0)	1	<0.01
Nepalese (1)	5	0.01
Pakistani (39)	51	0.08
Sri Lankan (2)	2	<0.01
Taiwanese (5)	5	0.01
Thai (18)	32	0.05
Vietnamese (72)	88	0.15
Hawaii Native/Pacific Islander (19)	52	0.09
Not Hispanic (17)	46	0.08
Hispanic (2)	6	0.01
Guamanian/Chamorro (5)	9	0.01
Native Hawaiian (7)	22	0.04
Samoan (1)	1	<0.01
White (52,396)	54,024	89.43
Not Hispanic (49,547)	50,645	83.83
Hispanic (2,849)	3,379	5.59

West Bend

Place Type: City
County: Washington
Population: 31,078†

Ancestry‡	Population	%
American (1,283)	1,283	4.17
Arab (15)	77	0.25
Lebanese (15)	29	0.09
Other Arab (0)	48	0.16
Australian (0)	21	0.07
Austrian (43)	162	0.53
Belgian (10)	109	0.35
British (29)	52	0.17
Canadian (10)	29	0.09
Croatian (25)	124	0.40
Czech (168)	598	1.94
Czechoslovakian (33)	33	0.11
Danish (47)	221	0.72
Dutch (117)	594	1.93
English (382)	1,825	5.93
European (229)	229	0.74
Finnish (163)	306	0.99
French, ex. Basque (118)	1,317	4.28
French Canadian (68)	209	0.68
German (9,491)	18,254	59.34
Greek (11)	19	0.06
Hungarian (39)	202	0.66
Irish (670)	3,491	11.35
Italian (245)	1,047	3.40

*Notes: † The Census 2010 population figure is used to calculate the percentages in the Hispanic Origin and Race categories. Ancestry percentages are based on the 2006-2010 American Community Survey population (not shown); ‡ Numbers in parentheses indicate the number of people reporting a single ancestry; * Numbers in parentheses indicate the number of persons reporting this race alone, not in combination with any other race; Please refer to the Explanation of Data for more information.*

Ancestry (continued)	Population	%
Latvian (0)	15	0.05
Lithuanian (29)	61	0.20
Luxemburger (0)	101	0.33
Norwegian (321)	1,284	4.17
Polish (687)	3,113	10.12
Portuguese (17)	17	0.06
Russian (78)	324	1.05
Scandinavian (26)	150	0.49
Scotch-Irish (10)	292	0.95
Scottish (138)	329	1.07
Serbian (59)	104	0.34
Slavic (0)	11	0.04
Slovak (15)	86	0.28
Slovene (0)	25	0.08
Swedish (49)	465	1.51
Swiss (27)	211	0.69
Ukrainian (8)	8	0.03
Welsh (21)	265	0.86
West Indian, ex. Hispanic (15)	96	0.31
Haitian (0)	81	0.26
Jamaican (15)	15	0.05
Yugoslavian (30)	43	0.14

Hispanic Origin	Population	%
Hispanic or Latino (of any race)	1,213	3.90
Central American, ex. Mexican	28	0.09
Costa Rican	1	<0.01
Guatemalan	20	0.06
Honduran	1	<0.01
Nicaraguan	1	<0.01
Panamanian	4	0.01
Salvadoran	1	<0.01
Cuban	18	0.06
Dominican Republic	6	0.02
Mexican	927	2.98
Puerto Rican	140	0.45
South American	13	0.04
Argentinean	1	<0.01
Chilean	4	0.01
Colombian	2	0.01
Ecuadorian	1	<0.01
Peruvian	5	0.02
Other Hispanic or Latino	81	0.26

Race*	Population	%
African-American/Black (296)	513	1.65
Not Hispanic (283)	476	1.53
Hispanic (13)	37	0.12
American Indian/Alaska Native (134)	272	0.88
Not Hispanic (119)	243	0.78
Hispanic (15)	29	0.09
Blackfeet (5)	5	0.02
Cherokee (2)	15	0.05
Chippewa (53)	79	0.25
Creek (0)	1	<0.01
Iroquois (16)	29	0.09
Menominee (5)	11	0.04
Mexican American Ind. (2)	6	0.02
Navajo (0)	1	<0.01
Ottawa (7)	12	0.04
Paiute (1)	3	0.01
Potawatomi (2)	3	0.01
Sioux (4)	8	0.03
Yaqui (0)	1	<0.01
Asian (241)	349	1.12
Not Hispanic (238)	321	1.03
Hispanic (3)	28	0.09
Burmese (5)	5	0.02
Cambodian (0)	1	<0.01
Chinese, ex. Taiwanese (51)	64	0.21
Filipino (58)	93	0.30
Hmong (7)	10	0.03
Indian (48)	56	0.18
Indonesian (1)	5	0.02
Japanese (6)	29	0.09
Korean (25)	45	0.14
Laotian (1)	1	<0.01
Pakistani (1)	1	<0.01
Sri Lankan (4)	4	0.01
Thai (5)	7	0.02
Vietnamese (15)	20	0.06
Hawaii Native/Pacific Islander (3)	16	0.05
Not Hispanic (3)	9	0.03
Hispanic (0)	7	0.02
Fijian (0)	2	0.01
Guamanian/Chamorro (1)	3	0.01
Native Hawaiian (2)	9	0.03
White (29,452)	29,952	96.38
Not Hispanic (28,816)	29,199	93.95
Hispanic (636)	753	2.42

Weston

Place Type: Village
County: Marathon
Population: 14,868†

Ancestry‡	Population	%
American (606)	606	4.21
Arab (0)	19	0.13
Syrian (0)	19	0.13
Austrian (35)	129	0.90
Belgian (0)	51	0.35
Brazilian (7)	14	0.10
British (12)	24	0.17
Croatian (40)	70	0.49
Czech (14)	203	1.41
Danish (15)	68	0.47
Dutch (33)	166	1.15
English (229)	695	4.83
European (53)	53	0.37
Finnish (68)	310	2.16
French, ex. Basque (109)	583	4.05
French Canadian (81)	188	1.31
German (3,339)	6,809	47.35
Greek (0)	126	0.88
Hungarian (0)	8	0.06
Irish (267)	1,120	7.79
Italian (172)	450	3.13
Lithuanian (0)	18	0.13
Luxemburger (0)	29	0.20
Norwegian (404)	852	5.92
Polish (668)	2,399	16.68
Portuguese (43)	57	0.40
Russian (8)	99	0.69
Scotch-Irish (39)	101	0.70
Scottish (48)	168	1.17
Slovak (0)	18	0.13
Slovene (0)	14	0.10
Swedish (53)	255	1.77
Swiss (14)	82	0.57
Ukrainian (14)	14	0.10
Welsh (7)	11	0.08

Hispanic Origin	Population	%
Hispanic or Latino (of any race)	301	2.02
Central American, ex. Mexican	19	0.13
Costa Rican	1	0.01
Guatemalan	5	0.03
Honduran	7	0.05
Panamanian	5	0.03
Salvadoran	1	0.01
Cuban	8	0.05
Dominican Republic	2	0.01
Mexican	194	1.30
Puerto Rican	27	0.18
South American	18	0.12
Argentinean	2	0.01
Bolivian	2	0.01
Colombian	1	0.01
Ecuadorian	1	0.01
Peruvian	9	0.06
Venezuelan	3	0.02
Other Hispanic or Latino	33	0.22

Race*	Population	%
African-American/Black (115)	188	1.26
Not Hispanic (112)	183	1.23
Hispanic (3)	5	0.03
American Indian/Alaska Native (61)	133	0.89
Not Hispanic (52)	118	0.79
Hispanic (9)	15	0.10
Apache (0)	2	0.01
Cherokee (0)	4	0.03
Chippewa (23)	38	0.26
Choctaw (1)	1	0.01
Comanche (1)	1	0.01
Iroquois (4)	8	0.05
Menominee (4)	10	0.07
Mexican American Ind. (3)	4	0.03
Navajo (1)	3	0.02
Ottawa (0)	1	0.01
Paiute (1)	1	0.01
Potawatomi (2)	5	0.03
Seminole (0)	1	0.01
Asian (1,299)	1,367	9.19
Not Hispanic (1,297)	1,362	9.16
Hispanic (2)	5	0.03
Burmese (0)	2	0.01
Cambodian (0)	3	0.02
Chinese, ex. Taiwanese (38)	49	0.33
Filipino (15)	25	0.17
Hmong (1,067)	1,089	7.32
Indian (31)	39	0.26
Indonesian (3)	3	0.02
Japanese (2)	12	0.08
Korean (12)	16	0.11
Laotian (28)	35	0.24
Malaysian (0)	2	0.01
Nepalese (1)	1	0.01
Pakistani (8)	8	0.05
Sri Lankan (2)	2	0.01
Taiwanese (1)	4	0.03
Thai (4)	8	0.05
Vietnamese (10)	15	0.10
Hawaii Native/Pacific Islander (2)	15	0.10
Not Hispanic (1)	14	0.09
Hispanic (1)	1	0.01
Guamanian/Chamorro (1)	1	0.01
Native Hawaiian (0)	1	0.01
Samoan (0)	2	0.01
White (13,038)	13,251	89.12
Not Hispanic (12,897)	13,080	87.97
Hispanic (141)	171	1.15

Whitefish Bay

Place Type: Village
County: Milwaukee
Population: 14,110†

Ancestry‡	Population	%
American (194)	194	1.39
Arab (32)	92	0.66
Arab (0)	38	0.27
Lebanese (20)	42	0.30
Other Arab (12)	12	0.09
Armenian (10)	23	0.16
Austrian (13)	63	0.45
Belgian (27)	54	0.39
British (36)	73	0.52
Croatian (37)	110	0.79
Czech (19)	224	1.60
Czechoslovakian (0)	30	0.21
Danish (21)	82	0.59
Dutch (9)	184	1.32
Eastern European (11)	11	0.08
English (260)	1,528	10.92
Estonian (0)	12	0.09
European (332)	344	2.46
Finnish (10)	67	0.48
French, ex. Basque (31)	573	4.10
French Canadian (21)	71	0.51
German (1,360)	5,437	38.87
Greek (63)	151	1.08
Hungarian (0)	74	0.53
Iranian (56)	56	0.40
Irish (641)	3,525	25.20
Israeli (16)	16	0.11
Italian (325)	1,685	12.05

*Notes: † The Census 2010 population figure is used to calculate the percentages in the Hispanic Origin and Race categories. Ancestry percentages are based on the 2006-2010 American Community Survey population (not shown); ‡ Numbers in parentheses indicate the number of people reporting a single ancestry; * Numbers in parentheses indicate the number of persons reporting this race alone, not in combination with any other race; Please refer to the Explanation of Data for more information.*

Lithuanian (12)	119	0.85
Luxemburger (0)	13	0.09
Macedonian (11)	11	0.08
Northern European (64)	64	0.46
Norwegian (90)	550	3.93
Pennsylvania German (14)	14	0.10
Polish (246)	1,172	8.38
Portuguese (9)	20	0.14
Romanian (0)	72	0.51
Russian (99)	229	1.64
Scandinavian (35)	64	0.46
Scotch-Irish (50)	198	1.42
Scottish (30)	365	2.61
Serbian (0)	9	0.06
Slavic (0)	9	0.06
Slovak (97)	188	1.34
Slovene (0)	55	0.39
Swedish (138)	550	3.93
Swiss (53)	187	1.34
Turkish (0)	13	0.09
Ukrainian (52)	75	0.54
Welsh (0)	76	0.54

Hispanic Origin	Population	%
Hispanic or Latino (of any race)	399	2.83
Central American, ex. Mexican	36	0.26
Costa Rican	5	0.04
Guatemalan	24	0.17
Honduran	2	0.01
Panamanian	4	0.03
Salvadoran	1	0.01
Cuban	7	0.05
Mexican	148	1.05
Puerto Rican	73	0.52
South American	83	0.59
Argentinean	23	0.16
Bolivian	4	0.03
Chilean	1	0.01
Colombian	37	0.26
Ecuadorian	3	0.02
Paraguayan	2	0.01
Peruvian	5	0.04
Uruguayan	1	0.01
Venezuelan	5	0.04
Other South American	2	0.01
Other Hispanic or Latino	52	0.37

Race*	Population	%
African-American/Black (270)	355	2.52
Not Hispanic (269)	345	2.45
Hispanic (1)	10	0.07
American Indian/Alaska Native (19)	57	0.40
Not Hispanic (15)	51	0.36
Hispanic (4)	6	0.04
Blackfeet (0)	4	0.03
Canadian/French Am. Ind. (0)	1	0.01
Cherokee (2)	9	0.06
Chippewa (7)	13	0.09
Choctaw (0)	4	0.03
Iroquois (2)	2	0.01
Menominee (4)	5	0.04
Mexican American Ind. (3)	6	0.04
Potawatomi (0)	2	0.01
Asian (516)	659	4.67
Not Hispanic (513)	649	4.60
Hispanic (3)	10	0.07
Bangladeshi (5)	7	0.05
Cambodian (1)	1	0.01
Chinese, ex. Taiwanese (178)	205	1.45
Filipino (35)	65	0.46
Hmong (2)	2	0.01
Indian (76)	89	0.63
Indonesian (3)	7	0.05
Japanese (16)	30	0.21
Korean (152)	176	1.25
Malaysian (1)	1	0.01
Nepalese (9)	10	0.07
Pakistani (4)	5	0.04
Taiwanese (11)	12	0.09
Thai (8)	12	0.09
Vietnamese (9)	19	0.13
Hawaii Native/Pacific Islander (0)	11	0.08
Not Hispanic (0)	11	0.08
Native Hawaiian (0)	6	0.04
White (12,973)	13,227	93.74
Not Hispanic (12,651)	12,882	91.30
Hispanic (322)	345	2.45

Whitewater

Place Type: City
County: Walworth
Population: 11,150†

Ancestry‡	Population	%
African, Sub-Saharan (27)	65	0.58
African (27)	65	0.58
Albanian (101)	101	0.91
American (143)	143	1.28
Arab (46)	46	0.41
Arab (14)	14	0.13
Lebanese (32)	32	0.29
Armenian (5)	5	0.04
Austrian (18)	71	0.64
Belgian (16)	89	0.80
British (17)	48	0.43
Croatian (13)	13	0.12
Czech (15)	181	1.62
Danish (21)	160	1.43
Dutch (23)	245	2.20
English (205)	956	8.57
European (15)	15	0.13
Finnish (0)	63	0.56
French, ex. Basque (26)	313	2.81
French Canadian (28)	97	0.87
German (2,154)	5,327	47.75
Greek (51)	51	0.46
Hungarian (15)	95	0.85
Irish (272)	1,533	13.74
Italian (223)	752	6.74
Lithuanian (35)	66	0.59
Luxemburger (9)	9	0.08
Norwegian (166)	662	5.93
Polish (168)	1,071	9.60
Russian (0)	48	0.43
Scandinavian (0)	32	0.29
Scotch-Irish (113)	188	1.69
Scottish (25)	245	2.20
Slovak (0)	15	0.13
Slovene (0)	20	0.18
Swedish (17)	299	2.68
Swiss (0)	90	0.81
Turkish (53)	69	0.62
Ukrainian (0)	14	0.13
Welsh (9)	58	0.52
West Indian, ex. Hispanic (11)	11	0.10
Jamaican (11)	11	0.10

Hispanic Origin	Population	%
Hispanic or Latino (of any race)	957	8.58
Central American, ex. Mexican	27	0.24
Costa Rican	5	0.04
Guatemalan	5	0.04
Honduran	2	0.02
Panamanian	3	0.03
Salvadoran	12	0.11
Cuban	5	0.04
Dominican Republic	6	0.05
Mexican	817	7.33
Puerto Rican	40	0.36
South American	18	0.16
Argentinean	1	0.01
Bolivian	1	0.01
Chilean	5	0.04
Colombian	4	0.04
Ecuadorian	1	0.01
Peruvian	4	0.04
Venezuelan	2	0.02
Other Hispanic or Latino	44	0.39

Race*	Population	%
African-American/Black (332)	413	3.70
Not Hispanic (326)	396	3.55
Hispanic (6)	17	0.15
American Indian/Alaska Native (28)	85	0.76
Not Hispanic (23)	70	0.63
Hispanic (5)	15	0.13
Aleut *(Alaska Native)* (0)	2	0.02
Apache (0)	2	0.02
Blackfeet (0)	1	0.01
Cherokee (0)	10	0.09
Chippewa (4)	15	0.13
Creek (0)	1	0.01
Delaware (0)	1	0.01
Hopi (1)	3	0.03
Iroquois (1)	3	0.03
Kiowa (1)	1	0.01
Menominee (1)	1	0.01
Ottawa (2)	2	0.02
Sioux (1)	1	0.01
South American Ind. (1)	1	0.01
Asian (212)	244	2.19
Not Hispanic (212)	240	2.15
Hispanic (0)	4	0.04
Cambodian (4)	4	0.04
Chinese, ex. Taiwanese (63)	70	0.63
Filipino (13)	19	0.17
Hmong (37)	37	0.33
Indian (30)	30	0.27
Indonesian (1)	1	0.01
Japanese (7)	17	0.15
Korean (17)	21	0.19
Pakistani (1)	1	0.01
Sri Lankan (5)	5	0.04
Thai (1)	2	0.02
Vietnamese (14)	15	0.13
Hawaii Native/Pacific Islander (10)	22	0.20
Not Hispanic (9)	21	0.19
Hispanic (1)	1	0.01
Fijian (1)	1	0.01
Guamanian/Chamorro (1)	7	0.06
Native Hawaiian (6)	9	0.08
Samoan (2)	2	0.02
White (9,946)	10,118	90.74
Not Hispanic (9,477)	9,610	86.19
Hispanic (469)	508	4.56

Whitewater

Place Type: City
County: Walworth
Population: 14,390†

Ancestry‡	Population	%
African, Sub-Saharan (27)	65	0.45
African (27)	65	0.45
Albanian (101)	101	0.71
American (158)	158	1.11
Arab (46)	46	0.32
Arab (14)	14	0.10
Lebanese (32)	32	0.22
Armenian (5)	5	0.03
Austrian (18)	107	0.75
Belgian (30)	143	1.00
British (17)	49	0.34
Croatian (13)	13	0.09
Czech (90)	352	2.46
Czechoslovakian (14)	14	0.10
Danish (21)	209	1.46
Dutch (33)	301	2.11
English (239)	1,137	7.96
European (15)	15	0.10
Finnish (0)	90	0.63
French, ex. Basque (54)	574	4.02
French Canadian (51)	197	1.38
German (2,646)	6,761	47.31
Greek (51)	65	0.45
Hungarian (15)	109	0.76
Irish (287)	1,904	13.32

*Notes: † The Census 2010 population figure is used to calculate the percentages in the Hispanic Origin and Race categories. Ancestry percentages are based on the 2006-2010 American Community Survey population (not shown); ‡ Numbers in parentheses indicate the number of people reporting a single ancestry; * Numbers in parentheses indicate the number of persons reporting this race alone, not in combination with any other race; Please refer to the Explanation of Data for more information.*

Italian (235)	867	6.07
Lithuanian (35)	66	0.46
Luxemburger (9)	9	0.06
Northern European (14)	14	0.10
Norwegian (189)	936	6.55
Pennsylvania German (0)	12	0.08
Polish (232)	1,393	9.75
Russian (0)	48	0.34
Scandinavian (0)	32	0.22
Scotch-Irish (167)	242	1.69
Scottish (25)	320	2.24
Slovak (0)	15	0.10
Slovene (0)	20	0.14
Swedish (17)	327	2.29
Swiss (20)	111	0.78
Turkish (53)	69	0.48
Ukrainian (0)	14	0.10
Welsh (9)	104	0.73
West Indian, ex. Hispanic (11)	11	0.08
Jamaican (11)	11	0.08

Hispanic Origin	Population	%
Hispanic or Latino (of any race)	1,372	9.53
Central American, ex. Mexican	34	0.24
Costa Rican	6	0.04
Guatemalan	6	0.04
Honduran	3	0.02
Panamanian	6	0.04
Salvadoran	13	0.09
Cuban	8	0.06
Dominican Republic	7	0.05
Mexican	1,194	8.30
Puerto Rican	54	0.38
South American	24	0.17
Argentinean	1	0.01
Bolivian	1	0.01
Chilean	5	0.03
Colombian	5	0.03
Ecuadorian	6	0.04
Peruvian	4	0.03
Venezuelan	2	0.01
Other Hispanic or Latino	51	0.35

Race*	Population	%
African-American/Black (505)	623	4.33
Not Hispanic (490)	595	4.13
Hispanic (15)	28	0.19
American Indian/Alaska Native (36)	106	0.74
Not Hispanic (29)	84	0.58
Hispanic (7)	22	0.15
Aleut *(Alaska Native)* (0)	2	0.01
Apache (0)	6	0.04
Blackfeet (0)	1	0.01
Cherokee (0)	12	0.08
Chippewa (6)	17	0.12
Choctaw (0)	1	0.01
Creek (0)	1	0.01
Delaware (0)	1	0.01
Hopi (2)	4	0.03
Iroquois (1)	4	0.03
Kiowa (1)	1	0.01
Menominee (1)	1	0.01
Ottawa (2)	2	0.01
Sioux (1)	2	0.01
South American Ind. (1)	1	0.01
Asian (280)	328	2.28
Not Hispanic (280)	323	2.24
Hispanic (0)	5	0.03
Cambodian (5)	6	0.04
Chinese, ex. Taiwanese (75)	84	0.58
Filipino (14)	24	0.17
Hmong (53)	53	0.37
Indian (43)	44	0.31
Indonesian (1)	1	0.01
Japanese (7)	21	0.15
Korean (24)	31	0.22
Pakistani (1)	2	0.01
Sri Lankan (5)	5	0.03
Thai (13)	17	0.12
Vietnamese (15)	17	0.12
Hawaii Native/Pacific Islander (10)	23	0.16
Not Hispanic (9)	22	0.15
Hispanic (1)	1	0.01
Fijian (1)	1	0.01
Guamanian/Chamorro (1)	7	0.05
Native Hawaiian (6)	9	0.06
Samoan (2)	3	0.02
White (12,657)	12,897	89.62
Not Hispanic (12,009)	12,190	84.71
Hispanic (648)	707	4.91

Wisconsin Rapids

Place Type: City
County: Wood
Population: 18,367†

Ancestry‡	Population	%
American (622)	622	3.39
Austrian (0)	38	0.21
Belgian (0)	38	0.21
British (0)	14	0.08
Croatian (43)	69	0.38
Czech (51)	162	0.88
Czechoslovakian (0)	35	0.19
Danish (86)	311	1.70
Dutch (342)	736	4.01
English (262)	1,147	6.26
European (27)	27	0.15
Finnish (43)	157	0.86
French, ex. Basque (83)	769	4.19
French Canadian (104)	258	1.41
German (3,562)	8,620	47.02
Hungarian (11)	82	0.45
Irish (337)	2,259	12.32
Italian (49)	220	1.20
Lithuanian (14)	51	0.28
Luxemburger (0)	40	0.22
Norwegian (289)	1,052	5.74
Pennsylvania German (0)	10	0.05
Polish (724)	2,590	14.13
Russian (0)	95	0.52
Scotch-Irish (11)	149	0.81
Scottish (143)	269	1.47
Slovene (13)	13	0.07
Swedish (101)	543	2.96
Swiss (56)	342	1.87
Ukrainian (16)	16	0.09
Welsh (15)	91	0.50

Hispanic Origin	Population	%
Hispanic or Latino (of any race)	535	2.91
Central American, ex. Mexican	5	0.03
Guatemalan	1	0.01
Honduran	3	0.02
Nicaraguan	1	0.01
Cuban	4	0.02
Mexican	400	2.18
Puerto Rican	44	0.24
South American	16	0.09
Chilean	1	0.01
Colombian	5	0.03
Ecuadorian	6	0.03
Peruvian	3	0.02
Venezuelan	1	0.01
Other Hispanic or Latino	66	0.36

Race*	Population	%
African-American/Black (133)	249	1.36
Not Hispanic (132)	234	1.27
Hispanic (1)	15	0.08
American Indian/Alaska Native (177)	267	1.45
Not Hispanic (164)	244	1.33
Hispanic (13)	23	0.13
Aleut *(Alaska Native)* (1)	1	0.01
Arapaho (0)	1	0.01
Blackfeet (1)	1	0.01
Cherokee (0)	7	0.04
Chippewa (17)	24	0.13
Cree (1)	2	0.01
Inupiat *(Alaska Native)* (1)	1	0.01
Iroquois (12)	22	0.12
Menominee (10)	10	0.05
Mexican American Ind. (0)	3	0.02
Navajo (3)	3	0.02
Potawatomi (10)	19	0.10
Sioux (5)	5	0.03
Tlingit-Haida *(Alaska Native)* (3)	4	0.02
Yaqui (1)	1	0.01
Asian (672)	704	3.83
Not Hispanic (664)	693	3.77
Hispanic (8)	11	0.06
Chinese, ex. Taiwanese (23)	24	0.13
Filipino (27)	35	0.19
Hmong (550)	562	3.06
Indian (9)	16	0.09
Japanese (5)	6	0.03
Korean (21)	25	0.14
Laotian (2)	7	0.04
Pakistani (7)	7	0.04
Thai (3)	7	0.04
Vietnamese (16)	17	0.09
Hawaii Native/Pacific Islander (3)	12	0.07
Not Hispanic (3)	12	0.07
Guamanian/Chamorro (0)	1	0.01
Native Hawaiian (2)	4	0.02
White (16,940)	17,194	93.61
Not Hispanic (16,646)	16,844	91.71
Hispanic (294)	350	1.91

*Notes: † The Census 2010 population figure is used to calculate the percentages in the Hispanic Origin and Race categories. Ancestry percentages are based on the 2006-2010 American Community Survey population (not shown); ‡ Numbers in parentheses indicate the number of people reporting a single ancestry; * Numbers in parentheses indicate the number of persons reporting this race alone, not in combination with any other race; Please refer to the Explanation of Data for more information.*

WYOMING

Place Type: State
Population: 563,626†

Ancestry‡	Population	%
Afghan (0)	5	<0.01
African, Sub-Saharan (194)	227	0.04
African (81)	114	0.02
Nigerian (18)	18	<0.01
South African (95)	95	0.02
Albanian (8)	42	0.01
Alsatian (19)	19	<0.01
American (37,568)	37,568	6.89
Arab (128)	457	0.08
Arab (0)	44	0.01
Egyptian (10)	10	<0.01
Jordanian (18)	18	<0.01
Lebanese (70)	270	0.05
Palestinian (9)	22	<0.01
Syrian (21)	93	0.02
Armenian (33)	95	0.02
Assyrian/Chaldean/Syriac (0)	25	<0.01
Australian (125)	259	0.05
Austrian (574)	1,740	0.32
Basque (527)	1,170	0.21
Belgian (235)	781	0.14
Brazilian (12)	60	0.01
British (833)	1,715	0.31
Bulgarian (114)	167	0.03
Cajun (32)	61	0.01
Canadian (292)	857	0.16
Celtic (111)	189	0.03
Croatian (133)	462	0.08
Czech (1,175)	4,732	0.87
Czechoslovakian (310)	776	0.14
Danish (2,582)	10,576	1.94
Dutch (2,566)	13,153	2.41
Eastern European (179)	228	0.04
English (28,754)	85,513	15.67
Estonian (17)	86	0.02
European (6,953)	7,865	1.44
Finnish (922)	2,944	0.54
French, ex. Basque (2,659)	18,748	3.44
French Canadian (975)	2,734	0.50
German (55,153)	156,305	28.65
German Russian (4)	44	0.01
Greek (1,198)	2,634	0.48
Hungarian (517)	1,951	0.36
Icelander (161)	286	0.05
Iranian (141)	155	0.03
Irish (20,471)	79,785	14.62
Israeli (10)	70	0.01
Italian (6,961)	18,943	3.47
Latvian (43)	55	0.01
Lithuanian (127)	361	0.07
Luxemburger (8)	39	0.01
Macedonian (10)	10	<0.01
New Zealander (12)	40	0.01
Northern European (946)	971	0.18
Norwegian (6,435)	19,401	3.56
Pennsylvania German (228)	484	0.09
Polish (3,439)	11,917	2.18
Portuguese (337)	1,285	0.24
Romanian (71)	164	0.03
Russian (971)	4,837	0.89
Scandinavian (1,506)	2,904	0.53
Scotch-Irish (6,402)	16,466	3.02
Scottish (6,012)	20,825	3.82
Serbian (54)	128	0.02
Slavic (243)	846	0.16
Slovak (249)	709	0.13
Slovene (190)	544	0.10
Swedish (5,173)	18,760	3.44
Swiss (641)	3,664	0.67
Turkish (226)	238	0.04
Ukrainian (123)	511	0.09
Welsh (1,255)	6,530	1.20
West Indian, ex. Hispanic (103)	103	0.02
Barbadian (2)	2	<0.01
Haitian (3)	3	<0.01
Jamaican (61)	61	0.01
West Indian (37)	37	0.01
Yugoslavian (374)	906	0.17

Hispanic Origin	Population	%
Hispanic or Latino (of any race)	50,231	8.91
Central American, ex. Mexican	977	0.17
Costa Rican	52	0.01
Guatemalan	418	0.07
Honduran	145	0.03
Nicaraguan	73	0.01
Panamanian	81	0.01
Salvadoran	198	0.04
Other Central American	10	<0.01
Cuban	275	0.05
Dominican Republic	45	0.01
Mexican	37,719	6.69
Puerto Rican	1,026	0.18
South American	852	0.15
Argentinean	76	0.01
Bolivian	43	0.01
Chilean	78	0.01
Colombian	178	0.03
Ecuadorian	81	0.01
Paraguayan	3	<0.01
Peruvian	305	0.05
Uruguayan	9	<0.01
Venezuelan	66	0.01
Other South American	13	<0.01
Other Hispanic or Latino	9,337	1.66

Race*	Population	%
African-American/Black (4,748)	7,285	1.29
Not Hispanic (4,351)	6,397	1.13
Hispanic (397)	888	0.16
American Indian/Alaska Native (13,336)	18,596	3.30
Not Hispanic (11,784)	15,988	2.84
Hispanic (1,552)	2,608	0.46
Alaska Athabascan *(Ala. Nat.)* (17)	34	0.01
Aleut *(Alaska Native)* (15)	29	0.01
Apache (86)	246	0.04
Arapaho (4,864)	5,224	0.93
Blackfeet (106)	262	0.05
Canadian/French Am. Ind. (20)	32	0.01
Central American Ind. (5)	10	<0.01
Cherokee (376)	1,282	0.23
Cheyenne (172)	233	0.04
Chickasaw (36)	67	0.01
Chippewa (260)	457	0.08
Choctaw (126)	277	0.05
Colville (2)	4	<0.01
Comanche (17)	59	0.01
Cree (7)	21	<0.01
Creek (24)	57	0.01
Crow (156)	239	0.04
Delaware (26)	40	0.01
Hopi (10)	17	<0.01
Houma (1)	1	<0.01
Inupiat *(Alaska Native)* (11)	29	0.01
Iroquois (43)	102	0.02
Kiowa (6)	10	<0.01
Lumbee (6)	13	<0.01
Menominee (3)	3	<0.01
Mexican American Ind. (124)	186	0.03
Navajo (358)	506	0.09
Osage (11)	30	0.01
Ottawa (8)	20	<0.01
Paiute (16)	26	<0.01
Pima (6)	10	<0.01
Potawatomi (29)	46	0.01
Pueblo (28)	58	0.01
Puget Sound Salish (8)	17	<0.01
Seminole (13)	28	<0.01
Shoshone (2,449)	2,818	0.50
Sioux (841)	1,408	0.25
South American Ind. (26)	31	0.01
Spanish American Ind. (29)	35	0.01
Tlingit-Haida *(Alaska Native)* (13)	40	0.01
Tohono O'Odham (12)	14	<0.01
Ute (41)	71	0.01
Yakama (5)	10	<0.01
Yaqui (18)	33	0.01
Yuman (4)	6	<0.01
Yup'ik *(Alaska Native)* (11)	21	<0.01
Asian (4,426)	6,729	1.19
Not Hispanic (4,279)	6,286	1.12
Hispanic (147)	443	0.08
Bangladeshi (14)	15	<0.01
Bhutanese (9)	10	<0.01
Burmese (6)	10	<0.01
Cambodian (28)	39	0.01
Chinese, ex. Taiwanese (1,013)	1,299	0.23
Filipino (901)	1,657	0.29
Hmong (5)	8	<0.01
Indian (589)	739	0.13
Indonesian (44)	85	0.02
Japanese (454)	982	0.17
Korean (508)	803	0.14
Laotian (32)	42	0.01
Malaysian (17)	22	<0.01
Nepalese (70)	71	0.01
Pakistani (74)	112	0.02
Sri Lankan (25)	31	0.01
Taiwanese (31)	41	0.01
Thai (174)	259	0.05
Vietnamese (191)	283	0.05
Hawaii Native/Pacific Islander (427)	1,063	0.19
Not Hispanic (365)	875	0.16
Hispanic (62)	188	0.03
Fijian (2)	8	<0.01
Guamanian/Chamorro (101)	174	0.03
Marshallese (9)	12	<0.01
Native Hawaiian (147)	457	0.08
Samoan (70)	151	0.03
Tongan (17)	32	0.01
White (511,279)	522,739	92.75
Not Hispanic (483,874)	491,793	87.26
Hispanic (27,405)	30,946	5.49

*Notes: † The Census 2010 population figure is used to calculate the percentages in the Hispanic Origin and Race categories. Ancestry percentages are based on the 2006-2010 American Community Survey population (not shown); ‡ Numbers in parentheses indicate the number of people reporting a single ancestry; * Numbers in parentheses indicate the number of persons reporting this race alone, not in combination with any other race; Please refer to the Explanation of Data for more information.*

Casper

Place Type: City
County: Natrona
Population: 55,316†

Ancestry‡	Population	%
American (5,099)	5,099	9.42
Arab (16)	108	0.20
Arab (0)	33	0.06
Lebanese (16)	16	0.03
Syrian (0)	59	0.11
Australian (40)	40	0.07
Austrian (18)	109	0.20
Basque (26)	62	0.11
Belgian (38)	76	0.14
Brazilian (12)	12	0.02
British (65)	170	0.31
Bulgarian (15)	15	0.03
Cajun (13)	13	0.02
Canadian (34)	48	0.09
Celtic (0)	13	0.02
Croatian (48)	82	0.15
Czech (143)	672	1.24
Czechoslovakian (21)	82	0.15
Danish (390)	955	1.76
Dutch (284)	1,385	2.56
Eastern European (16)	16	0.03
English (2,372)	6,732	12.43
European (550)	614	1.13
Finnish (106)	234	0.43
French, ex. Basque (484)	2,099	3.88
French Canadian (62)	313	0.58
German (5,626)	14,556	26.89
Greek (227)	588	1.09
Hungarian (33)	97	0.18
Iranian (77)	77	0.14
Irish (3,311)	8,579	15.85
Italian (1,176)	2,111	3.90
Lithuanian (0)	20	0.04
Norwegian (737)	2,288	4.23
Pennsylvania German (12)	12	0.02
Polish (305)	1,083	2.00
Portuguese (25)	152	0.28
Russian (22)	272	0.50
Scandinavian (98)	195	0.36
Scotch-Irish (469)	1,189	2.20
Scottish (550)	1,825	3.37
Serbian (9)	9	0.02
Slavic (0)	162	0.30
Slovak (32)	62	0.11
Slovene (12)	47	0.09
Swedish (442)	1,414	2.61
Swiss (59)	207	0.38
Turkish (0)	9	0.02
Ukrainian (28)	50	0.09
Welsh (101)	635	1.17
Yugoslavian (36)	69	0.13

Hispanic Origin	Population	%
Hispanic or Latino (of any race)	4,070	7.36
Central American, ex. Mexican	73	0.13
Costa Rican	2	<0.01
Guatemalan	31	0.06
Honduran	15	0.03
Nicaraguan	15	0.03
Panamanian	6	0.01
Salvadoran	4	0.01
Cuban	35	0.06
Dominican Republic	6	0.01
Mexican	3,039	5.49
Puerto Rican	76	0.14
South American	87	0.16
Argentinean	12	0.02
Bolivian	8	0.01
Chilean	6	0.01
Colombian	22	0.04
Ecuadorian	10	0.02
Peruvian	9	0.02
Venezuelan	14	0.03
Other South American	6	0.01
Other Hispanic or Latino	754	1.36

Race*	Population	%
African-American/Black (560)	998	1.80
Not Hispanic (523)	884	1.60
Hispanic (37)	114	0.21
American Indian/Alaska Native (521)	1,024	1.85
Not Hispanic (398)	782	1.41
Hispanic (123)	242	0.44
Alaska Athabascan *(Ala. Nat.)* (3)	5	0.01
Aleut *(Alaska Native)* (4)	4	0.01
Apache (12)	22	0.04
Arapaho (84)	113	0.20
Blackfeet (5)	28	0.05
Canadian/French Am. Ind. (2)	3	0.01
Cherokee (26)	95	0.17
Cheyenne (10)	12	0.02
Chickasaw (3)	3	0.01
Chippewa (40)	67	0.12
Choctaw (12)	23	0.04
Colville (0)	2	<0.01
Comanche (0)	3	0.01
Cree (1)	6	0.01
Creek (0)	3	0.01
Crow (3)	3	0.01
Delaware (0)	2	<0.01
Hopi (0)	1	<0.01
Inupiat *(Alaska Native)* (1)	4	0.01
Iroquois (3)	4	0.01
Lumbee (0)	1	<0.01
Mexican American Ind. (11)	21	0.04
Navajo (23)	30	0.05
Osage (0)	3	0.01
Ottawa (0)	5	0.01
Paiute (0)	1	<0.01
Potawatomi (2)	3	0.01
Pueblo (4)	8	0.01
Shoshone (26)	48	0.09
Sioux (45)	92	0.17
South American Ind. (1)	1	<0.01
Spanish American Ind. (5)	5	0.01
Tlingit-Haida *(Alaska Native)* (1)	1	<0.01
Tohono O'Odham (5)	6	0.01
Ute (2)	3	0.01
Yaqui (1)	6	0.01
Yup'ik *(Alaska Native)* (1)	1	<0.01
Asian (436)	664	1.20
Not Hispanic (407)	603	1.09
Hispanic (29)	61	0.11
Burmese (1)	1	<0.01
Cambodian (3)	7	0.01
Chinese, ex. Taiwanese (101)	123	0.22
Filipino (109)	194	0.35
Indian (51)	64	0.12
Indonesian (0)	11	0.02
Japanese (31)	78	0.14
Korean (33)	56	0.10
Laotian (17)	18	0.03
Malaysian (3)	3	0.01
Pakistani (2)	4	0.01
Sri Lankan (5)	8	0.01
Taiwanese (1)	1	<0.01
Thai (21)	33	0.06
Vietnamese (37)	52	0.09
Hawaii Native/Pacific Islander (26)	112	0.20
Not Hispanic (26)	100	0.18
Hispanic (0)	12	0.02
Fijian (1)	1	<0.01
Guamanian/Chamorro (4)	12	0.02
Native Hawaiian (6)	33	0.06
Samoan (3)	19	0.03
Tongan (5)	12	0.02
White (51,048)	52,369	94.67
Not Hispanic (48,886)	49,793	90.02
Hispanic (2,162)	2,576	4.66

Cheyenne

Place Type: City
County: Laramie
Population: 59,466†

Ancestry‡	Population	%
African, Sub-Saharan (37)	53	0.09
African (37)	53	0.09
American (2,433)	2,433	4.20
Arab (28)	82	0.14
Arab (0)	11	0.02
Lebanese (19)	62	0.11
Palestinian (9)	9	0.02
Armenian (6)	52	0.09
Austrian (108)	240	0.41
Basque (0)	15	0.03
Belgian (0)	73	0.13
British (115)	285	0.49
Canadian (28)	131	0.23
Celtic (43)	60	0.10
Croatian (0)	34	0.06
Czech (182)	612	1.06
Czechoslovakian (27)	56	0.10
Danish (126)	664	1.15
Dutch (224)	691	1.19
Eastern European (49)	49	0.08
English (2,107)	7,136	12.32
Estonian (0)	14	0.02
European (872)	1,088	1.88
Finnish (36)	303	0.52
French, ex. Basque (278)	1,628	2.81
French Canadian (100)	230	0.40
German (5,613)	17,210	29.71
German Russian (0)	13	0.02
Greek (209)	397	0.69
Hungarian (20)	116	0.20
Icelander (0)	9	0.02
Iranian (12)	12	0.02
Irish (1,808)	9,027	15.58
Israeli (0)	60	0.10
Italian (917)	2,263	3.91
Latvian (11)	23	0.04
Northern European (91)	91	0.16
Norwegian (739)	2,092	3.61
Pennsylvania German (28)	113	0.20
Polish (318)	1,300	2.24
Portuguese (148)	416	0.72
Russian (97)	631	1.09
Scandinavian (125)	313	0.54
Scotch-Irish (665)	1,698	2.93
Scottish (681)	2,248	3.88
Slavic (12)	66	0.11
Slovak (21)	97	0.17
Slovene (21)	153	0.26
Swedish (390)	1,450	2.50
Swiss (16)	182	0.31
Ukrainian (27)	51	0.09
Welsh (193)	724	1.25
Yugoslavian (106)	156	0.27

Hispanic Origin	Population	%
Hispanic or Latino (of any race)	8,594	14.45
Central American, ex. Mexican	88	0.15
Costa Rican	10	0.02
Guatemalan	18	0.03
Honduran	15	0.03
Nicaraguan	6	0.01
Panamanian	25	0.04
Salvadoran	14	0.02
Cuban	59	0.10
Dominican Republic	6	0.01
Mexican	5,803	9.76
Puerto Rican	267	0.45
South American	105	0.18
Argentinean	2	<0.01
Bolivian	4	0.01
Chilean	8	0.01
Colombian	26	0.04
Ecuadorian	4	0.01

*Notes: † The Census 2010 population figure is used to calculate the percentages in the Hispanic Origin and Race categories. Ancestry percentages are based on the 2006-2010 American Community Survey population (not shown); ‡ Numbers in parentheses indicate the number of people reporting a single ancestry; * Numbers in parentheses indicate the number of persons reporting this race alone, not in combination with any other race; Please refer to the Explanation of Data for more information.*

Peruvian	48	0.08
Uruguayan	1	<0.01
Venezuelan	10	0.02
Other South American	2	<0.01
Other Hispanic or Latino	2,266	3.81

Race*	Population	%
African-American/Black (1,715)	2,406	4.05
Not Hispanic (1,567)	2,107	3.54
Hispanic (148)	299	0.50
American Indian/Alaska Native (570)	1,181	1.99
Not Hispanic (371)	802	1.35
Hispanic (199)	379	0.64
Alaska Athabascan *(Ala. Nat.)* (1)	10	0.02
Aleut *(Alaska Native)* (6)	9	0.02
Apache (20)	53	0.09
Arapaho (31)	52	0.09
Blackfeet (9)	22	0.04
Canadian/French Am. Ind. (2)	5	0.01
Cherokee (48)	175	0.29
Cheyenne (4)	7	0.01
Chickasaw (4)	11	0.02
Chippewa (15)	36	0.06
Choctaw (2)	16	0.03
Comanche (0)	5	0.01
Creek (0)	3	0.01
Delaware (3)	3	0.01
Hopi (0)	3	0.01
Houma (1)	1	<0.01
Inupiat *(Alaska Native)* (1)	4	0.01
Iroquois (5)	14	0.02
Kiowa (1)	1	<0.01
Lumbee (0)	1	<0.01
Mexican American Ind. (10)	16	0.03
Navajo (29)	45	0.08
Osage (1)	1	<0.01
Ottawa (2)	2	<0.01
Pima (0)	1	<0.01
Potawatomi (0)	1	<0.01
Pueblo (1)	2	<0.01
Puget Sound Salish (0)	2	<0.01
Seminole (0)	3	0.01
Shoshone (24)	41	0.07
Sioux (86)	163	0.27
South American Ind. (15)	16	0.03
Spanish American Ind. (5)	5	0.01
Tlingit-Haida *(Alaska Native)* (1)	9	0.02
Tohono O'Odham (1)	1	<0.01
Ute (1)	1	<0.01
Yup'ik *(Alaska Native)* (1)	3	0.01
Asian (732)	1,163	1.96
Not Hispanic (698)	1,034	1.74
Hispanic (34)	129	0.22
Bangladeshi (5)	5	0.01
Bhutanese (1)	2	<0.01
Burmese (0)	2	<0.01
Cambodian (4)	4	0.01
Chinese, ex. Taiwanese (108)	151	0.25
Filipino (186)	348	0.59
Hmong (1)	1	<0.01
Indian (88)	109	0.18
Indonesian (1)	3	0.01
Japanese (84)	169	0.28
Korean (122)	203	0.34
Laotian (1)	2	<0.01
Nepalese (9)	9	0.02
Pakistani (18)	24	0.04
Taiwanese (4)	7	0.01
Thai (28)	42	0.07
Vietnamese (38)	53	0.09
Hawaii Native/Pacific Islander (118)	213	0.36
Not Hispanic (95)	166	0.28
Hispanic (23)	47	0.08
Fijian (0)	1	<0.01
Guamanian/Chamorro (44)	58	0.10
Native Hawaiian (42)	91	0.15
Samoan (12)	22	0.04
Tongan (2)	3	0.01
White (51,999)	53,749	90.39
Not Hispanic (46,818)	47,975	80.68
Hispanic (5,181)	5,774	9.71

Cody

Place Type: City
County: Park
Population: 9,520†

Ancestry‡	Population	%
American (825)	825	8.82
Armenian (7)	7	0.07
Austrian (0)	9	0.10
Belgian (15)	29	0.31
British (10)	10	0.11
Canadian (16)	27	0.29
Croatian (0)	11	0.12
Czech (0)	40	0.43
Danish (17)	165	1.76
Dutch (53)	295	3.15
Eastern European (0)	8	0.09
English (420)	1,421	15.18
European (268)	268	2.86
Finnish (21)	47	0.50
French, ex. Basque (53)	255	2.72
French Canadian (38)	56	0.60
German (1,061)	2,815	30.08
Hungarian (0)	47	0.50
Irish (253)	1,346	14.38
Italian (156)	293	3.13
Lithuanian (20)	20	0.21
Northern European (27)	37	0.40
Norwegian (118)	464	4.96
Polish (50)	241	2.58
Portuguese (0)	26	0.28
Russian (0)	183	1.96
Scandinavian (13)	58	0.62
Scotch-Irish (110)	301	3.22
Scottish (315)	454	4.85
Serbian (0)	31	0.33
Swedish (51)	291	3.11
Swiss (14)	95	1.02
Ukrainian (9)	50	0.53
Welsh (40)	101	1.08

Hispanic Origin	Population	%
Hispanic or Latino (of any race)	291	3.06
Central American, ex. Mexican	6	0.06
Guatemalan	4	0.04
Nicaraguan	2	0.02
Cuban	3	0.03
Dominican Republic	5	0.05
Mexican	228	2.39
Puerto Rican	6	0.06
South American	7	0.07
Chilean	2	0.02
Colombian	3	0.03
Uruguayan	2	0.02
Other Hispanic or Latino	36	0.38

Race*	Population	%
African-American/Black (16)	48	0.50
Not Hispanic (16)	45	0.47
Hispanic (0)	3	0.03
American Indian/Alaska Native (69)	162	1.70
Not Hispanic (60)	143	1.50
Hispanic (9)	19	0.20
Aleut *(Alaska Native)* (2)	6	0.06
Apache (0)	1	0.01
Arapaho (3)	8	0.08
Blackfeet (0)	2	0.02
Cherokee (4)	28	0.29
Chippewa (3)	7	0.07
Choctaw (9)	12	0.13
Cree (0)	1	0.01
Creek (2)	3	0.03
Inupiat *(Alaska Native)* (1)	3	0.03
Iroquois (5)	7	0.07
Kiowa (0)	2	0.02
Mexican American Ind. (0)	1	0.01
Navajo (1)	3	0.03
Potawatomi (0)	1	0.01
Pueblo (0)	2	0.02
Puget Sound Salish (0)	2	0.02
Seminole (2)	2	0.02
Shoshone (2)	4	0.04
Sioux (10)	20	0.21
Asian (41)	72	0.76
Not Hispanic (41)	71	0.75
Hispanic (0)	1	0.01
Chinese, ex. Taiwanese (9)	9	0.09
Filipino (7)	16	0.17
Indian (1)	3	0.03
Japanese (6)	18	0.19
Korean (6)	8	0.08
Thai (5)	7	0.07
Vietnamese (4)	4	0.04
Hawaii Native/Pacific Islander (9)	13	0.14
Not Hispanic (9)	13	0.14
Guamanian/Chamorro (4)	4	0.04
Native Hawaiian (1)	4	0.04
Samoan (3)	3	0.03
White (9,126)	9,287	97.55
Not Hispanic (8,959)	9,089	95.47
Hispanic (167)	198	2.08

Evanston

Place Type: City
County: Uinta
Population: 12,359†

Ancestry‡	Population	%
American (414)	414	3.45
Australian (36)	36	0.30
British (13)	13	0.11
Canadian (0)	15	0.12
Czech (0)	57	0.47
Danish (52)	524	4.36
Dutch (72)	362	3.01
English (1,073)	3,237	26.94
European (193)	205	1.71
French, ex. Basque (122)	776	6.46
French Canadian (63)	166	1.38
German (794)	2,635	21.93
Greek (0)	22	0.18
Hungarian (13)	172	1.43
Icelander (15)	38	0.32
Irish (220)	1,248	10.39
Italian (151)	298	2.48
Lithuanian (0)	8	0.07
Northern European (14)	14	0.12
Norwegian (63)	364	3.03
Polish (59)	246	2.05
Portuguese (0)	145	1.21
Russian (9)	30	0.25
Scandinavian (16)	16	0.13
Scotch-Irish (142)	553	4.60
Scottish (122)	652	5.43
Serbian (0)	13	0.11
Slovak (0)	10	0.08
Swedish (50)	204	1.70
Swiss (10)	46	0.38
Welsh (0)	425	3.54
Yugoslavian (10)	23	0.19

Hispanic Origin	Population	%
Hispanic or Latino (of any race)	1,526	12.35
Central American, ex. Mexican	37	0.30
Guatemalan	27	0.22
Honduran	4	0.03
Panamanian	4	0.03
Salvadoran	2	0.02
Cuban	4	0.03
Mexican	1,241	10.04
Puerto Rican	34	0.28
South American	66	0.53
Chilean	6	0.05
Colombian	4	0.03
Ecuadorian	4	0.03
Paraguayan	1	0.01

*Notes: † The Census 2010 population figure is used to calculate the percentages in the Hispanic Origin and Race categories. Ancestry percentages are based on the 2006-2010 American Community Survey population (not shown); ‡ Numbers in parentheses indicate the number of people reporting a single ancestry; * Numbers in parentheses indicate the number of persons reporting this race alone, not in combination with any other race; Please refer to the Explanation of Data for more information.*

Peruvian	47	0.38
Venezuelan	4	0.03
Other Hispanic or Latino	144	1.17

Race*	Population	%
African-American/Black (39)	85	0.69
Not Hispanic (32)	68	0.55
Hispanic (7)	17	0.14
American Indian/Alaska Native (119)	264	2.14
Not Hispanic (85)	206	1.67
Hispanic (34)	58	0.47
Apache (3)	11	0.09
Arapaho (5)	5	0.04
Blackfeet (2)	12	0.10
Canadian/French Am. Ind. (0)	1	0.01
Cherokee (5)	41	0.33
Cheyenne (0)	3	0.02
Chickasaw (1)	1	0.01
Chippewa (3)	5	0.04
Choctaw (2)	7	0.06
Comanche (0)	5	0.04
Crow (1)	4	0.03
Inupiat *(Alaska Native)* (2)	4	0.03
Iroquois (4)	4	0.03
Mexican American Ind. (2)	3	0.02
Navajo (15)	34	0.28
Ottawa (0)	1	0.01
Paiute (0)	1	0.01
Pueblo (0)	3	0.02
Seminole (0)	4	0.03
Shoshone (11)	17	0.14
Sioux (6)	18	0.15
South American Ind. (2)	2	0.02
Spanish American Ind. (1)	1	0.01
Ute (3)	4	0.03
Yakama (1)	1	0.01
Asian (36)	91	0.74
Not Hispanic (36)	88	0.71
Hispanic (0)	3	0.02
Chinese, ex. Taiwanese (6)	10	0.08
Filipino (6)	35	0.28
Indian (6)	7	0.06
Japanese (4)	12	0.10
Korean (4)	10	0.08
Pakistani (0)	5	0.04
Thai (3)	3	0.02
Vietnamese (4)	5	0.04
Hawaii Native/Pacific Islander (21)	45	0.36
Not Hispanic (19)	38	0.31
Hispanic (2)	7	0.06
Guamanian/Chamorro (1)	3	0.02
Marshallese (8)	10	0.08
Native Hawaiian (2)	15	0.12
Samoan (2)	6	0.05
Tongan (0)	1	0.01
White (11,095)	11,380	92.08
Not Hispanic (10,449)	10,642	86.11
Hispanic (646)	738	5.97

Gillette

Place Type: City
County: Campbell
Population: 29,087†

Ancestry‡	Population	%
American (1,447)	1,447	5.33
Arab (29)	84	0.31
Jordanian (18)	18	0.07
Lebanese (11)	66	0.24
Austrian (65)	74	0.27
Basque (69)	69	0.25
Belgian (10)	72	0.27
British (33)	52	0.19
Canadian (2)	2	0.01
Czech (135)	337	1.24
Czechoslovakian (47)	47	0.17
Danish (85)	391	1.44
Dutch (139)	582	2.14
English (716)	2,795	10.30
European (182)	182	0.67
Finnish (33)	230	0.85
French, ex. Basque (109)	1,006	3.71
French Canadian (22)	78	0.29
German (2,994)	7,892	29.08
Greek (0)	47	0.17
Hungarian (59)	79	0.29
Irish (1,212)	4,378	16.13
Italian (377)	785	2.89
Northern European (29)	29	0.11
Norwegian (502)	1,337	4.93
Pennsylvania German (0)	18	0.07
Polish (124)	572	2.11
Romanian (2)	2	0.01
Russian (14)	154	0.57
Scandinavian (26)	86	0.32
Scotch-Irish (206)	473	1.74
Scottish (135)	426	1.57
Slovak (12)	25	0.09
Slovene (0)	15	0.06
Swedish (251)	723	2.66
Swiss (28)	130	0.48
Ukrainian (0)	20	0.07
Welsh (0)	51	0.19
Yugoslavian (9)	9	0.03

Hispanic Origin	Population	%
Hispanic or Latino (of any race)	2,764	9.50
Central American, ex. Mexican	155	0.53
Costa Rican	1	<0.01
Guatemalan	77	0.26
Honduran	17	0.06
Nicaraguan	2	0.01
Panamanian	2	0.01
Salvadoran	53	0.18
Other Central American	3	0.01
Cuban	4	0.01
Dominican Republic	2	0.01
Mexican	2,163	7.44
Puerto Rican	79	0.27
South American	35	0.12
Argentinean	6	0.02
Bolivian	2	0.01
Chilean	2	0.01
Colombian	6	0.02
Ecuadorian	6	0.02
Peruvian	7	0.02
Venezuelan	6	0.02
Other Hispanic or Latino	326	1.12

Race*	Population	%
African-American/Black (123)	230	0.79
Not Hispanic (105)	197	0.68
Hispanic (18)	33	0.11
American Indian/Alaska Native (356)	629	2.16
Not Hispanic (268)	484	1.66
Hispanic (88)	145	0.50
Alaska Athabascan *(Ala. Nat.)* (2)	2	0.01
Aleut *(Alaska Native)* (0)	1	<0.01
Apache (0)	1	<0.01
Arapaho (6)	15	0.05
Blackfeet (6)	12	0.04
Canadian/French Am. Ind. (1)	4	0.01
Cherokee (14)	37	0.13
Cheyenne (16)	20	0.07
Chickasaw (4)	4	0.01
Chippewa (24)	39	0.13
Choctaw (11)	18	0.06
Comanche (1)	3	0.01
Cree (0)	1	<0.01
Creek (1)	2	0.01
Iroquois (1)	1	<0.01
Lumbee (1)	1	<0.01
Mexican American Ind. (6)	17	0.06
Navajo (30)	41	0.14
Ottawa (0)	3	0.01
Pima (0)	2	0.01
Potawatomi (0)	4	0.01
Seminole (0)	2	0.01
Shoshone (14)	25	0.09
Sioux (93)	153	0.53
Spanish American Ind. (3)	3	0.01
Tlingit-Haida *(Alaska Native)* (1)	1	<0.01
Ute (2)	10	0.03
Yup'ik *(Alaska Native)* (2)	2	0.01
Asian (200)	309	1.06
Not Hispanic (195)	292	1.00
Hispanic (5)	17	0.06
Cambodian (0)	2	0.01
Chinese, ex. Taiwanese (21)	31	0.11
Filipino (47)	81	0.28
Indian (39)	44	0.15
Indonesian (7)	9	0.03
Japanese (14)	43	0.15
Korean (11)	20	0.07
Laotian (1)	1	<0.01
Malaysian (1)	1	<0.01
Nepalese (1)	1	<0.01
Pakistani (21)	32	0.11
Thai (18)	22	0.08
Vietnamese (12)	16	0.06
Hawaii Native/Pacific Islander (13)	40	0.14
Not Hispanic (10)	29	0.10
Hispanic (3)	11	0.04
Guamanian/Chamorro (1)	4	0.01
Native Hawaiian (10)	21	0.07
Samoan (2)	6	0.02
Tongan (0)	2	0.01
White (26,831)	27,438	94.33
Not Hispanic (25,327)	25,720	88.42
Hispanic (1,504)	1,718	5.91

Green River

Place Type: City
County: Sweetwater
Population: 12,515†

Ancestry‡	Population	%
American (620)	620	5.06
Australian (0)	77	0.63
Austrian (14)	37	0.30
Basque (40)	90	0.73
Belgian (0)	15	0.12
British (18)	105	0.86
Canadian (21)	36	0.29
Czech (36)	50	0.41
Czechoslovakian (21)	31	0.25
Danish (25)	527	4.30
Dutch (44)	313	2.55
English (1,070)	2,794	22.79
European (45)	81	0.66
Finnish (0)	15	0.12
French, ex. Basque (17)	227	1.85
French Canadian (109)	161	1.31
German (745)	3,179	25.93
Greek (38)	89	0.73
Hungarian (0)	13	0.11
Irish (336)	1,418	11.57
Italian (271)	583	4.76
Lithuanian (0)	14	0.11
Northern European (23)	23	0.19
Norwegian (184)	353	2.88
Pennsylvania German (0)	6	0.05
Polish (23)	197	1.61
Portuguese (0)	22	0.18
Russian (42)	112	0.91
Scandinavian (24)	80	0.65
Scotch-Irish (63)	219	1.79
Scottish (120)	460	3.75
Slavic (0)	23	0.19
Slovak (0)	31	0.25
Swedish (40)	319	2.60
Swiss (0)	36	0.29
Ukrainian (21)	51	0.42
Welsh (40)	218	1.78

Hispanic Origin	Population	%
Hispanic or Latino (of any race)	1,682	13.44
Central American, ex. Mexican	28	0.22

*Notes: † The Census 2010 population figure is used to calculate the percentages in the Hispanic Origin and Race categories. Ancestry percentages are based on the 2006-2010 American Community Survey population (not shown); ‡ Numbers in parentheses indicate the number of people reporting a single ancestry; * Numbers in parentheses indicate the number of persons reporting this race alone, not in combination with any other race; Please refer to the Explanation of Data for more information.*

Costa Rican	4	0.03
Guatemalan	2	0.02
Honduran	4	0.03
Panamanian	2	0.02
Salvadoran	15	0.12
Other Central American	1	0.01
Cuban	2	0.02
Dominican Republic	3	0.02
Mexican	1,296	10.36
Puerto Rican	21	0.17
South American	6	0.05
Argentinean	2	0.02
Bolivian	1	0.01
Colombian	1	0.01
Peruvian	1	0.01
Venezuelan	1	0.01
Other Hispanic or Latino	326	2.60

Race*	Population	%
African-American/Black (53)	76	0.61
Not Hispanic (52)	75	0.60
Hispanic (1)	1	0.01
American Indian/Alaska Native (106)	175	1.40
Not Hispanic (78)	136	1.09
Hispanic (28)	39	0.31
Alaska Athabascan *(Ala. Nat.)* (0)	1	0.01
Apache (0)	1	0.01
Arapaho (1)	1	0.01
Blackfeet (3)	3	0.02
Central American Ind. (2)	2	0.02
Cherokee (8)	15	0.12
Chickasaw (1)	1	0.01
Chippewa (16)	22	0.18
Choctaw (2)	4	0.03
Cree (2)	3	0.02
Crow (1)	2	0.02
Delaware (0)	1	0.01
Inupiat *(Alaska Native)* (1)	2	0.02
Mexican American Ind. (2)	2	0.02
Navajo (28)	29	0.23
Paiute (2)	2	0.02
Shoshone (6)	15	0.12
Sioux (3)	8	0.06
Spanish American Ind. (1)	1	0.01
Yaqui (1)	3	0.02
Yup'ik *(Alaska Native)* (1)	4	0.03
Asian (61)	116	0.93
Not Hispanic (58)	104	0.83
Hispanic (3)	12	0.10
Chinese, ex. Taiwanese (10)	15	0.12
Filipino (15)	43	0.34
Indian (11)	12	0.10
Japanese (12)	26	0.21
Korean (5)	13	0.10
Laotian (1)	1	0.01
Malaysian (1)	1	0.01
Vietnamese (1)	1	0.01
Hawaii Native/Pacific Islander (8)	38	0.30
Not Hispanic (8)	26	0.21
Hispanic (0)	12	0.10
Guamanian/Chamorro (0)	2	0.02
Native Hawaiian (6)	18	0.14
Samoan (1)	1	0.01
Tongan (0)	1	0.01
White (11,521)	11,748	93.87
Not Hispanic (10,486)	10,615	84.82
Hispanic (1,035)	1,133	9.05

Jackson

Place Type: Town
County: Teton
Population: 9,577†

Ancestry‡	Population	%
American (550)	550	5.83
Austrian (24)	41	0.43
Canadian (0)	18	0.19
Danish (0)	53	0.56
Dutch (0)	94	1.00
English (666)	1,019	10.79
European (169)	191	2.02
French, ex. Basque (0)	106	1.12
French Canadian (19)	38	0.40
German (950)	2,310	24.47
Hungarian (26)	70	0.74
Irish (493)	1,013	10.73
Italian (51)	171	1.81
Norwegian (45)	158	1.67
Polish (152)	260	2.75
Portuguese (13)	26	0.28
Russian (36)	36	0.38
Scandinavian (70)	112	1.19
Scotch-Irish (105)	399	4.23
Scottish (136)	429	4.54
Slovak (0)	30	0.32
Slovene (19)	19	0.20
Swedish (211)	446	4.72
Swiss (0)	60	0.64
Welsh (32)	94	1.00

Hispanic Origin	Population	%
Hispanic or Latino (of any race)	2,607	27.22
Central American, ex. Mexican	74	0.77
Costa Rican	4	0.04
Guatemalan	27	0.28
Honduran	2	0.02
Nicaraguan	2	0.02
Panamanian	1	0.01
Salvadoran	34	0.36
Other Central American	4	0.04
Cuban	7	0.07
Mexican	2,285	23.86
Puerto Rican	21	0.22
South American	39	0.41
Argentinean	6	0.06
Chilean	2	0.02
Colombian	13	0.14
Ecuadorian	5	0.05
Peruvian	13	0.14
Other Hispanic or Latino	181	1.89

Race*	Population	%
African-American/Black (35)	54	0.56
Not Hispanic (19)	31	0.32
Hispanic (16)	23	0.24
American Indian/Alaska Native (78)	147	1.53
Not Hispanic (46)	88	0.92
Hispanic (32)	59	0.62
Arapaho (5)	7	0.07
Blackfeet (0)	2	0.02
Canadian/French Am. Ind. (1)	1	0.01
Central American Ind. (0)	3	0.03
Cherokee (2)	16	0.17
Chippewa (2)	3	0.03
Choctaw (0)	1	0.01
Creek (0)	1	0.01
Crow (1)	1	0.01
Iroquois (0)	1	0.01
Lumbee (1)	1	0.01
Mexican American Ind. (8)	9	0.09
Navajo (12)	12	0.13
Osage (1)	2	0.02
Paiute (1)	2	0.02
Pueblo (2)	2	0.02
Sioux (5)	11	0.11
Tlingit-Haida *(Alaska Native)* (1)	1	0.01
Asian (138)	185	1.93
Not Hispanic (132)	175	1.83
Hispanic (6)	10	0.10
Bhutanese (4)	4	0.04
Burmese (3)	3	0.03
Cambodian (2)	5	0.05
Chinese, ex. Taiwanese (29)	44	0.46
Filipino (29)	46	0.48
Indian (10)	15	0.16
Indonesian (3)	4	0.04
Japanese (8)	24	0.25
Korean (11)	12	0.13
Laotian (1)	1	0.01
Malaysian (0)	2	0.02
Nepalese (7)	7	0.07
Pakistani (6)	6	0.06
Taiwanese (0)	1	0.01
Thai (5)	5	0.05
Vietnamese (5)	6	0.06
Hawaii Native/Pacific Islander (12)	21	0.22
Not Hispanic (11)	19	0.20
Hispanic (1)	2	0.02
Guamanian/Chamorro (1)	1	0.01
Native Hawaiian (6)	13	0.14
Samoan (2)	2	0.02
Tongan (1)	1	0.01
White (7,645)	7,841	81.87
Not Hispanic (6,628)	6,720	70.17
Hispanic (1,017)	1,121	11.71

Laramie

Place Type: City
County: Albany
Population: 30,816†

Ancestry‡	Population	%
African, Sub-Saharan (95)	95	0.32
South African (95)	95	0.32
Albanian (8)	24	0.08
American (1,313)	1,313	4.43
Arab (10)	39	0.13
Egyptian (10)	10	0.03
Lebanese (0)	16	0.05
Palestinian (0)	13	0.04
Australian (0)	11	0.04
Austrian (64)	141	0.48
Belgian (0)	43	0.14
British (95)	155	0.52
Bulgarian (56)	71	0.24
Cajun (16)	16	0.05
Canadian (0)	6	0.02
Celtic (10)	10	0.03
Croatian (20)	91	0.31
Czech (79)	265	0.89
Czechoslovakian (44)	44	0.15
Danish (117)	593	2.00
Dutch (169)	481	1.62
Eastern European (16)	35	0.12
English (899)	3,484	11.74
Estonian (0)	10	0.03
European (631)	708	2.39
Finnish (23)	154	0.52
French, ex. Basque (104)	849	2.86
French Canadian (55)	230	0.78
German (3,666)	9,261	31.21
Greek (215)	375	1.26
Hungarian (15)	78	0.26
Icelander (0)	11	0.04
Iranian (27)	32	0.11
Irish (921)	4,207	14.18
Italian (512)	1,013	3.41
Latvian (6)	6	0.02
Lithuanian (14)	55	0.19
Luxemburger (5)	5	0.02
New Zealander (12)	31	0.10
Northern European (113)	113	0.38
Norwegian (414)	979	3.30
Pennsylvania German (6)	6	0.02
Polish (228)	740	2.49
Portuguese (0)	18	0.06
Romanian (21)	36	0.12
Russian (57)	291	0.98
Scandinavian (117)	135	0.45
Scotch-Irish (250)	703	2.37
Scottish (183)	1,102	3.71
Slovak (14)	77	0.26
Slovene (8)	19	0.06
Swedish (126)	1,380	4.65
Swiss (67)	157	0.53
Ukrainian (19)	66	0.22
Welsh (42)	422	1.42
Yugoslavian (0)	5	0.02

*Notes: † The Census 2010 population figure is used to calculate the percentages in the Hispanic Origin and Race categories. Ancestry percentages are based on the 2006-2010 American Community Survey population (not shown); ‡ Numbers in parentheses indicate the number of people reporting a single ancestry; * Numbers in parentheses indicate the number of persons reporting this race alone, not in combination with any other race; Please refer to the Explanation of Data for more information.*

Hispanic Origin	Population	%
Hispanic or Latino (of any race)	2,840	9.22
Central American, ex. Mexican	44	0.14
Costa Rican	7	0.02
Guatemalan	14	0.05
Honduran	3	0.01
Nicaraguan	12	0.04
Panamanian	3	0.01
Salvadoran	5	0.02
Cuban	18	0.06
Dominican Republic	4	0.01
Mexican	2,013	6.53
Puerto Rican	65	0.21
South American	47	0.15
Argentinean	10	0.03
Bolivian	4	0.01
Chilean	4	0.01
Colombian	5	0.02
Ecuadorian	7	0.02
Paraguayan	1	<0.01
Peruvian	7	0.02
Venezuelan	9	0.03
Other Hispanic or Latino	649	2.11

Race*	Population	%
African-American/Black (407)	578	1.88
Not Hispanic (377)	511	1.66
Hispanic (30)	67	0.22
American Indian/Alaska Native (207)	458	1.49
Not Hispanic (157)	340	1.10
Hispanic (50)	118	0.38
Apache (3)	14	0.05
Arapaho (29)	41	0.13
Blackfeet (2)	5	0.02
Canadian/French Am. Ind. (0)	1	<0.01
Cherokee (13)	48	0.16
Cheyenne (4)	4	0.01
Chickasaw (2)	5	0.02
Chippewa (5)	9	0.03
Choctaw (1)	12	0.04
Comanche (0)	3	0.01
Cree (0)	1	<0.01
Creek (0)	2	0.01
Crow (1)	5	0.02
Delaware (1)	1	<0.01
Hopi (1)	1	<0.01
Iroquois (0)	3	0.01
Lumbee (1)	1	<0.01
Mexican American Ind. (3)	3	0.01
Navajo (10)	23	0.07
Osage (1)	2	0.01
Paiute (0)	1	<0.01
Potawatomi (2)	4	0.01
Pueblo (4)	7	0.02
Seminole (2)	3	0.01
Shoshone (9)	22	0.07
Sioux (14)	38	0.12
South American Ind. (1)	3	0.01
Spanish American Ind. (1)	1	<0.01
Tlingit-Haida *(Alaska Native)* (1)	5	0.02
Tohono O'Odham (3)	3	0.01
Ute (7)	9	0.03
Yup'ik *(Alaska Native)* (3)	4	0.01
Asian (996)	1,260	4.09
Not Hispanic (984)	1,218	3.95
Hispanic (12)	42	0.14
Bangladeshi (9)	10	0.03
Bhutanese (1)	1	<0.01
Burmese (0)	1	<0.01
Chinese, ex. Taiwanese (409)	442	1.43
Filipino (42)	108	0.35
Hmong (1)	1	<0.01
Indian (180)	198	0.64
Indonesian (9)	10	0.03
Japanese (55)	125	0.41
Korean (103)	134	0.43
Laotian (5)	5	0.02
Malaysian (11)	11	0.04
Nepalese (49)	49	0.16
Pakistani (2)	2	0.01
Sri Lankan (19)	20	0.06
Taiwanese (20)	21	0.07
Thai (19)	28	0.09
Vietnamese (26)	33	0.11
Hawaii Native/Pacific Islander (20)	62	0.20
Not Hispanic (16)	47	0.15
Hispanic (4)	15	0.05
Guamanian/Chamorro (3)	9	0.03
Native Hawaiian (5)	26	0.08
Samoan (6)	11	0.04
Tongan (2)	4	0.01
White (27,571)	28,377	92.09
Not Hispanic (25,825)	26,376	85.59
Hispanic (1,746)	2,001	6.49

Rawlins

Place Type: City
County: Carbon
Population: 9,259†

Ancestry‡	Population	%
American (590)	590	6.50
Austrian (0)	11	0.12
Canadian (0)	2	0.02
Czech (0)	51	0.56
Czechoslovakian (0)	8	0.09
Danish (23)	256	2.82
Dutch (24)	209	2.30
English (370)	947	10.43
European (128)	160	1.76
Finnish (0)	16	0.18
French, ex. Basque (51)	205	2.26
French Canadian (39)	54	0.59
German (972)	2,174	23.95
Greek (9)	48	0.53
Hungarian (7)	15	0.17
Irish (254)	1,074	11.83
Italian (110)	265	2.92
Norwegian (44)	142	1.56
Pennsylvania German (0)	7	0.08
Polish (12)	97	1.07
Portuguese (0)	12	0.13
Scandinavian (57)	77	0.85
Scotch-Irish (58)	205	2.26
Scottish (87)	451	4.97
Slavic (13)	13	0.14
Swedish (108)	224	2.47
Swiss (0)	19	0.21
Ukrainian (0)	4	0.04
Welsh (20)	51	0.56
Yugoslavian (13)	31	0.34

Hispanic Origin	Population	%
Hispanic or Latino (of any race)	2,248	24.28
Central American, ex. Mexican	24	0.26
Guatemalan	5	0.05
Honduran	11	0.12
Nicaraguan	6	0.06
Salvadoran	2	0.02
Cuban	4	0.04
Dominican Republic	2	0.02
Mexican	1,597	17.25
Puerto Rican	11	0.12
South American	17	0.18
Chilean	1	0.01
Colombian	13	0.14
Ecuadorian	1	0.01
Peruvian	2	0.02
Other Hispanic or Latino	593	6.40

Race*	Population	%
African-American/Black (100)	141	1.52
Not Hispanic (98)	130	1.40
Hispanic (2)	11	0.12
American Indian/Alaska Native (119)	177	1.91
Not Hispanic (90)	129	1.39
Hispanic (29)	48	0.52
Apache (1)	2	0.02
Arapaho (26)	27	0.29
Blackfeet (1)	2	0.02
Cherokee (4)	19	0.21
Cheyenne (6)	7	0.08
Chippewa (5)	6	0.06
Choctaw (1)	4	0.04
Comanche (0)	2	0.02
Mexican American Ind. (3)	8	0.09
Navajo (5)	6	0.06
Osage (0)	2	0.02
Pueblo (0)	2	0.02
Seminole (0)	1	0.01
Shoshone (4)	4	0.04
Sioux (18)	20	0.22
South American Ind. (1)	1	0.01
Spanish American Ind. (2)	3	0.03
Tohono O'Odham (0)	1	0.01
Ute (2)	2	0.02
Asian (92)	120	1.30
Not Hispanic (86)	102	1.10
Hispanic (6)	18	0.19
Chinese, ex. Taiwanese (13)	14	0.15
Filipino (28)	36	0.39
Indian (26)	30	0.32
Indonesian (1)	1	0.01
Japanese (3)	5	0.05
Korean (9)	11	0.12
Laotian (0)	3	0.03
Pakistani (6)	8	0.09
Thai (2)	2	0.02
Vietnamese (0)	5	0.05
Hawaii Native/Pacific Islander (13)	16	0.17
Not Hispanic (12)	15	0.16
Hispanic (1)	1	0.01
Guamanian/Chamorro (2)	2	0.02
Native Hawaiian (4)	5	0.05
Samoan (6)	7	0.08
White (7,839)	8,067	87.13
Not Hispanic (6,622)	6,710	72.47
Hispanic (1,217)	1,357	14.66

Riverton

Place Type: City
County: Fremont
Population: 10,615†

Ancestry‡	Population	%
African, Sub-Saharan (12)	16	0.16
African (12)	16	0.16
American (963)	963	9.40
Australian (15)	15	0.15
Austrian (25)	111	1.08
Belgian (0)	13	0.13
British (14)	31	0.30
Bulgarian (16)	16	0.16
Celtic (13)	13	0.13
Croatian (0)	9	0.09
Czech (25)	85	0.83
Danish (77)	272	2.65
Dutch (44)	282	2.75
English (384)	1,193	11.64
European (191)	291	2.84
Finnish (0)	96	0.94
French, ex. Basque (3)	269	2.63
French Canadian (0)	33	0.32
German (1,007)	2,807	27.40
German Russian (0)	20	0.20
Hungarian (13)	13	0.13
Irish (250)	1,328	12.96
Italian (51)	135	1.32
Northern European (19)	19	0.19
Norwegian (75)	383	3.74
Pennsylvania German (0)	28	0.27
Polish (12)	123	1.20
Portuguese (0)	17	0.17
Russian (15)	31	0.30
Scandinavian (60)	82	0.80
Scotch-Irish (163)	319	3.11
Scottish (84)	353	3.45
Serbian (6)	6	0.06

*Notes: † The Census 2010 population figure is used to calculate the percentages in the Hispanic Origin and Race categories. Ancestry percentages are based on the 2006-2010 American Community Survey population (not shown); ‡ Numbers in parentheses indicate the number of people reporting a single ancestry; * Numbers in parentheses indicate the number of persons reporting this race alone, not in combination with any other race; Please refer to the Explanation of Data for more information.*

Slavic (0)	10	0.10
Slovak (0)	6	0.06
Swedish (146)	284	2.77
Swiss (0)	80	0.78
Welsh (14)	48	0.47
West Indian, ex. Hispanic (37)	37	0.36
Jamaican (37)	37	0.36
Yugoslavian (9)	35	0.34

Hispanic Origin	Population	%
Hispanic or Latino (of any race)	956	9.01
Central American, ex. Mexican	13	0.12
Guatemalan	8	0.08
Honduran	3	0.03
Panamanian	2	0.02
Cuban	2	0.02
Mexican	652	6.14
Puerto Rican	13	0.12
South American	6	0.06
Chilean	1	0.01
Colombian	4	0.04
Venezuelan	1	0.01
Other Hispanic or Latino	270	2.54

Race*	Population	%
African-American/Black (50)	85	0.80
Not Hispanic (41)	68	0.64
Hispanic (9)	17	0.16
American Indian/Alaska Native (1,099)	1,362	12.83
Not Hispanic (947)	1,167	10.99
Hispanic (152)	195	1.84
Alaska Athabascan *(Ala. Nat.)* (0)	1	0.01
Aleut *(Alaska Native)* (1)	1	0.01
Apache (2)	10	0.09
Arapaho (599)	666	6.27
Blackfeet (12)	13	0.12
Canadian/French Am. Ind. (1)	1	0.01
Cherokee (15)	41	0.39
Cheyenne (12)	14	0.13
Chickasaw (1)	2	0.02
Chippewa (6)	10	0.09
Choctaw (1)	5	0.05
Comanche (1)	4	0.04
Cree (1)	1	0.01
Creek (1)	2	0.02
Crow (3)	5	0.05
Hopi (5)	5	0.05
Iroquois (1)	5	0.05
Kiowa (0)	1	0.01
Mexican American Ind. (1)	2	0.02
Navajo (17)	26	0.24
Paiute (0)	1	0.01
Pima (0)	1	0.01
Potawatomi (4)	4	0.04
Pueblo (1)	1	0.01
Puget Sound Salish (0)	1	0.01
Shoshone (121)	173	1.63
Sioux (39)	57	0.54
Ute (1)	2	0.02
Yakama (0)	1	0.01
Yup'ik *(Alaska Native)* (0)	2	0.02
Asian (35)	61	0.57
Not Hispanic (32)	55	0.52
Hispanic (3)	6	0.06
Cambodian (1)	1	0.01
Chinese, ex. Taiwanese (8)	11	0.10
Filipino (8)	23	0.22
Indian (8)	8	0.08
Japanese (5)	14	0.13
Korean (3)	8	0.08
Vietnamese (0)	1	0.01
Hawaii Native/Pacific Islander (6)	12	0.11
Not Hispanic (4)	10	0.09
Hispanic (2)	2	0.02
Guamanian/Chamorro (2)	2	0.02
Native Hawaiian (4)	9	0.08
White (8,862)	9,211	86.77
Not Hispanic (8,354)	8,624	81.24
Hispanic (508)	587	5.53

Rock Springs

Place Type: City
County: Sweetwater
Population: 23,036†

Ancestry‡	Population	%
American (865)	865	3.93
Austrian (14)	73	0.33
Basque (25)	78	0.35
British (29)	98	0.45
Bulgarian (0)	12	0.05
Cajun (0)	16	0.07
Canadian (0)	5	0.02
Croatian (21)	138	0.63
Czech (13)	70	0.32
Czechoslovakian (14)	149	0.68
Danish (51)	394	1.79
Dutch (178)	540	2.45
Eastern European (0)	9	0.04
English (1,353)	3,940	17.90
European (204)	214	0.97
Finnish (92)	301	1.37
French, ex. Basque (107)	983	4.46
French Canadian (0)	10	0.05
German (1,441)	4,275	19.42
Greek (85)	115	0.52
Hungarian (8)	42	0.19
Icelander (23)	61	0.28
Irish (767)	2,870	13.04
Italian (668)	1,926	8.75
Lithuanian (0)	8	0.04
Northern European (101)	114	0.52
Norwegian (91)	470	2.13
Polish (144)	552	2.51
Portuguese (13)	28	0.13
Romanian (0)	18	0.08
Russian (8)	185	0.84
Scandinavian (0)	9	0.04
Scotch-Irish (528)	906	4.12
Scottish (228)	1,175	5.34
Serbian (7)	13	0.06
Slavic (59)	254	1.15
Slovak (25)	47	0.21
Slovene (89)	191	0.87
Swedish (114)	603	2.74
Swiss (5)	40	0.18
Ukrainian (0)	11	0.05
Welsh (9)	189	0.86
Yugoslavian (113)	302	1.37

Hispanic Origin	Population	%
Hispanic or Latino (of any race)	3,771	16.37
Central American, ex. Mexican	152	0.66
Costa Rican	6	0.03
Guatemalan	93	0.40
Honduran	23	0.10
Nicaraguan	3	0.01
Panamanian	3	0.01
Salvadoran	24	0.10
Cuban	11	0.05
Dominican Republic	4	0.02
Mexican	2,819	12.24
Puerto Rican	22	0.10
South American	68	0.30
Argentinean	3	0.01
Chilean	6	0.03
Colombian	25	0.11
Ecuadorian	17	0.07
Peruvian	7	0.03
Uruguayan	4	0.02
Venezuelan	6	0.03
Other Hispanic or Latino	695	3.02

Race*	Population	%
African-American/Black (323)	455	1.98
Not Hispanic (305)	415	1.80
Hispanic (18)	40	0.17
American Indian/Alaska Native (189)	376	1.63
Not Hispanic (133)	257	1.12
Hispanic (56)	119	0.52
Alaska Athabascan *(Ala. Nat.)* (1)	1	<0.01
Apache (1)	14	0.06
Arapaho (11)	13	0.06
Blackfeet (2)	7	0.03
Cherokee (15)	61	0.26
Cheyenne (1)	1	<0.01
Chickasaw (4)	4	0.02
Chippewa (7)	14	0.06
Choctaw (6)	22	0.10
Comanche (0)	2	0.01
Cree (0)	2	0.01
Creek (2)	2	0.01
Crow (5)	6	0.03
Delaware (2)	2	0.01
Inupiat *(Alaska Native)* (0)	1	<0.01
Mexican American Ind. (6)	7	0.03
Navajo (17)	18	0.08
Osage (0)	1	<0.01
Paiute (1)	1	<0.01
Pueblo (1)	5	0.02
Shoshone (5)	11	0.05
Sioux (7)	11	0.05
Spanish American Ind. (3)	4	0.02
Tlingit-Haida *(Alaska Native)* (1)	1	<0.01
Ute (2)	2	0.01
Yaqui (1)	1	<0.01
Asian (248)	331	1.44
Not Hispanic (244)	326	1.42
Hispanic (4)	5	0.02
Burmese (1)	1	<0.01
Cambodian (2)	2	0.01
Chinese, ex. Taiwanese (78)	96	0.42
Filipino (27)	52	0.23
Hmong (1)	2	0.01
Indian (36)	45	0.20
Indonesian (7)	13	0.06
Japanese (31)	41	0.18
Korean (22)	26	0.11
Malaysian (1)	1	<0.01
Pakistani (9)	9	0.04
Sri Lankan (1)	3	0.01
Thai (5)	9	0.04
Vietnamese (18)	21	0.09
Hawaii Native/Pacific Islander (29)	58	0.25
Not Hispanic (29)	52	0.23
Hispanic (0)	6	0.03
Fijian (1)	3	0.01
Guamanian/Chamorro (9)	14	0.06
Native Hawaiian (8)	20	0.09
Samoan (3)	5	0.02
Tongan (5)	5	0.02
White (19,907)	20,463	88.83
Not Hispanic (18,217)	18,523	80.41
Hispanic (1,690)	1,940	8.42

Sheridan

Place Type: City
County: Sheridan
Population: 17,444†

Ancestry‡	Population	%
American (1,317)	1,317	7.74
Austrian (5)	55	0.32
Basque (0)	8	0.05
Belgian (0)	20	0.12
British (13)	40	0.24
Cajun (0)	13	0.08
Canadian (0)	10	0.06
Celtic (0)	28	0.16
Croatian (10)	10	0.06
Czech (36)	252	1.48
Czechoslovakian (19)	19	0.11
Danish (113)	377	2.22
Dutch (46)	227	1.33
Eastern European (37)	37	0.22
English (564)	1,919	11.28
European (147)	160	0.94
Finnish (24)	88	0.52

*Notes: † The Census 2010 population figure is used to calculate the percentages in the Hispanic Origin and Race categories. Ancestry percentages are based on the 2006-2010 American Community Survey population (not shown); ‡ Numbers in parentheses indicate the number of people reporting a single ancestry; * Numbers in parentheses indicate the number of persons reporting this race alone, not in combination with any other race; Please refer to the Explanation of Data for more information.*

Ancestry	Population	%
French, ex. Basque (65)	894	5.26
French Canadian (62)	177	1.04
German (1,684)	5,283	31.06
Greek (34)	43	0.25
Hungarian (18)	94	0.55
Iranian (12)	21	0.12
Irish (599)	2,920	17.17
Italian (186)	486	2.86
Lithuanian (0)	10	0.06
New Zealander (0)	9	0.05
Northern European (33)	33	0.19
Norwegian (302)	993	5.84
Pennsylvania German (0)	14	0.08
Polish (430)	825	4.85
Portuguese (0)	15	0.09
Romanian (0)	19	0.11
Russian (6)	142	0.83
Scandinavian (56)	169	0.99
Scotch-Irish (378)	773	4.55
Scottish (115)	524	3.08
Slavic (0)	13	0.08
Slovak (8)	28	0.16
Swedish (112)	744	4.37
Swiss (0)	95	0.56
Welsh (59)	261	1.53
West Indian, ex. Hispanic (2)	2	0.01
Barbadian (2)	2	0.01
Yugoslavian (0)	7	0.04

Hispanic Origin	Population	%
Hispanic or Latino (of any race)	751	4.31
Central American, ex. Mexican	27	0.15
Guatemalan	18	0.10
Nicaraguan	2	0.01
Panamanian	1	0.01
Salvadoran	6	0.03
Cuban	14	0.08
Mexican	580	3.32
Puerto Rican	28	0.16
South American	15	0.09
Argentinean	1	0.01
Bolivian	2	0.01
Chilean	1	0.01
Colombian	4	0.02
Ecuadorian	1	0.01
Peruvian	4	0.02
Venezuelan	2	0.01
Other Hispanic or Latino	87	0.50

Race*	Population	%
African-American/Black (77)	122	0.70
Not Hispanic (68)	108	0.62
Hispanic (9)	14	0.08
American Indian/Alaska Native (176)	330	1.89
Not Hispanic (158)	294	1.69
Hispanic (18)	36	0.21
Alaska Athabascan *(Ala. Nat.)* (1)	1	0.01
Aleut *(Alaska Native)* (0)	2	0.01
Apache (0)	12	0.07
Arapaho (5)	10	0.06
Blackfeet (2)	9	0.05
Cherokee (10)	30	0.17
Cheyenne (18)	24	0.14
Chickasaw (1)	1	0.01
Chippewa (4)	14	0.08
Choctaw (6)	11	0.06
Cree (0)	1	0.01
Creek (0)	1	0.01
Crow (28)	43	0.25
Hopi (1)	1	0.01
Iroquois (0)	2	0.01
Mexican American Ind. (4)	7	0.04
Navajo (7)	12	0.07
Paiute (0)	1	0.01
Potawatomi (0)	2	0.01
Shoshone (4)	5	0.03
Sioux (29)	44	0.25
Spanish American Ind. (1)	1	0.01
Tlingit-Haida *(Alaska Native)* (0)	1	0.01
Yuman (1)	1	0.01
Asian (153)	236	1.35
Not Hispanic (153)	232	1.33
Hispanic (0)	4	0.02
Cambodian (1)	1	0.01
Chinese, ex. Taiwanese (27)	47	0.27
Filipino (32)	63	0.36
Indian (13)	18	0.10
Indonesian (3)	5	0.03
Japanese (9)	26	0.15
Korean (27)	41	0.24
Laotian (1)	3	0.02
Malaysian (0)	1	0.01
Nepalese (1)	2	0.01
Thai (8)	8	0.05
Vietnamese (7)	8	0.05
Hawaii Native/Pacific Islander (15)	28	0.16
Not Hispanic (8)	18	0.10
Hispanic (7)	10	0.06
Guamanian/Chamorro (3)	3	0.02
Native Hawaiian (5)	12	0.07
Samoan (3)	8	0.05
White (16,558)	16,852	96.61
Not Hispanic (16,052)	16,290	93.38
Hispanic (506)	562	3.22

*Notes: † The Census 2010 population figure is used to calculate the percentages in the Hispanic Origin and Race categories. Ancestry percentages are based on the 2006-2010 American Community Survey population (not shown); ‡ Numbers in parentheses indicate the number of people reporting a single ancestry; * Numbers in parentheses indicate the number of persons reporting this race alone, not in combination with any other race; Please refer to the Explanation of Data for more information.*

SECTION THREE:
Statistical Rankings

Ancestry Group Rankings

Introduction

In this section of this book, each ethnicity contains four tables. The first table is split into two parts. Part one ranks the U.S. and all 50 states plus the District of Columbia by ethnic population. Part two ranks the same areas by percent of the total population. The second table shows the top 150 places sorted by ethnic population (based on all places, regardless of total population), the third table shows the top 150 places sorted by percent of the total population (based on all places, regardless of total population), the fourth table shows the top 150 places sorted by percent of the total population (based on places with total population of 7,500 or more).

Within each table, column one displays the place name, the state, and the county (if a place spans more than one county, the county that holds the majority of the population is shown). Column one in the first table displays the state only. Column two displays the number of people reporting each ancestry (includes people reporting multiple ancestries). Column three is the percent of the total population reporting each ancestry. The 2006-2010 five-year estimated population figure from the American Community Survey is used to calculate the value in the "%" column.

Alphabetical Ancestry Cross-Reference Guide

Afghan *see* Ancestry–Afghan
African *see* Ancestry–African, Sub-Saharan: African
Albanian *see* Ancestry–Albanian
Alsatian *see* Ancestry–Alsatian
American *see* Ancestry–American
Arab: Other *see* Ancestry–Arab: Other
Arab *see* Ancestry–Arab: Arab
Armenian *see* Ancestry–Armenian
Assyrian *see* Ancestry–Assyrian/Chaldean/Syriac
Australian *see* Ancestry–Australian
Austrian *see* Ancestry–Austrian
Bahamian *see* Ancestry–West Indian: Bahamian, except Hispanic
Barbadian *see* Ancestry–West Indian: Barbadian, except Hispanic
Basque *see* Ancestry–Basque
Belgian *see* Ancestry–Belgian
Belizean *see* Ancestry–West Indian: Belizean, except Hispanic
Bermudan *see* Ancestry–West Indian: Bermudan, except Hispanic
Brazilian *see* Ancestry–Brazilian
British West Indian *see* Ancestry–West Indian: British West Indian, except Hispanic
British *see* Ancestry–British
Bulgarian *see* Ancestry–Bulgarian
Cajun *see* Ancestry–Cajun
Canadian *see* Ancestry–Canadian
Cape Verdean *see* Ancestry–African, Sub-Saharan: Cape Verdean
Carpatho Rusyn *see* Ancestry–Carpatho Rusyn
Celtic *see* Ancestry–Celtic
Chaldean *see* Ancestry–Assyrian/Chaldean/Syriac
Croatian *see* Ancestry–Croatian
Cypriot *see* Ancestry–Cypriot
Czech *see* Ancestry–Czech
Czechoslovakian *see* Ancestry–Czechoslovakian
Danish *see* Ancestry–Danish
Dutch West Indian *see* Ancestry–West Indian: Dutch West Indian, except Hispanic
Dutch *see* Ancestry–Dutch
Eastern European *see* Ancestry–Eastern European
Egyptian *see* Ancestry–Arab: Egyptian
English *see* Ancestry–English
Estonian *see* Ancestry–Estonian
Ethiopian *see* Ancestry–African, Sub-Saharan: Ethiopian
European *see* Ancestry–European
Finnish *see* Ancestry–Finnish
French (except Basque) *see* Ancestry–French, except Basque
French Canadian *see* Ancestry–French Canadian
German Russian *see* Ancestry–German Russian
German *see* Ancestry–German
Ghanaian *see* Ancestry–African, Sub-Saharan: Ghanaian
Greek *see* Ancestry–Greek
Guyanese *see* Ancestry–Guyanese
Haitian *see* Ancestry–West Indian: Haitian, except Hispanic
Hungarian *see* Ancestry–Hungarian
Icelander *see* Ancestry–Icelander
Iranian *see* Ancestry–Iranian
Iraqi *see* Ancestry–Arab: Iraqi
Irish *see* Ancestry–Irish
Israeli *see* Ancestry–Israeli
Italian *see* Ancestry–Italian
Jamaican *see* Ancestry–West Indian: Jamaican, except Hispanic
Jordanian *see* Ancestry–Arab: Jordanian
Kenyan *see* Ancestry–African, Sub-Saharan: Kenyan
Latvian *see* Ancestry–Latvian
Lebanese *see* Ancestry–Arab: Lebanese
Liberian *see* Ancestry–African, Sub-Saharan: Liberian
Lithuanian *see* Ancestry–Lithuanian
Luxemburger *see* Ancestry–Luxemburger
Macedonian *see* Ancestry–Macedonian
Maltese *see* Ancestry–Maltese
Moroccan *see* Ancestry–Arab: Moroccan
New Zealander *see* Ancestry–New Zealander
Nigerian *see* Ancestry–African, Sub-Saharan: Nigerian
Northern European *see* Ancestry–Northern European
Norwegian *see* Ancestry–Norwegian
Palestinian *see* Ancestry–Arab: Palestinian
Pennsylvania German *see* Ancestry–Pennsylvania German
Polish *see* Ancestry–Polish
Portuguese *see* Ancestry–Portuguese
Romanian *see* Ancestry–Romanian
Russian *see* Ancestry–Russian
Scandinavian *see* Ancestry–Scandinavian
Scotch-Irish *see* Ancestry–Scotch-Irish
Scottish *see* Ancestry–Scottish
Senegalese *see* Ancestry–African, Sub-Saharan: Senegalese
Serbian *see* Ancestry–Serbian
Sierra Leonean *see* Ancestry–African, Sub-Saharan: Sierra Leonean
Slavic *see* Ancestry–Slavic
Slovak *see* Ancestry–Slovak
Slovene *see* Ancestry–Slovene
Somalian *see* Ancestry–African, Sub-Saharan: Somalian
South African *see* Ancestry–African, Sub-Saharan: South African
Soviet Union *see* Ancestry–Soviet Union
Sub-Saharan African: Other *see* Ancestry–African, Sub-Saharan: Other
Sub-Saharan African *see* Ancestry–African, Sub-Saharan
Sudanese *see* Ancestry–African, Sub-Saharan: Sudanese
Swedish *see* Ancestry–Swedish
Swiss *see* Ancestry–Swiss
Syriac *see* Ancestry–Assyrian/Chaldean/Syriac
Syrian *see* Ancestry–Arab: Syrian
Trinidadian and Tobagonian *see* Ancestry–West Indian: Trinidadian and Tobagonian, except Hispanic
Turkish *see* Ancestry–Turkish
U.S. Virgin Islander *see* Ancestry–West Indian: U.S. Virgin Islander, except Hispanic
Ugandan *see* Ancestry–African, Sub-Saharan: Ugandan
Ukrainian *see* Ancestry–Ukrainian
Welsh *see* Ancestry–Welsh
West Indian (except Hispanic) *see* Ancestry–West Indian, except Hispanic
West Indian: Other *see* Ancestry–West Indian: Other, except Hispanic
West Indian *see* Ancestry–West Indian: West Indian, except Hispanic
Yugoslavian *see* Ancestry–Yugoslavian
Zimbabwean *see* Ancestry–African, Sub-Saharan: Zimbabwean

Please refer to the Explanation of Data in the front of the book for more detailed information.

Ancestry

Afghan

U.S. and 50 States Sorted by Population and Percent of Total Population

Place	Population	%
United States	**77,029**	**0.03**
California	33,216	0.09
Virginia	10,953	0.14
New York	10,755	0.06
New Jersey	2,907	0.03
Texas	2,204	0.01
Missouri	1,433	0.02
Arizona	1,386	0.02
Georgia	1,364	0.01
Colorado	1,111	0.02
Nevada	1,101	0.04
Florida	1,078	0.01
Illinois	1,058	0.01
Maryland	1,025	0.02
Pennsylvania	876	0.01
North Carolina	841	0.01
Massachusetts	723	0.01
Washington	693	0.01
Connecticut	478	0.01
Minnesota	452	0.01
Ohio	403	<0.01
Tennessee	329	0.01
Nebraska	287	0.02
Indiana	261	<0.01
Oregon	237	0.01
Iowa	202	0.01
Idaho	193	0.01
Maine	183	0.01
New Mexico	179	0.01
Michigan	174	<0.01
Utah	158	0.01
Kentucky	157	<0.01
District of Columbia	121	0.02
Kansas	95	<0.01
Louisiana	92	<0.01
Delaware	86	0.01
Wisconsin	78	<0.01
Alabama	59	<0.01
South Dakota	20	<0.01
Hawaii	13	<0.01
West Virginia	12	<0.01
Rhode Island	11	<0.01
Arkansas	10	<0.01
Vermont	10	<0.01
Wyoming	5	<0.01
Alaska	0	0.00
Mississippi	0	0.00
Montana	0	0.00
New Hampshire	0	0.00
North Dakota	0	0.00
Oklahoma	0	0.00
South Carolina	0	0.00

Place	Population	%
Virginia	10,953	0.14
California	33,216	0.09
New York	10,755	0.06
Nevada	1,101	0.04
United States	**77,029**	**0.03**
New Jersey	2,907	0.03
Missouri	1,433	0.02
Arizona	1,386	0.02
Colorado	1,111	0.02
Maryland	1,025	0.02
Nebraska	287	0.02
District of Columbia	121	0.02
Texas	2,204	0.01
Georgia	1,364	0.01
Florida	1,078	0.01
Illinois	1,058	0.01
Pennsylvania	876	0.01
North Carolina	841	0.01
Massachusetts	723	0.01
Washington	693	0.01
Connecticut	478	0.01
Minnesota	452	0.01
Tennessee	329	0.01
Oregon	237	0.01
Iowa	202	0.01
Idaho	193	0.01
Maine	183	0.01
New Mexico	179	0.01
Utah	158	0.01
Delaware	86	0.01
Ohio	403	<0.01
Indiana	261	<0.01
Michigan	174	<0.01
Kentucky	157	<0.01
Kansas	95	<0.01
Louisiana	92	<0.01
Wisconsin	78	<0.01
Alabama	59	<0.01
South Dakota	20	<0.01
Hawaii	13	<0.01
West Virginia	12	<0.01
Rhode Island	11	<0.01
Arkansas	10	<0.01
Vermont	10	<0.01
Wyoming	5	<0.01
Alaska	0	0.00
Mississippi	0	0.00
Montana	0	0.00
New Hampshire	0	0.00
North Dakota	0	0.00
Oklahoma	0	0.00
South Carolina	0	0.00

Please refer to the Explanation of Data in the front of the book for more detailed information.

Ancestry

Afghan

Top 150 Places Sorted by Population

Based on all places, regardless of total population

Place	Population	%
New York, NY (city) Kings County	6,470	0.08
Queens, NY (borough) Queens County	6,027	0.27
Fremont, CA (city) Alameda County	2,760	1.32
Los Angeles, CA (city) Los Angeles County	2,434	0.06
San Diego, CA (city) San Diego County	1,850	0.14
Concord, CA (city) Contra Costa County	1,655	1.36
Elk Grove, CA (city) Sacramento County	1,211	0.86
Irvine, CA (city) Orange County	1,177	0.59
Union City, CA (city) Alameda County	1,085	1.59
Tracy, CA (city) San Joaquin County	953	1.20
St. Louis, MO (city) St. Louis city County	926	0.29
San Jose, CA (city) Santa Clara County	925	0.10
Hayward, CA (city) Alameda County	826	0.58
Oyster Bay, NY (town) Nassau County	808	0.28
Antioch, CA (city) Contra Costa County	725	0.73
Alexandria, VA (ind. city) Alexandria independent city	701	0.52
Annandale, VA (cdp) Fairfax County	650	1.69
Simi Valley, CA (city) Ventura County	638	0.52
Parsippany-Troy Hills, NJ (township) Morris County	588	1.11
Sacramento, CA (city) Sacramento County	580	0.13
Oakland, CA (city) Alameda County	551	0.14
Phoenix, AZ (city) Maricopa County	516	0.04
Newark, NJ (city) Essex County	505	0.18
El Cajon, CA (city) San Diego County	484	0.49
Newark, CA (city) Alameda County	474	1.13
Milpitas, CA (city) Santa Clara County	454	0.70
South Riding, VA (cdp) Loudoun County	437	1.90
Garden Grove, CA (city) Orange County	434	0.26
Dublin, CA (city) Alameda County	428	1.00
Manteca, CA (city) San Joaquin County	416	0.64
Franconia, VA (cdp) Fairfax County	410	2.22
Hempstead, NY (town) Nassau County	399	0.05
Centreville, VA (cdp) Fairfax County	387	0.53
Cary, NC (town) Wake County	369	0.29
Gainesville, VA (cdp) Prince William County	353	3.27
Brooklyn, NY (borough) Kings County	344	0.01
Alameda, CA (city) Alameda County	337	0.46
Moreno Valley, CA (city) Riverside County	337	0.18
Hicksville, NY (cdp) Nassau County	323	0.77
Summerlin South, NV (cdp) Clark County	321	1.47
Tucson, AZ (city) Pima County	320	0.06
Schenectady, NY (city) Schenectady County	318	0.49
Raleigh, NC (city) Wake County	318	0.08
Castro Valley, CA (cdp) Alameda County	316	0.52
Huntington, NY (town) Suffolk County	314	0.16
Anaheim, CA (city) Orange County	308	0.09
Glen Ellyn, IL (village) DuPage County	305	1.11
Carlsbad, CA (city) San Diego County	302	0.30
Torrance, CA (city) Los Angeles County	298	0.21
Worcester, MA (city) Worcester County	291	0.16
Mountain House, CA (cdp) San Joaquin County	284	3.79
Fairfield, CA (city) Solano County	271	0.26
Kent, WA (city) King County	269	0.30
Huntington Station, NY (cdp) Suffolk County	268	0.85
Nashville-Davidson, TN (metro govt) Davidson County	266	0.05
Spring Valley, NV (cdp) Clark County	265	0.16
Islip, NY (town) Suffolk County	263	0.08
Aliso Viejo, CA (city) Orange County	262	0.57
Aurora, IL (city) Kane County	261	0.14
Ashburn, VA (cdp) Loudoun County	256	0.60
Modesto, CA (city) Stanislaus County	256	0.13
Ripon, CA (city) San Joaquin County	251	1.82
Omaha, NE (city) Douglas County	241	0.06
Temecula, CA (city) Riverside County	240	0.25
Fontana, CA (city) San Bernardino County	238	0.13
Fort Worth, TX (city) Tarrant County	235	0.03
Chicago, IL (city) Cook County	234	0.01
Kingstowne, VA (cdp) Fairfax County	229	1.58
East Lake-Orient Park, FL (cdp) Hillsborough County	229	0.96
Houston, TX (city) Harris County	224	0.01
Glendale, AZ (city) Maricopa County	223	0.10
Rancho Cucamonga, CA (city) San Bernardino County	219	0.14
Babylon, NY (town) Suffolk County	219	0.10
Rocklin, CA (city) Placer County	216	0.40
Paradise, NV (cdp) Clark County	215	0.10
Clifton Park, NY (town) Saratoga County	214	0.59
Redondo Beach, CA (city) Los Angeles County	210	0.32
Edison, NJ (township) Middlesex County	209	0.21
Boca Raton, FL (city) Palm Beach County	204	0.24
North Hempstead, NY (town) Nassau County	203	0.09
Brentwood, CA (city) Contra Costa County	200	0.43
Lake Ridge, VA (cdp) Prince William County	199	0.50
Franklin Farm, VA (cdp) Fairfax County	196	1.00
Burke, VA (cdp) Fairfax County	190	0.46
Springfield, VA (cdp) Fairfax County	189	0.62
Fullerton, CA (city) Orange County	188	0.14
Denver, CO (city) Denver County	188	0.03
Vista, CA (city) San Diego County	186	0.20
Mesa, AZ (city) Maricopa County	185	0.04
Glenn Dale, MD (cdp) Prince George's County	184	1.30
Fair Oaks, VA (cdp) Fairfax County	182	0.66
West Springfield, VA (cdp) Fairfax County	181	0.81
Malden, MA (city) Middlesex County	180	0.31
Santa Clarita, CA (city) Los Angeles County	180	0.10
Livermore, CA (city) Alameda County	179	0.23
Laguna Niguel, CA (city) Orange County	178	0.28
Buffalo, NY (city) Erie County	178	0.07
Jacksonville, FL (city) Duval County	178	0.02
Stockbridge, GA (city) Henry County	177	0.75
Penfield, NY (town) Monroe County	177	0.49
Shakopee, MN (city) Scott County	175	0.50
Muhlenberg, PA (township) Berks County	169	0.88
Murrieta, CA (city) Riverside County	165	0.17
Martinez, CA (city) Contra Costa County	163	0.46
Stone Ridge, VA (cdp) Loudoun County	161	2.67
Santa Clara, CA (city) Santa Clara County	160	0.14
Arlington, VA (cdp) Arlington County	160	0.08
Manassas Park, VA (ind. city) Manassas Park independent city	159	1.21
Portland, ME (city) Cumberland County	158	0.24
San Francisco, CA (city) San Francisco County	158	0.02
Contra Costa Centre, CA (cdp) Contra Costa County	155	2.77
West Sacramento, CA (city) Yolo County	155	0.34
Davis, CA (city) Yolo County	154	0.24
Dranesville, VA (cdp) Fairfax County	153	1.22
Pittsford, NY (town) Monroe County	153	0.53
Pleasanton, CA (city) Alameda County	153	0.22
Aurora, CO (city) Arapahoe County	153	0.05
Wolf Trap, VA (cdp) Fairfax County	152	0.91
Lake Forest, CA (city) Orange County	150	0.20
Stockton, CA (city) San Joaquin County	150	0.05
Teaneck, NJ (township) Bergen County	149	0.38
Columbia, MD (cdp) Howard County	148	0.15
Pittsburg, CA (city) Contra Costa County	147	0.24
Louisville-Jefferson County, KY (metro govt) Jefferson County	146	0.02
Irondequoit, NY (cdp/town) Monroe County	145	0.28
Kansas City, MO (city) Jackson County	145	0.03
Amherst, NY (town) Erie County	144	0.12
Reston, VA (cdp) Fairfax County	142	0.27
Eureka, CA (city) Humboldt County	141	0.52
Lathrop, CA (city) San Joaquin County	140	0.82
Malverne, NY (village) Nassau County	139	1.63
Chantilly, VA (cdp) Fairfax County	139	0.63
Atascocita, TX (cdp) Harris County	135	0.22
Thornton, CO (city) Adams County	135	0.12
Oakley, CA (city) Contra Costa County	133	0.40
Jericho, NY (cdp) Nassau County	129	0.99
Albuquerque, NM (city) Bernalillo County	129	0.02
Woodbury, NY (cdp) Nassau County	125	1.38
Ridgefield Park, NJ (village) Bergen County	125	0.99
Wyandanch, NY (cdp) Suffolk County	123	1.13
Belmont, VA (cdp) Loudoun County	121	2.30
Washington, DC (city) District of Columbia	121	0.02
Hyde Park, PA (cdp) Berks County	120	4.54
Alafaya, FL (cdp) Orange County	120	0.16
Groveton, VA (cdp) Fairfax County	119	0.87
McKinney, TX (city) Collin County	119	0.10
San Ramon, CA (city) Contra Costa County	118	0.18
Upper Darby, PA (township) Delaware County	115	0.14
Garland, TX (city) Dallas County	114	0.05
Pleasant Hill, CA (city) Contra Costa County	113	0.34

Please refer to the Explanation of Data in the front of the book for more detailed information.

Ancestry

Afghan

Top 150 Places Sorted by Percent of Total Population

Based on all places, regardless of total population

Place	Population	%
McFall, MO (city) Gentry County	20	9.35
Piney Mountain, VA (cdp) Albemarle County	77	5.74
Hyde Park, PA (cdp) Berks County	120	4.54
Mountain House, CA (cdp) San Joaquin County	284	3.79
Gainesville, VA (cdp) Prince William County	353	3.27
Contra Costa Centre, CA (cdp) Contra Costa County	155	2.77
Stone Ridge, VA (cdp) Loudoun County	161	2.67
Howard Lake, MN (city) Wright County	38	2.32
Belmont, VA (cdp) Loudoun County	121	2.30
Goshen, VA (town) Rockbridge County	11	2.30
Franconia, VA (cdp) Fairfax County	410	2.22
DeRuyter, NY (town) Madison County	27	2.14
San Antonio Heights, CA (cdp) San Bernardino County	79	1.99
South Riding, VA (cdp) Loudoun County	437	1.90
Ripon, CA (city) San Joaquin County	251	1.82
Pomona, NY (village) Rockland County	61	1.73
Annandale, VA (cdp) Fairfax County	650	1.69
Malverne, NY (village) Nassau County	139	1.63
Union City, CA (city) Alameda County	1,085	1.59
Kingstowne, VA (cdp) Fairfax County	229	1.58
Viola, NY (cdp) Rockland County	111	1.57
Summerlin South, NV (cdp) Clark County	321	1.47
Huntington Bay, NY (village) Suffolk County	21	1.47
Woodbury, NY (cdp) Nassau County	125	1.38
Concord, CA (city) Contra Costa County	1,655	1.36
Vinton, VA (town) Roanoke County	110	1.36
Fremont, CA (city) Alameda County	2,760	1.32
Glenn Dale, MD (cdp) Prince George's County	184	1.30
Dranesville, VA (cdp) Fairfax County	153	1.22
Laurel Hill, VA (cdp) Fairfax County	74	1.22
Sycamore Hills, MO (village) St. Louis County	8	1.22
Manassas Park, VA (ind. city) Manassas Park independent city	159	1.21
Lawrenceville, VA (town) Brunswick County	24	1.21
Thayne, WY (town) Lincoln County	5	1.21
Tracy, CA (city) San Joaquin County	953	1.20
Potomac Mills, VA (cdp) Prince William County	56	1.19
Westmore, VT (town) Orleans County	4	1.19
Twin Rivers, NJ (cdp) Mercer County	81	1.15
Newark, CA (city) Alameda County	474	1.13
Wyandanch, NY (cdp) Suffolk County	123	1.13
Lima, MI (township) Washtenaw County	36	1.13
Parsippany-Troy Hills, NJ (township) Morris County	588	1.11
Glen Ellyn, IL (village) DuPage County	305	1.11
Brigantine, NJ (city) Atlantic County	112	1.11
Cheshire Village, CT (cdp) New Haven County	57	1.07
New Salem, MA (town) Franklin County	10	1.07
Seven Corners, VA (cdp) Fairfax County	87	1.04
Dublin, CA (city) Alameda County	428	1.00
Franklin Farm, VA (cdp) Fairfax County	196	1.00
Triangle, VA (cdp) Prince William County	77	1.00
Jericho, NY (cdp) Nassau County	129	0.99
Ridgefield Park, NJ (village) Bergen County	125	0.99
Toro Canyon, CA (cdp) Santa Barbara County	13	0.97
East Lake-Orient Park, FL (cdp) Hillsborough County	229	0.96
Clinton, CT (cdp) Middlesex County	33	0.95
New Hyde Park, NY (village) Nassau County	89	0.93
Underwood-Petersville, AL (cdp) Lauderdale County	32	0.92
Wolf Trap, VA (cdp) Fairfax County	152	0.91
Fox Chapel, PA (borough) Allegheny County	49	0.91
Muhlenberg, PA (township) Berks County	169	0.88
Groveton, VA (cdp) Fairfax County	119	0.87
Upper Brookville, NY (village) Nassau County	13	0.87
Sunset Valley, TX (city) Travis County	4	0.87
Elk Grove, CA (city) Sacramento County	1,211	0.86
Lansdowne, VA (cdp) Loudoun County	84	0.86
Blackhawk, CA (cdp) Contra Costa County	83	0.86
Huntington Station, NY (cdp) Suffolk County	268	0.85
Lathrop, CA (city) San Joaquin County	140	0.82
West Springfield, VA (cdp) Fairfax County	181	0.81
Lake Luzerne, NY (cdp) Warren County	9	0.80
Fairview, CA (cdp) Alameda County	78	0.79
Hicksville, NY (cdp) Nassau County	323	0.77
Cedarhurst, NY (village) Nassau County	50	0.77
Bremen, GA (city) Haralson County	46	0.77
Stockbridge, GA (city) Henry County	177	0.75
Delhi, CA (cdp) Merced County	79	0.75
Antioch, CA (city) Contra Costa County	725	0.73
Lackland AFB, TX (cdp) Bexar County	55	0.73
Manorhaven, NY (village) Nassau County	46	0.72
Milpitas, CA (city) Santa Clara County	454	0.70
Muttontown, NY (village) Nassau County	24	0.70
Saranap, CA (cdp) Contra Costa County	34	0.69
Fairfax Station, VA (cdp) Fairfax County	80	0.68
Platte Center, NE (village) Platte County	3	0.68
East Islip, NY (cdp) Suffolk County	93	0.67
Fair Oaks, VA (cdp) Fairfax County	182	0.66
Bethpage, NY (cdp) Nassau County	109	0.66
Indiana, PA (township) Allegheny County	47	0.66
East Farmingdale, NY (cdp) Suffolk County	40	0.65
Montgomery, NY (village) Orange County	25	0.65
Manteca, CA (city) San Joaquin County	416	0.64
Abington, PA (township) Lackawanna County	11	0.64
Chantilly, VA (cdp) Fairfax County	139	0.63
Springfield, VA (cdp) Fairfax County	189	0.62
York, IN (town) Delaware County	57	0.62
Air Force Academy, CO (cdp) El Paso County	51	0.62
Urbana, MD (cdp) Frederick County	45	0.62
Ashburn, VA (cdp) Loudoun County	256	0.60
Lakeside, VA (cdp) Henrico County	72	0.60
Lafayette, PA (township) McKean County	15	0.60
Irvine, CA (city) Orange County	1,177	0.59
Clifton Park, NY (town) Saratoga County	214	0.59
Eastham, MA (town) Barnstable County	30	0.59
Hayward, CA (city) Alameda County	826	0.58
Burke Centre, VA (cdp) Fairfax County	99	0.58
Aliso Viejo, CA (city) Orange County	262	0.57
Newington Forest, VA (cdp) Fairfax County	73	0.56
Smyrna, DE (town) Kent County	52	0.56
Sappington, MO (cdp) St. Louis County	45	0.56
Centreville, VA (cdp) Fairfax County	387	0.53
Pittsford, NY (town) Monroe County	153	0.53
Ladera Ranch, CA (cdp) Orange County	97	0.53
Alexandria, VA (ind. city) Alexandria independent city	701	0.52
Simi Valley, CA (city) Ventura County	638	0.52
Castro Valley, CA (cdp) Alameda County	316	0.52
Eureka, CA (city) Humboldt County	141	0.52
White Oak, MD (cdp) Montgomery County	87	0.52
Hermosa Beach, CA (city) Los Angeles County	98	0.51
Flossmoor, IL (village) Cook County	47	0.51
Lake Ridge, VA (cdp) Prince William County	199	0.50
Shakopee, MN (city) Scott County	175	0.50
El Cajon, CA (city) San Diego County	484	0.49
Schenectady, NY (city) Schenectady County	318	0.49
Penfield, NY (town) Monroe County	177	0.49
Upper Saddle River, NJ (borough) Bergen County	39	0.48
New Milford, NJ (borough) Bergen County	77	0.47
Alameda, CA (city) Alameda County	337	0.46
Burke, VA (cdp) Fairfax County	190	0.46
Martinez, CA (city) Contra Costa County	163	0.46
Tukwila, WA (city) King County	86	0.46
Newington, VA (cdp) Fairfax County	61	0.46
Dexter, NM (town) Chaves County	6	0.46
Idylwood, VA (cdp) Fairfax County	70	0.45
Hybla Valley, VA (cdp) Fairfax County	66	0.45
Lorton, VA (cdp) Fairfax County	85	0.44
Brentwood, CA (city) Contra Costa County	200	0.43
Clarksburg, MD (cdp) Montgomery County	44	0.42
Rocklin, CA (city) Placer County	216	0.40
Oakley, CA (city) Contra Costa County	133	0.40
Vineyard, CA (cdp) Sacramento County	102	0.40
Fredericksburg, VA (ind. city) Fredericksburg independent city	93	0.40
Lone Tree, CO (city) Douglas County	40	0.40
Rose Hill, VA (cdp) Fairfax County	77	0.39
Riverdale, NJ (borough) Morris County	13	0.39
Winters, TX (city) Runnels County	10	0.39
Teaneck, NJ (township) Bergen County	149	0.38
Cockeysville, MD (cdp) Baltimore County	76	0.38
Long Branch, VA (cdp) Fairfax County	30	0.38
Saddle Rock, NY (village) Nassau County	4	0.38
West Falls Church, VA (cdp) Fairfax County	101	0.37

Please refer to the Explanation of Data in the front of the book for more detailed information.

Ancestry

Afghan

Top 150 Places Sorted by Percent of Total Population

Based on places with total population of 7,500 or more

Place	Population	%
Gainesville, VA (cdp) Prince William County	353	3.27
Franconia, VA (cdp) Fairfax County	410	2.22
South Riding, VA (cdp) Loudoun County	437	1.90
Ripon, CA (city) San Joaquin County	251	1.82
Annandale, VA (cdp) Fairfax County	650	1.69
Malverne, NY (village) Nassau County	139	1.63
Union City, CA (city) Alameda County	1,085	1.59
Kingstowne, VA (cdp) Fairfax County	229	1.58
Summerlin South, NV (cdp) Clark County	321	1.47
Woodbury, NY (cdp) Nassau County	125	1.38
Concord, CA (city) Contra Costa County	1,655	1.36
Vinton, VA (town) Roanoke County	110	1.36
Fremont, CA (city) Alameda County	2,760	1.32
Glenn Dale, MD (cdp) Prince George's County	184	1.30
Dranesville, VA (cdp) Fairfax County	153	1.22
Manassas Park, VA (ind. city) Manassas Park independent city	159	1.21
Tracy, CA (city) San Joaquin County	953	1.20
Newark, CA (city) Alameda County	474	1.13
Wyandanch, NY (cdp) Suffolk County	123	1.13
Parsippany-Troy Hills, NJ (township) Morris County	588	1.11
Glen Ellyn, IL (village) DuPage County	305	1.11
Brigantine, NJ (city) Atlantic County	112	1.11
Seven Corners, VA (cdp) Fairfax County	87	1.04
Dublin, CA (city) Alameda County	428	1.00
Franklin Farm, VA (cdp) Fairfax County	196	1.00
Triangle, VA (cdp) Prince William County	77	1.00
Jericho, NY (cdp) Nassau County	129	0.99
Ridgefield Park, NJ (village) Bergen County	125	0.99
East Lake-Orient Park, FL (cdp) Hillsborough County	229	0.96
New Hyde Park, NY (village) Nassau County	89	0.93
Wolf Trap, VA (cdp) Fairfax County	152	0.91
Muhlenberg, PA (township) Berks County	169	0.88
Groveton, VA (cdp) Fairfax County	119	0.87
Elk Grove, CA (city) Sacramento County	1,211	0.86
Lansdowne, VA (cdp) Loudoun County	84	0.86
Blackhawk, CA (cdp) Contra Costa County	83	0.86
Huntington Station, NY (cdp) Suffolk County	268	0.85
Lathrop, CA (city) San Joaquin County	140	0.82
West Springfield, VA (cdp) Fairfax County	181	0.81
Fairview, CA (cdp) Alameda County	78	0.79
Hicksville, NY (cdp) Nassau County	323	0.77
Stockbridge, GA (city) Henry County	177	0.75
Delhi, CA (cdp) Merced County	79	0.75
Antioch, CA (city) Contra Costa County	725	0.73
Lackland AFB, TX (cdp) Bexar County	55	0.73
Milpitas, CA (city) Santa Clara County	454	0.70
Fairfax Station, VA (cdp) Fairfax County	80	0.68
East Islip, NY (cdp) Suffolk County	93	0.67
Fair Oaks, VA (cdp) Fairfax County	182	0.66
Bethpage, NY (cdp) Nassau County	109	0.66
Manteca, CA (city) San Joaquin County	416	0.64
Chantilly, VA (cdp) Fairfax County	139	0.63
Springfield, VA (cdp) Fairfax County	189	0.62
York, IN (town) Delaware County	57	0.62
Air Force Academy, CO (cdp) El Paso County	51	0.62
Ashburn, VA (cdp) Loudoun County	256	0.60
Lakeside, VA (cdp) Henrico County	72	0.60
Irvine, CA (city) Orange County	1,177	0.59
Clifton Park, NY (town) Saratoga County	214	0.59
Hayward, CA (city) Alameda County	826	0.58
Burke Centre, VA (cdp) Fairfax County	99	0.58
Aliso Viejo, CA (city) Orange County	262	0.57
Newington Forest, VA (cdp) Fairfax County	73	0.56
Smyrna, DE (town) Kent County	52	0.56
Sappington, MO (cdp) St. Louis County	45	0.56
Centreville, VA (cdp) Fairfax County	387	0.53
Pittsford, NY (town) Monroe County	153	0.53
Ladera Ranch, CA (cdp) Orange County	97	0.53
Alexandria, VA (ind. city) Alexandria independent city	701	0.52
Simi Valley, CA (city) Ventura County	638	0.52
Castro Valley, CA (cdp) Alameda County	316	0.52
Eureka, CA (city) Humboldt County	141	0.52
White Oak, MD (cdp) Montgomery County	87	0.52
Hermosa Beach, CA (city) Los Angeles County	98	0.51
Flossmoor, IL (village) Cook County	47	0.51
Lake Ridge, VA (cdp) Prince William County	199	0.50
Shakopee, MN (city) Scott County	175	0.50
El Cajon, CA (city) San Diego County	484	0.49
Schenectady, NY (city) Schenectady County	318	0.49
Penfield, NY (town) Monroe County	177	0.49
Upper Saddle River, NJ (borough) Bergen County	39	0.48
New Milford, NJ (borough) Bergen County	77	0.47
Alameda, CA (city) Alameda County	337	0.46
Burke, VA (cdp) Fairfax County	190	0.46
Martinez, CA (city) Contra Costa County	163	0.46
Tukwila, WA (city) King County	86	0.46
Newington, VA (cdp) Fairfax County	61	0.46
Idylwood, VA (cdp) Fairfax County	70	0.45
Hybla Valley, VA (cdp) Fairfax County	66	0.45
Lorton, VA (cdp) Fairfax County	85	0.44
Brentwood, CA (city) Contra Costa County	200	0.43
Clarksburg, MD (cdp) Montgomery County	44	0.42
Rocklin, CA (city) Placer County	216	0.40
Oakley, CA (city) Contra Costa County	133	0.40
Vineyard, CA (cdp) Sacramento County	102	0.40
Fredericksburg, VA (ind. city) Fredericksburg independent city	93	0.40
Lone Tree, CO (city) Douglas County	40	0.40
Rose Hill, VA (cdp) Fairfax County	77	0.39
Teaneck, NJ (township) Bergen County	149	0.38
Cockeysville, MD (cdp) Baltimore County	76	0.38
Long Branch, VA (cdp) Fairfax County	30	0.38
West Falls Church, VA (cdp) Fairfax County	101	0.37
Tucker, GA (cdp) DeKalb County	100	0.37
Dunn Loring, VA (cdp) Fairfax County	33	0.36
Nutley, NJ (township) Essex County	97	0.35
Fairfax, VA (ind. city) Fairfax independent city	77	0.35
West Sacramento, CA (city) Yolo County	155	0.34
Pleasant Hill, CA (city) Contra Costa County	113	0.34
Linda, CA (cdp) Yuba County	60	0.34
Franklin Square, NY (cdp) Nassau County	97	0.33
San Carlos, CA (city) San Mateo County	92	0.33
Plainview, NY (cdp) Nassau County	85	0.33
Reedley, CA (city) Fresno County	78	0.33
Bethlehem, PA (city) Lehigh County	63	0.33
Orinda, CA (city) Contra Costa County	57	0.33
Fort Hunt, VA (cdp) Fairfax County	52	0.33
Redondo Beach, CA (city) Los Angeles County	210	0.32
Inglewood-Finn Hill, WA (cdp) King County	74	0.32
Sayville, NY (cdp) Suffolk County	52	0.32
George Mason, VA (cdp) Fairfax County	28	0.32
Malden, MA (city) Middlesex County	180	0.31
Moorpark, CA (city) Ventura County	106	0.31
Bellmore, NY (cdp) Nassau County	50	0.31
Buckhall, VA (cdp) Prince William County	48	0.31
Hickory Hills, IL (city) Cook County	44	0.31
University of California Davis, CA (cdp) Yolo County	24	0.31
Carlsbad, CA (city) San Diego County	302	0.30
Kent, WA (city) King County	269	0.30
East Windsor, NJ (township) Mercer County	81	0.30
North Decatur, GA (cdp) DeKalb County	52	0.30
St. Louis, MO (city) St. Louis city County	926	0.29
Cary, NC (town) Wake County	369	0.29
Oakton, VA (cdp) Fairfax County	97	0.29
Upper Allen, PA (township) Cumberland County	50	0.29
Oyster Bay, NY (town) Nassau County	808	0.28
Laguna Niguel, CA (city) Orange County	178	0.28
Irondequoit, NY (cdp/town) Monroe County	145	0.28
Hillsborough, NJ (township) Somerset County	107	0.28
San Lorenzo, CA (cdp) Alameda County	67	0.28
Rocky Hill, CT (town) Hartford County	54	0.28
Oswego, NY (city) Oswego County	50	0.28
Cherry Hill, VA (cdp) Prince William County	44	0.28
Westbury, NY (village) Nassau County	42	0.28
Wakefield, VA (cdp) Fairfax County	32	0.28
Cape Elizabeth, ME (town) Cumberland County	25	0.28
Queens, NY (borough) Queens County	6,027	0.27
Reston, VA (cdp) Fairfax County	142	0.27
Garden Grove, CA (city) Orange County	434	0.26
Fairfield, CA (city) Solano County	271	0.26
Bailey's Crossroads, VA (cdp) Fairfax County	54	0.26

SECTION THREE

Please refer to the Explanation of Data in the front of the book for more detailed information.

Ancestry

African, Sub-Saharan

U.S. and 50 States Sorted by Population and Percent of Total Population

Place	Population	%	Place	Population	%
United States	**2,783,033**	**0.92**	Rhode Island	31,531	2.98
California	265,745	0.73	Maryland	168,316	2.95
New York	240,909	1.25	District of Columbia	15,795	2.70
Texas	227,737	0.94	Virginia	157,765	2.01
Georgia	183,695	1.94	Georgia	183,695	1.94
Maryland	168,316	2.95	Minnesota	99,186	1.89
Virginia	157,765	2.01	Massachusetts	109,092	1.68
Florida	145,105	0.78	New York	240,909	1.25
Massachusetts	109,092	1.68	Indiana	79,021	1.23
Minnesota	99,186	1.89	Delaware	10,135	1.15
Ohio	98,709	0.86	New Jersey	89,531	1.03
New Jersey	89,531	1.03	Nevada	26,691	1.01
Pennsylvania	83,254	0.66	Texas	227,737	0.94
North Carolina	80,649	0.87	**United States**	**2,783,033**	**0.92**
Illinois	80,211	0.63	North Carolina	80,649	0.87
Indiana	79,021	1.23	South Carolina	39,304	0.87
Washington	56,489	0.86	Louisiana	38,611	0.87
Michigan	54,355	0.55	Ohio	98,709	0.86
Tennessee	40,669	0.65	Washington	56,489	0.86
South Carolina	39,304	0.87	Mississippi	24,715	0.84
Louisiana	38,611	0.87	Connecticut	28,542	0.80
Missouri	37,706	0.64	Florida	145,105	0.78
Alabama	35,394	0.75	Alabama	35,394	0.75
Rhode Island	31,531	2.98	California	265,745	0.73
Connecticut	28,542	0.80	Nebraska	12,490	0.69
Arizona	28,150	0.45	Pennsylvania	83,254	0.66
Colorado	27,233	0.56	Tennessee	40,669	0.65
Nevada	26,691	1.01	Missouri	37,706	0.64
Wisconsin	25,325	0.45	Illinois	80,211	0.63
Mississippi	24,715	0.84	Colorado	27,233	0.56
Kentucky	23,400	0.55	Kansas	15,821	0.56
Kansas	15,821	0.56	Michigan	54,355	0.55
District of Columbia	15,795	2.70	Kentucky	23,400	0.55
Iowa	15,454	0.51	Iowa	15,454	0.51
Oregon	15,318	0.41	Alaska	3,475	0.50
Oklahoma	15,106	0.41	Maine	6,088	0.46
Nebraska	12,490	0.69	Arizona	28,150	0.45
Arkansas	10,636	0.37	Wisconsin	25,325	0.45
Delaware	10,135	1.15	South Dakota	3,405	0.43
Utah	8,735	0.33	Oregon	15,318	0.41
Maine	6,088	0.46	Oklahoma	15,106	0.41
New Hampshire	4,912	0.37	Arkansas	10,636	0.37
West Virginia	4,094	0.22	New Hampshire	4,912	0.37
New Mexico	3,951	0.20	North Dakota	2,284	0.35
Alaska	3,475	0.50	Utah	8,735	0.33
South Dakota	3,405	0.43	Vermont	1,770	0.28
Idaho	2,939	0.19	West Virginia	4,094	0.22
North Dakota	2,284	0.35	New Mexico	3,951	0.20
Hawaii	1,881	0.14	Idaho	2,939	0.19
Vermont	1,770	0.28	Montana	1,477	0.15
Montana	1,477	0.15	Hawaii	1,881	0.14
Wyoming	227	0.04	Wyoming	227	0.04

Please refer to the Explanation of Data in the front of the book for more detailed information.

Ancestry

African, Sub-Saharan

Top 150 Places Sorted by Population

Based on all places, regardless of total population

Place	Population	%
New York, NY (city) Kings County	175,478	2.17
Brooklyn, NY (borough) Kings County	63,004	2.55
Bronx, NY (borough) Bronx County	55,928	4.10
Los Angeles, CA (city) Los Angeles County	51,431	1.36
Indianapolis, IN (city) Marion County	43,672	5.39
Houston, TX (city) Harris County	41,757	2.02
Chicago, IL (city) Cook County	36,226	1.34
Philadelphia, PA (city) Philadelphia County	29,046	1.93
Minneapolis, MN (city) Hennepin County	27,138	7.15
Columbus, OH (city) Franklin County	26,987	3.50
Queens, NY (borough) Queens County	25,166	1.14
Boston, MA (city) Suffolk County	24,343	4.04
Manhattan, NY (borough) New York County	24,146	1.52
Virginia Beach, VA (ind. city) Virginia Beach independent city	21,562	4.95
Dallas, TX (city) Dallas County	19,903	1.68
Fort Worth, TX (city) Tarrant County	18,558	2.63
Cincinnati, OH (city) Hamilton County	17,006	5.67
Baltimore, MD (city) Baltimore city County	15,989	2.58
Washington, DC (city) District of Columbia	15,795	2.70
San Diego, CA (city) San Diego County	15,315	1.19
Atlanta, GA (city) Fulton County	14,882	3.60
Seattle, WA (city) King County	14,788	2.48
Jacksonville, FL (city) Duval County	14,490	1.78
St. Paul, MN (city) Ramsey County	13,900	4.93
Fort Wayne, IN (city) Allen County	13,249	5.22
Brockton, MA (city) Plymouth County	13,116	13.97
Louisville-Jefferson County, KY (metro govt) Jefferson County	12,401	2.11
Raleigh, NC (city) Wake County	12,222	3.19
Detroit, MI (city) Wayne County	12,021	1.58
Pawtucket, RI (city) Providence County	11,509	16.06
Phoenix, AZ (city) Maricopa County	11,253	0.78
Charlotte, NC (city) Mecklenburg County	11,247	1.59
Nashville-Davidson, TN (metro govt) Davidson County	11,035	1.88
Long Beach, CA (city) Los Angeles County	10,870	2.35
Newark, NJ (city) Essex County	10,842	3.95
New Bedford, MA (city) Bristol County	10,738	11.31
Alexandria, VA (ind. city) Alexandria independent city	10,686	8.00
New Orleans, LA (city) Orleans Parish	10,425	3.53
Providence, RI (city) Providence County	10,380	5.82
Tallahassee, FL (city) Leon County	9,997	5.65
Memphis, TN (city) Shelby County	9,640	1.47
Arlington, TX (city) Tarrant County	8,945	2.49
Oakland, CA (city) Alameda County	8,436	2.18
Las Vegas, NV (city) Clark County	7,982	1.38
Rochester, NY (city) Monroe County	7,909	3.73
Denver, CO (city) Denver County	7,805	1.35
Brooklyn Park, MN (city) Hennepin County	7,751	10.53
Kansas City, MO (city) Jackson County	7,251	1.59
Staten Island, NY (borough) Richmond County	7,234	1.56
Milwaukee, WI (city) Milwaukee County	7,187	1.22
Norfolk, VA (ind. city) Norfolk independent city	7,047	2.91
Portland, OR (city) Multnomah County	6,834	1.21
St. Louis, MO (city) St. Louis city County	6,762	2.12
Aurora, CO (city) Arapahoe County	6,573	2.09
San Antonio, TX (city) Medina County	6,311	0.49
Greensboro, NC (city) Guilford County	6,270	2.38
Buffalo, NY (city) Erie County	6,085	2.29
Chesapeake, VA (ind. city) Chesapeake independent city	6,008	2.74
Richmond, CA (city) Contra Costa County	5,853	5.72
Hempstead, NY (town) Nassau County	5,844	0.78
San Jose, CA (city) Santa Clara County	5,552	0.60
Cleveland, OH (city) Cuyahoga County	5,454	1.33
Silver Spring, MD (cdp) Montgomery County	5,328	7.61
Worcester, MA (city) Worcester County	5,301	2.95
Douglasville, GA (city) Douglas County	5,296	18.03
Germantown, MD (cdp) Montgomery County	5,206	6.14
Paradise, NV (cdp) Clark County	5,153	2.36
Durham, NC (city) Durham County	5,147	2.34
Gulfport, MS (city) Harrison County	5,081	7.67
Madison, WI (city) Dane County	4,972	2.17
Augusta-Richmond County, GA (cons. govt) Richmond County	4,918	2.54
Arlington, VA (cdp) Arlington County	4,902	2.48
Tampa, FL (city) Hillsborough County	4,857	1.46
Omaha, NE (city) Douglas County	4,839	1.19
Carson, CA (city) Los Angeles County	4,806	5.26

Place	Population	%
Austin, TX (city) Travis County	4,779	0.63
Irving, TX (city) Dallas County	4,601	2.19
Shreveport, LA (city) Caddo Parish	4,579	2.31
Pittsburgh, PA (city) Allegheny County	4,577	1.49
Jersey City, NJ (city) Hudson County	4,569	1.88
Oklahoma City, OK (city) Oklahoma County	4,569	0.81
San Francisco, CA (city) San Francisco County	4,541	0.58
Tucson, AZ (city) Pima County	4,324	0.83
Erie, PA (city) Erie County	4,228	4.16
Compton, CA (city) Los Angeles County	4,191	4.38
Sacramento, CA (city) Sacramento County	4,175	0.91
Upper Darby, PA (township) Delaware County	4,163	5.05
Dale City, VA (cdp) Prince William County	4,147	6.52
Garland, TX (city) Dallas County	4,107	1.84
Columbia, MD (cdp) Howard County	4,023	4.09
Chillum, MD (cdp) Prince George's County	3,842	10.97
Cambridge, MA (city) Middlesex County	3,834	3.70
Lowell, MA (city) Middlesex County	3,805	3.62
Grand Prairie, TX (city) Dallas County	3,688	2.22
Plano, TX (city) Collin County	3,587	1.40
Vallejo, CA (city) Solano County	3,554	3.06
Rochester, MN (city) Olmsted County	3,552	3.41
Lincoln, NE (city) Lancaster County	3,548	1.40
St. Petersburg, FL (city) Pinellas County	3,479	1.42
Richmond, VA (ind. city) Richmond independent city	3,477	1.72
Bowie, MD (city) Prince George's County	3,354	6.18
Kent, WA (city) King County	3,346	3.74
Troy, AL (city) Pike County	3,299	19.17
Spring Valley, NV (cdp) Clark County	3,286	1.93
Hartford, CT (city/town) Hartford County	3,267	2.62
Toledo, OH (city) Lucas County	3,260	1.12
Champaign, IL (city) Champaign County	3,208	4.04
Trenton, NJ (city) Mercer County	3,208	3.77
Palmdale, CA (city) Los Angeles County	3,168	2.17
Fairland, MD (cdp) Montgomery County	3,150	13.64
Aspen Hill, MD (cdp) Montgomery County	3,142	6.68
Inglewood, CA (city) Los Angeles County	3,108	2.82
Sumter, SC (city) Sumter County	3,075	7.62
Bridgeport, CT (city/town) Fairfield County	3,053	2.14
Irvington, NJ (township) Essex County	3,030	5.53
Lincolnia, VA (cdp) Fairfax County	3,016	14.61
Reston, VA (cdp) Fairfax County	3,009	5.65
Brooklyn Center, MN (city) Hennepin County	2,998	10.10
Salt Lake City, UT (city) Salt Lake County	2,993	1.62
Birmingham, AL (city) Jefferson County	2,972	1.37
Yonkers, NY (city) Westchester County	2,939	1.51
Canton, OH (city) Stark County	2,852	3.83
Tacoma, WA (city) Pierce County	2,852	1.43
Brookhaven, NY (town) Suffolk County	2,832	0.59
Wichita, KS (city) Sedgwick County	2,816	0.75
Lithia Springs, GA (cdp) Douglas County	2,809	16.46
Hawthorne, CA (city) Los Angeles County	2,790	3.31
Missouri City, TX (city) Fort Bend County	2,774	4.30
Youngstown, OH (city) Mahoning County	2,765	3.97
City of Orange, NJ (township) Essex County	2,755	9.07
Takoma Park, MD (city) Montgomery County	2,750	16.32
Essex, MD (cdp) Baltimore County	2,745	7.08
Lynn, MA (city) Essex County	2,732	3.05
South Laurel, MD (cdp) Prince George's County	2,720	10.57
Newport News, VA (ind. city) Newport News independent city	2,685	1.48
Sioux Falls, SD (city) Minnehaha County	2,684	1.80
Baton Rouge, LA (city) East Baton Rouge Parish	2,652	1.16
Springfield, MA (city) Hampden County	2,648	1.73
White Oak, MD (cdp) Montgomery County	2,643	15.87
Milford Mill, MD (cdp) Baltimore County	2,633	9.15
East Providence, RI (city) Providence County	2,631	5.54
Tulsa, OK (city) Tulsa County	2,611	0.67
Knoxville, TN (city) Knox County	2,605	1.46
New Haven, CT (city/town) New Haven County	2,581	2.00
Grand Rapids, MI (city) Kent County	2,553	1.34
Sandy Springs, GA (city) Fulton County	2,544	2.80
Portland, ME (city) Cumberland County	2,505	3.79
Burnsville, MN (city) Dakota County	2,499	4.12
Sunrise Manor, NV (cdp) Clark County	2,479	1.28
Elk Grove, CA (city) Sacramento County	2,477	1.75

Ancestry

African, Sub-Saharan

Top 150 Places Sorted by Percent of Total Population

Based on all places, regardless of total population

Place	Population	%
Ebony, VA (cdp) Brunswick County	188	74.02
Bobtown, VA (cdp) Accomack County	307	58.81
Linwood, NY (cdp) Livingston County	64	48.85
Olancha, CA (cdp) Inyo County	89	43.84
Slickville, PA (cdp) Westmoreland County	168	43.30
Brundidge, AL (city) Pike County	988	40.23
Metompkin, VA (cdp) Accomack County	273	38.29
Southampton Meadows, VA (cdp) Southampton County	214	37.41
Makemie Park, VA (cdp) Accomack County	70	36.84
Fairview, VA (cdp) Mecklenburg County	80	35.24
Modest Town, VA (cdp) Accomack County	36	34.29
Oak Hall, VA (cdp) Accomack County	132	34.20
Nassawadox, VA (town) Northampton County	247	32.89
Mulberry, SC (cdp) Sumter County	104	31.52
Clarkston, GA (city) DeKalb County	2,338	30.95
Alberta, VA (town) Brunswick County	118	30.10
Boston, VA (cdp) Accomack County	204	29.82
Fredonia (Biscoe), AR (town) Prairie County	108	28.95
Gadsden, SC (cdp) Richland County	593	28.52
Nelsonia, VA (cdp) Accomack County	216	28.27
Horntown, VA (cdp) Accomack County	136	28.04
Urbancrest, OH (village) Franklin County	284	27.76
Gilliam, LA (village) Caddo Parish	53	27.32
Cats Bridge, VA (cdp) Accomack County	117	27.21
Colwyn, PA (borough) Delaware County	659	26.22
Jarratt, VA (town) Greensville County	186	25.98
Patterson, AR (city) Woodruff County	113	25.22
Keystone, WV (city) McDowell County	69	25.09
Lawrenceville, VA (town) Brunswick County	481	24.32
Sharon, GA (city) Taliaferro County	34	23.78
Pastoria, VA (cdp) Accomack County	146	23.74
Thynedale, VA (cdp) Mecklenburg County	22	23.66
Rocky Mound, TX (town) Camp County	17	23.61
Boydton, VA (town) Mecklenburg County	119	23.47
Keller, VA (town) Accomack County	51	23.18
Emporia, VA (ind. city) Emporia independent city	1,338	22.98
Horn, OK (town) Hughes County	28	22.76
Miesville, MN (city) Dakota County	24	22.64
St. Paul, AK (city) Aleutians West Census Area	234	21.97
Sun Valley, AZ (cdp) Navajo County	16	21.62
Chase City, VA (town) Mecklenburg County	561	21.53
Fort White, FL (town) Columbia County	149	21.13
Sciota, IL (village) McDonough County	8	21.05
Ideal, GA (city) Macon County	144	20.93
Stanardsville, VA (town) Greene County	58	20.64
Brantley, AL (town) Crenshaw County	229	20.50
Cotton Plant, AR (city) Woodruff County	134	20.40
Accomac, VA (town) Accomack County	108	20.22
Oakland, SC (cdp) Sumter County	273	20.06
Winton, NC (town) Hertford County	184	19.96
Clarksville, TX (city) Red River County	672	19.89
Akutan, AK (city) Aleutians East Borough	310	19.42
Troy, AL (city) Pike County	3,299	19.17
Jessup, MD (cdp) Anne Arundel County	2,087	18.84
Eastover, SC (town) Richland County	118	18.73
Apalachicola, FL (city) Franklin County	428	18.16
Douglasville, GA (city) Douglas County	5,296	18.03
Annona, TX (town) Red River County	57	17.92
East Spencer, NC (town) Rowan County	305	17.76
Barrett, TX (cdp) Harris County	401	17.56
East Lansing, MI (city) Clinton County	255	17.11
Courtland, VA (town) Southampton County	175	16.75
South Sumter, SC (cdp) Sumter County	403	16.69
Las Lomitas, TX (cdp) Jim Hogg County	49	16.55
Ridgeway, SC (town) Fairfield County	86	16.54
Lithia Springs, GA (cdp) Douglas County	2,809	16.46
Franklin, VA (ind. city) Franklin independent city	1,406	16.45
Takoma Park, MD (city) Montgomery County	2,750	16.32
Elba, AL (city) Coffee County	641	16.25
Pawtucket, RI (city) Providence County	11,509	16.06
Southview, PA (cdp) Washington County	24	16.00
White Oak, MD (cdp) Montgomery County	2,643	15.87
Rebecca, GA (town) Turner County	43	15.81
Dalzell, SC (cdp) Sumter County	496	15.38
Banks, AL (town) Pike County	46	15.28
Mappsville, VA (cdp) Accomack County	36	15.13
Voorhees, NJ (cdp) Somerset County	154	15.02
Adelphi, MD (cdp) Prince George's County	2,244	14.92
Springdale, MD (cdp) Prince George's County	375	14.87
Darby, PA (borough) Delaware County	1,568	14.79
Lincolnia, VA (cdp) Fairfax County	3,016	14.61
Lanham, MD (cdp) Prince George's County	1,301	14.57
Promised Land, SC (cdp) Greenwood County	69	14.47
Wheatley Heights, NY (cdp) Suffolk County	896	14.46
Luverne, AL (city) Crenshaw County	406	14.46
New Carrollton, MD (city) Prince George's County	1,748	14.42
Glenmont, MD (cdp) Montgomery County	1,936	14.39
Fairwood, MD (cdp) Prince George's County	663	14.26
Wakefield, VA (town) Sussex County	124	14.22
Leslie, GA (city) Sumter County	62	14.03
Brockton, MA (city) Plymouth County	13,116	13.97
Villa Heights, VA (cdp) Henry County	202	13.93
Wallace, SC (cdp) Marlboro County	122	13.90
De Valls Bluff, AR (city) Prairie County	79	13.84
Talbotton, GA (city) Talbot County	182	13.80
Mitchellville, MD (cdp) Prince George's County	1,606	13.78
Burtonsville, MD (cdp) Montgomery County	1,271	13.77
Lone Star, TX (city) Morris County	262	13.72
Parker's Crossroads, TN (city) Henderson County	40	13.70
Fairland, MD (cdp) Montgomery County	3,150	13.64
Rutledge, AL (town) Crenshaw County	91	13.58
Sherrill, AR (town) Jefferson County	6	13.33
Allison, PA (cdp) Fayette County	68	13.26
Yeadon, PA (borough) Delaware County	1,504	13.11
Wattsville, VA (cdp) Accomack County	168	13.09
Princeton, NC (town) Johnston County	170	13.04
Wallula, WA (cdp) Walla Walla County	12	13.04
Lake City, FL (city) Columbia County	1,604	13.03
Aucilla, FL (cdp) Jefferson County	40	13.03
Lockland, OH (village) Hamilton County	451	13.02
Union Level, VA (cdp) Mecklenburg County	57	12.90
Perry, FL (city) Taylor County	906	12.79
Largo, MD (cdp) Prince George's County	1,374	12.48
Poplar Hills, KY (city) Jefferson County	28	12.44
Shelter Cove, CA (cdp) Humboldt County	65	12.40
Crewe, VA (town) Nottoway County	319	12.31
Spencer, NC (town) Rowan County	400	12.17
Riverside, MN (township) Lac qui Parle County	39	12.15
Woodmore, MD (cdp) Prince George's County	423	12.08
Manistee, MI (township) Manistee County	489	12.06
Duquesne, PA (city) Allegheny County	696	11.95
Lake Arbor, MD (cdp) Prince George's County	1,227	11.90
Blackstone, VA (town) Nottoway County	421	11.61
Atlantic, VA (cdp) Accomack County	59	11.59
Kimball, WV (town) McDowell County	38	11.38
Brodnax, VA (town) Brunswick County	49	11.37
Winsor, MN (township) Clearwater County	10	11.36
Kenbridge, VA (town) Lunenburg County	135	11.32
New Bedford, MA (city) Bristol County	10,738	11.31
South Hill, VA (town) Mecklenburg County	523	11.25
Cape Charles, VA (town) Northampton County	125	11.24
Anmoore, WV (town) Harrison County	129	11.21
Seabrook, MD (cdp) Prince George's County	1,749	11.20
Onset, MA (cdp) Plymouth County	103	11.12
Hiram, GA (city) Paulding County	367	11.10
Grand View Estates, CO (cdp) Douglas County	30	11.07
Lovejoy, GA (city) Clayton County	637	11.00
Chillum, MD (cdp) Prince George's County	3,842	10.97
Halliday, ND (city) Dunn County	23	10.95
North Richmond, CA (cdp) Contra Costa County	326	10.87
Four Corners, TX (cdp) Fort Bend County	1,332	10.81
Riverdale Park, MD (town) Prince George's County	735	10.66
Moss Point, MS (city) Jackson County	1,483	10.62
Mason Neck, VA (cdp) Fairfax County	238	10.60
South Laurel, MD (cdp) Prince George's County	2,720	10.57
Newsoms, VA (town) Southampton County	29	10.55
Brooklyn Park, MN (city) Hennepin County	7,751	10.53
Rachel, NV (cdp) Lincoln County	8	10.53
Gary, WV (city) McDowell County	119	10.48
Glenn Dale, MD (cdp) Prince George's County	1,476	10.45

Ancestry

African, Sub-Saharan

Top 150 Places Sorted by Percent of Total Population

Based on places with total population of 7,500 or more

Place	Population	%
Clarkston, GA (city) DeKalb County	2,338	30.95
Troy, AL (city) Pike County	3,299	19.17
Jessup, MD (cdp) Anne Arundel County	2,087	18.84
Douglasville, GA (city) Douglas County	5,296	18.03
Lithia Springs, GA (cdp) Douglas County	2,809	16.46
Franklin, VA (ind. city) Franklin independent city	1,406	16.45
Takoma Park, MD (city) Montgomery County	2,750	16.32
Pawtucket, RI (city) Providence County	11,509	16.06
White Oak, MD (cdp) Montgomery County	2,643	15.87
Adelphi, MD (cdp) Prince George's County	2,244	14.92
Darby, PA (borough) Delaware County	1,568	14.79
Lincolnia, VA (cdp) Fairfax County	3,016	14.61
Lanham, MD (cdp) Prince George's County	1,301	14.57
New Carrollton, MD (city) Prince George's County	1,748	14.42
Glenmont, MD (cdp) Montgomery County	1,936	14.39
Brockton, MA (city) Plymouth County	13,116	13.97
Mitchellville, MD (cdp) Prince George's County	1,606	13.78
Burtonsville, MD (cdp) Montgomery County	1,271	13.77
Fairland, MD (cdp) Montgomery County	3,150	13.64
Yeadon, PA (borough) Delaware County	1,504	13.11
Lake City, FL (city) Columbia County	1,604	13.03
Largo, MD (cdp) Prince George's County	1,374	12.48
Lake Arbor, MD (cdp) Prince George's County	1,227	11.90
New Bedford, MA (city) Bristol County	10,738	11.31
Seabrook, MD (cdp) Prince George's County	1,749	11.20
Chillum, MD (cdp) Prince George's County	3,842	10.97
Four Corners, TX (cdp) Fort Bend County	1,332	10.81
Moss Point, MS (city) Jackson County	1,483	10.62
South Laurel, MD (cdp) Prince George's County	2,720	10.57
Brooklyn Park, MN (city) Hennepin County	7,751	10.53
Glenn Dale, MD (cdp) Prince George's County	1,476	10.45
Bladensburg, MD (town) Prince George's County	905	10.15
Brooklyn Center, MN (city) Hennepin County	2,998	10.10
Woodlawn, VA (cdp) Fairfax County	1,961	10.02
Brock Hall, MD (cdp) Prince George's County	817	10.02
Lorton, VA (cdp) Fairfax County	1,879	9.75
Dallas, GA (city) Paulding County	1,044	9.71
Kettering, MD (cdp) Prince George's County	1,191	9.49
Milford Mill, MD (cdp) Baltimore County	2,633	9.15
Knightdale, NC (town) Wake County	953	9.10
City of Orange, NJ (township) Essex County	2,755	9.07
Calverton, MD (cdp) Montgomery County	1,581	8.88
Columbia Heights, MN (city) Anoka County	1,720	8.82
SeaTac, WA (city) King County	2,295	8.68
Cherry Hill, VA (cdp) Prince William County	1,331	8.58
View Park-Windsor Hills, CA (cdp) Los Angeles County	894	8.30
Summerfield, MD (cdp) Prince George's County	923	8.29
Hybla Valley, VA (cdp) Fairfax County	1,203	8.23
Neabsco, VA (cdp) Prince William County	768	8.15
Alexandria, VA (ind. city) Alexandria independent city	10,686	8.00
Lochearn, MD (cdp) Baltimore County	2,010	7.81
Hyattsville, MD (city) Prince George's County	1,337	7.75
Gulfport, MS (city) Harrison County	5,081	7.67
Greenbelt, MD (city) Prince George's County	1,743	7.64
Sumter, SC (city) Sumter County	3,075	7.62
Silver Spring, MD (cdp) Montgomery County	5,328	7.61
Beltsville, MD (cdp) Prince George's County	1,164	7.54
Triangle, VA (cdp) Prince William County	557	7.24
Laurel, MD (city) Prince George's County	1,754	7.18
Minneapolis, MN (city) Hennepin County	27,138	7.15
Scottdale, GA (cdp) DeKalb County	699	7.15
Spanish Lake, MO (cdp) St. Louis County	1,547	7.10
Essex, MD (cdp) Baltimore County	2,745	7.08
East Riverdale, MD (cdp) Prince George's County	1,104	7.05
Marlboro Village, MD (cdp) Prince George's County	649	6.93
Newington, VA (cdp) Fairfax County	905	6.85
Central Falls, RI (city) Providence County	1,308	6.75
Hopkins, MN (city) Hennepin County	1,168	6.70
Aspen Hill, MD (cdp) Montgomery County	3,142	6.68
Maryland City, MD (cdp) Anne Arundel County	1,027	6.66
Randolph, MA (cdp/town) Norfolk County	2,078	6.56
North Bellport, NY (cdp) Suffolk County	737	6.54
Dale City, VA (cdp) Prince William County	4,147	6.52
Mission Bend, TX (cdp) Fort Bend County	2,467	6.52
Tukwila, WA (city) King County	1,197	6.45
Rosaryville, MD (cdp) Prince George's County	732	6.38
Montgomery Village, MD (cdp) Montgomery County	1,997	6.30
Friendly, MD (cdp) Prince George's County	624	6.26
Acworth, GA (city) Cobb County	1,204	6.23
Hillside, NJ (township) Union County	1,318	6.20
Bowie, MD (city) Prince George's County	3,354	6.18
Germantown, MD (cdp) Montgomery County	5,206	6.14
Landover, MD (cdp) Prince George's County	1,417	6.02
Bull Run, VA (cdp) Prince William County	776	6.02
Gautier, MS (city) Jackson County	1,087	6.01
West Athens, CA (cdp) Los Angeles County	499	6.01
Speedway, IN (town) Marion County	709	5.94
Coral Hills, MD (cdp) Prince George's County	566	5.86
Dunn, NC (city) Harnett County	534	5.85
Mount Pleasant, TX (city) Titus County	881	5.83
Providence, RI (city) Providence County	10,380	5.82
Old Jamestown, MO (cdp) St. Louis County	1,189	5.80
College Park, GA (city) Fulton County	810	5.80
Fayetteville, GA (city) Fayette County	880	5.77
Lemoore Station, CA (cdp) Kings County	455	5.77
Des Moines, WA (city) King County	1,689	5.74
McNair, VA (cdp) Fairfax County	871	5.73
Richmond, CA (city) Contra Costa County	5,853	5.72
Wareham, MA (town) Plymouth County	1,225	5.69
Cincinnati, OH (city) Hamilton County	17,006	5.67
Tallahassee, FL (city) Leon County	9,997	5.65
Reston, VA (cdp) Fairfax County	3,009	5.65
Fort Pierce, FL (city) St. Lucie County	2,399	5.65
Accokeek, MD (cdp) Prince George's County	594	5.65
Salisbury, NC (city) Rowan County	1,859	5.63
Stockbridge, GA (city) Henry County	1,327	5.60
Lakeside, VA (cdp) Henrico County	666	5.55
East Providence, RI (city) Providence County	2,631	5.54
Irvington, NJ (township) Essex County	3,030	5.53
Seven Corners, VA (cdp) Fairfax County	458	5.50
Colesville, MD (cdp) Montgomery County	777	5.47
Redan, GA (cdp) DeKalb County	1,869	5.46
Lexington, NE (city) Dawson County	551	5.45
Jefferson, LA (cdp) Jefferson Parish	652	5.41
Indianapolis, IN (city) Marion County	43,672	5.39
Atlantic City, NJ (city) Atlantic County	2,133	5.32
Union City, GA (city) Fulton County	951	5.32
Herndon, VA (town) Fairfax County	1,204	5.30
Donaldsonville, LA (city) Ascension Parish	396	5.27
Carson, CA (city) Los Angeles County	4,806	5.26
Texarkana, TX (city) Bowie County	1,888	5.25
Fort Wayne, IN (city) Allen County	13,249	5.22
Shively, KY (city) Jefferson County	789	5.21
Mount Rainier, MD (city) Prince George's County	421	5.17
Whitehall, OH (city) Franklin County	932	5.13
Willingboro, NJ (township) Burlington County	1,643	5.11
Kemp Mill, MD (cdp) Montgomery County	617	5.11
Camp Pendleton South, CA (cdp) San Diego County	684	5.10
Randallstown, MD (cdp) Baltimore County	1,659	5.09
Upper Darby, PA (township) Delaware County	4,163	5.05
Maplewood, NJ (township) Essex County	1,197	5.04
Franconia, VA (cdp) Fairfax County	926	5.02
Powder Springs, GA (city) Cobb County	691	5.02
Texarkana, AR (city) Miller County	1,488	5.00
Riverdale, GA (city) Clayton County	750	4.99
Glasgow, DE (cdp) New Castle County	779	4.98
Parkville, MD (cdp) Baltimore County	1,499	4.97
Oronoko, MI (charter township) Berrien County	459	4.97
Virginia Beach, VA (ind. city) Virginia Beach independent city	21,562	4.95
Americus, GA (city) Sumter County	843	4.95
St. Paul, MN (city) Ramsey County	13,900	4.93
Fort Morgan, CO (city) Morgan County	553	4.92
Cloverly, MD (cdp) Montgomery County	757	4.91
Belle Glade, FL (city) Palm Beach County	863	4.89
Jackson, MI (city) Jackson County	1,671	4.86
McDonough, GA (city) Henry County	980	4.86
Berkeley, MO (city) St. Louis County	444	4.86
Collingdale, PA (borough) Delaware County	426	4.86
Wheaton, MD (cdp) Montgomery County	2,184	4.84
Villa Rica, GA (city) Carroll County	605	4.84

Please refer to the Explanation of Data in the front of the book for more detailed information.

Ancestry

African, Sub-Saharan: African

U.S. and 50 States Sorted by Population and Percent of Total Population

Place	Population	%	Place	Population	%
United States	**1,731,621**	**0.57**	Maryland	90,411	1.59
California	181,250	0.49	District of Columbia	9,069	1.55
New York	142,623	0.74	Georgia	129,637	1.37
Texas	139,942	0.58	Virginia	101,824	1.30
Georgia	129,637	1.37	Indiana	68,814	1.07
Florida	116,581	0.63	Mississippi	23,459	0.80
Virginia	101,824	1.30	Louisiana	35,140	0.79
Maryland	90,411	1.59	South Carolina	35,276	0.78
Indiana	68,814	1.07	New York	142,623	0.74
Ohio	66,657	0.58	Delaware	6,305	0.72
North Carolina	55,748	0.60	Alabama	30,949	0.66
Pennsylvania	53,706	0.43	Nevada	17,448	0.66
Illinois	50,756	0.40	Florida	116,581	0.63
New Jersey	45,134	0.52	North Carolina	55,748	0.60
Michigan	39,842	0.40	Texas	139,942	0.58
South Carolina	35,276	0.78	Ohio	66,657	0.58
Louisiana	35,140	0.79	**United States**	**1,731,621**	**0.57**
Alabama	30,949	0.66	Minnesota	27,740	0.53
Minnesota	27,740	0.53	New Jersey	45,134	0.52
Missouri	26,968	0.46	California	181,250	0.49
Tennessee	26,128	0.42	Missouri	26,968	0.46
Massachusetts	25,563	0.39	Kentucky	19,102	0.45
Mississippi	23,459	0.80	Connecticut	15,637	0.44
Washington	23,144	0.35	Pennsylvania	53,706	0.43
Wisconsin	19,892	0.35	Tennessee	26,128	0.42
Kentucky	19,102	0.45	Illinois	50,756	0.40
Nevada	17,448	0.66	Michigan	39,842	0.40
Connecticut	15,637	0.44	Massachusetts	25,563	0.39
Arizona	13,653	0.22	Rhode Island	4,050	0.38
Colorado	12,605	0.26	Kansas	10,346	0.37
Iowa	10,567	0.35	Washington	23,144	0.35
Kansas	10,346	0.37	Wisconsin	19,892	0.35
Oklahoma	9,374	0.26	Iowa	10,567	0.35
Arkansas	9,178	0.32	Nebraska	6,278	0.35
District of Columbia	9,069	1.55	Arkansas	9,178	0.32
Oregon	8,398	0.22	Colorado	12,605	0.26
Delaware	6,305	0.72	Oklahoma	9,374	0.26
Nebraska	6,278	0.35	Alaska	1,717	0.25
Utah	4,330	0.16	Arizona	13,653	0.22
Rhode Island	4,050	0.38	Oregon	8,398	0.22
New Mexico	3,102	0.15	North Dakota	1,348	0.20
West Virginia	3,004	0.16	Utah	4,330	0.16
New Hampshire	1,861	0.14	West Virginia	3,004	0.16
Alaska	1,717	0.25	South Dakota	1,271	0.16
Idaho	1,433	0.09	New Mexico	3,102	0.15
North Dakota	1,348	0.20	New Hampshire	1,861	0.14
Maine	1,309	0.10	Vermont	765	0.12
South Dakota	1,271	0.16	Montana	1,091	0.11
Montana	1,091	0.11	Maine	1,309	0.10
Hawaii	1,082	0.08	Idaho	1,433	0.09
Vermont	765	0.12	Hawaii	1,082	0.08
Wyoming	114	0.02	Wyoming	114	0.02

Please refer to the Explanation of Data in the front of the book for more detailed information.

Ancestry

African, Sub-Saharan: African

Top 150 Places Sorted by Population

Based on all places, regardless of total population

Place	Population	%
New York, NY (city) Kings County	101,901	1.26
Brooklyn, NY (borough) Kings County	48,168	1.95
Los Angeles, CA (city) Los Angeles County	39,515	1.05
Indianapolis, IN (city) Marion County	38,288	4.73
Houston, TX (city) Harris County	24,810	1.20
Bronx, NY (borough) Bronx County	22,647	1.66
Chicago, IL (city) Cook County	21,971	0.81
Virginia Beach, VA (ind. city) Virginia Beach independent city	20,099	4.61
Philadelphia, PA (city) Philadelphia County	18,871	1.25
Fort Worth, TX (city) Tarrant County	16,247	2.30
Cincinnati, OH (city) Hamilton County	15,631	5.21
Queens, NY (borough) Queens County	14,083	0.64
Atlanta, GA (city) Fulton County	12,994	3.14
Manhattan, NY (borough) New York County	12,839	0.81
Fort Wayne, IN (city) Allen County	12,753	5.03
Jacksonville, FL (city) Duval County	11,387	1.40
Baltimore, MD (city) Baltimore city County	11,210	1.81
Columbus, OH (city) Franklin County	10,986	1.43
Dallas, TX (city) Dallas County	10,746	0.91
Louisville-Jefferson County, KY (metro govt) Jefferson County	10,026	1.71
New Orleans, LA (city) Orleans Parish	9,872	3.34
Detroit, MI (city) Wayne County	9,726	1.28
Long Beach, CA (city) Los Angeles County	9,464	2.05
Tallahassee, FL (city) Leon County	9,217	5.21
Washington, DC (city) District of Columbia	9,069	1.55
Minneapolis, MN (city) Hennepin County	8,873	2.34
Raleigh, NC (city) Wake County	7,836	2.05
Boston, MA (city) Suffolk County	6,993	1.16
Las Vegas, NV (city) Clark County	6,715	1.16
Memphis, TN (city) Shelby County	6,705	1.02
Rochester, NY (city) Monroe County	5,828	2.75
Norfolk, VA (ind. city) Norfolk independent city	5,828	2.41
Chesapeake, VA (ind. city) Chesapeake independent city	5,745	2.62
Milwaukee, WI (city) Milwaukee County	5,691	0.97
San Diego, CA (city) San Diego County	5,572	0.43
Charlotte, NC (city) Mecklenburg County	5,460	0.77
Phoenix, AZ (city) Maricopa County	5,295	0.37
Gulfport, MS (city) Harrison County	5,043	7.61
Douglasville, GA (city) Douglas County	5,008	17.05
Oakland, CA (city) Alameda County	4,978	1.29
Richmond, CA (city) Contra Costa County	4,973	4.86
Arlington, TX (city) Tarrant County	4,720	1.31
St. Louis, MO (city) St. Louis city County	4,621	1.45
Shreveport, LA (city) Caddo Parish	4,567	2.30
San Antonio, TX (city) Medina County	4,503	0.35
Augusta-Richmond County, GA (cons. govt) Richmond County	4,490	2.32
Carson, CA (city) Los Angeles County	4,332	4.74
Seattle, WA (city) King County	4,331	0.73
Cleveland, OH (city) Cuyahoga County	4,279	1.05
Buffalo, NY (city) Erie County	4,177	1.57
Staten Island, NY (borough) Richmond County	4,164	0.90
Kansas City, MO (city) Jackson County	4,120	0.91
Compton, CA (city) Los Angeles County	4,112	4.29
Newark, NJ (city) Essex County	4,089	1.49
Portland, OR (city) Multnomah County	3,921	0.69
Hempstead, NY (town) Nassau County	3,879	0.51
Nashville-Davidson, TN (metro govt) Davidson County	3,804	0.65
Tampa, FL (city) Hillsborough County	3,637	1.09
Erie, PA (city) Erie County	3,634	3.58
Denver, CO (city) Denver County	3,628	0.63
Pittsburgh, PA (city) Allegheny County	3,558	1.16
Madison, WI (city) Dane County	3,419	1.49
Durham, NC (city) Durham County	3,418	1.55
Troy, AL (city) Pike County	3,256	18.92
St. Petersburg, FL (city) Pinellas County	3,161	1.29
St. Paul, MN (city) Ramsey County	3,110	1.10
Vallejo, CA (city) Solano County	3,101	2.67
Sumter, SC (city) Sumter County	3,059	7.58
Alexandria, VA (ind. city) Alexandria independent city	3,054	2.29
Champaign, IL (city) Champaign County	3,045	3.83
San Francisco, CA (city) San Francisco County	3,031	0.38
Palmdale, CA (city) Los Angeles County	2,924	2.00
Greensboro, NC (city) Guilford County	2,798	1.06
Canton, OH (city) Stark County	2,713	3.64
Paradise, NV (cdp) Clark County	2,673	1.23
Youngstown, OH (city) Mahoning County	2,655	3.82
Oklahoma City, OK (city) Oklahoma County	2,648	0.47
Sacramento, CA (city) Sacramento County	2,618	0.57
Hartford, CT (city/town) Hartford County	2,605	2.09
Birmingham, AL (city) Jefferson County	2,600	1.20
Lithia Springs, GA (cdp) Douglas County	2,572	15.07
Brookhaven, NY (town) Suffolk County	2,533	0.53
Omaha, NE (city) Douglas County	2,433	0.60
Toledo, OH (city) Lucas County	2,419	0.83
Fort Pierce, FL (city) St. Lucie County	2,399	5.65
Tacoma, WA (city) Pierce County	2,387	1.20
Irving, TX (city) Dallas County	2,360	1.12
Lincoln, NE (city) Lancaster County	2,325	0.92
Sunrise Manor, NV (cdp) Clark County	2,303	1.19
Austin, TX (city) Travis County	2,290	0.30
Aurora, CO (city) Arapahoe County	2,285	0.73
Jackson, TN (city) Madison County	2,217	3.44
Knoxville, TN (city) Knox County	2,215	1.24
Inglewood, CA (city) Los Angeles County	2,163	1.97
Ocala, FL (city) Marion County	2,150	3.84
Columbia, MD (cdp) Howard County	2,146	2.18
Bowie, MD (city) Prince George's County	2,095	3.86
Jessup, MD (cdp) Anne Arundel County	2,087	18.84
Providence, RI (city) Providence County	2,075	1.16
Richmond, VA (ind. city) Richmond independent city	2,048	1.01
Fairfield, CA (city) Solano County	2,042	1.97
Akron, OH (city) Summit County	2,027	1.00
Vacaville, CA (city) Solano County	2,024	2.20
Trenton, NJ (city) Mercer County	2,000	2.35
San Jose, CA (city) Santa Clara County	1,999	0.22
Marietta, GA (city) Cobb County	1,961	3.43
Dayton, OH (city) Montgomery County	1,956	1.34
Tucson, AZ (city) Pima County	1,955	0.38
Baton Rouge, LA (city) East Baton Rouge Parish	1,898	0.83
Montgomery, AL (city) Montgomery County	1,891	0.92
Newport News, VA (ind. city) Newport News independent city	1,871	1.03
Chillum, MD (cdp) Prince George's County	1,865	5.32
Silver Spring, MD (cdp) Montgomery County	1,865	2.66
Columbia, SC (city) Richland County	1,837	1.44
Salisbury, NC (city) Rowan County	1,836	5.56
Arlington, VA (cdp) Arlington County	1,829	0.93
Fresno, CA (city) Fresno County	1,818	0.38
Wichita, KS (city) Sedgwick County	1,808	0.48
Lancaster, CA (city) Los Angeles County	1,803	1.20
Metairie, LA (cdp) Jefferson Parish	1,782	1.31
Dale City, VA (cdp) Prince William County	1,780	2.80
Mobile, AL (city) Mobile County	1,766	0.90
Essex, MD (cdp) Baltimore County	1,758	4.53
Racine, WI (city) Racine County	1,751	2.20
Texarkana, TX (city) Bowie County	1,748	4.86
Atlantic City, NJ (city) Atlantic County	1,745	4.35
Hawthorne, CA (city) Los Angeles County	1,719	2.04
Rancho Cucamonga, CA (city) San Bernardino County	1,716	1.07
Oceanside, CA (city) San Diego County	1,713	1.04
Fontana, CA (city) San Bernardino County	1,703	0.90
Antioch, CA (city) Contra Costa County	1,700	1.70
Waterbury, CT (city/town) New Haven County	1,693	1.54
Tulsa, OK (city) Tulsa County	1,671	0.43
Aspen Hill, MD (cdp) Montgomery County	1,657	3.52
Willowbrook, CA (cdp) Los Angeles County	1,646	4.68
Jackson, MI (city) Jackson County	1,634	4.76
Southfield, MI (city) Oakland County	1,632	2.24
Jackson, MS (city) Hinds County	1,624	0.93
Worcester, MA (city) Worcester County	1,614	0.90
Lake City, FL (city) Columbia County	1,604	13.03
Lawrence, IN (city) Marion County	1,595	3.59
Milford Mill, MD (cdp) Baltimore County	1,591	5.53
Colorado Springs, CO (city) El Paso County	1,583	0.39
Jersey City, NJ (city) Hudson County	1,581	0.65
Beloit, WI (city) Rock County	1,578	4.26
New Haven, CT (city/town) New Haven County	1,563	1.21
Little Rock, AR (city) Pulaski County	1,557	0.82
Lowell, MA (city) Middlesex County	1,552	1.48
Gary, IN (city) Lake County	1,527	1.81
Kansas City, KS (city) Wyandotte County	1,523	1.06

SECTION THREE

Please refer to the Explanation of Data in the front of the book for more detailed information.

Ancestry

African, Sub-Saharan: African

Top 150 Places Sorted by Percent of Total Population

Based on all places, regardless of total population

Place	Population	%
Ebony, VA (cdp) Brunswick County	188	74.02
Bobtown, VA (cdp) Accomack County	307	58.81
Olancha, CA (cdp) Inyo County	89	43.84
Slickville, PA (cdp) Westmoreland County	168	43.30
Brundidge, AL (city) Pike County	988	40.23
Metompkin, VA (cdp) Accomack County	273	38.29
Southampton Meadows, VA (cdp) Southampton County	214	37.41
Makemie Park, VA (cdp) Accomack County	70	36.84
Fairview, VA (cdp) Mecklenburg County	80	35.24
Modest Town, VA (cdp) Accomack County	36	34.29
Oak Hall, VA (cdp) Accomack County	132	34.20
Nassawadox, VA (town) Northampton County	247	32.89
Mulberry, SC (cdp) Sumter County	104	31.52
Alberta, VA (town) Brunswick County	118	30.10
Boston, VA (cdp) Accomack County	204	29.82
Fredonia (Biscoe), AR (town) Prairie County	108	28.95
Gadsden, SC (cdp) Richland County	593	28.52
Nelsonia, VA (cdp) Accomack County	216	28.27
Horntown, VA (cdp) Accomack County	136	28.04
Gilliam, LA (village) Caddo Parish	53	27.32
Cats Bridge, VA (cdp) Accomack County	117	27.21
Jarratt, VA (town) Greensville County	186	25.98
Patterson, AR (city) Woodruff County	113	25.22
Keystone, WV (city) McDowell County	69	25.09
Sharon, GA (city) Taliaferro County	34	23.78
Pastoria, VA (cdp) Accomack County	146	23.74
Thynedale, VA (cdp) Mecklenburg County	22	23.66
Rocky Mound, TX (town) Camp County	17	23.61
Boydton, VA (town) Mecklenburg County	119	23.47
Lawrenceville, VA (town) Brunswick County	463	23.41
Keller, VA (town) Accomack County	51	23.18
Emporia, VA (ind. city) Emporia independent city	1,330	22.84
Horn, OK (town) Hughes County	28	22.76
Sun Valley, AZ (cdp) Navajo County	16	21.62
Fort White, FL (town) Columbia County	149	21.13
Chase City, VA (town) Mecklenburg County	549	21.07
Sciota, IL (village) McDonough County	8	21.05
Ideal, GA (city) Macon County	144	20.93
Brantley, AL (town) Crenshaw County	229	20.50
Cotton Plant, AR (city) Woodruff County	134	20.40
Accomac, VA (town) Accomack County	108	20.22
Oakland, SC (cdp) Sumter County	273	20.06
Winton, NC (town) Hertford County	184	19.96
Clarksville, TX (city) Red River County	672	19.89
Troy, AL (city) Pike County	3,256	18.92
Jessup, MD (cdp) Anne Arundel County	2,087	18.84
Eastover, SC (town) Richland County	118	18.73
Apalachicola, FL (city) Franklin County	428	18.16
Annona, TX (town) Red River County	57	17.92
East Spencer, NC (town) Rowan County	305	17.76
Barrett, TX (cdp) Harris County	401	17.56
Douglasville, GA (city) Douglas County	5,008	17.05
Courtland, VA (town) Southampton County	175	16.75
South Sumter, SC (cdp) Sumter County	403	16.69
Las Lomitas, TX (cdp) Jim Hogg County	49	16.55
Ridgeway, SC (town) Fairfield County	86	16.54
Franklin, VA (ind. city) Franklin independent city	1,406	16.45
Elba, AL (city) Coffee County	641	16.25
Southview, PA (cdp) Washington County	24	16.00
Rebecca, GA (town) Turner County	43	15.81
Dalzell, SC (cdp) Sumter County	496	15.38
Banks, AL (town) Pike County	46	15.28
Mappsville, VA (cdp) Accomack County	36	15.13
Lithia Springs, GA (cdp) Douglas County	2,572	15.07
East Lansing, MI (city) Clinton County	219	14.70
Promised Land, SC (cdp) Greenwood County	69	14.47
Luverne, AL (city) Crenshaw County	406	14.46
Wakefield, VA (town) Sussex County	124	14.22
Leslie, GA (city) Sumter County	62	14.03
Villa Heights, VA (cdp) Henry County	202	13.93
Wallace, SC (cdp) Marlboro County	122	13.90
De Valls Bluff, AR (city) Prairie County	79	13.84
Talbotton, GA (city) Talbot County	182	13.80
Lone Star, TX (city) Morris County	262	13.72
Parker's Crossroads, TN (city) Henderson County	40	13.70
Rutledge, AL (town) Crenshaw County	91	13.58
Sherrill, AR (town) Jefferson County	6	13.33
Allison, PA (cdp) Fayette County	68	13.26
Wattsville, VA (cdp) Accomack County	168	13.09
Princeton, NC (town) Johnston County	170	13.04
Wallula, WA (cdp) Walla Walla County	12	13.04
Lake City, FL (city) Columbia County	1,604	13.03
Aucilla, FL (cdp) Jefferson County	40	13.03
Union Level, VA (cdp) Mecklenburg County	57	12.90
Perry, FL (city) Taylor County	906	12.79
Poplar Hills, KY (city) Jefferson County	28	12.44
Shelter Cove, CA (cdp) Humboldt County	65	12.40
Crewe, VA (town) Nottoway County	319	12.31
Spencer, NC (town) Rowan County	400	12.17
Manistee, MI (township) Manistee County	489	12.06
New Carrollton, MD (city) Prince George's County	1,461	12.05
Duquesne, PA (city) Allegheny County	696	11.95
Springdale, MD (cdp) Prince George's County	301	11.93
Blackstone, VA (town) Nottoway County	421	11.61
Atlantic, VA (cdp) Accomack County	59	11.59
Kimball, WV (town) McDowell County	38	11.38
Brodnax, VA (town) Brunswick County	49	11.37
Kenbridge, VA (town) Lunenburg County	135	11.32
South Hill, VA (town) Mecklenburg County	523	11.25
Cape Charles, VA (town) Northampton County	125	11.24
Anmoore, WV (town) Harrison County	129	11.21
Hiram, GA (city) Paulding County	367	11.10
North Richmond, CA (cdp) Contra Costa County	326	10.87
Moss Point, MS (city) Jackson County	1,483	10.62
Mason Neck, VA (cdp) Fairfax County	238	10.60
Newsoms, VA (town) Southampton County	29	10.55
Rachel, NV (cdp) Lincoln County	8	10.53
Gary, WV (city) McDowell County	119	10.48
Davenport, CA (cdp) Santa Cruz County	32	10.36
Royal Lakes, IL (village) Macoupin County	15	10.27
Woodland, GA (city) Talbot County	49	10.08
Burkeville, VA (town) Nottoway County	53	10.06
Naples, TX (city) Morris County	130	9.97
Belmont, NH (cdp) Belknap County	131	9.93
Onancock, VA (town) Accomack County	157	9.91
Kinloch, MO (city) St. Louis County	62	9.79
Middletown, CA (cdp) Lake County	161	9.78
Colwyn, PA (borough) Delaware County	243	9.67
Swansea, SC (town) Lexington County	78	9.67
Comstock, NE (village) Custer County	9	9.57
Rembert, SC (cdp) Sumter County	21	9.46
Lovejoy, GA (city) Clayton County	547	9.45
Warren Park, IN (town) Marion County	130	9.37
Hopkins, SC (cdp) Richland County	286	9.34
Paducah, TX (town) Cottle County	117	9.33
Anawalt, WV (town) McDowell County	26	9.29
Waverly Hall, GA (town) Harris County	99	9.26
Greensboro, GA (city) Greene County	310	9.25
Clarksville, VA (town) Mecklenburg County	112	9.18
Slayden, TN (town) Dickson County	23	9.13
Dallas, GA (city) Paulding County	979	9.10
Rankin, PA (borough) Allegheny County	185	9.09
Micro, NC (town) Johnston County	36	9.02
Mantoloking, NJ (borough) Ocean County	39	9.01
Cane Savannah, SC (cdp) Sumter County	126	9.00
Pittsburg, TX (city) Camp County	402	8.96
Creston, IL (village) Ogle County	70	8.96
Pineview, GA (town) Wilcox County	45	8.95
Victoria, VA (town) Lunenburg County	125	8.91
Kingston, GA (city) Bartow County	71	8.85
Largo, MD (cdp) Prince George's County	943	8.56
Cherryvale, SC (cdp) Sumter County	261	8.56
Uplands Park, MO (village) St. Louis County	37	8.47
Jasper, FL (city) Hamilton County	367	8.40
Marshallville, GA (city) Macon County	106	8.17
Lanham, MD (cdp) Prince George's County	729	8.16
Morgan, TX (city) Bosque County	42	8.14
Horace, KS (city) Greeley County	7	8.14
Laurel Park, VA (cdp) Henry County	42	8.05
White Springs, FL (town) Hamilton County	63	8.03

Please refer to the Explanation of Data in the front of the book for more detailed information.

Ancestry

African, Sub-Saharan: African

Top 150 Places Sorted by Percent of Total Population

Based on places with total population of 7,500 or more

Place	Population	%
Troy, AL (city) Pike County	3,256	18.92
Jessup, MD (cdp) Anne Arundel County	2,087	18.84
Douglasville, GA (city) Douglas County	5,008	17.05
Franklin, VA (ind. city) Franklin independent city	1,406	16.45
Lithia Springs, GA (cdp) Douglas County	2,572	15.07
Lake City, FL (city) Columbia County	1,604	13.03
New Carrollton, MD (city) Prince George's County	1,461	12.05
Moss Point, MS (city) Jackson County	1,483	10.62
Dallas, GA (city) Paulding County	979	9.10
Largo, MD (cdp) Prince George's County	943	8.56
Lanham, MD (cdp) Prince George's County	729	8.16
Gulfport, MS (city) Harrison County	5,043	7.61
Sumter, SC (city) Sumter County	3,059	7.58
Darby, PA (borough) Delaware County	777	7.33
Spanish Lake, MO (cdp) St. Louis County	1,512	6.93
Kettering, MD (cdp) Prince George's County	811	6.46
North Bellport, NY (cdp) Suffolk County	728	6.46
View Park-Windsor Hills, CA (cdp) Los Angeles County	694	6.45
Brock Hall, MD (cdp) Prince George's County	513	6.29
Clarkston, GA (city) DeKalb County	475	6.29
Fairland, MD (cdp) Montgomery County	1,444	6.25
Glenn Dale, MD (cdp) Prince George's County	876	6.20
White Oak, MD (cdp) Montgomery County	1,007	6.04
Rosaryville, MD (cdp) Prince George's County	685	5.97
Gautier, MS (city) Jackson County	1,074	5.94
Dunn, NC (city) Harnett County	534	5.85
Mount Pleasant, TX (city) Titus County	881	5.83
Lemoore Station, CA (cdp) Kings County	455	5.77
Fort Pierce, FL (city) St. Lucie County	2,399	5.65
Coral Hills, MD (cdp) Prince George's County	540	5.59
Salisbury, NC (city) Rowan County	1,836	5.56
Milford Mill, MD (cdp) Baltimore County	1,591	5.53
Lake Arbor, MD (cdp) Prince George's County	563	5.46
West Athens, CA (cdp) Los Angeles County	451	5.43
Jefferson, LA (cdp) Jefferson Parish	652	5.41
Chillum, MD (cdp) Prince George's County	1,865	5.32
Maryland City, MD (cdp) Anne Arundel County	821	5.32
Knightdale, NC (town) Wake County	556	5.31
Donaldsonville, LA (city) Ascension Parish	396	5.27
Adelphi, MD (cdp) Prince George's County	791	5.26
Lincolnia, VA (cdp) Fairfax County	1,078	5.22
Cincinnati, OH (city) Hamilton County	15,631	5.21
Tallahassee, FL (city) Leon County	9,217	5.21
Shively, KY (city) Jefferson County	789	5.21
Union City, GA (city) Fulton County	927	5.18
Marlboro Village, MD (cdp) Prince George's County	481	5.14
Takoma Park, MD (city) Montgomery County	861	5.11
Fort Wayne, IN (city) Allen County	12,753	5.03
Texarkana, AR (city) Miller County	1,488	5.00
Lochearn, MD (cdp) Baltimore County	1,272	4.95
Americus, GA (city) Sumter County	843	4.95
Speedway, IN (town) Marion County	581	4.87
Richmond, CA (city) Contra Costa County	4,973	4.86
Texarkana, TX (city) Bowie County	1,748	4.86
Camp Pendleton South, CA (cdp) San Diego County	652	4.86
Fayetteville, GA (city) Fayette County	739	4.84
Jackson, MI (city) Jackson County	1,634	4.76
Carson, CA (city) Los Angeles County	4,332	4.74
Indianapolis, IN (city) Marion County	38,288	4.73
Old Jamestown, MO (cdp) St. Louis County	967	4.72
Neabsco, VA (cdp) Prince William County	442	4.69
Willowbrook, CA (cdp) Los Angeles County	1,646	4.68
Belle Glade, FL (city) Palm Beach County	825	4.67
Berkeley, MO (city) St. Louis County	426	4.66
Virginia Beach, VA (ind. city) Virginia Beach independent city	20,099	4.61
Seabrook, MD (cdp) Prince George's County	717	4.59
Cherry Hill, VA (cdp) Prince William County	707	4.56
Lakeside, VA (cdp) Henrico County	547	4.56
Essex, MD (cdp) Baltimore County	1,758	4.53
College Park, GA (city) Fulton County	630	4.51
Oronoko, MI (charter township) Berrien County	414	4.49
Summerfield, MD (cdp) Prince George's County	493	4.43
South Laurel, MD (cdp) Prince George's County	1,123	4.36
Atlantic City, NJ (city) Atlantic County	1,745	4.35
Bryans Road, MD (cdp) Charles County	327	4.33
Compton, CA (city) Los Angeles County	4,112	4.29
Beloit, WI (city) Rock County	1,578	4.26
Key West, FL (city) Monroe County	1,035	4.24
Villa Rica, GA (city) Carroll County	530	4.24
Accokeek, MD (cdp) Prince George's County	438	4.17
Acworth, GA (city) Cobb County	805	4.16
Powder Springs, GA (city) Cobb County	572	4.15
Bladensburg, MD (town) Prince George's County	370	4.15
River Ridge, LA (cdp) Jefferson Parish	552	4.12
Fitchburg, WI (city) Dane County	1,004	4.10
Wilkinsburg, PA (borough) Allegheny County	655	4.01
Rodeo, CA (cdp) Contra Costa County	362	3.97
Lake Los Angeles, CA (cdp) Los Angeles County	495	3.96
Suisun City, CA (city) Solano County	1,089	3.93
Dentsville, SC (cdp) Richland County	528	3.92
Bowie, MD (city) Prince George's County	2,095	3.86
Ocala, FL (city) Marion County	2,150	3.84
Greenbelt, MD (city) Prince George's County	876	3.84
Champaign, IL (city) Champaign County	3,045	3.83
Youngstown, OH (city) Mahoning County	2,655	3.82
Laurel, MD (city) Prince George's County	923	3.78
Mitchellville, MD (cdp) Prince George's County	438	3.76
Redan, GA (cdp) DeKalb County	1,279	3.74
Winchester, NV (cdp) Clark County	1,000	3.68
Middle River, MD (cdp) Baltimore County	871	3.66
Canton, OH (city) Stark County	2,713	3.64
Lawrence, IN (city) Marion County	1,595	3.59
Erie, PA (city) Erie County	3,634	3.58
West Carson, CA (cdp) Los Angeles County	743	3.55
West Columbia, SC (city) Lexington County	521	3.55
Aspen Hill, MD (cdp) Montgomery County	1,657	3.52
Ferguson, MO (city) St. Louis County	749	3.51
Jeannette, PA (city) Westmoreland County	344	3.50
McNair, VA (cdp) Fairfax County	531	3.49
Columbia Heights, MN (city) Anoka County	676	3.47
Kinston, NC (city) Lenoir County	759	3.45
Robinwood, MD (cdp) Washington County	278	3.45
Jackson, TN (city) Madison County	2,217	3.44
Fife, WA (city) Pierce County	290	3.44
Marietta, GA (city) Cobb County	1,961	3.43
Yeadon, PA (borough) Delaware County	394	3.43
McDonough, GA (city) Henry County	691	3.42
Cordele, GA (city) Crisp County	379	3.38
Radcliff, KY (city) Hardin County	710	3.37
Bastrop, LA (city) Morehouse Parish	391	3.37
New Orleans, LA (city) Orleans Parish	9,872	3.34
Kinross, MI (charter township) Chippewa County	269	3.34
Urbana, IL (city) Champaign County	1,356	3.32
Sudley, VA (cdp) Prince William County	501	3.28
New Albany, MS (city) Union County	262	3.28
Brooklyn Center, MN (city) Hennepin County	970	3.27
Parkville, MD (cdp) Baltimore County	975	3.23
Pascagoula, MS (city) Jackson County	741	3.23
Colesville, MD (cdp) Montgomery County	459	3.23
Memphis, FL (cdp) Manatee County	274	3.21
Woodfield, SC (cdp) Richland County	322	3.20
Bridgeton, NJ (city) Cumberland County	799	3.19
Stockbridge, GA (city) Henry County	752	3.17
Tukwila, WA (city) King County	584	3.15
Gardere, LA (cdp) East Baton Rouge Parish	331	3.15
Atlanta, GA (city) Fulton County	12,994	3.14
Somerset, NJ (cdp) Somerset County	702	3.14
Montgomery Village, MD (cdp) Montgomery County	993	3.13
Glenmont, MD (cdp) Montgomery County	420	3.12
Burtonsville, MD (cdp) Montgomery County	288	3.12
Enterprise, AL (city) Coffee County	787	3.11
Jesup, GA (city) Wayne County	314	3.09
La Presa, CA (cdp) San Diego County	1,065	3.05
Burlington, IA (city) Des Moines County	781	3.05
Landover, MD (cdp) Prince George's County	719	3.05
Leavenworth, KS (city) Leavenworth County	1,071	3.04
Avon Park, FL (city) Highlands County	272	3.03
Beltsville, MD (cdp) Prince George's County	467	3.02
Randallstown, MD (cdp) Baltimore County	977	3.00
East Riverdale, MD (cdp) Prince George's County	470	3.00

Please refer to the Explanation of Data in the front of the book for more detailed information.

Ancestry

African, Sub-Saharan: Cape Verdean

U.S. and 50 States Sorted by Population and Percent of Total Population

Place	Population	%
United States	**92,936**	**0.03**
Massachusetts	53,174	0.82
Rhode Island	19,490	1.84
Connecticut	4,381	0.12
Florida	2,983	0.02
California	2,514	0.01
New Jersey	1,430	0.02
Virginia	1,059	0.01
Maryland	1,022	0.02
New York	844	<0.01
Georgia	802	0.01
North Carolina	568	0.01
Texas	514	<0.01
Nevada	401	0.02
Ohio	396	<0.01
South Carolina	378	0.01
Pennsylvania	355	<0.01
New Hampshire	311	0.02
Arizona	263	<0.01
Maine	218	0.02
Washington	217	<0.01
Illinois	197	<0.01
Oklahoma	187	0.01
Michigan	177	<0.01
Louisiana	117	<0.01
Oregon	98	<0.01
District of Columbia	93	0.02
Missouri	90	<0.01
Tennessee	78	<0.01
Idaho	76	<0.01
Hawaii	59	<0.01
Colorado	52	<0.01
New Mexico	52	<0.01
Utah	50	<0.01
Vermont	49	0.01
Delaware	47	0.01
West Virginia	43	<0.01
Kentucky	33	<0.01
Indiana	28	<0.01
Wisconsin	24	<0.01
Mississippi	17	<0.01
Kansas	13	<0.01
Alaska	10	<0.01
Minnesota	10	<0.01
Arkansas	8	<0.01
Nebraska	8	<0.01
Alabama	0	0.00
Iowa	0	0.00
Montana	0	0.00
North Dakota	0	0.00
South Dakota	0	0.00
Wyoming	0	0.00

Place	Population	%
Rhode Island	19,490	1.84
Massachusetts	53,174	0.82
Connecticut	4,381	0.12
United States	**92,936**	**0.03**
Florida	2,983	0.02
New Jersey	1,430	0.02
Maryland	1,022	0.02
Nevada	401	0.02
New Hampshire	311	0.02
Maine	218	0.02
District of Columbia	93	0.02
California	2,514	0.01
Virginia	1,059	0.01
Georgia	802	0.01
North Carolina	568	0.01
South Carolina	378	0.01
Oklahoma	187	0.01
Vermont	49	0.01
Delaware	47	0.01
New York	844	<0.01
Texas	514	<0.01
Ohio	396	<0.01
Pennsylvania	355	<0.01
Arizona	263	<0.01
Washington	217	<0.01
Illinois	197	<0.01
Michigan	177	<0.01
Louisiana	117	<0.01
Oregon	98	<0.01
Missouri	90	<0.01
Tennessee	78	<0.01
Idaho	76	<0.01
Hawaii	59	<0.01
Colorado	52	<0.01
New Mexico	52	<0.01
Utah	50	<0.01
West Virginia	43	<0.01
Kentucky	33	<0.01
Indiana	28	<0.01
Wisconsin	24	<0.01
Mississippi	17	<0.01
Kansas	13	<0.01
Alaska	10	<0.01
Minnesota	10	<0.01
Arkansas	8	<0.01
Nebraska	8	<0.01
Alabama	0	0.00
Iowa	0	0.00
Montana	0	0.00
North Dakota	0	0.00
South Dakota	0	0.00
Wyoming	0	0.00

Please refer to the Explanation of Data in the front of the book for more detailed information.

Ancestry

African, Sub-Saharan: Cape Verdean

Top 150 Places Sorted by Population

Based on all places, regardless of total population

Place	Population	%
Brockton, MA (city) Plymouth County	11,709	12.47
Boston, MA (city) Suffolk County	11,284	1.87
New Bedford, MA (city) Bristol County	10,262	10.81
Pawtucket, RI (city) Providence County	8,720	12.17
Providence, RI (city) Providence County	4,015	2.25
East Providence, RI (city) Providence County	2,265	4.77
Taunton, MA (city) Bristol County	1,852	3.31
Fall River, MA (city) Bristol County	1,574	1.76
Wareham, MA (town) Plymouth County	1,184	5.50
Central Falls, RI (city) Providence County	1,158	5.97
Bridgeport, CT (city/town) Fairfield County	1,080	0.76
Randolph, MA (cdp/town) Norfolk County	968	3.06
Cranston, RI (city) Providence County	739	0.92
Weymouth Town, MA (city) Norfolk County	595	1.12
New York, NY (city) Kings County	595	0.01
Dartmouth, MA (town) Bristol County	585	1.75
Plymouth, MA (town) Plymouth County	574	1.03
Newport, RI (city) Newport County	534	2.14
Norwich, CT (city/town) New London County	519	1.30
Jersey City, NJ (city) Hudson County	435	0.18
Chelsea, MA (city) Suffolk County	434	1.26
Mashpee, MA (town) Barnstable County	377	2.72
Cambridge, MA (city) Middlesex County	371	0.36
Waterbury, CT (city/town) New Haven County	353	0.32
Newton, MA (city) Middlesex County	345	0.41
Warwick, RI (city) Kent County	338	0.40
Barnstable Town, MA (city) Barnstable County	317	0.69
Marion, MA (town) Plymouth County	314	6.35
Attleboro, MA (city) Bristol County	313	0.72
Milton, MA (cdp/town) Norfolk County	307	1.15
Spring Valley, NV (cdp) Clark County	300	0.18
Sacramento, CA (city) Sacramento County	299	0.07
Somerville, MA (city) Middlesex County	282	0.37
Hanson, MA (town) Plymouth County	273	2.70
San Diego, CA (city) San Diego County	270	0.02
Scituate, MA (town) Plymouth County	268	1.48
Stoughton, MA (town) Norfolk County	265	0.99
Quincy, MA (city) Norfolk County	262	0.29
Everett, MA (city) Middlesex County	255	0.63
Carver, MA (town) Plymouth County	251	2.19
North Providence, RI (town) Providence County	249	0.77
Malden, MA (city) Middlesex County	249	0.43
Framingham, MA (cdp/town) Middlesex County	248	0.37
Dennis, MA (town) Barnstable County	246	1.69
Middleborough, MA (town) Plymouth County	243	1.08
Virginia Beach, VA (ind. city) Virginia Beach independent city	229	0.05
Falmouth, MA (town) Barnstable County	218	0.69
Lynn, MA (city) Essex County	215	0.24
West Haven, CT (city/town) New Haven County	214	0.39
Milford, CT (city) New Haven County	212	0.42
Milford, CT (town) New Haven County	212	0.40
Yarmouth, MA (town) Barnstable County	208	0.87
Cumberland, RI (town) Providence County	208	0.62
Manhattan, NY (borough) New York County	206	0.01
Poinciana, FL (cdp) Osceola County	202	0.40
Mansfield, MA (town) Bristol County	198	0.86
Los Angeles, CA (city) Los Angeles County	198	0.01
Lincoln, RI (town) Providence County	196	0.93
Yulee, FL (cdp) Nassau County	194	1.59
Apex, NC (town) Wake County	192	0.56
Fairhaven, MA (town) Bristol County	191	1.20
Weweantic, MA (cdp) Plymouth County	190	9.64
Easton, MA (town) Bristol County	188	0.82
Canton, MA (town) Norfolk County	187	0.88
Seekonk, MA (town) Bristol County	186	1.36
Worcester, MA (city) Worcester County	184	0.10
Lowell, MA (city) Middlesex County	183	0.17
West Wareham, MA (cdp) Plymouth County	178	8.54
Holbrook, MA (cdp/town) Norfolk County	166	1.55
Medford, MA (city) Middlesex County	165	0.30
New London, CT (city/town) New London County	163	0.59
Coventry, RI (town) Kent County	162	0.46
Bridgewater, MA (town) Plymouth County	159	0.60
Westport, MA (town) Bristol County	158	1.03
Danbury, CT (city/town) Fairfield County	158	0.20
South Dennis, MA (cdp) Barnstable County	157	4.13
Ledyard, CT (town) New London County	153	1.02
Springfield, MA (city) Hampden County	153	0.10
Brooklyn, NY (borough) Kings County	153	0.01
Hilton Head Island, SC (town) Beaufort County	149	0.41
Hillside, NJ (township) Union County	146	0.69
Freetown, MA (town) Bristol County	144	1.64
Woonsocket, RI (city) Providence County	144	0.35
Delray Beach, FL (city) Palm Beach County	144	0.24
Ansonia, CT (city/town) New Haven County	136	0.71
San Antonio, TX (city) Medina County	136	0.01
Wareham Center, MA (cdp) Plymouth County	135	4.70
Acushnet, MA (town) Bristol County	134	1.30
Montgomery, IL (village) Kendall County	134	0.84
New Britain, CT (city/town) Hartford County	133	0.18
Bowie, MD (city) Prince George's County	132	0.24
Newark, NJ (city) Essex County	132	0.05
Lakeville, MA (town) Plymouth County	131	1.25
Woburn, MA (city) Middlesex County	129	0.34
Philadelphia, PA (city) Philadelphia County	129	0.01
Bliss Corner, MA (cdp) Bristol County	127	2.25
Norfolk, VA (ind. city) Norfolk independent city	127	0.05
West Bridgewater, MA (town) Plymouth County	124	1.81
Amherst, MA (town) Hampshire County	124	0.33
Riverview, FL (cdp) Hillsborough County	124	0.19
Harwich, MA (town) Barnstable County	121	0.98
New Haven, CT (city/town) New Haven County	117	0.09
Queens, NY (borough) Queens County	117	0.01
Scituate, MA (cdp) Plymouth County	116	2.18
Lakewood, NJ (township) Ocean County	116	0.13
Oakland, CA (city) Alameda County	115	0.03
Concord, CA (city) Contra Costa County	114	0.09
Brookline, MA (cdp/town) Norfolk County	112	0.19
Naugatuck, CT (borough/town) New Haven County	110	0.35
Annapolis Neck, MD (cdp) Anne Arundel County	109	0.98
Holly Hill, FL (city) Volusia County	108	0.90
Raynham, MA (town) Bristol County	108	0.83
Bronx, NY (borough) Bronx County	108	0.01
Marshfield, MA (town) Plymouth County	106	0.42
Elk Grove, CA (city) Sacramento County	106	0.08
San Jose, CA (city) Santa Clara County	105	0.01
North Scituate, MA (cdp) Plymouth County	103	1.88
Webster, MA (cdp) Worcester County	103	0.90
Webster, MA (town) Worcester County	103	0.62
Stratford, CT (cdp/town) Fairfield County	103	0.20
South Yarmouth, MA (cdp) Barnstable County	102	0.89
West Springfield Town, MA (city) Hampden County	102	0.36
Plymouth, MA (cdp) Plymouth County	101	1.49
Smith Mills, MA (cdp) Bristol County	100	2.07
Leominster, MA (city) Worcester County	100	0.24
South Kingstown, RI (town) Washington County	99	0.33
Oak Bluffs, MA (town) Dukes County	97	2.22
Cheltenham, PA (township) Montgomery County	96	0.26
Revere, MA (city) Suffolk County	96	0.19
Nashua, NH (city) Hillsborough County	96	0.11
Fontana, CA (city) San Bernardino County	96	0.05
Buffalo, NY (city) Erie County	95	0.04
Raleigh, NC (city) Wake County	95	0.02
Englewood, OH (city) Montgomery County	94	0.71
Seattle, WA (city) King County	93	0.02
Washington, DC (city) District of Columbia	93	0.02
Sandwich, MA (town) Barnstable County	92	0.45
Onset, MA (cdp) Plymouth County	91	9.83
North Westport, MA (cdp) Bristol County	90	2.15
Amherst Center, MA (cdp) Hampshire County	89	0.46
West Orange, NJ (township) Essex County	87	0.19
Pembroke Pines, FL (city) Broward County	87	0.06
Chesapeake, VA (ind. city) Chesapeake independent city	87	0.04
White Marsh, MD (cdp) Baltimore County	86	0.90
North Attleborough, MA (town) Bristol County	85	0.30
Whitman, MA (town) Plymouth County	82	0.57
Bridgewater, MA (cdp) Plymouth County	81	1.11
Arlington, MA (cdp/town) Middlesex County	81	0.19
Cumberland Hill, RI (cdp) Providence County	78	1.00
Hypoluxo, FL (town) Palm Beach County	77	3.07

Please refer to the Explanation of Data in the front of the book for more detailed information.

Ancestry

African, Sub-Saharan: Cape Verdean

Top 150 Places Sorted by Percent of Total Population

Based on all places, regardless of total population

Place	Population	%
Brockton, MA (city) Plymouth County	11,709	12.47
Pawtucket, RI (city) Providence County	8,720	12.17
Grand View Estates, CO (cdp) Douglas County	30	11.07
New Bedford, MA (city) Bristol County	10,262	10.81
Onset, MA (cdp) Plymouth County	91	9.83
Weweantic, MA (cdp) Plymouth County	190	9.64
West Wareham, MA (cdp) Plymouth County	178	8.54
Aquinnah, MA (town) Dukes County	31	7.67
Providence, MN (township) Lac qui Parle County	8	7.08
Marion, MA (town) Plymouth County	314	6.35
Central Falls, RI (city) Providence County	1,158	5.97
Wareham, MA (town) Plymouth County	1,184	5.50
South Woodstock, CT (cdp) Windham County	57	4.99
East Providence, RI (city) Providence County	2,265	4.77
Wareham Center, MA (cdp) Plymouth County	135	4.70
South Dennis, MA (cdp) Barnstable County	157	4.13
Hamlin, ME (town) Aroostook County	12	3.99
Taunton, MA (city) Bristol County	1,852	3.31
Vershire, VT (town) Orange County	16	3.12
Hypoluxo, FL (town) Palm Beach County	77	3.07
Randolph, MA (cdp/town) Norfolk County	968	3.06
North Lakeville, MA (cdp) Plymouth County	62	2.88
West Burke, VT (village) Caledonia County	7	2.80
Mashpee, MA (town) Barnstable County	377	2.72
Hanson, MA (town) Plymouth County	273	2.70
The Pinehills, MA (cdp) Plymouth County	23	2.53
Bradford, RI (cdp) Washington County	40	2.35
Providence, RI (city) Providence County	4,015	2.25
Bliss Corner, MA (cdp) Bristol County	127	2.25
Oak Bluffs, MA (town) Dukes County	97	2.22
Dennis Port, MA (cdp) Barnstable County	76	2.21
Carver, MA (town) Plymouth County	251	2.19
Scituate, MA (cdp) Plymouth County	116	2.18
Smyrna, ME (town) Aroostook County	11	2.17
North Westport, MA (cdp) Bristol County	90	2.15
Newport, RI (city) Newport County	534	2.14
Smith Mills, MA (cdp) Bristol County	100	2.07
Harwich Center, MA (cdp) Barnstable County	35	1.97
North Scituate, MA (cdp) Plymouth County	103	1.88
Boston, MA (city) Suffolk County	11,284	1.87
West Bridgewater, MA (town) Plymouth County	124	1.81
Fall River, MA (city) Bristol County	1,574	1.76
Dartmouth, MA (town) Bristol County	585	1.75
Dennis, MA (town) Barnstable County	246	1.69
Acushnet Center, MA (cdp) Bristol County	44	1.69
Raynham Center, MA (cdp) Bristol County	68	1.67
Freetown, MA (town) Bristol County	144	1.64
Nesbit, MN (township) Polk County	2	1.61
Yulee, FL (cdp) Nassau County	194	1.59
Holbrook, MA (cdp/town) Norfolk County	166	1.55
Northwest Harwich, MA (cdp) Barnstable County	66	1.52
Plymouth, MA (cdp) Plymouth County	101	1.49
Scituate, MA (town) Plymouth County	268	1.48
Yarmouth Port, MA (cdp) Barnstable County	73	1.41
Marlboro Meadows, MD (cdp) Prince George's County	50	1.38
Seekonk, MA (town) Bristol County	186	1.36
Norwich, CT (city/town) New London County	519	1.30
Acushnet, MA (town) Bristol County	134	1.30
Grayson, GA (city) Gwinnett County	31	1.30
Chelsea, MA (city) Suffolk County	434	1.26
Lakeville, MA (town) Plymouth County	131	1.25
Fairhaven, MA (town) Bristol County	191	1.20
Silver Hill, MD (cdp) Prince George's County	72	1.18
Angwin, CA (cdp) Napa County	44	1.18
Lenox, MA (cdp) Berkshire County	17	1.18
Milton, MA (cdp/town) Norfolk County	307	1.15
Weymouth Town, MA (city) Norfolk County	595	1.12
Bridgewater, MA (cdp) Plymouth County	81	1.11
South Hackensack, NJ (township) Bergen County	25	1.11
Middleborough, MA (town) Plymouth County	243	1.08
Mexico, ME (cdp) Oxford County	23	1.07
Rochester, MA (town) Plymouth County	54	1.06
Kingston, MA (cdp) Plymouth County	59	1.04
Plymouth, MA (town) Plymouth County	574	1.03
Westport, MA (town) Bristol County	158	1.03
Mashpee Neck, MA (cdp) Barnstable County	11	1.03
Ledyard, CT (town) New London County	153	1.02
Arlington, KY (city) Carlisle County	4	1.02
Cumberland Hill, RI (cdp) Providence County	78	1.00
Preston, CT (town) New London County	47	1.00
Stoughton, MA (town) Norfolk County	265	0.99
Harwich, MA (town) Barnstable County	121	0.98
Annapolis Neck, MD (cdp) Anne Arundel County	109	0.98
Dighton, MA (town) Bristol County	68	0.98
Holland, MA (cdp) Hampden County	16	0.97
Lincoln, RI (town) Providence County	196	0.93
Dexter, ME (cdp) Penobscot County	17	0.93
Cranston, RI (city) Providence County	739	0.92
Phillipston, MA (town) Worcester County	17	0.92
Westborough, MA (cdp) Worcester County	36	0.91
Holly Hill, FL (city) Volusia County	108	0.90
Webster, MA (cdp) Worcester County	103	0.90
White Marsh, MD (cdp) Baltimore County	86	0.90
Tiverton, RI (cdp) Newport County	66	0.90
Hanson, MA (cdp) Plymouth County	17	0.90
South Yarmouth, MA (cdp) Barnstable County	102	0.89
Wilbraham, MA (cdp) Hampden County	29	0.89
Canton, MA (town) Norfolk County	187	0.88
Sandwich, MA (cdp) Barnstable County	26	0.88
Yarmouth, MA (town) Barnstable County	208	0.87
Mansfield, MA (town) Bristol County	198	0.86
East Falmouth, MA (cdp) Barnstable County	51	0.85
Warm Springs, CA (cdp) Riverside County	18	0.85
Montgomery, IL (village) Kendall County	134	0.84
Ocean Bluff-Brant Rock, MA (cdp) Plymouth County	41	0.84
Mexico, ME (town) Oxford County	23	0.84
Raynham, MA (town) Bristol County	108	0.83
Easton, MA (town) Bristol County	188	0.82
Rollinsford, NH (town) Strafford County	21	0.81
Plymouth, ME (town) Penobscot County	10	0.81
Marshfield, MA (cdp) Plymouth County	35	0.79
Plympton, MA (town) Plymouth County	22	0.79
North Providence, RI (town) Providence County	249	0.77
Worthington, MA (town) Hampshire County	9	0.77
Bridgeport, CT (city/town) Fairfield County	1,080	0.76
Holloman AFB, NM (cdp) Otero County	28	0.76
Hampton, CT (town) Windham County	14	0.75
South Windham, ME (cdp) Cumberland County	10	0.75
Peru, MA (town) Berkshire County	6	0.74
Attleboro, MA (city) Bristol County	313	0.72
Woodstock, CT (town) Windham County	57	0.72
Ansonia, CT (city/town) New Haven County	136	0.71
Englewood, OH (city) Montgomery County	94	0.71
Fort Polk South, LA (cdp) Vernon Parish	67	0.71
Bourne, MA (cdp) Barnstable County	9	0.71
Hadley, MA (town) Hampshire County	36	0.70
Barnstable Town, MA (city) Barnstable County	317	0.69
Falmouth, MA (town) Barnstable County	218	0.69
Hillside, NJ (township) Union County	146	0.69
Brooklyn, CT (cdp) Windham County	9	0.69
Falmouth, MA (cdp) Barnstable County	27	0.68
New Shoreham, RI (town) Washington County	6	0.66
Sharon, MA (cdp) Norfolk County	34	0.65
West Brookfield, MA (town) Worcester County	24	0.64
Tuftonboro, NH (town) Carroll County	16	0.64
West Dennis, MA (cdp) Barnstable County	13	0.64
Everett, MA (city) Middlesex County	255	0.63
Cumberland, RI (town) Providence County	208	0.62
Webster, MA (town) Worcester County	103	0.62
Mattapoisett, MA (town) Plymouth County	37	0.61
Holland, MA (town) Hampden County	16	0.61
Bridgewater, MA (town) Plymouth County	159	0.60
Dallas, GA (city) Paulding County	65	0.60
New London, CT (city/town) New London County	163	0.59
Kingston, RI (cdp) Washington County	36	0.59
Whitman, MA (town) Plymouth County	82	0.57
Tisbury, MA (town) Dukes County	22	0.57
Apex, NC (town) Wake County	192	0.56
Weston, MA (town) Middlesex County	61	0.55
West Yarmouth, MA (cdp) Barnstable County	33	0.54

Please refer to the Explanation of Data in the front of the book for more detailed information.

Ancestry

African, Sub-Saharan: Cape Verdean

Top 150 Places Sorted by Percent of Total Population

Based on places with total population of 7,500 or more

Place	Population	%
Brockton, MA (city) Plymouth County	11,709	12.47
Pawtucket, RI (city) Providence County	8,720	12.17
New Bedford, MA (city) Bristol County	10,262	10.81
Central Falls, RI (city) Providence County	1,158	5.97
Wareham, MA (town) Plymouth County	1,184	5.50
East Providence, RI (city) Providence County	2,265	4.77
Taunton, MA (city) Bristol County	1,852	3.31
Randolph, MA (cdp/town) Norfolk County	968	3.06
Mashpee, MA (town) Barnstable County	377	2.72
Hanson, MA (town) Plymouth County	273	2.70
Providence, RI (city) Providence County	4,015	2.25
Carver, MA (town) Plymouth County	251	2.19
Newport, RI (city) Newport County	534	2.14
Boston, MA (city) Suffolk County	11,284	1.87
Fall River, MA (city) Bristol County	1,574	1.76
Dartmouth, MA (town) Bristol County	585	1.75
Dennis, MA (town) Barnstable County	246	1.69
Freetown, MA (town) Bristol County	144	1.64
Yulee, FL (cdp) Nassau County	194	1.59
Holbrook, MA (cdp/town) Norfolk County	166	1.55
Scituate, MA (town) Plymouth County	268	1.48
Seekonk, MA (town) Bristol County	186	1.36
Norwich, CT (city/town) New London County	519	1.30
Acushnet, MA (town) Bristol County	134	1.30
Chelsea, MA (city) Suffolk County	434	1.26
Lakeville, MA (town) Plymouth County	131	1.25
Fairhaven, MA (town) Bristol County	191	1.20
Milton, MA (cdp/town) Norfolk County	307	1.15
Weymouth Town, MA (city) Norfolk County	595	1.12
Middleborough, MA (town) Plymouth County	243	1.08
Plymouth, MA (town) Plymouth County	574	1.03
Westport, MA (town) Bristol County	158	1.03
Ledyard, CT (town) New London County	153	1.02
Cumberland Hill, RI (cdp) Providence County	78	1.00
Stoughton, MA (town) Norfolk County	265	0.99
Harwich, MA (town) Barnstable County	121	0.98
Annapolis Neck, MD (cdp) Anne Arundel County	109	0.98
Lincoln, RI (town) Providence County	196	0.93
Cranston, RI (city) Providence County	739	0.92
Holly Hill, FL (city) Volusia County	108	0.90
Webster, MA (cdp) Worcester County	103	0.90
White Marsh, MD (cdp) Baltimore County	86	0.90
South Yarmouth, MA (cdp) Barnstable County	102	0.89
Canton, MA (town) Norfolk County	187	0.88
Yarmouth, MA (town) Barnstable County	208	0.87
Mansfield, MA (town) Bristol County	198	0.86
Montgomery, IL (village) Kendall County	134	0.84
Raynham, MA (town) Bristol County	108	0.83
Easton, MA (town) Bristol County	188	0.82
North Providence, RI (town) Providence County	249	0.77
Bridgeport, CT (city/town) Fairfield County	1,080	0.76
Attleboro, MA (city) Bristol County	313	0.72
Woodstock, CT (town) Windham County	57	0.72
Ansonia, CT (city/town) New Haven County	136	0.71
Englewood, OH (city) Montgomery County	94	0.71
Fort Polk South, LA (cdp) Vernon Parish	67	0.71
Barnstable Town, MA (city) Barnstable County	317	0.69
Falmouth, MA (town) Barnstable County	218	0.69
Hillside, NJ (township) Union County	146	0.69
Everett, MA (city) Middlesex County	255	0.63
Cumberland, RI (town) Providence County	208	0.62
Webster, MA (town) Worcester County	103	0.62
Bridgewater, MA (town) Plymouth County	159	0.60
Dallas, GA (city) Paulding County	65	0.60
New London, CT (city/town) New London County	163	0.59
Whitman, MA (town) Plymouth County	82	0.57
Apex, NC (town) Wake County	192	0.56
Weston, MA (town) Middlesex County	61	0.55
Lebanon, NH (city) Grafton County	69	0.53
Swansea, MA (town) Bristol County	76	0.48
Kingston, MA (town) Plymouth County	59	0.47
Coventry, RI (town) Kent County	162	0.46
Amherst Center, MA (cdp) Hampshire County	89	0.46
Sandwich, MA (town) Barnstable County	92	0.45
Wakefield-Peacedale, RI (cdp) Washington County	40	0.44
Malden, MA (city) Middlesex County	249	0.43
Milford, CT (city) New Haven County	212	0.42
Marshfield, MA (town) Plymouth County	106	0.42
Tiverton, RI (town) Newport County	66	0.42
Newton, MA (city) Middlesex County	345	0.41
Hilton Head Island, SC (town) Beaufort County	149	0.41
Warwick, RI (city) Kent County	338	0.40
Milford, CT (town) New Haven County	212	0.40
Poinciana, FL (cdp) Osceola County	202	0.40
West Haven, CT (city/town) New Haven County	214	0.39
Greenville, RI (cdp) Providence County	34	0.39
Somerville, MA (city) Middlesex County	282	0.37
Framingham, MA (cdp/town) Middlesex County	248	0.37
North Smithfield, RI (town) Providence County	44	0.37
Scituate, RI (town) Providence County	38	0.37
Cambridge, MA (city) Middlesex County	371	0.36
West Springfield Town, MA (city) Hampden County	102	0.36
Nanakuli, HI (cdp) Honolulu County	45	0.36
Woonsocket, RI (city) Providence County	144	0.35
Naugatuck, CT (borough/town) New Haven County	110	0.35
Barrington, RI (town) Bristol County	58	0.35
Woburn, MA (city) Middlesex County	129	0.34
Norfolk, MA (town) Norfolk County	38	0.34
Amherst, MA (town) Hampshire County	124	0.33
South Kingstown, RI (town) Washington County	99	0.33
Townsend, MA (town) Middlesex County	29	0.33
Waterbury, CT (city/town) New Haven County	353	0.32
La Riviera, CA (cdp) Sacramento County	35	0.31
Medford, MA (city) Middlesex County	165	0.30
North Attleborough, MA (town) Bristol County	85	0.30
Bellview, FL (cdp) Escambia County	73	0.30
Westerly, RI (town) Washington County	69	0.30
Hingham, MA (town) Plymouth County	66	0.30
Sand Springs, OK (city) Tulsa County	55	0.30
Georgetown, GA (cdp) Chatham County	37	0.30
Ware, MA (town) Hampshire County	30	0.30
Quincy, MA (city) Norfolk County	262	0.29
Smithfield, RI (town) Providence County	61	0.28
Havelock, NC (city) Craven County	55	0.27
Southbridge Town, MA (city) Worcester County	46	0.27
Seymour, CT (town) New Haven County	45	0.27
Cheltenham, PA (township) Montgomery County	96	0.26
Sharon, MA (town) Norfolk County	46	0.26
West Pensacola, FL (cdp) Escambia County	53	0.25
Oakdale, LA (city) Allen Parish	20	0.25
Lynn, MA (city) Essex County	215	0.24
Delray Beach, FL (city) Palm Beach County	144	0.24
Bowie, MD (city) Prince George's County	132	0.24
Leominster, MA (city) Worcester County	100	0.24
Ferry Pass, FL (cdp) Escambia County	66	0.24
Northbridge, MA (town) Worcester County	37	0.24
Charlestown, RI (town) Washington County	19	0.24
Marumsco, VA (cdp) Prince William County	76	0.23
Johnston, RI (town) Providence County	67	0.23
Parkland, FL (city) Broward County	51	0.23
Montville, CT (town) New London County	44	0.23
Valley Falls, RI (cdp) Providence County	26	0.23
Acton, MA (town) Middlesex County	48	0.22
Narragansett, RI (town) Washington County	36	0.22
Groton, CT (city) New London County	23	0.22
Tualatin, OR (city) Washington County	53	0.21
West Lealman, FL (cdp) Pinellas County	31	0.21
Wilbraham, MA (town) Hampden County	29	0.21
Uxbridge, MA (town) Worcester County	28	0.21
Ringwood, NJ (borough) Passaic County	26	0.21
Danbury, CT (city/town) Fairfield County	158	0.20
Stratford, CT (cdp/town) Fairfield County	103	0.20
West Warwick, RI (town) Kent County	59	0.20
Walpole, MA (town) Norfolk County	48	0.20
Westborough, MA (town) Worcester County	36	0.20
Halifax, MA (town) Plymouth County	15	0.20
Riverview, FL (cdp) Hillsborough County	124	0.19
Brookline, MA (cdp/town) Norfolk County	112	0.19
Revere, MA (city) Suffolk County	96	0.19
West Orange, NJ (township) Essex County	87	0.19

SECTION THREE

Please refer to the Explanation of Data in the front of the book for more detailed information.

Ancestry

African, Sub-Saharan: Ethiopian

U.S. and 50 States Sorted by Population and Percent of Total Population

Place	Population	%	Place	Population	%
United States	**172,984**	**0.06**	District of Columbia	2,601	0.45
California	24,586	0.07	Maryland	16,604	0.29
Virginia	19,180	0.24	Minnesota	14,183	0.27
Maryland	16,604	0.29	Virginia	19,180	0.24
Minnesota	14,183	0.27	Washington	13,093	0.20
Washington	13,093	0.20	Nevada	5,088	0.19
Texas	11,989	0.05	Colorado	6,547	0.13
Georgia	10,060	0.11	South Dakota	934	0.12
Colorado	6,547	0.13	Georgia	10,060	0.11
New York	5,107	0.03	California	24,586	0.07
Nevada	5,088	0.19	Massachusetts	4,593	0.07
Ohio	5,039	0.04	**United States**	**172,984**	**0.06**
Massachusetts	4,593	0.07	Texas	11,989	0.05
Florida	3,615	0.02	Tennessee	3,171	0.05
Pennsylvania	3,372	0.03	Oregon	1,812	0.05
Illinois	3,306	0.03	Ohio	5,039	0.04
Tennessee	3,171	0.05	Kansas	1,122	0.04
North Carolina	2,813	0.03	Alaska	260	0.04
District of Columbia	2,601	0.45	New York	5,107	0.03
Oregon	1,812	0.05	Pennsylvania	3,372	0.03
Michigan	1,696	0.02	Illinois	3,306	0.03
Arizona	1,489	0.02	North Carolina	2,813	0.03
Missouri	1,441	0.02	Iowa	798	0.03
Indiana	1,431	0.02	Maine	426	0.03
New Jersey	1,388	0.02	Florida	3,615	0.02
Kansas	1,122	0.04	Michigan	1,696	0.02
South Dakota	934	0.12	Arizona	1,489	0.02
Iowa	798	0.03	Missouri	1,441	0.02
Kentucky	651	0.02	Indiana	1,431	0.02
Wisconsin	597	0.01	New Jersey	1,388	0.02
Connecticut	481	0.01	Kentucky	651	0.02
South Carolina	429	0.01	West Virginia	306	0.02
Maine	426	0.03	Nebraska	277	0.02
Oklahoma	418	0.01	Delaware	218	0.02
West Virginia	306	0.02	Rhode Island	174	0.02
Nebraska	277	0.02	Vermont	155	0.02
Alaska	260	0.04	Wisconsin	597	0.01
Delaware	218	0.02	Connecticut	481	0.01
Alabama	217	<0.01	South Carolina	429	0.01
Idaho	201	0.01	Oklahoma	418	0.01
Utah	186	0.01	Idaho	201	0.01
Louisiana	181	<0.01	Utah	186	0.01
New Mexico	175	0.01	New Mexico	175	0.01
Rhode Island	174	0.02	New Hampshire	168	0.01
New Hampshire	168	0.01	Montana	106	0.01
Vermont	155	0.02	North Dakota	57	0.01
Arkansas	120	<0.01	Alabama	217	<0.01
Montana	106	0.01	Louisiana	181	<0.01
Hawaii	65	<0.01	Arkansas	120	<0.01
Mississippi	58	<0.01	Hawaii	65	<0.01
North Dakota	57	0.01	Mississippi	58	<0.01
Wyoming	0	0.00	Wyoming	0	0.00

Please refer to the Explanation of Data in the front of the book for more detailed information.

Ancestry

African, Sub-Saharan: Ethiopian

Top 150 Places Sorted by Population

Based on all places, regardless of total population

Place	Population	%
Seattle, WA (city) King County	4,391	0.74
Los Angeles, CA (city) Los Angeles County	3,896	0.10
St. Paul, MN (city) Ramsey County	3,839	1.36
Minneapolis, MN (city) Hennepin County	3,714	0.98
Alexandria, VA (ind. city) Alexandria independent city	3,617	2.71
Aurora, CO (city) Arapahoe County	2,877	0.92
New York, NY (city) Kings County	2,869	0.04
Dallas, TX (city) Dallas County	2,719	0.23
Washington, DC (city) District of Columbia	2,601	0.45
Houston, TX (city) Harris County	2,393	0.12
Chicago, IL (city) Cook County	2,224	0.08
Columbus, OH (city) Franklin County	2,207	0.29
San Jose, CA (city) Santa Clara County	2,008	0.22
San Diego, CA (city) San Diego County	1,985	0.15
Oakland, CA (city) Alameda County	1,983	0.51
Arlington, VA (cdp) Arlington County	1,974	1.00
Silver Spring, MD (cdp) Montgomery County	1,854	2.65
Nashville-Davidson, TN (metro govt) Davidson County	1,850	0.31
Denver, CO (city) Denver County	1,761	0.30
Paradise, NV (cdp) Clark County	1,756	0.81
Spring Valley, NV (cdp) Clark County	1,712	1.00
Philadelphia, PA (city) Philadelphia County	1,572	0.10
Cambridge, MA (city) Middlesex County	1,484	1.43
Jacksonville, FL (city) Duval County	1,185	0.15
Wheaton, MD (cdp) Montgomery County	1,145	2.54
Shoreline, WA (city) King County	1,085	2.07
Takoma Park, MD (city) Montgomery County	1,072	6.36
Manhattan, NY (borough) New York County	1,043	0.07
Lincolnia, VA (cdp) Fairfax County	1,026	4.97
Phoenix, AZ (city) Maricopa County	975	0.07
Baltimore, MD (city) Baltimore city County	965	0.16
Charlotte, NC (city) Mecklenburg County	954	0.14
Bronx, NY (borough) Bronx County	945	0.07
Portland, OR (city) Multnomah County	940	0.17
Garland, TX (city) Dallas County	863	0.39
Aspen Hill, MD (cdp) Montgomery County	833	1.77
Clarkston, GA (city) DeKalb County	824	10.91
Sioux Falls, SD (city) Minnehaha County	811	0.54
White Oak, MD (cdp) Montgomery County	809	4.86
Lynnwood, WA (city) Snohomish County	794	2.23
Boston, MA (city) Suffolk County	786	0.13
Brooklyn Center, MN (city) Hennepin County	742	2.50
Richmond, VA (ind. city) Richmond independent city	728	0.36
Eagan, MN (city) Dakota County	713	1.11
Memphis, TN (city) Shelby County	709	0.11
Franconia, VA (cdp) Fairfax County	700	3.79
Santa Clara, CA (city) Santa Clara County	692	0.62
Sacramento, CA (city) Sacramento County	692	0.15
Burien, WA (city) King County	643	1.96
Anaheim, CA (city) Orange County	642	0.19
Lorton, VA (cdp) Fairfax County	613	3.18
Des Moines, WA (city) King County	603	2.05
Herndon, VA (town) Fairfax County	597	2.63
Enterprise, NV (cdp) Clark County	596	0.60
Richardson, TX (city) Dallas County	590	0.61
San Francisco, CA (city) San Francisco County	585	0.07
Annandale, VA (cdp) Fairfax County	579	1.51
Plano, TX (city) Collin County	574	0.22
Whitehall, OH (city) Franklin County	565	3.11
SeaTac, WA (city) King County	547	2.07
Austin, TX (city) Travis County	530	0.07
Queens, NY (borough) Queens County	505	0.02
Atlanta, GA (city) Fulton County	499	0.12
Chillum, MD (cdp) Prince George's County	497	1.42
Elk Grove, CA (city) Sacramento County	492	0.35
Santa Rosa, CA (city) Sonoma County	491	0.30
Glenmont, MD (cdp) Montgomery County	487	3.62
Springfield, VA (cdp) Fairfax County	487	1.59
Federal Way, WA (city) King County	485	0.55
Richmond, CA (city) Contra Costa County	474	0.46
Cincinnati, OH (city) Hamilton County	458	0.15
Culver City, CA (city) Los Angeles County	456	1.17
Indianapolis, IN (city) Marion County	443	0.05
Upper Darby, PA (township) Delaware County	442	0.54
Fairland, MD (cdp) Montgomery County	432	1.87
Olney, MD (cdp) Montgomery County	432	1.30
Carrollton, TX (city) Denton County	432	0.37
Las Vegas, NV (city) Clark County	431	0.07
Adelphi, MD (cdp) Prince George's County	430	2.86
Bailey's Crossroads, VA (cdp) Fairfax County	429	2.06
Apple Valley, MN (city) Dakota County	422	0.87
Arlington, TX (city) Tarrant County	421	0.12
Louisville-Jefferson County, KY (metro govt) Jefferson County	418	0.07
Chelsea, MA (city) Suffolk County	415	1.20
Hawthorne, CA (city) Los Angeles County	409	0.49
Calverton, MD (cdp) Montgomery County	404	2.27
Inglewood, CA (city) Los Angeles County	399	0.36
Dale City, VA (cdp) Prince William County	383	0.60
Gaithersburg, MD (city) Montgomery County	372	0.64
Rockville, MD (city) Montgomery County	372	0.64
Vancouver, WA (city) Clark County	369	0.23
Palo Alto, CA (city) Santa Clara County	360	0.58
Kingstowne, VA (cdp) Fairfax County	357	2.46
Virginia Beach, VA (ind. city) Virginia Beach independent city	354	0.08
San Leandro, CA (city) Alameda County	350	0.42
Lake Ridge, VA (cdp) Prince William County	339	0.86
Kenmore, WA (city) King County	335	1.68
Grand Rapids, MI (city) Kent County	335	0.18
Oakton, VA (cdp) Fairfax County	331	0.99
Hayward, CA (city) Alameda County	331	0.23
Brooklyn, NY (borough) Kings County	330	0.01
Alameda, CA (city) Alameda County	326	0.45
Bull Run, VA (cdp) Prince William County	325	2.52
Olathe, KS (city) Johnson County	325	0.27
Raleigh, NC (city) Wake County	323	0.08
Hopkins, MN (city) Hennepin County	308	1.77
Wylie, TX (city) Collin County	308	0.83
Brooklyn Park, MN (city) Hennepin County	305	0.41
West Springfield, VA (cdp) Fairfax County	303	1.36
Shawnee, KS (city) Johnson County	302	0.50
Kansas City, MO (city) Jackson County	302	0.07
Burke, VA (cdp) Fairfax County	299	0.72
Reynoldsburg, OH (city) Franklin County	297	0.85
Hybla Valley, VA (cdp) Fairfax County	296	2.03
Germantown, MD (cdp) Montgomery County	282	0.33
Medford, MA (city) Middlesex County	275	0.50
Renton, WA (city) King County	266	0.31
High Point, NC (city) Guilford County	266	0.26
Stockton, CA (city) San Joaquin County	256	0.09
Catonsville, MD (cdp) Baltimore County	247	0.59
Newington, VA (cdp) Fairfax County	246	1.86
St. Louis, MO (city) St. Louis city County	246	0.08
Neabsco, VA (cdp) Prince William County	243	2.58
Columbia, MD (cdp) Howard County	243	0.25
Shelbyville, TN (city) Bedford County	242	1.22
Fresno, CA (city) Fresno County	240	0.05
Rochester, MN (city) Olmsted County	239	0.23
Edmonds, WA (city) Snohomish County	237	0.60
Irving, TX (city) Dallas County	236	0.11
Rose Hill, VA (cdp) Fairfax County	235	1.19
Oklahoma City, OK (city) Oklahoma County	235	0.04
Decatur, GA (city) DeKalb County	232	1.22
Woodbury, MN (city) Washington County	229	0.39
Long Beach, CA (city) Los Angeles County	229	0.05
Bryn Mawr-Skyway, WA (cdp) King County	227	1.59
Rochester, NY (city) Monroe County	227	0.11
Santa Monica, CA (city) Los Angeles County	225	0.25
Buffalo, NY (city) Erie County	223	0.08
Eden Prairie, MN (city) Hennepin County	222	0.37
Berkeley, CA (city) Alameda County	222	0.20
League City, TX (city) Galveston County	221	0.29
Kemp Mill, MD (cdp) Montgomery County	220	1.82
Five Forks, SC (cdp) Greenville County	217	1.65
Hyattsville, MD (city) Prince George's County	217	1.26
Antioch, CA (city) Contra Costa County	217	0.22
Lemon Grove, CA (city) San Diego County	213	0.85
Scottdale, GA (cdp) DeKalb County	210	2.15
West Orange, NJ (township) Essex County	210	0.46
Chula Vista, CA (city) San Diego County	209	0.09
Potomac, MD (cdp) Montgomery County	208	0.46

Please refer to the Explanation of Data in the front of the book for more detailed information.

SECTION THREE

Ancestry

African, Sub-Saharan: Ethiopian

Top 150 Places Sorted by Percent of Total Population

Based on all places, regardless of total population

Place	Population	%
Stanardsville, VA (town) Greene County	58	20.64
Clarkston, GA (city) DeKalb County	824	10.91
Springville, VA (cdp) Tazewell County	87	7.77
Tangelo Park, FL (cdp) Orange County	158	7.21
Arlington, VT (cdp) Bennington County	84	6.83
Grundy, VA (town) Buchanan County	58	6.39
Takoma Park, MD (city) Montgomery County	1,072	6.36
Elmer, MN (township) Pipestone County	18	6.23
Kilmarnock, VA (town) Lancaster County	79	5.07
Lincolnia, VA (cdp) Fairfax County	1,026	4.97
White Oak, MD (cdp) Montgomery County	809	4.86
Woodbury Center, CT (cdp) Litchfield County	70	4.74
Meadow View Addition, SD (cdp) Minnehaha County	21	4.31
Monroe, WI (town) Green County	50	3.87
Franconia, VA (cdp) Fairfax County	700	3.79
St. Paul, VA (town) Wise County	37	3.71
Glenmont, MD (cdp) Montgomery County	487	3.62
Spencerville, MD (cdp) Montgomery County	53	3.55
Lincoln Park, PA (cdp) Berks County	48	3.43
Arlington, VT (town) Bennington County	84	3.38
Poolesville, MD (town) Montgomery County	163	3.33
Pleasant Run Farm, OH (cdp) Hamilton County	141	3.19
Lorton, VA (cdp) Fairfax County	613	3.18
Whitehall, OH (city) Franklin County	565	3.11
Hillandale, MD (cdp) Montgomery County	196	3.06
Lloyd Harbor, NY (village) Suffolk County	110	3.00
Laurel Hill, VA (cdp) Fairfax County	177	2.92
Adelphi, MD (cdp) Prince George's County	430	2.86
Alexandria, VA (ind. city) Alexandria independent city	3,617	2.71
Silver Spring, MD (cdp) Montgomery County	1,854	2.65
Herndon, VA (town) Fairfax County	597	2.63
Neabsco, VA (cdp) Prince William County	243	2.58
Sheridan, MT (town) Madison County	19	2.55
Wheaton, MD (cdp) Montgomery County	1,145	2.54
Dayton, VA (town) Rockingham County	42	2.53
Bull Run, VA (cdp) Prince William County	325	2.52
Brooklyn Center, MN (city) Hennepin County	742	2.50
Kingstowne, VA (cdp) Fairfax County	357	2.46
Lauderdale, MN (city) Ramsey County	59	2.42
Beattystown, NJ (cdp) Warren County	112	2.40
Doraville, GA (city) DeKalb County	195	2.34
Cabana Colony, FL (cdp) Palm Beach County	55	2.33
Calverton, MD (cdp) Montgomery County	404	2.27
Lynnwood, WA (city) Snohomish County	794	2.23
Marlboro, VT (town) Windham County	22	2.22
Sweet, MN (township) Pipestone County	9	2.18
Scottdale, GA (cdp) DeKalb County	210	2.15
Meadowdale, WA (cdp) Snohomish County	61	2.15
Inverness, CA (cdp) Marin County	29	2.10
Shoreline, WA (city) King County	1,085	2.07
SeaTac, WA (city) King County	547	2.07
Greencastle, PA (borough) Franklin County	82	2.07
Bailey's Crossroads, VA (cdp) Fairfax County	429	2.06
Des Moines, WA (city) King County	603	2.05
Hybla Valley, VA (cdp) Fairfax County	296	2.03
Canton, MO (city) Lewis County	58	1.99
Unalaska, AK (city) Aleutians West Census Area	89	1.98
Dryden, MN (township) Sibley County	6	1.98
Burien, WA (city) King County	643	1.96
Strawberry, CA (cdp) Marin County	100	1.95
Vinita Park, MO (city) St. Louis County	32	1.92
Fairland, MD (cdp) Montgomery County	432	1.87
Newington, VA (cdp) Fairfax County	246	1.86
Jasper, NY (town) Steuben County	23	1.84
Kemp Mill, MD (cdp) Montgomery County	220	1.82
Burtonsville, MD (cdp) Montgomery County	167	1.81
Aspen Hill, MD (cdp) Montgomery County	833	1.77
Hopkins, MN (city) Hennepin County	308	1.77
Wormleysburg, PA (borough) Cumberland County	52	1.74
Fairwood, MD (cdp) Prince George's County	80	1.72
Leesburg, GA (city) Lee County	49	1.72
Kenmore, WA (city) King County	335	1.68
Five Forks, SC (cdp) Greenville County	217	1.65
Triangle, VA (cdp) Prince William County	125	1.62
Sparta, NY (town) Livingston County	27	1.62
Springfield, VA (cdp) Fairfax County	487	1.59
Bryn Mawr-Skyway, WA (cdp) King County	227	1.59
Urbancrest, OH (village) Franklin County	16	1.56
North Seekonk, MA (cdp) Bristol County	40	1.55
Crestview Hills, KY (city) Kenton County	48	1.54
Gilman, WI (village) Taylor County	8	1.54
Annandale, VA (cdp) Fairfax County	579	1.51
Deferiet, NY (village) Jefferson County	7	1.49
North Salem, NY (town) Westchester County	75	1.47
Quantico Base, VA (cdp) Prince William County	87	1.45
Barnesville, MD (town) Montgomery County	2	1.45
Cambridge, MA (city) Middlesex County	1,484	1.43
Chillum, MD (cdp) Prince George's County	497	1.42
Mansfield, NJ (township) Warren County	112	1.42
Fort Morgan, CO (city) Morgan County	157	1.40
Bern, WI (town) Marathon County	8	1.39
St. Paul, MN (city) Ramsey County	3,839	1.36
West Springfield, VA (cdp) Fairfax County	303	1.36
Olney, MD (cdp) Montgomery County	432	1.30
Spring Lake Park, MN (city) Anoka County	81	1.27
North Tunica, MS (cdp) Tunica County	8	1.27
Hyattsville, MD (city) Prince George's County	217	1.26
Cape Elizabeth, ME (town) Cumberland County	114	1.26
Spring Lake Park, MN (city) Anoka County	81	1.24
Norridgewock, ME (cdp) Somerset County	19	1.23
Shelbyville, TN (city) Bedford County	242	1.22
Decatur, GA (city) DeKalb County	232	1.22
Chelsea, MA (city) Suffolk County	415	1.20
Kenwood, OH (cdp) Hamilton County	87	1.20
Rose Hill, VA (cdp) Fairfax County	235	1.19
Boulevard Park, WA (cdp) King County	75	1.19
Lanham, MD (cdp) Prince George's County	105	1.18
Culver City, CA (city) Los Angeles County	456	1.17
McNair, VA (cdp) Fairfax County	177	1.16
Fairfield, IA (city) Jefferson County	108	1.14
Berwyn Heights, MD (town) Prince George's County	35	1.13
Oxford, GA (city) Newton County	29	1.13
Eagan, MN (city) Dakota County	713	1.11
Orange City, IA (city) Sioux County	66	1.11
Warwick, MA (town) Franklin County	6	1.10
Centreville, MD (town) Queen Anne's County	42	1.07
Elsmere, KY (city) Kenton County	88	1.05
North Kensington, MD (cdp) Montgomery County	100	1.04
Manhasset Hills, NY (cdp) Nassau County	38	1.03
Lilburn, GA (city) Gwinnett County	120	1.02
Norwich, MI (township) Newaygo County	6	1.02
Pinole, CA (city) Contra Costa County	187	1.01
Alexandria, MN (city) Douglas County	112	1.01
Arlington, VA (cdp) Arlington County	1,974	1.00
Spring Valley, NV (cdp) Clark County	1,712	1.00
Oakton, VA (cdp) Fairfax County	331	0.99
Minneapolis, MN (city) Hennepin County	3,714	0.98
St. Ann, MO (city) St. Louis County	128	0.98
Campbelltown, PA (cdp) Lebanon County	35	0.97
Pocomoke City, MD (city) Worcester County	40	0.95
Aurora, CO (city) Arapahoe County	2,877	0.92
Hollymead, VA (cdp) Albemarle County	74	0.92
Worthington, MN (city) Nobles County	112	0.91
Forest Glen, MD (cdp) Montgomery County	56	0.91
Largo, MD (cdp) Prince George's County	99	0.90
Empire, MN (township) Dakota County	20	0.90
Morgantown, PA (cdp) Berks County	8	0.90
Four Corners, MD (cdp) Montgomery County	71	0.89
Wedgefield, FL (cdp) Orange County	58	0.89
Forestville, OH (cdp) Hamilton County	96	0.88
Dumbarton, VA (cdp) Henrico County	59	0.88
Pomona, NY (village) Rockland County	31	0.88
Greenwood, LA (town) Caddo Parish	27	0.88
Apple Valley, MN (city) Dakota County	422	0.87
Lake Ridge, VA (cdp) Prince William County	339	0.86
Reynoldsburg, OH (city) Franklin County	297	0.85
Lemon Grove, CA (city) San Diego County	213	0.85
Tukwila, WA (city) King County	158	0.85
Walker Mill, MD (cdp) Prince George's County	98	0.85
Huntington, VA (cdp) Fairfax County	88	0.85

Please refer to the Explanation of Data in the front of the book for more detailed information.

Ancestry

African, Sub-Saharan: Ethiopian

Top 150 Places Sorted by Percent of Total Population

Based on places with total population of 7,500 or more

Place	Population	%
Clarkston, GA (city) DeKalb County	824	10.91
Takoma Park, MD (city) Montgomery County	1,072	6.36
Lincolnia, VA (cdp) Fairfax County	1,026	4.97
White Oak, MD (cdp) Montgomery County	809	4.86
Franconia, VA (cdp) Fairfax County	700	3.79
Glenmont, MD (cdp) Montgomery County	487	3.62
Lorton, VA (cdp) Fairfax County	613	3.18
Whitehall, OH (city) Franklin County	565	3.11
Adelphi, MD (cdp) Prince George's County	430	2.86
Alexandria, VA (ind. city) Alexandria independent city	3,617	2.71
Silver Spring, MD (cdp) Montgomery County	1,854	2.65
Herndon, VA (town) Fairfax County	597	2.63
Neabsco, VA (cdp) Prince William County	243	2.58
Wheaton, MD (cdp) Montgomery County	1,145	2.54
Bull Run, VA (cdp) Prince William County	325	2.52
Brooklyn Center, MN (city) Hennepin County	742	2.50
Kingstowne, VA (cdp) Fairfax County	357	2.46
Doraville, GA (city) DeKalb County	195	2.34
Calverton, MD (cdp) Montgomery County	404	2.27
Lynnwood, WA (city) Snohomish County	794	2.23
Scottdale, GA (cdp) DeKalb County	210	2.15
Shoreline, WA (city) King County	1,085	2.07
SeaTac, WA (city) King County	547	2.07
Bailey's Crossroads, VA (cdp) Fairfax County	429	2.06
Des Moines, WA (city) King County	603	2.05
Hybla Valley, VA (cdp) Fairfax County	296	2.03
Burien, WA (city) King County	643	1.96
Fairland, MD (cdp) Montgomery County	432	1.87
Newington, VA (cdp) Fairfax County	246	1.86
Kemp Mill, MD (cdp) Montgomery County	220	1.82
Burtonsville, MD (cdp) Montgomery County	167	1.81
Aspen Hill, MD (cdp) Montgomery County	833	1.77
Hopkins, MN (city) Hennepin County	308	1.77
Kenmore, WA (city) King County	335	1.68
Five Forks, SC (cdp) Greenville County	217	1.65
Triangle, VA (cdp) Prince William County	125	1.62
Springfield, VA (cdp) Fairfax County	487	1.59
Bryn Mawr-Skyway, WA (cdp) King County	227	1.59
Annandale, VA (cdp) Fairfax County	579	1.51
Cambridge, MA (city) Middlesex County	1,484	1.43
Chillum, MD (cdp) Prince George's County	497	1.42
Mansfield, NJ (township) Warren County	112	1.42
Fort Morgan, CO (city) Morgan County	157	1.40
St. Paul, MN (city) Ramsey County	3,839	1.36
West Springfield, VA (cdp) Fairfax County	303	1.36
Olney, MD (cdp) Montgomery County	432	1.30
Hyattsville, MD (city) Prince George's County	217	1.26
Cape Elizabeth, ME (town) Cumberland County	114	1.26
Shelbyville, TN (city) Bedford County	242	1.22
Decatur, GA (city) DeKalb County	232	1.22
Chelsea, MA (city) Suffolk County	415	1.20
Rose Hill, VA (cdp) Fairfax County	235	1.19
Lanham, MD (cdp) Prince George's County	105	1.18
Culver City, CA (city) Los Angeles County	456	1.17
McNair, VA (cdp) Fairfax County	177	1.16
Fairfield, IA (city) Jefferson County	108	1.14
Eagan, MN (city) Dakota County	713	1.11
Elsmere, KY (city) Kenton County	88	1.05
North Kensington, MD (cdp) Montgomery County	100	1.04
Lilburn, GA (city) Gwinnett County	120	1.02
Pinole, CA (city) Contra Costa County	187	1.01
Alexandria, MN (city) Douglas County	112	1.01
Arlington, VA (cdp) Arlington County	1,974	1.00
Spring Valley, NV (cdp) Clark County	1,712	1.00
Oakton, VA (cdp) Fairfax County	331	0.99
Minneapolis, MN (city) Hennepin County	3,714	0.98
St. Ann, MO (city) St. Louis County	128	0.98
Aurora, CO (city) Arapahoe County	2,877	0.92
Hollymead, VA (cdp) Albemarle County	74	0.92
Worthington, MN (city) Nobles County	112	0.91
Largo, MD (cdp) Prince George's County	99	0.90
Four Corners, MD (cdp) Montgomery County	71	0.89
Forestville, OH (cdp) Hamilton County	96	0.88
Apple Valley, MN (city) Dakota County	422	0.87
Lake Ridge, VA (cdp) Prince William County	339	0.86
Reynoldsburg, OH (city) Franklin County	297	0.85
Lemon Grove, CA (city) San Diego County	213	0.85
Tukwila, WA (city) King County	158	0.85
Walker Mill, MD (cdp) Prince George's County	98	0.85
Huntington, VA (cdp) Fairfax County	88	0.85
Wylie, TX (city) Collin County	308	0.83
Radford, VA (ind. city) Radford independent city	135	0.83
Robbinsville, NJ (township) Mercer County	108	0.83
Paradise, NV (cdp) Clark County	1,756	0.81
Leisure World, MD (cdp) Montgomery County	70	0.81
Kings Park West, VA (cdp) Fairfax County	115	0.80
Hercules, CA (city) Contra Costa County	182	0.79
Little Canada, MN (city) Ramsey County	75	0.78
Mountlake Terrace, WA (city) Snohomish County	153	0.77
Temple Hills, MD (cdp) Prince George's County	59	0.77
Beltsville, MD (cdp) Prince George's County	118	0.76
Mountain Park, GA (cdp) Gwinnett County	90	0.75
Seattle, WA (city) King County	4,391	0.74
Woodlawn, VA (cdp) Fairfax County	142	0.73
Burke, VA (cdp) Fairfax County	299	0.72
Clarksville, AR (city) Johnson County	65	0.72
La Palma, CA (city) Orange County	110	0.71
Falls Church, VA (ind. city) Falls Church independent city	81	0.71
Woodbury, CT (town) Litchfield County	70	0.71
Marina del Rey, CA (cdp) Los Angeles County	65	0.71
Sachse, TX (city) Dallas County	128	0.70
Mount Rainier, MD (city) Prince George's County	57	0.70
Matthews, NC (town) Mecklenburg County	181	0.68
Bedford, NY (town) Westchester County	117	0.67
Laurel, MD (city) Prince George's County	159	0.65
Gaithersburg, MD (city) Montgomery County	372	0.64
Rockville, MD (city) Montgomery County	372	0.64
New Brighton, MN (city) Ramsey County	134	0.63
Readington, NJ (township) Hunterdon County	103	0.63
Santa Clara, CA (city) Santa Clara County	692	0.62
Hillcrest Heights, MD (cdp) Prince George's County	98	0.62
Yeadon, PA (borough) Delaware County	71	0.62
Richardson, TX (city) Dallas County	590	0.61
North Potomac, MD (cdp) Montgomery County	153	0.61
Cherry Hill, VA (cdp) Prince William County	95	0.61
Enterprise, NV (cdp) Clark County	596	0.60
Dale City, VA (cdp) Prince William County	383	0.60
Edmonds, WA (city) Snohomish County	237	0.60
Milford Mill, MD (cdp) Baltimore County	173	0.60
Catonsville, MD (cdp) Baltimore County	247	0.59
Anoka, MN (city) Anoka County	103	0.59
Groveton, VA (cdp) Fairfax County	80	0.59
Marshall, MN (city) Lyon County	79	0.59
Friendly, MD (cdp) Prince George's County	59	0.59
Palo Alto, CA (city) Santa Clara County	360	0.58
Cloverly, MD (cdp) Montgomery County	90	0.58
Seven Corners, VA (cdp) Fairfax County	48	0.58
West St. Paul, MN (city) Dakota County	111	0.57
Langley Park, MD (cdp) Prince George's County	104	0.57
East Hill-Meridian, WA (cdp) King County	163	0.56
Maplewood, MO (city) St. Louis County	46	0.56
Federal Way, WA (city) King County	485	0.55
Picnic Point, WA (cdp) Snohomish County	47	0.55
Sioux Falls, SD (city) Minnehaha County	811	0.54
Upper Darby, PA (township) Delaware County	442	0.54
Home Gardens, CA (cdp) Riverside County	59	0.54
Fort Washington, MD (cdp) Prince George's County	134	0.53
Kingsgate, WA (cdp) King County	72	0.53
Chamblee, GA (city) DeKalb County	51	0.52
Oakland, CA (city) Alameda County	1,983	0.51
Romeoville, IL (village) Will County	192	0.51
Clinton, MD (cdp) Prince George's County	185	0.51
Pullman, WA (city) Whitman County	146	0.51
Forest Park, OH (city) Hamilton County	96	0.51
Wilkinsburg, PA (borough) Allegheny County	83	0.51
Shawnee, KS (city) Johnson County	302	0.50
Medford, MA (city) Middlesex County	275	0.50
Mill Creek, WA (city) Snohomish County	88	0.50
Kulpsville, PA (cdp) Montgomery County	39	0.50
Hawthorne, CA (city) Los Angeles County	409	0.49

Please refer to the Explanation of Data in the front of the book for more detailed information.

Ancestry

African, Sub-Saharan: Ghanaian

U.S. and 50 States Sorted by Population and Percent of Total Population

Place	Population	%
United States	**83,718**	**0.03**
New York	23,006	0.12
Virginia	9,289	0.12
New Jersey	9,071	0.10
Maryland	7,373	0.13
Illinois	3,934	0.03
Georgia	3,644	0.04
Massachusetts	3,276	0.05
Texas	2,981	0.01
Ohio	2,919	0.03
California	2,383	0.01
Pennsylvania	1,774	0.01
North Carolina	1,745	0.02
Connecticut	1,522	0.04
Florida	1,187	0.01
Minnesota	995	0.02
Rhode Island	874	0.08
Colorado	830	0.02
Arizona	625	0.01
Michigan	563	0.01
Tennessee	554	0.01
Washington	550	0.01
Delaware	544	0.06
Missouri	433	0.01
Oklahoma	411	0.01
District of Columbia	385	0.07
Oregon	341	0.01
Indiana	322	0.01
New Hampshire	267	0.02
Nevada	262	0.01
Mississippi	251	0.01
Nebraska	242	0.01
Utah	230	0.01
South Carolina	192	<0.01
Wisconsin	153	<0.01
Iowa	110	<0.01
Kentucky	94	<0.01
Alabama	93	<0.01
Arkansas	75	<0.01
West Virginia	47	<0.01
New Mexico	40	<0.01
Louisiana	38	<0.01
Kansas	33	<0.01
North Dakota	19	<0.01
Maine	15	<0.01
Hawaii	13	<0.01
Montana	7	<0.01
Vermont	6	<0.01
Alaska	0	0.00
Idaho	0	0.00
South Dakota	0	0.00
Wyoming	0	0.00

Place	Population	%
Maryland	7,373	0.13
New York	23,006	0.12
Virginia	9,289	0.12
New Jersey	9,071	0.10
Rhode Island	874	0.08
District of Columbia	385	0.07
Delaware	544	0.06
Massachusetts	3,276	0.05
Georgia	3,644	0.04
Connecticut	1,522	0.04
United States	**83,718**	**0.03**
Illinois	3,934	0.03
Ohio	2,919	0.03
North Carolina	1,745	0.02
Minnesota	995	0.02
Colorado	830	0.02
New Hampshire	267	0.02
Texas	2,981	0.01
California	2,383	0.01
Pennsylvania	1,774	0.01
Florida	1,187	0.01
Arizona	625	0.01
Michigan	563	0.01
Tennessee	554	0.01
Washington	550	0.01
Missouri	433	0.01
Oklahoma	411	0.01
Oregon	341	0.01
Indiana	322	0.01
Nevada	262	0.01
Mississippi	251	0.01
Nebraska	242	0.01
Utah	230	0.01
South Carolina	192	<0.01
Wisconsin	153	<0.01
Iowa	110	<0.01
Kentucky	94	<0.01
Alabama	93	<0.01
Arkansas	75	<0.01
West Virginia	47	<0.01
New Mexico	40	<0.01
Louisiana	38	<0.01
Kansas	33	<0.01
North Dakota	19	<0.01
Maine	15	<0.01
Hawaii	13	<0.01
Montana	7	<0.01
Vermont	6	<0.01
Alaska	0	0.00
Idaho	0	0.00
South Dakota	0	0.00
Wyoming	0	0.00

Please refer to the Explanation of Data in the front of the book for more detailed information.

Ancestry

African, Sub-Saharan: Ghanaian

Top 150 Places Sorted by Population

Based on all places, regardless of total population

Place	Population	%
New York, NY (city) Kings County	19,782	0.24
Bronx, NY (borough) Bronx County	13,490	0.99
Brooklyn, NY (borough) Kings County	3,898	0.16
Chicago, IL (city) Cook County	1,873	0.07
Worcester, MA (city) Worcester County	1,681	0.93
Newark, NJ (city) Essex County	1,420	0.52
Queens, NY (borough) Queens County	1,326	0.06
Columbus, OH (city) Franklin County	1,303	0.17
Alexandria, VA (ind. city) Alexandria independent city	923	0.69
Manhattan, NY (borough) New York County	818	0.05
Woodlawn, VA (cdp) Fairfax County	742	3.79
Germantown, MD (cdp) Montgomery County	708	0.83
Irvington, NJ (township) Essex County	692	1.26
Jersey City, NJ (city) Hudson County	624	0.26
Dale City, VA (cdp) Prince William County	608	0.96
City of Orange, NJ (township) Essex County	604	1.99
Los Angeles, CA (city) Los Angeles County	587	0.02
Yonkers, NY (city) Westchester County	585	0.30
Philadelphia, PA (city) Philadelphia County	584	0.04
Columbia, MD (cdp) Howard County	563	0.57
Charlotte, NC (city) Mecklenburg County	539	0.08
Arlington, TX (city) Tarrant County	478	0.13
Providence, RI (city) Providence County	462	0.26
North Brunswick, NJ (township) Middlesex County	385	0.96
Washington, DC (city) District of Columbia	385	0.07
Greensboro, NC (city) Guilford County	375	0.14
Calverton, MD (cdp) Montgomery County	369	2.07
Fairfield, OH (city) Butler County	368	0.86
Mount Vernon, NY (city) Westchester County	347	0.52
Marumsco, VA (cdp) Prince William County	346	1.07
East Orange, NJ (city) Essex County	345	0.53
South Brunswick, NJ (township) Middlesex County	342	0.81
Cherry Hill, VA (cdp) Prince William County	332	2.14
Aurora, CO (city) Arapahoe County	323	0.10
Bolingbrook, IL (village) Will County	314	0.43
Norfolk, VA (ind. city) Norfolk independent city	309	0.13
Hempstead, NY (town) Nassau County	306	0.04
Baltimore, MD (city) Baltimore city County	303	0.05
Trenton, NJ (city) Mercer County	300	0.35
Fairland, MD (cdp) Montgomery County	291	1.26
Kendall Park, NJ (cdp) Middlesex County	289	3.28
Bladensburg, MD (town) Prince George's County	284	3.18
Richmond, VA (ind. city) Richmond independent city	281	0.14
Woodridge, IL (village) DuPage County	276	0.85
Hybla Valley, VA (cdp) Fairfax County	271	1.85
Houston, TX (city) Harris County	271	0.01
Milford Mill, MD (cdp) Baltimore County	269	0.94
St. Paul, MN (city) Ramsey County	263	0.09
Westerville, OH (city) Franklin County	262	0.73
Clarksburg, MD (cdp) Montgomery County	261	2.48
Newington, VA (cdp) Fairfax County	261	1.98
Huntington, VA (cdp) Fairfax County	256	2.47
Mount Vernon, VA (cdp) Fairfax County	254	2.16
Staten Island, NY (borough) Richmond County	250	0.05
East Hartford, CT (cdp/town) Hartford County	249	0.49
Lake Ridge, VA (cdp) Prince William County	246	0.62
Pawtucket, RI (city) Providence County	244	0.34
Lincolnia, VA (cdp) Fairfax County	242	1.17
Nashville-Davidson, TN (metro govt) Davidson County	241	0.04
Linton Hall, VA (cdp) Prince William County	240	0.72
Groveton, VA (cdp) Fairfax County	239	1.75
Lorton, VA (cdp) Fairfax County	238	1.24
Peoria, IL (city) Peoria County	236	0.21
Hanover Park, IL (village) Cook County	233	0.62
Mesquite, TX (city) Dallas County	227	0.17
Elizabeth, NJ (city) Union County	224	0.18
Succasunna, NJ (cdp) Morris County	219	2.44
Roxbury, NJ (township) Morris County	219	0.94
Portland, OR (city) Multnomah County	217	0.04
Hillsborough, NJ (township) Somerset County	207	0.54
Reston, VA (cdp) Fairfax County	205	0.38
Oklahoma City, OK (city) Oklahoma County	205	0.04
Dallas, TX (city) Dallas County	205	0.02
Lowell, MA (city) Middlesex County	204	0.19
Grand Prairie, TX (city) Dallas County	201	0.12
Old Bridge, NJ (township) Middlesex County	197	0.31
Phoenix, AZ (city) Maricopa County	193	0.01
Omaha, NE (city) Douglas County	183	0.04
Hamilton, NJ (township) Mercer County	182	0.21
College Park, GA (city) Fulton County	180	1.29
Arlington, VA (cdp) Arlington County	175	0.09
Denver, CO (city) Denver County	172	0.03
Lakeview, NY (cdp) Nassau County	169	3.03
Cascades, VA (cdp) Loudoun County	164	1.36
Ewing, NJ (township) Mercer County	164	0.46
Aberdeen, MD (city) Harford County	161	1.08
Burtonsville, MD (cdp) Montgomery County	160	1.73
North Potomac, MD (cdp) Montgomery County	156	0.62
Sayreville, NJ (borough) Middlesex County	155	0.37
Frederick, MD (city) Frederick County	155	0.24
Woodbridge, NJ (township) Middlesex County	154	0.16
Indianapolis, IN (city) Marion County	154	0.02
Haverstraw, NY (town) Rockland County	149	0.42
Burke, VA (cdp) Fairfax County	149	0.36
Chicopee, MA (city) Hampden County	149	0.27
Lake Arbor, MD (cdp) Prince George's County	148	1.44
Fort Washington, MD (cdp) Prince George's County	147	0.58
Havre de Grace, MD (city) Harford County	145	1.13
Franklin, NJ (township) Somerset County	144	0.24
Vancouver, WA (city) Clark County	144	0.09
Durham, NC (city) Durham County	144	0.07
Olney, MD (cdp) Montgomery County	143	0.43
Albany, NY (city) Albany County	143	0.15
West Covina, CA (city) Los Angeles County	143	0.14
Cockeysville, MD (cdp) Baltimore County	140	0.71
Chandler, AZ (city) Maricopa County	140	0.06
Brooklyn Park, MN (city) Hennepin County	138	0.19
Jackson, MS (city) Hinds County	137	0.08
Redland, MD (cdp) Montgomery County	136	0.80
Boston, MA (city) Suffolk County	135	0.02
Upper Darby, PA (township) Delaware County	134	0.16
Gaithersburg, MD (city) Montgomery County	132	0.23
Memphis, TN (city) Shelby County	132	0.02
Hyattsville, MD (city) Prince George's County	131	0.76
Minneapolis, MN (city) Hennepin County	131	0.03
Las Vegas, NV (city) Clark County	131	0.02
Greenville, NC (city) Pitt County	129	0.16
Thousand Oaks, CA (city) Ventura County	128	0.10
Paterson, NJ (city) Passaic County	127	0.09
McLean, VA (cdp) Fairfax County	126	0.27
Sanatoga, PA (cdp) Montgomery County	124	1.50
Lower Pottsgrove, PA (township) Montgomery County	124	1.04
Severn, MD (cdp) Anne Arundel County	124	0.30
Bridgeport, CT (city/town) Fairfield County	124	0.09
Austin, TX (city) Travis County	124	0.02
East Point, GA (city) Fulton County	123	0.36
San Francisco, CA (city) San Francisco County	123	0.02
Burr Ridge, IL (village) DuPage County	122	1.16
West Haven, CT (city/town) New Haven County	122	0.22
Kennesaw, GA (city) Cobb County	119	0.42
Richfield, MN (city) Hennepin County	119	0.34
Hillside, NJ (township) Union County	117	0.55
North Hempstead, NY (town) Nassau County	117	0.05
Rockwall, TX (city) Rockwall County	116	0.33
Glenmont, MD (cdp) Montgomery County	115	0.85
Syracuse, NY (city) Onondaga County	113	0.08
Harvey, IL (city) Cook County	110	0.43
Clinton, MI (charter township) Macomb County	110	0.11
Victorville, CA (city) San Bernardino County	110	0.10
Naperville, IL (city) DuPage County	110	0.08
Chester, PA (township) Delaware County	109	2.68
Middle Smithfield, PA (township) Monroe County	109	0.70
Raleigh, NC (city) Wake County	109	0.03
White Marsh, MD (cdp) Baltimore County	108	1.13
West Haverstraw, NY (village) Rockland County	108	1.07
Piscataway, NJ (township) Middlesex County	108	0.20
Brockton, MA (city) Plymouth County	108	0.12
Fayetteville, NC (city) Cumberland County	106	0.05
Senoia, GA (city) Coweta County	105	3.43
Glasgow, DE (cdp) New Castle County	105	0.67

Please refer to the Explanation of Data in the front of the book for more detailed information.

Ancestry

African, Sub-Saharan: Ghanaian

Top 150 Places Sorted by Percent of Total Population

Based on all places, regardless of total population

Place	Population	%
Ford, MN (township) Kanabec County	19	8.64
Woodlawn, VA (cdp) Fairfax County	742	3.79
Seaside Park, NJ (borough) Ocean County	67	3.65
Senoia, GA (city) Coweta County	105	3.43
Kendall Park, NJ (cdp) Middlesex County	289	3.28
Bladensburg, MD (town) Prince George's County	284	3.18
Lakeview, NY (cdp) Nassau County	169	3.03
Pine Island, TX (town) Waller County	34	3.00
Chester, PA (township) Delaware County	109	2.68
Six Mile Run, NJ (cdp) Somerset County	91	2.50
Clarksburg, MD (cdp) Montgomery County	261	2.48
Huntington, VA (cdp) Fairfax County	256	2.47
Castle Hills, TX (city) Bexar County	102	2.47
Succasunna, NJ (cdp) Morris County	219	2.44
Dulles Town Center, VA (cdp) Loudoun County	85	2.19
Mount Vernon, VA (cdp) Fairfax County	254	2.16
Cherry Hill, VA (cdp) Prince William County	332	2.14
Calverton, MD (cdp) Montgomery County	369	2.07
Konterra, MD (cdp) Prince George's County	44	2.03
City of Orange, NJ (township) Essex County	604	1.99
Newington, VA (cdp) Fairfax County	261	1.98
Hybla Valley, VA (cdp) Fairfax County	271	1.85
Groveton, VA (cdp) Fairfax County	239	1.75
Burtonsville, MD (cdp) Montgomery County	160	1.73
South Blooming Grove, NY (village) Orange County	57	1.73
Missouri City, MO (city) Clay County	5	1.72
West Point, GA (city) Troup County	55	1.65
Belle Haven, VA (cdp) Fairfax County	102	1.56
Coxsackie, NY (village) Greene County	44	1.54
Tyndall AFB, FL (cdp) Bay County	60	1.51
Sanatoga, PA (cdp) Montgomery County	124	1.50
Lake Arbor, MD (cdp) Prince George's County	148	1.44
Oxford, GA (city) Newton County	36	1.40
Altavista, VA (town) Campbell County	47	1.37
Cascades, VA (cdp) Loudoun County	164	1.36
Katonah, NY (cdp) Westchester County	20	1.36
Madison Park, NJ (cdp) Middlesex County	89	1.30
Elliston, VA (cdp) Montgomery County	14	1.30
College Park, GA (city) Fulton County	180	1.29
Savage, MD (cdp) Howard County	86	1.27
Irvington, NJ (township) Essex County	692	1.26
Fairland, MD (cdp) Montgomery County	291	1.26
Springfield, PA (township) York County	62	1.25
Lorton, VA (cdp) Fairfax County	238	1.24
Washington, NJ (borough) Warren County	81	1.23
Absecon, NJ (city) Atlantic County	101	1.21
Franklin, NH (city) Merrimack County	103	1.20
Lincolnia, VA (cdp) Fairfax County	242	1.17
County Center, VA (cdp) Prince William County	39	1.17
University Center, VA (cdp) Loudoun County	38	1.17
Burr Ridge, IL (village) DuPage County	122	1.16
Waterford, CT (cdp) New London County	31	1.15
Havre de Grace, MD (city) Harford County	145	1.13
White Marsh, MD (cdp) Baltimore County	108	1.13
Aberdeen, MD (city) Harford County	161	1.08
Marumsco, VA (cdp) Prince William County	346	1.07
West Haverstraw, NY (village) Rockland County	108	1.07
Lower Pottsgrove, PA (township) Montgomery County	124	1.04
Orland Hills, IL (village) Cook County	73	1.04
Wheatley Heights, NY (cdp) Suffolk County	64	1.03
Woodmore, MD (cdp) Prince George's County	36	1.03
Oak Grove, VA (cdp) Loudoun County	17	1.00
Bronx, NY (borough) Bronx County	13,490	0.99
Auburn, GA (city) Barrow County	70	0.98
Dale City, VA (cdp) Prince William County	608	0.96
North Brunswick, NJ (township) Middlesex County	385	0.96
Milford Mill, MD (cdp) Baltimore County	269	0.94
Roxbury, NJ (township) Morris County	219	0.94
Hillcrest, NY (cdp) Rockland County	77	0.94
Worcester, MA (city) Worcester County	1,681	0.93
Sugarland Run, VA (cdp) Loudoun County	102	0.93
Lawrenceville, VA (town) Brunswick County	18	0.91
Fairfield, OH (city) Butler County	368	0.86
Yeadon, PA (borough) Delaware County	99	0.86
Freemansburg, PA (borough) Northampton County	22	0.86
Woodridge, IL (village) DuPage County	276	0.85
Glenmont, MD (cdp) Montgomery County	115	0.85
Twin Rivers, NJ (cdp) Mercer County	60	0.85
Fort Lee, VA (cdp) Prince George County	52	0.85
Flower Hill, NY (village) Nassau County	39	0.85
Buena Vista, MI (cdp) Saginaw County	55	0.84
Germantown, MD (cdp) Montgomery County	708	0.83
Mountain Park, GA (cdp) Gwinnett County	98	0.82
Central, SC (town) Pickens County	40	0.82
South Brunswick, NJ (township) Middlesex County	342	0.81
Redland, MD (cdp) Montgomery County	136	0.80
Williston, FL (city) Levy County	22	0.79
Hyattsville, MD (city) Prince George's County	131	0.76
Berwyn Heights, MD (town) Prince George's County	23	0.74
Westerville, OH (city) Franklin County	262	0.73
Riverdale Park, MD (town) Prince George's County	50	0.73
Linton Hall, VA (cdp) Prince William County	240	0.72
Cockeysville, MD (cdp) Baltimore County	140	0.71
Triangle, VA (cdp) Prince William County	55	0.71
Dayton, NJ (cdp) Middlesex County	53	0.71
Meridian Station, MS (cdp) Lauderdale County	18	0.71
Middle Smithfield, PA (township) Monroe County	109	0.70
Alexandria, VA (ind. city) Alexandria independent city	923	0.69
Mount Healthy, OH (city) Hamilton County	42	0.69
Excelsior, WI (town) Sauk County	10	0.69
Stone Ridge, VA (cdp) Loudoun County	41	0.68
Glasgow, DE (cdp) New Castle County	105	0.67
Fords, NJ (cdp) Middlesex County	101	0.67
SUNY Oswego, NY (cdp) Oswego County	30	0.67
Forsyth, IL (village) Macon County	22	0.67
McNair, VA (cdp) Fairfax County	97	0.64
Manassas Park, VA (ind. city) Manassas Park independent city	84	0.64
Carrollton, MO (city) Carroll County	24	0.63
Lake Ridge, VA (cdp) Prince William County	246	0.62
Hanover Park, IL (village) Cook County	233	0.62
North Potomac, MD (cdp) Montgomery County	156	0.62
Mount Ivy, NY (cdp) Rockland County	41	0.62
Buena Vista, MI (charter township) Saginaw County	55	0.61
Orange, VA (town) Orange County	29	0.61
Allegheny, PA (township) Cambria County	17	0.61
Mount Rainier, MD (city) Prince George's County	49	0.60
Adelphi, MD (cdp) Prince George's County	88	0.59
Fort Washington, MD (cdp) Prince George's County	147	0.58
Spencer, MA (cdp) Worcester County	33	0.58
Columbia, MD (cdp) Howard County	563	0.57
Antis, PA (township) Blair County	37	0.57
Nanuet, NY (cdp) Rockland County	99	0.56
East Garden City, NY (cdp) Nassau County	31	0.56
Hillside, NJ (township) Union County	117	0.55
Palmyra, NJ (borough) Burlington County	41	0.55
Hillsborough, NJ (township) Somerset County	207	0.54
Glenburn, PA (township) Lackawanna County	7	0.54
East Orange, NJ (city) Essex County	345	0.53
Neabsco, VA (cdp) Prince William County	50	0.53
Lake Dallas, TX (city) Denton County	37	0.53
Newark, NJ (city) Essex County	1,420	0.52
Mount Vernon, NY (city) Westchester County	347	0.52
Lithia Springs, GA (cdp) Douglas County	89	0.52
Westbury, NY (village) Nassau County	78	0.52
Norcross, GA (city) Gwinnett County	48	0.52
Mountain View, CO (town) Jefferson County	3	0.51
Ramtown, NJ (cdp) Monmouth County	30	0.50
East Hartford, CT (cdp/town) Hartford County	249	0.49
Bloomfield, CT (town) Hartford County	100	0.49
Coxsackie, NY (town) Greene County	44	0.49
Oaklawn-Sunview, KS (cdp) Sedgwick County	14	0.48
Morrisville, NY (village) Madison County	12	0.47
Ewing, NJ (township) Mercer County	164	0.46
Westphalia, MD (cdp) Prince George's County	28	0.46
Chase City, VA (town) Mecklenburg County	12	0.46
Roselle, NJ (borough) Union County	94	0.45
Bolingbrook, IL (village) Will County	314	0.43
Olney, MD (cdp) Montgomery County	143	0.43
Harvey, IL (city) Cook County	110	0.43
Winterville, NC (town) Pitt County	36	0.43

Please refer to the Explanation of Data in the front of the book for more detailed information.

Ancestry

African, Sub-Saharan: Ghanaian

Top 150 Places Sorted by Percent of Total Population

Based on places with total population of 7,500 or more

Place	Population	%
Woodlawn, VA (cdp) Fairfax County	742	3.79
Kendall Park, NJ (cdp) Middlesex County	289	3.28
Bladensburg, MD (town) Prince George's County	284	3.18
Clarksburg, MD (cdp) Montgomery County	261	2.48
Huntington, VA (cdp) Fairfax County	256	2.47
Succasunna, NJ (cdp) Morris County	219	2.44
Mount Vernon, VA (cdp) Fairfax County	254	2.16
Cherry Hill, VA (cdp) Prince William County	332	2.14
Calverton, MD (cdp) Montgomery County	369	2.07
City of Orange, NJ (township) Essex County	604	1.99
Newington, VA (cdp) Fairfax County	261	1.98
Hybla Valley, VA (cdp) Fairfax County	271	1.85
Groveton, VA (cdp) Fairfax County	239	1.75
Burtonsville, MD (cdp) Montgomery County	160	1.73
Sanatoga, PA (cdp) Montgomery County	124	1.50
Lake Arbor, MD (cdp) Prince George's County	148	1.44
Cascades, VA (cdp) Loudoun County	164	1.36
College Park, GA (city) Fulton County	180	1.29
Irvington, NJ (township) Essex County	692	1.26
Fairland, MD (cdp) Montgomery County	291	1.26
Lorton, VA (cdp) Fairfax County	238	1.24
Absecon, NJ (city) Atlantic County	101	1.21
Franklin, NH (city) Merrimack County	103	1.20
Lincolnia, VA (cdp) Fairfax County	242	1.17
Burr Ridge, IL (village) DuPage County	122	1.16
Havre de Grace, MD (city) Harford County	145	1.13
White Marsh, MD (cdp) Baltimore County	108	1.13
Aberdeen, MD (city) Harford County	161	1.08
Marumsco, VA (cdp) Prince William County	346	1.07
West Haverstraw, NY (village) Rockland County	108	1.07
Lower Pottsgrove, PA (township) Montgomery County	124	1.04
Bronx, NY (borough) Bronx County	13,490	0.99
Dale City, VA (cdp) Prince William County	608	0.96
North Brunswick, NJ (township) Middlesex County	385	0.96
Milford Mill, MD (cdp) Baltimore County	269	0.94
Roxbury, NJ (township) Morris County	219	0.94
Hillcrest, NY (cdp) Rockland County	77	0.94
Worcester, MA (city) Worcester County	1,681	0.93
Sugarland Run, VA (cdp) Loudoun County	102	0.93
Fairfield, OH (city) Butler County	368	0.86
Yeadon, PA (borough) Delaware County	99	0.86
Woodridge, IL (village) DuPage County	276	0.85
Glenmont, MD (cdp) Montgomery County	115	0.85
Germantown, MD (cdp) Montgomery County	708	0.83
Mountain Park, GA (cdp) Gwinnett County	98	0.82
South Brunswick, NJ (township) Middlesex County	342	0.81
Redland, MD (cdp) Montgomery County	136	0.80
Hyattsville, MD (city) Prince George's County	131	0.76
Westerville, OH (city) Franklin County	262	0.73
Linton Hall, VA (cdp) Prince William County	240	0.72
Cockeysville, MD (cdp) Baltimore County	140	0.71
Triangle, VA (cdp) Prince William County	55	0.71
Middle Smithfield, PA (township) Monroe County	109	0.70
Alexandria, VA (ind. city) Alexandria independent city	923	0.69
Glasgow, DE (cdp) New Castle County	105	0.67
Fords, NJ (cdp) Middlesex County	101	0.67
McNair, VA (cdp) Fairfax County	97	0.64
Manassas Park, VA (ind. city) Manassas Park independent city	84	0.64
Lake Ridge, VA (cdp) Prince William County	246	0.62
Hanover Park, IL (village) Cook County	233	0.62
North Potomac, MD (cdp) Montgomery County	156	0.62
Buena Vista, MI (charter township) Saginaw County	55	0.61
Mount Rainier, MD (city) Prince George's County	49	0.60
Adelphi, MD (cdp) Prince George's County	88	0.59
Fort Washington, MD (cdp) Prince George's County	147	0.58
Columbia, MD (cdp) Howard County	563	0.57
Nanuet, NY (cdp) Rockland County	99	0.56
Hillside, NJ (township) Union County	117	0.55
Hillsborough, NJ (township) Somerset County	207	0.54
East Orange, NJ (city) Essex County	345	0.53
Neabsco, VA (cdp) Prince William County	50	0.53
Newark, NJ (city) Essex County	1,420	0.52
Mount Vernon, NY (city) Westchester County	347	0.52
Lithia Springs, GA (cdp) Douglas County	89	0.52
Westbury, NY (village) Nassau County	78	0.52
Norcross, GA (city) Gwinnett County	48	0.52
East Hartford, CT (cdp/town) Hartford County	249	0.49
Bloomfield, CT (town) Hartford County	100	0.49
Coxsackie, NY (town) Greene County	44	0.49
Ewing, NJ (township) Mercer County	164	0.46
Roselle, NJ (borough) Union County	94	0.45
Bolingbrook, IL (village) Will County	314	0.43
Olney, MD (cdp) Montgomery County	143	0.43
Harvey, IL (city) Cook County	110	0.43
Winterville, NC (town) Pitt County	36	0.43
Haverstraw, NY (town) Rockland County	149	0.42
Kennesaw, GA (city) Cobb County	119	0.42
Princeton Meadows, NJ (cdp) Middlesex County	58	0.42
Franklin Park, NJ (cdp) Somerset County	53	0.42
Mansfield, CT (town) Tolland County	105	0.41
Rosaryville, MD (cdp) Prince George's County	47	0.41
Four Corners, MD (cdp) Montgomery County	33	0.41
Laurel, MD (city) Prince George's County	98	0.40
Elkridge, MD (cdp) Howard County	53	0.39
West Athens, CA (cdp) Los Angeles County	32	0.39
Reston, VA (cdp) Fairfax County	205	0.38
Oswego, NY (town) Oswego County	30	0.38
Sayreville, NJ (borough) Middlesex County	155	0.37
Milford, PA (township) Bucks County	36	0.37
New Windsor, NY (cdp) Orange County	34	0.37
Burke, VA (cdp) Fairfax County	149	0.36
East Point, GA (city) Fulton County	123	0.36
Seabrook, MD (cdp) Prince George's County	56	0.36
Trenton, NJ (city) Mercer County	300	0.35
Old Bridge, NJ (cdp) Middlesex County	82	0.35
Aberdeen, NJ (township) Monmouth County	64	0.35
North College Hill, OH (city) Hamilton County	33	0.35
Pawtucket, RI (city) Providence County	244	0.34
Richfield, MN (city) Hennepin County	119	0.34
Maplewood, NJ (township) Essex County	81	0.34
Fairfax Station, VA (cdp) Fairfax County	40	0.34
Lilburn, GA (city) Gwinnett County	40	0.34
Croydon, PA (cdp) Bucks County	34	0.34
Rockwall, TX (city) Rockwall County	116	0.33
Jollyville, TX (cdp) Williamson County	53	0.33
Beltsville, MD (cdp) Prince George's County	51	0.33
Oakdale, MN (city) Washington County	88	0.32
Fishkill, NY (town) Dutchess County	70	0.32
Blooming Grove, NY (town) Orange County	57	0.32
Wallingford Center, CT (cdp) New Haven County	57	0.32
La Vista, NE (city) Sarpy County	48	0.32
Clemson, SC (city) Pickens County	44	0.32
Signal Hill, CA (city) Los Angeles County	34	0.32
Hanover, NH (cdp) Grafton County	27	0.32
Orange, MA (town) Franklin County	25	0.32
Old Bridge, NJ (township) Middlesex County	197	0.31
Greenbelt, MD (city) Prince George's County	71	0.31
Falls Church, VA (ind. city) Falls Church independent city	36	0.31
Stony Brook University, NY (cdp) Suffolk County	26	0.31
Montvale, NJ (borough) Bergen County	24	0.31
Yonkers, NY (city) Westchester County	585	0.30
Severn, MD (cdp) Anne Arundel County	124	0.30
Lindenwold, NJ (borough) Camden County	52	0.30
Holden, MA (town) Worcester County	50	0.29
Marshall, MO (city) Saline County	37	0.29
Madison Heights, VA (cdp) Amherst County	32	0.29
Socorro, NM (city) Socorro County	26	0.29
Carteret, NJ (borough) Middlesex County	62	0.28
Spencer, MA (town) Worcester County	33	0.28
Fairburn, GA (city) Fulton County	32	0.28
Chicopee, MA (city) Hampden County	149	0.27
McLean, VA (cdp) Fairfax County	126	0.27
Burlington, NJ (township) Burlington County	60	0.27
Charlestown, RI (town) Washington County	21	0.27
Jersey City, NJ (city) Hudson County	624	0.26
Providence, RI (city) Providence County	462	0.26
Dover, NH (city) Strafford County	78	0.26
Plainsboro, NJ (township) Middlesex County	58	0.26
Elko, NV (city) Elko County	46	0.26
Takoma Park, MD (city) Montgomery County	44	0.26

SECTION THREE

Ancestry

African, Sub-Saharan: Kenyan

U.S. and 50 States Sorted by Population and Percent of Total Population

Place	Population	%
United States	**45,177**	**0.01**
Texas	5,989	0.02
Massachusetts	3,832	0.06
Minnesota	3,671	0.07
California	3,397	0.01
Maryland	2,458	0.04
Georgia	2,136	0.02
New Jersey	1,953	0.02
Washington	1,905	0.03
North Carolina	1,597	0.02
New York	1,324	0.01
Pennsylvania	1,277	0.01
Kansas	1,270	0.05
Virginia	1,135	0.01
Missouri	994	0.02
Ohio	948	0.01
Florida	925	<0.01
Alabama	921	0.02
Michigan	876	0.01
Illinois	863	0.01
Delaware	811	0.09
Oklahoma	769	0.02
Tennessee	755	0.01
Indiana	663	0.01
Arizona	616	0.01
Iowa	580	0.02
Connecticut	396	0.01
South Carolina	294	0.01
Nevada	285	0.01
Wisconsin	258	<0.01
Oregon	254	0.01
New Hampshire	243	0.02
West Virginia	214	0.01
District of Columbia	211	0.04
Kentucky	204	<0.01
Hawaii	192	0.01
Louisiana	187	<0.01
Colorado	132	<0.01
Arkansas	85	<0.01
Alaska	82	0.01
Maine	79	0.01
South Dakota	68	0.01
Utah	66	<0.01
Mississippi	60	<0.01
Rhode Island	52	<0.01
North Dakota	42	0.01
Nebraska	35	<0.01
New Mexico	35	<0.01
Vermont	26	<0.01
Idaho	12	<0.01
Montana	0	0.00
Wyoming	0	0.00

Place	Population	%
Delaware	811	0.09
Minnesota	3,671	0.07
Massachusetts	3,832	0.06
Kansas	1,270	0.05
Maryland	2,458	0.04
District of Columbia	211	0.04
Washington	1,905	0.03
Texas	5,989	0.02
Georgia	2,136	0.02
New Jersey	1,953	0.02
North Carolina	1,597	0.02
Missouri	994	0.02
Alabama	921	0.02
Oklahoma	769	0.02
Iowa	580	0.02
New Hampshire	243	0.02
United States	**45,177**	**0.01**
California	3,397	0.01
New York	1,324	0.01
Pennsylvania	1,277	0.01
Virginia	1,135	0.01
Ohio	948	0.01
Michigan	876	0.01
Illinois	863	0.01
Tennessee	755	0.01
Indiana	663	0.01
Arizona	616	0.01
Connecticut	396	0.01
South Carolina	294	0.01
Nevada	285	0.01
Oregon	254	0.01
West Virginia	214	0.01
Hawaii	192	0.01
Alaska	82	0.01
Maine	79	0.01
South Dakota	68	0.01
North Dakota	42	0.01
Florida	925	<0.01
Wisconsin	258	<0.01
Kentucky	204	<0.01
Louisiana	187	<0.01
Colorado	132	<0.01
Arkansas	85	<0.01
Utah	66	<0.01
Mississippi	60	<0.01
Rhode Island	52	<0.01
Nebraska	35	<0.01
New Mexico	35	<0.01
Vermont	26	<0.01
Idaho	12	<0.01
Montana	0	0.00
Wyoming	0	0.00

Please refer to the Explanation of Data in the front of the book for more detailed information.

Ancestry

African, Sub-Saharan: Kenyan

Top 150 Places Sorted by Population

Based on all places, regardless of total population

Place	Population	%
Lowell, MA (city) Middlesex County	1,309	1.25
Arlington, TX (city) Tarrant County	913	0.25
Raleigh, NC (city) Wake County	766	0.20
Plano, TX (city) Collin County	555	0.22
Columbus, OH (city) Franklin County	517	0.07
Seattle, WA (city) King County	513	0.09
Chicago, IL (city) Cook County	456	0.02
Wichita, KS (city) Sedgwick County	429	0.11
Dallas, TX (city) Dallas County	409	0.03
Worcester, MA (city) Worcester County	408	0.23
Brooklyn Park, MN (city) Hennepin County	404	0.55
Grand Prairie, TX (city) Dallas County	400	0.24
Olathe, KS (city) Johnson County	388	0.32
Lewisville, TX (city) Denton County	349	0.38
New York, NY (city) Kings County	344	<0.01
Denton, TX (city) Denton County	338	0.31
San Ramon, CA (city) Contra Costa County	336	0.50
Los Angeles, CA (city) Los Angeles County	336	0.01
Houston, TX (city) Harris County	331	0.02
Nashville-Davidson, TN (metro govt) Davidson County	288	0.05
Baltimore, MD (city) Baltimore city County	286	0.05
Detroit, MI (city) Wayne County	286	0.04
Irving, TX (city) Dallas County	284	0.14
Charlotte, NC (city) Mecklenburg County	282	0.04
McKinney, TX (city) Collin County	275	0.23
Tewksbury, MA (town) Middlesex County	274	0.96
Burnsville, MN (city) Dakota County	274	0.45
St. Louis, MO (city) St. Louis city County	266	0.08
St. Paul, MN (city) Ramsey County	262	0.09
Oklahoma City, OK (city) Oklahoma County	262	0.05
Jersey City, NJ (city) Hudson County	252	0.10
Silver Spring, MD (cdp) Montgomery County	247	0.35
Norman, OK (city) Cleveland County	236	0.22
Minnetonka, MN (city) Hennepin County	222	0.45
Federal Way, WA (city) King County	221	0.25
South Bend, IN (city) St. Joseph County	218	0.21
Acworth, GA (city) Cobb County	214	1.11
Washington, DC (city) District of Columbia	211	0.04
Kent, WA (city) King County	210	0.23
Memphis, TN (city) Shelby County	210	0.03
Arlington, VA (cdp) Arlington County	203	0.10
St. Louis Park, MN (city) Hennepin County	202	0.45
New Castle, DE (city) New Castle County	194	3.70
DeSoto, TX (city) Dallas County	187	0.40
Plymouth, MN (city) Hennepin County	175	0.25
Homewood, AL (city) Jefferson County	172	0.69
Austin, TX (city) Travis County	172	0.02
Eagan, MN (city) Dakota County	169	0.26
Murphy, TX (city) Collin County	168	1.10
Alabaster, AL (city) Shelby County	166	0.56
Fitchburg, MA (city) Worcester County	161	0.40
West Des Moines, IA (city) Polk County	161	0.29
Phoenix, AZ (city) Maricopa County	161	0.01
San Diego, CA (city) San Diego County	160	0.01
Essex, MD (cdp) Baltimore County	157	0.40
Portland, OR (city) Multnomah County	153	0.03
Tuckahoe, VA (cdp) Henrico County	150	0.33
Kenmore, WA (city) King County	148	0.74
Tempe, AZ (city) Maricopa County	147	0.09
Philadelphia, PA (city) Philadelphia County	147	0.01
Winston-Salem, NC (city) Forsyth County	145	0.06
Madison, WI (city) Dane County	144	0.06
Tulsa, OK (city) Tulsa County	144	0.04
Richardson, TX (city) Dallas County	142	0.15
Kansas City, MO (city) Jackson County	142	0.03
Trumbull, CT (cdp/town) Fairfield County	141	0.40
Burtonsville, MD (cdp) Montgomery County	140	1.52
Tucson, AZ (city) Pima County	138	0.03
Lynn, MA (city) Essex County	135	0.15
Columbia, MD (cdp) Howard County	135	0.14
Fairfield, CA (city) Solano County	135	0.13
Hoover, AL (city) Jefferson County	134	0.17
North Las Vegas, NV (city) Clark County	130	0.06
Rancho Cordova, CA (city) Sacramento County	129	0.20
St. Cloud, MN (city) Stearns County	128	0.25
St. Cloud, MN (city) Stearns County	128	0.20
Nashua, NH (city) Hillsborough County	128	0.15
Hillside, NJ (township) Union County	127	0.60
Oakdale, MN (city) Washington County	126	0.46
North Brunswick, NJ (township) Middlesex County	126	0.32
Des Moines, IA (city) Polk County	126	0.06
New Brighton, MN (city) Ramsey County	120	0.56
Pullman, WA (city) Whitman County	120	0.42
Lakeside, VA (cdp) Henrico County	119	0.99
Malden, MA (city) Middlesex County	118	0.20
Long Beach, CA (city) Los Angeles County	117	0.03
Columbia, MO (city) Boone County	115	0.11
Oakland, CA (city) Alameda County	115	0.03
Dracut, MA (town) Middlesex County	114	0.39
Woodburn, VA (cdp) Fairfax County	113	1.30
Albany, CA (city) Alameda County	113	0.63
Germantown, MD (cdp) Montgomery County	113	0.13
Overland Park, KS (city) Johnson County	112	0.07
Richfield, MN (city) Hennepin County	110	0.32
Amherst, MA (town) Hampshire County	108	0.29
Yonkers, NY (city) Westchester County	107	0.05
Foothill Farms, CA (cdp) Sacramento County	106	0.32
Cottage Grove, MN (city) Washington County	104	0.31
Sayreville, NJ (borough) Middlesex County	103	0.24
Peabody, MA (city) Essex County	102	0.20
North Plainfield, NJ (borough) Somerset County	101	0.46
Novato, CA (city) Marin County	101	0.20
Albany, NY (city) Albany County	101	0.10
Atlanta, GA (city) Fulton County	101	0.02
Riverside, CA (city) Riverside County	100	0.03
Glasgow, DE (cdp) New Castle County	98	0.63
Huntsville, AL (city) Madison County	98	0.06
Florissant, MO (city) St. Louis County	96	0.18
Queens, NY (borough) Queens County	96	<0.01
Rockville, MD (city) Montgomery County	95	0.16
Fort Worth, TX (city) Tarrant County	94	0.01
Mustang, OK (city) Canadian County	93	0.56
Champlin, MN (city) Hennepin County	93	0.41
Minneapolis, MN (city) Hennepin County	93	0.02
Orange, TX (city) Orange County	90	0.48
Dunwoody, GA (city) DeKalb County	90	0.20
The Colony, TX (city) Denton County	88	0.25
Schaumburg, IL (village) Cook County	88	0.12
Frisco, TX (city) Collin County	88	0.09
Santa Ana, CA (city) Orange County	88	0.03
Adrian, MI (city) Lenawee County	87	0.40
Lebanon, PA (city) Lebanon County	86	0.34
Tonawanda, NY (cdp) Erie County	86	0.15
Tonawanda, NY (town) Erie County	86	0.12
Everett, WA (city) Snohomish County	86	0.08
Las Vegas, NV (city) Clark County	86	0.01
Lake Butler, FL (cdp) Orange County	85	0.54
Waimalu, HI (cdp) Honolulu County	84	0.59
Bayonne, NJ (city) Hudson County	84	0.14
Avondale, AZ (city) Maricopa County	84	0.12
South Amherst, MA (cdp) Hampshire County	82	1.66
Irondale, AL (city) Jefferson County	82	0.67
Fairland, MD (cdp) Montgomery County	82	0.36
Woodbridge, NJ (township) Middlesex County	82	0.08
West End, NY (cdp) Otsego County	81	5.18
Oneonta, NY (town) Otsego County	81	1.56
Severn, MD (cdp) Anne Arundel County	80	0.19
Pratt, KS (city) Pratt County	79	1.16
Navarre, FL (cdp) Santa Rosa County	79	0.27
Willingboro, NJ (township) Burlington County	79	0.25
Franklin, TN (city) Williamson County	79	0.13
Edison, NJ (township) Middlesex County	79	0.08
Salida, CA (cdp) Stanislaus County	78	0.53
Renton, WA (city) King County	78	0.09
Newport News, VA (ind. city) Newport News independent city	78	0.04
Staten Island, NY (borough) Richmond County	78	0.02
Ludlow, MA (town) Hampden County	77	0.36
Urbandale, IA (city) Polk County	77	0.21
Coon Rapids, MN (city) Anoka County	77	0.12
Brooklyn, NY (borough) Kings County	77	<0.01

Ancestry

African, Sub-Saharan: Kenyan

Top 150 Places Sorted by Percent of Total Population

Based on all places, regardless of total population

Place	Population	%
Riverside, MN (township) Lac qui Parle County	39	12.15
Lacomb, OR (cdp) Linn County	36	9.35
West End, NY (cdp) Otsego County	81	5.18
Winsor, MN (township) Clearwater County	4	4.55
Elsah, IL (village) Jersey County	21	3.79
New Castle, DE (city) New Castle County	194	3.70
Lauderdale, MN (city) Ramsey County	70	2.87
Wanamingo, MN (city) Goodhue County	27	2.70
Midway, FL (cdp) Seminole County	40	2.37
Rose Hill, MN (township) Cottonwood County	4	2.00
Bryn Mawr, PA (cdp) Montgomery County	70	1.99
Wilmore, KY (city) Jessamine County	74	1.98
Unity Village, MO (village) Jackson County	2	1.96
Quentin, PA (cdp) Lebanon County	9	1.86
Blue Earth City, MN (township) Faribault County	7	1.78
South Amherst, MA (cdp) Hampshire County	82	1.66
Oneonta, NY (town) Otsego County	81	1.56
Cushing, MN (township) Morrison County	11	1.56
Burtonsville, MD (cdp) Montgomery County	140	1.52
North Westport, MA (cdp) Bristol County	59	1.41
Harvest, AL (cdp) Madison County	59	1.34
Salem, NJ (city) Salem County	70	1.32
Woodburn, VA (cdp) Fairfax County	113	1.30
Houghton, NY (cdp) Allegany County	22	1.29
Piermont, NY (village) Rockland County	32	1.27
Plumsteadville, PA (cdp) Bucks County	33	1.26
Lowell, MA (city) Middlesex County	1,309	1.25
Abbeville, SC (city) Abbeville County	64	1.19
Pratt, KS (city) Pratt County	79	1.16
Acworth, GA (city) Cobb County	214	1.11
Murphy, TX (city) Collin County	168	1.10
Huntington Woods, MI (city) Oakland County	66	1.06
Pine, PA (township) Mercer County	53	1.05
Biglerville, PA (borough) Adams County	11	1.05
East Petersburg, PA (borough) Lancaster County	45	1.00
Lakeside, VA (cdp) Henrico County	119	0.99
Paoli, PA (cdp) Chester County	52	0.99
Tewksbury, MA (town) Middlesex County	274	0.96
Caneadea, NY (town) Allegany County	22	0.86
St. Michaels, MD (town) Talbot County	9	0.82
Atkins, IA (city) Benton County	14	0.81
Austell, GA (city) Cobb County	51	0.80
Pleasant Run, OH (cdp) Hamilton County	38	0.80
Crestview Hills, KY (city) Kenton County	25	0.80
Clifton Heights, PA (borough) Delaware County	51	0.77
Mount Ivy, NY (cdp) Rockland County	50	0.76
Kenmore, WA (city) King County	148	0.74
Seven Corners, VA (cdp) Fairfax County	62	0.74
Leslie, MI (city) Ingham County	14	0.73
Burke, WI (town) Dane County	23	0.72
Davidson, NC (town) Mecklenburg County	72	0.70
Homewood, AL (city) Jefferson County	172	0.69
South Williamsport, PA (borough) Lycoming County	43	0.68
Irondale, AL (city) Jefferson County	82	0.67
Morganville, NJ (cdp) Monmouth County	31	0.67
Ellsworth, KS (city) Ellsworth County	20	0.65
Albany, CA (city) Alameda County	113	0.63
Glasgow, DE (cdp) New Castle County	98	0.63
Cambridge, MN (city) Isanti County	48	0.61
Horseheads, NY (village) Chemung County	39	0.61
Clearwater, MN (township) Wright County	8	0.61
Hillside, NJ (township) Union County	127	0.60
Hartford, KY (city) Ohio County	16	0.60
Waimalu, HI (cdp) Honolulu County	84	0.59
Accokeek, MD (cdp) Prince George's County	61	0.58
Mosinee, WI (town) Marathon County	12	0.58
Cocoa West, FL (cdp) Brevard County	34	0.57
Messiah College, PA (cdp) Cumberland County	14	0.57
Ellerslie, MD (cdp) Allegany County	2	0.57
Alabaster, AL (city) Shelby County	166	0.56
New Brighton, MN (city) Ramsey County	120	0.56
Mustang, OK (city) Canadian County	93	0.56
Woodstock, CT (town) Windham County	44	0.56
Brooklyn Park, MN (city) Hennepin County	404	0.55
Lake Butler, FL (cdp) Orange County	85	0.54
Edwardsville, KS (city) Wyandotte County	23	0.54
Salida, CA (cdp) Stanislaus County	78	0.53
Roseau, MN (city) Roseau County	14	0.52
Foley, MN (city) Benton County	13	0.51
Hanover, PA (township) Lehigh County	8	0.51
San Ramon, CA (city) Contra Costa County	336	0.50
Addison, TX (town) Dallas County	66	0.50
Homestead, PA (borough) Allegheny County	16	0.50
Goodwell, OK (town) Texas County	6	0.50
Montevallo, AL (city) Shelby County	30	0.49
Orange, TX (city) Orange County	90	0.48
Springdale, NJ (cdp) Camden County	70	0.48
Millersville, PA (borough) Lancaster County	39	0.48
Pennside, PA (cdp) Berks County	21	0.48
West Cornwall, PA (township) Lebanon County	9	0.47
Oakdale, MN (city) Washington County	126	0.46
North Plainfield, NJ (borough) Somerset County	101	0.46
Burnsville, MN (city) Dakota County	274	0.45
Minnetonka, MN (city) Hennepin County	222	0.45
St. Louis Park, MN (city) Hennepin County	202	0.45
Grandville, MI (city) Kent County	70	0.45
Woodlawn, MD (cdp) Prince George's County	28	0.43
Pullman, WA (city) Whitman County	120	0.42
Calvin, MI (township) Cass County	9	0.42
Youngstown, NY (village) Niagara County	8	0.42
Champlin, MN (city) Hennepin County	93	0.41
Fords, NJ (cdp) Middlesex County	62	0.41
Bryn Mawr-Skyway, WA (cdp) King County	59	0.41
DeSoto, TX (city) Dallas County	187	0.40
Fitchburg, MA (city) Worcester County	161	0.40
Essex, MD (cdp) Baltimore County	157	0.40
Trumbull, CT (cdp/town) Fairfield County	141	0.40
Adrian, MI (city) Lenawee County	87	0.40
Rock Valley, IA (city) Sioux County	13	0.40
Dracut, MA (town) Middlesex County	114	0.39
Westport, MA (town) Bristol County	59	0.39
Lewisville, TX (city) Denton County	349	0.38
Willistown, PA (township) Chester County	40	0.38
Nether Providence, PA (township) Delaware County	50	0.37
Savage, MD (cdp) Howard County	25	0.37
Fairland, MD (cdp) Montgomery County	82	0.36
Ludlow, MA (town) Hampden County	77	0.36
Ashton-Sandy Spring, MD (cdp) Montgomery County	19	0.36
Pagedale, MO (city) St. Louis County	12	0.36
Perkins, OK (city) Payne County	10	0.36
Silver Spring, MD (cdp) Montgomery County	247	0.35
White Oak, MD (cdp) Montgomery County	59	0.35
Wilbraham, MA (town) Hampden County	49	0.35
El Dorado, KS (city) Butler County	46	0.35
Blooming Grove, WI (town) Dane County	6	0.35
North Randall, OH (village) Cuyahoga County	3	0.35
Lebanon, PA (city) Lebanon County	86	0.34
Hopkins, MN (city) Hennepin County	60	0.34
Lantana, FL (town) Palm Beach County	35	0.34
St. Anthony, MN (city) Ramsey County	10	0.34
Tuckahoe, VA (cdp) Henrico County	150	0.33
Crystal, MN (city) Hennepin County	72	0.33
Olathe, KS (city) Johnson County	388	0.32
North Brunswick, NJ (township) Middlesex County	126	0.32
Richfield, MN (city) Hennepin County	110	0.32
Foothill Farms, CA (cdp) Sacramento County	106	0.32
Little Elm, TX (city) Denton County	71	0.32
Rosemount, MN (city) Dakota County	66	0.32
Angwin, CA (cdp) Napa County	12	0.32
Denton, TX (city) Denton County	338	0.31
Cottage Grove, MN (city) Washington County	104	0.31
Old Jamestown, MO (cdp) St. Louis County	63	0.31
Southbridge Town, MA (city) Worcester County	53	0.31
Mount Rainier, MD (city) Prince George's County	25	0.31
Joppatowne, MD (cdp) Harford County	38	0.30
Red Bank, NJ (borough) Monmouth County	36	0.30
Berrien, MI (township) Berrien County	15	0.30
West Des Moines, IA (city) Polk County	161	0.29
Amherst, MA (town) Hampshire County	108	0.29
Prospect Heights, IL (city) Cook County	47	0.29

Please refer to the Explanation of Data in the front of the book for more detailed information.

Ancestry

African, Sub-Saharan: Kenyan

Top 150 Places Sorted by Percent of Total Population

Based on places with total population of 7,500 or more

Place	Population	%
Burtonsville, MD (cdp) Montgomery County	140	1.52
Woodburn, VA (cdp) Fairfax County	113	1.30
Lowell, MA (city) Middlesex County	1,309	1.25
Acworth, GA (city) Cobb County	214	1.11
Murphy, TX (city) Collin County	168	1.10
Lakeside, VA (cdp) Henrico County	119	0.99
Tewksbury, MA (town) Middlesex County	274	0.96
Kenmore, WA (city) King County	148	0.74
Seven Corners, VA (cdp) Fairfax County	62	0.74
Davidson, NC (town) Mecklenburg County	72	0.70
Homewood, AL (city) Jefferson County	172	0.69
Irondale, AL (city) Jefferson County	82	0.67
Albany, CA (city) Alameda County	113	0.63
Glasgow, DE (cdp) New Castle County	98	0.63
Cambridge, MN (city) Isanti County	48	0.61
Hillside, NJ (township) Union County	127	0.60
Waimalu, HI (cdp) Honolulu County	84	0.59
Accokeek, MD (cdp) Prince George's County	61	0.58
Alabaster, AL (city) Shelby County	166	0.56
New Brighton, MN (city) Ramsey County	120	0.56
Mustang, OK (city) Canadian County	93	0.56
Woodstock, CT (town) Windham County	44	0.56
Brooklyn Park, MN (city) Hennepin County	404	0.55
Lake Butler, FL (cdp) Orange County	85	0.54
Salida, CA (cdp) Stanislaus County	78	0.53
San Ramon, CA (city) Contra Costa County	336	0.50
Addison, TX (town) Dallas County	66	0.50
Orange, TX (city) Orange County	90	0.48
Springdale, NJ (cdp) Camden County	70	0.48
Millersville, PA (borough) Lancaster County	39	0.48
Oakdale, MN (city) Washington County	126	0.46
North Plainfield, NJ (borough) Somerset County	101	0.46
Burnsville, MN (city) Dakota County	274	0.45
Minnetonka, MN (city) Hennepin County	222	0.45
St. Louis Park, MN (city) Hennepin County	202	0.45
Grandville, MI (city) Kent County	70	0.45
Pullman, WA (city) Whitman County	120	0.42
Champlin, MN (city) Hennepin County	93	0.41
Fords, NJ (cdp) Middlesex County	62	0.41
Bryn Mawr-Skyway, WA (cdp) King County	59	0.41
DeSoto, TX (city) Dallas County	187	0.40
Fitchburg, MA (city) Worcester County	161	0.40
Essex, MD (cdp) Baltimore County	157	0.40
Trumbull, CT (cdp/town) Fairfield County	141	0.40
Adrian, MI (city) Lenawee County	87	0.40
Dracut, MA (town) Middlesex County	114	0.39
Westport, MA (town) Bristol County	59	0.39
Lewisville, TX (city) Denton County	349	0.38
Willistown, PA (township) Chester County	40	0.38
Nether Providence, PA (township) Delaware County	50	0.37
Fairland, MD (cdp) Montgomery County	82	0.36
Ludlow, MA (town) Hampden County	77	0.36
Silver Spring, MD (cdp) Montgomery County	247	0.35
White Oak, MD (cdp) Montgomery County	59	0.35
Wilbraham, MA (town) Hampden County	49	0.35
El Dorado, KS (city) Butler County	46	0.35
Lebanon, PA (city) Lebanon County	86	0.34
Hopkins, MN (city) Hennepin County	60	0.34
Lantana, FL (town) Palm Beach County	35	0.34
Tuckahoe, VA (cdp) Henrico County	150	0.33
Crystal, MN (city) Hennepin County	72	0.33
Olathe, KS (city) Johnson County	388	0.32
North Brunswick, NJ (township) Middlesex County	126	0.32
Richfield, MN (city) Hennepin County	110	0.32
Foothill Farms, CA (cdp) Sacramento County	106	0.32
Little Elm, TX (city) Denton County	71	0.32
Rosemount, MN (city) Dakota County	66	0.32
Denton, TX (city) Denton County	338	0.31
Cottage Grove, MN (city) Washington County	104	0.31
Old Jamestown, MO (cdp) St. Louis County	63	0.31
Southbridge Town, MA (city) Worcester County	53	0.31
Mount Rainier, MD (city) Prince George's County	25	0.31
Joppatowne, MD (cdp) Harford County	38	0.30
Red Bank, NJ (borough) Monmouth County	36	0.30
West Des Moines, IA (city) Polk County	161	0.29
Amherst, MA (town) Hampshire County	108	0.29
Prospect Heights, IL (city) Cook County	47	0.29
Elkton, MD (town) Cecil County	44	0.29
Glassmanor, MD (cdp) Prince George's County	49	0.28
North St. Paul, MN (city) Ramsey County	32	0.28
Navarre, FL (cdp) Santa Rosa County	79	0.27
Ridgecrest, CA (city) Kern County	73	0.27
Hazelwood, MO (city) St. Louis County	70	0.27
Ossining, NY (village) Westchester County	66	0.27
Roselle, NJ (borough) Union County	56	0.27
Haslett, MI (cdp) Ingham County	53	0.27
Sycamore, IL (city) DeKalb County	46	0.27
Plumstead, PA (township) Bucks County	33	0.27
Eagan, MN (city) Dakota County	169	0.26
Balch Springs, TX (city) Dallas County	59	0.26
Coolbaugh, PA (township) Monroe County	53	0.26
Arlington, TX (city) Tarrant County	913	0.25
Federal Way, WA (city) King County	221	0.25
Plymouth, MN (city) Hennepin County	175	0.25
St. Cloud, MN (city) Stearns County	128	0.25
The Colony, TX (city) Denton County	88	0.25
Willingboro, NJ (township) Burlington County	79	0.25
Troy, AL (city) Pike County	43	0.25
Grand Prairie, TX (city) Dallas County	400	0.24
Sayreville, NJ (borough) Middlesex County	103	0.24
Brookside, DE (cdp) New Castle County	34	0.24
Calera, AL (city) Shelby County	25	0.24
Fife, WA (city) Pierce County	20	0.24
Worcester, MA (city) Worcester County	408	0.23
McKinney, TX (city) Collin County	275	0.23
Kent, WA (city) King County	210	0.23
Montgomery Village, MD (cdp) Montgomery County	72	0.23
Plano, TX (city) Collin County	555	0.22
Norman, OK (city) Cleveland County	236	0.22
Lebanon, MO (city) Laclede County	31	0.22
Bull Run, VA (cdp) Prince William County	28	0.22
Plaistow, NH (town) Rockingham County	17	0.22
South Bend, IN (city) St. Joseph County	218	0.21
Urbandale, IA (city) Polk County	77	0.21
Fairbanks, AK (city) Fairbanks North Star Borough	66	0.21
Savage, MN (city) Scott County	57	0.21
Mansfield, CT (town) Tolland County	55	0.21
Pleasant Hills, PA (borough) Allegheny County	17	0.21
Raleigh, NC (city) Wake County	766	0.20
Rancho Cordova, CA (city) Sacramento County	129	0.20
St. Cloud, MN (city) Stearns County	128	0.20
Malden, MA (city) Middlesex County	118	0.20
Peabody, MA (city) Essex County	102	0.20
Novato, CA (city) Marin County	101	0.20
Dunwoody, GA (city) DeKalb County	90	0.20
Woburn, MA (city) Middlesex County	76	0.20
Horseheads, NY (town) Chemung County	39	0.20
Madison, NJ (borough) Morris County	32	0.20
Waunakee, WI (village) Dane County	23	0.20
Oberlin, OH (city) Lorain County	17	0.20
Severn, MD (cdp) Anne Arundel County	80	0.19
Watertown Town, MA (city) Middlesex County	61	0.19
Parkville, MD (cdp) Baltimore County	57	0.19
Kennesaw, GA (city) Cobb County	55	0.19
Greer, SC (city) Greenville County	46	0.19
Ashland, CA (cdp) Alameda County	42	0.19
Warrensburg, MO (city) Johnson County	36	0.19
Palm Springs, FL (village) Palm Beach County	35	0.19
Wallington, NJ (borough) Bergen County	21	0.19
West Caldwell, NJ (township) Essex County	20	0.19
Florissant, MO (city) St. Louis County	96	0.18
Ossining, NY (town) Westchester County	66	0.18
Owings Mills, MD (cdp) Baltimore County	53	0.18
Garfield Heights, OH (city) Cuyahoga County	51	0.18
Green, OH (city) Summit County	46	0.18
Silverdale, WA (cdp) Kitsap County	34	0.18
East Lampeter, PA (township) Lancaster County	28	0.18
Speedway, IN (town) Marion County	22	0.18
Fairview, OR (city) Multnomah County	15	0.18
Hoover, AL (city) Jefferson County	134	0.17

Please refer to the Explanation of Data in the front of the book for more detailed information.

Ancestry

African, Sub-Saharan: Liberian

U.S. and 50 States Sorted by Population and Percent of Total Population

Place	Population	%
United States	**52,299**	**0.02**
Minnesota	7,611	0.15
Pennsylvania	7,515	0.06
New Jersey	4,445	0.05
Maryland	4,007	0.07
New York	3,006	0.02
Rhode Island	2,980	0.28
Georgia	2,368	0.03
Virginia	2,087	0.03
North Carolina	1,963	0.02
Texas	1,729	0.01
Massachusetts	1,636	0.03
Florida	1,287	0.01
California	1,184	<0.01
Ohio	939	0.01
Missouri	873	0.01
Michigan	830	0.01
Indiana	771	0.01
Arizona	690	0.01
Connecticut	662	0.02
Tennessee	551	0.01
Delaware	504	0.06
Illinois	439	<0.01
Kentucky	431	0.01
Wisconsin	414	0.01
Colorado	371	0.01
Iowa	322	0.01
Oklahoma	314	0.01
South Carolina	274	0.01
Oregon	262	0.01
Washington	246	<0.01
Nevada	221	0.01
New Hampshire	208	0.02
Louisiana	152	<0.01
Montana	151	0.02
North Dakota	107	0.02
Utah	98	<0.01
Alabama	97	<0.01
Hawaii	95	0.01
District of Columbia	91	0.02
South Dakota	84	0.01
Nebraska	83	<0.01
Arkansas	40	<0.01
Idaho	40	<0.01
Kansas	33	<0.01
Alaska	32	<0.01
West Virginia	28	<0.01
Mississippi	13	<0.01
New Mexico	11	<0.01
Vermont	4	<0.01
Maine	0	0.00
Wyoming	0	0.00

Place	Population	%
Rhode Island	2,980	0.28
Minnesota	7,611	0.15
Maryland	4,007	0.07
Pennsylvania	7,515	0.06
Delaware	504	0.06
New Jersey	4,445	0.05
Georgia	2,368	0.03
Virginia	2,087	0.03
Massachusetts	1,636	0.03
United States	**52,299**	**0.02**
New York	3,006	0.02
North Carolina	1,963	0.02
Connecticut	662	0.02
New Hampshire	208	0.02
Montana	151	0.02
North Dakota	107	0.02
District of Columbia	91	0.02
Texas	1,729	0.01
Florida	1,287	0.01
Ohio	939	0.01
Missouri	873	0.01
Michigan	830	0.01
Indiana	771	0.01
Arizona	690	0.01
Tennessee	551	0.01
Kentucky	431	0.01
Wisconsin	414	0.01
Colorado	371	0.01
Iowa	322	0.01
Oklahoma	314	0.01
South Carolina	274	0.01
Oregon	262	0.01
Nevada	221	0.01
Hawaii	95	0.01
South Dakota	84	0.01
California	1,184	<0.01
Illinois	439	<0.01
Washington	246	<0.01
Louisiana	152	<0.01
Utah	98	<0.01
Alabama	97	<0.01
Nebraska	83	<0.01
Arkansas	40	<0.01
Idaho	40	<0.01
Kansas	33	<0.01
Alaska	32	<0.01
West Virginia	28	<0.01
Mississippi	13	<0.01
New Mexico	11	<0.01
Vermont	4	<0.01
Maine	0	0.00
Wyoming	0	0.00

Please refer to the Explanation of Data in the front of the book for more detailed information.

Ancestry

African, Sub-Saharan: Liberian

Top 150 Places Sorted by Population

Based on all places, regardless of total population

Place	Population	%
Brooklyn Park, MN (city) Hennepin County	3,237	4.40
Philadelphia, PA (city) Philadelphia County	3,198	0.21
New York, NY (city) Kings County	1,991	0.02
Providence, RI (city) Providence County	1,682	0.94
Upper Darby, PA (township) Delaware County	1,530	1.86
Pawtucket, RI (city) Providence County	1,075	1.50
Newark, NJ (city) Essex County	918	0.33
Reston, VA (cdp) Fairfax County	836	1.57
Brooklyn Center, MN (city) Hennepin County	796	2.68
Minneapolis, MN (city) Hennepin County	791	0.21
Trenton, NJ (city) Mercer County	755	0.89
Indianapolis, IN (city) Marion County	687	0.08
Charlotte, NC (city) Mecklenburg County	633	0.09
Yeadon, PA (borough) Delaware County	612	5.33
Phoenix, AZ (city) Maricopa County	585	0.04
Germantown, MD (cdp) Montgomery County	574	0.68
Darby, PA (borough) Delaware County	566	5.34
Staten Island, NY (borough) Richmond County	532	0.11
Worcester, MA (city) Worcester County	529	0.29
West Haven, CT (city/town) New Haven County	524	0.95
Hamilton, NJ (township) Mercer County	495	0.56
Brooklyn, NY (borough) Kings County	452	0.02
Bronx, NY (borough) Bronx County	450	0.03
Boston, MA (city) Suffolk County	440	0.07
Willingboro, NJ (township) Burlington County	435	1.35
Louisville-Jefferson County, KY (metro govt) Jefferson County	395	0.07
Columbus, OH (city) Franklin County	384	0.05
Queens, NY (borough) Queens County	381	0.02
High Point, NC (city) Guilford County	376	0.37
Jacksonville, FL (city) Duval County	369	0.05
Kansas City, MO (city) Jackson County	356	0.08
Burlington, NJ (township) Burlington County	322	1.44
Houston, TX (city) Harris County	311	0.02
Grand Rapids, MI (city) Kent County	309	0.16
Babylon, NY (town) Suffolk County	309	0.14
Dallas, TX (city) Dallas County	307	0.03
Essex, MD (cdp) Baltimore County	287	0.74
St. Louis, MO (city) St. Louis city County	273	0.09
Durham, NC (city) Durham County	265	0.12
Lynn, MA (city) Essex County	263	0.29
Euless, TX (city) Tarrant County	256	0.51
Wheatley Heights, NY (cdp) Suffolk County	251	4.05
St. Paul, MN (city) Ramsey County	248	0.09
Syracuse, NY (city) Onondaga County	246	0.17
Bristol, PA (township) Bucks County	243	0.44
Worthington, MN (city) Nobles County	239	1.93
Alexandria, VA (ind. city) Alexandria independent city	235	0.18
Hybla Valley, VA (cdp) Fairfax County	231	1.58
Paradise, NV (cdp) Clark County	221	0.10
Crystal, MN (city) Hennepin County	219	0.99
Madison, WI (city) Dane County	209	0.09
St. Cloud, MN (city) Stearns County	207	0.32
Greensboro, NC (city) Guilford County	204	0.08
Collingdale, PA (borough) Delaware County	203	2.32
East Orange, NJ (city) Essex County	197	0.30
St. Michael, MN (city) Wright County	192	1.25
Elfers, FL (cdp) Pasco County	183	1.38
Manhattan, NY (borough) New York County	176	0.01
Atlantic City, NJ (city) Atlantic County	172	0.43
St. Cloud, MN (city) Stearns County	170	0.33
Mitchellville, MD (cdp) Prince George's County	166	1.42
Manchester, NH (city) Hillsborough County	164	0.15
Coon Rapids, MN (city) Anoka County	161	0.26
Ewing, NJ (township) Mercer County	160	0.45
Falls, PA (township) Bucks County	158	0.46
Austin, TX (city) Travis County	158	0.02
Woonsocket, RI (city) Providence County	157	0.38
Portland, OR (city) Multnomah County	157	0.03
Montgomery Village, MD (cdp) Montgomery County	156	0.49
Tulsa, OK (city) Tulsa County	153	0.04
Des Moines, IA (city) Polk County	152	0.08
New Hope, MN (city) Hennepin County	150	0.74
Nashville-Davidson, TN (metro govt) Davidson County	141	0.02
Plantation, FL (city) Broward County	137	0.16
Arlington, TX (city) Tarrant County	135	0.04
Burtonsville, MD (cdp) Montgomery County	129	1.40
Hayward, CA (city) Alameda County	129	0.09
Cleveland, OH (city) Cuyahoga County	128	0.03
Richfield, MN (city) Hennepin County	127	0.37
Leesburg, VA (town) Loudoun County	126	0.31
Severn, MD (cdp) Anne Arundel County	125	0.30
Andover, MN (city) Anoka County	124	0.41
Frederick, MD (city) Frederick County	123	0.19
Jersey City, NJ (city) Hudson County	123	0.05
Marlboro Meadows, MD (cdp) Prince George's County	120	3.30
Helena Valley West Central, MT (cdp) Lewis and Clark County	119	1.45
Ridley, PA (township) Delaware County	118	0.38
Golden Valley, MN (city) Hennepin County	115	0.57
Brock Hall, MD (cdp) Prince George's County	114	1.40
Aspen Hill, MD (cdp) Montgomery County	113	0.24
Brockton, MA (city) Plymouth County	111	0.12
Abilene, TX (city) Taylor County	111	0.10
Stockbridge, GA (city) Henry County	110	0.46
Johnson City, TN (city) Washington County	110	0.18
Baltimore, MD (city) Baltimore city County	110	0.02
Gaithersburg, MD (city) Montgomery County	109	0.19
Fairland, MD (cdp) Montgomery County	107	0.46
Oklahoma City, OK (city) Oklahoma County	107	0.02
Winston-Salem, NC (city) Forsyth County	106	0.05
Avondale, AZ (city) Maricopa County	105	0.15
Milpitas, CA (city) Santa Clara County	104	0.16
St. Petersburg, FL (city) Pinellas County	104	0.04
Apple Valley, MN (city) Dakota County	102	0.21
Columbia, MD (cdp) Howard County	102	0.10
Chicago, IL (city) Cook County	102	<0.01
Colwyn, PA (borough) Delaware County	101	4.02
Kent, WA (city) King County	100	0.11
Lowell, MA (city) Middlesex County	99	0.09
Hamtramck, MI (city) Wayne County	97	0.43
Urban Honolulu, HI (cdp) Honolulu County	95	0.03
Lakeland, FL (city) Polk County	94	0.10
San Jose, CA (city) Santa Clara County	94	0.01
Laurel, MD (city) Prince George's County	92	0.38
Maplewood, MN (city) Ramsey County	92	0.25
Stockton, CA (city) San Joaquin County	91	0.03
Washington, DC (city) District of Columbia	91	0.02
Lochearn, MD (cdp) Baltimore County	89	0.35
Knoxville, TN (city) Knox County	89	0.05
Rochester, NY (city) Monroe County	89	0.04
Oakland, CA (city) Alameda County	89	0.02
Urbandale, IA (city) Polk County	88	0.23
Utica, NY (city) Oneida County	88	0.14
Kemp Mill, MD (cdp) Montgomery County	85	0.70
Milford Mill, MD (cdp) Baltimore County	85	0.30
Silver Spring, MD (cdp) Montgomery County	85	0.12
Sioux Falls, SD (city) Minnehaha County	84	0.06
Leland Grove, IL (city) Sangamon County	83	5.14
New Orleans, LA (city) Orleans Parish	83	0.03
Lancaster, SC (city) Lancaster County	82	0.99
Fair Oaks, VA (cdp) Fairfax County	82	0.30
Fargo, ND (city) Cass County	82	0.08
Denver, CO (city) Denver County	81	0.01
Detroit, MI (city) Wayne County	81	0.01
Shakopee, MN (city) Scott County	80	0.23
Fairless Hills, PA (cdp) Bucks County	79	0.90
Orlando, FL (city) Orange County	78	0.03
Littleton, CO (city) Arapahoe County	77	0.19
Omaha, NE (city) Douglas County	76	0.02
Fort Worth, TX (city) Tarrant County	76	0.01
Los Angeles, CA (city) Los Angeles County	76	<0.01
Heron Bay, GA (cdp) Henry County	74	2.31
Toccoa, GA (city) Stephens County	74	0.86
Buffalo, NY (city) Erie County	74	0.03
Medford, MA (city) Middlesex County	72	0.13
Posen, IL (village) Cook County	71	1.25
Pittsburgh, PA (city) Allegheny County	71	0.02
Takoma Park, MD (city) Montgomery County	70	0.42
Milwaukee, WI (city) Milwaukee County	70	0.01
Wheaton, MD (cdp) Montgomery County	69	0.15
Wilmington, DE (city) New Castle County	69	0.10

Please refer to the Explanation of Data in the front of the book for more detailed information.

Ancestry

African, Sub-Saharan: Liberian

Top 150 Places Sorted by Percent of Total Population

Based on all places, regardless of total population

Place	Population	%
Shelocta, PA (borough) Indiana County	7	5.93
Darby, PA (borough) Delaware County	566	5.34
Yeadon, PA (borough) Delaware County	612	5.33
Leland Grove, IL (city) Sangamon County	83	5.14
Brooklyn Park, MN (city) Hennepin County	3,237	4.40
Wheatley Heights, NY (cdp) Suffolk County	251	4.05
Colwyn, PA (borough) Delaware County	101	4.02
Yogaville, VA (cdp) Buckingham County	10	3.97
Marlboro Meadows, MD (cdp) Prince George's County	120	3.30
Oneida, KY (cdp) Clay County	13	3.09
Pelican Lake, MN (township) Grant County	11	2.89
Brooklyn Center, MN (city) Hennepin County	796	2.68
Collingdale, PA (borough) Delaware County	203	2.32
Heron Bay, GA (cdp) Henry County	74	2.31
Akutan, AK (city) Aleutians East Borough	32	2.01
Worthington, MN (city) Nobles County	239	1.93
Clayton, DE (town) Kent County	51	1.93
Toftrees, PA (cdp) Centre County	42	1.92
Upper Darby, PA (township) Delaware County	1,530	1.86
Upland, PA (borough) Delaware County	56	1.76
Hybla Valley, VA (cdp) Fairfax County	231	1.58
Reston, VA (cdp) Fairfax County	836	1.57
Pawtucket, RI (city) Providence County	1,075	1.50
Hi-Nella, NJ (borough) Camden County	14	1.50
Helena Valley West Central, MT (cdp) Lewis and Clark County	119	1.45
Burlington, NJ (township) Burlington County	322	1.44
Mitchellville, MD (cdp) Prince George's County	166	1.42
Burtonsville, MD (cdp) Montgomery County	129	1.40
Brock Hall, MD (cdp) Prince George's County	114	1.40
Elfers, FL (cdp) Pasco County	183	1.38
Oxford, WI (village) Marquette County	7	1.38
Lockland, OH (village) Hamilton County	47	1.36
Willingboro, NJ (township) Burlington County	435	1.35
St. Michael, MN (city) Wright County	192	1.25
Posen, IL (village) Cook County	71	1.25
Huber Ridge, OH (cdp) Franklin County	56	1.25
Blowers, MN (township) Otter Tail County	4	1.24
Bayview, WI (town) Bayfield County	6	1.06
Crystal, MN (city) Hennepin County	219	0.99
Lancaster, SC (city) Lancaster County	82	0.99
West Haven, CT (city/town) New Haven County	524	0.95
Providence, RI (city) Providence County	1,682	0.94
Enola, PA (cdp) Cumberland County	62	0.94
Cairo, IL (city) Alexander County	27	0.91
Fairless Hills, PA (cdp) Bucks County	79	0.90
Trenton, NJ (city) Mercer County	755	0.89
Toccoa, GA (city) Stephens County	74	0.86
Morris, MN (city) Stevens County	45	0.86
Westville, NJ (borough) Gloucester County	37	0.85
Bethany, MI (township) Gratiot County	11	0.81
Cornwells Heights, PA (cdp) Bucks County	11	0.79
Essex, MD (cdp) Baltimore County	287	0.74
New Hope, MN (city) Hennepin County	150	0.74
Blakely, PA (borough) Lackawanna County	48	0.72
Kemp Mill, MD (cdp) Montgomery County	85	0.70
Germantown, MD (cdp) Montgomery County	574	0.68
Folcroft, PA (borough) Delaware County	44	0.66
Landover Hills, MD (town) Prince George's County	12	0.64
Richmond Heights, OH (city) Cuyahoga County	65	0.61
Golden Valley, MN (city) Hennepin County	115	0.57
Hamilton, NJ (township) Mercer County	495	0.56
Twin Rivers, NJ (cdp) Mercer County	38	0.54
Whiteman AFB, MO (cdp) Johnson County	18	0.54
Jackson, MN (township) Scott County	7	0.53
Euless, TX (city) Tarrant County	256	0.51
Montgomery Village, MD (cdp) Montgomery County	156	0.49
Falls, PA (township) Bucks County	158	0.46
Stockbridge, GA (city) Henry County	110	0.46
Fairland, MD (cdp) Montgomery County	107	0.46
Leola, PA (cdp) Lancaster County	33	0.46
Wayzata, MN (city) Hennepin County	17	0.46
Ewing, NJ (township) Mercer County	160	0.45
Otsego, MN (city) Wright County	56	0.45
Copake, NY (town) Columbia County	16	0.45
Bristol, PA (township) Bucks County	243	0.44
Atlantic City, NJ (city) Atlantic County	172	0.43
Hamtramck, MI (city) Wayne County	97	0.43
Takoma Park, MD (city) Montgomery County	70	0.42
Andover, MN (city) Anoka County	124	0.41
Pataskala, OH (city) Licking County	58	0.41
Glendale, CO (city) Arapahoe County	17	0.41
Raleigh Hills, OR (cdp) Washington County	26	0.39
Woonsocket, RI (city) Providence County	157	0.38
Ridley, PA (township) Delaware County	118	0.38
Laurel, MD (city) Prince George's County	92	0.38
Edgewater Park, NJ (township) Burlington County	33	0.38
Upper Leacock, PA (township) Lancaster County	33	0.38
Leonard, TX (city) Fannin County	9	0.38
High Point, NC (city) Guilford County	376	0.37
Richfield, MN (city) Hennepin County	127	0.37
Brown Deer, WI (village) Milwaukee County	44	0.37
Belmont, VA (cdp) Loudoun County	19	0.36
Penn Estates, PA (cdp) Monroe County	15	0.36
Collegeville, MN (township) Stearns County	12	0.36
Lochearn, MD (cdp) Baltimore County	89	0.35
Broadlands, VA (cdp) Loudoun County	37	0.35
Roseland, NJ (borough) Essex County	20	0.35
South Haven, MI (charter township) Van Buren County	14	0.35
Rosedale, MD (cdp) Baltimore County	65	0.34
Morrisville, PA (borough) Bucks County	31	0.34
Kingston, RI (cdp) Washington County	21	0.34
Barnard, VT (town) Windsor County	4	0.34
Newark, NJ (city) Essex County	918	0.33
St. Cloud, MN (city) Stearns County	170	0.33
Glenolden, PA (borough) Delaware County	24	0.33
Fox Lake, WI (town) Dodge County	10	0.33
St. Cloud, MN (city) Stearns County	207	0.32
Summerfield, MD (cdp) Prince George's County	36	0.32
St. Cloud, MN (city) Sherburne County	22	0.32
Leesburg, VA (town) Loudoun County	126	0.31
East Pennsboro, PA (township) Cumberland County	62	0.31
East Orange, NJ (city) Essex County	197	0.30
Severn, MD (cdp) Anne Arundel County	125	0.30
Milford Mill, MD (cdp) Baltimore County	85	0.30
Fair Oaks, VA (cdp) Fairfax County	82	0.30
Wyandanch, NY (cdp) Suffolk County	33	0.30
Lynwood, IL (village) Cook County	26	0.30
Worcester, MA (city) Worcester County	529	0.29
Lynn, MA (city) Essex County	263	0.29
Patton, PA (township) Centre County	42	0.29
Smithville, NY (town) Chenango County	4	0.29
South Coatesville, PA (borough) Chester County	4	0.29
Saddle Rock, NY (village) Nassau County	3	0.29
Riverdale Park, MD (town) Prince George's County	19	0.28
Danby, NY (town) Tompkins County	9	0.28
Rosemount, MN (city) Dakota County	56	0.27
Stone Mountain, GA (city) DeKalb County	16	0.27
Thompsontown, PA (borough) Juniata County	2	0.27
Coon Rapids, MN (city) Anoka County	161	0.26
Anoka, MN (city) Anoka County	45	0.26
South Orange Village, NJ (township) Essex County	42	0.26
Maplewood, MN (city) Ramsey County	92	0.25
Countryside, VA (cdp) Loudoun County	24	0.25
Port Jervis, NY (city) Orange County	22	0.25
Ettrick, VA (cdp) Chesterfield County	15	0.25
King George, VA (cdp) King George County	9	0.25
Aspen Hill, MD (cdp) Montgomery County	113	0.24
Ocean, NJ (township) Monmouth County	65	0.24
Alexander City, AL (city) Tallapoosa County	35	0.24
Downingtown, PA (borough) Chester County	19	0.24
Urbandale, IA (city) Polk County	88	0.23
Shakopee, MN (city) Scott County	80	0.23
Lawrenceville, GA (city) Gwinnett County	63	0.23
Inkster, MI (city) Wayne County	61	0.23
South Plainfield, NJ (borough) Middlesex County	52	0.23
Lithia Springs, GA (cdp) Douglas County	40	0.23
St. Cloud, MN (city) Benton County	15	0.23
Macungie, PA (borough) Lehigh County	7	0.23
Burlingame, CA (city) San Mateo County	62	0.22
Ontwa, MI (township) Cass County	14	0.22

Please refer to the Explanation of Data in the front of the book for more detailed information.

Ancestry

African, Sub-Saharan: Liberian

Top 150 Places Sorted by Percent of Total Population

Based on places with total population of 7,500 or more

Place	Population	%
Darby, PA (borough) Delaware County	566	5.34
Yeadon, PA (borough) Delaware County	612	5.33
Brooklyn Park, MN (city) Hennepin County	3,237	4.40
Brooklyn Center, MN (city) Hennepin County	796	2.68
Collingdale, PA (borough) Delaware County	203	2.32
Worthington, MN (city) Nobles County	239	1.93
Upper Darby, PA (township) Delaware County	1,530	1.86
Hybla Valley, VA (cdp) Fairfax County	231	1.58
Reston, VA (cdp) Fairfax County	836	1.57
Pawtucket, RI (city) Providence County	1,075	1.50
Helena Valley West Central, MT (cdp) Lewis and Clark County	119	1.45
Burlington, NJ (township) Burlington County	322	1.44
Mitchellville, MD (cdp) Prince George's County	166	1.42
Burtonsville, MD (cdp) Montgomery County	129	1.40
Brock Hall, MD (cdp) Prince George's County	114	1.40
Elfers, FL (cdp) Pasco County	183	1.38
Willingboro, NJ (township) Burlington County	435	1.35
St. Michael, MN (city) Wright County	192	1.25
Crystal, MN (city) Hennepin County	219	0.99
Lancaster, SC (city) Lancaster County	82	0.99
West Haven, CT (city/town) New Haven County	524	0.95
Providence, RI (city) Providence County	1,682	0.94
Fairless Hills, PA (cdp) Bucks County	79	0.90
Trenton, NJ (city) Mercer County	755	0.89
Toccoa, GA (city) Stephens County	74	0.86
Essex, MD (cdp) Baltimore County	287	0.74
New Hope, MN (city) Hennepin County	150	0.74
Kemp Mill, MD (cdp) Montgomery County	85	0.70
Germantown, MD (cdp) Montgomery County	574	0.68
Richmond Heights, OH (city) Cuyahoga County	65	0.61
Golden Valley, MN (city) Hennepin County	115	0.57
Hamilton, NJ (township) Mercer County	495	0.56
Euless, TX (city) Tarrant County	256	0.51
Montgomery Village, MD (cdp) Montgomery County	156	0.49
Falls, PA (township) Bucks County	158	0.46
Stockbridge, GA (city) Henry County	110	0.46
Fairland, MD (cdp) Montgomery County	107	0.46
Ewing, NJ (township) Mercer County	160	0.45
Otsego, MN (city) Wright County	56	0.45
Bristol, PA (township) Bucks County	243	0.44
Atlantic City, NJ (city) Atlantic County	172	0.43
Hamtramck, MI (city) Wayne County	97	0.43
Takoma Park, MD (city) Montgomery County	70	0.42
Andover, MN (city) Anoka County	124	0.41
Pataskala, OH (city) Licking County	58	0.41
Woonsocket, RI (city) Providence County	157	0.38
Ridley, PA (township) Delaware County	118	0.38
Laurel, MD (city) Prince George's County	92	0.38
Edgewater Park, NJ (township) Burlington County	33	0.38
Upper Leacock, PA (township) Lancaster County	33	0.38
High Point, NC (city) Guilford County	376	0.37
Richfield, MN (city) Hennepin County	127	0.37
Brown Deer, WI (village) Milwaukee County	44	0.37
Lochearn, MD (cdp) Baltimore County	89	0.35
Broadlands, VA (cdp) Loudoun County	37	0.35
Rosedale, MD (cdp) Baltimore County	65	0.34
Morrisville, PA (borough) Bucks County	31	0.34
Newark, NJ (city) Essex County	918	0.33
St. Cloud, MN (city) Stearns County	170	0.33
St. Cloud, MN (city) Stearns County	207	0.32
Summerfield, MD (cdp) Prince George's County	36	0.32
Leesburg, VA (town) Loudoun County	126	0.31
East Pennsboro, PA (township) Cumberland County	62	0.31
East Orange, NJ (city) Essex County	197	0.30
Severn, MD (cdp) Anne Arundel County	125	0.30
Milford Mill, MD (cdp) Baltimore County	85	0.30
Fair Oaks, VA (cdp) Fairfax County	82	0.30
Wyandanch, NY (cdp) Suffolk County	33	0.30
Lynwood, IL (village) Cook County	26	0.30
Worcester, MA (city) Worcester County	529	0.29
Lynn, MA (city) Essex County	263	0.29
Patton, PA (township) Centre County	42	0.29
Rosemount, MN (city) Dakota County	56	0.27
Coon Rapids, MN (city) Anoka County	161	0.26
Anoka, MN (city) Anoka County	45	0.26
South Orange Village, NJ (township) Essex County	42	0.26
Maplewood, MN (city) Ramsey County	92	0.25
Countryside, VA (cdp) Loudoun County	24	0.25
Port Jervis, NY (city) Orange County	22	0.25
Aspen Hill, MD (cdp) Montgomery County	113	0.24
Ocean, NJ (township) Monmouth County	65	0.24
Alexander City, AL (city) Tallapoosa County	35	0.24
Downingtown, PA (borough) Chester County	19	0.24
Urbandale, IA (city) Polk County	88	0.23
Shakopee, MN (city) Scott County	80	0.23
Lawrenceville, GA (city) Gwinnett County	63	0.23
Inkster, MI (city) Wayne County	61	0.23
South Plainfield, NJ (borough) Middlesex County	52	0.23
Lithia Springs, GA (cdp) Douglas County	40	0.23
Burlingame, CA (city) San Mateo County	62	0.22
Philadelphia, PA (city) Philadelphia County	3,198	0.21
Minneapolis, MN (city) Hennepin County	791	0.21
Apple Valley, MN (city) Dakota County	102	0.21
Wayne, MI (city) Wayne County	37	0.21
Maryland City, MD (cdp) Anne Arundel County	33	0.21
Adelphi, MD (cdp) Prince George's County	32	0.21
Orange, CT (cdp/town) New Haven County	29	0.21
Romulus, MI (city) Wayne County	47	0.20
Rose Hill, VA (cdp) Fairfax County	39	0.20
Lorton, VA (cdp) Fairfax County	38	0.20
Middle, DE (town) New Castle County	34	0.20
White Oak, MD (cdp) Montgomery County	33	0.20
Cloverly, MD (cdp) Montgomery County	31	0.20
New Carrollton, MD (city) Prince George's County	24	0.20
Frederick, MD (city) Frederick County	123	0.19
Gaithersburg, MD (city) Montgomery County	109	0.19
Littleton, CO (city) Arapahoe County	77	0.19
Suitland, MD (cdp) Prince George's County	49	0.19
Sterling, VA (cdp) Loudoun County	48	0.19
Champlin, MN (city) Hennepin County	44	0.19
Webster Groves, MO (city) St. Louis County	44	0.19
Altoona, IA (city) Polk County	26	0.19
Alexandria, VA (ind. city) Alexandria independent city	235	0.18
Johnson City, TN (city) Washington County	110	0.18
Maywood, IL (village) Cook County	45	0.18
University Heights, OH (city) Cuyahoga County	25	0.18
Syracuse, NY (city) Onondaga County	246	0.17
Chester, PA (city) Delaware County	57	0.17
Archdale, NC (city) Randolph County	19	0.17
Ventnor City, NJ (city) Atlantic County	19	0.17
Lanham, MD (cdp) Prince George's County	15	0.17
Grand Rapids, MI (city) Kent County	309	0.16
Plantation, FL (city) Broward County	137	0.16
Milpitas, CA (city) Santa Clara County	104	0.16
Scotch Plains, NJ (township) Union County	36	0.16
Manchester, NH (city) Hillsborough County	164	0.15
Avondale, AZ (city) Maricopa County	105	0.15
Wheaton, MD (cdp) Montgomery County	69	0.15
Woodlawn, MD (cdp) Baltimore County	57	0.15
University City, MO (city) St. Louis County	54	0.15
Foster City, CA (city) San Mateo County	46	0.15
Williamstown, MA (town) Berkshire County	12	0.15
Babylon, NY (town) Suffolk County	309	0.14
Utica, NY (city) Oneida County	88	0.14
East Windsor, NJ (township) Mercer County	38	0.14
Edgewood, MD (cdp) Harford County	36	0.14
South Laurel, MD (cdp) Prince George's County	36	0.14
Lincolnia, VA (cdp) Fairfax County	29	0.14
Woodlawn, VA (cdp) Fairfax County	28	0.14
North Amityville, NY (cdp) Suffolk County	25	0.14
Grand Rapids, MI (charter township) Kent County	23	0.14
Fallsburg, NY (town) Sullivan County	18	0.14
Hasbrouck Heights, NJ (borough) Bergen County	16	0.14
Marlboro Village, MD (cdp) Prince George's County	13	0.14
Decorah, IA (city) Winneshiek County	11	0.14
Groveland, FL (city) Lake County	11	0.14
Medford, MA (city) Middlesex County	72	0.13
The Hammocks, FL (cdp) Miami-Dade County	66	0.13
Dover, DE (city) Kent County	47	0.13
Montgomery, PA (township) Montgomery County	31	0.13

Ancestry

African, Sub-Saharan: Nigerian

U.S. and 50 States Sorted by Population and Percent of Total Population

Place	Population	%
United States	**250,819**	**0.08**
Texas	42,529	0.17
New York	28,991	0.15
Maryland	24,893	0.44
California	21,824	0.06
Georgia	19,679	0.21
New Jersey	16,851	0.19
Illinois	13,217	0.10
Florida	8,180	0.04
Pennsylvania	6,451	0.05
North Carolina	6,162	0.07
Minnesota	6,014	0.11
Massachusetts	5,678	0.09
Virginia	5,515	0.07
Ohio	5,051	0.04
Michigan	4,487	0.05
Indiana	3,311	0.05
Washington	2,896	0.04
Tennessee	2,540	0.04
Missouri	2,523	0.04
Oklahoma	2,222	0.06
Arizona	2,218	0.04
Rhode Island	2,106	0.20
Connecticut	2,078	0.06
Wisconsin	1,812	0.03
Louisiana	1,717	0.04
District of Columbia	1,682	0.29
Alabama	1,560	0.03
Delaware	1,100	0.12
Colorado	832	0.02
Nevada	716	0.03
South Carolina	699	0.02
Iowa	604	0.02
Oregon	541	0.01
Arkansas	534	0.02
Kansas	517	0.02
Nebraska	506	0.03
Mississippi	397	0.01
Kentucky	358	0.01
Utah	336	0.01
New Mexico	276	0.01
West Virginia	262	0.01
New Hampshire	220	0.02
Maine	208	0.02
Alaska	163	0.02
North Dakota	119	0.02
South Dakota	93	0.01
Montana	66	0.01
Vermont	29	<0.01
Hawaii	24	<0.01
Wyoming	18	<0.01
Idaho	14	<0.01

Place	Population	%
Maryland	24,893	0.44
District of Columbia	1,682	0.29
Georgia	19,679	0.21
Rhode Island	2,106	0.20
New Jersey	16,851	0.19
Texas	42,529	0.17
New York	28,991	0.15
Delaware	1,100	0.12
Minnesota	6,014	0.11
Illinois	13,217	0.10
Massachusetts	5,678	0.09
United States	**250,819**	**0.08**
North Carolina	6,162	0.07
Virginia	5,515	0.07
California	21,824	0.06
Oklahoma	2,222	0.06
Connecticut	2,078	0.06
Pennsylvania	6,451	0.05
Michigan	4,487	0.05
Indiana	3,311	0.05
Florida	8,180	0.04
Ohio	5,051	0.04
Washington	2,896	0.04
Tennessee	2,540	0.04
Missouri	2,523	0.04
Arizona	2,218	0.04
Louisiana	1,717	0.04
Wisconsin	1,812	0.03
Alabama	1,560	0.03
Nevada	716	0.03
Nebraska	506	0.03
Colorado	832	0.02
South Carolina	699	0.02
Iowa	604	0.02
Arkansas	534	0.02
Kansas	517	0.02
New Hampshire	220	0.02
Maine	208	0.02
Alaska	163	0.02
North Dakota	119	0.02
Oregon	541	0.01
Mississippi	397	0.01
Kentucky	358	0.01
Utah	336	0.01
New Mexico	276	0.01
West Virginia	262	0.01
South Dakota	93	0.01
Montana	66	0.01
Vermont	29	<0.01
Hawaii	24	<0.01
Wyoming	18	<0.01
Idaho	14	<0.01

Please refer to the Explanation of Data in the front of the book for more detailed information.

Ancestry

African, Sub-Saharan: Nigerian

Top 150 Places Sorted by Population

Based on all places, regardless of total population

Place	Population	%
New York, NY (city) Kings County	21,507	0.27
Houston, TX (city) Harris County	8,818	0.43
Queens, NY (borough) Queens County	6,304	0.29
Chicago, IL (city) Cook County	6,193	0.23
Brooklyn, NY (borough) Kings County	6,033	0.24
Bronx, NY (borough) Bronx County	5,538	0.41
Los Angeles, CA (city) Los Angeles County	3,268	0.09
Newark, NJ (city) Essex County	2,732	0.99
Dallas, TX (city) Dallas County	2,477	0.21
Indianapolis, IN (city) Marion County	2,048	0.25
Manhattan, NY (borough) New York County	1,953	0.12
Mission Bend, TX (cdp) Fort Bend County	1,903	5.03
Philadelphia, PA (city) Philadelphia County	1,877	0.12
Baltimore, MD (city) Baltimore city County	1,814	0.29
Missouri City, TX (city) Fort Bend County	1,795	2.78
Boston, MA (city) Suffolk County	1,775	0.29
Arlington, TX (city) Tarrant County	1,737	0.48
Washington, DC (city) District of Columbia	1,682	0.29
Staten Island, NY (borough) Richmond County	1,679	0.36
Brooklyn Park, MN (city) Hennepin County	1,642	2.23
Grand Prairie, TX (city) Dallas County	1,571	0.95
Nashville-Davidson, TN (metro govt) Davidson County	1,462	0.25
Union, NJ (township) Union County	1,428	2.56
Providence, RI (city) Providence County	1,388	0.78
Raleigh, NC (city) Wake County	1,375	0.36
Plano, TX (city) Collin County	1,355	0.53
South Laurel, MD (cdp) Prince George's County	1,307	5.08
Garland, TX (city) Dallas County	1,291	0.58
Detroit, MI (city) Wayne County	1,282	0.17
Charlotte, NC (city) Mecklenburg County	1,192	0.17
Hempstead, NY (town) Nassau County	1,115	0.15
Austin, TX (city) Travis County	1,038	0.14
Four Corners, TX (cdp) Fort Bend County	956	7.76
City of Orange, NJ (township) Essex County	910	2.99
Lewisville, TX (city) Denton County	882	0.95
Bowie, MD (city) Prince George's County	863	1.59
Columbus, OH (city) Franklin County	861	0.11
Irvington, NJ (township) Essex County	832	1.52
San Antonio, TX (city) Medina County	830	0.06
Jersey City, NJ (city) Hudson County	822	0.34
Norman, OK (city) Cleveland County	815	0.75
Irving, TX (city) Dallas County	789	0.38
Jacksonville, FL (city) Duval County	787	0.10
Mitchellville, MD (cdp) Prince George's County	776	6.66
San Leandro, CA (city) Alameda County	729	0.88
Kansas City, MO (city) Jackson County	727	0.16
Babylon, NY (town) Suffolk County	707	0.33
San Diego, CA (city) San Diego County	658	0.05
Landover, MD (cdp) Prince George's County	647	2.75
Toledo, OH (city) Lucas County	642	0.22
Virginia Beach, VA (ind. city) Virginia Beach independent city	610	0.14
Durham, NC (city) Durham County	604	0.27
Milwaukee, WI (city) Milwaukee County	599	0.10
Madison, WI (city) Dane County	571	0.25
Eastvale, CA (cdp) Riverside County	565	1.15
Oklahoma City, OK (city) Oklahoma County	559	0.10
Greensboro, NC (city) Guilford County	553	0.21
Tampa, FL (city) Hillsborough County	552	0.17
Riverdale, GA (city) Clayton County	550	3.66
Hayward, CA (city) Alameda County	543	0.38
Oakland, CA (city) Alameda County	542	0.14
Long Beach, CA (city) Los Angeles County	528	0.11
Seattle, WA (city) King County	523	0.09
El Paso, TX (city) El Paso County	523	0.08
Antioch, CA (city) Contra Costa County	522	0.52
Santa Clarita, CA (city) Los Angeles County	517	0.30
Randallstown, MD (cdp) Baltimore County	512	1.57
Mableton, GA (cdp) Cobb County	511	1.43
Baton Rouge, LA (city) East Baton Rouge Parish	509	0.22
Minneapolis, MN (city) Hennepin County	499	0.13
East Orange, NJ (city) Essex County	493	0.76
Germantown, MD (cdp) Montgomery County	492	0.58
Franklin, NJ (township) Somerset County	490	0.81
Lochearn, MD (cdp) Baltimore County	489	1.90
Memphis, TN (city) Shelby County	481	0.07
Milford Mill, MD (cdp) Baltimore County	480	1.67
Mansfield, TX (city) Tarrant County	478	0.94
Hamilton, NJ (township) Mercer County	470	0.53
Fort Worth, TX (city) Tarrant County	466	0.07
New Haven, CT (city/town) New Haven County	456	0.35
St. Paul, MN (city) Ramsey County	450	0.16
Hawthorne, CA (city) Los Angeles County	447	0.53
Miramar, FL (city) Broward County	446	0.39
Lynn, MA (city) Essex County	445	0.50
Yonkers, NY (city) Westchester County	442	0.23
Bakersfield, CA (city) Kern County	440	0.13
Randolph, MA (cdp/town) Norfolk County	434	1.37
Hempstead, NY (village) Nassau County	427	0.80
Phoenix, AZ (city) Maricopa County	422	0.03
Pembroke Pines, FL (city) Broward County	416	0.27
Inglewood, CA (city) Los Angeles County	415	0.38
Parkville, MD (cdp) Baltimore County	412	1.37
West Haven, CT (city/town) New Haven County	412	0.75
Fayetteville, NC (city) Cumberland County	412	0.21
Lanham, MD (cdp) Prince George's County	411	4.60
Edgewood, MD (cdp) Harford County	405	1.60
West Orange, NJ (township) Essex County	404	0.88
Bellflower, CA (city) Los Angeles County	402	0.53
Redan, GA (cdp) DeKalb County	397	1.16
Stafford, TX (city) Fort Bend County	395	2.33
Waldorf, MD (cdp) Charles County	395	0.59
Pittsburgh, PA (city) Allegheny County	391	0.13
Mesquite, TX (city) Dallas County	388	0.29
Glenn Dale, MD (cdp) Prince George's County	387	2.74
Hillside, NJ (township) Union County	378	1.78
Silver Spring, MD (cdp) Montgomery County	377	0.54
Stockbridge, GA (city) Henry County	376	1.59
Denver, CO (city) Denver County	375	0.06
Pflugerville, TX (city) Travis County	372	0.87
Aurora, IL (city) Kane County	372	0.20
Atlanta, GA (city) Fulton County	372	0.09
Milton, GA (city) Fulton County	370	1.27
Carson, CA (city) Los Angeles County	369	0.40
Sugar Land, TX (city) Fort Bend County	368	0.48
Elk Grove, CA (city) Sacramento County	363	0.26
Friendly, MD (cdp) Prince George's County	361	3.62
Sacramento, CA (city) Sacramento County	359	0.08
Laurel, MD (city) Prince George's County	358	1.47
Chillum, MD (cdp) Prince George's County	354	1.01
Worcester, MA (city) Worcester County	354	0.20
Lawrenceville, GA (city) Gwinnett County	352	1.27
Calumet City, IL (city) Cook County	352	0.95
Cleveland, OH (city) Cuyahoga County	352	0.09
Riverside, CA (city) Riverside County	351	0.12
Maplewood, NJ (township) Essex County	349	1.47
Yucaipa, CA (city) San Bernardino County	348	0.69
North Atlanta, GA (cdp) DeKalb County	345	0.93
Poughkeepsie, NY (city) Dutchess County	342	1.05
Huntley, IL (village) McHenry County	340	1.60
Ann Arbor, MI (city) Washtenaw County	338	0.29
Colton, CA (city) San Bernardino County	335	0.64
Largo, MD (cdp) Prince George's County	332	3.01
Beltsville, MD (cdp) Prince George's County	327	2.12
Fairland, MD (cdp) Montgomery County	327	1.42
St. Louis, MO (city) St. Louis city County	327	0.10
Richmond, CA (city) Contra Costa County	326	0.32
Omaha, NE (city) Douglas County	326	0.08
Palm Coast, FL (city) Flagler County	323	0.46
Little Rock, AR (city) Pulaski County	320	0.17
Dover, DE (city) Kent County	313	0.88
Chandler, AZ (city) Maricopa County	312	0.14
Kettering, MD (cdp) Prince George's County	310	2.47
Ontario, CA (city) San Bernardino County	307	0.19
Norfolk, VA (ind. city) Norfolk independent city	306	0.13
Calverton, MD (cdp) Montgomery County	304	1.71
Tallahassee, FL (city) Leon County	303	0.17
Sandy Springs, GA (city) Fulton County	302	0.33
Upper Darby, PA (township) Delaware County	300	0.36
Corpus Christi, TX (city) Nueces County	300	0.10
Woodlawn, MD (cdp) Baltimore County	299	0.79

Please refer to the Explanation of Data in the front of the book for more detailed information.

Ancestry

African, Sub-Saharan: Nigerian

Top 150 Places Sorted by Percent of Total Population

Based on all places, regardless of total population

Place	Population	%
Voorhees, NJ (cdp) Somerset County	154	15.02
Seven Oaks, TX (city) Polk County	15	9.15
Chatmoss, VA (cdp) Henry County	146	8.63
Springlake, TX (town) Lamb County	9	8.33
Four Corners, TX (cdp) Fort Bend County	956	7.76
Scottsville, TX (city) Harrison County	28	6.88
Jackson, PA (township) Butler County	251	6.83
Mitchellville, MD (cdp) Prince George's County	776	6.66
Brooklawn, NJ (borough) Camden County	105	6.19
Lockland, OH (village) Hamilton County	204	5.89
Aldan, PA (borough) Delaware County	241	5.77
Mettawa, IL (village) Lake County	34	5.70
South Laurel, MD (cdp) Prince George's County	1,307	5.08
Mission Bend, TX (cdp) Fort Bend County	1,903	5.03
Lincoln University, PA (cdp) Chester County	94	4.86
Lanham, MD (cdp) Prince George's County	411	4.60
Glenarden, MD (city) Prince George's County	278	4.58
Johnstown, WY (cdp) Fremont County	11	4.37
Fairwood, MD (cdp) Prince George's County	201	4.32
Southern Gateway, VA (cdp) Stafford County	145	4.12
West Buechel, KY (city) Jefferson County	45	4.03
Layhill, MD (cdp) Montgomery County	227	4.00
Medical Lake, WA (city) Spokane County	189	3.91
Marquette, WI (town) Green Lake County	21	3.80
Riverdale, GA (city) Clayton County	550	3.66
Friendly, MD (cdp) Prince George's County	361	3.62
Leesport, PA (borough) Berks County	72	3.53
Kenwood, OH (cdp) Hamilton County	239	3.31
Wesley Hills, NY (village) Rockland County	180	3.30
Largo, MD (cdp) Prince George's County	332	3.01
City of Orange, NJ (township) Essex County	910	2.99
Burtonsville, MD (cdp) Montgomery County	276	2.99
Auburn, GA (city) Barrow County	208	2.92
Cheverly, MD (town) Prince George's County	180	2.89
Hutchins, TX (city) Dallas County	141	2.89
Brandywine, MD (cdp) Prince George's County	173	2.87
Lawnside, NJ (borough) Camden County	81	2.80
Missouri City, TX (city) Fort Bend County	1,795	2.78
Austell, GA (city) Cobb County	178	2.78
Landover, MD (cdp) Prince George's County	647	2.75
Glenn Dale, MD (cdp) Prince George's County	387	2.74
Wheatley Heights, NY (cdp) Suffolk County	167	2.70
Springdale, MD (cdp) Prince George's County	65	2.58
Union, NJ (township) Union County	1,428	2.56
North Laurel, MD (cdp) Howard County	104	2.55
Kanabec, MN (township) Kanabec County	25	2.52
Kettering, MD (cdp) Prince George's County	310	2.47
Deerpark, NY (town) Orange County	196	2.47
Bel-Ridge, MO (village) St. Louis County	69	2.47
Flossmoor, IL (village) Cook County	221	2.40
Woodlawn, MD (cdp) Prince George's County	154	2.37
Lake Arbor, MD (cdp) Prince George's County	242	2.35
Woodmore, MD (cdp) Prince George's County	82	2.34
Stafford, TX (city) Fort Bend County	395	2.33
Brooklyn Park, MN (city) Hennepin County	1,642	2.23
Posen, IL (village) Cook County	127	2.23
Franklin Park, NJ (cdp) Somerset County	273	2.16
Riverdale Park, MD (town) Prince George's County	147	2.13
Lenox, IA (city) Taylor County	28	2.13
Beltsville, MD (cdp) Prince George's County	327	2.12
Myers Corner, NY (cdp) Dutchess County	134	2.10
Marietta, WI (town) Crawford County	9	2.05
Princeton Meadows, NJ (cdp) Middlesex County	279	2.03
Greencastle, PA (borough) Franklin County	80	2.02
Lemont, PA (cdp) Centre County	47	1.96
Lochearn, MD (cdp) Baltimore County	489	1.90
Knightdale, NC (town) Wake County	199	1.90
Bladensburg, MD (town) Prince George's County	166	1.86
Lower Oxford, PA (township) Chester County	94	1.86
Milford, IA (city) Dickinson County	53	1.86
Ashburn, GA (city) Turner County	75	1.79
Country Lake Estates, NJ (cdp) Burlington County	67	1.79
Hillside, NJ (township) Union County	378	1.78
Rising Sun, MD (town) Cecil County	47	1.77
Coldstream, KY (city) Jefferson County	22	1.74
Vinita Terrace, MO (village) St. Louis County	4	1.72
Calverton, MD (cdp) Montgomery County	304	1.71
Moose Lake, MN (city) Carlton County	46	1.71
Travilah, MD (cdp) Montgomery County	205	1.70
Brock Hall, MD (cdp) Prince George's County	137	1.68
Milford Mill, MD (cdp) Baltimore County	480	1.67
Seabrook, MD (cdp) Prince George's County	261	1.67
Chester, NY (village) Orange County	66	1.67
Hazel Crest, IL (village) Cook County	234	1.64
Mountain House, CA (cdp) San Joaquin County	123	1.64
Warr Acres, OK (city) Oklahoma County	163	1.63
Frankfort, IL (village) Will County	276	1.62
Adelphi, MD (cdp) Prince George's County	242	1.61
Edgewood, MD (cdp) Harford County	405	1.60
Huntley, IL (village) McHenry County	340	1.60
Kittery, ME (cdp) York County	79	1.60
Bowie, MD (city) Prince George's County	863	1.59
Stockbridge, GA (city) Henry County	376	1.59
Randallstown, MD (cdp) Baltimore County	512	1.57
Wyandanch, NY (cdp) Suffolk County	172	1.57
Fresno, TX (cdp) Fort Bend County	259	1.56
Haverford College, PA (cdp) Delaware County	18	1.56
Lovejoy, GA (city) Clayton County	90	1.55
Irvington, NJ (township) Essex County	832	1.52
Laurel, MD (city) Prince George's County	358	1.47
Maplewood, NJ (township) Essex County	349	1.47
California, MD (cdp) St. Mary's County	174	1.45
Rosedale, MD (cdp) Baltimore County	275	1.44
Frontenac, MO (city) St. Louis County	50	1.44
Mableton, GA (cdp) Cobb County	511	1.43
Lumberton, NJ (township) Burlington County	176	1.43
Fairland, MD (cdp) Montgomery County	327	1.42
Waverly, TN (city) Humphreys County	58	1.42
New Fairview, TX (city) Wise County	17	1.41
Lowes Island, VA (cdp) Loudoun County	160	1.40
Swissvale, PA (borough) Allegheny County	127	1.40
Conewago, PA (township) York County	100	1.40
Silver Lake, NC (cdp) New Hanover County	76	1.40
Coyle, OK (town) Logan County	4	1.40
Randolph, MA (cdp/town) Norfolk County	434	1.37
Parkville, MD (cdp) Baltimore County	412	1.37
Sinclair, WY (town) Carbon County	7	1.35
Russell, KY (city) Greenup County	45	1.32
Manchester, MO (city) St. Louis County	239	1.31
Champlin, MN (city) Hennepin County	293	1.29
Aberdeen, NJ (township) Monmouth County	231	1.28
North Valley Stream, NY (cdp) Nassau County	212	1.28
East Riverdale, MD (cdp) Prince George's County	200	1.28
Milton, GA (city) Fulton County	370	1.27
Lawrenceville, GA (city) Gwinnett County	352	1.27
Summerfield, MD (cdp) Prince George's County	141	1.27
View Park-Windsor Hills, CA (cdp) Los Angeles County	137	1.27
Orchard Park, NY (village) Erie County	41	1.26
Fairburn, GA (city) Fulton County	144	1.25
Plainsboro, NJ (township) Middlesex County	279	1.24
New Market, AL (cdp) Madison County	23	1.24
Rossville, MD (cdp) Baltimore County	185	1.23
East Fallowfield, PA (township) Chester County	87	1.23
Colwyn, PA (borough) Delaware County	31	1.23
State Line, PA (cdp) Franklin County	30	1.23
Auburndale, FL (city) Polk County	163	1.22
Cloverly, MD (cdp) Montgomery County	186	1.21
Rock Hill, NY (cdp) Sullivan County	20	1.21
Chesilhurst, NJ (borough) Camden County	19	1.21
Occoquan, VA (town) Prince William County	7	1.20
Country Club Hills, IL (city) Cook County	194	1.19
Sienna Plantation, TX (cdp) Fort Bend County	146	1.18
Pike Bay, MN (township) Cass County	19	1.18
Oak Park Heights, MN (city) Washington County	50	1.17
New Lebanon, NY (town) Columbia County	29	1.17
Landover Hills, MD (town) Prince George's County	22	1.17
Redan, GA (cdp) DeKalb County	397	1.16
Scaggsville, MD (cdp) Howard County	267	1.16
Harvest, AL (cdp) Madison County	51	1.16
Eastvale, CA (cdp) Riverside County	565	1.15

Please refer to the Explanation of Data in the front of the book for more detailed information.

Ancestry

African, Sub-Saharan: Nigerian

Top 150 Places Sorted by Percent of Total Population

Based on places with total population of 7,500 or more

Place	Population	%
Four Corners, TX (cdp) Fort Bend County	956	7.76
Mitchellville, MD (cdp) Prince George's County	776	6.66
South Laurel, MD (cdp) Prince George's County	1,307	5.08
Mission Bend, TX (cdp) Fort Bend County	1,903	5.03
Lanham, MD (cdp) Prince George's County	411	4.60
Riverdale, GA (city) Clayton County	550	3.66
Friendly, MD (cdp) Prince George's County	361	3.62
Largo, MD (cdp) Prince George's County	332	3.01
City of Orange, NJ (township) Essex County	910	2.99
Burtonsville, MD (cdp) Montgomery County	276	2.99
Missouri City, TX (city) Fort Bend County	1,795	2.78
Landover, MD (cdp) Prince George's County	647	2.75
Glenn Dale, MD (cdp) Prince George's County	387	2.74
Union, NJ (township) Union County	1,428	2.56
Kettering, MD (cdp) Prince George's County	310	2.47
Deerpark, NY (town) Orange County	196	2.47
Flossmoor, IL (village) Cook County	221	2.40
Lake Arbor, MD (cdp) Prince George's County	242	2.35
Stafford, TX (city) Fort Bend County	395	2.33
Brooklyn Park, MN (city) Hennepin County	1,642	2.23
Franklin Park, NJ (cdp) Somerset County	273	2.16
Beltsville, MD (cdp) Prince George's County	327	2.12
Princeton Meadows, NJ (cdp) Middlesex County	279	2.03
Lochearn, MD (cdp) Baltimore County	489	1.90
Knightdale, NC (town) Wake County	199	1.90
Bladensburg, MD (town) Prince George's County	166	1.86
Hillside, NJ (township) Union County	378	1.78
Calverton, MD (cdp) Montgomery County	304	1.71
Travilah, MD (cdp) Montgomery County	205	1.70
Brock Hall, MD (cdp) Prince George's County	137	1.68
Milford Mill, MD (cdp) Baltimore County	480	1.67
Seabrook, MD (cdp) Prince George's County	261	1.67
Hazel Crest, IL (village) Cook County	234	1.64
Warr Acres, OK (city) Oklahoma County	163	1.63
Frankfort, IL (village) Will County	276	1.62
Adelphi, MD (cdp) Prince George's County	242	1.61
Edgewood, MD (cdp) Harford County	405	1.60
Huntley, IL (village) McHenry County	340	1.60
Bowie, MD (city) Prince George's County	863	1.59
Stockbridge, GA (city) Henry County	376	1.59
Randallstown, MD (cdp) Baltimore County	512	1.57
Wyandanch, NY (cdp) Suffolk County	172	1.57
Fresno, TX (cdp) Fort Bend County	259	1.56
Irvington, NJ (township) Essex County	832	1.52
Laurel, MD (city) Prince George's County	358	1.47
Maplewood, NJ (township) Essex County	349	1.47
California, MD (cdp) St. Mary's County	174	1.45
Rosedale, MD (cdp) Baltimore County	275	1.44
Mableton, GA (cdp) Cobb County	511	1.43
Lumberton, NJ (township) Burlington County	176	1.43
Fairland, MD (cdp) Montgomery County	327	1.42
Lowes Island, VA (cdp) Loudoun County	160	1.40
Swissvale, PA (borough) Allegheny County	127	1.40
Randolph, MA (cdp/town) Norfolk County	434	1.37
Parkville, MD (cdp) Baltimore County	412	1.37
Manchester, MO (city) St. Louis County	239	1.31
Champlin, MN (city) Hennepin County	293	1.29
Aberdeen, NJ (township) Monmouth County	231	1.28
North Valley Stream, NY (cdp) Nassau County	212	1.28
East Riverdale, MD (cdp) Prince George's County	200	1.28
Milton, GA (city) Fulton County	370	1.27
Lawrenceville, GA (city) Gwinnett County	352	1.27
Summerfield, MD (cdp) Prince George's County	141	1.27
View Park-Windsor Hills, CA (cdp) Los Angeles County	137	1.27
Fairburn, GA (city) Fulton County	144	1.25
Plainsboro, NJ (township) Middlesex County	279	1.24
Rossville, MD (cdp) Baltimore County	185	1.23
Auburndale, FL (city) Polk County	163	1.22
Cloverly, MD (cdp) Montgomery County	186	1.21
Country Club Hills, IL (city) Cook County	194	1.19
Sienna Plantation, TX (cdp) Fort Bend County	146	1.18
Redan, GA (cdp) DeKalb County	397	1.16
Scaggsville, MD (cdp) Howard County	267	1.16
Eastvale, CA (cdp) Riverside County	565	1.15
Bordentown, NJ (township) Burlington County	126	1.15
Greenbelt, MD (city) Prince George's County	257	1.13
El Sobrante, CA (cdp) Contra Costa County	152	1.13
North Babylon, NY (cdp) Suffolk County	198	1.12
Bothell West, WA (cdp) Snohomish County	175	1.12
Colesville, MD (cdp) Montgomery County	159	1.12
Lynwood, IL (village) Cook County	96	1.10
Poughkeepsie, NY (city) Dutchess County	342	1.05
McDonough, GA (city) Henry County	212	1.05
Woodlawn, VA (cdp) Fairfax County	204	1.04
Evans, GA (cdp) Columbia County	285	1.03
Mount Rainier, MD (city) Prince George's County	83	1.02
Chillum, MD (cdp) Prince George's County	354	1.01
New Cassel, NY (cdp) Nassau County	127	1.01
Maryland City, MD (cdp) Anne Arundel County	154	1.00
Newark, NJ (city) Essex County	2,732	0.99
New Carrollton, MD (city) Prince George's County	120	0.99
Grand Prairie, TX (city) Dallas County	1,571	0.95
Lewisville, TX (city) Denton County	882	0.95
Calumet City, IL (city) Cook County	352	0.95
Oakdale, MN (city) Washington County	259	0.95
Fort Washington, MD (cdp) Prince George's County	240	0.95
Yeadon, PA (borough) Delaware County	109	0.95
Mansfield, TX (city) Tarrant County	478	0.94
Hyattsville, MD (city) Prince George's County	163	0.94
North Atlanta, GA (cdp) DeKalb County	345	0.93
Homewood, IL (village) Cook County	180	0.93
Greatwood, TX (cdp) Fort Bend County	109	0.93
Loma Linda, CA (city) San Bernardino County	205	0.90
San Leandro, CA (city) Alameda County	729	0.88
West Orange, NJ (township) Essex County	404	0.88
Dover, DE (city) Kent County	313	0.88
Inkster, MI (city) Wayne County	232	0.88
Sweden, NY (town) Monroe County	125	0.88
Pflugerville, TX (city) Travis County	372	0.87
Glasgow, DE (cdp) New Castle County	135	0.86
Marlton, MD (cdp) Prince George's County	77	0.85
Colonie, NY (village) Albany County	66	0.84
The Colony, TX (city) Denton County	289	0.83
Justice, IL (village) Cook County	105	0.83
Mounds View, MN (city) Ramsey County	101	0.83
Houma, LA (city) Terrebonne Parish	276	0.82
Wappinger, NY (town) Dutchess County	221	0.82
Opa-locka, FL (city) Miami-Dade County	124	0.82
Kittery, ME (town) York County	79	0.82
Franklin, NJ (township) Somerset County	490	0.81
Douglasville, GA (city) Douglas County	237	0.81
Hanover, PA (township) Northampton County	87	0.81
Hempstead, NY (village) Nassau County	427	0.80
Hercules, CA (city) Contra Costa County	184	0.80
West Manchester, PA (township) York County	150	0.80
Woodlawn, MD (cdp) Baltimore County	299	0.79
Palmer, PA (township) Northampton County	159	0.79
Sussex, WI (village) Waukesha County	81	0.79
Providence, RI (city) Providence County	1,388	0.78
Franklin Farm, VA (cdp) Fairfax County	151	0.77
Cloquet, MN (city) Carlton County	92	0.77
East Orange, NJ (city) Essex County	493	0.76
Park City, IL (city) Lake County	58	0.76
Norman, OK (city) Cleveland County	815	0.75
West Haven, CT (city/town) New Haven County	412	0.75
Murphy, TX (city) Collin County	115	0.75
Presque Isle, ME (city) Aroostook County	73	0.75
Wells Branch, TX (cdp) Travis County	86	0.74
Fairview, CA (cdp) Alameda County	73	0.74
Marlboro Village, MD (cdp) Prince George's County	69	0.74
Clinton, MD (cdp) Prince George's County	264	0.73
College Park, MD (city) Prince George's County	217	0.73
Uniondale, NY (cdp) Nassau County	179	0.73
Solon, OH (city) Cuyahoga County	168	0.73
Joppatowne, MD (cdp) Harford County	93	0.73
Parkland, WA (cdp) Pierce County	253	0.71
Cottage Grove, MN (city) Washington County	241	0.71
Oxon Hill, MD (cdp) Prince George's County	131	0.71
Crowley, TX (city) Tarrant County	83	0.70
Yucaipa, CA (city) San Bernardino County	348	0.69

Please refer to the Explanation of Data in the front of the book for more detailed information.

SECTION THREE

Ancestry

African, Sub-Saharan: Senegalese

U.S. and 50 States Sorted by Population and Percent of Total Population

Place	Population	%
United States	**10,055**	**<0.01**
New York	3,166	0.02
Maryland	782	0.01
California	644	<0.01
Virginia	551	0.01
Ohio	537	<0.01
Pennsylvania	477	<0.01
New Jersey	474	0.01
Michigan	396	<0.01
Texas	380	<0.01
Massachusetts	377	0.01
Rhode Island	370	0.04
Georgia	360	<0.01
Indiana	193	<0.01
District of Columbia	163	0.03
North Carolina	156	<0.01
Florida	147	<0.01
Kansas	131	<0.01
Colorado	108	<0.01
Kentucky	93	<0.01
Maine	72	0.01
Missouri	69	<0.01
Illinois	62	<0.01
Washington	55	<0.01
Tennessee	54	<0.01
South Carolina	40	<0.01
Minnesota	37	<0.01
Iowa	26	<0.01
Oregon	25	<0.01
Oklahoma	24	<0.01
Connecticut	19	<0.01
Idaho	19	<0.01
Wisconsin	18	<0.01
Arizona	15	<0.01
Alaska	11	<0.01
Delaware	4	<0.01
Alabama	0	0.00
Arkansas	0	0.00
Hawaii	0	0.00
Louisiana	0	0.00
Mississippi	0	0.00
Montana	0	0.00
Nebraska	0	0.00
Nevada	0	0.00
New Hampshire	0	0.00
New Mexico	0	0.00
North Dakota	0	0.00
South Dakota	0	0.00
Utah	0	0.00
Vermont	0	0.00
West Virginia	0	0.00
Wyoming	0	0.00

Place	Population	%
Rhode Island	370	0.04
District of Columbia	163	0.03
New York	3,166	0.02
Maryland	782	0.01
Virginia	551	0.01
New Jersey	474	0.01
Massachusetts	377	0.01
Maine	72	0.01
United States	**10,055**	**<0.01**
California	644	<0.01
Ohio	537	<0.01
Pennsylvania	477	<0.01
Michigan	396	<0.01
Texas	380	<0.01
Georgia	360	<0.01
Indiana	193	<0.01
North Carolina	156	<0.01
Florida	147	<0.01
Kansas	131	<0.01
Colorado	108	<0.01
Kentucky	93	<0.01
Missouri	69	<0.01
Illinois	62	<0.01
Washington	55	<0.01
Tennessee	54	<0.01
South Carolina	40	<0.01
Minnesota	37	<0.01
Iowa	26	<0.01
Oregon	25	<0.01
Oklahoma	24	<0.01
Connecticut	19	<0.01
Idaho	19	<0.01
Wisconsin	18	<0.01
Arizona	15	<0.01
Alaska	11	<0.01
Delaware	4	<0.01
Alabama	0	0.00
Arkansas	0	0.00
Hawaii	0	0.00
Louisiana	0	0.00
Mississippi	0	0.00
Montana	0	0.00
Nebraska	0	0.00
Nevada	0	0.00
New Hampshire	0	0.00
New Mexico	0	0.00
North Dakota	0	0.00
South Dakota	0	0.00
Utah	0	0.00
Vermont	0	0.00
West Virginia	0	0.00
Wyoming	0	0.00

Please refer to the Explanation of Data in the front of the book for more detailed information.

Ancestry

African, Sub-Saharan: Senegalese

Top 150 Places Sorted by Population

Based on all places, regardless of total population

Place	Population	%
New York, NY (city) Kings County	2,895	0.04
Manhattan, NY (borough) New York County	1,216	0.08
Bronx, NY (borough) Bronx County	1,068	0.08
Brooklyn, NY (borough) Kings County	401	0.02
Baltimore, MD (city) Baltimore city County	222	0.04
Cincinnati, OH (city) Hamilton County	195	0.06
Upper Darby, PA (township) Delaware County	191	0.23
Pawtucket, RI (city) Providence County	170	0.24
Newington, VA (cdp) Fairfax County	167	1.26
Los Angeles, CA (city) Los Angeles County	164	<0.01
Washington, DC (city) District of Columbia	163	0.03
Indianapolis, IN (city) Marion County	150	0.02
Houston, TX (city) Harris County	144	0.01
Springfield, MA (city) Hampden County	143	0.09
San Diego, CA (city) San Diego County	141	0.01
Triangle, VA (cdp) Prince William County	139	1.81
Philadelphia, PA (city) Philadelphia County	139	0.01
Finneytown, OH (cdp) Hamilton County	131	1.01
Monterey, CA (city) Monterey County	131	0.47
Staten Island, NY (borough) Richmond County	126	0.03
Bayonne, NJ (city) Hudson County	120	0.19
North Providence, RI (town) Providence County	106	0.33
Columbus, OH (city) Franklin County	104	0.01
Lynn, MA (city) Essex County	103	0.11
Boston, MA (city) Suffolk County	101	0.02
Kansas City, KS (city) Wyandotte County	97	0.07
Mitchellville, MD (cdp) Prince George's County	93	0.80
Silver Spring, MD (cdp) Montgomery County	90	0.13
Jersey City, NJ (city) Hudson County	90	0.04
Herndon, VA (town) Fairfax County	86	0.38
Haslett, MI (cdp) Ingham County	84	0.43
Meridian, MI (charter township) Ingham County	84	0.21
Queens, NY (borough) Queens County	84	<0.01
Claremont, CA (city) Los Angeles County	83	0.24
Lawrence, NJ (township) Mercer County	80	0.24
Westland, MI (city) Wayne County	74	0.09
Amarillo, TX (city) Potter County	73	0.04
Denver, CO (city) Denver County	73	0.01
Portland, ME (city) Cumberland County	72	0.11
Mahopac, NY (cdp) Putnam County	64	0.84
Carmel, NY (town) Putnam County	64	0.19
Gaithersburg, MD (city) Montgomery County	64	0.11
Fort Lauderdale, FL (city) Broward County	62	0.04
Roselle Park, NJ (borough) Union County	59	0.45
Louisville-Jefferson County, KY (metro govt) Jefferson County	56	0.01
Seattle, WA (city) King County	55	0.01
Hybla Valley, VA (cdp) Fairfax County	54	0.37
Spring, TX (cdp) Harris County	54	0.10
Mount Rainier, MD (city) Prince George's County	53	0.65
Haverstraw, NY (village) Rockland County	52	0.45
Aberdeen, NJ (township) Monmouth County	52	0.29
Haverstraw, NY (town) Rockland County	52	0.14
Romulus, MI (city) Wayne County	50	0.21
Woonsocket, RI (city) Providence County	50	0.12
Pontiac, MI (city) Oakland County	50	0.08
Norfolk, VA (ind. city) Norfolk independent city	50	0.02
Alexandria, VA (ind. city) Alexandria independent city	48	0.04
Charlotte, NC (city) Mecklenburg County	47	0.01
Raleigh, NC (city) Wake County	45	0.01
Peachtree City, GA (city) Fayette County	43	0.13
Bethlehem, PA (city) Northampton County	43	0.08
Bethlehem, PA (city) Northampton County	43	0.06
Orangeburg, SC (city) Orangeburg County	40	0.29
Schaumburg, IL (village) Cook County	39	0.05
Tallahassee, FL (city) Leon County	38	0.02
Takoma Park, MD (city) Montgomery County	37	0.22
Minneapolis, MN (city) Hennepin County	37	0.01
Pittsburgh, PA (city) Allegheny County	36	0.01
Glenmont, MD (cdp) Montgomery County	34	0.25
East Providence, RI (city) Providence County	34	0.07
Lawrence, KS (city) Douglas County	34	0.04
St. Joseph, MO (city) Buchanan County	34	0.04
Lyndon, KY (city) Jefferson County	33	0.31
Wheaton, MD (cdp) Montgomery County	33	0.07
Towson, MD (cdp) Baltimore County	33	0.06
San Leandro, CA (city) Alameda County	33	0.04
Kansas City, MO (city) Jackson County	29	0.01
South Kensington, MD (cdp) Montgomery County	28	0.34
Lewisville, TX (city) Denton County	28	0.03
Knoxville, TN (city) Knox County	28	0.02
Detroit, MI (city) Wayne County	28	<0.01
Wells Branch, TX (cdp) Travis County	27	0.23
Pittsford, NY (town) Monroe County	26	0.09
Portland, OR (city) Multnomah County	25	<0.01
Colesville, MD (cdp) Montgomery County	23	0.16
Bedford Heights, OH (city) Cuyahoga County	22	0.20
North Brunswick, NJ (township) Middlesex County	22	0.06
Redan, GA (cdp) DeKalb County	22	0.06
Ypsilanti, MI (charter township) Washtenaw County	22	0.04
Columbia, MD (cdp) Howard County	22	0.02
Yonkers, NY (city) Westchester County	21	0.01
Wyncote, PA (cdp) Montgomery County	20	0.63
Cheltenham, PA (township) Montgomery County	20	0.05
Germantown, MD (cdp) Montgomery County	20	0.02
Fort Collins, CO (city) Larimer County	20	0.01
Salinas, CA (city) Monterey County	20	0.01
Warren, MI (city) Macomb County	20	0.01
SUNY Oswego, NY (cdp) Oswego County	19	0.43
Oswego, NY (town) Oswego County	19	0.24
Moscow, ID (city) Latah County	19	0.08
Southfield, MI (city) Oakland County	19	0.03
Cattaraugus Reservation, NY (reservation) Erie County	18	0.96
Swatara, PA (township) Dauphin County	18	0.08
Milwaukee, WI (city) Milwaukee County	18	<0.01
Clayton, NY (village) Jefferson County	17	0.83
Clayton, NY (town) Jefferson County	17	0.34
Cusseta-Chattahoochee County, GA (unified govt) Chattahoochee County	17	0.15
Fairview Heights, IL (city) St. Clair County	17	0.10
Muscatine, IA (city) Muscatine County	17	0.07
Lakeland, FL (city) Polk County	17	0.02
Mission Viejo, CA (city) Orange County	17	0.02
Cleveland, OH (city) Cuyahoga County	17	<0.01
Memphis, TN (city) Shelby County	17	<0.01
Baltimore Highlands, MD (cdp) Baltimore County	16	0.22
South Hadley, MA (town) Hampshire County	16	0.09
Durham, NC (city) Durham County	16	0.01
Tampa, FL (city) Hillsborough County	16	<0.01
Englewood, CO (city) Arapahoe County	15	0.05
Holland, MI (charter township) Ottawa County	15	0.04
Toledo, OH (city) Lucas County	15	0.01
Atlanta, GA (city) Fulton County	15	<0.01
Tucson, AZ (city) Pima County	15	<0.01
Buena Vista, MI (cdp) Saginaw County	14	0.21
Twin Rivers, NJ (cdp) Mercer County	14	0.20
Los Altos Hills, CA (town) Santa Clara County	14	0.18
Buena Vista, MI (charter township) Saginaw County	14	0.16
Greencastle, IN (city) Putnam County	14	0.14
Northbrook, OH (cdp) Hamilton County	14	0.14
Plainsboro, NJ (township) Middlesex County	14	0.06
East Windsor, NJ (township) Mercer County	14	0.05
West Haven, CT (city/town) New Haven County	14	0.03
Jacksonville, FL (city) Duval County	14	<0.01
Lithia Springs, GA (cdp) Douglas County	13	0.08
Medina, OH (city) Medina County	13	0.05
Belleville, NJ (township) Essex County	13	0.04
Jackson, MI (city) Jackson County	13	0.04
Newark, CA (city) Alameda County	13	0.03
Fishers, IN (town) Hamilton County	13	0.02
Greensboro, NC (city) Guilford County	13	<0.01
Crown Heights, NY (cdp) Dutchess County	12	0.42
Geneseo, NY (village) Livingston County	12	0.15
Port Jervis, NY (city) Orange County	12	0.13
Geneseo, NY (town) Livingston County	12	0.12
Bethany, OK (city) Oklahoma County	12	0.06
Norristown, PA (borough) Montgomery County	12	0.04
Poughkeepsie, NY (town) Dutchess County	12	0.03
Edmond, OK (city) Oklahoma County	12	0.02
Jacksonville, NC (city) Onslow County	12	0.02
Mount Vernon, NY (city) Westchester County	12	0.02
Richardson, TX (city) Dallas County	12	0.01

Please refer to the Explanation of Data in the front of the book for more detailed information.

Ancestry

African, Sub-Saharan: Senegalese

Top 150 Places Sorted by Percent of Total Population

Based on all places, regardless of total population

Place	Population	%
Triangle, VA (cdp) Prince William County	139	1.81
Bonnieville, KY (city) Hart County	4	1.48
Newington, VA (cdp) Fairfax County	167	1.26
Finneytown, OH (cdp) Hamilton County	131	1.01
Cattaraugus Reservation, NY (reservation) Erie County	18	0.96
Mahopac, NY (cdp) Putnam County	64	0.84
Clayton, NY (village) Jefferson County	17	0.83
Mitchellville, MD (cdp) Prince George's County	93	0.80
Akutan, AK (city) Aleutians East Borough	11	0.69
Mount Rainier, MD (city) Prince George's County	53	0.65
Wyncote, PA (cdp) Montgomery County	20	0.63
Shutesbury, MA (town) Franklin County	10	0.53
Monterey, CA (city) Monterey County	131	0.47
Wayne, PA (township) Clinton County	8	0.47
Roselle Park, NJ (borough) Union County	59	0.45
Haverstraw, NY (village) Rockland County	52	0.45
Sackets Harbor, NY (village) Jefferson County	6	0.44
Haslett, MI (cdp) Ingham County	84	0.43
SUNY Oswego, NY (cdp) Oswego County	19	0.43
Crown Heights, NY (cdp) Dutchess County	12	0.42
Bel-Nor, MO (village) St. Louis County	6	0.39
Herndon, VA (town) Fairfax County	86	0.38
Hybla Valley, VA (cdp) Fairfax County	54	0.37
Cottage City, MD (town) Prince George's County	4	0.36
South Kensington, MD (cdp) Montgomery County	28	0.34
Clayton, NY (town) Jefferson County	17	0.34
North Providence, RI (town) Providence County	106	0.33
Lyndon, KY (city) Jefferson County	33	0.31
Aberdeen, NJ (township) Monmouth County	52	0.29
Orangeburg, SC (city) Orangeburg County	40	0.29
Glenmont, MD (cdp) Montgomery County	34	0.25
Pawtucket, RI (city) Providence County	170	0.24
Claremont, CA (city) Los Angeles County	83	0.24
Lawrence, NJ (township) Mercer County	80	0.24
Oswego, NY (town) Oswego County	19	0.24
Upper Darby, PA (township) Delaware County	191	0.23
Wells Branch, TX (cdp) Travis County	27	0.23
Takoma Park, MD (city) Montgomery County	37	0.22
Baltimore Highlands, MD (cdp) Baltimore County	16	0.22
Meridian, MI (charter township) Ingham County	84	0.21
Romulus, MI (city) Wayne County	50	0.21
Buena Vista, MI (cdp) Saginaw County	14	0.21
Bedford Heights, OH (city) Cuyahoga County	22	0.20
Twin Rivers, NJ (cdp) Mercer County	14	0.20
Bayonne, NJ (city) Hudson County	120	0.19
Carmel, NY (town) Putnam County	64	0.19
Los Altos Hills, CA (town) Santa Clara County	14	0.18
Hounsfield, NY (town) Jefferson County	6	0.18
Colesville, MD (cdp) Montgomery County	23	0.16
Buena Vista, MI (charter township) Saginaw County	14	0.16
Cusseta-Chattahoochee County, GA (unified govt) Chattahoochee County	17	0.15
Geneseo, NY (village) Livingston County	12	0.15
Williamsburg, MA (town) Hampshire County	4	0.15
Haverstraw, NY (town) Rockland County	52	0.14
Greencastle, IN (city) Putnam County	14	0.14
Northbrook, OH (cdp) Hamilton County	14	0.14
Silver Spring, MD (cdp) Montgomery County	90	0.13
Peachtree City, GA (city) Fayette County	43	0.13
Port Jervis, NY (city) Orange County	12	0.13
Woonsocket, RI (city) Providence County	50	0.12
Geneseo, NY (town) Livingston County	12	0.12
Lynn, MA (city) Essex County	103	0.11
Portland, ME (city) Cumberland County	72	0.11
Gaithersburg, MD (city) Montgomery County	64	0.11
Spring, TX (cdp) Harris County	54	0.10
Fairview Heights, IL (city) St. Clair County	17	0.10
Glocester, RI (town) Providence County	10	0.10
Springfield, MA (city) Hampden County	143	0.09
Westland, MI (city) Wayne County	74	0.09
Pittsford, NY (town) Monroe County	26	0.09
South Hadley, MA (town) Hampshire County	16	0.09
Manhattan, NY (borough) New York County	1,216	0.08
Bronx, NY (borough) Bronx County	1,068	0.08
Pontiac, MI (city) Oakland County	50	0.08
Bethlehem, PA (city) Northampton County	43	0.08
Moscow, ID (city) Latah County	19	0.08
Swatara, PA (township) Dauphin County	18	0.08
Lithia Springs, GA (cdp) Douglas County	13	0.08
Kansas City, KS (city) Wyandotte County	97	0.07
East Providence, RI (city) Providence County	34	0.07
Wheaton, MD (cdp) Montgomery County	33	0.07
Muscatine, IA (city) Muscatine County	17	0.07
Lansdowne, VA (cdp) Loudoun County	7	0.07
Cincinnati, OH (city) Hamilton County	195	0.06
Bethlehem, PA (city) Northampton County	43	0.06
Towson, MD (cdp) Baltimore County	33	0.06
North Brunswick, NJ (township) Middlesex County	22	0.06
Redan, GA (cdp) DeKalb County	22	0.06
Plainsboro, NJ (township) Middlesex County	14	0.06
Bethany, OK (city) Oklahoma County	12	0.06
Middletown, PA (township) Delaware County	10	0.06
Schaumburg, IL (village) Cook County	39	0.05
Cheltenham, PA (township) Montgomery County	20	0.05
Englewood, CO (city) Arapahoe County	15	0.05
East Windsor, NJ (township) Mercer County	14	0.05
Medina, OH (city) Medina County	13	0.05
New York, NY (city) Kings County	2,895	0.04
Baltimore, MD (city) Baltimore city County	222	0.04
Jersey City, NJ (city) Hudson County	90	0.04
Amarillo, TX (city) Potter County	73	0.04
Fort Lauderdale, FL (city) Broward County	62	0.04
Alexandria, VA (ind. city) Alexandria independent city	48	0.04
Lawrence, KS (city) Douglas County	34	0.04
St. Joseph, MO (city) Buchanan County	34	0.04
San Leandro, CA (city) Alameda County	33	0.04
Ypsilanti, MI (charter township) Washtenaw County	22	0.04
Holland, MI (charter township) Ottawa County	15	0.04
Belleville, NJ (township) Essex County	13	0.04
Jackson, MI (city) Jackson County	13	0.04
Norristown, PA (borough) Montgomery County	12	0.04
Washington, DC (city) District of Columbia	163	0.03
Staten Island, NY (borough) Richmond County	126	0.03
Lewisville, TX (city) Denton County	28	0.03
Southfield, MI (city) Oakland County	19	0.03
West Haven, CT (city/town) New Haven County	14	0.03
Newark, CA (city) Alameda County	13	0.03
Poughkeepsie, NY (town) Dutchess County	12	0.03
Brooklyn, NY (borough) Kings County	401	0.02
Indianapolis, IN (city) Marion County	150	0.02
Boston, MA (city) Suffolk County	101	0.02
Norfolk, VA (ind. city) Norfolk independent city	50	0.02
Tallahassee, FL (city) Leon County	38	0.02
Knoxville, TN (city) Knox County	28	0.02
Columbia, MD (cdp) Howard County	22	0.02
Germantown, MD (cdp) Montgomery County	20	0.02
Lakeland, FL (city) Polk County	17	0.02
Mission Viejo, CA (city) Orange County	17	0.02
Fishers, IN (town) Hamilton County	13	0.02
Edmond, OK (city) Oklahoma County	12	0.02
Jacksonville, NC (city) Onslow County	12	0.02
Mount Vernon, NY (city) Westchester County	12	0.02
Bethesda, MD (cdp) Montgomery County	10	0.02
Irvington, NJ (township) Essex County	10	0.02
Ames, IA (city) Story County	9	0.02
Mansfield, OH (city) Richland County	8	0.02
Palm Springs, CA (city) Riverside County	7	0.02
New London, CT (city/town) New London County	5	0.02
Houston, TX (city) Harris County	144	0.01
San Diego, CA (city) San Diego County	141	0.01
Philadelphia, PA (city) Philadelphia County	139	0.01
Columbus, OH (city) Franklin County	104	0.01
Denver, CO (city) Denver County	73	0.01
Louisville-Jefferson County, KY (metro govt) Jefferson County	56	0.01
Seattle, WA (city) King County	55	0.01
Charlotte, NC (city) Mecklenburg County	47	0.01
Raleigh, NC (city) Wake County	45	0.01
Minneapolis, MN (city) Hennepin County	37	0.01
Pittsburgh, PA (city) Allegheny County	36	0.01
Kansas City, MO (city) Jackson County	29	0.01
Yonkers, NY (city) Westchester County	21	0.01

Please refer to the Explanation of Data in the front of the book for more detailed information.

Ancestry

African, Sub-Saharan: Senegalese

Top 150 Places Sorted by Percent of Total Population

Based on places with total population of 7,500 or more

Place	Population	%
Triangle, VA (cdp) Prince William County	139	1.81
Newington, VA (cdp) Fairfax County	167	1.26
Finneytown, OH (cdp) Hamilton County	131	1.01
Mahopac, NY (cdp) Putnam County	64	0.84
Mitchellville, MD (cdp) Prince George's County	93	0.80
Mount Rainier, MD (city) Prince George's County	53	0.65
Monterey, CA (city) Monterey County	131	0.47
Roselle Park, NJ (borough) Union County	59	0.45
Haverstraw, NY (village) Rockland County	52	0.45
Haslett, MI (cdp) Ingham County	84	0.43
Herndon, VA (town) Fairfax County	86	0.38
Hybla Valley, VA (cdp) Fairfax County	54	0.37
South Kensington, MD (cdp) Montgomery County	28	0.34
North Providence, RI (town) Providence County	106	0.33
Lyndon, KY (city) Jefferson County	33	0.31
Aberdeen, NJ (township) Monmouth County	52	0.29
Orangeburg, SC (city) Orangeburg County	40	0.29
Glenmont, MD (cdp) Montgomery County	34	0.25
Pawtucket, RI (city) Providence County	170	0.24
Claremont, CA (city) Los Angeles County	83	0.24
Lawrence, NJ (township) Mercer County	80	0.24
Oswego, NY (town) Oswego County	19	0.24
Upper Darby, PA (township) Delaware County	191	0.23
Wells Branch, TX (cdp) Travis County	27	0.23
Takoma Park, MD (city) Montgomery County	37	0.22
Meridian, MI (charter township) Ingham County	84	0.21
Romulus, MI (city) Wayne County	50	0.21
Bedford Heights, OH (city) Cuyahoga County	22	0.20
Bayonne, NJ (city) Hudson County	120	0.19
Carmel, NY (town) Putnam County	64	0.19
Los Altos Hills, CA (town) Santa Clara County	14	0.18
Colesville, MD (cdp) Montgomery County	23	0.16
Buena Vista, MI (charter township) Saginaw County	14	0.16
Cusseta-Chattahoochee County, GA (unified govt) Chattahoochee County	17	0.15
Geneseo, NY (village) Livingston County	12	0.15
Haverstraw, NY (town) Rockland County	52	0.14
Greencastle, IN (city) Putnam County	14	0.14
Northbrook, OH (cdp) Hamilton County	14	0.14
Silver Spring, MD (cdp) Montgomery County	90	0.13
Peachtree City, GA (city) Fayette County	43	0.13
Port Jervis, NY (city) Orange County	12	0.13
Woonsocket, RI (city) Providence County	50	0.12
Geneseo, NY (town) Livingston County	12	0.12
Lynn, MA (city) Essex County	103	0.11
Portland, ME (city) Cumberland County	72	0.11
Gaithersburg, MD (city) Montgomery County	64	0.11
Spring, TX (cdp) Harris County	54	0.10
Fairview Heights, IL (city) St. Clair County	17	0.10
Glocester, RI (town) Providence County	10	0.10
Springfield, MA (city) Hampden County	143	0.09
Westland, MI (city) Wayne County	74	0.09
Pittsford, NY (town) Monroe County	26	0.09
South Hadley, MA (town) Hampshire County	16	0.09
Manhattan, NY (borough) New York County	1,216	0.08
Bronx, NY (borough) Bronx County	1,068	0.08
Pontiac, MI (city) Oakland County	50	0.08
Bethlehem, PA (city) Northampton County	43	0.08
Moscow, ID (city) Latah County	19	0.08
Swatara, PA (township) Dauphin County	18	0.08
Lithia Springs, GA (cdp) Douglas County	13	0.08
Kansas City, KS (city) Wyandotte County	97	0.07
East Providence, RI (city) Providence County	34	0.07
Wheaton, MD (cdp) Montgomery County	33	0.07
Muscatine, IA (city) Muscatine County	17	0.07
Lansdowne, VA (cdp) Loudoun County	7	0.07
Cincinnati, OH (city) Hamilton County	195	0.06
Bethlehem, PA (city) Northampton County	43	0.06
Towson, MD (cdp) Baltimore County	33	0.06
North Brunswick, NJ (township) Middlesex County	22	0.06
Redan, GA (cdp) DeKalb County	22	0.06
Plainsboro, NJ (township) Middlesex County	14	0.06
Bethany, OK (city) Oklahoma County	12	0.06
Middletown, PA (township) Delaware County	10	0.06
Schaumburg, IL (village) Cook County	39	0.05
Cheltenham, PA (township) Montgomery County	20	0.05
Englewood, CO (city) Arapahoe County	15	0.05
East Windsor, NJ (township) Mercer County	14	0.05
Medina, OH (city) Medina County	13	0.05
New York, NY (city) Kings County	2,895	0.04
Baltimore, MD (city) Baltimore city County	222	0.04
Jersey City, NJ (city) Hudson County	90	0.04
Amarillo, TX (city) Potter County	73	0.04
Fort Lauderdale, FL (city) Broward County	62	0.04
Alexandria, VA (ind. city) Alexandria independent city	48	0.04
Lawrence, KS (city) Douglas County	34	0.04
St. Joseph, MO (city) Buchanan County	34	0.04
San Leandro, CA (city) Alameda County	33	0.04
Ypsilanti, MI (charter township) Washtenaw County	22	0.04
Holland, MI (charter township) Ottawa County	15	0.04
Belleville, NJ (township) Essex County	13	0.04
Jackson, MI (city) Jackson County	13	0.04
Norristown, PA (borough) Montgomery County	12	0.04
Washington, DC (city) District of Columbia	163	0.03
Staten Island, NY (borough) Richmond County	126	0.03
Lewisville, TX (city) Denton County	28	0.03
Southfield, MI (city) Oakland County	19	0.03
West Haven, CT (city/town) New Haven County	14	0.03
Newark, CA (city) Alameda County	13	0.03
Poughkeepsie, NY (town) Dutchess County	12	0.03
Brooklyn, NY (borough) Kings County	401	0.02
Indianapolis, IN (city) Marion County	150	0.02
Boston, MA (city) Suffolk County	101	0.02
Norfolk, VA (ind. city) Norfolk independent city	50	0.02
Tallahassee, FL (city) Leon County	38	0.02
Knoxville, TN (city) Knox County	28	0.02
Columbia, MD (cdp) Howard County	22	0.02
Germantown, MD (cdp) Montgomery County	20	0.02
Lakeland, FL (city) Polk County	17	0.02
Mission Viejo, CA (city) Orange County	17	0.02
Fishers, IN (town) Hamilton County	13	0.02
Edmond, OK (city) Oklahoma County	12	0.02
Jacksonville, NC (city) Onslow County	12	0.02
Mount Vernon, NY (city) Westchester County	12	0.02
Bethesda, MD (cdp) Montgomery County	10	0.02
Irvington, NJ (township) Essex County	10	0.02
Ames, IA (city) Story County	9	0.02
Mansfield, OH (city) Richland County	8	0.02
Palm Springs, CA (city) Riverside County	7	0.02
New London, CT (city/town) New London County	5	0.02
Houston, TX (city) Harris County	144	0.01
San Diego, CA (city) San Diego County	141	0.01
Philadelphia, PA (city) Philadelphia County	139	0.01
Columbus, OH (city) Franklin County	104	0.01
Denver, CO (city) Denver County	73	0.01
Louisville-Jefferson County, KY (metro govt) Jefferson County	56	0.01
Seattle, WA (city) King County	55	0.01
Charlotte, NC (city) Mecklenburg County	47	0.01
Raleigh, NC (city) Wake County	45	0.01
Minneapolis, MN (city) Hennepin County	37	0.01
Pittsburgh, PA (city) Allegheny County	36	0.01
Kansas City, MO (city) Jackson County	29	0.01
Yonkers, NY (city) Westchester County	21	0.01
Fort Collins, CO (city) Larimer County	20	0.01
Salinas, CA (city) Monterey County	20	0.01
Warren, MI (city) Macomb County	20	0.01
Durham, NC (city) Durham County	16	0.01
Toledo, OH (city) Lucas County	15	0.01
Richardson, TX (city) Dallas County	12	0.01
Athens-Clarke County, GA (unified govt) Clarke County	11	0.01
Richmond, CA (city) Contra Costa County	11	0.01
College Station, TX (city) Brazos County	8	0.01
Gastonia, NC (city) Gaston County	8	0.01
West Bloomfield, MI (charter township) Oakland County	7	0.01
Moline, IL (city) Rock Island County	6	0.01
Los Angeles, CA (city) Los Angeles County	164	<0.01
Queens, NY (borough) Queens County	84	<0.01
Detroit, MI (city) Wayne County	28	<0.01
Portland, OR (city) Multnomah County	25	<0.01
Milwaukee, WI (city) Milwaukee County	18	<0.01
Cleveland, OH (city) Cuyahoga County	17	<0.01

Please refer to the Explanation of Data in the front of the book for more detailed information.

Ancestry

African, Sub-Saharan: Sierra Leonean

U.S. and 50 States Sorted by Population and Percent of Total Population

Place	Population	%
United States	**16,343**	**0.01**
Maryland	2,915	0.05
Virginia	2,475	0.03
New York	1,711	0.01
Pennsylvania	1,036	0.01
Georgia	1,003	0.01
Texas	954	<0.01
New Jersey	947	0.01
Massachusetts	913	0.01
California	667	<0.01
North Carolina	590	0.01
Ohio	558	<0.01
Illinois	497	<0.01
Minnesota	415	0.01
Florida	339	<0.01
District of Columbia	172	0.03
Missouri	149	<0.01
Washington	135	<0.01
Tennessee	127	<0.01
Utah	102	<0.01
Oregon	98	<0.01
Arizona	96	<0.01
Delaware	63	0.01
Rhode Island	51	<0.01
Alaska	41	0.01
Indiana	41	<0.01
Alabama	34	<0.01
Louisiana	34	<0.01
Connecticut	31	<0.01
Wisconsin	29	<0.01
Iowa	23	<0.01
Michigan	23	<0.01
Colorado	14	<0.01
South Carolina	12	<0.01
Arkansas	11	<0.01
Kansas	10	<0.01
Kentucky	10	<0.01
Nebraska	9	<0.01
Nevada	8	<0.01
Hawaii	0	0.00
Idaho	0	0.00
Maine	0	0.00
Mississippi	0	0.00
Montana	0	0.00
New Hampshire	0	0.00
New Mexico	0	0.00
North Dakota	0	0.00
Oklahoma	0	0.00
South Dakota	0	0.00
Vermont	0	0.00
West Virginia	0	0.00
Wyoming	0	0.00

Place	Population	%
Maryland	2,915	0.05
Virginia	2,475	0.03
District of Columbia	172	0.03
United States	**16,343**	**0.01**
New York	1,711	0.01
Pennsylvania	1,036	0.01
Georgia	1,003	0.01
New Jersey	947	0.01
Massachusetts	913	0.01
North Carolina	590	0.01
Minnesota	415	0.01
Delaware	63	0.01
Alaska	41	0.01
Texas	954	<0.01
California	667	<0.01
Ohio	558	<0.01
Illinois	497	<0.01
Florida	339	<0.01
Missouri	149	<0.01
Washington	135	<0.01
Tennessee	127	<0.01
Utah	102	<0.01
Oregon	98	<0.01
Arizona	96	<0.01
Rhode Island	51	<0.01
Indiana	41	<0.01
Alabama	34	<0.01
Louisiana	34	<0.01
Connecticut	31	<0.01
Wisconsin	29	<0.01
Iowa	23	<0.01
Michigan	23	<0.01
Colorado	14	<0.01
South Carolina	12	<0.01
Arkansas	11	<0.01
Kansas	10	<0.01
Kentucky	10	<0.01
Nebraska	9	<0.01
Nevada	8	<0.01
Hawaii	0	0.00
Idaho	0	0.00
Maine	0	0.00
Mississippi	0	0.00
Montana	0	0.00
New Hampshire	0	0.00
New Mexico	0	0.00
North Dakota	0	0.00
Oklahoma	0	0.00
South Dakota	0	0.00
Vermont	0	0.00
West Virginia	0	0.00
Wyoming	0	0.00

Please refer to the Explanation of Data in the front of the book for more detailed information.

Ancestry

African, Sub-Saharan: Sierra Leonean

Top 150 Places Sorted by Population

Based on all places, regardless of total population

Place	Population	%
New York, NY (city) Kings County	1,572	0.02
Alexandria, VA (ind. city) Alexandria independent city	863	0.65
Bronx, NY (borough) Bronx County	759	0.06
Columbus, OH (city) Franklin County	461	0.06
Boston, MA (city) Suffolk County	452	0.08
Manhattan, NY (borough) New York County	422	0.03
Reston, VA (cdp) Fairfax County	330	0.62
Randolph, MA (cdp/town) Norfolk County	316	1.00
Seabrook, MD (cdp) Prince George's County	311	1.99
Irondale, GA (cdp) Clayton County	237	3.18
Houston, TX (city) Harris County	235	0.01
Colwyn, PA (borough) Delaware County	231	9.19
Chicago, IL (city) Cook County	221	0.01
Fairland, MD (cdp) Montgomery County	214	0.93
Greensboro, NC (city) Guilford County	210	0.08
Takoma Park, MD (city) Montgomery County	204	1.21
Lake Arbor, MD (cdp) Prince George's County	201	1.95
Yeadon, PA (borough) Delaware County	197	1.72
Washington, DC (city) District of Columbia	172	0.03
Raleigh, NC (city) Wake County	161	0.04
East Orange, NJ (city) Essex County	160	0.25
Darby, PA (borough) Delaware County	156	1.47
Dale City, VA (cdp) Prince William County	150	0.24
Cherry Hill, VA (cdp) Prince William County	147	0.95
Brooklyn, NY (borough) Kings County	147	0.01
Lincolnia, VA (cdp) Fairfax County	144	0.70
Philadelphia, PA (city) Philadelphia County	144	0.01
Laurel Hill, VA (cdp) Fairfax County	140	2.31
Old Bridge, NJ (township) Middlesex County	138	0.21
Nashville-Davidson, TN (metro govt) Davidson County	127	0.02
Queens, NY (borough) Queens County	127	0.01
St. Louis, MO (city) St. Louis city County	125	0.04
Newark, NJ (city) Essex County	123	0.04
East Windsor, NJ (township) Mercer County	121	0.45
Valrico, FL (cdp) Hillsborough County	121	0.35
Los Angeles, CA (city) Los Angeles County	121	<0.01
Franklin, NJ (township) Somerset County	120	0.20
Baltimore, MD (city) Baltimore city County	120	0.02
Staten Island, NY (borough) Richmond County	117	0.03
San Jose, CA (city) Santa Clara County	117	0.01
Woodlawn, VA (cdp) Fairfax County	116	0.59
Upper Darby, PA (township) Delaware County	116	0.14
Beltsville, MD (cdp) Prince George's County	112	0.73
Ramsey, MN (city) Anoka County	112	0.49
Glenmont, MD (cdp) Montgomery County	110	0.82
Romeoville, IL (village) Will County	105	0.28
Waldorf, MD (cdp) Charles County	102	0.15
Dallas, TX (city) Dallas County	100	0.01
Garland, TX (city) Dallas County	97	0.04
St. Paul, MN (city) Ramsey County	95	0.03
Vacaville, CA (city) Solano County	91	0.10
Mitchellville, MD (cdp) Prince George's County	89	0.76
Jacksonville, FL (city) Duval County	87	0.01
Durham, NC (city) Durham County	83	0.04
Hyattsville, MD (city) Prince George's County	81	0.47
Federal Way, WA (city) King County	80	0.09
Gresham, OR (city) Multnomah County	78	0.08
Marlboro Village, MD (cdp) Prince George's County	76	0.81
Brooklyn Park, MN (city) Hennepin County	76	0.10
Danville, VA (ind. city) Danville independent city	72	0.16
Surprise, AZ (city) Maricopa County	72	0.07
Calverton, MD (cdp) Montgomery County	71	0.40
Murray, UT (city) Salt Lake County	71	0.15
Pennsauken, NJ (township) Camden County	70	0.19
Charlotte, NC (city) Mecklenburg County	70	0.01
East Franklin, NJ (cdp) Somerset County	67	0.87
Chillum, MD (cdp) Prince George's County	63	0.18
Fayetteville, GA (city) Fayette County	60	0.39
Hagerstown, MD (city) Washington County	59	0.15
Marietta, GA (city) Cobb County	58	0.10
Summerfield, MD (cdp) Prince George's County	57	0.51
Odenton, MD (cdp) Anne Arundel County	56	0.16
Pittsburgh, PA (city) Allegheny County	55	0.02
South Holland, IL (village) Cook County	54	0.25
Six Mile Run, NJ (cdp) Somerset County	53	1.46
Schaumburg, IL (village) Cook County	53	0.07
Castaic, CA (cdp) Los Angeles County	52	0.29
Wylie, TX (city) Collin County	52	0.14
Livermore, CA (city) Alameda County	52	0.07
Lowell, MA (city) Middlesex County	52	0.05
Providence, RI (city) Providence County	51	0.03
Allen, TX (city) Collin County	50	0.06
Pembroke Park, FL (town) Broward County	49	0.83
Scaggsville, MD (cdp) Howard County	49	0.21
Accokeek, MD (cdp) Prince George's County	46	0.44
Lorton, VA (cdp) Fairfax County	46	0.24
Kemp Mill, MD (cdp) Montgomery County	44	0.36
Owings Mills, MD (cdp) Baltimore County	44	0.15
Minneapolis, MN (city) Hennepin County	44	0.01
Olney, MD (cdp) Montgomery County	43	0.13
Bolingbrook, IL (village) Will County	43	0.06
Montgomery Village, MD (cdp) Montgomery County	42	0.13
Bowie, MD (city) Prince George's County	42	0.08
Nome, AK (city) Nome Census Area	41	1.17
Lanham, MD (cdp) Prince George's County	41	0.46
Holyoke, MA (city) Hampden County	41	0.10
Severn, MD (cdp) Anne Arundel County	39	0.09
Pearland, TX (city) Brazoria County	39	0.05
Edison, NJ (township) Middlesex County	39	0.04
Lake Darby, OH (cdp) Franklin County	38	0.82
Ashland, CA (cdp) Alameda County	38	0.17
Olmsted Falls, OH (city) Cuyahoga County	36	0.41
Fayetteville, NC (city) Cumberland County	36	0.02
Essex, MD (cdp) Baltimore County	35	0.09
Camden, NJ (city) Camden County	35	0.04
Columbia, MD (cdp) Howard County	35	0.04
Silver Spring, MD (cdp) Montgomery County	34	0.05
Tuscaloosa, AL (city) Tuscaloosa County	34	0.04
Glendale, CA (city) Los Angeles County	34	0.02
Baton Rouge, LA (city) East Baton Rouge Parish	34	0.01
East Riverdale, MD (cdp) Prince George's County	33	0.21
State College, PA (borough) Centre County	33	0.08
Aspen Hill, MD (cdp) Montgomery County	33	0.07
Fairwood, MD (cdp) Prince George's County	32	0.69
Asbury Park, NJ (city) Monmouth County	32	0.20
Inver Grove Heights, MN (city) Dakota County	31	0.09
Holly Springs, NC (town) Wake County	30	0.14
Little Elm, TX (city) Denton County	30	0.14
Sandy Springs, GA (city) Fulton County	30	0.03
New Castle, DE (city) New Castle County	29	0.55
Manteca, CA (city) San Joaquin County	28	0.04
Hawthorne, CA (city) Los Angeles County	27	0.03
Long Beach, CA (city) Los Angeles County	27	0.01
Hybla Valley, VA (cdp) Fairfax County	25	0.17
Sudley, VA (cdp) Prince William County	25	0.16
Tacoma, WA (city) Pierce County	25	0.01
Golden Valley, MN (city) Hennepin County	24	0.12
Egypt Lake-Leto, FL (cdp) Hillsborough County	24	0.07
Germantown, MD (cdp) Montgomery County	24	0.03
Phoenix, AZ (city) Maricopa County	24	<0.01
Fairfax Station, VA (cdp) Fairfax County	23	0.20
Streetsboro, OH (city) Portage County	23	0.15
Annapolis, MD (city) Anne Arundel County	23	0.06
Berkeley, CA (city) Alameda County	23	0.02
Des Moines, IA (city) Polk County	23	0.01
Worcester, MA (city) Worcester County	23	0.01
Marlboro Meadows, MD (cdp) Prince George's County	22	0.61
Dryden, NY (town) Tompkins County	22	0.15
Rossville, MD (cdp) Baltimore County	22	0.15
Tucker, GA (cdp) DeKalb County	22	0.08
Mount Vernon, NY (city) Westchester County	22	0.03
East Lansdowne, PA (borough) Delaware County	21	0.79
Riviera Beach, MD (cdp) Anne Arundel County	21	0.18
Monroeville, PA (municipality) Allegheny County	21	0.07
Mishawaka, IN (city) St. Joseph County	21	0.04
Potomac Mills, VA (cdp) Prince William County	20	0.42
New Carrollton, MD (city) Prince George's County	20	0.16
Brooklyn Center, MN (city) Hennepin County	20	0.07
Portland, OR (city) Multnomah County	20	<0.01
Edmonston, MD (town) Prince George's County	19	1.43

Please refer to the Explanation of Data in the front of the book for more detailed information.

Ancestry

African, Sub-Saharan: Sierra Leonean

Top 150 Places Sorted by Percent of Total Population

Based on all places, regardless of total population

Place	Population	%
Colwyn, PA (borough) Delaware County	231	9.19
Irondale, GA (cdp) Clayton County	237	3.18
Laurel Hill, VA (cdp) Fairfax County	140	2.31
Seabrook, MD (cdp) Prince George's County	311	1.99
Lake Arbor, MD (cdp) Prince George's County	201	1.95
Yeadon, PA (borough) Delaware County	197	1.72
Darby, PA (borough) Delaware County	156	1.47
Six Mile Run, NJ (cdp) Somerset County	53	1.46
Edmonston, MD (town) Prince George's County	19	1.43
Takoma Park, MD (city) Montgomery County	204	1.21
Nome, AK (city) Nome Census Area	41	1.17
Randolph, MA (cdp/town) Norfolk County	316	1.00
Cherry Hill, VA (cdp) Prince William County	147	0.95
Fairland, MD (cdp) Montgomery County	214	0.93
East Franklin, NJ (cdp) Somerset County	67	0.87
Pembroke Park, FL (town) Broward County	49	0.83
Glenmont, MD (cdp) Montgomery County	110	0.82
Lake Darby, OH (cdp) Franklin County	38	0.82
Marlboro Village, MD (cdp) Prince George's County	76	0.81
East Lansdowne, PA (borough) Delaware County	21	0.79
Mitchellville, MD (cdp) Prince George's County	89	0.76
Beltsville, MD (cdp) Prince George's County	112	0.73
Bonanza, GA (cdp) Clayton County	19	0.73
Lincolnia, VA (cdp) Fairfax County	144	0.70
Fairwood, MD (cdp) Prince George's County	32	0.69
Alexandria, VA (ind. city) Alexandria independent city	863	0.65
Reston, VA (cdp) Fairfax County	330	0.62
Marlboro Meadows, MD (cdp) Prince George's County	22	0.61
Woodlawn, VA (cdp) Fairfax County	116	0.59
How, WI (town) Oconto County	3	0.57
Kutztown University, PA (cdp) Berks County	14	0.56
New Castle, DE (city) New Castle County	29	0.55
Summerfield, MD (cdp) Prince George's County	57	0.51
Ramsey, MN (city) Anoka County	112	0.49
Hyattsville, MD (city) Prince George's County	81	0.47
Lanham, MD (cdp) Prince George's County	41	0.46
East Windsor, NJ (township) Mercer County	121	0.45
Accokeek, MD (cdp) Prince George's County	46	0.44
Potomac Mills, VA (cdp) Prince William County	20	0.42
Olmsted Falls, OH (city) Cuyahoga County	36	0.41
Calverton, MD (cdp) Montgomery County	71	0.40
Fayetteville, GA (city) Fayette County	60	0.39
Hopedale, MA (cdp) Worcester County	15	0.37
Kemp Mill, MD (cdp) Montgomery County	44	0.36
Brentwood, MD (town) Prince George's County	11	0.36
Springdale, MD (cdp) Prince George's County	9	0.36
Valrico, FL (cdp) Hillsborough County	121	0.35
Willernie, MN (city) Washington County	2	0.35
Hamilton, NY (village) Madison County	12	0.34
Kenvil, NJ (cdp) Morris County	10	0.34
Castaic, CA (cdp) Los Angeles County	52	0.29
Romeoville, IL (village) Will County	105	0.28
East Orange, NJ (city) Essex County	160	0.25
South Holland, IL (village) Cook County	54	0.25
Hopedale, MA (town) Worcester County	15	0.25
Dale City, VA (cdp) Prince William County	150	0.24
Lorton, VA (cdp) Fairfax County	46	0.24
Cocoa West, FL (cdp) Brevard County	14	0.23
Old Bridge, NJ (township) Middlesex County	138	0.21
Scaggsville, MD (cdp) Howard County	49	0.21
East Riverdale, MD (cdp) Prince George's County	33	0.21
Franklin, NJ (township) Somerset County	120	0.20
Asbury Park, NJ (city) Monmouth County	32	0.20
Fairfax Station, VA (cdp) Fairfax County	23	0.20
Brock Hall, MD (cdp) Prince George's County	16	0.20
Pennsauken, NJ (township) Camden County	70	0.19
Larkfield-Wikiup, CA (cdp) Sonoma County	16	0.19
Chillum, MD (cdp) Prince George's County	63	0.18
Riviera Beach, MD (cdp) Anne Arundel County	21	0.18
Maxatawny, PA (township) Berks County	14	0.18
Hamilton, NY (town) Madison County	12	0.18
Grass Lake, MI (charter township) Jackson County	10	0.18
Ashland, CA (cdp) Alameda County	38	0.17
Hybla Valley, VA (cdp) Fairfax County	25	0.17
George Mason, VA (cdp) Fairfax County	15	0.17
University of Virginia, VA (cdp) Albemarle County	12	0.17
Edgefield, SC (town) Edgefield County	8	0.17
Danville, VA (ind. city) Danville independent city	72	0.16
Odenton, MD (cdp) Anne Arundel County	56	0.16
Sudley, VA (cdp) Prince William County	25	0.16
New Carrollton, MD (city) Prince George's County	20	0.16
Manhasset, NY (cdp) Nassau County	13	0.16
Waldorf, MD (cdp) Charles County	102	0.15
Murray, UT (city) Salt Lake County	71	0.15
Hagerstown, MD (city) Washington County	59	0.15
Owings Mills, MD (cdp) Baltimore County	44	0.15
Streetsboro, OH (city) Portage County	23	0.15
Dryden, NY (town) Tompkins County	22	0.15
Rossville, MD (cdp) Baltimore County	22	0.15
Flushing, MI (city) Genesee County	13	0.15
Upper Darby, PA (township) Delaware County	116	0.14
Wylie, TX (city) Collin County	52	0.14
Holly Springs, NC (town) Wake County	30	0.14
Little Elm, TX (city) Denton County	30	0.14
Olney, MD (cdp) Montgomery County	43	0.13
Montgomery Village, MD (cdp) Montgomery County	42	0.13
Golden Valley, MN (city) Hennepin County	24	0.12
Adelphi, MD (cdp) Prince George's County	18	0.12
North Kensington, MD (cdp) Montgomery County	12	0.12
Neabsco, VA (cdp) Prince William County	11	0.12
Folcroft, PA (borough) Delaware County	8	0.12
Elk Plain, WA (cdp) Pierce County	16	0.11
Parkway, CA (cdp) Sacramento County	15	0.11
Coatesville, PA (city) Chester County	14	0.11
Princeton, NJ (borough) Mercer County	14	0.11
Vacaville, CA (city) Solano County	91	0.10
Brooklyn Park, MN (city) Hennepin County	76	0.10
Marietta, GA (city) Cobb County	58	0.10
Holyoke, MA (city) Hampden County	41	0.10
Coral Hills, MD (cdp) Prince George's County	10	0.10
Federal Way, WA (city) King County	80	0.09
Severn, MD (cdp) Anne Arundel County	39	0.09
Essex, MD (cdp) Baltimore County	35	0.09
Inver Grove Heights, MN (city) Dakota County	31	0.09
Cimarron Hills, CO (cdp) El Paso County	14	0.09
Kettering, MD (cdp) Prince George's County	11	0.09
Boston, MA (city) Suffolk County	452	0.08
Greensboro, NC (city) Guilford County	210	0.08
Gresham, OR (city) Multnomah County	78	0.08
Bowie, MD (city) Prince George's County	42	0.08
State College, PA (borough) Centre County	33	0.08
Tucker, GA (cdp) DeKalb County	22	0.08
White Oak, MD (cdp) Montgomery County	14	0.08
Mount Vernon, VA (cdp) Fairfax County	9	0.08
Surprise, AZ (city) Maricopa County	72	0.07
Schaumburg, IL (village) Cook County	53	0.07
Livermore, CA (city) Alameda County	52	0.07
Aspen Hill, MD (cdp) Montgomery County	33	0.07
Egypt Lake-Leto, FL (cdp) Hillsborough County	24	0.07
Monroeville, PA (municipality) Allegheny County	21	0.07
Brooklyn Center, MN (city) Hennepin County	20	0.07
Seguin, TX (city) Guadalupe County	18	0.07
Jasmine Estates, FL (cdp) Pasco County	13	0.07
Lindenwold, NJ (borough) Camden County	13	0.07
Stockton, WI (town) Portage County	2	0.07
Bronx, NY (borough) Bronx County	759	0.06
Columbus, OH (city) Franklin County	461	0.06
Allen, TX (city) Collin County	50	0.06
Bolingbrook, IL (village) Will County	43	0.06
Annapolis, MD (city) Anne Arundel County	23	0.06
South Laurel, MD (cdp) Prince George's County	16	0.06
Palmer, PA (township) Northampton County	12	0.06
Roselle, NJ (borough) Union County	12	0.06
Newington Forest, VA (cdp) Fairfax County	8	0.06
Lowell, MA (city) Middlesex County	52	0.05
Pearland, TX (city) Brazoria County	39	0.05
Silver Spring, MD (cdp) Montgomery County	34	0.05
Ewing, NJ (township) Mercer County	19	0.05
Mission Bend, TX (cdp) Fort Bend County	19	0.05
Northampton, MA (city) Hampshire County	14	0.05

Please refer to the Explanation of Data in the front of the book for more detailed information.

Ancestry

African, Sub-Saharan: Sierra Leonean

Top 150 Places Sorted by Percent of Total Population

Based on places with total population of 7,500 or more

Place	Population	%
Seabrook, MD (cdp) Prince George's County	311	1.99
Lake Arbor, MD (cdp) Prince George's County	201	1.95
Yeadon, PA (borough) Delaware County	197	1.72
Darby, PA (borough) Delaware County	156	1.47
Takoma Park, MD (city) Montgomery County	204	1.21
Randolph, MA (cdp/town) Norfolk County	316	1.00
Cherry Hill, VA (cdp) Prince William County	147	0.95
Fairland, MD (cdp) Montgomery County	214	0.93
East Franklin, NJ (cdp) Somerset County	67	0.87
Glenmont, MD (cdp) Montgomery County	110	0.82
Marlboro Village, MD (cdp) Prince George's County	76	0.81
Mitchellville, MD (cdp) Prince George's County	89	0.76
Beltsville, MD (cdp) Prince George's County	112	0.73
Lincolnia, VA (cdp) Fairfax County	144	0.70
Alexandria, VA (ind. city) Alexandria independent city	863	0.65
Reston, VA (cdp) Fairfax County	330	0.62
Woodlawn, VA (cdp) Fairfax County	116	0.59
Summerfield, MD (cdp) Prince George's County	57	0.51
Ramsey, MN (city) Anoka County	112	0.49
Hyattsville, MD (city) Prince George's County	81	0.47
Lanham, MD (cdp) Prince George's County	41	0.46
East Windsor, NJ (township) Mercer County	121	0.45
Accokeek, MD (cdp) Prince George's County	46	0.44
Olmsted Falls, OH (city) Cuyahoga County	36	0.41
Calverton, MD (cdp) Montgomery County	71	0.40
Fayetteville, GA (city) Fayette County	60	0.39
Kemp Mill, MD (cdp) Montgomery County	44	0.36
Valrico, FL (cdp) Hillsborough County	121	0.35
Castaic, CA (cdp) Los Angeles County	52	0.29
Romeoville, IL (village) Will County	105	0.28
East Orange, NJ (city) Essex County	160	0.25
South Holland, IL (village) Cook County	54	0.25
Dale City, VA (cdp) Prince William County	150	0.24
Lorton, VA (cdp) Fairfax County	46	0.24
Old Bridge, NJ (township) Middlesex County	138	0.21
Scaggsville, MD (cdp) Howard County	49	0.21
East Riverdale, MD (cdp) Prince George's County	33	0.21
Franklin, NJ (township) Somerset County	120	0.20
Asbury Park, NJ (city) Monmouth County	32	0.20
Fairfax Station, VA (cdp) Fairfax County	23	0.20
Brock Hall, MD (cdp) Prince George's County	16	0.20
Pennsauken, NJ (township) Camden County	70	0.19
Larkfield-Wikiup, CA (cdp) Sonoma County	16	0.19
Chillum, MD (cdp) Prince George's County	63	0.18
Riviera Beach, MD (cdp) Anne Arundel County	21	0.18
Maxatawny, PA (township) Berks County	14	0.18
Ashland, CA (cdp) Alameda County	38	0.17
Hybla Valley, VA (cdp) Fairfax County	25	0.17
George Mason, VA (cdp) Fairfax County	15	0.17
Danville, VA (ind. city) Danville independent city	72	0.16
Odenton, MD (cdp) Anne Arundel County	56	0.16
Sudley, VA (cdp) Prince William County	25	0.16
New Carrollton, MD (city) Prince George's County	20	0.16
Manhasset, NY (cdp) Nassau County	13	0.16
Waldorf, MD (cdp) Charles County	102	0.15
Murray, UT (city) Salt Lake County	71	0.15
Hagerstown, MD (city) Washington County	59	0.15
Owings Mills, MD (cdp) Baltimore County	44	0.15
Streetsboro, OH (city) Portage County	23	0.15
Dryden, NY (town) Tompkins County	22	0.15
Rossville, MD (cdp) Baltimore County	22	0.15
Flushing, MI (city) Genesee County	13	0.15
Upper Darby, PA (township) Delaware County	116	0.14
Wylie, TX (city) Collin County	52	0.14
Holly Springs, NC (town) Wake County	30	0.14
Little Elm, TX (city) Denton County	30	0.14
Olney, MD (cdp) Montgomery County	43	0.13
Montgomery Village, MD (cdp) Montgomery County	42	0.13
Golden Valley, MN (city) Hennepin County	24	0.12
Adelphi, MD (cdp) Prince George's County	18	0.12
North Kensington, MD (cdp) Montgomery County	12	0.12
Neabsco, VA (cdp) Prince William County	11	0.12
Elk Plain, WA (cdp) Pierce County	16	0.11
Parkway, CA (cdp) Sacramento County	15	0.11
Coatesville, PA (city) Chester County	14	0.11
Princeton, NJ (borough) Mercer County	14	0.11
Vacaville, CA (city) Solano County	91	0.10
Brooklyn Park, MN (city) Hennepin County	76	0.10
Marietta, GA (city) Cobb County	58	0.10
Holyoke, MA (city) Hampden County	41	0.10
Coral Hills, MD (cdp) Prince George's County	10	0.10
Federal Way, WA (city) King County	80	0.09
Severn, MD (cdp) Anne Arundel County	39	0.09
Essex, MD (cdp) Baltimore County	35	0.09
Inver Grove Heights, MN (city) Dakota County	31	0.09
Cimarron Hills, CO (cdp) El Paso County	14	0.09
Kettering, MD (cdp) Prince George's County	11	0.09
Boston, MA (city) Suffolk County	452	0.08
Greensboro, NC (city) Guilford County	210	0.08
Gresham, OR (city) Multnomah County	78	0.08
Bowie, MD (city) Prince George's County	42	0.08
State College, PA (borough) Centre County	33	0.08
Tucker, GA (cdp) DeKalb County	22	0.08
White Oak, MD (cdp) Montgomery County	14	0.08
Mount Vernon, VA (cdp) Fairfax County	9	0.08
Surprise, AZ (city) Maricopa County	72	0.07
Schaumburg, IL (village) Cook County	53	0.07
Livermore, CA (city) Alameda County	52	0.07
Aspen Hill, MD (cdp) Montgomery County	33	0.07
Egypt Lake-Leto, FL (cdp) Hillsborough County	24	0.07
Monroeville, PA (municipality) Allegheny County	21	0.07
Brooklyn Center, MN (city) Hennepin County	20	0.07
Seguin, TX (city) Guadalupe County	18	0.07
Jasmine Estates, FL (cdp) Pasco County	13	0.07
Lindenwold, NJ (borough) Camden County	13	0.07
Bronx, NY (borough) Bronx County	759	0.06
Columbus, OH (city) Franklin County	461	0.06
Allen, TX (city) Collin County	50	0.06
Bolingbrook, IL (village) Will County	43	0.06
Annapolis, MD (city) Anne Arundel County	23	0.06
South Laurel, MD (cdp) Prince George's County	16	0.06
Palmer, PA (township) Northampton County	12	0.06
Roselle, NJ (borough) Union County	12	0.06
Newington Forest, VA (cdp) Fairfax County	8	0.06
Lowell, MA (city) Middlesex County	52	0.05
Pearland, TX (city) Brazoria County	39	0.05
Silver Spring, MD (cdp) Montgomery County	34	0.05
Ewing, NJ (township) Mercer County	19	0.05
Mission Bend, TX (cdp) Fort Bend County	19	0.05
Northampton, MA (city) Hampshire County	14	0.05
Baldwin, NY (cdp) Nassau County	11	0.05
DuBois, PA (city) Clearfield County	4	0.05
Raleigh, NC (city) Wake County	161	0.04
St. Louis, MO (city) St. Louis city County	125	0.04
Newark, NJ (city) Essex County	123	0.04
Garland, TX (city) Dallas County	97	0.04
Durham, NC (city) Durham County	83	0.04
Edison, NJ (township) Middlesex County	39	0.04
Camden, NJ (city) Camden County	35	0.04
Columbia, MD (cdp) Howard County	35	0.04
Tuscaloosa, AL (city) Tuscaloosa County	34	0.04
Manteca, CA (city) San Joaquin County	28	0.04
Mishawaka, IN (city) St. Joseph County	21	0.04
North Brunswick, NJ (township) Middlesex County	15	0.04
College Park, MD (city) Prince George's County	12	0.04
Fredericksburg, VA (ind. city) Fredericksburg independent city	10	0.04
Roxbury, NJ (township) Morris County	10	0.04
Manhattan, NY (borough) New York County	422	0.03
Washington, DC (city) District of Columbia	172	0.03
Staten Island, NY (borough) Richmond County	117	0.03
St. Paul, MN (city) Ramsey County	95	0.03
Providence, RI (city) Providence County	51	0.03
Sandy Springs, GA (city) Fulton County	30	0.03
Hawthorne, CA (city) Los Angeles County	27	0.03
Germantown, MD (cdp) Montgomery County	24	0.03
Mount Vernon, NY (city) Westchester County	22	0.03
Logan, UT (city) Cache County	15	0.03
DeSoto, TX (city) Dallas County	14	0.03
Goshen, IN (city) Elkhart County	9	0.03
Glasgow, DE (cdp) New Castle County	5	0.03

Ancestry

African, Sub-Saharan: Somalian

U.S. and 50 States Sorted by Population and Percent of Total Population

Place	Population	%
United States	**100,011**	**0.03**
Minnesota	32,449	0.62
Ohio	10,078	0.09
Washington	9,543	0.15
California	7,150	0.02
Texas	3,601	0.01
Virginia	3,460	0.04
New York	3,053	0.02
Arizona	3,028	0.05
Massachusetts	2,663	0.04
Maine	2,462	0.19
Tennessee	2,211	0.04
Georgia	2,093	0.02
Oregon	2,061	0.05
Colorado	1,838	0.04
Missouri	1,366	0.02
Utah	1,348	0.05
North Carolina	1,308	0.01
Nebraska	1,300	0.07
Michigan	981	0.01
Kentucky	914	0.02
Illinois	839	0.01
Maryland	765	0.01
Wisconsin	701	0.01
Indiana	626	0.01
Connecticut	579	0.02
Kansas	478	0.02
Alaska	424	0.06
Nevada	368	0.01
Vermont	304	0.05
Idaho	300	0.02
North Dakota	256	0.04
South Dakota	253	0.03
Pennsylvania	250	<0.01
Iowa	239	0.01
New Jersey	233	<0.01
South Carolina	149	<0.01
Arkansas	114	<0.01
Louisiana	114	<0.01
Hawaii	38	<0.01
Montana	32	<0.01
District of Columbia	13	<0.01
Delaware	12	<0.01
Alabama	11	<0.01
Oklahoma	6	<0.01
Florida	0	0.00
Mississippi	0	0.00
New Hampshire	0	0.00
New Mexico	0	0.00
Rhode Island	0	0.00
West Virginia	0	0.00
Wyoming	0	0.00

Place	Population	%
Minnesota	32,449	0.62
Maine	2,462	0.19
Washington	9,543	0.15
Ohio	10,078	0.09
Nebraska	1,300	0.07
Alaska	424	0.06
Arizona	3,028	0.05
Oregon	2,061	0.05
Utah	1,348	0.05
Vermont	304	0.05
Virginia	3,460	0.04
Massachusetts	2,663	0.04
Tennessee	2,211	0.04
Colorado	1,838	0.04
North Dakota	256	0.04
United States	**100,011**	**0.03**
South Dakota	253	0.03
California	7,150	0.02
New York	3,053	0.02
Georgia	2,093	0.02
Missouri	1,366	0.02
Kentucky	914	0.02
Connecticut	579	0.02
Kansas	478	0.02
Idaho	300	0.02
Texas	3,601	0.01
North Carolina	1,308	0.01
Michigan	981	0.01
Illinois	839	0.01
Maryland	765	0.01
Wisconsin	701	0.01
Indiana	626	0.01
Nevada	368	0.01
Iowa	239	0.01
Pennsylvania	250	<0.01
New Jersey	233	<0.01
South Carolina	149	<0.01
Arkansas	114	<0.01
Louisiana	114	<0.01
Hawaii	38	<0.01
Montana	32	<0.01
District of Columbia	13	<0.01
Delaware	12	<0.01
Alabama	11	<0.01
Oklahoma	6	<0.01
Florida	0	0.00
Mississippi	0	0.00
New Hampshire	0	0.00
New Mexico	0	0.00
Rhode Island	0	0.00
West Virginia	0	0.00
Wyoming	0	0.00

Please refer to the Explanation of Data in the front of the book for more detailed information.

Ancestry

African, Sub-Saharan: Somalian

Top 150 Places Sorted by Population

Based on all places, regardless of total population

Place	Population	%
Minneapolis, MN (city) Hennepin County	12,303	3.24
Columbus, OH (city) Franklin County	9,093	1.18
St. Paul, MN (city) Ramsey County	4,697	1.67
San Diego, CA (city) San Diego County	4,090	0.32
Seattle, WA (city) King County	3,872	0.65
Rochester, MN (city) Olmsted County	2,488	2.39
Nashville-Davidson, TN (metro govt) Davidson County	1,880	0.32
Eden Prairie, MN (city) Hennepin County	1,636	2.76
Burnsville, MN (city) Dakota County	1,295	2.13
Phoenix, AZ (city) Maricopa County	1,261	0.09
Boston, MA (city) Suffolk County	1,186	0.20
Kent, WA (city) King County	1,051	1.18
Portland, OR (city) Multnomah County	1,004	0.18
Rochester, NY (city) Monroe County	980	0.46
Columbia Heights, MN (city) Anoka County	959	4.92
Portland, ME (city) Cumberland County	920	1.39
Bloomington, MN (city) Hennepin County	911	1.10
Salt Lake City, UT (city) Salt Lake County	908	0.49
Buffalo, NY (city) Erie County	858	0.32
SeaTac, WA (city) King County	823	3.11
Everett, WA (city) Snohomish County	787	0.77
Houston, TX (city) Harris County	784	0.04
Dallas, TX (city) Dallas County	780	0.07
Lewiston, ME (city) Androscoggin County	750	2.04
Louisville-Jefferson County, KY (metro govt) Jefferson County	680	0.12
St. Cloud, MN (city) Stearns County	657	1.27
St. Cloud, MN (city) Stearns County	657	1.01
Chicago, IL (city) Cook County	637	0.02
Tucson, AZ (city) Pima County	607	0.12
Hopkins, MN (city) Hennepin County	598	3.43
Chandler, AZ (city) Maricopa County	598	0.26
Renton, WA (city) King County	582	0.67
St. Louis Park, MN (city) Hennepin County	561	1.26
Alexandria, VA (ind. city) Alexandria independent city	560	0.42
Kansas City, MO (city) Jackson County	555	0.12
Denver, CO (city) Denver County	550	0.10
Springfield, MA (city) Hampden County	542	0.35
Fridley, MN (city) Anoka County	541	1.97
Des Moines, WA (city) King County	535	1.82
St. Louis, MO (city) St. Louis city County	533	0.17
New York, NY (city) Kings County	518	0.01
Irving, TX (city) Dallas County	514	0.24
Raleigh, NC (city) Wake County	496	0.13
Charlotte, NC (city) Mecklenburg County	485	0.07
Syracuse, NY (city) Onondaga County	478	0.33
Lexington, NE (city) Dawson County	464	4.59
Eagan, MN (city) Dakota County	459	0.71
Willmar, MN (city) Kandiyohi County	451	2.33
Indianapolis, IN (city) Marion County	432	0.05
San Antonio, TX (city) Medina County	412	0.03
Tukwila, WA (city) King County	407	2.19
Tempe, AZ (city) Maricopa County	404	0.25
Faribault, MN (city) Rice County	400	1.74
Fort Morgan, CO (city) Morgan County	396	3.53
Mankato, MN (city) Blue Earth County	395	1.03
Mankato, MN (city) Blue Earth County	395	1.03
Aurora, CO (city) Arapahoe County	394	0.13
Edina, MN (city) Hennepin County	390	0.82
La Presa, CA (cdp) San Diego County	388	1.11
Milwaukee, WI (city) Milwaukee County	381	0.06
Brooklyn Center, MN (city) Hennepin County	356	1.20
Millcreek, UT (cdp) Salt Lake County	342	0.56
San Jose, CA (city) Santa Clara County	324	0.04
Omaha, NE (city) Douglas County	322	0.08
Owatonna, MN (city) Steele County	321	1.27
Lansing, MI (city) Ingham County	316	0.29
Lansing, MI (city) Ingham County	316	0.27
Hartford, CT (city/town) Hartford County	315	0.25
Charlottesville, VA (ind. city) Charlottesville independent city	310	0.73
Scottdale, GA (cdp) DeKalb County	303	3.10
Richfield, MN (city) Hennepin County	300	0.86
East Riverdale, MD (cdp) Prince George's County	293	1.87
Cambridge, MA (city) Middlesex County	287	0.28
Westbrook, ME (city) Cumberland County	280	1.62
Lorton, VA (cdp) Fairfax County	280	1.45
Boise City, ID (city) Ada County	274	0.13
Savage, MN (city) Scott County	267	1.00
Brooklyn, NY (borough) Kings County	260	0.01
South Portland, ME (city) Cumberland County	258	1.04
Waite Park, MN (city) Stearns County	247	3.68
Auburn, ME (city) Androscoggin County	238	1.02
Decatur, GA (city) DeKalb County	236	1.24
Auburn, WA (city) King County	234	0.35
La Mesa, CA (city) San Diego County	233	0.41
Urbancrest, OH (village) Franklin County	223	21.80
South Sioux City, NE (city) Dakota County	217	1.67
Grand Island, NE (city) Hall County	216	0.46
Brooklyn Park, MN (city) Hennepin County	214	0.29
Arlington, TX (city) Tarrant County	214	0.06
Mountlake Terrace, WA (city) Snohomish County	211	1.06
Sioux Falls, SD (city) Minnehaha County	210	0.14
Fort Worth, TX (city) Tarrant County	209	0.03
Vallejo, CA (city) Solano County	203	0.17
Lemon Grove, CA (city) San Diego County	202	0.81
Hillsboro, OR (city) Washington County	199	0.23
Lynn, MA (city) Essex County	195	0.22
Des Moines, IA (city) Polk County	195	0.10
Amarillo, TX (city) Potter County	194	0.10
Minnetonka, MN (city) Hennepin County	193	0.39
Winooski, VT (city) Chittenden County	189	2.65
Bridgeport, CT (city/town) Fairfield County	188	0.13
Barron, WI (city) Barron County	186	5.46
White Center, WA (cdp) King County	186	1.47
Shakopee, MN (city) Scott County	186	0.53
Chantilly, VA (cdp) Fairfax County	182	0.82
New Hope, MN (city) Hennepin County	177	0.87
Unalaska, AK (city) Aleutians West Census Area	176	3.92
Hazel Dell, WA (cdp) Clark County	176	0.91
Shoreline, WA (city) King County	176	0.34
Shelbyville, TN (city) Bedford County	172	0.87
Dodge City, KS (city) Ford County	171	0.65
Coon Rapids, MN (city) Anoka County	168	0.27
Garden Home-Whitford, OR (cdp) Washington County	167	2.77
Moorhead, MN (city) Clay County	166	0.45
Marumsco, VA (cdp) Prince William County	160	0.49
Taylors, SC (cdp) Greenville County	149	0.69
Dale City, VA (cdp) Prince William County	148	0.23
Elk Grove, CA (city) Sacramento County	148	0.10
Grand Forks, ND (city) Grand Forks County	144	0.28
Centreville, VA (cdp) Fairfax County	144	0.20
Aloha, OR (cdp) Washington County	142	0.30
Tigard, OR (city) Washington County	139	0.29
Oceanside, CA (city) San Diego County	139	0.08
Corvallis, OR (city) Benton County	135	0.25
Wheaton, IL (city) DuPage County	134	0.25
Fayetteville, NC (city) Cumberland County	134	0.07
North Brunswick, NJ (township) Middlesex County	132	0.33
Hilliard, OH (city) Franklin County	130	0.47
San Marcos, CA (city) San Diego County	129	0.17
Seabrook, MD (cdp) Prince George's County	127	0.81
Florence, KY (city) Boone County	127	0.43
Ypsilanti, MI (charter township) Washtenaw County	127	0.24
Quincy, MA (city) Norfolk County	125	0.14
Manhattan, NY (borough) New York County	125	0.01
Olathe, KS (city) Johnson County	123	0.10
Garden City, KS (city) Finney County	120	0.46
Roseville, MN (city) Ramsey County	120	0.36
Warrensville Heights, OH (city) Cuyahoga County	119	0.87
Greeley, CO (city) Weld County	118	0.13
Greensboro, NC (city) Guilford County	118	0.04
East Hill-Meridian, WA (cdp) King County	116	0.40
Memphis, TN (city) Shelby County	116	0.02
Sunrise Manor, NV (cdp) Clark County	115	0.06
Beaverton, OR (city) Washington County	112	0.13
Madison, WI (city) Dane County	111	0.05
Tucker, GA (cdp) DeKalb County	108	0.40
Worcester, MA (city) Worcester County	108	0.06
Erlanger, KY (city) Kenton County	107	0.60
Burke Centre, VA (cdp) Fairfax County	106	0.62
Oakland, CA (city) Alameda County	105	0.03

SECTION THREE

Please refer to the Explanation of Data in the front of the book for more detailed information.

Ancestry

African, Sub-Saharan: Somalian

Top 150 Places Sorted by Percent of Total Population

Based on all places, regardless of total population

Place	Population	%
Urbancrest, OH (village) Franklin County	223	21.80
St. Paul, AK (city) Aleutians West Census Area	78	7.32
Barron, WI (city) Barron County	186	5.46
Columbia Heights, MN (city) Anoka County	959	4.92
Akutan, AK (city) Aleutians East Borough	76	4.76
Sand Point, AK (city) Aleutians East Borough	63	4.74
Lexington, NE (city) Dawson County	464	4.59
Lake Hamilton, AR (cdp) Garland County	79	4.10
Unalaska, AK (city) Aleutians West Census Area	176	3.92
Waite Park, MN (city) Stearns County	247	3.68
Fort Morgan, CO (city) Morgan County	396	3.53
Hopkins, MN (city) Hennepin County	598	3.43
Minneapolis, MN (city) Hennepin County	12,303	3.24
Oshkosh, MN (township) Yellow Medicine County	8	3.17
SeaTac, WA (city) King County	823	3.11
Scottdale, GA (cdp) DeKalb County	303	3.10
Garden Home-Whitford, OR (cdp) Washington County	167	2.77
Eden Prairie, MN (city) Hennepin County	1,636	2.76
Pelican Rapids, MN (city) Otter Tail County	73	2.72
Winooski, VT (city) Chittenden County	189	2.65
Rochester, MN (city) Olmsted County	2,488	2.39
Willmar, MN (city) Kandiyohi County	451	2.33
Tukwila, WA (city) King County	407	2.19
Burnsville, MN (city) Dakota County	1,295	2.13
Riverview, MO (village) St. Louis County	61	2.12
White Cloud, MI (city) Newaygo County	36	2.05
Lewiston, ME (city) Androscoggin County	750	2.04
Fridley, MN (city) Anoka County	541	1.97
East Riverdale, MD (cdp) Prince George's County	293	1.87
Des Moines, WA (city) King County	535	1.82
Faribault, MN (city) Rice County	400	1.74
St. Paul, MN (city) Ramsey County	4,697	1.67
South Sioux City, NE (city) Dakota County	217	1.67
Westbrook, ME (city) Cumberland County	280	1.62
Sunnyside, CA (cdp) Fresno County	70	1.54
White Center, WA (cdp) King County	186	1.47
Lorton, VA (cdp) Fairfax County	280	1.45
Red Lake Falls, MN (city) Red Lake County	21	1.43
Portland, ME (city) Cumberland County	920	1.39
Boys Town, NE (village) Douglas County	8	1.35
Huber Ridge, OH (cdp) Franklin County	57	1.28
St. Cloud, MN (city) Stearns County	657	1.27
Owatonna, MN (city) Steele County	321	1.27
St. Louis Park, MN (city) Hennepin County	561	1.26
Decatur, GA (city) DeKalb County	236	1.24
Brooklyn Center, MN (city) Hennepin County	356	1.20
Columbus, OH (city) Franklin County	9,093	1.18
Kent, WA (city) King County	1,051	1.18
Clarkston, GA (city) DeKalb County	89	1.18
Campo, CA (cdp) San Diego County	35	1.18
Point Hope, AK (city) North Slope Borough	16	1.13
La Presa, CA (cdp) San Diego County	388	1.11
Bloomington, MN (city) Hennepin County	911	1.10
Mountlake Terrace, WA (city) Snohomish County	211	1.06
South Portland, ME (city) Cumberland County	258	1.04
Mankato, MN (city) Blue Earth County	395	1.03
Mankato, MN (city) Blue Earth County	395	1.03
Schuyler, NE (city) Colfax County	61	1.03
Auburn, ME (city) Androscoggin County	238	1.02
St. Cloud, MN (city) Stearns County	657	1.01
Savage, MN (city) Scott County	267	1.00
Hazel Dell, WA (cdp) Clark County	176	0.91
Falcon Heights, MN (city) Ramsey County	48	0.91
Manchester, IL (village) Scott County	4	0.89
New Hope, MN (city) Hennepin County	177	0.87
Shelbyville, TN (city) Bedford County	172	0.87
Warrensville Heights, OH (city) Cuyahoga County	119	0.87
Richfield, MN (city) Hennepin County	300	0.86
St. John, MO (city) St. Louis County	55	0.84
Mendota Heights, MN (city) Dakota County	93	0.83
Edina, MN (city) Hennepin County	390	0.82
Chantilly, VA (cdp) Fairfax County	182	0.82
Lemon Grove, CA (city) San Diego County	202	0.81
Seabrook, MD (cdp) Prince George's County	127	0.81
East Lansdowne, PA (borough) Delaware County	21	0.79

Place	Population	%
Everett, WA (city) Snohomish County	787	0.77
Charlottesville, VA (ind. city) Charlottesville independent city	310	0.73
Carnation, WA (city) King County	15	0.72
Eagan, MN (city) Dakota County	459	0.71
Urbana, MD (cdp) Frederick County	52	0.71
Taylors, SC (cdp) Greenville County	149	0.69
Renton, WA (city) King County	582	0.67
Moose Lake, MN (city) Carlton County	18	0.67
Newington Forest, VA (cdp) Fairfax County	86	0.66
Seven Corners, VA (cdp) Fairfax County	55	0.66
Seattle, WA (city) King County	3,872	0.65
Dodge City, KS (city) Ford County	171	0.65
Newellton, LA (town) Tensas Parish	11	0.65
Burke Centre, VA (cdp) Fairfax County	106	0.62
Erlanger, KY (city) Kenton County	107	0.60
Buffalo, MN (city) Wright County	89	0.60
Millcreek, UT (cdp) Salt Lake County	342	0.56
Mahtomedi, MN (city) Washington County	43	0.56
Riverton, WA (cdp) King County	36	0.55
Lake Crystal, MN (city) Blue Earth County	14	0.55
Shakopee, MN (city) Scott County	186	0.53
Wilton, ND (city) McLean County	4	0.53
Kingstowne, VA (cdp) Fairfax County	76	0.52
Summerfield, MD (cdp) Prince George's County	58	0.52
Salem, IL (city) Marion County	39	0.52
Cannon Falls, MN (city) Goodhue County	21	0.52
Salt Lake City, UT (city) Salt Lake County	908	0.49
Marumsco, VA (cdp) Prince William County	160	0.49
Byron, MN (city) Olmsted County	23	0.49
Hilliard, OH (city) Franklin County	130	0.47
Rochester, NY (city) Monroe County	980	0.46
Grand Island, NE (city) Hall County	216	0.46
Garden City, KS (city) Finney County	120	0.46
Harrogate, TN (city) Claiborne County	20	0.46
Moorhead, MN (city) Clay County	166	0.45
Brandermill, VA (cdp) Chesterfield County	56	0.45
Florence, KY (city) Boone County	127	0.43
Alexandria, VA (ind. city) Alexandria independent city	560	0.42
La Mesa, CA (city) San Diego County	233	0.41
East Hill-Meridian, WA (cdp) King County	116	0.40
Tucker, GA (cdp) DeKalb County	108	0.40
Battlement Mesa, CO (cdp) Garfield County	20	0.40
Minnetonka, MN (city) Hennepin County	193	0.39
Prairieville, LA (cdp) Ascension Parish	103	0.39
Miles City, MT (city) Custer County	32	0.39
Fairwood, MD (cdp) Prince George's County	17	0.37
Roseville, MN (city) Ramsey County	120	0.36
Ypsilanti, MI (city) Washtenaw County	72	0.36
Lahaina, HI (cdp) Maui County	38	0.36
Springfield, MA (city) Hampden County	542	0.35
Auburn, WA (city) King County	234	0.35
Cascades, VA (cdp) Loudoun County	42	0.35
East Montpelier, VT (town) Washington County	9	0.35
Shoreline, WA (city) King County	176	0.34
Wakefield, VA (cdp) Fairfax County	39	0.34
St. Peter, MN (city) Nicollet County	38	0.34
Syracuse, NY (city) Onondaga County	478	0.33
North Brunswick, NJ (township) Middlesex County	132	0.33
Winchester, VA (ind. city) Winchester independent city	86	0.33
Champlin, MN (city) Hennepin County	75	0.33
San Diego, CA (city) San Diego County	4,090	0.32
Nashville-Davidson, TN (metro govt) Davidson County	1,880	0.32
Buffalo, NY (city) Erie County	858	0.32
Robbinsdale, MN (city) Hennepin County	43	0.31
Aloha, OR (cdp) Washington County	142	0.30
Lower Allen, PA (township) Cumberland County	54	0.30
Lansing, MI (city) Ingham County	316	0.29
Brooklyn Park, MN (city) Hennepin County	214	0.29
Tigard, OR (city) Washington County	139	0.29
East Point, GA (city) Fulton County	99	0.29
Port Jervis, NY (city) Orange County	26	0.29
Cambridge, MA (city) Middlesex County	287	0.28
Grand Forks, ND (city) Grand Forks County	144	0.28
Jollyville, TX (cdp) Williamson County	45	0.28
Lansing, MI (city) Ingham County	316	0.27

Please refer to the Explanation of Data in the front of the book for more detailed information.

Ancestry

African, Sub-Saharan: Somalian

Top 150 Places Sorted by Percent of Total Population

Based on places with total population of 7,500 or more

Place	Population	%
Columbia Heights, MN (city) Anoka County	959	4.92
Lexington, NE (city) Dawson County	464	4.59
Fort Morgan, CO (city) Morgan County	396	3.53
Hopkins, MN (city) Hennepin County	598	3.43
Minneapolis, MN (city) Hennepin County	12,303	3.24
SeaTac, WA (city) King County	823	3.11
Scottdale, GA (cdp) DeKalb County	303	3.10
Eden Prairie, MN (city) Hennepin County	1,636	2.76
Rochester, MN (city) Olmsted County	2,488	2.39
Willmar, MN (city) Kandiyohi County	451	2.33
Tukwila, WA (city) King County	407	2.19
Burnsville, MN (city) Dakota County	1,295	2.13
Lewiston, ME (city) Androscoggin County	750	2.04
Fridley, MN (city) Anoka County	541	1.97
East Riverdale, MD (cdp) Prince George's County	293	1.87
Des Moines, WA (city) King County	535	1.82
Faribault, MN (city) Rice County	400	1.74
St. Paul, MN (city) Ramsey County	4,697	1.67
South Sioux City, NE (city) Dakota County	217	1.67
Westbrook, ME (city) Cumberland County	280	1.62
White Center, WA (cdp) King County	186	1.47
Lorton, VA (cdp) Fairfax County	280	1.45
Portland, ME (city) Cumberland County	920	1.39
St. Cloud, MN (city) Stearns County	657	1.27
Owatonna, MN (city) Steele County	321	1.27
St. Louis Park, MN (city) Hennepin County	561	1.26
Decatur, GA (city) DeKalb County	236	1.24
Brooklyn Center, MN (city) Hennepin County	356	1.20
Columbus, OH (city) Franklin County	9,093	1.18
Kent, WA (city) King County	1,051	1.18
Clarkston, GA (city) DeKalb County	89	1.18
La Presa, CA (cdp) San Diego County	388	1.11
Bloomington, MN (city) Hennepin County	911	1.10
Mountlake Terrace, WA (city) Snohomish County	211	1.06
South Portland, ME (city) Cumberland County	258	1.04
Mankato, MN (city) Blue Earth County	395	1.03
Mankato, MN (city) Blue Earth County	395	1.03
Auburn, ME (city) Androscoggin County	238	1.02
St. Cloud, MN (city) Stearns County	657	1.01
Savage, MN (city) Scott County	267	1.00
Hazel Dell, WA (cdp) Clark County	176	0.91
New Hope, MN (city) Hennepin County	177	0.87
Shelbyville, TN (city) Bedford County	172	0.87
Warrensville Heights, OH (city) Cuyahoga County	119	0.87
Richfield, MN (city) Hennepin County	300	0.86
Mendota Heights, MN (city) Dakota County	93	0.83
Edina, MN (city) Hennepin County	390	0.82
Chantilly, VA (cdp) Fairfax County	182	0.82
Lemon Grove, CA (city) San Diego County	202	0.81
Seabrook, MD (cdp) Prince George's County	127	0.81
Everett, WA (city) Snohomish County	787	0.77
Charlottesville, VA (ind. city) Charlottesville independent city	310	0.73
Eagan, MN (city) Dakota County	459	0.71
Taylors, SC (cdp) Greenville County	149	0.69
Renton, WA (city) King County	582	0.67
Newington Forest, VA (cdp) Fairfax County	86	0.66
Seven Corners, VA (cdp) Fairfax County	55	0.66
Seattle, WA (city) King County	3,872	0.65
Dodge City, KS (city) Ford County	171	0.65
Burke Centre, VA (cdp) Fairfax County	106	0.62
Erlanger, KY (city) Kenton County	107	0.60
Buffalo, MN (city) Wright County	89	0.60
Millcreek, UT (cdp) Salt Lake County	342	0.56
Mahtomedi, MN (city) Washington County	43	0.56
Shakopee, MN (city) Scott County	186	0.53
Kingstowne, VA (cdp) Fairfax County	76	0.52
Summerfield, MD (cdp) Prince George's County	58	0.52
Salt Lake City, UT (city) Salt Lake County	908	0.49
Marumsco, VA (cdp) Prince William County	160	0.49
Hilliard, OH (city) Franklin County	130	0.47
Rochester, NY (city) Monroe County	980	0.46
Grand Island, NE (city) Hall County	216	0.46
Garden City, KS (city) Finney County	120	0.46
Moorhead, MN (city) Clay County	166	0.45
Brandermill, VA (cdp) Chesterfield County	56	0.45

Place	Population	%
Florence, KY (city) Boone County	127	0.43
Alexandria, VA (ind. city) Alexandria independent city	560	0.42
La Mesa, CA (city) San Diego County	233	0.41
East Hill-Meridian, WA (cdp) King County	116	0.40
Tucker, GA (cdp) DeKalb County	108	0.40
Minnetonka, MN (city) Hennepin County	193	0.39
Prairieville, LA (cdp) Ascension Parish	103	0.39
Miles City, MT (city) Custer County	32	0.39
Roseville, MN (city) Ramsey County	120	0.36
Ypsilanti, MI (city) Washtenaw County	72	0.36
Lahaina, HI (cdp) Maui County	38	0.36
Springfield, MA (city) Hampden County	542	0.35
Auburn, WA (city) King County	234	0.35
Cascades, VA (cdp) Loudoun County	42	0.35
Shoreline, WA (city) King County	176	0.34
Wakefield, VA (cdp) Fairfax County	39	0.34
St. Peter, MN (city) Nicollet County	38	0.34
Syracuse, NY (city) Onondaga County	478	0.33
North Brunswick, NJ (township) Middlesex County	132	0.33
Winchester, VA (ind. city) Winchester independent city	86	0.33
Champlin, MN (city) Hennepin County	75	0.33
San Diego, CA (city) San Diego County	4,090	0.32
Nashville-Davidson, TN (metro govt) Davidson County	1,880	0.32
Buffalo, NY (city) Erie County	858	0.32
Robbinsdale, MN (city) Hennepin County	43	0.31
Aloha, OR (cdp) Washington County	142	0.30
Lower Allen, PA (township) Cumberland County	54	0.30
Lansing, MI (city) Ingham County	316	0.29
Brooklyn Park, MN (city) Hennepin County	214	0.29
Tigard, OR (city) Washington County	139	0.29
East Point, GA (city) Fulton County	99	0.29
Port Jervis, NY (city) Orange County	26	0.29
Cambridge, MA (city) Middlesex County	287	0.28
Grand Forks, ND (city) Grand Forks County	144	0.28
Jollyville, TX (cdp) Williamson County	45	0.28
Lansing, MI (city) Ingham County	316	0.27
Coon Rapids, MN (city) Anoka County	168	0.27
Chandler, AZ (city) Maricopa County	598	0.26
Tempe, AZ (city) Maricopa County	404	0.25
Hartford, CT (city/town) Hartford County	315	0.25
Corvallis, OR (city) Benton County	135	0.25
Wheaton, IL (city) DuPage County	134	0.25
Irving, TX (city) Dallas County	514	0.24
Ypsilanti, MI (charter township) Washtenaw County	127	0.24
Burlington, VT (city) Chittenden County	102	0.24
Leesburg, VA (town) Loudoun County	97	0.24
Hillsboro, OR (city) Washington County	199	0.23
Dale City, VA (cdp) Prince William County	148	0.23
Westlake, OH (city) Cuyahoga County	76	0.23
Lynn, MA (city) Essex County	195	0.22
Bryn Mawr-Skyway, WA (cdp) King County	32	0.22
Apple Valley, MN (city) Dakota County	102	0.21
Pittsfield, MI (charter township) Washtenaw County	73	0.21
Boston, MA (city) Suffolk County	1,186	0.20
Centreville, VA (cdp) Fairfax County	144	0.20
Dublin, OH (city) Franklin County	77	0.20
West Springfield, VA (cdp) Fairfax County	44	0.20
Brookings, SD (city) Brookings County	43	0.20
Whitehall, OH (city) Franklin County	37	0.20
Reston, VA (cdp) Fairfax County	103	0.19
Portland, OR (city) Multnomah County	1,004	0.18
West St. Paul, MN (city) Dakota County	35	0.18
Skowhegan, ME (town) Somerset County	16	0.18
Cambridge, MN (city) Isanti County	14	0.18
St. Louis, MO (city) St. Louis city County	533	0.17
Vallejo, CA (city) Solano County	203	0.17
San Marcos, CA (city) San Diego County	129	0.17
Randolph, MA (cdp/town) Norfolk County	53	0.17
Lawrenceville, GA (city) Gwinnett County	46	0.17
Denison, IA (city) Crawford County	14	0.17
Utica, NY (city) Oneida County	99	0.16
Euless, TX (city) Tarrant County	79	0.16
Parkland, WA (cdp) Pierce County	58	0.16
Rosemount, MN (city) Dakota County	34	0.16
St. Peters, MO (city) St. Charles County	77	0.15

Ancestry

African, Sub-Saharan: South African

U.S. and 50 States Sorted by Population and Percent of Total Population

Place	Population	%
United States	**53,088**	**0.02**
California	8,602	0.02
Florida	5,723	0.03
New York	3,993	0.02
Texas	3,814	0.02
Georgia	3,424	0.04
New Jersey	2,127	0.02
North Carolina	1,690	0.02
Illinois	1,623	0.01
Arizona	1,570	0.03
Virginia	1,420	0.02
Massachusetts	1,360	0.02
Pennsylvania	1,323	0.01
Ohio	1,304	0.01
Washington	1,247	0.02
Colorado	1,094	0.02
Maryland	1,076	0.02
Michigan	1,042	0.01
Connecticut	943	0.03
South Carolina	853	0.02
Tennessee	797	0.01
Nevada	762	0.03
Oregon	715	0.02
Wisconsin	666	0.01
Indiana	600	0.01
Minnesota	536	0.01
Missouri	535	0.01
Utah	453	0.02
Louisiana	403	0.01
Alabama	378	0.01
Idaho	335	0.02
Kansas	318	0.01
Iowa	229	0.01
Kentucky	224	0.01
Oklahoma	191	0.01
Hawaii	184	0.01
District of Columbia	182	0.03
New Mexico	163	0.01
Nebraska	160	0.01
Delaware	132	0.01
Rhode Island	128	0.01
Arkansas	124	<0.01
Vermont	122	0.02
New Hampshire	96	0.01
Wyoming	95	0.02
Mississippi	84	<0.01
South Dakota	71	0.01
North Dakota	51	0.01
Maine	49	<0.01
West Virginia	36	<0.01
Montana	24	<0.01
Alaska	17	<0.01

Place	Population	%
Georgia	3,424	0.04
Florida	5,723	0.03
Arizona	1,570	0.03
Connecticut	943	0.03
Nevada	762	0.03
District of Columbia	182	0.03
United States	**53,088**	**0.02**
California	8,602	0.02
New York	3,993	0.02
Texas	3,814	0.02
New Jersey	2,127	0.02
North Carolina	1,690	0.02
Virginia	1,420	0.02
Massachusetts	1,360	0.02
Washington	1,247	0.02
Colorado	1,094	0.02
Maryland	1,076	0.02
South Carolina	853	0.02
Oregon	715	0.02
Utah	453	0.02
Idaho	335	0.02
Vermont	122	0.02
Wyoming	95	0.02
Illinois	1,623	0.01
Pennsylvania	1,323	0.01
Ohio	1,304	0.01
Michigan	1,042	0.01
Tennessee	797	0.01
Wisconsin	666	0.01
Indiana	600	0.01
Minnesota	536	0.01
Missouri	535	0.01
Louisiana	403	0.01
Alabama	378	0.01
Kansas	318	0.01
Iowa	229	0.01
Kentucky	224	0.01
Oklahoma	191	0.01
Hawaii	184	0.01
New Mexico	163	0.01
Nebraska	160	0.01
Delaware	132	0.01
Rhode Island	128	0.01
New Hampshire	96	0.01
South Dakota	71	0.01
North Dakota	51	0.01
Arkansas	124	<0.01
Mississippi	84	<0.01
Maine	49	<0.01
West Virginia	36	<0.01
Montana	24	<0.01
Alaska	17	<0.01

Please refer to the Explanation of Data in the front of the book for more detailed information.

Ancestry

African, Sub-Saharan: South African

Top 150 Places Sorted by Population

Based on all places, regardless of total population

Place	Population	%
New York, NY (city) Kings County	2,116	0.03
Los Angeles, CA (city) Los Angeles County	1,463	0.04
Manhattan, NY (borough) New York County	1,372	0.09
San Diego, CA (city) San Diego County	869	0.07
Houston, TX (city) Harris County	594	0.03
Dallas, TX (city) Dallas County	465	0.04
Phoenix, AZ (city) Maricopa County	395	0.03
Chicago, IL (city) Cook County	375	0.01
Queens, NY (borough) Queens County	356	0.02
Irvine, CA (city) Orange County	339	0.17
Brooklyn, NY (borough) Kings County	320	0.01
Reno, NV (city) Washoe County	297	0.13
Sandy Springs, GA (city) Fulton County	282	0.31
Seattle, WA (city) King County	281	0.05
Clarkston, GA (city) DeKalb County	267	3.53
Austin, TX (city) Travis County	258	0.03
San Francisco, CA (city) San Francisco County	247	0.03
Denver, CO (city) Denver County	242	0.04
Philadelphia, PA (city) Philadelphia County	235	0.02
Tampa, FL (city) Hillsborough County	229	0.07
Scottsdale, AZ (city) Maricopa County	226	0.10
Atlanta, GA (city) Fulton County	222	0.05
Maplewood, NJ (township) Essex County	216	0.91
Pembroke Pines, FL (city) Broward County	214	0.14
San Jose, CA (city) Santa Clara County	211	0.02
West Linn, OR (city) Clackamas County	201	0.82
Fullerton, CA (city) Orange County	198	0.15
Charlotte, NC (city) Mecklenburg County	194	0.03
Plano, TX (city) Collin County	190	0.07
Fort Lauderdale, FL (city) Broward County	187	0.11
Highlands Ranch, CO (cdp) Douglas County	182	0.19
Washington, DC (city) District of Columbia	182	0.03
New Rochelle, NY (city) Westchester County	179	0.24
Boca Raton, FL (city) Palm Beach County	179	0.21
Naperville, IL (city) DuPage County	179	0.13
Alpharetta, GA (city) Fulton County	175	0.32
Fort Worth, TX (city) Tarrant County	175	0.02
The Woodlands, TX (cdp) Montgomery County	169	0.18
Hollywood, FL (city) Broward County	165	0.12
Kansas City, MO (city) Jackson County	164	0.04
Montgomery, IL (village) Kendall County	163	1.02
Raleigh, NC (city) Wake County	163	0.04
Innsbrook, VA (cdp) Henrico County	159	2.17
Sarasota Springs, FL (cdp) Sarasota County	153	1.06
Carmichael, CA (cdp) Sacramento County	152	0.25
Sacramento, CA (city) Sacramento County	149	0.03
Peachtree City, GA (city) Fayette County	145	0.42
Waltham, MA (city) Middlesex County	141	0.24
Tucson, AZ (city) Pima County	139	0.03
Manhattan Beach, CA (city) Los Angeles County	138	0.40
Lower Merion, PA (township) Montgomery County	137	0.24
Carmel, IN (city) Hamilton County	137	0.18
Stamford, CT (city/town) Fairfield County	128	0.11
Milwaukee, WI (city) Milwaukee County	128	0.02
New Orleans, LA (city) Orleans Parish	127	0.04
Newport Beach, CA (city) Orange County	125	0.15
Flower Mound, TX (town) Denton County	124	0.20
Oakland, FL (town) Orange County	123	5.39
Ann Arbor, MI (city) Washtenaw County	123	0.11
Santa Clarita, CA (city) Los Angeles County	123	0.07
Boston, MA (city) Suffolk County	123	0.02
Cary, NC (town) Wake County	121	0.09
Murrieta, CA (city) Riverside County	118	0.12
Santa Ana, CA (city) Orange County	118	0.04
Catalina Foothills, AZ (cdp) Pima County	116	0.22
Coral Springs, FL (city) Broward County	116	0.10
Columbus, OH (city) Franklin County	115	0.01
Bloomingdale, FL (cdp) Hillsborough County	113	0.52
Crestline, CA (cdp) San Bernardino County	112	1.25
Mountain Home AFB, ID (cdp) Elmore County	110	3.04
Mount Pleasant, SC (town) Charleston County	108	0.17
Lincoln, NE (city) Lancaster County	108	0.04
Henderson, NV (city) Clark County	107	0.04
Cambridge, MA (city) Middlesex County	105	0.10
Hempstead, NY (town) Nassau County	104	0.01

Place	Population	%
Cheval, FL (cdp) Hillsborough County	103	1.00
Weston, FL (city) Broward County	103	0.16
Medford, OR (city) Jackson County	103	0.14
Las Vegas, NV (city) Clark County	103	0.02
Penn Forest, PA (township) Carbon County	102	1.15
Bluefield, VA (town) Tazewell County	101	1.86
Richmond, VA (ind. city) Richmond independent city	101	0.05
Concord, CA (city) Contra Costa County	100	0.08
Celebration, FL (cdp) Osceola County	99	1.28
Plantation, FL (city) Broward County	99	0.12
Palo Alto, CA (city) Santa Clara County	97	0.16
Laramie, WY (city) Albany County	95	0.32
Leawood, KS (city) Johnson County	95	0.30
Bullhead City, AZ (city) Mohave County	95	0.24
Griffin, GA (city) Spalding County	94	0.40
Miami Beach, FL (city) Miami-Dade County	94	0.11
Teaneck, NJ (township) Bergen County	93	0.24
White Oak, MD (cdp) Montgomery County	92	0.55
Newton, MA (city) Middlesex County	92	0.11
Berkeley, CA (city) Alameda County	92	0.08
Wellington, FL (village) Palm Beach County	91	0.17
Mine Hill, NJ (township) Morris County	90	2.46
Mequon, WI (city) Ozaukee County	90	0.39
Glen Burnie, MD (cdp) Anne Arundel County	90	0.14
Running Springs, CA (cdp) San Bernardino County	87	1.72
Cherry Creek, CO (cdp) Arapahoe County	86	0.80
Mercer Island, WA (city) King County	86	0.38
Derry, PA (township) Dauphin County	86	0.36
West Milford, NJ (township) Passaic County	86	0.33
Baltimore, MD (city) Baltimore city County	86	0.01
Margate, FL (city) Broward County	85	0.16
Clemmons, NC (village) Forsyth County	83	0.46
Dunwoody, GA (city) DeKalb County	83	0.19
Mountain View, CA (city) Santa Clara County	83	0.11
Palmdale, CA (city) Los Angeles County	83	0.06
Issaquah, WA (city) King County	82	0.29
Hillsborough, NJ (township) Somerset County	82	0.22
Apopka, FL (city) Orange County	82	0.21
Bothell, WA (city) King County	81	0.25
Beaverton, OR (city) Washington County	81	0.09
Scarsdale, NY (town/village) Westchester County	80	0.47
Clermont, FL (city) Lake County	80	0.31
Cortlandt, NY (town) Westchester County	80	0.20
Roswell, GA (city) Fulton County	80	0.09
Beachwood, OH (city) Cuyahoga County	79	0.66
Skokie, IL (village) Cook County	79	0.12
White Plains, NY (city) Westchester County	78	0.14
Laguna Niguel, CA (city) Orange County	78	0.12
Johns Creek, GA (city) Fulton County	78	0.11
Mount Pleasant, NY (town) Westchester County	77	0.18
Rocklin, CA (city) Placer County	77	0.14
Santa Monica, CA (city) Los Angeles County	77	0.09
Mission Viejo, CA (city) Orange County	77	0.08
Sutton, MA (town) Worcester County	76	0.86
Sammamish, WA (city) King County	76	0.18
Greenville, OH (city) Darke County	75	0.57
Pacifica, CA (city) San Mateo County	75	0.20
Tustin, CA (city) Orange County	75	0.10
West Palm Beach, FL (city) Palm Beach County	75	0.08
Lakewood, CO (city) Jefferson County	75	0.05
Durham, NC (city) Durham County	75	0.03
Detroit, MI (city) Wayne County	75	0.01
Northborough, MA (town) Worcester County	74	0.52
Harbor Bluffs, FL (cdp) Pinellas County	73	2.49
Franklin, TN (city) Williamson County	73	0.12
Virginia Beach, VA (ind. city) Virginia Beach independent city	73	0.02
Cave Spring, VA (cdp) Roanoke County	72	0.28
Chattanooga, TN (city) Hamilton County	72	0.04
Sarasota, FL (city) Sarasota County	71	0.13
Arlington, TX (city) Tarrant County	71	0.02
Signal Mountain, TN (town) Hamilton County	70	0.94
Poway, CA (city) San Diego County	70	0.15
Pocatello, ID (city) Bannock County	70	0.13
Jacksonville, FL (city) Duval County	70	0.01
Laguna Beach, CA (city) Orange County	69	0.30

Please refer to the Explanation of Data in the front of the book for more detailed information.

Ancestry

African, Sub-Saharan: South African

Top 150 Places Sorted by Percent of Total Population

Based on all places, regardless of total population

Place	Population	%
Linwood, NY (cdp) Livingston County	64	48.85
Miesville, MN (city) Dakota County	24	22.64
Halliday, ND (city) Dunn County	23	10.95
Dora, NM (village) Roosevelt County	19	8.19
Cleveland, ND (city) Stutsman County	12	7.10
McGregor, IA (city) Clayton County	47	5.51
Oakland, FL (town) Orange County	123	5.39
Westwood Shores, TX (cdp) Trinity County	54	5.31
Yogaville, VA (cdp) Buckingham County	12	4.76
Foster, MN (township) Faribault County	10	4.44
Naples, SD (town) Clark County	1	3.85
Dovray, MN (township) Murray County	6	3.82
Clarkston, GA (city) DeKalb County	267	3.53
Maunaloa, HI (cdp) Maui County	18	3.33
Schell City, MO (city) Vernon County	10	3.30
South Coventry, CT (cdp) Tolland County	44	3.24
Bird Island, MN (township) Renville County	6	3.19
Scotland, SD (city) Bon Homme County	27	3.18
Sylvanite, MT (cdp) Lincoln County	3	3.16
Laughlin AFB, TX (cdp) Val Verde County	43	3.11
Mountain Home AFB, ID (cdp) Elmore County	110	3.04
Clifton, KS (city) Washington County	14	3.03
Coy, AR (town) Lonoke County	3	2.83
Harbor Bluffs, FL (cdp) Pinellas County	73	2.49
Mine Hill, NJ (township) Morris County	90	2.46
East Lansing, MI (city) Clinton County	36	2.42
Lyon, MI (township) Roscommon County	36	2.39
Bishop, GA (town) Oconee County	7	2.27
Nora Springs, IA (city) Floyd County	35	2.25
Cobb, CA (cdp) Lake County	43	2.22
Cape Vincent, NY (village) Jefferson County	15	2.21
Innsbrook, VA (cdp) Henrico County	159	2.17
Vesta, MN (city) Redwood County	7	2.01
York, NY (town) Livingston County	64	1.89
Haw River, NC (town) Alamance County	35	1.89
Bluefield, VA (town) Tazewell County	101	1.86
Tripp, SD (city) Hutchinson County	11	1.83
Cienega Springs, AZ (cdp) La Paz County	52	1.81
Arlington, WI (town) Columbia County	17	1.75
Running Springs, CA (cdp) San Bernardino County	87	1.72
Kinderhook, NY (village) Columbia County	24	1.71
Golden Beach, FL (town) Miami-Dade County	14	1.71
Washburn, WI (town) Bayfield County	7	1.67
Cochiti Lake, NM (cdp) Sandoval County	8	1.63
Fremont, MI (township) Saginaw County	27	1.37
Woodsburgh, NY (village) Nassau County	10	1.34
Celebration, FL (cdp) Osceola County	99	1.28
Crestline, CA (cdp) San Bernardino County	112	1.25
Caliente, NV (city) Lincoln County	11	1.25
Marin City, CA (cdp) Marin County	35	1.24
Dalworthington Gardens, TX (city) Tarrant County	29	1.24
Sudan, TX (city) Lamb County	12	1.23
Greendale, MO (city) St. Louis County	8	1.16
Penn Forest, PA (township) Carbon County	102	1.15
Star City, WV (town) Monongalia County	20	1.14
Cherrytree, PA (township) Venango County	16	1.10
Sarasota Springs, FL (cdp) Sarasota County	153	1.06
Rhinebeck, NY (village) Dutchess County	29	1.05
Montgomery, IL (village) Kendall County	163	1.02
Davis Junction, IL (village) Ogle County	22	1.01
Cheval, FL (cdp) Hillsborough County	103	1.00
Buck, PA (township) Luzerne County	3	0.99
Lantana, TX (cdp) Denton County	57	0.97
Indian Hills, NV (cdp) Douglas County	54	0.97
Signal Mountain, TN (town) Hamilton County	70	0.94
Ligonier, IN (city) Noble County	40	0.93
Hudson Bend, TX (cdp) Travis County	28	0.93
Great Neck Estates, NY (village) Nassau County	25	0.92
Maplewood, NJ (township) Essex County	216	0.91
Montrose-Ghent, OH (cdp) Summit County	46	0.90
Biltmore Forest, NC (town) Buncombe County	14	0.90
Cambridge, ID (city) Washington County	3	0.90
Sutton, MA (town) Worcester County	76	0.86
University, MS (cdp) Lafayette County	37	0.85
Pomona, NY (village) Rockland County	30	0.85
Orange, OH (village) Cuyahoga County	28	0.85
West Linn, OR (city) Clackamas County	201	0.82
Lewiston, MN (city) Winona County	15	0.82
Waterbury, VT (village) Washington County	18	0.81
Cherry Creek, CO (cdp) Arapahoe County	86	0.80
Morton, WA (city) Lewis County	10	0.80
Pelham Manor, NY (village) Westchester County	43	0.79
Norton, MN (township) Winona County	5	0.78
Dunellen, NJ (borough) Middlesex County	55	0.77
Brookline, NH (town) Hillsborough County	37	0.76
Orangeburg, NY (cdp) Rockland County	33	0.76
Margaret, AL (town) St. Clair County	29	0.75
San Juan Bautista, CA (city) San Benito County	11	0.75
Lynn, MN (township) McLeod County	4	0.75
Collegeville, PA (borough) Montgomery County	38	0.74
Lockland, OH (village) Hamilton County	25	0.72
Hopewell, IL (village) Marshall County	3	0.72
Wood Village, OR (city) Multnomah County	26	0.71
Constable, NY (town) Franklin County	9	0.71
Northfield, OH (village) Summit County	26	0.70
Glenville, CT (cdp) Fairfield County	17	0.70
Ashland, KS (city) Clark County	8	0.70
Clear Lake, IN (town) Steuben County	3	0.70
Middlebury, VT (cdp) Addison County	45	0.69
Castle Hills, TX (city) Bexar County	28	0.68
Cedarhurst, NY (village) Nassau County	43	0.67
Beachwood, OH (city) Cuyahoga County	79	0.66
Gotha, FL (cdp) Orange County	13	0.66
Milford, PA (borough) Pike County	7	0.66
Martin's Additions, MD (village) Montgomery County	6	0.66
Eastgate, WA (cdp) King County	34	0.65
Wickenburg, AZ (town) Maricopa County	41	0.63
Ruckersville, VA (cdp) Greene County	7	0.63
Huntleigh, MO (city) St. Louis County	2	0.63
Otterbein, IN (town) Benton County	7	0.62
Pebble Creek, FL (cdp) Hillsborough County	46	0.61
White Rock, NM (cdp) Los Alamos County	36	0.61
Weaverville, NC (town) Buncombe County	19	0.61
Hamburg, NY (village) Erie County	57	0.60
Essex Village, CT (cdp) Middlesex County	15	0.60
Perry, MI (city) Shiawassee County	13	0.60
Knollwood, IL (cdp) Lake County	10	0.60
Bakersfield, VT (town) Franklin County	8	0.60
Beaver Dam, WI (town) Dodge County	23	0.59
Sleepy Hollow, IL (village) Kane County	20	0.59
Larchmont, NY (village) Westchester County	34	0.58
Silt, CO (town) Garfield County	16	0.58
Bannockburn, IL (village) Lake County	8	0.58
Greenville, OH (city) Darke County	75	0.57
Neptune Beach, FL (city) Duval County	40	0.57
White Oak, MD (cdp) Montgomery County	92	0.55
Rumson, NJ (borough) Monmouth County	39	0.55
Bamberg, SC (town) Bamberg County	20	0.55
Hansen, ID (city) Twin Falls County	5	0.55
Browns Point, WA (cdp) Pierce County	6	0.54
Middlebury, VT (town) Addison County	45	0.53
Manchester, VT (village) Bennington County	4	0.53
Bloomingdale, FL (cdp) Hillsborough County	113	0.52
Northborough, MA (town) Worcester County	74	0.52
Nelson, WI (village) Buffalo County	2	0.52
Short Hills, NJ (cdp) Essex County	67	0.51
Walthourville, GA (city) Liberty County	21	0.51
Courtland, MN (city) Nicollet County	3	0.51
Jewett City, CT (borough) New London County	17	0.50
Cape Vincent, NY (town) Jefferson County	15	0.50
Lake Mary, FL (city) Seminole County	67	0.49
Lone Tree, CO (city) Douglas County	48	0.49
Felton, CA (cdp) Santa Cruz County	22	0.49
Hope, NJ (township) Warren County	10	0.49
Springfield, NY (town) Otsego County	7	0.49
Lansdowne, PA (borough) Delaware County	51	0.48
Ludlow, VT (village) Windsor County	4	0.48
Oak City, UT (town) Millard County	3	0.48
Scarsdale, NY (town/village) Westchester County	80	0.47
Prairie du Chien, WI (city) Crawford County	28	0.47

Please refer to the Explanation of Data in the front of the book for more detailed information.

Ancestry

African, Sub-Saharan: South African

Top 150 Places Sorted by Percent of Total Population

Based on places with total population of 7,500 or more

Place	Population	%
Clarkston, GA (city) DeKalb County	267	3.53
Celebration, FL (cdp) Osceola County	99	1.28
Crestline, CA (cdp) San Bernardino County	112	1.25
Penn Forest, PA (township) Carbon County	102	1.15
Sarasota Springs, FL (cdp) Sarasota County	153	1.06
Montgomery, IL (village) Kendall County	163	1.02
Cheval, FL (cdp) Hillsborough County	103	1.00
Maplewood, NJ (township) Essex County	216	0.91
Sutton, MA (town) Worcester County	76	0.86
West Linn, OR (city) Clackamas County	201	0.82
Cherry Creek, CO (cdp) Arapahoe County	86	0.80
Beachwood, OH (city) Cuyahoga County	79	0.66
Pebble Creek, FL (cdp) Hillsborough County	46	0.61
Hamburg, NY (village) Erie County	57	0.60
Greenville, OH (city) Darke County	75	0.57
White Oak, MD (cdp) Montgomery County	92	0.55
Middlebury, VT (town) Addison County	45	0.53
Bloomingdale, FL (cdp) Hillsborough County	113	0.52
Northborough, MA (town) Worcester County	74	0.52
Short Hills, NJ (cdp) Essex County	67	0.51
Lake Mary, FL (city) Seminole County	67	0.49
Lone Tree, CO (city) Douglas County	48	0.49
Lansdowne, PA (borough) Delaware County	51	0.48
Scarsdale, NY (town/village) Westchester County	80	0.47
Clemmons, NC (village) Forsyth County	83	0.46
Lincoln Park, NJ (borough) Morris County	47	0.44
Ormond-by-the-Sea, FL (cdp) Volusia County	34	0.44
Peachtree City, GA (city) Fayette County	145	0.42
Lindon, UT (city) Utah County	41	0.42
Waimea, HI (cdp) Hawaii County	40	0.41
Manhattan Beach, CA (city) Los Angeles County	138	0.40
Griffin, GA (city) Spalding County	94	0.40
Middleton, WI (city) Dane County	68	0.40
Mequon, WI (city) Ozaukee County	90	0.39
Colonial Heights, VA (ind. city) Colonial Heights independent city	68	0.39
Hartland, MI (township) Livingston County	56	0.39
Mercer Island, WA (city) King County	86	0.38
Robbinsville, NJ (township) Mercer County	49	0.38
Douglas, MA (town) Worcester County	31	0.38
Rhinebeck, NY (town) Dutchess County	29	0.38
Bellaire, TX (city) Harris County	61	0.37
Waunakee, WI (village) Dane County	43	0.37
Upper Providence, PA (township) Delaware County	38	0.37
Derry, PA (township) Dauphin County	86	0.36
Southchase, FL (cdp) Orange County	59	0.36
Beaver Dam, WI (city) Dodge County	58	0.36
Coventry, CT (town) Tolland County	44	0.36
Nantucket, MA (cdp) Nantucket County	29	0.36
Mantua, NJ (township) Gloucester County	53	0.35
Pelham, NY (town) Westchester County	43	0.35
Lighthouse Point, FL (city) Broward County	37	0.35
Milford, NH (cdp) Hillsborough County	32	0.35
Woodlake, VA (cdp) Chesterfield County	28	0.35
Millburn, NJ (township) Essex County	67	0.34
Jollyville, TX (cdp) Williamson County	54	0.34
Pennfield, MI (charter township) Calhoun County	31	0.34
West Milford, NJ (township) Passaic County	86	0.33
Wyckoff, NJ (township) Bergen County	54	0.33
Pismo Beach, CA (city) San Luis Obispo County	26	0.33
Alpharetta, GA (city) Fulton County	175	0.32
Laramie, WY (city) Albany County	95	0.32
Sharon, MA (town) Norfolk County	55	0.32
New Fairfield, CT (town) Fairfield County	44	0.32
Travilah, MD (cdp) Montgomery County	39	0.32
Lehigh, PA (township) Northampton County	33	0.32
Franklin, LA (city) St. Mary Parish	25	0.32
Oradell, NJ (borough) Bergen County	25	0.32
Sandy Springs, GA (city) Fulton County	282	0.31
Clermont, FL (city) Lake County	80	0.31
Acworth, GA (city) Cobb County	59	0.31
Monfort Heights, OH (cdp) Hamilton County	36	0.31
Annapolis Neck, MD (cdp) Anne Arundel County	34	0.31
Leawood, KS (city) Johnson County	95	0.30
Laguna Beach, CA (city) Orange County	69	0.30
Easley, SC (city) Pickens County	60	0.30
Prospect Heights, IL (city) Cook County	49	0.30
Cloverly, MD (cdp) Montgomery County	47	0.30
Montecito, CA (cdp) Santa Barbara County	28	0.30
Issaquah, WA (city) King County	82	0.29
Nantucket, MA (town) Nantucket County	29	0.29
Cave Spring, VA (cdp) Roanoke County	72	0.28
Prairie Village, KS (city) Johnson County	61	0.28
Lake Butler, FL (cdp) Orange County	44	0.28
Clayton, MO (city) St. Louis County	43	0.28
Barton, NY (town) Tioga County	25	0.28
Kinderhook, NY (town) Columbia County	24	0.28
Holly Springs, GA (city) Cherokee County	23	0.28
Avon, CT (town) Hartford County	47	0.27
North Aurora, IL (village) Kane County	42	0.27
Solana Beach, CA (city) San Diego County	34	0.27
Roxborough Park, CO (cdp) Douglas County	25	0.27
Camas, WA (city) Clark County	47	0.26
New Territory, TX (cdp) Fort Bend County	43	0.26
Truckee, CA (town) Nevada County	41	0.26
Kettering, MD (cdp) Prince George's County	32	0.26
Collegedale, TN (city) Hamilton County	21	0.26
Broussard, LA (city) Lafayette Parish	20	0.26
Carmichael, CA (cdp) Sacramento County	152	0.25
Bothell, WA (city) King County	81	0.25
Ridgefield, CT (town) Fairfield County	60	0.25
Key Biscayne, FL (village) Miami-Dade County	30	0.25
New Rochelle, NY (city) Westchester County	179	0.24
Waltham, MA (city) Middlesex County	141	0.24
Lower Merion, PA (township) Montgomery County	137	0.24
Bullhead City, AZ (city) Mohave County	95	0.24
Teaneck, NJ (township) Bergen County	93	0.24
Parkland, FL (city) Broward County	54	0.24
Woodstock, GA (city) Cherokee County	53	0.24
Somerset, MA (cdp/town) Bristol County	44	0.24
Glasgow, DE (cdp) New Castle County	38	0.24
Sedona, AZ (city) Yavapai County	25	0.24
York, NE (city) York County	19	0.24
New Castle, NY (town) Westchester County	40	0.23
Morrisville, NC (town) Wake County	37	0.23
Meadville, PA (city) Crawford County	31	0.23
Brambleton, VA (cdp) Loudoun County	20	0.23
Mahtomedi, MN (city) Washington County	18	0.23
Catalina Foothills, AZ (cdp) Pima County	116	0.22
Hillsborough, NJ (township) Somerset County	82	0.22
Windsor, CT (town) Hartford County	64	0.22
Four Corners, FL (cdp) Lake County	57	0.22
Daphne, AL (city) Baldwin County	46	0.22
Ardmore, PA (cdp) Montgomery County	27	0.22
Weston, CT (town) Fairfield County	22	0.22
Boca Raton, FL (city) Palm Beach County	179	0.21
Apopka, FL (city) Orange County	82	0.21
Nacogdoches, TX (city) Nacogdoches County	68	0.21
Isla Vista, CA (cdp) Santa Barbara County	49	0.21
Raritan, NJ (township) Hunterdon County	47	0.21
Milford, NH (town) Hillsborough County	32	0.21
Fruitville, FL (cdp) Sarasota County	29	0.21
Catalina, AZ (cdp) Pima County	17	0.21
Flower Mound, TX (town) Denton County	124	0.20
Cortlandt, NY (town) Westchester County	80	0.20
Pacifica, CA (city) San Mateo County	75	0.20
Bridgewater, MA (town) Plymouth County	53	0.20
Wekiwa Springs, FL (cdp) Seminole County	46	0.20
Moraga, CA (town) Contra Costa County	32	0.20
Berkeley, MO (city) St. Louis County	18	0.20
Garrison, MD (cdp) Baltimore County	15	0.20
Highlands Ranch, CO (cdp) Douglas County	182	0.19
Dunwoody, GA (city) DeKalb County	83	0.19
Storrs, CT (cdp) Tolland County	27	0.19
Burtonsville, MD (cdp) Montgomery County	18	0.19
Lopatcong, NJ (township) Warren County	15	0.19
The Woodlands, TX (cdp) Montgomery County	169	0.18
Carmel, IN (city) Hamilton County	137	0.18
Mount Pleasant, NY (town) Westchester County	77	0.18
Sammamish, WA (city) King County	76	0.18
Lake Oswego, OR (city) Clackamas County	65	0.18

SECTION THREE

Please refer to the Explanation of Data in the front of the book for more detailed information.

Ancestry

African, Sub-Saharan: Sudanese

U.S. and 50 States Sorted by Population and Percent of Total Population

Place	Population	%
United States	**38,432**	**0.01**
Virginia	3,441	0.04
Texas	3,279	0.01
California	3,028	0.01
Nebraska	3,016	0.17
New York	2,137	0.01
North Carolina	1,880	0.02
Minnesota	1,787	0.03
Arizona	1,651	0.03
Tennessee	1,386	0.02
Colorado	1,202	0.02
Iowa	1,178	0.04
New Jersey	1,075	0.01
Pennsylvania	1,027	0.01
Florida	943	0.01
Michigan	846	0.01
New Hampshire	843	0.06
Maine	788	0.06
Utah	720	0.03
Missouri	707	0.01
Maryland	661	0.01
Illinois	585	<0.01
Alaska	558	0.08
Georgia	542	0.01
Massachusetts	483	0.01
Alabama	456	0.01
South Dakota	443	0.06
Indiana	433	0.01
Oklahoma	428	0.01
Ohio	385	<0.01
Kansas	362	0.01
Washington	350	0.01
Kentucky	316	0.01
Connecticut	292	0.01
Wisconsin	182	<0.01
Nevada	177	0.01
Mississippi	172	0.01
South Carolina	145	<0.01
Idaho	127	0.01
Oregon	97	<0.01
Rhode Island	82	0.01
Delaware	70	0.01
District of Columbia	51	0.01
North Dakota	43	0.01
Vermont	35	0.01
Arkansas	16	<0.01
Louisiana	7	<0.01
Hawaii	0	0.00
Montana	0	0.00
New Mexico	0	0.00
West Virginia	0	0.00
Wyoming	0	0.00

Place	Population	%
Nebraska	3,016	0.17
Alaska	558	0.08
New Hampshire	843	0.06
Maine	788	0.06
South Dakota	443	0.06
Virginia	3,441	0.04
Iowa	1,178	0.04
Minnesota	1,787	0.03
Arizona	1,651	0.03
Utah	720	0.03
North Carolina	1,880	0.02
Tennessee	1,386	0.02
Colorado	1,202	0.02
United States	**38,432**	**0.01**
Texas	3,279	0.01
California	3,028	0.01
New York	2,137	0.01
New Jersey	1,075	0.01
Pennsylvania	1,027	0.01
Florida	943	0.01
Michigan	846	0.01
Missouri	707	0.01
Maryland	661	0.01
Georgia	542	0.01
Massachusetts	483	0.01
Alabama	456	0.01
Indiana	433	0.01
Oklahoma	428	0.01
Kansas	362	0.01
Washington	350	0.01
Kentucky	316	0.01
Connecticut	292	0.01
Nevada	177	0.01
Mississippi	172	0.01
Idaho	127	0.01
Rhode Island	82	0.01
Delaware	70	0.01
District of Columbia	51	0.01
North Dakota	43	0.01
Vermont	35	0.01
Illinois	585	<0.01
Ohio	385	<0.01
Wisconsin	182	<0.01
South Carolina	145	<0.01
Oregon	97	<0.01
Arkansas	16	<0.01
Louisiana	7	<0.01
Hawaii	0	0.00
Montana	0	0.00
New Mexico	0	0.00
West Virginia	0	0.00
Wyoming	0	0.00

Please refer to the Explanation of Data in the front of the book for more detailed information.

Ancestry

African, Sub-Saharan: Sudanese

Top 150 Places Sorted by Population

Based on all places, regardless of total population

Place	Population	%
New York, NY (city) Kings County	1,303	0.02
Greensboro, NC (city) Guilford County	1,144	0.43
Phoenix, AZ (city) Maricopa County	1,144	0.08
Omaha, NE (city) Douglas County	1,060	0.26
San Diego, CA (city) San Diego County	1,036	0.08
Manchester, NH (city) Hillsborough County	843	0.77
Brooklyn, NY (borough) Kings County	731	0.03
Lincoln, NE (city) Lancaster County	703	0.28
Nashville-Davidson, TN (metro govt) Davidson County	653	0.11
Denver, CO (city) Denver County	634	0.11
Bellevue, NE (city) Sarpy County	628	1.25
Kansas City, MO (city) Jackson County	544	0.12
Houston, TX (city) Harris County	541	0.03
Reston, VA (cdp) Fairfax County	525	0.99
Euless, TX (city) Tarrant County	518	1.03
Dallas, TX (city) Dallas County	491	0.04
North Brunswick, NJ (township) Middlesex County	481	1.20
Salt Lake City, UT (city) Salt Lake County	466	0.25
Alexandria, VA (ind. city) Alexandria independent city	450	0.34
Jacksonville, FL (city) Duval County	425	0.05
Portland, ME (city) Cumberland County	416	0.63
Sioux Falls, SD (city) Minnehaha County	404	0.27
Des Moines, IA (city) Polk County	396	0.20
Oklahoma City, OK (city) Oklahoma County	385	0.07
Anchorage, AK (municipality) Anchorage Municipality	382	0.13
Indianapolis, IN (city) Marion County	376	0.05
High Point, NC (city) Guilford County	327	0.32
Grand Island, NE (city) Hall County	315	0.67
Tucson, AZ (city) Pima County	315	0.06
Arlington, VA (cdp) Arlington County	292	0.15
Queens, NY (borough) Queens County	286	0.01
Grand Rapids, MI (city) Kent County	285	0.15
South Portland, ME (city) Cumberland County	280	1.13
Auburn, AL (city) Lee County	273	0.53
Buffalo, NY (city) Erie County	268	0.10
Louisville-Jefferson County, KY (metro govt) Jefferson County	245	0.04
Amarillo, TX (city) Potter County	244	0.13
Lansing, MI (city) Ingham County	239	0.22
Lansing, MI (city) Ingham County	239	0.21
Lincolnia, VA (cdp) Fairfax County	235	1.14
Lake Barcroft, VA (cdp) Fairfax County	229	2.53
Irving, TX (city) Dallas County	229	0.11
Centreville, VA (cdp) Fairfax County	225	0.31
Chicago, IL (city) Cook County	225	0.01
Erie, PA (city) Erie County	221	0.22
Swatara, PA (township) Dauphin County	217	0.94
Richardson, TX (city) Dallas County	214	0.22
Newport News, VA (ind. city) Newport News independent city	208	0.11
Jersey City, NJ (city) Hudson County	203	0.08
Kansas City, KS (city) Wyandotte County	193	0.13
Mankato, MN (city) Blue Earth County	191	0.50
Mankato, MN (city) Blue Earth County	191	0.50
Rochester, MN (city) Olmsted County	189	0.18
St. Paul, MN (city) Ramsey County	188	0.07
Los Angeles, CA (city) Los Angeles County	184	<0.01
Lynn, MA (city) Essex County	183	0.20
Allen, TX (city) Collin County	181	0.23
Syracuse, NY (city) Onondaga County	177	0.12
Memphis, TN (city) Shelby County	171	0.03
Harrisonburg, VA (ind. city) Harrisonburg independent city	168	0.35
Philadelphia, PA (city) Philadelphia County	167	0.01
Baltimore, MD (city) Baltimore city County	164	0.03
Fort Worth, TX (city) Tarrant County	164	0.02
Burnsville, MN (city) Dakota County	162	0.27
Maryville, TN (city) Blount County	160	0.59
Athens-Clarke County, GA (unified govt) Clarke County	159	0.14
Glen Ellyn, IL (village) DuPage County	157	0.57
Bronx, NY (borough) Bronx County	149	0.01
Clarkston, GA (city) DeKalb County	144	1.91
Muscle Shoals, AL (city) Colbert County	143	1.10
Woodbury, MN (city) Washington County	143	0.24
Franconia, VA (cdp) Fairfax County	141	0.76
Manhattan, NY (borough) New York County	137	0.01
Fair Oaks, VA (cdp) Fairfax County	134	0.49
Durham, NC (city) Durham County	134	0.06
Olathe, KS (city) Johnson County	133	0.11
Hybla Valley, VA (cdp) Fairfax County	131	0.90
Minneapolis, MN (city) Hennepin County	131	0.03
Cedar Rapids, IA (city) Linn County	128	0.10
Sterling, VA (cdp) Loudoun County	127	0.50
Long Beach, CA (city) Los Angeles County	126	0.03
Bloomington, MN (city) Hennepin County	120	0.15
Nampa, ID (city) Canyon County	118	0.15
Rosemount, MN (city) Dakota County	115	0.56
Edina, MN (city) Hennepin County	115	0.24
West Hartford, CT (cdp/town) Hartford County	115	0.18
Fresno, CA (city) Fresno County	109	0.02
Bailey's Crossroads, VA (cdp) Fairfax County	107	0.51
Fayetteville, NC (city) Cumberland County	107	0.05
Rochester, NY (city) Monroe County	107	0.05
Austin, MN (city) Mower County	106	0.43
Millcreek, UT (cdp) Salt Lake County	106	0.17
Bridgeport, CT (city/town) Fairfield County	106	0.07
La Vista, NE (city) Sarpy County	105	0.70
White Oak, MD (cdp) Montgomery County	104	0.62
Gallatin, TN (city) Sumner County	104	0.36
Clive, IA (city) Polk County	103	0.69
Hawthorne, CA (city) Los Angeles County	102	0.12
Charlotte, NC (city) Mecklenburg County	101	0.01
Wells Branch, TX (cdp) Travis County	100	0.87
Silver Spring, MD (cdp) Montgomery County	96	0.14
Seekonk, MA (town) Bristol County	95	0.69
Ridgeland, MS (city) Madison County	94	0.40
Urbandale, IA (city) Polk County	94	0.25
La Vergne, TN (city) Rutherford County	93	0.31
SeaTac, WA (city) King County	92	0.35
Lewiston, ME (city) Androscoggin County	92	0.25
Columbus, OH (city) Franklin County	90	0.01
Marshalltown, IA (city) Marshall County	89	0.33
Laurel, VA (cdp) Henrico County	88	0.55
Oshkosh, WI (city) Winnebago County	88	0.13
Chadron, NE (city) Dawes County	87	1.50
Moorhead, MN (city) Clay County	86	0.23
Cleveland, OH (city) Cuyahoga County	86	0.02
City of Orange, NJ (township) Essex County	85	0.28
Union City, NJ (city) Hudson County	83	0.13
San Jose, CA (city) Santa Clara County	81	0.01
Lansdale, PA (borough) Montgomery County	79	0.49
St. Paul, AK (city) Aleutians West Census Area	78	7.32
Oakland, CA (city) Alameda County	78	0.02
Akutan, AK (city) Aleutians East Borough	77	4.82
North Miami Beach, FL (city) Miami-Dade County	77	0.19
Fort Washington, MD (cdp) Prince George's County	73	0.29
Taylorsville, UT (city) Salt Lake County	73	0.13
Portland, OR (city) Multnomah County	73	0.01
Paradise, NV (cdp) Clark County	71	0.03
Storm Lake, IA (city) Buena Vista County	70	0.68
Darnestown, MD (cdp) Montgomery County	69	1.06
Northfield, MN (city) Rice County	65	0.35
Northfield, MN (city) Rice County	65	0.33
Lincoln Park, MI (city) Wayne County	64	0.17
Cincinnati, OH (city) Hamilton County	63	0.02
Mountain House, CA (cdp) San Joaquin County	62	0.83
Santa Clara, CA (city) Santa Clara County	60	0.05
Inkster, MI (city) Wayne County	59	0.22
Linton Hall, VA (cdp) Prince William County	59	0.18
East Lansing, MI (city) Ingham County	58	0.12
East Lansing, MI (city) Ingham County	58	0.12
Iowa City, IA (city) Johnson County	57	0.09
Brockton, MA (city) Plymouth County	57	0.06
Peoria, AZ (city) Yavapai County	57	0.04
Renton, WA (city) King County	56	0.06
Yuma, AZ (city) Yuma County	56	0.06
Annandale, VA (cdp) Fairfax County	55	0.14
Elyria, OH (city) Lorain County	55	0.10
Temecula, CA (city) Riverside County	55	0.06
Chicago Ridge, IL (village) Cook County	54	0.38
Springfield, MA (city) Hampden County	54	0.04
Madison, WI (city) Dane County	53	0.02
West Haven, CT (city/town) New Haven County	51	0.09

Ancestry

African, Sub-Saharan: Sudanese

Top 150 Places Sorted by Percent of Total Population

Based on all places, regardless of total population

Place	Population	%
St. Paul, AK (city) Aleutians West Census Area	78	7.32
French Camp, MS (town) Choctaw County	7	5.19
Akutan, AK (city) Aleutians East Borough	77	4.82
Elk Creek, NE (village) Johnson County	5	4.81
Millbourne, PA (borough) Delaware County	44	4.18
Lake Barcroft, VA (cdp) Fairfax County	229	2.53
Dunnell, MN (city) Martin County	3	1.92
Clarkston, GA (city) DeKalb County	144	1.91
Elmore, MN (city) Faribault County	10	1.63
West Buechel, KY (city) Jefferson County	18	1.61
Chadron, NE (city) Dawes County	87	1.50
Pequot Lakes, MN (city) Crow Wing County	34	1.47
Worthing, SD (city) Lincoln County	11	1.41
Bellevue, NE (city) Sarpy County	628	1.25
North Brunswick, NJ (township) Middlesex County	481	1.20
Lincolnia, VA (cdp) Fairfax County	235	1.14
South Portland, ME (city) Cumberland County	280	1.13
Peru, NE (city) Nemaha County	12	1.11
Muscle Shoals, AL (city) Colbert County	143	1.10
Darnestown, MD (cdp) Montgomery County	69	1.06
Euless, TX (city) Tarrant County	518	1.03
Reston, VA (cdp) Fairfax County	525	0.99
Swatara, PA (township) Dauphin County	217	0.94
Hybla Valley, VA (cdp) Fairfax County	131	0.90
Glen Rose, TX (city) Somervell County	23	0.90
Wells Branch, TX (cdp) Travis County	100	0.87
Mountain House, CA (cdp) San Joaquin County	62	0.83
Princess Anne, MD (town) Somerset County	26	0.83
Manchester, NH (city) Hillsborough County	843	0.77
Franconia, VA (cdp) Fairfax County	141	0.76
La Vista, NE (city) Sarpy County	105	0.70
Oxford, GA (city) Newton County	18	0.70
Clive, IA (city) Polk County	103	0.69
Seekonk, MA (town) Bristol County	95	0.69
Storm Lake, IA (city) Buena Vista County	70	0.68
Norwood, KY (city) Jefferson County	2	0.68
Grand Island, NE (city) Hall County	315	0.67
Mahoning, PA (township) Montour County	27	0.65
Portland, ME (city) Cumberland County	416	0.63
White Oak, MD (cdp) Montgomery County	104	0.62
Northfield, VT (village) Washington County	21	0.61
Maryville, TN (city) Blount County	160	0.59
Leadwood, MO (city) St. Francois County	7	0.58
Glen Ellyn, IL (village) DuPage County	157	0.57
Rosemount, MN (city) Dakota County	115	0.56
Aurora, NE (city) Hamilton County	25	0.56
Laurel, VA (cdp) Henrico County	88	0.55
Hinton, OK (town) Caddo County	14	0.55
Auburn, AL (city) Lee County	273	0.53
Chillicothe, MO (city) Livingston County	47	0.53
Reed City, MI (city) Osceola County	14	0.52
Bailey's Crossroads, VA (cdp) Fairfax County	107	0.51
Mankato, MN (city) Blue Earth County	191	0.50
Mankato, MN (city) Blue Earth County	191	0.50
Sterling, VA (cdp) Loudoun County	127	0.50
Fair Oaks, VA (cdp) Fairfax County	134	0.49
Lansdale, PA (borough) Montgomery County	79	0.49
Northeast Ithaca, NY (cdp) Tompkins County	13	0.49
Amor, MN (township) Otter Tail County	3	0.48
Greensboro, NC (city) Guilford County	1,144	0.43
Austin, MN (city) Mower County	106	0.43
Morrisville, NY (village) Madison County	11	0.43
Riverside, MO (city) Platte County	12	0.41
Ridgeland, MS (city) Madison County	94	0.40
Unalaska, AK (city) Aleutians West Census Area	18	0.40
Mars Hill, NC (town) Madison County	11	0.40
Chicago Ridge, IL (village) Cook County	54	0.38
Lexington, NE (city) Dawson County	38	0.38
Gallatin, TN (city) Sumner County	104	0.36
Harrisonburg, VA (ind. city) Harrisonburg independent city	168	0.35
SeaTac, WA (city) King County	92	0.35
Northfield, MN (city) Rice County	65	0.35
Alexandria, VA (ind. city) Alexandria independent city	450	0.34
Northfield, VT (town) Washington County	21	0.34
Marshalltown, IA (city) Marshall County	89	0.33
Northfield, MN (city) Rice County	65	0.33
High Point, NC (city) Guilford County	327	0.32
Colonial Park, PA (cdp) Dauphin County	42	0.32
Centreville, VA (cdp) Fairfax County	225	0.31
La Vergne, TN (city) Rutherford County	93	0.31
Williamson, NY (town) Wayne County	21	0.30
Fort Washington, MD (cdp) Prince George's County	73	0.29
Deal, NJ (borough) Monmouth County	3	0.29
Lincoln, NE (city) Lancaster County	703	0.28
City of Orange, NJ (township) Essex County	85	0.28
Whitehall, OH (city) Franklin County	50	0.28
New Ellenton, SC (town) Aiken County	6	0.28
Sioux Falls, SD (city) Minnehaha County	404	0.27
Burnsville, MN (city) Dakota County	162	0.27
Coralville, IA (city) Johnson County	50	0.27
West Columbia, SC (city) Lexington County	39	0.27
Omaha, NE (city) Douglas County	1,060	0.26
Pleasant Hill, IA (city) Polk County	21	0.26
Salt Lake City, UT (city) Salt Lake County	466	0.25
Urbandale, IA (city) Polk County	94	0.25
Lewiston, ME (city) Androscoggin County	92	0.25
Dumas, TX (city) Moore County	35	0.25
Seven Corners, VA (cdp) Fairfax County	21	0.25
Wayne, NE (city) Wayne County	14	0.25
Woodbury, MN (city) Washington County	143	0.24
Edina, MN (city) Hennepin County	115	0.24
Middle, DE (town) New Castle County	40	0.24
Bluffton, OH (village) Allen County	10	0.24
Brockway, PA (borough) Jefferson County	5	0.24
Allen, TX (city) Collin County	181	0.23
Moorhead, MN (city) Clay County	86	0.23
Lansing, MI (city) Ingham County	239	0.22
Erie, PA (city) Erie County	221	0.22
Richardson, TX (city) Dallas County	214	0.22
Inkster, MI (city) Wayne County	59	0.22
Lebanon, MO (city) Laclede County	31	0.22
Lansing, MI (city) Ingham County	239	0.21
Crete, NE (city) Saline County	14	0.21
Eaton, NY (town) Madison County	11	0.21
Des Moines, IA (city) Polk County	396	0.20
Lynn, MA (city) Essex County	183	0.20
Kingstowne, VA (cdp) Fairfax County	29	0.20
North Miami Beach, FL (city) Miami-Dade County	77	0.19
Yeadon, PA (borough) Delaware County	22	0.19
Edgefield, SC (town) Edgefield County	9	0.19
Niagara, WI (city) Marinette County	3	0.19
Rochester, MN (city) Olmsted County	189	0.18
West Hartford, CT (cdp/town) Hartford County	115	0.18
Linton Hall, VA (cdp) Prince William County	59	0.18
Ben Lomond, CA (cdp) Santa Cruz County	11	0.18
Millcreek, UT (cdp) Salt Lake County	106	0.17
Lincoln Park, MI (city) Wayne County	64	0.17
Temple Terrace, FL (city) Hillsborough County	42	0.17
Campbellsville, KY (city) Taylor County	16	0.17
Woodlawn, MD (cdp) Prince George's County	11	0.17
Bisbee, AZ (city) Cochise County	10	0.17
Tredyffrin, PA (township) Chester County	47	0.16
Rosemont, CA (cdp) Sacramento County	36	0.16
Englishtown, NJ (borough) Monmouth County	3	0.16
Arlington, VA (cdp) Arlington County	292	0.15
Grand Rapids, MI (city) Kent County	285	0.15
Bloomington, MN (city) Hennepin County	120	0.15
Nampa, ID (city) Canyon County	118	0.15
Denison, IA (city) Crawford County	12	0.15
Newport, PA (township) Luzerne County	8	0.15
Athens-Clarke County, GA (unified govt) Clarke County	159	0.14
Silver Spring, MD (cdp) Montgomery County	96	0.14
Annandale, VA (cdp) Fairfax County	55	0.14
Shakopee, MN (city) Scott County	49	0.14
Chesterton, IN (town) Porter County	19	0.14
Greendale, WI (village) Milwaukee County	19	0.14
Henderson, TX (city) Rusk County	18	0.14
Portland, NY (town) Chautauqua County	7	0.14
Anchorage, AK (municipality) Anchorage Municipality	382	0.13
Amarillo, TX (city) Potter County	244	0.13

Please refer to the Explanation of Data in the front of the book for more detailed information.

Ancestry

African, Sub-Saharan: Sudanese

Top 150 Places Sorted by Percent of Total Population

Based on places with total population of 7,500 or more

Place	Population	%
Lake Barcroft, VA (cdp) Fairfax County	229	2.53
Clarkston, GA (city) DeKalb County	144	1.91
Bellevue, NE (city) Sarpy County	628	1.25
North Brunswick, NJ (township) Middlesex County	481	1.20
Lincolnia, VA (cdp) Fairfax County	235	1.14
South Portland, ME (city) Cumberland County	280	1.13
Muscle Shoals, AL (city) Colbert County	143	1.10
Euless, TX (city) Tarrant County	518	1.03
Reston, VA (cdp) Fairfax County	525	0.99
Swatara, PA (township) Dauphin County	217	0.94
Hybla Valley, VA (cdp) Fairfax County	131	0.90
Wells Branch, TX (cdp) Travis County	100	0.87
Manchester, NH (city) Hillsborough County	843	0.77
Franconia, VA (cdp) Fairfax County	141	0.76
La Vista, NE (city) Sarpy County	105	0.70
Clive, IA (city) Polk County	103	0.69
Seekonk, MA (town) Bristol County	95	0.69
Storm Lake, IA (city) Buena Vista County	70	0.68
Grand Island, NE (city) Hall County	315	0.67
Portland, ME (city) Cumberland County	416	0.63
White Oak, MD (cdp) Montgomery County	104	0.62
Maryville, TN (city) Blount County	160	0.59
Glen Ellyn, IL (village) DuPage County	157	0.57
Rosemount, MN (city) Dakota County	115	0.56
Laurel, VA (cdp) Henrico County	88	0.55
Auburn, AL (city) Lee County	273	0.53
Chillicothe, MO (city) Livingston County	47	0.53
Bailey's Crossroads, VA (cdp) Fairfax County	107	0.51
Mankato, MN (city) Blue Earth County	191	0.50
Mankato, MN (city) Blue Earth County	191	0.50
Sterling, VA (cdp) Loudoun County	127	0.50
Fair Oaks, VA (cdp) Fairfax County	134	0.49
Lansdale, PA (borough) Montgomery County	79	0.49
Greensboro, NC (city) Guilford County	1,144	0.43
Austin, MN (city) Mower County	106	0.43
Ridgeland, MS (city) Madison County	94	0.40
Chicago Ridge, IL (village) Cook County	54	0.38
Lexington, NE (city) Dawson County	38	0.38
Gallatin, TN (city) Sumner County	104	0.36
Harrisonburg, VA (ind. city) Harrisonburg independent city	168	0.35
SeaTac, WA (city) King County	92	0.35
Northfield, MN (city) Rice County	65	0.35
Alexandria, VA (ind. city) Alexandria independent city	450	0.34
Marshalltown, IA (city) Marshall County	89	0.33
Northfield, MN (city) Rice County	65	0.33
High Point, NC (city) Guilford County	327	0.32
Colonial Park, PA (cdp) Dauphin County	42	0.32
Centreville, VA (cdp) Fairfax County	225	0.31
La Vergne, TN (city) Rutherford County	93	0.31
Fort Washington, MD (cdp) Prince George's County	73	0.29
Lincoln, NE (city) Lancaster County	703	0.28
City of Orange, NJ (township) Essex County	85	0.28
Whitehall, OH (city) Franklin County	50	0.28
Sioux Falls, SD (city) Minnehaha County	404	0.27
Burnsville, MN (city) Dakota County	162	0.27
Coralville, IA (city) Johnson County	50	0.27
West Columbia, SC (city) Lexington County	39	0.27
Omaha, NE (city) Douglas County	1,060	0.26
Pleasant Hill, IA (city) Polk County	21	0.26
Salt Lake City, UT (city) Salt Lake County	466	0.25
Urbandale, IA (city) Polk County	94	0.25
Lewiston, ME (city) Androscoggin County	92	0.25
Dumas, TX (city) Moore County	35	0.25
Seven Corners, VA (cdp) Fairfax County	21	0.25
Woodbury, MN (city) Washington County	143	0.24
Edina, MN (city) Hennepin County	115	0.24
Middle, DE (town) New Castle County	40	0.24
Allen, TX (city) Collin County	181	0.23
Moorhead, MN (city) Clay County	86	0.23
Lansing, MI (city) Ingham County	239	0.22
Erie, PA (city) Erie County	221	0.22
Richardson, TX (city) Dallas County	214	0.22
Inkster, MI (city) Wayne County	59	0.22
Lebanon, MO (city) Laclede County	31	0.22
Lansing, MI (city) Ingham County	239	0.21
Des Moines, IA (city) Polk County	396	0.20
Lynn, MA (city) Essex County	183	0.20
Kingstowne, VA (cdp) Fairfax County	29	0.20
North Miami Beach, FL (city) Miami-Dade County	77	0.19
Yeadon, PA (borough) Delaware County	22	0.19
Rochester, MN (city) Olmsted County	189	0.18
West Hartford, CT (cdp/town) Hartford County	115	0.18
Linton Hall, VA (cdp) Prince William County	59	0.18
Millcreek, UT (cdp) Salt Lake County	106	0.17
Lincoln Park, MI (city) Wayne County	64	0.17
Temple Terrace, FL (city) Hillsborough County	42	0.17
Campbellsville, KY (city) Taylor County	16	0.17
Tredyffrin, PA (township) Chester County	47	0.16
Rosemont, CA (cdp) Sacramento County	36	0.16
Arlington, VA (cdp) Arlington County	292	0.15
Grand Rapids, MI (city) Kent County	285	0.15
Bloomington, MN (city) Hennepin County	120	0.15
Nampa, ID (city) Canyon County	118	0.15
Denison, IA (city) Crawford County	12	0.15
Athens-Clarke County, GA (unified govt) Clarke County	159	0.14
Silver Spring, MD (cdp) Montgomery County	96	0.14
Annandale, VA (cdp) Fairfax County	55	0.14
Shakopee, MN (city) Scott County	49	0.14
Chesterton, IN (town) Porter County	19	0.14
Greendale, WI (village) Milwaukee County	19	0.14
Henderson, TX (city) Rusk County	18	0.14
Anchorage, AK (municipality) Anchorage Municipality	382	0.13
Amarillo, TX (city) Potter County	244	0.13
Kansas City, KS (city) Wyandotte County	193	0.13
Oshkosh, WI (city) Winnebago County	88	0.13
Union City, NJ (city) Hudson County	83	0.13
Taylorsville, UT (city) Salt Lake County	73	0.13
Brighton, NY (cdp/town) Monroe County	47	0.13
Fort Dodge, IA (city) Webster County	33	0.13
Creston, IA (city) Union County	10	0.13
Kansas City, MO (city) Jackson County	544	0.12
Syracuse, NY (city) Onondaga County	177	0.12
Hawthorne, CA (city) Los Angeles County	102	0.12
East Lansing, MI (city) Ingham County	58	0.12
East Lansing, MI (city) Ingham County	58	0.12
Melrose Park, IL (village) Cook County	29	0.12
Pontiac, IL (city) Livingston County	15	0.12
Nashville-Davidson, TN (metro govt) Davidson County	653	0.11
Denver, CO (city) Denver County	634	0.11
Irving, TX (city) Dallas County	229	0.11
Newport News, VA (ind. city) Newport News independent city	208	0.11
Olathe, KS (city) Johnson County	133	0.11
Roseville, MN (city) Ramsey County	35	0.11
Agoura Hills, CA (city) Los Angeles County	23	0.11
Port Washington, NY (cdp) Nassau County	17	0.11
Hershey, PA (cdp) Dauphin County	14	0.11
Grinnell, IA (city) Poweshiek County	10	0.11
Buffalo, NY (city) Erie County	268	0.10
Cedar Rapids, IA (city) Linn County	128	0.10
Elyria, OH (city) Lorain County	55	0.10
Burlington, NC (city) Alamance County	48	0.10
Brigham City, UT (city) Box Elder County	18	0.10
Mead Valley, CA (cdp) Riverside County	18	0.10
East San Gabriel, CA (cdp) Los Angeles County	15	0.10
Newington, VA (cdp) Fairfax County	13	0.10
Iowa City, IA (city) Johnson County	57	0.09
West Haven, CT (city/town) New Haven County	51	0.09
Rocklin, CA (city) Placer County	48	0.09
Lower Paxton, PA (township) Dauphin County	42	0.09
University, FL (cdp) Hillsborough County	36	0.09
East Meadow, NY (cdp) Nassau County	33	0.09
Flint, MI (charter township) Genesee County	31	0.09
East Point, GA (city) Fulton County	30	0.09
Winchester, NV (cdp) Clark County	24	0.09
Phoenix, AZ (city) Maricopa County	1,144	0.08
San Diego, CA (city) San Diego County	1,036	0.08
Jersey City, NJ (city) Hudson County	203	0.08
Oakton, VA (cdp) Fairfax County	27	0.08
Norristown, PA (borough) Montgomery County	26	0.08
Harrisburg, NC (town) Cabarrus County	8	0.08

SECTION THREE

Ancestry

African, Sub-Saharan: Ugandan

U.S. and 50 States Sorted by Population and Percent of Total Population

Place	Population	%
United States	**8,565**	**<0.01**
Massachusetts	1,922	0.03
California	1,202	<0.01
Maryland	671	0.01
New York	464	<0.01
Minnesota	424	0.01
Virginia	416	0.01
Colorado	290	0.01
New Jersey	254	<0.01
Georgia	249	<0.01
Texas	226	<0.01
Pennsylvania	215	<0.01
Washington	194	<0.01
New Hampshire	182	0.01
Iowa	150	<0.01
Ohio	139	<0.01
Michigan	129	<0.01
Illinois	117	<0.01
Indiana	109	<0.01
Alabama	102	<0.01
Missouri	87	<0.01
Arizona	86	<0.01
Utah	79	<0.01
Kansas	76	<0.01
District of Columbia	74	0.01
Connecticut	73	<0.01
Oklahoma	73	<0.01
Nevada	72	<0.01
North Dakota	68	0.01
Wisconsin	62	<0.01
Florida	59	<0.01
West Virginia	50	<0.01
Nebraska	41	<0.01
Kentucky	40	<0.01
North Carolina	38	<0.01
Tennessee	30	<0.01
South Carolina	28	<0.01
Vermont	16	<0.01
South Dakota	15	<0.01
Delaware	12	<0.01
New Mexico	12	<0.01
Rhode Island	10	<0.01
Alaska	9	<0.01
Arkansas	0	0.00
Hawaii	0	0.00
Idaho	0	0.00
Louisiana	0	0.00
Maine	0	0.00
Mississippi	0	0.00
Montana	0	0.00
Oregon	0	0.00
Wyoming	0	0.00

Place	Population	%
Massachusetts	1,922	0.03
Maryland	671	0.01
Minnesota	424	0.01
Virginia	416	0.01
Colorado	290	0.01
New Hampshire	182	0.01
District of Columbia	74	0.01
North Dakota	68	0.01
United States	**8,565**	**<0.01**
California	1,202	<0.01
New York	464	<0.01
New Jersey	254	<0.01
Georgia	249	<0.01
Texas	226	<0.01
Pennsylvania	215	<0.01
Washington	194	<0.01
Iowa	150	<0.01
Ohio	139	<0.01
Michigan	129	<0.01
Illinois	117	<0.01
Indiana	109	<0.01
Alabama	102	<0.01
Missouri	87	<0.01
Arizona	86	<0.01
Utah	79	<0.01
Kansas	76	<0.01
Connecticut	73	<0.01
Oklahoma	73	<0.01
Nevada	72	<0.01
Wisconsin	62	<0.01
Florida	59	<0.01
West Virginia	50	<0.01
Nebraska	41	<0.01
Kentucky	40	<0.01
North Carolina	38	<0.01
Tennessee	30	<0.01
South Carolina	28	<0.01
Vermont	16	<0.01
South Dakota	15	<0.01
Delaware	12	<0.01
New Mexico	12	<0.01
Rhode Island	10	<0.01
Alaska	9	<0.01
Arkansas	0	0.00
Hawaii	0	0.00
Idaho	0	0.00
Louisiana	0	0.00
Maine	0	0.00
Mississippi	0	0.00
Montana	0	0.00
Oregon	0	0.00
Wyoming	0	0.00

Please refer to the Explanation of Data in the front of the book for more detailed information.

Ancestry

African, Sub-Saharan: Ugandan

Top 150 Places Sorted by Population

Based on all places, regardless of total population

Place	Population	%
Los Angeles, CA (city) Los Angeles County	491	0.01
Malden, MA (city) Middlesex County	481	0.83
Waltham, MA (city) Middlesex County	279	0.47
New York, NY (city) Kings County	256	<0.01
Aurora, CO (city) Arapahoe County	206	0.07
Dale City, VA (cdp) Prince William County	193	0.30
Boston, MA (city) Suffolk County	183	0.03
Melrose, MA (city) Middlesex County	174	0.65
Santa Rosa, CA (city) Sonoma County	146	0.09
Brooklyn Park, MN (city) Hennepin County	141	0.19
Roseville, MN (city) Ramsey County	132	0.40
Manhattan, NY (borough) New York County	125	0.01
Rock Valley, IA (city) Sioux County	121	3.70
Everett, MA (city) Middlesex County	115	0.28
Watertown Town, MA (city) Middlesex County	110	0.35
Rancho Cordova, CA (city) Sacramento County	108	0.17
Layhill, MD (cdp) Montgomery County	99	1.74
Salem, NH (town) Rockingham County	99	0.34
Fairland, MD (cdp) Montgomery County	96	0.42
Burlington, MA (cdp/town) Middlesex County	90	0.38
Spring Valley, NY (village) Rockland County	86	0.28
Ramapo, NY (town) Rockland County	86	0.07
Richmond, VA (ind. city) Richmond independent city	82	0.04
Queens, NY (borough) Queens County	77	<0.01
Temecula, CA (city) Riverside County	76	0.08
Washington, DC (city) District of Columbia	74	0.01
Maplewood, NJ (township) Essex County	73	0.31
St. Paul, MN (city) Ramsey County	73	0.03
Phoenix, AZ (city) Maricopa County	72	<0.01
Burtonsville, MD (cdp) Montgomery County	70	0.76
Baltimore, MD (city) Baltimore city County	69	0.01
Sayreville, NJ (borough) Middlesex County	68	0.16
Concord, CA (city) Contra Costa County	66	0.05
West Fargo, ND (city) Cass County	63	0.26
Garland, TX (city) Dallas County	63	0.03
Kalamazoo, MI (city) Kalamazoo County	61	0.08
Braddock Hills, PA (borough) Allegheny County	60	3.22
Germantown, MD (cdp) Montgomery County	59	0.07
Albany, GA (city) Dougherty County	58	0.08
Pittsburg, CA (city) Contra Costa County	55	0.09
Manchester, NH (city) Hillsborough County	55	0.05
Indianapolis, IN (city) Marion County	54	0.01
Brooklyn, NY (borough) Kings County	54	<0.01
Mount Olive, NJ (township) Morris County	52	0.19
Framingham, MA (cdp/town) Middlesex County	52	0.08
Horsham, PA (township) Montgomery County	51	0.20
North Bethesda, MD (cdp) Montgomery County	51	0.13
Tulsa, OK (city) Tulsa County	51	0.01
Federal Way, WA (city) King County	50	0.06
Cambridge, MA (city) Middlesex County	48	0.05
Plano, TX (city) Collin County	48	0.02
Dracut, MA (town) Middlesex County	47	0.16
Lowell, MA (city) Middlesex County	46	0.04
Provo, UT (city) Utah County	45	0.04
Somerville, MA (city) Middlesex County	44	0.06
Las Vegas, NV (city) Clark County	44	0.01
Bellevue, WA (city) King County	42	0.04
Evanston, IL (city) Cook County	41	0.06
Arden-Arcade, CA (cdp) Sacramento County	40	0.04
Manhattan, KS (city) Riley County	39	0.08
Chicago, IL (city) Cook County	39	<0.01
Esmont, VA (cdp) Albemarle County	38	3.68
Greensboro, NC (city) Guilford County	38	0.01
Hemet, CA (city) Riverside County	37	0.05
Old Jamestown, MO (cdp) St. Louis County	36	0.18
Arlington, MA (cdp/town) Middlesex County	36	0.09
Newton, MA (city) Middlesex County	36	0.04
St. Cloud, MN (city) Stearns County	35	0.07
St. Cloud, MN (city) Stearns County	35	0.05
Tuscaloosa, AL (city) Tuscaloosa County	35	0.04
Birmingham, AL (city) Jefferson County	35	0.02
Ayer, MA (town) Middlesex County	34	0.46
Woburn, MA (city) Middlesex County	34	0.09
Buffalo, NY (city) Erie County	33	0.01
Milwaukee, WI (city) Milwaukee County	33	0.01
Northport, AL (city) Tuscaloosa County	32	0.14
Lincoln, NE (city) Lancaster County	32	0.01
Simsbury Center, CT (cdp) Hartford County	30	0.50
Calverton, MD (cdp) Montgomery County	30	0.17
Tukwila, WA (city) King County	30	0.16
Simsbury, CT (town) Hartford County	30	0.13
Urbandale, IA (city) Polk County	29	0.08
Long Beach, CA (city) Los Angeles County	29	0.01
Wilkinson Heights, SC (cdp) Orangeburg County	28	1.23
Bloomfield, CT (town) Hartford County	28	0.14
Hudson, NH (town) Hillsborough County	28	0.12
Minneapolis, MN (city) Hennepin County	28	0.01
Syracuse, NY (city) Onondaga County	26	0.02
Louisville-Jefferson County, KY (metro govt) Jefferson County	26	<0.01
Roscoe, IL (village) Winnebago County	24	0.24
Ithaca, NY (town) Tompkins County	24	0.12
San Bernardino, CA (city) San Bernardino County	24	0.01
East Whiteland, PA (township) Chester County	23	0.22
Wichita, KS (city) Sedgwick County	23	0.01
Urbana, MD (cdp) Frederick County	22	0.30
Oklahoma City, OK (city) Oklahoma County	22	<0.01
Lower Paxton, PA (township) Dauphin County	21	0.04
Hayward, CA (city) Alameda County	21	0.01
Nashville-Davidson, TN (metro govt) Davidson County	21	<0.01
Seattle, WA (city) King County	21	<0.01
Oxford, MA (town) Worcester County	20	0.15
Moon, PA (township) Allegheny County	20	0.08
Martinez, GA (cdp) Columbia County	20	0.06
Chula Vista, CA (city) San Diego County	20	0.01
Torrance, CA (city) Los Angeles County	20	0.01
Cloverly, MD (cdp) Montgomery County	19	0.12
Mount Vernon, NY (city) Westchester County	19	0.03
Springfield, NJ (township) Union County	18	0.12
Atlantic City, NJ (city) Atlantic County	18	0.04
Florissant, MO (city) St. Louis County	18	0.03
Riverside, CA (city) Riverside County	18	0.01
San Jose, CA (city) Santa Clara County	18	<0.01
North Manchester, IN (town) Wabash County	17	0.28
Cottonwood Heights, UT (city) Salt Lake County	17	0.05
Logan, UT (city) Cache County	17	0.04
Canton, MI (charter township) Wayne County	17	0.02
Chesapeake, VA (ind. city) Chesapeake independent city	17	0.01
St. Mary of the Woods, IN (cdp) Vigo County	16	1.44
Charlotte, VT (town) Chittenden County	16	0.43
Glenmont, MD (cdp) Montgomery County	16	0.12
Salem, MA (city) Essex County	16	0.04
West Palm Beach, FL (city) Palm Beach County	16	0.02
Swarthmore, PA (borough) Delaware County	15	0.24
San Marcos, TX (city) Hays County	15	0.03
Rapid City, SD (city) Pennington County	15	0.02
Waterbury, CT (city/town) New Haven County	15	0.01
Bothell West, WA (cdp) Snohomish County	14	0.09
Reston, VA (cdp) Fairfax County	14	0.03
Rocklin, CA (city) Placer County	14	0.03
Evansville, IN (city) Vanderburgh County	14	0.01
Newark, NJ (city) Essex County	14	0.01
Topeka, KS (city) Shawnee County	14	0.01
Lexington-Fayette, KY (cons. govt) Fayette County	14	<0.01
Air Force Academy, CO (cdp) El Paso County	13	0.16
Brown Deer, WI (village) Milwaukee County	13	0.11
Superior, MI (charter township) Washtenaw County	13	0.10
Belmont, MA (cdp/town) Middlesex County	13	0.05
Carney, MD (cdp) Baltimore County	13	0.05
Superior, WI (city) Douglas County	13	0.05
Wellesley, MA (cdp/town) Norfolk County	13	0.05
Montgomery Village, MD (cdp) Montgomery County	13	0.04
Arlington, VA (cdp) Arlington County	13	0.01
Fair Oaks, VA (cdp) Fairfax County	12	0.04
Cleveland Heights, OH (city) Cuyahoga County	12	0.03
Denton, TX (city) Denton County	12	0.01
Sunrise Manor, NV (cdp) Clark County	12	0.01
Albuquerque, NM (city) Bernalillo County	12	<0.01
St. Louis, MO (city) St. Louis city County	12	<0.01
Hamilton, NY (village) Madison County	11	0.31
Hamilton, NY (town) Madison County	11	0.17

Please refer to the Explanation of Data in the front of the book for more detailed information.

Ancestry

African, Sub-Saharan: Ugandan

Top 150 Places Sorted by Percent of Total Population

Based on all places, regardless of total population

Place	Population	%
Port Alsworth, AK (cdp) Lake and Peninsula Borough	9	8.91
Rock Valley, IA (city) Sioux County	121	3.70
Esmont, VA (cdp) Albemarle County	38	3.68
Braddock Hills, PA (borough) Allegheny County	60	3.22
Layhill, MD (cdp) Montgomery County	99	1.74
St. Mary of the Woods, IN (cdp) Vigo County	16	1.44
Wilkinson Heights, SC (cdp) Orangeburg County	28	1.23
Hereim, MN (township) Roseau County	3	1.12
Harrisville, PA (borough) Butler County	8	0.87
Malden, MA (city) Middlesex County	481	0.83
Burtonsville, MD (cdp) Montgomery County	70	0.76
Melrose, MA (city) Middlesex County	174	0.65
Stubbs, WI (town) Rusk County	3	0.55
Simsbury Center, CT (cdp) Hartford County	30	0.50
Waltham, MA (city) Middlesex County	279	0.47
Ayer, MA (town) Middlesex County	34	0.46
Charlotte, VT (town) Chittenden County	16	0.43
Fairland, MD (cdp) Montgomery County	96	0.42
Roseville, MN (city) Ramsey County	132	0.40
Granby, CO (town) Grand County	8	0.39
Burlington, MA (cdp/town) Middlesex County	90	0.38
Watertown Town, MA (city) Middlesex County	110	0.35
Salem, NH (town) Rockingham County	99	0.34
Maplewood, NJ (township) Essex County	73	0.31
Hamilton, NY (village) Madison County	11	0.31
Dale City, VA (cdp) Prince William County	193	0.30
Urbana, MD (cdp) Frederick County	22	0.30
Everett, MA (city) Middlesex County	115	0.28
Spring Valley, NY (village) Rockland County	86	0.28
North Manchester, IN (town) Wabash County	17	0.28
West Fargo, ND (city) Cass County	63	0.26
Greenvale, MN (township) Dakota County	2	0.25
Roscoe, IL (village) Winnebago County	24	0.24
Swarthmore, PA (borough) Delaware County	15	0.24
East Whiteland, PA (township) Chester County	23	0.22
Horsham, PA (township) Montgomery County	51	0.20
Brooklyn Park, MN (city) Hennepin County	141	0.19
Mount Olive, NJ (township) Morris County	52	0.19
Everson, WA (city) Whatcom County	5	0.19
Old Jamestown, MO (cdp) St. Louis County	36	0.18
Rancho Cordova, CA (city) Sacramento County	108	0.17
Calverton, MD (cdp) Montgomery County	30	0.17
Hamilton, NY (town) Madison County	11	0.17
Sayreville, NJ (borough) Middlesex County	68	0.16
Dracut, MA (town) Middlesex County	47	0.16
Tukwila, WA (city) King County	30	0.16
Air Force Academy, CO (cdp) El Paso County	13	0.16
Dumbarton, VA (cdp) Henrico County	11	0.16
Oxford, MA (town) Worcester County	20	0.15
Northport, AL (city) Tuscaloosa County	32	0.14
Bloomfield, CT (town) Hartford County	28	0.14
North Bethesda, MD (cdp) Montgomery County	51	0.13
Simsbury, CT (town) Hartford County	30	0.13
Hudson, NH (town) Hillsborough County	28	0.12
Ithaca, NY (town) Tompkins County	24	0.12
Cloverly, MD (cdp) Montgomery County	19	0.12
Springfield, NJ (township) Union County	18	0.12
Glenmont, MD (cdp) Montgomery County	16	0.12
Brown Deer, WI (village) Milwaukee County	13	0.11
Superior, MI (charter township) Washtenaw County	13	0.10
Santa Rosa, CA (city) Sonoma County	146	0.09
Pittsburg, CA (city) Contra Costa County	55	0.09
Arlington, MA (cdp/town) Middlesex County	36	0.09
Woburn, MA (city) Middlesex County	34	0.09
Bothell West, WA (cdp) Snohomish County	14	0.09
Woodhaven, MI (city) Wayne County	11	0.09
Temecula, CA (city) Riverside County	76	0.08
Kalamazoo, MI (city) Kalamazoo County	61	0.08
Albany, GA (city) Dougherty County	58	0.08
Framingham, MA (cdp/town) Middlesex County	52	0.08
Manhattan, KS (city) Riley County	39	0.08
Urbandale, IA (city) Polk County	29	0.08
Moon, PA (township) Allegheny County	20	0.08
Northview, MI (cdp) Kent County	11	0.08
Aurora, CO (city) Arapahoe County	206	0.07
Ramapo, NY (town) Rockland County	86	0.07
Germantown, MD (cdp) Montgomery County	59	0.07
St. Cloud, MN (city) Stearns County	35	0.07
McNair, VA (cdp) Fairfax County	11	0.07
White Oak, MD (cdp) Montgomery County	11	0.07
North Union, PA (township) Fayette County	9	0.07
Federal Way, WA (city) King County	50	0.06
Somerville, MA (city) Middlesex County	44	0.06
Evanston, IL (city) Cook County	41	0.06
Martinez, GA (cdp) Columbia County	20	0.06
Concord, CA (city) Contra Costa County	66	0.05
Manchester, NH (city) Hillsborough County	55	0.05
Cambridge, MA (city) Middlesex County	48	0.05
Hemet, CA (city) Riverside County	37	0.05
St. Cloud, MN (city) Stearns County	35	0.05
Cottonwood Heights, UT (city) Salt Lake County	17	0.05
Belmont, MA (cdp/town) Middlesex County	13	0.05
Carney, MD (cdp) Baltimore County	13	0.05
Superior, WI (city) Douglas County	13	0.05
Wellesley, MA (cdp/town) Norfolk County	13	0.05
Acton, MA (town) Middlesex County	11	0.05
Rosemount, MN (city) Dakota County	10	0.05
Woodstock, GA (city) Cherokee County	10	0.05
Creve Coeur, MO (city) St. Louis County	9	0.05
Richmond, VA (ind. city) Richmond independent city	82	0.04
Lowell, MA (city) Middlesex County	46	0.04
Provo, UT (city) Utah County	45	0.04
Bellevue, WA (city) King County	42	0.04
Arden-Arcade, CA (cdp) Sacramento County	40	0.04
Newton, MA (city) Middlesex County	36	0.04
Tuscaloosa, AL (city) Tuscaloosa County	35	0.04
Lower Paxton, PA (township) Dauphin County	21	0.04
Atlantic City, NJ (city) Atlantic County	18	0.04
Logan, UT (city) Cache County	17	0.04
Salem, MA (city) Essex County	16	0.04
Montgomery Village, MD (cdp) Montgomery County	13	0.04
Fair Oaks, VA (cdp) Fairfax County	12	0.04
Cleburne, TX (city) Johnson County	11	0.04
Plainfield, MI (charter township) Kent County	11	0.04
West Springfield Town, MA (city) Hampden County	10	0.04
Denison, TX (city) Grayson County	9	0.04
Walpole, MA (town) Norfolk County	9	0.04
Oxford, OH (city) Butler County	8	0.04
Boston, MA (city) Suffolk County	183	0.03
St. Paul, MN (city) Ramsey County	73	0.03
Garland, TX (city) Dallas County	63	0.03
Mount Vernon, NY (city) Westchester County	19	0.03
Florissant, MO (city) St. Louis County	18	0.03
San Marcos, TX (city) Hays County	15	0.03
Reston, VA (cdp) Fairfax County	14	0.03
Rocklin, CA (city) Placer County	14	0.03
Cleveland Heights, OH (city) Cuyahoga County	12	0.03
Keller, TX (city) Tarrant County	11	0.03
Kearney, NE (city) Buffalo County	9	0.03
Athens, OH (city) Athens County	6	0.03
Greenbelt, MD (city) Prince George's County	6	0.03
Plano, TX (city) Collin County	48	0.02
Birmingham, AL (city) Jefferson County	35	0.02
Syracuse, NY (city) Onondaga County	26	0.02
Canton, MI (charter township) Wayne County	17	0.02
West Palm Beach, FL (city) Palm Beach County	16	0.02
Rapid City, SD (city) Pennington County	15	0.02
Revere, MA (city) Suffolk County	11	0.02
Rockville, MD (city) Montgomery County	10	0.02
Battle Creek, MI (city) Calhoun County	9	0.02
Lakewood, OH (city) Cuyahoga County	9	0.02
White Plains, NY (city) Westchester County	9	0.02
Mishawaka, IN (city) St. Joseph County	8	0.02
Southgate, MI (city) Wayne County	7	0.02
Maricopa, AZ (city) Pinal County	6	0.02
Olney, MD (cdp) Montgomery County	5	0.02
Bergenfield, NJ (borough) Bergen County	4	0.02
Los Angeles, CA (city) Los Angeles County	491	0.01
Manhattan, NY (borough) New York County	125	0.01
Washington, DC (city) District of Columbia	74	0.01

Please refer to the Explanation of Data in the front of the book for more detailed information.

Ancestry

African, Sub-Saharan: Ugandan

Top 150 Places Sorted by Percent of Total Population

Based on places with total population of 7,500 or more

Place	Population	%
Malden, MA (city) Middlesex County	481	0.83
Burtonsville, MD (cdp) Montgomery County	70	0.76
Melrose, MA (city) Middlesex County	174	0.65
Waltham, MA (city) Middlesex County	279	0.47
Fairland, MD (cdp) Montgomery County	96	0.42
Roseville, MN (city) Ramsey County	132	0.40
Burlington, MA (cdp/town) Middlesex County	90	0.38
Watertown Town, MA (city) Middlesex County	110	0.35
Salem, NH (town) Rockingham County	99	0.34
Maplewood, NJ (township) Essex County	73	0.31
Dale City, VA (cdp) Prince William County	193	0.30
Everett, MA (city) Middlesex County	115	0.28
Spring Valley, NY (village) Rockland County	86	0.28
West Fargo, ND (city) Cass County	63	0.26
Roscoe, IL (village) Winnebago County	24	0.24
East Whiteland, PA (township) Chester County	23	0.22
Horsham, PA (township) Montgomery County	51	0.20
Brooklyn Park, MN (city) Hennepin County	141	0.19
Mount Olive, NJ (township) Morris County	52	0.19
Old Jamestown, MO (cdp) St. Louis County	36	0.18
Rancho Cordova, CA (city) Sacramento County	108	0.17
Calverton, MD (cdp) Montgomery County	30	0.17
Sayreville, NJ (borough) Middlesex County	68	0.16
Dracut, MA (town) Middlesex County	47	0.16
Tukwila, WA (city) King County	30	0.16
Air Force Academy, CO (cdp) El Paso County	13	0.16
Oxford, MA (town) Worcester County	20	0.15
Northport, AL (city) Tuscaloosa County	32	0.14
Bloomfield, CT (town) Hartford County	28	0.14
North Bethesda, MD (cdp) Montgomery County	51	0.13
Simsbury, CT (town) Hartford County	30	0.13
Hudson, NH (town) Hillsborough County	28	0.12
Ithaca, NY (town) Tompkins County	24	0.12
Cloverly, MD (cdp) Montgomery County	19	0.12
Springfield, NJ (township) Union County	18	0.12
Glenmont, MD (cdp) Montgomery County	16	0.12
Brown Deer, WI (village) Milwaukee County	13	0.11
Superior, MI (charter township) Washtenaw County	13	0.10
Santa Rosa, CA (city) Sonoma County	146	0.09
Pittsburg, CA (city) Contra Costa County	55	0.09
Arlington, MA (cdp/town) Middlesex County	36	0.09
Woburn, MA (city) Middlesex County	34	0.09
Bothell West, WA (cdp) Snohomish County	14	0.09
Woodhaven, MI (city) Wayne County	11	0.09
Temecula, CA (city) Riverside County	76	0.08
Kalamazoo, MI (city) Kalamazoo County	61	0.08
Albany, GA (city) Dougherty County	58	0.08
Framingham, MA (cdp/town) Middlesex County	52	0.08
Manhattan, KS (city) Riley County	39	0.08
Urbandale, IA (city) Polk County	29	0.08
Moon, PA (township) Allegheny County	20	0.08
Northview, MI (cdp) Kent County	11	0.08
Aurora, CO (city) Arapahoe County	206	0.07
Ramapo, NY (town) Rockland County	86	0.07
Germantown, MD (cdp) Montgomery County	59	0.07
St. Cloud, MN (city) Stearns County	35	0.07
McNair, VA (cdp) Fairfax County	11	0.07
White Oak, MD (cdp) Montgomery County	11	0.07
North Union, PA (township) Fayette County	9	0.07
Federal Way, WA (city) King County	50	0.06
Somerville, MA (city) Middlesex County	44	0.06
Evanston, IL (city) Cook County	41	0.06
Martinez, GA (cdp) Columbia County	20	0.06
Concord, CA (city) Contra Costa County	66	0.05
Manchester, NH (city) Hillsborough County	55	0.05
Cambridge, MA (city) Middlesex County	48	0.05
Hemet, CA (city) Riverside County	37	0.05
St. Cloud, MN (city) Stearns County	35	0.05
Cottonwood Heights, UT (city) Salt Lake County	17	0.05
Belmont, MA (cdp/town) Middlesex County	13	0.05
Carney, MD (cdp) Baltimore County	13	0.05
Superior, WI (city) Douglas County	13	0.05
Wellesley, MA (cdp/town) Norfolk County	13	0.05
Acton, MA (town) Middlesex County	11	0.05
Rosemount, MN (city) Dakota County	10	0.05
Woodstock, GA (city) Cherokee County	10	0.05
Creve Coeur, MO (city) St. Louis County	9	0.05
Richmond, VA (ind. city) Richmond independent city	82	0.04
Lowell, MA (city) Middlesex County	46	0.04
Provo, UT (city) Utah County	45	0.04
Bellevue, WA (city) King County	42	0.04
Arden-Arcade, CA (cdp) Sacramento County	40	0.04
Newton, MA (city) Middlesex County	36	0.04
Tuscaloosa, AL (city) Tuscaloosa County	35	0.04
Lower Paxton, PA (township) Dauphin County	21	0.04
Atlantic City, NJ (city) Atlantic County	18	0.04
Logan, UT (city) Cache County	17	0.04
Salem, MA (city) Essex County	16	0.04
Montgomery Village, MD (cdp) Montgomery County	13	0.04
Fair Oaks, VA (cdp) Fairfax County	12	0.04
Cleburne, TX (city) Johnson County	11	0.04
Plainfield, MI (charter township) Kent County	11	0.04
West Springfield Town, MA (city) Hampden County	10	0.04
Denison, TX (city) Grayson County	9	0.04
Walpole, MA (town) Norfolk County	9	0.04
Oxford, OH (city) Butler County	8	0.04
Boston, MA (city) Suffolk County	183	0.03
St. Paul, MN (city) Ramsey County	73	0.03
Garland, TX (city) Dallas County	63	0.03
Mount Vernon, NY (city) Westchester County	19	0.03
Florissant, MO (city) St. Louis County	18	0.03
San Marcos, TX (city) Hays County	15	0.03
Reston, VA (cdp) Fairfax County	14	0.03
Rocklin, CA (city) Placer County	14	0.03
Cleveland Heights, OH (city) Cuyahoga County	12	0.03
Keller, TX (city) Tarrant County	11	0.03
Kearney, NE (city) Buffalo County	9	0.03
Athens, OH (city) Athens County	6	0.03
Greenbelt, MD (city) Prince George's County	6	0.03
Plano, TX (city) Collin County	48	0.02
Birmingham, AL (city) Jefferson County	35	0.02
Syracuse, NY (city) Onondaga County	26	0.02
Canton, MI (charter township) Wayne County	17	0.02
West Palm Beach, FL (city) Palm Beach County	16	0.02
Rapid City, SD (city) Pennington County	15	0.02
Revere, MA (city) Suffolk County	11	0.02
Rockville, MD (city) Montgomery County	10	0.02
Battle Creek, MI (city) Calhoun County	9	0.02
Lakewood, OH (city) Cuyahoga County	9	0.02
White Plains, NY (city) Westchester County	9	0.02
Mishawaka, IN (city) St. Joseph County	8	0.02
Southgate, MI (city) Wayne County	7	0.02
Maricopa, AZ (city) Pinal County	6	0.02
Olney, MD (cdp) Montgomery County	5	0.02
Bergenfield, NJ (borough) Bergen County	4	0.02
Los Angeles, CA (city) Los Angeles County	491	0.01
Manhattan, NY (borough) New York County	125	0.01
Washington, DC (city) District of Columbia	74	0.01
Baltimore, MD (city) Baltimore city County	69	0.01
Indianapolis, IN (city) Marion County	54	0.01
Tulsa, OK (city) Tulsa County	51	0.01
Las Vegas, NV (city) Clark County	44	0.01
Greensboro, NC (city) Guilford County	38	0.01
Buffalo, NY (city) Erie County	33	0.01
Milwaukee, WI (city) Milwaukee County	33	0.01
Lincoln, NE (city) Lancaster County	32	0.01
Long Beach, CA (city) Los Angeles County	29	0.01
Minneapolis, MN (city) Hennepin County	28	0.01
San Bernardino, CA (city) San Bernardino County	24	0.01
Wichita, KS (city) Sedgwick County	23	0.01
Hayward, CA (city) Alameda County	21	0.01
Chula Vista, CA (city) San Diego County	20	0.01
Torrance, CA (city) Los Angeles County	20	0.01
Riverside, CA (city) Riverside County	18	0.01
Chesapeake, VA (ind. city) Chesapeake independent city	17	0.01
Waterbury, CT (city/town) New Haven County	15	0.01
Evansville, IN (city) Vanderburgh County	14	0.01
Newark, NJ (city) Essex County	14	0.01
Topeka, KS (city) Shawnee County	14	0.01
Arlington, VA (cdp) Arlington County	13	0.01

SECTION THREE

Please refer to the Explanation of Data in the front of the book for more detailed information.

Ancestry

African, Sub-Saharan: Zimbabwean

U.S. and 50 States Sorted by Population and Percent of Total Population

Place	Population	%
United States	**6,098**	**<0.01**
California	726	<0.01
Texas	686	<0.01
New York	646	<0.01
Michigan	446	<0.01
Florida	442	<0.01
Ohio	381	<0.01
Maryland	242	<0.01
Georgia	208	<0.01
Pennsylvania	201	<0.01
New Hampshire	170	0.01
Indiana	162	<0.01
Tennessee	160	<0.01
Washington	158	<0.01
Illinois	146	<0.01
Virginia	141	<0.01
Minnesota	124	<0.01
New Jersey	121	<0.01
Missouri	108	<0.01
Massachusetts	103	<0.01
North Carolina	79	<0.01
Kansas	74	<0.01
Oregon	64	<0.01
Arizona	59	<0.01
Colorado	56	<0.01
Wisconsin	55	<0.01
Alabama	53	<0.01
Utah	51	<0.01
Louisiana	38	<0.01
Connecticut	27	<0.01
Iowa	27	<0.01
Hawaii	26	<0.01
Nevada	26	<0.01
Kentucky	25	<0.01
Oklahoma	18	<0.01
Idaho	15	<0.01
District of Columbia	13	<0.01
South Carolina	12	<0.01
Nebraska	9	<0.01
Alaska	0	0.00
Arkansas	0	0.00
Delaware	0	0.00
Maine	0	0.00
Mississippi	0	0.00
Montana	0	0.00
New Mexico	0	0.00
North Dakota	0	0.00
Rhode Island	0	0.00
South Dakota	0	0.00
Vermont	0	0.00
West Virginia	0	0.00
Wyoming	0	0.00

Place	Population	%
New Hampshire	170	0.01
United States	**6,098**	**<0.01**
California	726	<0.01
Texas	686	<0.01
New York	646	<0.01
Michigan	446	<0.01
Florida	442	<0.01
Ohio	381	<0.01
Maryland	242	<0.01
Georgia	208	<0.01
Pennsylvania	201	<0.01
Indiana	162	<0.01
Tennessee	160	<0.01
Washington	158	<0.01
Illinois	146	<0.01
Virginia	141	<0.01
Minnesota	124	<0.01
New Jersey	121	<0.01
Missouri	108	<0.01
Massachusetts	103	<0.01
North Carolina	79	<0.01
Kansas	74	<0.01
Oregon	64	<0.01
Arizona	59	<0.01
Colorado	56	<0.01
Wisconsin	55	<0.01
Alabama	53	<0.01
Utah	51	<0.01
Louisiana	38	<0.01
Connecticut	27	<0.01
Iowa	27	<0.01
Hawaii	26	<0.01
Nevada	26	<0.01
Kentucky	25	<0.01
Oklahoma	18	<0.01
Idaho	15	<0.01
District of Columbia	13	<0.01
South Carolina	12	<0.01
Nebraska	9	<0.01
Alaska	0	0.00
Arkansas	0	0.00
Delaware	0	0.00
Maine	0	0.00
Mississippi	0	0.00
Montana	0	0.00
New Mexico	0	0.00
North Dakota	0	0.00
Rhode Island	0	0.00
South Dakota	0	0.00
Vermont	0	0.00
West Virginia	0	0.00
Wyoming	0	0.00

Please refer to the Explanation of Data in the front of the book for more detailed information.

Ancestry

African, Sub-Saharan: Zimbabwean

Top 150 Places Sorted by Population

Based on all places, regardless of total population

Place	Population	%
New York, NY (city) Kings County	414	0.01
Comstock Northwest, MI (cdp) Kalamazoo County	175	2.74
Comstock, MI (charter township) Kalamazoo County	175	1.20
Blue Ash, OH (city) Hamilton County	172	1.43
Indianapolis, IN (city) Marion County	149	0.02
Laurel, FL (cdp) Sarasota County	147	1.83
Columbus, OH (city) Franklin County	125	0.02
Derry, NH (cdp) Rockingham County	122	0.53
Derry, NH (town) Rockingham County	122	0.36
Stockton, CA (city) San Joaquin County	118	0.04
Bronx, NY (borough) Bronx County	108	0.01
Chicago, IL (city) Cook County	107	<0.01
Queens, NY (borough) Queens County	107	<0.01
Pasadena, CA (city) Los Angeles County	105	0.08
Los Angeles, CA (city) Los Angeles County	101	<0.01
Manhattan, NY (borough) New York County	100	0.01
Brooklyn, NY (borough) Kings County	99	<0.01
Kirkland, WA (city) King County	95	0.20
Dallas, TX (city) Dallas County	90	0.01
Tampa, FL (city) Hillsborough County	86	0.03
Frisco, TX (city) Collin County	83	0.08
Coppell, TX (city) Dallas County	82	0.21
Garland, TX (city) Dallas County	79	0.04
Memphis, TN (city) Shelby County	79	0.01
Rochester, NY (city) Monroe County	76	0.04
Olathe, KS (city) Johnson County	74	0.06
Robbinsdale, MN (city) Hennepin County	68	0.49
Temecula, CA (city) Riverside County	68	0.07
Fairfax, VA (ind. city) Fairfax independent city	62	0.28
Garrison, MD (cdp) Baltimore County	61	0.80
Limerick, PA (township) Montgomery County	55	0.32
Cincinnati, OH (city) Hamilton County	53	0.02
Forney, TX (city) Kaufman County	52	0.40
Philadelphia, PA (city) Philadelphia County	51	<0.01
McKinney, TX (city) Collin County	50	0.04
Boston, MA (city) Suffolk County	50	0.01
Phoenix, AZ (city) Maricopa County	50	<0.01
Lincoln Beach, OR (cdp) Lincoln County	48	2.03
Okemos, MI (cdp) Ingham County	48	0.23
St. Cloud, FL (city) Osceola County	48	0.14
Meridian, MI (charter township) Ingham County	48	0.12
DeSoto, TX (city) Dallas County	46	0.10
Kalamazoo, MI (city) Kalamazoo County	46	0.06
Santa Monica, CA (city) Los Angeles County	46	0.05
Buffalo, NY (city) Erie County	45	0.02
San Lorenzo, CA (cdp) Alameda County	44	0.19
Baltimore, MD (city) Baltimore city County	44	0.01
Glenmont, MD (cdp) Montgomery County	42	0.31
Melbourne, FL (city) Brevard County	42	0.05
Fort Worth, TX (city) Tarrant County	41	0.01
Callicoon, NY (town) Sullivan County	40	1.30
West Jordan, UT (city) Salt Lake County	40	0.04
Chapel Hill, NC (town) Orange County	39	0.07
San Diego, CA (city) San Diego County	39	<0.01
Pembroke, NH (town) Merrimack County	37	0.52
Pittsburgh, PA (city) Allegheny County	36	0.01
Clayton, CA (city) Contra Costa County	35	0.32
South Laurel, MD (cdp) Prince George's County	33	0.13
North Bergen, NJ (township) Hudson County	33	0.06
San Ramon, CA (city) Contra Costa County	33	0.05
Camp Pendleton South, CA (cdp) San Diego County	32	0.24
Plainville, MA (town) Norfolk County	31	0.38
Alexandria, VA (ind. city) Alexandria independent city	31	0.02
Huntsville, AL (city) Madison County	31	0.02
Corona, CA (city) Riverside County	30	0.02
Waco, TX (city) McLennan County	30	0.02
Plantation Mobile Home Park, FL (cdp) Palm Beach County	29	2.34
Fern Prairie, WA (cdp) Clark County	29	1.62
Travilah, MD (cdp) Montgomery County	28	0.23
Rochester, MN (city) Olmsted County	28	0.03
Knoxville, TN (city) Knox County	28	0.02
Oneonta, NY (city) Otsego County	26	0.19
Hilo, HI (cdp) Hawaii County	26	0.05
Columbia, MO (city) Boone County	26	0.02
Paradise, NV (cdp) Clark County	26	0.01
Urbana, IL (city) Champaign County	25	0.06
West New York, NJ (town) Hudson County	25	0.05
St. Paul, TX (town) Collin County	24	2.20
East Ithaca, NY (cdp) Tompkins County	24	1.20
Ithaca, NY (town) Tompkins County	24	0.12
New Orleans, LA (city) Orleans Parish	24	0.01
St. Louis, MO (city) St. Louis city County	24	0.01
Laurel, VA (cdp) Henrico County	23	0.14
Webster Groves, MO (city) St. Louis County	23	0.10
Battle Creek, MI (city) Calhoun County	23	0.04
Loma Linda, CA (city) San Bernardino County	22	0.10
Seattle, WA (city) King County	22	<0.01
East Lansdowne, PA (borough) Delaware County	21	0.79
Cleveland, TN (city) Bradley County	21	0.05
East Lansing, MI (city) Ingham County	20	0.04
East Lansing, MI (city) Ingham County	20	0.04
Rochester Hills, MI (city) Oakland County	20	0.03
Milwaukee, WI (city) Milwaukee County	19	<0.01
Athens, PA (township) Bradford County	18	0.35
Short Hills, NJ (cdp) Essex County	18	0.14
Millburn, NJ (township) Essex County	18	0.09
Highlands Ranch, CO (cdp) Douglas County	18	0.02
Shelby, MI (charter township) Macomb County	18	0.02
Lexington-Fayette, KY (cons. govt) Fayette County	18	0.01
West Bloomfield, MI (charter township) Oakland County	17	0.03
Ames, IA (city) Story County	16	0.03
Waltham, MA (city) Middlesex County	16	0.03
Farmington Hills, MI (city) Oakland County	16	0.02
Passaic, NJ (city) Passaic County	16	0.02
Portland, OR (city) Multnomah County	16	<0.01
Glendale, WI (city) Milwaukee County	15	0.12
Smyrna, GA (city) Cobb County	15	0.03
Boise City, ID (city) Ada County	15	0.01
Pawcatuck, CT (cdp) New London County	14	0.24
Westwego, LA (city) Jefferson Parish	14	0.16
Davidson, NC (town) Mecklenburg County	14	0.14
Stonington, CT (town) New London County	14	0.08
Buffalo Grove, IL (village) Lake County	14	0.03
Richmond, VA (ind. city) Richmond independent city	14	0.01
Hopewell, TN (cdp) Bradley County	13	0.67
Canton, NY (village) St. Lawrence County	13	0.21
Canton, NY (town) St. Lawrence County	13	0.12
Beaver Dam, WI (city) Dodge County	13	0.08
Vernon, CT (town) Tolland County	13	0.04
Elkhart, IN (city) Elkhart County	13	0.03
Irvine, CA (city) Orange County	13	0.01
Washington, DC (city) District of Columbia	13	<0.01
Cibolo, TX (city) Guadalupe County	12	0.09
Takoma Park, MD (city) Montgomery County	12	0.07
Gaines, MI (charter township) Kent County	12	0.05
Manheim, PA (township) Lancaster County	12	0.03
Southfield, MI (city) Oakland County	12	0.02
Akron, OH (city) Summit County	12	0.01
Charleston, SC (city) Charleston County	12	0.01
Coral Springs, FL (city) Broward County	12	0.01
Edison, NJ (township) Middlesex County	12	0.01
Lewisville, TX (city) Denton County	12	0.01
Sunrise, FL (city) Broward County	12	0.01
Tacoma, WA (city) Pierce County	12	0.01
Plano, TX (city) Collin County	12	<0.01
Mount Vernon, IA (city) Linn County	11	0.25
Oregon, MI (township) Lapeer County	11	0.18
Lake Barcroft, VA (cdp) Fairfax County	11	0.12
Morrisville, NC (town) Wake County	11	0.07
Camp Springs, MD (cdp) Prince George's County	11	0.06
Northfield, MN (city) Rice County	11	0.06
Northfield, MN (city) Rice County	11	0.06
Saginaw, MI (charter township) Saginaw County	11	0.03
Lakeville, MN (city) Dakota County	11	0.02
South Jordan, UT (city) Salt Lake County	11	0.02
Wheaton, MD (cdp) Montgomery County	11	0.02
Manchester, NH (city) Hillsborough County	11	0.01
Monterey, CA (city) Monterey County	10	0.04
Rancho Santa Margarita, CA (city) Orange County	10	0.02
Boca Raton, FL (city) Palm Beach County	10	0.01

SECTION THREE

Please refer to the Explanation of Data in the front of the book for more detailed information.

Ancestry

African, Sub-Saharan: Zimbabwean

Top 150 Places Sorted by Percent of Total Population

Based on all places, regardless of total population

Place	Population	%
Comstock Northwest, MI (cdp) Kalamazoo County	175	2.74
Plantation Mobile Home Park, FL (cdp) Palm Beach County	29	2.34
St. Paul, TX (town) Collin County	24	2.20
Lincoln Beach, OR (cdp) Lincoln County	48	2.03
Laurel, FL (cdp) Sarasota County	147	1.83
Fern Prairie, WA (cdp) Clark County	29	1.62
Blue Ash, OH (city) Hamilton County	172	1.43
Callicoon, NY (town) Sullivan County	40	1.30
Union, NE (village) Cass County	3	1.24
Comstock, MI (charter township) Kalamazoo County	175	1.20
East Ithaca, NY (cdp) Tompkins County	24	1.20
Langston, OK (town) Logan County	8	0.88
Garrison, MD (cdp) Baltimore County	61	0.80
East Lansdowne, PA (borough) Delaware County	21	0.79
Hopewell, TN (cdp) Bradley County	13	0.67
Derry, NH (cdp) Rockingham County	122	0.53
Pembroke, NH (town) Merrimack County	37	0.52
Robbinsdale, MN (city) Hennepin County	68	0.49
Wayne, PA (township) Clinton County	8	0.47
Forney, TX (city) Kaufman County	52	0.40
Plainville, MA (town) Norfolk County	31	0.38
Derry, NH (town) Rockingham County	122	0.36
Athens, PA (township) Bradford County	18	0.35
Limerick, PA (township) Montgomery County	55	0.32
Clayton, CA (city) Contra Costa County	35	0.32
Glenmont, MD (cdp) Montgomery County	42	0.31
Fairfax, VA (ind. city) Fairfax independent city	62	0.28
Mount Vernon, IA (city) Linn County	11	0.25
Camp Pendleton South, CA (cdp) San Diego County	32	0.24
Pawcatuck, CT (cdp) New London County	14	0.24
Okemos, MI (cdp) Ingham County	48	0.23
Travilah, MD (cdp) Montgomery County	28	0.23
Coppell, TX (city) Dallas County	82	0.21
Canton, NY (village) St. Lawrence County	13	0.21
Kirkland, WA (city) King County	95	0.20
San Lorenzo, CA (cdp) Alameda County	44	0.19
Oneonta, NY (city) Otsego County	26	0.19
Oregon, MI (township) Lapeer County	11	0.18
Orrock, MN (township) Sherburne County	6	0.18
Westwego, LA (city) Jefferson Parish	14	0.16
Cuthbert, GA (city) Randolph County	6	0.16
St. Cloud, FL (city) Osceola County	48	0.14
Laurel, VA (cdp) Henrico County	23	0.14
Short Hills, NJ (cdp) Essex County	18	0.14
Davidson, NC (town) Mecklenburg County	14	0.14
South Laurel, MD (cdp) Prince George's County	33	0.13
Hamilton, MO (city) Caldwell County	3	0.13
Meridian, MI (charter township) Ingham County	48	0.12
Ithaca, NY (town) Tompkins County	24	0.12
Glendale, WI (city) Milwaukee County	15	0.12
Canton, NY (town) St. Lawrence County	13	0.12
Lake Barcroft, VA (cdp) Fairfax County	11	0.12
Tuscumbia, AL (city) Colbert County	9	0.11
Fair Plain, MI (cdp) Berrien County	8	0.11
DeSoto, TX (city) Dallas County	46	0.10
Webster Groves, MO (city) St. Louis County	23	0.10
Loma Linda, CA (city) San Bernardino County	22	0.10
Waupun, WI (city) Dodge County	8	0.10
Millburn, NJ (township) Essex County	18	0.09
Cibolo, TX (city) Guadalupe County	12	0.09
Pasadena, CA (city) Los Angeles County	105	0.08
Frisco, TX (city) Collin County	83	0.08
Stonington, CT (town) New London County	14	0.08
Beaver Dam, WI (city) Dodge County	13	0.08
Temecula, CA (city) Riverside County	68	0.07
Chapel Hill, NC (town) Orange County	39	0.07
Takoma Park, MD (city) Montgomery County	12	0.07
Morrisville, NC (town) Wake County	11	0.07
Waupun, WI (city) Dodge County	8	0.07
Olathe, KS (city) Johnson County	74	0.06
Kalamazoo, MI (city) Kalamazoo County	46	0.06
North Bergen, NJ (township) Hudson County	33	0.06
Urbana, IL (city) Champaign County	25	0.06
Camp Springs, MD (cdp) Prince George's County	11	0.06
Northfield, MN (city) Rice County	11	0.06
Northfield, MN (city) Rice County	11	0.06
Highland Village, TX (city) Denton County	9	0.06
Santa Monica, CA (city) Los Angeles County	46	0.05
Melbourne, FL (city) Brevard County	42	0.05
San Ramon, CA (city) Contra Costa County	33	0.05
Hilo, HI (cdp) Hawaii County	26	0.05
West New York, NJ (town) Hudson County	25	0.05
Cleveland, TN (city) Bradley County	21	0.05
Gaines, MI (charter township) Kent County	12	0.05
Benton, MI (charter township) Berrien County	8	0.05
Stockton, CA (city) San Joaquin County	118	0.04
Garland, TX (city) Dallas County	79	0.04
Rochester, NY (city) Monroe County	76	0.04
McKinney, TX (city) Collin County	50	0.04
West Jordan, UT (city) Salt Lake County	40	0.04
Battle Creek, MI (city) Calhoun County	23	0.04
East Lansing, MI (city) Ingham County	20	0.04
East Lansing, MI (city) Ingham County	20	0.04
Vernon, CT (town) Tolland County	13	0.04
Monterey, CA (city) Monterey County	10	0.04
Spring Hill, TN (city) Williamson County	9	0.04
Tampa, FL (city) Hillsborough County	86	0.03
Rochester, MN (city) Olmsted County	28	0.03
Rochester Hills, MI (city) Oakland County	20	0.03
West Bloomfield, MI (charter township) Oakland County	17	0.03
Ames, IA (city) Story County	16	0.03
Waltham, MA (city) Middlesex County	16	0.03
Smyrna, GA (city) Cobb County	15	0.03
Buffalo Grove, IL (village) Lake County	14	0.03
Elkhart, IN (city) Elkhart County	13	0.03
Manheim, PA (township) Lancaster County	12	0.03
Saginaw, MI (charter township) Saginaw County	11	0.03
Waxahachie, TX (city) Ellis County	9	0.03
Indianapolis, IN (city) Marion County	149	0.02
Columbus, OH (city) Franklin County	125	0.02
Cincinnati, OH (city) Hamilton County	53	0.02
Buffalo, NY (city) Erie County	45	0.02
Alexandria, VA (ind. city) Alexandria independent city	31	0.02
Huntsville, AL (city) Madison County	31	0.02
Corona, CA (city) Riverside County	30	0.02
Waco, TX (city) McLennan County	30	0.02
Knoxville, TN (city) Knox County	28	0.02
Columbia, MO (city) Boone County	26	0.02
Highlands Ranch, CO (cdp) Douglas County	18	0.02
Shelby, MI (charter township) Macomb County	18	0.02
Farmington Hills, MI (city) Oakland County	16	0.02
Passaic, NJ (city) Passaic County	16	0.02
Southfield, MI (city) Oakland County	12	0.02
Lakeville, MN (city) Dakota County	11	0.02
South Jordan, UT (city) Salt Lake County	11	0.02
Wheaton, MD (cdp) Montgomery County	11	0.02
Rancho Santa Margarita, CA (city) Orange County	10	0.02
Mansfield, TX (city) Tarrant County	9	0.02
Bethlehem, NY (town) Albany County	8	0.02
Oviedo, FL (city) Seminole County	6	0.02
New York, NY (city) Kings County	414	0.01
Bronx, NY (borough) Bronx County	108	0.01
Manhattan, NY (borough) New York County	100	0.01
Dallas, TX (city) Dallas County	90	0.01
Memphis, TN (city) Shelby County	79	0.01
Boston, MA (city) Suffolk County	50	0.01
Baltimore, MD (city) Baltimore city County	44	0.01
Fort Worth, TX (city) Tarrant County	41	0.01
Pittsburgh, PA (city) Allegheny County	36	0.01
Paradise, NV (cdp) Clark County	26	0.01
New Orleans, LA (city) Orleans Parish	24	0.01
St. Louis, MO (city) St. Louis city County	24	0.01
Lexington-Fayette, KY (cons. govt) Fayette County	18	0.01
Boise City, ID (city) Ada County	15	0.01
Richmond, VA (ind. city) Richmond independent city	14	0.01
Irvine, CA (city) Orange County	13	0.01
Akron, OH (city) Summit County	12	0.01
Charleston, SC (city) Charleston County	12	0.01
Coral Springs, FL (city) Broward County	12	0.01
Edison, NJ (township) Middlesex County	12	0.01

Please refer to the Explanation of Data in the front of the book for more detailed information.

Ancestry

African, Sub-Saharan: Zimbabwean

Top 150 Places Sorted by Percent of Total Population

Based on places with total population of 7,500 or more

Place	Population	%
Laurel, FL (cdp) Sarasota County	147	1.83
Blue Ash, OH (city) Hamilton County	172	1.43
Comstock, MI (charter township) Kalamazoo County	175	1.20
Garrison, MD (cdp) Baltimore County	61	0.80
Derry, NH (cdp) Rockingham County	122	0.53
Robbinsdale, MN (city) Hennepin County	68	0.49
Forney, TX (city) Kaufman County	52	0.40
Plainville, MA (town) Norfolk County	31	0.38
Derry, NH (town) Rockingham County	122	0.36
Limerick, PA (township) Montgomery County	55	0.32
Clayton, CA (city) Contra Costa County	35	0.32
Glenmont, MD (cdp) Montgomery County	42	0.31
Fairfax, VA (ind. city) Fairfax independent city	62	0.28
Camp Pendleton South, CA (cdp) San Diego County	32	0.24
Okemos, MI (cdp) Ingham County	48	0.23
Travilah, MD (cdp) Montgomery County	28	0.23
Coppell, TX (city) Dallas County	82	0.21
Kirkland, WA (city) King County	95	0.20
San Lorenzo, CA (cdp) Alameda County	44	0.19
Oneonta, NY (city) Otsego County	26	0.19
Westwego, LA (city) Jefferson Parish	14	0.16
St. Cloud, FL (city) Osceola County	48	0.14
Laurel, VA (cdp) Henrico County	23	0.14
Short Hills, NJ (cdp) Essex County	18	0.14
Davidson, NC (town) Mecklenburg County	14	0.14
South Laurel, MD (cdp) Prince George's County	33	0.13
Meridian, MI (charter township) Ingham County	48	0.12
Ithaca, NY (town) Tompkins County	24	0.12
Glendale, WI (city) Milwaukee County	15	0.12
Canton, NY (town) St. Lawrence County	13	0.12
Lake Barcroft, VA (cdp) Fairfax County	11	0.12
Tuscumbia, AL (city) Colbert County	9	0.11
DeSoto, TX (city) Dallas County	46	0.10
Webster Groves, MO (city) St. Louis County	23	0.10
Loma Linda, CA (city) San Bernardino County	22	0.10
Waupun, WI (city) Dodge County	8	0.10
Millburn, NJ (township) Essex County	18	0.09
Cibolo, TX (city) Guadalupe County	12	0.09
Pasadena, CA (city) Los Angeles County	105	0.08
Frisco, TX (city) Collin County	83	0.08
Stonington, CT (town) New London County	14	0.08
Beaver Dam, WI (city) Dodge County	13	0.08
Temecula, CA (city) Riverside County	68	0.07
Chapel Hill, NC (town) Orange County	39	0.07
Takoma Park, MD (city) Montgomery County	12	0.07
Morrisville, NC (town) Wake County	11	0.07
Waupun, WI (city) Dodge County	8	0.07
Olathe, KS (city) Johnson County	74	0.06
Kalamazoo, MI (city) Kalamazoo County	46	0.06
North Bergen, NJ (township) Hudson County	33	0.06
Urbana, IL (city) Champaign County	25	0.06
Camp Springs, MD (cdp) Prince George's County	11	0.06
Northfield, MN (city) Rice County	11	0.06
Northfield, MN (city) Rice County	11	0.06
Highland Village, TX (city) Denton County	9	0.06
Santa Monica, CA (city) Los Angeles County	46	0.05
Melbourne, FL (city) Brevard County	42	0.05
San Ramon, CA (city) Contra Costa County	33	0.05
Hilo, HI (cdp) Hawaii County	26	0.05
West New York, NJ (town) Hudson County	25	0.05
Cleveland, TN (city) Bradley County	21	0.05
Gaines, MI (charter township) Kent County	12	0.05
Benton, MI (charter township) Berrien County	8	0.05
Stockton, CA (city) San Joaquin County	118	0.04
Garland, TX (city) Dallas County	79	0.04
Rochester, NY (city) Monroe County	76	0.04
McKinney, TX (city) Collin County	50	0.04
West Jordan, UT (city) Salt Lake County	40	0.04
Battle Creek, MI (city) Calhoun County	23	0.04
East Lansing, MI (city) Ingham County	20	0.04
East Lansing, MI (city) Ingham County	20	0.04
Vernon, CT (town) Tolland County	13	0.04
Monterey, CA (city) Monterey County	10	0.04
Spring Hill, TN (city) Williamson County	9	0.04
Tampa, FL (city) Hillsborough County	86	0.03
Rochester, MN (city) Olmsted County	28	0.03
Rochester Hills, MI (city) Oakland County	20	0.03
West Bloomfield, MI (charter township) Oakland County	17	0.03
Ames, IA (city) Story County	16	0.03
Waltham, MA (city) Middlesex County	16	0.03
Smyrna, GA (city) Cobb County	15	0.03
Buffalo Grove, IL (village) Lake County	14	0.03
Elkhart, IN (city) Elkhart County	13	0.03
Manheim, PA (township) Lancaster County	12	0.03
Saginaw, MI (charter township) Saginaw County	11	0.03
Waxahachie, TX (city) Ellis County	9	0.03
Indianapolis, IN (city) Marion County	149	0.02
Columbus, OH (city) Franklin County	125	0.02
Cincinnati, OH (city) Hamilton County	53	0.02
Buffalo, NY (city) Erie County	45	0.02
Alexandria, VA (ind. city) Alexandria independent city	31	0.02
Huntsville, AL (city) Madison County	31	0.02
Corona, CA (city) Riverside County	30	0.02
Waco, TX (city) McLennan County	30	0.02
Knoxville, TN (city) Knox County	28	0.02
Columbia, MO (city) Boone County	26	0.02
Highlands Ranch, CO (cdp) Douglas County	18	0.02
Shelby, MI (charter township) Macomb County	18	0.02
Farmington Hills, MI (city) Oakland County	16	0.02
Passaic, NJ (city) Passaic County	16	0.02
Southfield, MI (city) Oakland County	12	0.02
Lakeville, MN (city) Dakota County	11	0.02
South Jordan, UT (city) Salt Lake County	11	0.02
Wheaton, MD (cdp) Montgomery County	11	0.02
Rancho Santa Margarita, CA (city) Orange County	10	0.02
Mansfield, TX (city) Tarrant County	9	0.02
Bethlehem, NY (town) Albany County	8	0.02
Oviedo, FL (city) Seminole County	6	0.02
New York, NY (city) Kings County	414	0.01
Bronx, NY (borough) Bronx County	108	0.01
Manhattan, NY (borough) New York County	100	0.01
Dallas, TX (city) Dallas County	90	0.01
Memphis, TN (city) Shelby County	79	0.01
Boston, MA (city) Suffolk County	50	0.01
Baltimore, MD (city) Baltimore city County	44	0.01
Fort Worth, TX (city) Tarrant County	41	0.01
Pittsburgh, PA (city) Allegheny County	36	0.01
Paradise, NV (cdp) Clark County	26	0.01
New Orleans, LA (city) Orleans Parish	24	0.01
St. Louis, MO (city) St. Louis city County	24	0.01
Lexington-Fayette, KY (cons. govt) Fayette County	18	0.01
Boise City, ID (city) Ada County	15	0.01
Richmond, VA (ind. city) Richmond independent city	14	0.01
Irvine, CA (city) Orange County	13	0.01
Akron, OH (city) Summit County	12	0.01
Charleston, SC (city) Charleston County	12	0.01
Coral Springs, FL (city) Broward County	12	0.01
Edison, NJ (township) Middlesex County	12	0.01
Lewisville, TX (city) Denton County	12	0.01
Sunrise, FL (city) Broward County	12	0.01
Tacoma, WA (city) Pierce County	12	0.01
Manchester, NH (city) Hillsborough County	11	0.01
Boca Raton, FL (city) Palm Beach County	10	0.01
Norman, OK (city) Cleveland County	10	0.01
Ann Arbor, MI (city) Washtenaw County	9	0.01
O'Fallon, MO (city) St. Charles County	9	0.01
Roswell, GA (city) Fulton County	8	0.01
Trenton, NJ (city) Mercer County	8	0.01
Bowling Green, KY (city) Warren County	7	0.01
Bellevue, NE (city) Sarpy County	6	0.01
Medford, MA (city) Middlesex County	6	0.01
Chicago, IL (city) Cook County	107	<0.01
Queens, NY (borough) Queens County	107	<0.01
Los Angeles, CA (city) Los Angeles County	101	<0.01
Brooklyn, NY (borough) Kings County	99	<0.01
Philadelphia, PA (city) Philadelphia County	51	<0.01
Phoenix, AZ (city) Maricopa County	50	<0.01
San Diego, CA (city) San Diego County	39	<0.01
Seattle, WA (city) King County	22	<0.01
Milwaukee, WI (city) Milwaukee County	19	<0.01

Ancestry

African, Sub-Saharan: Other

U.S. and 50 States Sorted by Population and Percent of Total Population

Place	Population	%
United States	**120,887**	**0.04**
New York	20,838	0.11
Maryland	14,436	0.25
Texas	9,124	0.04
Georgia	7,490	0.08
California	6,588	0.02
Virginia	5,772	0.07
North Carolina	4,312	0.05
Pennsylvania	4,275	0.03
New Jersey	4,028	0.05
Illinois	3,630	0.03
Massachusetts	3,519	0.05
Ohio	3,378	0.03
Minnesota	3,190	0.06
Washington	2,756	0.04
Florida	2,694	0.01
Tennessee	2,127	0.03
Arizona	2,091	0.03
Michigan	2,021	0.02
Indiana	1,517	0.02
Connecticut	1,421	0.04
Missouri	1,363	0.02
Colorado	1,262	0.03
Rhode Island	1,164	0.11
Kansas	1,038	0.04
District of Columbia	995	0.17
Kentucky	905	0.02
Nevada	857	0.03
Utah	686	0.03
Oklahoma	671	0.02
Iowa	601	0.02
Oregon	552	0.01
Nebraska	526	0.03
Alabama	523	0.01
South Carolina	523	0.01
Louisiana	483	0.01
Maine	462	0.03
Wisconsin	462	0.01
Idaho	367	0.02
New Hampshire	343	0.03
Arkansas	331	0.01
Delaware	313	0.04
Vermont	259	0.04
Mississippi	204	0.01
North Dakota	174	0.03
South Dakota	173	0.02
Alaska	151	0.02
West Virginia	104	0.01
Hawaii	103	0.01
New Mexico	85	<0.01
Montana	0	0.00
Wyoming	0	0.00

Place	Population	%
Maryland	14,436	0.25
District of Columbia	995	0.17
New York	20,838	0.11
Rhode Island	1,164	0.11
Georgia	7,490	0.08
Virginia	5,772	0.07
Minnesota	3,190	0.06
North Carolina	4,312	0.05
New Jersey	4,028	0.05
Massachusetts	3,519	0.05
United States	**120,887**	**0.04**
Texas	9,124	0.04
Washington	2,756	0.04
Connecticut	1,421	0.04
Kansas	1,038	0.04
Delaware	313	0.04
Vermont	259	0.04
Pennsylvania	4,275	0.03
Illinois	3,630	0.03
Ohio	3,378	0.03
Tennessee	2,127	0.03
Arizona	2,091	0.03
Colorado	1,262	0.03
Nevada	857	0.03
Utah	686	0.03
Nebraska	526	0.03
Maine	462	0.03
New Hampshire	343	0.03
North Dakota	174	0.03
California	6,588	0.02
Michigan	2,021	0.02
Indiana	1,517	0.02
Missouri	1,363	0.02
Kentucky	905	0.02
Oklahoma	671	0.02
Iowa	601	0.02
Idaho	367	0.02
South Dakota	173	0.02
Alaska	151	0.02
Florida	2,694	0.01
Oregon	552	0.01
Alabama	523	0.01
South Carolina	523	0.01
Louisiana	483	0.01
Wisconsin	462	0.01
Arkansas	331	0.01
Mississippi	204	0.01
West Virginia	104	0.01
Hawaii	103	0.01
New Mexico	85	<0.01
Montana	0	0.00
Wyoming	0	0.00

Please refer to the Explanation of Data in the front of the book for more detailed information.

Ancestry

African, Sub-Saharan: Other

Top 150 Places Sorted by Population

Based on all places, regardless of total population

Place	Population	%
New York, NY (city) Kings County	17,415	0.22
Bronx, NY (borough) Bronx County	10,539	0.77
Manhattan, NY (borough) New York County	3,545	0.22
Houston, TX (city) Harris County	2,449	0.12
Philadelphia, PA (city) Philadelphia County	1,902	0.13
Brooklyn, NY (borough) Kings County	1,881	0.08
Chicago, IL (city) Cook County	1,781	0.07
Germantown, MD (cdp) Montgomery County	1,430	1.69
Newark, NJ (city) Essex County	1,324	0.48
Charlotte, NC (city) Mecklenburg County	1,242	0.18
Queens, NY (borough) Queens County	1,219	0.06
Dallas, TX (city) Dallas County	1,077	0.09
Los Angeles, CA (city) Los Angeles County	1,031	0.03
Washington, DC (city) District of Columbia	995	0.17
Chillum, MD (cdp) Prince George's County	954	2.72
Memphis, TN (city) Shelby County	953	0.15
Fort Worth, TX (city) Tarrant County	844	0.12
Raleigh, NC (city) Wake County	839	0.22
Gaithersburg, MD (city) Montgomery County	792	1.36
Indianapolis, IN (city) Marion County	785	0.10
Boston, MA (city) Suffolk County	750	0.12
Columbus, OH (city) Franklin County	713	0.09
Dale City, VA (cdp) Prince William County	672	1.06
Greensboro, NC (city) Guilford County	670	0.25
Phoenix, AZ (city) Maricopa County	658	0.05
Adelphi, MD (cdp) Prince George's County	637	4.24
Glenmont, MD (cdp) Montgomery County	631	4.69
Bedford, TX (city) Tarrant County	612	1.30
St. Paul, MN (city) Ramsey County	608	0.22
Clarkston, GA (city) DeKalb County	539	7.13
Tucson, AZ (city) Pima County	534	0.10
Alexandria, VA (ind. city) Alexandria independent city	521	0.39
Silver Spring, MD (cdp) Montgomery County	517	0.74
Nashville-Davidson, TN (metro govt) Davidson County	516	0.09
Baltimore, MD (city) Baltimore city County	501	0.08
Seattle, WA (city) King County	495	0.08
Providence, RI (city) Providence County	493	0.28
Minneapolis, MN (city) Hennepin County	482	0.13
Louisville-Jefferson County, KY (metro govt) Jefferson County	453	0.08
White Oak, MD (cdp) Montgomery County	437	2.62
Irvington, NJ (township) Essex County	425	0.78
Greenbelt, MD (city) Prince George's County	416	1.82
Bridgeport, CT (city/town) Fairfield County	416	0.29
Kent, WA (city) King County	411	0.46
Salt Lake City, UT (city) Salt Lake County	401	0.22
Atlanta, GA (city) Fulton County	398	0.10
Glendale, AZ (city) Maricopa County	386	0.17
Pearland, TX (city) Brazoria County	383	0.46
San Diego, CA (city) San Diego County	376	0.03
Cincinnati, OH (city) Hamilton County	374	0.12
Columbia, MD (cdp) Howard County	367	0.37
Forest Park, OH (city) Hamilton County	366	1.96
New Rochelle, NY (city) Westchester County	365	0.48
Bayonet Point, FL (cdp) Pasco County	359	1.52
Montgomery Village, MD (cdp) Montgomery County	346	1.09
Kansas City, KS (city) Wyandotte County	346	0.24
Lexington-Fayette, KY (cons. govt) Fayette County	343	0.12
Potomac, MD (cdp) Montgomery County	329	0.73
Omaha, NE (city) Douglas County	329	0.08
Takoma Park, MD (city) Montgomery County	320	1.90
Worcester, MA (city) Worcester County	318	0.18
Watertown Town, MA (city) Middlesex County	315	1.00
Cleveland, OH (city) Cuyahoga County	315	0.08
Oakland, CA (city) Alameda County	310	0.08
Rose Hill, VA (cdp) Fairfax County	309	1.56
Rochester, NY (city) Monroe County	309	0.15
San Jose, CA (city) Santa Clara County	297	0.03
Arlington, VA (cdp) Arlington County	295	0.15
Lansing, MI (city) Ingham County	289	0.26
Lansing, MI (city) Ingham County	289	0.25
Boise City, ID (city) Ada County	283	0.14
East Orange, NJ (city) Essex County	282	0.43
San Antonio, TX (city) Medina County	282	0.02
North Bethesda, MD (cdp) Montgomery County	278	0.69
Denver, CO (city) Denver County	276	0.05
Hempstead, NY (town) Nassau County	275	0.04
St. Louis, MO (city) St. Louis city County	269	0.08
Pawtucket, RI (city) Providence County	268	0.37
Aurora, CO (city) Arapahoe County	261	0.08
Lake Ridge, VA (cdp) Prince William County	259	0.66
Detroit, MI (city) Wayne County	259	0.03
Madison, WI (city) Dane County	258	0.11
Wichita, KS (city) Sedgwick County	258	0.07
Woodlawn, VA (cdp) Fairfax County	254	1.30
Jersey City, NJ (city) Hudson County	247	0.10
Breckenridge Hills, MO (city) St. Louis County	238	5.01
Seabrook, MD (cdp) Prince George's County	238	1.52
Long Beach, CA (city) Los Angeles County	235	0.05
Staten Island, NY (borough) Richmond County	231	0.05
Sandy Springs, GA (city) Fulton County	229	0.25
Reno, NV (city) Washoe County	229	0.10
Arlington, TX (city) Tarrant County	229	0.06
Colorado Springs, CO (city) El Paso County	227	0.06
Erie, PA (city) Erie County	226	0.22
Woodmore, MD (cdp) Prince George's County	220	6.28
Bellevue, WA (city) King County	219	0.18
Grand Prairie, TX (city) Dallas County	219	0.13
Hyattsville, MD (city) Prince George's County	218	1.26
San Francisco, CA (city) San Francisco County	218	0.03
Lincolnia, VA (cdp) Fairfax County	217	1.05
Paradise, NV (cdp) Clark County	212	0.10
Overland Park, KS (city) Johnson County	209	0.12
Las Vegas, NV (city) Clark County	207	0.04
Pittsburg, CA (city) Contra Costa County	206	0.33
Bethesda, MD (cdp) Montgomery County	204	0.35
West Palm Beach, FL (city) Palm Beach County	202	0.21
Aurora, IL (city) Kane County	202	0.11
Middlesex, NJ (borough) Middlesex County	200	1.46
Sharon Hill, PA (borough) Delaware County	198	3.51
Knightdale, NC (town) Wake County	198	1.89
Owings Mills, MD (cdp) Baltimore County	197	0.66
Euless, TX (city) Tarrant County	197	0.39
Aspen Hill, MD (cdp) Montgomery County	195	0.41
Wheaton, MD (cdp) Montgomery County	193	0.43
Glenn Dale, MD (cdp) Prince George's County	192	1.36
St. Louis Park, MN (city) Hennepin County	192	0.43
Upper Darby, PA (township) Delaware County	192	0.23
Tallahassee, FL (city) Leon County	189	0.11
Anaheim, CA (city) Orange County	189	0.06
Burlington, VT (city) Chittenden County	187	0.45
Centreville, VA (cdp) Fairfax County	187	0.26
Austin, TX (city) Travis County	185	0.02
Price, PA (township) Monroe County	184	5.29
Port St. Lucie, FL (city) St. Lucie County	184	0.12
Mount Vernon, NY (city) Westchester County	180	0.27
City of Orange, NJ (township) Essex County	178	0.59
Manchester, NH (city) Hillsborough County	178	0.16
Portland, ME (city) Cumberland County	175	0.26
Roswell, GA (city) Fulton County	175	0.20
Dayton, OH (city) Montgomery County	175	0.12
Tulsa, OK (city) Tulsa County	175	0.05
Kansas City, MO (city) Jackson County	175	0.04
Sioux Falls, SD (city) Minnehaha County	173	0.12
Chicopee, MA (city) Hampden County	172	0.31
Berkeley, CA (city) Alameda County	172	0.16
Amherst, NY (town) Erie County	170	0.14
New Haven, CT (city/town) New Haven County	170	0.13
Beaumont, TX (city) Jefferson County	169	0.15
Cheverly, MD (town) Prince George's County	168	2.69
Piscataway, NJ (township) Middlesex County	168	0.31
Fort Wayne, IN (city) Allen County	164	0.06
Herndon, VA (town) Fairfax County	163	0.72
Troy, NY (city) Rensselaer County	159	0.32
Rockville, MD (city) Montgomery County	158	0.27
Fairland, MD (cdp) Montgomery County	157	0.68
Islip, NY (town) Suffolk County	155	0.05
Portland, OR (city) Multnomah County	155	0.03
Marina del Rey, CA (cdp) Los Angeles County	149	1.62
Fort Washington, MD (cdp) Prince George's County	148	0.59
North Andover, MA (town) Essex County	147	0.53

SECTION THREE

Please refer to the Explanation of Data in the front of the book for more detailed information.

Ancestry

African, Sub-Saharan: Other

Top 150 Places Sorted by Percent of Total Population

Based on all places, regardless of total population

Place	Population	%
Clarkston, GA (city) DeKalb County	539	7.13
Derwood, MD (cdp) Montgomery County	138	6.46
Woodmore, MD (cdp) Prince George's County	220	6.28
Kukuihaele, HI (cdp) Hawaii County	23	6.02
Price, PA (township) Monroe County	184	5.29
Breckenridge Hills, MO (city) St. Louis County	238	5.01
Glenmont, MD (cdp) Montgomery County	631	4.69
Tunica Resorts, MS (cdp) Tunica County	66	4.48
Lakewood, TN (city) Davidson County	100	4.25
Adelphi, MD (cdp) Prince George's County	637	4.24
Ophir, CO (town) San Miguel County	5	4.00
Epps, LA (village) West Carroll Parish	63	3.96
Ewing, NE (village) Holt County	20	3.94
Sharon Hill, PA (borough) Delaware County	198	3.51
Milford, ME (town) Penobscot County	99	3.24
Southern Gateway, VA (cdp) Stafford County	113	3.21
West Branch, PA (township) Potter County	12	2.90
Lathrup Village, MI (city) Oakland County	116	2.83
Chillum, MD (cdp) Prince George's County	954	2.72
Cheverly, MD (town) Prince George's County	168	2.69
Lockland, OH (village) Hamilton County	93	2.69
West Laurel, MD (cdp) Prince George's County	125	2.64
White Oak, MD (cdp) Montgomery County	437	2.62
Warm Springs, GA (city) Meriwether County	8	2.61
Fisher, MN (township) Polk County	4	2.44
Arnold Line, MS (cdp) Lamar County	38	2.41
Bon Air, AL (town) Talladega County	3	2.14
Colwyn, PA (borough) Delaware County	53	2.11
St. Anthony, MN (city) Ramsey County	61	2.08
Forest Park, OH (city) Hamilton County	366	1.96
Takoma Park, MD (city) Montgomery County	320	1.90
Savage, MD (cdp) Howard County	129	1.90
Millbourne, PA (borough) Delaware County	20	1.90
Knightdale, NC (town) Wake County	198	1.89
South Nyack, NY (village) Rockland County	105	1.89
Greenbelt, MD (city) Prince George's County	416	1.82
Keedysville, MD (town) Washington County	20	1.71
Machias, ME (cdp) Washington County	23	1.70
Germantown, MD (cdp) Montgomery County	1,430	1.69
Eucalyptus Hills, CA (cdp) San Diego County	99	1.69
Marina del Rey, CA (cdp) Los Angeles County	149	1.62
Rose Hill, VA (cdp) Fairfax County	309	1.56
Dumfries, VA (town) Prince William County	77	1.56
Hillsborough, NC (town) Orange County	92	1.54
Bayonet Point, FL (cdp) Pasco County	359	1.52
Seabrook, MD (cdp) Prince George's County	238	1.52
Belle Haven, VA (cdp) Fairfax County	100	1.52
Middlesex, NJ (borough) Middlesex County	200	1.46
Greendale, MO (city) St. Louis County	10	1.45
Fairwood, MD (cdp) Prince George's County	66	1.42
Gaithersburg, MD (city) Montgomery County	792	1.36
Glenn Dale, MD (cdp) Prince George's County	192	1.36
Angwin, CA (cdp) Napa County	51	1.36
Edmonston, MD (town) Prince George's County	18	1.36
Bedford, TX (city) Tarrant County	612	1.30
Woodlawn, VA (cdp) Fairfax County	254	1.30
Hyattsville, MD (city) Prince George's County	218	1.26
Summerfield, MD (cdp) Prince George's County	138	1.24
Litchfield Park, AZ (city) Maricopa County	64	1.21
French Gulch, CA (cdp) Shasta County	2	1.16
Baltimore Highlands, MD (cdp) Baltimore County	82	1.12
Finley, WA (cdp) Benton County	61	1.11
Highland, PA (township) Clarion County	7	1.11
Montgomery Village, MD (cdp) Montgomery County	346	1.09
Chamblee, GA (city) DeKalb County	105	1.08
Enfield, NH (town) Grafton County	50	1.08
Missouri Valley, IA (city) Harrison County	31	1.07
Dale City, VA (cdp) Prince William County	672	1.06
Porters Neck, NC (cdp) New Hanover County	53	1.06
Lincolnia, VA (cdp) Fairfax County	217	1.05
Fair Oaks, GA (cdp) Cobb County	66	1.03
Watertown Town, MA (city) Middlesex County	315	1.00
Pelham, NY (village) Westchester County	68	1.00
Westphalia, MD (cdp) Prince George's County	61	1.00
Yarmouth Port, MA (cdp) Barnstable County	52	1.00
West Buechel, KY (city) Jefferson County	11	0.98
Whittemore, IA (city) Kossuth County	6	0.96
Bladensburg, MD (town) Prince George's County	85	0.95
South Amherst, MA (cdp) Hampshire County	47	0.95
Machias, ME (town) Washington County	23	0.95
Wells Branch, TX (cdp) Travis County	109	0.94
Wayne, PA (township) Clinton County	16	0.94
Brentwood, PA (borough) Allegheny County	90	0.93
Beardstown, IL (city) Cass County	56	0.93
Layhill, MD (cdp) Montgomery County	53	0.93
Dellwood, MN (city) Washington County	10	0.93
Fraser, MI (city) Macomb County	136	0.92
Turpin Hills, OH (cdp) Hamilton County	45	0.91
Menands, NY (village) Albany County	36	0.90
Potomac Mills, VA (cdp) Prince William County	42	0.89
Helena, GA (city) Telfair County	26	0.88
Edgemoor, DE (cdp) New Castle County	46	0.86
Shiloh, PA (cdp) York County	97	0.85
Woodbury, NY (cdp) Nassau County	76	0.84
Mount Rainier, MD (city) Prince George's County	68	0.83
Hainesville, IL (village) Lake County	27	0.81
North Randall, OH (village) Cuyahoga County	7	0.81
Martha Lake, WA (cdp) Snohomish County	123	0.79
Cloverly, MD (cdp) Montgomery County	122	0.79
Emmaus, PA (borough) Lehigh County	89	0.79
Irvington, NJ (township) Essex County	425	0.78
West Hempstead, NY (cdp) Nassau County	143	0.78
Bronx, NY (borough) Bronx County	10,539	0.77
Colesville, MD (cdp) Montgomery County	109	0.77
Dayton, MN (city) Hennepin County	35	0.77
Scarborough, ME (town) Cumberland County	142	0.76
Laie, HI (cdp) Honolulu County	43	0.76
St. Anthony, MN (city) Hennepin and Ramsey Counties	61	0.75
Dayton, MN (city) Hennepin County	35	0.75
Silver Spring, MD (cdp) Montgomery County	517	0.74
Wheatley Heights, NY (cdp) Suffolk County	46	0.74
Pomona, NY (village) Rockland County	26	0.74
Point of Rocks, MD (cdp) Frederick County	10	0.74
Potomac, MD (cdp) Montgomery County	329	0.73
Conewago, PA (township) York County	52	0.73
Perryman, MD (cdp) Harford County	17	0.73
Hiram, OH (village) Portage County	9	0.73
Herndon, VA (town) Fairfax County	163	0.72
Lower Allen, PA (cdp) Cumberland County	50	0.72
Franklinton, NC (town) Franklin County	15	0.72
North Bethesda, MD (cdp) Montgomery County	278	0.69
Ravena, NY (village) Albany County	23	0.69
Fairland, MD (cdp) Montgomery County	157	0.68
Spring Ridge, MD (cdp) Frederick County	40	0.68
Fullerton, PA (cdp) Lehigh County	101	0.67
Glenville, WV (town) Gilmer County	15	0.67
Lake Ridge, VA (cdp) Prince William County	259	0.66
Owings Mills, MD (cdp) Baltimore County	197	0.66
Montgomery, IL (village) Kendall County	105	0.66
Glasgow, DE (cdp) New Castle County	103	0.66
Somerville, NJ (borough) Somerset County	81	0.66
Rockford, TN (city) Blount County	6	0.65
Morton Grove, IL (village) Cook County	146	0.64
Lorton, VA (cdp) Fairfax County	123	0.64
Champlin, MN (city) Hennepin County	143	0.63
Pelham, NY (town) Westchester County	76	0.62
Kinross, MI (charter township) Chippewa County	50	0.62
Port Allen, LA (city) West Baton Rouge Parish	32	0.62
Cockeysville, MD (cdp) Baltimore County	119	0.60
City of Orange, NJ (township) Essex County	178	0.59
Fort Washington, MD (cdp) Prince George's County	148	0.59
Grambling, LA (city) Lincoln Parish	29	0.59
Chadron, NE (city) Dawes County	34	0.58
Hillman, MI (village) Montmorency County	4	0.58
Baltic, OH (village) Tuscarawas County	3	0.58
Powder Springs, GA (city) Cobb County	78	0.57
White Center, WA (cdp) King County	72	0.57
St. Andrews, SC (cdp) Richland County	117	0.56
Mustang, OK (city) Canadian County	93	0.56
Lake Arbor, MD (cdp) Prince George's County	58	0.56

Please refer to the Explanation of Data in the front of the book for more detailed information.

Ancestry

African, Sub-Saharan: Other

Top 150 Places Sorted by Percent of Total Population

Based on places with total population of 7,500 or more

Place	Population	%
Clarkston, GA (city) DeKalb County	539	7.13
Glenmont, MD (cdp) Montgomery County	631	4.69
Adelphi, MD (cdp) Prince George's County	637	4.24
Chillum, MD (cdp) Prince George's County	954	2.72
White Oak, MD (cdp) Montgomery County	437	2.62
Forest Park, OH (city) Hamilton County	366	1.96
Takoma Park, MD (city) Montgomery County	320	1.90
Knightdale, NC (town) Wake County	198	1.89
Greenbelt, MD (city) Prince George's County	416	1.82
Germantown, MD (cdp) Montgomery County	1,430	1.69
Marina del Rey, CA (cdp) Los Angeles County	149	1.62
Rose Hill, VA (cdp) Fairfax County	309	1.56
Bayonet Point, FL (cdp) Pasco County	359	1.52
Seabrook, MD (cdp) Prince George's County	238	1.52
Middlesex, NJ (borough) Middlesex County	200	1.46
Gaithersburg, MD (city) Montgomery County	792	1.36
Glenn Dale, MD (cdp) Prince George's County	192	1.36
Bedford, TX (city) Tarrant County	612	1.30
Woodlawn, VA (cdp) Fairfax County	254	1.30
Hyattsville, MD (city) Prince George's County	218	1.26
Summerfield, MD (cdp) Prince George's County	138	1.24
Montgomery Village, MD (cdp) Montgomery County	346	1.09
Chamblee, GA (city) DeKalb County	105	1.08
Dale City, VA (cdp) Prince William County	672	1.06
Lincolnia, VA (cdp) Fairfax County	217	1.05
Watertown Town, MA (city) Middlesex County	315	1.00
Bladensburg, MD (town) Prince George's County	85	0.95
Wells Branch, TX (cdp) Travis County	109	0.94
Brentwood, PA (borough) Allegheny County	90	0.93
Fraser, MI (city) Macomb County	136	0.92
Shiloh, PA (cdp) York County	97	0.85
Woodbury, NY (cdp) Nassau County	76	0.84
Mount Rainier, MD (city) Prince George's County	68	0.83
Martha Lake, WA (cdp) Snohomish County	123	0.79
Cloverly, MD (cdp) Montgomery County	122	0.79
Emmaus, PA (borough) Lehigh County	89	0.79
Irvington, NJ (township) Essex County	425	0.78
West Hempstead, NY (cdp) Nassau County	143	0.78
Bronx, NY (borough) Bronx County	10,539	0.77
Colesville, MD (cdp) Montgomery County	109	0.77
Scarborough, ME (town) Cumberland County	142	0.76
St. Anthony, MN (city) Hennepin and Ramsey Counties	61	0.75
Silver Spring, MD (cdp) Montgomery County	517	0.74
Potomac, MD (cdp) Montgomery County	329	0.73
Herndon, VA (town) Fairfax County	163	0.72
North Bethesda, MD (cdp) Montgomery County	278	0.69
Fairland, MD (cdp) Montgomery County	157	0.68
Fullerton, PA (cdp) Lehigh County	101	0.67
Lake Ridge, VA (cdp) Prince William County	259	0.66
Owings Mills, MD (cdp) Baltimore County	197	0.66
Montgomery, IL (village) Kendall County	105	0.66
Glasgow, DE (cdp) New Castle County	103	0.66
Somerville, NJ (borough) Somerset County	81	0.66
Morton Grove, IL (village) Cook County	146	0.64
Lorton, VA (cdp) Fairfax County	123	0.64
Champlin, MN (city) Hennepin County	143	0.63
Pelham, NY (town) Westchester County	76	0.62
Kinross, MI (charter township) Chippewa County	50	0.62
Cockeysville, MD (cdp) Baltimore County	119	0.60
City of Orange, NJ (township) Essex County	178	0.59
Fort Washington, MD (cdp) Prince George's County	148	0.59
Powder Springs, GA (city) Cobb County	78	0.57
White Center, WA (cdp) King County	72	0.57
St. Andrews, SC (cdp) Richland County	117	0.56
Mustang, OK (city) Canadian County	93	0.56
Lake Arbor, MD (cdp) Prince George's County	58	0.56
North Andover, MA (town) Essex County	147	0.53
Portsmouth, RI (town) Newport County	92	0.53
Streetsboro, OH (city) Portage County	82	0.53
Clayton, NC (town) Johnston County	78	0.53
West Manchester, PA (township) York County	97	0.52
Caln, PA (township) Chester County	71	0.52
New Carrollton, MD (city) Prince George's County	63	0.52
Wappinger, NY (town) Dutchess County	137	0.51
Shelby, NC (city) Cleveland County	100	0.49
Newark, NJ (city) Essex County	1,324	0.48
New Rochelle, NY (city) Westchester County	365	0.48
Chantilly, VA (cdp) Fairfax County	107	0.48
Scottdale, GA (cdp) DeKalb County	47	0.48
North Druid Hills, GA (cdp) DeKalb County	86	0.47
Mentone, CA (cdp) San Bernardino County	42	0.47
North Star, DE (cdp) New Castle County	37	0.47
Kent, WA (city) King County	411	0.46
Pearland, TX (city) Brazoria County	383	0.46
Elkridge, MD (cdp) Howard County	62	0.46
Lansdowne, VA (cdp) Loudoun County	45	0.46
Burlington, VT (city) Chittenden County	187	0.45
Glen Ellyn, IL (village) DuPage County	122	0.45
Laurel, MD (city) Prince George's County	111	0.45
Brock Hall, MD (cdp) Prince George's County	37	0.45
North Providence, RI (town) Providence County	141	0.44
Des Moines, WA (city) King County	128	0.44
Imperial Beach, CA (city) San Diego County	116	0.44
Parma Heights, OH (city) Cuyahoga County	91	0.44
Lithia Springs, GA (cdp) Douglas County	75	0.44
Merrifield, VA (cdp) Fairfax County	63	0.44
East Franklin, NJ (cdp) Somerset County	34	0.44
East Orange, NJ (city) Essex County	282	0.43
Wheaton, MD (cdp) Montgomery County	193	0.43
St. Louis Park, MN (city) Hennepin County	192	0.43
Langley Park, MD (cdp) Prince George's County	78	0.43
East Riverdale, MD (cdp) Prince George's County	67	0.43
Chenango, NY (town) Broome County	49	0.43
Beltsville, MD (cdp) Prince George's County	65	0.42
Aspen Hill, MD (cdp) Montgomery County	195	0.41
South Laurel, MD (cdp) Prince George's County	105	0.41
Rainbow City, AL (city) Etowah County	38	0.40
Alexandria, VA (ind. city) Alexandria independent city	521	0.39
Euless, TX (city) Tarrant County	197	0.39
Randallstown, MD (cdp) Baltimore County	126	0.39
Orangeburg, SC (city) Orangeburg County	54	0.39
Whitehall, PA (township) Lehigh County	101	0.38
Rosemount, MN (city) Dakota County	79	0.38
McDonough, GA (city) Henry County	77	0.38
Shiloh, IL (village) St. Clair County	46	0.38
Columbia, MD (cdp) Howard County	367	0.37
Pawtucket, RI (city) Providence County	268	0.37
New Hope, MN (city) Hennepin County	75	0.37
Spring Lake, NC (town) Cumberland County	44	0.37
Fairfield, AL (city) Jefferson County	42	0.37
North Kensington, MD (cdp) Montgomery County	35	0.36
Dunn Loring, VA (cdp) Fairfax County	33	0.36
Bethesda, MD (cdp) Montgomery County	204	0.35
Little Canada, MN (city) Ramsey County	34	0.35
Hagerstown, MD (city) Washington County	135	0.34
Richfield, MN (city) Hennepin County	119	0.34
Canton, MA (town) Norfolk County	72	0.34
Vadnais Heights, MN (city) Ramsey County	42	0.34
Pittsburg, CA (city) Contra Costa County	206	0.33
Andover, MN (city) Anoka County	100	0.33
Amherst Center, MA (cdp) Hampshire County	64	0.33
Bellaire, TX (city) Harris County	55	0.33
Troy, NY (city) Rensselaer County	159	0.32
Kennesaw, GA (city) Cobb County	91	0.32
Ottumwa, IA (city) Wapello County	79	0.32
North Lynnwood, WA (cdp) Snohomish County	51	0.32
Westview, FL (cdp) Miami-Dade County	30	0.32
George Mason, VA (cdp) Fairfax County	28	0.32
Chicopee, MA (city) Hampden County	172	0.31
Piscataway, NJ (township) Middlesex County	168	0.31
Burke, VA (cdp) Fairfax County	130	0.31
Amherst, MA (town) Hampshire County	117	0.31
Brighton, NY (cdp/town) Monroe County	113	0.31
Warwick, PA (township) Lancaster County	54	0.31
View Park-Windsor Hills, CA (cdp) Los Angeles County	33	0.31
Webster, TX (city) Harris County	31	0.31
Durham, NH (cdp) Strafford County	28	0.31
Brooklyn Center, MN (city) Hennepin County	88	0.30
Sidney, OH (city) Shelby County	64	0.30
Lynnfield, MA (cdp/town) Essex County	35	0.30

SECTION THREE

Ancestry

Albanian

U.S. and 50 States Sorted by Population and Percent of Total Population

Place	Population	%
United States	**172,149**	**0.06**
New York	46,223	0.24
Michigan	22,903	0.23
Massachusetts	15,095	0.23
Florida	11,060	0.06
New Jersey	11,019	0.13
Connecticut	9,401	0.27
Pennsylvania	8,869	0.07
Illinois	8,794	0.07
Texas	4,654	0.02
Ohio	4,061	0.04
California	3,854	0.01
Wisconsin	2,903	0.05
Missouri	2,687	0.05
Arizona	2,656	0.04
Virginia	2,493	0.03
Georgia	1,477	0.02
New Hampshire	1,385	0.11
Maryland	1,365	0.02
Nevada	1,077	0.04
Washington	867	0.01
Maine	854	0.06
South Carolina	808	0.02
North Carolina	762	0.01
Indiana	703	0.01
Colorado	630	0.01
Iowa	606	0.02
Kentucky	581	0.01
Alaska	471	0.07
Utah	466	0.02
Oregon	369	0.01
Oklahoma	363	0.01
Tennessee	272	<0.01
Delaware	269	0.03
New Mexico	258	0.01
Rhode Island	249	0.02
Minnesota	239	<0.01
Vermont	228	0.04
District of Columbia	183	0.03
North Dakota	166	0.03
Alabama	164	<0.01
Louisiana	152	<0.01
Nebraska	139	0.01
Idaho	124	0.01
Kansas	107	<0.01
Wyoming	42	0.01
West Virginia	35	<0.01
Hawaii	20	<0.01
Arkansas	17	<0.01
Mississippi	15	<0.01
Montana	14	<0.01
South Dakota	0	0.00

Place	Population	%
Connecticut	9,401	0.27
New York	46,223	0.24
Michigan	22,903	0.23
Massachusetts	15,095	0.23
New Jersey	11,019	0.13
New Hampshire	1,385	0.11
Pennsylvania	8,869	0.07
Illinois	8,794	0.07
Alaska	471	0.07
United States	**172,149**	**0.06**
Florida	11,060	0.06
Maine	854	0.06
Wisconsin	2,903	0.05
Missouri	2,687	0.05
Ohio	4,061	0.04
Arizona	2,656	0.04
Nevada	1,077	0.04
Vermont	228	0.04
Virginia	2,493	0.03
Delaware	269	0.03
District of Columbia	183	0.03
North Dakota	166	0.03
Texas	4,654	0.02
Georgia	1,477	0.02
Maryland	1,365	0.02
South Carolina	808	0.02
Iowa	606	0.02
Utah	466	0.02
Rhode Island	249	0.02
California	3,854	0.01
Washington	867	0.01
North Carolina	762	0.01
Indiana	703	0.01
Colorado	630	0.01
Kentucky	581	0.01
Oregon	369	0.01
Oklahoma	363	0.01
New Mexico	258	0.01
Nebraska	139	0.01
Idaho	124	0.01
Wyoming	42	0.01
Tennessee	272	<0.01
Minnesota	239	<0.01
Alabama	164	<0.01
Louisiana	152	<0.01
Kansas	107	<0.01
West Virginia	35	<0.01
Hawaii	20	<0.01
Arkansas	17	<0.01
Mississippi	15	<0.01
Montana	14	<0.01
South Dakota	0	0.00

Please refer to the Explanation of Data in the front of the book for more detailed information.

Ancestry

Albanian

Top 150 Places Sorted by Population

Based on all places, regardless of total population

Place	Population	%
New York, NY (city) Kings County	31,056	0.38
Staten Island, NY (borough) Richmond County	8,108	1.75
Bronx, NY (borough) Bronx County	7,835	0.57
Brooklyn, NY (borough) Kings County	6,871	0.28
Queens, NY (borough) Queens County	6,624	0.30
Philadelphia, PA (city) Philadelphia County	3,892	0.26
Sterling Heights, MI (city) Macomb County	3,414	2.63
Worcester, MA (city) Worcester County	2,568	1.43
Jacksonville, FL (city) Duval County	2,515	0.31
Waterbury, CT (city/town) New Haven County	2,423	2.20
Yonkers, NY (city) Westchester County	2,270	1.16
Boston, MA (city) Suffolk County	2,022	0.34
Macomb, MI (township) Macomb County	2,016	2.69
Chicago, IL (city) Cook County	1,699	0.06
Manhattan, NY (borough) New York County	1,618	0.10
Shelby, MI (charter township) Macomb County	1,549	2.13
Hempstead, NY (town) Nassau County	1,052	0.14
Quincy, MA (city) Norfolk County	958	1.06
Farmington Hills, MI (city) Oakland County	866	1.08
Phoenix, AZ (city) Maricopa County	852	0.06
Rochester Hills, MI (city) Oakland County	831	1.18
Westland, MI (city) Wayne County	829	0.98
Garfield, NJ (city) Bergen County	826	2.74
Clearwater, FL (city) Pinellas County	796	0.74
Lakewood, OH (city) Cuyahoga County	766	1.45
Clinton, MI (charter township) Macomb County	757	0.78
Stamford, CT (city/town) Fairfield County	747	0.62
Dearborn, MI (city) Wayne County	666	0.68
Yorktown, NY (town) Westchester County	628	1.75
Houston, TX (city) Harris County	615	0.03
Troy, MI (city) Oakland County	612	0.76
Tempe, AZ (city) Maricopa County	592	0.36
St. Louis, MO (city) St. Louis city County	587	0.18
Clifton, NJ (city) Passaic County	543	0.66
Warren, MI (city) Macomb County	534	0.39
Addison, IL (village) DuPage County	526	1.43
Roswell, GA (city) Fulton County	525	0.61
Madison Heights, MI (city) Oakland County	514	1.72
Braintree Town, MA (city) Norfolk County	507	1.44
Dallas, TX (city) Dallas County	481	0.04
Largo, FL (city) Pinellas County	475	0.62
Grosse Pointe Park, MI (city) Wayne County	472	4.02
Oakland, MI (charter township) Oakland County	467	2.90
Aurora, IL (city) Kane County	467	0.25
Manchester, NH (city) Hillsborough County	456	0.42
Syracuse, NY (city) Onondaga County	455	0.31
Watertown, CT (town) Litchfield County	443	1.97
Lodi, NJ (borough) Bergen County	436	1.82
Livonia, MI (city) Wayne County	420	0.43
South Milwaukee, WI (city) Milwaukee County	419	2.00
Wayne, NJ (township) Passaic County	417	0.77
Colonie, NY (town) Albany County	405	0.50
Madison, WI (city) Dane County	404	0.18
Anchorage, AK (municipality) Anchorage Municipality	399	0.14
Farmington, NY (town) Ontario County	388	3.35
Washington, MI (township) Macomb County	386	1.59
Southgate, MI (city) Wayne County	386	1.28
Taylor, MI (city) Wayne County	385	0.60
Albany, NY (city) Albany County	384	0.39
New Rochelle, NY (city) Westchester County	370	0.49
Buffalo, NY (city) Erie County	369	0.14
Oyster Bay, NY (town) Nassau County	368	0.13
Old Bridge, NJ (township) Middlesex County	367	0.57
St. Petersburg, FL (city) Pinellas County	365	0.15
Carmel, NY (town) Putnam County	361	1.05
Spring Valley, NV (cdp) Clark County	355	0.21
St. Clair Shores, MI (city) Macomb County	351	0.58
Scottsdale, AZ (city) Maricopa County	345	0.16
Howell, NJ (township) Monmouth County	344	0.68
Temple Terrace, FL (city) Hillsborough County	342	1.41
West Des Moines, IA (city) Polk County	342	0.62
Oakville, CT (cdp) Litchfield County	339	3.61
Los Angeles, CA (city) Los Angeles County	335	0.01
Mansfield, TX (city) Tarrant County	332	0.65
Fair Lawn, NJ (borough) Bergen County	330	1.03
Rocky River, OH (city) Cuyahoga County	328	1.62
Clarkstown, NY (town) Rockland County	328	0.39
Ballwin, MO (city) St. Louis County	321	1.05
Hawthorne, NJ (borough) Passaic County	317	1.71
West Bloomfield, MI (charter township) Oakland County	315	0.49
Monroe, NY (village) Orange County	310	3.73
Monroe, NY (town) Orange County	310	0.80
Las Vegas, NV (city) Clark County	305	0.05
Akron, OH (city) Summit County	304	0.15
Mount Vernon, NY (city) Westchester County	303	0.45
North Hempstead, NY (town) Nassau County	296	0.13
Newton, MA (city) Middlesex County	295	0.35
Bridgeport, CT (city/town) Fairfield County	292	0.20
Columbus, OH (city) Franklin County	292	0.04
Lynn, MA (city) Essex County	289	0.32
Wethersfield, CT (cdp/town) Hartford County	287	1.08
Bruce, MI (township) Macomb County	281	3.24
Winthrop Town, MA (city) Suffolk County	280	1.62
Revere, MA (city) Suffolk County	279	0.56
Upper Darby, PA (township) Delaware County	278	0.34
Cresskill, NJ (borough) Bergen County	274	3.27
South Whitehall, PA (township) Lehigh County	267	1.40
Surprise, AZ (city) Maricopa County	263	0.25
Willow Springs, IL (village) Cook County	258	4.83
Brownville, NJ (cdp) Middlesex County	257	8.82
Commerce, MI (charter township) Oakland County	257	0.65
Chesterfield, MI (township) Macomb County	255	0.60
Fort Worth, TX (city) Tarrant County	254	0.04
Hartford, CT (city/town) Hartford County	250	0.20
Albuquerque, NM (city) Bernalillo County	249	0.05
Beaumont, TX (city) Jefferson County	247	0.21
Myrtle Beach, SC (city) Horry County	243	0.91
Affton, MO (cdp) St. Louis County	242	1.20
Orangetown, NY (town) Rockland County	241	0.50
Malden, MA (city) Middlesex County	241	0.41
Novi, MI (city) Oakland County	240	0.45
Prospect, CT (town) New Haven County	238	2.56
West Haven, CT (city/town) New Haven County	238	0.43
Royal Oak, MI (city) Oakland County	238	0.41
Roselle Park, NJ (borough) Union County	237	1.80
Huntington, NY (town) Suffolk County	237	0.12
East Fishkill, NY (town) Dutchess County	236	0.83
Valley Stream, NY (village) Nassau County	236	0.64
Wixom, MI (city) Oakland County	235	1.75
Des Plaines, IL (city) Cook County	234	0.41
Arlington, VA (cdp) Arlington County	234	0.12
Detroit, MI (city) Wayne County	233	0.03
Everett, MA (city) Middlesex County	227	0.56
Natick, MA (town) Middlesex County	226	0.70
Fairfield, CT (town) Fairfield County	226	0.38
Utica, MI (city) Macomb County	225	4.73
Naples Park, FL (cdp) Collier County	224	3.33
Emmaus, PA (borough) Lehigh County	223	1.98
Fairview Park, OH (city) Cuyahoga County	223	1.32
Pinellas Park, FL (city) Pinellas County	223	0.46
Somers, NY (town) Westchester County	221	1.11
Abilene, TX (city) Taylor County	221	0.19
Norwood, MA (cdp/town) Norfolk County	220	0.78
Enterprise, NV (cdp) Clark County	218	0.22
Little Falls, NJ (township) Passaic County	217	1.56
Fruit Cove, FL (cdp) St. Johns County	213	0.72
Canton, MI (charter township) Wayne County	213	0.24
Nutley, NJ (township) Essex County	212	0.76
Wheaton, IL (city) DuPage County	212	0.40
Guilderland, NY (town) Albany County	211	0.60
Wayne, MI (city) Wayne County	210	1.17
Bristol, CT (city/town) Hartford County	210	0.35
Frisco, TX (city) Collin County	210	0.20
Babylon, NY (town) Suffolk County	210	0.10
Putnam Valley, NY (town) Putnam County	209	1.79
Blacksburg, VA (town) Montgomery County	208	0.49
Anaheim, CA (city) Orange County	207	0.06
Salem, MA (city) Essex County	206	0.50
Hamtramck, MI (city) Wayne County	205	0.91
Franklin Square, NY (cdp) Nassau County	205	0.69

SECTION THREE

Please refer to the Explanation of Data in the front of the book for more detailed information.

Ancestry

Albanian

Top 150 Places Sorted by Percent of Total Population

Based on all places, regardless of total population

Place	Population	%
Springbrook, IA (city) Jackson County	31	23.13
Matlacha Isles-Matlacha Shores, FL (cdp) Lee County	28	14.58
Yorktown Heights, NY (cdp) Westchester County	170	10.19
North Lakeville, MA (cdp) Plymouth County	199	9.26
Brownville, NJ (cdp) Middlesex County	257	8.82
Milton, NY (cdp) Ulster County	101	8.68
Shrub Oak, NY (cdp) Westchester County	134	7.40
Seldovia, AK (city) Kenai Peninsula Borough	28	6.86
Albrightsville, PA (cdp) Carbon County	13	6.67
Lehman, PA (township) Luzerne County	204	5.88
Forreston, IL (village) Ogle County	91	5.86
Seymour, WI (town) Lafayette County	24	5.26
Cortland, IL (town) DeKalb County	186	4.89
Wauregan, CT (cdp) Windham County	44	4.87
Willow Springs, IL (village) Cook County	258	4.83
Bristol, NH (cdp) Grafton County	77	4.77
Utica, MI (city) Macomb County	225	4.73
Belleair Bluffs, FL (city) Pinellas County	91	4.35
Penney Farms, FL (town) Clay County	16	4.07
Grosse Pointe Park, MI (city) Wayne County	472	4.02
Port Royal, PA (borough) Juniata County	46	3.88
Brewster Hill, NY (cdp) Putnam County	91	3.78
Monroe, NY (village) Orange County	310	3.73
Badger, MN (city) Roseau County	15	3.70
Pantops, VA (cdp) Albemarle County	84	3.67
Oakville, CT (cdp) Litchfield County	339	3.61
Saltaire, NY (village) Suffolk County	2	3.45
Brodheadsville, PA (cdp) Monroe County	58	3.36
Farmington, NY (town) Ontario County	388	3.35
Honeyville, UT (city) Box Elder County	41	3.35
Naples Park, FL (cdp) Collier County	224	3.33
Cresskill, NJ (borough) Bergen County	274	3.27
Lattimer, PA (cdp) Luzerne County	13	3.25
Bruce, MI (township) Macomb County	281	3.24
Dix, NY (town) Schuyler County	126	3.20
Wind Gap, PA (borough) Northampton County	87	3.17
Tivoli, NY (village) Dutchess County	30	3.02
Oakland, MI (charter township) Oakland County	467	2.90
Milton, WI (town) Rock County	83	2.84
Peninsula, OH (village) Summit County	16	2.79
Marlborough, CT (town) Hartford County	174	2.77
Lake Mohawk, OH (cdp) Carroll County	48	2.76
Tariffville, CT (cdp) Hartford County	35	2.75
Garfield, NJ (city) Bergen County	826	2.74
West Hazleton, PA (borough) Luzerne County	120	2.72
Macomb, MI (township) Macomb County	2,016	2.69
Sterling Heights, MI (city) Macomb County	3,414	2.63
Keene, NY (town) Essex County	23	2.63
Sheridan, MO (town) Worth County	6	2.59
Marlborough, MO (village) St. Louis County	48	2.58
Prospect, CT (town) New Haven County	238	2.56
Hatfield, MA (cdp) Hampshire County	36	2.56
Newtown, CT (borough) Fairfield County	51	2.55
Bradenton Beach, FL (city) Manatee County	37	2.55
Bristol, NH (town) Grafton County	77	2.51
Hamilton, VA (town) Loudoun County	14	2.47
Sappington, MO (cdp) St. Louis County	196	2.46
Hilltop, WV (cdp) Fayette County	9	2.41
Hope, NY (town) Hamilton County	10	2.39
Washington, MA (town) Berkshire County	14	2.36
McKinley Heights, OH (cdp) Trumbull County	25	2.29
Tisbury, MA (town) Dukes County	88	2.26
Greig, NY (town) Lewis County	25	2.24
Waterbury, CT (city/town) New Haven County	2,423	2.20
Holly, MI (village) Oakland County	134	2.19
Porter, PA (township) Huntingdon County	43	2.14
Shelby, MI (charter township) Macomb County	1,549	2.13
Morris, CT (town) Litchfield County	52	2.11
Newfields, NH (cdp) Rockingham County	6	2.07
Marlborough, NY (town) Ulster County	180	2.06
Colonie, NY (village) Albany County	161	2.05
South Milwaukee, WI (city) Milwaukee County	419	2.00
Emmaus, PA (borough) Lehigh County	223	1.98
Linden, TN (town) Perry County	20	1.98
Watertown, CT (town) Litchfield County	443	1.97
Marlboro, NY (cdp) Ulster County	79	1.97
Mooers, NY (town) Clinton County	70	1.96
Catskill, NY (village) Greene County	80	1.93
Remington, VA (town) Fauquier County	14	1.93
Lakeville, MA (town) Plymouth County	199	1.90
Prospect Park, NJ (borough) Passaic County	111	1.90
Woodland, NJ (township) Burlington County	22	1.87
Vergennes, IL (village) Jackson County	7	1.87
Bethlehem Village, CT (cdp) Litchfield County	41	1.84
Schleswig, WI (town) Manitowoc County	40	1.84
Lincoln Park, NJ (borough) Morris County	195	1.83
Lodi, NJ (borough) Bergen County	436	1.82
Sorrento, FL (cdp) Lake County	15	1.82
Roselle Park, NJ (borough) Union County	237	1.80
Williamson, NY (town) Wayne County	125	1.80
Peach Lake, NY (cdp) Putnam County	29	1.80
Putnam Valley, NY (town) Putnam County	209	1.79
Mentz, NY (town) Cayuga County	36	1.78
Dahlonega, GA (city) Lumpkin County	89	1.76
Staten Island, NY (borough) Richmond County	8,108	1.75
Yorktown, NY (town) Westchester County	628	1.75
Wixom, MI (city) Oakland County	235	1.75
Fort Laramie, WY (town) Goshen County	3	1.74
Madison Heights, MI (city) Oakland County	514	1.72
Hollis, NH (town) Hillsborough County	131	1.72
Topsfield, MA (cdp) Essex County	49	1.72
Hawthorne, NJ (borough) Passaic County	317	1.71
Lake Orion, MI (village) Oakland County	50	1.70
Henry, IL (city) Marshall County	42	1.70
Cedarville, IL (village) Stephenson County	15	1.69
Rossville, IL (village) Vermilion County	21	1.66
Gustavus, AK (city) Hoonah-Angoon Census Area	7	1.65
Elwood, UT (town) Box Elder County	15	1.64
Flower Hill, NY (village) Nassau County	75	1.63
Tinmouth, VT (town) Rutland County	11	1.63
Rocky River, OH (city) Cuyahoga County	328	1.62
Winthrop Town, MA (city) Suffolk County	280	1.62
Washington, MI (township) Macomb County	386	1.59
Juliustown, NJ (cdp) Burlington County	5	1.57
Little Falls, NJ (township) Passaic County	217	1.56
Highland, NY (town) Sullivan County	39	1.54
Wickenburg, AZ (town) Maricopa County	100	1.53
Solebury, PA (township) Bucks County	129	1.51
Singac, NJ (cdp) Passaic County	61	1.51
Clawson, MI (city) Oakland County	180	1.50
Plymouth, WI (city) Sheboygan County	122	1.46
Lakewood, OH (city) Cuyahoga County	766	1.45
Brookdale, NJ (cdp) Essex County	133	1.45
Hartsdale, NY (cdp) Westchester County	75	1.45
Braintree Town, MA (city) Norfolk County	507	1.44
Milladore, WI (village) Wood County	4	1.44
Worcester, MA (city) Worcester County	2,568	1.43
Addison, IL (village) DuPage County	526	1.43
Collegeville, PA (borough) Montgomery County	73	1.42
North Middletown, NJ (cdp) Monmouth County	42	1.42
Temple Terrace, FL (city) Hillsborough County	342	1.41
South Whitehall, PA (township) Lehigh County	267	1.40
North Haledon, NJ (borough) Passaic County	115	1.40
Wadsworth, IL (village) Lake County	54	1.40
Greene, PA (township) Erie County	65	1.39
Scotts Corners, NY (cdp) Westchester County	7	1.39
Rockledge, PA (borough) Montgomery County	35	1.37
Webster, NH (town) Merrimack County	25	1.35
Shiremanstown, PA (borough) Cumberland County	20	1.33
Fairview Park, OH (city) Cuyahoga County	223	1.32
Bedminster, NJ (township) Somerset County	108	1.32
Gridley, IL (village) McLean County	20	1.32
Hillcrest, IL (village) Ogle County	17	1.32
Southampton, PA (township) Cumberland County	79	1.31
Old Bethpage, NY (cdp) Nassau County	73	1.31
Thornwood, NY (cdp) Westchester County	48	1.31
Harrietstown, NY (town) Franklin County	74	1.30
Fishkill, NY (village) Dutchess County	27	1.30
Southgate, MI (city) Wayne County	386	1.28
Saranac Lake, NY (village) Franklin County	74	1.28

Please refer to the Explanation of Data in the front of the book for more detailed information.

Ancestry

Albanian

Top 150 Places Sorted by Percent of Total Population

Based on places with total population of 7,500 or more

Place	Population	%
Grosse Pointe Park, MI (city) Wayne County	472	4.02
Monroe, NY (village) Orange County	310	3.73
Oakville, CT (cdp) Litchfield County	339	3.61
Farmington, NY (town) Ontario County	388	3.35
Cresskill, NJ (borough) Bergen County	274	3.27
Bruce, MI (township) Macomb County	281	3.24
Oakland, MI (charter township) Oakland County	467	2.90
Garfield, NJ (city) Bergen County	826	2.74
Macomb, MI (township) Macomb County	2,016	2.69
Sterling Heights, MI (city) Macomb County	3,414	2.63
Prospect, CT (town) New Haven County	238	2.56
Sappington, MO (cdp) St. Louis County	196	2.46
Waterbury, CT (city/town) New Haven County	2,423	2.20
Shelby, MI (charter township) Macomb County	1,549	2.13
Marlborough, NY (town) Ulster County	180	2.06
Colonie, NY (village) Albany County	161	2.05
South Milwaukee, WI (city) Milwaukee County	419	2.00
Emmaus, PA (borough) Lehigh County	223	1.98
Watertown, CT (town) Litchfield County	443	1.97
Lakeville, MA (town) Plymouth County	199	1.90
Lincoln Park, NJ (borough) Morris County	195	1.83
Lodi, NJ (borough) Bergen County	436	1.82
Roselle Park, NJ (borough) Union County	237	1.80
Putnam Valley, NY (town) Putnam County	209	1.79
Staten Island, NY (borough) Richmond County	8,108	1.75
Yorktown, NY (town) Westchester County	628	1.75
Wixom, MI (city) Oakland County	235	1.75
Madison Heights, MI (city) Oakland County	514	1.72
Hollis, NH (town) Hillsborough County	131	1.72
Hawthorne, NJ (borough) Passaic County	317	1.71
Rocky River, OH (city) Cuyahoga County	328	1.62
Winthrop Town, MA (city) Suffolk County	280	1.62
Washington, MI (township) Macomb County	386	1.59
Little Falls, NJ (township) Passaic County	217	1.56
Solebury, PA (township) Bucks County	129	1.51
Clawson, MI (city) Oakland County	180	1.50
Plymouth, WI (city) Sheboygan County	122	1.46
Lakewood, OH (city) Cuyahoga County	766	1.45
Brookdale, NJ (cdp) Essex County	133	1.45
Braintree Town, MA (city) Norfolk County	507	1.44
Worcester, MA (city) Worcester County	2,568	1.43
Addison, IL (village) DuPage County	526	1.43
Temple Terrace, FL (city) Hillsborough County	342	1.41
South Whitehall, PA (township) Lehigh County	267	1.40
North Haledon, NJ (borough) Passaic County	115	1.40
Fairview Park, OH (city) Cuyahoga County	223	1.32
Bedminster, NJ (township) Somerset County	108	1.32
Southgate, MI (city) Wayne County	386	1.28
Loganville, GA (city) Walton County	121	1.26
Guttenberg, NJ (town) Hudson County	137	1.25
Kent, NY (town) Putnam County	168	1.23
Milford, MI (charter township) Oakland County	190	1.22
Holly, MI (township) Oakland County	134	1.21
Affton, MO (cdp) St. Louis County	242	1.20
Rochester Hills, MI (city) Oakland County	831	1.18
Wayne, MI (city) Wayne County	210	1.17
Yonkers, NY (city) Westchester County	2,270	1.16
Fort Salonga, NY (cdp) Suffolk County	121	1.15
Broadlands, VA (cdp) Loudoun County	122	1.14
Conning Towers Nautilus Park, CT (cdp) New London County	105	1.14
Somers, NY (town) Westchester County	221	1.11
Farmington Hills, MI (city) Oakland County	866	1.08
Wethersfield, CT (cdp/town) Hartford County	287	1.08
Southeast, NY (town) Putnam County	198	1.08
Woodmere, NY (cdp) Nassau County	189	1.08
Grosse Pointe Woods, MI (city) Wayne County	175	1.07
North Castle, NY (town) Westchester County	124	1.07
Quincy, MA (city) Norfolk County	958	1.06
Hasbrouck Heights, NJ (borough) Bergen County	124	1.06
Beverly Hills, FL (cdp) Citrus County	90	1.06
Carmel, NY (town) Putnam County	361	1.05
Ballwin, MO (city) St. Louis County	321	1.05
Nanuet, NY (cdp) Rockland County	186	1.04
Fair Lawn, NJ (borough) Bergen County	330	1.03
Wolcott, CT (town) New Haven County	165	1.00
Overlea, MD (cdp) Baltimore County	125	0.99
Westland, MI (city) Wayne County	829	0.98
Thomaston, CT (town) Litchfield County	77	0.98
Concord, MO (cdp) St. Louis County	153	0.97
West Carrollton, OH (city) Montgomery County	129	0.97
Rantoul, IL (village) Champaign County	122	0.97
Willowick, OH (city) Lake County	132	0.93
Dickinson, TX (city) Galveston County	171	0.92
East Rockaway, NY (village) Nassau County	90	0.92
Myrtle Beach, SC (city) Horry County	243	0.91
Hamtramck, MI (city) Wayne County	205	0.91
Whitewater, WI (city) Walworth County	101	0.91
Culpeper, VA (town) Culpeper County	140	0.90
Mason, MI (city) Ingham County	73	0.90
Oxford, CT (town) New Haven County	109	0.89
Norwell, MA (town) Plymouth County	92	0.89
Birmingham, MI (city) Oakland County	173	0.87
Stoughton, WI (city) Dane County	108	0.86
Palmyra, NY (town) Wayne County	68	0.86
Elfers, FL (cdp) Pasco County	112	0.85
Cudahy, WI (city) Milwaukee County	153	0.84
Keansburg, NJ (borough) Monmouth County	86	0.84
East Fishkill, NY (town) Dutchess County	236	0.83
Schiller Park, IL (village) Cook County	97	0.83
Summit, IL (village) Cook County	90	0.83
Holden, MA (town) Worcester County	140	0.82
Pearl River, NY (cdp) Rockland County	120	0.82
Monroe, NY (town) Orange County	310	0.80
Congers, NY (cdp) Rockland County	63	0.80
Parma Heights, OH (city) Cuyahoga County	164	0.79
South Farmingdale, NY (cdp) Nassau County	117	0.79
Buxton, ME (town) York County	63	0.79
Garden City Park, NY (cdp) Nassau County	62	0.79
Clinton, MI (charter township) Macomb County	757	0.78
Norwood, MA (cdp/town) Norfolk County	220	0.78
Elmwood Park, NJ (borough) Bergen County	149	0.78
Short Hills, NJ (cdp) Essex County	103	0.78
Piedmont, CA (city) Alameda County	82	0.78
Kinnelon, NJ (borough) Morris County	79	0.78
Wayne, NJ (township) Passaic County	417	0.77
Lyon, MI (charter township) Oakland County	108	0.77
Hartford, WI (city) Washington County	106	0.77
Woodlyn, PA (cdp) Delaware County	70	0.77
Troy, MI (city) Oakland County	612	0.76
Nutley, NJ (township) Essex County	212	0.76
Villa Park, IL (village) DuPage County	168	0.76
Clearwater, FL (city) Pinellas County	796	0.74
Center Line, MI (city) Macomb County	62	0.74
Briarcliff Manor, NY (village) Westchester County	59	0.74
Fruit Cove, FL (cdp) St. Johns County	213	0.72
Farmers Branch, TX (city) Dallas County	204	0.72
Waverly, MI (cdp) Eaton County	179	0.72
Southbridge Town, MA (city) Worcester County	121	0.72
Harper Woods, MI (city) Wayne County	103	0.72
Succasunna, NJ (cdp) Morris County	65	0.72
Whitewater, WI (city) Walworth County	101	0.71
Natick, MA (town) Middlesex County	226	0.70
Franklin Square, NY (cdp) Nassau County	205	0.69
Brigham City, UT (city) Box Elder County	122	0.69
Holliston, MA (town) Middlesex County	93	0.69
Westtown, PA (township) Chester County	75	0.69
Mount Kisco, NY (town/village) Westchester County	73	0.69
West Boylston, MA (town) Worcester County	53	0.69
Dearborn, MI (city) Wayne County	666	0.68
Howell, NJ (township) Monmouth County	344	0.68
Catskill, NY (town) Greene County	80	0.67
Clifton, NJ (city) Passaic County	543	0.66
Palm Springs, FL (village) Palm Beach County	123	0.66
Mansfield, TX (city) Tarrant County	332	0.65
Commerce, MI (charter township) Oakland County	257	0.65
Cockeysville, MD (cdp) Baltimore County	128	0.65
Greenwich, CT (cdp) Fairfield County	86	0.65
Valley Stream, NY (village) Nassau County	236	0.64
Halfmoon, NY (town) Saratoga County	134	0.64
Huntington Station, NY (cdp) Suffolk County	199	0.63

SECTION THREE

Please refer to the Explanation of Data in the front of the book for more detailed information.

Ancestry

Alsatian

U.S. and 50 States Sorted by Population and Percent of Total Population

Place	Population	%
United States	**12,104**	**<0.01**
Texas	2,796	0.01
California	926	<0.01
New York	882	<0.01
Ohio	705	0.01
Illinois	669	0.01
Pennsylvania	599	<0.01
New Jersey	492	0.01
Florida	444	<0.01
Massachusetts	309	<0.01
Indiana	300	<0.01
Missouri	268	<0.01
Virginia	258	<0.01
North Carolina	255	<0.01
Colorado	254	0.01
Wisconsin	235	<0.01
Maryland	213	<0.01
Oregon	195	0.01
Nevada	148	0.01
Michigan	147	<0.01
Arizona	145	<0.01
Minnesota	145	<0.01
Kentucky	138	<0.01
Washington	138	<0.01
Georgia	136	<0.01
Louisiana	131	<0.01
Alabama	122	<0.01
South Carolina	113	<0.01
Connecticut	104	<0.01
Iowa	102	<0.01
Nebraska	72	<0.01
New Mexico	72	<0.01
Vermont	69	0.01
Rhode Island	46	<0.01
South Dakota	44	0.01
District of Columbia	39	0.01
Kansas	39	<0.01
New Hampshire	38	<0.01
Montana	35	<0.01
Mississippi	32	<0.01
Delaware	30	<0.01
Arkansas	27	<0.01
Maine	25	<0.01
Tennessee	25	<0.01
Utah	25	<0.01
Alaska	20	<0.01
Wyoming	19	<0.01
Idaho	18	<0.01
West Virginia	18	<0.01
North Dakota	15	<0.01
Oklahoma	14	<0.01
Hawaii	13	<0.01

Place	Population	%
Texas	2,796	0.01
Ohio	705	0.01
Illinois	669	0.01
New Jersey	492	0.01
Colorado	254	0.01
Oregon	195	0.01
Nevada	148	0.01
Vermont	69	0.01
South Dakota	44	0.01
District of Columbia	39	0.01
United States	**12,104**	**<0.01**
California	926	<0.01
New York	882	<0.01
Pennsylvania	599	<0.01
Florida	444	<0.01
Massachusetts	309	<0.01
Indiana	300	<0.01
Missouri	268	<0.01
Virginia	258	<0.01
North Carolina	255	<0.01
Wisconsin	235	<0.01
Maryland	213	<0.01
Michigan	147	<0.01
Arizona	145	<0.01
Minnesota	145	<0.01
Kentucky	138	<0.01
Washington	138	<0.01
Georgia	136	<0.01
Louisiana	131	<0.01
Alabama	122	<0.01
South Carolina	113	<0.01
Connecticut	104	<0.01
Iowa	102	<0.01
Nebraska	72	<0.01
New Mexico	72	<0.01
Rhode Island	46	<0.01
Kansas	39	<0.01
New Hampshire	38	<0.01
Montana	35	<0.01
Mississippi	32	<0.01
Delaware	30	<0.01
Arkansas	27	<0.01
Maine	25	<0.01
Tennessee	25	<0.01
Utah	25	<0.01
Alaska	20	<0.01
Wyoming	19	<0.01
Idaho	18	<0.01
West Virginia	18	<0.01
North Dakota	15	<0.01
Oklahoma	14	<0.01
Hawaii	13	<0.01

Please refer to the Explanation of Data in the front of the book for more detailed information.

Ancestry

Alsatian

Top 150 Places Sorted by Population

Based on all places, regardless of total population

Place	Population	%
San Antonio, TX (city) Medina County	662	0.05
New York, NY (city) Kings County	217	<0.01
Manhattan, NY (borough) New York County	129	0.01
Portland, OR (city) Multnomah County	122	0.02
Castroville, TX (city) Medina County	120	4.48
Austin, TX (city) Travis County	102	0.01
Chicago, IL (city) Cook County	96	<0.01
Pittsburgh, PA (city) Allegheny County	91	0.03
Los Angeles, CA (city) Los Angeles County	78	<0.01
Hondo, TX (city) Medina County	77	0.88
Medfield, MA (town) Norfolk County	73	0.61
Houston, TX (city) Harris County	72	<0.01
Ashland, OH (city) Ashland County	69	0.33
Cincinnati, OH (city) Hamilton County	67	0.02
Madison, WI (city) Dane County	66	0.03
LaCoste, TX (city) Medina County	61	4.38
San Jose, CA (city) Santa Clara County	61	0.01
Naperville, IL (city) DuPage County	59	0.04
Boerne, TX (city) Kendall County	58	0.60
Odessa, TX (city) Ector County	58	0.06
Eldorado, TX (city) Schleicher County	56	2.20
Spring Valley, NV (cdp) Clark County	55	0.03
Elk Grove Village, IL (village) Cook County	54	0.16
Philadelphia, PA (city) Philadelphia County	54	<0.01
Greendale, IN (city) Dearborn County	53	1.16
New Orleans, LA (city) Orleans Parish	52	0.02
Albany, NY (city) Albany County	51	0.05
New Bremen, NY (town) Lewis County	50	1.85
Mobile, AL (city) Mobile County	49	0.03
San Francisco, CA (city) San Francisco County	49	0.01
Aberdeen, IN (cdp) Porter County	48	2.20
St. Petersburg, FL (city) Pinellas County	46	0.02
Woodway, TX (city) McLennan County	45	0.54
Yardville, NJ (cdp) Mercer County	44	0.59
Hamilton, NJ (township) Mercer County	44	0.05
Lamar, PA (township) Clinton County	41	1.64
Fair Lawn, NJ (borough) Bergen County	41	0.13
Jacksonville, IL (city) Morgan County	40	0.21
Orchard Park, NY (town) Erie County	40	0.14
Oak Park, IL (village) Cook County	40	0.08
Arlington, VA (cdp) Arlington County	40	0.02
De Witt, NY (town) Onondaga County	39	0.15
Winter Springs, FL (city) Seminole County	39	0.12
Louisville-Jefferson County, KY (metro govt) Jefferson County	39	0.01
Washington, DC (city) District of Columbia	39	0.01
Mandeville, LA (city) St. Tammany Parish	37	0.32
Dallas, TX (city) Dallas County	37	<0.01
Queens, NY (borough) Queens County	37	<0.01
Holliston, MA (town) Middlesex County	36	0.27
Linden, NJ (city) Union County	36	0.09
Eureka, CA (city) Humboldt County	35	0.13
Fort Collins, CO (city) Larimer County	34	0.02
Lytle, TX (city) Atascosa County	33	1.16
Costa Mesa, CA (city) Orange County	33	0.03
Kansas City, MO (city) Jackson County	33	0.01
Mexia, TX (city) Limestone County	32	0.43
Amherst, NY (town) Erie County	32	0.03
Corpus Christi, TX (city) Nueces County	32	0.01
Laredo, TX (city) Webb County	32	0.01
Scottsdale, AZ (city) Maricopa County	32	0.01
Wabasso, FL (cdp) Indian River County	31	4.34
Worcester, PA (township) Montgomery County	31	0.33
Dent, OH (cdp) Hamilton County	30	0.31
Grove City, OH (city) Franklin County	30	0.09
Milwaukee, WI (city) Milwaukee County	30	0.01
Hempstead, NY (town) Nassau County	30	<0.01
Timberwood Park, TX (cdp) Bexar County	29	0.25
Ames, IA (city) Story County	29	0.05
Bethesda, MD (cdp) Montgomery County	29	0.05
Mount Prospect, IL (village) Cook County	29	0.05
Boulder, CO (city) Boulder County	29	0.03
Concord, CA (city) Contra Costa County	29	0.02
Garland, TX (city) Dallas County	29	0.01
Columbus, OH (city) Franklin County	29	<0.01
Honea Path, SC (town) Anderson County	27	0.71
Scenic Oaks, TX (cdp) Bexar County	27	0.54
Kirkwood, MO (city) St. Louis County	27	0.10
Monroeville, PA (municipality) Allegheny County	27	0.10
Rancho Palos Verdes, CA (city) Los Angeles County	27	0.07
Shelton, CT (city/town) Fairfield County	27	0.07
Hamburg, NY (town) Erie County	27	0.05
Enterprise, NV (cdp) Clark County	27	0.03
Yakima, WA (city) Yakima County	27	0.03
Brooklyn, NY (borough) Kings County	27	<0.01
Taylor Mill, KY (city) Kenton County	26	0.39
Clarence, NY (town) Erie County	26	0.09
Friendswood, TX (city) Galveston County	26	0.07
Akron, OH (city) Summit County	26	0.01
Salem Heights, OH (cdp) Hamilton County	25	0.63
McGregor, FL (cdp) Lee County	25	0.33
Upper Moreland, PA (township) Montgomery County	25	0.10
Medford, MA (city) Middlesex County	25	0.05
Ontario, CA (city) San Bernardino County	25	0.02
Thousand Oaks, CA (city) Ventura County	25	0.02
Overland Park, KS (city) Johnson County	25	0.01
St. Paul, MN (city) Ramsey County	25	0.01
Truchas, NM (cdp) Rio Arriba County	24	3.63
Archbold, OH (village) Fulton County	24	0.57
Goshen, IN (city) Elkhart County	24	0.08
Ewing, NJ (township) Mercer County	24	0.07
Tonawanda, NY (cdp) Erie County	24	0.04
Tonawanda, NY (town) Erie County	24	0.03
Reno, NV (city) Washoe County	24	0.01
Staten Island, NY (borough) Richmond County	24	0.01
Seattle, WA (city) King County	24	<0.01
Treasure Island, FL (city) Pinellas County	23	0.34
Morrisville, NC (town) Wake County	23	0.14
San Carlos, CA (city) San Mateo County	23	0.08
Oakland Park, FL (city) Broward County	23	0.06
Arden-Arcade, CA (cdp) Sacramento County	23	0.03
Alexandria, VA (ind. city) Alexandria independent city	23	0.02
Minneapolis, MN (city) Hennepin County	23	0.01
Las Vegas, NV (city) Clark County	23	<0.01
Long Hill, NJ (township) Morris County	22	0.25
Springfield, PA (township) Montgomery County	22	0.11
Brighton, NY (cdp/town) Monroe County	22	0.06
Muncie, IN (city) Delaware County	22	0.03
Baton Rouge, LA (city) East Baton Rouge Parish	22	0.01
Stonewall, TX (cdp) Gillespie County	21	2.51
West Lakeland, MN (township) Washington County	21	0.53
New London, PA (township) Chester County	21	0.38
East Aurora, NY (village) Erie County	21	0.33
Margate City, NJ (city) Atlantic County	21	0.31
Mayo, MD (cdp) Anne Arundel County	21	0.27
Corrales, NM (village) Sandoval County	21	0.26
Kirkland, NY (town) Oneida County	21	0.20
Aurora, NY (town) Erie County	21	0.15
Middletown, PA (township) Delaware County	21	0.13
Wantagh, NY (cdp) Nassau County	21	0.12
Athens, OH (city) Athens County	21	0.09
Marple, PA (township) Delaware County	21	0.09
Rifton, NY (cdp) Ulster County	20	3.31
Sterling, MA (town) Worcester County	20	0.26
Esopus, NY (town) Ulster County	20	0.22
White Oak, OH (cdp) Hamilton County	20	0.11
Maywood, IL (village) Cook County	20	0.08
Cape Coral, FL (city) Lee County	20	0.01
Lexington-Fayette, KY (cons. govt) Fayette County	20	0.01
Metairie, LA (cdp) Jefferson Parish	20	0.01
Phoenix, AZ (city) Maricopa County	20	<0.01
Falmouth, MA (cdp) Barnstable County	19	0.48
Tioga, NY (town) Tioga County	19	0.39
Ambler, PA (borough) Montgomery County	19	0.30
Beverly Hills, CA (city) Los Angeles County	19	0.06
Falmouth, MA (town) Barnstable County	19	0.06
Berkeley, CA (city) Alameda County	19	0.02
Bloomington, IN (city) Monroe County	19	0.02
Charlotte, NC (city) Mecklenburg County	19	<0.01
Woodlawn, NC (cdp) Alamance County	18	1.44
Telluride, CO (town) San Miguel County	18	0.70

SECTION THREE

Please refer to the Explanation of Data in the front of the book for more detailed information.

Ancestry

Alsatian

Top 150 Places Sorted by Percent of Total Population

Based on all places, regardless of total population

Place	Population	%
Castroville, TX (city) Medina County	120	4.48
LaCoste, TX (city) Medina County	61	4.38
Wabasso, FL (cdp) Indian River County	31	4.34
Truchas, NM (cdp) Rio Arriba County	24	3.63
Macdoel, CA (cdp) Siskiyou County	5	3.40
Rifton, NY (cdp) Ulster County	20	3.31
Pineland, FL (cdp) Lee County	11	2.70
Stonewall, TX (cdp) Gillespie County	21	2.51
Eldorado, TX (city) Schleicher County	56	2.20
Aberdeen, IN (cdp) Porter County	48	2.20
New Bremen, NY (town) Lewis County	50	1.85
Sister Bay, WI (village) Door County	11	1.68
Strawn, TX (city) Palo Pinto County	12	1.65
Lamar, PA (township) Clinton County	41	1.64
D'Hanis, TX (cdp) Medina County	12	1.53
Woodlawn, NC (cdp) Alamance County	18	1.44
Lake Waynoka, OH (cdp) Brown County	11	1.21
Greendale, IN (city) Dearborn County	53	1.16
Lytle, TX (city) Atascosa County	33	1.16
East Butler, PA (borough) Butler County	8	1.13
Apple Canyon Lake, IL (cdp) Jo Daviess County	6	1.07
Prescott, MN (township) Faribault County	2	1.06
Ogden, MI (township) Lenawee County	10	0.96
Winhall, VT (town) Bennington County	5	0.94
Liberty, MI (township) Wexford County	8	0.90
Congerville, IL (village) Woodford County	5	0.90
Hondo, TX (city) Medina County	77	0.88
Pittsford, NY (village) Monroe County	12	0.85
Shields, WI (town) Dodge County	4	0.78
Patch Grove, WI (village) Grant County	2	0.78
Gainesville, NY (village) Wyoming County	2	0.75
Honea Path, SC (town) Anderson County	27	0.71
Langlade, WI (town) Langlade County	4	0.71
Middleport, PA (borough) Schuylkill County	3	0.71
Telluride, CO (town) San Miguel County	18	0.70
Swedesboro, NJ (borough) Gloucester County	17	0.67
Silver Lake, OH (village) Summit County	17	0.66
Dousman, WI (village) Waukesha County	15	0.66
Murray Hill, KY (city) Jefferson County	3	0.66
Salem Heights, OH (cdp) Hamilton County	25	0.63
Aptos Hills-Larkin Valley, CA (cdp) Santa Cruz County	15	0.63
Cabana Colony, FL (cdp) Palm Beach County	15	0.63
Medfield, MA (town) Norfolk County	73	0.61
Boerne, TX (city) Kendall County	58	0.60
Lincolnville, ME (town) Waldo County	11	0.60
Pleasant Valley, WI (town) St. Croix County	3	0.60
Yardville, NJ (cdp) Mercer County	44	0.59
Holiday Heights, NJ (cdp) Ocean County	13	0.59
Archbold, OH (village) Fulton County	24	0.57
Yorktown, TX (city) DeWitt County	12	0.57
Patrick Springs, VA (cdp) Patrick County	9	0.56
Warren, PA (township) Franklin County	2	0.56
Castleton, VT (cdp) Rutland County	9	0.55
Woodway, TX (city) McLennan County	45	0.54
Scenic Oaks, TX (cdp) Bexar County	27	0.54
West Lakeland, MN (township) Washington County	21	0.53
Hollywood Park, TX (town) Bexar County	16	0.53
Barnes, WI (town) Bayfield County	4	0.53
Rehoboth Beach, DE (city) Sussex County	6	0.52
Burlington, PA (township) Bradford County	4	0.51
New Prague, MN (city) Le Sueur County	14	0.50
Murrayville, IL (village) Morgan County	3	0.50
Falmouth, MA (cdp) Barnstable County	19	0.48
Cassville, WI (village) Grant County	4	0.48
Stevens, PA (township) Bradford County	2	0.47
Moreland Hills, OH (village) Cuyahoga County	15	0.45
Barton, WI (town) Washington County	12	0.45
Muse, PA (cdp) Washington County	12	0.45
Somonauk, IL (village) DeKalb County	9	0.45
Mexia, TX (city) Limestone County	32	0.43
Del Mar, CA (city) San Diego County	18	0.43
Banner Elk, NC (town) Avery County	4	0.43
Riverwood, KY (city) Jefferson County	2	0.43
Orleans, IA (city) Dickinson County	3	0.42
Riverview Park, PA (cdp) Berks County	14	0.41

Place	Population	%
Wayne, NY (town) Steuben County	4	0.41
Freeman, WI (town) Crawford County	3	0.41
Surry, NH (town) Cheshire County	3	0.41
Sherwood, OH (cdp) Hamilton County	14	0.40
Fredericktown, OH (village) Knox County	10	0.40
Chenequa, WI (village) Waukesha County	3	0.40
Shirley, IN (town) Hancock County	3	0.40
Taylor Mill, KY (city) Kenton County	26	0.39
Tioga, NY (town) Tioga County	19	0.39
Sharon, WI (town) Walworth County	3	0.39
Washington, MN (township) Le Sueur County	3	0.39
New London, PA (township) Chester County	21	0.38
Wyncote, PA (cdp) Montgomery County	12	0.38
Cottonwood Falls, KS (city) Chase County	4	0.38
Berne, NY (town) Albany County	10	0.36
Pecatonica, IL (village) Winnebago County	9	0.36
Duxbury, VT (town) Washington County	5	0.35
Rouseville, PA (borough) Venango County	2	0.35
Sweden, ME (town) Oxford County	1	0.35
Treasure Island, FL (city) Pinellas County	23	0.34
Trego, WI (town) Washburn County	3	0.34
Ashland, OH (city) Ashland County	69	0.33
Worcester, PA (township) Montgomery County	31	0.33
McGregor, FL (cdp) Lee County	25	0.33
East Aurora, NY (village) Erie County	21	0.33
Conewango, PA (township) Warren County	12	0.33
Cottonwood, CA (cdp) Shasta County	10	0.33
Great Neck Estates, NY (village) Nassau County	9	0.33
Varick, NY (town) Seneca County	6	0.33
Mandeville, LA (city) St. Tammany Parish	37	0.32
Norwich, NY (town) Chenango County	13	0.32
Elizabeth, WV (town) Wirt County	4	0.32
Dent, OH (cdp) Hamilton County	30	0.31
Margate City, NJ (city) Atlantic County	21	0.31
Roxbury, CT (town) Litchfield County	7	0.31
Harrisville, NH (town) Cheshire County	3	0.31
Ambler, PA (borough) Montgomery County	19	0.30
Beecher, IL (village) Will County	14	0.30
East Lansdowne, PA (borough) Delaware County	8	0.30
Germany, PA (township) Adams County	8	0.30
Florida, NY (village) Orange County	8	0.29
Benton, WI (village) Lafayette County	3	0.29
Arlington, VT (town) Bennington County	7	0.28
Locke, NY (town) Cayuga County	5	0.28
Holliston, MA (town) Middlesex County	36	0.27
Mayo, MD (cdp) Anne Arundel County	21	0.27
San Miguel, CA (cdp) Contra Costa County	9	0.27
Bay, MI (township) Charlevoix County	4	0.27
Cambridge, NY (village) Washington County	4	0.27
Homeland, GA (city) Charlton County	4	0.27
Dike, IA (city) Grundy County	3	0.27
Corrales, NM (village) Sandoval County	21	0.26
Sterling, MA (town) Worcester County	20	0.26
Summit, WI (town) Waukesha County	12	0.26
Baileys Harbor, WI (town) Door County	3	0.26
Newark Valley, NY (village) Tioga County	3	0.26
Timberwood Park, TX (cdp) Bexar County	29	0.25
Long Hill, NJ (township) Morris County	22	0.25
Chevy Chase, MD (town) Montgomery County	7	0.25
Almond, NY (town) Allegany County	4	0.25
Argos, IN (town) Marshall County	4	0.25
Belgrade, MN (township) Nicollet County	3	0.25
Georgia, VT (town) Franklin County	11	0.24
Strafford, VT (town) Orange County	3	0.24
Sharon, MN (township) Le Sueur County	2	0.24
New Boston, NH (town) Hillsborough County	12	0.23
Port Aransas, TX (city) Nueces County	8	0.23
Oakland, PA (township) Butler County	7	0.23
Gibsonburg, OH (village) Sandusky County	6	0.23
Three Way, TN (city) Madison County	4	0.23
Beechwood Village, KY (city) Jefferson County	3	0.23
Manawa, WI (city) Waupaca County	3	0.23
Esopus, NY (town) Ulster County	20	0.22
Sardinia, NY (town) Erie County	6	0.22
Lake Como, NJ (borough) Monmouth County	4	0.22

Ancestry

Alsatian

Top 150 Places Sorted by Percent of Total Population

Based on places with total population of 7,500 or more

Place	Population	%
Hondo, TX (city) Medina County	77	0.88
Medfield, MA (town) Norfolk County	73	0.61
Boerne, TX (city) Kendall County	58	0.60
Yardville, NJ (cdp) Mercer County	44	0.59
Woodway, TX (city) McLennan County	45	0.54
Ashland, OH (city) Ashland County	69	0.33
Worcester, PA (township) Montgomery County	31	0.33
McGregor, FL (cdp) Lee County	25	0.33
Mandeville, LA (city) St. Tammany Parish	37	0.32
Dent, OH (cdp) Hamilton County	30	0.31
Holliston, MA (town) Middlesex County	36	0.27
Mayo, MD (cdp) Anne Arundel County	21	0.27
Corrales, NM (village) Sandoval County	21	0.26
Sterling, MA (town) Worcester County	20	0.26
Timberwood Park, TX (cdp) Bexar County	29	0.25
Long Hill, NJ (township) Morris County	22	0.25
Esopus, NY (town) Ulster County	20	0.22
Jacksonville, IL (city) Morgan County	40	0.21
Kirkland, NY (town) Oneida County	21	0.20
Pearsall, TX (city) Frio County	18	0.20
Des Peres, MO (city) St. Louis County	17	0.20
Bloomingdale, NJ (borough) Passaic County	15	0.20
Swissvale, PA (borough) Allegheny County	17	0.19
Alamosa, CO (city) Alamosa County	16	0.18
Smithfield, VA (town) Isle of Wight County	14	0.18
Elk Grove Village, IL (village) Cook County	54	0.16
Washington, NJ (township) Bergen County	14	0.16
De Witt, NY (town) Onondaga County	39	0.15
Aurora, NY (town) Erie County	21	0.15
Crestwood Village, NJ (cdp) Ocean County	12	0.15
Long Branch, VA (cdp) Fairfax County	12	0.15
Orchard Park, NY (town) Erie County	40	0.14
Morrisville, NC (town) Wake County	23	0.14
Granby, CT (town) Hartford County	16	0.14
Grosse Pointe Park, MI (city) Wayne County	16	0.14
Vashon, WA (cdp) King County	14	0.14
Chillicothe, MO (city) Livingston County	12	0.14
Herkimer, NY (village) Herkimer County	11	0.14
Hollis, NH (town) Hillsborough County	11	0.14
Fair Lawn, NJ (borough) Bergen County	41	0.13
Eureka, CA (city) Humboldt County	35	0.13
Middletown, PA (township) Delaware County	21	0.13
Astoria, OR (city) Clatsop County	12	0.13
Ladue, MO (city) St. Louis County	11	0.13
Sunset Hills, MO (city) St. Louis County	11	0.13
Iron Mountain, MI (city) Dickinson County	10	0.13
Rhinebeck, NY (town) Dutchess County	10	0.13
Winter Springs, FL (city) Seminole County	39	0.12
Wantagh, NY (cdp) Nassau County	21	0.12
Falmouth, ME (town) Cumberland County	13	0.12
Oak Hills, OR (cdp) Washington County	13	0.12
Sierra Madre, CA (city) Los Angeles County	13	0.12
Lambertville, MI (cdp) Monroe County	12	0.12
Summerfield, NC (town) Guilford County	12	0.12
Palm Beach, FL (town) Palm Beach County	10	0.12
South Lockport, NY (cdp) Niagara County	10	0.12
Springfield, PA (township) Montgomery County	22	0.11
White Oak, OH (cdp) Hamilton County	20	0.11
Pequannock, NJ (township) Morris County	17	0.11
Auburn, CA (city) Placer County	15	0.11
Tenafly, NJ (borough) Bergen County	15	0.11
Lewisville, NC (town) Forsyth County	14	0.11
Cecil, PA (township) Washington County	12	0.11
Gages Lake, IL (cdp) Lake County	11	0.11
Herkimer, NY (town) Herkimer County	11	0.11
Show Low, AZ (city) Navajo County	11	0.11
Hardyston, NJ (township) Sussex County	9	0.11
Kirkwood, MO (city) St. Louis County	27	0.10
Monroeville, PA (municipality) Allegheny County	27	0.10
Upper Moreland, PA (township) Montgomery County	25	0.10
North Myrtle Beach, SC (city) Horry County	14	0.10
Hot Springs Village, AR (cdp) Garland County	13	0.10
St. Ann, MO (city) St. Louis County	13	0.10
Auburn, IN (city) DeKalb County	12	0.10
Gloucester Point, VA (cdp) Gloucester County	10	0.10
Linden, NJ (city) Union County	36	0.09
Grove City, OH (city) Franklin County	30	0.09
Clarence, NY (town) Erie County	26	0.09
Athens, OH (city) Athens County	21	0.09
Marple, PA (township) Delaware County	21	0.09
Islip, NY (cdp) Suffolk County	18	0.09
Naples, FL (city) Collier County	18	0.09
Parole, MD (cdp) Anne Arundel County	14	0.09
Mill Valley, CA (city) Marin County	13	0.09
Finneytown, OH (cdp) Hamilton County	12	0.09
Elizabethtown, PA (borough) Lancaster County	11	0.09
Forestville, OH (cdp) Hamilton County	10	0.09
Progress, PA (cdp) Dauphin County	9	0.09
South Huntington, NY (cdp) Suffolk County	9	0.09
Oak Park, IL (village) Cook County	40	0.08
Goshen, IN (city) Elkhart County	24	0.08
San Carlos, CA (city) San Mateo County	23	0.08
Maywood, IL (village) Cook County	20	0.08
Venice, FL (city) Sarasota County	16	0.08
Canyon Lake, TX (cdp) Comal County	15	0.08
Trussville, AL (city) Jefferson County	14	0.08
East Greenbush, NY (town) Rensselaer County	13	0.08
Farmington, MO (city) St. Francois County	13	0.08
Druid Hills, GA (cdp) DeKalb County	12	0.08
Swampscott, MA (cdp/town) Essex County	11	0.08
Monfort Heights, OH (cdp) Hamilton County	9	0.08
Colts Neck, NJ (township) Monmouth County	8	0.08
Troy, MO (city) Lincoln County	8	0.08
Bellevue, OH (city) Sandusky County	7	0.08
Rock Falls, IL (city) Whiteside County	7	0.08
Rancho Palos Verdes, CA (city) Los Angeles County	27	0.07
Shelton, CT (city/town) Fairfield County	27	0.07
Friendswood, TX (city) Galveston County	26	0.07
Ewing, NJ (township) Mercer County	24	0.07
New Brighton, MN (city) Ramsey County	15	0.07
Muhlenberg, PA (township) Berks County	14	0.07
Decatur, GA (city) DeKalb County	13	0.07
Point Pleasant, NJ (borough) Ocean County	13	0.07
Barrington, RI (town) Bristol County	11	0.07
Overland, MO (city) St. Louis County	11	0.07
Tanque Verde, AZ (cdp) Pima County	11	0.07
Warren, NJ (township) Somerset County	11	0.07
Greensburg, PA (city) Westmoreland County	10	0.07
Blue Ash, OH (city) Hamilton County	9	0.07
Effingham, IL (city) Effingham County	9	0.07
Bath, NY (town) Steuben County	8	0.07
Bordentown, NJ (township) Burlington County	8	0.07
Alma, MI (city) Gratiot County	7	0.07
Willistown, PA (township) Chester County	7	0.07
Seven Corners, VA (cdp) Fairfax County	6	0.07
Odessa, TX (city) Ector County	58	0.06
Oakland Park, FL (city) Broward County	23	0.06
Brighton, NY (cdp/town) Monroe County	22	0.06
Beverly Hills, CA (city) Los Angeles County	19	0.06
Falmouth, MA (town) Barnstable County	19	0.06
Northampton, MA (city) Hampshire County	18	0.06
Clinton, MS (city) Hinds County	15	0.06
Whitemarsh, PA (township) Montgomery County	11	0.06
Boulder City, NV (city) Clark County	10	0.06
Norwalk, OH (city) Huron County	10	0.06
West Melbourne, FL (city) Brevard County	10	0.06
Lake St. Louis, MO (city) St. Charles County	9	0.06
Worthington, OH (city) Franklin County	8	0.06
Two Rivers, WI (city) Manitowoc County	7	0.06
Upper Montclair, NJ (cdp) Essex County	7	0.06
San Antonio, TX (city) Medina County	662	0.05
Albany, NY (city) Albany County	51	0.05
Hamilton, NJ (township) Mercer County	44	0.05
Ames, IA (city) Story County	29	0.05
Bethesda, MD (cdp) Montgomery County	29	0.05
Mount Prospect, IL (village) Cook County	29	0.05
Hamburg, NY (town) Erie County	27	0.05
Medford, MA (city) Middlesex County	25	0.05
Maryland Heights, MO (city) St. Louis County	15	0.05
Northbrook, IL (village) Cook County	15	0.05

Please refer to the Explanation of Data in the front of the book for more detailed information.

Ancestry

American

U.S. and 50 States Sorted by Population and Percent of Total Population

Place	Population	%
United States	**19,094,109**	**6.28**
Texas	1,367,253	5.62
Florida	1,269,765	6.86
Tennessee	1,075,817	17.25
North Carolina	1,066,458	11.50
Georgia	1,012,372	10.69
Ohio	911,201	7.91
California	889,435	2.43
Kentucky	846,598	19.75
Virginia	835,282	10.65
New York	689,298	3.58
Indiana	644,285	10.04
Alabama	629,152	13.35
Illinois	587,066	4.61
South Carolina	563,469	12.49
Missouri	552,994	9.34
Pennsylvania	550,441	4.36
Michigan	473,397	4.76
Louisiana	406,029	9.17
Oklahoma	351,499	9.56
Mississippi	349,153	11.87
Arkansas	309,378	10.77
New Jersey	280,724	3.22
Maryland	277,540	4.87
Arizona	272,761	4.37
Washington	268,313	4.09
West Virginia	246,632	13.40
Colorado	218,038	4.46
Massachusetts	211,558	3.27
Kansas	190,250	6.77
Oregon	183,475	4.88
Utah	171,689	6.46
Iowa	169,175	5.61
Wisconsin	168,101	2.98
Idaho	149,238	9.77
Minnesota	142,698	2.72
Nevada	99,327	3.77
Connecticut	94,674	2.67
Maine	92,362	6.96
New Mexico	67,803	3.37
Nebraska	65,793	3.66
Montana	59,349	6.09
New Hampshire	56,844	4.33
Vermont	42,304	6.78
Wyoming	37,568	6.89
Delaware	37,428	4.25
South Dakota	27,843	3.48
Alaska	24,459	3.54
Rhode Island	22,938	2.17
North Dakota	16,254	2.46
Hawaii	10,350	0.78
District of Columbia	8,279	1.42

Place	Population	%
Kentucky	846,598	19.75
Tennessee	1,075,817	17.25
West Virginia	246,632	13.40
Alabama	629,152	13.35
South Carolina	563,469	12.49
Mississippi	349,153	11.87
North Carolina	1,066,458	11.50
Arkansas	309,378	10.77
Georgia	1,012,372	10.69
Virginia	835,282	10.65
Indiana	644,285	10.04
Idaho	149,238	9.77
Oklahoma	351,499	9.56
Missouri	552,994	9.34
Louisiana	406,029	9.17
Ohio	911,201	7.91
Maine	92,362	6.96
Wyoming	37,568	6.89
Florida	1,269,765	6.86
Vermont	42,304	6.78
Kansas	190,250	6.77
Utah	171,689	6.46
United States	**19,094,109**	**6.28**
Montana	59,349	6.09
Texas	1,367,253	5.62
Iowa	169,175	5.61
Oregon	183,475	4.88
Maryland	277,540	4.87
Michigan	473,397	4.76
Illinois	587,066	4.61
Colorado	218,038	4.46
Arizona	272,761	4.37
Pennsylvania	550,441	4.36
New Hampshire	56,844	4.33
Delaware	37,428	4.25
Washington	268,313	4.09
Nevada	99,327	3.77
Nebraska	65,793	3.66
New York	689,298	3.58
Alaska	24,459	3.54
South Dakota	27,843	3.48
New Mexico	67,803	3.37
Massachusetts	211,558	3.27
New Jersey	280,724	3.22
Wisconsin	168,101	2.98
Minnesota	142,698	2.72
Connecticut	94,674	2.67
North Dakota	16,254	2.46
California	889,435	2.43
Rhode Island	22,938	2.17
District of Columbia	8,279	1.42
Hawaii	10,350	0.78

Please refer to the Explanation of Data in the front of the book for more detailed information.

Ancestry

American

Top 150 Places Sorted by Population

Based on all places, regardless of total population

Place	Population	%
New York, NY (city) Kings County	209,430	2.59
Brooklyn, NY (borough) Kings County	78,858	3.20
Los Angeles, CA (city) Los Angeles County	68,094	1.81
Louisville-Jefferson County, KY (metro govt) Jefferson County	61,150	10.42
Nashville-Davidson, TN (metro govt) Davidson County	58,785	10.00
Manhattan, NY (borough) New York County	54,694	3.45
Houston, TX (city) Harris County	54,678	2.64
Jacksonville, FL (city) Duval County	54,229	6.68
Indianapolis, IN (city) Marion County	52,433	6.47
Phoenix, AZ (city) Maricopa County	51,759	3.57
San Antonio, TX (city) Medina County	49,486	3.84
Kansas City, MO (city) Jackson County	48,909	10.75
Fort Worth, TX (city) Tarrant County	48,874	6.93
Virginia Beach, VA (ind. city) Virginia Beach independent city	47,698	10.94
Queens, NY (borough) Queens County	45,604	2.07
Raleigh, NC (city) Wake County	37,404	9.77
Oklahoma City, OK (city) Oklahoma County	36,023	6.39
Lexington-Fayette, KY (cons. govt) Fayette County	35,561	12.35
Chicago, IL (city) Cook County	34,496	1.28
Dallas, TX (city) Dallas County	33,684	2.84
San Diego, CA (city) San Diego County	32,627	2.54
Memphis, TN (city) Shelby County	32,233	4.92
Columbus, OH (city) Franklin County	31,925	4.14
Charlotte, NC (city) Mecklenburg County	30,441	4.31
Chesapeake, VA (ind. city) Chesapeake independent city	30,037	13.70
Tulsa, OK (city) Tulsa County	27,566	7.10
Baltimore, MD (city) Baltimore city County	27,486	4.43
Fort Wayne, IN (city) Allen County	25,688	10.12
Norfolk, VA (ind. city) Norfolk independent city	25,600	10.57
Springfield, MO (city) Christian County	25,097	15.79
Austin, TX (city) Travis County	24,492	3.21
Hempstead, NY (town) Nassau County	23,869	3.17
Portland, OR (city) Multnomah County	23,846	4.21
Evansville, IN (city) Vanderburgh County	23,162	19.60
Mesa, AZ (city) Maricopa County	22,368	5.09
El Paso, TX (city) El Paso County	22,367	3.56
Atlanta, GA (city) Fulton County	21,935	5.31
Chattanooga, TN (city) Hamilton County	21,415	13.02
Surprise, AZ (city) Maricopa County	21,370	20.59
Wichita, KS (city) Sedgwick County	21,334	5.71
Philadelphia, PA (city) Philadelphia County	20,637	1.37
Denver, CO (city) Denver County	19,324	3.34
Knoxville, TN (city) Knox County	19,205	10.78
Montgomery, AL (city) Montgomery County	18,629	9.10
Huntsville, AL (city) Madison County	18,369	10.47
Cincinnati, OH (city) Hamilton County	18,156	6.05
Arlington, TX (city) Tarrant County	18,145	5.05
Plano, TX (city) Collin County	17,867	6.98
Colorado Springs, CO (city) El Paso County	17,720	4.39
Mesquite, TX (city) Dallas County	17,131	12.60
Boise City, ID (city) Ada County	17,120	8.29
Cape Coral, FL (city) Lee County	17,041	11.38
Johnson City, TN (city) Washington County	16,607	26.89
Bronx, NY (borough) Bronx County	16,297	1.19
Aurora, CO (city) Arapahoe County	16,179	5.15
Wichita Falls, TX (city) Wichita County	16,094	15.47
Dayton, OH (city) Montgomery County	16,035	11.01
Peoria, AZ (city) Yavapai County	15,709	10.56
Owensboro, KY (city) Daviess County	15,563	27.53
Nampa, ID (city) Canyon County	15,510	19.80
Seattle, WA (city) King County	15,466	2.60
Wilmington, NC (city) New Hanover County	15,339	14.65
Hamilton, OH (city) Butler County	15,067	24.12
Augusta-Richmond County, GA (cons. govt) Richmond County	14,917	7.71
Las Vegas, NV (city) Clark County	14,662	2.53
Harrisonburg, VA (ind. city) Harrisonburg independent city	14,504	30.60
Mobile, AL (city) Mobile County	14,358	7.34
Staten Island, NY (borough) Richmond County	13,977	3.02
Albuquerque, NM (city) Bernalillo County	13,911	2.62
Lubbock, TX (city) Lubbock County	13,599	6.12
Clearwater, FL (city) Pinellas County	13,526	12.52
Murfreesboro, TN (city) Rutherford County	13,352	13.01
Amarillo, TX (city) Potter County	12,934	6.91
Clarksville, TN (city) Montgomery County	12,832	10.17
Greensboro, NC (city) Guilford County	12,778	4.85
Omaha, NE (city) Douglas County	12,470	3.06
Hawthorne, CA (city) Los Angeles County	12,456	14.79
Suffolk, VA (ind. city) Suffolk independent city	12,434	15.06
Alexandria, LA (city) Rapides Parish	12,391	26.05
Kingsport, TN (city) Sullivan County	12,357	25.82
Rockford, IL (city) Winnebago County	12,203	7.90
Ogden, UT (city) Weber County	12,144	14.98
Charleston, SC (city) Charleston County	12,018	10.33
Tampa, FL (city) Hillsborough County	12,011	3.60
San Jose, CA (city) Santa Clara County	11,998	1.30
McKinney, TX (city) Collin County	11,945	10.07
Fort Lauderdale, FL (city) Broward County	11,911	7.12
Columbus, GA (city) Muscogee County	11,893	6.34
Simi Valley, CA (city) Ventura County	11,845	9.74
Boston, MA (city) Suffolk County	11,829	1.96
Winston-Salem, NC (city) Forsyth County	11,710	5.21
Tucson, AZ (city) Pima County	11,664	2.25
Terre Haute, IN (city) Vigo County	11,657	19.29
Baton Rouge, LA (city) East Baton Rouge Parish	11,516	5.03
Decatur, IL (city) Macon County	11,484	15.03
Anchorage, AK (municipality) Anchorage Municipality	11,326	3.98
Roanoke, VA (ind. city) Roanoke independent city	11,233	11.73
Henderson, NV (city) Clark County	11,216	4.50
Hampton, VA (ind. city) Hampton independent city	11,117	8.00
St. Louis, MO (city) St. Louis city County	11,071	3.47
Paterson, NJ (city) Passaic County	11,070	7.59
Richardson, TX (city) Dallas County	10,636	10.91
Corpus Christi, TX (city) Nueces County	10,626	3.55
Lehigh Acres, FL (cdp) Lee County	10,490	12.42
Lakewood, NJ (township) Ocean County	10,480	11.95
Orange, CA (city) Orange County	10,395	7.72
Reno, NV (city) Washoe County	10,284	4.65
Scottsdale, AZ (city) Maricopa County	10,175	4.65
Toledo, OH (city) Lucas County	10,051	3.44
Brookhaven, NY (town) Suffolk County	10,016	2.09
Cleveland, OH (city) Cuyahoga County	9,836	2.40
Asheville, NC (city) Buncombe County	9,825	11.99
Orlando, FL (city) Orange County	9,820	4.20
Oyster Bay, NY (town) Nassau County	9,798	3.36
Shreveport, LA (city) Caddo Parish	9,705	4.89
Longview, TX (city) Gregg County	9,691	12.23
Portsmouth, VA (ind. city) Portsmouth independent city	9,562	9.88
Cary, NC (town) Wake County	9,424	7.39
Little Rock, AR (city) Pulaski County	9,399	4.93
Springfield, IL (city) Sangamon County	9,384	8.15
Overland Park, KS (city) Johnson County	9,285	5.45
Caldwell, ID (city) Canyon County	9,247	21.14
North Richland Hills, TX (city) Tarrant County	9,156	14.78
St. Petersburg, FL (city) Pinellas County	9,124	3.71
Dothan, AL (city) Houston County	9,085	14.13
Glendale, AZ (city) Maricopa County	9,053	3.94
Billings, MT (city) Yellowstone County	9,034	8.90
Independence, MO (city) Jackson County	9,002	7.79
Palm Bay, FL (city) Brevard County	8,953	8.90
Midland, TX (city) Midland County	8,789	8.17
Des Moines, IA (city) Polk County	8,780	4.34
Broken Arrow, OK (city) Tulsa County	8,737	9.22
Durham, NC (city) Durham County	8,730	3.96
Newport News, VA (ind. city) Newport News independent city	8,706	4.79
Hollywood, FL (city) Broward County	8,678	6.14
Lincoln, NE (city) Lancaster County	8,631	3.41
Fayetteville, NC (city) Cumberland County	8,601	4.32
Irving, TX (city) Dallas County	8,519	4.06
Spokane, WA (city) Spokane County	8,496	4.11
Lawton, OK (city) Comanche County	8,455	8.97
Washington, DC (city) District of Columbia	8,279	1.42
Akron, OH (city) Summit County	8,242	4.06
Bakersfield, CA (city) Kern County	8,205	2.47
Champaign, IL (city) Champaign County	8,172	10.29
Springfield, OH (city) Clark County	8,078	13.14
Birmingham, AL (city) Jefferson County	8,045	3.72
San Francisco, CA (city) San Francisco County	8,041	1.02
Garland, TX (city) Dallas County	8,029	3.60
Cookeville, TN (city) Putnam County	8,005	26.93
Bloomington, IL (city) McLean County	8,005	10.69

Please refer to the Explanation of Data in the front of the book for more detailed information.

Ancestry

American

Top 150 Places Sorted by Percent of Total Population

Based on all places, regardless of total population

Place	Population	%
Kingston, NM (cdp) Sierra County	242	100.00
Etna, WY (cdp) Lincoln County	176	100.00
Tillatoba, MS (town) Yalobusha County	107	100.00
Beaver Valley, AZ (cdp) Gila County	71	100.00
Mexican Hat, UT (cdp) San Juan County	63	100.00
Erin Springs, OK (town) Garvin County	59	100.00
Oasis, UT (cdp) Millard County	32	100.00
Islandton, SC (cdp) Colleton County	19	100.00
Mona, IA (cdp) Mitchell County	18	100.00
Brooktree Park, ND (cdp) Cass County	16	100.00
Malcolm, AL (cdp) Washington County	14	100.00
Hutton, MD (cdp) Garrett County	10	100.00
Gulfcrest, AL (cdp) Mobile County	9	100.00
Powder River, WY (cdp) Natrona County	7	100.00
Charleston Park, FL (cdp) Lee County	447	97.81
Leon, OK (town) Love County	103	97.17
Woodland, MD (cdp) Allegany County	104	93.69
Carolina, AL (town) Covington County	271	92.49
Eccles, WV (cdp) Raleigh County	416	87.03
Artemus, KY (cdp) Knox County	842	86.89
Libertyville, AL (town) Covington County	73	85.88
Boody, IL (cdp) Macon County	163	85.34
Fairford, AL (cdp) Washington County	99	85.34
Ezel, KY (cdp) Morgan County	167	85.20
San Antonio, NM (cdp) Socorro County	143	83.63
Windsor, SC (town) Aiken County	116	83.45
Steely Hollow, OK (cdp) Cherokee County	39	82.98
Fairview, KY (cdp) Christian County	250	82.78
Callaghan, VA (cdp) Alleghany County	275	81.85
Thackerville, OK (town) Love County	404	81.78
Williams, IN (cdp) Lawrence County	173	81.60
Rosine, KY (cdp) Ohio County	145	81.46
Ratliff City, OK (town) Carter County	60	80.00
Churchville, VA (cdp) Augusta County	177	79.02
Camden, IL (village) Schuyler County	75	78.95
Trafford, PA (borough) Allegheny County	30	78.95
Coldiron, KY (cdp) Harlan County	181	78.70
Bolt, WV (cdp) Raleigh County	404	77.84
Weogufka, AL (cdp) Coosa County	142	75.94
Edge Hill, GA (city) Glascock County	66	75.86
Rockingham, GA (cdp) Bacon County	150	75.76
Onton, KY (cdp) Webster County	30	75.00
Delta, LA (village) Madison Parish	220	73.33
Maybell, CO (cdp) Moffat County	55	73.33
Echo, UT (cdp) Summit County	69	72.63
Drew, ME (plantation) Penobscot County	33	71.74
Galloway, WV (cdp) Barbour County	95	70.90
Coronaca, SC (cdp) Greenwood County	277	70.13
Foster, OK (town) Garvin County	91	70.00
Noma, FL (town) Holmes County	214	69.93
Sophia, WV (town) Raleigh County	846	69.86
Cawood, KY (cdp) Harlan County	457	69.77
Schuyler, VA (cdp) Nelson County	224	69.57
Booneville, KY (city) Owsley County	67	69.07
Glenwood, NM (cdp) Catron County	147	68.69
Hollowayville, IL (village) Bureau County	41	68.33
Kilbourne, LA (village) West Carroll Parish	430	67.40
Coal City, WV (cdp) Raleigh County	1,113	67.25
Macon, NC (town) Warren County	376	66.67
McNary, LA (village) Rapides Parish	130	66.67
Montello, NV (cdp) Elko County	40	66.67
Fairgarden, TN (cdp) Sevier County	529	66.54
Wolf Summit, WV (cdp) Harrison County	181	66.30
Pine Lakes, FL (cdp) Lake County	540	65.93
Lamoille, NV (cdp) Elko County	25	65.79
Crellin, MD (cdp) Garrett County	38	65.52
Marshall, IN (town) Parke County	169	65.25
Sneedville, TN (town) Hancock County	1,133	65.15
Graball, TN (cdp) Sumner County	56	65.12
Lockhart, AL (town) Covington County	347	65.10
Iron City, GA (town) Seminole County	205	65.08
Biddle, MT (cdp) Powder River County	22	64.71
Buels, VT (gore) Chittenden County	11	64.71
Campton, KY (city) Wolfe County	225	64.66
Rhodell, WV (town) Raleigh County	97	64.24

Place	Population	%
Elmore City, OK (town) Garvin County	497	64.13
Foosland, IL (village) Champaign County	66	64.08
Springer, OK (town) Carter County	345	64.01
Katherine, AZ (cdp) Mohave County	115	63.89
Eldorado, MD (town) Dorchester County	65	63.73
Wiederkehr Village, AR (city) Franklin County	7	63.64
La Follette, TN (city) Campbell County	4,814	63.47
Tolu, KY (cdp) Crittenden County	12	63.16
Lowell, KS (cdp) Cherokee County	149	62.87
Osyka, MS (town) Pike County	324	62.55
Morristown, AZ (cdp) Maricopa County	115	62.50
Horn Hill, AL (town) Covington County	226	62.43
Wintergreen, VA (cdp) Nelson County	78	62.40
Flat Rock, OH (cdp) Seneca County	86	61.87
Walnut Grove, TN (cdp) Hardin County	250	61.73
Jalapa, IN (cdp) Grant County	122	61.62
Blaine, KY (city) Lawrence County	64	61.54
Oakhurst, TX (cdp) San Jacinto County	24	61.54
Cusseta, AL (town) Chambers County	35	61.40
Basye, VA (cdp) Shenandoah County	537	61.09
Flat Lick, KY (cdp) Knox County	589	60.91
Hysham, MT (town) Treasure County	246	60.89
Middletown, IL (village) Logan County	198	60.55
Huetter, ID (city) Kootenai County	80	60.15
Ghent, WV (cdp) Raleigh County	318	60.11
Wittmann, AZ (cdp) Maricopa County	496	60.05
Annada, MO (village) Pike County	3	60.00
Prospect, LA (cdp) Grant Parish	326	59.93
Katie, OK (town) Garvin County	137	59.83
Sandy Hook, KY (city) Elliott County	423	59.58
Kanauga, OH (cdp) Gallia County	75	59.52
Faxon, OK (town) Comanche County	141	59.49
Baxter, TN (town) Putnam County	860	59.11
Start, LA (cdp) Richland Parish	501	58.80
Haleburg, AL (town) Henry County	58	58.59
New River, VA (cdp) Pulaski County	120	58.54
MacArthur, WV (cdp) Raleigh County	842	58.43
Octa, OH (village) Fayette County	28	58.33
Mecca, IN (town) Parke County	207	57.66
Buchanan, VA (town) Botetourt County	777	57.56
Loco, OK (town) Stephens County	61	57.55
Mayhill, NM (cdp) Otero County	59	57.28
Spencer Mountain, NC (town) Gaston County	12	57.14
Nicasio, CA (cdp) Marin County	4	57.14
Nora, NE (village) Nuckolls County	4	57.14
Seven Points, TX (city) Henderson County	901	56.95
Lowgap, NC (cdp) Surry County	164	56.94
Good Hope, GA (city) Walton County	243	56.91
Troutville, VA (town) Botetourt County	326	56.89
Liberty, KY (city) Casey County	916	56.61
North Beltrami, MN (unorganized territory) Beltrami County	13	56.52
Fallis, OK (town) Lincoln County	22	56.41
Dickson, OK (town) Carter County	829	56.28
Kansas, OH (cdp) Seneca County	166	56.27
Rutledge, TN (town) Grainger County	866	56.20
Hustonville, KY (city) Lincoln County	213	56.20
Coinjock, NC (cdp) Currituck County	123	56.16
Perkins, GA (cdp) Jenkins County	138	56.10
Vansant, VA (cdp) Buchanan County	371	56.04
Carlin, NV (city) Elko County	1,486	55.93
Ray, AL (cdp) Coosa County	151	55.93
Somerville, OH (village) Butler County	147	55.89
Eubank, KY (city) Pulaski County	266	55.77
Creola, LA (village) Grant Parish	150	55.76
Babbie, AL (town) Covington County	379	55.57
Massanutten, VA (cdp) Rockingham County	1,091	55.30
Douds, IA (cdp) Van Buren County	63	55.26
Sanford, VA (cdp) Accomack County	69	55.20
Church Creek, MD (town) Dorchester County	50	54.95
Leonard, MN (city) Clearwater County	17	54.84
Frenchburg, KY (city) Menifee County	445	54.67
Jefferson, NC (town) Ashe County	876	54.65
Sanford, AL (town) Covington County	282	54.65
Junction City, KY (city) Boyle County	1,589	54.64
Maysville, OK (town) Garvin County	572	54.63

Ancestry

American

Top 150 Places Sorted by Percent of Total Population

Based on places with total population of 7,500 or more

Place	Population	%
La Follette, TN (city) Campbell County	4,814	63.47
Middlesborough, KY (city) Bell County	5,083	48.85
London, KY (city) Laurel County	2,924	36.88
Manchester, TN (city) Coffee County	3,290	33.24
Pell City, AL (city) St. Clair County	4,058	33.17
Sylacauga, AL (city) Talladega County	4,046	31.64
McMinnville, TN (city) Warren County	4,258	31.60
Harrodsburg, KY (city) Mercer County	2,608	31.35
Jefferson City, TN (city) Jefferson County	2,529	31.24
Harrisonburg, VA (ind. city) Harrisonburg independent city	14,504	30.60
Paragould, AR (city) Greene County	7,771	30.57
Sandy, PA (township) Clearfield County	3,282	30.33
Mount Washington, KY (city) Bullitt County	2,710	29.95
Yulee, FL (cdp) Nassau County	3,607	29.49
Shelbyville, TN (city) Bedford County	5,828	29.48
Hernando, FL (cdp) Citrus County	2,626	29.17
Andalusia, AL (city) Covington County	2,593	28.82
Shepherdsville, KY (city) Bullitt County	3,107	28.73
Lenoir City, TN (city) Loudon County	2,398	28.68
Bloomingdale, TN (cdp) Sullivan County	2,773	28.46
Ardmore, OK (city) Carter County	6,658	27.58
Owensboro, KY (city) Daviess County	15,563	27.53
Paris, KY (city) Bourbon County	2,344	27.22
Lewisburg, TN (city) Marshall County	2,965	27.07
Soddy-Daisy, TN (city) Hamilton County	3,348	27.02
Cookeville, TN (city) Putnam County	8,005	26.93
Fultondale, AL (city) Jefferson County	2,178	26.91
Johnson City, TN (city) Washington County	16,607	26.89
Goulds, FL (cdp) Miami-Dade County	2,438	26.49
Waynesville, NC (town) Haywood County	2,603	26.20
Alexandria, LA (city) Rapides Parish	12,391	26.05
Somerset, KY (city) Pulaski County	2,908	26.03
Hueytown, AL (city) Jefferson County	4,171	26.02
Norwood, OH (city) Hamilton County	5,029	25.84
Kingsport, TN (city) Sullivan County	12,357	25.82
Moreau, NY (town) Saratoga County	3,769	25.82
Sevierville, TN (city) Sevier County	3,710	25.63
Ellsworth, ME (city) Hancock County	1,906	25.23
Pittsburg, KS (city) Crawford County	5,054	25.19
Winchester, KY (city) Clark County	4,506	24.85
Ozark, MO (city) Christian County	4,054	24.39
Hamilton, OH (city) Butler County	15,067	24.12
Glasgow, KY (city) Barren County	3,358	24.12
Lawrenceburg, KY (city) Anderson County	2,462	24.12
Washington Terrace, UT (city) Weber County	2,144	24.04
Nicholasville, KY (city) Jessamine County	6,445	23.99
Cypress Gardens, FL (cdp) Polk County	2,293	23.90
La Grange, KY (city) Oldham County	1,834	23.63
Princeton, IN (city) Gibson County	2,023	23.44
Scottsboro, AL (city) Jackson County	3,458	23.37
Brazil, IN (city) Clay County	1,759	23.35
Bardstown, KY (city) Nelson County	2,681	23.21
Park City, UT (city) Summit County	1,753	23.21
Bristol, TN (city) Sullivan County	6,121	23.16
Moody, AL (city) St. Clair County	2,562	23.00
Elizabethton, TN (city) Carter County	3,272	22.87
Jacksonville, IL (city) Morgan County	4,436	22.86
Nixa, MO (city) Christian County	4,111	22.81
Atoka, TN (town) Tipton County	1,739	22.79
Beckley, WV (city) Raleigh County	3,981	22.74
Spring Creek, NV (cdp) Elko County	2,989	22.17
Clinton, TN (city) Anderson County	2,160	22.17
Hillview, KY (city) Bullitt County	1,782	22.10
Morristown, TN (city) Hamblen County	6,330	22.02
Winder, GA (city) Barrow County	3,012	22.00
Burkburnett, TX (city) Wichita County	2,372	21.99
Shelbyville, KY (city) Shelby County	2,945	21.97
Milledgeville, GA (city) Baldwin County	4,210	21.89
Woodward, OK (city) Woodward County	2,631	21.79
Garden City, SC (cdp) Horry County	1,925	21.72
Wabash, IN (city) Wabash County	2,352	21.68
La Vergne, TN (city) Rutherford County	6,573	21.65
Middle Valley, TN (cdp) Hamilton County	2,770	21.55
Covington, TN (city) Tipton County	1,933	21.44
Fort Scott, KS (city) Bourbon County	1,737	21.38
Danville, KY (city) Boyle County	3,416	21.28
Seagoville, TX (city) Dallas County	2,983	21.24
Crossville, TN (city) Cumberland County	2,255	21.22
El Mirage, AZ (city) Maricopa County	5,912	21.17
Caldwell, ID (city) Canyon County	9,247	21.14
St. Matthews, KY (city) Jefferson County	3,644	20.98
Smyrna, TN (town) Rutherford County	7,890	20.71
Greenfield, NY (town) Saratoga County	1,602	20.71
Red Bank, SC (cdp) Lexington County	2,086	20.69
Eustis, FL (city) Lake County	3,864	20.68
Stuarts Draft, VA (cdp) Augusta County	1,554	20.61
Surprise, AZ (city) Maricopa County	21,370	20.59
Timberlake, VA (cdp) Campbell County	2,895	20.58
Durant, OK (city) Bryan County	3,210	20.56
West Haven, UT (city) Weber County	1,852	20.45
McComb, MS (city) Pike County	2,637	20.39
Xenia, OH (city) Greene County	5,196	20.30
New Albany, MS (city) Union County	1,607	20.09
Staunton, VA (ind. city) Staunton independent city	4,752	19.96
Enterprise, AL (city) Coffee County	5,016	19.84
Nampa, ID (city) Canyon County	15,510	19.80
Dexter, MO (city) Stoddard County	1,544	19.66
Evansville, IN (city) Vanderburgh County	23,162	19.60
Citrus Springs, FL (cdp) Citrus County	1,496	19.60
London, OH (city) Madison County	1,892	19.49
Rye, NY (city) Westchester County	3,014	19.45
Kings Grant, NC (cdp) New Hanover County	1,620	19.41
Vinton, VA (town) Roanoke County	1,566	19.40
Clarksville, AR (city) Johnson County	1,738	19.30
DuBois, PA (city) Clearfield County	1,514	19.30
Terre Haute, IN (city) Vigo County	11,657	19.29
Georgetown, KY (city) Scott County	5,247	19.24
East Ridge, TN (city) Hamilton County	3,997	19.24
Millington, TN (city) Shelby County	1,982	19.15
Versailles, KY (city) Woodford County	1,614	19.13
Tavares, FL (city) Lake County	2,611	19.08
Berea, KY (city) Madison County	2,529	19.08
Senatobia, MS (city) Tate County	1,517	19.06
Petal, MS (city) Forrest County	1,955	18.98
West Perrine, FL (cdp) Miami-Dade County	1,900	18.98
Red Bank, TN (city) Hamilton County	2,210	18.95
Del Aire, CA (cdp) Los Angeles County	1,815	18.94
Parkersburg, WV (city) Wood County	6,009	18.93
Clanton, AL (city) Chilton County	1,615	18.88
Marion, NC (city) McDowell County	1,521	18.87
Fairborn, OH (city) Greene County	6,052	18.82
Columbia, TN (city) Maury County	6,485	18.81
Harrison, TN (cdp) Hamilton County	1,486	18.77
Lincoln, IL (city) Logan County	2,708	18.75
Clarksburg, WV (city) Harrison County	3,094	18.70
Bristol, VA (ind. city) Bristol independent city	3,296	18.62
North Ogden, UT (city) Weber County	3,110	18.54
Vernon, TX (city) Wilbarger County	2,045	18.53
Springfield, TN (city) Robertson County	2,979	18.51
Pulaski, TN (city) Giles County	1,455	18.43
Tifton, GA (city) Tift County	2,979	18.34
Crawfordsville, IN (city) Montgomery County	2,909	18.30
Winter Haven, FL (city) Polk County	6,048	18.26
East Peoria, IL (city) Tazewell County	4,226	18.20
Circleville, OH (city) Pickaway County	2,430	18.19
Bayou Blue, LA (cdp) Lafourche Parish	2,032	18.17
Park Hills, MO (city) St. Francois County	1,567	18.17
Morgan City, LA (city) St. Mary Parish	2,257	18.15
Union City, TN (city) Obion County	1,975	18.13
Greencastle, IN (city) Putnam County	1,877	18.12
Central, LA (city) East Baton Rouge Parish	4,864	18.09
Socastee, SC (cdp) Horry County	3,094	18.09
Riverside, OH (city) Montgomery County	4,612	18.08
Duncan, OK (city) Stephens County	4,167	17.99
Seymour, TN (cdp) Sevier County	1,863	17.95
Roy, UT (city) Weber County	6,424	17.92
Tillmans Corner, AL (cdp) Mobile County	2,946	17.90
White Settlement, TX (city) Tarrant County	2,841	17.88
Roscoe, IL (village) Winnebago County	1,805	17.76
Hartsville-Trousdale County, TN (cons. govt) Trousdale County	1,375	17.74

SECTION THREE

Please refer to the Explanation of Data in the front of the book for more detailed information.

Ancestry

Arab

U.S. and 50 States Sorted by Population and Percent of Total Population

Place	Population	%
United States	**1,547,365**	**0.51**
California	247,243	0.67
Michigan	152,212	1.53
New York	145,746	0.76
Florida	95,752	0.52
Texas	91,635	0.38
New Jersey	84,528	0.97
Illinois	71,622	0.56
Ohio	65,834	0.57
Massachusetts	63,448	0.98
Pennsylvania	61,004	0.48
Virginia	52,561	0.67
Arizona	29,862	0.48
North Carolina	29,140	0.31
Maryland	24,736	0.43
Georgia	24,675	0.26
Tennessee	22,034	0.35
Washington	20,528	0.31
Minnesota	18,803	0.36
Connecticut	18,013	0.51
Colorado	16,488	0.34
Missouri	16,327	0.28
Indiana	15,838	0.25
Louisiana	15,274	0.34
Oregon	14,161	0.38
Nevada	12,140	0.46
Oklahoma	10,688	0.29
Wisconsin	10,677	0.19
South Carolina	10,632	0.24
Alabama	10,369	0.22
Kentucky	9,623	0.22
Rhode Island	8,762	0.83
Kansas	7,880	0.28
New Hampshire	7,578	0.58
Mississippi	6,984	0.24
West Virginia	6,081	0.33
Nebraska	6,036	0.34
Iowa	5,304	0.18
New Mexico	4,972	0.25
Utah	4,815	0.18
Arkansas	4,529	0.16
District of Columbia	3,776	0.65
Maine	3,422	0.26
Delaware	2,836	0.32
Vermont	2,586	0.41
Idaho	1,900	0.12
Montana	1,880	0.19
Hawaii	1,853	0.14
North Dakota	1,534	0.23
South Dakota	1,380	0.17
Alaska	1,207	0.17
Wyoming	457	0.08

Place	Population	%
Michigan	152,212	1.53
Massachusetts	63,448	0.98
New Jersey	84,528	0.97
Rhode Island	8,762	0.83
New York	145,746	0.76
California	247,243	0.67
Virginia	52,561	0.67
District of Columbia	3,776	0.65
New Hampshire	7,578	0.58
Ohio	65,834	0.57
Illinois	71,622	0.56
Florida	95,752	0.52
United States	**1,547,365**	**0.51**
Connecticut	18,013	0.51
Pennsylvania	61,004	0.48
Arizona	29,862	0.48
Nevada	12,140	0.46
Maryland	24,736	0.43
Vermont	2,586	0.41
Texas	91,635	0.38
Oregon	14,161	0.38
Minnesota	18,803	0.36
Tennessee	22,034	0.35
Colorado	16,488	0.34
Louisiana	15,274	0.34
Nebraska	6,036	0.34
West Virginia	6,081	0.33
Delaware	2,836	0.32
North Carolina	29,140	0.31
Washington	20,528	0.31
Oklahoma	10,688	0.29
Missouri	16,327	0.28
Kansas	7,880	0.28
Georgia	24,675	0.26
Maine	3,422	0.26
Indiana	15,838	0.25
New Mexico	4,972	0.25
South Carolina	10,632	0.24
Mississippi	6,984	0.24
North Dakota	1,534	0.23
Alabama	10,369	0.22
Kentucky	9,623	0.22
Wisconsin	10,677	0.19
Montana	1,880	0.19
Iowa	5,304	0.18
Utah	4,815	0.18
South Dakota	1,380	0.17
Alaska	1,207	0.17
Arkansas	4,529	0.16
Hawaii	1,853	0.14
Idaho	1,900	0.12
Wyoming	457	0.08

Please refer to the Explanation of Data in the front of the book for more detailed information.

Ancestry

Arab

Top 150 Places Sorted by Population

Based on all places, regardless of total population

Place	Population	%
New York, NY (city) Kings County	82,165	1.02
Dearborn, MI (city) Wayne County	38,503	39.13
Brooklyn, NY (borough) Kings County	34,840	1.41
Los Angeles, CA (city) Los Angeles County	30,066	0.80
Queens, NY (borough) Queens County	19,669	0.89
Chicago, IL (city) Cook County	16,946	0.63
Manhattan, NY (borough) New York County	13,828	0.87
Houston, TX (city) Harris County	13,350	0.65
Dearborn Heights, MI (city) Wayne County	10,397	17.91
San Diego, CA (city) San Diego County	10,030	0.78
Nashville-Davidson, TN (metro govt) Davidson County	9,538	1.62
Staten Island, NY (borough) Richmond County	8,820	1.90
Detroit, MI (city) Wayne County	8,642	1.14
Sterling Heights, MI (city) Macomb County	8,488	6.54
Phoenix, AZ (city) Maricopa County	8,436	0.58
Philadelphia, PA (city) Philadelphia County	7,763	0.52
Jacksonville, FL (city) Duval County	7,436	0.92
Jersey City, NJ (city) Hudson County	6,852	2.82
Columbus, OH (city) Franklin County	6,451	0.84
Boston, MA (city) Suffolk County	6,307	1.05
San Francisco, CA (city) San Francisco County	5,672	0.72
Bronx, NY (borough) Bronx County	5,008	0.37
San Jose, CA (city) Santa Clara County	4,802	0.52
El Cajon, CA (city) San Diego County	4,795	4.90
West Bloomfield, MI (charter township) Oakland County	4,594	7.10
Austin, TX (city) Travis County	4,508	0.59
Charlotte, NC (city) Mecklenburg County	4,490	0.64
San Antonio, TX (city) Medina County	4,433	0.34
Fresno, CA (city) Fresno County	4,301	0.89
Hamtramck, MI (city) Wayne County	4,285	18.97
Glendale, CA (city) Los Angeles County	4,218	2.19
Hempstead, NY (town) Nassau County	4,218	0.56
Anaheim, CA (city) Orange County	4,077	1.22
Raleigh, NC (city) Wake County	3,836	1.00
Dallas, TX (city) Dallas County	3,820	0.32
Clifton, NJ (city) Passaic County	3,816	4.61
Washington, DC (city) District of Columbia	3,776	0.65
Arlington, TX (city) Tarrant County	3,607	1.00
Portland, OR (city) Multnomah County	3,494	0.62
Toledo, OH (city) Lucas County	3,428	1.17
San Bernardino, CA (city) San Bernardino County	3,403	1.63
Corona, CA (city) Riverside County	3,365	2.24
Cleveland, OH (city) Cuyahoga County	3,346	0.82
Tucson, AZ (city) Pima County	3,263	0.63
Irvine, CA (city) Orange County	3,229	1.62
Yonkers, NY (city) Westchester County	3,210	1.65
Allentown, PA (city) Lehigh County	3,112	2.67
Troy, MI (city) Oakland County	3,081	3.80
El Paso, TX (city) El Paso County	2,973	0.47
Arlington, VA (cdp) Arlington County	2,931	1.48
Pittsburgh, PA (city) Allegheny County	2,859	0.93
Warren, MI (city) Macomb County	2,804	2.06
Indianapolis, IN (city) Marion County	2,776	0.34
Paterson, NJ (city) Passaic County	2,774	1.90
Bayonne, NJ (city) Hudson County	2,773	4.47
Oak Lawn, IL (village) Cook County	2,764	4.95
Las Vegas, NV (city) Clark County	2,731	0.47
Bakersfield, CA (city) Kern County	2,702	0.81
Worcester, MA (city) Worcester County	2,701	1.50
Oklahoma City, OK (city) Oklahoma County	2,661	0.47
Denver, CO (city) Denver County	2,656	0.46
Oakland, CA (city) Alameda County	2,646	0.68
Tulsa, OK (city) Tulsa County	2,615	0.67
Seattle, WA (city) King County	2,600	0.44
Tampa, FL (city) Hillsborough County	2,508	0.75
Farmington Hills, MI (city) Oakland County	2,505	3.12
Canton, MI (charter township) Wayne County	2,465	2.80
Plano, TX (city) Collin County	2,465	0.96
Alexandria, VA (ind. city) Alexandria independent city	2,458	1.84
Huntington Beach, CA (city) Orange County	2,455	1.30
Louisville-Jefferson County, KY (metro govt) Jefferson County	2,417	0.41
Orland Park, IL (village) Cook County	2,393	4.34
Albuquerque, NM (city) Bernalillo County	2,393	0.45
Minneapolis, MN (city) Hennepin County	2,389	0.63
Livonia, MI (city) Wayne County	2,374	2.42
Fremont, CA (city) Alameda County	2,346	1.12
St. Louis, MO (city) St. Louis city County	2,332	0.73
Daly City, CA (city) San Mateo County	2,327	2.33
Wichita, KS (city) Sedgwick County	2,327	0.62
Revere, MA (city) Suffolk County	2,310	4.62
Long Beach, CA (city) Los Angeles County	2,244	0.49
Riverside, CA (city) Riverside County	2,242	0.75
Wayne, NJ (township) Passaic County	2,206	4.06
Milwaukee, WI (city) Milwaukee County	2,196	0.37
Kansas City, MO (city) Jackson County	2,176	0.48
Ann Arbor, MI (city) Washtenaw County	2,158	1.87
East Brunswick, NJ (township) Middlesex County	2,092	4.41
Shelby, MI (charter township) Macomb County	2,092	2.87
North Hempstead, NY (town) Nassau County	2,078	0.93
Omaha, NE (city) Douglas County	2,069	0.51
Rancho Cucamonga, CA (city) San Bernardino County	2,065	1.28
Aurora, CO (city) Arapahoe County	2,042	0.65
Scottsdale, AZ (city) Maricopa County	2,012	0.92
Bridgeview, IL (village) Cook County	2,010	12.45
Pasadena, CA (city) Los Angeles County	2,003	1.47
Metairie, LA (cdp) Jefferson Parish	1,998	1.47
Paradise, NV (cdp) Clark County	1,992	0.91
Sugar Land, TX (city) Fort Bend County	1,981	2.60
Tempe, AZ (city) Maricopa County	1,962	1.20
Gilbert, AZ (town) Maricopa County	1,948	1.00
Baltimore, MD (city) Baltimore city County	1,937	0.31
Miami, FL (city) Miami-Dade County	1,934	0.49
Memphis, TN (city) Shelby County	1,931	0.29
Methuen Town, MA (city) Essex County	1,897	4.09
Santa Clarita, CA (city) Los Angeles County	1,891	1.10
St. Petersburg, FL (city) Pinellas County	1,890	0.77
Sacramento, CA (city) Sacramento County	1,877	0.41
Lexington-Fayette, KY (cons. govt) Fayette County	1,875	0.65
Clinton, MI (charter township) Macomb County	1,873	1.93
Lincoln, NE (city) Lancaster County	1,863	0.74
Virginia Beach, VA (ind. city) Virginia Beach independent city	1,861	0.43
Henderson, NV (city) Clark County	1,830	0.73
Orlando, FL (city) Orange County	1,823	0.78
Buffalo, NY (city) Erie County	1,815	0.68
Burbank, CA (city) Los Angeles County	1,768	1.72
Naperville, IL (city) DuPage County	1,759	1.25
Lackawanna, NY (city) Erie County	1,753	9.61
Stockton, CA (city) San Joaquin County	1,750	0.61
Richardson, TX (city) Dallas County	1,710	1.75
Malden, MA (city) Middlesex County	1,671	2.87
Southfield, MI (city) Oakland County	1,650	2.26
Skokie, IL (village) Cook County	1,643	2.57
Fort Worth, TX (city) Tarrant County	1,628	0.23
Macomb, MI (township) Macomb County	1,625	2.17
Quincy, MA (city) Norfolk County	1,614	1.78
Chicago Ridge, IL (village) Cook County	1,605	11.35
Hickory Hills, IL (city) Cook County	1,595	11.39
Atlanta, GA (city) Fulton County	1,578	0.38
Old Bridge, NJ (township) Middlesex County	1,562	2.42
Burbank, IL (city) Cook County	1,558	5.48
Utica, NY (city) Oneida County	1,558	2.52
Palos Hills, IL (city) Cook County	1,536	8.84
Amherst, NY (town) Erie County	1,530	1.27
Glendale, AZ (city) Maricopa County	1,516	0.66
North Bergen, NJ (township) Hudson County	1,502	2.52
Colorado Springs, CO (city) El Paso County	1,502	0.37
Chino Hills, CA (city) San Bernardino County	1,497	2.01
Modesto, CA (city) Stanislaus County	1,485	0.74
Rochester Hills, MI (city) Oakland County	1,483	2.10
Cambridge, MA (city) Middlesex County	1,481	1.43
Lafayette, LA (city) Lafayette Parish	1,481	1.25
Bloomfield, MI (charter township) Oakland County	1,477	3.56
Madison Heights, MI (city) Oakland County	1,463	4.88
Chandler, AZ (city) Maricopa County	1,455	0.63
Islip, NY (town) Suffolk County	1,453	0.44
Lakewood, OH (city) Cuyahoga County	1,450	2.75
Elk Grove, CA (city) Sacramento County	1,444	1.02
Beaverton, OR (city) Washington County	1,419	1.61
Irving, TX (city) Dallas County	1,418	0.68
Torrance, CA (city) Los Angeles County	1,417	0.98

Please refer to the Explanation of Data in the front of the book for more detailed information.

Ancestry

Arab

Top 150 Places Sorted by Percent of Total Population

Based on all places, regardless of total population

Place	Population	%
McCoy, CO (cdp) Eagle County	13	56.52
Dearborn, MI (city) Wayne County	38,503	39.13
Boulevard, CA (cdp) San Diego County	11	35.48
Waitsfield, VT (cdp) Washington County	64	33.86
Cambridge, NH (township) Coos County	3	33.33
Claire City, SD (town) Roberts County	24	30.77
Deal, NJ (borough) Monmouth County	256	24.76
Cannondale, CT (cdp) Fairfield County	45	24.46
Stanchfield, MN (cdp) Isanti County	14	20.59
Atlantic Beach, SC (town) Horry County	53	19.00
Hamtramck, MI (city) Wayne County	4,285	18.97
Dearborn Heights, MI (city) Wayne County	10,397	17.91
Thompsons, TX (town) Fort Bend County	42	17.65
St. James, MI (cdp) Charlevoix County	27	14.36
Hat Creek, CA (cdp) Shasta County	31	14.35
Harrietta, MI (village) Wexford County	16	14.16
Victor, CA (cdp) San Joaquin County	37	13.50
Pottawattamie Park, IN (town) LaPorte County	26	13.13
Mayhill, NM (cdp) Otero County	13	12.62
Kenwood, CA (cdp) Sonoma County	58	12.55
Bridgeview, IL (village) Cook County	2,010	12.45
Ponce de Leon, FL (town) Holmes County	57	12.34
Crandon Lakes, NJ (cdp) Sussex County	158	12.23
Maybell, CO (cdp) Moffat County	9	12.00
Parklawn, CA (cdp) Stanislaus County	95	11.99
Vineland, MN (township) Polk County	15	11.72
Katherine, AZ (cdp) Mohave County	21	11.67
Hickory Hills, IL (city) Cook County	1,595	11.39
Chicago Ridge, IL (village) Cook County	1,605	11.35
Orland Hills, IL (village) Cook County	796	11.35
Utica, PA (borough) Venango County	18	11.32
Salmon Creek, CA (cdp) Sonoma County	9	10.84
St. James, MI (township) Charlevoix County	27	10.47
Falcon, NC (town) Cumberland County	27	10.23
Hokah, MN (city) Houston County	41	10.00
Heeney, CO (cdp) Summit County	7	10.00
Clark Mills, NY (cdp) Oneida County	109	9.71
Seven Hills, CO (cdp) Boulder County	17	9.66
Lackawanna, NY (city) Erie County	1,753	9.61
Rockingham, GA (cdp) Bacon County	19	9.60
Tunica, MS (town) Tunica County	116	9.44
Cuba, AL (town) Sumter County	37	9.34
Damascus, OH (cdp) Mahoning County	23	9.27
Highland, PA (township) Clarion County	58	9.16
Lake City, CO (town) Hinsdale County	22	9.09
Palos Hills, IL (city) Cook County	1,536	8.84
Baldwin, IL (village) Randolph County	32	8.82
Samoa, CA (cdp) Humboldt County	24	8.79
Fallon Station, NV (cdp) Churchill County	66	8.55
Bulger, PA (cdp) Washington County	41	8.42
Georgetown, MN (township) Clay County	14	8.28
Summerhaven, AZ (cdp) Pima County	8	8.25
Garden Prairie, IL (village) Boone County	15	8.11
Crown Point, NY (town) Essex County	167	8.06
Lake Bosworth, WA (cdp) Snohomish County	36	7.79
Rutland, IL (village) LaSalle County	26	7.54
Glenfield, PA (borough) Allegheny County	13	7.43
Jefferson City, MT (cdp) Jefferson County	27	7.24
Moodus, CT (cdp) Middlesex County	81	7.22
Little Falls, NJ (township) Passaic County	1,000	7.21
Sun Valley, PA (cdp) Monroe County	175	7.16
Eldorado Springs, CO (cdp) Boulder County	50	7.14
West Bloomfield, MI (charter township) Oakland County	4,594	7.10
Elkhorn, CA (cdp) Monterey County	122	7.09
Coldwater, MI (city) Branch County	775	7.06
Saddle Rock, NY (village) Nassau County	74	7.06
Springbrook, ND (city) Williams County	3	6.98
Old Bennington, VT (village) Bennington County	13	6.95
Fayetteville, PA (cdp) Franklin County	217	6.90
Melville, RI (cdp) Newport County	138	6.88
Hostetter, PA (cdp) Westmoreland County	50	6.83
Lenox, GA (town) Cook County	74	6.80
Mount Crawford, VA (town) Rockingham County	24	6.80
Ama, LA (cdp) St. Charles Parish	108	6.79
Elmer, OK (town) Jackson County	6	6.74
Kingston, NJ (cdp) Middlesex County	133	6.72
Port William, OH (village) Clinton County	17	6.67
West Long Branch, NJ (borough) Monmouth County	540	6.65
Marksboro, NJ (cdp) Warren County	6	6.59
Desoto Lakes, FL (cdp) Sarasota County	261	6.58
Village of Grosse Pointe Shores, MI (city) Wayne County	191	6.57
Sterling Heights, MI (city) Macomb County	8,488	6.54
Paxtang, PA (borough) Dauphin County	98	6.53
Copperton, UT (cdp) Salt Lake County	46	6.50
Village of Grosse Pointe Shores, MI (city) Wayne County	193	6.49
Georgetown, PA (cdp) Luzerne County	116	6.49
Vineyard Haven, MA (cdp) Dukes County	160	6.48
Melvindale, MI (city) Wayne County	685	6.37
Hewlett Bay Park, NY (village) Nassau County	33	6.36
Lake Barcroft, VA (cdp) Fairfax County	575	6.35
Newton, MS (city) Newton County	219	6.35
Hampton, NE (village) Hamilton County	30	6.34
Palo Alto, PA (borough) Schuylkill County	65	6.26
Hillsboro Beach, FL (town) Broward County	106	6.21
Woodland Park, NJ (borough) Passaic County	716	6.17
Hulbert, MI (township) Chippewa County	14	6.14
Herndon, KS (city) Rawlins County	12	6.12
Green Lane, PA (borough) Montgomery County	27	6.09
Columbia, NJ (cdp) Warren County	17	6.09
Ravena, NY (village) Albany County	200	6.03
Arvin, CA (city) Kern County	1,089	5.94
Prospect Park, NJ (borough) Passaic County	346	5.93
East Pasadena, CA (cdp) Los Angeles County	340	5.91
Brush Fork, WV (cdp) Mercer County	62	5.91
Brandt, MN (township) Polk County	3	5.88
Rougemont, NC (cdp) Durham County	46	5.87
Feasterville, PA (cdp) Bucks County	176	5.84
Upper Exeter, PA (cdp) Luzerne County	46	5.84
Oakwood, PA (cdp) Lawrence County	122	5.82
Pearl Beach, MI (cdp) St. Clair County	183	5.81
Grand Lake, CO (town) Grand County	15	5.79
East Uniontown, PA (cdp) Fayette County	143	5.78
Tysons Corner, VA (cdp) Fairfax County	983	5.75
Spring Valley Lake, CA (cdp) San Bernardino County	436	5.71
Fullerton, PA (cdp) Lehigh County	854	5.67
Goochland, VA (cdp) Goochland County	44	5.65
Jefferson, WV (cdp) Kanawha County	23	5.60
Orchard Lake Village, MI (city) Oakland County	119	5.59
Lanesboro, PA (borough) Susquehanna County	30	5.57
Robbinsville, NJ (cdp) Mercer County	124	5.53
Versailles, IN (town) Ripley County	97	5.50
Burbank, IL (city) Cook County	1,558	5.48
Deerfield, NY (town) Oneida County	230	5.48
Fort Chiswell, VA (cdp) Wythe County	52	5.47
Mulliken, MI (village) Eaton County	27	5.33
Justice, IL (village) Cook County	671	5.31
Ovilla, TX (city) Ellis County	189	5.31
Mackenzie, MO (village) St. Louis County	6	5.26
Stiles, PA (cdp) Lehigh County	51	5.23
Halls, TN (town) Lauderdale County	120	5.16
Oden, MI (cdp) Emmet County	26	5.16
Downsville, LA (village) Union Parish	8	5.16
Pimmit Hills, VA (cdp) Fairfax County	319	5.12
Ingalls, KS (city) Gray County	16	5.11
Toomsboro, GA (city) Wilkinson County	36	5.09
Tannersville, NY (village) Greene County	22	5.07
Riley, IN (town) Vigo County	11	5.07
Salladasburg, PA (borough) Lycoming County	12	5.06
Langeloth, PA (cdp) Washington County	22	5.02
North Kansas City, MO (city) Clay County	215	5.01
Millington, IL (village) LaSalle County	44	5.01
Firth, NE (village) Lancaster County	28	5.00
McDonald, PA (borough) Allegheny County	19	5.00
Clyde, NJ (cdp) Somerset County	12	5.00
Old Tappan, NJ (borough) Bergen County	283	4.99
Oak Lawn, IL (village) Cook County	2,764	4.95
El Cajon, CA (city) San Diego County	4,795	4.90
Paragon Estates, CO (cdp) Boulder County	51	4.89
Madison Heights, MI (city) Oakland County	1,463	4.88
Bruno, WV (cdp) Logan County	20	4.88

Ancestry

Arab

Top 150 Places Sorted by Percent of Total Population

Based on places with total population of 7,500 or more

Place	Population	%
Dearborn, MI (city) Wayne County	38,503	39.13
Hamtramck, MI (city) Wayne County	4,285	18.97
Dearborn Heights, MI (city) Wayne County	10,397	17.91
Bridgeview, IL (village) Cook County	2,010	12.45
Hickory Hills, IL (city) Cook County	1,595	11.39
Chicago Ridge, IL (village) Cook County	1,605	11.35
Lackawanna, NY (city) Erie County	1,753	9.61
Palos Hills, IL (city) Cook County	1,536	8.84
Little Falls, NJ (township) Passaic County	1,000	7.21
West Bloomfield, MI (charter township) Oakland County	4,594	7.10
Coldwater, MI (city) Branch County	775	7.06
West Long Branch, NJ (borough) Monmouth County	540	6.65
Sterling Heights, MI (city) Macomb County	8,488	6.54
Melvindale, MI (city) Wayne County	685	6.37
Lake Barcroft, VA (cdp) Fairfax County	575	6.35
Woodland Park, NJ (borough) Passaic County	716	6.17
Arvin, CA (city) Kern County	1,089	5.94
Tysons Corner, VA (cdp) Fairfax County	983	5.75
Spring Valley Lake, CA (cdp) San Bernardino County	436	5.71
Fullerton, PA (cdp) Lehigh County	854	5.67
Burbank, IL (city) Cook County	1,558	5.48
Justice, IL (village) Cook County	671	5.31
Oak Lawn, IL (village) Cook County	2,764	4.95
El Cajon, CA (city) San Diego County	4,795	4.90
Madison Heights, MI (city) Oakland County	1,463	4.88
Whitehall, PA (township) Lehigh County	1,261	4.76
Revere, MA (city) Suffolk County	2,310	4.62
Clifton, NJ (city) Passaic County	3,816	4.61
Bayonne, NJ (city) Hudson County	2,773	4.47
East Brunswick, NJ (township) Middlesex County	2,092	4.41
Orland Park, IL (village) Cook County	2,393	4.34
Blackstone, MA (town) Worcester County	387	4.30
Wallington, NJ (borough) Bergen County	476	4.20
Brookside, DE (cdp) New Castle County	598	4.16
Burr Ridge, IL (village) DuPage County	433	4.12
Methuen Town, MA (city) Essex County	1,897	4.09
Wayne, NJ (township) Passaic County	2,206	4.06
Lodi, NJ (borough) Bergen County	960	4.01
Ridgefield Park, NJ (village) Bergen County	506	3.99
Bailey's Crossroads, VA (cdp) Fairfax County	829	3.98
Hillsborough, CA (town) San Mateo County	422	3.96
Olmsted Falls, OH (city) Cuyahoga County	343	3.92
Cedar Grove, NJ (township) Essex County	474	3.85
Beverly Hills, CA (city) Los Angeles County	1,295	3.81
Pelham, NH (town) Hillsborough County	480	3.81
Troy, MI (city) Oakland County	3,081	3.80
Totowa, NJ (borough) Passaic County	403	3.80
Middleburg Heights, OH (city) Cuyahoga County	596	3.77
Farmington, MI (city) Oakland County	391	3.77
Norwood, MA (cdp/town) Norfolk County	1,066	3.76
North Olmsted, OH (city) Cuyahoga County	1,223	3.73
Northville, MI (township) Wayne County	1,008	3.70
Grosse Pointe Woods, MI (city) Wayne County	604	3.69
Pittsfield, MI (charter township) Washtenaw County	1,249	3.66
Westlake, OH (city) Cuyahoga County	1,183	3.66
Watertown Town, MA (city) Middlesex County	1,151	3.64
Kingstowne, VA (cdp) Fairfax County	526	3.62
Fair Lakes, VA (cdp) Fairfax County	285	3.58
Bloomfield, MI (charter township) Oakland County	1,477	3.56
San Dimas, CA (city) Los Angeles County	1,194	3.55
Rancho San Diego, CA (cdp) San Diego County	717	3.54
Fairview, NJ (borough) Bergen County	484	3.54
Uniontown, PA (city) Fayette County	374	3.49
Dunn Loring, VA (cdp) Fairfax County	322	3.48
Hampden, PA (township) Cumberland County	946	3.45
Princeton Meadows, NJ (cdp) Middlesex County	470	3.42
Paramus, NJ (borough) Bergen County	879	3.37
Seven Corners, VA (cdp) Fairfax County	280	3.36
Franconia, VA (cdp) Fairfax County	608	3.30
Southwick, MA (town) Hampden County	307	3.27
Bull Mountain, OR (cdp) Washington County	300	3.27
Cloverdale, CA (city) Sonoma County	268	3.26
Woodmere, NY (cdp) Nassau County	568	3.25
New Hartford, NY (town) Oneida County	710	3.23
Worth, IL (village) Cook County	344	3.22
Parma Heights, OH (city) Cuyahoga County	660	3.18
Woodburn, VA (cdp) Fairfax County	277	3.18
Farmington Hills, MI (city) Oakland County	2,505	3.12
Robbinsville, NJ (township) Mercer County	406	3.12
Seven Hills, OH (city) Cuyahoga County	368	3.12
Goodlettsville, TN (city) Davidson County	480	3.11
Hawthorne, NJ (borough) Passaic County	571	3.07
Wolf Trap, VA (cdp) Fairfax County	511	3.06
Doctor Phillips, FL (cdp) Orange County	342	3.05
Princeton, NJ (borough) Mercer County	381	3.04
Plainville, MA (town) Norfolk County	246	3.04
Washington, NJ (township) Bergen County	271	3.01
Temple Terrace, FL (city) Hillsborough County	723	2.98
Dedham, MA (cdp/town) Norfolk County	722	2.97
Middleton, MA (town) Essex County	259	2.97
Niagara, NY (town) Niagara County	250	2.96
Farmingdale, NY (village) Nassau County	242	2.96
Terrytown, LA (cdp) Jefferson Parish	666	2.94
North Union, PA (township) Fayette County	383	2.94
Fairview Park, OH (city) Cuyahoga County	495	2.93
Western Springs, IL (village) Cook County	369	2.92
Kirkland, NY (town) Oneida County	298	2.90
Mansfield, NJ (township) Burlington County	232	2.90
Whitestown, NY (town) Oneida County	538	2.89
Hastings-on-Hudson, NY (village) Westchester County	225	2.89
Shelby, MI (charter township) Macomb County	2,092	2.87
Malden, MA (city) Middlesex County	1,671	2.87
Hackensack, NJ (city) Bergen County	1,226	2.87
Oakdale, NY (cdp) Suffolk County	220	2.87
Millbrae, CA (city) San Mateo County	600	2.86
Greenwood, MS (city) Leflore County	450	2.84
New Scotland, NY (town) Albany County	246	2.84
Jersey City, NJ (city) Hudson County	6,852	2.82
Canton, MI (charter township) Wayne County	2,465	2.80
Mayfield Heights, OH (city) Cuyahoga County	529	2.77
Briarcliff Manor, NY (village) Westchester County	222	2.77
Lakewood, OH (city) Cuyahoga County	1,450	2.75
El Sobrante, CA (cdp) Riverside County	304	2.73
Lewiston, NY (town) Niagara County	441	2.72
Pompton Lakes, NJ (borough) Passaic County	298	2.72
Sylvania, OH (city) Lucas County	514	2.71
San Bruno, CA (city) San Mateo County	1,085	2.70
Plainsboro, NJ (township) Middlesex County	605	2.69
Hazel Park, MI (city) Oakland County	454	2.69
Fair Oaks, VA (cdp) Fairfax County	738	2.68
Wanaque, NJ (borough) Passaic County	292	2.68
Allentown, PA (city) Lehigh County	3,112	2.67
Ocean, NJ (township) Monmouth County	727	2.67
Fort Mohave, AZ (cdp) Mohave County	383	2.66
Rose Hill, VA (cdp) Fairfax County	524	2.65
Clay, MI (township) St. Clair County	247	2.64
Somerset, MA (cdp/town) Bristol County	478	2.63
Coeymans, NY (town) Albany County	200	2.63
Hasbrouck Heights, NJ (borough) Bergen County	308	2.62
Sugar Land, TX (city) Fort Bend County	1,981	2.60
Niles, IL (village) Cook County	765	2.60
West Hempstead, NY (cdp) Nassau County	480	2.60
Skokie, IL (village) Cook County	1,643	2.57
Calabasas, CA (city) Los Angeles County	581	2.56
Windham, NH (town) Rockingham County	337	2.55
McLean, VA (cdp) Fairfax County	1,172	2.54
La Verne, CA (city) Los Angeles County	793	2.54
Macedonia, OH (city) Summit County	275	2.53
New Baltimore, VA (cdp) Fauquier County	199	2.53
Utica, NY (city) Oneida County	1,558	2.52
North Bergen, NJ (township) Hudson County	1,502	2.52
Foster City, CA (city) San Mateo County	750	2.52
Auburn, MA (town) Worcester County	408	2.52
Mukilteo, WA (city) Snohomish County	499	2.51
Superior, MI (charter township) Washtenaw County	320	2.51
Cumberland, RI (town) Providence County	830	2.49
Southchase, FL (cdp) Orange County	411	2.49
Cliffside Park, NJ (borough) Bergen County	579	2.48
Tinley Park, IL (village) Cook County	1,358	2.47
Bostonia, CA (cdp) San Diego County	357	2.46

Please refer to the Explanation of Data in the front of the book for more detailed information.

Ancestry

Arab: Arab

U.S. and 50 States Sorted by Population and Percent of Total Population

Place	Population	%
United States	**259,644**	**0.09**
California	41,438	0.11
Michigan	34,741	0.35
New York	25,231	0.13
Illinois	19,609	0.15
Texas	16,323	0.07
Florida	15,315	0.08
New Jersey	11,398	0.13
Ohio	10,035	0.09
Virginia	9,329	0.12
Pennsylvania	6,995	0.06
North Carolina	5,243	0.06
Massachusetts	5,145	0.08
Arizona	4,690	0.08
Maryland	4,108	0.07
Missouri	3,669	0.06
Tennessee	3,630	0.06
Indiana	3,625	0.06
Oregon	3,593	0.10
Georgia	3,555	0.04
Louisiana	3,545	0.08
Washington	2,993	0.05
Minnesota	2,047	0.04
Colorado	1,994	0.04
Kentucky	1,858	0.04
Wisconsin	1,749	0.03
Oklahoma	1,596	0.04
Nevada	1,443	0.05
Kansas	1,382	0.05
Connecticut	1,375	0.04
Alabama	1,358	0.03
South Carolina	1,113	0.02
Arkansas	1,044	0.04
Nebraska	985	0.05
Mississippi	748	0.03
New Mexico	708	0.04
Iowa	696	0.02
Utah	668	0.03
District of Columbia	627	0.11
Rhode Island	598	0.06
New Hampshire	538	0.04
West Virginia	517	0.03
Delaware	483	0.05
Maine	461	0.03
Hawaii	418	0.03
Idaho	335	0.02
Montana	229	0.02
South Dakota	127	0.02
North Dakota	100	0.02
Vermont	98	0.02
Alaska	95	0.01
Wyoming	44	0.01

Place	Population	%
Michigan	34,741	0.35
Illinois	19,609	0.15
New York	25,231	0.13
New Jersey	11,398	0.13
Virginia	9,329	0.12
California	41,438	0.11
District of Columbia	627	0.11
Oregon	3,593	0.10
United States	**259,644**	**0.09**
Ohio	10,035	0.09
Florida	15,315	0.08
Massachusetts	5,145	0.08
Arizona	4,690	0.08
Louisiana	3,545	0.08
Texas	16,323	0.07
Maryland	4,108	0.07
Pennsylvania	6,995	0.06
North Carolina	5,243	0.06
Missouri	3,669	0.06
Tennessee	3,630	0.06
Indiana	3,625	0.06
Rhode Island	598	0.06
Washington	2,993	0.05
Nevada	1,443	0.05
Kansas	1,382	0.05
Nebraska	985	0.05
Delaware	483	0.05
Georgia	3,555	0.04
Minnesota	2,047	0.04
Colorado	1,994	0.04
Kentucky	1,858	0.04
Oklahoma	1,596	0.04
Connecticut	1,375	0.04
Arkansas	1,044	0.04
New Mexico	708	0.04
New Hampshire	538	0.04
Wisconsin	1,749	0.03
Alabama	1,358	0.03
Mississippi	748	0.03
Utah	668	0.03
West Virginia	517	0.03
Maine	461	0.03
Hawaii	418	0.03
South Carolina	1,113	0.02
Iowa	696	0.02
Idaho	335	0.02
Montana	229	0.02
South Dakota	127	0.02
North Dakota	100	0.02
Vermont	98	0.02
Alaska	95	0.01
Wyoming	44	0.01

Please refer to the Explanation of Data in the front of the book for more detailed information.

Ancestry

Arab: Arab

Top 150 Places Sorted by Population

Based on all places, regardless of total population

Place	Population	%
New York, NY (city) Kings County	15,160	0.19
Dearborn, MI (city) Wayne County	8,134	8.27
Brooklyn, NY (borough) Kings County	7,609	0.31
Detroit, MI (city) Wayne County	4,349	0.57
Chicago, IL (city) Cook County	4,311	0.16
Los Angeles, CA (city) Los Angeles County	3,096	0.08
Houston, TX (city) Harris County	3,016	0.15
Queens, NY (borough) Queens County	2,283	0.10
Hamtramck, MI (city) Wayne County	2,280	10.09
Philadelphia, PA (city) Philadelphia County	2,081	0.14
Jacksonville, FL (city) Duval County	2,036	0.25
Sterling Heights, MI (city) Macomb County	1,888	1.46
Staten Island, NY (borough) Richmond County	1,829	0.39
Fresno, CA (city) Fresno County	1,720	0.36
Manhattan, NY (borough) New York County	1,720	0.11
Bronx, NY (borough) Bronx County	1,719	0.13
Phoenix, AZ (city) Maricopa County	1,525	0.11
West Bloomfield, MI (charter township) Oakland County	1,506	2.33
Oak Lawn, IL (village) Cook County	1,415	2.53
Lackawanna, NY (city) Erie County	1,331	7.30
Clifton, NJ (city) Passaic County	1,177	1.42
Columbus, OH (city) Franklin County	1,109	0.14
San Francisco, CA (city) San Francisco County	1,106	0.14
Raleigh, NC (city) Wake County	1,105	0.29
Orland Park, IL (village) Cook County	1,104	2.00
Paterson, NJ (city) Passaic County	1,083	0.74
Bakersfield, CA (city) Kern County	1,040	0.31
Yonkers, NY (city) Westchester County	1,036	0.53
Portland, OR (city) Multnomah County	1,017	0.18
Livonia, MI (city) Wayne County	1,013	1.03
Dearborn Heights, MI (city) Wayne County	1,002	1.73
Daly City, CA (city) San Mateo County	991	0.99
San Diego, CA (city) San Diego County	944	0.07
Troy, MI (city) Oakland County	929	1.15
Tinley Park, IL (village) Cook County	902	1.64
Nashville-Davidson, TN (metro govt) Davidson County	890	0.15
Stockton, CA (city) San Joaquin County	879	0.31
Charlotte, NC (city) Mecklenburg County	840	0.12
Memphis, TN (city) Shelby County	807	0.12
Bridgeview, IL (village) Cook County	786	4.87
Arvin, CA (city) Kern County	782	4.27
Chicago Ridge, IL (village) Cook County	766	5.42
San Antonio, TX (city) Medina County	742	0.06
Hickory Hills, IL (city) Cook County	727	5.19
Arlington, VA (cdp) Arlington County	725	0.37
Canton, MI (charter township) Wayne County	709	0.81
San Jose, CA (city) Santa Clara County	698	0.08
Arlington, TX (city) Tarrant County	687	0.19
Irvine, CA (city) Orange County	667	0.33
Cleveland, OH (city) Cuyahoga County	663	0.16
Buffalo, NY (city) Erie County	644	0.24
Palos Hills, IL (city) Cook County	637	3.67
Tampa, FL (city) Hillsborough County	631	0.19
Washington, DC (city) District of Columbia	627	0.11
Louisville-Jefferson County, KY (metro govt) Jefferson County	618	0.11
Hackensack, NJ (city) Bergen County	617	1.44
Toledo, OH (city) Lucas County	614	0.21
Boston, MA (city) Suffolk County	609	0.10
Anaheim, CA (city) Orange County	607	0.18
Sacramento, CA (city) Sacramento County	597	0.13
Lexington-Fayette, KY (cons. govt) Fayette County	593	0.21
Austin, TX (city) Travis County	593	0.08
Farmington Hills, MI (city) Oakland County	587	0.73
Pittsfield, MI (charter township) Washtenaw County	582	1.71
Omaha, NE (city) Douglas County	580	0.14
Revere, MA (city) Suffolk County	578	1.16
Columbia, MO (city) Boone County	578	0.55
San Bernardino, CA (city) San Bernardino County	574	0.27
El Paso, TX (city) El Paso County	569	0.09
El Cajon, CA (city) San Diego County	560	0.57
Indianapolis, IN (city) Marion County	542	0.07
Baton Rouge, LA (city) East Baton Rouge Parish	539	0.24
Long Beach, CA (city) Los Angeles County	537	0.12
Westland, MI (city) Wayne County	536	0.63
Burbank, IL (city) Cook County	532	1.87
Kansas City, MO (city) Jackson County	528	0.12
Miami Beach, FL (city) Miami-Dade County	522	0.60
Oakland, CA (city) Alameda County	515	0.13
Madison Heights, MI (city) Oakland County	503	1.68
Oklahoma City, OK (city) Oklahoma County	499	0.09
San Dimas, CA (city) Los Angeles County	488	1.45
Tempe, AZ (city) Maricopa County	472	0.29
Irving, TX (city) Dallas County	472	0.22
Tulsa, OK (city) Tulsa County	470	0.12
Gilbert, AZ (town) Maricopa County	469	0.24
Corona, CA (city) Riverside County	463	0.31
Rancho Cucamonga, CA (city) San Bernardino County	454	0.28
North Olmsted, OH (city) Cuyahoga County	447	1.36
North Richland Hills, TX (city) Tarrant County	438	0.71
Cambridge, MA (city) Middlesex County	432	0.42
Tucson, AZ (city) Pima County	432	0.08
Sugar Land, TX (city) Fort Bend County	428	0.56
Glendale, CA (city) Los Angeles County	420	0.22
Lockport, IL (city) Will County	407	1.71
Chino Hills, CA (city) San Bernardino County	405	0.54
Denver, CO (city) Denver County	403	0.07
Woodland Park, NJ (borough) Passaic County	401	3.45
Shelby, MI (charter township) Macomb County	397	0.55
Rockford, IL (city) Winnebago County	397	0.26
Fremont, CA (city) Alameda County	396	0.19
Milwaukee, WI (city) Milwaukee County	396	0.07
Overland Park, KS (city) Johnson County	394	0.23
Novi, MI (city) Oakland County	392	0.73
Centreville, VA (cdp) Fairfax County	388	0.54
Metairie, LA (cdp) Jefferson Parish	388	0.29
Pittsburgh, PA (city) Allegheny County	388	0.13
Burbank, CA (city) Los Angeles County	383	0.37
Pasadena, CA (city) Los Angeles County	383	0.28
Lodi, NJ (borough) Bergen County	382	1.59
Hampton, VA (ind. city) Hampton independent city	369	0.27
Fontana, CA (city) San Bernardino County	368	0.19
Hurst, TX (city) Tarrant County	367	0.99
South San Francisco, CA (city) San Mateo County	363	0.59
Allentown, PA (city) Lehigh County	360	0.31
Orland Hills, IL (village) Cook County	357	5.09
Aurora, CO (city) Arapahoe County	353	0.11
Bailey's Crossroads, VA (cdp) Fairfax County	344	1.65
Kennesaw, GA (city) Cobb County	344	1.21
Westlake, OH (city) Cuyahoga County	344	1.06
Columbia, MD (cdp) Howard County	343	0.35
Jersey City, NJ (city) Hudson County	341	0.14
Dallas, TX (city) Dallas County	339	0.03
Fort Worth, TX (city) Tarrant County	335	0.05
Joliet, IL (city) Will County	331	0.23
Terrytown, LA (cdp) Jefferson Parish	330	1.46
Melvindale, MI (city) Wayne County	329	3.06
Ann Arbor, MI (city) Washtenaw County	327	0.28
Highland, IN (town) Lake County	326	1.37
Fridley, MN (city) Anoka County	326	1.19
Mission Viejo, CA (city) Orange County	324	0.35
Henrietta, NY (town) Monroe County	321	0.76
Gainesville, FL (city) Alachua County	319	0.26
Hempstead, NY (town) Nassau County	319	0.04
Homer Glen, IL (village) Will County	317	1.28
Eugene, OR (city) Lane County	317	0.21
Albuquerque, NM (city) Bernalillo County	317	0.06
Clinton, MI (charter township) Macomb County	312	0.32
Beaverton, OR (city) Washington County	311	0.35
Knoxville, TN (city) Knox County	311	0.17
Torrance, CA (city) Los Angeles County	310	0.22
Warren, MI (city) Macomb County	309	0.23
Pasadena, TX (city) Harris County	302	0.21
Southfield, MI (city) Oakland County	299	0.41
Wilson, NC (city) Wilson County	297	0.62
Portland, ME (city) Cumberland County	295	0.45
Fair Oaks, VA (cdp) Fairfax County	290	1.05
San Bruno, CA (city) San Mateo County	286	0.71
West Linn, OR (city) Clackamas County	285	1.16
Wayne, NJ (township) Passaic County	282	0.52
Justice, IL (village) Cook County	281	2.22

SECTION THREE

Please refer to the Explanation of Data in the front of the book for more detailed information.

Ancestry

Arab: Arab

Top 150 Places Sorted by Percent of Total Population

Based on all places, regardless of total population

Place	Population	%
Thompsons, TX (town) Fort Bend County	35	14.71
St. James, MI (cdp) Charlevoix County	27	14.36
Victor, CA (cdp) San Joaquin County	37	13.50
Parklawn, CA (cdp) Stanislaus County	95	11.99
Katherine, AZ (cdp) Mohave County	21	11.67
St. James, MI (township) Charlevoix County	27	10.47
Hamtramck, MI (city) Wayne County	2,280	10.09
Dearborn, MI (city) Wayne County	8,134	8.27
Lake Bosworth, WA (cdp) Snohomish County	36	7.79
Lackawanna, NY (city) Erie County	1,331	7.30
Moodus, CT (cdp) Middlesex County	81	7.22
Lenox, GA (town) Cook County	74	6.80
Elmer, OK (town) Jackson County	6	6.74
Hulbert, MI (township) Chippewa County	14	6.14
Goochland, VA (cdp) Goochland County	44	5.65
Chicago Ridge, IL (village) Cook County	766	5.42
Hickory Hills, IL (city) Cook County	727	5.19
Orland Hills, IL (village) Cook County	357	5.09
Toomsboro, GA (city) Wilkinson County	36	5.09
Bridgeview, IL (village) Cook County	786	4.87
Newton, MS (city) Newton County	162	4.70
State Line, MS (town) Greene County	22	4.67
Noble, IL (village) Richland County	28	4.61
Highland, PA (township) Clarion County	29	4.58
Frazier Park, CA (cdp) Kern County	108	4.51
Wanchese, NC (cdp) Dare County	79	4.51
Camanche North Shore, CA (cdp) Amador County	35	4.50
Ducor, CA (cdp) Tulare County	20	4.50
Sundown, TX (city) Hockley County	60	4.32
Arvin, CA (city) Kern County	782	4.27
Hardin, IL (village) Calhoun County	48	4.13
Akron, MN (township) Wilkin County	4	4.08
Green Lane, PA (borough) Montgomery County	18	4.06
South Rosemary, NC (cdp) Halifax County	117	3.75
Palos Hills, IL (city) Cook County	637	3.67
Strathmore, CA (cdp) Tulare County	119	3.61
Clatskanie, OR (city) Columbia County	63	3.57
Lake Shore, MN (city) Cass County	43	3.54
Woodland Park, NJ (borough) Passaic County	401	3.45
West Pittsburg, PA (cdp) Lawrence County	23	3.42
Alder, MT (cdp) Madison County	5	3.40
Lexington, OH (village) Richland County	168	3.25
Monee, IL (village) Will County	160	3.25
Grant-Valkaria, FL (town) Brevard County	122	3.24
Warren, TX (cdp) Tyler County	17	3.22
Mathews, VA (cdp) Mathews County	25	3.18
Dollar Bay, MI (cdp) Houghton County	26	3.17
Brinckerhoff, NY (cdp) Dutchess County	101	3.13
Melvindale, MI (city) Wayne County	329	3.06
Brogden, NC (cdp) Wayne County	76	3.05
Bethany, WV (town) Brooke County	22	3.03
Berlin, NJ (township) Camden County	161	3.02
Westminster, SC (city) Oconee County	70	2.95
Millbrook, NY (village) Dutchess County	48	2.94
Tunica, MS (town) Tunica County	36	2.93
Wattsburg, PA (borough) Erie County	11	2.93
Buckingham, FL (cdp) Lee County	125	2.92
Hebron, MD (town) Wicomico County	25	2.87
Columbia, ME (town) Washington County	11	2.87
Clark Mills, NY (cdp) Oneida County	32	2.85
Whitefish, MI (township) Chippewa County	16	2.84
Terre du Lac, MO (cdp) St. Francois County	61	2.80
Columbia, AL (town) Houston County	21	2.64
Morristown, NY (town) St. Lawrence County	71	2.59
Chevy Chase Section Five, MD (village) Montgomery County	19	2.59
Berry Hill, TN (city) Davidson County	12	2.57
Wilson, WI (town) Dunn County	12	2.55
Taylor, PA (township) Lawrence County	23	2.54
Oak Lawn, IL (village) Cook County	1,415	2.53
Pine Mountain Club, CA (cdp) Kern County	36	2.47
Stroudsburg, PA (borough) Monroe County	140	2.44
Wise, VA (town) Wise County	81	2.44
New Scotland, NY (town) Albany County	209	2.41
Orange, NY (town) Schuyler County	43	2.41
Bel Aire, KS (city) Sedgwick County	157	2.38
Excelsior, MI (township) Kalkaska County	21	2.35
West Bloomfield, MI (charter township) Oakland County	1,506	2.33
Washington, MI (township) Gratiot County	16	2.33
Old Jefferson, LA (cdp) East Baton Rouge Parish	144	2.27
Cherry Valley, NY (village) Otsego County	10	2.27
Parker, TX (city) Collin County	79	2.26
Justice, IL (village) Cook County	281	2.22
Del Norte, CO (town) Rio Grande County	36	2.16
Hilliard, FL (town) Nassau County	65	2.15
Potomac Mills, VA (cdp) Prince William County	101	2.14
Golden Hills, CA (cdp) Kern County	183	2.13
Bret Harte, CA (cdp) Stanislaus County	106	2.08
White Hall, AR (city) Jefferson County	111	2.06
Lake Barcroft, VA (cdp) Fairfax County	186	2.05
Spencerport, NY (village) Monroe County	72	2.02
Orland Park, IL (village) Cook County	1,104	2.00
Coldwater, MI (city) Branch County	218	1.99
Merrionette Park, IL (village) Cook County	44	1.96
University Park, NM (cdp) Do±a Ana County	60	1.93
Greenville, DE (cdp) New Castle County	47	1.92
Burr Ridge, IL (village) DuPage County	200	1.90
Somerton, AZ (city) Yuma County	250	1.89
Burbank, IL (city) Cook County	532	1.87
Crest, CA (cdp) San Diego County	40	1.87
Doctor Phillips, FL (cdp) Orange County	209	1.86
Rome, WI (town) Adams County	51	1.86
Hudson, NY (city) Columbia County	127	1.85
Spring Lake Park, MN (city) Anoka County	117	1.84
Crosspointe, VA (cdp) Fairfax County	103	1.83
Kansas, IL (village) Edgar County	17	1.83
Junction City, CA (cdp) Trinity County	22	1.80
Spring Lake Park, MN (city) Anoka County	117	1.79
Pickford, MI (township) Chippewa County	24	1.77
Cedar Bluff, AL (town) Cherokee County	33	1.76
Rose Hill Acres, TX (city) Hardin County	10	1.74
Dearborn Heights, MI (city) Wayne County	1,002	1.73
Meadow Lake, NM (cdp) Valencia County	101	1.72
Pittsfield, MI (charter township) Washtenaw County	582	1.71
Lockport, IL (city) Will County	407	1.71
Madison Heights, MI (city) Oakland County	503	1.68
Pompey, NY (town) Onondaga County	115	1.67
Bluewell, WV (cdp) Mercer County	38	1.67
Edinburgh, IN (town) Johnson County	65	1.66
Shorewood Forest, IN (cdp) Porter County	50	1.66
Bailey's Crossroads, VA (cdp) Fairfax County	344	1.65
Larkin, MI (charter township) Midland County	83	1.65
White Pine, TN (town) Jefferson County	35	1.65
Clayville, NY (village) Oneida County	7	1.65
Tinley Park, IL (village) Cook County	902	1.64
Prospect Park, NJ (borough) Passaic County	94	1.61
Lodi, NJ (borough) Bergen County	382	1.59
Brocton, IL (village) Edgar County	7	1.58
Moreland Hills, OH (village) Cuyahoga County	52	1.57
Emerson, NJ (borough) Bergen County	114	1.56
Plainsboro Center, NJ (cdp) Middlesex County	42	1.56
Newcastle, WA (city) King County	152	1.54
Floyd, VA (town) Floyd County	10	1.53
Martin, MI (village) Allegan County	6	1.48
Linndale, OH (village) Cuyahoga County	2	1.47
Sterling Heights, MI (city) Macomb County	1,888	1.46
Terrytown, LA (cdp) Jefferson Parish	330	1.46
San Dimas, CA (city) Los Angeles County	488	1.45
Hackensack, NJ (city) Bergen County	617	1.44
Union Grove, WI (village) Racine County	70	1.44
King George, VA (cdp) King George County	52	1.44
Lincoln Heights, OH (village) Hamilton County	49	1.44
Willowbrook, IL (village) DuPage County	122	1.43
Pleasant Valley, MO (city) Clay County	43	1.43
Osceola, MI (township) Houghton County	26	1.43
Waltonville, IL (village) Jefferson County	6	1.43
Clifton, NJ (city) Passaic County	1,177	1.42
Ormond-by-the-Sea, FL (cdp) Volusia County	110	1.42
Strattanville, PA (borough) Clarion County	9	1.42
Briarcliff Manor, NY (village) Westchester County	113	1.41
Litchfield, CT (borough) Litchfield County	17	1.41

Please refer to the Explanation of Data in the front of the book for more detailed information.

Ancestry

Arab: Arab

Top 150 Places Sorted by Percent of Total Population

Based on places with total population of 7,500 or more

Place	Population	%
Hamtramck, MI (city) Wayne County	2,280	10.09
Dearborn, MI (city) Wayne County	8,134	8.27
Lackawanna, NY (city) Erie County	1,331	7.30
Chicago Ridge, IL (village) Cook County	766	5.42
Hickory Hills, IL (city) Cook County	727	5.19
Bridgeview, IL (village) Cook County	786	4.87
Arvin, CA (city) Kern County	782	4.27
Palos Hills, IL (city) Cook County	637	3.67
Woodland Park, NJ (borough) Passaic County	401	3.45
Melvindale, MI (city) Wayne County	329	3.06
Oak Lawn, IL (village) Cook County	1,415	2.53
New Scotland, NY (town) Albany County	209	2.41
West Bloomfield, MI (charter township) Oakland County	1,506	2.33
Justice, IL (village) Cook County	281	2.22
Golden Hills, CA (cdp) Kern County	183	2.13
Lake Barcroft, VA (cdp) Fairfax County	186	2.05
Orland Park, IL (village) Cook County	1,104	2.00
Coldwater, MI (city) Branch County	218	1.99
Burr Ridge, IL (village) DuPage County	200	1.90
Somerton, AZ (city) Yuma County	250	1.89
Burbank, IL (city) Cook County	532	1.87
Doctor Phillips, FL (cdp) Orange County	209	1.86
Dearborn Heights, MI (city) Wayne County	1,002	1.73
Pittsfield, MI (charter township) Washtenaw County	582	1.71
Lockport, IL (city) Will County	407	1.71
Madison Heights, MI (city) Oakland County	503	1.68
Bailey's Crossroads, VA (cdp) Fairfax County	344	1.65
Tinley Park, IL (village) Cook County	902	1.64
Lodi, NJ (borough) Bergen County	382	1.59
Newcastle, WA (city) King County	152	1.54
Sterling Heights, MI (city) Macomb County	1,888	1.46
Terrytown, LA (cdp) Jefferson Parish	330	1.46
San Dimas, CA (city) Los Angeles County	488	1.45
Hackensack, NJ (city) Bergen County	617	1.44
Willowbrook, IL (village) DuPage County	122	1.43
Clifton, NJ (city) Passaic County	1,177	1.42
Ormond-by-the-Sea, FL (cdp) Volusia County	110	1.42
Briarcliff Manor, NY (village) Westchester County	113	1.41
Tarboro, NC (town) Edgecombe County	160	1.40
Highland, IN (town) Lake County	326	1.37
North Olmsted, OH (city) Cuyahoga County	447	1.36
Cedar Grove, NJ (township) Essex County	166	1.35
Franconia, VA (cdp) Fairfax County	247	1.34
Washington, NJ (township) Bergen County	120	1.33
Homer Glen, IL (village) Will County	317	1.28
Monsey, NY (cdp) Rockland County	191	1.27
Bridgeton, MO (city) St. Louis County	155	1.27
Chevy Chase, MD (cdp) Montgomery County	121	1.24
Richfield, MI (township) Genesee County	108	1.24
Kennesaw, GA (city) Cobb County	344	1.21
Jericho, NY (cdp) Nassau County	157	1.21
Fridley, MN (city) Anoka County	326	1.19
Blackfoot, ID (city) Bingham County	136	1.18
Revere, MA (city) Suffolk County	578	1.16
West Linn, OR (city) Clackamas County	285	1.16
Country Walk, FL (cdp) Miami-Dade County	185	1.16
Troy, MI (city) Oakland County	929	1.15
New Baltimore, VA (cdp) Fauquier County	88	1.12
East La Mirada, CA (cdp) Los Angeles County	112	1.10
Ridgefield Park, NJ (village) Bergen County	137	1.08
Glenvar Heights, FL (cdp) Miami-Dade County	163	1.07
Fairmount, NY (cdp) Onondaga County	108	1.07
Timberlane, LA (cdp) Jefferson Parish	103	1.07
Westlake, OH (city) Cuyahoga County	344	1.06
Riverbank, CA (city) Stanislaus County	231	1.06
Princeton, NJ (township) Mercer County	174	1.06
Middleton, MA (town) Essex County	92	1.06
Fair Oaks, VA (cdp) Fairfax County	290	1.05
Westminster, MD (city) Carroll County	195	1.05
Livonia, MI (city) Wayne County	1,013	1.03
Upper Gwynedd, PA (township) Montgomery County	158	1.03
Lansdowne, VA (cdp) Loudoun County	101	1.03
Pineville, LA (city) Rapides Parish	148	1.02
Grosse Ile, MI (township) Wayne County	107	1.02
Williamstown, MA (town) Berkshire County	80	1.02
Westmont, IL (village) DuPage County	246	1.00
Rose Hill, VA (cdp) Fairfax County	197	1.00
Daly City, CA (city) San Mateo County	991	0.99
Hurst, TX (city) Tarrant County	367	0.99
Manassas Park, VA (ind. city) Manassas Park independent city	127	0.96
Fairfax Station, VA (cdp) Fairfax County	112	0.96
Gold River, CA (cdp) Sacramento County	80	0.96
Rancho San Diego, CA (cdp) San Diego County	192	0.95
Smithfield, NC (town) Johnston County	101	0.92
East Haddam, CT (town) Middlesex County	81	0.90
South Abington, PA (township) Lackawanna County	81	0.90
Wolf Trap, VA (cdp) Fairfax County	149	0.89
Colesville, MD (cdp) Montgomery County	126	0.89
Bryant, AR (city) Saline County	138	0.88
Greencastle, IN (city) Putnam County	91	0.88
Ridgefield, CT (cdp) Fairfield County	68	0.88
Berea, SC (cdp) Greenville County	111	0.86
Inkster, MI (city) Wayne County	223	0.85
El Sobrante, CA (cdp) Riverside County	95	0.85
Niagara, NY (town) Niagara County	72	0.85
Ewa Gentry, HI (cdp) Honolulu County	181	0.84
Bethel, CT (cdp) Fairfield County	74	0.84
Upper Deerfield, NJ (township) Cumberland County	64	0.84
Butler, NJ (borough) Morris County	63	0.84
Upper Saddle River, NJ (borough) Bergen County	66	0.82
Canton, MI (charter township) Wayne County	709	0.81
Superior, MI (charter township) Washtenaw County	103	0.81
Happy Valley, OR (city) Clackamas County	102	0.81
Lincolnwood, IL (village) Cook County	99	0.80
Waldwick, NJ (borough) Bergen County	77	0.80
Avon, IN (town) Hendricks County	92	0.79
Richmond West, FL (cdp) Miami-Dade County	255	0.78
New Hope, MN (city) Hennepin County	156	0.77
Henrietta, NY (town) Monroe County	321	0.76
Schererville, IN (town) Lake County	216	0.76
Woodburn, VA (cdp) Fairfax County	66	0.76
Lackland AFB, TX (cdp) Bexar County	58	0.76
Fullerton, PA (cdp) Lehigh County	113	0.75
Bonita, CA (cdp) San Diego County	105	0.75
Paterson, NJ (city) Passaic County	1,083	0.74
Mundy, MI (township) Genesee County	109	0.74
Farmington Hills, MI (city) Oakland County	587	0.73
Novi, MI (city) Oakland County	392	0.73
Genesee, MI (charter township) Genesee County	162	0.73
Hawthorne, NJ (borough) Passaic County	136	0.73
North Babylon, NY (cdp) Suffolk County	130	0.73
Lynnfield, MA (cdp/town) Essex County	84	0.73
Van Buren, MI (charter township) Wayne County	201	0.72
La Palma, CA (city) Orange County	111	0.72
Wixom, MI (city) Oakland County	97	0.72
Perkasie, PA (borough) Bucks County	62	0.72
North Richland Hills, TX (city) Tarrant County	438	0.71
San Bruno, CA (city) San Mateo County	286	0.71
Parma Heights, OH (city) Cuyahoga County	148	0.71
Mansfield, CT (town) Tolland County	182	0.70
Plainsboro, NJ (township) Middlesex County	157	0.70
Terryville, NY (cdp) Suffolk County	83	0.70
Dinuba, CA (city) Tulare County	142	0.68
White Marsh, MD (cdp) Baltimore County	65	0.68
Hales Corners, WI (village) Milwaukee County	52	0.68
Paramus, NJ (borough) Bergen County	174	0.67
Seminole, FL (city) Pinellas County	116	0.67
Oak Park, MI (city) Oakland County	197	0.66
Auburn, CA (city) Placer County	89	0.66
Valley Falls, RI (cdp) Providence County	76	0.66
Big Rapids, MI (city) Mecosta County	70	0.65
Bloomfield, MI (charter township) Oakland County	264	0.64
North Weeki Wachee, FL (cdp) Hernando County	54	0.64
Westland, MI (city) Wayne County	536	0.63
South Pasadena, CA (city) Los Angeles County	161	0.63
Bedford, MA (town) Middlesex County	82	0.63
Hasbrouck Heights, NJ (borough) Bergen County	74	0.63
Wilson, NC (city) Wilson County	297	0.62
Flint, MI (charter township) Genesee County	201	0.62
University, FL (cdp) Orange County	132	0.62

Please refer to the Explanation of Data in the front of the book for more detailed information.

Ancestry

Arab: Egyptian

U.S. and 50 States Sorted by Population and Percent of Total Population

Place	Population	%
United States	**179,853**	**0.06**
California	37,531	0.10
New Jersey	28,164	0.32
New York	25,478	0.13
Florida	10,623	0.06
Texas	7,521	0.03
Pennsylvania	6,728	0.05
Virginia	6,649	0.08
Illinois	5,053	0.04
Ohio	4,801	0.04
Massachusetts	4,335	0.07
Tennessee	4,302	0.07
North Carolina	3,860	0.04
Maryland	3,816	0.07
Michigan	3,275	0.03
Washington	3,083	0.05
Minnesota	2,752	0.05
Georgia	2,085	0.02
Arizona	1,788	0.03
South Carolina	1,759	0.04
Oregon	1,582	0.04
Connecticut	1,396	0.04
Indiana	1,376	0.02
Nevada	1,310	0.05
Missouri	1,273	0.02
Wisconsin	900	0.02
Iowa	791	0.03
Kansas	777	0.03
Colorado	764	0.02
Alabama	757	0.02
Louisiana	618	0.01
Rhode Island	513	0.05
Oklahoma	477	0.01
Kentucky	462	0.01
West Virginia	408	0.02
Hawaii	335	0.03
District of Columbia	315	0.05
New Mexico	295	0.01
Mississippi	277	0.01
New Hampshire	250	0.02
Arkansas	248	0.01
Delaware	209	0.02
Nebraska	194	0.01
Idaho	174	0.01
Utah	162	0.01
Vermont	114	0.02
Alaska	81	0.01
Maine	79	0.01
North Dakota	75	0.01
South Dakota	16	<0.01
Montana	12	<0.01
Wyoming	10	<0.01

Place	Population	%
New Jersey	28,164	0.32
New York	25,478	0.13
California	37,531	0.10
Virginia	6,649	0.08
Massachusetts	4,335	0.07
Tennessee	4,302	0.07
Maryland	3,816	0.07
United States	**179,853**	**0.06**
Florida	10,623	0.06
Pennsylvania	6,728	0.05
Washington	3,083	0.05
Minnesota	2,752	0.05
Nevada	1,310	0.05
Rhode Island	513	0.05
District of Columbia	315	0.05
Illinois	5,053	0.04
Ohio	4,801	0.04
North Carolina	3,860	0.04
South Carolina	1,759	0.04
Oregon	1,582	0.04
Connecticut	1,396	0.04
Texas	7,521	0.03
Michigan	3,275	0.03
Arizona	1,788	0.03
Iowa	791	0.03
Kansas	777	0.03
Hawaii	335	0.03
Georgia	2,085	0.02
Indiana	1,376	0.02
Missouri	1,273	0.02
Wisconsin	900	0.02
Colorado	764	0.02
Alabama	757	0.02
West Virginia	408	0.02
New Hampshire	250	0.02
Delaware	209	0.02
Vermont	114	0.02
Louisiana	618	0.01
Oklahoma	477	0.01
Kentucky	462	0.01
New Mexico	295	0.01
Mississippi	277	0.01
Arkansas	248	0.01
Nebraska	194	0.01
Idaho	174	0.01
Utah	162	0.01
Alaska	81	0.01
Maine	79	0.01
North Dakota	75	0.01
South Dakota	16	<0.01
Montana	12	<0.01
Wyoming	10	<0.01

Please refer to the Explanation of Data in the front of the book for more detailed information.

Ancestry

Arab: Egyptian

Top 150 Places Sorted by Population

Based on all places, regardless of total population

Place	Population	%
New York, NY (city) Kings County	17,698	0.22
Queens, NY (borough) Queens County	6,551	0.30
Los Angeles, CA (city) Los Angeles County	6,033	0.16
Brooklyn, NY (borough) Kings County	5,231	0.21
Jersey City, NJ (city) Hudson County	4,507	1.85
Staten Island, NY (borough) Richmond County	3,292	0.71
Nashville-Davidson, TN (metro govt) Davidson County	3,050	0.52
Bayonne, NJ (city) Hudson County	2,608	4.20
Manhattan, NY (borough) New York County	1,906	0.12
East Brunswick, NJ (township) Middlesex County	1,893	3.99
Hempstead, NY (town) Nassau County	1,227	0.16
Old Bridge, NJ (township) Middlesex County	1,204	1.87
Corona, CA (city) Riverside County	1,103	0.73
Anaheim, CA (city) Orange County	1,072	0.32
Huntington Beach, CA (city) Orange County	1,048	0.55
Chicago, IL (city) Cook County	1,010	0.04
Columbus, OH (city) Franklin County	911	0.12
San Jose, CA (city) Santa Clara County	847	0.09
Houston, TX (city) Harris County	732	0.04
Bronx, NY (borough) Bronx County	718	0.05
Raleigh, NC (city) Wake County	703	0.18
Santa Clarita, CA (city) Los Angeles County	636	0.37
Charlotte, NC (city) Mecklenburg County	604	0.09
Downey, CA (city) Los Angeles County	603	0.54
Hampden, PA (township) Cumberland County	600	2.19
Philadelphia, PA (city) Philadelphia County	580	0.04
North Hempstead, NY (town) Nassau County	529	0.24
Clifton, NJ (city) Passaic County	502	0.61
Bellflower, CA (city) Los Angeles County	494	0.65
San Francisco, CA (city) San Francisco County	483	0.06
South Brunswick, NJ (township) Middlesex County	472	1.11
Irvine, CA (city) Orange County	463	0.23
Woodbridge, NJ (township) Middlesex County	460	0.46
Lynnwood, WA (city) Snohomish County	438	1.23
Brookhaven, NY (town) Suffolk County	435	0.09
Rancho Cucamonga, CA (city) San Bernardino County	434	0.27
San Antonio, TX (city) Medina County	432	0.03
San Diego, CA (city) San Diego County	430	0.03
Huntington, NY (town) Suffolk County	425	0.21
Woodmere, NY (cdp) Nassau County	418	2.39
Henderson, NV (city) Clark County	417	0.17
Las Vegas, NV (city) Clark County	408	0.07
Alexandria, VA (ind. city) Alexandria independent city	407	0.30
Jacksonville, FL (city) Duval County	398	0.05
Minneapolis, MN (city) Hennepin County	392	0.10
Fremont, CA (city) Alameda County	391	0.19
Plano, TX (city) Collin County	385	0.15
Reston, VA (cdp) Fairfax County	374	0.70
Chino Hills, CA (city) San Bernardino County	371	0.50
Greenville, NC (city) Pitt County	368	0.46
Paramount, CA (city) Los Angeles County	364	0.67
Bakersfield, CA (city) Kern County	364	0.11
Islip, NY (town) Suffolk County	364	0.11
Phoenix, AZ (city) Maricopa County	362	0.02
Dearborn, MI (city) Wayne County	356	0.36
Wayne, NJ (township) Passaic County	351	0.65
Riverside, CA (city) Riverside County	349	0.12
Torrance, CA (city) Los Angeles County	341	0.24
Lakewood, NJ (township) Ocean County	339	0.39
North Brunswick, NJ (township) Middlesex County	338	0.85
Sayreville, NJ (borough) Middlesex County	333	0.79
Coconut Creek, FL (city) Broward County	332	0.64
Hawthorne, CA (city) Los Angeles County	329	0.39
Glendale, CA (city) Los Angeles County	329	0.17
Rahway, NJ (city) Union County	328	1.22
Spokane, WA (city) Spokane County	327	0.16
Cleveland, OH (city) Cuyahoga County	326	0.08
Lansdale, PA (borough) Montgomery County	324	2.00
Revere, MA (city) Suffolk County	316	0.63
South River, NJ (borough) Middlesex County	315	1.99
Washington, DC (city) District of Columbia	315	0.05
Fresno, CA (city) Fresno County	313	0.06
Eastvale, CA (cdp) Riverside County	308	0.63
Westminster, CA (city) Orange County	306	0.34
Germantown, MD (cdp) Montgomery County	304	0.36
Edison, NJ (township) Middlesex County	304	0.31
Laurel, VA (cdp) Henrico County	303	1.88
Arlington, VA (cdp) Arlington County	299	0.15
Columbia, MD (cdp) Howard County	297	0.30
Ridgefield Park, NJ (village) Bergen County	294	2.32
Elizabeth, NJ (city) Union County	290	0.24
Troy, MI (city) Oakland County	286	0.35
Boston, MA (city) Suffolk County	284	0.05
Old Bridge, NJ (cdp) Middlesex County	283	1.21
Sterling Heights, MI (city) Macomb County	283	0.22
Belleville, NJ (township) Essex County	280	0.78
Aliso Viejo, CA (city) Orange County	279	0.60
Santa Monica, CA (city) Los Angeles County	278	0.31
Palmdale, CA (city) Los Angeles County	277	0.19
Blackstone, MA (town) Worcester County	276	3.07
Arcadia, CA (city) Los Angeles County	275	0.49
Hanahan, SC (city) Berkeley County	274	1.62
Cary, NC (town) Wake County	271	0.21
Moreno Valley, CA (city) Riverside County	271	0.14
Long Beach, CA (city) Los Angeles County	263	0.06
Justice, IL (village) Cook County	262	2.07
Lakewood, NJ (cdp) Ocean County	259	0.52
Hackensack, NJ (city) Bergen County	256	0.60
Dallas, TX (city) Dallas County	256	0.02
Wallington, NJ (borough) Bergen County	255	2.25
Clarkstown, NY (town) Rockland County	254	0.30
Portland, OR (city) Multnomah County	253	0.04
Stockton, CA (city) San Joaquin County	251	0.09
Roxbury, NJ (township) Morris County	250	1.07
Bardmoor, FL (cdp) Pinellas County	249	2.41
Coralville, IA (city) Johnson County	248	1.36
Monroe, NJ (township) Middlesex County	248	0.67
Quincy, MA (city) Norfolk County	248	0.27
Foster City, CA (city) San Mateo County	245	0.82
Burbank, CA (city) Los Angeles County	244	0.24
Arlington, TX (city) Tarrant County	244	0.07
Tempe, AZ (city) Maricopa County	243	0.15
Yonkers, NY (city) Westchester County	243	0.12
Franklin, NJ (township) Somerset County	242	0.40
Hamilton, NJ (township) Mercer County	242	0.27
Scotch Plains, NJ (township) Union County	241	1.04
Aurora, CO (city) Arapahoe County	238	0.08
Tampa, FL (city) Hillsborough County	236	0.07
San Ramon, CA (city) Contra Costa County	232	0.35
Bethlehem, PA (township) Northampton County	230	0.98
Tustin, CA (city) Orange County	230	0.31
Frisco, TX (city) Collin County	230	0.22
Cupertino, CA (city) Santa Clara County	227	0.40
Bridgeview, IL (village) Cook County	224	1.39
Simpsonville, SC (city) Greenville County	224	1.28
Perry Hall, MD (cdp) Baltimore County	224	0.79
Lower Paxton, PA (township) Dauphin County	224	0.48
Oyster Bay, NY (town) Nassau County	222	0.08
Santa Ana, CA (city) Orange County	222	0.07
Cloverdale, CA (city) Sonoma County	221	2.69
Oakdale, NY (cdp) Suffolk County	220	2.87
Cliffside Park, NJ (borough) Bergen County	220	0.94
Danville, CA (town) Contra Costa County	218	0.52
Tucson, AZ (city) Pima County	218	0.04
Eden Prairie, MN (city) Hennepin County	214	0.36
Newburgh, NY (town) Orange County	213	0.72
Rochester Hills, MI (city) Oakland County	213	0.30
Martin, TN (city) Weakley County	211	1.90
Avenel, NJ (cdp) Middlesex County	211	1.23
Laguna Niguel, CA (city) Orange County	211	0.34
Overland Park, KS (city) Johnson County	210	0.12
Gilbert, AZ (town) Maricopa County	210	0.11
Hickory Hills, IL (city) Cook County	209	1.49
Bridgewater, NJ (township) Somerset County	208	0.47
Rialto, CA (city) San Bernardino County	208	0.21
Upper Darby, PA (township) Delaware County	207	0.25
San Dimas, CA (city) Los Angeles County	206	0.61
Piscataway, NJ (township) Middlesex County	206	0.37
Antioch, CA (city) Contra Costa County	206	0.21
Costa Mesa, CA (city) Orange County	206	0.19

SECTION THREE

Please refer to the Explanation of Data in the front of the book for more detailed information.

Ancestry

Arab: Egyptian

Top 150 Places Sorted by Percent of Total Population

Based on all places, regardless of total population

Place	Population	%
Utica, PA (borough) Venango County	18	11.32
Fallon Station, NV (cdp) Churchill County	66	8.55
Ponce de Leon, FL (town) Holmes County	28	6.06
Paxtang, PA (borough) Dauphin County	81	5.40
Downsville, LA (village) Union Parish	8	5.16
Konterra, MD (cdp) Prince George's County	104	4.80
Ten Mile Run, NJ (cdp) Somerset County	86	4.80
Herndon, KS (city) Rawlins County	9	4.59
Highland, PA (township) Clarion County	29	4.58
Kerby, OR (cdp) Josephine County	20	4.26
Bayonne, NJ (city) Hudson County	2,608	4.20
South Toledo Bend, TX (cdp) Newton County	33	4.17
Philomath, OR (city) Benton County	187	4.14
Callicoon, NY (town) Sullivan County	125	4.05
East Brunswick, NJ (township) Middlesex County	1,893	3.99
Yogaville, VA (cdp) Buckingham County	10	3.97
Wrightsville, PA (borough) York County	89	3.87
Wormleysburg, PA (borough) Cumberland County	112	3.75
Versailles, IN (town) Ripley County	62	3.52
Noank, CT (cdp) New London County	62	3.44
Hatfield, PA (borough) Montgomery County	106	3.34
Kingston, NJ (cdp) Middlesex County	66	3.33
Leetsdale, PA (borough) Allegheny County	38	3.25
Seymour, WI (city) Outagamie County	110	3.19
Sterling City, TX (city) Sterling County	27	3.15
Blackstone, MA (town) Worcester County	276	3.07
Tullytown, PA (borough) Bucks County	56	2.99
Oakdale, NY (cdp) Suffolk County	220	2.87
Shiremanstown, PA (borough) Cumberland County	43	2.86
Campbellsburg, IN (town) Washington County	18	2.86
Glen Echo, MD (town) Montgomery County	7	2.81
Star City, WV (town) Monongalia County	49	2.78
Belleair Beach, FL (city) Pinellas County	39	2.73
Heathcote, NJ (cdp) Middlesex County	154	2.70
Cloverdale, CA (city) Sonoma County	221	2.69
Orange Lake, NY (cdp) Orange County	183	2.68
Singac, NJ (cdp) Passaic County	108	2.68
Robbinsville, NJ (cdp) Mercer County	59	2.63
Deerfield, NY (town) Oneida County	110	2.62
South Fulton, TN (city) Obion County	48	2.54
Northwest Ithaca, NY (cdp) Tompkins County	28	2.43
Bardmoor, FL (cdp) Pinellas County	249	2.41
Woodmere, NY (cdp) Nassau County	418	2.39
Gordon Heights, NY (cdp) Suffolk County	76	2.33
Ridgefield Park, NJ (village) Bergen County	294	2.32
Wallington, NJ (borough) Bergen County	255	2.25
Woodridge, NY (village) Sullivan County	20	2.23
Watchung, NJ (borough) Somerset County	125	2.20
Hampden, PA (township) Cumberland County	600	2.19
Carlisle, NY (town) Schoharie County	40	2.15
Woodside, CA (town) San Mateo County	112	2.14
Elsinboro, NJ (township) Salem County	25	2.12
Justice, IL (village) Cook County	262	2.07
Strasburg, IL (village) Shelby County	16	2.06
Monroe, PA (township) Snyder County	79	2.04
Lake Barcroft, VA (cdp) Fairfax County	183	2.02
Acres Green, CO (cdp) Douglas County	63	2.02
Lansdale, PA (borough) Montgomery County	324	2.00
Osage Beach, MO (city) Camden County	87	2.00
South River, NJ (borough) Middlesex County	315	1.99
Santa Rosa Valley, CA (cdp) Ventura County	62	1.92
Herricks, NY (cdp) Nassau County	75	1.91
Martin, TN (city) Weakley County	211	1.90
Linwood, NJ (city) Atlantic County	136	1.90
Laurel, VA (cdp) Henrico County	303	1.88
Old Bridge, NJ (township) Middlesex County	1,204	1.87
Citrus, CA (cdp) Los Angeles County	189	1.87
Jersey City, NJ (city) Hudson County	4,507	1.85
Sparkill, NY (cdp) Rockland County	25	1.81
Matawan, NJ (borough) Monmouth County	157	1.79
Montague, NJ (township) Sussex County	68	1.79
Dibble, OK (town) McClain County	32	1.78
Rocky Mount, VA (town) Franklin County	85	1.77
Alpha, NJ (borough) Warren County	44	1.77
Dayton, NJ (cdp) Middlesex County	131	1.76

Place	Population	%
Alexandria, PA (borough) Huntingdon County	7	1.76
Muttontown, NY (village) Nassau County	60	1.74
Tierra Verde, FL (cdp) Pinellas County	62	1.72
Oneida Castle, NY (village) Oneida County	9	1.72
Orange, OH (village) Cuyahoga County	56	1.70
North Great River, NY (cdp) Suffolk County	62	1.63
Hanahan, SC (city) Berkeley County	274	1.62
Spotswood, NJ (borough) Middlesex County	132	1.61
Sand Lake, MN (township) Itasca County	2	1.60
Manhasset Hills, NY (cdp) Nassau County	58	1.57
Trexlertown, PA (cdp) Lehigh County	29	1.56
Graysville, TN (town) Rhea County	17	1.55
Deal, NJ (borough) Monmouth County	16	1.55
Somerset, MD (town) Montgomery County	21	1.54
Green Knoll, NJ (cdp) Somerset County	85	1.53
Skippack, PA (cdp) Montgomery County	53	1.52
Del Aire, CA (cdp) Los Angeles County	145	1.51
Bancroft, MN (township) Freeborn County	18	1.51
Hickory Hills, IL (city) Cook County	209	1.49
Viera East, FL (cdp) Brevard County	177	1.49
Midway City, CA (cdp) Orange County	116	1.49
Upton, MA (cdp) Worcester County	42	1.49
Robbinsville, NJ (township) Mercer County	193	1.48
Madison Park, NJ (cdp) Middlesex County	101	1.48
Tiburon, CA (town) Marin County	130	1.47
Crump, TN (city) Hardin County	25	1.47
Manalapan, FL (town) Palm Beach County	4	1.47
Brooklyn Park, MD (cdp) Anne Arundel County	205	1.45
Blackwells Mills, NJ (cdp) Somerset County	10	1.43
Innsbrook, VA (cdp) Henrico County	104	1.42
Andover, NJ (borough) Sussex County	12	1.42
Lakeport, CA (city) Lake County	68	1.40
Bridgeview, IL (village) Cook County	224	1.39
Cottonwood, ID (city) Idaho County	18	1.39
West Menlo Park, CA (cdp) San Mateo County	47	1.38
Coralville, IA (city) Johnson County	248	1.36
Hunters Creek Village, TX (city) Harris County	59	1.36
Port Barre, LA (town) St. Landry Parish	29	1.36
South Abington, PA (township) Lackawanna County	121	1.35
Westbury, NY (village) Nassau County	199	1.33
South Hackensack, NJ (township) Bergen County	30	1.33
Industry, PA (borough) Beaver County	24	1.33
Robertsville, NJ (cdp) Monmouth County	145	1.31
Emmitsburg, MD (town) Frederick County	36	1.31
Laurence Harbor, NJ (cdp) Middlesex County	77	1.29
Simpsonville, SC (city) Greenville County	224	1.28
Cementon, PA (cdp) Lehigh County	21	1.28
Warrenton, NC (town) Warren County	14	1.28
Fair Lakes, VA (cdp) Fairfax County	101	1.27
Lynnwood, WA (city) Snohomish County	438	1.23
Avenel, NJ (cdp) Middlesex County	211	1.23
Rahway, NJ (city) Union County	328	1.22
Hanover, NJ (township) Morris County	166	1.22
Old Bridge, NJ (cdp) Middlesex County	283	1.21
Westfield, VT (town) Orleans County	6	1.21
South Amherst, MA (cdp) Hampshire County	59	1.20
Frederica, DE (town) Kent County	9	1.20
Halifax, VT (town) Windham County	10	1.19
Falcon Heights, MN (city) Ramsey County	62	1.18
Pine Castle, FL (cdp) Orange County	128	1.17
Sands Point, NY (village) Nassau County	31	1.17
Eatontown, NJ (borough) Monmouth County	150	1.16
West Long Branch, NJ (borough) Monmouth County	94	1.16
New Milford, CT (cdp) Litchfield County	74	1.15
North Plymouth, MA (cdp) Plymouth County	43	1.14
Lowville, NY (village) Lewis County	45	1.13
Crosspointe, VA (cdp) Fairfax County	63	1.12
South Brunswick, NJ (township) Middlesex County	472	1.11
Upper Deerfield, NJ (township) Cumberland County	85	1.11
Carlstadt, NJ (borough) Bergen County	67	1.11
Cresskill, NJ (borough) Bergen County	91	1.09
Crompond, NY (cdp) Westchester County	22	1.08
Hopkinton, NY (town) St. Lawrence County	11	1.08
Roxbury, NJ (township) Morris County	250	1.07
Swedesboro, NJ (borough) Gloucester County	27	1.07

Please refer to the Explanation of Data in the front of the book for more detailed information.

Ancestry

Arab: Egyptian

Top 150 Places Sorted by Percent of Total Population

Based on places with total population of 7,500 or more

Place	Population	%
Bayonne, NJ (city) Hudson County	2,608	4.20
East Brunswick, NJ (township) Middlesex County	1,893	3.99
Blackstone, MA (town) Worcester County	276	3.07
Oakdale, NY (cdp) Suffolk County	220	2.87
Cloverdale, CA (city) Sonoma County	221	2.69
Bardmoor, FL (cdp) Pinellas County	249	2.41
Woodmere, NY (cdp) Nassau County	418	2.39
Ridgefield Park, NJ (village) Bergen County	294	2.32
Wallington, NJ (borough) Bergen County	255	2.25
Hampden, PA (township) Cumberland County	600	2.19
Justice, IL (village) Cook County	262	2.07
Lake Barcroft, VA (cdp) Fairfax County	183	2.02
Lansdale, PA (borough) Montgomery County	324	2.00
South River, NJ (borough) Middlesex County	315	1.99
Martin, TN (city) Weakley County	211	1.90
Laurel, VA (cdp) Henrico County	303	1.88
Old Bridge, NJ (township) Middlesex County	1,204	1.87
Citrus, CA (cdp) Los Angeles County	189	1.87
Jersey City, NJ (city) Hudson County	4,507	1.85
Matawan, NJ (borough) Monmouth County	157	1.79
Hanahan, SC (city) Berkeley County	274	1.62
Spotswood, NJ (borough) Middlesex County	132	1.61
Del Aire, CA (cdp) Los Angeles County	145	1.51
Hickory Hills, IL (city) Cook County	209	1.49
Viera East, FL (cdp) Brevard County	177	1.49
Midway City, CA (cdp) Orange County	116	1.49
Robbinsville, NJ (township) Mercer County	193	1.48
Tiburon, CA (town) Marin County	130	1.47
Brooklyn Park, MD (cdp) Anne Arundel County	205	1.45
Bridgeview, IL (village) Cook County	224	1.39
Coralville, IA (city) Johnson County	248	1.36
South Abington, PA (township) Lackawanna County	121	1.35
Westbury, NY (village) Nassau County	199	1.33
Robertsville, NJ (cdp) Monmouth County	145	1.31
Simpsonville, SC (city) Greenville County	224	1.28
Fair Lakes, VA (cdp) Fairfax County	101	1.27
Lynnwood, WA (city) Snohomish County	438	1.23
Avenel, NJ (cdp) Middlesex County	211	1.23
Rahway, NJ (city) Union County	328	1.22
Hanover, NJ (township) Morris County	166	1.22
Old Bridge, NJ (cdp) Middlesex County	283	1.21
Pine Castle, FL (cdp) Orange County	128	1.17
Eatontown, NJ (borough) Monmouth County	150	1.16
West Long Branch, NJ (borough) Monmouth County	94	1.16
South Brunswick, NJ (township) Middlesex County	472	1.11
Upper Deerfield, NJ (township) Cumberland County	85	1.11
Cresskill, NJ (borough) Bergen County	91	1.09
Roxbury, NJ (township) Morris County	250	1.07
Bull Run, VA (cdp) Prince William County	136	1.06
Scotch Plains, NJ (township) Union County	241	1.04
El Sobrante, CA (cdp) Riverside County	114	1.02
Colonial Park, PA (cdp) Dauphin County	131	1.00
Wakefield-Peacedale, RI (cdp) Washington County	90	1.00
Ridgefield, NJ (borough) Bergen County	108	0.99
Philipstown, NY (town) Putnam County	96	0.99
Bethlehem, PA (township) Northampton County	230	0.98
Picnic Point, WA (cdp) Snohomish County	83	0.98
Hershey, PA (cdp) Dauphin County	125	0.96
Burr Ridge, IL (village) DuPage County	100	0.95
Cliffside Park, NJ (borough) Bergen County	220	0.94
Hamilton, PA (township) Monroe County	86	0.94
West St. Paul, MN (city) Dakota County	182	0.93
Pacific Grove, CA (city) Monterey County	138	0.93
Columbia, PA (borough) Lancaster County	97	0.93
South Huntington, NY (cdp) Suffolk County	91	0.92
Center Line, MI (city) Macomb County	76	0.91
Lake Wylie, SC (cdp) York County	75	0.90
Canyon Lake, CA (city) Riverside County	95	0.89
Skidaway Island, GA (cdp) Chatham County	72	0.89
Wood-Ridge, NJ (borough) Bergen County	66	0.87
North Brunswick, NJ (township) Middlesex County	338	0.85
Sutton, MA (town) Worcester County	75	0.85
Seven Corners, VA (cdp) Fairfax County	71	0.85
Knightdale, NC (town) Wake County	88	0.84
Foster City, CA (city) San Mateo County	245	0.82
Brookdale, NJ (cdp) Essex County	75	0.82
Carteret, NJ (borough) Middlesex County	179	0.80
Montgomeryville, PA (cdp) Montgomery County	105	0.80
Carver, MA (town) Plymouth County	92	0.80
Sayreville, NJ (borough) Middlesex County	333	0.79
Perry Hall, MD (cdp) Baltimore County	224	0.79
Belleville, NJ (township) Essex County	280	0.78
Little Falls, NJ (township) Passaic County	108	0.78
Woodbury, NY (village) Orange County	82	0.78
Leonia, NJ (borough) Bergen County	69	0.78
Hopkinton, MA (town) Middlesex County	111	0.77
Columbia Heights, MN (city) Anoka County	149	0.76
Ladera Ranch, CA (cdp) Orange County	139	0.76
Franklin Lakes, NJ (borough) Bergen County	80	0.76
Millstone, NJ (township) Monmouth County	78	0.76
Great Falls, VA (cdp) Fairfax County	120	0.75
Cedar Grove, NJ (township) Essex County	92	0.75
Upper Macungie, PA (township) Lehigh County	141	0.74
Highland Village, TX (city) Denton County	109	0.74
Woodbury, NY (town) Orange County	82	0.74
Corona, CA (city) Riverside County	1,103	0.73
Newburgh, NY (town) Orange County	213	0.72
Readington, NJ (township) Hunterdon County	117	0.72
Glen Carbon, IL (village) Madison County	88	0.72
Spring Valley Lake, CA (cdp) San Bernardino County	55	0.72
Staten Island, NY (borough) Richmond County	3,292	0.71
Reston, VA (cdp) Fairfax County	374	0.70
Nanuet, NY (cdp) Rockland County	124	0.70
East Whiteland, PA (township) Chester County	72	0.69
Baldwin, NY (cdp) Nassau County	162	0.68
Paramount, CA (city) Los Angeles County	364	0.67
Monroe, NJ (township) Middlesex County	248	0.67
Indian Harbour Beach, FL (city) Brevard County	56	0.67
Sterling, MA (town) Worcester County	52	0.67
Walnut, CA (city) Los Angeles County	194	0.66
North Arlington, NJ (borough) Bergen County	101	0.66
East Rockaway, NY (village) Nassau County	65	0.66
Bellflower, CA (city) Los Angeles County	494	0.65
Wayne, NJ (township) Passaic County	351	0.65
Los Altos, CA (city) Santa Clara County	186	0.65
Westmont, IL (village) DuPage County	160	0.65
Charlestown, RI (town) Washington County	51	0.65
Coconut Creek, FL (city) Broward County	332	0.64
Colleyville, TX (city) Tarrant County	143	0.64
Mukilteo, WA (city) Snohomish County	128	0.64
Manchester, VA (cdp) Chesterfield County	71	0.64
Revere, MA (city) Suffolk County	316	0.63
Eastvale, CA (cdp) Riverside County	308	0.63
East Pennsboro, PA (township) Cumberland County	122	0.62
Fort Drum, NY (cdp) Jefferson County	76	0.62
Worcester, PA (township) Montgomery County	58	0.62
Clifton, NJ (city) Passaic County	502	0.61
San Dimas, CA (city) Los Angeles County	206	0.61
Clinton, NJ (township) Hunterdon County	83	0.61
Webster, TX (city) Harris County	60	0.61
Harwood Heights, IL (village) Cook County	52	0.61
Aliso Viejo, CA (city) Orange County	279	0.60
Hackensack, NJ (city) Bergen County	256	0.60
Montgomery, PA (township) Montgomery County	145	0.60
Melville, NY (cdp) Suffolk County	114	0.60
Sylvania, OH (city) Lucas County	114	0.60
New Milford, NJ (borough) Bergen County	98	0.60
Woodstock, GA (city) Cherokee County	131	0.59
Fuquay-Varina, NC (town) Wake County	96	0.59
Echelon, NJ (cdp) Camden County	59	0.59
Great Neck, NY (village) Nassau County	58	0.59
Bergenfield, NJ (borough) Bergen County	155	0.58
Madison Heights, MI (city) Oakland County	172	0.57
Glassboro, NJ (borough) Gloucester County	108	0.57
Marlborough, NY (town) Ulster County	50	0.57
Bloomingdale, NJ (borough) Passaic County	43	0.57
Schererville, IN (town) Lake County	159	0.56
Castaic, CA (cdp) Los Angeles County	102	0.56
East Greenbush, NY (town) Rensselaer County	91	0.56
Huntington Beach, CA (city) Orange County	1,048	0.55

SECTION THREE

Please refer to the Explanation of Data in the front of the book for more detailed information.

Ancestry

Arab: Iraqi

U.S. and 50 States Sorted by Population and Percent of Total Population

Place	Population	%
United States	**73,896**	**0.02**
Michigan	19,942	0.20
California	15,029	0.04
Arizona	5,224	0.08
Illinois	4,332	0.03
Texas	3,770	0.02
New York	3,013	0.02
Tennessee	2,559	0.04
Virginia	1,958	0.02
Florida	1,718	0.01
Ohio	1,346	0.01
Massachusetts	1,255	0.02
Missouri	1,159	0.02
Nebraska	1,083	0.06
Georgia	963	0.01
Pennsylvania	955	0.01
Washington	920	0.01
Nevada	808	0.03
Colorado	730	0.01
Minnesota	620	0.01
Indiana	594	0.01
Louisiana	593	0.01
Maryland	553	0.01
New Jersey	471	0.01
Connecticut	437	0.01
Iowa	353	0.01
Utah	334	0.01
Oregon	320	0.01
Kentucky	315	0.01
Alabama	278	0.01
Kansas	262	0.01
North Carolina	241	<0.01
Arkansas	205	0.01
New Mexico	202	0.01
Vermont	194	0.03
Wisconsin	185	<0.01
North Dakota	132	0.02
Oklahoma	129	<0.01
District of Columbia	114	0.02
West Virginia	99	0.01
Rhode Island	88	0.01
South Dakota	81	0.01
Mississippi	74	<0.01
South Carolina	64	<0.01
New Hampshire	42	<0.01
Idaho	39	<0.01
Maine	35	<0.01
Alaska	34	<0.01
Montana	27	<0.01
Hawaii	16	<0.01
Delaware	1	<0.01
Wyoming	0	0.00

Place	Population	%
Michigan	19,942	0.20
Arizona	5,224	0.08
Nebraska	1,083	0.06
California	15,029	0.04
Tennessee	2,559	0.04
Illinois	4,332	0.03
Nevada	808	0.03
Vermont	194	0.03
United States	**73,896**	**0.02**
Texas	3,770	0.02
New York	3,013	0.02
Virginia	1,958	0.02
Massachusetts	1,255	0.02
Missouri	1,159	0.02
North Dakota	132	0.02
District of Columbia	114	0.02
Florida	1,718	0.01
Ohio	1,346	0.01
Georgia	963	0.01
Pennsylvania	955	0.01
Washington	920	0.01
Colorado	730	0.01
Minnesota	620	0.01
Indiana	594	0.01
Louisiana	593	0.01
Maryland	553	0.01
New Jersey	471	0.01
Connecticut	437	0.01
Iowa	353	0.01
Utah	334	0.01
Oregon	320	0.01
Kentucky	315	0.01
Alabama	278	0.01
Kansas	262	0.01
Arkansas	205	0.01
New Mexico	202	0.01
West Virginia	99	0.01
Rhode Island	88	0.01
South Dakota	81	0.01
North Carolina	241	<0.01
Wisconsin	185	<0.01
Oklahoma	129	<0.01
Mississippi	74	<0.01
South Carolina	64	<0.01
New Hampshire	42	<0.01
Idaho	39	<0.01
Maine	35	<0.01
Alaska	34	<0.01
Montana	27	<0.01
Hawaii	16	<0.01
Delaware	1	<0.01
Wyoming	0	0.00

Please refer to the Explanation of Data in the front of the book for more detailed information.

Ancestry

Arab: Iraqi

Top 150 Places Sorted by Population

Based on all places, regardless of total population

Place	Population	%
Sterling Heights, MI (city) Macomb County	4,199	3.24
El Cajon, CA (city) San Diego County	3,081	3.15
Dearborn, MI (city) Wayne County	2,820	2.87
Phoenix, AZ (city) Maricopa County	2,033	0.14
West Bloomfield, MI (charter township) Oakland County	1,775	2.74
Nashville-Davidson, TN (metro govt) Davidson County	1,707	0.29
Chicago, IL (city) Cook County	1,592	0.06
Los Angeles, CA (city) Los Angeles County	1,444	0.04
San Diego, CA (city) San Diego County	1,390	0.11
Southfield, MI (city) Oakland County	1,164	1.60
New York, NY (city) Kings County	1,137	0.01
Detroit, MI (city) Wayne County	1,125	0.15
Lincoln, NE (city) Lancaster County	992	0.39
Warren, MI (city) Macomb County	932	0.69
Skokie, IL (village) Cook County	898	1.41
Farmington Hills, MI (city) Oakland County	777	0.97
St. Louis, MO (city) St. Louis city County	723	0.23
Troy, MI (city) Oakland County	722	0.89
Glendale, CA (city) Los Angeles County	715	0.37
Glendale, AZ (city) Maricopa County	703	0.31
Tucson, AZ (city) Pima County	687	0.13
Arlington, TX (city) Tarrant County	652	0.18
Shelby, MI (charter township) Macomb County	639	0.88
Manhattan, NY (borough) New York County	583	0.04
Dearborn Heights, MI (city) Wayne County	578	1.00
Modesto, CA (city) Stanislaus County	547	0.27
Houston, TX (city) Harris County	532	0.03
North Hempstead, NY (town) Nassau County	500	0.22
Spring Valley, CA (cdp) San Diego County	475	1.74
Rancho San Diego, CA (cdp) San Diego County	459	2.27
Madison Heights, MI (city) Oakland County	424	1.42
Chandler, AZ (city) Maricopa County	403	0.18
Irving, TX (city) Dallas County	401	0.19
Commerce, MI (charter township) Oakland County	399	1.02
Niles, IL (village) Cook County	391	1.33
Fort Mohave, AZ (cdp) Mohave County	363	2.52
Jacksonville, FL (city) Duval County	363	0.04
Peoria, AZ (city) Yavapai County	339	0.23
Columbus, OH (city) Franklin County	334	0.04
Rochester Hills, MI (city) Oakland County	331	0.47
Bostonia, CA (cdp) San Diego County	322	2.22
Queens, NY (borough) Queens County	315	0.01
Worcester, MA (city) Worcester County	312	0.17
Kenner, LA (city) Jefferson Parish	309	0.46
Buffalo, NY (city) Erie County	288	0.11
Hempstead, NY (town) Nassau County	284	0.04
Hazel Park, MI (city) Oakland County	277	1.64
Norfolk, VA (ind. city) Norfolk independent city	270	0.11
Centerville, OH (city) Montgomery County	264	1.11
Arlington, VA (cdp) Arlington County	258	0.13
Riverside, CA (city) Riverside County	258	0.09
Bloomfield, MI (charter township) Oakland County	256	0.62
Louisville-Jefferson County, KY (metro govt) Jefferson County	254	0.04
Dallas, TX (city) Dallas County	250	0.02
Lansing, MI (city) Ingham County	246	0.22
Lansing, MI (city) Ingham County	246	0.21
Corona, CA (city) Riverside County	239	0.16
Short Pump, VA (cdp) Henrico County	232	0.97
Daly City, CA (city) San Mateo County	230	0.23
Goodlettsville, TN (city) Davidson County	221	1.43
Denver, CO (city) Denver County	218	0.04
Philadelphia, PA (city) Philadelphia County	218	0.01
Schaumburg, IL (village) Cook County	217	0.30
Des Moines, IA (city) Polk County	217	0.11
Salt Lake City, UT (city) Salt Lake County	211	0.11
Oak Park, MI (city) Oakland County	209	0.70
Mobile, AL (city) Mobile County	209	0.11
Novi, MI (city) Oakland County	208	0.39
Erie, PA (city) Erie County	208	0.20
Centreville, VA (cdp) Fairfax County	201	0.28
Winter Gardens, CA (cdp) San Diego County	200	0.99
Indianapolis, IN (city) Marion County	192	0.02
Albuquerque, NM (city) Bernalillo County	191	0.04
Paradise, NV (cdp) Clark County	184	0.08
Metairie, LA (cdp) Jefferson Parish	182	0.13
Norton Shores, MI (city) Muskegon County	181	0.76
Royal Oak, MI (city) Oakland County	181	0.31
Calabasas, CA (city) Los Angeles County	179	0.79
Bridgeport, CT (city/town) Fairfield County	178	0.12
Lower Moreland, PA (township) Montgomery County	177	1.40
San Jose, CA (city) Santa Clara County	177	0.02
Moorhead, MN (city) Clay County	175	0.48
Santa Clara, CA (city) Santa Clara County	174	0.15
Henderson, NV (city) Clark County	169	0.07
Winooski, VT (city) Chittenden County	168	2.36
Dix Hills, NY (cdp) Suffolk County	166	0.63
Huntington, NY (town) Suffolk County	166	0.08
Kansas City, MO (city) Jackson County	164	0.04
Fair Oaks, VA (cdp) Fairfax County	163	0.59
San Antonio, TX (city) Medina County	162	0.01
Haverhill, MA (city) Essex County	156	0.26
Memphis, TN (city) Shelby County	156	0.02
Spring Valley Lake, CA (cdp) San Bernardino County	154	2.02
Parma, OH (city) Cuyahoga County	153	0.19
Surprise, AZ (city) Maricopa County	150	0.14
Austin, TX (city) Travis County	150	0.02
Santee, CA (city) San Diego County	148	0.28
Las Vegas, NV (city) Clark County	147	0.03
Beverly Hills, CA (city) Los Angeles County	146	0.43
Junction City, KS (city) Geary County	145	0.70
Beaverton, OR (city) Washington County	145	0.16
Roseville, CA (city) Placer County	141	0.12
Oceanside, CA (city) San Diego County	141	0.09
La Presa, CA (cdp) San Diego County	138	0.40
Waterford, MI (charter township) Oakland County	135	0.19
Milwaukee, WI (city) Milwaukee County	135	0.02
Pacifica, CA (city) San Mateo County	134	0.36
Brooklyn, NY (borough) Kings County	134	0.01
Highland Park, IL (city) Lake County	132	0.44
Mesa, AZ (city) Maricopa County	130	0.03
Young, AZ (town) Maricopa County	126	2.22
Canton, MI (charter township) Wayne County	126	0.14
Winter Park, FL (city) Orange County	125	0.44
Lynnwood, WA (city) Snohomish County	125	0.35
Rockford, IL (city) Winnebago County	125	0.08
Macomb, MI (township) Macomb County	124	0.17
Thornton, CO (city) Adams County	123	0.11
Dayton, OH (city) Montgomery County	123	0.08
Northville, MI (township) Wayne County	122	0.45
Little Rock, AR (city) Pulaski County	122	0.06
Lynn Haven, FL (city) Bay County	121	0.68
Alexandria, VA (ind. city) Alexandria independent city	119	0.09
Boston, MA (city) Suffolk County	119	0.02
Mesquite, TX (city) Dallas County	116	0.09
San Bernardino, CA (city) San Bernardino County	114	0.05
Plano, TX (city) Collin County	114	0.04
Colorado Springs, CO (city) El Paso County	114	0.03
Washington, DC (city) District of Columbia	114	0.02
Temple Terrace, FL (city) Hillsborough County	113	0.47
West Hempstead, NY (cdp) Nassau County	112	0.61
Ludlow, MA (town) Hampden County	112	0.53
Washington, MI (township) Macomb County	111	0.46
Fremont, CA (city) Alameda County	110	0.05
Orchard Lake Village, MI (city) Oakland County	107	5.03
Seabrook, MD (cdp) Prince George's County	107	0.69
Simi Valley, CA (city) Ventura County	107	0.09
Pittsburgh, PA (city) Allegheny County	104	0.03
Yonkers, NY (city) Westchester County	103	0.05
Lakeside, CA (cdp) San Diego County	100	0.49
Hercules, CA (city) Contra Costa County	100	0.43
Redwood City, CA (city) San Mateo County	100	0.13
Cypress, CA (city) Orange County	99	0.21
Weston, FL (city) Broward County	99	0.16
Watauga, TX (city) Tarrant County	98	0.42
Walled Lake, MI (city) Oakland County	95	1.37
Clinton, MI (charter township) Macomb County	95	0.10
Hewlett, NY (cdp) Nassau County	94	1.40
Summerlin South, NV (cdp) Clark County	94	0.43
West Chicago, IL (city) DuPage County	91	0.35
Fargo, ND (city) Cass County	91	0.09

Ancestry

Arab: Iraqi

Top 150 Places Sorted by Percent of Total Population

Based on all places, regardless of total population

Place	Population	%
Hat Creek, CA (cdp) Shasta County	31	14.35
Jefferson City, MT (cdp) Jefferson County	27	7.24
Orchard Lake Village, MI (city) Oakland County	107	5.03
Saddle Rock, NY (village) Nassau County	46	4.39
Mount Crawford, VA (town) Rockingham County	14	3.97
Sterling Heights, MI (city) Macomb County	4,199	3.24
El Cajon, CA (city) San Diego County	3,081	3.15
Dearborn, MI (city) Wayne County	2,820	2.87
Cumberland City, TN (town) Stewart County	10	2.86
West Bloomfield, MI (charter township) Oakland County	1,775	2.74
Lennon, MI (village) Shiawassee County	17	2.63
Fort Mohave, AZ (cdp) Mohave County	363	2.52
Winooski, VT (city) Chittenden County	168	2.36
Kensington, NY (village) Nassau County	28	2.32
Pelican Rapids, MN (city) Otter Tail County	62	2.31
Rancho San Diego, CA (cdp) San Diego County	459	2.27
Bostonia, CA (cdp) San Diego County	322	2.22
Young, AZ (town) Maricopa County	126	2.22
Herricks, NY (cdp) Nassau County	86	2.18
Spring Valley Lake, CA (cdp) San Bernardino County	154	2.02
Dunsmuir, CA (city) Siskiyou County	36	2.02
Versailles, IN (town) Ripley County	35	1.99
Water Mill, NY (cdp) Suffolk County	28	1.83
East Lansing, MI (city) Clinton County	27	1.81
Great Neck Gardens, NY (cdp) Nassau County	16	1.76
Spring Valley, CA (cdp) San Diego County	475	1.74
Sharon, KS (city) Barber County	4	1.74
Indian Lake, TX (town) Cameron County	16	1.65
Hazel Park, MI (city) Oakland County	277	1.64
Manlius, MI (township) Allegan County	49	1.64
Southfield, MI (city) Oakland County	1,164	1.60
Robbinsville, NJ (cdp) Mercer County	34	1.52
East Pasadena, CA (cdp) Los Angeles County	86	1.50
Jamul, CA (cdp) San Diego County	78	1.47
Goodlettsville, TN (city) Davidson County	221	1.43
Madison Heights, MI (city) Oakland County	424	1.42
Skokie, IL (village) Cook County	898	1.41
Lower Moreland, PA (township) Montgomery County	177	1.40
Hewlett, NY (cdp) Nassau County	94	1.40
Walled Lake, MI (city) Oakland County	95	1.37
Niles, IL (village) Cook County	391	1.33
Birch Run, MI (village) Saginaw County	22	1.29
Granite Hills, CA (cdp) San Diego County	43	1.26
Sands Point, NY (village) Nassau County	33	1.24
Middleburgh, NY (town) Schoharie County	46	1.23
Elmer, MI (township) Oscoda County	15	1.16
Atlantic Beach, NY (village) Nassau County	21	1.13
Centerville, OH (city) Montgomery County	264	1.11
East Hills, NY (village) Nassau County	71	1.04
Lake Success, NY (village) Nassau County	30	1.04
Commerce, MI (charter township) Oakland County	399	1.02
Bagdad, AZ (cdp) Yavapai County	20	1.02
Searingtown, NY (cdp) Nassau County	46	1.01
Dearborn Heights, MI (city) Wayne County	578	1.00
Winter Gardens, CA (cdp) San Diego County	200	0.99
Washington, PA (township) Schuylkill County	29	0.98
Farmington Hills, MI (city) Oakland County	777	0.97
Short Pump, VA (cdp) Henrico County	232	0.97
Hewlett Bay Park, NY (village) Nassau County	5	0.96
Lincoln Beach, OR (cdp) Lincoln County	22	0.93
Troy, MI (city) Oakland County	722	0.89
Shelby, MI (charter township) Macomb County	639	0.88
Audubon, NJ (borough) Camden County	76	0.85
Lathrup Village, MI (city) Oakland County	35	0.85
Deepwater, MO (city) Henry County	4	0.83
Oakwood, GA (city) Hall County	32	0.81
Calabasas, CA (city) Los Angeles County	179	0.79
Norton Shores, MI (city) Muskegon County	181	0.76
Cohoctah, MI (township) Livingston County	26	0.76
Carle Place, NY (cdp) Nassau County	40	0.72
Stevensville, MI (village) Berrien County	8	0.72
Oak Park, MI (city) Oakland County	209	0.70
Junction City, KS (city) Geary County	145	0.70
Warren, MI (city) Macomb County	932	0.69
Seabrook, MD (cdp) Prince George's County	107	0.69
Mountain Park, GA (cdp) Gwinnett County	82	0.69
Iowa Falls, IA (city) Hardin County	36	0.69
Lynn Haven, FL (city) Bay County	121	0.68
Hedwig Village, TX (city) Harris County	17	0.68
Weston, MA (town) Middlesex County	75	0.67
Fairview, TN (city) Williamson County	50	0.67
White Center, WA (cdp) King County	83	0.66
Venice, MI (township) Shiawassee County	17	0.65
Oak Ridge, MO (town) Cape Girardeau County	2	0.65
Great Neck Plaza, NY (village) Nassau County	42	0.64
Dix Hills, NY (cdp) Suffolk County	166	0.63
Bloomfield, MI (charter township) Oakland County	256	0.62
West Hempstead, NY (cdp) Nassau County	112	0.61
Cabin John, MD (cdp) Montgomery County	12	0.61
Fair Oaks, VA (cdp) Fairfax County	163	0.59
Biltmore Forest, NC (town) Buncombe County	9	0.58
Osceola, MI (township) Houghton County	10	0.55
Millbury, MA (town) Worcester County	71	0.54
Ludlow, MA (town) Hampden County	112	0.53
Melvindale, MI (city) Wayne County	55	0.51
Bay Mills, MI (township) Chippewa County	8	0.50
Lakeside, CA (cdp) San Diego County	100	0.49
Moorhead, MN (city) Clay County	175	0.48
Rose, MI (township) Oakland County	30	0.48
University Gardens, NY (cdp) Nassau County	19	0.48
Rochester Hills, MI (city) Oakland County	331	0.47
Temple Terrace, FL (city) Hillsborough County	113	0.47
Norwich, VT (town) Windsor County	16	0.47
Hampton Falls, NH (town) Rockingham County	11	0.47
Kenner, LA (city) Jefferson Parish	309	0.46
Washington, MI (township) Macomb County	111	0.46
Gerrish, MI (township) Roscommon County	14	0.46
Evart, MI (city) Osceola County	8	0.46
Northville, MI (township) Wayne County	122	0.45
Casa de Oro-Mount Helix, CA (cdp) San Diego County	86	0.45
Tysons Corner, VA (cdp) Fairfax County	77	0.45
Highland Park, IL (city) Lake County	132	0.44
Winter Park, FL (city) Orange County	125	0.44
Branson, MO (city) Taney County	43	0.44
Indian Harbour Beach, FL (city) Brevard County	37	0.44
Speaker, MI (township) Sanilac County	6	0.44
Beverly Hills, CA (city) Los Angeles County	146	0.43
Hercules, CA (city) Contra Costa County	100	0.43
Summerlin South, NV (cdp) Clark County	94	0.43
Elk Plain, WA (cdp) Pierce County	62	0.43
Watauga, TX (city) Tarrant County	98	0.42
Oakland, MI (charter township) Oakland County	68	0.42
Farmington, MI (city) Oakland County	44	0.42
Rutledge, PA (borough) Delaware County	4	0.42
La Presa, CA (cdp) San Diego County	138	0.40
Lake Mathews, CA (cdp) Riverside County	24	0.40
Rosslyn Farms, PA (borough) Allegheny County	2	0.40
Crossgate, KY (city) Jefferson County	1	0.40
Lincoln, NE (city) Lancaster County	992	0.39
Novi, MI (city) Oakland County	208	0.39
Orinda, CA (city) Contra Costa County	66	0.38
Chevy Chase, MD (cdp) Montgomery County	37	0.38
Woodburn, VA (cdp) Fairfax County	33	0.38
Beetown, WI (town) Grant County	3	0.38
Sugar Island, MI (township) Chippewa County	3	0.38
Glendale, CA (city) Los Angeles County	715	0.37
Pacifica, CA (city) San Mateo County	134	0.36
Princeton, NJ (borough) Mercer County	45	0.36
Birch Run, MI (township) Saginaw County	22	0.36
Bradley Beach, NJ (borough) Monmouth County	16	0.36
Lake Holiday, IL (cdp) LaSalle County	16	0.36
Lynnwood, WA (city) Snohomish County	125	0.35
West Chicago, IL (city) DuPage County	91	0.35
Suffern, NY (village) Rockland County	37	0.35
White Bear Lake, MN (city) Ramsey County	79	0.34
White Bear Lake, MN (city) Ramsey County	79	0.34
North Lynnwood, WA (cdp) Snohomish County	54	0.34
East Riverdale, MD (cdp) Prince George's County	53	0.34
Kingstowne, VA (cdp) Fairfax County	50	0.34
Keedysville, MD (town) Washington County	4	0.34

Please refer to the Explanation of Data in the front of the book for more detailed information.

Ancestry

Arab: Iraqi

Top 150 Places Sorted by Percent of Total Population

Based on places with total population of 7,500 or more

Place	Population	%
Sterling Heights, MI (city) Macomb County	4,199	3.24
El Cajon, CA (city) San Diego County	3,081	3.15
Dearborn, MI (city) Wayne County	2,820	2.87
West Bloomfield, MI (charter township) Oakland County	1,775	2.74
Fort Mohave, AZ (cdp) Mohave County	363	2.52
Rancho San Diego, CA (cdp) San Diego County	459	2.27
Bostonia, CA (cdp) San Diego County	322	2.22
Spring Valley Lake, CA (cdp) San Bernardino County	154	2.02
Spring Valley, CA (cdp) San Diego County	475	1.74
Hazel Park, MI (city) Oakland County	277	1.64
Southfield, MI (city) Oakland County	1,164	1.60
Goodlettsville, TN (city) Davidson County	221	1.43
Madison Heights, MI (city) Oakland County	424	1.42
Skokie, IL (village) Cook County	898	1.41
Lower Moreland, PA (township) Montgomery County	177	1.40
Niles, IL (village) Cook County	391	1.33
Centerville, OH (city) Montgomery County	264	1.11
Commerce, MI (charter township) Oakland County	399	1.02
Dearborn Heights, MI (city) Wayne County	578	1.00
Winter Gardens, CA (cdp) San Diego County	200	0.99
Farmington Hills, MI (city) Oakland County	777	0.97
Short Pump, VA (cdp) Henrico County	232	0.97
Troy, MI (city) Oakland County	722	0.89
Shelby, MI (charter township) Macomb County	639	0.88
Audubon, NJ (borough) Camden County	76	0.85
Calabasas, CA (city) Los Angeles County	179	0.79
Norton Shores, MI (city) Muskegon County	181	0.76
Oak Park, MI (city) Oakland County	209	0.70
Junction City, KS (city) Geary County	145	0.70
Warren, MI (city) Macomb County	932	0.69
Seabrook, MD (cdp) Prince George's County	107	0.69
Mountain Park, GA (cdp) Gwinnett County	82	0.69
Lynn Haven, FL (city) Bay County	121	0.68
Weston, MA (town) Middlesex County	75	0.67
Fairview, TN (city) Williamson County	50	0.67
White Center, WA (cdp) King County	83	0.66
Dix Hills, NY (cdp) Suffolk County	166	0.63
Bloomfield, MI (charter township) Oakland County	256	0.62
West Hempstead, NY (cdp) Nassau County	112	0.61
Fair Oaks, VA (cdp) Fairfax County	163	0.59
Millbury, MA (town) Worcester County	71	0.54
Ludlow, MA (town) Hampden County	112	0.53
Melvindale, MI (city) Wayne County	55	0.51
Lakeside, CA (cdp) San Diego County	100	0.49
Moorhead, MN (city) Clay County	175	0.48
Rochester Hills, MI (city) Oakland County	331	0.47
Temple Terrace, FL (city) Hillsborough County	113	0.47
Kenner, LA (city) Jefferson Parish	309	0.46
Washington, MI (township) Macomb County	111	0.46
Northville, MI (township) Wayne County	122	0.45
Casa de Oro-Mount Helix, CA (cdp) San Diego County	86	0.45
Tysons Corner, VA (cdp) Fairfax County	77	0.45
Highland Park, IL (city) Lake County	132	0.44
Winter Park, FL (city) Orange County	125	0.44
Branson, MO (city) Taney County	43	0.44
Indian Harbour Beach, FL (city) Brevard County	37	0.44
Beverly Hills, CA (city) Los Angeles County	146	0.43
Hercules, CA (city) Contra Costa County	100	0.43
Summerlin South, NV (cdp) Clark County	94	0.43
Elk Plain, WA (cdp) Pierce County	62	0.43
Watauga, TX (city) Tarrant County	98	0.42
Oakland, MI (charter township) Oakland County	68	0.42
Farmington, MI (city) Oakland County	44	0.42
La Presa, CA (cdp) San Diego County	138	0.40
Lincoln, NE (city) Lancaster County	992	0.39
Novi, MI (city) Oakland County	208	0.39
Orinda, CA (city) Contra Costa County	66	0.38
Chevy Chase, MD (cdp) Montgomery County	37	0.38
Woodburn, VA (cdp) Fairfax County	33	0.38
Glendale, CA (city) Los Angeles County	715	0.37
Pacifica, CA (city) San Mateo County	134	0.36
Princeton, NJ (borough) Mercer County	45	0.36
Lynnwood, WA (city) Snohomish County	125	0.35
West Chicago, IL (city) DuPage County	91	0.35
Suffern, NY (village) Rockland County	37	0.35

Place	Population	%
White Bear Lake, MN (city) Ramsey County	79	0.34
White Bear Lake, MN (city) Ramsey County	79	0.34
North Lynnwood, WA (cdp) Snohomish County	54	0.34
East Riverdale, MD (cdp) Prince George's County	53	0.34
Kingstowne, VA (cdp) Fairfax County	50	0.34
La Cañada Flintridge, CA (city) Los Angeles County	67	0.33
Marina, CA (city) Monterey County	65	0.33
Kings Park, NY (cdp) Suffolk County	56	0.33
Wixom, MI (city) Oakland County	45	0.33
New Baltimore, MI (city) Macomb County	37	0.33
Yankton, SD (city) Yankton County	46	0.32
Glendale, AZ (city) Maricopa County	703	0.31
Royal Oak, MI (city) Oakland County	181	0.31
Morton Grove, IL (village) Cook County	72	0.31
Fort Salonga, NY (cdp) Suffolk County	33	0.31
Schaumburg, IL (village) Cook County	217	0.30
Idylwood, VA (cdp) Fairfax County	47	0.30
Fort Irwin, CA (cdp) San Bernardino County	27	0.30
Nashville-Davidson, TN (metro govt) Davidson County	1,707	0.29
Centreville, VA (cdp) Fairfax County	201	0.28
Santee, CA (city) San Diego County	148	0.28
Bainbridge Island, WA (city) Kitsap County	62	0.28
Garfield, MI (charter township) Grand Traverse County	44	0.28
Bonita, CA (cdp) San Diego County	40	0.28
Modesto, CA (city) Stanislaus County	547	0.27
South Salt Lake, UT (city) Salt Lake County	63	0.27
Haverhill, MA (city) Essex County	156	0.26
Pittsford, NY (town) Monroe County	75	0.26
Inkster, MI (city) Wayne County	68	0.26
Robbinsville, NJ (township) Mercer County	34	0.26
Sterling, VA (cdp) Loudoun County	63	0.25
Bethany, OK (city) Oklahoma County	48	0.25
South Venice, FL (cdp) Sarasota County	35	0.25
La Vergne, TN (city) Rutherford County	73	0.24
West Springfield Town, MA (city) Hampden County	69	0.24
St. Louis, MO (city) St. Louis city County	723	0.23
Peoria, AZ (city) Yavapai County	339	0.23
Daly City, CA (city) San Mateo County	230	0.23
Scio, MI (township) Washtenaw County	45	0.23
Dover, NJ (town) Morris County	42	0.23
Lilburn, GA (city) Gwinnett County	27	0.23
Holly, MI (township) Oakland County	26	0.23
North Hempstead, NY (town) Nassau County	500	0.22
Lansing, MI (city) Ingham County	246	0.22
Bedford, MI (township) Monroe County	68	0.22
Lansing, MI (city) Ingham County	246	0.21
Cypress, CA (city) Orange County	99	0.21
New Brighton, MN (city) Ramsey County	45	0.21
Agoura Hills, CA (city) Los Angeles County	42	0.21
Ojus, FL (cdp) Miami-Dade County	35	0.21
Clarendon Hills, IL (village) DuPage County	17	0.21
Erie, PA (city) Erie County	208	0.20
Danville, IL (city) Vermilion County	66	0.20
East Haven, CT (cdp/town) New Haven County	58	0.20
Durant, OK (city) Bryan County	31	0.20
Great Neck, NY (village) Nassau County	20	0.20
Irving, TX (city) Dallas County	401	0.19
Parma, OH (city) Cuyahoga County	153	0.19
Waterford, MI (charter township) Oakland County	135	0.19
McLean, VA (cdp) Fairfax County	87	0.19
Glenview, IL (village) Cook County	82	0.19
Bloomfield, CT (town) Hartford County	38	0.19
Springfield, NJ (township) Union County	30	0.19
Anderson, CA (city) Shasta County	19	0.19
Arlington, TX (city) Tarrant County	652	0.18
Chandler, AZ (city) Maricopa County	403	0.18
Farmington, CT (town) Hartford County	46	0.18
Lower Allen, PA (township) Cumberland County	33	0.18
Oxford, MS (city) Lafayette County	33	0.18
Sartell, MN (city) Stearns County	23	0.18
Lincolnwood, IL (village) Cook County	22	0.18
Worcester, MA (city) Worcester County	312	0.17
Macomb, MI (township) Macomb County	124	0.17
Lake Oswego, OR (city) Clackamas County	61	0.17
Pittsfield, MI (charter township) Washtenaw County	59	0.17

Please refer to the Explanation of Data in the front of the book for more detailed information.

Ancestry

Arab: Jordanian

U.S. and 50 States Sorted by Population and Percent of Total Population

Place	Population	%
United States	**60,056**	**0.02**
California	13,108	0.04
Texas	5,296	0.02
Illinois	4,755	0.04
New York	4,623	0.02
Michigan	3,841	0.04
New Jersey	3,112	0.04
Florida	2,907	0.02
Ohio	2,833	0.02
Pennsylvania	1,616	0.01
Virginia	1,610	0.02
North Carolina	1,457	0.02
Arizona	1,279	0.02
Massachusetts	1,005	0.02
Alabama	924	0.02
Tennessee	894	0.01
Louisiana	771	0.02
Georgia	736	0.01
Washington	702	0.01
Kentucky	684	0.02
Oklahoma	649	0.02
Wisconsin	642	0.01
Oregon	624	0.02
South Carolina	615	0.01
Indiana	596	0.01
Maryland	559	0.01
Missouri	475	0.01
Minnesota	442	0.01
Kansas	438	0.02
Arkansas	434	0.02
Colorado	411	0.01
Nebraska	303	0.02
Connecticut	248	0.01
Nevada	240	0.01
Mississippi	223	0.01
Rhode Island	177	0.02
Iowa	162	0.01
New Mexico	150	0.01
Utah	137	0.01
Delaware	122	0.01
Idaho	71	<0.01
West Virginia	44	<0.01
South Dakota	41	0.01
District of Columbia	28	<0.01
Montana	18	<0.01
Wyoming	18	<0.01
North Dakota	13	<0.01
Hawaii	12	<0.01
Maine	9	<0.01
Vermont	2	<0.01
Alaska	0	0.00
New Hampshire	0	0.00

Place	Population	%
California	13,108	0.04
Illinois	4,755	0.04
Michigan	3,841	0.04
New Jersey	3,112	0.04
United States	**60,056**	**0.02**
Texas	5,296	0.02
New York	4,623	0.02
Florida	2,907	0.02
Ohio	2,833	0.02
Virginia	1,610	0.02
North Carolina	1,457	0.02
Arizona	1,279	0.02
Massachusetts	1,005	0.02
Alabama	924	0.02
Louisiana	771	0.02
Kentucky	684	0.02
Oklahoma	649	0.02
Oregon	624	0.02
Kansas	438	0.02
Arkansas	434	0.02
Nebraska	303	0.02
Rhode Island	177	0.02
Pennsylvania	1,616	0.01
Tennessee	894	0.01
Georgia	736	0.01
Washington	702	0.01
Wisconsin	642	0.01
South Carolina	615	0.01
Indiana	596	0.01
Maryland	559	0.01
Missouri	475	0.01
Minnesota	442	0.01
Colorado	411	0.01
Connecticut	248	0.01
Nevada	240	0.01
Mississippi	223	0.01
Iowa	162	0.01
New Mexico	150	0.01
Utah	137	0.01
Delaware	122	0.01
South Dakota	41	0.01
Idaho	71	<0.01
West Virginia	44	<0.01
District of Columbia	28	<0.01
Montana	18	<0.01
Wyoming	18	<0.01
North Dakota	13	<0.01
Hawaii	12	<0.01
Maine	9	<0.01
Vermont	2	<0.01
Alaska	0	0.00
New Hampshire	0	0.00

Please refer to the Explanation of Data in the front of the book for more detailed information.

Ancestry

Arab: Jordanian

Top 150 Places Sorted by Population

Based on all places, regardless of total population

Place	Population	%
New York, NY (city) Kings County	1,298	0.02
Los Angeles, CA (city) Los Angeles County	1,238	0.03
Chicago, IL (city) Cook County	948	0.04
Philadelphia, PA (city) Philadelphia County	939	0.06
Yonkers, NY (city) Westchester County	907	0.47
Dearborn, MI (city) Wayne County	805	0.82
Arlington, TX (city) Tarrant County	787	0.22
Brooklyn, NY (borough) Kings County	752	0.03
Fresno, CA (city) Fresno County	708	0.15
Phoenix, AZ (city) Maricopa County	667	0.05
Columbus, OH (city) Franklin County	617	0.08
Paterson, NJ (city) Passaic County	596	0.41
Houston, TX (city) Harris County	595	0.03
Anaheim, CA (city) Orange County	575	0.17
Sugar Land, TX (city) Fort Bend County	451	0.59
Metairie, LA (cdp) Jefferson Parish	384	0.28
Riverside, CA (city) Riverside County	367	0.12
Pasadena, CA (city) Los Angeles County	356	0.26
San Francisco, CA (city) San Francisco County	353	0.04
Bakersfield, CA (city) Kern County	352	0.11
Beaverton, OR (city) Washington County	347	0.39
Milwaukee, WI (city) Milwaukee County	327	0.06
Orland Park, IL (village) Cook County	316	0.57
Bensenville, IL (village) DuPage County	307	1.65
Queens, NY (borough) Queens County	307	0.01
Oklahoma City, OK (city) Oklahoma County	303	0.05
Overland Park, KS (city) Johnson County	284	0.17
Alexandria, VA (ind. city) Alexandria independent city	281	0.21
South San Francisco, CA (city) San Mateo County	278	0.45
League City, TX (city) Galveston County	269	0.35
Hoover, AL (city) Jefferson County	269	0.34
Dearborn Heights, MI (city) Wayne County	265	0.46
Cutler Bay, FL (town) Miami-Dade County	262	0.68
Oak Lawn, IL (village) Cook County	254	0.45
Livermore, CA (city) Alameda County	250	0.32
San Bernardino, CA (city) San Bernardino County	250	0.12
Nashville-Davidson, TN (metro govt) Davidson County	249	0.04
Miramar, FL (city) Broward County	248	0.22
Millbrae, CA (city) San Mateo County	243	1.16
La Verne, CA (city) Los Angeles County	243	0.78
Irvine, CA (city) Orange County	239	0.12
Davie, FL (town) Broward County	235	0.26
Lodi, NJ (borough) Bergen County	234	0.98
Edison, NJ (township) Middlesex County	233	0.23
Bridgeview, IL (village) Cook County	225	1.39
Poughkeepsie, NY (town) Dutchess County	223	0.51
Orange, CA (city) Orange County	219	0.16
San Jose, CA (city) Santa Clara County	219	0.02
Livonia, MI (city) Wayne County	216	0.22
Carrollwood, FL (cdp) Hillsborough County	208	0.61
Mount Holly, NC (city) Gaston County	205	1.59
Hyde Park, NY (town) Dutchess County	204	0.94
Westminster, CA (city) Orange County	202	0.23
Austin, TX (city) Travis County	202	0.03
Oak Forest, IL (city) Cook County	201	0.73
Toledo, OH (city) Lucas County	201	0.07
Sacramento, CA (city) Sacramento County	199	0.04
Jersey City, NJ (city) Hudson County	198	0.08
Tulsa, OK (city) Tulsa County	189	0.05
Raleigh, NC (city) Wake County	186	0.05
San Diego, CA (city) San Diego County	185	0.01
Staten Island, NY (borough) Richmond County	183	0.04
Bailey's Crossroads, VA (cdp) Fairfax County	182	0.87
Indianapolis, IN (city) Marion County	182	0.02
Hickory Hills, IL (city) Cook County	180	1.29
West New York, NJ (town) Hudson County	180	0.37
Westland, MI (city) Wayne County	180	0.21
Lumberton, NC (city) Robeson County	179	0.83
Brownstown, MI (charter township) Wayne County	179	0.61
Brookhaven, NY (town) Suffolk County	178	0.04
Mesquite, TX (city) Dallas County	176	0.13
St. Petersburg, FL (city) Pinellas County	176	0.07
Sun Valley, PA (cdp) Monroe County	175	7.16
La Grange, NY (town) Dutchess County	175	1.12
Chestnuthill, PA (township) Monroe County	175	1.03
Warren, MI (city) Macomb County	174	0.13
San Antonio, TX (city) Medina County	173	0.01
Medford, MA (city) Middlesex County	172	0.31
Huntington Beach, CA (city) Orange County	171	0.09
Omaha, NE (city) Douglas County	169	0.04
Park Ridge, IL (city) Cook County	168	0.45
Nicholasville, KY (city) Jessamine County	167	0.62
Santa Clarita, CA (city) Los Angeles County	167	0.10
Rainbow City, AL (city) Etowah County	166	1.77
Menifee, CA (city) Riverside County	163	0.22
Sterling Heights, MI (city) Macomb County	161	0.12
Rancho Cucamonga, CA (city) San Bernardino County	161	0.10
Santee, CA (city) San Diego County	160	0.30
Greensboro, NC (city) Guilford County	159	0.06
Plant City, FL (city) Hillsborough County	154	0.45
Mukilteo, WA (city) Snohomish County	153	0.77
Wade Hampton, SC (cdp) Greenville County	153	0.75
Jonesboro, AR (city) Craighead County	151	0.23
Niagara, NY (town) Niagara County	149	1.77
Plymouth, MI (charter township) Wayne County	147	0.53
Grand Prairie, TX (city) Dallas County	147	0.09
Crestwood, IL (village) Cook County	143	1.31
Charter Oak, CA (cdp) Los Angeles County	142	1.53
Fair Lawn, NJ (borough) Bergen County	142	0.44
Buena Park, CA (city) Orange County	142	0.18
San Ramon, CA (city) Contra Costa County	141	0.21
Charleston, SC (city) Charleston County	140	0.12
Shreveport, LA (city) Caddo Parish	139	0.07
Fort Lauderdale, FL (city) Broward County	136	0.08
Dallas, TX (city) Dallas County	136	0.01
Clifton, NJ (city) Passaic County	135	0.16
San Mateo, CA (city) San Mateo County	134	0.14
Lewiston, NY (town) Niagara County	133	0.82
Plano, TX (city) Collin County	133	0.05
Wichita, KS (city) Sedgwick County	133	0.04
Lake Ronkonkoma, NY (cdp) Suffolk County	132	0.61
Lee, MI (township) Midland County	130	3.00
Chicago Ridge, IL (village) Cook County	130	0.92
McNair, VA (cdp) Fairfax County	130	0.85
Irving, TX (city) Dallas County	129	0.06
Smyrna, GA (city) Cobb County	128	0.25
Arlington, VA (cdp) Arlington County	128	0.06
Cincinnati, OH (city) Hamilton County	127	0.04
Woodbury, NY (village) Orange County	126	1.20
Woodbury, NY (town) Orange County	126	1.14
Waco, TX (city) McLennan County	126	0.10
Paramus, NJ (borough) Bergen County	125	0.48
Virginia Beach, VA (ind. city) Virginia Beach independent city	125	0.03
Pompton Lakes, NJ (borough) Passaic County	123	1.12
Kenner, LA (city) Jefferson Parish	123	0.18
Moorpark, CA (city) Ventura County	122	0.36
Islip, NY (town) Suffolk County	122	0.04
Miami, FL (city) Miami-Dade County	122	0.03
Simi Valley, CA (city) Ventura County	120	0.10
Palm Beach Gardens, FL (city) Palm Beach County	118	0.25
Placentia, CA (city) Orange County	118	0.24
Brooklyn Park, MN (city) Hennepin County	118	0.16
Liberty, NY (town) Sullivan County	117	1.18
Maple Grove, MN (city) Hennepin County	117	0.20
Charlotte, NC (city) Mecklenburg County	117	0.02
Detroit, MI (city) Wayne County	117	0.02
Atascadero, CA (city) San Luis Obispo County	116	0.41
Prospect Park, NJ (borough) Passaic County	115	1.97
Elk Grove, CA (city) Sacramento County	115	0.08
Cleveland, OH (city) Cuyahoga County	115	0.03
Little Ferry, NJ (borough) Bergen County	114	1.08
Palos Hills, IL (city) Cook County	114	0.66
Spokane Valley, WA (city) Spokane County	114	0.13
Fairfield, CA (city) Solano County	113	0.11
Melville, RI (cdp) Newport County	112	5.59
Middletown, RI (town) Newport County	112	0.68
Chandler, AZ (city) Maricopa County	112	0.05
Boston, MA (city) Suffolk County	112	0.02
Redlands, CA (city) San Bernardino County	111	0.16
Auburn Hills, MI (city) Oakland County	110	0.52

Ancestry

Arab: Jordanian

Top 150 Places Sorted by Percent of Total Population

Based on all places, regardless of total population

Place	Population	%
Sun Valley, PA (cdp) Monroe County	175	7.16
Melville, RI (cdp) Newport County	112	5.59
Rutland, IL (village) LaSalle County	13	3.77
Lee, MI (township) Midland County	130	3.00
Bowne, MI (township) Kent County	89	2.94
Woodway, WA (city) Snohomish County	35	2.46
Moundville, AL (town) Hale County	51	2.34
Fairview, NY (cdp) Dutchess County	108	2.32
Pingree Grove, IL (village) Kane County	83	2.20
Prospect Park, NJ (borough) Passaic County	115	1.97
James, MI (township) Saginaw County	37	1.90
New Burlington, OH (cdp) Hamilton County	99	1.87
Dahlgren Center, VA (cdp) King George County	32	1.84
Rainbow City, AL (city) Etowah County	166	1.77
Niagara, NY (town) Niagara County	149	1.77
Bensenville, IL (village) DuPage County	307	1.65
Newton, MS (city) Newton County	57	1.65
Fremont, NY (town) Sullivan County	20	1.62
Mount Holly, NC (city) Gaston County	205	1.59
Charter Oak, CA (cdp) Los Angeles County	142	1.53
Leonardo, NJ (cdp) Monmouth County	42	1.52
Shingletown, CA (cdp) Shasta County	31	1.49
Putnam Lake, NY (cdp) Putnam County	52	1.42
Dakota Dunes, SD (cdp) Union County	37	1.42
Bridgeview, IL (village) Cook County	225	1.39
Tyro, NC (cdp) Davidson County	53	1.35
Addison, MI (township) Oakland County	84	1.32
Crestwood, IL (village) Cook County	143	1.31
Dexter, MI (township) Washtenaw County	78	1.31
Hickory Hills, IL (city) Cook County	180	1.29
Woodbury, NY (village) Orange County	126	1.20
Taos, NM (town) Taos County	67	1.20
Liberty, NY (town) Sullivan County	117	1.18
Millbrae, CA (city) San Mateo County	243	1.16
Cave Creek, AZ (town) Maricopa County	57	1.16
Woodbury, NY (town) Orange County	126	1.14
Hainesville, IL (village) Lake County	38	1.14
La Grange, NY (town) Dutchess County	175	1.12
Pompton Lakes, NJ (borough) Passaic County	123	1.12
Little Ferry, NJ (borough) Bergen County	114	1.08
Bull Mountain, OR (cdp) Washington County	98	1.07
Old Bennington, VT (village) Bennington County	2	1.07
Baywood, NY (cdp) Suffolk County	82	1.04
Chestnuthill, PA (township) Monroe County	175	1.03
Warr Acres, OK (city) Oklahoma County	99	0.99
Lodi, NJ (borough) Bergen County	234	0.98
Hyde Park, NY (town) Dutchess County	204	0.94
Plains, PA (cdp) Luzerne County	37	0.93
Chicago Ridge, IL (village) Cook County	130	0.92
Woodside, CA (town) San Mateo County	48	0.92
Shannon Hills, AR (city) Saline County	27	0.92
Sherrill, NY (city) Oneida County	28	0.91
Sturtevant, WI (village) Racine County	59	0.89
Bailey's Crossroads, VA (cdp) Fairfax County	182	0.87
Pantops, VA (cdp) Albemarle County	20	0.87
McNair, VA (cdp) Fairfax County	130	0.85
Wilson, WI (town) Dunn County	4	0.85
Lumberton, NC (city) Robeson County	179	0.83
Dearborn, MI (city) Wayne County	805	0.82
Lewiston, NY (town) Niagara County	133	0.82
Ravenna, OH (city) Portage County	94	0.80
Willow Springs, IL (village) Cook County	43	0.80
La Verne, CA (city) Los Angeles County	243	0.78
Park Layne, OH (cdp) Clark County	35	0.78
Mukilteo, WA (city) Snohomish County	153	0.77
Genesee, ID (city) Latah County	7	0.76
Wade Hampton, SC (cdp) Greenville County	153	0.75
Oak Forest, IL (city) Cook County	201	0.73
Lemoore Station, CA (cdp) Kings County	55	0.70
Olpe, KS (city) Lyon County	4	0.70
Cutler Bay, FL (town) Miami-Dade County	262	0.68
Middletown, RI (town) Newport County	112	0.68
Palos Hills, IL (city) Cook County	114	0.66
East La Mirada, CA (cdp) Los Angeles County	67	0.66
West Caln, PA (township) Chester County	58	0.66
Glenmont, MD (cdp) Montgomery County	87	0.65
Cannon AFB, NM (cdp) Curry County	19	0.64
Fairview Park, OH (city) Cuyahoga County	107	0.63
Cherry Hill, VA (cdp) Prince William County	97	0.63
Bellefontaine, OH (city) Logan County	83	0.63
Nicholasville, KY (city) Jessamine County	167	0.62
Markesan, WI (city) Green Lake County	9	0.62
Carrollwood, FL (cdp) Hillsborough County	208	0.61
Brownstown, MI (charter township) Wayne County	179	0.61
Lake Ronkonkoma, NY (cdp) Suffolk County	132	0.61
Newport, SC (cdp) York County	24	0.61
Sugar Land, TX (city) Fort Bend County	451	0.59
Orland Park, IL (village) Cook County	316	0.57
Rio Pinar, FL (cdp) Orange County	30	0.57
Hanover, PA (township) Northampton County	59	0.55
Olmsted Falls, OH (city) Cuyahoga County	48	0.55
St. James, MN (city) Watonwan County	25	0.55
East Longmeadow, MA (town) Hampden County	83	0.54
Plymouth, MI (charter township) Wayne County	147	0.53
Miamisburg, OH (city) Montgomery County	105	0.53
Haledon, NJ (borough) Passaic County	44	0.53
Auburn Hills, MI (city) Oakland County	110	0.52
Gainesville, VA (cdp) Prince William County	56	0.52
Alondra Park, CA (cdp) Los Angeles County	46	0.52
Big Beaver, PA (borough) Beaver County	10	0.52
Poughkeepsie, NY (town) Dutchess County	223	0.51
Manchester, MO (city) St. Louis County	93	0.51
Shawnee Hills, OH (village) Delaware County	4	0.51
Goodlettsville, TN (city) Davidson County	77	0.50
Rosemont, IL (village) Cook County	20	0.50
Newkirk, OK (city) Kay County	11	0.50
Chico, WA (cdp) Kitsap County	12	0.49
Paramus, NJ (borough) Bergen County	125	0.48
Chowchilla, CA (city) Madera County	87	0.48
Ventnor City, NJ (city) Atlantic County	53	0.48
Sheboygan, WI (town) Sheboygan County	34	0.48
Merrimac, VA (cdp) Montgomery County	10	0.48
Yonkers, NY (city) Westchester County	907	0.47
Pearl River, NY (cdp) Rockland County	68	0.47
Hebron, TX (town) Denton County	3	0.47
Dearborn Heights, MI (city) Wayne County	265	0.46
Kenova, WV (city) Wayne County	15	0.46
Van, TX (city) Van Zandt County	12	0.46
South San Francisco, CA (city) San Mateo County	278	0.45
Oak Lawn, IL (village) Cook County	254	0.45
Park Ridge, IL (city) Cook County	168	0.45
Plant City, FL (city) Hillsborough County	154	0.45
Lumberton, NJ (township) Burlington County	55	0.45
Fair Lawn, NJ (borough) Bergen County	142	0.44
Irving, WI (town) Jackson County	4	0.44
Patterson, NY (town) Putnam County	52	0.43
East Milton, FL (cdp) Santa Rosa County	39	0.43
Franconia, VA (cdp) Fairfax County	77	0.42
Pea Ridge, WV (cdp) Cabell County	29	0.42
Posen, IL (village) Cook County	24	0.42
Paterson, NJ (city) Passaic County	596	0.41
Atascadero, CA (city) San Luis Obispo County	116	0.41
Beaverton, OR (city) Washington County	347	0.39
Murphy, TX (city) Collin County	59	0.39
Wood Dale, IL (city) DuPage County	54	0.39
Colma, CA (town) San Mateo County	6	0.39
East Fishkill, NY (town) Dutchess County	110	0.38
Bloomingdale, NJ (borough) Passaic County	29	0.38
West New York, NJ (town) Hudson County	180	0.37
Miller Place, NY (cdp) Suffolk County	46	0.37
Plains, PA (township) Luzerne County	37	0.37
Moorpark, CA (city) Ventura County	122	0.36
West Hempstead, NY (cdp) Nassau County	66	0.36
Hudson, WI (city) St. Croix County	44	0.36
Glen Rock, NJ (borough) Bergen County	42	0.36
League City, TX (city) Galveston County	269	0.35
Gaines, MI (charter township) Kent County	84	0.35
Birmingham, MI (city) Oakland County	69	0.35
Hoover, AL (city) Jefferson County	269	0.34
Loma Linda, CA (city) San Bernardino County	78	0.34

Please refer to the Explanation of Data in the front of the book for more detailed information.

Ancestry

Arab: Jordanian

Top 150 Places Sorted by Percent of Total Population

Based on places with total population of 7,500 or more

Place	Population	%
Rainbow City, AL (city) Etowah County	166	1.77
Niagara, NY (town) Niagara County	149	1.77
Bensenville, IL (village) DuPage County	307	1.65
Mount Holly, NC (city) Gaston County	205	1.59
Charter Oak, CA (cdp) Los Angeles County	142	1.53
Bridgeview, IL (village) Cook County	225	1.39
Crestwood, IL (village) Cook County	143	1.31
Hickory Hills, IL (city) Cook County	180	1.29
Woodbury, NY (village) Orange County	126	1.20
Liberty, NY (town) Sullivan County	117	1.18
Millbrae, CA (city) San Mateo County	243	1.16
Woodbury, NY (town) Orange County	126	1.14
La Grange, NY (town) Dutchess County	175	1.12
Pompton Lakes, NJ (borough) Passaic County	123	1.12
Little Ferry, NJ (borough) Bergen County	114	1.08
Bull Mountain, OR (cdp) Washington County	98	1.07
Baywood, NY (cdp) Suffolk County	82	1.04
Chestnuthill, PA (township) Monroe County	175	1.03
Warr Acres, OK (city) Oklahoma County	99	0.99
Lodi, NJ (borough) Bergen County	234	0.98
Hyde Park, NY (town) Dutchess County	204	0.94
Chicago Ridge, IL (village) Cook County	130	0.92
Bailey's Crossroads, VA (cdp) Fairfax County	182	0.87
McNair, VA (cdp) Fairfax County	130	0.85
Lumberton, NC (city) Robeson County	179	0.83
Dearborn, MI (city) Wayne County	805	0.82
Lewiston, NY (town) Niagara County	133	0.82
Ravenna, OH (city) Portage County	94	0.80
La Verne, CA (city) Los Angeles County	243	0.78
Mukilteo, WA (city) Snohomish County	153	0.77
Wade Hampton, SC (cdp) Greenville County	153	0.75
Oak Forest, IL (city) Cook County	201	0.73
Lemoore Station, CA (cdp) Kings County	55	0.70
Cutler Bay, FL (town) Miami-Dade County	262	0.68
Middletown, RI (town) Newport County	112	0.68
Palos Hills, IL (city) Cook County	114	0.66
East La Mirada, CA (cdp) Los Angeles County	67	0.66
West Caln, PA (township) Chester County	58	0.66
Glenmont, MD (cdp) Montgomery County	87	0.65
Fairview Park, OH (city) Cuyahoga County	107	0.63
Cherry Hill, VA (cdp) Prince William County	97	0.63
Bellefontaine, OH (city) Logan County	83	0.63
Nicholasville, KY (city) Jessamine County	167	0.62
Carrollwood, FL (cdp) Hillsborough County	208	0.61
Brownstown, MI (charter township) Wayne County	179	0.61
Lake Ronkonkoma, NY (cdp) Suffolk County	132	0.61
Sugar Land, TX (city) Fort Bend County	451	0.59
Orland Park, IL (village) Cook County	316	0.57
Hanover, PA (township) Northampton County	59	0.55
Olmsted Falls, OH (city) Cuyahoga County	48	0.55
East Longmeadow, MA (town) Hampden County	83	0.54
Plymouth, MI (charter township) Wayne County	147	0.53
Miamisburg, OH (city) Montgomery County	105	0.53
Haledon, NJ (borough) Passaic County	44	0.53
Auburn Hills, MI (city) Oakland County	110	0.52
Gainesville, VA (cdp) Prince William County	56	0.52
Alondra Park, CA (cdp) Los Angeles County	46	0.52
Poughkeepsie, NY (town) Dutchess County	223	0.51
Manchester, MO (city) St. Louis County	93	0.51
Goodlettsville, TN (city) Davidson County	77	0.50
Paramus, NJ (borough) Bergen County	125	0.48
Chowchilla, CA (city) Madera County	87	0.48
Ventnor City, NJ (city) Atlantic County	53	0.48
Yonkers, NY (city) Westchester County	907	0.47
Pearl River, NY (cdp) Rockland County	68	0.47
Dearborn Heights, MI (city) Wayne County	265	0.46
South San Francisco, CA (city) San Mateo County	278	0.45
Oak Lawn, IL (village) Cook County	254	0.45
Park Ridge, IL (city) Cook County	168	0.45
Plant City, FL (city) Hillsborough County	154	0.45
Lumberton, NJ (township) Burlington County	55	0.45
Fair Lawn, NJ (borough) Bergen County	142	0.44
Patterson, NY (town) Putnam County	52	0.43
East Milton, FL (cdp) Santa Rosa County	39	0.43
Franconia, VA (cdp) Fairfax County	77	0.42
Paterson, NJ (city) Passaic County	596	0.41
Atascadero, CA (city) San Luis Obispo County	116	0.41
Beaverton, OR (city) Washington County	347	0.39
Murphy, TX (city) Collin County	59	0.39
Wood Dale, IL (city) DuPage County	54	0.39
East Fishkill, NY (town) Dutchess County	110	0.38
Bloomingdale, NJ (borough) Passaic County	29	0.38
West New York, NJ (town) Hudson County	180	0.37
Miller Place, NY (cdp) Suffolk County	46	0.37
Plains, PA (township) Luzerne County	37	0.37
Moorpark, CA (city) Ventura County	122	0.36
West Hempstead, NY (cdp) Nassau County	66	0.36
Hudson, WI (city) St. Croix County	44	0.36
Glen Rock, NJ (borough) Bergen County	42	0.36
League City, TX (city) Galveston County	269	0.35
Gaines, MI (charter township) Kent County	84	0.35
Birmingham, MI (city) Oakland County	69	0.35
Hoover, AL (city) Jefferson County	269	0.34
Loma Linda, CA (city) San Bernardino County	78	0.34
Livermore, CA (city) Alameda County	250	0.32
Mauldin, SC (city) Greenville County	70	0.32
Worth, IL (village) Cook County	34	0.32
Webster, TX (city) Harris County	32	0.32
Medford, MA (city) Middlesex County	172	0.31
Niles, IL (village) Cook County	90	0.31
Evans, GA (cdp) Columbia County	86	0.31
Rocky River, OH (city) Cuyahoga County	62	0.31
Santee, CA (city) San Diego County	160	0.30
Coatesville, PA (city) Chester County	38	0.30
Randallstown, MD (cdp) Baltimore County	95	0.29
Belle Glade, FL (city) Palm Beach County	52	0.29
Sycamore, IL (city) DeKalb County	48	0.29
Bryant, AR (city) Saline County	46	0.29
Kingston, PA (borough) Luzerne County	39	0.29
Canyon Lake, CA (city) Riverside County	31	0.29
Metairie, LA (cdp) Jefferson Parish	384	0.28
Clinton, UT (city) Davis County	53	0.28
Linganore, MD (cdp) Frederick County	23	0.28
Pittsfield, MI (charter township) Washtenaw County	92	0.27
Indian Trail, NC (town) Union County	81	0.27
Bradley Gardens, NJ (cdp) Somerset County	39	0.27
Bedford, MA (town) Middlesex County	35	0.27
Pasadena, CA (city) Los Angeles County	356	0.26
Davie, FL (town) Broward County	235	0.26
Brentwood, TN (city) Williamson County	91	0.26
Smyrna, GA (city) Cobb County	128	0.25
Palm Beach Gardens, FL (city) Palm Beach County	118	0.25
Mehlville, MO (cdp) St. Louis County	69	0.25
Vernon Hills, IL (village) Lake County	61	0.25
Sylvania, OH (city) Lucas County	48	0.25
Bon Air, VA (cdp) Chesterfield County	39	0.25
Pine Castle, FL (cdp) Orange County	27	0.25
Placentia, CA (city) Orange County	118	0.24
Bell, CA (city) Los Angeles County	85	0.24
Dobbs Ferry, NY (village) Westchester County	26	0.24
Valencia West, AZ (cdp) Pima County	22	0.24
Hastings-on-Hudson, NY (village) Westchester County	19	0.24
Edison, NJ (township) Middlesex County	233	0.23
Westminster, CA (city) Orange County	202	0.23
Jonesboro, AR (city) Craighead County	151	0.23
North Olmsted, OH (city) Cuyahoga County	74	0.23
Poughkeepsie, NY (city) Dutchess County	73	0.23
Long Hill, NJ (township) Morris County	20	0.23
Arlington, TX (city) Tarrant County	787	0.22
Miramar, FL (city) Broward County	248	0.22
Livonia, MI (city) Wayne County	216	0.22
Menifee, CA (city) Riverside County	163	0.22
Tigard, OR (city) Washington County	106	0.22
Waxahachie, TX (city) Ellis County	61	0.22
Rosemount, MN (city) Dakota County	45	0.22
Alexandria, VA (ind. city) Alexandria independent city	281	0.21
Westland, MI (city) Wayne County	180	0.21
San Ramon, CA (city) Contra Costa County	141	0.21
Greenwood, IN (city) Johnson County	101	0.21
Sayreville, NJ (borough) Middlesex County	90	0.21

SECTION THREE

Please refer to the Explanation of Data in the front of the book for more detailed information.

Ancestry

Arab: Lebanese

U.S. and 50 States Sorted by Population and Percent of Total Population

Place	Population	%
United States	**485,917**	**0.16**
California	58,107	0.16
Michigan	57,876	0.58
Massachusetts	32,722	0.51
New York	32,642	0.17
Florida	32,346	0.17
Texas	31,584	0.13
Ohio	30,056	0.26
Pennsylvania	19,891	0.16
Virginia	14,509	0.19
New Jersey	12,869	0.15
Illinois	11,409	0.09
North Carolina	10,370	0.11
Arizona	9,427	0.15
Georgia	9,372	0.10
Connecticut	9,293	0.26
Minnesota	6,905	0.13
Washington	6,412	0.10
Louisiana	6,342	0.14
Maryland	6,284	0.11
Colorado	5,701	0.12
New Hampshire	5,264	0.40
Nevada	5,119	0.19
Missouri	5,118	0.09
Alabama	4,477	0.09
Oklahoma	4,427	0.12
Indiana	4,417	0.07
South Carolina	4,408	0.10
Tennessee	4,277	0.07
Mississippi	4,229	0.14
Kentucky	3,823	0.09
Oregon	3,731	0.10
Rhode Island	3,396	0.32
Kansas	3,196	0.11
West Virginia	3,189	0.17
Wisconsin	3,016	0.05
New Mexico	2,338	0.12
Maine	2,246	0.17
Nebraska	2,057	0.11
Iowa	1,976	0.07
Utah	1,730	0.07
Vermont	1,690	0.27
District of Columbia	1,243	0.21
Arkansas	1,145	0.04
Montana	1,016	0.10
North Dakota	803	0.12
Idaho	770	0.05
Alaska	692	0.10
Delaware	654	0.07
South Dakota	601	0.08
Hawaii	482	0.04
Wyoming	270	0.05

Place	Population	%
Michigan	57,876	0.58
Massachusetts	32,722	0.51
New Hampshire	5,264	0.40
Rhode Island	3,396	0.32
Vermont	1,690	0.27
Ohio	30,056	0.26
Connecticut	9,293	0.26
District of Columbia	1,243	0.21
Virginia	14,509	0.19
Nevada	5,119	0.19
New York	32,642	0.17
Florida	32,346	0.17
West Virginia	3,189	0.17
Maine	2,246	0.17
United States	**485,917**	**0.16**
California	58,107	0.16
Pennsylvania	19,891	0.16
New Jersey	12,869	0.15
Arizona	9,427	0.15
Louisiana	6,342	0.14
Mississippi	4,229	0.14
Texas	31,584	0.13
Minnesota	6,905	0.13
Colorado	5,701	0.12
Oklahoma	4,427	0.12
New Mexico	2,338	0.12
North Dakota	803	0.12
North Carolina	10,370	0.11
Maryland	6,284	0.11
Kansas	3,196	0.11
Nebraska	2,057	0.11
Georgia	9,372	0.10
Washington	6,412	0.10
South Carolina	4,408	0.10
Oregon	3,731	0.10
Montana	1,016	0.10
Alaska	692	0.10
Illinois	11,409	0.09
Missouri	5,118	0.09
Alabama	4,477	0.09
Kentucky	3,823	0.09
South Dakota	601	0.08
Indiana	4,417	0.07
Tennessee	4,277	0.07
Iowa	1,976	0.07
Utah	1,730	0.07
Delaware	654	0.07
Wisconsin	3,016	0.05
Idaho	770	0.05
Wyoming	270	0.05
Arkansas	1,145	0.04
Hawaii	482	0.04

Please refer to the Explanation of Data in the front of the book for more detailed information.

Ancestry

Arab: Lebanese

Top 150 Places Sorted by Population

Based on all places, regardless of total population

Place	Population	%
Dearborn, MI (city) Wayne County	18,812	19.12
New York, NY (city) Kings County	11,682	0.14
Los Angeles, CA (city) Los Angeles County	8,079	0.21
Dearborn Heights, MI (city) Wayne County	7,446	12.82
Brooklyn, NY (borough) Kings County	4,757	0.19
Houston, TX (city) Harris County	3,912	0.19
San Diego, CA (city) San Diego County	3,545	0.28
Manhattan, NY (borough) New York County	3,331	0.21
Boston, MA (city) Suffolk County	2,304	0.38
Queens, NY (borough) Queens County	2,228	0.10
Austin, TX (city) Travis County	2,130	0.28
Glendale, CA (city) Los Angeles County	2,062	1.07
Phoenix, AZ (city) Maricopa County	2,021	0.14
Chicago, IL (city) Cook County	1,936	0.07
Methuen Town, MA (city) Essex County	1,776	3.83
Dallas, TX (city) Dallas County	1,717	0.14
Toledo, OH (city) Lucas County	1,656	0.57
Columbus, OH (city) Franklin County	1,656	0.21
Jacksonville, FL (city) Duval County	1,636	0.20
Charlotte, NC (city) Mecklenburg County	1,598	0.23
San Antonio, TX (city) Medina County	1,449	0.11
Sterling Heights, MI (city) Macomb County	1,441	1.11
El Paso, TX (city) El Paso County	1,419	0.23
Wichita, KS (city) Sedgwick County	1,388	0.37
Worcester, MA (city) Worcester County	1,347	0.75
San Jose, CA (city) Santa Clara County	1,317	0.14
Las Vegas, NV (city) Clark County	1,259	0.22
Washington, DC (city) District of Columbia	1,243	0.21
Clinton, MI (charter township) Macomb County	1,184	1.22
Seattle, WA (city) King County	1,156	0.19
Fall River, MA (city) Bristol County	1,149	1.28
Cleveland, OH (city) Cuyahoga County	1,147	0.28
San Francisco, CA (city) San Francisco County	1,112	0.14
San Bernardino, CA (city) San Bernardino County	1,107	0.53
Portland, OR (city) Multnomah County	1,079	0.19
Plano, TX (city) Collin County	1,051	0.41
Staten Island, NY (borough) Richmond County	1,019	0.22
St. Louis, MO (city) St. Louis city County	1,013	0.32
Albuquerque, NM (city) Bernalillo County	999	0.19
Philadelphia, PA (city) Philadelphia County	991	0.07
Amherst, NY (town) Erie County	985	0.81
Canton, MI (charter township) Wayne County	969	1.10
Tucson, AZ (city) Pima County	951	0.18
Utica, NY (city) Oneida County	947	1.53
Pomona, CA (city) Los Angeles County	935	0.63
Pittsburgh, PA (city) Allegheny County	934	0.30
Oklahoma City, OK (city) Oklahoma County	928	0.16
Minneapolis, MN (city) Hennepin County	918	0.24
Akron, OH (city) Summit County	914	0.45
Lafayette, LA (city) Lafayette Parish	897	0.76
Warren, MI (city) Macomb County	891	0.66
Scottsdale, AZ (city) Maricopa County	879	0.40
Peoria, IL (city) Peoria County	874	0.77
Tulsa, OK (city) Tulsa County	874	0.23
Miami, FL (city) Miami-Dade County	856	0.22
Corona, CA (city) Riverside County	845	0.56
Raleigh, NC (city) Wake County	837	0.22
Paradise, NV (cdp) Clark County	836	0.38
Indianapolis, IN (city) Marion County	826	0.10
Anaheim, CA (city) Orange County	816	0.25
Parma, OH (city) Cuyahoga County	813	0.99
Watertown Town, MA (city) Middlesex County	811	2.57
Danbury, CT (city/town) Fairfield County	809	1.02
Macomb, MI (township) Macomb County	808	1.08
Riverside, CA (city) Riverside County	789	0.26
Tampa, FL (city) Hillsborough County	774	0.23
Enterprise, NV (cdp) Clark County	757	0.76
Troy, MI (city) Oakland County	752	0.93
Louisville-Jefferson County, KY (metro govt) Jefferson County	745	0.13
Norwood, MA (cdp/town) Norfolk County	742	2.61
Omaha, NE (city) Douglas County	723	0.18
Gilbert, AZ (town) Maricopa County	718	0.37
Colorado Springs, CO (city) El Paso County	712	0.18
Lakewood, OH (city) Cuyahoga County	706	1.34
Cincinnati, OH (city) Hamilton County	704	0.23
Shelby, MI (charter township) Macomb County	686	0.94
Arlington, VA (cdp) Arlington County	672	0.34
Livonia, MI (city) Wayne County	668	0.68
Denver, CO (city) Denver County	664	0.11
Irvine, CA (city) Orange County	661	0.33
Hempstead, NY (town) Nassau County	657	0.09
Bloomfield, MI (charter township) Oakland County	654	1.58
Tempe, AZ (city) Maricopa County	650	0.40
Virginia Beach, VA (ind. city) Virginia Beach independent city	647	0.15
Atlanta, GA (city) Fulton County	636	0.15
Kendall, FL (cdp) Miami-Dade County	627	0.82
Charleston, WV (city) Kanawha County	618	1.20
Dedham, MA (cdp/town) Norfolk County	592	2.43
Frisco, TX (city) Collin County	589	0.57
Long Beach, CA (city) Los Angeles County	588	0.13
St. Petersburg, FL (city) Pinellas County	582	0.24
Lexington-Fayette, KY (cons. govt) Fayette County	581	0.20
Lansing, MI (city) Ingham County	579	0.50
Reno, NV (city) Washoe County	568	0.26
Detroit, MI (city) Wayne County	566	0.07
Lansing, MI (city) Ingham County	565	0.51
Corpus Christi, TX (city) Nueces County	562	0.19
St. Clair Shores, MI (city) Macomb County	558	0.92
Redondo Beach, CA (city) Los Angeles County	545	0.83
Brockton, MA (city) Plymouth County	529	0.56
Richmond, VA (ind. city) Richmond independent city	526	0.26
Nashville-Davidson, TN (metro govt) Davidson County	524	0.09
St. Paul, MN (city) Ramsey County	509	0.18
Mission Viejo, CA (city) Orange County	507	0.55
McLean, VA (cdp) Fairfax County	504	1.09
Santa Clarita, CA (city) Los Angeles County	503	0.29
Manchester, NH (city) Hillsborough County	498	0.45
Whitestown, NY (town) Oneida County	495	2.66
Rancho Cucamonga, CA (city) San Bernardino County	495	0.31
Shreveport, LA (city) Caddo Parish	491	0.25
Salem, NH (town) Rockingham County	488	1.69
Mesa, AZ (city) Maricopa County	486	0.11
Marlborough, MA (city) Middlesex County	483	1.28
Buffalo, NY (city) Erie County	481	0.18
Middleburg Heights, OH (city) Cuyahoga County	479	3.03
Hoover, AL (city) Jefferson County	478	0.61
Gresham, OR (city) Multnomah County	476	0.47
Andover, MA (town) Essex County	475	1.45
Garland, TX (city) Dallas County	471	0.21
Burbank, CA (city) Los Angeles County	470	0.46
Northville, MI (township) Wayne County	468	1.72
Pasadena, CA (city) Los Angeles County	467	0.34
Taunton, MA (city) Bristol County	464	0.83
Spring Valley, NV (cdp) Clark County	463	0.27
Plantation, FL (city) Broward County	462	0.54
Lubbock, TX (city) Lubbock County	456	0.21
Glendora, CA (city) Los Angeles County	455	0.91
Somerset, MA (cdp/town) Bristol County	454	2.50
Fremont, CA (city) Alameda County	454	0.22
West Bloomfield, MI (charter township) Oakland County	453	0.70
Huntington Beach, CA (city) Orange County	453	0.24
Farmington Hills, MI (city) Oakland County	451	0.56
Thousand Oaks, CA (city) Ventura County	451	0.36
Hollywood, FL (city) Broward County	448	0.32
Chesapeake, VA (ind. city) Chesapeake independent city	448	0.20
Franklin Town, MA (city) Norfolk County	444	1.43
Bell, CA (city) Los Angeles County	444	1.25
Carlsbad, CA (city) San Diego County	443	0.44
Roseville, MI (city) Macomb County	440	0.92
West Haven, CT (city/town) New Haven County	440	0.80
New Orleans, LA (city) Orleans Parish	438	0.15
Arlington, TX (city) Tarrant County	438	0.12
Orlando, FL (city) Orange County	434	0.19
Shrewsbury, MA (town) Worcester County	433	1.24
Westlake, OH (city) Cuyahoga County	431	1.33
Sugar Land, TX (city) Fort Bend County	429	0.56
Tonawanda, NY (town) Erie County	428	0.58
Quincy, MA (city) Norfolk County	428	0.47
Chesterfield, MI (township) Macomb County	418	0.98
Cambridge, MA (city) Middlesex County	416	0.40

Please refer to the Explanation of Data in the front of the book for more detailed information.

Ancestry

Arab: Lebanese

Top 150 Places Sorted by Percent of Total Population

Based on all places, regardless of total population

Place	Population	%
Boulevard, CA (cdp) San Diego County	11	35.48
Stanchfield, MN (cdp) Isanti County	14	20.59
Dearborn, MI (city) Wayne County	18,812	19.12
Pottawattamie Park, IN (town) LaPorte County	26	13.13
Dearborn Heights, MI (city) Wayne County	7,446	12.82
Mayhill, NM (cdp) Otero County	13	12.62
Kenwood, CA (cdp) Sonoma County	58	12.55
Vineland, MN (township) Polk County	15	11.72
Salmon Creek, CA (cdp) Sonoma County	9	10.84
Heeney, CO (cdp) Summit County	7	10.00
Seven Hills, CO (cdp) Boulder County	17	9.66
Rockingham, GA (cdp) Bacon County	19	9.60
Damascus, OH (cdp) Mahoning County	23	9.27
Samoa, CA (cdp) Humboldt County	24	8.79
Summerhaven, AZ (cdp) Pima County	8	8.25
Garden Prairie, IL (village) Boone County	15	8.11
Hokah, MN (city) Houston County	31	7.56
Glenfield, PA (borough) Allegheny County	13	7.43
Eldorado Springs, CO (cdp) Boulder County	50	7.14
Springbrook, ND (city) Williams County	3	6.98
Ama, LA (cdp) St. Charles Parish	108	6.79
Port William, OH (village) Clinton County	17	6.67
Marksboro, NJ (cdp) Warren County	6	6.59
Desoto Lakes, FL (cdp) Sarasota County	261	6.58
Copperton, UT (cdp) Salt Lake County	46	6.50
Vineyard Haven, MA (cdp) Dukes County	160	6.48
Palo Alto, PA (borough) Schuylkill County	65	6.26
Hillsboro Beach, FL (town) Broward County	106	6.21
Village of Grosse Pointe Shores, MI (city) Wayne County	173	5.96
Village of Grosse Pointe Shores, MI (city) Wayne County	175	5.88
Old Bennington, VT (village) Bennington County	11	5.88
Brandt, MN (township) Polk County	3	5.88
Rougemont, NC (cdp) Durham County	46	5.87
Upper Exeter, PA (cdp) Luzerne County	46	5.84
Clark Mills, NY (cdp) Oneida County	65	5.79
Grand Lake, CO (town) Grand County	15	5.79
Hampton, NE (village) Hamilton County	27	5.71
Jefferson, WV (cdp) Kanawha County	23	5.60
Mulliken, MI (village) Eaton County	27	5.33
Mackenzie, MO (village) St. Louis County	6	5.26
Oden, MI (cdp) Emmet County	26	5.16
Langeloth, PA (cdp) Washington County	22	5.02
Millington, IL (village) LaSalle County	44	5.01
Clyde, NJ (cdp) Somerset County	12	5.00
Mooresboro, NC (town) Cleveland County	17	4.80
Lake Tomahawk, OH (cdp) Columbiana County	21	4.59
Climax, MN (city) Polk County	10	4.59
Roff, OK (town) Pontotoc County	33	4.55
Crown Point, NY (town) Essex County	94	4.54
Bloomingburg, OH (village) Fayette County	44	4.51
Logan, MI (township) Mason County	11	4.51
Oliver, PA (cdp) Fayette County	97	4.48
Morton, WA (city) Lewis County	55	4.41
Woodbury, VT (town) Washington County	41	4.36
Fifty-Six, AR (city) Stone County	14	4.35
New York Mills, NY (village) Oneida County	145	4.30
Lazy Y U, AZ (cdp) Mohave County	9	4.17
Tisbury, MA (town) Dukes County	160	4.12
Lohman, MO (city) Cole County	8	4.10
Hidden Spring, ID (cdp) Ada County	60	4.07
Pawleys Island, SC (town) Georgetown County	4	4.00
Ovilla, TX (city) Ellis County	139	3.90
Pearl Beach, MI (cdp) St. Clair County	122	3.88
Lewiston, NY (village) Niagara County	105	3.88
Montville, ME (town) Waldo County	43	3.88
Methuen Town, MA (city) Essex County	1,776	3.83
East Uniontown, PA (cdp) Fayette County	92	3.72
New Summerfield, TX (city) Cherokee County	45	3.72
Au Sable, MI (cdp) Iosco County	41	3.72
Ashland, ME (town) Aroostook County	54	3.69
Gordon, PA (borough) Schuylkill County	28	3.68
Laymantown, VA (cdp) Botetourt County	106	3.67
Ivins, UT (city) Washington County	240	3.64
Colquitt, GA (city) Miller County	86	3.63
Black Eagle, MT (cdp) Cascade County	31	3.62
Port Vincent, LA (village) Livingston Parish	28	3.61
Nashville, KS (city) Kingman County	3	3.61
Abington, PA (township) Lackawanna County	61	3.57
Uniontown, PA (city) Fayette County	374	3.49
Nottingham, NH (town) Rockingham County	161	3.48
Westwood, KY (city) Jefferson County	19	3.45
Cromwell, MN (city) Carlton County	4	3.45
Summerfield, MI (township) Monroe County	113	3.38
Patterson Heights, PA (borough) Beaver County	24	3.38
Five Points, OH (cdp) Warren County	65	3.37
Mulberry, OH (cdp) Clermont County	109	3.35
Bunker Hill Village, TX (city) Harris County	121	3.34
Williamsville, NY (village) Erie County	177	3.33
Freeport, ME (cdp) Cumberland County	51	3.33
Fountain Lake, AR (town) Garland County	21	3.21
Sunrise, MN (township) Chisago County	64	3.17
Washington, VA (town) Rappahannock County	4	3.15
Piney Point Village, TX (city) Harris County	98	3.14
Susquehanna, PA (township) Cambria County	67	3.14
Coarsegold, CA (cdp) Madera County	50	3.11
Robbinsville, NC (town) Graham County	31	3.11
East Pasadena, CA (cdp) Los Angeles County	178	3.09
Cathlamet, WA (town) Wahkiakum County	19	3.09
Ashland, ME (cdp) Aroostook County	27	3.08
Cedarville, MI (township) Menominee County	10	3.08
East Millstone, NJ (cdp) Somerset County	25	3.07
Camanche Village, CA (cdp) Amador County	18	3.06
Houston Acres, KY (city) Jefferson County	16	3.05
Middleburg Heights, OH (city) Cuyahoga County	479	3.03
Niantic, CT (cdp) New London County	89	3.03
Stanley, ND (city) Mountrail County	53	3.01
Wrangell, AK (borough) Wrangell City and Borough	70	2.99
Thompsons, TX (town) Fort Bend County	7	2.94
Marble Cliff, OH (village) Franklin County	17	2.91
Yorkville, NY (village) Oneida County	76	2.83
Eastborough, KS (city) Sedgwick County	23	2.83
Richland, TX (town) Navarro County	8	2.83
Village of Grosse Pointe Shores, MI (city) Macomb County	2	2.82
Bevil Oaks, TX (city) Jefferson County	36	2.80
Nicholson, PA (township) Fayette County	45	2.78
Jenkins, PA (township) Luzerne County	122	2.74
Ringsted, IA (city) Emmet County	13	2.73
Kempner, TX (city) Lampasas County	27	2.71
Fisher, LA (village) Sabine Parish	7	2.69
Vernon, NY (town) Oneida County	144	2.68
Savoy, MA (town) Berkshire County	20	2.68
Dune Acres, IN (town) Porter County	7	2.67
Whitestown, NY (town) Oneida County	495	2.66
New Folden, MN (township) Marshall County	7	2.65
Aptos, CA (cdp) Santa Cruz County	165	2.64
Port Carbon, PA (borough) Schuylkill County	49	2.64
Lacona, NY (village) Oswego County	16	2.63
Crandall, TX (city) Kaufman County	75	2.62
Willow River, MN (city) Pine County	10	2.62
Norwood, MA (cdp/town) Norfolk County	742	2.61
Hillsborough, CA (town) San Mateo County	278	2.61
Pultneyville, NY (cdp) Wayne County	20	2.61
Hannaford, ND (city) Griggs County	4	2.61
Skaneateles, NY (village) Onondaga County	61	2.59
Watertown Town, MA (city) Middlesex County	811	2.57
Schuyler, NY (town) Herkimer County	87	2.56
Newtown, PA (cdp) Schuylkill County	8	2.56
North Union, PA (township) Fayette County	332	2.55
Quonochontaug, RI (cdp) Washington County	12	2.55
North Bay Village, FL (city) Miami-Dade County	179	2.54
Davison, MI (city) Genesee County	135	2.54
Prestbury, IL (cdp) Kane County	46	2.54
Windham, NY (cdp) Greene County	11	2.53
Hungerford, TX (cdp) Wharton County	12	2.52
Green Valley, CA (cdp) Solano County	40	2.51
Somerset, MA (cdp/town) Bristol County	454	2.50
Grosse Pointe, MI (city) Wayne County	137	2.50
Fairbanks, MI (township) Delta County	9	2.49
Creedmoor, TX (city) Travis County	6	2.48
Bel Aire, KS (city) Sedgwick County	162	2.46

Please refer to the Explanation of Data in the front of the book for more detailed information.

Ancestry

Arab: Lebanese

Top 150 Places Sorted by Percent of Total Population

Based on places with total population of 7,500 or more

Place	Population	%
Dearborn, MI (city) Wayne County	18,812	19.12
Dearborn Heights, MI (city) Wayne County	7,446	12.82
Methuen Town, MA (city) Essex County	1,776	3.83
Uniontown, PA (city) Fayette County	374	3.49
Middleburg Heights, OH (city) Cuyahoga County	479	3.03
Whitestown, NY (town) Oneida County	495	2.66
Norwood, MA (cdp/town) Norfolk County	742	2.61
Hillsborough, CA (town) San Mateo County	278	2.61
Watertown Town, MA (city) Middlesex County	811	2.57
North Union, PA (township) Fayette County	332	2.55
Somerset, MA (cdp/town) Bristol County	454	2.50
Dedham, MA (cdp/town) Norfolk County	592	2.43
Seven Hills, OH (city) Cuyahoga County	259	2.20
Grosse Pointe Woods, MI (city) Wayne County	355	2.17
Windham, NH (town) Rockingham County	282	2.14
Plainville, MA (town) Norfolk County	173	2.14
Fair Lakes, VA (cdp) Fairfax County	168	2.11
Mayfield Heights, OH (city) Cuyahoga County	401	2.10
Highland Heights, OH (city) Cuyahoga County	171	2.07
Clay, MI (township) St. Clair County	186	1.99
Western Springs, IL (village) Cook County	251	1.98
Auburn, MA (town) Worcester County	319	1.97
Olean, NY (city) Cattaraugus County	284	1.95
Maltby, WA (cdp) Snohomish County	223	1.91
Tobyhanna, PA (township) Monroe County	159	1.91
Washington, IL (city) Tazewell County	274	1.90
Fullerton, PA (cdp) Lehigh County	283	1.88
Westwood, MA (town) Norfolk County	266	1.85
Hopewell, PA (township) Beaver County	234	1.85
Lewiston, NY (town) Niagara County	299	1.84
Marathon, FL (city) Monroe County	155	1.82
Fenton, MI (charter township) Genesee County	272	1.78
Southwick, MA (town) Hampden County	166	1.77
Greenwood, MS (city) Leflore County	278	1.75
Long Branch, VA (cdp) Fairfax County	139	1.75
Northville, MI (township) Wayne County	468	1.72
Farmington, MI (city) Oakland County	176	1.70
Salem, NH (town) Rockingham County	488	1.69
Grosse Pointe Farms, MI (city) Wayne County	162	1.69
Cascade, MI (charter township) Kent County	281	1.67
Pinehurst, NC (village) Moore County	206	1.65
Half Moon, NC (cdp) Onslow County	131	1.60
Upper Makefield, PA (township) Bucks County	129	1.60
Bloomfield, MI (charter township) Oakland County	654	1.58
Dallas, GA (city) Paulding County	169	1.57
North Greenbush, NY (town) Rensselaer County	185	1.56
Carnot-Moon, PA (cdp) Allegheny County	176	1.56
Pelham, NH (town) Hillsborough County	196	1.55
Oak Hills Place, LA (cdp) East Baton Rouge Parish	124	1.55
Calimesa, CA (city) Riverside County	122	1.55
Utica, NY (city) Oneida County	947	1.53
Hastings-on-Hudson, NY (village) Westchester County	117	1.50
South Lyon, MI (city) Oakland County	165	1.49
Burtonsville, MD (cdp) Montgomery County	138	1.49
New River, AZ (cdp) Maricopa County	173	1.48
Glen Allen, VA (cdp) Henrico County	227	1.46
Aliquippa, PA (city) Beaver County	143	1.46
Andover, MA (town) Essex County	475	1.45
Franklin Town, MA (city) Norfolk County	444	1.43
Marcy, NY (town) Oneida County	128	1.41
New Baltimore, VA (cdp) Fauquier County	111	1.41
New Britain, PA (township) Bucks County	154	1.39
Robbinsville, NJ (township) Mercer County	179	1.38
Hasbrouck Heights, NJ (borough) Bergen County	162	1.38
Parma Heights, OH (city) Cuyahoga County	285	1.37
Waverly, MI (cdp) Eaton County	336	1.36
Brook Park, OH (city) Cuyahoga County	263	1.35
Fuller Heights, FL (cdp) Polk County	105	1.35
Lakewood, OH (city) Cuyahoga County	706	1.34
Westlake, OH (city) Cuyahoga County	431	1.33
Southport, NY (cdp) Chemung County	101	1.33
Tysons Corner, VA (cdp) Fairfax County	226	1.32
Dumont, NJ (borough) Bergen County	227	1.31
Fairhaven, MA (town) Bristol County	208	1.31
Oregon, OH (city) Lucas County	261	1.30
Rolling Hills Estates, CA (city) Los Angeles County	104	1.30
Old Lyme, CT (town) New London County	99	1.30
Forest Hills, MI (cdp) Kent County	329	1.29
Pine, PA (township) Allegheny County	139	1.29
Fall River, MA (city) Bristol County	1,149	1.28
Marlborough, MA (city) Middlesex County	483	1.28
Millis, MA (town) Norfolk County	100	1.28
Waterville, ME (city) Kennebec County	201	1.27
Cheat Lake, WV (cdp) Monongalia County	97	1.27
Bell, CA (city) Los Angeles County	444	1.25
Wheeling, WV (city) Ohio County	360	1.25
North Andover, MA (town) Essex County	350	1.25
Mundy, MI (township) Genesee County	184	1.25
Dunmore, PA (borough) Lackawanna County	176	1.25
Shrewsbury, MA (town) Worcester County	433	1.24
Wheatfield, NY (town) Niagara County	214	1.24
New Hartford, NY (town) Oneida County	271	1.23
Flowood, MS (city) Rankin County	93	1.23
Clinton, MI (charter township) Macomb County	1,184	1.22
Oak Grove, OR (cdp) Clackamas County	206	1.22
Foster City, CA (city) San Mateo County	360	1.21
Redding, CT (town) Fairfield County	108	1.21
Charleston, WV (city) Kanawha County	618	1.20
Birmingham, MI (city) Oakland County	240	1.20
Grosse Pointe Park, MI (city) Wayne County	141	1.20
Kirkland, NY (town) Oneida County	123	1.20
Westlake Village, CA (city) Los Angeles County	99	1.20
Londonderry, NH (cdp) Rockingham County	130	1.19
Harrison, MI (charter township) Macomb County	293	1.18
Ledyard, CT (town) New London County	178	1.18
Whitehall, PA (township) Lehigh County	309	1.17
Granite Bay, CA (cdp) Placer County	266	1.17
Princeton, NJ (borough) Mercer County	147	1.17
Bull Mountain, OR (cdp) Washington County	107	1.17
University Heights, OH (city) Cuyahoga County	158	1.16
South Union, PA (township) Fayette County	125	1.16
Rockland, MA (town) Plymouth County	201	1.15
Boardman, OH (cdp) Mahoning County	402	1.14
North Smithfield, RI (town) Providence County	134	1.14
Moore, PA (township) Northampton County	104	1.14
Hanover, PA (township) Luzerne County	126	1.13
Sturbridge, MA (town) Worcester County	102	1.13
Andover, MA (cdp) Essex County	97	1.13
Walpole, MA (town) Norfolk County	265	1.12
Duarte, CA (city) Los Angeles County	239	1.12
Middlesborough, KY (city) Bell County	117	1.12
Lapeer, MI (city) Lapeer County	102	1.12
Sterling Heights, MI (city) Macomb County	1,441	1.11
Canton, MI (charter township) Wayne County	969	1.10
Scott, PA (township) Allegheny County	187	1.10
Little Falls, NJ (township) Passaic County	153	1.10
McLean, VA (cdp) Fairfax County	504	1.09
Delta, MI (charter township) Eaton County	351	1.09
North Potomac, MD (cdp) Montgomery County	272	1.09
Macomb, MI (township) Macomb County	808	1.08
Sedona, AZ (city) Yavapai County	111	1.08
The Village, OK (city) Oklahoma County	98	1.08
Northfield, MI (township) Washtenaw County	90	1.08
Molalla, OR (city) Clackamas County	83	1.08
Glendale, CA (city) Los Angeles County	2,062	1.07
East Longmeadow, MA (town) Hampden County	165	1.07
Union Park, FL (cdp) Orange County	109	1.07
Neshannock, PA (township) Lawrence County	102	1.07
Bridgeport, WV (city) Harrison County	85	1.07
Halifax, MA (town) Plymouth County	80	1.07
Easton, MA (town) Bristol County	244	1.06
Sylvania, OH (city) Lucas County	202	1.06
Rocky River, OH (city) Cuyahoga County	213	1.05
Medfield, MA (town) Norfolk County	126	1.05
Millbury, MA (town) Worcester County	137	1.04
Falmouth, ME (town) Cumberland County	115	1.04
Sugarland Run, VA (cdp) Loudoun County	114	1.04
River Vale, NJ (township) Bergen County	100	1.04
North Gates, NY (cdp) Monroe County	97	1.04
Adams, MA (town) Berkshire County	89	1.04

SECTION THREE

Please refer to the Explanation of Data in the front of the book for more detailed information.

Ancestry

Arab: Moroccan

U.S. and 50 States Sorted by Population and Percent of Total Population

Place	Population	%
United States	**74,908**	**0.02**
New York	12,364	0.06
Florida	8,858	0.05
California	8,147	0.02
Massachusetts	6,471	0.10
Virginia	4,839	0.06
New Jersey	4,481	0.05
Illinois	3,159	0.02
Pennsylvania	2,980	0.02
Texas	2,627	0.01
Maryland	2,306	0.04
North Carolina	1,893	0.02
Michigan	1,643	0.02
Colorado	1,560	0.03
Ohio	1,497	0.01
Connecticut	1,264	0.04
Minnesota	1,165	0.02
Georgia	992	0.01
Missouri	956	0.02
Nevada	825	0.03
Washington	614	0.01
Alabama	603	0.01
Indiana	571	0.01
Oklahoma	548	0.01
Arizona	490	0.01
Wisconsin	412	0.01
South Carolina	395	0.01
Oregon	388	0.01
District of Columbia	362	0.06
Kentucky	321	0.01
Kansas	310	0.01
Delaware	218	0.02
New Hampshire	200	0.02
Rhode Island	169	0.02
Louisiana	168	<0.01
Tennessee	146	<0.01
Arkansas	136	<0.01
Hawaii	118	0.01
Mississippi	118	<0.01
West Virginia	111	0.01
New Mexico	105	0.01
Iowa	90	<0.01
Utah	75	<0.01
Idaho	43	<0.01
Maine	42	<0.01
Alaska	41	0.01
Vermont	37	0.01
Nebraska	27	<0.01
South Dakota	23	<0.01
Montana	0	0.00
North Dakota	0	0.00
Wyoming	0	0.00

Place	Population	%
Massachusetts	6,471	0.10
New York	12,364	0.06
Virginia	4,839	0.06
District of Columbia	362	0.06
Florida	8,858	0.05
New Jersey	4,481	0.05
Maryland	2,306	0.04
Connecticut	1,264	0.04
Colorado	1,560	0.03
Nevada	825	0.03
United States	**74,908**	**0.02**
California	8,147	0.02
Illinois	3,159	0.02
Pennsylvania	2,980	0.02
North Carolina	1,893	0.02
Michigan	1,643	0.02
Minnesota	1,165	0.02
Missouri	956	0.02
Delaware	218	0.02
New Hampshire	200	0.02
Rhode Island	169	0.02
Texas	2,627	0.01
Ohio	1,497	0.01
Georgia	992	0.01
Washington	614	0.01
Alabama	603	0.01
Indiana	571	0.01
Oklahoma	548	0.01
Arizona	490	0.01
Wisconsin	412	0.01
South Carolina	395	0.01
Oregon	388	0.01
Kentucky	321	0.01
Kansas	310	0.01
Hawaii	118	0.01
West Virginia	111	0.01
New Mexico	105	0.01
Alaska	41	0.01
Vermont	37	0.01
Louisiana	168	<0.01
Tennessee	146	<0.01
Arkansas	136	<0.01
Mississippi	118	<0.01
Iowa	90	<0.01
Utah	75	<0.01
Idaho	43	<0.01
Maine	42	<0.01
Nebraska	27	<0.01
South Dakota	23	<0.01
Montana	0	0.00
North Dakota	0	0.00
Wyoming	0	0.00

Please refer to the Explanation of Data in the front of the book for more detailed information.

Ancestry

Arab: Moroccan

Top 150 Places Sorted by Population

Based on all places, regardless of total population

Place	Population	%
New York, NY (city) Kings County	8,987	0.11
Queens, NY (borough) Queens County	3,459	0.16
Brooklyn, NY (borough) Kings County	2,648	0.11
Los Angeles, CA (city) Los Angeles County	2,098	0.06
Manhattan, NY (borough) New York County	1,592	0.10
Boston, MA (city) Suffolk County	1,171	0.19
Chicago, IL (city) Cook County	1,014	0.04
Revere, MA (city) Suffolk County	792	1.58
Orlando, FL (city) Orange County	792	0.34
Houston, TX (city) Harris County	765	0.04
Jersey City, NJ (city) Hudson County	716	0.29
Philadelphia, PA (city) Philadelphia County	684	0.05
Malden, MA (city) Middlesex County	671	1.15
Bronx, NY (borough) Bronx County	667	0.05
Staten Island, NY (borough) Richmond County	621	0.13
San Diego, CA (city) San Diego County	611	0.05
Aurora, CO (city) Arapahoe County	590	0.19
Baltimore, MD (city) Baltimore city County	564	0.09
Lakewood, NJ (township) Ocean County	532	0.61
Lakewood, NJ (cdp) Ocean County	466	0.94
Quincy, MA (city) Norfolk County	465	0.51
St. Petersburg, FL (city) Pinellas County	458	0.19
Beverly Hills, CA (city) Los Angeles County	451	1.33
Denver, CO (city) Denver County	437	0.08
Detroit, MI (city) Wayne County	398	0.05
Charlotte, NC (city) Mecklenburg County	382	0.05
Hempstead, NY (town) Nassau County	376	0.05
Chelsea, MA (city) Suffolk County	364	1.05
Washington, DC (city) District of Columbia	362	0.06
Alexandria, VA (ind. city) Alexandria independent city	337	0.25
Kissimmee, FL (city) Osceola County	312	0.53
Pittsburgh, PA (city) Allegheny County	312	0.10
Columbus, OH (city) Franklin County	308	0.04
Cary, NC (town) Wake County	301	0.24
Franklin, NJ (township) Somerset County	298	0.49
Ramapo, NY (town) Rockland County	291	0.24
Newark, NJ (city) Essex County	289	0.11
Oakton, VA (cdp) Fairfax County	276	0.82
Lincolnia, VA (cdp) Fairfax County	264	1.28
Raleigh, NC (city) Wake County	258	0.07
Aventura, FL (city) Miami-Dade County	256	0.76
Worcester, MA (city) Worcester County	244	0.14
Oklahoma City, OK (city) Oklahoma County	244	0.04
Virginia Beach, VA (ind. city) Virginia Beach independent city	242	0.06
Buenaventura Lakes, FL (cdp) Osceola County	238	0.89
Naperville, IL (city) DuPage County	235	0.17
Richardson, TX (city) Dallas County	231	0.24
Paradise, NV (cdp) Clark County	227	0.10
Dale City, VA (cdp) Prince William County	224	0.35
Plano, TX (city) Collin County	222	0.09
Tampa, FL (city) Hillsborough County	222	0.07
Fayetteville, PA (cdp) Franklin County	217	6.90
Greene, PA (township) Franklin County	217	1.36
Everett, MA (city) Middlesex County	216	0.53
Lindenhurst, NY (village) Suffolk County	209	0.76
Babylon, NY (town) Suffolk County	209	0.10
Potomac, MD (cdp) Montgomery County	202	0.45
Huntington, NY (town) Suffolk County	192	0.09
Wichita, KS (city) Sedgwick County	192	0.05
Plantation, FL (city) Broward County	191	0.22
Miami Beach, FL (city) Miami-Dade County	189	0.22
Mamaroneck, NY (village) Westchester County	188	1.00
Mamaroneck, NY (town) Westchester County	188	0.65
Somerset, NJ (cdp) Somerset County	187	0.84
Burke, VA (cdp) Fairfax County	186	0.45
Palo Alto, CA (city) Santa Clara County	181	0.29
Richmond, VA (ind. city) Richmond independent city	180	0.09
Birmingham, AL (city) Jefferson County	178	0.08
Feasterville, PA (cdp) Bucks County	176	5.84
Lower Southampton, PA (township) Bucks County	176	0.92
Medford, MA (city) Middlesex County	176	0.32
Columbia Heights, MN (city) Anoka County	175	0.90
Arlington, VA (cdp) Arlington County	175	0.09
Torrance, CA (city) Los Angeles County	174	0.12
Carrollwood, FL (cdp) Hillsborough County	173	0.50

Place	Population	%
East Moline, IL (city) Rock Island County	172	0.80
Bridgeport, CT (city/town) Fairfield County	168	0.12
Minneapolis, MN (city) Hennepin County	168	0.04
Teaneck, NJ (township) Bergen County	167	0.42
Huntington, VA (cdp) Fairfax County	166	1.60
Kansas City, MO (city) Jackson County	166	0.04
Vestavia Hills, AL (city) Jefferson County	163	0.49
Kingstowne, VA (cdp) Fairfax County	162	1.12
Lakeland, FL (city) Polk County	160	0.17
Cambridge, MA (city) Middlesex County	160	0.15
North Miami Beach, FL (city) Miami-Dade County	158	0.38
Sandy Springs, GA (city) Fulton County	157	0.17
Westmont, CA (cdp) Los Angeles County	155	0.50
Waterbury, CT (city/town) New Haven County	155	0.14
Austin, TX (city) Travis County	155	0.02
Brighton, NY (cdp/town) Monroe County	154	0.42
Boca Raton, FL (city) Palm Beach County	154	0.18
Miami, FL (city) Miami-Dade County	153	0.04
Kinross, MI (charter township) Chippewa County	152	1.89
Brockton, MA (city) Plymouth County	151	0.16
Cherry Hill, NJ (township) Camden County	149	0.21
Lakewood, CA (city) Los Angeles County	149	0.19
Corona, CA (city) Riverside County	148	0.10
Azalea Park, FL (cdp) Orange County	147	1.12
Lakewood, CO (city) Jefferson County	147	0.10
Huntington Station, NY (cdp) Suffolk County	146	0.46
Scottsdale, AZ (city) Maricopa County	144	0.07
Milwaukee, WI (city) Milwaukee County	144	0.02
Centreville, VA (cdp) Fairfax County	143	0.20
Seattle, WA (city) King County	143	0.02
Southwick, MA (town) Hampden County	141	1.50
Islip, NY (town) Suffolk County	141	0.04
Indianapolis, IN (city) Marion County	141	0.02
Meriden, CT (city/town) New Haven County	140	0.23
Belleville, NJ (township) Essex County	137	0.38
Oak Lawn, IL (village) Cook County	137	0.25
Camden, NJ (city) Camden County	137	0.18
Berkeley, CA (city) Alameda County	136	0.12
Henderson, NV (city) Clark County	135	0.05
San Francisco, CA (city) San Francisco County	135	0.02
Irvine, CA (city) Orange County	133	0.07
Melrose, MA (city) Middlesex County	132	0.49
Fontana, CA (city) San Bernardino County	132	0.07
Franconia, VA (cdp) Fairfax County	131	0.71
Stamford, CT (city/town) Fairfield County	131	0.11
Oyster Bay, NY (town) Nassau County	131	0.04
Newport News, VA (ind. city) Newport News independent city	125	0.07
Dallas, TX (city) Dallas County	125	0.01
Lansing, IL (village) Cook County	123	0.44
Phoenix, AZ (city) Maricopa County	123	0.01
Winthrop Town, MA (city) Suffolk County	121	0.70
Annandale, VA (cdp) Fairfax County	121	0.31
Dearborn, MI (city) Wayne County	121	0.12
North Las Vegas, NV (city) Clark County	120	0.06
Greenwich, CT (town) Fairfield County	119	0.20
Alameda, CA (city) Alameda County	119	0.16
Monsey, NY (cdp) Rockland County	118	0.78
Salem, MA (city) Essex County	118	0.29
Lynn, MA (city) Essex County	118	0.13
Southchase, FL (cdp) Orange County	117	0.71
Four Corners, FL (cdp) Lake County	117	0.46
Lemoyne, PA (borough) Cumberland County	116	2.60
Long Branch, NJ (city) Monmouth County	115	0.37
Chula Vista, CA (city) San Diego County	113	0.05
Las Vegas, NV (city) Clark County	112	0.02
Colonie, NY (town) Albany County	111	0.14
South Bradenton, FL (cdp) Manatee County	110	0.50
Yonkers, NY (city) Westchester County	110	0.06
Airmont, NY (village) Rockland County	109	1.29
Rosedale, MD (cdp) Baltimore County	109	0.57
North Attleborough, MA (town) Bristol County	109	0.38
Novato, CA (city) Marin County	108	0.21
Garden Grove, CA (city) Orange County	108	0.06
Spokane, WA (city) Spokane County	108	0.05
Union City, NJ (city) Hudson County	107	0.16

SECTION THREE

Please refer to the Explanation of Data in the front of the book for more detailed information.

Ancestry

Arab: Moroccan

Top 150 Places Sorted by Percent of Total Population

Based on all places, regardless of total population

Place	Population	%
Atlantic Beach, SC (town) Horry County	53	19.00
Maybell, CO (cdp) Moffat County	9	12.00
Fayetteville, PA (cdp) Franklin County	217	6.90
Ponce de Leon, FL (town) Holmes County	29	6.28
Feasterville, PA (cdp) Bucks County	176	5.84
Brunswick, NC (town) Columbus County	43	3.86
Six Mile Run, NJ (cdp) Somerset County	100	2.75
Lemoyne, PA (borough) Cumberland County	116	2.60
Newton, TX (city) Newton County	66	2.54
Northwest Ithaca, NY (cdp) Tompkins County	28	2.43
Devon, PA (cdp) Chester County	34	2.20
Philmont, NY (village) Columbia County	24	2.07
McMillan, MI (township) Ontonagon County	10	2.02
Denmark, ME (town) Oxford County	21	1.94
Flagler Estates, FL (cdp) St. Johns County	55	1.91
Kinross, MI (charter township) Chippewa County	152	1.89
Tupper Lake, NY (village) Franklin County	68	1.77
Mammoth, PA (cdp) Westmoreland County	10	1.73
Hillsborough, NH (cdp) Hillsborough County	45	1.62
Huntington, VA (cdp) Fairfax County	166	1.60
Revere, MA (city) Suffolk County	792	1.58
Wilson's Mills, NC (town) Johnston County	33	1.56
Southwick, MA (town) Hampden County	141	1.50
South Valley Stream, NY (cdp) Nassau County	76	1.44
Greene, PA (township) Franklin County	217	1.36
Beverly Hills, CA (city) Los Angeles County	451	1.33
Poplar Hills, KY (city) Jefferson County	3	1.33
Hana, HI (cdp) Maui County	21	1.31
Airmont, NY (village) Rockland County	109	1.29
Lincolnia, VA (cdp) Fairfax County	264	1.28
Belle Haven, VA (cdp) Fairfax County	83	1.27
Spotsylvania Courthouse, VA (cdp) Spotsylvania County	50	1.26
Brookville, NY (village) Nassau County	43	1.24
Williamsburg, FL (cdp) Orange County	84	1.23
South Pasadena, FL (city) Pinellas County	61	1.21
Bayboro, NC (town) Pamlico County	17	1.21
Wheeler, NY (town) Steuben County	14	1.19
Mount Holly Springs, PA (borough) Cumberland County	23	1.17
Malden, MA (city) Middlesex County	671	1.15
Browndell, TX (city) Jasper County	3	1.15
Maplewood, MO (city) St. Louis County	94	1.14
Seven Corners, VA (cdp) Fairfax County	94	1.13
Tupper Lake, NY (town) Franklin County	68	1.13
Kingstowne, VA (cdp) Fairfax County	162	1.12
Azalea Park, FL (cdp) Orange County	147	1.12
Mechanicville, NY (city) Saratoga County	58	1.12
Gouverneur, NY (village) St. Lawrence County	44	1.10
Esperance, WA (cdp) Snohomish County	37	1.09
Riverside, MO (city) Platte County	32	1.09
Balmville, NY (cdp) Orange County	36	1.08
Lake Success, NY (village) Nassau County	31	1.07
Pentland, MI (township) Luce County	27	1.06
Chelsea, MA (city) Suffolk County	364	1.05
Marion Center, MA (cdp) Plymouth County	12	1.04
Watopa, MN (township) Wabasha County	3	1.04
Mamaroneck, NY (village) Westchester County	188	1.00
Commerce, GA (city) Jackson County	65	1.00
Hamlin, PA (township) McKean County	6	1.00
Somerset, MD (town) Montgomery County	13	0.95
Lakewood, NJ (cdp) Ocean County	466	0.94
Lower Southampton, PA (township) Bucks County	176	0.92
Coldwater, MI (township) Branch County	59	0.92
Pamelia, NY (town) Jefferson County	28	0.92
Columbia Heights, MN (city) Anoka County	175	0.90
Washington Grove, MD (town) Montgomery County	4	0.90
Buenaventura Lakes, FL (cdp) Osceola County	238	0.89
Greenbriar, VA (cdp) Fairfax County	68	0.89
Rollingwood, CA (cdp) Contra Costa County	26	0.89
Merrionette Park, IL (village) Cook County	20	0.89
Gas, KS (city) Allen County	5	0.88
New Chester, WI (town) Adams County	20	0.87
White Stone, VA (town) Lancaster County	3	0.87
Licking, MO (city) Texas County	30	0.85
Somerset, NJ (cdp) Somerset County	187	0.84
Marion, VA (town) Smyth County	50	0.83
Oakton, VA (cdp) Fairfax County	276	0.82
Waxhaw, NC (town) Union County	72	0.82
East Moline, IL (city) Rock Island County	172	0.80
Society Hill, NJ (cdp) Middlesex County	32	0.80
Harrington Park, NJ (borough) Bergen County	37	0.79
Monsey, NY (cdp) Rockland County	118	0.78
Mount Joy, PA (borough) Lancaster County	57	0.78
Gregg, PA (township) Union County	40	0.78
Chippewa Falls, MN (township) Pope County	2	0.78
St. Augustine Beach, FL (city) St. Johns County	46	0.77
Hillsborough, NH (town) Hillsborough County	45	0.77
Clio, AL (city) Barbour County	18	0.77
Aventura, FL (city) Miami-Dade County	256	0.76
Lindenhurst, NY (village) Suffolk County	209	0.76
Sharon Hill, PA (borough) Delaware County	43	0.76
Stafford Courthouse, VA (cdp) Stafford County	31	0.76
Pea Ridge, FL (cdp) Santa Rosa County	30	0.76
Waitsburg, WA (city) Walla Walla County	9	0.75
Russell Gardens, NY (village) Nassau County	7	0.73
Manalapan, FL (town) Palm Beach County	2	0.73
Moriah, NY (town) Essex County	35	0.72
Niwot, CO (cdp) Boulder County	28	0.72
Franconia, VA (cdp) Fairfax County	131	0.71
Southchase, FL (cdp) Orange County	117	0.71
Farmingdale, NY (village) Nassau County	58	0.71
Winthrop Town, MA (city) Suffolk County	121	0.70
Trexlertown, PA (cdp) Lehigh County	13	0.70
Battlefield, MO (city) Greene County	35	0.69
Siloam Springs, AR (city) Benton County	97	0.68
Helena, OK (town) Alfalfa County	11	0.68
Blountville, TN (cdp) Sullivan County	22	0.66
Dublin, PA (borough) Bucks County	15	0.66
Mamaroneck, NY (town) Westchester County	188	0.65
Butler, PA (township) Schuylkill County	34	0.65
Bay Pines, FL (cdp) Pinellas County	19	0.65
Sharpsburg, NC (town) Nash County	14	0.65
Fircrest, WA (city) Pierce County	40	0.63
Rossville, MD (cdp) Baltimore County	93	0.62
Gouverneur, NY (town) St. Lawrence County	44	0.62
Groesbeck, TX (city) Limestone County	27	0.62
Ellsworth, KS (city) Ellsworth County	19	0.62
Lakewood, NJ (township) Ocean County	532	0.61
Bay Hill, FL (cdp) Orange County	32	0.61
Tipton, MO (city) Moniteau County	20	0.61
Ionia, MI (city) Ionia County	72	0.60
Mount Kisco, NY (town/village) Westchester County	64	0.60
Lafayette, PA (township) McKean County	15	0.60
North Arlington, NJ (borough) Bergen County	90	0.59
Brainerd, MN (city) Crow Wing County	81	0.59
Dunn Loring, VA (cdp) Fairfax County	55	0.59
Edgecliff Village, TX (town) Tarrant County	16	0.59
Knightsen, CA (cdp) Contra Costa County	9	0.58
Swede Grove, MN (township) Meeker County	2	0.58
Rosedale, MD (cdp) Baltimore County	109	0.57
Ross, PA (township) Monroe County	34	0.57
Greenwich, PA (township) Berks County	21	0.57
Tysons Corner, VA (cdp) Fairfax County	95	0.56
Baywood, NY (cdp) Suffolk County	44	0.56
Rocky Mount, VA (town) Franklin County	27	0.56
Rush City, MN (city) Chisago County	17	0.56
Bee Ridge, FL (cdp) Sarasota County	55	0.55
Paradise Valley, AZ (town) Maricopa County	71	0.54
Viola, NY (cdp) Rockland County	38	0.54
Kelly, PA (township) Union County	29	0.54
South Amherst, OH (village) Lorain County	10	0.54
Kissimmee, FL (city) Osceola County	312	0.53
Everett, MA (city) Middlesex County	216	0.53
St. Louis, MI (city) Gratiot County	39	0.53
Cheraw, SC (town) Chesterfield County	31	0.53
Copake, NY (town) Columbia County	19	0.53
Prospect Heights, IL (city) Cook County	85	0.52
Ventnor City, NJ (city) Atlantic County	58	0.52
Riverside, MD (cdp) Harford County	34	0.52
Maugansville, MD (cdp) Washington County	16	0.52
Quincy, MA (city) Norfolk County	465	0.51

Please refer to the Explanation of Data in the front of the book for more detailed information.

Ancestry

Arab: Moroccan

Top 150 Places Sorted by Percent of Total Population

Based on places with total population of 7,500 or more

Place	Population	%
Kinross, MI (charter township) Chippewa County	152	1.89
Huntington, VA (cdp) Fairfax County	166	1.60
Revere, MA (city) Suffolk County	792	1.58
Southwick, MA (town) Hampden County	141	1.50
Greene, PA (township) Franklin County	217	1.36
Beverly Hills, CA (city) Los Angeles County	451	1.33
Airmont, NY (village) Rockland County	109	1.29
Lincolnia, VA (cdp) Fairfax County	264	1.28
Malden, MA (city) Middlesex County	671	1.15
Maplewood, MO (city) St. Louis County	94	1.14
Seven Corners, VA (cdp) Fairfax County	94	1.13
Kingstowne, VA (cdp) Fairfax County	162	1.12
Azalea Park, FL (cdp) Orange County	147	1.12
Chelsea, MA (city) Suffolk County	364	1.05
Mamaroneck, NY (village) Westchester County	188	1.00
Lakewood, NJ (cdp) Ocean County	466	0.94
Lower Southampton, PA (township) Bucks County	176	0.92
Columbia Heights, MN (city) Anoka County	175	0.90
Buenaventura Lakes, FL (cdp) Osceola County	238	0.89
Greenbriar, VA (cdp) Fairfax County	68	0.89
Somerset, NJ (cdp) Somerset County	187	0.84
Oakton, VA (cdp) Fairfax County	276	0.82
Waxhaw, NC (town) Union County	72	0.82
East Moline, IL (city) Rock Island County	172	0.80
Monsey, NY (cdp) Rockland County	118	0.78
Aventura, FL (city) Miami-Dade County	256	0.76
Lindenhurst, NY (village) Suffolk County	209	0.76
Franconia, VA (cdp) Fairfax County	131	0.71
Southchase, FL (cdp) Orange County	117	0.71
Farmingdale, NY (village) Nassau County	58	0.71
Winthrop Town, MA (city) Suffolk County	121	0.70
Siloam Springs, AR (city) Benton County	97	0.68
Mamaroneck, NY (town) Westchester County	188	0.65
Rossville, MD (cdp) Baltimore County	93	0.62
Lakewood, NJ (township) Ocean County	532	0.61
Ionia, MI (city) Ionia County	72	0.60
Mount Kisco, NY (town/village) Westchester County	64	0.60
North Arlington, NJ (borough) Bergen County	90	0.59
Brainerd, MN (city) Crow Wing County	81	0.59
Dunn Loring, VA (cdp) Fairfax County	55	0.59
Rosedale, MD (cdp) Baltimore County	109	0.57
Tysons Corner, VA (cdp) Fairfax County	95	0.56
Baywood, NY (cdp) Suffolk County	44	0.56
Bee Ridge, FL (cdp) Sarasota County	55	0.55
Paradise Valley, AZ (town) Maricopa County	71	0.54
Kissimmee, FL (city) Osceola County	312	0.53
Everett, MA (city) Middlesex County	216	0.53
Prospect Heights, IL (city) Cook County	85	0.52
Ventnor City, NJ (city) Atlantic County	58	0.52
Quincy, MA (city) Norfolk County	465	0.51
Carrollwood, FL (cdp) Hillsborough County	173	0.50
Westmont, CA (cdp) Los Angeles County	155	0.50
South Bradenton, FL (cdp) Manatee County	110	0.50
Franklin, NJ (township) Somerset County	298	0.49
Vestavia Hills, AL (city) Jefferson County	163	0.49
Melrose, MA (city) Middlesex County	132	0.49
Hickory Hills, IL (city) Cook County	69	0.49
Highland Park, NJ (borough) Middlesex County	68	0.49
Greentree, NJ (cdp) Camden County	56	0.49
Hamilton, PA (township) Monroe County	43	0.47
Huntington Station, NY (cdp) Suffolk County	146	0.46
Four Corners, FL (cdp) Lake County	117	0.46
Oak Brook, IL (village) DuPage County	36	0.46
Potomac, MD (cdp) Montgomery County	202	0.45
Burke, VA (cdp) Fairfax County	186	0.45
Westborough, MA (town) Worcester County	83	0.45
Merrifield, VA (cdp) Fairfax County	64	0.45
Hastings-on-Hudson, NY (village) Westchester County	35	0.45
Lansing, IL (village) Cook County	123	0.44
Park Forest Village, PA (cdp) Centre County	43	0.43
Teaneck, NJ (township) Bergen County	167	0.42
Brighton, NY (cdp/town) Monroe County	154	0.42
Helena, AL (city) Shelby County	65	0.42
West University Place, TX (city) Harris County	62	0.42
Windham, NH (town) Rockingham County	55	0.42
Aurora, OH (city) Portage County	63	0.41
North Middleton, PA (township) Cumberland County	45	0.41
South Laurel, MD (cdp) Prince George's County	102	0.40
Bridgeview, IL (village) Cook County	65	0.40
Harrison, NJ (town) Hudson County	54	0.40
Echelon, NJ (cdp) Camden County	39	0.39
North Miami Beach, FL (city) Miami-Dade County	158	0.38
Belleville, NJ (township) Essex County	137	0.38
North Attleborough, MA (town) Bristol County	109	0.38
Ansonia, CT (city/town) New Haven County	72	0.38
Fort Drum, NY (cdp) Jefferson County	47	0.38
Long Branch, NJ (city) Monmouth County	115	0.37
Cherry Hill Mall, NJ (cdp) Camden County	52	0.37
North Kensington, MD (cdp) Montgomery County	36	0.37
Ellisville, MO (city) St. Louis County	34	0.37
Dale City, VA (cdp) Prince William County	224	0.35
Old Bridge, NJ (cdp) Middlesex County	82	0.35
Spring Lake, NC (town) Cumberland County	41	0.35
Westview, FL (cdp) Miami-Dade County	33	0.35
Orlando, FL (city) Orange County	792	0.34
North Bellmore, NY (cdp) Nassau County	67	0.34
Hawaiian Gardens, CA (city) Los Angeles County	49	0.34
Silverton, OR (city) Marion County	30	0.34
Swatara, PA (township) Dauphin County	77	0.33
Scarsdale, NY (town/village) Westchester County	56	0.33
Kemp Mill, MD (cdp) Montgomery County	40	0.33
Tittabawassee, MI (township) Saginaw County	31	0.33
Medford, MA (city) Middlesex County	176	0.32
Pleasant Hill, CA (city) Contra Costa County	104	0.32
University, FL (cdp) Orange County	68	0.32
Easttown, PA (township) Chester County	34	0.32
Glocester, RI (town) Providence County	31	0.32
Annandale, VA (cdp) Fairfax County	121	0.31
Maynard, MA (cdp/town) Middlesex County	31	0.31
Lansdowne, VA (cdp) Loudoun County	30	0.31
Blackman, MI (charter township) Jackson County	72	0.30
Bailey's Crossroads, VA (cdp) Fairfax County	63	0.30
Englewood, OH (city) Montgomery County	39	0.30
Lapeer, MI (city) Lapeer County	27	0.30
Closter, NJ (borough) Bergen County	25	0.30
Jersey City, NJ (city) Hudson County	716	0.29
Palo Alto, CA (city) Santa Clara County	181	0.29
Salem, MA (city) Essex County	118	0.29
Reisterstown, MD (cdp) Baltimore County	77	0.29
Newtown, PA (township) Bucks County	56	0.29
Bexley, OH (city) Franklin County	38	0.29
Guttenberg, NJ (town) Hudson County	32	0.29
Sutton, MA (town) Worcester County	26	0.29
Springdale, NJ (cdp) Camden County	41	0.28
Forest City, FL (cdp) Seminole County	39	0.28
River Grove, IL (village) Cook County	29	0.28
Lenox, MI (township) Macomb County	28	0.28
Mill Creek, WA (city) Snohomish County	48	0.27
Pine Castle, FL (cdp) Orange County	29	0.27
Boonton, NJ (town) Morris County	23	0.27
Palmetto Bay, FL (village) Miami-Dade County	62	0.26
Chestnuthill, PA (township) Monroe County	45	0.26
Abington, MA (cdp/town) Plymouth County	41	0.26
Madison, NJ (borough) Morris County	41	0.26
Pacific Grove, CA (city) Monterey County	39	0.26
Piedmont, CA (city) Alameda County	27	0.26
Alexandria, VA (ind. city) Alexandria independent city	337	0.25
Oak Lawn, IL (village) Cook County	137	0.25
Radnor, PA (township) Delaware County	79	0.25
Ferguson, PA (township) Centre County	43	0.25
Hinsdale, IL (village) DuPage County	41	0.25
Farmington, MO (city) St. Francois County	40	0.25
Upper Southampton, PA (township) Bucks County	39	0.25
Hybla Valley, VA (cdp) Fairfax County	36	0.25
Dranesville, VA (cdp) Fairfax County	31	0.25
Cary, NC (town) Wake County	301	0.24
Ramapo, NY (town) Rockland County	291	0.24
Richardson, TX (city) Dallas County	231	0.24
Harvey, IL (city) Cook County	61	0.24
Milford, MA (cdp) Worcester County	60	0.24

Please refer to the Explanation of Data in the front of the book for more detailed information.

Ancestry

Arab: Palestinian

U.S. and 50 States Sorted by Population and Percent of Total Population

Place	Population	%
United States	**83,241**	**0.03**
California	18,442	0.05
Illinois	9,810	0.08
Texas	6,557	0.03
Florida	5,557	0.03
New York	5,501	0.03
Ohio	4,705	0.04
New Jersey	4,613	0.05
Michigan	4,576	0.05
Virginia	2,371	0.03
Pennsylvania	1,727	0.01
North Carolina	1,551	0.02
Maryland	1,434	0.03
Wisconsin	1,297	0.02
Tennessee	1,278	0.02
Minnesota	1,135	0.02
Washington	1,132	0.02
Georgia	986	0.01
Massachusetts	929	0.01
Indiana	885	0.01
Louisiana	872	0.02
Arizona	851	0.01
Missouri	744	0.01
Oregon	702	0.02
Colorado	653	0.01
Alabama	584	0.01
Kentucky	576	0.01
Oklahoma	485	0.01
Connecticut	379	0.01
Utah	357	0.01
South Carolina	320	0.01
Nevada	301	0.01
District of Columbia	261	0.04
Mississippi	258	0.01
Kansas	245	0.01
Arkansas	212	0.01
Iowa	206	0.01
Nebraska	133	0.01
Delaware	125	0.01
New Mexico	114	0.01
Alaska	54	0.01
Rhode Island	49	<0.01
Maine	44	<0.01
West Virginia	44	<0.01
Hawaii	36	<0.01
Idaho	36	<0.01
Vermont	33	0.01
Montana	33	<0.01
Wyoming	22	<0.01
New Hampshire	16	<0.01
South Dakota	10	<0.01
North Dakota	0	0.00

Place	Population	%
Illinois	9,810	0.08
California	18,442	0.05
New Jersey	4,613	0.05
Michigan	4,576	0.05
Ohio	4,705	0.04
District of Columbia	261	0.04
United States	**83,241**	**0.03**
Texas	6,557	0.03
Florida	5,557	0.03
New York	5,501	0.03
Virginia	2,371	0.03
Maryland	1,434	0.03
North Carolina	1,551	0.02
Wisconsin	1,297	0.02
Tennessee	1,278	0.02
Minnesota	1,135	0.02
Washington	1,132	0.02
Louisiana	872	0.02
Oregon	702	0.02
Pennsylvania	1,727	0.01
Georgia	986	0.01
Massachusetts	929	0.01
Indiana	885	0.01
Arizona	851	0.01
Missouri	744	0.01
Colorado	653	0.01
Alabama	584	0.01
Kentucky	576	0.01
Oklahoma	485	0.01
Connecticut	379	0.01
Utah	357	0.01
South Carolina	320	0.01
Nevada	301	0.01
Mississippi	258	0.01
Kansas	245	0.01
Arkansas	212	0.01
Iowa	206	0.01
Nebraska	133	0.01
Delaware	125	0.01
New Mexico	114	0.01
Alaska	54	0.01
Vermont	33	0.01
Rhode Island	49	<0.01
Maine	44	<0.01
West Virginia	44	<0.01
Hawaii	36	<0.01
Idaho	36	<0.01
Montana	33	<0.01
Wyoming	22	<0.01
New Hampshire	16	<0.01
South Dakota	10	<0.01
North Dakota	0	0.00

Please refer to the Explanation of Data in the front of the book for more detailed information.

Ancestry

Arab: Palestinian

Top 150 Places Sorted by Population

Based on all places, regardless of total population

Place	Population	%
New York, NY (city) Kings County	3,421	0.04
Chicago, IL (city) Cook County	2,219	0.08
Brooklyn, NY (borough) Kings County	1,482	0.06
Houston, TX (city) Harris County	949	0.05
Los Angeles, CA (city) Los Angeles County	947	0.03
San Diego, CA (city) San Diego County	828	0.06
Manhattan, NY (borough) New York County	794	0.05
Dearborn, MI (city) Wayne County	792	0.80
Oak Lawn, IL (village) Cook County	739	1.32
San Francisco, CA (city) San Francisco County	705	0.09
San Bernardino, CA (city) San Bernardino County	670	0.32
Queens, NY (borough) Queens County	638	0.03
Philadelphia, PA (city) Philadelphia County	621	0.04
Burbank, IL (city) Cook County	620	2.18
Jacksonville, FL (city) Duval County	616	0.08
Columbus, OH (city) Franklin County	604	0.08
Chicago Ridge, IL (village) Cook County	598	4.23
San Jose, CA (city) Santa Clara County	587	0.06
Orland Park, IL (village) Cook County	563	1.02
Daly City, CA (city) San Mateo County	555	0.56
Cleveland, OH (city) Cuyahoga County	553	0.14
Richmond, CA (city) Contra Costa County	539	0.53
Milwaukee, WI (city) Milwaukee County	507	0.09
Dallas, TX (city) Dallas County	500	0.04
Staten Island, NY (borough) Richmond County	479	0.10
Wayne, NJ (township) Passaic County	476	0.88
San Bruno, CA (city) San Mateo County	471	1.17
Lodi, CA (city) San Joaquin County	464	0.75
North Bergen, NJ (township) Hudson County	422	0.71
San Antonio, TX (city) Medina County	413	0.03
Ann Arbor, MI (city) Washtenaw County	410	0.36
Pembroke Pines, FL (city) Broward County	404	0.27
Elk Grove, CA (city) Sacramento County	396	0.28
Fremont, CA (city) Alameda County	391	0.19
Clifton, NJ (city) Passaic County	356	0.43
Pittsfield, MI (charter township) Washtenaw County	336	0.99
Naperville, IL (city) DuPage County	336	0.24
North Olmsted, OH (city) Cuyahoga County	331	1.01
Palos Hills, IL (city) Cook County	330	1.90
Paterson, NJ (city) Passaic County	323	0.22
South San Francisco, CA (city) San Mateo County	320	0.52
Schererville, IN (town) Lake County	293	1.03
Fairview, NJ (borough) Bergen County	291	2.13
Brooklyn Park, MN (city) Hennepin County	290	0.39
Bridgeview, IL (village) Cook County	284	1.76
Orland, CA (city) Glenn County	282	3.95
Hickory Hills, IL (city) Cook County	274	1.96
Modesto, CA (city) Stanislaus County	270	0.13
San Mateo, CA (city) San Mateo County	265	0.28
Lexington-Fayette, KY (cons. govt) Fayette County	263	0.09
Aspen Hill, MD (cdp) Montgomery County	261	0.56
Washington, DC (city) District of Columbia	261	0.04
Moreno Valley, CA (city) Riverside County	259	0.14
Canton, MI (charter township) Wayne County	255	0.29
Worth, IL (village) Cook County	249	2.33
Tucson, AZ (city) Pima County	240	0.05
Olive Branch, MS (city) DeSoto County	237	0.74
Tulsa, OK (city) Tulsa County	230	0.06
Antioch, CA (city) Contra Costa County	229	0.23
Spring Valley Lake, CA (cdp) San Bernardino County	227	2.97
Fairfield, CA (city) Solano County	226	0.22
Anaheim, CA (city) Orange County	226	0.07
Memphis, TN (city) Shelby County	224	0.03
Rocky Mount, NC (city) Nash County	222	0.38
Livonia, MI (city) Wayne County	220	0.22
Tamarac, FL (city) Broward County	218	0.36
Kansas City, MO (city) Jackson County	217	0.05
Sugar Land, TX (city) Fort Bend County	216	0.28
Santa Ana, CA (city) Orange County	216	0.07
Toledo, OH (city) Lucas County	216	0.07
Cliffside Park, NJ (borough) Bergen County	215	0.92
Macedonia, OH (city) Summit County	213	1.96
Strongsville, OH (city) Cuyahoga County	211	0.48
Worcester, MA (city) Worcester County	206	0.11
Nashville-Davidson, TN (metro govt) Davidson County	206	0.04
Terrytown, LA (cdp) Jefferson Parish	205	0.91
Ogden, UT (city) Weber County	204	0.25
Ravena, NY (village) Albany County	200	6.03
Coeymans, NY (town) Albany County	200	2.63
Galt, CA (city) Sacramento County	200	0.87
Tallmadge, OH (city) Summit County	199	1.15
Mesquite, TX (city) Dallas County	198	0.15
Dearborn Heights, MI (city) Wayne County	196	0.34
Portland, OR (city) Multnomah County	196	0.03
Corona, CA (city) Riverside County	195	0.13
Mountain View, CA (city) Santa Clara County	193	0.27
Richardson, TX (city) Dallas County	191	0.20
Poughkeepsie, NY (town) Dutchess County	183	0.42
Austin, TX (city) Travis County	182	0.02
Belle Glade, FL (city) Palm Beach County	180	1.02
Orland Hills, IL (village) Cook County	178	2.54
Virginia Beach, VA (ind. city) Virginia Beach independent city	177	0.04
Chino Hills, CA (city) San Bernardino County	175	0.24
Scottsdale, AZ (city) Maricopa County	175	0.08
Lumberton, NC (city) Robeson County	174	0.81
Phoenix, AZ (city) Maricopa County	174	0.01
Dalton, GA (city) Whitfield County	173	0.53
Elizabeth, NJ (city) Union County	170	0.14
Fresno, CA (city) Fresno County	170	0.04
Rosemount, MN (city) Dakota County	169	0.82
Germantown, MD (cdp) Montgomery County	169	0.20
Rancho Cucamonga, CA (city) San Bernardino County	168	0.10
Islip, NY (town) Suffolk County	166	0.05
Hayward, CA (city) Alameda County	165	0.12
Bakersfield, CA (city) Kern County	165	0.05
Seattle, WA (city) King County	162	0.03
Sacramento, CA (city) Sacramento County	159	0.03
Crandon Lakes, NJ (cdp) Sussex County	158	12.23
Stillwater, NJ (township) Sussex County	158	3.78
Little Falls, NJ (township) Passaic County	154	1.11
Rialto, CA (city) San Bernardino County	153	0.15
Fort Worth, TX (city) Tarrant County	153	0.02
Allen, TX (city) Collin County	152	0.20
Reston, VA (cdp) Fairfax County	151	0.28
North Arlington, NJ (borough) Bergen County	150	0.98
Louisville-Jefferson County, KY (metro govt) Jefferson County	149	0.03
Plant City, FL (city) Hillsborough County	147	0.43
Elmwood Park, IL (village) Cook County	145	0.59
Westlake, OH (city) Cuyahoga County	145	0.45
Bell, CA (city) Los Angeles County	144	0.40
Hazel Dell, WA (cdp) Clark County	142	0.74
Wheaton, MD (cdp) Montgomery County	142	0.32
Bartlett, TN (city) Shelby County	142	0.27
Tallahassee, FL (city) Leon County	142	0.08
Temple Terrace, FL (city) Hillsborough County	139	0.57
Suisun City, CA (city) Solano County	139	0.50
Yonkers, NY (city) Westchester County	139	0.07
Garden City, MI (city) Wayne County	138	0.49
Colorado Springs, CO (city) El Paso County	138	0.03
Oakland, CA (city) Alameda County	137	0.04
Perth Amboy, NJ (city) Middlesex County	136	0.27
Alameda, CA (city) Alameda County	136	0.19
Grand Blanc, MI (charter township) Genesee County	134	0.37
Alsip, IL (village) Cook County	132	0.69
Detroit, MI (city) Wayne County	132	0.02
Vestavia Hills, AL (city) Jefferson County	131	0.39
Fontana, CA (city) San Bernardino County	131	0.07
Blaine, MN (city) Anoka County	128	0.23
White Horse, NJ (cdp) Mercer County	127	1.39
Hercules, CA (city) Contra Costa County	127	0.55
Hamilton, NJ (township) Mercer County	127	0.14
Chowchilla, CA (city) Madera County	126	0.70
San Lorenzo, CA (cdp) Alameda County	125	0.53
Pacifica, CA (city) San Mateo County	125	0.34
Santa Clarita, CA (city) Los Angeles County	125	0.07
Rowlett, TX (city) Dallas County	124	0.23
Oak Creek, WI (city) Milwaukee County	123	0.37
Springfield, MA (city) Hampden County	123	0.08
Alexandria, VA (ind. city) Alexandria independent city	122	0.09
Charlotte, NC (city) Mecklenburg County	122	0.02

Ancestry

Arab: Palestinian

Top 150 Places Sorted by Percent of Total Population

Based on all places, regardless of total population

Place	Population	%
McCoy, CO (cdp) Eagle County	13	56.52
Crandon Lakes, NJ (cdp) Sussex County	158	12.23
Georgetown, MN (township) Clay County	14	8.28
Ravena, NY (village) Albany County	200	6.03
Chicago Ridge, IL (village) Cook County	598	4.23
Orland, CA (city) Glenn County	282	3.95
Stillwater, NJ (township) Sussex County	158	3.78
Miles, PA (township) Centre County	56	3.66
Crown Point, NY (town) Essex County	70	3.38
Spring Valley Lake, CA (cdp) San Bernardino County	227	2.97
Rosemont, IL (village) Cook County	117	2.94
Lowellville, OH (village) Mahoning County	33	2.86
Riverdale, NJ (borough) Morris County	93	2.76
Paragon Estates, CO (cdp) Boulder County	28	2.68
Coeymans, NY (town) Albany County	200	2.63
Orland Hills, IL (village) Cook County	178	2.54
Kingston, NJ (cdp) Middlesex County	47	2.37
Worth, IL (village) Cook County	249	2.33
Salem Heights, OH (cdp) Hamilton County	90	2.26
Pingree Grove, IL (village) Kane County	83	2.20
Burbank, IL (city) Cook County	620	2.18
Fairview, NJ (borough) Bergen County	291	2.13
Hickory Hills, IL (city) Cook County	274	1.96
Macedonia, OH (city) Summit County	213	1.96
Elkhart, IL (village) Logan County	7	1.92
Palos Hills, IL (city) Cook County	330	1.90
Huber Ridge, OH (cdp) Franklin County	83	1.86
Chouteau, OK (town) Mayes County	42	1.85
Bridgeview, IL (village) Cook County	284	1.76
San Leanna, TX (village) Travis County	10	1.66
Embarrass, WI (village) Waupaca County	6	1.65
Villa Park, CA (city) Orange County	95	1.63
Penryn, CA (cdp) Placer County	12	1.60
South Canaan, PA (township) Wayne County	28	1.58
Larch Way, WA (cdp) Snohomish County	55	1.54
Skyland Estates, VA (cdp) Warren County	12	1.54
Ann Arbor, MI (charter township) Washtenaw County	65	1.48
Lake of the Woods, IL (cdp) Champaign County	44	1.44
Van Etten, NY (town) Chemung County	18	1.43
White Horse, NJ (cdp) Mercer County	127	1.39
Haverford College, PA (cdp) Delaware County	16	1.39
Oak Lawn, IL (village) Cook County	739	1.32
Melville, RI (cdp) Newport County	26	1.30
Roslyn, NY (village) Nassau County	35	1.28
Ballard, UT (town) Uintah County	7	1.25
Lapeer, MI (township) Lapeer County	63	1.22
Sandy Lake, PA (township) Mercer County	16	1.20
Arlington Heights, PA (cdp) Monroe County	76	1.19
Stuyvesant, NY (town) Columbia County	24	1.19
San Bruno, CA (city) San Mateo County	471	1.17
Osage, IA (city) Mitchell County	42	1.17
Tallmadge, OH (city) Summit County	199	1.15
Ullin, IL (village) Pulaski County	7	1.13
Little Falls, NJ (township) Passaic County	154	1.11
Lasara, TX (cdp) Willacy County	9	1.10
Blakely, GA (city) Early County	56	1.08
St. Anthony, MN (city) Hennepin County	56	1.08
Oakfield, NY (village) Genesee County	22	1.07
Lompico, CA (cdp) Santa Cruz County	11	1.06
Schererville, IN (town) Lake County	293	1.03
Orland Park, IL (village) Cook County	563	1.02
Belle Glade, FL (city) Palm Beach County	180	1.02
Oak Grove, KY (city) Christian County	74	1.02
North Olmsted, OH (city) Cuyahoga County	331	1.01
Pittsfield, MI (charter township) Washtenaw County	336	0.99
North Arlington, NJ (borough) Bergen County	150	0.98
Seneca, SC (city) Oconee County	78	0.97
Minden, NV (cdp) Douglas County	29	0.96
Timberlane, LA (cdp) Jefferson Parish	91	0.94
Cliffside Park, NJ (borough) Bergen County	215	0.92
Terrytown, LA (cdp) Jefferson Parish	205	0.91
Wayne, NJ (township) Passaic County	476	0.88
Boyne City, MI (city) Charlevoix County	33	0.88
Galt, CA (city) Sacramento County	200	0.87
Silver Creek, NY (village) Chautauqua County	23	0.86
Justice, IL (village) Cook County	107	0.85
Fox Run, PA (cdp) Butler County	29	0.84
Doctor Phillips, FL (cdp) Orange County	93	0.83
New Albany, OH (village) Franklin County	59	0.83
Theodore, AL (cdp) Mobile County	51	0.83
Rosemount, MN (city) Dakota County	169	0.82
Salmon, ID (city) Lemhi County	26	0.82
Lumberton, NC (city) Robeson County	174	0.81
Milan, TN (city) Gibson County	63	0.81
Lower Grand Lagoon, FL (cdp) Bay County	40	0.81
Dearborn, MI (city) Wayne County	792	0.80
Hillsborough, CA (town) San Mateo County	84	0.79
Beloit, WI (town) Rock County	59	0.78
Sylvan, MI (township) Washtenaw County	22	0.78
Lodi, CA (city) San Joaquin County	464	0.75
Raleigh Hills, OR (cdp) Washington County	50	0.75
Olive Branch, MS (city) DeSoto County	237	0.74
Hazel Dell, WA (cdp) Clark County	142	0.74
Morada, CA (cdp) San Joaquin County	36	0.74
Indian Springs Village, AL (city) Shelby County	18	0.73
Lake Barrington, IL (village) Lake County	35	0.72
North Bergen, NJ (township) Hudson County	422	0.71
Channahon, IL (village) Will County	87	0.71
Tyrone, MI (township) Livingston County	71	0.71
Farmingdale, NY (village) Nassau County	58	0.71
Chowchilla, CA (city) Madera County	126	0.70
Atlas, MI (township) Genesee County	56	0.70
Bear Creek, TX (village) Hays County	3	0.70
Sorrento, ME (town) Hancock County	2	0.70
Alsip, IL (village) Cook County	132	0.69
Wallington, NJ (borough) Bergen County	78	0.69
St. Anthony, MN (city) Hennepin and Ramsey Counties	56	0.69
Bethany, WV (town) Brooke County	5	0.69
Oakfield, NY (town) Genesee County	22	0.68
Plandome Heights, NY (village) Nassau County	7	0.66
Milford, TX (town) Ellis County	4	0.66
Coto de Caza, CA (cdp) Orange County	97	0.63
Grand Terrace, CA (city) San Bernardino County	76	0.63
Prospect Park, NJ (borough) Passaic County	37	0.63
Garyville, LA (cdp) St. John the Baptist Parish	17	0.63
Hayes, MI (township) Charlevoix County	12	0.63
Hamilton, PA (township) Monroe County	57	0.62
Buzzards Bay, MA (cdp) Barnstable County	23	0.62
Bingham, MI (township) Leelanau County	16	0.62
Farmington, MS (town) Alcorn County	16	0.62
Countryside, VA (cdp) Loudoun County	58	0.61
New Paltz, NY (village) Ulster County	41	0.61
Norwood, NC (town) Stanly County	13	0.61
Brookfield, IL (village) Cook County	112	0.60
Laurel Springs, NJ (borough) Camden County	13	0.60
Elmwood Park, IL (village) Cook County	145	0.59
Bound Brook, NJ (borough) Somerset County	61	0.59
Southside Place, TX (city) Harris County	10	0.59
West Amwell, NJ (township) Hunterdon County	21	0.58
Temple Terrace, FL (city) Hillsborough County	139	0.57
Daly City, CA (city) San Mateo County	555	0.56
Aspen Hill, MD (cdp) Montgomery County	261	0.56
Fairview Park, OH (city) Cuyahoga County	94	0.56
Northlake, SC (cdp) Anderson County	20	0.56
Lafayette, PA (township) McKean County	14	0.56
Hercules, CA (city) Contra Costa County	127	0.55
Bull Mountain, OR (cdp) Washington County	50	0.55
Lyons, IL (village) Cook County	57	0.54
Clifton Heights, PA (borough) Delaware County	36	0.54
Richmond, CA (city) Contra Costa County	539	0.53
Dalton, GA (city) Whitfield County	173	0.53
San Lorenzo, CA (cdp) Alameda County	125	0.53
Millbrae, CA (city) San Mateo County	112	0.53
Dinuba, CA (city) Tulare County	110	0.53
South San Francisco, CA (city) San Mateo County	320	0.52
Milwaukie, OR (city) Clackamas County	107	0.52
Miamisburg, OH (city) Montgomery County	104	0.52
Harwood Heights, IL (village) Cook County	44	0.52
Pepper Pike, OH (city) Cuyahoga County	31	0.52
Cetronia, PA (cdp) Lehigh County	10	0.51

Ancestry

Arab: Palestinian

Top 150 Places Sorted by Percent of Total Population

Based on places with total population of 7,500 or more

Place	Population	%
Chicago Ridge, IL (village) Cook County	598	4.23
Spring Valley Lake, CA (cdp) San Bernardino County	227	2.97
Coeymans, NY (town) Albany County	200	2.63
Worth, IL (village) Cook County	249	2.33
Burbank, IL (city) Cook County	620	2.18
Fairview, NJ (borough) Bergen County	291	2.13
Hickory Hills, IL (city) Cook County	274	1.96
Macedonia, OH (city) Summit County	213	1.96
Palos Hills, IL (city) Cook County	330	1.90
Bridgeview, IL (village) Cook County	284	1.76
White Horse, NJ (cdp) Mercer County	127	1.39
Oak Lawn, IL (village) Cook County	739	1.32
San Bruno, CA (city) San Mateo County	471	1.17
Tallmadge, OH (city) Summit County	199	1.15
Little Falls, NJ (township) Passaic County	154	1.11
Schererville, IN (town) Lake County	293	1.03
Orland Park, IL (village) Cook County	563	1.02
Belle Glade, FL (city) Palm Beach County	180	1.02
North Olmsted, OH (city) Cuyahoga County	331	1.01
Pittsfield, MI (charter township) Washtenaw County	336	0.99
North Arlington, NJ (borough) Bergen County	150	0.98
Seneca, SC (city) Oconee County	78	0.97
Timberlane, LA (cdp) Jefferson Parish	91	0.94
Cliffside Park, NJ (borough) Bergen County	215	0.92
Terrytown, LA (cdp) Jefferson Parish	205	0.91
Wayne, NJ (township) Passaic County	476	0.88
Galt, CA (city) Sacramento County	200	0.87
Justice, IL (village) Cook County	107	0.85
Doctor Phillips, FL (cdp) Orange County	93	0.83
Rosemount, MN (city) Dakota County	169	0.82
Lumberton, NC (city) Robeson County	174	0.81
Milan, TN (city) Gibson County	63	0.81
Dearborn, MI (city) Wayne County	792	0.80
Hillsborough, CA (town) San Mateo County	84	0.79
Beloit, WI (town) Rock County	59	0.78
Lodi, CA (city) San Joaquin County	464	0.75
Olive Branch, MS (city) DeSoto County	237	0.74
Hazel Dell, WA (cdp) Clark County	142	0.74
North Bergen, NJ (township) Hudson County	422	0.71
Channahon, IL (village) Will County	87	0.71
Tyrone, MI (township) Livingston County	71	0.71
Farmingdale, NY (village) Nassau County	58	0.71
Chowchilla, CA (city) Madera County	126	0.70
Atlas, MI (township) Genesee County	56	0.70
Alsip, IL (village) Cook County	132	0.69
Wallington, NJ (borough) Bergen County	78	0.69
St. Anthony, MN (city) Hennepin and Ramsey Counties	56	0.69
Coto de Caza, CA (cdp) Orange County	97	0.63
Grand Terrace, CA (city) San Bernardino County	76	0.63
Hamilton, PA (township) Monroe County	57	0.62
Countryside, VA (cdp) Loudoun County	58	0.61
Brookfield, IL (village) Cook County	112	0.60
Elmwood Park, IL (village) Cook County	145	0.59
Bound Brook, NJ (borough) Somerset County	61	0.59
Temple Terrace, FL (city) Hillsborough County	139	0.57
Daly City, CA (city) San Mateo County	555	0.56
Aspen Hill, MD (cdp) Montgomery County	261	0.56
Fairview Park, OH (city) Cuyahoga County	94	0.56
Hercules, CA (city) Contra Costa County	127	0.55
Bull Mountain, OR (cdp) Washington County	50	0.55
Lyons, IL (village) Cook County	57	0.54
Richmond, CA (city) Contra Costa County	539	0.53
Dalton, GA (city) Whitfield County	173	0.53
San Lorenzo, CA (cdp) Alameda County	125	0.53
Millbrae, CA (city) San Mateo County	112	0.53
Dinuba, CA (city) Tulare County	110	0.53
South San Francisco, CA (city) San Mateo County	320	0.52
Milwaukie, OR (city) Clackamas County	107	0.52
Miamisburg, OH (city) Montgomery County	104	0.52
Harwood Heights, IL (village) Cook County	44	0.52
Suisun City, CA (city) Solano County	139	0.50
Garden City, MI (city) Wayne County	138	0.49
Darien, IL (city) DuPage County	109	0.49
Strongsville, OH (city) Cuyahoga County	211	0.48
Ventnor City, NJ (city) Atlantic County	53	0.48
Homer Glen, IL (village) Will County	114	0.46
Winterville, NC (town) Pitt County	39	0.46
Westlake, OH (city) Cuyahoga County	145	0.45
Washington, MI (township) Macomb County	106	0.44
Clifton, NJ (city) Passaic County	356	0.43
Plant City, FL (city) Hillsborough County	147	0.43
Shenandoah, LA (cdp) East Baton Rouge Parish	79	0.43
Round Lake, IL (village) Lake County	69	0.43
Dunn Loring, VA (cdp) Fairfax County	40	0.43
Emeryville, CA (city) Alameda County	40	0.43
Poughkeepsie, NY (town) Dutchess County	183	0.42
Hamilton, PA (township) Franklin County	44	0.42
Munster, IN (town) Lake County	96	0.41
Stroud, PA (township) Monroe County	76	0.41
Lake Arrowhead, CA (cdp) San Bernardino County	39	0.41
Bell, CA (city) Los Angeles County	144	0.40
Susquehanna, PA (township) Dauphin County	95	0.40
Brooklyn Park, MN (city) Hennepin County	290	0.39
Vestavia Hills, AL (city) Jefferson County	131	0.39
Hampden, PA (township) Cumberland County	106	0.39
Pinecrest, FL (village) Miami-Dade County	72	0.39
Shafter, CA (city) Kern County	64	0.39
Morrisville, NC (town) Wake County	63	0.39
Chalmette, LA (cdp) St. Bernard Parish	48	0.39
Linganore, MD (cdp) Frederick County	32	0.39
Rocky Mount, NC (city) Nash County	222	0.38
Pineville, LA (city) Rapides Parish	55	0.38
Seven Hills, OH (city) Cuyahoga County	45	0.38
Grand Blanc, MI (charter township) Genesee County	134	0.37
Oak Creek, WI (city) Milwaukee County	123	0.37
Mount Olive, NJ (township) Morris County	103	0.37
Lockport, IL (city) Will County	88	0.37
Stuart, FL (city) Martin County	58	0.37
Ann Arbor, MI (city) Washtenaw County	410	0.36
Tamarac, FL (city) Broward County	218	0.36
Punta Gorda, FL (city) Charlotte County	60	0.36
Evans, GA (cdp) Columbia County	98	0.35
New Territory, TX (cdp) Fort Bend County	59	0.35
Dearborn Heights, MI (city) Wayne County	196	0.34
Pacifica, CA (city) San Mateo County	125	0.34
Texas, MI (charter township) Kalamazoo County	48	0.34
Buford, GA (city) Gwinnett County	41	0.34
Little Ferry, NJ (borough) Bergen County	36	0.34
George Mason, VA (cdp) Fairfax County	30	0.34
Greenfield, WI (city) Milwaukee County	120	0.33
Oak Ridge, FL (cdp) Orange County	66	0.33
Middleburg Heights, OH (city) Cuyahoga County	52	0.33
Culpeper, VA (town) Culpeper County	51	0.33
Hunters Creek, FL (cdp) Orange County	47	0.33
Columbia City, IN (city) Whitley County	27	0.33
San Bernardino, CA (city) San Bernardino County	670	0.32
Wheaton, MD (cdp) Montgomery County	142	0.32
New Hope, MN (city) Hennepin County	65	0.32
Frankfort, IL (village) Will County	54	0.32
East Rockaway, NY (village) Nassau County	31	0.32
Annandale, VA (cdp) Fairfax County	120	0.31
Hazel Park, MI (city) Oakland County	52	0.31
St. John, IN (town) Lake County	43	0.31
Pike Creek, DE (cdp) New Castle County	24	0.30
University of California Davis, CA (cdp) Yolo County	23	0.30
Canton, MI (charter township) Wayne County	255	0.29
Sterling, VA (cdp) Loudoun County	73	0.29
Allendale, MI (charter township) Ottawa County	56	0.29
New Paltz, NY (town) Ulster County	41	0.29
Wauconda, IL (village) Lake County	38	0.29
Princeton, NJ (borough) Mercer County	36	0.29
Delavan, WI (city) Walworth County	25	0.29
Elk Grove, CA (city) Sacramento County	396	0.28
San Mateo, CA (city) San Mateo County	265	0.28
Sugar Land, TX (city) Fort Bend County	216	0.28
Reston, VA (cdp) Fairfax County	151	0.28
Weatherford, TX (city) Parker County	68	0.28
Ardmore, OK (city) Carter County	67	0.28
University, FL (cdp) Orange County	60	0.28
Forest Park, OH (city) Hamilton County	53	0.28

Please refer to the Explanation of Data in the front of the book for more detailed information.

Ancestry

Arab: Syrian

U.S. and 50 States Sorted by Population and Percent of Total Population

Place	Population	%
United States	**147,426**	**0.05**
California	19,307	0.05
Pennsylvania	14,843	0.12
New York	14,535	0.08
New Jersey	12,826	0.15
Florida	10,081	0.05
Michigan	8,240	0.08
Texas	7,835	0.03
Massachusetts	6,513	0.10
Ohio	6,042	0.05
Illinois	4,734	0.04
Rhode Island	3,519	0.33
Arizona	2,959	0.05
Virginia	2,769	0.04
Connecticut	2,249	0.06
Indiana	2,104	0.03
Georgia	2,099	0.02
Maryland	2,004	0.04
Washington	1,864	0.03
North Carolina	1,848	0.02
Oregon	1,366	0.04
Louisiana	1,362	0.03
Colorado	1,344	0.03
Missouri	1,200	0.02
Nevada	1,195	0.05
Oklahoma	1,065	0.03
West Virginia	1,035	0.06
Tennessee	1,025	0.02
South Carolina	995	0.02
Wisconsin	950	0.02
New Hampshire	930	0.07
Minnesota	921	0.02
Mississippi	721	0.02
Kentucky	692	0.02
Nebraska	650	0.04
Kansas	632	0.02
Iowa	582	0.02
Alabama	542	0.01
Arkansas	520	0.02
Utah	446	0.02
Maine	435	0.03
New Mexico	373	0.02
North Dakota	336	0.05
Vermont	325	0.05
South Dakota	282	0.04
District of Columbia	251	0.04
Hawaii	216	0.02
Idaho	178	0.01
Montana	160	0.02
Delaware	119	0.01
Alaska	114	0.02
Wyoming	93	0.02

Place	Population	%
Rhode Island	3,519	0.33
New Jersey	12,826	0.15
Pennsylvania	14,843	0.12
Massachusetts	6,513	0.10
New York	14,535	0.08
Michigan	8,240	0.08
New Hampshire	930	0.07
Connecticut	2,249	0.06
West Virginia	1,035	0.06
United States	**147,426**	**0.05**
California	19,307	0.05
Florida	10,081	0.05
Ohio	6,042	0.05
Arizona	2,959	0.05
Nevada	1,195	0.05
North Dakota	336	0.05
Vermont	325	0.05
Illinois	4,734	0.04
Virginia	2,769	0.04
Maryland	2,004	0.04
Oregon	1,366	0.04
Nebraska	650	0.04
South Dakota	282	0.04
District of Columbia	251	0.04
Texas	7,835	0.03
Indiana	2,104	0.03
Washington	1,864	0.03
Louisiana	1,362	0.03
Colorado	1,344	0.03
Oklahoma	1,065	0.03
Maine	435	0.03
Georgia	2,099	0.02
North Carolina	1,848	0.02
Missouri	1,200	0.02
Tennessee	1,025	0.02
South Carolina	995	0.02
Wisconsin	950	0.02
Minnesota	921	0.02
Mississippi	721	0.02
Kentucky	692	0.02
Kansas	632	0.02
Iowa	582	0.02
Arkansas	520	0.02
Utah	446	0.02
New Mexico	373	0.02
Hawaii	216	0.02
Montana	160	0.02
Alaska	114	0.02
Wyoming	93	0.02
Alabama	542	0.01
Idaho	178	0.01
Delaware	119	0.01

Please refer to the Explanation of Data in the front of the book for more detailed information.

Ancestry

Arab: Syrian

Top 150 Places Sorted by Population

Based on all places, regardless of total population

Place	Population	%
New York, NY (city) Kings County	8,198	0.10
Brooklyn, NY (borough) Kings County	5,890	0.24
Los Angeles, CA (city) Los Angeles County	2,954	0.08
Allentown, PA (city) Lehigh County	2,119	1.82
Jacksonville, FL (city) Duval County	1,637	0.20
Manhattan, NY (borough) New York County	1,112	0.07
Chicago, IL (city) Cook County	1,029	0.04
Houston, TX (city) Harris County	988	0.05
San Diego, CA (city) San Diego County	762	0.06
El Paso, TX (city) El Paso County	718	0.11
Whitehall, PA (township) Lehigh County	717	2.71
Wayne, NJ (township) Passaic County	715	1.32
Philadelphia, PA (city) Philadelphia County	637	0.04
Cumberland, RI (town) Providence County	611	1.84
Clifton, NJ (city) Passaic County	601	0.73
Staten Island, NY (borough) Richmond County	584	0.13
Little Falls, NJ (township) Passaic County	577	4.16
Tucson, AZ (city) Pima County	557	0.11
Boston, MA (city) Suffolk County	540	0.09
Lancaster, CA (city) Los Angeles County	536	0.36
Dearborn Heights, MI (city) Wayne County	512	0.88
Hempstead, NY (town) Nassau County	512	0.07
Pittsburgh, PA (city) Allegheny County	499	0.16
Phoenix, AZ (city) Maricopa County	455	0.03
Richardson, TX (city) Dallas County	442	0.45
Pasadena, CA (city) Los Angeles County	428	0.31
West Long Branch, NJ (borough) Monmouth County	427	5.26
Queens, NY (borough) Queens County	420	0.02
Pawtucket, RI (city) Providence County	419	0.58
Columbus, OH (city) Franklin County	415	0.05
Ocean, NJ (township) Monmouth County	410	1.50
Burbank, CA (city) Los Angeles County	409	0.40
Anaheim, CA (city) Orange County	399	0.12
Austin, TX (city) Travis County	384	0.05
Toledo, OH (city) Lucas County	381	0.13
Alexandria, VA (ind. city) Alexandria independent city	379	0.28
Fullerton, PA (cdp) Lehigh County	371	2.46
Fresno, CA (city) Fresno County	363	0.07
New Hartford, NY (town) Oneida County	351	1.60
Irvine, CA (city) Orange County	346	0.17
Glendale, CA (city) Los Angeles County	340	0.18
Paterson, NJ (city) Passaic County	336	0.23
South Whitehall, PA (township) Lehigh County	309	1.62
Dearborn, MI (city) Wayne County	309	0.31
Cranston, RI (city) Providence County	306	0.38
Lincoln, RI (town) Providence County	302	1.43
Arlington, TX (city) Tarrant County	300	0.08
Danbury, CT (city/town) Fairfield County	293	0.37
Totowa, NJ (borough) Passaic County	288	2.72
Glendora, CA (city) Los Angeles County	283	0.57
Orange, CA (city) Orange County	268	0.20
Flint, MI (charter township) Genesee County	267	0.82
Worcester, MA (city) Worcester County	259	0.14
Tulsa, OK (city) Tulsa County	259	0.07
South Hill, WA (cdp) Pierce County	257	0.49
Charlotte, NC (city) Mecklenburg County	254	0.04
Santa Clarita, CA (city) Los Angeles County	252	0.15
San Antonio, TX (city) Medina County	252	0.02
Long Branch, NJ (city) Monmouth County	251	0.81
Charleston, WV (city) Kanawha County	251	0.49
Washington, DC (city) District of Columbia	251	0.04
Lewisville, TX (city) Denton County	250	0.27
Utica, NY (city) Oneida County	248	0.40
Aventura, FL (city) Miami-Dade County	245	0.73
Old Tappan, NJ (borough) Bergen County	243	4.28
Scottsdale, AZ (city) Maricopa County	241	0.11
Indianapolis, IN (city) Marion County	239	0.03
Simi Valley, CA (city) Ventura County	236	0.19
Springfield, IL (city) Sangamon County	235	0.20
Paradise, NV (cdp) Clark County	235	0.11
Portland, OR (city) Multnomah County	235	0.04
Princeton Meadows, NJ (cdp) Middlesex County	233	1.70
Plainsboro, NJ (township) Middlesex County	233	1.04
Albuquerque, NM (city) Bernalillo County	232	0.04
Spring Hill, FL (cdp) Hernando County	231	0.24
West Covina, CA (city) Los Angeles County	231	0.22
Nashville-Davidson, TN (metro govt) Davidson County	230	0.04
Rancho Cucamonga, CA (city) San Bernardino County	225	0.14
Bethlehem, PA (city) Northampton County	224	0.30
Woodland Park, NJ (borough) Passaic County	220	1.90
Brookhaven, NY (town) Suffolk County	220	0.05
Allen Park, MI (city) Wayne County	219	0.77
Hollywood, FL (city) Broward County	217	0.15
Cedar Grove, NJ (township) Essex County	216	1.75
Woonsocket, RI (city) Providence County	213	0.51
Lakewood, OH (city) Cuyahoga County	213	0.40
Upper Darby, PA (township) Delaware County	213	0.26
Olmsted Falls, OH (city) Cuyahoga County	210	2.40
Redlands, CA (city) San Bernardino County	208	0.30
North Providence, RI (town) Providence County	207	0.64
Glendale, AZ (city) Maricopa County	205	0.09
Northampton, PA (borough) Northampton County	198	2.00
Leicester, MA (town) Worcester County	198	1.81
Salisbury, PA (township) Lehigh County	197	1.45
Dorneyville, PA (cdp) Lehigh County	193	4.30
Pembroke Pines, FL (city) Broward County	192	0.13
Dallas, TX (city) Dallas County	192	0.02
Bronx, NY (borough) Bronx County	192	0.01
Bloomfield, MI (charter township) Oakland County	191	0.46
Henderson, NV (city) Clark County	191	0.08
Providence, RI (city) Providence County	190	0.11
Las Vegas, NV (city) Clark County	189	0.03
Sterling Heights, MI (city) Macomb County	187	0.14
Wanaque, NJ (borough) Passaic County	184	1.69
Catalina Foothills, AZ (cdp) Pima County	182	0.35
Parsippany-Troy Hills, NJ (township) Morris County	181	0.34
Queensbury, NY (town) Warren County	180	0.65
Gilbert, AZ (town) Maricopa County	180	0.09
Valley Falls, RI (cdp) Providence County	179	1.55
Mount Lebanon, PA (township) Allegheny County	179	0.55
Spokane, WA (city) Spokane County	177	0.09
Kansas City, MO (city) Jackson County	177	0.04
Shelby, MI (charter township) Macomb County	176	0.24
Chino, CA (city) San Bernardino County	174	0.22
Farmington Hills, MI (city) Oakland County	174	0.22
Hempfield, PA (township) Westmoreland County	173	0.40
Canton, MI (charter township) Wayne County	173	0.20
Baltimore, MD (city) Baltimore city County	173	0.03
Greenwood, MS (city) Leflore County	172	1.08
Ann Arbor, MI (city) Washtenaw County	172	0.15
Omaha, NE (city) Douglas County	172	0.04
Rochester Hills, MI (city) Oakland County	171	0.24
Tampa, FL (city) Hillsborough County	171	0.05
San Jose, CA (city) Santa Clara County	171	0.02
Deal, NJ (borough) Monmouth County	169	16.34
Macomb, MI (township) Macomb County	169	0.23
Freehold, NJ (township) Monmouth County	164	0.46
Canton, OH (city) Stark County	164	0.22
Paramus, NJ (borough) Bergen County	163	0.62
Wilkes-Barre, PA (city) Luzerne County	163	0.39
Provo, UT (city) Utah County	162	0.15
Thousand Oaks, CA (city) Ventura County	162	0.13
Towson, MD (cdp) Baltimore County	160	0.30
Warren, MI (city) Macomb County	160	0.12
Rosedale, CA (cdp) Kern County	159	1.07
San Francisco, CA (city) San Francisco County	159	0.02
Skokie, IL (village) Cook County	158	0.25
Lafayette, LA (city) Lafayette Parish	158	0.13
Lower Burrell, PA (city) Westmoreland County	157	1.32
Seattle, WA (city) King County	157	0.03
Geneva, NY (city) Ontario County	155	1.16
Cleveland, OH (city) Cuyahoga County	155	0.04
Clinton, MI (charter township) Macomb County	154	0.16
North Whitehall, PA (township) Lehigh County	153	0.98
Chelmsford, MA (town) Middlesex County	153	0.46
Torrance, CA (city) Los Angeles County	153	0.11
Chandler, AZ (city) Maricopa County	153	0.07
North Bergen, NJ (township) Hudson County	152	0.26
South Elgin, IL (village) Kane County	151	0.71
Pelham, NH (town) Hillsborough County	150	1.19

Ancestry

Arab: Syrian

Top 150 Places Sorted by Percent of Total Population

Based on all places, regardless of total population

Place	Population	%
Waitsfield, VT (cdp) Washington County	64	33.86
Cambridge, NH (township) Coos County	3	33.33
Claire City, SD (town) Roberts County	24	30.77
Cannondale, CT (cdp) Fairfield County	45	24.46
Deal, NJ (borough) Monmouth County	169	16.34
Lake City, CO (town) Hinsdale County	22	9.09
Hostetter, PA (cdp) Westmoreland County	50	6.83
Georgetown, PA (cdp) Luzerne County	116	6.49
Columbia, NJ (cdp) Warren County	17	6.09
Bulger, PA (cdp) Washington County	29	5.95
Fort Chiswell, VA (cdp) Wythe County	52	5.47
West Long Branch, NJ (borough) Monmouth County	427	5.26
Stiles, PA (cdp) Lehigh County	51	5.23
Oakwood, PA (cdp) Lawrence County	109	5.20
Ingalls, KS (city) Gray County	16	5.11
Tannersville, NY (village) Greene County	22	5.07
Lanesboro, PA (borough) Susquehanna County	27	5.01
Firth, NE (village) Lancaster County	28	5.00
McDonald, PA (borough) Allegheny County	19	5.00
Bruno, WV (cdp) Logan County	20	4.88
Maddock, ND (city) Benson County	20	4.87
Chautauqua, NY (cdp) Chautauqua County	12	4.55
Shellsburg, IA (city) Benton County	39	4.44
Dorneyville, PA (cdp) Lehigh County	193	4.30
Old Tappan, NJ (borough) Bergen County	243	4.28
Little Falls, NJ (township) Passaic County	577	4.16
Mountain Lodge Park, NY (cdp) Orange County	74	3.98
Lamar, TX (cdp) Aransas County	23	3.95
Freedom, ME (town) Waldo County	26	3.89
Rosalia, KS (cdp) Butler County	10	3.89
Wilkes-Barre, PA (township) Luzerne County	116	3.86
Hamilton, ND (city) Pembina County	2	3.57
East Barre, VT (cdp) Washington County	22	3.55
Rosemount, OH (cdp) Scioto County	77	3.50
Waitsfield, VT (town) Washington County	64	3.47
Allenhurst, NJ (borough) Monmouth County	17	3.46
Mountain Lake, NJ (cdp) Warren County	26	3.42
Shavertown, PA (cdp) Luzerne County	64	3.22
Conneaut Lake, PA (borough) Crawford County	18	3.18
Grenora, ND (city) Williams County	8	3.15
North Catasauqua, PA (borough) Northampton County	88	3.07
Far Hills, NJ (borough) Somerset County	26	3.07
Indian Creek, FL (village) Miami-Dade County	3	3.00
Cutler, ME (town) Washington County	19	2.95
Manchester, NY (village) Ontario County	46	2.86
North Abington, PA (township) Lackawanna County	19	2.85
Carl, GA (town) Barrow County	14	2.82
West Logan, WV (town) Logan County	12	2.76
Pennsboro, WV (city) Ritchie County	36	2.74
Totowa, NJ (borough) Passaic County	288	2.72
Whitehall, PA (township) Lehigh County	717	2.71
Bear Creek Village, PA (borough) Luzerne County	7	2.71
Doniphan, NE (village) Hall County	23	2.68
Brevort, MI (township) Mackinac County	17	2.66
Union, PA (township) Lawrence County	137	2.65
Shorewood Forest, IN (cdp) Porter County	77	2.55
Graysville, TN (town) Rhea County	28	2.55
Silver Brook, MN (township) Carlton County	17	2.50
Sanford, MI (village) Midland County	27	2.47
Fullerton, PA (cdp) Lehigh County	371	2.46
Belcourt, ND (cdp) Rolette County	38	2.44
Hokah, MN (city) Houston County	10	2.44
Olmsted Falls, OH (city) Cuyahoga County	210	2.40
Oakhurst, NJ (cdp) Monmouth County	101	2.40
McConnellsburg, PA (borough) Fulton County	29	2.37
Bayview, CA (cdp) Contra Costa County	52	2.36
Worley, ID (city) Kootenai County	4	2.35
Walbridge, OH (village) Wood County	71	2.30
Brooklawn, NJ (borough) Camden County	39	2.30
Cetronia, PA (cdp) Lehigh County	44	2.27
Cuba, AL (town) Sumter County	9	2.27
Pickens, SC (city) Pickens County	70	2.23
Sheatown, PA (cdp) Luzerne County	11	2.22
Esko, MN (cdp) Carlton County	41	2.18
Cross Creek, PA (cdp) Washington County	3	2.17
Edmore, ND (city) Ramsey County	6	2.13
Thompsonville, PA (cdp) Washington County	85	2.12
East Uniontown, PA (cdp) Fayette County	51	2.06
Putnam, PA (township) Tioga County	11	2.06
Beaver Dam Lake, NY (cdp) Orange County	55	2.01
Northampton, PA (borough) Northampton County	198	2.00
Fort Montgomery, NY (cdp) Orange County	17	1.99
Murray, NE (village) Cass County	14	1.98
Taylor, NY (town) Cortland County	11	1.98
Pearl Beach, MI (cdp) St. Clair County	61	1.94
Dunn, WI (town) Dunn County	27	1.94
Foosland, IL (village) Champaign County	2	1.94
Woodland Park, NJ (borough) Passaic County	220	1.90
West Glens Falls, NY (cdp) Warren County	126	1.90
Pine Springs, MN (city) Washington County	7	1.90
Armada, MI (village) Macomb County	34	1.89
University Heights, IA (city) Johnson County	21	1.89
Ashland, PA (borough) Schuylkill County	54	1.87
Cumberland, RI (town) Providence County	611	1.84
Hokendauqua, PA (cdp) Lehigh County	66	1.84
Chadwicks, NY (cdp) Oneida County	22	1.84
Cumberland Hill, RI (cdp) Providence County	143	1.83
Coquille, OR (city) Coos County	72	1.83
Allentown, PA (city) Lehigh County	2,119	1.82
Paradise Heights, FL (cdp) Orange County	18	1.82
Leicester, MA (town) Worcester County	198	1.81
Boonton, NJ (township) Morris County	77	1.80
New Era, MI (village) Oceana County	11	1.78
Bronson, IA (city) Woodbury County	7	1.78
Export, PA (borough) Westmoreland County	16	1.76
Cedar Grove, NJ (township) Essex County	216	1.75
Malmstrom AFB, MT (cdp) Cascade County	84	1.74
East Lansing, MI (city) Clinton County	26	1.74
Whites, IN (town) Boone County	33	1.72
Bruin, PA (borough) Butler County	9	1.72
Mission Woods, KS (city) Johnson County	3	1.72
Princeton Meadows, NJ (cdp) Middlesex County	233	1.70
Kingston, PA (township) Luzerne County	119	1.70
New Castle Northwest, PA (cdp) Lawrence County	22	1.70
Shelby, IA (city) Shelby County	10	1.70
Wanaque, NJ (borough) Passaic County	184	1.69
Chouteau, OK (town) Mayes County	38	1.68
Sherwood Shores, TX (cdp) Grayson County	19	1.68
Byrnedale, PA (cdp) Elk County	8	1.67
Westville, IL (village) Vermilion County	53	1.66
Baldwin, PA (township) Allegheny County	33	1.66
Rock Springs, WI (village) Sauk County	6	1.65
Fillmore, NY (cdp) Allegany County	10	1.63
South Whitehall, PA (township) Lehigh County	309	1.62
German, PA (township) Fayette County	84	1.62
Ideal, MN (township) Crow Wing County	18	1.61
New Hartford, NY (town) Oneida County	351	1.60
North Haledon, NJ (borough) Passaic County	130	1.59
Yorklyn, PA (cdp) York County	29	1.59
Arnold, PA (city) Westmoreland County	83	1.58
West Bethlehem, PA (township) Washington County	21	1.58
Stroudsburg, PA (borough) Monroe County	90	1.57
Escalante, UT (city) Garfield County	14	1.56
Valley Falls, RI (cdp) Providence County	179	1.55
Highland Park, PA (cdp) Mifflin County	24	1.55
Glenview Hills, KY (city) Jefferson County	5	1.52
Ocean, NJ (township) Monmouth County	410	1.50
Hickory, PA (township) Lawrence County	37	1.49
Knightsville, IN (town) Clay County	13	1.47
Salisbury, PA (township) Lehigh County	197	1.45
Cairo, IL (city) Alexander County	43	1.45
Walpole, MA (cdp) Norfolk County	93	1.44
Lincoln, RI (town) Providence County	302	1.43
Arnold, CA (cdp) Calaveras County	49	1.42
Lowhill, PA (township) Lehigh County	31	1.42
Cathcart, WA (cdp) Snohomish County	30	1.42
Mill Village, PA (borough) Erie County	6	1.42
Ovilla, TX (city) Ellis County	50	1.40
Wadena, MN (township) Wadena County	12	1.39
Jennerstown, PA (borough) Somerset County	7	1.39

Please refer to the Explanation of Data in the front of the book for more detailed information.

Ancestry

Arab: Syrian

Top 150 Places Sorted by Percent of Total Population

Based on places with total population of 7,500 or more

Place	Population	%
West Long Branch, NJ (borough) Monmouth County	427	5.26
Little Falls, NJ (township) Passaic County	577	4.16
Totowa, NJ (borough) Passaic County	288	2.72
Whitehall, PA (township) Lehigh County	717	2.71
Fullerton, PA (cdp) Lehigh County	371	2.46
Olmsted Falls, OH (city) Cuyahoga County	210	2.40
Northampton, PA (borough) Northampton County	198	2.00
Woodland Park, NJ (borough) Passaic County	220	1.90
Cumberland, RI (town) Providence County	611	1.84
Cumberland Hill, RI (cdp) Providence County	143	1.83
Allentown, PA (city) Lehigh County	2,119	1.82
Leicester, MA (town) Worcester County	198	1.81
Cedar Grove, NJ (township) Essex County	216	1.75
Princeton Meadows, NJ (cdp) Middlesex County	233	1.70
Wanaque, NJ (borough) Passaic County	184	1.69
South Whitehall, PA (township) Lehigh County	309	1.62
New Hartford, NY (town) Oneida County	351	1.60
North Haledon, NJ (borough) Passaic County	130	1.59
Valley Falls, RI (cdp) Providence County	179	1.55
Ocean, NJ (township) Monmouth County	410	1.50
Salisbury, PA (township) Lehigh County	197	1.45
Lincoln, RI (town) Providence County	302	1.43
Wayne, NJ (township) Passaic County	715	1.32
Lower Burrell, PA (city) Westmoreland County	157	1.32
Pompton Lakes, NJ (borough) Passaic County	134	1.22
Pelham, NH (town) Hillsborough County	150	1.19
Middleton, MA (town) Essex County	103	1.18
Geneva, NY (city) Ontario County	155	1.16
Jupiter Farms, FL (cdp) Palm Beach County	138	1.15
Neshannock, PA (township) Lawrence County	109	1.14
Mechanicsburg, PA (borough) Cumberland County	100	1.11
Farmington, MI (city) Oakland County	114	1.10
Sienna Plantation, TX (cdp) Fort Bend County	136	1.09
Greenwood, MS (city) Leflore County	172	1.08
Cloquet, MN (city) Carlton County	130	1.08
Rosedale, CA (cdp) Kern County	159	1.07
Kingston, PA (borough) Luzerne County	139	1.05
Plainsboro, NJ (township) Middlesex County	233	1.04
Upper Saucon, PA (township) Lehigh County	148	1.03
Kinnelon, NJ (borough) Morris County	105	1.03
Franklin Lakes, NJ (borough) Bergen County	105	1.00
Wakefield-Peacedale, RI (cdp) Washington County	90	1.00
Cortez, CO (city) Montezuma County	84	1.00
Norfolk, MA (town) Norfolk County	109	0.99
North Whitehall, PA (township) Lehigh County	153	0.98
Woodburn, VA (cdp) Fairfax County	83	0.95
Wood-Ridge, NJ (borough) Bergen County	72	0.95
Rye, NY (city) Westchester County	146	0.94
Schiller Park, IL (village) Cook County	108	0.93
Happy Valley, OR (city) Clackamas County	114	0.91
Grosse Pointe Woods, MI (city) Wayne County	148	0.90
Watervliet, NY (city) Albany County	92	0.89
Dearborn Heights, MI (city) Wayne County	512	0.88
Winfield, IL (village) DuPage County	80	0.88
Wallington, NJ (borough) Bergen County	99	0.87
Haledon, NJ (borough) Passaic County	71	0.86
Plaistow, NH (town) Rockingham County	66	0.86
Foxborough, MA (town) Norfolk County	141	0.85
Hammonton, NJ (town) Atlantic County	123	0.84
Dent, OH (cdp) Hamilton County	82	0.84
Murphy, TX (city) Collin County	126	0.83
Flint, MI (charter township) Genesee County	267	0.82
Hernando, MS (city) DeSoto County	109	0.82
Salisbury, NY (cdp) Nassau County	96	0.82
Pleasant Hill, MO (city) Cass County	64	0.82
Long Branch, NJ (city) Monmouth County	251	0.81
Hartland, MI (township) Livingston County	115	0.80
Teays Valley, WV (cdp) Putnam County	107	0.78
Allen Park, MI (city) Wayne County	219	0.77
Dumont, NJ (borough) Bergen County	132	0.76
Northview, MI (cdp) Kent County	110	0.76
Tyngsborough, MA (town) Middlesex County	83	0.75
Enumclaw, WA (city) King County	80	0.75
Hillside, IL (village) Cook County	61	0.75
Hawthorne, NJ (borough) Passaic County	137	0.74
Clifton, NJ (city) Passaic County	601	0.73
Aventura, FL (city) Miami-Dade County	245	0.73
Fairview Park, OH (city) Cuyahoga County	123	0.73
Carnegie, PA (borough) Allegheny County	58	0.73
Bethlehem, PA (city) Lehigh County	140	0.72
Central Falls, RI (city) Providence County	140	0.72
Newtown, PA (township) Delaware County	87	0.72
South Elgin, IL (village) Kane County	151	0.71
Burrillville, RI (town) Providence County	111	0.70
West Mifflin, PA (borough) Allegheny County	141	0.69
Stevenson Ranch, CA (cdp) Los Angeles County	116	0.69
Burr Ridge, IL (village) DuPage County	73	0.69
Bonadelle Ranchos-Madera Ranchos, CA (cdp) Madera County	60	0.67
Oxford, MA (town) Worcester County	91	0.66
Port Jefferson Station, NY (cdp) Suffolk County	50	0.66
Queensbury, NY (town) Warren County	180	0.65
Elmwood Park, NJ (borough) Bergen County	125	0.65
Rostraver, PA (township) Westmoreland County	74	0.65
Clay, MI (township) St. Clair County	61	0.65
Manchester, NY (town) Ontario County	61	0.65
North Providence, RI (town) Providence County	207	0.64
Oakland, NJ (borough) Bergen County	81	0.64
Paramus, NJ (borough) Bergen County	163	0.62
Gaines, MI (charter township) Kent County	150	0.62
Fairview, NJ (borough) Bergen County	84	0.62
New Kensington, PA (city) Westmoreland County	83	0.62
Southchase, FL (cdp) Orange County	100	0.61
Hanover, PA (township) Northampton County	65	0.61
Waimea, HI (cdp) Hawaii County	60	0.61
Newport, RI (city) Newport County	148	0.59
New Castle, PA (city) Lawrence County	141	0.59
Forks, PA (township) Northampton County	81	0.59
Allegheny, PA (township) Westmoreland County	48	0.59
Pawtucket, RI (city) Providence County	419	0.58
Hamilton Square, NJ (cdp) Mercer County	78	0.58
Kearney, MO (city) Clay County	46	0.58
Glendora, CA (city) Los Angeles County	283	0.57
Washington, PA (city) Washington County	78	0.56
Waldwick, NJ (borough) Bergen County	54	0.56
Center, PA (township) Butler County	44	0.56
Mount Lebanon, PA (township) Allegheny County	179	0.55
Milton, MA (cdp/town) Norfolk County	147	0.55
Middle Smithfield, PA (township) Monroe County	86	0.55
East Hampton, CT (town) Middlesex County	71	0.55
Glen Rock, NJ (borough) Bergen County	63	0.55
Fallon, NV (city) Churchill County	47	0.55
Boonton, NJ (town) Morris County	46	0.55
Montpelier, VT (city) Washington County	42	0.53
Bloomingdale, NJ (borough) Passaic County	40	0.53
Hermosa Beach, CA (city) Los Angeles County	101	0.52
East Islip, NY (cdp) Suffolk County	73	0.52
North Smithfield, RI (town) Providence County	61	0.52
Woonsocket, RI (city) Providence County	213	0.51
Peters, PA (township) Washington County	104	0.51
Sanford, ME (cdp) York County	54	0.51
Millstone, NJ (township) Monmouth County	52	0.51
Lake Wylie, SC (cdp) York County	43	0.51
Canton, MA (town) Norfolk County	107	0.50
Greenwood, AR (city) Sebastian County	43	0.50
South Hill, WA (cdp) Pierce County	257	0.49
Charleston, WV (city) Kanawha County	251	0.49
Middle River, MD (cdp) Baltimore County	117	0.49
Walpole, MA (town) Norfolk County	117	0.49
Stonington, CT (town) New London County	90	0.49
Blooming Grove, NY (town) Orange County	89	0.49
New Milford, NJ (borough) Bergen County	79	0.49
Lincoln Park, NJ (borough) Morris County	52	0.49
Orange Park, FL (town) Clay County	43	0.49
Glocester, RI (town) Providence County	47	0.48
Monessen, PA (city) Westmoreland County	38	0.48
Clayton, MI (charter township) Genesee County	37	0.48
Johnston, RI (town) Providence County	134	0.47
Tysons Corner, VA (cdp) Fairfax County	81	0.47
Quartz Hill, CA (cdp) Los Angeles County	49	0.47
Burlington, CT (town) Hartford County	43	0.47

Please refer to the Explanation of Data in the front of the book for more detailed information.

Ancestry

Arab: Other

U.S. and 50 States Sorted by Population and Percent of Total Population

Place	Population	%
United States	**182,424**	**0.06**
California	36,134	0.10
New York	22,359	0.12
Michigan	18,078	0.18
Texas	10,122	0.04
Illinois	8,761	0.07
Virginia	8,527	0.11
Florida	8,347	0.05
New Jersey	6,594	0.08
Pennsylvania	5,269	0.04
Massachusetts	5,073	0.08
Ohio	4,519	0.04
Tennessee	3,923	0.06
Georgia	3,887	0.04
Maryland	3,672	0.06
Colorado	3,331	0.07
Arizona	3,154	0.05
Minnesota	2,816	0.05
Washington	2,808	0.04
North Carolina	2,677	0.03
Oregon	1,855	0.05
Missouri	1,733	0.03
Indiana	1,670	0.03
Wisconsin	1,526	0.03
Connecticut	1,372	0.04
Oklahoma	1,312	0.04
Louisiana	1,003	0.02
South Carolina	963	0.02
Utah	906	0.03
Delaware	905	0.10
Nevada	899	0.03
Kentucky	892	0.02
Alabama	846	0.02
New Mexico	687	0.03
Kansas	638	0.02
West Virginia	634	0.03
Nebraska	604	0.03
Arkansas	585	0.02
District of Columbia	575	0.10
Iowa	448	0.01
Montana	385	0.04
New Hampshire	338	0.03
Mississippi	336	0.01
Idaho	254	0.02
Rhode Island	253	0.02
Hawaii	220	0.02
South Dakota	199	0.02
Alaska	96	0.01
Vermont	93	0.01
North Dakota	75	0.01
Maine	71	0.01
Wyoming	0	0.00

Place	Population	%
Michigan	18,078	0.18
New York	22,359	0.12
Virginia	8,527	0.11
California	36,134	0.10
Delaware	905	0.10
District of Columbia	575	0.10
New Jersey	6,594	0.08
Massachusetts	5,073	0.08
Illinois	8,761	0.07
Colorado	3,331	0.07
United States	**182,424**	**0.06**
Tennessee	3,923	0.06
Maryland	3,672	0.06
Florida	8,347	0.05
Arizona	3,154	0.05
Minnesota	2,816	0.05
Oregon	1,855	0.05
Texas	10,122	0.04
Pennsylvania	5,269	0.04
Ohio	4,519	0.04
Georgia	3,887	0.04
Washington	2,808	0.04
Connecticut	1,372	0.04
Oklahoma	1,312	0.04
Montana	385	0.04
North Carolina	2,677	0.03
Missouri	1,733	0.03
Indiana	1,670	0.03
Wisconsin	1,526	0.03
Utah	906	0.03
Nevada	899	0.03
New Mexico	687	0.03
West Virginia	634	0.03
Nebraska	604	0.03
New Hampshire	338	0.03
Louisiana	1,003	0.02
South Carolina	963	0.02
Kentucky	892	0.02
Alabama	846	0.02
Kansas	638	0.02
Arkansas	585	0.02
Idaho	254	0.02
Rhode Island	253	0.02
Hawaii	220	0.02
South Dakota	199	0.02
Iowa	448	0.01
Mississippi	336	0.01
Alaska	96	0.01
Vermont	93	0.01
North Dakota	75	0.01
Maine	71	0.01
Wyoming	0	0.00

Please refer to the Explanation of Data in the front of the book for more detailed information.

Ancestry

Arab: Other

Top 150 Places Sorted by Population

Based on all places, regardless of total population

Place	Population	%
New York, NY (city) Kings County	14,584	0.18
Dearborn, MI (city) Wayne County	6,354	6.46
Brooklyn, NY (borough) Kings County	6,337	0.26
Los Angeles, CA (city) Los Angeles County	4,177	0.11
Queens, NY (borough) Queens County	3,468	0.16
Chicago, IL (city) Cook County	2,887	0.11
Manhattan, NY (borough) New York County	2,742	0.17
Nashville-Davidson, TN (metro govt) Davidson County	2,642	0.45
Hamtramck, MI (city) Wayne County	1,973	8.73
Houston, TX (city) Harris County	1,861	0.09
Detroit, MI (city) Wayne County	1,837	0.24
San Francisco, CA (city) San Francisco County	1,559	0.20
Oakland, CA (city) Alameda County	1,520	0.39
San Diego, CA (city) San Diego County	1,335	0.10
Bronx, NY (borough) Bronx County	1,256	0.09
Boston, MA (city) Suffolk County	1,136	0.19
Phoenix, AZ (city) Maricopa County	1,076	0.07
Philadelphia, PA (city) Philadelphia County	1,012	0.07
El Cajon, CA (city) San Diego County	958	0.98
Clifton, NJ (city) Passaic County	876	1.06
Staten Island, NY (borough) Richmond County	781	0.17
Jersey City, NJ (city) Hudson County	743	0.31
San Antonio, TX (city) Medina County	742	0.06
San Jose, CA (city) Santa Clara County	695	0.08
Denver, CO (city) Denver County	682	0.12
Hempstead, NY (town) Nassau County	664	0.09
Jacksonville, FL (city) Duval County	656	0.08
Irvine, CA (city) Orange County	600	0.30
Brookside, DE (cdp) New Castle County	598	4.16
Revere, MA (city) Suffolk County	592	1.18
Fremont, CA (city) Alameda County	590	0.28
Long Beach, CA (city) Los Angeles County	586	0.13
Washington, DC (city) District of Columbia	575	0.10
Charlotte, NC (city) Mecklenburg County	573	0.08
San Bernardino, CA (city) San Bernardino County	571	0.27
North Hempstead, NY (town) Nassau County	571	0.26
Portland, OR (city) Multnomah County	570	0.10
West Bloomfield, MI (charter township) Oakland County	567	0.88
Fresno, CA (city) Fresno County	564	0.12
Coldwater, MI (city) Branch County	557	5.07
Baltimore, MD (city) Baltimore city County	528	0.09
Austin, TX (city) Travis County	526	0.07
Ann Arbor, MI (city) Washtenaw County	522	0.45
Binghamton, NY (city) Broome County	521	1.10
Brooklyn Park, MN (city) Hennepin County	513	0.70
Minneapolis, MN (city) Hennepin County	505	0.13
Seattle, WA (city) King County	505	0.08
Santee, CA (city) San Diego County	498	0.94
Columbus, OH (city) Franklin County	497	0.06
Allen, TX (city) Collin County	483	0.62
Arlington, VA (cdp) Arlington County	478	0.24
Milwaukee, WI (city) Milwaukee County	457	0.08
Raleigh, NC (city) Wake County	456	0.12
Palos Hills, IL (city) Cook County	455	2.62
Indianapolis, IN (city) Marion County	451	0.06
Atlanta, GA (city) Fulton County	450	0.11
Pittsburgh, PA (city) Allegheny County	445	0.14
Oklahoma City, OK (city) Oklahoma County	437	0.08
Bridgeview, IL (village) Cook County	426	2.64
Arlington, TX (city) Tarrant County	423	0.12
Pearland, TX (city) Brazoria County	420	0.51
Tulsa, OK (city) Tulsa County	416	0.11
Farmington Hills, MI (city) Oakland County	412	0.51
Lackawanna, NY (city) Erie County	402	2.20
Salt Lake City, UT (city) Salt Lake County	402	0.22
Kent, WA (city) King County	398	0.44
Rochester, NY (city) Monroe County	390	0.18
Albuquerque, NM (city) Bernalillo County	384	0.07
Little Rock, AR (city) Pulaski County	379	0.20
Dearborn Heights, MI (city) Wayne County	371	0.64
Tempe, AZ (city) Maricopa County	369	0.22
Calexico, CA (city) Imperial County	365	1.01
Metairie, LA (cdp) Jefferson Parish	357	0.26
Burbank, IL (city) Cook County	339	1.19
Tysons Corner, VA (cdp) Fairfax County	338	1.98
Beverly Hills, CA (city) Los Angeles County	322	0.95
Kansas City, MO (city) Jackson County	320	0.07
Malden, MA (city) Middlesex County	316	0.54
Tampa, FL (city) Hillsborough County	315	0.09
Yonkers, NY (city) Westchester County	312	0.16
Arvin, CA (city) Kern County	307	1.67
Sacramento, CA (city) Sacramento County	306	0.07
Dallas, TX (city) Dallas County	305	0.03
Toledo, OH (city) Lucas County	304	0.10
Depew, NY (village) Erie County	303	1.96
Berkeley, CA (city) Alameda County	303	0.28
Fort Collins, CO (city) Larimer County	303	0.22
Fort Worth, TX (city) Tarrant County	302	0.04
Sterling Heights, MI (city) Macomb County	300	0.23
Madison, WI (city) Dane County	300	0.13
Newport Beach, CA (city) Orange County	297	0.36
Allentown, PA (city) Lehigh County	295	0.25
Melvindale, MI (city) Wayne County	292	2.71
Gates, NY (town) Monroe County	291	1.02
Sugar Land, TX (city) Fort Bend County	287	0.38
Quincy, MA (city) Norfolk County	279	0.31
Johns Creek, GA (city) Fulton County	277	0.38
Millcreek, UT (cdp) Salt Lake County	271	0.44
Bakersfield, CA (city) Kern County	271	0.08
Centreville, VA (cdp) Fairfax County	270	0.37
Amherst, NY (town) Erie County	270	0.22
Buffalo, NY (city) Erie County	270	0.10
Tredyffrin, PA (township) Chester County	269	0.91
Walnut Creek, CA (city) Contra Costa County	267	0.42
Sunnyvale, CA (city) Santa Clara County	267	0.20
Naperville, IL (city) DuPage County	267	0.19
Paterson, NJ (city) Passaic County	266	0.18
Columbia, MD (cdp) Howard County	264	0.27
Thousand Oaks, CA (city) Ventura County	264	0.21
Anaheim, CA (city) Orange County	262	0.08
Berkley, CO (cdp) Adams County	258	2.13
Modesto, CA (city) Stanislaus County	258	0.13
Las Vegas, NV (city) Clark County	258	0.04
San Mateo, CA (city) San Mateo County	257	0.27
Warren, MI (city) Macomb County	257	0.19
Gates, NY (cdp) Monroe County	256	4.76
Rose Hill, VA (cdp) Fairfax County	256	1.30
Oyster Bay, NY (town) Nassau County	255	0.09
Santa Clara, CA (city) Santa Clara County	254	0.23
Burlingame, CA (city) San Mateo County	253	0.90
Alexandria, VA (ind. city) Alexandria independent city	253	0.19
North Bergen, NJ (township) Hudson County	252	0.42
Plano, TX (city) Collin County	248	0.10
Cherry Hill, NJ (township) Camden County	246	0.35
Cheektowaga, NY (town) Erie County	244	0.27
Orlando, FL (city) Orange County	243	0.10
Terre Haute, IN (city) Vigo County	241	0.40
Coon Rapids, MN (city) Anoka County	241	0.39
Temple Terrace, FL (city) Hillsborough County	238	0.98
Corona, CA (city) Riverside County	238	0.16
Omaha, NE (city) Douglas County	237	0.06
Alafaya, FL (cdp) Orange County	236	0.31
Richmond, VA (ind. city) Richmond independent city	236	0.12
Lakeland, FL (city) Polk County	234	0.24
Huntsville, AL (city) Madison County	233	0.13
Friendship Heights Village, MD (cdp) Montgomery County	231	4.00
Tinley Park, IL (village) Cook County	231	0.42
Chula Vista, CA (city) San Diego County	231	0.10
Gilbert, AZ (town) Maricopa County	230	0.12
Orland Park, IL (village) Cook County	229	0.42
Upland, CA (city) San Bernardino County	227	0.31
Westminster, CA (city) Orange County	227	0.26
Cleveland, OH (city) Cuyahoga County	227	0.06
Glendale, CA (city) Los Angeles County	224	0.12
Lexington-Fayette, KY (cons. govt) Fayette County	224	0.08
San Juan Capistrano, CA (city) Orange County	223	0.65
Annandale, VA (cdp) Fairfax County	219	0.57
Cambridge, MA (city) Middlesex County	219	0.21
Clemson, SC (city) Pickens County	218	1.60
Santa Monica, CA (city) Los Angeles County	218	0.25

SECTION THREE

Please refer to the Explanation of Data in the front of the book for more detailed information.

Ancestry

Arab: Other

Top 150 Places Sorted by Percent of Total Population

Based on all places, regardless of total population

Place	Population	%
Harrietta, MI (village) Wexford County	16	14.16
Falcon, NC (town) Cumberland County	27	10.23
Baldwin, IL (village) Randolph County	32	8.82
Hamtramck, MI (city) Wayne County	1,973	8.73
Elkhorn, CA (cdp) Monterey County	122	7.09
Cuba, AL (town) Sumter County	28	7.07
Dearborn, MI (city) Wayne County	6,354	6.46
Tunica, MS (town) Tunica County	75	6.10
Brush Fork, WV (cdp) Mercer County	62	5.91
Halls, TN (town) Lauderdale County	120	5.16
Deal, NJ (borough) Monmouth County	53	5.13
Coldwater, MI (city) Branch County	557	5.07
Riley, IN (town) Vigo County	11	5.07
Salladasburg, PA (borough) Lycoming County	12	5.06
North Kansas City, MO (city) Clay County	215	5.01
Hewlett Bay Park, NY (village) Nassau County	26	5.01
Gates, NY (cdp) Monroe County	256	4.76
Rose Hills, CA (cdp) Los Angeles County	133	4.55
Logan, PA (township) Clinton County	30	4.44
Buttonwillow, CA (cdp) Kern County	71	4.24
Lyons, PA (borough) Berks County	19	4.19
Brookside, DE (cdp) New Castle County	598	4.16
South Shenango, PA (township) Crawford County	77	4.03
Friendship Heights Village, MD (cdp) Montgomery County	231	4.00
Enetai, WA (cdp) Kitsap County	87	3.97
Norris Canyon, CA (cdp) Contra Costa County	32	3.94
Harbor Bluffs, FL (cdp) Pinellas County	113	3.85
Rutland, IL (village) LaSalle County	13	3.77
Woodlands, CA (cdp) San Luis Obispo County	14	3.76
Gaston, NC (town) Northampton County	46	3.65
Orient, ME (town) Aroostook County	4	3.45
Lund, MN (township) Douglas County	9	3.37
Pymatuning Central, PA (cdp) Crawford County	77	3.25
Allenwood, PA (cdp) Union County	16	3.06
Topeka, IN (town) LaGrange County	38	3.02
Chesterbrook, PA (cdp) Chester County	126	2.84
Mount Crawford, VA (town) Rockingham County	10	2.83
East Tulare Villa, CA (cdp) Tulare County	35	2.80
Boon, MI (township) Wexford County	16	2.80
Pimmit Hills, VA (cdp) Fairfax County	170	2.73
St. Anthony, MN (city) Ramsey County	80	2.72
Melvindale, MI (city) Wayne County	292	2.71
Saddle Rock, NY (village) Nassau County	28	2.67
Bridgeview, IL (village) Cook County	426	2.64
Palos Hills, IL (city) Cook County	455	2.62
Del Rio, CA (cdp) Stanislaus County	30	2.53
Haskins, OH (village) Wood County	29	2.53
East Richmond Heights, CA (cdp) Contra Costa County	78	2.43
Alta Vista, KS (city) Wabaunsee County	11	2.32
Kokhanok, AK (cdp) Lake and Peninsula Borough	3	2.31
Holyrood, KS (city) Ellsworth County	12	2.25
Spring Lake Park, MN (city) Anoka County	141	2.21
Lackawanna, NY (city) Erie County	402	2.20
St. Wendel, MN (township) Stearns County	49	2.17
Spring Lake Park, MN (city) Anoka County	141	2.16
Lake Barcroft, VA (cdp) Fairfax County	195	2.15
Roscoe, MN (city) Stearns County	2	2.15
Berkley, CO (cdp) Adams County	258	2.13
New Galilee, PA (borough) Beaver County	9	2.12
Perrysville, IN (town) Vermillion County	12	2.11
Shelter Cove, CA (cdp) Humboldt County	11	2.10
Dunn Loring, VA (cdp) Fairfax County	193	2.09
Emerson, NE (village) Dixon County	16	2.08
St. Regis Mohawk Reservation, NY (reservation) Franklin County	65	2.07
East Jordan, MI (city) Charlevoix County	39	2.02
Orland Hills, IL (village) Cook County	141	2.01
Tysons Corner, VA (cdp) Fairfax County	338	1.98
New Egypt, NJ (cdp) Ocean County	43	1.97
Depew, NY (village) Erie County	303	1.96
Shady Shores, TX (town) Denton County	48	1.96
Garrett Park, MD (town) Montgomery County	18	1.96
Mansfield, NJ (township) Burlington County	156	1.95
Yorkshire, VA (cdp) Prince William County	128	1.88
Bellbrook, OH (city) Greene County	131	1.87
Vandalia, IL (city) Fayette County	109	1.87
Kings Point, NY (village) Nassau County	92	1.85
Central Heights-Midland City, AZ (cdp) Gila County	50	1.84
Pulaski, PA (township) Beaver County	27	1.84
Salem, CT (town) New London County	75	1.83
St. Pauls, NC (town) Robeson County	37	1.80
Rodeo, CA (cdp) Contra Costa County	163	1.79
Flourtown, PA (cdp) Montgomery County	81	1.79
Glendale, CO (city) Arapahoe County	72	1.73
Arvin, CA (city) Kern County	307	1.67
Bluewell, WV (cdp) Mercer County	38	1.67
Grass Lake, MI (charter township) Jackson County	92	1.66
Roslyn Heights, NY (cdp) Nassau County	107	1.65
Channel Islands Beach, CA (cdp) Ventura County	53	1.64
Warminster Heights, PA (cdp) Bucks County	74	1.63
Mill Neck, NY (village) Nassau County	13	1.61
Clemson, SC (city) Pickens County	218	1.60
Bloomfield Hills, MI (city) Oakland County	62	1.60
Hayfield, VA (cdp) Fairfax County	61	1.59
Lowes Island, VA (cdp) Loudoun County	180	1.58
North Fort Lewis, WA (cdp) Pierce County	45	1.55
Sands Point, NY (village) Nassau County	41	1.54
Firebaugh, CA (city) Fresno County	113	1.53
Socorro, NM (city) Socorro County	137	1.51
Chase, PA (cdp) Luzerne County	20	1.48
Manasquan, NJ (borough) Monmouth County	86	1.44
Oakhurst, NJ (cdp) Monmouth County	60	1.42
Greentown, OH (cdp) Stark County	45	1.40
Phoenix, OR (city) Jackson County	62	1.38
Bagdad, AZ (cdp) Yavapai County	27	1.38
Edgewood, FL (city) Orange County	33	1.35
Rose Hill, VA (cdp) Fairfax County	256	1.30
Hunters Creek Village, TX (city) Harris County	56	1.29
Somerset, MD (town) Montgomery County	17	1.24
Churchill, MI (township) Ogemaw County	25	1.23
Patton, PA (township) Centre County	179	1.22
Baldwin Harbor, NY (cdp) Nassau County	105	1.21
Madera Acres, CA (cdp) Madera County	109	1.20
Houghton, MI (city) Houghton County	91	1.20
Layhill, MD (cdp) Montgomery County	68	1.20
Osage, IA (city) Mitchell County	43	1.20
Burbank, IL (city) Cook County	339	1.19
Superior, MI (charter township) Washtenaw County	152	1.19
Potomac Mills, VA (cdp) Prince William County	56	1.19
Revere, MA (city) Suffolk County	592	1.18
French Camp, CA (cdp) San Joaquin County	68	1.18
Campo, CA (cdp) San Diego County	35	1.18
St. Marys, KS (city) Pottawatomie County	33	1.18
Far Hills, NJ (borough) Somerset County	10	1.18
Cary, WI (town) Wood County	6	1.18
Honea Path, SC (town) Anderson County	44	1.16
Mount Airy, MD (town) Carroll County	102	1.14
Sugar Creek, WI (town) Walworth County	44	1.13
Vero Beach, FL (city) Indian River County	178	1.12
Ridgefield, NJ (borough) Bergen County	123	1.12
Lynn, MI (township) St. Clair County	13	1.12
Lake George, NY (village) Warren County	11	1.12
Cherry Hill Mall, NJ (cdp) Camden County	155	1.11
Binghamton, NY (city) Broome County	521	1.10
Oakhurst, CA (cdp) Madera County	36	1.10
Frankfort, OH (village) Ross County	12	1.09
Progreso Lakes, TX (city) Hidalgo County	3	1.09
Goodlettsville, TN (city) Davidson County	165	1.07
Clifton, NJ (city) Passaic County	876	1.06
Islip Terrace, NY (cdp) Suffolk County	61	1.06
Rutland, WI (town) Dane County	21	1.06
Hoschton, GA (city) Jackson County	15	1.04
Lincoln Park, TX (town) Denton County	3	1.04
Park Forest Village, PA (cdp) Centre County	104	1.03
Seven Corners, VA (cdp) Fairfax County	86	1.03
Gates, NY (town) Monroe County	291	1.02
Broadmoor, CA (cdp) San Mateo County	40	1.02
McIntyre, PA (township) Lycoming County	5	1.02
Calexico, CA (city) Imperial County	365	1.01
Idylwood, VA (cdp) Fairfax County	159	1.01
Waynesville, OH (village) Warren County	29	1.01

Please refer to the Explanation of Data in the front of the book for more detailed information.

Ancestry

Arab: Other

Top 150 Places Sorted by Percent of Total Population

Based on places with total population of 7,500 or more

Place	Population	%
Hamtramck, MI (city) Wayne County	1,973	8.73
Dearborn, MI (city) Wayne County	6,354	6.46
Coldwater, MI (city) Branch County	557	5.07
Brookside, DE (cdp) New Castle County	598	4.16
Melvindale, MI (city) Wayne County	292	2.71
Bridgeview, IL (village) Cook County	426	2.64
Palos Hills, IL (city) Cook County	455	2.62
Lackawanna, NY (city) Erie County	402	2.20
Lake Barcroft, VA (cdp) Fairfax County	195	2.15
Berkley, CO (cdp) Adams County	258	2.13
Dunn Loring, VA (cdp) Fairfax County	193	2.09
Tysons Corner, VA (cdp) Fairfax County	338	1.98
Depew, NY (village) Erie County	303	1.96
Mansfield, NJ (township) Burlington County	156	1.95
Rodeo, CA (cdp) Contra Costa County	163	1.79
Arvin, CA (city) Kern County	307	1.67
Clemson, SC (city) Pickens County	218	1.60
Lowes Island, VA (cdp) Loudoun County	180	1.58
Socorro, NM (city) Socorro County	137	1.51
Rose Hill, VA (cdp) Fairfax County	256	1.30
Patton, PA (township) Centre County	179	1.22
Baldwin Harbor, NY (cdp) Nassau County	105	1.21
Madera Acres, CA (cdp) Madera County	109	1.20
Houghton, MI (city) Houghton County	91	1.20
Burbank, IL (city) Cook County	339	1.19
Superior, MI (charter township) Washtenaw County	152	1.19
Revere, MA (city) Suffolk County	592	1.18
Mount Airy, MD (town) Carroll County	102	1.14
Vero Beach, FL (city) Indian River County	178	1.12
Ridgefield, NJ (borough) Bergen County	123	1.12
Cherry Hill Mall, NJ (cdp) Camden County	155	1.11
Binghamton, NY (city) Broome County	521	1.10
Goodlettsville, TN (city) Davidson County	165	1.07
Clifton, NJ (city) Passaic County	876	1.06
Park Forest Village, PA (cdp) Centre County	104	1.03
Seven Corners, VA (cdp) Fairfax County	86	1.03
Gates, NY (town) Monroe County	291	1.02
Calexico, CA (city) Imperial County	365	1.01
Idylwood, VA (cdp) Fairfax County	159	1.01
St. Anthony, MN (city) Hennepin and Ramsey Counties	80	0.99
El Cajon, CA (city) San Diego County	958	0.98
Temple Terrace, FL (city) Hillsborough County	238	0.98
Hollymead, VA (cdp) Albemarle County	79	0.98
Hickory Hills, IL (city) Cook County	136	0.97
Pelham, NH (town) Hillsborough County	122	0.97
Kingstowne, VA (cdp) Fairfax County	140	0.96
Beverly Hills, CA (city) Los Angeles County	322	0.95
Santee, CA (city) San Diego County	498	0.94
Tredyffrin, PA (township) Chester County	269	0.91
Burlingame, CA (city) San Mateo County	253	0.90
Kirkland, NY (town) Oneida County	91	0.89
West Bloomfield, MI (charter township) Oakland County	567	0.88
Lansdowne, VA (cdp) Loudoun County	83	0.84
Woodbury, NY (cdp) Nassau County	76	0.84
Tenafly, NJ (borough) Bergen County	118	0.83
Wolf Trap, VA (cdp) Fairfax County	135	0.81
Sycamore, IL (city) DeKalb County	134	0.80
Falls Church, VA (ind. city) Falls Church independent city	91	0.79
Golden, CO (city) Jefferson County	144	0.78
Chicago Ridge, IL (village) Cook County	111	0.78
West Park, FL (city) Broward County	110	0.77
Farmingdale, NY (village) Nassau County	63	0.77
Briarcliff Manor, NY (village) Westchester County	62	0.77
Burke Centre, VA (cdp) Fairfax County	129	0.76
Glenmont, MD (cdp) Montgomery County	98	0.73
La Grange Park, IL (village) Cook County	95	0.71
McFarland, CA (city) Kern County	87	0.71
Brooklyn Park, MN (city) Hennepin County	513	0.70
King of Prussia, PA (cdp) Montgomery County	134	0.68
Vienna, VA (town) Fairfax County	104	0.68
Lincolnwood, IL (village) Cook County	85	0.68
Calabasas, CA (city) Los Angeles County	152	0.67
Riverbank, CA (city) Stanislaus County	146	0.67
Joppatowne, MD (cdp) Harford County	83	0.66
San Juan Capistrano, CA (city) Orange County	223	0.65
Cherry Hill, VA (cdp) Prince William County	101	0.65
Sugarland Run, VA (cdp) Loudoun County	71	0.65
Monroe, NY (village) Orange County	54	0.65
Dearborn Heights, MI (city) Wayne County	371	0.64
Sand Lake, NY (town) Rensselaer County	54	0.64
Athens, OH (city) Athens County	148	0.63
Warwick, PA (township) Bucks County	89	0.63
Allen, TX (city) Collin County	483	0.62
Hawthorne, NJ (borough) Passaic County	115	0.62
Ada, MI (township) Kent County	78	0.62
Lamont, CA (cdp) Kern County	93	0.61
Huntington, VA (cdp) Fairfax County	63	0.61
Streetsboro, OH (city) Portage County	93	0.60
West University Place, TX (city) Harris County	88	0.60
Winter Gardens, CA (cdp) San Diego County	120	0.59
Loma Linda, CA (city) San Bernardino County	133	0.58
West Hempstead, NY (cdp) Nassau County	107	0.58
Lemay, MO (cdp) St. Louis County	93	0.58
Annandale, VA (cdp) Fairfax County	219	0.57
Ashland, NJ (cdp) Camden County	49	0.57
San Carlos, CA (city) San Mateo County	155	0.56
Gainesville, VA (cdp) Prince William County	60	0.56
Bloomington, CA (cdp) San Bernardino County	137	0.55
Malden, MA (city) Middlesex County	316	0.54
Port Chester, NY (village) Westchester County	155	0.54
South Elgin, IL (village) Kane County	114	0.54
Bethany, OR (cdp) Washington County	106	0.54
North Fair Oaks, CA (cdp) San Mateo County	77	0.54
Solana Beach, CA (city) San Diego County	69	0.54
Lakeville, MA (town) Plymouth County	56	0.54
Great Neck, NY (village) Nassau County	53	0.54
Spring Valley, CA (cdp) San Diego County	145	0.53
Woodmere, NY (cdp) Nassau County	92	0.53
Ringwood, NJ (borough) Passaic County	64	0.53
Washington, NJ (township) Bergen County	48	0.53
Ashland, OH (city) Ashland County	108	0.52
Forks, PA (township) Northampton County	71	0.52
New Kensington, PA (city) Westmoreland County	69	0.52
Plumsted, NJ (township) Ocean County	43	0.52
Pearland, TX (city) Brazoria County	420	0.51
Farmington Hills, MI (city) Oakland County	412	0.51
Oakley, CA (city) Contra Costa County	172	0.51
Butte-Silver Bow, MT (cons. govt) Silver Bow County	167	0.51
Foothill Farms, CA (cdp) Sacramento County	166	0.51
De Pere, WI (city) Brown County	119	0.51
Leesburg, VA (town) Loudoun County	202	0.50
Bell, CA (city) Los Angeles County	177	0.50
Miami Shores, FL (village) Miami-Dade County	52	0.49
Heath, OH (city) Licking County	49	0.49
Lower Swatara, PA (township) Dauphin County	40	0.49
Brooksville, FL (city) Hernando County	39	0.49
Upper Merion, PA (township) Montgomery County	134	0.48
North Castle, NY (town) Westchester County	56	0.48
Scotts Valley, CA (city) Santa Cruz County	55	0.48
Smithfield, NC (town) Johnston County	53	0.48
Mount Kisco, NY (town/village) Westchester County	51	0.48
Bohemia, NY (cdp) Suffolk County	48	0.48
Ladue, MO (city) St. Louis County	41	0.48
Columbia Heights, MN (city) Anoka County	92	0.47
Whitemarsh, PA (township) Montgomery County	81	0.47
Shafter, CA (city) Kern County	77	0.47
Byram, MS (city) Hinds County	49	0.47
Springfield, VA (cdp) Fairfax County	139	0.46
Simpsonville, SC (city) Greenville County	81	0.46
Nashville-Davidson, TN (metro govt) Davidson County	2,642	0.45
Ann Arbor, MI (city) Washtenaw County	522	0.45
San Bruno, CA (city) San Mateo County	181	0.45
Mineola, NY (village) Nassau County	84	0.45
Great Falls, VA (cdp) Fairfax County	71	0.45
Overlea, MD (cdp) Baltimore County	57	0.45
Wanaque, NJ (borough) Passaic County	49	0.45
Timonium, MD (cdp) Baltimore County	44	0.45
Gettysburg, PA (borough) Adams County	35	0.45
Kent, WA (city) King County	398	0.44
Millcreek, UT (cdp) Salt Lake County	271	0.44

Please refer to the Explanation of Data in the front of the book for more detailed information.

Ancestry

Armenian

U.S. and 50 States Sorted by Population and Percent of Total Population

Place	Population	%
United States	**447,580**	**0.15**
California	241,323	0.66
Massachusetts	28,471	0.44
New York	24,803	0.13
Michigan	17,345	0.17
New Jersey	15,816	0.18
Florida	13,446	0.07
Pennsylvania	9,325	0.07
Illinois	8,357	0.07
Rhode Island	6,694	0.63
Washington	5,924	0.09
Connecticut	5,875	0.17
Arizona	5,863	0.09
Texas	5,754	0.02
Nevada	5,479	0.21
Virginia	5,208	0.07
Maryland	4,572	0.08
Ohio	4,333	0.04
North Carolina	3,644	0.04
Wisconsin	3,438	0.06
Georgia	2,964	0.03
New Hampshire	2,934	0.22
Colorado	2,877	0.06
Oregon	2,488	0.07
Utah	2,350	0.09
Missouri	2,260	0.04
Maine	1,384	0.10
Tennessee	1,348	0.02
Minnesota	1,299	0.02
Indiana	1,080	0.02
South Carolina	1,024	0.02
Oklahoma	967	0.03
Kentucky	931	0.02
Idaho	860	0.06
New Mexico	739	0.04
Vermont	672	0.11
Kansas	669	0.02
District of Columbia	574	0.10
Louisiana	523	0.01
Alabama	522	0.01
North Dakota	460	0.07
Delaware	448	0.05
Hawaii	428	0.03
Iowa	415	0.01
Arkansas	400	0.01
Alaska	271	0.04
South Dakota	238	0.03
West Virginia	196	0.01
Mississippi	179	0.01
Montana	175	0.02
Nebraska	140	0.01
Wyoming	95	0.02

Place	Population	%
California	241,323	0.66
Rhode Island	6,694	0.63
Massachusetts	28,471	0.44
New Hampshire	2,934	0.22
Nevada	5,479	0.21
New Jersey	15,816	0.18
Michigan	17,345	0.17
Connecticut	5,875	0.17
United States	**447,580**	**0.15**
New York	24,803	0.13
Vermont	672	0.11
Maine	1,384	0.10
District of Columbia	574	0.10
Washington	5,924	0.09
Arizona	5,863	0.09
Utah	2,350	0.09
Maryland	4,572	0.08
Florida	13,446	0.07
Pennsylvania	9,325	0.07
Illinois	8,357	0.07
Virginia	5,208	0.07
Oregon	2,488	0.07
North Dakota	460	0.07
Wisconsin	3,438	0.06
Colorado	2,877	0.06
Idaho	860	0.06
Delaware	448	0.05
Ohio	4,333	0.04
North Carolina	3,644	0.04
Missouri	2,260	0.04
New Mexico	739	0.04
Alaska	271	0.04
Georgia	2,964	0.03
Oklahoma	967	0.03
Hawaii	428	0.03
South Dakota	238	0.03
Texas	5,754	0.02
Tennessee	1,348	0.02
Minnesota	1,299	0.02
Indiana	1,080	0.02
South Carolina	1,024	0.02
Kentucky	931	0.02
Kansas	669	0.02
Montana	175	0.02
Wyoming	95	0.02
Louisiana	523	0.01
Alabama	522	0.01
Iowa	415	0.01
Arkansas	400	0.01
West Virginia	196	0.01
Mississippi	179	0.01
Nebraska	140	0.01

Please refer to the Explanation of Data in the front of the book for more detailed information.

Ancestry

Armenian

Top 150 Places Sorted by Population

Based on all places, regardless of total population

Place	Population	%
Los Angeles, CA (city) Los Angeles County	73,256	1.94
Glendale, CA (city) Los Angeles County	65,434	34.05
Burbank, CA (city) Los Angeles County	12,490	12.16
New York, NY (city) Kings County	10,159	0.13
Fresno, CA (city) Fresno County	7,000	1.45
Pasadena, CA (city) Los Angeles County	5,017	3.68
Queens, NY (borough) Queens County	4,658	0.21
San Diego, CA (city) San Diego County	3,045	0.24
Manhattan, NY (borough) New York County	2,653	0.17
Altadena, CA (cdp) Los Angeles County	2,354	5.18
Brooklyn, NY (borough) Kings County	2,300	0.09
La Crescenta-Montrose, CA (cdp) Los Angeles County	2,171	10.89
San Francisco, CA (city) San Francisco County	2,149	0.27
Watertown Town, MA (city) Middlesex County	2,036	6.44
Montebello, CA (city) Los Angeles County	1,885	3.02
Phoenix, AZ (city) Maricopa County	1,825	0.13
Cranston, RI (city) Providence County	1,691	2.10
San Jose, CA (city) Santa Clara County	1,585	0.17
Hempstead, NY (town) Nassau County	1,451	0.19
Worcester, MA (city) Worcester County	1,417	0.79
Santa Clarita, CA (city) Los Angeles County	1,403	0.81
Las Vegas, NV (city) Clark County	1,393	0.24
Oyster Bay, NY (town) Nassau County	1,383	0.47
Boston, MA (city) Suffolk County	1,356	0.23
Philadelphia, PA (city) Philadelphia County	1,315	0.09
Waltham, MA (city) Middlesex County	1,267	2.12
Chicago, IL (city) Cook County	1,256	0.05
Spring Valley, NV (cdp) Clark County	1,199	0.70
Belmont, MA (cdp/town) Middlesex County	1,126	4.62
Clovis, CA (city) Fresno County	984	1.08
Providence, RI (city) Providence County	966	0.54
La Cañada Flintridge, CA (city) Los Angeles County	925	4.57
Rancho Cordova, CA (city) Sacramento County	900	1.42
Long Beach, CA (city) Los Angeles County	889	0.19
Irvine, CA (city) Orange County	838	0.42
Houston, TX (city) Harris County	834	0.04
West Bloomfield, MI (charter township) Oakland County	814	1.26
Anaheim, CA (city) Orange County	802	0.24
Lexington, MA (cdp/town) Middlesex County	801	2.60
Orange, CA (city) Orange County	781	0.58
Palmdale, CA (city) Los Angeles County	776	0.53
Arlington, MA (cdp/town) Middlesex County	766	1.81
San Mateo, CA (city) San Mateo County	755	0.80
Bellevue, WA (city) King County	737	0.62
Sacramento, CA (city) Sacramento County	711	0.15
Whittier, CA (city) Los Angeles County	696	0.82
Huntington Beach, CA (city) Orange County	695	0.37
Costa Mesa, CA (city) Orange County	674	0.62
Redondo Beach, CA (city) Los Angeles County	659	1.00
Brookhaven, NY (town) Suffolk County	643	0.13
Cambridge, MA (city) Middlesex County	638	0.62
Scottsdale, AZ (city) Maricopa County	636	0.29
Seattle, WA (city) King County	634	0.11
North Hempstead, NY (town) Nassau County	631	0.28
Henderson, NV (city) Clark County	626	0.25
Charlotte, NC (city) Mecklenburg County	612	0.09
Simi Valley, CA (city) Ventura County	599	0.49
Bloomfield, MI (charter township) Oakland County	583	1.41
Rancho Palos Verdes, CA (city) Los Angeles County	581	1.40
Newport Beach, CA (city) Orange County	581	0.70
Livonia, MI (city) Wayne County	580	0.59
Thousand Oaks, CA (city) Ventura County	578	0.46
Lancaster, CA (city) Los Angeles County	576	0.38
Washington, DC (city) District of Columbia	574	0.10
Modesto, CA (city) Stanislaus County	565	0.28
Farmington Hills, MI (city) Oakland County	564	0.70
Bakersfield, CA (city) Kern County	557	0.17
Dearborn, MI (city) Wayne County	542	0.55
Warwick, RI (city) Kent County	540	0.65
Warren, MI (city) Macomb County	528	0.39
Huntington, NY (town) Suffolk County	525	0.26
Paramus, NJ (borough) Bergen County	510	1.96
Haverhill, MA (city) Essex County	499	0.83
Visalia, CA (city) Tulare County	492	0.41
Torrance, CA (city) Los Angeles County	485	0.34
Duarte, CA (city) Los Angeles County	473	2.21
Mission Viejo, CA (city) Orange County	462	0.50
Chandler, AZ (city) Maricopa County	458	0.20
Diamond Bar, CA (city) Los Angeles County	447	0.80
Racine, WI (city) Racine County	447	0.56
Rancho Cucamonga, CA (city) San Bernardino County	444	0.28
Waterford, MI (charter township) Oakland County	435	0.61
Nashua, NH (city) Hillsborough County	434	0.50
Shrewsbury, MA (town) Worcester County	432	1.23
Novi, MI (city) Oakland County	432	0.80
Cliffside Park, NJ (borough) Bergen County	425	1.82
Upper Darby, PA (township) Delaware County	423	0.51
Marple, PA (township) Delaware County	421	1.80
Westminster, CA (city) Orange County	419	0.47
Sunnyvale, CA (city) Santa Clara County	419	0.31
Troy, NY (city) Rensselaer County	418	0.84
Yonkers, NY (city) Westchester County	411	0.21
Billerica, MA (town) Middlesex County	406	1.03
Burlington, MA (cdp/town) Middlesex County	404	1.69
Albuquerque, NM (city) Bernalillo County	396	0.07
Paradise, NV (cdp) Clark County	391	0.18
Camarillo, CA (city) Ventura County	390	0.61
Laguna Niguel, CA (city) Orange County	387	0.62
Dallas, TX (city) Dallas County	387	0.03
Tempe, AZ (city) Maricopa County	386	0.24
Fort Lee, NJ (borough) Bergen County	385	1.09
Sandy, UT (city) Salt Lake County	384	0.44
Berkeley, CA (city) Alameda County	381	0.35
Covina, CA (city) Los Angeles County	379	0.80
Boca Raton, FL (city) Palm Beach County	379	0.45
Fountain Valley, CA (city) Orange County	378	0.69
Canton, MI (charter township) Wayne County	376	0.43
Skokie, IL (village) Cook County	372	0.58
Wellington, FL (village) Palm Beach County	367	0.68
Lowell, MA (city) Middlesex County	366	0.35
Oakland, CA (city) Alameda County	359	0.09
Riverside, CA (city) Riverside County	357	0.12
Southfield, MI (township) Oakland County	356	2.45
Newton, MA (city) Middlesex County	356	0.42
Royal Oak, MI (city) Oakland County	351	0.61
Portland, OR (city) Multnomah County	347	0.06
Durham, NC (city) Durham County	340	0.15
Troy, MI (city) Oakland County	338	0.42
Fullerton, CA (city) Orange County	338	0.25
Arden-Arcade, CA (cdp) Sacramento County	337	0.37
La Verne, CA (city) Los Angeles County	334	1.07
North Tustin, CA (cdp) Orange County	333	1.36
Franklin Town, MA (city) Norfolk County	331	1.07
San Antonio, TX (city) Medina County	323	0.03
Rowland Heights, CA (cdp) Los Angeles County	322	0.62
Kansas City, MO (city) Jackson County	321	0.07
Tucson, AZ (city) Pima County	321	0.06
Rockville, MD (city) Montgomery County	320	0.55
Yorba Linda, CA (city) Orange County	319	0.51
Austin, TX (city) Travis County	319	0.04
Millbrae, CA (city) San Mateo County	316	1.50
Bethesda, MD (cdp) Montgomery County	316	0.54
Glendora, CA (city) Los Angeles County	315	0.63
Fargo, ND (city) Cass County	314	0.31
North Providence, RI (town) Providence County	313	0.97
Corona, CA (city) Riverside County	313	0.21
Aurora, CO (city) Arapahoe County	312	0.10
Staten Island, NY (borough) Richmond County	311	0.07
Beverly Hills, MI (village) Oakland County	307	2.99
Moorpark, CA (city) Ventura County	305	0.90
Dana Point, CA (city) Orange County	304	0.91
Livermore, CA (city) Alameda County	304	0.39
Dearborn Heights, MI (city) Wayne County	303	0.52
Salt Lake City, UT (city) Salt Lake County	302	0.16
Barnstable Town, MA (city) Barnstable County	299	0.65
Newington, CT (cdp/town) Hartford County	297	0.98
Tampa, FL (city) Hillsborough County	297	0.09
Pawtucket, RI (city) Providence County	296	0.41
Walnut Creek, CA (city) Contra Costa County	291	0.46
Colorado Springs, CO (city) El Paso County	290	0.07

SECTION THREE

Please refer to the Explanation of Data in the front of the book for more detailed information.

Ancestry

Armenian

Top 150 Places Sorted by Percent of Total Population

Based on all places, regardless of total population

Place	Population	%
Glendale, CA (city) Los Angeles County	65,434	34.05
Leggett, CA (cdp) Mendocino County	13	19.12
Avery, CA (cdp) Calaveras County	59	15.49
Ronald, WA (cdp) Kittitas County	15	14.02
Petersham, MA (cdp) Worcester County	32	13.68
Harbor Hills, NY (cdp) Nassau County	67	13.54
Fort Snelling, MN (unorganized territory) Hennepin County	9	12.33
Burbank, CA (city) Los Angeles County	12,490	12.16
La Crescenta-Montrose, CA (cdp) Los Angeles County	2,171	10.89
Belleair Shore, FL (town) Pinellas County	7	9.59
Driscoll, ND (cdp) Burleigh County	9	9.57
Village of Grosse Pointe Shores, MI (city) Macomb County	6	8.45
Duxbury, MA (cdp) Plymouth County	137	8.19
Andover, VT (town) Windsor County	37	8.11
Tannersville, NY (village) Greene County	34	7.83
Kanarraville, UT (town) Iron County	31	7.54
Buffalo Gap, SD (town) Custer County	12	6.98
Kahlotus, WA (city) Franklin County	13	6.67
Duane Lake, NY (cdp) Schenectady County	16	6.61
Watertown Town, MA (city) Middlesex County	2,036	6.44
Bieber, CA (cdp) Lassen County	16	6.23
Klein, MT (cdp) Musselshell County	24	6.14
Castle Hill, CA (cdp) Contra Costa County	81	6.10
Lake Angelus, MI (city) Oakland County	17	5.78
Manchester, VT (village) Bennington County	43	5.70
Saddle River, NJ (borough) Bergen County	176	5.61
Amador City, CA (city) Amador County	7	5.47
Altadena, CA (cdp) Los Angeles County	2,354	5.18
Herron Island, WA (cdp) Pierce County	9	5.14
Pine Hill, NY (cdp) Ulster County	13	5.06
Lakeview, GA (cdp) Catoosa County	260	4.97
Pleasant Valley, NY (cdp) Dutchess County	41	4.95
Meadow Valley, CA (cdp) Plumas County	33	4.90
Hickory Flat, MS (town) Benton County	21	4.87
Manila, CA (cdp) Humboldt County	42	4.74
Belmont, MA (cdp/town) Middlesex County	1,126	4.62
La Cañada Flintridge, CA (city) Los Angeles County	925	4.57
Seabrook Beach, NH (cdp) Rockingham County	69	4.48
Yarnell, AZ (cdp) Yavapai County	26	4.46
Santa Venetia, CA (cdp) Marin County	227	4.45
Indian River, MI (cdp) Cheboygan County	77	4.44
Hasley Canyon, CA (cdp) Los Angeles County	42	4.35
Burlington, MI (township) Calhoun County	85	4.24
Healdton, OK (city) Carter County	117	4.21
East Burke, VT (cdp) Caledonia County	5	4.07
Central Hancock, ME (unorganized territory) Hancock County	4	4.00
Boylston, NY (town) Oswego County	19	3.98
Old Fig Garden, CA (cdp) Fresno County	201	3.93
Hewlett, NY (cdp) Nassau County	264	3.92
Munsey Park, NY (village) Nassau County	103	3.87
Double Spring, NV (cdp) Douglas County	8	3.83
McKinley Park, AK (cdp) Denali Borough	6	3.80
Waldoboro, ME (cdp) Lincoln County	40	3.79
Pittsford, NY (village) Monroe County	52	3.70
Queen Anne, MD (town) Queen Anne's County	9	3.70
Pasadena, CA (city) Los Angeles County	5,017	3.68
East Pasadena, CA (cdp) Los Angeles County	211	3.67
Orchard Lake Village, MI (city) Oakland County	77	3.62
Centerville, CA (cdp) Fresno County	11	3.58
San Pasqual, CA (cdp) Los Angeles County	72	3.51
Chenango Bridge, NY (cdp) Broome County	106	3.48
Barker Ten Mile, NC (cdp) Robeson County	41	3.48
West Sand Lake, NY (cdp) Rensselaer County	91	3.47
Naselle, WA (cdp) Pacific County	24	3.47
Bleecker, NY (town) Fulton County	15	3.40
Salton City, CA (cdp) Imperial County	47	3.36
Malinta, OH (village) Henry County	10	3.36
Willowbrook, KS (city) Reno County	4	3.25
Shrub Oak, NY (cdp) Westchester County	58	3.20
Exeter, RI (town) Washington County	205	3.14
Englewood Cliffs, NJ (borough) Bergen County	165	3.13
Delta Junction, AK (city) Southeast Fairbanks Census Area	32	3.12
Adams, WI (city) Adams County	55	3.08
Deltaville, VA (cdp) Middlesex County	25	3.05
Montebello, CA (city) Los Angeles County	1,885	3.02
Daytona Beach Shores, FL (city) Volusia County	131	3.02
Easton, NY (town) Washington County	79	3.00
Queen Anne, MD (cdp) Prince George's County	34	3.00
Beverly Hills, MI (village) Oakland County	307	2.99
Upper Brookville, NY (village) Nassau County	43	2.89
Sunnyside, CA (cdp) Fresno County	129	2.83
York Harbor, ME (cdp) York County	83	2.79
Blue Lake, CA (city) Humboldt County	36	2.78
Rutland, MA (cdp) Worcester County	64	2.76
Newfields, NH (cdp) Rockingham County	8	2.76
Port Hope, MI (village) Huron County	6	2.76
Bradner, OH (village) Wood County	33	2.67
Knox, ME (town) Waldo County	18	2.61
Lexington, MA (cdp/town) Middlesex County	801	2.60
South Run, VA (cdp) Fairfax County	175	2.60
Leona Valley, CA (cdp) Los Angeles County	42	2.60
Oradell, NJ (borough) Bergen County	204	2.57
Georgetown, NY (town) Madison County	23	2.57
South Oroville, CA (cdp) Butte County	171	2.56
Ross, CA (town) Marin County	51	2.55
Old Tappan, NJ (borough) Bergen County	144	2.54
Roslyn Harbor, NY (village) Nassau County	29	2.52
Humbird, WI (cdp) Clark County	7	2.52
Woodland Hills, UT (city) Utah County	33	2.51
Ridgefield, NJ (borough) Bergen County	274	2.50
Novi, MI (township) Oakland County	3	2.50
Tuscarora, MI (township) Cheboygan County	77	2.49
Orange, NH (town) Grafton County	8	2.48
Gray, ME (cdp) Cumberland County	18	2.47
Albright, WV (town) Preston County	8	2.46
Southfield, MI (township) Oakland County	356	2.45
East Marion, NY (cdp) Suffolk County	32	2.39
Petersham, MA (town) Worcester County	32	2.39
Lynnfield, MA (cdp/town) Essex County	273	2.38
Golf Manor, OH (village) Hamilton County	86	2.36
Sea Ranch Lakes, FL (village) Broward County	19	2.33
Franklin Lakes, NJ (borough) Bergen County	243	2.31
Weldon, CA (cdp) Kern County	52	2.26
Northvale, NJ (borough) Bergen County	103	2.25
Pullman, WV (town) Ritchie County	6	2.25
Montara, CA (cdp) San Mateo County	69	2.24
Wadsworth, IL (village) Lake County	86	2.23
Portland, CT (cdp) Middlesex County	132	2.22
Duarte, CA (city) Los Angeles County	473	2.21
Northwood, NH (town) Rockingham County	92	2.20
Harrington Park, NJ (borough) Bergen County	100	2.15
Tahoe Vista, CA (cdp) Placer County	33	2.14
Cody, NE (village) Cherry County	3	2.14
East Douglas, MA (cdp) Worcester County	49	2.13
Waltham, MA (city) Middlesex County	1,267	2.12
Cranston, RI (city) Providence County	1,691	2.10
Douglas, MA (town) Worcester County	172	2.09
Plainedge, NY (cdp) Nassau County	191	2.07
Indian Creek, IL (village) Lake County	11	2.06
Cumberland Head, NY (cdp) Clinton County	34	2.05
Mokelumne Hill, CA (cdp) Calaveras County	15	2.04
Narragansett Pier, RI (cdp) Washington County	71	2.03
Searsburg, VT (town) Bennington County	3	2.03
Del Rio, CA (cdp) Stanislaus County	24	2.02
Freeport, PA (township) Greene County	5	2.01
Langley, WA (city) Island County	21	2.00
Northfield, OH (village) Summit County	73	1.97
Paramus, NJ (borough) Bergen County	510	1.96
Silver Lake, NJ (cdp) Warren County	7	1.96
Plandome, NY (village) Nassau County	27	1.95
Los Angeles, CA (city) Los Angeles County	73,256	1.94
Fleischmanns, NY (village) Delaware County	4	1.94
Villa Park, CA (city) Orange County	112	1.93
Stafford, OR (cdp) Clackamas County	34	1.93
Royalton, MI (township) Berrien County	88	1.92
Alpine, NJ (borough) Bergen County	37	1.92
Wormleysburg, PA (borough) Cumberland County	57	1.91
Wind Point, WI (village) Racine County	32	1.89
Tariffville, CT (cdp) Hartford County	24	1.89
Fairplay, CO (town) Park County	12	1.89

Please refer to the Explanation of Data in the front of the book for more detailed information.

Ancestry

Armenian

Top 150 Places Sorted by Percent of Total Population

Based on places with total population of 7,500 or more

Place	Population	%
Glendale, CA (city) Los Angeles County	65,434	34.05
Burbank, CA (city) Los Angeles County	12,490	12.16
La Crescenta-Montrose, CA (cdp) Los Angeles County	2,171	10.89
Watertown Town, MA (city) Middlesex County	2,036	6.44
Altadena, CA (cdp) Los Angeles County	2,354	5.18
Belmont, MA (cdp/town) Middlesex County	1,126	4.62
La Cañada Flintridge, CA (city) Los Angeles County	925	4.57
Pasadena, CA (city) Los Angeles County	5,017	3.68
Montebello, CA (city) Los Angeles County	1,885	3.02
Beverly Hills, MI (village) Oakland County	307	2.99
Lexington, MA (cdp/town) Middlesex County	801	2.60
Oradell, NJ (borough) Bergen County	204	2.57
Ridgefield, NJ (borough) Bergen County	274	2.50
Southfield, MI (township) Oakland County	356	2.45
Lynnfield, MA (cdp/town) Essex County	273	2.38
Franklin Lakes, NJ (borough) Bergen County	243	2.31
Duarte, CA (city) Los Angeles County	473	2.21
Waltham, MA (city) Middlesex County	1,267	2.12
Cranston, RI (city) Providence County	1,691	2.10
Douglas, MA (town) Worcester County	172	2.09
Plainedge, NY (cdp) Nassau County	191	2.07
Paramus, NJ (borough) Bergen County	510	1.96
Los Angeles, CA (city) Los Angeles County	73,256	1.94
Bee Ridge, FL (cdp) Sarasota County	186	1.86
Palos Verdes Estates, CA (city) Los Angeles County	247	1.84
Cliffside Park, NJ (borough) Bergen County	425	1.82
Arlington, MA (cdp/town) Middlesex County	766	1.81
Horsham, PA (cdp) Montgomery County	261	1.81
Topanga, CA (cdp) Los Angeles County	154	1.81
Marple, PA (township) Delaware County	421	1.80
Fort Lewis, WA (cdp) Pierce County	244	1.78
Kensington, CT (cdp) Hartford County	153	1.75
Burlington, MA (cdp/town) Middlesex County	404	1.69
Charter Oak, CA (cdp) Los Angeles County	154	1.66
Bedford, MA (town) Middlesex County	206	1.58
Chesterton, IN (town) Porter County	207	1.57
Portland, CT (town) Middlesex County	148	1.57
Brown Deer, WI (village) Milwaukee County	184	1.55
Valley Center, CA (cdp) San Diego County	138	1.53
Sudbury, MA (town) Middlesex County	263	1.52
Wrentham, MA (town) Norfolk County	164	1.52
Mammoth Lakes, CA (town) Mono County	122	1.52
Lighthouse Point, FL (city) Broward County	158	1.51
Southwood Acres, CT (cdp) Hartford County	119	1.51
Millbrae, CA (city) San Mateo County	316	1.50
Fresno, CA (city) Fresno County	7,000	1.45
Haddam, CT (town) Middlesex County	117	1.43
Rancho Cordova, CA (city) Sacramento County	900	1.42
Glen Rock, NJ (borough) Bergen County	164	1.42
Bloomfield, MI (charter township) Oakland County	583	1.41
Rancho Palos Verdes, CA (city) Los Angeles County	581	1.40
North Greenbush, NY (town) Rensselaer County	166	1.40
Washington, NJ (township) Bergen County	125	1.39
Rodeo, CA (cdp) Contra Costa County	126	1.38
Cresskill, NJ (borough) Bergen County	115	1.37
North Tustin, CA (cdp) Orange County	333	1.36
Syosset, NY (cdp) Nassau County	257	1.36
Stoneham, MA (cdp/town) Middlesex County	285	1.34
Montecito, CA (cdp) Santa Barbara County	120	1.30
Norridge, IL (village) Cook County	186	1.29
Ramsey, NJ (borough) Bergen County	185	1.29
Seabrook, NH (town) Rockingham County	110	1.28
Millis, MA (town) Norfolk County	100	1.28
West Bloomfield, MI (charter township) Oakland County	814	1.26
Winchester, MA (cdp/town) Middlesex County	265	1.26
River Vale, NJ (township) Bergen County	121	1.26
Wyckoff, NJ (township) Bergen County	208	1.25
York, ME (town) York County	159	1.25
Weston, MA (town) Middlesex County	139	1.24
Hampstead, NH (town) Rockingham County	106	1.24
Shrewsbury, MA (town) Worcester County	432	1.23
Medway, MA (town) Norfolk County	155	1.23
Crete, IL (village) Will County	104	1.23
Hillsborough, CA (town) San Mateo County	130	1.22
Riverside, NJ (township) Burlington County	98	1.21
Ridgefield, CT (cdp) Fairfield County	93	1.20
Hermosa Beach, CA (city) Los Angeles County	230	1.19
Stevenson Ranch, CA (cdp) Los Angeles County	201	1.19
Rutland, MA (town) Worcester County	91	1.18
Kenmore, WA (city) King County	233	1.17
North Reading, MA (town) Middlesex County	170	1.17
Kingsburg, CA (city) Fresno County	129	1.17
Greenville, RI (cdp) Providence County	103	1.17
Park Ridge, NJ (borough) Bergen County	101	1.17
Agoura Hills, CA (city) Los Angeles County	234	1.15
Alamo, CA (cdp) Contra Costa County	174	1.15
West Boylston, MA (town) Worcester County	88	1.15
Brewster, MA (town) Barnstable County	112	1.13
Ashland, MA (town) Middlesex County	179	1.12
Weehawken, NJ (township) Hudson County	141	1.12
Broomall, PA (cdp) Delaware County	125	1.11
Westwood, MA (town) Norfolk County	159	1.10
Fort Lee, NJ (borough) Bergen County	385	1.09
Clovis, CA (city) Fresno County	984	1.08
North Kingstown, RI (town) Washington County	287	1.08
Sand Lake, NY (town) Rensselaer County	91	1.08
La Verne, CA (city) Los Angeles County	334	1.07
Franklin Town, MA (city) Norfolk County	331	1.07
Palisades Park, NJ (borough) Bergen County	203	1.06
Middleton, MA (town) Essex County	92	1.06
Narragansett, RI (town) Washington County	169	1.05
Kittery, ME (town) York County	101	1.05
Billerica, MA (town) Middlesex County	406	1.03
Genoa, MI (township) Livingston County	200	1.02
Burlingame, CA (city) San Mateo County	286	1.01
Horsham, PA (township) Montgomery County	261	1.01
East Hanover, NJ (township) Morris County	114	1.01
Redondo Beach, CA (city) Los Angeles County	659	1.00
Summerlin South, NV (cdp) Clark County	218	1.00
Hudson, MA (cdp) Middlesex County	147	1.00
Bonadelle Ranchos-Madera Ranchos, CA (cdp) Madera County	89	1.00
Upper Saddle River, NJ (borough) Bergen County	81	1.00
Pembroke, MA (town) Plymouth County	175	0.99
Concord, PA (township) Delaware County	160	0.99
Saddle Brook, NJ (township) Bergen County	134	0.99
South Lyon, MI (city) Oakland County	110	0.99
Newington, CT (cdp/town) Hartford County	297	0.98
Allen Park, MI (city) Wayne County	281	0.98
Milford, MA (cdp) Worcester County	245	0.98
Birmingham, MI (city) Oakland County	195	0.98
North Providence, RI (town) Providence County	313	0.97
Tamalpais-Homestead Valley, CA (cdp) Marin County	102	0.96
Wakefield-Peacedale, RI (cdp) Washington County	87	0.96
Oak Park, CA (cdp) Ventura County	134	0.95
Leicester, MA (town) Worcester County	104	0.95
Libertyville, IL (village) Lake County	193	0.94
Chenango, NY (town) Broome County	106	0.94
Milford, MA (town) Worcester County	260	0.93
Palm Valley, FL (cdp) St. Johns County	185	0.93
Orinda, CA (city) Contra Costa County	163	0.93
Lansing, NY (town) Tompkins County	102	0.93
Putnam, CT (cdp) Windham County	70	0.93
Drexel Hill, PA (cdp) Delaware County	265	0.92
East Massapequa, NY (cdp) Nassau County	164	0.92
Duxbury, MA (town) Plymouth County	137	0.92
Lake Villa, IL (village) Lake County	78	0.92
Dana Point, CA (city) Orange County	304	0.91
Windham, NH (town) Rockingham County	120	0.91
Algoma, MI (township) Kent County	87	0.91
Moorpark, CA (city) Ventura County	305	0.90
Wilmington, MA (cdp/town) Middlesex County	196	0.90
Truckee, CA (town) Nevada County	142	0.90
Newtown, PA (township) Delaware County	108	0.89
Melrose, MA (city) Middlesex County	234	0.88
Lincoln, RI (town) Providence County	185	0.88
Lynbrook, NY (village) Nassau County	171	0.88
Hebron, CT (town) Tolland County	84	0.88
Smithfield, RI (town) Providence County	186	0.87
New Canaan, CT (town) Fairfield County	168	0.86
Ridgefield Park, NJ (village) Bergen County	109	0.86

Please refer to the Explanation of Data in the front of the book for more detailed information.

Ancestry

Assyrian/Chaldean/Syriac

U.S. and 50 States Sorted by Population and Percent of Total Population

Place	Population	%
United States	**89,410**	**0.03**
Michigan	33,051	0.33
California	27,563	0.08
Illinois	17,225	0.14
Arizona	2,956	0.05
Florida	996	0.01
New Jersey	891	0.01
Connecticut	703	0.02
New York	644	<0.01
Nevada	555	0.02
Indiana	453	0.01
Virginia	438	0.01
Texas	406	<0.01
Ohio	389	<0.01
Pennsylvania	386	<0.01
Georgia	342	<0.01
Washington	227	<0.01
Massachusetts	223	<0.01
Maryland	196	<0.01
Tennessee	177	<0.01
Rhode Island	160	0.02
North Carolina	138	<0.01
Colorado	130	<0.01
New Mexico	118	0.01
Oregon	117	<0.01
Arkansas	110	<0.01
Wisconsin	97	<0.01
South Carolina	94	<0.01
Mississippi	92	<0.01
Minnesota	77	<0.01
Missouri	70	<0.01
Oklahoma	56	<0.01
Kentucky	42	<0.01
Alabama	32	<0.01
Kansas	30	<0.01
Maine	28	<0.01
Wyoming	25	<0.01
West Virginia	24	<0.01
Hawaii	18	<0.01
Utah	18	<0.01
Iowa	17	<0.01
Nebraska	15	<0.01
Alaska	14	<0.01
District of Columbia	14	<0.01
New Hampshire	13	<0.01
North Dakota	12	<0.01
Vermont	12	<0.01
Idaho	10	<0.01
Delaware	6	<0.01
Louisiana	0	0.00
Montana	0	0.00
South Dakota	0	0.00

Place	Population	%
Michigan	33,051	0.33
Illinois	17,225	0.14
California	27,563	0.08
Arizona	2,956	0.05
United States	**89,410**	**0.03**
Connecticut	703	0.02
Nevada	555	0.02
Rhode Island	160	0.02
Florida	996	0.01
New Jersey	891	0.01
Indiana	453	0.01
Virginia	438	0.01
New Mexico	118	0.01
New York	644	<0.01
Texas	406	<0.01
Ohio	389	<0.01
Pennsylvania	386	<0.01
Georgia	342	<0.01
Washington	227	<0.01
Massachusetts	223	<0.01
Maryland	196	<0.01
Tennessee	177	<0.01
North Carolina	138	<0.01
Colorado	130	<0.01
Oregon	117	<0.01
Arkansas	110	<0.01
Wisconsin	97	<0.01
South Carolina	94	<0.01
Mississippi	92	<0.01
Minnesota	77	<0.01
Missouri	70	<0.01
Oklahoma	56	<0.01
Kentucky	42	<0.01
Alabama	32	<0.01
Kansas	30	<0.01
Maine	28	<0.01
Wyoming	25	<0.01
West Virginia	24	<0.01
Hawaii	18	<0.01
Utah	18	<0.01
Iowa	17	<0.01
Nebraska	15	<0.01
Alaska	14	<0.01
District of Columbia	14	<0.01
New Hampshire	13	<0.01
North Dakota	12	<0.01
Vermont	12	<0.01
Idaho	10	<0.01
Delaware	6	<0.01
Louisiana	0	0.00
Montana	0	0.00
South Dakota	0	0.00

Please refer to the Explanation of Data in the front of the book for more detailed information.

Ancestry

Assyrian/Chaldean/Syriac

Top 150 Places Sorted by Population

Based on all places, regardless of total population

Place	Population	%
Sterling Heights, MI (city) Macomb County	8,026	6.19
Turlock, CA (city) Stanislaus County	5,798	8.61
West Bloomfield, MI (charter township) Oakland County	5,475	8.46
El Cajon, CA (city) San Diego County	4,776	4.88
Chicago, IL (city) Cook County	4,646	0.17
Skokie, IL (village) Cook County	3,833	6.01
Warren, MI (city) Macomb County	2,627	1.93
Modesto, CA (city) Stanislaus County	2,553	1.26
San Jose, CA (city) Santa Clara County	2,016	0.22
Troy, MI (city) Oakland County	1,643	2.03
Niles, IL (village) Cook County	1,483	5.03
Los Angeles, CA (city) Los Angeles County	1,479	0.04
Shelby, MI (charter township) Macomb County	1,454	2.00
Madison Heights, MI (city) Oakland County	1,310	4.37
Farmington Hills, MI (city) Oakland County	1,226	1.53
Phoenix, AZ (city) Maricopa County	1,205	0.08
Commerce, MI (charter township) Oakland County	1,119	2.85
Lincolnwood, IL (village) Cook County	905	7.29
Southfield, MI (city) Oakland County	863	1.18
Rancho San Diego, CA (cdp) San Diego County	776	3.83
Oak Park, MI (city) Oakland County	706	2.36
Detroit, MI (city) Wayne County	656	0.09
Des Plaines, IL (city) Cook County	614	1.07
Hazel Park, MI (city) Oakland County	561	3.32
Morton Grove, IL (village) Cook County	533	2.33
Waterford, MI (charter township) Oakland County	527	0.73
Rochester Hills, MI (city) Oakland County	500	0.71
Jamul, CA (cdp) San Diego County	465	8.74
San Diego, CA (city) San Diego County	463	0.04
Novi, MI (city) Oakland County	450	0.84
Spring Valley, CA (cdp) San Diego County	448	1.64
Macomb, MI (township) Macomb County	430	0.57
Hamlin, MI (township) Eaton County	410	12.42
Bloomfield, MI (charter township) Oakland County	367	0.89
Mount Prospect, IL (village) Cook County	355	0.66
Riverbank, CA (city) Stanislaus County	350	1.61
Pine Castle, FL (cdp) Orange County	333	3.05
Keego Harbor, MI (city) Oakland County	329	11.23
Scottsdale, AZ (city) Maricopa County	312	0.14
Glenview, IL (village) Cook County	303	0.69
Flint, MI (city) Genesee County	277	0.26
Peoria, AZ (city) Yavapai County	277	0.19
Glendale, AZ (city) Maricopa County	264	0.11
Elgin, IL (city) Kane County	263	0.25
Grand Blanc, MI (charter township) Genesee County	262	0.72
Ceres, CA (city) Stanislaus County	262	0.59
Park Ridge, IL (city) Cook County	255	0.69
Bonita, CA (cdp) San Diego County	242	1.72
Glendale, CA (city) Los Angeles County	235	0.12
Casa de Oro-Mount Helix, CA (cdp) San Diego County	228	1.19
New York, NY (city) Kings County	227	<0.01
Las Vegas, NV (city) Clark County	221	0.04
Santa Clara, CA (city) Santa Clara County	219	0.19
Northville, MI (township) Wayne County	214	0.79
Chandler, AZ (city) Maricopa County	214	0.09
New Britain, CT (city/town) Hartford County	213	0.29
San Francisco, CA (city) San Francisco County	196	0.02
Bartlett, IL (village) DuPage County	185	0.46
New Milford, NJ (borough) Bergen County	183	1.13
Bolingbrook, IL (village) Will County	172	0.24
Southington, CT (town) Hartford County	171	0.40
Cupertino, CA (city) Santa Clara County	168	0.30
Santa Clarita, CA (city) Los Angeles County	162	0.09
Yonkers, NY (city) Westchester County	157	0.08
Sacramento, CA (city) Sacramento County	151	0.03
Sunnyvale, CA (city) Santa Clara County	141	0.10
Manhattan, NY (borough) New York County	137	0.01
Georgetown, IL (city) Vermilion County	134	3.84
Augusta-Richmond County, GA (cons. govt) Richmond County	130	0.07
Palo Alto, CA (city) Santa Clara County	126	0.20
Burton, MI (city) Genesee County	125	0.41
Elk Grove Village, IL (village) Cook County	125	0.38
Poway, CA (city) San Diego County	121	0.25
Oakland, MI (charter township) Oakland County	120	0.74
Hanover Park, IL (village) Cook County	119	0.32
Royal Oak, MI (city) Oakland County	116	0.20
Flushing, MI (city) Genesee County	115	1.36
Orchard Lake Village, MI (city) Oakland County	114	5.36
Hoffman Estates, IL (village) Cook County	114	0.22
White Lake, MI (charter township) Oakland County	113	0.38
Canton, MI (charter township) Wayne County	113	0.13
Surprise, AZ (city) Maricopa County	113	0.11
Santee, CA (city) San Diego County	110	0.21
Roselle, IL (village) DuPage County	109	0.48
Clovis, CA (city) Fresno County	108	0.12
Bostonia, CA (cdp) San Diego County	106	0.73
Sunrise Manor, NV (cdp) Clark County	104	0.05
Empire, CA (cdp) Stanislaus County	103	2.74
South Elgin, IL (village) Kane County	101	0.48
Schiller Park, IL (village) Cook County	100	0.86
Young, AZ (town) Maricopa County	99	1.74
Riverside, CA (city) Riverside County	99	0.03
Santa Fe, NM (city) Santa Fe County	98	0.14
Roseville, CA (city) Placer County	98	0.09
Columbus, OH (city) Franklin County	97	0.01
Livonia, MI (city) Wayne County	95	0.10
La Mesa, CA (city) San Diego County	94	0.17
Red Bluff, CA (city) Tehama County	93	0.67
Irvine, CA (city) Orange County	87	0.04
Northbrook, IL (village) Cook County	86	0.26
La Habra, CA (city) Orange County	85	0.14
Anaheim, CA (city) Orange County	85	0.03
Wixom, MI (city) Oakland County	82	0.61
Prospect Heights, IL (city) Cook County	81	0.50
Cascade, MI (charter township) Kent County	81	0.48
Fremont, CA (city) Alameda County	81	0.04
Otisco, MI (township) Ionia County	80	3.13
Bonadelle Ranchos-Madera Ranchos, CA (cdp) Madera County	79	0.88
Fresno, CA (city) Fresno County	79	0.02
Southfield, MI (township) Oakland County	78	0.54
Gurnee, IL (village) Lake County	78	0.25
Westminster, CA (city) Orange County	78	0.09
Henderson, NV (city) Clark County	78	0.03
La Presa, CA (cdp) San Diego County	77	0.22
Ontario, CA (city) San Bernardino County	77	0.05
Lansdowne, VA (cdp) Loudoun County	76	0.77
Teaneck, NJ (township) Bergen County	76	0.19
Murrieta, CA (city) Riverside County	76	0.08
Mesa, AZ (city) Maricopa County	76	0.02
Marysville, MI (city) St. Clair County	75	0.75
Independence, MI (charter township) Oakland County	75	0.22
Haverford, PA (township) Delaware County	75	0.15
Burbank, CA (city) Los Angeles County	74	0.07
Naperville, IL (city) DuPage County	74	0.05
Berkley, MI (city) Oakland County	73	0.48
Bristol, CT (city/town) Hartford County	73	0.12
Rolling Meadows, IL (city) Cook County	72	0.31
Desert Hot Springs, CA (city) Riverside County	72	0.29
Visalia, CA (city) Tulare County	71	0.06
New Baltimore, MI (city) Macomb County	70	0.62
Yorba Linda, CA (city) Orange County	69	0.11
Bellflower, CA (city) Los Angeles County	69	0.09
Clayton, MI (charter township) Genesee County	68	0.89
Marina, CA (city) Monterey County	67	0.34
Los Gatos, CA (town) Santa Clara County	67	0.23
Danville, IL (city) Vermilion County	66	0.20
Streamwood, IL (village) Cook County	65	0.17
Long Beach, CA (city) Los Angeles County	65	0.01
Johnsburg, IL (village) McHenry County	64	1.02
Stanton, CA (city) Orange County	64	0.17
Hughson, CA (city) Stanislaus County	63	1.01
Lake in the Hills, IL (village) McHenry County	63	0.22
Bakersfield, CA (city) Kern County	63	0.02
Green Oak, MI (township) Livingston County	62	0.35
Ferndale, MI (city) Oakland County	62	0.31
Milpitas, CA (city) Santa Clara County	62	0.10
Livermore, CA (city) Alameda County	62	0.08
Aberdeen, IN (cdp) Porter County	61	2.79
Lathrup Village, MI (city) Oakland County	61	1.49
Virginia Beach, VA (ind. city) Virginia Beach independent city	61	0.01

Ancestry

Assyrian/Chaldean/Syriac

Top 150 Places Sorted by Percent of Total Population

Based on all places, regardless of total population

Place	Population	%
Hamlin, MI (township) Eaton County	410	12.42
Keego Harbor, MI (city) Oakland County	329	11.23
Jamul, CA (cdp) San Diego County	465	8.74
Turlock, CA (city) Stanislaus County	5,798	8.61
West Bloomfield, MI (charter township) Oakland County	5,475	8.46
Lincolnwood, IL (village) Cook County	905	7.29
Sterling Heights, MI (city) Macomb County	8,026	6.19
Skokie, IL (village) Cook County	3,833	6.01
Lamy, NM (cdp) Santa Fe County	20	5.99
Orchard Lake Village, MI (city) Oakland County	114	5.36
Niles, IL (village) Cook County	1,483	5.03
Millington, IL (village) LaSalle County	43	4.90
El Cajon, CA (city) San Diego County	4,776	4.88
Madison Heights, MI (city) Oakland County	1,310	4.37
Georgetown, IL (city) Vermilion County	134	3.84
Rancho San Diego, CA (cdp) San Diego County	776	3.83
Hazel Park, MI (city) Oakland County	561	3.32
Otisco, MI (township) Ionia County	80	3.13
Pine Castle, FL (cdp) Orange County	333	3.05
Commerce, MI (charter township) Oakland County	1,119	2.85
Aberdeen, IN (cdp) Porter County	61	2.79
Empire, CA (cdp) Stanislaus County	103	2.74
Crystal, WI (town) Washburn County	6	2.71
Rock River, MI (township) Alger County	35	2.49
Oak Park, MI (city) Oakland County	706	2.36
Morton Grove, IL (village) Cook County	533	2.33
Lily Lake, WI (cdp) Kenosha County	12	2.17
Bass Lake, CA (cdp) Madera County	10	2.16
Louisville, TN (city) Blount County	52	2.05
Troy, MI (city) Oakland County	1,643	2.03
Shelby, MI (charter township) Macomb County	1,454	2.00
Warren, MI (city) Macomb County	2,627	1.93
Young, AZ (town) Maricopa County	99	1.74
Bonita, CA (cdp) San Diego County	242	1.72
Cambrian Park, CA (cdp) Santa Clara County	54	1.66
Spring Valley, CA (cdp) San Diego County	448	1.64
Manlius, MI (township) Allegan County	49	1.64
Riverbank, CA (city) Stanislaus County	350	1.61
East Jordan, MI (city) Charlevoix County	31	1.61
Rio Verde, AZ (cdp) Maricopa County	28	1.59
Meridian Station, MS (cdp) Lauderdale County	39	1.55
Rose Valley, PA (borough) Delaware County	15	1.55
Farmington Hills, MI (city) Oakland County	1,226	1.53
Graton, CA (cdp) Sonoma County	24	1.50
Lathrup Village, MI (city) Oakland County	61	1.49
Flushing, MI (city) Genesee County	115	1.36
Big Pine Key, FL (cdp) Monroe County	50	1.33
Tilden, MI (township) Marquette County	15	1.33
Birch Run, MI (village) Saginaw County	22	1.29
Woodhull, MI (township) Shiawassee County	49	1.27
Modesto, CA (city) Stanislaus County	2,553	1.26
New Lothrop, MI (village) Shiawassee County	8	1.25
Casa de Oro-Mount Helix, CA (cdp) San Diego County	228	1.19
Southfield, MI (city) Oakland County	863	1.18
Keyes, CA (cdp) Stanislaus County	60	1.18
Franklin, MI (village) Oakland County	37	1.18
Sleepy Hollow, IL (village) Kane County	40	1.17
Emmett, MI (township) St. Clair County	31	1.16
Antrim, MI (township) Shiawassee County	30	1.15
New Milford, NJ (borough) Bergen County	183	1.13
Longbranch, WA (cdp) Pierce County	38	1.10
Shannon Hills, AR (city) Saline County	32	1.09
Venetian Village, IL (cdp) Lake County	33	1.08
Des Plaines, IL (city) Cook County	614	1.07
Johnsburg, IL (village) McHenry County	64	1.02
Hughson, CA (city) Stanislaus County	63	1.01
East Oakdale, CA (cdp) Stanislaus County	30	1.01
Egg Harbor, WI (village) Door County	2	0.98
Advance, NC (cdp) Davie County	11	0.96
Harrington Park, NJ (borough) Bergen County	44	0.95
Jordan, MI (township) Antrim County	9	0.94
Old Tappan, NJ (borough) Bergen County	53	0.93
Mohave Valley, AZ (cdp) Mohave County	21	0.93
Atglen, PA (borough) Chester County	12	0.93
Bloomfield, MI (charter township) Oakland County	367	0.89

Place	Population	%
Clayton, MI (charter township) Genesee County	68	0.89
Bonadelle Ranchos-Madera Ranchos, CA (cdp) Madera County	79	0.88
Schiller Park, IL (village) Cook County	100	0.86
Novi, MI (city) Oakland County	450	0.84
Northville, MI (township) Wayne County	214	0.79
Niederwald, TX (city) Hays County	3	0.79
Cambria, IL (village) Williamson County	9	0.78
Trout Lake, WA (cdp) Klickitat County	4	0.78
Lansdowne, VA (cdp) Loudoun County	76	0.77
Cohoctah, MI (township) Livingston County	26	0.76
Fabius, MI (township) St. Joseph County	25	0.76
Marysville, MI (city) St. Clair County	75	0.75
Oakland, MI (charter township) Oakland County	120	0.74
Waterford, MI (charter township) Oakland County	527	0.73
Bostonia, CA (cdp) San Diego County	106	0.73
Maple Ridge, MI (township) Delta County	7	0.73
Grand Blanc, MI (charter township) Genesee County	262	0.72
Downingtown, PA (borough) Chester County	57	0.72
Bowlus, MN (city) Morrison County	2	0.72
Rochester Hills, MI (city) Oakland County	500	0.71
Lake Villa, IL (village) Lake County	60	0.71
Saegertown, PA (borough) Crawford County	8	0.70
Glenview, IL (village) Cook County	303	0.69
Park Ridge, IL (city) Cook County	255	0.69
Morris Plains, NJ (borough) Morris County	38	0.68
Del Rey Oaks, CA (city) Monterey County	12	0.68
Red Bluff, CA (city) Tehama County	93	0.67
Mount Prospect, IL (village) Cook County	355	0.66
Esparto, CA (cdp) Yolo County	18	0.66
Greenville, MI (city) Montcalm County	55	0.65
New Baltimore, MI (city) Macomb County	70	0.62
South Barrington, IL (village) Cook County	27	0.62
Mountain Home, NC (cdp) Henderson County	20	0.62
Wixom, MI (city) Oakland County	82	0.61
Messiah College, PA (cdp) Cumberland County	15	0.61
Lake Bluff, IL (village) Lake County	36	0.60
Ceres, CA (city) Stanislaus County	262	0.59
Mineral, PA (township) Venango County	3	0.58
Macomb, MI (township) Macomb County	430	0.57
Blackhawk, CA (cdp) Contra Costa County	53	0.55
Chevy Chase Village, MD (town) Montgomery County	11	0.55
Osceola, MI (township) Houghton County	10	0.55
Southfield, MI (township) Oakland County	78	0.54
Stamford, VT (town) Bennington County	4	0.53
Washington, NJ (township) Bergen County	47	0.52
Midland Park, NJ (borough) Bergen County	36	0.51
Prospect Heights, IL (city) Cook County	81	0.50
Farmington, MI (city) Oakland County	52	0.50
Middlecreek, PA (township) Somerset County	5	0.50
Tuxedo Park, NY (village) Orange County	3	0.50
Rochester, MI (city) Oakland County	60	0.49
Haddam, CT (town) Middlesex County	40	0.49
Aroma Park, IL (village) Kankakee County	4	0.49
Roselle, IL (village) DuPage County	109	0.48
South Elgin, IL (village) Kane County	101	0.48
Cascade, MI (charter township) Kent County	81	0.48
Berkley, MI (city) Oakland County	73	0.48
Rose, MI (township) Oakland County	30	0.48
Island City, OR (city) Union County	5	0.48
Lexington, MI (village) Sanilac County	5	0.48
Potomac Mills, VA (cdp) Prince William County	22	0.47
Gold Key Lake, PA (cdp) Pike County	10	0.47
East Lansing, MI (city) Clinton County	7	0.47
Bartlett, IL (village) DuPage County	185	0.46
Gerrish, MI (township) Roscommon County	14	0.46
Raymond, NH (cdp) Rockingham County	13	0.46
Greatwood, TX (cdp) Fort Bend County	53	0.45
Kensington, CT (cdp) Hartford County	39	0.45
Odessa, MO (city) Lafayette County	23	0.44
Fox Island, WA (cdp) Pierce County	13	0.44
Saline, MI (township) Washtenaw County	9	0.44
Congers, NY (cdp) Rockland County	34	0.43
Richland, MI (township) Kalamazoo County	32	0.43
Strawberry, CA (cdp) Marin County	22	0.43
Kennedy, CA (cdp) San Joaquin County	14	0.43

Please refer to the Explanation of Data in the front of the book for more detailed information.

Ancestry

Assyrian/Chaldean/Syriac

Top 150 Places Sorted by Percent of Total Population

Based on places with total population of 7,500 or more

Place	Population	%
Turlock, CA (city) Stanislaus County	5,798	8.61
West Bloomfield, MI (charter township) Oakland County	5,475	8.46
Lincolnwood, IL (village) Cook County	905	7.29
Sterling Heights, MI (city) Macomb County	8,026	6.19
Skokie, IL (village) Cook County	3,833	6.01
Niles, IL (village) Cook County	1,483	5.03
El Cajon, CA (city) San Diego County	4,776	4.88
Madison Heights, MI (city) Oakland County	1,310	4.37
Rancho San Diego, CA (cdp) San Diego County	776	3.83
Hazel Park, MI (city) Oakland County	561	3.32
Pine Castle, FL (cdp) Orange County	333	3.05
Commerce, MI (charter township) Oakland County	1,119	2.85
Oak Park, MI (city) Oakland County	706	2.36
Morton Grove, IL (village) Cook County	533	2.33
Troy, MI (city) Oakland County	1,643	2.03
Shelby, MI (charter township) Macomb County	1,454	2.00
Warren, MI (city) Macomb County	2,627	1.93
Bonita, CA (cdp) San Diego County	242	1.72
Spring Valley, CA (cdp) San Diego County	448	1.64
Riverbank, CA (city) Stanislaus County	350	1.61
Farmington Hills, MI (city) Oakland County	1,226	1.53
Flushing, MI (city) Genesee County	115	1.36
Modesto, CA (city) Stanislaus County	2,553	1.26
Casa de Oro-Mount Helix, CA (cdp) San Diego County	228	1.19
Southfield, MI (city) Oakland County	863	1.18
New Milford, NJ (borough) Bergen County	183	1.13
Des Plaines, IL (city) Cook County	614	1.07
Bloomfield, MI (charter township) Oakland County	367	0.89
Clayton, MI (charter township) Genesee County	68	0.89
Bonadelle Ranchos-Madera Ranchos, CA (cdp) Madera County	79	0.88
Schiller Park, IL (village) Cook County	100	0.86
Novi, MI (city) Oakland County	450	0.84
Northville, MI (township) Wayne County	214	0.79
Lansdowne, VA (cdp) Loudoun County	76	0.77
Marysville, MI (city) St. Clair County	75	0.75
Oakland, MI (charter township) Oakland County	120	0.74
Waterford, MI (charter township) Oakland County	527	0.73
Bostonia, CA (cdp) San Diego County	106	0.73
Grand Blanc, MI (charter township) Genesee County	262	0.72
Downingtown, PA (borough) Chester County	57	0.72
Rochester Hills, MI (city) Oakland County	500	0.71
Lake Villa, IL (village) Lake County	60	0.71
Glenview, IL (village) Cook County	303	0.69
Park Ridge, IL (city) Cook County	255	0.69
Red Bluff, CA (city) Tehama County	93	0.67
Mount Prospect, IL (village) Cook County	355	0.66
Greenville, MI (city) Montcalm County	55	0.65
New Baltimore, MI (city) Macomb County	70	0.62
Wixom, MI (city) Oakland County	82	0.61
Ceres, CA (city) Stanislaus County	262	0.59
Macomb, MI (township) Macomb County	430	0.57
Blackhawk, CA (cdp) Contra Costa County	53	0.55
Southfield, MI (township) Oakland County	78	0.54
Washington, NJ (township) Bergen County	47	0.52
Prospect Heights, IL (city) Cook County	81	0.50
Farmington, MI (city) Oakland County	52	0.50
Rochester, MI (city) Oakland County	60	0.49
Haddam, CT (town) Middlesex County	40	0.49
Roselle, IL (village) DuPage County	109	0.48
South Elgin, IL (village) Kane County	101	0.48
Cascade, MI (charter township) Kent County	81	0.48
Berkley, MI (city) Oakland County	73	0.48
Bartlett, IL (village) DuPage County	185	0.46
Greatwood, TX (cdp) Fort Bend County	53	0.45
Kensington, CT (cdp) Hartford County	39	0.45
Congers, NY (cdp) Rockland County	34	0.43
Burton, MI (city) Genesee County	125	0.41
Southington, CT (town) Hartford County	171	0.40
Beverly Hills, MI (village) Oakland County	41	0.40
Elk Grove Village, IL (village) Cook County	125	0.38
White Lake, MI (charter township) Oakland County	113	0.38
Clawson, MI (city) Oakland County	46	0.38
Lakeland, TN (city) Shelby County	44	0.38
Winfield, IL (village) DuPage County	33	0.37
Maysville, KY (city) Mason County	32	0.36
Green Oak, MI (township) Livingston County	62	0.35
Harwood Heights, IL (village) Cook County	30	0.35
Marina, CA (city) Monterey County	67	0.34
Hanover Park, IL (village) Cook County	119	0.32
Rolling Meadows, IL (city) Cook County	72	0.31
Ferndale, MI (city) Oakland County	62	0.31
Cupertino, CA (city) Santa Clara County	168	0.30
Round Lake, IL (village) Lake County	48	0.30
Lincoln, MI (charter township) Berrien County	43	0.30
Oak Park, CA (cdp) Ventura County	42	0.30
New Britain, CT (city/town) Hartford County	213	0.29
Desert Hot Springs, CA (city) Riverside County	72	0.29
Ocean Springs, MS (city) Jackson County	50	0.29
Lincoln, RI (town) Providence County	57	0.27
Winter Gardens, CA (cdp) San Diego County	54	0.27
Flint, MI (city) Genesee County	277	0.26
Northbrook, IL (village) Cook County	86	0.26
Berlin, CT (town) Hartford County	50	0.26
Wood Dale, IL (city) DuPage County	36	0.26
Elgin, IL (city) Kane County	263	0.25
Poway, CA (city) San Diego County	121	0.25
Gurnee, IL (village) Lake County	78	0.25
Fairfax, VA (ind. city) Fairfax independent city	55	0.25
Lake Zurich, IL (village) Lake County	48	0.25
Big Bear City, CA (cdp) San Bernardino County	30	0.25
Bolingbrook, IL (village) Will County	172	0.24
Lyon, MI (charter township) Oakland County	33	0.24
Upper Saddle River, NJ (borough) Bergen County	19	0.24
Los Gatos, CA (town) Santa Clara County	67	0.23
Elmwood Park, IL (village) Cook County	58	0.23
La Riviera, CA (cdp) Sacramento County	26	0.23
St. Johns, MI (city) Clinton County	18	0.23
San Jose, CA (city) Santa Clara County	2,016	0.22
Hoffman Estates, IL (village) Cook County	114	0.22
La Presa, CA (cdp) San Diego County	77	0.22
Independence, MI (charter township) Oakland County	75	0.22
Lake in the Hills, IL (village) McHenry County	63	0.22
Wilmette, IL (village) Cook County	59	0.22
Oxford, MI (charter township) Oakland County	44	0.22
Vienna, MI (charter township) Genesee County	30	0.22
Livingston, CA (city) Merced County	28	0.22
Santee, CA (city) San Diego County	110	0.21
Alpine, CA (cdp) San Diego County	28	0.21
Clarendon Hills, IL (village) DuPage County	17	0.21
Palo Alto, CA (city) Santa Clara County	126	0.20
Royal Oak, MI (city) Oakland County	116	0.20
Danville, IL (city) Vermilion County	66	0.20
Cary, IL (village) McHenry County	36	0.20
Milford, MI (charter township) Oakland County	32	0.20
Atlas, MI (township) Genesee County	16	0.20
Peoria, AZ (city) Yavapai County	277	0.19
Santa Clara, CA (city) Santa Clara County	219	0.19
Teaneck, NJ (township) Bergen County	76	0.19
Lemont, IL (village) Cook County	29	0.19
Dallas, PA (township) Luzerne County	17	0.19
Forest Hills, MI (cdp) Kent County	46	0.18
Ballenger Creek, MD (cdp) Frederick County	34	0.18
Brandon, MI (charter township) Oakland County	27	0.18
Floris, VA (cdp) Fairfax County	15	0.18
Chicago, IL (city) Cook County	4,646	0.17
La Mesa, CA (city) San Diego County	94	0.17
Streamwood, IL (village) Cook County	65	0.17
Stanton, CA (city) Orange County	64	0.17
Newington, CT (cdp/town) Hartford County	52	0.17
La Grange Park, IL (village) Cook County	23	0.17
Emeryville, CA (city) Alameda County	16	0.17
Tiburon, CA (town) Marin County	15	0.17
Bloomingdale, NJ (borough) Passaic County	13	0.17
Burlingame, CA (city) San Mateo County	44	0.16
Lodi, NJ (borough) Bergen County	39	0.16
Birmingham, MI (city) Oakland County	32	0.16
Haverford, PA (township) Delaware County	75	0.15
Upper Arlington, OH (city) Franklin County	51	0.15
Hobart, IN (city) Lake County	42	0.15
Belmont, CA (city) San Mateo County	38	0.15

SECTION THREE

Please refer to the Explanation of Data in the front of the book for more detailed information.

Ancestry

Australian

U.S. and 50 States Sorted by Population and Percent of Total Population

Place	Population	%
United States	**94,368**	**0.03**
California	19,471	0.05
New York	7,418	0.04
Texas	5,952	0.02
Florida	5,111	0.03
Washington	4,271	0.07
Pennsylvania	2,907	0.02
Michigan	2,822	0.03
Illinois	2,719	0.02
Virginia	2,692	0.03
Colorado	2,509	0.05
Oregon	2,291	0.06
Ohio	2,134	0.02
New Jersey	2,090	0.02
North Carolina	2,088	0.02
Massachusetts	1,992	0.03
Utah	1,982	0.07
Arizona	1,965	0.03
Georgia	1,937	0.02
Missouri	1,495	0.03
Wisconsin	1,470	0.03
Connecticut	1,433	0.04
Maryland	1,424	0.02
Indiana	1,313	0.02
Minnesota	1,136	0.02
Nevada	1,087	0.04
Tennessee	1,029	0.02
Kentucky	1,012	0.02
Alabama	984	0.02
Oklahoma	980	0.03
Iowa	829	0.03
South Carolina	684	0.02
Idaho	664	0.04
Hawaii	644	0.05
Kansas	608	0.02
Alaska	593	0.09
Louisiana	552	0.01
New Mexico	503	0.02
Arkansas	500	0.02
New Hampshire	437	0.03
Nebraska	412	0.02
Maine	333	0.03
District of Columbia	295	0.05
Montana	290	0.03
Rhode Island	272	0.03
Wyoming	259	0.05
Mississippi	221	0.01
West Virginia	174	0.01
Vermont	146	0.02
North Dakota	105	0.02
South Dakota	83	0.01
Delaware	50	0.01

Place	Population	%
Alaska	593	0.09
Washington	4,271	0.07
Utah	1,982	0.07
Oregon	2,291	0.06
California	19,471	0.05
Colorado	2,509	0.05
Hawaii	644	0.05
District of Columbia	295	0.05
Wyoming	259	0.05
New York	7,418	0.04
Connecticut	1,433	0.04
Nevada	1,087	0.04
Idaho	664	0.04
United States	**94,368**	**0.03**
Florida	5,111	0.03
Michigan	2,822	0.03
Virginia	2,692	0.03
Massachusetts	1,992	0.03
Arizona	1,965	0.03
Missouri	1,495	0.03
Wisconsin	1,470	0.03
Oklahoma	980	0.03
Iowa	829	0.03
New Hampshire	437	0.03
Maine	333	0.03
Montana	290	0.03
Rhode Island	272	0.03
Texas	5,952	0.02
Pennsylvania	2,907	0.02
Illinois	2,719	0.02
Ohio	2,134	0.02
New Jersey	2,090	0.02
North Carolina	2,088	0.02
Georgia	1,937	0.02
Maryland	1,424	0.02
Indiana	1,313	0.02
Minnesota	1,136	0.02
Tennessee	1,029	0.02
Kentucky	1,012	0.02
Alabama	984	0.02
South Carolina	684	0.02
Kansas	608	0.02
New Mexico	503	0.02
Arkansas	500	0.02
Nebraska	412	0.02
Vermont	146	0.02
North Dakota	105	0.02
Louisiana	552	0.01
Mississippi	221	0.01
West Virginia	174	0.01
South Dakota	83	0.01
Delaware	50	0.01

Please refer to the Explanation of Data in the front of the book for more detailed information.

Ancestry

Australian

Top 150 Places Sorted by Population

Based on all places, regardless of total population

Place	Population	%
New York, NY (city) Kings County	3,906	0.05
Manhattan, NY (borough) New York County	2,719	0.17
Los Angeles, CA (city) Los Angeles County	2,486	0.07
San Diego, CA (city) San Diego County	1,114	0.09
San Francisco, CA (city) San Francisco County	954	0.12
Brooklyn, NY (borough) Kings County	832	0.03
Houston, TX (city) Harris County	690	0.03
Seattle, WA (city) King County	631	0.11
Chicago, IL (city) Cook County	561	0.02
Portland, OR (city) Multnomah County	455	0.08
Huntington Beach, CA (city) Orange County	391	0.21
Phoenix, AZ (city) Maricopa County	377	0.03
Albuquerque, NM (city) Bernalillo County	366	0.07
Sacramento, CA (city) Sacramento County	357	0.08
Raleigh, NC (city) Wake County	356	0.09
Austin, TX (city) Travis County	356	0.05
Huntsville, AL (city) Madison County	325	0.19
Anchorage, AK (municipality) Anchorage Municipality	324	0.11
Spokane, WA (city) Spokane County	321	0.16
Virginia Beach, VA (ind. city) Virginia Beach independent city	312	0.07
Denver, CO (city) Denver County	301	0.05
Murrieta, CA (city) Riverside County	295	0.31
Washington, DC (city) District of Columbia	295	0.05
The Woodlands, TX (cdp) Montgomery County	285	0.31
Queens, NY (borough) Queens County	285	0.01
Davis, CA (city) Yolo County	269	0.41
Indianapolis, IN (city) Marion County	258	0.03
Roseville, CA (city) Placer County	256	0.22
Irvine, CA (city) Orange County	256	0.13
Jersey City, NJ (city) Hudson County	255	0.10
Shiloh, IL (village) St. Clair County	250	2.08
Lexington-Fayette, KY (cons. govt) Fayette County	249	0.09
Meridian, ID (city) Ada County	243	0.35
Philadelphia, PA (city) Philadelphia County	243	0.02
Las Vegas, NV (city) Clark County	241	0.04
Reno, NV (city) Washoe County	236	0.11
Hempstead, NY (town) Nassau County	236	0.03
Chesterfield, MI (township) Macomb County	218	0.51
Warner Robins, GA (city) Houston County	218	0.34
Oakland, CA (city) Alameda County	216	0.06
Omaha, NE (city) Douglas County	215	0.05
Santa Barbara, CA (city) Santa Barbara County	212	0.24
Salt Lake City, UT (city) Salt Lake County	211	0.11
Arlington, TX (city) Tarrant County	203	0.06
Greenwich, CT (town) Fairfield County	196	0.32
Fort Worth, TX (city) Tarrant County	195	0.03
Trophy Club, TX (town) Denton County	191	2.38
Coconut Creek, FL (city) Broward County	191	0.37
Santa Monica, CA (city) Los Angeles County	188	0.21
Centennial, CO (city) Arapahoe County	182	0.18
Tucson, AZ (city) Pima County	179	0.03
Jacksonville, FL (city) Duval County	179	0.02
Victorville, CA (city) San Bernardino County	177	0.16
Salem, OR (city) Marion County	176	0.12
Boston, MA (city) Suffolk County	176	0.03
Coronado, CA (city) San Diego County	175	0.89
Thousand Oaks, CA (city) Ventura County	172	0.14
Lucerne, CA (cdp) Lake County	167	6.23
Santa Clarita, CA (city) Los Angeles County	166	0.10
Bellevue, WA (city) King County	165	0.14
Long Beach, CA (city) Los Angeles County	165	0.04
Urban Honolulu, HI (cdp) Honolulu County	162	0.05
Oklahoma City, OK (city) Oklahoma County	160	0.03
Minneapolis, MN (city) Hennepin County	159	0.04
Milwaukee, WI (city) Milwaukee County	159	0.03
Whitehall, OH (city) Franklin County	156	0.86
Westford, MA (town) Middlesex County	156	0.73
North Myrtle Beach, SC (city) Horry County	155	1.16
Columbus, OH (city) Franklin County	154	0.02
Avon, CO (town) Eagle County	152	2.40
Charlotte, NC (city) Mecklenburg County	152	0.02
Provo, UT (city) Utah County	151	0.14
Rancho Cucamonga, CA (city) San Bernardino County	150	0.09
Arlington, VA (cdp) Arlington County	150	0.08
Dallas, TX (city) Dallas County	149	0.01
Tacoma, WA (city) Pierce County	148	0.07
Urbandale, IA (city) Polk County	147	0.39
San Clemente, CA (city) Orange County	147	0.24
Hoboken, NJ (city) Hudson County	145	0.31
Danville, CA (town) Contra Costa County	143	0.34
Tulsa, OK (city) Tulsa County	142	0.04
Mesa, AZ (city) Maricopa County	141	0.03
West Jordan, UT (city) Salt Lake County	140	0.14
Norman, OK (city) Cleveland County	139	0.13
Fort Lauderdale, FL (city) Broward County	139	0.08
St. Joseph, MI (city) Berrien County	138	1.64
Sandy, UT (city) Salt Lake County	138	0.16
Plano, TX (city) Collin County	138	0.05
Germantown, TN (city) Shelby County	137	0.35
Encinitas, CA (city) San Diego County	133	0.23
West Linn, OR (city) Clackamas County	132	0.54
Ogden, UT (city) Weber County	132	0.16
Henderson, NV (city) Clark County	131	0.05
Marysville, WA (city) Snohomish County	130	0.22
Detroit, MI (city) Wayne County	129	0.02
Durham, NC (city) Durham County	127	0.06
Chandler, AZ (city) Maricopa County	126	0.05
Nashville-Davidson, TN (metro govt) Davidson County	125	0.02
San Antonio, TX (city) Medina County	125	0.01
Cotati, CA (city) Sonoma County	124	1.75
Cumberland, ME (town) Cumberland County	124	1.73
Princeton, IN (city) Gibson County	124	1.44
Roswell, GA (city) Fulton County	123	0.14
Torrance, CA (city) Los Angeles County	122	0.08
Valley Springs, CA (cdp) Calaveras County	121	3.00
San Anselmo, CA (town) Marin County	121	0.99
Walnut Creek, CA (city) Contra Costa County	121	0.19
Allentown, PA (city) Lehigh County	120	0.10
Wichita, KS (city) Sedgwick County	119	0.03
Tampa, FL (city) Hillsborough County	118	0.04
Louisville-Jefferson County, KY (metro govt) Jefferson County	118	0.02
Garden Home-Whitford, OR (cdp) Washington County	117	1.94
Yukon, OK (city) Canadian County	115	0.52
Naperville, IL (city) DuPage County	114	0.08
Hilton Head Island, SC (town) Beaufort County	113	0.31
Lake Forest, CA (city) Orange County	112	0.15
Marina del Rey, CA (cdp) Los Angeles County	110	1.20
Wellesley, MA (cdp/town) Norfolk County	110	0.40
Lakeland, FL (city) Polk County	110	0.11
Atlanta, GA (city) Fulton County	110	0.03
North Vernon, IN (city) Jennings County	109	1.71
Middle Smithfield, PA (township) Monroe County	109	0.70
Cambridge, MA (city) Middlesex County	108	0.10
Littleton, CO (city) Arapahoe County	107	0.26
Frisco, TX (city) Collin County	107	0.10
Baltimore, MD (city) Baltimore city County	107	0.02
Florence, KY (city) Boone County	106	0.36
Wilmington, NC (city) New Hanover County	106	0.10
Gainesville, FL (city) Alachua County	106	0.09
Vancouver, WA (city) Clark County	106	0.07
Windsor, CA (town) Sonoma County	105	0.41
Gilbert, AZ (town) Maricopa County	105	0.05
Colorado Springs, CO (city) El Paso County	105	0.03
Goleta, CA (city) Santa Barbara County	104	0.35
Milton, FL (city) Santa Rosa County	103	1.18
Brentwood, TN (city) Williamson County	103	0.29
Johns Creek, GA (city) Fulton County	103	0.14
Pembroke Pines, FL (city) Broward County	103	0.07
Spring Valley, NV (cdp) Clark County	103	0.06
Sitka, AK (borough) Sitka City and Borough	102	1.15
Red Oak, TX (city) Ellis County	102	1.03
Glendale, AZ (city) Maricopa County	102	0.04
Carlsbad, CA (city) San Diego County	101	0.10
Alexandria, VA (ind. city) Alexandria independent city	101	0.08
Huntington, NY (town) Suffolk County	101	0.05
Lake Worth, FL (city) Palm Beach County	100	0.28
Redlands, CA (city) San Bernardino County	100	0.15
Islip, NY (town) Suffolk County	100	0.03
Ewa Gentry, HI (cdp) Honolulu County	97	0.45
Wildwood, MO (city) St. Louis County	97	0.28

SECTION THREE

Please refer to the Explanation of Data in the front of the book for more detailed information.

Ancestry

Australian

Top 150 Places Sorted by Percent of Total Population

Based on all places, regardless of total population

Place	Population	%
La Sal, UT (cdp) San Juan County	31	28.70
Martell, CA (cdp) Amador County	40	26.14
Burton, NE (village) Keya Paha County	3	9.38
Farmington, CA (cdp) San Joaquin County	28	9.33
Lindisfarne, MT (cdp) Lake County	13	7.47
Bear Valley, CA (cdp) Alpine County	5	7.46
Cove, OR (city) Union County	35	7.00
Garfield, NM (cdp) Doña Ana County	13	6.95
Emery, UT (town) Emery County	24	6.94
Lucerne, CA (cdp) Lake County	167	6.23
Mount Crested Butte, CO (town) Gunnison County	34	6.08
Dazey, ND (city) Barnes County	5	5.68
Red Butte, WY (cdp) Natrona County	31	5.10
Glenwood, UT (town) Sevier County	26	4.95
Brooks, OR (cdp) Marion County	16	4.66
Mount Gretna, PA (borough) Lebanon County	7	4.61
Allenport, PA (cdp) Huntingdon County	22	4.55
Lafayette, OH (village) Allen County	13	4.55
Mount Olivet, KY (city) Robertson County	21	4.41
Correctionville, IA (city) Woodbury County	38	4.40
Carlsborg, WA (cdp) Clallam County	44	4.38
Custer, MT (cdp) Yellowstone County	8	4.06
Hallie, WI (town) Chippewa County	6	4.05
Great Bend, PA (borough) Susquehanna County	39	3.96
Cooksville, IL (village) McLean County	6	3.95
White Haven, MT (cdp) Lincoln County	22	3.83
Ellendale, DE (town) Sussex County	16	3.52
Adak, AK (city) Aleutians West Census Area	2	3.45
Colome, SD (city) Tripp County	14	3.35
Kawela Bay, HI (cdp) Honolulu County	10	3.34
Reardan, WA (town) Lincoln County	18	3.31
Shenandoah Retreat, VA (cdp) Clarke County	22	3.25
Fredericksburg, PA (cdp) Crawford County	20	3.24
Friendsville, PA (borough) Susquehanna County	4	3.20
Gerrard, CO (cdp) Rio Grande County	6	3.14
Valley Springs, CA (cdp) Calaveras County	121	3.00
Indio Hills, CA (cdp) Riverside County	41	2.95
Haverford College, PA (cdp) Delaware County	34	2.95
Hamilton, NC (town) Martin County	13	2.92
Chincoteague, VA (town) Accomack County	92	2.89
Keswick, CA (cdp) Shasta County	12	2.82
Ester, AK (cdp) Fairbanks North Star Borough	53	2.71
Belle Fontaine, AL (cdp) Mobile County	20	2.71
Brice, OH (village) Franklin County	3	2.70
Lake Ann, MI (village) Benzie County	8	2.61
Lily Lake, WI (cdp) Kenosha County	14	2.53
Rossie, IA (city) Clay County	2	2.53
Vienna, LA (town) Lincoln Parish	10	2.47
Lofall, WA (cdp) Kitsap County	62	2.43
Avon, CO (town) Eagle County	152	2.40
Trophy Club, TX (town) Denton County	191	2.38
Amador City, CA (city) Amador County	3	2.34
Holley, OR (cdp) Linn County	11	2.33
Bryn Athyn, PA (borough) Montgomery County	27	2.30
Sumner, WI (town) Jefferson County	19	2.30
Upper Exeter, PA (cdp) Luzerne County	18	2.29
Palmer, IA (city) Pocahontas County	3	2.26
Dickens, IA (city) Clay County	5	2.23
Benson, MN (city) Swift County	68	2.15
Shiloh, IL (village) St. Clair County	250	2.08
Meeteetse, WY (town) Park County	7	2.05
Inverness, CA (cdp) Marin County	28	2.03
Clifford, MI (village) Lapeer County	7	2.01
Bath, MI (cdp) Clinton County	45	1.98
Norris Canyon, CA (cdp) Contra Costa County	16	1.97
Canyon City, OR (town) Grant County	11	1.97
Beaverville, IL (village) Iroquois County	8	1.97
Rose Dell, MN (township) Rock County	3	1.96
Madge, WI (town) Washburn County	11	1.95
Garden Home-Whitford, OR (cdp) Washington County	117	1.94
Durham, CT (cdp) Middlesex County	51	1.94
Franklin, ID (city) Franklin County	13	1.92
Cape Vincent, NY (village) Jefferson County	13	1.91
Orick, CA (cdp) Humboldt County	6	1.90
Bazine, KS (city) Ness County	6	1.88
Rose Creek, MN (city) Mower County	8	1.87
Galway, NY (village) Saratoga County	2	1.85
Los Ranchos, CA (cdp) San Luis Obispo County	28	1.84
Newport, NY (village) Herkimer County	9	1.84
Pleasanton, NE (village) Buffalo County	7	1.84
Westport, OK (town) Pawnee County	5	1.81
Troy, NC (town) Montgomery County	58	1.80
Andes, NY (cdp) Delaware County	5	1.80
Los Berros, CA (cdp) San Luis Obispo County	11	1.79
Sibley, MO (village) Jackson County	6	1.79
Red River, NM (town) Taos County	13	1.78
Bovina, NY (town) Delaware County	9	1.76
Cotati, CA (city) Sonoma County	124	1.75
Bradbury, CA (city) Los Angeles County	17	1.74
Cumberland, ME (town) Cumberland County	124	1.73
Bolinas, CA (cdp) Marin County	20	1.72
North Vernon, IN (city) Jennings County	109	1.71
St. Joseph, MI (city) Berrien County	138	1.64
St. Augustine Beach, FL (city) St. Johns County	95	1.58
Colville, WA (city) Stevens County	75	1.58
Marlboro, NY (cdp) Ulster County	63	1.57
Montgomery, MN (city) Le Sueur County	47	1.56
Cedarville, NJ (cdp) Cumberland County	15	1.55
Fredonia, AZ (town) Coconino County	18	1.54
Merrill, OR (city) Klamath County	11	1.54
Geyserville, CA (cdp) Sonoma County	15	1.51
Windham, NY (town) Greene County	25	1.50
Fruitport, MI (village) Muskegon County	16	1.50
Sparta, MO (city) Christian County	26	1.49
Dulac, LA (cdp) Terrebonne Parish	17	1.48
Ovid, NY (village) Seneca County	7	1.47
Onawa, IA (city) Monona County	44	1.46
Princeton, IN (city) Gibson County	124	1.44
Crook, CO (town) Logan County	2	1.44
Concow, CA (cdp) Butte County	11	1.39
Cimarron, KS (city) Gray County	28	1.38
Magnolia, WI (town) Rock County	12	1.38
Fayette, MO (city) Howard County	37	1.37
Frenchtown, NJ (borough) Hunterdon County	19	1.36
Wolf Creek, UT (cdp) Weber County	13	1.36
Steele, ND (city) Kidder County	9	1.36
Pine Village, IN (town) Warren County	3	1.35
Cross Plains, TN (city) Robertson County	22	1.34
Butte Falls, OR (town) Jackson County	7	1.34
Creighton, NE (city) Knox County	17	1.33
Marathon, TX (cdp) Brewster County	6	1.32
Loudon, NH (cdp) Merrimack County	8	1.31
King Salmon, AK (cdp) Bristol Bay Borough	5	1.30
Alexandria Bay, NY (village) Jefferson County	14	1.28
Sheldon, IA (city) O'Brien County	64	1.27
Fredericktown, PA (cdp) Washington County	5	1.26
Acres Green, CO (cdp) Douglas County	39	1.25
Spurgeon, IN (town) Pike County	2	1.25
New Prague, MN (city) Le Sueur County	35	1.24
Bannockburn, IL (village) Lake County	17	1.24
Steilacoom, WA (town) Pierce County	75	1.23
Sleepy Hollow, CA (cdp) Marin County	30	1.23
Lake Isabella, CA (cdp) Kern County	40	1.22
Cassville, MO (city) Barry County	40	1.21
Loyola, CA (cdp) Santa Clara County	40	1.21
Hartford, AR (city) Sebastian County	10	1.21
Kensett, IA (city) Worth County	3	1.21
Marina del Rey, CA (cdp) Los Angeles County	110	1.20
Milton, FL (city) Santa Rosa County	103	1.18
Roodhouse, IL (city) Greene County	23	1.18
Kamas, UT (city) Summit County	22	1.18
Mayhew Lake, MN (township) Benton County	10	1.18
Gazelle, CA (cdp) Siskiyou County	2	1.18
North Myrtle Beach, SC (city) Horry County	155	1.16
East Pasadena, CA (cdp) Los Angeles County	67	1.16
Federalsburg, MD (town) Caroline County	32	1.16
Severance, MN (township) Sibley County	3	1.16
Sitka, AK (borough) Sitka City and Borough	102	1.15
Montague, MI (township) Muskegon County	20	1.15
Lyons, OR (city) Linn County	12	1.15

Please refer to the Explanation of Data in the front of the book for more detailed information.

Ancestry

Australian

Top 150 Places Sorted by Percent of Total Population

Based on places with total population of 7,500 or more

Place	Population	%
Trophy Club, TX (town) Denton County	191	2.38
Shiloh, IL (village) St. Clair County	250	2.08
St. Joseph, MI (city) Berrien County	138	1.64
Princeton, IN (city) Gibson County	124	1.44
Marina del Rey, CA (cdp) Los Angeles County	110	1.20
Milton, FL (city) Santa Rosa County	103	1.18
North Myrtle Beach, SC (city) Horry County	155	1.16
Sitka, AK (borough) Sitka City and Borough	102	1.15
Red Oak, TX (city) Ellis County	102	1.03
Riverside, CT (cdp) Fairfield County	87	1.03
San Anselmo, CA (town) Marin County	121	0.99
Coronado, CA (city) San Diego County	175	0.89
Whitehall, OH (city) Franklin County	156	0.86
University of California Davis, CA (cdp) Yolo County	64	0.83
Park City, UT (city) Summit County	62	0.82
Warrenton, VA (town) Fauquier County	75	0.81
Putnam Valley, NY (town) Putnam County	90	0.77
Westford, MA (town) Middlesex County	156	0.73
Redding, CT (town) Fairfield County	64	0.72
Marlborough, NY (town) Ulster County	63	0.72
Vashon, WA (cdp) King County	70	0.71
Middle Smithfield, PA (township) Monroe County	109	0.70
Purdue University, IN (cdp) Tippecanoe County	89	0.69
Allouez, WI (village) Brown County	94	0.66
Northampton, PA (borough) Northampton County	65	0.66
Green River, WY (city) Sweetwater County	77	0.63
Bedford, MI (charter township) Calhoun County	60	0.63
Walworth, NY (town) Wayne County	57	0.62
Upper Uwchlan, PA (township) Chester County	64	0.61
Tamalpais-Homestead Valley, CA (cdp) Marin County	64	0.60
Woodstock, CT (town) Windham County	47	0.60
Chesapeake Ranch Estates, MD (cdp) Calvert County	56	0.58
Scarsdale, NY (town/village) Westchester County	96	0.56
Rye, NY (city) Westchester County	86	0.55
Troy, IL (city) Madison County	54	0.55
Fairfield, IA (city) Jefferson County	52	0.55
West Linn, OR (city) Clackamas County	132	0.54
Yukon, OK (city) Canadian County	115	0.52
Chesterfield, MI (township) Macomb County	218	0.51
Canton, PA (township) Washington County	43	0.51
Monroe, NY (village) Orange County	42	0.50
Red Hook, NY (town) Dutchess County	55	0.49
Steamboat Springs, CO (city) Routt County	57	0.48
Oakdale, NY (cdp) Suffolk County	37	0.48
Jessup, MD (cdp) Anne Arundel County	52	0.47
Scotchtown, NY (cdp) Orange County	46	0.47
Shenandoah, LA (cdp) East Baton Rouge Parish	84	0.46
Ewa Gentry, HI (cdp) Honolulu County	97	0.45
San Marino, CA (city) Los Angeles County	59	0.45
Helena Valley Southeast, MT (cdp) Lewis and Clark County	36	0.45
Red Bluff, CA (city) Tehama County	62	0.44
Milford, PA (township) Bucks County	43	0.44
Kings Grant, NC (cdp) New Hanover County	37	0.44
Weehawken, NJ (township) Hudson County	54	0.43
Cross Lanes, WV (cdp) Kanawha County	40	0.43
Mount Joy, PA (township) Lancaster County	40	0.42
Montpelier, VT (city) Washington County	33	0.42
Summit, WA (cdp) Pierce County	33	0.42
Davis, CA (city) Yolo County	269	0.41
Windsor, CA (town) Sonoma County	105	0.41
West Hempfield, PA (township) Lancaster County	65	0.41
Bath, MI (charter township) Clinton County	45	0.41
Hollymead, VA (cdp) Albemarle County	33	0.41
Wellesley, MA (cdp/town) Norfolk County	110	0.40
Port Washington, NY (cdp) Nassau County	65	0.40
Rochester, MI (city) Oakland County	49	0.40
Greenfield, NY (town) Saratoga County	31	0.40
Urbandale, IA (city) Polk County	147	0.39
Holiday, FL (cdp) Pasco County	87	0.39
Franklin Park, PA (borough) Allegheny County	50	0.39
Wayland, MA (town) Middlesex County	50	0.39
Struthers, OH (city) Mahoning County	42	0.39
Harleysville, PA (cdp) Montgomery County	37	0.39
Bainbridge Island, WA (city) Kitsap County	86	0.38
Orinda, CA (city) Contra Costa County	67	0.38

Place	Population	%
Lawrenceburg, KY (city) Anderson County	39	0.38
Glocester, RI (town) Providence County	37	0.38
Somers, WI (town) Kenosha County	36	0.38
Mount Airy, MD (town) Carroll County	34	0.38
Redlands, CO (cdp) Mesa County	30	0.38
Coconut Creek, FL (city) Broward County	191	0.37
Florence, KY (city) Boone County	106	0.36
Yucca Valley, CA (town) San Bernardino County	74	0.36
Mill Valley, CA (city) Marin County	49	0.36
Claremont, NH (city) Sullivan County	48	0.36
Snoqualmie, WA (city) King County	33	0.36
Meridian, ID (city) Ada County	243	0.35
Germantown, TN (city) Shelby County	137	0.35
Goleta, CA (city) Santa Barbara County	104	0.35
Alvin, TX (city) Brazoria County	87	0.35
Bellevue, OH (city) Sandusky County	29	0.35
Warner Robins, GA (city) Houston County	218	0.34
Danville, CA (town) Contra Costa County	143	0.34
Lake Forest, IL (city) Lake County	65	0.34
Plumstead, PA (township) Bucks County	42	0.34
Rotonda, FL (cdp) Charlotte County	32	0.34
Holt, MI (cdp) Ingham County	77	0.33
Monroe, MI (city) Monroe County	70	0.33
Fenton, MI (charter township) Genesee County	51	0.33
Lake Mary, FL (city) Seminole County	45	0.33
Washington Terrace, UT (city) Weber County	29	0.33
Franklin, VA (ind. city) Franklin independent city	28	0.33
Greenwich, CT (town) Fairfield County	196	0.32
Princeton, NJ (township) Mercer County	52	0.32
Thompson, NY (town) Sullivan County	48	0.32
Murrieta, CA (city) Riverside County	295	0.31
The Woodlands, TX (cdp) Montgomery County	285	0.31
Hoboken, NJ (city) Hudson County	145	0.31
Hilton Head Island, SC (town) Beaufort County	113	0.31
Edgewater Park, NJ (township) Burlington County	27	0.31
Cedar Hills, OR (cdp) Washington County	26	0.31
Hastings-on-Hudson, NY (village) Westchester County	24	0.31
Midvale, UT (city) Salt Lake County	82	0.30
Delhi, MI (charter township) Ingham County	77	0.30
Mililani Mauka, HI (cdp) Honolulu County	62	0.30
Short Hills, NJ (cdp) Essex County	39	0.30
Malibu, CA (city) Los Angeles County	38	0.30
Evanston, WY (city) Uinta County	36	0.30
Superior, CO (town) Boulder County	36	0.30
Florida City, FL (city) Miami-Dade County	32	0.30
Maili, HI (cdp) Honolulu County	24	0.30
Brentwood, TN (city) Williamson County	103	0.29
American Canyon, CA (city) Napa County	52	0.29
Lebanon, NH (city) Grafton County	38	0.29
Pelham, NY (town) Westchester County	35	0.29
Lower Gwynedd, PA (township) Montgomery County	32	0.29
Westwood, NJ (borough) Bergen County	32	0.29
Wyomissing, PA (borough) Berks County	31	0.29
Placerville, CA (city) El Dorado County	30	0.29
Cloverdale, CA (city) Sonoma County	24	0.29
Baywood, NY (cdp) Suffolk County	23	0.29
Lake Worth, FL (city) Palm Beach County	100	0.28
Wildwood, MO (city) St. Louis County	97	0.28
Hingham, MA (town) Plymouth County	61	0.28
El Sobrante, CA (cdp) Contra Costa County	38	0.28
Richland, PA (township) Bucks County	35	0.28
Loveland, OH (city) Hamilton County	33	0.28
South Milwaukee, WI (city) Milwaukee County	57	0.27
Madison, CT (town) New Haven County	49	0.27
Rockland, MA (town) Plymouth County	47	0.27
Brenham, TX (city) Washington County	41	0.27
Robbinsdale, MN (city) Hennepin County	37	0.27
Lewisville, NC (town) Forsyth County	34	0.27
Klahanie, WA (cdp) King County	30	0.27
Union Park, FL (cdp) Orange County	27	0.27
Burtonsville, MD (cdp) Montgomery County	25	0.27
Charlotte, MI (city) Eaton County	25	0.27
Sandwich, IL (city) DeKalb County	21	0.27
Littleton, CO (city) Arapahoe County	107	0.26
Spanish Fork, UT (city) Utah County	84	0.26

Please refer to the Explanation of Data in the front of the book for more detailed information.

Ancestry

Austrian

U.S. and 50 States Sorted by Population and Percent of Total Population

Place	Population	%
United States	**766,033**	**0.25**
New York	91,260	0.47
California	81,470	0.22
Pennsylvania	59,263	0.47
Florida	57,024	0.31
Illinois	41,675	0.33
New Jersey	41,569	0.48
Ohio	28,071	0.24
Wisconsin	27,068	0.48
Texas	26,496	0.11
Michigan	22,990	0.23
Washington	20,651	0.31
Colorado	20,532	0.42
Minnesota	18,518	0.35
Massachusetts	17,069	0.26
Virginia	16,342	0.21
Maryland	16,287	0.29
Connecticut	15,059	0.42
Arizona	14,542	0.23
Georgia	12,371	0.13
Missouri	12,116	0.20
North Carolina	11,896	0.13
Oregon	11,540	0.31
Indiana	9,059	0.14
Nevada	7,045	0.27
Kansas	6,158	0.22
Tennessee	6,067	0.10
Montana	5,779	0.59
South Carolina	5,711	0.13
Utah	5,579	0.21
Iowa	4,718	0.16
Alabama	4,068	0.09
Oklahoma	3,679	0.10
Nebraska	3,603	0.20
Idaho	3,560	0.23
Kentucky	3,504	0.08
New Hampshire	3,059	0.23
New Mexico	2,966	0.15
Louisiana	2,926	0.07
Maine	2,418	0.18
Vermont	2,219	0.36
West Virginia	2,133	0.12
District of Columbia	2,131	0.36
Rhode Island	2,125	0.20
Alaska	2,075	0.30
Delaware	2,016	0.23
Arkansas	1,972	0.07
Hawaii	1,918	0.14
Wyoming	1,740	0.32
Mississippi	1,445	0.05
South Dakota	1,329	0.17
North Dakota	1,222	0.19

Place	Population	%
Montana	5,779	0.59
New Jersey	41,569	0.48
Wisconsin	27,068	0.48
New York	91,260	0.47
Pennsylvania	59,263	0.47
Colorado	20,532	0.42
Connecticut	15,059	0.42
Vermont	2,219	0.36
District of Columbia	2,131	0.36
Minnesota	18,518	0.35
Illinois	41,675	0.33
Wyoming	1,740	0.32
Florida	57,024	0.31
Washington	20,651	0.31
Oregon	11,540	0.31
Alaska	2,075	0.30
Maryland	16,287	0.29
Nevada	7,045	0.27
Massachusetts	17,069	0.26
United States	**766,033**	**0.25**
Ohio	28,071	0.24
Michigan	22,990	0.23
Arizona	14,542	0.23
Idaho	3,560	0.23
New Hampshire	3,059	0.23
Delaware	2,016	0.23
California	81,470	0.22
Kansas	6,158	0.22
Virginia	16,342	0.21
Utah	5,579	0.21
Missouri	12,116	0.20
Nebraska	3,603	0.20
Rhode Island	2,125	0.20
North Dakota	1,222	0.19
Maine	2,418	0.18
South Dakota	1,329	0.17
Iowa	4,718	0.16
New Mexico	2,966	0.15
Indiana	9,059	0.14
Hawaii	1,918	0.14
Georgia	12,371	0.13
North Carolina	11,896	0.13
South Carolina	5,711	0.13
West Virginia	2,133	0.12
Texas	26,496	0.11
Tennessee	6,067	0.10
Oklahoma	3,679	0.10
Alabama	4,068	0.09
Kentucky	3,504	0.08
Louisiana	2,926	0.07
Arkansas	1,972	0.07
Mississippi	1,445	0.05

Please refer to the Explanation of Data in the front of the book for more detailed information.

Ancestry

Austrian

Top 150 Places Sorted by Population

Based on all places, regardless of total population

Place	Population	%
New York, NY (city) Kings County	30,712	0.38
Manhattan, NY (borough) New York County	14,656	0.93
Los Angeles, CA (city) Los Angeles County	11,090	0.29
Queens, NY (borough) Queens County	7,523	0.34
Chicago, IL (city) Cook County	7,125	0.26
Brooklyn, NY (borough) Kings County	5,123	0.21
Hempstead, NY (town) Nassau County	4,963	0.66
San Diego, CA (city) San Diego County	3,861	0.30
San Francisco, CA (city) San Francisco County	3,588	0.45
Oyster Bay, NY (town) Nassau County	3,412	1.17
Brookhaven, NY (town) Suffolk County	2,867	0.60
North Hempstead, NY (town) Nassau County	2,782	1.24
Seattle, WA (city) King County	2,639	0.44
Philadelphia, PA (city) Philadelphia County	2,580	0.17
Phoenix, AZ (city) Maricopa County	2,553	0.18
Houston, TX (city) Harris County	2,488	0.12
Denver, CO (city) Denver County	2,416	0.42
Washington, DC (city) District of Columbia	2,131	0.36
Islip, NY (town) Suffolk County	2,019	0.61
Huntington, NY (town) Suffolk County	2,004	0.99
Milwaukee, WI (city) Milwaukee County	1,985	0.34
Colorado Springs, CO (city) El Paso County	1,947	0.48
Portland, OR (city) Multnomah County	1,912	0.34
Bronx, NY (borough) Bronx County	1,868	0.14
Pittsburgh, PA (city) Allegheny County	1,622	0.53
Las Vegas, NV (city) Clark County	1,545	0.27
Staten Island, NY (borough) Richmond County	1,542	0.33
Dallas, TX (city) Dallas County	1,538	0.13
Jacksonville, FL (city) Duval County	1,515	0.19
Austin, TX (city) Travis County	1,482	0.19
Minneapolis, MN (city) Hennepin County	1,469	0.39
Scottsdale, AZ (city) Maricopa County	1,456	0.67
Allentown, PA (city) Lehigh County	1,440	1.24
Columbus, OH (city) Franklin County	1,440	0.19
Ramapo, NY (town) Rockland County	1,328	1.08
Charlotte, NC (city) Mecklenburg County	1,273	0.18
San Antonio, TX (city) Medina County	1,252	0.10
St. Paul, MN (city) Ramsey County	1,232	0.44
Tampa, FL (city) Hillsborough County	1,167	0.35
Tucson, AZ (city) Pima County	1,160	0.22
Albuquerque, NM (city) Bernalillo County	1,155	0.22
Anchorage, AK (municipality) Anchorage Municipality	1,151	0.40
Boca Raton, FL (city) Palm Beach County	1,141	1.34
Arlington, VA (cdp) Arlington County	1,139	0.58
Greenburgh, NY (town) Westchester County	1,117	1.27
Indianapolis, IN (city) Marion County	1,084	0.13
Madison, WI (city) Dane County	1,082	0.47
San Jose, CA (city) Santa Clara County	1,045	0.11
Boston, MA (city) Suffolk County	1,039	0.17
Baltimore, MD (city) Baltimore city County	1,016	0.16
Amherst, NY (town) Erie County	1,014	0.84
St. Petersburg, FL (city) Pinellas County	1,012	0.41
Reno, NV (city) Washoe County	998	0.45
Louisville-Jefferson County, KY (metro govt) Jefferson County	933	0.16
Smithtown, NY (town) Suffolk County	930	0.79
Nashville-Davidson, TN (metro govt) Davidson County	904	0.15
Whitehall, PA (township) Lehigh County	902	3.40
Mesa, AZ (city) Maricopa County	876	0.20
Henderson, NV (city) Clark County	847	0.34
Oakland, CA (city) Alameda County	843	0.22
Thousand Oaks, CA (city) Ventura County	836	0.67
Omaha, NE (city) Douglas County	836	0.21
Butte-Silver Bow, MT (cons. govt) Silver Bow County	835	2.54
Clarkstown, NY (town) Rockland County	827	0.99
Babylon, NY (town) Suffolk County	808	0.38
Buffalo, NY (city) Erie County	799	0.30
Santa Monica, CA (city) Los Angeles County	793	0.89
Bethlehem, PA (city) Northampton County	783	1.05
Atlanta, GA (city) Fulton County	778	0.19
Kansas City, MO (city) Jackson County	766	0.17
St. Louis, MO (city) St. Louis city County	765	0.24
Paradise, NV (cdp) Clark County	758	0.35
Fort Lauderdale, FL (city) Broward County	748	0.45
Deerfield Beach, FL (city) Broward County	740	0.98
Arlington Heights, IL (village) Cook County	732	0.98
Huntington Beach, CA (city) Orange County	728	0.39
Cherry Hill, NJ (township) Camden County	720	1.01
Spokane, WA (city) Spokane County	720	0.35
Sacramento, CA (city) Sacramento County	709	0.15
Coral Springs, FL (city) Broward County	692	0.57
Alexandria, VA (ind. city) Alexandria independent city	689	0.52
Wauwatosa, WI (city) Milwaukee County	684	1.48
Hollywood, FL (city) Broward County	675	0.48
Raleigh, NC (city) Wake County	670	0.18
Naperville, IL (city) DuPage County	666	0.47
Fort Worth, TX (city) Tarrant County	665	0.09
Newton, MA (city) Middlesex County	650	0.77
Lower Merion, PA (township) Montgomery County	648	1.12
Fort Collins, CO (city) Larimer County	644	0.46
Aurora, CO (city) Arapahoe County	644	0.21
Virginia Beach, VA (ind. city) Virginia Beach independent city	636	0.15
Toledo, OH (city) Lucas County	628	0.22
Highlands Ranch, CO (cdp) Douglas County	623	0.66
Overland Park, KS (city) Johnson County	622	0.36
Southampton, NY (town) Suffolk County	621	1.10
Bethesda, MD (cdp) Montgomery County	619	1.06
Yonkers, NY (city) Westchester County	618	0.32
Flower Mound, TX (town) Denton County	617	0.98
Long Beach, CA (city) Los Angeles County	617	0.13
Boulder, CO (city) Boulder County	612	0.63
Anaheim, CA (city) Orange County	609	0.18
Riverside, CA (city) Riverside County	607	0.20
Toms River, NJ (cdp) Ocean County	602	0.68
Toms River, NJ (township) Ocean County	602	0.66
San Rafael, CA (city) Marin County	601	1.06
Newport Beach, CA (city) Orange County	601	0.72
Carlsbad, CA (city) San Diego County	596	0.60
West Palm Beach, FL (city) Palm Beach County	594	0.61
Clearwater, FL (city) Pinellas County	592	0.55
Cleveland, OH (city) Cuyahoga County	589	0.14
Plainview, NY (cdp) Nassau County	587	2.28
Manalapan, NJ (township) Monmouth County	584	1.54
Oklahoma City, OK (city) Oklahoma County	577	0.10
West Allis, WI (city) Milwaukee County	576	0.96
Wichita, KS (city) Sedgwick County	576	0.15
White Plains, NY (city) Westchester County	572	1.02
New Orleans, LA (city) Orleans Parish	572	0.19
Potomac, MD (cdp) Montgomery County	569	1.27
Tinley Park, IL (village) Cook County	566	1.03
Coconut Creek, FL (city) Broward County	564	1.09
Lower Macungie, PA (township) Lehigh County	559	1.95
Bend, OR (city) Deschutes County	557	0.75
Long Beach, NY (city) Nassau County	555	1.66
Beverly Hills, CA (city) Los Angeles County	554	1.63
Middletown, NJ (township) Monmouth County	550	0.82
New Rochelle, NY (city) Westchester County	547	0.72
Columbia, MD (cdp) Howard County	547	0.56
Plano, TX (city) Collin County	546	0.21
Bethlehem, PA (city) Northampton County	544	0.98
Arlington, TX (city) Tarrant County	540	0.15
Berkeley, CA (city) Alameda County	539	0.49
Livingston, NJ (township) Essex County	536	1.86
Bellevue, WA (city) King County	535	0.45
El Paso, TX (city) El Paso County	532	0.08
Lakewood, CO (city) Jefferson County	530	0.37
Lubbock, TX (city) Lubbock County	529	0.24
Evanston, IL (city) Cook County	528	0.71
Cambridge, MA (city) Middlesex County	528	0.51
Sterling Heights, MI (city) Macomb County	526	0.41
Monroe, NJ (township) Middlesex County	522	1.40
Orlando, FL (city) Orange County	522	0.22
Weston, FL (city) Broward County	520	0.83
Walnut Creek, CA (city) Contra Costa County	512	0.80
The Woodlands, TX (cdp) Montgomery County	509	0.55
Billings, MT (city) Yellowstone County	509	0.50
Aventura, FL (city) Miami-Dade County	507	1.50
Cincinnati, OH (city) Hamilton County	502	0.17
Plantation, FL (city) Broward County	501	0.59
Boise City, ID (city) Ada County	500	0.24
Centennial, CO (city) Arapahoe County	499	0.50

Please refer to the Explanation of Data in the front of the book for more detailed information.

Ancestry

Austrian

Top 150 Places Sorted by Percent of Total Population

Based on all places, regardless of total population

Place	Population	%
Great Meadows, NJ (cdp) Warren County	140	54.90
Floriston, CA (cdp) Nevada County	14	51.85
Preston, NV (cdp) White Pine County	56	42.75
Lima, WI (town) Pepin County	181	30.89
Creston, CA (cdp) San Luis Obispo County	19	28.36
Fishing Creek, MD (cdp) Dorchester County	18	22.50
Cannon, MN (township) Kittson County	4	22.22
Vicksburg, PA (cdp) Union County	48	21.24
Third River, MN (township) Itasca County	10	18.87
West Hampton Dunes, NY (village) Suffolk County	8	18.60
Round Top, TX (town) Fayette County	12	18.18
Canton, WI (town) Buffalo County	58	17.74
Durand, WI (town) Pepin County	122	16.94
Lafferty, OH (cdp) Belmont County	33	15.07
Eden, SD (town) Marshall County	14	14.43
Gallatin Gateway, MT (cdp) Gallatin County	129	14.16
Eau Galle, WI (town) Dunn County	123	13.93
Camptonville, CA (cdp) Yuba County	26	13.83
Daniel, UT (town) Wasatch County	152	13.77
Mountain Lake, MN (township) Cottonwood County	41	13.53
Jamison City, PA (cdp) Columbia County	14	13.33
Peru, WI (town) Dunn County	27	13.11
Fawn Lake, MN (township) Todd County	78	13.00
De Borgia, MT (cdp) Mineral County	12	12.77
Lenhartsville, PA (borough) Berks County	22	12.43
Durand, WI (city) Pepin County	232	12.15
Waubeek, WI (town) Pepin County	50	12.11
Bland, VA (cdp) Bland County	32	11.90
Cloverdale, OR (cdp) Tillamook County	53	11.80
Scofield, UT (town) Carbon County	2	11.76
Whitehaven, MD (cdp) Wicomico County	11	11.58
Maxville, WI (town) Buffalo County	37	11.49
Rock Creek, WI (town) Dunn County	98	11.38
Albany, WI (town) Pepin County	86	11.15
Cardwell, MT (cdp) Jefferson County	3	11.11
Herndon, KS (city) Rawlins County	21	10.71
Sedalia, CO (cdp) Douglas County	19	10.50
Sykeston, ND (city) Wells County	7	10.29
Rexford, MT (town) Lincoln County	8	10.26
Ocean City, WA (cdp) Grays Harbor County	18	10.11
Harbor Hills, NY (cdp) Nassau County	50	10.10
Taycheedah, WI (cdp) Fond du Lac County	56	9.82
Artesian, SD (town) Sanborn County	12	9.76
Powers, OR (city) Coos County	72	9.61
Rose Hill, MN (township) Cottonwood County	19	9.50
New Dosey, MN (township) Pine County	8	9.20
Elmer, MN (township) St. Louis County	14	9.03
Bivalve, MD (cdp) Wicomico County	16	8.84
Coplay, PA (borough) Lehigh County	286	8.82
Rock Elm, WI (town) Pierce County	44	8.80
Inman, NE (village) Holt County	8	8.79
Marksboro, NJ (cdp) Warren County	8	8.79
Oneida, PA (cdp) Schuylkill County	16	8.70
Grand Plain, MN (township) Marshall County	2	8.70
Wilson, WY (cdp) Teton County	122	8.68
La Crosse, MN (township) Jackson County	12	8.51
Linsell, MN (township) Marshall County	3	8.33
Haverford College, PA (cdp) Delaware County	95	8.24
Galatia, KS (city) Barton County	6	8.22
Edgewood, CA (cdp) Siskiyou County	4	8.16
Surprise, NE (village) Butler County	3	8.11
Sun Valley, ID (city) Blaine County	111	7.92
Tainter Lake, WI (cdp) Dunn County	197	7.87
Rutherford, CA (cdp) Napa County	15	7.85
North San Juan, CA (cdp) Nevada County	10	7.63
Kenwood, CA (cdp) Sonoma County	35	7.58
Deerfield, MA (cdp) Franklin County	14	7.49
Deer Lake, PA (borough) Schuylkill County	53	7.35
Odin, KS (cdp) Barton County	5	7.35
Menomonie, WI (town) Dunn County	245	7.32
Union, WI (town) Pierce County	50	7.25
Windsor, FL (cdp) Indian River County	15	7.25
Nuremberg, PA (cdp) Schuylkill County	27	7.24
Kilgore, NE (village) Cherry County	4	7.14
New Tripoli, PA (cdp) Lehigh County	58	7.09
Preston, NE (village) Richardson County	9	7.09
Nelson, WI (town) Buffalo County	41	7.06
Great Neck Gardens, NY (cdp) Nassau County	64	7.05
Plum City, WI (village) Pierce County	32	7.00
Stiles, PA (cdp) Lehigh County	68	6.97
Mondovi, WI (city) Buffalo County	193	6.96
Saltaire, NY (village) Suffolk County	4	6.90
Redway, CA (cdp) Humboldt County	70	6.84
Portland, CO (cdp) Ouray County	16	6.84
Manor Creek, KY (city) Jefferson County	11	6.83
Uniondale, IN (town) Wells County	12	6.78
Walpole, NH (cdp) Cheshire County	43	6.74
Alford, MA (town) Berkshire County	29	6.71
Glenbrook, NV (cdp) Douglas County	11	6.71
Weston, PA (cdp) Luzerne County	23	6.57
Rheems, PA (cdp) Lancaster County	86	6.55
Beaverton, AL (town) Lamar County	10	6.54
Moody AFB, GA (cdp) Lowndes County	71	6.53
Jeddo, PA (borough) Luzerne County	7	6.48
Rodanthe, NC (cdp) Dare County	27	6.46
Leopolis, WI (cdp) Shawano County	3	6.38
Grahamtown, MD (cdp) Allegany County	15	6.33
Fingal, ND (city) Barnes County	7	6.25
Port Washington, OH (village) Tuscarawas County	33	6.21
Java, SD (town) Walworth County	9	6.21
Palenville, NY (cdp) Greene County	70	6.17
Islip Terrace, NY (cdp) Suffolk County	353	6.15
La Grange, WY (town) Goshen County	31	6.15
Rico, CO (town) Dolores County	16	6.15
Helena West Side, MT (cdp) Lewis and Clark County	86	6.09
Macksville, KS (city) Stafford County	29	6.09
Cordova, MD (cdp) Talbot County	33	6.08
Waverly, WA (town) Spokane County	6	6.06
Twin Lakes, CO (cdp) Lake County	7	6.03
Asotin, WA (city) Asotin County	55	5.97
Malta Bend, MO (town) Saline County	13	5.96
Cochrane, WI (village) Buffalo County	28	5.94
Falling Waters, WV (cdp) Berkeley County	46	5.93
Dryville, PA (cdp) Berks County	39	5.90
Cascade, PA (township) Lycoming County	26	5.90
Dover, MO (town) Lafayette County	6	5.88
Hostetter, PA (cdp) Westmoreland County	43	5.87
Griggstown, NJ (cdp) Somerset County	52	5.86
Chebeague Island, ME (town) Cumberland County	14	5.83
Lumber, PA (township) Cameron County	12	5.83
Suffield Depot, CT (cdp) Hartford County	68	5.82
Bashaw, MN (township) Brown County	14	5.81
Ross, ND (city) Mountrail County	5	5.81
Cuylerville, NY (cdp) Livingston County	25	5.76
Black Butte Ranch, OR (cdp) Deschutes County	16	5.71
Bluewater, CA (cdp) San Bernardino County	10	5.71
Mount Charleston, NV (cdp) Clark County	11	5.70
Union, WV (town) Monroe County	29	5.69
Ferdinand, ID (city) Idaho County	11	5.67
Richmond, KS (city) Franklin County	29	5.65
Big Arm, MT (cdp) Lake County	18	5.64
Catlett, VA (cdp) Fauquier County	12	5.61
Parker, ID (city) Fremont County	15	5.60
Danbury, NC (town) Stokes County	8	5.56
Newell, PA (borough) Fayette County	31	5.52
Franklin, KS (cdp) Crawford County	18	5.50
Coleville, CA (cdp) Mono County	33	5.45
Lake Mack-Forest Hills, FL (cdp) Lake County	56	5.44
Waterville, WI (town) Pepin County	46	5.42
Sheppton, PA (cdp) Schuylkill County	12	5.41
Keswick, CA (cdp) Shasta County	23	5.40
Cooke City, MT (cdp) Park County	3	5.36
Ripley, IL (village) Brown County	3	5.36
Weston, WI (town) Dunn County	31	5.34
Kerby, OR (cdp) Josephine County	25	5.32
Belle Valley, OH (village) Noble County	19	5.31
High Falls, NY (cdp) Ulster County	45	5.23
Ocean Beach, NY (village) Suffolk County	6	5.22
Ellsburg, MN (township) St. Louis County	8	5.19
Esther, MN (township) Polk County	8	5.19

Please refer to the Explanation of Data in the front of the book for more detailed information.

Ancestry

Austrian

Top 150 Places Sorted by Percent of Total Population

Based on places with total population of 7,500 or more

Place	Population	%
Northampton, PA (borough) Northampton County	428	4.32
Whitehall, PA (township) Lehigh County	902	3.40
Hazle, PA (township) Luzerne County	306	3.26
Salisbury, PA (township) Lehigh County	433	3.20
North Whitehall, PA (township) Lehigh County	481	3.08
Briarcliff Manor, NY (village) Westchester County	238	2.97
Emmaus, PA (borough) Lehigh County	325	2.88
Bushkill, PA (township) Northampton County	223	2.77
Lehigh, PA (township) Northampton County	286	2.73
Woodmere, NY (cdp) Nassau County	475	2.72
Butler, PA (township) Luzerne County	230	2.61
Anaconda-Deer Lodge County, MT (special city) Deer Lodge County	241	2.60
Calimesa, CA (city) Riverside County	204	2.59
Butte-Silver Bow, MT (cons. govt) Silver Bow County	835	2.54
Riverside, IL (village) Cook County	222	2.54
Westwood, NJ (borough) Bergen County	274	2.52
Lewisboro, NY (town) Westchester County	309	2.51
Croton-on-Hudson, NY (village) Westchester County	191	2.42
Camp Hill, PA (borough) Cumberland County	188	2.40
East La Mirada, CA (cdp) Los Angeles County	238	2.34
Weston, CT (town) Fairfield County	235	2.33
Upper Saddle River, NJ (borough) Bergen County	188	2.33
Hollis, NH (town) Hillsborough County	176	2.31
Plainview, NY (cdp) Nassau County	587	2.28
Fullerton, PA (cdp) Lehigh County	338	2.25
New Castle, NY (town) Westchester County	386	2.21
Woodbury, NY (cdp) Nassau County	198	2.18
Fairmount, NY (cdp) Onondaga County	218	2.17
Cresskill, NJ (borough) Bergen County	182	2.17
Glen Rock, NJ (borough) Bergen County	249	2.16
Scarsdale, NY (town/village) Westchester County	355	2.07
Upper Macungie, PA (township) Lehigh County	392	2.06
Cascades, VA (cdp) Loudoun County	248	2.06
Uniontown, PA (city) Fayette County	221	2.06
Hartland, WI (village) Waukesha County	184	2.06
Springdale, NJ (cdp) Camden County	301	2.05
Greentree, NJ (cdp) Camden County	231	2.02
Geddes, NY (town) Onondaga County	341	1.99
Red Hook, NY (town) Dutchess County	222	1.98
Woodbury, CT (town) Litchfield County	194	1.96
River Vale, NJ (township) Bergen County	188	1.96
Lower Macungie, PA (township) Lehigh County	559	1.95
Watertown, WI (city) Dodge County	165	1.95
Short Hills, NJ (cdp) Essex County	256	1.94
Chatham, NJ (township) Morris County	202	1.94
Glencoe, IL (village) Cook County	167	1.94
South Whitehall, PA (township) Lehigh County	368	1.93
Tomah, WI (city) Monroe County	173	1.93
Jericho, NY (cdp) Nassau County	249	1.91
Esopus, NY (town) Ulster County	175	1.91
Hillsdale, NJ (borough) Bergen County	193	1.90
Washington, NJ (township) Bergen County	170	1.89
Livingston, NJ (township) Essex County	536	1.86
Hastings-on-Hudson, NY (village) Westchester County	144	1.85
Madison, CT (town) New Haven County	336	1.84
Montvale, NJ (borough) Bergen County	140	1.83
Kendall Park, NJ (cdp) Middlesex County	159	1.81
Laguna Woods, CA (city) Orange County	292	1.79
Readington, NJ (township) Hunterdon County	289	1.78
Millburn, NJ (township) Essex County	350	1.75
Dunmore, PA (borough) Lackawanna County	246	1.75
Valley Cottage, NY (cdp) Rockland County	164	1.74
Lake Grove, NY (village) Suffolk County	189	1.72
Pompton Lakes, NJ (borough) Passaic County	189	1.72
Gunbarrel, CO (cdp) Boulder County	163	1.72
Massapequa Park, NY (village) Nassau County	290	1.71
Topanga, CA (cdp) Los Angeles County	146	1.71
Westlake Village, CA (city) Los Angeles County	140	1.69
Avon, CT (town) Hartford County	297	1.68
Payson, UT (city) Utah County	287	1.67
Long Beach, NY (city) Nassau County	555	1.66
Princeton, NJ (borough) Mercer County	208	1.66
Hillsborough, CA (town) San Mateo County	177	1.66
Melville, NY (cdp) Suffolk County	315	1.65
Tarrytown, NY (village) Westchester County	185	1.65
Palm Beach, FL (town) Palm Beach County	142	1.64
Beverly Hills, CA (city) Los Angeles County	554	1.63
Crestwood Village, NJ (cdp) Ocean County	132	1.62
Ridgefield, CT (cdp) Fairfield County	125	1.62
Tenafly, NJ (borough) Bergen County	229	1.60
North New Hyde Park, NY (cdp) Nassau County	235	1.59
Haddonfield, NJ (borough) Camden County	181	1.56
Great Neck, NY (village) Nassau County	154	1.56
Oronoko, MI (charter township) Berrien County	144	1.56
West Freehold, NJ (cdp) Monmouth County	216	1.55
Manalapan, NJ (township) Monmouth County	584	1.54
Wheatfield, NY (town) Niagara County	267	1.54
East Whiteland, PA (township) Chester County	161	1.54
Lyndhurst, OH (city) Cuyahoga County	216	1.53
South Union, PA (township) Fayette County	165	1.53
Oceanside, NY (cdp) Nassau County	470	1.51
Succasunna, NJ (cdp) Morris County	136	1.51
Aventura, FL (city) Miami-Dade County	507	1.50
North Fayette, PA (township) Allegheny County	203	1.50
Wauwatosa, WI (city) Milwaukee County	684	1.48
Golden, CO (city) Jefferson County	271	1.47
Hanover, NH (cdp) Grafton County	125	1.47
Hazleton, PA (city) Luzerne County	364	1.46
Mantua, NJ (township) Gloucester County	221	1.46
Miller Place, NY (cdp) Suffolk County	179	1.46
Eaton, OH (city) Preble County	123	1.46
Bonham, TX (city) Fannin County	148	1.45
Stony Brook, NY (cdp) Suffolk County	196	1.44
Lincoln Park, NJ (borough) Morris County	153	1.44
Kingston, NY (city) Ulster County	342	1.43
Wyckoff, NJ (township) Bergen County	237	1.43
North Star, DE (cdp) New Castle County	113	1.43
Camillus, NY (town) Onondaga County	340	1.42
Scotch Plains, NJ (township) Union County	329	1.42
Lemont, IL (village) Cook County	218	1.42
Plainedge, NY (cdp) Nassau County	131	1.42
Scott, PA (township) Allegheny County	239	1.41
Bellevue, PA (borough) Allegheny County	118	1.41
Monroe, NJ (township) Middlesex County	522	1.40
Beekman, NY (town) Dutchess County	203	1.40
Endwell, NY (cdp) Broome County	164	1.40
Raritan, NJ (township) Hunterdon County	306	1.39
Ocean Pines, MD (cdp) Worcester County	153	1.39
Redding, CT (town) Fairfield County	124	1.39
Lake Villa, IL (village) Lake County	118	1.39
Hauppauge, NY (cdp) Suffolk County	289	1.38
Shasta Lake, CA (city) Shasta County	139	1.38
Holbrook, NY (cdp) Suffolk County	370	1.37
Upper St. Clair, PA (cdp/township) Allegheny County	263	1.37
Whitemarsh, PA (township) Montgomery County	236	1.37
Monsey, NY (cdp) Rockland County	206	1.37
North Massapequa, NY (cdp) Nassau County	253	1.36
Mamaroneck, NY (town) Westchester County	392	1.35
Jefferson Valley-Yorktown, NY (cdp) Westchester County	196	1.35
East Bradford, PA (township) Chester County	134	1.35
Bayport, NY (cdp) Suffolk County	120	1.35
Boca Raton, FL (city) Palm Beach County	1,141	1.34
Calabasas, CA (city) Los Angeles County	304	1.34
Dallas, GA (city) Paulding County	144	1.34
Golden Hills, CA (cdp) Kern County	115	1.34
Bedford, NY (town) Westchester County	232	1.33
St. Charles, IL (city) Kane County	426	1.32
Berkeley Heights, NJ (township) Union County	173	1.32
Corte Madera, CA (town) Marin County	120	1.32
Solon, OH (city) Cuyahoga County	300	1.31
Brewster, MA (town) Barnstable County	130	1.31
Massapequa, NY (cdp) Nassau County	296	1.30
Setauket-East Setauket, NY (cdp) Suffolk County	204	1.30
Southfield, MI (township) Oakland County	188	1.30
East Hanover, NJ (township) Morris County	146	1.30
Long Hill, NJ (township) Morris County	114	1.30
New Hyde Park, NY (village) Nassau County	124	1.29
Airmont, NY (village) Rockland County	109	1.29
Garrison, MD (cdp) Baltimore County	98	1.29
Ridgefield, CT (town) Fairfield County	310	1.28

Ancestry

Basque

U.S. and 50 States Sorted by Population and Percent of Total Population

Place	Population	%
United States	**59,586**	**0.02**
California	20,606	0.06
Idaho	7,264	0.48
Nevada	5,390	0.20
Oregon	3,233	0.09
Washington	2,847	0.04
Florida	1,998	0.01
Arizona	1,969	0.03
Texas	1,959	0.01
Colorado	1,653	0.03
Utah	1,598	0.06
New York	1,514	0.01
Wyoming	1,170	0.21
New Mexico	685	0.03
Montana	633	0.07
Illinois	569	<0.01
Pennsylvania	521	<0.01
New Jersey	520	0.01
Maryland	463	0.01
Virginia	319	<0.01
Hawaii	310	0.02
Nebraska	310	0.02
Michigan	301	<0.01
Arkansas	288	0.01
Missouri	258	<0.01
Oklahoma	251	0.01
North Carolina	245	<0.01
Wisconsin	235	<0.01
District of Columbia	222	0.04
Massachusetts	206	<0.01
Alaska	199	0.03
Louisiana	171	<0.01
Maine	150	0.01
Tennessee	146	<0.01
Georgia	135	<0.01
Minnesota	120	<0.01
Kentucky	113	<0.01
South Carolina	110	<0.01
Vermont	102	0.02
Kansas	99	<0.01
Connecticut	85	<0.01
Delaware	81	0.01
Indiana	81	<0.01
Alabama	68	<0.01
West Virginia	67	<0.01
Ohio	63	<0.01
South Dakota	58	0.01
Iowa	48	<0.01
North Dakota	47	0.01
Mississippi	47	<0.01
New Hampshire	46	<0.01
Rhode Island	13	<0.01

Place	Population	%
Idaho	7,264	0.48
Wyoming	1,170	0.21
Nevada	5,390	0.20
Oregon	3,233	0.09
Montana	633	0.07
California	20,606	0.06
Utah	1,598	0.06
Washington	2,847	0.04
District of Columbia	222	0.04
Arizona	1,969	0.03
Colorado	1,653	0.03
New Mexico	685	0.03
Alaska	199	0.03
United States	**59,586**	**0.02**
Hawaii	310	0.02
Nebraska	310	0.02
Vermont	102	0.02
Florida	1,998	0.01
Texas	1,959	0.01
New York	1,514	0.01
New Jersey	520	0.01
Maryland	463	0.01
Arkansas	288	0.01
Oklahoma	251	0.01
Maine	150	0.01
Delaware	81	0.01
South Dakota	58	0.01
North Dakota	47	0.01
Illinois	569	<0.01
Pennsylvania	521	<0.01
Virginia	319	<0.01
Michigan	301	<0.01
Missouri	258	<0.01
North Carolina	245	<0.01
Wisconsin	235	<0.01
Massachusetts	206	<0.01
Louisiana	171	<0.01
Tennessee	146	<0.01
Georgia	135	<0.01
Minnesota	120	<0.01
Kentucky	113	<0.01
South Carolina	110	<0.01
Kansas	99	<0.01
Connecticut	85	<0.01
Indiana	81	<0.01
Alabama	68	<0.01
West Virginia	67	<0.01
Ohio	63	<0.01
Iowa	48	<0.01
Mississippi	47	<0.01
New Hampshire	46	<0.01
Rhode Island	13	<0.01

Please refer to the Explanation of Data in the front of the book for more detailed information.

Ancestry

Basque

Top 150 Places Sorted by Population

Based on all places, regardless of total population

Place	Population	%
Boise City, ID (city) Ada County	1,763	0.85
Bakersfield, CA (city) Kern County	1,084	0.33
Reno, NV (city) Washoe County	1,065	0.48
New York, NY (city) Kings County	902	0.01
Los Angeles, CA (city) Los Angeles County	741	0.02
Meridian, ID (city) Ada County	683	0.99
San Francisco, CA (city) San Francisco County	508	0.06
San Diego, CA (city) San Diego County	498	0.04
Seattle, WA (city) King County	441	0.07
Winnemucca, NV (city) Humboldt County	432	6.05
Manhattan, NY (borough) New York County	428	0.03
Portland, OR (city) Multnomah County	409	0.07
Nampa, ID (city) Canyon County	407	0.52
Fresno, CA (city) Fresno County	359	0.07
Sparks, NV (city) Washoe County	300	0.34
Elko, NV (city) Elko County	292	1.64
Phoenix, AZ (city) Maricopa County	285	0.02
Stockton, CA (city) San Joaquin County	280	0.10
Santa Barbara, CA (city) Santa Barbara County	276	0.31
Tucson, AZ (city) Pima County	261	0.05
Twin Falls, ID (city) Twin Falls County	259	0.61
San Jose, CA (city) Santa Clara County	259	0.03
Chicago, IL (city) Cook County	259	0.01
Bend, OR (city) Deschutes County	253	0.34
Gilbert, AZ (town) Maricopa County	244	0.13
San Antonio, TX (city) Medina County	230	0.02
Houston, TX (city) Harris County	228	0.01
Kendall, FL (cdp) Miami-Dade County	226	0.29
Washington, DC (city) District of Columbia	222	0.04
Rancho Cucamonga, CA (city) San Bernardino County	221	0.14
Pacifica, CA (city) San Mateo County	213	0.58
Fayetteville, AR (city) Washington County	213	0.30
Mammoth Lakes, CA (town) Mono County	206	2.57
Rosedale, CA (cdp) Kern County	206	1.39
Fernley, NV (city) Lyon County	202	1.10
Upland, CA (city) San Bernardino County	202	0.27
Spring Creek, NV (cdp) Elko County	201	1.49
Mountain Home, ID (city) Elmore County	192	1.42
Paradise, NV (cdp) Clark County	188	0.09
Las Vegas, NV (city) Clark County	183	0.03
Albuquerque, NM (city) Bernalillo County	181	0.03
San Ramon, CA (city) Contra Costa County	176	0.26
Hayden, ID (city) Kootenai County	173	1.35
Medford, OR (city) Jackson County	165	0.22
West Jordan, UT (city) Salt Lake County	165	0.17
Santa Fe, NM (city) Santa Fe County	160	0.24
El Dorado Hills, CA (cdp) El Dorado County	159	0.37
Covina, CA (city) Los Angeles County	159	0.33
Arden-Arcade, CA (cdp) Sacramento County	159	0.17
Queens, NY (borough) Queens County	159	0.01
Tualatin, OR (city) Washington County	156	0.61
Livermore, CA (city) Alameda County	156	0.20
Long Beach, CA (city) Los Angeles County	153	0.03
Carlsbad, CA (city) San Diego County	152	0.15
Battle Mountain, NV (cdp) Lander County	149	3.91
Austin, TX (city) Travis County	148	0.02
Hemet, CA (city) Riverside County	146	0.19
Eugene, OR (city) Lane County	146	0.10
Martinez, CA (city) Contra Costa County	144	0.40
Norfolk, NE (city) Madison County	140	0.58
Spokane Valley, WA (city) Spokane County	140	0.16
Carson City, NV (ind. city) Carson City County	138	0.25
Spokane, WA (city) Spokane County	136	0.07
Tracy, CA (city) San Joaquin County	134	0.17
Salt Lake City, UT (city) Salt Lake County	134	0.07
Ontario, OR (city) Malheur County	133	1.18
Napa, CA (city) Napa County	130	0.17
Willows, CA (city) Glenn County	129	2.08
Brooklyn, NY (borough) Kings County	129	0.01
Woodland, CA (city) Yolo County	127	0.23
Fort Collins, CO (city) Larimer County	126	0.09
Fallon, NV (city) Churchill County	125	1.46
San Mateo, CA (city) San Mateo County	125	0.13
Berwick, ME (town) York County	123	1.72
Carmichael, CA (cdp) Sacramento County	123	0.20
Bellingham, WA (city) Whatcom County	122	0.15
Mission Viejo, CA (city) Orange County	122	0.13
Antioch, CA (city) Contra Costa County	122	0.12
North Hempstead, NY (town) Nassau County	121	0.05
Riverside, CA (city) Riverside County	120	0.04
Alameda, CA (city) Alameda County	119	0.16
Henderson, NV (city) Clark County	117	0.05
Santa Clara, CA (city) Santa Clara County	116	0.10
Ontario, CA (city) San Bernardino County	116	0.07
Modesto, CA (city) Stanislaus County	116	0.06
San Luis Obispo, CA (city) San Luis Obispo County	115	0.26
Rocklin, CA (city) Placer County	115	0.21
Summerlin South, NV (cdp) Clark County	111	0.51
Hollister, CA (city) San Benito County	111	0.32
Irvine, CA (city) Orange County	111	0.06
Bronx, NY (borough) Bronx County	109	0.01
Vacaville, CA (city) Solano County	108	0.12
Glendora, CA (city) Los Angeles County	106	0.21
Redding, CA (city) Shasta County	106	0.12
Chino, CA (city) San Bernardino County	103	0.13
Sacramento, CA (city) Sacramento County	101	0.02
Clovis, CA (city) Fresno County	100	0.11
Daly City, CA (city) San Mateo County	99	0.10
Spring Valley, NV (cdp) Clark County	99	0.06
Denver, CO (city) Denver County	99	0.02
Pinedale, WY (town) Sublette County	98	5.03
Lakewood, CO (city) Jefferson County	98	0.07
Colorado Springs, CO (city) El Paso County	96	0.02
White Oak, MD (cdp) Montgomery County	95	0.57
Orcutt, CA (cdp) Santa Barbara County	95	0.33
Miami Beach, FL (city) Miami-Dade County	95	0.11
Kuna, ID (city) Ada County	94	0.68
Alamo, CA (cdp) Contra Costa County	94	0.62
San Bruno, CA (city) San Mateo County	94	0.23
South Jordan, UT (city) Salt Lake County	94	0.20
Chandler, AZ (city) Maricopa County	92	0.04
Mesa, AZ (city) Maricopa County	92	0.02
Caldwell, ID (city) Canyon County	91	0.21
Green River, WY (city) Sweetwater County	90	0.73
Pocatello, ID (city) Bannock County	90	0.17
Pittsburg, CA (city) Contra Costa County	87	0.14
Hayesville, OR (cdp) Marion County	86	0.44
Marysville, CA (city) Yuba County	85	0.69
Menifee, CA (city) Riverside County	85	0.12
Millcreek, UT (cdp) Salt Lake County	84	0.14
Alamosa, CO (city) Alamosa County	83	0.95
Paradise Valley, NV (cdp) Humboldt County	82	35.34
Telluride, CO (town) San Miguel County	82	3.17
Meiners Oaks, CA (cdp) Ventura County	82	2.33
Rancho Palos Verdes, CA (city) Los Angeles County	82	0.20
Chula Vista, CA (city) San Diego County	80	0.03
Oklahoma City, OK (city) Oklahoma County	80	0.01
Highland, CA (city) San Bernardino County	79	0.15
Rock Springs, WY (city) Sweetwater County	78	0.35
West Linn, OR (city) Clackamas County	78	0.32
Novato, CA (city) Marin County	78	0.15
Davis, CA (city) Yolo County	77	0.12
Staten Island, NY (borough) Richmond County	77	0.02
Powell, WY (city) Park County	76	1.24
Lake Oswego, OR (city) Clackamas County	76	0.21
Minden, NV (cdp) Douglas County	75	2.49
Spanish Springs, NV (cdp) Washoe County	75	0.51
Issaquah, WA (city) King County	75	0.27
El Centro, CA (city) Imperial County	75	0.18
Durham, CA (cdp) Butte County	74	1.31
Traverse City, MI (city) Grand Traverse County	74	0.51
Traverse City, MI (city) Grand Traverse County	74	0.50
Potomac, MD (cdp) Montgomery County	74	0.17
Rancho Santa Margarita, CA (city) Orange County	74	0.16
Provo, UT (city) Utah County	74	0.07
Burlingame, CA (city) San Mateo County	73	0.26
Lewiston, ID (city) Nez Perce County	73	0.23
Santa Cruz, CA (city) Santa Cruz County	73	0.13
North Rock Springs, WY (cdp) Sweetwater County	72	2.21
Lafayette, CA (city) Contra Costa County	72	0.30

SECTION THREE

Ancestry

Basque

Top 150 Places Sorted by Percent of Total Population

Based on all places, regardless of total population

Place	Population	%
Orovada, NV (cdp) Humboldt County	23	37.10
Paradise Valley, NV (cdp) Humboldt County	82	35.34
Juntura, OR (cdp) Malheur County	7	15.22
Cotopaxi, CO (cdp) Fremont County	6	14.63
Elmira, CA (cdp) Solano County	22	14.38
Dillon Beach, CA (cdp) Marin County	23	14.11
Imlay, NV (cdp) Pershing County	11	13.25
Eden, WY (cdp) Sweetwater County	30	11.95
Stanley, ID (city) Custer County	5	11.90
Wooldridge, MO (village) Cooper County	2	9.09
Jordan Valley, OR (city) Malheur County	14	8.97
Cloverdale, OR (cdp) Tillamook County	36	8.02
Sereno del Mar, CA (cdp) Sonoma County	9	7.32
Brogan, OR (cdp) Malheur County	10	7.04
Tatitlek, AK (cdp) Valdez-Cordova Census Area	5	6.76
Encino, NM (village) Torrance County	4	6.25
Clearmont, WY (town) Sheridan County	5	6.10
Winnemucca, NV (city) Humboldt County	432	6.05
Acme, WA (cdp) Whatcom County	21	5.79
Smiths Ferry, ID (cdp) Valley County	14	5.67
Culbertson, MT (town) Roosevelt County	41	5.45
Keene, CA (cdp) Kern County	17	5.38
Clearview Acres, WY (cdp) Sweetwater County	23	5.15
Cowan, CA (cdp) Stanislaus County	18	5.14
Hastings, OK (town) Jefferson County	6	5.04
Pinedale, WY (town) Sublette County	98	5.03
Kaycee, WY (town) Johnson County	19	4.94
Fort Peck, MT (town) Valley County	10	4.41
Ruhenstroth, NV (cdp) Douglas County	39	3.96
Woodland, UT (cdp) Summit County	28	3.92
Battle Mountain, NV (cdp) Lander County	149	3.91
Davenport, CA (cdp) Santa Cruz County	12	3.88
Fortine, MT (cdp) Lincoln County	12	3.85
China Lake Acres, CA (cdp) Kern County	55	3.54
Idaho City, ID (city) Boise County	17	3.46
White Bird, ID (city) Idaho County	3	3.37
Glenns Ferry, ID (city) Elmore County	55	3.30
Council, ID (city) Adams County	32	3.20
Telluride, CO (town) San Miguel County	82	3.17
Onota, MI (township) Alger County	9	3.10
Litchfield, CA (cdp) Lassen County	3	2.91
Horseshoe Bend, ID (city) Boise County	27	2.76
Wamsutter, WY (town) Sweetwater County	9	2.76
Eureka, NV (cdp) Eureka County	13	2.75
Garden Valley, ID (cdp) Boise County	15	2.70
Mayberry, PA (township) Montour County	8	2.63
Tranquillity, CA (cdp) Fresno County	32	2.61
Cascade, ID (city) Valley County	29	2.61
Harlowton, MT (city) Wheatland County	23	2.59
Mammoth Lakes, CA (town) Mono County	206	2.57
Minden, NV (cdp) Douglas County	75	2.49
Quinton, OK (town) Pittsburg County	22	2.49
Cedar Crest, NM (cdp) Bernalillo County	34	2.48
Bass Lake, CA (cdp) Madera County	11	2.38
Meiners Oaks, CA (cdp) Ventura County	82	2.33
Vanceboro, ME (town) Washington County	3	2.33
Tyrone, MN (township) Le Sueur County	15	2.30
Sleepy Hollow, CA (cdp) Marin County	56	2.29
Riggins, ID (city) Idaho County	9	2.27
Kremlin, MT (cdp) Hill County	3	2.26
Pine, AZ (cdp) Gila County	48	2.25
Vale, OR (city) Malheur County	35	2.25
La Veta, CO (town) Huerfano County	17	2.23
North Rock Springs, WY (cdp) Sweetwater County	72	2.21
Shoshone, ID (city) Lincoln County	40	2.19
Big Piney, WY (town) Sublette County	15	2.16
Aleknagik, AK (city) Dillingham Census Area	6	2.11
Chapin, IA (cdp) Franklin County	2	2.11
Willows, CA (city) Glenn County	129	2.08
Wall Lane, AZ (cdp) Yuma County	9	2.08
Cawker City, KS (city) Mitchell County	12	2.04
Brady, NE (village) Lincoln County	9	1.99
Coats, NC (town) Harnett County	41	1.94
Lumber, PA (township) Cameron County	4	1.94
Greybull, WY (town) Big Horn County	32	1.92
Branson, CO (town) Las Animas County	2	1.90
Kanorado, KS (city) Sherman County	3	1.88
Julian, CA (cdp) San Diego County	28	1.86
Marsing, ID (city) Owyhee County	15	1.82
Hidden Spring, ID (cdp) Ada County	26	1.76
Benbow, CA (cdp) Humboldt County	10	1.76
Berwick, ME (town) York County	123	1.72
Island Park, ID (city) Fremont County	3	1.70
Weaverville, CA (cdp) Trinity County	67	1.68
Franklin, WV (town) Pendleton County	15	1.67
Elko, NV (city) Elko County	292	1.64
Platte Woods, MO (city) Platte County	5	1.56
Filer, ID (city) Twin Falls County	36	1.50
Spring Creek, NV (cdp) Elko County	201	1.49
Middlebush, NJ (cdp) Somerset County	30	1.49
Avilla Beach, CA (cdp) San Luis Obispo County	15	1.47
Fallon, NV (city) Churchill County	125	1.46
Bolinas, CA (cdp) Marin County	17	1.46
Mountain Home, ID (city) Elmore County	192	1.42
Columbus, NM (village) Luna County	18	1.40
Augusta, MT (cdp) Lewis and Clark County	4	1.40
Rosedale, CA (cdp) Kern County	206	1.39
Oak View, CA (cdp) Ventura County	55	1.39
Alford, MA (town) Berkshire County	6	1.39
Frazer, MT (cdp) Valley County	4	1.38
Linden, CA (cdp) San Joaquin County	26	1.37
Hayden, ID (city) Kootenai County	173	1.35
Parma, ID (city) Canyon County	28	1.35
Johnstonville, CA (cdp) Lassen County	7	1.35
Millwood, WA (town) Spokane County	22	1.33
Lake Prairie, MN (township) Nicollet County	7	1.32
Durham, CA (cdp) Butte County	74	1.31
Harper, OR (cdp) Malheur County	2	1.31
McSwain, CA (cdp) Merced County	52	1.30
Nevada City, CA (city) Nevada County	40	1.30
Sutter, CA (cdp) Sutter County	38	1.30
Forest Ranch, CA (cdp) Butte County	17	1.27
Buffalo, WY (city) Johnson County	56	1.25
Powell, WY (city) Park County	76	1.24
Fraser, CO (town) Grand County	17	1.23
Denair, CA (cdp) Stanislaus County	53	1.22
Douglas, WY (city) Converse County	71	1.20
Pine Canyon, CA (cdp) Monterey County	24	1.20
Ontario, OR (city) Malheur County	133	1.18
Evansville, WY (town) Natrona County	29	1.17
Moorcroft, WY (town) Crook County	15	1.17
Hartley, CA (cdp) Solano County	31	1.13
Westfir, OR (city) Lane County	3	1.12
Jamestown, CA (cdp) Tuolumne County	41	1.11
Fernley, NV (city) Lyon County	202	1.10
Tahoe Vista, CA (cdp) Placer County	17	1.10
Silver Springs, NV (cdp) Lyon County	55	1.09
Bellevue, ID (city) Blaine County	21	1.09
Irrigon, OR (city) Morrow County	21	1.09
Plattekill, NY (cdp) Ulster County	15	1.09
Island City, OR (city) Union County	11	1.07
Madras, OR (city) Jefferson County	64	1.06
Garrett, WA (cdp) Walla Walla County	14	1.04
Homedale, ID (city) Owyhee County	27	1.02
Potrero, CA (cdp) San Diego County	12	1.02
Clallam Bay, WA (cdp) Clallam County	9	1.02
Union, OR (city) Union County	21	1.01
Golden Valley, NV (cdp) Washoe County	16	1.01
Paulina, LA (cdp) St. James Parish	12	1.01
Graton, CA (cdp) Sonoma County	16	1.00
Meridian, ID (city) Ada County	683	0.99
Lemmon Valley, NV (cdp) Washoe County	51	0.99
Estacada, OR (city) Clackamas County	26	0.97
Hollister, ID (city) Twin Falls County	3	0.96
Alamosa, CO (city) Alamosa County	83	0.95
Lago Vista, TX (city) Travis County	53	0.93
Key Center, WA (cdp) Pierce County	28	0.93
Montague, CA (city) Siskiyou County	13	0.93
North Edwards, CA (cdp) Kern County	10	0.91
Monticello, GA (city) Jasper County	24	0.90

Please refer to the Explanation of Data in the front of the book for more detailed information.

Ancestry

Basque

Top 150 Places Sorted by Percent of Total Population

Based on places with total population of 7,500 or more

Place	Population	%
Mammoth Lakes, CA (town) Mono County	206	2.57
Elko, NV (city) Elko County	292	1.64
Spring Creek, NV (cdp) Elko County	201	1.49
Fallon, NV (city) Churchill County	125	1.46
Mountain Home, ID (city) Elmore County	192	1.42
Rosedale, CA (cdp) Kern County	206	1.39
Hayden, ID (city) Kootenai County	173	1.35
Ontario, OR (city) Malheur County	133	1.18
Fernley, NV (city) Lyon County	202	1.10
Meridian, ID (city) Ada County	683	0.99
Alamosa, CO (city) Alamosa County	83	0.95
Boise City, ID (city) Ada County	1,763	0.85
Green River, WY (city) Sweetwater County	90	0.73
Marysville, CA (city) Yuba County	85	0.69
Kuna, ID (city) Ada County	94	0.68
Garden City, ID (city) Ada County	70	0.63
Alamo, CA (cdp) Contra Costa County	94	0.62
Twin Falls, ID (city) Twin Falls County	259	0.61
Tualatin, OR (city) Washington County	156	0.61
Kalaoa, HI (cdp) Hawaii County	53	0.61
Redlands, CO (cdp) Mesa County	46	0.59
Pacifica, CA (city) San Mateo County	213	0.58
Norfolk, NE (city) Madison County	140	0.58
Lake of the Woods, VA (cdp) Orange County	45	0.58
White Oak, MD (cdp) Montgomery County	95	0.57
Croton-on-Hudson, NY (village) Westchester County	42	0.53
Nampa, ID (city) Canyon County	407	0.52
Summerlin South, NV (cdp) Clark County	111	0.51
Spanish Springs, NV (cdp) Washoe County	75	0.51
Traverse City, MI (city) Grand Traverse County	74	0.51
Larkfield-Wikiup, CA (cdp) Sonoma County	44	0.51
Traverse City, MI (city) Grand Traverse County	74	0.50
Pedley, CA (cdp) Riverside County	59	0.50
Reno, NV (city) Washoe County	1,065	0.48
Cape St. Claire, MD (cdp) Anne Arundel County	42	0.48
Beaufort, SC (city) Beaufort County	58	0.46
Grover Beach, CA (city) San Luis Obispo County	59	0.45
Hayesville, OR (cdp) Marion County	86	0.44
Taft, CA (city) Kern County	41	0.44
Trinidad, CO (city) Las Animas County	41	0.44
Sonoma, CA (city) Sonoma County	42	0.41
Martinez, CA (city) Contra Costa County	144	0.40
Jennings Lodge, OR (cdp) Clackamas County	31	0.40
Pacific Grove, CA (city) Monterey County	56	0.38
El Dorado Hills, CA (cdp) El Dorado County	159	0.37
El Sobrante, CA (cdp) Contra Costa County	50	0.37
Grantsville, UT (city) Tooele County	31	0.37
Rock Springs, WY (city) Sweetwater County	78	0.35
Upper St. Clair, PA (cdp/township) Allegheny County	67	0.35
Guttenberg, NJ (town) Hudson County	38	0.35
Tiburon, CA (town) Marin County	31	0.35
Sparks, NV (city) Washoe County	300	0.34
Bend, OR (city) Deschutes County	253	0.34
Gardnerville Ranchos, NV (cdp) Douglas County	40	0.34
East Whiteland, PA (township) Chester County	36	0.34
Jerome, ID (city) Jerome County	35	0.34
Bakersfield, CA (city) Kern County	1,084	0.33
Covina, CA (city) Los Angeles County	159	0.33
Orcutt, CA (cdp) Santa Barbara County	95	0.33
Hollister, CA (city) San Benito County	111	0.32
West Linn, OR (city) Clackamas County	78	0.32
Santa Barbara, CA (city) Santa Barbara County	276	0.31
Fayetteville, AR (city) Washington County	213	0.30
Lafayette, CA (city) Contra Costa County	72	0.30
Berkley, CO (cdp) Adams County	36	0.30
Soquel, CA (cdp) Santa Cruz County	28	0.30
Kendall, FL (cdp) Miami-Dade County	226	0.29
Lemoore, CA (city) Kings County	70	0.29
Mineola, NY (village) Nassau County	54	0.29
Monmouth, OR (city) Polk County	27	0.29
Lamar, CO (city) Prowers County	23	0.29
Chowchilla, CA (city) Madera County	51	0.28
Frederickson, WA (cdp) Pierce County	49	0.28
Vashon, WA (cdp) King County	28	0.28
Upland, CA (city) San Bernardino County	202	0.27
Issaquah, WA (city) King County	75	0.27
Dinuba, CA (city) Tulare County	57	0.27
Ellensburg, WA (city) Kittitas County	49	0.27
Cold Springs, NV (cdp) Washoe County	25	0.27
Yreka, CA (city) Siskiyou County	21	0.27
San Ramon, CA (city) Contra Costa County	176	0.26
San Luis Obispo, CA (city) San Luis Obispo County	115	0.26
Burlingame, CA (city) San Mateo County	73	0.26
Moscow, ID (city) Latah County	60	0.26
Pendleton, OR (city) Umatilla County	44	0.26
Mill Valley, CA (city) Marin County	35	0.26
Tamalpais-Homestead Valley, CA (cdp) Marin County	28	0.26
Woodbury, NY (village) Orange County	27	0.26
Carson City, NV (ind. city) Carson City County	138	0.25
Gillette, WY (city) Campbell County	69	0.25
Post Falls, ID (city) Kootenai County	65	0.25
La Riviera, CA (cdp) Sacramento County	28	0.25
Cortez, CO (city) Montezuma County	21	0.25
Santa Fe, NM (city) Santa Fe County	160	0.24
Redmond, OR (city) Deschutes County	60	0.24
Short Hills, NJ (cdp) Essex County	32	0.24
Woodbury, NY (town) Orange County	27	0.24
Newcastle, WA (city) King County	24	0.24
Prineville, OR (city) Crook County	23	0.24
Woodland, CA (city) Yolo County	127	0.23
San Bruno, CA (city) San Mateo County	94	0.23
Lewiston, ID (city) Nez Perce County	73	0.23
Ramona, CA (cdp) San Diego County	50	0.23
Bethany, OR (cdp) Washington County	44	0.23
Opa-locka, FL (city) Miami-Dade County	35	0.23
Cornelius, OR (city) Washington County	26	0.23
Medford, OR (city) Jackson County	165	0.22
Seal Beach, CA (city) Orange County	53	0.22
Dixon, CA (city) Solano County	40	0.22
Colchester, VT (town) Chittenden County	38	0.22
Susanville, CA (city) Lassen County	38	0.22
Paradise Valley, AZ (town) Maricopa County	29	0.22
Oak Hills, OR (cdp) Washington County	24	0.22
Cheney, WA (city) Spokane County	23	0.22
Piedmont, CA (city) Alameda County	23	0.22
Corte Madera, CA (town) Marin County	20	0.22
Templeton, CA (cdp) San Luis Obispo County	18	0.22
Rocklin, CA (city) Placer County	115	0.21
Glendora, CA (city) Los Angeles County	106	0.21
Caldwell, ID (city) Canyon County	91	0.21
Lake Oswego, OR (city) Clackamas County	76	0.21
Moorpark, CA (city) Ventura County	70	0.21
Juneau, AK (borough) Juneau City and Borough	64	0.21
Mililani Town, HI (cdp) Honolulu County	63	0.21
Rye, NY (city) Westchester County	32	0.21
Lakeland North, WA (cdp) King County	25	0.21
North Wantagh, NY (cdp) Nassau County	24	0.21
Sierra Madre, CA (city) Los Angeles County	23	0.21
Enumclaw, WA (city) King County	22	0.21
Livermore, CA (city) Alameda County	156	0.20
Carmichael, CA (cdp) Sacramento County	123	0.20
South Jordan, UT (city) Salt Lake County	94	0.20
Rancho Palos Verdes, CA (city) Los Angeles County	82	0.20
Libertyville, IL (village) Lake County	41	0.20
Eagle, ID (city) Ada County	38	0.20
Oakland, MI (charter township) Oakland County	32	0.20
Hutto, TX (city) Williamson County	24	0.20
Woodbury, NJ (city) Gloucester County	21	0.20
Roxborough Park, CO (cdp) Douglas County	18	0.20
East Foothills, CA (cdp) Santa Clara County	15	0.20
Hemet, CA (city) Riverside County	146	0.19
South Salt Lake, UT (city) Salt Lake County	43	0.19
Crowley, TX (city) Tarrant County	23	0.19
Emeryville, CA (city) Alameda County	18	0.19
Woodmoor, CO (cdp) El Paso County	17	0.19
Golden Valley, AZ (cdp) Mohave County	16	0.19
El Centro, CA (city) Imperial County	75	0.18
San Carlos, CA (city) San Mateo County	51	0.18
Oak Grove, OR (cdp) Clackamas County	30	0.18
Princeton, NJ (township) Mercer County	30	0.18

SECTION THREE

Please refer to the Explanation of Data in the front of the book for more detailed information.

Ancestry

Belgian

U.S. and 50 States Sorted by Population and Percent of Total Population

Place	Population	%
United States	**386,694**	**0.13**
Wisconsin	57,524	1.02
Michigan	56,212	0.56
Illinois	33,847	0.27
California	27,884	0.08
Minnesota	16,141	0.31
Florida	15,450	0.08
New York	13,929	0.07
Indiana	13,481	0.21
Texas	12,067	0.05
Ohio	10,037	0.09
Pennsylvania	9,754	0.08
Washington	9,226	0.14
Iowa	8,265	0.27
Colorado	7,111	0.15
New Jersey	6,706	0.08
Arizona	6,568	0.11
Oregon	5,731	0.15
Missouri	5,561	0.09
Massachusetts	5,453	0.08
North Carolina	5,418	0.06
Virginia	5,213	0.07
Kansas	5,165	0.18
Georgia	5,063	0.05
Louisiana	4,531	0.10
Maryland	3,928	0.07
Connecticut	3,118	0.09
Tennessee	2,654	0.04
Montana	2,361	0.24
Nevada	2,236	0.08
Nebraska	2,089	0.12
South Carolina	2,062	0.05
South Dakota	1,683	0.21
New Hampshire	1,673	0.13
Oklahoma	1,559	0.04
Idaho	1,520	0.10
Utah	1,514	0.06
New Mexico	1,452	0.07
Kentucky	1,445	0.03
Alabama	1,332	0.03
West Virginia	1,311	0.07
Arkansas	1,275	0.04
Rhode Island	1,120	0.11
North Dakota	1,047	0.16
Maine	992	0.07
Wyoming	781	0.14
Hawaii	664	0.05
Mississippi	656	0.02
Alaska	616	0.09
District of Columbia	496	0.08
Vermont	470	0.08
Delaware	303	0.03

Place	Population	%
Wisconsin	57,524	1.02
Michigan	56,212	0.56
Minnesota	16,141	0.31
Illinois	33,847	0.27
Iowa	8,265	0.27
Montana	2,361	0.24
Indiana	13,481	0.21
South Dakota	1,683	0.21
Kansas	5,165	0.18
North Dakota	1,047	0.16
Colorado	7,111	0.15
Oregon	5,731	0.15
Washington	9,226	0.14
Wyoming	781	0.14
United States	**386,694**	**0.13**
New Hampshire	1,673	0.13
Nebraska	2,089	0.12
Arizona	6,568	0.11
Rhode Island	1,120	0.11
Louisiana	4,531	0.10
Idaho	1,520	0.10
Ohio	10,037	0.09
Missouri	5,561	0.09
Connecticut	3,118	0.09
Alaska	616	0.09
California	27,884	0.08
Florida	15,450	0.08
Pennsylvania	9,754	0.08
New Jersey	6,706	0.08
Massachusetts	5,453	0.08
Nevada	2,236	0.08
District of Columbia	496	0.08
Vermont	470	0.08
New York	13,929	0.07
Virginia	5,213	0.07
Maryland	3,928	0.07
New Mexico	1,452	0.07
West Virginia	1,311	0.07
Maine	992	0.07
North Carolina	5,418	0.06
Utah	1,514	0.06
Texas	12,067	0.05
Georgia	5,063	0.05
South Carolina	2,062	0.05
Hawaii	664	0.05
Tennessee	2,654	0.04
Oklahoma	1,559	0.04
Arkansas	1,275	0.04
Kentucky	1,445	0.03
Alabama	1,332	0.03
Delaware	303	0.03
Mississippi	656	0.02

Please refer to the Explanation of Data in the front of the book for more detailed information.

Ancestry

Belgian

Top 150 Places Sorted by Population

Based on all places, regardless of total population

Place	Population	%
Green Bay, WI (city) Brown County	9,328	8.97
New York, NY (city) Kings County	4,472	0.06
Moline, IL (city) Rock Island County	2,722	6.28
Chicago, IL (city) Cook County	2,597	0.10
Manhattan, NY (borough) New York County	2,470	0.16
St. Clair Shores, MI (city) Macomb County	2,178	3.58
Los Angeles, CA (city) Los Angeles County	2,001	0.05
Macomb, MI (township) Macomb County	1,860	2.48
De Pere, WI (city) Brown County	1,847	7.95
Clinton, MI (charter township) Macomb County	1,840	1.89
Sterling Heights, MI (city) Macomb County	1,835	1.41
Mishawaka, IN (city) St. Joseph County	1,831	3.82
Warren, MI (city) Macomb County	1,678	1.24
Ashwaubenon, WI (village) Brown County	1,666	9.74
San Diego, CA (city) San Diego County	1,571	0.12
Bellevue, WI (village) Brown County	1,555	11.07
Rock Island, IL (city) Rock Island County	1,408	3.63
Phoenix, AZ (city) Maricopa County	1,393	0.10
Howard, WI (village) Brown County	1,379	8.24
Shelby, MI (charter township) Macomb County	1,336	1.84
Sturgeon Bay, WI (city) Door County	1,335	14.51
Chesterfield, MI (township) Macomb County	1,276	2.99
Suamico, WI (village) Brown County	1,268	11.67
San Antonio, TX (city) Medina County	1,182	0.09
Milwaukee, WI (city) Milwaukee County	1,121	0.19
Luxemburg, WI (village) Kewaunee County	1,040	42.96
Allouez, WI (village) Brown County	1,032	7.24
Davenport, IA (city) Scott County	1,023	1.04
Brooklyn, NY (borough) Kings County	1,012	0.04
Portland, OR (city) Multnomah County	995	0.18
Roseville, MI (city) Macomb County	978	2.04
Minneapolis, MN (city) Hennepin County	962	0.25
Marshall, MN (city) Lyon County	933	6.95
Seattle, WA (city) King County	909	0.15
Houston, TX (city) Harris County	887	0.04
Denver, CO (city) Denver County	876	0.15
South Bend, IN (city) St. Joseph County	871	0.85
Indianapolis, IN (city) Marion County	866	0.11
East Moline, IL (city) Rock Island County	816	3.82
Appleton, WI (city) Outagamie County	816	1.12
Red River, WI (town) Kewaunee County	799	52.88
Appleton, WI (city) Outagamie County	799	1.33
San Francisco, CA (city) San Francisco County	783	0.10
Grosse Pointe Woods, MI (city) Wayne County	776	4.74
Madison, WI (city) Dane County	759	0.33
Kansas City, MO (city) Jackson County	753	0.17
Ramapo, NY (town) Rockland County	751	0.61
Green Bay, WI (town) Brown County	743	36.80
Scott, WI (town) Brown County	740	21.41
Austin, TX (city) Travis County	723	0.09
Troy, MI (city) Oakland County	722	0.89
Columbus, OH (city) Franklin County	699	0.09
San Jose, CA (city) Santa Clara County	693	0.07
Luxemburg, WI (town) Kewaunee County	691	44.13
Charlotte, NC (city) Mecklenburg County	690	0.10
Olathe, KS (city) Johnson County	659	0.55
Geneseo, IL (city) Henry County	628	9.70
Ann Arbor, MI (city) Washtenaw County	605	0.53
Queens, NY (borough) Queens County	593	0.03
Rochester Hills, MI (city) Oakland County	586	0.83
St. Paul, MN (city) Ramsey County	582	0.21
Overland Park, KS (city) Johnson County	575	0.34
Kewanee, IL (city) Henry County	560	4.30
Las Vegas, NV (city) Clark County	558	0.10
Harrison, MI (charter township) Macomb County	553	2.24
Jacksonville, FL (city) Duval County	548	0.07
New Baltimore, MI (city) Macomb County	532	4.70
Brussels, WI (town) Door County	528	48.00
Ira, MI (township) St. Clair County	528	9.45
Bruce, MI (township) Macomb County	507	5.85
Algoma, WI (city) Kewaunee County	505	15.70
Omaha, NE (city) Douglas County	497	0.12
Washington, DC (city) District of Columbia	496	0.08
Little Suamico, WI (town) Oconto County	483	10.29
Bettendorf, IA (city) Scott County	473	1.46
Virginia Beach, VA (ind. city) Virginia Beach independent city	473	0.11
Peoria, IL (city) Peoria County	465	0.41
Lenox, MI (township) Macomb County	461	4.54
Washington, MI (township) Macomb County	457	1.89
Cedar Rapids, IA (city) Linn County	454	0.36
Humboldt, WI (town) Brown County	448	33.84
Naperville, IL (city) DuPage County	443	0.31
Tucson, AZ (city) Pima County	442	0.09
Union, WI (town) Door County	441	44.10
Silvis, IL (city) Rock Island County	433	5.82
Eastpointe, MI (city) Macomb County	432	1.31
Des Moines, IA (city) Polk County	430	0.21
Royal Oak, MI (city) Oakland County	424	0.73
Detroit, MI (city) Wayne County	422	0.06
Fraser, MI (city) Macomb County	420	2.85
Oceanside, CA (city) San Diego County	420	0.25
Eugene, OR (city) Lane County	409	0.27
Lincoln, WI (town) Kewaunee County	405	43.88
Hempstead, NY (town) Nassau County	405	0.05
Albuquerque, NM (city) Bernalillo County	401	0.08
Brookhaven, NY (town) Suffolk County	401	0.08
Monsey, NY (cdp) Rockland County	400	2.66
Orchards, WA (cdp) Clark County	399	1.97
Alexandria, LA (city) Rapides Parish	397	0.83
Sioux Falls, SD (city) Minnehaha County	393	0.26
Hillsboro, OR (city) Washington County	383	0.43
Orion, MI (charter township) Oakland County	382	1.09
Colorado Springs, CO (city) El Paso County	380	0.09
Fort Lauderdale, FL (city) Broward County	374	0.22
Arvada, CO (city) Jefferson County	372	0.35
Oakland, CA (city) Alameda County	370	0.10
Evanston, IL (city) Cook County	369	0.50
Shawnee, KS (city) Johnson County	365	0.61
Ledgeview, WI (town) Brown County	356	5.94
Carmel, IN (city) Hamilton County	352	0.46
Kaukauna, WI (city) Outagamie County	351	2.33
Marquette, MI (city) Marquette County	351	1.65
Henderson, NV (city) Clark County	351	0.14
Chandler, AZ (city) Maricopa County	350	0.15
Fort Collins, CO (city) Larimer County	349	0.25
Granger, IN (cdp) St. Joseph County	347	1.22
Dallas, TX (city) Dallas County	346	0.03
Cary, NC (town) Wake County	343	0.27
Lakewood, CO (city) Jefferson County	340	0.24
Dearborn, MI (city) Wayne County	339	0.34
Grand Rapids, MI (city) Kent County	335	0.18
Aurora, CO (city) Arapahoe County	335	0.11
Billings, MT (city) Yellowstone County	332	0.33
Nasewaupee, WI (town) Door County	330	15.41
Canton, MI (charter township) Wayne County	329	0.37
Islip, NY (town) Suffolk County	328	0.10
Lansing, MI (city) Ingham County	326	0.29
Lansing, MI (city) Ingham County	326	0.28
Scottsdale, AZ (city) Maricopa County	323	0.15
Monroe, MI (charter township) Monroe County	322	2.21
Superior, WI (city) Douglas County	322	1.18
Wausau, WI (city) Marathon County	320	0.82
Nashville-Davidson, TN (metro govt) Davidson County	319	0.05
Livonia, MI (city) Wayne County	314	0.32
Minneota, MN (city) Lyon County	311	26.07
Salem, OR (city) Marion County	310	0.20
Cartersville, GA (city) Bartow County	306	1.58
Oshkosh, WI (city) Winnebago County	305	0.47
Waukesha, WI (city) Waukesha County	305	0.44
Escanaba, MI (township) Delta County	303	8.68
Lenexa, KS (city) Johnson County	303	0.64
St. Louis, MO (city) St. Louis city County	302	0.09
Gardner, WI (town) Door County	301	26.90
Kenosha, WI (city) Kenosha County	301	0.31
Duluth, MN (city) St. Louis County	300	0.35
Santa Monica, CA (city) Los Angeles County	300	0.34
Cambridge, MA (city) Middlesex County	297	0.29
Lincoln, NE (city) Lancaster County	297	0.12
Novi, MI (city) Oakland County	295	0.55
Boston, MA (city) Suffolk County	293	0.05

Ancestry

Belgian

Top 150 Places Sorted by Percent of Total Population

Based on all places, regardless of total population

Place	Population	%
Gloster, LA (cdp) De Soto Parish	15	55.56
Red River, WI (town) Kewaunee County	799	52.88
Brussels, WI (town) Door County	528	48.00
Luxemburg, WI (town) Kewaunee County	691	44.13
Union, WI (town) Door County	441	44.10
Lincoln, WI (town) Kewaunee County	405	43.88
Luxemburg, WI (village) Kewaunee County	1,040	42.96
Eidsvold, MN (township) Lyon County	115	41.67
Grandview, MN (township) Lyon County	121	40.74
Casco, WI (village) Kewaunee County	228	39.38
Bowman, TN (cdp) Cumberland County	13	37.14
Green Bay, WI (town) Brown County	743	36.80
Minnesota Lake, MN (city) Blue Earth County	6	35.29
Dyckesville, WI (cdp) Brown County	174	34.39
Humboldt, WI (town) Brown County	448	33.84
Westerheim, MN (township) Lyon County	95	31.25
Nordland, MN (township) Lyon County	57	30.81
West Branch, MI (township) Dickinson County	11	28.95
Milroy, MN (city) Redwood County	70	28.23
Fairview, MN (township) Lyon County	105	27.49
Little Sturgeon, WI (cdp) Door County	42	27.10
Gardner, WI (town) Door County	301	26.90
Vallers, MN (township) Lyon County	75	26.69
Normania, MN (township) Yellow Medicine County	60	26.67
Atkinson, IL (town) Henry County	248	26.41
Ahnapee, WI (town) Kewaunee County	250	26.10
Minneota, MN (city) Lyon County	311	26.07
Lucas, MN (township) Lyon County	78	25.16
Rocky Point, MT (cdp) Lake County	14	24.56
Plumwood, OH (cdp) Madison County	43	24.02
Annawan, IL (town) Henry County	214	22.86
Stanley, MN (township) Lyon County	60	22.73
Casco, WI (town) Kewaunee County	236	22.61
Forestville, WI (town) Door County	235	21.58
Scott, WI (town) Brown County	740	21.41
Forestville, WI (village) Door County	107	21.06
Ghent, MN (city) Lyon County	76	19.24
Eaton, WI (town) Brown County	291	19.21
Underwood, MN (township) Redwood County	32	18.60
Lake Stay, MN (township) Lincoln County	35	17.77
West Kewaunee, WI (town) Kewaunee County	239	17.73
Lyons, MN (township) Lyon County	33	17.55
Guernsey, IA (city) Poweshiek County	10	17.24
Taunton, MN (city) Lyon County	30	16.67
Algoma, WI (city) Kewaunee County	505	15.70
Montpelier, WI (town) Kewaunee County	222	15.69
Nasewaupee, WI (town) Door County	330	15.41
Porter, MN (city) Yellow Medicine County	29	15.26
Granite Rock, MN (township) Redwood County	28	14.97
Amiret, MN (township) Lyon County	27	14.67
New Denmark, WI (town) Brown County	227	14.63
Sturgeon Bay, WI (city) Door County	1,335	14.51
Limestone, MN (township) Lincoln County	18	14.40
Burton, MN (township) Yellow Medicine County	23	14.20
Island Lake, MN (township) Lyon County	18	13.85
Gourley, MI (township) Menominee County	46	13.81
Rockland, WI (town) Brown County	245	13.65
Pierce, WI (town) Kewaunee County	115	13.64
Clifton, MN (township) Lyon County	34	13.23
Marshfield, MN (township) Lincoln County	30	12.88
McDonald, PA (borough) Allegheny County	48	12.63
DeKalb Junction, NY (cdp) St. Lawrence County	41	12.58
Alta Vista, MN (township) Lincoln County	19	12.50
Glenmore, WI (town) Brown County	139	12.38
Westline, MN (township) Redwood County	18	12.24
Cleveland, WI (town) Jackson County	58	12.11
Lena, WI (town) Oconto County	90	12.08
Bulger, PA (cdp) Washington County	58	11.91
Custer, MN (township) Lyon County	21	11.73
Oconto, WI (town) Oconto County	152	11.71
Suamico, WI (village) Brown County	1,268	11.67
Holly, MN (township) Murray County	14	11.38
Brandt, SD (town) Deuel County	10	11.36
Lena, WI (village) Oconto County	53	11.30
Swede Prairie, MN (township) Yellow Medicine County	13	11.30
Norman, MN (township) Yellow Medicine County	34	11.22
Vesta, MN (township) Redwood County	24	11.21
Lynd, MN (township) Lyon County	49	11.09
Bellevue, WI (village) Brown County	1,555	11.07
Holiday Lake, IA (cdp) Poweshiek County	74	10.79
Stiles, WI (town) Oconto County	172	10.78
Monroe, MN (township) Lyon County	25	10.78
Stephenson, MI (township) Menominee County	75	10.64
Willow Lake, MN (township) Redwood County	19	10.61
Franklin, WI (town) Kewaunee County	105	10.57
Little Suamico, WI (town) Oconto County	483	10.29
Edgar, MT (cdp) Carbon County	16	10.19
Eden, MN (township) Polk County	20	10.15
Coon Creek, MN (township) Lyon County	30	10.10
Miami, TX (city) Roberts County	53	10.04
Lake Marshall, MN (township) Lyon County	51	10.02
Ashwaubenon, WI (village) Brown County	1,666	9.74
Geneseo, IL (city) Henry County	628	9.70
Kewaunee, WI (city) Kewaunee County	279	9.46
Ira, MI (township) St. Clair County	528	9.45
Sturgeon Bay, WI (town) Door County	74	9.30
Piehl, WI (town) Oneida County	7	9.21
Sodus, MN (township) Lyon County	29	9.18
St. Leo, MN (city) Yellow Medicine County	14	9.15
Emmett, MI (village) St. Clair County	30	9.12
Coffee City, TX (town) Henderson County	27	9.09
Green Bay, WI (city) Brown County	9,328	8.97
Clay Banks, WI (town) Door County	37	8.96
Hartwick, IA (city) Poweshiek County	5	8.93
Mineral, IL (village) Bureau County	21	8.79
Akron, MN (township) Big Stone County	12	8.76
Coyne Center, IL (cdp) Rock Island County	63	8.74
Cleveland, IL (village) Henry County	14	8.70
Escanaba, MI (township) Delta County	303	8.68
Carlton, WI (town) Kewaunee County	76	8.67
Pensaukee, WI (town) Oconto County	109	8.57
Sheffield, IL (village) Bureau County	84	8.55
Pulcifer, WI (cdp) Shawano County	14	8.54
Hansonville, MN (township) Lincoln County	7	8.43
Victor, IA (city) Iowa County	67	8.36
Wrightstown, WI (town) Brown County	175	8.33
Cold Bay, AK (city) Aleutians East Borough	3	8.33
Gales, MN (township) Redwood County	17	8.29
Howard, WI (village) Brown County	1,379	8.24
Coal Valley, IL (village) Rock Island County	284	8.22
Maribel, WI (village) Manitowoc County	25	8.22
Abrams, WI (town) Oconto County	155	8.12
Russell, MN (city) Lyon County	27	8.06
Maple Grove, WI (town) Shawano County	70	8.02
Vesta, MN (city) Redwood County	28	8.02
New Liberty, IA (city) Scott County	12	8.00
Florence, MN (city) Lyon County	2	8.00
Maple Falls, WA (cdp) Whatcom County	40	7.98
De Pere, WI (city) Brown County	1,847	7.95
Langdon, KS (city) Reno County	3	7.89
Cottonwood, MN (city) Lyon County	78	7.85
Royal, MN (township) Lincoln County	12	7.79
Park View, IA (cdp) Scott County	189	7.78
Tyro, MN (township) Yellow Medicine County	16	7.77
Orion, IL (village) Henry County	145	7.74
Forest, WI (town) St. Croix County	46	7.67
Riverview, WI (town) Oconto County	57	7.48
Hillsdale, IL (village) Rock Island County	37	7.37
Niagara, WI (town) Marinette County	57	7.35
Joffre, PA (cdp) Washington County	46	7.31
Meire Grove, MN (city) Stearns County	8	7.27
Kenneth, MN (city) Rock County	5	7.25
Allouez, WI (village) Brown County	1,032	7.24
Sherrard, IL (village) Mercer County	60	7.24
Pittsfield, WI (town) Brown County	187	7.23
Sobieski, WI (cdp) Oconto County	20	7.12
Rock Lake, MN (township) Lyon County	19	7.09
Brampton, MI (township) Delta County	79	7.00
Vienna, MN (township) Rock County	6	6.98
Angelica, WI (cdp) Shawano County	8	6.96

Please refer to the Explanation of Data in the front of the book for more detailed information.

Ancestry

Belgian

Top 150 Places Sorted by Percent of Total Population

Based on places with total population of 7,500 or more

Place	Population	%
Sturgeon Bay, WI (city) Door County	1,335	14.51
Suamico, WI (village) Brown County	1,268	11.67
Bellevue, WI (village) Brown County	1,555	11.07
Ashwaubenon, WI (village) Brown County	1,666	9.74
Green Bay, WI (city) Brown County	9,328	8.97
Howard, WI (village) Brown County	1,379	8.24
De Pere, WI (city) Brown County	1,847	7.95
Allouez, WI (village) Brown County	1,032	7.24
Marshall, MN (city) Lyon County	933	6.95
Moline, IL (city) Rock Island County	2,722	6.28
Bruce, MI (township) Macomb County	507	5.85
Grosse Pointe Woods, MI (city) Wayne County	776	4.74
New Baltimore, MI (city) Macomb County	532	4.70
Lenox, MI (township) Macomb County	461	4.54
Kewanee, IL (city) Henry County	560	4.30
Mishawaka, IN (city) St. Joseph County	1,831	3.82
East Moline, IL (city) Rock Island County	816	3.82
Rock Island, IL (city) Rock Island County	1,408	3.63
St. Clair Shores, MI (city) Macomb County	2,178	3.58
Chesterfield, MI (township) Macomb County	1,276	2.99
Fraser, MI (city) Macomb County	420	2.85
Menominee, MI (city) Menominee County	242	2.79
Monsey, NY (cdp) Rockland County	400	2.66
Macomb, MI (township) Macomb County	1,860	2.48
Kaukauna, WI (city) Outagamie County	351	2.33
Grosse Pointe Farms, MI (city) Wayne County	217	2.27
Clay, MI (township) St. Clair County	212	2.27
Harrison, MI (charter township) Macomb County	553	2.24
Monroe, MI (charter township) Monroe County	322	2.21
Escanaba, MI (city) Delta County	275	2.16
Little Chute, WI (village) Outagamie County	217	2.07
Fort Gratiot, MI (charter township) St. Clair County	231	2.06
Roseville, MI (city) Macomb County	978	2.04
Harrison, WI (town) Calumet County	203	2.03
Orchards, WA (cdp) Clark County	399	1.97
Clinton, MI (charter township) Macomb County	1,840	1.89
Washington, MI (township) Macomb County	457	1.89
Clarendon Hills, IL (village) DuPage County	155	1.87
Shelby, MI (charter township) Macomb County	1,336	1.84
Grafton, WI (village) Ozaukee County	206	1.82
Grosse Pointe Park, MI (city) Wayne County	210	1.79
Harper Woods, MI (city) Wayne County	255	1.78
Two Rivers, WI (city) Manitowoc County	208	1.75
Fox Lake, IL (village) Lake County	184	1.75
Marinette, WI (city) Marinette County	189	1.70
Harrison, PA (township) Allegheny County	174	1.66
Marquette, MI (city) Marquette County	351	1.65
East Bay, MI (township) Grand Traverse County	171	1.61
Cartersville, GA (city) Bartow County	306	1.58
Port Huron, MI (charter township) St. Clair County	161	1.54
Plymouth, WI (city) Sheboygan County	129	1.54
St. Peter, MN (city) Nicollet County	167	1.52
Fort Drum, NY (cdp) Jefferson County	185	1.51
Rochester, MI (city) Oakland County	182	1.48
Bettendorf, IA (city) Scott County	473	1.46
Iron Mountain, MI (city) Dickinson County	114	1.46
Sterling Heights, MI (city) Macomb County	1,835	1.41
Mount Clemens, MI (city) Macomb County	235	1.41
Greenville, WI (town) Outagamie County	136	1.40
Detroit Lakes, MN (city) Becker County	119	1.40
Long Lake, MI (township) Grand Traverse County	119	1.39
Falmouth, ME (town) Cumberland County	152	1.37
Hudson, WI (city) St. Croix County	166	1.35
Appleton, WI (city) Outagamie County	799	1.33
Eastpointe, MI (city) Macomb County	432	1.31
Frenchtown, MI (township) Monroe County	272	1.31
Northfield, MI (township) Washtenaw County	108	1.30
Bridgeport, WV (city) Harrison County	103	1.29
Gulf Hills, MS (cdp) Jackson County	102	1.29
Cedarburg, WI (city) Ozaukee County	142	1.25
Warren, MI (city) Macomb County	1,678	1.24
Birmingham, MI (city) Oakland County	248	1.24
Granger, IN (cdp) St. Joseph County	347	1.22
Superior, WI (city) Douglas County	322	1.18
Brighton, MI (city) Livingston County	88	1.17
Menomonie, WI (city) Dunn County	186	1.16
Rostraver, PA (township) Westmoreland County	133	1.16
Hampton, MI (charter township) Bay County	113	1.16
Oregon, WI (village) Dane County	103	1.15
Pewaukee, WI (city) Waukesha County	146	1.13
Piedmont, CA (city) Alameda County	119	1.13
Comstock Park, MI (cdp) Kent County	117	1.13
Appleton, WI (city) Outagamie County	816	1.12
Alpine, MI (township) Kent County	151	1.12
Marathon, FL (city) Monroe County	95	1.12
Houghton, MI (city) Houghton County	85	1.12
Orion, MI (charter township) Oakland County	382	1.09
Brandon, MI (charter township) Oakland County	164	1.09
Bedford, MI (charter township) Calhoun County	103	1.09
Kimball, MI (township) St. Clair County	102	1.09
Fenton, MI (charter township) Genesee County	164	1.07
Waukee, IA (city) Dallas County	132	1.07
Cecil, PA (township) Washington County	118	1.07
Rockport, TX (city) Aransas County	92	1.06
Waukesha, WI (town) Waukesha County	95	1.05
Davenport, IA (city) Scott County	1,023	1.04
Lincoln, MI (charter township) Berrien County	151	1.04
Waunakee, WI (village) Dane County	119	1.03
Shawano, WI (city) Shawano County	95	1.03
Whitewater, WI (city) Walworth County	143	1.00
Verona, WI (city) Dane County	100	1.00
Gloucester Point, VA (cdp) Gloucester County	103	0.99
Menasha, WI (city) Winnebago County	149	0.98
Saline, MI (city) Washtenaw County	86	0.98
Putnam, MI (township) Livingston County	82	0.98
Highland, MI (charter township) Oakland County	183	0.95
South Fayette, PA (township) Allegheny County	132	0.95
Wauconda, IL (village) Lake County	124	0.95
Oakland, MI (charter township) Oakland County	151	0.94
Fairview, OR (city) Multnomah County	80	0.94
Redlands, CO (cdp) Mesa County	73	0.94
Monroe, MI (city) Monroe County	198	0.93
Neenah, WI (city) Winnebago County	234	0.92
Frankfort Square, IL (cdp) Will County	87	0.91
Hermantown, MN (city) St. Louis County	83	0.91
St. Charles, IL (city) Kane County	292	0.90
Troy, MI (city) Oakland County	722	0.89
Thompsonville, CT (cdp) Hartford County	79	0.89
Le Ray, NY (town) Jefferson County	192	0.88
East Grand Forks, MN (city) Polk County	74	0.88
Grand Chute, WI (town) Outagamie County	178	0.87
Menasha, WI (city) Winnebago County	149	0.87
Atlas, MI (township) Genesee County	68	0.86
South Bend, IN (city) St. Joseph County	871	0.85
Wixom, MI (city) Oakland County	114	0.85
Willistown, PA (township) Chester County	88	0.84
Rochester Hills, MI (city) Oakland County	586	0.83
Alexandria, LA (city) Rapides Parish	397	0.83
Shawangunk, NY (town) Ulster County	116	0.83
Wausau, WI (city) Marathon County	320	0.82
Summit, MI (township) Jackson County	183	0.81
Auburn Hills, MI (city) Oakland County	171	0.81
Dunbar, WV (city) Kanawha County	64	0.81
Whitewater, WI (city) Walworth County	89	0.80
Oconomowoc, WI (town) Waukesha County	66	0.80
Madison Heights, MI (city) Oakland County	236	0.79
Frankfort, IL (village) Will County	134	0.79
Fruitvale, CO (cdp) Mesa County	61	0.79
Kalamazoo, MI (charter township) Kalamazoo County	169	0.78
DeForest, WI (village) Dane County	68	0.78
Stallings, NC (town) Union County	98	0.77
Ringwood, NJ (borough) Passaic County	94	0.77
Hamburg, MI (township) Livingston County	165	0.76
East Bethel, MN (city) Anoka County	88	0.76
Gateway, FL (cdp) Lee County	67	0.76
Laconia, NH (city) Belknap County	121	0.75
Center Line, MI (city) Macomb County	63	0.75
Sun Prairie, WI (city) Dane County	206	0.74
Hartford, WI (city) Washington County	102	0.74
Springfield, MI (charter township) Oakland County	102	0.74

SECTION THREE

Please refer to the Explanation of Data in the front of the book for more detailed information.

Ancestry

Brazilian

U.S. and 50 States Sorted by Population and Percent of Total Population

Place	Population	%
United States	**347,346**	**0.11**
Florida	73,827	0.40
Massachusetts	65,170	1.01
New Jersey	35,800	0.41
California	30,167	0.08
New York	26,401	0.14
Connecticut	17,330	0.49
Texas	12,012	0.05
Georgia	11,684	0.12
Pennsylvania	7,831	0.06
Maryland	7,043	0.12
Illinois	5,648	0.04
Virginia	5,078	0.06
North Carolina	4,247	0.05
Utah	3,931	0.15
Washington	2,999	0.05
New Hampshire	2,783	0.21
Michigan	2,563	0.03
Ohio	2,500	0.02
South Carolina	2,413	0.05
Nevada	2,295	0.09
Colorado	2,229	0.05
Arizona	2,220	0.04
Louisiana	2,113	0.05
Indiana	1,706	0.03
Rhode Island	1,617	0.15
Missouri	1,530	0.03
Minnesota	1,383	0.03
Tennessee	1,288	0.02
Oregon	1,235	0.03
Wisconsin	1,014	0.02
Hawaii	876	0.07
Alabama	864	0.02
Kansas	851	0.03
Kentucky	788	0.02
Oklahoma	731	0.02
Iowa	629	0.02
District of Columbia	616	0.11
Arkansas	547	0.02
New Mexico	443	0.02
Alaska	432	0.06
Nebraska	384	0.02
Idaho	373	0.02
Mississippi	300	0.01
Montana	272	0.03
Vermont	270	0.04
West Virginia	237	0.01
Maine	236	0.02
Delaware	221	0.03
North Dakota	93	0.01
South Dakota	66	0.01
Wyoming	60	0.01

Place	Population	%
Massachusetts	65,170	1.01
Connecticut	17,330	0.49
New Jersey	35,800	0.41
Florida	73,827	0.40
New Hampshire	2,783	0.21
Utah	3,931	0.15
Rhode Island	1,617	0.15
New York	26,401	0.14
Georgia	11,684	0.12
Maryland	7,043	0.12
United States	**347,346**	**0.11**
District of Columbia	616	0.11
Nevada	2,295	0.09
California	30,167	0.08
Hawaii	876	0.07
Pennsylvania	7,831	0.06
Virginia	5,078	0.06
Alaska	432	0.06
Texas	12,012	0.05
North Carolina	4,247	0.05
Washington	2,999	0.05
South Carolina	2,413	0.05
Colorado	2,229	0.05
Louisiana	2,113	0.05
Illinois	5,648	0.04
Arizona	2,220	0.04
Vermont	270	0.04
Michigan	2,563	0.03
Indiana	1,706	0.03
Missouri	1,530	0.03
Minnesota	1,383	0.03
Oregon	1,235	0.03
Kansas	851	0.03
Montana	272	0.03
Delaware	221	0.03
Ohio	2,500	0.02
Tennessee	1,288	0.02
Wisconsin	1,014	0.02
Alabama	864	0.02
Kentucky	788	0.02
Oklahoma	731	0.02
Iowa	629	0.02
Arkansas	547	0.02
New Mexico	443	0.02
Nebraska	384	0.02
Idaho	373	0.02
Maine	236	0.02
Mississippi	300	0.01
West Virginia	237	0.01
North Dakota	93	0.01
South Dakota	66	0.01
Wyoming	60	0.01

Please refer to the Explanation of Data in the front of the book for more detailed information.

Ancestry

Brazilian

Top 150 Places Sorted by Population

Based on all places, regardless of total population

Place	Population	%
New York, NY (city) Kings County	13,119	0.16
Newark, NJ (city) Essex County	9,232	3.36
Deerfield Beach, FL (city) Broward County	7,233	9.61
Framingham, MA (cdp/town) Middlesex County	7,030	10.44
Queens, NY (borough) Queens County	6,175	0.28
Orlando, FL (city) Orange County	5,755	2.46
Boston, MA (city) Suffolk County	5,461	0.91
Manhattan, NY (borough) New York County	4,541	0.29
Danbury, CT (city/town) Fairfield County	4,363	5.50
Los Angeles, CA (city) Los Angeles County	3,962	0.11
Bridgeport, CT (city/town) Fairfield County	3,942	2.76
Somerville, MA (city) Middlesex County	3,547	4.72
Everett, MA (city) Middlesex County	3,406	8.40
Worcester, MA (city) Worcester County	3,363	1.87
Malden, MA (city) Middlesex County	3,303	5.68
Pompano Beach, FL (city) Broward County	2,923	2.91
Lowell, MA (city) Middlesex County	2,774	2.64
Long Branch, NJ (city) Monmouth County	2,702	8.76
Philadelphia, PA (city) Philadelphia County	2,622	0.17
Coconut Creek, FL (city) Broward County	2,476	4.80
Elizabeth, NJ (city) Union County	2,462	2.00
San Diego, CA (city) San Diego County	2,350	0.18
Milford, MA (town) Worcester County	2,271	8.15
Milford, MA (cdp) Worcester County	2,230	8.94
Miami, FL (city) Miami-Dade County	2,185	0.56
Kearny, NJ (town) Hudson County	2,074	5.16
Mount Vernon, NY (city) Westchester County	2,013	3.00
Sandy Springs, GA (city) Fulton County	1,816	2.00
Brooklyn, NY (borough) Kings County	1,719	0.07
Revere, MA (city) Suffolk County	1,616	3.23
San Francisco, CA (city) San Francisco County	1,569	0.20
Peabody, MA (city) Essex County	1,505	2.98
Boca Raton, FL (city) Palm Beach County	1,485	1.75
Chicago, IL (city) Cook County	1,439	0.05
Marlborough, MA (city) Middlesex County	1,412	3.75
Charlotte, NC (city) Mecklenburg County	1,399	0.20
Leominster, MA (city) Worcester County	1,390	3.40
Houston, TX (city) Harris County	1,370	0.07
Jacksonville, FL (city) Duval County	1,313	0.16
Nashua, NH (city) Hillsborough County	1,248	1.43
Brockton, MA (city) Plymouth County	1,238	1.32
Barnstable Town, MA (city) Barnstable County	1,214	2.65
Coral Springs, FL (city) Broward County	1,206	1.00
Fall River, MA (city) Bristol County	1,197	1.34
Medford, MA (city) Middlesex County	1,180	2.13
Stoughton, MA (town) Norfolk County	1,177	4.39
Doral, FL (city) Miami-Dade County	1,174	2.85
Pembroke Pines, FL (city) Broward County	1,118	0.73
Port St. Lucie, FL (city) St. Lucie County	1,029	0.66
New Bedford, MA (city) Bristol County	997	1.05
Marietta, GA (city) Cobb County	986	1.72
Austin, TX (city) Travis County	966	0.13
Quincy, MA (city) Norfolk County	949	1.05
Rye, NY (town) Westchester County	929	2.05
Weymouth Town, MA (city) Norfolk County	907	1.70
Islip, NY (town) Suffolk County	895	0.27
Miami Beach, FL (city) Miami-Dade County	886	1.01
Dallas, TX (city) Dallas County	850	0.07
Fort Lauderdale, FL (city) Broward County	816	0.49
Hollywood, FL (city) Broward County	805	0.57
Port Chester, NY (village) Westchester County	803	2.81
Union, NJ (township) Union County	774	1.39
Riverside, NJ (township) Burlington County	764	9.40
The Hammocks, FL (cdp) Miami-Dade County	764	1.53
Greenwich, CT (town) Fairfield County	760	1.25
Hartford, CT (city/town) Hartford County	756	0.61
Kissimmee, FL (city) Osceola County	746	1.26
Hillside, NJ (township) Union County	734	3.45
New Rochelle, NY (city) Westchester County	728	0.96
Waterbury, CT (city/town) New Haven County	725	0.66
South River, NJ (borough) Middlesex County	709	4.47
Plymouth, MA (town) Plymouth County	698	1.26
Weston, FL (city) Broward County	698	1.11
Oakland Park, FL (city) Broward County	695	1.67
Harrison, NJ (town) Hudson County	692	5.10
Stamford, CT (city/town) Fairfield County	692	0.57
San Jose, CA (city) Santa Clara County	683	0.07
Kendall West, FL (cdp) Miami-Dade County	681	1.93
Taunton, MA (city) Bristol County	669	1.20
Fort Myers, FL (city) Lee County	667	1.07
Southchase, FL (cdp) Orange County	662	4.02
Miramar, FL (city) Broward County	657	0.58
Cape Coral, FL (city) Lee County	654	0.44
Fountainebleau, FL (cdp) Miami-Dade County	642	1.09
Phoenix, AZ (city) Maricopa County	636	0.04
Washington, DC (city) District of Columbia	616	0.11
North Hempstead, NY (town) Nassau County	613	0.27
Yarmouth, MA (town) Barnstable County	608	2.53
Sunrise, FL (city) Broward County	582	0.68
Shrewsbury, MA (town) Worcester County	575	1.64
Roswell, GA (city) Fulton County	567	0.66
Randolph, MA (cdp/town) Norfolk County	562	1.78
Norwood, MA (cdp/town) Norfolk County	558	1.97
Lehigh Acres, FL (cdp) Lee County	558	0.66
Key Biscayne, FL (village) Miami-Dade County	555	4.63
Las Vegas, NV (city) Clark County	552	0.10
Richmond, CA (city) Contra Costa County	547	0.53
Tampa, FL (city) Hillsborough County	537	0.16
Lynn, MA (city) Essex County	520	0.58
Woburn, MA (city) Middlesex County	517	1.38
Plano, TX (city) Collin County	515	0.20
Salem, MA (city) Essex County	511	1.25
Germantown, MD (cdp) Montgomery County	509	0.60
Provo, UT (city) Utah County	505	0.46
Greenwich, CT (cdp) Fairfield County	494	3.72
North Miami, FL (city) Miami-Dade County	484	0.82
Hempstead, NY (town) Nassau County	479	0.06
Rockville, MD (city) Montgomery County	477	0.82
New Milford, CT (town) Litchfield County	474	1.68
Metairie, LA (cdp) Jefferson Parish	472	0.35
Watertown Town, MA (city) Middlesex County	459	1.45
Chelsea, MA (city) Suffolk County	458	1.33
Melrose, MA (city) Middlesex County	451	1.69
Harrison, NY (town/village) Westchester County	450	1.68
Huntington Beach, CA (city) Orange County	450	0.24
Raleigh, NC (city) Wake County	444	0.12
Gainesville, FL (city) Alachua County	441	0.35
White Plains, NY (city) Westchester County	440	0.79
San Bruno, CA (city) San Mateo County	438	1.09
Margate, FL (city) Broward County	438	0.82
Brookhaven, NY (town) Suffolk County	436	0.09
South Yarmouth, MA (cdp) Barnstable County	432	3.77
Vineyard Haven, MA (cdp) Dukes County	430	17.41
Tisbury, MA (town) Dukes County	430	11.07
Yonkers, NY (city) Westchester County	422	0.22
Brentwood, NY (cdp) Suffolk County	418	0.76
Ojus, FL (cdp) Miami-Dade County	413	2.43
Salt Lake City, UT (city) Salt Lake County	412	0.22
Orlovista, FL (cdp) Orange County	402	5.47
Town 'n' Country, FL (cdp) Hillsborough County	399	0.52
Bronx, NY (borough) Bronx County	397	0.03
Seattle, WA (city) King County	394	0.07
Reno, NV (city) Washoe County	391	0.18
Anaheim, CA (city) Orange County	387	0.12
New Orleans, LA (city) Orleans Parish	385	0.13
Saugus, MA (cdp/town) Essex County	383	1.45
Davie, FL (town) Broward County	383	0.42
Burlingame, CA (city) San Mateo County	381	1.35
Henderson, NV (city) Clark County	381	0.15
Hudson, MA (town) Middlesex County	380	2.04
Scaggsville, MD (cdp) Howard County	379	1.65
Coral Gables, FL (city) Miami-Dade County	377	0.82
Jersey City, NJ (city) Hudson County	370	0.15
Oyster Bay, NY (town) Nassau County	370	0.13
Milford, CT (town) New Haven County	353	0.67
Linden, NJ (city) Union County	351	0.88
Clovis, CA (city) Fresno County	350	0.38
Baltimore, MD (city) Baltimore city County	350	0.06
Delray Beach, FL (city) Palm Beach County	348	0.57
Fort Worth, TX (city) Tarrant County	348	0.05

Please refer to the Explanation of Data in the front of the book for more detailed information.

Ancestry

Brazilian

Top 150 Places Sorted by Percent of Total Population

Based on all places, regardless of total population

Place	Population	%
Ortley, SD (town) Roberts County	9	20.00
Vineyard Haven, MA (cdp) Dukes County	430	17.41
Page Park, FL (cdp) Lee County	121	17.04
Carrick, CA (cdp) Siskiyou County	20	11.76
Hillsboro Pines, FL (cdp) Broward County	37	11.67
Urie, WY (cdp) Uinta County	23	11.62
Tisbury, MA (town) Dukes County	430	11.07
Buras, LA (cdp) Plaquemines Parish	67	10.62
Framingham, MA (cdp/town) Middlesex County	7,030	10.44
Three Mile Bay, NY (cdp) Jefferson County	21	9.95
Deerfield Beach, FL (city) Broward County	7,233	9.61
Riverside, NJ (township) Burlington County	764	9.40
Milford, MA (cdp) Worcester County	2,230	8.94
Long Branch, NJ (city) Monmouth County	2,702	8.76
East Newark, NJ (borough) Hudson County	208	8.75
Everett, MA (city) Middlesex County	3,406	8.40
Milford, MA (town) Worcester County	2,271	8.15
Fairview, OH (village) Guernsey County	4	6.56
Saddle Rock Estates, NY (cdp) Nassau County	33	6.30
North Plymouth, MA (cdp) Plymouth County	225	5.95
Mexico Beach, FL (city) Bay County	68	5.76
Malden, MA (city) Middlesex County	3,303	5.68
Danbury, CT (city/town) Fairfield County	4,363	5.50
Orlovista, FL (cdp) Orange County	402	5.47
Canaan, CT (cdp) Litchfield County	75	5.39
Adelino, NM (cdp) Valencia County	44	5.35
Kearny, NJ (town) Hudson County	2,074	5.16
Dewey-Humboldt, AZ (town) Yavapai County	201	5.11
Harrison, NJ (town) Hudson County	692	5.10
Edgartown, MA (town) Dukes County	203	5.10
Lompico, CA (cdp) Santa Cruz County	52	5.01
Coconut Creek, FL (city) Broward County	2,476	4.80
Jan Phyl Village, FL (cdp) Polk County	246	4.80
Snowmass Village, CO (town) Pitkin County	124	4.79
Somerville, MA (city) Middlesex County	3,547	4.72
Savoy, MA (town) Berkshire County	35	4.69
Key Biscayne, FL (village) Miami-Dade County	555	4.63
South River, NJ (borough) Middlesex County	709	4.47
Tyringham, MA (town) Berkshire County	18	4.41
Stoughton, MA (town) Norfolk County	1,177	4.39
Sagaponack, NY (village) Suffolk County	11	4.30
Bicknell, UT (town) Wayne County	15	4.20
Alba, MI (cdp) Antrim County	12	4.20
New Seabury, MA (cdp) Barnstable County	37	4.19
Southchase, FL (cdp) Orange County	662	4.02
Westborough, MA (cdp) Worcester County	157	3.96
Stowe, VT (cdp) Lamoille County	35	3.95
West Sand Lake, NY (cdp) Rensselaer County	101	3.85
Williamsburg, FL (cdp) Orange County	259	3.78
Middleborough Center, MA (cdp) Plymouth County	252	3.78
South Yarmouth, MA (cdp) Barnstable County	432	3.77
Marlborough, MA (city) Middlesex County	1,412	3.75
Greenwich, CT (cdp) Fairfield County	494	3.72
Underwood, MN (city) Otter Tail County	15	3.68
Kawela Bay, HI (cdp) Honolulu County	11	3.68
Corwin Springs, MT (cdp) Park County	3	3.61
Raynham Center, MA (cdp) Bristol County	147	3.60
Tuckerton, NJ (borough) Ocean County	122	3.58
Smoke Rise, AL (cdp) Blount County	83	3.53
Clinton, CT (cdp) Middlesex County	122	3.52
Chestonia, MI (township) Antrim County	12	3.49
Hillside, NJ (township) Union County	734	3.45
Spring Ridge, FL (cdp) Gilchrist County	10	3.44
Leominster, MA (city) Worcester County	1,390	3.40
Newark, NJ (city) Essex County	9,232	3.36
Watergate, FL (cdp) Palm Beach County	95	3.36
Revere, MA (city) Suffolk County	1,616	3.23
Port LaBelle, FL (cdp) Hendry County	119	3.12
Mount Vernon, NY (city) Westchester County	2,013	3.00
Edgewater Park, NJ (township) Burlington County	262	3.00
Potomac Mills, VA (cdp) Prince William County	141	2.99
Peabody, MA (city) Essex County	1,505	2.98
Castle Rock, WA (city) Cowlitz County	69	2.97
Rocksbury, MN (township) Pennington County	39	2.97
Diamondville, WY (town) Lincoln County	23	2.94
Pompano Beach, FL (city) Broward County	2,923	2.91
Durham, PA (township) Bucks County	35	2.89
West Yarmouth, MA (cdp) Barnstable County	176	2.88
Doral, FL (city) Miami-Dade County	1,174	2.85
Port Chester, NY (village) Westchester County	803	2.81
Mount Pocono, PA (borough) Monroe County	89	2.81
Saw Creek, PA (cdp) Pike County	141	2.78
Cold Bay, AK (city) Aleutians East Borough	1	2.78
University at Buffalo, NY (cdp) Erie County	156	2.77
Magnolia, NJ (borough) Camden County	121	2.77
Hunts Point, WA (town) King County	12	2.77
Bridgeport, CT (city/town) Fairfield County	3,942	2.76
Taft, FL (cdp) Orange County	51	2.76
Bull Run Mountain Estates, VA (cdp) Prince William County	25	2.69
Flanders, NY (cdp) Suffolk County	120	2.66
Barnstable Town, MA (city) Barnstable County	1,214	2.65
Silver Lake, NJ (cdp) Essex County	99	2.65
Lowell, MA (city) Middlesex County	2,774	2.64
Scituate, MA (cdp) Plymouth County	140	2.63
Ipswich, MA (cdp) Essex County	102	2.55
Fulton, MD (cdp) Howard County	50	2.54
Yarmouth, MA (town) Barnstable County	608	2.53
Elsah, IL (village) Jersey County	14	2.53
Orlando, FL (city) Orange County	5,755	2.46
Ojus, FL (cdp) Miami-Dade County	413	2.43
Pohatcong, NJ (township) Warren County	82	2.41
Paia, HI (cdp) Maui County	71	2.37
Cresaptown, MD (cdp) Allegany County	81	2.34
New Milford, CT (cdp) Litchfield County	150	2.33
Plymouth, MA (cdp) Plymouth County	157	2.32
Pupukea, HI (cdp) Honolulu County	102	2.31
Temple, NH (town) Hillsborough County	33	2.31
Popple, MN (township) Clearwater County	10	2.30
North Westport, MA (cdp) Bristol County	96	2.29
Sun Valley, ID (city) Blaine County	32	2.28
Napanoch, NY (cdp) Ulster County	24	2.26
Clinton, MA (cdp) Worcester County	162	2.25
Surfside, FL (town) Miami-Dade County	125	2.25
North Canaan, CT (town) Litchfield County	75	2.24
Darnen, MN (township) Stevens County	7	2.24
East York, PA (cdp) York County	205	2.23
Cragsmoor, NY (cdp) Ulster County	8	2.22
Holbrook, MA (cdp/town) Norfolk County	236	2.21
Arcanum, OH (village) Darke County	53	2.21
Tuckahoe, NY (cdp) Suffolk County	31	2.20
Hoffman, MN (city) Grant County	13	2.19
West Long Branch, NJ (borough) Monmouth County	176	2.17
Stone Harbor, NJ (borough) Cape May County	20	2.15
Richland, PA (township) Bucks County	267	2.14
Horizon West, FL (cdp) Orange County	216	2.14
Medford, MA (city) Middlesex County	1,180	2.13
North Arlington, NJ (borough) Bergen County	324	2.12
Bay Hill, FL (cdp) Orange County	111	2.11
Williamsburg, KY (city) Whitley County	111	2.11
Spring Valley, KY (city) Jefferson County	14	2.11
Red Rock, AZ (cdp) Pinal County	21	2.10
Hudson, MA (cdp) Middlesex County	306	2.09
Fairview, NJ (borough) Bergen County	285	2.09
Marshfield, MA (cdp) Plymouth County	92	2.07
Rye, NY (town) Westchester County	929	2.05
Hudson, MA (town) Middlesex County	380	2.04
Elizabeth, NJ (city) Union County	2,462	2.00
Sandy Springs, GA (city) Fulton County	1,816	2.00
Harwood Heights, IL (village) Cook County	169	2.00
Ayer, MA (town) Middlesex County	146	2.00
South Patrick Shores, FL (cdp) Brevard County	114	2.00
Fishers Island, NY (cdp) Suffolk County	5	2.00
Rockwell, AR (cdp) Garland County	76	1.99
Northborough, MA (town) Worcester County	281	1.98
Eatontown, NJ (borough) Monmouth County	256	1.98
Norwood, MA (cdp/town) Norfolk County	558	1.97
Slater-Marietta, SC (cdp) Greenville County	45	1.96
Valhalla, NY (cdp) Westchester County	60	1.95
Mashpee, MA (town) Barnstable County	269	1.94
Kendall West, FL (cdp) Miami-Dade County	681	1.93

Please refer to the Explanation of Data in the front of the book for more detailed information.

Ancestry

Brazilian

Top 150 Places Sorted by Percent of Total Population

Based on places with total population of 7,500 or more

Place	Population	%
Framingham, MA (cdp/town) Middlesex County	7,030	10.44
Deerfield Beach, FL (city) Broward County	7,233	9.61
Riverside, NJ (township) Burlington County	764	9.40
Milford, MA (cdp) Worcester County	2,230	8.94
Long Branch, NJ (city) Monmouth County	2,702	8.76
Everett, MA (city) Middlesex County	3,406	8.40
Milford, MA (town) Worcester County	2,271	8.15
Malden, MA (city) Middlesex County	3,303	5.68
Danbury, CT (city/town) Fairfield County	4,363	5.50
Kearny, NJ (town) Hudson County	2,074	5.16
Harrison, NJ (town) Hudson County	692	5.10
Coconut Creek, FL (city) Broward County	2,476	4.80
Somerville, MA (city) Middlesex County	3,547	4.72
Key Biscayne, FL (village) Miami-Dade County	555	4.63
South River, NJ (borough) Middlesex County	709	4.47
Stoughton, MA (town) Norfolk County	1,177	4.39
Southchase, FL (cdp) Orange County	662	4.02
South Yarmouth, MA (cdp) Barnstable County	432	3.77
Marlborough, MA (city) Middlesex County	1,412	3.75
Greenwich, CT (cdp) Fairfield County	494	3.72
Hillside, NJ (township) Union County	734	3.45
Leominster, MA (city) Worcester County	1,390	3.40
Newark, NJ (city) Essex County	9,232	3.36
Revere, MA (city) Suffolk County	1,616	3.23
Mount Vernon, NY (city) Westchester County	2,013	3.00
Edgewater Park, NJ (township) Burlington County	262	3.00
Peabody, MA (city) Essex County	1,505	2.98
Pompano Beach, FL (city) Broward County	2,923	2.91
Doral, FL (city) Miami-Dade County	1,174	2.85
Port Chester, NY (village) Westchester County	803	2.81
Bridgeport, CT (city/town) Fairfield County	3,942	2.76
Barnstable Town, MA (city) Barnstable County	1,214	2.65
Lowell, MA (city) Middlesex County	2,774	2.64
Yarmouth, MA (town) Barnstable County	608	2.53
Orlando, FL (city) Orange County	5,755	2.46
Ojus, FL (cdp) Miami-Dade County	413	2.43
East York, PA (cdp) York County	205	2.23
Holbrook, MA (cdp/town) Norfolk County	236	2.21
West Long Branch, NJ (borough) Monmouth County	176	2.17
Richland, PA (township) Bucks County	267	2.14
Horizon West, FL (cdp) Orange County	216	2.14
Medford, MA (city) Middlesex County	1,180	2.13
North Arlington, NJ (borough) Bergen County	324	2.12
Hudson, MA (cdp) Middlesex County	306	2.09
Fairview, NJ (borough) Bergen County	285	2.09
Rye, NY (town) Westchester County	929	2.05
Hudson, MA (town) Middlesex County	380	2.04
Elizabeth, NJ (city) Union County	2,462	2.00
Sandy Springs, GA (city) Fulton County	1,816	2.00
Harwood Heights, IL (village) Cook County	169	2.00
Northborough, MA (town) Worcester County	281	1.98
Eatontown, NJ (borough) Monmouth County	256	1.98
Norwood, MA (cdp/town) Norfolk County	558	1.97
Mashpee, MA (town) Barnstable County	269	1.94
Kendall West, FL (cdp) Miami-Dade County	681	1.93
Grafton, MA (town) Worcester County	331	1.92
Worcester, MA (city) Worcester County	3,363	1.87
Delran, NJ (township) Burlington County	314	1.87
Redding, CT (town) Fairfield County	162	1.81
Randolph, MA (cdp/town) Norfolk County	562	1.78
Pompton Lakes, NJ (borough) Passaic County	195	1.78
Lehman, PA (township) Pike County	183	1.76
Boca Raton, FL (city) Palm Beach County	1,485	1.75
Marietta, GA (city) Cobb County	986	1.72
Weymouth Town, MA (city) Norfolk County	907	1.70
Melrose, MA (city) Middlesex County	451	1.69
New Milford, CT (town) Litchfield County	474	1.68
Harrison, NY (town/village) Westchester County	450	1.68
Oakland Park, FL (city) Broward County	695	1.67
Scaggsville, MD (cdp) Howard County	379	1.65
Shrewsbury, MA (town) Worcester County	575	1.64
Ashland, MA (town) Middlesex County	250	1.56
Whitman, MA (town) Plymouth County	222	1.54
Greenbriar, VA (cdp) Fairfax County	118	1.54
The Hammocks, FL (cdp) Miami-Dade County	764	1.53
Robinwood, MD (cdp) Washington County	123	1.53
Milford, NH (cdp) Hillsborough County	136	1.50
Middle Island, NY (cdp) Suffolk County	149	1.46
Templeton, MA (town) Worcester County	114	1.46
Watertown Town, MA (city) Middlesex County	459	1.45
Saugus, MA (cdp/town) Essex County	383	1.45
Clinton, MA (town) Worcester County	198	1.45
Nashua, NH (city) Hillsborough County	1,248	1.43
Lyndhurst, NJ (township) Bergen County	283	1.40
Union, NJ (township) Union County	774	1.39
Woburn, MA (city) Middlesex County	517	1.38
Gulf Shores, AL (city) Baldwin County	125	1.38
Linganore, MD (cdp) Frederick County	114	1.37
Burlingame, CA (city) San Mateo County	381	1.35
Florida Ridge, FL (cdp) Indian River County	228	1.35
Fall River, MA (city) Bristol County	1,197	1.34
Chelsea, MA (city) Suffolk County	458	1.33
Brockton, MA (city) Plymouth County	1,238	1.32
Rockland, MA (town) Plymouth County	230	1.31
Westborough, MA (town) Worcester County	238	1.30
Huntington, VA (cdp) Fairfax County	134	1.29
Rio del Mar, CA (cdp) Santa Cruz County	122	1.29
Abington, MA (cdp/town) Plymouth County	200	1.27
Kissimmee, FL (city) Osceola County	746	1.26
Plymouth, MA (town) Plymouth County	698	1.26
Jupiter Farms, FL (cdp) Palm Beach County	151	1.26
Brooksville, FL (city) Hernando County	99	1.26
Greenwich, CT (town) Fairfield County	760	1.25
Salem, MA (city) Essex County	511	1.25
Auburn, MA (town) Worcester County	203	1.25
Budd Lake, NJ (cdp) Morris County	105	1.25
Mineola, NY (village) Nassau County	232	1.24
Weehawken, NJ (township) Hudson County	156	1.24
Bensenville, IL (village) DuPage County	227	1.22
Hopatcong, NJ (borough) Sussex County	188	1.22
Taunton, MA (city) Bristol County	669	1.20
Sand Lake, NY (town) Rensselaer County	101	1.19
Raynham, MA (town) Bristol County	154	1.18
Doctor Phillips, FL (cdp) Orange County	131	1.17
Crestwood, IL (village) Cook County	128	1.17
Oronoko, MI (charter township) Berrien County	107	1.16
Parkland, FL (city) Broward County	258	1.15
Chalmette, LA (cdp) St. Bernard Parish	143	1.15
Putnam, CT (cdp) Windham County	86	1.15
Bethlehem, PA (township) Northampton County	266	1.13
Middleborough, MA (town) Plymouth County	252	1.12
Hanahan, SC (city) Berkeley County	189	1.12
Weston, FL (city) Broward County	698	1.11
Fountainebleau, FL (cdp) Miami-Dade County	642	1.09
San Bruno, CA (city) San Mateo County	438	1.09
Mamaroneck, NY (village) Westchester County	205	1.09
Fort Myers, FL (city) Lee County	667	1.07
Capitola, CA (city) Santa Cruz County	104	1.06
New Bedford, MA (city) Bristol County	997	1.05
Quincy, MA (city) Norfolk County	949	1.05
Suffern, NY (village) Rockland County	112	1.05
Bethel, CT (cdp) Fairfield County	92	1.05
Southgate, FL (cdp) Sarasota County	82	1.05
Newburyport, MA (city) Essex County	179	1.04
Hastings-on-Hudson, NY (village) Westchester County	81	1.04
Lake Jackson, TX (city) Brazoria County	277	1.03
Mamaroneck, NY (town) Westchester County	296	1.02
Ronkonkoma, NY (cdp) Suffolk County	202	1.02
Ives Estates, FL (cdp) Miami-Dade County	180	1.02
Miami Beach, FL (city) Miami-Dade County	886	1.01
Newport East, RI (cdp) Newport County	117	1.01
Watervliet, NY (city) Albany County	104	1.01
Coral Springs, FL (city) Broward County	1,206	1.00
Acton, MA (town) Middlesex County	213	1.00
Palmetto Bay, FL (village) Miami-Dade County	230	0.98
Rodeo, CA (cdp) Contra Costa County	89	0.98
Gloucester, MA (city) Essex County	281	0.97
New Rochelle, NY (city) Westchester County	728	0.96
Springettsbury, PA (township) York County	250	0.95
Westchase, FL (cdp) Hillsborough County	200	0.95

SECTION THREE

Please refer to the Explanation of Data in the front of the book for more detailed information.

Ancestry

British

U.S. and 50 States Sorted by Population and Percent of Total Population

Place	Population	%	Place	Population	%
United States	**1,223,541**	**0.40**	Utah	37,360	1.41
California	150,588	0.41	District of Columbia	4,625	0.79
Florida	89,770	0.48	Vermont	4,561	0.73
Texas	82,805	0.34	Washington	44,417	0.68
New York	58,548	0.30	Virginia	51,637	0.66
Virginia	51,637	0.66	Oregon	24,488	0.65
Washington	44,417	0.68	Alaska	4,363	0.63
Georgia	43,905	0.46	New Hampshire	8,211	0.62
North Carolina	43,114	0.47	Idaho	9,256	0.61
Ohio	42,018	0.36	Colorado	27,593	0.56
Pennsylvania	39,949	0.32	Maine	7,274	0.55
Utah	37,360	1.41	Delaware	4,508	0.51
Illinois	36,600	0.29	Florida	89,770	0.48
Michigan	33,670	0.34	Maryland	27,502	0.48
Massachusetts	29,647	0.46	Connecticut	16,877	0.48
Colorado	27,593	0.56	North Carolina	43,114	0.47
Maryland	27,502	0.48	Georgia	43,905	0.46
Tennessee	26,831	0.43	Massachusetts	29,647	0.46
Arizona	25,456	0.41	Tennessee	26,831	0.43
New Jersey	25,400	0.29	California	150,588	0.41
Oregon	24,488	0.65	Arizona	25,456	0.41
Indiana	23,647	0.37	South Carolina	18,348	0.41
Missouri	19,268	0.33	**United States**	**1,223,541**	**0.40**
South Carolina	18,348	0.41	Kentucky	17,099	0.40
Alabama	17,673	0.38	Alabama	17,673	0.38
Kentucky	17,099	0.40	Kansas	10,664	0.38
Connecticut	16,877	0.48	Indiana	23,647	0.37
Minnesota	14,024	0.27	Arkansas	10,712	0.37
Wisconsin	13,311	0.24	Nevada	9,693	0.37
Oklahoma	12,462	0.34	Ohio	42,018	0.36
Arkansas	10,712	0.37	New Mexico	7,049	0.35
Kansas	10,664	0.38	Texas	82,805	0.34
Nevada	9,693	0.37	Michigan	33,670	0.34
Louisiana	9,341	0.21	Oklahoma	12,462	0.34
Idaho	9,256	0.61	Missouri	19,268	0.33
New Hampshire	8,211	0.62	Rhode Island	3,451	0.33
Iowa	7,841	0.26	Pennsylvania	39,949	0.32
Mississippi	7,308	0.25	Montana	3,148	0.32
Maine	7,274	0.55	Wyoming	1,715	0.31
New Mexico	7,049	0.35	New York	58,548	0.30
West Virginia	5,294	0.29	Illinois	36,600	0.29
Nebraska	4,810	0.27	New Jersey	25,400	0.29
District of Columbia	4,625	0.79	West Virginia	5,294	0.29
Vermont	4,561	0.73	Minnesota	14,024	0.27
Delaware	4,508	0.51	Nebraska	4,810	0.27
Alaska	4,363	0.63	Iowa	7,841	0.26
Hawaii	3,458	0.26	Hawaii	3,458	0.26
Rhode Island	3,451	0.33	Mississippi	7,308	0.25
Montana	3,148	0.32	Wisconsin	13,311	0.24
Wyoming	1,715	0.31	Louisiana	9,341	0.21
North Dakota	1,229	0.19	North Dakota	1,229	0.19
South Dakota	1,023	0.13	South Dakota	1,023	0.13

Please refer to the Explanation of Data in the front of the book for more detailed information.

Ancestry

British

Top 150 Places Sorted by Population

Based on all places, regardless of total population

Place	Population	%
New York, NY (city) Kings County	21,065	0.26
Los Angeles, CA (city) Los Angeles County	12,180	0.32
Manhattan, NY (borough) New York County	12,129	0.77
Houston, TX (city) Harris County	7,594	0.37
Seattle, WA (city) King County	6,970	1.17
San Diego, CA (city) San Diego County	6,683	0.52
San Francisco, CA (city) San Francisco County	6,050	0.77
Chicago, IL (city) Cook County	5,392	0.20
Portland, OR (city) Multnomah County	5,218	0.92
Dallas, TX (city) Dallas County	4,910	0.41
Phoenix, AZ (city) Maricopa County	4,800	0.33
Austin, TX (city) Travis County	4,770	0.62
Brooklyn, NY (borough) Kings County	4,749	0.19
Washington, DC (city) District of Columbia	4,625	0.79
Charlotte, NC (city) Mecklenburg County	3,557	0.50
Indianapolis, IN (city) Marion County	3,547	0.44
Jacksonville, FL (city) Duval County	3,347	0.41
Nashville-Davidson, TN (metro govt) Davidson County	3,331	0.57
Columbus, OH (city) Franklin County	3,242	0.42
San Antonio, TX (city) Medina County	3,160	0.24
San Jose, CA (city) Santa Clara County	3,157	0.34
Atlanta, GA (city) Fulton County	3,155	0.76
Salt Lake City, UT (city) Salt Lake County	2,957	1.60
Virginia Beach, VA (ind. city) Virginia Beach independent city	2,913	0.67
Raleigh, NC (city) Wake County	2,874	0.75
Denver, CO (city) Denver County	2,850	0.49
Boston, MA (city) Suffolk County	2,755	0.46
Colorado Springs, CO (city) El Paso County	2,744	0.68
Provo, UT (city) Utah County	2,706	2.46
Louisville-Jefferson County, KY (metro govt) Jefferson County	2,671	0.46
Oklahoma City, OK (city) Oklahoma County	2,582	0.46
Philadelphia, PA (city) Philadelphia County	2,578	0.17
Mesa, AZ (city) Maricopa County	2,465	0.56
Queens, NY (borough) Queens County	2,457	0.11
Tucson, AZ (city) Pima County	2,300	0.44
Albuquerque, NM (city) Bernalillo County	2,194	0.41
Arlington, VA (cdp) Arlington County	2,177	1.10
Las Vegas, NV (city) Clark County	1,999	0.34
Anchorage, AK (municipality) Anchorage Municipality	1,984	0.70
Fort Worth, TX (city) Tarrant County	1,934	0.27
Lexington-Fayette, KY (cons. govt) Fayette County	1,889	0.66
Minneapolis, MN (city) Hennepin County	1,812	0.48
Sandy, UT (city) Salt Lake County	1,810	2.08
Oakland, CA (city) Alameda County	1,790	0.46
Tampa, FL (city) Hillsborough County	1,784	0.54
Memphis, TN (city) Shelby County	1,756	0.27
Greensboro, NC (city) Guilford County	1,727	0.66
Scottsdale, AZ (city) Maricopa County	1,682	0.77
Baltimore, MD (city) Baltimore city County	1,646	0.27
Long Beach, CA (city) Los Angeles County	1,611	0.35
Boise City, ID (city) Ada County	1,576	0.76
Miami, FL (city) Miami-Dade County	1,572	0.40
Millcreek, UT (cdp) Salt Lake County	1,516	2.49
Thousand Oaks, CA (city) Ventura County	1,514	1.21
Arlington, TX (city) Tarrant County	1,509	0.42
Durham, NC (city) Durham County	1,500	0.68
Boulder, CO (city) Boulder County	1,498	1.54
Sacramento, CA (city) Sacramento County	1,493	0.32
St. Petersburg, FL (city) Pinellas County	1,467	0.60
Orem, UT (city) Utah County	1,439	1.66
Alexandria, VA (ind. city) Alexandria independent city	1,439	1.08
Plano, TX (city) Collin County	1,431	0.56
Richmond, VA (ind. city) Richmond independent city	1,398	0.69
Madison, WI (city) Dane County	1,387	0.61
Eugene, OR (city) Lane County	1,376	0.90
Fremont, CA (city) Alameda County	1,345	0.64
Cincinnati, OH (city) Hamilton County	1,314	0.44
Aurora, CO (city) Arapahoe County	1,295	0.41
Ann Arbor, MI (city) Washtenaw County	1,287	1.12
Lubbock, TX (city) Lubbock County	1,274	0.57
Cambridge, MA (city) Middlesex County	1,239	1.20
Bellevue, WA (city) King County	1,238	1.04
Greenwich, CT (town) Fairfield County	1,236	2.03
Brookhaven, NY (town) Suffolk County	1,235	0.26
Chapel Hill, NC (town) Orange County	1,225	2.22
Kansas City, MO (city) Jackson County	1,211	0.27
Mission Viejo, CA (city) Orange County	1,204	1.30
Reno, NV (city) Washoe County	1,200	0.54
Tulsa, OK (city) Tulsa County	1,200	0.31
Hempstead, NY (town) Nassau County	1,197	0.16
Overland Park, KS (city) Johnson County	1,191	0.70
Cary, NC (town) Wake County	1,185	0.93
Huntington Beach, CA (city) Orange County	1,185	0.63
Irvine, CA (city) Orange County	1,176	0.59
Wichita, KS (city) Sedgwick County	1,174	0.31
Huntsville, AL (city) Madison County	1,159	0.66
Henderson, NV (city) Clark County	1,154	0.46
Pittsburgh, PA (city) Allegheny County	1,143	0.37
Bronx, NY (borough) Bronx County	1,115	0.08
Orlando, FL (city) Orange County	1,113	0.48
Tallahassee, FL (city) Leon County	1,112	0.63
Vancouver, WA (city) Clark County	1,110	0.69
Naperville, IL (city) DuPage County	1,104	0.78
Spokane, WA (city) Spokane County	1,092	0.53
The Woodlands, TX (cdp) Montgomery County	1,088	1.18
Centennial, CO (city) Arapahoe County	1,082	1.08
Omaha, NE (city) Douglas County	1,065	0.26
Winston-Salem, NC (city) Forsyth County	1,064	0.47
Knoxville, TN (city) Knox County	1,053	0.59
Roswell, GA (city) Fulton County	1,036	1.21
Norfolk, VA (ind. city) Norfolk independent city	1,031	0.43
Bethesda, MD (cdp) Montgomery County	1,028	1.76
Athens-Clarke County, GA (unified govt) Clarke County	1,015	0.89
Palo Alto, CA (city) Santa Clara County	1,004	1.61
Tacoma, WA (city) Pierce County	1,001	0.50
St. Paul, MN (city) Ramsey County	996	0.35
Chesapeake, VA (ind. city) Chesapeake independent city	983	0.45
Chandler, AZ (city) Maricopa County	979	0.43
Fort Lauderdale, FL (city) Broward County	976	0.58
Berkeley, CA (city) Alameda County	975	0.89
Lincoln, NE (city) Lancaster County	967	0.38
Simi Valley, CA (city) Ventura County	962	0.79
Newport News, VA (ind. city) Newport News independent city	961	0.53
South Jordan, UT (city) Salt Lake County	958	2.07
Little Rock, AR (city) Pulaski County	942	0.49
McLean, VA (cdp) Fairfax County	941	2.04
Bountiful, UT (city) Davis County	931	2.20
Mountain View, CA (city) Santa Clara County	927	1.28
Santa Monica, CA (city) Los Angeles County	914	1.03
Sandy Springs, GA (city) Fulton County	904	1.00
Glendale, CA (city) Los Angeles County	895	0.47
Chula Vista, CA (city) San Diego County	895	0.39
New Orleans, LA (city) Orleans Parish	892	0.30
Lake Forest, CA (city) Orange County	891	1.16
Tempe, AZ (city) Maricopa County	873	0.53
Urban Honolulu, HI (cdp) Honolulu County	871	0.26
Rancho Santa Margarita, CA (city) Orange County	868	1.83
Santa Rosa, CA (city) Sonoma County	857	0.53
Clearwater, FL (city) Pinellas County	855	0.79
Paradise, NV (cdp) Clark County	846	0.39
Fresno, CA (city) Fresno County	841	0.17
Huntington, NY (town) Suffolk County	840	0.42
Gilbert, AZ (town) Maricopa County	838	0.43
Sunnyvale, CA (city) Santa Clara County	836	0.61
Santa Clarita, CA (city) Los Angeles County	831	0.48
Bellingham, WA (city) Whatcom County	829	1.05
Costa Mesa, CA (city) Orange County	826	0.76
Beaverton, OR (city) Washington County	816	0.93
Sugar Land, TX (city) Fort Bend County	812	1.07
Pasadena, CA (city) Los Angeles County	812	0.60
Layton, UT (city) Davis County	809	1.23
Charleston, SC (city) Charleston County	801	0.69
Montgomery, AL (city) Montgomery County	799	0.39
Lakewood, CO (city) Jefferson County	795	0.56
Gainesville, FL (city) Alachua County	789	0.63
Toledo, OH (city) Lucas County	785	0.27
Oceanside, CA (city) San Diego County	781	0.47
Laguna Niguel, CA (city) Orange County	778	1.24
Glendale, AZ (city) Maricopa County	777	0.34
Santa Barbara, CA (city) Santa Barbara County	773	0.88

Ancestry

British

Top 150 Places Sorted by Percent of Total Population

Based on all places, regardless of total population

Place	Population	%
Johnsville, CA (cdp) Plumas County	67	79.76
Clarksburg, IN (cdp) Decatur County	60	49.18
Victoria, AR (town) Mississippi County	29	49.15
Kennedy Meadows, CA (cdp) Tulare County	9	47.37
Sallis, MS (town) Attala County	114	46.34
Oceola, OH (cdp) Crawford County	100	45.66
Waldo, KS (city) Russell County	13	39.39
Bear Valley, CA (cdp) Mariposa County	95	34.93
Twain, CA (cdp) Plumas County	22	32.84
Lushton, NE (village) York County	6	31.58
Claire City, SD (town) Roberts County	24	30.77
Ogden, AR (city) Little River County	62	27.80
Glenbrook, NV (cdp) Douglas County	39	23.78
Pierrepont Manor, NY (cdp) Jefferson County	28	22.95
Jacumba, CA (cdp) San Diego County	138	21.97
Hoytsville, UT (cdp) Summit County	125	21.85
Rock Creek Park, CO (cdp) El Paso County	15	20.55
Deepstep, GA (town) Washington County	32	20.38
Iatan, MO (village) Platte County	12	20.34
Oswego, SC (cdp) Sumter County	9	20.00
Burdette, AR (town) Mississippi County	76	18.86
Seven Springs, NC (town) Wayne County	25	18.66
Union Valley, TX (city) Hunt County	69	17.92
Elmira, CA (cdp) Solano County	25	16.34
Pilgrim, MI (cdp) Benzie County	3	15.79
Hazard, NE (village) Sherman County	10	15.63
Quinby, VA (cdp) Accomack County	23	15.54
Salton Sea Beach, CA (cdp) Imperial County	64	13.79
Outlook, MT (town) Sheridan County	10	13.51
Jensen, UT (cdp) Uintah County	61	13.38
Stokes, NC (cdp) Pitt County	32	13.33
Wylie, MN (township) Red Lake County	8	13.33
Ten Broeck, KY (city) Jefferson County	12	12.77
Salisbury Mills, NY (cdp) Orange County	36	12.33
Struble, IA (city) Plymouth County	8	12.12
Rockville, SC (town) Charleston County	19	11.95
Belknap, MT (cdp) Sanders County	12	11.88
Farmington, PA (cdp) Fayette County	80	11.38
Canalou, MO (city) New Madrid County	28	11.24
Sunshine, CO (cdp) Boulder County	35	11.15
Northwest Stanwood, WA (cdp) Snohomish County	9	11.11
Andersonville, TN (cdp) Anderson County	18	10.98
Aneta, ND (city) Nelson County	39	10.60
Randolph AFB, TX (cdp) Bexar County	110	10.51
Custer, WA (cdp) Whatcom County	55	10.34
Bay View, MI (cdp) Emmet County	10	10.10
Launiupoko, HI (cdp) Maui County	47	10.02
Peter, UT (cdp) Cache County	42	9.86
Bohemia, MI (township) Ontonagon County	4	9.76
Baring, ME (plantation) Washington County	30	9.49
Chilhowee, MO (town) Johnson County	31	9.42
Woodlands, CA (cdp) San Luis Obispo County	35	9.41
Riverside, WY (town) Carbon County	3	9.38
Mill Spring, MO (village) Wayne County	14	9.33
Clifton, ID (city) Franklin County	31	9.09
Port Alexander, AK (city) Petersburg Census Area	6	9.09
Toomsuba, MS (cdp) Lauderdale County	39	9.07
Wasola, MO (cdp) Ozark County	17	9.04
Pike, CA (cdp) Sierra County	14	8.92
West Havre, MT (cdp) Hill County	17	8.90
Gouglersville, PA (cdp) Berks County	22	8.66
Ranburne, AL (town) Cleburne County	47	8.58
Georgetown, MN (city) Clay County	20	8.55
Leigh, MN (township) Morrison County	25	8.42
Charleston, UT (town) Wasatch County	43	8.27
Northwest Piscataquis, ME (unorganized territory) Piscataquis County	8	8.16
Noblestown, PA (cdp) Allegheny County	25	8.12
Gorham, NY (cdp) Ontario County	47	8.08
Brookside, CO (town) Fremont County	22	8.06
North Hartland, VT (cdp) Windsor County	9	8.04
Kenwood, CA (cdp) Sonoma County	37	8.01
Swan Quarter, NC (cdp) Hyde County	34	7.93
Minor Hill, TN (city) Giles County	33	7.93
Marked Tree, AR (city) Poinsett County	205	7.89
Sandy Valley, NV (cdp) Clark County	81	7.80
Hamilton, MO (city) Caldwell County	175	7.77
Maalaea, HI (cdp) Maui County	29	7.71
Mingoville, PA (cdp) Centre County	28	7.63
Stone Lake, WI (cdp) Sawyer County	10	7.58
Allensville, KY (city) Todd County	15	7.54
Macdoel, CA (cdp) Siskiyou County	11	7.48
Eagle Grove, GA (cdp) Hart County	12	7.45
Sandy River, ME (plantation) Franklin County	7	7.45
Lake Wilderness, VA (cdp) Spotsylvania County	174	7.44
Bristol, TX (cdp) Ellis County	30	7.41
High Rolls, NM (cdp) Otero County	51	7.39
Tampico, WA (cdp) Yakima County	8	7.27
Atwood, CO (cdp) Logan County	14	7.25
Downieville-Lawson-Dumont, CO (cdp) Clear Creek County	23	7.23
Beaux Arts Village, WA (town) King County	27	7.20
Pylesville, MD (cdp) Harford County	42	7.14
Franktown, CO (cdp) Douglas County	31	7.08
Olinda, HI (cdp) Maui County	93	7.07
Etowah, AR (town) Mississippi County	15	7.04
Melbourne, KY (city) Campbell County	35	7.03
Richmond, VT (cdp) Chittenden County	34	6.94
Gilmore City, IA (city) Humboldt County	34	6.87
Norfork, AR (city) Baxter County	34	6.81
Ketchum, ID (city) Blaine County	189	6.76
Delta, AL (cdp) Clay County	16	6.75
Hot Springs, VA (cdp) Bath County	41	6.74
Ripton, VT (town) Addison County	35	6.72
Chazy, NY (cdp) Clinton County	34	6.71
Ward, SD (town) Moody County	4	6.67
Canal Lewisville, OH (cdp) Coshocton County	23	6.65
Tusayan, AZ (cdp) Coconino County	12	6.63
East Cook, MN (unorganized territory) Cook County	71	6.62
Nanticoke, MD (cdp) Wicomico County	11	6.59
Pine Brook Hill, CO (cdp) Boulder County	70	6.54
Wabasso Beach, FL (cdp) Indian River County	116	6.39
Zephyr Cove, NV (cdp) Douglas County	16	6.35
Verdunville, WV (cdp) Logan County	37	6.29
Big Lake, MO (village) Holt County	11	6.25
Greenville, VA (cdp) Augusta County	46	6.24
Minden, IA (city) Pottawattamie County	35	6.21
Whitewater, CA (cdp) Riverside County	41	6.20
Pleasant Plain, OH (village) Warren County	9	6.16
Dawson, MD (cdp) Allegany County	11	6.15
El Lago, TX (city) Harris County	169	6.12
Montague, NY (town) Lewis County	6	6.12
Rosedale, NM (cdp) Grant County	18	6.08
Centerville, WI (town) Manitowoc County	43	6.06
West Glacier, MT (cdp) Flathead County	12	6.06
Wingville, WI (town) Grant County	25	6.04
Darlington, MO (village) Gentry County	7	6.03
Glen Echo, MD (town) Montgomery County	15	6.02
Pawleys Island, SC (town) Georgetown County	6	6.00
Kupreanof, AK (city) Petersburg Census Area	3	6.00
Campbell Station, AR (city) Jackson County	19	5.96
Minerva, MN (township) Clearwater County	9	5.96
Jacksonport, AR (town) Jackson County	8	5.93
Hugo, CO (town) Lincoln County	44	5.84
Keiser, AR (city) Mississippi County	46	5.74
Rabbit Hash, KY (cdp) Boone County	17	5.74
Alexander, ND (city) McKenzie County	17	5.72
Stokes, MN (township) Roseau County	9	5.70
Coffee Creek, CA (cdp) Trinity County	10	5.65
New Deal, TN (cdp) Sumner County	35	5.64
Spring Lake, FL (cdp) Hernando County	27	5.63
Sherwood, OH (village) Defiance County	31	5.61
Bay View, WA (cdp) Skagit County	38	5.58
Seabrook, MA (cdp) Barnstable County	17	5.47
Rachel, WV (cdp) Marion County	9	5.42
South Duxbury, MA (cdp) Plymouth County	182	5.39
Northeast St. Louis, MN (unorganized territory) St. Louis County	14	5.38
White Hall, WV (town) Marion County	28	5.34
Perkinsville, VT (village) Windsor County	7	5.34
Juliustown, NJ (cdp) Burlington County	17	5.33
New Suffolk, NY (cdp) Suffolk County	10	5.32
Nickerson, MN (township) Pine County	5	5.32

Please refer to the Explanation of Data in the front of the book for more detailed information.

Ancestry

British

Top 150 Places Sorted by Percent of Total Population

Based on places with total population of 7,500 or more

Place	Population	%
Park City, UT (city) Summit County	350	4.63
Clarendon Hills, IL (village) DuPage County	373	4.51
Palm Beach, FL (town) Palm Beach County	369	4.25
Wynne, AR (city) Cross County	349	4.15
Coto de Caza, CA (cdp) Orange County	614	3.97
Cedar Hills, UT (city) Utah County	292	3.41
Tiburon, CA (town) Marin County	284	3.22
Hanover, NH (town) Grafton County	357	3.17
Montecito, CA (cdp) Santa Barbara County	288	3.12
Hanover, NH (cdp) Grafton County	257	3.03
Highland Park, TX (town) Dallas County	250	2.93
Boxford, MA (town) Essex County	228	2.88
Princeton, NJ (borough) Mercer County	360	2.87
Key Biscayne, FL (village) Miami-Dade County	344	2.87
Smithfield, UT (city) Cache County	250	2.79
North Logan, UT (city) Cache County	209	2.69
Castle Pines North, CO (city) Douglas County	250	2.66
Holladay, UT (city) Salt Lake County	690	2.62
Highland, UT (city) Utah County	364	2.59
Woodburn, VA (cdp) Fairfax County	222	2.55
Grantsville, UT (city) Tooele County	214	2.53
Millcreek, UT (cdp) Salt Lake County	1,516	2.49
Hollis, NH (town) Hillsborough County	189	2.48
Provo, UT (city) Utah County	2,706	2.46
South Riding, VA (cdp) Loudoun County	565	2.46
Farmington, UT (city) Davis County	421	2.45
Centerville, UT (city) Davis County	371	2.44
Bow, NH (town) Merrimack County	185	2.44
Druid Hills, GA (cdp) DeKalb County	351	2.40
Clayton, CA (city) Contra Costa County	256	2.37
Old Lyme, CT (town) New London County	180	2.37
Walworth, NY (town) Wayne County	217	2.34
Kaysville, UT (city) Davis County	608	2.33
Chatham, NJ (township) Morris County	243	2.33
Soquel, CA (cdp) Santa Cruz County	218	2.32
Upper Uwchlan, PA (township) Chester County	237	2.26
Cedar Mill, OR (cdp) Washington County	327	2.25
Lindon, UT (city) Utah County	218	2.25
Edgewood, WA (city) Pierce County	211	2.25
Chapel Hill, NC (town) Orange County	1,225	2.22
Bountiful, UT (city) Davis County	931	2.20
South Kensington, MD (cdp) Montgomery County	179	2.20
Cottonwood Heights, UT (city) Salt Lake County	731	2.18
Paradise Valley, AZ (town) Maricopa County	288	2.18
Hurricane, UT (city) Washington County	287	2.17
Seabrook, TX (city) Harris County	249	2.17
Perkiomen, PA (township) Montgomery County	190	2.17
Rexburg, ID (city) Madison County	526	2.15
Wilton, CT (town) Fairfield County	382	2.14
Montpelier, VT (city) Washington County	169	2.14
West Point, UT (city) Davis County	190	2.13
Idylwood, VA (cdp) Fairfax County	332	2.12
Bedford, MA (town) Middlesex County	276	2.11
Spanish Fork, UT (city) Utah County	669	2.10
Mill Valley, CA (city) Marin County	288	2.10
Upper Montclair, NJ (cdp) Essex County	244	2.10
Rockwood, VA (cdp) Chesterfield County	164	2.09
Sandy, UT (city) Salt Lake County	1,810	2.08
South Jordan, UT (city) Salt Lake County	958	2.07
Brigham City, UT (city) Box Elder County	366	2.07
Waxhaw, NC (town) Union County	181	2.07
Badger, AK (cdp) Fairbanks North Star Borough	374	2.06
Pawling, NY (town) Dutchess County	171	2.05
McLean, VA (cdp) Fairfax County	941	2.04
Chamblee, GA (city) DeKalb County	199	2.04
Corrales, NM (village) Sandoval County	166	2.04
Pike Creek, DE (cdp) New Castle County	164	2.04
Greenwich, CT (town) Fairfield County	1,236	2.03
University Park, TX (city) Dallas County	466	2.03
Chalco, NE (cdp) Sarpy County	217	2.02
Essex Junction, VT (village) Chittenden County	184	2.01
Scotts Valley, CA (city) Santa Cruz County	226	1.99
Upper Saddle River, NJ (borough) Bergen County	161	1.99
Greenbriar, VA (cdp) Fairfax County	153	1.99
Brazil, IN (city) Clay County	150	1.99
North Salt Lake, UT (city) Davis County	296	1.98
Briarcliff Manor, NY (village) Westchester County	159	1.98
Rossmoor, CA (cdp) Orange County	207	1.97
Alpine, UT (city) Utah County	177	1.95
Dranesville, VA (cdp) Fairfax County	244	1.94
Clemson, SC (city) Pickens County	262	1.93
Rotonda, FL (cdp) Charlotte County	184	1.93
Snohomish, WA (city) Snohomish County	175	1.93
Concord, MA (town) Middlesex County	333	1.92
Falls Church, VA (ind. city) Falls Church independent city	220	1.92
Groton, MA (town) Middlesex County	198	1.92
Branson, MO (city) Taney County	188	1.91
Morehead City, NC (town) Carteret County	162	1.90
Brighton, MI (city) Livingston County	141	1.88
Syracuse, UT (city) Davis County	406	1.87
Mason, MI (city) Ingham County	151	1.87
Fort Hunt, VA (cdp) Fairfax County	297	1.86
Chester, NJ (township) Morris County	144	1.86
Bainbridge Island, WA (city) Kitsap County	417	1.85
Naples, FL (city) Collier County	377	1.85
Annapolis Neck, MD (cdp) Anne Arundel County	205	1.85
Darien, CT (cdp/town) Fairfield County	375	1.84
Princeton, NJ (township) Mercer County	301	1.84
Superior, CO (town) Boulder County	218	1.84
Rancho Santa Margarita, CA (city) Orange County	868	1.83
Louisville, CO (city) Boulder County	338	1.83
Broussard, LA (city) Lafayette Parish	142	1.83
Union Hill-Novelty Hill, WA (cdp) King County	334	1.82
Minneola, FL (city) Lake County	164	1.82
San Anselmo, CA (town) Marin County	221	1.81
Farragut, TN (town) Knox County	363	1.80
Weddington, NC (town) Union County	166	1.80
Cottage Lake, WA (cdp) King County	398	1.79
Palmer Town, MA (city) Hampden County	218	1.79
Springfield, MI (charter township) Oakland County	246	1.78
West Point, NY (cdp) Orange County	168	1.78
Bethesda, MD (cdp) Montgomery County	1,028	1.76
Riverton, UT (city) Salt Lake County	634	1.76
Cinco Ranch, TX (cdp) Fort Bend County	320	1.76
Celebration, FL (cdp) Osceola County	136	1.75
Waterboro, ME (town) York County	131	1.75
Seal Beach, CA (city) Orange County	419	1.74
Hopewell, NJ (township) Mercer County	299	1.74
St. Simons, GA (cdp) Glynn County	224	1.74
Menlo Park, CA (city) San Mateo County	540	1.72
Lexington, MA (cdp/town) Middlesex County	525	1.70
Seminole, FL (city) Pinellas County	294	1.70
Oxford, AL (city) Calhoun County	355	1.69
Indian Harbour Beach, FL (city) Brevard County	140	1.67
Orem, UT (city) Utah County	1,439	1.66
Essex, VT (town) Chittenden County	323	1.66
Payson, UT (city) Utah County	286	1.66
Morrisville, NC (town) Wake County	268	1.66
Stanford, CA (cdp) Santa Clara County	235	1.65
Clinton, CT (town) Middlesex County	219	1.64
Coshocton, OH (city) Coshocton County	186	1.64
North Myrtle Beach, SC (city) Horry County	219	1.63
Malibu, CA (city) Los Angeles County	208	1.63
Montgomery, OH (city) Hamilton County	165	1.63
Wells, ME (town) York County	158	1.63
Templeton, CA (cdp) San Luis Obispo County	131	1.63
Four Corners, FL (cdp) Lake County	413	1.62
Huntington, VA (cdp) Fairfax County	168	1.62
Palo Alto, CA (city) Santa Clara County	1,004	1.61
Vestavia Hills, AL (city) Jefferson County	537	1.61
American Fork, UT (city) Utah County	409	1.61
Bellaire, TX (city) Harris County	267	1.61
Exeter, NH (town) Rockingham County	232	1.61
Forks, PA (township) Northampton County	220	1.61
Ballston, NY (town) Saratoga County	155	1.61
Salt Lake City, UT (city) Salt Lake County	2,957	1.60
Kennebunk, ME (town) York County	173	1.59
Dunwoody, GA (city) DeKalb County	707	1.58
Tooele, UT (city) Tooele County	478	1.58
El Segundo, CA (city) Los Angeles County	261	1.58

SECTION THREE

Please refer to the Explanation of Data in the front of the book for more detailed information.

Ancestry

Bulgarian

U.S. and 50 States Sorted by Population and Percent of Total Population

Place	Population	%
United States	**89,808**	**0.03**
Illinois	14,058	0.11
California	11,242	0.03
New York	8,210	0.04
Florida	6,029	0.03
Michigan	3,473	0.03
Washington	3,286	0.05
Massachusetts	3,166	0.05
Ohio	2,864	0.02
Texas	2,749	0.01
New Jersey	2,697	0.03
Pennsylvania	2,544	0.02
Nevada	2,352	0.09
Maryland	2,338	0.04
Colorado	2,078	0.04
Virginia	1,989	0.03
Georgia	1,866	0.02
Arizona	1,750	0.03
Oregon	1,633	0.04
Missouri	1,611	0.03
North Carolina	1,544	0.02
Indiana	1,359	0.02
Wisconsin	1,113	0.02
Connecticut	932	0.03
Minnesota	868	0.02
South Carolina	769	0.02
Oklahoma	750	0.02
Iowa	584	0.02
Kentucky	432	0.01
Louisiana	416	0.01
Utah	395	0.01
Kansas	383	0.01
Tennessee	362	0.01
Alabama	346	0.01
North Dakota	340	0.05
District of Columbia	309	0.05
Hawaii	294	0.02
Arkansas	284	0.01
New Mexico	275	0.01
Maine	274	0.02
Delaware	230	0.03
Alaska	224	0.03
Idaho	220	0.01
Rhode Island	193	0.02
West Virginia	188	0.01
Wyoming	167	0.03
New Hampshire	151	0.01
Montana	149	0.02
South Dakota	111	0.01
Mississippi	94	<0.01
Vermont	67	0.01
Nebraska	50	<0.01

Place	Population	%
Illinois	14,058	0.11
Nevada	2,352	0.09
Washington	3,286	0.05
Massachusetts	3,166	0.05
North Dakota	340	0.05
District of Columbia	309	0.05
New York	8,210	0.04
Maryland	2,338	0.04
Colorado	2,078	0.04
Oregon	1,633	0.04
United States	**89,808**	**0.03**
California	11,242	0.03
Florida	6,029	0.03
Michigan	3,473	0.03
New Jersey	2,697	0.03
Virginia	1,989	0.03
Arizona	1,750	0.03
Missouri	1,611	0.03
Connecticut	932	0.03
Delaware	230	0.03
Alaska	224	0.03
Wyoming	167	0.03
Ohio	2,864	0.02
Pennsylvania	2,544	0.02
Georgia	1,866	0.02
North Carolina	1,544	0.02
Indiana	1,359	0.02
Wisconsin	1,113	0.02
Minnesota	868	0.02
South Carolina	769	0.02
Oklahoma	750	0.02
Iowa	584	0.02
Hawaii	294	0.02
Maine	274	0.02
Rhode Island	193	0.02
Montana	149	0.02
Texas	2,749	0.01
Kentucky	432	0.01
Louisiana	416	0.01
Utah	395	0.01
Kansas	383	0.01
Tennessee	362	0.01
Alabama	346	0.01
Arkansas	284	0.01
New Mexico	275	0.01
Idaho	220	0.01
West Virginia	188	0.01
New Hampshire	151	0.01
South Dakota	111	0.01
Vermont	67	0.01
Mississippi	94	<0.01
Nebraska	50	<0.01

Please refer to the Explanation of Data in the front of the book for more detailed information.

Ancestry

Bulgarian

Top 150 Places Sorted by Population

Based on all places, regardless of total population

Place	Population	%
New York, NY (city) Kings County	5,011	0.06
Chicago, IL (city) Cook County	3,223	0.12
Los Angeles, CA (city) Los Angeles County	2,293	0.06
Queens, NY (borough) Queens County	2,090	0.10
Manhattan, NY (borough) New York County	1,272	0.08
Brooklyn, NY (borough) Kings County	1,128	0.05
Mount Prospect, IL (village) Cook County	926	1.72
Spring Valley, NV (cdp) Clark County	898	0.53
Arlington Heights, IL (village) Cook County	754	1.01
Phoenix, AZ (city) Maricopa County	716	0.05
Portland, OR (city) Multnomah County	665	0.12
St. Petersburg, FL (city) Pinellas County	584	0.24
Bronx, NY (borough) Bronx County	521	0.04
Seattle, WA (city) King County	506	0.09
San Diego, CA (city) San Diego County	474	0.04
San Francisco, CA (city) San Francisco County	468	0.06
Las Vegas, NV (city) Clark County	466	0.08
Boston, MA (city) Suffolk County	453	0.08
Woburn, MA (city) Middlesex County	429	1.14
Des Plaines, IL (city) Cook County	389	0.68
Thornton, CO (city) Adams County	362	0.32
Wheeling, IL (village) Cook County	351	0.95
Schiller Park, IL (village) Cook County	318	2.73
Washington, DC (city) District of Columbia	309	0.05
Sunnyvale, CA (city) Santa Clara County	308	0.23
Bellevue, WA (city) King County	304	0.25
Sacramento, CA (city) Sacramento County	304	0.07
Concord, CA (city) Contra Costa County	294	0.24
Plano, TX (city) Collin County	288	0.11
Palatine, IL (village) Cook County	267	0.40
Fruitville, FL (cdp) Sarasota County	265	1.91
San Jose, CA (city) Santa Clara County	264	0.03
Paradise, NV (cdp) Clark County	263	0.12
Ballwin, MO (city) St. Louis County	258	0.85
Enterprise, NV (cdp) Clark County	255	0.26
Rolling Meadows, IL (city) Cook County	246	1.04
Clearwater, FL (city) Pinellas County	239	0.22
Oklahoma City, OK (city) Oklahoma County	234	0.04
Cockeysville, MD (cdp) Baltimore County	231	1.16
Austin, TX (city) Travis County	231	0.03
Dallas, TX (city) Dallas County	226	0.02
Palm Coast, FL (city) Flagler County	217	0.31
Toledo, OH (city) Lucas County	217	0.07
Cary, NC (town) Wake County	215	0.17
Glendale Heights, IL (village) DuPage County	212	0.63
Schaumburg, IL (village) Cook County	207	0.28
Lakeside, CA (cdp) San Diego County	205	1.00
Skokie, IL (village) Cook County	205	0.32
Granite City, IL (city) Madison County	202	0.66
Buffalo, NY (city) Erie County	201	0.08
Cambridge, MA (city) Middlesex County	193	0.19
Hamburg, NY (town) Erie County	192	0.34
Chico, CA (city) Butte County	187	0.22
Carrollwood, FL (cdp) Hillsborough County	184	0.54
Hempstead, NY (town) Nassau County	181	0.02
Atlanta, GA (city) Fulton County	180	0.04
Arlington, TX (city) Tarrant County	178	0.05
Shelby, MI (charter township) Macomb County	174	0.24
Baltimore, MD (city) Baltimore city County	174	0.03
Tucson, AZ (city) Pima County	174	0.03
Streamwood, IL (village) Cook County	171	0.44
Garfield, NJ (city) Bergen County	169	0.56
Houston, TX (city) Harris County	168	0.01
Fort Collins, CO (city) Larimer County	164	0.12
Willowbrook, IL (village) DuPage County	162	1.90
Wixom, MI (city) Oakland County	162	1.20
Roselle, IL (village) DuPage County	161	0.71
Fort Wayne, IN (city) Allen County	156	0.06
Mundelein, IL (village) Lake County	155	0.50
Bethesda, MD (cdp) Montgomery County	154	0.26
Laurel, MD (city) Prince George's County	153	0.63
Franklin Town, MA (city) Norfolk County	152	0.49
Spokane, WA (city) Spokane County	152	0.07
Fort Worth, TX (city) Tarrant County	152	0.02
Philadelphia, PA (city) Philadelphia County	150	0.01
Winchester, VA (ind. city) Winchester independent city	148	0.57
El Dorado Hills, CA (cdp) El Dorado County	148	0.34
Overland Park, KS (city) Johnson County	147	0.09
Anaheim, CA (city) Orange County	147	0.04
North Lynnwood, WA (cdp) Snohomish County	144	0.91
Albuquerque, NM (city) Bernalillo County	144	0.03
Pompano Beach, FL (city) Broward County	143	0.14
St. Louis, MO (city) St. Louis city County	143	0.04
West Hempstead, NY (cdp) Nassau County	142	0.77
Northglenn, CO (city) Adams County	142	0.40
Elk Grove Village, IL (village) Cook County	141	0.43
Irvine, CA (city) Orange County	141	0.07
Waimea, HI (cdp) Hawaii County	140	1.43
Plainfield, IL (village) Will County	140	0.39
Germantown, MD (cdp) Montgomery County	139	0.16
Tulsa, OK (city) Tulsa County	139	0.04
Denver, CO (city) Denver County	139	0.02
Bismarck, ND (city) Burleigh County	138	0.23
Silver Spring, MD (cdp) Montgomery County	138	0.20
Henderson, NV (city) Clark County	138	0.06
Nantucket, MA (cdp) Nantucket County	137	1.72
Nantucket, MA (town) Nantucket County	137	1.36
Arvada, CO (city) Jefferson County	136	0.13
Happy Valley, OR (city) Clackamas County	135	1.07
Lexington-Fayette, KY (cons. govt) Fayette County	135	0.05
Rosemont, IL (village) Cook County	131	3.29
Beaverton, OR (city) Washington County	131	0.15
Jersey City, NJ (city) Hudson County	131	0.05
Marietta, GA (city) Cobb County	130	0.23
Riverside, CA (city) Riverside County	130	0.04
Columbus, OH (city) Franklin County	130	0.02
Edwardsville, IL (city) Madison County	129	0.55
Brookhaven, NY (town) Suffolk County	128	0.03
Norman, OK (city) Cleveland County	127	0.12
Pittsburgh, PA (city) Allegheny County	127	0.04
Montgomery, NY (town) Orange County	126	0.56
Deerfield, IL (village) Lake County	125	0.68
Dayton, OH (city) Montgomery County	125	0.09
Ithaca, NY (city) Tompkins County	123	0.41
Miami Beach, FL (city) Miami-Dade County	123	0.14
Charlotte, NC (city) Mecklenburg County	123	0.02
Harwood Heights, IL (village) Cook County	121	1.43
Minneapolis, MN (city) Hennepin County	120	0.03
North Bethesda, MD (cdp) Montgomery County	119	0.29
Hollywood, FL (city) Broward County	119	0.08
Oak Harbor, WA (city) Island County	118	0.54
Pasadena, CA (city) Los Angeles County	116	0.09
New Milford, NJ (borough) Bergen County	115	0.71
Gilbert, AZ (town) Maricopa County	115	0.06
Glendale, CA (city) Los Angeles County	115	0.06
Hoboken, NJ (city) Hudson County	114	0.24
Walnut Creek, CA (city) Contra Costa County	114	0.18
Tuckahoe, VA (cdp) Henrico County	113	0.25
St. Peters, MO (city) St. Charles County	113	0.21
Parma Heights, OH (city) Cuyahoga County	112	0.54
Kansas City, MO (city) Jackson County	112	0.02
Montevallo, AL (city) Shelby County	111	1.82
Union Hill-Novelty Hill, WA (cdp) King County	110	0.60
Gaithersburg, MD (city) Montgomery County	108	0.19
Mountain View, CA (city) Santa Clara County	108	0.15
Waterford, MI (charter township) Oakland County	108	0.15
Fairview Park, OH (city) Cuyahoga County	107	0.63
Carpentersville, IL (village) Kane County	107	0.29
Clifton, NJ (city) Passaic County	107	0.13
Wilmette, IL (village) Cook County	106	0.39
Chesterfield, MO (city) St. Louis County	106	0.22
Oxnard, CA (city) Ventura County	106	0.06
Tampa, FL (city) Hillsborough County	106	0.03
Bedford, NY (town) Westchester County	105	0.60
Danville, PA (borough) Montour County	104	2.21
East Stroudsburg, PA (borough) Monroe County	104	1.04
Baton Rouge, LA (city) East Baton Rouge Parish	104	0.05
Highland Park, NJ (borough) Middlesex County	103	0.74
Front Royal, VA (town) Warren County	103	0.71
Lynnwood, WA (city) Snohomish County	103	0.29

SECTION THREE

Please refer to the Explanation of Data in the front of the book for more detailed information.

Ancestry

Bulgarian

Top 150 Places Sorted by Percent of Total Population

Based on all places, regardless of total population

Place	Population	%
Anchor Bay, CA (cdp) Mendocino County	50	15.67
Unity, OR (city) Baker County	6	11.11
Skagway, AK (cdp) Skagway Municipality	97	8.79
Hollister, OK (town) Tillman County	11	8.03
Dupuyer, MT (cdp) Pondera County	3	5.77
Marmarth, ND (city) Slope County	10	5.71
Bishop Hill, IL (village) Henry County	6	5.66
Cannonville, UT (town) Garfield County	9	5.59
Monroe, PA (township) Bradford County	62	4.94
Cheriton, VA (town) Northampton County	31	4.71
Silver Creek, MO (village) Newton County	32	4.43
Leland, MI (cdp) Leelanau County	14	4.39
Baldwin, IA (city) Jackson County	4	4.04
Woodmere, OH (village) Cuyahoga County	36	3.91
Stevens, MN (township) Stevens County	2	3.77
Forest Lake, IL (cdp) Lake County	63	3.47
Meadow Valley, CA (cdp) Plumas County	23	3.41
Wind Gap, PA (borough) Northampton County	93	3.38
Parker, WA (cdp) Yakima County	17	3.35
Rosemont, IL (village) Cook County	131	3.29
Friendship, MD (cdp) Anne Arundel County	13	3.16
Tappen, ND (city) Kidder County	8	3.13
Bedford Hills, NY (cdp) Westchester County	99	3.04
Polk City, FL (town) Polk County	52	2.95
Hanna City, IL (village) Peoria County	37	2.82
Streeter, ND (city) Stutsman County	3	2.78
Vance, AL (town) Tuscaloosa County	38	2.75
Schiller Park, IL (village) Cook County	318	2.73
Wales, NY (town) Erie County	81	2.72
Skagen, MN (township) Roseau County	6	2.63
Berlin, MI (township) St. Clair County	86	2.61
Fairfield, NY (town) Herkimer County	42	2.49
Chengwatana, MN (township) Pine County	17	2.47
Clyde, WI (town) Iowa County	9	2.45
Log Cabin, TX (city) Henderson County	20	2.42
Carpio, ND (city) Ward County	3	2.36
Lake Delton, WI (village) Sauk County	63	2.29
Bramwell, WV (town) Mercer County	10	2.28
Knollwood, IL (cdp) Lake County	38	2.27
San Francisco, MN (township) Carver County	20	2.26
Rantoul, KS (city) Franklin County	4	2.26
Danville, PA (borough) Montour County	104	2.21
Middletown, CA (cdp) Lake County	36	2.19
Alleghenyville, PA (cdp) Berks County	18	2.17
Clinton, WI (village) Rock County	41	2.15
Meadview, AZ (cdp) Mohave County	27	2.10
DeLand Southwest, FL (cdp) Volusia County	19	2.04
Appleton, MN (township) Swift County	4	2.03
Monroeville, OH (village) Huron County	27	2.02
Cathlamet, WA (town) Wahkiakum County	12	1.95
Pembroke, NY (town) Genesee County	83	1.92
Fruitville, FL (cdp) Sarasota County	265	1.91
Timber Lake, SD (city) Dewey County	9	1.91
Willowbrook, IL (village) DuPage County	162	1.90
Pomona, KS (city) Franklin County	16	1.88
North Star, MN (township) St. Louis County	4	1.88
Effort, PA (cdp) Monroe County	32	1.84
Montevallo, AL (city) Shelby County	111	1.82
McConnellsburg, PA (borough) Fulton County	22	1.80
Penndel, PA (borough) Bucks County	42	1.79
Bolton, MA (town) Worcester County	85	1.78
Blue Ball, PA (cdp) Lancaster County	14	1.78
Iron River, MI (city) Iron County	54	1.75
Mount Prospect, IL (village) Cook County	926	1.72
Nantucket, MA (cdp) Nantucket County	137	1.72
Ross, PA (township) Monroe County	97	1.62
Dubois, WY (town) Fremont County	14	1.62
Wolf Creek, UT (cdp) Weber County	15	1.57
Diamond Bluff, WI (town) Pierce County	9	1.55
Blowers, MN (township) Otter Tail County	5	1.55
Johnstown, MI (township) Barry County	46	1.51
Rancho Viejo, TX (town) Cameron County	35	1.50
Gambier, OH (village) Knox County	33	1.50
Maybrook, NY (village) Orange County	44	1.48
Fort Polk North, LA (cdp) Vernon Parish	38	1.46
Akron, MN (township) Big Stone County	2	1.46
Bay City, WI (village) Pierce County	7	1.44
Waimea, HI (cdp) Hawaii County	140	1.43
Harwood Heights, IL (village) Cook County	121	1.43
Sleepy Hollow, IL (village) Kane County	48	1.41
Spencerville, MD (cdp) Montgomery County	21	1.41
Belle Valley, OH (village) Noble County	5	1.40
Nantucket, MA (town) Nantucket County	137	1.36
Oak Bluffs, MA (town) Dukes County	59	1.35
Oakwood Park, MO (village) Clay County	2	1.34
Wildwood Lake, TN (cdp) Bradley County	43	1.28
Bristol, SD (city) Day County	5	1.28
Crompond, NY (cdp) Westchester County	26	1.27
Trappe, PA (borough) Montgomery County	43	1.25
Remerton, GA (city) Lowndes County	15	1.25
Augusta, IL (village) Hancock County	10	1.24
Amherst, ME (town) Hancock County	3	1.24
California, PA (borough) Washington County	81	1.23
Hector, AR (town) Pope County	4	1.21
Wixom, MI (city) Oakland County	162	1.20
Long Point, IL (village) Livingston County	3	1.20
Walden, NY (village) Orange County	82	1.19
Voluntown, CT (town) New London County	31	1.19
Hilton, NY (village) Monroe County	69	1.18
Mettawa, IL (village) Lake County	7	1.17
Cockeysville, MD (cdp) Baltimore County	231	1.16
Sugar Island, MI (township) Chippewa County	9	1.15
Parkdale, MO (village) Jefferson County	2	1.15
Woburn, MA (city) Middlesex County	429	1.14
Smithville, NJ (cdp) Atlantic County	69	1.14
Reading, MI (township) Hillsdale County	23	1.13
Proctorsville, VT (cdp) Windsor County	4	1.12
Baileys Harbor, WI (cdp) Door County	3	1.12
Tiverton, RI (cdp) Newport County	80	1.10
Cameron, OK (town) Le Flore County	4	1.10
Happy Valley, OR (city) Clackamas County	135	1.07
Hesperia, MI (village) Oceana County	11	1.06
Ontwa, MI (township) Cass County	68	1.05
Lincoln Village, CA (cdp) San Joaquin County	47	1.05
Rolling Meadows, IL (city) Cook County	246	1.04
East Stroudsburg, PA (borough) Monroe County	104	1.04
Belvedere, CA (city) Marin County	22	1.04
Pimmit Hills, VA (cdp) Fairfax County	64	1.03
Chester, MD (town) Kent County	53	1.03
Coon Rapids, IA (city) Carroll County	12	1.02
Orbisonia, PA (borough) Huntingdon County	8	1.02
Arlington Heights, IL (village) Cook County	754	1.01
Johns, CO (town) Weld County	87	1.01
Archie, MO (city) Cass County	12	1.01
Clear Lake Shores, TX (city) Galveston County	11	1.01
Troy, WI (town) Sauk County	7	1.01
Lakeside, CA (cdp) San Diego County	205	1.00
Grandwood Park, IL (cdp) Lake County	50	1.00
Hollister, MO (city) Taney County	43	1.00
Hayward, WI (town) Sawyer County	35	0.99
Seaside Park, NJ (borough) Ocean County	18	0.98
West Chester, IA (city) Washington County	1	0.97
Hampshire, IL (village) Kane County	49	0.96
Franklin, WI (town) Sauk County	7	0.96
Wheeling, IL (village) Cook County	351	0.95
St. Anthony, MN (city) Ramsey County	28	0.95
Glasco, NY (cdp) Ulster County	22	0.95
Cleveland, WI (town) Chippewa County	9	0.95
Kimmel, PA (township) Bedford County	14	0.92
Riverside, MI (township) Missaukee County	11	0.92
Alden, IA (city) Hardin County	8	0.92
Mayfield, NY (village) Fulton County	8	0.92
North Lynnwood, WA (cdp) Snohomish County	144	0.91
Devon, PA (cdp) Chester County	14	0.91
West Yellowstone, MT (town) Gallatin County	10	0.91
Greenville, CA (cdp) Plumas County	9	0.91
Rosewood Heights, IL (cdp) Madison County	39	0.90
Stambaugh, MI (township) Iron County	10	0.90
Whitefish, MI (township) Chippewa County	5	0.89
Tropic, UT (town) Garfield County	6	0.88

Please refer to the Explanation of Data in the front of the book for more detailed information.

Ancestry

Bulgarian

Top 150 Places Sorted by Percent of Total Population

Based on places with total population of 7,500 or more

Place	Population	%
Schiller Park, IL (village) Cook County	318	2.73
Fruitville, FL (cdp) Sarasota County	265	1.91
Willowbrook, IL (village) DuPage County	162	1.90
Mount Prospect, IL (village) Cook County	926	1.72
Nantucket, MA (cdp) Nantucket County	137	1.72
Waimea, HI (cdp) Hawaii County	140	1.43
Harwood Heights, IL (village) Cook County	121	1.43
Nantucket, MA (town) Nantucket County	137	1.36
Wixom, MI (city) Oakland County	162	1.20
Cockeysville, MD (cdp) Baltimore County	231	1.16
Woburn, MA (city) Middlesex County	429	1.14
Happy Valley, OR (city) Clackamas County	135	1.07
Rolling Meadows, IL (city) Cook County	246	1.04
East Stroudsburg, PA (borough) Monroe County	104	1.04
Arlington Heights, IL (village) Cook County	754	1.01
Johns, CO (town) Weld County	87	1.01
Lakeside, CA (cdp) San Diego County	205	1.00
Wheeling, IL (village) Cook County	351	0.95
North Lynnwood, WA (cdp) Snohomish County	144	0.91
Itasca, IL (village) DuPage County	73	0.87
Ballwin, MO (city) St. Louis County	258	0.85
Pine, PA (township) Allegheny County	88	0.82
River Falls, WI (city) Pierce County	93	0.80
Long Hill, NJ (township) Morris County	69	0.79
West Hempstead, NY (cdp) Nassau County	142	0.77
Highland Park, NJ (borough) Middlesex County	103	0.74
Olivette, MO (city) St. Louis County	57	0.74
Roselle, IL (village) DuPage County	161	0.71
New Milford, NJ (borough) Bergen County	115	0.71
Front Royal, VA (town) Warren County	103	0.71
Des Plaines, IL (city) Cook County	389	0.68
Deerfield, IL (village) Lake County	125	0.68
Wantage, NJ (township) Sussex County	77	0.68
Granite City, IL (city) Madison County	202	0.66
Orange Park, FL (town) Clay County	57	0.65
Glendale Heights, IL (village) DuPage County	212	0.63
Laurel, MD (city) Prince George's County	153	0.63
Fairview Park, OH (city) Cuyahoga County	107	0.63
River Falls, WI (city) Pierce County	93	0.63
Lyndon, KY (city) Jefferson County	68	0.63
Lexington, SC (town) Lexington County	102	0.62
Prospect Heights, IL (city) Cook County	99	0.61
Mount Airy, NC (city) Surry County	64	0.61
Union Hill-Novelty Hill, WA (cdp) King County	110	0.60
Bedford, NY (town) Westchester County	105	0.60
Rochester, MI (city) Oakland County	71	0.58
Elwood, NY (cdp) Suffolk County	65	0.58
Winchester, VA (ind. city) Winchester independent city	148	0.57
Garfield, NJ (city) Bergen County	169	0.56
Montgomery, NY (town) Orange County	126	0.56
Edwardsville, IL (city) Madison County	129	0.55
Corte Madera, CA (town) Marin County	50	0.55
Carrollwood, FL (cdp) Hillsborough County	184	0.54
Oak Harbor, WA (city) Island County	118	0.54
Parma Heights, OH (city) Cuyahoga County	112	0.54
Spring Valley, NV (cdp) Clark County	898	0.53
River Grove, IL (village) Cook County	54	0.53
Tiverton, RI (town) Newport County	80	0.51
Mundelein, IL (village) Lake County	155	0.50
Dobbs Ferry, NY (village) Westchester County	54	0.50
Fallston, MD (cdp) Harford County	40	0.50
Franklin Town, MA (city) Norfolk County	152	0.49
Franklin Park, IL (village) Cook County	88	0.48
Stanford, CA (cdp) Santa Clara County	69	0.48
Beckett Ridge, OH (cdp) Butler County	43	0.48
Forestville, OH (cdp) Hamilton County	51	0.47
Delafield, WI (town) Waukesha County	39	0.47
Garden City Park, NY (cdp) Nassau County	37	0.47
Carrboro, NC (town) Orange County	88	0.46
Suffield, CT (town) Hartford County	71	0.46
Holbrook, MA (cdp/town) Norfolk County	49	0.46
Parma, NY (town) Monroe County	69	0.45
Herrin, IL (city) Williamson County	55	0.45
Pike Creek Valley, DE (cdp) New Castle County	51	0.45
Fairview, CA (cdp) Alameda County	44	0.45
Streamwood, IL (village) Cook County	171	0.44
Elk Grove Village, IL (village) Cook County	141	0.43
Avon, OH (city) Lorain County	84	0.43
Vermilion, OH (city) Lorain County	46	0.43
Key West, FL (city) Monroe County	102	0.42
East Rutherford, NJ (borough) Bergen County	37	0.42
Leonia, NJ (borough) Bergen County	37	0.42
Briarcliff Manor, NY (village) Westchester County	34	0.42
Downingtown, PA (borough) Chester County	33	0.42
Ithaca, NY (city) Tompkins County	123	0.41
Laconia, NH (city) Belknap County	67	0.41
Succasunna, NJ (cdp) Morris County	37	0.41
Palatine, IL (village) Cook County	267	0.40
Northglenn, CO (city) Adams County	142	0.40
Ashland, OR (city) Jackson County	81	0.40
The Village, OK (city) Oklahoma County	36	0.40
Vinings, GA (cdp) Cobb County	34	0.40
Plainfield, IL (village) Will County	140	0.39
Wilmette, IL (village) Cook County	106	0.39
Lake Zurich, IL (village) Lake County	77	0.39
Wading River, NY (cdp) Suffolk County	32	0.39
Oregon, OH (city) Lucas County	77	0.38
Kirksville, MO (city) Adair County	67	0.38
Red Hook, NY (town) Dutchess County	43	0.38
Adelphi, MD (cdp) Prince George's County	56	0.37
New Kingman-Butler, AZ (cdp) Mohave County	53	0.37
Geneva, NY (city) Ontario County	49	0.37
Massena, NY (village) St. Lawrence County	42	0.37
Riverside, IL (village) Cook County	32	0.37
Andover, MA (cdp) Essex County	31	0.36
Celebration, FL (cdp) Osceola County	28	0.36
Saugerties, NY (town) Ulster County	68	0.35
Gulfport, FL (city) Pinellas County	42	0.35
Harrison, TN (cdp) Hamilton County	28	0.35
St. Anthony, MN (city) Hennepin and Ramsey Counties	28	0.35
Plaistow, NH (town) Rockingham County	27	0.35
Hamburg, NY (town) Erie County	192	0.34
El Dorado Hills, CA (cdp) El Dorado County	148	0.34
Grayslake, IL (village) Lake County	71	0.34
Lebanon, IN (city) Boone County	54	0.34
Temperance, MI (cdp) Monroe County	29	0.34
Bloomingdale, IL (village) DuPage County	72	0.33
Verona, NJ (township) Essex County	44	0.33
Massena, NY (town) St. Lawrence County	42	0.33
Glen Carbon, IL (village) Madison County	40	0.33
Big Rapids, MI (city) Mecosta County	35	0.33
Menominee, MI (city) Menominee County	29	0.33
Thornton, CO (city) Adams County	362	0.32
Skokie, IL (village) Cook County	205	0.32
La Crescenta-Montrose, CA (cdp) Los Angeles County	63	0.32
Bensenville, IL (village) DuPage County	60	0.32
North Druid Hills, GA (cdp) DeKalb County	58	0.32
Moraga, CA (town) Contra Costa County	51	0.32
Setauket-East Setauket, NY (cdp) Suffolk County	51	0.32
Larkspur, CA (city) Marin County	38	0.32
Palm Coast, FL (city) Flagler County	217	0.31
Upper Chichester, PA (township) Delaware County	51	0.31
Great Falls, VA (cdp) Fairfax County	50	0.31
Palos Verdes Estates, CA (city) Los Angeles County	42	0.31
Newtown, PA (township) Delaware County	38	0.31
Lowes Island, VA (cdp) Loudoun County	35	0.31
Colonial Heights, VA (ind. city) Colonial Heights independent city	53	0.30
Middle Island, NY (cdp) Suffolk County	31	0.30
Winchendon, MA (town) Worcester County	31	0.30
Cross Lanes, WV (cdp) Kanawha County	28	0.30
George Mason, VA (cdp) Fairfax County	27	0.30
North Bethesda, MD (cdp) Montgomery County	119	0.29
Carpentersville, IL (village) Kane County	107	0.29
Lynnwood, WA (city) Snohomish County	103	0.29
Paramus, NJ (borough) Bergen County	75	0.29
Anoka, MN (city) Anoka County	50	0.29
Capitola, CA (city) Santa Cruz County	28	0.29
Brockport, NY (village) Monroe County	24	0.29
Schaumburg, IL (village) Cook County	207	0.28
Yarmouth, MA (town) Barnstable County	68	0.28

SECTION THREE

Please refer to the Explanation of Data in the front of the book for more detailed information.

Ancestry

Cajun

U.S. and 50 States Sorted by Population and Percent of Total Population

Place	Population	%	Place	Population	%
United States	**108,696**	**0.04**	Louisiana	49,469	1.12
Louisiana	49,469	1.12	Texas	23,705	0.10
Texas	23,705	0.10	Mississippi	2,097	0.07
Florida	3,242	0.02	Maine	983	0.07
California	2,987	0.01	Arkansas	1,619	0.06
Mississippi	2,097	0.07	**United States**	**108,696**	**0.04**
Georgia	2,024	0.02	Oklahoma	1,293	0.04
Arkansas	1,619	0.06	Montana	357	0.04
Alabama	1,592	0.03	Alabama	1,592	0.03
Tennessee	1,556	0.02	Colorado	1,314	0.03
North Carolina	1,416	0.02	Florida	3,242	0.02
Colorado	1,314	0.03	Georgia	2,024	0.02
Virginia	1,295	0.02	Tennessee	1,556	0.02
Oklahoma	1,293	0.04	North Carolina	1,416	0.02
Missouri	1,267	0.02	Virginia	1,295	0.02
Arizona	1,101	0.02	Missouri	1,267	0.02
Maine	983	0.07	Arizona	1,101	0.02
Washington	956	0.01	South Carolina	768	0.02
New York	897	<0.01	Oregon	614	0.02
South Carolina	768	0.02	Kansas	577	0.02
Indiana	666	0.01	Nevada	416	0.02
Oregon	614	0.02	New Mexico	355	0.02
Illinois	612	<0.01	Alaska	123	0.02
Massachusetts	585	0.01	California	2,987	0.01
Kansas	577	0.02	Washington	956	0.01
Ohio	558	<0.01	Indiana	666	0.01
Michigan	547	0.01	Massachusetts	585	0.01
Kentucky	459	0.01	Michigan	547	0.01
Pennsylvania	425	<0.01	Kentucky	459	0.01
Nevada	416	0.02	Maryland	404	0.01
Maryland	404	0.01	Iowa	348	0.01
Montana	357	0.04	Connecticut	273	0.01
New Mexico	355	0.02	Nebraska	229	0.01
Iowa	348	0.01	West Virginia	171	0.01
Connecticut	273	0.01	Idaho	150	0.01
Wisconsin	246	<0.01	New Hampshire	112	0.01
Nebraska	229	0.01	Hawaii	110	0.01
New Jersey	176	<0.01	Delaware	86	0.01
West Virginia	171	0.01	Vermont	80	0.01
Idaho	150	0.01	District of Columbia	73	0.01
Utah	125	<0.01	Wyoming	61	0.01
Alaska	123	0.02	New York	897	<0.01
Minnesota	121	<0.01	Illinois	612	<0.01
New Hampshire	112	0.01	Ohio	558	<0.01
Hawaii	110	0.01	Pennsylvania	425	<0.01
Delaware	86	0.01	Wisconsin	246	<0.01
Vermont	80	0.01	New Jersey	176	<0.01
District of Columbia	73	0.01	Utah	125	<0.01
Wyoming	61	0.01	Minnesota	121	<0.01
North Dakota	29	<0.01	North Dakota	29	<0.01
South Dakota	27	<0.01	South Dakota	27	<0.01
Rhode Island	0	0.00	Rhode Island	0	0.00

Please refer to the Explanation of Data in the front of the book for more detailed information.

Ancestry

Cajun

Top 150 Places Sorted by Population

Based on all places, regardless of total population

Place	Population	%
Lafayette, LA (city) Lafayette Parish	3,304	2.78
Baton Rouge, LA (city) East Baton Rouge Parish	1,586	0.69
Houston, TX (city) Harris County	1,358	0.07
Lake Charles, LA (city) Calcasieu Parish	1,050	1.47
New Orleans, LA (city) Orleans Parish	712	0.24
Nederland, TX (city) Jefferson County	668	3.84
Austin, TX (city) Travis County	660	0.09
Metairie, LA (cdp) Jefferson Parish	651	0.48
Beaumont, TX (city) Jefferson County	616	0.53
Scott, LA (city) Lafayette Parish	586	6.95
New Iberia, LA (city) Iberia Parish	575	1.85
Moss Bluff, LA (cdp) Calcasieu Parish	554	4.74
Houma, LA (city) Terrebonne Parish	520	1.55
Sulphur, LA (city) Calcasieu Parish	486	2.40
Port Neches, TX (city) Jefferson County	476	3.67
Broussard, LA (city) Lafayette Parish	463	5.97
Bayou Cane, LA (cdp) Terrebonne Parish	459	2.31
Central, LA (city) East Baton Rouge Parish	452	1.68
Dallas, TX (city) Dallas County	444	0.04
Eunice, LA (city) St. Landry Parish	439	4.24
Jennings, LA (city) Jefferson Davis Parish	433	4.14
New York, NY (city) Kings County	432	0.01
San Antonio, TX (city) Medina County	426	0.03
Abbeville, LA (city) Vermilion Parish	420	3.44
Galliano, LA (cdp) Lafourche Parish	384	4.85
Colorado Springs, CO (city) El Paso County	381	0.09
Kenner, LA (city) Jefferson Parish	380	0.57
Carencro, LA (city) Lafayette Parish	367	4.99
Groves, TX (city) Jefferson County	359	2.25
Port Arthur, TX (city) Jefferson County	343	0.64
Carlyss, LA (cdp) Calcasieu Parish	341	7.14
Cut Off, LA (cdp) Lafourche Parish	341	6.67
Thibodaux, LA (city) Lafourche Parish	336	2.32
Shreveport, LA (city) Caddo Parish	331	0.17
Orange, TX (city) Orange County	326	1.72
Jacksonville, FL (city) Duval County	305	0.04
Phoenix, AZ (city) Maricopa County	302	0.02
Youngsville, LA (city) Lafayette Parish	289	3.94
Estelle, LA (cdp) Jefferson Parish	283	1.67
Prien, LA (cdp) Calcasieu Parish	277	3.88
Shenandoah, LA (cdp) East Baton Rouge Parish	269	1.47
Old Jefferson, LA (cdp) East Baton Rouge Parish	254	4.00
Crowley, LA (city) Acadia Parish	237	1.77
Tulsa, OK (city) Tulsa County	237	0.06
Kaplan, LA (city) Vermilion Parish	226	4.79
Manhattan, NY (borough) New York County	224	0.01
Alexandria, LA (city) Rapides Parish	223	0.47
Chauvin, LA (cdp) Terrebonne Parish	220	6.83
Fort Worth, TX (city) Tarrant County	219	0.03
San Francisco, CA (city) San Francisco County	219	0.03
Franklin, LA (city) St. Mary Parish	218	2.80
The Woodlands, TX (cdp) Montgomery County	218	0.24
San Diego, CA (city) San Diego County	217	0.02
Raceland, LA (cdp) Lafourche Parish	216	2.02
Prairieville, LA (cdp) Ascension Parish	216	0.83
La Porte, TX (city) Harris County	216	0.65
Vidor, TX (city) Orange County	212	1.99
Lacombe, LA (cdp) St. Tammany Parish	210	2.71
Larose, LA (cdp) Lafourche Parish	209	3.25
Charlotte, NC (city) Mecklenburg County	208	0.03
Morgan City, LA (city) St. Mary Parish	207	1.66
Atascocita, TX (cdp) Harris County	207	0.34
Montgomery, AL (city) Montgomery County	203	0.10
Denver, CO (city) Denver County	202	0.03
Deer Park, TX (city) Harris County	198	0.63
Rayne, LA (city) Acadia Parish	190	2.36
Pearland, TX (city) Brazoria County	188	0.23
Pasadena, TX (city) Harris County	187	0.13
Mobile, AL (city) Mobile County	186	0.10
St. Petersburg, FL (city) Pinellas County	184	0.07
Golden Meadow, LA (town) Lafourche Parish	182	7.04
Lumberton, TX (city) Hardin County	178	1.57
League City, TX (city) Galveston County	176	0.23
Presquille, LA (cdp) Terrebonne Parish	175	13.06
Brooklyn, NY (borough) Kings County	175	0.01
Mathews, LA (cdp) Lafourche Parish	174	7.59
Cedar Park, TX (city) Williamson County	171	0.38
Oklahoma City, OK (city) Oklahoma County	168	0.03
Reserve, LA (cdp) St. John the Baptist Parish	167	1.76
Westwego, LA (city) Jefferson Parish	166	1.88
Central Gardens, TX (cdp) Jefferson County	165	3.36
Galveston, TX (city) Galveston County	163	0.33
Long Beach, CA (city) Los Angeles County	157	0.03
Tucson, AZ (city) Pima County	156	0.03
Los Angeles, CA (city) Los Angeles County	153	<0.01
Bossier City, LA (city) Bossier Parish	152	0.25
Universal City, TX (city) Bexar County	148	0.84
River Ridge, LA (cdp) Jefferson Parish	145	1.08
Longmont, CO (city) Boulder County	145	0.17
Fort Hood, TX (cdp) Bell County	143	0.42
Breaux Bridge, LA (city) St. Martin Parish	142	1.76
Iowa, LA (town) Calcasieu Parish	141	4.85
Catahoula, LA (cdp) St. Martin Parish	139	8.71
Corpus Christi, TX (city) Nueces County	139	0.05
Bakersfield, CA (city) Kern County	139	0.04
Abilene, TX (city) Taylor County	136	0.12
Stillwater, OK (city) Payne County	135	0.30
Bridge City, TX (city) Orange County	134	1.68
Copperas Cove, TX (city) Coryell County	133	0.42
Zachary, LA (city) East Baton Rouge Parish	132	0.92
Portland, OR (city) Multnomah County	132	0.02
Fannett, TX (cdp) Jefferson County	130	4.95
Columbia, SC (city) Richland County	130	0.10
Huntsville, AL (city) Madison County	130	0.07
Orlando, FL (city) Orange County	129	0.06
Laplace, LA (cdp) St. John the Baptist Parish	128	0.41
St. Martinville, LA (city) St. Martin Parish	127	2.02
Livonia, LA (town) Pointe Coupee Parish	125	8.37
Mauriceville, TX (cdp) Orange County	125	4.07
Eagleton Village, TN (cdp) Blount County	122	2.66
Bayou Blue, LA (cdp) Lafourche Parish	120	1.07
Ville Platte, LA (city) Evangeline Parish	119	1.55
Texas City, TX (city) Galveston County	119	0.27
Van Buren, ME (town) Aroostook County	118	4.56
Lake Arthur, LA (town) Jefferson Davis Parish	118	4.24
Lake Jackson, TX (city) Brazoria County	118	0.44
Luling, LA (cdp) St. Charles Parish	117	0.91
Slidell, LA (city) St. Tammany Parish	117	0.43
Berwick, LA (town) St. Mary Parish	116	2.39
Alexandria, VA (ind. city) Alexandria independent city	115	0.09
Chackbay, LA (cdp) Lafourche Parish	109	1.88
Friendswood, TX (city) Galveston County	109	0.31
Westlake, LA (city) Calcasieu Parish	108	2.38
Dartmouth, MA (town) Bristol County	107	0.32
Arlington, TX (city) Tarrant County	106	0.03
Poteau, OK (city) Le Flore County	105	1.25
Thomasville, NC (city) Davidson County	105	0.40
Marrero, LA (cdp) Jefferson Parish	104	0.32
Athens-Clarke County, GA (unified govt) Clarke County	103	0.09
Garland, TX (city) Dallas County	103	0.05
Vinton, LA (town) Calcasieu Parish	102	3.18
Gulfport, MS (city) Harrison County	100	0.15
Welsh, LA (town) Jefferson Davis Parish	99	3.05
Druid Hills, GA (cdp) DeKalb County	99	0.68
Missouri City, TX (city) Fort Bend County	99	0.15
Chicago, IL (city) Cook County	99	<0.01
Longview, TX (city) Gregg County	98	0.12
McKinney, TX (city) Collin County	98	0.08
Waco, TX (city) McLennan County	98	0.08
Biloxi, MS (city) Harrison County	95	0.22
Madawaska, ME (town) Aroostook County	94	2.27
Murfreesboro, TN (city) Rutherford County	94	0.09
Sunrise Manor, NV (cdp) Clark County	93	0.05
Terrytown, LA (cdp) Jefferson Parish	92	0.41
Opelousas, LA (city) St. Landry Parish	90	0.51
Baltimore, MD (city) Baltimore city County	90	0.01
Bayou Gauche, LA (cdp) St. Charles Parish	88	3.44
Madawaska, ME (cdp) Aroostook County	88	2.55
Laguna Beach, FL (cdp) Bay County	88	2.44
Gonzales, LA (city) Ascension Parish	88	0.92

Ancestry

Cajun

Top 150 Places Sorted by Percent of Total Population

Based on all places, regardless of total population

Place	Population	%
Douglassville, TX (town) Cass County	80	22.04
Manley Hot Springs, AK (cdp) Yukon-Koyukuk Census Area	15	20.00
Hester, LA (cdp) St. James Parish	67	16.30
Conway, IA (city) Taylor County	6	15.38
Hayes, LA (cdp) Calcasieu Parish	68	13.36
Presquille, LA (cdp) Terrebonne Parish	175	13.06
Roeville, FL (cdp) Santa Rosa County	63	12.26
Latham, KS (city) Butler County	25	12.02
Tradewinds, TX (cdp) San Patricio County	20	10.31
Winterville, ME (plantation) Aroostook County	14	9.93
Eagle Village, AK (cdp) Southeast Fairbanks Census Area	4	9.76
Morganza, LA (village) Pointe Coupee Parish	59	9.53
Catahoula, LA (cdp) St. Martin Parish	139	8.71
Sylvanite, MT (cdp) Lincoln County	8	8.42
Livonia, LA (town) Pointe Coupee Parish	125	8.37
Fordoche, LA (town) Pointe Coupee Parish	71	8.35
Mathews, LA (cdp) Lafourche Parish	174	7.59
Calverton, VA (cdp) Fauquier County	9	7.44
Barataria, LA (cdp) Jefferson Parish	53	7.17
Carlyss, LA (cdp) Calcasieu Parish	341	7.14
Keachi, LA (town) De Soto Parish	14	7.07
Golden Meadow, LA (town) Lafourche Parish	182	7.04
Scott, LA (city) Lafayette Parish	586	6.95
Chauvin, LA (cdp) Terrebonne Parish	220	6.83
Cut Off, LA (cdp) Lafourche Parish	341	6.67
Joyce, LA (cdp) Winn Parish	25	6.67
State Line, MS (town) Greene County	31	6.58
Lisbon, LA (village) Claiborne Parish	17	5.99
Broussard, LA (city) Lafayette Parish	463	5.97
Grand Isle, ME (town) Aroostook County	31	5.83
Melville, LA (town) St. Landry Parish	64	5.81
Atlanta, LA (village) Winn Parish	7	5.74
Kraemer, LA (cdp) Lafourche Parish	63	5.50
Montegut, LA (cdp) Terrebonne Parish	57	5.28
Turin, GA (town) Coweta County	17	5.14
Carencro, LA (city) Lafayette Parish	367	4.99
Fannett, TX (cdp) Jefferson County	130	4.95
Cooper, ME (town) Washington County	10	4.95
Galliano, LA (cdp) Lafourche Parish	384	4.85
Iowa, LA (town) Calcasieu Parish	141	4.85
Wallagrass, ME (town) Aroostook County	34	4.84
Kaplan, LA (city) Vermilion Parish	226	4.79
Moss Bluff, LA (cdp) Calcasieu Parish	554	4.74
Mineral, WA (cdp) Lewis County	10	4.57
Van Buren, ME (town) Aroostook County	118	4.56
Dulac, LA (cdp) Terrebonne Parish	51	4.43
Lacassine, LA (cdp) Jefferson Davis Parish	19	4.36
Eunice, LA (city) St. Landry Parish	439	4.24
Lake Arthur, LA (town) Jefferson Davis Parish	118	4.24
Raleigh, MS (town) Smith County	67	4.17
Jennings, LA (city) Jefferson Davis Parish	433	4.14
Lydia, LA (cdp) Iberia Parish	37	4.13
Vander, NC (cdp) Cumberland County	41	4.12
Mauriceville, TX (cdp) Orange County	125	4.07
Old Jefferson, LA (cdp) East Baton Rouge Parish	254	4.00
Youngsville, LA (city) Lafayette Parish	289	3.94
Delcambre, LA (town) Vermilion Parish	57	3.93
Woodloch, TX (town) Montgomery County	6	3.92
Gueydan, LA (town) Vermilion Parish	59	3.90
Prien, LA (cdp) Calcasieu Parish	277	3.88
Nederland, TX (city) Jefferson County	668	3.84
Eagle Nest, NM (village) Colfax County	11	3.82
Bevil Oaks, TX (city) Jefferson County	49	3.80
Braden, TN (town) Fayette County	12	3.76
St. Agatha, ME (town) Aroostook County	31	3.72
Port Neches, TX (city) Jefferson County	476	3.67
Jonestown, TX (city) Travis County	75	3.62
Evergreen, LA (town) Avoyelles Parish	12	3.61
Henderson, LA (town) St. Martin Parish	60	3.59
Pearl River, LA (town) St. Tammany Parish	87	3.54
Moline, KS (city) Elk County	13	3.50
Cade, LA (cdp) St. Martin Parish	51	3.48
Patton Village, TX (city) Montgomery County	42	3.45
Frenchville, ME (town) Aroostook County	36	3.45
Abbeville, LA (city) Vermilion Parish	420	3.44
Bayou Gauche, LA (cdp) St. Charles Parish	88	3.44
New Canada, ME (town) Aroostook County	9	3.42
Central Gardens, TX (cdp) Jefferson County	165	3.36
Rose City, TX (city) Orange County	21	3.34
Edom, TX (city) Van Zandt County	12	3.33
Van Buren, ME (cdp) Aroostook County	76	3.32
Rivanna, VA (cdp) Albemarle County	57	3.29
Morse, LA (village) Acadia Parish	23	3.27
Larose, LA (cdp) Lafourche Parish	209	3.25
Devers, TX (city) Liberty County	15	3.23
Erath, LA (town) Vermilion Parish	74	3.21
Vinton, LA (town) Calcasieu Parish	102	3.18
Grand Isle, LA (town) Jefferson Parish	19	3.18
Estherwood, LA (village) Acadia Parish	31	3.15
Lula, MS (town) Coahoma County	9	3.15
Damon, TX (cdp) Brazoria County	10	3.13
Welsh, LA (town) Jefferson Davis Parish	99	3.05
Watson, LA (cdp) Livingston Parish	44	3.05
Lafourche Crossing, LA (cdp) Lafourche Parish	63	3.02
Independence, WI (city) Trempealeau County	37	2.98
Cranberry Isles, ME (town) Hancock County	3	2.97
Cecilia, LA (cdp) St. Martin Parish	61	2.85
Franklin, LA (city) St. Mary Parish	218	2.80
Lafayette, LA (city) Lafayette Parish	3,304	2.78
Sour Lake, TX (city) Hardin County	53	2.76
Taylor Landing, TX (city) Jefferson County	8	2.73
Lacombe, LA (cdp) St. Tammany Parish	210	2.71
Eagleton Village, TN (cdp) Blount County	122	2.66
Branch, LA (cdp) Acadia Parish	15	2.66
Hamlin, ME (town) Aroostook County	8	2.66
Reddell, LA (cdp) Evangeline Parish	16	2.59
Madawaska, ME (cdp) Aroostook County	88	2.55
Square Lake, ME (unorganized territory) Aroostook County	17	2.49
Laguna Beach, FL (cdp) Bay County	88	2.44
Sunset, LA (town) St. Landry Parish	68	2.43
Sulphur, LA (city) Calcasieu Parish	486	2.40
Berwick, LA (town) St. Mary Parish	116	2.39
Westlake, LA (city) Calcasieu Parish	108	2.38
Woodworth, LA (town) Rapides Parish	40	2.37
Rayne, LA (city) Acadia Parish	190	2.36
Martindale, TX (city) Caldwell County	32	2.36
Paincourtville, LA (cdp) Assumption Parish	35	2.34
Jamestown, LA (village) Bienville Parish	3	2.33
Thibodaux, LA (city) Lafourche Parish	336	2.32
Bayou Cane, LA (cdp) Terrebonne Parish	459	2.31
Baldwin, LA (town) St. Mary Parish	57	2.30
Hull, TX (cdp) Liberty County	10	2.30
Sylvania, PA (township) Potter County	2	2.30
Randolph AFB, TX (cdp) Bexar County	24	2.29
Madawaska, ME (town) Aroostook County	94	2.27
Mildred, TX (town) Navarro County	9	2.26
Groves, TX (city) Jefferson County	359	2.25
Hornbeck, LA (town) Vernon Parish	14	2.25
Matoaca, VA (cdp) Chesterfield County	54	2.24
Bayou Goula, LA (cdp) Iberville Parish	7	2.23
Lithopolis, OH (village) Fairfield County	14	2.22
Sky Valley, CA (cdp) Riverside County	40	2.18
Duson, LA (town) Lafayette Parish	33	2.13
Faxon, PA (cdp) Lycoming County	31	2.08
Raceland, LA (cdp) Lafourche Parish	216	2.02
St. Martinville, LA (city) St. Martin Parish	127	2.02
Cankton, LA (village) St. Landry Parish	11	2.00
Vidor, TX (city) Orange County	212	1.99
Pinewood Estates, TX (cdp) Hardin County	36	1.99
Pinehurst, TX (city) Orange County	40	1.96
Spearsville, LA (village) Union Parish	3	1.96
Holiday Island, AR (cdp) Carroll County	46	1.95
Labadieville, LA (cdp) Assumption Parish	32	1.92
Rose Hill Acres, TX (city) Hardin County	11	1.91
Westwego, LA (city) Jefferson Parish	166	1.88
Chackbay, LA (cdp) Lafourche Parish	109	1.88
Young, AZ (cdp) Gila County	7	1.86
New Iberia, LA (city) Iberia Parish	575	1.85
Church Point, LA (town) Acadia Parish	85	1.85
Fort Kent, ME (cdp) Aroostook County	54	1.85

Please refer to the Explanation of Data in the front of the book for more detailed information.

Ancestry

Cajun

Top 150 Places Sorted by Percent of Total Population

Based on places with total population of 7,500 or more

Place	Population	%
Scott, LA (city) Lafayette Parish	586	6.95
Broussard, LA (city) Lafayette Parish	463	5.97
Galliano, LA (cdp) Lafourche Parish	384	4.85
Moss Bluff, LA (cdp) Calcasieu Parish	554	4.74
Eunice, LA (city) St. Landry Parish	439	4.24
Jennings, LA (city) Jefferson Davis Parish	433	4.14
Nederland, TX (city) Jefferson County	668	3.84
Port Neches, TX (city) Jefferson County	476	3.67
Abbeville, LA (city) Vermilion Parish	420	3.44
Franklin, LA (city) St. Mary Parish	218	2.80
Lafayette, LA (city) Lafayette Parish	3,304	2.78
Lacombe, LA (cdp) St. Tammany Parish	210	2.71
Sulphur, LA (city) Calcasieu Parish	486	2.40
Rayne, LA (city) Acadia Parish	190	2.36
Thibodaux, LA (city) Lafourche Parish	336	2.32
Bayou Cane, LA (cdp) Terrebonne Parish	459	2.31
Groves, TX (city) Jefferson County	359	2.25
Raceland, LA (cdp) Lafourche Parish	216	2.02
Vidor, TX (city) Orange County	212	1.99
Westwego, LA (city) Jefferson Parish	166	1.88
New Iberia, LA (city) Iberia Parish	575	1.85
Crowley, LA (city) Acadia Parish	237	1.77
Reserve, LA (cdp) St. John the Baptist Parish	167	1.76
Breaux Bridge, LA (city) St. Martin Parish	142	1.76
Orange, TX (city) Orange County	326	1.72
Central, LA (city) East Baton Rouge Parish	452	1.68
Bridge City, TX (city) Orange County	134	1.68
Estelle, LA (cdp) Jefferson Parish	283	1.67
Morgan City, LA (city) St. Mary Parish	207	1.66
Lumberton, TX (city) Hardin County	178	1.57
Houma, LA (city) Terrebonne Parish	520	1.55
Ville Platte, LA (city) Evangeline Parish	119	1.55
Lake Charles, LA (city) Calcasieu Parish	1,050	1.47
Shenandoah, LA (cdp) East Baton Rouge Parish	269	1.47
Poteau, OK (city) Le Flore County	105	1.25
River Ridge, LA (cdp) Jefferson Parish	145	1.08
Bayou Blue, LA (cdp) Lafourche Parish	120	1.07
Zachary, LA (city) East Baton Rouge Parish	132	0.92
Gonzales, LA (city) Ascension Parish	88	0.92
Luling, LA (cdp) St. Charles Parish	117	0.91
Universal City, TX (city) Bexar County	148	0.84
Prairieville, LA (cdp) Ascension Parish	216	0.83
Lawrenceburg, TN (city) Lawrence County	87	0.83
Branson, MO (city) Taney County	78	0.79
Destrehan, LA (cdp) St. Charles Parish	84	0.74
Harahan, LA (city) Jefferson Parish	68	0.73
Claiborne, LA (cdp) Ouachita Parish	81	0.70
Baton Rouge, LA (city) East Baton Rouge Parish	1,586	0.69
Jasper, TX (city) Jasper County	52	0.69
Druid Hills, GA (cdp) DeKalb County	99	0.68
Denham Springs, LA (city) Livingston Parish	69	0.68
La Porte, TX (city) Harris County	216	0.65
Oak Hill, WV (city) Fayette County	50	0.65
Port Arthur, TX (city) Jefferson County	343	0.64
Kirby, TX (city) Bexar County	52	0.64
Deer Park, TX (city) Harris County	198	0.63
Tecumseh, MI (city) Lenawee County	52	0.60
Elgin, TX (city) Bastrop County	49	0.60
Haiku-Pauwela, HI (cdp) Maui County	48	0.60
Pleasant Hill, MO (city) Cass County	46	0.59
Pineville, LA (city) Rapides Parish	84	0.58
Kenner, LA (city) Jefferson Parish	380	0.57
Mandeville, LA (city) St. Tammany Parish	65	0.57
West Point, NY (cdp) Orange County	54	0.57
Helena Valley West Central, MT (cdp) Lewis and Clark County	47	0.57
Kinross, MI (charter township) Chippewa County	45	0.56
Camp Pendleton South, CA (cdp) San Diego County	74	0.55
Beaumont, TX (city) Jefferson County	616	0.53
Catskill, NY (town) Greene County	62	0.52
Opelousas, LA (city) St. Landry Parish	90	0.51
Caribou, ME (city) Aroostook County	40	0.49
Metairie, LA (cdp) Jefferson Parish	651	0.48
Cornelius, OR (city) Washington County	55	0.48
Alexandria, LA (city) Rapides Parish	223	0.47
Andover, KS (city) Butler County	52	0.47
Rendon, TX (cdp) Tarrant County	57	0.46
Webster, TX (city) Harris County	45	0.46
Bridge City, LA (cdp) Jefferson Parish	42	0.46
Gretna, LA (city) Jefferson Parish	80	0.45
Fort Leonard Wood, MO (cdp) Pulaski County	69	0.45
Covington, GA (city) Newton County	60	0.45
Chalmette, LA (cdp) St. Bernard Parish	56	0.45
Lake Jackson, TX (city) Brazoria County	118	0.44
Slidell, LA (city) St. Tammany Parish	117	0.43
Highlands, NY (town) Orange County	54	0.43
Robinson, TX (city) McLennan County	43	0.43
Fort Hood, TX (cdp) Bell County	143	0.42
Copperas Cove, TX (city) Coryell County	133	0.42
Laplace, LA (cdp) St. John the Baptist Parish	128	0.41
Terrytown, LA (cdp) Jefferson Parish	92	0.41
Oakdale, LA (city) Allen Parish	32	0.41
Thomasville, NC (city) Davidson County	105	0.40
Kingsland, GA (city) Camden County	60	0.40
Greatwood, TX (cdp) Fort Bend County	47	0.40
Pecan Grove, TX (cdp) Fort Bend County	61	0.39
Cedar Park, TX (city) Williamson County	171	0.38
Covington, LA (city) St. Tammany Parish	34	0.38
Hammond, LA (city) Tangipahoa Parish	73	0.37
Belle Chasse, LA (cdp) Plaquemines Parish	55	0.37
West Monroe, LA (city) Ouachita Parish	49	0.37
Oak Hills Place, LA (cdp) East Baton Rouge Parish	29	0.36
Timberwood Park, TX (cdp) Bexar County	41	0.35
Arlington, TN (town) Shelby County	35	0.35
Wells, ME (town) York County	34	0.35
Atascocita, TX (cdp) Harris County	207	0.34
Millington, TN (city) Shelby County	35	0.34
Maysville, KY (city) Mason County	31	0.34
Vail, AZ (cdp) Pima County	31	0.34
Galveston, TX (city) Galveston County	163	0.33
Midway, FL (cdp) Santa Rosa County	51	0.33
Dartmouth, MA (town) Bristol County	107	0.32
Marrero, LA (cdp) Jefferson Parish	104	0.32
Ruston, LA (city) Lincoln Parish	69	0.32
Ocean Springs, MS (city) Jackson County	56	0.32
Friendswood, TX (city) Galveston County	109	0.31
Milan, TN (city) Gibson County	24	0.31
Stillwater, OK (city) Payne County	135	0.30
Stuttgart, AR (city) Arkansas County	28	0.30
DeRidder, LA (city) Beauregard Parish	30	0.29
Gardere, LA (cdp) East Baton Rouge Parish	30	0.29
Highland Park, TX (town) Dallas County	25	0.29
Alvin, TX (city) Brazoria County	68	0.28
Daphne, AL (city) Baldwin County	59	0.28
Dickinson, TX (city) Galveston County	51	0.28
Saraland, AL (city) Mobile County	37	0.28
Sienna Plantation, TX (cdp) Fort Bend County	35	0.28
Loyalsock, PA (township) Lycoming County	31	0.28
Cleveland, TX (city) Liberty County	22	0.28
North Star, DE (cdp) New Castle County	22	0.28
Texas City, TX (city) Galveston County	119	0.27
Des Moines, WA (city) King County	80	0.27
Belton, MO (city) Cass County	62	0.27
Coralville, IA (city) Johnson County	49	0.27
Long Beach, MS (city) Harrison County	40	0.27
Warrington, FL (cdp) Escambia County	40	0.27
Kyle, TX (city) Hays County	63	0.26
Brownwood, TX (city) Brown County	51	0.26
Jefferson, LA (cdp) Jefferson Parish	31	0.26
Keokuk, IA (city) Lee County	28	0.26
Vashon, WA (cdp) King County	26	0.26
Bossier City, LA (city) Bossier Parish	152	0.25
Diamondhead, MS (cdp) Hancock County	20	0.25
Lackland AFB, TX (cdp) Bexar County	19	0.25
New Orleans, LA (city) Orleans Parish	712	0.24
The Woodlands, TX (cdp) Montgomery County	218	0.24
Clarksville, IN (town) Clark County	55	0.24
Perry, GA (city) Houston County	32	0.24
Santa Fe, TX (city) Galveston County	29	0.24
Cheval, FL (cdp) Hillsborough County	25	0.24
Fort Mill, SC (town) York County	25	0.24

Please refer to the Explanation of Data in the front of the book for more detailed information.

Ancestry

Canadian

U.S. and 50 States Sorted by Population and Percent of Total Population

Place	Population	%
United States	**716,067**	**0.24**
California	90,905	0.25
Florida	71,240	0.38
Massachusetts	59,793	0.92
Michigan	50,490	0.51
New York	50,059	0.26
Texas	31,732	0.13
Washington	31,516	0.48
Arizona	20,054	0.32
Connecticut	18,069	0.51
New Hampshire	17,068	1.30
Ohio	15,625	0.14
Illinois	15,620	0.12
Maine	15,595	1.17
North Carolina	15,051	0.16
Pennsylvania	14,976	0.12
Virginia	14,555	0.19
Oregon	14,475	0.38
New Jersey	12,750	0.15
Georgia	12,702	0.13
Colorado	12,644	0.26
Utah	9,976	0.38
Indiana	9,085	0.14
Nevada	8,634	0.33
Maryland	8,086	0.14
Minnesota	7,405	0.14
Wisconsin	6,962	0.12
Missouri	6,463	0.11
Vermont	6,324	1.01
Tennessee	6,232	0.10
South Carolina	6,175	0.14
Louisiana	5,310	0.12
Idaho	5,158	0.34
Rhode Island	5,044	0.48
Oklahoma	3,818	0.10
Alabama	3,696	0.08
Kentucky	3,661	0.09
Kansas	3,517	0.13
Iowa	3,406	0.11
New Mexico	2,667	0.13
Alaska	2,616	0.38
Montana	2,526	0.26
Arkansas	2,252	0.08
Hawaii	2,006	0.15
Delaware	1,825	0.21
Nebraska	1,785	0.10
Mississippi	1,725	0.06
North Dakota	1,242	0.19
West Virginia	1,179	0.06
District of Columbia	972	0.17
Wyoming	857	0.16
South Dakota	544	0.07

Place	Population	%
New Hampshire	17,068	1.30
Maine	15,595	1.17
Vermont	6,324	1.01
Massachusetts	59,793	0.92
Michigan	50,490	0.51
Connecticut	18,069	0.51
Washington	31,516	0.48
Rhode Island	5,044	0.48
Florida	71,240	0.38
Oregon	14,475	0.38
Utah	9,976	0.38
Alaska	2,616	0.38
Idaho	5,158	0.34
Nevada	8,634	0.33
Arizona	20,054	0.32
New York	50,059	0.26
Colorado	12,644	0.26
Montana	2,526	0.26
California	90,905	0.25
United States	**716,067**	**0.24**
Delaware	1,825	0.21
Virginia	14,555	0.19
North Dakota	1,242	0.19
District of Columbia	972	0.17
North Carolina	15,051	0.16
Wyoming	857	0.16
New Jersey	12,750	0.15
Hawaii	2,006	0.15
Ohio	15,625	0.14
Indiana	9,085	0.14
Maryland	8,086	0.14
Minnesota	7,405	0.14
South Carolina	6,175	0.14
Texas	31,732	0.13
Georgia	12,702	0.13
Kansas	3,517	0.13
New Mexico	2,667	0.13
Illinois	15,620	0.12
Pennsylvania	14,976	0.12
Wisconsin	6,962	0.12
Louisiana	5,310	0.12
Missouri	6,463	0.11
Iowa	3,406	0.11
Tennessee	6,232	0.10
Oklahoma	3,818	0.10
Nebraska	1,785	0.10
Kentucky	3,661	0.09
Alabama	3,696	0.08
Arkansas	2,252	0.08
South Dakota	544	0.07
Mississippi	1,725	0.06
West Virginia	1,179	0.06

Please refer to the Explanation of Data in the front of the book for more detailed information.

Ancestry

Canadian

Top 150 Places Sorted by Population

Based on all places, regardless of total population

Place	Population	%
New York, NY (city) Kings County	10,989	0.14
Los Angeles, CA (city) Los Angeles County	7,817	0.21
Manhattan, NY (borough) New York County	5,646	0.36
San Diego, CA (city) San Diego County	3,425	0.27
Seattle, WA (city) King County	3,240	0.54
Brooklyn, NY (borough) Kings County	3,116	0.13
Phoenix, AZ (city) Maricopa County	3,054	0.21
Boston, MA (city) Suffolk County	2,864	0.48
Houston, TX (city) Harris County	2,415	0.12
Mesa, AZ (city) Maricopa County	2,400	0.55
Chicago, IL (city) Cook County	2,179	0.08
Portland, OR (city) Multnomah County	2,161	0.38
San Jose, CA (city) Santa Clara County	1,796	0.19
Austin, TX (city) Travis County	1,759	0.23
Scottsdale, AZ (city) Maricopa County	1,742	0.80
San Francisco, CA (city) San Francisco County	1,697	0.22
Hollywood, FL (city) Broward County	1,525	1.08
Charlotte, NC (city) Mecklenburg County	1,520	0.22
Manchester, NH (city) Hillsborough County	1,399	1.27
Indianapolis, IN (city) Marion County	1,392	0.17
Colorado Springs, CO (city) El Paso County	1,389	0.34
Las Vegas, NV (city) Clark County	1,377	0.24
Lynn, MA (city) Essex County	1,312	1.46
Queens, NY (borough) Queens County	1,308	0.06
Nashua, NH (city) Hillsborough County	1,290	1.48
San Antonio, TX (city) Medina County	1,260	0.10
Henderson, NV (city) Clark County	1,230	0.49
Virginia Beach, VA (ind. city) Virginia Beach independent city	1,216	0.28
Tampa, FL (city) Hillsborough County	1,176	0.35
Philadelphia, PA (city) Philadelphia County	1,094	0.07
Irvine, CA (city) Orange County	1,087	0.55
Hempstead, NY (town) Nassau County	1,084	0.14
Anchorage, AK (municipality) Anchorage Municipality	1,067	0.38
Brockton, MA (city) Plymouth County	1,046	1.11
Denver, CO (city) Denver County	1,045	0.18
Largo, FL (city) Pinellas County	1,037	1.34
Fort Worth, TX (city) Tarrant County	1,026	0.15
Quincy, MA (city) Norfolk County	1,024	1.13
Columbus, OH (city) Franklin County	1,023	0.13
Jacksonville, FL (city) Duval County	1,013	0.12
Tucson, AZ (city) Pima County	1,007	0.19
Brookhaven, NY (town) Suffolk County	999	0.21
Washington, DC (city) District of Columbia	972	0.17
St. Petersburg, FL (city) Pinellas County	968	0.39
Reno, NV (city) Washoe County	959	0.43
Fort Lauderdale, FL (city) Broward County	952	0.57
Waltham, MA (city) Middlesex County	908	1.52
Bristol, CT (city/town) Hartford County	905	1.50
Albuquerque, NM (city) Bernalillo County	894	0.17
Plano, TX (city) Collin County	891	0.35
Arlington, MA (cdp/town) Middlesex County	889	2.10
Long Beach, CA (city) Los Angeles County	887	0.19
Haverhill, MA (city) Essex County	885	1.47
Livonia, MI (city) Wayne County	885	0.90
Dallas, TX (city) Dallas County	883	0.07
Fresno, CA (city) Fresno County	874	0.18
Coral Springs, FL (city) Broward County	849	0.70
Lowell, MA (city) Middlesex County	840	0.80
Chandler, AZ (city) Maricopa County	834	0.36
The Woodlands, TX (cdp) Montgomery County	826	0.90
Durham, NC (city) Durham County	821	0.37
Bellingham, WA (city) Whatcom County	799	1.01
Huntington Beach, CA (city) Orange County	799	0.42
Weymouth Town, MA (city) Norfolk County	785	1.47
Minneapolis, MN (city) Hennepin County	784	0.21
Torrance, CA (city) Los Angeles County	769	0.53
Westland, MI (city) Wayne County	768	0.91
Tulsa, OK (city) Tulsa County	761	0.20
Deerfield Beach, FL (city) Broward County	759	1.01
Anaheim, CA (city) Orange County	756	0.23
Port St. Lucie, FL (city) St. Lucie County	751	0.48
Huntington, NY (town) Suffolk County	743	0.37
Detroit, MI (city) Wayne County	743	0.10
Raleigh, NC (city) Wake County	740	0.19
Sunnyvale, CA (city) Santa Clara County	738	0.54
Naperville, IL (city) DuPage County	734	0.52
Rochester Hills, MI (city) Oakland County	733	1.04
Somerville, MA (city) Middlesex County	731	0.97
Spokane, WA (city) Spokane County	730	0.35
Lewiston, ME (city) Androscoggin County	725	1.98
Thousand Oaks, CA (city) Ventura County	725	0.58
St. Clair Shores, MI (city) Macomb County	716	1.18
Nashville-Davidson, TN (metro govt) Davidson County	711	0.12
Billerica, MA (town) Middlesex County	704	1.78
Orlando, FL (city) Orange County	702	0.30
Salt Lake City, UT (city) Salt Lake County	689	0.37
Taunton, MA (city) Bristol County	688	1.23
Spring Valley, NV (cdp) Clark County	687	0.40
Fort Wayne, IN (city) Allen County	681	0.27
Ramapo, NY (town) Rockland County	680	0.55
Boise City, ID (city) Ada County	678	0.33
Clearwater, FL (city) Pinellas County	671	0.62
Sammamish, WA (city) King County	662	1.53
Vancouver, WA (city) Clark County	656	0.41
Braintree Town, MA (city) Norfolk County	653	1.86
Pompano Beach, FL (city) Broward County	651	0.65
Grand Rapids, MI (city) Kent County	649	0.34
Highlands Ranch, CO (cdp) Douglas County	644	0.68
Palm Desert, CA (city) Riverside County	641	1.32
Ann Arbor, MI (city) Washtenaw County	638	0.55
Newton, MA (city) Middlesex County	636	0.76
Warren, MI (city) Macomb County	635	0.47
Peoria, AZ (city) Yavapai County	635	0.43
Sacramento, CA (city) Sacramento County	634	0.14
Lancaster, CA (city) Los Angeles County	631	0.42
Medford, MA (city) Middlesex County	625	1.13
Waterford, MI (charter township) Oakland County	625	0.87
Riverside, CA (city) Riverside County	620	0.21
Woburn, MA (city) Middlesex County	615	1.64
Gilbert, AZ (town) Maricopa County	614	0.31
Leominster, MA (city) Worcester County	612	1.49
Clinton, MI (charter township) Macomb County	612	0.63
West Bloomfield, MI (charter township) Oakland County	611	0.94
West Palm Beach, FL (city) Palm Beach County	609	0.62
Temecula, CA (city) Riverside County	608	0.63
Bellevue, WA (city) King County	608	0.51
Sterling Heights, MI (city) Macomb County	604	0.47
Pembroke Pines, FL (city) Broward County	602	0.40
League City, TX (city) Galveston County	599	0.78
Bakersfield, CA (city) Kern County	598	0.18
Shelby, MI (charter township) Macomb County	597	0.82
Orem, UT (city) Utah County	594	0.68
Cambridge, MA (city) Middlesex County	593	0.57
Santa Monica, CA (city) Los Angeles County	592	0.67
Eugene, OR (city) Lane County	591	0.39
Surprise, AZ (city) Maricopa County	589	0.57
Amherst, NY (town) Erie County	589	0.49
Derry, NH (town) Rockingham County	583	1.74
Babylon, NY (town) Suffolk County	581	0.27
Fitchburg, MA (city) Worcester County	578	1.44
Newport News, VA (ind. city) Newport News independent city	574	0.32
Canton, MI (charter township) Wayne County	572	0.65
Macomb, MI (township) Macomb County	571	0.76
Simi Valley, CA (city) Ventura County	571	0.47
Bedford, NH (town) Hillsborough County	564	2.71
Royal Oak, MI (city) Oakland County	559	0.97
Mission Viejo, CA (city) Orange County	559	0.60
Tacoma, WA (city) Pierce County	558	0.28
Buffalo, NY (city) Erie County	558	0.21
Aurora, CO (city) Arapahoe County	558	0.18
Oakland, CA (city) Alameda County	558	0.14
Plymouth, MA (town) Plymouth County	555	1.00
Salem, OR (city) Marion County	554	0.36
Atlanta, GA (city) Fulton County	552	0.13
Rochester, NY (city) Monroe County	550	0.26
Staten Island, NY (borough) Richmond County	544	0.12
Salem, NH (town) Rockingham County	543	1.88
Boca Raton, FL (city) Palm Beach County	542	0.64
Santa Clarita, CA (city) Los Angeles County	540	0.31
Novato, CA (city) Marin County	539	1.07

Please refer to the Explanation of Data in the front of the book for more detailed information.

Ancestry

Canadian

Top 150 Places Sorted by Percent of Total Population

Based on all places, regardless of total population

Place	Population	%
Hidden Lake, CO (cdp) Boulder County	15	35.71
East Verde Estates, AZ (cdp) Gila County	20	33.33
Danville, WA (cdp) Ferry County	11	32.35
Seconsett Island, MA (cdp) Barnstable County	8	32.00
Corning, MO (town) Holt County	5	29.41
Charlos Heights, MT (cdp) Ravalli County	22	25.88
Suissevale, NH (cdp) Carroll County	23	25.84
North Franklin, ME (unorganized territory) Franklin County	21	24.14
Pease, MN (city) Mille Lacs County	30	21.28
Clam Lake, WI (cdp) Ashland County	14	20.90
Round Valley, AZ (cdp) Gila County	31	20.67
Dayton, MT (cdp) Lake County	11	20.37
Donald, WA (cdp) Yakima County	36	20.11
Fair Oaks, OR (cdp) Douglas County	49	19.44
Fishers Landing, NY (cdp) Jefferson County	10	18.87
Oto, IA (city) Woodbury County	20	18.69
Southside Chesconessex, VA (cdp) Accomack County	19	18.10
Prescott, MI (village) Ogemaw County	37	17.62
Rochester, VT (cdp) Windsor County	43	17.06
Northeast Somerset, ME (unorganized territory) Somerset County	78	16.74
Negley, OH (cdp) Columbiana County	40	16.74
Gillett Grove, IA (city) Clay County	7	15.91
Butterfield, MN (township) Watonwan County	40	14.87
Vanceboro, ME (town) Washington County	19	14.73
Leggett, CA (cdp) Mendocino County	10	14.71
Natural Bridge, NY (cdp) Jefferson County	58	14.36
La Fargeville, NY (cdp) Jefferson County	99	14.14
Anchor Bay, CA (cdp) Mendocino County	42	13.17
Crisman, CO (cdp) Boulder County	16	12.90
Fenwood, WI (village) Marathon County	30	12.50
Cyr, ME (plantation) Aroostook County	12	12.37
Nile, WA (cdp) Yakima County	18	12.24
Myhre, MN (township) Lake of the Woods County	24	12.12
Northwest Stanwood, WA (cdp) Snohomish County	9	11.11
Turtle River, MN (city) Beltrami County	3	11.11
Huntsville, OH (village) Logan County	44	11.08
Buffalo, IN (cdp) White County	74	10.72
Greenville, NH (cdp) Hillsborough County	128	9.88
North Walpole, NH (cdp) Cheshire County	119	9.86
Libby, MN (township) Aitkin County	3	9.38
Coral, PA (cdp) Indiana County	29	9.32
Albion, ID (city) Cassia County	29	9.29
Great Pond, ME (town) Hancock County	2	9.09
Plymouth, UT (town) Box Elder County	30	8.85
Simpson, IL (village) Johnson County	2	8.70
Buck Creek, IN (cdp) Tippecanoe County	30	8.57
Mayo, SC (cdp) Spartanburg County	127	8.43
Haynesville, ME (town) Aroostook County	12	8.33
Cold Bay, AK (city) Aleutians East Borough	3	8.33
West Forks, ME (plantation) Somerset County	2	8.33
Pleasant Ridge, ME (plantation) Somerset County	8	8.25
Kingston, UT (town) Piute County	9	8.11
Ithaca, NE (village) Saunders County	10	8.06
Grass Valley, NV (cdp) Pershing County	63	8.01
Farmington, PA (cdp) Fayette County	56	7.97
Clay Springs, AZ (cdp) Navajo County	53	7.85
Cumminsville, NY (cdp) Livingston County	9	7.76
Maple Grove, MI (cdp) Benzie County	8	7.69
Danforth, ME (town) Washington County	49	7.67
Shadow Lake, WA (cdp) King County	152	7.65
Pleasanton, NM (cdp) Catron County	14	7.57
Perry, ME (town) Washington County	70	7.42
Nelsonville, WI (village) Portage County	17	7.39
Donnybrook, ND (city) Ward County	7	7.37
Meddybemps, ME (town) Washington County	10	7.35
Central Aroostook, ME (unorganized territory) Aroostook County	8	7.34
Codyville, ME (plantation) Washington County	4	7.27
New Limerick, ME (town) Aroostook County	39	7.16
Lake View, ME (plantation) Piscataquis County	7	7.00
East Valley, MN (township) Marshall County	3	6.98
Fern Forest, HI (cdp) Hawaii County	45	6.94
Caswell, ME (town) Aroostook County	23	6.76
Eagleville, PA (cdp) Centre County	16	6.72
Alburg, VT (village) Grand Isle County	40	6.67
Moody AFB, GA (cdp) Lowndes County	72	6.62
Wedgewood, MI (cdp) Wexford County	14	6.45
Ferdinand, VT (town) Essex County	2	6.45
Dover, MA (cdp) Norfolk County	154	6.44
Crawford, ME (town) Washington County	7	6.42
Fleming, CO (town) Logan County	32	6.39
East Central Penobscot, ME (unorganized territory) Penobscot County	16	6.30
Popponesset, MA (cdp) Barnstable County	12	6.25
Amherst, ME (town) Hancock County	15	6.20
Coplin, ME (plantation) Franklin County	6	6.19
Orleans, NY (town) Jefferson County	164	6.09
Red Butte, WY (cdp) Natrona County	37	6.09
Jay, ME (town) Franklin County	297	6.07
Willimantic, ME (town) Piscataquis County	8	6.06
Masthope, PA (cdp) Pike County	30	5.94
Kiester, MN (township) Faribault County	18	5.88
Copalis Beach, WA (cdp) Grays Harbor County	15	5.88
Epping, ND (city) Williams County	3	5.88
Chebeague Island, ME (town) Cumberland County	14	5.83
Manistique, MI (city) Schoolcraft County	190	5.82
Yankee Lake, OH (village) Trumbull County	4	5.80
Netarts, OR (cdp) Tillamook County	43	5.70
Terminous, CA (cdp) San Joaquin County	23	5.62
Greenville, NH (town) Hillsborough County	137	5.61
Milton, VT (cdp) Chittenden County	108	5.61
Littleton Common, MA (cdp) Middlesex County	161	5.57
St. John, ME (plantation) Aroostook County	15	5.56
Highlands, NJ (borough) Monmouth County	281	5.55
Chateaugay, NY (village) Franklin County	31	5.54
Birdsall, NY (town) Allegany County	17	5.54
Walpole, NH (town) Cheshire County	208	5.53
Alburg, VT (town) Grand Isle County	97	5.53
Stannard, VT (town) Caledonia County	13	5.53
Grafton, VT (town) Windham County	27	5.51
Bradley, ME (town) Penobscot County	78	5.49
Weston, ME (town) Aroostook County	9	5.49
Rosalia, WA (town) Whitman County	37	5.47
Wheatland, MI (township) Sanilac County	24	5.47
Greenhorn, CA (cdp) Plumas County	11	5.42
Belt, MT (town) Cascade County	37	5.41
Garden Prairie, IL (village) Boone County	10	5.41
Canaan, VT (town) Essex County	62	5.38
South Hills, MT (cdp) Jefferson County	12	5.36
Holland, VT (town) Orleans County	38	5.35
Perkinsville, VT (village) Windsor County	7	5.34
Upton, ME (town) Oxford County	4	5.33
Kennebunkport, ME (cdp) York County	59	5.32
Providence, MN (township) Lac qui Parle County	6	5.31
Apple Valley, UT (town) Washington County	33	5.30
Michiana, MI (village) Berrien County	8	5.30
Cambridge, ME (town) Somerset County	23	5.29
South Barre, VT (cdp) Washington County	53	5.27
Goldfield, NV (cdp) Esmeralda County	13	5.24
Marion, MT (cdp) Flathead County	25	5.23
Cave Junction, OR (city) Josephine County	89	5.22
Bear Creek, WI (town) Waupaca County	48	5.20
Beddington, ME (town) Washington County	4	5.19
Ucon, ID (city) Bonneville County	65	5.15
Waddington, NY (village) St. Lawrence County	37	5.13
Richville, NY (village) St. Lawrence County	15	5.12
Whitestone, AK (cdp) Southeast Fairbanks Census Area	8	5.10
Haverhill, NH (town) Grafton County	238	5.09
Machias, NY (cdp) Cattaraugus County	37	5.08
Sterling, UT (town) Sanpete County	16	5.06
Plainfield, VT (cdp) Washington County	15	5.05
Gordon, WI (town) Ashland County	14	5.05
St. Anne, IL (village) Kankakee County	63	5.04
Whiting, VT (town) Addison County	24	5.04
Paradise Park, CA (cdp) Santa Cruz County	23	5.04
Milburn, OK (town) Johnston County	19	5.04
Garner, AR (town) White County	11	5.02
Easton, ME (town) Aroostook County	56	4.99
Concord, GA (city) Pike County	18	4.97
Cactus Flats, AZ (cdp) Graham County	75	4.95
Rhodhiss, NC (town) Burke County	63	4.95
Pinedale, AZ (cdp) Navajo County	11	4.93

Please refer to the Explanation of Data in the front of the book for more detailed information.

Ancestry

Canadian

Top 150 Places Sorted by Percent of Total Population

Based on places with total population of 7,500 or more

Place	Population	%
Mansfield Center, MA (cdp) Bristol County	285	3.75
Fort Gratiot, MI (charter township) St. Clair County	341	3.04
Milton, VT (town) Chittenden County	294	2.88
Glens Falls North, NY (cdp) Warren County	245	2.80
Putnam, CT (town) Windham County	263	2.75
Bedford, NH (town) Hillsborough County	564	2.71
Monsey, NY (cdp) Rockland County	404	2.68
Weare, NH (town) Hillsborough County	224	2.59
Citrus Springs, FL (cdp) Citrus County	198	2.59
Littleton, MA (town) Middlesex County	224	2.58
Knik-Fairview, AK (cdp) Matanuska-Susitna Borough	313	2.56
Topsham, ME (town) Sagadahoc County	221	2.47
Raynham, MA (town) Bristol County	322	2.46
Rehoboth, MA (town) Bristol County	277	2.44
Waterboro, ME (town) York County	183	2.44
South Lyon, MI (city) Oakland County	261	2.36
Claremont, NH (city) Sullivan County	317	2.35
Wilmington, MA (cdp/town) Middlesex County	505	2.31
Auburn, ME (city) Androscoggin County	518	2.23
Lakewood Park, FL (cdp) St. Lucie County	264	2.23
Grosse Ile, MI (township) Wayne County	234	2.23
Bow, NH (town) Merrimack County	167	2.21
Rockland, MA (town) Plymouth County	386	2.20
Paradise Valley, AZ (town) Maricopa County	288	2.18
Goffstown, NH (town) Hillsborough County	378	2.14
Arlington, MA (cdp/town) Middlesex County	889	2.10
Clawson, MI (city) Oakland County	252	2.10
Lancaster, MA (town) Worcester County	163	2.10
Falmouth, ME (town) Cumberland County	227	2.05
Presque Isle, ME (city) Aroostook County	198	2.05
Avon Park, FL (city) Highlands County	184	2.05
Bellingham, MA (town) Norfolk County	325	2.03
Lynden, WA (city) Whatcom County	235	2.03
Holualoa, HI (cdp) Hawaii County	195	2.01
Hampstead, NH (town) Rockingham County	172	2.01
Londonderry, NH (town) Rockingham County	481	1.99
Easthampton Town, MA (city) Hampshire County	319	1.99
Lewiston, ME (city) Androscoggin County	725	1.98
Old Orchard Beach, ME (cdp/town) York County	171	1.95
Pembroke, MA (town) Plymouth County	342	1.94
Grafton, MA (town) Worcester County	336	1.94
Hooksett, NH (town) Merrimack County	258	1.94
Old Lyme, CT (town) New London County	146	1.92
Berlin, NH (city) Coos County	195	1.91
Hazel Park, MI (city) Oakland County	320	1.90
Lemoore Station, CA (cdp) Kings County	150	1.90
Salem, NH (town) Rockingham County	543	1.88
Braintree Town, MA (city) Norfolk County	653	1.86
Newfane, NY (town) Niagara County	178	1.85
Half Moon, NC (cdp) Onslow County	150	1.84
Marshfield, MA (town) Plymouth County	458	1.83
DeBary, FL (city) Volusia County	349	1.83
Sandy, OR (city) Clackamas County	161	1.82
Camas, WA (city) Clark County	333	1.81
Newton, NJ (town) Sussex County	146	1.80
Billerica, MA (town) Middlesex County	704	1.78
Holliston, MA (town) Middlesex County	236	1.76
Massena, NY (village) St. Lawrence County	198	1.76
Derry, NH (town) Rockingham County	583	1.74
Bridgewater, MA (town) Plymouth County	458	1.74
Melrose, MA (city) Middlesex County	463	1.73
Amesbury Town, MA (city) Essex County	280	1.73
Valley Center, CA (cdp) San Diego County	156	1.73
Sanford, ME (town) York County	360	1.71
Winthrop Town, MA (city) Suffolk County	294	1.70
Fort Salonga, NY (cdp) Suffolk County	178	1.70
Winchendon, MA (town) Worcester County	174	1.70
Medfield, MA (town) Norfolk County	202	1.69
Putnam, CT (cdp) Windham County	125	1.67
Norton, MA (town) Bristol County	311	1.65
Windsor, CO (town) Weld County	286	1.65
Burrillville, RI (town) Providence County	264	1.65
Waterville, ME (city) Kennebec County	260	1.65
Somers, CT (town) Tolland County	188	1.65
Keansburg, NJ (borough) Monmouth County	169	1.65
Woburn, MA (city) Middlesex County	615	1.64
Somersworth, NH (city) Strafford County	194	1.64
Brighton, MI (city) Livingston County	123	1.64
Holly, MI (township) Oakland County	181	1.63
Merrimack, NH (town) Hillsborough County	414	1.62
Sanford, ME (cdp) York County	172	1.62
Brandon, MI (charter township) Oakland County	241	1.60
Bath, ME (city) Sagadahoc County	140	1.60
Middleborough, MA (town) Plymouth County	358	1.59
Carver, MA (town) Plymouth County	182	1.59
North Gates, NY (cdp) Monroe County	148	1.59
Fallsburg, NY (town) Sullivan County	204	1.58
Seabrook, NH (town) Rockingham County	136	1.58
Salisbury, MA (town) Essex County	129	1.58
Laurel, FL (cdp) Sarasota County	127	1.58
Belchertown, MA (town) Hampshire County	225	1.57
Ipswich, MA (town) Essex County	205	1.57
Port Huron, MI (city) St. Clair County	485	1.56
Dedham, MA (cdp/town) Norfolk County	380	1.56
Truckee, CA (town) Nevada County	248	1.56
Milford, NH (town) Hillsborough County	233	1.56
Freeport, ME (town) Cumberland County	123	1.56
Fish Hawk, FL (cdp) Hillsborough County	200	1.55
Lone Tree, CO (city) Douglas County	153	1.55
Oakland, MI (charter township) Oakland County	248	1.54
Massena, NY (town) St. Lawrence County	198	1.54
Southborough, MA (town) Worcester County	148	1.54
Sammamish, WA (city) King County	662	1.53
Dania Beach, FL (city) Broward County	449	1.53
Mansfield, MA (town) Bristol County	353	1.53
Southbury, CT (town) New Haven County	301	1.53
Berlin, CT (town) Hartford County	299	1.53
Millbury, MA (town) Worcester County	202	1.53
Waltham, MA (city) Middlesex County	908	1.52
Wells, ME (town) York County	147	1.52
Gray, ME (town) Cumberland County	116	1.52
Holbrook, MA (cdp/town) Norfolk County	161	1.51
Lisbon, ME (town) Androscoggin County	137	1.51
Bristol, CT (city/town) Hartford County	905	1.50
St. Johns, MI (city) Clinton County	119	1.50
Leominster, MA (city) Worcester County	612	1.49
Colchester, VT (town) Chittenden County	254	1.49
Lebanon, NH (city) Grafton County	195	1.49
Corte Madera, CA (town) Marin County	136	1.49
York, MI (charter township) Washtenaw County	128	1.49
North Londonderry, PA (township) Lebanon County	117	1.49
Spring Valley Lake, CA (cdp) San Bernardino County	114	1.49
Nashua, NH (city) Hillsborough County	1,290	1.48
Haverhill, MA (city) Essex County	885	1.47
Weymouth Town, MA (city) Norfolk County	785	1.47
North Andover, MA (town) Essex County	412	1.47
Milford, MI (charter township) Oakland County	230	1.47
Rochester, MI (city) Oakland County	181	1.47
Buxton, ME (town) York County	118	1.47
Lynn, MA (city) Essex County	1,312	1.46
North Reading, MA (town) Middlesex County	212	1.46
Lakeside, VA (cdp) Henrico County	175	1.46
Woods Cross, UT (city) Davis County	134	1.46
Washington, MI (township) Macomb County	351	1.45
Westford, MA (town) Middlesex County	311	1.45
Kennebunk, ME (town) York County	158	1.45
Londonderry, NH (cdp) Rockingham County	158	1.45
Barre, VT (town) Washington County	114	1.45
Fitchburg, MA (city) Worcester County	578	1.44
Gardner, MA (city) Worcester County	293	1.44
Plainville, CT (town) Hartford County	254	1.44
Mount Dora, FL (city) Lake County	178	1.44
Boxford, MA (town) Essex County	114	1.44
Hudson, NH (town) Hillsborough County	347	1.43
North Smithfield, RI (town) Providence County	168	1.43
Panama City Beach, FL (city) Bay County	163	1.43
Bennington, VT (cdp) Bennington County	128	1.43
Brooklyn, CT (town) Windham County	116	1.43
Cumberland Hill, RI (cdp) Providence County	112	1.43
Randolph, MA (cdp/town) Norfolk County	449	1.42

SECTION THREE

Please refer to the Explanation of Data in the front of the book for more detailed information.

Ancestry

Carpatho Rusyn

U.S. and 50 States Sorted by Population and Percent of Total Population

Place	Population	%
United States	**7,501**	**<0.01**
Pennsylvania	2,480	0.02
Ohio	959	0.01
New York	741	<0.01
New Jersey	402	<0.01
California	374	<0.01
Florida	320	<0.01
Michigan	269	<0.01
Minnesota	250	<0.01
Connecticut	149	<0.01
Georgia	129	<0.01
Maryland	126	<0.01
Alaska	117	0.02
Virginia	112	<0.01
Texas	107	<0.01
Illinois	91	<0.01
Arizona	85	<0.01
Washington	79	<0.01
North Carolina	70	<0.01
Indiana	62	<0.01
Hawaii	57	<0.01
Tennessee	51	<0.01
Oklahoma	50	<0.01
Wisconsin	48	<0.01
District of Columbia	40	0.01
Massachusetts	40	<0.01
Oregon	40	<0.01
West Virginia	35	<0.01
South Carolina	27	<0.01
Alabama	26	<0.01
Colorado	23	<0.01
Idaho	20	<0.01
Iowa	20	<0.01
Montana	18	<0.01
Arkansas	15	<0.01
Kentucky	15	<0.01
Vermont	13	<0.01
Louisiana	12	<0.01
Missouri	9	<0.01
Delaware	8	<0.01
Nevada	5	<0.01
South Dakota	4	<0.01
North Dakota	3	<0.01
Kansas	0	0.00
Maine	0	0.00
Mississippi	0	0.00
Nebraska	0	0.00
New Hampshire	0	0.00
New Mexico	0	0.00
Rhode Island	0	0.00
Utah	0	0.00
Wyoming	0	0.00

Place	Population	%
Pennsylvania	2,480	0.02
Alaska	117	0.02
Ohio	959	0.01
District of Columbia	40	0.01
United States	**7,501**	**<0.01**
New York	741	<0.01
New Jersey	402	<0.01
California	374	<0.01
Florida	320	<0.01
Michigan	269	<0.01
Minnesota	250	<0.01
Connecticut	149	<0.01
Georgia	129	<0.01
Maryland	126	<0.01
Virginia	112	<0.01
Texas	107	<0.01
Illinois	91	<0.01
Arizona	85	<0.01
Washington	79	<0.01
North Carolina	70	<0.01
Indiana	62	<0.01
Hawaii	57	<0.01
Tennessee	51	<0.01
Oklahoma	50	<0.01
Wisconsin	48	<0.01
Massachusetts	40	<0.01
Oregon	40	<0.01
West Virginia	35	<0.01
South Carolina	27	<0.01
Alabama	26	<0.01
Colorado	23	<0.01
Idaho	20	<0.01
Iowa	20	<0.01
Montana	18	<0.01
Arkansas	15	<0.01
Kentucky	15	<0.01
Vermont	13	<0.01
Louisiana	12	<0.01
Missouri	9	<0.01
Delaware	8	<0.01
Nevada	5	<0.01
South Dakota	4	<0.01
North Dakota	3	<0.01
Kansas	0	0.00
Maine	0	0.00
Mississippi	0	0.00
Nebraska	0	0.00
New Hampshire	0	0.00
New Mexico	0	0.00
Rhode Island	0	0.00
Utah	0	0.00
Wyoming	0	0.00

Please refer to the Explanation of Data in the front of the book for more detailed information.

Ancestry

Carpatho Rusyn

Top 150 Places Sorted by Population

Based on all places, regardless of total population

Place	Population	%
New York, NY (city) Kings County	249	<0.01
Parma, OH (city) Cuyahoga County	116	0.14
Pittsburgh, PA (city) Allegheny County	116	0.04
Manhattan, NY (borough) New York County	112	0.01
Union, NY (town) Broome County	101	0.18
Anchorage, AK (municipality) Anchorage Municipality	98	0.03
Windber, PA (borough) Somerset County	88	2.10
Los Angeles, CA (city) Los Angeles County	80	<0.01
Dunmore, PA (borough) Lackawanna County	69	0.49
Aurora, OH (city) Portage County	65	0.43
Hermitage, PA (city) Mercer County	64	0.40
Staten Island, NY (borough) Richmond County	63	0.01
Flushing, MI (city) Genesee County	57	0.67
Los Altos, CA (city) Santa Clara County	57	0.20
Brooklyn, NY (borough) Kings County	53	<0.01
Elizabeth, PA (township) Allegheny County	52	0.39
Donora, PA (borough) Washington County	51	1.03
Tallmadge, OH (city) Summit County	51	0.29
Lawton, OK (city) Comanche County	50	0.05
Plains, PA (cdp) Luzerne County	49	1.23
Glassport, PA (borough) Allegheny County	49	1.08
Plains, PA (township) Luzerne County	49	0.49
Escondido, CA (city) San Diego County	49	0.03
Stratford, CT (cdp/town) Fairfield County	47	0.09
Manville, NJ (borough) Somerset County	46	0.44
Philadelphia, PA (city) Philadelphia County	46	<0.01
Greenock, PA (cdp) Allegheny County	44	2.33
Starke, FL (city) Bradford County	44	0.79
Penn Hills, PA (township) Allegheny County	43	0.10
Mansfield, OH (city) Richland County	43	0.09
Scottsdale, AZ (city) Maricopa County	43	0.02
St. Paul, MN (city) Ramsey County	42	0.01
Canfield, OH (city) Mahoning County	41	0.55
Kaneohe, HI (cdp) Honolulu County	40	0.12
Yonkers, NY (city) Westchester County	40	0.02
Washington, DC (city) District of Columbia	40	0.01
Johnson City, NY (village) Broome County	39	0.26
Royal Oak, MI (city) Oakland County	39	0.07
Erie, PA (city) Erie County	37	0.04
Oakland, CA (city) Alameda County	37	0.01
Fenton, MI (charter township) Genesee County	36	0.24
Millcreek, PA (township) Erie County	36	0.07
Hempstead, NY (town) Nassau County	36	<0.01
Pleasant Valley, WV (city) Marion County	35	1.12
Scranton, PA (city) Lackawanna County	35	0.05
Columbus, OH (city) Franklin County	35	<0.01
McKees Rocks, PA (borough) Allegheny County	34	0.55
Clifton, NJ (city) Passaic County	34	0.04
Long Beach, CA (city) Los Angeles County	34	0.01
Taylor, PA (borough) Lackawanna County	33	0.52
Newberry, PA (township) York County	31	0.20
Bloomingdale, FL (cdp) Hillsborough County	31	0.14
Wall, NJ (township) Monmouth County	31	0.12
Wayne, NJ (township) Passaic County	31	0.06
Olyphant, PA (borough) Lackawanna County	30	0.59
Ruskin, FL (cdp) Hillsborough County	30	0.21
Fairview Park, OH (city) Cuyahoga County	30	0.18
Nashville-Davidson, TN (metro govt) Davidson County	30	0.01
Baltimore, MD (city) Baltimore city County	30	<0.01
Carbondale, PA (city) Lackawanna County	29	0.32
Glenshaw, PA (cdp) Allegheny County	29	0.32
Shaler, PA (township) Allegheny County	29	0.10
East Fallowfield, PA (township) Chester County	28	0.40
Oswego, NY (town) Oswego County	28	0.35
Westerville, OH (city) Franklin County	28	0.08
Hempfield, PA (township) Westmoreland County	28	0.07
Eagan, MN (city) Dakota County	28	0.04
Austin, TX (city) Travis County	28	<0.01
Watertown, MI (charter township) Clinton County	27	0.57
Stowe, PA (township) Allegheny County	27	0.42
Peters, PA (township) Washington County	27	0.13
North Belle Vernon, PA (borough) Westmoreland County	26	1.37
Southmont, PA (borough) Cambria County	26	1.10
Lower Yoder, PA (township) Cambria County	26	0.95
Fallowfield, PA (township) Washington County	26	0.60
Rostraver, PA (township) Westmoreland County	26	0.23
Hauppauge, NY (cdp) Suffolk County	26	0.12
Johnstown, PA (city) Cambria County	26	0.12
Bethel Park, PA (municipality) Allegheny County	26	0.08
Lorain, OH (city) Lorain County	26	0.04
Smithtown, NY (town) Suffolk County	26	0.02
Arnold City, PA (cdp) Fayette County	25	2.98
Washington, PA (township) Fayette County	25	0.63
Munhall, PA (borough) Allegheny County	25	0.22
Lakewood, OH (city) Cuyahoga County	25	0.05
Akron, OH (city) Summit County	25	0.01
Chicago, IL (city) Cook County	25	<0.01
South Huntingdon, PA (township) Westmoreland County	24	0.41
Cambria, PA (township) Cambria County	24	0.39
Baldwin, PA (borough) Allegheny County	24	0.12
Monroeville, PA (municipality) Allegheny County	24	0.08
Gang Mills, NY (cdp) Steuben County	23	0.55
Erwin, NY (town) Steuben County	23	0.29
Richland, PA (township) Allegheny County	23	0.22
Margate City, NJ (city) Atlantic County	22	0.33
Poughkeepsie, NY (town) Dutchess County	21	0.05
Southington, CT (town) Hartford County	21	0.05
Brockton, MA (city) Plymouth County	21	0.02
Minneapolis, MN (city) Hennepin County	21	0.01
Shenorock, NY (cdp) Westchester County	20	1.02
Derby, CT (city/town) New Haven County	20	0.16
White, PA (township) Indiana County	20	0.13
Huntington, NY (cdp) Suffolk County	20	0.11
Somers, NY (town) Westchester County	20	0.10
North Huntingdon, PA (township) Westmoreland County	20	0.07
Mechanicsville, VA (cdp) Hanover County	20	0.06
Parker, CO (town) Douglas County	20	0.05
Youngstown, OH (city) Mahoning County	20	0.03
Boise City, ID (city) Ada County	20	0.01
Huntington, NY (town) Suffolk County	20	0.01
Cranbury, NJ (cdp) Middlesex County	19	0.86
Muse, PA (cdp) Washington County	19	0.71
Cranbury, NJ (township) Middlesex County	19	0.51
Avalon, PA (borough) Allegheny County	19	0.40
Chino Valley, AZ (town) Yavapai County	19	0.18
Cecil, PA (township) Washington County	19	0.17
West Mifflin, PA (borough) Allegheny County	19	0.09
Boardman, OH (cdp) Mahoning County	19	0.05
Mankato, MN (city) Blue Earth County	19	0.05
Mankato, MN (city) Blue Earth County	19	0.05
Lower Paxton, PA (township) Dauphin County	19	0.04
Bristol, PA (township) Bucks County	19	0.03
Citrus Heights, CA (city) Sacramento County	19	0.02
Paterson, NJ (city) Passaic County	19	0.01
Baden, PA (borough) Beaver County	18	0.43
North Salem, NY (town) Westchester County	18	0.35
Belgrade, MT (city) Gallatin County	18	0.25
DuBois, PA (city) Clearfield County	18	0.23
Uniontown, PA (city) Fayette County	18	0.17
Cypress Lake, FL (cdp) Lee County	18	0.15
Saddle Brook, NJ (township) Bergen County	18	0.13
Broadview Heights, OH (city) Cuyahoga County	18	0.10
Vestal, NY (town) Broome County	18	0.06
San Bruno, CA (city) San Mateo County	18	0.04
North Miami, FL (city) Miami-Dade County	18	0.03
Greenville, NC (city) Pitt County	18	0.02
Versailles, PA (borough) Allegheny County	17	1.10
Sylvan Lake, MI (city) Oakland County	17	0.94
Portage, PA (township) Cambria County	17	0.46
McMurray, PA (cdp) Washington County	17	0.35
Campbell, OH (city) Mahoning County	17	0.20
Hanover, PA (township) Northampton County	17	0.16
La Grange, NY (town) Dutchess County	17	0.11
New Port Richey, FL (city) Pasco County	17	0.11
Sachse, TX (city) Dallas County	17	0.09
Somerset, NJ (cdp) Somerset County	17	0.08
Ross, PA (township) Allegheny County	17	0.05
Hillsborough, NJ (township) Somerset County	17	0.04
Franklin, NJ (township) Somerset County	17	0.03
Danbury, CT (city/town) Fairfield County	17	0.02

Ancestry

Carpatho Rusyn

Top 150 Places Sorted by Percent of Total Population

Based on all places, regardless of total population

Place	Population	%
Evansville, AK (cdp) Yukon-Koyukuk Census Area	4	16.67
Arnold City, PA (cdp) Fayette County	25	2.98
Greenock, PA (cdp) Allegheny County	44	2.33
Deer Lake, PA (cdp) Fayette County	14	2.11
Windber, PA (borough) Somerset County	88	2.10
Norman, MN (township) Pine County	5	1.85
Elco, PA (borough) Washington County	5	1.78
Lublin, WI (village) Taylor County	3	1.69
North Belle Vernon, PA (borough) Westmoreland County	26	1.37
Enlow, PA (cdp) Allegheny County	10	1.32
Plains, PA (cdp) Luzerne County	49	1.23
Paint, PA (borough) Somerset County	11	1.16
Grand Marais, MN (city) Cook County	14	1.14
Pleasant Valley, WV (city) Marion County	35	1.12
Southmont, PA (borough) Cambria County	26	1.10
Versailles, PA (borough) Allegheny County	17	1.10
Glassport, PA (borough) Allegheny County	49	1.08
Donora, PA (borough) Washington County	51	1.03
Shenorock, NY (cdp) Westchester County	20	1.02
Salix, PA (cdp) Cambria County	13	0.99
Lower Yoder, PA (township) Cambria County	26	0.95
Sylvan Lake, MI (city) Oakland County	17	0.94
Cranbury, NJ (cdp) Middlesex County	19	0.86
Christiana, PA (borough) Lancaster County	12	0.83
New Vernon, PA (township) Mercer County	4	0.82
East Pittsburgh, PA (borough) Allegheny County	16	0.81
Starke, FL (city) Bradford County	44	0.79
New Hartford, NY (village) Oneida County	15	0.78
Paris, PA (cdp) Washington County	6	0.76
Forest City, PA (borough) Susquehanna County	13	0.74
Muse, PA (cdp) Washington County	19	0.71
Springboro, PA (borough) Crawford County	3	0.71
Toftrees, PA (cdp) Centre County	15	0.69
Oakland, PA (cdp) Cambria County	11	0.69
Chinchilla, PA (cdp) Lackawanna County	12	0.68
West Brownsville, PA (borough) Washington County	6	0.68
Flushing, MI (city) Genesee County	57	0.67
Dunlevy, PA (borough) Washington County	2	0.66
Dushore, PA (borough) Sullivan County	4	0.65
West Shenango, PA (township) Crawford County	4	0.65
Washington, PA (township) Fayette County	25	0.63
East McKeesport, PA (borough) Allegheny County	14	0.61
Jenkins, MN (township) Crow Wing County	2	0.61
Fallowfield, PA (township) Washington County	26	0.60
Stewart Manor, NY (village) Nassau County	13	0.60
Field, MN (township) St. Louis County	2	0.60
Olyphant, PA (borough) Lackawanna County	30	0.59
Lathrop, PA (township) Susquehanna County	4	0.59
Watertown, MI (charter township) Clinton County	27	0.57
Clymer, PA (borough) Indiana County	8	0.56
Canfield, OH (city) Mahoning County	41	0.55
McKees Rocks, PA (borough) Allegheny County	34	0.55
Gang Mills, NY (cdp) Steuben County	23	0.55
Holiday Heights, NJ (cdp) Ocean County	12	0.54
Braddock Hills, PA (borough) Allegheny County	10	0.54
Palmdale, PA (cdp) Dauphin County	11	0.53
Taylor, PA (borough) Lackawanna County	33	0.52
Cranbury, NJ (township) Middlesex County	19	0.51
Henry Clay, PA (township) Fayette County	10	0.50
Dunmore, PA (borough) Lackawanna County	69	0.49
Plains, PA (township) Luzerne County	49	0.49
Lynnwood-Pricedale, PA (cdp) Westmoreland County	10	0.49
Central City, PA (borough) Somerset County	6	0.47
Portage, PA (township) Cambria County	17	0.46
Churchill, PA (borough) Allegheny County	14	0.46
Laflin, PA (borough) Luzerne County	7	0.46
Bayfield, WI (town) Bayfield County	3	0.45
Pennsbury Village, PA (borough) Allegheny County	3	0.45
New Castle, PA (township) Schuylkill County	2	0.45
Manville, NJ (borough) Somerset County	46	0.44
Aurora, OH (city) Portage County	65	0.43
Baden, PA (borough) Beaver County	18	0.43
Liberty, PA (borough) Allegheny County	11	0.43
Pleasant City, OH (village) Guernsey County	2	0.43
Stowe, PA (township) Allegheny County	27	0.42

Place	Population	%
Sunset Beach, NC (town) Brunswick County	14	0.42
Parryville, PA (borough) Carbon County	2	0.42
South Huntingdon, PA (township) Westmoreland County	24	0.41
Hermitage, PA (city) Mercer County	64	0.40
East Fallowfield, PA (township) Chester County	28	0.40
Avalon, PA (borough) Allegheny County	19	0.40
Elizabeth, PA (township) Allegheny County	52	0.39
Cambria, PA (township) Cambria County	24	0.39
Wharton, PA (township) Fayette County	14	0.38
Stonycreek, PA (township) Cambria County	11	0.38
Huntington, PA (township) Adams County	9	0.38
Dale, PA (borough) Cambria County	5	0.38
Scalp Level, PA (borough) Cambria County	3	0.38
Jenner, PA (township) Somerset County	15	0.36
Oswego, NY (town) Oswego County	28	0.35
North Salem, NY (town) Westchester County	18	0.35
McMurray, PA (cdp) Washington County	17	0.35
Cass, PA (township) Schuylkill County	7	0.35
Faison, NC (town) Duplin County	4	0.34
Margate City, NJ (city) Atlantic County	22	0.33
Perry, PA (township) Mercer County	5	0.33
Buck, PA (township) Luzerne County	1	0.33
Carbondale, PA (city) Lackawanna County	29	0.32
Glenshaw, PA (cdp) Allegheny County	29	0.32
Chisholm, MN (city) St. Louis County	16	0.32
Singac, NJ (cdp) Passaic County	13	0.32
Shutesbury, MA (town) Franklin County	6	0.32
Weatherly, PA (borough) Carbon County	8	0.31
Knife Lake, MN (township) Kanabec County	3	0.30
Tallmadge, OH (city) Summit County	51	0.29
Erwin, NY (town) Steuben County	23	0.29
Harwinton, CT (town) Litchfield County	16	0.28
Turtle Creek, PA (borough) Allegheny County	15	0.28
Whitaker, PA (borough) Allegheny County	4	0.28
Columbus, PA (cdp) Warren County	2	0.28
Upper Yoder, PA (township) Cambria County	15	0.27
Almena, MI (township) Van Buren County	13	0.27
South Barrington, IL (village) Cook County	12	0.27
Perry, PA (township) Fayette County	7	0.27
Roaring Brook, PA (township) Lackawanna County	4	0.27
Johnson City, NY (village) Broome County	39	0.26
Brittany Farms-The Highlands, PA (cdp) Bucks County	10	0.26
Forward, PA (township) Allegheny County	9	0.26
Stanley, WI (city) Chippewa County	9	0.26
Stanley, WI (city) Chippewa County	9	0.26
Walker, PA (township) Juniata County	7	0.26
Belgrade, MT (city) Gallatin County	18	0.25
Jackson, PA (township) Cambria County	11	0.25
Thompsonville, PA (cdp) Washington County	10	0.25
Fenton, MI (charter township) Genesee County	36	0.24
Mountain Lakes, NJ (borough) Morris County	10	0.24
South Coventry, PA (township) Chester County	6	0.24
Rostraver, PA (township) Westmoreland County	26	0.23
DuBois, PA (city) Clearfield County	18	0.23
Mount Olive, AL (cdp) Jefferson County	9	0.23
Mecosta, MI (township) Mecosta County	6	0.23
Waterford, PA (borough) Erie County	3	0.23
Wilmington, PA (township) Mercer County	3	0.23
Munhall, PA (borough) Allegheny County	25	0.22
Richland, PA (township) Allegheny County	23	0.22
North Caldwell, NJ (borough) Essex County	14	0.22
Adams, PA (township) Cambria County	13	0.22
Elba, MI (township) Lapeer County	12	0.22
Fairview, NY (cdp) Dutchess County	10	0.22
Honesdale, PA (borough) Wayne County	10	0.22
Hanover, PA (township) Washington County	6	0.22
Ruskin, FL (cdp) Hillsborough County	30	0.21
Georges, PA (township) Fayette County	14	0.21
Anamosa, IA (city) Jones County	12	0.21
Cross Creek, PA (township) Washington County	3	0.21
Los Altos, CA (city) Santa Clara County	57	0.20
Newberry, PA (township) York County	31	0.20
Campbell, OH (city) Mahoning County	17	0.20
Wellington, OH (village) Lorain County	10	0.20
Persia, NY (town) Cattaraugus County	5	0.20

Please refer to the Explanation of Data in the front of the book for more detailed information.

Ancestry

Carpatho Rusyn

Top 150 Places Sorted by Percent of Total Population

Based on places with total population of 7,500 or more

Place	Population	%
Flushing, MI (city) Genesee County	57	0.67
Dunmore, PA (borough) Lackawanna County	69	0.49
Plains, PA (township) Luzerne County	49	0.49
Manville, NJ (borough) Somerset County	46	0.44
Aurora, OH (city) Portage County	65	0.43
Hermitage, PA (city) Mercer County	64	0.40
Elizabeth, PA (township) Allegheny County	52	0.39
Oswego, NY (town) Oswego County	28	0.35
Carbondale, PA (city) Lackawanna County	29	0.32
Glenshaw, PA (cdp) Allegheny County	29	0.32
Tallmadge, OH (city) Summit County	51	0.29
Erwin, NY (town) Steuben County	23	0.29
Johnson City, NY (village) Broome County	39	0.26
Fenton, MI (charter township) Genesee County	36	0.24
Rostraver, PA (township) Westmoreland County	26	0.23
DuBois, PA (city) Clearfield County	18	0.23
Munhall, PA (borough) Allegheny County	25	0.22
Richland, PA (township) Allegheny County	23	0.22
Ruskin, FL (cdp) Hillsborough County	30	0.21
Los Altos, CA (city) Santa Clara County	57	0.20
Newberry, PA (township) York County	31	0.20
Campbell, OH (city) Mahoning County	17	0.20
Union, NY (town) Broome County	101	0.18
Fairview Park, OH (city) Cuyahoga County	30	0.18
Chino Valley, AZ (town) Yavapai County	19	0.18
Cresskill, NJ (borough) Bergen County	15	0.18
Maxatawny, PA (township) Berks County	14	0.18
Cecil, PA (township) Washington County	19	0.17
Uniontown, PA (city) Fayette County	18	0.17
Tanaina, AK (cdp) Matanuska-Susitna Borough	15	0.17
Oberlin, OH (city) Lorain County	14	0.17
Camp Hill, PA (borough) Cumberland County	13	0.17
Derby, CT (city/town) New Haven County	20	0.16
Hanover, PA (township) Northampton County	17	0.16
Montpelier, VT (city) Washington County	13	0.16
Cypress Lake, FL (cdp) Lee County	18	0.15
Plymouth, MI (city) Wayne County	14	0.15
South Strabane, PA (township) Washington County	14	0.15
Parma, OH (city) Cuyahoga County	116	0.14
Bloomingdale, FL (cdp) Hillsborough County	31	0.14
College, PA (township) Centre County	13	0.14
O'Hara, PA (township) Allegheny County	12	0.14
Peters, PA (township) Washington County	27	0.13
White, PA (township) Indiana County	20	0.13
Saddle Brook, NJ (township) Bergen County	18	0.13
East Whiteland, PA (township) Chester County	14	0.13
Economy, PA (borough) Beaver County	12	0.13
South Abington, PA (township) Lackawanna County	12	0.13
Tobyhanna, PA (township) Monroe County	11	0.13
Kaneohe, HI (cdp) Honolulu County	40	0.12
Wall, NJ (township) Monmouth County	31	0.12
Hauppauge, NY (cdp) Suffolk County	26	0.12
Johnstown, PA (city) Cambria County	26	0.12
Baldwin, PA (borough) Allegheny County	24	0.12
Brighton, PA (township) Beaver County	10	0.12
Grove City, PA (borough) Mercer County	10	0.12
Pleasant Hills, PA (borough) Allegheny County	10	0.12
Huntington, NY (cdp) Suffolk County	20	0.11
La Grange, NY (town) Dutchess County	17	0.11
New Port Richey, FL (city) Pasco County	17	0.11
Flossmoor, IL (village) Cook County	10	0.11
Old Forge, PA (borough) Lackawanna County	9	0.11
Penn Hills, PA (township) Allegheny County	43	0.10
Shaler, PA (township) Allegheny County	29	0.10
Somers, NY (town) Westchester County	20	0.10
Broadview Heights, OH (city) Cuyahoga County	18	0.10
Hammonton, NJ (town) Atlantic County	15	0.10
Patton, PA (township) Centre County	15	0.10
Bloomsburg, PA (town) Columbia County	14	0.10
Sun Lakes, AZ (cdp) Maricopa County	14	0.10
Whitehall, PA (borough) Allegheny County	14	0.10
Clemson, SC (city) Pickens County	13	0.10
Salem, OH (city) Columbiana County	12	0.10
Berwick, PA (borough) Columbia County	11	0.10
Southwood Acres, CT (cdp) Hartford County	8	0.10
Stratford, CT (cdp/town) Fairfield County	47	0.09
Mansfield, OH (city) Richland County	43	0.09
West Mifflin, PA (borough) Allegheny County	19	0.09
Sachse, TX (city) Dallas County	17	0.09
Scott, PA (township) Allegheny County	15	0.09
Little Falls, NJ (township) Passaic County	13	0.09
Richland, PA (township) Cambria County	12	0.09
Endwell, NY (cdp) Broome County	11	0.09
Norton, OH (city) Summit County	11	0.09
New Britain, PA (township) Bucks County	10	0.09
Wantage, NJ (township) Sussex County	10	0.09
Millersville, PA (borough) Lancaster County	7	0.09
Westerville, OH (city) Franklin County	28	0.08
Bethel Park, PA (municipality) Allegheny County	26	0.08
Monroeville, PA (municipality) Allegheny County	24	0.08
Somerset, NJ (cdp) Somerset County	17	0.08
Butler, PA (township) Butler County	14	0.08
Kenmore, NY (village) Erie County	13	0.08
Greensburg, PA (city) Westmoreland County	12	0.08
Clarksburg, MD (cdp) Montgomery County	8	0.08
Herkimer, NY (town) Herkimer County	8	0.08
Richmond Heights, OH (city) Cuyahoga County	8	0.08
Royal Oak, MI (city) Oakland County	39	0.07
Millcreek, PA (township) Erie County	36	0.07
Hempfield, PA (township) Westmoreland County	28	0.07
North Huntingdon, PA (township) Westmoreland County	20	0.07
McKeesport, PA (city) Allegheny County	15	0.07
New Hartford, NY (town) Oneida County	15	0.07
Okemos, MI (cdp) Ingham County	15	0.07
Rocky River, OH (city) Cuyahoga County	14	0.07
Farmington, MN (city) Dakota County	13	0.07
North Fayette, PA (township) Allegheny County	10	0.07
Worthington, OH (city) Franklin County	10	0.07
Brandermill, VA (cdp) Chesterfield County	9	0.07
St. John, IN (town) Lake County	9	0.07
Coshocton, OH (city) Coshocton County	8	0.07
Wayne, NJ (township) Passaic County	31	0.06
Mechanicsville, VA (cdp) Hanover County	20	0.06
Vestal, NY (town) Broome County	18	0.06
Lincolnia, VA (cdp) Fairfax County	13	0.06
Bailey's Crossroads, VA (cdp) Fairfax County	12	0.06
Murrysville, PA (municipality) Westmoreland County	12	0.06
Columbia Heights, MN (city) Anoka County	11	0.06
Penn, PA (township) Westmoreland County	11	0.06
South Whitehall, PA (township) Lehigh County	11	0.06
Bemidji, MN (city) Beltrami County	8	0.06
Upper Saucon, PA (township) Lehigh County	8	0.06
Seven Hills, OH (city) Cuyahoga County	7	0.06
Lawton, OK (city) Comanche County	50	0.05
Scranton, PA (city) Lackawanna County	35	0.05
Lakewood, OH (city) Cuyahoga County	25	0.05
Poughkeepsie, NY (town) Dutchess County	21	0.05
Southington, CT (town) Hartford County	21	0.05
Parker, CO (town) Douglas County	20	0.05
Boardman, OH (cdp) Mahoning County	19	0.05
Mankato, MN (city) Blue Earth County	19	0.05
Mankato, MN (city) Blue Earth County	19	0.05
Ross, PA (township) Allegheny County	17	0.05
Florence, KY (city) Boone County	15	0.05
Sherwood, AR (city) Pulaski County	15	0.05
Batavia, IL (city) Kane County	14	0.05
Schererville, IN (town) Lake County	13	0.05
Rockledge, FL (city) Brevard County	12	0.05
Rockville Centre, NY (village) Nassau County	12	0.05
Springfield, PA (township) Delaware County	12	0.05
Citrus Park, FL (cdp) Hillsborough County	11	0.05
Derry, PA (township) Dauphin County	11	0.05
Laurel, MD (city) Prince George's County	11	0.05
Merrick, NY (cdp) Nassau County	11	0.05
Munster, IN (town) Lake County	11	0.05
Solon, OH (city) Cuyahoga County	11	0.05
Ashland, OR (city) Jackson County	10	0.05
Saugerties, NY (town) Ulster County	10	0.05
Hyattsville, MD (city) Prince George's County	8	0.05
East Wenatchee, WA (city) Douglas County	7	0.05

SECTION THREE

Please refer to the Explanation of Data in the front of the book for more detailed information.

Ancestry

Celtic

U.S. and 50 States Sorted by Population and Percent of Total Population

Place	Population	%
United States	**52,937**	**0.02**
California	7,889	0.02
Texas	3,860	0.02
Florida	2,843	0.02
Washington	2,693	0.04
New York	2,324	0.01
Massachusetts	2,317	0.04
Colorado	1,935	0.04
Virginia	1,825	0.02
Ohio	1,824	0.02
Pennsylvania	1,798	0.01
North Carolina	1,789	0.02
Michigan	1,510	0.02
Oregon	1,382	0.04
Georgia	1,295	0.01
Arizona	1,245	0.02
New Jersey	1,079	0.01
Illinois	980	0.01
New Mexico	939	0.05
Tennessee	910	0.01
Maryland	895	0.02
Missouri	734	0.01
South Carolina	727	0.02
Alabama	666	0.01
Indiana	636	0.01
Connecticut	617	0.02
Nevada	600	0.02
Minnesota	582	0.01
Kentucky	553	0.01
Utah	520	0.02
Alaska	504	0.07
Mississippi	488	0.02
Idaho	459	0.03
Wisconsin	451	0.01
Oklahoma	420	0.01
Arkansas	391	0.01
Maine	348	0.03
Louisiana	302	0.01
Iowa	299	0.01
New Hampshire	292	0.02
Kansas	286	0.01
West Virginia	238	0.01
Rhode Island	226	0.02
Nebraska	213	0.01
Vermont	192	0.03
Wyoming	189	0.03
Hawaii	187	0.01
Montana	169	0.02
South Dakota	122	0.02
Delaware	107	0.01
District of Columbia	48	0.01
North Dakota	39	0.01

Place	Population	%
Alaska	504	0.07
New Mexico	939	0.05
Washington	2,693	0.04
Massachusetts	2,317	0.04
Colorado	1,935	0.04
Oregon	1,382	0.04
Idaho	459	0.03
Maine	348	0.03
Vermont	192	0.03
Wyoming	189	0.03
United States	**52,937**	**0.02**
California	7,889	0.02
Texas	3,860	0.02
Florida	2,843	0.02
Virginia	1,825	0.02
Ohio	1,824	0.02
North Carolina	1,789	0.02
Michigan	1,510	0.02
Arizona	1,245	0.02
Maryland	895	0.02
South Carolina	727	0.02
Connecticut	617	0.02
Nevada	600	0.02
Utah	520	0.02
Mississippi	488	0.02
New Hampshire	292	0.02
Rhode Island	226	0.02
Montana	169	0.02
South Dakota	122	0.02
New York	2,324	0.01
Pennsylvania	1,798	0.01
Georgia	1,295	0.01
New Jersey	1,079	0.01
Illinois	980	0.01
Tennessee	910	0.01
Missouri	734	0.01
Alabama	666	0.01
Indiana	636	0.01
Minnesota	582	0.01
Kentucky	553	0.01
Wisconsin	451	0.01
Oklahoma	420	0.01
Arkansas	391	0.01
Louisiana	302	0.01
Iowa	299	0.01
Kansas	286	0.01
West Virginia	238	0.01
Nebraska	213	0.01
Hawaii	187	0.01
Delaware	107	0.01
District of Columbia	48	0.01
North Dakota	39	0.01

Please refer to the Explanation of Data in the front of the book for more detailed information.

Ancestry

Celtic

Top 150 Places Sorted by Population

Based on all places, regardless of total population

Place	Population	%
Los Angeles, CA (city) Los Angeles County	654	0.02
New York, NY (city) Kings County	564	0.01
Seattle, WA (city) King County	321	0.05
Anchorage, AK (municipality) Anchorage Municipality	308	0.11
Manhattan, NY (borough) New York County	304	0.02
Austin, TX (city) Travis County	302	0.04
East Bridgewater, MA (town) Plymouth County	287	2.10
San Jose, CA (city) Santa Clara County	243	0.03
Oakland, CA (city) Alameda County	235	0.06
Portland, OR (city) Multnomah County	226	0.04
San Diego, CA (city) San Diego County	224	0.02
Glendale, AZ (city) Maricopa County	223	0.10
Phoenix, AZ (city) Maricopa County	223	0.02
Arden-Arcade, CA (cdp) Sacramento County	205	0.23
Poway, CA (city) San Diego County	204	0.43
San Francisco, CA (city) San Francisco County	194	0.02
Albuquerque, NM (city) Bernalillo County	192	0.04
Westminster, CO (city) Adams County	184	0.18
Vancouver, WA (city) Clark County	183	0.11
Fresno, CA (city) Fresno County	183	0.04
San Antonio, TX (city) Medina County	173	0.01
Long Beach, CA (city) Los Angeles County	170	0.04
Virginia Beach, VA (ind. city) Virginia Beach independent city	170	0.04
Queens, NY (borough) Queens County	169	0.01
Houston, TX (city) Harris County	164	0.01
Minneapolis, MN (city) Hennepin County	160	0.04
Methuen Town, MA (city) Essex County	158	0.34
Santa Clarita, CA (city) Los Angeles County	157	0.09
Chicago, IL (city) Cook County	155	0.01
Ashland, MA (town) Middlesex County	153	0.95
Colorado Springs, CO (city) El Paso County	150	0.04
Paw Paw, MI (township) Van Buren County	145	2.05
Arlington, TX (city) Tarrant County	145	0.04
Tucson, AZ (city) Pima County	140	0.03
Fort Worth, TX (city) Tarrant County	136	0.02
Dallas, TX (city) Dallas County	132	0.01
Denver, CO (city) Denver County	126	0.02
Durham, NC (city) Durham County	119	0.05
Everett, MA (city) Middlesex County	115	0.28
Flower Mound, TX (town) Denton County	115	0.18
Redwood City, CA (city) San Mateo County	115	0.15
Englewood, FL (cdp) Sarasota County	114	0.72
Fullerton, CA (city) Orange County	111	0.08
Flint, MI (charter township) Genesee County	109	0.33
Alexandria, VA (ind. city) Alexandria independent city	108	0.08
Oceanside, CA (city) San Diego County	103	0.06
Hornell, NY (city) Steuben County	102	1.18
Boise City, ID (city) Ada County	102	0.05
Charlotte, NC (city) Mecklenburg County	100	0.01
Fernley, NV (city) Lyon County	98	0.53
Reno, NV (city) Washoe County	98	0.04
Sacramento, CA (city) Sacramento County	97	0.02
New Braunfels, TX (city) Comal County	95	0.18
Columbus, OH (city) Franklin County	95	0.01
Lakewood, CO (city) Jefferson County	94	0.07
Arlington, VA (cdp) Arlington County	94	0.05
Spokane, WA (city) Spokane County	93	0.05
Whitehall, PA (township) Lehigh County	91	0.34
El Cerro, NM (cdp) Valencia County	90	2.65
Salem, MA (city) Essex County	89	0.22
Santa Cruz, CA (city) Santa Cruz County	89	0.15
Boston, MA (city) Suffolk County	88	0.01
Thornton, CO (city) Adams County	87	0.08
Berkeley, CA (city) Alameda County	86	0.08
Bakersfield, CA (city) Kern County	86	0.03
Sherwood, OR (city) Washington County	84	0.49
Asheville, NC (city) Buncombe County	84	0.10
Springfield, PA (township) Delaware County	83	0.35
Tigard, OR (city) Washington County	83	0.18
Sparks, NV (city) Washoe County	83	0.10
Huntsville, AL (city) Madison County	83	0.05
Aurora, CO (city) Arapahoe County	82	0.03
Bayonne, NJ (city) Hudson County	81	0.13
Anaheim, CA (city) Orange County	81	0.02
Fremont, CA (city) Alameda County	80	0.04
Shrewsbury, MA (town) Worcester County	79	0.23
Las Vegas, NV (city) Clark County	79	0.01
Mill Valley, CA (city) Marin County	78	0.57
Los Lunas, NM (village) Valencia County	78	0.56
Saratoga Springs, UT (city) Utah County	78	0.53
Brea, CA (city) Orange County	78	0.20
Four Corners, OR (cdp) Marion County	77	0.49
Melbourne, FL (city) Brevard County	77	0.10
Bellevue, WA (city) King County	77	0.06
Louisville-Jefferson County, KY (metro govt) Jefferson County	77	0.01
Johnson City, TN (city) Washington County	75	0.12
Gold River, CA (cdp) Sacramento County	74	0.89
Tacoma, WA (city) Pierce County	74	0.04
Roanoke, VA (ind. city) Roanoke independent city	73	0.08
Richmond, CA (city) Contra Costa County	73	0.07
Salt Lake City, UT (city) Salt Lake County	73	0.04
Tempe, AZ (city) Maricopa County	73	0.04
Toledo, OH (city) Lucas County	73	0.03
Mount Vernon, WA (city) Skagit County	72	0.23
McAllen, TX (city) Hidalgo County	71	0.06
Kansas City, MO (city) Jackson County	71	0.02
Indian Point, MO (village) Stone County	70	6.16
Toronto, OH (city) Jefferson County	70	1.40
Bremen, GA (city) Haralson County	70	1.17
Hershey, PA (cdp) Dauphin County	70	0.54
Derry, PA (township) Dauphin County	70	0.29
Corpus Christi, TX (city) Nueces County	70	0.02
Briar, TX (cdp) Tarrant County	69	1.14
Odessa, TX (city) Ector County	69	0.07
Madison, WI (city) Dane County	69	0.03
Jacksonville, FL (city) Duval County	69	0.01
Tulsa, OK (city) Tulsa County	68	0.02
Bristol, PA (borough) Bucks County	67	0.68
Versailles, KY (city) Woodford County	66	0.78
Lake Ridge, VA (cdp) Prince William County	66	0.17
Glendora, CA (city) Los Angeles County	66	0.13
Estes Park, CO (town) Larimer County	65	1.12
Forest City, NC (town) Rutherford County	65	0.87
Hamilton, MA (town) Essex County	65	0.83
Centennial, CO (city) Arapahoe County	65	0.07
Huntington, NY (town) Suffolk County	65	0.03
Damascus, MD (cdp) Montgomery County	64	0.41
Niles, OH (city) Trumbull County	64	0.33
Babylon, NY (town) Suffolk County	64	0.03
Winston-Salem, NC (city) Forsyth County	64	0.03
Franklin Town, MA (city) Norfolk County	63	0.20
Tampa, FL (city) Hillsborough County	63	0.02
Carrboro, NC (town) Orange County	62	0.33
Weatherford, TX (city) Parker County	62	0.26
Edmond, OK (city) Oklahoma County	62	0.08
Lexington-Fayette, KY (cons. govt) Fayette County	62	0.02
Oak Grove, SC (cdp) Lexington County	61	0.58
Little Rock, AR (city) Pulaski County	61	0.03
Omaha, NE (city) Douglas County	61	0.01
Mount Repose, OH (cdp) Clermont County	60	1.41
Stafford, TX (city) Fort Bend County	60	0.35
Cheyenne, WY (city) Laramie County	60	0.10
Bend, OR (city) Deschutes County	60	0.08
Troy, MI (city) Oakland County	60	0.07
Rochester, MN (city) Olmsted County	60	0.06
Salem, OR (city) Marion County	60	0.04
Overland Park, KS (city) Johnson County	59	0.03
Lower Southampton, PA (township) Bucks County	57	0.30
Lawrence, KS (city) Douglas County	57	0.07
Miami, FL (city) Miami-Dade County	57	0.01
Blackwood, NJ (cdp) Camden County	56	1.11
Prescott Valley, AZ (town) Yavapai County	56	0.15
Gloucester, NJ (township) Camden County	56	0.09
Waterford, MI (charter township) Oakland County	56	0.08
Duluth, MN (city) St. Louis County	56	0.07
Highlands Ranch, CO (cdp) Douglas County	56	0.06
Columbus, GA (city) Muscogee County	55	0.03
Oyster Bay, NY (town) Nassau County	55	0.02
Rapid City, SD (city) Pennington County	54	0.08
Jessup, MD (cdp) Anne Arundel County	53	0.48

SECTION THREE

Please refer to the Explanation of Data in the front of the book for more detailed information.

Ancestry

Celtic

Top 150 Places Sorted by Percent of Total Population

Based on all places, regardless of total population

Place	Population	%
Fallis, OK (town) Lincoln County	12	30.77
Comptche, CA (cdp) Mendocino County	21	21.88
Omena, MI (cdp) Leelanau County	35	12.54
Lakeville, ME (town) Penobscot County	6	8.33
Carrick, CA (cdp) Siskiyou County	13	7.65
Indian Point, MO (village) Stone County	70	6.16
Keswick, CA (cdp) Shasta County	24	5.63
Custer, WA (cdp) Whatcom County	27	5.08
Leipsic, DE (town) Kent County	6	4.76
Clontarf, MN (city) Swift County	7	4.58
Clare, IA (city) Webster County	5	4.42
Athena, OR (city) Umatilla County	44	4.28
Ventura, NM (cdp) Luna County	17	4.26
Dennison, MN (city) Goodhue County	6	3.80
Dennison, MN (city) Goodhue County	6	3.80
Brooks, OR (cdp) Marion County	13	3.79
Boys Ranch, TX (cdp) Oldham County	8	3.57
Bellewood, KY (city) Jefferson County	11	3.37
Tupman, CA (cdp) Kern County	4	3.36
East Millstone, NJ (cdp) Somerset County	26	3.19
Wilton, NH (cdp) Hillsborough County	32	3.01
Rocky Point, NC (cdp) Pender County	52	2.87
Sycamore, SC (town) Allendale County	4	2.80
Lane, OK (cdp) Atoka County	10	2.75
Mount Lena, MD (cdp) Washington County	12	2.70
Kim, CO (town) Las Animas County	3	2.70
Hoyt, KS (city) Jackson County	16	2.66
El Cerro, NM (cdp) Valencia County	90	2.65
Mount Gretna, PA (borough) Lebanon County	4	2.63
Wing, ND (city) Burleigh County	5	2.55
Gales Ferry, CT (cdp) New London County	26	2.52
Beckwourth, CA (cdp) Plumas County	10	2.41
Napanoch, NY (cdp) Ulster County	25	2.35
Kamiah, ID (city) Lewis County	33	2.29
Dillsboro, NC (town) Jackson County	3	2.26
Shenandoah Shores, VA (cdp) Warren County	15	2.16
Crane, OR (cdp) Harney County	4	2.15
East Bridgewater, MA (town) Plymouth County	287	2.10
Paw Paw, MI (township) Van Buren County	145	2.05
Virgin, UT (town) Washington County	7	1.94
McRae, AR (city) White County	15	1.92
Mission Hill, SD (town) Yankton County	5	1.92
Leelanau, MI (township) Leelanau County	35	1.90
Hosston, LA (village) Caddo Parish	6	1.87
Athens, MI (township) Calhoun County	48	1.86
Fall City, WA (cdp) King County	38	1.84
Olive Hill, KY (city) Carter County	34	1.83
Corralitos, CA (cdp) Santa Cruz County	49	1.82
Mogul, NV (cdp) Washoe County	28	1.78
Stockton, KS (city) Rooks County	26	1.76
Brooklin, ME (town) Hancock County	18	1.76
Tidmore Bend, AL (cdp) Etowah County	16	1.76
Roberta, GA (city) Crawford County	15	1.76
North Lynbrook, NY (cdp) Nassau County	13	1.75
Bassett, NE (city) Rock County	11	1.74
Chiloquin, OR (city) Klamath County	12	1.73
Eldridge, CA (cdp) Sonoma County	30	1.71
Eagleswood, NJ (township) Ocean County	25	1.71
Chimney Rock Village, NC (village) Rutherford County	3	1.63
Columbia, NC (town) Tyrrell County	15	1.61
Buffalo Soapstone, AK (cdp) Matanuska-Susitna Borough	11	1.60
Cowley, WY (town) Big Horn County	9	1.59
Indian Hills, NM (cdp) Torrance County	17	1.57
Bishop Hills, TX (town) Potter County	4	1.55
Stagecoach, TX (town) Montgomery County	7	1.54
Montour, IA (city) Tama County	4	1.53
Lynn, MN (township) McLeod County	8	1.51
Bell Buckle, TN (town) Bedford County	6	1.51
Katonah, NY (cdp) Westchester County	22	1.50
Sheridan, WI (town) Dunn County	7	1.50
Okarche, OK (town) Kingfisher County	16	1.46
University Heights, IA (city) Johnson County	16	1.44
Nelson, IL (village) Lee County	3	1.42
Mount Repose, OH (cdp) Clermont County	60	1.41
Mount Penn, PA (borough) Berks County	44	1.41
Lewis, NY (town) Essex County	18	1.41
Sunset Village, GA (cdp) Upson County	15	1.41
Toronto, OH (city) Jefferson County	70	1.40
Newville, PA (borough) Cumberland County	18	1.39
Kekoskee, WI (village) Dodge County	2	1.37
Cutten, CA (cdp) Humboldt County	41	1.35
Silverstreet, SC (town) Newberry County	3	1.35
Seymour, TX (city) Baylor County	37	1.34
Bishop, CA (city) Inyo County	51	1.33
St. Armand, NY (town) Essex County	17	1.33
Brandon, VT (cdp) Rutland County	24	1.32
Cayuga, NY (village) Cayuga County	6	1.32
Home, MI (township) Newaygo County	3	1.32
Sugar Bush Knolls, OH (village) Portage County	2	1.32
Pipestone, MI (township) Berrien County	28	1.28
Cuyamungue, NM (cdp) Santa Fe County	6	1.28
Taloga, OK (town) Dewey County	7	1.27
Dover Beaches North, NJ (cdp) Ocean County	19	1.26
Foreman, AR (city) Little River County	14	1.22
Plymouth, CA (city) Amador County	11	1.22
Story, WY (cdp) Sheridan County	10	1.22
Caryville, TN (town) Campbell County	27	1.20
Laura, OH (village) Miami County	7	1.20
Granville South, OH (cdp) Licking County	19	1.19
Hornell, NY (city) Steuben County	102	1.18
Bremen, GA (city) Haralson County	70	1.17
Star Valley, AZ (town) Gila County	28	1.17
Friend, NE (city) Saline County	11	1.17
Briar, TX (cdp) Tarrant County	69	1.14
Monmouth Beach, NJ (borough) Monmouth County	38	1.13
Beloit, OH (village) Mahoning County	14	1.13
Estes Park, CO (town) Larimer County	65	1.12
Riverside, IA (city) Washington County	10	1.12
Blackwood, NJ (cdp) Camden County	56	1.11
Kanab, UT (city) Kane County	46	1.11
Cottage Grove, WI (town) Dane County	43	1.11
Mount Calvary, WI (village) Fond du Lac County	5	1.10
West Union, WV (town) Doddridge County	9	1.09
Koshkonong, MO (town) Oregon County	3	1.08
Rose Hill, NC (town) Duplin County	15	1.07
Mansfield, MI (township) Iron County	2	1.07
East Side, PA (borough) Carbon County	4	1.06
Clinton, NY (town) Dutchess County	45	1.05
Beloit, KS (city) Mitchell County	40	1.05
Nash, TX (city) Bowie County	30	1.05
Homosassa, FL (cdp) Citrus County	26	1.04
Chesterfield, NY (town) Essex County	25	1.04
Ferrum, VA (cdp) Franklin County	17	1.04
Matthews, MO (city) New Madrid County	9	1.04
Riverlea, OH (village) Franklin County	5	1.04
Waverly, AL (town) Chambers County	2	1.03
New Britain, PA (borough) Bucks County	32	1.02
McLeansville, NC (cdp) Guilford County	8	1.02
Charlo, MT (cdp) Lake County	4	1.02
Delanson, NY (village) Schenectady County	3	1.02
Lewiston, NY (village) Niagara County	27	1.00
Marlinton, WV (town) Pocahontas County	14	1.00
Coal Creek, CO (cdp) Jefferson County	24	0.99
Munch, MN (township) Pine County	2	0.99
Edgewood, NM (town) Santa Fe County	36	0.98
Monterey, TN (town) Putnam County	28	0.98
Mariaville, ME (town) Hancock County	6	0.98
Lake Montezuma, AZ (cdp) Yavapai County	40	0.97
Merton, WI (village) Waukesha County	30	0.97
Walton Hills, OH (village) Cuyahoga County	22	0.97
Jackson, NC (town) Northampton County	5	0.97
Emma, MO (city) Saline County	4	0.97
Ashland, MA (town) Middlesex County	153	0.95
Eielson AFB, AK (cdp) Fairbanks North Star Borough	40	0.95
Forestbrook, SC (cdp) Horry County	40	0.95
Spring Ridge, PA (cdp) Berks County	10	0.95
Eddington, ME (town) Penobscot County	19	0.94
Stansberry Lake, WA (cdp) Pierce County	17	0.94
Friendsville, TN (city) Blount County	10	0.94
Nashville, AR (city) Howard County	43	0.93

Please refer to the Explanation of Data in the front of the book for more detailed information.

Ancestry

Celtic

Top 150 Places Sorted by Percent of Total Population

Based on places with total population of 7,500 or more

Place	Population	%
East Bridgewater, MA (town) Plymouth County	287	2.10
Hornell, NY (city) Steuben County	102	1.18
Ashland, MA (town) Middlesex County	153	0.95
Gold River, CA (cdp) Sacramento County	74	0.89
Hamilton, MA (town) Essex County	65	0.83
Versailles, KY (city) Woodford County	66	0.78
Englewood, FL (cdp) Sarasota County	114	0.72
Bristol, PA (borough) Bucks County	67	0.68
Oak Grove, SC (cdp) Lexington County	61	0.58
Mill Valley, CA (city) Marin County	78	0.57
Los Lunas, NM (village) Valencia County	78	0.56
Hershey, PA (cdp) Dauphin County	70	0.54
Fernley, NV (city) Lyon County	98	0.53
Saratoga Springs, UT (city) Utah County	78	0.53
Stonegate, CO (cdp) Douglas County	46	0.53
Fairview, CA (cdp) Alameda County	49	0.50
Yreka, CA (city) Siskiyou County	38	0.50
Sherwood, OR (city) Washington County	84	0.49
Four Corners, OR (cdp) Marion County	77	0.49
Jessup, MD (cdp) Anne Arundel County	53	0.48
Villas, FL (cdp) Lee County	52	0.47
Struthers, OH (city) Mahoning County	51	0.47
Socorro, NM (city) Socorro County	43	0.47
Sterling, MA (town) Worcester County	36	0.47
Poway, CA (city) San Diego County	204	0.43
Damascus, MD (cdp) Montgomery County	64	0.41
Kemp Mill, MD (cdp) Montgomery County	50	0.41
Bethel, CT (cdp) Fairfield County	35	0.40
Carneys Point, NJ (township) Salem County	31	0.39
Clinton, CT (town) Middlesex County	50	0.38
Los Alamos, NM (cdp) Los Alamos County	46	0.38
Chatham, IL (village) Sangamon County	42	0.38
Weston, MA (town) Middlesex County	42	0.38
Winslow, ME (cdp/town) Kennebec County	30	0.38
Holualoa, HI (cdp) Hawaii County	36	0.37
East Bradford, PA (township) Chester County	36	0.36
Maurice River, NJ (township) Cumberland County	29	0.36
Springfield, PA (township) Delaware County	83	0.35
Stafford, TX (city) Fort Bend County	60	0.35
Emmaus, PA (borough) Lehigh County	39	0.35
Methuen Town, MA (city) Essex County	158	0.34
Whitehall, PA (township) Lehigh County	91	0.34
Dunn Loring, VA (cdp) Fairfax County	31	0.34
Flint, MI (charter township) Genesee County	109	0.33
Niles, OH (city) Trumbull County	64	0.33
Carrboro, NC (town) Orange County	62	0.33
Long Hill, NJ (township) Morris County	29	0.33
Litchfield, NH (town) Hillsborough County	27	0.33
Overland, MO (city) St. Louis County	52	0.32
Cusseta-Chattahoochee County, GA (unified govt) Chattahoochee County	37	0.32
Hamburg, NY (village) Erie County	30	0.32
Leisure World, MD (cdp) Montgomery County	28	0.32
Smithfield, VA (town) Isle of Wight County	25	0.32
Fullerton, PA (cdp) Lehigh County	46	0.31
Park Forest Village, PA (cdp) Centre County	31	0.31
Lower Southampton, PA (township) Bucks County	57	0.30
Wolf Trap, VA (cdp) Fairfax County	50	0.30
Berkeley Heights, NJ (township) Union County	40	0.30
Jupiter Farms, FL (cdp) Palm Beach County	36	0.30
Lantana, FL (town) Palm Beach County	31	0.30
Demopolis, AL (city) Marengo County	23	0.30
Derry, PA (township) Dauphin County	70	0.29
Olivehurst, CA (cdp) Yuba County	38	0.29
Winchester, CT (town) Litchfield County	33	0.29
Palm Beach, FL (town) Palm Beach County	25	0.29
Everett, MA (city) Middlesex County	115	0.28
Trussville, AL (city) Jefferson County	53	0.28
Denville, NJ (township) Morris County	47	0.28
Uxbridge, MA (town) Worcester County	36	0.28
Northwest Harborcreek, PA (cdp) Erie County	25	0.28
Larkspur, CA (city) Marin County	32	0.27
Chenango, NY (town) Broome County	30	0.27
North Bend, OR (city) Coos County	26	0.27
Weatherford, TX (city) Parker County	62	0.26
Caln, PA (township) Chester County	36	0.26
Floris, VA (cdp) Fairfax County	21	0.26
Atlantic Beach, FL (city) Duval County	33	0.25
Medfield, MA (town) Norfolk County	30	0.25
Forestdale, AL (cdp) Jefferson County	27	0.25
Birch Bay, WA (cdp) Whatcom County	20	0.25
Springdale, NJ (cdp) Camden County	35	0.24
Phelan, CA (cdp) San Bernardino County	33	0.24
Spring Creek, NV (cdp) Elko County	33	0.24
Tarboro, NC (town) Edgecombe County	27	0.24
Jerome, ID (city) Jerome County	25	0.24
Liberty, NY (town) Sullivan County	24	0.24
Prineville, OR (city) Crook County	23	0.24
Woodlyn, PA (cdp) Delaware County	22	0.24
Arden-Arcade, CA (cdp) Sacramento County	205	0.23
Shrewsbury, MA (town) Worcester County	79	0.23
Mount Vernon, WA (city) Skagit County	72	0.23
Shelton, WA (city) Mason County	22	0.23
Fairview, TN (city) Williamson County	17	0.23
Salem, MA (city) Essex County	89	0.22
Milwaukie, OR (city) Clackamas County	44	0.22
Mashpee, MA (town) Barnstable County	30	0.22
Bull Run, VA (cdp) Prince William County	29	0.22
Elwood, NY (cdp) Suffolk County	24	0.22
Cape Canaveral, FL (city) Brevard County	22	0.22
St. Marys, OH (city) Auglaize County	18	0.22
Summit, NJ (city) Union County	45	0.21
Rocky River, OH (city) Cuyahoga County	42	0.21
Glassboro, NJ (borough) Gloucester County	40	0.21
South Burlington, VT (city) Chittenden County	36	0.21
Patton, PA (township) Centre County	31	0.21
Antioch, IL (village) Lake County	29	0.21
North Weeki Wachee, FL (cdp) Hernando County	18	0.21
Ketchikan, AK (city) Ketchikan Gateway Borough	17	0.21
Brea, CA (city) Orange County	78	0.20
Franklin Town, MA (city) Norfolk County	63	0.20
Eagle Pass, TX (city) Maverick County	50	0.20
Burlington, MA (cdp/town) Middlesex County	48	0.20
Key West, FL (city) Monroe County	48	0.20
Ruston, LA (city) Lincoln Parish	44	0.20
Tonawanda, NY (city) Erie County	31	0.20
Leoni, MI (township) Jackson County	28	0.20
Aurora, NY (town) Erie County	27	0.20
Scottdale, GA (cdp) DeKalb County	20	0.20
Center Line, MI (city) Macomb County	17	0.20
Black Mountain, NC (town) Buncombe County	16	0.20
Bethel, CT (town) Fairfield County	35	0.19
Easthampton Town, MA (city) Hampshire County	31	0.19
Parma, NY (town) Monroe County	30	0.19
Wawarsing, NY (town) Ulster County	25	0.19
Riverview, MI (city) Wayne County	24	0.19
Somers Point, NJ (city) Atlantic County	21	0.19
Fairview, PA (township) Erie County	19	0.19
Rye Brook, NY (village) Westchester County	17	0.19
Trophy Club, TX (town) Denton County	15	0.19
Westminster, CO (city) Adams County	184	0.18
Flower Mound, TX (town) Denton County	115	0.18
New Braunfels, TX (city) Comal County	95	0.18
Tigard, OR (city) Washington County	83	0.18
Edgewater, FL (city) Volusia County	38	0.18
Mountain Brook, AL (city) Jefferson County	36	0.18
Duxbury, MA (town) Plymouth County	27	0.18
Halawa, HI (cdp) Honolulu County	25	0.18
Westwood, MI (cdp) Kalamazoo County	16	0.18
Bow, NH (town) Merrimack County	14	0.18
Monessen, PA (city) Westmoreland County	14	0.18
Lake Ridge, VA (cdp) Prince William County	66	0.17
Fairbanks, AK (city) Fairbanks North Star Borough	53	0.17
Port Angeles, WA (city) Clallam County	32	0.17
Mount Vernon, OH (city) Knox County	29	0.17
Lewiston, NY (town) Niagara County	27	0.17
Ledyard, CT (town) New London County	26	0.17
Hendersonville, NC (city) Henderson County	22	0.17
Sonoma, CA (city) Sonoma County	18	0.17
Thomaston, GA (city) Upson County	16	0.17
West Point, UT (city) Davis County	15	0.17

Please refer to the Explanation of Data in the front of the book for more detailed information.

Ancestry

Croatian

U.S. and 50 States Sorted by Population and Percent of Total Population

Place	Population	%
United States	**417,130**	**0.14**
Pennsylvania	50,995	0.40
California	45,537	0.12
Illinois	44,065	0.35
Ohio	41,430	0.36
New York	26,607	0.14
Michigan	20,547	0.21
Florida	16,360	0.09
Wisconsin	15,775	0.28
Indiana	13,306	0.21
Washington	13,268	0.20
New Jersey	13,154	0.15
Missouri	9,856	0.17
Texas	9,186	0.04
Arizona	8,595	0.14
Minnesota	8,558	0.16
Colorado	6,570	0.13
Kansas	6,494	0.23
Virginia	6,245	0.08
Oregon	5,124	0.14
North Carolina	4,404	0.05
Georgia	4,167	0.04
Iowa	3,961	0.13
Nevada	3,875	0.15
Maryland	3,390	0.06
Connecticut	3,218	0.09
Massachusetts	3,017	0.05
Louisiana	2,921	0.07
West Virginia	2,396	0.13
Utah	2,318	0.09
Montana	2,213	0.23
South Carolina	2,097	0.05
Nebraska	2,051	0.11
Tennessee	1,689	0.03
Idaho	1,388	0.09
Alabama	1,305	0.03
New Mexico	1,298	0.06
Kentucky	1,291	0.03
Mississippi	1,054	0.04
Alaska	852	0.12
Oklahoma	843	0.02
Arkansas	826	0.03
New Hampshire	783	0.06
Hawaii	723	0.05
South Dakota	641	0.08
District of Columbia	611	0.10
Delaware	487	0.06
Wyoming	462	0.08
Maine	334	0.03
Rhode Island	330	0.03
Vermont	267	0.04
North Dakota	246	0.04

Place	Population	%
Pennsylvania	50,995	0.40
Ohio	41,430	0.36
Illinois	44,065	0.35
Wisconsin	15,775	0.28
Kansas	6,494	0.23
Montana	2,213	0.23
Michigan	20,547	0.21
Indiana	13,306	0.21
Washington	13,268	0.20
Missouri	9,856	0.17
Minnesota	8,558	0.16
New Jersey	13,154	0.15
Nevada	3,875	0.15
United States	**417,130**	**0.14**
New York	26,607	0.14
Arizona	8,595	0.14
Oregon	5,124	0.14
Colorado	6,570	0.13
Iowa	3,961	0.13
West Virginia	2,396	0.13
California	45,537	0.12
Alaska	852	0.12
Nebraska	2,051	0.11
District of Columbia	611	0.10
Florida	16,360	0.09
Connecticut	3,218	0.09
Utah	2,318	0.09
Idaho	1,388	0.09
Virginia	6,245	0.08
South Dakota	641	0.08
Wyoming	462	0.08
Louisiana	2,921	0.07
Maryland	3,390	0.06
New Mexico	1,298	0.06
New Hampshire	783	0.06
Delaware	487	0.06
North Carolina	4,404	0.05
Massachusetts	3,017	0.05
South Carolina	2,097	0.05
Hawaii	723	0.05
Texas	9,186	0.04
Georgia	4,167	0.04
Mississippi	1,054	0.04
Vermont	267	0.04
North Dakota	246	0.04
Tennessee	1,689	0.03
Alabama	1,305	0.03
Kentucky	1,291	0.03
Arkansas	826	0.03
Maine	334	0.03
Rhode Island	330	0.03
Oklahoma	843	0.02

Please refer to the Explanation of Data in the front of the book for more detailed information.

Ancestry

Croatian

Top 150 Places Sorted by Population

Based on all places, regardless of total population

Place	Population	%
New York, NY (city) Kings County	11,304	0.14
Chicago, IL (city) Cook County	7,104	0.26
Queens, NY (borough) Queens County	7,054	0.32
Los Angeles, CA (city) Los Angeles County	6,277	0.17
Pittsburgh, PA (city) Allegheny County	2,304	0.75
Manhattan, NY (borough) New York County	2,164	0.14
Phoenix, AZ (city) Maricopa County	1,912	0.13
Seattle, WA (city) King County	1,828	0.31
Mentor, OH (city) Lake County	1,797	3.77
Kansas City, KS (city) Wyandotte County	1,767	1.23
San Jose, CA (city) Santa Clara County	1,692	0.18
Milwaukee, WI (city) Milwaukee County	1,587	0.27
Cleveland, OH (city) Cuyahoga County	1,547	0.38
San Francisco, CA (city) San Francisco County	1,466	0.19
San Diego, CA (city) San Diego County	1,378	0.11
Kansas City, MO (city) Jackson County	1,349	0.30
Portland, OR (city) Multnomah County	1,270	0.22
Joliet, IL (city) Will County	1,196	0.82
Columbus, OH (city) Franklin County	1,158	0.15
Overland Park, KS (city) Johnson County	1,131	0.66
Parma, OH (city) Cuyahoga County	1,112	1.36
Euclid, OH (city) Cuyahoga County	1,084	2.20
Hempstead, NY (town) Nassau County	1,033	0.14
Naperville, IL (city) DuPage County	1,020	0.72
Oyster Bay, NY (town) Nassau County	1,002	0.34
Brooklyn, NY (borough) Kings County	998	0.04
Rancho Palos Verdes, CA (city) Los Angeles County	990	2.38
Jacksonville, FL (city) Duval County	974	0.12
Omaha, NE (city) Douglas County	961	0.24
Las Vegas, NV (city) Clark County	937	0.16
Philadelphia, PA (city) Philadelphia County	916	0.06
North Huntingdon, PA (township) Westmoreland County	911	3.01
Hammond, IN (city) Lake County	908	1.12
St. Louis, MO (city) St. Louis city County	875	0.27
Staten Island, NY (borough) Richmond County	869	0.19
Orland Park, IL (village) Cook County	840	1.52
Shaler, PA (township) Allegheny County	834	2.91
Tucson, AZ (city) Pima County	785	0.15
Huntington, NY (town) Suffolk County	781	0.39
Willoughby, OH (city) Lake County	769	3.46
Cliffside Park, NJ (borough) Bergen County	750	3.21
Boardman, OH (cdp) Mahoning County	733	2.07
West Allis, WI (city) Milwaukee County	731	1.22
McCandless, PA (township) Allegheny County	725	2.56
Willowick, OH (city) Lake County	705	4.96
Swatara, PA (township) Dauphin County	692	2.99
Eastlake, OH (city) Lake County	689	3.65
Youngstown, OH (city) Mahoning County	688	0.99
Mesa, AZ (city) Maricopa County	687	0.16
Ross, PA (township) Allegheny County	678	2.18
North Hempstead, NY (town) Nassau County	672	0.30
Allison Park, PA (cdp) Allegheny County	668	3.00
Lower Paxton, PA (township) Dauphin County	668	1.43
Schererville, IN (town) Lake County	664	2.33
Highland, IN (town) Lake County	663	2.80
Tacoma, WA (city) Pierce County	628	0.32
Huntington Beach, CA (city) Orange County	618	0.33
Charlotte, NC (city) Mecklenburg County	618	0.09
Denver, CO (city) Denver County	615	0.11
Washington, DC (city) District of Columbia	611	0.10
Greenburgh, NY (town) Westchester County	609	0.69
Austin, TX (city) Travis County	606	0.08
Austintown, OH (cdp) Mahoning County	596	1.97
Fairview, NJ (borough) Bergen County	594	4.35
Brookhaven, NY (town) Suffolk County	588	0.12
Crown Point, IN (city) Lake County	585	2.24
Akron, OH (city) Summit County	584	0.29
Wickliffe, OH (city) Lake County	580	4.51
Monroeville, PA (municipality) Allegheny County	578	2.04
Oak Lawn, IL (village) Cook County	577	1.03
Lorain, OH (city) Lorain County	569	0.87
Lakewood, OH (city) Cuyahoga County	563	1.07
Minneapolis, MN (city) Hennepin County	558	0.15
Mount Pleasant, NY (town) Westchester County	554	1.28
Arlington, VA (cdp) Arlington County	550	0.28

Place	Population	%
McKeesport, PA (city) Allegheny County	538	2.64
Bellingham, WA (city) Whatcom County	538	0.68
North Olmsted, OH (city) Cuyahoga County	525	1.60
Penn Hills, PA (township) Allegheny County	518	1.21
Henderson, NV (city) Clark County	518	0.21
Houston, TX (city) Harris County	518	0.03
Munster, IN (town) Lake County	516	2.22
Gilbert, AZ (town) Maricopa County	510	0.26
Willoughby Hills, OH (city) Lake County	505	5.38
Hampton, PA (township) Allegheny County	503	2.79
Westlake, OH (city) Cuyahoga County	498	1.54
Hempfield, PA (township) Westmoreland County	496	1.15
Buffalo, NY (city) Erie County	487	0.18
Dallas, TX (city) Dallas County	487	0.04
Long Beach, CA (city) Los Angeles County	485	0.11
Hobart, IN (city) Lake County	483	1.70
Sacramento, CA (city) Sacramento County	483	0.11
West Mifflin, PA (borough) Allegheny County	482	2.35
Hopewell, PA (township) Beaver County	477	3.77
Scottsdale, AZ (city) Maricopa County	476	0.22
San Antonio, TX (city) Medina County	476	0.04
Lansing, IL (village) Cook County	471	1.68
Arden-Arcade, CA (cdp) Sacramento County	471	0.52
Spokane, WA (city) Spokane County	455	0.22
Oakland, CA (city) Alameda County	455	0.12
New Berlin, WI (city) Waukesha County	452	1.14
Channahon, IL (village) Will County	446	3.65
Downers Grove, IL (village) DuPage County	446	0.93
Franklin, WI (city) Milwaukee County	437	1.28
Center, PA (township) Beaver County	434	3.72
Hibbing, MN (city) St. Louis County	434	2.65
Spring Valley, NV (cdp) Clark County	432	0.25
Belle Chasse, LA (cdp) Plaquemines Parish	431	2.89
Santa Monica, CA (city) Los Angeles County	427	0.48
Baldwin, PA (borough) Allegheny County	424	2.16
Duluth, MN (city) St. Louis County	423	0.49
Colorado Springs, CO (city) El Paso County	422	0.10
Hermitage, PA (city) Mercer County	416	2.58
Madison, WI (city) Dane County	415	0.18
Indianapolis, IN (city) Marion County	412	0.05
Penn, PA (township) Westmoreland County	410	2.06
New Lenox, IL (village) Will County	407	1.70
Bethel Park, PA (municipality) Allegheny County	407	1.26
Warren, MI (city) Macomb County	406	0.30
Shawnee, KS (city) Johnson County	404	0.67
Independence, MO (city) Jackson County	398	0.34
Thousand Oaks, CA (city) Ventura County	398	0.32
Tinley Park, IL (village) Cook County	394	0.72
Lockport, IL (city) Will County	393	1.65
Amherst, NY (town) Erie County	393	0.32
Torrance, CA (city) Los Angeles County	390	0.27
Sunnyvale, CA (city) Santa Clara County	388	0.28
Shorewood, IL (village) Will County	385	2.62
Des Moines, IA (city) Polk County	385	0.19
Unity, PA (township) Westmoreland County	384	1.72
Fort Worth, TX (city) Tarrant County	384	0.05
West Deer, PA (township) Allegheny County	382	3.29
Reno, NV (city) Washoe County	380	0.17
Cranberry, PA (township) Butler County	375	1.37
Lombard, IL (village) DuPage County	374	0.88
Albuquerque, NM (city) Bernalillo County	367	0.07
Paradise, NV (cdp) Clark County	366	0.17
Barberton, OH (city) Summit County	364	1.36
North Royalton, OH (city) Cuyahoga County	364	1.21
Granite City, IL (city) Madison County	363	1.19
Merrillville, IN (town) Lake County	359	1.04
Bellevue, WA (city) King County	358	0.30
Nashville-Davidson, TN (metro govt) Davidson County	354	0.06
Lomita, CA (city) Los Angeles County	352	1.74
Erie, PA (city) Erie County	352	0.35
Des Plaines, IL (city) Cook County	351	0.61
Lakewood, CO (city) Jefferson County	351	0.25
Oakville, MO (cdp) St. Louis County	349	0.99
Franklin Park, PA (borough) Allegheny County	348	2.68
Wheeling, WV (city) Ohio County	347	1.20

Please refer to the Explanation of Data in the front of the book for more detailed information.

Ancestry

Croatian

Top 150 Places Sorted by Percent of Total Population

Based on all places, regardless of total population

Place	Population	%
Venice, LA (cdp) Plaquemines Parish	48	50.53
Bonanza, CO (town) Saguache County	3	50.00
Hendersonville, PA (cdp) Washington County	72	36.73
La Cueva, NM (cdp) Sandoval County	33	31.43
Crown, PA (cdp) Clarion County	26	22.03
Kingston, WI (town) Juneau County	14	18.18
McCook, IL (village) Cook County	66	18.08
Enhaut, PA (cdp) Dauphin County	148	16.39
Kirkville, IA (city) Wapello County	19	16.24
Rathbun, IA (city) Appanoose County	10	14.49
Yankee Lake, OH (village) Trumbull County	10	14.49
Lowell, KS (cdp) Cherokee County	34	14.35
Harrison City, PA (cdp) Westmoreland County	16	14.16
Ronald, WA (cdp) Kittitas County	15	14.02
Riverside, OR (cdp) Umatilla County	21	13.46
Bressler, PA (cdp) Dauphin County	189	13.00
Nebish, MN (township) Beltrami County	22	12.79
Alger, WA (cdp) Skagit County	31	12.50
West Sunbury, PA (borough) Butler County	23	12.23
Ashland, WI (town) Ashland County	93	12.03
Lublin, WI (village) Taylor County	21	11.86
Ahmeek, MI (village) Keweenaw County	21	11.60
Buras, LA (cdp) Plaquemines Parish	72	11.41
Radnor, OH (cdp) Delaware County	16	11.35
Mystic, IA (city) Appanoose County	56	10.63
Russellton, PA (cdp) Allegheny County	146	10.47
Gingles, WI (town) Ashland County	67	10.23
Numa, IA (city) Appanoose County	10	10.10
Ensign, MI (township) Delta County	86	9.90
Avon, NC (cdp) Dare County	22	9.69
Naomi, PA (cdp) Fayette County	11	9.65
Bairdford, PA (cdp) Allegheny County	65	9.64
Lake Santee, IN (cdp) Decatur County	61	9.52
Wawina, MN (township) Itasca County	6	9.52
Gilson, IL (cdp) Knox County	9	9.09
Bulger, PA (cdp) Washington County	44	9.03
Goldfield, NV (cdp) Esmeralda County	22	8.87
Cassville, WV (cdp) Monongalia County	66	8.80
Piney Mountain, VA (cdp) Albemarle County	117	8.72
Empire, LA (cdp) Plaquemines Parish	58	8.64
Millsboro, PA (cdp) Washington County	40	8.60
Fayette City, PA (borough) Fayette County	34	8.48
East Rochester, PA (borough) Beaver County	58	8.37
Crucible, PA (cdp) Greene County	53	8.36
Lincoln, WI (town) Bayfield County	21	8.20
Bessemer, PA (borough) Lawrence County	96	8.08
Sidman, PA (cdp) Cambria County	21	8.08
Mansfield, MI (township) Iron County	15	8.02
Cornucopia, WI (cdp) Bayfield County	5	7.81
Parker, SD (city) Turner County	83	7.42
Ellsworth, PA (borough) Washington County	74	7.33
White City, IL (village) Macoupin County	18	7.26
Homewood, PA (borough) Beaver County	9	7.20
Williamson, IA (city) Lucas County	9	7.20
Lincoln, WI (town) Vilas County	158	7.07
Mason, WI (town) Bayfield County	17	7.00
Stanton, MI (township) Houghton County	86	6.96
Garfield, MI (township) Mackinac County	86	6.95
Reedsville, PA (cdp) Mifflin County	30	6.90
Wilsonville, IL (village) Macoupin County	35	6.89
McKinley Heights, OH (cdp) Trumbull County	75	6.88
Indian Springs, TX (cdp) Polk County	72	6.84
Etna, PA (borough) Allegheny County	237	6.76
Boston, PA (cdp) Allegheny County	28	6.67
Allenport, PA (borough) Washington County	29	6.65
Allouez, MI (township) Keweenaw County	103	6.60
Essex, IL (village) Kankakee County	38	6.53
Cohassett Beach, WA (cdp) Grays Harbor County	37	6.51
Montmorenci, IN (cdp) Tippecanoe County	11	6.51
Lake Linden, MI (village) Houghton County	63	6.47
Anderson, WI (town) Iron County	6	6.45
Braddock Hills, PA (borough) Allegheny County	120	6.44
Poydras, LA (cdp) St. Bernard Parish	121	6.40
Bridgewater, PA (borough) Beaver County	43	6.39
Ellisville, IL (village) Fulton County	6	6.32
Hunker, PA (borough) Westmoreland County	20	6.31
Barksdale, WI (town) Bayfield County	47	6.30
Iron Range, MN (township) Itasca County	36	6.29
Gilbert, MN (city) St. Louis County	110	6.21
Grant Town, WV (town) Marion County	32	6.18
Emlenton, PA (borough) Venango County	44	6.11
Reserve, PA (township) Allegheny County	208	6.09
St. David, IL (village) Fulton County	31	6.08
Arrowhead, MN (township) St. Louis County	9	6.08
Versailles, PA (borough) Allegheny County	93	6.03
Emlenton, PA (borough) Venango County	44	6.03
Conway, PA (borough) Beaver County	127	5.96
Adams, MI (township) Houghton County	153	5.93
Swan Lake, MT (cdp) Lake County	7	5.83
Sun Valley Lake, IA (cdp) Ringgold County	11	5.79
Hagali, MN (township) Beltrami County	17	5.78
Inverness, CA (cdp) Marin County	79	5.72
Promise City, IA (city) Wayne County	8	5.67
Centerville, IA (city) Appanoose County	316	5.65
Gleed, WA (cdp) Yakima County	143	5.61
Seventh Mountain, OR (cdp) Deschutes County	19	5.60
White Pine, MI (cdp) Ontonagon County	23	5.58
Fredericktown, PA (cdp) Washington County	22	5.56
Smock, PA (cdp) Fayette County	36	5.51
Hometown, IL (city) Cook County	237	5.48
Kelly, WI (town) Bayfield County	28	5.48
Venice, NE (cdp) Douglas County	6	5.45
Castorland, NY (village) Lewis County	21	5.44
Wiota, IA (city) Cass County	8	5.44
Clyde, WI (town) Iowa County	20	5.43
Aberdeen, IN (cdp) Porter County	118	5.40
Willoughby Hills, OH (city) Lake County	505	5.38
Taconite, MN (city) Itasca County	17	5.38
Nason, IL (city) Jefferson County	10	5.35
Harmony, NJ (cdp) Warren County	21	5.33
Sawyerville, IL (village) Macoupin County	14	5.32
Shooks, MN (township) Beltrami County	12	5.31
Fayal, MN (township) St. Louis County	85	5.30
Ben Avon Heights, PA (borough) Allegheny County	21	5.30
Lakeline, OH (village) Lake County	8	5.30
Beallsville, PA (borough) Washington County	23	5.26
Belgium, WI (town) Ozaukee County	73	5.20
Waite Hill, OH (village) Lake County	25	5.17
Laurium, MI (village) Houghton County	111	5.16
South Range, MI (village) Houghton County	21	5.16
Farmington, WV (town) Marion County	19	5.15
Schoolcraft, MI (township) Houghton County	91	5.14
Oconee, IL (village) Shelby County	9	5.14
Grand View, WI (cdp) Bayfield County	4	5.13
South Beaver, PA (township) Beaver County	140	5.10
Perry, PA (township) Armstrong County	21	5.10
New Auburn, MN (city) Sibley County	28	5.08
Port Vue, PA (borough) Allegheny County	194	5.05
Cincinnati, IA (city) Appanoose County	18	5.04
Webster, PA (cdp) Westmoreland County	16	5.00
Peeksville, WI (town) Ashland County	7	5.00
Willowick, OH (city) Lake County	705	4.96
Austinburg, OH (cdp) Ashtabula County	40	4.96
Goodfield, IL (village) Woodford County	55	4.92
McDavitt, MN (township) St. Louis County	20	4.90
Greenock, PA (cdp) Allegheny County	91	4.81
Claysville, PA (borough) Washington County	30	4.81
Buhl, MN (city) St. Louis County	42	4.71
Cattle Creek, CO (cdp) Garfield County	40	4.71
Elderon, WI (village) Marathon County	8	4.71
Yukon, PA (cdp) Westmoreland County	25	4.70
Cokeburg, PA (borough) Washington County	33	4.67
Wylandville, PA (cdp) Washington County	16	4.60
Thiensville, WI (village) Ozaukee County	148	4.56
Spring Ridge, PA (cdp) Berks County	48	4.56
Baden, PA (borough) Beaver County	189	4.55
Somo, WI (town) Lincoln County	5	4.55
Bass Lake, CA (cdp) Madera County	21	4.54
Alango, MN (township) St. Louis County	12	4.53
Ehrenfeld, PA (borough) Cambria County	9	4.52

Please refer to the Explanation of Data in the front of the book for more detailed information.

Ancestry

Croatian

Top 150 Places Sorted by Percent of Total Population

Based on places with total population of 7,500 or more

Place	Population	%
Willoughby Hills, OH (city) Lake County	505	5.38
Willowick, OH (city) Lake County	705	4.96
Wickliffe, OH (city) Lake County	580	4.51
Kennedy, PA (township) Allegheny County	340	4.47
Fairview, NJ (borough) Bergen County	594	4.35
Mentor, OH (city) Lake County	1,797	3.77
Hopewell, PA (township) Beaver County	477	3.77
Sunset Hills, MO (city) St. Louis County	318	3.77
Center, PA (township) Beaver County	434	3.72
Eastlake, OH (city) Lake County	689	3.65
Channahon, IL (village) Will County	446	3.65
Economy, PA (borough) Beaver County	328	3.64
Willoughby, OH (city) Lake County	769	3.46
West Deer, PA (township) Allegheny County	382	3.29
Highland Heights, OH (city) Cuyahoga County	268	3.25
Cliffside Park, NJ (borough) Bergen County	750	3.21
North Huntingdon, PA (township) Westmoreland County	911	3.01
Allison Park, PA (cdp) Allegheny County	668	3.00
Swatara, PA (township) Dauphin County	692	2.99
Shaler, PA (township) Allegheny County	834	2.91
Belle Chasse, LA (cdp) Plaquemines Parish	431	2.89
Virginia, MN (city) St. Louis County	251	2.86
Lakes of the Four Seasons, IN (cdp) Lake County	216	2.86
Jefferson Hills, PA (borough) Allegheny County	293	2.82
Highland, IN (town) Lake County	663	2.80
Hampton, PA (township) Allegheny County	503	2.79
Franklin Park, PA (borough) Allegheny County	348	2.68
Hibbing, MN (city) St. Louis County	434	2.65
McKeesport, PA (city) Allegheny County	538	2.64
Ridgefield, NJ (borough) Bergen County	289	2.64
Shorewood, IL (village) Will County	385	2.62
Hermitage, PA (city) Mercer County	416	2.58
McCandless, PA (township) Allegheny County	725	2.56
Hubbard, OH (city) Trumbull County	203	2.56
Willowbrook, IL (village) DuPage County	218	2.55
Cecil, PA (township) Washington County	277	2.52
White Oak, PA (borough) Allegheny County	199	2.52
Struthers, OH (city) Mahoning County	269	2.47
O'Hara, PA (township) Allegheny County	203	2.42
Elizabeth, PA (township) Allegheny County	319	2.40
Macedonia, OH (city) Summit County	261	2.40
St. John, IN (town) Lake County	328	2.39
Schroeppel, NY (town) Oswego County	203	2.39
Campbell, OH (city) Mahoning County	202	2.39
Rancho Palos Verdes, CA (city) Los Angeles County	990	2.38
West Mifflin, PA (borough) Allegheny County	482	2.35
Schererville, IN (town) Lake County	664	2.33
Ashland, WI (city) Ashland County	193	2.33
Mentor-on-the-Lake, OH (city) Lake County	177	2.33
Aliquippa, PA (city) Beaver County	223	2.28
Crown Point, IN (city) Lake County	585	2.24
Pleasant Hills, PA (borough) Allegheny County	185	2.24
Munster, IN (town) Lake County	516	2.22
Euclid, OH (city) Cuyahoga County	1,084	2.20
Swissvale, PA (borough) Allegheny County	199	2.20
Ross, PA (township) Allegheny County	678	2.18
Baldwin, PA (borough) Allegheny County	424	2.16
Pine, PA (township) Allegheny County	229	2.13
Lemont, IL (village) Cook County	322	2.10
Boardman, OH (cdp) Mahoning County	733	2.07
Penn, PA (township) Westmoreland County	410	2.06
Seabrook, TX (city) Harris County	236	2.06
Monroeville, PA (municipality) Allegheny County	578	2.04
Munhall, PA (borough) Allegheny County	231	2.02
Lincolnwood, IL (village) Cook County	249	2.00
South Union, PA (township) Fayette County	216	2.00
Austintown, OH (cdp) Mahoning County	596	1.97
Escanaba, MI (city) Delta County	244	1.92
Monessen, PA (city) Westmoreland County	151	1.92
Delafield, WI (town) Waukesha County	157	1.89
Lyons, IL (village) Cook County	198	1.88
Brighton, PA (township) Beaver County	151	1.85
Brooklyn, OH (city) Cuyahoga County	205	1.84
Bellevue, PA (borough) Allegheny County	153	1.83
Grosse Pointe Park, MI (city) Wayne County	214	1.82
Houghton, MI (city) Houghton County	138	1.82
Lomita, CA (city) Los Angeles County	352	1.74
Unity, PA (township) Westmoreland County	384	1.72
Hobart, IN (city) Lake County	483	1.70
New Lenox, IL (village) Will County	407	1.70
Crest Hill, IL (city) Will County	344	1.69
Lansing, IL (village) Cook County	471	1.68
Anaconda-Deer Lodge County, MT (special city) Deer Lodge County	155	1.67
Ellwood City, PA (borough) Lawrence County	137	1.67
Lockport, IL (city) Will County	393	1.65
Sharon, PA (city) Mercer County	235	1.63
Uniontown, PA (city) Fayette County	175	1.63
Dobbs Ferry, NY (village) Westchester County	175	1.62
Long Branch, VA (cdp) Fairfax County	128	1.61
North Olmsted, OH (city) Cuyahoga County	525	1.60
La Grange, IL (village) Cook County	244	1.58
West Hanover, PA (township) Dauphin County	139	1.58
South Fayette, PA (township) Allegheny County	219	1.57
Lower Swatara, PA (township) Dauphin County	127	1.55
Westlake, OH (city) Cuyahoga County	498	1.54
Orland Park, IL (village) Cook County	840	1.52
North Strabane, PA (township) Washington County	195	1.52
Larkspur, CA (city) Marin County	180	1.52
Easthampton Town, MA (city) Hampshire County	241	1.50
Fernway, PA (cdp) Butler County	184	1.50
Sappington, MO (cdp) St. Louis County	120	1.50
Richland, PA (township) Allegheny County	159	1.49
Aberdeen, WA (city) Grays Harbor County	250	1.48
Palisades Park, NJ (borough) Bergen County	279	1.46
Lower Paxton, PA (township) Dauphin County	668	1.43
Burr Ridge, IL (village) DuPage County	150	1.43
Dyer, IN (town) Lake County	227	1.42
Maxatawny, PA (township) Berks County	109	1.41
Greensburg, PA (city) Westmoreland County	210	1.40
Chicago Ridge, IL (village) Cook County	198	1.40
Cedar Lake, IN (town) Lake County	155	1.39
Neshannock, PA (township) Lawrence County	132	1.39
Peters, PA (township) Washington County	283	1.38
Hinsdale, IL (village) DuPage County	230	1.38
Cranberry, PA (township) Butler County	375	1.37
Geneva, IL (city) Kane County	294	1.37
Parma, OH (city) Cuyahoga County	1,112	1.36
Barberton, OH (city) Summit County	364	1.36
Johnstown, PA (city) Cambria County	291	1.36
Rostraver, PA (township) Westmoreland County	155	1.36
Fox Lake, IL (village) Lake County	143	1.36
Sachse, TX (city) Dallas County	248	1.35
Murrysville, PA (municipality) Westmoreland County	264	1.33
La Grange Park, IL (village) Cook County	178	1.33
Oak Brook, IL (village) DuPage County	105	1.33
Wood River, IL (city) Madison County	143	1.32
Lowell, IN (town) Lake County	118	1.32
Park Ridge, NJ (borough) Bergen County	114	1.32
St. Joseph, MI (city) Berrien County	111	1.32
Mukwonago, WI (town) Waukesha County	103	1.32
Parma Heights, OH (city) Cuyahoga County	272	1.31
Shenango, PA (township) Lawrence County	98	1.31
Millstone, NJ (township) Monmouth County	134	1.30
Weirton, WV (city) Hancock County	255	1.29
Oradell, NJ (borough) Bergen County	102	1.29
Mount Pleasant, NY (town) Westchester County	554	1.28
Franklin, WI (city) Milwaukee County	437	1.28
Lackawanna, NY (city) Erie County	233	1.28
Bethel Park, PA (municipality) Allegheny County	407	1.26
Moon, PA (township) Allegheny County	297	1.26
Glen Rock, NJ (borough) Bergen County	146	1.26
Frankfort Square, IL (cdp) Will County	120	1.26
Closter, NJ (borough) Bergen County	105	1.26
Whitehall, PA (borough) Allegheny County	172	1.24
Seven Hills, OH (city) Cuyahoga County	146	1.24
Kansas City, KS (city) Wyandotte County	1,767	1.23
Affton, MO (cdp) St. Louis County	247	1.23
Bethpage, NY (cdp) Nassau County	204	1.23
West Allis, WI (city) Milwaukee County	731	1.22
Canton, IL (city) Fulton County	180	1.22

SECTION THREE

Please refer to the Explanation of Data in the front of the book for more detailed information.

Ancestry

Cypriot

U.S. and 50 States Sorted by Population and Percent of Total Population

Place	Population	%
United States	**5,843**	**<0.01**
New York	1,721	0.01
New Jersey	693	0.01
California	604	<0.01
Pennsylvania	375	<0.01
Massachusetts	267	<0.01
Virginia	246	<0.01
Maryland	201	<0.01
Illinois	171	<0.01
Ohio	141	<0.01
Texas	137	<0.01
Florida	135	<0.01
North Carolina	135	<0.01
Connecticut	110	<0.01
Indiana	88	<0.01
Missouri	87	<0.01
Colorado	85	<0.01
Michigan	82	<0.01
Wisconsin	81	<0.01
Washington	75	<0.01
Arizona	54	<0.01
Vermont	42	0.01
South Carolina	40	<0.01
Georgia	30	<0.01
Idaho	26	<0.01
New Mexico	25	<0.01
Arkansas	22	<0.01
West Virginia	21	<0.01
Kentucky	19	<0.01
Iowa	16	<0.01
Kansas	16	<0.01
Tennessee	16	<0.01
Minnesota	15	<0.01
Louisiana	13	<0.01
Oregon	13	<0.01
Hawaii	12	<0.01
District of Columbia	11	<0.01
Maine	9	<0.01
Rhode Island	9	<0.01
Alabama	0	0.00
Alaska	0	0.00
Delaware	0	0.00
Mississippi	0	0.00
Montana	0	0.00
Nebraska	0	0.00
Nevada	0	0.00
New Hampshire	0	0.00
North Dakota	0	0.00
Oklahoma	0	0.00
South Dakota	0	0.00
Utah	0	0.00
Wyoming	0	0.00

Place	Population	%
New York	1,721	0.01
New Jersey	693	0.01
Vermont	42	0.01
United States	**5,843**	**<0.01**
California	604	<0.01
Pennsylvania	375	<0.01
Massachusetts	267	<0.01
Virginia	246	<0.01
Maryland	201	<0.01
Illinois	171	<0.01
Ohio	141	<0.01
Texas	137	<0.01
Florida	135	<0.01
North Carolina	135	<0.01
Connecticut	110	<0.01
Indiana	88	<0.01
Missouri	87	<0.01
Colorado	85	<0.01
Michigan	82	<0.01
Wisconsin	81	<0.01
Washington	75	<0.01
Arizona	54	<0.01
South Carolina	40	<0.01
Georgia	30	<0.01
Idaho	26	<0.01
New Mexico	25	<0.01
Arkansas	22	<0.01
West Virginia	21	<0.01
Kentucky	19	<0.01
Iowa	16	<0.01
Kansas	16	<0.01
Tennessee	16	<0.01
Minnesota	15	<0.01
Louisiana	13	<0.01
Oregon	13	<0.01
Hawaii	12	<0.01
District of Columbia	11	<0.01
Maine	9	<0.01
Rhode Island	9	<0.01
Alabama	0	0.00
Alaska	0	0.00
Delaware	0	0.00
Mississippi	0	0.00
Montana	0	0.00
Nebraska	0	0.00
Nevada	0	0.00
New Hampshire	0	0.00
North Dakota	0	0.00
Oklahoma	0	0.00
South Dakota	0	0.00
Utah	0	0.00
Wyoming	0	0.00

Please refer to the Explanation of Data in the front of the book for more detailed information.

Ancestry

Cypriot

Top 150 Places Sorted by Population

Based on all places, regardless of total population

Place	Population	%
New York, NY (city) Kings County	960	0.01
Queens, NY (borough) Queens County	644	0.03
Hempstead, NY (town) Nassau County	254	0.03
Manhattan, NY (borough) New York County	216	0.01
Chicago, IL (city) Cook County	122	<0.01
Lawrenceville, NJ (cdp) Mercer County	116	3.26
Lawrence, NJ (township) Mercer County	116	0.35
Santa Clara, CA (city) Santa Clara County	115	0.10
Pittsburgh, PA (city) Allegheny County	102	0.03
Long Beach, CA (city) Los Angeles County	94	0.02
Oceanside, NY (cdp) Nassau County	90	0.29
Holmdel, NJ (township) Monmouth County	83	0.50
Huntington, NY (town) Suffolk County	82	0.04
Boston, MA (city) Suffolk County	77	0.01
Philadelphia, PA (city) Philadelphia County	75	<0.01
Los Angeles, CA (city) Los Angeles County	69	<0.01
Valley Stream, NY (village) Nassau County	68	0.18
Franklin Square, NY (cdp) Nassau County	67	0.23
Lower Merion, PA (township) Montgomery County	66	0.11
Yorktown, NY (town) Westchester County	65	0.18
North Hempstead, NY (town) Nassau County	64	0.03
Oyster Bay, NY (town) Nassau County	63	0.02
Brooklyn, NY (borough) Kings County	62	<0.01
West Lafayette, IN (city) Tippecanoe County	61	0.21
Greenlawn, NY (cdp) Suffolk County	56	0.43
Stoneham, MA (cdp/town) Middlesex County	55	0.26
Rotterdam, NY (town) Schenectady County	54	0.19
Alameda, CA (city) Alameda County	51	0.07
Brookhaven, NY (town) Suffolk County	51	0.01
San Diego, CA (city) San Diego County	51	<0.01
San Francisco, CA (city) San Francisco County	50	0.01
Creve Coeur, MO (city) St. Louis County	47	0.27
Kennewick, WA (city) Benton County	46	0.07
Cambridge, MA (city) Middlesex County	46	0.04
Brick, NJ (township) Ocean County	45	0.06
West Hartford, CT (cdp/town) Hartford County	43	0.07
Olney, MD (cdp) Montgomery County	40	0.12
Wayne, NJ (township) Passaic County	40	0.07
Lake Grove, NY (village) Suffolk County	39	0.35
Union, NJ (township) Union County	38	0.07
Virginia Beach, VA (ind. city) Virginia Beach independent city	38	0.01
Bronx, NY (borough) Bronx County	38	<0.01
Berkeley, NJ (township) Ocean County	36	0.09
Aurora, CO (city) Arapahoe County	36	0.01
Georgia, VT (town) Franklin County	34	0.75
Elon, NC (town) Alamance County	34	0.38
South San Francisco, CA (city) San Mateo County	34	0.05
South Brunswick, NJ (township) Middlesex County	33	0.08
Phoenix, AZ (city) Maricopa County	32	<0.01
Hampton, VA (ind. city) Hampton independent city	31	0.02
Malden, MA (city) Middlesex County	30	0.05
Rye, NY (town) Westchester County	28	0.06
Centennial, CO (city) Arapahoe County	28	0.03
Grosse Pointe Woods, MI (city) Wayne County	27	0.17
Mineola, NY (village) Nassau County	27	0.14
South Pasadena, CA (city) Los Angeles County	27	0.11
Brookline, MA (cdp/town) Norfolk County	27	0.05
Jersey City, NJ (city) Hudson County	27	0.01
Madison, WI (city) Dane County	27	0.01
Raleigh, NC (city) Wake County	27	0.01
Pocatello, ID (city) Bannock County	26	0.05
Islip, NY (town) Suffolk County	25	0.01
Elk, NJ (township) Gloucester County	24	0.58
Arlington Heights, PA (cdp) Monroe County	24	0.38
Upper Freehold, NJ (township) Monmouth County	24	0.37
Stroud, PA (township) Monroe County	24	0.13
Raritan, NJ (township) Hunterdon County	24	0.11
Coral Gables, FL (city) Miami-Dade County	24	0.05
Harrisonburg, VA (ind. city) Harrisonburg independent city	24	0.05
St. Louis, MO (city) St. Louis city County	24	0.01
Lake of the Woods, VA (cdp) Orange County	23	0.29
Newington, CT (cdp/town) Hartford County	23	0.08
Parsippany-Troy Hills, NJ (township) Morris County	23	0.04
El Paso, TX (city) El Paso County	23	<0.01
Kinnelon, NJ (borough) Morris County	22	0.22
Rancho Cordova, CA (city) Sacramento County	22	0.03
Norfolk, VA (ind. city) Norfolk independent city	22	0.01
Richmond, VA (ind. city) Richmond independent city	21	0.01
Burlington, KY (cdp) Boone County	19	0.12
Rotterdam, NY (cdp) Schenectady County	19	0.09
Tarpon Springs, FL (city) Pinellas County	19	0.08
Severna Park, MD (cdp) Anne Arundel County	19	0.05
Jacksonville, NC (city) Onslow County	19	0.03
Carle Place, NY (cdp) Nassau County	18	0.32
DeForest, WI (village) Dane County	18	0.21
Wayne, MI (city) Wayne County	18	0.10
Monroe, MI (city) Monroe County	18	0.08
Carlsbad, CA (city) San Diego County	18	0.02
Clarence Center, NY (cdp) Erie County	17	0.79
Bryn Mawr, PA (cdp) Montgomery County	17	0.48
Centre, PA (township) Berks County	17	0.43
Clarence, NY (town) Erie County	17	0.06
Hamden, CT (town) New Haven County	17	0.03
Hinsdale, MA (town) Berkshire County	16	0.72
Sea Cliff, NY (village) Nassau County	16	0.32
South Hill, NY (cdp) Tompkins County	16	0.24
Mamaroneck, NY (village) Westchester County	16	0.09
Ithaca, NY (town) Tompkins County	16	0.08
Arnold, MD (cdp) Anne Arundel County	16	0.07
Annapolis, MD (city) Anne Arundel County	16	0.04
Des Moines, IA (city) Polk County	16	0.01
Tierra Verde, FL (cdp) Pinellas County	15	0.42
Madison, WI (town) Dane County	15	0.24
Antis, PA (township) Blair County	15	0.23
Midland Park, NJ (borough) Bergen County	15	0.21
Middle Smithfield, PA (township) Monroe County	15	0.10
North Canton, OH (city) Stark County	15	0.09
Carbondale, IL (city) Jackson County	15	0.06
Bentonville, AR (city) Benton County	15	0.05
Ewing, NJ (township) Mercer County	15	0.04
Austin, TX (city) Travis County	15	<0.01
Marseilles, IL (city) LaSalle County	14	0.27
Stratford, NJ (borough) Camden County	14	0.20
Hasbrouck Heights, NJ (borough) Bergen County	14	0.12
Five Forks, SC (cdp) Greenville County	14	0.11
Highland Village, TX (city) Denton County	14	0.10
Storrs, CT (cdp) Tolland County	14	0.10
North Bay Shore, NY (cdp) Suffolk County	14	0.07
Mansfield, CT (town) Tolland County	14	0.05
Oakton, VA (cdp) Fairfax County	14	0.04
Renton, WA (city) King County	14	0.02
Columbus, OH (city) Franklin County	14	<0.01
Balmville, NY (cdp) Orange County	13	0.39
Muttontown, NY (village) Nassau County	13	0.38
Paradise Hills, NM (cdp) Bernalillo County	13	0.25
Williamsburg, VA (ind. city) Williamsburg independent city	13	0.10
Lancaster, PA (township) Lancaster County	13	0.08
Ansonia, CT (city/town) New Haven County	13	0.07
Newtown, PA (township) Bucks County	13	0.07
North Bellmore, NY (cdp) Nassau County	13	0.07
Reisterstown, MD (cdp) Baltimore County	13	0.05
Newburgh, NY (town) Orange County	13	0.04
Westfield, NJ (town) Union County	13	0.04
Hillsboro, OR (city) Washington County	13	0.01
Minneapolis, MN (city) Hennepin County	13	<0.01
Eatons Neck, NY (cdp) Suffolk County	12	0.89
Maitland, FL (city) Orange County	12	0.08
East Patchogue, NY (cdp) Suffolk County	12	0.06
Eastchester, NY (cdp) Westchester County	12	0.06
Eastchester, NY (town) Westchester County	12	0.04
Garfield, NJ (city) Bergen County	12	0.04
Port Chester, NY (village) Westchester County	12	0.04
Lakewood, OH (city) Cuyahoga County	12	0.02
Missouri City, TX (city) Fort Bend County	12	0.02
Oak Park, IL (village) Cook County	12	0.02
Palm Harbor, FL (cdp) Pinellas County	12	0.02
Hamilton, NJ (township) Mercer County	12	0.01
Santa Barbara, CA (city) Santa Barbara County	12	0.01
Albuquerque, NM (city) Bernalillo County	12	<0.01
Manchester, TN (city) Coffee County	11	0.11

SECTION THREE

Please refer to the Explanation of Data in the front of the book for more detailed information.

Ancestry

Cypriot

Top 150 Places Sorted by Percent of Total Population

Based on all places, regardless of total population

Place	Population	%
Lawrenceville, NJ (cdp) Mercer County	116	3.26
Hillside, NY (cdp) Ulster County	8	1.06
Jones, MN (township) Beltrami County	2	0.96
Eatons Neck, NY (cdp) Suffolk County	12	0.89
Lake Nebagamon, WI (village) Douglas County	10	0.83
Clarence Center, NY (cdp) Erie County	17	0.79
Georgia, VT (town) Franklin County	34	0.75
Vienna, LA (town) Lincoln Parish	3	0.74
Hinsdale, MA (town) Berkshire County	16	0.72
Weir, KS (city) Cherokee County	5	0.65
Hewlett Harbor, NY (village) Nassau County	7	0.60
Garland, ME (town) Penobscot County	6	0.59
Elk, NJ (township) Gloucester County	24	0.58
Holmdel, NJ (township) Monmouth County	83	0.50
Bryn Mawr, PA (cdp) Montgomery County	17	0.48
Greenlawn, NY (cdp) Suffolk County	56	0.43
Centre, PA (township) Berks County	17	0.43
Tierra Verde, FL (cdp) Pinellas County	15	0.42
Laurel Hollow, NY (village) Nassau County	8	0.42
Balmville, NY (cdp) Orange County	13	0.39
Elon, NC (town) Alamance County	34	0.38
Arlington Heights, PA (cdp) Monroe County	24	0.38
Muttontown, NY (village) Nassau County	13	0.38
Upper Freehold, NJ (township) Monmouth County	24	0.37
Lawrence, NJ (township) Mercer County	116	0.35
Lake Grove, NY (village) Suffolk County	39	0.35
Roslyn, NY (village) Nassau County	9	0.33
Carle Place, NY (cdp) Nassau County	18	0.32
Sea Cliff, NY (village) Nassau County	16	0.32
North East, NY (town) Dutchess County	9	0.30
Oceanside, NY (cdp) Nassau County	90	0.29
Lake of the Woods, VA (cdp) Orange County	23	0.29
Locust Valley, NY (cdp) Nassau County	9	0.29
Lafayette, NJ (township) Sussex County	7	0.28
Huntington Bay, NY (village) Suffolk County	4	0.28
Creve Coeur, MO (city) St. Louis County	47	0.27
Marseilles, IL (city) LaSalle County	14	0.27
Underhill, VT (town) Chittenden County	8	0.27
Stewartstown, PA (borough) York County	6	0.27
Stoneham, MA (cdp/town) Middlesex County	55	0.26
Paradise Hills, NM (cdp) Bernalillo County	13	0.25
Parkesburg, PA (borough) Chester County	9	0.25
South Hill, NY (cdp) Tompkins County	16	0.24
Madison, WI (town) Dane County	15	0.24
Oyster Bay Cove, NY (village) Nassau County	6	0.24
Franklin Square, NY (cdp) Nassau County	67	0.23
Antis, PA (township) Blair County	15	0.23
Kinnelon, NJ (borough) Morris County	22	0.22
Farmingdale, NJ (borough) Monmouth County	3	0.22
West Lafayette, IN (city) Tippecanoe County	61	0.21
DeForest, WI (village) Dane County	18	0.21
Midland Park, NJ (borough) Bergen County	15	0.21
Haworth, NJ (borough) Bergen County	7	0.21
Stratford, NJ (borough) Camden County	14	0.20
Rotterdam, NY (town) Schenectady County	54	0.19
Jean Lafitte, LA (town) Jefferson Parish	4	0.19
Palermo, ME (town) Waldo County	3	0.19
Valley Stream, NY (village) Nassau County	68	0.18
Yorktown, NY (town) Westchester County	65	0.18
Old Brookville, NY (village) Nassau County	4	0.18
Grosse Pointe Woods, MI (city) Wayne County	27	0.17
Chevy Chase Village, MD (town) Montgomery County	3	0.15
Plymouth, OH (village) Richland County	3	0.15
Mineola, NY (village) Nassau County	27	0.14
Lutherville, MD (cdp) Baltimore County	9	0.14
Stroud, PA (township) Monroe County	24	0.13
Olney, MD (cdp) Montgomery County	40	0.12
Burlington, KY (cdp) Boone County	19	0.12
Hasbrouck Heights, NJ (borough) Bergen County	14	0.12
Lower Merion, PA (township) Montgomery County	66	0.11
South Pasadena, CA (city) Los Angeles County	27	0.11
Raritan, NJ (township) Hunterdon County	24	0.11
Five Forks, SC (cdp) Greenville County	14	0.11
Manchester, TN (city) Coffee County	11	0.11
Santa Clara, CA (city) Santa Clara County	115	0.10
Wayne, MI (city) Wayne County	18	0.10
Middle Smithfield, PA (township) Monroe County	15	0.10
Highland Village, TX (city) Denton County	14	0.10
Storrs, CT (cdp) Tolland County	14	0.10
Williamsburg, VA (ind. city) Williamsburg independent city	13	0.10
Hanover, PA (township) Northampton County	11	0.10
South Huntington, NY (cdp) Suffolk County	10	0.10
Bayville, NY (village) Nassau County	7	0.10
Berkeley, NJ (township) Ocean County	36	0.09
Rotterdam, NY (cdp) Schenectady County	19	0.09
Mamaroneck, NY (village) Westchester County	16	0.09
North Canton, OH (city) Stark County	15	0.09
South Brunswick, NJ (township) Middlesex County	33	0.08
Newington, CT (cdp/town) Hartford County	23	0.08
Tarpon Springs, FL (city) Pinellas County	19	0.08
Monroe, MI (city) Monroe County	18	0.08
Ithaca, NY (town) Tompkins County	16	0.08
Lancaster, PA (township) Lancaster County	13	0.08
Maitland, FL (city) Orange County	12	0.08
Alameda, CA (city) Alameda County	51	0.07
Kennewick, WA (city) Benton County	46	0.07
West Hartford, CT (cdp/town) Hartford County	43	0.07
Wayne, NJ (township) Passaic County	40	0.07
Union, NJ (township) Union County	38	0.07
Arnold, MD (cdp) Anne Arundel County	16	0.07
North Bay Shore, NY (cdp) Suffolk County	14	0.07
Ansonia, CT (city/town) New Haven County	13	0.07
Newtown, PA (township) Bucks County	13	0.07
North Bellmore, NY (cdp) Nassau County	13	0.07
Fort Hunt, VA (cdp) Fairfax County	11	0.07
Sayville, NY (cdp) Suffolk County	11	0.07
Stanford, CA (cdp) Santa Clara County	10	0.07
Brick, NJ (township) Ocean County	45	0.06
Rye, NY (town) Westchester County	28	0.06
Clarence, NY (town) Erie County	17	0.06
Carbondale, IL (city) Jackson County	15	0.06
East Patchogue, NY (cdp) Suffolk County	12	0.06
Eastchester, NY (cdp) Westchester County	12	0.06
Cloverly, MD (cdp) Montgomery County	10	0.06
Port Washington, NY (cdp) Nassau County	10	0.06
Ulster, NY (town) Ulster County	8	0.06
South San Francisco, CA (city) San Mateo County	34	0.05
Malden, MA (city) Middlesex County	30	0.05
Brookline, MA (cdp/town) Norfolk County	27	0.05
Pocatello, ID (city) Bannock County	26	0.05
Coral Gables, FL (city) Miami-Dade County	24	0.05
Harrisonburg, VA (ind. city) Harrisonburg independent city	24	0.05
Severna Park, MD (cdp) Anne Arundel County	19	0.05
Bentonville, AR (city) Benton County	15	0.05
Mansfield, CT (town) Tolland County	14	0.05
Reisterstown, MD (cdp) Baltimore County	13	0.05
Carrboro, NC (town) Orange County	10	0.05
Towamencin, PA (township) Montgomery County	9	0.05
Huntington, NY (town) Suffolk County	82	0.04
Cambridge, MA (city) Middlesex County	46	0.04
Parsippany-Troy Hills, NJ (township) Morris County	23	0.04
Annapolis, MD (city) Anne Arundel County	16	0.04
Ewing, NJ (township) Mercer County	15	0.04
Oakton, VA (cdp) Fairfax County	14	0.04
Newburgh, NY (town) Orange County	13	0.04
Westfield, NJ (town) Union County	13	0.04
Eastchester, NY (town) Westchester County	12	0.04
Garfield, NJ (city) Bergen County	12	0.04
Port Chester, NY (village) Westchester County	12	0.04
Somerset, NJ (cdp) Somerset County	8	0.04
Queens, NY (borough) Queens County	644	0.03
Hempstead, NY (town) Nassau County	254	0.03
Pittsburgh, PA (city) Allegheny County	102	0.03
North Hempstead, NY (town) Nassau County	64	0.03
Centennial, CO (city) Arapahoe County	28	0.03
Rancho Cordova, CA (city) Sacramento County	22	0.03
Jacksonville, NC (city) Onslow County	19	0.03
Hamden, CT (town) New Haven County	17	0.03
Boardman, OH (cdp) Mahoning County	11	0.03
Buckeye, AZ (town) Maricopa County	11	0.03

Ancestry

Cypriot

Top 150 Places Sorted by Percent of Total Population

Based on places with total population of 7,500 or more

Place	Population	%
Holmdel, NJ (township) Monmouth County	83	0.50
Greenlawn, NY (cdp) Suffolk County	56	0.43
Elon, NC (town) Alamance County	34	0.38
Lawrence, NJ (township) Mercer County	116	0.35
Lake Grove, NY (village) Suffolk County	39	0.35
Oceanside, NY (cdp) Nassau County	90	0.29
Lake of the Woods, VA (cdp) Orange County	23	0.29
Creve Coeur, MO (city) St. Louis County	47	0.27
Stoneham, MA (cdp/town) Middlesex County	55	0.26
Franklin Square, NY (cdp) Nassau County	67	0.23
Kinnelon, NJ (borough) Morris County	22	0.22
West Lafayette, IN (city) Tippecanoe County	61	0.21
DeForest, WI (village) Dane County	18	0.21
Rotterdam, NY (town) Schenectady County	54	0.19
Valley Stream, NY (village) Nassau County	68	0.18
Yorktown, NY (town) Westchester County	65	0.18
Grosse Pointe Woods, MI (city) Wayne County	27	0.17
Mineola, NY (village) Nassau County	27	0.14
Stroud, PA (township) Monroe County	24	0.13
Olney, MD (cdp) Montgomery County	40	0.12
Burlington, KY (cdp) Boone County	19	0.12
Hasbrouck Heights, NJ (borough) Bergen County	14	0.12
Lower Merion, PA (township) Montgomery County	66	0.11
South Pasadena, CA (city) Los Angeles County	27	0.11
Raritan, NJ (township) Hunterdon County	24	0.11
Five Forks, SC (cdp) Greenville County	14	0.11
Manchester, TN (city) Coffee County	11	0.11
Santa Clara, CA (city) Santa Clara County	115	0.10
Wayne, MI (city) Wayne County	18	0.10
Middle Smithfield, PA (township) Monroe County	15	0.10
Highland Village, TX (city) Denton County	14	0.10
Storrs, CT (cdp) Tolland County	14	0.10
Williamsburg, VA (ind. city) Williamsburg independent city	13	0.10
Hanover, PA (township) Northampton County	11	0.10
South Huntington, NY (cdp) Suffolk County	10	0.10
Berkeley, NJ (township) Ocean County	36	0.09
Rotterdam, NY (cdp) Schenectady County	19	0.09
Mamaroneck, NY (village) Westchester County	16	0.09
North Canton, OH (city) Stark County	15	0.09
South Brunswick, NJ (township) Middlesex County	33	0.08
Newington, CT (cdp/town) Hartford County	23	0.08
Tarpon Springs, FL (city) Pinellas County	19	0.08
Monroe, MI (city) Monroe County	18	0.08
Ithaca, NY (town) Tompkins County	16	0.08
Lancaster, PA (township) Lancaster County	13	0.08
Maitland, FL (city) Orange County	12	0.08
Alameda, CA (city) Alameda County	51	0.07
Kennewick, WA (city) Benton County	46	0.07
West Hartford, CT (cdp/town) Hartford County	43	0.07
Wayne, NJ (township) Passaic County	40	0.07
Union, NJ (township) Union County	38	0.07
Arnold, MD (cdp) Anne Arundel County	16	0.07
North Bay Shore, NY (cdp) Suffolk County	14	0.07
Ansonia, CT (city/town) New Haven County	13	0.07
Newtown, PA (township) Bucks County	13	0.07
North Bellmore, NY (cdp) Nassau County	13	0.07
Fort Hunt, VA (cdp) Fairfax County	11	0.07
Sayville, NY (cdp) Suffolk County	11	0.07
Stanford, CA (cdp) Santa Clara County	10	0.07
Brick, NJ (township) Ocean County	45	0.06
Rye, NY (town) Westchester County	28	0.06
Clarence, NY (town) Erie County	17	0.06
Carbondale, IL (city) Jackson County	15	0.06
East Patchogue, NY (cdp) Suffolk County	12	0.06
Eastchester, NY (cdp) Westchester County	12	0.06
Cloverly, MD (cdp) Montgomery County	10	0.06
Port Washington, NY (cdp) Nassau County	10	0.06
Ulster, NY (town) Ulster County	8	0.06
South San Francisco, CA (city) San Mateo County	34	0.05
Malden, MA (city) Middlesex County	30	0.05
Brookline, MA (cdp/town) Norfolk County	27	0.05
Pocatello, ID (city) Bannock County	26	0.05
Coral Gables, FL (city) Miami-Dade County	24	0.05
Harrisonburg, VA (ind. city) Harrisonburg independent city	24	0.05
Severna Park, MD (cdp) Anne Arundel County	19	0.05

Place	Population	%
Bentonville, AR (city) Benton County	15	0.05
Mansfield, CT (town) Tolland County	14	0.05
Reisterstown, MD (cdp) Baltimore County	13	0.05
Carrboro, NC (town) Orange County	10	0.05
Towamencin, PA (township) Montgomery County	9	0.05
Huntington, NY (town) Suffolk County	82	0.04
Cambridge, MA (city) Middlesex County	46	0.04
Parsippany-Troy Hills, NJ (township) Morris County	23	0.04
Annapolis, MD (city) Anne Arundel County	16	0.04
Ewing, NJ (township) Mercer County	15	0.04
Oakton, VA (cdp) Fairfax County	14	0.04
Newburgh, NY (town) Orange County	13	0.04
Westfield, NJ (town) Union County	13	0.04
Eastchester, NY (town) Westchester County	12	0.04
Garfield, NJ (city) Bergen County	12	0.04
Port Chester, NY (village) Westchester County	12	0.04
Somerset, NJ (cdp) Somerset County	8	0.04
Queens, NY (borough) Queens County	644	0.03
Hempstead, NY (town) Nassau County	254	0.03
Pittsburgh, PA (city) Allegheny County	102	0.03
North Hempstead, NY (town) Nassau County	64	0.03
Centennial, CO (city) Arapahoe County	28	0.03
Rancho Cordova, CA (city) Sacramento County	22	0.03
Jacksonville, NC (city) Onslow County	19	0.03
Hamden, CT (town) New Haven County	17	0.03
Boardman, OH (cdp) Mahoning County	11	0.03
Buckeye, AZ (town) Maricopa County	11	0.03
Fort Lee, NJ (borough) Bergen County	10	0.03
Burlingame, CA (city) San Mateo County	9	0.03
Highland Park, IL (city) Lake County	8	0.03
Fairfax, VA (ind. city) Fairfax independent city	6	0.03
Long Beach, CA (city) Los Angeles County	94	0.02
Oyster Bay, NY (town) Nassau County	63	0.02
Hampton, VA (ind. city) Hampton independent city	31	0.02
Carlsbad, CA (city) San Diego County	18	0.02
Renton, WA (city) King County	14	0.02
Lakewood, OH (city) Cuyahoga County	12	0.02
Missouri City, TX (city) Fort Bend County	12	0.02
Oak Park, IL (village) Cook County	12	0.02
Palm Harbor, FL (cdp) Pinellas County	12	0.02
Appleton, WI (city) Outagamie County	11	0.02
Appleton, WI (city) Outagamie County	11	0.02
Davis, CA (city) Yolo County	11	0.02
Bethesda, MD (cdp) Montgomery County	10	0.02
Royal Oak, MI (city) Oakland County	10	0.02
San Bruno, CA (city) San Mateo County	10	0.02
East Brunswick, NJ (township) Middlesex County	9	0.02
Hempstead, NY (village) Nassau County	9	0.02
Fitchburg, MA (city) Worcester County	8	0.02
Freehold, NJ (township) Monmouth County	8	0.02
Hoboken, NJ (city) Hudson County	8	0.02
Natick, MA (town) Middlesex County	8	0.02
Tuckahoe, VA (cdp) Henrico County	8	0.02
Wheaton, MD (cdp) Montgomery County	7	0.02
Anacortes, WA (city) Skagit County	3	0.02
New York, NY (city) Kings County	960	0.01
Manhattan, NY (borough) New York County	216	0.01
Boston, MA (city) Suffolk County	77	0.01
Brookhaven, NY (town) Suffolk County	51	0.01
San Francisco, CA (city) San Francisco County	50	0.01
Virginia Beach, VA (ind. city) Virginia Beach independent city	38	0.01
Aurora, CO (city) Arapahoe County	36	0.01
Jersey City, NJ (city) Hudson County	27	0.01
Madison, WI (city) Dane County	27	0.01
Raleigh, NC (city) Wake County	27	0.01
Islip, NY (town) Suffolk County	25	0.01
St. Louis, MO (city) St. Louis city County	24	0.01
Norfolk, VA (ind. city) Norfolk independent city	22	0.01
Richmond, VA (ind. city) Richmond independent city	21	0.01
Des Moines, IA (city) Polk County	16	0.01
Hillsboro, OR (city) Washington County	13	0.01
Hamilton, NJ (township) Mercer County	12	0.01
Santa Barbara, CA (city) Santa Barbara County	12	0.01
Columbia, SC (city) Richland County	11	0.01
Gilbert, AZ (town) Maricopa County	11	0.01

Please refer to the Explanation of Data in the front of the book for more detailed information.

Ancestry

Czech

U.S. and 50 States Sorted by Population and Percent of Total Population

Place	Population	%
United States	**1,597,950**	**0.53**
Texas	215,461	0.89
Illinois	128,879	1.01
Minnesota	100,809	1.92
Wisconsin	100,716	1.79
Nebraska	97,986	5.45
California	94,047	0.26
Ohio	73,775	0.64
Iowa	62,486	2.07
Florida	60,744	0.33
Pennsylvania	57,652	0.46
New York	57,264	0.30
Michigan	52,092	0.52
Colorado	38,207	0.78
New Jersey	32,426	0.37
Washington	31,684	0.48
Missouri	30,187	0.51
Arizona	29,168	0.47
Kansas	26,489	0.94
Virginia	24,760	0.32
Maryland	23,982	0.42
Oregon	21,728	0.58
South Dakota	18,627	2.33
Indiana	18,523	0.29
North Carolina	18,171	0.20
Oklahoma	16,698	0.45
Connecticut	15,840	0.45
Georgia	15,034	0.16
Massachusetts	13,668	0.21
North Dakota	12,732	1.93
Nevada	10,271	0.39
Tennessee	9,921	0.16
Montana	8,637	0.89
Idaho	8,079	0.53
South Carolina	7,444	0.17
Arkansas	6,665	0.23
Utah	6,122	0.23
New Mexico	5,868	0.29
Alabama	5,484	0.12
Louisiana	5,251	0.12
Kentucky	5,009	0.12
Wyoming	4,732	0.87
West Virginia	3,834	0.21
Alaska	3,516	0.51
New Hampshire	3,311	0.25
Vermont	2,529	0.41
Delaware	2,392	0.27
Maine	2,259	0.17
Hawaii	2,175	0.16
Mississippi	1,975	0.07
District of Columbia	1,392	0.24
Rhode Island	1,249	0.12

Place	Population	%
Nebraska	97,986	5.45
South Dakota	18,627	2.33
Iowa	62,486	2.07
North Dakota	12,732	1.93
Minnesota	100,809	1.92
Wisconsin	100,716	1.79
Illinois	128,879	1.01
Kansas	26,489	0.94
Texas	215,461	0.89
Montana	8,637	0.89
Wyoming	4,732	0.87
Colorado	38,207	0.78
Ohio	73,775	0.64
Oregon	21,728	0.58
United States	**1,597,950**	**0.53**
Idaho	8,079	0.53
Michigan	52,092	0.52
Missouri	30,187	0.51
Alaska	3,516	0.51
Washington	31,684	0.48
Arizona	29,168	0.47
Pennsylvania	57,652	0.46
Oklahoma	16,698	0.45
Connecticut	15,840	0.45
Maryland	23,982	0.42
Vermont	2,529	0.41
Nevada	10,271	0.39
New Jersey	32,426	0.37
Florida	60,744	0.33
Virginia	24,760	0.32
New York	57,264	0.30
Indiana	18,523	0.29
New Mexico	5,868	0.29
Delaware	2,392	0.27
California	94,047	0.26
New Hampshire	3,311	0.25
District of Columbia	1,392	0.24
Arkansas	6,665	0.23
Utah	6,122	0.23
Massachusetts	13,668	0.21
West Virginia	3,834	0.21
North Carolina	18,171	0.20
South Carolina	7,444	0.17
Maine	2,259	0.17
Georgia	15,034	0.16
Tennessee	9,921	0.16
Hawaii	2,175	0.16
Alabama	5,484	0.12
Louisiana	5,251	0.12
Kentucky	5,009	0.12
Rhode Island	1,249	0.12
Mississippi	1,975	0.07

Please refer to the Explanation of Data in the front of the book for more detailed information.

Ancestry

Czech

Top 150 Places Sorted by Population

Based on all places, regardless of total population

Place	Population	%
Omaha, NE (city) Douglas County	16,370	4.02
Lincoln, NE (city) Lancaster County	15,960	6.31
New York, NY (city) Kings County	12,800	0.16
Chicago, IL (city) Cook County	12,642	0.47
Houston, TX (city) Harris County	11,531	0.56
Cedar Rapids, IA (city) Linn County	8,665	6.91
Austin, TX (city) Travis County	7,696	1.01
Los Angeles, CA (city) Los Angeles County	6,899	0.18
San Antonio, TX (city) Medina County	6,245	0.48
Phoenix, AZ (city) Maricopa County	6,161	0.42
Minneapolis, MN (city) Hennepin County	5,254	1.38
San Diego, CA (city) San Diego County	5,144	0.40
Manhattan, NY (borough) New York County	4,820	0.30
Dallas, TX (city) Dallas County	4,600	0.39
Milwaukee, WI (city) Milwaukee County	3,843	0.65
Seattle, WA (city) King County	3,837	0.64
St. Paul, MN (city) Ramsey County	3,697	1.31
Denver, CO (city) Denver County	3,635	0.63
Naperville, IL (city) DuPage County	3,566	2.53
Portland, OR (city) Multnomah County	3,510	0.62
Queens, NY (borough) Queens County	3,464	0.16
Brooklyn, NY (borough) Kings County	3,393	0.14
Fort Worth, TX (city) Tarrant County	3,259	0.46
Victoria, TX (city) Victoria County	3,189	5.15
Brookhaven, NY (town) Suffolk County	3,121	0.65
Colorado Springs, CO (city) El Paso County	3,019	0.75
Columbus, OH (city) Franklin County	2,996	0.39
Oklahoma City, OK (city) Oklahoma County	2,994	0.53
San Francisco, CA (city) San Francisco County	2,987	0.38
Madison, WI (city) Dane County	2,835	1.24
Cleveland, OH (city) Cuyahoga County	2,835	0.69
Sioux Falls, SD (city) Minnehaha County	2,644	1.78
Manitowoc, WI (city) Manitowoc County	2,632	7.79
Wichita, KS (city) Sedgwick County	2,469	0.66
Hempstead, NY (town) Nassau County	2,447	0.32
Arlington, TX (city) Tarrant County	2,426	0.67
Corpus Christi, TX (city) Nueces County	2,403	0.80
Tucson, AZ (city) Pima County	2,371	0.46
Bellevue, NE (city) Sarpy County	2,355	4.69
Scottsdale, AZ (city) Maricopa County	2,352	1.08
Las Vegas, NV (city) Clark County	2,336	0.40
Green Bay, WI (city) Brown County	2,282	2.20
Downers Grove, IL (village) DuPage County	2,278	4.75
Iowa City, IA (city) Johnson County	2,243	3.36
Parma, OH (city) Cuyahoga County	2,231	2.72
Philadelphia, PA (city) Philadelphia County	2,209	0.15
College Station, TX (city) Brazos County	2,125	2.40
Mesa, AZ (city) Maricopa County	2,078	0.47
Islip, NY (town) Suffolk County	2,026	0.61
Des Moines, IA (city) Polk County	2,013	1.00
Jacksonville, FL (city) Duval County	2,003	0.25
Fremont, NE (city) Dodge County	1,953	7.45
Grand Island, NE (city) Hall County	1,865	3.97
Berwyn, IL (city) Cook County	1,864	3.35
Marion, IA (city) Linn County	1,778	5.34
Anchorage, AK (municipality) Anchorage Municipality	1,771	0.62
Overland Park, KS (city) Johnson County	1,736	1.02
Boise City, ID (city) Ada County	1,692	0.82
Columbus, NE (city) Platte County	1,679	7.76
Pittsburgh, PA (city) Allegheny County	1,676	0.54
Baltimore, MD (city) Baltimore city County	1,668	0.27
St. Louis, MO (city) St. Louis city County	1,655	0.52
Charlotte, NC (city) Mecklenburg County	1,654	0.23
San Jose, CA (city) Santa Clara County	1,653	0.18
Brookfield, IL (village) Cook County	1,651	8.78
Albuquerque, NM (city) Bernalillo County	1,642	0.31
Kansas City, MO (city) Jackson County	1,638	0.36
Rochester, MN (city) Olmsted County	1,637	1.57
Fort Collins, CO (city) Larimer County	1,625	1.16
Virginia Beach, VA (ind. city) Virginia Beach independent city	1,563	0.36
Fargo, ND (city) Cass County	1,537	1.50
Aurora, CO (city) Arapahoe County	1,519	0.48
Indianapolis, IN (city) Marion County	1,484	0.18
Joliet, IL (city) Will County	1,474	1.02
Temple, TX (city) Bell County	1,468	2.31
Eagan, MN (city) Dakota County	1,438	2.23
New Prague, MN (city) Scott County	1,436	20.46
Aurora, IL (city) Kane County	1,429	0.75
Bloomington, MN (city) Hennepin County	1,412	1.71
Tinley Park, IL (village) Cook County	1,409	2.56
Bryan, TX (city) Brazos County	1,405	1.91
Chandler, AZ (city) Maricopa County	1,395	0.61
Washington, DC (city) District of Columbia	1,392	0.24
Kearney, NE (city) Buffalo County	1,385	4.58
Owatonna, MN (city) Steele County	1,381	5.45
Oyster Bay, NY (town) Nassau County	1,379	0.47
Plano, TX (city) Collin County	1,343	0.52
Two Rivers, WI (city) Manitowoc County	1,321	11.13
Eau Claire, WI (city) Eau Claire County	1,307	2.01
Racine, WI (city) Racine County	1,306	1.64
Pasadena, TX (city) Harris County	1,283	0.87
Darien, IL (city) DuPage County	1,274	5.75
Minnetonka, MN (city) Hennepin County	1,271	2.56
Huntington, NY (town) Suffolk County	1,271	0.63
Eau Claire, WI (city) Eau Claire County	1,266	2.01
Lubbock, TX (city) Lubbock County	1,266	0.57
North Royalton, OH (city) Cuyahoga County	1,263	4.21
Boulder, CO (city) Boulder County	1,263	1.30
The Woodlands, TX (cdp) Montgomery County	1,260	1.37
Waco, TX (city) McLennan County	1,243	1.02
Strongsville, OH (city) Cuyahoga County	1,236	2.79
Nashville-Davidson, TN (metro govt) Davidson County	1,226	0.21
St. Petersburg, FL (city) Pinellas County	1,213	0.49
Taylor, TX (city) Williamson County	1,189	7.96
Norfolk, NE (city) Madison County	1,184	4.94
Blaine, MN (city) Anoka County	1,180	2.13
Henderson, NV (city) Clark County	1,176	0.47
Waterloo, IA (city) Black Hawk County	1,174	1.73
Ames, IA (city) Story County	1,167	2.04
Boston, MA (city) Suffolk County	1,167	0.19
Sacramento, CA (city) Sacramento County	1,164	0.25
Arlington Heights, IL (village) Cook County	1,161	1.55
Orland Park, IL (village) Cook County	1,159	2.10
Schaumburg, IL (village) Cook County	1,159	1.58
La Crosse, WI (city) La Crosse County	1,156	2.26
Centennial, CO (city) Arapahoe County	1,144	1.14
Westmont, IL (village) DuPage County	1,135	4.63
Lombard, IL (village) DuPage County	1,128	2.64
Dickinson, ND (city) Stark County	1,125	6.55
Grand Forks, ND (city) Grand Forks County	1,119	2.14
Olathe, KS (city) Johnson County	1,119	0.93
Plainfield, IL (village) Will County	1,111	3.11
Round Rock, TX (city) Williamson County	1,109	1.19
Waukesha, WI (city) Waukesha County	1,105	1.58
Spokane, WA (city) Spokane County	1,105	0.54
Burnsville, MN (city) Dakota County	1,084	1.79
Davenport, IA (city) Scott County	1,082	1.10
Rapid City, SD (city) Pennington County	1,081	1.63
Bolingbrook, IL (village) Will County	1,080	1.49
Huntington Beach, CA (city) Orange County	1,079	0.57
Arlington, VA (cdp) Arlington County	1,076	0.54
Woodridge, IL (village) DuPage County	1,067	3.29
West Allis, WI (city) Milwaukee County	1,066	1.78
El Campo, TX (city) Wharton County	1,063	9.22
Paradise, NV (cdp) Clark County	1,062	0.49
Appleton, WI (city) Outagamie County	1,057	1.46
Maple Grove, MN (city) Hennepin County	1,056	1.79
Lakeville, MN (city) Dakota County	1,054	1.95
St. Cloud, MN (city) Stearns County	1,053	1.62
Garland, TX (city) Dallas County	1,038	0.47
Wahoo, NE (city) Saunders County	1,013	22.93
Caledonia, WI (village) Racine County	1,011	4.12
Pearland, TX (city) Brazoria County	1,010	1.22
Bartlett, IL (village) DuPage County	1,006	2.51
Oak Lawn, IL (village) Cook County	1,005	1.80
Eden Prairie, MN (city) Hennepin County	996	1.68
Glen Ellyn, IL (village) DuPage County	993	3.62
Council Bluffs, IA (city) Pottawattamie County	990	1.61
La Vista, NE (city) Sarpy County	986	6.55
Plymouth, MN (city) Hennepin County	985	1.42

SECTION THREE

Ancestry

Czech

Top 150 Places Sorted by Percent of Total Population

Based on all places, regardless of total population

Place	Population	%
Dwight, NE (village) Butler County	201	72.04
Verdel, NE (village) Knox County	51	65.38
Lawton, ND (city) Ramsey County	15	65.22
Loretto, NE (cdp) Boone County	96	63.58
Morse Bluff, NE (village) Saunders County	98	60.49
Tippecanoe, OH (cdp) Harrison County	47	60.26
Colon, NE (village) Saunders County	50	58.14
Ola, SD (cdp) Brule County	12	57.14
Raeville, NE (cdp) Boone County	4	57.14
Abie, NE (village) Butler County	33	55.93
Running Water, SD (cdp) Bon Homme County	31	55.36
Brainard, NE (village) Butler County	201	52.76
Dragoon, AZ (cdp) Cochise County	106	51.21
Verdigre, NE (village) Knox County	234	50.98
Prague, NE (village) Saunders County	172	50.59
Conway, ND (city) Walsh County	10	50.00
Danville, MO (cdp) Montgomery County	9	50.00
Vining, IA (city) Tama County	29	49.15
Toqua, MN (township) Big Stone County	25	46.30
Lake Roberts Heights, NM (cdp) Grant County	31	46.27
Malmo, NE (village) Saunders County	64	46.04
Linwood, NE (village) Butler County	52	46.02
Jackson Junction, IA (city) Winneshiek County	45	45.92
Jennings, KS (city) Decatur County	78	44.32
Spillville, IA (city) Winneshiek County	127	44.25
Davidson, MN (unorganized territory) Aitkin County	48	44.04
Weston, NE (village) Saunders County	132	43.85
Irvington, IA (cdp) Kossuth County	7	43.75
Clarkson, NE (city) Colfax County	314	43.55
Deweese, NE (village) Clay County	14	42.42
Protivin, IA (city) Howard County	126	42.14
Doran, MN (city) Wilkin County	8	42.11
Moulton, TX (town) Lavaca County	421	41.32
Tyndall, SD (city) Bon Homme County	504	41.14
Garrison, NE (village) Butler County	17	40.48
Pisek, ND (city) Walsh County	38	40.43
Milligan, NE (village) Fillmore County	99	40.24
Wood, SD (town) Mellette County	40	40.00
Gross, NE (village) Boyd County	2	40.00
Valparaiso, NE (village) Saunders County	222	38.28
Octavia, NE (village) Butler County	54	38.03
Ulysses, NE (village) Butler County	67	37.85
Geddes, SD (city) Charles Mix County	96	36.36
Lankin, ND (city) Walsh County	50	36.23
Henryville, MN (township) Renville County	101	35.44
Lewistown Heights, MT (cdp) Fergus County	119	35.21
Defiance, MO (cdp) St. Charles County	32	34.78
Yuba, WI (village) Richland County	27	34.18
Manning, ND (cdp) Dunn County	16	34.04
Royalton, MN (city) Benton County	3	33.33
Elberon, IA (city) Tama County	76	32.90
Cuba, KS (city) Republic County	55	32.74
Pohlitz, MN (township) Roseau County	12	32.43
Tabor, SD (town) Bon Homme County	135	32.14
Dorchester, NE (village) Saline County	151	32.06
Shiner, TX (city) Lavaca County	743	31.83
Dante, SD (town) Charles Mix County	26	31.71
Lanesburgh, MN (township) Le Sueur County	606	31.33
Castle Rock, WI (town) Grant County	94	31.23
Two Creeks, WI (town) Manitowoc County	146	31.20
East Bernard, TX (city) Wharton County	753	30.95
Leroy, TX (city) McLennan County	94	30.13
Clutier, IA (city) Tama County	77	30.08
Howells, NE (village) Colfax County	162	30.06
Wilber, NE (city) Saline County	549	30.03
Butte Meadows, CA (cdp) Butte County	9	30.00
Dorchester, TX (city) Grayson County	42	29.79
Carlton, WI (town) Kewaunee County	261	29.76
West, TX (city) McLennan County	829	29.73
Mahaska, KS (city) Washington County	26	29.55
Erin, MN (township) Rice County	216	29.39
Abbott, TX (city) Hill County	122	28.77
Franklin, WI (town) Kewaunee County	280	28.20
Bee, NE (village) Seward County	50	27.93
Letcher, SD (town) Sanborn County	48	27.91
Wheatland, MN (township) Rice County	417	27.76
Vanderbilt, TX (cdp) Jackson County	95	27.70
Lexington, MN (township) Le Sueur County	220	27.60
Bow Valley, NE (cdp) Cedar County	53	27.60
David City, NE (city) Butler County	773	27.44
Louise, TX (cdp) Wharton County	276	27.38
La Ward, TX (city) Jackson County	46	27.38
New Cambria, KS (city) Saline County	35	27.34
Lazy Lake, FL (village) Broward County	3	27.27
Fairchilds, TX (village) Fort Bend County	146	27.19
Tierra Grande, TX (cdp) Nueces County	16	27.12
Kellnersville, WI (village) Manitowoc County	84	27.10
Parnell, MN (township) Traverse County	13	27.08
Berlin, WI (city) Waushara County	10	27.03
Montgomery, MN (township) Le Sueur County	161	26.83
Northland, MN (township) Polk County	41	26.80
Fort Atkinson, IA (city) Winneshiek County	101	26.58
Silver Lake, MN (city) McLeod County	172	26.50
Heidelberg, MN (city) Le Sueur County	36	26.09
Middle Amana, IA (cdp) Iowa County	280	26.05
Park, MN (township) Pine County	13	26.00
Conchas Dam, NM (cdp) San Miguel County	44	25.88
Guernsey, IA (city) Poweshiek County	15	25.86
Niobrara, NE (village) Knox County	102	25.76
New Pine Creek, CA (cdp) Modoc County	29	25.66
Cow Creek, SD (cdp) Sully County	11	25.58
Fayetteville, TX (city) Fayette County	99	25.13
Chelsea, IA (city) Tama County	73	25.09
Tabor, MN (township) Polk County	41	25.00
Falcon Village, TX (cdp) Starr County	18	24.66
Hallettsville, TX (city) Lavaca County	628	24.36
Nordick, MN (township) Wilkin County	26	24.07
Swanton, NE (village) Saline County	26	24.07
Hungerford, TX (cdp) Wharton County	114	23.95
Roscoe, NE (cdp) Keith County	20	23.81
Utica, SD (town) Yankton County	10	23.81
Krupp, WA (town) Grant County	5	23.81
Sunol, NE (cdp) Cheyenne County	5	23.81
White Pine, MN (township) Aitkin County	5	23.81
Merriman, NE (village) Cherry County	35	23.49
Mishicot, WI (town) Manitowoc County	317	23.33
Spring Creek, MN (township) Becker County	49	23.22
Orchard, TX (city) Fort Bend County	115	23.05
Wahoo, NE (city) Saunders County	1,013	22.93
Munden, KS (city) Republic County	19	22.89
Ganado, TX (city) Jackson County	420	22.79
Center Junction, IA (city) Jones County	36	22.64
Wauzeka, WI (town) Crawford County	83	22.49
Tobias, NE (village) Saline County	37	22.29
Montpelier, WI (town) Kewaunee County	315	22.26
Snook, TX (city) Burleson County	115	22.24
Inez, TX (cdp) Victoria County	513	21.91
Enterprise, MN (township) Jackson County	47	21.86
Hordville, NE (village) Hamilton County	29	21.80
West Kewaunee, WI (town) Kewaunee County	293	21.74
Price, WI (town) Langlade County	56	21.71
Worcester, WI (town) Price County	356	21.62
Summit, MN (township) Steele County	98	21.59
Eastman, WI (village) Crawford County	78	21.55
Schulenburg, TX (city) Fayette County	605	21.30
Penelope, TX (town) Hill County	52	21.22
Truxton, MO (village) Lincoln County	8	21.05
New Prague, MN (city) Scott County	882	21.01
Wagner, SD (city) Charles Mix County	358	21.00
Ceresco, NE (village) Saunders County	227	20.96
Forest View, IL (village) Cook County	174	20.86
Angus, MN (township) Polk County	15	20.83
Bristow, NE (village) Boyd County	16	20.78
Gibson, WI (town) Manitowoc County	277	20.73
Maribel, WI (village) Manitowoc County	63	20.72
Montfort, WI (village) Iowa County	18	20.69
Vining, MN (city) Otter Tail County	12	20.69
Campbell, MN (township) Wilkin County	13	20.63
Yoder, WY (town) Goshen County	58	20.57
Barnett, MN (township) Roseau County	31	20.53

Please refer to the Explanation of Data in the front of the book for more detailed information.

Ancestry

Czech

Top 150 Places Sorted by Percent of Total Population

Based on places with total population of 7,500 or more

Place	Population	%
Two Rivers, WI (city) Manitowoc County	1,321	11.13
El Campo, TX (city) Wharton County	1,063	9.22
Brookfield, IL (village) Cook County	1,651	8.78
Riverside, IL (village) Cook County	725	8.30
Taylor, TX (city) Williamson County	1,189	7.96
Antigo, WI (city) Langlade County	661	7.95
Manitowoc, WI (city) Manitowoc County	2,632	7.79
Columbus, NE (city) Platte County	1,679	7.76
Wharton, TX (city) Wharton County	671	7.58
Fremont, NE (city) Dodge County	1,953	7.45
La Grange Park, IL (village) Cook County	966	7.22
Cedar Rapids, IA (city) Linn County	8,665	6.91
Dickinson, ND (city) Stark County	1,125	6.55
La Vista, NE (city) Sarpy County	986	6.55
Seven Hills, OH (city) Cuyahoga County	756	6.41
Lincoln, NE (city) Lancaster County	15,960	6.31
Chalco, NE (cdp) Sarpy County	623	5.81
Darien, IL (city) DuPage County	1,274	5.75
Lyons, IL (village) Cook County	604	5.74
Owatonna, MN (city) Steele County	1,381	5.45
Beatrice, NE (city) Gage County	676	5.37
Marion, IA (city) Linn County	1,778	5.34
Owosso, MI (city) Shiawassee County	816	5.28
Yankton, SD (city) Yankton County	752	5.28
Ennis, TX (city) Ellis County	946	5.18
Victoria, TX (city) Victoria County	3,189	5.15
Westchester, IL (village) Cook County	836	5.05
Bay City, TX (city) Matagorda County	880	4.98
Norfolk, NE (city) Madison County	1,184	4.94
York, NE (city) York County	375	4.77
Downers Grove, IL (village) DuPage County	2,278	4.75
La Grange, IL (village) Cook County	731	4.74
Lemont, IL (village) Cook County	726	4.74
Bellevue, NE (city) Sarpy County	2,355	4.69
Willowbrook, IL (village) DuPage County	397	4.65
Westmont, IL (village) DuPage County	1,135	4.63
Papillion, NE (city) Sarpy County	871	4.63
Waconia, MN (city) Carver County	470	4.63
Kearney, NE (city) Buffalo County	1,385	4.58
Island Lake, IL (village) McHenry County	374	4.55
North Royalton, OH (city) Cuyahoga County	1,263	4.21
Frankfort Square, IL (cdp) Will County	401	4.21
Caledonia, WI (village) Racine County	1,011	4.12
Pecan Grove, TX (cdp) Fort Bend County	645	4.08
Murphy, MO (cdp) Jefferson County	364	4.08
Omaha, NE (city) Douglas County	16,370	4.02
Hastings, NE (city) Adams County	983	3.98
Grand Island, NE (city) Hall County	1,865	3.97
Brecksville, OH (city) Cuyahoga County	533	3.93
Hickory Hills, IL (city) Cook County	543	3.88
Justice, IL (village) Cook County	489	3.87
North Liberty, IA (city) Johnson County	456	3.84
Lisbon, WI (town) Waukesha County	381	3.79
River Falls, WI (city) Pierce County	549	3.74
Rice Lake, WI (city) Barron County	311	3.68
Wahpeton, ND (city) Richland County	288	3.67
Glen Ellyn, IL (village) DuPage County	993	3.62
Ashwaubenon, WI (village) Brown County	613	3.58
Western Springs, IL (village) Cook County	450	3.56
Bedford, OH (city) Cuyahoga County	461	3.49
Brooklyn, OH (city) Cuyahoga County	386	3.46
Pierre, SD (city) Hughes County	464	3.41
Rocky River, OH (city) Cuyahoga County	687	3.40
Hutto, TX (city) Williamson County	419	3.40
Lisle, IL (village) DuPage County	753	3.38
St. Johns, MI (city) Clinton County	268	3.38
Iowa City, IA (city) Johnson County	2,243	3.36
Clear Lake, IA (city) Cerro Gordo County	262	3.36
Berwyn, IL (city) Cook County	1,864	3.35
Hutchinson, MN (city) McLeod County	474	3.34
Faribault, MN (city) Rice County	765	3.32
Thief River Falls, MN (city) Pennington County	283	3.31
Woodridge, IL (village) DuPage County	1,067	3.29
Solon, OH (city) Cuyahoga County	754	3.28
McFarland, WI (village) Dane County	247	3.26
Garfield Heights, OH (city) Cuyahoga County	945	3.25
Berea, OH (city) Cuyahoga County	613	3.23
Midlothian, TX (city) Ellis County	532	3.21
Worth, IL (village) Cook County	343	3.21
Mitchell, SD (city) Davison County	482	3.18
River Falls, WI (city) Pierce County	370	3.18
Plainfield, IL (village) Will County	1,111	3.11
Homer Glen, IL (village) Will County	768	3.11
Allouez, WI (village) Brown County	443	3.11
Broadview Heights, OH (city) Cuyahoga County	578	3.10
Chanhassen, MN (city) Carver County	703	3.08
Macedonia, OH (city) Summit County	333	3.07
Mendota Heights, MN (city) Dakota County	341	3.04
Decorah, IA (city) Winneshiek County	246	3.03
Gold Canyon, AZ (cdp) Pinal County	337	3.02
Fairview Park, OH (city) Cuyahoga County	509	3.01
Aurora, OH (city) Portage County	456	3.00
Greendale, WI (village) Milwaukee County	419	3.00
Otsego, MN (city) Wright County	376	3.00
North Olmsted, OH (city) Cuyahoga County	982	2.99
Warrenton, MO (city) Warren County	227	2.99
West Livingston, TX (cdp) Polk County	224	2.98
New Lenox, IL (village) Will County	711	2.97
Waunakee, WI (village) Dane County	343	2.97
East Grand Forks, MN (city) Polk County	248	2.96
McCook, NE (city) Red Willow County	229	2.96
Fort Dodge, IA (city) Webster County	748	2.95
Miller Place, NY (cdp) Suffolk County	363	2.95
Greatwood, TX (cdp) Fort Bend County	346	2.95
Big Lake, MN (city) Sherburne County	283	2.93
Angleton, TX (city) Brazoria County	548	2.91
Howard, WI (village) Brown County	487	2.91
Robinson, TX (city) McLennan County	287	2.88
Savage, MN (city) Scott County	764	2.87
Woodway, TX (city) McLennan County	239	2.86
Parma Heights, OH (city) Cuyahoga County	593	2.85
Monona, WI (city) Dane County	215	2.83
Suamico, WI (village) Brown County	306	2.82
Strongsville, OH (city) Cuyahoga County	1,236	2.79
Concord, MO (cdp) St. Louis County	440	2.78
Wellington, KS (city) Sumner County	227	2.77
Beacon Square, FL (cdp) Pasco County	210	2.76
Batavia, IL (city) Kane County	712	2.75
Bohemia, NY (cdp) Suffolk County	271	2.74
Twinsburg, OH (city) Summit County	505	2.73
East Bethel, MN (city) Anoka County	317	2.73
Parma, OH (city) Cuyahoga County	2,231	2.72
Northfield, MN (city) Rice County	529	2.72
Villa Park, IL (village) DuPage County	603	2.71
Sartell, MN (city) Stearns County	342	2.71
Prior Lake, MN (city) Scott County	599	2.70
Crest Hill, IL (city) Will County	549	2.70
Oak Brook, IL (village) DuPage County	213	2.69
Hales Corners, WI (village) Milwaukee County	205	2.68
Windsor, PA (township) York County	447	2.67
Richmond, TX (city) Fort Bend County	311	2.67
Long Hill, NJ (township) Morris County	233	2.67
Milton, FL (city) Santa Rosa County	232	2.67
Mandan, ND (city) Morton County	474	2.66
North Platte, NE (city) Lincoln County	654	2.65
Bloomingdale, IL (village) DuPage County	580	2.65
Palos Hills, IL (city) Cook County	460	2.65
Bemidji, MN (city) Beltrami County	350	2.65
Salem, WI (town) Kenosha County	311	2.65
Lombard, IL (village) DuPage County	1,128	2.64
Rosenberg, TX (city) Fort Bend County	774	2.64
Clarendon Hills, IL (village) DuPage County	218	2.63
Brushy Creek, TX (cdp) Williamson County	582	2.62
Mount Pleasant, WI (village) Racine County	667	2.60
Maple Heights, OH (city) Cuyahoga County	612	2.60
Northfield, MN (city) Rice County	479	2.60
Shawano, WI (city) Shawano County	240	2.60
Shoreview, MN (city) Ramsey County	645	2.59
Geneva, IL (city) Kane County	552	2.57
Tinley Park, IL (village) Cook County	1,409	2.56

Please refer to the Explanation of Data in the front of the book for more detailed information.

Ancestry

Czechoslovakian

U.S. and 50 States Sorted by Population and Percent of Total Population

Place	Population	%
United States	**320,161**	**0.11**
California	25,946	0.07
Texas	24,660	0.10
Pennsylvania	23,548	0.19
New York	22,547	0.12
Ohio	18,742	0.16
Illinois	17,974	0.14
Florida	17,795	0.10
Michigan	16,698	0.17
New Jersey	12,038	0.14
Minnesota	10,843	0.21
Wisconsin	9,277	0.16
Washington	8,284	0.13
Arizona	6,850	0.11
Colorado	6,821	0.14
Nebraska	6,161	0.34
Connecticut	6,136	0.17
Virginia	5,977	0.08
Missouri	5,759	0.10
Iowa	5,659	0.19
North Carolina	5,381	0.06
Maryland	5,207	0.09
Indiana	5,115	0.08
Oregon	4,612	0.12
Georgia	4,341	0.05
Kansas	3,873	0.14
Massachusetts	3,825	0.06
Oklahoma	3,045	0.08
Nevada	2,396	0.09
Montana	2,198	0.23
Tennessee	2,123	0.03
South Carolina	2,098	0.05
Arkansas	2,087	0.07
South Dakota	1,937	0.24
Alabama	1,883	0.04
Utah	1,853	0.07
Idaho	1,760	0.12
New Mexico	1,685	0.08
West Virginia	1,634	0.09
North Dakota	1,354	0.21
Louisiana	1,277	0.03
Alaska	1,237	0.18
Kentucky	1,076	0.03
New Hampshire	1,016	0.08
Delaware	966	0.11
Maine	947	0.07
Wyoming	776	0.14
Mississippi	688	0.02
Vermont	665	0.11
Rhode Island	562	0.05
Hawaii	551	0.04
District of Columbia	278	0.05

Place	Population	%
Nebraska	6,161	0.34
South Dakota	1,937	0.24
Montana	2,198	0.23
Minnesota	10,843	0.21
North Dakota	1,354	0.21
Pennsylvania	23,548	0.19
Iowa	5,659	0.19
Alaska	1,237	0.18
Michigan	16,698	0.17
Connecticut	6,136	0.17
Ohio	18,742	0.16
Wisconsin	9,277	0.16
Illinois	17,974	0.14
New Jersey	12,038	0.14
Colorado	6,821	0.14
Kansas	3,873	0.14
Wyoming	776	0.14
Washington	8,284	0.13
New York	22,547	0.12
Oregon	4,612	0.12
Idaho	1,760	0.12
United States	**320,161**	**0.11**
Arizona	6,850	0.11
Delaware	966	0.11
Vermont	665	0.11
Texas	24,660	0.10
Florida	17,795	0.10
Missouri	5,759	0.10
Maryland	5,207	0.09
Nevada	2,396	0.09
West Virginia	1,634	0.09
Virginia	5,977	0.08
Indiana	5,115	0.08
Oklahoma	3,045	0.08
New Mexico	1,685	0.08
New Hampshire	1,016	0.08
California	25,946	0.07
Arkansas	2,087	0.07
Utah	1,853	0.07
Maine	947	0.07
North Carolina	5,381	0.06
Massachusetts	3,825	0.06
Georgia	4,341	0.05
South Carolina	2,098	0.05
Rhode Island	562	0.05
District of Columbia	278	0.05
Alabama	1,883	0.04
Hawaii	551	0.04
Tennessee	2,123	0.03
Louisiana	1,277	0.03
Kentucky	1,076	0.03
Mississippi	688	0.02

Please refer to the Explanation of Data in the front of the book for more detailed information.

Ancestry

Czechoslovakian

Top 150 Places Sorted by Population

Based on all places, regardless of total population

Place	Population	%
New York, NY (city) Kings County	4,870	0.06
Chicago, IL (city) Cook County	2,450	0.09
Los Angeles, CA (city) Los Angeles County	1,806	0.05
Brooklyn, NY (borough) Kings County	1,684	0.07
Houston, TX (city) Harris County	1,568	0.08
Queens, NY (borough) Queens County	1,467	0.07
Omaha, NE (city) Douglas County	1,311	0.32
Manhattan, NY (borough) New York County	1,256	0.08
Phoenix, AZ (city) Maricopa County	1,066	0.07
Hempstead, NY (town) Nassau County	1,054	0.14
San Diego, CA (city) San Diego County	1,044	0.08
San Antonio, TX (city) Medina County	1,035	0.08
Lincoln, NE (city) Lancaster County	1,016	0.40
Brookhaven, NY (town) Suffolk County	917	0.19
Austin, TX (city) Travis County	839	0.11
Columbus, OH (city) Franklin County	819	0.11
Pittsburgh, PA (city) Allegheny County	773	0.25
Charlotte, NC (city) Mecklenburg County	759	0.11
Philadelphia, PA (city) Philadelphia County	721	0.05
Portland, OR (city) Multnomah County	720	0.13
Ramapo, NY (town) Rockland County	654	0.53
Wichita, KS (city) Sedgwick County	651	0.17
Virginia Beach, VA (ind. city) Virginia Beach independent city	631	0.14
Seattle, WA (city) King County	629	0.11
Colorado Springs, CO (city) El Paso County	622	0.15
Oyster Bay, NY (town) Nassau County	618	0.21
Dallas, TX (city) Dallas County	611	0.05
Islip, NY (town) Suffolk County	596	0.18
Jacksonville, FL (city) Duval County	596	0.07
Minneapolis, MN (city) Hennepin County	586	0.15
Denver, CO (city) Denver County	586	0.10
Cleveland, OH (city) Cuyahoga County	553	0.14
Cedar Rapids, IA (city) Linn County	551	0.44
Corpus Christi, TX (city) Nueces County	546	0.18
Fort Worth, TX (city) Tarrant County	546	0.08
Tucson, AZ (city) Pima County	545	0.11
Anchorage, AK (municipality) Anchorage Municipality	505	0.18
North Hempstead, NY (town) Nassau County	493	0.22
San Jose, CA (city) Santa Clara County	484	0.05
Las Vegas, NV (city) Clark County	483	0.08
Albuquerque, NM (city) Bernalillo County	473	0.09
Mesa, AZ (city) Maricopa County	470	0.11
Fort Collins, CO (city) Larimer County	468	0.33
Oklahoma City, OK (city) Oklahoma County	459	0.08
Sterling Heights, MI (city) Macomb County	456	0.35
Scottsdale, AZ (city) Maricopa County	454	0.21
Madison, WI (city) Dane County	445	0.19
Babylon, NY (town) Suffolk County	438	0.21
Huntington, NY (town) Suffolk County	435	0.22
San Francisco, CA (city) San Francisco County	422	0.05
Milwaukee, WI (city) Milwaukee County	411	0.07
Gilbert, AZ (town) Maricopa County	398	0.20
Indianapolis, IN (city) Marion County	393	0.05
Long Beach, CA (city) Los Angeles County	369	0.08
Sioux Falls, SD (city) Minnehaha County	367	0.25
Union, NY (town) Broome County	364	0.65
Ames, IA (city) Story County	355	0.62
Toms River, NJ (township) Ocean County	355	0.39
Yonkers, NY (city) Westchester County	354	0.18
Gresham, OR (city) Multnomah County	349	0.34
Berwyn, IL (city) Cook County	346	0.62
Toms River, NJ (cdp) Ocean County	345	0.39
Arlington, TX (city) Tarrant County	345	0.10
Kansas City, MO (city) Jackson County	344	0.08
Hamilton, NJ (township) Mercer County	340	0.38
Henderson, NV (city) Clark County	340	0.14
Allentown, PA (city) Lehigh County	338	0.29
Tacoma, WA (city) Pierce County	328	0.16
St. Paul, MN (city) Ramsey County	326	0.12
Aurora, CO (city) Arapahoe County	326	0.10
Tampa, FL (city) Hillsborough County	326	0.10
Great Falls, MT (city) Cascade County	321	0.55
Overland Park, KS (city) Johnson County	318	0.19
Elyria, OH (city) Lorain County	312	0.57
Smithtown, NY (town) Suffolk County	310	0.26
St. Louis, MO (city) St. Louis city County	307	0.10
Boston, MA (city) Suffolk County	307	0.05
Toledo, OH (city) Lucas County	304	0.10
Parma, OH (city) Cuyahoga County	299	0.37
Tulsa, OK (city) Tulsa County	298	0.08
Sacramento, CA (city) Sacramento County	294	0.06
Downers Grove, IL (village) DuPage County	291	0.61
Pasadena, TX (city) Harris County	288	0.20
Lincoln Park, MI (city) Wayne County	280	0.73
Washington, DC (city) District of Columbia	278	0.05
Apple Valley, MN (city) Dakota County	277	0.57
Warren, MI (city) Macomb County	276	0.20
Clovis, CA (city) Fresno County	275	0.30
Spring Hill, FL (cdp) Hernando County	275	0.28
Baltimore, MD (city) Baltimore city County	274	0.04
Cape Coral, FL (city) Lee County	271	0.18
Milford, CT (town) New Haven County	269	0.51
Lakewood, NJ (township) Ocean County	269	0.31
Lynnwood, WA (city) Snohomish County	268	0.75
Milford, CT (city) New Haven County	266	0.52
Naperville, IL (city) DuPage County	266	0.19
Burnsville, MN (city) Dakota County	265	0.44
Mansfield, OH (city) Richland County	260	0.53
Orem, UT (city) Utah County	260	0.30
Yuba City, CA (city) Sutter County	259	0.41
Troy, MI (city) Oakland County	258	0.32
Miami Beach, FL (city) Miami-Dade County	256	0.29
Stamford, CT (city/town) Fairfield County	254	0.21
Boise City, ID (city) Ada County	253	0.12
Millcreek, PA (township) Erie County	250	0.47
North Salt Lake, UT (city) Davis County	245	1.63
Aurora, IL (city) Kane County	244	0.13
Irving, TX (city) Dallas County	244	0.12
Reston, VA (cdp) Fairfax County	243	0.46
Port St. Lucie, FL (city) St. Lucie County	242	0.16
Grand Forks, ND (city) Grand Forks County	240	0.46
Westminster, CO (city) Adams County	239	0.23
Plano, TX (city) Collin County	239	0.09
Denton, TX (city) Denton County	238	0.22
Saginaw, MI (charter township) Saginaw County	237	0.58
Staten Island, NY (borough) Richmond County	237	0.05
Pinetop Country Club, AZ (cdp) Navajo County	236	9.41
Washington, MI (township) Macomb County	236	0.97
Brick, NJ (township) Ocean County	236	0.31
Spokane, WA (city) Spokane County	236	0.11
Redding, CA (city) Shasta County	235	0.26
Anaheim, CA (city) Orange County	234	0.07
Maple Grove, MN (city) Hennepin County	233	0.39
Akron, OH (city) Summit County	233	0.11
Buffalo, NY (city) Erie County	231	0.09
New Prague, MN (city) Scott County	230	3.28
Woodbridge, NJ (township) Middlesex County	230	0.23
Thornton, CO (city) Adams County	230	0.20
Danbury, CT (city/town) Fairfield County	227	0.29
Lawton, OK (city) Comanche County	227	0.24
Little Rock, AR (city) Pulaski County	227	0.12
Bronx, NY (borough) Bronx County	226	0.02
Davenport, IA (city) Scott County	224	0.23
St. Petersburg, FL (city) Pinellas County	224	0.09
Russellville, AR (city) Pope County	223	0.82
Norman, OK (city) Cleveland County	223	0.21
Cuyahoga Falls, OH (city) Summit County	222	0.45
Taylor, MI (city) Wayne County	222	0.35
Billings, MT (city) Yellowstone County	221	0.22
Flint, MI (charter township) Genesee County	220	0.67
Clifton, NJ (city) Passaic County	220	0.27
Waco, TX (city) McLennan County	220	0.18
Renton, WA (city) King County	219	0.25
Clinton, MI (charter township) Macomb County	218	0.22
Strongsville, OH (city) Cuyahoga County	217	0.49
Topeka, KS (city) Shawnee County	217	0.17
Grand Rapids, MI (city) Kent County	217	0.11
Duluth, MN (city) St. Louis County	216	0.25
Huntington Beach, CA (city) Orange County	214	0.11
Westchester, IL (village) Cook County	213	1.29

SECTION THREE

Ancestry

Czechoslovakian

Top 150 Places Sorted by Percent of Total Population

Based on all places, regardless of total population

Place	Population	%
Bonanza, CO (town) Saguache County	3	50.00
Swanville, MN (city) Todd County	4	44.44
White Hills, AZ (cdp) Mohave County	60	36.81
Brownlee, NE (cdp) Cherry County	4	26.67
Spiritwood, ND (cdp) Stutsman County	7	25.93
Dragoon, AZ (cdp) Cochise County	49	23.67
Pecan Park, NM (cdp) Luna County	20	22.47
Lower Elochoman, WA (cdp) Wahkiakum County	20	21.51
Smallwood, NY (cdp) Sullivan County	145	21.08
Lytle Creek, CA (cdp) San Bernardino County	148	20.00
Polonia, MN (township) Roseau County	2	20.00
Brewer, MO (cdp) Perry County	54	19.15
East Keating, PA (township) Clinton County	3	17.65
Abie, NE (village) Butler County	10	16.95
Willow Creek, AK (cdp) Valdez-Cordova Census Area	14	16.47
Arcola, MO (village) Dade County	7	16.28
Clacks Canyon, AZ (cdp) Mohave County	20	13.89
Harrison City, PA (cdp) Westmoreland County	15	13.27
College City, CA (cdp) Colusa County	12	13.04
Timken, KS (city) Rush County	6	12.77
Minocqua, WI (cdp) Oneida County	61	12.60
Beaver Creek, MT (cdp) Hill County	36	12.54
Roland, AR (cdp) Pulaski County	132	12.43
Dante, SD (town) Charles Mix County	10	12.20
Oxbow Estates, AZ (cdp) Gila County	18	11.18
Lamy, NM (cdp) Santa Fe County	37	11.08
Smoky Hollow, MN (township) Cass County	7	10.77
Englewood, PA (cdp) Schuylkill County	51	10.49
Whitestone, AK (cdp) Southeast Fairbanks Census Area	16	10.19
Pinetop Country Club, AZ (cdp) Navajo County	236	9.41
Bucyrus, ND (city) Adams County	2	9.09
Irvington, IL (village) Washington County	54	8.91
Okahumpka, FL (cdp) Lake County	14	8.81
Snoqualmie Pass, WA (cdp) Kittitas County	9	8.57
Ponderosa Pines, MT (cdp) Gallatin County	26	8.52
Blairsburg, IA (city) Hamilton County	16	8.47
Westerville, NE (cdp) Custer County	4	8.33
Denham, MN (city) Pine County	3	8.33
Harlingen, NJ (cdp) Somerset County	35	8.27
Rock Falls, IA (city) Cerro Gordo County	12	8.22
Ingleside on the Bay, TX (city) San Patricio County	55	8.17
Hometown, PA (cdp) Schuylkill County	118	8.08
Ness, MN (township) St. Louis County	5	8.06
Berea, NE (cdp) Box Butte County	2	8.00
Washington, VA (town) Rappahannock County	10	7.87
Sawyerville, IL (village) Macoupin County	20	7.60
Cedar Rapids, WI (town) Rusk County	3	7.50
Flensburg, MN (city) Morrison County	19	7.48
Potshot Lake, MN (unorganized territory) St. Louis County	2	7.14
Imperial, TX (cdp) Pecos County	13	7.07
Medaryville, IN (town) Pulaski County	34	6.83
Ellisburg, NY (village) Jefferson County	17	6.75
Vicksburg, AZ (cdp) La Paz County	24	6.72
Monroe, SD (town) Turner County	10	6.49
Dorchester, TX (city) Grayson County	9	6.38
Lynch, NE (village) Boyd County	11	6.32
Allport, PA (cdp) Clearfield County	15	6.15
Arthur, MN (township) Traverse County	4	6.15
Lanesburgh, MN (township) Le Sueur County	118	6.10
Milligan, NE (village) Fillmore County	15	6.10
Dry Creek, OK (cdp) Cherokee County	13	6.10
Elk, PA (township) Tioga County	2	6.06
Yorkshire, NY (cdp) Cattaraugus County	75	5.96
Farley, MN (township) Polk County	2	5.88
Twining, MI (village) Arenac County	11	5.85
Sand Coulee, MT (cdp) Cascade County	11	5.82
Aguanga, CA (cdp) Riverside County	82	5.73
Santa Susana, CA (cdp) Ventura County	73	5.61
Rangeley, ME (plantation) Franklin County	6	5.50
Flemington, MO (village) Polk County	4	5.41
Cuba, KS (city) Republic County	9	5.36
Rush Center, KS (city) Rush County	11	5.31
Brighton, ME (plantation) Somerset County	2	5.26
Bartlett, NH (cdp) Carroll County	19	5.25
Walker Valley, NY (cdp) Ulster County	28	5.22
Mi-Wuk Village, CA (cdp) Tuolumne County	44	5.19
White Bear Lake, MN (city) Washington County	12	5.15
Sumter, MN (township) McLeod County	29	5.12
Faithorn, MI (township) Menominee County	12	5.11
Happy Valley, NM (cdp) Eddy County	16	5.06
New Prague, MN (city) Scott County	212	5.05
Point of Rocks, MD (cdp) Frederick County	68	5.05
Bee, NE (village) Seward County	9	5.03
Beurys Lake, PA (cdp) Schuylkill County	9	5.00
New Salem, PA (cdp) Fayette County	32	4.89
Lake McMurray, WA (cdp) Skagit County	6	4.76
Lauderdale Lakes, WI (cdp) Walworth County	55	4.71
Buffalo, OH (cdp) Guernsey County	18	4.68
Kensington, NY (village) Nassau County	56	4.65
St. Paul, IA (city) Lee County	4	4.60
Valle Crucis, NC (cdp) Watauga County	29	4.59
Isabel, SD (town) Dewey County	13	4.58
Branchdale, PA (cdp) Schuylkill County	12	4.58
Mahaska, KS (city) Washington County	4	4.55
Palmyra, UT (cdp) Utah County	27	4.51
Montgomery, MN (township) Le Sueur County	27	4.50
Powers, MN (township) Cass County	41	4.49
Flaxton, ND (city) Burke County	4	4.44
Fullerton, ND (city) Dickey County	3	4.41
Pathfork, KY (cdp) Harlan County	16	4.40
Keystone, MN (township) Polk County	5	4.39
Pilger, NE (village) Stanton County	17	4.36
Narka, KS (city) Republic County	5	4.35
Vienna, MD (town) Dorchester County	11	4.31
Tabor, SD (town) Bon Homme County	18	4.29
Metaline, WA (town) Pend Oreille County	7	4.29
Derrynane, MN (township) Le Sueur County	19	4.28
Hubbard, WI (town) Rusk County	7	4.27
May Creek, WA (cdp) Snohomish County	38	4.26
Pisek, ND (city) Walsh County	4	4.26
Fairdale, ND (city) Walsh County	2	4.26
Forest, MN (township) Rice County	53	4.23
Box Elder, MT (cdp) Hill County	4	4.21
Lakota, ND (city) Nelson County	25	4.17
Harmony, WI (town) Price County	10	4.15
Brady, MI (township) Saginaw County	95	4.10
Bremen, MN (township) Pine County	13	4.10
Janette Lake, MN (unorganized territory) St. Louis County	10	4.10
Captains Cove, VA (cdp) Accomack County	18	4.01
Portal, ND (city) Burke County	4	4.00
Flatwoods, WV (town) Braxton County	7	3.98
Edgerton, MO (city) Platte County	26	3.96
Verdigre, NE (village) Knox County	18	3.92
Greenville, NY (cdp) Greene County	34	3.91
Dixon, MT (cdp) Sanders County	16	3.90
Hamilton, IA (city) Marion County	3	3.90
Snook, TX (city) Burleson County	20	3.87
East Rocky Hill, NJ (cdp) Somerset County	12	3.87
Luray, MO (village) Clark County	4	3.85
Hegins, PA (cdp) Schuylkill County	29	3.74
South Heights, PA (borough) Beaver County	15	3.74
Porter, PA (township) Huntingdon County	75	3.73
Dundas, MN (city) Rice County	39	3.70
Shannondale, WV (cdp) Jefferson County	93	3.68
Sheldon, WI (village) Rusk County	9	3.67
Glasgow, WV (town) Kanawha County	29	3.65
Bethel, NY (town) Sullivan County	156	3.62
Munden, KS (city) Republic County	3	3.61
Tyndall, SD (city) Bon Homme County	44	3.59
Twin Forks, NM (cdp) Otero County	11	3.58
Henderson, MI (township) Wexford County	6	3.57
Hamilton, ND (city) Pembina County	2	3.57
Des Moines River, MN (township) Murray County	5	3.55
Foscoe, NC (cdp) Watauga County	29	3.54
Seadrift, TX (city) Calhoun County	36	3.53
Carrolton, MN (township) Fillmore County	9	3.53
Lawrence, WI (town) Rusk County	9	3.52
Craig, IA (city) Plymouth County	2	3.51
Ross, ND (city) Mountrail County	3	3.49
Sharon, KS (city) Barber County	8	3.48

Please refer to the Explanation of Data in the front of the book for more detailed information.

Ancestry

Czechoslovakian

Top 150 Places Sorted by Percent of Total Population

Based on places with total population of 7,500 or more

Place	Population	%
Thomaston, CT (town) Litchfield County	175	2.22
Pebble Creek, FL (cdp) Hillsborough County	145	1.92
Grandview, WA (city) Yakima County	183	1.76
North Salt Lake, UT (city) Davis County	245	1.63
Riverside, IL (village) Cook County	134	1.53
East Grand Forks, MN (city) Polk County	113	1.35
Storm Lake, IA (city) Buena Vista County	136	1.31
Iron Mountain, MI (city) Dickinson County	102	1.31
Westchester, IL (village) Cook County	213	1.29
St. Johns, MI (city) Clinton County	101	1.28
Catalina, AZ (cdp) Pima County	104	1.27
Molalla, OR (city) Clackamas County	96	1.25
Knik-Fairview, AK (cdp) Matanuska-Susitna Borough	150	1.23
Streator, IL (city) LaSalle County	161	1.22
North Greenbush, NY (town) Rensselaer County	144	1.21
Pottsville, PA (city) Schuylkill County	166	1.14
Robinson, TX (city) McLennan County	114	1.14
Lake Morton-Berrydale, WA (cdp) King County	109	1.12
Monessen, PA (city) Westmoreland County	88	1.12
Houghton, MI (city) Houghton County	83	1.10
Roscoe, IL (village) Winnebago County	111	1.09
Chalco, NE (cdp) Sarpy County	115	1.07
Bohemia, NY (cdp) Suffolk County	106	1.07
Chenango, NY (town) Broome County	119	1.06
La Grange, IL (village) Cook County	159	1.03
Crestwood Village, NJ (cdp) Ocean County	82	1.01
Stoneham, MA (cdp/town) Middlesex County	213	1.00
Mira Monte, CA (cdp) Ventura County	78	1.00
Washington, MI (township) Macomb County	236	0.97
Dayton, TX (city) Liberty County	75	0.96
Beacon Square, FL (cdp) Pasco County	73	0.96
Brighton, MI (city) Livingston County	72	0.96
La Grange Park, IL (village) Cook County	127	0.95
Ennis, TX (city) Ellis County	171	0.94
Lehigh, PA (township) Northampton County	98	0.94
Richland, PA (township) Cambria County	118	0.93
Cresskill, NJ (borough) Bergen County	78	0.93
Boulder City, NV (city) Clark County	141	0.92
Lakeland South, WA (cdp) King County	103	0.92
Bayport, NY (cdp) Suffolk County	82	0.92
Grand Blanc, MI (city) Genesee County	77	0.92
Pleasant Hills, PA (borough) Allegheny County	76	0.92
Warrenton, MO (city) Warren County	70	0.92
Broadlands, VA (cdp) Loudoun County	96	0.90
Darien, IL (city) DuPage County	198	0.89
Geneva, IL (city) Kane County	190	0.89
North Strabane, PA (township) Washington County	114	0.89
Woodmoor, CO (cdp) El Paso County	79	0.89
Eagle Point, OR (city) Jackson County	70	0.89
Brecksville, OH (city) Cuyahoga County	119	0.88
Fort Leonard Wood, MO (cdp) Pulaski County	133	0.87
Big Rapids, MI (city) Mecosta County	93	0.87
Olivette, MO (city) St. Louis County	67	0.87
Cedar Mill, OR (cdp) Washington County	125	0.86
Brainerd, MN (city) Crow Wing County	118	0.86
Ladera Ranch, CA (cdp) Orange County	154	0.85
Cimarron Hills, CO (cdp) El Paso County	132	0.85
Endwell, NY (cdp) Broome County	98	0.84
Summit, WA (cdp) Pierce County	67	0.84
Pewaukee, WI (city) Waukesha County	108	0.83
Crestwood, IL (village) Cook County	91	0.83
Farmingdale, NY (village) Nassau County	68	0.83
Russellville, AR (city) Pope County	223	0.82
Pequannock, NJ (township) Morris County	125	0.82
Tolland, CT (town) Tolland County	121	0.82
Upper Saucon, PA (township) Lehigh County	117	0.82
Munhall, PA (borough) Allegheny County	94	0.82
Jeannette, PA (city) Westmoreland County	81	0.82
McKeesport, PA (city) Allegheny County	165	0.81
Papillion, NE (city) Sarpy County	152	0.81
Johnson City, NY (village) Broome County	123	0.81
New Kingman-Butler, AZ (cdp) Mohave County	117	0.81
D'Iberville, MS (city) Harrison County	72	0.81
Midlothian, TX (city) Ellis County	133	0.80
Terryville, NY (cdp) Suffolk County	95	0.80
Kendall Park, NJ (cdp) Middlesex County	70	0.80
Larkfield-Wikiup, CA (cdp) Sonoma County	69	0.80
Long Hill, NJ (township) Morris County	69	0.79
Ellington, CT (town) Tolland County	119	0.78
Bedford, OH (city) Cuyahoga County	103	0.78
Lenox, NY (town) Madison County	71	0.78
Rolla, MO (city) Phelps County	148	0.77
Great Bend, KS (city) Barton County	121	0.77
Mounds View, MN (city) Ramsey County	93	0.77
Leon Valley, TX (city) Bexar County	77	0.77
Helena Valley Southeast, MT (cdp) Lewis and Clark County	61	0.77
Horseheads, NY (town) Chemung County	148	0.76
Lynnwood, WA (city) Snohomish County	268	0.75
Buckingham, PA (township) Bucks County	147	0.75
Dickinson, ND (city) Stark County	128	0.75
Brookfield, CT (town) Fairfield County	121	0.75
Monsey, NY (cdp) Rockland County	113	0.75
Winfield, IL (village) DuPage County	68	0.75
Morehead City, NC (town) Carteret County	64	0.75
Nipomo, CA (cdp) San Luis Obispo County	119	0.74
Owosso, MI (city) Shiawassee County	114	0.74
Lake Mary, FL (city) Seminole County	100	0.74
Zephyrhills, FL (city) Pasco County	99	0.74
Lincoln Park, MI (city) Wayne County	280	0.73
Martinsville, NJ (cdp) Somerset County	84	0.73
Lansing, NY (town) Tompkins County	80	0.73
Tomball, TX (city) Harris County	76	0.73
Soquel, CA (cdp) Santa Cruz County	69	0.73
Hot Springs Village, AR (cdp) Garland County	90	0.72
North Lebanon, PA (township) Lebanon County	81	0.72
Woodbury, NY (village) Orange County	75	0.72
Lake St. Louis, MO (city) St. Charles County	99	0.71
Brigantine, NJ (city) Atlantic County	72	0.71
Alma, MI (city) Gratiot County	67	0.71
White Horse, NJ (cdp) Mercer County	65	0.71
Poteau, OK (city) Le Flore County	60	0.71
Wickliffe, OH (city) Lake County	90	0.70
Alexandria, MN (city) Douglas County	78	0.70
St. Albans, WV (city) Kanawha County	77	0.70
Lake Mohawk, NJ (cdp) Sussex County	70	0.70
Avon, OH (city) Lorain County	134	0.69
Country Club Hills, IL (city) Cook County	113	0.69
Grandville, MI (city) Kent County	107	0.69
Mundy, MI (township) Genesee County	102	0.69
Waukee, IA (city) Dallas County	85	0.69
Fredonia, NY (village) Chautauqua County	77	0.69
Scotia, NY (village) Schenectady County	53	0.69
Mount Pleasant, WI (village) Racine County	174	0.68
Rock Springs, WY (city) Sweetwater County	149	0.68
Lower Gwynedd, PA (township) Montgomery County	76	0.68
Woodbury, NY (town) Orange County	75	0.68
Floris, VA (cdp) Fairfax County	55	0.68
Flint, MI (charter township) Genesee County	220	0.67
Point Pleasant, NJ (borough) Ocean County	126	0.67
Stroud, PA (township) Monroe County	125	0.67
Socastee, SC (cdp) Horry County	115	0.67
North Fayette, PA (township) Allegheny County	91	0.67
Brandon, SD (city) Minnehaha County	55	0.67
Conshohocken, PA (borough) Montgomery County	52	0.67
University of California Davis, CA (cdp) Yolo County	52	0.67
Copiague, NY (cdp) Suffolk County	136	0.66
Twinsburg, OH (city) Summit County	122	0.66
Clark, NJ (township) Union County	96	0.66
Western Springs, IL (village) Cook County	83	0.66
Fernway, PA (cdp) Butler County	81	0.66
Grand Rapids, MN (city) Itasca County	71	0.66
Douglas, MA (town) Worcester County	54	0.66
Union, NY (town) Broome County	364	0.65
North Huntingdon, PA (township) Westmoreland County	197	0.65
Westmont, IL (village) DuPage County	159	0.65
Whitehall, PA (borough) Allegheny County	90	0.65
University Heights, OH (city) Cuyahoga County	88	0.65
Putnam, MI (township) Livingston County	54	0.65
Cascade, MI (charter township) Kent County	108	0.64
Scotts Valley, CA (city) Santa Cruz County	73	0.64

Please refer to the Explanation of Data in the front of the book for more detailed information.

Ancestry

Danish

U.S. and 50 States Sorted by Population and Percent of Total Population

Place	Population	%
United States	**1,453,897**	**0.48**
California	194,960	0.53
Utah	155,362	5.85
Minnesota	86,508	1.65
Washington	75,185	1.15
Wisconsin	68,154	1.21
Iowa	66,290	2.20
Illinois	53,218	0.42
Texas	52,181	0.21
Nebraska	50,896	2.83
Florida	47,700	0.26
Colorado	46,668	0.95
Arizona	45,625	0.73
Michigan	44,243	0.44
Oregon	43,160	1.15
Idaho	37,041	2.43
New York	35,247	0.18
Missouri	20,826	0.35
Nevada	20,157	0.77
New Jersey	19,832	0.23
Virginia	19,482	0.25
Pennsylvania	19,001	0.15
South Dakota	18,778	2.35
Ohio	18,632	0.16
Kansas	16,188	0.58
North Carolina	15,824	0.17
Massachusetts	15,620	0.24
Montana	14,452	1.48
Connecticut	13,331	0.38
Indiana	13,281	0.21
Georgia	13,099	0.14
Maryland	11,776	0.21
Wyoming	10,576	1.94
Tennessee	9,312	0.15
Oklahoma	8,389	0.23
North Dakota	7,925	1.20
New Mexico	7,207	0.36
Maine	6,354	0.48
South Carolina	6,353	0.14
Arkansas	5,934	0.21
Alaska	5,778	0.84
Alabama	4,771	0.10
Kentucky	4,682	0.11
Louisiana	4,178	0.09
Hawaii	4,172	0.31
New Hampshire	3,796	0.29
Mississippi	2,760	0.09
Vermont	2,144	0.34
Rhode Island	2,127	0.20
Delaware	1,776	0.20
District of Columbia	1,495	0.26
West Virginia	1,451	0.08

Place	Population	%
Utah	155,362	5.85
Nebraska	50,896	2.83
Idaho	37,041	2.43
South Dakota	18,778	2.35
Iowa	66,290	2.20
Wyoming	10,576	1.94
Minnesota	86,508	1.65
Montana	14,452	1.48
Wisconsin	68,154	1.21
North Dakota	7,925	1.20
Washington	75,185	1.15
Oregon	43,160	1.15
Colorado	46,668	0.95
Alaska	5,778	0.84
Nevada	20,157	0.77
Arizona	45,625	0.73
Kansas	16,188	0.58
California	194,960	0.53
United States	**1,453,897**	**0.48**
Maine	6,354	0.48
Michigan	44,243	0.44
Illinois	53,218	0.42
Connecticut	13,331	0.38
New Mexico	7,207	0.36
Missouri	20,826	0.35
Vermont	2,144	0.34
Hawaii	4,172	0.31
New Hampshire	3,796	0.29
Florida	47,700	0.26
District of Columbia	1,495	0.26
Virginia	19,482	0.25
Massachusetts	15,620	0.24
New Jersey	19,832	0.23
Oklahoma	8,389	0.23
Texas	52,181	0.21
Indiana	13,281	0.21
Maryland	11,776	0.21
Arkansas	5,934	0.21
Rhode Island	2,127	0.20
Delaware	1,776	0.20
New York	35,247	0.18
North Carolina	15,824	0.17
Ohio	18,632	0.16
Pennsylvania	19,001	0.15
Tennessee	9,312	0.15
Georgia	13,099	0.14
South Carolina	6,353	0.14
Kentucky	4,682	0.11
Alabama	4,771	0.10
Louisiana	4,178	0.09
Mississippi	2,760	0.09
West Virginia	1,451	0.08

Please refer to the Explanation of Data in the front of the book for more detailed information.

Ancestry

Danish

Top 150 Places Sorted by Population

Based on all places, regardless of total population

Place	Population	%
Omaha, NE (city) Douglas County	10,484	2.57
Los Angeles, CA (city) Los Angeles County	9,510	0.25
Salt Lake City, UT (city) Salt Lake County	8,002	4.34
New York, NY (city) Kings County	7,018	0.09
Provo, UT (city) Utah County	6,933	6.29
Seattle, WA (city) King County	6,649	1.12
Phoenix, AZ (city) Maricopa County	6,271	0.43
Portland, OR (city) Multnomah County	6,203	1.09
San Diego, CA (city) San Diego County	5,944	0.46
Sandy, UT (city) Salt Lake County	5,910	6.78
Orem, UT (city) Utah County	5,572	6.42
Chicago, IL (city) Cook County	5,565	0.21
Lincoln, NE (city) Lancaster County	5,511	2.18
West Jordan, UT (city) Salt Lake County	5,433	5.51
Minneapolis, MN (city) Hennepin County	5,219	1.37
Mesa, AZ (city) Maricopa County	5,214	1.19
West Valley City, UT (city) Salt Lake County	4,543	3.63
Manhattan, NY (borough) New York County	4,095	0.26
Racine, WI (city) Racine County	3,974	4.99
Council Bluffs, IA (city) Pottawattamie County	3,910	6.37
St. George, UT (city) Washington County	3,742	5.26
San Francisco, CA (city) San Francisco County	3,739	0.47
Bountiful, UT (city) Davis County	3,631	8.57
Layton, UT (city) Davis County	3,630	5.53
Millcreek, UT (cdp) Salt Lake County	3,590	5.89
Boise City, ID (city) Ada County	3,555	1.72
Logan, UT (city) Cache County	3,533	7.61
Denver, CO (city) Denver County	3,528	0.61
Colorado Springs, CO (city) El Paso County	3,493	0.86
Sioux Falls, SD (city) Minnehaha County	3,392	2.28
San Jose, CA (city) Santa Clara County	3,362	0.36
St. Paul, MN (city) Ramsey County	3,307	1.17
Houston, TX (city) Harris County	3,200	0.15
Las Vegas, NV (city) Clark County	3,165	0.55
Madison, WI (city) Dane County	3,128	1.36
Draper, UT (city) Salt Lake County	2,854	7.27
Austin, TX (city) Travis County	2,849	0.37
Murray, UT (city) Salt Lake County	2,847	6.15
Taylorsville, UT (city) Salt Lake County	2,806	4.81
Henderson, NV (city) Clark County	2,803	1.12
South Jordan, UT (city) Salt Lake County	2,796	6.03
Gilbert, AZ (town) Maricopa County	2,731	1.40
Lehi, UT (city) Utah County	2,669	6.35
Tucson, AZ (city) Pima County	2,604	0.50
Pleasant Grove, UT (city) Utah County	2,556	8.13
Ogden, UT (city) Weber County	2,476	3.05
Des Moines, IA (city) Polk County	2,393	1.18
Riverton, UT (city) Salt Lake County	2,347	6.52
Pocatello, ID (city) Bannock County	2,334	4.38
Spokane, WA (city) Spokane County	2,307	1.12
Spanish Fork, UT (city) Utah County	2,293	7.20
Fresno, CA (city) Fresno County	2,292	0.47
Anchorage, AK (municipality) Anchorage Municipality	2,291	0.81
Albuquerque, NM (city) Bernalillo County	2,273	0.43
Santa Rosa, CA (city) Sonoma County	2,234	1.37
Chandler, AZ (city) Maricopa County	2,230	0.97
Eugene, OR (city) Lane County	2,211	1.44
San Antonio, TX (city) Medina County	2,087	0.16
Reno, NV (city) Washoe County	2,069	0.94
Kansas City, MO (city) Jackson County	2,006	0.44
Huntington Beach, CA (city) Orange County	1,987	1.05
Dallas, TX (city) Dallas County	1,958	0.16
Kenosha, WI (city) Kenosha County	1,951	1.98
Sacramento, CA (city) Sacramento County	1,908	0.42
Brigham City, UT (city) Box Elder County	1,901	10.78
Vancouver, WA (city) Clark County	1,881	1.17
Cottonwood Heights, UT (city) Salt Lake County	1,868	5.57
Idaho Falls, ID (city) Bonneville County	1,858	3.34
Kaysville, UT (city) Davis County	1,856	7.12
Milwaukee, WI (city) Milwaukee County	1,843	0.31
American Fork, UT (city) Utah County	1,842	7.26
Sioux City, IA (city) Woodbury County	1,835	2.23
Scottsdale, AZ (city) Maricopa County	1,820	0.83
Ames, IA (city) Story County	1,819	3.17
Lakewood, CO (city) Jefferson County	1,798	1.27
Fort Collins, CO (city) Larimer County	1,773	1.27
Holladay, UT (city) Salt Lake County	1,765	6.71
Aurora, CO (city) Arapahoe County	1,738	0.55
Cedar Rapids, IA (city) Linn County	1,715	1.37
Mount Pleasant, WI (village) Racine County	1,671	6.50
Tooele, UT (city) Tooele County	1,648	5.46
Wichita, KS (city) Sedgwick County	1,639	0.44
Jacksonville, FL (city) Duval County	1,631	0.20
Springville, UT (city) Utah County	1,620	5.86
Tacoma, WA (city) Pierce County	1,617	0.81
Rexburg, ID (city) Madison County	1,597	6.51
Overland Park, KS (city) Johnson County	1,595	0.94
Roseville, CA (city) Placer County	1,567	1.38
Salem, OR (city) Marion County	1,560	1.03
Oceanside, CA (city) San Diego County	1,549	0.94
Grand Island, NE (city) Hall County	1,497	3.19
Washington, DC (city) District of Columbia	1,495	0.26
Loveland, CO (city) Larimer County	1,488	2.32
Billings, MT (city) Yellowstone County	1,486	1.46
Charlotte, NC (city) Mecklenburg County	1,486	0.21
Cedar City, UT (city) Iron County	1,485	5.36
Indianapolis, IN (city) Marion County	1,483	0.18
Kearns, UT (cdp) Salt Lake County	1,449	4.17
Carlsbad, CA (city) San Diego County	1,413	1.42
Glendale, AZ (city) Maricopa County	1,409	0.61
Tempe, AZ (city) Maricopa County	1,408	0.86
Farmington, UT (city) Davis County	1,406	8.18
Thousand Oaks, CA (city) Ventura County	1,405	1.13
Bakersfield, CA (city) Kern County	1,382	0.42
Caledonia, WI (village) Racine County	1,378	5.62
Fort Worth, TX (city) Tarrant County	1,378	0.20
Rochester, MN (city) Olmsted County	1,374	1.32
Blair, NE (city) Washington County	1,373	17.21
Bellevue, NE (city) Sarpy County	1,369	2.72
Waterloo, IA (city) Black Hawk County	1,353	1.99
Centerville, UT (city) Davis County	1,342	8.82
Magna, UT (cdp) Salt Lake County	1,341	4.98
Oklahoma City, OK (city) Oklahoma County	1,333	0.24
Highlands Ranch, CO (cdp) Douglas County	1,332	1.40
Grand Rapids, MI (city) Kent County	1,324	0.70
Green Bay, WI (city) Brown County	1,267	1.22
Brooklyn, NY (borough) Kings County	1,267	0.05
Bloomington, MN (city) Hennepin County	1,261	1.53
Albert Lea, MN (city) Freeborn County	1,249	6.91
Bellevue, WA (city) King County	1,239	1.04
Brookhaven, NY (town) Suffolk County	1,229	0.26
Syracuse, UT (city) Davis County	1,223	5.64
Spokane Valley, WA (city) Spokane County	1,223	1.39
Oakland, CA (city) Alameda County	1,221	0.32
Highland, UT (city) Utah County	1,220	8.66
Kearney, NE (city) Buffalo County	1,218	4.03
Plymouth, MN (city) Hennepin County	1,215	1.76
Boulder, CO (city) Boulder County	1,215	1.25
Columbus, OH (city) Franklin County	1,200	0.16
San Buenaventura (Ventura), CA (city) Ventura County	1,189	1.13
Chico, CA (city) Butte County	1,185	1.39
Long Beach, CA (city) Los Angeles County	1,179	0.26
Edina, MN (city) Hennepin County	1,176	2.48
Paradise, NV (cdp) Clark County	1,175	0.54
Roy, UT (city) Weber County	1,173	3.27
Arvada, CO (city) Jefferson County	1,173	1.12
Bellingham, WA (city) Whatcom County	1,165	1.47
Fremont, NE (city) Dodge County	1,156	4.41
Maple Grove, MN (city) Hennepin County	1,152	1.95
Minnetonka, MN (city) Hennepin County	1,143	2.31
Missoula, MT (city) Missoula County	1,143	1.75
Cedar Falls, IA (city) Black Hawk County	1,134	2.97
Eagle Mountain, UT (city) Utah County	1,124	6.28
Citrus Heights, CA (city) Sacramento County	1,123	1.33
Gresham, OR (city) Multnomah County	1,109	1.09
Livermore, CA (city) Alameda County	1,107	1.41
Virginia Beach, VA (ind. city) Virginia Beach independent city	1,106	0.25
Centennial, CO (city) Arapahoe County	1,092	1.09
Atlantic, IA (city) Cass County	1,086	15.34
Riverside, CA (city) Riverside County	1,079	0.36

Ancestry

Danish

Top 150 Places Sorted by Percent of Total Population

Based on all places, regardless of total population

Place	Population	%
Mendeltna, AK (cdp) Valdez-Cordova Census Area	20	100.00
Gann Valley, SD (cdp) Buffalo County	5	100.00
Albee, SD (town) Grant County	3	100.00
Luverne, ND (city) Steele County	14	82.35
New Auburn, WI (village) Barron County	8	72.73
Washam, WY (cdp) Sweetwater County	36	66.67
Edna, CA (cdp) San Luis Obispo County	20	66.67
Brayton, IA (city) Audubon County	96	58.18
North Marysville, WA (cdp) Snohomish County	22	57.89
Berlin, ND (city) LaMoure County	19	55.88
Cache, UT (cdp) Cache County	10	52.63
Albany, WY (cdp) Albany County	9	50.00
Leamington, UT (town) Millard County	93	49.47
Washington, CA (cdp) Nevada County	18	48.65
Moorefield, NE (village) Frontier County	9	47.37
Elk Horn, IA (city) Shelby County	234	46.71
Spring City, UT (city) Sanpete County	517	42.24
Cruzville, NM (cdp) Catron County	16	42.11
Cowles, NE (village) Webster County	10	41.67
Osino, NV (cdp) Elko County	167	41.03
Ward, SD (town) Moody County	24	40.00
Exira, IA (city) Audubon County	316	39.01
Merrifield, MN (cdp) Crow Wing County	95	35.45
Correll, MN (city) Big Stone County	26	35.14
Audubon, IA (city) Audubon County	743	34.13
Utica, SD (town) Yankton County	14	33.33
Eldora, CO (cdp) Boulder County	13	33.33
Snyder, CO (cdp) Morgan County	56	31.64
McGrew, NE (village) Scotts Bluff County	13	30.95
Virden, NM (village) Hidalgo County	36	30.77
Shoshone, CA (cdp) Inyo County	10	30.30
Butte Meadows, CA (cdp) Butte County	9	30.00
Tintah, MN (township) Traverse County	6	30.00
Ward, CO (town) Boulder County	20	29.85
Keeler, CA (cdp) Inyo County	8	29.63
West Wood, UT (cdp) Carbon County	200	28.86
Elsinore, UT (town) Sevier County	281	28.76
Otter Tail Peninsula, MN (township) Cass County	11	28.21
Hope, MN (township) Lincoln County	82	28.08
White Earth, ND (city) Mountrail County	16	28.07
Badger, SD (town) Kingsbury County	26	27.96
Deweyville, UT (town) Box Elder County	99	27.35
Gasquet, CA (cdp) Del Norte County	154	26.92
Teasdale, UT (cdp) Wayne County	7	26.92
Urie, WY (cdp) Uinta County	53	26.77
Manfred, MN (township) Lac qui Parle County	20	26.67
Crane, MT (cdp) Richland County	16	26.67
Dry Valley, NV (cdp) Lincoln County	9	26.47
Friendship, MD (cdp) Anne Arundel County	108	26.21
Gray, IA (city) Audubon County	19	25.33
North Loup, NE (village) Valley County	94	25.27
Castle Dale, UT (city) Emery County	416	25.17
Otranto, IA (cdp) Mitchell County	7	25.00
Obert, NE (village) Cedar County	4	25.00
Mantua, UT (town) Box Elder County	170	24.67
Kimballton, IA (city) Audubon County	91	24.59
Hobson, MT (city) Judith Basin County	49	24.02
Florence, MN (city) Lyon County	6	24.00
Redmond, UT (town) Sevier County	120	23.81
Manchester, MN (city) Freeborn County	5	23.81
St. Joseph, MN (township) Kittson County	5	23.81
Mayfield, UT (town) Sanpete County	104	23.69
Anita, IA (city) Cass County	246	23.45
Carlston, MN (township) Freeborn County	61	23.37
Liberty, MN (township) Polk County	33	22.45
Montpelier, ND (city) Stutsman County	28	22.40
Lamar, NE (village) Chase County	2	22.22
Comptche, CA (cdp) Mendocino County	21	21.88
Central Valley, UT (town) Sevier County	61	21.79
Cordova, NE (village) Seward County	10	21.74
Moroni, UT (city) Sanpete County	261	21.71
St. Helena, NE (village) Cedar County	11	21.57
Elba, NE (village) Howard County	64	21.55
Auburn, WY (cdp) Lincoln County	53	21.54
Elwood, UT (town) Box Elder County	195	21.36
Riverside, UT (cdp) Box Elder County	133	21.18
Lynndyl, UT (town) Millard County	28	21.05
Lyons, NE (city) Burt County	186	20.95
Coram, MT (cdp) Flathead County	86	20.82
Wintergreen, VA (cdp) Nelson County	26	20.80
Tyler, MN (city) Lincoln County	209	20.75
Elmo, UT (town) Emery County	55	20.75
Sterling, UT (town) Sanpete County	65	20.57
Howell, UT (town) Box Elder County	36	20.57
Rock Creek Park, CO (cdp) El Paso County	15	20.55
Mount Pleasant, UT (city) Sanpete County	641	20.41
Westphalia, IA (city) Shelby County	12	20.34
Emerald, WI (cdp) St. Croix County	18	20.00
Kirkman, IA (city) Shelby County	11	20.00
Conway, ND (city) Walsh County	4	20.00
False Pass, AK (city) Aleutians East Borough	3	20.00
Viborg, SD (city) Turner County	166	19.98
Craig, NE (village) Burt County	43	19.91
Alsea, OR (cdp) Benton County	41	19.71
Levan, UT (town) Juab County	215	19.65
Cornish, MN (township) Aitkin County	9	19.57
Diamond Lake, MN (township) Lincoln County	62	19.31
St. Benedict, IA (cdp) Kossuth County	5	19.23
Fountain Green, UT (city) Sanpete County	169	19.20
Thurston, NE (village) Thurston County	16	19.05
Artois, CA (cdp) Glenn County	27	19.01
Pacific Beach, WA (cdp) Grays Harbor County	83	18.99
Sanford, CO (town) Conejos County	167	18.98
Aetna, MN (township) Pipestone County	28	18.79
Arlington, NE (village) Washington County	279	18.76
Bear River City, UT (city) Box Elder County	182	18.74
Seven Springs, NC (town) Wayne County	25	18.66
Plush, OR (cdp) Lake County	11	18.64
Erwin, SD (town) Kingsbury County	7	18.42
Garden City, UT (town) Rich County	68	18.33
Rogers, MN (township) Cass County	11	18.33
Smithfield, NE (village) Gosper County	11	18.33
Bridgewater, IA (city) Adair County	26	18.18
Volin, SD (town) Yankton County	34	18.09
Camp Crook, SD (town) Harding County	17	18.09
Greenwater, WA (cdp) Pierce County	20	17.86
Annabella, UT (town) Sevier County	118	17.77
Cotesfield, NE (village) Howard County	14	17.72
Mona, UT (city) Juab County	193	17.69
Osmond, WY (cdp) Lincoln County	69	17.69
Scipio, UT (town) Millard County	34	17.62
New Holland, SD (cdp) Douglas County	20	17.54
Irene, SD (city) Turner County	97	17.51
Red Corral, CA (cdp) Amador County	300	17.47
Tuttletown, CA (cdp) Tuolumne County	147	17.40
Hetland, SD (town) Kingsbury County	5	17.24
Richfield, KS (city) Morton County	5	17.24
Blair, NE (city) Washington County	1,373	17.21
Hazard, NE (village) Sherman County	11	17.19
Ferron, UT (city) Emery County	260	17.07
Three Lakes, MN (township) Redwood County	29	17.06
Downieville-Lawson-Dumont, CO (cdp) Clear Creek County	54	16.98
Vining, IA (city) Tama County	10	16.95
Dayton, ID (city) Franklin County	74	16.70
Simpson, KS (city) Mitchell County	17	16.67
Cooperton, OK (town) Kiowa County	2	16.67
Kanosh, UT (town) Millard County	99	16.56
Eden, MN (township) Brown County	49	16.55
Joseph, UT (town) Sevier County	58	16.52
Soldier, IA (city) Monona County	38	16.52
Bancroft, MN (township) Freeborn County	196	16.43
Moorhead, IA (city) Monona County	32	16.33
Captiva, FL (cdp) Lee County	24	16.33
Askov, MN (city) Pine County	66	16.30
Lake Stay, MN (township) Lincoln County	32	16.24
Rutherford, CA (cdp) Napa County	31	16.23
Kilgore, NE (village) Cherry County	9	16.07
Coulterville, CA (cdp) Mariposa County	26	16.05
New Pine Creek, CA (cdp) Modoc County	18	15.93
Gillett Grove, IA (city) Clay County	7	15.91

Ancestry

Danish

Top 150 Places Sorted by Percent of Total Population

Based on places with total population of 7,500 or more

Place	Population	%
Blair, NE (city) Washington County	1,373	17.21
Brigham City, UT (city) Box Elder County	1,901	10.78
Mapleton, UT (city) Utah County	753	9.98
Centerville, UT (city) Davis County	1,342	8.82
Highland, UT (city) Utah County	1,220	8.66
Bountiful, UT (city) Davis County	3,631	8.57
Farmington, UT (city) Davis County	1,406	8.18
Pleasant Grove, UT (city) Utah County	2,556	8.13
Alpine, UT (city) Utah County	693	7.65
Logan, UT (city) Cache County	3,533	7.61
Lindon, UT (city) Utah County	733	7.56
Draper, UT (city) Salt Lake County	2,854	7.27
American Fork, UT (city) Utah County	1,842	7.26
Spanish Fork, UT (city) Utah County	2,293	7.20
Kaysville, UT (city) Davis County	1,856	7.12
Albert Lea, MN (city) Freeborn County	1,249	6.91
West Point, UT (city) Davis County	606	6.80
Sandy, UT (city) Salt Lake County	5,910	6.78
Holladay, UT (city) Salt Lake County	1,765	6.71
Santaquin, UT (city) Utah County	550	6.58
Price, UT (city) Carbon County	554	6.54
North Logan, UT (city) Cache County	507	6.53
Riverton, UT (city) Salt Lake County	2,347	6.52
Rexburg, ID (city) Madison County	1,597	6.51
Mount Pleasant, WI (village) Racine County	1,671	6.50
Orem, UT (city) Utah County	5,572	6.42
Council Bluffs, IA (city) Pottawattamie County	3,910	6.37
Lehi, UT (city) Utah County	2,669	6.35
Provo, UT (city) Utah County	6,933	6.29
Eagle Mountain, UT (city) Utah County	1,124	6.28
Murray, UT (city) Salt Lake County	2,847	6.15
Smithfield, UT (city) Cache County	549	6.13
Blackfoot, ID (city) Bingham County	697	6.05
South Jordan, UT (city) Salt Lake County	2,796	6.03
Millcreek, UT (cdp) Salt Lake County	3,590	5.89
Springville, UT (city) Utah County	1,620	5.86
Syracuse, UT (city) Davis County	1,223	5.64
Caledonia, WI (village) Racine County	1,378	5.62
Cottonwood Heights, UT (city) Salt Lake County	1,868	5.57
Layton, UT (city) Davis County	3,630	5.53
West Jordan, UT (city) Salt Lake County	5,433	5.51
Tooele, UT (city) Tooele County	1,648	5.46
North Ogden, UT (city) Weber County	915	5.45
North Salt Lake, UT (city) Davis County	816	5.45
Cedar City, UT (city) Iron County	1,485	5.36
Ludington, MI (city) Mason County	431	5.28
St. George, UT (city) Washington County	3,742	5.26
Chalco, NE (cdp) Sarpy County	562	5.24
Saratoga Springs, UT (city) Utah County	756	5.14
Washington Terrace, UT (city) Weber County	451	5.06
Heber, UT (city) Wasatch County	541	5.03
Racine, WI (city) Racine County	3,974	4.99
Magna, UT (cdp) Salt Lake County	1,341	4.98
Greenville, MI (city) Montcalm County	419	4.95
Payson, UT (city) Utah County	843	4.90
Taylorsville, UT (city) Salt Lake County	2,806	4.81
Fremont, NE (city) Dodge County	1,156	4.41
Pocatello, ID (city) Bannock County	2,334	4.38
Evanston, WY (city) Uinta County	524	4.36
Salt Lake City, UT (city) Salt Lake County	8,002	4.34
Green River, WY (city) Sweetwater County	527	4.30
Kearns, UT (cdp) Salt Lake County	1,449	4.17
Cedar Hills, UT (city) Utah County	352	4.11
Grantsville, UT (city) Tooele County	343	4.06
Kearney, NE (city) Buffalo County	1,218	4.03
West Haven, UT (city) Weber County	361	3.99
Fairmont, MN (city) Martin County	421	3.96
Norwalk, IA (city) Warren County	329	3.82
Clinton, UT (city) Davis County	723	3.80
Spencer, IA (city) Clay County	423	3.78
Chubbuck, ID (city) Bannock County	483	3.71
Woods Cross, UT (city) Davis County	335	3.65
West Valley City, UT (city) Salt Lake County	4,543	3.63
Ammon, ID (city) Bonneville County	449	3.61
South Ogden, UT (city) Weber County	575	3.60
Herriman, UT (city) Salt Lake County	652	3.56
Burley, ID (city) Cassia County	352	3.56
Marshall, MN (city) Lyon County	471	3.51
North Mankato, MN (city) Nicollet County	456	3.47
Owatonna, MN (city) Steele County	851	3.36
Idaho Falls, ID (city) Bonneville County	1,858	3.34
Riverdale, UT (city) Weber County	273	3.33
Roy, UT (city) Weber County	1,173	3.27
Diamond Springs, CA (cdp) El Dorado County	370	3.27
Yankton, SD (city) Yankton County	464	3.26
Grand Island, NE (city) Hall County	1,497	3.19
Vernal, UT (city) Uintah County	280	3.19
Ames, IA (city) Story County	1,819	3.17
Spanish Springs, NV (cdp) Washoe County	466	3.16
Beloit, WI (town) Rock County	240	3.16
Bothell West, WA (cdp) Snohomish County	492	3.15
Lake Morton-Berrydale, WA (cdp) King County	298	3.08
Hutchinson, MN (city) McLeod County	436	3.07
Ogden, UT (city) Weber County	2,476	3.05
Clinton, IA (city) Clinton County	824	3.05
Mitchell, SD (city) Davison County	461	3.04
Blackhawk, CA (cdp) Contra Costa County	292	3.04
Midvale, UT (city) Salt Lake County	833	3.02
Hurricane, UT (city) Washington County	394	2.98
Webster City, IA (city) Hamilton County	242	2.98
Cedar Falls, IA (city) Black Hawk County	1,134	2.97
Brookings, SD (city) Brookings County	637	2.97
Carroll, IA (city) Carroll County	298	2.97
York, NE (city) York County	234	2.97
Live Oak, CA (city) Sutter County	241	2.96
Washington, UT (city) Washington County	514	2.95
Burlington, WA (city) Skagit County	238	2.91
Mira Monte, CA (cdp) Ventura County	226	2.90
Mukilteo, WA (city) Snohomish County	572	2.88
Johnston, IA (city) Polk County	448	2.85
Cottage Lake, WA (cdp) King County	628	2.82
Rawlins, WY (city) Carbon County	256	2.82
Denison, IA (city) Crawford County	226	2.80
Waverly, IA (city) Bremer County	272	2.79
Paradise, CA (town) Butte County	731	2.77
Rosemount, MN (city) Dakota County	567	2.74
Taft, CA (city) Kern County	257	2.74
Bellevue, NE (city) Sarpy County	1,369	2.72
Maple Valley, WA (city) King County	568	2.71
Northfield, MN (city) Rice County	526	2.71
South Sioux City, NE (city) Dakota County	352	2.71
El Campo, TX (city) Wharton County	309	2.68
Riverton, WY (city) Fremont County	272	2.65
White Bear Lake, MN (city) Ramsey County	613	2.64
Washougal, WA (city) Clark County	349	2.64
Salem, WI (town) Kenosha County	310	2.64
Burlington, WI (city) Racine County	274	2.64
Clearfield, UT (city) Davis County	775	2.63
Pismo Beach, CA (city) San Luis Obispo County	205	2.63
Mason City, IA (city) Cerro Gordo County	736	2.62
Snohomish, WA (city) Snohomish County	237	2.62
White Bear Lake, MN (city) Ramsey County	613	2.61
Oconomowoc, WI (town) Waukesha County	214	2.59
Indianola, IA (city) Warren County	375	2.58
Omaha, NE (city) Douglas County	10,484	2.57
Ramsey, MN (city) Anoka County	586	2.56
Oregon, WI (village) Dane County	229	2.56
Hudson, WI (town) St. Croix County	211	2.56
Storm Lake, IA (city) Buena Vista County	262	2.53
Papillion, NE (city) Sarpy County	472	2.51
Brandon, SD (city) Minnehaha County	207	2.51
North Platte, NE (city) Lincoln County	619	2.50
Dover, NY (town) Dutchess County	218	2.50
Kingsgate, WA (cdp) King County	340	2.49
Sturgeon Bay, WI (city) Door County	229	2.49
Edina, MN (city) Hennepin County	1,176	2.48
Woodmoor, CO (cdp) El Paso County	221	2.48
St. Anthony, MN (city) Hennepin and Ramsey Counties	201	2.48
Pewaukee, WI (city) Waukesha County	320	2.47
Enumclaw, WA (city) King County	263	2.47

SECTION THREE

Ancestry

Dutch

U.S. and 50 States Sorted by Population and Percent of Total Population

Place	Population	%
United States	**4,950,629**	**1.63**
Michigan	515,229	5.18
California	422,077	1.15
New York	277,731	1.44
Pennsylvania	268,376	2.13
Texas	242,507	1.00
Florida	232,801	1.26
Ohio	207,492	1.80
Illinois	201,329	1.58
Washington	161,947	2.47
Wisconsin	153,363	2.72
Iowa	147,978	4.91
Indiana	144,391	2.25
North Carolina	119,440	1.29
Missouri	115,789	1.96
New Jersey	110,584	1.27
Minnesota	106,516	2.03
Arizona	103,144	1.65
Colorado	96,824	1.98
Oregon	95,959	2.55
Virginia	91,260	1.16
Georgia	86,949	0.92
Tennessee	84,418	1.35
Oklahoma	80,729	2.20
Kansas	66,230	2.36
Utah	64,113	2.41
Maryland	59,254	1.04
Kentucky	58,584	1.37
Alabama	56,214	1.19
Arkansas	54,436	1.89
Massachusetts	47,023	0.73
West Virginia	46,046	2.50
South Carolina	45,122	1.00
Nebraska	38,931	2.16
South Dakota	38,184	4.78
Idaho	36,548	2.39
Nevada	34,972	1.33
Connecticut	30,302	0.85
Louisiana	27,195	0.61
Montana	26,514	2.72
New Mexico	23,258	1.16
Mississippi	23,177	0.79
Alaska	15,428	2.23
Delaware	14,189	1.61
Maine	13,889	1.05
Wyoming	13,153	2.41
New Hampshire	12,562	0.96
Hawaii	10,187	0.76
Vermont	9,815	1.57
North Dakota	9,198	1.39
Rhode Island	5,604	0.53
District of Columbia	3,668	0.63

Place	Population	%
Michigan	515,229	5.18
Iowa	147,978	4.91
South Dakota	38,184	4.78
Wisconsin	153,363	2.72
Montana	26,514	2.72
Oregon	95,959	2.55
West Virginia	46,046	2.50
Washington	161,947	2.47
Utah	64,113	2.41
Wyoming	13,153	2.41
Idaho	36,548	2.39
Kansas	66,230	2.36
Indiana	144,391	2.25
Alaska	15,428	2.23
Oklahoma	80,729	2.20
Nebraska	38,931	2.16
Pennsylvania	268,376	2.13
Minnesota	106,516	2.03
Colorado	96,824	1.98
Missouri	115,789	1.96
Arkansas	54,436	1.89
Ohio	207,492	1.80
Arizona	103,144	1.65
United States	**4,950,629**	**1.63**
Delaware	14,189	1.61
Illinois	201,329	1.58
Vermont	9,815	1.57
New York	277,731	1.44
North Dakota	9,198	1.39
Kentucky	58,584	1.37
Tennessee	84,418	1.35
Nevada	34,972	1.33
North Carolina	119,440	1.29
New Jersey	110,584	1.27
Florida	232,801	1.26
Alabama	56,214	1.19
Virginia	91,260	1.16
New Mexico	23,258	1.16
California	422,077	1.15
Maine	13,889	1.05
Maryland	59,254	1.04
Texas	242,507	1.00
South Carolina	45,122	1.00
New Hampshire	12,562	0.96
Georgia	86,949	0.92
Connecticut	30,302	0.85
Mississippi	23,177	0.79
Hawaii	10,187	0.76
Massachusetts	47,023	0.73
District of Columbia	3,668	0.63
Louisiana	27,195	0.61
Rhode Island	5,604	0.53

Please refer to the Explanation of Data in the front of the book for more detailed information.

Ancestry

Dutch

Top 150 Places Sorted by Population

Based on all places, regardless of total population

Place	Population	%
Grand Rapids, MI (city) Kent County	29,229	15.35
New York, NY (city) Kings County	23,151	0.29
Georgetown, MI (charter township) Ottawa County	19,742	42.55
Phoenix, AZ (city) Maricopa County	17,964	1.24
Los Angeles, CA (city) Los Angeles County	17,897	0.47
Wyoming, MI (city) Kent County	16,185	22.54
San Diego, CA (city) San Diego County	14,365	1.12
Chicago, IL (city) Cook County	14,116	0.52
Seattle, WA (city) King County	11,744	1.97
Indianapolis, IN (city) Marion County	11,553	1.43
Portland, OR (city) Multnomah County	11,114	1.96
Columbus, OH (city) Franklin County	10,822	1.40
Houston, TX (city) Harris County	10,740	0.52
Manhattan, NY (borough) New York County	10,414	0.66
Oklahoma City, OK (city) Oklahoma County	10,020	1.78
Sioux Falls, SD (city) Minnehaha County	9,552	6.42
Holland, MI (charter township) Ottawa County	9,456	27.26
Holland, MI (city) Ottawa County	9,167	27.20
Jacksonville, FL (city) Duval County	9,104	1.12
Kentwood, MI (city) Kent County	8,913	18.48
Denver, CO (city) Denver County	8,389	1.45
Wichita, KS (city) Sedgwick County	8,318	2.23
Louisville-Jefferson County, KY (metro govt) Jefferson County	8,249	1.41
Des Moines, IA (city) Polk County	8,169	4.04
Colorado Springs, CO (city) El Paso County	7,669	1.90
Charlotte, NC (city) Mecklenburg County	7,656	1.08
Mesa, AZ (city) Maricopa County	7,556	1.72
Austin, TX (city) Travis County	7,521	0.98
San Jose, CA (city) Santa Clara County	7,446	0.80
San Francisco, CA (city) San Francisco County	7,416	0.94
Tucson, AZ (city) Pima County	7,333	1.41
Byron, MI (township) Kent County	7,207	36.27
Jenison, MI (cdp) Ottawa County	7,138	41.41
Tulsa, OK (city) Tulsa County	7,047	1.82
Virginia Beach, VA (ind. city) Virginia Beach independent city	6,989	1.60
Dallas, TX (city) Dallas County	6,964	0.59
San Antonio, TX (city) Medina County	6,824	0.53
Holland, MI (city) Ottawa County	6,776	25.45
Omaha, NE (city) Douglas County	6,723	1.65
Nashville-Davidson, TN (metro govt) Davidson County	6,654	1.13
Fort Worth, TX (city) Tarrant County	6,572	0.93
Gaines, MI (charter township) Kent County	6,541	26.89
Kansas City, MO (city) Jackson County	6,489	1.43
Lincoln, NE (city) Lancaster County	6,306	2.49
Albuquerque, NM (city) Bernalillo County	6,233	1.17
Plainfield, MI (charter township) Kent County	6,200	20.05
Kalamazoo, MI (city) Kalamazoo County	6,165	8.30
Anchorage, AK (municipality) Anchorage Municipality	6,141	2.16
Las Vegas, NV (city) Clark County	6,095	1.05
Walker, MI (city) Kent County	5,992	25.73
Minneapolis, MN (city) Hennepin County	5,978	1.57
Park, MI (township) Ottawa County	5,929	33.10
Philadelphia, PA (city) Philadelphia County	5,855	0.39
Brooklyn, NY (borough) Kings County	5,664	0.23
Zeeland, MI (charter township) Ottawa County	5,488	56.97
Grandville, MI (city) Kent County	5,342	34.25
Appleton, WI (city) Outagamie County	5,229	7.20
Portage, MI (city) Kalamazoo County	5,214	11.36
Allendale, MI (charter township) Ottawa County	4,973	25.50
Madison, WI (city) Dane County	4,872	2.13
Sacramento, CA (city) Sacramento County	4,826	1.05
Forest Hills, MI (cdp) Kent County	4,743	18.65
Fresno, CA (city) Fresno County	4,720	0.98
Long Beach, CA (city) Los Angeles County	4,630	1.00
Huntington Beach, CA (city) Orange County	4,608	2.44
Henderson, NV (city) Clark County	4,574	1.84
Chandler, AZ (city) Maricopa County	4,546	1.98
Pella, IA (city) Marion County	4,538	43.81
Scottsdale, AZ (city) Maricopa County	4,409	2.02
Appleton, WI (city) Outagamie County	4,342	7.24
Cedar Rapids, IA (city) Linn County	4,245	3.38
Spokane, WA (city) Spokane County	4,231	2.05
Allendale, MI (cdp) Ottawa County	4,184	25.13
Milwaukee, WI (city) Milwaukee County	4,173	0.71
Raleigh, NC (city) Wake County	4,068	1.06
Brookhaven, NY (town) Suffolk County	4,038	0.84
Modesto, CA (city) Stanislaus County	4,037	2.00
Bakersfield, CA (city) Kern County	4,032	1.21
Jamestown, MI (charter township) Ottawa County	4,013	59.63
Sioux Center, IA (city) Sioux County	4,004	57.89
Green Bay, WI (city) Brown County	4,002	3.85
Boise City, ID (city) Ada County	3,976	1.93
Cutlerville, MI (cdp) Kent County	3,950	28.25
Lexington-Fayette, KY (cons. govt) Fayette County	3,928	1.36
Vancouver, WA (city) Clark County	3,903	2.44
Reno, NV (city) Washoe County	3,861	1.75
Lynden, WA (city) Whatcom County	3,829	33.07
Aurora, CO (city) Arapahoe County	3,806	1.21
Gilbert, AZ (town) Maricopa County	3,780	1.94
Eugene, OR (city) Lane County	3,771	2.46
Lansing, MI (city) Ingham County	3,759	3.39
Lansing, MI (city) Ingham County	3,759	3.25
Glendale, AZ (city) Maricopa County	3,754	1.63
Arlington, TX (city) Tarrant County	3,739	1.04
Fort Collins, CO (city) Larimer County	3,677	2.62
Washington, DC (city) District of Columbia	3,668	0.63
Riverside, CA (city) Riverside County	3,659	1.22
Salt Lake City, UT (city) Salt Lake County	3,648	1.98
Hudsonville, MI (city) Ottawa County	3,637	50.65
Fort Wayne, IN (city) Allen County	3,612	1.42
St. Paul, MN (city) Ramsey County	3,582	1.27
Toledo, OH (city) Lucas County	3,569	1.22
Overland Park, KS (city) Johnson County	3,555	2.08
Norton Shores, MI (city) Muskegon County	3,547	14.83
Queens, NY (borough) Queens County	3,516	0.16
Springfield, MO (city) Christian County	3,470	2.18
Sioux City, IA (city) Woodbury County	3,449	4.20
Blendon, MI (township) Ottawa County	3,432	59.09
Everett, WA (city) Snohomish County	3,363	3.31
Grand Haven, MI (charter township) Ottawa County	3,354	22.42
Colonie, NY (town) Albany County	3,334	4.09
Spring Lake, MI (township) Ottawa County	3,279	23.09
Memphis, TN (city) Shelby County	3,241	0.49
Orange City, IA (city) Sioux County	3,238	54.27
St. Petersburg, FL (city) Pinellas County	3,222	1.31
Salem, OR (city) Marion County	3,203	2.11
Tampa, FL (city) Hillsborough County	3,201	0.96
Grand Rapids, MI (charter township) Kent County	3,169	19.51
Hempstead, NY (town) Nassau County	3,142	0.42
Tacoma, WA (city) Pierce County	3,136	1.58
Olathe, KS (city) Johnson County	3,129	2.59
Zeeland, MI (city) Ottawa County	3,110	55.44
Bellingham, WA (city) Whatcom County	3,095	3.92
Little Chute, WI (village) Outagamie County	2,988	28.48
Kalamazoo, MI (charter township) Kalamazoo County	2,979	13.67
Tempe, AZ (city) Maricopa County	2,935	1.79
Knoxville, TN (city) Knox County	2,933	1.65
Rochester, NY (city) Monroe County	2,898	1.37
Greece, NY (town) Monroe County	2,890	3.03
Cleveland, OH (city) Cuyahoga County	2,881	0.70
Peoria, AZ (city) Yavapai County	2,869	1.93
Cincinnati, OH (city) Hamilton County	2,867	0.96
West Jordan, UT (city) Salt Lake County	2,863	2.90
Sheboygan, WI (city) Sheboygan County	2,853	5.74
Caledonia, MI (township) Kent County	2,846	24.18
Akron, OH (city) Summit County	2,805	1.38
Cascade, MI (charter township) Kent County	2,786	16.56
Lakewood, CO (city) Jefferson County	2,767	1.95
Highlands Ranch, CO (cdp) Douglas County	2,762	2.90
Ada, MI (township) Kent County	2,744	21.79
Topeka, KS (city) Shawnee County	2,729	2.16
Independence, MO (city) Jackson County	2,728	2.36
Baltimore, MD (city) Baltimore city County	2,727	0.44
Anaheim, CA (city) Orange County	2,724	0.82
Allentown, PA (city) Lehigh County	2,721	2.34
Rancho Cucamonga, CA (city) San Bernardino County	2,719	1.69
Oshtemo, MI (charter township) Kalamazoo County	2,665	12.82
Lansing, IL (village) Cook County	2,662	9.51
Amarillo, TX (city) Potter County	2,642	1.41
Oceanside, CA (city) San Diego County	2,641	1.60

Ancestry

Dutch

Top 150 Places Sorted by Percent of Total Population

Based on all places, regardless of total population

Place	Population	%
Jeffrey City, WY (cdp) Fremont County	75	100.00
Escondida, NM (cdp) Socorro County	40	100.00
Loraine, ND (city) Renville County	19	100.00
Duran, NM (cdp) Torrance County	5	100.00
Leota, MN (cdp) Nobles County	103	92.79
Calvin, ND (city) Cavalier County	10	83.33
Winfred, SD (cdp) Lake County	67	79.76
Okaton, SD (cdp) Jones County	32	72.73
Doon, IA (city) Lyon County	344	71.22
Moulton, MN (township) Murray County	167	70.76
Leota, MN (township) Nobles County	186	68.89
Le Sueur, MN (city) Nicollet County	17	68.00
Osborne, MN (township) Pipestone County	163	67.08
Hull, IA (city) Sioux County	1,311	67.06
Prinsburg, MN (city) Kandiyohi County	314	65.42
Edgerton, MN (city) Pipestone County	769	64.89
Sully, IA (city) Jasper County	639	63.46
Alvord, IA (city) Lyon County	99	61.88
Rock Valley, IA (city) Sioux County	2,009	61.36
Overisel, MI (township) Allegan County	1,733	60.13
Jamestown, MI (charter township) Ottawa County	4,013	59.63
Corsica, SD (city) Douglas County	350	59.22
Blendon, MI (township) Ottawa County	3,432	59.09
Sioux Center, IA (city) Sioux County	4,004	57.89
Maurice, IA (city) Sioux County	161	57.71
Loco Hills, NM (cdp) Eddy County	30	57.69
Tonsina, AK (cdp) Valdez-Cordova Census Area	44	57.14
Cottonwood, SD (town) Jackson County	4	57.14
Zeeland, MI (charter township) Ottawa County	5,488	56.97
Zeeland, MI (city) Ottawa County	3,110	55.44
Frytown, IA (cdp) Johnson County	28	54.90
Sims Chapel, AL (cdp) Washington County	59	54.63
Battle Plain, MN (township) Rock County	108	54.55
Orange City, IA (city) Sioux County	3,238	54.27
Randolph, WI (town) Columbia County	388	54.04
Boyden, IA (city) Sioux County	388	53.22
Hachita, NM (cdp) Grant County	30	52.63
Jefferson, OK (town) Grant County	17	51.52
South Haven, MI (city) Allegan County	17	51.52
Terlton, OK (town) Pawnee County	35	51.47
Gibbsville, WI (cdp) Sheboygan County	245	51.26
Burke, MN (township) Pipestone County	115	51.11
Hudsonville, MI (city) Ottawa County	3,637	50.65
Bucyrus, ND (city) Adams County	11	50.00
Oostburg, WI (village) Sheboygan County	1,423	49.84
Leighton, IA (city) Mahaska County	104	47.71
Trosky, MN (city) Pipestone County	45	47.37
Tuscarora, NY (cdp) Livingston County	36	46.75
Ferney, SD (cdp) Brown County	28	46.67
North Central Cass, MN (unorganized territory) Cass County	53	46.49
Archer, IA (city) O'Brien County	39	46.43
McBaine, MO (town) Boone County	12	46.15
New Holland, SD (cdp) Douglas County	52	45.61
Foundryville, PA (cdp) Columbia County	89	45.41
Holland, MN (township) Kandiyohi County	158	45.27
Soldier Creek, SD (cdp) Todd County	32	45.07
Hospers, IA (city) Sioux County	333	45.00
Olive, MI (township) Ottawa County	2,124	44.38
Celeryville, OH (cdp) Huron County	59	44.36
Laketown, MI (township) Allegan County	2,459	44.12
Edna Bay, AK (cdp) Prince of Wales-Hyder Census Area	26	44.07
Pella, IA (city) Marion County	4,538	43.81
Alamo Lake, AZ (cdp) La Paz County	17	43.59
Alto, WI (town) Fond du Lac County	474	43.57
Fillmore, MI (township) Allegan County	1,186	43.55
Weott, CA (cdp) Humboldt County	76	43.18
Richland, MI (township) Missaukee County	629	43.02
Mount Carbon, PA (borough) Schuylkill County	43	43.00
Leeds, MN (township) Murray County	91	42.92
Georgetown, MI (charter township) Ottawa County	19,742	42.55
Chandler, MN (city) Murray County	95	42.22
Ralston, WY (cdp) Park County	74	41.81
Hatfield, MN (city) Pipestone County	20	41.67
Fountain Prairie, MN (township) Pipestone County	81	41.54
Jenison, MI (cdp) Ottawa County	7,138	41.41
Fenton, MN (township) Murray County	61	40.94
Tipton, PA (cdp) Blair County	440	40.89
Port Sheldon, MI (township) Ottawa County	1,742	40.49
McBain, MI (city) Missaukee County	280	40.17
Kimberly, WV (cdp) Fayette County	119	40.07
Byron Center, MI (cdp) Kent County	2,019	40.03
Van Dyne, WI (cdp) Fond du Lac County	150	39.89
Chanarambie, MN (township) Murray County	82	39.81
Bird-in-Hand, PA (cdp) Lancaster County	121	39.54
Lynnville, IA (city) Jasper County	154	39.39
Pulaski, OH (cdp) Williams County	26	39.39
Heath, MI (township) Allegan County	1,299	39.36
Monterey Park Tract, CA (cdp) Stanislaus County	109	39.07
Aetna, MN (township) Pipestone County	58	38.93
Inwood, IA (city) Lyon County	334	38.84
Churchill, MT (cdp) Gallatin County	300	38.46
Weston, IA (cdp) Pottawattamie County	57	38.26
Southbrook, MN (township) Cottonwood County	21	38.18
Hollandale, MN (city) Freeborn County	86	37.89
Pungoteague, VA (cdp) Accomack County	91	37.76
Little Orleans, MD (cdp) Allegany County	9	37.50
West Amana, IA (cdp) Iowa County	56	37.33
Oasis, NM (cdp) Sierra County	96	37.07
Ireton, IA (city) Sioux County	274	36.93
Manlius, MI (township) Allegan County	1,099	36.88
Platte, SD (city) Charles Mix County	474	36.69
Leighton, MI (township) Allegan County	1,731	36.57
Friesland, WI (village) Columbia County	135	36.39
Norrie, CO (cdp) Pitkin County	16	36.36
Byron, MI (township) Kent County	7,207	36.27
Grange, MN (township) Pipestone County	65	36.11
Siglerville, PA (cdp) Mifflin County	30	35.29
Steen, MN (city) Rock County	58	35.15
Dorr, MI (township) Allegan County	2,578	35.00
Prairie View, KS (city) Phillips County	42	35.00
Stickney, SD (town) Aurora County	65	34.95
Dailey, WV (cdp) Randolph County	15	34.88
Enterprise, MI (township) Missaukee County	78	34.82
Sanborn, IA (city) O'Brien County	452	34.72
Clinton, MN (township) Rock County	104	34.55
McDermitt, NV (cdp) Humboldt County	41	34.45
Magnolia, MN (township) Rock County	64	34.41
Aetna, MI (township) Missaukee County	148	34.26
Grandville, MI (city) Kent County	5,342	34.25
Holland, MI (city) Allegan County	2,391	33.78
Garcon Point, FL (cdp) Santa Rosa County	161	33.75
Tallmadge, MI (charter township) Ottawa County	2,517	33.52
Mound, MN (township) Rock County	70	33.49
Struble, IA (city) Plymouth County	22	33.33
Browns Creek, MN (township) Red Lake County	14	33.33
Sheldon, IA (city) O'Brien County	1,680	33.29
Fulton, IL (city) Whiteside County	1,189	33.20
Park, MI (township) Ottawa County	5,929	33.10
Lynden, WA (city) Whatcom County	3,829	33.07
Vandenbroek, WI (town) Outagamie County	480	33.01
Mina, NV (cdp) Mineral County	29	32.95
Indian Springs, MT (cdp) Lincoln County	23	32.86
Sportsmen Acres, OK (town) Mayes County	118	32.51
Harrison, SD (cdp) Douglas County	13	32.50
Kennedyville, MD (cdp) Kent County	51	32.28
Beechwood, MI (cdp) Ottawa County	1,067	32.25
Martin, MN (township) Rock County	108	32.24
Malden-on-Hudson, NY (cdp) Ulster County	104	32.20
Hollister, OK (town) Tillman County	44	32.12
Polkton, MI (charter township) Ottawa County	747	31.99
Randolph, WI (village) Dodge County	592	31.93
Apache Creek, NM (cdp) Catron County	22	31.43
Robinson, MI (township) Ottawa County	1,895	31.37
Cardiff, AL (town) Jefferson County	21	31.34
Chester, WI (town) Dodge County	220	31.29
Highland, MI (township) Osceola County	435	31.25
Udell, IA (city) Appanoose County	14	31.11
Randolph, WI (village) Dodge County	725	31.08
Naples, SD (town) Clark County	8	30.77
Ridgely, MO (village) Platte County	43	30.71

Please refer to the Explanation of Data in the front of the book for more detailed information.

Ancestry

Dutch

Top 150 Places Sorted by Percent of Total Population

Based on places with total population of 7,500 or more

Place	Population	%
Zeeland, MI (charter township) Ottawa County	5,488	56.97
Pella, IA (city) Marion County	4,538	43.81
Georgetown, MI (charter township) Ottawa County	19,742	42.55
Jenison, MI (cdp) Ottawa County	7,138	41.41
Byron, MI (township) Kent County	7,207	36.27
Grandville, MI (city) Kent County	5,342	34.25
Tallmadge, MI (charter township) Ottawa County	2,517	33.52
Park, MI (township) Ottawa County	5,929	33.10
Lynden, WA (city) Whatcom County	3,829	33.07
Little Chute, WI (village) Outagamie County	2,988	28.48
Cutlerville, MI (cdp) Kent County	3,950	28.25
Holland, MI (charter township) Ottawa County	9,456	27.26
Holland, MI (city) Ottawa County	9,167	27.20
Gaines, MI (charter township) Kent County	6,541	26.89
Thornapple, MI (township) Barry County	2,027	26.03
Walker, MI (city) Kent County	5,992	25.73
Allendale, MI (charter township) Ottawa County	4,973	25.50
Holland, MI (city) Ottawa County	6,776	25.45
Allendale, MI (cdp) Ottawa County	4,184	25.13
Caledonia, MI (township) Kent County	2,846	24.18
Spring Lake, MI (township) Ottawa County	3,279	23.09
Grand Haven, MI (city) Ottawa County	2,413	22.68
Wyoming, MI (city) Kent County	16,185	22.54
Grand Haven, MI (charter township) Ottawa County	3,354	22.42
Ada, MI (township) Kent County	2,744	21.79
Algoma, MI (township) Kent County	2,022	21.19
Plainfield, MI (charter township) Kent County	6,200	20.05
Grand Rapids, MI (charter township) Kent County	3,169	19.51
Waupun, WI (city) Dodge County	2,184	19.19
Cannon, MI (township) Kent County	2,469	18.79
Forest Hills, MI (cdp) Kent County	4,743	18.65
East Grand Rapids, MI (city) Kent County	1,985	18.49
Kentwood, MI (city) Kent County	8,913	18.48
Cooper, MI (charter township) Kalamazoo County	1,815	18.45
Fruitport, MI (charter township) Muskegon County	2,383	17.63
Arcadia, NY (town) Wayne County	2,484	17.31
Comstock, MI (charter township) Kalamazoo County	2,519	17.21
Waupun, WI (city) Dodge County	1,343	16.90
Kaukauna, WI (city) Outagamie County	2,534	16.81
Northview, MI (cdp) Kent County	2,401	16.64
Cascade, MI (charter township) Kent County	2,786	16.56
Oskaloosa, IA (city) Mahaska County	1,882	16.52
Sodus, NY (town) Wayne County	1,373	16.20
Schoolcraft, MI (township) Kalamazoo County	1,299	16.18
Newark, NY (village) Wayne County	1,482	16.14
Comstock Park, MI (cdp) Kent County	1,609	15.59
Grand Rapids, MI (city) Kent County	29,229	15.35
Westwood, MI (cdp) Kalamazoo County	1,365	15.07
Norton Shores, MI (city) Muskegon County	3,547	14.83
Alpine, MI (township) Kent County	1,999	14.82
North Haledon, NJ (borough) Passaic County	1,213	14.82
Sparta, MI (township) Kent County	1,313	14.41
Palmyra, NY (town) Wayne County	1,132	14.32
Dalton, MI (township) Muskegon County	1,278	13.97
Kalamazoo, MI (charter township) Kalamazoo County	2,979	13.67
Texas, MI (charter township) Kalamazoo County	1,885	13.48
Oshtemo, MI (charter township) Kalamazoo County	2,665	12.82
Macedon, NY (town) Wayne County	1,138	12.61
Harrison, WI (town) Calumet County	1,247	12.47
Antwerp, MI (township) Van Buren County	1,481	12.35
Laketon, MI (township) Muskegon County	927	12.20
Manchester, NY (town) Ontario County	1,103	11.81
Portage, MI (city) Kalamazoo County	5,214	11.36
Ontario, NY (town) Wayne County	1,092	10.87
Muskegon, MI (charter township) Muskegon County	1,891	10.53
Pottsville, PA (city) Schuylkill County	1,491	10.27
Greenville, MI (city) Montcalm County	853	10.07
Wantage, NJ (township) Sussex County	1,107	9.80
Lansing, IL (village) Cook County	2,662	9.51
West Milford, NJ (township) Passaic County	2,396	9.30
Hawthorne, NJ (borough) Passaic County	1,699	9.15
St. John, IN (town) Lake County	1,255	9.14
Le Mars, IA (city) Plymouth County	880	9.05
Schodack, NY (town) Rensselaer County	1,158	9.04
Pleasant Hill, IA (city) Polk County	731	9.02
St. Joseph, MI (city) Berrien County	742	8.84
Brandon, SD (city) Minnehaha County	716	8.70
Coal, PA (township) Northumberland County	895	8.66
Sheboygan Falls, WI (city) Sheboygan County	659	8.66
Coeymans, NY (town) Albany County	652	8.58
Cadillac, MI (city) Wexford County	878	8.46
Rensselaer, NY (city) Rensselaer County	775	8.46
Douglass, PA (township) Montgomery County	839	8.40
Altoona, IA (city) Polk County	1,147	8.34
Kalamazoo, MI (city) Kalamazoo County	6,165	8.30
Saugerties, NY (town) Ulster County	1,603	8.23
Kinderhook, NY (town) Columbia County	696	8.21
Ripon, CA (city) San Joaquin County	1,123	8.14
De Pere, WI (city) Brown County	1,863	8.02
Big Rapids, MI (city) Mecosta County	856	8.00
Appleton, WI (city) Calumet County	869	7.78
Berwick, PA (borough) Columbia County	821	7.76
Palos Heights, IL (city) Cook County	924	7.58
Menasha, WI (town) Winnebago County	1,348	7.48
East Bay, MI (township) Grand Traverse County	790	7.44
Highland, IN (town) Lake County	1,729	7.29
Grand Chute, WI (town) Outagamie County	1,494	7.29
Appleton, WI (city) Outagamie County	4,342	7.24
Bedford, MI (charter township) Calhoun County	684	7.24
Crete, IL (village) Will County	610	7.23
Esopus, NY (town) Ulster County	660	7.22
Appleton, WI (city) Outagamie County	5,229	7.20
Hardyston, NJ (township) Sussex County	566	7.14
Egelston, MI (township) Muskegon County	701	7.07
Catskill, NY (town) Greene County	838	7.05
Newton, IA (city) Jasper County	1,077	7.01
Ludington, MI (city) Mason County	572	7.00
Dyer, IN (town) Lake County	1,096	6.87
Bellevue, WI (village) Brown County	965	6.87
Bath, NY (town) Steuben County	845	6.87
Lehigh, PA (township) Northampton County	719	6.87
Vernon, NJ (township) Sussex County	1,651	6.77
Howard, WI (village) Brown County	1,128	6.74
Canandaigua, NY (city) Ontario County	713	6.68
Muskegon, MI (city) Muskegon County	2,594	6.65
Butler, PA (township) Luzerne County	583	6.62
Norwalk, IA (city) Warren County	569	6.60
Ferndale, WA (city) Whatcom County	724	6.59
Spring Arbor, MI (township) Jackson County	542	6.58
Bloomingdale, NJ (borough) Passaic County	499	6.58
Birch Bay, WA (cdp) Whatcom County	516	6.55
Uniontown, PA (city) Fayette County	701	6.53
Suamico, WI (village) Brown County	706	6.50
Ashwaubenon, WI (village) Brown County	1,105	6.46
Connellsville, PA (city) Fayette County	507	6.43
Sioux Falls, SD (city) Minnehaha County	9,552	6.42
Lincoln, MI (charter township) Berrien County	925	6.37
Delavan, WI (city) Walworth County	544	6.37
New Scotland, NY (town) Albany County	551	6.36
Rhinebeck, NY (town) Dutchess County	485	6.34
Waukee, IA (city) Dallas County	771	6.27
Clinton, IA (city) Clinton County	1,679	6.21
Niles, MI (township) Berrien County	864	6.18
Newberg, OR (city) Yamhill County	1,322	6.17
Farmington, NY (town) Ontario County	709	6.12
Johnstown, NY (city) Fulton County	535	6.12
Red Hook, NY (town) Dutchess County	680	6.06
Crawford, NY (town) Orange County	554	6.06
Spencer, IA (city) Clay County	676	6.04
Waterloo, NY (town) Seneca County	466	6.02
Moore, PA (township) Northampton County	550	6.00
Newton, NJ (town) Sussex County	484	5.96
Emmett, MI (charter township) Calhoun County	704	5.94
Long Lake, MI (township) Grand Traverse County	508	5.93
Pennfield, MI (charter township) Calhoun County	535	5.92
Hyde Park, NY (town) Dutchess County	1,270	5.88
Ulster, NY (town) Ulster County	729	5.85
Butler, NJ (borough) Morris County	440	5.85
Wanaque, NJ (borough) Passaic County	636	5.84
Pequannock, NJ (township) Morris County	888	5.82

SECTION THREE

Please refer to the Explanation of Data in the front of the book for more detailed information.

Ancestry

Eastern European

U.S. and 50 States Sorted by Population and Percent of Total Population

Place	Population	%
United States	**419,221**	**0.14**
New York	89,540	0.47
California	56,408	0.15
New Jersey	35,149	0.40
Massachusetts	23,919	0.37
Florida	22,944	0.12
Pennsylvania	22,509	0.18
Maryland	19,110	0.34
Illinois	18,969	0.15
Connecticut	11,000	0.31
Ohio	10,672	0.09
Texas	10,443	0.04
Virginia	9,708	0.12
Michigan	8,444	0.08
Georgia	7,570	0.08
Washington	7,317	0.11
Colorado	6,705	0.14
Arizona	5,805	0.09
Minnesota	5,504	0.10
North Carolina	5,437	0.06
Oregon	4,436	0.12
District of Columbia	3,934	0.67
Missouri	3,436	0.06
Wisconsin	2,877	0.05
Indiana	2,605	0.04
Tennessee	2,311	0.04
Nevada	2,003	0.08
New Mexico	1,723	0.09
Kentucky	1,576	0.04
New Hampshire	1,520	0.12
Kansas	1,471	0.05
Rhode Island	1,423	0.13
South Carolina	1,405	0.03
Vermont	1,400	0.22
Maine	1,166	0.09
Delaware	1,108	0.13
Louisiana	1,015	0.02
Alabama	887	0.02
Utah	864	0.03
Iowa	852	0.03
Oklahoma	697	0.02
West Virginia	536	0.03
Nebraska	499	0.03
Idaho	483	0.03
Alaska	460	0.07
Hawaii	340	0.03
Montana	326	0.03
Arkansas	252	0.01
Wyoming	228	0.04
Mississippi	129	<0.01
North Dakota	67	0.01
South Dakota	39	<0.01

Place	Population	%
District of Columbia	3,934	0.67
New York	89,540	0.47
New Jersey	35,149	0.40
Massachusetts	23,919	0.37
Maryland	19,110	0.34
Connecticut	11,000	0.31
Vermont	1,400	0.22
Pennsylvania	22,509	0.18
California	56,408	0.15
Illinois	18,969	0.15
United States	**419,221**	**0.14**
Colorado	6,705	0.14
Rhode Island	1,423	0.13
Delaware	1,108	0.13
Florida	22,944	0.12
Virginia	9,708	0.12
Oregon	4,436	0.12
New Hampshire	1,520	0.12
Washington	7,317	0.11
Minnesota	5,504	0.10
Ohio	10,672	0.09
Arizona	5,805	0.09
New Mexico	1,723	0.09
Maine	1,166	0.09
Michigan	8,444	0.08
Georgia	7,570	0.08
Nevada	2,003	0.08
Alaska	460	0.07
North Carolina	5,437	0.06
Missouri	3,436	0.06
Wisconsin	2,877	0.05
Kansas	1,471	0.05
Texas	10,443	0.04
Indiana	2,605	0.04
Tennessee	2,311	0.04
Kentucky	1,576	0.04
Wyoming	228	0.04
South Carolina	1,405	0.03
Utah	864	0.03
Iowa	852	0.03
West Virginia	536	0.03
Nebraska	499	0.03
Idaho	483	0.03
Hawaii	340	0.03
Montana	326	0.03
Louisiana	1,015	0.02
Alabama	887	0.02
Oklahoma	697	0.02
Arkansas	252	0.01
North Dakota	67	0.01
Mississippi	129	<0.01
South Dakota	39	<0.01

Please refer to the Explanation of Data in the front of the book for more detailed information.

Ancestry

Eastern European

Top 150 Places Sorted by Population

Based on all places, regardless of total population

Place	Population	%
New York, NY (city) Kings County	44,970	0.56
Manhattan, NY (borough) New York County	25,277	1.60
Los Angeles, CA (city) Los Angeles County	14,001	0.37
Brooklyn, NY (borough) Kings County	12,941	0.52
Chicago, IL (city) Cook County	5,967	0.22
Hempstead, NY (town) Nassau County	5,775	0.77
Queens, NY (borough) Queens County	4,673	0.21
Washington, DC (city) District of Columbia	3,934	0.67
San Francisco, CA (city) San Francisco County	3,844	0.49
Oyster Bay, NY (town) Nassau County	3,841	1.32
North Hempstead, NY (town) Nassau County	3,769	1.69
Philadelphia, PA (city) Philadelphia County	3,363	0.22
Seattle, WA (city) King County	2,615	0.44
San Diego, CA (city) San Diego County	2,599	0.20
Boston, MA (city) Suffolk County	2,474	0.41
Newton, MA (city) Middlesex County	2,236	2.66
Huntington, NY (town) Suffolk County	2,012	1.00
Greenburgh, NY (town) Westchester County	2,009	2.29
Lower Merion, PA (township) Montgomery County	1,986	3.42
Lakewood, NJ (township) Ocean County	1,765	2.01
Oakland, CA (city) Alameda County	1,717	0.44
Portland, OR (city) Multnomah County	1,654	0.29
Bronx, NY (borough) Bronx County	1,646	0.12
Houston, TX (city) Harris County	1,613	0.08
Denver, CO (city) Denver County	1,565	0.27
Bethesda, MD (cdp) Montgomery County	1,513	2.58
Potomac, MD (cdp) Montgomery County	1,483	3.31
Lakewood, NJ (cdp) Ocean County	1,442	2.90
Dallas, TX (city) Dallas County	1,384	0.12
Baltimore, MD (city) Baltimore city County	1,371	0.22
Brookline, MA (cdp/town) Norfolk County	1,361	2.35
Arlington, VA (cdp) Arlington County	1,323	0.67
Cambridge, MA (city) Middlesex County	1,313	1.27
Livingston, NJ (township) Essex County	1,284	4.46
Clarkstown, NY (town) Rockland County	1,282	1.54
Plainview, NY (cdp) Nassau County	1,224	4.75
Scarsdale, NY (town/village) Westchester County	1,208	7.06
Phoenix, AZ (city) Maricopa County	1,201	0.08
Rockville, MD (city) Montgomery County	1,196	2.05
Pittsburgh, PA (city) Allegheny County	1,195	0.39
New Castle, NY (town) Westchester County	1,178	6.76
San Jose, CA (city) Santa Clara County	1,162	0.13
Austin, TX (city) Travis County	1,156	0.15
Ramapo, NY (town) Rockland County	1,144	0.93
Highland Park, NJ (borough) Middlesex County	1,124	8.03
Atlanta, GA (city) Fulton County	1,101	0.27
Pikesville, MD (cdp) Baltimore County	1,085	3.53
Minneapolis, MN (city) Hennepin County	1,072	0.28
Berkeley, CA (city) Alameda County	1,046	0.96
Mamaroneck, NY (town) Westchester County	1,042	3.60
Teaneck, NJ (township) Bergen County	1,026	2.60
Stamford, CT (city/town) Fairfield County	1,022	0.85
Hoboken, NJ (city) Hudson County	991	2.09
Santa Monica, CA (city) Los Angeles County	988	1.11
Westport, CT (cdp/town) Fairfield County	982	3.76
Highland Park, IL (city) Lake County	980	3.26
Millburn, NJ (township) Essex County	945	4.73
Scottsdale, AZ (city) Maricopa County	941	0.43
Cherry Hill, NJ (township) Camden County	931	1.31
Woodmere, NY (cdp) Nassau County	897	5.14
West Hartford, CT (cdp/town) Hartford County	894	1.42
New City, NY (cdp) Rockland County	890	2.66
New Rochelle, NY (city) Westchester County	870	1.15
Columbus, OH (city) Franklin County	867	0.11
Boulder, CO (city) Boulder County	866	0.89
Charlotte, NC (city) Mecklenburg County	862	0.12
Evanston, IL (city) Cook County	854	1.16
Irvine, CA (city) Orange County	851	0.43
West Bloomfield, MI (charter township) Oakland County	842	1.30
Boca Raton, FL (city) Palm Beach County	840	0.99
Silver Spring, MD (cdp) Montgomery County	795	1.13
Jericho, NY (cdp) Nassau County	776	5.96
Coral Springs, FL (city) Broward County	762	0.63
Sharon, MA (town) Norfolk County	742	4.26
Amherst, MA (town) Hampshire County	731	1.95
Brookhaven, NY (town) Suffolk County	728	0.15
Ann Arbor, MI (city) Washtenaw County	719	0.62
Tucson, AZ (city) Pima County	714	0.14
Rye, NY (town) Westchester County	699	1.54
Edison, NJ (township) Middlesex County	677	0.68
Columbia, MD (cdp) Howard County	676	0.69
Thousand Oaks, CA (city) Ventura County	674	0.54
East Brunswick, NJ (township) Middlesex County	669	1.41
Somerville, MA (city) Middlesex County	666	0.89
Agoura Hills, CA (city) Los Angeles County	663	3.26
Sandy Springs, GA (city) Fulton County	661	0.73
Minnetonka, MN (city) Hennepin County	657	1.33
Melville, NY (cdp) Suffolk County	654	3.43
Tenafly, NJ (borough) Bergen County	653	4.57
Smithtown, NY (town) Suffolk County	651	0.55
Montclair, NJ (township) Essex County	649	1.72
North Bethesda, MD (cdp) Montgomery County	623	1.54
West Orange, NJ (township) Essex County	623	1.36
Deerfield, IL (village) Lake County	618	3.36
Needham, MA (cdp/town) Norfolk County	618	2.15
Dunwoody, GA (city) DeKalb County	609	1.36
Providence, RI (city) Providence County	609	0.34
Glenview, IL (village) Cook County	596	1.37
Skokie, IL (village) Cook County	592	0.93
Northampton, PA (township) Bucks County	591	1.48
San Antonio, TX (city) Medina County	586	0.05
Merrick, NY (cdp) Nassau County	582	2.73
Northbrook, IL (village) Cook County	578	1.76
Buffalo Grove, IL (village) Lake County	577	1.38
Amherst, NY (town) Erie County	575	0.48
Cheltenham, PA (township) Montgomery County	566	1.54
Madison, WI (city) Dane County	564	0.25
White Plains, NY (city) Westchester County	557	1.00
Springdale, NJ (cdp) Camden County	550	3.74
Short Hills, NJ (cdp) Essex County	549	4.16
Raleigh, NC (city) Wake County	549	0.14
Beachwood, OH (city) Cuyahoga County	546	4.58
Upper Dublin, PA (township) Montgomery County	546	2.13
Shaker Heights, OH (city) Cuyahoga County	545	1.92
Aventura, FL (city) Miami-Dade County	544	1.61
Framingham, MA (cdp/town) Middlesex County	538	0.80
Beverly Hills, CA (city) Los Angeles County	535	1.57
Fair Lawn, NJ (borough) Bergen County	531	1.65
Alexandria, VA (ind. city) Alexandria independent city	531	0.40
Albuquerque, NM (city) Bernalillo County	526	0.10
Miami Beach, FL (city) Miami-Dade County	525	0.60
East Hills, NY (village) Nassau County	523	7.63
Plano, TX (city) Collin County	520	0.20
St. Paul, MN (city) Ramsey County	520	0.18
Harrison, NY (town/village) Westchester County	507	1.89
New Haven, CT (city/town) New Haven County	505	0.39
Weston, FL (city) Broward County	503	0.80
Syosset, NY (cdp) Nassau County	502	2.66
Farmington Hills, MI (city) Oakland County	501	0.62
Lexington, MA (cdp/town) Middlesex County	494	1.60
Virginia Beach, VA (ind. city) Virginia Beach independent city	493	0.11
Westfield, NJ (town) Union County	489	1.63
Manalapan, NJ (township) Monmouth County	487	1.28
North Castle, NY (town) Westchester County	484	4.18
Greensboro, NC (city) Guilford County	476	0.18
Cleveland Heights, OH (city) Cuyahoga County	475	1.02
Plantation, FL (city) Broward County	468	0.55
Hamden, CT (town) New Haven County	466	0.77
Princeton, NJ (township) Mercer County	464	2.83
St. Louis Park, MN (city) Hennepin County	463	1.04
Memphis, TN (city) Shelby County	463	0.07
Northampton, MA (city) Hampshire County	461	1.61
Yonkers, NY (city) Westchester County	458	0.24
University Heights, OH (city) Cuyahoga County	457	3.37
Santa Fe, NM (city) Santa Fe County	455	0.67
Wayne, NJ (township) Passaic County	452	0.83
Palo Alto, CA (city) Santa Clara County	452	0.72
South Brunswick, NJ (township) Middlesex County	448	1.06
Natick, MA (town) Middlesex County	442	1.36
Jersey City, NJ (city) Hudson County	441	0.18

Please refer to the Explanation of Data in the front of the book for more detailed information.

Ancestry

Eastern European

Top 150 Places Sorted by Percent of Total Population

Based on all places, regardless of total population

Place	Population	%
Tall Timber, CO (cdp) Boulder County	117	42.86
Butters, NC (cdp) Bladen County	84	35.29
Valeria, IA (city) Jasper County	15	22.73
River Forest, IN (town) Madison County	7	18.92
Great Neck Gardens, NY (cdp) Nassau County	106	11.67
Saddle Rock Estates, NY (cdp) Nassau County	60	11.45
Marietta, MN (city) Lac qui Parle County	25	11.26
Annetta North, TX (town) Parker County	46	9.37
Hewlett Harbor, NY (village) Nassau County	109	9.29
Harbor Hills, NY (cdp) Nassau County	44	8.89
Highland Park, NJ (borough) Middlesex County	1,124	8.03
Martin's Additions, MD (village) Montgomery County	70	7.74
East Hills, NY (village) Nassau County	523	7.63
Wilmore, PA (borough) Cambria County	10	7.58
Old Westbury, NY (village) Nassau County	297	7.54
Greenvale, NY (cdp) Nassau County	33	7.35
Hewlett Neck, NY (village) Nassau County	34	7.26
Round Hill Village, NV (cdp) Douglas County	66	7.24
Wallingford, VT (cdp) Rutland County	61	7.24
Scarsdale, NY (town/village) Westchester County	1,208	7.06
Matinecock, NY (village) Nassau County	54	7.05
Warner, NH (cdp) Merrimack County	38	6.87
New Castle, NY (town) Westchester County	1,178	6.76
Duck Key, FL (cdp) Monroe County	46	6.58
North Chevy Chase, MD (village) Montgomery County	36	6.43
Sumpter, OR (city) Baker County	9	6.25
Upper Nyack, NY (village) Rockland County	123	6.13
Eyers Grove, PA (cdp) Columbia County	6	6.00
Jericho, NY (cdp) Nassau County	776	5.96
Bal Harbour, FL (village) Miami-Dade County	157	5.94
Chokoloskee, FL (cdp) Collier County	14	5.93
Roslyn Estates, NY (village) Nassau County	73	5.91
South Amherst, MA (cdp) Hampshire County	290	5.88
Great Neck Estates, NY (village) Nassau County	155	5.67
Lido Beach, NY (cdp) Nassau County	148	5.67
Poquott, NY (village) Suffolk County	65	5.57
Chevy Chase Section Three, MD (village) Montgomery County	39	5.49
Brookville, NY (village) Nassau County	188	5.44
Hallam, NE (village) Lancaster County	7	5.34
Port Leyden, NY (village) Lewis County	37	5.21
Thomaston, NY (village) Nassau County	136	5.20
Woodmere, NY (cdp) Nassau County	897	5.14
Devon, PA (cdp) Chester County	79	5.12
Kensington, NY (village) Nassau County	61	5.06
Woodcliff Lake, NJ (borough) Bergen County	287	5.04
Coldspring, NY (town) Cattaraugus County	38	4.99
Huntington Woods, MI (city) Oakland County	309	4.98
Chevy Chase Section Five, MD (village) Montgomery County	36	4.90
Pine Brook Hill, CO (cdp) Boulder County	52	4.86
Franklin, MI (village) Oakland County	151	4.81
Lawrence, NY (village) Nassau County	309	4.79
Lake Success, NY (village) Nassau County	138	4.76
Plainview, NY (cdp) Nassau County	1,224	4.75
Millburn, NJ (township) Essex County	945	4.73
Greenville, NY (cdp) Westchester County	322	4.68
Wallingford, VT (town) Rutland County	105	4.67
Larchmont, NY (village) Westchester County	271	4.62
Northeast St. Louis, MN (unorganized territory) St. Louis County	12	4.62
Beachwood, OH (city) Cuyahoga County	546	4.58
Tenafly, NJ (borough) Bergen County	653	4.57
Willow Lake, MN (township) Redwood County	8	4.47
Livingston, NJ (township) Essex County	1,284	4.46
Rye Brook, NY (village) Westchester County	399	4.36
Atlantic Beach, NY (village) Nassau County	81	4.36
Tumalo, OR (cdp) Deschutes County	18	4.28
Barton Hills, MI (village) Washtenaw County	12	4.27
Sharon, MA (town) Norfolk County	742	4.26
Chevy Chase, MD (town) Montgomery County	117	4.19
North Castle, NY (town) Westchester County	484	4.18
West Hurley, NY (cdp) Ulster County	64	4.17
Short Hills, NJ (cdp) Essex County	549	4.16
North Hills, NY (village) Nassau County	203	4.11
Beaver, MN (township) Fillmore County	8	4.10
Hastings-on-Hudson, NY (village) Westchester County	316	4.06
Penn Wynne, PA (cdp) Montgomery County	235	4.04
Great Neck, NY (village) Nassau County	396	4.02
Weston, CT (town) Fairfield County	395	3.92
Salem, PA (township) Westmoreland County	258	3.88
Sands Point, NY (village) Nassau County	102	3.83
Aquilla, OH (village) Geauga County	14	3.83
Pepper Pike, OH (city) Cuyahoga County	227	3.81
Cedarhurst, NY (village) Nassau County	245	3.79
Kelayres, PA (cdp) Schuylkill County	21	3.79
James, SC (town) Berkeley County	2	3.77
Westport, CT (cdp/town) Fairfield County	982	3.76
Springdale, NJ (cdp) Camden County	550	3.74
Sleepy Hollow, CA (cdp) Marin County	91	3.72
Landisville, PA (cdp) Lancaster County	69	3.61
Mamaroneck, NY (town) Westchester County	1,042	3.60
Shenorock, NY (cdp) Westchester County	70	3.58
Parks, AZ (cdp) Coconino County	32	3.56
East Rockaway, NY (village) Nassau County	349	3.55
Paragon Estates, CO (cdp) Boulder County	37	3.55
Pikesville, MD (cdp) Baltimore County	1,085	3.53
Kemp Mill, MD (cdp) Montgomery County	416	3.44
Waverly, PA (cdp) Lackawanna County	18	3.44
Melville, NY (cdp) Suffolk County	654	3.43
Lower Merion, PA (township) Montgomery County	1,986	3.42
Old Bethpage, NY (cdp) Nassau County	190	3.41
University Heights, OH (city) Cuyahoga County	457	3.37
Irvington, NY (village) Westchester County	216	3.37
Chappaqua, NY (cdp) Westchester County	35	3.37
Sea Ranch, CA (cdp) Sonoma County	27	3.37
Deerfield, IL (village) Lake County	618	3.36
Ardsley, NY (village) Westchester County	147	3.35
Katonah, NY (cdp) Westchester County	49	3.34
Roscoe, PA (borough) Washington County	22	3.34
Potomac, MD (cdp) Montgomery County	1,483	3.31
Glenville, CT (cdp) Fairfield County	80	3.27
Highland Park, IL (city) Lake County	980	3.26
Agoura Hills, CA (city) Los Angeles County	663	3.26
Copake Lake, NY (cdp) Columbia County	24	3.25
Pound Ridge, NY (town) Westchester County	162	3.24
Reilly, PA (township) Schuylkill County	23	3.22
Dayton, NJ (cdp) Middlesex County	239	3.21
Roslyn Harbor, NY (village) Nassau County	37	3.21
Orange, OH (village) Cuyahoga County	105	3.20
Mansfield Center, CT (cdp) Tolland County	32	3.17
Landgrove, VT (town) Bennington County	6	3.17
Muir Beach, CA (cdp) Marin County	9	3.11
Hewlett, NY (cdp) Nassau County	209	3.10
Monterey, MA (town) Berkshire County	24	3.10
Thiells, NY (cdp) Rockland County	158	3.09
Upper Montclair, NJ (cdp) Essex County	354	3.05
Sharon, MA (cdp) Norfolk County	158	3.04
Bull Valley, IL (village) McHenry County	35	3.03
Northwest Ithaca, NY (cdp) Tompkins County	35	3.03
Dobbs Ferry, NY (village) Westchester County	323	3.00
Moss Beach, CA (cdp) San Mateo County	68	2.97
Effort, PA (cdp) Monroe County	51	2.94
Burlington, IN (town) Carroll County	21	2.94
Bendersville, PA (borough) Adams County	14	2.94
Bentleyville, OH (village) Cuyahoga County	31	2.93
Riverside, PA (cdp) Cambria County	13	2.93
Russell Gardens, NY (village) Nassau County	28	2.91
Lakewood, NJ (cdp) Ocean County	1,442	2.90
Haworth, NJ (borough) Bergen County	97	2.87
Polk, PA (township) Monroe County	223	2.86
Corralitos, CA (cdp) Santa Cruz County	77	2.86
Great Barrington, MA (town) Berkshire County	203	2.84
Lyonsdale, NY (town) Lewis County	37	2.84
Princeton, NJ (township) Mercer County	464	2.83
South Deerfield, MA (cdp) Franklin County	51	2.83
Wayland, MA (town) Middlesex County	363	2.82
Glen Echo, MD (town) Montgomery County	7	2.81
Briarcliff Manor, NY (village) Westchester County	225	2.80
Lorraine, NY (cdp) Jefferson County	6	2.79
Coalfield, TN (cdp) Morgan County	53	2.76
Eureka, NV (cdp) Eureka County	13	2.75
Great Neck Plaza, NY (village) Nassau County	181	2.74

Please refer to the Explanation of Data in the front of the book for more detailed information.

Ancestry

Eastern European

Top 150 Places Sorted by Percent of Total Population

Based on places with total population of 7,500 or more

Place	Population	%
Highland Park, NJ (borough) Middlesex County	1,124	8.03
Scarsdale, NY (town/village) Westchester County	1,208	7.06
New Castle, NY (town) Westchester County	1,178	6.76
Jericho, NY (cdp) Nassau County	776	5.96
Woodmere, NY (cdp) Nassau County	897	5.14
Plainview, NY (cdp) Nassau County	1,224	4.75
Millburn, NJ (township) Essex County	945	4.73
Beachwood, OH (city) Cuyahoga County	546	4.58
Tenafly, NJ (borough) Bergen County	653	4.57
Livingston, NJ (township) Essex County	1,284	4.46
Rye Brook, NY (village) Westchester County	399	4.36
Sharon, MA (town) Norfolk County	742	4.26
North Castle, NY (town) Westchester County	484	4.18
Short Hills, NJ (cdp) Essex County	549	4.16
Hastings-on-Hudson, NY (village) Westchester County	316	4.06
Great Neck, NY (village) Nassau County	396	4.02
Weston, CT (town) Fairfield County	395	3.92
Westport, CT (cdp/town) Fairfield County	982	3.76
Springdale, NJ (cdp) Camden County	550	3.74
Mamaroneck, NY (town) Westchester County	1,042	3.60
East Rockaway, NY (village) Nassau County	349	3.55
Pikesville, MD (cdp) Baltimore County	1,085	3.53
Kemp Mill, MD (cdp) Montgomery County	416	3.44
Melville, NY (cdp) Suffolk County	654	3.43
Lower Merion, PA (township) Montgomery County	1,986	3.42
University Heights, OH (city) Cuyahoga County	457	3.37
Deerfield, IL (village) Lake County	618	3.36
Potomac, MD (cdp) Montgomery County	1,483	3.31
Highland Park, IL (city) Lake County	980	3.26
Agoura Hills, CA (city) Los Angeles County	663	3.26
Upper Montclair, NJ (cdp) Essex County	354	3.05
Dobbs Ferry, NY (village) Westchester County	323	3.00
Lakewood, NJ (cdp) Ocean County	1,442	2.90
Polk, PA (township) Monroe County	223	2.86
Princeton, NJ (township) Mercer County	464	2.83
Wayland, MA (town) Middlesex County	363	2.82
Briarcliff Manor, NY (village) Westchester County	225	2.80
Merrick, NY (cdp) Nassau County	582	2.73
Port Washington, NY (cdp) Nassau County	437	2.71
Woodbury, NY (cdp) Nassau County	244	2.69
Newton, MA (city) Middlesex County	2,236	2.66
New City, NY (cdp) Rockland County	890	2.66
Syosset, NY (cdp) Nassau County	502	2.66
Teaneck, NJ (township) Bergen County	1,026	2.60
Bethesda, MD (cdp) Montgomery County	1,513	2.58
Closter, NJ (borough) Bergen County	209	2.51
Brookline, MA (cdp/town) Norfolk County	1,361	2.35
Glencoe, IL (village) Cook County	201	2.33
Woodbridge, CT (town) New Haven County	208	2.31
Greenburgh, NY (town) Westchester County	2,009	2.29
Stanford, CA (cdp) Santa Clara County	327	2.29
Mantua, VA (cdp) Fairfax County	172	2.29
Ashland, MA (town) Middlesex County	357	2.22
Mamaroneck, NY (village) Westchester County	412	2.20
Travilah, MD (cdp) Montgomery County	260	2.16
Needham, MA (cdp/town) Norfolk County	618	2.15
South Orange Village, NJ (township) Essex County	347	2.14
Upper Dublin, PA (township) Montgomery County	546	2.13
Chevy Chase, MD (cdp) Montgomery County	206	2.11
Hoboken, NJ (city) Hudson County	991	2.09
Lewisboro, NY (town) Westchester County	254	2.06
Rockville, MD (city) Montgomery County	1,196	2.05
West Freehold, NJ (cdp) Monmouth County	282	2.03
Lakewood, NJ (township) Ocean County	1,765	2.01
Amherst, MA (town) Hampshire County	731	1.95
Triangle, VA (cdp) Prince William County	149	1.94
Shaker Heights, OH (city) Cuyahoga County	545	1.92
Weston, MA (town) Middlesex County	215	1.92
Tamalpais-Homestead Valley, CA (cdp) Marin County	203	1.91
Harrison, NY (town/village) Westchester County	507	1.89
Four Corners, MD (cdp) Montgomery County	149	1.86
Croton-on-Hudson, NY (village) Westchester County	146	1.85
Solon, OH (city) Cuyahoga County	420	1.83
Calabasas, CA (city) Los Angeles County	416	1.83
Tiburon, CA (town) Marin County	160	1.81
North Druid Hills, GA (cdp) DeKalb County	331	1.80
Sudbury, MA (town) Middlesex County	311	1.80
Northbrook, IL (village) Cook County	578	1.76
Garrison, MD (cdp) Baltimore County	134	1.76
Metuchen, NJ (borough) Middlesex County	233	1.73
Montclair, NJ (township) Essex County	649	1.72
North Hempstead, NY (town) Nassau County	3,769	1.69
Greenlawn, NY (cdp) Suffolk County	216	1.68
Fair Lawn, NJ (borough) Bergen County	531	1.65
Mahwah, NJ (township) Bergen County	418	1.64
Westfield, NJ (town) Union County	489	1.63
Suffern, NY (village) Rockland County	175	1.63
Long Grove, IL (village) Lake County	128	1.63
Aventura, FL (city) Miami-Dade County	544	1.61
Northampton, MA (city) Hampshire County	461	1.61
Concord, MA (town) Middlesex County	280	1.61
Manhattan, NY (borough) New York County	25,277	1.60
Lexington, MA (cdp/town) Middlesex County	494	1.60
Dix Hills, NY (cdp) Suffolk County	424	1.60
Pelham, NY (town) Westchester County	195	1.60
Corte Madera, CA (town) Marin County	145	1.59
Piedmont, CA (city) Alameda County	167	1.58
Beverly Hills, CA (city) Los Angeles County	535	1.57
Upper Saddle River, NJ (borough) Bergen County	126	1.56
Clarkstown, NY (town) Rockland County	1,282	1.54
Rye, NY (town) Westchester County	699	1.54
North Bethesda, MD (cdp) Montgomery County	623	1.54
Cheltenham, PA (township) Montgomery County	566	1.54
Southfield, MI (township) Oakland County	222	1.53
Rossmoor, CA (cdp) Orange County	161	1.53
Monsey, NY (cdp) Rockland County	229	1.52
Oakland, NJ (borough) Bergen County	192	1.52
Springfield, NJ (township) Union County	234	1.51
North Potomac, MD (cdp) Montgomery County	372	1.49
Northampton, PA (township) Bucks County	591	1.48
Warren, NJ (township) Somerset County	224	1.48
Hanover, NH (cdp) Grafton County	123	1.45
Mill Valley, CA (city) Marin County	197	1.44
West Hartford, CT (cdp/town) Hartford County	894	1.42
Martinsville, NJ (cdp) Somerset County	163	1.42
East Brunswick, NJ (township) Middlesex County	669	1.41
Scotch Plains, NJ (township) Union County	323	1.39
Buffalo Grove, IL (village) Lake County	577	1.38
Glenview, IL (village) Cook County	596	1.37
Maplewood, NJ (township) Essex County	325	1.37
Montecito, CA (cdp) Santa Barbara County	127	1.37
West Orange, NJ (township) Essex County	623	1.36
Dunwoody, GA (city) DeKalb County	609	1.36
Natick, MA (town) Middlesex County	442	1.36
Tarrytown, NY (village) Westchester County	152	1.36
Southborough, MA (town) Worcester County	130	1.35
Southbury, CT (town) New Haven County	264	1.34
Minnetonka, MN (city) Hennepin County	657	1.33
Lower Gwynedd, PA (township) Montgomery County	149	1.33
Cherry Creek, CO (cdp) Arapahoe County	142	1.33
Oyster Bay, NY (town) Nassau County	3,841	1.32
Bedford, MA (town) Middlesex County	173	1.32
Cherry Hill, NJ (township) Camden County	931	1.31
West Windsor, NJ (township) Mercer County	343	1.31
Cherry Hill Mall, NJ (cdp) Camden County	183	1.31
West Bloomfield, MI (charter township) Oakland County	842	1.30
Wilmette, IL (village) Cook County	349	1.30
Barrington, RI (town) Bristol County	215	1.30
Glastonbury, CT (town) Hartford County	440	1.29
Creve Coeur, MO (city) St. Louis County	227	1.29
North Merrick, NY (cdp) Nassau County	160	1.29
Manalapan, NJ (township) Monmouth County	487	1.28
Cambridge, MA (city) Middlesex County	1,313	1.27
Marblehead, MA (cdp/town) Essex County	249	1.26
Marina del Rey, CA (cdp) Los Angeles County	116	1.26
Takoma Park, MD (city) Montgomery County	210	1.25
Bellaire, TX (city) Harris County	207	1.25
Somers, NY (town) Westchester County	248	1.24
South Whitehall, PA (township) Lehigh County	236	1.24
Bellmore, NY (cdp) Nassau County	199	1.23

SECTION THREE

Ancestry

English

U.S. and 50 States Sorted by Population and Percent of Total Population

Place	Population	%
United States	**27,404,243**	**9.02**
California	2,482,263	6.78
Texas	1,774,733	7.30
Florida	1,629,852	8.80
New York	1,180,365	6.14
Ohio	1,112,280	9.66
Pennsylvania	1,052,986	8.35
Michigan	1,034,184	10.39
North Carolina	981,696	10.59
Virginia	921,368	11.75
Georgia	858,272	9.06
Illinois	836,287	6.56
Washington	794,895	12.11
Massachusetts	747,497	11.54
Utah	719,492	27.08
Tennessee	655,572	10.51
Arizona	630,710	10.10
Indiana	623,154	9.71
Missouri	613,509	10.36
Colorado	581,842	11.91
Oregon	508,156	13.51
New Jersey	505,484	5.80
Maryland	504,354	8.85
Kentucky	494,312	11.53
Alabama	451,869	9.59
South Carolina	423,815	9.39
Wisconsin	371,912	6.60
Connecticut	363,910	10.26
Minnesota	328,807	6.27
Oklahoma	324,282	8.82
Kansas	312,695	11.13
Maine	307,666	23.17
Iowa	297,232	9.85
Louisiana	296,110	6.68
Arkansas	294,987	10.27
Idaho	269,570	17.66
Mississippi	251,326	8.54
New Hampshire	247,177	18.81
Nevada	244,546	9.29
West Virginia	225,960	12.28
Nebraska	171,698	9.54
New Mexico	160,177	7.96
Rhode Island	135,087	12.79
Montana	126,682	13.01
Vermont	113,280	18.15
Delaware	108,450	12.31
Wyoming	85,513	15.67
Alaska	69,363	10.04
Hawaii	59,810	4.48
South Dakota	57,338	7.17
North Dakota	31,409	4.76
District of Columbia	30,309	5.19

Place	Population	%
Utah	719,492	27.08
Maine	307,666	23.17
New Hampshire	247,177	18.81
Vermont	113,280	18.15
Idaho	269,570	17.66
Wyoming	85,513	15.67
Oregon	508,156	13.51
Montana	126,682	13.01
Rhode Island	135,087	12.79
Delaware	108,450	12.31
West Virginia	225,960	12.28
Washington	794,895	12.11
Colorado	581,842	11.91
Virginia	921,368	11.75
Massachusetts	747,497	11.54
Kentucky	494,312	11.53
Kansas	312,695	11.13
North Carolina	981,696	10.59
Tennessee	655,572	10.51
Michigan	1,034,184	10.39
Missouri	613,509	10.36
Arkansas	294,987	10.27
Connecticut	363,910	10.26
Arizona	630,710	10.10
Alaska	69,363	10.04
Iowa	297,232	9.85
Indiana	623,154	9.71
Ohio	1,112,280	9.66
Alabama	451,869	9.59
Nebraska	171,698	9.54
South Carolina	423,815	9.39
Nevada	244,546	9.29
Georgia	858,272	9.06
United States	**27,404,243**	**9.02**
Maryland	504,354	8.85
Oklahoma	324,282	8.82
Florida	1,629,852	8.80
Mississippi	251,326	8.54
Pennsylvania	1,052,986	8.35
New Mexico	160,177	7.96
Texas	1,774,733	7.30
South Dakota	57,338	7.17
California	2,482,263	6.78
Louisiana	296,110	6.68
Wisconsin	371,912	6.60
Illinois	836,287	6.56
Minnesota	328,807	6.27
New York	1,180,365	6.14
New Jersey	505,484	5.80
District of Columbia	30,309	5.19
North Dakota	31,409	4.76
Hawaii	59,810	4.48

Please refer to the Explanation of Data in the front of the book for more detailed information.

Ancestry

English

Top 150 Places Sorted by Population

Based on all places, regardless of total population

Place	Population	%
New York, NY (city) Kings County	146,525	1.81
Los Angeles, CA (city) Los Angeles County	129,873	3.44
Phoenix, AZ (city) Maricopa County	104,093	7.18
San Diego, CA (city) San Diego County	92,418	7.20
Houston, TX (city) Harris County	92,025	4.45
Manhattan, NY (borough) New York County	77,799	4.91
Jacksonville, FL (city) Duval County	71,352	8.79
Austin, TX (city) Travis County	70,206	9.19
Seattle, WA (city) King County	68,827	11.56
Indianapolis, IN (city) Marion County	67,644	8.35
Portland, OR (city) Multnomah County	65,820	11.61
Chicago, IL (city) Cook County	64,585	2.39
Dallas, TX (city) Dallas County	64,225	5.41
Mesa, AZ (city) Maricopa County	59,240	13.47
San Antonio, TX (city) Medina County	59,155	4.58
Columbus, OH (city) Franklin County	58,155	7.55
Charlotte, NC (city) Mecklenburg County	58,078	8.23
Louisville-Jefferson County, KY (metro govt) Jefferson County	54,761	9.33
Nashville-Davidson, TN (metro govt) Davidson County	52,395	8.91
Colorado Springs, CO (city) El Paso County	51,939	12.86
Fort Worth, TX (city) Tarrant County	50,261	7.13
Denver, CO (city) Denver County	49,616	8.58
Virginia Beach, VA (ind. city) Virginia Beach independent city	47,398	10.87
Philadelphia, PA (city) Philadelphia County	47,303	3.14
Oklahoma City, OK (city) Oklahoma County	47,135	8.36
San Francisco, CA (city) San Francisco County	45,268	5.74
Tucson, AZ (city) Pima County	42,792	8.25
San Jose, CA (city) Santa Clara County	42,150	4.56
Las Vegas, NV (city) Clark County	41,166	7.10
Albuquerque, NM (city) Bernalillo County	40,798	7.68
Raleigh, NC (city) Wake County	39,630	10.35
Wichita, KS (city) Sedgwick County	39,129	10.47
Tulsa, OK (city) Tulsa County	38,383	9.89
Lexington-Fayette, KY (cons. govt) Fayette County	38,127	13.24
Kansas City, MO (city) Jackson County	38,104	8.38
Salt Lake City, UT (city) Salt Lake County	37,181	20.15
Omaha, NE (city) Douglas County	34,668	8.51
Memphis, TN (city) Shelby County	33,489	5.11
Boise City, ID (city) Ada County	32,660	15.82
Brooklyn, NY (borough) Kings County	32,407	1.31
Boston, MA (city) Suffolk County	32,191	5.34
Provo, UT (city) Utah County	30,420	27.60
Washington, DC (city) District of Columbia	30,309	5.19
Brookhaven, NY (town) Suffolk County	30,089	6.27
Atlanta, GA (city) Fulton County	30,071	7.27
Henderson, NV (city) Clark County	29,502	11.84
Scottsdale, AZ (city) Maricopa County	28,279	12.93
Sacramento, CA (city) Sacramento County	28,086	6.11
Knoxville, TN (city) Knox County	27,870	15.64
Anchorage, AK (municipality) Anchorage Municipality	27,836	9.79
Gilbert, AZ (town) Maricopa County	27,216	13.95
Spokane, WA (city) Spokane County	26,107	12.64
St. Petersburg, FL (city) Pinellas County	25,968	10.57
Lincoln, NE (city) Lancaster County	25,732	10.17
Arlington, TX (city) Tarrant County	25,578	7.12
Orem, UT (city) Utah County	25,177	28.99
Sandy, UT (city) Salt Lake County	24,864	28.52
Tampa, FL (city) Hillsborough County	24,468	7.34
Fresno, CA (city) Fresno County	24,262	5.01
Minneapolis, MN (city) Hennepin County	24,174	6.37
Plano, TX (city) Collin County	24,040	9.39
Chesapeake, VA (ind. city) Chesapeake independent city	23,701	10.81
Overland Park, KS (city) Johnson County	23,474	13.77
West Jordan, UT (city) Salt Lake County	23,430	23.76
Long Beach, CA (city) Los Angeles County	23,359	5.06
Aurora, CO (city) Arapahoe County	23,298	7.42
Baltimore, MD (city) Baltimore city County	23,236	3.74
Reno, NV (city) Washoe County	23,056	10.43
Greensboro, NC (city) Guilford County	22,926	8.71
Eugene, OR (city) Lane County	22,769	14.85
Chandler, AZ (city) Maricopa County	22,635	9.86
Winston-Salem, NC (city) Forsyth County	22,468	10.00
Arlington, VA (cdp) Arlington County	22,268	11.28
Huntington Beach, CA (city) Orange County	21,837	11.56
Hempstead, NY (town) Nassau County	21,808	2.89
Bakersfield, CA (city) Kern County	21,066	6.35
St. George, UT (city) Washington County	20,786	29.22
West Valley City, UT (city) Salt Lake County	20,612	16.49
Madison, WI (city) Dane County	20,405	8.90
Queens, NY (borough) Queens County	20,267	0.92
Glendale, AZ (city) Maricopa County	20,114	8.76
Salem, OR (city) Marion County	20,013	13.18
Fort Wayne, IN (city) Allen County	19,734	7.78
Vancouver, WA (city) Clark County	19,703	12.30
Huntsville, AL (city) Madison County	19,637	11.19
Lubbock, TX (city) Lubbock County	19,524	8.78
Des Moines, IA (city) Polk County	19,201	9.50
Little Rock, AR (city) Pulaski County	19,158	10.05
Riverside, CA (city) Riverside County	18,993	6.32
Toledo, OH (city) Lucas County	18,826	6.45
Fort Collins, CO (city) Larimer County	18,471	13.19
Lakewood, CO (city) Jefferson County	18,422	12.97
Millcreek, UT (cdp) Salt Lake County	18,283	29.97
Durham, NC (city) Durham County	18,137	8.23
Springfield, MO (city) Christian County	17,952	11.29
Layton, UT (city) Davis County	17,949	27.33
Richmond, VA (ind. city) Richmond independent city	17,923	8.88
Cary, NC (town) Wake County	17,916	14.04
Santa Clarita, CA (city) Los Angeles County	17,821	10.35
Tacoma, WA (city) Pierce County	17,591	8.85
Norfolk, VA (ind. city) Norfolk independent city	17,520	7.24
Tempe, AZ (city) Maricopa County	17,066	10.40
Centennial, CO (city) Arapahoe County	16,957	16.96
Pittsburgh, PA (city) Allegheny County	16,692	5.42
Bountiful, UT (city) Davis County	16,637	39.27
Tallahassee, FL (city) Leon County	16,491	9.33
Amarillo, TX (city) Potter County	16,417	8.77
Carlsbad, CA (city) San Diego County	16,407	16.45
Cincinnati, OH (city) Hamilton County	16,011	5.33
Oakland, CA (city) Alameda County	15,955	4.12
Corpus Christi, TX (city) Nueces County	15,937	5.32
Paradise, NV (cdp) Clark County	15,932	7.31
Santa Rosa, CA (city) Sonoma County	15,897	9.77
Peoria, AZ (city) Yavapai County	15,893	10.69
Akron, OH (city) Summit County	15,829	7.80
Orlando, FL (city) Orange County	15,676	6.71
Arvada, CO (city) Jefferson County	15,551	14.83
Boulder, CO (city) Boulder County	15,511	15.98
Milwaukee, WI (city) Milwaukee County	15,507	2.63
Roseville, CA (city) Placer County	15,474	13.60
St. Paul, MN (city) Ramsey County	15,435	5.47
Newport News, VA (ind. city) Newport News independent city	15,413	8.48
Anaheim, CA (city) Orange County	15,386	4.62
El Paso, TX (city) El Paso County	14,883	2.37
Warwick, RI (city) Kent County	14,842	17.74
St. Louis, MO (city) St. Louis city County	14,777	4.64
Highlands Ranch, CO (cdp) Douglas County	14,728	15.49
Modesto, CA (city) Stanislaus County	14,727	7.29
Baton Rouge, LA (city) East Baton Rouge Parish	14,633	6.39
Mobile, AL (city) Mobile County	14,542	7.43
Charleston, SC (city) Charleston County	14,530	12.49
Garland, TX (city) Dallas County	14,518	6.51
Newport Beach, CA (city) Orange County	14,515	17.37
Alexandria, VA (ind. city) Alexandria independent city	14,500	10.85
Olathe, KS (city) Johnson County	14,439	11.96
Independence, MO (city) Jackson County	14,387	12.45
South Jordan, UT (city) Salt Lake County	14,244	30.72
Oceanside, CA (city) San Diego County	14,231	8.64
Cape Coral, FL (city) Lee County	14,168	9.46
Taylorsville, UT (city) Salt Lake County	14,138	24.23
Thousand Oaks, CA (city) Ventura County	14,138	11.34
Grand Rapids, MI (city) Kent County	14,001	7.35
Islip, NY (town) Suffolk County	13,963	4.18
New Orleans, LA (city) Orleans Parish	13,945	4.72
Wilmington, NC (city) New Hanover County	13,829	13.20
Norman, OK (city) Cleveland County	13,827	12.77
Cleveland, OH (city) Cuyahoga County	13,765	3.36
Rochester, NY (city) Monroe County	13,510	6.37
Ann Arbor, MI (city) Washtenaw County	13,447	11.67
The Woodlands, TX (cdp) Montgomery County	13,370	14.52

Please refer to the Explanation of Data in the front of the book for more detailed information.

Ancestry

English

Top 150 Places Sorted by Percent of Total Population

Based on all places, regardless of total population

Place	Population	%
North Light Plant, NM (cdp) San Juan County	277	100.00
Day, FL (cdp) Lafayette County	145	100.00
Pine Valley, UT (cdp) Washington County	134	100.00
Rancho Grande, NM (cdp) Catron County	101	100.00
Zarephath, NJ (cdp) Somerset County	95	100.00
Tabernash, CO (cdp) Grand County	86	100.00
Strawberry, CA (cdp) Tuolumne County	64	100.00
Glacier, WA (cdp) Whatcom County	52	100.00
Chesapeake, MO (cdp) Lawrence County	42	100.00
Siasconset, MA (cdp) Nantucket County	42	100.00
Escondida, NM (cdp) Socorro County	40	100.00
Eureka Roadhouse, AK (cdp) Matanuska-Susitna Borough	38	100.00
Indian Falls, CA (cdp) Plumas County	35	100.00
South Fork Estates, TX (cdp) Jim Hogg County	31	100.00
Indianola, OK (cdp) Delaware County	30	100.00
Yellow Pine, ID (cdp) Valley County	24	100.00
Lance Creek, WY (cdp) Niobrara County	23	100.00
Austin, NV (cdp) Lander County	21	100.00
Villa del Sol, TX (cdp) Cameron County	21	100.00
Albany, WY (cdp) Albany County	18	100.00
Trona, CA (cdp) Inyo County	17	100.00
Lonetree, WY (cdp) Uinta County	15	100.00
Organ, NM (cdp) Doña Ana County	15	100.00
Chicken, AK (cdp) Southeast Fairbanks Census Area	12	100.00
Whitehawk, CA (cdp) Plumas County	12	100.00
Cave, MO (town) Lincoln County	11	100.00
Dot Lake, AK (cdp) Southeast Fairbanks Census Area	11	100.00
Oasis, NV (cdp) Elko County	11	100.00
Scotland, IN (cdp) Greene County	11	100.00
Vantage, WA (cdp) Kittitas County	10	100.00
New Amsterdam, IN (town) Harrison County	6	100.00
Gann Valley, SD (cdp) Buffalo County	5	100.00
Grano, ND (city) Renville County	4	100.00
Winigan, MO (cdp) Sullivan County	76	88.37
Centennial Park, AZ (cdp) Mohave County	734	88.33
Amado, AZ (cdp) Santa Cruz County	81	86.17
Gerlach, NV (cdp) Washoe County	165	83.76
New Auburn, WI (village) Barron County	9	81.82
Spencer, ID (city) Clark County	35	81.40
Wintersburg, AZ (cdp) Maricopa County	40	80.00
Oak Hill, AL (town) Wilcox County	4	80.00
Hildale, UT (city) Washington County	2,058	77.37
Hillsboro, NM (cdp) Sierra County	140	76.50
Dry Valley, NV (cdp) Lincoln County	26	76.47
State Line, ID (city) Kootenai County	13	76.47
Padroni, CO (cdp) Logan County	107	75.89
Lee Mont, VA (cdp) Accomack County	99	75.00
Nikep, MD (cdp) Allegany County	29	74.36
No Name, CO (cdp) Garfield County	62	73.81
San Acacio, CO (cdp) Costilla County	27	72.97
Graceton, PA (cdp) Indiana County	263	72.85
Buckhorn, NM (cdp) Grant County	158	72.15
East Hancock, ME (unorganized territory) Hancock County	44	72.13
Amistad, TX (cdp) Val Verde County	18	72.00
Waves, NC (cdp) Dare County	74	71.84
Sweetwater, OK (town) Beckham County	115	70.55
Orient, WA (cdp) Ferry County	14	70.00
Coleman, GA (cdp) Randolph County	191	69.96
Ute Park, NM (cdp) Colfax County	51	69.86
Shoshone, CA (cdp) Inyo County	23	69.70
Talmage, KS (cdp) Dickinson County	71	69.61
Brodhead, WI (city) Rock County	16	69.57
Little River, CA (cdp) Mendocino County	200	68.97
Matinicus Isle, ME (plantation) Knox County	61	68.54
Bayport, FL (cdp) Hernando County	28	68.29
Miller, IA (cdp) Hancock County	46	67.65
Talmadge, ME (town) Washington County	27	67.50
Clawson, UT (town) Emery County	120	67.42
Coulterville, CA (cdp) Mariposa County	109	67.28
Antelope, OR (city) Wasco County	30	66.67
Old Hundred, NC (cdp) Scotland County	26	66.67
Barada, NE (village) Richardson County	24	66.67
West Forks, ME (plantation) Somerset County	16	66.67
Clay Springs, AZ (cdp) Navajo County	448	66.37
Grover, WY (cdp) Lincoln County	51	66.23
Matthews, GA (cdp) Jefferson County	64	65.98
Plantation Island, FL (cdp) Collier County	126	65.97
Isle au Haut, ME (town) Knox County	56	65.88
Johnson Village, CO (cdp) Chaffee County	224	65.50
Silerton, TN (town) Hardeman County	83	65.35
Bransford, TN (cdp) Sumner County	136	65.07
Campo Bonito, AZ (cdp) Pinal County	26	65.00
Covenant Life, AK (cdp) Haines Borough	38	64.41
Elk City, ID (cdp) Idaho County	171	64.29
Elgin, TN (cdp) Scott County	205	64.26
Henrieville, UT (town) Garfield County	164	63.81
Rodanthe, NC (cdp) Dare County	266	63.64
Mount Laguna, CA (cdp) San Diego County	42	63.64
Codyville, ME (plantation) Washington County	35	63.64
St. Charles, ID (city) Bear Lake County	64	63.37
Freedom Acres, AZ (cdp) Gila County	76	62.81
Colorado City, AZ (town) Mohave County	2,964	62.77
Deseret, UT (cdp) Millard County	146	62.66
Westerville, NE (cdp) Custer County	30	62.50
Elliott, MD (cdp) Dorchester County	20	62.50
Terlingua, TX (cdp) Brewster County	20	62.50
Roderfield, WV (cdp) McDowell County	48	62.34
Brumley, MO (town) Miller County	112	62.22
Woodruff, UT (town) Rich County	95	62.09
Deblois, ME (town) Washington County	31	62.00
Thompson Springs, UT (cdp) Grand County	13	61.90
Eola, OR (cdp) Polk County	16	61.54
Yarrowsburg, MD (cdp) Washington County	97	61.39
Urbanna, VA (town) Middlesex County	377	60.90
Pecan Park, NM (cdp) Luna County	54	60.67
Archer, NE (cdp) Merrick County	92	60.53
Valley Ford, CA (cdp) Sonoma County	52	60.47
Novice, TX (city) Coleman County	96	60.38
Emison, IN (cdp) Knox County	47	60.26
Waite, ME (town) Washington County	36	60.00
Escudilla Bonita, NM (cdp) Catron County	15	60.00
Lambert, OK (town) Alfalfa County	3	60.00
Jakes Corner, AZ (cdp) Gila County	61	59.80
Chauncey, GA (city) Dodge County	220	59.78
Gwynn, VA (cdp) Mathews County	320	59.59
East Burke, VT (cdp) Caledonia County	73	59.35
Lake, UT (town) Rich County	175	59.32
Ada, KS (cdp) Ottawa County	32	59.26
Greensboro, VT (cdp) Orleans County	71	59.17
Pinesdale, MT (town) Ravalli County	385	59.14
St. Charles, SD (cdp) Gregory County	13	59.09
Smoot, WY (cdp) Lincoln County	82	58.99
Princeton, SC (cdp) Laurens County	20	58.82
Bluebell, UT (cdp) Duchesne County	157	58.58
Leisure Lake, MO (cdp) Grundy County	59	58.42
Hartland, VT (cdp) Windsor County	255	58.22
Harkers Island, NC (cdp) Carteret County	634	58.01
Bishopville, MD (cdp) Worcester County	262	57.96
Caryville, FL (town) Washington County	288	57.72
Central, AZ (cdp) Graham County	251	57.70
Seville, GA (cdp) Wilcox County	100	57.47
Oakvale, WV (town) Mercer County	66	57.39
Alamo, NV (cdp) Lincoln County	720	57.32
Ola, SD (cdp) Brule County	12	57.14
Northwest Hancock, ME (unorganized territory) Hancock County	4	57.14
Rocky Ridge, UT (town) Juab County	429	57.12
Pinedale, AZ (cdp) Navajo County	127	56.95
Catherine, CO (cdp) Garfield County	107	56.61
Wanship, UT (cdp) Summit County	155	56.57
River Pines, CA (cdp) Amador County	322	56.10
Dayton, AL (town) Marengo County	23	56.10
Escalante, UT (city) Garfield County	503	56.08
Lake Roberts, NM (cdp) Grant County	14	56.00
Sawpit, CO (town) San Miguel County	38	55.88
Sherrill, AR (town) Jefferson County	25	55.56
Fairview, WY (cdp) Lincoln County	107	55.44
Hackberry, AZ (cdp) Mohave County	21	55.26
Ophir, UT (town) Tooele County	21	55.26
Meadow, UT (town) Millard County	149	55.19
Mountain View, WY (town) Uinta County	573	54.99

Please refer to the Explanation of Data in the front of the book for more detailed information.

Ancestry

English

Top 150 Places Sorted by Percent of Total Population

Based on places with total population of 7,500 or more

Place	Population	%
Mapleton, UT (city) Utah County	3,438	45.58
Alpine, UT (city) Utah County	3,898	43.02
Bountiful, UT (city) Davis County	16,637	39.27
Kaysville, UT (city) Davis County	9,929	38.11
Farmington, UT (city) Davis County	6,447	37.51
Centerville, UT (city) Davis County	5,663	37.22
North Salt Lake, UT (city) Davis County	5,556	37.07
American Fork, UT (city) Utah County	9,231	36.39
Rexburg, ID (city) Madison County	8,722	35.58
North Logan, UT (city) Cache County	2,744	35.34
Freeport, ME (town) Cumberland County	2,754	34.90
Holladay, UT (city) Salt Lake County	9,009	34.26
Springville, UT (city) Utah County	9,347	33.83
Highland, UT (city) Utah County	4,738	33.65
Lindon, UT (city) Utah County	3,217	33.17
Hurricane, UT (city) Washington County	4,323	32.67
Grantsville, UT (city) Tooele County	2,755	32.57
Woods Cross, UT (city) Davis County	2,964	32.34
Cedar Hills, UT (city) Utah County	2,762	32.24
Spanish Fork, UT (city) Utah County	10,230	32.12
North Ogden, UT (city) Weber County	5,359	31.94
Washington, UT (city) Washington County	5,555	31.91
Cedar City, UT (city) Iron County	8,751	31.57
Pleasant Grove, UT (city) Utah County	9,869	31.37
Cottonwood Heights, UT (city) Salt Lake County	10,398	31.00
South Jordan, UT (city) Salt Lake County	14,244	30.72
Conway, NH (town) Carroll County	3,058	30.60
Riverton, UT (city) Salt Lake County	10,945	30.41
Millcreek, UT (cdp) Salt Lake County	18,283	29.97
South Ogden, UT (city) Weber County	4,756	29.78
Smithfield, UT (city) Cache County	2,622	29.27
St. George, UT (city) Washington County	20,786	29.22
Orem, UT (city) Utah County	25,177	28.99
Highland Park, TX (town) Dallas County	2,447	28.68
Sandy, UT (city) Salt Lake County	24,864	28.52
Murray, UT (city) Salt Lake County	13,181	28.49
Richmond, RI (town) Washington County	2,179	28.40
Lehi, UT (city) Utah County	11,900	28.30
Brigham City, UT (city) Box Elder County	4,974	28.20
Scituate, RI (town) Providence County	2,915	28.20
Herriman, UT (city) Salt Lake County	5,134	28.01
Topsham, ME (town) Sagadahoc County	2,487	27.83
Provo, UT (city) Utah County	30,420	27.60
Layton, UT (city) Davis County	17,949	27.33
Charlestown, RI (town) Washington County	2,137	27.13
Syracuse, UT (city) Davis County	5,883	27.12
Eagle Mountain, UT (city) Utah County	4,852	27.12
Santaquin, UT (city) Utah County	2,268	27.11
Barrington, NH (town) Strafford County	2,287	27.05
Evanston, WY (city) Uinta County	3,237	26.94
Gloucester Point, VA (cdp) Gloucester County	2,792	26.83
Buxton, ME (town) York County	2,136	26.64
Wakefield-Peacedale, RI (cdp) Washington County	2,400	26.60
Price, UT (city) Carbon County	2,233	26.35
Draper, UT (city) Salt Lake County	10,324	26.30
Falmouth, ME (town) Cumberland County	2,905	26.20
Yarmouth, ME (town) Cumberland County	2,196	26.17
Saratoga Springs, UT (city) Utah County	3,816	25.97
Exeter, NH (cdp) Rockingham County	2,454	25.97
Green Valley, AZ (cdp) Pima County	5,447	25.45
McGregor, FL (cdp) Lee County	1,950	25.42
Clinton, UT (city) Davis County	4,831	25.38
Cape Elizabeth, ME (town) Cumberland County	2,277	25.14
Washington Terrace, UT (city) Weber County	2,242	25.14
Hamilton, MA (town) Essex County	1,967	25.14
Scarborough, ME (town) Cumberland County	4,681	25.12
Payson, UT (city) Utah County	4,305	25.05
Exeter, NH (town) Rockingham County	3,558	24.72
Brunswick, ME (cdp) Cumberland County	3,657	24.67
Hartford, VT (town) Windsor County	2,465	24.58
Brewer, ME (city) Penobscot County	2,312	24.51
Farmington, ME (town) Franklin County	1,884	24.39
Skidaway Island, GA (cdp) Chatham County	1,969	24.38
Kennebunk, ME (town) York County	2,649	24.34
Ammon, ID (city) Bonneville County	3,021	24.28
St. Simons, GA (cdp) Glynn County	3,116	24.24
Taylorsville, UT (city) Salt Lake County	14,138	24.23
Logan, UT (city) Cache County	11,240	24.22
West Point, UT (city) Davis County	2,146	24.09
Mountain Brook, AL (city) Jefferson County	4,865	23.87
Weare, NH (town) Hillsborough County	2,061	23.80
West Jordan, UT (city) Salt Lake County	23,430	23.76
Mayo, MD (cdp) Anne Arundel County	1,845	23.73
Brunswick, ME (town) Cumberland County	4,834	23.52
Danville, IN (town) Hendricks County	2,044	23.52
Gorham, ME (town) Cumberland County	3,777	23.51
Tooele, UT (city) Tooele County	7,067	23.43
Standish, ME (town) Cumberland County	2,291	23.34
Orinda, CA (city) Contra Costa County	4,072	23.29
Glocester, RI (town) Providence County	2,278	23.23
Auburn, CA (city) Placer County	3,120	23.20
Auburn, ME (city) Androscoggin County	5,342	22.95
Lake Monticello, VA (cdp) Fluvanna County	2,440	22.95
Spring Arbor, MI (township) Jackson County	1,889	22.94
Lunenburg, MA (town) Worcester County	2,290	22.93
Tuckahoe, VA (cdp) Henrico County	10,349	22.91
Clearfield, UT (city) Davis County	6,741	22.84
Green River, WY (city) Sweetwater County	2,794	22.79
Pocatello, ID (city) Bannock County	12,111	22.74
Canandaigua, NY (town) Ontario County	2,169	22.64
Roy, UT (city) Weber County	8,101	22.60
Colonial Heights, VA (ind. city) Colonial Heights independent city	3,948	22.60
York, ME (town) York County	2,874	22.59
Old Lyme, CT (town) New London County	1,712	22.56
Brattleboro, VT (town) Windham County	2,706	22.47
South Portland, ME (city) Cumberland County	5,570	22.46
East Greenwich, RI (town) Kent County	2,960	22.45
Bath, ME (city) Sagadahoc County	1,965	22.43
Pepperell, MA (town) Middlesex County	2,526	22.36
Granby, CT (town) Hartford County	2,468	22.19
Lake of the Woods, VA (cdp) Orange County	1,735	22.17
East Bradford, PA (township) Chester County	2,197	22.14
Brewster, MA (town) Barnstable County	2,190	22.14
Southport, NY (cdp) Chemung County	1,672	22.08
Waterboro, ME (town) York County	1,656	22.07
Idaho Falls, ID (city) Bonneville County	12,269	22.05
University Park, TX (city) Dallas County	5,057	22.01
Woodbury, CT (town) Litchfield County	2,181	22.01
Milford, NH (town) Hillsborough County	3,279	21.99
Chester, VA (cdp) Chesterfield County	4,378	21.98
Ocean Pines, MD (cdp) Worcester County	2,422	21.97
Newfane, NY (town) Niagara County	2,112	21.97
Caribou, ME (city) Aroostook County	1,803	21.89
Lakeland Highlands, FL (cdp) Polk County	2,519	21.85
Fairview, TN (city) Williamson County	1,637	21.83
Sanford, ME (cdp) York County	2,303	21.74
Florence, OR (city) Lane County	1,796	21.73
Newport, OR (city) Lincoln County	2,156	21.69
Vestavia Hills, AL (city) Jefferson County	7,214	21.66
Mason, MI (city) Ingham County	1,747	21.64
Boxford, MA (town) Essex County	1,707	21.56
Magna, UT (cdp) Salt Lake County	5,797	21.55
Augusta, ME (city) Kennebec County	4,115	21.49
San Diego Country Estates, CA (cdp) San Diego County	2,279	21.39
Wells, ME (town) York County	2,063	21.35
Waterloo, NY (town) Seneca County	1,651	21.34
Dennis, MA (town) Barnstable County	3,100	21.30
Pinehurst, NC (village) Moore County	2,658	21.23
Wyndham, VA (cdp) Henrico County	1,984	21.23
Waterville, ME (city) Kennebec County	3,342	21.18
Parma, NY (town) Monroe County	3,262	21.16
Chubbuck, ID (city) Bannock County	2,757	21.15
Hanover, NH (town) Grafton County	2,381	21.14
Medway, MA (town) Norfolk County	2,659	21.11
Granite Bay, CA (cdp) Placer County	4,781	21.08
Portsmouth, NH (city) Rockingham County	4,416	21.07
Solebury, PA (township) Bucks County	1,789	20.99
Davidson, NC (town) Mecklenburg County	2,164	20.97
Fallon, NV (city) Churchill County	1,795	20.97
Harwich, MA (town) Barnstable County	2,574	20.94

SECTION THREE

Ancestry

Estonian

U.S. and 50 States Sorted by Population and Percent of Total Population

Place	Population	%
United States	**28,312**	**0.01**
California	3,744	0.01
New York	3,462	0.02
Florida	1,990	0.01
New Jersey	1,770	0.02
Washington	1,536	0.02
Pennsylvania	1,136	0.01
Maryland	998	0.02
Texas	977	<0.01
Illinois	947	0.01
Virginia	917	0.01
Colorado	832	0.02
Connecticut	779	0.02
Massachusetts	705	0.01
Oregon	683	0.02
Ohio	663	0.01
Minnesota	594	0.01
Wisconsin	560	0.01
Michigan	461	<0.01
North Carolina	450	<0.01
Missouri	423	0.01
Georgia	415	<0.01
Arizona	395	0.01
Indiana	365	0.01
Delaware	348	0.04
New Hampshire	295	0.02
Utah	233	0.01
Tennessee	200	<0.01
Montana	192	0.02
New Mexico	185	0.01
Nebraska	181	0.01
District of Columbia	177	0.03
Alaska	166	0.02
Kentucky	142	<0.01
Maine	135	0.01
Arkansas	120	<0.01
Iowa	117	<0.01
South Carolina	104	<0.01
Idaho	98	0.01
Nevada	94	<0.01
Rhode Island	89	0.01
Wyoming	86	0.02
Alabama	81	<0.01
Louisiana	75	<0.01
Hawaii	67	0.01
Oklahoma	65	<0.01
North Dakota	64	0.01
Kansas	57	<0.01
West Virginia	40	<0.01
Vermont	38	0.01
South Dakota	33	<0.01
Mississippi	28	<0.01

Place	Population	%
Delaware	348	0.04
District of Columbia	177	0.03
New York	3,462	0.02
New Jersey	1,770	0.02
Washington	1,536	0.02
Maryland	998	0.02
Colorado	832	0.02
Connecticut	779	0.02
Oregon	683	0.02
New Hampshire	295	0.02
Montana	192	0.02
Alaska	166	0.02
Wyoming	86	0.02
United States	**28,312**	**0.01**
California	3,744	0.01
Florida	1,990	0.01
Pennsylvania	1,136	0.01
Illinois	947	0.01
Virginia	917	0.01
Massachusetts	705	0.01
Ohio	663	0.01
Minnesota	594	0.01
Wisconsin	560	0.01
Missouri	423	0.01
Arizona	395	0.01
Indiana	365	0.01
Utah	233	0.01
New Mexico	185	0.01
Nebraska	181	0.01
Maine	135	0.01
Idaho	98	0.01
Rhode Island	89	0.01
Hawaii	67	0.01
North Dakota	64	0.01
Vermont	38	0.01
Texas	977	<0.01
Michigan	461	<0.01
North Carolina	450	<0.01
Georgia	415	<0.01
Tennessee	200	<0.01
Kentucky	142	<0.01
Arkansas	120	<0.01
Iowa	117	<0.01
South Carolina	104	<0.01
Nevada	94	<0.01
Alabama	81	<0.01
Louisiana	75	<0.01
Oklahoma	65	<0.01
Kansas	57	<0.01
West Virginia	40	<0.01
South Dakota	33	<0.01
Mississippi	28	<0.01

Please refer to the Explanation of Data in the front of the book for more detailed information.

Ancestry

Estonian

Top 150 Places Sorted by Population

Based on all places, regardless of total population

Place	Population	%
New York, NY (city) Kings County	1,057	0.01
Manhattan, NY (borough) New York County	424	0.03
Los Angeles, CA (city) Los Angeles County	347	0.01
Brooklyn, NY (borough) Kings County	340	0.01
Lee's Summit, MO (city) Jackson County	270	0.31
San Francisco, CA (city) San Francisco County	227	0.03
Seattle, WA (city) King County	213	0.04
Boulder, CO (city) Boulder County	205	0.21
Chicago, IL (city) Cook County	202	0.01
Queens, NY (borough) Queens County	198	0.01
Santaquin, UT (city) Utah County	177	2.12
Washington, DC (city) District of Columbia	177	0.03
Islip, NY (town) Suffolk County	175	0.05
Hempstead, NY (town) Nassau County	175	0.02
Houston, TX (city) Harris County	171	0.01
San Diego, CA (city) San Diego County	164	0.01
Philadelphia, PA (city) Philadelphia County	147	0.01
Phoenix, AZ (city) Maricopa County	144	0.01
Auburn, MA (town) Worcester County	140	0.86
Huntington, NY (town) Suffolk County	140	0.07
Austin, TX (city) Travis County	136	0.02
Riverbank, CA (city) Stanislaus County	135	0.62
Oyster Bay, NY (town) Nassau County	130	0.04
Bloomingdale, FL (cdp) Hillsborough County	128	0.59
Denver, CO (city) Denver County	125	0.02
Anchorage, AK (municipality) Anchorage Municipality	124	0.04
Albuquerque, NM (city) Bernalillo County	124	0.02
Lancaster, CA (city) Los Angeles County	110	0.07
Orlando, FL (city) Orange County	109	0.05
Brookhaven, NY (town) Suffolk County	102	0.02
Ocean, NJ (township) Monmouth County	100	0.37
Indianapolis, IN (city) Marion County	99	0.01
Jupiter, FL (town) Palm Beach County	98	0.19
Madison, WI (city) Dane County	95	0.04
Jackson, NJ (township) Ocean County	90	0.17
Cincinnati, OH (city) Hamilton County	86	0.03
Bronx, NY (borough) Bronx County	85	0.01
Lancaster, NY (town) Erie County	83	0.20
Lower Saucon, PA (township) Northampton County	82	0.76
Colorado Springs, CO (city) El Paso County	81	0.02
Trumbull, CT (cdp/town) Fairfield County	80	0.23
St. Paul, MN (city) Ramsey County	80	0.03
Pike Creek Valley, DE (cdp) New Castle County	79	0.69
Clarence, NY (cdp) Erie County	78	2.64
Clarence, NY (town) Erie County	78	0.26
Cheektowaga, NY (cdp) Erie County	78	0.10
Cheektowaga, NY (town) Erie County	78	0.09
Raleigh, NC (city) Wake County	77	0.02
Lawrence, NJ (township) Mercer County	76	0.23
Redwood City, CA (city) San Mateo County	76	0.10
Spokane, WA (city) Spokane County	76	0.04
Hackensack, NJ (city) Bergen County	74	0.17
Issaquah, WA (city) King County	73	0.26
Evanston, IL (city) Cook County	73	0.10
Pawcatuck, CT (cdp) New London County	72	1.24
Stonington, CT (town) New London County	72	0.39
Minneapolis, MN (city) Hennepin County	72	0.02
Sebastian, FL (city) Indian River County	69	0.32
Edmonds, WA (city) Snohomish County	69	0.17
Richland, WA (city) Benton County	69	0.15
Jersey City, NJ (city) Hudson County	67	0.03
Garner, NC (town) Wake County	66	0.27
Wilton, CT (town) Fairfield County	65	0.36
Racine, WI (city) Racine County	65	0.08
Oakland, CA (city) Alameda County	65	0.02
Fayetteville, NC (city) Cumberland County	64	0.03
Dallas, TX (city) Dallas County	64	0.01
Conway, NH (cdp) Carroll County	63	3.45
Mound, MN (city) Hennepin County	63	0.70
Conway, NH (town) Carroll County	63	0.63
Scaggsville, MD (cdp) Howard County	63	0.27
Paragould, AR (city) Greene County	63	0.25
Pinellas Park, FL (city) Pinellas County	62	0.13
Port Orange, FL (city) Volusia County	62	0.11
Lincoln, NE (city) Lancaster County	62	0.02
Cedar Mill, OR (cdp) Washington County	61	0.42
Los Gatos, CA (town) Santa Clara County	61	0.21
Mercer Island, WA (city) King County	60	0.27
St. Louis Park, MN (city) Hennepin County	60	0.13
Lynchburg, VA (ind. city) Lynchburg independent city	60	0.08
Roseburg, OR (city) Douglas County	59	0.28
Louisville-Jefferson County, KY (metro govt) Jefferson County	58	0.01
Portland, OR (city) Multnomah County	58	0.01
Torrington, CT (city/town) Litchfield County	57	0.16
Greenburgh, NY (town) Westchester County	57	0.07
Berkeley, CA (city) Alameda County	57	0.05
Lakewood, CO (city) Jefferson County	57	0.04
Chanhassen, MN (city) Carver County	56	0.25
Gaithersburg, MD (city) Montgomery County	56	0.10
Lexington-Fayette, KY (cons. govt) Fayette County	56	0.02
Fort Montgomery, NY (cdp) Orange County	55	6.44
Bohemia, NY (cdp) Suffolk County	55	0.56
Highlands, NY (town) Orange County	55	0.44
Berkeley, NJ (township) Ocean County	55	0.13
Rockville, MD (city) Montgomery County	55	0.09
Inglewood, CA (city) Los Angeles County	55	0.05
Tacoma, WA (city) Pierce County	55	0.03
Baltimore, MD (city) Baltimore city County	55	0.01
Carmel-by-the-Sea, CA (city) Monterey County	54	1.45
West Islip, NY (cdp) Suffolk County	54	0.19
Alexandria, VA (ind. city) Alexandria independent city	54	0.04
Modesto, CA (city) Stanislaus County	54	0.03
Milwaukee, WI (city) Milwaukee County	54	0.01
San Jose, CA (city) Santa Clara County	54	0.01
Virginia Beach, VA (ind. city) Virginia Beach independent city	54	0.01
North Fort Myers, FL (cdp) Lee County	53	0.13
Lakewood, NJ (cdp) Ocean County	53	0.11
Towson, MD (cdp) Baltimore County	53	0.10
Terre Haute, IN (city) Vigo County	53	0.09
Lakewood, NJ (township) Ocean County	53	0.06
Santa Clara, CA (city) Santa Clara County	53	0.05
Yonkers, NY (city) Westchester County	53	0.03
Lakeway, TX (city) Travis County	52	0.48
Bozeman, MT (city) Gallatin County	52	0.14
Boston, MA (city) Suffolk County	52	0.01
La Grange, IL (village) Cook County	50	0.32
Melville, NY (cdp) Suffolk County	50	0.26
Newtown, CT (town) Fairfield County	50	0.19
Bethesda, MD (cdp) Montgomery County	50	0.09
Nashville-Davidson, TN (metro govt) Davidson County	50	0.01
Parole, MD (cdp) Anne Arundel County	48	0.32
Oceanside, NY (cdp) Nassau County	48	0.15
Ramapo, NY (town) Rockland County	48	0.04
Torrance, CA (city) Los Angeles County	48	0.03
North Hempstead, NY (town) Nassau County	48	0.02
Yaphank, NY (cdp) Suffolk County	47	0.76
Lake Barcroft, VA (cdp) Fairfax County	47	0.52
Greenville, NY (cdp) Westchester County	46	0.67
Aliquippa, PA (city) Beaver County	46	0.47
Seabrook, MD (cdp) Prince George's County	46	0.29
Hobart, WA (cdp) King County	45	0.71
Solebury, PA (township) Bucks County	45	0.53
Mount Vernon, NY (city) Westchester County	45	0.07
San Antonio, TX (city) Medina County	45	<0.01
Rockcreek, OR (cdp) Washington County	44	0.45
Cheltenham, PA (township) Montgomery County	44	0.12
Stratford, CT (cdp/town) Fairfield County	44	0.09
San Marcos, CA (city) San Diego County	44	0.06
Tuscaloosa, AL (city) Tuscaloosa County	44	0.05
Plano, TX (city) Collin County	44	0.02
Garrison, MD (cdp) Baltimore County	43	0.56
Twin Falls, ID (city) Twin Falls County	43	0.10
Des Moines, IA (city) Polk County	43	0.02
Durham, NC (city) Durham County	43	0.02
Rivanna, VA (cdp) Albemarle County	42	2.42
Roselle Park, NJ (borough) Union County	42	0.32
Englewood, NJ (city) Bergen County	42	0.16
Pittsford, NY (town) Monroe County	42	0.14
McAllen, TX (city) Hidalgo County	42	0.03
Cottage Grove, OR (city) Lane County	41	0.43

SECTION THREE

Please refer to the Explanation of Data in the front of the book for more detailed information.

Ancestry

Estonian

Top 150 Places Sorted by Percent of Total Population

Based on all places, regardless of total population

Place	Population	%
Meservey, IA (city) Cerro Gordo County	27	10.38
Redford, NY (cdp) Clinton County	31	6.47
Fort Montgomery, NY (cdp) Orange County	55	6.44
Knik River, AK (cdp) Matanuska-Susitna Borough	35	4.88
Evansville, MN (township) Douglas County	10	3.76
Conway, NH (cdp) Carroll County	63	3.45
Pine Haven, WY (town) Crook County	10	3.23
Warren, NY (town) Herkimer County	36	3.18
Iron River, WI (town) Bayfield County	28	2.85
Maxville, WI (town) Buffalo County	9	2.80
Bryn Athyn, PA (borough) Montgomery County	32	2.73
Graham, AL (cdp) Randolph County	8	2.68
Melrose, OR (cdp) Douglas County	18	2.65
Clarence, NY (cdp) Erie County	78	2.64
Lincoln, MI (village) Alcona County	9	2.54
Rivanna, VA (cdp) Albemarle County	42	2.42
Crows Nest, IN (town) Marion County	2	2.41
Ryan, IA (city) Delaware County	11	2.36
Paddock, MN (township) Otter Tail County	6	2.22
Alta, CA (cdp) Placer County	11	2.14
Santaquin, UT (city) Utah County	177	2.12
Jupiter Island, FL (town) Martin County	10	2.04
Moose Lake, MN (township) Beltrami County	6	1.97
Hillsboro Pines, FL (cdp) Broward County	6	1.89
Ryderwood, WA (cdp) Cowlitz County	6	1.82
Preston, PA (township) Wayne County	16	1.72
Ransom Canyon, TX (town) Lubbock County	20	1.70
Appleton, WI (city) Winnebago County	24	1.66
Jeffers Gardens, OR (cdp) Clatsop County	9	1.56
Shingobee, MN (township) Cass County	26	1.54
Freedom, NH (town) Carroll County	16	1.50
Carmel-by-the-Sea, CA (city) Monterey County	54	1.45
Jaffrey, NH (cdp) Cheshire County	32	1.34
Woodcock, PA (borough) Crawford County	3	1.30
Sheridan, MO (town) Worth County	3	1.29
Mendota, MN (city) Dakota County	2	1.28
Harrisville, NH (town) Cheshire County	12	1.25
Pawcatuck, CT (cdp) New London County	72	1.24
Bear Creek, WI (town) Sauk County	6	1.17
Seven Points, TX (city) Henderson County	18	1.14
Gustin, MI (township) Alcona County	9	1.12
Warner, NH (cdp) Merrimack County	6	1.08
Chenango Bridge, NY (cdp) Broome County	32	1.05
Edgecomb, ME (town) Lincoln County	12	1.05
Yalaha, FL (cdp) Lake County	12	1.05
Dedham, ME (town) Hancock County	22	1.03
Anson, ME (town) Somerset County	26	1.02
Third Lake, IL (village) Lake County	15	1.00
Varnam, NC (town) Brunswick County	6	1.00
Rossmoor, NJ (cdp) Middlesex County	28	0.98
Albany, PA (township) Berks County	15	0.97
Red Hook, NY (village) Dutchess County	18	0.96
Edgmont, PA (township) Delaware County	37	0.93
Preston, NY (town) Chenango County	9	0.93
River Road, WA (cdp) Clallam County	5	0.92
Montville, ME (town) Waldo County	10	0.90
Warren Park, IN (town) Marion County	12	0.87
Pe Ell, WA (town) Lewis County	4	0.87
Auburn, MA (town) Worcester County	140	0.86
Carsonville, MN (township) Becker County	2	0.84
Orient, NY (cdp) Suffolk County	5	0.83
Carnation, WA (city) King County	17	0.82
Elmer, NJ (borough) Salem County	10	0.82
Chester, CA (cdp) Plumas County	15	0.81
Saylorsburg, PA (cdp) Monroe County	17	0.80
Seaside Heights, NJ (borough) Ocean County	23	0.78
Lake Hamilton, AR (cdp) Garland County	15	0.78
Saranac, NY (town) Clinton County	31	0.77
Genola, UT (town) Utah County	9	0.77
Lower Saucon, PA (township) Northampton County	82	0.76
Yaphank, NY (cdp) Suffolk County	47	0.76
Shelburne Falls, MA (cdp) Franklin County	13	0.75
Heritage Pines, FL (cdp) Pasco County	14	0.73
Bayfield, CO (town) La Plata County	15	0.72
Hobart, WA (cdp) King County	45	0.71
Lyndeborough, NH (town) Hillsborough County	10	0.71
Mound, MN (city) Hennepin County	63	0.70
Georgetown, CT (cdp) Fairfield County	11	0.70
Grand View-on-Hudson, NY (village) Rockland County	2	0.70
Pike Creek Valley, DE (cdp) New Castle County	79	0.69
Oakdale, PA (borough) Allegheny County	9	0.68
Deal, NJ (borough) Monmouth County	7	0.68
Greenville, NY (cdp) Westchester County	46	0.67
Stock Island, FL (cdp) Monroe County	24	0.67
West Simsbury, CT (cdp) Hartford County	18	0.67
Milan, NY (town) Dutchess County	17	0.67
Williston, FL (city) Levy County	18	0.65
Sands, MI (township) Marquette County	16	0.65
Lusby, MD (cdp) Calvert County	15	0.65
Cameron, WI (village) Barron County	10	0.64
Highland, WI (town) Douglas County	2	0.64
Conway, NH (town) Carroll County	63	0.63
Atlantic Highlands, NJ (borough) Monmouth County	28	0.63
Riverbank, CA (city) Stanislaus County	135	0.62
Ahwahnee, CA (cdp) Madera County	13	0.62
Hickman, NE (city) Lancaster County	9	0.61
Bloomingdale, FL (cdp) Hillsborough County	128	0.59
Verona Walk, FL (cdp) Collier County	11	0.59
West Stockbridge, MA (town) Berkshire County	9	0.59
Jaffrey, NH (town) Cheshire County	32	0.58
Isle of Hope, GA (cdp) Chatham County	13	0.57
Brownstown, PA (cdp) Lancaster County	12	0.57
Bohemia, NY (cdp) Suffolk County	55	0.56
Garrison, MD (cdp) Baltimore County	43	0.56
Middleburgh, NY (town) Schoharie County	21	0.56
Fife Heights, WA (cdp) Pierce County	12	0.56
Kingfield, ME (town) Franklin County	6	0.56
Dallas, WI (village) Barron County	3	0.56
South Hill, NY (cdp) Tompkins County	36	0.55
Danby, VT (town) Rutland County	8	0.55
Tilden, WI (town) Chippewa County	6	0.55
Groton Long Point, CT (borough) New London County	3	0.55
Cazadero, CA (cdp) Sonoma County	2	0.55
Bayville, NY (village) Nassau County	36	0.54
Wailea, HI (cdp) Maui County	35	0.54
Chevy Chase Section Five, MD (village) Montgomery County	4	0.54
Solebury, PA (township) Bucks County	45	0.53
Mahopac, NY (cdp) Putnam County	40	0.53
Watchung, NJ (borough) Somerset County	30	0.53
Washburn, ND (city) McLean County	7	0.53
Lake Barcroft, VA (cdp) Fairfax County	47	0.52
Cambridge, MI (township) Lenawee County	30	0.52
Bellemeade, KY (city) Jefferson County	4	0.52
Pacific, WA (city) King County	33	0.51
Valentine, NE (city) Cherry County	14	0.51
Marble Cliff, OH (village) Franklin County	3	0.51
Woods Creek, WA (cdp) Snohomish County	30	0.50
Lake California, CA (cdp) Tehama County	13	0.50
Raleigh Hills, OR (cdp) Washington County	33	0.49
Watertown, WI (town) Jefferson County	9	0.49
North Collins, NY (village) Erie County	5	0.49
Valders, WI (village) Manitowoc County	4	0.49
Lakeway, TX (city) Travis County	52	0.48
Nelsonville, NY (village) Putnam County	3	0.48
Aliquippa, PA (city) Beaver County	46	0.47
Mantua, VA (cdp) Fairfax County	35	0.47
New Hartford, NY (village) Oneida County	9	0.47
Hallock, MN (city) Kittson County	5	0.47
Linwood, NJ (city) Atlantic County	33	0.46
Lindale, GA (cdp) Floyd County	22	0.46
Port Aransas, TX (city) Nueces County	16	0.46
Hanover, IL (village) Jo Daviess County	4	0.46
Rockcreek, OR (cdp) Washington County	44	0.45
Upper Deerfield, NJ (township) Cumberland County	34	0.45
Stephentown, NY (town) Rensselaer County	13	0.45
Litchfield, PA (township) Bradford County	6	0.45
Highlands, NY (town) Orange County	55	0.44
Lafayette, PA (township) McKean County	11	0.44
Cottage Grove, OR (city) Lane County	41	0.43
Island Heights, NJ (borough) Ocean County	6	0.43

Please refer to the Explanation of Data in the front of the book for more detailed information.

Ancestry

Estonian

Top 150 Places Sorted by Percent of Total Population

Based on places with total population of 7,500 or more

Place	Population	%
Santaquin, UT (city) Utah County	177	2.12
Auburn, MA (town) Worcester County	140	0.86
Lower Saucon, PA (township) Northampton County	82	0.76
Mound, MN (city) Hennepin County	63	0.70
Pike Creek Valley, DE (cdp) New Castle County	79	0.69
Conway, NH (town) Carroll County	63	0.63
Riverbank, CA (city) Stanislaus County	135	0.62
Bloomingdale, FL (cdp) Hillsborough County	128	0.59
Bohemia, NY (cdp) Suffolk County	55	0.56
Garrison, MD (cdp) Baltimore County	43	0.56
Solebury, PA (township) Bucks County	45	0.53
Mahopac, NY (cdp) Putnam County	40	0.53
Lake Barcroft, VA (cdp) Fairfax County	47	0.52
Lakeway, TX (city) Travis County	52	0.48
Aliquippa, PA (city) Beaver County	46	0.47
Mantua, VA (cdp) Fairfax County	35	0.47
Rockcreek, OR (cdp) Washington County	44	0.45
Upper Deerfield, NJ (township) Cumberland County	34	0.45
Highlands, NY (town) Orange County	55	0.44
Cottage Grove, OR (city) Lane County	41	0.43
Cedar Mill, OR (cdp) Washington County	61	0.42
Stonington, CT (town) New London County	72	0.39
Ocean, NJ (township) Monmouth County	100	0.37
Mount Joy, PA (township) Lancaster County	35	0.37
Wilton, CT (town) Fairfield County	65	0.36
Broadlands, VA (cdp) Loudoun County	38	0.36
Larkfield-Wikiup, CA (cdp) Sonoma County	31	0.36
Athol, MA (cdp) Worcester County	29	0.36
Sebastian, FL (city) Indian River County	69	0.32
La Grange, IL (village) Cook County	50	0.32
Parole, MD (cdp) Anne Arundel County	48	0.32
Roselle Park, NJ (borough) Union County	42	0.32
Lee's Summit, MO (city) Jackson County	270	0.31
Larkspur, CA (city) Marin County	37	0.31
World Golf Village, FL (cdp) St. Johns County	30	0.31
Woodburn, VA (cdp) Fairfax County	26	0.30
Seabrook, MD (cdp) Prince George's County	46	0.29
East Renton Highlands, WA (cdp) King County	32	0.29
Roseburg, OR (city) Douglas County	59	0.28
Chenango, NY (town) Broome County	32	0.28
Northwest Harborcreek, PA (cdp) Erie County	25	0.28
Garner, NC (town) Wake County	66	0.27
Scaggsville, MD (cdp) Howard County	63	0.27
Mercer Island, WA (city) King County	60	0.27
Clarence, NY (town) Erie County	78	0.26
Issaquah, WA (city) King County	73	0.26
Melville, NY (cdp) Suffolk County	50	0.26
Fort Lewis, WA (cdp) Pierce County	35	0.26
Fairview, PA (township) Erie County	26	0.26
Hartland, WI (village) Waukesha County	23	0.26
Harvard, IL (city) McHenry County	22	0.26
Paragould, AR (city) Greene County	63	0.25
Chanhassen, MN (city) Carver County	56	0.25
Athol, MA (town) Worcester County	29	0.25
Clarksburg, MD (cdp) Montgomery County	26	0.25
Camp Pendleton North, CA (cdp) San Diego County	25	0.25
Little Canada, MN (city) Ramsey County	24	0.25
Trumbull, CT (cdp/town) Fairfield County	80	0.23
Lawrence, NJ (township) Mercer County	76	0.23
Bothell West, WA (cdp) Snohomish County	36	0.23
Peru, IL (city) LaSalle County	24	0.23
Montvale, NJ (borough) Bergen County	18	0.23
Redlands, CO (cdp) Mesa County	18	0.23
Barrington, RI (town) Bristol County	36	0.22
University Heights, OH (city) Cuyahoga County	30	0.22
La Riviera, CA (cdp) Sacramento County	24	0.22
Boulder, CO (city) Boulder County	205	0.21
Los Gatos, CA (town) Santa Clara County	61	0.21
Mineola, NY (village) Nassau County	40	0.21
Tanque Verde, AZ (cdp) Pima County	35	0.21
Westport, MA (town) Bristol County	32	0.21
Jefferson Valley-Yorktown, NY (cdp) Westchester County	30	0.21
Red Bank, NJ (borough) Monmouth County	25	0.21
Lancaster, NY (town) Erie County	83	0.20
Mukilteo, WA (city) Snohomish County	40	0.20
Seaford, NY (cdp) Nassau County	31	0.20
Oak Park, CA (cdp) Ventura County	28	0.20
Malibu, CA (city) Los Angeles County	25	0.20
Scotts Valley, CA (city) Santa Cruz County	23	0.20
Huntington, VA (cdp) Fairfax County	21	0.20
Jupiter, FL (town) Palm Beach County	98	0.19
West Islip, NY (cdp) Suffolk County	54	0.19
Newtown, CT (town) Fairfield County	50	0.19
Syosset, NY (cdp) Nassau County	35	0.19
Summit, IL (village) Cook County	21	0.19
Hamilton, PA (township) Monroe County	17	0.19
Niskayuna, NY (town) Schenectady County	39	0.18
Mira Loma, CA (cdp) Riverside County	37	0.18
Ithaca, NY (town) Tompkins County	36	0.18
Carlisle, PA (borough) Cumberland County	33	0.18
Niles, MI (township) Berrien County	25	0.18
Woodbury, NY (village) Orange County	19	0.18
Edgewater Park, NJ (township) Burlington County	16	0.18
Lancaster, MA (town) Worcester County	14	0.18
Jackson, NJ (township) Ocean County	90	0.17
Hackensack, NJ (city) Bergen County	74	0.17
Edmonds, WA (city) Snohomish County	69	0.17
Lodi, NJ (borough) Bergen County	41	0.17
Idylwood, VA (cdp) Fairfax County	27	0.17
Maitland, FL (city) Orange County	26	0.17
East Hanover, NJ (township) Morris County	19	0.17
Woodbury, NY (town) Orange County	19	0.17
Orono, ME (cdp) Penobscot County	15	0.17
East Grand Forks, MN (city) Polk County	14	0.17
Mayo, MD (cdp) Anne Arundel County	13	0.17
Torrington, CT (city/town) Litchfield County	57	0.16
Englewood, NJ (city) Bergen County	42	0.16
Bloomingdale, IL (village) DuPage County	36	0.16
Kihei, HI (cdp) Maui County	32	0.16
Islip, NY (cdp) Suffolk County	31	0.16
Massapequa Park, NY (village) Nassau County	27	0.16
Washington, PA (township) Franklin County	22	0.16
Henderson, TX (city) Rusk County	21	0.16
East Windsor, CT (town) Hartford County	18	0.16
Red Hook, NY (town) Dutchess County	18	0.16
Byram, MS (city) Hinds County	17	0.16
College Place, WA (city) Walla Walla County	14	0.16
Kendall Park, NJ (cdp) Middlesex County	14	0.16
Bogota, NJ (borough) Bergen County	13	0.16
West Earl, PA (township) Lancaster County	12	0.16
Richland, WA (city) Benton County	69	0.15
Oceanside, NY (cdp) Nassau County	48	0.15
Horsham, PA (township) Montgomery County	39	0.15
Neenah, WI (city) Winnebago County	37	0.15
Harborcreek, PA (township) Erie County	25	0.15
Oakland, MI (charter township) Oakland County	24	0.15
Kings Park West, VA (cdp) Fairfax County	22	0.15
Mill Valley, CA (city) Marin County	21	0.15
Lemon Hill, CA (cdp) Sacramento County	20	0.15
Pelham, NY (town) Westchester County	18	0.15
Woodinville, WA (city) King County	16	0.15
Lambertville, MI (cdp) Monroe County	15	0.15
Orono, ME (town) Penobscot County	15	0.15
Winchendon, MA (town) Worcester County	15	0.15
Malverne, NY (village) Nassau County	13	0.15
Bedminster, NJ (township) Somerset County	12	0.15
Briarcliff Manor, NY (village) Westchester County	12	0.15
Pike Creek, DE (cdp) New Castle County	12	0.15
Bozeman, MT (city) Gallatin County	52	0.14
Pittsford, NY (town) Monroe County	42	0.14
East Hill-Meridian, WA (cdp) King County	41	0.14
Monterey, CA (city) Monterey County	40	0.14
Munster, IN (town) Lake County	33	0.14
Bailey's Crossroads, VA (cdp) Fairfax County	29	0.14
Broadview Heights, OH (city) Cuyahoga County	27	0.14
Lorton, VA (cdp) Fairfax County	27	0.14
Lackawanna, NY (city) Erie County	26	0.14
St. Matthews, KY (city) Jefferson County	24	0.14
Gainesville, VA (cdp) Prince William County	15	0.14
Town and Country, MO (city) St. Louis County	15	0.14

SECTION THREE

Please refer to the Explanation of Data in the front of the book for more detailed information.

Ancestry

European

U.S. and 50 States Sorted by Population and Percent of Total Population

Place	Population	%
United States	**3,074,695**	**1.01**
California	469,275	1.28
Texas	181,386	0.75
Florida	167,285	0.90
New York	157,939	0.82
Washington	138,348	2.11
Illinois	107,785	0.85
Virginia	101,514	1.29
Ohio	98,058	0.85
North Carolina	95,883	1.03
Georgia	94,610	1.00
Utah	93,786	3.53
Colorado	88,809	1.82
Michigan	86,424	0.87
Oregon	85,676	2.28
Pennsylvania	79,980	0.63
Missouri	64,904	1.10
Arizona	63,900	1.02
Maryland	61,268	1.08
Minnesota	60,621	1.16
Tennessee	58,594	0.94
Indiana	58,511	0.91
Oklahoma	57,453	1.56
New Jersey	55,373	0.63
Massachusetts	50,608	0.78
Wisconsin	42,467	0.75
Alabama	38,692	0.82
South Carolina	36,969	0.82
Kansas	35,572	1.27
Kentucky	32,836	0.77
Iowa	29,301	0.97
Idaho	29,128	1.91
Nevada	27,065	1.03
Connecticut	24,255	0.68
Arkansas	21,677	0.75
Mississippi	19,577	0.67
Louisiana	18,769	0.42
Nebraska	17,510	0.97
New Mexico	17,217	0.86
Alaska	14,134	2.04
Montana	12,265	1.26
West Virginia	11,343	0.62
New Hampshire	9,595	0.73
Maine	9,177	0.69
Vermont	8,825	1.41
Wyoming	7,865	1.44
District of Columbia	7,573	1.30
Hawaii	7,362	0.55
South Dakota	5,432	0.68
Delaware	5,354	0.61
Rhode Island	3,799	0.36
North Dakota	2,946	0.45

Place	Population	%
Utah	93,786	3.53
Oregon	85,676	2.28
Washington	138,348	2.11
Alaska	14,134	2.04
Idaho	29,128	1.91
Colorado	88,809	1.82
Oklahoma	57,453	1.56
Wyoming	7,865	1.44
Vermont	8,825	1.41
District of Columbia	7,573	1.30
Virginia	101,514	1.29
California	469,275	1.28
Kansas	35,572	1.27
Montana	12,265	1.26
Minnesota	60,621	1.16
Missouri	64,904	1.10
Maryland	61,268	1.08
North Carolina	95,883	1.03
Nevada	27,065	1.03
Arizona	63,900	1.02
United States	**3,074,695**	**1.01**
Georgia	94,610	1.00
Iowa	29,301	0.97
Nebraska	17,510	0.97
Tennessee	58,594	0.94
Indiana	58,511	0.91
Florida	167,285	0.90
Michigan	86,424	0.87
New Mexico	17,217	0.86
Illinois	107,785	0.85
Ohio	98,058	0.85
New York	157,939	0.82
Alabama	38,692	0.82
South Carolina	36,969	0.82
Massachusetts	50,608	0.78
Kentucky	32,836	0.77
Texas	181,386	0.75
Wisconsin	42,467	0.75
Arkansas	21,677	0.75
New Hampshire	9,595	0.73
Maine	9,177	0.69
Connecticut	24,255	0.68
South Dakota	5,432	0.68
Mississippi	19,577	0.67
Pennsylvania	79,980	0.63
New Jersey	55,373	0.63
West Virginia	11,343	0.62
Delaware	5,354	0.61
Hawaii	7,362	0.55
North Dakota	2,946	0.45
Louisiana	18,769	0.42
Rhode Island	3,799	0.36

Please refer to the Explanation of Data in the front of the book for more detailed information.

Ancestry

European

Top 150 Places Sorted by Population

Based on all places, regardless of total population

Place	Population	%
New York, NY (city) Kings County	66,267	0.82
Los Angeles, CA (city) Los Angeles County	33,149	0.88
Manhattan, NY (borough) New York County	27,846	1.76
Brooklyn, NY (borough) Kings County	27,499	1.11
Seattle, WA (city) King County	20,109	3.38
San Diego, CA (city) San Diego County	19,955	1.56
Chicago, IL (city) Cook County	17,169	0.64
San Francisco, CA (city) San Francisco County	15,818	2.00
Tulsa, OK (city) Tulsa County	15,267	3.93
Portland, OR (city) Multnomah County	14,432	2.55
Houston, TX (city) Harris County	13,040	0.63
Phoenix, AZ (city) Maricopa County	11,745	0.81
Dallas, TX (city) Dallas County	10,354	0.87
Austin, TX (city) Travis County	9,853	1.29
San Jose, CA (city) Santa Clara County	9,840	1.06
Indianapolis, IN (city) Marion County	9,215	1.14
Denver, CO (city) Denver County	8,938	1.55
Ramapo, NY (town) Rockland County	8,814	7.18
Colorado Springs, CO (city) El Paso County	8,253	2.04
Fort Worth, TX (city) Tarrant County	7,768	1.10
Washington, DC (city) District of Columbia	7,573	1.30
Provo, UT (city) Utah County	7,164	6.50
Columbus, OH (city) Franklin County	7,099	0.92
Oklahoma City, OK (city) Oklahoma County	6,973	1.24
Tucson, AZ (city) Pima County	6,941	1.34
Minneapolis, MN (city) Hennepin County	6,854	1.81
San Antonio, TX (city) Medina County	6,683	0.52
Queens, NY (borough) Queens County	6,584	0.30
Santa Rosa, CA (city) Sonoma County	6,559	4.03
Charlotte, NC (city) Mecklenburg County	6,521	0.92
Albuquerque, NM (city) Bernalillo County	6,436	1.21
Oakland, CA (city) Alameda County	6,403	1.65
Jacksonville, FL (city) Duval County	6,325	0.78
St. Louis, MO (city) St. Louis city County	6,123	1.92
Nashville-Davidson, TN (metro govt) Davidson County	5,959	1.01
Atlanta, GA (city) Fulton County	5,928	1.43
Hempstead, NY (town) Nassau County	5,650	0.75
Eugene, OR (city) Lane County	5,529	3.61
Long Beach, CA (city) Los Angeles County	5,522	1.20
Edmond, OK (city) Oklahoma County	5,462	6.95
Salt Lake City, UT (city) Salt Lake County	5,451	2.95
Raleigh, NC (city) Wake County	5,405	1.41
Sacramento, CA (city) Sacramento County	5,277	1.15
Anchorage, AK (municipality) Anchorage Municipality	5,161	1.82
Las Vegas, NV (city) Clark County	5,130	0.88
Fort Collins, CO (city) Larimer County	4,997	3.57
Boston, MA (city) Suffolk County	4,962	0.82
Philadelphia, PA (city) Philadelphia County	4,939	0.33
Omaha, NE (city) Douglas County	4,808	1.18
Louisville-Jefferson County, KY (metro govt) Jefferson County	4,703	0.80
Wichita, KS (city) Sedgwick County	4,651	1.24
Virginia Beach, VA (ind. city) Virginia Beach independent city	4,603	1.06
Mesa, AZ (city) Maricopa County	4,591	1.04
West Jordan, UT (city) Salt Lake County	4,258	4.32
Kansas City, MO (city) Jackson County	4,255	0.94
Spokane, WA (city) Spokane County	4,189	2.03
Plano, TX (city) Collin County	4,179	1.63
Arlington, TX (city) Tarrant County	4,105	1.14
Boulder, CO (city) Boulder County	4,098	4.22
Lexington-Fayette, KY (cons. govt) Fayette County	4,060	1.41
Memphis, TN (city) Shelby County	4,012	0.61
Boise City, ID (city) Ada County	3,968	1.92
Arlington, VA (cdp) Arlington County	3,919	1.98
Bakersfield, CA (city) Kern County	3,718	1.12
Aurora, CO (city) Arapahoe County	3,566	1.14
Temecula, CA (city) Riverside County	3,436	3.59
St. Petersburg, FL (city) Pinellas County	3,434	1.40
Tacoma, WA (city) Pierce County	3,412	1.72
Orem, UT (city) Utah County	3,386	3.90
Monsey, NY (cdp) Rockland County	3,363	22.35
St. Paul, MN (city) Ramsey County	3,305	1.17
Sandy, UT (city) Salt Lake County	3,293	3.78
Corvallis, OR (city) Benton County	3,268	6.12
Irvine, CA (city) Orange County	3,236	1.63
Huntington Beach, CA (city) Orange County	3,207	1.70
Gilbert, AZ (town) Maricopa County	3,197	1.64
Cary, NC (town) Wake County	3,166	2.48
Norman, OK (city) Cleveland County	3,162	2.92
Chandler, AZ (city) Maricopa County	3,099	1.35
Scottsdale, AZ (city) Maricopa County	3,094	1.41
Madison, WI (city) Dane County	3,091	1.35
Lakewood, NJ (township) Ocean County	3,076	3.51
Davis, CA (city) Yolo County	3,038	4.69
Fresno, CA (city) Fresno County	3,030	0.63
Bellevue, WA (city) King County	3,016	2.52
Baltimore, MD (city) Baltimore city County	3,008	0.48
Milwaukee, WI (city) Milwaukee County	2,989	0.51
Lincoln, NE (city) Lancaster County	2,985	1.18
Lawton, OK (city) Comanche County	2,956	3.14
Thousand Oaks, CA (city) Ventura County	2,952	2.37
Santa Clarita, CA (city) Los Angeles County	2,946	1.71
Oyster Bay, NY (town) Nassau County	2,919	1.00
Berkeley, CA (city) Alameda County	2,914	2.66
Reno, NV (city) Washoe County	2,903	1.31
Overland Park, KS (city) Johnson County	2,886	1.69
Vallejo, CA (city) Solano County	2,852	2.46
Greensboro, NC (city) Guilford County	2,845	1.08
Salem, OR (city) Marion County	2,750	1.81
Henderson, NV (city) Clark County	2,716	1.09
Palo Alto, CA (city) Santa Clara County	2,712	4.34
Carlsbad, CA (city) San Diego County	2,706	2.71
Tampa, FL (city) Hillsborough County	2,706	0.81
Oceanside, CA (city) San Diego County	2,689	1.63
Ann Arbor, MI (city) Washtenaw County	2,664	2.31
Naperville, IL (city) DuPage County	2,659	1.89
Longmont, CO (city) Boulder County	2,652	3.17
Vancouver, WA (city) Clark County	2,603	1.62
Cambridge, MA (city) Middlesex County	2,585	2.50
Roseville, CA (city) Placer County	2,574	2.26
Lawrence, KS (city) Douglas County	2,565	2.97
Durham, NC (city) Durham County	2,559	1.16
Cincinnati, OH (city) Hamilton County	2,521	0.84
Richmond, VA (ind. city) Richmond independent city	2,494	1.24
South Jordan, UT (city) Salt Lake County	2,477	5.34
Murrieta, CA (city) Riverside County	2,477	2.59
Newport Beach, CA (city) Orange County	2,427	2.90
Vacaville, CA (city) Solano County	2,390	2.60
Lehi, UT (city) Utah County	2,389	5.68
Millcreek, UT (cdp) Salt Lake County	2,379	3.90
Lakewood, NJ (cdp) Ocean County	2,375	4.77
Champaign, IL (city) Champaign County	2,373	2.99
Beaverton, OR (city) Washington County	2,357	2.68
Santa Cruz, CA (city) Santa Cruz County	2,354	4.04
Chesapeake, VA (ind. city) Chesapeake independent city	2,336	1.07
Huntsville, AL (city) Madison County	2,332	1.33
Centennial, CO (city) Arapahoe County	2,327	2.33
Winston-Salem, NC (city) Forsyth County	2,316	1.03
Rancho Cucamonga, CA (city) San Bernardino County	2,309	1.44
Pittsburgh, PA (city) Allegheny County	2,300	0.75
Bronx, NY (borough) Bronx County	2,270	0.17
Olathe, KS (city) Johnson County	2,267	1.88
Arvada, CO (city) Jefferson County	2,264	2.16
Lakewood, CO (city) Jefferson County	2,264	1.59
Belleville, IL (city) St. Clair County	2,261	5.15
New Orleans, LA (city) Orleans Parish	2,260	0.77
Olympia, WA (city) Thurston County	2,239	4.90
Sunnyvale, CA (city) Santa Clara County	2,236	1.64
Oviedo, FL (city) Seminole County	2,222	6.85
Springfield, MO (city) Christian County	2,217	1.39
Concord, CA (city) Contra Costa County	2,204	1.82
Bellingham, WA (city) Whatcom County	2,191	2.77
Huntington, NY (town) Suffolk County	2,177	1.08
Newton, MA (city) Middlesex County	2,164	2.58
Knoxville, TN (city) Knox County	2,161	1.21
Alexandria, VA (ind. city) Alexandria independent city	2,158	1.61
Bend, OR (city) Deschutes County	2,148	2.89
Altamonte Springs, FL (city) Seminole County	2,147	5.10
San Luis Obispo, CA (city) San Luis Obispo County	2,135	4.75
Highlands Ranch, CO (cdp) Douglas County	2,121	2.23
Brookhaven, NY (town) Suffolk County	2,098	0.44

Please refer to the Explanation of Data in the front of the book for more detailed information.

Ancestry

European

Top 150 Places Sorted by Percent of Total Population

Based on all places, regardless of total population

Place	Population	%
Mound, LA (village) Madison Parish	30	83.33
Motley, MN (city) Cass County	29	80.56
Amorita, OK (town) Alfalfa County	26	74.29
Mylo, ND (city) Rolette County	10	62.50
Santiago, WA (cdp) Grays Harbor County	9	52.94
Bentley, IL (town) Hancock County	10	52.63
Modest Town, VA (cdp) Accomack County	51	48.57
Rockford, ID (cdp) Bingham County	51	48.11
Shell, WY (cdp) Big Horn County	16	47.06
Lookout, CA (cdp) Modoc County	11	44.00
Buffalo Gap, SD (town) Custer County	66	38.37
Markleeville, CA (cdp) Alpine County	100	36.50
Alder, WA (cdp) Pierce County	104	35.99
Garberville, CA (cdp) Humboldt County	231	35.87
Danville, WA (cdp) Ferry County	12	35.29
Metaline, WA (town) Pend Oreille County	57	34.97
Byron, CA (cdp) Contra Costa County	417	34.75
June Lake, CA (cdp) Mono County	198	33.67
Mono City, CA (cdp) Mono County	26	33.33
Catharine, KS (cdp) Ellis County	11	31.43
Downieville, CA (cdp) Sierra County	64	30.05
Mount Charleston, NV (cdp) Clark County	58	30.05
Bellfountain, OR (cdp) Benton County	12	30.00
Parksville, SC (town) McCormick County	30	29.70
Shamrock, OK (town) Creek County	24	29.63
Cliffdell, WA (cdp) Yakima County	8	29.63
Kaser, NY (village) Rockland County	1,293	29.15
Shelter Cove, CA (cdp) Humboldt County	149	28.44
Weatherby, MO (town) DeKalb County	22	28.21
Mason, WI (village) Bayfield County	16	27.59
Lowes, KY (cdp) Graves County	14	26.92
Westbrook, MN (township) Cottonwood County	62	26.50
Hidden Lake, CO (cdp) Boulder County	11	26.19
Scotia, CA (cdp) Humboldt County	169	25.92
Davidson, OK (town) Tillman County	61	25.63
Ophir, CO (town) San Miguel County	32	25.60
Meadow Valley, CA (cdp) Plumas County	170	25.22
Indian Creek, FL (village) Miami-Dade County	25	25.00
Blue Lake, CA (city) Humboldt County	320	24.75
Charlos Heights, MT (cdp) Ravalli County	21	24.71
Manitou, OK (town) Tillman County	54	24.43
Hillsboro, VA (town) Loudoun County	14	24.14
Deming, WA (cdp) Whatcom County	68	23.78
Belleair Shore, FL (town) Pinellas County	17	23.29
Belden, CA (cdp) Plumas County	18	23.08
Redway, CA (cdp) Humboldt County	233	22.75
Monsey, NY (cdp) Rockland County	3,363	22.35
Popponesset Island, MA (cdp) Barnstable County	22	22.22
Medicine Park, OK (town) Comanche County	64	22.07
Hyder, AK (cdp) Prince of Wales-Hyder Census Area	27	21.60
Devol, OK (town) Cotton County	43	21.18
Hollis, AK (cdp) Prince of Wales-Hyder Census Area	30	21.13
Silver Plume, CO (town) Clear Creek County	34	20.99
Naukati Bay, AK (cdp) Prince of Wales-Hyder Census Area	13	20.97
Mud Bay, AK (cdp) Haines Borough	20	20.83
Phillipsville, CA (cdp) Humboldt County	16	20.78
Earl, NC (town) Cleveland County	48	20.69
Wilderness Rim, WA (cdp) King County	275	20.66
Alderpoint, CA (cdp) Humboldt County	43	20.48
Dayton, MT (cdp) Lake County	11	20.37
Randlett, OK (town) Cotton County	90	20.27
Ruth, CA (cdp) Trinity County	30	19.87
Avon, UT (cdp) Cache County	73	19.52
Torrey, MN (township) Cass County	30	19.48
Marysville, MT (cdp) Lewis and Clark County	13	19.40
Weott, CA (cdp) Humboldt County	34	19.32
El Portal, CA (cdp) Mariposa County	73	19.31
Homestead, IA (cdp) Iowa County	32	19.28
Livonia, MO (village) Putnam County	10	19.23
Brick Center, CO (cdp) Arapahoe County	14	18.92
Mammoth, WY (cdp) Park County	41	18.81
Idun, MN (township) Aitkin County	65	18.73
Chuluota, FL (cdp) Seminole County	444	18.59
Whale Pass, AK (cdp) Prince of Wales-Hyder Census Area	11	18.33
Silver Springs, AK (cdp) Valdez-Cordova Census Area	20	18.18

Place	Population	%
Cape Meares, OR (cdp) Tillamook County	14	17.95
Crescent Beach, FL (cdp) St. Johns County	206	17.93
New Square, NY (village) Rockland County	1,147	17.76
Homeworth, OH (cdp) Columbiana County	163	17.70
Neihart, MT (town) Cascade County	15	17.65
Lake Hughes, CA (cdp) Los Angeles County	137	17.61
Lewiston, MI (cdp) Montmorency County	249	17.52
Gentry, MO (village) Gentry County	13	17.11
Klickitat, WA (cdp) Klickitat County	60	17.09
Victor, MT (cdp) Ravalli County	122	17.04
South Taft, CA (cdp) Kern County	364	16.72
Mad River, CA (cdp) Trinity County	61	16.67
Neosho Falls, KS (city) Woodson County	29	16.67
Boone, MN (township) Lake of the Woods County	7	16.67
Pensacola, OK (town) Mayes County	7	16.67
White Plains, AL (cdp) Calhoun County	126	16.56
Pinopolis, SC (cdp) Berkeley County	217	16.51
Tabiona, UT (town) Duchesne County	42	16.41
Monroe, MA (town) Franklin County	18	16.36
Black Hammock, FL (cdp) Seminole County	143	16.25
Woodland Hills, UT (city) Utah County	213	16.17
Carnelian Bay, CA (cdp) Placer County	47	16.15
Rackerby, CA (cdp) Butte County	35	16.06
Florence, MN (city) Lyon County	4	16.00
Norrie, CO (cdp) Pitkin County	7	15.91
Sauget, IL (village) St. Clair County	38	15.64
Henrieville, UT (town) Garfield County	40	15.56
Brislet, MN (township) Polk County	9	15.52
Cimarron City, OK (town) Logan County	32	15.38
St. Benedict, IA (cdp) Kossuth County	4	15.38
Farmington, CA (cdp) San Joaquin County	46	15.33
Mockingbird Valley, KY (city) Jefferson County	19	15.32
LaPlace, IL (cdp) Piatt County	33	15.28
Caberfae, MI (cdp) Wexford County	19	14.96
Pinal, AZ (cdp) Gila County	74	14.92
Kramer, ND (city) Bottineau County	4	14.81
Proberta, CA (cdp) Tehama County	30	14.49
Fortuna, CA (city) Humboldt County	1,684	14.46
Adair Village, OR (city) Benton County	129	14.32
Strand, MN (township) Norman County	13	14.29
Lake City, CA (cdp) Modoc County	11	14.29
Castor, LA (village) Bienville Parish	22	14.19
Willow Creek, CA (cdp) Humboldt County	181	14.18
Norge, OK (town) Grady County	25	14.04
West Hampton Dunes, NY (village) Suffolk County	6	13.95
Towner, CO (cdp) Kiowa County	4	13.79
Holley, OR (cdp) Linn County	65	13.77
Hallam, NE (village) Lancaster County	18	13.74
Chilcoot-Vinton, CA (cdp) Plumas County	83	13.67
Alvo, NE (village) Cass County	12	13.64
Wisconsin Dells, WI (city) Juneau County	3	13.64
Holcomb, MS (cdp) Grenada County	74	13.58
Bracey, VA (cdp) Mecklenburg County	167	13.50
Samak, UT (cdp) Summit County	63	13.46
St. David, AZ (cdp) Cochise County	243	13.44
Byars, OK (town) McClain County	29	13.43
Loleta, CA (cdp) Humboldt County	113	13.39
Bald Head Island, NC (village) Brunswick County	10	13.33
Apple Valley, UT (town) Washington County	83	13.32
Cedarville, NJ (cdp) Cumberland County	128	13.24
Piedmont, SD (city) Meade County	5	13.16
Orrum, NC (town) Robeson County	12	13.04
Pelican, AK (city) Hoonah-Angoon Census Area	12	13.04
Camp Dennison, OH (cdp) Hamilton County	61	13.01
Coyle, OK (town) Logan County	37	12.94
Ithaca, OH (village) Darke County	10	12.82
Chalfant, CA (cdp) Mono County	99	12.69
Richmond Dale, OH (cdp) Ross County	26	12.62
Fayston, VT (town) Washington County	154	12.55
East Earl, PA (cdp) Lancaster County	194	12.52
Trinity Village, CA (cdp) Trinity County	16	12.50
Comptche, CA (cdp) Mendocino County	12	12.50
Spaulding, OK (town) Hughes County	11	12.50
Burton, NE (village) Keya Paha County	4	12.50
Loveland, OK (town) Tillman County	4	12.50

Please refer to the Explanation of Data in the front of the book for more detailed information.

Ancestry

European

Top 150 Places Sorted by Percent of Total Population

Based on places with total population of 7,500 or more

Place	Population	%
Monsey, NY (cdp) Rockland County	3,363	22.35
Fortuna, CA (city) Humboldt County	1,684	14.46
Arcata, CA (city) Humboldt County	1,637	9.57
Saratoga Springs, UT (city) Utah County	1,322	9.00
Eagle Mountain, UT (city) Utah County	1,585	8.86
Joshua Tree, CA (cdp) San Bernardino County	675	8.74
Cedar Hills, UT (city) Utah County	709	8.28
McKinleyville, CA (cdp) Humboldt County	1,276	7.55
Greenbriar, VA (cdp) Fairfax County	568	7.40
Cahokia, IL (village) St. Clair County	1,138	7.39
Longwood, FL (city) Seminole County	1,010	7.19
Ramapo, NY (town) Rockland County	8,814	7.18
Wekiwa Springs, FL (cdp) Seminole County	1,586	7.06
Kiryas Joel, NY (village) Orange County	1,340	7.02
Edmond, OK (city) Oklahoma County	5,462	6.95
Oviedo, FL (city) Seminole County	2,222	6.85
Provo, UT (city) Utah County	7,164	6.50
Riverdale, UT (city) Weber County	526	6.42
Kaysville, UT (city) Davis County	1,625	6.24
Highland, UT (city) Utah County	871	6.19
Corvallis, OR (city) Benton County	3,268	6.12
Magalia, CA (cdp) Butte County	694	5.96
Tamalpais-Homestead Valley, CA (cdp) Marin County	632	5.96
Upper Saddle River, NJ (borough) Bergen County	482	5.96
Pleasant Grove, UT (city) Utah County	1,858	5.91
Tiburon, CA (town) Marin County	520	5.89
El Sobrante, CA (cdp) Contra Costa County	792	5.87
Forest City, FL (cdp) Seminole County	808	5.81
Woods Cross, UT (city) Davis County	527	5.75
Black Forest, CO (cdp) El Paso County	768	5.71
Farmington, UT (city) Davis County	980	5.70
Lehi, UT (city) Utah County	2,389	5.68
Lake Mary, FL (city) Seminole County	767	5.66
Lindon, UT (city) Utah County	545	5.62
North Logan, UT (city) Cache County	436	5.61
Rosedale, CA (cdp) Kern County	828	5.58
Eureka, CA (city) Humboldt County	1,496	5.55
Mapleton, UT (city) Utah County	415	5.50
Springville, UT (city) Utah County	1,510	5.46
Juneau, AK (borough) Juneau City and Borough	1,675	5.41
Dixon, CA (city) Solano County	964	5.38
South Jordan, UT (city) Salt Lake County	2,477	5.34
Spanish Fork, UT (city) Utah County	1,690	5.31
Edwards, CO (cdp) Eagle County	476	5.30
Payson, UT (city) Utah County	899	5.23
Firestone, CO (town) Weld County	463	5.22
Belleville, IL (city) St. Clair County	2,261	5.15
Centerville, UT (city) Davis County	783	5.15
Altamonte Springs, FL (city) Seminole County	2,147	5.10
Union Hill-Novelty Hill, WA (cdp) King County	931	5.07
Topanga, CA (cdp) Los Angeles County	427	5.01
Orinda, CA (city) Contra Costa County	866	4.95
Olympia, WA (city) Thurston County	2,239	4.90
Birch Bay, WA (cdp) Whatcom County	385	4.89
Oak Hills, CA (cdp) San Bernardino County	392	4.87
Rockcreek, OR (cdp) Washington County	474	4.85
Vernal, UT (city) Uintah County	425	4.85
West Point, UT (city) Davis County	427	4.79
Lakewood, NJ (cdp) Ocean County	2,375	4.77
San Luis Obispo, CA (city) San Luis Obispo County	2,135	4.75
Cortlandville, NY (town) Cortland County	400	4.74
Swansea, IL (village) St. Clair County	612	4.73
Davis, CA (city) Yolo County	3,038	4.69
Capitola, CA (city) Santa Cruz County	453	4.62
Poulsbo, WA (city) Kitsap County	406	4.62
Stanford, CA (cdp) Santa Clara County	655	4.59
Winter Springs, FL (city) Seminole County	1,526	4.58
Fair Lawn, NJ (borough) Bergen County	1,469	4.57
Martha Lake, WA (cdp) Snohomish County	714	4.57
Rossmoor, CA (cdp) Orange County	478	4.56
Santaquin, UT (city) Utah County	379	4.53
Lincoln City, OR (city) Lincoln County	356	4.51
Albany, CA (city) Alameda County	807	4.50
Summit Park, UT (cdp) Summit County	336	4.48
Gunbarrel, CO (cdp) Boulder County	422	4.45
Logan, UT (city) Cache County	2,062	4.44
Clayton, CA (city) Contra Costa County	480	4.44
Piedmont, CA (city) Alameda County	468	4.43
Cheat Lake, WV (cdp) Monongalia County	335	4.39
Eagle, ID (city) Ada County	821	4.38
Cedar Mill, OR (cdp) Washington County	637	4.38
Vashon, WA (cdp) King County	434	4.37
Falls Church, VA (ind. city) Falls Church independent city	500	4.36
Palo Alto, CA (city) Santa Clara County	2,712	4.34
Menlo Park, CA (city) San Mateo County	1,356	4.33
San Carlos, CA (city) San Mateo County	1,204	4.33
Ladue, MO (city) St. Louis County	367	4.33
West Jordan, UT (city) Salt Lake County	4,258	4.32
Oatfield, OR (cdp) Clackamas County	588	4.32
Dranesville, VA (cdp) Fairfax County	541	4.31
Westwood, NJ (borough) Bergen County	467	4.30
Lewisboro, NY (town) Westchester County	526	4.27
Grantsville, UT (city) Tooele County	360	4.26
Mantua, VA (cdp) Fairfax County	319	4.25
Smithfield, UT (city) Cache County	380	4.24
Boulder, CO (city) Boulder County	4,098	4.22
Lake Oswego, OR (city) Clackamas County	1,541	4.21
Maitland, FL (city) Orange County	661	4.20
Glencoe, IL (village) Cook County	358	4.15
Troutdale, OR (city) Multnomah County	630	4.11
Louisville, CO (city) Boulder County	758	4.10
Milford, MI (charter township) Oakland County	641	4.10
Knik-Fairview, AK (cdp) Matanuska-Susitna Borough	502	4.10
Ham Lake, MN (city) Anoka County	611	4.09
North Castle, NY (town) Westchester County	473	4.08
Tooele, UT (city) Tooele County	1,228	4.07
Keizer, OR (city) Marion County	1,449	4.06
Webster Groves, MO (city) St. Louis County	933	4.06
Malibu, CA (city) Los Angeles County	519	4.06
Bainbridge Island, WA (city) Kitsap County	911	4.05
Santa Cruz, CA (city) Santa Cruz County	2,354	4.04
Riverton, UT (city) Salt Lake County	1,453	4.04
Oak Grove, MN (city) Anoka County	318	4.04
Ojai, CA (city) Ventura County	304	4.04
Santa Rosa, CA (city) Sonoma County	6,559	4.03
Montecito, CA (cdp) Santa Barbara County	369	3.99
Picnic Point, WA (cdp) Snohomish County	339	3.98
Pinole, CA (city) Contra Costa County	731	3.96
Tulsa, OK (city) Tulsa County	15,267	3.93
Rexburg, ID (city) Madison County	962	3.92
Orem, UT (city) Utah County	3,386	3.90
Millcreek, UT (cdp) Salt Lake County	2,379	3.90
Vinings, GA (cdp) Cobb County	335	3.90
Lakewood Park, FL (cdp) St. Lucie County	460	3.88
Cherry Creek, CO (cdp) Arapahoe County	415	3.88
Cheney, WA (city) Spokane County	397	3.86
Oak Park, CA (cdp) Ventura County	541	3.85
Soquel, CA (cdp) Santa Cruz County	361	3.84
Sammamish, WA (city) King County	1,651	3.81
Kemp Mill, MD (cdp) Montgomery County	460	3.81
Woodinville, WA (city) King County	406	3.81
Sanford, FL (city) Seminole County	1,953	3.80
Sandy, UT (city) Salt Lake County	3,293	3.78
Chestnut Ridge, NY (village) Rockland County	297	3.78
Manhattan Beach, CA (city) Los Angeles County	1,314	3.77
Los Alamos, NM (cdp) Los Alamos County	453	3.77
Chevy Chase, MD (cdp) Montgomery County	367	3.77
Heber, UT (city) Wasatch County	405	3.76
Mahwah, NJ (township) Bergen County	954	3.75
Mountain Brook, AL (city) Jefferson County	764	3.75
Clinton, UT (city) Davis County	714	3.75
Cape St. Claire, MD (cdp) Anne Arundel County	324	3.74
Draper, UT (city) Salt Lake County	1,462	3.72
Port Townsend, WA (city) Jefferson County	338	3.72
Suwanee, GA (city) Gwinnett County	535	3.68
Herriman, UT (city) Salt Lake County	672	3.67
Monroe, NY (town) Orange County	1,414	3.66
Montpelier, VT (city) Washington County	289	3.66
Los Altos, CA (city) Santa Clara County	1,037	3.65
Hales Corners, WI (village) Milwaukee County	278	3.64

Please refer to the Explanation of Data in the front of the book for more detailed information.

Ancestry

Finnish

U.S. and 50 States Sorted by Population and Percent of Total Population

Place	Population	%
United States	**677,272**	**0.22**
Michigan	111,010	1.12
Minnesota	103,159	1.97
California	54,331	0.15
Washington	48,045	0.73
Wisconsin	40,565	0.72
Florida	28,029	0.15
Massachusetts	26,973	0.42
Oregon	23,213	0.62
Ohio	19,872	0.17
Illinois	18,771	0.15
New York	16,941	0.09
Texas	15,486	0.06
Arizona	13,597	0.22
Colorado	11,951	0.24
New Hampshire	8,741	0.67
Pennsylvania	8,401	0.07
Virginia	7,593	0.10
Montana	7,362	0.76
Maine	7,205	0.54
Connecticut	6,699	0.19
Georgia	6,420	0.07
New Jersey	6,396	0.07
North Carolina	6,261	0.07
Utah	5,409	0.20
Indiana	5,241	0.08
Idaho	5,134	0.34
Maryland	4,905	0.09
Nevada	4,856	0.18
Alaska	4,418	0.64
Missouri	4,359	0.07
South Carolina	4,080	0.09
South Dakota	4,001	0.50
Tennessee	3,989	0.06
North Dakota	3,921	0.59
Iowa	3,043	0.10
Wyoming	2,944	0.54
New Mexico	2,510	0.12
Alabama	2,304	0.05
Kentucky	2,243	0.05
Oklahoma	2,060	0.06
Kansas	2,010	0.07
Nebraska	1,933	0.11
Vermont	1,907	0.31
Rhode Island	1,869	0.18
Hawaii	1,477	0.11
Arkansas	1,435	0.05
Louisiana	1,093	0.02
Mississippi	1,061	0.04
West Virginia	796	0.04
District of Columbia	778	0.13
Delaware	475	0.05

Place	Population	%
Minnesota	103,159	1.97
Michigan	111,010	1.12
Montana	7,362	0.76
Washington	48,045	0.73
Wisconsin	40,565	0.72
New Hampshire	8,741	0.67
Alaska	4,418	0.64
Oregon	23,213	0.62
North Dakota	3,921	0.59
Maine	7,205	0.54
Wyoming	2,944	0.54
South Dakota	4,001	0.50
Massachusetts	26,973	0.42
Idaho	5,134	0.34
Vermont	1,907	0.31
Colorado	11,951	0.24
United States	**677,272**	**0.22**
Arizona	13,597	0.22
Utah	5,409	0.20
Connecticut	6,699	0.19
Nevada	4,856	0.18
Rhode Island	1,869	0.18
Ohio	19,872	0.17
California	54,331	0.15
Florida	28,029	0.15
Illinois	18,771	0.15
District of Columbia	778	0.13
New Mexico	2,510	0.12
Nebraska	1,933	0.11
Hawaii	1,477	0.11
Virginia	7,593	0.10
Iowa	3,043	0.10
New York	16,941	0.09
Maryland	4,905	0.09
South Carolina	4,080	0.09
Indiana	5,241	0.08
Pennsylvania	8,401	0.07
Georgia	6,420	0.07
New Jersey	6,396	0.07
North Carolina	6,261	0.07
Missouri	4,359	0.07
Kansas	2,010	0.07
Texas	15,486	0.06
Tennessee	3,989	0.06
Oklahoma	2,060	0.06
Alabama	2,304	0.05
Kentucky	2,243	0.05
Arkansas	1,435	0.05
Delaware	475	0.05
Mississippi	1,061	0.04
West Virginia	796	0.04
Louisiana	1,093	0.02

Please refer to the Explanation of Data in the front of the book for more detailed information.

Ancestry

Finnish

Top 150 Places Sorted by Population

Based on all places, regardless of total population

Place	Population	%
Duluth, MN (city) St. Louis County	5,228	6.07
Minneapolis, MN (city) Hennepin County	3,786	1.00
Portland, OR (city) Multnomah County	3,748	0.66
New York, NY (city) Kings County	3,519	0.04
Seattle, WA (city) King County	3,089	0.52
Los Angeles, CA (city) Los Angeles County	2,919	0.08
Calumet, MI (charter township) Houghton County	2,757	42.38
Chicago, IL (city) Cook County	2,609	0.10
Marquette, MI (city) Marquette County	2,593	12.20
Phoenix, AZ (city) Maricopa County	2,568	0.18
San Diego, CA (city) San Diego County	2,374	0.19
St. Paul, MN (city) Ramsey County	2,347	0.83
Ishpeming, MI (city) Marquette County	2,142	32.95
Livonia, MI (city) Wayne County	2,019	2.06
Hibbing, MN (city) St. Louis County	2,018	12.31
Cloquet, MN (city) Carlton County	1,993	16.58
Vancouver, WA (city) Clark County	1,892	1.18
Superior, WI (city) Douglas County	1,885	6.93
Anchorage, AK (municipality) Anchorage Municipality	1,830	0.64
Virginia, MN (city) St. Louis County	1,733	19.77
Milwaukee, WI (city) Milwaukee County	1,685	0.29
Manhattan, NY (borough) New York County	1,658	0.10
Hancock, MI (city) Houghton County	1,552	33.98
Adams, MI (township) Houghton County	1,526	59.17
Plymouth, MN (city) Hennepin County	1,357	1.96
Bloomington, MN (city) Hennepin County	1,324	1.60
Negaunee, MI (city) Marquette County	1,313	28.77
Coon Rapids, MN (city) Anoka County	1,264	2.04
San Francisco, CA (city) San Francisco County	1,264	0.16
Ishpeming, MI (township) Marquette County	1,243	35.40
New Ipswich, NH (town) Hillsborough County	1,231	24.70
Spokane, WA (city) Spokane County	1,221	0.59
Longview, WA (city) Cowlitz County	1,211	3.31
Negaunee, MI (township) Marquette County	1,200	39.95
Fitchburg, MA (city) Worcester County	1,167	2.90
Ironwood, MI (city) Gogebic County	1,164	21.20
Thomson, MN (township) Carlton County	1,142	23.19
Portage, MI (charter township) Houghton County	1,123	35.67
Colorado Springs, CO (city) El Paso County	1,122	0.28
Tacoma, WA (city) Pierce County	1,082	0.54
Chocolay, MI (charter township) Marquette County	1,070	18.10
Worcester, MA (city) Worcester County	1,066	0.59
West Ishpeming, MI (cdp) Marquette County	1,061	36.94
Mesa, AZ (city) Maricopa County	1,047	0.24
Forsyth, MI (township) Marquette County	1,046	17.70
Eugene, OR (city) Lane County	1,044	0.68
Brooklyn Park, MN (city) Hennepin County	1,008	1.37
Maple Grove, MN (city) Hennepin County	997	1.69
Albuquerque, NM (city) Bernalillo County	985	0.19
Warren, MI (city) Macomb County	969	0.71
Blaine, MN (city) Anoka County	951	1.72
Madison, WI (city) Dane County	947	0.41
Houston, TX (city) Harris County	936	0.05
Laurium, MI (village) Houghton County	923	42.91
Las Vegas, NV (city) Clark County	921	0.16
Ashtabula, OH (city) Ashtabula County	914	4.69
Novi, MI (city) Oakland County	894	1.66
San Jose, CA (city) Santa Clara County	892	0.10
Chassell, MI (township) Houghton County	886	50.69
Gardner, MA (city) Worcester County	886	4.35
Waukegan, IL (city) Lake County	886	0.99
Jacksonville, FL (city) Duval County	886	0.11
Tucson, AZ (city) Pima County	881	0.17
Stanton, MI (township) Houghton County	874	70.77
Fargo, ND (city) Cass County	865	0.84
Columbus, OH (city) Franklin County	858	0.11
Sterling Heights, MI (city) Macomb County	854	0.66
L'Anse, MI (township) Baraga County	849	21.98
Green Bay, WI (city) Brown County	846	0.81
Hermantown, MN (city) St. Louis County	842	9.20
Redding, CA (city) Shasta County	836	0.94
Westland, MI (city) Wayne County	835	0.98
Denver, CO (city) Denver County	828	0.14
Eveleth, MN (city) St. Louis County	827	22.19
Butte-Silver Bow, MT (cons. govt) Silver Bow County	827	2.52

Place	Population	%
Rochester, MN (city) Olmsted County	827	0.79
Baraga, MI (township) Baraga County	810	20.61
Austin, TX (city) Travis County	802	0.10
Allouez, MI (township) Keweenaw County	801	51.35
Ann Arbor, MI (city) Washtenaw County	786	0.68
Rindge, NH (town) Cheshire County	782	13.05
Farmington Hills, MI (city) Oakland County	779	0.97
Washington, DC (city) District of Columbia	778	0.13
Houghton, MI (city) Houghton County	762	10.06
White, MN (township) St. Louis County	760	23.35
Boston, MA (city) Suffolk County	757	0.13
Bellingham, WA (city) Whatcom County	751	0.95
Eagan, MN (city) Dakota County	748	1.16
Royal Oak, MI (city) Oakland County	747	1.29
Ironwood, MI (charter township) Gogebic County	736	33.68
Mountain Iron, MN (city) St. Louis County	721	25.07
Torch Lake, MI (township) Houghton County	719	33.23
Kenosha, WI (city) Kenosha County	719	0.73
St. Louis Park, MN (city) Hennepin County	710	1.59
Beaverton, OR (city) Washington County	707	0.80
Brookhaven, NY (town) Suffolk County	706	0.15
Grand Rapids, MI (city) Kent County	703	0.37
Battle Ground, WA (city) Clark County	701	4.29
Iron Mountain, MI (city) Dickinson County	697	8.95
Queens, NY (borough) Queens County	693	0.03
Osceola, MI (township) Houghton County	692	38.17
Brooklyn, NY (borough) Kings County	692	0.03
Waterford, MI (charter township) Oakland County	690	0.96
Conneaut, OH (city) Ashtabula County	688	5.38
Shelby, MI (charter township) Macomb County	685	0.94
Aurora, CO (city) Arapahoe County	683	0.22
Escanaba, MI (city) Delta County	681	5.35
St. Cloud, MN (city) Stearns County	680	1.04
Ely, MI (township) Marquette County	677	34.90
Troy, MI (city) Oakland County	674	0.83
Gilbert, AZ (town) Maricopa County	669	0.34
Chisholm, MN (city) St. Louis County	668	13.48
Appleton, WI (city) Outagamie County	667	0.92
Burnsville, MN (city) Dakota County	666	1.10
Redford, MI (charter township) Wayne County	665	1.35
Virginia Beach, VA (ind. city) Virginia Beach independent city	654	0.15
Hempstead, NY (town) Nassau County	647	0.09
Edina, MN (city) Hennepin County	642	1.35
Fresno, CA (city) Fresno County	640	0.13
Commerce, MI (charter township) Oakland County	635	1.62
Minnetonka, MN (city) Hennepin County	634	1.28
Westminster, MA (town) Worcester County	631	8.73
St. Cloud, MN (city) Stearns County	626	1.21
Detroit, MI (city) Wayne County	624	0.08
Scottsdale, AZ (city) Maricopa County	622	0.28
Boise City, ID (city) Ada County	620	0.30
Great Falls, MT (city) Cascade County	619	1.07
Sault Ste. Marie, MI (city) Chippewa County	618	4.30
Leominster, MA (city) Worcester County	616	1.50
Nashville-Davidson, TN (metro govt) Davidson County	613	0.10
Woodbury, MN (city) Washington County	612	1.03
Brooklyn Center, MN (city) Hennepin County	605	2.04
Waukesha, WI (city) Waukesha County	603	0.86
San Antonio, TX (city) Medina County	602	0.05
Billings, MT (city) Yellowstone County	599	0.59
Hamburg, MI (township) Livingston County	587	2.71
Andover, MN (city) Anoka County	586	1.95
Clinton, MI (charter township) Macomb County	585	0.60
L'Anse, MI (village) Baraga County	584	24.47
Ely, MN (city) St. Louis County	574	16.31
Madison Heights, MI (city) Oakland County	571	1.91
Dallas, TX (city) Dallas County	571	0.05
Sacramento, CA (city) Sacramento County	567	0.12
Appleton, WI (city) Outagamie County	564	0.94
Ontonagon, MI (township) Ontonagon County	561	21.09
Cokato, MN (city) Wright County	556	20.20
Rochester Hills, MI (city) Oakland County	550	0.78
Rice Lake, MN (township) St. Louis County	548	13.43
Barnstable Town, MA (city) Barnstable County	548	1.20
Canton, MI (charter township) Wayne County	547	0.62

Ancestry

Finnish

Top 150 Places Sorted by Percent of Total Population

Based on all places, regardless of total population

Place	Population	%
Wolf Lake, MN (city) Becker County	34	94.44
Bohemia, MI (township) Ontonagon County	34	82.93
Wolf Lake, MN (township) Becker County	145	76.32
Stanton, MI (township) Houghton County	874	70.77
Hancock, MI (township) Houghton County	341	59.82
Adams, MI (township) Houghton County	1,526	59.17
Cedar Valley, MN (township) St. Louis County	118	57.00
Irvington, IA (cdp) Kossuth County	9	56.25
South Range, MI (village) Houghton County	225	55.28
Covington, MI (township) Baraga County	333	54.95
Humboldt, MI (township) Marquette County	245	54.44
Winton, MN (city) St. Louis County	103	54.21
Green Valley, MN (township) Becker County	203	53.00
Quincy, MI (township) Houghton County	182	52.00
Allouez, MI (township) Keweenaw County	801	51.35
Spruce Grove, MN (township) Becker County	170	51.20
Chassell, MI (township) Houghton County	886	50.69
Laird, MI (township) Houghton County	208	50.61
Effie, MN (city) Itasca County	66	50.38
Salo, MN (township) Aitkin County	37	50.00
Colvin, MN (township) St. Louis County	148	49.83
Richmond, MI (township) Marquette County	444	48.21
Eagle, MN (township) Carlton County	237	47.49
Vermilion Lake, MN (township) St. Louis County	141	47.32
Wakefield, MI (township) Gogebic County	143	47.19
Clark, MN (township) Aitkin County	72	47.06
Prairie Lake, MN (township) St. Louis County	14	46.67
Pike, MN (township) St. Louis County	193	45.31
Republic, MI (township) Marquette County	431	45.04
Interior, MI (township) Ontonagon County	198	45.00
Geyser, MT (cdp) Judith Basin County	8	44.44
Palmer, MI (cdp) Marquette County	244	44.20
Greenland, MI (township) Ontonagon County	307	43.98
Sandy, MN (township) St. Louis County	155	43.91
Republic, MI (cdp) Marquette County	244	43.26
Dollar Bay, MI (cdp) Houghton County	354	43.12
Laurium, MI (village) Houghton County	923	42.91
Calumet, MI (charter township) Houghton County	2,757	42.38
Houghton, MI (township) Keweenaw County	38	42.22
Clinton, MN (township) St. Louis County	531	42.11
Ault, MN (township) St. Louis County	69	42.07
Menahga, MN (city) Wadena County	473	41.78
Stannard, MI (township) Ontonagon County	341	41.28
Lakeview, MN (township) Carlton County	78	40.00
Negaunee, MI (township) Marquette County	1,200	39.95
Elm River, MI (township) Houghton County	57	39.86
Runeberg, MN (township) Becker County	212	39.63
Tilden, MI (township) Marquette County	445	39.31
Franklin, MI (township) Houghton County	542	39.13
Beseman, MN (township) Carlton County	62	38.27
Marengo, WI (town) Ashland County	147	38.18
Osceola, MI (township) Houghton County	692	38.17
Ahmeek, MI (village) Keweenaw County	69	38.12
Newton, MN (township) Otter Tail County	227	37.58
Blueberry, MN (township) Wadena County	284	37.57
Sturgeon, MN (township) St. Louis County	52	37.41
Kettle River, MN (city) Carlton County	73	37.24
Calumet, MI (village) Houghton County	269	37.10
West Ishpeming, MI (cdp) Marquette County	1,061	36.94
Blowers, MN (township) Otter Tail County	118	36.65
Eagle River, MI (cdp) Keweenaw County	24	36.36
Brule, WI (town) Douglas County	161	36.10
McMillan, MI (township) Ontonagon County	178	35.89
Embarrass, MN (township) St. Louis County	221	35.70
Portage, MI (charter township) Houghton County	1,123	35.67
Paddock, MN (township) Otter Tail County	96	35.56
Amasa, MI (cdp) Iron County	119	35.42
Ishpeming, MI (township) Marquette County	1,243	35.40
Halden, MN (township) St. Louis County	57	35.40
Jasper, MN (city) Rock County	31	35.23
Wuori, MN (township) St. Louis County	187	35.15
Copper City, MI (village) Houghton County	71	35.15
Ely, MI (township) Marquette County	677	34.90
Spurr, MI (township) Baraga County	62	34.83
Hematite, MI (township) Iron County	126	34.71
Arrowhead, MN (township) St. Louis County	51	34.46
Turin, MI (township) Marquette County	28	34.15
White River, WI (town) Ashland County	279	34.11
Hancock, MI (city) Houghton County	1,552	33.98
Haight, MI (township) Ontonagon County	71	33.81
Ironwood, MI (charter township) Gogebic County	736	33.68
Van Buren, MN (township) St. Louis County	61	33.52
Floodwood, MN (township) St. Louis County	83	33.47
Ludden, ND (city) Dickey County	13	33.33
Torch Lake, MI (township) Houghton County	719	33.23
Deep River, WA (cdp) Wahkiakum County	59	32.96
Ishpeming, MI (city) Marquette County	2,142	32.95
Duncan, MI (township) Houghton County	75	32.61
Automba, MN (township) Carlton County	50	32.47
Floodwood, MN (city) St. Louis County	157	32.24
Chatham, MI (village) Alger County	77	32.22
Alango, MN (township) St. Louis County	85	32.08
Kimball, WI (town) Iron County	166	31.86
Linden Grove, MN (township) St. Louis County	33	31.73
Seneca, SD (town) Faulk County	17	31.48
Oulu, WI (town) Bayfield County	171	31.09
Fairbanks, MN (township) St. Louis County	18	31.03
Knox, WI (town) Price County	96	30.97
Little Sand Lake, MN (unorganized territory) Itasca County	87	30.74
Rock River, MI (township) Alger County	431	30.72
Champion, MI (township) Marquette County	81	30.68
Maple Ridge, MI (township) Delta County	293	30.58
Vienna, SD (town) Clark County	28	30.43
Sherman, MI (township) Keweenaw County	27	30.34
Cokato, MN (township) Wright County	423	29.75
Ewing, MI (township) Marquette County	33	29.73
Angora, MN (township) St. Louis County	63	29.44
Maple, WI (town) Douglas County	219	29.32
Cromwell, MN (city) Carlton County	34	29.31
Schoolcraft, MI (township) Houghton County	516	29.15
River, MN (township) Red Lake County	41	29.08
Brule, WI (cdp) Douglas County	52	29.05
Negaunee, MI (city) Marquette County	1,313	28.77
Esko, MN (cdp) Carlton County	541	28.76
Oyehut, WA (cdp) Grays Harbor County	16	28.57
Erwin, MI (township) Gogebic County	93	28.18
Rockland, MI (township) Ontonagon County	64	27.95
Eagle Harbor, MI (cdp) Keweenaw County	18	27.69
Camp Crook, SD (town) Harding County	26	27.66
Red Eye, MN (township) Wadena County	113	27.36
Kalevala, MN (township) Carlton County	88	27.33
Lake Linden, MI (village) Houghton County	265	27.24
Michigamme, MI (cdp) Marquette County	78	27.18
Naselle, WA (cdp) Pacific County	188	27.17
Breitung, MN (township) St. Louis County	178	27.13
Fine Lakes, MN (township) St. Louis County	35	27.13
Soudan, MN (cdp) St. Louis County	121	26.83
Rice River, MN (township) Aitkin County	22	26.83
Ashland, WI (town) Ashland County	207	26.78
Tripp, WI (town) Bayfield County	61	26.29
Owens, MN (township) St. Louis County	72	26.09
Bergland, MI (township) Ontonagon County	142	26.06
Limestone, MI (township) Alger County	96	26.02
Hubbell, MI (cdp) Houghton County	326	25.98
Cherry, MN (township) St. Louis County	232	25.95
Max, MN (township) Itasca County	34	25.95
Kingston, MN (city) Meeker County	28	25.93
Wakefield, MI (city) Gogebic County	501	25.56
Fayal, MN (township) St. Louis County	409	25.51
Michigamme, MI (township) Marquette County	89	25.28
Felch, MI (township) Dickinson County	194	25.23
Kinney, MN (city) St. Louis County	33	25.19
North San Juan, CA (cdp) Nevada County	33	25.19
Rosburg, WA (cdp) Wahkiakum County	64	25.10
Mountain Iron, MN (city) St. Louis County	721	25.07
Monomoscoy Island, MA (cdp) Barnstable County	33	24.81
Great Scott, MN (township) St. Louis County	115	24.73
New Ipswich, NH (town) Hillsborough County	1,231	24.70
Lavell, MN (township) St. Louis County	79	24.61
Grant, MI (township) Keweenaw County	30	24.59

Please refer to the Explanation of Data in the front of the book for more detailed information.

Ancestry

Finnish

Top 150 Places Sorted by Percent of Total Population

Based on places with total population of 7,500 or more

Place	Population	%
Virginia, MN (city) St. Louis County	1,733	19.77
Cloquet, MN (city) Carlton County	1,993	16.58
Hibbing, MN (city) St. Louis County	2,018	12.31
Marquette, MI (city) Marquette County	2,593	12.20
Houghton, MI (city) Houghton County	762	10.06
Hermantown, MN (city) St. Louis County	842	9.20
Iron Mountain, MI (city) Dickinson County	697	8.95
Superior, WI (city) Douglas County	1,885	6.93
Templeton, MA (town) Worcester County	508	6.51
Duluth, MN (city) St. Louis County	5,228	6.07
Ashland, WI (city) Ashland County	449	5.42
Conneaut, OH (city) Ashtabula County	688	5.38
Escanaba, MI (city) Delta County	681	5.35
Winchendon, MA (town) Worcester County	488	4.78
Grand Rapids, MN (city) Itasca County	513	4.77
Ashtabula, OH (city) Ashtabula County	914	4.69
Astoria, OR (city) Clatsop County	429	4.49
Gardner, MA (city) Worcester County	886	4.35
Sault Ste. Marie, MI (city) Chippewa County	618	4.30
Battle Ground, WA (city) Clark County	701	4.29
Brighton, MI (city) Livingston County	282	3.76
Rogers, MN (city) Hennepin County	274	3.58
Buffalo, MN (city) Wright County	507	3.43
Longview, WA (city) Cowlitz County	1,211	3.31
Hartland, MI (township) Livingston County	475	3.30
Beach Park, IL (village) Lake County	421	3.16
Lunenburg, MA (town) Worcester County	316	3.16
Maynard, MA (cdp/town) Middlesex County	310	3.09
Sterling, MA (town) Worcester County	235	3.04
Bemidji, MN (city) Beltrami County	395	2.99
Fitchburg, MA (city) Worcester County	1,167	2.90
Oceola, MI (township) Livingston County	327	2.83
Brighton, MI (township) Livingston County	512	2.81
Detroit Lakes, MN (city) Becker County	234	2.76
Hamburg, MI (township) Livingston County	587	2.71
Lantana, FL (town) Palm Beach County	278	2.69
Sauk Rapids, MN (city) Benton County	318	2.55
Butte-Silver Bow, MT (cons. govt) Silver Bow County	827	2.52
Lancaster, MA (town) Worcester County	196	2.52
Marion, MI (township) Livingston County	243	2.51
Big Lake, MN (city) Sherburne County	242	2.51
North Madison, OH (cdp) Lake County	226	2.51
Wixom, MI (city) Oakland County	326	2.42
Menominee, MI (city) Menominee County	210	2.42
Berkley, MI (city) Oakland County	360	2.39
Hales Corners, WI (village) Milwaukee County	182	2.38
Thief River Falls, MN (city) Pennington County	200	2.34
Champlin, MN (city) Hennepin County	528	2.32
Lino Lakes, MN (city) Anoka County	455	2.30
Hoquiam, WA (city) Grays Harbor County	202	2.29
Egelston, MI (township) Muskegon County	226	2.28
Fenton, MI (charter township) Genesee County	335	2.19
Ramsey, MN (city) Anoka County	497	2.17
Weston, WI (village) Marathon County	310	2.16
Grand Chute, WI (town) Outagamie County	440	2.15
Green Oak, MI (township) Livingston County	378	2.15
Hutchinson, MN (city) McLeod County	302	2.13
Athol, MA (town) Worcester County	246	2.13
Alpena, MI (city) Alpena County	226	2.12
Otsego, MN (city) Wright County	264	2.11
Cumberland Hill, RI (cdp) Providence County	163	2.08
Livonia, MI (city) Wayne County	2,019	2.06
Coon Rapids, MN (city) Anoka County	1,264	2.04
Brooklyn Center, MN (city) Hennepin County	605	2.04
Milford, MI (charter township) Oakland County	315	2.02
Traverse City, MI (city) Grand Traverse County	290	1.99
Knik-Fairview, AK (cdp) Matanuska-Susitna Borough	243	1.99
Plymouth, MN (city) Hennepin County	1,357	1.96
White Bear Lake, MN (city) Ramsey County	455	1.96
Traverse City, MI (city) Grand Traverse County	290	1.96
East Renton Highlands, WA (cdp) King County	216	1.96
Mapleton, UT (city) Utah County	148	1.96
Andover, MN (city) Anoka County	586	1.95
White Bear Lake, MN (city) Ramsey County	455	1.94
East Bethel, MN (city) Anoka County	225	1.94
Pembroke, MA (town) Plymouth County	340	1.93
St. Francis, WI (city) Milwaukee County	177	1.93
Grand Haven, MI (city) Ottawa County	204	1.92
Madison Heights, MI (city) Oakland County	571	1.91
South Lyon, MI (city) Oakland County	212	1.91
Robbinsdale, MN (city) Hennepin County	263	1.90
Athol, MA (cdp) Worcester County	152	1.90
Farmington, MI (city) Oakland County	196	1.89
Gloucester, MA (city) Essex County	537	1.86
Kinross, MI (charter township) Chippewa County	149	1.85
Blair, MI (township) Grand Traverse County	147	1.85
Faribault, MN (city) Rice County	421	1.83
Highland, MI (charter township) Oakland County	352	1.83
Flushing, MI (charter township) Genesee County	195	1.82
Rice Lake, WI (city) Barron County	154	1.82
Gladstone, OR (city) Clackamas County	209	1.81
Westwood, MI (cdp) Kalamazoo County	163	1.80
New Brighton, MN (city) Ramsey County	381	1.79
Dryden, NY (town) Tompkins County	254	1.78
Port Angeles, WA (city) Clallam County	338	1.77
Genoa, MI (township) Livingston County	347	1.76
Clay, MI (township) St. Clair County	164	1.75
East Bay, MI (township) Grand Traverse County	184	1.73
Harrison, WI (town) Calumet County	173	1.73
Poulsbo, WA (city) Kitsap County	152	1.73
Blaine, MN (city) Anoka County	951	1.72
Brooklyn, CT (town) Windham County	139	1.72
Ash, MI (township) Monroe County	135	1.72
Anoka, MN (city) Anoka County	298	1.71
Elk River, MN (city) Sherburne County	382	1.70
Milford, NH (cdp) Hillsborough County	154	1.70
Maple Grove, MN (city) Hennepin County	997	1.69
Tumwater, WA (city) Thurston County	282	1.68
Fergus Falls, MN (city) Otter Tail County	224	1.68
Mound, MN (city) Hennepin County	152	1.68
Ashland, OR (city) Jackson County	335	1.67
Lyon, MI (charter township) Oakland County	233	1.67
Novi, MI (city) Oakland County	894	1.66
Plainfield, CT (town) Windham County	255	1.66
Wahpeton, ND (city) Richland County	129	1.64
Milford, NH (town) Hillsborough County	243	1.63
Long Lake, MI (township) Grand Traverse County	140	1.63
Commerce, MI (charter township) Oakland County	635	1.62
White Bear, MN (township) Ramsey County	175	1.61
Greenville, MI (city) Montcalm County	136	1.61
Bloomington, MN (city) Hennepin County	1,324	1.60
St. Louis Park, MN (city) Hennepin County	710	1.59
Millbury, MA (town) Worcester County	210	1.59
Union, MI (charter township) Isabella County	192	1.59
Beverly Hills, MI (village) Oakland County	164	1.59
Crystal, MN (city) Hennepin County	349	1.58
Suamico, WI (village) Brown County	172	1.58
York, MI (charter township) Washtenaw County	135	1.58
St. Michael, MN (city) Wright County	237	1.54
Lake Worth, FL (city) Palm Beach County	542	1.53
Tittabawassee, MI (township) Saginaw County	144	1.53
St. Peter, MN (city) Nicollet County	168	1.52
Vashon, WA (cdp) King County	151	1.52
Painesville, OH (city) Lake County	290	1.51
Hugo, MN (city) Washington County	183	1.51
Rapid Valley, SD (cdp) Pennington County	123	1.51
Leominster, MA (city) Worcester County	616	1.50
Waukesha, WI (town) Waukesha County	136	1.50
Howard, WI (village) Brown County	250	1.49
Wyoming, MN (city) Chisago County	114	1.48
Ypsilanti, MI (city) Washtenaw County	296	1.47
Auburn, MA (town) Worcester County	236	1.46
Rhinelander, WI (city) Oneida County	115	1.46
Los Altos Hills, CA (town) Santa Clara County	113	1.44
Ripon, WI (city) Fond du Lac County	111	1.44
South Milwaukee, WI (city) Milwaukee County	300	1.43
Allendale, MI (cdp) Ottawa County	238	1.43
Woodlyn, PA (cdp) Delaware County	130	1.43
West St. Paul, MN (city) Dakota County	278	1.42
Spring Lake, MI (township) Ottawa County	201	1.42

Please refer to the Explanation of Data in the front of the book for more detailed information.

Ancestry

French, except Basque

U.S. and 50 States Sorted by Population and Percent of Total Population

Place	Population	%	Place	Population	%
United States	**9,326,380**	**3.07**	Maine	232,390	17.50
California	775,213	2.12	New Hampshire	217,353	16.54
Louisiana	668,253	15.08	Vermont	96,627	15.48
Texas	579,204	2.38	Louisiana	668,253	15.08
Massachusetts	544,113	8.40	Rhode Island	131,396	12.44
Michigan	509,548	5.12	Massachusetts	544,113	8.40
New York	505,680	2.63	Connecticut	225,310	6.35
Florida	504,650	2.73	Michigan	509,548	5.12
Ohio	284,589	2.47	North Dakota	27,396	4.15
Illinois	272,074	2.13	Montana	39,850	4.09
Washington	248,969	3.79	Minnesota	214,073	4.08
Pennsylvania	234,946	1.86	Missouri	225,631	3.81
Maine	232,390	17.50	Wisconsin	214,749	3.81
Missouri	225,631	3.81	Washington	248,969	3.79
Connecticut	225,310	6.35	Oregon	138,537	3.68
New Hampshire	217,353	16.54	Alaska	24,258	3.51
Wisconsin	214,749	3.81	Wyoming	18,748	3.44
Minnesota	214,073	4.08	Colorado	164,476	3.37
Arizona	179,366	2.87	Kansas	93,887	3.34
North Carolina	170,948	1.84	Idaho	47,063	3.08
Indiana	167,332	2.61	**United States**	**9,326,380**	**3.07**
Virginia	166,835	2.13	Mississippi	85,806	2.92
Colorado	164,476	3.37	Arizona	179,366	2.87
Georgia	153,685	1.62	South Dakota	22,853	2.86
Oregon	138,537	3.68	Florida	504,650	2.73
Rhode Island	131,396	12.44	Nebraska	49,173	2.73
New Jersey	120,116	1.38	Iowa	81,806	2.71
Tennessee	113,844	1.83	New York	505,680	2.63
Maryland	108,376	1.90	Nevada	69,177	2.63
Vermont	96,627	15.48	Indiana	167,332	2.61
Kansas	93,887	3.34	Ohio	284,589	2.47
Alabama	90,000	1.91	Oklahoma	89,301	2.43
Oklahoma	89,301	2.43	Texas	579,204	2.38
South Carolina	89,148	1.98	Arkansas	66,023	2.30
Mississippi	85,806	2.92	Delaware	19,289	2.19
Iowa	81,806	2.71	Utah	57,011	2.15
Kentucky	79,830	1.86	New Mexico	43,256	2.15
Nevada	69,177	2.63	Illinois	272,074	2.13
Arkansas	66,023	2.30	Virginia	166,835	2.13
Utah	57,011	2.15	California	775,213	2.12
Nebraska	49,173	2.73	South Carolina	89,148	1.98
Idaho	47,063	3.08	Alabama	90,000	1.91
New Mexico	43,256	2.15	Maryland	108,376	1.90
Montana	39,850	4.09	Pennsylvania	234,946	1.86
West Virginia	31,698	1.72	Kentucky	79,830	1.86
North Dakota	27,396	4.15	North Carolina	170,948	1.84
Alaska	24,258	3.51	Tennessee	113,844	1.83
Hawaii	22,963	1.72	West Virginia	31,698	1.72
South Dakota	22,853	2.86	Hawaii	22,963	1.72
Delaware	19,289	2.19	District of Columbia	9,561	1.64
Wyoming	18,748	3.44	Georgia	153,685	1.62
District of Columbia	9,561	1.64	New Jersey	120,116	1.38

Please refer to the Explanation of Data in the front of the book for more detailed information.

Ancestry

French, except Basque

Top 150 Places Sorted by Population

Based on all places, regardless of total population

Place	Population	%
New York, NY (city) Kings County	67,195	0.83
Los Angeles, CA (city) Los Angeles County	46,698	1.24
Houston, TX (city) Harris County	35,661	1.72
Phoenix, AZ (city) Maricopa County	34,228	2.36
San Diego, CA (city) San Diego County	32,028	2.50
Manhattan, NY (borough) New York County	31,783	2.01
Metairie, LA (cdp) Jefferson Parish	30,479	22.43
Lafayette, LA (city) Lafayette Parish	27,086	22.80
Chicago, IL (city) Cook County	25,053	0.93
Manchester, NH (city) Hillsborough County	23,578	21.48
San Antonio, TX (city) Medina County	21,902	1.70
Austin, TX (city) Travis County	21,636	2.83
Portland, OR (city) Multnomah County	20,676	3.65
Baton Rouge, LA (city) East Baton Rouge Parish	20,513	8.95
New Orleans, LA (city) Orleans Parish	19,655	6.66
Seattle, WA (city) King County	18,860	3.17
Jacksonville, FL (city) Duval County	17,794	2.19
San Francisco, CA (city) San Francisco County	17,757	2.25
Worcester, MA (city) Worcester County	17,457	9.70
Dallas, TX (city) Dallas County	17,325	1.46
Indianapolis, IN (city) Marion County	15,735	1.94
Denver, CO (city) Denver County	15,585	2.70
Colorado Springs, CO (city) El Paso County	14,928	3.70
Tucson, AZ (city) Pima County	14,770	2.85
Columbus, OH (city) Franklin County	14,605	1.90
Fall River, MA (city) Bristol County	14,459	16.16
Brooklyn, NY (borough) Kings County	14,137	0.57
San Jose, CA (city) Santa Clara County	14,068	1.52
Boston, MA (city) Suffolk County	13,866	2.30
Las Vegas, NV (city) Clark County	13,806	2.38
Toledo, OH (city) Lucas County	13,787	4.72
Oklahoma City, OK (city) Oklahoma County	12,990	2.30
Minneapolis, MN (city) Hennepin County	12,885	3.39
Woonsocket, RI (city) Providence County	12,573	30.16
Fort Worth, TX (city) Tarrant County	12,534	1.78
Queens, NY (borough) Queens County	12,532	0.57
Louisville-Jefferson County, KY (metro govt) Jefferson County	12,472	2.12
Albuquerque, NM (city) Bernalillo County	12,304	2.32
Mesa, AZ (city) Maricopa County	12,261	2.79
Nashua, NH (city) Hillsborough County	12,233	14.05
Warwick, RI (city) Kent County	12,183	14.56
Chicopee, MA (city) Hampden County	12,103	21.94
Charlotte, NC (city) Mecklenburg County	12,074	1.71
Virginia Beach, VA (ind. city) Virginia Beach independent city	12,038	2.76
Philadelphia, PA (city) Philadelphia County	12,027	0.80
Springfield, MA (city) Hampden County	11,383	7.44
Wichita, KS (city) Sedgwick County	11,359	3.04
Kenner, LA (city) Jefferson Parish	11,139	16.71
Bristol, CT (city/town) Hartford County	11,084	18.33
Omaha, NE (city) Douglas County	11,071	2.72
Nashville-Davidson, TN (metro govt) Davidson County	11,069	1.88
Anchorage, AK (municipality) Anchorage Municipality	10,635	3.74
Kansas City, MO (city) Jackson County	10,371	2.28
Tulsa, OK (city) Tulsa County	10,197	2.63
Milwaukee, WI (city) Milwaukee County	10,118	1.72
Shreveport, LA (city) Caddo Parish	10,074	5.08
St. Paul, MN (city) Ramsey County	10,020	3.55
Fort Wayne, IN (city) Allen County	9,917	3.91
Sacramento, CA (city) Sacramento County	9,645	2.10
Lowell, MA (city) Middlesex County	9,625	9.16
Washington, DC (city) District of Columbia	9,561	1.64
New Bedford, MA (city) Bristol County	9,256	9.75
Pawtucket, RI (city) Providence County	9,245	12.90
Lewiston, ME (city) Androscoggin County	9,130	24.89
Brookhaven, NY (town) Suffolk County	8,961	1.87
Spokane, WA (city) Spokane County	8,862	4.29
St. Louis, MO (city) St. Louis city County	8,663	2.72
Lake Charles, LA (city) Calcasieu Parish	8,608	12.09
St. Petersburg, FL (city) Pinellas County	8,590	3.50
Vancouver, WA (city) Clark County	8,494	5.30
Haverhill, MA (city) Essex County	8,478	14.08
Long Beach, CA (city) Los Angeles County	8,425	1.82
Hempstead, NY (town) Nassau County	8,239	1.09
Scottsdale, AZ (city) Maricopa County	8,225	3.76
Houma, LA (city) Terrebonne Parish	8,023	23.86
Coventry, RI (town) Kent County	7,797	22.25
Fresno, CA (city) Fresno County	7,784	1.61
Cranston, RI (city) Providence County	7,738	9.60
Arlington, TX (city) Tarrant County	7,574	2.11
Henderson, NV (city) Clark County	7,568	3.04
Portland, ME (city) Cumberland County	7,416	11.21
Tampa, FL (city) Hillsborough County	7,410	2.22
Riverside, CA (city) Riverside County	7,394	2.46
Reno, NV (city) Washoe County	7,226	3.27
Warren, MI (city) Macomb County	7,214	5.31
Atlanta, GA (city) Fulton County	7,173	1.73
Marrero, LA (cdp) Jefferson Parish	7,170	21.77
Chandler, AZ (city) Maricopa County	7,166	3.12
Raleigh, NC (city) Wake County	7,025	1.84
Pittsfield, MA (city) Berkshire County	6,960	15.54
Madison, WI (city) Dane County	6,955	3.03
Memphis, TN (city) Shelby County	6,875	1.05
Plano, TX (city) Collin County	6,844	2.67
Enfield, CT (town) Hartford County	6,826	15.24
Huntington Beach, CA (city) Orange County	6,793	3.60
Overland Park, KS (city) Johnson County	6,763	3.97
Lincoln, NE (city) Lancaster County	6,760	2.67
Prairieville, LA (cdp) Ascension Parish	6,754	25.85
Aurora, CO (city) Arapahoe County	6,691	2.13
Boise City, ID (city) Ada County	6,632	3.21
Lexington-Fayette, KY (cons. govt) Fayette County	6,600	2.29
Tacoma, WA (city) Pierce County	6,584	3.31
Providence, RI (city) Providence County	6,529	3.66
Gilbert, AZ (town) Maricopa County	6,475	3.32
Taunton, MA (city) Bristol County	6,431	11.49
Fitchburg, MA (city) Worcester County	6,411	15.94
Concord, NH (city) Merrimack County	6,341	14.76
Cumberland, RI (town) Providence County	6,277	18.85
Leominster, MA (city) Worcester County	6,262	15.30
Syracuse, NY (city) Onondaga County	6,182	4.27
New Iberia, LA (city) Iberia Parish	6,165	19.87
Beaumont, TX (city) Jefferson County	6,139	5.29
Sterling Heights, MI (city) Macomb County	6,116	4.72
Lynn, MA (city) Essex County	6,087	6.79
Attleboro, MA (city) Bristol County	5,966	13.76
Mobile, AL (city) Mobile County	5,957	3.05
Eugene, OR (city) Lane County	5,920	3.86
Glendale, AZ (city) Maricopa County	5,863	2.55
Dracut, MA (town) Middlesex County	5,859	20.23
Green Bay, WI (city) Brown County	5,835	5.61
Corpus Christi, TX (city) Nueces County	5,816	1.94
Colonie, NY (town) Albany County	5,795	7.11
Sulphur, LA (city) Calcasieu Parish	5,782	28.60
Waterbury, CT (city/town) New Haven County	5,775	5.25
Rochester, NH (city) Strafford County	5,720	19.19
Salem, OR (city) Marion County	5,620	3.70
Biddeford, ME (city) York County	5,619	26.15
Sanford, ME (town) York County	5,617	26.70
Anaheim, CA (city) Orange County	5,575	1.67
Modesto, CA (city) Stanislaus County	5,489	2.72
Grand Rapids, MI (city) Kent County	5,485	2.88
Methuen Town, MA (city) Essex County	5,483	11.82
Burlington, VT (city) Chittenden County	5,481	13.07
Baltimore, MD (city) Baltimore city County	5,463	0.88
Lakewood, CO (city) Jefferson County	5,382	3.79
Oakland, CA (city) Alameda County	5,368	1.39
Tempe, AZ (city) Maricopa County	5,367	3.27
Springfield, MO (city) Christian County	5,365	3.38
Garland, TX (city) Dallas County	5,340	2.40
Derry, NH (town) Rockingham County	5,308	15.81
Bakersfield, CA (city) Kern County	5,286	1.59
West Warwick, RI (town) Kent County	5,269	17.95
Santa Clarita, CA (city) Los Angeles County	5,259	3.05
Cincinnati, OH (city) Hamilton County	5,247	1.75
Cape Coral, FL (city) Lee County	5,201	3.47
Norfolk, VA (ind. city) Norfolk independent city	5,155	2.13
Westfield, MA (city) Hampden County	5,147	12.56
Central, LA (city) East Baton Rouge Parish	5,142	19.12
Bangor, ME (city) Penobscot County	5,142	15.63
Slidell, LA (city) St. Tammany Parish	5,129	18.95

Please refer to the Explanation of Data in the front of the book for more detailed information.

Ancestry

French, except Basque

Top 150 Places Sorted by Percent of Total Population

Based on all places, regardless of total population

Place	Population	%
Beluga, AK (cdp) Kenai Peninsula Borough	42	100.00
Ketron Island, WA (cdp) Pierce County	14	100.00
Denio, NV (cdp) Humboldt County	12	100.00
Nottoway Court House, VA (cdp) Nottoway County	5	100.00
Millsfield, NH (township) Coos County	4	100.00
Tenney, MN (city) Wilkin County	4	100.00
Nenzel, NE (village) Cherry County	6	85.71
Raglesville, IN (cdp) Daviess County	44	84.62
Hansboro, ND (city) Towner County	5	83.33
Redstone, CO (cdp) Pitkin County	32	72.73
Frank, WV (cdp) Pocahontas County	141	71.94
Pondsville, MD (cdp) Washington County	109	70.78
Witherbee, NY (cdp) Essex County	175	70.56
Egan, LA (cdp) Acadia Parish	321	70.39
Reddell, LA (cdp) Evangeline Parish	426	69.04
Seconsett Island, MA (cdp) Barnstable County	17	68.00
Cambridge, NH (township) Coos County	6	66.67
Matthews, GA (cdp) Jefferson County	64	65.98
Winterville, ME (plantation) Aroostook County	93	65.96
Oakville, CA (cdp) Napa County	81	65.85
Port Murray, NJ (cdp) Warren County	48	64.86
Wheatland, ND (cdp) Cass County	70	61.95
Warren's, VT (gore) Essex County	16	61.54
Lacassine, LA (cdp) Jefferson Davis Parish	263	60.32
Morse, LA (village) Acadia Parish	417	59.23
Portage Lake, ME (town) Aroostook County	164	58.99
Chazy, NY (cdp) Clinton County	293	57.79
St. Francis, ME (town) Aroostook County	268	57.14
Paradis, LA (cdp) St. Charles Parish	567	56.53
South Fork, MO (cdp) Howell County	138	56.33
Crystal Mountain, MI (cdp) Benzie County	18	56.25
Lake Roberts, NM (cdp) Grant County	14	56.00
Bordelonville, LA (cdp) Avoyelles Parish	637	55.88
Frenchville, ME (town) Aroostook County	582	55.75
Bennett Springs, NV (cdp) Lincoln County	16	55.17
Monhegan, ME (plantation) Lincoln County	22	55.00
Jean Lafitte, LA (town) Jefferson Parish	1,150	54.95
Frye Island, ME (town) Cumberland County	46	54.12
Redford, NY (cdp) Clinton County	255	53.24
Estherwood, LA (village) Acadia Parish	511	51.98
Hessmer, LA (village) Avoyelles Parish	445	51.93
Pierre Part, LA (cdp) Assumption Parish	1,929	51.34
Eagle Lake, ME (cdp) Aroostook County	246	51.14
Redwood, NY (cdp) Jefferson County	158	51.13
Milton, ME (unorganized territory) Oxford County	73	50.69
Mermentau, LA (village) Acadia Parish	351	50.58
Grand Isle, LA (town) Jefferson Parish	299	50.08
Aurora, KS (city) Cloud County	34	50.00
Bancroft, ME (town) Aroostook County	31	50.00
Lowman, ID (cdp) Boise County	3	50.00
Damar, KS (city) Rooks County	146	49.32
Grand Point, LA (cdp) St. James Parish	1,140	49.24
Roanoke, LA (cdp) Jefferson Davis Parish	294	49.00
Ball Club, MN (cdp) Itasca County	105	48.84
Beulah, WY (cdp) Crook County	85	48.57
Onstad, MN (township) Polk County	16	48.48
Hackberry, LA (cdp) Cameron Parish	578	48.25
Fort Kent, ME (town) Aroostook County	1,969	47.66
Black Springs, AR (town) Montgomery County	85	47.49
Wallagrass, ME (town) Aroostook County	333	47.37
Eagle Lake, ME (town) Aroostook County	334	47.31
Cecilia, LA (cdp) St. Martin Parish	1,006	47.08
Lake No. 1, MN (unorganized territory) Lake County	39	46.99
Bantry, ND (city) McHenry County	7	46.67
Iota, LA (town) Acadia Parish	626	46.65
The Forks, ME (plantation) Somerset County	13	46.43
Hester, LA (cdp) St. James Parish	190	46.23
Renfrow, OK (town) Grant County	6	46.15
Sarles, ND (city) Cavalier County	6	46.15
Errol, NH (town) Coos County	124	46.10
Miranda, CA (cdp) Humboldt County	155	45.99
St. John, ME (plantation) Aroostook County	124	45.93
Aguilares, TX (cdp) Webb County	5	45.45
Plaucheville, LA (village) Avoyelles Parish	129	45.26
Browns Creek, MN (township) Red Lake County	19	45.24
Buras, LA (cdp) Plaquemines Parish	285	45.17
Turkey Creek, LA (village) Evangeline Parish	150	44.91
Dummer, NH (town) Coos County	175	44.53
Butler, SD (town) Day County	8	44.44
Piney, OK (cdp) Adair County	33	44.00
Wentworth, NH (location) Coos County	11	44.00
Mamou, LA (town) Evangeline Parish	1,451	43.77
Russia, MN (township) Polk County	21	43.75
Drummond, ID (city) Fremont County	14	43.75
Magnet, NE (village) Cedar County	7	43.75
River Bend, MO (village) Jackson County	7	43.75
Bourg, LA (cdp) Terrebonne Parish	1,020	43.65
Cyr, ME (plantation) Aroostook County	42	43.30
Free Union, VA (cdp) Albemarle County	160	42.90
St. Agatha, ME (town) Aroostook County	356	42.74
Albion, CA (cdp) Mendocino County	94	41.96
Cankton, LA (village) St. Landry Parish	230	41.89
Square Lake, ME (unorganized territory) Aroostook County	285	41.79
Saranac, NY (town) Clinton County	1,685	41.73
Fort Kent, ME (cdp) Aroostook County	1,215	41.64
Blandville, KY (city) Ballard County	89	41.59
Ashland, ME (cdp) Aroostook County	364	41.51
Wyoming, RI (cdp) Washington County	70	41.42
Maple Grove, MI (cdp) Benzie County	43	41.35
Stratford, NH (town) Coos County	390	41.14
Venice, LA (cdp) Plaquemines Parish	39	41.05
Bayou Gauche, LA (cdp) St. Charles Parish	1,050	41.03
Cliffdell, WA (cdp) Yakima County	11	40.74
Broaddus, TX (town) San Augustine County	96	40.68
Reeves, LA (village) Allen Parish	80	40.61
Mendes, GA (cdp) Tattnall County	15	40.54
Wasola, MO (cdp) Ozark County	76	40.43
Fontanelle, NE (cdp) Washington County	21	40.38
Cameron, LA (cdp) Cameron Parish	216	40.22
Wanger, MN (township) Marshall County	10	40.00
Kingsbury, ME (plantation) Piscataquis County	4	40.00
Duson, LA (town) Lafayette Parish	618	39.85
Elk Creek, CA (cdp) Glenn County	47	39.83
Bellmont, NY (town) Franklin County	720	39.80
Paulina, LA (cdp) St. James Parish	471	39.61
Valley Ford, CA (cdp) Sonoma County	34	39.53
Ashland, ME (town) Aroostook County	577	39.47
Tasley, VA (cdp) Accomack County	45	39.47
Gentilly, MN (township) Polk County	137	39.26
Harborton, VA (cdp) Accomack County	34	39.08
Center Point, LA (cdp) Avoyelles Parish	196	39.04
Alton, ME (town) Penobscot County	312	39.00
Helvetia, WV (cdp) Randolph County	14	38.89
Mooers, NY (cdp) Clinton County	218	38.86
Gueydan, LA (town) Vermilion Parish	586	38.76
Caswell, ME (town) Aroostook County	131	38.53
Maplewood Park, OH (cdp) Trumbull County	112	38.49
Evergreen, LA (town) Avoyelles Parish	127	38.25
Russia, OH (village) Shelby County	243	38.15
Barstow, WA (cdp) Ferry County	8	38.10
Shell Valley, ND (cdp) Rolette County	472	37.94
Three Mile Bay, NY (cdp) Jefferson County	80	37.91
Hart's Location, NH (town) Carroll County	14	37.84
Lorenzo, NE (cdp) Cheyenne County	14	37.84
Byersville, NY (cdp) Livingston County	23	37.70
Milton, LA (cdp) Lafayette Parish	999	37.58
Brusly, LA (town) West Baton Rouge Parish	930	37.53
West Stewartstown, NH (cdp) Coos County	158	37.53
Centennial, WY (cdp) Albany County	138	37.50
Pine Prairie, LA (village) Evangeline Parish	603	37.43
Mattawamkeag, ME (town) Penobscot County	404	37.41
North Grosvenor Dale, CT (cdp) Windham County	660	37.27
Clarksville, NH (town) Coos County	124	37.13
Norfolk, NY (cdp) St. Lawrence County	461	37.12
Wauregan, CT (cdp) Windham County	335	37.10
Bangor, NY (town) Franklin County	951	36.75
Bennington, NH (cdp) Hillsborough County	87	36.71
Sorrento, LA (town) Ascension Parish	496	36.55
Stewartstown, NH (town) Coos County	403	36.54
Fenwick, WV (cdp) Nicholas County	42	36.52

Please refer to the Explanation of Data in the front of the book for more detailed information.

Ancestry

French, except Basque

Top 150 Places Sorted by Percent of Total Population

Based on places with total population of 7,500 or more

Place	Population	%
Westwego, LA (city) Jefferson Parish	3,186	36.12
Waterboro, ME (town) York County	2,469	32.91
Skowhegan, ME (town) Somerset County	2,837	32.68
North Smithfield, RI (town) Providence County	3,838	32.61
Eunice, LA (city) St. Landry Parish	3,336	32.23
Burrillville, RI (town) Providence County	5,117	32.04
Caribou, ME (city) Aroostook County	2,579	31.32
Broussard, LA (city) Lafayette Parish	2,400	30.92
Harahan, LA (city) Jefferson Parish	2,848	30.71
Galliano, LA (cdp) Lafourche Parish	2,419	30.54
Ware, MA (town) Hampshire County	3,010	30.53
Thompson, CT (town) Windham County	2,872	30.44
Woonsocket, RI (city) Providence County	12,573	30.16
Spencer, MA (town) Worcester County	3,456	29.48
Bayou Blue, LA (cdp) Lafourche Parish	3,237	28.94
Webster, MA (cdp) Worcester County	3,296	28.93
Oxford, MA (town) Worcester County	3,917	28.61
Sulphur, LA (city) Calcasieu Parish	5,782	28.60
Adams, MA (town) Berkshire County	2,410	28.30
Sanford, ME (cdp) York County	2,990	28.22
Claremont, NH (city) Sullivan County	3,784	28.09
Berlin, NH (city) Coos County	2,840	27.82
Winslow, ME (cdp/town) Kennebec County	2,176	27.82
Killingly, CT (town) Windham County	4,805	27.70
Webster, MA (town) Worcester County	4,615	27.56
Destrehan, LA (cdp) St. Charles Parish	3,147	27.56
Rayne, LA (city) Acadia Parish	2,205	27.40
Scott, LA (city) Lafayette Parish	2,258	26.78
Sanford, ME (town) York County	5,617	26.70
Plattsburgh, NY (town) Clinton County	3,119	26.33
Biddeford, ME (city) York County	5,619	26.15
Plainfield, CT (town) Windham County	4,019	26.12
Crowley, LA (city) Acadia Parish	3,483	25.95
Prairieville, LA (cdp) Ascension Parish	6,754	25.85
Blackstone, MA (town) Worcester County	2,311	25.67
Saco, ME (city) York County	4,676	25.42
Luling, LA (cdp) St. Charles Parish	3,245	25.30
Lewiston, ME (city) Androscoggin County	9,130	24.89
River Ridge, LA (cdp) Jefferson Parish	3,331	24.84
Old Town, ME (city) Penobscot County	1,959	24.84
North Adams, MA (city) Berkshire County	3,416	24.66
Winchendon, MA (town) Worcester County	2,514	24.62
Glocester, RI (town) Providence County	2,407	24.55
Templeton, MA (town) Worcester County	1,912	24.51
Ville Platte, LA (city) Evangeline Parish	1,871	24.40
Estelle, LA (cdp) Jefferson Parish	4,088	24.14
Bayou Cane, LA (cdp) Terrebonne Parish	4,742	23.87
Houma, LA (city) Terrebonne Parish	8,023	23.86
Massena, NY (town) St. Lawrence County	3,068	23.82
Massena, NY (village) St. Lawrence County	2,657	23.58
Orange, MA (town) Franklin County	1,813	23.26
Augusta, ME (city) Kennebec County	4,441	23.19
Franklin, NH (city) Merrimack County	1,982	23.09
Douglas, MA (town) Worcester County	1,899	23.05
Raymond, NH (town) Rockingham County	2,318	22.86
Lafayette, LA (city) Lafayette Parish	27,086	22.80
Thibodaux, LA (city) Lafourche Parish	3,267	22.51
Metairie, LA (cdp) Jefferson Parish	30,479	22.43
Barre, VT (city) Washington County	2,042	22.41
Brooklyn, CT (town) Windham County	1,806	22.32
Coventry, RI (town) Kent County	7,797	22.25
Leicester, MA (town) Worcester County	2,420	22.18
Charlton, MA (town) Worcester County	2,814	22.14
Timberlane, LA (cdp) Jefferson Parish	2,132	22.11
Buxton, ME (town) York County	1,767	22.04
Chicopee, MA (city) Hampden County	12,103	21.94
Southbridge Town, MA (city) Worcester County	3,697	21.94
Palmer Town, MA (city) Hampden County	2,673	21.92
Dudley, MA (town) Worcester County	2,447	21.90
Marrero, LA (cdp) Jefferson Parish	7,170	21.77
Millbury, MA (town) Worcester County	2,878	21.77
Weare, NH (town) Hillsborough County	1,882	21.73
Belle Chasse, LA (cdp) Plaquemines Parish	3,227	21.63
Montague, MA (town) Franklin County	1,822	21.55
Manchester, NH (city) Hillsborough County	23,578	21.48
Monson, MA (town) Hampden County	1,832	21.47
Groves, TX (city) Jefferson County	3,431	21.46
Swansea, MA (town) Bristol County	3,407	21.43
Jennings, LA (city) Jefferson Davis Parish	2,241	21.42
Jefferson, LA (cdp) Jefferson Parish	2,573	21.36
Sturbridge, MA (town) Worcester County	1,924	21.29
Presque Isle, ME (city) Aroostook County	2,056	21.26
Old Orchard Beach, ME (cdp/town) York County	1,862	21.26
Woodstock, CT (town) Windham County	1,672	21.19
Athol, MA (cdp) Worcester County	1,696	21.15
Cumberland Hill, RI (cdp) Providence County	1,636	20.92
Plattsburgh, NY (city) Clinton County	4,160	20.83
Putnam, CT (cdp) Windham County	1,553	20.69
Newmarket, NH (town) Rockingham County	1,827	20.64
Gardner, MA (city) Worcester County	4,170	20.46
Athol, MA (town) Worcester County	2,357	20.39
Goffstown, NH (town) Hillsborough County	3,594	20.38
Oak Hills Place, LA (cdp) East Baton Rouge Parish	1,629	20.38
Somerset, MA (cdp/town) Bristol County	3,687	20.27
Dracut, MA (town) Middlesex County	5,859	20.23
Rutland, MA (town) Worcester County	1,553	20.17
Barrington, NH (town) Strafford County	1,702	20.13
Laconia, NH (city) Belknap County	3,261	20.11
Lunenburg, MA (town) Worcester County	1,995	19.98
New Iberia, LA (city) Iberia Parish	6,165	19.87
Pelham, NH (town) Hillsborough County	2,502	19.84
Hopkinton, RI (town) Washington County	1,606	19.66
Valley Falls, RI (cdp) Providence County	2,261	19.63
Sutton, MA (town) Worcester County	1,741	19.63
Lacombe, LA (cdp) St. Tammany Parish	1,522	19.61
Kingsbury, NY (town) Washington County	2,431	19.56
Putnam, CT (town) Windham County	1,860	19.45
Gray, ME (town) Cumberland County	1,480	19.40
Shenandoah, LA (cdp) East Baton Rouge Parish	3,535	19.32
Escanaba, MI (city) Delta County	2,458	19.30
Rochester, NH (city) Strafford County	5,720	19.19
Colchester, VT (town) Chittenden County	3,275	19.19
Griswold, CT (town) New London County	2,259	19.19
Auburn, MA (town) Worcester County	3,103	19.17
Auburn, ME (city) Androscoggin County	4,460	19.16
Bridge City, LA (cdp) Jefferson Parish	1,749	19.14
Central, LA (city) East Baton Rouge Parish	5,142	19.12
Covington, LA (city) St. Tammany Parish	1,700	19.01
Moss Bluff, LA (cdp) Calcasieu Parish	2,220	19.00
Slidell, LA (city) St. Tammany Parish	5,129	18.95
Uxbridge, MA (town) Worcester County	2,478	18.94
Port Neches, TX (city) Jefferson County	2,452	18.91
Barre, VT (town) Washington County	1,486	18.86
Cumberland, RI (town) Providence County	6,277	18.85
Cohoes, NY (city) Albany County	3,016	18.71
Belchertown, MA (town) Hampshire County	2,670	18.60
Merrimack, NH (town) Hillsborough County	4,752	18.58
Waterford, NY (town) Saratoga County	1,574	18.57
Abbeville, LA (city) Vermilion Parish	2,269	18.56
South Hadley, MA (town) Hampshire County	3,237	18.50
Rutland, VT (city) Rutland County	3,096	18.50
Richmond, RI (town) Washington County	1,413	18.42
Ludlow, MA (town) Hampden County	3,889	18.38
Bristol, CT (city/town) Hartford County	11,084	18.33
Tiverton, RI (town) Newport County	2,873	18.33
Easthampton Town, MA (city) Hampshire County	2,919	18.18
Chalmette, LA (cdp) St. Bernard Parish	2,264	18.18
Westport, MA (town) Bristol County	2,757	18.02
Waterville, ME (city) Kennebec County	2,836	17.98
Somersworth, NH (city) Strafford County	2,125	17.97
West Warwick, RI (town) Kent County	5,269	17.95
Ogdensburg, NY (city) St. Lawrence County	2,035	17.90
Acushnet, MA (town) Bristol County	1,842	17.90
Standish, ME (town) Cumberland County	1,745	17.78
Plaistow, NH (town) Rockingham County	1,369	17.77
Hudson, NH (town) Hillsborough County	4,314	17.74
Gonzales, LA (city) Ascension Parish	1,695	17.66
Fairhaven, MA (town) Bristol County	2,810	17.64
Coventry, CT (town) Tolland County	2,178	17.63
Southwood Acres, CT (cdp) Hartford County	1,386	17.61

SECTION THREE

Please refer to the Explanation of Data in the front of the book for more detailed information.

Ancestry

French Canadian

U.S. and 50 States Sorted by Population and Percent of Total Population

Place	Population	%
United States	**2,138,601**	**0.70**
Massachusetts	268,348	4.14
Michigan	177,875	1.79
New York	134,420	0.70
Florida	119,700	0.65
California	117,231	0.32
New Hampshire	113,567	8.64
Louisiana	112,549	2.54
Connecticut	104,750	2.95
Maine	100,089	7.54
Texas	73,747	0.30
Wisconsin	61,687	1.09
Washington	54,989	0.84
Minnesota	54,739	1.04
Rhode Island	52,379	4.96
Vermont	51,659	8.28
Illinois	37,197	0.29
Arizona	34,483	0.55
North Carolina	32,892	0.35
Ohio	32,522	0.28
Virginia	32,231	0.41
Pennsylvania	30,828	0.24
Colorado	29,127	0.60
Oregon	27,843	0.74
Georgia	24,648	0.26
New Jersey	24,006	0.28
Maryland	20,545	0.36
Indiana	17,621	0.27
Tennessee	15,974	0.26
Missouri	15,717	0.27
South Carolina	15,434	0.34
Nevada	12,651	0.48
North Dakota	12,068	1.83
Alabama	10,509	0.22
Kansas	10,270	0.37
Iowa	10,232	0.34
Montana	9,681	0.99
Oklahoma	9,274	0.25
Idaho	8,675	0.57
Kentucky	8,390	0.20
Alaska	7,044	1.02
Mississippi	6,902	0.23
Utah	6,485	0.24
Arkansas	6,437	0.22
New Mexico	6,320	0.31
Nebraska	5,985	0.33
South Dakota	4,471	0.56
Delaware	3,283	0.37
West Virginia	3,272	0.18
Hawaii	3,205	0.24
Wyoming	2,734	0.50
District of Columbia	1,916	0.33

Place	Population	%
New Hampshire	113,567	8.64
Vermont	51,659	8.28
Maine	100,089	7.54
Rhode Island	52,379	4.96
Massachusetts	268,348	4.14
Connecticut	104,750	2.95
Louisiana	112,549	2.54
North Dakota	12,068	1.83
Michigan	177,875	1.79
Wisconsin	61,687	1.09
Minnesota	54,739	1.04
Alaska	7,044	1.02
Montana	9,681	0.99
Washington	54,989	0.84
Oregon	27,843	0.74
United States	**2,138,601**	**0.70**
New York	134,420	0.70
Florida	119,700	0.65
Colorado	29,127	0.60
Idaho	8,675	0.57
South Dakota	4,471	0.56
Arizona	34,483	0.55
Wyoming	2,734	0.50
Nevada	12,651	0.48
Virginia	32,231	0.41
Kansas	10,270	0.37
Delaware	3,283	0.37
Maryland	20,545	0.36
North Carolina	32,892	0.35
South Carolina	15,434	0.34
Iowa	10,232	0.34
Nebraska	5,985	0.33
District of Columbia	1,916	0.33
California	117,231	0.32
New Mexico	6,320	0.31
Texas	73,747	0.30
Illinois	37,197	0.29
Ohio	32,522	0.28
New Jersey	24,006	0.28
Indiana	17,621	0.27
Missouri	15,717	0.27
Georgia	24,648	0.26
Tennessee	15,974	0.26
Oklahoma	9,274	0.25
Pennsylvania	30,828	0.24
Utah	6,485	0.24
Hawaii	3,205	0.24
Mississippi	6,902	0.23
Alabama	10,509	0.22
Arkansas	6,437	0.22
Kentucky	8,390	0.20
West Virginia	3,272	0.18

Please refer to the Explanation of Data in the front of the book for more detailed information.

Ancestry

French Canadian

Top 150 Places Sorted by Population

Based on all places, regardless of total population

Place	Population	%
Manchester, NH (city) Hillsborough County	12,622	11.50
New York, NY (city) Kings County	11,393	0.14
Lewiston, ME (city) Androscoggin County	8,580	23.39
Nashua, NH (city) Hillsborough County	8,465	9.73
Boston, MA (city) Suffolk County	7,407	1.23
Los Angeles, CA (city) Los Angeles County	6,978	0.18
Woonsocket, RI (city) Providence County	6,905	16.57
Phoenix, AZ (city) Maricopa County	6,161	0.42
Lowell, MA (city) Middlesex County	5,733	5.46
Chicopee, MA (city) Hampden County	5,392	9.77
Worcester, MA (city) Worcester County	5,259	2.92
Manhattan, NY (borough) New York County	5,246	0.33
San Diego, CA (city) San Diego County	5,134	0.40
Lafayette, LA (city) Lafayette Parish	4,911	4.13
Seattle, WA (city) King County	4,894	0.82
Chicago, IL (city) Cook County	4,592	0.17
Fall River, MA (city) Bristol County	4,538	5.07
Houston, TX (city) Harris County	4,357	0.21
Auburn, ME (city) Androscoggin County	4,350	18.69
Fitchburg, MA (city) Worcester County	4,262	10.60
Leominster, MA (city) Worcester County	4,102	10.02
Biddeford, ME (city) York County	4,022	18.72
Haverhill, MA (city) Essex County	3,997	6.64
Jacksonville, FL (city) Duval County	3,992	0.49
Springfield, MA (city) Hampden County	3,965	2.59
Concord, NH (city) Merrimack County	3,950	9.19
Bristol, CT (city/town) Hartford County	3,692	6.11
Portland, OR (city) Multnomah County	3,683	0.65
New Bedford, MA (city) Bristol County	3,628	3.82
Dracut, MA (town) Middlesex County	3,531	12.19
Cumberland, RI (town) Providence County	3,447	10.35
Pawtucket, RI (city) Providence County	3,308	4.62
Colorado Springs, CO (city) El Paso County	3,287	0.81
Virginia Beach, VA (ind. city) Virginia Beach independent city	3,266	0.75
Burlington, VT (city) Chittenden County	3,131	7.47
Attleboro, MA (city) Bristol County	3,102	7.15
Methuen Town, MA (city) Essex County	3,038	6.55
Green Bay, WI (city) Brown County	3,037	2.92
Austin, TX (city) Travis County	2,998	0.39
Mesa, AZ (city) Maricopa County	2,994	0.68
Brooklyn, NY (borough) Kings County	2,974	0.12
Enfield, CT (town) Hartford County	2,971	6.63
Livonia, MI (city) Wayne County	2,931	2.99
Portland, ME (city) Cumberland County	2,906	4.39
Warren, MI (city) Macomb County	2,892	2.13
Anchorage, AK (municipality) Anchorage Municipality	2,807	0.99
Lake Charles, LA (city) Calcasieu Parish	2,800	3.93
Berlin, NH (city) Coos County	2,776	27.19
Warwick, RI (city) Kent County	2,751	3.29
Hudson, NH (town) Hillsborough County	2,735	11.24
San Francisco, CA (city) San Francisco County	2,726	0.35
Burrillville, RI (town) Providence County	2,716	17.01
Minneapolis, MN (city) Hennepin County	2,697	0.71
Providence, RI (city) Providence County	2,675	1.50
San Antonio, TX (city) Medina County	2,643	0.20
Dover, NH (city) Strafford County	2,633	8.87
Milwaukee, WI (city) Milwaukee County	2,607	0.44
Salem, MA (city) Essex County	2,603	6.35
St. Paul, MN (city) Ramsey County	2,602	0.92
Spokane, WA (city) Spokane County	2,559	1.24
Killingly, CT (town) Windham County	2,541	14.65
Tucson, AZ (city) Pima County	2,501	0.48
Salem, NH (town) Rockingham County	2,500	8.65
Charlotte, NC (city) Mecklenburg County	2,489	0.35
Rochester, NH (city) Strafford County	2,488	8.35
Lincoln, RI (town) Providence County	2,483	11.76
Brookhaven, NY (town) Suffolk County	2,478	0.52
Gardner, MA (city) Worcester County	2,477	12.15
Sanford, ME (town) York County	2,475	11.77
Baton Rouge, LA (city) East Baton Rouge Parish	2,470	1.08
Agawam Town, MA (city) Hampden County	2,448	8.62
Coventry, RI (town) Kent County	2,444	6.97
Albuquerque, NM (city) Bernalillo County	2,420	0.46
Goffstown, NH (town) Hillsborough County	2,402	13.62
Derry, NH (town) Rockingham County	2,399	7.15
Brockton, MA (city) Plymouth County	2,396	2.55
Plainfield, CT (town) Windham County	2,392	15.55
Taunton, MA (city) Bristol County	2,377	4.25
Saco, ME (city) York County	2,361	12.83
Pittsfield, MA (city) Berkshire County	2,303	5.14
Cranston, RI (city) Providence County	2,296	2.85
Denver, CO (city) Denver County	2,280	0.39
Peabody, MA (city) Essex County	2,268	4.50
Houma, LA (city) Terrebonne Parish	2,267	6.74
Merrimack, NH (town) Hillsborough County	2,260	8.84
North Attleborough, MA (town) Bristol County	2,258	7.93
Quincy, MA (city) Norfolk County	2,249	2.48
Lynn, MA (city) Essex County	2,232	2.49
Waltham, MA (city) Middlesex County	2,192	3.67
Hooksett, NH (town) Merrimack County	2,174	16.31
Manchester, CT (town) Hartford County	2,168	3.76
Westfield, MA (city) Hampden County	2,134	5.21
Chelmsford, MA (town) Middlesex County	2,133	6.39
Las Vegas, NV (city) Clark County	2,086	0.36
Plymouth, MA (town) Plymouth County	2,035	3.66
Bangor, ME (city) Penobscot County	2,026	6.16
Toledo, OH (city) Lucas County	2,025	0.69
Keene, NH (city) Cheshire County	2,022	8.59
Queens, NY (borough) Queens County	2,020	0.09
Southbridge Town, MA (city) Worcester County	2,005	11.90
North Smithfield, RI (town) Providence County	1,990	16.91
Augusta, ME (city) Kennebec County	1,986	10.37
Sterling Heights, MI (city) Macomb County	1,986	1.53
Framingham, MA (cdp/town) Middlesex County	1,985	2.95
Colchester, VT (town) Chittenden County	1,974	11.57
Southington, CT (town) Hartford County	1,953	4.60
Bedford, NH (town) Hillsborough County	1,947	9.36
Essex, VT (town) Chittenden County	1,944	10.00
Billerica, MA (town) Middlesex County	1,941	4.90
Londonderry, NH (town) Rockingham County	1,916	7.92
Washington, DC (city) District of Columbia	1,916	0.33
Derry, NH (cdp) Rockingham County	1,905	8.32
Marlborough, MA (city) Middlesex County	1,899	5.04
South Burlington, VT (city) Chittenden County	1,896	10.92
Norwich, CT (city/town) New London County	1,892	4.75
Columbus, OH (city) Franklin County	1,886	0.24
Windham, CT (town) Windham County	1,873	7.48
Lawrence, MA (city) Essex County	1,858	2.47
West Springfield Town, MA (city) Hampden County	1,848	6.53
Smithfield, RI (town) Providence County	1,836	8.55
Taylor, MI (city) Wayne County	1,822	2.85
Clinton, MI (charter township) Macomb County	1,822	1.87
Beverly, MA (city) Essex County	1,808	4.59
Somerville, MA (city) Middlesex County	1,800	2.39
Waterbury, CT (city/town) New Haven County	1,796	1.63
Northbridge, MA (town) Worcester County	1,787	11.69
Syracuse, NY (city) Onondaga County	1,782	1.23
Pelham, NH (town) Hillsborough County	1,779	14.10
Hempstead, NY (town) Nassau County	1,779	0.24
Dearborn, MI (city) Wayne County	1,773	1.80
New Orleans, LA (city) Orleans Parish	1,755	0.59
Easthampton Town, MA (city) Hampshire County	1,748	10.89
San Jose, CA (city) Santa Clara County	1,741	0.19
Dallas, TX (city) Dallas County	1,729	0.15
Dartmouth, MA (town) Bristol County	1,696	5.06
Cambridge, MA (city) Middlesex County	1,695	1.64
Brunswick, ME (town) Cumberland County	1,693	8.24
Shrewsbury, MA (town) Worcester County	1,685	4.81
Meriden, CT (city/town) New Haven County	1,681	2.78
Henderson, NV (city) Clark County	1,654	0.66
St. Petersburg, FL (city) Pinellas County	1,651	0.67
Philadelphia, PA (city) Philadelphia County	1,636	0.11
Sabattus, ME (town) Androscoggin County	1,630	33.58
Milford, NH (town) Hillsborough County	1,613	10.82
Tewksbury, MA (town) Middlesex County	1,611	5.63
East Providence, RI (city) Providence County	1,611	3.39
Medford, MA (city) Middlesex County	1,608	2.90
St. Clair Shores, MI (city) Macomb County	1,601	2.63
Putnam, CT (town) Windham County	1,599	16.72
Colonie, NY (town) Albany County	1,591	1.95

SECTION THREE

Please refer to the Explanation of Data in the front of the book for more detailed information.

Ancestry

French Canadian

Top 150 Places Sorted by Percent of Total Population

Based on all places, regardless of total population

Place	Population	%
Green Acres, ND (cdp) Rolette County	14	100.00
Funkley, MN (city) Beltrami County	3	100.00
Somerset, VT (town) Windham County	3	100.00
East Dunseith, ND (cdp) Rolette County	301	62.32
St. John, ND (city) Rolette County	239	54.32
Belcourt, ND (cdp) Rolette County	836	53.66
Shell Valley, ND (cdp) Rolette County	659	52.97
North Franklin, ME (unorganized territory) Franklin County	45	51.72
Troy, VT (cdp) Orleans County	165	46.74
Dunseith, ND (city) Rolette County	322	45.54
Irasburg, VT (cdp) Orleans County	101	45.50
Melvin Village, NH (cdp) Carroll County	125	43.71
Phillipsville, CA (cdp) Humboldt County	32	41.56
Kertsonville, MN (township) Polk County	26	38.24
Oyens, IA (city) Plymouth County	21	38.18
Elliott, ND (city) Ransom County	6	37.50
Princeton, MN (city) Sherburne County	12	34.29
New Canada, ME (town) Aroostook County	89	33.84
Arnaudville, LA (town) St. Landry Parish	404	33.67
Sabattus, ME (town) Androscoggin County	1,630	33.58
Rolette, ND (city) Rolette County	186	33.57
Madawaska, ME (cdp) Aroostook County	1,153	33.40
Madawaska, ME (town) Aroostook County	1,361	32.87
Palmetto, LA (village) St. Landry Parish	75	32.75
Jordan Hill, LA (cdp) Winn Parish	167	32.68
Troy, VT (town) Orleans County	580	31.68
Readsboro, VT (cdp) Bennington County	104	31.52
Ihlen, MN (city) Pipestone County	16	31.37
North Troy, VT (village) Orleans County	233	30.82
Kingsbury, ME (plantation) Piscataquis County	3	30.00
Divide, CO (cdp) Teller County	25	29.41
Ventress, LA (cdp) Pointe Coupee Parish	305	29.30
Lowell, VT (cdp) Orleans County	71	27.73
Grand Isle, ME (town) Aroostook County	146	27.44
Egeland, ND (city) Towner County	3	27.27
Berlin, NH (city) Coos County	2,776	27.19
Wellington, ME (town) Piscataquis County	70	27.03
Brunswick, VT (town) Essex County	32	26.67
Gorham, NH (cdp) Coos County	399	26.55
Gorham, NH (town) Coos County	751	26.00
Derby Line, VT (village) Orleans County	261	26.00
Wales, ME (town) Androscoggin County	470	25.87
Leeds, ME (town) Androscoggin County	532	25.78
Irasburg, VT (town) Orleans County	305	25.61
Bartlett, NH (cdp) Carroll County	90	24.86
St. Agatha, ME (town) Aroostook County	200	24.01
Rodeo, NM (cdp) Hidalgo County	17	23.61
Pinardville, NH (cdp) Hillsborough County	887	23.58
Deerfield, MA (cdp) Franklin County	44	23.53
Lewiston, ME (city) Androscoggin County	8,580	23.39
Northwest Aitkin, MN (unorganized territory) Aitkin County	82	23.36
Charleston, VT (town) Orleans County	198	23.35
Rolla, ND (city) Rolette County	280	23.22
Eddyville, IL (village) Pope County	20	22.99
Derby Center, VT (village) Orleans County	177	22.87
Kendrick, OK (town) Lincoln County	44	22.80
Livermore Falls, ME (cdp) Androscoggin County	408	22.78
Newport, VT (city) Orleans County	1,057	22.48
Dorset, VT (cdp) Bennington County	70	22.44
Orleans, VT (village) Orleans County	188	22.43
Mooers, NY (cdp) Clinton County	124	22.10
Kratka, MN (township) Pennington County	51	22.08
Jay, VT (town) Orleans County	101	22.00
Minot, ME (town) Androscoggin County	559	21.82
Fort Kent, ME (cdp) Aroostook County	626	21.45
Choctaw, LA (cdp) Lafourche Parish	238	21.38
Cut Off, LA (cdp) Lafourche Parish	1,080	21.12
Minocqua, WI (cdp) Oneida County	102	21.07
Turner, ME (town) Androscoggin County	1,185	20.98
Newport, VT (town) Orleans County	314	20.86
Brownington, VT (town) Orleans County	176	20.85
Arizona Village, AZ (cdp) Mohave County	224	20.68
Dot Lake Village, AK (cdp) Southeast Fairbanks Census Area	14	20.59
Wilson, LA (village) East Feliciana Parish	112	20.44
King Arthur Park, MT (cdp) Gallatin County	115	20.43

Place	Population	%
Barton, VT (village) Orleans County	164	20.42
Derby, VT (town) Orleans County	947	20.34
Kremlin, MT (cdp) Hill County	27	20.30
Beecher Falls, VT (cdp) Essex County	34	20.12
Leonville, LA (town) St. Landry Parish	235	20.02
Petersham, MA (town) Worcester County	268	20.01
St. John, ME (plantation) Aroostook County	54	20.00
Van Buren, ME (town) Aroostook County	516	19.93
Branch, LA (cdp) Acadia Parish	112	19.89
Jeffersonville, VT (village) Lamoille County	125	19.87
Graniteville, VT (cdp) Washington County	147	19.86
Jacksonville, VT (village) Windham County	37	19.68
Port Barre, LA (town) St. Landry Parish	420	19.63
West Swanzey, NH (cdp) Cheshire County	226	19.60
Dummer, NH (town) Coos County	77	19.59
Newport Center, VT (cdp) Orleans County	37	19.58
Danville, VT (cdp) Caledonia County	70	19.55
Kraemer, LA (cdp) Lafourche Parish	220	19.20
Milan, NH (town) Coos County	252	19.19
North Brookfield, MA (cdp) Worcester County	385	19.18
Van Buren, ME (cdp) Aroostook County	438	19.13
Rosebud, MT (cdp) Rosebud County	16	19.05
Barton, VT (town) Orleans County	536	19.02
Damar, KS (city) Rooks County	56	18.92
Sentinel Butte, ND (city) Golden Valley County	10	18.87
Pequaywan, MN (township) St. Louis County	39	18.84
Fort Kent, ME (town) Aroostook County	777	18.81
Au Sable, MI (township) Roscommon County	61	18.77
Biddeford, ME (city) York County	4,022	18.72
Auburn, ME (city) Androscoggin County	4,350	18.69
Champlain, NY (town) Clinton County	1,079	18.59
Websterville, VT (cdp) Washington County	103	18.53
Beaver, MN (township) Roseau County	26	18.31
Livermore, ME (town) Androscoggin County	383	18.24
Greene, ME (town) Androscoggin County	792	18.23
Coventry, VT (town) Orleans County	213	18.21
North Grosvenor Dale, CT (cdp) Windham County	322	18.18
Roxbury, ME (town) Oxford County	64	18.18
South Hooksett, NH (cdp) Merrimack County	981	18.09
Sorrel, LA (cdp) St. Mary Parish	127	18.04
Granby, MA (town) Hampshire County	1,109	17.80
Galliano, LA (cdp) Lafourche Parish	1,409	17.79
Long Pine, NE (city) Brown County	66	17.79
Granby, MA (cdp) Hampshire County	218	17.77
Swanton, VT (village) Franklin County	434	17.69
Lyndonville, VT (village) Caledonia County	214	17.60
Moosup, CT (cdp) Windham County	513	17.51
Guildhall, VT (town) Essex County	39	17.49
Moose River, ME (town) Somerset County	33	17.37
Swanton, VT (town) Franklin County	1,113	17.34
Upton, ME (town) Oxford County	13	17.33
Ocean Grove, MA (cdp) Bristol County	531	17.27
Cromwell, MN (city) Carlton County	20	17.24
Putnam, CT (cdp) Windham County	1,288	17.16
Mooers, NY (town) Clinton County	614	17.16
Burrillville, RI (town) Providence County	2,716	17.01
Rose City, TX (city) Orange County	107	17.01
Milton, VT (cdp) Chittenden County	327	16.99
Poland, ME (town) Androscoggin County	902	16.92
North Smithfield, RI (town) Providence County	1,990	16.91
Readsboro, VT (town) Bennington County	131	16.86
Pioneer, CA (cdp) Amador County	182	16.74
Putnam, CT (town) Windham County	1,599	16.72
Kenton, DE (town) Kent County	13	16.67
St. Francis, ME (town) Aroostook County	78	16.63
Faithorn, MI (township) Menominee County	39	16.60
Woonsocket, RI (city) Providence County	6,905	16.57
Bloomington, NE (village) Franklin County	28	16.57
Union, NH (cdp) Carroll County	63	16.54
Krotz Springs, LA (town) St. Landry Parish	184	16.50
Canaan, VT (town) Essex County	188	16.32
Hooksett, NH (town) Merrimack County	2,174	16.31
Livermore Falls, ME (town) Androscoggin County	523	16.23
Lisbon, ME (town) Androscoggin County	1,468	16.15
Leicester, VT (town) Addison County	179	16.14

Please refer to the Explanation of Data in the front of the book for more detailed information.

Ancestry

French Canadian

Top 150 Places Sorted by Percent of Total Population

Based on places with total population of 7,500 or more

Place	Population	%
Berlin, NH (city) Coos County	2,776	27.19
Lewiston, ME (city) Androscoggin County	8,580	23.39
Biddeford, ME (city) York County	4,022	18.72
Auburn, ME (city) Androscoggin County	4,350	18.69
Galliano, LA (cdp) Lafourche Parish	1,409	17.79
Putnam, CT (cdp) Windham County	1,288	17.16
Burrillville, RI (town) Providence County	2,716	17.01
North Smithfield, RI (town) Providence County	1,990	16.91
Putnam, CT (town) Windham County	1,599	16.72
Woonsocket, RI (city) Providence County	6,905	16.57
Hooksett, NH (town) Merrimack County	2,174	16.31
Lisbon, ME (town) Androscoggin County	1,468	16.15
Plainfield, CT (town) Windham County	2,392	15.55
Thompson, CT (town) Windham County	1,463	15.51
Blackstone, MA (town) Worcester County	1,337	14.85
Cumberland Hill, RI (cdp) Providence County	1,161	14.85
Killingly, CT (town) Windham County	2,541	14.65
Pelham, NH (town) Hillsborough County	1,779	14.10
Winslow, ME (cdp/town) Kennebec County	1,083	13.84
Goffstown, NH (town) Hillsborough County	2,402	13.62
Topsham, ME (town) Sagadahoc County	1,183	13.24
Barre, VT (town) Washington County	1,030	13.07
Saco, ME (city) York County	2,361	12.83
Sanford, ME (cdp) York County	1,326	12.52
Barre, VT (city) Washington County	1,113	12.21
Dracut, MA (town) Middlesex County	3,531	12.19
Gardner, MA (city) Worcester County	2,477	12.15
Freetown, MA (town) Bristol County	1,062	12.07
Southbridge Town, MA (city) Worcester County	2,005	11.90
Sanford, ME (town) York County	2,475	11.77
Lincoln, RI (town) Providence County	2,483	11.76
Northbridge, MA (town) Worcester County	1,787	11.69
Colchester, VT (town) Chittenden County	1,974	11.57
St. Johnsbury, VT (town) Caledonia County	885	11.57
Manchester, NH (city) Hillsborough County	12,622	11.50
Spencer, MA (town) Worcester County	1,346	11.48
Ware, MA (town) Hampshire County	1,115	11.31
Monson, MA (town) Hampden County	961	11.26
Hudson, NH (town) Hillsborough County	2,735	11.24
South Burlington, VT (city) Chittenden County	1,896	10.92
Easthampton Town, MA (city) Hampshire County	1,748	10.89
Milford, NH (town) Hillsborough County	1,613	10.82
Bow, NH (town) Merrimack County	815	10.77
Litchfield, NH (town) Hillsborough County	872	10.70
Acushnet, MA (town) Bristol County	1,095	10.64
Fitchburg, MA (city) Worcester County	4,262	10.60
Plaistow, NH (town) Rockingham County	816	10.59
Charlton, MA (town) Worcester County	1,336	10.51
Milton, VT (town) Chittenden County	1,063	10.43
Sturbridge, MA (town) Worcester County	943	10.43
Templeton, MA (town) Worcester County	814	10.43
Brooklyn, CT (town) Windham County	843	10.42
Augusta, ME (city) Kennebec County	1,986	10.37
Cumberland, RI (town) Providence County	3,447	10.35
Plattsburgh, NY (town) Clinton County	1,225	10.34
Old Orchard Beach, ME (cdp/town) York County	898	10.25
Milford, NH (cdp) Hillsborough County	916	10.11
Griswold, CT (town) New London County	1,183	10.05
Leominster, MA (city) Worcester County	4,102	10.02
Essex, VT (town) Chittenden County	1,944	10.00
Winchendon, MA (town) Worcester County	1,008	9.87
Athol, MA (town) Worcester County	1,140	9.86
Chicopee, MA (city) Hampden County	5,392	9.77
Raceland, LA (cdp) Lafourche Parish	1,039	9.74
Nashua, NH (city) Hillsborough County	8,465	9.73
Franklin, NH (city) Merrimack County	835	9.73
Somersworth, NH (city) Strafford County	1,117	9.45
Weare, NH (town) Hillsborough County	818	9.45
Amesbury Town, MA (city) Essex County	1,521	9.37
Bedford, NH (town) Hillsborough County	1,947	9.36
Westport, MA (town) Bristol County	1,415	9.25
Concord, NH (city) Merrimack County	3,950	9.19
Williston, VT (town) Chittenden County	777	9.15
Newmarket, NH (town) Rockingham County	805	9.10
Laconia, NH (city) Belknap County	1,467	9.04
Uxbridge, MA (town) Worcester County	1,181	9.03
Old Town, ME (city) Penobscot County	711	9.02
Webster, MA (town) Worcester County	1,502	8.97
Dover, NH (city) Strafford County	2,633	8.87
Essex Junction, VT (village) Chittenden County	811	8.86
Ogdensburg, NY (city) St. Lawrence County	1,006	8.85
Merrimack, NH (town) Hillsborough County	2,260	8.84
Glocester, RI (town) Providence County	863	8.80
Athol, MA (cdp) Worcester County	705	8.79
Belchertown, MA (town) Hampshire County	1,250	8.71
Salem, NH (town) Rockingham County	2,500	8.65
Hollis, NH (town) Hillsborough County	657	8.63
Agawam Town, MA (city) Hampden County	2,448	8.62
Keene, NH (city) Cheshire County	2,022	8.59
Dudley, MA (town) Worcester County	960	8.59
Smithfield, RI (town) Providence County	1,836	8.55
Montague, MA (town) Franklin County	721	8.53
Somerset, MA (cdp/town) Bristol County	1,550	8.52
Bellingham, MA (town) Norfolk County	1,355	8.46
Swansea, MA (town) Bristol County	1,342	8.44
Rehoboth, MA (town) Bristol County	950	8.37
Waterboro, ME (town) York County	627	8.36
Rochester, NH (city) Strafford County	2,488	8.35
Derry, NH (cdp) Rockingham County	1,905	8.32
Colchester, CT (town) New London County	1,308	8.25
Brunswick, ME (town) Cumberland County	1,693	8.24
Lunenburg, MA (town) Worcester County	819	8.20
Wells, ME (town) York County	792	8.20
Abbeville, LA (city) Vermilion Parish	994	8.13
North Attleborough, MA (town) Bristol County	2,258	7.93
Londonderry, NH (town) Rockingham County	1,916	7.92
Massena, NY (village) St. Lawrence County	888	7.88
Leicester, MA (town) Worcester County	858	7.86
Sterling, MA (town) Worcester County	605	7.84
Escanaba, MI (city) Delta County	995	7.81
Adams, MA (town) Berkshire County	665	7.81
South Hadley, MA (town) Hampshire County	1,364	7.80
Woodstock, CT (town) Windham County	614	7.78
Caribou, ME (city) Aroostook County	637	7.74
Orono, ME (town) Penobscot County	786	7.71
Kittery, ME (town) York County	737	7.67
Westbrook, ME (city) Cumberland County	1,327	7.66
Fairhaven, MA (town) Bristol County	1,220	7.66
Plainville, MA (town) Norfolk County	618	7.64
Tyngsborough, MA (town) Middlesex County	848	7.62
Kennebunk, ME (town) York County	828	7.61
Skowhegan, ME (town) Somerset County	661	7.61
Waterville, ME (city) Kennebec County	1,199	7.60
Durham, NH (town) Strafford County	1,086	7.60
Raymond, NH (town) Rockingham County	770	7.59
Brunswick, ME (cdp) Cumberland County	1,123	7.58
Sutton, MA (town) Worcester County	671	7.57
Hebron, CT (town) Tolland County	721	7.53
Pepperell, MA (town) Middlesex County	850	7.52
Webster, MA (cdp) Worcester County	855	7.50
Palmer Town, MA (city) Hampden County	914	7.49
Windham, CT (town) Windham County	1,873	7.48
Burlington, VT (city) Chittenden County	3,131	7.47
Ludlow, MA (town) Hampden County	1,579	7.46
Bayou Blue, LA (cdp) Lafourche Parish	825	7.38
Durham, NH (cdp) Strafford County	660	7.38
Hampstead, NH (town) Rockingham County	632	7.38
Massena, NY (town) St. Lawrence County	945	7.34
Hampton, NH (cdp) Rockingham County	643	7.25
Boxford, MA (town) Essex County	573	7.24
Vidor, TX (city) Orange County	768	7.21
Willimantic, CT (cdp) Windham County	1,259	7.20
Millbury, MA (town) Worcester County	946	7.16
Orono, ME (cdp) Penobscot County	640	7.16
Attleboro, MA (city) Bristol County	3,102	7.15
Derry, NH (town) Rockingham County	2,399	7.15
Rutland, MA (town) Worcester County	548	7.12
Marinette, WI (city) Marinette County	784	7.07
Greenville, RI (cdp) Providence County	614	7.00
Coventry, RI (town) Kent County	2,444	6.97

SECTION THREE

Please refer to the Explanation of Data in the front of the book for more detailed information.

Ancestry

German

U.S. and 50 States Sorted by Population and Percent of Total Population

Place	Population	%
United States	**49,840,035**	**16.40**
Pennsylvania	3,533,978	28.02
California	3,506,466	9.57
Ohio	3,220,180	27.97
Texas	2,670,955	10.99
Illinois	2,634,885	20.67
Wisconsin	2,500,074	44.34
Michigan	2,254,107	22.65
New York	2,238,521	11.64
Florida	2,212,580	11.95
Minnesota	1,959,455	37.38
Indiana	1,692,418	26.37
Missouri	1,605,541	27.11
Washington	1,331,078	20.29
Iowa	1,195,559	39.64
Colorado	1,120,643	22.93
North Carolina	1,078,399	11.63
New Jersey	1,069,417	12.26
Arizona	1,011,650	16.19
Virginia	1,011,507	12.90
Maryland	924,581	16.23
Kansas	863,661	30.74
Oregon	824,204	21.91
Georgia	758,945	8.02
Nebraska	746,586	41.50
Kentucky	682,836	15.93
Tennessee	655,948	10.52
Oklahoma	567,850	15.45
South Carolina	464,530	10.30
Massachusetts	436,061	6.73
Louisiana	384,565	8.68
West Virginia	364,092	19.78
Alabama	364,083	7.73
Connecticut	361,307	10.19
Nevada	353,500	13.42
Arkansas	350,425	12.20
South Dakota	349,067	43.66
Utah	323,162	12.16
North Dakota	309,500	46.90
Idaho	309,212	20.25
Montana	283,211	29.08
New Mexico	209,559	10.41
Mississippi	179,323	6.10
Wyoming	156,305	28.65
Delaware	141,172	16.02
Alaska	134,424	19.45
New Hampshire	124,609	9.48
Maine	111,073	8.37
Hawaii	89,726	6.73
Rhode Island	65,504	6.20
Vermont	64,779	10.38
District of Columbia	38,822	6.64

Place	Population	%
North Dakota	309,500	46.90
Wisconsin	2,500,074	44.34
South Dakota	349,067	43.66
Nebraska	746,586	41.50
Iowa	1,195,559	39.64
Minnesota	1,959,455	37.38
Kansas	863,661	30.74
Montana	283,211	29.08
Wyoming	156,305	28.65
Pennsylvania	3,533,978	28.02
Ohio	3,220,180	27.97
Missouri	1,605,541	27.11
Indiana	1,692,418	26.37
Colorado	1,120,643	22.93
Michigan	2,254,107	22.65
Oregon	824,204	21.91
Illinois	2,634,885	20.67
Washington	1,331,078	20.29
Idaho	309,212	20.25
West Virginia	364,092	19.78
Alaska	134,424	19.45
United States	**49,840,035**	**16.40**
Maryland	924,581	16.23
Arizona	1,011,650	16.19
Delaware	141,172	16.02
Kentucky	682,836	15.93
Oklahoma	567,850	15.45
Nevada	353,500	13.42
Virginia	1,011,507	12.90
New Jersey	1,069,417	12.26
Arkansas	350,425	12.20
Utah	323,162	12.16
Florida	2,212,580	11.95
New York	2,238,521	11.64
North Carolina	1,078,399	11.63
Texas	2,670,955	10.99
Tennessee	655,948	10.52
New Mexico	209,559	10.41
Vermont	64,779	10.38
South Carolina	464,530	10.30
Connecticut	361,307	10.19
California	3,506,466	9.57
New Hampshire	124,609	9.48
Louisiana	384,565	8.68
Maine	111,073	8.37
Georgia	758,945	8.02
Alabama	364,083	7.73
Massachusetts	436,061	6.73
Hawaii	89,726	6.73
District of Columbia	38,822	6.64
Rhode Island	65,504	6.20
Mississippi	179,323	6.10

Please refer to the Explanation of Data in the front of the book for more detailed information.

Ancestry

German

Top 150 Places Sorted by Population

Based on all places, regardless of total population

Place	Population	%
New York, NY (city) Kings County	272,827	3.38
Chicago, IL (city) Cook County	205,863	7.61
Phoenix, AZ (city) Maricopa County	188,756	13.02
Los Angeles, CA (city) Los Angeles County	177,061	4.69
Columbus, OH (city) Franklin County	163,383	21.21
Indianapolis, IN (city) Marion County	149,656	18.48
San Diego, CA (city) San Diego County	140,941	10.99
Houston, TX (city) Harris County	122,874	5.94
Philadelphia, PA (city) Philadelphia County	122,783	8.16
Omaha, NE (city) Douglas County	122,060	29.97
Milwaukee, WI (city) Milwaukee County	116,547	19.76
San Antonio, TX (city) Medina County	112,963	8.76
Louisville-Jefferson County, KY (metro govt) Jefferson County	112,194	19.11
Lincoln, NE (city) Lancaster County	110,551	43.69
Portland, OR (city) Multnomah County	108,939	19.22
Manhattan, NY (borough) New York County	107,666	6.80
Austin, TX (city) Travis County	97,420	12.75
Seattle, WA (city) King County	97,270	16.34
Colorado Springs, CO (city) El Paso County	90,925	22.51
Wichita, KS (city) Sedgwick County	89,797	24.03
Brookhaven, NY (town) Suffolk County	89,711	18.69
Minneapolis, MN (city) Hennepin County	88,406	23.29
Denver, CO (city) Denver County	86,183	14.91
Jacksonville, FL (city) Duval County	84,470	10.40
Kansas City, MO (city) Jackson County	82,136	18.06
Madison, WI (city) Dane County	81,466	35.54
Oklahoma City, OK (city) Oklahoma County	78,776	13.98
Hempstead, NY (town) Nassau County	78,518	10.42
Mesa, AZ (city) Maricopa County	77,211	17.56
Toledo, OH (city) Lucas County	76,635	26.26
Fort Wayne, IN (city) Allen County	76,622	30.20
Dallas, TX (city) Dallas County	73,347	6.18
Tucson, AZ (city) Pima County	73,191	14.12
Charlotte, NC (city) Mecklenburg County	71,671	10.15
Queens, NY (borough) Queens County	70,399	3.20
Las Vegas, NV (city) Clark County	67,142	11.58
St. Paul, MN (city) Ramsey County	67,025	23.76
Pittsburgh, PA (city) Allegheny County	66,031	21.44
Fort Worth, TX (city) Tarrant County	65,149	9.24
San Francisco, CA (city) San Francisco County	65,133	8.25
Albuquerque, NM (city) Bernalillo County	63,293	11.91
Sioux Falls, SD (city) Minnehaha County	63,160	42.43
San Jose, CA (city) Santa Clara County	61,487	6.65
Virginia Beach, VA (ind. city) Virginia Beach independent city	59,578	13.66
Cincinnati, OH (city) Hamilton County	59,441	19.80
Nashville-Davidson, TN (metro govt) Davidson County	57,440	9.77
Tulsa, OK (city) Tulsa County	54,997	14.17
Anchorage, AK (municipality) Anchorage Municipality	54,988	19.34
Brooklyn, NY (borough) Kings County	52,798	2.14
Spokane, WA (city) Spokane County	52,196	25.27
St. Louis, MO (city) St. Louis city County	51,664	16.21
Overland Park, KS (city) Johnson County	51,466	30.18
Cedar Rapids, IA (city) Linn County	49,660	39.59
Des Moines, IA (city) Polk County	49,043	24.27
Islip, NY (town) Suffolk County	48,335	14.48
Baltimore, MD (city) Baltimore city County	45,914	7.40
Scottsdale, AZ (city) Maricopa County	45,292	20.70
Aurora, CO (city) Arapahoe County	45,040	14.34
Fargo, ND (city) Cass County	44,410	43.32
Fort Collins, CO (city) Larimer County	44,033	31.43
Henderson, NV (city) Clark County	43,626	17.50
Chandler, AZ (city) Maricopa County	43,260	18.85
Lexington-Fayette, KY (cons. govt) Fayette County	42,920	14.90
Gilbert, AZ (town) Maricopa County	42,680	21.88
Sacramento, CA (city) Sacramento County	41,408	9.01
Oyster Bay, NY (town) Nassau County	41,381	14.19
Cleveland, OH (city) Cuyahoga County	40,200	9.82
Boise City, ID (city) Ada County	39,868	19.31
Akron, OH (city) Summit County	39,722	19.59
Fresno, CA (city) Fresno County	39,420	8.14
Arlington, TX (city) Tarrant County	38,903	10.82
Washington, DC (city) District of Columbia	38,822	6.64
Raleigh, NC (city) Wake County	38,247	9.99
Olathe, KS (city) Johnson County	37,323	30.90
Vancouver, WA (city) Clark County	36,923	23.05
Appleton, WI (city) Outagamie County	36,784	50.65
Bismarck, ND (city) Burleigh County	36,206	60.36
St. Petersburg, FL (city) Pinellas County	35,808	14.57
Buffalo, NY (city) Erie County	35,760	13.44
Springfield, MO (city) Christian County	35,757	22.50
Oshkosh, WI (city) Winnebago County	35,453	54.12
Topeka, KS (city) Shawnee County	35,431	28.09
Reno, NV (city) Washoe County	35,389	16.01
Rochester, MN (city) Olmsted County	35,337	33.91
Plano, TX (city) Collin County	35,329	13.80
Glendale, AZ (city) Maricopa County	35,213	15.33
Green Bay, WI (city) Brown County	35,077	33.74
Lakewood, CO (city) Jefferson County	34,745	24.46
Tampa, FL (city) Hillsborough County	34,654	10.40
Davenport, IA (city) Scott County	34,092	34.67
Evansville, IN (city) Vanderburgh County	33,828	28.62
Huntington, NY (town) Suffolk County	33,758	16.70
Salem, OR (city) Marion County	33,574	22.12
Tacoma, WA (city) Pierce County	33,501	16.85
Billings, MT (city) Yellowstone County	33,137	32.63
Long Beach, CA (city) Los Angeles County	33,099	7.17
Naperville, IL (city) DuPage County	32,930	23.38
Waukesha, WI (city) Waukesha County	32,644	46.67
Huntington Beach, CA (city) Orange County	32,622	17.27
Eugene, OR (city) Lane County	32,438	21.16
Bakersfield, CA (city) Kern County	31,918	9.62
Babylon, NY (town) Suffolk County	31,578	14.78
Aurora, IL (city) Kane County	31,118	16.34
Arvada, CO (city) Jefferson County	30,908	29.47
Springfield, IL (city) Sangamon County	30,854	26.80
Amherst, NY (town) Erie County	30,579	25.28
Grand Rapids, MI (city) Kent County	30,522	16.03
Columbia, MO (city) Boone County	30,374	29.03
Appleton, WI (city) Outagamie County	29,980	49.97
Rockford, IL (city) Winnebago County	29,971	19.40
Dubuque, IA (city) Dubuque County	29,864	51.93
O'Fallon, MO (city) St. Charles County	29,723	39.75
St. Cloud, MN (city) Stearns County	29,609	45.44
Corpus Christi, TX (city) Nueces County	29,575	9.88
Riverside, CA (city) Riverside County	29,153	9.70
Peoria, AZ (city) Yavapai County	28,619	19.25
Eau Claire, WI (city) Eau Claire County	28,452	43.68
Tempe, AZ (city) Maricopa County	28,371	17.28
Kenosha, WI (city) Kenosha County	28,280	28.77
Memphis, TN (city) Shelby County	28,260	4.32
Boston, MA (city) Suffolk County	28,158	4.67
Erie, PA (city) Erie County	27,772	27.33
Eau Claire, WI (city) Eau Claire County	27,764	44.06
Atlanta, GA (city) Fulton County	27,301	6.60
Metairie, LA (cdp) Jefferson Parish	26,905	19.80
St. Charles, MO (city) St. Charles County	26,831	41.04
Lawrence, KS (city) Douglas County	26,767	30.97
Cape Coral, FL (city) Lee County	26,747	17.86
Santa Clarita, CA (city) Los Angeles County	26,730	15.52
Sioux City, IA (city) Woodbury County	26,728	32.55
Knoxville, TN (city) Knox County	26,566	14.91
Janesville, WI (city) Rock County	26,507	41.78
Arlington, VA (cdp) Arlington County	26,481	13.41
Warren, MI (city) Macomb County	26,458	19.48
Peoria, IL (city) Peoria County	26,263	23.07
West Allis, WI (city) Milwaukee County	26,168	43.61
Cheektowaga, NY (town) Erie County	26,125	29.39
Greece, NY (town) Monroe County	25,631	26.85
Sheboygan, WI (city) Sheboygan County	25,594	51.46
Centennial, CO (city) Arapahoe County	25,563	25.56
Lubbock, TX (city) Lubbock County	25,521	11.48
Bloomington, MN (city) Hennepin County	25,491	30.85
Staten Island, NY (borough) Richmond County	25,477	5.50
Independence, MO (city) Jackson County	25,265	21.86
El Paso, TX (city) El Paso County	25,193	4.01
Highlands Ranch, CO (cdp) Douglas County	24,806	26.08
Rapid City, SD (city) Pennington County	24,788	37.48
Lee's Summit, MO (city) Jackson County	24,716	28.40
Chesapeake, VA (ind. city) Chesapeake independent city	24,649	11.24
Waterloo, IA (city) Black Hawk County	24,591	36.22

Please refer to the Explanation of Data in the front of the book for more detailed information.

Ancestry

German

Top 150 Places Sorted by Percent of Total Population

Based on all places, regardless of total population

Place	Population	%
Miamiville, OH (cdp) Clermont County	226	100.00
Iago, TX (cdp) Wharton County	135	100.00
Winfred, SD (cdp) Lake County	84	100.00
Chase, AK (cdp) Matanuska-Susitna Borough	79	100.00
Gorman, MD (cdp) Garrett County	79	100.00
Jeffrey City, WY (cdp) Fremont County	75	100.00
Parshall, CO (cdp) Grand County	74	100.00
Big Spring, MO (cdp) Montgomery County	73	100.00
Strawberry, CA (cdp) Tuolumne County	64	100.00
Port Colden, NJ (cdp) Warren County	63	100.00
Ferney, SD (cdp) Brown County	60	100.00
Paderborn, IL (cdp) St. Clair County	59	100.00
Reid, MD (cdp) Washington County	49	100.00
Harmon, ND (cdp) Morton County	46	100.00
Lakeview North, WY (cdp) Platte County	46	100.00
Arlington, WY (cdp) Carbon County	44	100.00
Tetherow, OR (cdp) Deschutes County	43	100.00
Beluga, AK (cdp) Kenai Peninsula Borough	42	100.00
Websters Crossing, NY (cdp) Livingston County	42	100.00
Bayport, FL (cdp) Hernando County	41	100.00
Gheen, MN (unorganized territory) St. Louis County	34	100.00
Tamora, NE (cdp) Seward County	34	100.00
Lowell Point, AK (cdp) Kenai Peninsula Borough	33	100.00
McConnico, AZ (cdp) Mohave County	33	100.00
Jacksonville, IA (cdp) Shelby County	32	100.00
South Fork Estates, TX (cdp) Jim Hogg County	31	100.00
Farmer, SD (town) Hanson County	30	100.00
Newkirk, NM (cdp) Guadalupe County	29	100.00
Onaka, SD (town) Faulk County	29	100.00
St. Joseph, IA (cdp) Kossuth County	29	100.00
Regan, ND (city) Burleigh County	26	100.00
Toeterville, IA (cdp) Mitchell County	24	100.00
Bucks Lake, CA (cdp) Plumas County	23	100.00
Golden, NM (cdp) Santa Fe County	23	100.00
Big Pool, MD (cdp) Washington County	22	100.00
Mendeltna, AK (cdp) Valdez-Cordova Census Area	20	100.00
Loraine, ND (city) Renville County	19	100.00
Moorefield, NE (village) Frontier County	19	100.00
Tarrants, MO (village) Pike County	19	100.00
Danville, MO (cdp) Montgomery County	18	100.00
Milltown, SD (cdp) Hutchinson County	18	100.00
Huntley, WY (cdp) Goshen County	17	100.00
Jessie, ND (cdp) Griggs County	16	100.00
Wisconsin Dells, WI (city) Adams County	16	100.00
Colona, CO (cdp) Ouray County	15	100.00
Bridgeville, NJ (cdp) Warren County	14	100.00
Pine Valley, NJ (borough) Camden County	13	100.00
Cazenovia, WI (village) Sauk County	12	100.00
Crystal Bay, NV (cdp) Washoe County	12	100.00
Kaylor, SD (cdp) Hutchinson County	12	100.00
Roy Lake, MN (cdp) Clearwater County	12	100.00
Asherville, KS (cdp) Mitchell County	11	100.00
Emlenton, PA (borough) Clarion County	10	100.00
Marion, WI (city) Shawano County	10	100.00
Time, IL (village) Pike County	10	100.00
Cold Spring, PA (township) Lebanon County	9	100.00
Midway, MN (cdp) Mahnomen County	9	100.00
Royalton, MN (city) Benton County	9	100.00
Bankston, IA (city) Dubuque County	8	100.00
Alzada, MT (cdp) Carter County	7	100.00
De Lamere, ND (cdp) Sargent County	7	100.00
Mappsburg, VA (cdp) Accomack County	7	100.00
Meyer, IA (cdp) Mitchell County	7	100.00
Miltonsburg, OH (village) Monroe County	7	100.00
Nenzel, NE (village) Cherry County	7	100.00
Barry, MN (city) Big Stone County	6	100.00
Elysian, MN (city) Waseca County	6	100.00
Lutak, AK (cdp) Haines Borough	6	100.00
Rapid River, MN (township) Lake of the Woods County	6	100.00
Gross, NE (village) Boyd County	5	100.00
Lambert, OK (town) Alfalfa County	5	100.00
Nottoway Court House, VA (cdp) Nottoway County	5	100.00
Wetonka, SD (town) McPherson County	5	100.00
Seven Springs, PA (borough) Fayette County	4	100.00
Tenney, MN (city) Wilkin County	4	100.00

Place	Population	%
Albee, SD (town) Grant County	3	100.00
Funkley, MN (city) Beltrami County	3	100.00
Valley-Hi, PA (borough) Fulton County	3	100.00
Verdon, SD (town) Brown County	3	100.00
Crocker, SD (cdp) Clark County	2	100.00
Shady Grove, OK (town) Pawnee County	2	100.00
Lake City, SD (town) Marshall County	46	97.87
Jewett, MN (unorganized territory) Aitkin County	76	97.44
Walnut Creek, OH (cdp) Holmes County	373	96.38
Clare, MI (city) Isabella County	89	95.70
Foster, NE (village) Pierce County	66	95.65
Golva, ND (city) Golden Valley County	52	94.55
Altamont, SD (town) Deuel County	34	94.44
Pendleton, MO (village) Warren County	83	94.32
Marienthal, KS (cdp) Wichita County	138	92.62
Harris, KS (cdp) Anderson County	72	92.31
Greenwald, MN (city) Stearns County	161	92.00
Holiday City, OH (village) Williams County	45	91.84
Selz, ND (cdp) Pierce County	157	91.81
Burr, NE (village) Otoe County	76	91.57
McLean, NE (village) Pierce County	31	91.18
Waverly, SD (cdp) Codington County	30	90.91
Stately, MN (township) Brown County	169	90.86
Akaska, SD (town) Walworth County	89	90.82
Richland, SD (cdp) Union County	69	90.79
Palmer, KS (city) Washington County	86	90.53
Whittlesey, WI (cdp) Taylor County	124	90.51
East Amana, IA (cdp) Iowa County	85	90.43
Virginia, NE (village) Gage County	65	90.28
Mantador, ND (city) Richland County	37	90.24
Bancroft, SD (town) Kingsbury County	27	90.00
Stockham, NE (village) Hamilton County	52	89.66
Dodge, ND (city) Dunn County	126	89.36
Home, KS (cdp) Marshall County	179	89.05
Regal, MN (city) Kandiyohi County	24	88.89
Johnson, MN (city) Big Stone County	16	88.89
High Amana, IA (cdp) Iowa County	87	88.78
Brownsville, MD (cdp) Washington County	296	88.36
Kekoskee, WI (village) Dodge County	129	88.36
Dumont, MN (city) Traverse County	75	88.24
Streeter, ND (city) Stutsman County	95	87.96
Sioux Valley, MN (township) Jackson County	174	87.88
Brentford, SD (town) Spink County	105	87.50
Comfrey, MN (city) Cottonwood County	14	87.50
Clark, MN (township) Faribault County	313	87.19
Beaver, IA (city) Boone County	27	87.10
Millwood, MN (township) Stearns County	830	87.09
Strandburg, SD (town) Grant County	67	87.01
Glandorf, OH (village) Putnam County	869	86.99
Foxholm, ND (cdp) Ward County	53	86.89
Belvidere, NE (village) Thayer County	66	86.84
Jackson Junction, IA (city) Winneshiek County	85	86.73
Martin, ND (city) Sheridan County	39	86.67
Frystown, PA (cdp) Berks County	468	86.51
Balta, ND (city) Pierce County	57	86.36
Huntley, NE (village) Harlan County	19	86.36
Zion, MN (township) Stearns County	278	86.34
Prairie City, SD (cdp) Perkins County	82	86.32
Wolford, ND (city) Pierce County	62	86.11
Fish Lake, MN (cdp) Jackson County	31	86.11
Mulligan, MN (township) Brown County	197	86.03
Houghton, IA (city) Lee County	98	85.96
Wales, ND (city) Cavalier County	18	85.71
Fredonia, ND (city) Logan County	12	85.71
Spring Hill, MN (township) Stearns County	356	85.37
Buckman, MN (city) Morrison County	192	85.33
Orient, SD (town) Faulk County	73	84.88
Richfield, NE (cdp) Sarpy County	117	84.78
Loretto, NE (cdp) Boone County	128	84.77
Edna Bay, AK (cdp) Prince of Wales-Hyder Census Area	50	84.75
Luxemburg, IA (city) Dubuque County	144	84.71
New Haven, IA (cdp) Mitchell County	82	84.54
Luxemburg, MN (township) Stearns County	555	84.47
Miller City, OH (village) Putnam County	87	84.47
Round Lake, MN (township) Jackson County	189	84.38

Please refer to the Explanation of Data in the front of the book for more detailed information.

Ancestry

German

Top 150 Places Sorted by Percent of Total Population

Based on places with total population of 7,500 or more

Place	Population	%
Watertown, WI (city) Dodge County	5,575	66.05
New Ulm, MN (city) Brown County	8,740	64.70
Merrill, WI (city) Lincoln County	6,302	64.31
Richfield, WI (village) Washington County	7,127	63.49
Sussex, WI (village) Waukesha County	6,496	63.30
Mandan, ND (city) Morton County	11,268	63.26
Sheboygan Falls, WI (city) Sheboygan County	4,792	62.99
Plymouth, WI (city) Sheboygan County	5,139	61.38
Bismarck, ND (city) Burleigh County	36,206	60.36
Germantown, WI (village) Washington County	11,784	60.09
Carroll, IA (city) Carroll County	5,986	59.58
West Bend, WI (city) Washington County	18,254	59.34
Watertown, WI (city) Jefferson County	13,927	59.01
Mack, OH (cdp) Hamilton County	6,720	58.65
Bridgetown, OH (cdp) Hamilton County	8,375	58.41
St. Marys, PA (city) Elk County	7,779	58.41
Cedarburg, WI (city) Ozaukee County	6,639	58.33
Dickinson, ND (city) Stark County	10,005	58.28
Waunakee, WI (village) Dane County	6,722	58.16
Greenville, WI (town) Outagamie County	5,639	58.06
Merton, WI (town) Waukesha County	4,821	57.99
Lisbon, WI (town) Waukesha County	5,808	57.83
Waukesha, WI (town) Waukesha County	5,189	57.27
Kaukauna, WI (city) Outagamie County	8,603	57.07
Harrison, WI (town) Calumet County	5,692	56.93
Fond du Lac, WI (city) Fond du Lac County	24,411	56.90
Pewaukee, WI (city) Waukesha County	7,372	56.87
Oconomowoc, WI (city) Waukesha County	8,673	56.82
Marshfield, WI (city) Wood County	10,323	56.78
Marshfield, WI (city) Wood County	10,606	56.65
Vernon, WI (town) Waukesha County	4,290	56.57
Hays, KS (city) Ellis County	11,456	56.55
North Codorus, PA (township) York County	4,960	56.49
Mukwonago, WI (town) Waukesha County	4,406	56.49
Waverly, IA (city) Bremer County	5,480	56.18
Delafield, WI (town) Waukesha County	4,675	56.16
Menasha, WI (town) Winnebago County	10,106	56.05
Port Washington, WI (city) Ozaukee County	6,230	55.89
DeForest, WI (village) Dane County	4,827	55.68
Sartell, MN (city) Stearns County	8,210	55.64
Wapakoneta, OH (city) Auglaize County	5,472	55.30
Sartell, MN (city) Stearns County	6,966	55.19
Watertown, WI (city) Jefferson County	8,352	55.09
Neenah, WI (city) Winnebago County	13,932	55.01
Fairmont, MN (city) Martin County	5,847	55.01
Sauk Rapids, MN (city) Benton County	6,858	54.94
Jamestown, ND (city) Stutsman County	8,379	54.79
Jefferson, WI (city) Jefferson County	4,330	54.72
Hudson, WI (town) St. Croix County	4,511	54.70
Beaver Dam, WI (city) Dodge County	8,808	54.60
Appleton, WI (city) Calumet County	6,090	54.51
Grand Chute, WI (town) Outagamie County	11,164	54.46
Columbia, IL (city) Monroe County	5,142	54.30
Oshkosh, WI (city) Winnebago County	35,453	54.12
Hartford, WI (city) Washington County	7,426	54.02
Le Mars, IA (city) Plymouth County	5,246	53.98
White Oak, OH (cdp) Hamilton County	10,268	53.93
Menomonee Falls, WI (village) Waukesha County	18,977	53.88
North Mankato, MN (city) Nicollet County	7,044	53.58
Norway, WI (town) Racine County	4,235	53.55
Pewaukee, WI (village) Waukesha County	4,348	53.40
Oconomowoc, WI (town) Waukesha County	4,415	53.33
Muskego, WI (city) Waukesha County	12,615	53.17
Watertown, SD (city) Codington County	11,335	53.17
Monfort Heights, OH (cdp) Hamilton County	6,127	53.08
Norfolk, NE (city) Madison County	12,691	52.97
Hutchinson, MN (city) McLeod County	7,509	52.93
Waseca, MN (city) Waseca County	4,977	52.80
Grand Rapids, WI (town) Wood County	4,025	52.63
Oakville, MO (cdp) St. Louis County	18,478	52.42
Platteville, WI (city) Grant County	5,734	52.36
Jasper, IN (city) Dubois County	7,627	52.34
Aberdeen, SD (city) Brown County	13,450	52.31
Dubuque, IA (city) Dubuque County	29,864	51.93
Grafton, WI (village) Ozaukee County	5,887	51.92
Napoleon, OH (city) Henry County	4,409	51.86
Bryan, OH (city) Williams County	4,464	51.78
Menasha, WI (city) Winnebago County	7,864	51.76
Harrison, OH (city) Hamilton County	4,837	51.49
Sheboygan, WI (city) Sheboygan County	25,594	51.46
Menasha, WI (city) Winnebago County	8,713	51.15
Ripon, WI (city) Fond du Lac County	3,920	51.00
Sappington, MO (cdp) St. Louis County	4,065	50.93
Fort Atkinson, WI (city) Jefferson County	6,253	50.83
Highland, IL (city) Madison County	4,785	50.82
Tiffin, OH (city) Seneca County	9,113	50.81
Manitowoc, WI (city) Manitowoc County	17,143	50.73
Appleton, WI (city) Outagamie County	36,784	50.65
Mankato, MN (city) Blue Earth County	19,218	50.33
Mankato, MN (city) Blue Earth County	19,218	50.33
Suamico, WI (village) Brown County	5,468	50.32
Washington, MO (city) Franklin County	7,008	50.17
New Berlin, WI (city) Waukesha County	19,800	50.10
Charles City, IA (city) Floyd County	3,841	50.10
Appleton, WI (city) Outagamie County	29,980	49.97
Concord, MO (cdp) St. Louis County	7,910	49.94
Mitchell, SD (city) Davison County	7,574	49.94
West Fargo, ND (city) Cass County	11,892	49.82
Waconia, MN (city) Carver County	5,055	49.76
Baraboo, WI (city) Sauk County	5,892	49.68
Brandon, SD (city) Minnehaha County	4,086	49.63
River Falls, WI (city) Pierce County	5,762	49.57
Beatrice, NE (city) Gage County	6,232	49.52
Little Chute, WI (village) Outagamie County	5,195	49.51
York, NE (city) York County	3,893	49.47
Antigo, WI (city) Langlade County	4,099	49.31
Reedsburg, WI (city) Sauk County	4,427	49.29
Waterloo, IL (city) Monroe County	4,732	49.09
River Falls, WI (city) Pierce County	7,210	49.06
Wauwatosa, WI (city) Milwaukee County	22,644	49.04
Newberry, PA (township) York County	7,462	49.04
Penn, PA (township) Lancaster County	4,181	49.03
Fremont, NE (city) Dodge County	12,838	48.96
Brookfield, WI (city) Waukesha County	18,690	48.93
Crestwood, MO (city) St. Louis County	5,819	48.93
North Londonderry, PA (township) Lebanon County	3,842	48.92
Hartland, WI (village) Waukesha County	4,337	48.58
Yankton, SD (city) Yankton County	6,889	48.37
Madeira, OH (city) Hamilton County	4,193	48.34
Wausau, WI (city) Marathon County	18,828	48.23
Dent, OH (cdp) Hamilton County	4,721	48.21
Spearfish, SD (city) Lawrence County	4,910	48.16
Hales Corners, WI (village) Milwaukee County	3,672	48.02
Columbus, NE (city) Platte County	10,390	48.01
Portage, WI (city) Columbia County	4,916	47.94
Wyoming, MN (city) Chisago County	3,678	47.89
Plover, WI (village) Portage County	5,664	47.88
Dover, PA (township) York County	9,883	47.81
Brookings, SD (city) Brookings County	10,250	47.75
Whitewater, WI (city) Walworth County	5,327	47.75
Cheviot, OH (city) Hamilton County	4,015	47.72
Two Rivers, WI (city) Manitowoc County	5,661	47.68
Tomah, WI (city) Monroe County	4,268	47.55
St. Marys, OH (city) Auglaize County	3,954	47.54
Hastings, NE (city) Adams County	11,745	47.52
Greendale, WI (village) Milwaukee County	6,642	47.51
Weston, WI (village) Marathon County	6,809	47.35
Mount Joy, PA (township) Lancaster County	4,517	47.35
Whitewater, WI (city) Walworth County	6,761	47.31
Hastings, MN (city) Dakota County	10,210	47.29
St. Francis, WI (city) Milwaukee County	4,320	47.13
Sturgeon Bay, WI (city) Door County	4,333	47.11
Wisconsin Rapids, WI (city) Wood County	8,620	47.02
Menomonie, WI (city) Dunn County	7,542	46.96
Waukesha, WI (city) Waukesha County	32,644	46.67
La Crosse, WI (city) La Crosse County	23,911	46.67
St. Michael, MN (city) Wright County	7,166	46.58
Perryville, MO (city) Perry County	3,805	46.54
Fort Thomas, KY (city) Campbell County	7,511	46.42
Southampton, PA (township) Franklin County	3,575	46.40

SECTION THREE

Please refer to the Explanation of Data in the front of the book for more detailed information.

Ancestry

German Russian

U.S. and 50 States Sorted by Population and Percent of Total Population

Place	Population	%	Place	Population	%
United States	**16,037**	**0.01**	North Dakota	986	0.15
Kansas	1,650	0.06	Kansas	1,650	0.06
California	1,616	<0.01	Nebraska	273	0.02
North Dakota	986	0.15	South Dakota	138	0.02
Texas	869	<0.01	**United States**	**16,037**	**0.01**
Wisconsin	679	0.01	Wisconsin	679	0.01
New York	587	<0.01	Washington	576	0.01
Washington	576	0.01	Colorado	560	0.01
Colorado	560	0.01	Minnesota	470	0.01
Illinois	523	<0.01	Virginia	457	0.01
Ohio	481	<0.01	Maryland	412	0.01
Minnesota	470	0.01	Arizona	406	0.01
Florida	462	<0.01	Oklahoma	371	0.01
Virginia	457	0.01	Missouri	369	0.01
Michigan	417	<0.01	Oregon	302	0.01
Maryland	412	0.01	Nevada	175	0.01
Arizona	406	0.01	Montana	130	0.01
Georgia	373	<0.01	Alaska	99	0.01
Oklahoma	371	0.01	Idaho	91	0.01
Missouri	369	0.01	Wyoming	44	0.01
North Carolina	350	<0.01	Vermont	34	0.01
Pennsylvania	320	<0.01	California	1,616	<0.01
Oregon	302	0.01	Texas	869	<0.01
Nebraska	273	0.02	New York	587	<0.01
Kentucky	206	<0.01	Illinois	523	<0.01
New Jersey	199	<0.01	Ohio	481	<0.01
Indiana	194	<0.01	Florida	462	<0.01
Nevada	175	0.01	Michigan	417	<0.01
Tennessee	174	<0.01	Georgia	373	<0.01
Louisiana	139	<0.01	North Carolina	350	<0.01
South Dakota	138	0.02	Pennsylvania	320	<0.01
Alabama	134	<0.01	Kentucky	206	<0.01
South Carolina	134	<0.01	New Jersey	199	<0.01
Montana	130	0.01	Indiana	194	<0.01
Utah	103	<0.01	Tennessee	174	<0.01
Iowa	101	<0.01	Louisiana	139	<0.01
Alaska	99	0.01	Alabama	134	<0.01
Idaho	91	0.01	South Carolina	134	<0.01
Arkansas	71	<0.01	Utah	103	<0.01
Connecticut	67	<0.01	Iowa	101	<0.01
West Virginia	64	<0.01	Arkansas	71	<0.01
Massachusetts	55	<0.01	Connecticut	67	<0.01
Wyoming	44	0.01	West Virginia	64	<0.01
New Mexico	44	<0.01	Massachusetts	55	<0.01
Rhode Island	43	<0.01	New Mexico	44	<0.01
Mississippi	41	<0.01	Rhode Island	43	<0.01
Vermont	34	0.01	Mississippi	41	<0.01
Hawaii	23	<0.01	Hawaii	23	<0.01
New Hampshire	13	<0.01	New Hampshire	13	<0.01
Maine	12	<0.01	Maine	12	<0.01
Delaware	0	0.00	Delaware	0	0.00
District of Columbia	0	0.00	District of Columbia	0	0.00

Please refer to the Explanation of Data in the front of the book for more detailed information.

Ancestry

German Russian

Top 150 Places Sorted by Population

Based on all places, regardless of total population

Place	Population	%
Milwaukee, WI (city) Milwaukee County	376	0.06
Hays, KS (city) Ellis County	308	1.52
Tucson, AZ (city) Pima County	222	0.04
Topeka, KS (city) Shawnee County	220	0.17
New York, NY (city) Kings County	204	<0.01
Bismarck, ND (city) Burleigh County	178	0.30
Wichita, KS (city) Sedgwick County	174	0.05
Aurora, CO (city) Arapahoe County	152	0.05
Los Angeles, CA (city) Los Angeles County	145	<0.01
Houston, TX (city) Harris County	142	0.01
Minneapolis, MN (city) Hennepin County	128	0.03
Olathe, KS (city) Johnson County	127	0.11
Detroit, MI (city) Wayne County	119	0.02
Stockton, CA (city) San Joaquin County	117	0.04
West Fargo, ND (city) Cass County	115	0.48
Chicago, IL (city) Cook County	106	<0.01
Lincoln, NE (city) Lancaster County	105	0.04
Anchorage, AK (municipality) Anchorage Municipality	99	0.03
San Antonio, TX (city) Medina County	97	0.01
West Milwaukee, WI (village) Milwaukee County	95	2.29
Minot AFB, ND (cdp) Ward County	93	1.63
Selma, AL (city) Dallas County	93	0.45
Carson, CA (city) Los Angeles County	88	0.10
West Covina, CA (city) Los Angeles County	88	0.08
Billings, MT (city) Yellowstone County	83	0.08
Fargo, ND (city) Cass County	80	0.08
Akron, OH (city) Summit County	78	0.04
Queens, NY (borough) Queens County	78	<0.01
Mount Dora, FL (city) Lake County	75	0.61
Oklahoma City, OK (city) Oklahoma County	75	0.01
Dallas, OR (city) Polk County	74	0.52
West Valley City, UT (city) Salt Lake County	74	0.06
Maple Heights, OH (city) Cuyahoga County	68	0.29
Rockford, IL (city) Winnebago County	68	0.04
Baltimore, MD (city) Baltimore city County	67	0.01
Troy, NY (city) Rensselaer County	65	0.13
Panther Valley, NJ (cdp) Warren County	63	1.92
Allamuchy, NJ (township) Warren County	63	1.47
Abilene, TX (city) Taylor County	63	0.05
Evanston, IL (city) Cook County	62	0.08
Colorado Springs, CO (city) El Paso County	62	0.02
Redding, CA (city) Shasta County	61	0.07
McPherson, KS (city) McPherson County	60	0.45
Pineville, LA (city) Rapides Parish	60	0.41
Butler, MO (city) Bates County	58	1.36
Sierra Vista, AZ (city) Cochise County	57	0.13
Tacoma, WA (city) Pierce County	56	0.03
St. John, MO (city) St. Louis County	55	0.84
Elkton, MD (town) Cecil County	55	0.37
Norwood, MA (cdp/town) Norfolk County	55	0.19
Denver, CO (city) Denver County	55	0.01
Brooklyn, NY (borough) Kings County	55	<0.01
Webster Groves, MO (city) St. Louis County	53	0.23
Asheville, NC (city) Buncombe County	53	0.06
Las Vegas, NV (city) Clark County	53	0.01
San Diego, CA (city) San Diego County	53	<0.01
Lakewood, WA (city) Pierce County	51	0.09
Racine, WI (city) Racine County	51	0.06
Victoria, KS (city) Ellis County	50	4.07
Matoaca, VA (cdp) Chesterfield County	50	2.07
Baxter, MN (city) Crow Wing County	50	0.68
Foothill Farms, CA (cdp) Sacramento County	50	0.15
Arlington, TX (city) Tarrant County	50	0.01
Long Beach, CA (city) Los Angeles County	50	0.01
Portland, OR (city) Multnomah County	50	0.01
Southgate, MI (city) Wayne County	49	0.16
Spokane, LA (cdp) Concordia Parish	48	13.11
McKees Rocks, PA (borough) Allegheny County	48	0.78
St. Matthews, KY (city) Jefferson County	48	0.28
Owatonna, MN (city) Steele County	48	0.19
Silver Spring, MD (cdp) Montgomery County	48	0.07
Simonton Lake, IN (cdp) Elkhart County	47	0.93
Rocky Mount, NC (city) Nash County	47	0.08
Durham, NC (city) Durham County	47	0.02
Lubbock, TX (city) Lubbock County	47	0.02
Edmond, OK (city) Oklahoma County	46	0.06
Ellsworth, KS (city) Ellsworth County	45	1.46
Dumfries, VA (town) Prince William County	45	0.91
Beaverton, OR (city) Washington County	45	0.05
Omaha, NE (city) Douglas County	45	0.01
Laguna Beach, FL (cdp) Bay County	43	1.19
Pocahontas, AR (city) Randolph County	43	0.65
Newport, RI (city) Newport County	43	0.17
La Mesa, CA (city) San Diego County	43	0.08
Lower Macungie, PA (township) Lehigh County	42	0.15
Greeley, CO (city) Weld County	41	0.04
Buffalo, NY (city) Erie County	41	0.02
Kansas City, MO (city) Jackson County	41	0.01
Manhattan, NY (borough) New York County	41	<0.01
Boulder Hill, IL (cdp) Kendall County	40	0.46
Mastic, NY (cdp) Suffolk County	40	0.28
Paradise, NV (cdp) Clark County	40	0.02
Brookhaven, NY (town) Suffolk County	40	0.01
Lochearn, MD (cdp) Baltimore County	39	0.15
Delray Beach, FL (city) Palm Beach County	38	0.06
Sacramento, CA (city) Sacramento County	38	0.01
Niceville, FL (city) Okaloosa County	37	0.29
Ann Arbor, MI (city) Washtenaw County	37	0.03
Des Moines, IA (city) Polk County	37	0.02
Vancouver, WA (city) Clark County	37	0.02
St. Paul, MN (city) Ramsey County	37	0.01
Kinston, NC (city) Lenoir County	36	0.16
Bel Air North, MD (cdp) Harford County	36	0.12
Tonganoxie, KS (city) Leavenworth County	35	0.76
Walla Walla, WA (city) Walla Walla County	35	0.11
Valdosta, GA (city) Lowndes County	35	0.07
Graeagle, CA (cdp) Plumas County	34	3.73
Leitchfield, KY (city) Grayson County	34	0.51
Dunbar, WV (city) Kanawha County	34	0.43
Williston, VT (town) Chittenden County	34	0.40
New Haven, CT (city/town) New Haven County	34	0.03
Cincinnati, OH (city) Hamilton County	34	0.01
East Nottingham, PA (township) Chester County	33	0.40
Sterling, CO (city) Logan County	33	0.23
Tonawanda, NY (city) Erie County	33	0.22
Matteson, IL (village) Cook County	33	0.19
Patterson, CA (city) Stanislaus County	33	0.17
Columbus, OH (city) Franklin County	33	<0.01
Wheaton, MD (cdp) Montgomery County	32	0.07
Mandan, ND (city) Morton County	31	0.17
Bremerton, WA (city) Kitsap County	31	0.08
Wyoming, MN (city) Chisago County	30	0.39
Flossmoor, IL (village) Cook County	30	0.33
New Carrollton, MD (city) Prince George's County	30	0.25
Bronx, NY (borough) Bronx County	30	<0.01
Dallas, TX (city) Dallas County	30	<0.01
Bethany, OK (city) Oklahoma County	29	0.15
Ferguson, MO (city) St. Louis County	29	0.14
Duncan, OK (city) Stephens County	29	0.13
Grove City, OH (city) Franklin County	29	0.09
Panama City, FL (city) Bay County	29	0.08
Spartanburg, SC (city) Spartanburg County	29	0.08
Victorville, CA (city) San Bernardino County	29	0.03
Joliet, IL (city) Will County	29	0.02
Five Corners, WA (cdp) Clark County	28	0.16
Garfield Heights, OH (city) Cuyahoga County	28	0.10
Irondequoit, NY (cdp/town) Monroe County	28	0.05
Macomb, MI (township) Macomb County	28	0.04
Aberdeen, SD (city) Brown County	27	0.11
Hinesville, GA (city) Liberty County	27	0.08
Salina, KS (city) Saline County	27	0.06
Waukesha, WI (city) Waukesha County	27	0.04
Portsmouth, VA (ind. city) Portsmouth independent city	27	0.03
Lancaster, CA (city) Los Angeles County	27	0.02
Overland Park, KS (city) Johnson County	27	0.02
Newport News, VA (ind. city) Newport News independent city	27	0.01
Phoenix, AZ (city) Maricopa County	27	<0.01
Hilldale, PA (cdp) Luzerne County	26	1.81
Auberry, CA (cdp) Fresno County	26	1.18
Peppermill Village, MD (cdp) Prince George's County	26	0.54

Please refer to the Explanation of Data in the front of the book for more detailed information.

Ancestry

German Russian

Top 150 Places Sorted by Percent of Total Population

Based on all places, regardless of total population

Place	Population	%
Heil, ND (cdp) Grant County	9	56.25
Spokane, LA (cdp) Concordia Parish	48	13.11
Denhoff, ND (cdp) Sheridan County	2	10.53
Hazelton, ND (city) Emmons County	13	4.74
Sykeston, ND (city) Wells County	3	4.41
Victoria, KS (city) Ellis County	50	4.07
Berthold, ND (city) Ward County	20	3.85
Graeagle, CA (cdp) Plumas County	34	3.73
Schoenchen, KS (city) Ellis County	6	2.33
West Milwaukee, WI (village) Milwaukee County	95	2.29
La Jara, CO (town) Conejos County	20	2.15
Melbeta, NE (village) Scotts Bluff County	2	2.08
Matoaca, VA (cdp) Chesterfield County	50	2.07
Panther Valley, NJ (cdp) Warren County	63	1.92
Hilldale, PA (cdp) Luzerne County	26	1.81
Grand Mound, IA (city) Clinton County	12	1.72
Minot AFB, ND (cdp) Ward County	93	1.63
Leven, MN (township) Pope County	9	1.57
Hansen, ID (city) Twin Falls County	14	1.54
Hays, KS (city) Ellis County	308	1.52
Allamuchy, NJ (township) Warren County	63	1.47
Ellsworth, KS (city) Ellsworth County	45	1.46
Butler, MO (city) Bates County	58	1.36
Glen Ullin, ND (city) Morton County	11	1.34
Linton, ND (city) Emmons County	13	1.28
Arthur, ND (city) Cass County	4	1.28
North Randall, OH (village) Cuyahoga County	11	1.27
Pocahontas, VA (town) Tazewell County	5	1.27
Laguna Beach, FL (cdp) Bay County	43	1.19
Auberry, CA (cdp) Fresno County	26	1.18
Agency, MO (village) Buchanan County	8	1.08
Clallam Bay, WA (cdp) Clallam County	9	1.02
New Leipzig, ND (city) Grant County	2	1.00
Indianola, CA (cdp) Humboldt County	10	0.97
Canute, OK (town) Washita County	5	0.97
Union, OR (city) Union County	20	0.96
Holton, MI (township) Muskegon County	24	0.94
Hazen, ND (city) Mercer County	23	0.94
Vega, TX (city) Oldham County	9	0.94
Luray, KS (city) Russell County	2	0.94
Simonton Lake, IN (cdp) Elkhart County	47	0.93
Carbondale, KS (city) Osage County	14	0.93
Turpin, OK (cdp) Beaver County	4	0.92
Dumfries, VA (town) Prince William County	45	0.91
Van Buren, IN (town) Grant County	8	0.91
Lawn, TX (town) Taylor County	4	0.91
Lisbon, ND (city) Ransom County	19	0.86
Hettinger, ND (city) Adams County	10	0.85
Ridgeway, OH (village) Hardin County	4	0.85
St. John, MO (city) St. Louis County	55	0.84
Valley Hi, OH (village) Logan County	2	0.81
McClusky, ND (city) Sheridan County	3	0.80
McKees Rocks, PA (borough) Allegheny County	48	0.78
Lake Park, NC (village) Union County	25	0.77
Greensburg, KS (city) Kiowa County	8	0.77
Tonganoxie, KS (city) Leavenworth County	35	0.76
Jefferson, WI (town) Vernon County	10	0.76
Little River, KS (city) Rice County	4	0.76
Boronda, CA (cdp) Monterey County	13	0.73
Otis, KS (city) Rush County	2	0.73
Oakland, OK (town) Marshall County	6	0.72
Payne Springs, TX (town) Henderson County	5	0.72
Center, ND (city) Oliver County	4	0.71
Baxter, MN (city) Crow Wing County	50	0.68
Flasher, ND (city) Morton County	2	0.68
Polk, NE (village) Polk County	2	0.68
Ashley, ND (city) McIntosh County	5	0.67
Wilton, ND (city) McLean County	5	0.67
Gilby, ND (city) Grand Forks County	2	0.66
Pocahontas, AR (city) Randolph County	43	0.65
Salton City, CA (cdp) Imperial County	9	0.64
Mount Dora, FL (city) Lake County	75	0.61
Northchase, NC (cdp) New Hanover County	18	0.61
Ross, MN (township) Roseau County	3	0.61
Wishek, ND (city) McIntosh County	6	0.59
St. John, KS (city) Stafford County	8	0.58
Fort Laramie, WY (town) Goshen County	1	0.58
Harrisburg, SD (city) Lincoln County	20	0.56
Jacobus, PA (borough) York County	10	0.56
Patterson Heights, PA (borough) Beaver County	4	0.56
Peppermill Village, MD (cdp) Prince George's County	26	0.54
Holton, KS (city) Jackson County	18	0.54
Garrison, ND (city) McLean County	7	0.54
Pine Lake, GA (city) DeKalb County	4	0.53
Scranton, KS (city) Osage County	4	0.53
Dallas, OR (city) Polk County	74	0.52
Ellis, KS (city) Ellis County	10	0.52
Garfield, MN (township) Polk County	2	0.52
Leitchfield, KY (city) Grayson County	34	0.51
West Fargo, ND (city) Cass County	115	0.48
Ness City, KS (city) Ness County	7	0.48
Quinter, KS (city) Gove County	4	0.47
Boulder Hill, IL (cdp) Kendall County	40	0.46
Gorham, KS (city) Russell County	2	0.46
Selma, AL (city) Dallas County	93	0.45
McPherson, KS (city) McPherson County	60	0.45
Lake George, NY (town) Warren County	16	0.45
Dunbar, WV (city) Kanawha County	34	0.43
Macksville, KS (city) Stafford County	2	0.42
Pineville, LA (city) Rapides Parish	60	0.41
Sunnyslope, CA (cdp) Riverside County	20	0.41
Adrian, MO (city) Bates County	8	0.41
Bangor, MI (township) Van Buren County	8	0.41
Rouse, CA (cdp) Stanislaus County	8	0.41
Williston, VT (town) Chittenden County	34	0.40
East Nottingham, PA (township) Chester County	33	0.40
Coraopolis, PA (borough) Allegheny County	23	0.40
Springfield, PA (township) York County	20	0.40
Wyoming, MN (city) Chisago County	30	0.39
Castlewood, VA (cdp) Russell County	8	0.39
Parachute, CO (town) Garfield County	4	0.39
Healy, KS (cdp) Lane County	1	0.39
Manistee, MI (city) Manistee County	24	0.38
Clancy, MT (cdp) Jefferson County	7	0.38
West Liberty, OH (village) Logan County	7	0.38
Lake St. Croix Beach, MN (city) Washington County	4	0.38
Wilson, KS (city) Ellsworth County	3	0.38
Elkton, MD (town) Cecil County	55	0.37
Aquia Harbour, VA (cdp) Stafford County	24	0.37
Lake Hallie, WI (village) Chippewa County	22	0.36
De Soto, KS (city) Johnson County	20	0.36
Hagers, IN (town) Wayne County	6	0.36
Washington, KS (city) Washington County	4	0.36
Elgin, ND (city) Grant County	2	0.35
Otsego, MI (township) Allegan County	19	0.34
Lake, MN (township) Roseau County	8	0.34
Flossmoor, IL (village) Cook County	30	0.33
Garden City Park, NY (cdp) Nassau County	26	0.33
Hoisington, KS (city) Barton County	9	0.33
Pratt, KS (city) Pratt County	22	0.32
Loomis, CA (town) Placer County	21	0.32
Tunkhannock, PA (borough) Wyoming County	6	0.32
Alma, NE (city) Harlan County	4	0.32
Benton, KS (city) Butler County	3	0.32
Bismarck, ND (city) Burleigh County	178	0.30
Skiatook, OK (town) Osage County	22	0.30
Experiment, GA (cdp) Spalding County	9	0.30
Capac, MI (village) St. Clair County	6	0.30
Mapleton, ND (city) Cass County	2	0.30
Maple Heights, OH (city) Cuyahoga County	68	0.29
Niceville, FL (city) Okaloosa County	37	0.29
Silverton, OH (city) Hamilton County	14	0.29
Rugby, ND (city) Pierce County	8	0.29
St. Matthews, KY (city) Jefferson County	48	0.28
Mastic, NY (cdp) Suffolk County	40	0.28
North Kansas City, MO (city) Clay County	12	0.28
Chapman, KS (city) Dickinson County	4	0.28
Mount Vernon, IA (city) Linn County	12	0.27
Plains, PA (township) Luzerne County	26	0.26
Midland, WA (cdp) Pierce County	25	0.26

Please refer to the Explanation of Data in the front of the book for more detailed information.

Ancestry

German Russian

Top 150 Places Sorted by Percent of Total Population

Based on places with total population of 7,500 or more

Place	Population	%
Hays, KS (city) Ellis County	308	1.52
Mount Dora, FL (city) Lake County	75	0.61
Dallas, OR (city) Polk County	74	0.52
West Fargo, ND (city) Cass County	115	0.48
Boulder Hill, IL (cdp) Kendall County	40	0.46
Selma, AL (city) Dallas County	93	0.45
McPherson, KS (city) McPherson County	60	0.45
Dunbar, WV (city) Kanawha County	34	0.43
Pineville, LA (city) Rapides Parish	60	0.41
Williston, VT (town) Chittenden County	34	0.40
East Nottingham, PA (township) Chester County	33	0.40
Wyoming, MN (city) Chisago County	30	0.39
Elkton, MD (town) Cecil County	55	0.37
Flossmoor, IL (village) Cook County	30	0.33
Garden City Park, NY (cdp) Nassau County	26	0.33
Bismarck, ND (city) Burleigh County	178	0.30
Maple Heights, OH (city) Cuyahoga County	68	0.29
Niceville, FL (city) Okaloosa County	37	0.29
St. Matthews, KY (city) Jefferson County	48	0.28
Mastic, NY (cdp) Suffolk County	40	0.28
Plains, PA (township) Luzerne County	26	0.26
Midland, WA (cdp) Pierce County	25	0.26
New Carrollton, MD (city) Prince George's County	30	0.25
Vashon, WA (cdp) King County	25	0.25
Alderwood Manor, WA (cdp) Snohomish County	19	0.24
Webster Groves, MO (city) St. Louis County	53	0.23
Sterling, CO (city) Logan County	33	0.23
Tonawanda, NY (city) Erie County	33	0.22
Riverton, WY (city) Fremont County	20	0.20
Norwood, MA (cdp/town) Norfolk County	55	0.19
Owatonna, MN (city) Steele County	48	0.19
Matteson, IL (village) Cook County	33	0.19
Guthrie, OK (city) Logan County	19	0.19
Crookston, MN (city) Polk County	15	0.19
Havre de Grace, MD (city) Harford County	23	0.18
Topeka, KS (city) Shawnee County	220	0.17
Newport, RI (city) Newport County	43	0.17
Patterson, CA (city) Stanislaus County	33	0.17
Mandan, ND (city) Morton County	31	0.17
Cloverly, MD (cdp) Montgomery County	26	0.17
Ottawa, KS (city) Franklin County	21	0.17
Triangle, VA (cdp) Prince William County	13	0.17
Southgate, MI (city) Wayne County	49	0.16
Kinston, NC (city) Lenoir County	36	0.16
Five Corners, WA (cdp) Clark County	28	0.16
Washington Court House, OH (city) Fayette County	23	0.16
Miles City, MT (city) Custer County	13	0.16
Foothill Farms, CA (cdp) Sacramento County	50	0.15
Lower Macungie, PA (township) Lehigh County	42	0.15
Lochearn, MD (cdp) Baltimore County	39	0.15
Bethany, OK (city) Oklahoma County	29	0.15
Hanover, NH (cdp) Grafton County	13	0.15
Princeton, IL (city) Bureau County	12	0.15
Wilson, PA (borough) Northampton County	12	0.15
Ferguson, MO (city) St. Louis County	29	0.14
Lindenwold, NJ (borough) Camden County	25	0.14
Fort Drum, NY (cdp) Jefferson County	17	0.14
Redlands, CO (cdp) Mesa County	11	0.14
Temple Hills, MD (cdp) Prince George's County	11	0.14
Troy, NY (city) Rensselaer County	65	0.13
Sierra Vista, AZ (city) Cochise County	57	0.13
Duncan, OK (city) Stephens County	29	0.13
Bel Air North, MD (cdp) Harford County	36	0.12
Hastings, MN (city) Dakota County	26	0.12
Waynesboro, VA (ind. city) Waynesboro independent city	26	0.12
Hopkins, MN (city) Hennepin County	21	0.12
Dickinson, ND (city) Stark County	20	0.12
Hope Mills, NC (town) Cumberland County	17	0.12
Dobbs Ferry, NY (village) Westchester County	13	0.12
Hanover, NH (town) Grafton County	13	0.12
Holualoa, HI (cdp) Hawaii County	12	0.12
Bonadelle Ranchos-Madera Ranchos, CA (cdp) Madera County	11	0.12
Olathe, KS (city) Johnson County	127	0.11
Walla Walla, WA (city) Walla Walla County	35	0.11
Aberdeen, SD (city) Brown County	27	0.11
Ashland, OH (city) Ashland County	22	0.11
Orangeburg, SC (city) Orangeburg County	15	0.11
Thompsonville, CT (cdp) Hartford County	10	0.11
Carson, CA (city) Los Angeles County	88	0.10
Garfield Heights, OH (city) Cuyahoga County	28	0.10
Sun City Center, FL (cdp) Hillsborough County	20	0.10
Central Point, OR (city) Jackson County	16	0.10
Grover Beach, CA (city) San Luis Obispo County	13	0.10
Sartell, MN (city) Stearns County	13	0.10
Haverstraw, NY (village) Rockland County	12	0.10
Gages Lake, IL (cdp) Lake County	10	0.10
Socorro, NM (city) Socorro County	9	0.10
Lakewood, WA (city) Pierce County	51	0.09
Grove City, OH (city) Franklin County	29	0.09
Zion, IL (city) Lake County	23	0.09
Old Jamestown, MO (cdp) St. Louis County	18	0.09
Wantagh, NY (cdp) Nassau County	17	0.09
Pacific Grove, CA (city) Monterey County	14	0.09
Sartell, MN (city) Stearns County	13	0.09
Independence, KS (city) Montgomery County	9	0.09
St. Joseph, MI (charter township) Berrien County	9	0.09
Dalton, MI (township) Muskegon County	8	0.09
West Covina, CA (city) Los Angeles County	88	0.08
Billings, MT (city) Yellowstone County	83	0.08
Fargo, ND (city) Cass County	80	0.08
Evanston, IL (city) Cook County	62	0.08
Rocky Mount, NC (city) Nash County	47	0.08
La Mesa, CA (city) San Diego County	43	0.08
Bremerton, WA (city) Kitsap County	31	0.08
Panama City, FL (city) Bay County	29	0.08
Spartanburg, SC (city) Spartanburg County	29	0.08
Hinesville, GA (city) Liberty County	27	0.08
Kankakee, IL (city) Kankakee County	21	0.08
Lebanon, PA (city) Lebanon County	21	0.08
Le Ray, NY (town) Jefferson County	17	0.08
North Augusta, SC (city) Aiken County	17	0.08
Sahuarita, AZ (town) Pima County	17	0.08
Marina, CA (city) Monterey County	15	0.08
Murray, KY (city) Calloway County	14	0.08
Stafford, TX (city) Fort Bend County	13	0.08
Brunswick, ME (cdp) Cumberland County	12	0.08
Bellevue, WI (village) Brown County	11	0.08
Atchison, KS (city) Atchison County	9	0.08
Redding, CA (city) Shasta County	61	0.07
Silver Spring, MD (cdp) Montgomery County	48	0.07
Valdosta, GA (city) Lowndes County	35	0.07
Wheaton, MD (cdp) Montgomery County	32	0.07
Clifton Park, NY (town) Saratoga County	26	0.07
Gurnee, IL (village) Lake County	22	0.07
Springville, UT (city) Utah County	19	0.07
West St. Paul, MN (city) Dakota County	14	0.07
Colonial Heights, VA (ind. city) Colonial Heights independent city	12	0.07
Snellville, GA (city) Gwinnett County	12	0.07
Lebanon, OR (city) Linn County	11	0.07
Pierre, SD (city) Hughes County	10	0.07
Vermillion, SD (city) Clay County	7	0.07
Delta, CO (city) Delta County	6	0.07
Milwaukee, WI (city) Milwaukee County	376	0.06
West Valley City, UT (city) Salt Lake County	74	0.06
Asheville, NC (city) Buncombe County	53	0.06
Racine, WI (city) Racine County	51	0.06
Edmond, OK (city) Oklahoma County	46	0.06
Delray Beach, FL (city) Palm Beach County	38	0.06
Salina, KS (city) Saline County	27	0.06
Muskogee, OK (city) Muskogee County	22	0.06
Alton, IL (city) Madison County	16	0.06
Paducah, KY (city) McCracken County	16	0.06
Maplewood, NJ (township) Essex County	14	0.06
Pleasantville, NJ (city) Atlantic County	13	0.06
Brunswick, ME (town) Cumberland County	12	0.06
Radcliff, KY (city) Hardin County	12	0.06
Salmon Creek, WA (cdp) Clark County	12	0.06
Marshfield, WI (city) Wood County	11	0.06
Marshfield, WI (city) Wood County	11	0.06
Rio Linda, CA (cdp) Sacramento County	9	0.06

Ancestry

Greek

U.S. and 50 States Sorted by Population and Percent of Total Population

Place	Population	%
United States	**1,337,576**	**0.44**
New York	163,796	0.85
California	138,194	0.38
Illinois	105,569	0.83
Florida	94,742	0.51
Massachusetts	85,195	1.32
Pennsylvania	66,404	0.53
New Jersey	65,156	0.75
Ohio	58,649	0.51
Michigan	46,165	0.46
Texas	43,145	0.18
Virginia	34,660	0.44
Maryland	33,952	0.60
Connecticut	31,649	0.89
North Carolina	25,926	0.28
Washington	25,865	0.39
Arizona	24,950	0.40
Indiana	23,572	0.37
New Hampshire	21,025	1.60
Georgia	19,761	0.21
Colorado	19,656	0.40
Wisconsin	19,155	0.34
Missouri	15,635	0.26
South Carolina	13,475	0.30
Oregon	13,213	0.35
Utah	13,047	0.49
Minnesota	12,277	0.23
Nevada	11,346	0.43
Tennessee	11,234	0.18
Alabama	8,986	0.19
Rhode Island	7,603	0.72
Iowa	7,202	0.24
Maine	6,702	0.50
Kentucky	6,669	0.16
Louisiana	5,914	0.13
Oklahoma	5,871	0.16
West Virginia	5,595	0.30
New Mexico	5,103	0.25
Delaware	4,820	0.55
Idaho	4,723	0.31
Kansas	4,147	0.15
Nebraska	3,713	0.21
Arkansas	3,592	0.13
Mississippi	3,217	0.11
Montana	3,090	0.32
Wyoming	2,634	0.48
Vermont	2,600	0.42
Alaska	2,244	0.32
District of Columbia	2,120	0.36
Hawaii	1,957	0.15
South Dakota	1,025	0.13
North Dakota	636	0.10

Place	Population	%
New Hampshire	21,025	1.60
Massachusetts	85,195	1.32
Connecticut	31,649	0.89
New York	163,796	0.85
Illinois	105,569	0.83
New Jersey	65,156	0.75
Rhode Island	7,603	0.72
Maryland	33,952	0.60
Delaware	4,820	0.55
Pennsylvania	66,404	0.53
Florida	94,742	0.51
Ohio	58,649	0.51
Maine	6,702	0.50
Utah	13,047	0.49
Wyoming	2,634	0.48
Michigan	46,165	0.46
United States	**1,337,576**	**0.44**
Virginia	34,660	0.44
Nevada	11,346	0.43
Vermont	2,600	0.42
Arizona	24,950	0.40
Colorado	19,656	0.40
Washington	25,865	0.39
California	138,194	0.38
Indiana	23,572	0.37
District of Columbia	2,120	0.36
Oregon	13,213	0.35
Wisconsin	19,155	0.34
Montana	3,090	0.32
Alaska	2,244	0.32
Idaho	4,723	0.31
South Carolina	13,475	0.30
West Virginia	5,595	0.30
North Carolina	25,926	0.28
Missouri	15,635	0.26
New Mexico	5,103	0.25
Iowa	7,202	0.24
Minnesota	12,277	0.23
Georgia	19,761	0.21
Nebraska	3,713	0.21
Alabama	8,986	0.19
Texas	43,145	0.18
Tennessee	11,234	0.18
Kentucky	6,669	0.16
Oklahoma	5,871	0.16
Kansas	4,147	0.15
Hawaii	1,957	0.15
Louisiana	5,914	0.13
Arkansas	3,592	0.13
South Dakota	1,025	0.13
Mississippi	3,217	0.11
North Dakota	636	0.10

Please refer to the Explanation of Data in the front of the book for more detailed information.

Ancestry

Greek

Top 150 Places Sorted by Population

Based on all places, regardless of total population

Place	Population	%
New York, NY (city) Kings County	76,597	0.95
Queens, NY (borough) Queens County	41,654	1.89
Chicago, IL (city) Cook County	17,672	0.65
Brooklyn, NY (borough) Kings County	14,075	0.57
Manhattan, NY (borough) New York County	13,078	0.83
Los Angeles, CA (city) Los Angeles County	12,497	0.33
Hempstead, NY (town) Nassau County	10,033	1.33
Oyster Bay, NY (town) Nassau County	6,908	2.37
Brookhaven, NY (town) Suffolk County	5,703	1.19
Phoenix, AZ (city) Maricopa County	5,234	0.36
San Diego, CA (city) San Diego County	5,154	0.40
Houston, TX (city) Harris County	5,132	0.25
Boston, MA (city) Suffolk County	4,794	0.80
Seattle, WA (city) King County	4,462	0.75
Philadelphia, PA (city) Philadelphia County	4,288	0.28
San Francisco, CA (city) San Francisco County	4,216	0.53
Staten Island, NY (borough) Richmond County	4,183	0.90
Charlotte, NC (city) Mecklenburg County	4,046	0.57
Manchester, NH (city) Hillsborough County	3,676	3.35
Bronx, NY (borough) Bronx County	3,607	0.26
North Hempstead, NY (town) Nassau County	3,568	1.60
Peabody, MA (city) Essex County	3,419	6.78
Huntington, NY (town) Suffolk County	3,284	1.62
Virginia Beach, VA (ind. city) Virginia Beach independent city	3,185	0.73
Islip, NY (town) Suffolk County	3,126	0.94
Smithtown, NY (town) Suffolk County	3,078	2.62
San Jose, CA (city) Santa Clara County	3,018	0.33
Columbus, OH (city) Franklin County	2,987	0.39
Tarpon Springs, FL (city) Pinellas County	2,892	12.54
Lowell, MA (city) Middlesex County	2,821	2.68
Lynn, MA (city) Essex County	2,729	3.04
Portland, OR (city) Multnomah County	2,676	0.47
Jacksonville, FL (city) Duval County	2,672	0.33
Baltimore, MD (city) Baltimore city County	2,621	0.42
Las Vegas, NV (city) Clark County	2,578	0.44
Denver, CO (city) Denver County	2,504	0.43
Norwalk, CT (city/town) Fairfield County	2,483	2.93
Indianapolis, IN (city) Marion County	2,372	0.29
Austin, TX (city) Travis County	2,359	0.31
Stamford, CT (city/town) Fairfield County	2,296	1.90
Clearwater, FL (city) Pinellas County	2,266	2.10
Dallas, TX (city) Dallas County	2,251	0.19
Sacramento, CA (city) Sacramento County	2,242	0.49
Worcester, MA (city) Worcester County	2,240	1.24
Babylon, NY (town) Suffolk County	2,182	1.02
Tucson, AZ (city) Pima County	2,136	0.41
Washington, DC (city) District of Columbia	2,120	0.36
Pittsburgh, PA (city) Allegheny County	2,108	0.68
San Antonio, TX (city) Medina County	1,914	0.15
Naperville, IL (city) DuPage County	1,872	1.33
Albuquerque, NM (city) Bernalillo County	1,797	0.34
Orland Park, IL (village) Cook County	1,744	3.17
Tampa, FL (city) Hillsborough County	1,723	0.52
Nashua, NH (city) Hillsborough County	1,698	1.95
Scottsdale, AZ (city) Maricopa County	1,675	0.77
Skokie, IL (village) Cook County	1,666	2.61
Arlington Heights, IL (village) Cook County	1,599	2.13
Long Beach, CA (city) Los Angeles County	1,580	0.34
Milwaukee, WI (city) Milwaukee County	1,571	0.27
Des Plaines, IL (city) Cook County	1,559	2.72
Salt Lake City, UT (city) Salt Lake County	1,542	0.84
Haverhill, MA (city) Essex County	1,493	2.48
Henderson, NV (city) Clark County	1,492	0.60
Paradise, NV (cdp) Clark County	1,444	0.66
Chandler, AZ (city) Maricopa County	1,441	0.63
Cleveland, OH (city) Cuyahoga County	1,435	0.35
Mesa, AZ (city) Maricopa County	1,412	0.32
Salem, MA (city) Essex County	1,400	3.42
Campbell, OH (city) Mahoning County	1,393	16.50
Oklahoma City, OK (city) Oklahoma County	1,392	0.25
Arlington, VA (cdp) Arlington County	1,390	0.70
Raleigh, NC (city) Wake County	1,389	0.36
Dracut, MA (town) Middlesex County	1,362	4.70
Glenview, IL (village) Cook County	1,332	3.05
Norfolk, VA (ind. city) Norfolk independent city	1,328	0.55
Minneapolis, MN (city) Hennepin County	1,326	0.35
Schaumburg, IL (village) Cook County	1,317	1.80
Mount Prospect, IL (village) Cook County	1,303	2.42
Palos Hills, IL (city) Cook County	1,289	7.42
Upper Darby, PA (township) Delaware County	1,276	1.55
Livonia, MI (city) Wayne County	1,272	1.30
Yonkers, NY (city) Westchester County	1,272	0.65
Arlington, MA (cdp/town) Middlesex County	1,253	2.97
Oakland, CA (city) Alameda County	1,246	0.32
Santa Clarita, CA (city) Los Angeles County	1,243	0.72
Commack, NY (cdp) Suffolk County	1,230	3.40
St. Petersburg, FL (city) Pinellas County	1,228	0.50
Joliet, IL (city) Will County	1,225	0.84
Gilbert, AZ (town) Maricopa County	1,217	0.62
Glendale, CA (city) Los Angeles County	1,214	0.63
Fort Worth, TX (city) Tarrant County	1,211	0.17
Colorado Springs, CO (city) El Paso County	1,203	0.30
Greenburgh, NY (town) Westchester County	1,202	1.37
Huntington Beach, CA (city) Orange County	1,199	0.63
Nashville-Davidson, TN (metro govt) Davidson County	1,199	0.20
Palm Harbor, FL (cdp) Pinellas County	1,194	2.05
Spring Valley, NV (cdp) Clark County	1,183	0.69
Oak Lawn, IL (village) Cook County	1,162	2.08
Ann Arbor, MI (city) Washtenaw County	1,161	1.01
Canton, OH (city) Stark County	1,154	1.55
Sterling Heights, MI (city) Macomb County	1,148	0.89
Orangetown, NY (town) Rockland County	1,141	2.35
Park Ridge, IL (city) Cook County	1,134	3.06
Akron, OH (city) Summit County	1,127	0.56
Kansas City, MO (city) Jackson County	1,124	0.25
Winston-Salem, NC (city) Forsyth County	1,114	0.50
Morton Grove, IL (village) Cook County	1,109	4.85
Niles, IL (village) Cook County	1,107	3.76
Levittown, NY (cdp) Nassau County	1,100	2.06
Parma, OH (city) Cuyahoga County	1,087	1.33
Brookline, MA (cdp/town) Norfolk County	1,082	1.87
Fresno, CA (city) Fresno County	1,082	0.22
Beverly, MA (city) Essex County	1,068	2.71
Fort Lauderdale, FL (city) Broward County	1,067	0.64
Tinley Park, IL (village) Cook County	1,065	1.94
Aurora, IL (city) Kane County	1,065	0.56
Troy, MI (city) Oakland County	1,057	1.31
Newton, MA (city) Middlesex County	1,056	1.26
Reno, NV (city) Washoe County	1,055	0.48
Somerville, MA (city) Middlesex County	1,054	1.40
Greenwich, CT (town) Fairfield County	1,047	1.72
Cape Coral, FL (city) Lee County	1,037	0.69
Roseville, CA (city) Placer County	1,029	0.90
Bakersfield, CA (city) Kern County	1,029	0.31
Louisville-Jefferson County, KY (metro govt) Jefferson County	1,023	0.17
Cambridge, MA (city) Middlesex County	1,020	0.99
Northbrook, IL (village) Cook County	1,011	3.07
Plano, TX (city) Collin County	1,006	0.39
San Tan Valley, AZ (cdp) Pinal County	1,003	1.57
Shelby, MI (charter township) Macomb County	996	1.37
Southampton, NY (town) Suffolk County	995	1.76
Toms River, NJ (township) Ocean County	986	1.08
Memphis, TN (city) Shelby County	985	0.15
Brockton, MA (city) Plymouth County	978	1.04
Toms River, NJ (cdp) Ocean County	976	1.10
Fort Collins, CO (city) Larimer County	965	0.69
Lincolnwood, IL (village) Cook County	964	7.76
Atlanta, GA (city) Fulton County	956	0.23
Chesapeake, VA (ind. city) Chesapeake independent city	955	0.44
Santa Rosa, CA (city) Sonoma County	939	0.58
Danvers, MA (cdp/town) Essex County	937	3.59
Anchorage, AK (municipality) Anchorage Municipality	935	0.33
Fort Lee, NJ (borough) Bergen County	933	2.65
Thousand Oaks, CA (city) Ventura County	929	0.75
Spokane, WA (city) Spokane County	924	0.45
Addison, IL (village) DuPage County	921	2.51
Aurora, CO (city) Arapahoe County	920	0.29
Arvada, CO (city) Jefferson County	919	0.88
Madison, WI (city) Dane County	919	0.40
Tallahassee, FL (city) Leon County	917	0.52

SECTION THREE

Please refer to the Explanation of Data in the front of the book for more detailed information.

Ancestry

Greek

Top 150 Places Sorted by Percent of Total Population

Based on all places, regardless of total population

Place	Population	%
Sarona, WI (town) Washburn County	250	35.66
Cassel, CA (cdp) Shasta County	154	33.62
Floris, IA (city) Davis County	32	24.81
Timken, KS (city) Rush County	10	21.28
Silvana, WA (cdp) Snohomish County	13	20.97
Truchas, NM (cdp) Rio Arriba County	126	19.03
Harbor Hills, NY (cdp) Nassau County	94	18.99
Martins Creek, PA (cdp) Northampton County	110	17.83
Kingvale, CA (cdp) Nevada County	28	16.87
Campbell, OH (city) Mahoning County	1,393	16.50
Grand Pass, MO (village) Saline County	4	16.00
Cheshire, MA (cdp) Berkshire County	96	15.89
Tampico, WA (cdp) Yakima County	16	14.55
Ackworth, IA (city) Warren County	8	14.55
Walloon Lake, MI (cdp) Charlevoix County	32	14.16
Harding-Birch Lakes, AK (cdp) Fairbanks North Star Borough	32	13.62
Prosper, MN (township) Lake of the Woods County	6	13.04
Tarpon Springs, FL (city) Pinellas County	2,892	12.54
Cucumber, WV (cdp) McDowell County	12	12.37
Timothy, MN (township) Crow Wing County	18	12.16
Rennerdale, PA (cdp) Allegheny County	170	11.96
James, CO (town) Boulder County	33	11.87
Deer Lake, PA (cdp) Fayette County	78	11.78
Plandome Manor, NY (village) Nassau County	97	11.02
Winifred, MT (town) Fergus County	12	10.81
Lake Mohawk, OH (cdp) Carroll County	187	10.77
Shorewood Forest, IN (cdp) Porter County	320	10.61
Bell Buckle, TN (town) Bedford County	41	10.30
Manilla, IN (cdp) Rush County	33	10.28
High Amana, IA (cdp) Iowa County	10	10.20
Milton Mills, NH (cdp) Strafford County	16	10.06
Brogan, OR (cdp) Malheur County	14	9.86
Fort Shaw, MT (cdp) Cascade County	41	9.83
Horseshoe Beach, FL (town) Dixie County	19	9.74
Seven Hills, CO (cdp) Boulder County	17	9.66
Three Lakes, WI (cdp) Oneida County	58	9.46
Venango, PA (borough) Crawford County	19	9.36
Gene Autry, OK (town) Carter County	7	9.33
Lake Buckhorn, OH (cdp) Holmes County	32	9.30
Foster, PA (township) Luzerne County	316	9.23
South Barrington, IL (village) Cook County	403	9.19
Manhasset Hills, NY (cdp) Nassau County	328	8.90
Rochester, VT (cdp) Windsor County	22	8.73
Emlyn, KY (cdp) Whitley County	16	8.70
Aristes, PA (cdp) Columbia County	25	8.62
La Honda, CA (cdp) San Mateo County	103	8.52
Hagali, MN (township) Beltrami County	25	8.50
Old Brookville, NY (village) Nassau County	189	8.49
Mount Orab, OH (village) Brown County	334	8.47
Woods Landing-Jelm, WY (cdp) Albany County	12	8.45
Inverness, IL (village) Cook County	591	8.29
Sparkill, NY (cdp) Rockland County	114	8.25
Cumbola, PA (cdp) Schuylkill County	32	8.12
Eden, WY (cdp) Sweetwater County	20	7.97
Pilot Mound, IA (city) Boone County	14	7.95
Lincolnwood, IL (village) Cook County	964	7.76
Twin Lakes, CO (cdp) Lake County	9	7.76
Gila, NM (cdp) Grant County	34	7.74
Low Moor, VA (cdp) Alleghany County	27	7.69
Grandin, MO (city) Carter County	29	7.67
Rocky Ripple, IN (town) Marion County	49	7.61
Ocean Gate, NJ (borough) Ocean County	122	7.59
Langeloth, PA (cdp) Washington County	33	7.53
Halcott, NY (town) Greene County	20	7.52
Dixon, NM (cdp) Rio Arriba County	78	7.51
Palos Hills, IL (city) Cook County	1,289	7.42
Shinnecock Hills, NY (cdp) Suffolk County	133	7.25
Branson West, MO (city) Stone County	48	7.23
Pleasant Plains, NJ (cdp) Somerset County	58	7.21
High Falls, NY (cdp) Ulster County	62	7.20
Zephyr Cove, NV (cdp) Douglas County	18	7.14
Deer Island, OR (cdp) Columbia County	12	7.14
Beulah Valley, CO (cdp) Pueblo County	32	7.11
Bethany, IN (town) Morgan County	9	7.03
Meeteetse, WY (town) Park County	24	7.02
Northfield, ME (town) Washington County	12	7.02
Dover, MO (town) Lafayette County	7	6.86
Glendo, WY (town) Platte County	17	6.85
Somers, IA (city) Calhoun County	7	6.80
Peabody, MA (city) Essex County	3,419	6.78
Belleair, FL (town) Pinellas County	266	6.78
Bellerose, NY (village) Nassau County	84	6.75
Mattituck, NY (cdp) Suffolk County	279	6.73
Yorkville, OH (village) Jefferson County	86	6.71
Virgin, UT (town) Washington County	24	6.67
Chickaloon, AK (cdp) Matanuska-Susitna Borough	9	6.67
Walpack, NJ (township) Sussex County	2	6.67
Antares, AZ (cdp) Mohave County	10	6.54
Onaway, ID (city) Latah County	20	6.45
East Marion, NY (cdp) Suffolk County	86	6.43
Hill Country Village, TX (city) Bexar County	63	6.43
New Salem, PA (cdp) Fayette County	42	6.41
Edesville, MD (cdp) Kent County	13	6.40
Blauvelt, NY (cdp) Rockland County	335	6.34
Amherst, NH (cdp) Hillsborough County	49	6.31
Rockville, SC (town) Charleston County	10	6.29
Glen Ridge, FL (town) Palm Beach County	15	6.28
Plandome Heights, NY (village) Nassau County	66	6.27
Elma Center, NY (cdp) Erie County	171	6.25
Rhinecliff, NY (cdp) Dutchess County	23	6.20
Upper Brookville, NY (village) Nassau County	92	6.18
Princeton, MA (town) Worcester County	210	6.17
Sylvester, WV (town) Boone County	8	6.15
Dorrington, CA (cdp) Calaveras County	35	6.10
Cape May, NJ (city) Cape May County	224	6.08
Brodheadsville, PA (cdp) Monroe County	105	6.08
Belle Terre, NY (village) Suffolk County	56	6.03
Rensselaer, MO (village) Ralls County	8	6.02
Southview, PA (cdp) Washington County	9	6.00
Mount Carbon, PA (borough) Schuylkill County	6	6.00
Ipswich, MA (town) Essex County	780	5.97
Bedford Park, IL (village) Cook County	34	5.92
Thorne Bay, AK (city) Prince of Wales-Hyder Census Area	29	5.92
East Sandwich, MA (cdp) Barnstable County	225	5.89
Westwood, CA (cdp) Lassen County	63	5.84
Duncan, PA (township) Tioga County	10	5.81
Branchville, NJ (borough) Sussex County	53	5.77
Columbia, NJ (cdp) Warren County	16	5.73
Newark, VT (town) Caledonia County	26	5.71
Blodgett Landing, NH (cdp) Merrimack County	6	5.71
Despard, WV (cdp) Harrison County	42	5.68
Hiles, WI (town) Forest County	20	5.67
Masaryktown, FL (cdp) Hernando County	64	5.66
Effingham, NH (town) Carroll County	72	5.64
Segundo, CO (cdp) Las Animas County	4	5.63
Ayer, MA (cdp) Middlesex County	132	5.62
Bannockburn, IL (village) Lake County	77	5.62
Bethania, NC (town) Forsyth County	16	5.61
Rehoboth Beach, DE (city) Sussex County	65	5.60
Porter, PA (township) Pike County	19	5.60
Parker Strip, AZ (cdp) La Paz County	52	5.59
West Pocomoke, MD (cdp) Somerset County	25	5.59
Gulf Breeze, FL (city) Santa Rosa County	327	5.58
Harleigh, PA (cdp) Luzerne County	60	5.56
Lake Telemark, NJ (cdp) Morris County	75	5.52
Spafford, NY (town) Onondaga County	109	5.51
Belmar, NE (cdp) Keith County	13	5.51
Southworth, WA (cdp) Kitsap County	142	5.50
Littlejohn Island, ME (cdp) Cumberland County	8	5.48
Brownville, NE (village) Nemaha County	6	5.45
Glen Head, NY (cdp) Nassau County	247	5.42
Dyer, AR (city) Crawford County	34	5.42
River Forest, IN (town) Madison County	2	5.41
Delavan Lake, WI (cdp) Walworth County	149	5.38
South Hampton, NH (town) Rockingham County	39	5.38
Pinesdale, MT (town) Ravalli County	35	5.38
Chauncey, WV (cdp) Logan County	39	5.37
Old Bennington, VT (village) Bennington County	10	5.35
Dixville, NH (township) Coos County	4	5.33
Middletown, CA (cdp) Lake County	87	5.29

Please refer to the Explanation of Data in the front of the book for more detailed information.

Ancestry

Greek

Top 150 Places Sorted by Percent of Total Population

Based on places with total population of 7,500 or more

Place	Population	%
Campbell, OH (city) Mahoning County	1,393	16.50
Tarpon Springs, FL (city) Pinellas County	2,892	12.54
Lincolnwood, IL (village) Cook County	964	7.76
Palos Hills, IL (city) Cook County	1,289	7.42
Peabody, MA (city) Essex County	3,419	6.78
Ipswich, MA (town) Essex County	780	5.97
Norridge, IL (village) Cook County	719	4.99
Morton Grove, IL (village) Cook County	1,109	4.85
Dracut, MA (town) Middlesex County	1,362	4.70
Pelham, NH (town) Hillsborough County	579	4.59
Upper Saddle River, NJ (borough) Bergen County	358	4.43
Riverside, CT (cdp) Fairfield County	369	4.39
Montvale, NJ (borough) Bergen County	331	4.32
Lynnfield, MA (cdp/town) Essex County	493	4.29
North Massapequa, NY (cdp) Nassau County	783	4.20
Lake Grove, NY (village) Suffolk County	447	4.06
Farmingdale, NY (village) Nassau County	332	4.06
Oak Brook, IL (village) DuPage County	321	4.06
Manhasset, NY (cdp) Nassau County	326	3.97
Port Jefferson, NY (village) Suffolk County	310	3.96
Boxford, MA (town) Essex County	308	3.89
Schiller Park, IL (village) Cook County	453	3.88
Bellmore, NY (cdp) Nassau County	627	3.87
White Oak, PA (borough) Allegheny County	303	3.83
Tyngsborough, MA (town) Middlesex County	419	3.77
Niles, IL (village) Cook County	1,107	3.76
Island Lake, IL (village) McHenry County	309	3.76
Southborough, MA (town) Worcester County	361	3.75
Port Jefferson Station, NY (cdp) Suffolk County	281	3.74
Hastings-on-Hudson, NY (village) Westchester County	288	3.70
Garden City Park, NY (cdp) Nassau County	288	3.69
Westwood, MA (town) Norfolk County	527	3.66
Timonium, MD (cdp) Baltimore County	356	3.64
Syosset, NY (cdp) Nassau County	685	3.62
Danvers, MA (cdp/town) Essex County	937	3.59
Middleton, MA (town) Essex County	313	3.59
Salisbury, MA (town) Essex County	290	3.56
Palos Heights, IL (city) Cook County	433	3.55
Mira Monte, CA (cdp) Ventura County	277	3.55
River Vale, NJ (township) Bergen County	337	3.52
Sugar Grove, IL (village) Kane County	287	3.50
Bethpage, NY (cdp) Nassau County	574	3.45
Eastchester, NY (cdp) Westchester County	664	3.44
Salem, MA (city) Essex County	1,400	3.42
Commack, NY (cdp) Suffolk County	1,230	3.40
Bloomingdale, IL (village) DuPage County	744	3.40
Dormont, PA (borough) Allegheny County	293	3.39
Munster, IN (town) Lake County	784	3.37
Manchester, NH (city) Hillsborough County	3,676	3.35
Weare, NH (town) Hillsborough County	288	3.33
Broomall, PA (cdp) Delaware County	373	3.31
Clarendon Hills, IL (village) DuPage County	271	3.27
Holiday, FL (cdp) Pasco County	728	3.26
North Reading, MA (town) Middlesex County	470	3.23
Orland Park, IL (village) Cook County	1,744	3.17
Tenafly, NJ (borough) Bergen County	451	3.16
Handy, MI (township) Livingston County	253	3.15
Smithtown, NY (cdp) Suffolk County	820	3.13
Park Ridge, NJ (borough) Bergen County	270	3.13
Itasca, IL (village) DuPage County	263	3.13
Bedford, NH (town) Hillsborough County	642	3.09
Burr Ridge, IL (village) DuPage County	325	3.09
Northbrook, IL (village) Cook County	1,011	3.07
Park Ridge, IL (city) Cook County	1,134	3.06
Glenview, IL (village) Cook County	1,332	3.05
Lynn, MA (city) Essex County	2,729	3.04
Barrington, IL (village) Cook County	322	3.02
Maynard, MA (cdp/town) Middlesex County	302	3.01
Woodbury, NY (cdp) Nassau County	272	3.00
Elmwood Park, IL (village) Cook County	740	2.99
Arlington, MA (cdp/town) Middlesex County	1,253	2.97
Price, UT (city) Carbon County	252	2.97
Norwalk, CT (city/town) Fairfield County	2,483	2.93
Hudson, NH (town) Hillsborough County	702	2.89
Tysons Corner, VA (cdp) Fairfax County	494	2.89
Canonsburg, PA (borough) Washington County	258	2.89
Cumberland Hill, RI (cdp) Providence County	226	2.89
Newmarket, NH (town) Rockingham County	255	2.88
Newton, NJ (town) Sussex County	233	2.87
Hanover, PA (township) Northampton County	302	2.82
Monessen, PA (city) Westmoreland County	221	2.81
Nesconset, NY (cdp) Suffolk County	380	2.79
Weston, MA (town) Middlesex County	311	2.78
Dedham, MA (cdp/town) Norfolk County	668	2.75
Winchester, MA (cdp/town) Middlesex County	576	2.74
Des Plaines, IL (city) Cook County	1,559	2.72
Hingham, MA (town) Plymouth County	591	2.72
West Long Branch, NJ (borough) Monmouth County	221	2.72
Beverly, MA (city) Essex County	1,068	2.71
Frankfort, IL (village) Will County	462	2.71
Marple, PA (township) Delaware County	632	2.70
Garden City, NY (village) Nassau County	596	2.69
Lowell, MA (city) Middlesex County	2,821	2.68
Southold, NY (town) Suffolk County	584	2.68
Seaford, NY (cdp) Nassau County	414	2.68
Mukwonago, WI (town) Waukesha County	209	2.68
Franklin Square, NY (cdp) Nassau County	788	2.66
Portsmouth, NH (city) Rockingham County	558	2.66
Fort Lee, NJ (borough) Bergen County	933	2.65
South Farmingdale, NY (cdp) Nassau County	391	2.65
Millis, MA (town) Norfolk County	207	2.65
Triangle, VA (cdp) Prince William County	203	2.64
Sandwich, MA (town) Barnstable County	543	2.63
Succasunna, NJ (cdp) Morris County	236	2.63
Smithtown, NY (town) Suffolk County	3,078	2.62
Oldsmar, FL (city) Pinellas County	350	2.62
Skokie, IL (village) Cook County	1,666	2.61
Eastchester, NY (town) Westchester County	835	2.61
Kings Park, NY (cdp) Suffolk County	441	2.60
Kinderhook, NY (town) Columbia County	220	2.59
Brighton, PA (township) Beaver County	211	2.59
Wade Hampton, SC (cdp) Greenville County	524	2.58
Newtown, PA (township) Delaware County	312	2.58
Cliffside Park, NJ (borough) Bergen County	598	2.56
Newburyport, MA (city) Essex County	442	2.56
Medway, MA (town) Norfolk County	323	2.56
South Huntington, NY (cdp) Suffolk County	253	2.56
Watertown Town, MA (city) Middlesex County	805	2.55
Stony Brook, NY (cdp) Suffolk County	348	2.55
Short Pump, VA (cdp) Henrico County	610	2.54
Prospect Heights, IL (city) Cook County	413	2.54
Crown Point, IN (city) Lake County	661	2.53
Shiloh, IL (village) St. Clair County	304	2.53
White Marsh, MD (cdp) Baltimore County	241	2.53
Hamilton, MA (town) Essex County	197	2.52
Addison, IL (village) DuPage County	921	2.51
Rocky Point, NY (cdp) Suffolk County	341	2.51
Milford, NH (cdp) Hillsborough County	227	2.51
Mokena, IL (village) Will County	455	2.50
Elfers, FL (cdp) Pasco County	331	2.50
Middletown, PA (township) Delaware County	394	2.49
Brecksville, OH (city) Cuyahoga County	338	2.49
Haverhill, MA (city) Essex County	1,493	2.48
Dix Hills, NY (cdp) Suffolk County	659	2.48
Hazleton, PA (city) Luzerne County	616	2.48
Belmont, MA (cdp/town) Middlesex County	605	2.48
Plainview, NY (cdp) Nassau County	636	2.47
Rehoboth, MA (town) Bristol County	280	2.47
Lake Geneva, WI (city) Walworth County	190	2.47
Vernon, WI (town) Waukesha County	187	2.47
Weirton, WV (city) Hancock County	486	2.46
Wilmington, MA (cdp/town) Middlesex County	531	2.43
Mount Prospect, IL (village) Cook County	1,303	2.42
St. John, IN (town) Lake County	333	2.42
San Carlos, CA (city) San Mateo County	671	2.41
New Territory, TX (cdp) Fort Bend County	405	2.41
Hasbrouck Heights, NJ (borough) Bergen County	283	2.41
Aliquippa, PA (city) Beaver County	236	2.41
Airmont, NY (village) Rockland County	203	2.41
East Lake, FL (cdp) Pinellas County	750	2.40

Ancestry

Guyanese

U.S. and 50 States Sorted by Population and Percent of Total Population

Place	Population	%
United States	**202,258**	**0.07**
New York	123,809	0.64
Florida	21,902	0.12
New Jersey	17,871	0.20
Georgia	7,485	0.08
Maryland	5,981	0.10
Connecticut	3,650	0.10
California	2,932	0.01
Pennsylvania	2,750	0.02
North Carolina	2,234	0.02
Virginia	2,032	0.03
Texas	1,935	0.01
Massachusetts	1,440	0.02
Minnesota	1,294	0.02
Ohio	1,203	0.01
Illinois	897	0.01
Delaware	506	0.06
Tennessee	499	0.01
Michigan	366	<0.01
South Carolina	365	0.01
District of Columbia	355	0.06
Arizona	299	<0.01
Nevada	254	0.01
Washington	236	<0.01
Mississippi	197	0.01
Missouri	180	<0.01
Indiana	158	<0.01
Alabama	149	<0.01
Kansas	145	0.01
Kentucky	131	<0.01
Oregon	119	<0.01
Louisiana	115	<0.01
Colorado	109	<0.01
Rhode Island	83	0.01
New Mexico	81	<0.01
Oklahoma	74	<0.01
Iowa	72	<0.01
Hawaii	59	<0.01
New Hampshire	53	<0.01
West Virginia	46	<0.01
Alaska	45	0.01
Wisconsin	41	<0.01
Vermont	38	0.01
Maine	30	<0.01
Idaho	23	<0.01
Utah	8	<0.01
North Dakota	7	<0.01
Arkansas	0	0.00
Montana	0	0.00
Nebraska	0	0.00
South Dakota	0	0.00
Wyoming	0	0.00

Place	Population	%
New York	123,809	0.64
New Jersey	17,871	0.20
Florida	21,902	0.12
Maryland	5,981	0.10
Connecticut	3,650	0.10
Georgia	7,485	0.08
United States	**202,258**	**0.07**
Delaware	506	0.06
District of Columbia	355	0.06
Virginia	2,032	0.03
Pennsylvania	2,750	0.02
North Carolina	2,234	0.02
Massachusetts	1,440	0.02
Minnesota	1,294	0.02
California	2,932	0.01
Texas	1,935	0.01
Ohio	1,203	0.01
Illinois	897	0.01
Tennessee	499	0.01
South Carolina	365	0.01
Nevada	254	0.01
Mississippi	197	0.01
Kansas	145	0.01
Rhode Island	83	0.01
Alaska	45	0.01
Vermont	38	0.01
Michigan	366	<0.01
Arizona	299	<0.01
Washington	236	<0.01
Missouri	180	<0.01
Indiana	158	<0.01
Alabama	149	<0.01
Kentucky	131	<0.01
Oregon	119	<0.01
Louisiana	115	<0.01
Colorado	109	<0.01
New Mexico	81	<0.01
Oklahoma	74	<0.01
Iowa	72	<0.01
Hawaii	59	<0.01
New Hampshire	53	<0.01
West Virginia	46	<0.01
Wisconsin	41	<0.01
Maine	30	<0.01
Idaho	23	<0.01
Utah	8	<0.01
North Dakota	7	<0.01
Arkansas	0	0.00
Montana	0	0.00
Nebraska	0	0.00
South Dakota	0	0.00
Wyoming	0	0.00

Please refer to the Explanation of Data in the front of the book for more detailed information.

Ancestry

Guyanese

Top 150 Places Sorted by Population

Based on all places, regardless of total population

Place	Population	%
New York, NY (city) Kings County	107,972	1.34
Queens, NY (borough) Queens County	53,961	2.45
Brooklyn, NY (borough) Kings County	38,963	1.58
Bronx, NY (borough) Bronx County	11,837	0.87
Hempstead, NY (town) Nassau County	3,520	0.47
Jersey City, NJ (city) Hudson County	3,025	1.24
East Orange, NJ (city) Essex County	2,746	4.23
Manhattan, NY (borough) New York County	2,259	0.14
Newark, NJ (city) Essex County	2,202	0.80
Schenectady, NY (city) Schenectady County	1,915	2.93
Hartford, CT (city/town) Hartford County	1,086	0.87
Irvington, NJ (township) Essex County	993	1.81
Staten Island, NY (borough) Richmond County	952	0.21
Pine Hills, FL (cdp) Orange County	881	1.33
Valley Stream, NY (village) Nassau County	840	2.27
Clermont, FL (city) Lake County	775	2.96
Babylon, NY (town) Suffolk County	747	0.35
Boston, MA (city) Suffolk County	667	0.11
Philadelphia, PA (city) Philadelphia County	638	0.04
South Miami Heights, FL (cdp) Miami-Dade County	611	1.67
Miramar, FL (city) Broward County	609	0.54
Elmont, NY (cdp) Nassau County	581	1.68
Jacksonville, FL (city) Duval County	578	0.07
Pembroke Pines, FL (city) Broward County	557	0.37
Buffalo, NY (city) Erie County	529	0.20
Yonkers, NY (city) Westchester County	526	0.27
Houston, TX (city) Harris County	510	0.02
Orlovista, FL (cdp) Orange County	500	6.80
Islip, NY (town) Suffolk County	499	0.15
Baltimore, MD (city) Baltimore city County	491	0.08
Albany, NY (city) Albany County	483	0.49
City of Orange, NJ (township) Essex County	481	1.58
Redan, GA (cdp) DeKalb County	473	1.38
Waterbury, CT (city/town) New Haven County	468	0.43
Brookhaven, NY (town) Suffolk County	441	0.09
Los Angeles, CA (city) Los Angeles County	437	0.01
South Plainfield, NJ (borough) Middlesex County	413	1.79
North Hempstead, NY (town) Nassau County	405	0.18
Tamarac, FL (city) Broward County	398	0.67
Elizabeth, NJ (city) Union County	381	0.31
Rochester, NY (city) Monroe County	381	0.18
Ramapo, NY (town) Rockland County	371	0.30
Cleveland, OH (city) Cuyahoga County	370	0.09
Coral Springs, FL (city) Broward County	367	0.30
Mount Vernon, NY (city) Westchester County	360	0.54
Washington, DC (city) District of Columbia	355	0.06
North Valley Stream, NY (cdp) Nassau County	344	2.08
Lehigh Acres, FL (cdp) Lee County	333	0.39
Freeport, NY (village) Nassau County	324	0.76
Orlando, FL (city) Orange County	324	0.14
Miami Gardens, FL (city) Miami-Dade County	322	0.30
Plainfield, NJ (city) Union County	321	0.65
Coconut Creek, FL (city) Broward County	317	0.62
Winter Garden, FL (city) Orange County	307	0.98
Hempstead, NY (village) Nassau County	307	0.58
New Haven, CT (city/town) New Haven County	305	0.24
Bloomfield, NJ (township) Essex County	302	0.64
Charlotte, NC (city) Mecklenburg County	298	0.04
Alafaya, FL (cdp) Orange County	291	0.38
Long Beach, NY (city) Nassau County	289	0.86
Bridgeport, CT (city/town) Fairfield County	284	0.20
Port St. Lucie, FL (city) St. Lucie County	281	0.18
Hillcrest, NY (cdp) Rockland County	280	3.42
Linden, NJ (city) Union County	277	0.69
North Amityville, NY (cdp) Suffolk County	275	1.54
Chicago, IL (city) Cook County	272	0.01
Deerfield Beach, FL (city) Broward County	269	0.36
West Orange, NJ (township) Essex County	260	0.57
Concord, NC (city) Cabarrus County	260	0.35
San Diego, CA (city) San Diego County	260	0.02
Ocoee, FL (city) Orange County	255	0.75
Landover, MD (cdp) Prince George's County	254	1.08
Atlanta, GA (city) Fulton County	249	0.06
Woodbridge, NJ (township) Middlesex County	248	0.25
Lakewood, NJ (cdp) Ocean County	245	0.49

Place	Population	%
Lakewood, NJ (township) Ocean County	245	0.28
Palm Bay, FL (city) Brevard County	244	0.24
Tampa, FL (city) Hillsborough County	240	0.07
Richfield, MN (city) Hennepin County	236	0.68
Middletown, NJ (township) Monmouth County	236	0.35
Kearny, NJ (town) Hudson County	235	0.58
Franklin Square, NY (cdp) Nassau County	234	0.79
Greenburgh, NY (town) Westchester County	226	0.26
West Haven, CT (city/town) New Haven County	224	0.41
Pinellas Park, FL (city) Pinellas County	222	0.46
Edison, NJ (township) Middlesex County	221	0.22
Greensboro, NC (city) Guilford County	209	0.08
High Point, NC (city) Guilford County	207	0.21
Virginia Beach, VA (ind. city) Virginia Beach independent city	207	0.05
Raleigh, NC (city) Wake County	202	0.05
South Orange Village, NJ (township) Essex County	195	1.20
Union, NY (town) Broome County	191	0.34
Essex, MD (cdp) Baltimore County	189	0.49
Minneapolis, MN (city) Hennepin County	189	0.05
Austin, TX (city) Travis County	188	0.02
Oyster Bay, NY (town) Nassau County	187	0.06
Stroud, PA (township) Monroe County	186	0.99
Brandon, FL (cdp) Hillsborough County	186	0.19
Chillum, MD (cdp) Prince George's County	185	0.53
Hollywood, FL (city) Broward County	184	0.13
Huntington, NY (town) Suffolk County	180	0.09
Tallahassee, FL (city) Leon County	178	0.10
St. Petersburg, FL (city) Pinellas County	178	0.07
Taunton, MA (city) Bristol County	176	0.31
White Plains, NY (city) Westchester County	175	0.31
Bethlehem, PA (city) Northampton County	173	0.23
Batavia, NY (town) Genesee County	172	2.60
Sunrise, FL (city) Broward County	170	0.20
Watertown, NY (city) Jefferson County	169	0.63
Piscataway, NJ (township) Middlesex County	169	0.31
Deltona, FL (city) Volusia County	168	0.20
Floral Park, NY (village) Nassau County	167	1.04
Bogota, NJ (borough) Bergen County	166	2.03
Kendale Lakes, FL (cdp) Miami-Dade County	166	0.30
Arlington Heights, PA (cdp) Monroe County	164	2.56
Stockbridge, GA (city) Henry County	164	0.69
Deer Park, NY (cdp) Suffolk County	164	0.58
St. Regis Mohawk Reservation, NY (reservation) Franklin County	162	5.17
Southampton, NJ (township) Burlington County	162	1.54
Elkton, MD (town) Cecil County	162	1.08
Greenville, NY (town) Orange County	161	3.57
Indiantown, FL (cdp) Martin County	159	2.68
South Kensington, MD (cdp) Montgomery County	158	1.94
Syracuse, NY (city) Onondaga County	158	0.11
Bay Shore, NY (cdp) Suffolk County	157	0.56
Lighthouse Point, FL (city) Broward County	156	1.49
St. James, MD (cdp) Washington County	155	5.07
Kissimmee, FL (city) Osceola County	153	0.26
Fridley, MN (city) Anoka County	151	0.55
Highland, NY (cdp) Ulster County	149	2.62
Lloyd, NY (town) Ulster County	149	1.38
Cherry Hill, VA (cdp) Prince William County	148	0.95
Franklin, NJ (township) Somerset County	148	0.25
Clinton, MD (cdp) Prince George's County	147	0.41
Riverview, FL (cdp) Hillsborough County	146	0.22
Arlington, VA (cdp) Arlington County	146	0.07
Peekskill, NY (city) Westchester County	144	0.62
Town 'n' Country, FL (cdp) Hillsborough County	144	0.19
Brooklyn Center, MN (city) Hennepin County	142	0.48
Clarksville, TN (city) Montgomery County	142	0.11
Bayonne, NJ (city) Hudson County	140	0.23
Fayetteville, NC (city) Cumberland County	139	0.07
Brentwood, NY (cdp) Suffolk County	138	0.25
Palm Coast, FL (city) Flagler County	138	0.19
Colonie, NY (town) Albany County	137	0.17
Valrico, FL (cdp) Hillsborough County	136	0.39
North Lauderdale, FL (city) Broward County	136	0.33
Pennsauken, NJ (township) Camden County	135	0.38
Columbus, OH (city) Franklin County	135	0.02
San Antonio, TX (city) Medina County	135	0.01

SECTION THREE

Ancestry

Guyanese

Top 150 Places Sorted by Percent of Total Population

Based on all places, regardless of total population

Place	Population	%
Orlovista, FL (cdp) Orange County	500	6.80
Tusayan, AZ (cdp) Coconino County	11	6.08
St. Regis Mohawk Reservation, NY (reservation) Franklin County	162	5.17
St. James, MD (cdp) Washington County	155	5.07
Clarcona, FL (cdp) Orange County	112	4.33
Olga, FL (cdp) Lee County	75	4.33
East Orange, NJ (city) Essex County	2,746	4.23
Greenville, NY (town) Orange County	161	3.57
Hillcrest, NY (cdp) Rockland County	280	3.42
Zephyrhills North, FL (cdp) Pasco County	71	3.05
Clermont, FL (city) Lake County	775	2.96
Schenectady, NY (city) Schenectady County	1,915	2.93
Manhasset Hills, NY (cdp) Nassau County	102	2.77
Ballville, OH (cdp) Sandusky County	88	2.77
Indiantown, FL (cdp) Martin County	159	2.68
Highland, NY (cdp) Ulster County	149	2.62
Batavia, NY (town) Genesee County	172	2.60
Arlington Heights, PA (cdp) Monroe County	164	2.56
Queens, NY (borough) Queens County	53,961	2.45
Menands, NY (village) Albany County	97	2.43
Lincoln University, PA (cdp) Chester County	44	2.28
Valley Stream, NY (village) Nassau County	840	2.27
Heron Bay, GA (cdp) Henry County	71	2.22
Tangerine, FL (cdp) Orange County	39	2.22
Elmsford, NY (village) Westchester County	102	2.21
North Valley Stream, NY (cdp) Nassau County	344	2.08
Bogota, NJ (borough) Bergen County	166	2.03
South Kensington, MD (cdp) Montgomery County	158	1.94
Gotha, FL (cdp) Orange County	37	1.87
Irvington, NJ (township) Essex County	993	1.81
Yoe, PA (borough) York County	16	1.80
South Plainfield, NJ (borough) Middlesex County	413	1.79
Diana, NY (town) Lewis County	36	1.74
Watergate, FL (cdp) Palm Beach County	48	1.70
Elmont, NY (cdp) Nassau County	581	1.68
South Miami Heights, FL (cdp) Miami-Dade County	611	1.67
Oakland, FL (town) Orange County	38	1.66
Bozrah, CT (town) New London County	42	1.62
Brooklyn, NY (borough) Kings County	38,963	1.58
City of Orange, NJ (township) Essex County	481	1.58
Groveland, FL (city) Lake County	125	1.58
Calcium, NY (cdp) Jefferson County	56	1.58
Indian Lake, NY (town) Hamilton County	21	1.58
North Amityville, NY (cdp) Suffolk County	275	1.54
Southampton, NJ (township) Burlington County	162	1.54
Two Harbors, MN (city) Lake County	56	1.51
Lighthouse Point, FL (city) Broward County	156	1.49
Friendship, NY (cdp) Allegany County	18	1.48
Blountstown, FL (city) Calhoun County	37	1.46
Riverdale Park, MD (town) Prince George's County	97	1.41
South Floral Park, NY (village) Nassau County	22	1.41
Redan, GA (cdp) DeKalb County	473	1.38
Lloyd, NY (town) Ulster County	149	1.38
Mount Rainier, MD (city) Prince George's County	110	1.35
New York, NY (city) Kings County	107,972	1.34
Pine Hills, FL (cdp) Orange County	881	1.33
Pembroke, NY (town) Genesee County	57	1.32
Stony Brook University, NY (cdp) Suffolk County	109	1.30
Rodney Village, DE (cdp) Kent County	23	1.30
Odessa, FL (cdp) Pasco County	88	1.26
North Beach, MD (town) Calvert County	20	1.25
Cochecton, NY (town) Sullivan County	17	1.25
Jersey City, NJ (city) Hudson County	3,025	1.24
Medford Lakes, NJ (borough) Burlington County	51	1.22
South Orange Village, NJ (township) Essex County	195	1.20
Social Circle, GA (city) Walton County	50	1.19
Mascotte, FL (city) Lake County	56	1.16
South Hempstead, NY (cdp) Nassau County	37	1.16
Hillandale, MD (cdp) Montgomery County	73	1.14
Bridgewater, CT (town) Litchfield County	19	1.11
Landover, MD (cdp) Prince George's County	254	1.08
Elkton, MD (town) Cecil County	162	1.08
Cliffwood Beach, NJ (cdp) Monmouth County	33	1.08
Greentree, NJ (cdp) Camden County	121	1.06
Factoryville, PA (borough) Wyoming County	12	1.05
Floral Park, NY (village) Nassau County	167	1.04
Whitesboro, NY (village) Oneida County	39	1.03
Forestville, MD (cdp) Prince George's County	125	1.02
Rensselaer, NY (city) Rensselaer County	93	1.02
Tusculum, TN (city) Greene County	26	1.01
Flying Hills, PA (cdp) Berks County	25	1.01
Stroud, PA (township) Monroe County	186	0.99
Lakeview, NY (cdp) Nassau County	55	0.99
Winter Garden, FL (city) Orange County	307	0.98
Wrightstown, NJ (borough) Burlington County	7	0.98
Cherry Hill, VA (cdp) Prince William County	148	0.95
Burtonsville, MD (cdp) Montgomery County	87	0.94
Chesnee, SC (city) Spartanburg County	7	0.94
Lady Lake, FL (town) Lake County	131	0.93
Eau Claire, MI (village) Berrien County	5	0.93
Endicott, NY (village) Broome County	121	0.91
North Brentwood, MD (town) Prince George's County	5	0.90
Wyandanch, NY (cdp) Suffolk County	97	0.89
Hokendauqua, PA (cdp) Lehigh County	32	0.89
Rising Sun-Lebanon, DE (cdp) Kent County	25	0.89
Mitchellville, MD (cdp) Prince George's County	102	0.88
New Hyde Park, NY (village) Nassau County	85	0.88
South Bound Brook, NJ (borough) Somerset County	40	0.88
Bronx, NY (borough) Bronx County	11,837	0.87
Hartford, CT (city/town) Hartford County	1,086	0.87
Lower Oxford, PA (township) Chester County	44	0.87
Long Beach, NY (city) Nassau County	289	0.86
Jackson, PA (township) Monroe County	60	0.86
Wharton, NJ (borough) Morris County	56	0.86
Sky Lake, FL (cdp) Orange County	42	0.86
Friendship, NY (town) Allegany County	18	0.86
Newport, NC (town) Carteret County	34	0.85
South Valley Stream, NY (cdp) Nassau County	44	0.84
Spry, PA (cdp) York County	41	0.84
Roosevelt, NJ (borough) Monmouth County	6	0.84
Tavares, FL (city) Lake County	113	0.83
Wedgefield, FL (cdp) Orange County	53	0.82
Silver Hill, MD (cdp) Prince George's County	50	0.82
Argyle, NY (town) Washington County	31	0.82
Newark, NJ (city) Essex County	2,202	0.80
Northeast Ithaca, NY (cdp) Tompkins County	21	0.80
Hypoluxo, FL (town) Palm Beach County	20	0.80
Franklin Square, NY (cdp) Nassau County	234	0.79
South Huntington, NY (cdp) Suffolk County	78	0.79
Milton, FL (city) Santa Rosa County	69	0.79
East Garden City, NY (cdp) Nassau County	44	0.79
Old Bethpage, NY (cdp) Nassau County	44	0.79
St. Leo, FL (town) Pasco County	5	0.79
Farmington, NY (town) Ontario County	90	0.78
Thompsonville, CT (cdp) Hartford County	69	0.78
Gregg, PA (township) Union County	40	0.78
Dormont, PA (borough) Allegheny County	67	0.77
Freeport, NY (village) Nassau County	324	0.76
Ocoee, FL (city) Orange County	255	0.75
Bellerive, MO (village) St. Louis County	2	0.74
Mineville, NY (cdp) Essex County	10	0.73
Mount Vernon, OH (city) Knox County	120	0.71
Franklin Park, NJ (cdp) Somerset County	89	0.71
Paola, KS (city) Miami County	39	0.71
Ettrick, VA (cdp) Chesterfield County	41	0.70
Hartford, NY (town) Washington County	16	0.70
Linden, NJ (city) Union County	277	0.69
Stockbridge, GA (city) Henry County	164	0.69
Dunellen, NJ (borough) Middlesex County	49	0.69
Florence, NJ (cdp) Burlington County	32	0.69
Watchtower, NY (cdp) Ulster County	11	0.69
Richfield, MN (city) Hennepin County	236	0.68
Lanham, MD (cdp) Prince George's County	61	0.68
Sodus, NY (village) Wayne County	14	0.68
Tamarac, FL (city) Broward County	398	0.67
Mantua, NJ (township) Gloucester County	101	0.67
Richmond Heights, FL (cdp) Miami-Dade County	60	0.66
Bladensburg, MD (town) Prince George's County	59	0.66
Plainfield, NJ (city) Union County	321	0.65
East Rockingham, NC (cdp) Richmond County	26	0.65

Ancestry

Guyanese

Top 150 Places Sorted by Percent of Total Population

Based on places with total population of 7,500 or more

Place	Population	%
East Orange, NJ (city) Essex County	2,746	4.23
Hillcrest, NY (cdp) Rockland County	280	3.42
Clermont, FL (city) Lake County	775	2.96
Schenectady, NY (city) Schenectady County	1,915	2.93
Queens, NY (borough) Queens County	53,961	2.45
Valley Stream, NY (village) Nassau County	840	2.27
North Valley Stream, NY (cdp) Nassau County	344	2.08
Bogota, NJ (borough) Bergen County	166	2.03
South Kensington, MD (cdp) Montgomery County	158	1.94
Irvington, NJ (township) Essex County	993	1.81
South Plainfield, NJ (borough) Middlesex County	413	1.79
Elmont, NY (cdp) Nassau County	581	1.68
South Miami Heights, FL (cdp) Miami-Dade County	611	1.67
Brooklyn, NY (borough) Kings County	38,963	1.58
City of Orange, NJ (township) Essex County	481	1.58
Groveland, FL (city) Lake County	125	1.58
North Amityville, NY (cdp) Suffolk County	275	1.54
Southampton, NJ (township) Burlington County	162	1.54
Lighthouse Point, FL (city) Broward County	156	1.49
Redan, GA (cdp) DeKalb County	473	1.38
Lloyd, NY (town) Ulster County	149	1.38
Mount Rainier, MD (city) Prince George's County	110	1.35
New York, NY (city) Kings County	107,972	1.34
Pine Hills, FL (cdp) Orange County	881	1.33
Stony Brook University, NY (cdp) Suffolk County	109	1.30
Jersey City, NJ (city) Hudson County	3,025	1.24
South Orange Village, NJ (township) Essex County	195	1.20
Landover, MD (cdp) Prince George's County	254	1.08
Elkton, MD (town) Cecil County	162	1.08
Greentree, NJ (cdp) Camden County	121	1.06
Floral Park, NY (village) Nassau County	167	1.04
Forestville, MD (cdp) Prince George's County	125	1.02
Rensselaer, NY (city) Rensselaer County	93	1.02
Stroud, PA (township) Monroe County	186	0.99
Winter Garden, FL (city) Orange County	307	0.98
Cherry Hill, VA (cdp) Prince William County	148	0.95
Burtonsville, MD (cdp) Montgomery County	87	0.94
Lady Lake, FL (town) Lake County	131	0.93
Endicott, NY (village) Broome County	121	0.91
Wyandanch, NY (cdp) Suffolk County	97	0.89
Mitchellville, MD (cdp) Prince George's County	102	0.88
New Hyde Park, NY (village) Nassau County	85	0.88
Bronx, NY (borough) Bronx County	11,837	0.87
Hartford, CT (city/town) Hartford County	1,086	0.87
Long Beach, NY (city) Nassau County	289	0.86
Tavares, FL (city) Lake County	113	0.83
Newark, NJ (city) Essex County	2,202	0.80
Franklin Square, NY (cdp) Nassau County	234	0.79
South Huntington, NY (cdp) Suffolk County	78	0.79
Milton, FL (city) Santa Rosa County	69	0.79
Farmington, NY (town) Ontario County	90	0.78
Thompsonville, CT (cdp) Hartford County	69	0.78
Dormont, PA (borough) Allegheny County	67	0.77
Freeport, NY (village) Nassau County	324	0.76
Ocoee, FL (city) Orange County	255	0.75
Mount Vernon, OH (city) Knox County	120	0.71
Franklin Park, NJ (cdp) Somerset County	89	0.71
Linden, NJ (city) Union County	277	0.69
Stockbridge, GA (city) Henry County	164	0.69
Richfield, MN (city) Hennepin County	236	0.68
Lanham, MD (cdp) Prince George's County	61	0.68
Tamarac, FL (city) Broward County	398	0.67
Mantua, NJ (township) Gloucester County	101	0.67
Richmond Heights, FL (cdp) Miami-Dade County	60	0.66
Bladensburg, MD (town) Prince George's County	59	0.66
Plainfield, NJ (city) Union County	321	0.65
Bloomfield, NJ (township) Essex County	302	0.64
Jefferson Valley-Yorktown, NY (cdp) Westchester County	92	0.64
East Hanover, NJ (township) Morris County	72	0.64
Watertown, NY (city) Jefferson County	169	0.63
Calverton, MD (cdp) Montgomery County	113	0.63
Coconut Creek, FL (city) Broward County	317	0.62
Peekskill, NY (city) Westchester County	144	0.62
Southchase, FL (cdp) Orange County	102	0.62
Bensville, MD (cdp) Charles County	71	0.61
Summerfield, MD (cdp) Prince George's County	67	0.60
Hempstead, NY (village) Nassau County	307	0.58
Kearny, NJ (town) Hudson County	235	0.58
Deer Park, NY (cdp) Suffolk County	164	0.58
Brookdale, NJ (cdp) Essex County	53	0.58
Boonton, NJ (town) Morris County	49	0.58
West Orange, NJ (township) Essex County	260	0.57
Bay Shore, NY (cdp) Suffolk County	157	0.56
Leesburg, FL (city) Lake County	113	0.56
Haines City, FL (city) Polk County	110	0.56
Milford, NH (cdp) Hillsborough County	51	0.56
Fridley, MN (city) Anoka County	151	0.55
Miramar, FL (city) Broward County	609	0.54
Mount Vernon, NY (city) Westchester County	360	0.54
Miami Springs, FL (city) Miami-Dade County	74	0.54
Chillum, MD (cdp) Prince George's County	185	0.53
Centerville, OH (city) Montgomery County	123	0.52
New Cassel, NY (cdp) Nassau County	63	0.50
Albany, NY (city) Albany County	483	0.49
Lakewood, NJ (cdp) Ocean County	245	0.49
Essex, MD (cdp) Baltimore County	189	0.49
Brooklyn Center, MN (city) Hennepin County	142	0.48
Hillside, NJ (township) Union County	103	0.48
Princeton, FL (cdp) Miami-Dade County	100	0.48
Mastic, NY (cdp) Suffolk County	69	0.48
Red Hook, NY (town) Dutchess County	54	0.48
Hempstead, NY (town) Nassau County	3,520	0.47
Robbinsville, NJ (township) Mercer County	61	0.47
Pinellas Park, FL (city) Pinellas County	222	0.46
Carteret, NJ (borough) Middlesex County	104	0.46
Johnson City, NY (village) Broome County	70	0.46
Palmetto Estates, FL (cdp) Miami-Dade County	62	0.46
Lantana, FL (town) Palm Beach County	48	0.46
Englewood, NJ (city) Bergen County	120	0.45
Moore, PA (township) Northampton County	41	0.45
Camp Hill, PA (borough) Cumberland County	35	0.45
Butler, NJ (borough) Morris County	34	0.45
Fairburn, GA (city) Fulton County	51	0.44
Waterbury, CT (city/town) New Haven County	468	0.43
Scaggsville, MD (cdp) Howard County	98	0.43
Nanuet, NY (cdp) Rockland County	77	0.43
Lilburn, GA (city) Gwinnett County	51	0.43
Elmwood Park, NJ (borough) Bergen County	81	0.42
Patton, PA (township) Centre County	61	0.42
Florence, NJ (township) Burlington County	50	0.42
Jupiter Farms, FL (cdp) Palm Beach County	50	0.42
Rockville, CT (cdp) Tolland County	32	0.42
West Haven, CT (city/town) New Haven County	224	0.41
Clinton, MD (cdp) Prince George's County	147	0.41
Roselle, NJ (borough) Union County	85	0.41
Brookfield, CT (town) Fairfield County	66	0.41
Woodbridge, NJ (cdp) Middlesex County	77	0.40
Lehigh Acres, FL (cdp) Lee County	333	0.39
Valrico, FL (cdp) Hillsborough County	136	0.39
Newburgh, NY (city) Orange County	113	0.39
Fort Washington, MD (cdp) Prince George's County	98	0.39
Middle Smithfield, PA (township) Monroe County	60	0.39
Alafaya, FL (cdp) Orange County	291	0.38
Pennsauken, NJ (township) Camden County	135	0.38
Copiague, NY (cdp) Suffolk County	79	0.38
Rocky Hill, CT (town) Hartford County	74	0.38
Dover, NY (town) Dutchess County	33	0.38
Four Corners, MD (cdp) Montgomery County	30	0.38
Bithlo, FL (cdp) Orange County	29	0.38
Pembroke Pines, FL (city) Broward County	557	0.37
Belleville, NJ (township) Essex County	132	0.37
Deerfield Beach, FL (city) Broward County	269	0.36
East Meadow, NY (cdp) Nassau County	134	0.36
Lauderdale Lakes, FL (city) Broward County	117	0.36
Adelphi, MD (cdp) Prince George's County	54	0.36
Rosaryville, MD (cdp) Prince George's County	41	0.36
East Windsor, CT (town) Hartford County	39	0.36
Baywood, NY (cdp) Suffolk County	28	0.36
Babylon, NY (town) Suffolk County	747	0.35
Concord, NC (city) Cabarrus County	260	0.35

SECTION THREE

Please refer to the Explanation of Data in the front of the book for more detailed information.

Ancestry

Hungarian

U.S. and 50 States Sorted by Population and Percent of Total Population

Place	Population	%
United States	**1,537,238**	**0.51**
Ohio	210,625	1.83
New York	154,481	0.80
Pennsylvania	144,444	1.15
California	131,741	0.36
New Jersey	109,305	1.25
Florida	106,462	0.58
Michigan	104,987	1.05
Illinois	55,195	0.43
Connecticut	40,489	1.14
Indiana	38,908	0.61
Texas	36,107	0.15
Arizona	30,350	0.49
Virginia	29,610	0.38
Maryland	27,773	0.49
Wisconsin	26,169	0.46
North Carolina	25,192	0.27
Washington	23,840	0.36
Colorado	21,113	0.43
Massachusetts	21,035	0.32
Georgia	19,963	0.21
Missouri	14,513	0.25
Oregon	14,213	0.38
Nevada	14,122	0.54
Minnesota	13,958	0.27
Tennessee	12,297	0.20
South Carolina	10,608	0.24
West Virginia	9,727	0.53
Kentucky	6,878	0.16
Louisiana	5,280	0.12
Oklahoma	5,046	0.14
New Mexico	4,935	0.25
Delaware	4,921	0.56
Alabama	4,869	0.10
Utah	4,409	0.17
Kansas	4,340	0.15
Maine	4,207	0.32
Iowa	4,143	0.14
New Hampshire	4,074	0.31
Idaho	4,009	0.26
Arkansas	3,909	0.14
Montana	3,432	0.35
Nebraska	3,420	0.19
Hawaii	3,216	0.24
Vermont	3,115	0.50
North Dakota	2,728	0.41
Alaska	2,671	0.39
Rhode Island	2,662	0.25
Mississippi	2,297	0.08
District of Columbia	2,196	0.38
Wyoming	1,951	0.36
South Dakota	1,303	0.16

Place	Population	%
Ohio	210,625	1.83
New Jersey	109,305	1.25
Pennsylvania	144,444	1.15
Connecticut	40,489	1.14
Michigan	104,987	1.05
New York	154,481	0.80
Indiana	38,908	0.61
Florida	106,462	0.58
Delaware	4,921	0.56
Nevada	14,122	0.54
West Virginia	9,727	0.53
United States	**1,537,238**	**0.51**
Vermont	3,115	0.50
Arizona	30,350	0.49
Maryland	27,773	0.49
Wisconsin	26,169	0.46
Illinois	55,195	0.43
Colorado	21,113	0.43
North Dakota	2,728	0.41
Alaska	2,671	0.39
Virginia	29,610	0.38
Oregon	14,213	0.38
District of Columbia	2,196	0.38
California	131,741	0.36
Washington	23,840	0.36
Wyoming	1,951	0.36
Montana	3,432	0.35
Massachusetts	21,035	0.32
Maine	4,207	0.32
New Hampshire	4,074	0.31
North Carolina	25,192	0.27
Minnesota	13,958	0.27
Idaho	4,009	0.26
Missouri	14,513	0.25
New Mexico	4,935	0.25
Rhode Island	2,662	0.25
South Carolina	10,608	0.24
Hawaii	3,216	0.24
Georgia	19,963	0.21
Tennessee	12,297	0.20
Nebraska	3,420	0.19
Utah	4,409	0.17
Kentucky	6,878	0.16
South Dakota	1,303	0.16
Texas	36,107	0.15
Kansas	4,340	0.15
Oklahoma	5,046	0.14
Iowa	4,143	0.14
Arkansas	3,909	0.14
Louisiana	5,280	0.12
Alabama	4,869	0.10
Mississippi	2,297	0.08

Please refer to the Explanation of Data in the front of the book for more detailed information.

Ancestry

Hungarian

Top 150 Places Sorted by Population

Based on all places, regardless of total population

Place	Population	%
New York, NY (city) Kings County	55,459	0.69
Brooklyn, NY (borough) Kings County	26,607	1.08
Los Angeles, CA (city) Los Angeles County	16,285	0.43
Manhattan, NY (borough) New York County	14,667	0.93
Queens, NY (borough) Queens County	9,470	0.43
Chicago, IL (city) Cook County	8,760	0.32
Hempstead, NY (town) Nassau County	6,992	0.93
Cleveland, OH (city) Cuyahoga County	6,822	1.67
Ramapo, NY (town) Rockland County	6,804	5.54
Columbus, OH (city) Franklin County	6,569	0.85
Phoenix, AZ (city) Maricopa County	6,414	0.44
San Diego, CA (city) San Diego County	6,397	0.50
Toledo, OH (city) Lucas County	6,352	2.18
Monroe, NY (town) Orange County	5,591	14.45
Kiryas Joel, NY (village) Orange County	5,471	28.66
Philadelphia, PA (city) Philadelphia County	5,463	0.36
Akron, OH (city) Summit County	4,508	2.22
Pittsburgh, PA (city) Allegheny County	4,477	1.45
Brookhaven, NY (town) Suffolk County	4,390	0.91
Parma, OH (city) Cuyahoga County	4,239	5.18
Lakewood, NJ (township) Ocean County	3,772	4.30
Jacksonville, FL (city) Duval County	3,540	0.44
Seattle, WA (city) King County	3,531	0.59
Bethlehem, PA (city) Northampton County	3,458	4.63
Woodbridge, NJ (township) Middlesex County	3,418	3.45
San Francisco, CA (city) San Francisco County	3,416	0.43
Oyster Bay, NY (town) Nassau County	3,138	1.08
Lorain, OH (city) Lorain County	3,113	4.77
Las Vegas, NV (city) Clark County	3,106	0.54
Fairfield, CT (town) Fairfield County	3,015	5.13
Huntington, NY (town) Suffolk County	3,005	1.49
Mentor, OH (city) Lake County	2,998	6.29
Indianapolis, IN (city) Marion County	2,960	0.37
Hamilton, NJ (township) Mercer County	2,948	3.33
South Bend, IN (city) St. Joseph County	2,904	2.85
North Hempstead, NY (town) Nassau County	2,628	1.18
Bethlehem, PA (city) Northampton County	2,523	4.55
Portland, OR (city) Multnomah County	2,509	0.44
Lakewood, NJ (cdp) Ocean County	2,502	5.02
Lakewood, OH (city) Cuyahoga County	2,499	4.74
Bronx, NY (borough) Bronx County	2,427	0.18
Houston, TX (city) Harris County	2,396	0.12
Elyria, OH (city) Lorain County	2,358	4.29
Denver, CO (city) Denver County	2,348	0.41
Edison, NJ (township) Middlesex County	2,322	2.33
Mesa, AZ (city) Maricopa County	2,315	0.53
Staten Island, NY (borough) Richmond County	2,288	0.49
Colorado Springs, CO (city) El Paso County	2,249	0.56
Lincoln Park, MI (city) Wayne County	2,225	5.76
Scottsdale, AZ (city) Maricopa County	2,210	1.01
Buffalo, NY (city) Erie County	2,201	0.83
Washington, DC (city) District of Columbia	2,196	0.38
Tucson, AZ (city) Pima County	2,169	0.42
Milwaukee, WI (city) Milwaukee County	2,141	0.36
Taylor, MI (city) Wayne County	2,139	3.35
Islip, NY (town) Suffolk County	2,067	0.62
Charlotte, NC (city) Mecklenburg County	2,059	0.29
Baltimore, MD (city) Baltimore city County	2,050	0.33
San Antonio, TX (city) Medina County	1,998	0.15
Henderson, NV (city) Clark County	1,979	0.79
Virginia Beach, VA (ind. city) Virginia Beach independent city	1,964	0.45
Austin, TX (city) Travis County	1,960	0.26
Livonia, MI (city) Wayne County	1,923	1.96
Huntington Beach, CA (city) Orange County	1,920	1.02
Boston, MA (city) Suffolk County	1,882	0.31
San Jose, CA (city) Santa Clara County	1,873	0.20
Ann Arbor, MI (city) Washtenaw County	1,847	1.60
Allentown, PA (city) Lehigh County	1,829	1.57
Long Beach, CA (city) Los Angeles County	1,825	0.40
Dallas, TX (city) Dallas County	1,814	0.15
Brunswick, OH (city) Medina County	1,802	5.24
Albuquerque, NM (city) Bernalillo County	1,798	0.34
New Square, NY (village) Rockland County	1,787	27.67
North Olmsted, OH (city) Cuyahoga County	1,755	5.35
Norwalk, CT (city/town) Fairfield County	1,736	2.05
Oregon, OH (city) Lucas County	1,686	8.38
Toms River, NJ (township) Ocean County	1,678	1.83
Southgate, MI (city) Wayne County	1,630	5.40
North Ridgeville, OH (city) Lorain County	1,613	5.70
Strongsville, OH (city) Cuyahoga County	1,610	3.63
Hollywood, FL (city) Broward County	1,601	1.13
Milford, CT (town) New Haven County	1,573	2.98
Dearborn, MI (city) Wayne County	1,569	1.59
Toms River, NJ (cdp) Ocean County	1,568	1.76
Nashville-Davidson, TN (metro govt) Davidson County	1,567	0.27
Bridgeport, CT (city/town) Fairfield County	1,551	1.09
Farmington Hills, MI (city) Oakland County	1,546	1.93
Milford, CT (city) New Haven County	1,533	3.00
Brownstown, MI (charter township) Wayne County	1,529	5.21
Tampa, FL (city) Hillsborough County	1,529	0.46
Cuyahoga Falls, OH (city) Summit County	1,514	3.05
Monsey, NY (cdp) Rockland County	1,483	9.85
Stratford, CT (cdp/town) Fairfield County	1,477	2.91
Allen Park, MI (city) Wayne County	1,456	5.10
Chandler, AZ (city) Maricopa County	1,451	0.63
Broadview Heights, OH (city) Cuyahoga County	1,418	7.59
Westlake, OH (city) Cuyahoga County	1,410	4.36
Youngstown, OH (city) Mahoning County	1,409	2.02
Green, OH (city) Summit County	1,380	5.47
Jackson, NJ (township) Ocean County	1,365	2.57
Irvine, CA (city) Orange County	1,365	0.69
Port St. Lucie, FL (city) St. Lucie County	1,349	0.87
Mishawaka, IN (city) St. Joseph County	1,337	2.79
Solon, OH (city) Cuyahoga County	1,333	5.80
Brick, NJ (township) Ocean County	1,333	1.76
Arlington, VA (cdp) Arlington County	1,325	0.67
Cincinnati, OH (city) Hamilton County	1,319	0.44
Shelton, CT (city/town) Fairfield County	1,299	3.33
Boardman, OH (cdp) Mahoning County	1,296	3.66
Franklin, NJ (township) Somerset County	1,295	2.15
Boca Raton, FL (city) Palm Beach County	1,294	1.52
North Huntingdon, PA (township) Westmoreland County	1,284	4.24
Barberton, OH (city) Summit County	1,283	4.78
Louisville-Jefferson County, KY (metro govt) Jefferson County	1,283	0.22
Warren, MI (city) Macomb County	1,275	0.94
Madison, WI (city) Dane County	1,275	0.56
Paradise, NV (cdp) Clark County	1,261	0.58
Minneapolis, MN (city) Hennepin County	1,261	0.33
Smithtown, NY (town) Suffolk County	1,257	1.07
Santa Clarita, CA (city) Los Angeles County	1,257	0.73
East Brunswick, NJ (township) Middlesex County	1,255	2.65
Clifton, NJ (city) Passaic County	1,249	1.51
Greenburgh, NY (town) Westchester County	1,242	1.42
North Royalton, OH (city) Cuyahoga County	1,230	4.10
Euclid, OH (city) Cuyahoga County	1,228	2.49
Cleveland Heights, OH (city) Cuyahoga County	1,224	2.62
Gilbert, AZ (town) Maricopa County	1,214	0.62
Bethlehem, PA (township) Northampton County	1,213	5.17
Anchorage, AK (municipality) Anchorage Municipality	1,203	0.42
West Bloomfield, MI (charter township) Oakland County	1,200	1.85
Spring Hill, FL (cdp) Hernando County	1,198	1.24
Sterling Heights, MI (city) Macomb County	1,195	0.92
Amherst, NY (town) Erie County	1,194	0.99
Trumbull, CT (cdp/town) Fairfield County	1,193	3.36
Sacramento, CA (city) Sacramento County	1,189	0.26
Tonawanda, NY (town) Erie County	1,188	1.60
Trenton, MI (city) Wayne County	1,187	6.23
Stow, OH (city) Summit County	1,184	3.43
Middletown, NJ (township) Monmouth County	1,180	1.77
Medina, OH (city) Medina County	1,176	4.41
Twinsburg, OH (city) Summit County	1,158	6.26
Santa Monica, CA (city) Los Angeles County	1,147	1.29
Atlanta, GA (city) Fulton County	1,147	0.28
Detroit, MI (city) Wayne County	1,137	0.15
Austintown, OH (cdp) Mahoning County	1,136	3.76
St. Paul, MN (city) Ramsey County	1,133	0.40
Coral Springs, FL (city) Broward County	1,126	0.93
Thousand Oaks, CA (city) Ventura County	1,124	0.90
Omaha, NE (city) Douglas County	1,124	0.28
St. Petersburg, FL (city) Pinellas County	1,123	0.46

Ancestry

Hungarian

Top 150 Places Sorted by Percent of Total Population

Based on all places, regardless of total population

Place	Population	%
McGee Creek, CA (cdp) Mono County	17	58.62
Grand Island, MI (township) Alger County	27	48.21
Crestone, CO (town) Saguache County	41	43.62
Balfour, ND (city) McHenry County	8	40.00
South Lima, NY (cdp) Livingston County	72	35.47
Government Camp, OR (cdp) Clackamas County	19	33.93
Natural Bridge, NY (cdp) Jefferson County	137	33.91
Belle Mead, NJ (cdp) Somerset County	42	33.87
Dailey, WV (cdp) Randolph County	14	32.56
Zilwaukee, MI (township) Saginaw County	20	31.75
East Fultonham, OH (cdp) Muskingum County	47	29.94
Moskowite Corner, CA (cdp) Napa County	39	29.77
Kiryas Joel, NY (village) Orange County	5,471	28.66
Martins Creek, PA (cdp) Northampton County	173	28.04
New Square, NY (village) Rockland County	1,787	27.67
Taylorsville, CA (cdp) Plumas County	31	25.41
Hutchinson, NJ (cdp) Warren County	38	24.52
Kaser, NY (village) Rockland County	1,034	23.31
Carolina, WV (cdp) Marion County	94	22.54
Copalis Beach, WA (cdp) Grays Harbor County	53	20.78
Juliustown, NJ (cdp) Burlington County	65	20.38
Williston, OH (cdp) Ottawa County	75	20.27
Crystal Rock, OH (cdp) Erie County	14	19.72
Prosper, MN (township) Lake of the Woods County	9	19.57
Hostetter, PA (cdp) Westmoreland County	140	19.13
Deep Creek, VA (cdp) Accomack County	16	19.05
Pigeon Creek, OH (cdp) Summit County	135	18.96
Hiller, PA (cdp) Fayette County	235	18.08
Buels, VT (gore) Chittenden County	3	17.65
Maysville, CO (cdp) Chaffee County	25	17.61
Harmon, ND (cdp) Morton County	8	17.39
Fort Bridger, WY (cdp) Uinta County	38	17.19
Black Butte Ranch, OR (cdp) Deschutes County	48	17.14
Rush, PA (township) Dauphin County	40	17.02
Slatedale, PA (cdp) Lehigh County	76	16.67
Arbela, MO (town) Scotland County	3	16.67
Lac La Belle, WI (village) Jefferson County	2	16.67
Blackwells Mills, NJ (cdp) Somerset County	113	16.19
Oceanside, OR (cdp) Tillamook County	33	16.18
Centerville, PA (borough) Washington County	520	15.87
Cohasset, CA (cdp) Butte County	124	15.84
Sula, MT (cdp) Ravalli County	12	15.79
New Schaefferstown, PA (cdp) Berks County	23	15.65
Fairport Harbor, OH (village) Lake County	487	15.59
Van Voorhis, PA (cdp) Washington County	64	15.24
Brookside, CO (town) Fremont County	41	15.02
Monroe, NY (town) Orange County	5,591	14.45
Summerhaven, AZ (cdp) Pima County	14	14.43
Fairhope, PA (cdp) Fayette County	136	14.29
Conway, MI (cdp) Emmet County	21	14.19
Summit, OR (cdp) Benton County	12	14.12
Takilma, OR (cdp) Josephine County	35	13.89
Dillard, OR (cdp) Douglas County	49	13.69
Allison, PA (cdp) Fayette County	68	13.26
Coal Center, PA (borough) Washington County	37	13.26
Brave, PA (cdp) Greene County	27	13.04
Prattsville, NY (cdp) Greene County	41	12.85
Manston, MN (township) Wilkin County	3	12.50
River Bend, MO (village) Jackson County	2	12.50
Bolivar, OH (village) Tuscarawas County	144	11.94
Chalkhill, PA (cdp) Fayette County	10	11.90
Paint, PA (borough) Somerset County	113	11.89
Cairnbrook, PA (cdp) Somerset County	53	11.73
Milltown, NJ (borough) Middlesex County	807	11.70
Clifton, OH (village) Greene County	27	11.64
Yankee Lake, OH (village) Trumbull County	8	11.59
Lawrence, NY (village) Nassau County	746	11.57
James, SC (town) Berkeley County	6	11.32
Moreland Hills, OH (village) Cuyahoga County	373	11.27
West Hills, PA (cdp) Armstrong County	175	11.23
Bairdford, PA (cdp) Allegheny County	75	11.13
Cardwell, MT (cdp) Jefferson County	3	11.11
Idamay, WV (cdp) Marion County	56	11.00
Barnett, PA (township) Jefferson County	22	10.84
Rayland, OH (village) Jefferson County	42	10.82
Fisher Island, FL (cdp) Miami-Dade County	21	10.82
Fostoria, MI (cdp) Tuscola County	79	10.79
Jamaica, IA (city) Guthrie County	29	10.78
Edenburg, PA (cdp) Berks County	80	10.70
Groveland, ID (cdp) Bingham County	69	10.68
Spelter, WV (cdp) Harrison County	27	10.63
Frye Island, ME (town) Cumberland County	9	10.59
Corning, OH (village) Perry County	74	10.51
Sheakleyville, PA (borough) Mercer County	16	10.46
Victory, PA (township) Venango County	42	10.42
Greene, PA (township) Greene County	51	10.37
Martinsburg, OH (village) Knox County	19	10.33
Beallsville, PA (borough) Washington County	45	10.30
Chesterland, OH (cdp) Geauga County	249	10.29
Grand Marsh, WI (cdp) Adams County	8	10.26
Y-O Ranch, WY (cdp) Platte County	24	10.21
Abeytas, NM (cdp) Socorro County	16	10.19
Kinsman Center, OH (cdp) Trumbull County	76	10.13
North Lawrence, OH (cdp) Stark County	18	10.06
Plumwood, OH (cdp) Madison County	18	10.06
Walton Hills, OH (village) Cuyahoga County	226	10.00
Bigelow, MO (village) Holt County	4	10.00
Robinette, WV (cdp) Logan County	42	9.98
Middletown, PA (cdp) Northampton County	716	9.94
Monsey, NY (cdp) Rockland County	1,483	9.85
Savannah, OH (village) Ashland County	30	9.80
Mabie, CA (cdp) Plumas County	16	9.70
Tiltonsville, OH (village) Jefferson County	136	9.69
Backus, MI (township) Roscommon County	24	9.68
Corwin Springs, MT (cdp) Park County	8	9.64
West Brownsville, PA (borough) Washington County	84	9.55
Maybeury, WV (cdp) McDowell County	37	9.54
Sewaren, NJ (cdp) Middlesex County	247	9.46
Limestone, PA (township) Warren County	25	9.43
Lake Sherwood, WI (cdp) Adams County	31	9.39
Harmony, NJ (township) Warren County	250	9.24
Annandale, NJ (cdp) Hunterdon County	112	9.24
Brandonville, WV (town) Preston County	6	9.23
Lansing, OH (cdp) Belmont County	34	9.21
New Dosey, MN (township) Pine County	8	9.20
Munhall, PA (borough) Allegheny County	1,051	9.17
Saddle Rock Estates, NY (cdp) Nassau County	48	9.16
Roebling, NJ (cdp) Burlington County	360	9.15
Bibo, NM (cdp) Cibola County	14	9.15
Northwood, OH (city) Wood County	480	9.01
Eyers Grove, PA (cdp) Columbia County	9	9.00
Tarentum, PA (borough) Allegheny County	410	8.98
Neapolis, OH (cdp) Lucas County	42	8.96
Wyano, PA (cdp) Westmoreland County	29	8.95
Avery, CA (cdp) Calaveras County	34	8.92
Hokendauqua, PA (cdp) Lehigh County	319	8.91
Roberta, GA (city) Crawford County	76	8.90
Register, GA (town) Bulloch County	13	8.90
Walland, TN (cdp) Blount County	13	8.78
Wakeman, OH (village) Huron County	100	8.73
Brunswick Station, ME (cdp) Cumberland County	109	8.71
Sandyville, OH (cdp) Tuscarawas County	27	8.68
Westport, NY (town) Essex County	109	8.67
Orange, OH (village) Cuyahoga County	283	8.61
Mount Hermon, NJ (cdp) Warren County	13	8.61
Viola, NY (cdp) Rockland County	604	8.57
Leaf River, IL (village) Ogle County	33	8.57
Union, WA (cdp) Mason County	45	8.56
Luis Lopez, NM (cdp) Socorro County	14	8.54
Windber, PA (borough) Somerset County	358	8.53
Holmes, MI (township) Menominee County	25	8.53
Greenview, CA (cdp) Siskiyou County	31	8.52
Altoona, KS (city) Wilson County	33	8.51
Canadian, OK (town) Pittsburg County	20	8.51
East Avon, NY (cdp) Livingston County	49	8.49
Jefferson, OH (village) Ashtabula County	272	8.41
Hills and Dales, OH (village) Stark County	20	8.40
Murray City, OH (village) Hocking County	36	8.39
Oregon, OH (city) Lucas County	1,686	8.38
East Millstone, NJ (cdp) Somerset County	68	8.35

Please refer to the Explanation of Data in the front of the book for more detailed information.

Ancestry

Hungarian

Top 150 Places Sorted by Percent of Total Population

Based on places with total population of 7,500 or more

Place	Population	%
Kiryas Joel, NY (village) Orange County	5,471	28.66
Monroe, NY (town) Orange County	5,591	14.45
Monsey, NY (cdp) Rockland County	1,483	9.85
Munhall, PA (borough) Allegheny County	1,051	9.17
Oregon, OH (city) Lucas County	1,686	8.38
Macedonia, OH (city) Summit County	905	8.33
Florence, NJ (township) Burlington County	962	8.03
Amherst, OH (city) Lorain County	938	7.80
Mentor-on-the-Lake, OH (city) Lake County	589	7.77
Broadview Heights, OH (city) Cuyahoga County	1,418	7.59
Norton, OH (city) Summit County	837	6.97
White Horse, NJ (cdp) Mercer County	615	6.73
Sheffield Lake, OH (city) Lorain County	591	6.41
Lyndhurst, OH (city) Cuyahoga County	904	6.39
Yardville, NJ (cdp) Mercer County	478	6.36
Aurora, OH (city) Portage County	965	6.35
Mentor, OH (city) Lake County	2,998	6.29
Twinsburg, OH (city) Summit County	1,158	6.26
Trenton, MI (city) Wayne County	1,187	6.23
Beachwood, OH (city) Cuyahoga County	733	6.14
Brecksville, OH (city) Cuyahoga County	830	6.13
Woodbridge, CT (town) New Haven County	550	6.11
Seven Hills, OH (city) Cuyahoga County	707	5.99
Fords, NJ (cdp) Middlesex County	900	5.97
Olmsted Falls, OH (city) Cuyahoga County	522	5.96
New Franklin, OH (city) Summit County	850	5.94
Solon, OH (city) Cuyahoga County	1,333	5.80
Lincoln Park, MI (city) Wayne County	2,225	5.76
North Ridgeville, OH (city) Lorain County	1,613	5.70
Northampton, PA (borough) Northampton County	562	5.67
Woodhaven, MI (city) Wayne County	726	5.64
Hubbard, OH (city) Trumbull County	446	5.63
Elizabeth, PA (township) Allegheny County	742	5.59
Bordentown, NJ (township) Burlington County	607	5.55
Ramapo, NY (town) Rockland County	6,804	5.54
Green, OH (city) Summit County	1,380	5.47
Southgate, MI (city) Wayne County	1,630	5.40
North Olmsted, OH (city) Cuyahoga County	1,755	5.35
Fairview Park, OH (city) Cuyahoga County	889	5.26
Brunswick, OH (city) Medina County	1,802	5.24
Brownstown, MI (charter township) Wayne County	1,529	5.21
Parma, OH (city) Cuyahoga County	4,239	5.18
Bethlehem, PA (township) Northampton County	1,213	5.17
Riverview, MI (city) Wayne County	653	5.17
Rocky River, OH (city) Cuyahoga County	1,041	5.15
Fairfield, CT (town) Fairfield County	3,015	5.13
Bedford, OH (city) Cuyahoga County	674	5.11
Allen Park, MI (city) Wayne County	1,456	5.10
North Madison, OH (cdp) Lake County	458	5.09
Avon, OH (city) Lorain County	984	5.04
Parma Heights, OH (city) Cuyahoga County	1,046	5.03
Lakewood, NJ (cdp) Ocean County	2,502	5.02
Eastlake, OH (city) Lake County	942	4.99
Lower Saucon, PA (township) Northampton County	535	4.98
Mayfield Heights, OH (city) Cuyahoga County	939	4.91
Avon Lake, OH (city) Lorain County	1,062	4.85
Bethlehem, PA (city) Lehigh County	935	4.84
Barberton, OH (city) Summit County	1,283	4.78
Lorain, OH (city) Lorain County	3,113	4.77
University Heights, OH (city) Cuyahoga County	647	4.77
Lakewood, OH (city) Cuyahoga County	2,499	4.74
Huron, MI (charter township) Wayne County	727	4.68
West Mifflin, PA (borough) Allegheny County	952	4.64
Bethlehem, PA (city) Northampton County	3,458	4.63
Middleburg Heights, OH (city) Cuyahoga County	730	4.62
Bay Village, OH (city) Cuyahoga County	723	4.62
Hudson, OH (city) Summit County	1,021	4.57
Struthers, OH (city) Mahoning County	497	4.56
Bethlehem, PA (city) Northampton County	2,523	4.55
Hanover, PA (township) Northampton County	487	4.54
Lehigh, PA (township) Northampton County	475	4.54
South Fayette, PA (township) Allegheny County	630	4.53
White Oak, PA (borough) Allegheny County	357	4.52
Jefferson Hills, PA (borough) Allegheny County	467	4.50
Painesville, OH (city) Lake County	851	4.43

Place	Population	%
Medina, OH (city) Medina County	1,176	4.41
Brook Park, OH (city) Cuyahoga County	855	4.39
Willowick, OH (city) Lake County	621	4.37
Berlin, MI (charter township) Monroe County	392	4.37
Westlake, OH (city) Cuyahoga County	1,410	4.36
Grosse Ile, MI (township) Wayne County	457	4.35
Wilson, PA (borough) Northampton County	342	4.32
Lakewood, NJ (township) Ocean County	3,772	4.30
Elyria, OH (city) Lorain County	2,358	4.29
North Huntingdon, PA (township) Westmoreland County	1,284	4.24
Rostraver, PA (township) Westmoreland County	482	4.22
Streetsboro, OH (city) Portage County	647	4.21
Wyandotte, MI (city) Wayne County	1,107	4.20
Mansfield, NJ (township) Burlington County	333	4.16
Berea, OH (city) Cuyahoga County	782	4.12
North Royalton, OH (city) Cuyahoga County	1,230	4.10
Salisbury, PA (township) Lehigh County	551	4.07
Hermitage, PA (city) Mercer County	642	3.97
Ash, MI (township) Monroe County	312	3.97
Readington, NJ (township) Hunterdon County	639	3.94
Manville, NJ (borough) Somerset County	406	3.92
Woodbridge, NJ (cdp) Middlesex County	735	3.82
Austintown, OH (cdp) Mahoning County	1,136	3.76
Brooklyn, OH (city) Cuyahoga County	419	3.76
Whitehall, PA (township) Lehigh County	993	3.75
Bushkill, PA (township) Northampton County	298	3.71
North Whitehall, PA (township) Lehigh County	577	3.70
Middlesex, NJ (borough) Middlesex County	503	3.68
Boardman, OH (cdp) Mahoning County	1,296	3.66
Lambertville, MI (cdp) Monroe County	374	3.65
Strongsville, OH (city) Cuyahoga County	1,610	3.63
Dix Hills, NY (cdp) Suffolk County	954	3.59
Highland Heights, OH (city) Cuyahoga County	296	3.59
Wadsworth, OH (city) Medina County	755	3.56
Pleasant Hills, PA (borough) Allegheny County	289	3.50
Willoughby, OH (city) Lake County	775	3.49
Mercerville, NJ (cdp) Mercer County	440	3.47
McKeesport, PA (city) Allegheny County	703	3.46
Amity, PA (township) Berks County	414	3.46
Monessen, PA (city) Westmoreland County	272	3.46
Woodbridge, NJ (township) Middlesex County	3,418	3.45
Kent, OH (city) Portage County	994	3.45
Stow, OH (city) Summit County	1,184	3.43
Vermilion, OH (city) Lorain County	368	3.41
Flat Rock, MI (city) Wayne County	329	3.40
Garfield Heights, OH (city) Cuyahoga County	986	3.39
Salem, OH (city) Columbiana County	419	3.38
Trumbull, CT (cdp/town) Fairfield County	1,193	3.36
Oberlin, OH (city) Lorain County	279	3.36
Taylor, MI (city) Wayne County	2,139	3.35
Hamilton, NJ (township) Mercer County	2,948	3.33
Shelton, CT (city/town) Fairfield County	1,299	3.33
Oak Hill, WV (city) Fayette County	255	3.33
Monroe, CT (town) Fairfield County	641	3.32
Highland Park, NJ (borough) Middlesex County	465	3.32
Conneaut, OH (city) Ashtabula County	421	3.29
Perkasie, PA (borough) Bucks County	283	3.29
Hopewell, NJ (township) Mercer County	562	3.28
Phillipsburg, NJ (town) Warren County	499	3.28
Byram, NJ (township) Sussex County	276	3.27
Perrysburg, OH (city) Wood County	659	3.25
Maumee, OH (city) Lucas County	468	3.25
Carbondale, PA (city) Lackawanna County	292	3.24
Chartiers, PA (township) Washington County	249	3.23
Vernon, NJ (township) Sussex County	781	3.20
Thompson, NY (town) Sullivan County	488	3.20
Polk, PA (township) Monroe County	250	3.20
Wickliffe, OH (city) Lake County	409	3.18
Upper Saucon, PA (township) Lehigh County	454	3.16
Fernway, PA (cdp) Butler County	387	3.15
Maple Heights, OH (city) Cuyahoga County	736	3.12
Richland, PA (township) Cambria County	397	3.12
Spotswood, NJ (borough) Middlesex County	254	3.10
Derby, CT (city/town) New Haven County	396	3.09
Kendall Park, NJ (cdp) Middlesex County	272	3.09

Ancestry

Icelander

U.S. and 50 States Sorted by Population and Percent of Total Population

Place	Population	%
United States	**51,234**	**0.02**
California	7,372	0.02
Washington	6,800	0.10
Minnesota	3,875	0.07
Utah	3,861	0.15
North Dakota	2,840	0.43
Florida	2,368	0.01
Texas	1,835	0.01
New York	1,528	0.01
Oregon	1,456	0.04
Arizona	1,449	0.02
Colorado	1,337	0.03
Virginia	1,216	0.02
Illinois	1,165	0.01
Massachusetts	1,058	0.02
Michigan	1,022	0.01
North Carolina	946	0.01
Wisconsin	927	0.02
Ohio	808	0.01
New Jersey	698	0.01
Idaho	694	0.05
Georgia	683	0.01
Pennsylvania	638	0.01
Nevada	551	0.02
Missouri	515	0.01
Maryland	490	0.01
Connecticut	445	0.01
Kansas	437	0.02
Montana	356	0.04
Tennessee	355	0.01
Oklahoma	310	0.01
Indiana	292	<0.01
Wyoming	286	0.05
South Carolina	270	0.01
Iowa	249	0.01
Nebraska	238	0.01
New Mexico	233	0.01
Louisiana	226	0.01
South Dakota	198	0.02
Alabama	173	<0.01
Mississippi	162	0.01
Alaska	160	0.02
Hawaii	129	0.01
Vermont	109	0.02
Arkansas	90	<0.01
Maine	68	0.01
West Virginia	66	<0.01
New Hampshire	64	<0.01
District of Columbia	59	0.01
Delaware	52	0.01
Kentucky	51	<0.01
Rhode Island	24	<0.01

Place	Population	%
North Dakota	2,840	0.43
Utah	3,861	0.15
Washington	6,800	0.10
Minnesota	3,875	0.07
Idaho	694	0.05
Wyoming	286	0.05
Oregon	1,456	0.04
Montana	356	0.04
Colorado	1,337	0.03
United States	**51,234**	**0.02**
California	7,372	0.02
Arizona	1,449	0.02
Virginia	1,216	0.02
Massachusetts	1,058	0.02
Wisconsin	927	0.02
Nevada	551	0.02
Kansas	437	0.02
South Dakota	198	0.02
Alaska	160	0.02
Vermont	109	0.02
Florida	2,368	0.01
Texas	1,835	0.01
New York	1,528	0.01
Illinois	1,165	0.01
Michigan	1,022	0.01
North Carolina	946	0.01
Ohio	808	0.01
New Jersey	698	0.01
Georgia	683	0.01
Pennsylvania	638	0.01
Missouri	515	0.01
Maryland	490	0.01
Connecticut	445	0.01
Tennessee	355	0.01
Oklahoma	310	0.01
South Carolina	270	0.01
Iowa	249	0.01
Nebraska	238	0.01
New Mexico	233	0.01
Louisiana	226	0.01
Mississippi	162	0.01
Hawaii	129	0.01
Maine	68	0.01
District of Columbia	59	0.01
Delaware	52	0.01
Indiana	292	<0.01
Alabama	173	<0.01
Arkansas	90	<0.01
West Virginia	66	<0.01
New Hampshire	64	<0.01
Kentucky	51	<0.01
Rhode Island	24	<0.01

Please refer to the Explanation of Data in the front of the book for more detailed information.

Ancestry

Icelander

Top 150 Places Sorted by Population

Based on all places, regardless of total population

Place	Population	%
Seattle, WA (city) King County	893	0.15
Grand Forks, ND (city) Grand Forks County	626	1.20
New York, NY (city) Kings County	572	0.01
Spanish Fork, UT (city) Utah County	544	1.71
Yucaipa, CA (city) San Bernardino County	484	0.96
San Diego, CA (city) San Diego County	408	0.03
Manhattan, NY (borough) New York County	382	0.02
Portland, OR (city) Multnomah County	380	0.07
Los Angeles, CA (city) Los Angeles County	380	0.01
Fargo, ND (city) Cass County	330	0.32
San Francisco, CA (city) San Francisco County	223	0.03
Phoenix, AZ (city) Maricopa County	217	0.01
Chicago, IL (city) Cook County	207	0.01
Cavalier, ND (city) Pembina County	206	12.80
Bellingham, WA (city) Whatcom County	204	0.26
Palmdale, CA (city) Los Angeles County	204	0.14
Sacramento, CA (city) Sacramento County	189	0.04
Murray, UT (city) Salt Lake County	187	0.40
Payson, UT (city) Utah County	180	1.05
Everett, WA (city) Snohomish County	180	0.18
Minneapolis, MN (city) Hennepin County	174	0.05
Jacksonville, FL (city) Duval County	169	0.02
St. George, UT (city) Washington County	162	0.23
Boise City, ID (city) Ada County	158	0.08
Taylor Lake Village, TX (city) Harris County	156	4.40
Mount Vernon, WA (city) Skagit County	155	0.50
Newton, MA (city) Middlesex County	155	0.18
Jamul, CA (cdp) San Diego County	152	2.86
Colorado Springs, CO (city) El Paso County	149	0.04
Ephrata, WA (city) Grant County	147	1.98
Logan, UT (city) Cache County	147	0.32
Ormond Beach, FL (city) Volusia County	145	0.38
Norfolk, VA (ind. city) Norfolk independent city	145	0.06
Springville, UT (city) Utah County	144	0.52
Bismarck, ND (city) Burleigh County	144	0.24
Chandler, AZ (city) Maricopa County	143	0.06
Salt Lake City, UT (city) Salt Lake County	142	0.08
Sandy, UT (city) Salt Lake County	141	0.16
St. Paul, MN (city) Ramsey County	141	0.05
Birch Bay, WA (cdp) Whatcom County	140	1.78
West Fargo, ND (city) Cass County	139	0.58
Austin, TX (city) Travis County	139	0.02
Waseca, MN (city) Waseca County	137	1.45
Eden Prairie, MN (city) Hennepin County	137	0.23
Shawnee, KS (city) Johnson County	136	0.23
Eagan, MN (city) Dakota County	135	0.21
Denver, CO (city) Denver County	135	0.02
Orem, UT (city) Utah County	132	0.15
Tampa, FL (city) Hillsborough County	132	0.04
Las Vegas, NV (city) Clark County	132	0.02
Kenmore, WA (city) King County	130	0.65
Burien, WA (city) King County	129	0.39
Provo, UT (city) Utah County	128	0.12
Kingsland, TX (cdp) Llano County	127	2.30
Duluth, MN (city) St. Louis County	127	0.15
San Jose, CA (city) Santa Clara County	121	0.01
China Lake Acres, CA (cdp) Kern County	120	7.73
Houston, TX (city) Harris County	119	0.01
Jamestown, WA (cdp) Clallam County	117	22.20
San Ramon, CA (city) Contra Costa County	116	0.17
Virginia Beach, VA (ind. city) Virginia Beach independent city	110	0.03
Maple Grove, MN (city) Hennepin County	107	0.18
Kirkland, WA (city) King County	106	0.22
Weymouth Town, MA (city) Norfolk County	106	0.20
Glendale, AZ (city) Maricopa County	106	0.05
Urbana, IL (city) Champaign County	105	0.26
Frederick, CO (town) Weld County	104	1.35
East Hartford, CT (cdp/town) Hartford County	104	0.20
Brandon, FL (cdp) Hillsborough County	104	0.10
Brooklyn, NY (borough) Kings County	103	<0.01
Fircrest, WA (city) Pierce County	102	1.59
South Salt Lake, UT (city) Salt Lake County	102	0.44
Wichita, KS (city) Sedgwick County	102	0.03
Edmonds, WA (city) Snohomish County	100	0.25
West Jordan, UT (city) Salt Lake County	100	0.10
Lacey, NJ (township) Ocean County	97	0.35
Fort Lauderdale, FL (city) Broward County	97	0.06
Baytown, TX (city) Harris County	96	0.14
Modesto, CA (city) Stanislaus County	96	0.05
Woodbury, MN (city) Washington County	95	0.16
San Antonio, TX (city) Medina County	95	0.01
Madison, WI (city) Dane County	92	0.04
Hempstead, NY (town) Nassau County	92	0.01
Issaquah, WA (city) King County	91	0.33
Tacoma, WA (city) Pierce County	91	0.05
Puyallup, WA (city) Pierce County	89	0.24
South Jordan, UT (city) Salt Lake County	89	0.19
Albuquerque, NM (city) Bernalillo County	89	0.02
Grafton, ND (city) Walsh County	88	2.04
Carmichael, CA (cdp) Sacramento County	88	0.14
Arlington, VA (cdp) Arlington County	88	0.04
Billings, MT (city) Yellowstone County	87	0.09
Rancho Cucamonga, CA (city) San Bernardino County	87	0.05
Brooklyn Park, MN (city) Hennepin County	86	0.12
Philadelphia, PA (city) Philadelphia County	86	0.01
Northern, MN (township) Beltrami County	85	1.87
Brigham City, UT (city) Box Elder County	85	0.48
Providence, TX (cdp) Denton County	83	1.91
Farmington, UT (city) Davis County	83	0.48
Carlsbad, CA (city) San Diego County	83	0.08
Walhalla, ND (city) Pembina County	80	7.35
Sudden Valley, WA (cdp) Whatcom County	80	1.19
Mapleton, UT (city) Utah County	80	1.06
Fort Collins, CO (city) Larimer County	80	0.06
Peoria, AZ (city) Yavapai County	80	0.05
Anchorage, AK (municipality) Anchorage Municipality	79	0.03
Boston, MA (city) Suffolk County	79	0.01
Red Hill, SC (cdp) Horry County	78	0.56
Mukilteo, WA (city) Snohomish County	78	0.39
Niles, IL (village) Cook County	78	0.26
Ann Arbor, MI (city) Washtenaw County	78	0.07
Aurora, CO (city) Arapahoe County	78	0.02
Salem, UT (city) Utah County	77	1.27
Memphis, TN (city) Shelby County	77	0.01
Blaine, WA (city) Whatcom County	76	1.67
Inglewood-Finn Hill, WA (cdp) King County	76	0.33
Millcreek, UT (cdp) Salt Lake County	76	0.12
Long Beach, CA (city) Los Angeles County	76	0.02
Benjamin, UT (cdp) Utah County	75	7.60
Gambier, OH (village) Knox County	75	3.41
Hutchinson, MN (city) McLeod County	75	0.53
Ontario, CA (city) San Bernardino County	75	0.05
Lake Forest Park, WA (city) King County	73	0.58
Bellevue, WA (city) King County	73	0.06
Hollywood, FL (city) Broward County	73	0.05
Urban Honolulu, HI (cdp) Honolulu County	73	0.02
Tulsa, OK (city) Tulsa County	72	0.02
Lexington Park, MD (cdp) St. Mary's County	71	0.65
Salmon Creek, WA (cdp) Clark County	71	0.35
Rancho Santa Margarita, CA (city) Orange County	71	0.15
Mesa, AZ (city) Maricopa County	71	0.02
Boone, NC (town) Watauga County	69	0.42
Mill Creek, WA (city) Snohomish County	69	0.39
Novi, MI (city) Oakland County	69	0.13
Oklahoma City, OK (city) Oklahoma County	69	0.01
Dublin, CA (city) Alameda County	68	0.16
Marysville, WA (city) Snohomish County	68	0.12
Bloomington, MN (city) Hennepin County	68	0.08
Berkeley, CA (city) Alameda County	68	0.06
Greenfield, WI (city) Milwaukee County	67	0.19
Olathe, KS (city) Johnson County	67	0.06
Henderson, NV (city) Clark County	67	0.03
Raleigh, NC (city) Wake County	67	0.02
Tucson, AZ (city) Pima County	67	0.01
Dundee, OR (city) Yamhill County	66	2.14
Post Falls, ID (city) Kootenai County	66	0.25
Longview, TX (city) Gregg County	66	0.08
Athens-Clarke County, GA (unified govt) Clarke County	66	0.06
Florence, CO (city) Fremont County	65	1.68
Kingman, AZ (city) Mohave County	65	0.23

SECTION THREE

Please refer to the Explanation of Data in the front of the book for more detailed information.

Ancestry

Icelander

Top 150 Places Sorted by Percent of Total Population

Based on all places, regardless of total population

Place	Population	%
Hamilton, ND (city) Pembina County	14	25.00
Jamestown, WA (cdp) Clallam County	117	22.20
Canton City, ND (city) Pembina County	7	20.59
Mountain, ND (city) Pembina County	7	15.22
Edinburg, ND (city) Walsh County	27	12.92
Cavalier, ND (city) Pembina County	206	12.80
Woodruff, UT (town) Rich County	19	12.42
Milton, ND (city) Cavalier County	9	11.25
Skamokawa Valley, WA (cdp) Wahkiakum County	33	9.79
Limestone, MN (township) Lincoln County	11	8.80
Swede Prairie, MN (township) Yellow Medicine County	9	7.83
Kranzburg, SD (town) Codington County	12	7.79
China Lake Acres, CA (cdp) Kern County	120	7.73
Benjamin, UT (cdp) Utah County	75	7.60
Gold Hill, CO (cdp) Boulder County	15	7.43
Walhalla, ND (city) Pembina County	80	7.35
Mammoth, WY (cdp) Park County	16	7.34
Divide, CO (cdp) Teller County	6	7.06
Nassau, MN (city) Lac qui Parle County	7	6.80
Gardner, ND (city) Cass County	5	6.76
Upham, ND (city) McHenry County	10	6.41
Toronto, SD (town) Deuel County	19	6.33
Hammond, MN (township) Polk County	3	6.12
Skane, MN (township) Kittson County	3	5.88
Marble, MN (township) Lincoln County	11	5.73
Bertha, MN (city) Todd County	30	5.43
Bicknell, UT (town) Wayne County	19	5.32
Colman, SD (city) Moody County	42	5.02
Hoople, ND (city) Walsh County	18	4.93
Purdy, WA (cdp) Pierce County	62	4.84
Teien, MN (township) Kittson County	3	4.55
Dickey, ND (city) LaMoure County	2	4.55
Grugan, PA (township) Clinton County	3	4.48
Taylor Lake Village, TX (city) Harris County	156	4.40
Osnabrock, ND (city) Cavalier County	7	4.32
Fenwick, CT (borough) Middlesex County	3	4.29
Washington, WI (town) Door County	29	4.18
St. Thomas, ND (city) Pembina County	14	4.13
Westerheim, MN (township) Lyon County	12	3.95
Alta Vista, MN (township) Lincoln County	6	3.95
Taunton, MN (city) Lyon County	7	3.89
Atherton, MN (township) Wilkin County	5	3.79
Crystal, ND (city) Pembina County	5	3.79
Flaxville, MT (town) Daniels County	3	3.75
Newark, VT (town) Caledonia County	17	3.74
Logan, ND (cdp) Ward County	9	3.66
Alger, WA (cdp) Skagit County	9	3.63
Petersburg, ND (city) Nelson County	6	3.51
Potamo, MN (township) Lake of the Woods County	3	3.49
Farmington, WA (town) Whitman County	7	3.48
Minneota, MN (city) Lyon County	41	3.44
Gambier, OH (village) Knox County	75	3.41
Thayne, WY (town) Lincoln County	14	3.38
May Creek, WA (cdp) Snohomish County	29	3.25
White Haven, MT (cdp) Lincoln County	18	3.14
Henderson, IA (city) Mills County	4	3.05
Green River, UT (city) Emery County	28	2.88
Jamul, CA (cdp) San Diego County	152	2.86
Starkweather, ND (city) Ramsey County	4	2.84
Finley, ND (city) Steele County	13	2.65
Lake Roesiger, WA (cdp) Snohomish County	9	2.65
Elm Creek, MN (township) Martin County	5	2.58
Lone Pine, MN (township) Itasca County	11	2.54
Horace, ND (city) Cass County	57	2.53
Cobb, CA (cdp) Lake County	49	2.53
Towner, ND (city) McHenry County	14	2.45
Mentor, MN (city) Polk County	4	2.45
Jadis, MN (township) Roseau County	13	2.39
Hettinger, ND (city) Adams County	28	2.37
Stafford, MN (township) Roseau County	7	2.36
Preston, MD (town) Caroline County	12	2.34
Sawyer, ND (city) Ward County	8	2.33
Kingsland, TX (cdp) Llano County	127	2.30
Genola, UT (town) Utah County	26	2.23
Spruce, MN (township) Roseau County	15	2.22
Westport, MN (township) Pope County	5	2.21
Ceresco, MN (township) Blue Earth County	5	2.20
Rivergrove, OR (city) Clackamas County	5	2.17
Park River, ND (city) Walsh County	31	2.16
Dundee, OR (city) Yamhill County	66	2.14
Linden, MN (township) Brown County	6	2.13
Fairview, MN (township) Lyon County	8	2.09
Clitherall, MN (township) Otter Tail County	11	2.08
Atlanta, NE (village) Phelps County	3	2.07
Neche, ND (city) Pembina County	8	2.06
Grafton, ND (city) Walsh County	88	2.04
Euclid, MN (township) Polk County	3	2.03
Richardville, MN (township) Kittson County	3	2.03
Ephrata, WA (city) Grant County	147	1.98
Rippey, IA (city) Greene County	6	1.95
Cascade, MT (town) Cascade County	10	1.94
Sigurd, UT (town) Sevier County	8	1.93
Providence, TX (cdp) Denton County	83	1.91
Hitterdal, MN (city) Clay County	4	1.90
Bayfield, WI (city) Bayfield County	10	1.89
Stanley, MN (township) Lyon County	5	1.89
Northern, MN (township) Beltrami County	85	1.87
Brenda, AZ (cdp) La Paz County	7	1.85
Burton, MN (township) Yellow Medicine County	3	1.85
Nordick, MN (township) Wilkin County	2	1.85
Palmyra, UT (cdp) Utah County	11	1.84
Glennallen, AK (cdp) Valdez-Cordova Census Area	10	1.81
Tryon, NE (cdp) McPherson County	3	1.80
Nezperce, ID (city) Lewis County	6	1.79
Birch Bay, WA (cdp) Whatcom County	140	1.78
Weston, NJ (cdp) Somerset County	19	1.77
Zumbrota, MN (city) Goodhue County	55	1.73
Drayton, ND (city) Pembina County	12	1.72
Buzzle, MN (township) Beltrami County	4	1.72
Marshfield, MN (township) Lincoln County	4	1.72
Spanish Fork, UT (city) Utah County	544	1.71
Elk Ridge, UT (city) Utah County	37	1.70
Lake Riverside, CA (cdp) Riverside County	24	1.70
Ivanhoe, MN (city) Lincoln County	9	1.70
Lewiston, MI (cdp) Montmorency County	24	1.69
Florence, CO (city) Fremont County	65	1.68
Langdon, ND (city) Cavalier County	30	1.68
Sister Bay, WI (village) Door County	11	1.68
Blaine, WA (city) Whatcom County	76	1.67
Woodside East, DE (cdp) Kent County	32	1.61
Acalanes Ridge, CA (cdp) Contra Costa County	26	1.61
Fircrest, WA (city) Pierce County	102	1.59
Flagler Estates, FL (cdp) St. Johns County	46	1.59
Tunsberg, MN (township) Chippewa County	2	1.59
Nidaros, MN (township) Otter Tail County	5	1.55
Lake Benton, MN (township) Lincoln County	3	1.55
Adams, ND (city) Walsh County	2	1.55
Todd Creek, CO (cdp) Adams County	57	1.52
Shell Ridge, CA (cdp) Contra Costa County	21	1.52
Westhaven-Moonstone, CA (cdp) Humboldt County	13	1.52
Lake Stay, MN (township) Lincoln County	3	1.52
Fort Ransom, ND (city) Ransom County	1	1.49
Sparta, MN (township) Chippewa County	11	1.46
Camp Douglas, WI (village) Juneau County	8	1.46
Waseca, MN (city) Waseca County	137	1.45
Lankin, ND (city) Walsh County	2	1.45
Meraux, LA (cdp) St. Bernard Parish	62	1.43
Hardin, MO (city) Ray County	7	1.42
Portage, PA (township) Potter County	3	1.42
Lambert, MN (township) Red Lake County	2	1.41
Palmyra, MO (city) Marion County	50	1.40
Morrison, CO (town) Jefferson County	4	1.40
Rome, WI (town) Adams County	38	1.38
Wildwood, MN (township) Itasca County	2	1.38
Franklin, MN (township) Wright County	38	1.37
Frederick, CO (town) Weld County	104	1.35
Harlowton, MT (city) Wheatland County	12	1.35
Huntsville, MN (township) Polk County	7	1.35
New London, MN (township) Kandiyohi County	39	1.33
Pixley, CA (cdp) Tulare County	39	1.32

Ancestry

Icelander

Top 150 Places Sorted by Percent of Total Population

Based on places with total population of 7,500 or more

Place	Population	%
Birch Bay, WA (cdp) Whatcom County	140	1.78
Spanish Fork, UT (city) Utah County	544	1.71
Waseca, MN (city) Waseca County	137	1.45
Frederick, CO (town) Weld County	104	1.35
Grand Forks, ND (city) Grand Forks County	626	1.20
Mapleton, UT (city) Utah County	80	1.06
Payson, UT (city) Utah County	180	1.05
Yucaipa, CA (city) San Bernardino County	484	0.96
Kenmore, WA (city) King County	130	0.65
Lexington Park, MD (cdp) St. Mary's County	71	0.65
Alpine, UT (city) Utah County	55	0.61
West Fargo, ND (city) Cass County	139	0.58
Lake Forest Park, WA (city) King County	73	0.58
Grosse Pointe Farms, MI (city) Wayne County	55	0.58
Red Hill, SC (cdp) Horry County	78	0.56
Perry, IA (city) Dallas County	42	0.55
Hutchinson, MN (city) McLeod County	75	0.53
Sturgeon Bay, WI (city) Door County	49	0.53
Springville, UT (city) Utah County	144	0.52
Corte Madera, CA (town) Marin County	47	0.52
Mount Vernon, WA (city) Skagit County	155	0.50
Winchester, TN (city) Franklin County	41	0.49
Brigham City, UT (city) Box Elder County	85	0.48
Farmington, UT (city) Davis County	83	0.48
Colts Neck, NJ (township) Monmouth County	49	0.48
Olney, IL (city) Richland County	40	0.46
South Salt Lake, UT (city) Salt Lake County	102	0.44
Gainesville, VA (cdp) Prince William County	47	0.44
Mammoth Lakes, CA (town) Mono County	35	0.44
Gold Canyon, AZ (cdp) Pinal County	48	0.43
Boone, NC (town) Watauga County	69	0.42
Cloquet, MN (city) Carlton County	51	0.42
Fergus Falls, MN (city) Otter Tail County	55	0.41
Murray, UT (city) Salt Lake County	187	0.40
Medfield, MA (town) Norfolk County	48	0.40
Gardnerville Ranchos, NV (cdp) Douglas County	47	0.40
Burien, WA (city) King County	129	0.39
Mukilteo, WA (city) Snohomish County	78	0.39
Mill Creek, WA (city) Snohomish County	69	0.39
Fuller Heights, FL (cdp) Polk County	30	0.39
Ormond Beach, FL (city) Volusia County	145	0.38
Sartell, MN (city) Stearns County	47	0.37
Hurricane, UT (city) Washington County	47	0.36
Union, MI (charter township) Isabella County	43	0.36
Newcastle, WA (city) King County	36	0.36
Lacey, NJ (township) Ocean County	97	0.35
Salmon Creek, WA (cdp) Clark County	71	0.35
Washougal, WA (city) Clark County	46	0.35
Blooming Grove, NY (town) Orange County	62	0.34
Fernley, NV (city) Lyon County	62	0.34
Sauk Rapids, MN (city) Benton County	43	0.34
Suamico, WI (village) Brown County	37	0.34
Issaquah, WA (city) King County	91	0.33
Inglewood-Finn Hill, WA (cdp) King County	76	0.33
Mandan, ND (city) Morton County	59	0.33
Westwood, MA (town) Norfolk County	47	0.33
Fargo, ND (city) Cass County	330	0.32
Logan, UT (city) Cache County	147	0.32
Sartell, MN (city) Stearns County	47	0.32
Evanston, WY (city) Uinta County	38	0.32
Price, UT (city) Carbon County	27	0.32
Monroe, CT (town) Fairfield County	60	0.31
Casa de Oro-Mount Helix, CA (cdp) San Diego County	59	0.31
Enumclaw, WA (city) King County	33	0.31
Detroit Lakes, MN (city) Becker County	26	0.31
Golden Valley, MN (city) Hennepin County	61	0.30
Anthem, AZ (cdp) Maricopa County	59	0.30
Monfort Heights, OH (cdp) Hamilton County	35	0.30
Cadillac, MI (city) Wexford County	31	0.30
Harrison, WI (town) Calumet County	30	0.30
Ives Estates, FL (cdp) Miami-Dade County	51	0.29
Ferndale, WA (city) Whatcom County	32	0.29
Woodmoor, CO (cdp) El Paso County	26	0.29
Alderwood Manor, WA (cdp) Snohomish County	23	0.29
Rock Springs, WY (city) Sweetwater County	61	0.28
Hermosa Beach, CA (city) Los Angeles County	55	0.28
Malibu, CA (city) Los Angeles County	36	0.28
Soquel, CA (cdp) Santa Cruz County	26	0.28
Stoneham, MA (cdp/town) Middlesex County	57	0.27
Santaquin, UT (city) Utah County	23	0.27
Bellingham, WA (city) Whatcom County	204	0.26
Urbana, IL (city) Champaign County	105	0.26
Niles, IL (village) Cook County	78	0.26
Lockport, NY (town) Niagara County	52	0.26
Bonney Lake, WA (city) Pierce County	42	0.26
Alpine, CA (cdp) San Diego County	35	0.26
East Wenatchee, WA (city) Douglas County	33	0.26
Ardmore, PA (cdp) Montgomery County	32	0.26
Lynden, WA (city) Whatcom County	30	0.26
Chino Valley, AZ (town) Yavapai County	28	0.26
Plainedge, NY (cdp) Nassau County	24	0.26
Edmonds, WA (city) Snohomish County	100	0.25
Post Falls, ID (city) Kootenai County	66	0.25
Gunbarrel, CO (cdp) Boulder County	24	0.25
Rapid Valley, SD (cdp) Pennington County	20	0.25
Brighton, MI (city) Livingston County	19	0.25
Bismarck, ND (city) Burleigh County	144	0.24
Puyallup, WA (city) Pierce County	89	0.24
Altamont, OR (cdp) Klamath County	48	0.24
Ukiah, CA (city) Mendocino County	39	0.24
Charlton, MA (town) Worcester County	31	0.24
East Grand Forks, MN (city) Polk County	20	0.24
Croton-on-Hudson, NY (village) Westchester County	19	0.24
New Hanover, NJ (township) Burlington County	19	0.24
St. George, UT (city) Washington County	162	0.23
Eden Prairie, MN (city) Hennepin County	137	0.23
Shawnee, KS (city) Johnson County	136	0.23
Kingman, AZ (city) Mohave County	65	0.23
Magna, UT (cdp) Salt Lake County	63	0.23
New Lenox, IL (village) Will County	55	0.23
Fairwood, WA (cdp) King County	44	0.23
New Port Richey, FL (city) Pasco County	35	0.23
Sedro-Woolley, WA (city) Skagit County	24	0.23
Kirkland, WA (city) King County	106	0.22
Pittsford, NY (town) Monroe County	63	0.22
Riverbank, CA (city) Stanislaus County	47	0.22
Miamisburg, OH (city) Montgomery County	43	0.22
Columbia Heights, MN (city) Anoka County	42	0.22
Hopkins, MN (city) Hennepin County	38	0.22
Lake Tapps, WA (cdp) Pierce County	25	0.22
Independence, OR (city) Polk County	18	0.22
Wyoming, MN (city) Chisago County	17	0.22
Eagan, MN (city) Dakota County	135	0.21
Silver Firs, WA (cdp) Snohomish County	46	0.21
Ellensburg, WA (city) Kittitas County	38	0.21
Albany, CA (city) Alameda County	37	0.21
North Ogden, UT (city) Weber County	35	0.21
Berkley, MI (city) Oakland County	32	0.21
East San Gabriel, CA (cdp) Los Angeles County	32	0.21
La Grande, OR (city) Union County	27	0.21
Gloucester City, NJ (city) Camden County	24	0.21
Vernal, UT (city) Uintah County	18	0.21
Weymouth Town, MA (city) Norfolk County	106	0.20
East Hartford, CT (cdp/town) Hartford County	104	0.20
Bothell, WA (city) King County	64	0.20
Milton, MA (cdp/town) Norfolk County	53	0.20
Woodstock, GA (city) Cherokee County	44	0.20
New Brighton, MN (city) Ramsey County	43	0.20
Ashland, OR (city) Jackson County	41	0.20
Melville, NY (cdp) Suffolk County	38	0.20
Saratoga Springs, UT (city) Utah County	30	0.20
North St. Paul, MN (city) Ramsey County	23	0.20
West Point, UT (city) Davis County	18	0.20
Gold River, CA (cdp) Sacramento County	17	0.20
Crookston, MN (city) Polk County	16	0.20
Diamondhead, MS (cdp) Hancock County	16	0.20
South Jordan, UT (city) Salt Lake County	89	0.19
Greenfield, WI (city) Milwaukee County	67	0.19
Burlingame, CA (city) San Mateo County	54	0.19
Ferry Pass, FL (cdp) Escambia County	53	0.19

SECTION THREE

Please refer to the Explanation of Data in the front of the book for more detailed information.

Ancestry

Iranian

U.S. and 50 States Sorted by Population and Percent of Total Population

Place	Population	%
United States	**425,587**	**0.14**
California	203,656	0.56
Texas	29,906	0.12
New York	27,773	0.14
Virginia	18,768	0.24
Maryland	14,561	0.26
Florida	12,999	0.07
Illinois	9,708	0.08
Washington	8,943	0.14
Georgia	8,865	0.09
Massachusetts	7,989	0.12
New Jersey	7,366	0.08
Arizona	7,024	0.11
Pennsylvania	4,863	0.04
Nevada	4,677	0.18
Oregon	4,567	0.12
Colorado	4,419	0.09
Michigan	4,305	0.04
North Carolina	4,273	0.05
Ohio	4,038	0.04
Oklahoma	3,720	0.10
Tennessee	3,176	0.05
Missouri	3,078	0.05
Minnesota	2,467	0.05
Connecticut	2,460	0.07
Indiana	2,332	0.04
Alabama	1,940	0.04
Utah	1,669	0.06
Kansas	1,633	0.06
Kentucky	1,627	0.04
Wisconsin	1,534	0.03
South Carolina	1,406	0.03
District of Columbia	1,262	0.22
Louisiana	1,249	0.03
New Mexico	1,146	0.06
Iowa	891	0.03
Arkansas	685	0.02
Mississippi	661	0.02
Delaware	599	0.07
Nebraska	509	0.03
New Hampshire	500	0.04
Hawaii	395	0.03
Idaho	393	0.03
Rhode Island	380	0.04
West Virginia	288	0.02
Vermont	199	0.03
Maine	164	0.01
Wyoming	155	0.03
Alaska	137	0.02
Montana	137	0.01
South Dakota	54	0.01
North Dakota	41	0.01

Place	Population	%
California	203,656	0.56
Maryland	14,561	0.26
Virginia	18,768	0.24
District of Columbia	1,262	0.22
Nevada	4,677	0.18
United States	**425,587**	**0.14**
New York	27,773	0.14
Washington	8,943	0.14
Texas	29,906	0.12
Massachusetts	7,989	0.12
Oregon	4,567	0.12
Arizona	7,024	0.11
Oklahoma	3,720	0.10
Georgia	8,865	0.09
Colorado	4,419	0.09
Illinois	9,708	0.08
New Jersey	7,366	0.08
Florida	12,999	0.07
Connecticut	2,460	0.07
Delaware	599	0.07
Utah	1,669	0.06
Kansas	1,633	0.06
New Mexico	1,146	0.06
North Carolina	4,273	0.05
Tennessee	3,176	0.05
Missouri	3,078	0.05
Minnesota	2,467	0.05
Pennsylvania	4,863	0.04
Michigan	4,305	0.04
Ohio	4,038	0.04
Indiana	2,332	0.04
Alabama	1,940	0.04
Kentucky	1,627	0.04
New Hampshire	500	0.04
Rhode Island	380	0.04
Wisconsin	1,534	0.03
South Carolina	1,406	0.03
Louisiana	1,249	0.03
Iowa	891	0.03
Nebraska	509	0.03
Hawaii	395	0.03
Idaho	393	0.03
Vermont	199	0.03
Wyoming	155	0.03
Arkansas	685	0.02
Mississippi	661	0.02
West Virginia	288	0.02
Alaska	137	0.02
Maine	164	0.01
Montana	137	0.01
South Dakota	54	0.01
North Dakota	41	0.01

Please refer to the Explanation of Data in the front of the book for more detailed information.

Ancestry

Iranian

Top 150 Places Sorted by Population

Based on all places, regardless of total population

Place	Population	%
Los Angeles, CA (city) Los Angeles County	51,547	1.37
New York, NY (city) Kings County	10,204	0.13
Glendale, CA (city) Los Angeles County	10,199	5.31
North Hempstead, NY (town) Nassau County	9,262	4.14
Beverly Hills, CA (city) Los Angeles County	9,158	26.95
Irvine, CA (city) Orange County	7,908	3.97
San Diego, CA (city) San Diego County	7,595	0.59
San Jose, CA (city) Santa Clara County	7,389	0.80
Houston, TX (city) Harris County	4,582	0.22
Manhattan, NY (borough) New York County	4,256	0.27
Queens, NY (borough) Queens County	3,707	0.17
Plano, TX (city) Collin County	3,435	1.34
Laguna Niguel, CA (city) Orange County	3,258	5.20
Santa Monica, CA (city) Los Angeles County	2,587	2.92
Mission Viejo, CA (city) Orange County	2,460	2.66
Great Neck, NY (village) Nassau County	2,382	24.20
Newport Beach, CA (city) Orange County	2,378	2.85
San Francisco, CA (city) San Francisco County	2,263	0.29
Chicago, IL (city) Cook County	2,222	0.08
Kings Point, NY (village) Nassau County	2,070	41.62
Anaheim, CA (city) Orange County	2,070	0.62
Dallas, TX (city) Dallas County	2,012	0.17
Aliso Viejo, CA (city) Orange County	1,977	4.27
Austin, TX (city) Travis County	1,872	0.24
Brooklyn, NY (borough) Kings County	1,822	0.07
Calabasas, CA (city) Los Angeles County	1,747	7.70
Phoenix, AZ (city) Maricopa County	1,585	0.11
Burbank, CA (city) Los Angeles County	1,583	1.54
Thousand Oaks, CA (city) Ventura County	1,536	1.23
Johns Creek, GA (city) Fulton County	1,508	2.07
Oyster Bay, NY (town) Nassau County	1,464	0.50
Potomac, MD (cdp) Montgomery County	1,336	2.98
Las Vegas, NV (city) Clark County	1,319	0.23
Scottsdale, AZ (city) Maricopa County	1,314	0.60
Oklahoma City, OK (city) Oklahoma County	1,297	0.23
Washington, DC (city) District of Columbia	1,262	0.22
Seattle, WA (city) King County	1,225	0.21
Rockville, MD (city) Montgomery County	1,210	2.08
Rancho Palos Verdes, CA (city) Los Angeles County	1,182	2.85
Lake Forest, CA (city) Orange County	1,167	1.52
Bellevue, WA (city) King County	1,139	0.95
Sunnyvale, CA (city) Santa Clara County	1,120	0.82
Saratoga, CA (city) Santa Clara County	1,119	3.79
Torrance, CA (city) Los Angeles County	1,102	0.77
Henderson, NV (city) Clark County	1,089	0.44
San Antonio, TX (city) Medina County	1,074	0.08
Corona, CA (city) Riverside County	1,065	0.71
Oakland, CA (city) Alameda County	1,056	0.27
Laguna Hills, CA (city) Orange County	1,043	3.43
Arlington, TX (city) Tarrant County	1,042	0.29
Frisco, TX (city) Collin County	1,039	1.01
San Mateo, CA (city) San Mateo County	1,015	1.07
Walnut Creek, CA (city) Contra Costa County	1,013	1.59
Nashville-Davidson, TN (metro govt) Davidson County	1,008	0.17
Cupertino, CA (city) Santa Clara County	1,005	1.78
Sacramento, CA (city) Sacramento County	1,001	0.22
Fresno, CA (city) Fresno County	995	0.21
San Ramon, CA (city) Contra Costa County	973	1.46
Berkeley, CA (city) Alameda County	925	0.85
Rancho Cucamonga, CA (city) San Bernardino County	903	0.56
Germantown, MD (cdp) Montgomery County	902	1.06
Gaithersburg, MD (city) Montgomery County	893	1.54
Pleasanton, CA (city) Alameda County	870	1.28
Arlington, VA (cdp) Arlington County	865	0.44
Wolf Trap, VA (cdp) Fairfax County	853	5.11
Great Falls, VA (cdp) Fairfax County	800	5.02
Fremont, CA (city) Alameda County	800	0.38
Santa Clarita, CA (city) Los Angeles County	799	0.46
Upland, CA (city) San Bernardino County	798	1.08
Denver, CO (city) Denver County	794	0.14
Yorba Linda, CA (city) Orange County	789	1.25
Newton, MA (city) Middlesex County	788	0.94
Baltimore, MD (city) Baltimore city County	788	0.13
Bethesda, MD (cdp) Montgomery County	786	1.34
Charlotte, NC (city) Mecklenburg County	786	0.11

Place	Population	%
Roseville, CA (city) Placer County	767	0.67
Simi Valley, CA (city) Ventura County	767	0.63
Boston, MA (city) Suffolk County	739	0.12
North Bethesda, MD (cdp) Montgomery County	732	1.81
Reston, VA (cdp) Fairfax County	727	1.37
Turlock, CA (city) Stanislaus County	721	1.07
Palo Alto, CA (city) Santa Clara County	720	1.15
North Potomac, MD (cdp) Montgomery County	718	2.87
Ashburn, VA (cdp) Loudoun County	715	1.69
Concord, CA (city) Contra Costa County	714	0.59
Santa Clara, CA (city) Santa Clara County	713	0.63
Tustin, CA (city) Orange County	677	0.92
West Hollywood, CA (city) Los Angeles County	674	1.94
Great Neck Plaza, NY (village) Nassau County	673	10.18
Redondo Beach, CA (city) Los Angeles County	672	1.02
Albuquerque, NM (city) Bernalillo County	672	0.13
Philadelphia, PA (city) Philadelphia County	665	0.04
Alexandria, VA (ind. city) Alexandria independent city	658	0.49
Portland, OR (city) Multnomah County	648	0.11
Bakersfield, CA (city) Kern County	641	0.19
West Bloomfield, MI (charter township) Oakland County	640	0.99
Tucson, AZ (city) Pima County	634	0.12
Columbia, MD (cdp) Howard County	632	0.64
Orange, CA (city) Orange County	626	0.47
Jacksonville, FL (city) Duval County	620	0.08
Sandy Springs, GA (city) Fulton County	615	0.68
Dublin, CA (city) Alameda County	614	1.44
Long Beach, CA (city) Los Angeles County	613	0.13
El Dorado Hills, CA (cdp) El Dorado County	609	1.41
Danville, CA (town) Contra Costa County	607	1.45
Mountain View, CA (city) Santa Clara County	606	0.84
Carlsbad, CA (city) San Diego County	598	0.60
Paradise, NV (cdp) Clark County	588	0.27
Santa Rosa, CA (city) Sonoma County	586	0.36
Rancho Santa Margarita, CA (city) Orange County	579	1.22
Pasadena, CA (city) Los Angeles County	573	0.42
Louisville-Jefferson County, KY (metro govt) Jefferson County	573	0.10
Foster City, CA (city) San Mateo County	572	1.92
Great Neck Estates, NY (village) Nassau County	566	20.72
Virginia Beach, VA (ind. city) Virginia Beach independent city	555	0.13
Modesto, CA (city) Stanislaus County	554	0.27
Vacaville, CA (city) Solano County	541	0.59
Hempstead, NY (town) Nassau County	539	0.07
Overland Park, KS (city) Johnson County	538	0.32
Fullerton, CA (city) Orange County	537	0.40
Spring Valley, NV (cdp) Clark County	537	0.31
Tempe, AZ (city) Maricopa County	536	0.33
Campbell, CA (city) Santa Clara County	532	1.37
Raleigh, NC (city) Wake County	532	0.14
Folsom, CA (city) Sacramento County	531	0.77
Davis, CA (city) Yolo County	530	0.82
San Dimas, CA (city) Los Angeles County	522	1.55
Tulsa, OK (city) Tulsa County	516	0.13
Atlanta, GA (city) Fulton County	516	0.12
Naperville, IL (city) DuPage County	510	0.36
Pomona, CA (city) Los Angeles County	508	0.34
Allen, TX (city) Collin County	501	0.64
Novato, CA (city) Marin County	500	0.99
Escondido, CA (city) San Diego County	500	0.35
Irving, TX (city) Dallas County	498	0.24
McLean, VA (cdp) Fairfax County	497	1.08
Redwood City, CA (city) San Mateo County	491	0.65
Richmond, CA (city) Contra Costa County	485	0.47
La Crescenta-Montrose, CA (cdp) Los Angeles County	478	2.40
Huntington Beach, CA (city) Orange County	478	0.25
Huntington, NY (town) Suffolk County	471	0.23
Ladera Ranch, CA (cdp) Orange County	468	2.58
Norman, OK (city) Cleveland County	466	0.43
Columbus, OH (city) Franklin County	466	0.06
San Clemente, CA (city) Orange County	465	0.77
McKinney, TX (city) Collin County	464	0.39
Arden-Arcade, CA (cdp) Sacramento County	461	0.51
Riverside, CA (city) Riverside County	456	0.15
Indianapolis, IN (city) Marion County	455	0.06
Roslyn Heights, NY (cdp) Nassau County	452	6.97

SECTION THREE

Ancestry

Iranian

Top 150 Places Sorted by Percent of Total Population

Based on all places, regardless of total population

Place	Population	%
Kings Point, NY (village) Nassau County	2,070	41.62
Saddle Rock, NY (village) Nassau County	380	36.26
Drytown, CA (cdp) Amador County	76	36.19
Beverly Hills, CA (city) Los Angeles County	9,158	26.95
Great Neck, NY (village) Nassau County	2,382	24.20
Great Neck Estates, NY (village) Nassau County	566	20.72
Ruth, CA (cdp) Trinity County	27	17.88
Saddle Rock Estates, NY (cdp) Nassau County	90	17.18
Pinal, AZ (cdp) Gila County	78	15.73
Kensington, NY (village) Nassau County	180	14.94
Maharishi Vedic City, IA (city) Jefferson County	23	14.38
Great Neck Plaza, NY (village) Nassau County	673	10.18
Golf, IL (village) Cook County	58	9.78
Lexington Hills, CA (cdp) Santa Clara County	193	8.12
Calabasas, CA (city) Los Angeles County	1,747	7.70
Roslyn Heights, NY (cdp) Nassau County	452	6.97
Fairbanks Ranch, CA (cdp) San Diego County	136	6.88
Piney Point Village, TX (city) Harris County	211	6.76
Acalanes Ridge, CA (cdp) Contra Costa County	104	6.45
North Hills, NY (village) Nassau County	316	6.40
Flower Hill, NY (village) Nassau County	294	6.38
Camino Tassajara, CA (cdp) Contra Costa County	109	6.32
Roslyn, NY (village) Nassau County	169	6.20
Glendale, CA (city) Los Angeles County	10,199	5.31
Middleburg, VA (town) Loudoun County	25	5.27
Double Oak, TX (town) Denton County	147	5.22
Laguna Niguel, CA (city) Orange County	3,258	5.20
Wolf Trap, VA (cdp) Fairfax County	853	5.11
Mountain View, CO (town) Jefferson County	30	5.06
Great Falls, VA (cdp) Fairfax County	800	5.02
Cathcart, WA (cdp) Snohomish County	104	4.92
Fairview Beach, VA (cdp) King George County	28	4.88
Sands Point, NY (village) Nassau County	129	4.85
Great Neck Gardens, NY (cdp) Nassau County	43	4.74
Friendship Heights Village, MD (cdp) Montgomery County	273	4.73
Strawberry, CA (cdp) Marin County	241	4.69
Barton Creek, TX (cdp) Travis County	112	4.69
Rock Hill, NY (cdp) Sullivan County	76	4.60
Albertson, NY (cdp) Nassau County	259	4.53
Metzger, OR (cdp) Washington County	155	4.46
Sherwood Shores, TX (cdp) Grayson County	50	4.42
Lake Sherwood, CA (cdp) Ventura County	61	4.39
Aliso Viejo, CA (city) Orange County	1,977	4.27
North Hempstead, NY (town) Nassau County	9,262	4.14
San Antonio Heights, CA (cdp) San Bernardino County	164	4.12
Thomaston, NY (village) Nassau County	107	4.09
Prairie Rose, ND (city) Cass County	5	4.07
Asharoken, NY (village) Suffolk County	27	3.99
Irvine, CA (city) Orange County	7,908	3.97
Roslyn Estates, NY (village) Nassau County	49	3.97
Ten Mile Run, NJ (cdp) Somerset County	71	3.96
Aromas, CA (cdp) Monterey County	91	3.93
Bell Canyon, CA (cdp) Ventura County	96	3.91
Marin City, CA (cdp) Marin County	110	3.89
Old Westbury, NY (village) Nassau County	152	3.86
Saratoga, CA (city) Santa Clara County	1,119	3.79
Las Flores, CA (cdp) Orange County	236	3.76
Loyola, CA (cdp) Santa Clara County	124	3.74
East Hills, NY (village) Nassau County	255	3.72
Bertsch-Oceanview, CA (cdp) Del Norte County	96	3.71
Ivy, VA (cdp) Albemarle County	12	3.66
Lucas, TX (city) Collin County	171	3.52
Hillsborough, NH (cdp) Hillsborough County	97	3.50
Lomax, IL (village) Henderson County	17	3.46
Laguna Hills, CA (city) Orange County	1,043	3.43
Bannockburn, IL (village) Lake County	47	3.43
Pendleton, SC (town) Anderson County	100	3.38
Fair Lakes, VA (cdp) Fairfax County	268	3.37
Bluefield, VA (town) Tazewell County	183	3.37
Remington, OH (cdp) Hamilton County	8	3.35
Fruitdale, CA (cdp) Santa Clara County	32	3.31
Hickory Creek, TX (town) Denton County	99	3.23
Schuyler Falls, NY (town) Clinton County	167	3.21
Cannon Beach, OR (city) Clatsop County	35	3.20
Highlands-Baywood Park, CA (cdp) San Mateo County	132	3.18
Lowes Island, VA (cdp) Loudoun County	360	3.16
Upper Brookville, NY (village) Nassau County	47	3.16
Wisconsin, MN (township) Jackson County	8	3.13
Marina del Rey, CA (cdp) Los Angeles County	287	3.12
Oak Brook, IL (village) DuPage County	244	3.09
Brookville, NY (village) Nassau County	105	3.04
Marshall, VA (cdp) Fauquier County	46	2.99
Potomac, MD (cdp) Montgomery County	1,336	2.98
Roslyn Harbor, NY (village) Nassau County	34	2.95
Walker, CA (cdp) Mono County	20	2.95
Vienna, VA (town) Fairfax County	452	2.94
Santa Monica, CA (city) Los Angeles County	2,587	2.92
Los Altos Hills, CA (town) Santa Clara County	228	2.90
Bloomfield Hills, MI (city) Oakland County	112	2.89
North Potomac, MD (cdp) Montgomery County	718	2.87
Monte Sereno, CA (city) Santa Clara County	95	2.87
Newport Beach, CA (city) Orange County	2,378	2.85
Rancho Palos Verdes, CA (city) Los Angeles County	1,182	2.85
Cottonwood, CA (cdp) Shasta County	87	2.83
Westlake Village, CA (city) Los Angeles County	232	2.80
Manton, CA (cdp) Tehama County	8	2.80
Oak Park, CA (cdp) Ventura County	388	2.76
Dove Valley, CO (cdp) Arapahoe County	161	2.68
Old Bethpage, NY (cdp) Nassau County	149	2.67
Mission Viejo, CA (city) Orange County	2,460	2.66
Webster, TX (city) Harris County	262	2.66
Kaanapali, HI (cdp) Maui County	29	2.64
Lansdowne, VA (cdp) Loudoun County	254	2.59
Ladera Ranch, CA (cdp) Orange County	468	2.58
Georgetown, CT (cdp) Fairfield County	40	2.55
Van Alstyne, TX (city) Grayson County	75	2.54
Weed, CA (city) Siskiyou County	74	2.51
Penhook, VA (cdp) Franklin County	13	2.50
Williams Creek, IN (town) Marion County	10	2.50
Middle, MD (town) Frederick County	97	2.49
Santa Rosa Valley, CA (cdp) Ventura County	80	2.48
Burns Harbor, IN (town) Porter County	31	2.48
Port Vincent, LA (village) Livingston Parish	19	2.45
Sugarland Run, VA (cdp) Loudoun County	265	2.43
La Crescenta-Montrose, CA (cdp) Los Angeles County	478	2.40
Spring Hill, IN (town) Marion County	2	2.38
Contra Costa Centre, CA (cdp) Contra Costa County	131	2.34
Oakland, PA (cdp) Cambria County	37	2.34
Corte Madera, CA (town) Marin County	211	2.32
Wattsville, VA (cdp) Accomack County	29	2.26
Laughlin AFB, TX (cdp) Val Verde County	31	2.24
Kendall, WI (town) Lafayette County	10	2.23
Hillsborough, CA (town) San Mateo County	235	2.21
University Gardens, NY (cdp) Nassau County	88	2.21
Reliez Valley, CA (cdp) Contra Costa County	64	2.21
Manvel, TX (city) Brazoria County	106	2.20
West Haven-Sylvan, OR (cdp) Washington County	154	2.19
North Fort Lewis, WA (cdp) Pierce County	63	2.17
Barnesville, MD (town) Montgomery County	3	2.17
Modena, PA (borough) Chester County	10	2.15
Paradise Valley, AZ (town) Maricopa County	281	2.13
Carolina Beach, NC (town) New Hanover County	120	2.12
Pomona, NY (village) Rockland County	75	2.12
Idylwood, VA (cdp) Fairfax County	331	2.11
Alamo, CA (cdp) Contra Costa County	320	2.11
Mayfield, NY (town) Fulton County	137	2.11
Muttontown, NY (village) Nassau County	72	2.09
Rockville, MD (city) Montgomery County	1,210	2.08
Prospect, KY (city) Jefferson County	97	2.08
Johns Creek, GA (city) Fulton County	1,508	2.07
Pemberwick, CT (cdp) Fairfield County	69	2.03
Glenolden, PA (borough) Delaware County	145	2.02
Blackhawk, CA (cdp) Contra Costa County	193	2.01
San Leanna, TX (village) Travis County	12	1.99
Tysons Corner, VA (cdp) Fairfax County	337	1.97
Pickering, MO (town) Nodaway County	4	1.96
West Hollywood, CA (city) Los Angeles County	674	1.94
Foster City, CA (city) San Mateo County	572	1.92
Broomall, PA (cdp) Delaware County	216	1.92
Lincoln, MA (town) Middlesex County	126	1.92

Please refer to the Explanation of Data in the front of the book for more detailed information.

Ancestry

Iranian

Top 150 Places Sorted by Percent of Total Population

Based on places with total population of 7,500 or more

Place	Population	%
Beverly Hills, CA (city) Los Angeles County	9,158	26.95
Great Neck, NY (village) Nassau County	2,382	24.20
Calabasas, CA (city) Los Angeles County	1,747	7.70
Glendale, CA (city) Los Angeles County	10,199	5.31
Laguna Niguel, CA (city) Orange County	3,258	5.20
Wolf Trap, VA (cdp) Fairfax County	853	5.11
Great Falls, VA (cdp) Fairfax County	800	5.02
Aliso Viejo, CA (city) Orange County	1,977	4.27
North Hempstead, NY (town) Nassau County	9,262	4.14
Irvine, CA (city) Orange County	7,908	3.97
Saratoga, CA (city) Santa Clara County	1,119	3.79
Laguna Hills, CA (city) Orange County	1,043	3.43
Fair Lakes, VA (cdp) Fairfax County	268	3.37
Lowes Island, VA (cdp) Loudoun County	360	3.16
Marina del Rey, CA (cdp) Los Angeles County	287	3.12
Oak Brook, IL (village) DuPage County	244	3.09
Potomac, MD (cdp) Montgomery County	1,336	2.98
Vienna, VA (town) Fairfax County	452	2.94
Santa Monica, CA (city) Los Angeles County	2,587	2.92
Los Altos Hills, CA (town) Santa Clara County	228	2.90
North Potomac, MD (cdp) Montgomery County	718	2.87
Newport Beach, CA (city) Orange County	2,378	2.85
Rancho Palos Verdes, CA (city) Los Angeles County	1,182	2.85
Westlake Village, CA (city) Los Angeles County	232	2.80
Oak Park, CA (cdp) Ventura County	388	2.76
Mission Viejo, CA (city) Orange County	2,460	2.66
Webster, TX (city) Harris County	262	2.66
Lansdowne, VA (cdp) Loudoun County	254	2.59
Ladera Ranch, CA (cdp) Orange County	468	2.58
Sugarland Run, VA (cdp) Loudoun County	265	2.43
La Crescenta-Montrose, CA (cdp) Los Angeles County	478	2.40
Corte Madera, CA (town) Marin County	211	2.32
Hillsborough, CA (town) San Mateo County	235	2.21
Paradise Valley, AZ (town) Maricopa County	281	2.13
Idylwood, VA (cdp) Fairfax County	331	2.11
Alamo, CA (cdp) Contra Costa County	320	2.11
Rockville, MD (city) Montgomery County	1,210	2.08
Johns Creek, GA (city) Fulton County	1,508	2.07
Blackhawk, CA (cdp) Contra Costa County	193	2.01
Tysons Corner, VA (cdp) Fairfax County	337	1.97
West Hollywood, CA (city) Los Angeles County	674	1.94
Foster City, CA (city) San Mateo County	572	1.92
Broomall, PA (cdp) Delaware County	216	1.92
Laguna Woods, CA (city) Orange County	306	1.88
Gold River, CA (cdp) Sacramento County	156	1.87
North Bethesda, MD (cdp) Montgomery County	732	1.81
Cupertino, CA (city) Santa Clara County	1,005	1.78
Albany, CA (city) Alameda County	318	1.77
El Cerrito, CA (city) Contra Costa County	409	1.75
Ashburn, VA (cdp) Loudoun County	715	1.69
Belmont, CA (city) San Mateo County	424	1.68
Franklin Lakes, NJ (borough) Bergen County	177	1.68
Granite Bay, CA (cdp) Placer County	379	1.67
Coto de Caza, CA (cdp) Orange County	258	1.67
Bull Mountain, OR (cdp) Washington County	152	1.66
Franklin Farm, VA (cdp) Fairfax County	322	1.65
University of California Davis, CA (cdp) Yolo County	126	1.63
Broadlands, VA (cdp) Loudoun County	173	1.62
Manhasset, NY (cdp) Nassau County	132	1.61
Walnut Creek, CA (city) Contra Costa County	1,013	1.59
Westwood, MA (town) Norfolk County	227	1.58
Rossmoor, CA (cdp) Orange County	166	1.58
San Dimas, CA (city) Los Angeles County	522	1.55
Burbank, CA (city) Los Angeles County	1,583	1.54
Gaithersburg, MD (city) Montgomery County	893	1.54
Los Gatos, CA (town) Santa Clara County	446	1.54
Chestnut Ridge, NY (village) Rockland County	121	1.54
Moraga, CA (town) Contra Costa County	244	1.53
Lake Forest, CA (city) Orange County	1,167	1.52
La Cañada Flintridge, CA (city) Los Angeles County	307	1.52
Kingsgate, WA (cdp) King County	208	1.52
Rolling Hills Estates, CA (city) Los Angeles County	122	1.52
San Anselmo, CA (town) Marin County	184	1.51
Dunn Loring, VA (cdp) Fairfax County	139	1.50
San Ramon, CA (city) Contra Costa County	973	1.46
Countryside, VA (cdp) Loudoun County	140	1.46
Danville, CA (town) Contra Costa County	607	1.45
Dublin, CA (city) Alameda County	614	1.44
Garrison, MD (cdp) Baltimore County	110	1.44
Sierra Madre, CA (city) Los Angeles County	154	1.42
Clarksburg, MD (cdp) Montgomery County	150	1.42
El Dorado Hills, CA (cdp) El Dorado County	609	1.41
Lone Tree, CO (city) Douglas County	139	1.41
Clayton, CA (city) Contra Costa County	152	1.40
Floris, VA (cdp) Fairfax County	113	1.39
Los Angeles, CA (city) Los Angeles County	51,547	1.37
Reston, VA (cdp) Fairfax County	727	1.37
Campbell, CA (city) Santa Clara County	532	1.37
Malibu, CA (city) Los Angeles County	175	1.37
Greenbriar, VA (cdp) Fairfax County	104	1.36
San Carlos, CA (city) San Mateo County	377	1.35
Travilah, MD (cdp) Montgomery County	163	1.35
Plano, TX (city) Collin County	3,435	1.34
Bethesda, MD (cdp) Montgomery County	786	1.34
Los Altos, CA (city) Santa Clara County	379	1.33
Lake Butler, FL (cdp) Orange County	208	1.33
Pike Creek, DE (cdp) New Castle County	104	1.30
Cinco Ranch, TX (cdp) Fort Bend County	234	1.29
Philipstown, NY (town) Putnam County	125	1.29
Topanga, CA (cdp) Los Angeles County	110	1.29
Pleasanton, CA (city) Alameda County	870	1.28
La Verne, CA (city) Los Angeles County	396	1.27
Weston, MA (town) Middlesex County	142	1.27
Oakton, VA (cdp) Fairfax County	421	1.26
Yorba Linda, CA (city) Orange County	789	1.25
Chantilly, VA (cdp) Fairfax County	274	1.24
Thousand Oaks, CA (city) Ventura County	1,536	1.23
Rancho Santa Margarita, CA (city) Orange County	579	1.22
South Riding, VA (cdp) Loudoun County	281	1.22
West Hempstead, NY (cdp) Nassau County	222	1.20
South Huntington, NY (cdp) Suffolk County	118	1.19
Tiburon, CA (town) Marin County	105	1.19
Mount Airy, MD (town) Carroll County	105	1.18
Laguna Beach, CA (city) Orange County	266	1.17
Palo Alto, CA (city) Santa Clara County	720	1.15
Mays Chapel, MD (cdp) Baltimore County	137	1.15
Plainview, NY (cdp) Nassau County	294	1.14
Lake Oswego, OR (city) Clackamas County	408	1.12
Burlingame, CA (city) San Mateo County	313	1.11
Cascades, VA (cdp) Loudoun County	134	1.11
Larkspur, CA (city) Marin County	131	1.11
Neabsco, VA (cdp) Prince William County	104	1.10
Upland, CA (city) San Bernardino County	798	1.08
McLean, VA (cdp) Fairfax County	497	1.08
Groves, TX (city) Jefferson County	172	1.08
Ridgefield, NJ (borough) Bergen County	118	1.08
San Mateo, CA (city) San Mateo County	1,015	1.07
Turlock, CA (city) Stanislaus County	721	1.07
Menlo Park, CA (city) San Mateo County	336	1.07
Germantown, MD (cdp) Montgomery County	902	1.06
Scotts Valley, CA (city) Santa Cruz County	120	1.06
Marple, PA (township) Delaware County	245	1.05
Pleasant Hill, CA (city) Contra Costa County	340	1.04
Redondo Beach, CA (city) Los Angeles County	672	1.02
La Riviera, CA (cdp) Sacramento County	114	1.02
Fairfield, IA (city) Jefferson County	96	1.02
Frisco, TX (city) Collin County	1,039	1.01
Watertown Town, MA (city) Middlesex County	316	1.00
Agoura Hills, CA (city) Los Angeles County	203	1.00
West Bloomfield, MI (charter township) Oakland County	640	0.99
Novato, CA (city) Marin County	500	0.99
Town and Country, MO (city) St. Louis County	107	0.99
Morgan Hill, CA (city) Santa Clara County	357	0.97
Short Pump, VA (cdp) Henrico County	233	0.97
Lathrop, CA (city) San Joaquin County	165	0.97
Loma Linda, CA (city) San Bernardino County	219	0.96
Bellevue, WA (city) King County	1,139	0.95
Orinda, CA (city) Contra Costa County	166	0.95
Newton, MA (city) Middlesex County	788	0.94
Aloha, OR (cdp) Washington County	445	0.94

Please refer to the Explanation of Data in the front of the book for more detailed information.

Ancestry

Irish

U.S. and 50 States Sorted by Population and Percent of Total Population

Place	Population	%
United States	**35,751,251**	**11.76**
California	2,748,155	7.50
New York	2,565,928	13.34
Pennsylvania	2,251,268	17.85
Florida	1,979,058	10.69
Texas	1,911,738	7.86
Ohio	1,666,746	14.48
Illinois	1,648,856	12.94
Massachusetts	1,516,227	23.41
New Jersey	1,370,783	15.72
Michigan	1,186,068	11.92
North Carolina	879,734	9.49
Missouri	876,760	14.80
Georgia	862,101	9.10
Virginia	845,204	10.78
Indiana	827,853	12.90
Washington	806,898	12.30
Tennessee	704,259	11.30
Maryland	693,953	12.18
Arizona	667,632	10.69
Wisconsin	660,884	11.72
Colorado	628,929	12.87
Connecticut	614,767	17.34
Minnesota	599,902	11.44
Kentucky	586,154	13.68
Alabama	491,029	10.42
Oregon	487,695	12.96
Oklahoma	478,190	13.01
Iowa	464,920	15.41
South Carolina	435,909	9.66
Kansas	387,825	13.80
Arkansas	381,337	13.27
Louisiana	358,347	8.09
New Hampshire	292,826	22.29
Mississippi	285,021	9.69
West Virginia	278,642	15.14
Nevada	271,932	10.33
Nebraska	264,065	14.68
Maine	237,955	17.92
Rhode Island	211,879	20.06
Idaho	165,249	10.82
Utah	164,050	6.17
Delaware	160,416	18.20
Montana	157,032	16.13
New Mexico	151,945	7.55
Vermont	111,761	17.90
South Dakota	88,995	11.13
Alaska	85,326	12.34
Wyoming	79,785	14.62
Hawaii	66,244	4.97
North Dakota	53,397	8.09
District of Columbia	39,622	6.78

Place	Population	%
Massachusetts	1,516,227	23.41
New Hampshire	292,826	22.29
Rhode Island	211,879	20.06
Delaware	160,416	18.20
Maine	237,955	17.92
Vermont	111,761	17.90
Pennsylvania	2,251,268	17.85
Connecticut	614,767	17.34
Montana	157,032	16.13
New Jersey	1,370,783	15.72
Iowa	464,920	15.41
West Virginia	278,642	15.14
Missouri	876,760	14.80
Nebraska	264,065	14.68
Wyoming	79,785	14.62
Ohio	1,666,746	14.48
Kansas	387,825	13.80
Kentucky	586,154	13.68
New York	2,565,928	13.34
Arkansas	381,337	13.27
Oklahoma	478,190	13.01
Oregon	487,695	12.96
Illinois	1,648,856	12.94
Indiana	827,853	12.90
Colorado	628,929	12.87
Alaska	85,326	12.34
Washington	806,898	12.30
Maryland	693,953	12.18
Michigan	1,186,068	11.92
United States	**35,751,251**	**11.76**
Wisconsin	660,884	11.72
Minnesota	599,902	11.44
Tennessee	704,259	11.30
South Dakota	88,995	11.13
Idaho	165,249	10.82
Virginia	845,204	10.78
Florida	1,979,058	10.69
Arizona	667,632	10.69
Alabama	491,029	10.42
Nevada	271,932	10.33
Mississippi	285,021	9.69
South Carolina	435,909	9.66
North Carolina	879,734	9.49
Georgia	862,101	9.10
Louisiana	358,347	8.09
North Dakota	53,397	8.09
Texas	1,911,738	7.86
New Mexico	151,945	7.55
California	2,748,155	7.50
District of Columbia	39,622	6.78
Utah	164,050	6.17
Hawaii	66,244	4.97

Please refer to the Explanation of Data in the front of the book for more detailed information.

Ancestry

Irish

Top 150 Places Sorted by Population

Based on all places, regardless of total population

Place	Population	%
New York, NY (city) Kings County	410,889	5.09
Chicago, IL (city) Cook County	201,693	7.46
Philadelphia, PA (city) Philadelphia County	195,849	13.01
Los Angeles, CA (city) Los Angeles County	147,342	3.91
Phoenix, AZ (city) Maricopa County	130,005	8.96
Hempstead, NY (town) Nassau County	125,911	16.71
Brookhaven, NY (town) Suffolk County	122,200	25.45
Manhattan, NY (borough) New York County	117,355	7.41
San Diego, CA (city) San Diego County	108,215	8.44
Queens, NY (borough) Queens County	105,348	4.79
Columbus, OH (city) Franklin County	99,000	12.85
Boston, MA (city) Suffolk County	98,905	16.41
Indianapolis, IN (city) Marion County	93,959	11.60
Brooklyn, NY (borough) Kings County	84,945	3.44
Houston, TX (city) Harris County	84,899	4.11
Jacksonville, FL (city) Duval County	83,146	10.24
Louisville-Jefferson County, KY (metro govt) Jefferson County	80,713	13.75
Portland, OR (city) Multnomah County	72,114	12.73
Seattle, WA (city) King County	71,012	11.93
Islip, NY (town) Suffolk County	68,763	20.61
Omaha, NE (city) Douglas County	68,484	16.81
Austin, TX (city) Travis County	66,161	8.66
San Antonio, TX (city) Medina County	65,920	5.11
Staten Island, NY (borough) Richmond County	64,762	13.97
San Francisco, CA (city) San Francisco County	64,487	8.17
Oklahoma City, OK (city) Oklahoma County	62,334	11.06
Oyster Bay, NY (town) Nassau County	59,765	20.49
Denver, CO (city) Denver County	58,273	10.08
Dallas, TX (city) Dallas County	57,324	4.83
Nashville-Davidson, TN (metro govt) Davidson County	54,980	9.35
Charlotte, NC (city) Mecklenburg County	54,824	7.77
Virginia Beach, VA (ind. city) Virginia Beach independent city	54,157	12.42
Colorado Springs, CO (city) El Paso County	53,519	13.25
Kansas City, MO (city) Jackson County	53,239	11.70
Tucson, AZ (city) Pima County	52,307	10.09
Fort Worth, TX (city) Tarrant County	52,236	7.41
Pittsburgh, PA (city) Allegheny County	51,563	16.74
Las Vegas, NV (city) Clark County	50,836	8.77
Mesa, AZ (city) Maricopa County	46,956	10.68
Albuquerque, NM (city) Bernalillo County	46,146	8.68
San Jose, CA (city) Santa Clara County	46,086	4.98
Huntington, NY (town) Suffolk County	45,750	22.63
Tulsa, OK (city) Tulsa County	45,390	11.69
Wichita, KS (city) Sedgwick County	45,232	12.10
Babylon, NY (town) Suffolk County	42,364	19.83
Minneapolis, MN (city) Hennepin County	42,359	11.16
Washington, DC (city) District of Columbia	39,622	6.78
Baltimore, MD (city) Baltimore city County	39,501	6.37
Lexington-Fayette, KY (cons. govt) Fayette County	39,145	13.59
Bronx, NY (borough) Bronx County	38,479	2.82
Milwaukee, WI (city) Milwaukee County	37,577	6.37
Cleveland, OH (city) Cuyahoga County	37,296	9.11
Anchorage, AK (municipality) Anchorage Municipality	35,919	12.64
Sacramento, CA (city) Sacramento County	35,916	7.82
Lincoln, NE (city) Lancaster County	35,533	14.04
Memphis, TN (city) Shelby County	34,871	5.32
Toledo, OH (city) Lucas County	34,827	11.93
St. Paul, MN (city) Ramsey County	34,326	12.17
Buffalo, NY (city) Erie County	34,103	12.82
Spokane, WA (city) Spokane County	33,567	16.25
St. Petersburg, FL (city) Pinellas County	32,964	13.42
Cincinnati, OH (city) Hamilton County	32,799	10.93
Smithtown, NY (town) Suffolk County	31,963	27.18
Madison, WI (city) Dane County	31,932	13.93
Worcester, MA (city) Worcester County	31,857	17.70
Scottsdale, AZ (city) Maricopa County	31,781	14.53
Henderson, NV (city) Clark County	31,572	12.67
St. Louis, MO (city) St. Louis city County	31,486	9.88
Raleigh, NC (city) Wake County	31,339	8.19
Arlington, TX (city) Tarrant County	30,767	8.56
Tampa, FL (city) Hillsborough County	30,312	9.09
Quincy, MA (city) Norfolk County	29,819	32.85
Des Moines, IA (city) Polk County	29,511	14.60
Overland Park, KS (city) Johnson County	28,990	17.00
Fort Wayne, IN (city) Allen County	28,352	11.17
Reno, NV (city) Washoe County	28,213	12.77
Chandler, AZ (city) Maricopa County	27,549	12.00
Long Beach, CA (city) Los Angeles County	27,445	5.94
North Hempstead, NY (town) Nassau County	27,339	12.22
Fresno, CA (city) Fresno County	26,731	5.52
Gilbert, AZ (town) Maricopa County	26,594	13.63
Arlington, VA (cdp) Arlington County	26,567	13.45
Aurora, CO (city) Arapahoe County	26,508	8.44
Akron, OH (city) Summit County	26,458	13.05
Boise City, ID (city) Ada County	26,177	12.68
Plano, TX (city) Collin County	26,087	10.19
Naperville, IL (city) DuPage County	25,848	18.35
Bakersfield, CA (city) Kern County	25,483	7.68
Warwick, RI (city) Kent County	24,927	29.79
Huntington Beach, CA (city) Orange County	24,675	13.06
Chesapeake, VA (ind. city) Chesapeake independent city	23,626	10.77
Middletown, NJ (township) Monmouth County	23,587	35.36
Cedar Rapids, IA (city) Linn County	23,304	18.58
Tacoma, WA (city) Pierce County	23,291	11.71
Scranton, PA (city) Lackawanna County	23,274	30.60
Weymouth Town, MA (city) Norfolk County	23,257	43.60
Colonie, NY (town) Albany County	23,049	28.27
Springfield, MO (city) Christian County	22,991	14.46
Manchester, NH (city) Hillsborough County	22,788	20.76
Glendale, AZ (city) Maricopa County	22,705	9.89
Upper Darby, PA (township) Delaware County	22,488	27.30
Toms River, NJ (township) Ocean County	22,448	24.48
Atlanta, GA (city) Fulton County	22,432	5.43
Syracuse, NY (city) Onondaga County	22,387	15.47
Brick, NJ (township) Ocean County	22,344	29.44
Yonkers, NY (city) Westchester County	22,187	11.38
Amherst, NY (town) Erie County	22,106	18.28
Cape Coral, FL (city) Lee County	21,849	14.59
Eugene, OR (city) Lane County	21,708	14.16
Toms River, NJ (cdp) Ocean County	21,555	24.26
Lubbock, TX (city) Lubbock County	21,166	9.52
Lakewood, CO (city) Jefferson County	21,132	14.88
Joliet, IL (city) Will County	21,088	14.54
Fort Collins, CO (city) Larimer County	20,965	14.97
Riverside, CA (city) Riverside County	20,754	6.91
Port St. Lucie, FL (city) St. Lucie County	20,714	13.36
Vancouver, WA (city) Clark County	20,712	12.93
Knoxville, TN (city) Knox County	20,484	11.49
Nashua, NH (city) Hillsborough County	20,134	23.13
Orlando, FL (city) Orange County	19,764	8.46
Rochester, NY (city) Monroe County	19,595	9.24
Paradise, NV (cdp) Clark County	19,493	8.94
Tempe, AZ (city) Maricopa County	19,332	11.78
Modesto, CA (city) Stanislaus County	19,237	9.53
Santa Clarita, CA (city) Los Angeles County	19,220	11.16
Greece, NY (town) Monroe County	19,015	19.92
Tallahassee, FL (city) Leon County	19,003	10.75
Oakland, CA (city) Alameda County	18,855	4.87
Santa Rosa, CA (city) Sonoma County	18,711	11.50
Norfolk, VA (ind. city) Norfolk independent city	18,649	7.70
Grand Rapids, MI (city) Kent County	18,575	9.75
Haverford, PA (township) Delaware County	18,506	38.12
Salem, OR (city) Marion County	18,415	12.13
Plymouth, MA (town) Plymouth County	18,408	33.10
Aurora, IL (city) Kane County	18,380	9.65
Spring Hill, FL (cdp) Hernando County	18,343	18.97
Gloucester, NJ (township) Camden County	18,330	28.42
Corpus Christi, TX (city) Nueces County	18,284	6.11
Olathe, KS (city) Johnson County	18,267	15.12
Greensboro, NC (city) Guilford County	18,092	6.87
Lowell, MA (city) Middlesex County	18,066	17.19
Sioux Falls, SD (city) Minnehaha County	18,059	12.13
Roseville, CA (city) Placer County	18,023	15.83
Peoria, AZ (city) Yavapai County	17,928	12.06
Metairie, LA (cdp) Jefferson Parish	17,826	13.12
Albany, NY (city) Albany County	17,818	18.19
Levittown, PA (cdp) Bucks County	17,768	34.18
Amarillo, TX (city) Potter County	17,692	9.45
Erie, PA (city) Erie County	17,685	17.40
Anaheim, CA (city) Orange County	17,503	5.26

SECTION THREE

Please refer to the Explanation of Data in the front of the book for more detailed information.

Ancestry

Irish

Top 150 Places Sorted by Percent of Total Population

Based on all places, regardless of total population

Place	Population	%
Day, FL (cdp) Lafayette County	145	100.00
Tabernash, CO (cdp) Grand County	86	100.00
Johnsville, CA (cdp) Plumas County	84	100.00
Parshall, CO (cdp) Grand County	74	100.00
Reid, MD (cdp) Washington County	49	100.00
McConnico, AZ (cdp) Mohave County	33	100.00
Jacksonville, IA (cdp) Shelby County	32	100.00
Megargel, AL (cdp) Monroe County	31	100.00
Allamuchy, NJ (cdp) Warren County	25	100.00
Prattville, CA (cdp) Plumas County	21	100.00
Bridgeville, NJ (cdp) Warren County	14	100.00
Ketron Island, WA (cdp) Pierce County	14	100.00
Whitehawk, CA (cdp) Plumas County	12	100.00
Lake Davis, CA (cdp) Plumas County	11	100.00
Lazy Lake, FL (village) Broward County	11	100.00
Oasis, NV (cdp) Elko County	11	100.00
Cold Spring, PA (township) Lebanon County	9	100.00
Maish Vaya, AZ (cdp) Pima County	9	100.00
Miltonsburg, OH (village) Monroe County	7	100.00
Elysian, MN (city) Waseca County	6	100.00
Verdon, SD (town) Brown County	3	100.00
Shady Grove, OK (town) Pawnee County	2	100.00
Milford, CA (cdp) Lassen County	41	87.23
Zortman, MT (cdp) Phillips County	61	85.92
Jakes Corner, AZ (cdp) Gila County	86	84.31
Amado, AZ (cdp) Santa Cruz County	78	82.98
St. Charles, SD (cdp) Gregory County	18	81.82
Brick Center, CO (cdp) Arapahoe County	60	81.08
Ute Park, NM (cdp) Colfax County	59	80.82
Wetonka, SD (town) McPherson County	4	80.00
Edenborn, PA (cdp) Fayette County	81	79.41
Ballou, OK (cdp) Mayes County	41	78.85
Kemps Mill, MD (cdp) Washington County	63	77.78
Monterey Park Tract, CA (cdp) Stanislaus County	215	77.06
Nikep, MD (cdp) Allegany County	30	76.92
Mabie, CA (cdp) Plumas County	125	75.76
Powellville, MD (cdp) Wicomico County	50	75.76
Bankston, IA (city) Dubuque County	6	75.00
Kilbourne, OH (cdp) Delaware County	136	74.73
Beaconsfield, IA (city) Ringgold County	44	74.58
Cannondale, CT (cdp) Fairfield County	137	74.46
Van Voorhis, PA (cdp) Washington County	312	74.29
Miamiville, OH (cdp) Clermont County	166	73.45
Oak Beach-Captree, NY (cdp) Suffolk County	348	73.26
Ronald, WA (cdp) Kittitas County	77	71.96
Grugan, PA (township) Clinton County	48	71.64
Slana, AK (cdp) Valdez-Cordova Census Area	200	71.17
El Dara, IL (village) Pike County	88	70.97
Mendes, GA (cdp) Tattnall County	26	70.27
Eldora, CO (cdp) Boulder County	27	69.23
Camas, MT (cdp) Sanders County	64	68.82
Le Sueur, MN (city) Nicollet County	17	68.00
Seconsett Island, MA (cdp) Barnstable County	17	68.00
Hartly, DE (town) Kent County	97	67.83
Volcano, CA (cdp) Amador County	120	67.80
Daphnedale Park, CA (cdp) Modoc County	33	67.35
Crayne, KY (cdp) Crittenden County	78	67.24
Pin Oak Acres, OK (cdp) Mayes County	269	67.08
New Haven, IA (cdp) Mitchell County	65	67.01
Regina, NM (cdp) Sandoval County	64	66.67
Pulaski, OH (cdp) Williams County	44	66.67
Grover, CO (town) Weld County	47	66.20
McCool, MS (town) Attala County	139	66.19
Bergoo, WV (cdp) Webster County	28	65.12
Clow, MN (township) Kittson County	13	65.00
Pueblo, NM (cdp) San Miguel County	37	64.91
Springhill, MT (cdp) Gallatin County	57	64.77
Deerfield, MO (village) Vernon County	36	64.29
Jefferson, OK (town) Grant County	21	63.64
Grenville, NM (village) Union County	7	63.64
Maloy, IA (city) Ringgold County	19	63.33
Bartow, WV (cdp) Pocahontas County	82	63.08
Saddle Butte, MT (cdp) Hill County	139	62.90
Wickliffe, OK (cdp) Mayes County	50	62.50
Bigelow, MO (village) Holt County	25	62.50
Wallace, KS (city) Wallace County	25	62.50
Bentley, IA (cdp) Pottawattamie County	48	62.34
Hopewell Junction, NY (cdp) Dutchess County	290	61.97
Eola, OR (cdp) Polk County	16	61.54
Hendley, NE (village) Furnas County	14	60.87
Wightmans Grove, OH (cdp) Sandusky County	20	60.61
Foster, KY (city) Bracken County	15	60.00
Gross, NE (village) Boyd County	3	60.00
Hazel Green, WI (village) Lafayette County	3	60.00
Point Lookout, NY (cdp) Nassau County	763	59.98
Vaughnsville, OH (cdp) Putnam County	82	59.85
Tioga, WV (cdp) Nicholas County	78	59.54
Walker Valley, NY (cdp) Ulster County	319	59.51
Columbia, NJ (cdp) Warren County	166	59.50
Gibraltar, PA (cdp) Berks County	351	59.29
Anderson, IA (cdp) Fremont County	29	59.18
Alpine, CO (cdp) Rio Grande County	10	58.82
Wortham, MO (cdp) St. Francois County	157	58.80
Radersburg, MT (cdp) Broadwater County	31	58.49
Rye, AR (cdp) Cleveland County	71	58.20
Stanley, LA (village) De Soto Parish	99	57.56
San Fidel, NM (cdp) Cibola County	23	57.50
Knowles, OK (town) Beaver County	4	57.14
Birch River, WV (cdp) Nicholas County	93	57.06
Brandonville, WV (town) Preston County	37	56.92
Iron Horse, CA (cdp) Plumas County	155	56.78
Webster, ME (plantation) Penobscot County	38	56.72
Archer, NE (cdp) Merrick County	86	56.58
Cora, WY (cdp) Sublette County	153	56.46
Stoutsville, MO (village) Monroe County	9	56.25
Burchard, NE (village) Pawnee County	41	56.16
Phillipstown, IL (village) White County	43	55.84
Corinth, KY (city) Grant County	140	55.78
Bernard, IA (city) Dubuque County	75	55.56
Doyle, TX (cdp) San Patricio County	36	55.38
Pondsville, MD (cdp) Washington County	85	55.19
The Rock, GA (cdp) Upson County	103	55.08
Stotesbury, MO (town) Vernon County	11	55.00
Great Meadows, NJ (cdp) Warren County	140	54.90
Alamillo, NM (cdp) Socorro County	74	54.81
Downieville-Lawson-Dumont, CO (cdp) Clear Creek County	174	54.72
Big Pool, MD (cdp) Washington County	12	54.55
Sattley, CA (cdp) Sierra County	12	54.55
Cave, MO (town) Lincoln County	6	54.55
Sholes, NE (village) Wayne County	6	54.55
Felt, OK (cdp) Cimarron County	37	54.41
Aquilla, TX (city) Hill County	44	54.32
Hublersburg, PA (cdp) Centre County	27	54.00
Sylvarena, MS (village) Smith County	75	53.96
Coleman, GA (cdp) Randolph County	146	53.48
Alcova, WY (cdp) Natrona County	16	53.33
National, MD (cdp) Allegany County	16	53.33
Bud, WV (cdp) Wyoming County	157	53.22
Chase, AK (cdp) Matanuska-Susitna Borough	42	53.16
Lynnville, IL (village) Morgan County	70	53.03
Corinne, WV (cdp) Wyoming County	178	52.98
Adin, CA (cdp) Modoc County	198	52.94
Eddystone, PA (borough) Delaware County	1,301	52.67
Stockdale, OH (cdp) Pike County	91	52.60
Halltown, MO (village) Lawrence County	82	52.56
Pearl River, NY (cdp) Rockland County	7,647	52.46
Buford, OH (cdp) Highland County	146	52.33
Glencoe, OH (cdp) Belmont County	45	52.33
Staatsburg, NY (cdp) Dutchess County	274	52.29
St. Michael, PA (cdp) Cambria County	146	52.14
North Scituate, MA (cdp) Plymouth County	2,863	52.12
Bellerose, NY (village) Nassau County	648	52.09
Byers, KS (city) Pratt County	40	51.95
Heckscherville, PA (cdp) Schuylkill County	150	51.90
Maunie, IL (village) White County	71	51.82
Fair Oaks, OK (town) Wagoner County	29	51.79
Learned, MS (town) Hinds County	46	51.69
Newry, SC (cdp) Oconee County	46	51.69
Strathmere, NJ (cdp) Cape May County	124	51.67
Ferndale, FL (cdp) Lake County	79	51.63

Please refer to the Explanation of Data in the front of the book for more detailed information.

Ancestry

Irish

Top 150 Places Sorted by Percent of Total Population

Based on places with total population of 7,500 or more

Place	Population	%
Pearl River, NY (cdp) Rockland County	7,647	52.46
Hull, MA (cdp/town) Plymouth County	4,949	47.50
Folsom, PA (cdp) Delaware County	3,937	46.67
Scituate, MA (town) Plymouth County	8,427	46.62
Abington, MA (cdp/town) Plymouth County	7,156	45.57
Walpole, MA (town) Norfolk County	10,722	45.29
Marshfield, MA (town) Plymouth County	11,111	44.50
Pembroke, MA (town) Plymouth County	7,836	44.37
Braintree Town, MA (city) Norfolk County	15,564	44.31
Weymouth Town, MA (city) Norfolk County	23,257	43.60
Milton, MA (cdp/town) Norfolk County	11,589	43.46
Springfield, PA (township) Delaware County	10,435	43.38
Hingham, MA (town) Plymouth County	9,400	43.26
Ridley, PA (township) Delaware County	13,171	42.85
Hanover, MA (town) Plymouth County	5,810	42.28
Whitman, MA (town) Plymouth County	6,041	42.04
Haddon Heights, NJ (borough) Camden County	3,130	41.73
Norwell, MA (town) Plymouth County	4,309	41.55
Duxbury, MA (town) Plymouth County	6,141	41.22
Hanson, MA (town) Plymouth County	4,150	41.11
Audubon, NJ (borough) Camden County	3,561	40.01
Halifax, MA (town) Plymouth County	3,000	39.96
Holbrook, MA (cdp/town) Norfolk County	4,250	39.74
Mansfield Center, MA (cdp) Bristol County	3,021	39.74
Drexel Hill, PA (cdp) Delaware County	11,374	39.69
Foxborough, MA (town) Norfolk County	6,535	39.32
Raynham, MA (town) Bristol County	5,096	38.95
Gloucester City, NJ (city) Camden County	4,447	38.74
Dedham, MA (cdp/town) Norfolk County	9,299	38.23
Bridgewater, MA (town) Plymouth County	10,084	38.20
Haverford, PA (township) Delaware County	18,506	38.12
Sound Beach, NY (cdp) Suffolk County	2,887	38.09
Wilmington, MA (cdp/town) Middlesex County	8,301	37.92
Woodlyn, PA (cdp) Delaware County	3,434	37.87
Winthrop Town, MA (city) Suffolk County	6,534	37.74
Villas, NJ (cdp) Cape May County	3,552	37.62
Canton, MA (town) Norfolk County	7,967	37.50
Rockland, MA (town) Plymouth County	6,511	37.18
Floral Park, NY (village) Nassau County	5,928	37.02
Lower, NJ (township) Cape May County	8,399	36.94
Philipstown, NY (town) Putnam County	3,569	36.91
Garden City, NY (village) Nassau County	8,078	36.52
Norwood, MA (cdp/town) Norfolk County	10,354	36.49
Point Pleasant, NJ (borough) Ocean County	6,824	36.48
Kingston, MA (town) Plymouth County	4,543	36.43
Mansfield, MA (town) Bristol County	8,373	36.32
Manorville, NY (cdp) Suffolk County	4,894	36.21
Westwood, MA (town) Norfolk County	5,188	36.02
Sayville, NY (cdp) Suffolk County	5,796	35.98
Bristol, PA (borough) Bucks County	3,537	35.98
Carbondale, PA (city) Lackawanna County	3,237	35.96
Easton, MA (town) Bristol County	8,252	35.85
Tewksbury, MA (town) Middlesex County	10,258	35.84
Middletown, NJ (township) Monmouth County	23,587	35.36
Chatham, NJ (borough) Morris County	3,144	35.36
Reading, MA (cdp/town) Middlesex County	8,574	35.34
Medfield, MA (town) Norfolk County	4,228	35.30
Westtown, PA (township) Chester County	3,812	35.26
West Islip, NY (cdp) Suffolk County	10,102	35.21
North Reading, MA (town) Middlesex County	5,114	35.18
Haddon, NJ (township) Camden County	5,181	35.15
Village Green-Green Ridge, PA (cdp) Delaware County	2,705	35.14
Babylon, NY (village) Suffolk County	4,264	34.77
Narragansett, RI (town) Washington County	5,550	34.61
East Islip, NY (cdp) Suffolk County	4,821	34.59
East Northport, NY (cdp) Suffolk County	7,238	34.54
Rockville Centre, NY (village) Nassau County	8,256	34.48
Woburn, MA (city) Middlesex County	12,938	34.47
Hampton, NH (cdp) Rockingham County	3,033	34.20
Levittown, PA (cdp) Bucks County	17,768	34.18
Melrose, MA (city) Middlesex County	9,118	34.14
Aston, PA (township) Delaware County	5,606	34.05
Georgetown, MA (town) Essex County	2,722	34.05
Wakefield-Peacedale, RI (cdp) Washington County	3,059	33.91
Hopkinton, MA (town) Middlesex County	4,899	33.85
Hampton, NH (town) Rockingham County	5,240	33.84
Ocean City, NJ (city) Cape May County	4,152	33.79
Burlington, MA (cdp/town) Middlesex County	8,065	33.71
Waterford, NJ (township) Camden County	3,587	33.62
Kings Park, NY (cdp) Suffolk County	5,687	33.49
Northfield, NJ (city) Atlantic County	2,866	33.49
Hazlet, NJ (township) Monmouth County	6,871	33.45
Camillus, NY (town) Onondaga County	7,994	33.43
Upper Providence, PA (township) Delaware County	3,402	33.39
Cornwall, NY (town) Orange County	4,238	33.36
Bayport, NY (cdp) Suffolk County	2,972	33.33
East Bridgewater, MA (town) Plymouth County	4,521	33.15
Plymouth, MA (town) Plymouth County	18,408	33.10
Millis, MA (town) Norfolk County	2,585	33.04
Southborough, MA (town) Worcester County	3,176	33.02
Harrison, NJ (township) Gloucester County	3,915	32.99
Sandwich, MA (town) Barnstable County	6,794	32.94
Brunswick, NY (town) Rensselaer County	3,925	32.89
Lynnfield, MA (cdp/town) Essex County	3,776	32.87
Pike Creek, DE (cdp) New Castle County	2,638	32.87
Quincy, MA (city) Norfolk County	29,819	32.85
Wakefield, MA (cdp/town) Middlesex County	8,078	32.81
Hornell, NY (city) Steuben County	2,836	32.80
Oakdale, NY (cdp) Suffolk County	2,518	32.80
Auburn, MA (town) Worcester County	5,301	32.75
Croydon, PA (cdp) Bucks County	3,306	32.73
Pepperell, MA (town) Middlesex County	3,690	32.66
Massapequa Park, NY (village) Nassau County	5,535	32.63
Wall, NJ (township) Monmouth County	8,480	32.60
Cinnaminson, NJ (township) Burlington County	5,052	32.52
Tyngsborough, MA (town) Middlesex County	3,612	32.47
Beachwood, NJ (borough) Ocean County	3,561	32.33
North Andover, MA (town) Essex County	9,039	32.32
Denville, NJ (township) Morris County	5,335	32.26
Middletown, PA (township) Delaware County	5,100	32.24
Dunmore, PA (borough) Lackawanna County	4,541	32.22
Butte-Silver Bow, MT (cons. govt) Silver Bow County	10,583	32.21
Bethel, PA (township) Delaware County	2,693	32.21
Lake Carmel, NY (cdp) Putnam County	2,550	32.19
Wrentham, MA (town) Norfolk County	3,476	32.15
North Greenbush, NY (town) Rensselaer County	3,818	32.12
Norton, MA (town) Bristol County	6,063	32.11
East Goshen, PA (township) Chester County	5,772	32.11
Fallston, MD (cdp) Harford County	2,586	32.08
Newtown, PA (township) Delaware County	3,875	32.01
Billerica, MA (town) Middlesex County	12,640	31.94
Upper Southampton, PA (township) Bucks County	4,893	31.91
Newburyport, MA (city) Essex County	5,514	31.89
Ocean Acres, NJ (cdp) Ocean County	5,025	31.86
Winchester, MA (cdp/town) Middlesex County	6,677	31.77
Londonderry, NH (cdp) Rockingham County	3,463	31.73
Clinton, MA (town) Worcester County	4,313	31.69
Franklin Town, MA (city) Norfolk County	9,826	31.67
Londonderry, NH (town) Rockingham County	7,647	31.60
Charlestown, RI (town) Washington County	2,483	31.53
Chelmsford, MA (town) Middlesex County	10,488	31.43
Orangetown, NY (town) Rockland County	15,284	31.41
West Deptford, NJ (township) Gloucester County	6,726	31.36
Runnemede, NJ (borough) Camden County	2,661	31.35
Darby, PA (township) Delaware County	2,916	31.34
Schuylkill, PA (township) Chester County	2,602	31.33
Pitman, NJ (borough) Gloucester County	2,865	31.30
Groton, MA (town) Middlesex County	3,226	31.24
Warwick, NY (town) Orange County	10,015	31.23
Western Springs, IL (village) Cook County	3,953	31.23
Schodack, NY (town) Rensselaer County	3,996	31.21
Springfield, PA (township) Montgomery County	6,071	31.20
Des Peres, MO (city) St. Louis County	2,615	31.14
Williamstown, NJ (cdp) Gloucester County	4,416	31.03
Lake Ronkonkoma, NY (cdp) Suffolk County	6,669	31.01
Perkiomen, PA (township) Montgomery County	2,714	30.95
Vernon, NJ (township) Sussex County	7,540	30.93
Maynard, MA (cdp/town) Middlesex County	3,103	30.92
Upper Moreland, PA (township) Montgomery County	7,493	30.91
Conshohocken, PA (borough) Montgomery County	2,400	30.81

SECTION THREE

Please refer to the Explanation of Data in the front of the book for more detailed information.

Ancestry

Israeli

U.S. and 50 States Sorted by Population and Percent of Total Population

Place	Population	%
United States	**136,351**	**0.04**
New York	36,808	0.19
California	28,074	0.08
Florida	16,091	0.09
New Jersey	10,026	0.11
Texas	6,005	0.02
Massachusetts	4,349	0.07
Illinois	4,197	0.03
Pennsylvania	3,461	0.03
Maryland	3,268	0.06
Michigan	1,908	0.02
Georgia	1,795	0.02
Ohio	1,650	0.01
Arizona	1,625	0.03
Washington	1,596	0.02
Virginia	1,494	0.02
Nevada	1,367	0.05
Connecticut	1,210	0.03
Colorado	1,208	0.02
North Carolina	1,071	0.01
Minnesota	894	0.02
Oregon	755	0.02
Missouri	726	0.01
South Carolina	596	0.01
Tennessee	585	0.01
Louisiana	495	0.01
Wisconsin	495	0.01
Indiana	483	0.01
New Mexico	439	0.02
New Hampshire	385	0.03
Alabama	353	0.01
Iowa	331	0.01
District of Columbia	279	0.05
Oklahoma	254	0.01
Utah	245	0.01
Maine	237	0.02
Arkansas	196	0.01
Rhode Island	190	0.02
Kansas	155	0.01
Hawaii	148	0.01
Nebraska	119	0.01
Delaware	117	0.01
Kentucky	113	<0.01
West Virginia	110	0.01
Alaska	109	0.02
Idaho	95	0.01
Vermont	70	0.01
Wyoming	70	0.01
Mississippi	66	<0.01
South Dakota	23	<0.01
Montana	15	<0.01
North Dakota	0	0.00

Place	Population	%
New York	36,808	0.19
New Jersey	10,026	0.11
Florida	16,091	0.09
California	28,074	0.08
Massachusetts	4,349	0.07
Maryland	3,268	0.06
Nevada	1,367	0.05
District of Columbia	279	0.05
United States	**136,351**	**0.04**
Illinois	4,197	0.03
Pennsylvania	3,461	0.03
Arizona	1,625	0.03
Connecticut	1,210	0.03
New Hampshire	385	0.03
Texas	6,005	0.02
Michigan	1,908	0.02
Georgia	1,795	0.02
Washington	1,596	0.02
Virginia	1,494	0.02
Colorado	1,208	0.02
Minnesota	894	0.02
Oregon	755	0.02
New Mexico	439	0.02
Maine	237	0.02
Rhode Island	190	0.02
Alaska	109	0.02
Ohio	1,650	0.01
North Carolina	1,071	0.01
Missouri	726	0.01
South Carolina	596	0.01
Tennessee	585	0.01
Louisiana	495	0.01
Wisconsin	495	0.01
Indiana	483	0.01
Alabama	353	0.01
Iowa	331	0.01
Oklahoma	254	0.01
Utah	245	0.01
Arkansas	196	0.01
Kansas	155	0.01
Hawaii	148	0.01
Nebraska	119	0.01
Delaware	117	0.01
West Virginia	110	0.01
Idaho	95	0.01
Vermont	70	0.01
Wyoming	70	0.01
Kentucky	113	<0.01
Mississippi	66	<0.01
South Dakota	23	<0.01
Montana	15	<0.01
North Dakota	0	0.00

Please refer to the Explanation of Data in the front of the book for more detailed information.

Ancestry

Israeli

Top 150 Places Sorted by Population

Based on all places, regardless of total population

Place	Population	%
New York, NY (city) Kings County	21,872	0.27
Los Angeles, CA (city) Los Angeles County	12,294	0.33
Brooklyn, NY (borough) Kings County	9,707	0.39
Manhattan, NY (borough) New York County	6,624	0.42
Queens, NY (borough) Queens County	4,164	0.19
Ramapo, NY (town) Rockland County	3,342	2.72
Hempstead, NY (town) Nassau County	2,558	0.34
North Hempstead, NY (town) Nassau County	1,853	0.83
Hollywood, FL (city) Broward County	1,625	1.15
Chicago, IL (city) Cook County	1,411	0.05
Aventura, FL (city) Miami-Dade County	1,402	4.15
Houston, TX (city) Harris County	1,071	0.05
San Diego, CA (city) San Diego County	990	0.08
Kiryas Joel, NY (village) Orange County	949	4.97
Monroe, NY (town) Orange County	949	2.45
Dallas, TX (city) Dallas County	947	0.08
Plantation, FL (city) Broward County	939	1.10
Beverly Hills, CA (city) Los Angeles County	920	2.71
Woodmere, NY (cdp) Nassau County	879	5.04
Philadelphia, PA (city) Philadelphia County	861	0.06
Sunnyvale, CA (city) Santa Clara County	796	0.58
Viola, NY (cdp) Rockland County	792	11.23
Lakewood, NJ (township) Ocean County	777	0.89
Staten Island, NY (borough) Richmond County	759	0.16
Fair Lawn, NJ (borough) Bergen County	746	2.32
Oyster Bay, NY (town) Nassau County	663	0.23
Newton, MA (city) Middlesex County	651	0.78
San Jose, CA (city) Santa Clara County	641	0.07
Bronx, NY (borough) Bronx County	618	0.05
Monsey, NY (cdp) Rockland County	608	4.04
Lakewood, NJ (cdp) Ocean County	589	1.18
Miami Beach, FL (city) Miami-Dade County	565	0.65
Boston, MA (city) Suffolk County	554	0.09
Brookhaven, NY (town) Suffolk County	545	0.11
Kaser, NY (village) Rockland County	540	12.17
Brookline, MA (cdp/town) Norfolk County	531	0.92
Irvine, CA (city) Orange County	525	0.26
Austin, TX (city) Travis County	519	0.07
Tenafly, NJ (borough) Bergen County	498	3.49
Skokie, IL (village) Cook County	497	0.78
Coral Springs, FL (city) Broward County	481	0.40
Spring Valley, NY (village) Rockland County	473	1.56
Seattle, WA (city) King County	466	0.08
Denver, CO (city) Denver County	462	0.08
Ojus, FL (cdp) Miami-Dade County	447	2.63
Calabasas, CA (city) Los Angeles County	443	1.95
Pembroke Pines, FL (city) Broward County	443	0.29
San Francisco, CA (city) San Francisco County	437	0.06
Sunny Isles Beach, FL (city) Miami-Dade County	432	2.18
Cooper City, FL (city) Broward County	425	1.48
Palo Alto, CA (city) Santa Clara County	421	0.67
Plano, TX (city) Collin County	420	0.16
Las Vegas, NV (city) Clark County	405	0.07
East Brunswick, NJ (township) Middlesex County	397	0.84
Thousand Oaks, CA (city) Ventura County	384	0.31
League City, TX (city) Galveston County	383	0.50
Teaneck, NJ (township) Bergen County	378	0.96
Lower Merion, PA (township) Montgomery County	377	0.65
Potomac, MD (cdp) Montgomery County	367	0.82
Cupertino, CA (city) Santa Clara County	363	0.64
Baltimore, MD (city) Baltimore city County	355	0.06
Cherry Hill, NJ (township) Camden County	344	0.48
Cambridge, MA (city) Middlesex County	341	0.33
Nashville-Davidson, TN (metro govt) Davidson County	329	0.06
Great Neck, NY (village) Nassau County	326	3.31
Livingston, NJ (township) Essex County	311	1.08
Pikesville, MD (cdp) Baltimore County	300	0.98
Hoboken, NJ (city) Hudson County	298	0.63
San Antonio, TX (city) Medina County	292	0.02
Phoenix, AZ (city) Maricopa County	288	0.02
Huntington, NY (town) Suffolk County	285	0.14
Washington, DC (city) District of Columbia	279	0.05
Santa Monica, CA (city) Los Angeles County	277	0.31
Portland, OR (city) Multnomah County	277	0.05
Henderson, NV (city) Clark County	273	0.11
South Valley Stream, NY (cdp) Nassau County	268	5.09
West Bloomfield, MI (charter township) Oakland County	268	0.41
Oakhurst, CA (cdp) Madera County	260	7.97
Daytona Beach, FL (city) Volusia County	257	0.41
Weston, FL (city) Broward County	250	0.40
Albuquerque, NM (city) Bernalillo County	249	0.05
Clarkstown, NY (town) Rockland County	247	0.30
Fort Lee, NJ (borough) Bergen County	245	0.70
Coconut Creek, FL (city) Broward County	244	0.47
Homer Glen, IL (village) Will County	241	0.97
Sunrise, FL (city) Broward County	238	0.28
New Haven, CT (city/town) New Haven County	236	0.18
Oakland, CA (city) Alameda County	235	0.06
Fort Pierce South, FL (cdp) St. Lucie County	233	4.09
Wesley Hills, NY (village) Rockland County	231	4.24
North Bethesda, MD (cdp) Montgomery County	231	0.57
Fresno, CA (city) Fresno County	231	0.05
Davie, FL (town) Broward County	230	0.25
Boca Raton, FL (city) Palm Beach County	229	0.27
New City, NY (cdp) Rockland County	226	0.68
Greenburgh, NY (town) Westchester County	225	0.26
Marlboro, NJ (township) Monmouth County	221	0.56
Springdale, NJ (cdp) Camden County	217	1.48
Jersey City, NJ (city) Hudson County	216	0.09
Agoura Hills, CA (city) Los Angeles County	215	1.06
Berkeley, CA (city) Alameda County	214	0.20
Scottsdale, AZ (city) Maricopa County	213	0.10
Pittsburgh, PA (city) Allegheny County	210	0.07
Long Beach, CA (city) Los Angeles County	208	0.05
Kendall, FL (cdp) Miami-Dade County	205	0.27
Plainview, NY (cdp) Nassau County	204	0.79
Brighton, NY (cdp/town) Monroe County	204	0.56
Johns Creek, GA (city) Fulton County	201	0.28
Pleasant Hill, CA (city) Contra Costa County	200	0.61
Palm Beach Gardens, FL (city) Palm Beach County	199	0.43
West Hollywood, CA (city) Los Angeles County	198	0.57
Huntington Beach, CA (city) Orange County	197	0.10
Fort Lauderdale, FL (city) Broward County	195	0.12
Salisbury, NY (cdp) Nassau County	193	1.64
Flint, MI (charter township) Genesee County	192	0.59
Rockville, MD (city) Montgomery County	189	0.32
Woodbridge, NJ (township) Middlesex County	185	0.19
Spring Valley, NV (cdp) Clark County	182	0.11
White Plains, NY (city) Westchester County	181	0.32
New Square, NY (village) Rockland County	180	2.79
Smithtown, NY (town) Suffolk County	180	0.15
Buffalo, NY (city) Erie County	180	0.07
Cedarhurst, NY (village) Nassau County	178	2.75
Hallandale Beach, FL (city) Broward County	177	0.48
Tucson, AZ (city) Pima County	175	0.03
Manalapan, NJ (township) Monmouth County	174	0.46
Mount Vernon, NY (city) Westchester County	174	0.26
Lake Success, NY (village) Nassau County	172	5.94
Babylon, NY (town) Suffolk County	172	0.08
Chandler, AZ (city) Maricopa County	170	0.07
Yorktown, NY (town) Westchester County	169	0.47
Bloomington, IN (city) Monroe County	168	0.21
New Hempstead, NY (village) Rockland County	165	3.29
Dania Beach, FL (city) Broward County	165	0.56
Dunwoody, GA (city) DeKalb County	165	0.37
Miami, FL (city) Miami-Dade County	165	0.04
Manorhaven, NY (village) Nassau County	164	2.55
Boulder, CO (city) Boulder County	163	0.17
Fort Worth, TX (city) Tarrant County	162	0.02
Los Altos, CA (city) Santa Clara County	158	0.56
Santa Clarita, CA (city) Los Angeles County	157	0.09
College Park, MD (city) Prince George's County	155	0.52
North Miami Beach, FL (city) Miami-Dade County	154	0.37
Saddle Rock, NY (village) Nassau County	153	14.60
Commack, NY (cdp) Suffolk County	153	0.42
Atlanta, GA (city) Fulton County	153	0.04
Union, NJ (township) Union County	152	0.27
Waltham, MA (city) Middlesex County	152	0.25
Summerlin South, NV (cdp) Clark County	151	0.69
Bellevue, WA (city) King County	151	0.13

Please refer to the Explanation of Data in the front of the book for more detailed information.

SECTION THREE

Ancestry

Israeli

Top 150 Places Sorted by Percent of Total Population

Based on all places, regardless of total population

Place	Population	%
Saddle Rock, NY (village) Nassau County	153	14.60
Kaser, NY (village) Rockland County	540	12.17
Viola, NY (cdp) Rockland County	792	11.23
Union, NH (cdp) Carroll County	40	10.50
Oakhurst, CA (cdp) Madera County	260	7.97
Greenvale, NY (cdp) Nassau County	32	7.13
Jamesport, MO (city) Daviess County	42	6.85
Newtown, PA (borough) Bucks County	135	5.99
Cuba, MN (township) Becker County	15	5.98
Lake Success, NY (village) Nassau County	172	5.94
Scotch Meadows, NC (cdp) Scotland County	46	5.61
Postville, IA (city) Allamakee County	103	5.16
South Valley Stream, NY (cdp) Nassau County	268	5.09
Woodmere, NY (cdp) Nassau County	879	5.04
Kiryas Joel, NY (village) Orange County	949	4.97
Woodloch, TX (town) Montgomery County	7	4.58
Petros, TN (cdp) Morgan County	33	4.49
Schnecksville, PA (cdp) Lehigh County	118	4.25
Wesley Hills, NY (village) Rockland County	231	4.24
Eagleville, PA (cdp) Centre County	10	4.20
Aventura, FL (city) Miami-Dade County	1,402	4.15
Fort Pierce South, FL (cdp) St. Lucie County	233	4.09
Monsey, NY (cdp) Rockland County	608	4.04
Halifax, VT (town) Windham County	32	3.82
Great Neck Estates, NY (village) Nassau County	103	3.77
Trexlertown, PA (cdp) Lehigh County	68	3.66
Tenafly, NJ (borough) Bergen County	498	3.49
Haverford College, PA (cdp) Delaware County	39	3.38
Wilton, NH (town) Hillsborough County	123	3.32
Great Neck, NY (village) Nassau County	326	3.31
New Hempstead, NY (village) Rockland County	165	3.29
Searingtown, NY (cdp) Nassau County	146	3.21
Thomaston, NY (village) Nassau County	83	3.17
Leipsic, DE (town) Kent County	4	3.17
Meadowview Estates, KY (city) Jefferson County	17	2.94
Bradford, NY (town) Steuben County	30	2.85
North Hills, NY (village) Nassau County	139	2.81
Indian Creek, IL (village) Lake County	15	2.81
New Square, NY (village) Rockland County	180	2.79
Bar Harbor, ME (town) Hancock County	144	2.77
Cedarhurst, NY (village) Nassau County	178	2.75
Abbottstown, PA (borough) Adams County	26	2.73
Ramapo, NY (town) Rockland County	3,342	2.72
Beverly Hills, CA (city) Los Angeles County	920	2.71
Ojus, FL (cdp) Miami-Dade County	447	2.63
Atlantic Beach, NY (village) Nassau County	48	2.58
Manorhaven, NY (village) Nassau County	164	2.55
Russell Gardens, NY (village) Nassau County	24	2.49
Hewlett Harbor, NY (village) Nassau County	29	2.47
Monroe, NY (town) Orange County	949	2.45
Golden Beach, FL (town) Miami-Dade County	20	2.45
Glen Echo, MD (town) Montgomery County	6	2.41
Newington, NH (town) Rockingham County	17	2.36
Fair Lawn, NJ (borough) Bergen County	746	2.32
Cresaptown, MD (cdp) Allegany County	79	2.28
Deal, NJ (borough) Monmouth County	23	2.22
Sunny Isles Beach, FL (city) Miami-Dade County	432	2.18
Kensington, NY (village) Nassau County	26	2.16
Upper Brookville, NY (village) Nassau County	32	2.15
Head of the Harbor, NY (village) Suffolk County	30	2.14
Union Bridge, MD (town) Carroll County	17	2.03
Demarest, NJ (borough) Bergen County	98	2.02
Cayuga Heights, NY (village) Tompkins County	74	1.99
Surfside, FL (town) Miami-Dade County	110	1.98
Calabasas, CA (city) Los Angeles County	443	1.95
Frontenac, MO (city) St. Louis County	65	1.88
Juliustown, NJ (cdp) Burlington County	6	1.88
Sadler, TX (city) Grayson County	5	1.88
Hebron, TX (town) Denton County	12	1.87
Water Mill, NY (cdp) Suffolk County	28	1.83
Hana, HI (cdp) Maui County	29	1.80
Verplanck, NY (cdp) Westchester County	10	1.72
East Richmond Heights, CA (cdp) Contra Costa County	55	1.71
Greenville, NY (cdp) Westchester County	114	1.66
Lawrence, NY (village) Nassau County	107	1.66
Cambrian Park, CA (cdp) Santa Clara County	54	1.66
Southside Place, TX (city) Harris County	28	1.66
Salisbury, NY (cdp) Nassau County	193	1.64
Pomona, NY (village) Rockland County	58	1.64
Collingdale, PA (borough) Delaware County	143	1.63
Spring Valley, NY (village) Rockland County	473	1.56
Searsport, ME (cdp) Waldo County	16	1.55
Hopedale, MA (cdp) Worcester County	61	1.52
Woodbury, NY (cdp) Nassau County	137	1.51
Lanesboro, MN (city) Fillmore County	11	1.49
Cooper City, FL (city) Broward County	425	1.48
Springdale, NJ (cdp) Camden County	217	1.48
Markleeville, CA (cdp) Alpine County	4	1.46
Wattsville, VA (cdp) Accomack County	18	1.40
Margate City, NJ (city) Atlantic County	94	1.39
Boonton, NJ (township) Morris County	58	1.36
Woodsburgh, NY (village) Nassau County	10	1.34
Flower Hill, NY (village) Nassau County	61	1.32
Kyle, SD (cdp) Shannon County	13	1.28
Cordaville, MA (cdp) Worcester County	35	1.27
Suffern, NY (village) Rockland County	135	1.26
Myers Corner, NY (cdp) Dutchess County	80	1.26
Closter, NJ (borough) Bergen County	103	1.24
Lansing, NY (village) Tompkins County	43	1.23
Port Washington North, NY (village) Nassau County	37	1.22
Bal Harbour, FL (village) Miami-Dade County	32	1.21
Terryville, NY (cdp) Suffolk County	143	1.20
Great Neck Plaza, NY (village) Nassau County	79	1.19
Orange, MI (township) Kalkaska County	14	1.19
Lakewood, NJ (cdp) Ocean County	589	1.18
Narberth, PA (borough) Montgomery County	50	1.17
Bay Pines, FL (cdp) Pinellas County	34	1.16
Hollywood, FL (city) Broward County	1,625	1.15
Plantation, FL (city) Broward County	939	1.10
Ashland, NJ (cdp) Camden County	94	1.09
Kings Point, NY (village) Nassau County	54	1.09
Livingston, NJ (township) Essex County	311	1.08
Carmichaels, PA (borough) Greene County	5	1.08
Haworth, NJ (borough) Bergen County	36	1.07
Annandale, NJ (cdp) Hunterdon County	13	1.07
Agoura Hills, CA (city) Los Angeles County	215	1.06
Great Barrington, MA (cdp) Berkshire County	25	1.05
Brookville, NY (village) Nassau County	36	1.04
Marion Center, MA (cdp) Plymouth County	12	1.04
Hopedale, MA (town) Worcester County	61	1.03
Gulf Gate Estates, FL (cdp) Sarasota County	111	1.02
Jefferson Valley-Yorktown, NY (cdp) Westchester County	144	1.00
Tower Hill, IL (village) Shelby County	8	1.00
Chestnut Ridge, NY (village) Rockland County	78	0.99
Pikesville, MD (cdp) Baltimore County	300	0.98
Homer Glen, IL (village) Will County	241	0.97
Teaneck, NJ (township) Bergen County	378	0.96
Lyndhurst, OH (city) Cuyahoga County	136	0.96
Lompico, CA (cdp) Santa Cruz County	10	0.96
Hewlett Bay Park, NY (village) Nassau County	5	0.96
East Garden City, NY (cdp) Nassau County	52	0.94
Columbine Valley, CO (town) Arapahoe County	12	0.94
Armour, SD (city) Douglas County	6	0.94
Falcon Heights, MN (city) Ramsey County	49	0.93
East Norwich, NY (cdp) Nassau County	24	0.93
Brookline, MA (cdp/town) Norfolk County	531	0.92
Thorndale, PA (cdp) Chester County	31	0.92
Lakewood, NJ (township) Ocean County	777	0.89
Highland Park, NJ (borough) Middlesex County	124	0.89
Dayton, NJ (cdp) Middlesex County	66	0.89
Sandia Heights, NM (cdp) Bernalillo County	32	0.88
Red Hill, PA (borough) Montgomery County	22	0.88
Washougal, WA (city) Clark County	115	0.87
Lewisboro, NY (town) Westchester County	107	0.87
River Vale, NJ (township) Bergen County	83	0.87
Los Altos Hills, CA (town) Santa Clara County	68	0.87
Woodstock, NY (cdp) Ulster County	21	0.87
Blythedale, MO (village) Harrison County	2	0.87
Wixon Valley, TX (city) Brazos County	2	0.87
Roslyn Heights, NY (cdp) Nassau County	56	0.86

Please refer to the Explanation of Data in the front of the book for more detailed information.

Ancestry

Israeli

Top 150 Places Sorted by Percent of Total Population

Based on places with total population of 7,500 or more

Place	Population	%
Woodmere, NY (cdp) Nassau County	879	5.04
Kiryas Joel, NY (village) Orange County	949	4.97
Aventura, FL (city) Miami-Dade County	1,402	4.15
Monsey, NY (cdp) Rockland County	608	4.04
Tenafly, NJ (borough) Bergen County	498	3.49
Great Neck, NY (village) Nassau County	326	3.31
Ramapo, NY (town) Rockland County	3,342	2.72
Beverly Hills, CA (city) Los Angeles County	920	2.71
Ojus, FL (cdp) Miami-Dade County	447	2.63
Monroe, NY (town) Orange County	949	2.45
Fair Lawn, NJ (borough) Bergen County	746	2.32
Sunny Isles Beach, FL (city) Miami-Dade County	432	2.18
Calabasas, CA (city) Los Angeles County	443	1.95
Salisbury, NY (cdp) Nassau County	193	1.64
Collingdale, PA (borough) Delaware County	143	1.63
Spring Valley, NY (village) Rockland County	473	1.56
Woodbury, NY (cdp) Nassau County	137	1.51
Cooper City, FL (city) Broward County	425	1.48
Springdale, NJ (cdp) Camden County	217	1.48
Suffern, NY (village) Rockland County	135	1.26
Closter, NJ (borough) Bergen County	103	1.24
Terryville, NY (cdp) Suffolk County	143	1.20
Lakewood, NJ (cdp) Ocean County	589	1.18
Hollywood, FL (city) Broward County	1,625	1.15
Plantation, FL (city) Broward County	939	1.10
Ashland, NJ (cdp) Camden County	94	1.09
Livingston, NJ (township) Essex County	311	1.08
Agoura Hills, CA (city) Los Angeles County	215	1.06
Gulf Gate Estates, FL (cdp) Sarasota County	111	1.02
Jefferson Valley-Yorktown, NY (cdp) Westchester County	144	1.00
Chestnut Ridge, NY (village) Rockland County	78	0.99
Pikesville, MD (cdp) Baltimore County	300	0.98
Homer Glen, IL (village) Will County	241	0.97
Teaneck, NJ (township) Bergen County	378	0.96
Lyndhurst, OH (city) Cuyahoga County	136	0.96
Brookline, MA (cdp/town) Norfolk County	531	0.92
Lakewood, NJ (township) Ocean County	777	0.89
Highland Park, NJ (borough) Middlesex County	124	0.89
Washougal, WA (city) Clark County	115	0.87
Lewisboro, NY (town) Westchester County	107	0.87
River Vale, NJ (township) Bergen County	83	0.87
Los Altos Hills, CA (town) Santa Clara County	68	0.87
East Brunswick, NJ (township) Middlesex County	397	0.84
North Hempstead, NY (town) Nassau County	1,853	0.83
Potomac, MD (cdp) Montgomery County	367	0.82
Plainview, NY (cdp) Nassau County	204	0.79
Newton, MA (city) Middlesex County	651	0.78
Skokie, IL (village) Cook County	497	0.78
North Whitehall, PA (township) Lehigh County	118	0.76
Metuchen, NJ (borough) Middlesex County	101	0.75
West Freehold, NJ (cdp) Monmouth County	102	0.73
Forest City, FL (cdp) Seminole County	99	0.71
Fort Lee, NJ (borough) Bergen County	245	0.70
Avenel, NJ (cdp) Middlesex County	119	0.70
Summerlin South, NV (cdp) Clark County	151	0.69
New City, NY (cdp) Rockland County	226	0.68
Palo Alto, CA (city) Santa Clara County	421	0.67
Lexington, SC (town) Lexington County	110	0.67
Miami Beach, FL (city) Miami-Dade County	565	0.65
Lower Merion, PA (township) Montgomery County	377	0.65
Cupertino, CA (city) Santa Clara County	363	0.64
Marina del Rey, CA (cdp) Los Angeles County	59	0.64
Cresskill, NJ (borough) Bergen County	54	0.64
Hoboken, NJ (city) Hudson County	298	0.63
Kemp Mill, MD (cdp) Montgomery County	75	0.62
Pleasant Hill, CA (city) Contra Costa County	200	0.61
Glencoe, IL (village) Cook County	53	0.61
Kings Park West, VA (cdp) Fairfax County	87	0.60
Lincolnwood, IL (village) Cook County	75	0.60
Flint, MI (charter township) Genesee County	192	0.59
Isla Vista, CA (cdp) Santa Barbara County	140	0.59
Southborough, MA (town) Worcester County	57	0.59
Sunnyvale, CA (city) Santa Clara County	796	0.58
Ojai, CA (city) Ventura County	44	0.58
North Bethesda, MD (cdp) Montgomery County	231	0.57
West Hollywood, CA (city) Los Angeles County	198	0.57
Hudson, MA (cdp) Middlesex County	83	0.57
Marlboro, NJ (township) Monmouth County	221	0.56
Brighton, NY (cdp/town) Monroe County	204	0.56
Dania Beach, FL (city) Broward County	165	0.56
Los Altos, CA (city) Santa Clara County	158	0.56
Port Washington, NY (cdp) Nassau County	90	0.56
Merrick, NY (cdp) Nassau County	118	0.55
Oak Park, CA (cdp) Ventura County	77	0.55
Englewood, NJ (city) Bergen County	146	0.54
Solon, OH (city) Cuyahoga County	124	0.54
Albany, CA (city) Alameda County	97	0.54
Jollyville, TX (cdp) Williamson County	85	0.53
Cheney, WA (city) Spokane County	54	0.53
College Park, MD (city) Prince George's County	155	0.52
Briarcliff Manor, NY (village) Westchester County	42	0.52
Ocean, NJ (township) Monmouth County	140	0.51
Kalamazoo, MI (charter township) Kalamazoo County	111	0.51
League City, TX (city) Galveston County	383	0.50
Pittsford, NY (town) Monroe County	146	0.50
Terrytown, LA (cdp) Jefferson Parish	114	0.50
Stony Brook, NY (cdp) Suffolk County	68	0.50
Cherry Creek, CO (cdp) Arapahoe County	53	0.50
Lone Tree, CO (city) Douglas County	49	0.50
North Tustin, CA (cdp) Orange County	121	0.49
Aberdeen, WA (city) Grays Harbor County	82	0.49
Scotchtown, NY (cdp) Orange County	48	0.49
Cherry Hill, NJ (township) Camden County	344	0.48
Hallandale Beach, FL (city) Broward County	177	0.48
Highland Park, IL (city) Lake County	143	0.48
Saratoga Springs, NY (city) Saratoga County	127	0.48
Rutherford, NJ (borough) Bergen County	86	0.48
Short Hills, NJ (cdp) Essex County	63	0.48
Eatontown, NJ (borough) Monmouth County	62	0.48
Tarrytown, NY (village) Westchester County	54	0.48
Coconut Creek, FL (city) Broward County	244	0.47
Yorktown, NY (town) Westchester County	169	0.47
Lexington, MA (cdp/town) Middlesex County	146	0.47
Copiague, NY (cdp) Suffolk County	97	0.47
Melville, NY (cdp) Suffolk County	89	0.47
Stanford, CA (cdp) Santa Clara County	67	0.47
Martin, TN (city) Weakley County	52	0.47
Sonoma, CA (city) Sonoma County	48	0.47
Manalapan, NJ (township) Monmouth County	174	0.46
Oak Hills, CA (cdp) San Bernardino County	37	0.46
Millburn, NJ (township) Essex County	89	0.45
Hudson, MA (town) Middlesex County	83	0.45
Fairview, NJ (borough) Bergen County	62	0.45
Mission, KS (city) Johnson County	43	0.45
Oberlin, OH (city) Lorain County	37	0.45
Glen Cove, NY (city) Nassau County	118	0.44
Ithaca, NY (town) Tompkins County	86	0.44
Dumont, NJ (borough) Bergen County	77	0.44
Franklin Lakes, NJ (borough) Bergen County	46	0.44
Manhasset, NY (cdp) Nassau County	36	0.44
Athol, MA (cdp) Worcester County	35	0.44
Palm Beach Gardens, FL (city) Palm Beach County	199	0.43
Princeton, NJ (township) Mercer County	70	0.43
Moraga, CA (town) Contra Costa County	69	0.43
Manhattan, NY (borough) New York County	6,624	0.42
Commack, NY (cdp) Suffolk County	153	0.42
Fairfield, IA (city) Jefferson County	40	0.42
West Bloomfield, MI (charter township) Oakland County	268	0.41
Daytona Beach, FL (city) Volusia County	257	0.41
Acworth, GA (city) Cobb County	79	0.41
Lake Wales, FL (city) Polk County	57	0.41
Blue Ash, OH (city) Hamilton County	50	0.41
Upper Montclair, NJ (cdp) Essex County	47	0.41
Coral Springs, FL (city) Broward County	481	0.40
Weston, FL (city) Broward County	250	0.40
Grand Blanc, MI (charter township) Genesee County	145	0.40
Long Beach, NY (city) Nassau County	135	0.40
Dix Hills, NY (cdp) Suffolk County	106	0.40
Belmont, MA (cdp/town) Middlesex County	98	0.40
Canton, MA (town) Norfolk County	86	0.40

SECTION THREE

Please refer to the Explanation of Data in the front of the book for more detailed information.

Ancestry

Italian

U.S. and 50 States Sorted by Population and Percent of Total Population

Place	Population	%
United States	**17,571,808**	**5.78**
New York	2,731,316	14.20
Pennsylvania	1,577,604	12.51
California	1,543,300	4.21
New Jersey	1,521,527	17.45
Florida	1,215,631	6.57
Massachusetts	902,713	13.94
Illinois	810,398	6.36
Ohio	748,397	6.50
Connecticut	675,399	19.05
Michigan	478,974	4.81
Texas	466,610	1.92
Virginia	317,539	4.05
Maryland	311,872	5.47
Arizona	290,274	4.65
North Carolina	284,213	3.07
Colorado	253,097	5.18
Washington	238,187	3.63
Louisiana	224,434	5.07
Georgia	218,715	2.31
Missouri	215,204	3.63
Rhode Island	202,100	19.13
Wisconsin	201,496	3.57
Indiana	185,128	2.88
Nevada	169,273	6.43
Oregon	142,467	3.79
New Hampshire	137,298	10.45
Tennessee	129,067	2.07
Minnesota	128,278	2.45
South Carolina	120,326	2.67
Kentucky	88,876	2.07
Delaware	86,944	9.87
West Virginia	85,791	4.66
Alabama	83,808	1.78
Utah	76,864	2.89
Maine	75,833	5.71
Iowa	66,844	2.22
Kansas	65,265	2.32
Oklahoma	62,365	1.70
Mississippi	52,821	1.80
New Mexico	50,703	2.52
Nebraska	50,059	2.78
Arkansas	48,955	1.70
Vermont	46,857	7.51
Idaho	46,471	3.04
Montana	35,206	3.62
Hawaii	28,149	2.11
Alaska	25,157	3.64
Wyoming	18,943	3.47
District of Columbia	17,817	3.05
South Dakota	10,084	1.26
North Dakota	7,159	1.08

Place	Population	%
Rhode Island	202,100	19.13
Connecticut	675,399	19.05
New Jersey	1,521,527	17.45
New York	2,731,316	14.20
Massachusetts	902,713	13.94
Pennsylvania	1,577,604	12.51
New Hampshire	137,298	10.45
Delaware	86,944	9.87
Vermont	46,857	7.51
Florida	1,215,631	6.57
Ohio	748,397	6.50
Nevada	169,273	6.43
Illinois	810,398	6.36
United States	**17,571,808**	**5.78**
Maine	75,833	5.71
Maryland	311,872	5.47
Colorado	253,097	5.18
Louisiana	224,434	5.07
Michigan	478,974	4.81
West Virginia	85,791	4.66
Arizona	290,274	4.65
California	1,543,300	4.21
Virginia	317,539	4.05
Oregon	142,467	3.79
Alaska	25,157	3.64
Washington	238,187	3.63
Missouri	215,204	3.63
Montana	35,206	3.62
Wisconsin	201,496	3.57
Wyoming	18,943	3.47
North Carolina	284,213	3.07
District of Columbia	17,817	3.05
Idaho	46,471	3.04
Utah	76,864	2.89
Indiana	185,128	2.88
Nebraska	50,059	2.78
South Carolina	120,326	2.67
New Mexico	50,703	2.52
Minnesota	128,278	2.45
Kansas	65,265	2.32
Georgia	218,715	2.31
Iowa	66,844	2.22
Hawaii	28,149	2.11
Tennessee	129,067	2.07
Kentucky	88,876	2.07
Texas	466,610	1.92
Mississippi	52,821	1.80
Alabama	83,808	1.78
Oklahoma	62,365	1.70
Arkansas	48,955	1.70
South Dakota	10,084	1.26
North Dakota	7,159	1.08

Please refer to the Explanation of Data in the front of the book for more detailed information.

Ancestry

Italian

Top 150 Places Sorted by Population

Based on all places, regardless of total population

Place	Population	%
New York, NY (city) Kings County	625,004	7.74
Hempstead, NY (town) Nassau County	164,467	21.82
Queens, NY (borough) Queens County	159,812	7.27
Staten Island, NY (borough) Richmond County	156,288	33.72
Brookhaven, NY (town) Suffolk County	155,749	32.44
Brooklyn, NY (borough) Kings County	152,814	6.19
Philadelphia, PA (city) Philadelphia County	125,080	8.31
Chicago, IL (city) Cook County	102,842	3.80
Los Angeles, CA (city) Los Angeles County	101,064	2.68
Manhattan, NY (borough) New York County	98,563	6.22
Oyster Bay, NY (town) Nassau County	88,723	30.43
Islip, NY (town) Suffolk County	84,360	25.28
Babylon, NY (town) Suffolk County	61,852	28.95
San Diego, CA (city) San Diego County	61,669	4.81
Phoenix, AZ (city) Maricopa County	59,753	4.12
Bronx, NY (borough) Bronx County	57,527	4.21
Huntington, NY (town) Suffolk County	56,013	27.70
Boston, MA (city) Suffolk County	49,847	8.27
Smithtown, NY (town) Suffolk County	45,388	38.60
Pittsburgh, PA (city) Allegheny County	41,352	13.43
San Jose, CA (city) Santa Clara County	40,876	4.42
North Hempstead, NY (town) Nassau County	40,182	17.97
San Francisco, CA (city) San Francisco County	38,913	4.93
Columbus, OH (city) Franklin County	38,883	5.05
Las Vegas, NV (city) Clark County	38,013	6.56
Yonkers, NY (city) Westchester County	32,142	16.49
Houston, TX (city) Harris County	31,661	1.53
Jacksonville, FL (city) Duval County	31,420	3.87
Buffalo, NY (city) Erie County	30,606	11.51
Toms River, NJ (township) Ocean County	30,325	33.07
Toms River, NJ (cdp) Ocean County	29,313	32.99
Virginia Beach, VA (ind. city) Virginia Beach independent city	29,188	6.69
Charlotte, NC (city) Mecklenburg County	28,643	4.06
Cranston, RI (city) Providence County	27,317	33.90
Greece, NY (town) Monroe County	26,121	27.36
Seattle, WA (city) King County	25,949	4.36
Portland, OR (city) Multnomah County	24,417	4.31
San Antonio, TX (city) Medina County	24,332	1.89
Brick, NJ (township) Ocean County	24,022	31.65
Denver, CO (city) Denver County	24,012	4.15
Amherst, NY (town) Erie County	23,615	19.53
Mesa, AZ (city) Maricopa County	22,441	5.10
Tucson, AZ (city) Pima County	22,347	4.31
Metairie, LA (cdp) Jefferson Parish	22,255	16.38
Henderson, NV (city) Clark County	21,945	8.80
Worcester, MA (city) Worcester County	21,873	12.15
Tampa, FL (city) Hillsborough County	21,394	6.42
Austin, TX (city) Travis County	21,105	2.76
Hamilton, NJ (township) Mercer County	21,077	23.84
Port St. Lucie, FL (city) St. Lucie County	20,962	13.52
Colorado Springs, CO (city) El Paso County	20,646	5.11
Indianapolis, IN (city) Marion County	20,396	2.52
Waterbury, CT (city/town) New Haven County	20,320	18.48
Middletown, NJ (township) Monmouth County	20,292	30.42
Warwick, RI (city) Kent County	19,973	23.87
Providence, RI (city) Providence County	19,741	11.07
Rochester, NY (city) Monroe County	19,728	9.31
Omaha, NE (city) Douglas County	19,346	4.75
Tonawanda, NY (town) Erie County	19,213	25.93
Cleveland, OH (city) Cuyahoga County	19,033	4.65
Baltimore, MD (city) Baltimore city County	18,894	3.04
Sacramento, CA (city) Sacramento County	18,754	4.08
Syracuse, NY (city) Onondaga County	18,571	12.83
Stamford, CT (city/town) Fairfield County	18,300	15.14
Scottsdale, AZ (city) Maricopa County	18,298	8.36
Gloucester, NJ (township) Camden County	18,256	28.31
Albuquerque, NM (city) Bernalillo County	18,032	3.39
Washington, DC (city) District of Columbia	17,817	3.05
Levittown, NY (cdp) Nassau County	17,446	32.62
Dallas, TX (city) Dallas County	17,246	1.45
Cape Coral, FL (city) Lee County	17,100	11.42
Washington, NJ (township) Gloucester County	17,036	34.76
West Babylon, NY (cdp) Suffolk County	16,931	38.00
Norwalk, CT (city/town) Fairfield County	16,929	20.01
Spring Hill, FL (cdp) Hernando County	16,923	17.50
Clarkstown, NY (town) Rockland County	16,766	20.10
Milwaukee, WI (city) Milwaukee County	16,628	2.82
Howell, NJ (township) Monmouth County	16,618	32.73
Reno, NV (city) Washoe County	16,423	7.43
Woodbridge, NJ (township) Middlesex County	16,422	16.57
Colonie, NY (town) Albany County	16,393	20.11
Greenburgh, NY (town) Westchester County	16,339	18.64
Kansas City, MO (city) Jackson County	16,306	3.58
St. Petersburg, FL (city) Pinellas County	16,213	6.60
Fresno, CA (city) Fresno County	16,181	3.34
Scranton, PA (city) Lackawanna County	16,031	21.08
Erie, PA (city) Erie County	15,798	15.54
Hamden, CT (town) New Haven County	15,740	26.11
Revere, MA (city) Suffolk County	15,677	31.35
Jackson, NJ (township) Ocean County	15,576	29.33
Louisville-Jefferson County, KY (metro govt) Jefferson County	15,482	2.64
Old Bridge, NJ (township) Middlesex County	15,376	23.84
Sterling Heights, MI (city) Macomb County	15,325	11.82
Huntington Beach, CA (city) Orange County	15,311	8.10
Akron, OH (city) Summit County	15,000	7.40
West Haven, CT (city/town) New Haven County	14,769	26.82
Wayne, NJ (township) Passaic County	14,760	27.16
Naperville, IL (city) DuPage County	14,744	10.47
Johnston, RI (town) Providence County	14,729	51.23
Long Beach, CA (city) Los Angeles County	14,721	3.19
Raleigh, NC (city) Wake County	14,642	3.83
Cheektowaga, NY (town) Erie County	14,630	16.46
Irondequoit, NY (cdp/town) Monroe County	14,566	28.22
Clinton, MI (charter township) Macomb County	14,389	14.79
East Haven, CT (cdp/town) New Haven County	14,372	49.43
New Rochelle, NY (city) Westchester County	14,355	18.93
Tonawanda, NY (cdp) Erie County	14,269	24.37
Utica, NY (city) Oneida County	14,163	22.90
Wallingford, CT (town) New Haven County	13,926	31.09
Medford, MA (city) Middlesex County	13,886	25.04
Chandler, AZ (city) Maricopa County	13,856	6.04
Milford, CT (town) New Haven County	13,786	26.13
Paradise, NV (cdp) Clark County	13,644	6.26
Nashville-Davidson, TN (metro govt) Davidson County	13,591	2.31
Warren, MI (city) Macomb County	13,557	9.98
Fort Lauderdale, FL (city) Broward County	13,550	8.10
Berkeley, NJ (township) Ocean County	13,530	32.70
Franklin Square, NY (cdp) Nassau County	13,514	45.54
Macomb, MI (township) Macomb County	13,499	18.03
Milford, CT (city) New Haven County	13,306	26.08
Commack, NY (cdp) Suffolk County	13,261	36.68
Clay, NY (town) Onondaga County	13,235	22.78
Joliet, IL (city) Will County	13,198	9.10
Fort Worth, TX (city) Tarrant County	13,182	1.87
Santa Clarita, CA (city) Los Angeles County	13,153	7.64
Southington, CT (town) Hartford County	13,107	30.85
Vineland, NJ (city) Cumberland County	12,932	21.59
Upper Darby, PA (township) Delaware County	12,902	15.66
Bristol, CT (city/town) Hartford County	12,861	21.27
Albany, NY (city) Albany County	12,860	13.13
Gilbert, AZ (town) Maricopa County	12,802	6.56
North Providence, RI (town) Providence County	12,717	39.44
Cherry Hill, NJ (township) Camden County	12,695	17.89
Coral Springs, FL (city) Broward County	12,634	10.43
Hollywood, FL (city) Broward County	12,552	8.89
Jersey City, NJ (city) Hudson County	12,466	5.12
Fairfield, CT (town) Fairfield County	12,403	21.12
Carmel, NY (town) Putnam County	12,369	36.13
Cheektowaga, NY (cdp) Erie County	12,314	16.26
Riverside, CA (city) Riverside County	12,257	4.08
Santa Rosa, CA (city) Sonoma County	12,226	7.52
Orlando, FL (city) Orange County	12,187	5.21
New Haven, CT (city/town) New Haven County	12,171	9.44
Clifton, NJ (city) Passaic County	12,158	14.69
West Islip, NY (cdp) Suffolk County	12,015	41.88
Evesham, NJ (township) Burlington County	11,983	26.43
Danbury, CT (city/town) Fairfield County	11,954	15.06
Spring Valley, NV (cdp) Clark County	11,913	6.98
Yorktown, NY (town) Westchester County	11,883	33.09
Mount Pleasant, NY (town) Westchester County	11,847	27.28

Please refer to the Explanation of Data in the front of the book for more detailed information.

Ancestry

Italian

Top 150 Places Sorted by Percent of Total Population

Based on all places, regardless of total population

Place	Population	%
Colona, CO (cdp) Ouray County	15	100.00
Pierpoint, CA (cdp) Tulare County	12	100.00
Vantage, WA (cdp) Kittitas County	10	100.00
Playas, NM (cdp) Hidalgo County	57	83.82
Preston, NV (cdp) White Pine County	98	74.81
Westland, PA (cdp) Washington County	71	70.30
Emlenton, PA (borough) Clarion County	7	70.00
Kilbourne, OH (cdp) Delaware County	123	67.58
Atlasburg, PA (cdp) Washington County	144	62.88
Powhatan, LA (village) Natchitoches Parish	37	61.67
Wightmans Grove, OH (cdp) Sandusky County	20	60.61
Witherbee, NY (cdp) Essex County	149	60.08
Escudilla Bonita, NM (cdp) Catron County	15	60.00
Valmont, CO (cdp) Boulder County	74	59.68
Deputy, IN (cdp) Jefferson County	16	59.26
McGee Creek, CA (cdp) Mono County	17	58.62
Blodgett Landing, NH (cdp) Merrimack County	61	58.10
Northwest Hancock, ME (unorganized territory) Hancock County	4	57.14
Carrick, CA (cdp) Siskiyou County	93	54.71
Bagnell, MO (town) Miller County	43	52.44
Milton Mills, NH (cdp) Strafford County	83	52.20
Yatesville, PA (borough) Luzerne County	360	51.87
Bridgeport, CA (cdp) Mono County	207	51.49
Meadowlands, PA (cdp) Washington County	208	51.36
Hillside Lake, NY (cdp) Dutchess County	350	51.32
Johnston, RI (town) Providence County	14,729	51.23
North Massapequa, NY (cdp) Nassau County	9,384	50.28
Frankfort, NY (village) Herkimer County	1,299	50.17
Lake Buena Vista, FL (city) Orange County	3	50.00
East Kingston, NY (cdp) Ulster County	170	49.56
East Haven, CT (cdp/town) New Haven County	14,372	49.43
Great River, NY (cdp) Suffolk County	803	48.78
East Hanover, NJ (township) Morris County	5,463	48.64
Glacier, WA (cdp) Whatcom County	25	48.08
Allamuchy, NJ (cdp) Warren County	12	48.00
Makena, HI (cdp) Maui County	108	47.79
Cache, UT (cdp) Cache County	9	47.37
Baidland, PA (cdp) Washington County	1,092	47.27
Leeds, NY (cdp) Greene County	151	47.19
Fowlerville, NY (cdp) Livingston County	116	46.96
Moriches, NY (cdp) Suffolk County	1,413	46.85
Chase, AK (cdp) Matanuska-Susitna Borough	37	46.84
Fairfield, NJ (township) Essex County	3,443	46.72
Alcova, WY (cdp) Natrona County	14	46.67
Lafferty, OH (cdp) Belmont County	102	46.58
Masthope, PA (cdp) Pike County	235	46.53
Myers Flat, CA (cdp) Humboldt County	42	46.15
Hublersburg, PA (cdp) Centre County	23	46.00
Holiday Heights, NJ (cdp) Ocean County	1,020	45.90
Browntown, PA (cdp) Luzerne County	689	45.87
Elmira, CA (cdp) Solano County	70	45.75
Franklin Square, NY (cdp) Nassau County	13,514	45.54
Jenner, CA (cdp) Sonoma County	45	45.45
Nordic, WY (cdp) Lincoln County	56	45.16
Hammonton, NJ (town) Atlantic County	6,599	45.03
Delaware, NJ (cdp) Warren County	77	45.03
Yorktown Heights, NY (cdp) Westchester County	747	44.76
Gloster, LA (cdp) De Soto Parish	12	44.44
Thornburg, IA (city) Keokuk County	4	44.44
Brainards, NJ (cdp) Warren County	129	44.33
Baileyville, PA (cdp) Centre County	97	43.89
Lowellville, OH (village) Mahoning County	506	43.81
Duane Lake, NY (cdp) Schenectady County	106	43.80
Dover Beaches South, NJ (cdp) Ocean County	589	43.79
North Haven, CT (cdp/town) New Haven County	10,432	43.60
Massapequa, NY (cdp) Nassau County	9,908	43.53
Pardeesville, PA (cdp) Luzerne County	312	43.45
Sunny Slopes, CA (cdp) Mono County	86	43.43
Benton, CA (cdp) Mono County	125	43.25
Arrowhead Springs, WY (cdp) Sweetwater County	54	43.20
Malverne Park Oaks, NY (cdp) Nassau County	193	42.89
Northboro, IA (city) Page County	38	42.70
Nesconset, NY (cdp) Suffolk County	5,807	42.68
Lake Grove, NY (village) Suffolk County	4,700	42.66
Farmingville, NY (cdp) Suffolk County	6,818	42.57

Place	Population	%
Eastchester, NY (cdp) Westchester County	8,201	42.49
Holtsville, NY (cdp) Suffolk County	8,178	42.42
Hopewell Junction, NY (cdp) Dutchess County	198	42.31
Roseland, NJ (borough) Essex County	2,392	42.07
Head of the Harbor, NY (village) Suffolk County	587	41.96
Massapequa Park, NY (village) Nassau County	7,117	41.95
West Islip, NY (cdp) Suffolk County	12,015	41.88
Greenbackville, VA (cdp) Accomack County	63	41.72
Holbrook, NY (cdp) Suffolk County	11,251	41.70
St. James, NY (cdp) Suffolk County	5,324	41.68
Totowa, NJ (borough) Passaic County	4,411	41.64
Moonachie, NJ (borough) Bergen County	1,126	41.61
Cedar Glen West, NJ (cdp) Ocean County	544	41.50
Weott, CA (cdp) Humboldt County	73	41.48
Bradenville, PA (cdp) Westmoreland County	206	41.45
Hughestown, PA (borough) Luzerne County	551	41.43
Old Forge, PA (borough) Lackawanna County	3,455	41.26
Crabtree, PA (cdp) Westmoreland County	189	41.18
New Morgan, PA (borough) Berks County	7	41.18
Oakland, PA (cdp) Lawrence County	811	41.13
New Castle Northwest, PA (cdp) Lawrence County	530	40.90
Scotts Corners, NY (cdp) Westchester County	205	40.76
Saybrook Manor, CT (cdp) Middlesex County	540	40.75
Lattimer, PA (cdp) Luzerne County	163	40.75
Genoa, WI (village) Vernon County	77	40.74
Seaford, NY (cdp) Nassau County	6,290	40.68
West Sayville, NY (cdp) Suffolk County	2,116	40.56
Dillon Beach, CA (cdp) Marin County	66	40.49
Thornwood, NY (cdp) Westchester County	1,485	40.44
Hawthorne, NY (cdp) Westchester County	1,821	40.21
Malverne, NY (village) Nassau County	3,425	40.20
Jakes Corner, AZ (cdp) Gila County	41	40.20
Ellwood City, PA (borough) Beaver County	323	40.12
Montgomery Creek, CA (cdp) Shasta County	30	40.00
Weedville, PA (cdp) Elk County	187	39.96
Garden City South, NY (cdp) Nassau County	1,510	39.86
Lincolndale, NY (cdp) Westchester County	534	39.85
North Branford, CT (town) New Haven County	5,710	39.84
Selden, NY (cdp) Suffolk County	7,803	39.83
Kings Park, NY (cdp) Suffolk County	6,750	39.75
Ramtown, NJ (cdp) Monmouth County	2,363	39.53
Brady, PA (township) Clarion County	34	39.53
Roseto, PA (borough) Northampton County	596	39.52
North Providence, RI (town) Providence County	12,717	39.44
Pence, WI (cdp) Iron County	52	39.39
Ronkonkoma, NY (cdp) Suffolk County	7,783	39.35
South Farmingdale, NY (cdp) Nassau County	5,805	39.32
Newfield, NJ (borough) Gloucester County	663	39.30
Glendora, NJ (cdp) Camden County	1,917	39.23
Tickfaw, LA (village) Tangipahoa Parish	243	39.19
Pelham Manor, NY (village) Westchester County	2,121	38.92
East Norwich, NY (cdp) Nassau County	1,007	38.88
Lindenhurst, NY (village) Suffolk County	10,641	38.86
Sparkill, NY (cdp) Rockland County	535	38.74
Smithtown, NY (town) Suffolk County	45,388	38.60
Grier City, PA (cdp) Schuylkill County	44	38.60
North Wantagh, NY (cdp) Nassau County	4,516	38.59
Lyncourt, NY (cdp) Onondaga County	1,699	38.58
Saddle Brook, NJ (township) Bergen County	5,201	38.56
Pocono Mountain Lake Estates, PA (cdp) Pike County	392	38.54
South Hackensack, NJ (township) Bergen County	869	38.45
Islip Terrace, NY (cdp) Suffolk County	2,207	38.44
Peach Lake, NY (cdp) Putnam County	617	38.35
Fairview, WY (cdp) Lincoln County	74	38.34
Nutley, NJ (township) Essex County	10,739	38.33
Mahopac, NY (cdp) Putnam County	2,912	38.31
Watertown, CT (cdp) Litchfield County	1,399	38.16
Tribes Hill, NY (cdp) Montgomery County	445	38.16
Pence, WI (town) Iron County	58	38.16
Laurel, NY (cdp) Suffolk County	410	38.14
Websters Crossing, NY (cdp) Livingston County	16	38.10
Ocean Acres, NJ (cdp) Ocean County	5,997	38.02
West Babylon, NY (cdp) Suffolk County	16,931	38.00
Gold Key Lake, PA (cdp) Pike County	804	37.98
East Shoreham, NY (cdp) Suffolk County	2,420	37.88

Ancestry

Italian

Top 150 Places Sorted by Percent of Total Population

Based on places with total population of 7,500 or more

Place	Population	%
Johnston, RI (town) Providence County	14,729	51.23
North Massapequa, NY (cdp) Nassau County	9,384	50.28
East Haven, CT (cdp/town) New Haven County	14,372	49.43
East Hanover, NJ (township) Morris County	5,463	48.64
Franklin Square, NY (cdp) Nassau County	13,514	45.54
Hammonton, NJ (town) Atlantic County	6,599	45.03
North Haven, CT (cdp/town) New Haven County	10,432	43.60
Massapequa, NY (cdp) Nassau County	9,908	43.53
Nesconset, NY (cdp) Suffolk County	5,807	42.68
Lake Grove, NY (village) Suffolk County	4,700	42.66
Farmingville, NY (cdp) Suffolk County	6,818	42.57
Eastchester, NY (cdp) Westchester County	8,201	42.49
Holtsville, NY (cdp) Suffolk County	8,178	42.42
Massapequa Park, NY (village) Nassau County	7,117	41.95
West Islip, NY (cdp) Suffolk County	12,015	41.88
Holbrook, NY (cdp) Suffolk County	11,251	41.70
St. James, NY (cdp) Suffolk County	5,324	41.68
Totowa, NJ (borough) Passaic County	4,411	41.64
Old Forge, PA (borough) Lackawanna County	3,455	41.26
Seaford, NY (cdp) Nassau County	6,290	40.68
Malverne, NY (village) Nassau County	3,425	40.20
North Branford, CT (town) New Haven County	5,710	39.84
Selden, NY (cdp) Suffolk County	7,803	39.83
Kings Park, NY (cdp) Suffolk County	6,750	39.75
North Providence, RI (town) Providence County	12,717	39.44
Ronkonkoma, NY (cdp) Suffolk County	7,783	39.35
South Farmingdale, NY (cdp) Nassau County	5,805	39.32
Lindenhurst, NY (village) Suffolk County	10,641	38.86
Smithtown, NY (town) Suffolk County	45,388	38.60
North Wantagh, NY (cdp) Nassau County	4,516	38.59
Saddle Brook, NJ (township) Bergen County	5,201	38.56
Nutley, NJ (township) Essex County	10,739	38.33
Mahopac, NY (cdp) Putnam County	2,912	38.31
Ocean Acres, NJ (cdp) Ocean County	5,997	38.02
West Babylon, NY (cdp) Suffolk County	16,931	38.00
Bayport, NY (cdp) Suffolk County	3,375	37.85
Smithtown, NY (cdp) Suffolk County	9,899	37.78
Plainedge, NY (cdp) Nassau County	3,490	37.75
Frankfort, NY (town) Herkimer County	2,823	37.28
East Islip, NY (cdp) Suffolk County	5,173	37.11
Bohemia, NY (cdp) Suffolk County	3,670	37.08
Shirley, NY (cdp) Suffolk County	10,346	36.86
Kensington, CT (cdp) Hartford County	3,226	36.82
Commack, NY (cdp) Suffolk County	13,261	36.68
Wantagh, NY (cdp) Nassau County	6,573	36.56
Oakdale, NY (cdp) Suffolk County	2,804	36.52
Ridge, NY (cdp) Suffolk County	4,783	36.31
Lake Carmel, NY (cdp) Putnam County	2,872	36.25
Kent, NY (town) Putnam County	4,939	36.15
North Merrick, NY (cdp) Nassau County	4,476	36.14
Carmel, NY (town) Putnam County	12,369	36.13
Mastic, NY (cdp) Suffolk County	5,233	36.13
Deer Park, NY (cdp) Suffolk County	10,193	36.03
Centereach, NY (cdp) Suffolk County	11,413	36.02
Stoneham, MA (cdp/town) Middlesex County	7,672	35.98
Westerly, RI (cdp) Washington County	6,300	35.89
Cedar Grove, NJ (township) Essex County	4,411	35.83
Hazlet, NJ (township) Monmouth County	7,344	35.75
Dunmore, PA (borough) Lackawanna County	5,026	35.67
Wood-Ridge, NJ (borough) Bergen County	2,692	35.55
East Northport, NY (cdp) Suffolk County	7,443	35.52
Holiday City-Berkeley, NJ (cdp) Ocean County	4,467	35.51
Watertown, CT (town) Litchfield County	7,992	35.49
Ellwood City, PA (borough) Lawrence County	2,912	35.49
Lake Ronkonkoma, NY (cdp) Suffolk County	7,628	35.47
West Caldwell, NJ (township) Essex County	3,819	35.45
North Gates, NY (cdp) Monroe County	3,304	35.42
Hauppauge, NY (cdp) Suffolk County	7,401	35.37
Neshannock, PA (township) Lawrence County	3,369	35.36
Bethpage, NY (cdp) Nassau County	5,861	35.25
Lynbrook, NY (village) Nassau County	6,815	35.17
Manorville, NY (cdp) Suffolk County	4,731	35.01
Rocky Point, NY (cdp) Suffolk County	4,736	34.91
Stafford, NJ (township) Ocean County	9,068	34.84
East Fishkill, NY (town) Dutchess County	9,947	34.80
Washington, NJ (township) Gloucester County	17,036	34.76
Somers, NY (town) Westchester County	6,889	34.54
Saugus, MA (cdp/town) Essex County	9,094	34.46
Mount Sinai, NY (cdp) Suffolk County	4,006	34.46
Jefferson Valley-Yorktown, NY (cdp) Westchester County	4,984	34.44
Buena Vista, NJ (township) Atlantic County	2,621	34.41
Hasbrouck Heights, NJ (borough) Bergen County	4,027	34.30
East Rockaway, NY (village) Nassau County	3,374	34.30
Eastchester, NY (town) Westchester County	10,979	34.27
Medford, NY (cdp) Suffolk County	8,430	34.22
Bethel, PA (township) Delaware County	2,855	34.15
North Lindenhurst, NY (cdp) Suffolk County	3,969	34.14
Brookdale, NJ (cdp) Essex County	3,122	33.99
Wolcott, CT (town) New Haven County	5,587	33.97
Cranston, RI (city) Providence County	27,317	33.90
Miller Place, NY (cdp) Suffolk County	4,158	33.82
Winthrop Town, MA (city) Suffolk County	5,847	33.78
North Babylon, NY (cdp) Suffolk County	5,987	33.76
Staten Island, NY (borough) Richmond County	156,288	33.72
Lyndhurst, NJ (township) Bergen County	6,819	33.69
Farmingdale, NY (village) Nassau County	2,750	33.66
Pequannock, NJ (township) Morris County	5,105	33.49
Kenilworth, NJ (borough) Union County	2,613	33.46
Pittston, PA (city) Luzerne County	2,595	33.38
Putnam Valley, NY (town) Putnam County	3,892	33.36
Berlin, CT (town) Hartford County	6,520	33.28
South Huntington, NY (cdp) Suffolk County	3,278	33.16
Yorktown, NY (town) Westchester County	11,883	33.09
Toms River, NJ (township) Ocean County	30,325	33.07
Toms River, NJ (cdp) Ocean County	29,313	32.99
Westerly, RI (town) Washington County	7,569	32.98
Sayville, NY (cdp) Suffolk County	5,301	32.91
Pine Lake Park, NJ (cdp) Ocean County	2,667	32.77
Howell, NJ (township) Monmouth County	16,618	32.73
Berkeley, NJ (township) Ocean County	13,530	32.70
Levittown, NY (cdp) Nassau County	17,446	32.62
Islip, NY (cdp) Suffolk County	6,167	32.51
Brookhaven, NY (town) Suffolk County	155,749	32.44
Lacey, NJ (township) Ocean County	8,890	32.36
Gates, NY (town) Monroe County	9,171	32.21
North Bellmore, NY (cdp) Nassau County	6,303	32.20
Rotterdam, NY (town) Schenectady County	9,310	32.15
West Freehold, NJ (cdp) Monmouth County	4,467	32.10
Rotterdam, NY (cdp) Schenectady County	6,567	32.00
Oakville, CT (cdp) Litchfield County	2,998	31.96
Maywood, NJ (borough) Bergen County	3,028	31.86
Kenmore, NY (village) Erie County	4,944	31.80
Wading River, NY (cdp) Suffolk County	2,594	31.80
Caldwell, NJ (borough) Essex County	2,457	31.72
Brick, NJ (township) Ocean County	24,022	31.65
Folsom, PA (cdp) Delaware County	2,662	31.56
Hawthorne, NJ (borough) Passaic County	5,860	31.55
Monroe, CT (town) Fairfield County	6,078	31.47
Revere, MA (city) Suffolk County	15,677	31.35
Butler, NJ (borough) Morris County	2,356	31.35
Babylon, NY (village) Suffolk County	3,837	31.29
Lloyd, NY (town) Ulster County	3,369	31.29
Colts Neck, NJ (township) Monmouth County	3,179	31.25
New Castle, PA (city) Lawrence County	7,442	31.22
Lynnfield, MA (cdp/town) Essex County	3,582	31.18
Springfield, PA (township) Delaware County	7,492	31.15
Wallingford, CT (town) New Haven County	13,926	31.09
East Massapequa, NY (cdp) Nassau County	5,539	31.06
Marlborough, NY (town) Ulster County	2,718	31.06
North Haledon, NJ (borough) Passaic County	2,541	31.04
Wethersfield, CT (cdp/town) Hartford County	8,241	30.97
Trumbull, CT (cdp/town) Fairfield County	10,988	30.96
Southington, CT (town) Hartford County	13,107	30.85
Elwood, NY (cdp) Suffolk County	3,432	30.82
Prospect, CT (town) New Haven County	2,853	30.74
Cromwell, CT (town) Middlesex County	4,247	30.58
Waldwick, NJ (borough) Bergen County	2,928	30.56
Bellmore, NY (cdp) Nassau County	4,938	30.50
Runnemede, NJ (borough) Camden County	2,587	30.48
Oyster Bay, NY (town) Nassau County	88,723	30.43

SECTION THREE

Ancestry

Latvian

U.S. and 50 States Sorted by Population and Percent of Total Population

Place	Population	%
United States	**91,096**	**0.03**
California	11,443	0.03
New York	9,194	0.05
Illinois	6,982	0.05
Florida	4,921	0.03
Massachusetts	4,706	0.07
Michigan	4,265	0.04
New Jersey	3,946	0.05
Pennsylvania	3,754	0.03
Washington	3,380	0.05
Maryland	3,289	0.06
Minnesota	3,010	0.06
Wisconsin	2,810	0.05
Ohio	2,580	0.02
Texas	2,300	0.01
Colorado	2,142	0.04
Virginia	1,911	0.02
Connecticut	1,876	0.05
Oregon	1,701	0.05
Georgia	1,603	0.02
Arizona	1,588	0.03
Indiana	1,490	0.02
North Carolina	1,364	0.01
Iowa	942	0.03
Nevada	820	0.03
Missouri	792	0.01
Tennessee	666	0.01
South Carolina	625	0.01
Kentucky	530	0.01
New Hampshire	521	0.04
Maine	495	0.04
Nebraska	479	0.03
New Mexico	411	0.02
Idaho	376	0.02
Vermont	357	0.06
Hawaii	338	0.03
Montana	337	0.03
Kansas	327	0.01
Alabama	317	0.01
Oklahoma	304	0.01
Utah	300	0.01
District of Columbia	297	0.05
Louisiana	265	0.01
Alaska	252	0.04
Mississippi	196	0.01
Arkansas	187	0.01
Delaware	180	0.02
South Dakota	147	0.02
Rhode Island	127	0.01
North Dakota	102	0.02
West Virginia	96	0.01
Wyoming	55	0.01

Place	Population	%
Massachusetts	4,706	0.07
Maryland	3,289	0.06
Minnesota	3,010	0.06
Vermont	357	0.06
New York	9,194	0.05
Illinois	6,982	0.05
New Jersey	3,946	0.05
Washington	3,380	0.05
Wisconsin	2,810	0.05
Connecticut	1,876	0.05
Oregon	1,701	0.05
District of Columbia	297	0.05
Michigan	4,265	0.04
Colorado	2,142	0.04
New Hampshire	521	0.04
Maine	495	0.04
Alaska	252	0.04
United States	**91,096**	**0.03**
California	11,443	0.03
Florida	4,921	0.03
Pennsylvania	3,754	0.03
Arizona	1,588	0.03
Iowa	942	0.03
Nevada	820	0.03
Nebraska	479	0.03
Hawaii	338	0.03
Montana	337	0.03
Ohio	2,580	0.02
Virginia	1,911	0.02
Georgia	1,603	0.02
Indiana	1,490	0.02
New Mexico	411	0.02
Idaho	376	0.02
Delaware	180	0.02
South Dakota	147	0.02
North Dakota	102	0.02
Texas	2,300	0.01
North Carolina	1,364	0.01
Missouri	792	0.01
Tennessee	666	0.01
South Carolina	625	0.01
Kentucky	530	0.01
Kansas	327	0.01
Alabama	317	0.01
Oklahoma	304	0.01
Utah	300	0.01
Louisiana	265	0.01
Mississippi	196	0.01
Arkansas	187	0.01
Rhode Island	127	0.01
West Virginia	96	0.01
Wyoming	55	0.01

Please refer to the Explanation of Data in the front of the book for more detailed information.

Ancestry

Latvian

Top 150 Places Sorted by Population

Based on all places, regardless of total population

Place	Population	%
New York, NY (city) Kings County	3,302	0.04
Los Angeles, CA (city) Los Angeles County	2,043	0.05
Manhattan, NY (borough) New York County	1,822	0.12
Chicago, IL (city) Cook County	1,505	0.06
Boston, MA (city) Suffolk County	694	0.12
Brooklyn, NY (borough) Kings County	667	0.03
San Francisco, CA (city) San Francisco County	632	0.08
Seattle, WA (city) King County	624	0.10
San Diego, CA (city) San Diego County	596	0.05
Philadelphia, PA (city) Philadelphia County	570	0.04
Queens, NY (borough) Queens County	568	0.03
Portland, OR (city) Multnomah County	500	0.09
Minneapolis, MN (city) Hennepin County	453	0.12
Hempstead, NY (town) Nassau County	438	0.06
Milwaukee, WI (city) Milwaukee County	413	0.07
Houston, TX (city) Harris County	344	0.02
Edina, MN (city) Hennepin County	317	0.67
Washington, DC (city) District of Columbia	297	0.05
Naperville, IL (city) DuPage County	283	0.20
Newton, MA (city) Middlesex County	281	0.33
Indianapolis, IN (city) Marion County	275	0.03
St. Paul, MN (city) Ramsey County	262	0.09
Atlanta, GA (city) Fulton County	261	0.06
North Hempstead, NY (town) Nassau County	254	0.11
Virginia Beach, VA (ind. city) Virginia Beach independent city	239	0.05
Oyster Bay, NY (town) Nassau County	235	0.08
Mundelein, IL (village) Lake County	229	0.74
Phoenix, AZ (city) Maricopa County	227	0.02
Baltimore, MD (city) Baltimore city County	226	0.04
Des Moines, IA (city) Polk County	224	0.11
Jersey City, NJ (city) Hudson County	216	0.09
Austin, TX (city) Travis County	215	0.03
Columbus, OH (city) Franklin County	214	0.03
Grand Rapids, MI (city) Kent County	204	0.11
Oakland, CA (city) Alameda County	201	0.05
Lincoln, NE (city) Lancaster County	196	0.08
Huntington, NY (town) Suffolk County	193	0.10
Denver, CO (city) Denver County	191	0.03
Oak Park, IL (village) Cook County	190	0.37
Northbrook, IL (village) Cook County	183	0.56
Brookhaven, NY (town) Suffolk County	182	0.04
Scottsdale, AZ (city) Maricopa County	181	0.08
Dallas, TX (city) Dallas County	180	0.02
Ramapo, NY (town) Rockland County	174	0.14
Dedham, MA (cdp/town) Norfolk County	172	0.71
Louisville-Jefferson County, KY (metro govt) Jefferson County	171	0.03
Olney, MD (cdp) Montgomery County	170	0.51
Buffalo Grove, IL (village) Lake County	170	0.41
Noblesville, IN (city) Hamilton County	167	0.34
Gaithersburg, MD (city) Montgomery County	164	0.28
Urban Honolulu, HI (cdp) Honolulu County	163	0.05
Omaha, NE (city) Douglas County	163	0.04
Elk Grove Village, IL (village) Cook County	162	0.49
Chandler, AZ (city) Maricopa County	162	0.07
Coral Springs, FL (city) Broward County	158	0.13
Tucson, AZ (city) Pima County	157	0.03
Walnut Creek, CA (city) Contra Costa County	155	0.24
San Jose, CA (city) Santa Clara County	155	0.02
Fabius, MI (township) St. Joseph County	153	4.66
Greenburgh, NY (town) Westchester County	153	0.17
Lower Merion, PA (township) Montgomery County	151	0.26
Appleton, WI (city) Outagamie County	150	0.25
Appleton, WI (city) Outagamie County	150	0.21
Boulder, CO (city) Boulder County	150	0.15
Middletown, PA (township) Bucks County	149	0.33
Madison, WI (city) Dane County	149	0.06
Spring Valley, NV (cdp) Clark County	148	0.09
Fort Lauderdale, FL (city) Broward County	147	0.09
Kalamazoo, MI (city) Kalamazoo County	146	0.20
Manitou Springs, CO (city) El Paso County	145	2.92
Vacaville, CA (city) Solano County	143	0.16
Staten Island, NY (borough) Richmond County	142	0.03
Skokie, IL (village) Cook County	140	0.22
Albuquerque, NM (city) Bernalillo County	140	0.03
Pittsburgh, PA (city) Allegheny County	138	0.04
Colorado Springs, CO (city) El Paso County	138	0.03
Elmhurst, IL (city) DuPage County	137	0.31
Santa Monica, CA (city) Los Angeles County	136	0.15
Ann Arbor, MI (city) Washtenaw County	136	0.12
South Windsor, CT (town) Hartford County	135	0.53
Las Vegas, NV (city) Clark County	135	0.02
Airmont, NY (village) Rockland County	132	1.57
Agoura Hills, CA (city) Los Angeles County	131	0.64
Miami Beach, FL (city) Miami-Dade County	131	0.15
Irvine, CA (city) Orange County	131	0.07
Fort Collins, CO (city) Larimer County	130	0.09
Anchorage, AK (municipality) Anchorage Municipality	130	0.05
Wallkill, NY (town) Orange County	129	0.48
Carmel, IN (city) Hamilton County	129	0.17
Eden Prairie, MN (city) Hennepin County	128	0.22
Longmont, CO (city) Boulder County	128	0.15
Cambridge, MA (city) Middlesex County	126	0.12
Edgewater, NJ (borough) Bergen County	124	1.15
Beverly Hills, CA (city) Los Angeles County	124	0.36
Maple Grove, MN (city) Hennepin County	123	0.21
Pikesville, MD (cdp) Baltimore County	121	0.39
Delray Beach, FL (city) Palm Beach County	121	0.20
Memphis, TN (city) Shelby County	121	0.02
Germantown, WI (village) Washington County	120	0.61
St. Louis Park, MN (city) Hennepin County	120	0.27
Raleigh, NC (city) Wake County	119	0.03
Rumson, NJ (borough) Monmouth County	118	1.65
Terre Haute, IN (city) Vigo County	118	0.20
Aurora, IL (city) Kane County	116	0.06
Portage, MI (city) Kalamazoo County	115	0.25
Berwick, ME (cdp) York County	113	5.12
Berwick, ME (town) York County	113	1.58
Orange, CA (city) Orange County	113	0.08
Arden on the Severn, MD (cdp) Anne Arundel County	112	5.83
Torrance, CA (city) Los Angeles County	112	0.08
The Woodlands, TX (cdp) Montgomery County	109	0.12
Reno, NV (city) Washoe County	109	0.05
Tredyffrin, PA (township) Chester County	108	0.37
Cedar Rapids, IA (city) Linn County	108	0.09
West Valley City, UT (city) Salt Lake County	108	0.09
Marblehead, MA (cdp/town) Essex County	107	0.54
Biddeford, ME (city) York County	107	0.50
Redmond, WA (city) King County	106	0.20
Stanford, CA (cdp) Santa Clara County	105	0.74
Deerfield, IL (village) Lake County	105	0.57
Park Ridge, IL (city) Cook County	105	0.28
Oceanside, CA (city) San Diego County	105	0.06
Charlotte, NC (city) Mecklenburg County	105	0.01
Shoreline, WA (city) King County	104	0.20
Norwalk, CA (city) Los Angeles County	104	0.10
Coppell, TX (city) Dallas County	103	0.27
Wheaton, IL (city) DuPage County	103	0.19
Bronx, NY (borough) Bronx County	103	0.01
Glenview, IL (village) Cook County	102	0.23
Ellicott City, MD (cdp) Howard County	102	0.16
Winston-Salem, NC (city) Forsyth County	102	0.05
Lincolnwood, IL (village) Cook County	101	0.81
Kalamazoo, MI (charter township) Kalamazoo County	101	0.46
Toms River, NJ (township) Ocean County	101	0.11
Vancouver, WA (city) Clark County	101	0.06
Sacramento, CA (city) Sacramento County	101	0.02
Berkeley, CA (city) Alameda County	100	0.09
McAllen, TX (city) Hidalgo County	99	0.08
Cleveland, OH (city) Cuyahoga County	99	0.02
Long Beach, CA (city) Los Angeles County	99	0.02
East Hill-Meridian, WA (cdp) King County	96	0.33
Fishkill, NY (town) Dutchess County	95	0.44
Lake Oswego, OR (city) Clackamas County	95	0.26
Redondo Beach, CA (city) Los Angeles County	95	0.14
Columbia, MO (city) Boone County	95	0.09
Middleburg Heights, OH (city) Cuyahoga County	94	0.60
North Bethesda, MD (cdp) Montgomery County	94	0.23
West Allis, WI (city) Milwaukee County	94	0.16
Tampa, FL (city) Hillsborough County	94	0.03
Falmouth, MA (town) Barnstable County	93	0.29

SECTION THREE

Ancestry

Latvian

Top 150 Places Sorted by Percent of Total Population

Based on all places, regardless of total population

Place	Population	%
Pine Island, FL (cdp) Hernando County	39	27.46
Iatan, MO (village) Platte County	5	8.47
Braden, TN (town) Fayette County	26	8.15
Lake Hart, FL (cdp) Orange County	29	7.06
Arden on the Severn, MD (cdp) Anne Arundel County	112	5.83
Berwick, ME (cdp) York County	113	5.12
Odessa, MN (city) Big Stone County	6	4.80
Weidman, MI (cdp) Isabella County	39	4.76
Fabius, MI (township) St. Joseph County	153	4.66
Knik River, AK (cdp) Matanuska-Susitna Borough	33	4.60
Moose Pass, AK (cdp) Kenai Peninsula Borough	13	4.29
Stonyford, CA (cdp) Colusa County	5	4.20
Elba, MN (city) Winona County	6	4.11
Lake View, ME (plantation) Piscataquis County	4	4.00
South Koochiching, MN (unorganized territory) Koochiching County	7	3.95
Shelter Cove, CA (cdp) Humboldt County	20	3.82
Sorrento, ME (town) Hancock County	10	3.50
Westwood, CA (cdp) Lassen County	36	3.34
Arnett, OK (town) Ellis County	18	3.33
Wainaku, HI (cdp) Hawaii County	47	3.32
Pine Brook Hill, CO (cdp) Boulder County	35	3.27
New Preston, CT (cdp) Litchfield County	33	3.26
Durham, PA (township) Bucks County	38	3.14
Big Rock, IL (village) Kane County	36	3.13
Lake Dalecarlia, IN (cdp) Lake County	47	3.10
Daisytown, PA (borough) Cambria County	9	3.03
Merrimac, WI (village) Sauk County	10	2.95
Manitou Springs, CO (city) El Paso County	145	2.92
Los Ranchos, CA (cdp) San Luis Obispo County	44	2.90
Long Beach, MN (city) Pope County	13	2.80
Westby, MT (town) Sheridan County	4	2.80
Benton, NH (town) Grafton County	8	2.76
Tolland, MA (town) Hampden County	13	2.63
Williamson, NY (cdp) Wayne County	62	2.61
Halesite, NY (cdp) Suffolk County	55	2.61
Stony Creek, NY (town) Warren County	24	2.61
Camanche Village, CA (cdp) Amador County	15	2.55
Village of Grosse Pointe Shores, MI (city) Wayne County	71	2.44
Village of Grosse Pointe Shores, MI (city) Wayne County	71	2.39
Esperance, WA (cdp) Snohomish County	77	2.28
Lake, MI (township) Menominee County	15	2.28
Tofte, MN (township) Cook County	5	2.25
Rusk, WI (town) Rusk County	10	2.21
Cedar Glen West, NJ (cdp) Ocean County	28	2.14
Trout Lake, WA (cdp) Klickitat County	11	2.14
Conconully, WA (town) Okanogan County	4	2.13
Acalanes Ridge, CA (cdp) Contra Costa County	34	2.11
La Mesa, NM (cdp) Doña Ana County	11	2.08
Bemus Point, NY (village) Chautauqua County	6	2.05
Michiana, MI (village) Berrien County	3	1.99
Wolfeboro, NH (cdp) Carroll County	47	1.95
Spirit, WI (town) Price County	6	1.92
Saukville, WI (village) Ozaukee County	84	1.91
Fulton, MD (cdp) Howard County	37	1.88
Ryderwood, WA (cdp) Cowlitz County	6	1.82
Harmony, NJ (cdp) Warren County	7	1.78
Woods Bay, MT (cdp) Lake County	13	1.73
Rumson, NJ (borough) Monmouth County	118	1.65
Mason, WI (town) Bayfield County	4	1.65
Campbellsport, WI (village) Fond du Lac County	37	1.64
Kingston, MN (township) Meeker County	25	1.63
Somerset, MD (town) Montgomery County	22	1.61
Freeborn, MN (township) Freeborn County	5	1.61
Berwick, ME (town) York County	113	1.58
Airmont, NY (village) Rockland County	132	1.57
Pleasant Valley, NY (cdp) Dutchess County	13	1.57
Odessa, MN (township) Big Stone County	2	1.54
Tully, NY (village) Onondaga County	13	1.52
Sheffield, MA (town) Berkshire County	49	1.50
Winnebago, MN (township) Houston County	3	1.50
Teaticket, MA (cdp) Barnstable County	25	1.47
Tabor, SD (town) Bon Homme County	6	1.43
Haring, MI (cdp) Wexford County	5	1.43
Potterville, MI (city) Eaton County	36	1.41
Buckland, MA (town) Franklin County	29	1.40
Washington, PA (township) Berks County	52	1.39
Dexter, MI (village) Washtenaw County	53	1.37
Prospect, ME (town) Waldo County	12	1.36
Lauderdale, MN (city) Ramsey County	33	1.35
Esperance, NY (village) Schoharie County	6	1.34
Sherman, MI (township) Isabella County	39	1.33
LaFayette, NY (town) Onondaga County	65	1.32
Coarsegold, CA (cdp) Madera County	21	1.31
Makanda, IL (village) Jackson County	7	1.30
Fraser, IA (city) Boone County	2	1.29
Jamul, CA (cdp) San Diego County	67	1.26
Parker, SD (city) Turner County	14	1.25
Ardentown, DE (village) New Castle County	3	1.25
Jarrettsville, MD (cdp) Harford County	39	1.24
Volo, IL (village) Lake County	23	1.24
Chincoteague, VA (town) Accomack County	39	1.23
Sylvan, MI (township) Washtenaw County	35	1.23
San Antonio Heights, CA (cdp) San Bernardino County	48	1.21
San Pablo, NM (cdp) Doña Ana County	15	1.20
North Hills, NY (village) Nassau County	59	1.19
Pohatcong, NJ (township) Warren County	40	1.18
Lake Emma, MN (township) Hubbard County	13	1.18
Mountain Village, CO (town) San Miguel County	13	1.18
Mount Shasta, CA (city) Siskiyou County	40	1.17
Weatherby Lake, MO (city) Platte County	23	1.17
Lake Nacimiento, CA (cdp) San Luis Obispo County	28	1.16
Sycamore, KY (city) Jefferson County	2	1.16
Edgewater, NJ (borough) Bergen County	124	1.15
Home Lake, MN (township) Norman County	2	1.15
Strafford, VT (town) Orange County	14	1.14
Lansing, IA (city) Allamakee County	11	1.13
Winhall, VT (town) Bennington County	6	1.13
Bothell East, WA (cdp) Snohomish County	76	1.12
Toivola, MN (township) St. Louis County	2	1.12
Kandota, MN (township) Todd County	9	1.11
Morrill, MN (township) Morrison County	7	1.11
Falmouth, MA (cdp) Barnstable County	44	1.10
Waterville, OH (village) Lucas County	59	1.09
South Blooming Grove, NY (village) Orange County	36	1.09
Oxford, GA (city) Newton County	28	1.09
Richmond, NH (town) Cheshire County	15	1.08
Forest Hills, KY (city) Jefferson County	4	1.08
Rothschild, WI (village) Marathon County	55	1.06
Chilton, WI (town) Calumet County	16	1.06
Milton, WI (city) Rock County	58	1.05
Morris, MN (city) Stevens County	55	1.05
Walnut Creek, NC (village) Wayne County	10	1.05
German Valley, IL (village) Stephenson County	7	1.05
Liberty, PA (borough) Tioga County	3	1.05
Bainbridge, MI (township) Berrien County	30	1.04
Turtle, WI (town) Rock County	24	1.04
Hillsdale, NY (town) Columbia County	20	1.04
Hagaman, NY (village) Montgomery County	11	1.04
Lake Benton, MN (township) Lincoln County	2	1.04
Mullica Hill, NJ (cdp) Gloucester County	49	1.03
Hide-A-Way Lake, MS (cdp) Pearl River County	16	1.03
Shenorock, NY (cdp) Westchester County	20	1.02
Bloomfield, WI (town) Waushara County	10	1.02
Knox, NY (town) Albany County	27	1.01
Monroe, WI (town) Green County	13	1.01
Newcomb, NY (town) Essex County	5	1.01
Ben Avon Heights, PA (borough) Allegheny County	4	1.01
Leicester, VT (town) Addison County	11	0.99
Smolan, KS (city) Saline County	2	0.99
Thurman, IA (city) Fremont County	2	0.99
Lebanon Junction, KY (city) Bullitt County	16	0.98
Molalla, OR (city) Clackamas County	75	0.97
Melbourne Beach, FL (town) Brevard County	31	0.97
Plympton, MA (town) Plymouth County	27	0.97
Tyhee, ID (cdp) Bannock County	10	0.97
Northrop, MN (city) Martin County	2	0.97
Lawai, HI (cdp) Kauai County	20	0.96
Eldorado, WI (town) Fond du Lac County	12	0.96
Woodstock, NY (cdp) Ulster County	23	0.95
Bentleyville, OH (village) Cuyahoga County	10	0.95

Please refer to the Explanation of Data in the front of the book for more detailed information.

Ancestry

Latvian

Top 150 Places Sorted by Percent of Total Population

Based on places with total population of 7,500 or more

Place	Population	%
Airmont, NY (village) Rockland County	132	1.57
Edgewater, NJ (borough) Bergen County	124	1.15
Molalla, OR (city) Clackamas County	75	0.97
Lincolnwood, IL (village) Cook County	101	0.81
Westwood, MI (cdp) Kalamazoo County	73	0.81
Upper Saddle River, NJ (borough) Bergen County	65	0.80
Burley, ID (city) Cassia County	74	0.75
Mundelein, IL (village) Lake County	229	0.74
Stanford, CA (cdp) Santa Clara County	105	0.74
Dedham, MA (cdp/town) Norfolk County	172	0.71
Cypress Lake, FL (cdp) Lee County	84	0.70
Sonoma, CA (city) Sonoma County	71	0.69
Glendale, WI (city) Milwaukee County	87	0.68
Edina, MN (city) Hennepin County	317	0.67
Echelon, NJ (cdp) Camden County	67	0.67
Port Townsend, WA (city) Jefferson County	60	0.66
Agoura Hills, CA (city) Los Angeles County	131	0.64
Beaufort, SC (city) Beaufort County	78	0.62
Spotswood, NJ (borough) Middlesex County	51	0.62
Germantown, WI (village) Washington County	120	0.61
Middleburg Heights, OH (city) Cuyahoga County	94	0.60
Zeeland, MI (charter township) Ottawa County	57	0.59
Hanover, NH (cdp) Grafton County	50	0.59
Lake Geneva, WI (city) Walworth County	45	0.59
Westwood, MA (town) Norfolk County	83	0.58
Western Springs, IL (village) Cook County	74	0.58
Pine Castle, FL (cdp) Orange County	63	0.58
Deerfield, IL (village) Lake County	105	0.57
Northfield, MI (township) Washtenaw County	47	0.57
Northbrook, IL (village) Cook County	183	0.56
Shorewood, WI (village) Milwaukee County	73	0.56
Caledonia, MI (township) Kent County	65	0.55
Marblehead, MA (cdp/town) Essex County	107	0.54
Oconomowoc, WI (town) Waukesha County	45	0.54
South Windsor, CT (town) Hartford County	135	0.53
Port Washington, NY (cdp) Nassau County	86	0.53
Waldwick, NJ (borough) Bergen County	51	0.53
Clayton, MO (city) St. Louis County	79	0.52
Olney, MD (cdp) Montgomery County	170	0.51
Yorkville, IL (city) Kendall County	77	0.51
Biddeford, ME (city) York County	107	0.50
Elk Grove Village, IL (village) Cook County	162	0.49
Grand Haven, MI (charter township) Ottawa County	74	0.49
Madera Acres, CA (cdp) Madera County	44	0.49
Wallkill, NY (town) Orange County	129	0.48
Cinnaminson, NJ (township) Burlington County	73	0.47
Kingsgate, WA (cdp) King County	64	0.47
Marion, NC (city) McDowell County	38	0.47
Kalamazoo, MI (charter township) Kalamazoo County	101	0.46
Tarrytown, NY (village) Westchester County	52	0.46
Newmarket, NH (town) Rockingham County	41	0.46
Williamstown, MA (town) Berkshire County	36	0.46
Scio, MI (township) Washtenaw County	87	0.45
Cascade, MI (charter township) Kent County	75	0.45
Travilah, MD (cdp) Montgomery County	54	0.45
Fort Gratiot, MI (charter township) St. Clair County	50	0.45
Fishkill, NY (town) Dutchess County	95	0.44
Bethany, OR (cdp) Washington County	85	0.44
Stony Brook, NY (cdp) Suffolk County	60	0.44
Hanover, NH (town) Grafton County	50	0.44
Harleysville, PA (cdp) Montgomery County	42	0.44
Coronado, CA (city) San Diego County	85	0.43
South Strabane, PA (township) Washington County	39	0.43
Boonton, NJ (town) Morris County	36	0.43
Byram, NJ (township) Sussex County	36	0.43
Francisville, KY (cdp) Boone County	33	0.43
Summit Park, UT (cdp) Summit County	32	0.43
Richfield, WI (village) Washington County	47	0.42
Buffalo Grove, IL (village) Lake County	170	0.41
Harrison, NJ (township) Gloucester County	49	0.41
Maynard, MA (cdp/town) Middlesex County	41	0.41
Chaska, MN (city) Carver County	92	0.40
Plumstead, PA (township) Bucks County	49	0.40
Rockcreek, OR (cdp) Washington County	39	0.40
Monmouth, OR (city) Polk County	37	0.40
North Star, DE (cdp) New Castle County	32	0.40
Pikesville, MD (cdp) Baltimore County	121	0.39
Mount Kisco, NY (town/village) Westchester County	42	0.39
Allegheny, PA (township) Westmoreland County	32	0.39
Olivette, MO (city) St. Louis County	30	0.39
Jefferson Valley-Yorktown, NY (cdp) Westchester County	55	0.38
Williston, VT (town) Chittenden County	32	0.38
Oak Park, IL (village) Cook County	190	0.37
Tredyffrin, PA (township) Chester County	108	0.37
Scaggsville, MD (cdp) Howard County	85	0.37
Summerlin South, NV (cdp) Clark County	81	0.37
Brandermill, VA (cdp) Chesterfield County	46	0.37
Weston, MA (town) Middlesex County	41	0.37
Scotchtown, NY (cdp) Orange County	36	0.37
Marina del Rey, CA (cdp) Los Angeles County	34	0.37
Beverly Hills, CA (city) Los Angeles County	124	0.36
Eastchester, NY (cdp) Westchester County	70	0.36
Oberlin, OH (city) Lorain County	30	0.36
Upper Providence, PA (township) Montgomery County	70	0.35
Round Lake, IL (village) Lake County	56	0.35
Troutdale, OR (city) Multnomah County	53	0.35
Highland Park, NJ (borough) Middlesex County	49	0.35
Carver, MA (town) Plymouth County	40	0.35
East Bradford, PA (township) Chester County	35	0.35
Oakwood, OH (city) Montgomery County	32	0.35
Oregon, WI (village) Dane County	31	0.35
Itasca, IL (village) DuPage County	29	0.35
Bushkill, PA (township) Northampton County	28	0.35
Noblesville, IN (city) Hamilton County	167	0.34
Batavia, IL (city) Kane County	87	0.34
New Windsor, NY (town) Orange County	86	0.34
Foxborough, MA (town) Norfolk County	57	0.34
East Bridgewater, MA (town) Plymouth County	47	0.34
Wood Dale, IL (city) DuPage County	46	0.34
Haddonfield, NJ (borough) Camden County	39	0.34
Lakeland, TN (city) Shelby County	39	0.34
York, MI (charter township) Washtenaw County	29	0.34
Newton, MA (city) Middlesex County	281	0.33
Middletown, PA (township) Bucks County	149	0.33
East Hill-Meridian, WA (cdp) King County	96	0.33
Oshtemo, MI (charter township) Kalamazoo County	69	0.33
Golden Valley, MN (city) Hennepin County	66	0.33
South Burlington, VT (city) Chittenden County	58	0.33
Kings Park, NY (cdp) Suffolk County	56	0.33
Northview, MI (cdp) Kent County	47	0.33
Cannon, MI (township) Kent County	43	0.33
Gardnerville Ranchos, NV (cdp) Douglas County	39	0.33
Lapeer, MI (city) Lapeer County	30	0.33
Moore, PA (township) Northampton County	30	0.33
Malverne, NY (village) Nassau County	28	0.33
Crestwood Village, NJ (cdp) Ocean County	27	0.33
University Park, TX (city) Dallas County	74	0.32
Niskayuna, NY (town) Schenectady County	68	0.32
Milton, NY (town) Saratoga County	59	0.32
Scituate, MA (town) Plymouth County	58	0.32
Ringwood, NJ (borough) Passaic County	39	0.32
Elmhurst, IL (city) DuPage County	137	0.31
Comstock, MI (charter township) Kalamazoo County	45	0.31
St. Joseph, MI (charter township) Berrien County	31	0.31
New Baltimore, VA (cdp) Fauquier County	24	0.31
Garden City, NY (village) Nassau County	67	0.30
Waterford, CT (town) New London County	58	0.30
North Reading, MA (town) Middlesex County	43	0.30
Dobbs Ferry, NY (village) Westchester County	32	0.30
White Meadow Lake, NJ (cdp) Morris County	25	0.30
Falmouth, MA (town) Barnstable County	93	0.29
Lexington, MA (cdp/town) Middlesex County	88	0.29
Mansfield, CT (town) Tolland County	76	0.29
Walker, MI (city) Kent County	68	0.29
Wilton, CT (town) Fairfield County	51	0.29
Lower Salford, PA (township) Montgomery County	42	0.29
New Paltz, NY (town) Ulster County	40	0.29
University Heights, OH (city) Cuyahoga County	39	0.29
Short Hills, NJ (cdp) Essex County	38	0.29
Briarcliff Manor, NY (village) Westchester County	23	0.29

SECTION THREE

Ancestry

Lithuanian

U.S. and 50 States Sorted by Population and Percent of Total Population

Place	Population	%
United States	**708,860**	**0.23**
Illinois	92,913	0.73
Pennsylvania	82,290	0.65
Massachusetts	53,895	0.83
California	51,747	0.14
New York	48,825	0.25
Florida	43,399	0.23
New Jersey	35,622	0.41
Connecticut	32,136	0.91
Michigan	31,966	0.32
Ohio	24,321	0.21
Maryland	19,582	0.34
Texas	15,098	0.06
Virginia	14,636	0.19
Wisconsin	14,584	0.26
Arizona	13,206	0.21
Indiana	11,699	0.18
Washington	10,573	0.16
Colorado	10,148	0.21
North Carolina	9,457	0.10
New Hampshire	8,433	0.64
Georgia	8,215	0.09
Minnesota	6,775	0.13
Missouri	6,141	0.10
Maine	5,487	0.41
Oregon	5,342	0.14
Tennessee	4,522	0.07
Nevada	4,432	0.17
Rhode Island	4,291	0.41
South Carolina	3,690	0.08
Iowa	2,882	0.10
Delaware	2,741	0.31
Nebraska	2,702	0.15
Vermont	2,392	0.38
Kansas	2,177	0.08
New Mexico	2,154	0.11
Utah	1,971	0.07
West Virginia	1,960	0.11
Kentucky	1,924	0.04
Louisiana	1,888	0.04
Oklahoma	1,755	0.05
Alabama	1,560	0.03
Idaho	1,509	0.10
District of Columbia	1,441	0.25
Montana	1,276	0.13
Arkansas	1,202	0.04
Alaska	968	0.14
Hawaii	961	0.07
Mississippi	769	0.03
South Dakota	584	0.07
Wyoming	361	0.07
North Dakota	258	0.04

Place	Population	%
Connecticut	32,136	0.91
Massachusetts	53,895	0.83
Illinois	92,913	0.73
Pennsylvania	82,290	0.65
New Hampshire	8,433	0.64
New Jersey	35,622	0.41
Maine	5,487	0.41
Rhode Island	4,291	0.41
Vermont	2,392	0.38
Maryland	19,582	0.34
Michigan	31,966	0.32
Delaware	2,741	0.31
Wisconsin	14,584	0.26
New York	48,825	0.25
District of Columbia	1,441	0.25
United States	**708,860**	**0.23**
Florida	43,399	0.23
Ohio	24,321	0.21
Arizona	13,206	0.21
Colorado	10,148	0.21
Virginia	14,636	0.19
Indiana	11,699	0.18
Nevada	4,432	0.17
Washington	10,573	0.16
Nebraska	2,702	0.15
California	51,747	0.14
Oregon	5,342	0.14
Alaska	968	0.14
Minnesota	6,775	0.13
Montana	1,276	0.13
New Mexico	2,154	0.11
West Virginia	1,960	0.11
North Carolina	9,457	0.10
Missouri	6,141	0.10
Iowa	2,882	0.10
Idaho	1,509	0.10
Georgia	8,215	0.09
South Carolina	3,690	0.08
Kansas	2,177	0.08
Tennessee	4,522	0.07
Utah	1,971	0.07
Hawaii	961	0.07
South Dakota	584	0.07
Wyoming	361	0.07
Texas	15,098	0.06
Oklahoma	1,755	0.05
Kentucky	1,924	0.04
Louisiana	1,888	0.04
Arkansas	1,202	0.04
North Dakota	258	0.04
Alabama	1,560	0.03
Mississippi	769	0.03

Please refer to the Explanation of Data in the front of the book for more detailed information.

Ancestry

Lithuanian

Top 150 Places Sorted by Population

Based on all places, regardless of total population

Place	Population	%
New York, NY (city) Kings County	12,774	0.16
Chicago, IL (city) Cook County	12,503	0.46
Los Angeles, CA (city) Los Angeles County	6,875	0.18
Manhattan, NY (borough) New York County	5,775	0.36
Philadelphia, PA (city) Philadelphia County	5,334	0.35
Worcester, MA (city) Worcester County	3,290	1.83
Queens, NY (borough) Queens County	3,131	0.14
San Diego, CA (city) San Diego County	2,852	0.22
Naperville, IL (city) DuPage County	2,734	1.94
Boston, MA (city) Suffolk County	2,722	0.45
Brooklyn, NY (borough) Kings County	2,676	0.11
Phoenix, AZ (city) Maricopa County	2,661	0.18
Hempstead, NY (town) Nassau County	2,538	0.34
Oak Lawn, IL (village) Cook County	2,267	4.06
Pittsburgh, PA (city) Allegheny County	2,260	0.73
Seattle, WA (city) King County	2,126	0.36
Brookhaven, NY (town) Suffolk County	1,898	0.40
San Francisco, CA (city) San Francisco County	1,821	0.23
Baltimore, MD (city) Baltimore city County	1,693	0.27
Joliet, IL (city) Will County	1,678	1.16
Scranton, PA (city) Lackawanna County	1,584	2.08
Brockton, MA (city) Plymouth County	1,550	1.65
Tinley Park, IL (village) Cook County	1,503	2.74
Waterbury, CT (city/town) New Haven County	1,489	1.35
Houston, TX (city) Harris County	1,489	0.07
Washington, DC (city) District of Columbia	1,441	0.25
Orland Park, IL (village) Cook County	1,425	2.59
Denver, CO (city) Denver County	1,309	0.23
Portland, OR (city) Multnomah County	1,309	0.23
Grand Rapids, MI (city) Kent County	1,236	0.65
Woodridge, IL (village) DuPage County	1,229	3.78
Omaha, NE (city) Douglas County	1,226	0.30
Austin, TX (city) Travis County	1,213	0.16
Lakewood, NJ (township) Ocean County	1,181	1.35
Cleveland, OH (city) Cuyahoga County	1,180	0.29
Indianapolis, IN (city) Marion County	1,175	0.15
Homer Glen, IL (village) Will County	1,167	4.72
Scottsdale, AZ (city) Maricopa County	1,161	0.53
Lemont, IL (village) Cook County	1,131	7.38
Wilkes-Barre, PA (city) Luzerne County	1,109	2.67
Santa Monica, CA (city) Los Angeles County	1,080	1.22
Oyster Bay, NY (town) Nassau County	1,079	0.37
Virginia Beach, VA (ind. city) Virginia Beach independent city	1,067	0.24
St. Petersburg, FL (city) Pinellas County	1,041	0.42
Las Vegas, NV (city) Clark County	1,029	0.18
Columbus, OH (city) Franklin County	1,022	0.13
Palos Hills, IL (city) Cook County	1,012	5.83
Oak Forest, IL (city) Cook County	1,001	3.62
Arlington, VA (cdp) Arlington County	997	0.50
Aurora, IL (city) Kane County	979	0.51
Springfield, IL (city) Sangamon County	973	0.85
Huntington, NY (town) Suffolk County	956	0.47
Colorado Springs, CO (city) El Paso County	943	0.23
Tucson, AZ (city) Pima County	931	0.18
San Antonio, TX (city) Medina County	920	0.07
Minneapolis, MN (city) Hennepin County	913	0.24
Jacksonville, FL (city) Duval County	912	0.11
Watertown, CT (town) Litchfield County	892	3.96
Albuquerque, NM (city) Bernalillo County	889	0.17
Kenosha, WI (city) Kenosha County	885	0.90
Newton, MA (city) Middlesex County	866	1.03
Downers Grove, IL (village) DuPage County	865	1.80
Charlotte, NC (city) Mecklenburg County	856	0.12
Darien, IL (city) DuPage County	853	3.85
Burbank, IL (city) Cook County	845	2.97
Wheaton, IL (city) DuPage County	835	1.57
Rockford, IL (city) Winnebago County	827	0.54
Nashua, NH (city) Hillsborough County	823	0.95
Lakewood, NJ (cdp) Ocean County	800	1.61
Islip, NY (town) Suffolk County	799	0.24
Cambridge, MA (city) Middlesex County	792	0.77
Mesa, AZ (city) Maricopa County	758	0.17
New Lenox, IL (village) Will County	735	3.07
North Hempstead, NY (town) Nassau County	718	0.32
Pottsville, PA (city) Schuylkill County	715	4.92
Weymouth Town, MA (city) Norfolk County	714	1.34
Manchester, CT (town) Hartford County	708	1.23
Toms River, NJ (township) Ocean County	701	0.76
Oakland, CA (city) Alameda County	701	0.18
Brookline, MA (cdp/town) Norfolk County	697	1.20
Shrewsbury, MA (town) Worcester County	694	1.98
Hanover, PA (township) Luzerne County	693	6.24
Haverhill, MA (city) Essex County	682	1.13
Knoxville, TN (city) Knox County	679	0.38
Henderson, NV (city) Clark County	673	0.27
Boca Raton, FL (city) Palm Beach County	662	0.78
Toms River, NJ (cdp) Ocean County	658	0.74
Lockport, IL (city) Will County	645	2.71
Staten Island, NY (borough) Richmond County	645	0.14
San Jose, CA (city) Santa Clara County	644	0.07
Milwaukee, WI (city) Milwaukee County	643	0.11
Babylon, NY (town) Suffolk County	642	0.30
Bolingbrook, IL (village) Will County	640	0.88
Livonia, MI (city) Wayne County	637	0.65
West Mahanoy, PA (township) Schuylkill County	636	21.94
Huntington Beach, CA (city) Orange County	629	0.33
Smithtown, NY (town) Suffolk County	627	0.53
Kingston, PA (borough) Luzerne County	625	4.72
Wallingford, CT (town) New Haven County	613	1.37
Parma, OH (city) Cuyahoga County	613	0.75
Naugatuck, CT (borough/town) New Haven County	610	1.92
Milford, CT (town) New Haven County	609	1.15
Bristol, CT (city/town) Hartford County	607	1.00
Warren, MI (city) Macomb County	597	0.44
Barnstable Town, MA (city) Barnstable County	596	1.30
Boulder, CO (city) Boulder County	594	0.61
Milford, CT (city) New Haven County	593	1.16
Sacramento, CA (city) Sacramento County	593	0.13
Glastonbury, CT (town) Hartford County	588	1.73
Nashville-Davidson, TN (metro govt) Davidson County	588	0.10
Southington, CT (town) Hartford County	586	1.38
Norwood, MA (cdp/town) Norfolk County	584	2.06
Farmington Hills, MI (city) Oakland County	584	0.73
Mount Lebanon, PA (township) Allegheny County	583	1.78
Paradise, NV (cdp) Clark County	579	0.27
Kingston, PA (township) Luzerne County	575	8.22
Dallas, TX (city) Dallas County	573	0.05
New Britain, CT (city/town) Hartford County	572	0.78
Alexandria, VA (ind. city) Alexandria independent city	570	0.43
Euclid, OH (city) Cuyahoga County	568	1.15
Raleigh, NC (city) Wake County	566	0.15
Trumbull, CT (cdp/town) Fairfield County	564	1.59
Quincy, MA (city) Norfolk County	564	0.62
West Hartford, CT (cdp/town) Hartford County	563	0.90
Torrington, CT (city/town) Litchfield County	560	1.54
Hamden, CT (town) New Haven County	558	0.93
Mahanoy City, PA (borough) Schuylkill County	556	13.13
Atlanta, GA (city) Fulton County	556	0.13
Skokie, IL (village) Cook County	550	0.86
Shenandoah, PA (borough) Schuylkill County	548	10.62
Palos Heights, IL (city) Cook County	547	4.49
Bronx, NY (borough) Bronx County	547	0.04
Madison, WI (city) Dane County	545	0.24
Greece, NY (town) Monroe County	543	0.57
Tampa, FL (city) Hillsborough County	542	0.16
Kansas City, MO (city) Jackson County	542	0.12
Pikesville, MD (cdp) Baltimore County	541	1.76
Worth, IL (village) Cook County	540	5.06
Ramapo, NY (town) Rockland County	538	0.44
Torrance, CA (city) Los Angeles County	536	0.37
Methuen Town, MA (city) Essex County	532	1.15
Dearborn, MI (city) Wayne County	528	0.54
Bridgewater, MA (town) Plymouth County	525	1.99
Evanston, IL (city) Cook County	524	0.71
Woodbridge, NJ (township) Middlesex County	522	0.53
Fort Worth, TX (city) Tarrant County	518	0.07
Bartlett, IL (village) DuPage County	515	1.28
Lower Merion, PA (township) Montgomery County	514	0.89
Norwalk, CT (city/town) Fairfield County	513	0.61
Arlington Heights, IL (village) Cook County	510	0.68

SECTION THREE

Please refer to the Explanation of Data in the front of the book for more detailed information.

Ancestry

Lithuanian

Top 150 Places Sorted by Percent of Total Population

Based on all places, regardless of total population

Place	Population	%
Seven Springs, PA (borough) Fayette County	4	100.00
Chewsville, MD (cdp) Washington County	31	34.07
Force, PA (cdp) Elk County	65	33.16
Amberg, WI (cdp) Marinette County	76	32.76
Altamont, PA (cdp) Schuylkill County	239	32.34
Seltzer, PA (cdp) Schuylkill County	95	32.09
New Philadelphia, PA (borough) Schuylkill County	306	27.06
Livonia, MO (village) Putnam County	13	25.00
Fiddletown, CA (cdp) Amador County	20	24.10
Brandonville, PA (cdp) Schuylkill County	40	23.26
West Mahanoy, PA (township) Schuylkill County	636	21.94
Beverly Shores, IN (town) Porter County	144	21.30
Cumbola, PA (cdp) Schuylkill County	69	17.51
Byron, ME (town) Oxford County	21	17.21
Shenandoah Heights, PA (cdp) Schuylkill County	212	16.71
Calpine, CA (cdp) Sierra County	20	16.39
Lyon Mountain, NY (cdp) Clinton County	61	16.05
Dargan, MD (cdp) Washington County	46	15.70
Quintana, TX (town) Brazoria County	5	13.89
Middleport, PA (borough) Schuylkill County	58	13.78
Branch, PA (township) Schuylkill County	256	13.54
Park Crest, PA (cdp) Schuylkill County	94	13.30
Weston, PA (cdp) Luzerne County	46	13.14
Mahanoy City, PA (borough) Schuylkill County	556	13.13
Blythe, PA (township) Schuylkill County	109	13.01
Norwegian, PA (township) Schuylkill County	264	12.37
Girardville, PA (borough) Schuylkill County	188	12.34
Fort Snelling, MN (unorganized territory) Hennepin County	9	12.33
Callimont, PA (borough) Somerset County	5	12.20
Swall Meadows, CA (cdp) Mono County	46	11.59
Minersville, PA (borough) Schuylkill County	508	11.56
Shavertown, PA (cdp) Luzerne County	226	11.36
Union, PA (township) Schuylkill County	154	11.36
Tuscarora, PA (cdp) Schuylkill County	93	11.27
Forestville, PA (cdp) Schuylkill County	41	11.11
Helvetia, WV (cdp) Randolph County	4	11.11
Lamy, NM (cdp) Santa Fe County	37	11.08
Big Bend, CA (cdp) Shasta County	10	10.99
Browntown, PA (cdp) Luzerne County	164	10.92
Shenandoah, PA (borough) Schuylkill County	548	10.62
Schuylkill, PA (township) Schuylkill County	98	10.55
Frackville, PA (borough) Schuylkill County	405	10.44
Port Carbon, PA (borough) Schuylkill County	191	10.31
Weedville, PA (cdp) Elk County	47	10.04
Gilberton, PA (borough) Schuylkill County	83	9.96
West Havre, MT (cdp) Hill County	19	9.95
Luzerne, PA (borough) Luzerne County	282	9.88
Poydras, LA (cdp) St. Bernard Parish	182	9.62
Cormant, MN (township) Beltrami County	22	9.44
Beurys Lake, PA (cdp) Schuylkill County	17	9.44
East Union, PA (township) Schuylkill County	138	9.38
Panorama Park, IA (city) Scott County	13	9.35
Cressona, PA (borough) Schuylkill County	157	9.10
Pondsville, MD (cdp) Washington County	14	9.09
Cherry Valley, PA (borough) Butler County	5	9.09
Seven Springs, PA (borough) Fayette County	4	9.09
Thomaston, CT (cdp) Litchfield County	139	8.96
Foster, PA (township) Schuylkill County	16	8.84
Amberg, WI (town) Marinette County	76	8.83
Maxeys, GA (town) Oglethorpe County	14	8.81
Michiana Shores, IN (town) LaPorte County	36	8.76
New Castle, PA (township) Schuylkill County	39	8.69
Simpson, PA (cdp) Lackawanna County	124	8.67
Garden Grove, FL (cdp) Hernando County	62	8.41
Monomoscoy Island, MA (cdp) Barnstable County	11	8.27
West Abington, PA (township) Lackawanna County	18	8.26
Kingston, PA (township) Luzerne County	575	8.22
Tilden, TX (cdp) McMullen County	21	8.20
Palos Park, IL (village) Cook County	392	8.19
Whaleyville, MD (cdp) Worcester County	13	8.18
Dorrance, PA (township) Luzerne County	160	8.16
Noxen, PA (cdp) Wyoming County	57	8.13
Sheppton, PA (cdp) Schuylkill County	18	8.11
Pittston, PA (township) Luzerne County	270	8.03
Michiana, MI (village) Berrien County	12	7.95
Solana, FL (cdp) Charlotte County	39	7.93
Pikes Creek, PA (cdp) Luzerne County	22	7.91
Cass, PA (township) Schuylkill County	157	7.90
Curlew Lake, WA (cdp) Ferry County	35	7.87
Waumandee, WI (cdp) Buffalo County	4	7.84
Willow Springs, IL (village) Cook County	416	7.78
Nanticoke, MD (cdp) Wicomico County	13	7.78
Oklahoma, PA (cdp) Clearfield County	63	7.72
Fifth Ward, LA (cdp) Avoyelles Parish	54	7.66
Ringtown, PA (borough) Schuylkill County	55	7.63
Quemado, NM (cdp) Catron County	27	7.56
Powers Lake, WI (cdp) Kenosha County	107	7.50
Inkerman, PA (cdp) Luzerne County	141	7.40
Lemont, IL (village) Cook County	1,131	7.38
Tokeland, WA (cdp) Pacific County	10	7.30
Jenkins, PA (township) Luzerne County	324	7.29
Windsor, FL (cdp) Indian River County	15	7.25
Wynantskill, NY (cdp) Rensselaer County	256	7.24
Ravine, PA (cdp) Schuylkill County	71	7.18
Indian Head Park, IL (village) Cook County	272	7.17
St. Clair, PA (borough) Schuylkill County	215	7.08
Noxen, PA (township) Wyoming County	67	7.07
Warrior Run, PA (borough) Luzerne County	45	7.01
Olivet, IL (cdp) Vermilion County	29	7.00
McKeansburg, PA (cdp) Schuylkill County	12	6.98
Laflin, PA (borough) Luzerne County	106	6.93
Exeter, PA (borough) Luzerne County	389	6.84
Downsville, WI (cdp) Dunn County	8	6.78
Elk, MI (township) Lake County	59	6.77
Nicholson, PA (borough) Wyoming County	55	6.65
Exeter, PA (township) Luzerne County	148	6.63
Trucksville, PA (cdp) Luzerne County	133	6.59
Tall Timber, CO (cdp) Boulder County	18	6.59
Defiance, PA (cdp) Bedford County	20	6.56
Penn Lake Park, PA (borough) Luzerne County	22	6.49
Newtown, PA (cdp) Schuylkill County	20	6.39
North Bend, WA (city) King County	357	6.28
Bethlehem, CT (town) Litchfield County	225	6.26
Hanover, PA (township) Luzerne County	693	6.24
East Norwegian, PA (township) Schuylkill County	57	6.18
Merrionette Park, IL (village) Cook County	138	6.14
Barry, PA (township) Schuylkill County	64	6.01
Plymouth, PA (borough) Luzerne County	361	6.00
Smithton, PA (borough) Westmoreland County	33	5.94
Ryan, PA (township) Schuylkill County	141	5.91
Fell, PA (township) Lackawanna County	130	5.87
Bolivia, NC (town) Brunswick County	8	5.84
Palos Hills, IL (city) Cook County	1,012	5.83
Fraser, IA (city) Boone County	9	5.81
New Tripoli, PA (cdp) Lehigh County	47	5.75
Refton, PA (cdp) Lancaster County	12	5.74
Gordon, PA (borough) Schuylkill County	43	5.66
Belview, VA (cdp) Montgomery County	43	5.64
Delano, PA (cdp) Schuylkill County	21	5.63
Ross, PA (township) Luzerne County	162	5.61
June Lake, CA (cdp) Mono County	33	5.61
Flying Hills, PA (cdp) Berks County	139	5.60
Wagon Wheel, AZ (cdp) Navajo County	128	5.60
Montgomery, VT (town) Franklin County	53	5.60
Friendsville, PA (borough) Susquehanna County	7	5.60
Blacksville, WV (town) Monongalia County	7	5.56
Mexico, ME (cdp) Oxford County	119	5.53
Sugar Notch, PA (borough) Luzerne County	60	5.51
Fountain, MI (village) Mason County	9	5.49
Hardwick, MA (town) Worcester County	160	5.47
Amador City, CA (city) Amador County	7	5.47
Rocklake, ND (city) Towner County	7	5.47
Delano, PA (township) Schuylkill County	29	5.45
West Wareham, MA (cdp) Plymouth County	113	5.42
Hadley, MN (city) Murray County	4	5.41
Marion, NY (cdp) Wayne County	102	5.38
Marlin, PA (cdp) Schuylkill County	35	5.37
Dune Acres, IN (town) Porter County	14	5.34
Mount Tabor, VT (town) Rutland County	11	5.34
Buck Run, PA (cdp) Schuylkill County	7	5.34

Please refer to the Explanation of Data in the front of the book for more detailed information.

Ancestry

Lithuanian

Top 150 Places Sorted by Percent of Total Population

Based on places with total population of 7,500 or more

Place	Population	%
Lemont, IL (village) Cook County	1,131	7.38
Hanover, PA (township) Luzerne County	693	6.24
Palos Hills, IL (city) Cook County	1,012	5.83
Worth, IL (village) Cook County	540	5.06
Pottsville, PA (city) Schuylkill County	715	4.92
Athol, MA (cdp) Worcester County	382	4.76
Homer Glen, IL (village) Will County	1,167	4.72
Kingston, PA (borough) Luzerne County	625	4.72
Palos Heights, IL (city) Cook County	547	4.49
Riverside, IL (village) Cook County	365	4.18
Athol, MA (town) Worcester County	480	4.15
Oak Lawn, IL (village) Cook County	2,267	4.06
Watertown, CT (town) Litchfield County	892	3.96
Templeton, MA (town) Worcester County	308	3.95
Darien, IL (city) DuPage County	853	3.85
Willowbrook, IL (village) DuPage County	327	3.83
Woodridge, IL (village) DuPage County	1,229	3.78
Thomaston, CT (town) Litchfield County	289	3.67
Oak Forest, IL (city) Cook County	1,001	3.62
Millbury, MA (town) Worcester County	473	3.58
Pittston, PA (city) Luzerne County	277	3.56
Lakes of the Four Seasons, IN (cdp) Lake County	265	3.51
Hickory Hills, IL (city) Cook County	490	3.50
Sutton, MA (town) Worcester County	305	3.44
Mansfield, NJ (township) Warren County	267	3.38
Glencoe, IL (village) Cook County	289	3.35
Frankfort Square, IL (cdp) Will County	310	3.25
Oakville, CT (cdp) Litchfield County	305	3.25
St. Pete Beach, FL (city) Pinellas County	306	3.22
Nanticoke, PA (city) Luzerne County	331	3.15
Burr Ridge, IL (village) DuPage County	328	3.12
New Lenox, IL (village) Will County	735	3.07
Burbank, IL (city) Cook County	845	2.97
Burlington, CT (town) Hartford County	264	2.90
Prospect, CT (town) New Haven County	258	2.78
East Windsor, CT (town) Hartford County	301	2.76
Tinley Park, IL (village) Cook County	1,503	2.74
Lockport, IL (city) Will County	645	2.71
Lyons, IL (village) Cook County	284	2.70
Plains, PA (township) Luzerne County	271	2.69
Colonie, NY (village) Albany County	211	2.69
Wilkes-Barre, PA (city) Luzerne County	1,109	2.67
Dallas, PA (township) Luzerne County	235	2.67
Orland Park, IL (village) Cook County	1,425	2.59
Hanson, MA (town) Plymouth County	261	2.59
Dunmore, PA (borough) Lackawanna County	362	2.57
Oxford, CT (town) New Haven County	312	2.56
Mokena, IL (village) Will County	463	2.55
La Grange, IL (village) Cook County	389	2.52
Oxford, MA (town) Worcester County	343	2.51
Beachwood, OH (city) Cuyahoga County	299	2.51
Leicester, MA (town) Worcester County	272	2.49
Hanover, MA (town) Plymouth County	340	2.47
Crestwood, IL (village) Cook County	270	2.47
Mountain Top, PA (cdp) Luzerne County	260	2.46
Evergreen Park, IL (village) Cook County	476	2.40
Alsip, IL (village) Cook County	455	2.38
DuBois, PA (city) Clearfield County	185	2.36
Plumstead, PA (township) Bucks County	288	2.35
North Greenbush, NY (town) Rensselaer County	277	2.33
Ocean Pines, MD (cdp) Worcester County	250	2.27
Hamlin, NY (town) Monroe County	206	2.27
Midlothian, IL (village) Cook County	327	2.24
Plymouth, CT (town) Litchfield County	272	2.23
Hebron, CT (town) Tolland County	213	2.23
Berlin, CT (town) Hartford County	434	2.22
Willowick, OH (city) Lake County	316	2.22
Rutland, MA (town) Worcester County	168	2.18
Halifax, MA (town) Plymouth County	162	2.16
Easton, MA (town) Bristol County	489	2.12
Northborough, MA (town) Worcester County	300	2.12
Brentwood, PA (borough) Allegheny County	205	2.11
Middleborough, MA (town) Plymouth County	472	2.09
Chicago Ridge, IL (village) Cook County	295	2.09
Scranton, PA (city) Lackawanna County	1,584	2.08
Winchendon, MA (town) Worcester County	212	2.08
Pepperell, MA (town) Middlesex County	234	2.07
Norwood, MA (cdp/town) Norfolk County	584	2.06
Crest Hill, IL (city) Will County	411	2.02
Frankfort, IL (village) Will County	345	2.02
Bridgewater, MA (town) Plymouth County	525	1.99
Holden, MA (town) Worcester County	340	1.99
Butler, PA (township) Luzerne County	175	1.99
Shrewsbury, MA (town) Worcester County	694	1.98
Southwood Acres, CT (cdp) Hartford County	154	1.96
Naperville, IL (city) DuPage County	2,734	1.94
Wolcott, CT (town) New Haven County	319	1.94
Suffern, NY (village) Rockland County	208	1.94
Canton, CT (town) Hartford County	195	1.94
Harrisburg, IL (city) Saline County	173	1.94
La Grange Park, IL (village) Cook County	258	1.93
Naugatuck, CT (borough/town) New Haven County	610	1.92
Sandy, PA (township) Clearfield County	208	1.92
Pembroke, MA (town) Plymouth County	337	1.91
Carneys Point, NJ (township) Salem County	152	1.90
Westmont, IL (village) DuPage County	463	1.89
Robinson, PA (township) Allegheny County	247	1.89
Brookfield, IL (village) Cook County	354	1.88
Hinsdale, IL (village) DuPage County	313	1.88
New River, AZ (cdp) Maricopa County	220	1.88
Auburn, MA (town) Worcester County	303	1.87
Northbridge, MA (town) Worcester County	286	1.87
Amsterdam, NY (city) Montgomery County	344	1.86
Clarendon Hills, IL (village) DuPage County	154	1.86
Hobe Sound, FL (cdp) Martin County	219	1.85
Grafton, MA (town) Worcester County	318	1.84
Lyndhurst, OH (city) Cuyahoga County	260	1.84
Worcester, MA (city) Worcester County	3,290	1.83
Charlton, MA (town) Worcester County	233	1.83
Sound Beach, NY (cdp) Suffolk County	139	1.83
Downers Grove, IL (village) DuPage County	865	1.80
Mount Lebanon, PA (township) Allegheny County	583	1.78
Tolland, CT (town) Tolland County	264	1.78
Pikesville, MD (cdp) Baltimore County	541	1.76
St. John, IN (town) Lake County	242	1.76
Beach Park, IL (village) Lake County	235	1.76
Wrentham, MA (town) Norfolk County	190	1.76
Gardner, MA (city) Worcester County	357	1.75
Spencer, MA (town) Worcester County	205	1.75
Portage, WI (city) Columbia County	179	1.75
Glastonbury, CT (town) Hartford County	588	1.73
Rocky Hill, CT (town) Hartford County	336	1.73
Delran, NJ (township) Burlington County	290	1.73
Old Forge, PA (borough) Lackawanna County	145	1.73
Wareham, MA (town) Plymouth County	370	1.72
University Heights, OH (city) Cuyahoga County	234	1.72
Justice, IL (village) Cook County	217	1.72
Montague, MA (town) Franklin County	145	1.72
Winthrop Town, MA (city) Suffolk County	296	1.71
North Reading, MA (town) Middlesex County	248	1.71
Westwood, MA (town) Norfolk County	246	1.71
Winchester, CT (town) Litchfield County	192	1.71
Port Salerno, FL (cdp) Martin County	171	1.71
Walker, MI (city) Kent County	395	1.70
Norwell, MA (town) Plymouth County	176	1.70
Litchfield, CT (town) Litchfield County	145	1.70
Acton, MA (town) Middlesex County	360	1.68
Woodstock, CT (town) Windham County	132	1.67
Pelham, NH (town) Hillsborough County	210	1.66
Munhall, PA (borough) Allegheny County	190	1.66
Manteno, IL (village) Kankakee County	142	1.66
Brockton, MA (city) Plymouth County	1,550	1.65
Farmington, CT (town) Hartford County	413	1.65
Scott, PA (township) Allegheny County	280	1.65
Pinehurst, NC (village) Moore County	206	1.65
Plaistow, NH (town) Rockingham County	127	1.65
Orange, MA (town) Franklin County	128	1.64
Hudson, NH (town) Hillsborough County	397	1.63
Webster, MA (cdp) Worcester County	186	1.63
Litchfield, NH (town) Hillsborough County	133	1.63

Please refer to the Explanation of Data in the front of the book for more detailed information.

Ancestry

Luxemburger

U.S. and 50 States Sorted by Population and Percent of Total Population

Place	Population	%
United States	**45,597**	**0.02**
Illinois	6,688	0.05
Wisconsin	6,313	0.11
Iowa	5,983	0.20
Minnesota	5,789	0.11
California	2,948	0.01
Arizona	1,492	0.02
Washington	1,417	0.02
Florida	1,222	0.01
Texas	1,129	<0.01
Nebraska	951	0.05
Colorado	910	0.02
South Dakota	782	0.10
Michigan	781	0.01
Ohio	665	0.01
Indiana	591	0.01
New York	582	<0.01
Virginia	551	0.01
New Jersey	515	0.01
Kansas	511	0.02
Missouri	505	0.01
Maryland	500	0.01
Oregon	450	0.01
Pennsylvania	415	<0.01
Nevada	338	0.01
North Dakota	312	0.05
Georgia	311	<0.01
Montana	275	0.03
Massachusetts	269	<0.01
Connecticut	246	0.01
Alabama	220	<0.01
North Carolina	220	<0.01
Tennessee	178	<0.01
Kentucky	176	<0.01
Utah	173	0.01
Idaho	161	0.01
Arkansas	131	<0.01
District of Columbia	127	0.02
Alaska	124	0.02
Oklahoma	117	<0.01
New Mexico	109	0.01
South Carolina	79	<0.01
Rhode Island	73	0.01
Maine	48	<0.01
Louisiana	42	<0.01
Delaware	41	<0.01
Wyoming	39	0.01
Mississippi	35	<0.01
Hawaii	34	<0.01
Vermont	16	<0.01
West Virginia	13	<0.01
New Hampshire	0	0.00

Place	Population	%
Iowa	5,983	0.20
Wisconsin	6,313	0.11
Minnesota	5,789	0.11
South Dakota	782	0.10
Illinois	6,688	0.05
Nebraska	951	0.05
North Dakota	312	0.05
Montana	275	0.03
United States	**45,597**	**0.02**
Arizona	1,492	0.02
Washington	1,417	0.02
Colorado	910	0.02
Kansas	511	0.02
District of Columbia	127	0.02
Alaska	124	0.02
California	2,948	0.01
Florida	1,222	0.01
Michigan	781	0.01
Ohio	665	0.01
Indiana	591	0.01
Virginia	551	0.01
New Jersey	515	0.01
Missouri	505	0.01
Maryland	500	0.01
Oregon	450	0.01
Nevada	338	0.01
Connecticut	246	0.01
Utah	173	0.01
Idaho	161	0.01
New Mexico	109	0.01
Rhode Island	73	0.01
Wyoming	39	0.01
Texas	1,129	<0.01
New York	582	<0.01
Pennsylvania	415	<0.01
Georgia	311	<0.01
Massachusetts	269	<0.01
Alabama	220	<0.01
North Carolina	220	<0.01
Tennessee	178	<0.01
Kentucky	176	<0.01
Arkansas	131	<0.01
Oklahoma	117	<0.01
South Carolina	79	<0.01
Maine	48	<0.01
Louisiana	42	<0.01
Delaware	41	<0.01
Mississippi	35	<0.01
Hawaii	34	<0.01
Vermont	16	<0.01
West Virginia	13	<0.01
New Hampshire	0	0.00

Please refer to the Explanation of Data in the front of the book for more detailed information.

Ancestry

Luxemburger

Top 150 Places Sorted by Population

Based on all places, regardless of total population

Place	Population	%
Chicago, IL (city) Cook County	657	0.02
Aurora, IL (city) Kane County	608	0.32
Dubuque, IA (city) Dubuque County	563	0.98
Remsen, IA (city) Plymouth County	454	22.50
Le Mars, IA (city) Plymouth County	419	4.31
Sioux City, IA (city) Woodbury County	412	0.50
Port Washington, WI (city) Ozaukee County	361	3.24
Phoenix, AZ (city) Maricopa County	338	0.02
Rochester, MN (city) Olmsted County	299	0.29
Los Angeles, CA (city) Los Angeles County	253	0.01
Omaha, NE (city) Douglas County	239	0.06
Cedar Rapids, IA (city) Linn County	233	0.19
Des Moines, IA (city) Polk County	222	0.11
Milwaukee, WI (city) Milwaukee County	219	0.04
St. Paul, MN (city) Ramsey County	218	0.08
Sheboygan, WI (city) Sheboygan County	208	0.42
Sioux Falls, SD (city) Minnehaha County	207	0.14
Minneapolis, MN (city) Hennepin County	194	0.05
Belgium, WI (village) Ozaukee County	193	8.74
New York, NY (city) Kings County	193	<0.01
Shoreline, WA (city) King County	188	0.36
Tucson, AZ (city) Pima County	182	0.04
Belgium, WI (town) Ozaukee County	181	12.89
Mesa, AZ (city) Maricopa County	177	0.04
Port Washington, WI (town) Ozaukee County	170	11.62
Denver, CO (city) Denver County	169	0.03
San Jose, CA (city) Santa Clara County	168	0.02
Seattle, WA (city) King County	166	0.03
Portland, OR (city) Multnomah County	153	0.03
Algona, IA (city) Kossuth County	146	2.62
Des Plaines, IL (city) Cook County	144	0.25
Fredonia, WI (village) Ozaukee County	141	6.91
Random Lake, WI (village) Sheboygan County	140	9.25
Winona, MN (city) Winona County	136	0.49
Saukville, WI (village) Ozaukee County	135	3.06
Minnetonka, MN (city) Hennepin County	135	0.27
Evanston, IL (city) Cook County	132	0.18
San Diego, CA (city) San Diego County	130	0.01
Elmhurst, IL (city) DuPage County	129	0.29
Washington, DC (city) District of Columbia	127	0.02
San Francisco, CA (city) San Francisco County	126	0.02
Cedar Falls, IA (city) Black Hawk County	124	0.32
Monticello, IA (city) Jones County	123	3.25
Arlington Heights, IL (village) Cook County	122	0.16
St. Cloud, MN (city) Stearns County	121	0.19
Sherman, WI (town) Sheboygan County	118	7.85
Fredonia, WI (town) Ozaukee County	116	4.96
Overland Park, KS (city) Johnson County	114	0.07
Bloomington, MN (city) Hennepin County	110	0.13
Elgin, IL (city) Kane County	106	0.10
Roselle, IL (village) DuPage County	104	0.46
West Bend, WI (city) Washington County	101	0.33
Austin, TX (city) Travis County	101	0.01
Las Vegas, NV (city) Clark County	98	0.02
Bellevue, IA (city) Jackson County	97	4.24
Indianapolis, IN (city) Marion County	97	0.01
Ames, IA (city) Story County	93	0.16
Anchorage, AK (municipality) Anchorage Municipality	93	0.03
Centennial, CO (city) Arapahoe County	92	0.09
Naperville, IL (city) DuPage County	92	0.07
Cedar Grove, WI (village) Sheboygan County	91	4.61
Summit, WI (town) Waukesha County	91	1.95
Drum Point, MD (cdp) Calvert County	89	2.68
Hoffman Estates, IL (village) Cook County	86	0.17
Glendale, CA (city) Los Angeles County	86	0.04
Englewood, NJ (city) Bergen County	85	0.32
Yakima, WA (city) Yakima County	85	0.10
Bothell West, WA (cdp) Snohomish County	84	0.54
Green Bay, WI (city) Brown County	84	0.08
St. Cloud, MN (city) Stearns County	83	0.16
Morton Grove, IL (village) Cook County	80	0.35
Elk Grove Village, IL (village) Cook County	80	0.24
Eagan, MN (city) Dakota County	80	0.12
Rollingstone, MN (city) Winona County	79	10.14
Winnetka, IL (village) Cook County	79	0.65
Plymouth, WI (city) Sheboygan County	78	0.93
Coconut Creek, FL (city) Broward County	78	0.15
Plymouth, MN (city) Hennepin County	77	0.11
Lawrence, KS (city) Douglas County	76	0.09
Wichita, KS (city) Sedgwick County	76	0.02
Houston, TX (city) Harris County	76	<0.01
Richfield, WI (village) Washington County	75	0.67
Woodbury, MN (city) Washington County	74	0.12
Hillsborough, NC (town) Orange County	73	1.22
Wauwatosa, WI (city) Milwaukee County	73	0.16
Palatine, IL (village) Cook County	73	0.11
Huntington Beach, CA (city) Orange County	73	0.04
Colorado Springs, CO (city) El Paso County	73	0.02
Mendota Heights, MN (city) Dakota County	72	0.64
La Grange Park, IL (village) Cook County	72	0.54
St. Charles, IL (city) Kane County	72	0.22
Cedarburg, WI (city) Ozaukee County	69	0.61
Chanhassen, MN (city) Carver County	69	0.30
Schaumburg, IL (village) Cook County	69	0.09
St. Louis Park, MN (city) Hennepin County	68	0.15
Manhattan, NY (borough) New York County	68	<0.01
Spring Valley, NV (cdp) Clark County	67	0.04
Boston, MA (city) Suffolk County	66	0.01
San Antonio, TX (city) Medina County	66	0.01
Pinole, CA (city) Contra Costa County	64	0.35
Cedar Park, TX (city) Williamson County	64	0.14
Kenosha, WI (city) Kenosha County	64	0.07
Chandler, AZ (city) Maricopa County	64	0.03
Lincoln, NE (city) Lancaster County	64	0.03
Dallas, TX (city) Dallas County	64	0.01
Urbandale, IA (city) Polk County	63	0.17
Rolling Meadows, IL (city) Cook County	62	0.26
Glen Ellyn, IL (village) DuPage County	62	0.23
Wheaton, IL (city) DuPage County	62	0.12
Peoria, IL (city) Peoria County	62	0.05
Rochester, NY (city) Monroe County	62	0.03
Chalco, NE (cdp) Sarpy County	61	0.57
New Brighton, MN (city) Ramsey County	61	0.29
Shoreview, MN (city) Ramsey County	61	0.24
Fort Lee, NJ (borough) Bergen County	61	0.17
La Crosse, WI (city) La Crosse County	61	0.12
Eden Prairie, MN (city) Hennepin County	61	0.10
Brookfield, IL (village) Cook County	60	0.32
Fargo, ND (city) Cass County	60	0.06
Fond du Lac, WI (city) Fond du Lac County	59	0.14
Niles, IL (village) Cook County	58	0.20
Eau Claire, WI (city) Eau Claire County	58	0.09
Eau Claire, WI (city) Eau Claire County	58	0.09
Brooklyn, NY (borough) Kings County	58	<0.01
David City, NE (city) Butler County	57	2.02
Wilton, CT (town) Fairfield County	57	0.32
Lake Zurich, IL (village) Lake County	57	0.29
Madison, WI (city) Dane County	57	0.02
North Aurora, IL (village) Kane County	56	0.36
Tiffin, OH (city) Seneca County	56	0.31
Orangevale, CA (cdp) Sacramento County	56	0.16
Waukesha, WI (city) Waukesha County	56	0.08
Tampa, FL (city) Hillsborough County	55	0.02
Fort Worth, TX (city) Tarrant County	55	0.01
Steubenville, OH (city) Jefferson County	54	0.29
Woodstock, IL (city) McHenry County	54	0.22
Bellevue, NE (city) Sarpy County	54	0.11
Great Falls, MT (city) Cascade County	54	0.09
Staten Island, NY (borough) Richmond County	54	0.01
Lake Elmo, MN (city) Washington County	53	0.67
Robbinsdale, MN (city) Hennepin County	53	0.38
Brookings, SD (city) Brookings County	53	0.25
Shakopee, MN (city) Scott County	53	0.15
Sun City, AZ (cdp) Maricopa County	53	0.14
Lakeville, MN (city) Dakota County	53	0.10
Reno, NV (city) Washoe County	53	0.02
Manchester, IA (city) Delaware County	52	1.00
Iowa City, IA (city) Johnson County	52	0.08
Holland, WI (town) Sheboygan County	51	2.15
Columbia, SC (city) Richland County	51	0.04

Please refer to the Explanation of Data in the front of the book for more detailed information.

Ancestry

Luxemburger

Top 150 Places Sorted by Percent of Total Population

Based on all places, regardless of total population

Place	Population	%
Centralia, IA (city) Dubuque County	48	32.21
St. Donatus, IA (city) Jackson County	34	25.00
Luxemburg, IA (city) Dubuque County	41	24.12
Remsen, IA (city) Plymouth County	454	22.50
Minneiska, MN (city) Winona County	6	13.64
Belgium, WI (town) Ozaukee County	181	12.89
Port Washington, WI (town) Ozaukee County	170	11.62
Whitewater, MN (township) Winona County	24	10.86
Elmer, MN (township) Pipestone County	30	10.38
La Motte, IA (city) Jackson County	24	10.34
Rollingstone, MN (city) Winona County	79	10.14
Random Lake, WI (village) Sheboygan County	140	9.25
Mount Vernon, MN (township) Winona County	24	9.23
Springbrook, IA (city) Jackson County	12	8.96
Belgium, WI (village) Ozaukee County	193	8.74
Sherman, WI (town) Sheboygan County	118	7.85
Houlton, WI (cdp) St. Croix County	29	7.67
Murray, MN (township) Murray County	14	7.65
Fredonia, WI (village) Ozaukee County	141	6.91
Mayville, MN (township) Houston County	29	6.68
Altura, MN (city) Winona County	27	6.60
Bellechester, MN (city) Goodhue County	10	6.49
La Crosse, MN (township) Jackson County	9	6.38
Hill River, MN (township) Polk County	13	5.83
Guilford, MO (town) Nodaway County	3	5.66
Bassett, MN (township) St. Louis County	4	5.63
Ridgely, MN (township) Nicollet County	4	5.63
Newburg, MN (township) Fillmore County	21	5.51
Elba, MN (township) Winona County	11	5.29
Granville, IA (city) Sioux County	22	5.24
Fredonia, WI (town) Ozaukee County	116	4.96
Primrose, NE (village) Boone County	3	4.84
Bellechester, MN (city) Goodhue County	10	4.76
Chester, MN (township) Polk County	5	4.76
Rollingstone, MN (township) Winona County	28	4.71
Norton, MN (township) Winona County	30	4.65
Cedar Grove, WI (village) Sheboygan County	91	4.61
Cameron, MN (township) Murray County	9	4.52
Balltown, IA (city) Dubuque County	3	4.41
Le Mars, IA (city) Plymouth County	419	4.31
Waumandee, WI (town) Buffalo County	20	4.30
Bellevue, IA (city) Jackson County	97	4.24
Redwood Falls, MN (township) Redwood County	9	4.17
Elba, MN (city) Winona County	6	4.11
Quincy, MN (township) Olmsted County	13	4.09
Alton, IA (city) Sioux County	43	3.99
Mazeppa, MN (city) Wabasha County	26	3.87
Woodstock, MN (city) Pipestone County	5	3.79
Minneiska, MN (city) Wabasha County	6	3.77
Woodlands, CA (cdp) San Luis Obispo County	14	3.76
Hersey, MN (township) Nobles County	9	3.72
Preston, IA (city) Jackson County	37	3.71
Cushing, IA (city) Woodbury County	7	3.59
Newhalen, AK (city) Lake and Peninsula Borough	6	3.59
Kaneville, IL (village) Kane County	13	3.54
Dover, MN (township) Olmsted County	12	3.32
Gull Lake, WI (town) Washburn County	8	3.32
Hope, ND (city) Steele County	8	3.29
Owens, MN (township) St. Louis County	9	3.26
Monticello, IA (city) Jones County	123	3.25
Port Washington, WI (city) Ozaukee County	361	3.24
Hillsdale, MN (township) Winona County	21	3.10
Saukville, WI (village) Ozaukee County	135	3.06
Marcus, IA (city) Cherokee County	30	3.06
Struble, IA (city) Plymouth County	2	3.03
Mercer, WI (cdp) Iron County	17	3.01
La Bolt, SD (town) Grant County	2	2.99
Greenwood, MI (township) Oscoda County	39	2.95
Moose Creek, MN (township) Clearwater County	5	2.91
Kanaranzi, MN (township) Rock County	9	2.85
Bancroft, IA (city) Kossuth County	19	2.84
Vermillion, MN (city) Dakota County	11	2.82
Octavia, NE (village) Butler County	4	2.82
Adell, WI (village) Sheboygan County	14	2.81
Rosburg, WA (cdp) Wahkiakum County	7	2.75
Hospers, IA (city) Sioux County	20	2.70
Drum Point, MD (cdp) Calvert County	89	2.68
Rockford, IA (city) Floyd County	28	2.66
Home, MN (township) Brown County	15	2.65
Westport, MN (township) Pope County	6	2.65
Fleming, MN (township) Pine County	4	2.65
Algona, IA (city) Kossuth County	146	2.62
Wiscoy, MN (township) Winona County	6	2.58
White River, WI (town) Ashland County	21	2.57
Boulder Flats, WY (cdp) Fremont County	12	2.56
Granite, MN (township) Morrison County	12	2.48
Prairie Rose, ND (city) Cass County	3	2.44
Lewiston, MN (city) Winona County	44	2.40
Grenora, ND (city) Williams County	6	2.36
Waubeka, WI (cdp) Ozaukee County	19	2.32
Lytton, IA (city) Sac County	6	2.32
Norman, MN (township) Yellow Medicine County	7	2.31
Beaverdale, IA (cdp) Des Moines County	22	2.24
Middletown, MN (township) Jackson County	6	2.24
Waukenabo, MN (township) Aitkin County	4	2.22
Camino Tassajara, CA (cdp) Contra Costa County	38	2.20
Benton, WI (town) Lafayette County	10	2.18
Morristown, AZ (cdp) Maricopa County	4	2.17
Chester, MN (township) Wabasha County	12	2.16
Holland, WI (town) Sheboygan County	51	2.15
Merrill, IA (city) Plymouth County	17	2.12
Cascade, IA (city) Dubuque County	48	2.11
Pemberton, MN (city) Blue Earth County	6	2.11
Eagle Bend, MN (city) Todd County	10	2.08
Thompson, MN (township) Kittson County	3	2.04
David City, NE (city) Butler County	57	2.02
Warren, MN (township) Winona County	10	2.02
Summit, WI (town) Waukesha County	91	1.95
Sandy Hook, WI (cdp) Grant County	6	1.95
Ottawa, MN (township) Le Sueur County	5	1.95
Pleasant Hill, MN (township) Winona County	13	1.94
Vermillion, MN (township) Dakota County	22	1.92
Lismore, MN (township) Nobles County	5	1.91
Fremont, MN (township) Winona County	7	1.90
Glencoe, WI (town) Buffalo County	9	1.89
Elgin, MN (township) Wabasha County	14	1.83
Glasgow, MN (township) Wabasha County	6	1.82
Manyaska, MN (township) Martin County	6	1.82
Oyens, IA (city) Plymouth County	1	1.82
Bondin, MN (township) Murray County	5	1.81
Solomons, MD (cdp) Calvert County	36	1.79
Hazelhurst, WI (town) Oneida County	24	1.79
Sutherland, IA (city) O'Brien County	11	1.78
Billings, OK (town) Noble County	7	1.78
Bayview, WI (town) Bayfield County	10	1.76
Sherman, WI (town) Iron County	6	1.74
Rushford, MN (city) Fillmore County	36	1.71
Union, WA (cdp) Mason County	9	1.71
Homer, MN (township) Winona County	23	1.69
Hardwick, MN (city) Rock County	3	1.69
Taylors Falls, MN (city) Chisago County	17	1.67
Mazeppa, MN (township) Wabasha County	8	1.66
Eden, WI (village) Fond du Lac County	14	1.64
Dayton, WI (town) Richland County	11	1.64
Orienta, WI (town) Bayfield County	2	1.64
Mount Hope, KS (city) Sedgwick County	13	1.63
Worthington, IA (city) Dubuque County	6	1.62
Prestbury, IL (cdp) Kane County	29	1.60
Cape Royale, TX (cdp) San Jacinto County	6	1.59
Andrew, IA (city) Jackson County	6	1.57
McKinley Heights, OH (cdp) Trumbull County	17	1.56
Charter Oak, IA (city) Crawford County	7	1.56
Hoff, MN (township) Pope County	2	1.56
Oostburg, WI (village) Sheboygan County	44	1.54
Iona, MN (township) Murray County	2	1.53
Kingsley, IA (city) Plymouth County	20	1.52
Clam Falls, WI (town) Polk County	8	1.50
West Bend, IA (city) Palo Alto County	10	1.49
Prairieville, MN (township) Brown County	4	1.49
Opheim, MT (town) Valley County	2	1.49

Ancestry

Luxemburger

Top 150 Places Sorted by Percent of Total Population

Based on places with total population of 7,500 or more

Place	Population	%
Le Mars, IA (city) Plymouth County	419	4.31
Port Washington, WI (city) Ozaukee County	361	3.24
Dubuque, IA (city) Dubuque County	563	0.98
Plymouth, WI (city) Sheboygan County	78	0.93
Richfield, WI (village) Washington County	75	0.67
Lake Elmo, MN (city) Washington County	53	0.67
Winnetka, IL (village) Cook County	79	0.65
Mendota Heights, MN (city) Dakota County	72	0.64
Cedarburg, WI (city) Ozaukee County	69	0.61
McFarland, WI (village) Dane County	46	0.61
Chalco, NE (cdp) Sarpy County	61	0.57
Bothell West, WA (cdp) Snohomish County	84	0.54
La Grange Park, IL (village) Cook County	72	0.54
Sioux City, IA (city) Woodbury County	412	0.50
Winona, MN (city) Winona County	136	0.49
Roselle, IL (village) DuPage County	104	0.46
Sheboygan, WI (city) Sheboygan County	208	0.42
Oregon, WI (village) Dane County	38	0.42
Barrington, IL (village) Cook County	44	0.41
Flushing, MI (city) Genesee County	35	0.41
Robbinsdale, MN (city) Hennepin County	53	0.38
Arden Hills, MN (city) Ramsey County	36	0.38
Shoreline, WA (city) King County	188	0.36
North Aurora, IL (village) Kane County	56	0.36
Pewaukee, WI (city) Waukesha County	47	0.36
Valley Falls, RI (cdp) Providence County	42	0.36
Morton Grove, IL (village) Cook County	80	0.35
Pinole, CA (city) Contra Costa County	64	0.35
North Mankato, MN (city) Nicollet County	46	0.35
Grafton, WI (village) Ozaukee County	40	0.35
Little Chute, WI (village) Outagamie County	37	0.35
College Park, GA (city) Fulton County	47	0.34
Marshall, MN (city) Lyon County	45	0.34
Little Canada, MN (city) Ramsey County	33	0.34
Pewaukee, WI (village) Waukesha County	28	0.34
West Bend, WI (city) Washington County	101	0.33
Marinette, WI (city) Marinette County	37	0.33
Aurora, IL (city) Kane County	608	0.32
Cedar Falls, IA (city) Black Hawk County	124	0.32
Englewood, NJ (city) Bergen County	85	0.32
Brookfield, IL (village) Cook County	60	0.32
Wilton, CT (town) Fairfield County	57	0.32
New River, AZ (cdp) Maricopa County	38	0.32
North St. Paul, MN (city) Ramsey County	36	0.32
Sheboygan Falls, WI (city) Sheboygan County	24	0.32
Tiffin, OH (city) Seneca County	56	0.31
Dranesville, VA (cdp) Fairfax County	39	0.31
Worthington, MN (city) Nobles County	38	0.31
Riverside, IL (village) Cook County	27	0.31
Chanhassen, MN (city) Carver County	69	0.30
Greendale, WI (village) Milwaukee County	42	0.30
Black Forest, CO (cdp) El Paso County	40	0.30
Hamilton, PA (township) Franklin County	31	0.30
Lenox, NY (town) Madison County	27	0.30
Rochester, MN (city) Olmsted County	299	0.29
Elmhurst, IL (city) DuPage County	129	0.29
New Brighton, MN (city) Ramsey County	61	0.29
Lake Zurich, IL (village) Lake County	57	0.29
Steubenville, OH (city) Jefferson County	54	0.29
Clarendon Hills, IL (village) DuPage County	24	0.29
East Grand Rapids, MI (city) Kent County	30	0.28
Crookston, MN (city) Polk County	22	0.28
Minnetonka, MN (city) Hennepin County	135	0.27
St. Matthews, KY (city) Jefferson County	47	0.27
Durango, CO (city) La Plata County	45	0.27
Gold Canyon, AZ (cdp) Pinal County	30	0.27
Campton Hills, IL (village) Kane County	29	0.27
Rolling Meadows, IL (city) Cook County	62	0.26
Des Plaines, IL (city) Cook County	144	0.25
Brookings, SD (city) Brookings County	53	0.25
South St. Paul, MN (city) Dakota County	50	0.25
St. Peter, MN (city) Nicollet County	28	0.25
Elk Grove Village, IL (village) Cook County	80	0.24
Shoreview, MN (city) Ramsey County	61	0.24
East Hemet, CA (cdp) Riverside County	48	0.24
Escanaba, MI (city) Delta County	31	0.24
St. Stephens, NC (cdp) Catawba County	22	0.24
Hoquiam, WA (city) Grays Harbor County	21	0.24
Glen Ellyn, IL (village) DuPage County	62	0.23
Geneva, IL (city) Kane County	50	0.23
Orono, ME (cdp) Penobscot County	21	0.23
St. Charles, IL (city) Kane County	72	0.22
Woodstock, IL (city) McHenry County	54	0.22
Hastings, MN (city) Dakota County	47	0.22
Wisconsin Rapids, WI (city) Wood County	40	0.22
Yorkville, IL (city) Kendall County	33	0.22
South Fayette, PA (township) Allegheny County	30	0.22
St. Francis, WI (city) Milwaukee County	20	0.22
Orono, ME (town) Penobscot County	21	0.21
Sugar Grove, IL (village) Kane County	17	0.21
Niles, IL (village) Cook County	58	0.20
Muskego, WI (city) Waukesha County	48	0.20
Darien, CT (cdp/town) Fairfield County	41	0.20
Willmar, MN (city) Kandiyohi County	39	0.20
Montgomery, IL (village) Kendall County	32	0.20
Weston, WI (village) Marathon County	29	0.20
Shorewood, WI (village) Milwaukee County	26	0.20
Sauk Rapids, MN (city) Benton County	25	0.20
Cedar Rapids, IA (city) Linn County	233	0.19
St. Cloud, MN (city) Stearns County	121	0.19
Huntley, IL (village) McHenry County	40	0.19
Plymouth, PA (township) Montgomery County	32	0.19
Wood Dale, IL (city) DuPage County	26	0.19
Appleton, WI (city) Calumet County	21	0.19
Storm Lake, IA (city) Buena Vista County	20	0.19
Evanston, IL (city) Cook County	132	0.18
Oak Forest, IL (city) Cook County	50	0.18
Homewood, IL (village) Cook County	34	0.18
Menasha, WI (city) Winnebago County	28	0.18
Nether Providence, PA (township) Delaware County	24	0.18
The Dalles, OR (city) Wasco County	24	0.18
Fairview, OR (city) Multnomah County	15	0.18
Harwood Heights, IL (village) Cook County	15	0.18
Thief River Falls, MN (city) Pennington County	15	0.18
Hoffman Estates, IL (village) Cook County	86	0.17
Urbandale, IA (city) Polk County	63	0.17
Fort Lee, NJ (borough) Bergen County	61	0.17
Webster Groves, MO (city) St. Louis County	38	0.17
Point Pleasant, NJ (borough) Ocean County	32	0.17
La Grange, IL (village) Cook County	27	0.17
Fairhope, AL (city) Baldwin County	26	0.17
Fox Lake, IL (village) Lake County	18	0.17
Blackhawk, CA (cdp) Contra Costa County	16	0.17
Boulder Hill, IL (cdp) Kendall County	15	0.17
George Mason, VA (cdp) Fairfax County	15	0.17
Saddlebrooke, AZ (cdp) Pinal County	15	0.17
Arlington Heights, IL (village) Cook County	122	0.16
Ames, IA (city) Story County	93	0.16
St. Cloud, MN (city) Stearns County	83	0.16
Wauwatosa, WI (city) Milwaukee County	73	0.16
Orangevale, CA (cdp) Sacramento County	56	0.16
Anniston, AL (city) Calhoun County	37	0.16
Lake Forest, IL (city) Lake County	31	0.16
Coralville, IA (city) Johnson County	30	0.16
Stillwater, MN (city) Washington County	29	0.16
Menasha, WI (city) Winnebago County	28	0.16
Waunakee, WI (village) Dane County	19	0.16
Olympia Heights, FL (cdp) Miami-Dade County	18	0.16
Calumet Park, IL (village) Cook County	13	0.16
Decorah, IA (city) Winneshiek County	13	0.16
McGregor, FL (cdp) Lee County	12	0.16
Coconut Creek, FL (city) Broward County	78	0.15
St. Louis Park, MN (city) Hennepin County	68	0.15
Shakopee, MN (city) Scott County	53	0.15
Franklin, WI (city) Milwaukee County	50	0.15
Mahwah, NJ (township) Bergen County	39	0.15
Owatonna, MN (city) Steele County	38	0.15
Western Springs, IL (village) Cook County	19	0.15
Terryville, NY (cdp) Suffolk County	18	0.15
Chatham, NJ (township) Morris County	16	0.15

Please refer to the Explanation of Data in the front of the book for more detailed information.

SECTION THREE

Ancestry

Macedonian

U.S. and 50 States Sorted by Population and Percent of Total Population

Place	Population	%
United States	**52,386**	**0.02**
Michigan	10,155	0.10
New York	7,783	0.04
Indiana	5,064	0.08
New Jersey	4,858	0.06
Ohio	4,613	0.04
Illinois	4,372	0.03
California	2,776	0.01
Florida	2,426	0.01
Pennsylvania	1,117	0.01
Texas	1,066	<0.01
Connecticut	910	0.03
Virginia	676	0.01
Massachusetts	618	0.01
Missouri	615	0.01
Nevada	567	0.02
Wisconsin	554	0.01
Arizona	542	0.01
Oregon	311	0.01
Colorado	291	0.01
North Carolina	269	<0.01
Washington	258	<0.01
Minnesota	243	<0.01
New Mexico	238	0.01
Georgia	230	<0.01
Alaska	215	0.03
Maryland	195	<0.01
Kansas	193	0.01
South Carolina	182	<0.01
Tennessee	127	<0.01
District of Columbia	125	0.02
Alabama	101	<0.01
Oklahoma	93	<0.01
Maine	67	0.01
Hawaii	62	<0.01
Louisiana	58	<0.01
Mississippi	55	<0.01
Kentucky	54	<0.01
West Virginia	47	<0.01
Iowa	46	<0.01
Arkansas	42	<0.01
Nebraska	40	<0.01
Utah	33	<0.01
South Dakota	32	<0.01
Idaho	17	<0.01
Vermont	15	<0.01
Delaware	13	<0.01
Wyoming	10	<0.01
Montana	8	<0.01
North Dakota	4	<0.01
New Hampshire	0	0.00
Rhode Island	0	0.00

Place	Population	%
Michigan	10,155	0.10
Indiana	5,064	0.08
New Jersey	4,858	0.06
New York	7,783	0.04
Ohio	4,613	0.04
Illinois	4,372	0.03
Connecticut	910	0.03
Alaska	215	0.03
United States	**52,386**	**0.02**
Nevada	567	0.02
District of Columbia	125	0.02
California	2,776	0.01
Florida	2,426	0.01
Pennsylvania	1,117	0.01
Virginia	676	0.01
Massachusetts	618	0.01
Missouri	615	0.01
Wisconsin	554	0.01
Arizona	542	0.01
Oregon	311	0.01
Colorado	291	0.01
New Mexico	238	0.01
Kansas	193	0.01
Maine	67	0.01
Texas	1,066	<0.01
North Carolina	269	<0.01
Washington	258	<0.01
Minnesota	243	<0.01
Georgia	230	<0.01
Maryland	195	<0.01
South Carolina	182	<0.01
Tennessee	127	<0.01
Alabama	101	<0.01
Oklahoma	93	<0.01
Hawaii	62	<0.01
Louisiana	58	<0.01
Mississippi	55	<0.01
Kentucky	54	<0.01
West Virginia	47	<0.01
Iowa	46	<0.01
Arkansas	42	<0.01
Nebraska	40	<0.01
Utah	33	<0.01
South Dakota	32	<0.01
Idaho	17	<0.01
Vermont	15	<0.01
Delaware	13	<0.01
Wyoming	10	<0.01
Montana	8	<0.01
North Dakota	4	<0.01
New Hampshire	0	0.00
Rhode Island	0	0.00

Please refer to the Explanation of Data in the front of the book for more detailed information.

Ancestry

Macedonian

Top 150 Places Sorted by Population

Based on all places, regardless of total population

Place	Population	%
New York, NY (city) Kings County	4,911	0.06
Staten Island, NY (borough) Richmond County	1,590	0.34
Sterling Heights, MI (city) Macomb County	1,382	1.07
Macomb, MI (township) Macomb County	1,123	1.50
Queens, NY (borough) Queens County	1,109	0.05
Manhattan, NY (borough) New York County	1,086	0.07
Crown Point, IN (city) Lake County	901	3.46
Garfield, NJ (city) Bergen County	826	2.74
Shelby, MI (charter township) Macomb County	639	0.88
Bronx, NY (borough) Bronx County	628	0.05
Fort Wayne, IN (city) Allen County	580	0.23
Brooklyn, NY (borough) Kings County	498	0.02
Chicago, IL (city) Cook County	495	0.02
Los Angeles, CA (city) Los Angeles County	473	0.01
Wayne, NJ (township) Passaic County	461	0.85
Waterbury, CT (city/town) New Haven County	403	0.37
Schererville, IN (town) Lake County	401	1.41
Dearborn Heights, MI (city) Wayne County	393	0.68
Bloomingdale, NJ (borough) Passaic County	391	5.16
Winfield, IN (town) Lake County	385	9.73
Washington, MI (township) Macomb County	342	1.41
Mansfield, TX (city) Tarrant County	309	0.61
Columbus, OH (city) Franklin County	307	0.04
Naperville, IL (city) DuPage County	295	0.21
Livonia, MI (city) Wayne County	293	0.30
Irondequoit, NY (cdp/town) Monroe County	266	0.52
Indianapolis, IN (city) Marion County	265	0.03
Clinton, MI (charter township) Macomb County	242	0.25
Yonkers, NY (city) Westchester County	236	0.12
Clifton, NJ (city) Passaic County	230	0.28
Skokie, IL (village) Cook County	229	0.36
Fairfield, NJ (township) Essex County	227	3.08
Elmwood Park, NJ (borough) Bergen County	224	1.17
Troy, MI (city) Oakland County	223	0.28
Brunswick, OH (city) Medina County	222	0.65
Hobart, IN (city) Lake County	221	0.78
Rochester Hills, MI (city) Oakland County	217	0.31
Willowbrook, IL (village) DuPage County	214	2.50
Streamwood, IL (village) Cook County	204	0.52
Affton, MO (cdp) St. Louis County	194	0.96
Battle Creek, MI (city) Calhoun County	194	0.37
Clay, NY (town) Onondaga County	185	0.32
Albuquerque, NM (city) Bernalillo County	183	0.03
Wyoming, MI (city) Kent County	182	0.25
Portage, IN (city) Porter County	181	0.50
New Rochelle, NY (city) Westchester County	177	0.23
Paterson, NJ (city) Passaic County	175	0.12
Commerce, MI (charter township) Oakland County	174	0.44
Wheeler, IN (cdp) Porter County	172	38.22
Darien, IL (city) DuPage County	169	0.76
Dearborn, MI (city) Wayne County	165	0.17
Merrillville, IN (town) Lake County	158	0.46
San Francisco, CA (city) San Francisco County	156	0.02
Villas, NJ (cdp) Cape May County	150	1.59
Lower, NJ (township) Cape May County	150	0.66
Hamburg, NY (town) Erie County	149	0.26
Granite City, IL (city) Madison County	148	0.49
Tyrone, MI (township) Livingston County	147	1.47
Chesterfield, MI (township) Macomb County	146	0.34
Parsippany-Troy Hills, NJ (township) Morris County	146	0.28
Munster, IN (town) Lake County	145	0.62
Northville, MI (township) Wayne County	145	0.53
Springfield, OH (city) Clark County	145	0.24
Woodridge, IL (village) DuPage County	139	0.43
South River, NJ (borough) Middlesex County	137	0.86
La Grange, IL (village) Cook County	128	0.83
Carlsbad, CA (city) San Diego County	127	0.13
Milwaukee, WI (city) Milwaukee County	127	0.02
Phoenix, AZ (city) Maricopa County	127	0.01
New Baltimore, MI (city) Macomb County	126	1.11
Blackman, MI (charter township) Jackson County	126	0.52
Plymouth, MI (charter township) Wayne County	126	0.46
Madison, WI (city) Dane County	126	0.05
Las Vegas, NV (city) Clark County	126	0.02
Downers Grove, IL (village) DuPage County	125	0.26
Washington, DC (city) District of Columbia	125	0.02
White Oak, OH (cdp) Hamilton County	123	0.65
Johnstown, OH (village) Licking County	122	2.47
Wixom, MI (city) Oakland County	119	0.88
Greece, NY (town) Monroe County	119	0.12
Shorewood Forest, IN (cdp) Porter County	118	3.91
Gresham, OR (city) Multnomah County	118	0.12
Oakland, MI (charter township) Oakland County	116	0.72
Pickerington, OH (city) Fairfield County	116	0.68
Rockford, IL (city) Winnebago County	116	0.08
Warren, MI (city) Macomb County	114	0.08
Canton, MI (charter township) Wayne County	113	0.13
Green Oak, MI (township) Livingston County	112	0.64
Bailey's Crossroads, VA (cdp) Fairfax County	112	0.54
St. John, IN (town) Lake County	109	0.79
Enterprise, NV (cdp) Clark County	107	0.11
Carmel, IN (city) Hamilton County	104	0.14
Princeton Meadows, NJ (cdp) Middlesex County	103	0.75
Plainsboro, NJ (township) Middlesex County	103	0.46
Gahanna, OH (city) Franklin County	103	0.32
Lawrence, IN (city) Marion County	103	0.23
Seattle, WA (city) King County	102	0.02
Totowa, NJ (borough) Passaic County	100	0.94
Lorain, OH (city) Lorain County	97	0.15
Mishawaka, IN (city) St. Joseph County	96	0.20
Valparaiso, IN (city) Porter County	95	0.31
Elyria, OH (city) Lorain County	95	0.17
Wanaque, NJ (borough) Passaic County	94	0.86
Lincoln Park, NJ (borough) Morris County	93	0.87
Richmond, IN (city) Wayne County	93	0.25
Anchorage, AK (municipality) Anchorage Municipality	90	0.03
Topeka, KS (city) Shawnee County	89	0.07
West Milford, NJ (township) Passaic County	87	0.34
Anaheim, CA (city) Orange County	87	0.03
Henderson, NV (city) Clark County	87	0.03
Larkspur, CA (city) Marin County	85	0.72
St. Clair Shores, MI (city) Macomb County	84	0.14
Plainfield, IL (village) Will County	83	0.23
West Springfield Town, MA (city) Hampden County	82	0.29
Miami, FL (city) Miami-Dade County	82	0.02
Pompton Lakes, NJ (borough) Passaic County	81	0.74
Jersey City, NJ (city) Hudson County	81	0.03
Kinnelon, NJ (borough) Morris County	80	0.79
Grand Blanc, MI (charter township) Genesee County	80	0.22
Bartlett, IL (village) DuPage County	80	0.20
Webster, NY (town) Monroe County	80	0.19
Lakes of the Four Seasons, IN (cdp) Lake County	79	1.05
Vienna, VA (town) Fairfax County	79	0.51
Denver, CO (city) Denver County	78	0.01
Rochester, MI (city) Oakland County	77	0.63
Allen Park, MI (city) Wayne County	77	0.27
Brookfield, CT (town) Fairfield County	76	0.47
Norwalk, OH (city) Huron County	76	0.45
Passaic, NJ (city) Passaic County	76	0.11
Paradise, NV (cdp) Clark County	76	0.03
Austin, TX (city) Travis County	76	0.01
Genoa, MI (township) Livingston County	75	0.38
Orland Park, IL (village) Cook County	75	0.14
Norridge, IL (village) Cook County	74	0.51
Mack, OH (cdp) Hamilton County	72	0.63
Columbia, MO (city) Boone County	71	0.07
Rolling Meadows, IL (city) Cook County	70	0.30
Palm Coast, FL (city) Flagler County	70	0.10
Lynchburg, VA (ind. city) Lynchburg independent city	70	0.09
Dallas, TX (city) Dallas County	70	0.01
Harper Woods, MI (city) Wayne County	69	0.48
Hackensack, NJ (city) Bergen County	69	0.16
Egg Harbor, NJ (township) Atlantic County	68	0.16
Reno, NV (city) Washoe County	68	0.03
Syracuse, NY (city) Onondaga County	67	0.05
Summit, MI (township) Jackson County	66	0.29
Trumbull, CT (cdp/town) Fairfield County	65	0.18
Middletown, CT (city/town) Middlesex County	65	0.14
San Jose, CA (city) Santa Clara County	65	0.01
Stickney, IL (village) Cook County	64	0.97

Ancestry

Macedonian

Top 150 Places Sorted by Percent of Total Population

Based on all places, regardless of total population

Place	Population	%
Wheeler, IN (cdp) Porter County	172	38.22
Emmett, KS (city) Pottawatomie County	32	12.50
Winfield, IN (town) Lake County	385	9.73
Sunset Bay, NY (cdp) Chautauqua County	50	5.55
Bloomingdale, NJ (borough) Passaic County	391	5.16
Southwest Harbor, ME (cdp) Hancock County	30	4.37
Shorewood Forest, IN (cdp) Porter County	118	3.91
West Manchester, OH (village) Preble County	17	3.82
Crown Point, IN (city) Lake County	901	3.46
Fairfield, NJ (township) Essex County	227	3.08
Brewster, MA (cdp) Barnstable County	59	2.80
Garfield, NJ (city) Bergen County	826	2.74
Hannibal, NY (village) Oswego County	15	2.65
Andrew, IA (city) Jackson County	10	2.62
Willowbrook, IL (village) DuPage County	214	2.50
Bromley, KY (city) Kenton County	14	2.50
Johnstown, OH (village) Licking County	122	2.47
Onota, MI (township) Alger County	7	2.41
Kistler, PA (borough) Mifflin County	8	2.11
Laurel Hill, FL (city) Okaloosa County	12	2.00
Krakow, WI (cdp) Shawano County	7	1.97
Nocatee, FL (cdp) St. Johns County	63	1.94
Juniata, PA (township) Huntingdon County	10	1.91
Village of Grosse Pointe Shores, MI (city) Wayne County	54	1.86
Village of Grosse Pointe Shores, MI (city) Wayne County	54	1.81
Southwest Harbor, ME (town) Hancock County	30	1.74
Reeder, MI (township) Missaukee County	19	1.69
Novi, MI (township) Oakland County	2	1.67
Villas, NJ (cdp) Cape May County	150	1.59
Cold Brook, NY (village) Herkimer County	6	1.59
North Lakeport, CA (cdp) Lake County	56	1.58
Towamensing Trails, PA (cdp) Carbon County	10	1.56
Macomb, MI (township) Macomb County	1,123	1.50
Seabeck, WA (cdp) Kitsap County	12	1.50
Ashley, IL (city) Washington County	8	1.48
Tyrone, MI (township) Livingston County	147	1.47
Au Gres, MI (township) Arenac County	14	1.46
Shannon, IL (village) Carroll County	13	1.42
Schererville, IN (town) Lake County	401	1.41
Washington, MI (township) Macomb County	342	1.41
Lake Mohawk, OH (cdp) Carroll County	24	1.38
East Jordan, MI (city) Charlevoix County	26	1.35
Cedar Lake, WI (town) Barron County	13	1.30
Village Green, NY (cdp) Onondaga County	56	1.25
Chappaqua, NY (cdp) Westchester County	13	1.25
White City, IL (village) Macoupin County	3	1.21
Union Vale, NY (town) Dutchess County	57	1.18
Elmwood Park, NJ (borough) Bergen County	224	1.17
Northville, MI (city) Oakland County	38	1.16
Lake Fenton, MI (cdp) Genesee County	60	1.13
New Baltimore, MI (city) Macomb County	126	1.11
Riga, NY (town) Monroe County	61	1.10
Sterling Heights, MI (city) Macomb County	1,382	1.07
Lakes of the Four Seasons, IN (cdp) Lake County	79	1.05
Orbisonia, PA (borough) Huntingdon County	8	1.02
Black Lick, PA (township) Indiana County	12	1.01
Third Lake, IL (village) Lake County	15	1.00
Stickney, IL (village) Cook County	64	0.97
Affton, MO (cdp) St. Louis County	194	0.96
Mancos, CO (town) Montezuma County	10	0.95
Reed Point, MT (cdp) Stillwater County	2	0.95
Totowa, NJ (borough) Passaic County	100	0.94
Lewistown, IL (city) Fulton County	21	0.94
Brockway, MI (township) St. Clair County	19	0.94
Broadview, MT (town) Yellowstone County	2	0.93
Bingham Farms, MI (village) Oakland County	10	0.92
Countryside, IL (city) Cook County	53	0.91
Rives, MI (township) Jackson County	42	0.89
Shelby, MI (charter township) Macomb County	639	0.88
Wixom, MI (city) Oakland County	119	0.88
Olivet, MI (city) Eaton County	14	0.88
Alanson, MI (village) Emmet County	6	0.88
Lincoln Park, NJ (borough) Morris County	93	0.87
South River, NJ (borough) Middlesex County	137	0.86
Wanaque, NJ (borough) Passaic County	94	0.86
Angola on the Lake, NY (cdp) Erie County	12	0.86
Wayne, NJ (township) Passaic County	461	0.85
West Middlesex, PA (borough) Mercer County	7	0.85
Shenango, PA (township) Mercer County	33	0.84
La Grange, IL (village) Cook County	128	0.83
Churchill, OH (cdp) Trumbull County	22	0.83
Marietta-Alderwood, WA (cdp) Whatcom County	34	0.82
Fulton, IL (city) Whiteside County	29	0.81
Shawneetown, IL (city) Gallatin County	9	0.81
Milton, WI (city) Rock County	44	0.80
St. John, IN (town) Lake County	109	0.79
Kinnelon, NJ (borough) Morris County	80	0.79
Thomson, MN (township) Carlton County	39	0.79
Boylston, MA (town) Worcester County	34	0.79
Hobart, IN (city) Lake County	221	0.78
Pulaski, NY (village) Oswego County	19	0.78
Darien, IL (city) DuPage County	169	0.76
Divernon, IL (village) Sangamon County	10	0.76
Dune Acres, IN (town) Porter County	2	0.76
Princeton Meadows, NJ (cdp) Middlesex County	103	0.75
Puako, HI (cdp) Hawaii County	7	0.75
Pompton Lakes, NJ (borough) Passaic County	81	0.74
Beverly Shores, IN (town) Porter County	5	0.74
Oakland, MI (charter township) Oakland County	116	0.72
Larkspur, CA (city) Marin County	85	0.72
Resort, MI (township) Emmet County	19	0.71
Filer, ID (city) Twin Falls County	17	0.71
Sigel, WI (town) Chippewa County	7	0.71
Grimes, AL (town) Dale County	3	0.71
Hanover, NY (town) Chautauqua County	50	0.70
Elmwood, MI (township) Tuscola County	8	0.70
Paw Paw, MI (village) Van Buren County	24	0.69
Ford City, PA (borough) Armstrong County	21	0.69
Dearborn Heights, MI (city) Wayne County	393	0.68
Pickerington, OH (city) Fairfield County	116	0.68
Zeeland, MI (city) Ottawa County	38	0.68
Sunnyslope, WA (cdp) Chelan County	23	0.67
Liberty, MI (township) Wexford County	6	0.67
Bearinger, MI (township) Presque Isle County	2	0.67
Lower, NJ (township) Cape May County	150	0.66
Wyoming, WI (town) Iowa County	2	0.66
Brunswick, OH (city) Medina County	222	0.65
White Oak, OH (cdp) Hamilton County	123	0.65
Green Oak, MI (township) Livingston County	112	0.64
Greene, PA (township) Mercer County	8	0.64
Rochester, MI (city) Oakland County	77	0.63
Mack, OH (cdp) Hamilton County	72	0.63
Northville, MI (city) Oakland County	38	0.63
Munster, IN (town) Lake County	145	0.62
Ellwood City, PA (borough) Lawrence County	46	0.62
New Albany, OH (village) Franklin County	44	0.62
South Run, VA (cdp) Fairfax County	42	0.62
Poland, OH (village) Mahoning County	16	0.62
Mansfield, TX (city) Tarrant County	309	0.61
Grand Blanc, MI (city) Genesee County	51	0.61
Spring Arbor, MI (township) Jackson County	50	0.61
Hayes, MI (township) Otsego County	16	0.61
Brewster, MA (town) Barnstable County	59	0.60
Staunton, IL (city) Macoupin County	29	0.60
Southern Shores, NC (town) Dare County	16	0.60
Country Club, MO (village) Andrew County	13	0.59
Bells, TX (town) Grayson County	10	0.59
Windsor, MI (charter township) Eaton County	40	0.58
Marcellus, NY (town) Onondaga County	36	0.58
Conway, MI (township) Livingston County	20	0.57
North River Shores, FL (cdp) Martin County	20	0.57
St. James, NC (town) Brunswick County	16	0.57
Franklin, CT (town) New London County	11	0.57
Minerva Park, OH (village) Franklin County	7	0.57
Powell, OH (city) Delaware County	60	0.56
Ellwood City, PA (borough) Lawrence County	46	0.56
Sheffield, OH (village) Lorain County	21	0.56
Hebron, PA (township) Potter County	4	0.56
Pigeon Creek, OH (cdp) Summit County	4	0.56
Schiller Park, IL (village) Cook County	64	0.55

Please refer to the Explanation of Data in the front of the book for more detailed information.

Ancestry

Macedonian

Top 150 Places Sorted by Percent of Total Population

Based on places with total population of 7,500 or more

Place	Population	%
Bloomingdale, NJ (borough) Passaic County	391	5.16
Crown Point, IN (city) Lake County	901	3.46
Garfield, NJ (city) Bergen County	826	2.74
Willowbrook, IL (village) DuPage County	214	2.50
Villas, NJ (cdp) Cape May County	150	1.59
Macomb, MI (township) Macomb County	1,123	1.50
Tyrone, MI (township) Livingston County	147	1.47
Schererville, IN (town) Lake County	401	1.41
Washington, MI (township) Macomb County	342	1.41
Elmwood Park, NJ (borough) Bergen County	224	1.17
New Baltimore, MI (city) Macomb County	126	1.11
Sterling Heights, MI (city) Macomb County	1,382	1.07
Lakes of the Four Seasons, IN (cdp) Lake County	79	1.05
Affton, MO (cdp) St. Louis County	194	0.96
Totowa, NJ (borough) Passaic County	100	0.94
Shelby, MI (charter township) Macomb County	639	0.88
Wixom, MI (city) Oakland County	119	0.88
Lincoln Park, NJ (borough) Morris County	93	0.87
South River, NJ (borough) Middlesex County	137	0.86
Wanaque, NJ (borough) Passaic County	94	0.86
Wayne, NJ (township) Passaic County	461	0.85
La Grange, IL (village) Cook County	128	0.83
St. John, IN (town) Lake County	109	0.79
Kinnelon, NJ (borough) Morris County	80	0.79
Hobart, IN (city) Lake County	221	0.78
Darien, IL (city) DuPage County	169	0.76
Princeton Meadows, NJ (cdp) Middlesex County	103	0.75
Pompton Lakes, NJ (borough) Passaic County	81	0.74
Oakland, MI (charter township) Oakland County	116	0.72
Larkspur, CA (city) Marin County	85	0.72
Dearborn Heights, MI (city) Wayne County	393	0.68
Pickerington, OH (city) Fairfield County	116	0.68
Lower, NJ (township) Cape May County	150	0.66
Brunswick, OH (city) Medina County	222	0.65
White Oak, OH (cdp) Hamilton County	123	0.65
Green Oak, MI (township) Livingston County	112	0.64
Rochester, MI (city) Oakland County	77	0.63
Mack, OH (cdp) Hamilton County	72	0.63
Munster, IN (town) Lake County	145	0.62
Mansfield, TX (city) Tarrant County	309	0.61
Grand Blanc, MI (city) Genesee County	51	0.61
Spring Arbor, MI (township) Jackson County	50	0.61
Brewster, MA (town) Barnstable County	59	0.60
Powell, OH (city) Delaware County	60	0.56
Ellwood City, PA (borough) Lawrence County	46	0.56
Schiller Park, IL (village) Cook County	64	0.55
Bailey's Crossroads, VA (cdp) Fairfax County	112	0.54
Northville, MI (township) Wayne County	145	0.53
Butler, NJ (borough) Morris County	40	0.53
Irondequoit, NY (cdp/town) Monroe County	266	0.52
Streamwood, IL (village) Cook County	204	0.52
Blackman, MI (charter township) Jackson County	126	0.52
Vienna, VA (town) Fairfax County	79	0.51
Norridge, IL (village) Cook County	74	0.51
Portage, IN (city) Porter County	181	0.50
Granite City, IL (city) Madison County	148	0.49
Harper Woods, MI (city) Wayne County	69	0.48
Emmett, MI (charter township) Calhoun County	57	0.48
Lakes, AK (cdp) Matanuska-Susitna Borough	44	0.48
Hubbard, OH (city) Trumbull County	38	0.48
Brookfield, CT (town) Fairfield County	76	0.47
Merrillville, IN (town) Lake County	158	0.46
Plymouth, MI (charter township) Wayne County	126	0.46
Plainsboro, NJ (township) Middlesex County	103	0.46
Norwalk, OH (city) Huron County	76	0.45
Commerce, MI (charter township) Oakland County	174	0.44
Woodridge, IL (village) DuPage County	139	0.43
Van Buren, NY (town) Onondaga County	56	0.43
Hasbrouck Heights, NJ (borough) Bergen County	50	0.43
Plymouth, MI (city) Wayne County	39	0.43
Monona, WI (city) Dane County	32	0.42
Cheval, FL (cdp) Hillsborough County	41	0.40
Clarendon Hills, IL (village) DuPage County	33	0.40
Fenton, MI (charter township) Genesee County	60	0.39
Roselle Park, NJ (borough) Union County	51	0.39
Sierra Madre, CA (city) Los Angeles County	42	0.39
Sitka, AK (borough) Sitka City and Borough	35	0.39
Genoa, MI (township) Livingston County	75	0.38
Sheffield Lake, OH (city) Lorain County	35	0.38
Chatham, NJ (borough) Morris County	34	0.38
Concord, NY (town) Erie County	32	0.38
Waterbury, CT (city/town) New Haven County	403	0.37
Battle Creek, MI (city) Calhoun County	194	0.37
Hopatcong, NJ (borough) Sussex County	57	0.37
Lambertville, MI (cdp) Monroe County	38	0.37
Bruce, MI (township) Macomb County	32	0.37
Skokie, IL (village) Cook County	229	0.36
Bridgeview, IL (village) Cook County	56	0.35
North Strabane, PA (township) Washington County	45	0.35
Staten Island, NY (borough) Richmond County	1,590	0.34
Chesterfield, MI (township) Macomb County	146	0.34
West Milford, NJ (township) Passaic County	87	0.34
Easttown, PA (township) Chester County	35	0.33
Camp Hill, PA (borough) Cumberland County	26	0.33
Clay, NY (town) Onondaga County	185	0.32
Gahanna, OH (city) Franklin County	103	0.32
Hunters Creek, FL (cdp) Orange County	46	0.32
Rochester Hills, MI (city) Oakland County	217	0.31
Valparaiso, IN (city) Porter County	95	0.31
Bethany, OK (city) Oklahoma County	60	0.31
Mamakating, NY (town) Sullivan County	37	0.31
Webster, MA (cdp) Worcester County	35	0.31
Briarcliff Manor, NY (village) Westchester County	25	0.31
Livonia, MI (city) Wayne County	293	0.30
Rolling Meadows, IL (city) Cook County	70	0.30
Hampton, PA (township) Allegheny County	54	0.30
Farmington, NY (town) Ontario County	35	0.30
West Springfield Town, MA (city) Hampden County	82	0.29
Summit, MI (township) Jackson County	66	0.29
Clifton, NJ (city) Passaic County	230	0.28
Troy, MI (city) Oakland County	223	0.28
Parsippany-Troy Hills, NJ (township) Morris County	146	0.28
Pecan Grove, TX (cdp) Fort Bend County	45	0.28
Keansburg, NJ (borough) Monmouth County	29	0.28
Allen Park, MI (city) Wayne County	77	0.27
Brighton, MI (township) Livingston County	49	0.27
Springfield, MI (charter township) Oakland County	38	0.27
Babylon, NY (village) Suffolk County	33	0.27
Somers Point, NJ (city) Atlantic County	30	0.27
Corrales, NM (village) Sandoval County	22	0.27
Highland Heights, OH (city) Cuyahoga County	22	0.27
Hamburg, NY (town) Erie County	149	0.26
Downers Grove, IL (village) DuPage County	125	0.26
Sodus, NY (town) Wayne County	22	0.26
Clinton, MI (charter township) Macomb County	242	0.25
Wyoming, MI (city) Kent County	182	0.25
Richmond, IN (city) Wayne County	93	0.25
Parkland, FL (city) Broward County	56	0.25
New Fairfield, CT (town) Fairfield County	35	0.25
Springfield, OH (city) Clark County	145	0.24
Allison Park, PA (cdp) Allegheny County	54	0.24
Ogden, NY (town) Monroe County	47	0.24
Wolcott, CT (town) New Haven County	40	0.24
Montgomery, IL (village) Kendall County	38	0.24
Fort Wayne, IN (city) Allen County	580	0.23
New Rochelle, NY (city) Westchester County	177	0.23
Lawrence, IN (city) Marion County	103	0.23
Plainfield, IL (village) Will County	83	0.23
Kirkwood, MO (city) St. Louis County	63	0.23
Clermont, FL (city) Lake County	60	0.23
Homer Glen, IL (village) Will County	57	0.23
Onondaga, NY (town) Onondaga County	51	0.23
Warrenville, IL (city) DuPage County	31	0.23
Girard, OH (city) Trumbull County	24	0.23
Grand Blanc, MI (charter township) Genesee County	80	0.22
Lodi, NJ (borough) Bergen County	53	0.22
Wayne, MI (city) Wayne County	39	0.22
Little Falls, NJ (township) Passaic County	31	0.22
Naperville, IL (city) DuPage County	295	0.21
Fairview Park, OH (city) Cuyahoga County	36	0.21

Please refer to the Explanation of Data in the front of the book for more detailed information.

Ancestry

Maltese

U.S. and 50 States Sorted by Population and Percent of Total Population

Place	Population	%
United States	**43,082**	**0.01**
Michigan	12,447	0.13
New York	7,645	0.04
California	7,582	0.02
Florida	2,930	0.02
New Jersey	1,562	0.02
Texas	1,084	<0.01
Arizona	985	0.02
Nevada	712	0.03
Pennsylvania	703	0.01
Washington	663	0.01
North Carolina	623	0.01
Ohio	516	<0.01
Virginia	510	0.01
Connecticut	463	0.01
Colorado	430	0.01
Massachusetts	379	0.01
Illinois	356	<0.01
Georgia	329	<0.01
Maryland	274	<0.01
Oregon	230	0.01
South Carolina	210	<0.01
Indiana	197	<0.01
Hawaii	176	0.01
Alaska	169	0.02
New Hampshire	157	0.01
Oklahoma	134	<0.01
Utah	131	<0.01
Missouri	126	<0.01
Maine	123	0.01
Alabama	122	<0.01
Tennessee	113	<0.01
Minnesota	104	<0.01
Kentucky	100	<0.01
Idaho	94	0.01
Mississippi	85	<0.01
Rhode Island	65	0.01
Delaware	63	0.01
Nebraska	62	<0.01
Wisconsin	61	<0.01
Louisiana	59	<0.01
Kansas	50	<0.01
Montana	49	0.01
Arkansas	48	<0.01
Iowa	43	<0.01
West Virginia	32	<0.01
District of Columbia	24	<0.01
Vermont	23	<0.01
New Mexico	20	<0.01
South Dakota	19	<0.01
North Dakota	0	0.00
Wyoming	0	0.00

Place	Population	%
Michigan	12,447	0.13
New York	7,645	0.04
Nevada	712	0.03
California	7,582	0.02
Florida	2,930	0.02
New Jersey	1,562	0.02
Arizona	985	0.02
Alaska	169	0.02
United States	**43,082**	**0.01**
Pennsylvania	703	0.01
Washington	663	0.01
North Carolina	623	0.01
Virginia	510	0.01
Connecticut	463	0.01
Colorado	430	0.01
Massachusetts	379	0.01
Oregon	230	0.01
Hawaii	176	0.01
New Hampshire	157	0.01
Maine	123	0.01
Idaho	94	0.01
Rhode Island	65	0.01
Delaware	63	0.01
Montana	49	0.01
Texas	1,084	<0.01
Ohio	516	<0.01
Illinois	356	<0.01
Georgia	329	<0.01
Maryland	274	<0.01
South Carolina	210	<0.01
Indiana	197	<0.01
Oklahoma	134	<0.01
Utah	131	<0.01
Missouri	126	<0.01
Alabama	122	<0.01
Tennessee	113	<0.01
Minnesota	104	<0.01
Kentucky	100	<0.01
Mississippi	85	<0.01
Nebraska	62	<0.01
Wisconsin	61	<0.01
Louisiana	59	<0.01
Kansas	50	<0.01
Arkansas	48	<0.01
Iowa	43	<0.01
West Virginia	32	<0.01
District of Columbia	24	<0.01
Vermont	23	<0.01
New Mexico	20	<0.01
South Dakota	19	<0.01
North Dakota	0	0.00
Wyoming	0	0.00

Please refer to the Explanation of Data in the front of the book for more detailed information.

Ancestry

Maltese

Top 150 Places Sorted by Population

Based on all places, regardless of total population

Place	Population	%
New York, NY (city) Kings County	3,102	0.04
Queens, NY (borough) Queens County	1,565	0.07
Livonia, MI (city) Wayne County	845	0.86
Manhattan, NY (borough) New York County	840	0.05
Brookhaven, NY (town) Suffolk County	686	0.14
Dearborn, MI (city) Wayne County	662	0.67
San Francisco, CA (city) San Francisco County	608	0.08
Oyster Bay, NY (town) Nassau County	579	0.20
Hempstead, NY (town) Nassau County	540	0.07
Redford, MI (charter township) Wayne County	432	0.88
Babylon, NY (town) Suffolk County	378	0.18
Canton, MI (charter township) Wayne County	366	0.42
Las Vegas, NV (city) Clark County	365	0.06
Brooklyn, NY (borough) Kings County	362	0.01
Taylor, MI (city) Wayne County	342	0.54
Warren, MI (city) Macomb County	320	0.24
Islip, NY (town) Suffolk County	292	0.09
Staten Island, NY (borough) Richmond County	290	0.06
Westland, MI (city) Wayne County	287	0.34
Dearborn Heights, MI (city) Wayne County	286	0.49
Los Angeles, CA (city) Los Angeles County	279	0.01
San Bruno, CA (city) San Mateo County	275	0.68
Detroit, MI (city) Wayne County	266	0.04
West Babylon, NY (cdp) Suffolk County	252	0.57
North Hempstead, NY (town) Nassau County	248	0.11
Sterling Heights, MI (city) Macomb County	235	0.18
Allen Park, MI (city) Wayne County	232	0.81
Garden City, MI (city) Wayne County	228	0.81
Rochester Hills, MI (city) Oakland County	221	0.31
East Patchogue, NY (cdp) Suffolk County	220	1.04
Farmington Hills, MI (city) Oakland County	220	0.27
Danville, CA (town) Contra Costa County	217	0.52
Phoenix, AZ (city) Maricopa County	217	0.01
Smithtown, NY (town) Suffolk County	206	0.18
East Port Orchard, WA (cdp) Kitsap County	205	3.57
San Mateo, CA (city) San Mateo County	203	0.21
Macomb, MI (township) Macomb County	192	0.26
Millbrae, CA (city) San Mateo County	191	0.91
St. Clair Shores, MI (city) Macomb County	191	0.31
Northville, MI (township) Wayne County	185	0.68
Clinton, MI (charter township) Macomb County	183	0.19
Roseville, CA (city) Placer County	181	0.16
San Jose, CA (city) Santa Clara County	179	0.02
Commerce, MI (charter township) Oakland County	178	0.45
Riverview, MI (city) Wayne County	177	1.40
Green Oak, MI (township) Livingston County	176	1.00
Margate, FL (city) Broward County	171	0.32
Concord, CA (city) Contra Costa County	166	0.14
Scottsdale, AZ (city) Maricopa County	165	0.08
Lake Morton-Berrydale, WA (cdp) King County	164	1.69
Mesa, AZ (city) Maricopa County	156	0.04
Charlotte, NC (city) Mecklenburg County	156	0.02
Plainview, NY (cdp) Nassau County	155	0.60
Boardman, OH (cdp) Mahoning County	152	0.43
Miami, FL (city) Miami-Dade County	146	0.04
San Diego, CA (city) San Diego County	146	0.01
West Islip, NY (cdp) Suffolk County	142	0.49
Hicksville, NY (cdp) Nassau County	142	0.34
Colts Neck, NJ (township) Monmouth County	140	1.38
Virginia Beach, VA (ind. city) Virginia Beach independent city	139	0.03
Deerfield Beach, FL (city) Broward County	138	0.18
East Lansing, MI (city) Ingham County	132	0.28
East Lansing, MI (city) Ingham County	132	0.27
Jacksonville, FL (city) Duval County	127	0.02
Half Moon Bay, CA (city) San Mateo County	126	1.13
Waterford, MI (charter township) Oakland County	125	0.17
Redwood City, CA (city) San Mateo County	121	0.16
Roseville, MI (city) Macomb County	120	0.25
Novi, MI (city) Oakland County	120	0.22
Hillsborough, CA (town) San Mateo County	116	1.09
Grosse Ile, MI (township) Wayne County	115	1.09
Chesterfield, MI (township) Macomb County	115	0.27
Brighton, MI (township) Livingston County	113	0.62
Brownstown, MI (charter township) Wayne County	110	0.37
Franklin Square, NY (cdp) Nassau County	110	0.37
Lake Ronkonkoma, NY (cdp) Suffolk County	109	0.51
Tucson, AZ (city) Pima County	105	0.02
Hamptonburgh, NY (town) Orange County	103	1.89
Broomfield, CO (city) Broomfield County	102	0.19
Lincoln Park, MI (city) Wayne County	101	0.26
South San Francisco, CA (city) San Mateo County	100	0.16
Spring Hill, FL (cdp) Hernando County	100	0.10
Rochester, NY (city) Monroe County	100	0.05
Petaluma, CA (city) Sonoma County	99	0.17
Genoa, MI (township) Livingston County	96	0.49
Levittown, NY (cdp) Nassau County	96	0.18
South Lyon, MI (city) Oakland County	95	0.86
Bloomfield, MI (charter township) Oakland County	95	0.23
Romulus, MI (city) Wayne County	94	0.39
Riverside, CA (city) Riverside County	94	0.03
Raleigh, NC (city) Wake County	94	0.02
Tuxedo, NY (town) Orange County	93	2.59
East Palo Alto, CA (city) San Mateo County	93	0.33
Elmont, NY (cdp) Nassau County	93	0.27
Ann Arbor, MI (city) Washtenaw County	92	0.08
Troy, MI (city) Oakland County	90	0.11
Drum Point, MD (cdp) Calvert County	89	2.68
Royal Oak, MI (city) Oakland County	88	0.15
Huntington, NY (town) Suffolk County	88	0.04
Houston, TX (city) Harris County	88	<0.01
Winter Gardens, CA (cdp) San Diego County	87	0.43
Harrison, MI (charter township) Macomb County	85	0.34
Orion, MI (charter township) Oakland County	85	0.24
Miller Place, NY (cdp) Suffolk County	84	0.68
North Bellmore, NY (cdp) Nassau County	84	0.43
Pacifica, CA (city) San Mateo County	84	0.23
Plymouth, MI (charter township) Wayne County	81	0.29
Paradise, NV (cdp) Clark County	79	0.04
Montgomery, PA (township) Montgomery County	78	0.32
Carle Place, NY (cdp) Nassau County	77	1.38
Stockton, CA (city) San Joaquin County	77	0.03
Johnson Lane, NV (cdp) Douglas County	74	1.09
Addison, MI (township) Oakland County	73	1.15
San Carlos, CA (city) San Mateo County	73	0.26
Wallingford, CT (town) New Haven County	73	0.16
Chico, CA (city) Butte County	73	0.09
Yonkers, NY (city) Westchester County	73	0.04
Howell, NJ (township) Monmouth County	72	0.14
White Lake, MI (charter township) Oakland County	71	0.24
Portland, OR (city) Multnomah County	71	0.01
Iosco, MI (township) Livingston County	70	1.86
Huron, MI (charter township) Wayne County	70	0.45
Cathedral City, CA (city) Riverside County	70	0.14
Chicago, IL (city) Cook County	70	<0.01
Wyandotte, MI (city) Wayne County	69	0.26
Cypress, CA (city) Orange County	69	0.15
Kapaa, HI (cdp) Kauai County	68	0.68
Massapequa Park, NY (village) Nassau County	68	0.40
Anchorage, AK (municipality) Anchorage Municipality	68	0.02
Enterprise, NV (cdp) Clark County	67	0.07
Hartland, MI (township) Livingston County	66	0.46
Wixom, MI (city) Oakland County	65	0.48
Shelby, MI (charter township) Macomb County	65	0.09
Commack, NY (cdp) Suffolk County	64	0.18
Norwalk, CT (city/town) Fairfield County	64	0.08
Naperville, IL (city) DuPage County	64	0.05
Bohemia, NY (cdp) Suffolk County	63	0.64
Ypsilanti, MI (charter township) Washtenaw County	63	0.12
Plantation, FL (city) Broward County	63	0.07
Melvindale, MI (city) Wayne County	62	0.58
Clayton, CA (city) Contra Costa County	62	0.57
Trenton, MI (city) Wayne County	62	0.33
East Brunswick, NJ (township) Middlesex County	62	0.13
Holtsville, NY (cdp) Suffolk County	61	0.32
Martinez, CA (city) Contra Costa County	61	0.17
Madison, MI (charter township) Lenawee County	60	0.71
Bayonet Point, FL (cdp) Pasco County	60	0.25
Port Huron, MI (city) St. Clair County	60	0.19
Independence, MI (charter township) Oakland County	60	0.17
Old Bridge, NJ (township) Middlesex County	59	0.09

SECTION THREE

Please refer to the Explanation of Data in the front of the book for more detailed information.

Ancestry

Maltese

Top 150 Places Sorted by Percent of Total Population

Based on all places, regardless of total population

Place	Population	%
Wells, MI (township) Marquette County	21	8.86
Walland, TN (cdp) Blount County	13	8.78
Felsenthal, AR (town) Union County	8	7.27
Millen, MI (township) Alcona County	15	5.40
East Port Orchard, WA (cdp) Kitsap County	205	3.57
Pioneer, CA (cdp) Amador County	37	3.40
Wedgewood, MI (cdp) Wexford County	7	3.23
West Falmouth, MA (cdp) Barnstable County	48	3.17
Caseville, MI (village) Huron County	22	3.16
Springdale, MI (township) Manistee County	25	2.74
Drum Point, MD (cdp) Calvert County	89	2.68
Tuxedo, NY (town) Orange County	93	2.59
Wilson, MI (township) Charlevoix County	45	2.35
Trout Lake, MI (township) Chippewa County	9	2.17
Sleepy Hollow, CA (cdp) Marin County	49	2.01
Timber Cove, CA (cdp) Sonoma County	3	2.01
Hamptonburgh, NY (town) Orange County	103	1.89
Iosco, MI (township) Livingston County	70	1.86
Whitefish, MI (township) Chippewa County	10	1.78
Lake Morton-Berrydale, WA (cdp) King County	164	1.69
Grant, MI (township) Grand Traverse County	17	1.64
Alhambra Valley, CA (cdp) Contra Costa County	13	1.58
Knoxville, AR (town) Johnson County	16	1.56
Au Sable, MI (cdp) Iosco County	16	1.45
Plandome Heights, NY (village) Nassau County	15	1.42
Sebewaing, MI (village) Huron County	25	1.41
Riverview, MI (city) Wayne County	177	1.40
Springerville, AZ (town) Apache County	37	1.39
Colts Neck, NJ (township) Monmouth County	140	1.38
Carle Place, NY (cdp) Nassau County	77	1.38
Cazadero, CA (cdp) Sonoma County	5	1.38
Summerfield, MI (township) Monroe County	44	1.32
Marshfield Hills, MA (cdp) Plymouth County	32	1.30
Quentin, PA (cdp) Lebanon County	6	1.24
Ludlow, ME (town) Aroostook County	5	1.23
Logan, MI (township) Mason County	3	1.23
Waretown, NJ (cdp) Ocean County	16	1.21
Lost Lake Woods, MI (cdp) Alcona County	4	1.21
Hillside Lake, NY (cdp) Dutchess County	8	1.17
Addison, MI (township) Oakland County	73	1.15
Anna, IL (city) Union County	53	1.15
Murphys Estates, SC (cdp) Edgefield County	26	1.15
Central Lake, MI (village) Antrim County	12	1.15
Magnolia, DE (town) Kent County	1	1.15
Half Moon Bay, CA (city) San Mateo County	126	1.13
Elk Rapids, MI (village) Antrim County	21	1.13
Wright, NY (town) Schoharie County	21	1.11
Brownville, NJ (cdp) Middlesex County	32	1.10
Hillsborough, CA (town) San Mateo County	116	1.09
Grosse Ile, MI (township) Wayne County	115	1.09
Johnson Lane, NV (cdp) Douglas County	74	1.09
East Patchogue, NY (cdp) Suffolk County	220	1.04
Au Train, MI (township) Alger County	12	1.04
San Antonio Heights, CA (cdp) San Bernardino County	41	1.03
Astatula, FL (town) Lake County	26	1.03
Milton, NY (cdp) Ulster County	12	1.03
Bunker Hill, MI (township) Ingham County	21	1.02
Malcolm, NE (village) Lancaster County	4	1.01
Green Oak, MI (township) Livingston County	176	1.00
Imlay City, MI (city) Lapeer County	37	1.00
Kodiak, AK (city) Kodiak Island Borough	58	0.96
Chelsea, MI (city) Washtenaw County	47	0.96
Horton, MI (township) Ogemaw County	8	0.95
Sparkill, NY (cdp) Rockland County	13	0.94
Manatee Road, FL (cdp) Levy County	20	0.92
Shickshinny, PA (borough) Luzerne County	8	0.92
Millbrae, CA (city) San Mateo County	191	0.91
Wailua Homesteads, HI (cdp) Kauai County	49	0.90
Sebewaing, MI (township) Huron County	25	0.90
Au Sable, MI (charter township) Iosco County	16	0.90
Brewerton, NY (cdp) Onondaga County	36	0.89
Redford, MI (charter township) Wayne County	432	0.88
Mount Ivy, NY (cdp) Rockland County	58	0.88
Manchester, MI (village) Washtenaw County	19	0.88
Kenockee, MI (township) St. Clair County	21	0.87
Livonia, MI (city) Wayne County	845	0.86
South Lyon, MI (city) Oakland County	95	0.86
Caseville, MI (township) Huron County	22	0.85
Potter Valley, CA (cdp) Mendocino County	7	0.85
Fruitport, MI (village) Muskegon County	9	0.84
Boyes Hot Springs, CA (cdp) Sonoma County	57	0.82
Allen Park, MI (city) Wayne County	232	0.81
Garden City, MI (city) Wayne County	228	0.81
Munsons Corners, NY (cdp) Cortland County	22	0.81
Trexlertown, PA (cdp) Lehigh County	15	0.81
Bagley, MI (township) Otsego County	48	0.80
Lake Katrine, NY (cdp) Ulster County	19	0.80
Verdi, NV (cdp) Washoe County	11	0.80
Adrian, MI (township) Lenawee County	47	0.78
Elk Rapids, MI (township) Antrim County	21	0.78
Central Lake, MI (township) Antrim County	19	0.78
Sharon, MI (township) Washtenaw County	14	0.78
Lynn, MI (township) St. Clair County	9	0.78
Bethel Acres, OK (town) Pottawatomie County	22	0.77
Emerson, MI (township) Gratiot County	7	0.76
Pleasant Ridge, MI (city) Oakland County	19	0.74
Palmyra, NY (town) Wayne County	58	0.73
Richmond, MI (city) Macomb County	41	0.73
Richmond, MI (city) Macomb County	41	0.73
Castle Hills, TX (city) Bexar County	30	0.73
Belleville, MI (city) Wayne County	29	0.73
Nunn, CO (town) Weld County	3	0.73
Metamora, MI (village) Lapeer County	4	0.72
Madison, MI (charter township) Lenawee County	60	0.71
Beckett, NJ (cdp) Gloucester County	34	0.71
Evendale, OH (village) Hamilton County	20	0.71
Laureldale, PA (borough) Berks County	27	0.69
San Bruno, CA (city) San Mateo County	275	0.68
Northville, MI (township) Wayne County	185	0.68
Miller Place, NY (cdp) Suffolk County	84	0.68
Kapaa, HI (cdp) Kauai County	68	0.68
Dearborn, MI (city) Wayne County	662	0.67
Copperopolis, CA (cdp) Calaveras County	27	0.67
Centerport, NY (cdp) Suffolk County	37	0.66
Algonac, MI (city) St. Clair County	28	0.66
Crown Heights, NY (cdp) Dutchess County	19	0.66
Hyde Park, NY (cdp) Dutchess County	14	0.66
Penn, PA (township) Chester County	32	0.65
Alfred, NY (village) Allegany County	27	0.65
Milan, MI (township) Monroe County	11	0.65
Big Sky, MT (cdp) Gallatin County	10	0.65
Bohemia, NY (cdp) Suffolk County	63	0.64
Manchester, MI (township) Washtenaw County	29	0.64
Sims, MI (township) Arenac County	7	0.64
Gleneagle, CO (cdp) El Paso County	42	0.63
Pocopson, PA (township) Chester County	28	0.63
East Williston, NY (village) Nassau County	16	0.63
Brighton, MI (township) Livingston County	113	0.62
Centerville, MI (township) Leelanau County	8	0.62
Hubbard Lake, MI (cdp) Alcona County	6	0.62
Wolfforth, TX (city) Lubbock County	21	0.61
Winter Beach, FL (cdp) Indian River County	9	0.61
Plainview, NY (cdp) Nassau County	155	0.60
Salem, MI (township) Washtenaw County	34	0.60
Ballville, OH (cdp) Sandusky County	19	0.60
Penngrove, CA (cdp) Sonoma County	18	0.60
Flemington, NJ (borough) Hunterdon County	27	0.59
Silver Lake, NJ (cdp) Essex County	22	0.59
Clinton, MI (village) Lenawee County	15	0.59
Melvindale, MI (city) Wayne County	62	0.58
Scipio, MI (township) Hillsdale County	11	0.58
West Babylon, NY (cdp) Suffolk County	252	0.57
Clayton, CA (city) Contra Costa County	62	0.57
Krakow, MI (township) Presque Isle County	4	0.57
Logan, NJ (township) Gloucester County	34	0.56
Denton, MI (township) Roscommon County	32	0.56
Oak Ridge North, TX (city) Montgomery County	17	0.56
Crested Butte, CO (town) Gunnison County	8	0.56
East Quogue, NY (cdp) Suffolk County	26	0.55
Village of Clarkston, MI (city) Oakland County	4	0.55

Please refer to the Explanation of Data in the front of the book for more detailed information.

Ancestry

Maltese

Top 150 Places Sorted by Percent of Total Population

Based on places with total population of 7,500 or more

Place	Population	%
Lake Morton-Berrydale, WA (cdp) King County	164	1.69
Riverview, MI (city) Wayne County	177	1.40
Colts Neck, NJ (township) Monmouth County	140	1.38
Half Moon Bay, CA (city) San Mateo County	126	1.13
Hillsborough, CA (town) San Mateo County	116	1.09
Grosse Ile, MI (township) Wayne County	115	1.09
East Patchogue, NY (cdp) Suffolk County	220	1.04
Green Oak, MI (township) Livingston County	176	1.00
Millbrae, CA (city) San Mateo County	191	0.91
Redford, MI (charter township) Wayne County	432	0.88
Livonia, MI (city) Wayne County	845	0.86
South Lyon, MI (city) Oakland County	95	0.86
Allen Park, MI (city) Wayne County	232	0.81
Garden City, MI (city) Wayne County	228	0.81
Palmyra, NY (town) Wayne County	58	0.73
Madison, MI (charter township) Lenawee County	60	0.71
San Bruno, CA (city) San Mateo County	275	0.68
Northville, MI (township) Wayne County	185	0.68
Miller Place, NY (cdp) Suffolk County	84	0.68
Kapaa, HI (cdp) Kauai County	68	0.68
Dearborn, MI (city) Wayne County	662	0.67
Bohemia, NY (cdp) Suffolk County	63	0.64
Brighton, MI (township) Livingston County	113	0.62
Plainview, NY (cdp) Nassau County	155	0.60
Melvindale, MI (city) Wayne County	62	0.58
West Babylon, NY (cdp) Suffolk County	252	0.57
Clayton, CA (city) Contra Costa County	62	0.57
Taylor, MI (city) Wayne County	342	0.54
Plymouth, MI (city) Wayne County	49	0.54
Danville, CA (town) Contra Costa County	217	0.52
Lake Ronkonkoma, NY (cdp) Suffolk County	109	0.51
Dearborn Heights, MI (city) Wayne County	286	0.49
West Islip, NY (cdp) Suffolk County	142	0.49
Genoa, MI (township) Livingston County	96	0.49
Wixom, MI (city) Oakland County	65	0.48
Taft, CA (city) Kern County	44	0.47
Handy, MI (township) Livingston County	38	0.47
Hartland, MI (township) Livingston County	66	0.46
Commerce, MI (charter township) Oakland County	178	0.45
Huron, MI (charter township) Wayne County	70	0.45
Maltby, WA (cdp) Snohomish County	51	0.44
Boardman, OH (cdp) Mahoning County	152	0.43
Winter Gardens, CA (cdp) San Diego County	87	0.43
North Bellmore, NY (cdp) Nassau County	84	0.43
Lake of the Woods, VA (cdp) Orange County	34	0.43
Spring Valley Lake, CA (cdp) San Bernardino County	33	0.43
Canton, MI (charter township) Wayne County	366	0.42
Chester, NJ (township) Morris County	32	0.41
Massapequa Park, NY (village) Nassau County	68	0.40
Woodhaven, MI (city) Wayne County	52	0.40
Richfield, MI (township) Genesee County	35	0.40
York, MI (charter township) Washtenaw County	34	0.40
Romulus, MI (city) Wayne County	94	0.39
Lyon, MI (charter township) Oakland County	54	0.39
Audubon, NJ (borough) Camden County	35	0.39
Barrington, NH (town) Strafford County	32	0.38
Montvale, NJ (borough) Bergen County	29	0.38
Brownstown, MI (charter township) Wayne County	110	0.37
Franklin Square, NY (cdp) Nassau County	110	0.37
Clearlake, CA (city) Lake County	54	0.36
Upper Saucon, PA (township) Lehigh County	52	0.36
Pinehurst, NC (village) Moore County	45	0.36
Toppenish, WA (city) Yakima County	31	0.35
Westland, MI (city) Wayne County	287	0.34
Hicksville, NY (cdp) Nassau County	142	0.34
Harrison, MI (charter township) Macomb County	85	0.34
Milford, MI (charter township) Oakland County	53	0.34
Solebury, PA (township) Bucks County	29	0.34
East Palo Alto, CA (city) San Mateo County	93	0.33
Trenton, MI (city) Wayne County	62	0.33
Midlothian, TX (city) Ellis County	55	0.33
Parole, MD (cdp) Anne Arundel County	49	0.33
Woodbury, NY (village) Orange County	35	0.33
Margate, FL (city) Broward County	171	0.32
Montgomery, PA (township) Montgomery County	78	0.32
Holtsville, NY (cdp) Suffolk County	61	0.32
Stallings, NC (town) Union County	41	0.32
Woodbury, NY (town) Orange County	35	0.32
Rochester Hills, MI (city) Oakland County	221	0.31
St. Clair Shores, MI (city) Macomb County	191	0.31
Bruce, MI (township) Macomb County	27	0.31
Stuart, FL (city) Martin County	47	0.30
Mastic, NY (cdp) Suffolk County	43	0.30
Plymouth, MI (charter township) Wayne County	81	0.29
Tittabawassee, MI (township) Saginaw County	27	0.29
East Lansing, MI (city) Ingham County	132	0.28
South Farmingdale, NY (cdp) Nassau County	41	0.28
South Daytona, FL (city) Volusia County	36	0.28
Pocono, PA (township) Monroe County	31	0.28
Ash, MI (township) Monroe County	22	0.28
Laketon, MI (township) Muskegon County	21	0.28
Farmington Hills, MI (city) Oakland County	220	0.27
East Lansing, MI (city) Ingham County	132	0.27
Chesterfield, MI (township) Macomb County	115	0.27
Elmont, NY (cdp) Nassau County	93	0.27
Hamburg, MI (township) Livingston County	58	0.27
Wantagh, NY (cdp) Nassau County	48	0.27
Fraser, MI (city) Macomb County	40	0.27
Derby, CT (city/town) New Haven County	35	0.27
Putnam Valley, NY (town) Putnam County	32	0.27
New Baltimore, MI (city) Macomb County	31	0.27
Blackstone, MA (town) Worcester County	24	0.27
Larkfield-Wikiup, CA (cdp) Sonoma County	23	0.27
Macomb, MI (township) Macomb County	192	0.26
Lincoln Park, MI (city) Wayne County	101	0.26
San Carlos, CA (city) San Mateo County	73	0.26
Wyandotte, MI (city) Wayne County	69	0.26
Brandon, MI (charter township) Oakland County	39	0.26
Lapeer, MI (city) Lapeer County	24	0.26
Cortlandville, NY (town) Cortland County	22	0.26
Roseville, MI (city) Macomb County	120	0.25
Bayonet Point, FL (cdp) Pasco County	60	0.25
Farmingville, NY (cdp) Suffolk County	40	0.25
Robertsville, NJ (cdp) Monmouth County	28	0.25
Bardmoor, FL (cdp) Pinellas County	26	0.25
Brighton, MI (city) Livingston County	19	0.25
Warren, MI (city) Macomb County	320	0.24
Orion, MI (charter township) Oakland County	85	0.24
White Lake, MI (charter township) Oakland County	71	0.24
Ridgefield, CT (town) Fairfield County	58	0.24
Sebastian, FL (city) Indian River County	51	0.24
Clinton, NJ (township) Hunterdon County	33	0.24
Rocky Point, NY (cdp) Suffolk County	33	0.24
Terryville, NY (cdp) Suffolk County	29	0.24
Plattsburgh, NY (town) Clinton County	28	0.24
Doctor Phillips, FL (cdp) Orange County	27	0.24
Houghton, MI (city) Houghton County	18	0.24
Bloomfield, MI (charter township) Oakland County	95	0.23
Pacifica, CA (city) San Mateo County	84	0.23
Babylon, NY (village) Suffolk County	28	0.23
Berlin, MI (charter township) Monroe County	21	0.23
Matawan, NJ (borough) Monmouth County	20	0.23
Novi, MI (city) Oakland County	120	0.22
Moraga, CA (town) Contra Costa County	35	0.22
Merrifield, VA (cdp) Fairfax County	32	0.22
Flat Rock, MI (city) Wayne County	21	0.22
Tecumseh, MI (city) Lenawee County	19	0.22
San Mateo, CA (city) San Mateo County	203	0.21
Clinton, MA (town) Worcester County	29	0.21
Lake Mary, FL (city) Seminole County	29	0.21
Cornwall, NY (town) Orange County	27	0.21
Jericho, NY (cdp) Nassau County	27	0.21
Ringwood, NJ (borough) Passaic County	26	0.21
Grand Haven, MI (city) Ottawa County	22	0.21
Morehead City, NC (town) Carteret County	18	0.21
Celebration, FL (cdp) Osceola County	16	0.21
East Franklin, NJ (cdp) Somerset County	16	0.21
Oyster Bay, NY (town) Nassau County	579	0.20
Van Buren, MI (charter township) Wayne County	57	0.20
Spanaway, WA (cdp) Pierce County	56	0.20

SECTION THREE

Please refer to the Explanation of Data in the front of the book for more detailed information.

Ancestry

New Zealander

U.S. and 50 States Sorted by Population and Percent of Total Population

Place	Population	%
United States	**19,197**	**0.01**
California	4,604	0.01
Texas	1,131	<0.01
New York	1,002	0.01
Florida	990	0.01
Washington	927	0.01
Virginia	716	0.01
Colorado	713	0.01
North Carolina	562	0.01
Oregon	546	0.01
Utah	542	0.02
Illinois	542	<0.01
Arizona	495	0.01
Missouri	439	0.01
Massachusetts	432	0.01
Maryland	394	0.01
Ohio	387	<0.01
Pennsylvania	346	<0.01
Nevada	339	0.01
Tennessee	327	0.01
Indiana	318	<0.01
New Jersey	316	<0.01
Michigan	286	<0.01
Alabama	215	<0.01
Georgia	208	<0.01
Idaho	205	0.01
Connecticut	176	<0.01
District of Columbia	174	0.03
Wisconsin	164	<0.01
Hawaii	157	0.01
New Mexico	140	0.01
Minnesota	134	<0.01
Oklahoma	127	<0.01
Kansas	126	<0.01
Alaska	121	0.02
South Carolina	116	<0.01
Kentucky	103	<0.01
Iowa	85	<0.01
Vermont	79	0.01
Rhode Island	78	0.01
Maine	76	0.01
New Hampshire	74	0.01
Nebraska	64	<0.01
Louisiana	61	<0.01
Wyoming	40	0.01
Mississippi	37	<0.01
North Dakota	28	<0.01
Delaware	22	<0.01
Arkansas	20	<0.01
West Virginia	10	<0.01
South Dakota	3	<0.01
Montana	0	0.00

Place	Population	%
District of Columbia	174	0.03
Utah	542	0.02
Alaska	121	0.02
United States	**19,197**	**0.01**
California	4,604	0.01
New York	1,002	0.01
Florida	990	0.01
Washington	927	0.01
Virginia	716	0.01
Colorado	713	0.01
North Carolina	562	0.01
Oregon	546	0.01
Arizona	495	0.01
Missouri	439	0.01
Massachusetts	432	0.01
Maryland	394	0.01
Nevada	339	0.01
Tennessee	327	0.01
Idaho	205	0.01
Hawaii	157	0.01
New Mexico	140	0.01
Vermont	79	0.01
Rhode Island	78	0.01
Maine	76	0.01
New Hampshire	74	0.01
Wyoming	40	0.01
Texas	1,131	<0.01
Illinois	542	<0.01
Ohio	387	<0.01
Pennsylvania	346	<0.01
Indiana	318	<0.01
New Jersey	316	<0.01
Michigan	286	<0.01
Alabama	215	<0.01
Georgia	208	<0.01
Connecticut	176	<0.01
Wisconsin	164	<0.01
Minnesota	134	<0.01
Oklahoma	127	<0.01
Kansas	126	<0.01
South Carolina	116	<0.01
Kentucky	103	<0.01
Iowa	85	<0.01
Nebraska	64	<0.01
Louisiana	61	<0.01
Mississippi	37	<0.01
North Dakota	28	<0.01
Delaware	22	<0.01
Arkansas	20	<0.01
West Virginia	10	<0.01
South Dakota	3	<0.01
Montana	0	0.00

Please refer to the Explanation of Data in the front of the book for more detailed information.

Ancestry

New Zealander

Top 150 Places Sorted by Population

Based on all places, regardless of total population

Place	Population	%
New York, NY (city) Kings County	584	0.01
Los Angeles, CA (city) Los Angeles County	502	0.01
Manhattan, NY (borough) New York County	405	0.03
Chicago, IL (city) Cook County	205	0.01
Seattle, WA (city) King County	197	0.03
San Diego, CA (city) San Diego County	193	0.02
Washington, DC (city) District of Columbia	174	0.03
Provo, UT (city) Utah County	163	0.15
Torrance, CA (city) Los Angeles County	154	0.11
Houston, TX (city) Harris County	144	0.01
Brooklyn, NY (borough) Kings County	140	0.01
Colorado Springs, CO (city) El Paso County	138	0.03
Dallas, TX (city) Dallas County	132	0.01
American Canyon, CA (city) Napa County	129	0.73
Sammamish, WA (city) King County	129	0.30
Mesa, AZ (city) Maricopa County	129	0.03
Centennial, CO (city) Arapahoe County	127	0.13
San Francisco, CA (city) San Francisco County	123	0.02
Cinco Ranch, TX (cdp) Fort Bend County	115	0.63
Palo Alto, CA (city) Santa Clara County	103	0.16
Truckee, CA (town) Nevada County	98	0.62
Santa Rosa, CA (city) Sonoma County	96	0.06
Spring Valley, NV (cdp) Clark County	96	0.06
North Amherst, MA (cdp) Hampshire County	94	1.42
Amherst, MA (town) Hampshire County	94	0.25
Memphis, TN (city) Shelby County	92	0.01
Madison, AL (city) Madison County	91	0.23
Eugene, OR (city) Lane County	86	0.06
Denver, CO (city) Denver County	86	0.01
Upper Grand Lagoon, FL (cdp) Bay County	85	0.68
Mill Valley, CA (city) Marin County	83	0.61
Sedalia, MO (city) Pettis County	82	0.39
Huntington Beach, CA (city) Orange County	80	0.04
San Antonio, TX (city) Medina County	80	0.01
Henderson, NV (city) Clark County	78	0.03
Mayfair, CA (cdp) Fresno County	76	1.88
Santa Monica, CA (city) Los Angeles County	76	0.09
Riverside, CA (city) Riverside County	73	0.02
Charlotte, NC (city) Mecklenburg County	72	0.01
Ionia, MI (township) Ionia County	71	1.87
Boise City, ID (city) Ada County	70	0.03
Catalina Foothills, AZ (cdp) Pima County	69	0.13
Lafayette, IN (city) Tippecanoe County	68	0.10
Bolingbrook, IL (village) Will County	68	0.09
Arlington, VA (cdp) Arlington County	68	0.03
La Cañada Flintridge, CA (city) Los Angeles County	67	0.33
Avon, CO (town) Eagle County	66	1.04
Hillsboro, OR (city) Washington County	65	0.07
Cambridge, MA (city) Middlesex County	65	0.06
Warwick, RI (city) Kent County	64	0.08
Oakland, CA (city) Alameda County	63	0.02
Ballville, OH (cdp) Sandusky County	62	1.95
Laie, HI (cdp) Honolulu County	62	1.09
Alameda, CA (city) Alameda County	62	0.09
Beaumont, TX (city) Jefferson County	62	0.05
Wichita, KS (city) Sedgwick County	62	0.02
Glendale, MO (city) St. Louis County	60	1.02
Laguna Niguel, CA (city) Orange County	60	0.10
Tucson, AZ (city) Pima County	60	0.01
San Jose, CA (city) Santa Clara County	59	0.01
Scottsdale, AZ (city) Maricopa County	58	0.03
Hanford, CA (city) Kings County	57	0.11
Palmyra, PA (township) Pike County	55	1.63
Chagrin Falls, OH (village) Cuyahoga County	55	1.35
Monsey, NY (cdp) Rockland County	55	0.37
Costa Mesa, CA (city) Orange County	55	0.05
Ramapo, NY (town) Rockland County	55	0.04
Baltimore, MD (city) Baltimore city County	55	0.01
Deep River Center, CT (cdp) Middlesex County	53	2.02
Deep River, CT (town) Middlesex County	53	1.14
Wayne, NJ (township) Passaic County	53	0.10
O'Fallon, MO (city) St. Charles County	53	0.07
Clearwater, FL (city) Pinellas County	53	0.05
Reno, NV (city) Washoe County	53	0.02
Jacksonville, FL (city) Duval County	52	0.01
Philadelphia, PA (city) Philadelphia County	52	<0.01
El Dorado Hills, CA (cdp) El Dorado County	51	0.12
Fullerton, CA (city) Orange County	51	0.04
Nashville-Davidson, TN (metro govt) Davidson County	51	0.01
St. Albans, VT (town) Franklin County	50	0.84
West Haven, UT (city) Weber County	50	0.55
Estero, FL (cdp) Lee County	50	0.23
Salt Lake City, UT (city) Salt Lake County	50	0.03
Chapel Hill, NC (town) Orange County	49	0.09
Towson, MD (cdp) Baltimore County	49	0.09
Austin, TX (city) Travis County	49	0.01
Columbus, OH (city) Franklin County	48	0.01
Richmond, VA (ind. city) Richmond independent city	47	0.02
Telluride, CO (town) San Miguel County	46	1.78
Lubbock, TX (city) Lubbock County	46	0.02
Ithaca, NY (city) Tompkins County	45	0.15
San Dimas, CA (city) Los Angeles County	45	0.13
Watsonville, CA (city) Santa Cruz County	45	0.09
Bellevue, WA (city) King County	45	0.04
Lisbon, ME (town) Androscoggin County	44	0.48
Ripon, CA (city) San Joaquin County	44	0.32
Syracuse, UT (city) Davis County	44	0.20
Mooresville, NC (town) Iredell County	44	0.14
Coeur d'Alene, ID (city) Kootenai County	44	0.10
Miami Beach, FL (city) Miami-Dade County	44	0.05
Hendersonville, TN (city) Sumner County	43	0.09
Royal Oak, MI (city) Oakland County	43	0.07
Francisville, KY (cdp) Boone County	42	0.54
Columbine, CO (cdp) Jefferson County	42	0.18
Fresno, CA (city) Fresno County	42	0.01
Middle Inlet, WI (town) Marinette County	41	4.96
Biscayne Park, FL (village) Miami-Dade County	41	1.33
Trophy Club, TX (town) Denton County	41	0.51
Hastings, MN (city) Dakota County	41	0.19
Lawton, OK (city) Comanche County	41	0.04
Englewood, CO (city) Arapahoe County	40	0.13
Menlo Park, CA (city) San Mateo County	40	0.13
Montclair, NJ (township) Essex County	40	0.11
Leesburg, VA (town) Loudoun County	40	0.10
Lake Elsinore, CA (city) Riverside County	40	0.08
Woodcrest, CA (cdp) Riverside County	39	0.27
New Territory, TX (cdp) Fort Bend County	39	0.23
Norwalk, CT (city/town) Fairfield County	39	0.05
Mount Pulaski, IL (city) Logan County	38	2.38
Barrow, AK (city) North Slope Borough	38	0.92
Stone Ridge, VA (cdp) Loudoun County	38	0.63
Antioch, CA (city) Contra Costa County	38	0.04
Ester, AK (cdp) Fairbanks North Star Borough	37	1.89
Los Alamos, NM (cdp) Los Alamos County	37	0.31
Portales, NM (city) Roosevelt County	37	0.31
Monroe, WA (city) Snohomish County	37	0.22
Kannapolis, NC (city) Cabarrus County	37	0.09
Chandler, AZ (city) Maricopa County	37	0.02
Ladera Ranch, CA (cdp) Orange County	36	0.20
Hopkinsville, KY (city) Christian County	36	0.12
San Bruno, CA (city) San Mateo County	36	0.09
Bristol, CT (city/town) Hartford County	36	0.06
Berkeley, CA (city) Alameda County	36	0.03
Las Vegas, NV (city) Clark County	36	0.01
Milan, NY (town) Dutchess County	35	1.38
Lisbon Falls, ME (cdp) Androscoggin County	35	0.82
Sausalito, CA (city) Marin County	35	0.50
Deerpark, NY (town) Orange County	35	0.44
Princeton, IN (city) Gibson County	35	0.41
Salem, OR (city) Marion County	35	0.02
Indianapolis, IN (city) Marion County	35	<0.01
Kings Grant, NC (cdp) New Hanover County	34	0.41
Annandale, VA (cdp) Fairfax County	34	0.09
Pleasanton, CA (city) Alameda County	34	0.05
West Valley City, UT (city) Salt Lake County	34	0.03
Hoquiam, WA (city) Grays Harbor County	33	0.37
Newburyport, MA (city) Essex County	33	0.19
Thomasville, GA (city) Thomas County	33	0.18
Altadena, CA (cdp) Los Angeles County	33	0.07
Rocklin, CA (city) Placer County	33	0.06

SECTION THREE

Please refer to the Explanation of Data in the front of the book for more detailed information.

Ancestry

New Zealander

Top 150 Places Sorted by Percent of Total Population

Based on all places, regardless of total population

Place	Population	%
Middle Inlet, WI (town) Marinette County	41	4.96
Torrey, UT (town) Wayne County	7	2.86
Marion, OR (cdp) Marion County	9	2.53
Mount Pulaski, IL (city) Logan County	38	2.38
Deep River Center, CT (cdp) Middlesex County	53	2.02
Ballville, OH (cdp) Sandusky County	62	1.95
Ester, AK (cdp) Fairbanks North Star Borough	37	1.89
Mayfair, CA (cdp) Fresno County	76	1.88
Ionia, MI (township) Ionia County	71	1.87
Telluride, CO (town) San Miguel County	46	1.78
Palmyra, PA (township) Pike County	55	1.63
North Amherst, MA (cdp) Hampshire County	94	1.42
Shamokin Dam, PA (borough) Snyder County	27	1.40
Milan, NY (town) Dutchess County	35	1.38
Chagrin Falls, OH (village) Cuyahoga County	55	1.35
Biscayne Park, FL (village) Miami-Dade County	41	1.33
Belle Prairie, MN (township) Morrison County	15	1.20
Lake Summerset, IL (cdp) Winnebago County	21	1.19
Deep River, CT (town) Middlesex County	53	1.14
Cherry, MN (township) St. Louis County	10	1.12
Laie, HI (cdp) Honolulu County	62	1.09
Avon, CO (town) Eagle County	66	1.04
Glendale, MO (city) St. Louis County	60	1.02
South Bristol, ME (town) Lincoln County	10	1.02
Lake Junaluska, NC (cdp) Haywood County	27	0.99
Sunnyside, UT (city) Carbon County	6	0.97
Spring Creek, PA (township) Warren County	8	0.96
Bancroft, KY (city) Jefferson County	5	0.94
Birmingham, IA (city) Van Buren County	4	0.94
Barrow, AK (city) North Slope Borough	38	0.92
Belleville, AR (city) Yell County	4	0.92
Francis, UT (town) Summit County	11	0.90
Northville, MI (city) Wayne County	25	0.89
Rivergrove, OR (city) Clackamas County	2	0.87
St. Albans, VT (town) Franklin County	50	0.84
Ardentown, DE (village) New Castle County	2	0.83
Lisbon Falls, ME (cdp) Androscoggin County	35	0.82
Cochiti Lake, NM (cdp) Sandoval County	4	0.81
Day Valley, CA (cdp) Santa Cruz County	26	0.80
Patagonia, AZ (town) Santa Cruz County	5	0.80
St. James, MO (city) Phelps County	32	0.77
Banks, OR (city) Washington County	15	0.75
Newell, IA (city) Buena Vista County	6	0.75
American Canyon, CA (city) Napa County	129	0.73
Shady Shores, TX (town) Denton County	18	0.73
Hancock, NH (town) Hillsborough County	12	0.69
Upper Grand Lagoon, FL (cdp) Bay County	85	0.68
Bagdad, FL (cdp) Santa Rosa County	24	0.67
Shelburne, MA (town) Franklin County	13	0.64
Craftsbury, VT (town) Orleans County	8	0.64
Cinco Ranch, TX (cdp) Fort Bend County	115	0.63
Stone Ridge, VA (cdp) Loudoun County	38	0.63
Embden, ME (town) Somerset County	6	0.63
Truckee, CA (town) Nevada County	98	0.62
Mill Valley, CA (city) Marin County	83	0.61
Millis-Clicquot, MA (cdp) Norfolk County	27	0.60
Jackson, NH (town) Carroll County	5	0.56
Holland, VT (town) Orleans County	4	0.56
West Haven, UT (city) Weber County	50	0.55
Deer Creek, MN (township) Otter Tail County	2	0.55
Francisville, KY (cdp) Boone County	42	0.54
Boulder Creek, CA (cdp) Santa Cruz County	29	0.54
St. Marys, KS (city) Pottawatomie County	15	0.54
Oriskany Falls, NY (village) Oneida County	4	0.53
Willow River, MN (city) Pine County	2	0.52
Trophy Club, TX (town) Denton County	41	0.51
Castlewood, SD (city) Hamlin County	3	0.51
Sausalito, CA (city) Marin County	35	0.50
Redwood, OR (cdp) Josephine County	16	0.50
Owings, MD (cdp) Calvert County	11	0.49
Williamsfield, IL (village) Knox County	3	0.49
Lisbon, ME (town) Androscoggin County	44	0.48
McCord, OK (cdp) Osage County	9	0.46
Lynd, MN (city) Lyon County	2	0.46
Deerpark, NY (town) Orange County	35	0.44
Londonderry, PA (township) Dauphin County	23	0.44
Cleveland, FL (cdp) Charlotte County	16	0.44
Jackson, PA (township) Tioga County	8	0.44
Cassian, WI (town) Oneida County	4	0.44
West Haven-Sylvan, OR (cdp) Washington County	30	0.43
Monument Beach, MA (cdp) Barnstable County	11	0.42
Shaver Lake, CA (cdp) Fresno County	3	0.42
Princeton, IN (city) Gibson County	35	0.41
Kings Grant, NC (cdp) New Hanover County	34	0.41
Savage, MD (cdp) Howard County	28	0.41
Northville, MI (city) Oakland County	25	0.41
Fayette, IA (city) Fayette County	6	0.41
Empire, WI (town) Fond du Lac County	11	0.40
Tuftonboro, NH (town) Carroll County	10	0.40
Sedalia, MO (city) Pettis County	82	0.39
Niskayuna, NY (cdp) Schenectady County	18	0.39
Westport, NC (cdp) Lincoln County	13	0.39
Snyderville, UT (cdp) Summit County	20	0.38
Hampstead, NC (cdp) Pender County	14	0.38
Christiana, WI (town) Vernon County	3	0.38
Monsey, NY (cdp) Rockland County	55	0.37
Hoquiam, WA (city) Grays Harbor County	33	0.37
Overfield, PA (township) Wyoming County	5	0.37
Monroeville, AL (city) Monroe County	24	0.36
Edgerton, KS (city) Johnson County	6	0.36
Lowell, OR (city) Lane County	3	0.36
Millis, MA (town) Norfolk County	27	0.35
Good Hope, AL (town) Cullman County	8	0.35
Shelburne Falls, MA (cdp) Franklin County	6	0.35
Tega Cay, SC (city) York County	24	0.34
Willard, MO (city) Greene County	17	0.34
Topsham, VT (town) Orange County	4	0.34
La Cañada Flintridge, CA (city) Los Angeles County	67	0.33
Del Monte Forest, CA (cdp) Monterey County	14	0.33
Ripon, CA (city) San Joaquin County	44	0.32
Lake Fenton, MI (cdp) Genesee County	17	0.32
Chalfant, PA (borough) Allegheny County	3	0.32
Los Alamos, NM (cdp) Los Alamos County	37	0.31
Portales, NM (city) Roosevelt County	37	0.31
Sammamish, WA (city) King County	129	0.30
Chatham, NJ (township) Morris County	31	0.30
Loyola, CA (cdp) Santa Clara County	10	0.30
El Jebel, CO (cdp) Eagle County	14	0.29
Swannanoa, NC (cdp) Buncombe County	12	0.29
Bunk Foss, WA (cdp) Snohomish County	11	0.29
Aurelius, MI (township) Ingham County	10	0.29
Morgan, UT (city) Morgan County	10	0.29
Klahanie, WA (cdp) King County	32	0.28
Parkville, MO (city) Platte County	15	0.28
Royersford, PA (borough) Montgomery County	13	0.28
Canterbury, NH (town) Merrimack County	7	0.28
North Harmony, NY (town) Chautauqua County	6	0.28
Cooperstown, NY (village) Otsego County	5	0.28
Schwenksville, PA (borough) Montgomery County	4	0.28
Woodcrest, CA (cdp) Riverside County	39	0.27
Granville, OH (village) Licking County	15	0.27
Wellington, CO (town) Larimer County	15	0.27
Shamrock, MN (township) Aitkin County	3	0.27
Satellite Beach, FL (city) Brevard County	28	0.26
Morehead City, NC (town) Carteret County	22	0.26
Bedminster, NJ (township) Somerset County	21	0.26
Oakland, FL (town) Orange County	6	0.26
Bel-Nor, MO (village) St. Louis County	4	0.26
Franklin, GA (city) Heard County	3	0.26
Amherst, MA (town) Hampshire County	94	0.25
Big Bear City, CA (cdp) San Bernardino County	30	0.25
Montecito, CA (cdp) Santa Barbara County	23	0.25
Atherton, CA (town) San Mateo County	17	0.25
Crozet, VA (cdp) Albemarle County	13	0.25
Oak View, CA (cdp) Ventura County	10	0.25
St. Robert, MO (city) Pulaski County	10	0.25
Ridgeway, AK (cdp) Kenai Peninsula Borough	6	0.25
Countryside, VA (cdp) Loudoun County	23	0.24
South Sarasota, FL (cdp) Sarasota County	11	0.24
Castle Hills, TX (city) Bexar County	10	0.24

Please refer to the Explanation of Data in the front of the book for more detailed information.

Ancestry

New Zealander

Top 150 Places Sorted by Percent of Total Population

Based on places with total population of 7,500 or more

Place	Population	%
American Canyon, CA (city) Napa County	129	0.73
Upper Grand Lagoon, FL (cdp) Bay County	85	0.68
Cinco Ranch, TX (cdp) Fort Bend County	115	0.63
Truckee, CA (town) Nevada County	98	0.62
Mill Valley, CA (city) Marin County	83	0.61
West Haven, UT (city) Weber County	50	0.55
Francisville, KY (cdp) Boone County	42	0.54
Trophy Club, TX (town) Denton County	41	0.51
Lisbon, ME (town) Androscoggin County	44	0.48
Deerpark, NY (town) Orange County	35	0.44
Princeton, IN (city) Gibson County	35	0.41
Kings Grant, NC (cdp) New Hanover County	34	0.41
Sedalia, MO (city) Pettis County	82	0.39
Monsey, NY (cdp) Rockland County	55	0.37
Hoquiam, WA (city) Grays Harbor County	33	0.37
Millis, MA (town) Norfolk County	27	0.35
La Cañada Flintridge, CA (city) Los Angeles County	67	0.33
Ripon, CA (city) San Joaquin County	44	0.32
Los Alamos, NM (cdp) Los Alamos County	37	0.31
Portales, NM (city) Roosevelt County	37	0.31
Sammamish, WA (city) King County	129	0.30
Chatham, NJ (township) Morris County	31	0.30
Klahanie, WA (cdp) King County	32	0.28
Woodcrest, CA (cdp) Riverside County	39	0.27
Satellite Beach, FL (city) Brevard County	28	0.26
Morehead City, NC (town) Carteret County	22	0.26
Bedminster, NJ (township) Somerset County	21	0.26
Amherst, MA (town) Hampshire County	94	0.25
Big Bear City, CA (cdp) San Bernardino County	30	0.25
Montecito, CA (cdp) Santa Barbara County	23	0.25
Countryside, VA (cdp) Loudoun County	23	0.24
Madison, AL (city) Madison County	91	0.23
Estero, FL (cdp) Lee County	50	0.23
New Territory, TX (cdp) Fort Bend County	39	0.23
Monroe, WA (city) Snohomish County	37	0.22
Waipio, HI (cdp) Honolulu County	27	0.21
Princeton, NJ (borough) Mercer County	26	0.21
Syracuse, UT (city) Davis County	44	0.20
Ladera Ranch, CA (cdp) Orange County	36	0.20
Sitka, AK (borough) Sitka City and Borough	18	0.20
Long Grove, IL (village) Lake County	16	0.20
Hastings, MN (city) Dakota County	41	0.19
Newburyport, MA (city) Essex County	33	0.19
Columbine, CO (cdp) Jefferson County	42	0.18
Thomasville, GA (city) Thomas County	33	0.18
Astoria, OR (city) Clatsop County	17	0.18
Eggertsville, NY (cdp) Erie County	26	0.17
Miami Shores, FL (village) Miami-Dade County	18	0.17
Ashland, WI (city) Ashland County	14	0.17
Palo Alto, CA (city) Santa Clara County	103	0.16
University Heights, OH (city) Cuyahoga County	22	0.16
Speedway, IN (town) Marion County	19	0.16
Stony Brook University, NY (cdp) Suffolk County	13	0.16
Provo, UT (city) Utah County	163	0.15
Ithaca, NY (city) Tompkins County	45	0.15
Glassmanor, MD (cdp) Prince George's County	27	0.15
Centralia, WA (city) Lewis County	25	0.15
Middleton, WI (city) Dane County	25	0.15
Rye, NY (city) Westchester County	23	0.15
Lower Saucon, PA (township) Northampton County	16	0.15
Silver City, NM (town) Grant County	16	0.15
Storm Lake, IA (city) Buena Vista County	16	0.15
Mooresville, NC (town) Iredell County	44	0.14
Casa de Oro-Mount Helix, CA (cdp) San Diego County	27	0.14
Huntington, NY (cdp) Suffolk County	26	0.14
Wakefield, VA (cdp) Fairfax County	16	0.14
Centennial, CO (city) Arapahoe County	127	0.13
Catalina Foothills, AZ (cdp) Pima County	69	0.13
San Dimas, CA (city) Los Angeles County	45	0.13
Englewood, CO (city) Arapahoe County	40	0.13
Menlo Park, CA (city) San Mateo County	40	0.13
Westminster, MD (city) Carroll County	25	0.13
Aberdeen, MD (city) Harford County	20	0.13
Rosedale, CA (cdp) Kern County	19	0.13
Stanford, CA (cdp) Santa Clara County	19	0.13
Dardenne Prairie, MO (city) St. Charles County	13	0.13
El Dorado Hills, CA (cdp) El Dorado County	51	0.12
Hopkinsville, KY (city) Christian County	36	0.12
Belmont, MA (cdp/town) Middlesex County	30	0.12
Parkland, FL (city) Broward County	28	0.12
Golden, CO (city) Jefferson County	22	0.12
Thompson, NY (town) Sullivan County	18	0.12
San Anselmo, CA (town) Marin County	15	0.12
Steger, IL (village) Will County	12	0.12
Cold Springs, NV (cdp) Washoe County	11	0.12
Oakwood, OH (city) Montgomery County	11	0.12
Rice Lake, WI (city) Barron County	10	0.12
Torrance, CA (city) Los Angeles County	154	0.11
Hanford, CA (city) Kings County	57	0.11
Montclair, NJ (township) Essex County	40	0.11
East Palo Alto, CA (city) San Mateo County	31	0.11
West Milford, NJ (township) Passaic County	28	0.11
Lafayette, CA (city) Contra Costa County	27	0.11
Isla Vista, CA (cdp) Santa Barbara County	25	0.11
Keene, NH (city) Cheshire County	25	0.11
Kenmore, WA (city) King County	22	0.11
Salmon Creek, WA (cdp) Clark County	22	0.11
Fenton, MI (charter township) Genesee County	17	0.11
Hopkinton, MA (town) Middlesex County	16	0.11
North Salt Lake, UT (city) Davis County	16	0.11
Hudson, WI (city) St. Croix County	14	0.11
Irondale, AL (city) Jefferson County	13	0.11
Horizon West, FL (cdp) Orange County	11	0.11
Lafayette, IN (city) Tippecanoe County	68	0.10
Laguna Niguel, CA (city) Orange County	60	0.10
Wayne, NJ (township) Passaic County	53	0.10
Coeur d'Alene, ID (city) Kootenai County	44	0.10
Leesburg, VA (town) Loudoun County	40	0.10
Oregon City, OR (city) Clackamas County	32	0.10
Laramie, WY (city) Albany County	31	0.10
Cleburne, TX (city) Johnson County	28	0.10
Reisterstown, MD (cdp) Baltimore County	27	0.10
Spring Valley, CA (cdp) San Diego County	27	0.10
Ardmore, OK (city) Carter County	24	0.10
Granite Bay, CA (cdp) Placer County	23	0.10
Ennis, TX (city) Ellis County	19	0.10
Belton, TX (city) Bell County	17	0.10
Makakilo, HI (cdp) Honolulu County	17	0.10
New Port Richey, FL (city) Pasco County	16	0.10
Cedar Mill, OR (cdp) Washington County	14	0.10
Greenwich, CT (cdp) Fairfield County	13	0.10
Muscle Shoals, AL (city) Colbert County	13	0.10
Taylorville, IL (city) Christian County	13	0.10
Williamsburg, VA (ind. city) Williamsburg independent city	13	0.10
Zionsville, IN (town) Boone County	13	0.10
Lahaina, HI (cdp) Maui County	11	0.10
Chevy Chase, MD (cdp) Montgomery County	10	0.10
Rockport, TX (city) Aransas County	9	0.10
Camp Hill, PA (borough) Cumberland County	8	0.10
Santa Monica, CA (city) Los Angeles County	76	0.09
Bolingbrook, IL (village) Will County	68	0.09
Alameda, CA (city) Alameda County	62	0.09
Chapel Hill, NC (town) Orange County	49	0.09
Towson, MD (cdp) Baltimore County	49	0.09
Watsonville, CA (city) Santa Cruz County	45	0.09
Hendersonville, TN (city) Sumner County	43	0.09
Kannapolis, NC (city) Cabarrus County	37	0.09
San Bruno, CA (city) San Mateo County	36	0.09
Annandale, VA (cdp) Fairfax County	34	0.09
Pacifica, CA (city) San Mateo County	32	0.09
Manhattan Beach, CA (city) Los Angeles County	31	0.09
Delaware, OH (city) Delaware County	29	0.09
East Lake, FL (cdp) Pinellas County	29	0.09
West Lafayette, IN (city) Tippecanoe County	26	0.09
Concord, MA (town) Middlesex County	15	0.09
Glenvar Heights, FL (cdp) Miami-Dade County	14	0.09
Oconomowoc, WI (city) Waukesha County	14	0.09
Solana Beach, CA (city) San Diego County	12	0.09
Mays Chapel, MD (cdp) Baltimore County	11	0.09
Clarksburg, MD (cdp) Montgomery County	10	0.09

SECTION THREE

Please refer to the Explanation of Data in the front of the book for more detailed information.

Ancestry

Northern European

U.S. and 50 States Sorted by Population and Percent of Total Population

Place	Population	%	Place	Population	%
United States	**230,027**	**0.08**	Washington	19,819	0.30
California	45,938	0.13	Oregon	9,578	0.25
Washington	19,819	0.30	Alaska	1,579	0.23
Minnesota	11,416	0.22	Minnesota	11,416	0.22
New York	10,116	0.05	Utah	4,897	0.18
Texas	10,021	0.04	Montana	1,730	0.18
Oregon	9,578	0.25	Wyoming	971	0.18
Colorado	8,513	0.17	Colorado	8,513	0.17
Virginia	7,054	0.09	Vermont	1,055	0.17
Florida	7,003	0.04	Idaho	2,127	0.14
Illinois	6,547	0.05	California	45,938	0.13
Massachusetts	5,883	0.09	Iowa	3,242	0.11
Michigan	5,448	0.05	Maine	1,466	0.11
Arizona	5,102	0.08	New Mexico	2,060	0.10
Utah	4,897	0.18	District of Columbia	610	0.10
Pennsylvania	4,622	0.04	Virginia	7,054	0.09
Georgia	4,554	0.05	Massachusetts	5,883	0.09
Maryland	4,406	0.08	**United States**	**230,027**	**0.08**
Wisconsin	4,302	0.08	Arizona	5,102	0.08
North Carolina	4,055	0.04	Maryland	4,406	0.08
Ohio	3,939	0.03	Wisconsin	4,302	0.08
Missouri	3,384	0.06	Kansas	2,156	0.08
Indiana	3,363	0.05	Connecticut	2,619	0.07
Iowa	3,242	0.11	Nevada	1,929	0.07
New Jersey	2,983	0.03	New Hampshire	930	0.07
Connecticut	2,619	0.07	Missouri	3,384	0.06
Tennessee	2,477	0.04	Nebraska	1,074	0.06
Kansas	2,156	0.08	Hawaii	789	0.06
Idaho	2,127	0.14	South Dakota	468	0.06
New Mexico	2,060	0.10	North Dakota	417	0.06
Nevada	1,929	0.07	New York	10,116	0.05
South Carolina	1,865	0.04	Illinois	6,547	0.05
Montana	1,730	0.18	Michigan	5,448	0.05
Alaska	1,579	0.23	Georgia	4,554	0.05
Maine	1,466	0.11	Indiana	3,363	0.05
Alabama	1,401	0.03	Texas	10,021	0.04
Oklahoma	1,267	0.03	Florida	7,003	0.04
Nebraska	1,074	0.06	Pennsylvania	4,622	0.04
Vermont	1,055	0.17	North Carolina	4,055	0.04
Kentucky	1,049	0.02	Tennessee	2,477	0.04
Wyoming	971	0.18	South Carolina	1,865	0.04
Arkansas	955	0.03	Rhode Island	463	0.04
New Hampshire	930	0.07	Ohio	3,939	0.03
Mississippi	881	0.03	New Jersey	2,983	0.03
Hawaii	789	0.06	Alabama	1,401	0.03
Louisiana	767	0.02	Oklahoma	1,267	0.03
District of Columbia	610	0.10	Arkansas	955	0.03
South Dakota	468	0.06	Mississippi	881	0.03
Rhode Island	463	0.04	Delaware	286	0.03
West Virginia	451	0.02	Kentucky	1,049	0.02
North Dakota	417	0.06	Louisiana	767	0.02
Delaware	286	0.03	West Virginia	451	0.02

Please refer to the Explanation of Data in the front of the book for more detailed information.

Ancestry

Northern European

Top 150 Places Sorted by Population

Based on all places, regardless of total population

Place	Population	%
Seattle, WA (city) King County	4,576	0.77
New York, NY (city) Kings County	3,043	0.04
Portland, OR (city) Multnomah County	2,177	0.38
San Francisco, CA (city) San Francisco County	2,060	0.26
Los Angeles, CA (city) Los Angeles County	1,975	0.05
Chicago, IL (city) Cook County	1,551	0.06
San Diego, CA (city) San Diego County	1,520	0.12
Manhattan, NY (borough) New York County	1,485	0.09
Phoenix, AZ (city) Maricopa County	1,234	0.09
Santa Cruz, CA (city) Santa Cruz County	1,071	1.84
Denver, CO (city) Denver County	1,069	0.18
San Jose, CA (city) Santa Clara County	1,065	0.12
Fort Collins, CO (city) Larimer County	1,013	0.72
Houston, TX (city) Harris County	997	0.05
Brooklyn, NY (borough) Kings County	961	0.04
Albuquerque, NM (city) Bernalillo County	949	0.18
Minneapolis, MN (city) Hennepin County	881	0.23
Oakland, CA (city) Alameda County	853	0.22
Austin, TX (city) Travis County	837	0.11
St. Paul, MN (city) Ramsey County	785	0.28
Salt Lake City, UT (city) Salt Lake County	743	0.40
Madison, WI (city) Dane County	737	0.32
Eugene, OR (city) Lane County	734	0.48
Alexandria, VA (ind. city) Alexandria independent city	646	0.48
Washington, DC (city) District of Columbia	610	0.10
Dallas, TX (city) Dallas County	596	0.05
Bellevue, WA (city) King County	594	0.50
Arlington, VA (cdp) Arlington County	592	0.30
Indianapolis, IN (city) Marion County	584	0.07
San Antonio, TX (city) Medina County	518	0.04
Anchorage, AK (municipality) Anchorage Municipality	515	0.18
Hempstead, NY (town) Nassau County	514	0.07
Boulder, CO (city) Boulder County	512	0.53
Queens, NY (borough) Queens County	512	0.02
Lafayette, CA (city) Contra Costa County	511	2.15
Sacramento, CA (city) Sacramento County	493	0.11
Spokane, WA (city) Spokane County	488	0.24
Long Beach, CA (city) Los Angeles County	485	0.11
Tacoma, WA (city) Pierce County	477	0.24
Colorado Springs, CO (city) El Paso County	476	0.12
Kansas City, MO (city) Jackson County	472	0.10
Boise City, ID (city) Ada County	471	0.23
Tucson, AZ (city) Pima County	471	0.09
Salem, OR (city) Marion County	443	0.29
Shoreline, WA (city) King County	435	0.83
Maplewood, MN (city) Ramsey County	429	1.16
Cambridge, MA (city) Middlesex County	420	0.41
Walnut Creek, CA (city) Contra Costa County	409	0.64
Jacksonville, FL (city) Duval County	395	0.05
Mesa, AZ (city) Maricopa County	393	0.09
Fresno, CA (city) Fresno County	387	0.08
Boston, MA (city) Suffolk County	383	0.06
Edmonds, WA (city) Snohomish County	381	0.96
Palo Alto, CA (city) Santa Clara County	369	0.59
Philadelphia, PA (city) Philadelphia County	361	0.02
Sunnyvale, CA (city) Santa Clara County	360	0.26
Martinez, CA (city) Contra Costa County	359	1.01
Charlotte, NC (city) Mecklenburg County	357	0.05
Overland Park, KS (city) Johnson County	354	0.21
Coon Rapids, MN (city) Anoka County	352	0.57
Vancouver, WA (city) Clark County	344	0.21
Omaha, NE (city) Douglas County	341	0.08
Plymouth, MN (city) Hennepin County	340	0.49
Davis, CA (city) Yolo County	337	0.52
Bend, OR (city) Deschutes County	332	0.45
Bellingham, WA (city) Whatcom County	330	0.42
Santa Rosa, CA (city) Sonoma County	330	0.20
Oklahoma City, OK (city) Oklahoma County	330	0.06
Mill Valley, CA (city) Marin County	326	2.38
Apple Valley, MN (city) Dakota County	318	0.65
The Woodlands, TX (cdp) Montgomery County	311	0.34
Lakewood, CO (city) Jefferson County	311	0.22
Blaine, MN (city) Anoka County	308	0.56
Woodbury, MN (city) Washington County	306	0.51
Vashon, WA (cdp) King County	305	3.07
Berkeley, CA (city) Alameda County	305	0.28
Fort Worth, TX (city) Tarrant County	301	0.04
White Bear Lake, MN (city) Ramsey County	300	1.29
White Bear Lake, MN (city) Ramsey County	300	1.28
Fremont, CA (city) Alameda County	297	0.14
Riverside, CA (city) Riverside County	295	0.10
Los Altos, CA (city) Santa Clara County	294	1.03
Nashville-Davidson, TN (metro govt) Davidson County	290	0.05
Shoreview, MN (city) Ramsey County	286	1.15
Arden-Arcade, CA (cdp) Sacramento County	285	0.31
Las Vegas, NV (city) Clark County	278	0.05
Catalina Foothills, AZ (cdp) Pima County	276	0.53
Scottsdale, AZ (city) Maricopa County	276	0.13
Redding, CA (city) Shasta County	275	0.31
Los Gatos, CA (town) Santa Clara County	273	0.95
Huntington Beach, CA (city) Orange County	273	0.14
Alameda, CA (city) Alameda County	269	0.37
Atlanta, GA (city) Fulton County	269	0.07
Beaverton, OR (city) Washington County	268	0.30
Brea, CA (city) Orange County	267	0.69
Durham, NC (city) Durham County	261	0.12
Raleigh, NC (city) Wake County	261	0.07
Hillsboro, OR (city) Washington County	254	0.29
Thousand Oaks, CA (city) Ventura County	252	0.20
Brookhaven, NY (town) Suffolk County	249	0.05
Provo, UT (city) Utah County	246	0.22
Eden Prairie, MN (city) Hennepin County	244	0.41
Pasadena, CA (city) Los Angeles County	242	0.18
Henderson, NV (city) Clark County	242	0.10
Lakeville, MN (city) Dakota County	241	0.45
Corvallis, OR (city) Benton County	239	0.45
Columbia, MO (city) Boone County	238	0.23
San Ramon, CA (city) Contra Costa County	237	0.35
Cary, NC (town) Wake County	236	0.18
Iowa City, IA (city) Johnson County	235	0.35
Des Moines, WA (city) King County	234	0.80
Pleasanton, CA (city) Alameda County	234	0.34
Sandy, UT (city) Salt Lake County	231	0.27
Stockton, CA (city) San Joaquin County	231	0.08
Lexington-Fayette, KY (cons. govt) Fayette County	230	0.08
Roseville, CA (city) Placer County	229	0.20
Baltimore, MD (city) Baltimore city County	229	0.04
Rochester, MN (city) Olmsted County	226	0.22
Santa Clarita, CA (city) Los Angeles County	226	0.13
Milwaukee, WI (city) Milwaukee County	225	0.04
Lawrence, KS (city) Douglas County	224	0.26
Alamo, CA (cdp) Contra Costa County	222	1.46
Jupiter, FL (town) Palm Beach County	222	0.42
Carson City, NV (ind. city) Carson City County	222	0.40
St. Petersburg, FL (city) Pinellas County	221	0.09
Burbank, CA (city) Los Angeles County	220	0.21
Columbus, OH (city) Franklin County	220	0.03
Lake Arrowhead, CA (cdp) San Bernardino County	217	2.27
Tualatin, OR (city) Washington County	217	0.85
Eagan, MN (city) Dakota County	217	0.34
Duluth, MN (city) St. Louis County	217	0.25
Soquel, CA (cdp) Santa Cruz County	216	2.30
Oceanside, CA (city) San Diego County	213	0.13
Tulsa, OK (city) Tulsa County	212	0.05
Federal Way, WA (city) King County	210	0.24
Danville, CA (town) Contra Costa County	209	0.50
Ames, IA (city) Story County	208	0.36
Renton, WA (city) King County	206	0.24
Ann Arbor, MI (city) Washtenaw County	203	0.18
Rio del Mar, CA (cdp) Santa Cruz County	201	2.13
Tempe, AZ (city) Maricopa County	201	0.12
Virginia Beach, VA (ind. city) Virginia Beach independent city	201	0.05
Elk Grove, CA (city) Sacramento County	200	0.14
Sparks, NV (city) Washoe County	197	0.23
Centennial, CO (city) Arapahoe County	197	0.20
New Haven, CT (city/town) New Haven County	196	0.15
Memphis, TN (city) Shelby County	195	0.03
Severna Park, MD (cdp) Anne Arundel County	193	0.52
Logan, UT (city) Cache County	193	0.42
Santa Monica, CA (city) Los Angeles County	193	0.22

Please refer to the Explanation of Data in the front of the book for more detailed information.

Ancestry

Northern European

Top 150 Places Sorted by Percent of Total Population

Based on all places, regardless of total population

Place	Population	%
Little Grass Valley, CA (cdp) Plumas County	23	100.00
Freeport, CA (cdp) Sacramento County	10	50.00
Youngsville, NM (cdp) Rio Arriba County	7	25.93
Oxbow, ME (plantation) Aroostook County	15	25.42
Curlew, WA (cdp) Ferry County	17	25.00
Kerrick, MN (city) Pine County	11	17.19
Gales, MD (town) Dorchester County	8	14.04
Silver Gate, MT (cdp) Park County	2	12.50
Crisman, CO (cdp) Boulder County	15	12.10
Duanesburg, NY (cdp) Schenectady County	21	12.00
Schenevus, NY (cdp) Otsego County	32	11.64
Bivalve, MD (cdp) Wicomico County	21	11.60
La Grange, WY (town) Goshen County	54	10.71
Jefferson, MN (township) Houston County	6	10.71
Moose Park, MN (township) Itasca County	4	10.53
Salvisa, KY (cdp) Mercer County	35	10.48
Bridgetown, MS (cdp) DeSoto County	184	9.90
Parkdale, OR (cdp) Hood River County	27	9.41
Monument, PA (cdp) Centre County	13	9.35
Brinsmade, ND (city) Benson County	3	9.09
Eyers Grove, PA (cdp) Columbia County	9	9.00
Seventh Mountain, OR (cdp) Deschutes County	30	8.85
Brookhurst, WY (cdp) Natrona County	15	8.33
Bonanza Mountain Estates, CO (cdp) Boulder County	18	7.73
Cable, WI (cdp) Bayfield County	10	7.63
Betterton, MD (town) Kent County	34	7.56
West Valley, NY (cdp) Cattaraugus County	33	7.37
Skyland, NV (cdp) Douglas County	16	7.24
Nellieburg, MS (cdp) Lauderdale County	135	6.80
Wabana, MN (township) Itasca County	37	6.79
Evan, MN (city) Brown County	4	6.67
Tenakee Springs, AK (city) Hoonah-Angoon Census Area	5	6.41
Bechtelsville, PA (borough) Berks County	50	6.32
Valley Acres, CA (cdp) Kern County	35	6.23
Twin Lakes, IA (cdp) Calhoun County	19	5.83
Michigan City, ND (city) Nelson County	17	5.70
Prathersville, MO (village) Clay County	7	5.56
Oldham, SD (city) Kingsbury County	10	5.49
The Rock, GA (cdp) Upson County	10	5.35
Osceola, MN (township) Renville County	9	5.26
Woodlawn Park, OK (town) Oklahoma County	8	5.26
Fall City, WA (cdp) King County	107	5.17
Glenview Manor, KY (city) Jefferson County	9	5.14
New Kent, VA (cdp) New Kent County	8	5.06
Wishram, WA (cdp) Klickitat County	15	5.05
Eads, CO (town) Kiowa County	42	4.99
Platte Woods, MO (city) Platte County	16	4.98
Golden Valley, NV (cdp) Washoe County	78	4.95
Golf, FL (village) Palm Beach County	15	4.87
Alhambra Valley, CA (cdp) Contra Costa County	40	4.85
Dorset, VT (cdp) Bennington County	15	4.81
Hanalei, HI (cdp) Kauai County	32	4.79
Rehobeth, AL (town) Houston County	72	4.78
Fernan Lake Village, ID (city) Kootenai County	8	4.73
Kragero, MN (township) Chippewa County	5	4.59
Chacra, CO (cdp) Garfield County	20	4.58
Mahtowa, MN (cdp) Carlton County	15	4.50
May Creek, WA (cdp) Snohomish County	40	4.48
Newfield Hamlet, NY (cdp) Tompkins County	30	4.48
Sheridan, MN (township) Redwood County	7	4.46
Milton, ME (unorganized territory) Oxford County	6	4.17
Falling Water, TN (cdp) Hamilton County	46	4.16
Indian Village, IN (town) St. Joseph County	4	4.08
Outlook, MT (town) Sheridan County	3	4.05
Plainfield, VT (cdp) Washington County	12	4.04
Woodacre, CA (cdp) Marin County	50	4.00
Naches, WA (town) Yakima County	26	4.00
Long Lake, NY (cdp) Hamilton County	21	3.92
Montcalm, WV (cdp) Mercer County	20	3.91
Montana, WI (town) Buffalo County	12	3.90
Mulino, OR (cdp) Clackamas County	85	3.89
Cutler, ME (town) Washington County	25	3.88
Sheldon, MN (township) Houston County	10	3.75
Moorcroft, WY (town) Crook County	48	3.74
Old Bennington, VT (village) Bennington County	7	3.74

Place	Population	%
Pasatiempo, CA (cdp) Santa Cruz County	45	3.71
Big Bend, WI (town) Rusk County	18	3.71
Doland, SD (city) Spink County	6	3.68
Woods Hole, MA (cdp) Barnstable County	24	3.66
Lytle Creek, CA (cdp) San Bernardino County	27	3.65
Puako, HI (cdp) Hawaii County	34	3.64
Rochester, VT (cdp) Windsor County	9	3.57
Lonepine, MT (cdp) Sanders County	8	3.57
Oakdale, WI (town) Monroe County	23	3.54
Wallace, ID (city) Shoshone County	34	3.53
Milburn, OK (town) Johnston County	13	3.45
North Bay, WI (village) Racine County	11	3.35
Hornbrook, CA (cdp) Siskiyou County	9	3.33
Ruth, CA (cdp) Trinity County	5	3.31
Sonoita, AZ (cdp) Santa Cruz County	22	3.29
Deerfield, PA (township) Tioga County	25	3.28
Guilford, NY (town) Chenango County	97	3.27
Petersburg, AK (city) Petersburg Census Area	95	3.24
Max Meadows, VA (cdp) Wythe County	17	3.24
Gates, OR (city) Marion County	22	3.21
New Suffolk, NY (cdp) Suffolk County	6	3.19
Washington, VA (town) Rappahannock County	4	3.15
Burley, WA (cdp) Kitsap County	66	3.14
Summerland, CA (cdp) Santa Barbara County	34	3.14
Cascade Locks, OR (city) Hood River County	30	3.14
Anchor Bay, CA (cdp) Mendocino County	10	3.13
Butternut Valley, MN (township) Blue Earth County	12	3.12
Blue Hill, ME (cdp) Hancock County	33	3.08
Vashon, WA (cdp) King County	305	3.07
Georgetown, CA (cdp) El Dorado County	73	3.07
Brookdale, CA (cdp) Santa Cruz County	56	3.07
Lemitar, NM (cdp) Socorro County	10	3.07
Basin, MT (cdp) Jefferson County	5	3.05
Crozet, VA (cdp) Albemarle County	157	3.03
Goldendale, WA (city) Klickitat County	105	3.03
Ketchum, ID (city) Blaine County	84	3.00
Hot Sulphur Springs, CO (town) Grand County	28	2.97
Richmond, MN (township) Winona County	19	2.93
Brooksville, ME (town) Hancock County	29	2.89
Cornish, MN (township) Sibley County	6	2.88
Fenwick, CT (borough) Middlesex County	2	2.86
Apison, TN (cdp) Hamilton County	74	2.85
Scott, NY (town) Cortland County	36	2.85
Honomu, HI (cdp) Hawaii County	17	2.84
Nashotah, WI (village) Waukesha County	44	2.83
Bruno, MN (city) Pine County	2	2.82
Yarrow Point, WA (town) King County	24	2.81
Long Lake, NY (town) Hamilton County	21	2.80
Proctorsville, VT (cdp) Windsor County	10	2.80
Laurel, NY (cdp) Suffolk County	30	2.79
Kent Narrows, MD (cdp) Queen Anne's County	16	2.72
St. Leo, FL (town) Pasco County	17	2.70
Honner, MN (township) Redwood County	2	2.70
Pleasant Valley, MN (township) Mower County	10	2.69
Cold Springs, CA (cdp) El Dorado County	15	2.67
Rockport, ME (town) Knox County	91	2.66
Acton, CA (cdp) Los Angeles County	189	2.64
Maple Heights-Lake Desire, WA (cdp) King County	79	2.64
Mason Neck, VA (cdp) Fairfax County	59	2.63
Upper Brookville, NY (village) Nassau County	39	2.62
College Springs, IA (city) Page County	6	2.61
St. Leo, MN (city) Yellow Medicine County	4	2.61
Wiscoy, MN (township) Winona County	6	2.58
Duncan Falls, OH (cdp) Muskingum County	22	2.57
Hewitt, MN (city) Todd County	7	2.57
Poneto, IN (town) Wells County	5	2.54
Hazelton, MI (township) Shiawassee County	57	2.53
Duluth, WA (cdp) Clark County	40	2.53
Barnes Lake-Millers Lake, MI (cdp) Lapeer County	27	2.50
Dufur, OR (city) Wasco County	14	2.49
Dover, ID (city) Bonner County	12	2.49
Barton Hills, MI (village) Washtenaw County	7	2.49
Blowers, MN (township) Otter Tail County	8	2.48
Melvin, IA (city) Osceola County	5	2.48
Plainfield, NH (cdp) Sullivan County	5	2.48

Please refer to the Explanation of Data in the front of the book for more detailed information.

Ancestry

Northern European

Top 150 Places Sorted by Percent of Total Population

Based on places with total population of 7,500 or more

Place	Population	%
Vashon, WA (cdp) King County	305	3.07
Mill Valley, CA (city) Marin County	326	2.38
Soquel, CA (cdp) Santa Cruz County	216	2.30
Lake Arrowhead, CA (cdp) San Bernardino County	217	2.27
Lafayette, CA (city) Contra Costa County	511	2.15
Rio del Mar, CA (cdp) Santa Cruz County	201	2.13
Santa Cruz, CA (city) Santa Cruz County	1,071	1.84
Summit Park, UT (cdp) Summit County	133	1.77
Linthicum, MD (cdp) Anne Arundel County	178	1.70
Capitola, CA (city) Santa Cruz County	162	1.65
Lake Los Angeles, CA (cdp) Los Angeles County	188	1.50
Alamo, CA (cdp) Contra Costa County	222	1.46
Scotia, NY (village) Schenectady County	111	1.44
Triangle, VA (cdp) Prince William County	111	1.44
Solana Beach, CA (city) San Diego County	179	1.40
White Bear Lake, MN (city) Ramsey County	300	1.29
Antigo, WI (city) Langlade County	107	1.29
White Bear Lake, MN (city) Ramsey County	300	1.28
Hopkinton, MA (town) Middlesex County	178	1.23
Piedmont, CA (city) Alameda County	125	1.18
Maplewood, MN (city) Ramsey County	429	1.16
Shoreview, MN (city) Ramsey County	286	1.15
Mahtomedi, MN (city) Washington County	87	1.13
Oak Brook, IL (village) DuPage County	85	1.08
Evergreen, CO (cdp) Jefferson County	97	1.06
Palos Verdes Estates, CA (city) Los Angeles County	139	1.04
Los Altos, CA (city) Santa Clara County	294	1.03
Sonoma, CA (city) Sonoma County	105	1.02
Pitman, NJ (borough) Gloucester County	93	1.02
Martinez, CA (city) Contra Costa County	359	1.01
Casa de Oro-Mount Helix, CA (cdp) San Diego County	185	0.97
Edmonds, WA (city) Snohomish County	381	0.96
Clayton, CA (city) Contra Costa County	104	0.96
Los Gatos, CA (town) Santa Clara County	273	0.95
Half Moon Bay, CA (city) San Mateo County	106	0.95
Hudson, WI (town) St. Croix County	78	0.95
Snoqualmie, WA (city) King County	85	0.94
Anacortes, WA (city) Skagit County	145	0.93
San Marino, CA (city) Los Angeles County	122	0.93
Crestwood, MO (city) St. Louis County	108	0.91
Agoura Hills, CA (city) Los Angeles County	180	0.89
Colesville, MD (cdp) Montgomery County	127	0.89
Lake Forest Park, WA (city) King County	112	0.89
Los Altos Hills, CA (town) Santa Clara County	70	0.89
Traverse City, MI (city) Grand Traverse County	128	0.88
Traverse City, MI (city) Grand Traverse County	128	0.87
Tamalpais-Homestead Valley, CA (cdp) Marin County	92	0.87
Steamboat Springs, CO (city) Routt County	101	0.86
Eureka, MO (city) St. Louis County	83	0.86
Tualatin, OR (city) Washington County	217	0.85
Depew, NY (village) Erie County	130	0.84
West University Place, TX (city) Harris County	123	0.84
Shoreline, WA (city) King County	435	0.83
Laguna Beach, CA (city) Orange County	190	0.83
Cedar Mill, OR (cdp) Washington County	120	0.83
Mounds View, MN (city) Ramsey County	99	0.82
Pine Lake Park, NJ (cdp) Ocean County	66	0.81
Francisville, KY (cdp) Boone County	63	0.81
Des Moines, WA (city) King County	234	0.80
Eagle Mountain, UT (city) Utah County	144	0.80
Haddonfield, NJ (borough) Camden County	90	0.78
Lamar, CO (city) Prowers County	62	0.78
Seattle, WA (city) King County	4,576	0.77
Chanhassen, MN (city) Carver County	176	0.77
Golden Valley, MN (city) Hennepin County	156	0.77
Grand Blanc, MI (city) Genesee County	65	0.77
Concord, MA (town) Middlesex County	132	0.76
Setauket-East Setauket, NY (cdp) Suffolk County	120	0.76
Enumclaw, WA (city) King County	81	0.76
Big Bear City, CA (cdp) San Bernardino County	90	0.75
Pacific Grove, CA (city) Monterey County	110	0.74
East Foothills, CA (cdp) Santa Clara County	57	0.74
Little Canada, MN (city) Ramsey County	71	0.73
Fort Collins, CO (city) Larimer County	1,013	0.72
Wayland, MA (town) Middlesex County	93	0.72
Dallas, GA (city) Paulding County	77	0.72
Kapaa, HI (cdp) Kauai County	72	0.72
Cortlandville, NY (town) Cortland County	61	0.72
Cusseta-Chattahoochee County, GA (unified govt) Chattahoochee County	83	0.71
Darien, CT (cdp/town) Fairfield County	143	0.70
Brea, CA (city) Orange County	267	0.69
Clemmons, NC (village) Forsyth County	126	0.69
College, AK (cdp) Fairbanks North Star Borough	92	0.69
Weston, CT (town) Fairfield County	70	0.69
Fairview, CA (cdp) Alameda County	68	0.69
Live Oak, CA (cdp) Santa Cruz County	112	0.68
Lower Swatara, PA (township) Dauphin County	56	0.68
Yreka, CA (city) Siskiyou County	52	0.68
Paradise, CA (town) Butte County	178	0.67
Oceano, CA (cdp) San Luis Obispo County	53	0.67
Hermosa Beach, CA (city) Los Angeles County	127	0.66
Apple Valley, MN (city) Dakota County	318	0.65
Mountlake Terrace, WA (city) Snohomish County	130	0.65
Williamstown, MA (town) Berkshire County	51	0.65
Walnut Creek, CA (city) Contra Costa County	409	0.64
Wilton, CT (town) Fairfield County	114	0.64
Sweden, NY (town) Monroe County	90	0.64
Baker City, OR (city) Baker County	63	0.64
Beatrice, NE (city) Gage County	79	0.63
Morro Bay, CA (city) San Luis Obispo County	65	0.63
Chatham, NJ (borough) Morris County	56	0.63
West Point, UT (city) Davis County	56	0.63
Jollyville, TX (cdp) Williamson County	100	0.62
Medfield, MA (town) Norfolk County	74	0.62
Caledonia, MI (township) Kent County	73	0.62
Doctor Phillips, FL (cdp) Orange County	70	0.62
Woodmoor, CO (cdp) El Paso County	55	0.62
Helena Valley West Central, MT (cdp) Lewis and Clark County	51	0.62
Holladay, UT (city) Salt Lake County	161	0.61
Franconia, VA (cdp) Fairfax County	113	0.61
Covington, GA (city) Newton County	80	0.61
Athol, MA (cdp) Worcester County	49	0.61
East Hempfield, PA (township) Lancaster County	139	0.60
Coto de Caza, CA (cdp) Orange County	92	0.60
Allouez, WI (village) Brown County	86	0.60
Warwick, PA (township) Bucks County	85	0.60
Vadnais Heights, MN (city) Ramsey County	74	0.60
Grain Valley, MO (city) Jackson County	68	0.60
Lake Elmo, MN (city) Washington County	47	0.60
Palo Alto, CA (city) Santa Clara County	369	0.59
Fair Oaks, CA (cdp) Sacramento County	181	0.59
Superior, CO (town) Boulder County	70	0.59
Newcastle, WA (city) King County	58	0.59
Standish, ME (town) Cumberland County	58	0.59
Howell, MI (city) Livingston County	57	0.59
Mira Monte, CA (cdp) Ventura County	46	0.59
Seaside, CA (city) Monterey County	188	0.58
Monterey, CA (city) Monterey County	161	0.58
Lake Stevens, WA (city) Snohomish County	156	0.58
North Tustin, CA (cdp) Orange County	142	0.58
Bothell West, WA (cdp) Snohomish County	90	0.58
Centerville, UT (city) Davis County	89	0.58
La Grande, OR (city) Union County	75	0.58
Fulton, MO (city) Callaway County	73	0.58
Lowes Island, VA (cdp) Loudoun County	66	0.58
Cedar Lake, IN (town) Lake County	65	0.58
Corte Madera, CA (town) Marin County	53	0.58
Coon Rapids, MN (city) Anoka County	352	0.57
Sedro-Woolley, WA (city) Skagit County	59	0.57
Blaine, MN (city) Anoka County	308	0.56
Windsor, CA (town) Sonoma County	143	0.56
Bainbridge Island, WA (city) Kitsap County	126	0.56
Westford, MA (town) Middlesex County	120	0.56
Mountain Brook, AL (city) Jefferson County	115	0.56
Greenville, WI (town) Outagamie County	54	0.56
Mercer Island, WA (city) King County	123	0.55
Louisville, CO (city) Boulder County	102	0.55
Burke Centre, VA (cdp) Fairfax County	93	0.55
Vienna, VA (town) Fairfax County	85	0.55
Grand Haven, MI (city) Ottawa County	59	0.55

SECTION THREE

Ancestry

Norwegian

U.S. and 50 States Sorted by Population and Percent of Total Population

Place	Population	%
United States	**4,602,337**	**1.51**
Minnesota	866,785	16.54
Wisconsin	466,309	8.27
California	401,548	1.10
Washington	396,418	6.04
North Dakota	198,244	30.04
Illinois	173,334	1.36
Iowa	169,885	5.63
Oregon	151,447	4.03
Texas	132,828	0.55
South Dakota	119,341	14.93
Florida	118,894	0.64
Arizona	117,455	1.88
Colorado	114,313	2.34
Montana	95,971	9.86
Michigan	87,020	0.87
New York	85,859	0.45
Utah	65,960	2.48
Idaho	53,092	3.48
Virginia	50,733	0.65
Missouri	45,415	0.77
North Carolina	43,446	0.47
Pennsylvania	43,252	0.34
New Jersey	42,793	0.49
Ohio	42,773	0.37
Nevada	41,941	1.59
Nebraska	37,936	2.11
Indiana	36,566	0.57
Georgia	35,864	0.38
Massachusetts	33,943	0.52
Kansas	31,788	1.13
Maryland	29,174	0.51
Alaska	28,598	4.14
Tennessee	27,199	0.44
Oklahoma	23,782	0.65
Connecticut	19,891	0.56
Wyoming	19,401	3.56
New Mexico	19,139	0.95
South Carolina	17,246	0.38
Alabama	15,596	0.33
Kentucky	13,878	0.32
Arkansas	13,691	0.48
New Hampshire	12,016	0.91
Louisiana	11,962	0.27
Hawaii	10,203	0.77
Maine	10,090	0.76
Mississippi	6,939	0.24
Vermont	5,306	0.85
Delaware	4,636	0.53
Rhode Island	4,523	0.43
West Virginia	4,093	0.22
District of Columbia	3,821	0.65

Place	Population	%
North Dakota	198,244	30.04
Minnesota	866,785	16.54
South Dakota	119,341	14.93
Montana	95,971	9.86
Wisconsin	466,309	8.27
Washington	396,418	6.04
Iowa	169,885	5.63
Alaska	28,598	4.14
Oregon	151,447	4.03
Wyoming	19,401	3.56
Idaho	53,092	3.48
Utah	65,960	2.48
Colorado	114,313	2.34
Nebraska	37,936	2.11
Arizona	117,455	1.88
Nevada	41,941	1.59
United States	**4,602,337**	**1.51**
Illinois	173,334	1.36
Kansas	31,788	1.13
California	401,548	1.10
New Mexico	19,139	0.95
New Hampshire	12,016	0.91
Michigan	87,020	0.87
Vermont	5,306	0.85
Missouri	45,415	0.77
Hawaii	10,203	0.77
Maine	10,090	0.76
Virginia	50,733	0.65
Oklahoma	23,782	0.65
District of Columbia	3,821	0.65
Florida	118,894	0.64
Indiana	36,566	0.57
Connecticut	19,891	0.56
Texas	132,828	0.55
Delaware	4,636	0.53
Massachusetts	33,943	0.52
Maryland	29,174	0.51
New Jersey	42,793	0.49
Arkansas	13,691	0.48
North Carolina	43,446	0.47
New York	85,859	0.45
Tennessee	27,199	0.44
Rhode Island	4,523	0.43
Georgia	35,864	0.38
South Carolina	17,246	0.38
Ohio	42,773	0.37
Pennsylvania	43,252	0.34
Alabama	15,596	0.33
Kentucky	13,878	0.32
Louisiana	11,962	0.27
Mississippi	6,939	0.24
West Virginia	4,093	0.22

Please refer to the Explanation of Data in the front of the book for more detailed information.

Ancestry

Norwegian

Top 150 Places Sorted by Population

Based on all places, regardless of total population

Place	Population	%
Minneapolis, MN (city) Hennepin County	41,603	10.96
Fargo, ND (city) Cass County	36,248	35.35
Seattle, WA (city) King County	30,449	5.12
Sioux Falls, SD (city) Minnehaha County	24,722	16.61
St. Paul, MN (city) Ramsey County	24,039	8.52
Portland, OR (city) Multnomah County	23,053	4.07
Madison, WI (city) Dane County	22,465	9.80
New York, NY (city) Kings County	21,894	0.27
Los Angeles, CA (city) Los Angeles County	20,565	0.55
Phoenix, AZ (city) Maricopa County	19,701	1.36
Grand Forks, ND (city) Grand Forks County	17,361	33.20
San Diego, CA (city) San Diego County	16,955	1.32
Rochester, MN (city) Olmsted County	15,760	15.12
Spokane, WA (city) Spokane County	14,582	7.06
Chicago, IL (city) Cook County	14,090	0.52
Duluth, MN (city) St. Louis County	14,060	16.34
Moorhead, MN (city) Clay County	13,231	36.03
Eau Claire, WI (city) Eau Claire County	13,218	20.29
Bloomington, MN (city) Hennepin County	13,151	15.92
Eau Claire, WI (city) Eau Claire County	12,789	20.30
Mesa, AZ (city) Maricopa County	12,530	2.85
Bismarck, ND (city) Burleigh County	12,463	20.78
Milwaukee, WI (city) Milwaukee County	12,450	2.11
Minot, ND (city) Ward County	12,251	31.37
Plymouth, MN (city) Hennepin County	11,572	16.73
Colorado Springs, CO (city) El Paso County	11,336	2.81
Anchorage, AK (municipality) Anchorage Municipality	11,185	3.93
Tacoma, WA (city) Pierce County	11,116	5.59
Coon Rapids, MN (city) Anoka County	10,318	16.64
Eagan, MN (city) Dakota County	10,229	15.86
Maple Grove, MN (city) Hennepin County	10,177	17.24
Billings, MT (city) Yellowstone County	10,157	10.00
La Crosse, WI (city) La Crosse County	9,468	18.48
Burnsville, MN (city) Dakota County	9,298	15.32
Lakeville, MN (city) Dakota County	9,186	17.02
West Fargo, ND (city) Cass County	8,756	36.69
Denver, CO (city) Denver County	8,645	1.50
Blaine, MN (city) Anoka County	8,556	15.44
Omaha, NE (city) Douglas County	8,514	2.09
Janesville, WI (city) Rock County	8,447	13.31
Eden Prairie, MN (city) Hennepin County	8,151	13.76
Apple Valley, MN (city) Dakota County	8,144	16.71
Boise City, ID (city) Ada County	8,127	3.94
San Jose, CA (city) Santa Clara County	8,087	0.87
Vancouver, WA (city) Clark County	7,639	4.77
San Francisco, CA (city) San Francisco County	7,582	0.96
Tucson, AZ (city) Pima County	7,557	1.46
Woodbury, MN (city) Washington County	7,461	12.55
Rapid City, SD (city) Pennington County	7,457	11.27
Manhattan, NY (borough) New York County	7,445	0.47
Everett, WA (city) Snohomish County	7,415	7.29
Brooklyn Park, MN (city) Hennepin County	7,255	9.85
Des Moines, IA (city) Polk County	7,129	3.53
St. Cloud, MN (city) Stearns County	7,126	10.94
Minnetonka, MN (city) Hennepin County	7,112	14.35
Albuquerque, NM (city) Bernalillo County	7,108	1.34
Edina, MN (city) Hennepin County	7,074	14.91
Las Vegas, NV (city) Clark County	6,993	1.21
Houston, TX (city) Harris County	6,888	0.33
Eugene, OR (city) Lane County	6,754	4.41
Cedar Rapids, IA (city) Linn County	6,543	5.22
Salem, OR (city) Marion County	6,482	4.27
St. Louis Park, MN (city) Hennepin County	6,374	14.27
Mankato, MN (city) Blue Earth County	6,337	16.59
Mankato, MN (city) Blue Earth County	6,337	16.59
Great Falls, MT (city) Cascade County	6,293	10.87
Albert Lea, MN (city) Freeborn County	6,275	34.69
Austin, TX (city) Travis County	6,273	0.82
Spokane Valley, WA (city) Spokane County	6,078	6.90
Williston, ND (city) Williams County	6,065	43.78
Scottsdale, AZ (city) Maricopa County	6,064	2.77
Bellingham, WA (city) Whatcom County	6,023	7.63
St. Cloud, MN (city) Stearns County	5,997	11.57
Brooklyn, NY (borough) Kings County	5,982	0.24
Andover, MN (city) Anoka County	5,614	18.65
Austin, MN (city) Mower County	5,562	22.76
Salt Lake City, UT (city) Salt Lake County	5,504	2.98
Fort Collins, CO (city) Larimer County	5,465	3.90
Sacramento, CA (city) Sacramento County	5,382	1.17
Fergus Falls, MN (city) Otter Tail County	5,327	39.89
Roseville, MN (city) Ramsey County	5,311	15.97
San Antonio, TX (city) Medina County	5,211	0.40
Staten Island, NY (borough) Richmond County	5,135	1.11
Missoula, MT (city) Missoula County	5,083	7.77
Brookhaven, NY (town) Suffolk County	5,078	1.06
Marysville, WA (city) Snohomish County	5,047	8.72
Reno, NV (city) Washoe County	5,037	2.28
Lincoln, NE (city) Lancaster County	5,033	1.99
Chandler, AZ (city) Maricopa County	5,027	2.19
Henderson, NV (city) Clark County	4,967	1.99
Fort Worth, TX (city) Tarrant County	4,959	0.70
Watertown, SD (city) Codington County	4,938	23.16
Dallas, TX (city) Dallas County	4,919	0.41
Bellevue, WA (city) King County	4,786	4.01
Sioux City, IA (city) Woodbury County	4,767	5.81
Inver Grove Heights, MN (city) Dakota County	4,761	14.27
Brookings, SD (city) Brookings County	4,759	22.17
Savage, MN (city) Scott County	4,644	17.45
Willmar, MN (city) Kandiyohi County	4,617	23.88
Richfield, MN (city) Hennepin County	4,548	13.08
Rockford, IL (city) Winnebago County	4,532	2.93
Aurora, CO (city) Arapahoe County	4,525	1.44
Maplewood, MN (city) Ramsey County	4,522	12.19
Cottage Grove, MN (city) Washington County	4,472	13.14
Jacksonville, FL (city) Duval County	4,449	0.55
Owatonna, MN (city) Steele County	4,433	17.51
Winona, MN (city) Winona County	4,421	15.98
Superior, WI (city) Douglas County	4,344	15.97
Ames, IA (city) Story County	4,339	7.57
Jamestown, ND (city) Stutsman County	4,306	28.16
Champlin, MN (city) Hennepin County	4,306	18.93
Long Beach, CA (city) Los Angeles County	4,263	0.92
Mason City, IA (city) Cerro Gordo County	4,218	15.00
Gilbert, AZ (town) Maricopa County	4,178	2.14
Gresham, OR (city) Multnomah County	4,152	4.09
Edmonds, WA (city) Snohomish County	4,133	10.42
Shakopee, MN (city) Scott County	4,065	11.59
Shoreview, MN (city) Ramsey County	4,048	16.26
Kansas City, MO (city) Jackson County	4,020	0.88
Federal Way, WA (city) King County	4,011	4.57
Ramsey, MN (city) Anoka County	3,996	17.43
Northfield, MN (city) Rice County	3,994	20.57
Huntington Beach, CA (city) Orange County	3,981	2.11
Renton, WA (city) King County	3,952	4.58
Thief River Falls, MN (city) Pennington County	3,930	45.94
Onalaska, WI (city) La Crosse County	3,897	22.74
Appleton, WI (city) Outagamie County	3,880	5.34
Kent, WA (city) King County	3,872	4.33
Peoria, AZ (city) Yavapai County	3,872	2.60
Washington, DC (city) District of Columbia	3,821	0.65
Ankeny, IA (city) Polk County	3,796	8.99
Auburn, WA (city) King County	3,770	5.63
South Hill, WA (cdp) Pierce County	3,747	7.14
Elk River, MN (city) Sherburne County	3,721	16.53
Chanhassen, MN (city) Carver County	3,714	16.25
Aberdeen, SD (city) Brown County	3,665	14.25
Wichita, KS (city) Sedgwick County	3,662	0.98
Oklahoma City, OK (city) Oklahoma County	3,656	0.65
Shoreline, WA (city) King County	3,651	6.95
Indianapolis, IN (city) Marion County	3,636	0.45
Northfield, MN (city) Rice County	3,634	19.73
Waukesha, WI (city) Waukesha County	3,623	5.18
Green Bay, WI (city) Brown County	3,611	3.47
Oakdale, MN (city) Washington County	3,610	13.19
Prior Lake, MN (city) Scott County	3,596	16.20
Columbus, OH (city) Franklin County	3,594	0.47
Lakewood, CO (city) Jefferson County	3,582	2.52
Fridley, MN (city) Anoka County	3,536	12.87
Kirkland, WA (city) King County	3,534	7.41
Beloit, WI (city) Rock County	3,526	9.52

Ancestry

Norwegian

Top 150 Places Sorted by Percent of Total Population

Based on all places, regardless of total population

Place	Population	%
Caledonia, ND (cdp) Traill County	41	100.00
Blanchard, ND (cdp) Traill County	35	100.00
Battle, MN (township) Beltrami County	26	100.00
Toeterville, IA (cdp) Mitchell County	24	100.00
Auburn, ND (cdp) Walsh County	18	100.00
Antelope, MT (cdp) Sheridan County	17	100.00
Hamre, MN (township) Beltrami County	8	100.00
De Lamere, ND (cdp) Sargent County	7	100.00
Rapid River, MN (township) Lake of the Woods County	6	100.00
Scandia, MN (township) Polk County	28	93.33
Spruce Grove, MN (township) Beltrami County	88	91.67
Linsell, MN (township) Marshall County	33	91.67
Landa, ND (city) Bottineau County	32	88.89
Alamo, ND (city) Williams County	34	87.18
Wadena, MN (city) Otter Tail County	107	85.60
Whiteford, MN (township) Marshall County	32	84.21
Mayfield, MN (township) Pennington County	41	83.67
Mary, MN (township) Norman County	66	83.54
Springbrook, ND (city) Williams County	35	81.40
Holt, MN (city) Marshall County	59	80.82
Lessor, MN (township) Polk County	133	80.61
Reis, MN (township) Polk County	80	80.00
Edmore, ND (city) Ramsey County	223	79.08
Nereson, MN (township) Roseau County	34	79.07
Goodridge, MN (township) Pennington County	56	78.87
Eckvoll, MN (township) Marshall County	52	78.79
Hubbard, MN (township) Polk County	44	78.57
Ambrose, ND (city) Divide County	11	78.57
Angle, MN (township) Lake of the Woods County	54	78.26
Angle Inlet, MN (cdp) Lake of the Woods County	54	78.26
Equality, MN (township) Red Lake County	79	78.22
Midway, MN (cdp) Mahnomen County	7	77.78
Strandquist, MN (city) Marshall County	51	77.27
Soler, MN (township) Roseau County	64	77.11
Anthony, MN (township) Norman County	40	76.92
Storla, SD (cdp) Aurora County	10	76.92
Colfax, ND (city) Richland County	72	76.60
Kathryn, ND (city) Barnes County	42	76.36
White Earth, ND (city) Mountrail County	43	75.44
Erhard, MN (city) Otter Tail County	91	75.21
Hannaford, ND (city) Griggs County	115	75.16
Hagen, MN (township) Clay County	149	74.87
Lengby, MN (city) Polk County	85	74.56
Higdem, MN (township) Polk County	76	74.51
Rutland, ND (city) Sargent County	106	74.13
Hammond, MN (township) Polk County	36	73.47
Carpio, ND (city) Ward County	92	72.44
York, ND (city) Benson County	34	72.34
Litchville, ND (city) Barnes County	141	72.31
Johnson, MN (township) Polk County	26	72.22
Liberty, MN (township) Polk County	106	72.11
Oak Park, MN (township) Marshall County	104	71.72
Wyandotte, MN (township) Pennington County	101	71.63
Hantho, MN (township) Lac qui Parle County	80	71.43
Nunda, SD (town) Lake County	35	71.43
Camp 5, MN (township) St. Louis County	5	71.43
Tolna, ND (city) Nelson County	158	70.85
Good Hope, MN (township) Norman County	29	70.73
McVille, ND (city) Nelson County	182	70.27
Beltrami, MN (city) Polk County	33	70.21
Keene, MN (township) Clay County	98	70.00
Trail, MN (city) Polk County	28	70.00
Grenville, SD (town) Day County	46	69.70
Leal, ND (city) Barnes County	23	69.70
Hampden, ND (city) Ramsey County	43	69.35
Gully, MN (township) Polk County	95	69.34
Garden, MN (township) Polk County	129	68.98
Lockhart, MN (township) Norman County	46	68.66
Powers Lake, ND (city) Burke County	173	68.65
Berthold, ND (city) Ward County	355	68.40
Trondhjem, MN (township) Otter Tail County	114	68.26
Blue Mounds, MN (township) Pope County	128	68.09
Benedict, ND (city) McLean County	36	67.92
Prosper, MN (township) Lake of the Woods County	31	67.39
Wanamingo, MN (township) Goodhue County	327	67.28
Gary, MN (city) Norman County	86	67.19
Brandsvold, MN (township) Polk County	149	66.82
Tansem, MN (township) Clay County	185	66.79
Bejou, MN (city) Mahnomen County	66	66.67
Warrenton, MN (township) Marshall County	60	66.67
West Roy Lake, MN (cdp) Mahnomen County	4	66.67
White Rock, SD (town) Roberts County	2	66.67
Norway, MN (township) Fillmore County	206	66.45
Ulen, MN (township) Clay County	99	66.44
Langhei, MN (township) Pope County	122	66.30
Norwegian Grove, MN (township) Otter Tail County	222	66.27
Lambert, MN (township) Red Lake County	94	66.20
Huntly, MN (township) Marshall County	46	65.71
Sibley, ND (city) Barnes County	15	65.22
Helgeland, MN (township) Polk County	26	65.00
Silverton, MN (township) Pennington County	117	64.64
Sunburg, MN (city) Kandiyohi County	84	64.62
Edinburg, ND (city) Walsh County	135	64.59
Rome, MN (township) Faribault County	102	64.56
Spring Creek, MN (township) Norman County	38	64.41
Arendahl, MN (township) Fillmore County	168	64.37
Golden Valley, MN (township) Roseau County	109	64.12
Oscar, MN (township) Otter Tail County	114	63.69
Perth, ND (city) Towner County	14	63.64
Lac qui Parle, MN (township) Lac qui Parle County	92	63.45
Lakewood, MN (township) Lake of the Woods County	71	63.39
Felton, MN (township) Clay County	50	63.29
Glenfield, ND (city) Foster County	82	63.08
Pingree, ND (city) Stutsman County	46	63.01
Mabel, MN (city) Fillmore County	441	63.00
New Maine, MN (township) Marshall County	170	62.96
Newfolden, MN (city) Marshall County	212	62.91
Adams, ND (city) Walsh County	81	62.79
Portland, ND (city) Traill County	410	62.69
Como, MN (township) Marshall County	42	62.69
Hickory, MN (township) Pennington County	30	62.50
Shotley Brook, MN (unorganized territory) Beltrami County	5	62.50
McHenry, ND (city) Foster County	66	62.26
Akron, MN (township) Wilkin County	61	62.24
Newburg, MN (township) Fillmore County	237	62.20
Gully, MN (city) Polk County	23	62.16
Tumuli, MN (township) Otter Tail County	350	62.06
Myrtle, MN (city) Freeborn County	39	61.90
Delaware, MN (township) Grant County	45	61.64
Hitterdal, MN (city) Clay County	130	61.61
Kratka, MN (township) Pennington County	142	61.47
Hill River, MN (township) Polk County	137	61.43
Dazey, ND (city) Barnes County	54	61.36
Garfield, MN (township) Lac qui Parle County	122	61.31
McDonaldsville, MN (township) Norman County	106	61.27
Climax, MN (city) Polk County	133	61.01
Reiner, MN (township) Pennington County	39	60.94
Tioga, ND (city) Williams County	743	60.80
Binford, ND (city) Griggs County	121	60.80
Epping, ND (city) Williams County	31	60.78
Unity, WI (town) Trempealeau County	328	60.63
Middle River, MN (city) Marshall County	189	60.58
Russia, MN (township) Polk County	29	60.42
Emmons, MN (city) Freeborn County	211	60.29
Star, MN (township) Pennington County	44	60.27
Winsor, MN (township) Clearwater County	53	60.23
Winchester, MN (township) Norman County	48	60.00
Wendell, MN (city) Grant County	92	59.74
Camp Release, MN (township) Lac qui Parle County	201	59.64
Kragero, MN (township) Chippewa County	65	59.63
Hendrum, MN (city) Norman County	133	59.38
Voltaire, ND (city) McHenry County	19	59.38
Spring Grove, MN (township) Houston County	219	59.35
Garnes, MN (township) Red Lake County	93	59.24
Sundal, MN (township) Norman County	45	59.21
Andover, MN (township) Polk County	104	59.09
Pelican, MN (township) Otter Tail County	310	59.05
Pigeon Falls, WI (village) Trempealeau County	183	59.03
Bygland, MN (township) Polk County	152	58.91
Fertile, MN (city) Polk County	500	58.89

Please refer to the Explanation of Data in the front of the book for more detailed information.

Ancestry

Norwegian

Top 150 Places Sorted by Percent of Total Population

Based on places with total population of 7,500 or more

Place	Population	%
Thief River Falls, MN (city) Pennington County	3,930	45.94
Williston, ND (city) Williams County	6,065	43.78
Fergus Falls, MN (city) Otter Tail County	5,327	39.89
West Fargo, ND (city) Cass County	8,756	36.69
Moorhead, MN (city) Clay County	13,231	36.03
Fargo, ND (city) Cass County	36,248	35.35
Crookston, MN (city) Polk County	2,767	35.03
East Grand Forks, MN (city) Polk County	2,937	35.02
Albert Lea, MN (city) Freeborn County	6,275	34.69
Grand Forks, ND (city) Grand Forks County	17,361	33.20
Wahpeton, ND (city) Richland County	2,545	32.41
Minot, ND (city) Ward County	12,251	31.37
Detroit Lakes, MN (city) Becker County	2,517	29.71
Decorah, IA (city) Winneshiek County	2,395	29.51
Jamestown, ND (city) Stutsman County	4,306	28.16
Stoughton, WI (city) Dane County	3,477	27.60
Alexandria, MN (city) Douglas County	2,772	24.99
Holmen, WI (village) La Crosse County	2,069	24.47
Willmar, MN (city) Kandiyohi County	4,617	23.88
Brandon, SD (city) Minnehaha County	1,932	23.47
Watertown, SD (city) Codington County	4,938	23.16
Austin, MN (city) Mower County	5,562	22.76
Onalaska, WI (city) La Crosse County	3,897	22.74
Brookings, SD (city) Brookings County	4,759	22.17
Waseca, MN (city) Waseca County	2,028	21.51
Grand Rapids, MN (city) Itasca County	2,261	21.01
Havre, MT (city) Hill County	1,933	20.87
Sparta, WI (city) Monroe County	1,958	20.85
Bismarck, ND (city) Burleigh County	12,463	20.78
Northfield, MN (city) Rice County	3,994	20.57
Eau Claire, WI (city) Eau Claire County	12,789	20.30
Eau Claire, WI (city) Eau Claire County	13,218	20.29
Cambridge, MN (city) Isanti County	1,596	20.28
Rogers, MN (city) Hennepin County	1,538	20.08
Northfield, MN (city) Rice County	3,634	19.73
Waconia, MN (city) Carver County	1,976	19.45
Bemidji, MN (city) Beltrami County	2,522	19.09
Big Lake, MN (city) Sherburne County	1,842	19.07
Rice Lake, WI (city) Barron County	1,612	19.07
Champlin, MN (city) Hennepin County	4,306	18.93
Red Wing, MN (city) Goodhue County	3,114	18.93
St. Peter, MN (city) Nicollet County	2,084	18.92
East Bethel, MN (city) Anoka County	2,177	18.77
Ham Lake, MN (city) Anoka County	2,805	18.76
Andover, MN (city) Anoka County	5,614	18.65
La Crosse, WI (city) La Crosse County	9,468	18.48
Otsego, MN (city) Wright County	2,287	18.27
Hudson, WI (city) St. Croix County	2,239	18.15
River Falls, WI (city) Pierce County	2,664	18.13
Oak Grove, MN (city) Anoka County	1,427	18.11
St. Michael, MN (city) Wright County	2,766	17.98
White Bear, MN (township) Ramsey County	1,946	17.94
DeForest, WI (village) Dane County	1,555	17.94
Monticello, MN (city) Wright County	2,167	17.72
Chippewa Falls, WI (city) Chippewa County	2,412	17.68
Owatonna, MN (city) Steele County	4,433	17.51
Savage, MN (city) Scott County	4,644	17.45
Ramsey, MN (city) Anoka County	3,996	17.43
Marshall, MN (city) Lyon County	2,339	17.42
Lino Lakes, MN (city) Anoka County	3,444	17.41
Mounds View, MN (city) Ramsey County	2,100	17.35
Maple Grove, MN (city) Hennepin County	10,177	17.24
Brainerd, MN (city) Crow Wing County	2,362	17.19
St. Anthony, MN (city) Hennepin and Ramsey Counties	1,384	17.07
Lakeville, MN (city) Dakota County	9,186	17.02
Hutchinson, MN (city) McLeod County	2,403	16.94
Plymouth, MN (city) Hennepin County	11,572	16.73
Apple Valley, MN (city) Dakota County	8,144	16.71
Coon Rapids, MN (city) Anoka County	10,318	16.64
Anoka, MN (city) Anoka County	2,901	16.63
Sioux Falls, SD (city) Minnehaha County	24,722	16.61
Mankato, MN (city) Blue Earth County	6,337	16.59
Mankato, MN (city) Blue Earth County	6,337	16.59
Elk River, MN (city) Sherburne County	3,721	16.53
Sartell, MN (city) Stearns County	2,087	16.53

Place	Population	%
Buffalo, MN (city) Wright County	2,440	16.52
Farmington, MN (city) Dakota County	3,246	16.51
New Richmond, WI (city) St. Croix County	1,353	16.39
Mound, MN (city) Hennepin County	1,479	16.37
Duluth, MN (city) St. Louis County	14,060	16.34
Shoreview, MN (city) Ramsey County	4,048	16.26
Oregon, WI (village) Dane County	1,454	16.26
Chanhassen, MN (city) Carver County	3,714	16.25
Menomonie, WI (city) Dunn County	2,607	16.23
Prior Lake, MN (city) Scott County	3,596	16.20
Fairmont, MN (city) Martin County	1,715	16.14
Winona, MN (city) Winona County	4,421	15.98
Roseville, MN (city) Ramsey County	5,311	15.97
Superior, WI (city) Douglas County	4,344	15.97
Yankton, SD (city) Yankton County	2,273	15.96
Bloomington, MN (city) Hennepin County	13,151	15.92
Eagan, MN (city) Dakota County	10,229	15.86
Mandan, ND (city) Morton County	2,814	15.80
Sartell, MN (city) Stearns County	2,328	15.78
Hermantown, MN (city) St. Louis County	1,441	15.75
McFarland, WI (village) Dane County	1,191	15.72
Rosemount, MN (city) Dakota County	3,248	15.68
Monona, WI (city) Dane County	1,186	15.61
River Falls, WI (city) Pierce County	1,804	15.52
Blaine, MN (city) Anoka County	8,556	15.44
Burnsville, MN (city) Dakota County	9,298	15.32
Rochester, MN (city) Olmsted County	15,760	15.12
Hopkins, MN (city) Hennepin County	2,623	15.06
Mason City, IA (city) Cerro Gordo County	4,218	15.00
North Branch, MN (city) Chisago County	1,494	14.97
Forest Lake, MN (city) Washington County	2,647	14.92
Edina, MN (city) Hennepin County	7,074	14.91
Stillwater, MN (city) Washington County	2,652	14.90
North Mankato, MN (city) Nicollet County	1,959	14.90
Arden Hills, MN (city) Ramsey County	1,410	14.85
North St. Paul, MN (city) Ramsey County	1,690	14.84
Cloquet, MN (city) Carlton County	1,781	14.82
Vermillion, SD (city) Clay County	1,555	14.79
Hastings, MN (city) Dakota County	3,184	14.75
White Bear Lake, MN (city) Ramsey County	3,420	14.72
Dickinson, ND (city) Stark County	2,516	14.66
Golden Valley, MN (city) Hennepin County	2,949	14.61
New Hope, MN (city) Hennepin County	2,962	14.60
White Bear Lake, MN (city) Ramsey County	3,420	14.58
Chaska, MN (city) Carver County	3,348	14.56
Minnetonka, MN (city) Hennepin County	7,112	14.35
Lake Elmo, MN (city) Washington County	1,126	14.29
St. Louis Park, MN (city) Hennepin County	6,374	14.27
Inver Grove Heights, MN (city) Dakota County	4,761	14.27
Wyoming, MN (city) Chisago County	1,095	14.26
Aberdeen, SD (city) Brown County	3,665	14.25
Robbinsdale, MN (city) Hennepin County	1,977	14.25
Faribault, MN (city) Rice County	3,257	14.14
Vadnais Heights, MN (city) Ramsey County	1,728	14.07
New Brighton, MN (city) Ramsey County	2,996	14.05
Monroe, WI (city) Green County	1,523	14.02
Crystal, MN (city) Hennepin County	3,082	13.97
Miles City, MT (city) Custer County	1,160	13.96
Webster City, IA (city) Hamilton County	1,133	13.94
Hibbing, MN (city) St. Louis County	2,278	13.89
Clear Lake, IA (city) Cerro Gordo County	1,078	13.82
Hudson, WI (town) St. Croix County	1,136	13.77
Eden Prairie, MN (city) Hennepin County	8,151	13.76
Waunakee, WI (village) Dane County	1,561	13.51
Janesville, WI (city) Rock County	8,447	13.31
Little Falls, MN (city) Morrison County	1,109	13.28
Oakdale, MN (city) Washington County	3,610	13.19
Cottage Grove, MN (city) Washington County	4,472	13.14
Richfield, MN (city) Hennepin County	4,548	13.08
Huron, SD (city) Beadle County	1,571	12.97
Fridley, MN (city) Anoka County	3,536	12.87
Pierre, SD (city) Hughes County	1,735	12.75
Little Canada, MN (city) Ramsey County	1,233	12.75
Woodbury, MN (city) Washington County	7,461	12.55
Sun Prairie, WI (city) Dane County	3,481	12.52

SECTION THREE

Please refer to the Explanation of Data in the front of the book for more detailed information.

Ancestry

Pennsylvania German

U.S. and 50 States Sorted by Population and Percent of Total Population

Place	Population	%
United States	**346,187**	**0.11**
Pennsylvania	173,129	1.37
Ohio	32,246	0.28
New York	13,519	0.07
Indiana	13,018	0.20
Florida	10,545	0.06
Michigan	9,478	0.10
California	7,691	0.02
Wisconsin	7,015	0.12
New Jersey	6,854	0.08
Illinois	5,327	0.04
Texas	4,717	0.02
Iowa	4,659	0.15
Missouri	4,172	0.07
Maryland	4,035	0.07
Kansas	3,826	0.14
Arizona	3,475	0.06
Washington	3,453	0.05
Virginia	3,235	0.04
Delaware	3,020	0.34
North Carolina	2,855	0.03
Oregon	2,702	0.07
Colorado	2,598	0.05
Nebraska	2,567	0.14
Minnesota	2,396	0.05
South Carolina	1,877	0.04
Kentucky	1,724	0.04
Oklahoma	1,635	0.04
Tennessee	1,594	0.03
Georgia	1,325	0.01
West Virginia	1,048	0.06
Arkansas	925	0.03
Massachusetts	901	0.01
Connecticut	874	0.02
Montana	798	0.08
Nevada	770	0.03
South Dakota	719	0.09
Idaho	632	0.04
Alabama	595	0.01
New Mexico	511	0.03
Alaska	496	0.07
Wyoming	484	0.09
New Hampshire	446	0.03
Vermont	398	0.06
Louisiana	357	0.01
Maine	351	0.03
North Dakota	263	0.04
Rhode Island	233	0.02
Utah	225	0.01
Mississippi	214	0.01
Hawaii	193	0.01
District of Columbia	67	0.01

Place	Population	%
Pennsylvania	173,129	1.37
Delaware	3,020	0.34
Ohio	32,246	0.28
Indiana	13,018	0.20
Iowa	4,659	0.15
Kansas	3,826	0.14
Nebraska	2,567	0.14
Wisconsin	7,015	0.12
United States	**346,187**	**0.11**
Michigan	9,478	0.10
South Dakota	719	0.09
Wyoming	484	0.09
New Jersey	6,854	0.08
Montana	798	0.08
New York	13,519	0.07
Missouri	4,172	0.07
Maryland	4,035	0.07
Oregon	2,702	0.07
Alaska	496	0.07
Florida	10,545	0.06
Arizona	3,475	0.06
West Virginia	1,048	0.06
Vermont	398	0.06
Washington	3,453	0.05
Colorado	2,598	0.05
Minnesota	2,396	0.05
Illinois	5,327	0.04
Virginia	3,235	0.04
South Carolina	1,877	0.04
Kentucky	1,724	0.04
Oklahoma	1,635	0.04
Idaho	632	0.04
North Dakota	263	0.04
North Carolina	2,855	0.03
Tennessee	1,594	0.03
Arkansas	925	0.03
Nevada	770	0.03
New Mexico	511	0.03
New Hampshire	446	0.03
Maine	351	0.03
California	7,691	0.02
Texas	4,717	0.02
Connecticut	874	0.02
Rhode Island	233	0.02
Georgia	1,325	0.01
Massachusetts	901	0.01
Alabama	595	0.01
Louisiana	357	0.01
Utah	225	0.01
Mississippi	214	0.01
Hawaii	193	0.01
District of Columbia	67	0.01

Please refer to the Explanation of Data in the front of the book for more detailed information.

Ancestry

Pennsylvania German

Top 150 Places Sorted by Population

Based on all places, regardless of total population

Place	Population	%
Allentown, PA (city) Lehigh County	4,292	3.69
Bethlehem, PA (city) Northampton County	2,599	3.48
Reading, PA (city) Berks County	2,056	2.35
Philadelphia, PA (city) Philadelphia County	1,967	0.13
Bethlehem, PA (city) Northampton County	1,688	3.04
Lehigh, PA (township) Northampton County	1,634	15.60
North Whitehall, PA (township) Lehigh County	1,556	9.97
Salisbury, PA (township) Lancaster County	1,526	14.01
Washington, PA (township) Lehigh County	1,238	18.66
Muhlenberg, PA (township) Berks County	1,161	6.04
South Whitehall, PA (township) Lehigh County	1,117	5.86
Whitehall, PA (township) Lehigh County	1,093	4.13
Lower Macungie, PA (township) Lehigh County	1,065	3.72
Lebanon, PA (city) Lebanon County	1,014	3.99
Earl, PA (township) Lancaster County	991	14.43
Pottstown, PA (borough) Montgomery County	986	4.42
Emmaus, PA (borough) Lehigh County	939	8.33
Palmerton, PA (borough) Carbon County	921	16.99
Moore, PA (township) Northampton County	920	10.04
Bethlehem, PA (city) Lehigh County	911	4.72
Upper Milford, PA (township) Lehigh County	898	12.37
Williamsport, PA (city) Lycoming County	823	2.79
Lower Saucon, PA (township) Northampton County	749	6.98
Exeter, PA (township) Berks County	748	3.00
Pottsville, PA (city) Schuylkill County	745	5.13
Catasauqua, PA (borough) Lehigh County	741	11.45
Longswamp, PA (township) Berks County	738	13.09
Berwick, PA (borough) Columbia County	721	6.81
Easton, PA (city) Northampton County	711	2.64
Upper Macungie, PA (township) Lehigh County	703	3.69
Salisbury, PA (township) Lehigh County	696	5.14
Bart, PA (township) Lancaster County	688	22.36
Cumru, PA (township) Berks County	682	4.54
Spring, PA (township) Berks County	668	2.50
Rapho, PA (township) Lancaster County	643	6.36
Colerain, PA (township) Lancaster County	637	17.83
West Earl, PA (township) Lancaster County	628	8.21
Northampton, PA (borough) Northampton County	624	6.29
West Penn, PA (township) Schuylkill County	612	14.20
Clinton, WI (town) Vernon County	608	51.35
Maidencreek, PA (township) Berks County	584	6.70
Palmer, PA (township) Northampton County	580	2.88
Richland, PA (township) Bucks County	576	4.62
Maxatawny, PA (township) Berks County	574	7.43
Plainfield, PA (township) Northampton County	563	9.19
Wichita, KS (city) Sedgwick County	557	0.15
Paradise, PA (township) Lancaster County	554	10.92
Upper Leacock, PA (township) Lancaster County	544	6.29
Upper Saucon, PA (township) Lehigh County	535	3.73
Phoenix, AZ (city) Maricopa County	535	0.04
Lower Paxton, PA (township) Dauphin County	528	1.13
Fullerton, PA (cdp) Lehigh County	522	3.47
Perkasie, PA (borough) Bucks County	519	6.03
Farmersville, PA (cdp) Lancaster County	514	31.08
Altoona, PA (city) Blair County	509	1.09
Lower Towamensing, PA (township) Carbon County	502	15.48
East Lampeter, PA (township) Lancaster County	495	3.11
Oley, PA (township) Berks County	492	13.54
Ross, PA (township) Monroe County	489	8.16
Mahoning, PA (township) Carbon County	487	11.38
West Mahoning, PA (township) Indiana County	486	34.01
Bethlehem, PA (township) Northampton County	486	2.07
Lynn, PA (township) Lehigh County	485	11.63
Towamensing, PA (township) Carbon County	482	11.01
Wilson, PA (borough) Northampton County	480	6.07
Bushkill, PA (township) Northampton County	465	5.79
New York, NY (city) Kings County	465	0.01
East Pennsboro, PA (township) Cumberland County	450	2.27
Portland, OR (city) Multnomah County	450	0.08
Akron, OH (city) Summit County	444	0.22
Omaha, NE (city) Douglas County	444	0.11
Allen, PA (township) Northampton County	443	11.01
Wilkes-Barre, PA (city) Luzerne County	442	1.06
Blandon, PA (cdp) Berks County	441	6.19
Los Angeles, CA (city) Los Angeles County	440	0.01
Wayne, PA (township) Schuylkill County	437	8.69
York, PA (city) York County	436	1.00
Morristown, NY (town) St. Lawrence County	433	15.79
Honey Brook, PA (township) Chester County	428	5.76
Lehighton, PA (borough) Carbon County	418	7.53
Forks, PA (township) Northampton County	416	3.04
Franconia, PA (township) Montgomery County	413	3.25
Franklin, PA (township) Carbon County	410	9.65
Bangor, PA (borough) Northampton County	408	7.67
Middletown, PA (cdp) Northampton County	403	5.59
Leacock, PA (township) Lancaster County	399	7.73
Conemaugh, PA (township) Somerset County	398	5.44
Bath, PA (borough) Northampton County	396	14.55
Slatington, PA (borough) Lehigh County	395	9.21
Bern, PA (township) Berks County	395	5.76
Colebrookdale, PA (township) Berks County	391	7.60
Pittsburgh, PA (city) Allegheny County	385	0.12
Heidelberg, PA (township) Lehigh County	380	11.16
Polk, PA (township) Monroe County	376	4.81
Upper Pottsgrove, PA (township) Montgomery County	374	7.34
North Lebanon, PA (township) Lebanon County	373	3.33
Douglass, PA (township) Berks County	371	11.11
Tucson, AZ (city) Pima County	371	0.07
Hamburg, PA (borough) Berks County	370	8.63
Lewis, PA (township) Northumberland County	369	19.37
Clifton, WI (town) Monroe County	367	40.78
Hereford, PA (township) Berks County	367	12.03
South Londonderry, PA (township) Lebanon County	366	5.45
Topton, PA (borough) Berks County	365	15.30
Alburtis, PA (borough) Lehigh County	360	16.06
Milford, PA (township) Bucks County	359	3.67
Columbus, OH (city) Franklin County	359	0.05
Chestnuthill, PA (township) Monroe County	358	2.10
Lower Providence, PA (township) Montgomery County	355	1.43
Indianapolis, IN (city) Marion County	355	0.04
Bridge Creek, WI (town) Eau Claire County	352	18.75
Schuylkill Haven, PA (borough) Schuylkill County	350	6.44
Elkhart, IN (city) Elkhart County	347	0.67
Douglass, PA (township) Montgomery County	344	3.45
Troupsburg, NY (town) Steuben County	341	23.32
Boyertown, PA (borough) Berks County	338	8.33
West Rockhill, PA (township) Bucks County	338	6.61
Hellertown, PA (borough) Northampton County	338	5.74
Pennside, PA (cdp) Berks County	337	7.64
Derry, PA (township) Dauphin County	337	1.40
Abington, PA (township) Montgomery County	336	0.61
Albuquerque, NM (city) Bernalillo County	333	0.06
Menno, PA (township) Mifflin County	332	15.95
Birdsboro, PA (borough) Berks County	331	6.39
East Nottingham, PA (township) Chester County	331	4.05
Johnstown, PA (city) Cambria County	330	1.54
Scranton, PA (city) Lackawanna County	330	0.43
Erie, PA (city) Erie County	329	0.32
Logan, PA (township) Blair County	327	2.71
Manhattan, NY (borough) New York County	327	0.02
Tamaqua, PA (borough) Schuylkill County	326	4.59
West Brandywine, PA (township) Chester County	326	4.42
Sadsbury, PA (township) Lancaster County	325	9.75
Hilltown, PA (township) Bucks County	325	2.23
East Allen, PA (township) Northampton County	324	6.59
Bloomsburg, PA (town) Columbia County	324	2.27
Lower Salford, PA (township) Montgomery County	324	2.22
Union, PA (township) Mifflin County	323	9.44
Adams, PA (township) Cambria County	322	5.34
Weisenberg, PA (township) Lehigh County	321	6.69
Towamencin, PA (township) Montgomery County	321	1.83
Earl, PA (township) Berks County	318	9.95
Lackawannock, PA (township) Mercer County	316	11.68
East Penn, PA (township) Carbon County	315	11.15
Kutztown, PA (borough) Berks County	315	6.31
Lower Pottsgrove, PA (township) Montgomery County	315	2.65
Upper Providence, PA (township) Montgomery County	314	1.56
Chambersburg, PA (borough) Franklin County	313	1.57
Richmond, PA (township) Berks County	312	9.18
Bedminster, PA (township) Bucks County	312	4.97

SECTION THREE

Please refer to the Explanation of Data in the front of the book for more detailed information.

Ancestry

Pennsylvania German

Top 150 Places Sorted by Percent of Total Population

Based on all places, regardless of total population

Place	Population	%
Hublersburg, PA (cdp) Centre County	50	100.00
Clinton, WI (town) Vernon County	608	51.35
Kirkwood, PA (cdp) Lancaster County	164	49.25
Burns City, IN (cdp) Martin County	63	43.45
Knowles, OK (town) Beaver County	3	42.86
Winger, MN (township) Polk County	107	41.47
Clifton, WI (town) Monroe County	367	40.78
Sidman, PA (cdp) Cambria County	102	39.23
Slatedale, PA (cdp) Lehigh County	175	38.38
Ronks, PA (cdp) Lancaster County	99	37.22
Whites Landing, OH (cdp) Erie County	136	35.70
West Mahoning, PA (township) Indiana County	486	34.01
Capron, OK (town) Woods County	2	33.33
Richford, WI (town) Waushara County	197	32.78
Webster, WI (town) Vernon County	251	32.51
Farmersville, PA (cdp) Lancaster County	514	31.08
Hickory Grove, WI (town) Grant County	136	27.81
Atlantic, PA (cdp) Crawford County	13	26.00
Fort Indiantown Gap, PA (cdp) Lebanon County	31	25.83
Greenwood, WI (town) Vernon County	230	25.00
Tonsina, AK (cdp) Valdez-Cordova Census Area	19	24.68
Wilburton Population Two, PA (cdp) Columbia County	20	24.10
Krupp, WA (town) Grant County	5	23.81
Sheldon, WI (town) Monroe County	150	23.77
Troupsburg, NY (town) Steuben County	341	23.32
Running Water, SD (cdp) Bon Homme County	13	23.21
Grazierville, PA (cdp) Blair County	131	23.02
Bart, PA (township) Lancaster County	688	22.36
Mohrsville, PA (cdp) Berks County	73	22.32
Jefferson, WI (town) Monroe County	202	22.00
Redpath, MN (township) Traverse County	21	21.65
West Milton, PA (cdp) Union County	140	21.64
Virginville, PA (cdp) Berks County	60	21.35
Lake, PA (township) Mercer County	160	20.33
Wellington, WI (town) Monroe County	133	20.06
Shartlesville, PA (cdp) Berks County	98	19.80
Lewis, PA (township) Northumberland County	369	19.37
Ursina, PA (borough) Somerset County	79	19.36
Hainesburg, NJ (cdp) Warren County	35	19.23
Bridge Creek, WI (town) Eau Claire County	352	18.75
Washington, PA (township) Lehigh County	1,238	18.66
Altoona, FL (cdp) Lake County	16	18.18
Conewango, NY (town) Cattaraugus County	262	18.04
Colerain, PA (township) Lancaster County	637	17.83
Greene, PA (township) Clinton County	295	17.47
Shoemakersville, PA (borough) Berks County	259	17.42
Idaville, PA (cdp) Adams County	34	17.26
Kendall, WI (town) Lafayette County	77	17.19
Palmerton, PA (borough) Carbon County	921	16.99
South Mahoning, PA (township) Indiana County	266	16.96
Strausstown, PA (borough) Berks County	60	16.95
Barree, PA (township) Huntingdon County	91	16.82
Alburtis, PA (borough) Lehigh County	360	16.06
Upper Mahantongo, PA (township) Schuylkill County	106	16.06
Klingerstown, PA (cdp) Schuylkill County	17	16.04
Menno, PA (township) Mifflin County	332	15.95
Morristown, NY (town) St. Lawrence County	433	15.79
Lehigh, PA (township) Northampton County	1,634	15.60
Lower Towamensing, PA (township) Carbon County	502	15.48
Bally, PA (borough) Berks County	148	15.42
Springfield, WI (town) Jackson County	109	15.42
Liberty, WI (town) Grant County	115	15.37
De Peyster, NY (town) St. Lawrence County	147	15.34
Topton, PA (borough) Berks County	365	15.30
Anthony, PA (township) Montour County	228	15.24
Toboyne, PA (township) Perry County	64	15.20
Clifton, WI (town) Grant County	69	14.87
Oley, PA (cdp) Berks County	217	14.77
Oneida, PA (cdp) Schuylkill County	27	14.67
Bath, PA (borough) Northampton County	396	14.55
McKeansburg, PA (cdp) Schuylkill County	25	14.53
Fairview, PA (township) Mercer County	146	14.51
Delano, PA (cdp) Schuylkill County	54	14.48
Kingston, WI (town) Green Lake County	131	14.44
Earl, PA (township) Lancaster County	991	14.43
West Penn, PA (township) Schuylkill County	612	14.20
Wilmington, PA (township) Mercer County	184	14.06
Salisbury, PA (township) Lancaster County	1,526	14.01
Witmer, PA (cdp) Lancaster County	80	13.89
Hubley, PA (township) Schuylkill County	122	13.85
Gap, PA (cdp) Lancaster County	172	13.80
East Fallowfield, PA (township) Crawford County	183	13.79
Oley, PA (township) Berks County	492	13.54
Coyville, KS (city) Wilson County	5	13.51
Laporte, PA (township) Sullivan County	39	13.45
Lyons, PA (borough) Berks County	61	13.44
Sugar Grove, PA (township) Mercer County	140	13.27
Harmony, MN (township) Fillmore County	57	13.26
Ravine, PA (cdp) Schuylkill County	131	13.25
Canton, MN (city) Fillmore County	50	13.19
Parryville, PA (borough) Carbon County	63	13.13
Longswamp, PA (township) Berks County	738	13.09
Bowmanstown, PA (borough) Carbon County	119	12.99
Jeddo, PA (borough) Luzerne County	14	12.96
Lime Ridge, PA (cdp) Columbia County	133	12.85
Bethel, PA (cdp) Berks County	55	12.85
Flynn, MI (township) Sanilac County	126	12.84
Gibraltar, PA (cdp) Berks County	76	12.84
Pillow, PA (borough) Dauphin County	30	12.82
Crab Orchard, NE (village) Johnson County	7	12.73
Algansee, MI (township) Branch County	262	12.71
Weissport, PA (borough) Carbon County	64	12.67
Trumbauersville, PA (borough) Bucks County	122	12.63
Madison, PA (borough) Westmoreland County	47	12.60
Wilton, WI (town) Monroe County	102	12.59
Dana, IA (city) Greene County	8	12.50
Wallace, KS (city) Wallace County	5	12.50
Centerport, PA (borough) Berks County	66	12.48
Upper Milford, PA (township) Lehigh County	898	12.37
Upper Bern, PA (township) Berks County	169	12.31
Canton, MN (township) Fillmore County	71	12.31
New Ringgold, PA (borough) Schuylkill County	37	12.21
Hopewell, PA (township) Cumberland County	298	12.08
Hereford, PA (township) Berks County	367	12.03
Napoli, NY (town) Cattaraugus County	181	11.95
Northwood, PA (cdp) Blair County	40	11.94
Albany, PA (township) Berks County	184	11.85
Branchdale, PA (cdp) Schuylkill County	31	11.83
Lykens, PA (township) Dauphin County	129	11.71
Lackawannock, PA (township) Mercer County	316	11.68
Lynn, PA (township) Lehigh County	485	11.63
Brandonville, PA (cdp) Schuylkill County	20	11.63
Stouchsburg, PA (cdp) Berks County	68	11.60
York, WI (town) Clark County	112	11.51
Catasauqua, PA (borough) Lehigh County	741	11.45
Mahoning, PA (township) Carbon County	487	11.38
Eldred, PA (township) Schuylkill County	59	11.32
Georgetown, PA (cdp) Lancaster County	113	11.31
Nescopeck, PA (borough) Luzerne County	188	11.29
Saratoga, MN (township) Winona County	62	11.25
Walnutport, PA (borough) Northampton County	241	11.24
Fannett, PA (township) Franklin County	282	11.18
Heidelberg, PA (township) Lehigh County	380	11.16
West Hamburg, PA (cdp) Berks County	224	11.16
East Penn, PA (township) Carbon County	315	11.15
Douglass, PA (township) Berks County	371	11.11
Dudley, PA (borough) Huntingdon County	17	11.11
Prompton, PA (borough) Wayne County	22	11.06
Towamensing, PA (township) Carbon County	482	11.01
Allen, PA (township) Northampton County	443	11.01
East Union, PA (township) Schuylkill County	162	11.01
Paradise, PA (township) Lancaster County	554	10.92
Henderson, PA (township) Jefferson County	178	10.91
West Cameron, PA (township) Northumberland County	58	10.90
Cherryville, PA (cdp) Northampton County	155	10.88
Whitestown, WI (town) Vernon County	56	10.85
Mertztown, PA (cdp) Berks County	81	10.77
Hume, NY (town) Allegany County	219	10.74
Woodbury, PA (township) Bedford County	148	10.72
East Brunswick, PA (township) Schuylkill County	192	10.58

Please refer to the Explanation of Data in the front of the book for more detailed information.

Ancestry

Pennsylvania German

Top 150 Places Sorted by Percent of Total Population

Based on places with total population of 7,500 or more

Place	Population	%
Lehigh, PA (township) Northampton County	1,634	15.60
Salisbury, PA (township) Lancaster County	1,526	14.01
Moore, PA (township) Northampton County	920	10.04
North Whitehall, PA (township) Lehigh County	1,556	9.97
Emmaus, PA (borough) Lehigh County	939	8.33
West Earl, PA (township) Lancaster County	628	8.21
Maxatawny, PA (township) Berks County	574	7.43
Lower Saucon, PA (township) Northampton County	749	6.98
Berwick, PA (borough) Columbia County	721	6.81
Maidencreek, PA (township) Berks County	584	6.70
Rapho, PA (township) Lancaster County	643	6.36
Northampton, PA (borough) Northampton County	624	6.29
Upper Leacock, PA (township) Lancaster County	544	6.29
Wilson, PA (borough) Northampton County	480	6.07
Muhlenberg, PA (township) Berks County	1,161	6.04
Perkasie, PA (borough) Bucks County	519	6.03
South Whitehall, PA (township) Lehigh County	1,117	5.86
Bushkill, PA (township) Northampton County	465	5.79
Salisbury, PA (township) Lehigh County	696	5.14
Pottsville, PA (city) Schuylkill County	745	5.13
Polk, PA (township) Monroe County	376	4.81
Bethlehem, PA (city) Lehigh County	911	4.72
Richland, PA (township) Bucks County	576	4.62
Cumru, PA (township) Berks County	682	4.54
Pottstown, PA (borough) Montgomery County	986	4.42
Whitehall, PA (township) Lehigh County	1,093	4.13
East Nottingham, PA (township) Chester County	331	4.05
Lebanon, PA (city) Lebanon County	1,014	3.99
Upper Saucon, PA (township) Lehigh County	535	3.73
Lower Macungie, PA (township) Lehigh County	1,065	3.72
Allentown, PA (city) Lehigh County	4,292	3.69
Upper Macungie, PA (township) Lehigh County	703	3.69
Milford, PA (township) Bucks County	359	3.67
North Coventry, PA (township) Chester County	274	3.49
Bethlehem, PA (city) Northampton County	2,599	3.48
Fullerton, PA (cdp) Lehigh County	522	3.47
Douglass, PA (township) Montgomery County	344	3.45
Middletown, PA (borough) Dauphin County	309	3.44
North Lebanon, PA (township) Lebanon County	373	3.33
Ephrata, PA (township) Lancaster County	303	3.30
Franconia, PA (township) Montgomery County	413	3.25
East Lampeter, PA (township) Lancaster County	495	3.11
Hamilton, PA (township) Monroe County	281	3.08
Bethlehem, PA (city) Northampton County	1,688	3.04
Forks, PA (township) Northampton County	416	3.04
New Hanover, PA (township) Montgomery County	310	3.01
Exeter, PA (township) Berks County	748	3.00
Palmer, PA (township) Northampton County	580	2.88
Jackson, PA (township) Lebanon County	219	2.80
Williamsport, PA (city) Lycoming County	823	2.79
Dallas, PA (township) Luzerne County	242	2.75
Logan, PA (township) Blair County	327	2.71
Sunbury, PA (city) Northumberland County	272	2.71
Quakertown, PA (borough) Bucks County	242	2.67
Lower Pottsgrove, PA (township) Montgomery County	315	2.65
Easton, PA (city) Northampton County	711	2.64
East Cocalico, PA (township) Lancaster County	266	2.60
Amity, PA (township) Berks County	306	2.56
Hanover, PA (township) Northampton County	270	2.52
Spring, PA (township) Berks County	668	2.50
Reading, PA (city) Berks County	2,056	2.35
Tobyhanna, PA (township) Monroe County	195	2.34
East Pennsboro, PA (township) Cumberland County	450	2.27
Bloomsburg, PA (town) Columbia County	324	2.27
Harleysville, PA (cdp) Montgomery County	214	2.26
Hilltown, PA (township) Bucks County	325	2.23
Lower Salford, PA (township) Montgomery County	324	2.22
West Caln, PA (township) Chester County	194	2.22
Penn Forest, PA (township) Carbon County	197	2.21
Coal, PA (township) Northumberland County	222	2.15
Sanatoga, PA (cdp) Montgomery County	176	2.13
Chestnuthill, PA (township) Monroe County	358	2.10
Perkiomen, PA (township) Montgomery County	182	2.08
Bethlehem, PA (township) Northampton County	486	2.07
Wyomissing, PA (borough) Berks County	205	1.95
West Hanover, PA (township) Dauphin County	167	1.89
Towamencin, PA (township) Montgomery County	321	1.83
Lower Swatara, PA (township) Dauphin County	150	1.83
Limerick, PA (township) Montgomery County	281	1.63
Progress, PA (cdp) Dauphin County	154	1.61
Audubon, PA (cdp) Montgomery County	131	1.61
Conshohocken, PA (borough) Montgomery County	125	1.60
Chambersburg, PA (borough) Franklin County	313	1.57
Newberry, PA (township) York County	239	1.57
Hershey, PA (cdp) Dauphin County	206	1.57
Upper Providence, PA (township) Montgomery County	314	1.56
North Codorus, PA (township) York County	136	1.55
Connellsville, PA (city) Fayette County	122	1.55
Johnstown, PA (city) Cambria County	330	1.54
East Huntingdon, PA (township) Westmoreland County	122	1.54
Phillipsburg, NJ (town) Warren County	232	1.53
Nanticoke, PA (city) Luzerne County	156	1.49
Lower Allen, PA (township) Cumberland County	265	1.48
Mammoth Lakes, CA (town) Mono County	118	1.47
Lock Haven, PA (city) Clinton County	140	1.45
Lower Providence, PA (township) Montgomery County	355	1.43
Penn, PA (township) Westmoreland County	283	1.42
South Lebanon, PA (township) Lebanon County	131	1.41
Derry, PA (township) Dauphin County	337	1.40
Southport, NY (cdp) Chemung County	105	1.39
Lansdale, PA (borough) Montgomery County	224	1.38
Ashland, OH (city) Ashland County	283	1.37
New Garden, PA (township) Chester County	157	1.36
Gettysburg, PA (borough) Adams County	104	1.35
Phoenixville, PA (borough) Chester County	216	1.33
Hanover, PA (borough) York County	203	1.33
Upper Allen, PA (township) Cumberland County	228	1.30
Perry Heights, OH (cdp) Stark County	109	1.26
Shiloh, PA (cdp) York County	140	1.23
Windsor, PA (township) York County	202	1.20
Warwick, PA (township) Bucks County	169	1.20
Somerset, PA (township) Somerset County	144	1.20
Elizabethtown, PA (borough) Lancaster County	137	1.18
Dover, PA (township) York County	242	1.17
Upper Gwynedd, PA (township) Montgomery County	180	1.17
Ocean Pines, MD (cdp) Worcester County	129	1.17
Barton, NY (town) Tioga County	104	1.17
Upper Uwchlan, PA (township) Chester County	122	1.16
Dingman, PA (township) Pike County	134	1.15
Hanover, PA (township) Luzerne County	128	1.15
Carlisle, PA (borough) Cumberland County	211	1.14
Lower Paxton, PA (township) Dauphin County	528	1.13
Skippack, PA (township) Montgomery County	145	1.12
Ocean City, NJ (city) Cape May County	138	1.12
East York, PA (cdp) York County	103	1.12
West Donegal, PA (township) Lancaster County	89	1.12
Ephrata, PA (borough) Lancaster County	149	1.11
East Stroudsburg, PA (borough) Monroe County	110	1.10
Altoona, PA (city) Blair County	509	1.09
Holly Hill, FL (city) Volusia County	131	1.09
Westtown, PA (township) Chester County	118	1.09
Mountain Top, PA (cdp) Luzerne County	115	1.09
Butler, PA (township) Luzerne County	95	1.08
Wilkes-Barre, PA (city) Luzerne County	442	1.06
West Manchester, PA (township) York County	194	1.04
Southport, NY (town) Chemung County	114	1.04
Willow Grove, PA (cdp) Montgomery County	170	1.03
Derry, PA (township) Westmoreland County	147	1.02
Washington, PA (township) Franklin County	138	1.01
Richland, PA (township) Cambria County	128	1.01
York, PA (city) York County	436	1.00
Lower Southampton, PA (township) Bucks County	189	0.99
Hatfield, PA (township) Montgomery County	170	0.99
Loyalsock, PA (township) Lycoming County	109	0.99
Warren, PA (city) Warren County	96	0.98
Glenshaw, PA (cdp) Allegheny County	90	0.98
Millersville, PA (borough) Lancaster County	79	0.98
Oceano, CA (cdp) San Luis Obispo County	77	0.98
Kulpsville, PA (cdp) Montgomery County	76	0.98
Hampden, PA (township) Cumberland County	266	0.97

SECTION THREE

Please refer to the Explanation of Data in the front of the book for more detailed information.

Ancestry

Polish

U.S. and 50 States Sorted by Population and Percent of Total Population

Place	Population	%
United States	**9,835,471**	**3.24**
New York	1,007,597	5.24
Illinois	979,781	7.69
Michigan	900,446	9.05
Pennsylvania	880,890	6.98
New Jersey	565,484	6.48
Wisconsin	538,214	9.55
California	515,633	1.41
Florida	511,229	2.76
Ohio	462,815	4.02
Massachusetts	339,044	5.23
Connecticut	297,615	8.39
Texas	278,519	1.15
Minnesota	257,292	4.91
Indiana	210,729	3.28
Maryland	200,092	3.51
Arizona	161,575	2.59
Virginia	155,128	1.98
North Carolina	131,740	1.42
Washington	125,635	1.91
Colorado	123,913	2.54
Missouri	108,835	1.84
Georgia	103,243	1.09
Nebraska	67,899	3.77
Oregon	67,107	1.78
Tennessee	64,764	1.04
Nevada	60,741	2.31
South Carolina	58,211	1.29
New Hampshire	58,124	4.42
Delaware	45,593	5.17
Rhode Island	44,019	4.17
Iowa	40,744	1.35
Kentucky	40,567	0.95
Kansas	40,253	1.43
West Virginia	34,920	1.90
Alabama	33,111	0.70
Oklahoma	32,979	0.90
Maine	30,427	2.29
Arkansas	24,848	0.86
Vermont	24,566	3.94
Utah	23,897	0.90
New Mexico	23,528	1.17
Louisiana	22,235	0.50
Montana	20,558	2.11
Idaho	20,544	1.35
North Dakota	17,488	2.65
Alaska	17,329	2.51
Mississippi	15,189	0.52
Hawaii	13,836	1.04
South Dakota	12,884	1.61
Wyoming	11,917	2.18
District of Columbia	11,744	2.01

Place	Population	%
Wisconsin	538,214	9.55
Michigan	900,446	9.05
Connecticut	297,615	8.39
Illinois	979,781	7.69
Pennsylvania	880,890	6.98
New Jersey	565,484	6.48
New York	1,007,597	5.24
Massachusetts	339,044	5.23
Delaware	45,593	5.17
Minnesota	257,292	4.91
New Hampshire	58,124	4.42
Rhode Island	44,019	4.17
Ohio	462,815	4.02
Vermont	24,566	3.94
Nebraska	67,899	3.77
Maryland	200,092	3.51
Indiana	210,729	3.28
United States	**9,835,471**	**3.24**
Florida	511,229	2.76
North Dakota	17,488	2.65
Arizona	161,575	2.59
Colorado	123,913	2.54
Alaska	17,329	2.51
Nevada	60,741	2.31
Maine	30,427	2.29
Wyoming	11,917	2.18
Montana	20,558	2.11
District of Columbia	11,744	2.01
Virginia	155,128	1.98
Washington	125,635	1.91
West Virginia	34,920	1.90
Missouri	108,835	1.84
Oregon	67,107	1.78
South Dakota	12,884	1.61
Kansas	40,253	1.43
North Carolina	131,740	1.42
California	515,633	1.41
Iowa	40,744	1.35
Idaho	20,544	1.35
South Carolina	58,211	1.29
New Mexico	23,528	1.17
Texas	278,519	1.15
Georgia	103,243	1.09
Tennessee	64,764	1.04
Hawaii	13,836	1.04
Kentucky	40,567	0.95
Oklahoma	32,979	0.90
Utah	23,897	0.90
Arkansas	24,848	0.86
Alabama	33,111	0.70
Mississippi	15,189	0.52
Louisiana	22,235	0.50

Please refer to the Explanation of Data in the front of the book for more detailed information.

Ancestry

Polish

Top 150 Places Sorted by Population

Based on all places, regardless of total population

Place	Population	%
New York, NY (city) Kings County	216,891	2.68
Chicago, IL (city) Cook County	176,295	6.52
Brooklyn, NY (borough) Kings County	66,792	2.71
Manhattan, NY (borough) New York County	64,078	4.05
Los Angeles, CA (city) Los Angeles County	60,010	1.59
Queens, NY (borough) Queens County	59,757	2.72
Philadelphia, PA (city) Philadelphia County	58,395	3.88
Milwaukee, WI (city) Milwaukee County	47,271	8.02
Hempstead, NY (town) Nassau County	35,774	4.75
Phoenix, AZ (city) Maricopa County	33,636	2.32
Cheektowaga, NY (town) Erie County	31,456	35.39
Buffalo, NY (city) Erie County	28,108	10.57
Brookhaven, NY (town) Suffolk County	27,233	5.67
Warren, MI (city) Macomb County	26,655	19.63
San Diego, CA (city) San Diego County	26,533	2.07
Cheektowaga, NY (cdp) Erie County	26,237	34.63
Toledo, OH (city) Lucas County	25,480	8.73
Pittsburgh, PA (city) Allegheny County	24,743	8.03
Sterling Heights, MI (city) Macomb County	23,071	17.79
Oyster Bay, NY (town) Nassau County	19,395	6.65
Houston, TX (city) Harris County	19,181	0.93
Staten Island, NY (borough) Richmond County	18,430	3.98
Cleveland, OH (city) Cuyahoga County	18,227	4.45
Omaha, NE (city) Douglas County	18,043	4.43
Columbus, OH (city) Franklin County	17,936	2.33
Clinton, MI (charter township) Macomb County	17,913	18.41
Livonia, MI (city) Wayne County	17,428	17.80
Amherst, NY (town) Erie County	17,104	14.14
San Francisco, CA (city) San Francisco County	16,127	2.04
Boston, MA (city) Suffolk County	15,708	2.61
Macomb, MI (township) Macomb County	15,670	20.93
Naperville, IL (city) DuPage County	15,623	11.09
Las Vegas, NV (city) Clark County	15,542	2.68
San Antonio, TX (city) Medina County	15,204	1.18
Grand Rapids, MI (city) Kent County	15,189	7.98
Baltimore, MD (city) Baltimore city County	15,080	2.43
Lancaster, NY (town) Erie County	15,025	36.65
Seattle, WA (city) King County	14,995	2.52
Islip, NY (town) Suffolk County	14,896	4.46
New Britain, CT (city/town) Hartford County	14,770	20.25
Parma, OH (city) Cuyahoga County	14,703	17.95
Minneapolis, MN (city) Hennepin County	14,605	3.85
Joliet, IL (city) Will County	14,334	9.89
Jacksonville, FL (city) Duval County	13,924	1.72
North Hempstead, NY (town) Nassau County	13,352	5.97
West Seneca, NY (cdp/town) Erie County	13,252	29.63
Huntington, NY (town) Suffolk County	13,208	6.53
Hamburg, NY (town) Erie County	13,189	23.31
Erie, PA (city) Erie County	12,920	12.71
Shelby, MI (charter township) Macomb County	12,829	17.63
Portland, OR (city) Multnomah County	12,757	2.25
Indianapolis, IN (city) Marion County	12,731	1.57
Austin, TX (city) Travis County	12,686	1.66
Madison, WI (city) Dane County	12,532	5.47
Babylon, NY (town) Suffolk County	12,444	5.82
Tucson, AZ (city) Pima County	12,427	2.40
Arlington Heights, IL (village) Cook County	12,420	16.57
St. Clair Shores, MI (city) Macomb County	12,345	20.31
Denver, CO (city) Denver County	12,238	2.12
Charlotte, NC (city) Mecklenburg County	12,055	1.71
Chicopee, MA (city) Hampden County	11,927	21.62
Schaumburg, IL (village) Cook County	11,923	16.26
Virginia Beach, VA (ind. city) Virginia Beach independent city	11,914	2.73
Oak Lawn, IL (village) Cook County	11,843	21.21
Washington, DC (city) District of Columbia	11,744	2.01
West Allis, WI (city) Milwaukee County	11,608	19.34
Mesa, AZ (city) Maricopa County	11,558	2.63
Canton, MI (charter township) Wayne County	11,542	13.12
Tonawanda, NY (town) Erie County	11,479	15.49
Scranton, PA (city) Lackawanna County	10,984	14.44
Green Bay, WI (city) Brown County	10,763	10.35
Dearborn, MI (city) Wayne County	10,629	10.80
Detroit, MI (city) Wayne County	10,573	1.39
Scottsdale, AZ (city) Maricopa County	10,499	4.80
Colorado Springs, CO (city) El Paso County	10,470	2.59
South Bend, IN (city) St. Joseph County	10,370	10.16
Tinley Park, IL (village) Cook County	10,148	18.47
Dallas, TX (city) Dallas County	10,063	0.85
Orland Park, IL (village) Cook County	10,058	18.25
Hamilton, NJ (township) Mercer County	9,949	11.25
St. Paul, MN (city) Ramsey County	9,921	3.52
Mount Prospect, IL (village) Cook County	9,709	18.03
Worcester, MA (city) Worcester County	9,684	5.38
Des Plaines, IL (city) Cook County	9,648	16.82
Palatine, IL (village) Cook County	9,622	14.27
Westland, MI (city) Wayne County	9,616	11.34
Toms River, NJ (township) Ocean County	9,531	10.39
Ramapo, NY (town) Rockland County	9,453	7.70
Burbank, IL (city) Cook County	9,415	33.12
Aurora, IL (city) Kane County	9,369	4.92
Chesterfield, MI (township) Macomb County	9,296	21.81
Dearborn Heights, MI (city) Wayne County	9,260	15.95
Toms River, NJ (cdp) Ocean County	9,250	10.41
Woodbridge, NJ (township) Middlesex County	9,183	9.26
Troy, MI (city) Oakland County	9,135	11.28
Tonawanda, NY (cdp) Erie County	9,014	15.40
Henderson, NV (city) Clark County	8,939	3.59
San Jose, CA (city) Santa Clara County	8,895	0.96
Bristol, CT (city/town) Hartford County	8,846	14.63
Albuquerque, NM (city) Bernalillo County	8,841	1.66
Clifton, NJ (city) Passaic County	8,833	10.67
Farmington Hills, MI (city) Oakland County	8,787	10.96
Smithtown, NY (town) Suffolk County	8,707	7.40
Roseville, MI (city) Macomb County	8,671	18.13
Greenfield, WI (city) Milwaukee County	8,647	23.88
Bayonne, NJ (city) Hudson County	8,533	13.76
Kenosha, WI (city) Kenosha County	8,503	8.65
New Berlin, WI (city) Waukesha County	8,398	21.25
Oak Creek, WI (city) Milwaukee County	8,339	25.22
Wilkes-Barre, PA (city) Luzerne County	8,088	19.44
Anchorage, AK (municipality) Anchorage Municipality	8,074	2.84
St. Petersburg, FL (city) Pinellas County	8,031	3.27
Rochester Hills, MI (city) Oakland County	7,882	11.16
Ann Arbor, MI (city) Washtenaw County	7,858	6.82
Royal Oak, MI (city) Oakland County	7,841	13.58
Bronx, NY (borough) Bronx County	7,834	0.57
Franklin, WI (city) Milwaukee County	7,698	22.60
Waukesha, WI (city) Waukesha County	7,678	10.98
Park Ridge, IL (city) Cook County	7,624	20.54
Hammond, IN (city) Lake County	7,497	9.22
Downers Grove, IL (village) DuPage County	7,492	15.63
Lincoln, NE (city) Lancaster County	7,459	2.95
Brick, NJ (township) Ocean County	7,418	9.77
Raleigh, NC (city) Wake County	7,411	1.94
Chandler, AZ (city) Maricopa County	7,404	3.23
Stevens Point, WI (city) Portage County	7,335	27.70
Meriden, CT (city/town) New Haven County	7,331	12.12
Syracuse, NY (city) Onondaga County	7,273	5.03
Hoffman Estates, IL (village) Cook County	7,198	14.06
Fort Worth, TX (city) Tarrant County	7,162	1.02
Springfield, MA (city) Hampden County	7,121	4.66
Bay City, MI (city) Bay County	7,089	20.12
Bolingbrook, IL (village) Will County	7,074	9.74
Gilbert, AZ (town) Maricopa County	7,033	3.61
Southington, CT (town) Hartford County	6,969	16.40
Homer Glen, IL (village) Will County	6,952	28.12
Colonie, NY (town) Albany County	6,915	8.48
Elk Grove Village, IL (village) Cook County	6,843	20.69
Lakewood, NJ (township) Ocean County	6,788	7.74
Redford, MI (charter township) Wayne County	6,762	13.77
Niles, IL (village) Cook County	6,747	22.90
Dundalk, MD (cdp) Baltimore County	6,728	10.77
Arlington, VA (cdp) Arlington County	6,664	3.37
Millcreek, PA (township) Erie County	6,656	12.57
Stamford, CT (city/town) Fairfield County	6,643	5.49
Taylor, MI (city) Wayne County	6,619	10.37
Jersey City, NJ (city) Hudson County	6,577	2.70
Nashville-Davidson, TN (metro govt) Davidson County	6,574	1.12
North Tonawanda, NY (city) Niagara County	6,499	20.49
Tampa, FL (city) Hillsborough County	6,411	1.92

SECTION THREE

Please refer to the Explanation of Data in the front of the book for more detailed information.

Ancestry

Polish

Top 150 Places Sorted by Percent of Total Population

Based on all places, regardless of total population

Place	Population	%
Eagle Lake, PA (cdp) Lackawanna County	20	100.00
Posen, MI (village) Presque Isle County	201	78.82
Posen, MI (township) Presque Isle County	689	77.16
Du Bois, IL (village) Washington County	149	73.04
Belva, WV (cdp) Nicholas County	35	68.63
Pulawski, MI (township) Presque Isle County	231	68.55
Royalton, MN (city) Benton County	6	66.67
Polonia, WI (cdp) Portage County	339	64.94
Bevent, WI (town) Marathon County	774	62.72
Sharon, WI (town) Portage County	1,282	62.69
Clare, MI (city) Isabella County	58	62.37
Nelson Park, MN (township) Marshall County	73	61.86
Falls City, TX (city) Karnes County	228	61.79
Byram Center, NJ (cdp) Sussex County	8	61.54
Linwood, WI (town) Portage County	852	61.43
Burnside, WI (town) Trempealeau County	408	60.27
Polonia, MN (township) Roseau County	6	60.00
Dewey, WI (town) Portage County	633	59.72
Radom, IL (village) Washington County	122	59.22
Metz, MI (township) Presque Isle County	157	58.15
St. Joseph, MN (township) Kittson County	12	57.14
Angelica, WI (cdp) Shawano County	65	56.52
Diamond Beach, NJ (cdp) Cape May County	64	56.14
Reid, WI (town) Marathon County	693	55.71
Two Rivers, MN (township) Morrison County	344	53.75
Pulaski, WI (village) Shawano County	267	53.29
Minnesota Lake, MN (city) Blue Earth County	9	52.94
Grier City, PA (cdp) Schuylkill County	59	51.75
Sobieski, MN (city) Morrison County	101	51.01
Carson, WI (town) Portage County	588	51.00
Franzen, WI (town) Marathon County	245	50.83
Littlejohn Island, ME (cdp) Cumberland County	74	50.68
Pinon, NM (cdp) Otero County	14	50.00
Hill, MN (township) Kittson County	2	50.00
Tavistock, NJ (borough) Camden County	2	50.00
Sloan, NY (village) Erie County	1,831	49.88
Guenther, WI (town) Marathon County	141	49.82
Alban, WI (town) Portage County	376	49.60
Rosholt, WI (village) Portage County	214	49.08
Stockton, WI (town) Portage County	1,425	48.90
Ball Club, MN (cdp) Itasca County	105	48.84
Dupont, PA (borough) Luzerne County	1,319	48.78
Royal, MN (township) Lincoln County	75	48.70
Alberta, MN (township) Benton County	378	48.65
South Haven, MI (city) Allegan County	16	48.48
Armstrong Creek, WI (town) Forest County	199	47.84
Middle River, MN (township) Marshall County	31	47.69
Wright, MN (township) Marshall County	59	47.58
Willow Island, NE (cdp) Dawson County	18	47.37
Wallington, NJ (borough) Bergen County	5,307	46.85
Marshallton, PA (cdp) Northumberland County	772	46.12
Berlin, WI (city) Waushara County	17	45.95
Paris, MI (township) Huron County	179	45.78
Geronimo Estates, AZ (cdp) Gila County	21	45.65
Franklin, AZ (cdp) Greenlee County	10	45.45
Dodge, WI (town) Trempealeau County	219	45.44
Sobieski, WI (cdp) Oconto County	127	45.20
Summit Station, PA (cdp) Schuylkill County	56	45.16
Dodge, WI (cdp) Trempealeau County	59	44.70
Elmdale, MN (city) Morrison County	36	44.44
Cedar, MI (cdp) Leelanau County	41	43.62
Parkdale, MI (cdp) Manistee County	221	43.50
Lublin, WI (village) Taylor County	77	43.50
Sheatown, PA (cdp) Luzerne County	215	43.43
Slater, WY (cdp) Platte County	22	43.14
Amherst, WI (town) Portage County	587	43.13
Pelan, MN (township) Kittson County	17	42.50
Georgetown, MN (city) Clay County	99	42.31
Hillman, MN (city) Morrison County	22	42.31
Hull, WI (town) Portage County	2,246	42.19
West Nanticoke, PA (cdp) Luzerne County	229	42.10
Arcadia, WI (town) Trempealeau County	678	42.06
Bingham, MI (township) Huron County	744	42.01
Nanticoke, PA (city) Luzerne County	4,390	41.84
Swan River, MN (township) Morrison County	274	41.77
Amherst Junction, WI (village) Portage County	124	41.75
Georgetown, PA (cdp) Luzerne County	745	41.67
South Fork, WI (town) Rusk County	35	41.67
Duryea, PA (borough) Luzerne County	2,010	41.49
Ashton, NE (village) Sherman County	155	41.44
Krakow, MI (township) Presque Isle County	287	41.12
Dwight, MI (township) Huron County	350	40.94
Plumwood, OH (cdp) Madison County	73	40.78
Glen Lyon, PA (cdp) Luzerne County	817	40.37
Wanger, MN (township) Marshall County	10	40.00
Bowlus, MN (city) Morrison County	111	39.78
Alleghany, CA (cdp) Sierra County	21	39.62
Austin, MI (township) Sanilac County	256	39.51
Cuyahoga Heights, OH (village) Cuyahoga County	216	39.49
Independence, WI (city) Trempealeau County	488	39.35
Krakow, WI (cdp) Shawano County	140	39.33
Warrior Run, PA (borough) Luzerne County	251	39.10
Bellevue, MN (township) Morrison County	481	38.95
Shenandoah Heights, PA (cdp) Schuylkill County	494	38.93
Depew, NY (village) Erie County	5,979	38.69
Glencoe, WI (town) Buffalo County	184	38.57
Roosevelt, WI (town) Taylor County	172	38.39
Plymouth, PA (township) Luzerne County	666	38.32
Stronach, MI (cdp) Manistee County	59	38.06
Newport, PA (township) Luzerne County	2,002	37.87
Ubly, MI (village) Huron County	295	37.87
Tilghmanton, MD (cdp) Washington County	222	37.82
Pittston, PA (township) Luzerne County	1,271	37.78
Force, PA (cdp) Elk County	74	37.76
Phillipsville, CA (cdp) Humboldt County	29	37.66
Morrill, MN (township) Morrison County	236	37.46
Buck Run, PA (cdp) Schuylkill County	49	37.40
Laurel Run, PA (borough) Luzerne County	183	37.27
Nuangola, PA (borough) Luzerne County	369	37.12
Flensburg, MN (city) Morrison County	94	37.01
Swoyersville, PA (borough) Luzerne County	1,868	36.91
Sugar Notch, PA (borough) Luzerne County	401	36.82
Buckman, MN (township) Morrison County	271	36.77
Wanamie, PA (cdp) Luzerne County	262	36.75
Piffard, NY (cdp) Livingston County	22	36.67
Lancaster, NY (town) Erie County	15,025	36.65
Sigel, MI (township) Huron County	170	36.64
Independence, OH (city) Cuyahoga County	2,591	36.60
Dickson City, PA (borough) Lackawanna County	2,223	36.57
Ranshaw, PA (cdp) Northumberland County	205	36.48
Whiting, WI (village) Portage County	582	36.42
Roxbury, KS (cdp) McPherson County	12	36.36
Pringle, PA (borough) Luzerne County	341	36.35
Avoca, PA (borough) Luzerne County	970	36.23
Maple Grove, WI (town) Shawano County	314	35.97
Larksville, PA (borough) Luzerne County	1,623	35.94
Angelica, WI (town) Shawano County	649	35.94
Throop, PA (borough) Lackawanna County	1,452	35.85
Alpine Northwest, WY (cdp) Lincoln County	134	35.45
Cheektowaga, NY (town) Erie County	31,456	35.39
Pulaski, MN (township) Morrison County	139	35.37
Ashley, PA (borough) Luzerne County	986	35.32
Lincoln, MI (township) Huron County	299	35.18
Norridge, IL (village) Cook County	5,070	35.17
Pulaski, WI (village) Brown County	1,325	35.16
Marilla, NY (town) Erie County	1,884	35.06
Ali Chukson, AZ (cdp) Pima County	24	34.78
Amherst, WI (village) Portage County	358	34.72
Grapeville, PA (cdp) Westmoreland County	170	34.69
Carbondale, PA (township) Lackawanna County	373	34.67
Cheektowaga, NY (cdp) Erie County	26,237	34.63
Plymouth, PA (borough) Luzerne County	2,079	34.58
Oak Hill, MI (cdp) Manistee County	152	34.55
Buffalo, WI (town) Buffalo County	242	34.33
Filer City, MI (cdp) Manistee County	51	34.23
Rockville, NE (village) Sherman County	29	34.12
Platte Center, NE (village) Platte County	151	34.09
Rietbrock, WI (town) Marathon County	336	34.08
Chewsville, MD (cdp) Washington County	31	34.07
Silver Creek, NE (village) Merrick County	95	34.05

Please refer to the Explanation of Data in the front of the book for more detailed information.

Ancestry

Polish

Top 150 Places Sorted by Percent of Total Population

Based on places with total population of 7,500 or more

Place	Population	%
Wallington, NJ (borough) Bergen County	5,307	46.85
Nanticoke, PA (city) Luzerne County	4,390	41.84
Depew, NY (village) Erie County	5,979	38.69
Lancaster, NY (town) Erie County	15,025	36.65
Cheektowaga, NY (town) Erie County	31,456	35.39
Norridge, IL (village) Cook County	5,070	35.17
Cheektowaga, NY (cdp) Erie County	26,237	34.63
Burbank, IL (city) Cook County	9,415	33.12
River Grove, IL (village) Cook County	3,374	33.08
Lemont, IL (village) Cook County	4,685	30.58
Plains, PA (township) Luzerne County	3,066	30.46
Hanover, PA (township) Luzerne County	3,378	30.42
Lancaster, NY (village) Erie County	3,134	29.99
Wood Dale, IL (city) DuPage County	4,061	29.69
West Seneca, NY (cdp/town) Erie County	13,252	29.63
Alden, NY (town) Erie County	3,165	29.34
Justice, IL (village) Cook County	3,666	29.02
Hickory Hills, IL (city) Cook County	4,052	28.93
Dunkirk, NY (city) Chautauqua County	3,610	28.63
Cudahy, WI (city) Milwaukee County	5,166	28.50
Ware, MA (town) Hampshire County	2,803	28.43
Homer Glen, IL (village) Will County	6,952	28.12
Stevens Point, WI (city) Portage County	7,335	27.70
Adams, MA (town) Berkshire County	2,347	27.56
Harwood Heights, IL (village) Cook County	2,319	27.40
Alpena, MI (township) Alpena County	2,473	26.87
Hales Corners, WI (village) Milwaukee County	2,052	26.83
Schiller Park, IL (village) Cook County	3,034	26.00
Bridgeview, IL (village) Cook County	4,156	25.74
Lackawanna, NY (city) Erie County	4,681	25.66
South Milwaukee, WI (city) Milwaukee County	5,374	25.63
Palmer Town, MA (city) Hampden County	3,106	25.47
Oak Creek, WI (city) Milwaukee County	8,339	25.22
Plover, WI (village) Portage County	2,954	24.97
Lockport, IL (city) Will County	5,937	24.90
Monitor, MI (charter township) Bay County	2,612	24.62
Frankfort Square, IL (cdp) Will County	2,334	24.50
Dudley, MA (town) Worcester County	2,727	24.41
Evans, NY (town) Erie County	4,024	24.36
Norway, WI (town) Racine County	1,912	24.17
Palos Hills, IL (city) Cook County	4,193	24.14
Northwest Harborcreek, PA (cdp) Erie County	2,185	24.13
Elmwood Park, IL (village) Cook County	5,916	23.94
Greenfield, WI (city) Milwaukee County	8,647	23.88
Worth, IL (village) Cook County	2,539	23.78
Coal, PA (township) Northumberland County	2,422	23.43
Muskego, WI (city) Waukesha County	5,534	23.32
Hamburg, NY (town) Erie County	13,189	23.31
Greendale, WI (village) Milwaukee County	3,243	23.20
Boston, NY (town) Erie County	1,848	23.20
Niles, IL (village) Cook County	6,747	22.90
Alpena, MI (city) Alpena County	2,416	22.69
Franklin, WI (city) Milwaukee County	7,698	22.60
Old Forge, PA (borough) Lackawanna County	1,890	22.57
St. Francis, WI (city) Milwaukee County	2,053	22.40
Mountain Top, PA (cdp) Luzerne County	2,321	21.98
Eden, NY (town) Erie County	1,696	21.97
Chesterfield, MI (township) Macomb County	9,296	21.81
Fox Lake, IL (village) Lake County	2,292	21.80
Seven Hills, OH (city) Cuyahoga County	2,569	21.78
Chicopee, MA (city) Hampden County	11,927	21.62
Manville, NJ (borough) Somerset County	2,226	21.48
New Berlin, WI (city) Waukesha County	8,398	21.25
Oak Lawn, IL (village) Cook County	11,843	21.21
Garfield, NJ (city) Bergen County	6,403	21.21
Center Line, MI (city) Macomb County	1,767	21.10
Fraser, MI (city) Macomb County	3,109	21.09
Vernon, WI (town) Waukesha County	1,593	21.01
Pittston, PA (city) Luzerne County	1,629	20.95
Macomb, MI (township) Macomb County	15,670	20.93
Orchard Park, NY (town) Erie County	5,998	20.91
Elk Grove Village, IL (village) Cook County	6,843	20.69
Garfield Heights, OH (city) Cuyahoga County	6,009	20.68
Park Ridge, IL (city) Cook County	7,624	20.54
Elma, NY (town) Erie County	2,306	20.53
North Tonawanda, NY (city) Niagara County	6,499	20.49
Webster, MA (cdp) Worcester County	2,330	20.45
St. Clair Shores, MI (city) Macomb County	12,345	20.31
Mokena, IL (village) Will County	3,684	20.28
Broadview Heights, OH (city) Cuyahoga County	3,784	20.26
New Britain, CT (city/town) Hartford County	14,770	20.25
Hampton, MI (charter township) Bay County	1,963	20.23
Berlin, CT (town) Hartford County	3,945	20.14
Riverhead, NY (cdp) Suffolk County	2,558	20.14
Webster, MA (town) Worcester County	3,370	20.13
Bay City, MI (city) Bay County	7,089	20.12
Wyandotte, MI (city) Wayne County	5,299	20.10
Garden City, MI (city) Wayne County	5,657	20.06
Hazle, PA (township) Luzerne County	1,882	20.06
Fredonia, NY (village) Chautauqua County	2,212	19.88
New Baltimore, MI (city) Macomb County	2,241	19.78
Kingston, PA (borough) Luzerne County	2,610	19.71
Harborcreek, PA (township) Erie County	3,341	19.66
Warren, MI (city) Macomb County	26,655	19.63
Wilkes-Barre, PA (city) Luzerne County	8,088	19.44
West Allis, WI (city) Milwaukee County	11,608	19.34
Pomfret, NY (town) Chautauqua County	2,876	19.31
North Royalton, OH (city) Cuyahoga County	5,749	19.19
Frankfort, IL (village) Will County	3,261	19.12
Roselle, IL (village) DuPage County	4,344	19.11
Clay, MI (township) St. Clair County	1,781	19.04
Bangor, MI (charter township) Bay County	2,815	19.02
Harrison, PA (township) Allegheny County	1,986	18.96
Lower Burrell, PA (city) Westmoreland County	2,256	18.95
Brecksville, OH (city) Cuyahoga County	2,565	18.93
Lenox, MI (township) Macomb County	1,919	18.89
Plainville, CT (town) Hartford County	3,325	18.87
Newstead, NY (town) Erie County	1,604	18.83
South Amboy, NJ (city) Middlesex County	1,601	18.83
Spotswood, NJ (borough) Middlesex County	1,542	18.81
Easthampton Town, MA (city) Hampshire County	3,016	18.79
Aurora, NY (town) Erie County	2,573	18.70
Franklin Park, IL (village) Cook County	3,424	18.66
New Lenox, IL (village) Will County	4,463	18.64
Whitestown, NY (town) Oneida County	3,472	18.63
Prospect Heights, IL (city) Cook County	3,028	18.63
Allen Park, MI (city) Wayne County	5,275	18.48
Tinley Park, IL (village) Cook County	10,148	18.47
Lyons, IL (village) Cook County	1,945	18.47
Riverside, IL (village) Cook County	1,613	18.46
Dallas, PA (township) Luzerne County	1,625	18.45
Clinton, MI (charter township) Macomb County	17,913	18.41
Seymour, CT (town) New Haven County	3,003	18.35
Thompson, CT (town) Windham County	1,729	18.33
Orland Park, IL (village) Cook County	10,058	18.25
Washington, MI (township) Macomb County	4,410	18.21
Butler, PA (township) Luzerne County	1,597	18.14
Roseville, MI (city) Macomb County	8,671	18.13
Crestwood, IL (village) Cook County	1,977	18.10
Lake in the Hills, IL (village) McHenry County	5,160	18.04
Mount Prospect, IL (village) Cook County	9,709	18.03
Itasca, IL (village) DuPage County	1,508	17.97
Parma, OH (city) Cuyahoga County	14,703	17.95
Wheatfield, NY (town) Niagara County	3,083	17.81
Livonia, MI (city) Wayne County	17,428	17.80
Sterling Heights, MI (city) Macomb County	23,071	17.79
Peru, IL (city) LaSalle County	1,807	17.65
Shelby, MI (charter township) Macomb County	12,829	17.63
Ludlow, MA (town) Hampden County	3,723	17.60
Oceola, MI (township) Livingston County	2,036	17.60
Oak Forest, IL (city) Cook County	4,867	17.58
Kensington, CT (cdp) Hartford County	1,535	17.52
Woodhaven, MI (city) Wayne County	2,249	17.49
Schererville, IN (town) Lake County	4,977	17.48
St. John, IN (town) Lake County	2,401	17.48
Alsip, IL (village) Cook County	3,334	17.42
Chicago Ridge, IL (village) Cook County	2,464	17.42
Harrison, MI (charter township) Macomb County	4,305	17.40
Lake Zurich, IL (village) Lake County	3,385	17.31
South River, NJ (borough) Middlesex County	2,728	17.20

SECTION THREE

Please refer to the Explanation of Data in the front of the book for more detailed information.

Ancestry

Portuguese

U.S. and 50 States Sorted by Population and Percent of Total Population

Place	Population	%
United States	**1,426,867**	**0.47**
California	374,875	1.02
Massachusetts	312,022	4.82
Rhode Island	101,178	9.58
New Jersey	79,514	0.91
Florida	69,509	0.38
Hawaii	58,791	4.41
Connecticut	54,496	1.54
New York	52,967	0.28
Texas	26,974	0.11
Washington	22,051	0.34
Oregon	20,812	0.55
Pennsylvania	19,008	0.15
New Hampshire	18,526	1.41
Nevada	16,905	0.64
Arizona	16,847	0.27
Virginia	15,036	0.19
Georgia	12,995	0.14
North Carolina	11,957	0.13
Maryland	11,577	0.20
Colorado	10,527	0.22
Ohio	9,658	0.08
Illinois	9,579	0.08
Maine	8,246	0.62
Idaho	7,916	0.52
Michigan	6,093	0.06
Missouri	5,981	0.10
Tennessee	5,608	0.09
South Carolina	5,466	0.12
Louisiana	5,041	0.11
Indiana	4,720	0.07
Utah	4,433	0.17
Alabama	4,011	0.09
New Mexico	3,975	0.20
Oklahoma	3,923	0.11
Minnesota	3,749	0.07
Vermont	3,158	0.51
Kentucky	2,944	0.07
Wisconsin	2,905	0.05
Kansas	2,693	0.10
Arkansas	2,665	0.09
Alaska	2,567	0.37
Montana	2,543	0.26
Iowa	2,120	0.07
Nebraska	1,926	0.11
Delaware	1,897	0.22
Mississippi	1,505	0.05
Wyoming	1,285	0.24
District of Columbia	1,209	0.21
West Virginia	1,161	0.06
North Dakota	732	0.11
South Dakota	591	0.07

Place	Population	%
Rhode Island	101,178	9.58
Massachusetts	312,022	4.82
Hawaii	58,791	4.41
Connecticut	54,496	1.54
New Hampshire	18,526	1.41
California	374,875	1.02
New Jersey	79,514	0.91
Nevada	16,905	0.64
Maine	8,246	0.62
Oregon	20,812	0.55
Idaho	7,916	0.52
Vermont	3,158	0.51
United States	**1,426,867**	**0.47**
Florida	69,509	0.38
Alaska	2,567	0.37
Washington	22,051	0.34
New York	52,967	0.28
Arizona	16,847	0.27
Montana	2,543	0.26
Wyoming	1,285	0.24
Colorado	10,527	0.22
Delaware	1,897	0.22
District of Columbia	1,209	0.21
Maryland	11,577	0.20
New Mexico	3,975	0.20
Virginia	15,036	0.19
Utah	4,433	0.17
Pennsylvania	19,008	0.15
Georgia	12,995	0.14
North Carolina	11,957	0.13
South Carolina	5,466	0.12
Texas	26,974	0.11
Louisiana	5,041	0.11
Oklahoma	3,923	0.11
Nebraska	1,926	0.11
North Dakota	732	0.11
Missouri	5,981	0.10
Kansas	2,693	0.10
Tennessee	5,608	0.09
Alabama	4,011	0.09
Arkansas	2,665	0.09
Ohio	9,658	0.08
Illinois	9,579	0.08
Indiana	4,720	0.07
Minnesota	3,749	0.07
Kentucky	2,944	0.07
Iowa	2,120	0.07
South Dakota	591	0.07
Michigan	6,093	0.06
West Virginia	1,161	0.06
Wisconsin	2,905	0.05
Mississippi	1,505	0.05

Please refer to the Explanation of Data in the front of the book for more detailed information.

Ancestry

Portuguese

Top 150 Places Sorted by Population

Based on all places, regardless of total population

Place	Population	%
Fall River, MA (city) Bristol County	41,494	46.37
New Bedford, MA (city) Bristol County	38,632	40.69
Taunton, MA (city) Bristol County	17,002	30.39
East Providence, RI (city) Providence County	15,725	33.11
San Jose, CA (city) Santa Clara County	15,480	1.67
Newark, NJ (city) Essex County	14,175	5.16
New York, NY (city) Kings County	13,201	0.16
Dartmouth, MA (town) Bristol County	13,152	39.24
San Diego, CA (city) San Diego County	9,505	0.74
Pawtucket, RI (city) Providence County	8,114	11.32
Los Angeles, CA (city) Los Angeles County	7,722	0.20
Somerset, MA (cdp/town) Bristol County	7,714	42.42
Bristol, RI (town) Bristol County	7,346	31.68
Elizabeth, NJ (city) Union County	7,274	5.91
Modesto, CA (city) Stanislaus County	7,250	3.59
Sacramento, CA (city) Sacramento County	7,182	1.56
Urban Honolulu, HI (cdp) Honolulu County	6,667	2.02
Warwick, RI (city) Kent County	6,472	7.73
Westport, MA (town) Bristol County	6,339	41.44
Boston, MA (city) Suffolk County	6,162	1.02
Lowell, MA (city) Middlesex County	6,158	5.86
Swansea, MA (town) Bristol County	5,981	37.62
Providence, RI (city) Providence County	5,586	3.13
Tiverton, RI (town) Newport County	5,574	35.56
Cranston, RI (city) Providence County	5,508	6.84
Fresno, CA (city) Fresno County	5,315	1.10
Fairhaven, MA (town) Bristol County	5,225	32.79
Turlock, CA (city) Stanislaus County	5,184	7.69
Attleboro, MA (city) Bristol County	4,963	11.45
Cumberland, RI (town) Providence County	4,806	14.44
Fremont, CA (city) Alameda County	4,754	2.27
Queens, NY (borough) Queens County	4,727	0.21
Somerville, MA (city) Middlesex County	4,650	6.18
Acushnet, MA (town) Bristol County	4,606	44.77
San Francisco, CA (city) San Francisco County	4,497	0.57
Hayward, CA (city) Alameda County	4,390	3.10
Tulare, CA (city) Tulare County	4,347	7.63
Ludlow, MA (town) Hampden County	4,330	20.47
Hilo, HI (cdp) Hawaii County	4,207	8.62
Union, NJ (township) Union County	4,077	7.32
Danbury, CT (city/town) Fairfield County	4,065	5.12
Brockton, MA (city) Plymouth County	4,006	4.27
West Warwick, RI (town) Kent County	3,992	13.60
North Hempstead, NY (town) Nassau County	3,978	1.78
Kearny, NJ (town) Hudson County	3,917	9.74
Warren, RI (town) Bristol County	3,885	35.94
Manhattan, NY (borough) New York County	3,862	0.24
Tracy, CA (city) San Joaquin County	3,855	4.85
Brookhaven, NY (town) Suffolk County	3,802	0.79
Seekonk, MA (town) Bristol County	3,784	27.65
Bridgeport, CT (city/town) Fairfield County	3,709	2.60
Santa Clara, CA (city) Santa Clara County	3,654	3.25
Peabody, MA (city) Essex County	3,541	7.02
Coventry, RI (town) Kent County	3,429	9.79
San Leandro, CA (city) Alameda County	3,314	4.00
Manteca, CA (city) San Joaquin County	3,310	5.10
Bliss Corner, MA (cdp) Bristol County	3,303	58.47
Stockton, CA (city) San Joaquin County	3,256	1.13
Philadelphia, PA (city) Philadelphia County	3,158	0.21
Hanford, CA (city) Kings County	3,147	6.02
Plymouth, MA (town) Plymouth County	3,065	5.51
Phoenix, AZ (city) Maricopa County	3,044	0.21
Freetown, MA (town) Bristol County	3,007	34.19
Waterbury, CT (city/town) New Haven County	2,996	2.73
Livermore, CA (city) Alameda County	2,934	3.74
Brooklyn, NY (borough) Kings County	2,882	0.12
Portsmouth, RI (town) Newport County	2,857	16.50
Gloucester, MA (city) Essex County	2,840	9.83
Hempstead, NY (town) Nassau County	2,805	0.37
North Providence, RI (town) Providence County	2,755	8.54
Elk Grove, CA (city) Sacramento County	2,750	1.95
Valley Falls, RI (cdp) Providence County	2,748	23.86
Stoughton, MA (town) Norfolk County	2,721	10.16
Reno, NV (city) Washoe County	2,717	1.23
Tiverton, RI (cdp) Newport County	2,699	36.99
Yonkers, NY (city) Westchester County	2,670	1.37
Castro Valley, CA (cdp) Alameda County	2,665	4.40
Newport, RI (city) Newport County	2,644	10.59
Kailua, HI (cdp) Honolulu County	2,619	6.80
Falmouth, MA (town) Barnstable County	2,589	8.14
Hudson, MA (town) Middlesex County	2,576	13.82
Dighton, MA (town) Bristol County	2,436	35.19
Everett, MA (city) Middlesex County	2,434	6.00
Santa Rosa, CA (city) Sonoma County	2,415	1.48
Visalia, CA (city) Tulare County	2,411	2.02
Mineola, NY (village) Nassau County	2,368	12.67
Chico, CA (city) Butte County	2,352	2.76
Hudson, MA (cdp) Middlesex County	2,337	15.95
Concord, CA (city) Contra Costa County	2,291	1.89
Oakland, CA (city) Alameda County	2,276	0.59
Lincoln, RI (town) Providence County	2,260	10.70
Naugatuck, CT (borough/town) New Haven County	2,253	7.10
Smith Mills, MA (cdp) Bristol County	2,210	45.80
Cambridge, MA (city) Middlesex County	2,208	2.13
Marlborough, MA (city) Middlesex County	2,192	5.82
Barnstable Town, MA (city) Barnstable County	2,172	4.74
Rehoboth, MA (town) Bristol County	2,161	19.04
Brentwood, CA (city) Contra Costa County	2,149	4.64
Roseville, CA (city) Placer County	2,134	1.87
Johnston, RI (town) Providence County	2,130	7.41
Portland, OR (city) Multnomah County	2,108	0.37
Billerica, MA (town) Middlesex County	2,073	5.24
Middleborough, MA (town) Plymouth County	2,040	9.05
Hilmar-Irwin, CA (cdp) Merced County	2,015	40.32
Antioch, CA (city) Contra Costa County	1,994	2.00
Jacksonville, FL (city) Duval County	1,985	0.24
Milford, MA (town) Worcester County	1,977	7.10
Islip, NY (town) Suffolk County	1,977	0.59
Dublin, CA (city) Alameda County	1,945	4.56
Kahului, HI (cdp) Maui County	1,938	7.84
Bridgewater, MA (town) Plymouth County	1,921	7.28
Nashua, NH (city) Hillsborough County	1,878	2.16
Los Banos, CA (city) Merced County	1,870	5.41
North Westport, MA (cdp) Bristol County	1,862	44.41
Las Vegas, NV (city) Clark County	1,855	0.32
Medford, MA (city) Middlesex County	1,853	3.34
San Ramon, CA (city) Contra Costa County	1,836	2.75
Shelton, CT (city/town) Fairfield County	1,827	4.68
Seattle, WA (city) King County	1,823	0.31
Berkley, MA (town) Bristol County	1,787	28.34
South Kingstown, RI (town) Washington County	1,776	5.88
Middletown, RI (town) Newport County	1,757	10.74
Petaluma, CA (city) Sonoma County	1,755	3.10
Wareham, MA (town) Plymouth County	1,752	8.14
Central Falls, RI (city) Providence County	1,733	8.94
Pleasanton, CA (city) Alameda County	1,733	2.54
Woodbridge, NJ (township) Middlesex County	1,723	1.74
Houston, TX (city) Harris County	1,699	0.08
North Attleborough, MA (town) Bristol County	1,694	5.95
Milford, MA (cdp) Worcester County	1,691	6.78
South River, NJ (borough) Middlesex County	1,679	10.59
Springfield, MA (city) Hampden County	1,678	1.10
Columbus, OH (city) Franklin County	1,667	0.22
Malden, MA (city) Middlesex County	1,655	2.84
Merced, CA (city) Merced County	1,645	2.13
Citrus Heights, CA (city) Sacramento County	1,645	1.95
Newark, CA (city) Alameda County	1,640	3.91
Kaneohe, HI (cdp) Honolulu County	1,630	4.74
Vacaville, CA (city) Solano County	1,625	1.77
Pearl City, HI (cdp) Honolulu County	1,620	3.64
Palm Coast, FL (city) Flagler County	1,613	2.27
Bakersfield, CA (city) Kern County	1,586	0.48
Oakley, CA (city) Contra Costa County	1,582	4.72
Framingham, MA (cdp/town) Middlesex County	1,560	2.32
Dracut, MA (town) Middlesex County	1,553	5.36
San Antonio, TX (city) Medina County	1,549	0.12
Danville, CA (town) Contra Costa County	1,538	3.68
Woburn, MA (city) Middlesex County	1,522	4.05
Port St. Lucie, FL (city) St. Lucie County	1,500	0.97
Carmichael, CA (cdp) Sacramento County	1,497	2.42

SECTION THREE

Ancestry

Portuguese

Top 150 Places Sorted by Percent of Total Population

Based on all places, regardless of total population

Place	Population	%
Wyman, ME (unorganized territory) Franklin County	6	100.00
Acampo, CA (cdp) San Joaquin County	17	68.00
Bliss Corner, MA (cdp) Bristol County	3,303	58.47
Fall River, MA (city) Bristol County	41,494	46.37
Wallace, CA (cdp) Calaveras County	74	46.25
Smith Mills, MA (cdp) Bristol County	2,210	45.80
Acushnet, MA (town) Bristol County	4,606	44.77
North Westport, MA (cdp) Bristol County	1,862	44.41
Walpack, NJ (township) Sussex County	13	43.33
Cartago, CA (cdp) Inyo County	23	42.59
Acushnet Center, MA (cdp) Bristol County	1,108	42.44
Somerset, MA (cdp/town) Bristol County	7,714	42.42
Westport, MA (town) Bristol County	6,339	41.44
New Bedford, MA (city) Bristol County	38,632	40.69
Hilmar-Irwin, CA (cdp) Merced County	2,015	40.32
Dartmouth, MA (town) Bristol County	13,152	39.24
Swansea, MA (town) Bristol County	5,981	37.62
Tiverton, RI (cdp) Newport County	2,699	36.99
Warren, RI (town) Bristol County	3,885	35.94
Grangeville, CA (cdp) Kings County	215	35.89
Tiverton, RI (town) Newport County	5,574	35.56
Dighton, MA (town) Bristol County	2,436	35.19
Stevinson, CA (cdp) Merced County	82	34.31
Freetown, MA (town) Bristol County	3,007	34.19
East Providence, RI (city) Providence County	15,725	33.11
Fairhaven, MA (town) Bristol County	5,225	32.79
Princeton, CA (cdp) Colusa County	80	32.79
Ocean Grove, MA (cdp) Bristol County	1,000	32.53
Bristol, RI (town) Bristol County	7,346	31.68
Taunton, MA (city) Bristol County	17,002	30.39
Berkley, MA (town) Bristol County	1,787	28.34
Sunny Slopes, CA (cdp) Mono County	56	28.28
Trowbridge, CA (cdp) Sutter County	42	27.81
Seekonk, MA (town) Bristol County	3,784	27.65
Rodman, IA (city) Palo Alto County	9	25.00
Hardwick, CA (cdp) Kings County	23	24.73
Goodrich, TX (city) Polk County	98	23.90
Valley Falls, RI (cdp) Providence County	2,748	23.86
Honomu, HI (cdp) Hawaii County	140	23.41
Skillman, NJ (cdp) Somerset County	31	22.79
Rochester, MA (town) Plymouth County	1,131	22.14
West Goshen, CA (cdp) Tulare County	76	21.17
North Plymouth, MA (cdp) Plymouth County	787	20.81
Keokea, HI (cdp) Maui County	288	20.66
Ludlow, MA (town) Hampden County	4,330	20.47
Dana, IA (city) Greene County	13	20.31
Whitley Gardens, CA (cdp) San Luis Obispo County	74	19.89
Mohawk Vista, CA (cdp) Plumas County	33	19.76
Artois, CA (cdp) Glenn County	28	19.72
Paauilo, HI (cdp) Hawaii County	160	19.54
Naukati Bay, AK (cdp) Prince of Wales-Hyder Census Area	12	19.35
Gustine, CA (city) Merced County	1,045	19.22
Truro, MA (town) Barnstable County	350	19.12
Freedom Plains, NY (cdp) Dutchess County	134	19.06
Rehoboth, MA (town) Bristol County	2,161	19.04
Kalaheo, HI (cdp) Kauai County	894	18.76
Johannesburg, CA (cdp) Kern County	45	17.93
Mountain View, HI (cdp) Hawaii County	557	17.50
Hawaiian Beaches, HI (cdp) Hawaii County	738	17.33
Makaha Valley, HI (cdp) Honolulu County	243	17.10
Tisbury, MA (town) Dukes County	649	16.70
Portsmouth, RI (town) Newport County	2,857	16.50
McCarr, KY (cdp) Pike County	42	16.41
Papaikou, HI (cdp) Hawaii County	234	16.15
Thomson, MN (city) Carlton County	32	16.08
Smith Corner, CA (cdp) Kern County	46	16.03
Mattapoisett, MA (town) Plymouth County	970	15.96
Hudson, MA (cdp) Middlesex County	2,337	15.95
North Seekonk, MA (cdp) Bristol County	407	15.73
Tuttletown, CA (cdp) Tuolumne County	129	15.27
Moskowite Corner, CA (cdp) Napa County	20	15.27
Vineyard Haven, MA (cdp) Dukes County	376	15.22
Dos Palos Y, CA (cdp) Merced County	56	15.05
Marion, MA (town) Plymouth County	733	14.81
Provincetown, MA (cdp) Barnstable County	417	14.63
Provincetown, MA (town) Barnstable County	443	14.58
Laupahoehoe, HI (cdp) Hawaii County	72	14.55
Little Compton, RI (town) Newport County	507	14.45
Cumberland, RI (town) Providence County	4,806	14.44
Elkhorn, CA (cdp) Monterey County	244	14.19
Oak Bluffs, MA (town) Dukes County	618	14.16
Honokaa, HI (cdp) Hawaii County	400	14.09
Haena, HI (cdp) Kauai County	33	13.98
Worth, MO (village) Worth County	10	13.89
Hudson, MA (town) Middlesex County	2,576	13.82
Onset, MA (cdp) Plymouth County	128	13.82
Lower Lake, CA (cdp) Lake County	171	13.71
West Warwick, RI (town) Kent County	3,992	13.60
Makaha, HI (cdp) Honolulu County	1,047	13.57
Kurtistown, HI (cdp) Hawaii County	128	13.43
Waikane, HI (cdp) Honolulu County	101	13.41
Pukalani, HI (cdp) Maui County	1,065	13.19
Wainaku, HI (cdp) Hawaii County	181	12.80
Wareham Center, MA (cdp) Plymouth County	366	12.73
Mineola, NY (village) Nassau County	2,368	12.67
Marion Center, MA (cdp) Plymouth County	146	12.64
Makawao, HI (cdp) Maui County	872	12.63
Kukuihaele, HI (cdp) Hawaii County	48	12.57
Blairstown, NJ (cdp) Warren County	94	12.52
Alger, WA (cdp) Skagit County	31	12.50
Chinese Camp, CA (cdp) Tuolumne County	16	12.50
East Newark, NJ (borough) Hudson County	297	12.49
Ainaloa, HI (cdp) Hawaii County	319	12.38
Woodbury Center, CT (cdp) Litchfield County	182	12.33
Hickman, CA (cdp) Stanislaus County	54	12.30
North Lakeville, MA (cdp) Plymouth County	264	12.28
Black Point-Green Point, CA (cdp) Marin County	155	12.07
Honaunau-Napoopoo, HI (cdp) Hawaii County	324	11.97
Halaula, HI (cdp) Hawaii County	63	11.93
Mattapoisett Center, MA (cdp) Plymouth County	343	11.80
New Morgan, PA (borough) Berks County	2	11.76
Atwood, OK (town) Hughes County	13	11.71
Urie, WY (cdp) Uinta County	23	11.62
River Pines, CA (cdp) Amador County	66	11.50
Attleboro, MA (city) Bristol County	4,963	11.45
Pepeekeo, HI (cdp) Hawaii County	216	11.36
Omao, HI (cdp) Kauai County	157	11.34
Pawtucket, RI (city) Providence County	8,114	11.32
Sierra City, CA (cdp) Sierra County	67	11.15
Carnelian Bay, CA (cdp) Placer County	32	11.00
Raynham, MA (town) Bristol County	1,437	10.98
Hawaiian Paradise Park, HI (cdp) Hawaii County	854	10.89
Edgartown, MA (town) Dukes County	433	10.87
Mountain View, CA (cdp) Contra Costa County	228	10.86
Garden Farms, CA (cdp) San Luis Obispo County	49	10.86
Eden Roc, HI (cdp) Hawaii County	59	10.85
Riverdale Park, CA (cdp) Stanislaus County	125	10.83
Benson, PA (borough) Somerset County	19	10.80
Hanamaulu, HI (cdp) Kauai County	419	10.77
Denair, CA (cdp) Stanislaus County	466	10.76
Middletown, RI (town) Newport County	1,757	10.74
Bridgewater, MA (cdp) Plymouth County	787	10.74
Maili, HI (cdp) Honolulu County	865	10.73
Lincoln, RI (town) Providence County	2,260	10.70
McSwain, CA (cdp) Merced County	423	10.60
Newport, RI (city) Newport County	2,644	10.59
South River, NJ (borough) Middlesex County	1,679	10.59
Paukaa, HI (cdp) Hawaii County	43	10.54
Clayville, RI (cdp) Providence County	23	10.50
Chautauqua, KS (city) Chautauqua County	9	10.47
Newport East, RI (cdp) Newport County	1,217	10.46
Richfield, CA (cdp) Tehama County	28	10.45
Pahala, HI (cdp) Hawaii County	149	10.43
Argyle, MO (town) Osage County	17	10.37
Williams, OR (cdp) Josephine County	141	10.33
Kalaeloa, HI (cdp) Honolulu County	13	10.32
Olinda, HI (cdp) Maui County	135	10.27
Terminous, CA (cdp) San Joaquin County	42	10.27
Kapaau, HI (cdp) Hawaii County	167	10.26
Olowalu, HI (cdp) Maui County	10	10.20

Please refer to the Explanation of Data in the front of the book for more detailed information.

Ancestry

Portuguese

Top 150 Places Sorted by Percent of Total Population

Based on places with total population of 7,500 or more

Place	Population	%
Fall River, MA (city) Bristol County	41,494	46.37
Acushnet, MA (town) Bristol County	4,606	44.77
Somerset, MA (cdp/town) Bristol County	7,714	42.42
Westport, MA (town) Bristol County	6,339	41.44
New Bedford, MA (city) Bristol County	38,632	40.69
Dartmouth, MA (town) Bristol County	13,152	39.24
Swansea, MA (town) Bristol County	5,981	37.62
Warren, RI (town) Bristol County	3,885	35.94
Tiverton, RI (town) Newport County	5,574	35.56
Freetown, MA (town) Bristol County	3,007	34.19
East Providence, RI (city) Providence County	15,725	33.11
Fairhaven, MA (town) Bristol County	5,225	32.79
Bristol, RI (town) Bristol County	7,346	31.68
Taunton, MA (city) Bristol County	17,002	30.39
Seekonk, MA (town) Bristol County	3,784	27.65
Valley Falls, RI (cdp) Providence County	2,748	23.86
Ludlow, MA (town) Hampden County	4,330	20.47
Rehoboth, MA (town) Bristol County	2,161	19.04
Portsmouth, RI (town) Newport County	2,857	16.50
Hudson, MA (cdp) Middlesex County	2,337	15.95
Cumberland, RI (town) Providence County	4,806	14.44
Hudson, MA (town) Middlesex County	2,576	13.82
West Warwick, RI (town) Kent County	3,992	13.60
Makaha, HI (cdp) Honolulu County	1,047	13.57
Pukalani, HI (cdp) Maui County	1,065	13.19
Mineola, NY (village) Nassau County	2,368	12.67
Attleboro, MA (city) Bristol County	4,963	11.45
Pawtucket, RI (city) Providence County	8,114	11.32
Raynham, MA (town) Bristol County	1,437	10.98
Hawaiian Paradise Park, HI (cdp) Hawaii County	854	10.89
Middletown, RI (town) Newport County	1,757	10.74
Maili, HI (cdp) Honolulu County	865	10.73
Lincoln, RI (town) Providence County	2,260	10.70
Newport, RI (city) Newport County	2,644	10.59
South River, NJ (borough) Middlesex County	1,679	10.59
Newport East, RI (cdp) Newport County	1,217	10.46
Stoughton, MA (town) Norfolk County	2,721	10.16
Harrison, NJ (town) Hudson County	1,362	10.04
Newman, CA (city) Stanislaus County	978	9.97
Gloucester, MA (city) Essex County	2,840	9.83
Coventry, RI (town) Kent County	3,429	9.79
Kearny, NJ (town) Hudson County	3,917	9.74
Lakeville, MA (town) Plymouth County	967	9.24
Middleborough, MA (town) Plymouth County	2,040	9.05
Central Falls, RI (city) Providence County	1,733	8.94
Mansfield Center, MA (cdp) Bristol County	671	8.83
Hilo, HI (cdp) Hawaii County	4,207	8.62
North Providence, RI (town) Providence County	2,755	8.54
Artesia, CA (city) Los Angeles County	1,378	8.36
Falmouth, MA (town) Barnstable County	2,589	8.14
Wareham, MA (town) Plymouth County	1,752	8.14
Kahului, HI (cdp) Maui County	1,938	7.84
Barrington, RI (town) Bristol County	1,293	7.84
Richmond, RI (town) Washington County	597	7.78
Warwick, RI (city) Kent County	6,472	7.73
Turlock, CA (city) Stanislaus County	5,184	7.69
Tulare, CA (city) Tulare County	4,347	7.63
Glocester, RI (town) Providence County	748	7.63
Waianae, HI (cdp) Honolulu County	958	7.58
Greenville, RI (cdp) Providence County	657	7.49
Johnston, RI (town) Providence County	2,130	7.41
Waimea, HI (cdp) Hawaii County	718	7.34
Union, NJ (township) Union County	4,077	7.32
Bridgewater, MA (town) Plymouth County	1,921	7.28
Oakdale, CA (city) Stanislaus County	1,461	7.28
Naugatuck, CT (borough/town) New Haven County	2,253	7.10
Milford, MA (town) Worcester County	1,977	7.10
Haiku-Pauwela, HI (cdp) Maui County	566	7.06
Peabody, MA (city) Essex County	3,541	7.02
Stonington, CT (town) New London County	1,295	7.00
Cumberland Hill, RI (cdp) Providence County	547	6.99
Farmingville, NY (cdp) Suffolk County	1,109	6.92
Cranston, RI (city) Providence County	5,508	6.84
Kailua, HI (cdp) Honolulu County	2,619	6.80
Milford, MA (cdp) Worcester County	1,691	6.78

Place	Population	%
Kailua, HI (cdp) Hawaii County	879	6.73
Waihee-Waiehu, HI (cdp) Maui County	623	6.72
Wakefield-Peacedale, RI (cdp) Washington County	598	6.63
Wailuku, HI (cdp) Maui County	1,017	6.55
Hillside, NJ (township) Union County	1,385	6.51
Ewa Beach, HI (cdp) Honolulu County	959	6.27
Fairview, CA (cdp) Alameda County	611	6.23
Somerville, MA (city) Middlesex County	4,650	6.18
Scituate, RI (town) Providence County	634	6.13
Hanford, CA (city) Kings County	3,147	6.02
Everett, MA (city) Middlesex County	2,434	6.00
North Attleborough, MA (town) Bristol County	1,694	5.95
Kenilworth, NJ (borough) Union County	464	5.94
Elizabeth, NJ (city) Union County	7,274	5.91
North Arlington, NJ (borough) Bergen County	901	5.90
South Kingstown, RI (town) Washington County	1,776	5.88
San Lorenzo, CA (cdp) Alameda County	1,383	5.87
Lowell, MA (city) Middlesex County	6,158	5.86
Marlborough, MA (city) Middlesex County	2,192	5.82
Norton, MA (town) Bristol County	1,094	5.79
Kapaa, HI (cdp) Kauai County	581	5.78
Kalaoa, HI (cdp) Hawaii County	500	5.77
Carver, MA (town) Plymouth County	649	5.67
Grover Beach, CA (city) San Luis Obispo County	727	5.53
Discovery Bay, CA (cdp) Contra Costa County	632	5.53
Plymouth, MA (town) Plymouth County	3,065	5.51
Los Banos, CA (city) Merced County	1,870	5.41
Smithfield, RI (town) Providence County	1,161	5.41
Cherryland, CA (cdp) Alameda County	717	5.38
Dracut, MA (town) Middlesex County	1,553	5.36
Dayton, NV (cdp) Lyon County	526	5.35
Nantucket, MA (cdp) Nantucket County	424	5.33
Ripon, CA (city) San Joaquin County	732	5.31
Billerica, MA (town) Middlesex County	2,073	5.24
Newark, NJ (city) Essex County	14,175	5.16
Danbury, CT (city/town) Fairfield County	4,065	5.12
Manteca, CA (city) San Joaquin County	3,310	5.10
Middleton, MA (town) Essex County	431	4.94
Patterson, CA (city) Stanislaus County	932	4.88
Tracy, CA (city) San Joaquin County	3,855	4.85
Tewksbury, MA (town) Middlesex County	1,386	4.84
Mansfield, MA (town) Bristol County	1,106	4.80
Barnstable Town, MA (city) Barnstable County	2,172	4.74
Kaneohe, HI (cdp) Honolulu County	1,630	4.74
North Kingstown, RI (town) Washington County	1,258	4.73
Oakley, CA (city) Contra Costa County	1,582	4.72
North Smithfield, RI (town) Providence County	554	4.71
Nantucket, MA (town) Nantucket County	473	4.70
Shelton, CT (city/town) Fairfield County	1,827	4.68
Brentwood, CA (city) Contra Costa County	2,149	4.64
Westerly, RI (cdp) Washington County	804	4.58
Dublin, CA (city) Alameda County	1,945	4.56
Colonia, NJ (cdp) Middlesex County	812	4.49
Nanakuli, HI (cdp) Honolulu County	567	4.48
Warren, NJ (township) Somerset County	675	4.45
East Bridgewater, MA (town) Plymouth County	603	4.42
Castro Valley, CA (cdp) Alameda County	2,665	4.40
Ahuimanu, HI (cdp) Honolulu County	427	4.38
Harwich, MA (town) Barnstable County	530	4.31
East Foothills, CA (cdp) Santa Clara County	331	4.31
Brockton, MA (city) Plymouth County	4,006	4.27
Mashpee, MA (town) Barnstable County	592	4.27
Salida, CA (cdp) Stanislaus County	622	4.25
Newington, CT (cdp/town) Hartford County	1,283	4.23
Wahiawa, HI (cdp) Honolulu County	724	4.21
Norwood, MA (cdp/town) Norfolk County	1,192	4.20
Westerly, RI (town) Washington County	965	4.20
Windham, NH (town) Rockingham County	552	4.18
Hull, MA (cdp/town) Plymouth County	436	4.18
Pinole, CA (city) Contra Costa County	759	4.11
Clark, NJ (township) Union County	594	4.07
Woburn, MA (city) Middlesex County	1,522	4.05
Abington, MA (cdp/town) Plymouth County	635	4.04
San Leandro, CA (city) Alameda County	3,314	4.00
Dennis, MA (town) Barnstable County	582	4.00

Ancestry

Romanian

U.S. and 50 States Sorted by Population and Percent of Total Population

Place	Population	%
United States	**468,281**	**0.15**
California	67,491	0.18
New York	56,605	0.29
Florida	35,837	0.19
Illinois	34,691	0.27
Michigan	30,320	0.30
Ohio	29,751	0.26
New Jersey	20,608	0.24
Pennsylvania	19,304	0.15
Texas	15,958	0.07
Washington	15,804	0.24
Arizona	13,286	0.21
Georgia	11,109	0.12
Oregon	10,676	0.28
Massachusetts	8,711	0.13
Indiana	8,644	0.13
Virginia	8,442	0.11
Maryland	8,183	0.14
North Carolina	7,511	0.08
Minnesota	6,304	0.12
Connecticut	6,264	0.18
Colorado	5,560	0.11
Missouri	5,220	0.09
Wisconsin	5,184	0.09
Nevada	4,127	0.16
Tennessee	3,962	0.06
South Carolina	2,497	0.06
Kentucky	1,836	0.04
Louisiana	1,701	0.04
Utah	1,673	0.06
New Hampshire	1,641	0.12
Alabama	1,435	0.03
Idaho	1,431	0.09
Iowa	1,394	0.05
Delaware	1,323	0.15
Arkansas	1,270	0.04
Kansas	1,230	0.04
Nebraska	1,180	0.07
District of Columbia	1,068	0.18
Oklahoma	1,033	0.03
New Mexico	1,016	0.05
Maine	911	0.07
Montana	890	0.09
West Virginia	829	0.05
Hawaii	816	0.06
Alaska	804	0.12
Vermont	795	0.13
Rhode Island	741	0.07
North Dakota	490	0.07
Mississippi	314	0.01
South Dakota	247	0.03
Wyoming	164	0.03

Place	Population	%
Michigan	30,320	0.30
New York	56,605	0.29
Oregon	10,676	0.28
Illinois	34,691	0.27
Ohio	29,751	0.26
New Jersey	20,608	0.24
Washington	15,804	0.24
Arizona	13,286	0.21
Florida	35,837	0.19
California	67,491	0.18
Connecticut	6,264	0.18
District of Columbia	1,068	0.18
Nevada	4,127	0.16
United States	**468,281**	**0.15**
Pennsylvania	19,304	0.15
Delaware	1,323	0.15
Maryland	8,183	0.14
Massachusetts	8,711	0.13
Indiana	8,644	0.13
Vermont	795	0.13
Georgia	11,109	0.12
Minnesota	6,304	0.12
New Hampshire	1,641	0.12
Alaska	804	0.12
Virginia	8,442	0.11
Colorado	5,560	0.11
Missouri	5,220	0.09
Wisconsin	5,184	0.09
Idaho	1,431	0.09
Montana	890	0.09
North Carolina	7,511	0.08
Texas	15,958	0.07
Nebraska	1,180	0.07
Maine	911	0.07
Rhode Island	741	0.07
North Dakota	490	0.07
Tennessee	3,962	0.06
South Carolina	2,497	0.06
Utah	1,673	0.06
Hawaii	816	0.06
Iowa	1,394	0.05
New Mexico	1,016	0.05
West Virginia	829	0.05
Kentucky	1,836	0.04
Louisiana	1,701	0.04
Arkansas	1,270	0.04
Kansas	1,230	0.04
Alabama	1,435	0.03
Oklahoma	1,033	0.03
South Dakota	247	0.03
Wyoming	164	0.03
Mississippi	314	0.01

Please refer to the Explanation of Data in the front of the book for more detailed information.

Ancestry

Romanian

Top 150 Places Sorted by Population

Based on all places, regardless of total population

Place	Population	%
New York, NY (city) Kings County	29,552	0.37
Queens, NY (borough) Queens County	11,686	0.53
Los Angeles, CA (city) Los Angeles County	10,676	0.28
Chicago, IL (city) Cook County	9,121	0.34
Brooklyn, NY (borough) Kings County	8,046	0.33
Manhattan, NY (borough) New York County	7,692	0.49
Portland, OR (city) Multnomah County	3,976	0.70
Phoenix, AZ (city) Maricopa County	3,727	0.26
Hempstead, NY (town) Nassau County	2,811	0.37
Houston, TX (city) Harris County	2,664	0.13
Monroe, NY (town) Orange County	2,439	6.31
Kiryas Joel, NY (village) Orange County	2,293	12.01
Philadelphia, PA (city) Philadelphia County	2,101	0.14
San Diego, CA (city) San Diego County	2,000	0.16
San Francisco, CA (city) San Francisco County	1,943	0.25
Hollywood, FL (city) Broward County	1,788	1.27
Anaheim, CA (city) Orange County	1,744	0.52
Ramapo, NY (town) Rockland County	1,695	1.38
Sterling Heights, MI (city) Macomb County	1,620	1.25
Skokie, IL (village) Cook County	1,582	2.48
Oyster Bay, NY (town) Nassau County	1,492	0.51
North Hempstead, NY (town) Nassau County	1,434	0.64
Seattle, WA (city) King County	1,402	0.24
Gresham, OR (city) Multnomah County	1,399	1.38
Huntington, NY (town) Suffolk County	1,364	0.67
San Jose, CA (city) Santa Clara County	1,307	0.14
Cleveland, OH (city) Cuyahoga County	1,296	0.32
Aurora, IL (city) Kane County	1,266	0.66
Bellevue, WA (city) King County	1,262	1.06
Columbus, OH (city) Franklin County	1,256	0.16
Charlotte, NC (city) Mecklenburg County	1,248	0.18
Brookhaven, NY (town) Suffolk County	1,216	0.25
Troy, MI (city) Oakland County	1,184	1.46
Las Vegas, NV (city) Clark County	1,179	0.20
Bronx, NY (borough) Bronx County	1,164	0.09
Sacramento, CA (city) Sacramento County	1,087	0.24
Washington, DC (city) District of Columbia	1,068	0.18
Riverside, CA (city) Riverside County	1,063	0.35
Dallas, TX (city) Dallas County	1,061	0.09
Huntington Beach, CA (city) Orange County	1,012	0.54
Indianapolis, IN (city) Marion County	1,001	0.12
Peoria, AZ (city) Yavapai County	994	0.67
Staten Island, NY (borough) Richmond County	964	0.21
Warren, MI (city) Macomb County	955	0.70
Austin, TX (city) Travis County	947	0.12
Denver, CO (city) Denver County	923	0.16
Dearborn, MI (city) Wayne County	916	0.93
Vancouver, WA (city) Clark County	895	0.56
Des Plaines, IL (city) Cook County	867	1.51
Surprise, AZ (city) Maricopa County	855	0.82
Scottsdale, AZ (city) Maricopa County	835	0.38
Glendale, AZ (city) Maricopa County	816	0.36
Clinton, MI (charter township) Macomb County	810	0.83
Hallandale Beach, FL (city) Broward County	797	2.17
Farmington Hills, MI (city) Oakland County	794	0.99
Modesto, CA (city) Stanislaus County	791	0.39
Jacksonville, FL (city) Duval County	765	0.09
San Antonio, TX (city) Medina County	765	0.06
Parma, OH (city) Cuyahoga County	761	0.93
Asheville, NC (city) Buncombe County	759	0.93
Pembroke Pines, FL (city) Broward County	756	0.50
Boston, MA (city) Suffolk County	729	0.12
Shelby, MI (charter township) Macomb County	728	1.00
Antelope, CA (cdp) Sacramento County	714	1.56
Smithtown, NY (town) Suffolk County	707	0.60
Tamarac, FL (city) Broward County	706	1.18
Canton, MI (charter township) Wayne County	699	0.79
Boca Raton, FL (city) Palm Beach County	689	0.81
Rancho Cordova, CA (city) Sacramento County	682	1.08
Canton, OH (city) Stark County	682	0.92
Fullerton, CA (city) Orange County	663	0.50
Ann Arbor, MI (city) Washtenaw County	650	0.56
Rochester Hills, MI (city) Oakland County	642	0.91
Baltimore, MD (city) Baltimore city County	634	0.10
Carmichael, CA (cdp) Sacramento County	629	1.02

Place	Population	%
Nashville-Davidson, TN (metro govt) Davidson County	628	0.11
Morton Grove, IL (village) Cook County	624	2.73
Westland, MI (city) Wayne County	623	0.73
Macomb, MI (township) Macomb County	621	0.83
Long Beach, CA (city) Los Angeles County	621	0.13
Miami Beach, FL (city) Miami-Dade County	617	0.70
Irvine, CA (city) Orange County	617	0.31
Paradise, NV (cdp) Clark County	617	0.28
Detroit, MI (city) Wayne County	608	0.08
Lincolnwood, IL (village) Cook County	605	4.87
Chandler, AZ (city) Maricopa County	604	0.26
Sunnyvale, CA (city) Santa Clara County	594	0.44
Fort Worth, TX (city) Tarrant County	594	0.08
Mission Viejo, CA (city) Orange County	592	0.64
Olivehurst, CA (cdp) Yuba County	587	4.41
St. Paul, MN (city) Ramsey County	587	0.21
Virginia Beach, VA (ind. city) Virginia Beach independent city	580	0.13
Glendale, CA (city) Los Angeles County	576	0.30
Dix Hills, NY (cdp) Suffolk County	565	2.13
Akron, OH (city) Summit County	564	0.28
Dearborn Heights, MI (city) Wayne County	560	0.96
Pittsburgh, PA (city) Allegheny County	559	0.18
Minneapolis, MN (city) Hennepin County	557	0.15
Parma Heights, OH (city) Cuyahoga County	549	2.64
Orange, CA (city) Orange County	549	0.41
Arlington Heights, IL (village) Cook County	548	0.73
Davie, FL (town) Broward County	546	0.60
Clarkstown, NY (town) Rockland County	544	0.65
Tacoma, WA (city) Pierce County	538	0.27
Citrus Heights, CA (city) Sacramento County	533	0.63
Highland Park, IL (city) Lake County	530	1.76
Cambridge, MA (city) Middlesex County	530	0.51
Livonia, MI (city) Wayne County	524	0.54
Madison Heights, MI (city) Oakland County	522	1.74
Pasadena, CA (city) Los Angeles County	517	0.38
Loma Linda, CA (city) San Bernardino County	512	2.24
Cherry Hill, NJ (township) Camden County	509	0.72
Stamford, CT (city/town) Fairfield County	506	0.42
Santa Monica, CA (city) Los Angeles County	500	0.56
Evanston, IL (city) Cook County	499	0.68
Plantation, FL (city) Broward County	499	0.59
Kaser, NY (village) Rockland County	497	11.20
Thousand Oaks, CA (city) Ventura County	494	0.40
Madison, WI (city) Dane County	490	0.21
Greenburgh, NY (town) Westchester County	489	0.56
Bethesda, MD (cdp) Montgomery County	485	0.83
Lower Merion, PA (township) Montgomery County	478	0.82
Mesa, AZ (city) Maricopa County	475	0.11
Mount Prospect, IL (village) Cook County	474	0.88
Tucson, AZ (city) Pima County	471	0.09
West Bloomfield, MI (charter township) Oakland County	469	0.72
Strongsville, OH (city) Cuyahoga County	468	1.06
Islip, NY (town) Suffolk County	467	0.14
Buffalo Grove, IL (village) Lake County	466	1.11
Oakland, CA (city) Alameda County	466	0.12
Gainesville, FL (city) Alachua County	458	0.37
East Hill-Meridian, WA (cdp) King County	455	1.57
Henderson, NV (city) Clark County	454	0.18
Colorado Springs, CO (city) El Paso County	451	0.11
Berkeley, CA (city) Alameda County	449	0.41
Northbrook, IL (village) Cook County	445	1.35
Chaska, MN (city) Carver County	444	1.93
Lake in the Hills, IL (village) McHenry County	443	1.55
Sammamish, WA (city) King County	441	1.02
Spring Valley, NV (cdp) Clark County	440	0.26
Aventura, FL (city) Miami-Dade County	439	1.30
Reading, PA (city) Berks County	436	0.50
Toledo, OH (city) Lucas County	436	0.15
Fair Oaks, CA (cdp) Sacramento County	430	1.40
Lexington-Fayette, KY (cons. govt) Fayette County	430	0.15
San Rafael, CA (city) Marin County	425	0.75
Miami, FL (city) Miami-Dade County	423	0.11
Anchorage, AK (municipality) Anchorage Municipality	422	0.15
Laguna Niguel, CA (city) Orange County	421	0.67
Durham, NC (city) Durham County	421	0.19

Please refer to the Explanation of Data in the front of the book for more detailed information.

Ancestry

Romanian

Top 150 Places Sorted by Percent of Total Population

Based on all places, regardless of total population

Place	Population	%
Bryce Canyon City, UT (town) Garfield County	29	52.73
Plush, OR (cdp) Lake County	14	23.73
Sunset Beach, CA (cdp) Orange County	239	19.07
Grey Cloud Island, MN (township) Washington County	45	15.85
Kiryas Joel, NY (village) Orange County	2,293	12.01
Double Spring, NV (cdp) Douglas County	24	11.48
Kaser, NY (village) Rockland County	497	11.20
Halsey, OR (city) Linn County	98	10.76
Bibo, NM (cdp) Cibola County	14	9.15
Pocono Springs, PA (cdp) Wayne County	71	8.03
Greenview, CA (cdp) Siskiyou County	29	7.97
Deer Creek, AZ (cdp) Gila County	11	7.64
Duluth, WA (cdp) Clark County	119	7.51
Smoketown, PA (cdp) Lancaster County	27	7.16
Roosevelt, WA (cdp) Klickitat County	8	7.08
Remington, OH (cdp) Hamilton County	16	6.69
Grand Portage, MN (unorganized territory) Cook County	31	6.60
Montgomery, MA (town) Hampden County	48	6.56
Moores Hill, IN (town) Dearborn County	52	6.54
Avoca, IN (cdp) Lawrence County	34	6.46
Monroe, NY (town) Orange County	2,439	6.31
Clyde, NJ (cdp) Somerset County	15	6.25
Vienna Center, OH (cdp) Trumbull County	44	6.14
Kaneville, IL (village) Kane County	21	5.72
South Royalton, VT (cdp) Windsor County	27	5.66
West Milton, PA (cdp) Union County	36	5.56
Penns Creek, PA (cdp) Snyder County	28	5.47
Westwood, KY (city) Jefferson County	30	5.45
Harbor Hills, NY (cdp) Nassau County	27	5.45
University Gardens, NY (cdp) Nassau County	217	5.44
Deer Lake, PA (cdp) Fayette County	36	5.44
Dixonville, FL (cdp) Santa Rosa County	10	5.41
Celeryville, OH (cdp) Huron County	7	5.26
Tall Timber, CO (cdp) Boulder County	14	5.13
Manley, NE (village) Cass County	7	5.11
Boulder, WY (cdp) Sublette County	12	5.00
Maharishi Vedic City, IA (city) Jefferson County	8	5.00
Leonidas, MN (city) St. Louis County	4	5.00
Ravenna, TX (city) Fannin County	10	4.95
South Fork, MO (cdp) Howell County	12	4.90
Lincolnwood, IL (village) Cook County	605	4.87
Millbrook, IL (village) Kendall County	11	4.82
Kennedy, MN (city) Kittson County	7	4.76
Bar Harbor, ME (cdp) Hancock County	121	4.68
Smallwood, NY (cdp) Sullivan County	32	4.65
Cameron, SC (town) Calhoun County	21	4.61
Forest Lake, IL (cdp) Lake County	83	4.58
North Bay, WI (village) Racine County	15	4.57
Olivehurst, CA (cdp) Yuba County	587	4.41
Lashmeet, WV (cdp) Mercer County	11	4.38
Ward, PA (township) Tioga County	6	4.35
Pardeesville, PA (cdp) Luzerne County	31	4.32
Conashaugh Lakes, PA (cdp) Pike County	29	4.30
Gamble, PA (township) Lycoming County	37	4.28
Boswell's Corner, VA (cdp) Stafford County	63	4.23
New Trenton, IN (cdp) Franklin County	19	4.22
Rozel, KS (city) Pawnee County	4	4.21
Weymouth, NJ (township) Atlantic County	112	4.20
North Robinson, OH (village) Crawford County	8	4.17
Vineyard Lake, MI (cdp) Jackson County	31	4.16
Milford, NY (village) Otsego County	21	4.12
Port Henry, NY (village) Essex County	74	4.11
Pepper Pike, OH (city) Cuyahoga County	243	4.08
North Conway, NH (cdp) Carroll County	104	4.02
Derby, IA (city) Lucas County	5	4.00
Sand Lake, MN (township) Itasca County	5	4.00
Cedar Hill Lakes, MO (village) Jefferson County	9	3.88
Lorena, TX (city) McLennan County	78	3.86
Medaryville, IN (town) Pulaski County	19	3.82
Victor, MT (cdp) Ravalli County	27	3.77
Stevinson, CA (cdp) Merced County	9	3.77
Big Rock, IL (village) Kane County	43	3.74
Lehigh, PA (township) Wayne County	71	3.71
Dunbarton, NH (town) Merrimack County	100	3.70
East Norwich, NY (cdp) Nassau County	95	3.67
Pine Ridge, PA (cdp) Pike County	79	3.66
Rochelle Park, NJ (township) Bergen County	200	3.64
York, MI (charter township) Washtenaw County	311	3.63
Cooke City, MT (cdp) Park County	2	3.57
Rosedale, IN (town) Parke County	31	3.55
Braddock Heights, MD (cdp) Frederick County	96	3.54
Paloma Creek, TX (cdp) Denton County	92	3.54
Dennison, PA (township) Luzerne County	43	3.51
Eaton, IN (town) Delaware County	66	3.50
Barker, NY (town) Broome County	95	3.48
Wampum, PA (borough) Lawrence County	29	3.45
York Haven, PA (borough) York County	24	3.43
Trappe, PA (borough) Montgomery County	118	3.42
Fairlawn, OH (city) Summit County	254	3.40
Ho-Ho-Kus, NJ (borough) Bergen County	138	3.40
Gordon Heights, NY (cdp) Suffolk County	110	3.37
Airport, CA (cdp) Stanislaus County	53	3.33
Hartstown, PA (cdp) Crawford County	6	3.33
Lake Latonka, PA (cdp) Mercer County	30	3.30
Red Rock, AZ (cdp) Pinal County	33	3.29
Sparkill, NY (cdp) Rockland County	45	3.26
Hidden Hills, CA (city) Los Angeles County	82	3.25
Davenport, CA (cdp) Santa Cruz County	10	3.24
Brookdale, CA (cdp) Santa Cruz County	59	3.23
Walnut Grove, GA (city) Walton County	58	3.23
Pioneer, MI (township) Missaukee County	12	3.20
Port Byron, NY (village) Cayuga County	31	3.17
Sugar Camp, WI (town) Oneida County	62	3.15
Big Sky, MT (cdp) Gallatin County	48	3.14
Newburgh Heights, OH (village) Cuyahoga County	66	3.13
Oneida, KY (cdp) Clay County	13	3.09
East Dundee, IL (village) Kane County	90	3.07
Jonesboro, ME (town) Washington County	20	3.06
Steen, MN (city) Rock County	5	3.03
Cresson, TX (city) Parker County	17	3.02
Mokelumne Hill, CA (cdp) Calaveras County	22	2.99
Valier, MT (town) Pondera County	19	2.99
Pinewood Estates, TX (cdp) Hardin County	54	2.98
West Perry, PA (township) Snyder County	26	2.96
Dacula, GA (city) Gwinnett County	130	2.94
Saddlebrooke, MO (village) Christian County	9	2.93
University Center, VA (cdp) Loudoun County	94	2.90
Clarksville, VA (town) Mecklenburg County	35	2.87
Springmont, PA (cdp) Berks County	14	2.86
Castlewood, VA (cdp) Russell County	57	2.81
Bandon, OR (city) Coos County	86	2.80
Lancaster, KY (city) Garrard County	97	2.75
Dunbar, WI (cdp) Marinette County	2	2.74
Morton Grove, IL (village) Cook County	624	2.73
Vernon Center, NJ (cdp) Sussex County	56	2.73
Andes, NY (town) Delaware County	26	2.73
Turtle Lake, WI (village) Polk County	3	2.73
Springfield, NH (town) Sullivan County	27	2.72
Fairview, NC (cdp) Buncombe County	74	2.71
Sulphur Rock, AR (town) Independence County	13	2.69
Doyle, CA (cdp) Lassen County	10	2.69
Boyne Falls, MI (village) Charlevoix County	8	2.68
Eastgate, WA (cdp) King County	139	2.67
Michiana, MI (village) Berrien County	4	2.65
Trowbridge, CA (cdp) Sutter County	4	2.65
Parma Heights, OH (city) Cuyahoga County	549	2.64
Stockbridge, MI (village) Ingham County	29	2.64
Twin Oaks, MO (village) St. Louis County	10	2.64
Topeka, IL (village) Mason County	1	2.63
Rockwell, AR (cdp) Garland County	100	2.62
Markesan, WI (city) Green Lake County	38	2.62
Airmont, NY (village) Rockland County	219	2.60
Russell Gardens, NY (village) Nassau County	25	2.60
Maxbass, ND (city) Bottineau County	2	2.60
Campo, CA (cdp) San Diego County	76	2.57
Arenac, MI (township) Arenac County	22	2.57
Surfside, FL (town) Miami-Dade County	142	2.56
Brimfield, OH (cdp) Portage County	85	2.56
Hampton Beach, NH (cdp) Rockingham County	70	2.55
Secretary, MD (town) Dorchester County	17	2.55

Please refer to the Explanation of Data in the front of the book for more detailed information.

Ancestry

Romanian

Top 150 Places Sorted by Percent of Total Population

Based on places with total population of 7,500 or more

Place	Population	%
Kiryas Joel, NY (village) Orange County	2,293	12.01
Monroe, NY (town) Orange County	2,439	6.31
Lincolnwood, IL (village) Cook County	605	4.87
Olivehurst, CA (cdp) Yuba County	587	4.41
York, MI (charter township) Washtenaw County	311	3.63
Morton Grove, IL (village) Cook County	624	2.73
Parma Heights, OH (city) Cuyahoga County	549	2.64
Airmont, NY (village) Rockland County	219	2.60
Skokie, IL (village) Cook County	1,582	2.48
Highland Park, NJ (borough) Middlesex County	323	2.31
Monsey, NY (cdp) Rockland County	340	2.26
Loma Linda, CA (city) San Bernardino County	512	2.24
Hallandale Beach, FL (city) Broward County	797	2.17
Dix Hills, NY (cdp) Suffolk County	565	2.13
Highland Heights, OH (city) Cuyahoga County	175	2.12
Palm Beach, FL (town) Palm Beach County	177	2.04
Wood-Ridge, NJ (borough) Bergen County	154	2.03
Midland, WA (cdp) Pierce County	192	2.00
Great Neck, NY (village) Nassau County	192	1.95
Chaska, MN (city) Carver County	444	1.93
Seven Hills, OH (city) Cuyahoga County	227	1.92
Woodmere, NY (cdp) Nassau County	322	1.84
Middlesex, NJ (borough) Middlesex County	248	1.82
Flat Rock, MI (city) Wayne County	171	1.77
Highland Park, IL (city) Lake County	530	1.76
Madison Heights, MI (city) Oakland County	522	1.74
Highland Park, TX (town) Dallas County	146	1.71
Alderwood Manor, WA (cdp) Snohomish County	132	1.67
Struthers, OH (city) Mahoning County	180	1.65
Progress, PA (cdp) Dauphin County	156	1.63
East Hill-Meridian, WA (cdp) King County	455	1.57
Antelope, CA (cdp) Sacramento County	714	1.56
Alliance, OH (city) Stark County	351	1.56
Lebanon, NH (city) Grafton County	205	1.56
New Hyde Park, NY (village) Nassau County	150	1.56
Bath, ME (city) Sagadahoc County	137	1.56
Lake in the Hills, IL (village) McHenry County	443	1.55
Jericho, NY (cdp) Nassau County	198	1.52
Del Aire, CA (cdp) Los Angeles County	146	1.52
Des Plaines, IL (city) Cook County	867	1.51
Irmo, SC (town) Richland County	167	1.51
Groton, CT (city) New London County	152	1.49
El Sobrante, CA (cdp) Riverside County	165	1.48
Troy, MI (city) Oakland County	1,184	1.46
Mansfield, NJ (township) Burlington County	115	1.44
Beaver Falls, PA (city) Beaver County	130	1.43
Springdale, NJ (cdp) Camden County	207	1.41
Boulder Hill, IL (cdp) Kendall County	122	1.41
Fair Oaks, CA (cdp) Sacramento County	430	1.40
Ramapo, NY (town) Rockland County	1,695	1.38
Gresham, OR (city) Multnomah County	1,399	1.38
Glencoe, IL (village) Cook County	119	1.38
White Meadow Lake, NJ (cdp) Morris County	114	1.36
Northbrook, IL (village) Cook County	445	1.35
Scarsdale, NY (town/village) Westchester County	229	1.34
Pocono, PA (township) Monroe County	148	1.34
Troutdale, OR (city) Multnomah County	204	1.33
Mead Valley, CA (cdp) Riverside County	231	1.31
Lower Gwynedd, PA (township) Montgomery County	147	1.31
Aventura, FL (city) Miami-Dade County	439	1.30
Briarcliff Manor, NY (village) Westchester County	104	1.30
Schererville, IN (town) Lake County	368	1.29
Redding, CT (town) Fairfield County	115	1.29
Foothill Farms, CA (cdp) Sacramento County	420	1.28
Hollywood, FL (city) Broward County	1,788	1.27
Clinton, TN (city) Anderson County	124	1.27
Garden City, MI (city) Wayne County	356	1.26
Wood Dale, IL (city) DuPage County	173	1.26
Sterling Heights, MI (city) Macomb County	1,620	1.25
Middleburg Heights, OH (city) Cuyahoga County	195	1.23
Niles, IL (village) Cook County	358	1.22
Northville, MI (township) Wayne County	332	1.22
Bolivar, MO (city) Polk County	125	1.22
North Olmsted, OH (city) Cuyahoga County	398	1.21
Bexley, OH (city) Franklin County	157	1.21
Kenilworth, NJ (borough) Union County	94	1.20
Tamarac, FL (city) Broward County	706	1.18
Smithtown, NY (cdp) Suffolk County	308	1.18
Norridge, IL (village) Cook County	170	1.18
Wilmette, IL (village) Cook County	313	1.16
Camas, WA (city) Clark County	213	1.16
Marco Island, FL (city) Collier County	192	1.16
Hillsdale, NJ (borough) Bergen County	117	1.15
Ardmore, PA (cdp) Montgomery County	143	1.14
Conway, NH (town) Carroll County	114	1.14
Leoni, MI (township) Jackson County	157	1.13
Fair Lawn, NJ (borough) Bergen County	359	1.12
Buffalo Grove, IL (village) Lake County	466	1.11
Massillon, OH (city) Stark County	355	1.11
Holly, MI (township) Oakland County	123	1.11
LaSalle, IL (city) LaSalle County	108	1.11
Oradell, NJ (borough) Bergen County	87	1.10
Syosset, NY (cdp) Nassau County	206	1.09
Woodbury, NY (cdp) Nassau County	99	1.09
Rancho Cordova, CA (city) Sacramento County	682	1.08
North Royalton, OH (city) Cuyahoga County	323	1.08
Oceanside, NY (cdp) Nassau County	334	1.07
Twinsburg, OH (city) Summit County	199	1.07
Deerfield, IL (village) Lake County	197	1.07
Mack, OH (cdp) Hamilton County	123	1.07
Bellevue, WA (city) King County	1,262	1.06
Strongsville, OH (city) Cuyahoga County	468	1.06
Ashland, NJ (cdp) Camden County	92	1.06
Mundelein, IL (village) Lake County	326	1.05
Greenfield Town, MA (city) Franklin County	185	1.05
Croton-on-Hudson, NY (village) Westchester County	83	1.05
Ives Estates, FL (cdp) Miami-Dade County	183	1.04
Beachwood, OH (city) Cuyahoga County	124	1.04
Plymouth, MI (city) Wayne County	95	1.04
Hanover, NH (town) Grafton County	116	1.03
Carmichael, CA (cdp) Sacramento County	629	1.02
Sammamish, WA (city) King County	441	1.02
Prospect, CT (town) New Haven County	95	1.02
Mercer Island, WA (city) King County	226	1.01
Franklin Park, IL (village) Cook County	186	1.01
Shelby, MI (charter township) Macomb County	728	1.00
Nutley, NJ (township) Essex County	281	1.00
Kingsgate, WA (cdp) King County	137	1.00
Suffern, NY (village) Rockland County	107	1.00
Louisville, OH (city) Stark County	91	1.00
Farmington Hills, MI (city) Oakland County	794	0.99
New City, NY (cdp) Rockland County	332	0.99
Rocky River, OH (city) Cuyahoga County	199	0.99
Mill Valley, CA (city) Marin County	135	0.99
Richland, PA (township) Cambria County	126	0.99
Superior, MI (charter township) Washtenaw County	126	0.99
Lower Southampton, PA (township) Bucks County	187	0.98
Wyndham, VA (cdp) Henrico County	92	0.98
Price, UT (city) Carbon County	83	0.98
Woodcrest, CA (cdp) Riverside County	139	0.97
Powell, OH (city) Delaware County	105	0.97
Northfield, NJ (city) Atlantic County	83	0.97
Dearborn Heights, MI (city) Wayne County	560	0.96
Westmont, IL (village) DuPage County	234	0.96
Port Washington, NY (cdp) Nassau County	155	0.96
Westport, CT (cdp/town) Fairfield County	248	0.95
Golden Valley, MN (city) Hennepin County	191	0.95
Shorewood, WI (village) Milwaukee County	125	0.95
New Baltimore, MI (city) Macomb County	108	0.95
Maynard, MA (cdp/town) Middlesex County	95	0.95
Perry Heights, OH (cdp) Stark County	82	0.95
Itasca, IL (village) DuPage County	80	0.95
Cortlandt, NY (town) Westchester County	383	0.94
Livingston, NJ (township) Essex County	270	0.94
Melville, NY (cdp) Suffolk County	179	0.94
Incline Village, NV (cdp) Washoe County	81	0.94
Ellwood City, PA (borough) Lawrence County	77	0.94
Four Corners, MD (cdp) Montgomery County	75	0.94
Dearborn, MI (city) Wayne County	916	0.93
Parma, OH (city) Cuyahoga County	761	0.93

SECTION THREE

Please refer to the Explanation of Data in the front of the book for more detailed information.

Ancestry

Russian

U.S. and 50 States Sorted by Population and Percent of Total Population

Place	Population	%
United States	**3,072,756**	**1.01**
New York	474,184	2.47
California	446,376	1.22
Florida	239,314	1.29
Pennsylvania	202,430	1.60
New Jersey	197,299	2.26
Illinois	136,208	1.07
Massachusetts	120,438	1.86
Washington	86,098	1.31
Maryland	82,950	1.46
Texas	81,869	0.34
Ohio	80,848	0.70
Michigan	78,153	0.79
Connecticut	71,159	2.01
Colorado	60,224	1.23
Arizona	58,691	0.94
Virginia	55,000	0.70
Oregon	51,468	1.37
Georgia	44,575	0.47
Minnesota	44,525	0.85
Wisconsin	41,891	0.74
North Carolina	41,674	0.45
Missouri	31,898	0.54
Nevada	27,290	1.04
Indiana	25,824	0.40
North Dakota	25,211	3.82
Kansas	23,465	0.84
Tennessee	18,228	0.29
South Carolina	15,467	0.34
New Hampshire	13,211	1.01
South Dakota	13,055	1.63
Nebraska	12,966	0.72
Rhode Island	11,523	1.09
Oklahoma	10,943	0.30
Iowa	10,765	0.36
Utah	10,505	0.40
Kentucky	10,491	0.24
Alaska	10,011	1.45
Montana	9,911	1.02
Maine	9,751	0.73
New Mexico	9,662	0.48
District of Columbia	9,585	1.64
Idaho	9,298	0.61
Alabama	8,648	0.18
Vermont	8,473	1.36
Louisiana	7,899	0.18
Delaware	7,508	0.85
West Virginia	6,836	0.37
Hawaii	5,605	0.42
Arkansas	5,047	0.18
Wyoming	4,837	0.89
Mississippi	3,469	0.12

Place	Population	%
North Dakota	25,211	3.82
New York	474,184	2.47
New Jersey	197,299	2.26
Connecticut	71,159	2.01
Massachusetts	120,438	1.86
District of Columbia	9,585	1.64
South Dakota	13,055	1.63
Pennsylvania	202,430	1.60
Maryland	82,950	1.46
Alaska	10,011	1.45
Oregon	51,468	1.37
Vermont	8,473	1.36
Washington	86,098	1.31
Florida	239,314	1.29
Colorado	60,224	1.23
California	446,376	1.22
Rhode Island	11,523	1.09
Illinois	136,208	1.07
Nevada	27,290	1.04
Montana	9,911	1.02
United States	**3,072,756**	**1.01**
New Hampshire	13,211	1.01
Arizona	58,691	0.94
Wyoming	4,837	0.89
Minnesota	44,525	0.85
Delaware	7,508	0.85
Kansas	23,465	0.84
Michigan	78,153	0.79
Wisconsin	41,891	0.74
Maine	9,751	0.73
Nebraska	12,966	0.72
Ohio	80,848	0.70
Virginia	55,000	0.70
Idaho	9,298	0.61
Missouri	31,898	0.54
New Mexico	9,662	0.48
Georgia	44,575	0.47
North Carolina	41,674	0.45
Hawaii	5,605	0.42
Indiana	25,824	0.40
Utah	10,505	0.40
West Virginia	6,836	0.37
Iowa	10,765	0.36
Texas	81,869	0.34
South Carolina	15,467	0.34
Oklahoma	10,943	0.30
Tennessee	18,228	0.29
Kentucky	10,491	0.24
Alabama	8,648	0.18
Louisiana	7,899	0.18
Arkansas	5,047	0.18
Mississippi	3,469	0.12

Please refer to the Explanation of Data in the front of the book for more detailed information.

Ancestry

Russian

Top 150 Places Sorted by Population

Based on all places, regardless of total population

Place	Population	%
New York, NY (city) Kings County	240,690	2.98
Los Angeles, CA (city) Los Angeles County	96,251	2.55
Brooklyn, NY (borough) Kings County	88,579	3.59
Manhattan, NY (borough) New York County	82,983	5.24
Queens, NY (borough) Queens County	44,676	2.03
Chicago, IL (city) Cook County	28,264	1.05
Hempstead, NY (town) Nassau County	26,754	3.55
Philadelphia, PA (city) Philadelphia County	25,520	1.70
San Francisco, CA (city) San Francisco County	21,435	2.72
San Diego, CA (city) San Diego County	18,222	1.42
Staten Island, NY (borough) Richmond County	16,388	3.54
North Hempstead, NY (town) Nassau County	14,712	6.58
Oyster Bay, NY (town) Nassau County	14,554	4.99
Phoenix, AZ (city) Maricopa County	13,664	0.94
Portland, OR (city) Multnomah County	13,188	2.33
Brookhaven, NY (town) Suffolk County	12,073	2.51
Boston, MA (city) Suffolk County	11,209	1.86
Seattle, WA (city) King County	9,615	1.62
Washington, DC (city) District of Columbia	9,585	1.64
Huntington, NY (town) Suffolk County	9,499	4.70
Houston, TX (city) Harris County	9,363	0.45
Denver, CO (city) Denver County	8,670	1.50
Bronx, NY (borough) Bronx County	8,064	0.59
Las Vegas, NV (city) Clark County	7,526	1.30
Newton, MA (city) Middlesex County	7,389	8.80
Dallas, TX (city) Dallas County	7,373	0.62
Scottsdale, AZ (city) Maricopa County	6,802	3.11
Austin, TX (city) Travis County	6,655	0.87
Baltimore, MD (city) Baltimore city County	6,362	1.03
Buffalo Grove, IL (village) Lake County	6,299	15.05
Lower Merion, PA (township) Montgomery County	6,253	10.77
Pittsburgh, PA (city) Allegheny County	6,191	2.01
San Jose, CA (city) Santa Clara County	6,163	0.67
Boca Raton, FL (city) Palm Beach County	6,136	7.21
Ramapo, NY (town) Rockland County	6,069	4.95
Highland Park, IL (city) Lake County	6,049	20.11
Coral Springs, FL (city) Broward County	5,962	4.92
Charlotte, NC (city) Mecklenburg County	5,549	0.79
Columbus, OH (city) Franklin County	5,392	0.70
Oakland, CA (city) Alameda County	5,358	1.38
Smithtown, NY (town) Suffolk County	5,319	4.52
Clarkstown, NY (town) Rockland County	5,317	6.38
Tucson, AZ (city) Pima County	5,201	1.00
Cherry Hill, NJ (township) Camden County	5,175	7.29
Santa Monica, CA (city) Los Angeles County	5,142	5.80
Jacksonville, FL (city) Duval County	5,097	0.63
Greenburgh, NY (town) Westchester County	5,042	5.75
Islip, NY (town) Suffolk County	5,019	1.50
Pikesville, MD (cdp) Baltimore County	5,008	16.30
Bismarck, ND (city) Burleigh County	4,970	8.28
Sacramento, CA (city) Sacramento County	4,916	1.07
West Bloomfield, MI (charter township) Oakland County	4,873	7.53
Brookline, MA (cdp/town) Norfolk County	4,869	8.40
Skokie, IL (village) Cook County	4,794	7.51
Stamford, CT (city/town) Fairfield County	4,722	3.91
Long Beach, CA (city) Los Angeles County	4,610	1.00
West Hollywood, CA (city) Los Angeles County	4,501	12.99
Thousand Oaks, CA (city) Ventura County	4,469	3.58
Minneapolis, MN (city) Hennepin County	4,282	1.13
Northbrook, IL (village) Cook County	4,261	12.94
Santa Clarita, CA (city) Los Angeles County	4,252	2.47
Arlington, VA (cdp) Arlington County	4,145	2.10
Berkeley, CA (city) Alameda County	4,125	3.77
Irvine, CA (city) Orange County	4,120	2.07
Bethesda, MD (cdp) Montgomery County	4,117	7.03
Anchorage, AK (municipality) Anchorage Municipality	3,927	1.38
Atlanta, GA (city) Fulton County	3,892	0.94
Virginia Beach, VA (ind. city) Virginia Beach independent city	3,863	0.89
Cambridge, MA (city) Middlesex County	3,852	3.72
Babylon, NY (town) Suffolk County	3,774	1.77
Henderson, NV (city) Clark County	3,752	1.51
San Antonio, TX (city) Medina County	3,645	0.28
Potomac, MD (cdp) Montgomery County	3,628	8.10
Marlboro, NJ (township) Monmouth County	3,591	9.11
Vancouver, WA (city) Clark County	3,529	2.20
East Brunswick, NJ (township) Middlesex County	3,518	7.42
Tampa, FL (city) Hillsborough County	3,488	1.05
Aventura, FL (city) Miami-Dade County	3,483	10.31
Aurora, CO (city) Arapahoe County	3,483	1.11
Amherst, NY (town) Erie County	3,468	2.87
Nashville-Davidson, TN (metro govt) Davidson County	3,447	0.59
Huntington Beach, CA (city) Orange County	3,421	1.81
Hollywood, FL (city) Broward County	3,407	2.41
Farmington Hills, MI (city) Oakland County	3,395	4.23
West Hartford, CT (cdp/town) Hartford County	3,388	5.39
Beverly Hills, CA (city) Los Angeles County	3,343	9.84
Miami Beach, FL (city) Miami-Dade County	3,331	3.80
Deerfield, IL (village) Lake County	3,318	18.03
Albuquerque, NM (city) Bernalillo County	3,282	0.62
Indianapolis, IN (city) Marion County	3,280	0.41
Evanston, IL (city) Cook County	3,244	4.39
Ann Arbor, MI (city) Washtenaw County	3,214	2.79
Colorado Springs, CO (city) El Paso County	3,208	0.79
Plainview, NY (cdp) Nassau County	3,204	12.43
Framingham, MA (cdp/town) Middlesex County	3,180	4.72
Fort Lauderdale, FL (city) Broward County	3,176	1.90
Omaha, NE (city) Douglas County	3,148	0.77
New Rochelle, NY (city) Westchester County	3,102	4.09
Plantation, FL (city) Broward County	3,102	3.65
Fresno, CA (city) Fresno County	3,100	0.64
Manalapan, NJ (township) Monmouth County	3,099	8.17
Fair Lawn, NJ (borough) Bergen County	3,083	9.59
Overland Park, KS (city) Johnson County	3,050	1.79
Madison, WI (city) Dane County	3,045	1.33
Boulder, CO (city) Boulder County	3,025	3.12
Milwaukee, WI (city) Milwaukee County	3,017	0.51
Louisville-Jefferson County, KY (metro govt) Jefferson County	2,994	0.51
New City, NY (cdp) Rockland County	2,957	8.85
Plano, TX (city) Collin County	2,957	1.15
North Bethesda, MD (cdp) Montgomery County	2,942	7.27
Rockville, MD (city) Montgomery County	2,935	5.03
Scarsdale, NY (town/village) Westchester County	2,929	17.12
Weston, FL (city) Broward County	2,926	4.66
Lincoln, NE (city) Lancaster County	2,914	1.15
Spokane, WA (city) Spokane County	2,911	1.41
Wheeling, IL (village) Cook County	2,904	7.84
Livingston, NJ (township) Essex County	2,881	10.00
Pembroke Pines, FL (city) Broward County	2,834	1.86
Bellevue, WA (city) King County	2,825	2.36
Yonkers, NY (city) Westchester County	2,804	1.44
Monroe, NJ (township) Middlesex County	2,769	7.45
Providence, RI (city) Providence County	2,749	1.54
Lakewood, NJ (township) Ocean County	2,742	3.13
Tamarac, FL (city) Broward County	2,736	4.58
Fort Lee, NJ (borough) Bergen County	2,695	7.66
Scranton, PA (city) Lackawanna County	2,676	3.52
Sandy Springs, GA (city) Fulton County	2,673	2.94
Pompano Beach, FL (city) Broward County	2,603	2.59
Needham, MA (cdp/town) Norfolk County	2,587	9.02
Mesa, AZ (city) Maricopa County	2,582	0.59
St. Paul, MN (city) Ramsey County	2,579	0.91
Commack, NY (cdp) Suffolk County	2,576	7.13
Coconut Creek, FL (city) Broward County	2,576	5.00
Northampton, PA (township) Bucks County	2,533	6.36
Oceanside, NY (cdp) Nassau County	2,531	8.14
Calabasas, CA (city) Los Angeles County	2,509	11.06
Columbia, MD (cdp) Howard County	2,500	2.54
Sharon, MA (town) Norfolk County	2,498	14.33
Westport, CT (cdp/town) Fairfield County	2,494	9.55
Palm Beach Gardens, FL (city) Palm Beach County	2,484	5.32
Cheltenham, PA (township) Montgomery County	2,477	6.73
Glenview, IL (village) Cook County	2,477	5.67
Fargo, ND (city) Cass County	2,475	2.41
Tacoma, WA (city) Pierce County	2,468	1.24
Reno, NV (city) Washoe County	2,458	1.11
Paradise, NV (cdp) Clark County	2,457	1.13
Jersey City, NJ (city) Hudson County	2,439	1.00
Palo Alto, CA (city) Santa Clara County	2,425	3.88
Raleigh, NC (city) Wake County	2,411	0.63
Simi Valley, CA (city) Ventura County	2,408	1.98

Ancestry

Russian

Top 150 Places Sorted by Percent of Total Population

Based on all places, regardless of total population

Place	Population	%
Tavistock, NJ (borough) Camden County	4	100.00
Fox River, AK (cdp) Kenai Peninsula Borough	696	88.55
Raleigh, ND (cdp) Grant County	17	60.71
Lehr, ND (city) McIntosh County	61	57.01
Nikolaevsk, AK (cdp) Kenai Peninsula Borough	138	56.56
Chapin, IA (cdp) Franklin County	48	50.53
Auburn, ND (cdp) Walsh County	9	50.00
Ugashik, AK (cdp) Lake and Peninsula Borough	3	50.00
Thurmond, WV (town) Fayette County	2	50.00
Spring Lake, FL (cdp) Hernando County	213	44.38
Hendersonville, PA (cdp) Washington County	82	41.84
Bayside, WI (village) Ozaukee County	23	40.35
Haynes, ND (city) Adams County	12	38.71
Kendall, WA (cdp) Whatcom County	159	37.68
Piffard, NY (cdp) Livingston County	22	36.67
Copper Mountain, CO (cdp) Summit County	47	33.57
Voltaire, ND (city) McHenry County	10	31.25
Hewlett Bay Park, NY (village) Nassau County	155	29.87
Creston, CA (cdp) San Luis Obispo County	20	29.85
Cayuga, ND (city) Sargent County	12	29.27
Galisteo, NM (cdp) Santa Fe County	93	29.25
Ashley, ND (city) McIntosh County	213	28.63
Hosmer, SD (city) Edmunds County	51	28.49
Great Neck Gardens, NY (cdp) Nassau County	258	28.41
Hewlett Harbor, NY (village) Nassau County	331	28.22
Rocky Point, MT (cdp) Lake County	16	28.07
Moclips, WA (cdp) Grays Harbor County	39	27.27
Cleveland, ND (city) Stutsman County	46	27.22
Lakeridge, NV (cdp) Douglas County	47	26.86
Roslyn Estates, NY (village) Nassau County	327	26.48
Richmond, VT (cdp) Chittenden County	126	25.71
Zeeland, ND (city) McIntosh County	13	25.49
East Liberty, OH (cdp) Logan County	81	25.23
Leola, SD (city) McPherson County	95	23.93
San Cristobal, NM (cdp) Taos County	38	23.90
Woodsburgh, NY (village) Nassau County	178	23.89
Selma, OR (cdp) Josephine County	151	23.27
Dunlap, KS (city) Morris County	10	23.26
Sletten, MN (township) Polk County	30	22.73
Sandy Ridge, PA (cdp) Centre County	50	22.62
Vilas, SD (town) Miner County	6	22.22
Grand View-on-Hudson, NY (village) Rockland County	62	21.83
Tolstoy, SD (town) Potter County	5	21.74
Knute, MN (township) Polk County	149	21.66
Morris, SD (town) Corson County	18	21.43
Fredonia, ND (city) Logan County	3	21.43
Eureka, SD (city) McPherson County	207	21.36
Evansville, AK (cdp) Yukon-Koyukuk Census Area	5	20.83
Wishek, ND (city) McIntosh County	210	20.73
Hewlett Neck, NY (village) Nassau County	97	20.73
Vista, MO (village) St. Clair County	12	20.69
Russell Gardens, NY (village) Nassau County	199	20.66
Whittingham, NJ (cdp) Middlesex County	510	20.29
Scotts Corners, NY (cdp) Westchester County	102	20.28
East Hills, NY (village) Nassau County	1,385	20.21
Badger, MN (township) Polk County	22	20.18
Highland Park, IL (city) Lake County	6,049	20.11
Big Delta, AK (cdp) Southeast Fairbanks Census Area	107	20.00
Unity, ME (unorganized territory) Kennebec County	14	20.00
Laird, CO (cdp) Yuma County	6	20.00
Trail, OR (cdp) Jackson County	65	19.94
Williston, MD (cdp) Caroline County	38	19.79
Richardton, ND (city) Stark County	96	19.75
Tokeland, WA (cdp) Pacific County	27	19.71
Buffington, PA (cdp) Fayette County	31	19.50
Strasburg, ND (city) Emmons County	98	19.14
Bakerhill, AL (town) Barbour County	63	19.09
Concordia, NJ (cdp) Middlesex County	607	18.95
Hookstown, PA (borough) Beaver County	37	18.88
Hatfield, MN (city) Pipestone County	9	18.75
Bark Ranch, CO (cdp) Boulder County	45	18.60
Dorset, VT (cdp) Bennington County	58	18.59
Thomaston, NY (village) Nassau County	485	18.55
Deerfield, IL (village) Lake County	3,318	18.03
Brush Prairie, WA (cdp) Clark County	427	18.03
Lamy, NM (cdp) Santa Fe County	60	17.96
Genoa, NV (cdp) Douglas County	170	17.93
Napoleon, ND (city) Logan County	154	17.89
Sands Point, NY (village) Nassau County	475	17.86
Kensington, NY (village) Nassau County	214	17.76
Talmage, KS (cdp) Dickinson County	18	17.65
Selz, ND (cdp) Pierce County	30	17.54
Great Neck Estates, NY (village) Nassau County	476	17.42
Lipscomb, TX (cdp) Lipscomb County	5	17.24
Glencoe, IL (village) Cook County	1,479	17.14
Scarsdale, NY (town/village) Westchester County	2,929	17.12
Kulm, ND (city) LaMoure County	49	17.07
Mount Gretna Heights, PA (cdp) Lebanon County	28	17.07
Benedict, ND (city) McLean County	9	16.98
Athol, KS (city) Smith County	10	16.95
Rachel, WV (cdp) Marion County	28	16.87
Danbury, NE (village) Red Willow County	14	16.67
Artas, SD (town) Campbell County	2	16.67
Riverwoods, IL (village) Lake County	651	16.61
North Hills, NY (village) Nassau County	813	16.46
Linton, ND (city) Emmons County	166	16.31
Pikesville, MD (cdp) Baltimore County	5,008	16.30
Grindstone, PA (cdp) Fayette County	121	16.24
Hidden Hills, CA (city) Los Angeles County	408	16.18
Beachwood, OH (city) Cuyahoga County	1,926	16.14
Fritz Creek, AK (cdp) Kenai Peninsula Borough	276	15.96
Liebenthal, KS (city) Rush County	12	15.79
Nord, CA (cdp) Butte County	50	15.77
Frannie, WY (town) Big Horn County	25	15.72
Great Neck Plaza, NY (village) Nassau County	1,034	15.64
Deep Creek, VA (cdp) Accomack County	13	15.48
Sereno del Mar, CA (cdp) Sonoma County	19	15.45
South Naknek, AK (cdp) Bristol Bay Borough	14	15.38
Sharon, MA (cdp) Norfolk County	797	15.33
Buffalo Grove, IL (village) Lake County	6,299	15.05
Hope, ID (city) Bonner County	12	15.00
Nikolski, AK (cdp) Aleutians West Census Area	3	15.00
Steele, ND (city) Kidder County	98	14.83
Schoenchen, KS (city) Ellis County	38	14.79
Coal Center, PA (borough) Washington County	41	14.70
Charlestown, NH (cdp) Sullivan County	122	14.61
Sharon, MA (town) Norfolk County	2,498	14.33
Pajaro Dunes, CA (cdp) Santa Cruz County	43	14.33
Venango, NE (village) Perkins County	21	14.29
La Salle, MN (city) Watonwan County	12	14.29
Green Hills, PA (borough) Washington County	2	14.29
Wyncote, PA (cdp) Montgomery County	452	14.28
Herreid, SD (city) Campbell County	56	13.97
South Palm Beach, FL (town) Palm Beach County	180	13.96
Lyon Mountain, NY (cdp) Clinton County	53	13.95
Great Neck, NY (village) Nassau County	1,371	13.93
Summerville, OR (town) Union County	25	13.81
Mound City, SD (town) Campbell County	8	13.79
Nisland, SD (town) Butte County	26	13.76
Flasher, ND (city) Morton County	40	13.70
King Arthur Park, MT (cdp) Gallatin County	77	13.68
Naper, NE (village) Boyd County	16	13.68
Ranier, MN (city) Koochiching County	18	13.53
Weston, CT (town) Fairfield County	1,356	13.44
South Heart, ND (city) Stark County	29	13.43
Mayfield, PA (borough) Lackawanna County	249	13.41
Selby, SD (city) Walworth County	106	13.37
Bayside, WI (village) Milwaukee County	571	13.33
Somerset, MD (town) Montgomery County	181	13.24
Old Harbor, AK (city) Kodiak Island Borough	34	13.23
Burtrum, MN (city) Todd County	24	13.19
University Gardens, NY (cdp) Nassau County	524	13.14
East Atlantic Beach, NY (cdp) Nassau County	239	13.00
West Hollywood, CA (city) Los Angeles County	4,501	12.99
Bayside, WI (village) Milwaukee County	548	12.96
Cartago, CA (cdp) Inyo County	7	12.96
Northbrook, IL (village) Cook County	4,261	12.94
Vaughn, WA (cdp) Pierce County	55	12.94
Cairnbrook, PA (cdp) Somerset County	58	12.83
Lower Moreland, PA (township) Montgomery County	1,614	12.75

Ancestry

Russian

Top 150 Places Sorted by Percent of Total Population

Based on places with total population of 7,500 or more

Place	Population	%
Highland Park, IL (city) Lake County	6,049	20.11
Deerfield, IL (village) Lake County	3,318	18.03
Glencoe, IL (village) Cook County	1,479	17.14
Scarsdale, NY (town/village) Westchester County	2,929	17.12
Pikesville, MD (cdp) Baltimore County	5,008	16.30
Beachwood, OH (city) Cuyahoga County	1,926	16.14
Buffalo Grove, IL (village) Lake County	6,299	15.05
Sharon, MA (town) Norfolk County	2,498	14.33
Great Neck, NY (village) Nassau County	1,371	13.93
Weston, CT (town) Fairfield County	1,356	13.44
West Hollywood, CA (city) Los Angeles County	4,501	12.99
Northbrook, IL (village) Cook County	4,261	12.94
Lower Moreland, PA (township) Montgomery County	1,614	12.75
Springdale, NJ (cdp) Camden County	1,859	12.65
Garrison, MD (cdp) Baltimore County	963	12.63
Plainview, NY (cdp) Nassau County	3,204	12.43
Robertsville, NJ (cdp) Monmouth County	1,346	12.19
Jericho, NY (cdp) Nassau County	1,457	11.20
Calabasas, CA (city) Los Angeles County	2,509	11.06
New Castle, NY (town) Westchester County	1,879	10.78
Lower Merion, PA (township) Montgomery County	6,253	10.77
Short Hills, NJ (cdp) Essex County	1,416	10.72
Tenafly, NJ (borough) Bergen County	1,503	10.53
Hastings-on-Hudson, NY (village) Westchester County	808	10.38
Aventura, FL (city) Miami-Dade County	3,483	10.31
Rye Brook, NY (village) Westchester County	932	10.18
Merrick, NY (cdp) Nassau County	2,169	10.17
Woodbury, NY (cdp) Nassau County	922	10.16
Mandan, ND (city) Morton County	1,802	10.12
Livingston, NJ (township) Essex County	2,881	10.00
White Meadow Lake, NJ (cdp) Morris County	832	9.93
Woodmere, NY (cdp) Nassau County	1,721	9.86
Beverly Hills, CA (city) Los Angeles County	3,343	9.84
Millburn, NJ (township) Essex County	1,963	9.84
Fair Lawn, NJ (borough) Bergen County	3,083	9.59
Westport, CT (cdp/town) Fairfield County	2,494	9.55
Springfield, NJ (township) Union County	1,474	9.52
Palm Beach, FL (town) Palm Beach County	825	9.51
Sunny Isles Beach, FL (city) Miami-Dade County	1,839	9.30
Bexley, OH (city) Franklin County	1,210	9.29
Woodbridge, CT (town) New Haven County	836	9.28
Oak Park, CA (cdp) Ventura County	1,297	9.24
Marlboro, NJ (township) Monmouth County	3,591	9.11
Briarcliff Manor, NY (village) Westchester County	730	9.10
Needham, MA (cdp/town) Norfolk County	2,587	9.02
Long Grove, IL (village) Lake County	704	8.95
New City, NY (cdp) Rockland County	2,957	8.85
Ojus, FL (cdp) Miami-Dade County	1,499	8.83
Newton, MA (city) Middlesex County	7,389	8.80
Parkland, FL (city) Broward County	1,951	8.69
Old Forge, PA (borough) Lackawanna County	720	8.60
Marina del Rey, CA (cdp) Los Angeles County	789	8.58
Vernon Hills, IL (village) Lake County	2,089	8.57
Agoura Hills, CA (city) Los Angeles County	1,725	8.49
Airmont, NY (village) Rockland County	715	8.49
Five Corners, WA (cdp) Clark County	1,468	8.42
Melville, NY (cdp) Suffolk County	1,602	8.41
Brookline, MA (cdp/town) Norfolk County	4,869	8.40
Upper Dublin, PA (township) Montgomery County	2,127	8.31
Lower Southampton, PA (township) Bucks County	1,580	8.29
Bismarck, ND (city) Burleigh County	4,970	8.28
Wayland, MA (town) Middlesex County	1,061	8.25
Manalapan, NJ (township) Monmouth County	3,099	8.17
Oceanside, NY (cdp) Nassau County	2,531	8.14
Highland Park, NJ (borough) Middlesex County	1,135	8.11
Potomac, MD (cdp) Montgomery County	3,628	8.10
Whitemarsh, PA (township) Montgomery County	1,370	7.96
Olivette, MO (city) St. Louis County	608	7.94
Swampscott, MA (cdp/town) Essex County	1,085	7.85
Wheeling, IL (village) Cook County	2,904	7.84
Upper Makefield, PA (township) Bucks County	629	7.83
Creve Coeur, MO (city) St. Louis County	1,375	7.82
Cherry Hill Mall, NJ (cdp) Camden County	1,089	7.79
Upper Montclair, NJ (cdp) Essex County	899	7.75
Fort Lee, NJ (borough) Bergen County	2,695	7.66
Dickinson, ND (city) Stark County	1,303	7.59
West Bloomfield, MI (charter township) Oakland County	4,873	7.53
Skokie, IL (village) Cook County	4,794	7.51
Monroe, NJ (township) Middlesex County	2,769	7.45
East Brunswick, NJ (township) Middlesex County	3,518	7.42
Cherry Hill, NJ (township) Camden County	5,175	7.29
Leisure World, MD (cdp) Montgomery County	631	7.28
North Bethesda, MD (cdp) Montgomery County	2,942	7.27
Dix Hills, NY (cdp) Suffolk County	1,928	7.26
Boca Raton, FL (city) Palm Beach County	6,136	7.21
Shorewood, WI (village) Milwaukee County	943	7.17
Commack, NY (cdp) Suffolk County	2,576	7.13
Bethesda, MD (cdp) Montgomery County	4,117	7.03
Long Beach, NY (city) Nassau County	2,351	7.03
Greentree, NJ (cdp) Camden County	804	7.02
Mamaroneck, NY (town) Westchester County	2,006	6.93
Aberdeen, SD (city) Brown County	1,780	6.92
Lyndhurst, OH (city) Cuyahoga County	973	6.88
Pinecrest, FL (village) Miami-Dade County	1,255	6.84
Port Jefferson, NY (village) Suffolk County	532	6.80
Cheltenham, PA (township) Montgomery County	2,477	6.73
Orchards, WA (cdp) Clark County	1,348	6.66
North Hempstead, NY (town) Nassau County	14,712	6.58
Solon, OH (city) Cuyahoga County	1,498	6.52
Ashland, NJ (cdp) Camden County	556	6.44
Leonia, NJ (borough) Bergen County	571	6.42
Clarkstown, NY (town) Rockland County	5,317	6.38
Northampton, PA (township) Bucks County	2,533	6.36
Ferndale, WA (city) Whatcom County	691	6.29
Syosset, NY (cdp) Nassau County	1,188	6.28
Bellmore, NY (cdp) Nassau County	1,015	6.27
Greenwood Village, CO (city) Arapahoe County	837	6.26
Mayfield Heights, OH (city) Cuyahoga County	1,185	6.20
Princeton, NJ (township) Mercer County	1,014	6.19
Plains, PA (township) Luzerne County	623	6.19
Kemp Mill, MD (cdp) Montgomery County	744	6.16
North Castle, NY (town) Westchester County	713	6.15
Wilmette, IL (village) Cook County	1,650	6.13
Ashland, MA (town) Middlesex County	984	6.13
Minnehaha, WA (cdp) Clark County	590	6.12
Verona, NJ (township) Essex County	813	6.11
Princeton, NJ (borough) Mercer County	766	6.11
Port Washington, NY (cdp) Nassau County	979	6.07
Setauket-East Setauket, NY (cdp) Suffolk County	953	6.07
Marblehead, MA (cdp/town) Essex County	1,198	6.05
Lincolnwood, IL (village) Cook County	750	6.04
Croton-on-Hudson, NY (village) Westchester County	477	6.04
West Windsor, NJ (township) Mercer County	1,584	6.03
Warwick, PA (township) Bucks County	845	6.01
Wantagh, NY (cdp) Nassau County	1,075	5.98
Seaford, NY (cdp) Nassau County	924	5.98
Topanga, CA (cdp) Los Angeles County	506	5.94
River Vale, NJ (township) Bergen County	561	5.86
Mill Valley, CA (city) Marin County	802	5.85
Longmeadow, MA (cdp/town) Hampden County	916	5.81
Santa Monica, CA (city) Los Angeles County	5,142	5.80
Bedford, NY (town) Westchester County	1,008	5.79
Greenburgh, NY (town) Westchester County	5,042	5.75
Westfield, NJ (town) Union County	1,723	5.75
Montclair, NJ (township) Essex County	2,154	5.72
Piedmont, CA (city) Alameda County	605	5.72
Glenview, IL (village) Cook County	2,477	5.67
Closter, NJ (borough) Bergen County	471	5.66
Montville, NJ (township) Morris County	1,210	5.64
Monsey, NY (cdp) Rockland County	849	5.64
Laguna Woods, CA (city) Orange County	918	5.63
Richmond Hill, GA (city) Bryan County	497	5.59
O'Hara, PA (township) Allegheny County	467	5.58
West Springfield Town, MA (city) Hampden County	1,571	5.55
Valley Cottage, NY (cdp) Rockland County	522	5.52
Upper Southampton, PA (township) Bucks County	844	5.50
Westlake Village, CA (city) Los Angeles County	454	5.49
Upper Saddle River, NJ (borough) Bergen County	442	5.47
Malibu, CA (city) Los Angeles County	699	5.46
Sudbury, MA (town) Middlesex County	943	5.45

SECTION THREE

Please refer to the Explanation of Data in the front of the book for more detailed information.

Ancestry

Scandinavian

U.S. and 50 States Sorted by Population and Percent of Total Population

Place	Population	%
United States	**582,549**	**0.19**
Minnesota	77,745	1.48
California	67,697	0.18
Washington	51,902	0.79
Utah	33,337	1.25
Oregon	23,693	0.63
Texas	23,366	0.10
Wisconsin	20,652	0.37
Florida	20,098	0.11
Arizona	18,210	0.29
Colorado	18,006	0.37
Illinois	16,473	0.13
Michigan	14,042	0.14
New York	12,891	0.07
Virginia	10,867	0.14
Idaho	9,884	0.65
Iowa	9,463	0.31
Ohio	8,810	0.08
North Dakota	8,787	1.33
North Carolina	8,125	0.09
Georgia	7,986	0.08
Massachusetts	7,961	0.12
Pennsylvania	7,796	0.06
Montana	7,736	0.79
Missouri	7,357	0.12
Indiana	6,406	0.10
South Dakota	6,361	0.80
Nevada	6,213	0.24
New Jersey	5,569	0.06
Maryland	5,403	0.09
Tennessee	5,027	0.08
Nebraska	4,494	0.25
Alaska	4,300	0.62
Connecticut	3,916	0.11
South Carolina	3,863	0.09
Kansas	3,774	0.13
New Mexico	3,757	0.19
Oklahoma	3,624	0.10
Alabama	3,322	0.07
Arkansas	3,145	0.11
Maine	2,909	0.22
Wyoming	2,904	0.53
Kentucky	2,634	0.06
New Hampshire	2,212	0.17
Hawaii	2,056	0.15
Louisiana	1,776	0.04
Mississippi	1,349	0.05
Vermont	1,216	0.19
West Virginia	1,064	0.06
District of Columbia	895	0.15
Rhode Island	756	0.07
Delaware	720	0.08

Place	Population	%
Minnesota	77,745	1.48
North Dakota	8,787	1.33
Utah	33,337	1.25
South Dakota	6,361	0.80
Washington	51,902	0.79
Montana	7,736	0.79
Idaho	9,884	0.65
Oregon	23,693	0.63
Alaska	4,300	0.62
Wyoming	2,904	0.53
Wisconsin	20,652	0.37
Colorado	18,006	0.37
Iowa	9,463	0.31
Arizona	18,210	0.29
Nebraska	4,494	0.25
Nevada	6,213	0.24
Maine	2,909	0.22
United States	**582,549**	**0.19**
New Mexico	3,757	0.19
Vermont	1,216	0.19
California	67,697	0.18
New Hampshire	2,212	0.17
Hawaii	2,056	0.15
District of Columbia	895	0.15
Michigan	14,042	0.14
Virginia	10,867	0.14
Illinois	16,473	0.13
Kansas	3,774	0.13
Massachusetts	7,961	0.12
Missouri	7,357	0.12
Florida	20,098	0.11
Connecticut	3,916	0.11
Arkansas	3,145	0.11
Texas	23,366	0.10
Indiana	6,406	0.10
Oklahoma	3,624	0.10
North Carolina	8,125	0.09
Maryland	5,403	0.09
South Carolina	3,863	0.09
Ohio	8,810	0.08
Georgia	7,986	0.08
Tennessee	5,027	0.08
Delaware	720	0.08
New York	12,891	0.07
Alabama	3,322	0.07
Rhode Island	756	0.07
Pennsylvania	7,796	0.06
New Jersey	5,569	0.06
Kentucky	2,634	0.06
West Virginia	1,064	0.06
Mississippi	1,349	0.05
Louisiana	1,776	0.04

Please refer to the Explanation of Data in the front of the book for more detailed information.

Ancestry

Scandinavian

Top 150 Places Sorted by Population

Based on all places, regardless of total population

Place	Population	%
Minneapolis, MN (city) Hennepin County	4,614	1.22
Seattle, WA (city) King County	4,424	0.74
Los Angeles, CA (city) Los Angeles County	4,130	0.11
Portland, OR (city) Multnomah County	3,477	0.61
New York, NY (city) Kings County	3,434	0.04
Phoenix, AZ (city) Maricopa County	3,409	0.24
San Diego, CA (city) San Diego County	2,796	0.22
St. Paul, MN (city) Ramsey County	2,612	0.93
Duluth, MN (city) St. Louis County	2,182	2.54
Salt Lake City, UT (city) Salt Lake County	2,060	1.12
Anchorage, AK (municipality) Anchorage Municipality	1,980	0.70
Fargo, ND (city) Cass County	1,826	1.78
Chicago, IL (city) Cook County	1,792	0.07
Provo, UT (city) Utah County	1,775	1.61
Manhattan, NY (borough) New York County	1,731	0.11
Mesa, AZ (city) Maricopa County	1,725	0.39
Orem, UT (city) Utah County	1,689	1.94
Sandy, UT (city) Salt Lake County	1,603	1.84
Houston, TX (city) Harris County	1,548	0.07
Denver, CO (city) Denver County	1,543	0.27
Tacoma, WA (city) Pierce County	1,465	0.74
Spokane, WA (city) Spokane County	1,455	0.70
Albuquerque, NM (city) Bernalillo County	1,442	0.27
Austin, TX (city) Travis County	1,413	0.18
Tucson, AZ (city) Pima County	1,378	0.27
Eagan, MN (city) Dakota County	1,335	2.07
Colorado Springs, CO (city) El Paso County	1,306	0.32
Bloomington, MN (city) Hennepin County	1,292	1.56
Sioux Falls, SD (city) Minnehaha County	1,270	0.85
Vancouver, WA (city) Clark County	1,246	0.78
Plymouth, MN (city) Hennepin County	1,235	1.79
Lakeville, MN (city) Dakota County	1,202	2.23
Burnsville, MN (city) Dakota County	1,202	1.98
Indianapolis, IN (city) Marion County	1,199	0.15
Boise City, ID (city) Ada County	1,166	0.56
Millcreek, UT (cdp) Salt Lake County	1,133	1.86
Madison, WI (city) Dane County	1,128	0.49
Edina, MN (city) Hennepin County	1,110	2.34
San Antonio, TX (city) Medina County	1,106	0.09
Blaine, MN (city) Anoka County	1,099	1.98
San Francisco, CA (city) San Francisco County	1,088	0.14
Omaha, NE (city) Douglas County	1,062	0.26
Columbus, OH (city) Franklin County	1,042	0.14
Billings, MT (city) Yellowstone County	1,038	1.02
Bountiful, UT (city) Davis County	1,031	2.43
Las Vegas, NV (city) Clark County	1,029	0.18
Minnetonka, MN (city) Hennepin County	1,012	2.04
Eugene, OR (city) Lane County	1,005	0.66
Jacksonville, FL (city) Duval County	993	0.12
Sacramento, CA (city) Sacramento County	989	0.22
San Jose, CA (city) Santa Clara County	980	0.11
Fort Collins, CO (city) Larimer County	977	0.70
Virginia Beach, VA (ind. city) Virginia Beach independent city	961	0.22
Dallas, TX (city) Dallas County	958	0.08
St. Louis Park, MN (city) Hennepin County	949	2.12
Eden Prairie, MN (city) Hennepin County	943	1.59
Maple Grove, MN (city) Hennepin County	917	1.55
Hillsboro, OR (city) Washington County	909	1.03
St. Cloud, MN (city) Stearns County	906	1.39
Bismarck, ND (city) Burleigh County	902	1.50
Washington, DC (city) District of Columbia	895	0.15
Brooklyn, NY (borough) Kings County	882	0.04
Salem, OR (city) Marion County	874	0.58
West Jordan, UT (city) Salt Lake County	870	0.88
Des Moines, IA (city) Polk County	867	0.43
Rochester, MN (city) Olmsted County	840	0.81
Scottsdale, AZ (city) Maricopa County	840	0.38
Woodbury, MN (city) Washington County	832	1.40
Chandler, AZ (city) Maricopa County	824	0.36
Minot, ND (city) Ward County	806	2.06
Bellingham, WA (city) Whatcom County	792	1.00
Layton, UT (city) Davis County	791	1.20
Bellevue, WA (city) King County	790	0.66
Kansas City, MO (city) Jackson County	775	0.17
Gilbert, AZ (town) Maricopa County	772	0.40
St. Cloud, MN (city) Stearns County	768	1.48
Fort Worth, TX (city) Tarrant County	762	0.11
Reno, NV (city) Washoe County	760	0.34
Coon Rapids, MN (city) Anoka County	758	1.22
Aurora, CO (city) Arapahoe County	754	0.24
Meridian, ID (city) Ada County	753	1.09
Rapid City, SD (city) Pennington County	745	1.13
Riverton, UT (city) Salt Lake County	729	2.03
Henderson, NV (city) Clark County	727	0.29
Andover, MN (city) Anoka County	707	2.35
West Fargo, ND (city) Cass County	703	2.95
St. George, UT (city) Washington County	701	0.99
Corona, CA (city) Riverside County	681	0.45
Elk River, MN (city) Sherburne County	679	3.02
Cottonwood Heights, UT (city) Salt Lake County	675	2.01
Milwaukee, WI (city) Milwaukee County	660	0.11
South Jordan, UT (city) Salt Lake County	659	1.42
Everett, WA (city) Snohomish County	657	0.65
Bend, OR (city) Deschutes County	646	0.87
Centennial, CO (city) Arapahoe County	639	0.64
Kaysville, UT (city) Davis County	622	2.39
Fridley, MN (city) Anoka County	619	2.25
Marysville, WA (city) Snohomish County	614	1.06
Charlotte, NC (city) Mecklenburg County	609	0.09
Brooklyn Park, MN (city) Hennepin County	607	0.82
Lincoln, NE (city) Lancaster County	598	0.24
Logan, UT (city) Cache County	596	1.28
Rockford, IL (city) Winnebago County	588	0.38
Olympia, WA (city) Thurston County	583	1.28
Apple Valley, MN (city) Dakota County	583	1.20
Wichita, KS (city) Sedgwick County	568	0.15
Moorhead, MN (city) Clay County	564	1.54
Tempe, AZ (city) Maricopa County	564	0.34
Long Beach, CA (city) Los Angeles County	561	0.12
Boulder, CO (city) Boulder County	555	0.57
Peoria, AZ (city) Yavapai County	554	0.37
Pocatello, ID (city) Bannock County	553	1.04
Boston, MA (city) Suffolk County	551	0.09
Riverside, CA (city) Riverside County	548	0.18
Queens, NY (borough) Queens County	545	0.02
Bakersfield, CA (city) Kern County	543	0.16
Santa Rosa, CA (city) Sonoma County	542	0.33
Chanhassen, MN (city) Carver County	540	2.36
Huntington Beach, CA (city) Orange County	539	0.29
Beaverton, OR (city) Washington County	533	0.61
Alpine, UT (city) Utah County	532	5.87
Edmonds, WA (city) Snohomish County	525	1.32
West Valley City, UT (city) Salt Lake County	524	0.42
Oklahoma City, OK (city) Oklahoma County	524	0.09
Lino Lakes, MN (city) Anoka County	522	2.64
Missoula, MT (city) Missoula County	518	0.79
Concord, CA (city) Contra Costa County	517	0.43
Shakopee, MN (city) Scott County	510	1.45
Shoreview, MN (city) Ramsey County	508	2.04
Washington, UT (city) Washington County	506	2.91
Philadelphia, PA (city) Philadelphia County	504	0.03
Sioux City, IA (city) Woodbury County	503	0.61
Fresno, CA (city) Fresno County	487	0.10
Overland Park, KS (city) Johnson County	484	0.28
Corvallis, OR (city) Benton County	481	0.90
Arden-Arcade, CA (cdp) Sacramento County	481	0.53
Rexburg, ID (city) Madison County	479	1.95
Costa Mesa, CA (city) Orange County	473	0.43
Murray, UT (city) Salt Lake County	467	1.01
Torrance, CA (city) Los Angeles County	466	0.32
Inver Grove Heights, MN (city) Dakota County	462	1.39
Glendale, AZ (city) Maricopa County	461	0.20
Santa Clarita, CA (city) Los Angeles County	459	0.27
American Fork, UT (city) Utah County	458	1.81
Highlands Ranch, CO (cdp) Douglas County	454	0.48
Shoreline, WA (city) King County	452	0.86
Santa Cruz, CA (city) Santa Cruz County	451	0.77
Grand Forks, ND (city) Grand Forks County	449	0.86
Baxter, MN (city) Crow Wing County	448	6.10
Mankato, MN (city) Blue Earth County	448	1.17

Please refer to the Explanation of Data in the front of the book for more detailed information.

Ancestry

Scandinavian

Top 150 Places Sorted by Percent of Total Population

Based on all places, regardless of total population

Place	Population	%
Palmville, MN (township) Roseau County	21	91.30
Luis Lopez, NM (cdp) Socorro County	79	48.17
Fremont, UT (cdp) Wayne County	21	45.65
Ola, SD (cdp) Brule County	9	42.86
San Fidel, NM (cdp) Cibola County	17	42.50
Millward, MN (township) Aitkin County	17	38.64
Redpath, MN (township) Traverse County	36	37.11
Foldahl, MN (township) Marshall County	35	35.71
Nash, ND (cdp) Walsh County	5	35.71
Donnelly, MN (township) Marshall County	5	31.25
Alton, UT (town) Kane County	65	29.15
Walls, MN (township) Traverse County	13	28.89
Bassett, MN (township) St. Louis County	20	28.17
La Grande, WA (cdp) Pierce County	20	27.78
Bay Center, WA (cdp) Pacific County	66	27.73
McKinley, MN (unorganized territory) Kittson County	12	24.49
Sinnott, MN (township) Marshall County	5	22.73
North River, ND (city) Cass County	13	21.67
Nelson Lagoon, AK (cdp) Aleutians East Borough	5	20.00
Motley, MN (city) Cass County	7	19.44
Windsor, MN (township) Traverse County	10	19.23
South Koochiching, MN (unorganized territory) Koochiching County	33	18.64
East Cook, MN (unorganized territory) Cook County	193	18.00
Nelson, NV (cdp) Clark County	16	17.78
Jupiter, MN (township) Kittson County	16	17.58
Marengo, WI (town) Ashland County	67	17.40
Butteville, OR (cdp) Marion County	20	17.39
Windsor, NH (town) Hillsborough County	18	16.98
Johnson, MN (township) Polk County	6	16.67
Fort Ransom, ND (city) Ransom County	11	16.42
Spruce Valley, MN (township) Marshall County	31	16.23
Umber View Heights, MO (village) Cedar County	5	16.13
Forestburg, SD (cdp) Sanborn County	9	16.07
Avery, CA (cdp) Calaveras County	61	16.01
McKinley, MN (city) St. Louis County	7	15.91
Second Assessment, MN (unorganized territory) Crow Wing County	10	15.63
Libby, MN (township) Aitkin County	5	15.63
Dudley, MN (township) Clearwater County	60	15.35
Port Wing, WI (cdp) Bayfield County	35	15.35
Reine, MN (township) Roseau County	18	15.13
Slana, AK (cdp) Valdez-Cordova Census Area	42	14.95
Louisburg, MN (city) Lac qui Parle County	8	14.81
Baker, MN (township) Stevens County	20	14.71
Arveson, MN (township) Kittson County	14	14.58
Mitchell, MN (township) Wilkin County	8	14.29
Omena, MI (cdp) Leelanau County	39	13.98
Leadore, ID (city) Lemhi County	12	13.95
Takilma, OR (cdp) Josephine County	35	13.89
Sunburg, MN (city) Kandiyohi County	18	13.85
Star, MN (township) Pennington County	10	13.70
New Folden, MN (township) Marshall County	36	13.64
Hazelton, MN (township) Kittson County	15	13.64
Lincoln, MN (township) Marshall County	10	13.51
Oriska, ND (city) Barnes County	17	13.49
Colton, WA (town) Whitman County	32	13.22
Holyoke, MN (township) Carlton County	23	13.14
Grand Plain, MN (township) Marshall County	3	13.04
Emery, UT (town) Emery County	45	13.01
Wisconsin Dells, WI (city) Sauk County	30	12.88
Rico, CO (town) Dolores County	33	12.69
Lakeridge, NV (cdp) Douglas County	22	12.57
Tanberg, MN (township) Wilkin County	19	12.50
City Point, WI (town) Jackson County	25	12.44
Sterling, UT (town) Sanpete County	39	12.34
Brookhurst, WY (cdp) Natrona County	22	12.22
Craig, MT (cdp) Lewis and Clark County	5	12.20
Bowstring, MN (township) Itasca County	24	11.94
Belt, MT (town) Cascade County	81	11.84
South Greenfield, MO (village) Dade County	8	11.76
Farley, MN (township) Polk County	4	11.76
Winifred, MT (town) Fergus County	13	11.71
Lind, MN (township) Roseau County	7	11.67
North Puyallup, WA (cdp) Pierce County	188	11.48
Bay View, WA (cdp) Skagit County	78	11.45
Layton, FL (city) Monroe County	18	11.39
Huss, MN (township) Roseau County	19	11.38
Lynndyl, UT (town) Millard County	15	11.28
Gudrid, MN (township) Lake of the Woods County	19	11.18
Orwell, MN (township) Otter Tail County	17	11.11
Martin Lake, MN (cdp) Anoka County	72	11.04
Clear Creek, MN (unorganized territory) Carlton County	18	11.04
Fairview, WY (cdp) Lincoln County	21	10.88
Soler, MN (township) Roseau County	9	10.84
Lake Norden, SD (city) Hamlin County	50	10.78
Bailey, TX (city) Fannin County	21	10.71
Cooke City, MT (cdp) Park County	6	10.71
North Ottawa, MN (township) Grant County	8	10.53
Moose Creek, MN (township) Clearwater County	18	10.47
Black River, MN (township) Pennington County	7	10.45
Lockhart, MN (township) Norman County	7	10.45
Montpelier, ND (city) Stutsman County	13	10.40
Northeast St. Louis, MN (unorganized territory) St. Louis County	27	10.38
Tabor, MN (township) Polk County	17	10.37
Tripp, WI (town) Bayfield County	24	10.34
Fort Shaw, MT (cdp) Cascade County	43	10.31
Stanchfield, MN (cdp) Isanti County	7	10.29
Gales, MN (township) Redwood County	21	10.24
Grygla, MN (city) Marshall County	27	10.19
Walhalla, MN (township) Lake of the Woods County	24	10.13
McKinley Park, AK (cdp) Denali Borough	16	10.13
Gorst, WA (cdp) Kitsap County	53	10.11
Fulton, IN (town) Fulton County	18	10.00
Attu Station, AK (cdp) Aleutians West Census Area	12	9.92
Spring Brook, MN (township) Kittson County	7	9.72
Leadville North, CO (cdp) Lake County	168	9.70
Leon, MN (township) Clearwater County	28	9.66
Correll, MN (city) Big Stone County	7	9.46
Pelican, MN (township) Crow Wing County	55	9.45
Kelsey, MN (township) St. Louis County	15	9.43
Stephen, MN (city) Marshall County	66	9.35
Grimstad, MN (township) Roseau County	16	9.30
Crosby, MN (township) Pine County	9	9.28
Deerwood, MN (township) Kittson County	10	9.26
Seventh Mountain, OR (cdp) Deschutes County	31	9.14
Dieter, MN (township) Roseau County	20	9.13
Automba, MN (township) Carlton County	14	9.09
Two Inlets, MN (township) Becker County	14	8.97
Eschbach, WA (cdp) Yakima County	38	8.94
Hingham, MT (town) Hill County	10	8.85
Grafton, MN (township) Sibley County	23	8.81
Prairie View, MN (township) Wilkin County	20	8.70
Lindisfarne, MT (cdp) Lake County	15	8.62
Batavia, MT (cdp) Flathead County	31	8.61
Glenwood, UT (town) Sevier County	45	8.57
Clifton, ID (city) Franklin County	29	8.50
Northome, MN (unorganized territory) Koochiching County	58	8.49
Tenstrike, MN (city) Beltrami County	16	8.47
Otrey, MN (township) Big Stone County	7	8.43
Shooks, MN (township) Beltrami County	19	8.41
Land, MN (township) Grant County	22	8.40
Truesdale, MO (city) Warren County	55	8.38
Braggs, OK (town) Muskogee County	30	8.36
Reno, MN (township) Pope County	29	8.36
Wolverton, MN (township) Wilkin County	10	8.26
Elderon, WI (village) Marathon County	14	8.24
Plainview, MN (township) Wabasha County	47	8.20
Chistochina, AK (cdp) Valdez-Cordova Census Area	10	8.13
Hanover, MN (city) Hennepin County	51	8.07
Hampden, ND (city) Ramsey County	5	8.06
Birch Creek, MN (township) Pine County	24	8.05
Maskell, NE (village) Dixon County	7	8.05
Frontier, ND (city) Cass County	20	8.03
Randolph AFB, TX (cdp) Bexar County	84	8.02
Sharon, NH (town) Hillsborough County	30	8.02
Jenkins, MN (city) Crow Wing County	21	7.98
Alvarado, MN (city) Marshall County	31	7.97
Briarwood, ND (city) Cass County	6	7.89
Southeast Roseau, MN (unorganized territory) Roseau County	6	7.89
Moose Park, MN (township) Itasca County	3	7.89
Yellow Bank, MN (township) Lac qui Parle County	14	7.87

Please refer to the Explanation of Data in the front of the book for more detailed information.

Ancestry

Scandinavian

Top 150 Places Sorted by Percent of Total Population

Based on places with total population of 7,500 or more

Place	Population	%
Alpine, UT (city) Utah County	532	5.87
Smithfield, UT (city) Cache County	377	4.21
Ferndale, WA (city) Whatcom County	433	3.94
Big Lake, MN (city) Sherburne County	343	3.55
Wyoming, MN (city) Chisago County	261	3.40
Hermantown, MN (city) St. Louis County	307	3.36
Arden Hills, MN (city) Ramsey County	312	3.28
Rogers, MN (city) Hennepin County	233	3.04
Oak Grove, MN (city) Anoka County	239	3.03
Elk River, MN (city) Sherburne County	679	3.02
Hugo, MN (city) Washington County	365	3.01
West Fargo, ND (city) Cass County	703	2.95
Washington, UT (city) Washington County	506	2.91
Wahpeton, ND (city) Richland County	216	2.75
Lino Lakes, MN (city) Anoka County	522	2.64
Duluth, MN (city) St. Louis County	2,182	2.54
Stillwater, MN (city) Washington County	441	2.48
Bountiful, UT (city) Davis County	1,031	2.43
Brainerd, MN (city) Crow Wing County	334	2.43
Kaysville, UT (city) Davis County	622	2.39
Chanhassen, MN (city) Carver County	540	2.36
Andover, MN (city) Anoka County	707	2.35
Edina, MN (city) Hennepin County	1,110	2.34
Fridley, MN (city) Anoka County	619	2.25
North Salt Lake, UT (city) Davis County	335	2.24
Damascus, OR (city) Clackamas County	230	2.24
Lakeville, MN (city) Dakota County	1,202	2.23
Payson, UT (city) Utah County	382	2.22
Astoria, OR (city) Clatsop County	210	2.20
Olivehurst, CA (cdp) Yuba County	289	2.17
Mahtomedi, MN (city) Washington County	167	2.17
Red Wing, MN (city) Goodhue County	355	2.16
Centerville, UT (city) Davis County	328	2.16
Mukilteo, WA (city) Snohomish County	427	2.15
Rapid Valley, SD (cdp) Pennington County	173	2.13
St. Louis Park, MN (city) Hennepin County	949	2.12
Snohomish, WA (city) Snohomish County	190	2.10
River Falls, WI (city) Pierce County	242	2.08
Eagan, MN (city) Dakota County	1,335	2.07
Anoka, MN (city) Anoka County	361	2.07
Minot, ND (city) Ward County	806	2.06
Cedar Hills, UT (city) Utah County	176	2.05
Minnetonka, MN (city) Hennepin County	1,012	2.04
Shoreview, MN (city) Ramsey County	508	2.04
Vermillion, SD (city) Clay County	215	2.04
Riverton, UT (city) Salt Lake County	729	2.03
Cottonwood Heights, UT (city) Salt Lake County	675	2.01
Crystal, MN (city) Hennepin County	442	2.00
Highland, UT (city) Utah County	282	2.00
Bemidji, MN (city) Beltrami County	264	2.00
Hudson, WI (city) St. Croix County	246	1.99
Haiku-Pauwela, HI (cdp) Maui County	160	1.99
Burnsville, MN (city) Dakota County	1,202	1.98
Blaine, MN (city) Anoka County	1,099	1.98
Rosemount, MN (city) Dakota County	408	1.97
Rexburg, ID (city) Madison County	479	1.95
Orem, UT (city) Utah County	1,689	1.94
Vashon, WA (cdp) King County	193	1.94
Edgewood, WA (city) Pierce County	179	1.91
Lindon, UT (city) Utah County	181	1.87
Millcreek, UT (cdp) Salt Lake County	1,133	1.86
Ramsey, MN (city) Anoka County	423	1.85
Sandy, UT (city) Salt Lake County	1,603	1.84
Hopkins, MN (city) Hennepin County	318	1.83
American Fork, UT (city) Utah County	458	1.81
Plymouth, MN (city) Hennepin County	1,235	1.79
East Renton Highlands, WA (cdp) King County	198	1.79
Fargo, ND (city) Cass County	1,826	1.78
Herriman, UT (city) Salt Lake County	322	1.76
Cloquet, MN (city) Carlton County	212	1.76
Northfield, MN (city) Rice County	321	1.74
East Grand Forks, MN (city) Polk County	146	1.74
North Logan, UT (city) Cache County	135	1.74
River Falls, WI (city) Pierce County	254	1.73
St. Peter, MN (city) Nicollet County	190	1.72
Champlin, MN (city) Hennepin County	390	1.71
Northfield, MN (city) Rice County	332	1.71
Hutchinson, MN (city) McLeod County	240	1.69
White Bear, MN (township) Ramsey County	183	1.69
New Hope, MN (city) Hennepin County	336	1.66
Kings Park West, VA (cdp) Fairfax County	236	1.64
Fergus Falls, MN (city) Otter Tail County	219	1.64
Battle Ground, WA (city) Clark County	267	1.63
Mounds View, MN (city) Ramsey County	197	1.63
Brigham City, UT (city) Box Elder County	285	1.62
Provo, UT (city) Utah County	1,775	1.61
Springville, UT (city) Utah County	441	1.60
Eden Prairie, MN (city) Hennepin County	943	1.59
Lake Forest Park, WA (city) King County	199	1.58
New Brighton, MN (city) Ramsey County	334	1.57
Bloomington, MN (city) Hennepin County	1,292	1.56
Cottage Lake, WA (cdp) King County	347	1.56
Maple Grove, MN (city) Hennepin County	917	1.55
St. Michael, MN (city) Wright County	238	1.55
Moorhead, MN (city) Clay County	564	1.54
Prior Lake, MN (city) Scott County	342	1.54
Saratoga Springs, UT (city) Utah County	227	1.54
Gering, NE (city) Scotts Bluff County	127	1.54
Birch Bay, WA (cdp) Whatcom County	121	1.54
North Mankato, MN (city) Nicollet County	201	1.53
Artondale, WA (cdp) Pierce County	172	1.52
Fife, WA (city) Pierce County	128	1.52
Santaquin, UT (city) Utah County	127	1.52
Savage, MN (city) Scott County	402	1.51
Bismarck, ND (city) Burleigh County	902	1.50
White Bear Lake, MN (city) Ramsey County	346	1.49
Cambridge, MN (city) Isanti County	117	1.49
St. Cloud, MN (city) Stearns County	768	1.48
Hazel Dell, WA (cdp) Clark County	286	1.48
Port Orchard, WA (city) Kitsap County	159	1.48
New Richmond, WI (city) St. Croix County	122	1.48
Helena Valley West Central, MT (cdp) Lewis and Clark County	121	1.48
White Bear Lake, MN (city) Ramsey County	346	1.47
Eagle, ID (city) Ada County	276	1.47
Lake Tapps, WA (cdp) Pierce County	166	1.47
West Linn, OR (city) Clackamas County	360	1.46
Shakopee, MN (city) Scott County	510	1.45
Winfield, IL (village) DuPage County	131	1.45
Old Town, ME (city) Penobscot County	114	1.45
Otsego, MN (city) Wright County	180	1.44
Maple Valley, WA (city) King County	299	1.43
Golden Valley, MN (city) Hennepin County	288	1.43
Waconia, MN (city) Carver County	145	1.43
South Jordan, UT (city) Salt Lake County	659	1.42
Holladay, UT (city) Salt Lake County	373	1.42
North Lynnwood, WA (cdp) Snohomish County	225	1.42
Magna, UT (cdp) Salt Lake County	378	1.41
Woodbury, MN (city) Washington County	832	1.40
Marshfield, WI (city) Wood County	254	1.40
Ringwood, NJ (borough) Passaic County	170	1.40
St. Cloud, MN (city) Stearns County	906	1.39
Inver Grove Heights, MN (city) Dakota County	462	1.39
Spanish Fork, UT (city) Utah County	440	1.38
Tooele, UT (city) Tooele County	417	1.38
Walnut Grove, WA (cdp) Clark County	122	1.38
Albert Lea, MN (city) Freeborn County	247	1.37
Marshfield, WI (city) Wood County	254	1.36
Los Osos, CA (cdp) San Luis Obispo County	201	1.35
Menominee, MI (city) Menominee County	117	1.35
Grand Rapids, MN (city) Itasca County	144	1.34
Edmonds, WA (city) Snohomish County	525	1.32
St. Helens, OR (city) Columbia County	166	1.32
Rice Lake, WI (city) Barron County	112	1.32
Buffalo, MN (city) Wright County	193	1.31
Garrison, MD (cdp) Baltimore County	100	1.31
Superior, WI (city) Douglas County	350	1.29
Farmington, MN (city) Dakota County	253	1.29
Logan, UT (city) Cache County	596	1.28
Olympia, WA (city) Thurston County	583	1.28
Cottage Grove, MN (city) Washington County	437	1.28

SECTION THREE

Please refer to the Explanation of Data in the front of the book for more detailed information.

Ancestry

Scotch-Irish

U.S. and 50 States Sorted by Population and Percent of Total Population

Place	Population	%	Place	Population	%
United States	**5,227,887**	**1.72**	Maine	49,422	3.72
California	435,810	1.19	North Carolina	340,482	3.67
Texas	402,443	1.66	South Carolina	151,637	3.36
North Carolina	340,482	3.67	Tennessee	199,359	3.20
Florida	289,491	1.56	Wyoming	16,466	3.02
Pennsylvania	251,093	1.99	West Virginia	52,433	2.85
Virginia	201,730	2.57	Vermont	16,765	2.69
Tennessee	199,359	3.20	New Hampshire	34,354	2.61
Ohio	190,369	1.65	Montana	25,373	2.61
Georgia	183,779	1.94	Virginia	201,730	2.57
New York	164,725	0.86	Oregon	96,630	2.57
Washington	162,034	2.47	Washington	162,034	2.47
Michigan	156,935	1.58	Alabama	113,138	2.40
South Carolina	151,637	3.36	Alaska	16,456	2.38
Illinois	142,246	1.12	Mississippi	66,784	2.27
Massachusetts	123,361	1.90	Colorado	108,078	2.21
Missouri	115,144	1.94	Kentucky	90,125	2.10
Alabama	113,138	2.40	Kansas	57,792	2.06
Colorado	108,078	2.21	Arkansas	58,485	2.04
Arizona	103,566	1.66	Idaho	30,722	2.01
Oregon	96,630	2.57	Pennsylvania	251,093	1.99
Indiana	95,439	1.49	Georgia	183,779	1.94
Kentucky	90,125	2.10	Missouri	115,144	1.94
New Jersey	83,028	0.95	Massachusetts	123,361	1.90
Maryland	81,798	1.44	Oklahoma	68,107	1.85
Oklahoma	68,107	1.85	Delaware	15,385	1.75
Mississippi	66,784	2.27	**United States**	**5,227,887**	**1.72**
Arkansas	58,485	2.04	Texas	402,443	1.66
Kansas	57,792	2.06	Arizona	103,566	1.66
Louisiana	57,163	1.29	Ohio	190,369	1.65
Minnesota	52,686	1.01	New Mexico	32,039	1.59
West Virginia	52,433	2.85	Michigan	156,935	1.58
Maine	49,422	3.72	Nebraska	28,504	1.58
Connecticut	48,840	1.38	Florida	289,491	1.56
Wisconsin	48,166	0.85	Iowa	46,067	1.53
Iowa	46,067	1.53	Indiana	95,439	1.49
Nevada	36,943	1.40	Rhode Island	15,267	1.45
Utah	35,636	1.34	Maryland	81,798	1.44
New Hampshire	34,354	2.61	Nevada	36,943	1.40
New Mexico	32,039	1.59	Connecticut	48,840	1.38
Idaho	30,722	2.01	Utah	35,636	1.34
Nebraska	28,504	1.58	Louisiana	57,163	1.29
Montana	25,373	2.61	California	435,810	1.19
Vermont	16,765	2.69	North Dakota	7,878	1.19
Wyoming	16,466	3.02	South Dakota	9,400	1.18
Alaska	16,456	2.38	Illinois	142,246	1.12
Delaware	15,385	1.75	Minnesota	52,686	1.01
Rhode Island	15,267	1.45	District of Columbia	5,907	1.01
Hawaii	12,407	0.93	New Jersey	83,028	0.95
South Dakota	9,400	1.18	Hawaii	12,407	0.93
North Dakota	7,878	1.19	New York	164,725	0.86
District of Columbia	5,907	1.01	Wisconsin	48,166	0.85

Please refer to the Explanation of Data in the front of the book for more detailed information.

Ancestry

Scotch-Irish

Top 150 Places Sorted by Population

Based on all places, regardless of total population

Place	Population	%
New York, NY (city) Kings County	27,337	0.34
Charlotte, NC (city) Mecklenburg County	25,971	3.68
Los Angeles, CA (city) Los Angeles County	21,996	0.58
Houston, TX (city) Harris County	21,460	1.04
Austin, TX (city) Travis County	18,418	2.41
Nashville-Davidson, TN (metro govt) Davidson County	18,192	3.09
San Diego, CA (city) San Diego County	17,899	1.40
Phoenix, AZ (city) Maricopa County	17,582	1.21
Jacksonville, FL (city) Duval County	16,183	1.99
Dallas, TX (city) Dallas County	15,332	1.29
Seattle, WA (city) King County	14,973	2.52
Portland, OR (city) Multnomah County	14,767	2.61
San Antonio, TX (city) Medina County	14,143	1.10
Chicago, IL (city) Cook County	13,218	0.49
Manhattan, NY (borough) New York County	13,158	0.83
Raleigh, NC (city) Wake County	12,189	3.18
Columbus, OH (city) Franklin County	12,017	1.56
Fort Worth, TX (city) Tarrant County	11,727	1.66
Indianapolis, IN (city) Marion County	10,956	1.35
Virginia Beach, VA (ind. city) Virginia Beach independent city	10,850	2.49
Memphis, TN (city) Shelby County	10,576	1.61
Louisville-Jefferson County, KY (metro govt) Jefferson County	10,354	1.76
Colorado Springs, CO (city) El Paso County	10,315	2.55
Denver, CO (city) Denver County	10,302	1.78
Oklahoma City, OK (city) Oklahoma County	9,958	1.77
Philadelphia, PA (city) Philadelphia County	9,813	0.65
Albuquerque, NM (city) Bernalillo County	9,382	1.77
Lexington-Fayette, KY (cons. govt) Fayette County	8,882	3.08
Tucson, AZ (city) Pima County	8,731	1.68
Greensboro, NC (city) Guilford County	8,719	3.31
San Francisco, CA (city) San Francisco County	8,480	1.07
Kansas City, MO (city) Jackson County	8,013	1.76
Mesa, AZ (city) Maricopa County	8,003	1.82
Wichita, KS (city) Sedgwick County	7,956	2.13
Tulsa, OK (city) Tulsa County	7,681	1.98
Knoxville, TN (city) Knox County	7,606	4.27
Atlanta, GA (city) Fulton County	7,472	1.81
San Jose, CA (city) Santa Clara County	7,094	0.77
Omaha, NE (city) Douglas County	6,825	1.68
Arlington, TX (city) Tarrant County	6,774	1.88
Anchorage, AK (municipality) Anchorage Municipality	6,714	2.36
Winston-Salem, NC (city) Forsyth County	6,601	2.94
Boston, MA (city) Suffolk County	6,305	1.05
Las Vegas, NV (city) Clark County	6,246	1.08
Durham, NC (city) Durham County	6,163	2.80
Brooklyn, NY (borough) Kings County	6,090	0.25
Washington, DC (city) District of Columbia	5,907	1.01
Spokane, WA (city) Spokane County	5,621	2.72
Pittsburgh, PA (city) Allegheny County	5,558	1.80
Fayetteville, NC (city) Cumberland County	5,414	2.72
Wilmington, NC (city) New Hanover County	5,317	5.08
Sacramento, CA (city) Sacramento County	5,314	1.16
Huntsville, AL (city) Madison County	5,287	3.01
Arlington, VA (cdp) Arlington County	5,275	2.67
Lubbock, TX (city) Lubbock County	5,240	2.36
Brookhaven, NY (town) Suffolk County	5,102	1.06
Long Beach, CA (city) Los Angeles County	4,933	1.07
Boise City, ID (city) Ada County	4,913	2.38
Chesapeake, VA (ind. city) Chesapeake independent city	4,910	2.24
Reno, NV (city) Washoe County	4,901	2.22
St. Petersburg, FL (city) Pinellas County	4,877	1.98
Mobile, AL (city) Mobile County	4,869	2.49
Asheville, NC (city) Buncombe County	4,845	5.91
Plano, TX (city) Collin County	4,836	1.89
Hempstead, NY (town) Nassau County	4,788	0.64
Little Rock, AR (city) Pulaski County	4,785	2.51
Tacoma, WA (city) Pierce County	4,764	2.40
Columbia, SC (city) Richland County	4,743	3.72
Henderson, NV (city) Clark County	4,608	1.85
Queens, NY (borough) Queens County	4,602	0.21
Cary, NC (town) Wake County	4,549	3.57
Tallahassee, FL (city) Leon County	4,512	2.55
Chattanooga, TN (city) Hamilton County	4,509	2.74
Tampa, FL (city) Hillsborough County	4,470	1.34
Minneapolis, MN (city) Hennepin County	4,463	1.18
Fresno, CA (city) Fresno County	4,450	0.92
Scottsdale, AZ (city) Maricopa County	4,446	2.03
Richmond, VA (ind. city) Richmond independent city	4,401	2.18
Aurora, CO (city) Arapahoe County	4,343	1.38
Vancouver, WA (city) Clark County	4,328	2.70
Corpus Christi, TX (city) Nueces County	4,241	1.42
Lincoln, NE (city) Lancaster County	4,199	1.66
Charleston, SC (city) Charleston County	4,145	3.56
Fort Collins, CO (city) Larimer County	4,113	2.94
Baltimore, MD (city) Baltimore city County	4,103	0.66
Overland Park, KS (city) Johnson County	4,101	2.41
Eugene, OR (city) Lane County	4,061	2.65
Springfield, MO (city) Christian County	4,020	2.53
Roanoke, VA (ind. city) Roanoke independent city	3,985	4.16
Norfolk, VA (ind. city) Norfolk independent city	3,980	1.64
Santa Clarita, CA (city) Los Angeles County	3,817	2.22
Huntington Beach, CA (city) Orange County	3,816	2.02
Murfreesboro, TN (city) Rutherford County	3,807	3.71
Montgomery, AL (city) Montgomery County	3,794	1.85
Chandler, AZ (city) Maricopa County	3,742	1.63
Baton Rouge, LA (city) East Baton Rouge Parish	3,664	1.60
Gilbert, AZ (town) Maricopa County	3,608	1.85
Bakersfield, CA (city) Kern County	3,607	1.09
Alexandria, VA (ind. city) Alexandria independent city	3,602	2.70
Des Moines, IA (city) Polk County	3,594	1.78
Amarillo, TX (city) Potter County	3,584	1.91
Tempe, AZ (city) Maricopa County	3,553	2.16
Shreveport, LA (city) Caddo Parish	3,479	1.75
Riverside, CA (city) Riverside County	3,461	1.15
Lakewood, CO (city) Jefferson County	3,460	2.44
Gastonia, NC (city) Gaston County	3,416	4.83
Modesto, CA (city) Stanislaus County	3,409	1.69
Orlando, FL (city) Orange County	3,361	1.44
Santa Rosa, CA (city) Sonoma County	3,352	2.06
Akron, OH (city) Summit County	3,342	1.65
Garland, TX (city) Dallas County	3,317	1.49
Hoover, AL (city) Jefferson County	3,272	4.17
Oakland, CA (city) Alameda County	3,269	0.84
Columbus, GA (city) Muscogee County	3,256	1.74
Cincinnati, OH (city) Hamilton County	3,249	1.08
Franklin, TN (city) Williamson County	3,235	5.40
Concord, NC (city) Cabarrus County	3,224	4.29
Salem, OR (city) Marion County	3,213	2.12
El Paso, TX (city) El Paso County	3,199	0.51
Independence, MO (city) Jackson County	3,196	2.77
Madison, WI (city) Dane County	3,171	1.38
Rock Hill, SC (city) York County	3,164	5.01
Portland, ME (city) Cumberland County	3,162	4.78
High Point, NC (city) Guilford County	3,160	3.13
Islip, NY (town) Suffolk County	3,159	0.95
Fort Wayne, IN (city) Allen County	3,125	1.23
Newport News, VA (ind. city) Newport News independent city	3,100	1.70
Athens-Clarke County, GA (unified govt) Clarke County	3,049	2.68
Columbia, MO (city) Boone County	3,044	2.91
Denton, TX (city) Denton County	3,013	2.76
St. Louis, MO (city) St. Louis city County	3,000	0.94
Birmingham, AL (city) Jefferson County	2,982	1.38
Norman, OK (city) Cleveland County	2,960	2.73
Cleveland, OH (city) Cuyahoga County	2,928	0.72
Mount Pleasant, SC (town) Charleston County	2,909	4.53
St. Paul, MN (city) Ramsey County	2,890	1.02
Centennial, CO (city) Arapahoe County	2,887	2.89
Glendale, AZ (city) Maricopa County	2,882	1.25
Irving, TX (city) Dallas County	2,863	1.36
Topeka, KS (city) Shawnee County	2,853	2.26
Augusta-Richmond County, GA (cons. govt) Richmond County	2,850	1.47
Abilene, TX (city) Taylor County	2,845	2.44
Olathe, KS (city) Johnson County	2,838	2.35
Oceanside, CA (city) San Diego County	2,838	1.72
Bellevue, WA (city) King County	2,817	2.36
Boulder, CO (city) Boulder County	2,807	2.89
Chapel Hill, NC (town) Orange County	2,806	5.09
College Station, TX (city) Brazos County	2,796	3.16
Newport Beach, CA (city) Orange County	2,750	3.29
Lakeland, FL (city) Polk County	2,747	2.84

Please refer to the Explanation of Data in the front of the book for more detailed information.

Ancestry

Scotch-Irish

Top 150 Places Sorted by Percent of Total Population

Based on all places, regardless of total population

Place	Population	%
Chesapeake, MO (cdp) Lawrence County	42	100.00
Indian Falls, CA (cdp) Plumas County	35	100.00
Oatman, AZ (cdp) Mohave County	34	100.00
San Lorenzo, NM (cdp) Grant County	21	100.00
Loma Linda, TX (cdp) San Patricio County	19	100.00
Sunwest, AZ (cdp) La Paz County	7	100.00
Oak Hill, AL (town) Wilcox County	5	100.00
Padroni, CO (cdp) Logan County	120	85.11
Calvin, ND (city) Cavalier County	10	83.33
Plantation Island, FL (cdp) Collier County	126	65.97
Westerville, NE (cdp) Custer County	30	62.50
Jessie, ND (cdp) Griggs County	9	56.25
San Luis, NM (cdp) Sandoval County	18	54.55
Louviers, CO (cdp) Douglas County	91	54.49
Onondaga Nation Reservation, NY (reservation) Onondaga County	8	53.33
Huson, MT (cdp) Missoula County	45	52.94
Shell, WY (cdp) Big Horn County	18	52.94
Flowing Springs, AZ (cdp) Gila County	41	51.90
Buttzville, NJ (cdp) Warren County	103	51.76
Susitna, AK (cdp) Matanuska-Susitna Borough	17	51.52
Kings Valley, OR (cdp) Benton County	12	50.00
Homestead, NM (cdp) Catron County	11	50.00
Hill, MN (township) Kittson County	2	50.00
Le Roy, IA (city) Decatur County	2	50.00
Imlay, NV (cdp) Pershing County	40	48.19
Big Pool, MD (cdp) Washington County	10	45.45
McCoy, CO (cdp) Eagle County	10	43.48
Bowman, TN (cdp) Cumberland County	15	42.86
Tatum, SC (town) Marlboro County	27	42.19
Piedmont, SD (city) Meade County	16	42.11
Martinez Lake, AZ (cdp) Yuma County	46	41.07
Clipper Mills, CA (cdp) Butte County	40	40.82
Box Canyon, TX (cdp) Val Verde County	6	40.00
Rickreall, OR (cdp) Polk County	14	38.89
Barstow, WA (cdp) Ferry County	8	38.10
Lower Elochoman, WA (cdp) Wahkiakum County	35	37.63
Purple Sage, WY (cdp) Sweetwater County	146	36.68
Sierra Village, CA (cdp) Tuolumne County	55	36.18
Scofield, UT (town) Carbon County	6	35.29
St. Joseph, IA (cdp) Kossuth County	10	34.48
St. Cloud, MO (village) Crawford County	6	33.33
Kingston, NV (cdp) Lander County	24	32.88
Apache Creek, NM (cdp) Catron County	23	32.86
Daphnedale Park, CA (cdp) Modoc County	16	32.65
Iliamna, AK (cdp) Lake and Peninsula Borough	26	32.10
Milton, ME (unorganized territory) Oxford County	46	31.94
Twin Lakes, CO (cdp) Lake County	37	31.90
Justice, WV (cdp) Mingo County	166	31.20
May, OK (town) Harper County	9	31.03
San Pedro, NM (cdp) Santa Fe County	27	30.68
Snyder, CO (cdp) Morgan County	54	30.51
Hebgen Lake Estates, MT (cdp) Gallatin County	20	30.30
Roxbury, KS (cdp) McPherson County	10	30.30
West Alexander, PA (cdp) Washington County	248	30.02
Ward, CO (town) Boulder County	20	29.85
Pentress, WV (cdp) Monongalia County	86	29.45
Bessemer Bend, WY (cdp) Natrona County	66	28.95
Catherine, CO (cdp) Garfield County	54	28.57
Mamers, NC (cdp) Harnett County	265	28.25
Bland, VA (cdp) Bland County	76	28.25
Uehling, NE (village) Dodge County	104	27.81
Dixie, WV (cdp) Nicholas County	107	27.72
Chimney Rock Village, NC (village) Rutherford County	51	27.72
Sierra Brooks, CA (cdp) Sierra County	58	27.62
Wallowa Lake, OR (cdp) Wallowa County	11	27.50
Lazy Y U, AZ (cdp) Mohave County	59	27.31
Cliffside, NC (cdp) Rutherford County	109	27.25
Westfield, ME (town) Aroostook County	125	27.06
Lupus, MO (town) Moniteau County	10	27.03
Forbestown, CA (cdp) Butte County	95	26.76
Orchard, CO (cdp) Morgan County	25	26.32
Beulah, WY (cdp) Crook County	46	26.29
White Oak, NC (cdp) Bladen County	37	26.06
Waco, GA (city) Haralson County	124	26.05
Kent, IN (cdp) Jefferson County	50	26.04
Silver Gate, MT (cdp) Park County	4	25.00
Pine Lake, AZ (cdp) Mohave County	25	24.75
Panacea, FL (cdp) Wakulla County	229	24.60
Dayton, AL (town) Marengo County	10	24.39
Fitzpatrick, AL (cdp) Bullock County	35	24.31
Phenix, VA (town) Charlotte County	83	24.27
Tennant, IA (city) Shelby County	13	24.07
Garden City, SD (town) Clark County	12	24.00
Hatton, AL (cdp) Lawrence County	36	23.84
Leonard, MO (village) Shelby County	15	23.81
Dublin, NC (town) Bladen County	49	23.44
West Scio, OR (cdp) Linn County	35	23.33
Walpack, NJ (township) Sussex County	7	23.33
Cassville, WV (cdp) Monongalia County	174	23.20
Heimdal, ND (cdp) Wells County	3	23.08
Tiawah, OK (cdp) Rogers County	40	22.99
Ballantine, MT (cdp) Yellowstone County	33	22.92
Arrow Rock, MO (town) Saline County	11	22.92
King William, VA (cdp) King William County	49	22.90
Murphy, ID (cdp) Owyhee County	8	22.86
Cherry Log, GA (cdp) Gilmer County	21	22.83
Smoketown, PA (cdp) Lancaster County	86	22.81
Pleasanton, IA (city) Decatur County	10	22.73
Smartsville, CA (cdp) Yuba County	50	22.62
Hodges, SC (town) Greenwood County	36	22.22
Roe, AR (town) Monroe County	18	22.22
Lamar, NE (village) Chase County	2	22.22
Byron, OK (town) Alfalfa County	13	22.03
Victoria, AR (town) Mississippi County	13	22.03
Triumph, LA (cdp) Plaquemines Parish	7	21.88
Belgreen, AL (cdp) Franklin County	17	21.79
Clio, IA (city) Wayne County	26	21.67
Mina, NV (cdp) Mineral County	19	21.59
Birmingham, PA (borough) Huntingdon County	22	21.57
Hessville, OH (cdp) Sandusky County	17	21.52
Valley Head, WV (cdp) Randolph County	64	21.48
Bigfoot, TX (cdp) Frio County	32	21.33
Lacomb, OR (cdp) Linn County	82	21.30
Hillsdale, NC (cdp) Davie County	117	21.27
Ravalli, MT (cdp) Lake County	17	21.25
Max, NE (cdp) Dundy County	7	21.21
Donegal, PA (township) Washington County	580	21.19
Gasburg, VA (cdp) Brunswick County	80	21.11
Bradley, SC (cdp) Greenwood County	33	21.02
Leonore, IL (village) LaSalle County	18	20.93
Lytle Creek, CA (cdp) San Bernardino County	153	20.68
Chaplin, KY (cdp) Nelson County	73	20.68
Pinedale, AZ (cdp) Navajo County	46	20.63
Springhill, FL (cdp) Santa Rosa County	29	20.57
Verdi, CA (cdp) Sierra County	38	20.54
Whitten, IA (city) Hardin County	8	20.51
Kunkle, OH (cdp) Williams County	29	20.42
Northeast Somerset, ME (unorganized territory) Somerset County	95	20.39
Pitkin, CO (town) Gunnison County	17	20.24
Mount Croghan, SC (town) Chesterfield County	37	20.22
Galisteo, NM (cdp) Santa Fe County	64	20.13
Edwardsville, AL (town) Cleburne County	47	20.09
Time, IL (village) Pike County	2	20.00
Kirby, WY (town) Hot Springs County	24	19.83
Berrydale, FL (cdp) Santa Rosa County	75	19.69
Webster, NC (town) Jackson County	108	19.60
Cibola, AZ (cdp) La Paz County	55	19.57
Cross Creek, PA (cdp) Washington County	27	19.57
Van, WV (cdp) Boone County	38	19.49
Lake Junaluska, NC (cdp) Haywood County	527	19.40
Christie, OK (cdp) Adair County	44	19.38
Clayton, KS (city) Norton County	21	19.27
Jenner, CA (cdp) Sonoma County	19	19.19
Brewer, MO (cdp) Perry County	54	19.15
Richvale, CA (cdp) Butte County	39	19.12
Amanda Park, WA (cdp) Grays Harbor County	30	18.99
Naples, IL (town) Scott County	15	18.99
Brady, MT (cdp) Pondera County	36	18.95
Marshallberg, NC (cdp) Carteret County	61	18.83
West Union, IL (cdp) Clark County	79	18.76

Please refer to the Explanation of Data in the front of the book for more detailed information.

Ancestry

Scotch-Irish

Top 150 Places Sorted by Percent of Total Population

Based on places with total population of 7,500 or more

Place	Population	%
Forest Acres, SC (city) Richland County	944	9.07
Meadowbrook, AL (cdp) Shelby County	768	8.76
Belmont, NC (city) Gaston County	837	8.52
Canton, PA (township) Washington County	675	7.97
Abingdon, VA (town) Washington County	647	7.96
Canonsburg, PA (borough) Washington County	695	7.79
Alcoa, TN (city) Blount County	660	7.79
Hendersonville, NC (city) Henderson County	968	7.50
Waynesville, NC (town) Haywood County	741	7.46
Mint Hill, NC (town) Mecklenburg County	1,625	7.41
Black Mountain, NC (town) Buncombe County	579	7.41
Mountain Brook, AL (city) Jefferson County	1,474	7.23
Lake Wylie, SC (cdp) York County	600	7.18
Oxford, MS (city) Lafayette County	1,279	7.11
Maryville, TN (city) Blount County	1,912	7.10
Boone, NC (town) Watauga County	1,169	7.06
Washington, PA (city) Washington County	983	7.06
Lancaster, SC (city) Lancaster County	583	7.04
Grove City, PA (borough) Mercer County	574	6.92
Weddington, NC (town) Union County	629	6.83
Red Bank, TN (city) Hamilton County	784	6.72
Farragut, TN (town) Knox County	1,329	6.59
Old Orchard Beach, ME (cdp/town) York County	572	6.53
Staunton, VA (ind. city) Staunton independent city	1,505	6.32
East Bridgewater, MA (town) Plymouth County	843	6.18
North Myrtle Beach, SC (city) Horry County	824	6.15
Florence, SC (city) Florence County	2,209	6.13
Hollymead, VA (cdp) Albemarle County	490	6.11
Leland, NC (town) Brunswick County	725	6.08
Ruidoso, NM (village) Lincoln County	493	6.05
York, SC (city) York County	457	6.00
Vestavia Hills, AL (city) Jefferson County	1,994	5.99
Kennebunk, ME (town) York County	650	5.97
Orange Park, FL (town) Clay County	520	5.97
Beaver Falls, PA (city) Beaver County	541	5.95
Little River, SC (cdp) Horry County	516	5.95
Clemson, SC (city) Pickens County	807	5.94
Asheville, NC (city) Buncombe County	4,845	5.91
Bangor, ME (city) Penobscot County	1,941	5.90
Decatur, GA (city) DeKalb County	1,114	5.84
North Decatur, GA (cdp) DeKalb County	1,021	5.83
Matthews, NC (town) Mecklenburg County	1,544	5.81
Homewood, AL (city) Jefferson County	1,449	5.78
Sevierville, TN (city) Sevier County	829	5.73
Hamilton, MA (town) Essex County	447	5.71
Easley, SC (city) Pickens County	1,120	5.68
Hampton, NH (cdp) Rockingham County	504	5.68
Bothell West, WA (cdp) Snohomish County	877	5.62
Morehead City, NC (town) Carteret County	477	5.60
Gloucester Point, VA (cdp) Gloucester County	582	5.59
Bridgeport, WV (city) Harrison County	445	5.58
Harrisburg, NC (town) Cabarrus County	574	5.56
D'Iberville, MS (city) Harrison County	494	5.55
White House, TN (city) Sumner County	539	5.52
Port Townsend, WA (city) Jefferson County	501	5.52
New Baltimore, VA (cdp) Fauquier County	427	5.44
Pembroke, MA (town) Plymouth County	958	5.42
Franklin, TN (city) Williamson County	3,235	5.40
Indian Trail, NC (town) Union County	1,640	5.40
Shenango, PA (township) Lawrence County	405	5.40
Ocean Springs, MS (city) Jackson County	930	5.39
West Frankfort, IL (city) Franklin County	467	5.37
North Strabane, PA (township) Washington County	686	5.36
Downingtown, PA (borough) Chester County	424	5.36
Butler, PA (township) Butler County	927	5.34
Ellwood City, PA (borough) Lawrence County	438	5.34
Vinton, VA (town) Roanoke County	430	5.33
Kings Mountain, NC (city) Cleveland County	565	5.31
Morganton, NC (city) Burke County	899	5.30
Neshannock, PA (township) Lawrence County	504	5.29
Derry, PA (township) Westmoreland County	761	5.26
Flowood, MS (city) Rankin County	398	5.25
Waxhaw, NC (town) Union County	458	5.23
Leander, TX (city) Williamson County	1,216	5.22
Cornelius, NC (town) Mecklenburg County	1,194	5.20
Standish, ME (town) Cumberland County	510	5.20
Hanson, MA (town) Plymouth County	524	5.19
St. Albans, WV (city) Kanawha County	573	5.18
Southern Pines, NC (town) Moore County	626	5.17
South Strabane, PA (township) Washington County	471	5.17
Clay, AL (city) Jefferson County	492	5.16
Mission, KS (city) Johnson County	488	5.15
Powdersville, SC (cdp) Anderson County	412	5.15
Washougal, WA (city) Clark County	679	5.13
Mount Holly, NC (city) Gaston County	662	5.13
Southside, AL (city) Etowah County	428	5.13
Sun Lakes, AZ (cdp) Maricopa County	690	5.11
Guilford, PA (township) Franklin County	731	5.10
Chapel Hill, NC (town) Orange County	2,806	5.09
Wilmington, NC (city) New Hanover County	5,317	5.08
Indiana, PA (borough) Indiana County	713	5.07
Gulf Shores, AL (city) Baldwin County	457	5.06
Woodway, TX (city) McLennan County	423	5.05
Oak Ridge, TN (city) Anderson County	1,453	5.02
Rock Hill, SC (city) York County	3,164	5.01
Germantown, TN (city) Shelby County	1,936	5.01
Lincolnton, NC (city) Lincoln County	522	5.00
Hot Springs Village, AR (cdp) Garland County	625	4.99
Druid Hills, GA (cdp) DeKalb County	725	4.96
Graham, NC (city) Alamance County	691	4.96
Northbridge, MA (town) Worcester County	755	4.94
Carnegie, PA (borough) Allegheny County	394	4.94
South Kensington, MD (cdp) Montgomery County	401	4.92
Brentwood, TN (city) Williamson County	1,730	4.90
Trussville, AL (city) Jefferson County	911	4.90
Chartiers, PA (township) Washington County	376	4.87
East Nottingham, PA (township) Chester County	397	4.86
Freeport, ME (town) Cumberland County	383	4.85
Mount Airy, NC (city) Surry County	509	4.84
Gastonia, NC (city) Gaston County	3,416	4.83
Ferry Pass, FL (cdp) Escambia County	1,309	4.80
Portland, ME (city) Cumberland County	3,162	4.78
St. Simons, GA (cdp) Glynn County	614	4.78
Glenshaw, PA (cdp) Allegheny County	440	4.78
Clemmons, NC (village) Forsyth County	866	4.77
Bolivar, MO (city) Polk County	488	4.77
Huntersville, NC (town) Mecklenburg County	2,052	4.76
Highland Park, TX (town) Dallas County	406	4.76
Scarborough, ME (town) Cumberland County	886	4.75
Wyndham, VA (cdp) Henrico County	444	4.75
Uwchlan, PA (township) Chester County	851	4.74
Lakeland Highlands, FL (cdp) Polk County	546	4.74
Statesville, NC (city) Iredell County	1,165	4.73
Madison, MS (city) Madison County	1,102	4.73
Uxbridge, MA (town) Worcester County	619	4.73
Greenville, SC (city) Greenville County	2,731	4.72
Paradise, CA (town) Butte County	1,238	4.68
Lakes, AK (cdp) Matanuska-Susitna Borough	427	4.68
Enumclaw, WA (city) King County	498	4.67
Cave Spring, VA (cdp) Roanoke County	1,188	4.65
Seven Oaks, SC (cdp) Lexington County	760	4.65
Anderson, SC (city) Anderson County	1,231	4.63
Lewisville, NC (town) Forsyth County	579	4.63
Bluefield, WV (city) Mercer County	488	4.63
Oakwood, OH (city) Montgomery County	425	4.63
West Columbia, SC (city) Lexington County	677	4.62
Abington, MA (cdp/town) Plymouth County	723	4.60
Evanston, WY (city) Uinta County	553	4.60
Kingsport, TN (city) Sullivan County	2,197	4.59
Danville, KY (city) Boyle County	736	4.58
Teays Valley, WV (cdp) Putnam County	625	4.58
South Charleston, WV (city) Kanawha County	613	4.58
Jefferson City, TN (city) Jefferson County	371	4.58
North Druid Hills, GA (cdp) DeKalb County	838	4.56
Lawrenceburg, TN (city) Lawrence County	475	4.56
Sheridan, WY (city) Sheridan County	773	4.55
Alachua, FL (city) Alachua County	396	4.55
Waterboro, ME (town) York County	341	4.55
Lexington, SC (town) Lexington County	745	4.54
Hope Mills, NC (town) Cumberland County	654	4.54

SECTION THREE

Ancestry

Scottish

U.S. and 50 States Sorted by Population and Percent of Total Population

Place	Population	%	Place	Population	%
United States	**5,821,321**	**1.92**	Maine	74,329	5.60
California	565,334	1.54	Vermont	30,724	4.92
Texas	389,832	1.60	New Hampshire	63,006	4.80
Florida	335,948	1.81	Utah	123,661	4.65
North Carolina	246,993	2.66	Wyoming	20,825	3.82
Michigan	245,563	2.47	Oregon	129,950	3.45
Ohio	229,371	1.99	Idaho	52,306	3.43
New York	227,255	1.18	Montana	32,395	3.33
Washington	212,424	3.24	Washington	212,424	3.24
Pennsylvania	210,517	1.67	Alaska	22,096	3.20
Virginia	188,707	2.41	Colorado	139,848	2.86
Georgia	184,525	1.95	North Carolina	246,993	2.66
Massachusetts	172,593	2.66	Massachusetts	172,593	2.66
Illinois	160,166	1.26	Michigan	245,563	2.47
Tennessee	140,810	2.26	Virginia	188,707	2.41
Colorado	139,848	2.86	Tennessee	140,810	2.26
Arizona	130,243	2.08	Rhode Island	23,453	2.22
Oregon	129,950	3.45	Kansas	61,226	2.18
Indiana	123,773	1.93	South Carolina	97,162	2.15
Utah	123,661	4.65	West Virginia	39,458	2.14
Missouri	111,202	1.88	Alabama	99,232	2.11
New Jersey	104,979	1.20	Arizona	130,243	2.08
Maryland	100,292	1.76	Connecticut	72,788	2.05
Alabama	99,232	2.11	Kentucky	85,608	2.00
South Carolina	97,162	2.15	Ohio	229,371	1.99
Kentucky	85,608	2.00	Georgia	184,525	1.95
Maine	74,329	5.60	Indiana	123,773	1.93
Connecticut	72,788	2.05	Oklahoma	71,037	1.93
Oklahoma	71,037	1.93	Nevada	50,899	1.93
Minnesota	68,934	1.32	Delaware	16,995	1.93
Wisconsin	64,470	1.14	**United States**	**5,821,321**	**1.92**
New Hampshire	63,006	4.80	Missouri	111,202	1.88
Kansas	61,226	2.18	Arkansas	53,087	1.85
Arkansas	53,087	1.85	Florida	335,948	1.81
Idaho	52,306	3.43	Maryland	100,292	1.76
Nevada	50,899	1.93	New Mexico	34,572	1.72
Iowa	50,647	1.68	Iowa	50,647	1.68
Mississippi	47,248	1.61	Pennsylvania	210,517	1.67
Louisiana	45,283	1.02	Mississippi	47,248	1.61
West Virginia	39,458	2.14	Texas	389,832	1.60
New Mexico	34,572	1.72	California	565,334	1.54
Montana	32,395	3.33	Nebraska	27,303	1.52
Vermont	30,724	4.92	District of Columbia	7,961	1.36
Nebraska	27,303	1.52	North Dakota	8,803	1.33
Rhode Island	23,453	2.22	Minnesota	68,934	1.32
Alaska	22,096	3.20	South Dakota	10,344	1.29
Wyoming	20,825	3.82	Illinois	160,166	1.26
Delaware	16,995	1.93	New Jersey	104,979	1.20
Hawaii	15,144	1.14	New York	227,255	1.18
South Dakota	10,344	1.29	Wisconsin	64,470	1.14
North Dakota	8,803	1.33	Hawaii	15,144	1.14
District of Columbia	7,961	1.36	Louisiana	45,283	1.02

Please refer to the Explanation of Data in the front of the book for more detailed information.

Ancestry

Scottish

Top 150 Places Sorted by Population

Based on all places, regardless of total population

Place	Population	%
New York, NY (city) Kings County	38,000	0.47
Los Angeles, CA (city) Los Angeles County	29,120	0.77
San Diego, CA (city) San Diego County	24,212	1.89
Phoenix, AZ (city) Maricopa County	22,689	1.56
Seattle, WA (city) King County	22,301	3.75
Houston, TX (city) Harris County	21,995	1.06
Portland, OR (city) Multnomah County	19,960	3.52
Manhattan, NY (borough) New York County	19,553	1.23
Austin, TX (city) Travis County	18,914	2.48
Charlotte, NC (city) Mecklenburg County	17,085	2.42
Jacksonville, FL (city) Duval County	16,504	2.03
Chicago, IL (city) Cook County	16,230	0.60
Dallas, TX (city) Dallas County	15,251	1.28
San Antonio, TX (city) Medina County	14,856	1.15
Indianapolis, IN (city) Marion County	14,050	1.73
Columbus, OH (city) Franklin County	13,797	1.79
San Francisco, CA (city) San Francisco County	13,167	1.67
Nashville-Davidson, TN (metro govt) Davidson County	13,002	2.21
Fort Worth, TX (city) Tarrant County	12,780	1.81
Colorado Springs, CO (city) El Paso County	11,825	2.93
Virginia Beach, VA (ind. city) Virginia Beach independent city	11,456	2.63
Denver, CO (city) Denver County	11,109	1.92
Tucson, AZ (city) Pima County	10,796	2.08
Raleigh, NC (city) Wake County	10,633	2.78
Oklahoma City, OK (city) Oklahoma County	10,551	1.87
Mesa, AZ (city) Maricopa County	10,547	2.40
Albuquerque, NM (city) Bernalillo County	10,368	1.95
Louisville-Jefferson County, KY (metro govt) Jefferson County	9,762	1.66
Tulsa, OK (city) Tulsa County	9,394	2.42
Las Vegas, NV (city) Clark County	9,277	1.60
Anchorage, AK (municipality) Anchorage Municipality	9,274	3.26
San Jose, CA (city) Santa Clara County	9,176	0.99
Brooklyn, NY (borough) Kings County	8,809	0.36
Philadelphia, PA (city) Philadelphia County	8,768	0.58
Lexington-Fayette, KY (cons. govt) Fayette County	8,625	2.99
Boston, MA (city) Suffolk County	8,580	1.42
Atlanta, GA (city) Fulton County	8,305	2.01
Kansas City, MO (city) Jackson County	8,260	1.82
Washington, DC (city) District of Columbia	7,961	1.36
Spokane, WA (city) Spokane County	7,802	3.78
Sacramento, CA (city) Sacramento County	7,694	1.67
Memphis, TN (city) Shelby County	7,654	1.17
Boise City, ID (city) Ada County	7,350	3.56
Salt Lake City, UT (city) Salt Lake County	7,160	3.88
Wichita, KS (city) Sedgwick County	7,087	1.90
Scottsdale, AZ (city) Maricopa County	6,598	3.02
Arlington, TX (city) Tarrant County	6,592	1.83
Plano, TX (city) Collin County	6,560	2.56
Greensboro, NC (city) Guilford County	6,491	2.46
Provo, UT (city) Utah County	6,448	5.85
Henderson, NV (city) Clark County	6,213	2.49
Aurora, CO (city) Arapahoe County	6,166	1.96
St. Petersburg, FL (city) Pinellas County	6,164	2.51
Minneapolis, MN (city) Hennepin County	6,097	1.61
Long Beach, CA (city) Los Angeles County	6,072	1.31
Tampa, FL (city) Hillsborough County	5,811	1.74
Omaha, NE (city) Douglas County	5,728	1.41
Queens, NY (borough) Queens County	5,718	0.26
Brookhaven, NY (town) Suffolk County	5,703	1.19
Orem, UT (city) Utah County	5,672	6.53
Salem, OR (city) Marion County	5,618	3.70
Arlington, VA (cdp) Arlington County	5,607	2.84
Eugene, OR (city) Lane County	5,572	3.63
Vancouver, WA (city) Clark County	5,534	3.45
Reno, NV (city) Washoe County	5,267	2.38
Lubbock, TX (city) Lubbock County	5,187	2.33
Knoxville, TN (city) Knox County	5,075	2.85
Huntington Beach, CA (city) Orange County	5,014	2.65
Fresno, CA (city) Fresno County	4,988	1.03
Winston-Salem, NC (city) Forsyth County	4,986	2.22
Tacoma, WA (city) Pierce County	4,962	2.50
Chandler, AZ (city) Maricopa County	4,917	2.14
Fayetteville, NC (city) Cumberland County	4,887	2.46
Overland Park, KS (city) Johnson County	4,880	2.86
Chesapeake, VA (ind. city) Chesapeake independent city	4,830	2.20
Durham, NC (city) Durham County	4,809	2.18
Pittsburgh, PA (city) Allegheny County	4,798	1.56
Bakersfield, CA (city) Kern County	4,779	1.44
Baltimore, MD (city) Baltimore city County	4,773	0.77
Fort Wayne, IN (city) Allen County	4,615	1.82
Fort Collins, CO (city) Larimer County	4,607	3.29
Richmond, VA (ind. city) Richmond independent city	4,564	2.26
Gilbert, AZ (town) Maricopa County	4,530	2.32
Lincoln, NE (city) Lancaster County	4,525	1.79
Madison, WI (city) Dane County	4,523	1.97
Tallahassee, FL (city) Leon County	4,424	2.50
Springfield, MO (city) Christian County	4,372	2.75
Santa Rosa, CA (city) Sonoma County	4,346	2.67
Santa Clarita, CA (city) Los Angeles County	4,327	2.51
Oakland, CA (city) Alameda County	4,325	1.12
Huntsville, AL (city) Madison County	4,308	2.46
Lakewood, CO (city) Jefferson County	4,273	3.01
Boulder, CO (city) Boulder County	4,251	4.38
Charleston, SC (city) Charleston County	4,177	3.59
Norman, OK (city) Cleveland County	4,134	3.82
Livonia, MI (city) Wayne County	4,098	4.19
Corpus Christi, TX (city) Nueces County	4,071	1.36
Paradise, NV (cdp) Clark County	3,987	1.83
West Valley City, UT (city) Salt Lake County	3,977	3.18
Centennial, CO (city) Arapahoe County	3,946	3.95
Cary, NC (town) Wake County	3,944	3.09
Athens-Clarke County, GA (unified govt) Clarke County	3,930	3.46
Norfolk, VA (ind. city) Norfolk independent city	3,912	1.62
Hempstead, NY (town) Nassau County	3,831	0.51
Cincinnati, OH (city) Hamilton County	3,828	1.28
Sandy, UT (city) Salt Lake County	3,786	4.34
Glendale, AZ (city) Maricopa County	3,774	1.64
Arvada, CO (city) Jefferson County	3,761	3.59
Portland, ME (city) Cumberland County	3,739	5.65
Bellingham, WA (city) Whatcom County	3,739	4.73
St. Paul, MN (city) Ramsey County	3,738	1.33
Des Moines, IA (city) Polk County	3,712	1.84
Highlands Ranch, CO (cdp) Douglas County	3,704	3.89
Layton, UT (city) Davis County	3,697	5.63
Alexandria, VA (ind. city) Alexandria independent city	3,670	2.75
Orlando, FL (city) Orange County	3,660	1.57
Toledo, OH (city) Lucas County	3,645	1.25
Manchester, NH (city) Hillsborough County	3,642	3.32
Little Rock, AR (city) Pulaski County	3,635	1.91
McKinney, TX (city) Collin County	3,607	3.04
Ann Arbor, MI (city) Washtenaw County	3,574	3.10
Bellevue, WA (city) King County	3,541	2.96
Columbia, SC (city) Richland County	3,524	2.76
Amarillo, TX (city) Potter County	3,505	1.87
Mobile, AL (city) Mobile County	3,505	1.79
Wilmington, NC (city) New Hanover County	3,498	3.34
Chattanooga, TN (city) Hamilton County	3,484	2.12
Asheville, NC (city) Buncombe County	3,480	4.25
West Jordan, UT (city) Salt Lake County	3,464	3.51
Newport News, VA (ind. city) Newport News independent city	3,422	1.88
St. George, UT (city) Washington County	3,421	4.81
New Orleans, LA (city) Orleans Parish	3,369	1.14
Billings, MT (city) Yellowstone County	3,331	3.28
Montgomery, AL (city) Montgomery County	3,294	1.61
Thousand Oaks, CA (city) Ventura County	3,283	2.63
Riverside, CA (city) Riverside County	3,263	1.09
El Paso, TX (city) El Paso County	3,254	0.52
Millcreek, UT (cdp) Salt Lake County	3,225	5.29
The Woodlands, TX (cdp) Montgomery County	3,208	3.48
Bend, OR (city) Deschutes County	3,198	4.30
Peoria, AZ (city) Yavapai County	3,189	2.14
Roseville, CA (city) Placer County	3,159	2.78
Nashua, NH (city) Hillsborough County	3,108	3.57
Olathe, KS (city) Johnson County	3,104	2.57
Oceanside, CA (city) San Diego County	3,104	1.88
Cleveland, OH (city) Cuyahoga County	3,093	0.76
Mount Pleasant, SC (town) Charleston County	3,089	4.81
Birmingham, AL (city) Jefferson County	3,017	1.39
Rochester, NY (city) Monroe County	3,002	1.42
Milwaukee, WI (city) Milwaukee County	2,988	0.51

Please refer to the Explanation of Data in the front of the book for more detailed information.

Ancestry

Scottish

Top 150 Places Sorted by Percent of Total Population

Based on all places, regardless of total population

Place	Population	%
Young Place, NM (cdp) San Juan County	40	100.00
Villa del Sol, TX (cdp) Cameron County	21	100.00
Nutrioso, AZ (cdp) Apache County	15	100.00
Cass, WV (cdp) Pocahontas County	14	100.00
Chicken, AK (cdp) Southeast Fairbanks Census Area	12	100.00
Lake Lindsey, FL (cdp) Hernando County	9	100.00
Hansboro, ND (city) Towner County	5	83.33
Nanafalia, AL (cdp) Marengo County	49	83.05
Spencer, ID (city) Clark County	33	76.74
Coyville, KS (city) Wilson County	28	75.68
Mount Laguna, CA (cdp) San Diego County	42	63.64
Newkirk, NM (cdp) Guadalupe County	18	62.07
Spokane Creek, MT (cdp) Broadwater County	77	60.63
Rillito, AZ (cdp) Pima County	31	58.49
Pine Grove, WA (cdp) Ferry County	57	57.00
Myers Flat, CA (cdp) Humboldt County	49	53.85
Oakley, WY (cdp) Lincoln County	37	51.39
Mazie, OK (cdp) Mayes County	20	50.00
Triumph, LA (cdp) Plaquemines Parish	16	50.00
Weed, NM (cdp) Otero County	12	50.00
Churchs Ferry, ND (city) Ramsey County	2	50.00
Mulat, FL (cdp) Santa Rosa County	17	48.57
Goodyears Bar, CA (cdp) Sierra County	94	47.47
Vickery, OH (cdp) Sandusky County	43	47.25
Darwin, CA (cdp) Inyo County	14	46.67
Henderson Point, MS (cdp) Harrison County	14	46.67
Collegeville, IN (cdp) Jasper County	22	45.83
Murphy, ID (cdp) Owyhee County	16	45.71
Pinos Altos, NM (cdp) Grant County	16	44.44
Lupus, MO (town) Moniteau County	16	43.24
La Due, MO (village) Henry County	3	42.86
Bettles, AK (city) Yukon-Koyukuk Census Area	9	40.91
Cliff Village, MO (village) Newton County	42	40.78
Hazel Green, WI (village) Lafayette County	2	40.00
Whitehaven, MD (cdp) Wicomico County	37	38.95
Elmira, MO (village) Ray County	24	38.71
Conchas Dam, NM (cdp) San Miguel County	65	38.24
Thompson Springs, UT (cdp) Grand County	8	38.10
Likely, CA (cdp) Modoc County	23	36.51
Colburn, IN (cdp) Tippecanoe County	39	36.45
Rickreall, OR (cdp) Polk County	13	36.11
Robertson, WY (cdp) Uinta County	35	36.08
Pierpont, MO (village) Boone County	23	35.94
Fields Landing, CA (cdp) Humboldt County	93	35.91
Chelyan, WV (cdp) Kanawha County	197	34.87
McDermitt, NV (cdp) Humboldt County	41	34.45
Indian Springs, MT (cdp) Lincoln County	24	34.29
Dixon, WY (town) Carbon County	40	33.90
Nesbitt, TX (town) Harrison County	77	33.62
Lonetree, WY (cdp) Uinta County	5	33.33
Seboomook Lake, ME (unorganized territory) Somerset County	5	33.33
Dutch John, UT (cdp) Daggett County	42	32.81
Carlton, KS (city) Dickinson County	16	32.00
Great Pond, ME (town) Hancock County	7	31.82
Lewis, CO (cdp) Montezuma County	95	31.56
Dering Harbor, NY (village) Suffolk County	5	31.25
Moro, ME (plantation) Aroostook County	5	31.25
Landgrove, VT (town) Bennington County	59	31.22
Ritchey, MO (town) Newton County	15	30.61
Calpine, CA (cdp) Sierra County	37	30.33
Mount Moriah, MO (town) Harrison County	12	30.00
Northwest Somerset, ME (unorganized territory) Somerset County	6	30.00
Soda Springs, CA (cdp) Nevada County	38	29.69
Huntersville, WV (cdp) Pocahontas County	64	29.63
Brandon, CO (cdp) Kiowa County	8	29.63
Northwest Piscataquis, ME (unorganized territory) Piscataquis County	29	29.59
Sugartown, LA (cdp) Beauregard Parish	14	29.17
Carmet, CA (cdp) Sonoma County	9	29.03
Skykomish, WA (town) King County	36	28.80
Gold Hill, CO (cdp) Boulder County	58	28.71
Cranberry Isles, ME (town) Hancock County	29	28.71
Salvo, NC (cdp) Dare County	25	28.41
Hermleigh, TX (cdp) Scurry County	95	28.11
Gann, OH (village) Knox County	31	27.93
Veteran, WY (cdp) Goshen County	16	27.59
Max, NE (cdp) Dundy County	9	27.27
Suissevale, NH (cdp) Carroll County	24	26.97
Plumas Eureka, CA (cdp) Plumas County	63	26.92
Chelsea, SD (town) Faulk County	11	26.83
Lake Medina Shores, TX (cdp) Bandera County	379	26.73
Crestone, CO (town) Saguache County	25	26.60
Dotyville, OK (cdp) Ottawa County	26	26.53
Avon, UT (cdp) Cache County	98	26.20
Green Valley, MN (township) Becker County	99	25.85
Wade, ME (town) Aroostook County	82	25.71
Hingham, MT (town) Hill County	29	25.66
Shawmut, MT (cdp) Wheatland County	10	25.64
Idalia, CO (cdp) Yuma County	11	25.58
Slater, WY (cdp) Platte County	13	25.49
La Porte, CA (cdp) Plumas County	9	25.00
Hannah, ND (city) Cavalier County	3	25.00
Bivalve, MD (cdp) Wicomico County	45	24.86
Whitfield, FL (cdp) Santa Rosa County	82	24.62
Corriganville, MD (cdp) Allegany County	122	24.45
Plainville, OH (cdp) Hamilton County	54	24.22
Snowville, VA (cdp) Pulaski County	24	24.00
Curlew, IA (city) Palo Alto County	12	24.00
Amistad, TX (cdp) Val Verde County	6	24.00
Bennington, ID (cdp) Bear Lake County	52	23.74
Martell, CA (cdp) Amador County	36	23.53
Dana, IA (city) Greene County	15	23.44
Hustler, WI (village) Juneau County	48	23.41
Evergreen, MO (village) Laclede County	7	23.33
Rhinecliff, NY (cdp) Dutchess County	86	23.18
Canby, CA (cdp) Modoc County	46	23.12
Conway, IA (city) Taylor County	9	23.08
Teasdale, UT (cdp) Wayne County	6	23.08
East Hancock, ME (unorganized territory) Hancock County	14	22.95
Lake Roesiger, WA (cdp) Snohomish County	78	22.94
Shipman, VA (cdp) Nelson County	93	22.91
Kingvale, CA (cdp) Nevada County	38	22.89
Port Alexander, AK (city) Petersburg Census Area	15	22.73
Peoria, CO (cdp) Arapahoe County	37	22.56
Folsom, NM (village) Union County	25	22.52
Rest Haven, GA (town) Gwinnett County	27	22.31
Manzanita, OR (city) Tillamook County	80	22.28
Bon Aqua Junction, TN (cdp) Hickman County	209	22.16
Oxbow, ME (plantation) Aroostook County	13	22.03
Caratunk, ME (town) Somerset County	14	21.88
Sena, NM (cdp) San Miguel County	14	21.88
Juntura, OR (cdp) Malheur County	10	21.74
Edmond, KS (city) Norton County	12	21.43
Carbonado, WA (town) Pierce County	130	21.35
Scarbro, WV (cdp) Fayette County	86	21.34
Brinsmade, ND (city) Benson County	7	21.21
Catherine, CO (cdp) Garfield County	40	21.16
Crawford, ME (town) Washington County	23	21.10
Stockville, NE (village) Frontier County	8	21.05
Game Creek, AK (cdp) Hoonah-Angoon Census Area	4	21.05
Deercroft, NC (cdp) Scotland County	95	21.02
New Bedford, IL (village) Bureau County	13	20.63
North Haven, ME (town) Knox County	95	20.61
Pittman, FL (cdp) Lake County	59	20.56
Dunlo, PA (cdp) Cambria County	45	20.55
Dresden, KS (city) Decatur County	10	20.41
Clear Creek, CA (cdp) Lassen County	34	20.24
Lloyd, FL (cdp) Jefferson County	143	20.17
Hickman, CA (cdp) Stanislaus County	88	20.05
Gerton, NC (cdp) Henderson County	78	20.00
Gracey, KY (cdp) Christian County	9	20.00
Oswego, SC (cdp) Sumter County	9	20.00
Long Island, ME (town) Cumberland County	52	19.92
Deerfield, VA (cdp) Augusta County	22	19.82
Raymond, OH (cdp) Union County	52	19.77
Hot Springs Landing, NM (cdp) Sierra County	34	19.77
Bertram, IA (city) Linn County	62	19.75
Bishopville, MD (cdp) Worcester County	89	19.69
Westphalia, KS (city) Anderson County	21	19.63
Boyd, MT (cdp) Carbon County	9	19.57
Weston, ME (town) Aroostook County	32	19.51

Please refer to the Explanation of Data in the front of the book for more detailed information.

Ancestry

Scottish

Top 150 Places Sorted by Percent of Total Population

Based on places with total population of 7,500 or more

Place	Population	%
Mapleton, UT (city) Utah County	768	10.18
Conway, NH (town) Carroll County	908	9.08
Vashon, WA (cdp) King County	874	8.80
Exeter, NH (town) Rockingham County	1,245	8.65
Bath, ME (city) Sagadahoc County	732	8.36
Falmouth, ME (town) Cumberland County	895	8.07
Black Mountain, NC (town) Buncombe County	622	7.97
Pleasant Grove, UT (city) Utah County	2,468	7.85
Barre, VT (town) Washington County	616	7.82
Buxton, ME (town) York County	621	7.75
Exeter, NH (cdp) Rockingham County	729	7.71
Skidaway Island, GA (cdp) Chatham County	622	7.70
Mountain Brook, AL (city) Jefferson County	1,550	7.61
Cedar City, UT (city) Iron County	2,090	7.54
Springville, UT (city) Utah County	2,073	7.50
Woods Cross, UT (city) Davis County	678	7.40
Gorham, ME (town) Cumberland County	1,173	7.30
Kennebunk, ME (town) York County	784	7.20
University Park, TX (city) Dallas County	1,611	7.01
Dayton, NV (cdp) Lyon County	689	7.01
Brewer, ME (city) Penobscot County	659	6.99
Brunswick, ME (cdp) Cumberland County	1,035	6.98
St. Johnsbury, VT (town) Caledonia County	532	6.95
Newburyport, MA (city) Essex County	1,200	6.94
Montpelier, VT (city) Washington County	547	6.92
Pinehurst, NC (village) Moore County	861	6.88
Freeport, ME (town) Cumberland County	542	6.87
Coos Bay, OR (city) Coos County	1,093	6.86
Highland Park, TX (town) Dallas County	585	6.86
York, ME (town) York County	871	6.85
Holladay, UT (city) Salt Lake County	1,799	6.84
Canton, NY (town) St. Lawrence County	734	6.74
Standish, ME (town) Cumberland County	662	6.74
Boone, NC (town) Watauga County	1,112	6.71
Hamilton, MA (town) Essex County	520	6.65
Madison, CT (town) New Haven County	1,211	6.64
Wells, ME (town) York County	640	6.62
Georgetown, MA (town) Essex County	528	6.60
Weare, NH (town) Hillsborough County	571	6.59
Ipswich, MA (town) Essex County	858	6.56
Brewster, MA (town) Barnstable County	647	6.54
Orem, UT (city) Utah County	5,672	6.53
Adams, MA (town) Berkshire County	554	6.50
Barre, VT (city) Washington County	587	6.44
Hanover, NH (town) Grafton County	719	6.38
Payson, UT (city) Utah County	1,095	6.37
Kittery, ME (town) York County	608	6.33
Salisbury, MA (town) Essex County	516	6.33
Bainbridge Island, WA (city) Kitsap County	1,421	6.32
Heber, UT (city) Wasatch County	674	6.26
Port Huron, MI (charter township) St. Clair County	643	6.15
Syracuse, UT (city) Davis County	1,320	6.09
South Portland, ME (city) Cumberland County	1,505	6.07
Darien, CT (cdp/town) Fairfield County	1,236	6.05
Mill Valley, CA (city) Marin County	824	6.01
Brunswick, ME (town) Cumberland County	1,234	6.00
Southern Pines, NC (town) Moore County	727	6.00
Old Orchard Beach, ME (cdp/town) York County	523	5.97
Lehi, UT (city) Utah County	2,502	5.95
Hot Springs Village, AR (cdp) Garland County	744	5.94
Port Townsend, WA (city) Jefferson County	539	5.94
Ellsworth, ME (city) Hancock County	446	5.90
Leeds, AL (city) Jefferson County	666	5.89
South Ogden, UT (city) Weber County	939	5.88
Madison, MS (city) Madison County	1,367	5.87
Washington, UT (city) Washington County	1,020	5.86
Provo, UT (city) Utah County	6,448	5.85
Tooele, UT (city) Tooele County	1,759	5.83
Farmington, UT (city) Davis County	1,000	5.82
West University Place, TX (city) Harris County	849	5.81
Harwich, MA (town) Barnstable County	714	5.81
Blackfoot, ID (city) Bingham County	667	5.79
Saline, MI (city) Washtenaw County	505	5.78
Lake of the Woods, VA (cdp) Orange County	451	5.76
Evergreen, CO (cdp) Jefferson County	525	5.74
Mayfield, MI (township) Lapeer County	462	5.74
Portsmouth, NH (city) Rockingham County	1,198	5.71
Scarborough, ME (town) Cumberland County	1,064	5.71
Bountiful, UT (city) Davis County	2,410	5.69
Cape Elizabeth, ME (town) Cumberland County	514	5.68
Fort Gratiot, MI (charter township) St. Clair County	635	5.67
Portland, ME (city) Cumberland County	3,739	5.65
Rockwood, VA (cdp) Chesterfield County	443	5.65
Bow, NH (town) Merrimack County	428	5.65
Murray, UT (city) Salt Lake County	2,611	5.64
Layton, UT (city) Davis County	3,697	5.63
Whitman, MA (town) Plymouth County	807	5.62
Gunbarrel, CO (cdp) Boulder County	532	5.62
Sandy, OR (city) Clackamas County	498	5.62
Vestavia Hills, AL (city) Jefferson County	1,870	5.61
Hartford, VT (town) Windsor County	562	5.60
East Bradford, PA (township) Chester County	553	5.57
Middlebury, VT (town) Addison County	472	5.57
Bangor, ME (city) Penobscot County	1,823	5.54
Riverdale, UT (city) Weber County	454	5.54
Discovery Bay, CA (cdp) Contra Costa County	632	5.53
Summit, WA (cdp) Pierce County	439	5.53
Cottonwood Heights, UT (city) Salt Lake County	1,851	5.52
West Point, UT (city) Davis County	492	5.52
Williamstown, MA (town) Berkshire County	435	5.52
Concord, NH (city) Merrimack County	2,368	5.51
Spanish Fork, UT (city) Utah County	1,754	5.51
Rochester, NH (city) Strafford County	1,641	5.51
Camas, WA (city) Clark County	1,005	5.48
Barrington, NH (town) Strafford County	463	5.48
Helena Valley Southeast, MT (cdp) Lewis and Clark County	434	5.48
Highland, UT (city) Utah County	770	5.47
North Logan, UT (city) Cache County	425	5.47
Louisville, CO (city) Boulder County	1,009	5.46
Brentwood, TN (city) Williamson County	1,926	5.45
Chesapeake Ranch Estates, MD (cdp) Calvert County	531	5.45
Cannon, MI (township) Kent County	713	5.43
Evanston, WY (city) Uinta County	652	5.43
South Lyon, MI (city) Oakland County	600	5.42
Yarmouth, ME (town) Cumberland County	455	5.42
Topanga, CA (cdp) Los Angeles County	461	5.41
Matthews, NC (town) Mecklenburg County	1,433	5.40
Lafayette, CO (city) Boulder County	1,307	5.40
Merrimack, NH (town) Hillsborough County	1,379	5.39
North Salt Lake, UT (city) Davis County	806	5.38
Hampstead, NH (town) Rockingham County	460	5.38
Summit Park, UT (cdp) Summit County	403	5.37
Grosse Pointe Farms, MI (city) Wayne County	512	5.36
Rock Springs, WY (city) Sweetwater County	1,175	5.34
Brandermill, VA (cdp) Chesterfield County	667	5.31
Millcreek, UT (cdp) Salt Lake County	3,225	5.29
Mayo, MD (cdp) Anne Arundel County	410	5.27
Amesbury Town, MA (city) Essex County	854	5.26
Kingsbury, NY (town) Washington County	651	5.24
Mountain Park, GA (cdp) Gwinnett County	624	5.23
East Grand Rapids, MI (city) Kent County	561	5.23
Inglewood-Finn Hill, WA (cdp) King County	1,208	5.22
Corrales, NM (village) Sandoval County	425	5.21
Presque Isle, ME (city) Aroostook County	503	5.20
Cimarron Hills, CO (cdp) El Paso County	807	5.17
Rockland, MA (town) Plymouth County	904	5.16
Newberg, OR (city) Yamhill County	1,102	5.14
Lakes, AK (cdp) Matanuska-Susitna Borough	469	5.14
Marblehead, MA (cdp/town) Essex County	1,014	5.12
Lansdowne, VA (cdp) Loudoun County	501	5.10
Canton, GA (city) Cherokee County	1,058	5.09
Topsham, ME (town) Sagadahoc County	455	5.09
Ketchikan, AK (city) Ketchikan Gateway Borough	406	5.08
Cave Spring, VA (cdp) Roanoke County	1,296	5.07
Lake Oswego, OR (city) Clackamas County	1,847	5.05
Woodmoor, CO (cdp) El Paso County	450	5.05
Payson, AZ (town) Gila County	756	5.03
Chapel Hill, NC (town) Orange County	2,770	5.02
Clinton, UT (city) Davis County	956	5.02
Germantown, TN (city) Shelby County	1,937	5.01

Please refer to the Explanation of Data in the front of the book for more detailed information.

Ancestry

Serbian

U.S. and 50 States Sorted by Population and Percent of Total Population

Place	Population	%
United States	**175,165**	**0.06**
Illinois	21,258	0.17
Pennsylvania	19,549	0.15
Ohio	17,530	0.15
California	15,315	0.04
Indiana	11,326	0.18
Michigan	9,458	0.10
Florida	8,922	0.05
Wisconsin	8,548	0.15
New York	8,499	0.04
Arizona	4,909	0.08
Minnesota	4,348	0.08
New Jersey	3,833	0.04
Texas	3,567	0.01
Virginia	3,514	0.04
Nevada	3,114	0.12
North Carolina	2,490	0.03
Missouri	2,448	0.04
Maryland	2,382	0.04
Colorado	2,263	0.05
Washington	2,232	0.03
Georgia	1,868	0.02
West Virginia	1,507	0.08
Massachusetts	1,469	0.02
Oregon	1,313	0.03
South Carolina	1,084	0.02
Connecticut	1,053	0.03
Iowa	1,043	0.03
Utah	937	0.04
Kansas	856	0.03
Nebraska	838	0.05
Tennessee	825	0.01
Montana	745	0.08
Louisiana	526	0.01
Maine	470	0.04
Hawaii	445	0.03
New Mexico	440	0.02
Arkansas	406	0.01
Kentucky	401	0.01
Idaho	396	0.03
Oklahoma	385	0.01
District of Columbia	330	0.06
North Dakota	329	0.05
Vermont	304	0.05
Alaska	304	0.04
Alabama	277	0.01
New Hampshire	270	0.02
Delaware	223	0.03
South Dakota	216	0.03
Mississippi	166	0.01
Wyoming	128	0.02
Rhode Island	106	0.01

Place	Population	%
Indiana	11,326	0.18
Illinois	21,258	0.17
Pennsylvania	19,549	0.15
Ohio	17,530	0.15
Wisconsin	8,548	0.15
Nevada	3,114	0.12
Michigan	9,458	0.10
Arizona	4,909	0.08
Minnesota	4,348	0.08
West Virginia	1,507	0.08
Montana	745	0.08
United States	**175,165**	**0.06**
District of Columbia	330	0.06
Florida	8,922	0.05
Colorado	2,263	0.05
Nebraska	838	0.05
North Dakota	329	0.05
Vermont	304	0.05
California	15,315	0.04
New York	8,499	0.04
New Jersey	3,833	0.04
Virginia	3,514	0.04
Missouri	2,448	0.04
Maryland	2,382	0.04
Utah	937	0.04
Maine	470	0.04
Alaska	304	0.04
North Carolina	2,490	0.03
Washington	2,232	0.03
Oregon	1,313	0.03
Connecticut	1,053	0.03
Iowa	1,043	0.03
Kansas	856	0.03
Hawaii	445	0.03
Idaho	396	0.03
Delaware	223	0.03
South Dakota	216	0.03
Georgia	1,868	0.02
Massachusetts	1,469	0.02
South Carolina	1,084	0.02
New Mexico	440	0.02
New Hampshire	270	0.02
Wyoming	128	0.02
Texas	3,567	0.01
Tennessee	825	0.01
Louisiana	526	0.01
Arkansas	406	0.01
Kentucky	401	0.01
Oklahoma	385	0.01
Alabama	277	0.01
Mississippi	166	0.01
Rhode Island	106	0.01

Please refer to the Explanation of Data in the front of the book for more detailed information.

Ancestry

Serbian

Top 150 Places Sorted by Population

Based on all places, regardless of total population

Place	Population	%
Chicago, IL (city) Cook County	5,286	0.20
New York, NY (city) Kings County	4,911	0.06
Queens, NY (borough) Queens County	2,438	0.11
Milwaukee, WI (city) Milwaukee County	2,035	0.35
Parma, OH (city) Cuyahoga County	1,778	2.17
Phoenix, AZ (city) Maricopa County	1,547	0.11
Manhattan, NY (borough) New York County	1,526	0.10
Los Angeles, CA (city) Los Angeles County	1,315	0.03
Pittsburgh, PA (city) Allegheny County	993	0.32
Munster, IN (town) Lake County	984	4.23
Akron, OH (city) Summit County	945	0.47
Spring Valley, NV (cdp) Clark County	941	0.55
San Diego, CA (city) San Diego County	935	0.07
Schererville, IN (town) Lake County	859	3.02
Indianapolis, IN (city) Marion County	777	0.10
Greenfield, WI (city) Milwaukee County	737	2.04
Hobart, IN (city) Lake County	614	2.16
Hammond, IN (city) Lake County	572	0.70
St. Petersburg, FL (city) Pinellas County	572	0.23
Reno, NV (city) Washoe County	539	0.24
Mesa, AZ (city) Maricopa County	536	0.12
Cleveland, OH (city) Cuyahoga County	529	0.13
Franklin, WI (city) Milwaukee County	526	1.54
Jacksonville, FL (city) Duval County	525	0.06
Brooklyn, NY (borough) Kings County	520	0.02
Columbus, OH (city) Franklin County	511	0.07
Niles, IL (village) Cook County	498	1.69
Philadelphia, PA (city) Philadelphia County	493	0.03
Orland Park, IL (village) Cook County	457	0.83
North Huntingdon, PA (township) Westmoreland County	453	1.49
Lansing, IL (village) Cook County	441	1.57
St. John, IN (town) Lake County	439	3.20
Omaha, NE (city) Douglas County	437	0.11
San Francisco, CA (city) San Francisco County	435	0.06
North Royalton, OH (city) Cuyahoga County	433	1.45
Hopewell, PA (township) Beaver County	423	3.34
Valparaiso, IN (city) Porter County	421	1.36
Kenosha, WI (city) Kenosha County	409	0.42
Portland, OR (city) Multnomah County	405	0.07
Brunswick, OH (city) Medina County	399	1.16
Las Vegas, NV (city) Clark County	398	0.07
San Jose, CA (city) Santa Clara County	398	0.04
Scottsdale, AZ (city) Maricopa County	392	0.18
Seattle, WA (city) King County	386	0.06
Rochester Hills, MI (city) Oakland County	382	0.54
Hibbing, MN (city) St. Louis County	374	2.28
Sterling Heights, MI (city) Macomb County	369	0.28
Charlotte, NC (city) Mecklenburg County	362	0.05
Hempfield, PA (township) Westmoreland County	360	0.84
Barberton, OH (city) Summit County	358	1.33
Countryside, IL (city) Cook County	351	6.03
Crown Point, IN (city) Lake County	337	1.29
Austin, TX (city) Travis County	336	0.04
Troy, MI (city) Oakland County	333	0.41
Washington, DC (city) District of Columbia	330	0.06
Skokie, IL (village) Cook County	325	0.51
Weirton, WV (city) Hancock County	324	1.64
Harwood Heights, IL (village) Cook County	319	3.77
Minneapolis, MN (city) Hennepin County	318	0.08
Hermitage, PA (city) Mercer County	317	1.96
Denver, CO (city) Denver County	313	0.05
Sacramento, CA (city) Sacramento County	312	0.07
Houston, TX (city) Harris County	309	0.01
Arlington Heights, IL (village) Cook County	307	0.41
Joliet, IL (city) Will County	305	0.21
Penn, PA (township) Westmoreland County	302	1.52
Naperville, IL (city) DuPage County	301	0.21
Arlington, VA (cdp) Arlington County	301	0.15
Northbrook, IL (village) Cook County	300	0.91
Center, PA (township) Beaver County	296	2.53
Buffalo, NY (city) Erie County	291	0.11
Carlsbad, CA (city) San Diego County	288	0.29
Cranberry, PA (township) Butler County	283	1.03
Portland, ME (city) Cumberland County	283	0.43
Des Plaines, IL (city) Cook County	282	0.49
Duluth, MN (city) St. Louis County	282	0.33
Hamburg, NY (town) Erie County	279	0.49
West Allis, WI (city) Milwaukee County	279	0.46
Enterprise, NV (cdp) Clark County	276	0.28
New Berlin, WI (city) Waukesha County	275	0.70
Baldwin, PA (borough) Allegheny County	271	1.38
Paterson, NJ (city) Passaic County	271	0.19
Portage, IN (city) Porter County	268	0.74
Macomb, MI (township) Macomb County	268	0.36
Urban Honolulu, HI (cdp) Honolulu County	268	0.08
Shelby, MI (charter township) Macomb County	265	0.36
Cuyahoga Falls, OH (city) Summit County	264	0.53
Royal Oak, MI (city) Oakland County	264	0.46
Long Beach, CA (city) Los Angeles County	263	0.06
Highland, IN (town) Lake County	259	1.09
Monroeville, PA (municipality) Allegheny County	255	0.90
Paradise, NV (cdp) Clark County	255	0.12
Virginia Beach, VA (ind. city) Virginia Beach independent city	254	0.06
Livonia, MI (city) Wayne County	253	0.26
High Point, NC (city) Guilford County	250	0.25
Orchard Park, NY (town) Erie County	247	0.86
Merrillville, IN (town) Lake County	247	0.72
Clinton, MI (charter township) Macomb County	246	0.25
Kansas City, MO (city) Jackson County	246	0.05
Swatara, PA (township) Dauphin County	244	1.05
Midland, PA (borough) Beaver County	241	8.91
St. Louis, MO (city) St. Louis city County	241	0.08
Staten Island, NY (borough) Richmond County	240	0.05
Warren, MI (city) Macomb County	237	0.17
Oak Park, IL (village) Cook County	236	0.46
Parma Heights, OH (city) Cuyahoga County	234	1.13
New Smyrna Beach, FL (city) Volusia County	231	1.02
Broadview Heights, OH (city) Cuyahoga County	230	1.23
Steubenville, OH (city) Jefferson County	226	1.22
Stratford, CT (cdp/town) Fairfield County	225	0.44
Waukegan, IL (city) Lake County	225	0.25
Bolingbrook, IL (village) Will County	224	0.31
Fort Collins, CO (city) Larimer County	224	0.16
Irvine, CA (city) Orange County	223	0.11
Tucson, AZ (city) Pima County	223	0.04
Peoria, IL (city) Peoria County	222	0.19
Libertyville, IL (village) Lake County	219	1.07
Gilbert, AZ (town) Maricopa County	219	0.11
Anchorage, AK (municipality) Anchorage Municipality	219	0.08
Darien, IL (city) DuPage County	217	0.98
Albuquerque, NM (city) Bernalillo County	212	0.04
Baltimore, MD (city) Baltimore city County	207	0.03
Lincolnwood, IL (village) Cook County	206	1.66
Lorain, OH (city) Lorain County	206	0.32
Salt Lake City, UT (city) Salt Lake County	206	0.11
Norton, OH (city) Summit County	205	1.71
Cedar Lake, IN (town) Lake County	204	1.83
Norfolk, VA (ind. city) Norfolk independent city	201	0.08
San Antonio, TX (city) Medina County	201	0.02
Ohioville, PA (borough) Beaver County	200	5.61
Machesney Park, IL (village) Winnebago County	200	0.87
Racine, WI (city) Racine County	200	0.25
South Milwaukee, WI (city) Milwaukee County	199	0.95
Burbank, CA (city) Los Angeles County	198	0.19
Fort Lee, NJ (borough) Bergen County	197	0.56
Independence, MO (city) Jackson County	197	0.17
Farmington Hills, MI (city) Oakland County	195	0.24
Upper St. Clair, PA (cdp/township) Allegheny County	194	1.01
Fernway, PA (cdp) Butler County	193	1.57
Tempe, AZ (city) Maricopa County	190	0.12
Dalzell, SC (cdp) Sumter County	187	5.80
Santa Clara, CA (city) Santa Clara County	187	0.17
Bronx, NY (borough) Bronx County	187	0.01
Jupiter, FL (town) Palm Beach County	186	0.35
Glendale, AZ (city) Maricopa County	185	0.08
Fort Worth, TX (city) Tarrant County	185	0.03
Morton Grove, IL (village) Cook County	183	0.80
Lakewood, OH (city) Cuyahoga County	183	0.35
Sunnyvale, CA (city) Santa Clara County	183	0.13
Clifton, NJ (city) Passaic County	182	0.22

SECTION THREE

Please refer to the Explanation of Data in the front of the book for more detailed information.

Ancestry

Serbian

Top 150 Places Sorted by Percent of Total Population

Based on all places, regardless of total population

Place	Population	%
Hendricks, MI (township) Mackinac County	20	15.63
Glasgow, PA (borough) Beaver County	8	15.38
Vilas, SD (town) Miner County	3	11.11
Slovan, PA (cdp) Washington County	43	10.67
Crouch, ID (city) Boise County	33	10.54
Mabie, CA (cdp) Plumas County	16	9.70
Skamokawa Valley, WA (cdp) Wahkiakum County	32	9.50
Midland, PA (borough) Beaver County	241	8.91
Plainville, OH (cdp) Hamilton County	18	8.07
Wall, PA (borough) Allegheny County	41	7.51
Wilder, VT (cdp) Windsor County	109	7.06
Carpenter, MN (township) Itasca County	14	6.93
Foxfield, CO (town) Arapahoe County	58	6.78
Crescent Valley, NV (cdp) Eureka County	27	6.73
Hastings, IA (city) Mills County	13	6.63
Memphis, MI (city) Macomb County	47	6.55
Brightwood, VA (cdp) Madison County	57	6.51
Glacier View, AK (cdp) Matanuska-Susitna Borough	21	6.50
Homewood, PA (borough) Beaver County	8	6.40
Countryside, IL (city) Cook County	351	6.03
Dalzell, SC (cdp) Sumter County	187	5.80
Newburg, PA (borough) Cumberland County	19	5.65
Ohioville, PA (borough) Beaver County	200	5.61
Keene, CA (cdp) Kern County	17	5.38
Manchester, IL (village) Scott County	22	4.89
Shorewood Forest, IN (cdp) Porter County	139	4.61
Ideal, MN (township) Crow Wing County	51	4.56
Riverside, PA (cdp) Cambria County	20	4.50
Export, PA (borough) Westmoreland County	40	4.40
Hollister, OK (town) Tillman County	6	4.38
Munster, IN (town) Lake County	984	4.23
Middle Branch, MI (township) Osceola County	33	4.17
Memphis, MI (city) Macomb County	47	4.15
Metamora, MI (village) Lapeer County	23	4.13
Ellwood City, PA (borough) Beaver County	33	4.10
Indian Head Park, IL (village) Cook County	153	4.03
Franklin, PA (borough) Cambria County	14	3.93
Bodega Bay, CA (cdp) Sonoma County	30	3.83
Lawrence, MN (township) Itasca County	19	3.80
Harwood Heights, IL (village) Cook County	319	3.77
Stevens, MN (township) Stevens County	2	3.77
Industry, PA (borough) Beaver County	67	3.72
Raccoon, PA (township) Beaver County	113	3.63
Rosslyn Farms, PA (borough) Allegheny County	18	3.61
University of Pittsburgh Johnstown, PA (cdp) Cambria County	62	3.58
Edmore, ND (city) Ramsey County	10	3.55
Level Green, PA (cdp) Westmoreland County	126	3.39
Hopewell, PA (township) Beaver County	423	3.34
Armington, IL (village) Tazewell County	13	3.32
Reynolds, IN (town) White County	20	3.29
New Stanton, PA (borough) Westmoreland County	95	3.28
Verona, PA (borough) Allegheny County	87	3.28
Vanport, PA (township) Beaver County	46	3.27
Davidsville, PA (cdp) Somerset County	48	3.22
St. John, IN (town) Lake County	439	3.20
Campbell, MN (city) Wilkin County	7	3.17
Port Vue, PA (borough) Allegheny County	121	3.15
Marlin, PA (cdp) Schuylkill County	20	3.07
Rockville, UT (town) Washington County	7	3.03
Pottawattamie Park, IN (town) LaPorte County	6	3.03
Schererville, IN (town) Lake County	859	3.02
Grand Canyon Village, AZ (cdp) Coconino County	36	3.02
Wuori, MN (township) St. Louis County	16	3.01
Marshall, WI (village) Dane County	113	2.98
East Conemaugh, PA (borough) Cambria County	40	2.98
Leith-Hatfield, PA (cdp) Fayette County	83	2.95
Agar, SD (town) Sully County	2	2.94
South Beaver, PA (township) Beaver County	79	2.88
Blanford, IN (cdp) Vermillion County	10	2.88
Elco, PA (borough) Washington County	8	2.85
East McKeesport, PA (borough) Allegheny County	65	2.84
Calumet, MN (city) Itasca County	9	2.80
Shingletown, CA (cdp) Shasta County	58	2.78
Tower Lakes, IL (village) Lake County	41	2.78
Buffington, PA (township) Indiana County	38	2.75
Silver Lake, OH (village) Summit County	70	2.73
Bear Rocks, PA (cdp) Fayette County	29	2.65
Trommald, MN (city) Crow Wing County	2	2.63
Bovey, MN (city) Itasca County	20	2.60
Gilbertville, IA (city) Black Hawk County	19	2.60
East Rochester, PA (borough) Beaver County	18	2.60
Meadow Acres, WY (cdp) Natrona County	7	2.60
Pennwyn, PA (cdp) Berks County	18	2.59
Buhl, MN (city) St. Louis County	23	2.58
Center, PA (township) Beaver County	296	2.53
Oberlin, PA (cdp) Dauphin County	15	2.52
Bethany, WV (town) Brooke County	18	2.48
Knollwood, IL (cdp) Lake County	41	2.45
Blaine, PA (township) Washington County	12	2.44
Greenway, MN (township) Itasca County	42	2.42
Alleghenyville, PA (cdp) Berks County	20	2.42
Onota, MI (township) Alger County	7	2.41
Hooverson Heights, WV (cdp) Brooke County	74	2.40
Pleasant Gap, PA (cdp) Centre County	66	2.40
North Crows Nest, IN (town) Marion County	1	2.38
New Galilee, PA (borough) Beaver County	10	2.36
Mitchell, MI (township) Alcona County	7	2.35
Verdi, NV (cdp) Washoe County	32	2.33
Duncan, AZ (town) Greenlee County	13	2.33
Whitaker, PA (borough) Allegheny County	33	2.32
Trafford, PA (borough) Westmoreland County	72	2.30
Allenport, PA (borough) Washington County	10	2.29
Hibbing, MN (city) St. Louis County	374	2.28
Murphys, CA (cdp) Calaveras County	53	2.28
Fern, WI (town) Florence County	5	2.28
Trafford, PA (borough) Westmoreland County	72	2.27
Fairview Beach, VA (cdp) King George County	13	2.26
Silver Summit, UT (cdp) Summit County	66	2.25
Franklin Furnace, OH (cdp) Scioto County	37	2.21
Parma, OH (city) Cuyahoga County	1,778	2.17
Rutherford, PA (cdp) Dauphin County	89	2.17
Haverford College, PA (cdp) Delaware County	25	2.17
Daniel, UT (town) Wasatch County	24	2.17
Mercer, ND (city) McLean County	2	2.17
Hobart, IN (city) Lake County	614	2.16
Shenango, PA (township) Mercer County	85	2.15
Detroit Beach, MI (cdp) Monroe County	38	2.15
Fallowfield, PA (township) Washington County	93	2.14
Mingo Junction, OH (village) Jefferson County	74	2.14
Salton City, CA (cdp) Imperial County	30	2.14
Roscoe, PA (borough) Washington County	14	2.12
Long Branch, PA (borough) Washington County	13	2.12
Garnett, KS (city) Anderson County	72	2.11
Madison, PA (township) Armstrong County	14	2.09
Chisholm, MN (city) St. Louis County	103	2.08
West Almond, NY (town) Allegany County	6	2.08
Superior, WI (town) Douglas County	43	2.07
Plum Springs, KY (city) Warren County	9	2.07
Fox Run, PA (cdp) Butler County	71	2.06
Wood-Ridge, NJ (borough) Bergen County	155	2.05
Clinton, WI (town) Rock County	18	2.05
Greenfield, WI (city) Milwaukee County	737	2.04
Orange, OH (village) Cuyahoga County	67	2.04
Lake Angelus, MI (city) Oakland County	6	2.04
Cohasset, MN (city) Itasca County	54	2.03
Belmont, WI (town) Lafayette County	14	2.01
Hermitage, PA (city) Mercer County	317	1.96
Glen Osborne, PA (borough) Allegheny County	9	1.96
Orangeville, OH (village) Trumbull County	3	1.96
Whiting, IN (city) Lake County	98	1.95
Middlesex, PA (township) Butler County	105	1.93
Daugherty, PA (township) Beaver County	62	1.93
Bermuda Dunes, CA (cdp) Riverside County	132	1.92
Manor, PA (borough) Westmoreland County	60	1.91
Lindsey, OH (village) Sandusky County	9	1.91
Lebanon South, PA (cdp) Lebanon County	41	1.90
Kipton, OH (village) Lorain County	6	1.90
Rices Landing, PA (borough) Greene County	9	1.89
Slippery Rock, PA (township) Lawrence County	61	1.88
Springwater, WI (town) Waushara County	30	1.88

Please refer to the Explanation of Data in the front of the book for more detailed information.

Ancestry

Serbian

Top 150 Places Sorted by Percent of Total Population

Based on places with total population of 7,500 or more

Place	Population	%
Munster, IN (town) Lake County	984	4.23
Harwood Heights, IL (village) Cook County	319	3.77
Hopewell, PA (township) Beaver County	423	3.34
St. John, IN (town) Lake County	439	3.20
Schererville, IN (town) Lake County	859	3.02
Center, PA (township) Beaver County	296	2.53
Hibbing, MN (city) St. Louis County	374	2.28
Parma, OH (city) Cuyahoga County	1,778	2.17
Hobart, IN (city) Lake County	614	2.16
Wood-Ridge, NJ (borough) Bergen County	155	2.05
Greenfield, WI (city) Milwaukee County	737	2.04
Hermitage, PA (city) Mercer County	317	1.96
Cedar Lake, IN (town) Lake County	204	1.83
White Oak, PA (borough) Allegheny County	142	1.80
Norton, OH (city) Summit County	205	1.71
Niles, IL (village) Cook County	498	1.69
Brighton, PA (township) Beaver County	136	1.67
Lincolnwood, IL (village) Cook County	206	1.66
Weirton, WV (city) Hancock County	324	1.64
North Versailles, PA (township) Allegheny County	167	1.62
Aliquippa, PA (city) Beaver County	158	1.62
Lansing, IL (village) Cook County	441	1.57
Fernway, PA (cdp) Butler County	193	1.57
Lowell, IN (town) Lake County	141	1.57
Franklin, WI (city) Milwaukee County	526	1.54
Penn, PA (township) Westmoreland County	302	1.52
North Huntingdon, PA (township) Westmoreland County	453	1.49
North Royalton, OH (city) Cuyahoga County	433	1.45
Baldwin, PA (borough) Allegheny County	271	1.38
Valparaiso, IN (city) Porter County	421	1.36
Easttown, PA (township) Chester County	142	1.35
South Amboy, NJ (city) Middlesex County	114	1.34
Barberton, OH (city) Summit County	358	1.33
Wanaque, NJ (borough) Passaic County	145	1.33
Pleasant Hills, PA (borough) Allegheny County	109	1.32
Crown Point, IN (city) Lake County	337	1.29
Grand Rapids, MN (city) Itasca County	134	1.25
Broadview Heights, OH (city) Cuyahoga County	230	1.23
Adams, PA (township) Butler County	133	1.23
Steubenville, OH (city) Jefferson County	226	1.22
Gulf Gate Estates, FL (cdp) Sarasota County	131	1.20
Lakes of the Four Seasons, IN (cdp) Lake County	90	1.19
Brunswick, OH (city) Medina County	399	1.16
Parma Heights, OH (city) Cuyahoga County	234	1.13
Lyons, IL (village) Cook County	118	1.12
Beaver Falls, PA (city) Beaver County	102	1.12
Matawan, NJ (borough) Monmouth County	98	1.12
Highland, IN (town) Lake County	259	1.09
Hartford, VT (town) Windsor County	109	1.09
Libertyville, IL (village) Lake County	219	1.07
Swatara, PA (township) Dauphin County	244	1.05
Richland, PA (township) Cambria County	133	1.04
Cranberry, PA (township) Butler County	283	1.03
Lincoln Park, NJ (borough) Morris County	109	1.03
New Smyrna Beach, FL (city) Volusia County	231	1.02
Upper St. Clair, PA (cdp/township) Allegheny County	194	1.01
Cudahy, WI (city) Milwaukee County	180	0.99
Darien, IL (city) DuPage County	217	0.98
South Milwaukee, WI (city) Milwaukee County	199	0.95
Dyer, IN (town) Lake County	152	0.95
North Kensington, MD (cdp) Montgomery County	91	0.95
Olmsted Falls, OH (city) Cuyahoga County	83	0.95
St. Pete Beach, FL (city) Pinellas County	88	0.93
Northbrook, IL (village) Cook County	300	0.91
Greendale, WI (village) Milwaukee County	127	0.91
Vermilion, OH (city) Lorain County	98	0.91
Monroeville, PA (municipality) Allegheny County	255	0.90
Whitehall, PA (borough) Allegheny County	125	0.90
South Union, PA (township) Fayette County	97	0.90
Jeannette, PA (city) Westmoreland County	89	0.90
Hamilton, PA (township) Franklin County	93	0.89
Elwood, IN (city) Madison County	78	0.88
Machesney Park, IL (village) Winnebago County	200	0.87
Middleburg Heights, OH (city) Cuyahoga County	138	0.87
Orchard Park, NY (town) Erie County	247	0.86
La Grange Park, IL (village) Cook County	115	0.86
West Mifflin, PA (borough) Allegheny County	174	0.85
Avon, OH (city) Lorain County	166	0.85
Hempfield, PA (township) Westmoreland County	360	0.84
Pleasant Prairie, WI (village) Kenosha County	161	0.84
Tonawanda, NY (city) Erie County	128	0.84
Lake Station, IN (city) Lake County	108	0.84
Totowa, NJ (borough) Passaic County	89	0.84
Lower Swatara, PA (township) Dauphin County	69	0.84
Orland Park, IL (village) Cook County	457	0.83
Girard, OH (city) Trumbull County	83	0.81
Morton Grove, IL (village) Cook County	183	0.80
Tallmadge, OH (city) Summit County	138	0.80
Haledon, NJ (borough) Passaic County	66	0.80
Norway, WI (town) Racine County	63	0.80
Chartiers, PA (township) Washington County	62	0.80
Wadsworth, OH (city) Medina County	168	0.79
Red Hook, NY (town) Dutchess County	87	0.78
Long Hill, NJ (township) Morris County	68	0.78
Lisle, IL (village) DuPage County	172	0.77
Maplewood, MO (city) St. Louis County	63	0.77
Johnstown, PA (city) Cambria County	164	0.76
Englewood, OH (city) Montgomery County	99	0.75
Vernon, WI (town) Waukesha County	57	0.75
Portage, IN (city) Porter County	268	0.74
Willoughby, OH (city) Lake County	165	0.74
Robinson, PA (township) Allegheny County	97	0.74
Carnot-Moon, PA (cdp) Allegheny County	83	0.74
West Hanover, PA (township) Dauphin County	64	0.73
Merrillville, IN (town) Lake County	247	0.72
Lackawanna, NY (city) Erie County	131	0.72
Kennedy, PA (township) Allegheny County	54	0.71
Hammond, IN (city) Lake County	572	0.70
New Berlin, WI (city) Waukesha County	275	0.70
St. Joseph, MI (city) Berrien County	59	0.70
Hamburg, NY (village) Erie County	66	0.69
Mount Airy, MD (town) Carroll County	61	0.68
Mount Pleasant, WI (village) Racine County	171	0.67
Green, OH (city) Summit County	170	0.67
Silverdale, WA (cdp) Kitsap County	126	0.67
Chamblee, GA (city) DeKalb County	65	0.67
Plymouth, MI (city) Wayne County	61	0.67
Frenchtown, MI (township) Monroe County	136	0.65
Bull Mountain, OR (cdp) Washington County	60	0.65
South Lebanon, PA (township) Lebanon County	60	0.65
Wahpeton, ND (city) Richland County	51	0.65
Murrysville, PA (municipality) Westmoreland County	128	0.64
Cecil, PA (township) Washington County	70	0.64
Cheat Lake, WV (cdp) Monongalia County	49	0.64
Mason City, IA (city) Cerro Gordo County	176	0.63
Fairmount, NY (cdp) Onondaga County	63	0.63
Rio del Mar, CA (cdp) Santa Cruz County	59	0.63
Prospect Heights, IL (city) Cook County	100	0.62
Brooklyn, OH (city) Cuyahoga County	69	0.62
Derby, CT (city/town) New Haven County	78	0.61
North Strabane, PA (township) Washington County	78	0.61
Larkspur, CA (city) Marin County	72	0.61
Mack, OH (cdp) Hamilton County	70	0.61
McKeesport, PA (city) Allegheny County	122	0.60
Seven Hills, OH (city) Cuyahoga County	71	0.60
Powell, OH (city) Delaware County	64	0.59
Long Branch, VA (cdp) Fairfax County	47	0.59
Peters, PA (township) Washington County	119	0.58
Washington, MI (township) Macomb County	137	0.57
Greensburg, PA (city) Westmoreland County	86	0.57
Barrington, IL (village) Cook County	61	0.57
Moundsville, WV (city) Marshall County	54	0.57
Fort Lee, NJ (borough) Bergen County	197	0.56
Fairview Park, OH (city) Cuyahoga County	94	0.56
La Grange, IL (village) Cook County	87	0.56
Lindenhurst, IL (village) Lake County	80	0.56
Spring Valley, NV (cdp) Clark County	941	0.55
Butte-Silver Bow, MT (cons. govt) Silver Bow County	181	0.55
Westlake, OH (city) Cuyahoga County	178	0.55
Griffith, IN (town) Lake County	93	0.55

SECTION THREE

Please refer to the Explanation of Data in the front of the book for more detailed information.

Ancestry

Slavic

U.S. and 50 States Sorted by Population and Percent of Total Population

Place	Population	%
United States	**136,830**	**0.05**
Pennsylvania	17,175	0.14
California	13,137	0.04
New York	9,898	0.05
Ohio	8,235	0.07
New Jersey	7,764	0.09
Florida	6,656	0.04
Michigan	6,334	0.06
Illinois	5,900	0.05
Minnesota	4,296	0.08
Texas	4,227	0.02
Virginia	4,021	0.05
Colorado	3,852	0.08
Wisconsin	3,684	0.07
Washington	3,287	0.05
Maryland	3,039	0.05
North Carolina	2,554	0.03
Arizona	2,540	0.04
Indiana	2,352	0.04
Connecticut	2,028	0.06
Georgia	2,026	0.02
Oregon	1,847	0.05
Massachusetts	1,651	0.03
Missouri	1,643	0.03
Tennessee	1,522	0.02
South Carolina	1,340	0.03
Nevada	1,230	0.05
Montana	1,123	0.12
West Virginia	1,048	0.06
Kansas	1,024	0.04
New Mexico	955	0.05
Mississippi	913	0.03
Wyoming	846	0.16
Utah	838	0.03
Nebraska	807	0.04
Alabama	698	0.01
Louisiana	690	0.02
Kentucky	661	0.02
Oklahoma	655	0.02
Maine	640	0.05
Delaware	583	0.07
Iowa	576	0.02
Idaho	546	0.04
Arkansas	445	0.02
Alaska	420	0.06
North Dakota	260	0.04
New Hampshire	214	0.02
Vermont	209	0.03
Hawaii	153	0.01
District of Columbia	134	0.02
South Dakota	80	0.01
Rhode Island	74	0.01

Place	Population	%
Wyoming	846	0.16
Pennsylvania	17,175	0.14
Montana	1,123	0.12
New Jersey	7,764	0.09
Minnesota	4,296	0.08
Colorado	3,852	0.08
Ohio	8,235	0.07
Wisconsin	3,684	0.07
Delaware	583	0.07
Michigan	6,334	0.06
Connecticut	2,028	0.06
West Virginia	1,048	0.06
Alaska	420	0.06
United States	**136,830**	**0.05**
New York	9,898	0.05
Illinois	5,900	0.05
Virginia	4,021	0.05
Washington	3,287	0.05
Maryland	3,039	0.05
Oregon	1,847	0.05
Nevada	1,230	0.05
New Mexico	955	0.05
Maine	640	0.05
California	13,137	0.04
Florida	6,656	0.04
Arizona	2,540	0.04
Indiana	2,352	0.04
Kansas	1,024	0.04
Nebraska	807	0.04
Idaho	546	0.04
North Dakota	260	0.04
North Carolina	2,554	0.03
Massachusetts	1,651	0.03
Missouri	1,643	0.03
South Carolina	1,340	0.03
Mississippi	913	0.03
Utah	838	0.03
Vermont	209	0.03
Texas	4,227	0.02
Georgia	2,026	0.02
Tennessee	1,522	0.02
Louisiana	690	0.02
Kentucky	661	0.02
Oklahoma	655	0.02
Iowa	576	0.02
Arkansas	445	0.02
New Hampshire	214	0.02
District of Columbia	134	0.02
Alabama	698	0.01
Hawaii	153	0.01
South Dakota	80	0.01
Rhode Island	74	0.01

Please refer to the Explanation of Data in the front of the book for more detailed information.

Ancestry

Slavic

Top 150 Places Sorted by Population

Based on all places, regardless of total population

Place	Population	%
New York, NY (city) Kings County	1,962	0.02
Chicago, IL (city) Cook County	1,157	0.04
Queens, NY (borough) Queens County	765	0.03
Los Angeles, CA (city) Los Angeles County	742	0.02
San Francisco, CA (city) San Francisco County	627	0.08
Brooklyn, NY (borough) Kings County	564	0.02
Phoenix, AZ (city) Maricopa County	541	0.04
Philadelphia, PA (city) Philadelphia County	498	0.03
San Diego, CA (city) San Diego County	468	0.04
Columbus, OH (city) Franklin County	458	0.06
Indianapolis, IN (city) Marion County	455	0.06
Jacksonville, FL (city) Duval County	448	0.06
Seattle, WA (city) King County	444	0.07
Pittsburgh, PA (city) Allegheny County	428	0.14
Portland, OR (city) Multnomah County	412	0.07
Omaha, NE (city) Douglas County	408	0.10
Manhattan, NY (borough) New York County	400	0.03
D'Iberville, MS (city) Harrison County	392	4.40
Bayonne, NJ (city) Hudson County	347	0.56
Charlotte, NC (city) Mecklenburg County	340	0.05
Minneapolis, MN (city) Hennepin County	308	0.08
Union, NY (town) Broome County	291	0.52
Austin, TX (city) Travis County	289	0.04
Paradise, NV (cdp) Clark County	288	0.13
Hamilton, NJ (township) Mercer County	286	0.32
Milwaukee, WI (city) Milwaukee County	281	0.05
Denver, CO (city) Denver County	269	0.05
Duluth, MN (city) St. Louis County	256	0.30
Colorado Springs, CO (city) El Paso County	255	0.06
Rock Springs, WY (city) Sweetwater County	254	1.15
Murfreesboro, TN (city) Rutherford County	244	0.24
Houston, TX (city) Harris County	242	0.01
Tucson, AZ (city) Pima County	241	0.05
Greece, NY (town) Monroe County	240	0.25
Yonkers, NY (city) Westchester County	237	0.12
San Jose, CA (city) Santa Clara County	235	0.03
Lower Paxton, PA (township) Dauphin County	232	0.50
Cleveland, OH (city) Cuyahoga County	232	0.06
Las Vegas, NV (city) Clark County	232	0.04
Sunnyvale, CA (city) Santa Clara County	228	0.17
Oklahoma City, OK (city) Oklahoma County	223	0.04
Mesa, AZ (city) Maricopa County	222	0.05
Biloxi, MS (city) Harrison County	216	0.49
North Tonawanda, NY (city) Niagara County	209	0.66
Macomb, MI (township) Macomb County	204	0.27
Rancho Palos Verdes, CA (city) Los Angeles County	203	0.49
Anchorage, AK (municipality) Anchorage Municipality	203	0.07
Chesapeake, VA (ind. city) Chesapeake independent city	200	0.09
Derry, PA (township) Dauphin County	198	0.82
Boise City, ID (city) Ada County	195	0.09
North Hempstead, NY (town) Nassau County	195	0.09
Madison, WI (city) Dane County	194	0.08
Albuquerque, NM (city) Bernalillo County	194	0.04
Tacoma, WA (city) Pierce County	193	0.10
Louisville-Jefferson County, KY (metro govt) Jefferson County	189	0.03
Fargo, ND (city) Cass County	187	0.18
San Antonio, TX (city) Medina County	184	0.01
Hempfield, PA (township) Westmoreland County	183	0.43
Alexandria, VA (ind. city) Alexandria independent city	176	0.13
Aurora, CO (city) Arapahoe County	176	0.06
Independence, MI (charter township) Oakland County	174	0.51
Oyster Bay, NY (town) Nassau County	173	0.06
Corvallis, OR (city) Benton County	172	0.32
New Rochelle, NY (city) Westchester County	171	0.23
Mahwah, NJ (township) Bergen County	168	0.66
Santa Monica, CA (city) Los Angeles County	167	0.19
Hempstead, NY (town) Nassau County	166	0.02
Casper, WY (city) Natrona County	162	0.30
Gilbert, AZ (town) Maricopa County	161	0.08
Sacramento, CA (city) Sacramento County	161	0.04
San Clemente, CA (city) Orange County	160	0.26
Coral Springs, FL (city) Broward County	158	0.13
East Haven, CT (cdp/town) New Haven County	157	0.54
Thornton, CO (city) Adams County	157	0.14
Long Beach, CA (city) Los Angeles County	157	0.03
South Riding, VA (cdp) Loudoun County	156	0.68
Hibbing, MN (city) St. Louis County	155	0.95
Canton, MI (charter township) Wayne County	154	0.18
San Buenaventura (Ventura), CA (city) Ventura County	153	0.15
Pueblo, CO (city) Pueblo County	153	0.14
Amherst, NY (town) Erie County	153	0.13
Joliet, IL (city) Will County	153	0.11
St. Paul, MN (city) Ramsey County	152	0.05
Billings, MT (city) Yellowstone County	150	0.15
Virginia Beach, VA (ind. city) Virginia Beach independent city	148	0.03
Edison, NJ (township) Middlesex County	147	0.15
Millcreek, PA (township) Erie County	145	0.27
Parma, OH (city) Cuyahoga County	145	0.18
Cottonwood Heights, UT (city) Salt Lake County	144	0.43
Beaverton, OR (city) Washington County	144	0.16
Fresno, CA (city) Fresno County	144	0.03
Delta, MI (charter township) Eaton County	143	0.44
Catalina Foothills, AZ (cdp) Pima County	143	0.27
Staten Island, NY (borough) Richmond County	143	0.03
Shaler, PA (township) Allegheny County	141	0.49
Scottsdale, AZ (city) Maricopa County	140	0.06
Eden Prairie, MN (city) Hennepin County	139	0.23
Alafaya, FL (cdp) Orange County	139	0.18
Troy, MI (city) Oakland County	139	0.17
Dallas, TX (city) Dallas County	139	0.01
North Braddock, PA (borough) Allegheny County	138	2.72
Hopewell, PA (township) Beaver County	135	1.07
New Castle, PA (city) Lawrence County	135	0.57
McCandless, PA (township) Allegheny County	135	0.48
Hamden, CT (town) New Haven County	135	0.22
Washington, DC (city) District of Columbia	134	0.02
Cuyahoga Falls, OH (city) Summit County	132	0.27
Roanoke, VA (ind. city) Roanoke independent city	132	0.14
Centennial, CO (city) Arapahoe County	132	0.13
Evesham, NJ (township) Burlington County	131	0.29
Vestal, NY (town) Broome County	130	0.46
Binghamton, NY (city) Broome County	130	0.27
Springfield, IL (city) Sangamon County	129	0.11
Washington, NJ (borough) Warren County	128	1.94
Waverly, MI (cdp) Eaton County	128	0.52
Berkeley, CA (city) Alameda County	128	0.12
Fairfield, CA (city) Solano County	128	0.12
Nashville-Davidson, TN (metro govt) Davidson County	128	0.02
Gorham, ME (town) Cumberland County	127	0.79
Land O' Lakes, FL (cdp) Pasco County	127	0.39
Erie, PA (city) Erie County	127	0.12
Lyon, MI (charter township) Oakland County	123	0.88
Tonawanda, NY (town) Erie County	123	0.17
Chapel Hill, NC (town) Orange County	122	0.22
Elizabeth, PA (township) Allegheny County	121	0.91
Leawood, KS (city) Johnson County	121	0.39
Spring Valley, NV (cdp) Clark County	121	0.07
Gorham, ME (cdp) Cumberland County	120	1.65
Niles, IL (village) Cook County	120	0.41
Zionsville, IN (town) Boone County	119	0.89
Penn, PA (township) Westmoreland County	119	0.60
Columbia, SC (city) Richland County	119	0.09
Boston, MA (city) Suffolk County	119	0.02
Lawrenceville, GA (city) Gwinnett County	118	0.43
Lawrence, KS (city) Douglas County	118	0.14
Lemont, IL (village) Cook County	117	0.76
Brunswick, OH (city) Medina County	117	0.34
Laguna Niguel, CA (city) Orange County	117	0.19
Manteca, CA (city) San Joaquin County	117	0.18
Summerville, SC (town) Dorchester County	116	0.29
Smithtown, NY (town) Suffolk County	116	0.10
Chandler, AZ (city) Maricopa County	116	0.05
Norfolk, VA (ind. city) Norfolk independent city	116	0.05
Woodbridge, NJ (township) Middlesex County	115	0.12
Everett, WA (city) Snohomish County	115	0.11
Glenshaw, PA (cdp) Allegheny County	114	1.24
Sayreville, NJ (borough) Middlesex County	114	0.27
Woodbury, MN (city) Washington County	113	0.19
Green Bay, WI (city) Brown County	113	0.11
Nokesville, VA (cdp) Prince William County	112	8.28

Please refer to the Explanation of Data in the front of the book for more detailed information.

SECTION THREE

Ancestry

Slavic

Top 150 Places Sorted by Percent of Total Population

Based on all places, regardless of total population

Place	Population	%
Port Colden, NJ (cdp) Warren County	48	76.19
Swiftwater, MN (township) Lake of the Woods County	17	42.50
Jesterville, MD (cdp) Wicomico County	79	23.30
Geyser, MT (cdp) Judith Basin County	3	16.67
Lafferty, OH (cdp) Belmont County	35	15.98
Brown City, MI (city) Lapeer County	4	13.79
Sand Coulee, MT (cdp) Cascade County	24	12.70
Kerrtown, PA (cdp) Crawford County	38	11.55
Groveland, CA (cdp) Tuolumne County	31	8.76
Chisholm, ME (cdp) Franklin County	103	8.38
Nokesville, VA (cdp) Prince William County	112	8.28
Cinnamon Lake, OH (cdp) Ashland County	74	8.15
Hatton, AL (cdp) Lawrence County	12	7.95
Washingtonville, OH (village) Columbiana County	62	6.87
Hobson, MT (city) Judith Basin County	14	6.86
McKinley, MN (city) St. Louis County	3	6.82
Southview, PA (cdp) Washington County	10	6.67
Burr Oak, IA (cdp) Winneshiek County	12	6.56
Seltzer, PA (cdp) Schuylkill County	19	6.42
Calumet, PA (cdp) Westmoreland County	61	5.99
Lakeside, MT (cdp) Flathead County	93	5.78
Palmdale, PA (cdp) Dauphin County	107	5.17
Sullivan, PA (township) Tioga County	74	5.07
Dunlo, PA (cdp) Cambria County	11	5.02
Lake of the Woods, CA (cdp) Kern County	46	4.67
Exeter, PA (township) Luzerne County	102	4.57
Hoffman, MN (city) Grant County	27	4.55
Blaine, PA (township) Washington County	22	4.47
D'Iberville, MS (city) Harrison County	392	4.40
Fall Lake, MN (township) Lake County	27	4.38
Buras, LA (cdp) Plaquemines Parish	27	4.28
Watertown, FL (cdp) Columbia County	98	4.24
Knowlton, WI (cdp) Marathon County	6	4.23
Potter, NE (village) Cheyenne County	16	4.22
Spring Hill, PA (cdp) Cambria County	41	3.96
Finlayson, MN (city) Pine County	12	3.96
Knox, PA (township) Clearfield County	22	3.93
Slickville, PA (cdp) Westmoreland County	15	3.87
Gilbert, MN (city) St. Louis County	67	3.79
Mount Crested Butte, CO (town) Gunnison County	21	3.76
Thomas, WV (city) Tucker County	17	3.76
Emery, UT (town) Emery County	13	3.76
Cavetown, MD (cdp) Washington County	48	3.70
Rupert, VT (town) Bennington County	36	3.68
Gales, MD (town) Dorchester County	2	3.51
Tannersville, NY (village) Greene County	15	3.46
Mason, WI (village) Bayfield County	2	3.45
South Deerfield, MA (cdp) Franklin County	62	3.44
Valencia, NM (cdp) Valencia County	83	3.43
Reliance, WY (cdp) Sweetwater County	24	3.39
Kugler, MN (township) St. Louis County	5	3.38
Bethany, PA (borough) Wayne County	13	3.28
Port Vincent, LA (village) Livingston Parish	25	3.23
Rhinecliff, NY (cdp) Dutchess County	12	3.23
Elgin, PA (borough) Erie County	8	3.20
Miller, PA (township) Huntingdon County	13	3.17
Biwabik, MN (city) St. Louis County	34	3.16
Summerhill, PA (borough) Cambria County	12	3.10
Cassandra, PA (borough) Cambria County	4	3.10
Aquadale, NC (cdp) Stanly County	15	3.06
Sharon, CT (cdp) Litchfield County	21	3.02
Brockway, PA (borough) Jefferson County	63	2.98
Eaton, WI (town) Clark County	24	2.96
Castle Pines, CO (cdp) Douglas County	106	2.92
Amity, PA (township) Erie County	29	2.90
Sea Girt, NJ (borough) Monmouth County	55	2.82
Janesville, CA (cdp) Lassen County	34	2.82
Vaughn, WA (cdp) Pierce County	12	2.82
Coffee Creek, CA (cdp) Trinity County	5	2.82
South Coventry, CT (cdp) Tolland County	38	2.80
Makinen, MN (unorganized territory) St. Louis County	34	2.80
Madisonburg, PA (cdp) Centre County	3	2.80
Stony River, MN (township) Lake County	6	2.75
North Braddock, PA (borough) Allegheny County	138	2.72
Ruby, WI (town) Chippewa County	16	2.72
Depauville, NY (cdp) Jefferson County	12	2.70
Fayal, MN (township) St. Louis County	43	2.68
Oxford, NJ (cdp) Warren County	31	2.66
Lilly, PA (borough) Cambria County	24	2.65
Limestone, PA (township) Warren County	7	2.64
Winton, MN (city) St. Louis County	5	2.63
Marshallville, OH (village) Wayne County	21	2.62
Calumet, MI (village) Houghton County	19	2.62
West Finley, PA (township) Washington County	20	2.56
Gaskill, PA (township) Jefferson County	19	2.56
Laurys Station, PA (cdp) Lehigh County	33	2.52
Jefferson Heights, NY (cdp) Greene County	40	2.51
Tresckow, PA (cdp) Carbon County	21	2.47
Dalton, WI (cdp) Green Lake County	4	2.47
Collinsburg, PA (cdp) Westmoreland County	28	2.46
Parkton, NC (town) Robeson County	11	2.45
Sharpsburg, MD (town) Washington County	16	2.42
Bear Creek, WI (village) Outagamie County	11	2.42
Superior, WI (town) Douglas County	50	2.41
Seneca, WI (town) Green Lake County	11	2.41
East Berwick, PA (cdp) Luzerne County	46	2.37
McConnell, WV (cdp) Logan County	15	2.37
Millsboro, PA (cdp) Washington County	11	2.37
Merlin, OR (cdp) Josephine County	45	2.36
Oberlin, PA (cdp) Dauphin County	14	2.35
North Star, MN (township) St. Louis County	5	2.35
Norvelt, PA (cdp) Westmoreland County	22	2.34
So-Hi, AZ (cdp) Mohave County	21	2.28
Lenkerville, PA (cdp) Dauphin County	13	2.28
Bryantown, MD (cdp) Charles County	15	2.27
Blooming Valley, PA (borough) Crawford County	10	2.26
Wilmot, NH (town) Merrimack County	28	2.24
Silver Lake, WI (village) Kenosha County	54	2.23
Joffre, PA (cdp) Washington County	14	2.23
Soudan, MN (cdp) St. Louis County	10	2.22
Long Beach, IN (town) LaPorte County	32	2.19
Anderson, WI (town) Iron County	2	2.15
Shannondale, WV (cdp) Jefferson County	54	2.14
La Barge, WY (town) Lincoln County	11	2.14
Millston, WI (cdp) Jackson County	2	2.13
Anson, ME (cdp) Somerset County	20	2.12
Big Falls, MN (city) Koochiching County	5	2.12
Jay, ME (town) Franklin County	103	2.11
Au Train, MI (township) Alger County	24	2.08
Beaverdale, PA (cdp) Cambria County	23	2.07
Shorewood Forest, IN (cdp) Porter County	62	2.06
Beallsville, PA (borough) Washington County	9	2.06
Spring Creek, PA (township) Warren County	17	2.04
Leadville, CO (city) Lake County	53	2.01
Sand Creek, WI (town) Dunn County	10	1.98
Marklesburg, PA (borough) Huntingdon County	4	1.98
Sand Lake, MN (unorganized territory) St. Louis County	19	1.97
Humphrey, NE (city) Platte County	17	1.97
Randolph, MN (city) Dakota County	7	1.97
Harmony, NY (town) Chautauqua County	44	1.96
Apalachin, NY (cdp) Tioga County	22	1.96
Cedar Grove, NM (cdp) Santa Fe County	11	1.96
Dixon, MT (cdp) Sanders County	8	1.95
Washington, NJ (borough) Warren County	128	1.94
Edom, TX (city) Van Zandt County	7	1.94
Boswell, PA (borough) Somerset County	28	1.91
Laflin, PA (borough) Luzerne County	29	1.90
Middleport, PA (borough) Schuylkill County	8	1.90
Riverside, NY (cdp) Suffolk County	53	1.89
Sykesville, PA (borough) Jefferson County	25	1.88
Oakwood, PA (cdp) Lawrence County	39	1.86
Farley, MO (village) Platte County	6	1.86
Lazy Mountain, AK (cdp) Matanuska-Susitna Borough	18	1.85
Florence, NJ (cdp) Burlington County	85	1.84
Johnsonburg, PA (borough) Elk County	50	1.84
Amber, MI (township) Mason County	45	1.83
Swoyersville, PA (borough) Luzerne County	92	1.82
Lewisville, WA (cdp) Clark County	37	1.82
Boggs, PA (township) Centre County	54	1.81
Ogema, MN (city) Becker County	3	1.81

Please refer to the Explanation of Data in the front of the book for more detailed information.

Ancestry

Slavic

Top 150 Places Sorted by Percent of Total Population

Based on places with total population of 7,500 or more

Place	Population	%
D'Iberville, MS (city) Harrison County	392	4.40
Cheat Lake, WV (cdp) Monongalia County	102	1.34
Glenshaw, PA (cdp) Allegheny County	114	1.24
Rock Springs, WY (city) Sweetwater County	254	1.15
Kulpsville, PA (cdp) Montgomery County	88	1.13
Millis, MA (town) Norfolk County	87	1.11
Hopewell, PA (township) Beaver County	135	1.07
Grove City, PA (borough) Mercer County	82	0.99
West Point, UT (city) Davis County	87	0.98
Mount Pleasant, PA (township) Westmoreland County	105	0.96
Hibbing, MN (city) St. Louis County	155	0.95
Woodland Park, NJ (borough) Passaic County	108	0.93
New Hyde Park, NY (village) Nassau County	89	0.93
Latrobe, PA (city) Westmoreland County	79	0.93
Elizabeth, PA (township) Allegheny County	121	0.91
Los Alamos, NM (cdp) Los Alamos County	108	0.90
Zionsville, IN (town) Boone County	119	0.89
Lyon, MI (charter township) Oakland County	123	0.88
Bridgeport, WV (city) Harrison County	70	0.88
Butler, PA (township) Luzerne County	76	0.86
Robbinsville, NJ (township) Mercer County	110	0.85
Ojai, CA (city) Ventura County	63	0.84
Derry, PA (township) Dauphin County	198	0.82
Florence, NJ (township) Burlington County	96	0.80
Gorham, ME (town) Cumberland County	127	0.79
Economy, PA (borough) Beaver County	71	0.79
Northampton, PA (borough) Northampton County	77	0.78
Lemont, IL (village) Cook County	117	0.76
Hazle, PA (township) Luzerne County	71	0.76
Succasunna, NJ (cdp) Morris County	67	0.75
West Deer, PA (township) Allegheny County	86	0.74
Sheboygan Falls, WI (city) Sheboygan County	56	0.74
Metuchen, NJ (borough) Middlesex County	97	0.72
Worcester, PA (township) Montgomery County	67	0.71
Hershey, PA (cdp) Dauphin County	91	0.70
Glenwood Springs, CO (city) Garfield County	66	0.70
Spring Garden, PA (township) York County	85	0.69
Rostraver, PA (township) Westmoreland County	79	0.69
Moore, PA (township) Northampton County	63	0.69
South Riding, VA (cdp) Loudoun County	156	0.68
DuBois, PA (city) Clearfield County	53	0.68
Mayo, MD (cdp) Anne Arundel County	53	0.68
Grand Ledge, MI (city) Eaton County	53	0.67
Grand Ledge, MI (city) Eaton County	53	0.67
North Tonawanda, NY (city) Niagara County	209	0.66
Mahwah, NJ (township) Bergen County	168	0.66
Cecil, PA (township) Washington County	71	0.65
Sweet Home, OR (city) Linn County	56	0.64
Oneida, NY (city) Madison County	72	0.63
Penn, PA (township) Westmoreland County	119	0.60
Lower Burrell, PA (city) Westmoreland County	70	0.59
Minooka, IL (village) Grundy County	56	0.59
Mansfield, NJ (township) Burlington County	47	0.59
Dormont, PA (borough) Allegheny County	50	0.58
New Castle, PA (city) Lawrence County	135	0.57
Pell City, AL (city) St. Clair County	70	0.57
Bayonne, NJ (city) Hudson County	347	0.56
Hamilton, PA (township) Monroe County	51	0.56
Half Moon, NC (cdp) Onslow County	46	0.56
Conway, SC (city) Horry County	91	0.55
Virginia, MN (city) St. Louis County	48	0.55
Bernalillo, NM (town) Sandoval County	44	0.55
East Haven, CT (cdp/town) New Haven County	157	0.54
Kings Park West, VA (cdp) Fairfax County	78	0.54
Cascades, VA (cdp) Loudoun County	65	0.54
Lower Swatara, PA (township) Dauphin County	44	0.54
Scarsdale, NY (town/village) Westchester County	91	0.53
Meadville, PA (city) Crawford County	72	0.53
Wood-Ridge, NJ (borough) Bergen County	40	0.53
Union, NY (town) Broome County	291	0.52
Waverly, MI (cdp) Eaton County	128	0.52
St. Marys, PA (city) Elk County	69	0.52
New Richmond, WI (city) St. Croix County	43	0.52
Ocean, NJ (township) Ocean County	42	0.52
Mantua, VA (cdp) Fairfax County	39	0.52
Independence, MI (charter township) Oakland County	174	0.51
West Mifflin, PA (borough) Allegheny County	104	0.51
Louisville, CO (city) Boulder County	94	0.51
Hamilton Square, NJ (cdp) Mercer County	68	0.51
South Union, PA (township) Fayette County	55	0.51
Evergreen, CO (cdp) Jefferson County	47	0.51
Sodus, NY (town) Wayne County	43	0.51
Pleasant Hills, PA (borough) Allegheny County	42	0.51
Lower Paxton, PA (township) Dauphin County	232	0.50
Towamencin, PA (township) Montgomery County	88	0.50
Kemp Mill, MD (cdp) Montgomery County	60	0.50
Lake Mohawk, NJ (cdp) Sussex County	50	0.50
Fairview, CA (cdp) Alameda County	49	0.50
Marina del Rey, CA (cdp) Los Angeles County	46	0.50
Monona, WI (city) Dane County	38	0.50
Biloxi, MS (city) Harrison County	216	0.49
Rancho Palos Verdes, CA (city) Los Angeles County	203	0.49
Shaler, PA (township) Allegheny County	141	0.49
Oil City, PA (city) Venango County	52	0.49
Northwest Harborcreek, PA (cdp) Erie County	44	0.49
Camp Hill, PA (borough) Cumberland County	38	0.49
McCandless, PA (township) Allegheny County	135	0.48
Eastlake, OH (city) Lake County	91	0.48
Denville, NJ (township) Morris County	80	0.48
New Paltz, NY (town) Ulster County	67	0.48
Mount Vernon, VA (cdp) Fairfax County	56	0.48
Marlborough, NY (town) Ulster County	42	0.48
Doylestown, PA (borough) Bucks County	40	0.48
Oconomowoc, WI (town) Waukesha County	40	0.48
Holmdel, NJ (township) Monmouth County	78	0.47
Wickliffe, OH (city) Lake County	61	0.47
Byram, NJ (township) Sussex County	40	0.47
Vestal, NY (town) Broome County	130	0.46
Waukee, IA (city) Dallas County	57	0.46
Pontiac, IL (city) Livingston County	56	0.46
Milford, PA (township) Bucks County	45	0.46
The Village, OK (city) Oklahoma County	42	0.46
Lamar, CO (city) Prowers County	36	0.46
Catskill, NY (town) Greene County	53	0.45
Capitola, CA (city) Santa Cruz County	44	0.45
Charlotte, MI (city) Eaton County	41	0.45
Lopatcong, NJ (township) Warren County	35	0.45
Delta, MI (charter township) Eaton County	143	0.44
Haledon, NJ (borough) Passaic County	36	0.44
Mapleton, UT (city) Utah County	33	0.44
Hempfield, PA (township) Westmoreland County	183	0.43
Cottonwood Heights, UT (city) Salt Lake County	144	0.43
Lawrenceville, GA (city) Gwinnett County	118	0.43
Stafford, NJ (township) Ocean County	112	0.43
Estero, FL (cdp) Lee County	91	0.43
Upper Providence, PA (township) Montgomery County	87	0.43
Aliquippa, PA (city) Beaver County	42	0.43
Zanesville, OH (city) Muskingum County	108	0.42
Willoughby, OH (city) Lake County	94	0.42
Chantilly, VA (cdp) Fairfax County	93	0.42
Kuna, ID (city) Ada County	58	0.42
Robinson, PA (township) Allegheny County	55	0.42
North Strabane, PA (township) Washington County	54	0.42
Farmington, MI (city) Oakland County	44	0.42
Blackhawk, CA (cdp) Contra Costa County	40	0.42
St. Pete Beach, FL (city) Pinellas County	40	0.42
Topanga, CA (cdp) Los Angeles County	36	0.42
North Star, DE (cdp) New Castle County	33	0.42
Mahtomedi, MN (city) Washington County	32	0.42
Waikele, HI (cdp) Honolulu County	32	0.42
Niles, IL (village) Cook County	120	0.41
Lenoir, NC (city) Caldwell County	75	0.41
Willow Grove, PA (cdp) Montgomery County	68	0.41
Kenmore, NY (village) Erie County	64	0.41
Fraser, MI (city) Macomb County	60	0.41
Loveland, OH (city) Hamilton County	48	0.41
Stuarts Draft, VA (cdp) Augusta County	31	0.41
Wilton, NY (town) Saratoga County	62	0.40
South Fayette, PA (township) Allegheny County	55	0.40
Cedar Grove, NJ (township) Essex County	49	0.40

SECTION THREE

Please refer to the Explanation of Data in the front of the book for more detailed information.

Ancestry

Slovak

U.S. and 50 States Sorted by Population and Percent of Total Population

Place	Population	%
United States	**805,282**	**0.26**
Pennsylvania	244,706	1.94
Ohio	144,300	1.25
Illinois	41,893	0.33
New Jersey	41,166	0.47
New York	35,389	0.18
Florida	33,763	0.18
Michigan	27,400	0.28
California	24,859	0.07
Connecticut	22,283	0.63
Indiana	21,051	0.33
Virginia	15,111	0.19
Wisconsin	14,101	0.25
Maryland	12,869	0.23
Texas	10,918	0.04
North Carolina	10,408	0.11
Arizona	10,327	0.17
Colorado	9,132	0.19
Minnesota	8,206	0.16
Massachusetts	7,448	0.11
Georgia	6,996	0.07
Washington	6,718	0.10
Missouri	5,031	0.08
South Carolina	4,937	0.11
West Virginia	4,579	0.25
Tennessee	3,915	0.06
Oregon	3,684	0.10
Nevada	3,617	0.14
Kentucky	2,743	0.06
Delaware	1,961	0.22
Maine	1,960	0.15
Iowa	1,878	0.06
New Mexico	1,836	0.09
New Hampshire	1,718	0.13
Kansas	1,606	0.06
Alabama	1,596	0.03
Utah	1,503	0.06
Oklahoma	1,425	0.04
Montana	1,203	0.12
Louisiana	1,187	0.03
Nebraska	1,125	0.06
Rhode Island	1,124	0.11
Arkansas	1,056	0.04
Vermont	1,037	0.17
District of Columbia	930	0.16
Alaska	925	0.13
Idaho	922	0.06
Mississippi	796	0.03
Wyoming	709	0.13
Hawaii	596	0.04
South Dakota	353	0.04
North Dakota	286	0.04

Place	Population	%
Pennsylvania	244,706	1.94
Ohio	144,300	1.25
Connecticut	22,283	0.63
New Jersey	41,166	0.47
Illinois	41,893	0.33
Indiana	21,051	0.33
Michigan	27,400	0.28
United States	**805,282**	**0.26**
Wisconsin	14,101	0.25
West Virginia	4,579	0.25
Maryland	12,869	0.23
Delaware	1,961	0.22
Virginia	15,111	0.19
Colorado	9,132	0.19
New York	35,389	0.18
Florida	33,763	0.18
Arizona	10,327	0.17
Vermont	1,037	0.17
Minnesota	8,206	0.16
District of Columbia	930	0.16
Maine	1,960	0.15
Nevada	3,617	0.14
New Hampshire	1,718	0.13
Alaska	925	0.13
Wyoming	709	0.13
Montana	1,203	0.12
North Carolina	10,408	0.11
Massachusetts	7,448	0.11
South Carolina	4,937	0.11
Rhode Island	1,124	0.11
Washington	6,718	0.10
Oregon	3,684	0.10
New Mexico	1,836	0.09
Missouri	5,031	0.08
California	24,859	0.07
Georgia	6,996	0.07
Tennessee	3,915	0.06
Kentucky	2,743	0.06
Iowa	1,878	0.06
Kansas	1,606	0.06
Utah	1,503	0.06
Nebraska	1,125	0.06
Idaho	922	0.06
Texas	10,918	0.04
Oklahoma	1,425	0.04
Arkansas	1,056	0.04
Hawaii	596	0.04
South Dakota	353	0.04
North Dakota	286	0.04
Alabama	1,596	0.03
Louisiana	1,187	0.03
Mississippi	796	0.03

Please refer to the Explanation of Data in the front of the book for more detailed information.

Ancestry

Slovak

Top 150 Places Sorted by Population

Based on all places, regardless of total population

Place	Population	%
Cleveland, OH (city) Cuyahoga County	7,074	1.73
New York, NY (city) Kings County	6,785	0.08
Parma, OH (city) Cuyahoga County	6,760	8.25
Pittsburgh, PA (city) Allegheny County	5,935	1.93
Chicago, IL (city) Cook County	4,761	0.18
Columbus, OH (city) Franklin County	3,380	0.44
Youngstown, OH (city) Mahoning County	3,113	4.47
North Huntingdon, PA (township) Westmoreland County	3,038	10.02
Union, NY (town) Broome County	3,003	5.33
Strongsville, OH (city) Cuyahoga County	2,962	6.68
West Mifflin, PA (borough) Allegheny County	2,921	14.25
Boardman, OH (cdp) Mahoning County	2,764	7.81
Stratford, CT (cdp/town) Fairfield County	2,753	5.42
Hempfield, PA (township) Westmoreland County	2,694	6.27
Bethlehem, PA (city) Northampton County	2,574	3.44
Philadelphia, PA (city) Philadelphia County	2,480	0.16
Lakewood, OH (city) Cuyahoga County	2,432	4.62
Manhattan, NY (borough) New York County	2,298	0.15
Austintown, OH (cdp) Mahoning County	2,267	7.50
Phoenix, AZ (city) Maricopa County	2,214	0.15
Akron, OH (city) Summit County	2,164	1.07
Hazleton, PA (city) Luzerne County	2,045	8.22
North Olmsted, OH (city) Cuyahoga County	2,024	6.17
Los Angeles, CA (city) Los Angeles County	1,904	0.05
Lorain, OH (city) Lorain County	1,882	2.89
Queens, NY (borough) Queens County	1,882	0.09
Brooklyn, NY (borough) Kings County	1,826	0.07
Brunswick, OH (city) Medina County	1,800	5.23
Hammond, IN (city) Lake County	1,791	2.20
North Royalton, OH (city) Cuyahoga County	1,719	5.74
Johnstown, PA (city) Cambria County	1,712	7.98
Unity, PA (township) Westmoreland County	1,706	7.63
Munhall, PA (borough) Allegheny County	1,676	14.63
Bethlehem, PA (city) Northampton County	1,659	2.99
Joliet, IL (city) Will County	1,601	1.10
Streator, IL (city) LaSalle County	1,596	12.10
Bethel Park, PA (municipality) Allegheny County	1,579	4.90
Elyria, OH (city) Lorain County	1,549	2.82
Allentown, PA (city) Lehigh County	1,543	1.33
Hamilton, NJ (township) Mercer County	1,508	1.71
Erie, PA (city) Erie County	1,499	1.47
Wilkes-Barre, PA (city) Luzerne County	1,497	3.60
Harrison, PA (township) Allegheny County	1,475	14.08
San Diego, CA (city) San Diego County	1,472	0.11
Struthers, OH (city) Mahoning County	1,441	13.23
Charlotte, NC (city) Mecklenburg County	1,441	0.20
North Ridgeville, OH (city) Lorain County	1,428	5.05
Milford, CT (town) New Haven County	1,428	2.71
Hermitage, PA (city) Mercer County	1,409	8.72
Milford, CT (city) New Haven County	1,397	2.74
Bridgeport, CT (city/town) Fairfield County	1,376	0.97
Ross, PA (township) Allegheny County	1,359	4.37
Shelton, CT (city/town) Fairfield County	1,351	3.46
Scranton, PA (city) Lackawanna County	1,344	1.77
Binghamton, NY (city) Broome County	1,334	2.81
North Union, PA (township) Fayette County	1,323	10.16
Rostraver, PA (township) Westmoreland County	1,315	11.51
South Union, PA (township) Fayette County	1,286	11.92
Monroeville, PA (municipality) Allegheny County	1,285	4.54
Avon, OH (city) Lorain County	1,282	6.57
Mentor, OH (city) Lake County	1,279	2.68
Westlake, OH (city) Cuyahoga County	1,268	3.92
Mount Pleasant, PA (township) Westmoreland County	1,256	11.48
Brook Park, OH (city) Cuyahoga County	1,255	6.45
Garfield Heights, OH (city) Cuyahoga County	1,253	4.31
Penn, PA (township) Westmoreland County	1,225	6.15
Plum, PA (borough) Allegheny County	1,214	4.52
Whitehall, PA (township) Lehigh County	1,204	4.54
Derry, PA (township) Westmoreland County	1,164	8.04
Colorado Springs, CO (city) El Paso County	1,163	0.29
Warren, OH (city) Trumbull County	1,161	2.72
Milwaukee, WI (city) Milwaukee County	1,159	0.20
McKeesport, PA (city) Allegheny County	1,158	5.69
Woodbridge, NJ (township) Middlesex County	1,139	1.15
Baldwin, PA (borough) Allegheny County	1,136	5.79
Cranberry, PA (township) Butler County	1,119	4.09
Hopewell, PA (township) Beaver County	1,103	8.72
North Versailles, PA (township) Allegheny County	1,098	10.67
McCandless, PA (township) Allegheny County	1,094	3.87
Indianapolis, IN (city) Marion County	1,058	0.13
Seattle, WA (city) King County	1,056	0.18
Elizabeth, PA (township) Allegheny County	1,052	7.92
Schererville, IN (town) Lake County	1,051	3.69
Hazle, PA (township) Luzerne County	1,049	11.18
Richland, PA (township) Cambria County	1,049	8.24
Euclid, OH (city) Cuyahoga County	1,043	2.11
Sterling Heights, MI (city) Macomb County	1,027	0.79
Parma Heights, OH (city) Cuyahoga County	1,023	4.92
Avon Lake, OH (city) Lorain County	1,021	4.67
Naperville, IL (city) DuPage County	1,015	0.72
Penn Hills, PA (township) Allegheny County	1,005	2.35
Broadview Heights, OH (city) Cuyahoga County	997	5.34
Middleburg Heights, OH (city) Cuyahoga County	971	6.15
Toledo, OH (city) Lucas County	945	0.32
Murrysville, PA (municipality) Westmoreland County	931	4.69
Washington, DC (city) District of Columbia	930	0.16
Trumbull, CT (cdp/town) Fairfield County	919	2.59
Bethlehem, PA (city) Lehigh County	915	4.74
Clifton, NJ (city) Passaic County	913	1.10
Johnson City, NY (village) Broome County	908	5.96
Linden, NJ (city) Union County	900	2.25
Lower Burrell, PA (city) Westmoreland County	898	7.54
Highland, IN (town) Lake County	896	3.78
Campbell, OH (city) Mahoning County	892	10.56
Rocky River, OH (city) Cuyahoga County	892	4.42
Fairview Park, OH (city) Cuyahoga County	891	5.27
Millcreek, PA (township) Erie County	886	1.67
Peters, PA (township) Washington County	885	4.31
Brecksville, OH (city) Cuyahoga County	882	6.51
Whitehall, PA (borough) Allegheny County	880	6.32
Mount Lebanon, PA (township) Allegheny County	879	2.68
White Oak, PA (borough) Allegheny County	878	11.11
Medina, OH (city) Medina County	873	3.27
San Francisco, CA (city) San Francisco County	861	0.11
Brooklyn, OH (city) Cuyahoga County	860	7.71
Minneapolis, MN (city) Hennepin County	857	0.23
Lower Macungie, PA (township) Lehigh County	856	2.99
Sharon, PA (city) Mercer County	848	5.87
South Whitehall, PA (township) Lehigh County	847	4.45
Jacksonville, FL (city) Duval County	847	0.10
Seven Hills, OH (city) Cuyahoga County	845	7.16
Stamford, CT (city/town) Fairfield County	836	0.69
Solon, OH (city) Cuyahoga County	824	3.59
Warren, MI (city) Macomb County	821	0.60
Munster, IN (town) Lake County	814	3.50
Upper Yoder, PA (township) Cambria County	810	14.73
Torrington, CT (city/town) Litchfield County	805	2.21
West Deer, PA (township) Allegheny County	803	6.91
Tucson, AZ (city) Pima County	803	0.15
Jefferson Hills, PA (borough) Allegheny County	795	7.66
Denver, CO (city) Denver County	794	0.14
Butler, PA (township) Butler County	791	4.56
Willoughby, OH (city) Lake County	789	3.55
Greensburg, PA (city) Westmoreland County	784	5.21
Bayonne, NJ (city) Hudson County	782	1.26
Houston, TX (city) Harris County	775	0.04
Virginia Beach, VA (ind. city) Virginia Beach independent city	774	0.18
Plains, PA (township) Luzerne County	772	7.67
New Kensington, PA (city) Westmoreland County	770	5.76
Portage, IN (city) Porter County	766	2.11
Mesa, AZ (city) Maricopa County	760	0.17
Barberton, OH (city) Summit County	759	2.83
Adams, PA (township) Cambria County	756	12.54
Shaler, PA (township) Allegheny County	756	2.63
White, PA (township) Indiana County	753	4.87
Endwell, NY (cdp) Broome County	740	6.33
Austin, TX (city) Travis County	732	0.10
Aurora, OH (city) Portage County	724	4.76
Robinson, PA (township) Allegheny County	723	5.53
Kingston, PA (borough) Luzerne County	723	5.46

Please refer to the Explanation of Data in the front of the book for more detailed information.

Ancestry

Slovak

Top 150 Places Sorted by Percent of Total Population

Based on all places, regardless of total population

Place	Population	%
Jeddo, PA (borough) Luzerne County	44	40.74
Mammoth, PA (cdp) Westmoreland County	234	40.55
Dicksonville, PA (cdp) Indiana County	167	35.68
Tresckow, PA (cdp) Carbon County	258	30.32
Norvelt, PA (cdp) Westmoreland County	275	29.19
Madrid, NM (cdp) Santa Fe County	24	27.27
Hawk Run, PA (cdp) Clearfield County	84	27.01
Dayton, MN (city) Wright County	26	26.80
Yankee Lake, OH (village) Trumbull County	18	26.09
Lattimer, PA (cdp) Luzerne County	103	25.75
Sutersville, PA (borough) Westmoreland County	156	24.61
Banks, PA (township) Carbon County	304	24.34
Beaver Meadows, PA (borough) Carbon County	195	24.10
Gorman, MD (cdp) Garrett County	19	24.05
Pilsen, WI (town) Bayfield County	36	24.00
Beaverdale, PA (cdp) Cambria County	266	23.90
Atwood, PA (borough) Armstrong County	32	23.02
Crabtree, PA (cdp) Westmoreland County	99	21.57
Stockdale, PA (borough) Washington County	120	21.43
Whitaker, PA (borough) Allegheny County	298	20.91
Brownstown, PA (borough) Cambria County	170	20.61
Edenborn, PA (cdp) Fayette County	21	20.59
South Versailles, PA (township) Allegheny County	68	19.10
Clarence, PA (cdp) Centre County	116	18.99
Leith-Hatfield, PA (cdp) Fayette County	529	18.79
Chase, PA (cdp) Luzerne County	246	18.24
Nesquehoning, PA (borough) Carbon County	606	18.04
Hostetter, PA (cdp) Westmoreland County	129	17.62
Kylertown, PA (cdp) Clearfield County	82	17.52
Lower Yoder, PA (township) Cambria County	478	17.43
Grassflat, PA (cdp) Clearfield County	87	17.26
Fowlerville, NY (cdp) Livingston County	42	17.00
Bobtown, PA (cdp) Greene County	176	16.89
Las Nutrias, NM (cdp) Socorro County	15	16.85
Roseville, PA (borough) Tioga County	26	16.77
Elrama, PA (cdp) Washington County	49	16.72
New Freeport, PA (cdp) Greene County	13	16.67
Brookfield Center, OH (cdp) Trumbull County	244	16.58
Jefferson, PA (township) Fayette County	372	16.54
Port Vue, PA (borough) Allegheny County	631	16.43
Cassandra, PA (borough) Cambria County	21	16.28
Snow Shoe, PA (township) Centre County	299	16.26
Webster, PA (cdp) Westmoreland County	52	16.25
Perryopolis, PA (borough) Fayette County	294	16.24
Covington, PA (township) Clearfield County	86	16.17
Ronco, PA (cdp) Fayette County	42	16.03
Hometown, PA (cdp) Schuylkill County	234	16.02
West Homestead, PA (borough) Allegheny County	327	15.98
Tuscarora, PA (cdp) Schuylkill County	131	15.88
Pardeesville, PA (cdp) Luzerne County	114	15.88
Perry, PA (township) Fayette County	411	15.87
New Middletown, OH (village) Mahoning County	293	15.86
Silkworth, PA (cdp) Luzerne County	129	15.83
Lawrence, PA (cdp) Washington County	69	15.83
Cooper, PA (township) Clearfield County	428	15.80
Loyalhanna, PA (cdp) Westmoreland County	516	15.72
Atlasburg, PA (cdp) Washington County	36	15.72
Morris, PA (township) Clearfield County	463	15.63
Star Junction, PA (cdp) Fayette County	123	15.61
Baumstown, PA (cdp) Berks County	71	15.43
Lansford, PA (borough) Carbon County	618	15.41
West Leechburg, PA (borough) Westmoreland County	227	15.41
Calumet, PA (cdp) Westmoreland County	155	15.23
Schuylkill, PA (township) Schuylkill County	139	14.96
Hudson, PA (cdp) Luzerne County	221	14.93
Elim, PA (cdp) Cambria County	578	14.90
Smock, PA (cdp) Fayette County	97	14.85
Upper Yoder, PA (township) Cambria County	810	14.73
Munhall, PA (borough) Allegheny County	1,676	14.63
Weston, PA (cdp) Luzerne County	51	14.57
Mount Union, IA (city) Henry County	16	14.55
Harleigh, PA (cdp) Luzerne County	156	14.46
Summit Hill, PA (borough) Carbon County	442	14.44
Put-in-Bay, OH (village) Ottawa County	20	14.39
Meadowlands, MN (city) St. Louis County	17	14.29
Middle Taylor, PA (township) Cambria County	98	14.26
West Mifflin, PA (borough) Allegheny County	2,921	14.25
Sidman, PA (cdp) Cambria County	37	14.23
Hunker, PA (borough) Westmoreland County	45	14.20
Harrison, PA (township) Allegheny County	1,475	14.08
East McKeesport, PA (borough) Allegheny County	322	14.07
Menallen, PA (township) Fayette County	599	14.01
Rush, PA (township) Schuylkill County	478	13.86
Greenock, PA (cdp) Allegheny County	261	13.79
Manorville, PA (borough) Armstrong County	52	13.72
Bigler, PA (cdp) Clearfield County	24	13.71
Paint, PA (borough) Somerset County	130	13.68
Oneida, PA (cdp) Schuylkill County	25	13.59
Oklahoma, PA (borough) Westmoreland County	109	13.42
Meadowlands, PA (cdp) Washington County	54	13.33
Struthers, OH (city) Mahoning County	1,441	13.23
Frazer, PA (township) Allegheny County	147	13.13
Ford Cliff, PA (borough) Armstrong County	60	13.04
Salix, PA (cdp) Cambria County	169	12.87
Lowellville, OH (village) Mahoning County	148	12.81
Brackenridge, PA (borough) Allegheny County	419	12.80
Sykesville, PA (borough) Jefferson County	170	12.80
South Uniontown, PA (cdp) Fayette County	175	12.77
Swoyersville, PA (borough) Luzerne County	644	12.72
Bentleyville, PA (borough) Washington County	332	12.72
Ashley, PA (borough) Luzerne County	352	12.61
Plymouth, PA (township) Luzerne County	219	12.60
Stratton, OH (village) Jefferson County	35	12.59
Adams, PA (township) Cambria County	756	12.54
East Deer, PA (township) Allegheny County	169	12.45
Donora, PA (borough) Washington County	608	12.32
Vandling, PA (borough) Lackawanna County	71	12.28
Pringle, PA (borough) Luzerne County	115	12.26
Delano, PA (township) Schuylkill County	65	12.22
Streator, IL (city) LaSalle County	1,596	12.10
South Pymatuning, PA (township) Mercer County	329	12.07
Kline, PA (township) Schuylkill County	197	12.04
Ogle, PA (township) Somerset County	76	12.03
South Union, PA (township) Fayette County	1,286	11.92
Lincoln, PA (borough) Allegheny County	124	11.90
Scalp Level, PA (borough) Cambria County	93	11.88
Greensboro, PA (borough) Greene County	31	11.83
Shippingport, PA (borough) Beaver County	23	11.79
Seavey, MN (township) Aitkin County	2	11.76
Summerhill, PA (township) Cambria County	311	11.75
Coaldale, PA (borough) Schuylkill County	308	11.65
Whiting, IN (city) Lake County	584	11.63
Park Crest, PA (cdp) Schuylkill County	82	11.60
McAdoo, PA (borough) Schuylkill County	285	11.55
Rostraver, PA (township) Westmoreland County	1,315	11.51
Mount Pleasant, PA (township) Westmoreland County	1,256	11.48
Grindstone, PA (cdp) Fayette County	85	11.41
Ridgely, MD (town) Caroline County	256	11.34
Dravosburg, PA (borough) Allegheny County	208	11.32
West Wyoming, PA (borough) Luzerne County	308	11.26
Hazle, PA (township) Luzerne County	1,049	11.18
Rowes Run, PA (cdp) Fayette County	98	11.14
Mingo Junction, OH (village) Jefferson County	385	11.12
White Oak, PA (borough) Allegheny County	878	11.11
Springdale, PA (township) Allegheny County	164	10.98
Pleasant View, PA (cdp) Armstrong County	117	10.87
Kelayres, PA (cdp) Schuylkill County	60	10.83
Cementon, PA (cdp) Lehigh County	177	10.79
Anderson, WI (town) Iron County	10	10.75
Larksville, PA (borough) Luzerne County	484	10.72
Rayne, PA (township) Indiana County	328	10.72
Marblehead, OH (village) Ottawa County	86	10.71
Noblestown, PA (cdp) Allegheny County	33	10.71
Elliston, MT (cdp) Powell County	21	10.71
Highland, ME (plantation) Somerset County	6	10.71
Russellton, PA (cdp) Allegheny County	149	10.69
North Versailles, PA (township) Allegheny County	1,098	10.67
North Philipsburg, PA (cdp) Centre County	102	10.66
Campbell, OH (city) Mahoning County	892	10.56
Pine Glen, PA (cdp) Centre County	14	10.53

Please refer to the Explanation of Data in the front of the book for more detailed information.

Ancestry

Slovak

Top 150 Places Sorted by Percent of Total Population

Based on places with total population of 7,500 or more

Place	Population	%
Munhall, PA (borough) Allegheny County	1,676	14.63
West Mifflin, PA (borough) Allegheny County	2,921	14.25
Harrison, PA (township) Allegheny County	1,475	14.08
Struthers, OH (city) Mahoning County	1,441	13.23
Streator, IL (city) LaSalle County	1,596	12.10
South Union, PA (township) Fayette County	1,286	11.92
Rostraver, PA (township) Westmoreland County	1,315	11.51
Mount Pleasant, PA (township) Westmoreland County	1,256	11.48
Hazle, PA (township) Luzerne County	1,049	11.18
White Oak, PA (borough) Allegheny County	878	11.11
North Versailles, PA (township) Allegheny County	1,098	10.67
Campbell, OH (city) Mahoning County	892	10.56
North Union, PA (township) Fayette County	1,323	10.16
North Huntingdon, PA (township) Westmoreland County	3,038	10.02
Hermitage, PA (city) Mercer County	1,409	8.72
Hopewell, PA (township) Beaver County	1,103	8.72
Parma, OH (city) Cuyahoga County	6,760	8.25
Richland, PA (township) Cambria County	1,049	8.24
Hazleton, PA (city) Luzerne County	2,045	8.22
Allegheny, PA (township) Westmoreland County	666	8.19
Latrobe, PA (city) Westmoreland County	687	8.11
Derry, PA (township) Westmoreland County	1,164	8.04
Johnstown, PA (city) Cambria County	1,712	7.98
Elizabeth, PA (township) Allegheny County	1,052	7.92
Monessen, PA (city) Westmoreland County	621	7.90
Boardman, OH (cdp) Mahoning County	2,764	7.81
Pleasant Hills, PA (borough) Allegheny County	643	7.79
Butler, PA (township) Luzerne County	682	7.74
Brooklyn, OH (city) Cuyahoga County	860	7.71
Plains, PA (township) Luzerne County	772	7.67
Jefferson Hills, PA (borough) Allegheny County	795	7.66
Unity, PA (township) Westmoreland County	1,706	7.63
Lower Burrell, PA (city) Westmoreland County	898	7.54
Austintown, OH (cdp) Mahoning County	2,267	7.50
Hubbard, OH (city) Trumbull County	569	7.18
Seven Hills, OH (city) Cuyahoga County	845	7.16
West Deer, PA (township) Allegheny County	803	6.91
Northampton, PA (borough) Northampton County	673	6.79
Kennedy, PA (township) Allegheny County	514	6.76
Strongsville, OH (city) Cuyahoga County	2,962	6.68
Avon, OH (city) Lorain County	1,282	6.57
Brecksville, OH (city) Cuyahoga County	882	6.51
Mountain Top, PA (cdp) Luzerne County	683	6.47
Brook Park, OH (city) Cuyahoga County	1,255	6.45
Uniontown, PA (city) Fayette County	680	6.34
Endwell, NY (cdp) Broome County	740	6.33
Whitehall, PA (borough) Allegheny County	880	6.32
Hempfield, PA (township) Westmoreland County	2,694	6.27
North Olmsted, OH (city) Cuyahoga County	2,024	6.17
Penn, PA (township) Westmoreland County	1,225	6.15
Middleburg Heights, OH (city) Cuyahoga County	971	6.15
East Huntingdon, PA (township) Westmoreland County	476	5.99
Center, PA (township) Beaver County	698	5.98
Connellsville, PA (city) Fayette County	471	5.98
Johnson City, NY (village) Broome County	908	5.96
Amherst, OH (city) Lorain County	714	5.93
Sharon, PA (city) Mercer County	848	5.87
Economy, PA (borough) Beaver County	522	5.80
Baldwin, PA (borough) Allegheny County	1,136	5.79
New Kensington, PA (city) Westmoreland County	770	5.76
North Royalton, OH (city) Cuyahoga County	1,719	5.74
McKeesport, PA (city) Allegheny County	1,158	5.69
Chartiers, PA (township) Washington County	429	5.56
Robinson, PA (township) Allegheny County	723	5.53
Kingston, PA (borough) Luzerne County	723	5.46
Stratford, CT (cdp/town) Fairfield County	2,753	5.42
Broadview Heights, OH (city) Cuyahoga County	997	5.34
Union, NY (town) Broome County	3,003	5.33
Castle Shannon, PA (borough) Allegheny County	438	5.28
Fairview Park, OH (city) Cuyahoga County	891	5.27
Brunswick, OH (city) Medina County	1,800	5.23
Greensburg, PA (city) Westmoreland County	784	5.21
Dallas, PA (township) Luzerne County	457	5.19
South Strabane, PA (township) Washington County	471	5.17
Cecil, PA (township) Washington County	567	5.16
North Ridgeville, OH (city) Lorain County	1,428	5.05
Lower Saucon, PA (township) Northampton County	537	5.00
Nanticoke, PA (city) Luzerne County	518	4.94
Parma Heights, OH (city) Cuyahoga County	1,023	4.92
Bethel Park, PA (municipality) Allegheny County	1,579	4.90
White, PA (township) Indiana County	753	4.87
South Park Township, PA (cdp) Allegheny County	654	4.86
South Park, PA (township) Allegheny County	654	4.86
Hanover, PA (township) Luzerne County	531	4.78
Aurora, OH (city) Portage County	724	4.76
Endicott, NY (village) Broome County	634	4.76
Wickliffe, OH (city) Lake County	612	4.76
Bethlehem, PA (city) Lehigh County	915	4.74
Murrysville, PA (municipality) Westmoreland County	931	4.69
Avon Lake, OH (city) Lorain County	1,021	4.67
Lakewood, OH (city) Cuyahoga County	2,432	4.62
Butler, PA (township) Butler County	791	4.56
Monroeville, PA (municipality) Allegheny County	1,285	4.54
Whitehall, PA (township) Lehigh County	1,204	4.54
Plum, PA (borough) Allegheny County	1,214	4.52
Bay Village, OH (city) Cuyahoga County	706	4.51
Swissvale, PA (borough) Allegheny County	408	4.51
Youngstown, OH (city) Mahoning County	3,113	4.47
South Whitehall, PA (township) Lehigh County	847	4.45
Rocky River, OH (city) Cuyahoga County	892	4.42
Fernway, PA (cdp) Butler County	539	4.39
Dunmore, PA (borough) Lackawanna County	617	4.38
Ross, PA (township) Allegheny County	1,359	4.37
Garfield Heights, OH (city) Cuyahoga County	1,253	4.31
Peters, PA (township) Washington County	885	4.31
South Fayette, PA (township) Allegheny County	591	4.25
Cranberry, PA (township) Butler County	1,119	4.09
South Abington, PA (township) Lackawanna County	367	4.09
Canonsburg, PA (borough) Washington County	364	4.08
Moore, PA (township) Northampton County	371	4.05
Salisbury, PA (township) Lehigh County	534	3.94
Westlake, OH (city) Cuyahoga County	1,268	3.92
North Strabane, PA (township) Washington County	501	3.92
McCandless, PA (township) Allegheny County	1,094	3.87
Macedonia, OH (city) Summit County	420	3.87
Girard, OH (city) Trumbull County	391	3.81
Highland, IN (town) Lake County	896	3.78
Olmsted Falls, OH (city) Cuyahoga County	331	3.78
Streetsboro, OH (city) Portage County	578	3.76
Willowick, OH (city) Lake County	531	3.74
Emmaus, PA (borough) Lehigh County	417	3.70
Schererville, IN (town) Lake County	1,051	3.69
Berea, OH (city) Cuyahoga County	698	3.68
Manville, NJ (borough) Somerset County	378	3.65
Center, PA (township) Butler County	289	3.65
Wilkes-Barre, PA (city) Luzerne County	1,497	3.60
Sandy, PA (township) Clearfield County	390	3.60
Solon, OH (city) Cuyahoga County	824	3.59
Niles, OH (city) Trumbull County	698	3.59
Highland Heights, OH (city) Cuyahoga County	296	3.59
Twinsburg, OH (city) Summit County	663	3.58
Chenango, NY (town) Broome County	401	3.56
Willoughby, OH (city) Lake County	789	3.55
Munster, IN (town) Lake County	814	3.50
Phoenixville, PA (borough) Chester County	569	3.50
Sheffield Lake, OH (city) Lorain County	322	3.49
Brentwood, PA (borough) Allegheny County	337	3.47
Shelton, CT (city/town) Fairfield County	1,351	3.46
Bethlehem, PA (city) Northampton County	2,574	3.44
Richland, PA (township) Allegheny County	367	3.44
Folsom, PA (cdp) Delaware County	278	3.30
Glenshaw, PA (cdp) Allegheny County	303	3.29
Eastlake, OH (city) Lake County	619	3.28
Medina, OH (city) Medina County	873	3.27
Mentor-on-the-Lake, OH (city) Lake County	246	3.24
Upper Saucon, PA (township) Lehigh County	460	3.20
Lower Swatara, PA (township) Dauphin County	263	3.20
Pottsville, PA (city) Schuylkill County	463	3.19
Pine, PA (township) Allegheny County	343	3.19
Scott, PA (township) Allegheny County	534	3.15

Please refer to the Explanation of Data in the front of the book for more detailed information.

Ancestry

Slovene

U.S. and 50 States Sorted by Population and Percent of Total Population

Place	Population	%
United States	**174,808**	**0.06**
Ohio	55,482	0.48
Pennsylvania	16,861	0.13
Illinois	14,745	0.12
Minnesota	9,800	0.19
Wisconsin	9,199	0.16
California	8,956	0.02
Colorado	5,966	0.12
Florida	5,739	0.03
New York	4,802	0.02
Michigan	4,617	0.05
Texas	4,306	0.02
Virginia	2,934	0.04
Indiana	2,873	0.04
Arizona	2,595	0.04
Washington	2,254	0.03
Maryland	1,946	0.03
North Carolina	1,847	0.02
New Jersey	1,586	0.02
Connecticut	1,374	0.04
Kansas	1,358	0.05
Missouri	1,336	0.02
Georgia	1,305	0.01
Massachusetts	1,284	0.02
Oregon	1,079	0.03
Utah	936	0.04
South Carolina	855	0.02
Tennessee	817	0.01
Montana	809	0.08
Nevada	743	0.03
Wyoming	544	0.10
New Mexico	527	0.03
Kentucky	515	0.01
Iowa	512	0.02
West Virginia	432	0.02
Idaho	355	0.02
Nebraska	346	0.02
Alabama	345	0.01
Oklahoma	336	0.01
District of Columbia	334	0.06
Vermont	329	0.05
Hawaii	292	0.02
Maine	226	0.02
Mississippi	218	0.01
Louisiana	190	<0.01
Delaware	183	0.02
New Hampshire	181	0.01
Alaska	155	0.02
Rhode Island	120	0.01
South Dakota	107	0.01
Arkansas	102	<0.01
North Dakota	55	0.01

Place	Population	%
Ohio	55,482	0.48
Minnesota	9,800	0.19
Wisconsin	9,199	0.16
Pennsylvania	16,861	0.13
Illinois	14,745	0.12
Colorado	5,966	0.12
Wyoming	544	0.10
Montana	809	0.08
United States	**174,808**	**0.06**
District of Columbia	334	0.06
Michigan	4,617	0.05
Kansas	1,358	0.05
Vermont	329	0.05
Virginia	2,934	0.04
Indiana	2,873	0.04
Arizona	2,595	0.04
Connecticut	1,374	0.04
Utah	936	0.04
Florida	5,739	0.03
Washington	2,254	0.03
Maryland	1,946	0.03
Oregon	1,079	0.03
Nevada	743	0.03
New Mexico	527	0.03
California	8,956	0.02
New York	4,802	0.02
Texas	4,306	0.02
North Carolina	1,847	0.02
New Jersey	1,586	0.02
Missouri	1,336	0.02
Massachusetts	1,284	0.02
South Carolina	855	0.02
Iowa	512	0.02
West Virginia	432	0.02
Idaho	355	0.02
Nebraska	346	0.02
Hawaii	292	0.02
Maine	226	0.02
Delaware	183	0.02
Alaska	155	0.02
Georgia	1,305	0.01
Tennessee	817	0.01
Kentucky	515	0.01
Alabama	345	0.01
Oklahoma	336	0.01
Mississippi	218	0.01
New Hampshire	181	0.01
Rhode Island	120	0.01
South Dakota	107	0.01
North Dakota	55	0.01
Louisiana	190	<0.01
Arkansas	102	<0.01

Please refer to the Explanation of Data in the front of the book for more detailed information.

Ancestry

Slovene

Top 150 Places Sorted by Population

Based on all places, regardless of total population

Place	Population	%
Cleveland, OH (city) Cuyahoga County	3,214	0.79
Mentor, OH (city) Lake County	3,037	6.38
Euclid, OH (city) Cuyahoga County	2,895	5.87
Willoughby, OH (city) Lake County	1,861	8.37
Joliet, IL (city) Will County	1,830	1.26
Parma, OH (city) Cuyahoga County	1,677	2.05
Eastlake, OH (city) Lake County	1,595	8.45
New York, NY (city) Kings County	1,476	0.02
Chicago, IL (city) Cook County	1,432	0.05
Columbus, OH (city) Franklin County	1,380	0.18
Willowick, OH (city) Lake County	1,273	8.96
Wickliffe, OH (city) Lake County	1,137	8.85
Pueblo, CO (city) Pueblo County	1,107	1.04
Milwaukee, WI (city) Milwaukee County	851	0.14
Lakewood, OH (city) Cuyahoga County	761	1.44
Pittsburgh, PA (city) Allegheny County	739	0.24
Willoughby Hills, OH (city) Lake County	736	7.84
Los Angeles, CA (city) Los Angeles County	730	0.02
Strongsville, OH (city) Cuyahoga County	726	1.64
Garfield Heights, OH (city) Cuyahoga County	717	2.47
Phoenix, AZ (city) Maricopa County	713	0.05
Hibbing, MN (city) St. Louis County	702	4.28
Manhattan, NY (borough) New York County	695	0.04
North Royalton, OH (city) Cuyahoga County	666	2.22
Mentor-on-the-Lake, OH (city) Lake County	601	7.92
Akron, OH (city) Summit County	588	0.29
Kirtland, OH (city) Lake County	581	8.50
Westlake, OH (city) Cuyahoga County	555	1.72
Lorain, OH (city) Lorain County	546	0.84
Seattle, WA (city) King County	536	0.09
Indianapolis, IN (city) Marion County	497	0.06
Highland Heights, OH (city) Cuyahoga County	476	5.77
Queens, NY (borough) Queens County	468	0.02
Sheboygan, WI (city) Sheboygan County	462	0.93
Twinsburg, OH (city) Summit County	460	2.48
Mayfield Heights, OH (city) Cuyahoga County	455	2.38
San Diego, CA (city) San Diego County	455	0.04
Denver, CO (city) Denver County	453	0.08
North Olmsted, OH (city) Cuyahoga County	438	1.34
Minneapolis, MN (city) Hennepin County	437	0.12
Brunswick, OH (city) Medina County	432	1.26
Avon Lake, OH (city) Lorain County	431	1.97
Broadview Heights, OH (city) Cuyahoga County	420	2.25
Austin, TX (city) Travis County	415	0.05
San Francisco, CA (city) San Francisco County	400	0.05
Lyndhurst, OH (city) Cuyahoga County	398	2.81
Greenfield, WI (city) Milwaukee County	398	1.10
Solon, OH (city) Cuyahoga County	394	1.71
West Allis, WI (city) Milwaukee County	388	0.65
Aurora, OH (city) Portage County	384	2.53
Eveleth, MN (city) St. Louis County	383	10.28
Duluth, MN (city) St. Louis County	371	0.43
Ely, MN (city) St. Louis County	356	10.11
Shorewood, IL (village) Will County	352	2.39
Independence, OH (city) Cuyahoga County	349	4.93
Virginia, MN (city) St. Louis County	347	3.96
Crest Hill, IL (city) Will County	346	1.70
Parma Heights, OH (city) Cuyahoga County	346	1.66
Chisholm, MN (city) St. Louis County	341	6.88
Washington, DC (city) District of Columbia	334	0.06
Barberton, OH (city) Summit County	332	1.24
Hempfield, PA (township) Westmoreland County	328	0.76
Maple Heights, OH (city) Cuyahoga County	318	1.35
Bethlehem, PA (city) Northampton County	316	0.42
Avon, OH (city) Lorain County	311	1.59
Mayfield, OH (village) Cuyahoga County	305	8.90
Brecksville, OH (city) Cuyahoga County	304	2.24
Waukegan, IL (city) Lake County	304	0.34
Lemont, IL (village) Cook County	303	1.98
Seven Hills, OH (city) Cuyahoga County	299	2.53
Middleburg Heights, OH (city) Cuyahoga County	296	1.87
South Euclid, OH (city) Cuyahoga County	295	1.32
Kansas City, KS (city) Wyandotte County	283	0.20
Colorado Springs, CO (city) El Paso County	281	0.07
Stow, OH (city) Summit County	279	0.81

Place	Population	%
Oak Creek, WI (city) Milwaukee County	277	0.84
St. Paul, MN (city) Ramsey County	277	0.10
Portland, OR (city) Multnomah County	275	0.05
Centennial, CO (city) Arapahoe County	273	0.27
Philadelphia, PA (city) Philadelphia County	273	0.02
Richmond Heights, OH (city) Cuyahoga County	271	2.56
Channahon, IL (village) Will County	268	2.19
North Strabane, PA (township) Washington County	265	2.07
Peters, PA (township) Washington County	264	1.29
Painesville, OH (city) Lake County	260	1.35
Geneva, OH (city) Ashtabula County	259	4.12
Fairview Park, OH (city) Cuyahoga County	259	1.53
Mesa, AZ (city) Maricopa County	259	0.06
Charlotte, NC (city) Mecklenburg County	255	0.04
Fort Collins, CO (city) Larimer County	247	0.18
North Fayette, PA (township) Allegheny County	246	1.82
Madison, WI (city) Dane County	243	0.11
San Antonio, TX (city) Medina County	239	0.02
Jacksonville, FL (city) Duval County	238	0.03
Houston, TX (city) Harris County	233	0.01
Bethlehem, PA (city) Northampton County	231	0.42
Cecil, PA (township) Washington County	225	2.05
Penn, PA (township) Westmoreland County	224	1.12
North Ridgeville, OH (city) Lorain County	223	0.79
Portage, IN (city) Porter County	218	0.60
Virginia Beach, VA (ind. city) Virginia Beach independent city	218	0.05
Robinson, PA (township) Allegheny County	215	1.64
Muskego, WI (city) Waukesha County	212	0.89
LaSalle, IL (city) LaSalle County	209	2.16
Oak Park, IL (village) Cook County	208	0.40
Cleveland Heights, OH (city) Cuyahoga County	204	0.44
North Madison, OH (cdp) Lake County	203	2.26
Mountain Iron, MN (city) St. Louis County	202	7.02
Bay Village, OH (city) Cuyahoga County	201	1.28
Buffalo Grove, IL (village) Lake County	201	0.48
Brookfield, WI (city) Waukesha County	198	0.52
Cuyahoga Falls, OH (city) Summit County	198	0.40
Hudson, OH (city) Summit County	196	0.88
Berea, OH (city) Cuyahoga County	195	1.03
Lockport, IL (city) Will County	194	0.81
Rock Springs, WY (city) Sweetwater County	191	0.87
California, PA (borough) Washington County	190	2.88
Norton, OH (city) Summit County	190	1.58
Fairfield, CT (town) Fairfield County	190	0.32
Bethel Park, PA (municipality) Allegheny County	186	0.58
Farmington Hills, MI (city) Oakland County	185	0.23
Aurora, CO (city) Arapahoe County	185	0.06
Arlington, VA (cdp) Arlington County	184	0.09
South Park Township, PA (cdp) Allegheny County	183	1.36
South Park, PA (township) Allegheny County	183	1.36
Macedonia, OH (city) Summit County	181	1.67
Rocky River, OH (city) Cuyahoga County	180	0.89
Penn Hills, PA (township) Allegheny County	180	0.42
Naperville, IL (city) DuPage County	178	0.13
Franklin, WI (city) Milwaukee County	176	0.52
Overland Park, KS (city) Johnson County	174	0.10
Lakewood, CO (city) Jefferson County	172	0.12
Chartiers, PA (township) Washington County	171	2.22
Moreland Hills, OH (village) Cuyahoga County	170	5.14
South Fayette, PA (township) Allegheny County	169	1.21
Pembroke Pines, FL (city) Broward County	169	0.11
Boulder, CO (city) Boulder County	168	0.17
Gurnee, IL (village) Lake County	167	0.54
New Berlin, WI (city) Waukesha County	166	0.42
Elyria, OH (city) Lorain County	165	0.30
Wilson, WI (town) Sheboygan County	164	4.98
Pueblo West, CO (cdp) Pueblo County	164	0.59
Chardon, OH (city) Geauga County	163	3.15
Medina, OH (city) Medina County	163	0.61
Minnetonka, MN (city) Hennepin County	163	0.33
Brooklyn, NY (borough) Kings County	160	0.01
Huntington Beach, CA (city) Orange County	159	0.08
Sewickley, PA (township) Westmoreland County	158	2.62
Santa Cruz, CA (city) Santa Cruz County	158	0.27
Albuquerque, NM (city) Bernalillo County	156	0.03

Please refer to the Explanation of Data in the front of the book for more detailed information.

Ancestry

Slovene

Top 150 Places Sorted by Percent of Total Population

Based on all places, regardless of total population

Place	Population	%
Lake No. 1, MN (unorganized territory) Lake County	31	37.35
McKinley, MN (city) St. Louis County	7	15.91
El Moro, CO (cdp) Las Animas County	53	14.68
Lakeline, OH (village) Lake County	22	14.57
Hendren, WI (town) Clark County	70	14.11
Grand River, OH (village) Lake County	48	13.68
Kirtland Hills, OH (village) Lake County	94	12.30
Southview, PA (cdp) Washington County	17	11.33
Tower, MN (city) St. Louis County	42	10.77
Eveleth, MN (city) St. Louis County	383	10.28
McCormack, MN (unorganized territory) St. Louis County	25	10.12
Ely, MN (city) St. Louis County	356	10.11
Willowick, OH (city) Lake County	1,273	8.96
Balkan, MN (township) St. Louis County	73	8.92
Mayfield, OH (village) Cuyahoga County	305	8.90
Wickliffe, OH (city) Lake County	1,137	8.85
Fall Lake, MN (township) Lake County	54	8.77
Sand Lake, MN (unorganized territory) St. Louis County	82	8.51
Kirtland, OH (city) Lake County	581	8.50
Vandling, PA (borough) Lackawanna County	49	8.48
Eastlake, OH (city) Lake County	1,595	8.45
Willoughby, OH (city) Lake County	1,861	8.37
Soudan, MN (cdp) St. Louis County	36	7.98
Mentor-on-the-Lake, OH (city) Lake County	601	7.92
Mount Clare, IL (village) Macoupin County	85	7.92
Willoughby Hills, OH (city) Lake County	736	7.84
Yukon, PA (cdp) Westmoreland County	40	7.52
Pilsen, WI (town) Bayfield County	11	7.33
Dunlo, PA (cdp) Cambria County	16	7.31
Rowes Run, PA (cdp) Fayette County	63	7.16
Breitung, MN (township) St. Louis County	47	7.16
Mountain Iron, MN (city) St. Louis County	202	7.02
Forest City, PA (borough) Susquehanna County	121	6.93
Chisholm, MN (city) St. Louis County	341	6.88
North Perry, OH (village) Lake County	66	6.86
Winton, MN (city) St. Louis County	13	6.84
Livingston Wheeler, NM (cdp) Eddy County	59	6.77
North Ottawa, MN (township) Grant County	5	6.58
Clinton, PA (township) Wayne County	116	6.56
Aurora, MN (city) St. Louis County	97	6.55
St. Stephen, MN (city) Stearns County	54	6.55
Foster, MN (township) Big Stone County	11	6.51
Mentor, OH (city) Lake County	3,037	6.38
Fayal, MN (township) St. Louis County	102	6.36
Babbitt, MN (city) St. Louis County	86	6.34
Seven Hills, CO (cdp) Boulder County	11	6.25
Harrietta, MI (village) Wexford County	7	6.19
Euclid, OH (city) Cuyahoga County	2,895	5.87
Goochland, VA (cdp) Goochland County	45	5.78
Highland Heights, OH (city) Cuyahoga County	476	5.77
French, MN (township) St. Louis County	23	5.50
Morse, MN (township) St. Louis County	68	5.38
Hickory, PA (township) Forest County	34	5.29
Johnson Creek, WI (village) Jefferson County	134	5.25
Mead, WI (town) Clark County	13	5.20
Imperial, PA (cdp) Allegheny County	120	5.16
Moreland Hills, OH (village) Cuyahoga County	170	5.14
Wilson, WI (town) Sheboygan County	164	4.98
Riverside, PA (cdp) Cambria County	22	4.95
Independence, OH (city) Cuyahoga County	349	4.93
Alango, MN (township) St. Louis County	13	4.91
Biwabik, MN (township) St. Louis County	43	4.88
Brook Park, MN (city) Pine County	7	4.86
Decatur, NY (town) Otsego County	15	4.78
Bedford, NY (cdp) Westchester County	86	4.73
Boon, MI (cdp) Wexford County	8	4.71
Valley View, OH (village) Cuyahoga County	90	4.62
Gilbert, MN (city) St. Louis County	81	4.58
Biwabik, MN (city) St. Louis County	49	4.55
Fairfield, WA (town) Spokane County	38	4.43
Whittlesey, WI (cdp) Taylor County	6	4.38
McGovern, PA (cdp) Washington County	132	4.37
Vermilion Lake, MN (township) St. Louis County	13	4.36
Limestone, MI (township) Alger County	16	4.34
Sturgeon, MN (township) St. Louis County	6	4.32
St. Paul, KS (city) Neosho County	30	4.29
Hibbing, MN (city) St. Louis County	702	4.28
Hills and Dales, OH (village) Stark County	10	4.20
Kersey, PA (cdp) Elk County	40	4.15
Wuori, MN (township) St. Louis County	22	4.14
Geneva, OH (city) Ashtabula County	259	4.12
Mathias, MI (township) Alger County	19	4.12
Grant, MI (township) Keweenaw County	5	4.10
Hunting Valley, OH (village) Cuyahoga County	26	4.04
Madison, OH (village) Lake County	125	3.98
Chesterland, OH (cdp) Geauga County	96	3.97
Slovan, PA (cdp) Washington County	16	3.97
Virginia, MN (city) St. Louis County	347	3.96
Bovina, NY (town) Delaware County	20	3.92
Linden Grove, MN (township) St. Louis County	4	3.85
New Bedford, PA (cdp) Lawrence County	25	3.83
Buhl, MN (city) St. Louis County	34	3.82
West Wood, UT (cdp) Carbon County	26	3.75
Burton, MN (township) Yellow Medicine County	6	3.70
Conkling Park, ID (cdp) Kootenai County	3	3.70
White, MN (township) St. Louis County	120	3.69
Portage, MN (township) St. Louis County	7	3.66
Rock Creek, OH (village) Ashtabula County	26	3.64
Walpole, NH (cdp) Cheshire County	23	3.61
Warner, WI (town) Clark County	24	3.60
Metamora, MI (village) Lapeer County	20	3.59
Seventh Mountain, OR (cdp) Deschutes County	12	3.54
Westfield Center, OH (village) Medina County	38	3.52
Birch Lake, MN (unorganized territory) St. Louis County	18	3.52
Sheffield, OH (village) Lorain County	132	3.49
Roaming Shores, OH (village) Ashtabula County	66	3.48
Wylandville, PA (cdp) Washington County	12	3.45
Summit, PA (township) Potter County	4	3.45
Packwaukee, WI (cdp) Marquette County	8	3.43
Edie, PA (cdp) Somerset County	3	3.37
Sherman, MI (township) Keweenaw County	3	3.37
Greentown, OH (cdp) Stark County	108	3.36
Bratenahl, OH (village) Cuyahoga County	46	3.36
Roseland, KS (city) Cherokee County	4	3.36
Eagles Nest, MN (township) St. Louis County	6	3.35
Independence, UT (town) Wasatch County	8	3.31
Brookside, CO (town) Fremont County	9	3.30
Worcester, NY (cdp) Otsego County	51	3.24
Perry, OH (village) Lake County	52	3.23
Hawk Run, PA (cdp) Clearfield County	10	3.22
North Utica, IL (village) LaSalle County	38	3.20
Eaton, WI (town) Clark County	26	3.20
Rockdale, IL (village) Will County	62	3.17
Chardon, OH (city) Geauga County	163	3.15
Boon, MI (township) Wexford County	18	3.15
Waite Hill, OH (village) Lake County	15	3.10
Spring Glen, UT (cdp) Carbon County	29	3.08
North Bay, WI (village) Racine County	10	3.05
Bearville, MN (township) Itasca County	4	3.05
Woodcock, PA (borough) Crawford County	7	3.03
Keystone, WI (town) Bayfield County	13	3.02
Russellton, PA (cdp) Allegheny County	42	3.01
Great Scott, MN (township) St. Louis County	14	3.01
Gastonville, PA (cdp) Washington County	84	2.99
Edwards AFB, CA (cdp) Kern County	104	2.92
California, PA (borough) Washington County	190	2.88
Northfield, OH (village) Summit County	107	2.88
Little Falls, NY (town) Herkimer County	41	2.88
Greenwood, WI (city) Clark County	29	2.88
Timberlake, OH (village) Lake County	18	2.85
Muse, PA (cdp) Washington County	75	2.82
Middlefield, OH (village) Geauga County	74	2.82
North Philipsburg, PA (cdp) Centre County	27	2.82
Lyndhurst, OH (city) Cuyahoga County	398	2.81
Hilltop, OH (cdp) Trumbull County	20	2.77
Titusville, NY (cdp) Dutchess County	13	2.72
Burton, OH (village) Geauga County	36	2.70
Conemaugh, PA (township) Cambria County	55	2.69
Loyal, WI (city) Clark County	32	2.65
Sewickley, PA (township) Westmoreland County	158	2.62

Please refer to the Explanation of Data in the front of the book for more detailed information.

Ancestry

Slovene

Top 150 Places Sorted by Percent of Total Population

Based on places with total population of 7,500 or more

Place	Population	%
Willowick, OH (city) Lake County	1,273	8.96
Wickliffe, OH (city) Lake County	1,137	8.85
Eastlake, OH (city) Lake County	1,595	8.45
Willoughby, OH (city) Lake County	1,861	8.37
Mentor-on-the-Lake, OH (city) Lake County	601	7.92
Willoughby Hills, OH (city) Lake County	736	7.84
Mentor, OH (city) Lake County	3,037	6.38
Euclid, OH (city) Cuyahoga County	2,895	5.87
Highland Heights, OH (city) Cuyahoga County	476	5.77
Hibbing, MN (city) St. Louis County	702	4.28
Virginia, MN (city) St. Louis County	347	3.96
Lyndhurst, OH (city) Cuyahoga County	398	2.81
Richmond Heights, OH (city) Cuyahoga County	271	2.56
Aurora, OH (city) Portage County	384	2.53
Seven Hills, OH (city) Cuyahoga County	299	2.53
Twinsburg, OH (city) Summit County	460	2.48
Garfield Heights, OH (city) Cuyahoga County	717	2.47
Shorewood, IL (village) Will County	352	2.39
Mayfield Heights, OH (city) Cuyahoga County	455	2.38
North Madison, OH (cdp) Lake County	203	2.26
Broadview Heights, OH (city) Cuyahoga County	420	2.25
Brecksville, OH (city) Cuyahoga County	304	2.24
North Royalton, OH (city) Cuyahoga County	666	2.22
Chartiers, PA (township) Washington County	171	2.22
Channahon, IL (village) Will County	268	2.19
LaSalle, IL (city) LaSalle County	209	2.16
North Strabane, PA (township) Washington County	265	2.07
Parma, OH (city) Cuyahoga County	1,677	2.05
Cecil, PA (township) Washington County	225	2.05
Lemont, IL (village) Cook County	303	1.98
Avon Lake, OH (city) Lorain County	431	1.97
Middleburg Heights, OH (city) Cuyahoga County	296	1.87
North Fayette, PA (township) Allegheny County	246	1.82
Westlake, OH (city) Cuyahoga County	555	1.72
Solon, OH (city) Cuyahoga County	394	1.71
Crest Hill, IL (city) Will County	346	1.70
Macedonia, OH (city) Summit County	181	1.67
Parma Heights, OH (city) Cuyahoga County	346	1.66
Strongsville, OH (city) Cuyahoga County	726	1.64
Robinson, PA (township) Allegheny County	215	1.64
Avon, OH (city) Lorain County	311	1.59
Norton, OH (city) Summit County	190	1.58
Fairview Park, OH (city) Cuyahoga County	259	1.53
Olmsted Falls, OH (city) Cuyahoga County	133	1.52
Canonsburg, PA (borough) Washington County	134	1.50
Lakewood, OH (city) Cuyahoga County	761	1.44
South Park Township, PA (cdp) Allegheny County	183	1.36
South Park, PA (township) Allegheny County	183	1.36
Maple Heights, OH (city) Cuyahoga County	318	1.35
Painesville, OH (city) Lake County	260	1.35
North Olmsted, OH (city) Cuyahoga County	438	1.34
South Euclid, OH (city) Cuyahoga County	295	1.32
Peters, PA (township) Washington County	264	1.29
Bay Village, OH (city) Cuyahoga County	201	1.28
Joliet, IL (city) Will County	1,830	1.26
Brunswick, OH (city) Medina County	432	1.26
Barberton, OH (city) Summit County	332	1.24
South Fayette, PA (township) Allegheny County	169	1.21
Franklin Park, PA (borough) Allegheny County	152	1.17
West Deer, PA (township) Allegheny County	134	1.15
Brooklyn, OH (city) Cuyahoga County	127	1.14
Penn, PA (township) Westmoreland County	224	1.12
Greenfield, WI (city) Milwaukee County	398	1.10
North Union, PA (township) Fayette County	138	1.06
Amherst, OH (city) Lorain County	126	1.05
Pueblo, CO (city) Pueblo County	1,107	1.04
Berea, OH (city) Cuyahoga County	195	1.03
Peru, IL (city) LaSalle County	105	1.03
Glendale, WI (city) Milwaukee County	131	1.02
Des Peres, MO (city) St. Louis County	84	1.00
Sheboygan Falls, WI (city) Sheboygan County	76	1.00
Streetsboro, OH (city) Portage County	148	0.96
La Grange Park, IL (village) Cook County	128	0.96
Bedford, OH (city) Cuyahoga County	127	0.96
Rostraver, PA (township) Westmoreland County	108	0.95
Girard, OH (city) Trumbull County	96	0.94
Sheffield Lake, OH (city) Lorain County	87	0.94
Sheboygan, WI (city) Sheboygan County	462	0.93
University Heights, OH (city) Cuyahoga County	124	0.91
Muskego, WI (city) Waukesha County	212	0.89
Rocky River, OH (city) Cuyahoga County	180	0.89
Hudson, OH (city) Summit County	196	0.88
Vienna, VA (town) Fairfax County	135	0.88
Rock Springs, WY (city) Sweetwater County	191	0.87
Hartland, WI (village) Waukesha County	78	0.87
Minooka, IL (village) Grundy County	82	0.86
Lorain, OH (city) Lorain County	546	0.84
Oak Creek, WI (city) Milwaukee County	277	0.84
Stow, OH (city) Summit County	279	0.81
Lockport, IL (city) Will County	194	0.81
Beachwood, OH (city) Cuyahoga County	97	0.81
Wauconda, IL (village) Lake County	104	0.80
Powell, OH (city) Delaware County	86	0.80
Cleveland, OH (city) Cuyahoga County	3,214	0.79
North Ridgeville, OH (city) Lorain County	223	0.79
Greendale, WI (village) Milwaukee County	111	0.79
Vermilion, OH (city) Lorain County	84	0.78
Tenafly, NJ (borough) Bergen County	110	0.77
Riverside, IL (village) Cook County	67	0.77
Hempfield, PA (township) Westmoreland County	328	0.76
New Franklin, OH (city) Summit County	108	0.75
East Bradford, PA (township) Chester County	74	0.75
Pleasant Prairie, WI (village) Kenosha County	137	0.72
Beach Park, IL (village) Lake County	96	0.72
Greenwich, CT (cdp) Fairfield County	96	0.72
Conneaut, OH (city) Ashtabula County	92	0.72
Winfield, IL (village) DuPage County	65	0.72
Carnegie, PA (borough) Allegheny County	55	0.69
Pewaukee, WI (village) Waukesha County	54	0.66
West Allis, WI (city) Milwaukee County	388	0.65
Clarendon Hills, IL (village) DuPage County	54	0.65
Yreka, CA (city) Siskiyou County	50	0.65
Newberry, PA (township) York County	97	0.64
Glenshaw, PA (cdp) Allegheny County	59	0.64
Pine, PA (township) Allegheny County	68	0.63
Richland, PA (township) Cambria County	79	0.62
Medina, OH (city) Medina County	163	0.61
Marathon, FL (city) Monroe County	52	0.61
Vernon, WI (town) Waukesha County	46	0.61
Portage, IN (city) Porter County	218	0.60
Bernardsville, NJ (borough) Somerset County	46	0.60
Pueblo West, CO (cdp) Pueblo County	164	0.59
Murrysville, PA (municipality) Westmoreland County	118	0.59
Oconomowoc, WI (city) Waukesha County	90	0.59
Bethel Park, PA (municipality) Allegheny County	186	0.58
Grand Rapids, MN (city) Itasca County	62	0.58
Lake of the Woods, VA (cdp) Orange County	45	0.58
Fort Washington, MD (cdp) Prince George's County	143	0.57
Mequon, WI (city) Ozaukee County	132	0.57
Columbia City, IN (city) Whitley County	46	0.56
Hubbard, OH (city) Trumbull County	44	0.56
Bedford, NY (town) Westchester County	96	0.55
Frankfort, IL (village) Will County	93	0.55
Choctaw, OK (city) Oklahoma County	59	0.55
Glenwood Springs, CO (city) Garfield County	52	0.55
O'Hara, PA (township) Allegheny County	46	0.55
Gurnee, IL (village) Lake County	167	0.54
Hampton, PA (township) Allegheny County	97	0.54
South Strabane, PA (township) Washington County	49	0.54
Price, UT (city) Carbon County	46	0.54
Niles, OH (city) Trumbull County	103	0.53
Scott, PA (township) Allegheny County	89	0.53
Mount Pleasant, PA (township) Westmoreland County	58	0.53
Lakes of the Four Seasons, IN (cdp) Lake County	40	0.53
Brookfield, WI (city) Waukesha County	198	0.52
Franklin, WI (city) Milwaukee County	176	0.52
Brook Park, OH (city) Cuyahoga County	102	0.52
Upper St. Clair, PA (cdp/township) Allegheny County	100	0.52
Minnehaha, WA (cdp) Clark County	49	0.51
Sturgeon Bay, WI (city) Door County	47	0.51

SECTION THREE

Ancestry

Soviet Union

U.S. and 50 States Sorted by Population and Percent of Total Population

Place	Population	%
United States	**2,123**	**<0.01**
New York	458	<0.01
New Jersey	353	<0.01
California	334	<0.01
Washington	168	<0.01
Florida	134	<0.01
Massachusetts	104	<0.01
Illinois	102	<0.01
Pennsylvania	59	<0.01
Michigan	52	<0.01
Virginia	47	<0.01
Nevada	38	<0.01
Ohio	36	<0.01
Oregon	33	<0.01
South Carolina	26	<0.01
Texas	25	<0.01
Tennessee	24	<0.01
Connecticut	23	<0.01
Minnesota	18	<0.01
Missouri	18	<0.01
Georgia	17	<0.01
North Carolina	14	<0.01
Maryland	13	<0.01
Wisconsin	12	<0.01
Utah	9	<0.01
Arkansas	6	<0.01
Alabama	0	0.00
Alaska	0	0.00
Arizona	0	0.00
Colorado	0	0.00
Delaware	0	0.00
District of Columbia	0	0.00
Hawaii	0	0.00
Idaho	0	0.00
Indiana	0	0.00
Iowa	0	0.00
Kansas	0	0.00
Kentucky	0	0.00
Louisiana	0	0.00
Maine	0	0.00
Mississippi	0	0.00
Montana	0	0.00
Nebraska	0	0.00
New Hampshire	0	0.00
New Mexico	0	0.00
North Dakota	0	0.00
Oklahoma	0	0.00
Rhode Island	0	0.00
South Dakota	0	0.00
Vermont	0	0.00
West Virginia	0	0.00
Wyoming	0	0.00

Place	Population	%
United States	**2,123**	**<0.01**
New York	458	<0.01
New Jersey	353	<0.01
California	334	<0.01
Washington	168	<0.01
Florida	134	<0.01
Massachusetts	104	<0.01
Illinois	102	<0.01
Pennsylvania	59	<0.01
Michigan	52	<0.01
Virginia	47	<0.01
Nevada	38	<0.01
Ohio	36	<0.01
Oregon	33	<0.01
South Carolina	26	<0.01
Texas	25	<0.01
Tennessee	24	<0.01
Connecticut	23	<0.01
Minnesota	18	<0.01
Missouri	18	<0.01
Georgia	17	<0.01
North Carolina	14	<0.01
Maryland	13	<0.01
Wisconsin	12	<0.01
Utah	9	<0.01
Arkansas	6	<0.01
Alabama	0	0.00
Alaska	0	0.00
Arizona	0	0.00
Colorado	0	0.00
Delaware	0	0.00
District of Columbia	0	0.00
Hawaii	0	0.00
Idaho	0	0.00
Indiana	0	0.00
Iowa	0	0.00
Kansas	0	0.00
Kentucky	0	0.00
Louisiana	0	0.00
Maine	0	0.00
Mississippi	0	0.00
Montana	0	0.00
Nebraska	0	0.00
New Hampshire	0	0.00
New Mexico	0	0.00
North Dakota	0	0.00
Oklahoma	0	0.00
Rhode Island	0	0.00
South Dakota	0	0.00
Vermont	0	0.00
West Virginia	0	0.00
Wyoming	0	0.00

Please refer to the Explanation of Data in the front of the book for more detailed information.

Ancestry

Soviet Union

Top 150 Places Sorted by Population

Based on all places, regardless of total population

Place	Population	%
New York, NY (city) Kings County	419	0.01
Brooklyn, NY (borough) Kings County	219	0.01
Tenafly, NJ (borough) Bergen County	180	1.26
Los Angeles, CA (city) Los Angeles County	105	<0.01
Kirkland, WA (city) King County	104	0.22
San Francisco, CA (city) San Francisco County	75	0.01
Queens, NY (borough) Queens County	71	<0.01
Seattle, WA (city) King County	64	0.01
Staten Island, NY (borough) Richmond County	63	0.01
Manhattan, NY (borough) New York County	54	<0.01
Long Lake, MI (township) Grand Traverse County	52	0.61
Boston, MA (city) Suffolk County	50	0.01
Fair Lawn, NJ (borough) Bergen County	43	0.13
Old Bridge, NJ (township) Middlesex County	43	0.07
Hemet, CA (city) Riverside County	34	0.04
Aventura, FL (city) Miami-Dade County	30	0.09
Weston, MA (town) Middlesex County	27	0.24
East Brunswick, NJ (township) Middlesex County	27	0.06
Arlington, VA (cdp) Arlington County	26	0.01
San Diego, CA (city) San Diego County	25	<0.01
Clifton, NJ (city) Passaic County	23	0.03
New Haven, CT (city/town) New Haven County	23	0.02
Lower Merion, PA (township) Montgomery County	22	0.04
Morton Grove, IL (village) Cook County	21	0.09
Bernards, NJ (township) Somerset County	21	0.08
Portland, OR (city) Multnomah County	21	<0.01
Skokie, IL (village) Cook County	20	0.03
Santa Monica, CA (city) Los Angeles County	20	0.02
Pahrump, NV (cdp) Nye County	19	0.05
Paradise, NV (cdp) Clark County	19	0.01
Chicago, IL (city) Cook County	19	<0.01
Buffalo Grove, IL (village) Lake County	18	0.04
Northampton, PA (township) Bucks County	17	0.04
Champlin, MN (city) Hennepin County	16	0.07
Hallandale Beach, FL (city) Broward County	16	0.04
Marlboro, NJ (township) Monmouth County	16	0.04
Cincinnati, OH (city) Hamilton County	15	<0.01
Laguna Woods, CA (city) Orange County	14	0.09
Duarte, CA (city) Los Angeles County	14	0.07
Evanston, IL (city) Cook County	14	0.02
Mount Pleasant, SC (town) Charleston County	14	0.02
Cambridge, MA (city) Middlesex County	14	0.01
Yonkers, NY (city) Westchester County	14	0.01
Perry Heights, OH (cdp) Stark County	13	0.15
World Golf Village, FL (cdp) St. Johns County	13	0.13
Manhattan Beach, CA (city) Los Angeles County	13	0.04
Brookline, MA (cdp/town) Norfolk County	13	0.02
Hornell, NY (city) Steuben County	12	0.14
Socastee, SC (cdp) Horry County	12	0.07
Petersburg, VA (ind. city) Petersburg independent city	12	0.04
Bronx, NY (borough) Bronx County	12	<0.01
Bryn Mawr, PA (cdp) Montgomery County	11	0.31
Dania Beach, FL (city) Broward County	11	0.04
Vernon Hills, IL (village) Lake County	10	0.04
Oceanside, NY (cdp) Nassau County	10	0.03
Bensalem, PA (township) Bucks County	10	0.02
Allentown, PA (city) Lehigh County	10	0.01
Boca Raton, FL (city) Palm Beach County	10	0.01
Columbia, MO (city) Boone County	10	0.01
Hempstead, NY (town) Nassau County	10	<0.01
Ben Lomond, CA (cdp) Santa Cruz County	9	0.15
Ojai, CA (city) Ventura County	9	0.12
Ogden, UT (city) Weber County	9	0.01
Palo Alto, CA (city) Santa Clara County	9	0.01
Richmond, VA (ind. city) Richmond independent city	9	<0.01
Suwanee, GA (city) Gwinnett County	8	0.06
Brookfield, WI (city) Waukesha County	8	0.02
St. Louis, MO (city) St. Louis city County	8	<0.01
Gulfport, FL (city) Pinellas County	7	0.06
Fairfield, CA (city) Solano County	7	0.01
Merton, WI (town) Waukesha County	4	0.05
Wainscott, NY (cdp) Suffolk County	3	0.69
Corvallis, OR (city) Benton County	3	0.01
East Hampton, NY (town) Suffolk County	3	0.01
Norden, MN (township) Pennington County	2	0.47

Place	Population	%
Aaronsburg, PA (cdp) Centre County	0	0.00
Aaronsburg, PA (cdp) Washington County	0	0.00
Aastad, MN (township) Otter Tail County	0	0.00
Abanda, AL (cdp) Chambers County	0	0.00
Abbeville, AL (city) Henry County	0	0.00
Abbeville, GA (city) Wilcox County	0	0.00
Abbeville, LA (city) Vermilion Parish	0	0.00
Abbeville, MS (town) Lafayette County	0	0.00
Abbeville, SC (city) Abbeville County	0	0.00
Abbot, ME (town) Piscataquis County	0	0.00
Abbotsford, WI (city) Clark County	0	0.00
Abbotsford, WI (city) Clark County	0	0.00
Abbotsford, WI (city) Marathon County	0	0.00
Abbott, TX (city) Hill County	0	0.00
Abbott, PA (township) Potter County	0	0.00
Abbottstown, PA (borough) Adams County	0	0.00
Abbyville, KS (city) Reno County	0	0.00
Abercrombie, ND (city) Richland County	0	0.00
Aberdeen, ID (city) Bingham County	0	0.00
Aberdeen, IN (cdp) Porter County	0	0.00
Aberdeen, MD (city) Harford County	0	0.00
Aberdeen, MS (city) Monroe County	0	0.00
Aberdeen, NC (town) Moore County	0	0.00
Aberdeen, OH (village) Brown County	0	0.00
Aberdeen, SD (city) Brown County	0	0.00
Aberdeen, WA (city) Grays Harbor County	0	0.00
Aberdeen, NJ (township) Monmouth County	0	0.00
Aberdeen Gardens, WA (cdp) Grays Harbor County	0	0.00
Aberdeen Proving Ground, MD (cdp) Harford County	0	0.00
Abernathy, TX (city) Hale County	0	0.00
Abeytas, NM (cdp) Socorro County	0	0.00
Abie, NE (village) Butler County	0	0.00
Abilene, KS (city) Dickinson County	0	0.00
Abilene, TX (city) Taylor County	0	0.00
Abingdon, IL (city) Knox County	0	0.00
Abingdon, VA (town) Washington County	0	0.00
Abington, MA (cdp/town) Plymouth County	0	0.00
Abington, PA (township) Lackawanna County	0	0.00
Abington, PA (township) Montgomery County	0	0.00
Abiquiu, NM (cdp) Rio Arriba County	0	0.00
Abita Springs, LA (town) St. Tammany Parish	0	0.00
Abram, TX (cdp) Hidalgo County	0	0.00
Abrams, WI (cdp) Oconto County	0	0.00
Abrams, WI (town) Oconto County	0	0.00
Absarokee, MT (cdp) Stillwater County	0	0.00
Absecon, NJ (city) Atlantic County	0	0.00
Acacia Villas, FL (cdp) Palm Beach County	0	0.00
Acalanes Ridge, CA (cdp) Contra Costa County	0	0.00
Acampo, CA (cdp) San Joaquin County	0	0.00
Accident, MD (town) Garrett County	0	0.00
Accokeek, MD (cdp) Prince George's County	0	0.00
Accomac, VA (town) Accomack County	0	0.00
Accord, NY (cdp) Ulster County	0	0.00
Accoville, WV (cdp) Logan County	0	0.00
Acequia, ID (city) Minidoka County	0	0.00
Achille, OK (town) Bryan County	0	0.00
Ackerly, TX (city) Dawson County	0	0.00
Ackerman, MS (town) Choctaw County	0	0.00
Ackermanville, PA (cdp) Northampton County	0	0.00
Ackley, IA (city) Hardin County	0	0.00
Ackley, WI (town) Langlade County	0	0.00
Ackworth, IA (city) Warren County	0	0.00
Acme, WA (cdp) Whatcom County	0	0.00
Acme, MI (township) Grand Traverse County	0	0.00
Acoma, MN (township) McLeod County	0	0.00
Acomita Lake, NM (cdp) Cibola County	0	0.00
Acres Green, CO (cdp) Douglas County	0	0.00
Acton, CA (cdp) Los Angeles County	0	0.00
Acton, ME (town) York County	0	0.00
Acton, MA (town) Middlesex County	0	0.00
Acton, MN (township) Meeker County	0	0.00
Acushnet, MA (town) Bristol County	0	0.00
Acushnet Center, MA (cdp) Bristol County	0	0.00
Acworth, GA (city) Cobb County	0	0.00
Acworth, NH (town) Sullivan County	0	0.00

Ancestry

Soviet Union

Top 150 Places Sorted by Percent of Total Population

Based on all places, regardless of total population

Place	Population	%
Tenafly, NJ (borough) Bergen County	180	1.26
Wainscott, NY (cdp) Suffolk County	3	0.69
Long Lake, MI (township) Grand Traverse County	52	0.61
Norden, MN (township) Pennington County	2	0.47
Bryn Mawr, PA (cdp) Montgomery County	11	0.31
Weston, MA (town) Middlesex County	27	0.24
Kirkland, WA (city) King County	104	0.22
Perry Heights, OH (cdp) Stark County	13	0.15
Ben Lomond, CA (cdp) Santa Cruz County	9	0.15
Hornell, NY (city) Steuben County	12	0.14
Fair Lawn, NJ (borough) Bergen County	43	0.13
World Golf Village, FL (cdp) St. Johns County	13	0.13
Ojai, CA (city) Ventura County	9	0.12
Aventura, FL (city) Miami-Dade County	30	0.09
Morton Grove, IL (village) Cook County	21	0.09
Laguna Woods, CA (city) Orange County	14	0.09
Bernards, NJ (township) Somerset County	21	0.08
Old Bridge, NJ (township) Middlesex County	43	0.07
Champlin, MN (city) Hennepin County	16	0.07
Duarte, CA (city) Los Angeles County	14	0.07
Socastee, SC (cdp) Horry County	12	0.07
East Brunswick, NJ (township) Middlesex County	27	0.06
Suwanee, GA (city) Gwinnett County	8	0.06
Gulfport, FL (city) Pinellas County	7	0.06
Pahrump, NV (cdp) Nye County	19	0.05
Merton, WI (town) Waukesha County	4	0.05
Hemet, CA (city) Riverside County	34	0.04
Lower Merion, PA (township) Montgomery County	22	0.04
Buffalo Grove, IL (village) Lake County	18	0.04
Northampton, PA (township) Bucks County	17	0.04
Hallandale Beach, FL (city) Broward County	16	0.04
Marlboro, NJ (township) Monmouth County	16	0.04
Manhattan Beach, CA (city) Los Angeles County	13	0.04
Petersburg, VA (ind. city) Petersburg independent city	12	0.04
Dania Beach, FL (city) Broward County	11	0.04
Vernon Hills, IL (village) Lake County	10	0.04
Clifton, NJ (city) Passaic County	23	0.03
Skokie, IL (village) Cook County	20	0.03
Oceanside, NY (cdp) Nassau County	10	0.03
New Haven, CT (city/town) New Haven County	23	0.02
Santa Monica, CA (city) Los Angeles County	20	0.02
Evanston, IL (city) Cook County	14	0.02
Mount Pleasant, SC (town) Charleston County	14	0.02
Brookline, MA (cdp/town) Norfolk County	13	0.02
Bensalem, PA (township) Bucks County	10	0.02
Brookfield, WI (city) Waukesha County	8	0.02
New York, NY (city) Kings County	419	0.01
Brooklyn, NY (borough) Kings County	219	0.01
San Francisco, CA (city) San Francisco County	75	0.01
Seattle, WA (city) King County	64	0.01
Staten Island, NY (borough) Richmond County	63	0.01
Boston, MA (city) Suffolk County	50	0.01
Arlington, VA (cdp) Arlington County	26	0.01
Paradise, NV (cdp) Clark County	19	0.01
Cambridge, MA (city) Middlesex County	14	0.01
Yonkers, NY (city) Westchester County	14	0.01
Allentown, PA (city) Lehigh County	10	0.01
Boca Raton, FL (city) Palm Beach County	10	0.01
Columbia, MO (city) Boone County	10	0.01
Ogden, UT (city) Weber County	9	0.01
Palo Alto, CA (city) Santa Clara County	9	0.01
Fairfield, CA (city) Solano County	7	0.01
Corvallis, OR (city) Benton County	3	0.01
East Hampton, NY (town) Suffolk County	3	0.01
Los Angeles, CA (city) Los Angeles County	105	<0.01
Queens, NY (borough) Queens County	71	<0.01
Manhattan, NY (borough) New York County	54	<0.01
San Diego, CA (city) San Diego County	25	<0.01
Portland, OR (city) Multnomah County	21	<0.01
Chicago, IL (city) Cook County	19	<0.01
Cincinnati, OH (city) Hamilton County	15	<0.01
Bronx, NY (borough) Bronx County	12	<0.01
Hempstead, NY (town) Nassau County	10	<0.01
Richmond, VA (ind. city) Richmond independent city	9	<0.01
St. Louis, MO (city) St. Louis city County	8	<0.01

Place	Population	%
Aaronsburg, PA (cdp) Centre County	0	0.00
Aaronsburg, PA (cdp) Washington County	0	0.00
Aastad, MN (township) Otter Tail County	0	0.00
Abanda, AL (cdp) Chambers County	0	0.00
Abbeville, AL (city) Henry County	0	0.00
Abbeville, GA (city) Wilcox County	0	0.00
Abbeville, LA (city) Vermilion Parish	0	0.00
Abbeville, MS (town) Lafayette County	0	0.00
Abbeville, SC (city) Abbeville County	0	0.00
Abbot, ME (town) Piscataquis County	0	0.00
Abbotsford, WI (city) Clark County	0	0.00
Abbotsford, WI (city) Clark County	0	0.00
Abbotsford, WI (city) Marathon County	0	0.00
Abbott, TX (city) Hill County	0	0.00
Abbott, PA (township) Potter County	0	0.00
Abbottstown, PA (borough) Adams County	0	0.00
Abbyville, KS (city) Reno County	0	0.00
Abercrombie, ND (city) Richland County	0	0.00
Aberdeen, ID (city) Bingham County	0	0.00
Aberdeen, IN (cdp) Porter County	0	0.00
Aberdeen, MD (city) Harford County	0	0.00
Aberdeen, MS (city) Monroe County	0	0.00
Aberdeen, NC (town) Moore County	0	0.00
Aberdeen, OH (village) Brown County	0	0.00
Aberdeen, SD (city) Brown County	0	0.00
Aberdeen, WA (city) Grays Harbor County	0	0.00
Aberdeen, NJ (township) Monmouth County	0	0.00
Aberdeen Gardens, WA (cdp) Grays Harbor County	0	0.00
Aberdeen Proving Ground, MD (cdp) Harford County	0	0.00
Abernathy, TX (city) Hale County	0	0.00
Abeytas, NM (cdp) Socorro County	0	0.00
Abie, NE (village) Butler County	0	0.00
Abilene, KS (city) Dickinson County	0	0.00
Abilene, TX (city) Taylor County	0	0.00
Abingdon, IL (city) Knox County	0	0.00
Abingdon, VA (town) Washington County	0	0.00
Abington, MA (cdp/town) Plymouth County	0	0.00
Abington, PA (township) Lackawanna County	0	0.00
Abington, PA (township) Montgomery County	0	0.00
Abiquiu, NM (cdp) Rio Arriba County	0	0.00
Abita Springs, LA (town) St. Tammany Parish	0	0.00
Abram, TX (cdp) Hidalgo County	0	0.00
Abrams, WI (cdp) Oconto County	0	0.00
Abrams, WI (town) Oconto County	0	0.00
Absarokee, MT (cdp) Stillwater County	0	0.00
Absecon, NJ (city) Atlantic County	0	0.00
Acacia Villas, FL (cdp) Palm Beach County	0	0.00
Acalanes Ridge, CA (cdp) Contra Costa County	0	0.00
Acampo, CA (cdp) San Joaquin County	0	0.00
Accident, MD (town) Garrett County	0	0.00
Accokeek, MD (cdp) Prince George's County	0	0.00
Accomac, VA (town) Accomack County	0	0.00
Accord, NY (cdp) Ulster County	0	0.00
Accoville, WV (cdp) Logan County	0	0.00
Acequia, ID (city) Minidoka County	0	0.00
Achille, OK (town) Bryan County	0	0.00
Ackerly, TX (city) Dawson County	0	0.00
Ackerman, MS (town) Choctaw County	0	0.00
Ackermanville, PA (cdp) Northampton County	0	0.00
Ackley, IA (city) Hardin County	0	0.00
Ackley, WI (town) Langlade County	0	0.00
Ackworth, IA (city) Warren County	0	0.00
Acme, WA (cdp) Whatcom County	0	0.00
Acme, MI (township) Grand Traverse County	0	0.00
Acoma, MN (township) McLeod County	0	0.00
Acomita Lake, NM (cdp) Cibola County	0	0.00
Acres Green, CO (cdp) Douglas County	0	0.00
Acton, CA (cdp) Los Angeles County	0	0.00
Acton, ME (town) York County	0	0.00
Acton, MA (town) Middlesex County	0	0.00
Acton, MN (township) Meeker County	0	0.00
Acushnet, MA (town) Bristol County	0	0.00
Acushnet Center, MA (cdp) Bristol County	0	0.00
Acworth, GA (city) Cobb County	0	0.00
Acworth, NH (town) Sullivan County	0	0.00

Please refer to the Explanation of Data in the front of the book for more detailed information.

Ancestry

Soviet Union

Top 150 Places Sorted by Percent of Total Population

Based on places with total population of 7,500 or more

Place	Population	%
Tenafly, NJ (borough) Bergen County	180	1.26
Long Lake, MI (township) Grand Traverse County	52	0.61
Weston, MA (town) Middlesex County	27	0.24
Kirkland, WA (city) King County	104	0.22
Perry Heights, OH (cdp) Stark County	13	0.15
Hornell, NY (city) Steuben County	12	0.14
Fair Lawn, NJ (borough) Bergen County	43	0.13
World Golf Village, FL (cdp) St. Johns County	13	0.13
Ojai, CA (city) Ventura County	9	0.12
Aventura, FL (city) Miami-Dade County	30	0.09
Morton Grove, IL (village) Cook County	21	0.09
Laguna Woods, CA (city) Orange County	14	0.09
Bernards, NJ (township) Somerset County	21	0.08
Old Bridge, NJ (township) Middlesex County	43	0.07
Champlin, MN (city) Hennepin County	16	0.07
Duarte, CA (city) Los Angeles County	14	0.07
Socastee, SC (cdp) Horry County	12	0.07
East Brunswick, NJ (township) Middlesex County	27	0.06
Suwanee, GA (city) Gwinnett County	8	0.06
Gulfport, FL (city) Pinellas County	7	0.06
Pahrump, NV (cdp) Nye County	19	0.05
Merton, WI (town) Waukesha County	4	0.05
Hemet, CA (city) Riverside County	34	0.04
Lower Merion, PA (township) Montgomery County	22	0.04
Buffalo Grove, IL (village) Lake County	18	0.04
Northampton, PA (township) Bucks County	17	0.04
Hallandale Beach, FL (city) Broward County	16	0.04
Marlboro, NJ (township) Monmouth County	16	0.04
Manhattan Beach, CA (city) Los Angeles County	13	0.04
Petersburg, VA (ind. city) Petersburg independent city	12	0.04
Dania Beach, FL (city) Broward County	11	0.04
Vernon Hills, IL (village) Lake County	10	0.04
Clifton, NJ (city) Passaic County	23	0.03
Skokie, IL (village) Cook County	20	0.03
Oceanside, NY (cdp) Nassau County	10	0.03
New Haven, CT (city/town) New Haven County	23	0.02
Santa Monica, CA (city) Los Angeles County	20	0.02
Evanston, IL (city) Cook County	14	0.02
Mount Pleasant, SC (town) Charleston County	14	0.02
Brookline, MA (cdp/town) Norfolk County	13	0.02
Bensalem, PA (township) Bucks County	10	0.02
Brookfield, WI (city) Waukesha County	8	0.02
New York, NY (city) Kings County	419	0.01
Brooklyn, NY (borough) Kings County	219	0.01
San Francisco, CA (city) San Francisco County	75	0.01
Seattle, WA (city) King County	64	0.01
Staten Island, NY (borough) Richmond County	63	0.01
Boston, MA (city) Suffolk County	50	0.01
Arlington, VA (cdp) Arlington County	26	0.01
Paradise, NV (cdp) Clark County	19	0.01
Cambridge, MA (city) Middlesex County	14	0.01
Yonkers, NY (city) Westchester County	14	0.01
Allentown, PA (city) Lehigh County	10	0.01
Boca Raton, FL (city) Palm Beach County	10	0.01
Columbia, MO (city) Boone County	10	0.01
Ogden, UT (city) Weber County	9	0.01
Palo Alto, CA (city) Santa Clara County	9	0.01
Fairfield, CA (city) Solano County	7	0.01
Corvallis, OR (city) Benton County	3	0.01
East Hampton, NY (town) Suffolk County	3	0.01
Los Angeles, CA (city) Los Angeles County	105	<0.01
Queens, NY (borough) Queens County	71	<0.01
Manhattan, NY (borough) New York County	54	<0.01
San Diego, CA (city) San Diego County	25	<0.01
Portland, OR (city) Multnomah County	21	<0.01
Chicago, IL (city) Cook County	19	<0.01
Cincinnati, OH (city) Hamilton County	15	<0.01
Bronx, NY (borough) Bronx County	12	<0.01
Hempstead, NY (town) Nassau County	10	<0.01
Richmond, VA (ind. city) Richmond independent city	9	<0.01
St. Louis, MO (city) St. Louis city County	8	<0.01
Abbeville, LA (city) Vermilion Parish	0	0.00
Aberdeen, MD (city) Harford County	0	0.00
Aberdeen, SD (city) Brown County	0	0.00
Aberdeen, WA (city) Grays Harbor County	0	0.00
Aberdeen, NJ (township) Monmouth County	0	0.00
Abilene, TX (city) Taylor County	0	0.00
Abingdon, VA (town) Washington County	0	0.00
Abington, MA (cdp/town) Plymouth County	0	0.00
Abington, PA (township) Montgomery County	0	0.00
Absecon, NJ (city) Atlantic County	0	0.00
Accokeek, MD (cdp) Prince George's County	0	0.00
Acton, MA (town) Middlesex County	0	0.00
Acushnet, MA (town) Bristol County	0	0.00
Acworth, GA (city) Cobb County	0	0.00
Ada, OK (city) Pontotoc County	0	0.00
Ada, MI (township) Kent County	0	0.00
Adams, MA (town) Berkshire County	0	0.00
Adams, PA (township) Butler County	0	0.00
Addison, IL (village) DuPage County	0	0.00
Addison, TX (town) Dallas County	0	0.00
Adelanto, CA (city) San Bernardino County	0	0.00
Adelphi, MD (cdp) Prince George's County	0	0.00
Adrian, MI (city) Lenawee County	0	0.00
Affton, MO (cdp) St. Louis County	0	0.00
Agawam Town, MA (city) Hampden County	0	0.00
Agoura Hills, CA (city) Los Angeles County	0	0.00
Ahuimanu, HI (cdp) Honolulu County	0	0.00
Aiea, HI (cdp) Honolulu County	0	0.00
Aiken, SC (city) Aiken County	0	0.00
Air Force Academy, CO (cdp) El Paso County	0	0.00
Airmont, NY (village) Rockland County	0	0.00
Akron, OH (city) Summit County	0	0.00
Alabaster, AL (city) Shelby County	0	0.00
Alachua, FL (city) Alachua County	0	0.00
Alafaya, FL (cdp) Orange County	0	0.00
Alameda, CA (city) Alameda County	0	0.00
Alamo, CA (cdp) Contra Costa County	0	0.00
Alamo, TX (city) Hidalgo County	0	0.00
Alamogordo, NM (city) Otero County	0	0.00
Alamosa, CO (city) Alamosa County	0	0.00
Albany, CA (city) Alameda County	0	0.00
Albany, GA (city) Dougherty County	0	0.00
Albany, NY (city) Albany County	0	0.00
Albany, OR (city) Linn County	0	0.00
Albemarle, NC (city) Stanly County	0	0.00
Albert Lea, MN (city) Freeborn County	0	0.00
Albertville, AL (city) Marshall County	0	0.00
Albion, MI (city) Calhoun County	0	0.00
Albion, NY (town) Orleans County	0	0.00
Albuquerque, NM (city) Bernalillo County	0	0.00
Alcoa, TN (city) Blount County	0	0.00
Alden, NY (town) Erie County	0	0.00
Alderwood Manor, WA (cdp) Snohomish County	0	0.00
Aldine, TX (cdp) Harris County	0	0.00
Alexander City, AL (city) Tallapoosa County	0	0.00
Alexandria, KY (city) Campbell County	0	0.00
Alexandria, LA (city) Rapides Parish	0	0.00
Alexandria, MN (city) Douglas County	0	0.00
Alexandria, VA (ind. city) Alexandria independent city	0	0.00
Algoma, MI (township) Kent County	0	0.00
Algonquin, IL (village) McHenry County	0	0.00
Alhambra, CA (city) Los Angeles County	0	0.00
Alice, TX (city) Jim Wells County	0	0.00
Aliquippa, PA (city) Beaver County	0	0.00
Aliso Viejo, CA (city) Orange County	0	0.00
Allegany, NY (town) Cattaraugus County	0	0.00
Allegheny, PA (township) Westmoreland County	0	0.00
Allen, TX (city) Collin County	0	0.00
Allen Park, MI (city) Wayne County	0	0.00
Allendale, MI (cdp) Ottawa County	0	0.00
Allendale, MI (charter township) Ottawa County	0	0.00
Alliance, NE (city) Box Butte County	0	0.00
Alliance, OH (city) Stark County	0	0.00
Allison Park, PA (cdp) Allegheny County	0	0.00
Allouez, WI (village) Brown County	0	0.00
Alma, MI (city) Gratiot County	0	0.00
Aloha, OR (cdp) Washington County	0	0.00
Alondra Park, CA (cdp) Los Angeles County	0	0.00
Alpena, MI (city) Alpena County	0	0.00

SECTION THREE

Ancestry

Swedish

U.S. and 50 States Sorted by Population and Percent of Total Population

Place	Population	%
United States	**4,293,208**	**1.41**
Minnesota	496,174	9.47
California	456,603	1.25
Illinois	302,369	2.37
Washington	244,773	3.73
Michigan	172,043	1.73
Florida	164,461	0.89
Wisconsin	158,306	2.81
Texas	158,259	0.65
Colorado	137,182	2.81
New York	132,781	0.69
Massachusetts	122,801	1.90
Oregon	117,209	3.12
Pennsylvania	114,312	0.91
Arizona	109,020	1.75
Utah	108,734	4.09
Iowa	98,447	3.26
Nebraska	89,083	4.95
Ohio	78,498	0.68
Kansas	69,209	2.46
Connecticut	66,693	1.88
Indiana	65,409	1.02
Missouri	64,889	1.10
Virginia	60,352	0.77
New Jersey	54,488	0.62
North Carolina	52,952	0.57
Idaho	51,884	3.40
Georgia	44,257	0.47
Nevada	39,042	1.48
Maryland	37,285	0.65
Tennessee	35,031	0.56
Montana	33,389	3.43
North Dakota	31,513	4.78
South Dakota	30,517	3.82
Oklahoma	28,013	0.76
New Hampshire	26,728	2.03
Maine	25,098	1.89
South Carolina	23,186	0.51
Rhode Island	18,996	1.80
Alaska	18,842	2.73
Wyoming	18,760	3.44
Arkansas	18,687	0.65
New Mexico	18,667	0.93
Alabama	18,238	0.39
Kentucky	18,107	0.42
Louisiana	12,729	0.29
Vermont	11,399	1.83
Hawaii	10,414	0.78
Mississippi	8,572	0.29
West Virginia	7,471	0.41
Delaware	7,281	0.83
District of Columbia	4,055	0.69

Place	Population	%
Minnesota	496,174	9.47
Nebraska	89,083	4.95
North Dakota	31,513	4.78
Utah	108,734	4.09
South Dakota	30,517	3.82
Washington	244,773	3.73
Wyoming	18,760	3.44
Montana	33,389	3.43
Idaho	51,884	3.40
Iowa	98,447	3.26
Oregon	117,209	3.12
Wisconsin	158,306	2.81
Colorado	137,182	2.81
Alaska	18,842	2.73
Kansas	69,209	2.46
Illinois	302,369	2.37
New Hampshire	26,728	2.03
Massachusetts	122,801	1.90
Maine	25,098	1.89
Connecticut	66,693	1.88
Vermont	11,399	1.83
Rhode Island	18,996	1.80
Arizona	109,020	1.75
Michigan	172,043	1.73
Nevada	39,042	1.48
United States	**4,293,208**	**1.41**
California	456,603	1.25
Missouri	64,889	1.10
Indiana	65,409	1.02
New Mexico	18,667	0.93
Pennsylvania	114,312	0.91
Florida	164,461	0.89
Delaware	7,281	0.83
Hawaii	10,414	0.78
Virginia	60,352	0.77
Oklahoma	28,013	0.76
New York	132,781	0.69
District of Columbia	4,055	0.69
Ohio	78,498	0.68
Texas	158,259	0.65
Maryland	37,285	0.65
Arkansas	18,687	0.65
New Jersey	54,488	0.62
North Carolina	52,952	0.57
Tennessee	35,031	0.56
South Carolina	23,186	0.51
Georgia	44,257	0.47
Kentucky	18,107	0.42
West Virginia	7,471	0.41
Alabama	18,238	0.39
Louisiana	12,729	0.29
Mississippi	8,572	0.29

Please refer to the Explanation of Data in the front of the book for more detailed information.

Ancestry

Swedish

Top 150 Places Sorted by Population

Based on all places, regardless of total population

Place	Population	%
Minneapolis, MN (city) Hennepin County	30,230	7.96
Chicago, IL (city) Cook County	26,075	0.96
Los Angeles, CA (city) Los Angeles County	23,723	0.63
Seattle, WA (city) King County	21,937	3.69
New York, NY (city) Kings County	20,940	0.26
St. Paul, MN (city) Ramsey County	18,089	6.41
Phoenix, AZ (city) Maricopa County	17,706	1.22
San Diego, CA (city) San Diego County	17,467	1.36
Portland, OR (city) Multnomah County	17,319	3.06
Omaha, NE (city) Douglas County	15,444	3.79
Lincoln, NE (city) Lancaster County	13,266	5.24
Rockford, IL (city) Winnebago County	12,535	8.11
Duluth, MN (city) St. Louis County	12,102	14.06
Denver, CO (city) Denver County	11,437	1.98
Manhattan, NY (borough) New York County	10,408	0.66
Colorado Springs, CO (city) El Paso County	9,674	2.39
Bloomington, MN (city) Hennepin County	9,528	11.53
Mesa, AZ (city) Maricopa County	9,428	2.14
San Francisco, CA (city) San Francisco County	8,924	1.13
San Jose, CA (city) Santa Clara County	8,620	0.93
Austin, TX (city) Travis County	8,572	1.12
Houston, TX (city) Harris County	7,900	0.38
Spokane, WA (city) Spokane County	7,476	3.62
Plymouth, MN (city) Hennepin County	7,210	10.42
Salt Lake City, UT (city) Salt Lake County	7,051	3.82
Coon Rapids, MN (city) Anoka County	7,001	11.29
Tacoma, WA (city) Pierce County	6,871	3.46
Anchorage, AK (municipality) Anchorage Municipality	6,636	2.33
Maple Grove, MN (city) Hennepin County	6,556	11.10
Madison, WI (city) Dane County	6,536	2.85
Tucson, AZ (city) Pima County	6,478	1.25
Blaine, MN (city) Anoka County	6,373	11.50
Fargo, ND (city) Cass County	6,328	6.17
Las Vegas, NV (city) Clark County	6,296	1.09
Albuquerque, NM (city) Bernalillo County	6,215	1.17
Kansas City, MO (city) Jackson County	6,140	1.35
Dallas, TX (city) Dallas County	6,140	0.52
Boise City, ID (city) Ada County	6,126	2.97
Minnetonka, MN (city) Hennepin County	6,106	12.32
San Antonio, TX (city) Medina County	6,093	0.47
Scottsdale, AZ (city) Maricopa County	5,842	2.67
Jamestown, NY (city) Chautauqua County	5,809	18.63
Wichita, KS (city) Sedgwick County	5,808	1.55
Edina, MN (city) Hennepin County	5,740	12.10
Milwaukee, WI (city) Milwaukee County	5,711	0.97
Sacramento, CA (city) Sacramento County	5,613	1.22
Indianapolis, IN (city) Marion County	5,593	0.69
Fort Collins, CO (city) Larimer County	5,589	3.99
Eden Prairie, MN (city) Hennepin County	5,463	9.23
Sioux Falls, SD (city) Minnehaha County	5,345	3.59
Burnsville, MN (city) Dakota County	5,316	8.76
Boston, MA (city) Suffolk County	5,313	0.88
Vancouver, WA (city) Clark County	5,301	3.31
Eagan, MN (city) Dakota County	5,297	8.21
Lakeville, MN (city) Dakota County	5,268	9.76
Des Moines, IA (city) Polk County	5,226	2.59
Aurora, CO (city) Arapahoe County	5,208	1.66
Brooklyn, NY (borough) Kings County	5,185	0.21
Rochester, MN (city) Olmsted County	5,106	4.90
Woodbury, MN (city) Washington County	5,100	8.58
Provo, UT (city) Utah County	5,073	4.60
Overland Park, KS (city) Johnson County	5,063	2.97
Brooklyn Park, MN (city) Hennepin County	5,012	6.81
Fort Worth, TX (city) Tarrant County	4,965	0.70
Gilbert, AZ (town) Maricopa County	4,884	2.50
Henderson, NV (city) Clark County	4,820	1.93
Worcester, MA (city) Worcester County	4,756	2.64
St. Louis Park, MN (city) Hennepin County	4,663	10.44
West Jordan, UT (city) Salt Lake County	4,599	4.66
Sandy, UT (city) Salt Lake County	4,524	5.19
Columbus, OH (city) Franklin County	4,492	0.58
Fresno, CA (city) Fresno County	4,491	0.93
Lakewood, CO (city) Jefferson County	4,401	3.10
Oklahoma City, OK (city) Oklahoma County	4,355	0.77
Naperville, IL (city) DuPage County	4,354	3.09
St. Cloud, MN (city) Stearns County	4,319	6.63
Jacksonville, FL (city) Duval County	4,315	0.53
Huntington Beach, CA (city) Orange County	4,208	2.23
Long Beach, CA (city) Los Angeles County	4,170	0.90
Chandler, AZ (city) Maricopa County	4,164	1.81
Arvada, CO (city) Jefferson County	4,149	3.96
Eugene, OR (city) Lane County	4,137	2.70
Charlotte, NC (city) Mecklenburg County	4,136	0.59
Apple Valley, MN (city) Dakota County	4,120	8.45
Santa Clarita, CA (city) Los Angeles County	4,096	2.38
Bakersfield, CA (city) Kern County	4,065	1.22
Washington, DC (city) District of Columbia	4,055	0.69
Brookhaven, NY (town) Suffolk County	4,045	0.84
Salem, OR (city) Marion County	4,012	2.64
Virginia Beach, VA (ind. city) Virginia Beach independent city	4,008	0.92
Everett, WA (city) Snohomish County	3,941	3.88
Hempstead, NY (town) Nassau County	3,930	0.52
Tulsa, OK (city) Tulsa County	3,856	0.99
Centennial, CO (city) Arapahoe County	3,818	3.82
Roseville, MN (city) Ramsey County	3,809	11.45
Andover, MN (city) Anoka County	3,749	12.46
Philadelphia, PA (city) Philadelphia County	3,719	0.25
Bellingham, WA (city) Whatcom County	3,705	4.69
Nashville-Davidson, TN (metro govt) Davidson County	3,661	0.62
Oakland, CA (city) Alameda County	3,653	0.94
Maplewood, MN (city) Ramsey County	3,646	9.83
Bellevue, WA (city) King County	3,603	3.02
St. Cloud, MN (city) Stearns County	3,563	6.88
Orem, UT (city) Utah County	3,563	4.10
Reno, NV (city) Washoe County	3,513	1.59
West Valley City, UT (city) Salt Lake County	3,499	2.80
Spokane Valley, WA (city) Spokane County	3,481	3.95
Westminster, CO (city) Adams County	3,446	3.29
Boulder, CO (city) Boulder County	3,434	3.54
Superior, WI (city) Douglas County	3,428	12.61
Grand Rapids, MI (city) Kent County	3,385	1.78
Richfield, MN (city) Hennepin County	3,383	9.73
Riverside, CA (city) Riverside County	3,367	1.12
Billings, MT (city) Yellowstone County	3,328	3.28
Moline, IL (city) Rock Island County	3,277	7.56
Modesto, CA (city) Stanislaus County	3,260	1.61
Highlands Ranch, CO (cdp) Douglas County	3,199	3.36
Arlington Heights, IL (village) Cook County	3,191	4.26
Aurora, IL (city) Kane County	3,178	1.67
Thousand Oaks, CA (city) Ventura County	3,155	2.53
Galesburg, IL (city) Knox County	3,141	9.76
Olathe, KS (city) Johnson County	3,130	2.59
Tempe, AZ (city) Maricopa County	3,121	1.90
St. Petersburg, FL (city) Pinellas County	3,112	1.27
Bend, OR (city) Deschutes County	3,094	4.16
Santa Rosa, CA (city) Sonoma County	3,092	1.90
Glendale, AZ (city) Maricopa County	3,079	1.34
Redding, CA (city) Shasta County	3,053	3.42
Moorhead, MN (city) Clay County	3,044	8.29
Beaverton, OR (city) Washington County	2,976	3.38
Plano, TX (city) Collin County	2,970	1.16
Cottage Grove, MN (city) Washington County	2,939	8.64
Shoreview, MN (city) Ramsey County	2,915	11.71
Chanhassen, MN (city) Carver County	2,897	12.68
Edmonds, WA (city) Snohomish County	2,872	7.24
Queens, NY (borough) Queens County	2,862	0.13
Topeka, KS (city) Shawnee County	2,854	2.26
Davenport, IA (city) Scott County	2,848	2.90
Carlsbad, CA (city) San Diego County	2,833	2.84
Cedar Rapids, IA (city) Linn County	2,828	2.25
Irvine, CA (city) Orange County	2,808	1.41
Sioux City, IA (city) Woodbury County	2,805	3.42
Anaheim, CA (city) Orange County	2,803	0.84
Peoria, IL (city) Peoria County	2,798	2.46
Roseville, CA (city) Placer County	2,780	2.44
St. George, UT (city) Washington County	2,753	3.87
Elk River, MN (city) Sherburne County	2,741	12.17
White Bear Lake, MN (city) Ramsey County	2,726	11.62
Kent, WA (city) King County	2,722	3.04
Kenosha, WI (city) Kenosha County	2,719	2.77

SECTION THREE

Ancestry

Swedish

Top 150 Places Sorted by Percent of Total Population

Based on all places, regardless of total population

Place	Population	%
Angle, MN (township) Lake of the Woods County	69	100.00
Angle Inlet, MN (cdp) Lake of the Woods County	69	100.00
Kohls Ranch, AZ (cdp) Gila County	26	100.00
Hogans Corner, WA (cdp) Grays Harbor County	13	100.00
Poole, NE (cdp) Buffalo County	12	100.00
Northeast Aitkin, MN (unorganized territory) Aitkin County	3	100.00
South Red River, MN (township) Kittson County	20	90.91
Prairie City, SD (cdp) Perkins County	79	83.16
Minnie, MN (township) Beltrami County	4	80.00
East Cass, MN (unorganized territory) Cass County	30	76.92
Skane, MN (township) Kittson County	39	76.47
Mountain View, WY (cdp) Natrona County	30	66.67
White Rock, SD (town) Roberts County	2	66.67
Shotley Brook, MN (unorganized territory) Beltrami County	5	62.50
Barstow, WA (cdp) Ferry County	13	61.90
Springfield, WI (cdp) Walworth County	66	61.68
Lind, MN (township) Roseau County	37	61.67
Jupiter, MN (township) Kittson County	56	61.54
Denham, MN (city) Pine County	22	61.11
Linsell, MN (township) Marshall County	22	61.11
Edenborn, PA (cdp) Fayette County	62	60.78
Cane Beds, AZ (cdp) Mohave County	128	60.66
Onyx, CA (cdp) Kern County	78	60.47
Calio, ND (city) Cavalier County	6	60.00
Berlin, ND (city) LaMoure County	20	58.82
Davis, MN (township) Kittson County	32	58.18
Richfield, NE (cdp) Sarpy County	78	56.52
Irvington, IA (cdp) Kossuth County	9	56.25
Sattley, CA (cdp) Sierra County	12	54.55
Lake Roberts Heights, NM (cdp) Grant County	36	53.73
Hay Lake, MN (unorganized territory) St. Louis County	22	53.66
Verdi, CA (cdp) Sierra County	98	52.97
Goodland, FL (cdp) Collier County	192	52.46
Effie, MN (city) Itasca County	68	51.91
Naples, SD (town) Clark County	13	50.00
Donnelly, MN (township) Marshall County	8	50.00
Hill, MN (township) Kittson County	2	50.00
Tegner, MN (township) Kittson County	23	48.94
Zemple, MN (city) Itasca County	33	48.53
Hazelton, MN (township) Kittson County	53	48.18
Heimdal, ND (cdp) Wells County	6	46.15
Hollenberg, KS (city) Washington County	16	45.71
Kroschel, MN (township) Kanabec County	82	45.56
San Luis, NM (cdp) Sandoval County	15	45.45
Chautauqua, NY (cdp) Chautauqua County	119	45.08
Oxford, ID (city) Franklin County	26	44.83
Johnson, MN (township) Polk County	16	44.44
Turtle River, MN (city) Beltrami County	12	44.44
Swan Lake, MT (cdp) Lake County	53	44.17
Palmyra, MN (township) Renville County	67	44.08
Orin, WY (cdp) Converse County	53	43.80
Pembine, WI (cdp) Marinette County	94	43.72
Chilgren, MN (township) Lake of the Woods County	98	42.98
Armstrong, OK (town) Bryan County	28	42.42
Bartlett, IA (cdp) Fremont County	8	42.11
Deerwood, MN (township) Kittson County	45	41.67
Poppleton, MN (township) Kittson County	46	41.44
Silesia, MT (cdp) Carbon County	31	41.33
Bray, MN (township) Pennington County	21	41.18
Royal, NE (village) Antelope County	16	41.03
Funk, NE (village) Phelps County	76	40.43
Wausa, NE (village) Knox County	210	40.38
New Sweden, ME (town) Aroostook County	206	40.16
Lee, MN (township) Aitkin County	30	40.00
Pelan, MN (township) Kittson County	16	40.00
Prairie Lake, MN (township) St. Louis County	12	40.00
Richardville, MN (township) Kittson County	58	39.19
Max, MN (township) Itasca County	51	38.93
Jasper, MN (city) Rock County	34	38.64
Martinsburg, NE (village) Dixon County	27	38.57
Mud Bay, AK (cdp) Haines Borough	37	38.54
Rock Island Arsenal, IL (cdp) Rock Island County	30	38.46
Manning, ND (cdp) Dunn County	18	38.30
Forest, MN (township) Becker County	47	38.21
Quamba, MN (city) Kanabec County	34	38.20

Place	Population	%
Morcom, MN (township) St. Louis County	50	38.17
Henriette, MN (city) Pine County	16	38.10
Beaver, MN (township) Roseau County	54	38.03
Percy, MN (township) Kittson County	11	37.93
Logan, MN (township) Aitkin County	62	37.80
Black River, MN (township) Pennington County	25	37.31
Strathcona, MN (city) Roseau County	20	37.04
Mickinock, MN (township) Roseau County	101	37.00
Maysville, AR (cdp) Benton County	48	36.92
Beaulieu, MN (cdp) Mahnomen County	38	36.89
West Branch, MI (township) Dickinson County	14	36.84
Cherry Grove, PA (township) Warren County	89	36.78
Ogema, WI (cdp) Price County	75	36.76
Maple Ridge, MN (township) Isanti County	256	36.73
Lake Bronson, MN (city) Kittson County	89	36.33
Vining, MN (city) Otter Tail County	21	36.21
Chinook, WA (cdp) Pacific County	110	36.18
Felch, MI (township) Dickinson County	277	36.02
Hill, WI (town) Price County	133	35.95
Rollis, MN (township) Marshall County	30	35.71
Ambrose, ND (city) Divide County	5	35.71
Donaldson, MN (city) Kittson County	28	35.44
Kennedy, MN (city) Kittson County	52	35.37
Northland, MN (township) Polk County	54	35.29
Malung, MN (township) Roseau County	137	35.04
Northland, MN (township) St. Louis County	48	35.04
Hallock, MN (township) Kittson County	47	34.81
Owens, MN (township) St. Louis County	96	34.78
Oakland, NE (city) Burt County	473	34.73
Warrenton, MN (township) Marshall County	31	34.44
Hallock, MN (city) Kittson County	364	34.37
Bear Valley, CA (cdp) Alpine County	23	34.33
Como, MN (township) Marshall County	23	34.33
Malta, MN (township) Big Stone County	32	34.04
Beltrami, MN (city) Polk County	16	34.04
Bishop Hill, IL (village) Henry County	36	33.96
Little Pine, MN (township) Crow Wing County	18	33.96
Cloverleaf, MN (township) Pennington County	25	33.78
Grimstad, MN (township) Roseau County	58	33.72
Stafford, MN (township) Roseau County	99	33.45
Englevale, ND (cdp) Ransom County	22	33.33
Roxbury, KS (cdp) McPherson County	11	33.33
Lewis, MN (township) Mille Lacs County	9	33.33
Grattan, MN (township) Itasca County	8	33.33
New Albany, KS (city) Wilson County	3	33.33
Cedar, MN (township) Martin County	70	33.18
Quinnesec, MI (cdp) Dickinson County	333	33.00
Pillsbury, MN (township) Swift County	72	32.88
Odin, MN (township) Watonwan County	52	32.70
Amador, MN (township) Chisago County	322	32.69
Radisson, WI (village) Sawyer County	79	32.51
Comfort, MN (township) Kanabec County	376	32.50
Balsam, MN (township) Aitkin County	13	32.50
Blue Mounds, MN (township) Pope County	61	32.45
Kiantone, NY (town) Chautauqua County	482	32.44
Falun, MN (township) Roseau County	60	32.43
Wright, KS (cdp) Ford County	66	32.35
Big Woods, MN (township) Marshall County	44	32.35
Arveson, MN (township) Kittson County	31	32.29
Bay de Noc, MI (township) Delta County	122	32.28
Beaver, MN (township) Aitkin County	10	32.26
Government Camp, OR (cdp) Clackamas County	18	32.14
Glen, MN (township) Aitkin County	129	32.01
Acampo, CA (cdp) San Joaquin County	8	32.00
Cambridge, MN (township) Isanti County	816	31.99
Spring Brook, MN (township) Kittson County	23	31.94
Naponee, NE (village) Franklin County	38	31.93
Valley Ranch, CA (cdp) Plumas County	38	31.93
Spruce, MN (township) Roseau County	215	31.85
Malmo, MN (township) Aitkin County	135	31.84
Strandquist, MN (city) Marshall County	21	31.82
Lake Johanna, MN (township) Pope County	47	31.76
Stanchfield, MN (township) Isanti County	368	31.72
Southeast Roseau, MN (unorganized territory) Roseau County	24	31.58
Polk Centre, MN (township) Pennington County	23	31.51

Please refer to the Explanation of Data in the front of the book for more detailed information.

Ancestry

Swedish

Top 150 Places Sorted by Percent of Total Population

Based on places with total population of 7,500 or more

Place	Population	%
Ellicott, NY (town) Chautauqua County	2,238	25.52
Cambridge, MN (city) Isanti County	1,497	19.03
Jamestown, NY (city) Chautauqua County	5,809	18.63
Hermantown, MN (city) St. Louis County	1,687	18.44
North Branch, MN (city) Chisago County	1,739	17.43
Wyoming, MN (city) Chisago County	1,276	16.61
Thief River Falls, MN (city) Pennington County	1,304	15.24
Oak Grove, MN (city) Anoka County	1,200	15.23
Princeton, IL (city) Bureau County	1,179	14.95
Arden Hills, MN (city) Ramsey County	1,410	14.85
Vadnais Heights, MN (city) Ramsey County	1,786	14.54
Mounds View, MN (city) Ramsey County	1,717	14.18
Duluth, MN (city) St. Louis County	12,102	14.06
Alexandria, MN (city) Douglas County	1,551	13.98
Forest Lake, MN (city) Washington County	2,479	13.97
Iron Mountain, MI (city) Dickinson County	1,082	13.89
White Bear, MN (township) Ramsey County	1,491	13.74
Ham Lake, MN (city) Anoka County	2,045	13.68
Red Wing, MN (city) Goodhue County	2,237	13.60
Virginia, MN (city) St. Louis County	1,146	13.07
St. Anthony, MN (city) Hennepin and Ramsey Counties	1,058	13.05
Warren, PA (city) Warren County	1,264	12.93
Buffalo, MN (city) Wright County	1,901	12.87
Chanhassen, MN (city) Carver County	2,897	12.68
Superior, WI (city) Douglas County	3,428	12.61
Mound, MN (city) Hennepin County	1,136	12.57
New Brighton, MN (city) Ramsey County	2,664	12.49
Andover, MN (city) Anoka County	3,749	12.46
Lake Elmo, MN (city) Washington County	974	12.36
East Bethel, MN (city) Anoka County	1,430	12.33
Minnetonka, MN (city) Hennepin County	6,106	12.32
Elk River, MN (city) Sherburne County	2,741	12.17
Edina, MN (city) Hennepin County	5,740	12.10
Grand Rapids, MN (city) Itasca County	1,294	12.02
St. Peter, MN (city) Nicollet County	1,320	11.98
Champlin, MN (city) Hennepin County	2,715	11.94
Detroit Lakes, MN (city) Becker County	1,003	11.84
Shoreview, MN (city) Ramsey County	2,915	11.71
White Bear Lake, MN (city) Ramsey County	2,726	11.62
Bloomington, MN (city) Hennepin County	9,528	11.53
Blaine, MN (city) Anoka County	6,373	11.50
White Bear Lake, MN (city) Ramsey County	2,669	11.49
Stillwater, MN (city) Washington County	2,046	11.49
North St. Paul, MN (city) Ramsey County	1,305	11.46
Roseville, MN (city) Ramsey County	3,809	11.45
Willmar, MN (city) Kandiyohi County	2,195	11.35
Prior Lake, MN (city) Scott County	2,511	11.31
Coon Rapids, MN (city) Anoka County	7,001	11.29
Mahtomedi, MN (city) Washington County	863	11.21
Rosemount, MN (city) Dakota County	2,317	11.19
Big Lake, MN (city) Sherburne County	1,077	11.15
Hibbing, MN (city) St. Louis County	1,821	11.11
Maple Grove, MN (city) Hennepin County	6,556	11.10
Lino Lakes, MN (city) Anoka County	2,169	10.96
Boone, IA (city) Boone County	1,398	10.95
Cloquet, MN (city) Carlton County	1,316	10.95
Ramsey, MN (city) Anoka County	2,508	10.94
Otsego, MN (city) Wright County	1,363	10.89
Robbinsdale, MN (city) Hennepin County	1,510	10.88
Little Falls, MN (city) Morrison County	904	10.83
East Grand Forks, MN (city) Polk County	904	10.78
Escanaba, MI (city) Delta County	1,359	10.67
Hudson, WI (town) St. Croix County	872	10.57
St. Louis Park, MN (city) Hennepin County	4,663	10.44
Northfield, MN (city) Rice County	2,025	10.43
Plymouth, MN (city) Hennepin County	7,210	10.42
Hugo, MN (city) Washington County	1,261	10.40
Northfield, MN (city) Rice County	1,879	10.20
Golden Valley, MN (city) Hennepin County	2,054	10.18
Anoka, MN (city) Anoka County	1,772	10.16
New Hope, MN (city) Hennepin County	2,021	9.96
St. Michael, MN (city) Wright County	1,530	9.95
Maplewood, MN (city) Ramsey County	3,646	9.83
Lakeville, MN (city) Dakota County	5,268	9.76
Galesburg, IL (city) Knox County	3,141	9.76
Richfield, MN (city) Hennepin County	3,383	9.73
Rogers, MN (city) Hennepin County	730	9.53
Auburn, MA (town) Worcester County	1,518	9.38
Farmington, MN (city) Dakota County	1,838	9.35
Eden Prairie, MN (city) Hennepin County	5,463	9.23
Waconia, MN (city) Carver County	937	9.22
Loves Park, IL (city) Winnebago County	2,154	9.08
Fridley, MN (city) Anoka County	2,472	9.00
Little Canada, MN (city) Ramsey County	865	8.95
Fergus Falls, MN (city) Otter Tail County	1,192	8.93
Hudson, WI (city) St. Croix County	1,096	8.89
Marquette, MI (city) Marquette County	1,868	8.79
Burnsville, MN (city) Dakota County	5,316	8.76
Crystal, MN (city) Hennepin County	1,931	8.75
Oakdale, MN (city) Washington County	2,389	8.73
Cottage Grove, MN (city) Washington County	2,939	8.64
Vashon, WA (cdp) King County	858	8.64
Woodbury, MN (city) Washington County	5,100	8.58
Columbia Heights, MN (city) Anoka County	1,665	8.54
Brooklyn Center, MN (city) Hennepin County	2,522	8.50
Marinette, WI (city) Marinette County	942	8.49
Apple Valley, MN (city) Dakota County	4,120	8.45
Eagle Mountain, UT (city) Utah County	1,512	8.45
Moorhead, MN (city) Clay County	3,044	8.29
Machesney Park, IL (village) Winnebago County	1,904	8.25
Eagan, MN (city) Dakota County	5,297	8.21
Ashland, WI (city) Ashland County	678	8.19
Hopkins, MN (city) Hennepin County	1,422	8.16
Rockford, IL (city) Winnebago County	12,535	8.11
Monticello, MN (city) Wright County	984	8.05
Chaska, MN (city) Carver County	1,841	8.01
Sycamore, IL (city) DeKalb County	1,341	7.98
Minneapolis, MN (city) Hennepin County	30,230	7.96
Mendota Heights, MN (city) Dakota County	887	7.91
Hastings, MN (city) Dakota County	1,706	7.90
Savage, MN (city) Scott County	2,091	7.86
West St. Paul, MN (city) Dakota County	1,542	7.85
Rutland, MA (town) Worcester County	597	7.75
Hutchinson, MN (city) McLeod County	1,084	7.64
Moline, IL (city) Rock Island County	3,277	7.56
Sauk Rapids, MN (city) Benton County	942	7.55
Sutton, MA (town) Worcester County	667	7.52
Menominee, MI (city) Menominee County	653	7.52
Inver Grove Heights, MN (city) Dakota County	2,486	7.45
Enumclaw, WA (city) King County	794	7.45
Santaquin, UT (city) Utah County	616	7.36
Blair, NE (city) Washington County	587	7.36
Batavia, IL (city) Kane County	1,906	7.35
Kewanee, IL (city) Henry County	956	7.35
Centerville, UT (city) Davis County	1,114	7.32
River Falls, WI (city) Pierce County	1,069	7.27
Edmonds, WA (city) Snohomish County	2,872	7.24
Highland, UT (city) Utah County	1,012	7.19
Monroe, WA (city) Snohomish County	1,199	7.18
Kearney, NE (city) Buffalo County	2,160	7.15
Holden, MA (town) Worcester County	1,221	7.15
Bemidji, MN (city) Beltrami County	940	7.12
Laketon, MI (township) Muskegon County	541	7.12
Fremont, NE (city) Dodge County	1,862	7.10
Waseca, MN (city) Waseca County	658	6.98
East Haddam, CT (town) Middlesex County	623	6.89
St. Cloud, MN (city) Stearns County	3,563	6.88
Geneva, IL (city) Kane County	1,469	6.85
North Mankato, MN (city) Nicollet County	898	6.83
Inglewood-Finn Hill, WA (cdp) King County	1,577	6.82
Brooklyn Park, MN (city) Hennepin County	5,012	6.81
Brainerd, MN (city) Crow Wing County	935	6.80
Herriman, UT (city) Salt Lake County	1,238	6.75
Roscoe, IL (village) Winnebago County	678	6.67
New Richmond, WI (city) St. Croix County	548	6.64
St. Cloud, MN (city) Stearns County	4,319	6.63
Grinnell, IA (city) Poweshiek County	612	6.61
Sandy, OR (city) Clackamas County	586	6.61
Monmouth, IL (city) Warren County	619	6.59
Grimes, IA (city) Polk County	504	6.59

Please refer to the Explanation of Data in the front of the book for more detailed information.

Ancestry

Swiss

U.S. and 50 States Sorted by Population and Percent of Total Population

Place	Population	%
United States	**1,003,505**	**0.33**
California	114,687	0.31
Ohio	78,114	0.68
Pennsylvania	71,887	0.57
Wisconsin	60,339	1.07
Indiana	44,777	0.70
Illinois	41,435	0.33
New York	39,241	0.20
Florida	38,285	0.21
Washington	37,409	0.57
Texas	33,911	0.14
Utah	33,898	1.28
Oregon	30,820	0.82
Colorado	25,250	0.52
Missouri	24,908	0.42
Michigan	24,617	0.25
Minnesota	23,180	0.44
Virginia	20,872	0.27
Arizona	20,063	0.32
New Jersey	18,304	0.21
Iowa	15,924	0.53
North Carolina	15,605	0.17
Kansas	15,153	0.54
Maryland	13,369	0.23
Idaho	12,781	0.84
Massachusetts	12,578	0.19
Georgia	12,015	0.13
Tennessee	11,563	0.19
Kentucky	10,855	0.25
Connecticut	10,239	0.29
Nevada	9,396	0.36
South Carolina	8,780	0.19
Nebraska	7,954	0.44
Oklahoma	7,635	0.21
Montana	6,302	0.65
Arkansas	5,805	0.20
Alabama	4,476	0.09
New Mexico	4,417	0.22
West Virginia	3,806	0.21
Wyoming	3,664	0.67
Louisiana	3,249	0.07
Alaska	3,164	0.46
South Dakota	2,925	0.37
Hawaii	2,868	0.22
New Hampshire	2,841	0.22
Maine	2,496	0.19
Mississippi	2,359	0.08
Delaware	2,262	0.26
North Dakota	2,149	0.33
Vermont	2,092	0.34
District of Columbia	1,732	0.30
Rhode Island	1,054	0.10

Place	Population	%
Utah	33,898	1.28
Wisconsin	60,339	1.07
Idaho	12,781	0.84
Oregon	30,820	0.82
Indiana	44,777	0.70
Ohio	78,114	0.68
Wyoming	3,664	0.67
Montana	6,302	0.65
Pennsylvania	71,887	0.57
Washington	37,409	0.57
Kansas	15,153	0.54
Iowa	15,924	0.53
Colorado	25,250	0.52
Alaska	3,164	0.46
Minnesota	23,180	0.44
Nebraska	7,954	0.44
Missouri	24,908	0.42
South Dakota	2,925	0.37
Nevada	9,396	0.36
Vermont	2,092	0.34
United States	**1,003,505**	**0.33**
Illinois	41,435	0.33
North Dakota	2,149	0.33
Arizona	20,063	0.32
California	114,687	0.31
District of Columbia	1,732	0.30
Connecticut	10,239	0.29
Virginia	20,872	0.27
Delaware	2,262	0.26
Michigan	24,617	0.25
Kentucky	10,855	0.25
Maryland	13,369	0.23
New Mexico	4,417	0.22
Hawaii	2,868	0.22
New Hampshire	2,841	0.22
Florida	38,285	0.21
New Jersey	18,304	0.21
Oklahoma	7,635	0.21
West Virginia	3,806	0.21
New York	39,241	0.20
Arkansas	5,805	0.20
Massachusetts	12,578	0.19
Tennessee	11,563	0.19
South Carolina	8,780	0.19
Maine	2,496	0.19
North Carolina	15,605	0.17
Texas	33,911	0.14
Georgia	12,015	0.13
Rhode Island	1,054	0.10
Alabama	4,476	0.09
Mississippi	2,359	0.08
Louisiana	3,249	0.07

Please refer to the Explanation of Data in the front of the book for more detailed information.

Ancestry

Swiss

Top 150 Places Sorted by Population

Based on all places, regardless of total population

Place	Population	%
New York, NY (city) Kings County	8,135	0.10
Los Angeles, CA (city) Los Angeles County	5,328	0.14
Manhattan, NY (borough) New York County	4,962	0.31
Portland, OR (city) Multnomah County	4,649	0.82
San Diego, CA (city) San Diego County	4,165	0.32
Seattle, WA (city) King County	3,689	0.62
Madison, WI (city) Dane County	3,652	1.59
Chicago, IL (city) Cook County	3,481	0.13
San Francisco, CA (city) San Francisco County	3,264	0.41
Denver, CO (city) Denver County	3,029	0.52
Phoenix, AZ (city) Maricopa County	2,842	0.20
Columbus, OH (city) Franklin County	2,745	0.36
Houston, TX (city) Harris County	2,669	0.13
Monroe, WI (city) Green County	2,626	24.17
San Jose, CA (city) Santa Clara County	2,530	0.27
Fort Wayne, IN (city) Allen County	2,499	0.98
Louisville-Jefferson County, KY (metro govt) Jefferson County	2,422	0.41
Indianapolis, IN (city) Marion County	2,276	0.28
Austin, TX (city) Travis County	2,023	0.26
Mesa, AZ (city) Maricopa County	1,916	0.44
Philadelphia, PA (city) Philadelphia County	1,886	0.13
Salt Lake City, UT (city) Salt Lake County	1,861	1.01
Washington, DC (city) District of Columbia	1,732	0.30
Charlotte, NC (city) Mecklenburg County	1,724	0.24
Minneapolis, MN (city) Hennepin County	1,707	0.45
Sacramento, CA (city) Sacramento County	1,686	0.37
Milwaukee, WI (city) Milwaukee County	1,595	0.27
Provo, UT (city) Utah County	1,574	1.43
Colorado Springs, CO (city) El Paso County	1,558	0.39
Kansas City, MO (city) Jackson County	1,546	0.34
Brooklyn, NY (borough) Kings County	1,491	0.06
Goshen, IN (city) Elkhart County	1,482	4.74
Scottsdale, AZ (city) Maricopa County	1,463	0.67
Oklahoma City, OK (city) Oklahoma County	1,461	0.26
St. George, UT (city) Washington County	1,428	2.01
Tucson, AZ (city) Pima County	1,426	0.28
Salem, OR (city) Marion County	1,425	0.94
Boston, MA (city) Suffolk County	1,406	0.23
Boise City, ID (city) Ada County	1,404	0.68
Dallas, TX (city) Dallas County	1,387	0.12
Henderson, NV (city) Clark County	1,372	0.55
Brookhaven, NY (town) Suffolk County	1,356	0.28
Las Vegas, NV (city) Clark County	1,327	0.23
Sandy, UT (city) Salt Lake County	1,319	1.51
Anchorage, AK (municipality) Anchorage Municipality	1,313	0.46
Wichita, KS (city) Sedgwick County	1,300	0.35
Omaha, NE (city) Douglas County	1,276	0.31
Jacksonville, FL (city) Duval County	1,260	0.16
Queens, NY (borough) Queens County	1,260	0.06
Nashville-Davidson, TN (metro govt) Davidson County	1,234	0.21
Albuquerque, NM (city) Bernalillo County	1,201	0.23
Hempstead, NY (town) Nassau County	1,183	0.16
West Jordan, UT (city) Salt Lake County	1,159	1.18
Overland Park, KS (city) Johnson County	1,151	0.68
Toledo, OH (city) Lucas County	1,134	0.39
San Antonio, TX (city) Medina County	1,111	0.09
Virginia Beach, VA (ind. city) Virginia Beach independent city	1,090	0.25
Orem, UT (city) Utah County	1,084	1.25
Modesto, CA (city) Stanislaus County	1,072	0.53
Fort Collins, CO (city) Larimer County	1,059	0.76
Spokane, WA (city) Spokane County	1,057	0.51
Reno, NV (city) Washoe County	1,057	0.48
Fort Worth, TX (city) Tarrant County	1,038	0.15
Brecknock, PA (township) Lancaster County	1,027	14.39
Fresno, CA (city) Fresno County	1,010	0.21
Berne, IN (city) Adams County	1,005	24.67
Harrisonburg, VA (ind. city) Harrisonburg independent city	999	2.11
West Valley City, UT (city) Salt Lake County	991	0.79
Lincoln, NE (city) Lancaster County	989	0.39
Janesville, WI (city) Rock County	957	1.51
Aurora, CO (city) Arapahoe County	951	0.30
St. Paul, MN (city) Ramsey County	945	0.34
Eugene, OR (city) Lane County	930	0.61
Santa Rosa, CA (city) Sonoma County	924	0.57
Tacoma, WA (city) Pierce County	915	0.46

Place	Population	%
Logan, UT (city) Cache County	909	1.96
Vancouver, WA (city) Clark County	903	0.56
Santa Clarita, CA (city) Los Angeles County	896	0.52
Highlands Ranch, CO (cdp) Douglas County	862	0.91
Oakland, CA (city) Alameda County	856	0.22
Tulsa, OK (city) Tulsa County	851	0.22
Raleigh, NC (city) Wake County	846	0.22
East Earl, PA (township) Lancaster County	838	13.17
Pittsburgh, PA (city) Allegheny County	838	0.27
Beaverton, OR (city) Washington County	837	0.95
Irvine, CA (city) Orange County	835	0.42
South Jordan, UT (city) Salt Lake County	831	1.79
Bellevue, WA (city) King County	818	0.68
Cincinnati, OH (city) Hamilton County	796	0.27
St. Petersburg, FL (city) Pinellas County	789	0.32
Arlington, VA (cdp) Arlington County	787	0.40
Cedar Rapids, IA (city) Linn County	786	0.63
Ephrata, PA (township) Lancaster County	785	8.54
Berkeley, CA (city) Alameda County	784	0.72
Bountiful, UT (city) Davis County	773	1.82
Lakewood, CO (city) Jefferson County	769	0.54
Centennial, CO (city) Arapahoe County	767	0.77
Long Beach, CA (city) Los Angeles County	763	0.17
Waukesha, WI (city) Waukesha County	761	1.09
St. Louis, MO (city) St. Louis city County	758	0.24
East Lampeter, PA (township) Lancaster County	756	4.75
Bakersfield, CA (city) Kern County	750	0.23
Pocatello, ID (city) Bannock County	737	1.38
Millcreek, UT (cdp) Salt Lake County	737	1.21
Chandler, AZ (city) Maricopa County	735	0.32
Newport Beach, CA (city) Orange County	730	0.87
Peoria, IL (city) Peoria County	729	0.64
Layton, UT (city) Davis County	726	1.11
Wooster, OH (city) Wayne County	722	2.77
Davis, CA (city) Yolo County	722	1.11
Lancaster, PA (city) Lancaster County	714	1.21
Gilbert, AZ (town) Maricopa County	711	0.36
Lexington-Fayette, KY (cons. govt) Fayette County	708	0.25
San Luis Obispo, CA (city) San Luis Obispo County	703	1.56
Petaluma, CA (city) Sonoma County	697	1.23
Ellington, CT (town) Tolland County	692	4.54
Roseville, CA (city) Placer County	691	0.61
Kaysville, UT (city) Davis County	690	2.65
Akron, OH (city) Summit County	690	0.34
Huntington Beach, CA (city) Orange County	688	0.36
Oyster Bay, NY (town) Nassau County	686	0.24
Columbia, MO (city) Boone County	683	0.65
Olathe, KS (city) Johnson County	674	0.56
Ephrata, PA (borough) Lancaster County	673	5.03
Tempe, AZ (city) Maricopa County	670	0.41
St. Joseph, MO (city) Buchanan County	660	0.87
Baltimore, MD (city) Baltimore city County	660	0.11
West Lampeter, PA (township) Lancaster County	647	4.36
Pleasant Grove, UT (city) Utah County	647	2.06
Naperville, IL (city) DuPage County	647	0.46
Santa Barbara, CA (city) Santa Barbara County	644	0.73
Rochester, MN (city) Olmsted County	643	0.62
Riverside, CA (city) Riverside County	643	0.21
Grand Rapids, MI (city) Kent County	639	0.34
San Buenaventura (Ventura), CA (city) Ventura County	637	0.61
Des Moines, IA (city) Polk County	632	0.31
Huntington, NY (town) Suffolk County	632	0.31
Warwick, PA (township) Lancaster County	628	3.60
Manheim, PA (township) Lancaster County	625	1.67
Rockford, IL (city) Winnebago County	625	0.40
Orrville, OH (city) Wayne County	622	7.37
Earl, PA (township) Lancaster County	620	9.02
New Philadelphia, OH (city) Tuscarawas County	620	3.59
Islip, NY (town) Suffolk County	619	0.19
Arvada, CO (city) Jefferson County	613	0.58
Casas Adobes, AZ (cdp) Pima County	608	0.90
Penn, PA (township) Lancaster County	602	7.06
Lawrence, KS (city) Douglas County	597	0.69
Clovis, CA (city) Fresno County	596	0.65
Gresham, OR (city) Multnomah County	592	0.58

SECTION THREE

Ancestry

Swiss

Top 150 Places Sorted by Percent of Total Population

Based on all places, regardless of total population

Place	Population	%
Little America, WY (cdp) Sweetwater County	16	72.73
Belleville, NY (cdp) Jefferson County	79	67.52
Bay Lake, FL (city) Orange County	12	63.16
Pickens, WV (cdp) Randolph County	44	53.66
Churchs Ferry, ND (city) Ramsey County	2	50.00
Wolford, ND (city) Pierce County	34	47.22
Lebam, WA (cdp) Pacific County	68	43.87
Mays Lick, KY (cdp) Mason County	59	43.38
Harris, KS (cdp) Anderson County	33	42.31
Berlin, OH (cdp) Holmes County	390	41.40
Van Tassell, WY (town) Niobrara County	2	40.00
Helvetia, WV (cdp) Randolph County	14	38.89
Wineglass, MT (cdp) Park County	28	32.56
Washington, WI (town) Green County	232	32.09
Sylvester, WI (town) Green County	325	30.35
Goodville, PA (cdp) Lancaster County	78	30.35
Monticello, WI (village) Green County	362	30.34
Adams, WI (town) Green County	156	29.94
New Glarus, WI (village) Green County	549	29.45
Minnesota Lake, MN (city) Blue Earth County	5	29.41
Mount Eaton, OH (village) Wayne County	70	29.05
Sterling, OH (cdp) Wayne County	96	28.24
Garden, UT (cdp) Rich County	11	28.21
Picks, SD (town) Charles Mix County	24	27.91
Veteran, WY (cdp) Goshen County	16	27.59
Monroe, WI (town) Green County	348	26.93
Clarno, WI (town) Green County	321	26.82
Monterey, KY (city) Owen County	60	26.79
Woodford, WI (cdp) Lafayette County	16	26.67
Berne, IN (city) Adams County	1,005	24.67
Bern, KS (city) Nemaha County	41	24.55
Kidron, OH (cdp) Wayne County	253	24.33
Monroe, WI (city) Green County	2,626	24.17
Bradley, SD (town) Clark County	12	23.53
Horton, MN (township) Stevens County	49	23.44
Antioch, OH (village) Monroe County	50	23.04
Mount Pleasant, WI (town) Green County	112	22.95
Nicolaus, CA (cdp) Sutter County	38	22.22
Taos Ski Valley, NM (village) Taos County	10	22.22
New Glarus, WI (town) Green County	304	21.98
Wilmot, OH (village) Stark County	51	21.98
Thorp, WI (town) Clark County	193	21.76
Cadiz, WI (town) Green County	200	21.74
Longwood, WI (town) Clark County	173	21.31
Blanchardville, WI (village) Iowa County	36	21.30
Walnut Creek, OH (cdp) Holmes County	82	21.19
Gratiot, WI (town) Lafayette County	117	21.16
Pelham, TN (cdp) Grundy County	78	20.86
Manston, MN (township) Wilkin County	5	20.83
Wayne, WI (town) Lafayette County	104	20.68
Wallula, WA (cdp) Walla Walla County	19	20.65
Laurel Mountain, PA (borough) Westmoreland County	48	20.51
Sugarcreek, OH (village) Tuscarawas County	448	20.06
Browntown, WI (village) Green County	48	19.67
Jefferson, WI (town) Green County	230	19.52
Allensville, PA (cdp) Mifflin County	80	18.74
Moscow, WI (town) Iowa County	96	18.60
Blue Ball, PA (cdp) Lancaster County	146	18.58
Elgin, IA (city) Fayette County	136	18.55
Wiederkehr Village, AR (city) Franklin County	2	18.18
Brooklyn, WI (town) Green County	186	18.16
Pandora, OH (village) Putnam County	205	17.95
Juntura, OR (cdp) Malheur County	8	17.39
Bingham, PA (township) Potter County	121	17.36
Rendsville, MN (township) Stevens County	27	17.20
Blanchardville, WI (village) Lafayette County	126	17.19
Gilboa, OH (village) Putnam County	24	17.14
Turnerville, WY (cdp) Lincoln County	46	17.10
Exeter, WI (town) Green County	303	17.06
Spring Grove, WI (town) Green County	180	16.97
Antelope Hills, WY (cdp) Natrona County	17	16.83
Drowning Creek, OK (cdp) Delaware County	20	16.81
Parnell, MN (township) Traverse County	8	16.67
Guys Mills, PA (cdp) Crawford County	26	16.46
Yale, IL (village) Jasper County	11	16.42
Montana, WI (town) Buffalo County	50	16.23
Primrose, WI (town) Dane County	115	16.02
Blanchardville, WI (village) Lafayette County	90	15.96
Steinauer, NE (village) Pawnee County	12	15.79
Congerville, IL (village) Woodford County	87	15.70
Farmington, PA (cdp) Fayette County	110	15.65
Trinity Village, CA (cdp) Trinity County	20	15.63
Alma, WI (town) Buffalo County	46	15.38
McGregor, MN (township) Aitkin County	8	15.38
Hamer, ID (city) Jefferson County	4	15.38
Bryant, IN (town) Jay County	46	15.33
Beaver, PA (township) Crawford County	118	15.28
Marrowbone, KY (cdp) Cumberland County	70	15.28
Millerton, PA (cdp) Tioga County	47	15.26
Bloomington, ID (city) Bear Lake County	32	15.17
Wiota, WI (town) Lafayette County	141	15.15
Osterdock, IA (city) Clayton County	10	15.15
Argyle, WI (town) Lafayette County	60	15.08
Monroe, IN (town) Adams County	137	15.02
Central Valley, UT (town) Sevier County	42	15.00
Montrose, WI (town) Dane County	142	14.99
Soudersburg, PA (cdp) Lancaster County	79	14.99
Lincoln, WI (town) Buffalo County	28	14.81
Argyle, WI (village) Lafayette County	151	14.79
Jordan, WI (town) Green County	76	14.79
Monticello, WI (town) Lafayette County	28	14.74
Pettisville, OH (cdp) Fulton County	71	14.70
Cane Beds, AZ (cdp) Mohave County	31	14.69
Juda, WI (cdp) Green County	63	14.55
Harmony, MN (township) Fillmore County	62	14.42
Brecknock, PA (township) Lancaster County	1,027	14.39
Parral, OH (village) Tuscarawas County	35	14.29
Baileyville, KS (cdp) Nemaha County	31	14.29
Nash, ND (cdp) Walsh County	2	14.29
Spanish Valley, UT (cdp) San Juan County	30	14.22
Brodhead, WI (city) Green County	457	14.17
Buffalo, PA (township) Union County	494	14.13
Brodhead, WI (city) Green County	457	14.07
South Wayne, WI (village) Lafayette County	66	14.07
Rush, PA (township) Dauphin County	33	14.04
Virginville, PA (cdp) Berks County	39	13.88
Terre Hill, PA (borough) Lancaster County	147	13.78
Green Grove, WI (town) Clark County	110	13.73
Albany, WI (town) Green County	142	13.67
Smyrna, ME (town) Aroostook County	69	13.58
Grand Lake Towne, OK (town) Mayes County	22	13.58
Riceville, PA (cdp) Crawford County	8	13.56
Chinook, WA (cdp) Pacific County	41	13.49
Blanchard, WI (town) Lafayette County	28	13.40
Elk Lick, PA (township) Somerset County	298	13.35
Chapman, PA (township) Snyder County	229	13.35
East Earl, PA (township) Lancaster County	838	13.17
Sierra City, CA (cdp) Sierra County	79	13.14
Whittlesey, WI (cdp) Taylor County	18	13.14
Bluebell, UT (cdp) Duchesne County	35	13.06
Witmer, PA (cdp) Lancaster County	75	13.02
Albany, WI (village) Green County	141	12.96
Idaville, OR (cdp) Tillamook County	57	12.95
Verlot, WA (cdp) Snohomish County	30	12.93
Waldwick, WI (town) Iowa County	62	12.92
Belleville, WI (village) Green County	97	12.88
Fairfield, MT (town) Teton County	71	12.79
York, WI (town) Green County	103	12.67
Withee, WI (town) Clark County	137	12.51
Sunrise Beach, MO (village) Camden County	56	12.50
McIntire, IA (city) Mitchell County	12	12.50
Trinidad, CA (city) Humboldt County	32	12.36
Orangeville, IL (village) Stephenson County	110	12.35
Bluffton, OH (village) Allen County	509	12.32
Schoeneck, PA (cdp) Lancaster County	106	12.31
Patterson, OH (village) Hardin County	14	12.28
Spring Valley, WI (town) Rock County	98	11.84
Morris, MN (township) Stevens County	58	11.84
Belleville, WI (village) Dane County	307	11.78
Deaver, WY (town) Big Horn County	22	11.76

Please refer to the Explanation of Data in the front of the book for more detailed information.

Ancestry

Swiss

Top 150 Places Sorted by Percent of Total Population

Based on places with total population of 7,500 or more

Place	Population	%
Monroe, WI (city) Green County	2,626	24.17
Ephrata, PA (township) Lancaster County	785	8.54
Orrville, OH (city) Wayne County	622	7.37
Penn, PA (township) Lancaster County	602	7.06
West Earl, PA (township) Lancaster County	535	6.99
Highland, IL (city) Madison County	576	6.12
Verona, WI (city) Dane County	587	5.85
East Cocalico, PA (township) Lancaster County	578	5.64
Bluffton, IN (city) Wells County	526	5.52
West Donegal, PA (township) Lancaster County	438	5.49
Upper Leacock, PA (township) Lancaster County	446	5.16
Ephrata, PA (borough) Lancaster County	673	5.03
East Lampeter, PA (township) Lancaster County	756	4.75
Goshen, IN (city) Elkhart County	1,482	4.74
Ellington, CT (town) Tolland County	692	4.54
West Lampeter, PA (township) Lancaster County	647	4.36
Dover, OH (city) Tuscarawas County	541	4.23
Franconia, PA (township) Montgomery County	510	4.01
Beloit, WI (town) Rock County	276	3.64
Warwick, PA (township) Lancaster County	628	3.60
Rapho, PA (township) Lancaster County	364	3.60
New Philadelphia, OH (city) Tuscarawas County	620	3.59
Sunset Hills, MO (city) St. Louis County	297	3.53
McFarland, WI (village) Dane County	266	3.51
Elizabethtown, PA (borough) Lancaster County	388	3.35
Decatur, IN (city) Adams County	332	3.35
Centerville, UT (city) Davis County	506	3.33
Highland, UT (city) Utah County	461	3.27
Jackson, PA (township) Lebanon County	249	3.19
Payson, UT (city) Utah County	535	3.11
Salisbury, PA (township) Lancaster County	338	3.10
West Hempfield, PA (township) Lancaster County	492	3.07
Lititz, PA (borough) Lancaster County	279	3.00
Manor, PA (township) Lancaster County	564	2.96
Alpine, UT (city) Utah County	267	2.95
Grand Rapids, WI (town) Wood County	220	2.88
Perry Heights, OH (cdp) Stark County	247	2.86
Wooster, OH (city) Wayne County	722	2.77
Los Alamos, NM (cdp) Los Alamos County	332	2.76
Kaysville, UT (city) Davis County	690	2.65
Ormond-by-the-Sea, FL (cdp) Volusia County	198	2.55
Southampton, PA (township) Franklin County	194	2.52
Oroville East, CA (cdp) Butte County	214	2.49
Prairie Village, KS (city) Johnson County	537	2.47
Ripon, CA (city) San Joaquin County	340	2.47
Oregon, WI (village) Dane County	221	2.47
Truckee, CA (town) Nevada County	387	2.44
Mount Joy, PA (township) Lancaster County	233	2.44
Monona, WI (city) Dane County	185	2.43
North Logan, UT (city) Cache County	188	2.42
Alliance, OH (city) Stark County	540	2.40
South Lebanon, PA (township) Lebanon County	221	2.38
Steamboat Springs, CO (city) Routt County	280	2.37
Lindon, UT (city) Utah County	225	2.32
Napoleon, OH (city) Henry County	197	2.32
Middleton, WI (city) Dane County	390	2.27
North Ogden, UT (city) Weber County	381	2.27
Fitchburg, WI (city) Dane County	554	2.26
Antrim, PA (township) Franklin County	328	2.26
Blackfoot, ID (city) Bingham County	260	2.26
East Hempfield, PA (township) Lancaster County	519	2.24
Wilton, CT (town) Fairfield County	390	2.18
Maxatawny, PA (township) Berks County	167	2.16
Westlake Village, CA (city) Los Angeles County	175	2.12
Harrisonburg, VA (ind. city) Harrisonburg independent city	999	2.11
Heber, UT (city) Wasatch County	227	2.11
Waunakee, WI (village) Dane County	241	2.09
Pleasant Grove, UT (city) Utah County	647	2.06
Louisville, OH (city) Stark County	187	2.05
Upper Montclair, NJ (cdp) Essex County	235	2.03
Rexburg, ID (city) Madison County	495	2.02
St. George, UT (city) Washington County	1,428	2.01
Platteville, WI (city) Grant County	219	2.00
Salem, OH (city) Columbiana County	245	1.98
Logan, UT (city) Cache County	909	1.96
Wadsworth, OH (city) Medina County	413	1.95
Upper Macungie, PA (township) Lehigh County	370	1.94
Pryor Creek, OK (city) Mayes County	180	1.91
Greene, PA (township) Franklin County	301	1.89
Merrill, WI (city) Lincoln County	185	1.89
Bath, MI (charter township) Clinton County	206	1.88
Wisconsin Rapids, WI (city) Wood County	342	1.87
Morton, IL (village) Tazewell County	297	1.86
Cedar Hills, UT (city) Utah County	159	1.86
Ellensburg, WA (city) Kittitas County	328	1.84
St. Matthews, KY (city) Jefferson County	320	1.84
Pewaukee, WI (city) Waukesha County	237	1.83
Bountiful, UT (city) Davis County	773	1.82
Snohomish, WA (city) Snohomish County	165	1.82
Clarendon Hills, IL (village) DuPage County	151	1.82
Perrysburg, OH (city) Wood County	364	1.80
Waukee, IA (city) Dallas County	221	1.80
South Jordan, UT (city) Salt Lake County	831	1.79
Doylestown, PA (borough) Bucks County	148	1.76
Springville, UT (city) Utah County	483	1.75
Anderson, CA (city) Shasta County	172	1.74
Smithfield, UT (city) Cache County	153	1.71
Arcata, CA (city) Humboldt County	290	1.70
Stoughton, WI (city) Dane County	214	1.70
Tamalpais-Homestead Valley, CA (cdp) Marin County	180	1.70
Mapleton, UT (city) Utah County	128	1.70
Hartford, WI (city) Washington County	232	1.69
North Londonderry, PA (township) Lebanon County	133	1.69
Manheim, PA (township) Lancaster County	625	1.67
McPherson, KS (city) McPherson County	220	1.66
Gulfport, FL (city) Pinellas County	202	1.66
Columbus, NE (city) Platte County	356	1.65
Cedar City, UT (city) Iron County	453	1.63
American Fork, UT (city) Utah County	414	1.63
Mount Dora, FL (city) Lake County	201	1.63
North Codorus, PA (township) York County	142	1.62
Oatfield, OR (cdp) Clackamas County	219	1.61
Corte Madera, CA (town) Marin County	147	1.61
Monterey, CA (city) Monterey County	446	1.60
Madison, WI (city) Dane County	3,652	1.59
Solana Beach, CA (city) San Diego County	203	1.59
Freeport, IL (city) Stephenson County	406	1.58
Concord, MO (cdp) St. Louis County	251	1.58
South Middleton, PA (township) Cumberland County	228	1.58
Rio del Mar, CA (cdp) Santa Cruz County	149	1.58
San Luis Obispo, CA (city) San Luis Obispo County	703	1.56
Golden, CO (city) Jefferson County	287	1.56
Tiffin, OH (city) Seneca County	280	1.56
Weston, CT (town) Fairfield County	157	1.56
Upper Arlington, OH (city) Franklin County	521	1.55
Lancaster, PA (township) Lancaster County	245	1.55
Placerville, CA (city) El Dorado County	161	1.55
Columbine, CO (cdp) Jefferson County	369	1.54
Winnetka, IL (village) Cook County	186	1.54
Tecumseh, MI (city) Lenawee County	133	1.54
Syracuse, UT (city) Davis County	332	1.53
Sarasota Springs, FL (cdp) Sarasota County	222	1.53
Saratoga Springs, UT (city) Utah County	223	1.52
Incline Village, NV (cdp) Washoe County	131	1.52
Sandy, UT (city) Salt Lake County	1,319	1.51
Janesville, WI (city) Rock County	957	1.51
Lake Forest Park, WA (city) King County	190	1.51
Knik-Fairview, AK (cdp) Matanuska-Susitna Borough	185	1.51
Hugo, MN (city) Washington County	183	1.51
Adams, PA (township) Butler County	163	1.51
Columbia City, IN (city) Whitley County	124	1.51
Edgewood, WA (city) Pierce County	141	1.50
Saddlebrooke, AZ (cdp) Pinal County	135	1.50
New Haven, IN (city) Allen County	207	1.49
Town and Country, MO (city) St. Louis County	161	1.49
Milwaukie, OR (city) Clackamas County	302	1.48
Beaver Dam, WI (city) Dodge County	238	1.48
Guilford, PA (township) Franklin County	212	1.48
Cheney, WA (city) Spokane County	152	1.48
Vernal, UT (city) Uintah County	130	1.48

Please refer to the Explanation of Data in the front of the book for more detailed information.

Ancestry

Turkish

U.S. and 50 States Sorted by Population and Percent of Total Population

Place	Population	%
United States	**177,841**	**0.06**
New York	29,907	0.16
California	22,091	0.06
New Jersey	16,830	0.19
Florida	15,289	0.08
Texas	9,221	0.04
Virginia	8,040	0.10
Pennsylvania	6,319	0.05
Illinois	5,949	0.05
Massachusetts	5,933	0.09
Washington	5,149	0.08
Maryland	5,049	0.09
Ohio	4,399	0.04
Georgia	4,126	0.04
North Carolina	3,355	0.04
Connecticut	3,256	0.09
Michigan	2,589	0.03
Arizona	2,477	0.04
South Carolina	1,758	0.04
Colorado	1,702	0.03
Nevada	1,696	0.06
Missouri	1,633	0.03
Indiana	1,592	0.02
Oregon	1,472	0.04
Tennessee	1,396	0.02
Wisconsin	1,395	0.02
Alabama	1,393	0.03
Minnesota	1,123	0.02
Louisiana	1,092	0.02
Kentucky	1,030	0.02
Oklahoma	977	0.03
Utah	956	0.04
Iowa	820	0.03
Kansas	739	0.03
New Mexico	712	0.04
Idaho	687	0.04
Delaware	652	0.07
Rhode Island	645	0.06
New Hampshire	587	0.04
West Virginia	585	0.03
District of Columbia	511	0.09
Arkansas	438	0.02
Hawaii	362	0.03
Nebraska	316	0.02
Vermont	295	0.05
Maine	278	0.02
Mississippi	245	0.01
Wyoming	238	0.04
Alaska	173	0.03
Montana	126	0.01
South Dakota	120	0.02
North Dakota	118	0.02

Place	Population	%
New Jersey	16,830	0.19
New York	29,907	0.16
Virginia	8,040	0.10
Massachusetts	5,933	0.09
Maryland	5,049	0.09
Connecticut	3,256	0.09
District of Columbia	511	0.09
Florida	15,289	0.08
Washington	5,149	0.08
Delaware	652	0.07
United States	**177,841**	**0.06**
California	22,091	0.06
Nevada	1,696	0.06
Rhode Island	645	0.06
Pennsylvania	6,319	0.05
Illinois	5,949	0.05
Vermont	295	0.05
Texas	9,221	0.04
Ohio	4,399	0.04
Georgia	4,126	0.04
North Carolina	3,355	0.04
Arizona	2,477	0.04
South Carolina	1,758	0.04
Oregon	1,472	0.04
Utah	956	0.04
New Mexico	712	0.04
Idaho	687	0.04
New Hampshire	587	0.04
Wyoming	238	0.04
Michigan	2,589	0.03
Colorado	1,702	0.03
Missouri	1,633	0.03
Alabama	1,393	0.03
Oklahoma	977	0.03
Iowa	820	0.03
Kansas	739	0.03
West Virginia	585	0.03
Hawaii	362	0.03
Alaska	173	0.03
Indiana	1,592	0.02
Tennessee	1,396	0.02
Wisconsin	1,395	0.02
Minnesota	1,123	0.02
Louisiana	1,092	0.02
Kentucky	1,030	0.02
Arkansas	438	0.02
Nebraska	316	0.02
Maine	278	0.02
South Dakota	120	0.02
North Dakota	118	0.02
Mississippi	245	0.01
Montana	126	0.01

Please refer to the Explanation of Data in the front of the book for more detailed information.

Ancestry

Turkish

Top 150 Places Sorted by Population

Based on all places, regardless of total population

Place	Population	%
New York, NY (city) Kings County	14,927	0.18
Brooklyn, NY (borough) Kings County	5,164	0.21
Queens, NY (borough) Queens County	3,767	0.17
Manhattan, NY (borough) New York County	3,703	0.23
Los Angeles, CA (city) Los Angeles County	3,354	0.09
Houston, TX (city) Harris County	2,090	0.10
Brookhaven, NY (town) Suffolk County	1,935	0.40
Staten Island, NY (borough) Richmond County	1,607	0.35
Chicago, IL (city) Cook County	1,598	0.06
San Diego, CA (city) San Diego County	1,280	0.10
Oyster Bay, NY (town) Nassau County	1,232	0.42
Hempstead, NY (town) Nassau County	1,202	0.16
Paterson, NJ (city) Passaic County	1,148	0.79
Clifton, NJ (city) Passaic County	1,122	1.36
Babylon, NY (town) Suffolk County	939	0.44
Boston, MA (city) Suffolk County	876	0.15
Austin, TX (city) Travis County	820	0.11
Charlotte, NC (city) Mecklenburg County	809	0.11
Philadelphia, PA (city) Philadelphia County	786	0.05
Seattle, WA (city) King County	736	0.12
San Francisco, CA (city) San Francisco County	721	0.09
Bronx, NY (borough) Bronx County	686	0.05
Dallas, TX (city) Dallas County	625	0.05
Irvine, CA (city) Orange County	612	0.31
Rochester, NY (city) Monroe County	612	0.29
Columbus, OH (city) Franklin County	601	0.08
Miami Beach, FL (city) Miami-Dade County	584	0.67
Oakland, CA (city) Alameda County	575	0.15
Wayne, NJ (township) Passaic County	569	1.05
Greece, NY (town) Monroe County	561	0.59
Plano, TX (city) Collin County	558	0.22
San Jose, CA (city) Santa Clara County	539	0.06
Washington, DC (city) District of Columbia	511	0.09
Phoenix, AZ (city) Maricopa County	505	0.03
Huntington, NY (town) Suffolk County	502	0.25
San Mateo, CA (city) San Mateo County	501	0.53
Portland, OR (city) Multnomah County	499	0.09
Pittsburgh, PA (city) Allegheny County	485	0.16
Salt Lake City, UT (city) Salt Lake County	480	0.26
Tampa, FL (city) Hillsborough County	478	0.14
Tukwila, WA (city) King County	460	2.48
Albuquerque, NM (city) Bernalillo County	460	0.09
Torrance, CA (city) Los Angeles County	459	0.32
Jersey City, NJ (city) Hudson County	453	0.19
Kent, WA (city) King County	445	0.50
Fair Oaks, VA (cdp) Fairfax County	444	1.61
Jacksonville, FL (city) Duval County	432	0.05
Atlanta, GA (city) Fulton County	411	0.10
North Hempstead, NY (town) Nassau County	408	0.18
Las Vegas, NV (city) Clark County	408	0.07
Virginia Beach, VA (ind. city) Virginia Beach independent city	407	0.09
Potomac, MD (cdp) Montgomery County	391	0.87
East Patchogue, NY (cdp) Suffolk County	388	1.84
Islip, NY (town) Suffolk County	384	0.12
Denver, CO (city) Denver County	384	0.07
Reno, NV (city) Washoe County	380	0.17
Enterprise, NV (cdp) Clark County	375	0.38
Ann Arbor, MI (city) Washtenaw County	373	0.32
Lyndhurst, NJ (township) Bergen County	362	1.79
Cliffside Park, NJ (borough) Bergen County	360	1.54
Arlington, VA (cdp) Arlington County	355	0.18
Roswell, GA (city) Fulton County	353	0.41
Buffalo, NY (city) Erie County	350	0.13
San Antonio, TX (city) Medina County	340	0.03
Baltimore, MD (city) Baltimore city County	334	0.05
Louisville-Jefferson County, KY (metro govt) Jefferson County	330	0.06
Raleigh, NC (city) Wake County	329	0.09
Tempe, AZ (city) Maricopa County	326	0.20
Orlando, FL (city) Orange County	321	0.14
Alexandria, VA (ind. city) Alexandria independent city	317	0.24
Richmond, VA (ind. city) Richmond independent city	314	0.16
Fort Lauderdale, FL (city) Broward County	309	0.18
Deer Park, NY (cdp) Suffolk County	308	1.09
West New York, NJ (town) Hudson County	308	0.64
Baton Rouge, LA (city) East Baton Rouge Parish	301	0.13
Boise City, ID (city) Ada County	300	0.15
Fairview, NJ (borough) Bergen County	297	2.17
Plantation, FL (city) Broward County	294	0.35
Margate, FL (city) Broward County	291	0.54
West Springfield Town, MA (city) Hampden County	290	1.03
St. Louis, MO (city) St. Louis city County	290	0.09
Pembroke Pines, FL (city) Broward County	289	0.19
Long Beach, CA (city) Los Angeles County	288	0.06
Lodi, NJ (borough) Bergen County	286	1.19
Charlottesville, VA (ind. city) Charlottesville independent city	285	0.67
Ellicott City, MD (cdp) Howard County	284	0.44
Redwood City, CA (city) San Mateo County	283	0.38
Chandler, AZ (city) Maricopa County	282	0.12
Syracuse, NY (city) Onondaga County	279	0.19
Sacramento, CA (city) Sacramento County	279	0.06
Boca Raton, FL (city) Palm Beach County	277	0.33
West Haven, CT (city/town) New Haven County	276	0.50
Woodland Park, NJ (borough) Passaic County	275	2.37
Quincy, MA (city) Norfolk County	275	0.30
Weston, FL (city) Broward County	272	0.43
Cambridge, MA (city) Middlesex County	267	0.26
Aventura, FL (city) Miami-Dade County	263	0.78
Champaign, IL (city) Champaign County	263	0.33
Durham, NC (city) Durham County	262	0.12
Delran, NJ (township) Burlington County	258	1.54
Northdale, FL (cdp) Hillsborough County	258	1.11
Shirley, NY (cdp) Suffolk County	257	0.92
Orchards, WA (cdp) Clark County	256	1.26
New Castle, NY (town) Westchester County	255	1.46
Clearwater, FL (city) Pinellas County	254	0.24
Nashville-Davidson, TN (metro govt) Davidson County	254	0.04
Methuen Town, MA (city) Essex County	253	0.55
Edgewater, NJ (borough) Bergen County	249	2.31
Bellevue, WA (city) King County	246	0.21
Irondequoit, NY (cdp/town) Monroe County	245	0.47
Howell, NJ (township) Monmouth County	243	0.48
Mobile, AL (city) Mobile County	243	0.12
Indianapolis, IN (city) Marion County	243	0.03
Johns Creek, GA (city) Fulton County	241	0.33
Edison, NJ (township) Middlesex County	240	0.24
Brighton, NY (cdp/town) Monroe County	239	0.66
Brookline, MA (cdp/town) Norfolk County	239	0.41
Towson, MD (cdp) Baltimore County	237	0.44
Hanover, NJ (township) Morris County	236	1.73
Webster, NY (town) Monroe County	234	0.56
Tucson, AZ (city) Pima County	232	0.04
Renton, WA (city) King County	231	0.27
Iowa City, IA (city) Johnson County	226	0.34
Santa Barbara, CA (city) Santa Barbara County	226	0.26
Lake Butler, FL (cdp) Orange County	224	1.43
Whitehall, PA (borough) Allegheny County	223	1.60
Oakton, VA (cdp) Fairfax County	223	0.67
Lakewood, OH (city) Cuyahoga County	222	0.42
Gainesville, FL (city) Alachua County	218	0.18
Hollywood, FL (city) Broward County	217	0.15
Providence, RI (city) Providence County	216	0.12
Centennial, CO (city) Arapahoe County	214	0.21
Scottsdale, AZ (city) Maricopa County	214	0.10
East Massapequa, NY (cdp) Nassau County	212	1.19
Melrose, MA (city) Middlesex County	212	0.79
Commack, NY (cdp) Suffolk County	211	0.58
Tallahassee, FL (city) Leon County	211	0.12
Fort Worth, TX (city) Tarrant County	210	0.03
Henrietta, NY (town) Monroe County	209	0.50
Levittown, PA (cdp) Bucks County	209	0.40
Milwaukee, WI (city) Milwaukee County	209	0.04
Dunedin, FL (city) Pinellas County	207	0.58
Troy, NY (city) Rensselaer County	207	0.41
Sandy Springs, GA (city) Fulton County	207	0.23
Newport Beach, CA (city) Orange County	204	0.24
Smithtown, NY (town) Suffolk County	204	0.17
Waterbury, CT (city/town) New Haven County	203	0.18
Dayton, OH (city) Montgomery County	203	0.14
Cinnaminson, NJ (township) Burlington County	202	1.30
Bristol, PA (township) Bucks County	201	0.37

SECTION THREE

Ancestry

Turkish

Top 150 Places Sorted by Percent of Total Population

Based on all places, regardless of total population

Place	Population	%
Megargel, AL (cdp) Monroe County	31	100.00
Dering Harbor, NY (village) Suffolk County	5	31.25
Pine Island, FL (cdp) Hernando County	38	26.76
Marietta, IL (village) Fulton County	18	14.17
Parnell, MO (city) Nodaway County	10	6.62
Agenda, KS (city) Republic County	6	6.12
Matlacha, FL (cdp) Lee County	45	5.97
Dunfermline, IL (village) Fulton County	11	5.42
New Trier, MN (city) Dakota County	5	5.15
Dell Grove, MN (township) Pine County	32	4.89
Birmingham, PA (township) Chester County	198	4.67
Jeffersonville, NY (village) Sullivan County	15	4.66
Barnegat, NJ (cdp) Ocean County	130	4.56
Wedgefield, SC (cdp) Sumter County	61	4.39
Manchester, KS (city) Dickinson County	7	4.32
Delanco, NJ (township) Burlington County	164	3.97
Mount Calm, TX (city) Hill County	11	3.90
South Fork, MO (cdp) Howell County	9	3.67
Deal, NJ (borough) Monmouth County	37	3.58
Universal, IN (town) Vermillion County	13	3.40
Orient, NY (cdp) Suffolk County	20	3.33
Port Washington North, NY (village) Nassau County	100	3.29
Sandgate, VT (town) Bennington County	12	3.28
Tyro, KS (city) Montgomery County	8	3.15
Hilldale, PA (cdp) Luzerne County	45	3.14
Port Monmouth, NJ (cdp) Monmouth County	138	3.09
Freemansburg, PA (borough) Northampton County	76	2.98
Clinchco, VA (town) Dickenson County	14	2.94
Summerland, CA (cdp) Santa Barbara County	31	2.86
Perryville, MD (town) Cecil County	120	2.78
Benson, IL (village) Woodford County	11	2.78
Allegheny, PA (township) Venango County	11	2.72
Greenwich, NJ (cdp) Warren County	71	2.67
Mantua, VA (cdp) Fairfax County	194	2.58
Loudoun Valley Estates, VA (cdp) Loudoun County	62	2.58
Tukwila, WA (city) King County	460	2.48
Crystal Lake Park, MO (city) St. Louis County	12	2.44
Califon, NJ (borough) Hunterdon County	31	2.42
Woodland Park, NJ (borough) Passaic County	275	2.37
Granby, MA (cdp) Hampshire County	29	2.36
Newberry, FL (city) Alachua County	113	2.34
Edgewater, NJ (borough) Bergen County	249	2.31
Walton, NY (village) Delaware County	61	2.31
Bal Harbour, FL (village) Miami-Dade County	60	2.27
Winsor, MN (township) Clearwater County	2	2.27
Wading River, NY (cdp) Suffolk County	178	2.18
Fairview, NJ (borough) Bergen County	297	2.17
Princeton Junction, NJ (cdp) Mercer County	50	2.17
Moore, ID (city) Butte County	5	2.17
Northport, NY (village) Suffolk County	161	2.16
Clayton, NJ (borough) Gloucester County	171	2.12
Van Buren, OH (village) Hancock County	7	2.12
Deltana, AK (cdp) Southeast Fairbanks Census Area	37	2.10
Edgewater Park, NJ (township) Burlington County	180	2.06
Phil Campbell, AL (town) Franklin County	18	2.06
Piermont, NY (village) Rockland County	50	1.99
Newtonsville, OH (village) Clermont County	6	1.99
Friendship Heights Village, MD (cdp) Montgomery County	114	1.98
Linneus, ME (town) Aroostook County	17	1.98
Glendale, CO (city) Arapahoe County	80	1.92
Bayville, NY (village) Nassau County	128	1.91
Delmar, DE (town) Sussex County	30	1.89
Neeses, SC (town) Orangeburg County	5	1.89
Saybrook, IL (village) McLean County	12	1.88
Highgate, VT (town) Franklin County	66	1.87
Bear Creek, TX (village) Hays County	8	1.86
East Patchogue, NY (cdp) Suffolk County	388	1.84
Cross Timber, TX (town) Johnson County	4	1.83
Lyndhurst, NJ (township) Bergen County	362	1.79
South Floral Park, NY (village) Nassau County	28	1.79
Idaville, IN (cdp) White County	9	1.77
Bowers, DE (town) Kent County	5	1.76
Herrick, PA (township) Susquehanna County	14	1.74
Hanover, NJ (township) Morris County	236	1.73
Harmony, IN (town) Clay County	11	1.73
Pimmit Hills, VA (cdp) Fairfax County	107	1.72
Contra Costa Centre, CA (cdp) Contra Costa County	96	1.72
Thomaston, NY (village) Nassau County	45	1.72
Gages Lake, IL (cdp) Lake County	167	1.64
Lincolnville, SC (town) Charleston County	24	1.62
Fair Oaks, VA (cdp) Fairfax County	444	1.61
Whitehall, PA (borough) Allegheny County	223	1.60
Cheval, FL (cdp) Hillsborough County	164	1.59
Southold, NY (cdp) Suffolk County	91	1.57
Shorewood Hills, WI (village) Dane County	25	1.57
Hancock, WI (town) Waushara County	8	1.55
Cliffside Park, NJ (borough) Bergen County	360	1.54
Delran, NJ (township) Burlington County	258	1.54
Carter Springs, NV (cdp) Douglas County	9	1.54
Rougemont, NC (cdp) Durham County	12	1.53
Avalon, PA (borough) Allegheny County	72	1.51
Gerber, CA (cdp) Tehama County	14	1.51
Dallas, WI (village) Barron County	8	1.51
Webster, NY (village) Monroe County	80	1.49
Pennsbury Village, PA (borough) Allegheny County	10	1.49
Greenport West, NY (cdp) Suffolk County	29	1.48
New Castle, NY (town) Westchester County	255	1.46
Jerome, AZ (town) Yavapai County	6	1.45
Lake Butler, FL (cdp) Orange County	224	1.43
Williamsburg, FL (cdp) Orange County	98	1.43
Lakeview, GA (cdp) Catoosa County	75	1.43
Sag Harbor, NY (village) Suffolk County	28	1.43
Eatontown, NJ (borough) Monmouth County	184	1.42
Strattanville, PA (borough) Clarion County	9	1.42
New Paltz, NY (village) Ulster County	95	1.41
Manchester Center, VT (cdp) Bennington County	29	1.41
Carlstadt, NJ (borough) Bergen County	84	1.39
Indian Shores, FL (town) Pinellas County	20	1.38
Clifton, NJ (city) Passaic County	1,122	1.36
Little Ferry, NJ (borough) Bergen County	143	1.35
Great Neck Plaza, NY (village) Nassau County	89	1.35
Hiltonia, GA (town) Screven County	4	1.35
Hepburn, PA (township) Lycoming County	37	1.34
Cinnaminson, NJ (township) Burlington County	202	1.30
North Lindenhurst, NY (cdp) Suffolk County	150	1.29
Belle Terre, NY (village) Suffolk County	12	1.29
Greenwich, NJ (township) Warren County	71	1.28
Holbrook, NE (village) Furnas County	2	1.28
Orchards, WA (cdp) Clark County	256	1.26
Franklin Lakes, NJ (borough) Bergen County	132	1.26
Fulton, IL (city) Whiteside County	45	1.26
McChord AFB, WA (cdp) Pierce County	39	1.25
Fairhope, AL (city) Baldwin County	184	1.23
Lockwood, MO (city) Dade County	12	1.23
Telford, PA (borough) Montgomery County	32	1.22
Bee Cave, TX (city) Travis County	41	1.21
Lodi, NJ (borough) Bergen County	286	1.19
East Massapequa, NY (cdp) Nassau County	212	1.19
Port Jefferson, NY (village) Suffolk County	93	1.19
Mashpee, MA (town) Barnstable County	164	1.18
Westminster, SC (city) Oconee County	28	1.18
Shalimar, FL (town) Okaloosa County	10	1.16
Holmdel, NJ (township) Monmouth County	191	1.15
Middle Island, NY (cdp) Suffolk County	118	1.15
Clallam Bay, WA (cdp) Clallam County	10	1.13
Vero Beach, FL (city) Indian River County	178	1.12
North Bay Village, FL (city) Miami-Dade County	79	1.12
Blue Ridge, VA (cdp) Botetourt County	36	1.12
Brentwood, MD (town) Prince George's County	34	1.12
Northdale, FL (cdp) Hillsborough County	258	1.11
Martha Lake, WA (cdp) Snohomish County	174	1.11
Bay Harbor Islands, FL (town) Miami-Dade County	62	1.11
Deer Park, NY (cdp) Suffolk County	308	1.09
Highland Park, NJ (borough) Middlesex County	152	1.09
Walton, NY (town) Delaware County	61	1.09
Norwood, CO (town) San Miguel County	8	1.09
Sarasota Springs, FL (cdp) Sarasota County	157	1.08
Netcong, NJ (borough) Morris County	35	1.08
Bethpage, NY (cdp) Nassau County	178	1.07
Hanover, PA (township) Northampton County	115	1.07

Please refer to the Explanation of Data in the front of the book for more detailed information.

Ancestry

Turkish

Top 150 Places Sorted by Percent of Total Population

Based on places with total population of 7,500 or more

Place	Population	%
Mantua, VA (cdp) Fairfax County	194	2.58
Tukwila, WA (city) King County	460	2.48
Woodland Park, NJ (borough) Passaic County	275	2.37
Edgewater, NJ (borough) Bergen County	249	2.31
Wading River, NY (cdp) Suffolk County	178	2.18
Fairview, NJ (borough) Bergen County	297	2.17
Clayton, NJ (borough) Gloucester County	171	2.12
Edgewater Park, NJ (township) Burlington County	180	2.06
East Patchogue, NY (cdp) Suffolk County	388	1.84
Lyndhurst, NJ (township) Bergen County	362	1.79
Hanover, NJ (township) Morris County	236	1.73
Gages Lake, IL (cdp) Lake County	167	1.64
Fair Oaks, VA (cdp) Fairfax County	444	1.61
Whitehall, PA (borough) Allegheny County	223	1.60
Cheval, FL (cdp) Hillsborough County	164	1.59
Cliffside Park, NJ (borough) Bergen County	360	1.54
Delran, NJ (township) Burlington County	258	1.54
New Castle, NY (town) Westchester County	255	1.46
Lake Butler, FL (cdp) Orange County	224	1.43
Eatontown, NJ (borough) Monmouth County	184	1.42
Clifton, NJ (city) Passaic County	1,122	1.36
Little Ferry, NJ (borough) Bergen County	143	1.35
Cinnaminson, NJ (township) Burlington County	202	1.30
North Lindenhurst, NY (cdp) Suffolk County	150	1.29
Orchards, WA (cdp) Clark County	256	1.26
Franklin Lakes, NJ (borough) Bergen County	132	1.26
Fairhope, AL (city) Baldwin County	184	1.23
Lodi, NJ (borough) Bergen County	286	1.19
East Massapequa, NY (cdp) Nassau County	212	1.19
Port Jefferson, NY (village) Suffolk County	93	1.19
Mashpee, MA (town) Barnstable County	164	1.18
Holmdel, NJ (township) Monmouth County	191	1.15
Middle Island, NY (cdp) Suffolk County	118	1.15
Vero Beach, FL (city) Indian River County	178	1.12
Northdale, FL (cdp) Hillsborough County	258	1.11
Martha Lake, WA (cdp) Snohomish County	174	1.11
Deer Park, NY (cdp) Suffolk County	308	1.09
Highland Park, NJ (borough) Middlesex County	152	1.09
Sarasota Springs, FL (cdp) Sarasota County	157	1.08
Bethpage, NY (cdp) Nassau County	178	1.07
Hanover, PA (township) Northampton County	115	1.07
Wayne, NJ (township) Passaic County	569	1.05
Fuquay-Varina, NC (town) Wake County	168	1.04
West Springfield Town, MA (city) Hampden County	290	1.03
St. Albans, WV (city) Kanawha County	114	1.03
St. Matthews, KY (city) Jefferson County	175	1.01
Coventry, CT (town) Tolland County	123	1.00
Patchogue, NY (village) Suffolk County	118	1.00
North Babylon, NY (cdp) Suffolk County	170	0.96
Capitola, CA (city) Santa Cruz County	91	0.93
Shirley, NY (cdp) Suffolk County	257	0.92
Lutz, FL (cdp) Hillsborough County	180	0.91
Glassboro, NJ (borough) Gloucester County	169	0.90
Guttenberg, NJ (town) Hudson County	99	0.90
Chantilly, VA (cdp) Fairfax County	196	0.89
Potomac, MD (cdp) Montgomery County	391	0.87
Perrysburg, OH (city) Wood County	176	0.87
Totowa, NJ (borough) Passaic County	89	0.84
Franklin Farm, VA (cdp) Fairfax County	162	0.83
Pampa, TX (city) Gray County	148	0.83
Islip, NY (cdp) Suffolk County	155	0.82
Westwood, NJ (borough) Bergen County	89	0.82
Lake Barcroft, VA (cdp) Fairfax County	74	0.82
Elwood, IN (city) Madison County	73	0.82
Castle Shannon, PA (borough) Allegheny County	67	0.81
Wallingford Center, CT (cdp) New Haven County	144	0.80
Paterson, NJ (city) Passaic County	1,148	0.79
Melrose, MA (city) Middlesex County	212	0.79
Aventura, FL (city) Miami-Dade County	263	0.78
West Hempstead, NY (cdp) Nassau County	143	0.78
Troy, AL (city) Pike County	132	0.77
Upper Deerfield, NJ (township) Cumberland County	58	0.76
Medina, OH (city) Medina County	199	0.75
Mount Airy, MD (town) Carroll County	67	0.75
Tysons Corner, VA (cdp) Fairfax County	127	0.74
Ventnor City, NJ (city) Atlantic County	82	0.74
Mill Creek East, WA (cdp) Snohomish County	102	0.73
Massapequa, NY (cdp) Nassau County	164	0.72
Gibsonton, FL (cdp) Hillsborough County	94	0.72
Trinity, FL (cdp) Pasco County	78	0.72
Wyndham, VA (cdp) Henrico County	67	0.72
Lincoln, RI (town) Providence County	151	0.71
Ludlow, MA (town) Hampden County	150	0.71
Jericho, NY (cdp) Nassau County	93	0.71
Bellmawr, NJ (borough) Camden County	83	0.71
Richmond Heights, OH (city) Cuyahoga County	75	0.71
Spearfish, SD (city) Lawrence County	72	0.71
Plainview, NY (cdp) Nassau County	181	0.70
Mantua, NJ (township) Gloucester County	106	0.70
Southold, NY (town) Suffolk County	150	0.69
Farmingville, NY (cdp) Suffolk County	111	0.69
Chicago Ridge, IL (village) Cook County	97	0.69
Hasbrouck Heights, NJ (borough) Bergen County	81	0.69
O'Hara, PA (township) Allegheny County	58	0.69
New Paltz, NY (town) Ulster County	95	0.68
Brookhaven, PA (borough) Delaware County	54	0.68
Miami Beach, FL (city) Miami-Dade County	584	0.67
Charlottesville, VA (ind. city) Charlottesville independent city	285	0.67
Oakton, VA (cdp) Fairfax County	223	0.67
Clemson, SC (city) Pickens County	91	0.67
Brighton, NY (cdp/town) Monroe County	239	0.66
Estelle, LA (cdp) Jefferson Parish	111	0.66
Seven Corners, VA (cdp) Fairfax County	55	0.66
Mehlville, MO (cdp) St. Louis County	177	0.65
Barnegat, NJ (township) Ocean County	130	0.65
Echelon, NJ (cdp) Camden County	65	0.65
West New York, NJ (town) Hudson County	308	0.64
Burlingame, CA (city) San Mateo County	181	0.64
Sunny Isles Beach, FL (city) Miami-Dade County	126	0.64
Graham, WA (cdp) Pierce County	136	0.63
South Portland, ME (city) Cumberland County	155	0.62
Bear, DE (cdp) New Castle County	116	0.62
Bryant, AR (city) Saline County	98	0.62
Whitewater, WI (city) Walworth County	69	0.62
North Tustin, CA (cdp) Orange County	149	0.61
Halfway, MD (cdp) Washington County	62	0.61
Woodbury, NY (cdp) Nassau County	55	0.61
Parkland, FL (city) Broward County	135	0.60
Camas, WA (city) Clark County	110	0.60
Radford, VA (ind. city) Radford independent city	98	0.60
Johnson City, NY (village) Broome County	92	0.60
West Freehold, NJ (cdp) Monmouth County	84	0.60
East Rockaway, NY (village) Nassau County	59	0.60
Greece, NY (town) Monroe County	561	0.59
Farmington, CT (town) Hartford County	148	0.59
Gonzalez, FL (cdp) Escambia County	73	0.59
Commack, NY (cdp) Suffolk County	211	0.58
Dunedin, FL (city) Pinellas County	207	0.58
Wantagh, NY (cdp) Nassau County	105	0.58
Pooler, GA (city) Chatham County	96	0.58
Kings Park West, VA (cdp) Fairfax County	84	0.58
Los Alamos, NM (cdp) Los Alamos County	70	0.58
North Gates, NY (cdp) Monroe County	53	0.57
Port Jefferson Station, NY (cdp) Suffolk County	43	0.57
Webster, NY (town) Monroe County	234	0.56
SeaTac, WA (city) King County	147	0.56
Weehawken, NJ (township) Hudson County	70	0.56
Shasta Lake, CA (city) Shasta County	56	0.56
Triangle, VA (cdp) Prince William County	43	0.56
Methuen Town, MA (city) Essex County	253	0.55
Riverhead, NY (town) Suffolk County	178	0.55
Stafford, TX (city) Fort Bend County	94	0.55
Bull Run, VA (cdp) Prince William County	71	0.55
Huntington, VA (cdp) Fairfax County	57	0.55
Colts Neck, NJ (township) Monmouth County	56	0.55
Maywood, NJ (borough) Bergen County	52	0.55
Margate, FL (city) Broward County	291	0.54
Closter, NJ (borough) Bergen County	45	0.54
San Mateo, CA (city) San Mateo County	501	0.53
North Bellmore, NY (cdp) Nassau County	103	0.53

Please refer to the Explanation of Data in the front of the book for more detailed information.

Ancestry

Ukrainian

U.S. and 50 States Sorted by Population and Percent of Total Population

Place	Population	%
United States	**956,909**	**0.31**
New York	133,633	0.69
Pennsylvania	117,955	0.94
California	93,449	0.26
New Jersey	71,894	0.82
Illinois	50,346	0.40
Florida	48,668	0.26
Washington	47,100	0.72
Ohio	46,993	0.41
Michigan	41,842	0.42
Massachusetts	23,908	0.37
Connecticut	22,353	0.63
Maryland	21,727	0.38
Oregon	21,179	0.56
Texas	19,625	0.08
Virginia	18,941	0.24
North Carolina	15,628	0.17
Minnesota	15,132	0.29
Arizona	14,120	0.23
Colorado	13,260	0.27
Georgia	12,538	0.13
Wisconsin	9,752	0.17
Indiana	9,005	0.14
Missouri	7,893	0.13
South Carolina	7,313	0.16
Tennessee	7,311	0.12
Delaware	5,892	0.67
Nevada	5,306	0.20
Kentucky	3,837	0.09
North Dakota	3,813	0.58
New Hampshire	3,774	0.29
Utah	3,140	0.12
Iowa	2,825	0.09
Kansas	2,823	0.10
Idaho	2,766	0.18
Oklahoma	2,676	0.07
Rhode Island	2,653	0.25
Montana	2,630	0.27
Alabama	2,410	0.05
New Mexico	2,259	0.11
Maine	2,222	0.17
Louisiana	2,128	0.05
District of Columbia	1,967	0.34
Nebraska	1,959	0.11
West Virginia	1,952	0.11
Vermont	1,750	0.28
Alaska	1,634	0.24
Arkansas	1,286	0.04
Hawaii	1,236	0.09
South Dakota	1,186	0.15
Mississippi	709	0.02
Wyoming	511	0.09

Place	Population	%
Pennsylvania	117,955	0.94
New Jersey	71,894	0.82
Washington	47,100	0.72
New York	133,633	0.69
Delaware	5,892	0.67
Connecticut	22,353	0.63
North Dakota	3,813	0.58
Oregon	21,179	0.56
Michigan	41,842	0.42
Ohio	46,993	0.41
Illinois	50,346	0.40
Maryland	21,727	0.38
Massachusetts	23,908	0.37
District of Columbia	1,967	0.34
United States	**956,909**	**0.31**
Minnesota	15,132	0.29
New Hampshire	3,774	0.29
Vermont	1,750	0.28
Colorado	13,260	0.27
Montana	2,630	0.27
California	93,449	0.26
Florida	48,668	0.26
Rhode Island	2,653	0.25
Virginia	18,941	0.24
Alaska	1,634	0.24
Arizona	14,120	0.23
Nevada	5,306	0.20
Idaho	2,766	0.18
North Carolina	15,628	0.17
Wisconsin	9,752	0.17
Maine	2,222	0.17
South Carolina	7,313	0.16
South Dakota	1,186	0.15
Indiana	9,005	0.14
Georgia	12,538	0.13
Missouri	7,893	0.13
Tennessee	7,311	0.12
Utah	3,140	0.12
New Mexico	2,259	0.11
Nebraska	1,959	0.11
West Virginia	1,952	0.11
Kansas	2,823	0.10
Kentucky	3,837	0.09
Iowa	2,825	0.09
Hawaii	1,236	0.09
Wyoming	511	0.09
Texas	19,625	0.08
Oklahoma	2,676	0.07
Alabama	2,410	0.05
Louisiana	2,128	0.05
Arkansas	1,286	0.04
Mississippi	709	0.02

Please refer to the Explanation of Data in the front of the book for more detailed information.

Ancestry

Ukrainian

Top 150 Places Sorted by Population

Based on all places, regardless of total population

Place	Population	%
New York, NY (city) Kings County	48,714	0.60
Brooklyn, NY (borough) Kings County	25,046	1.02
Philadelphia, PA (city) Philadelphia County	13,262	0.88
Chicago, IL (city) Cook County	12,513	0.46
Los Angeles, CA (city) Los Angeles County	11,493	0.30
Manhattan, NY (borough) New York County	8,849	0.56
Queens, NY (borough) Queens County	8,375	0.38
Portland, OR (city) Multnomah County	7,584	1.34
San Francisco, CA (city) San Francisco County	4,917	0.62
Parma, OH (city) Cuyahoga County	4,857	5.93
Staten Island, NY (borough) Richmond County	4,836	1.04
San Diego, CA (city) San Diego County	3,425	0.27
Antelope, CA (cdp) Sacramento County	3,301	7.22
Vancouver, WA (city) Clark County	3,056	1.91
Phoenix, AZ (city) Maricopa County	3,010	0.21
Pittsburgh, PA (city) Allegheny County	2,972	0.96
Rancho Cordova, CA (city) Sacramento County	2,814	4.45
Hempstead, NY (town) Nassau County	2,806	0.37
Auburn, WA (city) King County	2,463	3.68
Seattle, WA (city) King County	2,427	0.41
North Highlands, CA (cdp) Sacramento County	2,401	5.63
Brookhaven, NY (town) Suffolk County	2,350	0.49
Kent, WA (city) King County	2,259	2.53
Sacramento, CA (city) Sacramento County	2,189	0.48
Tacoma, WA (city) Pierce County	2,166	1.09
Boston, MA (city) Suffolk County	2,138	0.35
Cleveland, OH (city) Cuyahoga County	2,072	0.51
Everett, WA (city) Snohomish County	2,019	1.99
Warren, MI (city) Macomb County	1,999	1.47
Washington, DC (city) District of Columbia	1,967	0.34
Columbus, OH (city) Franklin County	1,935	0.25
Charlotte, NC (city) Mecklenburg County	1,867	0.26
Houston, TX (city) Harris County	1,858	0.09
Citrus Heights, CA (city) Sacramento County	1,833	2.17
Oyster Bay, NY (town) Nassau County	1,774	0.61
Greece, NY (town) Monroe County	1,758	1.84
San Jose, CA (city) Santa Clara County	1,748	0.19
Huntington, NY (town) Suffolk County	1,742	0.86
Denver, CO (city) Denver County	1,742	0.30
Buffalo, NY (city) Erie County	1,739	0.65
Federal Way, WA (city) King County	1,665	1.90
Minneapolis, MN (city) Hennepin County	1,628	0.43
Baltimore, MD (city) Baltimore city County	1,608	0.26
Bronx, NY (borough) Bronx County	1,608	0.12
Five Corners, WA (cdp) Clark County	1,598	9.16
Jacksonville, FL (city) Duval County	1,510	0.19
Yonkers, NY (city) Westchester County	1,494	0.77
Clifton, NJ (city) Passaic County	1,493	1.80
Spokane, WA (city) Spokane County	1,433	0.69
Sterling Heights, MI (city) Macomb County	1,410	1.09
Ramapo, NY (town) Rockland County	1,403	1.14
Arlington, VA (cdp) Arlington County	1,375	0.70
Woodbridge, NJ (township) Middlesex County	1,370	1.38
Bensalem, PA (township) Bucks County	1,352	2.24
Webster, NY (town) Monroe County	1,334	3.20
Las Vegas, NV (city) Clark County	1,333	0.23
Rochester, NY (city) Monroe County	1,325	0.63
Buffalo Grove, IL (village) Lake County	1,311	3.13
Northampton, PA (township) Bucks County	1,274	3.20
Islip, NY (town) Suffolk County	1,272	0.38
Auburn, NY (city) Cayuga County	1,247	4.48
Skokie, IL (village) Cook County	1,223	1.92
Tucson, AZ (city) Pima County	1,223	0.24
Virginia Beach, VA (ind. city) Virginia Beach independent city	1,201	0.28
Scottsdale, AZ (city) Maricopa County	1,173	0.54
Irondequoit, NY (cdp/town) Monroe County	1,169	2.27
Gresham, OR (city) Multnomah County	1,136	1.12
Allentown, PA (city) Lehigh County	1,122	0.96
Nashville-Davidson, TN (metro govt) Davidson County	1,119	0.19
North Royalton, OH (city) Cuyahoga County	1,113	3.71
West Springfield Town, MA (city) Hampden County	1,111	3.93
Westfield, MA (city) Hampden County	1,111	2.71
Rochester Hills, MI (city) Oakland County	1,108	1.57
Syracuse, NY (city) Onondaga County	1,095	0.76
Foothill Farms, CA (cdp) Sacramento County	1,082	3.30
Amherst, NY (town) Erie County	1,074	0.89
Fresno, CA (city) Fresno County	1,067	0.22
Scranton, PA (city) Lackawanna County	1,060	1.39
Farmington Hills, MI (city) Oakland County	1,053	1.31
Livonia, MI (city) Wayne County	1,041	1.06
Austin, TX (city) Travis County	1,008	0.13
Hollywood, FL (city) Broward County	1,005	0.71
North Hempstead, NY (town) Nassau County	1,005	0.45
Stamford, CT (city/town) Fairfield County	1,004	0.83
Dallas, TX (city) Dallas County	999	0.08
Dearborn, MI (city) Wayne County	988	1.00
Toms River, NJ (township) Ocean County	986	1.08
Camillus, NY (town) Onondaga County	975	4.08
Aurora, CO (city) Arapahoe County	968	0.31
Toms River, NJ (cdp) Ocean County	965	1.09
St. Petersburg, FL (city) Pinellas County	965	0.39
Santa Monica, CA (city) Los Angeles County	957	1.08
West Hollywood, CA (city) Los Angeles County	956	2.76
Fair Lawn, NJ (borough) Bergen County	952	2.96
Hamilton, NJ (township) Mercer County	944	1.07
Brighton, NY (cdp/town) Monroe County	940	2.58
Colorado Springs, CO (city) El Paso County	938	0.23
Renton, WA (city) King County	936	1.08
Overland Park, KS (city) Johnson County	918	0.54
Naperville, IL (city) DuPage County	915	0.65
Mesa, AZ (city) Maricopa County	913	0.21
North Port, FL (city) Sarasota County	905	1.74
Babylon, NY (town) Suffolk County	905	0.42
Newton, MA (city) Middlesex County	903	1.08
Abington, PA (township) Montgomery County	885	1.60
Parma Heights, OH (city) Cuyahoga County	883	4.25
Jersey City, NJ (city) Hudson County	883	0.36
West Seneca, NY (cdp/town) Erie County	881	1.97
Fair Oaks, CA (cdp) Sacramento County	869	2.83
Bethlehem, PA (city) Northampton County	864	1.16
Erie, PA (city) Erie County	864	0.85
Colonie, NY (town) Albany County	860	1.05
Raleigh, NC (city) Wake County	846	0.22
Troy, MI (city) Oakland County	845	1.04
West Hartford, CT (cdp/town) Hartford County	837	1.33
Pikesville, MD (cdp) Baltimore County	834	2.71
Carlsbad, CA (city) San Diego County	832	0.83
Roseville, CA (city) Placer County	830	0.73
Milwaukee, WI (city) Milwaukee County	830	0.14
Lower Southampton, PA (township) Bucks County	827	4.34
Troy, NY (city) Rensselaer County	819	1.64
Carmichael, CA (cdp) Sacramento County	819	1.33
Reisterstown, MD (cdp) Baltimore County	803	2.98
Indianapolis, IN (city) Marion County	792	0.10
Albuquerque, NM (city) Bernalillo County	791	0.15
Geddes, NY (town) Onondaga County	780	4.54
Cambridge, MA (city) Middlesex County	775	0.75
San Antonio, TX (city) Medina County	774	0.06
Spokane Valley, WA (city) Spokane County	770	0.87
Rosemont, CA (cdp) Sacramento County	768	3.36
East Brunswick, NJ (township) Middlesex County	768	1.62
Penfield, NY (town) Monroe County	765	2.13
Henderson, NV (city) Clark County	762	0.31
Arden-Arcade, CA (cdp) Sacramento County	761	0.84
Salem, OR (city) Marion County	759	0.50
Lakewood, NJ (township) Ocean County	755	0.86
Happy Valley, OR (city) Clackamas County	753	5.98
Levittown, PA (cdp) Bucks County	752	1.45
Asheville, NC (city) Buncombe County	745	0.91
Glenview, IL (village) Cook County	741	1.70
Strongsville, OH (city) Cuyahoga County	741	1.67
Tampa, FL (city) Hillsborough County	741	0.22
Huntington Beach, CA (city) Orange County	732	0.39
Bethlehem, PA (city) Northampton County	724	1.31
Palm Coast, FL (city) Flagler County	723	1.02
Old Bridge, NJ (township) Middlesex County	717	1.11
Middletown, PA (township) Bucks County	716	1.58
West Sacramento, CA (city) Yolo County	716	1.56
Coon Rapids, MN (city) Anoka County	714	1.15
Bristol, PA (township) Bucks County	704	1.28

Please refer to the Explanation of Data in the front of the book for more detailed information.

Ancestry

Ukrainian

Top 150 Places Sorted by Percent of Total Population

Based on all places, regardless of total population

Place	Population	%
Forestville, PA (cdp) Schuylkill County	176	47.70
Camp 5, MN (township) St. Louis County	2	28.57
Macedonia, IL (village) Franklin County	6	25.00
Seltzer, PA (cdp) Schuylkill County	72	24.32
Cairnbrook, PA (cdp) Somerset County	106	23.45
Evergreen, MO (village) Laclede County	7	23.33
Springbrook, IA (city) Jackson County	31	23.13
Negley, OH (cdp) Columbiana County	48	20.08
Sandia Park, NM (cdp) Bernalillo County	14	20.00
Cass, PA (township) Schuylkill County	387	19.48
Butte, ND (city) McLean County	25	18.80
Bergen, ND (city) McHenry County	3	17.65
Washington Mills, NY (cdp) Oneida County	186	17.30
Thompson, MN (township) Kittson County	25	17.01
Fort Hill, OR (cdp) Polk County	14	16.67
Kerhonkson, NY (cdp) Ulster County	202	15.97
Smithfield, IL (village) Fulton County	46	15.81
New Schaefferstown, PA (cdp) Berks County	23	15.65
Yorktown, VA (cdp) York County	27	15.52
Cross Village, MI (cdp) Emmet County	11	15.49
Altamont, PA (cdp) Schuylkill County	112	15.16
Clifton, SC (cdp) Spartanburg County	101	13.91
Roca, NE (village) Lancaster County	42	13.91
Herbster, WI (cdp) Bayfield County	6	13.64
Gilberton, PA (borough) Schuylkill County	112	13.45
Slickville, PA (cdp) Westmoreland County	52	13.40
Nome, ND (city) Barnes County	5	12.82
Delta Junction, AK (city) Southeast Fairbanks Census Area	131	12.76
Bathgate, ND (city) Pembina County	8	12.70
South Fork, MO (cdp) Howell County	31	12.65
Elverta, CA (cdp) Sacramento County	634	12.57
Kendall, WA (cdp) Whatcom County	53	12.56
Heckscherville, PA (cdp) Schuylkill County	36	12.46
Potlicker Flats, PA (cdp) Mifflin County	34	12.01
Cragsmoor, NY (cdp) Ulster County	43	11.94
Kennedy, MN (city) Kittson County	17	11.56
Beaver Creek, MD (cdp) Washington County	21	11.48
Pajaro Dunes, CA (cdp) Santa Cruz County	34	11.33
Goodridge, MN (township) Pennington County	8	11.27
Dicksonville, PA (cdp) Indiana County	52	11.11
Mulino, OR (cdp) Clackamas County	242	11.09
Skillman, NJ (cdp) Somerset County	15	11.03
Granville, MN (township) Kittson County	14	10.94
Marion Heights, PA (borough) Northumberland County	64	10.85
Bonanza Mountain Estates, CO (cdp) Boulder County	25	10.73
Atlasburg, PA (cdp) Washington County	24	10.48
Clarendon, NY (town) Orleans County	374	10.35
Wilburton Population One, PA (cdp) Columbia County	21	10.24
Norwegian, PA (township) Schuylkill County	216	10.12
Harrison, SD (cdp) Douglas County	4	10.00
Scandia, MN (township) Polk County	3	10.00
Webster, NY (village) Monroe County	531	9.90
Redwood, NY (cdp) Jefferson County	30	9.71
Schuyler, NY (town) Herkimer County	321	9.46
Minersville, PA (borough) Schuylkill County	415	9.44
Mountain Lodge Park, NY (cdp) Orange County	175	9.41
Crabtree, PA (cdp) Westmoreland County	43	9.37
Marlin, PA (cdp) Schuylkill County	60	9.20
Five Corners, WA (cdp) Clark County	1,598	9.16
Matamoras, PA (borough) Pike County	200	9.08
Vallecito, CA (cdp) Calaveras County	48	8.92
Belmont Estates, VA (cdp) Rockingham County	113	8.81
Belfield, ND (city) Stark County	57	8.74
Machias, WA (cdp) Snohomish County	94	8.71
Hookstown, PA (borough) Beaver County	17	8.67
Soap Lake, WA (city) Grant County	101	8.54
Muir Beach, CA (cdp) Marin County	24	8.30
Baden, PA (borough) Beaver County	343	8.26
New Castle, PA (township) Schuylkill County	37	8.24
Ramey, PA (borough) Clearfield County	36	8.20
Charleston, TN (city) Bradley County	59	8.16
Deer Park, MN (township) Pennington County	18	8.14
West Mahanoy, PA (township) Schuylkill County	235	8.11
Parnell, MN (township) Polk County	3	8.11
Lambs Grove, IA (city) Jasper County	17	8.02

Place	Population	%
Cherryville, PA (cdp) Northampton County	114	8.00
Jacksonville, PA (cdp) Indiana County	48	7.97
Big Lagoon, CA (cdp) Humboldt County	15	7.94
Cayuga, NY (village) Cayuga County	36	7.93
Collins, OH (cdp) Huron County	41	7.84
Walker Valley, NY (cdp) Ulster County	41	7.65
Englewood, PA (cdp) Schuylkill County	37	7.61
Vienna, NJ (cdp) Warren County	55	7.58
Brooks, OR (cdp) Marion County	26	7.58
Hinsdale, NH (cdp) Cheshire County	133	7.45
Mill Village, PA (borough) Erie County	31	7.33
Kenneth, MN (city) Rock County	5	7.25
Antelope, CA (cdp) Sacramento County	3,301	7.22
Harmony, PA (township) Beaver County	231	7.19
Kinghurst, MN (township) Itasca County	6	7.14
Harmony, NJ (cdp) Warren County	28	7.11
Summit, WI (town) Juneau County	42	7.07
Westwood, PA (cdp) Chester County	41	7.02
Deltana, AK (cdp) Southeast Fairbanks Census Area	123	6.99
Alvarado, MN (city) Marshall County	27	6.94
Branch, PA (township) Schuylkill County	131	6.93
Nedrow, NY (cdp) Onondaga County	157	6.92
Percy, MN (township) Kittson County	2	6.90
McAdoo, PA (borough) Schuylkill County	169	6.85
McDonald, PA (borough) Allegheny County	26	6.84
Lakeville, NY (cdp) Livingston County	41	6.81
Union Springs, NY (village) Cayuga County	76	6.71
Niantic, CT (cdp) New London County	196	6.68
Oxford, NJ (cdp) Warren County	78	6.68
Frackville, PA (borough) Schuylkill County	256	6.60
Wynantskill, NY (cdp) Rensselaer County	232	6.56
Gulich, PA (township) Clearfield County	84	6.55
Canton Valley, CT (cdp) Hartford County	92	6.50
Betterton, MD (town) Kent County	29	6.44
Mount Hood, OR (cdp) Hood River County	19	6.42
Conyngham, PA (township) Columbia County	44	6.40
Lumberland, NY (town) Sullivan County	161	6.37
Hoople, ND (city) Walsh County	23	6.30
Balfour, NC (cdp) Henderson County	68	6.28
Lopatcong Overlook, NJ (cdp) Warren County	55	6.27
Lake City, PA (borough) Erie County	186	6.25
Pierpont, MO (village) Boone County	4	6.25
Aquasco, MD (cdp) Prince George's County	52	6.22
Ford City, PA (borough) Armstrong County	189	6.20
Prescott, MI (village) Ogemaw County	13	6.19
Boiling Springs, SC (cdp) Spartanburg County	510	6.18
Cementon, PA (cdp) Lehigh County	101	6.15
Reinerton, PA (cdp) Schuylkill County	31	6.14
Foundryville, PA (cdp) Columbia County	12	6.12
Bell Canyon, CA (cdp) Ventura County	150	6.11
Mather, CA (cdp) Sacramento County	274	6.09
Deblois, ME (town) Washington County	3	6.00
Happy Valley, OR (city) Clackamas County	753	5.98
Hunter, NY (town) Greene County	164	5.96
Norris, IL (village) Fulton County	9	5.96
Parma, OH (city) Cuyahoga County	4,857	5.93
Ferndale, FL (cdp) Lake County	9	5.88
Fullerton, ND (city) Dickey County	4	5.88
Avella, PA (cdp) Washington County	42	5.87
Landgrove, VT (town) Bennington County	11	5.82
Fife Heights, WA (cdp) Pierce County	125	5.81
Walnut Grove, WA (cdp) Clark County	509	5.77
Fairmount, NY (cdp) Onondaga County	578	5.75
Hometown, PA (cdp) Schuylkill County	84	5.75
North Highlands, CA (cdp) Sacramento County	2,401	5.63
Lexington, NY (town) Greene County	51	5.63
Roosevelt, WI (town) Taylor County	25	5.58
Caribou, MN (township) Kittson County	2	5.56
Solvay, NY (village) Onondaga County	366	5.54
North Manheim, PA (township) Schuylkill County	206	5.53
Independence, OH (city) Cuyahoga County	390	5.51
Olyphant, PA (borough) Lackawanna County	281	5.50
Bigler, PA (township) Clearfield County	67	5.47
Heidelberg, PA (borough) Allegheny County	70	5.45
Cross Village, MI (township) Emmet County	11	5.45

Please refer to the Explanation of Data in the front of the book for more detailed information.

Ancestry

Ukrainian

Top 150 Places Sorted by Percent of Total Population

Based on places with total population of 7,500 or more

Place	Population	%
Five Corners, WA (cdp) Clark County	1,598	9.16
Antelope, CA (cdp) Sacramento County	3,301	7.22
Boiling Springs, SC (cdp) Spartanburg County	510	6.18
Happy Valley, OR (city) Clackamas County	753	5.98
Parma, OH (city) Cuyahoga County	4,857	5.93
Walnut Grove, WA (cdp) Clark County	509	5.77
Fairmount, NY (cdp) Onondaga County	578	5.75
North Highlands, CA (cdp) Sacramento County	2,401	5.63
Carnegie, PA (borough) Allegheny County	429	5.38
Economy, PA (borough) Beaver County	447	4.96
Geddes, NY (town) Onondaga County	780	4.54
Auburn, NY (city) Cayuga County	1,247	4.48
Rancho Cordova, CA (city) Sacramento County	2,814	4.45
Northampton, PA (borough) Northampton County	435	4.39
Lower Southampton, PA (township) Bucks County	827	4.34
Upper Southampton, PA (township) Bucks County	662	4.32
Parma Heights, OH (city) Cuyahoga County	883	4.25
Camillus, NY (town) Onondaga County	975	4.08
Hanover, NJ (township) Morris County	554	4.07
Cohoes, NY (city) Albany County	642	3.98
West Springfield Town, MA (city) Hampden County	1,111	3.93
Lower Pottsgrove, PA (township) Montgomery County	457	3.84
Lakeland North, WA (cdp) King County	464	3.81
North Royalton, OH (city) Cuyahoga County	1,113	3.71
Auburn, WA (city) King County	2,463	3.68
Hanover, PA (township) Luzerne County	408	3.67
Picnic Point, WA (cdp) Snohomish County	306	3.60
Coal, PA (township) Northumberland County	365	3.53
North Greenbush, NY (town) Rensselaer County	418	3.52
Kennedy, PA (township) Allegheny County	265	3.49
Bedminster, NJ (township) Somerset County	285	3.48
Battle Ground, WA (city) Clark County	561	3.43
Mayfield Heights, OH (city) Cuyahoga County	649	3.40
Sanatoga, PA (cdp) Montgomery County	281	3.40
Rosemont, CA (cdp) Sacramento County	768	3.36
Seven Hills, OH (city) Cuyahoga County	394	3.34
Manville, NJ (borough) Somerset County	344	3.32
Plymouth, WI (city) Sheboygan County	278	3.32
Foothill Farms, CA (cdp) Sacramento County	1,082	3.30
Middleburg Heights, OH (city) Cuyahoga County	517	3.27
Webster, NY (town) Monroe County	1,334	3.20
Northampton, PA (township) Bucks County	1,274	3.20
Center, PA (township) Butler County	253	3.20
Deerpark, NY (town) Orange County	251	3.16
Buffalo Grove, IL (village) Lake County	1,311	3.13
Butler, PA (township) Butler County	543	3.13
West Caldwell, NJ (township) Essex County	329	3.05
Warwick, PA (township) Bucks County	423	3.01
Reisterstown, MD (cdp) Baltimore County	803	2.98
Fair Lawn, NJ (borough) Bergen County	952	2.96
Branchburg, NJ (township) Somerset County	428	2.96
Salisbury, PA (township) Lehigh County	400	2.95
Pottsville, PA (city) Schuylkill County	427	2.94
Yardville, NJ (cdp) Mercer County	221	2.94
Berwick, PA (borough) Columbia County	310	2.93
Lehigh, PA (township) Northampton County	304	2.90
Brookhaven, PA (borough) Delaware County	229	2.87
Princeton, NJ (borough) Mercer County	358	2.86
Upper Chichester, PA (township) Delaware County	474	2.84
Mansfield, NJ (township) Warren County	224	2.84
Fair Oaks, CA (cdp) Sacramento County	869	2.83
Saddle Brook, NJ (township) Bergen County	378	2.80
Phoenixville, PA (borough) Chester County	454	2.79
Swampscott, MA (cdp/town) Essex County	385	2.79
Broadview Heights, OH (city) Cuyahoga County	520	2.78
Carteret, NJ (borough) Middlesex County	621	2.77
West Hollywood, CA (city) Los Angeles County	956	2.76
Upper Saddle River, NJ (borough) Bergen County	222	2.75
Upper Makefield, PA (township) Bucks County	220	2.74
Westfield, MA (city) Hampden County	1,111	2.71
Pikesville, MD (cdp) Baltimore County	834	2.71
Fulton, NY (city) Oswego County	318	2.67
Harwood Heights, IL (village) Cook County	224	2.65
Colonia, NJ (cdp) Middlesex County	474	2.62
Big Flats, NY (town) Chemung County	199	2.62
Woodland Park, NJ (borough) Passaic County	303	2.61
Onondaga, NY (town) Onondaga County	589	2.60
Monessen, PA (city) Westmoreland County	204	2.59
Brighton, NY (cdp/town) Monroe County	940	2.58
Whitehall, PA (township) Lehigh County	684	2.58
Troutdale, OR (city) Multnomah County	395	2.57
South Park Township, PA (cdp) Allegheny County	344	2.56
South Park, PA (township) Allegheny County	344	2.56
Warrington, PA (township) Bucks County	574	2.55
Kent, WA (city) King County	2,259	2.53
Village Green-Green Ridge, PA (cdp) Delaware County	195	2.53
North Strabane, PA (township) Washington County	320	2.50
Tanaina, AK (cdp) Matanuska-Susitna Borough	215	2.49
Orchards, WA (cdp) Clark County	502	2.48
Lower Moreland, PA (township) Montgomery County	311	2.46
Alderwood Manor, WA (cdp) Snohomish County	194	2.46
Clark, NJ (township) Union County	358	2.45
Moore, PA (township) Northampton County	223	2.43
Ansonia, CT (city/town) New Haven County	459	2.40
Hamlin, NY (town) Monroe County	218	2.40
Spotswood, NJ (borough) Middlesex County	196	2.39
East Lyme, CT (town) New London County	454	2.38
Seymour, CT (town) New Haven County	389	2.38
Woodburn, OR (city) Marion County	549	2.36
Whitemarsh, PA (township) Montgomery County	403	2.34
Emmaus, PA (borough) Lehigh County	264	2.34
Springfield, NJ (township) Union County	360	2.33
River Grove, IL (village) Cook County	238	2.33
Bellevue, PA (borough) Allegheny County	195	2.33
Vernon Hills, IL (village) Lake County	565	2.32
Eastmont, WA (cdp) Snohomish County	449	2.32
Lower Saucon, PA (township) Northampton County	248	2.31
Prospect Heights, IL (city) Cook County	373	2.30
Hamilton, PA (township) Monroe County	210	2.30
Irondequoit, NY (cdp/town) Monroe County	1,169	2.27
Trinity, FL (cdp) Pasco County	243	2.25
Bensalem, PA (township) Bucks County	1,352	2.24
East Hill-Meridian, WA (cdp) King County	647	2.24
Worcester, PA (township) Montgomery County	209	2.23
Austintown, OH (cdp) Mahoning County	666	2.20
Citrus Heights, CA (city) Sacramento County	1,833	2.17
Minnehaha, WA (cdp) Clark County	209	2.17
Dallas, PA (township) Luzerne County	190	2.16
Spring Valley, NY (village) Rockland County	648	2.14
Fairless Hills, PA (cdp) Bucks County	187	2.14
Penfield, NY (town) Monroe County	765	2.13
Verona, NJ (township) Essex County	283	2.13
Ferndale, WA (city) Whatcom County	234	2.13
Martinsville, NJ (cdp) Somerset County	241	2.10
Upper Dublin, PA (township) Montgomery County	536	2.09
Solebury, PA (township) Bucks County	178	2.09
Dickinson, ND (city) Stark County	357	2.08
Willowbrook, IL (village) DuPage County	177	2.07
South Venice, FL (cdp) Sarasota County	286	2.05
Elmwood Park, IL (village) Cook County	503	2.04
Robbinsville, NJ (township) Mercer County	266	2.04
Hebron, CT (town) Tolland County	195	2.04
Livonia, NY (town) Livingston County	158	2.04
Wawarsing, NY (town) Ulster County	270	2.02
Schaghticoke, NY (town) Rensselaer County	153	2.00
Everett, WA (city) Snohomish County	2,019	1.99
Northbrook, IL (village) Cook County	655	1.99
Willimantic, CT (cdp) Windham County	346	1.98
West Seneca, NY (cdp/town) Erie County	881	1.97
Coeymans, NY (town) Albany County	150	1.97
Cranford, NJ (township) Union County	439	1.96
Ephrata, PA (borough) Lancaster County	262	1.96
Wilson, PA (borough) Northampton County	155	1.96
Horseheads, NY (town) Chemung County	378	1.95
Skokie, IL (village) Cook County	1,223	1.92
South Fayette, PA (township) Allegheny County	267	1.92
Vancouver, WA (city) Clark County	3,056	1.91
Federal Way, WA (city) King County	1,665	1.90
Lackawanna, NY (city) Erie County	346	1.90
Warminster, PA (township) Bucks County	615	1.89

Please refer to the Explanation of Data in the front of the book for more detailed information.

SECTION THREE

Ancestry

Welsh

U.S. and 50 States Sorted by Population and Percent of Total Population

Place	Population	%
United States	**1,922,914**	**0.63**
Pennsylvania	187,607	1.49
California	180,792	0.49
Ohio	135,998	1.18
Texas	102,101	0.42
Florida	101,857	0.55
New York	88,255	0.46
Washington	70,800	1.08
Virginia	58,256	0.74
Utah	58,155	2.19
North Carolina	54,197	0.58
Illinois	52,576	0.41
Michigan	51,799	0.52
Colorado	46,949	0.96
Arizona	44,751	0.72
Oregon	42,581	1.13
Maryland	41,924	0.74
Georgia	41,220	0.44
Missouri	40,759	0.69
Indiana	38,925	0.61
New Jersey	38,268	0.44
Tennessee	34,433	0.55
Wisconsin	28,171	0.50
Massachusetts	26,359	0.41
Minnesota	25,064	0.48
Iowa	22,794	0.76
Kansas	22,702	0.81
Kentucky	22,649	0.53
Idaho	22,464	1.47
South Carolina	22,370	0.50
Oklahoma	19,204	0.52
Nevada	18,227	0.69
Alabama	18,106	0.38
Connecticut	14,946	0.42
West Virginia	14,347	0.78
Arkansas	13,110	0.46
Nebraska	11,660	0.65
Maine	11,608	0.87
New Mexico	11,089	0.55
Louisiana	10,645	0.24
Montana	10,263	1.05
Delaware	9,396	1.07
Mississippi	9,225	0.31
New Hampshire	8,677	0.66
Vermont	7,758	1.24
Wyoming	6,530	1.20
Alaska	6,512	0.94
Hawaii	5,166	0.39
South Dakota	3,937	0.49
Rhode Island	3,185	0.30
District of Columbia	2,671	0.46
North Dakota	1,876	0.28

Place	Population	%
Utah	58,155	2.19
Pennsylvania	187,607	1.49
Idaho	22,464	1.47
Vermont	7,758	1.24
Wyoming	6,530	1.20
Ohio	135,998	1.18
Oregon	42,581	1.13
Washington	70,800	1.08
Delaware	9,396	1.07
Montana	10,263	1.05
Colorado	46,949	0.96
Alaska	6,512	0.94
Maine	11,608	0.87
Kansas	22,702	0.81
West Virginia	14,347	0.78
Iowa	22,794	0.76
Virginia	58,256	0.74
Maryland	41,924	0.74
Arizona	44,751	0.72
Missouri	40,759	0.69
Nevada	18,227	0.69
New Hampshire	8,677	0.66
Nebraska	11,660	0.65
United States	**1,922,914**	**0.63**
Indiana	38,925	0.61
North Carolina	54,197	0.58
Florida	101,857	0.55
Tennessee	34,433	0.55
New Mexico	11,089	0.55
Kentucky	22,649	0.53
Michigan	51,799	0.52
Oklahoma	19,204	0.52
Wisconsin	28,171	0.50
South Carolina	22,370	0.50
California	180,792	0.49
South Dakota	3,937	0.49
Minnesota	25,064	0.48
New York	88,255	0.46
Arkansas	13,110	0.46
District of Columbia	2,671	0.46
Georgia	41,220	0.44
New Jersey	38,268	0.44
Texas	102,101	0.42
Connecticut	14,946	0.42
Illinois	52,576	0.41
Massachusetts	26,359	0.41
Hawaii	5,166	0.39
Alabama	18,106	0.38
Mississippi	9,225	0.31
Rhode Island	3,185	0.30
North Dakota	1,876	0.28
Louisiana	10,645	0.24

Please refer to the Explanation of Data in the front of the book for more detailed information.

Ancestry

Welsh

Top 150 Places Sorted by Population

Based on all places, regardless of total population

Place	Population	%
New York, NY (city) Kings County	11,219	0.14
Los Angeles, CA (city) Los Angeles County	10,583	0.28
Columbus, OH (city) Franklin County	10,220	1.33
San Diego, CA (city) San Diego County	8,167	0.64
Seattle, WA (city) King County	7,475	1.26
Phoenix, AZ (city) Maricopa County	7,431	0.51
Portland, OR (city) Multnomah County	7,213	1.27
Manhattan, NY (borough) New York County	6,000	0.38
Houston, TX (city) Harris County	5,944	0.29
Chicago, IL (city) Cook County	5,904	0.22
Austin, TX (city) Travis County	5,568	0.73
Charlotte, NC (city) Mecklenburg County	4,719	0.67
Indianapolis, IN (city) Marion County	4,603	0.57
Colorado Springs, CO (city) El Paso County	4,586	1.14
Scranton, PA (city) Lackawanna County	4,539	5.97
Denver, CO (city) Denver County	4,528	0.78
Philadelphia, PA (city) Philadelphia County	4,345	0.29
Dallas, TX (city) Dallas County	4,109	0.35
Jacksonville, FL (city) Duval County	4,080	0.50
Virginia Beach, VA (ind. city) Virginia Beach independent city	3,937	0.90
San Antonio, TX (city) Medina County	3,900	0.30
Salt Lake City, UT (city) Salt Lake County	3,831	2.08
Boise City, ID (city) Ada County	3,812	1.85
Nashville-Davidson, TN (metro govt) Davidson County	3,812	0.65
San Francisco, CA (city) San Francisco County	3,806	0.48
Albuquerque, NM (city) Bernalillo County	3,720	0.70
Tucson, AZ (city) Pima County	3,631	0.70
Mesa, AZ (city) Maricopa County	3,484	0.79
Kansas City, MO (city) Jackson County	3,415	0.75
San Jose, CA (city) Santa Clara County	3,304	0.36
Las Vegas, NV (city) Clark County	3,194	0.55
Provo, UT (city) Utah County	3,138	2.85
Raleigh, NC (city) Wake County	3,130	0.82
Fort Worth, TX (city) Tarrant County	3,065	0.43
Oklahoma City, OK (city) Oklahoma County	2,967	0.53
Louisville-Jefferson County, KY (metro govt) Jefferson County	2,824	0.48
Wichita, KS (city) Sedgwick County	2,768	0.74
Pittsburgh, PA (city) Allegheny County	2,729	0.89
Minneapolis, MN (city) Hennepin County	2,689	0.71
Tulsa, OK (city) Tulsa County	2,688	0.69
Washington, DC (city) District of Columbia	2,671	0.46
Brooklyn, NY (borough) Kings County	2,606	0.11
Omaha, NE (city) Douglas County	2,490	0.61
Madison, WI (city) Dane County	2,470	1.08
Anchorage, AK (municipality) Anchorage Municipality	2,452	0.86
Orem, UT (city) Utah County	2,447	2.82
Lexington-Fayette, KY (cons. govt) Fayette County	2,350	0.82
Wilkes-Barre, PA (city) Luzerne County	2,318	5.57
Sacramento, CA (city) Sacramento County	2,314	0.50
Eugene, OR (city) Lane County	2,309	1.51
Spokane, WA (city) Spokane County	2,279	1.10
Overland Park, KS (city) Johnson County	2,249	1.32
Henderson, NV (city) Clark County	2,051	0.82
Cincinnati, OH (city) Hamilton County	2,038	0.68
Akron, OH (city) Summit County	2,022	1.00
Boston, MA (city) Suffolk County	2,022	0.34
Fresno, CA (city) Fresno County	1,973	0.41
Baltimore, MD (city) Baltimore city County	1,970	0.32
Lincoln, NE (city) Lancaster County	1,968	0.78
Vancouver, WA (city) Clark County	1,965	1.23
Memphis, TN (city) Shelby County	1,935	0.30
Scottsdale, AZ (city) Maricopa County	1,906	0.87
Atlanta, GA (city) Fulton County	1,888	0.46
Long Beach, CA (city) Los Angeles County	1,823	0.39
Winston-Salem, NC (city) Forsyth County	1,806	0.80
Tacoma, WA (city) Pierce County	1,803	0.91
West Jordan, UT (city) Salt Lake County	1,797	1.82
Tempe, AZ (city) Maricopa County	1,791	1.09
Huntington Beach, CA (city) Orange County	1,786	0.95
Plano, TX (city) Collin County	1,786	0.70
Tampa, FL (city) Hillsborough County	1,777	0.53
Arlington, VA (cdp) Arlington County	1,767	0.89
Arlington, TX (city) Tarrant County	1,699	0.47
West Valley City, UT (city) Salt Lake County	1,691	1.35
Des Moines, IA (city) Polk County	1,677	0.83
Aurora, CO (city) Arapahoe County	1,675	0.53
Glendale, AZ (city) Maricopa County	1,672	0.73
Queens, NY (borough) Queens County	1,666	0.08
Chandler, AZ (city) Maricopa County	1,641	0.71
Sandy, UT (city) Salt Lake County	1,612	1.85
Tallahassee, FL (city) Leon County	1,611	0.91
Cleveland, OH (city) Cuyahoga County	1,575	0.38
Fort Collins, CO (city) Larimer County	1,548	1.11
Knoxville, TN (city) Knox County	1,534	0.86
Reno, NV (city) Washoe County	1,524	0.69
Modesto, CA (city) Stanislaus County	1,523	0.75
Santa Clarita, CA (city) Los Angeles County	1,502	0.87
St. George, UT (city) Washington County	1,498	2.11
Chesapeake, VA (ind. city) Chesapeake independent city	1,492	0.68
Bethlehem, PA (city) Northampton County	1,433	1.92
Lakewood, CO (city) Jefferson County	1,424	1.00
Millcreek, UT (cdp) Salt Lake County	1,423	2.33
Pocatello, ID (city) Bannock County	1,418	2.66
Salem, OR (city) Marion County	1,418	0.93
Alexandria, VA (ind. city) Alexandria independent city	1,404	1.05
Durham, NC (city) Durham County	1,397	0.63
Richmond, VA (ind. city) Richmond independent city	1,390	0.69
Norfolk, VA (ind. city) Norfolk independent city	1,390	0.57
Cary, NC (town) Wake County	1,388	1.09
Fort Wayne, IN (city) Allen County	1,388	0.55
St. Petersburg, FL (city) Pinellas County	1,382	0.56
Union, NY (town) Broome County	1,372	2.44
Ogden, UT (city) Weber County	1,358	1.68
Oakland, CA (city) Alameda County	1,353	0.35
South Jordan, UT (city) Salt Lake County	1,336	2.88
Rancho Cucamonga, CA (city) San Bernardino County	1,323	0.82
Orlando, FL (city) Orange County	1,309	0.56
Toledo, OH (city) Lucas County	1,296	0.44
Layton, UT (city) Davis County	1,288	1.96
Milwaukee, WI (city) Milwaukee County	1,285	0.22
Highlands Ranch, CO (cdp) Douglas County	1,282	1.35
St. Paul, MN (city) Ramsey County	1,272	0.45
Lehi, UT (city) Utah County	1,270	3.02
St. Louis, MO (city) St. Louis city County	1,263	0.40
Centennial, CO (city) Arapahoe County	1,261	1.26
Bountiful, UT (city) Davis County	1,258	2.97
Lubbock, TX (city) Lubbock County	1,248	0.56
Bakersfield, CA (city) Kern County	1,244	0.37
Springfield, MO (city) Christian County	1,243	0.78
Santa Rosa, CA (city) Sonoma County	1,242	0.76
Greensboro, NC (city) Guilford County	1,239	0.47
Olathe, KS (city) Johnson County	1,225	1.01
Norman, OK (city) Cleveland County	1,207	1.11
Columbia, MO (city) Boone County	1,194	1.14
Brookhaven, NY (town) Suffolk County	1,189	0.25
Riverside, CA (city) Riverside County	1,170	0.39
Gilbert, AZ (town) Maricopa County	1,169	0.60
Paradise, NV (cdp) Clark County	1,144	0.52
Newport Beach, CA (city) Orange County	1,134	1.36
Newport News, VA (ind. city) Newport News independent city	1,112	0.61
Asheville, NC (city) Buncombe County	1,103	1.35
Murray, UT (city) Salt Lake County	1,098	2.37
Hillsboro, OR (city) Washington County	1,096	1.24
Billings, MT (city) Yellowstone County	1,095	1.08
Cottonwood Heights, UT (city) Salt Lake County	1,094	3.26
Boulder, CO (city) Boulder County	1,080	1.11
Boardman, OH (cdp) Mahoning County	1,078	3.04
Draper, UT (city) Salt Lake County	1,075	2.74
Santa Monica, CA (city) Los Angeles County	1,075	1.21
Topeka, KS (city) Shawnee County	1,070	0.85
Ann Arbor, MI (city) Washtenaw County	1,064	0.92
Syracuse, NY (city) Onondaga County	1,060	0.73
Idaho Falls, ID (city) Bonneville County	1,059	1.90
Huntsville, AL (city) Madison County	1,058	0.60
Cedar Rapids, IA (city) Linn County	1,056	0.84
Oceanside, CA (city) San Diego County	1,055	0.64
Allentown, PA (city) Lehigh County	1,050	0.90
Logan, UT (city) Cache County	1,042	2.25
Independence, MO (city) Jackson County	1,031	0.89
Denton, TX (city) Denton County	1,030	0.94

SECTION THREE

Please refer to the Explanation of Data in the front of the book for more detailed information.

Ancestry

Welsh

Top 150 Places Sorted by Percent of Total Population

Based on all places, regardless of total population

Place	Population	%
Prattville, CA (cdp) Plumas County	21	100.00
Crystal Bay, NV (cdp) Washoe County	12	100.00
Alpine Northeast, WY (cdp) Lincoln County	8	100.00
Valley-Hi, PA (borough) Fulton County	3	100.00
Winigan, MO (cdp) Sullivan County	61	70.93
Gheen, MN (unorganized territory) St. Louis County	22	64.71
Ophir, UT (town) Tooele County	22	57.89
National, MD (cdp) Allegany County	16	53.33
Middle Frisco, NM (cdp) Catron County	17	53.13
Parc, NY (cdp) Clinton County	22	52.38
Siasconset, MA (cdp) Nantucket County	22	52.38
Primrose, AK (cdp) Kenai Peninsula Borough	9	50.00
Genoa City, WI (village) Kenosha County	3	50.00
Little River, CA (cdp) Mendocino County	138	47.59
Magnet, NE (village) Cedar County	7	43.75
Glencoe, OH (cdp) Belmont County	37	43.02
Maple Grove, MI (cdp) Benzie County	43	41.35
Pinedale, AZ (cdp) Navajo County	87	39.01
Elliott, MD (cdp) Dorchester County	12	37.50
Boyd, MT (cdp) Carbon County	17	36.96
Likely, CA (cdp) Modoc County	23	36.51
Jacksonburg, WV (cdp) Wetzel County	16	36.36
Hidden Lake, CO (cdp) Boulder County	15	35.71
River Sioux, IA (cdp) Harrison County	15	34.88
Fedora, SD (cdp) Miner County	8	33.33
Pentress, WV (cdp) Monongalia County	88	30.14
Pilgrim, MI (cdp) Benzie County	5	26.32
Moore, ID (city) Butte County	59	25.65
Pageton, WV (cdp) McDowell County	24	25.53
Passaic, MO (town) Bates County	2	25.00
Jacksonville, PA (cdp) Centre County	25	24.75
Tony, WI (village) Rusk County	26	24.53
Barneveld, NY (village) Oneida County	74	24.10
Ivanhoe North, TX (city) Tyler County	24	23.76
Vaughnsville, OH (cdp) Putnam County	32	23.36
Beseman, MN (township) Carlton County	37	22.84
Butte, ND (city) McLean County	30	22.56
King Lake, NE (cdp) Douglas County	28	21.88
Montello, NV (cdp) Elko County	13	21.67
La Paz Valley, AZ (cdp) La Paz County	109	21.54
Judson, MN (township) Blue Earth County	131	21.51
Deerfield, MO (village) Vernon County	12	21.43
Randsburg, CA (cdp) Kern County	9	21.43
Hackberry, AZ (cdp) Mohave County	8	21.05
Silvana, WA (cdp) Snohomish County	13	20.97
Wintergreen, VA (cdp) Nelson County	26	20.80
Wintersburg, AZ (cdp) Maricopa County	10	20.00
Gandy, NE (village) Logan County	9	19.57
Canaan, NH (cdp) Grafton County	171	19.28
Crestone, CO (town) Saguache County	18	19.15
Jamison City, PA (cdp) Columbia County	20	19.05
Oak, NE (village) Nuckolls County	13	18.84
Anchor Bay, CA (cdp) Mendocino County	60	18.81
Vineyard, UT (town) Utah County	36	18.75
Pointe Aux Barques, MI (township) Huron County	2	18.18
La Platte, NE (cdp) Sarpy County	15	18.07
Malad City, ID (city) Oneida County	442	18.03
Camp Sherman, OR (cdp) Jefferson County	46	17.90
Millerton, IA (city) Wayne County	16	17.58
Dunlo, PA (cdp) Cambria County	38	17.35
Silver Lake, OR (cdp) Lake County	19	17.27
Pine Valley, UT (cdp) Washington County	23	17.16
Timber Hills, PA (cdp) Lebanon County	55	16.52
Saratoga, IN (town) Randolph County	31	16.49
Vicksburg, PA (cdp) Union County	37	16.37
Vallecito, CA (cdp) Calaveras County	87	16.17
Duanesburg, NY (cdp) Schenectady County	28	16.00
Dundee, MN (city) Nobles County	11	15.94
Sylvanite, MT (cdp) Lincoln County	15	15.79
Green, KS (city) Clay County	20	15.75
St. Mary's, CO (cdp) Clear Creek County	28	15.30
Marion, UT (cdp) Summit County	56	15.26
Edna Bay, AK (cdp) Prince of Wales-Hyder Census Area	9	15.25
Oneida, KS (city) Nemaha County	9	15.25
Lucerne, MO (village) Putnam County	7	15.22
Valley Acres, CA (cdp) Kern County	85	15.12
Hideout, UT (town) Wasatch County	37	14.98
Hartline, WA (town) Grant County	15	14.71
Matlacha Isles-Matlacha Shores, FL (cdp) Lee County	28	14.58
Waverly, PA (cdp) Lackawanna County	76	14.53
Ragsdale, IN (cdp) Knox County	16	14.41
Hepzibah, WV (cdp) Harrison County	86	14.38
Catherine, CO (cdp) Garfield County	27	14.29
Atomic City, ID (city) Bingham County	4	14.29
Gascoyne, ND (city) Bowman County	3	14.29
Green Hills, PA (borough) Washington County	2	14.29
Venedocia, OH (village) Van Wert County	16	14.16
Remsen, NY (town) Oneida County	274	14.13
West Winfield, NY (village) Herkimer County	112	14.11
Newton, PA (township) Lackawanna County	395	14.09
Grier City, PA (cdp) Schuylkill County	16	14.04
Benton, PA (township) Lackawanna County	231	14.01
Bradford, VT (cdp) Orange County	95	13.99
Hildale, UT (city) Washington County	372	13.98
Winfield, NY (town) Herkimer County	268	13.96
Dunlap, KS (city) Morris County	6	13.95
Remsen, NY (village) Oneida County	76	13.89
Peeples Valley, AZ (cdp) Yavapai County	69	13.66
Lewis, CO (cdp) Montezuma County	41	13.62
Wales, UT (town) Sanpete County	46	13.61
Tanacross, AK (cdp) Southeast Fairbanks Census Area	16	13.56
Holland Patent, NY (village) Oneida County	75	13.54
Samak, UT (cdp) Summit County	63	13.46
Ransom, PA (township) Lackawanna County	190	13.37
Brady, MT (cdp) Pondera County	25	13.16
Newton, UT (town) Cache County	85	13.14
Middletown, PA (township) Susquehanna County	49	13.10
Grover, WY (cdp) Lincoln County	10	12.99
Courtdale, PA (borough) Luzerne County	96	12.96
Grand View Estates, CO (cdp) Douglas County	35	12.92
Harveys Lake, PA (borough) Luzerne County	355	12.82
Joyce, LA (cdp) Winn Parish	48	12.80
Rush, PA (township) Dauphin County	30	12.77
Charleston, UT (town) Wasatch County	66	12.69
West Falls, PA (cdp) Wyoming County	66	12.67
Eagarville, IL (village) Macoupin County	10	12.66
Madison, NY (village) Madison County	49	12.47
Fountain Springs, PA (cdp) Schuylkill County	44	12.43
Smeltertown, CO (cdp) Chaffee County	13	12.38
La Plume, PA (township) Lackawanna County	90	12.33
Hiller, PA (cdp) Fayette County	160	12.31
Dillon Beach, CA (cdp) Marin County	20	12.27
Sandyville, OH (cdp) Tuscarawas County	38	12.22
Dalton, PA (borough) Lackawanna County	147	12.12
Central, AK (cdp) Yukon-Koyukuk Census Area	16	12.12
Placerville, ID (city) Boise County	4	12.12
Coburn, PA (cdp) Centre County	14	12.07
Bannock, OH (cdp) Belmont County	25	12.02
Lincoln, MN (township) Blue Earth County	27	12.00
Allerton, IA (city) Wayne County	60	11.90
Pitkin, CO (town) Gunnison County	10	11.90
Honcut, CA (cdp) Butte County	68	11.89
Belknap, MT (cdp) Sanders County	12	11.88
Weston, CO (cdp) Las Animas County	7	11.86
Pomeroy, PA (cdp) Chester County	41	11.85
Martins Creek, PA (cdp) Northampton County	73	11.83
Thousand Island Park, NY (cdp) Jefferson County	13	11.71
Waitsfield, VT (cdp) Washington County	22	11.64
Douglassville, PA (cdp) Berks County	28	11.62
Hamer, ID (city) Jefferson County	3	11.54
Beaver Creek, MD (cdp) Washington County	21	11.48
Noyes, PA (township) Clinton County	37	11.46
Elberta, UT (cdp) Utah County	34	11.37
Bangor, CA (cdp) Butte County	42	11.35
Franklin, PA (township) Luzerne County	209	11.32
Mulford, CO (cdp) Garfield County	15	11.28
Gallatin River Ranch, MT (cdp) Gallatin County	10	11.24
Watch Hill, RI (cdp) Washington County	29	11.20
Kempton, PA (cdp) Berks County	17	11.18
Clifford, PA (township) Susquehanna County	241	11.12

Please refer to the Explanation of Data in the front of the book for more detailed information.

Ancestry

Welsh

Top 150 Places Sorted by Percent of Total Population

Based on places with total population of 7,500 or more

Place	Population	%
Dallas, PA (township) Luzerne County	820	9.31
Hanover, PA (township) Luzerne County	890	8.01
Old Forge, PA (borough) Lackawanna County	664	7.93
Kingston, PA (borough) Luzerne County	841	6.35
South Abington, PA (township) Lackawanna County	544	6.07
Scranton, PA (city) Lackawanna County	4,539	5.97
Wilkes-Barre, PA (city) Luzerne County	2,318	5.57
San Diego Country Estates, CA (cdp) San Diego County	563	5.28
Nanticoke, PA (city) Luzerne County	541	5.16
Mountain Top, PA (cdp) Luzerne County	531	5.03
Plains, PA (township) Luzerne County	466	4.63
Maltby, WA (cdp) Snohomish County	539	4.62
Niles, OH (city) Trumbull County	898	4.61
Dunmore, PA (borough) Lackawanna County	600	4.26
Brentwood, PA (borough) Allegheny County	403	4.15
Centerville, UT (city) Davis County	626	4.11
Rexburg, ID (city) Madison County	971	3.96
Bloomsburg, PA (town) Columbia County	566	3.96
Mapleton, UT (city) Utah County	298	3.95
Whitestown, NY (town) Oneida County	718	3.85
York, MI (charter township) Washtenaw County	330	3.85
Chenango, NY (town) Broome County	419	3.72
Kirkland, NY (town) Oneida County	378	3.68
Worthington, OH (city) Franklin County	506	3.67
New Hartford, NY (town) Oneida County	804	3.66
Pittston, PA (city) Luzerne County	282	3.63
Frankfort, NY (town) Herkimer County	271	3.58
Phoenixville, PA (borough) Chester County	575	3.54
Evanston, WY (city) Uinta County	425	3.54
Cedar Hills, OR (cdp) Washington County	295	3.54
Folsom, PA (cdp) Delaware County	291	3.45
Farmington, UT (city) Davis County	592	3.44
Camp Hill, PA (borough) Cumberland County	262	3.35
Davidson, NC (town) Mecklenburg County	344	3.33
Emmaus, PA (borough) Lehigh County	371	3.29
Endwell, NY (cdp) Broome County	383	3.28
Cottonwood Heights, UT (city) Salt Lake County	1,094	3.26
Woods Cross, UT (city) Davis County	298	3.25
Salisbury, PA (township) Lehigh County	436	3.22
Boone, IA (city) Boone County	411	3.22
Herriman, UT (city) Salt Lake County	586	3.20
East Bradford, PA (township) Chester County	318	3.20
Fallon, NV (city) Churchill County	272	3.18
Forks, PA (township) Northampton County	432	3.16
Wyomissing, PA (borough) Berks County	333	3.16
East Liverpool, OH (city) Columbiana County	361	3.13
Frostburg, MD (city) Allegany County	273	3.11
Munhall, PA (borough) Allegheny County	355	3.10
Ilion, NY (village) Herkimer County	250	3.08
Cedar City, UT (city) Iron County	846	3.05
Black Forest, CO (cdp) El Paso County	411	3.05
Boardman, OH (cdp) Mahoning County	1,078	3.04
Moscow, ID (city) Latah County	708	3.04
Lehi, UT (city) Utah County	1,270	3.02
Upper Macungie, PA (township) Lehigh County	571	3.00
Bountiful, UT (city) Davis County	1,258	2.97
Carbondale, PA (city) Lackawanna County	267	2.97
Delaware, OH (city) Delaware County	998	2.96
Alpine, UT (city) Utah County	267	2.95
Upper Arlington, OH (city) Franklin County	983	2.92
South Jordan, UT (city) Salt Lake County	1,336	2.88
Middlebury, VT (town) Addison County	243	2.87
Doylestown, PA (borough) Bucks County	241	2.87
Provo, UT (city) Utah County	3,138	2.85
Upper Allen, PA (township) Cumberland County	499	2.85
Milford, PA (township) Bucks County	279	2.85
Greenville, MI (city) Montcalm County	241	2.85
Alderwood Manor, WA (cdp) Snohomish County	225	2.85
Gahanna, OH (city) Franklin County	927	2.84
Orem, UT (city) Utah County	2,447	2.82
Hampden, PA (township) Cumberland County	769	2.81
North Logan, UT (city) Cache County	217	2.79
Holladay, UT (city) Salt Lake County	725	2.76
Draper, UT (city) Salt Lake County	1,075	2.74
Kenton, OH (city) Hardin County	228	2.73

Place	Population	%
Park City, UT (city) Summit County	206	2.73
Springville, UT (city) Utah County	742	2.69
Wanaque, NJ (borough) Passaic County	293	2.69
Cumru, PA (township) Berks County	402	2.68
Bryan, OH (city) Williams County	231	2.68
Upper Saucon, PA (township) Lehigh County	383	2.67
Kelso, WA (city) Cowlitz County	320	2.67
Pocatello, ID (city) Bannock County	1,418	2.66
East Grand Rapids, MI (city) Kent County	286	2.66
Endicott, NY (village) Broome County	352	2.64
German Flatts, NY (town) Herkimer County	351	2.64
Rome, NY (city) Oneida County	891	2.63
Rostraver, PA (township) Westmoreland County	300	2.63
Towamencin, PA (township) Montgomery County	461	2.62
White Oak, PA (borough) Allegheny County	207	2.62
Warwick, PA (township) Lancaster County	455	2.61
Silver Spring, PA (township) Cumberland County	342	2.61
Derry, PA (township) Dauphin County	625	2.60
Bethlehem, PA (city) Lehigh County	502	2.60
Elkton, MD (town) Cecil County	387	2.58
North Canton, OH (city) Stark County	444	2.56
Spanish Fork, UT (city) Utah County	812	2.55
Lawrence, PA (township) Clearfield County	197	2.55
Summit Park, UT (cdp) Summit County	191	2.55
North Whitehall, PA (township) Lehigh County	394	2.53
Snoqualmie, WA (city) King County	229	2.53
Linganore, MD (cdp) Frederick County	210	2.53
Lower Salford, PA (township) Montgomery County	367	2.52
Owego, NY (town) Tioga County	503	2.51
Pottsville, PA (city) Schuylkill County	365	2.51
Dover, OH (city) Tuscarawas County	320	2.50
Santaquin, UT (city) Utah County	208	2.49
Garden City, ID (city) Ada County	274	2.48
Skowhegan, ME (town) Somerset County	215	2.48
Hilliard, OH (city) Franklin County	680	2.47
Allison Park, PA (cdp) Allegheny County	551	2.47
Oak Hills, OR (cdp) Washington County	269	2.47
Knightdale, NC (town) Wake County	259	2.47
Neshannock, PA (township) Lawrence County	235	2.47
North Ogden, UT (city) Weber County	413	2.46
Lehigh, PA (township) Northampton County	258	2.46
Summerfield, NC (town) Guilford County	237	2.46
Fairless Hills, PA (cdp) Bucks County	215	2.46
Kaysville, UT (city) Davis County	638	2.45
Schroeppel, NY (town) Oswego County	208	2.45
Boxford, MA (town) Essex County	194	2.45
Union, NY (town) Broome County	1,372	2.44
Austintown, OH (cdp) Mahoning County	737	2.44
Mendota Heights, MN (city) Dakota County	274	2.44
Big Flats, NY (town) Chemung County	185	2.44
Horseheads, NY (town) Chemung County	471	2.43
Salem, OH (city) Columbiana County	301	2.43
Polk, PA (township) Monroe County	190	2.43
South Whitehall, PA (township) Lehigh County	460	2.42
Burlington, WA (city) Skagit County	198	2.42
New Britain, PA (township) Bucks County	266	2.41
Prairie Village, KS (city) Johnson County	521	2.40
Penn, PA (township) Westmoreland County	477	2.39
Hollymead, VA (cdp) Albemarle County	192	2.39
Murray, UT (city) Salt Lake County	1,098	2.37
Payson, UT (city) Utah County	407	2.37
Van Buren, NY (town) Onondaga County	309	2.37
Richland, PA (township) Cambria County	299	2.35
Sitka, AK (borough) Sitka City and Borough	209	2.35
Brigham City, UT (city) Box Elder County	412	2.34
Millcreek, UT (cdp) Salt Lake County	1,423	2.33
Palos Verdes Estates, CA (city) Los Angeles County	311	2.32
Grove City, OH (city) Franklin County	784	2.31
Kearns, UT (cdp) Salt Lake County	800	2.30
Colleyville, TX (city) Tarrant County	510	2.30
Marysville, OH (city) Union County	490	2.30
Eagle, ID (city) Ada County	431	2.30
North Fayette, PA (township) Allegheny County	307	2.27
Worcester, PA (township) Montgomery County	212	2.26
Montecito, CA (cdp) Santa Barbara County	209	2.26

Please refer to the Explanation of Data in the front of the book for more detailed information.

Ancestry

West Indian, excluding Hispanic

U.S. and 50 States Sorted by Population and Percent of Total Population

Place	Population	%
United States	**2,548,218**	**0.84**
New York	790,170	4.11
Florida	750,598	4.05
New Jersey	148,178	1.70
Massachusetts	111,104	1.72
Georgia	102,553	1.08
Connecticut	80,311	2.26
California	73,694	0.20
Maryland	67,574	1.19
Pennsylvania	63,964	0.51
Texas	61,097	0.25
Virginia	35,551	0.45
North Carolina	31,296	0.34
Illinois	29,090	0.23
Oklahoma	23,128	0.63
Ohio	17,473	0.15
Michigan	13,682	0.14
South Carolina	10,670	0.24
Washington	9,017	0.14
Delaware	8,678	0.98
Tennessee	8,270	0.13
District of Columbia	8,198	1.40
Alabama	7,971	0.17
Arizona	7,702	0.12
Louisiana	7,057	0.16
Missouri	6,838	0.12
Nevada	6,573	0.25
Colorado	6,514	0.13
Indiana	6,151	0.10
Rhode Island	6,025	0.57
Arkansas	4,974	0.17
Kentucky	4,830	0.11
Wisconsin	4,801	0.09
Minnesota	4,756	0.09
Oregon	3,580	0.10
New Hampshire	3,499	0.27
Kansas	3,056	0.11
Mississippi	2,403	0.08
New Mexico	2,284	0.11
West Virginia	2,079	0.11
Hawaii	2,051	0.15
Iowa	1,944	0.06
Maine	1,690	0.13
Utah	1,680	0.06
Alaska	1,523	0.22
Nebraska	1,258	0.07
Idaho	875	0.06
Vermont	575	0.09
Montana	398	0.04
North Dakota	369	0.06
South Dakota	363	0.05
Wyoming	103	0.02

Place	Population	%
New York	790,170	4.11
Florida	750,598	4.05
Connecticut	80,311	2.26
Massachusetts	111,104	1.72
New Jersey	148,178	1.70
District of Columbia	8,198	1.40
Maryland	67,574	1.19
Georgia	102,553	1.08
Delaware	8,678	0.98
United States	**2,548,218**	**0.84**
Oklahoma	23,128	0.63
Rhode Island	6,025	0.57
Pennsylvania	63,964	0.51
Virginia	35,551	0.45
North Carolina	31,296	0.34
New Hampshire	3,499	0.27
Texas	61,097	0.25
Nevada	6,573	0.25
South Carolina	10,670	0.24
Illinois	29,090	0.23
Alaska	1,523	0.22
California	73,694	0.20
Alabama	7,971	0.17
Arkansas	4,974	0.17
Louisiana	7,057	0.16
Ohio	17,473	0.15
Hawaii	2,051	0.15
Michigan	13,682	0.14
Washington	9,017	0.14
Tennessee	8,270	0.13
Colorado	6,514	0.13
Maine	1,690	0.13
Arizona	7,702	0.12
Missouri	6,838	0.12
Kentucky	4,830	0.11
Kansas	3,056	0.11
New Mexico	2,284	0.11
West Virginia	2,079	0.11
Indiana	6,151	0.10
Oregon	3,580	0.10
Wisconsin	4,801	0.09
Minnesota	4,756	0.09
Vermont	575	0.09
Mississippi	2,403	0.08
Nebraska	1,258	0.07
Iowa	1,944	0.06
Utah	1,680	0.06
Idaho	875	0.06
North Dakota	369	0.06
South Dakota	363	0.05
Montana	398	0.04
Wyoming	103	0.02

Please refer to the Explanation of Data in the front of the book for more detailed information.

Ancestry

West Indian, excluding Hispanic

Top 150 Places Sorted by Population

Based on all places, regardless of total population

Place	Population	%
New York, NY (city) Kings County	598,504	7.41
Brooklyn, NY (borough) Kings County	306,541	12.43
Queens, NY (borough) Queens County	147,460	6.71
Bronx, NY (borough) Bronx County	107,527	7.87
Hempstead, NY (town) Nassau County	45,733	6.07
Boston, MA (city) Suffolk County	37,235	6.18
Manhattan, NY (borough) New York County	30,009	1.90
Miramar, FL (city) Broward County	27,767	24.42
North Miami, FL (city) Miami-Dade County	26,808	45.58
Philadelphia, PA (city) Philadelphia County	25,436	1.69
Lauderhill, FL (city) Broward County	24,371	36.31
Miami, FL (city) Miami-Dade County	22,133	5.65
Miami Gardens, FL (city) Miami-Dade County	22,012	20.84
Pine Hills, FL (cdp) Orange County	18,274	27.60
Sunrise, FL (city) Broward County	18,263	21.47
Los Angeles, CA (city) Los Angeles County	17,886	0.47
Pembroke Pines, FL (city) Broward County	17,733	11.64
Fort Lauderdale, FL (city) Broward County	16,929	10.12
Lauderdale Lakes, FL (city) Broward County	14,867	45.68
Golden Glades, FL (cdp) Miami-Dade County	14,555	44.15
North Lauderdale, FL (city) Broward County	14,218	34.83
Bridgeport, CT (city/town) Fairfield County	13,990	9.81
Hartford, CT (city/town) Hartford County	13,498	10.82
Mount Vernon, NY (city) Westchester County	13,279	19.80
Orlando, FL (city) Orange County	12,816	5.48
Ramapo, NY (town) Rockland County	12,710	10.36
Brockton, MA (city) Plymouth County	12,651	13.48
North Miami Beach, FL (city) Miami-Dade County	12,390	29.96
Jacksonville, FL (city) Duval County	11,629	1.43
Coral Springs, FL (city) Broward County	11,510	9.50
Port St. Lucie, FL (city) St. Lucie County	11,418	7.37
Irvington, NJ (township) Essex County	11,355	20.71
Hollywood, FL (city) Broward County	11,302	8.00
Babylon, NY (town) Suffolk County	11,187	5.24
Chicago, IL (city) Cook County	11,174	0.41
Boynton Beach, FL (city) Palm Beach County	10,890	16.11
Pompano Beach, FL (city) Broward County	10,664	10.62
Islip, NY (town) Suffolk County	10,274	3.08
Plantation, FL (city) Broward County	9,883	11.61
Newark, NJ (city) Essex County	9,871	3.59
Elmont, NY (cdp) Nassau County	9,499	27.54
Tampa, FL (city) Hillsborough County	9,430	2.83
East Orange, NJ (city) Essex County	9,005	13.87
Houston, TX (city) Harris County	9,005	0.44
Deerfield Beach, FL (city) Broward County	8,681	11.53
Yonkers, NY (city) Westchester County	8,578	4.40
Stamford, CT (city/town) Fairfield County	8,540	7.06
Washington, DC (city) District of Columbia	8,198	1.40
Baltimore, MD (city) Baltimore city County	8,122	1.31
Delray Beach, FL (city) Palm Beach County	8,076	13.22
West Palm Beach, FL (city) Palm Beach County	8,010	8.19
Spring Valley, NY (village) Rockland County	7,957	26.24
Palm Bay, FL (city) Brevard County	7,918	7.87
Jersey City, NJ (city) Hudson County	7,300	3.00
Lehigh Acres, FL (cdp) Lee County	7,052	8.35
Staten Island, NY (borough) Richmond County	6,967	1.50
Tamarac, FL (city) Broward County	6,937	11.60
Margate, FL (city) Broward County	6,566	12.25
Hempstead, NY (village) Nassau County	6,463	12.11
Brookhaven, NY (town) Suffolk County	6,377	1.33
Poinciana, FL (cdp) Osceola County	6,118	12.22
Randolph, MA (cdp/town) Norfolk County	6,103	19.28
City of Orange, NJ (township) Essex County	6,099	20.07
Ives Estates, FL (cdp) Miami-Dade County	5,425	30.82
Paterson, NJ (city) Passaic County	5,356	3.67
Springfield, MA (city) Hampden County	5,251	3.43
Rochester, NY (city) Monroe County	5,230	2.47
Uniondale, NY (cdp) Nassau County	5,218	21.30
Elizabeth, NJ (city) Union County	5,042	4.09
Oakland Park, FL (city) Broward County	4,977	11.93
Pinewood, FL (cdp) Miami-Dade County	4,875	30.55
Tallahassee, FL (city) Leon County	4,789	2.71
New Rochelle, NY (city) Westchester County	4,597	6.06
Charlotte, NC (city) Mecklenburg County	4,254	0.60
North Valley Stream, NY (cdp) Nassau County	4,249	25.74
Lake Worth, FL (city) Palm Beach County	4,230	11.95
Virginia Beach, VA (ind. city) Virginia Beach independent city	4,166	0.96
North Hempstead, NY (town) Nassau County	4,095	1.83
Freeport, NY (village) Nassau County	3,970	9.30
Bloomfield, CT (town) Hartford County	3,968	19.51
Columbus, OH (city) Franklin County	3,944	0.51
Fort Myers, FL (city) Lee County	3,917	6.28
Coconut Creek, FL (city) Broward County	3,889	7.55
Cambridge, MA (city) Middlesex County	3,852	3.72
North Amityville, NY (cdp) Suffolk County	3,825	21.47
Poughkeepsie, NY (city) Dutchess County	3,810	11.74
Valley Stream, NY (village) Nassau County	3,754	10.15
Union, NJ (township) Union County	3,727	6.69
Riviera Beach, FL (city) Palm Beach County	3,715	11.44
West Little River, FL (cdp) Miami-Dade County	3,693	11.34
Baldwin, NY (cdp) Nassau County	3,673	15.49
Atlanta, GA (city) Fulton County	3,668	0.89
South Miami Heights, FL (cdp) Miami-Dade County	3,633	9.92
Malden, MA (city) Middlesex County	3,580	6.15
Greenburgh, NY (town) Westchester County	3,562	4.06
Brentwood, NY (cdp) Suffolk County	3,472	6.33
Windsor, CT (town) Hartford County	3,451	11.92
New Haven, CT (city/town) New Haven County	3,422	2.66
Albany, NY (city) Albany County	3,298	3.37
Oak Ridge, FL (cdp) Orange County	3,240	16.15
Waterbury, CT (city/town) New Haven County	3,170	2.88
Wellington, FL (village) Palm Beach County	3,156	5.87
Providence, RI (city) Providence County	3,133	1.76
Everett, MA (city) Middlesex County	3,103	7.65
The Acreage, FL (cdp) Palm Beach County	3,061	8.08
Davie, FL (town) Broward County	3,019	3.33
Port Charlotte, FL (cdp) Charlotte County	3,012	5.33
Trenton, NJ (city) Mercer County	3,010	3.53
Norwalk, CT (city/town) Fairfield County	2,966	3.51
Plainfield, NJ (city) Union County	2,945	6.00
Norfolk, VA (ind. city) Norfolk independent city	2,941	1.21
Cutler Bay, FL (town) Miami-Dade County	2,932	7.63
Huntington, NY (town) Suffolk County	2,882	1.43
Fort Pierce, FL (city) St. Lucie County	2,869	6.75
Roselle, NJ (borough) Union County	2,851	13.61
Clarkstown, NY (town) Rockland County	2,834	3.40
Royal Palm Beach, FL (village) Palm Beach County	2,831	8.79
University, FL (cdp) Hillsborough County	2,802	6.92
East Hartford, CT (cdp/town) Hartford County	2,797	5.49
Hillcrest, NY (cdp) Rockland County	2,791	34.04
Greenacres, FL (city) Palm Beach County	2,775	7.65
Buffalo, NY (city) Erie County	2,773	1.04
Teaneck, NJ (township) Bergen County	2,628	6.66
Cape Coral, FL (city) Lee County	2,621	1.75
Lynn, MA (city) Essex County	2,618	2.92
Detroit, MI (city) Wayne County	2,609	0.34
San Diego, CA (city) San Diego County	2,607	0.20
Oklahoma City, OK (city) Oklahoma County	2,596	0.46
Immokalee, FL (cdp) Collier County	2,594	13.70
San Antonio, TX (city) Medina County	2,588	0.20
Palm Coast, FL (city) Flagler County	2,571	3.63
Belle Glade, FL (city) Palm Beach County	2,549	14.43
Central Islip, NY (cdp) Suffolk County	2,523	7.03
Homestead, FL (city) Miami-Dade County	2,508	4.55
West Orange, NJ (township) Essex County	2,506	5.48
Evanston, IL (city) Cook County	2,476	3.35
Fayetteville, NC (city) Cumberland County	2,462	1.24
Lake Park, FL (town) Palm Beach County	2,448	29.82
Dania Beach, FL (city) Broward County	2,429	8.26
Willingboro, NJ (township) Burlington County	2,365	7.35
Worcester, MA (city) Worcester County	2,360	1.31
Maplewood, NJ (township) Essex County	2,332	9.83
Oyster Bay, NY (town) Nassau County	2,311	0.79
Pembroke Park, FL (town) Broward County	2,285	38.81
Durham, NC (city) Durham County	2,283	1.04
Raleigh, NC (city) Wake County	2,282	0.60
Hallandale Beach, FL (city) Broward County	2,278	6.20
Westview, FL (cdp) Miami-Dade County	2,276	24.34
Daytona Beach, FL (city) Volusia County	2,253	3.58
Kendall, FL (cdp) Miami-Dade County	2,243	2.93

Ancestry

West Indian, excluding Hispanic

Top 150 Places Sorted by Percent of Total Population

Based on all places, regardless of total population

Place	Population	%
Ballou, OK (cdp) Mayes County	41	78.85
Lauderdale Lakes, FL (city) Broward County	14,867	45.68
North Miami, FL (city) Miami-Dade County	26,808	45.58
Golden Glades, FL (cdp) Miami-Dade County	14,555	44.15
Blue Hills, CT (cdp) Hartford County	1,191	41.18
Pembroke Park, FL (town) Broward County	2,285	38.81
Lauderhill, FL (city) Broward County	24,371	36.31
North Lauderdale, FL (city) Broward County	14,218	34.83
Juntura, OR (cdp) Malheur County	16	34.78
Slickville, PA (cdp) Westmoreland County	134	34.54
San Castle, FL (cdp) Palm Beach County	1,065	34.29
Hillcrest, NY (cdp) Rockland County	2,791	34.04
Stacey Street, FL (cdp) Palm Beach County	408	33.58
Dodge, OK (cdp) Delaware County	21	32.31
Ives Estates, FL (cdp) Miami-Dade County	5,425	30.82
Loco Hills, NM (cdp) Eddy County	16	30.77
Pinewood, FL (cdp) Miami-Dade County	4,875	30.55
North Miami Beach, FL (city) Miami-Dade County	12,390	29.96
Lake Park, FL (town) Palm Beach County	2,448	29.82
Albrightsville, PA (cdp) Carbon County	54	27.69
Pine Hills, FL (cdp) Orange County	18,274	27.60
Elmont, NY (cdp) Nassau County	9,499	27.54
Spring Valley, NY (village) Rockland County	7,957	26.24
North Valley Stream, NY (cdp) Nassau County	4,249	25.74
Bradley Junction, FL (cdp) Polk County	45	25.42
Miramar, FL (city) Broward County	27,767	24.42
Westview, FL (cdp) Miami-Dade County	2,276	24.34
El Portal, FL (village) Miami-Dade County	568	23.73
Sunrise, FL (city) Broward County	18,263	21.47
North Amityville, NY (cdp) Suffolk County	3,825	21.47
Seminole Manor, FL (cdp) Palm Beach County	557	21.31
Uniondale, NY (cdp) Nassau County	5,218	21.30
Slaughter Beach, DE (town) Sussex County	22	21.15
Miami Gardens, FL (city) Miami-Dade County	22,012	20.84
Irvington, NJ (township) Essex County	11,355	20.71
Lely Resort, FL (cdp) Collier County	1,002	20.14
City of Orange, NJ (township) Essex County	6,099	20.07
Limestone Creek, FL (cdp) Palm Beach County	159	19.83
Mount Vernon, NY (city) Westchester County	13,279	19.80
Bloomfield, CT (town) Hartford County	3,968	19.51
Randolph, MA (cdp/town) Norfolk County	6,103	19.28
Rosedale, OK (town) McClain County	15	19.23
Mangonia Park, FL (town) Palm Beach County	319	19.01
Washington Park, FL (cdp) Broward County	271	18.47
Lakeview, NY (cdp) Nassau County	1,015	18.22
Portage, MI (township) Mackinac County	155	18.07
Parker, MN (township) Marshall County	6	17.65
Tioga, WV (cdp) Nicholas County	23	17.56
South Floral Park, NY (village) Nassau County	271	17.35
Fowlerton, TX (cdp) La Salle County	43	16.73
Wheatley Heights, NY (cdp) Suffolk County	1,036	16.72
Hillburn, NY (village) Rockland County	155	16.33
Oak Ridge, FL (cdp) Orange County	3,240	16.15
Boynton Beach, FL (city) Palm Beach County	10,890	16.11
Pin Oak Acres, OK (cdp) Mayes County	64	15.96
Briggs, OK (cdp) Cherokee County	33	15.71
Palmetto Estates, FL (cdp) Miami-Dade County	2,124	15.59
Baldwin, NY (cdp) Nassau County	3,673	15.49
Lantana, FL (town) Palm Beach County	1,581	15.28
Martha, OK (town) Jackson County	29	15.10
West Park, FL (city) Broward County	2,100	14.73
Belle Glade, FL (city) Palm Beach County	2,549	14.43
Harlem Heights, FL (cdp) Lee County	226	14.26
East Orange, NJ (city) Essex County	9,005	13.87
East Lansdowne, PA (borough) Delaware County	365	13.80
Immokalee, FL (cdp) Collier County	2,594	13.70
Roselle, NJ (borough) Union County	2,851	13.61
Ravia, OK (town) Johnston County	67	13.51
Brockton, MA (city) Plymouth County	12,651	13.48
Delray Beach, FL (city) Palm Beach County	8,076	13.22
Foxholm, ND (cdp) Ward County	8	13.11
Brooklyn, NY (borough) Kings County	306,541	12.43
Margate, FL (city) Broward County	6,566	12.25
Royal Palm Estates, FL (cdp) Palm Beach County	448	12.24
Miami Shores, FL (village) Miami-Dade County	1,286	12.23
West Perrine, FL (cdp) Miami-Dade County	1,224	12.23
Poinciana, FL (cdp) Osceola County	6,118	12.22
Westgate, FL (cdp) Palm Beach County	903	12.21
Naranja, FL (cdp) Miami-Dade County	775	12.14
Fort Pierce South, FL (cdp) St. Lucie County	691	12.14
Hempstead, NY (village) Nassau County	6,463	12.11
Asbury Park, NJ (city) Monmouth County	1,964	12.07
Country Walk, FL (cdp) Miami-Dade County	1,913	12.03
Stonewall, OK (town) Pontotoc County	50	11.99
Lake Worth, FL (city) Palm Beach County	4,230	11.95
Nyack, NY (village) Rockland County	832	11.95
Oakland Park, FL (city) Broward County	4,977	11.93
Windsor, CT (town) Hartford County	3,451	11.92
New Cassel, NY (cdp) Nassau County	1,491	11.87
Poughkeepsie, NY (city) Dutchess County	3,810	11.74
Fairview, NY (cdp) Westchester County	278	11.65
Pembroke Pines, FL (city) Broward County	17,733	11.64
Plantation, FL (city) Broward County	9,883	11.61
Tamarac, FL (city) Broward County	6,937	11.60
Haverhill, FL (town) Palm Beach County	237	11.59
Westbury, NY (village) Nassau County	1,722	11.55
Deerfield Beach, FL (city) Broward County	8,681	11.53
Riviera Beach, FL (city) Palm Beach County	3,715	11.44
Keller, VA (town) Accomack County	25	11.36
Mannsville, OK (town) Johnston County	99	11.35
West Little River, FL (cdp) Miami-Dade County	3,693	11.34
Florida City, FL (city) Miami-Dade County	1,194	11.26
Spencerville, MD (cdp) Montgomery County	167	11.18
Naples Manor, FL (cdp) Collier County	583	11.05
Saxapahaw, NC (cdp) Alamance County	124	10.99
Bridge Creek, OK (town) Grady County	45	10.84
Hartford, CT (city/town) Hartford County	13,498	10.82
Roosevelt, NY (cdp) Nassau County	1,613	10.72
Lakewood Gardens, FL (cdp) Palm Beach County	87	10.69
Pompano Beach, FL (city) Broward County	10,664	10.62
South Valley Stream, NY (cdp) Nassau County	556	10.56
Mead, OK (town) Bryan County	16	10.53
Ramapo, NY (town) Rockland County	12,710	10.36
Lake Belvedere Estates, FL (cdp) Palm Beach County	334	10.35
Madison, FL (city) Madison County	300	10.24
Kenwood Estates, FL (cdp) Palm Beach County	113	10.22
Morrisville, NY (village) Madison County	258	10.19
Valley Stream, NY (village) Nassau County	3,754	10.15
Fort Lauderdale, FL (city) Broward County	16,929	10.12
Pomona, NY (village) Rockland County	356	10.07
Oceola, OH (cdp) Crawford County	22	10.05
Kingston, NJ (cdp) Middlesex County	198	10.00
South Bay, FL (city) Palm Beach County	475	9.95
South Miami Heights, FL (cdp) Miami-Dade County	3,633	9.92
Chestnut Ridge, NY (village) Rockland County	775	9.87
Stock Island, FL (cdp) Monroe County	354	9.86
Maplewood, NJ (township) Essex County	2,332	9.83
Bridgeport, CT (city/town) Fairfield County	13,990	9.81
Zena, OK (cdp) Delaware County	12	9.76
Grainola, OK (town) Osage County	6	9.68
Coral Springs, FL (city) Broward County	11,510	9.50
Tupelo, OK (city) Coal County	25	9.47
Vilas, CO (town) Baca County	5	9.43
Islandia, NY (village) Suffolk County	310	9.39
Oak Bluffs, MA (town) Dukes County	408	9.35
Freeport, NY (village) Nassau County	3,970	9.30
Bonanza, GA (cdp) Clayton County	238	9.18
Pine Castle, FL (cdp) Orange County	994	9.10
Winter Beach, FL (cdp) Indian River County	133	9.05
Curtin, PA (township) Centre County	56	8.95
Dougherty, OK (town) Murray County	17	8.90
Baldwin Harbor, NY (cdp) Nassau County	771	8.87
Royal Palm Beach, FL (village) Palm Beach County	2,831	8.79
Belford, NJ (cdp) Monmouth County	121	8.67
Opa-locka, FL (city) Miami-Dade County	1,307	8.65
Delmar, DE (town) Sussex County	137	8.62
Lincoln University, PA (cdp) Chester County	166	8.58
Minneola, FL (city) Lake County	772	8.57
East Farmingdale, NY (cdp) Suffolk County	522	8.53
Blue Mountain, AR (town) Logan County	19	8.48

Please refer to the Explanation of Data in the front of the book for more detailed information.

Ancestry

West Indian, excluding Hispanic

Top 150 Places Sorted by Percent of Total Population

Based on places with total population of 7,500 or more

Place	Population	%
Lauderdale Lakes, FL (city) Broward County	14,867	45.68
North Miami, FL (city) Miami-Dade County	26,808	45.58
Golden Glades, FL (cdp) Miami-Dade County	14,555	44.15
Lauderhill, FL (city) Broward County	24,371	36.31
North Lauderdale, FL (city) Broward County	14,218	34.83
Hillcrest, NY (cdp) Rockland County	2,791	34.04
Ives Estates, FL (cdp) Miami-Dade County	5,425	30.82
Pinewood, FL (cdp) Miami-Dade County	4,875	30.55
North Miami Beach, FL (city) Miami-Dade County	12,390	29.96
Lake Park, FL (town) Palm Beach County	2,448	29.82
Pine Hills, FL (cdp) Orange County	18,274	27.60
Elmont, NY (cdp) Nassau County	9,499	27.54
Spring Valley, NY (village) Rockland County	7,957	26.24
North Valley Stream, NY (cdp) Nassau County	4,249	25.74
Miramar, FL (city) Broward County	27,767	24.42
Westview, FL (cdp) Miami-Dade County	2,276	24.34
Sunrise, FL (city) Broward County	18,263	21.47
North Amityville, NY (cdp) Suffolk County	3,825	21.47
Uniondale, NY (cdp) Nassau County	5,218	21.30
Miami Gardens, FL (city) Miami-Dade County	22,012	20.84
Irvington, NJ (township) Essex County	11,355	20.71
City of Orange, NJ (township) Essex County	6,099	20.07
Mount Vernon, NY (city) Westchester County	13,279	19.80
Bloomfield, CT (town) Hartford County	3,968	19.51
Randolph, MA (cdp/town) Norfolk County	6,103	19.28
Oak Ridge, FL (cdp) Orange County	3,240	16.15
Boynton Beach, FL (city) Palm Beach County	10,890	16.11
Palmetto Estates, FL (cdp) Miami-Dade County	2,124	15.59
Baldwin, NY (cdp) Nassau County	3,673	15.49
Lantana, FL (town) Palm Beach County	1,581	15.28
West Park, FL (city) Broward County	2,100	14.73
Belle Glade, FL (city) Palm Beach County	2,549	14.43
East Orange, NJ (city) Essex County	9,005	13.87
Immokalee, FL (cdp) Collier County	2,594	13.70
Roselle, NJ (borough) Union County	2,851	13.61
Brockton, MA (city) Plymouth County	12,651	13.48
Delray Beach, FL (city) Palm Beach County	8,076	13.22
Brooklyn, NY (borough) Kings County	306,541	12.43
Margate, FL (city) Broward County	6,566	12.25
Miami Shores, FL (village) Miami-Dade County	1,286	12.23
West Perrine, FL (cdp) Miami-Dade County	1,224	12.23
Poinciana, FL (cdp) Osceola County	6,118	12.22
Hempstead, NY (village) Nassau County	6,463	12.11
Asbury Park, NJ (city) Monmouth County	1,964	12.07
Country Walk, FL (cdp) Miami-Dade County	1,913	12.03
Lake Worth, FL (city) Palm Beach County	4,230	11.95
Oakland Park, FL (city) Broward County	4,977	11.93
Windsor, CT (town) Hartford County	3,451	11.92
New Cassel, NY (cdp) Nassau County	1,491	11.87
Poughkeepsie, NY (city) Dutchess County	3,810	11.74
Pembroke Pines, FL (city) Broward County	17,733	11.64
Plantation, FL (city) Broward County	9,883	11.61
Tamarac, FL (city) Broward County	6,937	11.60
Westbury, NY (village) Nassau County	1,722	11.55
Deerfield Beach, FL (city) Broward County	8,681	11.53
Riviera Beach, FL (city) Palm Beach County	3,715	11.44
West Little River, FL (cdp) Miami-Dade County	3,693	11.34
Florida City, FL (city) Miami-Dade County	1,194	11.26
Hartford, CT (city/town) Hartford County	13,498	10.82
Roosevelt, NY (cdp) Nassau County	1,613	10.72
Pompano Beach, FL (city) Broward County	10,664	10.62
Ramapo, NY (town) Rockland County	12,710	10.36
Valley Stream, NY (village) Nassau County	3,754	10.15
Fort Lauderdale, FL (city) Broward County	16,929	10.12
South Miami Heights, FL (cdp) Miami-Dade County	3,633	9.92
Chestnut Ridge, NY (village) Rockland County	775	9.87
Maplewood, NJ (township) Essex County	2,332	9.83
Bridgeport, CT (city/town) Fairfield County	13,990	9.81
Coral Springs, FL (city) Broward County	11,510	9.50
Freeport, NY (village) Nassau County	3,970	9.30
Pine Castle, FL (cdp) Orange County	994	9.10
Baldwin Harbor, NY (cdp) Nassau County	771	8.87
Royal Palm Beach, FL (village) Palm Beach County	2,831	8.79
Opa-locka, FL (city) Miami-Dade County	1,307	8.65
Minneola, FL (city) Lake County	772	8.57
Hillside, NJ (township) Union County	1,789	8.41
Lehigh Acres, FL (cdp) Lee County	7,052	8.35
Dania Beach, FL (city) Broward County	2,429	8.26
West Palm Beach, FL (city) Palm Beach County	8,010	8.19
Wilton Manors, FL (city) Broward County	969	8.16
The Acreage, FL (cdp) Palm Beach County	3,061	8.08
Hollywood, FL (city) Broward County	11,302	8.00
Golden Gate, FL (cdp) Collier County	1,914	7.93
Bronx, NY (borough) Bronx County	107,527	7.87
Palm Bay, FL (city) Brevard County	7,918	7.87
Wyandanch, NY (cdp) Suffolk County	855	7.82
Everett, MA (city) Middlesex County	3,103	7.65
Greenacres, FL (city) Palm Beach County	2,775	7.65
Cutler Bay, FL (town) Miami-Dade County	2,932	7.63
Coconut Creek, FL (city) Broward County	3,889	7.55
Richmond Heights, FL (cdp) Miami-Dade County	682	7.53
Nantucket, MA (cdp) Nantucket County	597	7.51
New York, NY (city) Kings County	598,504	7.41
Port St. Lucie, FL (city) St. Lucie County	11,418	7.37
Palm Springs, FL (village) Palm Beach County	1,376	7.37
Nanuet, NY (cdp) Rockland County	1,313	7.37
Willingboro, NJ (township) Burlington County	2,365	7.35
Oronoko, MI (charter township) Berrien County	678	7.35
East Lake-Orient Park, FL (cdp) Hillsborough County	1,734	7.23
Englewood, NJ (city) Bergen County	1,933	7.21
Stamford, CT (city/town) Fairfield County	8,540	7.06
Central Islip, NY (cdp) Suffolk County	2,523	7.03
University, FL (cdp) Hillsborough County	2,802	6.92
North Bay Shore, NY (cdp) Suffolk County	1,332	6.83
The Crossings, FL (cdp) Miami-Dade County	1,618	6.82
Southchase, FL (cdp) Orange County	1,114	6.76
Fort Pierce, FL (city) St. Lucie County	2,869	6.75
Pebble Creek, FL (cdp) Hillsborough County	510	6.75
Queens, NY (borough) Queens County	147,460	6.71
Yeadon, PA (borough) Delaware County	770	6.71
Union, NJ (township) Union County	3,727	6.69
Leisure City, FL (cdp) Miami-Dade County	1,442	6.67
Teaneck, NJ (township) Bergen County	2,628	6.66
Pleasantville, NJ (city) Atlantic County	1,341	6.64
McDonough, GA (city) Henry County	1,321	6.55
Boonton, NJ (town) Morris County	549	6.53
Rockville, CT (cdp) Tolland County	503	6.53
Three Lakes, FL (cdp) Miami-Dade County	919	6.37
Brentwood, NY (cdp) Suffolk County	3,472	6.33
East Massapequa, NY (cdp) Nassau County	1,128	6.33
Fort Myers, FL (city) Lee County	3,917	6.28
Hallandale Beach, FL (city) Broward County	2,278	6.20
Boston, MA (city) Suffolk County	37,235	6.18
Malden, MA (city) Middlesex County	3,580	6.15
Scotchtown, NY (cdp) Orange County	597	6.13
Hempstead, NY (town) Nassau County	45,733	6.07
New Rochelle, NY (city) Westchester County	4,597	6.06
Plainfield, NJ (city) Union County	2,945	6.00
Nantucket, MA (town) Nantucket County	597	5.93
West Haverstraw, NY (village) Rockland County	597	5.92
Wellington, FL (village) Palm Beach County	3,156	5.87
Haines City, FL (city) Polk County	1,146	5.79
Chillum, MD (cdp) Prince George's County	1,995	5.69
Goulds, FL (cdp) Miami-Dade County	521	5.66
Miami, FL (city) Miami-Dade County	22,133	5.65
Stockbridge, GA (city) Henry County	1,334	5.63
Avon Park, FL (city) Highlands County	504	5.62
East Hartford, CT (cdp/town) Hartford County	2,797	5.49
Orlando, FL (city) Orange County	12,816	5.48
West Orange, NJ (township) Essex County	2,506	5.48
Linden, NJ (city) Union County	2,184	5.46
Baywood, NY (cdp) Suffolk County	425	5.40
Lansdowne, PA (borough) Delaware County	571	5.36
Port Charlotte, FL (cdp) Charlotte County	3,012	5.33
Norwich, CT (city/town) New London County	2,123	5.33
Clermont, FL (city) Lake County	1,385	5.30
Princeton, FL (cdp) Miami-Dade County	1,091	5.29
Country Club, FL (cdp) Miami-Dade County	2,093	5.27
Adelphi, MD (cdp) Prince George's County	793	5.27
Amityville, NY (village) Suffolk County	503	5.27

Please refer to the Explanation of Data in the front of the book for more detailed information.

Ancestry

West Indian: Bahamian, excluding Hispanic

U.S. and 50 States Sorted by Population and Percent of Total Population

Place	Population	%
United States	**41,029**	**0.01**
Florida	24,810	0.13
Georgia	2,871	0.03
New York	1,796	0.01
Texas	1,010	<0.01
North Carolina	974	0.01
New Jersey	867	0.01
California	775	<0.01
Maryland	766	0.01
Massachusetts	740	0.01
South Carolina	581	0.01
Virginia	534	0.01
Pennsylvania	516	<0.01
Tennessee	418	0.01
Ohio	396	<0.01
Connecticut	365	0.01
Illinois	333	<0.01
Michigan	326	<0.01
Missouri	314	0.01
Oklahoma	288	0.01
Alabama	264	0.01
Oregon	180	<0.01
Minnesota	169	<0.01
Arkansas	168	0.01
Iowa	129	<0.01
District of Columbia	120	0.02
Mississippi	120	<0.01
Arizona	118	<0.01
Washington	117	<0.01
Indiana	109	<0.01
Colorado	108	<0.01
Louisiana	92	<0.01
Hawaii	89	0.01
Nevada	86	<0.01
Utah	72	<0.01
Nebraska	71	<0.01
Wisconsin	70	<0.01
Kentucky	67	<0.01
Alaska	62	0.01
New Mexico	50	<0.01
Maine	35	<0.01
West Virginia	26	<0.01
Kansas	12	<0.01
Idaho	7	<0.01
North Dakota	5	<0.01
New Hampshire	3	<0.01
Delaware	0	0.00
Montana	0	0.00
Rhode Island	0	0.00
South Dakota	0	0.00
Vermont	0	0.00
Wyoming	0	0.00

Place	Population	%
Florida	24,810	0.13
Georgia	2,871	0.03
District of Columbia	120	0.02
United States	**41,029**	**0.01**
New York	1,796	0.01
North Carolina	974	0.01
New Jersey	867	0.01
Maryland	766	0.01
Massachusetts	740	0.01
South Carolina	581	0.01
Virginia	534	0.01
Tennessee	418	0.01
Connecticut	365	0.01
Missouri	314	0.01
Oklahoma	288	0.01
Alabama	264	0.01
Arkansas	168	0.01
Hawaii	89	0.01
Alaska	62	0.01
Texas	1,010	<0.01
California	775	<0.01
Pennsylvania	516	<0.01
Ohio	396	<0.01
Illinois	333	<0.01
Michigan	326	<0.01
Oregon	180	<0.01
Minnesota	169	<0.01
Iowa	129	<0.01
Mississippi	120	<0.01
Arizona	118	<0.01
Washington	117	<0.01
Indiana	109	<0.01
Colorado	108	<0.01
Louisiana	92	<0.01
Nevada	86	<0.01
Utah	72	<0.01
Nebraska	71	<0.01
Wisconsin	70	<0.01
Kentucky	67	<0.01
New Mexico	50	<0.01
Maine	35	<0.01
West Virginia	26	<0.01
Kansas	12	<0.01
Idaho	7	<0.01
North Dakota	5	<0.01
New Hampshire	3	<0.01
Delaware	0	0.00
Montana	0	0.00
Rhode Island	0	0.00
South Dakota	0	0.00
Vermont	0	0.00
Wyoming	0	0.00

Please refer to the Explanation of Data in the front of the book for more detailed information.

Ancestry

West Indian: Bahamian, excluding Hispanic

Top 150 Places Sorted by Population

Based on all places, regardless of total population

Place	Population	%
Miami Gardens, FL (city) Miami-Dade County	1,706	1.61
Miami, FL (city) Miami-Dade County	1,673	0.43
New York, NY (city) Kings County	1,147	0.01
Hollywood, FL (city) Broward County	922	0.65
Fort Lauderdale, FL (city) Broward County	644	0.38
Jacksonville, FL (city) Duval County	631	0.08
Sunrise, FL (city) Broward County	576	0.68
Pinewood, FL (cdp) Miami-Dade County	558	3.50
North Lauderdale, FL (city) Broward County	539	1.32
North Miami, FL (city) Miami-Dade County	512	0.87
Pembroke Pines, FL (city) Broward County	499	0.33
Manhattan, NY (borough) New York County	457	0.03
Opa-locka, FL (city) Miami-Dade County	435	2.88
Miramar, FL (city) Broward County	414	0.36
Lauderhill, FL (city) Broward County	410	0.61
Port St. Lucie, FL (city) St. Lucie County	398	0.26
Lauderdale Lakes, FL (city) Broward County	393	1.21
Tallahassee, FL (city) Leon County	349	0.20
Delray Beach, FL (city) Palm Beach County	346	0.57
Golden Glades, FL (cdp) Miami-Dade County	317	0.96
West Little River, FL (cdp) Miami-Dade County	314	0.96
Richmond Heights, FL (cdp) Miami-Dade County	308	3.40
Goulds, FL (cdp) Miami-Dade County	299	3.25
Oakland Park, FL (city) Broward County	290	0.69
Brooklyn, NY (borough) Kings County	266	0.01
North Miami Beach, FL (city) Miami-Dade County	251	0.61
Ives Estates, FL (cdp) Miami-Dade County	250	1.42
Pembroke Park, FL (town) Broward County	249	4.23
West Park, FL (city) Broward County	247	1.73
Boynton Beach, FL (city) Palm Beach County	228	0.34
West Palm Beach, FL (city) Palm Beach County	226	0.23
Orlando, FL (city) Orange County	224	0.10
Pebble Creek, FL (cdp) Hillsborough County	223	2.95
Rochester, NY (city) Monroe County	218	0.10
Bronx, NY (borough) Bronx County	208	0.02
Dania Beach, FL (city) Broward County	204	0.69
Pine Hills, FL (cdp) Orange County	201	0.30
McDonough, GA (city) Henry County	200	0.99
Riviera Beach, FL (city) Palm Beach County	200	0.62
Queens, NY (borough) Queens County	185	0.01
Raleigh, NC (city) Wake County	184	0.05
Golden Gate, FL (cdp) Collier County	179	0.74
Margate, FL (city) Broward County	179	0.33
Los Angeles, CA (city) Los Angeles County	166	<0.01
Houston, TX (city) Harris County	165	0.01
Westview, FL (cdp) Miami-Dade County	164	1.75
Palm Beach Gardens, FL (city) Palm Beach County	163	0.35
San Antonio, TX (city) Medina County	162	0.01
Tiptonville, TN (town) Lake County	159	3.57
Palm Springs, FL (village) Palm Beach County	158	0.85
Deerfield Beach, FL (city) Broward County	158	0.21
High Point, NC (city) Guilford County	155	0.15
Forest Park, GA (city) Clayton County	154	0.80
Royal Palm Beach, FL (village) Palm Beach County	154	0.48
Atlanta, GA (city) Fulton County	154	0.04
St. Petersburg, FL (city) Pinellas County	152	0.06
Pompano Beach, FL (city) Broward County	147	0.15
Princeton, FL (cdp) Miami-Dade County	146	0.71
Pittsfield, MA (city) Berkshire County	144	0.32
Roanoke Rapids, NC (city) Halifax County	141	0.89
Gloucester, NJ (township) Camden County	138	0.21
Greenwich, CT (cdp) Fairfield County	135	1.02
Palmetto Estates, FL (cdp) Miami-Dade County	135	0.99
Greenwich, CT (town) Fairfield County	135	0.22
University, FL (cdp) Orange County	128	0.60
Daytona Beach, FL (city) Volusia County	128	0.20
North Sarasota, FL (cdp) Sarasota County	126	1.70
Fall River, MA (city) Bristol County	126	0.14
Hallandale Beach, FL (city) Broward County	125	0.34
North Decatur, GA (cdp) DeKalb County	124	0.71
Davie, FL (town) Broward County	124	0.14
Everett, MA (city) Middlesex County	123	0.30
Oviedo, FL (city) Seminole County	122	0.38
Charlotte, NC (city) Mecklenburg County	122	0.02
South Miami Heights, FL (cdp) Miami-Dade County	121	0.33
Nashville-Davidson, TN (metro govt) Davidson County	121	0.02
Washington, DC (city) District of Columbia	120	0.02
Brent, FL (cdp) Escambia County	118	0.50
The Hammocks, FL (cdp) Miami-Dade County	118	0.24
Fort Pierce, FL (city) St. Lucie County	112	0.26
Portland, OR (city) Multnomah County	110	0.02
Braintree Town, MA (city) Norfolk County	109	0.31
Forest City, FL (cdp) Seminole County	107	0.77
Lake Worth, FL (city) Palm Beach County	106	0.30
Tampa, FL (city) Hillsborough County	105	0.03
Philadelphia, PA (city) Philadelphia County	104	0.01
Woodbury, NJ (city) Gloucester County	103	1.00
Pickerington, OH (city) Fairfield County	100	0.59
Tamarac, FL (city) Broward County	100	0.17
Pleasantville, NJ (city) Atlantic County	98	0.48
Jefferson City, MO (city) Cole County	98	0.23
Coral Springs, FL (city) Broward County	98	0.08
Galesburg, IL (city) Knox County	97	0.30
Columbia, SC (city) Richland County	97	0.08
Pittsfield, MI (charter township) Washtenaw County	96	0.28
Country Club, FL (cdp) Miami-Dade County	93	0.23
Columbus, OH (city) Franklin County	93	0.01
Edmond, OK (city) Oklahoma County	92	0.12
Somerville, MA (city) Middlesex County	92	0.12
Long Beach, CA (city) Los Angeles County	92	0.02
Haines City, FL (city) Polk County	91	0.46
Richmond West, FL (cdp) Miami-Dade County	91	0.28
Dale City, VA (cdp) Prince William County	91	0.14
Whitpain, PA (township) Montgomery County	90	0.48
Germantown, MD (cdp) Montgomery County	90	0.11
Peachtree City, GA (city) Fayette County	89	0.26
Lehigh Acres, FL (cdp) Lee County	89	0.11
North Amityville, NY (cdp) Suffolk County	88	0.49
Inglewood, CA (city) Los Angeles County	88	0.08
Babylon, NY (town) Suffolk County	88	0.04
Lantana, FL (town) Palm Beach County	87	0.84
Schofield Barracks, HI (cdp) Honolulu County	87	0.72
Gifford, FL (cdp) Indian River County	83	0.80
Poinciana, FL (cdp) Osceola County	79	0.16
The Crossings, FL (cdp) Miami-Dade County	78	0.33
Baltimore, MD (city) Baltimore city County	78	0.01
Palm River-Clair Mel, FL (cdp) Hillsborough County	77	0.37
Plantation, FL (city) Broward County	75	0.09
Fort Washington, MD (cdp) Prince George's County	74	0.29
San Diego, CA (city) San Diego County	74	0.01
Kennesaw, GA (city) Cobb County	72	0.25
Ocala, FL (city) Marion County	72	0.13
Brandon, FL (cdp) Hillsborough County	70	0.07
Paulsboro, NJ (borough) Gloucester County	69	1.12
Fort Pierce North, FL (cdp) St. Lucie County	69	0.98
West Perrine, FL (cdp) Miami-Dade County	69	0.69
Woodmere, LA (cdp) Jefferson Parish	68	0.59
Belle Glade, FL (city) Palm Beach County	68	0.39
Summerlin South, NV (cdp) Clark County	67	0.31
Clovis, CA (city) Fresno County	66	0.07
Tulsa, OK (city) Tulsa County	66	0.02
Camp Springs, MD (cdp) Prince George's County	65	0.35
Miami Shores, FL (village) Miami-Dade County	64	0.61
Gainesville, FL (city) Alachua County	64	0.05
Des Moines, IA (city) Polk County	64	0.03
Worthington, OH (city) Franklin County	63	0.46
Oklahoma City, OK (city) Oklahoma County	63	0.01
Rockledge, FL (city) Brevard County	61	0.25
Phoenix, AZ (city) Maricopa County	61	<0.01
Port Wentworth, GA (city) Chatham County	60	1.22
Norwalk, CT (city/town) Fairfield County	60	0.07
Denton, TX (city) Denton County	60	0.05
Anderson, SC (city) Anderson County	59	0.22
Trenton, NJ (city) Mercer County	59	0.07
Frisco, TX (city) Collin County	59	0.06
Detroit, MI (city) Wayne County	59	0.01
Union City, GA (city) Fulton County	58	0.32
Georgetown, GA (cdp) Chatham County	57	0.47
Highland Springs, VA (cdp) Henrico County	57	0.35
Florida Ridge, FL (cdp) Indian River County	57	0.34

Please refer to the Explanation of Data in the front of the book for more detailed information.

Ancestry

West Indian: Bahamian, excluding Hispanic

Top 150 Places Sorted by Percent of Total Population

Based on all places, regardless of total population

Place	Population	%
Mead, OK (town) Bryan County	16	10.53
Pembroke Park, FL (town) Broward County	249	4.23
Seville, FL (cdp) Volusia County	13	3.75
Tiptonville, TN (town) Lake County	159	3.57
Pinewood, FL (cdp) Miami-Dade County	558	3.50
Richmond Heights, FL (cdp) Miami-Dade County	308	3.40
Goulds, FL (cdp) Miami-Dade County	299	3.25
Pebble Creek, FL (cdp) Hillsborough County	223	2.95
Opa-locka, FL (city) Miami-Dade County	435	2.88
Molino, FL (cdp) Escambia County	35	2.73
Pleasant Plains, NJ (cdp) Somerset County	18	2.24
Port Carbon, PA (borough) Schuylkill County	41	2.21
Homestead Base, FL (cdp) Miami-Dade County	14	1.87
Westview, FL (cdp) Miami-Dade County	164	1.75
West Park, FL (city) Broward County	247	1.73
North Sarasota, FL (cdp) Sarasota County	126	1.70
Miami Gardens, FL (city) Miami-Dade County	1,706	1.61
Queenland, MD (cdp) Prince George's County	34	1.59
Ives Estates, FL (cdp) Miami-Dade County	250	1.42
North Lauderdale, FL (city) Broward County	539	1.32
Whitakers, NC (town) Edgecombe County	8	1.23
Port Wentworth, GA (city) Chatham County	60	1.22
Gulf Stream, FL (town) Palm Beach County	9	1.22
Lauderdale Lakes, FL (city) Broward County	393	1.21
Paulsboro, NJ (borough) Gloucester County	69	1.12
Bangor Base, WA (cdp) Kitsap County	43	1.03
Bethel Manor, VA (cdp) York County	42	1.03
Greenwich, CT (cdp) Fairfield County	135	1.02
Woodbury, NJ (city) Gloucester County	103	1.00
McDonough, GA (city) Henry County	200	0.99
Palmetto Estates, FL (cdp) Miami-Dade County	135	0.99
Fort Pierce North, FL (cdp) St. Lucie County	69	0.98
Golden Glades, FL (cdp) Miami-Dade County	317	0.96
West Little River, FL (cdp) Miami-Dade County	314	0.96
Emmett, MI (township) St. Clair County	24	0.90
Roanoke Rapids, NC (city) Halifax County	141	0.89
North Miami, FL (city) Miami-Dade County	512	0.87
Palm Springs, FL (village) Palm Beach County	158	0.85
Lantana, FL (town) Palm Beach County	87	0.84
Burnham, ME (town) Waldo County	10	0.84
Avondale Estates, GA (city) DeKalb County	24	0.81
Rewey, WI (village) Iowa County	2	0.81
Forest Park, GA (city) Clayton County	154	0.80
Gifford, FL (cdp) Indian River County	83	0.80
Cornwells Heights, PA (cdp) Bucks County	11	0.79
Forest City, FL (cdp) Seminole County	107	0.77
De Funiak Springs, FL (city) Walton County	40	0.76
Palm Shores, FL (town) Brevard County	6	0.75
Golden Gate, FL (cdp) Collier County	179	0.74
Schofield Barracks, HI (cdp) Honolulu County	87	0.72
Princeton, FL (cdp) Miami-Dade County	146	0.71
North Decatur, GA (cdp) DeKalb County	124	0.71
Oxford, GA (city) Newton County	18	0.70
Boulevard Gardens, FL (cdp) Broward County	12	0.70
Clio, SC (town) Marlboro County	6	0.70
Oakland Park, FL (city) Broward County	290	0.69
Dania Beach, FL (city) Broward County	204	0.69
West Perrine, FL (cdp) Miami-Dade County	69	0.69
Canaan, ME (town) Somerset County	15	0.69
Sunrise, FL (city) Broward County	576	0.68
Wyndmoor, PA (cdp) Montgomery County	39	0.66
Hollywood, FL (city) Broward County	922	0.65
Riviera Beach, FL (city) Palm Beach County	200	0.62
Guyton, GA (city) Effingham County	10	0.62
Lauderhill, FL (city) Broward County	410	0.61
North Miami Beach, FL (city) Miami-Dade County	251	0.61
Miami Shores, FL (village) Miami-Dade County	64	0.61
Quincy, FL (city) Gadsden County	48	0.61
University, FL (cdp) Orange County	128	0.60
Marion, WI (town) Juneau County	3	0.60
Pickerington, OH (city) Fairfield County	100	0.59
Woodmere, LA (cdp) Jefferson Parish	68	0.59
Wedgefield, FL (cdp) Orange County	38	0.59
Delray Beach, FL (city) Palm Beach County	346	0.57
North Kensington, MD (cdp) Montgomery County	55	0.57
Newburgh, IN (town) Warrick County	18	0.55
Homosassa, FL (cdp) Citrus County	13	0.52
Parkville, MO (city) Platte County	27	0.51
Somerset, MN (township) Steele County	4	0.51
Brent, FL (cdp) Escambia County	118	0.50
North Amityville, NY (cdp) Suffolk County	88	0.49
Dade City, FL (city) Pasco County	33	0.49
Cisco, TX (city) Eastland County	19	0.49
Biscayne Park, FL (village) Miami-Dade County	15	0.49
Ashland, AL (town) Clay County	13	0.49
Royal Palm Beach, FL (village) Palm Beach County	154	0.48
Pleasantville, NJ (city) Atlantic County	98	0.48
Whitpain, PA (township) Montgomery County	90	0.48
Hellertown, PA (borough) Northampton County	28	0.48
Mangonia Park, FL (town) Palm Beach County	8	0.48
Georgetown, GA (cdp) Chatham County	57	0.47
Acworth, NH (town) Sullivan County	3	0.47
Haines City, FL (city) Polk County	91	0.46
Worthington, OH (city) Franklin County	63	0.46
Ettrick, VA (cdp) Chesterfield County	27	0.46
North Kansas City, MO (city) Clay County	19	0.44
Miami, FL (city) Miami-Dade County	1,673	0.43
Marshall, MO (city) Saline County	55	0.43
Whitewater, MI (township) Grand Traverse County	11	0.43
Whitesboro, NJ (cdp) Cape May County	10	0.43
East Butler, PA (borough) Butler County	3	0.43
Headland, AL (city) Henry County	18	0.41
Elgin, OK (city) Comanche County	8	0.40
Belle Glade, FL (city) Palm Beach County	68	0.39
Fort Lauderdale, FL (city) Broward County	644	0.38
Oviedo, FL (city) Seminole County	122	0.38
Miller Place, NY (cdp) Suffolk County	47	0.38
Wheatland, WI (town) Kenosha County	13	0.38
Kimball, WI (town) Iron County	2	0.38
Palm River-Clair Mel, FL (cdp) Hillsborough County	77	0.37
Beaufort, SC (city) Beaufort County	46	0.37
Fort Shawnee, OH (village) Allen County	14	0.37
Miramar, FL (city) Broward County	414	0.36
Brownsville, FL (cdp) Miami-Dade County	47	0.36
Pineville, NC (town) Mecklenburg County	26	0.36
Denmark, SC (city) Bamberg County	13	0.36
Collegeville, MN (township) Stearns County	12	0.36
Palm Beach Gardens, FL (city) Palm Beach County	163	0.35
Camp Springs, MD (cdp) Prince George's County	65	0.35
Highland Springs, VA (cdp) Henrico County	57	0.35
Seffner, FL (cdp) Hillsborough County	26	0.35
Boynton Beach, FL (city) Palm Beach County	228	0.34
Hallandale Beach, FL (city) Broward County	125	0.34
Florida Ridge, FL (cdp) Indian River County	57	0.34
Vienna, GA (city) Dooly County	13	0.34
Elmwood, WI (village) Pierce County	3	0.34
Boys Town, NE (village) Douglas County	2	0.34
Pembroke Pines, FL (city) Broward County	499	0.33
Margate, FL (city) Broward County	179	0.33
South Miami Heights, FL (cdp) Miami-Dade County	121	0.33
The Crossings, FL (cdp) Miami-Dade County	78	0.33
Jupiter Farms, FL (cdp) Palm Beach County	40	0.33
El Portal, FL (village) Miami-Dade County	8	0.33
Pittsfield, MA (city) Berkshire County	144	0.32
Union City, GA (city) Fulton County	58	0.32
South Floral Park, NY (village) Nassau County	5	0.32
Braintree Town, MA (city) Norfolk County	109	0.31
Summerlin South, NV (cdp) Clark County	67	0.31
Woodmore, MD (cdp) Prince George's County	11	0.31
Pine Hills, FL (cdp) Orange County	201	0.30
Everett, MA (city) Middlesex County	123	0.30
Lake Worth, FL (city) Palm Beach County	106	0.30
Galesburg, IL (city) Knox County	97	0.30
Middle, NJ (township) Cape May County	56	0.30
Lake Wales, FL (city) Polk County	42	0.30
Fort Knox, KY (cdp) Hardin County	36	0.30
Holly Hill, FL (city) Volusia County	36	0.30
Avon Park, FL (city) Highlands County	27	0.30
Brambleton, VA (cdp) Loudoun County	26	0.30
Fircrest, WA (city) Pierce County	19	0.30

Please refer to the Explanation of Data in the front of the book for more detailed information.

Ancestry

West Indian: Bahamian, excluding Hispanic

Top 150 Places Sorted by Percent of Total Population

Based on places with total population of 7,500 or more

Place	Population	%
Pinewood, FL (cdp) Miami-Dade County	558	3.50
Richmond Heights, FL (cdp) Miami-Dade County	308	3.40
Goulds, FL (cdp) Miami-Dade County	299	3.25
Pebble Creek, FL (cdp) Hillsborough County	223	2.95
Opa-locka, FL (city) Miami-Dade County	435	2.88
Westview, FL (cdp) Miami-Dade County	164	1.75
West Park, FL (city) Broward County	247	1.73
Miami Gardens, FL (city) Miami-Dade County	1,706	1.61
Ives Estates, FL (cdp) Miami-Dade County	250	1.42
North Lauderdale, FL (city) Broward County	539	1.32
Lauderdale Lakes, FL (city) Broward County	393	1.21
Greenwich, CT (cdp) Fairfield County	135	1.02
Woodbury, NJ (city) Gloucester County	103	1.00
McDonough, GA (city) Henry County	200	0.99
Palmetto Estates, FL (cdp) Miami-Dade County	135	0.99
Golden Glades, FL (cdp) Miami-Dade County	317	0.96
West Little River, FL (cdp) Miami-Dade County	314	0.96
Roanoke Rapids, NC (city) Halifax County	141	0.89
North Miami, FL (city) Miami-Dade County	512	0.87
Palm Springs, FL (village) Palm Beach County	158	0.85
Lantana, FL (town) Palm Beach County	87	0.84
Forest Park, GA (city) Clayton County	154	0.80
Gifford, FL (cdp) Indian River County	83	0.80
Forest City, FL (cdp) Seminole County	107	0.77
Golden Gate, FL (cdp) Collier County	179	0.74
Schofield Barracks, HI (cdp) Honolulu County	87	0.72
Princeton, FL (cdp) Miami-Dade County	146	0.71
North Decatur, GA (cdp) DeKalb County	124	0.71
Oakland Park, FL (city) Broward County	290	0.69
Dania Beach, FL (city) Broward County	204	0.69
West Perrine, FL (cdp) Miami-Dade County	69	0.69
Sunrise, FL (city) Broward County	576	0.68
Hollywood, FL (city) Broward County	922	0.65
Riviera Beach, FL (city) Palm Beach County	200	0.62
Lauderhill, FL (city) Broward County	410	0.61
North Miami Beach, FL (city) Miami-Dade County	251	0.61
Miami Shores, FL (village) Miami-Dade County	64	0.61
Quincy, FL (city) Gadsden County	48	0.61
University, FL (cdp) Orange County	128	0.60
Pickerington, OH (city) Fairfield County	100	0.59
Woodmere, LA (cdp) Jefferson Parish	68	0.59
Delray Beach, FL (city) Palm Beach County	346	0.57
North Kensington, MD (cdp) Montgomery County	55	0.57
Brent, FL (cdp) Escambia County	118	0.50
North Amityville, NY (cdp) Suffolk County	88	0.49
Royal Palm Beach, FL (village) Palm Beach County	154	0.48
Pleasantville, NJ (city) Atlantic County	98	0.48
Whitpain, PA (township) Montgomery County	90	0.48
Georgetown, GA (cdp) Chatham County	57	0.47
Haines City, FL (city) Polk County	91	0.46
Worthington, OH (city) Franklin County	63	0.46
Miami, FL (city) Miami-Dade County	1,673	0.43
Marshall, MO (city) Saline County	55	0.43
Belle Glade, FL (city) Palm Beach County	68	0.39
Fort Lauderdale, FL (city) Broward County	644	0.38
Oviedo, FL (city) Seminole County	122	0.38
Miller Place, NY (cdp) Suffolk County	47	0.38
Palm River-Clair Mel, FL (cdp) Hillsborough County	77	0.37
Beaufort, SC (city) Beaufort County	46	0.37
Miramar, FL (city) Broward County	414	0.36
Brownsville, FL (cdp) Miami-Dade County	47	0.36
Palm Beach Gardens, FL (city) Palm Beach County	163	0.35
Camp Springs, MD (cdp) Prince George's County	65	0.35
Highland Springs, VA (cdp) Henrico County	57	0.35
Boynton Beach, FL (city) Palm Beach County	228	0.34
Hallandale Beach, FL (city) Broward County	125	0.34
Florida Ridge, FL (cdp) Indian River County	57	0.34
Pembroke Pines, FL (city) Broward County	499	0.33
Margate, FL (city) Broward County	179	0.33
South Miami Heights, FL (cdp) Miami-Dade County	121	0.33
The Crossings, FL (cdp) Miami-Dade County	78	0.33
Jupiter Farms, FL (cdp) Palm Beach County	40	0.33
Pittsfield, MA (city) Berkshire County	144	0.32
Union City, GA (city) Fulton County	58	0.32
Braintree Town, MA (city) Norfolk County	109	0.31
Summerlin South, NV (cdp) Clark County	67	0.31
Pine Hills, FL (cdp) Orange County	201	0.30
Everett, MA (city) Middlesex County	123	0.30
Lake Worth, FL (city) Palm Beach County	106	0.30
Galesburg, IL (city) Knox County	97	0.30
Middle, NJ (township) Cape May County	56	0.30
Lake Wales, FL (city) Polk County	42	0.30
Fort Knox, KY (cdp) Hardin County	36	0.30
Holly Hill, FL (city) Volusia County	36	0.30
Avon Park, FL (city) Highlands County	27	0.30
Brambleton, VA (cdp) Loudoun County	26	0.30
Fort Washington, MD (cdp) Prince George's County	74	0.29
Seven Oaks, SC (cdp) Lexington County	47	0.29
Uniontown, PA (city) Fayette County	31	0.29
Pittsfield, MI (charter township) Washtenaw County	96	0.28
Richmond West, FL (cdp) Miami-Dade County	91	0.28
Punta Gorda, FL (city) Charlotte County	44	0.27
Rosaryville, MD (cdp) Prince George's County	31	0.27
Port St. Lucie, FL (city) St. Lucie County	398	0.26
Fort Pierce, FL (city) St. Lucie County	112	0.26
Peachtree City, GA (city) Fayette County	89	0.26
Seabrook, TX (city) Harris County	30	0.26
South Miami, FL (city) Miami-Dade County	30	0.26
Groton, CT (city) New London County	27	0.26
Sumner, WA (city) Pierce County	24	0.26
Kennesaw, GA (city) Cobb County	72	0.25
Rockledge, FL (city) Brevard County	61	0.25
Cocoa, FL (city) Brevard County	43	0.25
Florida City, FL (city) Miami-Dade County	26	0.25
The Hammocks, FL (cdp) Miami-Dade County	118	0.24
Huntington, VA (cdp) Fairfax County	25	0.24
West Palm Beach, FL (city) Palm Beach County	226	0.23
Jefferson City, MO (city) Cole County	98	0.23
Country Club, FL (cdp) Miami-Dade County	93	0.23
Greenwich, CT (town) Fairfield County	135	0.22
Anderson, SC (city) Anderson County	59	0.22
Stockbridge, GA (city) Henry County	51	0.22
Converse, TX (city) Bexar County	38	0.22
Concord, PA (township) Delaware County	35	0.22
Jefferson, GA (city) Jackson County	19	0.22
Deerfield Beach, FL (city) Broward County	158	0.21
Gloucester, NJ (township) Camden County	138	0.21
Bloomingdale, FL (cdp) Hillsborough County	45	0.21
La Marque, TX (city) Galveston County	31	0.21
Winder, GA (city) Barrow County	29	0.21
Redding, CT (town) Fairfield County	19	0.21
Tallahassee, FL (city) Leon County	349	0.20
Daytona Beach, FL (city) Volusia County	128	0.20
Bellview, FL (cdp) Escambia County	49	0.20
Springfield, PA (township) Montgomery County	39	0.20
East Stroudsburg, PA (borough) Monroe County	20	0.20
Fort Valley, GA (city) Peach County	19	0.20
Wyndham, VA (cdp) Henrico County	19	0.20
Rodeo, CA (cdp) Contra Costa County	18	0.20
Humboldt, TN (city) Gibson County	17	0.20
Hamilton, NJ (township) Atlantic County	48	0.19
Leesburg, FL (city) Lake County	39	0.19
Vincennes, IN (city) Knox County	34	0.19
Palmetto Bay, FL (village) Miami-Dade County	41	0.18
New Smyrna Beach, FL (city) Volusia County	40	0.18
Mount Rainier, MD (city) Prince George's County	15	0.18
Tamarac, FL (city) Broward County	100	0.17
Laurel, MD (city) Prince George's County	42	0.17
Northdale, FL (cdp) Hillsborough County	40	0.17
Marshall, MN (city) Lyon County	23	0.17
Powder Springs, GA (city) Cobb County	23	0.17
Knightdale, NC (town) Wake County	18	0.17
Poinciana, FL (cdp) Osceola County	79	0.16
Pemberton, NJ (township) Burlington County	44	0.16
East Lyme, CT (town) New London County	31	0.16
Melville, NY (cdp) Suffolk County	31	0.16
Bayshore Gardens, FL (cdp) Manatee County	26	0.16
Cocoa Beach, FL (city) Brevard County	19	0.16
High Point, NC (city) Guilford County	155	0.15
Pompano Beach, FL (city) Broward County	147	0.15

SECTION THREE

Please refer to the Explanation of Data in the front of the book for more detailed information.

Ancestry

West Indian: Barbadian, excluding Hispanic

U.S. and 50 States Sorted by Population and Percent of Total Population

Place	Population	%
United States	**57,742**	**0.02**
New York	27,200	0.14
Florida	5,629	0.03
Massachusetts	4,733	0.07
New Jersey	3,790	0.04
Georgia	2,230	0.02
Pennsylvania	2,183	0.02
Maryland	1,314	0.02
Texas	1,268	0.01
California	1,235	<0.01
Connecticut	1,210	0.03
Virginia	960	0.01
North Carolina	877	0.01
Rhode Island	528	0.05
Illinois	506	<0.01
Ohio	480	<0.01
Michigan	356	<0.01
Washington	321	<0.01
Kansas	283	0.01
District of Columbia	267	0.05
Kentucky	256	0.01
South Carolina	253	0.01
Tennessee	221	<0.01
Arizona	193	<0.01
Delaware	136	0.02
Wisconsin	136	<0.01
Hawaii	123	0.01
Alabama	105	<0.01
Oregon	102	<0.01
Indiana	97	<0.01
Nevada	90	<0.01
Arkansas	84	<0.01
Minnesota	84	<0.01
New Hampshire	81	0.01
Colorado	72	<0.01
Missouri	58	<0.01
Louisiana	57	<0.01
Maine	55	<0.01
Oklahoma	54	<0.01
Utah	33	<0.01
Iowa	30	<0.01
New Mexico	28	<0.01
Mississippi	12	<0.01
Vermont	7	<0.01
North Dakota	3	<0.01
Wyoming	2	<0.01
Alaska	0	0.00
Idaho	0	0.00
Montana	0	0.00
Nebraska	0	0.00
South Dakota	0	0.00
West Virginia	0	0.00

Place	Population	%
New York	27,200	0.14
Massachusetts	4,733	0.07
Rhode Island	528	0.05
District of Columbia	267	0.05
New Jersey	3,790	0.04
Florida	5,629	0.03
Connecticut	1,210	0.03
United States	**57,742**	**0.02**
Georgia	2,230	0.02
Pennsylvania	2,183	0.02
Maryland	1,314	0.02
Delaware	136	0.02
Texas	1,268	0.01
Virginia	960	0.01
North Carolina	877	0.01
Kansas	283	0.01
Kentucky	256	0.01
South Carolina	253	0.01
Hawaii	123	0.01
New Hampshire	81	0.01
California	1,235	<0.01
Illinois	506	<0.01
Ohio	480	<0.01
Michigan	356	<0.01
Washington	321	<0.01
Tennessee	221	<0.01
Arizona	193	<0.01
Wisconsin	136	<0.01
Alabama	105	<0.01
Oregon	102	<0.01
Indiana	97	<0.01
Nevada	90	<0.01
Arkansas	84	<0.01
Minnesota	84	<0.01
Colorado	72	<0.01
Missouri	58	<0.01
Louisiana	57	<0.01
Maine	55	<0.01
Oklahoma	54	<0.01
Utah	33	<0.01
Iowa	30	<0.01
New Mexico	28	<0.01
Mississippi	12	<0.01
Vermont	7	<0.01
North Dakota	3	<0.01
Wyoming	2	<0.01
Alaska	0	0.00
Idaho	0	0.00
Montana	0	0.00
Nebraska	0	0.00
South Dakota	0	0.00
West Virginia	0	0.00

Please refer to the Explanation of Data in the front of the book for more detailed information.

Ancestry

West Indian: Barbadian, excluding Hispanic

Top 150 Places Sorted by Population

Based on all places, regardless of total population

Place	Population	%
New York, NY (city) Kings County	22,550	0.28
Brooklyn, NY (borough) Kings County	14,916	0.60
Queens, NY (borough) Queens County	5,021	0.23
Boston, MA (city) Suffolk County	2,090	0.35
Bronx, NY (borough) Bronx County	1,612	0.12
Hempstead, NY (town) Nassau County	1,279	0.17
Manhattan, NY (borough) New York County	907	0.06
Philadelphia, PA (city) Philadelphia County	635	0.04
Newark, NJ (city) Essex County	590	0.21
Freeport, NY (village) Nassau County	447	1.05
Jacksonville, FL (city) Duval County	399	0.05
Cambridge, MA (city) Middlesex County	338	0.33
Providence, RI (city) Providence County	322	0.18
Pembroke Pines, FL (city) Broward County	320	0.21
New Rochelle, NY (city) Westchester County	316	0.42
Brockton, MA (city) Plymouth County	305	0.32
Washington, DC (city) District of Columbia	267	0.05
Miramar, FL (city) Broward County	261	0.23
Jersey City, NJ (city) Hudson County	239	0.10
Springfield, MA (city) Hampden County	234	0.15
Rochester, NY (city) Monroe County	230	0.11
Winston-Salem, NC (city) Forsyth County	222	0.10
Louisville-Jefferson County, KY (metro govt) Jefferson County	214	0.04
Mount Vernon, NY (city) Westchester County	208	0.31
Hartford, CT (city/town) Hartford County	208	0.17
Los Angeles, CA (city) Los Angeles County	202	0.01
Baltimore, MD (city) Baltimore city County	199	0.03
Virginia Beach, VA (ind. city) Virginia Beach independent city	198	0.05
North Hempstead, NY (town) Nassau County	184	0.08
Carthage, NY (village) Jefferson County	183	4.92
Wilna, NY (town) Jefferson County	183	2.87
Babylon, NY (town) Suffolk County	183	0.09
Randolph, MA (cdp/town) Norfolk County	179	0.57
Plainfield, NJ (city) Union County	174	0.35
Uniondale, NY (cdp) Nassau County	168	0.69
Palm Bay, FL (city) Brevard County	166	0.16
Coconut Creek, FL (city) Broward County	165	0.32
Irvington, NJ (township) Essex County	160	0.29
Rialto, CA (city) San Bernardino County	159	0.16
Fort Lauderdale, FL (city) Broward County	157	0.09
Yonkers, NY (city) Westchester County	157	0.08
Greenburgh, NY (town) Westchester County	155	0.18
Atlanta, GA (city) Fulton County	155	0.04
Chicago, IL (city) Cook County	154	0.01
Hempstead, NY (village) Nassau County	153	0.29
Charlotte, NC (city) Mecklenburg County	148	0.02
East Orange, NJ (city) Essex County	141	0.22
Deerfield Beach, FL (city) Broward County	140	0.19
Keansburg, NJ (borough) Monmouth County	138	1.35
Columbus, OH (city) Franklin County	132	0.02
Westbury, NY (village) Nassau County	129	0.87
Maywood, IL (village) Cook County	129	0.53
Dallas, TX (city) Dallas County	129	0.01
Burlington, NJ (township) Burlington County	127	0.57
Willingboro, NJ (township) Burlington County	126	0.39
Winslow, NJ (township) Camden County	124	0.32
Urban Honolulu, HI (cdp) Honolulu County	123	0.04
Lauderhill, FL (city) Broward County	122	0.18
Waterbury, CT (city/town) New Haven County	118	0.11
Bridgeport, CT (city/town) Fairfield County	117	0.08
Country Walk, FL (cdp) Miami-Dade County	116	0.73
Middletown, CT (city/town) Middlesex County	116	0.24
Bellingham, MA (cdp) Norfolk County	112	2.45
Bellingham, MA (town) Norfolk County	112	0.70
The Hammocks, FL (cdp) Miami-Dade County	112	0.22
North Amityville, NY (cdp) Suffolk County	110	0.62
Kansas City, KS (city) Wyandotte County	107	0.07
Gardner, MA (city) Worcester County	106	0.52
Worcester, MA (city) Worcester County	106	0.06
South Nyack, NY (village) Rockland County	105	1.89
Orangetown, NY (town) Rockland County	105	0.22
Boynton Beach, FL (city) Palm Beach County	102	0.15
The Colony, TX (city) Denton County	100	0.29
Delran, NJ (township) Burlington County	99	0.59
Malden, MA (city) Middlesex County	99	0.17
Bensalem, PA (township) Bucks County	99	0.16
San Antonio, TX (city) Medina County	98	0.01
Fairland, MD (cdp) Montgomery County	96	0.42
Syracuse, NY (city) Onondaga County	96	0.07
Montgomery, NJ (township) Somerset County	95	0.44
Shawnee, KS (city) Johnson County	95	0.16
Schenectady, NY (city) Schenectady County	94	0.14
Staten Island, NY (borough) Richmond County	94	0.02
Hornell, NY (city) Steuben County	93	1.08
Antioch, CA (city) Contra Costa County	93	0.09
Newport News, VA (ind. city) Newport News independent city	93	0.05
East Hill-Meridian, WA (cdp) King County	90	0.31
Pawtucket, RI (city) Providence County	90	0.13
Lakeview, NY (cdp) Nassau County	89	1.60
Woburn, MA (city) Middlesex County	89	0.24
Bloomfield, NJ (township) Essex County	87	0.18
Asbury Park, NJ (city) Monmouth County	85	0.52
Upper Darby, PA (township) Delaware County	85	0.10
Montclair, NJ (township) Essex County	83	0.22
Farmington, CT (town) Hartford County	81	0.32
City of Orange, NJ (township) Essex County	80	0.26
Whitemarsh, PA (township) Montgomery County	79	0.46
Baldwin, NY (cdp) Nassau County	79	0.33
East Hartford, CT (cdp/town) Hartford County	79	0.15
Lynn, MA (city) Essex County	79	0.09
Seattle, WA (city) King County	79	0.01
Newport East, RI (cdp) Newport County	78	0.67
Middletown, RI (town) Newport County	78	0.48
Middletown, NJ (township) Monmouth County	78	0.12
Hollywood, FL (city) Broward County	78	0.06
Pittsburgh, PA (city) Allegheny County	77	0.02
Nashville-Davidson, TN (metro govt) Davidson County	76	0.01
Colwyn, PA (borough) Delaware County	75	2.98
North Olmsted, OH (city) Cuyahoga County	74	0.23
Teaneck, NJ (township) Bergen County	74	0.19
Germantown, MD (cdp) Montgomery County	74	0.09
Chesapeake, VA (ind. city) Chesapeake independent city	74	0.03
South Valley Stream, NY (cdp) Nassau County	73	1.39
Wilmington Island, GA (cdp) Chatham County	73	0.46
Wichita, KS (city) Sedgwick County	73	0.02
Fallsburg, NY (town) Sullivan County	72	0.56
Hampton, VA (ind. city) Hampton independent city	72	0.05
Fontana, CA (city) San Bernardino County	72	0.04
Linglestown, PA (cdp) Dauphin County	71	1.04
Fort Pierce, FL (city) St. Lucie County	71	0.17
Lower Paxton, PA (township) Dauphin County	71	0.15
Bradenton, FL (city) Manatee County	71	0.14
Port Charlotte, FL (cdp) Charlotte County	71	0.13
Houston, TX (city) Harris County	71	<0.01
Palm Coast, FL (city) Flagler County	70	0.10
Monticello, NY (village) Sullivan County	68	1.01
Baldwin Harbor, NY (cdp) Nassau County	68	0.78
Thompson, NY (town) Sullivan County	68	0.45
Barnegat, NJ (township) Ocean County	68	0.34
Gates, NY (town) Monroe County	68	0.24
Reading, PA (city) Berks County	68	0.08
Portland, OR (city) Multnomah County	68	0.01
Dranesville, VA (cdp) Fairfax County	67	0.53
New Haven, CT (city/town) New Haven County	67	0.05
Hackensack, NJ (city) Bergen County	66	0.15
Silver Spring, MD (cdp) Montgomery County	66	0.09
Scaggsville, MD (cdp) Howard County	65	0.28
Manchester, CT (town) Hartford County	64	0.11
Royal Oak, MI (city) Oakland County	64	0.11
Piscataway, NJ (township) Middlesex County	63	0.11
Glen Burnie, MD (cdp) Anne Arundel County	63	0.10
Islip, NY (town) Suffolk County	63	0.02
Stroudsburg, PA (borough) Monroe County	62	1.08
Hinesville, GA (city) Liberty County	62	0.19
Indiantown, FL (cdp) Martin County	61	1.03
Fox Point, WI (village) Milwaukee County	61	0.91
Scottdale, GA (cdp) DeKalb County	61	0.62
Bloomfield, CT (town) Hartford County	61	0.30
Carteret, NJ (borough) Middlesex County	60	0.27
Elmont, NY (cdp) Nassau County	60	0.17

SECTION THREE

Please refer to the Explanation of Data in the front of the book for more detailed information.

Ancestry

West Indian: Barbadian, excluding Hispanic

Top 150 Places Sorted by Percent of Total Population

Based on all places, regardless of total population

Place	Population	%
Slickville, PA (cdp) Westmoreland County	43	11.08
Orrtanna, PA (cdp) Adams County	10	6.17
Carthage, NY (village) Jefferson County	183	4.92
Homewood, PA (borough) Beaver County	6	4.80
East Arcadia, NC (town) Bladen County	22	4.40
Wallace, SC (cdp) Marlboro County	36	4.10
Culver, MN (township) St. Louis County	16	3.94
Colwyn, PA (borough) Delaware County	75	2.98
Wilna, NY (town) Jefferson County	183	2.87
Savannah, TX (cdp) Denton County	53	2.50
Bellingham, MA (cdp) Norfolk County	112	2.45
Southwest Harbor, ME (cdp) Hancock County	14	2.04
South Nyack, NY (village) Rockland County	105	1.89
Harriman, NY (village) Orange County	44	1.86
Lakeview, NY (cdp) Nassau County	89	1.60
Mathews, VA (cdp) Mathews County	11	1.40
South Valley Stream, NY (cdp) Nassau County	73	1.39
Keansburg, NJ (borough) Monmouth County	138	1.35
Highland, PA (township) Adams County	10	1.15
Hornell, NY (city) Steuben County	93	1.08
Stroudsburg, PA (borough) Monroe County	62	1.08
Freeport, NY (village) Nassau County	447	1.05
Linglestown, PA (cdp) Dauphin County	71	1.04
Indiantown, FL (cdp) Martin County	61	1.03
Monticello, NY (village) Sullivan County	68	1.01
Kensington, MN (city) Douglas County	4	0.99
Fox Point, WI (village) Milwaukee County	61	0.91
Sierra View, PA (cdp) Monroe County	50	0.88
Westbury, NY (village) Nassau County	129	0.87
Tangelo Park, FL (cdp) Orange County	19	0.87
Tri-Lakes, IN (cdp) Whitley County	14	0.85
Southwest Harbor, ME (town) Hancock County	14	0.81
Rolesville, NC (town) Wake County	26	0.79
St. Leo, FL (town) Pasco County	5	0.79
Baldwin Harbor, NY (cdp) Nassau County	68	0.78
Lincoln University, PA (cdp) Chester County	15	0.78
Cochituate, MA (cdp) Middlesex County	49	0.77
Warm Springs, OR (cdp) Jefferson County	24	0.76
Adams, NY (village) Jefferson County	14	0.75
Pocono Woodland Lakes, PA (cdp) Pike County	21	0.74
Country Walk, FL (cdp) Miami-Dade County	116	0.73
Milltown, NJ (borough) Middlesex County	50	0.73
Warwick, MA (town) Franklin County	4	0.73
Bellingham, MA (town) Norfolk County	112	0.70
Ellenville, NY (village) Ulster County	29	0.70
Uniondale, NY (cdp) Nassau County	168	0.69
Crompond, NY (cdp) Westchester County	14	0.68
Newport East, RI (cdp) Newport County	78	0.67
Salem, PA (township) Westmoreland County	43	0.65
Harlem, FL (cdp) Hendry County	20	0.64
Black Earth, WI (village) Dane County	8	0.64
North Amityville, NY (cdp) Suffolk County	110	0.62
Scottdale, GA (cdp) DeKalb County	61	0.62
Brooklyn, NY (borough) Kings County	14,916	0.60
Gravette, AR (city) Benton County	12	0.60
Delran, NJ (township) Burlington County	99	0.59
Randolph, MA (cdp/town) Norfolk County	179	0.57
Burlington, NJ (township) Burlington County	127	0.57
Victory Gardens, NJ (borough) Morris County	10	0.57
Fallsburg, NY (town) Sullivan County	72	0.56
Millvale, PA (borough) Allegheny County	21	0.56
Brock Hall, MD (cdp) Prince George's County	45	0.55
Lake Park, FL (town) Palm Beach County	45	0.55
Nantucket, MA (cdp) Nantucket County	44	0.55
Wyndmoor, PA (cdp) Montgomery County	33	0.55
Scotchtown, NY (cdp) Orange County	53	0.54
Carle Place, NY (cdp) Nassau County	30	0.54
Norton Center, MA (cdp) Bristol County	14	0.54
Maywood, IL (village) Cook County	129	0.53
Dranesville, VA (cdp) Fairfax County	67	0.53
Hamilton, PA (township) Monroe County	48	0.53
Lake Odessa, MI (village) Ionia County	12	0.53
Gardner, MA (city) Worcester County	106	0.52
Asbury Park, NJ (city) Monmouth County	85	0.52
Wyoming, OH (city) Hamilton County	41	0.49
Fox River Grove, IL (village) McHenry County	25	0.49
Rossmoor, NJ (cdp) Middlesex County	14	0.49
Middletown, RI (town) Newport County	78	0.48
Kirby, TX (city) Bexar County	39	0.48
Tye, TX (city) Taylor County	5	0.48
Whitemarsh, PA (township) Montgomery County	79	0.46
Wilmington Island, GA (cdp) Chatham County	73	0.46
Medulla, FL (cdp) Polk County	38	0.46
Port Ludlow, WA (cdp) Jefferson County	14	0.46
Thompson, NY (town) Sullivan County	68	0.45
Pembina, ND (city) Pembina County	3	0.45
Montgomery, NJ (township) Somerset County	95	0.44
Nantucket, MA (town) Nantucket County	44	0.44
New Rochelle, NY (city) Westchester County	316	0.42
Fairland, MD (cdp) Montgomery County	96	0.42
Lawrenceville, NJ (cdp) Mercer County	15	0.42
New Haven, NY (town) Oswego County	12	0.42
Riverview, MO (village) St. Louis County	12	0.42
Friendly, MD (cdp) Prince George's County	41	0.41
Pahokee, FL (city) Palm Beach County	24	0.41
Palmetto Estates, FL (cdp) Miami-Dade County	54	0.40
Loughman, FL (cdp) Polk County	11	0.40
Willingboro, NJ (township) Burlington County	126	0.39
Wayland, MA (town) Middlesex County	49	0.38
South Bay, FL (city) Palm Beach County	18	0.38
Stewart Manor, NY (village) Nassau County	8	0.37
Shrewsbury, NJ (township) Monmouth County	4	0.37
New Milford, CT (cdp) Litchfield County	23	0.36
Indian Rocks Beach, FL (city) Pinellas County	15	0.36
Old Westbury, NY (village) Nassau County	14	0.36
South Beach, FL (cdp) Indian River County	13	0.36
Highland, NY (town) Sullivan County	9	0.36
Richmond, PA (township) Tioga County	9	0.36
Boston, MA (city) Suffolk County	2,090	0.35
Plainfield, NJ (city) Union County	174	0.35
Woodbury, NY (village) Orange County	37	0.35
Barnegat, NJ (township) Ocean County	68	0.34
Bladensburg, MD (town) Prince George's County	30	0.34
Nicholls, GA (city) Coffee County	9	0.34
Walton, NY (village) Delaware County	9	0.34
Cambridge, MA (city) Middlesex County	338	0.33
Baldwin, NY (cdp) Nassau County	79	0.33
Woodbury, NY (town) Orange County	37	0.33
Lansdowne, PA (borough) Delaware County	35	0.33
Brockton, MA (city) Plymouth County	305	0.32
Coconut Creek, FL (city) Broward County	165	0.32
Winslow, NJ (township) Camden County	124	0.32
Farmington, CT (town) Hartford County	81	0.32
Forrest City, AR (city) St. Francis County	48	0.32
Port Royal, SC (town) Beaufort County	33	0.32
George Mason, VA (cdp) Fairfax County	28	0.32
Hampton, GA (city) Henry County	21	0.32
Sheldon, VT (town) Franklin County	7	0.32
Mount Vernon, NY (city) Westchester County	208	0.31
East Hill-Meridian, WA (cdp) King County	90	0.31
Chestnut Ridge, NY (village) Rockland County	24	0.31
Roslyn Heights, NY (cdp) Nassau County	20	0.31
Odessa, MI (township) Ionia County	12	0.31
Cleveland, GA (city) White County	10	0.31
Bradbury, CA (city) Los Angeles County	3	0.31
Bloomfield, CT (town) Hartford County	61	0.30
Lower Oxford, PA (township) Chester County	15	0.30
East Lansdowne, PA (borough) Delaware County	8	0.30
Irvington, NJ (township) Essex County	160	0.29
Hempstead, NY (village) Nassau County	153	0.29
The Colony, TX (city) Denton County	100	0.29
Chestnuthill, PA (township) Monroe County	50	0.29
New York, NY (city) Kings County	22,550	0.28
Scaggsville, MD (cdp) Howard County	65	0.28
Waconia, MN (city) Carver County	28	0.28
Adams, NY (town) Jefferson County	14	0.28
Hollywood, SC (town) Charleston County	13	0.28
Hatfield, MA (town) Hampshire County	9	0.28
Plandome Heights, NY (village) Nassau County	3	0.28
Carteret, NJ (borough) Middlesex County	60	0.27

Please refer to the Explanation of Data in the front of the book for more detailed information.

Ancestry

West Indian: Barbadian, excluding Hispanic

Top 150 Places Sorted by Percent of Total Population

Based on places with total population of 7,500 or more

Place	Population	%
Keansburg, NJ (borough) Monmouth County	138	1.35
Hornell, NY (city) Steuben County	93	1.08
Freeport, NY (village) Nassau County	447	1.05
Westbury, NY (village) Nassau County	129	0.87
Baldwin Harbor, NY (cdp) Nassau County	68	0.78
Country Walk, FL (cdp) Miami-Dade County	116	0.73
Bellingham, MA (town) Norfolk County	112	0.70
Uniondale, NY (cdp) Nassau County	168	0.69
Newport East, RI (cdp) Newport County	78	0.67
North Amityville, NY (cdp) Suffolk County	110	0.62
Scottdale, GA (cdp) DeKalb County	61	0.62
Brooklyn, NY (borough) Kings County	14,916	0.60
Delran, NJ (township) Burlington County	99	0.59
Randolph, MA (cdp/town) Norfolk County	179	0.57
Burlington, NJ (township) Burlington County	127	0.57
Fallsburg, NY (town) Sullivan County	72	0.56
Brock Hall, MD (cdp) Prince George's County	45	0.55
Lake Park, FL (town) Palm Beach County	45	0.55
Nantucket, MA (cdp) Nantucket County	44	0.55
Scotchtown, NY (cdp) Orange County	53	0.54
Maywood, IL (village) Cook County	129	0.53
Dranesville, VA (cdp) Fairfax County	67	0.53
Hamilton, PA (township) Monroe County	48	0.53
Gardner, MA (city) Worcester County	106	0.52
Asbury Park, NJ (city) Monmouth County	85	0.52
Wyoming, OH (city) Hamilton County	41	0.49
Middletown, RI (town) Newport County	78	0.48
Kirby, TX (city) Bexar County	39	0.48
Whitemarsh, PA (township) Montgomery County	79	0.46
Wilmington Island, GA (cdp) Chatham County	73	0.46
Medulla, FL (cdp) Polk County	38	0.46
Thompson, NY (town) Sullivan County	68	0.45
Montgomery, NJ (township) Somerset County	95	0.44
Nantucket, MA (town) Nantucket County	44	0.44
New Rochelle, NY (city) Westchester County	316	0.42
Fairland, MD (cdp) Montgomery County	96	0.42
Friendly, MD (cdp) Prince George's County	41	0.41
Palmetto Estates, FL (cdp) Miami-Dade County	54	0.40
Willingboro, NJ (township) Burlington County	126	0.39
Wayland, MA (town) Middlesex County	49	0.38
Boston, MA (city) Suffolk County	2,090	0.35
Plainfield, NJ (city) Union County	174	0.35
Woodbury, NY (village) Orange County	37	0.35
Barnegat, NJ (township) Ocean County	68	0.34
Bladensburg, MD (town) Prince George's County	30	0.34
Cambridge, MA (city) Middlesex County	338	0.33
Baldwin, NY (cdp) Nassau County	79	0.33
Woodbury, NY (town) Orange County	37	0.33
Lansdowne, PA (borough) Delaware County	35	0.33
Brockton, MA (city) Plymouth County	305	0.32
Coconut Creek, FL (city) Broward County	165	0.32
Winslow, NJ (township) Camden County	124	0.32
Farmington, CT (town) Hartford County	81	0.32
Forrest City, AR (city) St. Francis County	48	0.32
Port Royal, SC (town) Beaufort County	33	0.32
George Mason, VA (cdp) Fairfax County	28	0.32
Mount Vernon, NY (city) Westchester County	208	0.31
East Hill-Meridian, WA (cdp) King County	90	0.31
Chestnut Ridge, NY (village) Rockland County	24	0.31
Bloomfield, CT (town) Hartford County	61	0.30
Irvington, NJ (township) Essex County	160	0.29
Hempstead, NY (village) Nassau County	153	0.29
The Colony, TX (city) Denton County	100	0.29
Chestnuthill, PA (township) Monroe County	50	0.29
New York, NY (city) Kings County	22,550	0.28
Scaggsville, MD (cdp) Howard County	65	0.28
Waconia, MN (city) Carver County	28	0.28
Carteret, NJ (borough) Middlesex County	60	0.27
Denville, NJ (township) Morris County	45	0.27
Pine Ridge, FL (cdp) Citrus County	24	0.27
City of Orange, NJ (township) Essex County	80	0.26
Somerset, NJ (cdp) Somerset County	59	0.26
DeBary, FL (city) Volusia County	49	0.26
Hatfield, PA (township) Montgomery County	45	0.26
Blooming Grove, NY (town) Orange County	46	0.25
Middletown, CT (city/town) Middlesex County	116	0.24
Woburn, MA (city) Middlesex County	89	0.24
Gates, NY (town) Monroe County	68	0.24
North Valley Stream, NY (cdp) Nassau County	39	0.24
Temple Hills, MD (cdp) Prince George's County	18	0.24
Queens, NY (borough) Queens County	5,021	0.23
Miramar, FL (city) Broward County	261	0.23
North Olmsted, OH (city) Cuyahoga County	74	0.23
University, FL (cdp) Orange County	49	0.23
Fuller Heights, FL (cdp) Polk County	18	0.23
East Orange, NJ (city) Essex County	141	0.22
The Hammocks, FL (cdp) Miami-Dade County	112	0.22
Orangetown, NY (town) Rockland County	105	0.22
Montclair, NJ (township) Essex County	83	0.22
Stoughton, MA (town) Norfolk County	58	0.22
Snellville, GA (city) Gwinnett County	41	0.22
Auburndale, FL (city) Polk County	29	0.22
Wawarsing, NY (town) Ulster County	29	0.22
Jensen Beach, FL (cdp) Martin County	27	0.22
Newark, NJ (city) Essex County	590	0.21
Pembroke Pines, FL (city) Broward County	320	0.21
Camp Pendleton North, CA (cdp) San Diego County	21	0.21
Wallkill, NY (town) Orange County	53	0.20
Middletown, PA (township) Delaware County	32	0.20
Maurice River, NJ (township) Cumberland County	16	0.20
Deerfield Beach, FL (city) Broward County	140	0.19
Teaneck, NJ (township) Bergen County	74	0.19
Hinesville, GA (city) Liberty County	62	0.19
Azalea Park, FL (cdp) Orange County	25	0.19
Roselle Park, NJ (borough) Union County	25	0.19
Sunset Hills, MO (city) St. Louis County	16	0.19
Providence, RI (city) Providence County	322	0.18
Greenburgh, NY (town) Westchester County	155	0.18
Lauderhill, FL (city) Broward County	122	0.18
Bloomfield, NJ (township) Essex County	87	0.18
Mamaroneck, NY (town) Westchester County	51	0.18
Auburn, ME (city) Androscoggin County	41	0.18
Kinston, NC (city) Lenoir County	40	0.18
Canton, MA (town) Norfolk County	38	0.18
Silver Firs, WA (cdp) Snohomish County	38	0.18
Amherst Center, MA (cdp) Hampshire County	35	0.18
Highland Springs, VA (cdp) Henrico County	30	0.18
Dingman, PA (township) Pike County	21	0.18
Cecil, PA (township) Washington County	20	0.18
Gettysburg, PA (borough) Adams County	14	0.18
Hempstead, NY (town) Nassau County	1,279	0.17
Hartford, CT (city/town) Hartford County	208	0.17
Malden, MA (city) Middlesex County	99	0.17
Fort Pierce, FL (city) St. Lucie County	71	0.17
Elmont, NY (cdp) Nassau County	60	0.17
Richmond West, FL (cdp) Miami-Dade County	56	0.17
Copiague, NY (cdp) Suffolk County	36	0.17
Springfield, PA (township) Montgomery County	33	0.17
North Babylon, NY (cdp) Suffolk County	30	0.17
Union City, GA (city) Fulton County	30	0.17
El Segundo, CA (city) Los Angeles County	28	0.17
Mastic Beach, NY (cdp) Suffolk County	22	0.17
Ardmore, PA (cdp) Montgomery County	21	0.17
Clayton, NJ (borough) Gloucester County	14	0.17
Palm Bay, FL (city) Brevard County	166	0.16
Rialto, CA (city) San Bernardino County	159	0.16
Bensalem, PA (township) Bucks County	99	0.16
Shawnee, KS (city) Johnson County	95	0.16
Cheltenham, PA (township) Montgomery County	59	0.16
Lauderdale Lakes, FL (city) Broward County	52	0.16
Londonderry, NH (cdp) Rockingham County	18	0.16
Tuskegee, AL (city) Macon County	16	0.16
Washington, NC (city) Beaufort County	16	0.16
South Abington, PA (township) Lackawanna County	14	0.16
Springfield, MA (city) Hampden County	234	0.15
Boynton Beach, FL (city) Palm Beach County	102	0.15
East Hartford, CT (cdp/town) Hartford County	79	0.15
Lower Paxton, PA (township) Dauphin County	71	0.15
Hackensack, NJ (city) Bergen County	66	0.15
Spartanburg, SC (city) Spartanburg County	58	0.15

SECTION THREE

Please refer to the Explanation of Data in the front of the book for more detailed information.

Ancestry

West Indian: Belizean, excluding Hispanic

U.S. and 50 States Sorted by Population and Percent of Total Population

Place	Population	%
United States	**49,872**	**0.02**
California	19,627	0.05
New York	7,037	0.04
Illinois	4,851	0.04
Florida	4,237	0.02
Texas	3,677	0.02
New Jersey	1,185	0.01
Virginia	988	0.01
Georgia	937	0.01
Nevada	830	0.03
Louisiana	628	0.01
Pennsylvania	624	<0.01
North Carolina	459	<0.01
Arizona	441	0.01
Washington	367	0.01
Colorado	340	0.01
Massachusetts	302	<0.01
Wisconsin	293	0.01
Rhode Island	292	0.03
Maryland	262	<0.01
Missouri	241	<0.01
Ohio	214	<0.01
Oklahoma	200	0.01
Michigan	188	<0.01
Connecticut	172	<0.01
Tennessee	161	<0.01
South Carolina	152	<0.01
Indiana	147	<0.01
Alabama	116	<0.01
Minnesota	107	<0.01
District of Columbia	101	0.02
Utah	91	<0.01
South Dakota	88	0.01
Mississippi	83	<0.01
Oregon	71	<0.01
Kentucky	69	<0.01
Iowa	52	<0.01
Montana	34	<0.01
Alaska	33	<0.01
New Mexico	30	<0.01
Delaware	28	<0.01
Hawaii	28	<0.01
Idaho	21	<0.01
Vermont	18	<0.01
Arkansas	12	<0.01
Kansas	12	<0.01
New Hampshire	12	<0.01
West Virginia	11	<0.01
Nebraska	3	<0.01
Maine	0	0.00
North Dakota	0	0.00
Wyoming	0	0.00

Place	Population	%
California	19,627	0.05
New York	7,037	0.04
Illinois	4,851	0.04
Nevada	830	0.03
Rhode Island	292	0.03
United States	**49,872**	**0.02**
Florida	4,237	0.02
Texas	3,677	0.02
District of Columbia	101	0.02
New Jersey	1,185	0.01
Virginia	988	0.01
Georgia	937	0.01
Louisiana	628	0.01
Arizona	441	0.01
Washington	367	0.01
Colorado	340	0.01
Wisconsin	293	0.01
Oklahoma	200	0.01
South Dakota	88	0.01
Pennsylvania	624	<0.01
North Carolina	459	<0.01
Massachusetts	302	<0.01
Maryland	262	<0.01
Missouri	241	<0.01
Ohio	214	<0.01
Michigan	188	<0.01
Connecticut	172	<0.01
Tennessee	161	<0.01
South Carolina	152	<0.01
Indiana	147	<0.01
Alabama	116	<0.01
Minnesota	107	<0.01
Utah	91	<0.01
Mississippi	83	<0.01
Oregon	71	<0.01
Kentucky	69	<0.01
Iowa	52	<0.01
Montana	34	<0.01
Alaska	33	<0.01
New Mexico	30	<0.01
Delaware	28	<0.01
Hawaii	28	<0.01
Idaho	21	<0.01
Vermont	18	<0.01
Arkansas	12	<0.01
Kansas	12	<0.01
New Hampshire	12	<0.01
West Virginia	11	<0.01
Nebraska	3	<0.01
Maine	0	0.00
North Dakota	0	0.00
Wyoming	0	0.00

Please refer to the Explanation of Data in the front of the book for more detailed information.

Ancestry

West Indian: Belizean, excluding Hispanic

Top 150 Places Sorted by Population

Based on all places, regardless of total population

Place	Population	%
Los Angeles, CA (city) Los Angeles County	8,719	0.23
New York, NY (city) Kings County	5,674	0.07
Chicago, IL (city) Cook County	2,273	0.08
Brooklyn, NY (borough) Kings County	2,026	0.08
Bronx, NY (borough) Bronx County	1,493	0.11
Houston, TX (city) Harris County	1,482	0.07
Queens, NY (borough) Queens County	1,344	0.06
Lancaster, CA (city) Los Angeles County	876	0.59
Manhattan, NY (borough) New York County	735	0.05
Inglewood, CA (city) Los Angeles County	711	0.65
Westmont, CA (cdp) Los Angeles County	574	1.83
Waukegan, IL (city) Lake County	536	0.60
Evanston, IL (city) Cook County	358	0.48
Hawthorne, CA (city) Los Angeles County	341	0.41
Long Beach, CA (city) Los Angeles County	336	0.07
Las Vegas, NV (city) Clark County	335	0.06
Dallas, TX (city) Dallas County	335	0.03
San Pablo, CA (city) Contra Costa County	330	1.13
Miramar, FL (city) Broward County	324	0.28
Compton, CA (city) Los Angeles County	308	0.32
Hollywood, FL (city) Broward County	267	0.19
Newport News, VA (ind. city) Newport News independent city	261	0.14
Providence, RI (city) Providence County	255	0.14
Moreno Valley, CA (city) Riverside County	236	0.13
Rialto, CA (city) San Bernardino County	231	0.23
Dale City, VA (cdp) Prince William County	227	0.36
North Chicago, IL (city) Lake County	217	0.66
Jacksonville, FL (city) Duval County	211	0.03
Gardena, CA (city) Los Angeles County	203	0.35
Kingston, NJ (cdp) Middlesex County	198	10.00
South Brunswick, NJ (township) Middlesex County	198	0.47
Fontana, CA (city) San Bernardino County	198	0.10
Jersey City, NJ (city) Hudson County	195	0.08
Missouri City, TX (city) Fort Bend County	182	0.28
Rancho Cucamonga, CA (city) San Bernardino County	179	0.11
West Rancho Dominguez, CA (cdp) Los Angeles County	178	3.09
Sierra View, PA (cdp) Monroe County	175	3.09
Chestnuthill, PA (township) Monroe County	175	1.03
Elizabeth, NJ (city) Union County	175	0.14
Cutler Bay, FL (town) Miami-Dade County	173	0.45
Rochester, NY (city) Monroe County	171	0.08
Stevenson Ranch, CA (cdp) Los Angeles County	167	0.99
Victorville, CA (city) San Bernardino County	167	0.15
Cape Coral, FL (city) Lee County	161	0.11
Bremerton, WA (city) Kitsap County	155	0.41
Culver City, CA (city) Los Angeles County	155	0.40
White Plains, NY (city) Westchester County	155	0.28
Ontario, CA (city) San Bernardino County	155	0.09
Kenner, LA (city) Jefferson Parish	153	0.23
Lakewood, CA (city) Los Angeles County	153	0.19
Kenosha, WI (city) Kenosha County	150	0.15
Denver, CO (city) Denver County	149	0.03
New Orleans, LA (city) Orleans Parish	146	0.05
Santa Clarita, CA (city) Los Angeles County	145	0.08
San Francisco, CA (city) San Francisco County	140	0.02
Windsor, CT (town) Hartford County	139	0.48
Phoenix, AZ (city) Maricopa County	139	0.01
San Antonio, TX (city) Medina County	134	0.01
Montclair, CA (city) San Bernardino County	131	0.36
Palmdale, CA (city) Los Angeles County	128	0.09
North Las Vegas, NV (city) Clark County	127	0.06
Altadena, CA (cdp) Los Angeles County	126	0.28
North Miami Beach, FL (city) Miami-Dade County	125	0.30
DeSoto, TX (city) Dallas County	125	0.27
Paradise, NV (cdp) Clark County	125	0.06
Covina, CA (city) Los Angeles County	123	0.26
Gurnee, IL (village) Lake County	122	0.39
San Diego, CA (city) San Diego County	122	0.01
Menifee, CA (city) Riverside County	121	0.17
South Nyack, NY (village) Rockland County	120	2.16
Orangetown, NY (town) Rockland County	120	0.25
Fort Pierce South, FL (cdp) St. Lucie County	118	2.07
Mount Vernon, NY (city) Westchester County	118	0.18
Hempstead, NY (town) Nassau County	118	0.02
Cheltenham, PA (township) Montgomery County	117	0.32
Chino Hills, CA (city) San Bernardino County	116	0.16
Miami Gardens, FL (city) Miami-Dade County	112	0.11
Lake Elsinore, CA (city) Riverside County	111	0.23
St. Charles, MO (city) St. Charles County	111	0.17
Metairie, LA (cdp) Jefferson Parish	107	0.08
Tuckahoe, VA (cdp) Henrico County	104	0.23
Sacramento, CA (city) Sacramento County	104	0.02
Zion, IL (city) Lake County	102	0.42
Washington, DC (city) District of Columbia	101	0.02
Adelanto, CA (city) San Bernardino County	100	0.34
Hempfield, PA (township) Mercer County	99	2.62
Seaside, CA (city) Monterey County	97	0.30
Colton, CA (city) San Bernardino County	96	0.18
Sunrise Manor, NV (cdp) Clark County	95	0.05
Arlington, TX (city) Tarrant County	95	0.03
Kenmore, WA (city) King County	94	0.47
Windsor, CA (town) Sonoma County	94	0.36
Aventura, FL (city) Miami-Dade County	93	0.28
Chino, CA (city) San Bernardino County	93	0.12
Brockton, MA (city) Plymouth County	92	0.10
Kingman, AZ (city) Mohave County	89	0.32
Torrance, CA (city) Los Angeles County	88	0.06
Chili, NY (town) Monroe County	85	0.30
Northampton, MA (city) Hampshire County	85	0.30
Tamarac, FL (city) Broward County	82	0.14
North Hempstead, NY (town) Nassau County	81	0.04
Middletown, NY (city) Orange County	80	0.29
Poughkeepsie, NY (city) Dutchess County	80	0.25
Perris, CA (city) Riverside County	80	0.13
Lake Alfred, FL (city) Polk County	79	1.61
Teaneck, NJ (township) Bergen County	79	0.20
Mount Olive, NJ (township) Morris County	78	0.28
Paramount, CA (city) Los Angeles County	77	0.14
Roswell, GA (city) Fulton County	77	0.09
Staten Island, NY (borough) Richmond County	76	0.02
Harwood Heights, IL (village) Cook County	75	0.89
Austin, TX (city) Travis County	74	0.01
Westlake Village, CA (city) Los Angeles County	73	0.88
Lawndale, CA (city) Los Angeles County	73	0.22
Stockton, CA (city) San Joaquin County	73	0.03
Westmont, IL (village) DuPage County	72	0.29
Richardson, TX (city) Dallas County	72	0.07
San Bernardino, CA (city) San Bernardino County	72	0.03
Herlong, CA (cdp) Lassen County	70	5.00
Longwood, FL (city) Seminole County	70	0.50
New Bern, NC (city) Craven County	70	0.25
Foothill Farms, CA (cdp) Sacramento County	69	0.21
Cicero, IL (town) Cook County	68	0.08
Vincent, CA (cdp) Los Angeles County	67	0.41
Ives Estates, FL (cdp) Miami-Dade County	67	0.38
Pinellas Park, FL (city) Pinellas County	67	0.14
Pomona, CA (city) Los Angeles County	67	0.05
Hinesville, GA (city) Liberty County	66	0.20
La Mesa, CA (city) San Diego County	65	0.12
Bolingbrook, IL (village) Will County	64	0.09
Fort Lauderdale, FL (city) Broward County	64	0.04
Salem, OR (city) Marion County	64	0.04
Richmond West, FL (cdp) Miami-Dade County	63	0.19
West Palm Beach, FL (city) Palm Beach County	63	0.06
Myrtle Grove, FL (cdp) Escambia County	62	0.39
Killeen, TX (city) Bell County	62	0.05
Franklin Grove, IL (village) Lee County	61	4.39
Chesapeake, VA (ind. city) Chesapeake independent city	61	0.03
Henderson, NV (city) Clark County	61	0.02
Oakland, CA (city) Alameda County	61	0.02
Tampa, FL (city) Hillsborough County	61	0.02
Tucson, AZ (city) Pima County	61	0.01
Villas, FL (cdp) Lee County	60	0.55
Grapevine, TX (city) Tarrant County	60	0.13
North Port, FL (city) Sarasota County	58	0.11
Modesto, CA (city) Stanislaus County	58	0.03
Boulder, CO (city) Boulder County	57	0.06
Hampton, VA (ind. city) Hampton independent city	57	0.04
Oakdale, MN (city) Washington County	56	0.20
Racine, WI (city) Racine County	56	0.07

SECTION THREE

Please refer to the Explanation of Data in the front of the book for more detailed information.

Ancestry

West Indian: Belizean, excluding Hispanic

Top 150 Places Sorted by Percent of Total Population

Based on all places, regardless of total population

Place	Population	%
Kingston, NJ (cdp) Middlesex County	198	10.00
Herlong, CA (cdp) Lassen County	70	5.00
Franklin Grove, IL (village) Lee County	61	4.39
Turbett, PA (township) Juniata County	29	3.82
West Rancho Dominguez, CA (cdp) Los Angeles County	178	3.09
Sierra View, PA (cdp) Monroe County	175	3.09
Bearden, OK (town) Okfuskee County	5	3.05
Diggins, MO (village) Webster County	9	2.94
Hempfield, PA (township) Mercer County	99	2.62
South Nyack, NY (village) Rockland County	120	2.16
Fort Pierce South, FL (cdp) St. Lucie County	118	2.07
Westmont, CA (cdp) Los Angeles County	574	1.83
Long Lake, IL (cdp) Lake County	53	1.73
Lake Alfred, FL (city) Polk County	79	1.61
Black River, NY (village) Jefferson County	22	1.41
Pineville, WV (town) Wyoming County	11	1.36
Panama, NY (village) Chautauqua County	6	1.26
East Lake Lillian, MN (township) Kandiyohi County	2	1.19
San Pablo, CA (city) Contra Costa County	330	1.13
Pioche, NV (cdp) Lincoln County	9	1.13
Royal Palm Estates, FL (cdp) Palm Beach County	38	1.04
Chestnuthill, PA (township) Monroe County	175	1.03
Stevenson Ranch, CA (cdp) Los Angeles County	167	0.99
Herricks, NY (cdp) Nassau County	37	0.94
Dugway, UT (cdp) Tooele County	11	0.92
Harwood Heights, IL (village) Cook County	75	0.89
Westlake Village, CA (city) Los Angeles County	73	0.88
New Sarpy, LA (cdp) St. Charles Parish	13	0.87
Woodfin, NC (town) Buncombe County	50	0.85
Armona, CA (cdp) Kings County	25	0.82
Wilmington, VT (town) Windham County	18	0.81
Bonners Ferry, ID (city) Boundary County	21	0.80
Cooper, TN (town) Robertson County	31	0.76
Tyrone, GA (town) Fayette County	48	0.75
Rutland, NY (town) Jefferson County	22	0.73
Saluda, NC (city) Polk County	5	0.71
New Castle, CO (town) Garfield County	28	0.68
Garden Ridge, TX (city) Comal County	20	0.67
North Chicago, IL (city) Lake County	217	0.66
Inglewood, CA (city) Los Angeles County	711	0.65
Cattaraugus Reservation, NY (reservation) Erie County	12	0.64
Prentiss, MS (town) Jefferson Davis County	9	0.64
Waukegan, IL (city) Lake County	536	0.60
Lancaster, CA (city) Los Angeles County	876	0.59
Naples Park, FL (cdp) Collier County	40	0.59
Villas, FL (cdp) Lee County	60	0.55
Park City, IL (city) Lake County	40	0.53
Longwood, FL (city) Seminole County	70	0.50
Evanston, IL (city) Cook County	358	0.48
Windsor, CT (town) Hartford County	139	0.48
St. Leo, FL (town) Pasco County	3	0.48
South Brunswick, NJ (township) Middlesex County	198	0.47
Kenmore, WA (city) King County	94	0.47
Carthage, NY (village) Jefferson County	17	0.46
Cutler Bay, FL (town) Miami-Dade County	173	0.45
Zeeland, MI (charter township) Ottawa County	43	0.45
Chestnut Ridge, NY (village) Rockland County	35	0.45
Naples Manor, FL (cdp) Collier County	23	0.44
The Meadows, FL (cdp) Sarasota County	19	0.44
Newport, NC (town) Carteret County	17	0.43
Zion, IL (city) Lake County	102	0.42
Hawthorne, CA (city) Los Angeles County	341	0.41
Bremerton, WA (city) Kitsap County	155	0.41
Vincent, CA (cdp) Los Angeles County	67	0.41
Culver City, CA (city) Los Angeles County	155	0.40
Gurnee, IL (village) Lake County	122	0.39
Myrtle Grove, FL (cdp) Escambia County	62	0.39
Ives Estates, FL (cdp) Miami-Dade County	67	0.38
Kewanee, IL (city) Henry County	50	0.38
Blackwood, NJ (cdp) Camden County	19	0.38
Melissa, TX (city) Collin County	16	0.38
Brookville, NY (village) Nassau County	13	0.38
Leilani Estates, HI (cdp) Hawaii County	6	0.38
Dale City, VA (cdp) Prince William County	227	0.36
Montclair, CA (city) San Bernardino County	131	0.36
Windsor, CA (town) Sonoma County	94	0.36
Riverton, NJ (borough) Burlington County	10	0.36
Gardena, CA (city) Los Angeles County	203	0.35
Mantua, VA (cdp) Fairfax County	26	0.35
Vine Hill, CA (cdp) Contra Costa County	12	0.35
Adelanto, CA (city) San Bernardino County	100	0.34
New Brockton, AL (town) Coffee County	5	0.34
Compton, CA (city) Los Angeles County	308	0.32
Cheltenham, PA (township) Montgomery County	117	0.32
Kingman, AZ (city) Mohave County	89	0.32
Woodlake, VA (cdp) Chesterfield County	25	0.32
Round Lake Heights, IL (village) Lake County	9	0.31
North Miami Beach, FL (city) Miami-Dade County	125	0.30
Seaside, CA (city) Monterey County	97	0.30
Chili, NY (town) Monroe County	85	0.30
Northampton, MA (city) Hampshire County	85	0.30
Westbury, NY (village) Nassau County	44	0.30
Middletown, NY (city) Orange County	80	0.29
Westmont, IL (village) DuPage County	72	0.29
St. Francis, WI (city) Milwaukee County	27	0.29
Gulf Breeze, FL (city) Santa Rosa County	17	0.29
Elkton, VA (town) Rockingham County	8	0.29
Eagle, NE (village) Cass County	3	0.29
Miramar, FL (city) Broward County	324	0.28
Missouri City, TX (city) Fort Bend County	182	0.28
White Plains, NY (city) Westchester County	155	0.28
Altadena, CA (cdp) Los Angeles County	126	0.28
Aventura, FL (city) Miami-Dade County	93	0.28
Mount Olive, NJ (township) Morris County	78	0.28
Urbana, IA (city) Benton County	4	0.28
DeSoto, TX (city) Dallas County	125	0.27
Ridgefield Park, NJ (village) Bergen County	34	0.27
Wilna, NY (town) Jefferson County	17	0.27
Harmony, NY (town) Chautauqua County	6	0.27
Covina, CA (city) Los Angeles County	123	0.26
Lewisburg, TN (city) Marshall County	29	0.26
Shohola, PA (township) Pike County	7	0.26
Orangetown, NY (town) Rockland County	120	0.25
Poughkeepsie, NY (city) Dutchess County	80	0.25
New Bern, NC (city) Craven County	70	0.25
Tuskegee, AL (city) Macon County	25	0.25
Palm Shores, FL (town) Brevard County	2	0.25
Miami Springs, FL (city) Miami-Dade County	33	0.24
Jefferson, LA (cdp) Jefferson Parish	29	0.24
Los Angeles, CA (city) Los Angeles County	8,719	0.23
Rialto, CA (city) San Bernardino County	231	0.23
Kenner, LA (city) Jefferson Parish	153	0.23
Lake Elsinore, CA (city) Riverside County	111	0.23
Tuckahoe, VA (cdp) Henrico County	104	0.23
Bridgeton, MO (city) St. Louis County	28	0.23
Brockport, NY (village) Monroe County	19	0.23
Lawndale, CA (city) Los Angeles County	73	0.22
Green Cove Springs, FL (city) Clay County	15	0.22
Winthrop Harbor, IL (village) Lake County	15	0.22
Foothill Farms, CA (cdp) Sacramento County	69	0.21
Temple Terrace, FL (city) Hillsborough County	52	0.21
Sunset, FL (cdp) Miami-Dade County	35	0.21
Meadows Place, TX (city) Fort Bend County	10	0.21
Wheeler AFB, HI (cdp) Honolulu County	5	0.21
Teaneck, NJ (township) Bergen County	79	0.20
Hinesville, GA (city) Liberty County	66	0.20
Oakdale, MN (city) Washington County	56	0.20
Roosevelt, NY (cdp) Nassau County	30	0.20
Forney, TX (city) Kaufman County	26	0.20
East Garden City, NY (cdp) Nassau County	11	0.20
Edgewood, FL (city) Orange County	5	0.20
Hollywood, FL (city) Broward County	267	0.19
Lakewood, CA (city) Los Angeles County	153	0.19
Richmond West, FL (cdp) Miami-Dade County	63	0.19
Lake Magdalene, FL (cdp) Hillsborough County	55	0.19
Inkster, MI (city) Wayne County	50	0.19
Dickinson, TX (city) Galveston County	36	0.19
Beach Park, IL (village) Lake County	25	0.19
Westview, FL (cdp) Miami-Dade County	18	0.19
Alondra Park, CA (cdp) Los Angeles County	17	0.19

Please refer to the Explanation of Data in the front of the book for more detailed information.

Ancestry

West Indian: Belizean, excluding Hispanic

Top 150 Places Sorted by Percent of Total Population

Based on places with total population of 7,500 or more

Place	Population	%
Westmont, CA (cdp) Los Angeles County	574	1.83
San Pablo, CA (city) Contra Costa County	330	1.13
Chestnuthill, PA (township) Monroe County	175	1.03
Stevenson Ranch, CA (cdp) Los Angeles County	167	0.99
Harwood Heights, IL (village) Cook County	75	0.89
Westlake Village, CA (city) Los Angeles County	73	0.88
North Chicago, IL (city) Lake County	217	0.66
Inglewood, CA (city) Los Angeles County	711	0.65
Waukegan, IL (city) Lake County	536	0.60
Lancaster, CA (city) Los Angeles County	876	0.59
Villas, FL (cdp) Lee County	60	0.55
Park City, IL (city) Lake County	40	0.53
Longwood, FL (city) Seminole County	70	0.50
Evanston, IL (city) Cook County	358	0.48
Windsor, CT (town) Hartford County	139	0.48
South Brunswick, NJ (township) Middlesex County	198	0.47
Kenmore, WA (city) King County	94	0.47
Cutler Bay, FL (town) Miami-Dade County	173	0.45
Zeeland, MI (charter township) Ottawa County	43	0.45
Chestnut Ridge, NY (village) Rockland County	35	0.45
Zion, IL (city) Lake County	102	0.42
Hawthorne, CA (city) Los Angeles County	341	0.41
Bremerton, WA (city) Kitsap County	155	0.41
Vincent, CA (cdp) Los Angeles County	67	0.41
Culver City, CA (city) Los Angeles County	155	0.40
Gurnee, IL (village) Lake County	122	0.39
Myrtle Grove, FL (cdp) Escambia County	62	0.39
Ives Estates, FL (cdp) Miami-Dade County	67	0.38
Kewanee, IL (city) Henry County	50	0.38
Dale City, VA (cdp) Prince William County	227	0.36
Montclair, CA (city) San Bernardino County	131	0.36
Windsor, CA (town) Sonoma County	94	0.36
Gardena, CA (city) Los Angeles County	203	0.35
Mantua, VA (cdp) Fairfax County	26	0.35
Adelanto, CA (city) San Bernardino County	100	0.34
Compton, CA (city) Los Angeles County	308	0.32
Cheltenham, PA (township) Montgomery County	117	0.32
Kingman, AZ (city) Mohave County	89	0.32
Woodlake, VA (cdp) Chesterfield County	25	0.32
North Miami Beach, FL (city) Miami-Dade County	125	0.30
Seaside, CA (city) Monterey County	97	0.30
Chili, NY (town) Monroe County	85	0.30
Northampton, MA (city) Hampshire County	85	0.30
Westbury, NY (village) Nassau County	44	0.30
Middletown, NY (city) Orange County	80	0.29
Westmont, IL (village) DuPage County	72	0.29
St. Francis, WI (city) Milwaukee County	27	0.29
Miramar, FL (city) Broward County	324	0.28
Missouri City, TX (city) Fort Bend County	182	0.28
White Plains, NY (city) Westchester County	155	0.28
Altadena, CA (cdp) Los Angeles County	126	0.28
Aventura, FL (city) Miami-Dade County	93	0.28
Mount Olive, NJ (township) Morris County	78	0.28
DeSoto, TX (city) Dallas County	125	0.27
Ridgefield Park, NJ (village) Bergen County	34	0.27
Covina, CA (city) Los Angeles County	123	0.26
Lewisburg, TN (city) Marshall County	29	0.26
Orangetown, NY (town) Rockland County	120	0.25
Poughkeepsie, NY (city) Dutchess County	80	0.25
New Bern, NC (city) Craven County	70	0.25
Tuskegee, AL (city) Macon County	25	0.25
Miami Springs, FL (city) Miami-Dade County	33	0.24
Jefferson, LA (cdp) Jefferson Parish	29	0.24
Los Angeles, CA (city) Los Angeles County	8,719	0.23
Rialto, CA (city) San Bernardino County	231	0.23
Kenner, LA (city) Jefferson Parish	153	0.23
Lake Elsinore, CA (city) Riverside County	111	0.23
Tuckahoe, VA (cdp) Henrico County	104	0.23
Bridgeton, MO (city) St. Louis County	28	0.23
Brockport, NY (village) Monroe County	19	0.23
Lawndale, CA (city) Los Angeles County	73	0.22
Foothill Farms, CA (cdp) Sacramento County	69	0.21
Temple Terrace, FL (city) Hillsborough County	52	0.21
Sunset, FL (cdp) Miami-Dade County	35	0.21
Teaneck, NJ (township) Bergen County	79	0.20
Hinesville, GA (city) Liberty County	66	0.20
Oakdale, MN (city) Washington County	56	0.20
Roosevelt, NY (cdp) Nassau County	30	0.20
Forney, TX (city) Kaufman County	26	0.20
Hollywood, FL (city) Broward County	267	0.19
Lakewood, CA (city) Los Angeles County	153	0.19
Richmond West, FL (cdp) Miami-Dade County	63	0.19
Lake Magdalene, FL (cdp) Hillsborough County	55	0.19
Inkster, MI (city) Wayne County	50	0.19
Dickinson, TX (city) Galveston County	36	0.19
Beach Park, IL (village) Lake County	25	0.19
Westview, FL (cdp) Miami-Dade County	18	0.19
Alondra Park, CA (cdp) Los Angeles County	17	0.19
Perkiomen, PA (township) Montgomery County	17	0.19
Mount Vernon, NY (city) Westchester County	118	0.18
Colton, CA (city) San Bernardino County	96	0.18
Radcliff, KY (city) Hardin County	38	0.18
Bostonia, CA (cdp) San Diego County	26	0.18
West Columbia, SC (city) Lexington County	26	0.18
Markham, IL (city) Cook County	22	0.18
Menifee, CA (city) Riverside County	121	0.17
St. Charles, MO (city) St. Charles County	111	0.17
La Verne, CA (city) Los Angeles County	54	0.17
Cockeysville, MD (cdp) Baltimore County	34	0.17
Round Lake, IL (village) Lake County	27	0.17
Kaneohe Station, HI (cdp) Honolulu County	17	0.17
Chino Hills, CA (city) San Bernardino County	116	0.16
Lake Jackson, TX (city) Brazoria County	44	0.16
Lemon Grove, CA (city) San Diego County	40	0.16
Havelock, NC (city) Craven County	32	0.16
Warrensburg, MO (city) Johnson County	29	0.16
Floral Park, NY (village) Nassau County	25	0.16
Clearlake, CA (city) Lake County	24	0.16
Accokeek, MD (cdp) Prince George's County	17	0.16
Oronoko, MI (charter township) Berrien County	15	0.16
Victorville, CA (city) San Bernardino County	167	0.15
Kenosha, WI (city) Kenosha County	150	0.15
Golden Glades, FL (cdp) Miami-Dade County	49	0.15
Aberdeen, SD (city) Brown County	38	0.15
Dolton, IL (village) Cook County	36	0.15
Seal Beach, CA (city) Orange County	36	0.15
French Valley, CA (cdp) Riverside County	31	0.15
North Augusta, SC (city) Aiken County	30	0.15
Glenwood, IL (village) Cook County	13	0.15
Newport News, VA (ind. city) Newport News independent city	261	0.14
Providence, RI (city) Providence County	255	0.14
Elizabeth, NJ (city) Union County	175	0.14
Tamarac, FL (city) Broward County	82	0.14
Paramount, CA (city) Los Angeles County	77	0.14
Pinellas Park, FL (city) Pinellas County	67	0.14
Lennox, CA (cdp) Los Angeles County	31	0.14
Avocado Heights, CA (cdp) Los Angeles County	21	0.14
Shiloh, PA (cdp) York County	16	0.14
West Long Branch, NJ (borough) Monmouth County	11	0.14
Moreno Valley, CA (city) Riverside County	236	0.13
Perris, CA (city) Riverside County	80	0.13
Grapevine, TX (city) Tarrant County	60	0.13
Burleson, TX (city) Johnson County	44	0.13
San Juan Capistrano, CA (city) Orange County	43	0.13
Wake Forest, NC (town) Wake County	35	0.13
Munster, IN (town) Lake County	31	0.13
Sweden, NY (town) Monroe County	19	0.13
Forest Park, IL (village) Cook County	18	0.13
Okmulgee, OK (city) Okmulgee County	16	0.13
Chester, IL (city) Randolph County	11	0.13
Chino, CA (city) San Bernardino County	93	0.12
La Mesa, CA (city) San Diego County	65	0.12
Aliso Viejo, CA (city) Orange County	55	0.12
Soledad, CA (city) Monterey County	30	0.12
Terrytown, LA (cdp) Jefferson Parish	28	0.12
Coralville, IA (city) Johnson County	21	0.12
Lakeland North, WA (cdp) King County	15	0.12
Lakewood Park, FL (cdp) St. Lucie County	14	0.12
Harleysville, PA (cdp) Montgomery County	11	0.12
Attica, NY (town) Wyoming County	9	0.12

Please refer to the Explanation of Data in the front of the book for more detailed information.

Ancestry

West Indian: Bermudan, excluding Hispanic

U.S. and 50 States Sorted by Population and Percent of Total Population

Place	Population	%
United States	**6,728**	**<0.01**
Florida	1,077	0.01
New York	672	<0.01
Massachusetts	538	0.01
Texas	481	<0.01
New Jersey	452	0.01
Georgia	452	<0.01
Pennsylvania	423	<0.01
Maryland	356	0.01
California	308	<0.01
Virginia	233	<0.01
South Carolina	215	<0.01
Michigan	153	<0.01
North Carolina	141	<0.01
Ohio	128	<0.01
Connecticut	117	<0.01
Mississippi	109	<0.01
Washington	103	<0.01
Alabama	96	<0.01
Arizona	78	<0.01
Illinois	59	<0.01
Louisiana	47	<0.01
Indiana	42	<0.01
District of Columbia	41	0.01
New Hampshire	41	<0.01
Oklahoma	41	<0.01
Rhode Island	37	<0.01
Colorado	33	<0.01
Delaware	31	<0.01
West Virginia	28	<0.01
Kansas	25	<0.01
Hawaii	22	<0.01
Minnesota	20	<0.01
New Mexico	20	<0.01
Missouri	18	<0.01
Tennessee	18	<0.01
Kentucky	13	<0.01
Oregon	13	<0.01
Arkansas	12	<0.01
Maine	10	<0.01
Iowa	7	<0.01
Vermont	7	<0.01
Utah	6	<0.01
Wisconsin	5	<0.01
Alaska	0	0.00
Idaho	0	0.00
Montana	0	0.00
Nebraska	0	0.00
Nevada	0	0.00
North Dakota	0	0.00
South Dakota	0	0.00
Wyoming	0	0.00

Place	Population	%
Florida	1,077	0.01
Massachusetts	538	0.01
New Jersey	452	0.01
Maryland	356	0.01
District of Columbia	41	0.01
United States	**6,728**	**<0.01**
New York	672	<0.01
Texas	481	<0.01
Georgia	452	<0.01
Pennsylvania	423	<0.01
California	308	<0.01
Virginia	233	<0.01
South Carolina	215	<0.01
Michigan	153	<0.01
North Carolina	141	<0.01
Ohio	128	<0.01
Connecticut	117	<0.01
Mississippi	109	<0.01
Washington	103	<0.01
Alabama	96	<0.01
Arizona	78	<0.01
Illinois	59	<0.01
Louisiana	47	<0.01
Indiana	42	<0.01
New Hampshire	41	<0.01
Oklahoma	41	<0.01
Rhode Island	37	<0.01
Colorado	33	<0.01
Delaware	31	<0.01
West Virginia	28	<0.01
Kansas	25	<0.01
Hawaii	22	<0.01
Minnesota	20	<0.01
New Mexico	20	<0.01
Missouri	18	<0.01
Tennessee	18	<0.01
Kentucky	13	<0.01
Oregon	13	<0.01
Arkansas	12	<0.01
Maine	10	<0.01
Iowa	7	<0.01
Vermont	7	<0.01
Utah	6	<0.01
Wisconsin	5	<0.01
Alaska	0	0.00
Idaho	0	0.00
Montana	0	0.00
Nebraska	0	0.00
Nevada	0	0.00
North Dakota	0	0.00
South Dakota	0	0.00
Wyoming	0	0.00

Please refer to the Explanation of Data in the front of the book for more detailed information.

Ancestry

West Indian: Bermudan, excluding Hispanic

Top 150 Places Sorted by Population

Based on all places, regardless of total population

Place	Population	%
New York, NY (city) Kings County	518	0.01
Bronx, NY (borough) Bronx County	198	0.01
Haltom City, TX (city) Tarrant County	196	0.47
Queens, NY (borough) Queens County	177	0.01
Progress, PA (cdp) Dauphin County	165	1.72
Susquehanna, PA (township) Dauphin County	165	0.70
Boston, MA (city) Suffolk County	157	0.03
Natick, MA (town) Middlesex County	132	0.41
Lauderdale Lakes, FL (city) Broward County	131	0.40
Manhattan, NY (borough) New York County	127	0.01
Los Angeles, CA (city) Los Angeles County	118	<0.01
Jacksonville, FL (city) Duval County	101	0.01
Pontiac, MI (city) Oakland County	89	0.15
Olympia, WA (city) Thurston County	79	0.17
Newark, NJ (city) Essex County	70	0.03
San Antonio, TX (city) Medina County	68	0.01
Sanford, FL (city) Seminole County	67	0.13
Pembroke Pines, FL (city) Broward County	67	0.04
Hackensack, NJ (city) Bergen County	64	0.15
Forest Oaks, NC (cdp) Guilford County	58	1.71
Socastee, SC (cdp) Horry County	57	0.33
Hempstead, NY (town) Nassau County	52	0.01
Miami, FL (city) Miami-Dade County	52	0.01
Baltimore, MD (city) Baltimore city County	48	0.01
Salem, PA (township) Wayne County	47	1.12
Suitland, MD (cdp) Prince George's County	47	0.19
Tallahassee, FL (city) Leon County	47	0.03
San Diego, CA (city) San Diego County	46	<0.01
North Royalton, OH (city) Cuyahoga County	45	0.15
Cedar Hill, TX (city) Dallas County	45	0.11
Worcester, MA (city) Worcester County	45	0.03
West Palm Beach, FL (city) Palm Beach County	44	0.04
Roosevelt, NY (cdp) Nassau County	43	0.29
Exton, PA (cdp) Chester County	42	0.92
West Whiteland, PA (township) Chester County	42	0.23
Plainfield, NJ (city) Union County	42	0.09
Haverhill, MA (city) Essex County	42	0.07
Peoria, AZ (city) Yavapai County	42	0.03
Ardmore, OK (city) Carter County	41	0.17
Clearwater, FL (city) Pinellas County	41	0.04
Washington, DC (city) District of Columbia	41	0.01
Bloomfield, NJ (township) Essex County	40	0.08
Huntsville, AL (city) Madison County	39	0.02
Oakland, CA (city) Alameda County	39	0.01
South Lancaster, MA (cdp) Worcester County	38	2.17
Lancaster, MA (town) Worcester County	38	0.49
Pascagoula, MS (city) Jackson County	37	0.16
Pittsburgh, PA (city) Allegheny County	37	0.01
Albany, NY (city) Albany County	36	0.04
Bowie, MD (city) Prince George's County	35	0.06
Centereach, NY (cdp) Suffolk County	34	0.11
Oakland Park, FL (city) Broward County	34	0.08
Pearland, TX (city) Brazoria County	34	0.04
Brookhaven, NY (town) Suffolk County	34	0.01
Greensboro, NC (city) Guilford County	34	0.01
Melbourne Beach, FL (town) Brevard County	32	1.00
Chesapeake, VA (ind. city) Chesapeake independent city	32	0.01
Birmingham, AL (city) Jefferson County	30	0.01
Waco, TX (city) McLennan County	29	0.02
Philadelphia, PA (city) Philadelphia County	29	<0.01
Viera East, FL (cdp) Brevard County	28	0.24
East Orange, NJ (city) Essex County	28	0.04
Beckett, NJ (cdp) Gloucester County	27	0.57
Logan, NJ (township) Gloucester County	27	0.44
Lantana, FL (town) Palm Beach County	27	0.26
Iselin, NJ (cdp) Middlesex County	27	0.14
Lutz, FL (cdp) Hillsborough County	27	0.14
Woodbridge, NJ (township) Middlesex County	27	0.03
Providence, RI (city) Providence County	27	0.02
Chester, SC (city) Chester County	26	0.45
South Kensington, MD (cdp) Montgomery County	26	0.32
Scaggsville, MD (cdp) Howard County	26	0.11
West Hartford, CT (cdp/town) Hartford County	26	0.04
Glendale, AZ (city) Maricopa County	26	0.01
Raymond, NH (cdp) Rockingham County	25	0.89
Raymond, NH (town) Rockingham County	25	0.25
Englewood, NJ (city) Bergen County	25	0.09
North Branch, MI (village) Lapeer County	24	2.60
North Branch, MI (township) Lapeer County	24	0.65
Fitzgerald, GA (city) Ben Hill County	24	0.26
Salisbury, MD (city) Wicomico County	24	0.08
New Haven, CT (city/town) New Haven County	24	0.02
Virginia Beach, VA (ind. city) Virginia Beach independent city	24	0.01
Chicago, IL (city) Cook County	24	<0.01
Lochearn, MD (cdp) Baltimore County	22	0.09
Schertz, TX (city) Guadalupe County	22	0.08
Norfolk, VA (ind. city) Norfolk independent city	21	0.01
Watchung, NJ (borough) Somerset County	20	0.35
Pebble Creek, FL (cdp) Hillsborough County	20	0.26
Cayce, SC (city) Lexington County	20	0.16
East Hartford, CT (cdp/town) Hartford County	20	0.04
Noblesville, IN (city) Hamilton County	19	0.04
Urban Honolulu, HI (cdp) Honolulu County	19	0.01
Houston, TX (city) Harris County	19	<0.01
Glenarden, MD (city) Prince George's County	18	0.30
Clayton, OH (city) Montgomery County	18	0.14
Goldenrod, FL (cdp) Orange County	18	0.13
Jenison, MI (cdp) Ottawa County	18	0.10
Georgetown, MI (charter township) Ottawa County	18	0.04
Shoreline, WA (city) King County	18	0.03
Johns Creek, GA (city) Fulton County	18	0.02
Cibolo, TX (city) Guadalupe County	17	0.13
Cumru, PA (township) Berks County	17	0.11
Parkville, MD (cdp) Baltimore County	17	0.06
Santee, CA (city) San Diego County	17	0.03
Temple, TX (city) Bell County	17	0.03
Alexandria, VA (ind. city) Alexandria independent city	17	0.01
Fremont, NH (town) Rockingham County	16	0.38
Fern Park, FL (cdp) Seminole County	16	0.22
Takoma Park, MD (city) Montgomery County	16	0.09
West Falls Church, VA (cdp) Fairfax County	16	0.06
Hilton Head Island, SC (town) Beaufort County	16	0.04
Towson, MD (cdp) Baltimore County	16	0.03
Brandon, FL (cdp) Hillsborough County	16	0.02
Brooklyn, NY (borough) Kings County	16	<0.01
Charlotte, NC (city) Mecklenburg County	16	<0.01
Groton, MA (cdp) Middlesex County	15	1.12
Groton, MA (town) Middlesex County	15	0.15
Malden, MA (city) Middlesex County	15	0.03
Cambridge, MA (city) Middlesex County	15	0.01
Elk Grove, CA (city) Sacramento County	15	0.01
Gulf Breeze, FL (city) Santa Rosa County	14	0.24
Fairfax, CA (town) Marin County	14	0.19
Maxatawny, PA (township) Berks County	14	0.18
South Boston, VA (town) Halifax County	14	0.17
Kettering, MD (cdp) Prince George's County	14	0.11
Concord, MA (town) Middlesex County	14	0.08
Medford, MA (city) Middlesex County	14	0.03
Largo, FL (city) Pinellas County	14	0.02
Centennial, CO (city) Arapahoe County	14	0.01
Killeen, TX (city) Bell County	14	0.01
St. Louis, MO (city) St. Louis city County	14	<0.01
Green Island, NY (town/village) Albany County	13	0.51
Old Westbury, NY (village) Nassau County	13	0.33
Prospect, KY (city) Jefferson County	13	0.28
University of Virginia, VA (cdp) Albemarle County	13	0.19
Calimesa, CA (city) Riverside County	13	0.17
Greenbriar, VA (cdp) Fairfax County	13	0.17
Brooklyn Park, MD (cdp) Anne Arundel County	13	0.09
West Park, FL (city) Broward County	13	0.09
Berea, OH (city) Cuyahoga County	13	0.07
King of Prussia, PA (cdp) Montgomery County	13	0.07
New Castle, PA (city) Lawrence County	13	0.05
Stoughton, MA (town) Norfolk County	13	0.05
Upper Merion, PA (township) Montgomery County	13	0.05
Oyster Bay, NY (town) Nassau County	13	<0.01
Portland, OR (city) Multnomah County	13	<0.01
Thompsonville, IL (village) Franklin County	12	2.13
Bethany, CT (town) New Haven County	12	0.22
Thompson, CT (town) Windham County	12	0.13

Please refer to the Explanation of Data in the front of the book for more detailed information.

Ancestry

West Indian: Bermudan, excluding Hispanic

Top 150 Places Sorted by Percent of Total Population

Based on all places, regardless of total population

Place	Population	%
North Branch, MI (village) Lapeer County	24	2.60
South Lancaster, MA (cdp) Worcester County	38	2.17
Thompsonville, IL (village) Franklin County	12	2.13
Benson, VT (cdp) Rutland County	7	1.95
Montrose Manor, PA (cdp) Berks County	8	1.74
Progress, PA (cdp) Dauphin County	165	1.72
Forest Oaks, NC (cdp) Guilford County	58	1.71
Ozawkie, KS (city) Jefferson County	8	1.22
Salem, PA (township) Wayne County	47	1.12
Groton, MA (cdp) Middlesex County	15	1.12
Melbourne Beach, FL (town) Brevard County	32	1.00
Exton, PA (cdp) Chester County	42	0.92
Raymond, NH (cdp) Rockingham County	25	0.89
Susquehanna, PA (township) Dauphin County	165	0.70
Benson, VT (town) Rutland County	7	0.67
North Branch, MI (township) Lapeer County	24	0.65
Houston, DE (town) Kent County	3	0.58
Beckett, NJ (cdp) Gloucester County	27	0.57
Green Island, NY (town/village) Albany County	13	0.51
Lancaster, MA (town) Worcester County	38	0.49
Haltom City, TX (city) Tarrant County	196	0.47
Chester, SC (city) Chester County	26	0.45
Logan, NJ (township) Gloucester County	27	0.44
Natick, MA (town) Middlesex County	132	0.41
Lauderdale Lakes, FL (city) Broward County	131	0.40
Fremont, NH (town) Rockingham County	16	0.38
Watchung, NJ (borough) Somerset County	20	0.35
Monaghan, PA (township) York County	9	0.35
Socastee, SC (cdp) Horry County	57	0.33
Old Westbury, NY (village) Nassau County	13	0.33
South Kensington, MD (cdp) Montgomery County	26	0.32
Glenarden, MD (city) Prince George's County	18	0.30
Roosevelt, NY (cdp) Nassau County	43	0.29
Ellsworth, KS (city) Ellsworth County	9	0.29
Prospect, KY (city) Jefferson County	13	0.28
Lantana, FL (town) Palm Beach County	27	0.26
Fitzgerald, GA (city) Ben Hill County	24	0.26
Pebble Creek, FL (cdp) Hillsborough County	20	0.26
Bel-Nor, MO (village) St. Louis County	4	0.26
Raymond, NH (town) Rockingham County	25	0.25
Viera East, FL (cdp) Brevard County	28	0.24
Gulf Breeze, FL (city) Santa Rosa County	14	0.24
Lawnside, NJ (borough) Camden County	7	0.24
West Whiteland, PA (township) Chester County	42	0.23
Fern Park, FL (cdp) Seminole County	16	0.22
Bethany, CT (town) New Haven County	12	0.22
Colwyn, PA (borough) Delaware County	5	0.20
Suitland, MD (cdp) Prince George's County	47	0.19
Fairfax, CA (town) Marin County	14	0.19
University of Virginia, VA (cdp) Albemarle County	13	0.19
West Newbury, MA (town) Essex County	8	0.19
Maxatawny, PA (township) Berks County	14	0.18
Osceola, WI (town) Polk County	5	0.18
Olympia, WA (city) Thurston County	79	0.17
Ardmore, OK (city) Carter County	41	0.17
South Boston, VA (town) Halifax County	14	0.17
Calimesa, CA (city) Riverside County	13	0.17
Greenbriar, VA (cdp) Fairfax County	13	0.17
Los Ranchos de Albuquerque, NM (village) Bernalillo County	10	0.17
Pascagoula, MS (city) Jackson County	37	0.16
Cayce, SC (city) Lexington County	20	0.16
Pontiac, MI (city) Oakland County	89	0.15
Hackensack, NJ (city) Bergen County	64	0.15
North Royalton, OH (city) Cuyahoga County	45	0.15
Groton, MA (town) Middlesex County	15	0.15
Clermont, NY (town) Columbia County	3	0.15
Upper Nyack, NY (village) Rockland County	3	0.15
Iselin, NJ (cdp) Middlesex County	27	0.14
Lutz, FL (cdp) Hillsborough County	27	0.14
Clayton, OH (city) Montgomery County	18	0.14
Sanford, FL (city) Seminole County	67	0.13
Goldenrod, FL (cdp) Orange County	18	0.13
Cibolo, TX (city) Guadalupe County	17	0.13
Thompson, CT (town) Windham County	12	0.13
Diamondhead, MS (cdp) Hancock County	10	0.13
Mount Holly, NJ (township) Burlington County	12	0.12
Ocean, NJ (township) Ocean County	10	0.12
Cedar Hill, TX (city) Dallas County	45	0.11
Centereach, NY (cdp) Suffolk County	34	0.11
Scaggsville, MD (cdp) Howard County	26	0.11
Cumru, PA (township) Berks County	17	0.11
Kettering, MD (cdp) Prince George's County	14	0.11
Lanham, MD (cdp) Prince George's County	10	0.11
Iroquois Point, HI (cdp) Honolulu County	3	0.11
Jenison, MI (cdp) Ottawa County	18	0.10
Rossmoor, CA (cdp) Orange County	10	0.10
Woodbury, NJ (city) Gloucester County	10	0.10
Nevada, IA (city) Story County	7	0.10
Plainfield, NJ (city) Union County	42	0.09
Englewood, NJ (city) Bergen County	25	0.09
Lochearn, MD (cdp) Baltimore County	22	0.09
Takoma Park, MD (city) Montgomery County	16	0.09
Brooklyn Park, MD (cdp) Anne Arundel County	13	0.09
West Park, FL (city) Broward County	13	0.09
Short Hills, NJ (cdp) Essex County	12	0.09
Somers Point, NJ (city) Atlantic County	10	0.09
Horizon West, FL (cdp) Orange County	9	0.09
Bloomfield, NJ (township) Essex County	40	0.08
Oakland Park, FL (city) Broward County	34	0.08
Salisbury, MD (city) Wicomico County	24	0.08
Schertz, TX (city) Guadalupe County	22	0.08
Concord, MA (town) Middlesex County	14	0.08
Lower Gwynedd, PA (township) Montgomery County	9	0.08
Macedonia, OH (city) Summit County	9	0.08
Litchfield, CT (town) Litchfield County	7	0.08
Woodlyn, PA (cdp) Delaware County	7	0.08
Haverhill, MA (city) Essex County	42	0.07
Berea, OH (city) Cuyahoga County	13	0.07
King of Prussia, PA (cdp) Montgomery County	13	0.07
Tuskegee, AL (city) Macon County	7	0.07
Bowie, MD (city) Prince George's County	35	0.06
Parkville, MD (cdp) Baltimore County	17	0.06
West Falls Church, VA (cdp) Fairfax County	16	0.06
Millburn, NJ (township) Essex County	12	0.06
New Castle, PA (city) Lawrence County	13	0.05
Stoughton, MA (town) Norfolk County	13	0.05
Upper Merion, PA (township) Montgomery County	13	0.05
Augusta, ME (city) Kennebec County	10	0.05
Canton, MA (town) Norfolk County	10	0.05
Norton, MA (town) Bristol County	10	0.05
South Orange Village, NJ (township) Essex County	8	0.05
Travilah, MD (cdp) Montgomery County	6	0.05
Delaware, PA (township) Pike County	4	0.05
Pembroke Pines, FL (city) Broward County	67	0.04
West Palm Beach, FL (city) Palm Beach County	44	0.04
Clearwater, FL (city) Pinellas County	41	0.04
Albany, NY (city) Albany County	36	0.04
Pearland, TX (city) Brazoria County	34	0.04
East Orange, NJ (city) Essex County	28	0.04
West Hartford, CT (cdp/town) Hartford County	26	0.04
East Hartford, CT (cdp/town) Hartford County	20	0.04
Noblesville, IN (city) Hamilton County	19	0.04
Georgetown, MI (charter township) Ottawa County	18	0.04
Hilton Head Island, SC (town) Beaufort County	16	0.04
Middleborough, MA (town) Plymouth County	10	0.04
Newport, RI (city) Newport County	10	0.04
Old Bridge, NJ (cdp) Middlesex County	10	0.04
Shaker Heights, OH (city) Cuyahoga County	10	0.04
Red Bank, NJ (borough) Monmouth County	5	0.04
Marshall, PA (township) Allegheny County	3	0.04
Boston, MA (city) Suffolk County	157	0.03
Newark, NJ (city) Essex County	70	0.03
Tallahassee, FL (city) Leon County	47	0.03
Worcester, MA (city) Worcester County	45	0.03
Peoria, AZ (city) Yavapai County	42	0.03
Woodbridge, NJ (township) Middlesex County	27	0.03
Shoreline, WA (city) King County	18	0.03
Santee, CA (city) San Diego County	17	0.03
Temple, TX (city) Bell County	17	0.03
Towson, MD (cdp) Baltimore County	16	0.03

Please refer to the Explanation of Data in the front of the book for more detailed information.

Ancestry

West Indian: Bermudan, excluding Hispanic

Top 150 Places Sorted by Percent of Total Population

Based on places with total population of 7,500 or more

Place	Population	%
Progress, PA (cdp) Dauphin County	165	1.72
Susquehanna, PA (township) Dauphin County	165	0.70
Lancaster, MA (town) Worcester County	38	0.49
Haltom City, TX (city) Tarrant County	196	0.47
Natick, MA (town) Middlesex County	132	0.41
Lauderdale Lakes, FL (city) Broward County	131	0.40
Socastee, SC (cdp) Horry County	57	0.33
South Kensington, MD (cdp) Montgomery County	26	0.32
Roosevelt, NY (cdp) Nassau County	43	0.29
Lantana, FL (town) Palm Beach County	27	0.26
Fitzgerald, GA (city) Ben Hill County	24	0.26
Pebble Creek, FL (cdp) Hillsborough County	20	0.26
Raymond, NH (town) Rockingham County	25	0.25
Viera East, FL (cdp) Brevard County	28	0.24
West Whiteland, PA (township) Chester County	42	0.23
Suitland, MD (cdp) Prince George's County	47	0.19
Maxatawny, PA (township) Berks County	14	0.18
Olympia, WA (city) Thurston County	79	0.17
Ardmore, OK (city) Carter County	41	0.17
South Boston, VA (town) Halifax County	14	0.17
Calimesa, CA (city) Riverside County	13	0.17
Greenbriar, VA (cdp) Fairfax County	13	0.17
Pascagoula, MS (city) Jackson County	37	0.16
Cayce, SC (city) Lexington County	20	0.16
Pontiac, MI (city) Oakland County	89	0.15
Hackensack, NJ (city) Bergen County	64	0.15
North Royalton, OH (city) Cuyahoga County	45	0.15
Groton, MA (town) Middlesex County	15	0.15
Iselin, NJ (cdp) Middlesex County	27	0.14
Lutz, FL (cdp) Hillsborough County	27	0.14
Clayton, OH (city) Montgomery County	18	0.14
Sanford, FL (city) Seminole County	67	0.13
Goldenrod, FL (cdp) Orange County	18	0.13
Cibolo, TX (city) Guadalupe County	17	0.13
Thompson, CT (town) Windham County	12	0.13
Diamondhead, MS (cdp) Hancock County	10	0.13
Mount Holly, NJ (township) Burlington County	12	0.12
Ocean, NJ (township) Ocean County	10	0.12
Cedar Hill, TX (city) Dallas County	45	0.11
Centereach, NY (cdp) Suffolk County	34	0.11
Scaggsville, MD (cdp) Howard County	26	0.11
Cumru, PA (township) Berks County	17	0.11
Kettering, MD (cdp) Prince George's County	14	0.11
Lanham, MD (cdp) Prince George's County	10	0.11
Jenison, MI (cdp) Ottawa County	18	0.10
Rossmoor, CA (cdp) Orange County	10	0.10
Woodbury, NJ (city) Gloucester County	10	0.10
Plainfield, NJ (city) Union County	42	0.09
Englewood, NJ (city) Bergen County	25	0.09
Lochearn, MD (cdp) Baltimore County	22	0.09
Takoma Park, MD (city) Montgomery County	16	0.09
Brooklyn Park, MD (cdp) Anne Arundel County	13	0.09
West Park, FL (city) Broward County	13	0.09
Short Hills, NJ (cdp) Essex County	12	0.09
Somers Point, NJ (city) Atlantic County	10	0.09
Horizon West, FL (cdp) Orange County	9	0.09
Bloomfield, NJ (township) Essex County	40	0.08
Oakland Park, FL (city) Broward County	34	0.08
Salisbury, MD (city) Wicomico County	24	0.08
Schertz, TX (city) Guadalupe County	22	0.08
Concord, MA (town) Middlesex County	14	0.08
Lower Gwynedd, PA (township) Montgomery County	9	0.08
Macedonia, OH (city) Summit County	9	0.08
Litchfield, CT (town) Litchfield County	7	0.08
Woodlyn, PA (cdp) Delaware County	7	0.08
Haverhill, MA (city) Essex County	42	0.07
Berea, OH (city) Cuyahoga County	13	0.07
King of Prussia, PA (cdp) Montgomery County	13	0.07
Tuskegee, AL (city) Macon County	7	0.07
Bowie, MD (city) Prince George's County	35	0.06
Parkville, MD (cdp) Baltimore County	17	0.06
West Falls Church, VA (cdp) Fairfax County	16	0.06
Millburn, NJ (township) Essex County	12	0.06
New Castle, PA (city) Lawrence County	13	0.05
Stoughton, MA (town) Norfolk County	13	0.05
Upper Merion, PA (township) Montgomery County	13	0.05
Augusta, ME (city) Kennebec County	10	0.05
Canton, MA (town) Norfolk County	10	0.05
Norton, MA (town) Bristol County	10	0.05
South Orange Village, NJ (township) Essex County	8	0.05
Travilah, MD (cdp) Montgomery County	6	0.05
Pembroke Pines, FL (city) Broward County	67	0.04
West Palm Beach, FL (city) Palm Beach County	44	0.04
Clearwater, FL (city) Pinellas County	41	0.04
Albany, NY (city) Albany County	36	0.04
Pearland, TX (city) Brazoria County	34	0.04
East Orange, NJ (city) Essex County	28	0.04
West Hartford, CT (cdp/town) Hartford County	26	0.04
East Hartford, CT (cdp/town) Hartford County	20	0.04
Noblesville, IN (city) Hamilton County	19	0.04
Georgetown, MI (charter township) Ottawa County	18	0.04
Hilton Head Island, SC (town) Beaufort County	16	0.04
Middleborough, MA (town) Plymouth County	10	0.04
Newport, RI (city) Newport County	10	0.04
Old Bridge, NJ (cdp) Middlesex County	10	0.04
Shaker Heights, OH (city) Cuyahoga County	10	0.04
Red Bank, NJ (borough) Monmouth County	5	0.04
Boston, MA (city) Suffolk County	157	0.03
Newark, NJ (city) Essex County	70	0.03
Tallahassee, FL (city) Leon County	47	0.03
Worcester, MA (city) Worcester County	45	0.03
Peoria, AZ (city) Yavapai County	42	0.03
Woodbridge, NJ (township) Middlesex County	27	0.03
Shoreline, WA (city) King County	18	0.03
Santee, CA (city) San Diego County	17	0.03
Temple, TX (city) Bell County	17	0.03
Towson, MD (cdp) Baltimore County	16	0.03
Malden, MA (city) Middlesex County	15	0.03
Medford, MA (city) Middlesex County	14	0.03
Moorhead, MN (city) Clay County	12	0.03
Glenview, IL (village) Cook County	11	0.03
Hinesville, GA (city) Liberty County	11	0.03
Apex, NC (town) Wake County	10	0.03
Carney, MD (cdp) Baltimore County	9	0.03
Michigan City, IN (city) LaPorte County	9	0.03
Warminster, PA (township) Bucks County	9	0.03
Nutley, NJ (township) Essex County	8	0.03
Cranford, NJ (township) Union County	7	0.03
Princeton, FL (cdp) Miami-Dade County	6	0.03
Huntsville, AL (city) Madison County	39	0.02
Waco, TX (city) McLennan County	29	0.02
Providence, RI (city) Providence County	27	0.02
New Haven, CT (city/town) New Haven County	24	0.02
Johns Creek, GA (city) Fulton County	18	0.02
Brandon, FL (cdp) Hillsborough County	16	0.02
Largo, FL (city) Pinellas County	14	0.02
Fayetteville, AR (city) Washington County	12	0.02
Union City, CA (city) Alameda County	12	0.02
Cleveland Heights, OH (city) Cuyahoga County	11	0.02
Charlottesville, VA (ind. city) Charlottesville independent city	10	0.02
Old Bridge, NJ (township) Middlesex County	10	0.02
Union, NJ (township) Union County	10	0.02
Hempstead, NY (village) Nassau County	9	0.02
Wesley Chapel, FL (cdp) Pasco County	9	0.02
Bedford, TX (city) Tarrant County	8	0.02
Maplewood, MN (city) Ramsey County	8	0.02
Milford, CT (city) New Haven County	8	0.02
Milford, CT (town) New Haven County	8	0.02
Ridley, PA (township) Delaware County	7	0.02
New York, NY (city) Kings County	518	0.01
Bronx, NY (borough) Bronx County	198	0.01
Queens, NY (borough) Queens County	177	0.01
Manhattan, NY (borough) New York County	127	0.01
Jacksonville, FL (city) Duval County	101	0.01
San Antonio, TX (city) Medina County	68	0.01
Hempstead, NY (town) Nassau County	52	0.01
Miami, FL (city) Miami-Dade County	52	0.01
Baltimore, MD (city) Baltimore city County	48	0.01
Washington, DC (city) District of Columbia	41	0.01
Oakland, CA (city) Alameda County	39	0.01

Please refer to the Explanation of Data in the front of the book for more detailed information.

SECTION THREE

Ancestry

West Indian: British West Indian, excluding Hispanic

U.S. and 50 States Sorted by Population and Percent of Total Population

Place	Population	%
United States	**91,048**	**0.03**
New York	49,916	0.26
Florida	12,326	0.07
New Jersey	5,719	0.07
Georgia	3,105	0.03
Maryland	2,637	0.05
Massachusetts	2,076	0.03
Texas	2,023	0.01
California	1,757	<0.01
Connecticut	1,702	0.05
Pennsylvania	1,596	0.01
Virginia	1,335	0.02
North Carolina	1,029	0.01
Ohio	457	<0.01
Louisiana	389	0.01
Indiana	347	0.01
Illinois	345	<0.01
Michigan	301	<0.01
District of Columbia	296	0.05
Arizona	276	<0.01
Missouri	262	<0.01
Colorado	250	0.01
South Carolina	242	0.01
Alaska	231	0.03
Washington	215	<0.01
Tennessee	209	<0.01
Delaware	204	0.02
Oklahoma	189	0.01
Rhode Island	188	0.02
Alabama	183	<0.01
Iowa	158	0.01
Wisconsin	158	<0.01
Nevada	130	<0.01
Mississippi	115	<0.01
New Mexico	107	0.01
New Hampshire	91	0.01
Kansas	91	<0.01
Minnesota	79	<0.01
Nebraska	59	<0.01
Oregon	52	<0.01
Maine	51	<0.01
Arkansas	40	<0.01
West Virginia	39	<0.01
Kentucky	34	<0.01
Utah	28	<0.01
Vermont	6	<0.01
North Dakota	5	<0.01
Hawaii	0	0.00
Idaho	0	0.00
Montana	0	0.00
South Dakota	0	0.00
Wyoming	0	0.00

Place	Population	%
New York	49,916	0.26
Florida	12,326	0.07
New Jersey	5,719	0.07
Maryland	2,637	0.05
Connecticut	1,702	0.05
District of Columbia	296	0.05
United States	**91,048**	**0.03**
Georgia	3,105	0.03
Massachusetts	2,076	0.03
Alaska	231	0.03
Virginia	1,335	0.02
Delaware	204	0.02
Rhode Island	188	0.02
Texas	2,023	0.01
Pennsylvania	1,596	0.01
North Carolina	1,029	0.01
Louisiana	389	0.01
Indiana	347	0.01
Colorado	250	0.01
South Carolina	242	0.01
Oklahoma	189	0.01
Iowa	158	0.01
New Mexico	107	0.01
New Hampshire	91	0.01
California	1,757	<0.01
Ohio	457	<0.01
Illinois	345	<0.01
Michigan	301	<0.01
Arizona	276	<0.01
Missouri	262	<0.01
Washington	215	<0.01
Tennessee	209	<0.01
Alabama	183	<0.01
Wisconsin	158	<0.01
Nevada	130	<0.01
Mississippi	115	<0.01
Kansas	91	<0.01
Minnesota	79	<0.01
Nebraska	59	<0.01
Oregon	52	<0.01
Maine	51	<0.01
Arkansas	40	<0.01
West Virginia	39	<0.01
Kentucky	34	<0.01
Utah	28	<0.01
Vermont	6	<0.01
North Dakota	5	<0.01
Hawaii	0	0.00
Idaho	0	0.00
Montana	0	0.00
South Dakota	0	0.00
Wyoming	0	0.00

Please refer to the Explanation of Data in the front of the book for more detailed information.

Ancestry

West Indian: British West Indian, excluding Hispanic

Top 150 Places Sorted by Population

Based on all places, regardless of total population

Place	Population	%
New York, NY (city) Kings County	44,326	0.55
Brooklyn, NY (borough) Kings County	30,607	1.24
Bronx, NY (borough) Bronx County	7,136	0.52
Queens, NY (borough) Queens County	4,689	0.21
Manhattan, NY (borough) New York County	1,658	0.10
Hempstead, NY (town) Nassau County	972	0.13
Boston, MA (city) Suffolk County	798	0.13
Perth Amboy, NJ (city) Middlesex County	735	1.46
Jersey City, NJ (city) Hudson County	638	0.26
Philadelphia, PA (city) Philadelphia County	541	0.04
Yonkers, NY (city) Westchester County	497	0.26
Islip, NY (town) Suffolk County	470	0.14
Bridgeport, CT (city/town) Fairfield County	453	0.32
Miami Gardens, FL (city) Miami-Dade County	438	0.41
Pine Hills, FL (cdp) Orange County	425	0.64
Mount Vernon, NY (city) Westchester County	348	0.52
Orlando, FL (city) Orange County	342	0.15
Miami, FL (city) Miami-Dade County	338	0.09
Fayetteville, NC (city) Cumberland County	333	0.17
Hollywood, FL (city) Broward County	329	0.23
Fort Lauderdale, FL (city) Broward County	318	0.19
East Orange, NJ (city) Essex County	310	0.48
Los Angeles, CA (city) Los Angeles County	308	0.01
Virginia Beach, VA (ind. city) Virginia Beach independent city	302	0.07
Irvington, NJ (township) Essex County	300	0.55
Jacksonville, FL (city) Duval County	300	0.04
Wallkill, NY (town) Orange County	296	1.09
Washington, DC (city) District of Columbia	296	0.05
Miramar, FL (city) Broward County	292	0.26
Newark, NJ (city) Essex County	291	0.11
East Lake-Orient Park, FL (cdp) Hillsborough County	275	1.15
Wawayanda, NY (town) Orange County	271	3.79
North Lauderdale, FL (city) Broward County	265	0.65
Bay Shore, NY (cdp) Suffolk County	253	0.91
Ramapo, NY (town) Rockland County	253	0.21
Hempstead, NY (village) Nassau County	250	0.47
Plantation, FL (city) Broward County	250	0.29
Pembroke Pines, FL (city) Broward County	246	0.16
Deerfield Beach, FL (city) Broward County	242	0.32
Staten Island, NY (borough) Richmond County	236	0.05
Golden Glades, FL (cdp) Miami-Dade County	230	0.70
Brockton, MA (city) Plymouth County	230	0.25
New Britain, CT (city/town) Hartford County	228	0.31
Rochester, NY (city) Monroe County	223	0.11
Scotchtown, NY (cdp) Orange County	222	2.28
Titusville, FL (city) Brevard County	215	0.49
Albany, NY (city) Albany County	210	0.21
Hartford, CT (city/town) Hartford County	209	0.17
Temecula, CA (city) Riverside County	198	0.21
Garland, TX (city) Dallas County	196	0.09
University, FL (cdp) Hillsborough County	194	0.48
Baltimore, MD (city) Baltimore city County	194	0.03
Valrico, FL (cdp) Hillsborough County	186	0.54
Lauderhill, FL (city) Broward County	185	0.28
Covington, GA (city) Newton County	184	1.39
Asbury Park, NJ (city) Monmouth County	183	1.12
Grambling, LA (city) Lincoln Parish	182	3.71
Franklin, NJ (township) Somerset County	182	0.30
South Miami Heights, FL (cdp) Miami-Dade County	180	0.49
Princeton, NJ (township) Mercer County	179	1.09
Anchorage, AK (municipality) Anchorage Municipality	177	0.06
Springfield, MA (city) Hampden County	176	0.12
Hackensack, NJ (city) Bergen County	171	0.40
Baytown, TX (city) Harris County	171	0.24
Margate, FL (city) Broward County	170	0.32
Maplewood, NJ (township) Essex County	168	0.71
Uniondale, NY (cdp) Nassau County	166	0.68
Columbus, OH (city) Franklin County	165	0.02
Bradenton, FL (city) Manatee County	159	0.31
Chandler, AZ (city) Maricopa County	158	0.07
West Palm Beach, FL (city) Palm Beach County	157	0.16
Oyster Bay, NY (town) Nassau County	157	0.05
West Orange, NJ (township) Essex County	156	0.34
Scaggsville, MD (cdp) Howard County	154	0.67
New Rochelle, NY (city) Westchester County	153	0.20
West Deptford, NJ (township) Gloucester County	151	0.70
Kansas City, MO (city) Jackson County	148	0.03
Montgomery Village, MD (cdp) Montgomery County	147	0.46
Tamarac, FL (city) Broward County	147	0.25
Silver Spring, MD (cdp) Montgomery County	146	0.21
Roanoke Rapids, NC (city) Halifax County	142	0.90
Woodbridge, NJ (township) Middlesex County	142	0.14
Maitland, FL (city) Orange County	140	0.89
Valley Stream, NY (village) Nassau County	139	0.38
Atlanta, GA (city) Fulton County	139	0.03
West Park, FL (city) Broward County	137	0.96
Ensley, FL (cdp) Escambia County	136	0.75
Norfolk, VA (ind. city) Norfolk independent city	136	0.06
Tampa, FL (city) Hillsborough County	131	0.04
Spring Valley, NY (village) Rockland County	130	0.43
Houston, TX (city) Harris County	130	0.01
North Fort Myers, FL (cdp) Lee County	123	0.30
Meadowbrook, VA (cdp) Chesterfield County	122	0.63
Coral Springs, FL (city) Broward County	121	0.10
Augusta-Richmond County, GA (cons. govt) Richmond County	120	0.06
North Amityville, NY (cdp) Suffolk County	119	0.67
Babylon, NY (town) Suffolk County	119	0.06
Boca Raton, FL (city) Palm Beach County	117	0.14
St. Petersburg, FL (city) Pinellas County	115	0.05
Buffalo, NY (city) Erie County	115	0.04
Randolph, MA (cdp/town) Norfolk County	114	0.36
Montclair, NJ (township) Essex County	114	0.30
Town 'n' Country, FL (cdp) Hillsborough County	114	0.15
Chillum, MD (cdp) Prince George's County	113	0.32
Dallas, TX (city) Dallas County	113	0.01
San Diego, CA (city) San Diego County	112	0.01
Holly Springs, GA (city) Cherokee County	111	1.33
Hyattsville, MD (city) Prince George's County	108	0.63
Sunrise, FL (city) Broward County	108	0.13
Ontario, CA (city) San Bernardino County	107	0.06
Seattle, WA (city) King County	107	0.02
Lompoc, CA (city) Santa Barbara County	103	0.25
Chicago, IL (city) Cook County	103	<0.01
Elizabeth, NJ (city) Union County	101	0.08
New Haven, CT (city/town) New Haven County	101	0.08
City of Orange, NJ (township) Essex County	100	0.33
West Haven, CT (city/town) New Haven County	100	0.18
Kettering, MD (cdp) Prince George's County	99	0.79
Opa-locka, FL (city) Miami-Dade County	99	0.66
Wheaton, MD (cdp) Montgomery County	99	0.22
Buenaventura Lakes, FL (cdp) Osceola County	97	0.36
Palm Bay, FL (city) Brevard County	97	0.10
Baldwin, NY (cdp) Nassau County	96	0.40
Hillcrest, NY (cdp) Rockland County	93	1.13
Delray Beach, FL (city) Palm Beach County	93	0.15
Slickville, PA (cdp) Westmoreland County	91	23.45
Salem, PA (township) Westmoreland County	91	1.37
Crofton, MD (cdp) Anne Arundel County	91	0.33
Wichita Falls, TX (city) Wichita County	91	0.09
Newport News, VA (ind. city) Newport News independent city	91	0.05
Hicksville, NY (cdp) Nassau County	90	0.22
Freeport, NY (village) Nassau County	90	0.21
Taunton, MA (city) Bristol County	90	0.16
Ocean, NJ (township) Monmouth County	89	0.33
Brandon, FL (cdp) Hillsborough County	89	0.09
Stockbridge, GA (city) Henry County	88	0.37
Ames, IA (city) Story County	88	0.15
North Miami, FL (city) Miami-Dade County	88	0.15
Lawton, OK (city) Comanche County	88	0.09
Providence, RI (city) Providence County	88	0.05
Madison Park, NJ (cdp) Middlesex County	87	1.27
Franklin Park, NJ (cdp) Somerset County	87	0.69
Montclair, VA (cdp) Prince William County	87	0.45
Old Bridge, NJ (township) Middlesex County	87	0.13
Miami Shores, FL (village) Miami-Dade County	86	0.82
Teaneck, NJ (township) Bergen County	86	0.22
Fish Hawk, FL (cdp) Hillsborough County	85	0.66
Central Islip, NY (cdp) Suffolk County	85	0.24
The Acreage, FL (cdp) Palm Beach County	84	0.22
East Hartford, CT (cdp/town) Hartford County	84	0.16

SECTION THREE

Please refer to the Explanation of Data in the front of the book for more detailed information.

Ancestry

West Indian: British West Indian, excluding Hispanic

Top 150 Places Sorted by Percent of Total Population

Based on all places, regardless of total population

Place	Population	%
Slickville, PA (cdp) Westmoreland County	91	23.45
Thompson, PA (township) Susquehanna County	26	5.18
Iowa Colony, TX (village) Brazoria County	56	4.22
Wawayanda, NY (town) Orange County	271	3.79
Grambling, LA (city) Lincoln Parish	182	3.71
Flemington, GA (city) Liberty County	28	2.86
Clarcona, FL (cdp) Orange County	72	2.79
Scotchtown, NY (cdp) Orange County	222	2.28
Price, PA (township) Monroe County	75	2.15
Jarales, NM (cdp) Valencia County	44	2.12
Marlboro Meadows, MD (cdp) Prince George's County	76	2.09
Amagansett, NY (cdp) Suffolk County	17	1.90
South Lancaster, MA (cdp) Worcester County	32	1.83
Kenwood Estates, FL (cdp) Palm Beach County	17	1.54
Cumberland Head, NY (cdp) Clinton County	25	1.51
Perth Amboy, NJ (city) Middlesex County	735	1.46
Watertown, MN (township) Carver County	15	1.40
Covington, GA (city) Newton County	184	1.39
Salem, PA (township) Westmoreland County	91	1.37
Harvest, AL (cdp) Madison County	59	1.34
Holly Springs, GA (city) Cherokee County	111	1.33
Madison Park, NJ (cdp) Middlesex County	87	1.27
Brooklyn, NY (borough) Kings County	30,607	1.24
Packer, PA (township) Carbon County	12	1.23
West Ocean City, MD (cdp) Worcester County	55	1.21
East Lake-Orient Park, FL (cdp) Hillsborough County	275	1.15
Pembroke Park, FL (town) Broward County	67	1.14
Hillcrest, NY (cdp) Rockland County	93	1.13
Asbury Park, NJ (city) Monmouth County	183	1.12
Franklin Center, NJ (cdp) Somerset County	43	1.10
Wallkill, NY (town) Orange County	296	1.09
Princeton, NJ (township) Mercer County	179	1.09
Norton Center, MA (cdp) Bristol County	28	1.08
Palo Alto, PA (borough) Schuylkill County	11	1.06
El Portal, FL (village) Miami-Dade County	25	1.04
McConnell AFB, KS (cdp) Sedgwick County	17	0.99
Pigeon Falls, WI (village) Trempealeau County	3	0.97
West Park, FL (city) Broward County	137	0.96
Bay Shore, NY (cdp) Suffolk County	253	0.91
Roanoke Rapids, NC (city) Halifax County	142	0.90
Maitland, FL (city) Orange County	140	0.89
Preston, WI (town) Trempealeau County	9	0.87
Highland, NY (cdp) Ulster County	49	0.86
Mechanicstown, NY (cdp) Orange County	63	0.84
Maywood, NJ (borough) Bergen County	79	0.83
Miami Shores, FL (village) Miami-Dade County	86	0.82
Royal Palm Estates, FL (cdp) Palm Beach County	30	0.82
Kettering, MD (cdp) Prince George's County	99	0.79
Belfast, NY (cdp) Allegany County	7	0.79
Middletown, NY (town) Delaware County	29	0.76
Ensley, FL (cdp) Escambia County	136	0.75
Greenville, NY (town) Orange County	34	0.75
Big Flats, NY (cdp) Chemung County	41	0.74
Bridge City, LA (cdp) Jefferson Parish	67	0.73
Mineville, NY (cdp) Essex County	10	0.73
Maplewood, NJ (township) Essex County	168	0.71
North Great River, NY (cdp) Suffolk County	27	0.71
Golden Glades, FL (cdp) Miami-Dade County	230	0.70
West Deptford, NJ (township) Gloucester County	151	0.70
Pleasant Valley, NY (town) Dutchess County	67	0.70
Franklin Park, NJ (cdp) Somerset County	87	0.69
Golden Grove, SC (cdp) Greenville County	21	0.69
Uniondale, NY (cdp) Nassau County	166	0.68
Woodlawn, MD (cdp) Prince George's County	44	0.68
Rosemount, OH (cdp) Scioto County	15	0.68
Scaggsville, MD (cdp) Howard County	154	0.67
North Amityville, NY (cdp) Suffolk County	119	0.67
Westview, FL (cdp) Miami-Dade County	63	0.67
Oronoko, MI (charter township) Berrien County	62	0.67
Opa-locka, FL (city) Miami-Dade County	99	0.66
Fish Hawk, FL (cdp) Hillsborough County	85	0.66
Avon, IN (town) Hendricks County	77	0.66
Downingtown, PA (borough) Chester County	52	0.66
North Lauderdale, FL (city) Broward County	265	0.65
Richmond Hill, GA (city) Bryan County	58	0.65

Place	Population	%
Pine Hills, FL (cdp) Orange County	425	0.64
New Carrollton, MD (city) Prince George's County	77	0.64
Laurens, SC (city) Laurens County	59	0.64
Landover Hills, MD (town) Prince George's County	12	0.64
Meadowbrook, VA (cdp) Chesterfield County	122	0.63
Hyattsville, MD (city) Prince George's County	108	0.63
Indian Mountain Lake, PA (cdp) Monroe County	32	0.63
East New Market, MD (town) Dorchester County	2	0.63
McChord AFB, WA (cdp) Pierce County	19	0.61
Brooklyn, CT (cdp) Windham County	8	0.61
Upper Montclair, NJ (cdp) Essex County	68	0.59
Cheverly, MD (town) Prince George's County	36	0.58
Hillsdale, NY (town) Columbia County	11	0.57
New York, NY (city) Kings County	44,326	0.55
Irvington, NJ (township) Essex County	300	0.55
Valrico, FL (cdp) Hillsborough County	186	0.54
Bogota, NJ (borough) Bergen County	44	0.54
Big Flats, NY (town) Chemung County	41	0.54
Mount Rainier, MD (city) Prince George's County	43	0.53
Bronx, NY (borough) Bronx County	7,136	0.52
Mount Vernon, NY (city) Westchester County	348	0.52
Perkiomen, PA (township) Montgomery County	46	0.52
Nyack, NY (village) Rockland County	36	0.52
East Garden City, NY (cdp) Nassau County	29	0.52
Manvel, TX (city) Brazoria County	25	0.52
Titusville, FL (city) Brevard County	215	0.49
South Miami Heights, FL (cdp) Miami-Dade County	180	0.49
Stroudsburg, PA (borough) Monroe County	28	0.49
East Orange, NJ (city) Essex County	310	0.48
University, FL (cdp) Hillsborough County	194	0.48
Oakville, CT (cdp) Litchfield County	45	0.48
Clewiston, FL (city) Hendry County	34	0.48
Hempstead, NY (village) Nassau County	250	0.47
Sadsbury, PA (township) Chester County	16	0.47
Montgomery Village, MD (cdp) Montgomery County	147	0.46
Lloyd, NY (town) Ulster County	49	0.46
Montclair, VA (cdp) Prince William County	87	0.45
South Floral Park, NY (village) Nassau County	7	0.45
Brownsville, FL (cdp) Miami-Dade County	58	0.44
Belfast, NY (town) Allegany County	7	0.44
Spring Valley, NY (village) Rockland County	130	0.43
Colonia, NJ (cdp) Middlesex County	78	0.43
South Valley Stream, NY (cdp) Nassau County	22	0.42
Miami Gardens, FL (city) Miami-Dade County	438	0.41
Marlboro Village, MD (cdp) Prince George's County	38	0.41
Lancaster, MA (town) Worcester County	32	0.41
Norwood Court, MO (town) St. Louis County	4	0.41
Hackensack, NJ (city) Bergen County	171	0.40
Baldwin, NY (cdp) Nassau County	96	0.40
Williamstown, NJ (cdp) Gloucester County	57	0.40
Jefferson, LA (cdp) Jefferson Parish	48	0.40
Wysox, PA (township) Bradford County	7	0.40
Shelburne, MA (town) Franklin County	8	0.39
Garrison, ND (city) McLean County	5	0.39
Valley Stream, NY (village) Nassau County	139	0.38
Clayton, DE (town) Kent County	10	0.38
Stockbridge, GA (city) Henry County	88	0.37
Binghamton University, NY (cdp) Broome County	26	0.37
Randolph, MA (cdp/town) Norfolk County	114	0.36
Buenaventura Lakes, FL (cdp) Osceola County	97	0.36
West Orange, NJ (township) Essex County	156	0.34
Groveton, VA (cdp) Fairfax County	46	0.34
Greentree, NJ (cdp) Camden County	39	0.34
Woodland, WA (city) Cowlitz County	18	0.34
Port Reading, NJ (cdp) Middlesex County	12	0.34
Horicon, NY (town) Warren County	5	0.34
City of Orange, NJ (township) Essex County	100	0.33
Crofton, MD (cdp) Anne Arundel County	91	0.33
Ocean, NJ (township) Monmouth County	89	0.33
Rotterdam, NY (cdp) Schenectady County	68	0.33
Silver Springs Shores, FL (cdp) Marion County	23	0.33
Wesley Hills, NY (village) Rockland County	18	0.33
Bridgeport, CT (city/town) Fairfield County	453	0.32
Deerfield Beach, FL (city) Broward County	242	0.32
Margate, FL (city) Broward County	170	0.32

Ancestry

West Indian: British West Indian, excluding Hispanic

Top 150 Places Sorted by Percent of Total Population

Based on places with total population of 7,500 or more

Place	Population	%
Scotchtown, NY (cdp) Orange County	222	2.28
Perth Amboy, NJ (city) Middlesex County	735	1.46
Covington, GA (city) Newton County	184	1.39
Holly Springs, GA (city) Cherokee County	111	1.33
Brooklyn, NY (borough) Kings County	30,607	1.24
East Lake-Orient Park, FL (cdp) Hillsborough County	275	1.15
Hillcrest, NY (cdp) Rockland County	93	1.13
Asbury Park, NJ (city) Monmouth County	183	1.12
Wallkill, NY (town) Orange County	296	1.09
Princeton, NJ (township) Mercer County	179	1.09
West Park, FL (city) Broward County	137	0.96
Bay Shore, NY (cdp) Suffolk County	253	0.91
Roanoke Rapids, NC (city) Halifax County	142	0.90
Maitland, FL (city) Orange County	140	0.89
Maywood, NJ (borough) Bergen County	79	0.83
Miami Shores, FL (village) Miami-Dade County	86	0.82
Kettering, MD (cdp) Prince George's County	99	0.79
Ensley, FL (cdp) Escambia County	136	0.75
Bridge City, LA (cdp) Jefferson Parish	67	0.73
Maplewood, NJ (township) Essex County	168	0.71
Golden Glades, FL (cdp) Miami-Dade County	230	0.70
West Deptford, NJ (township) Gloucester County	151	0.70
Pleasant Valley, NY (town) Dutchess County	67	0.70
Franklin Park, NJ (cdp) Somerset County	87	0.69
Uniondale, NY (cdp) Nassau County	166	0.68
Scaggsville, MD (cdp) Howard County	154	0.67
North Amityville, NY (cdp) Suffolk County	119	0.67
Westview, FL (cdp) Miami-Dade County	63	0.67
Oronoko, MI (charter township) Berrien County	62	0.67
Opa-locka, FL (city) Miami-Dade County	99	0.66
Fish Hawk, FL (cdp) Hillsborough County	85	0.66
Avon, IN (town) Hendricks County	77	0.66
Downingtown, PA (borough) Chester County	52	0.66
North Lauderdale, FL (city) Broward County	265	0.65
Richmond Hill, GA (city) Bryan County	58	0.65
Pine Hills, FL (cdp) Orange County	425	0.64
New Carrollton, MD (city) Prince George's County	77	0.64
Laurens, SC (city) Laurens County	59	0.64
Meadowbrook, VA (cdp) Chesterfield County	122	0.63
Hyattsville, MD (city) Prince George's County	108	0.63
Upper Montclair, NJ (cdp) Essex County	68	0.59
New York, NY (city) Kings County	44,326	0.55
Irvington, NJ (township) Essex County	300	0.55
Valrico, FL (cdp) Hillsborough County	186	0.54
Bogota, NJ (borough) Bergen County	44	0.54
Big Flats, NY (town) Chemung County	41	0.54
Mount Rainier, MD (city) Prince George's County	43	0.53
Bronx, NY (borough) Bronx County	7,136	0.52
Mount Vernon, NY (city) Westchester County	348	0.52
Perkiomen, PA (township) Montgomery County	46	0.52
Titusville, FL (city) Brevard County	215	0.49
South Miami Heights, FL (cdp) Miami-Dade County	180	0.49
East Orange, NJ (city) Essex County	310	0.48
University, FL (cdp) Hillsborough County	194	0.48
Oakville, CT (cdp) Litchfield County	45	0.48
Hempstead, NY (village) Nassau County	250	0.47
Montgomery Village, MD (cdp) Montgomery County	147	0.46
Lloyd, NY (town) Ulster County	49	0.46
Montclair, VA (cdp) Prince William County	87	0.45
Brownsville, FL (cdp) Miami-Dade County	58	0.44
Spring Valley, NY (village) Rockland County	130	0.43
Colonia, NJ (cdp) Middlesex County	78	0.43
Miami Gardens, FL (city) Miami-Dade County	438	0.41
Marlboro Village, MD (cdp) Prince George's County	38	0.41
Lancaster, MA (town) Worcester County	32	0.41
Hackensack, NJ (city) Bergen County	171	0.40
Baldwin, NY (cdp) Nassau County	96	0.40
Williamstown, NJ (cdp) Gloucester County	57	0.40
Jefferson, LA (cdp) Jefferson Parish	48	0.40
Valley Stream, NY (village) Nassau County	139	0.38
Stockbridge, GA (city) Henry County	88	0.37
Randolph, MA (cdp/town) Norfolk County	114	0.36
Buenaventura Lakes, FL (cdp) Osceola County	97	0.36
West Orange, NJ (township) Essex County	156	0.34
Groveton, VA (cdp) Fairfax County	46	0.34
Greentree, NJ (cdp) Camden County	39	0.34
City of Orange, NJ (township) Essex County	100	0.33
Crofton, MD (cdp) Anne Arundel County	91	0.33
Ocean, NJ (township) Monmouth County	89	0.33
Rotterdam, NY (cdp) Schenectady County	68	0.33
Bridgeport, CT (city/town) Fairfield County	453	0.32
Deerfield Beach, FL (city) Broward County	242	0.32
Margate, FL (city) Broward County	170	0.32
Chillum, MD (cdp) Prince George's County	113	0.32
Farmington, MI (city) Oakland County	33	0.32
Weston, CT (town) Fairfield County	32	0.32
Orange Park, FL (town) Clay County	28	0.32
New Britain, CT (city/town) Hartford County	228	0.31
Bradenton, FL (city) Manatee County	159	0.31
Landover, MD (cdp) Prince George's County	72	0.31
Bedford Heights, OH (city) Cuyahoga County	34	0.31
Heath, OH (city) Licking County	31	0.31
Franklin, NJ (township) Somerset County	182	0.30
North Fort Myers, FL (cdp) Lee County	123	0.30
Montclair, NJ (township) Essex County	114	0.30
Avenel, NJ (cdp) Middlesex County	52	0.30
Plantation, FL (city) Broward County	250	0.29
San Carlos Park, FL (cdp) Lee County	51	0.29
Apollo Beach, FL (cdp) Hillsborough County	39	0.29
Lauderhill, FL (city) Broward County	185	0.28
Bergenfield, NJ (borough) Bergen County	75	0.28
Roosevelt, NY (cdp) Nassau County	42	0.28
Middletown, NY (city) Orange County	75	0.27
Jersey City, NJ (city) Hudson County	638	0.26
Yonkers, NY (city) Westchester County	497	0.26
Miramar, FL (city) Broward County	292	0.26
Westbury, NY (village) Nassau County	39	0.26
Brunswick, ME (cdp) Cumberland County	38	0.26
Collegedale, TN (city) Hamilton County	21	0.26
Brockton, MA (city) Plymouth County	230	0.25
Tamarac, FL (city) Broward County	147	0.25
Lompoc, CA (city) Santa Barbara County	103	0.25
Nanuet, NY (cdp) Rockland County	45	0.25
South Farmingdale, NY (cdp) Nassau County	37	0.25
Florida City, FL (city) Miami-Dade County	26	0.25
Baytown, TX (city) Harris County	171	0.24
Central Islip, NY (cdp) Suffolk County	85	0.24
Hinesville, GA (city) Liberty County	78	0.24
Setauket-East Setauket, NY (cdp) Suffolk County	38	0.24
Maryland City, MD (cdp) Anne Arundel County	37	0.24
Tenafly, NJ (borough) Bergen County	34	0.24
Hollywood, FL (city) Broward County	329	0.23
Rotterdam, NY (town) Schenectady County	68	0.23
Temple Terrace, FL (city) Hillsborough County	55	0.23
Somerset, NJ (cdp) Somerset County	52	0.23
Farmington, NY (town) Ontario County	27	0.23
Pike Creek Valley, DE (cdp) New Castle County	26	0.23
Wheaton, MD (cdp) Montgomery County	99	0.22
Hicksville, NY (cdp) Nassau County	90	0.22
Teaneck, NJ (township) Bergen County	86	0.22
The Acreage, FL (cdp) Palm Beach County	84	0.22
Chestnuthill, PA (township) Monroe County	38	0.22
Groton, CT (city) New London County	22	0.22
Queens, NY (borough) Queens County	4,689	0.21
Ramapo, NY (town) Rockland County	253	0.21
Albany, NY (city) Albany County	210	0.21
Temecula, CA (city) Riverside County	198	0.21
Silver Spring, MD (cdp) Montgomery County	146	0.21
Freeport, NY (village) Nassau County	90	0.21
Redan, GA (cdp) DeKalb County	73	0.21
East Chicago, IN (city) Lake County	64	0.21
Manchester, CT (cdp) Hartford County	64	0.21
Plattsburgh, NY (town) Clinton County	25	0.21
New Rochelle, NY (city) Westchester County	153	0.20
The Colony, TX (city) Denton County	70	0.20
Watertown, CT (town) Litchfield County	45	0.20
Gladeview, FL (cdp) Miami-Dade County	22	0.20
Horizon West, FL (cdp) Orange County	20	0.20
Lackland AFB, TX (cdp) Bexar County	15	0.20
Fort Lauderdale, FL (city) Broward County	318	0.19

Please refer to the Explanation of Data in the front of the book for more detailed information.

Ancestry

West Indian: Dutch West Indian, excluding Hispanic

U.S. and 50 States Sorted by Population and Percent of Total Population

Place	Population	%
United States	**61,278**	**0.02**
Oklahoma	20,181	0.55
Texas	15,988	0.07
Arkansas	3,076	0.11
California	2,806	0.01
Florida	2,022	0.01
New York	1,887	0.01
Tennessee	1,701	0.03
Missouri	984	0.02
New Mexico	908	0.05
Georgia	850	0.01
Alabama	774	0.02
Arizona	751	0.01
West Virginia	689	0.04
Ohio	676	0.01
North Carolina	653	0.01
Oregon	628	0.02
Kansas	622	0.02
Kentucky	509	0.01
New Jersey	488	0.01
Louisiana	447	0.01
Colorado	335	0.01
Mississippi	327	0.01
Washington	324	<0.01
Virginia	310	<0.01
Indiana	294	<0.01
Alaska	293	0.04
Michigan	284	<0.01
Pennsylvania	267	<0.01
South Carolina	259	0.01
Illinois	259	<0.01
Connecticut	207	0.01
Iowa	185	0.01
Idaho	184	0.01
Wisconsin	172	<0.01
Minnesota	161	<0.01
Maryland	145	<0.01
Massachusetts	130	<0.01
Nevada	107	<0.01
Delaware	100	0.01
Hawaii	72	0.01
Utah	61	<0.01
Montana	43	<0.01
Nebraska	41	<0.01
District of Columbia	26	<0.01
Maine	24	<0.01
Vermont	14	<0.01
North Dakota	10	<0.01
South Dakota	3	<0.01
New Hampshire	1	<0.01
Rhode Island	0	0.00
Wyoming	0	0.00

Place	Population	%
Oklahoma	20,181	0.55
Arkansas	3,076	0.11
Texas	15,988	0.07
New Mexico	908	0.05
West Virginia	689	0.04
Alaska	293	0.04
Tennessee	1,701	0.03
United States	**61,278**	**0.02**
Missouri	984	0.02
Alabama	774	0.02
Oregon	628	0.02
Kansas	622	0.02
California	2,806	0.01
Florida	2,022	0.01
New York	1,887	0.01
Georgia	850	0.01
Arizona	751	0.01
Ohio	676	0.01
North Carolina	653	0.01
Kentucky	509	0.01
New Jersey	488	0.01
Louisiana	447	0.01
Colorado	335	0.01
Mississippi	327	0.01
South Carolina	259	0.01
Connecticut	207	0.01
Iowa	185	0.01
Idaho	184	0.01
Delaware	100	0.01
Hawaii	72	0.01
Washington	324	<0.01
Virginia	310	<0.01
Indiana	294	<0.01
Michigan	284	<0.01
Pennsylvania	267	<0.01
Illinois	259	<0.01
Wisconsin	172	<0.01
Minnesota	161	<0.01
Maryland	145	<0.01
Massachusetts	130	<0.01
Nevada	107	<0.01
Utah	61	<0.01
Montana	43	<0.01
Nebraska	41	<0.01
District of Columbia	26	<0.01
Maine	24	<0.01
Vermont	14	<0.01
North Dakota	10	<0.01
South Dakota	3	<0.01
New Hampshire	1	<0.01
Rhode Island	0	0.00
Wyoming	0	0.00

Please refer to the Explanation of Data in the front of the book for more detailed information.

Ancestry

West Indian: Dutch West Indian, excluding Hispanic

Top 150 Places Sorted by Population

Based on all places, regardless of total population

Place	Population	%
Oklahoma City, OK (city) Oklahoma County	2,248	0.40
New York, NY (city) Kings County	1,167	0.01
Tulsa, OK (city) Tulsa County	944	0.24
Ada, OK (city) Pontotoc County	436	2.64
Fort Worth, TX (city) Tarrant County	435	0.06
Brooklyn, NY (borough) Kings County	424	0.02
Moore, OK (city) Cleveland County	409	0.78
San Antonio, TX (city) Medina County	400	0.03
Amarillo, TX (city) Potter County	332	0.18
Chickasha, OK (city) Grady County	303	1.87
Manhattan, NY (borough) New York County	276	0.02
Austin, TX (city) Travis County	255	0.03
Norman, OK (city) Cleveland County	251	0.23
Lubbock, TX (city) Lubbock County	249	0.11
Anchorage, AK (municipality) Anchorage Municipality	249	0.09
Pace, FL (cdp) Santa Rosa County	235	1.21
Ruidoso, NM (village) Lincoln County	226	2.77
Broken Arrow, OK (city) Tulsa County	221	0.23
Midwest City, OK (city) Oklahoma County	210	0.39
Bellville, TX (city) Austin County	206	5.04
Oildale, CA (cdp) Kern County	206	0.63
Queens, NY (borough) Queens County	206	0.01
Bakersfield, CA (city) Kern County	201	0.06
Hempstead, NY (town) Nassau County	199	0.03
Lawton, OK (city) Comanche County	192	0.20
Odessa, TX (city) Ector County	189	0.19
Yukon, OK (city) Canadian County	175	0.79
Dallas, TX (city) Dallas County	173	0.01
Bronx, NY (borough) Bronx County	172	0.01
Euless, TX (city) Tarrant County	170	0.34
Owasso, OK (city) Tulsa County	163	0.61
Paris, TX (city) Lamar County	161	0.64
McAlester, OK (city) Pittsburg County	160	0.87
Coral Springs, FL (city) Broward County	157	0.13
Houston, TX (city) Harris County	157	0.01
Fort Smith, AR (city) Sebastian County	156	0.18
Wichita Falls, TX (city) Wichita County	152	0.15
Okemah, OK (city) Okfuskee County	149	4.70
Ventnor City, NJ (city) Atlantic County	149	1.34
Blanchard, OK (city) McClain County	148	2.05
Clinton, OK (city) Custer County	147	1.66
Grand Prairie, TX (city) Dallas County	142	0.09
Edmond, OK (city) Oklahoma County	139	0.18
Wichita, KS (city) Sedgwick County	137	0.04
North Valley Stream, NY (cdp) Nassau County	134	0.81
Fresno, CA (city) Fresno County	133	0.03
Vinita, OK (city) Craig County	131	2.26
Ranger, TX (city) Eastland County	127	4.37
Sulphur, OK (city) Murray County	126	2.59
Muskogee, OK (city) Muskogee County	125	0.32
Phoenix, AZ (city) Maricopa County	122	0.01
Garland, TX (city) Dallas County	121	0.05
Corpus Christi, TX (city) Nueces County	121	0.04
Rush Springs, OK (town) Grady County	120	7.50
Sapulpa, OK (city) Creek County	118	0.58
Henryetta, OK (city) Okmulgee County	116	1.94
Carrollton, TX (city) Denton County	116	0.10
Alcoa, TN (city) Blount County	114	1.35
Gainesville, TX (city) Cooke County	113	0.70
Portland, OR (city) Multnomah County	113	0.02
Duncan, OK (city) Stephens County	111	0.48
Big Spring, TX (city) Howard County	111	0.42
Marlow, OK (city) Stephens County	109	2.36
Porterville, CA (city) Tulare County	109	0.21
Sand Springs, OK (city) Tulsa County	107	0.58
Texanna, OK (cdp) McIntosh County	106	4.81
Purcell, OK (city) McClain County	106	1.83
Del City, OK (city) Oklahoma County	106	0.50
Liberty, TX (city) Liberty County	103	1.23
Craigsville, WV (cdp) Nicholas County	102	3.26
Poteau, OK (city) Le Flore County	102	1.21
Tucson, AZ (city) Pima County	102	0.02
Mannsville, OK (town) Johnston County	99	11.35
Mannford, OK (town) Creek County	93	3.03
Frederick, OK (city) Tillman County	92	2.28
Miami, OK (city) Ottawa County	92	0.67
Pampa, TX (city) Gray County	91	0.51
Canyon, TX (city) Randall County	90	0.69
Bixby, OK (city) Tulsa County	90	0.46
Bartlesville, OK (city) Washington County	89	0.25
Plano, TX (city) Collin County	89	0.03
Staten Island, NY (borough) Richmond County	89	0.02
Collinsville, OK (city) Tulsa County	87	1.58
Artesia, NM (city) Eddy County	87	0.79
Stroud, OK (city) Lincoln County	85	3.14
Nanticoke, PA (city) Luzerne County	84	0.80
Durant, OK (city) Bryan County	82	0.53
Mustang, OK (city) Canadian County	82	0.50
Victoria, TX (city) Victoria County	82	0.13
Weatherford, OK (city) Custer County	81	0.77
Roseburg North, OR (cdp) Douglas County	80	1.16
Borger, TX (city) Hutchinson County	80	0.61
Shawnee, OK (city) Pottawatomie County	80	0.27
Stillwater, OK (city) Payne County	80	0.18
Whitehouse, TX (city) Smith County	79	1.07
Chippewa Falls, WI (city) Chippewa County	79	0.58
Jacksonville, AR (city) Pulaski County	79	0.28
Fayetteville, AR (city) Washington County	79	0.11
Albany, NY (city) Albany County	79	0.08
Monahans, TX (city) Ward County	78	1.15
Pryor Creek, OK (city) Mayes County	76	0.81
Zachary, LA (city) East Baton Rouge Parish	75	0.53
San Buenaventura (Ventura), CA (city) Ventura County	75	0.07
Knoxville, TN (city) Knox County	75	0.04
Santa Clarita, CA (city) Los Angeles County	75	0.04
San Diego, CA (city) San Diego County	74	0.01
Elk City, OK (city) Beckham County	72	0.62
Alice, TX (city) Jim Wells County	72	0.38
El Paso, TX (city) El Paso County	72	0.01
Ninnekah, OK (town) Grady County	71	6.31
Brownville, NY (town) Jefferson County	71	1.16
Midlothian, TX (city) Ellis County	71	0.43
Los Angeles, CA (city) Los Angeles County	71	<0.01
Russellville, AR (city) Pope County	70	0.26
Irving, TX (city) Dallas County	70	0.03
Antlers, OK (city) Pushmataha County	69	2.81
Glenpool, OK (city) Tulsa County	69	0.67
League City, TX (city) Galveston County	69	0.09
Harrah, OK (city) Oklahoma County	68	1.34
Addison, TX (town) Dallas County	68	0.52
Ravia, OK (town) Johnston County	67	13.51
Bristow, OK (city) Creek County	67	1.59
Westbury, NY (village) Nassau County	65	0.44
North Hempstead, NY (town) Nassau County	65	0.03
Pin Oak Acres, OK (cdp) Mayes County	64	15.96
Spring Valley, AZ (cdp) Yavapai County	64	5.16
Hearne, TX (city) Robertson County	64	1.41
Denison, TX (city) Grayson County	64	0.28
Fort Hood, TX (cdp) Bell County	63	0.18
Madison, WI (city) Dane County	63	0.03
Mariposa, CA (cdp) Mariposa County	62	2.92
Brady, TX (city) McCulloch County	62	1.13
Andrews, TX (city) Andrews County	62	0.59
Converse, TX (city) Bexar County	62	0.37
Stanton, TX (city) Martin County	61	2.27
Forney, TX (city) Kaufman County	61	0.46
Bergenfield, NJ (borough) Bergen County	61	0.23
Enid, OK (city) Garfield County	61	0.13
Frisco, TX (city) Collin County	61	0.06
Six Shooter Canyon, AZ (cdp) Gila County	60	5.83
Ardmore, OK (city) Carter County	60	0.25
Nashville-Davidson, TN (metro govt) Davidson County	60	0.01
Maud, OK (city) Pottawatomie County	59	5.41
Horatio, AR (city) Sevier County	59	4.68
Ovilla, TX (city) Ellis County	59	1.66
West Odessa, TX (cdp) Ector County	59	0.27
Hobbs, NM (city) Lea County	59	0.18
Dewey, OK (city) Washington County	58	1.70
Grove, OK (city) Delaware County	58	0.90
Soddy-Daisy, TN (city) Hamilton County	58	0.47

Please refer to the Explanation of Data in the front of the book for more detailed information.

Ancestry

West Indian: Dutch West Indian, excluding Hispanic

Top 150 Places Sorted by Percent of Total Population

Based on all places, regardless of total population

Place	Population	%
Ballou, OK (cdp) Mayes County	41	78.85
Dodge, OK (cdp) Delaware County	21	32.31
Loco Hills, NM (cdp) Eddy County	16	30.77
Rosedale, OK (town) McClain County	15	19.23
Tioga, WV (cdp) Nicholas County	23	17.56
Fowlerton, TX (cdp) La Salle County	43	16.73
Pin Oak Acres, OK (cdp) Mayes County	64	15.96
Briggs, OK (cdp) Cherokee County	33	15.71
Martha, OK (town) Jackson County	29	15.10
Ravia, OK (town) Johnston County	67	13.51
Foxholm, ND (cdp) Ward County	8	13.11
Stonewall, OK (town) Pontotoc County	50	11.99
Mannsville, OK (town) Johnston County	99	11.35
Bridge Creek, OK (town) Grady County	45	10.84
Zena, OK (cdp) Delaware County	12	9.76
Grainola, OK (town) Osage County	6	9.68
Tupelo, OK (city) Coal County	25	9.47
Vilas, CO (town) Baca County	5	9.43
Curtin, PA (township) Centre County	56	8.95
Dougherty, OK (town) Murray County	17	8.90
Blue Mountain, AR (town) Logan County	19	8.48
Wickett, TX (town) Ward County	37	8.45
Rush Springs, OK (town) Grady County	120	7.50
Beersheba Springs, TN (town) Grundy County	43	6.53
Pyote, TX (town) Ward County	8	6.45
Yeager, OK (town) Hughes County	5	6.41
Ninnekah, OK (town) Grady County	71	6.31
Deport, TX (city) Lamar County	42	6.16
Wapanucka, OK (town) Johnston County	26	5.92
Six Shooter Canyon, AZ (cdp) Gila County	60	5.83
Hawley, TX (city) Jones County	37	5.76
Phillips, OK (town) Coal County	12	5.69
Norge, OK (town) Grady County	10	5.62
Eldon, OK (cdp) Cherokee County	36	5.50
Peggs, OK (cdp) Cherokee County	39	5.45
Orlando, OK (town) Logan County	9	5.42
Maud, OK (city) Pottawatomie County	59	5.41
Pine Harbor, TX (cdp) Marion County	47	5.39
Rule, TX (town) Haskell County	32	5.27
Spring Valley, AZ (cdp) Yavapai County	64	5.16
Tryon, OK (town) Lincoln County	22	5.13
Bellville, TX (city) Austin County	206	5.04
Lehigh, OK (city) Coal County	24	4.95
Calvin, OK (town) Hughes County	8	4.94
Texanna, OK (cdp) McIntosh County	106	4.81
Indianola, OK (town) Pittsburg County	8	4.76
Kemp, OK (town) Bryan County	5	4.76
Okemah, OK (city) Okfuskee County	149	4.70
Horatio, AR (city) Sevier County	59	4.68
Denning, AR (town) Franklin County	10	4.52
Bernice, OK (town) Delaware County	23	4.45
Bluejacket, OK (town) Craig County	6	4.41
Ranger, TX (city) Eastland County	127	4.37
Clarksville City, TX (city) Gregg County	26	4.36
Fanshawe, OK (town) Le Flore County	11	4.28
Silverton, TX (city) Briscoe County	37	4.18
Taloga, OK (town) Dewey County	23	4.18
Adair, OK (town) Mayes County	31	4.11
Ripley, OK (town) Payne County	21	4.07
Ratcliff, AR (city) Logan County	7	4.07
Millerton, OK (town) McCurtain County	12	4.05
Dierks, AR (city) Howard County	39	3.96
Shady Grove, OK (cdp) Cherokee County	28	3.89
Picher, OK (city) Ottawa County	17	3.85
Kiefer, OK (town) Creek County	53	3.84
Faxon, OK (town) Comanche County	9	3.80
Wilton, AR (city) Little River County	24	3.78
Derby Acres, CA (cdp) Kern County	15	3.74
Washington, OK (town) McClain County	22	3.73
Shaniko, OR (city) Wasco County	1	3.70
Albion, OK (town) Pushmataha County	4	3.64
Saddle Butte, MT (cdp) Hill County	8	3.62
Depew, OK (town) Creek County	18	3.60
Western Grove, AR (town) Newton County	16	3.58
Bokchito, OK (town) Bryan County	14	3.57
Gardendale, TX (cdp) Ector County	46	3.54
Geronimo, OK (town) Comanche County	53	3.52
Gillham, AR (town) Sevier County	5	3.50
Paoli, OK (town) Garvin County	19	3.48
Oolitic, IN (town) Lawrence County	47	3.45
Sadler, TX (city) Grayson County	9	3.38
Bowlegs, OK (town) Seminole County	11	3.34
Damascus, VA (town) Washington County	31	3.31
Craigsville, WV (cdp) Nicholas County	102	3.26
Verden, OK (town) Grady County	18	3.25
Formoso, KS (city) Jewell County	4	3.25
Windom, TX (town) Fannin County	8	3.20
Weleetka, OK (town) Okfuskee County	23	3.19
Stroud, OK (city) Lincoln County	85	3.14
Bradley, OK (town) Grady County	6	3.06
Arenas Valley, NM (cdp) Grant County	49	3.05
Gail, TX (cdp) Borden County	6	3.05
Mannford, OK (town) Creek County	93	3.03
Whitesboro, OK (cdp) Le Flore County	6	3.03
Stinnett, TX (city) Hutchinson County	55	2.99
Wade, MS (cdp) Jackson County	23	2.99
Canadian, OK (town) Pittsburg County	7	2.98
La Ward, TX (city) Jackson County	5	2.98
Cromwell, OK (town) Seminole County	8	2.96
Exeter, MO (city) Barry County	30	2.95
Fitzhugh, OK (town) Pontotoc County	5	2.94
Mariposa, CA (cdp) Mariposa County	62	2.92
Roosevelt, OK (town) Kiowa County	6	2.91
Westport, OK (town) Pawnee County	8	2.90
Garvin, OK (town) McCurtain County	7	2.89
Antlers, OK (city) Pushmataha County	69	2.81
Schulter, OK (town) Okmulgee County	16	2.79
Francis, OK (town) Pontotoc County	5	2.79
Ruidoso, NM (village) Lincoln County	226	2.77
Melrose, NM (village) Curry County	20	2.77
Keota, OK (town) Haskell County	11	2.77
Wenden, AZ (cdp) La Paz County	18	2.76
Roff, OK (town) Pontotoc County	20	2.75
Crowder, OK (town) Pittsburg County	15	2.75
Bromide, OK (town) Johnston County	5	2.75
Pocasset, OK (town) Grady County	4	2.74
Henning, IL (village) Vermilion County	7	2.73
Dewar, OK (town) Okmulgee County	28	2.72
Konawa, OK (city) Seminole County	47	2.70
Randlett, OK (town) Cotton County	12	2.70
Hardin, TX (city) Liberty County	21	2.69
Carter, OK (town) Beckham County	7	2.67
Pritchett, CO (town) Baca County	6	2.67
Burrton, KS (city) Harvey County	26	2.66
Hitchita, OK (town) McIntosh County	5	2.66
Warren, TX (cdp) Tyler County	14	2.65
Smithville, OK (town) McCurtain County	6	2.65
Ada, OK (city) Pontotoc County	436	2.64
Colmesneil, TX (city) Tyler County	15	2.62
Foreman, AR (city) Little River County	30	2.61
Savanna, OK (town) Pittsburg County	15	2.61
Sulphur, OK (city) Murray County	126	2.59
Woodville, AL (town) Jackson County	22	2.54
Alta Vista, KS (city) Wabaunsee County	12	2.53
Fruitvale, TX (city) Van Zandt County	12	2.53
Christoval, TX (cdp) Tom Green County	11	2.47
Afton, OK (town) Ottawa County	20	2.44
Stonewall, MS (town) Clarke County	26	2.42
Fritch, TX (city) Hutchinson County	53	2.38
Apache, OK (town) Caddo County	36	2.37
Alpine, AZ (cdp) Apache County	4	2.37
Marlow, OK (city) Stephens County	109	2.36
West Jefferson, AL (town) Jefferson County	9	2.33
Bogata, TX (city) Red River County	31	2.29
Binger, OK (town) Caddo County	19	2.29
Frederick, OK (city) Tillman County	92	2.28
Stanton, TX (city) Martin County	61	2.27
Winthrop, AR (city) Little River County	4	2.27
Vinita, OK (city) Craig County	131	2.26
Buna, TX (cdp) Jasper County	46	2.24

Ancestry

West Indian: Dutch West Indian, excluding Hispanic

Top 150 Places Sorted by Percent of Total Population

Based on places with total population of 7,500 or more

Place	Population	%
Ruidoso, NM (village) Lincoln County	226	2.77
Ada, OK (city) Pontotoc County	436	2.64
Chickasha, OK (city) Grady County	303	1.87
Clinton, OK (city) Custer County	147	1.66
Alcoa, TN (city) Blount County	114	1.35
Ventnor City, NJ (city) Atlantic County	149	1.34
Liberty, TX (city) Liberty County	103	1.23
Pace, FL (cdp) Santa Rosa County	235	1.21
Poteau, OK (city) Le Flore County	102	1.21
McAlester, OK (city) Pittsburg County	160	0.87
North Valley Stream, NY (cdp) Nassau County	134	0.81
Pryor Creek, OK (city) Mayes County	76	0.81
Nanticoke, PA (city) Luzerne County	84	0.80
Yukon, OK (city) Canadian County	175	0.79
Artesia, NM (city) Eddy County	87	0.79
Moore, OK (city) Cleveland County	409	0.78
Weatherford, OK (city) Custer County	81	0.77
Aurora, MO (city) Lawrence County	55	0.73
Gainesville, TX (city) Cooke County	113	0.70
Canyon, TX (city) Randall County	90	0.69
Miami, OK (city) Ottawa County	92	0.67
Glenpool, OK (city) Tulsa County	69	0.67
Paris, TX (city) Lamar County	161	0.64
Oildale, CA (cdp) Kern County	206	0.63
Elk City, OK (city) Beckham County	72	0.62
Owasso, OK (city) Tulsa County	163	0.61
Borger, TX (city) Hutchinson County	80	0.61
Andrews, TX (city) Andrews County	62	0.59
Sapulpa, OK (city) Creek County	118	0.58
Sand Springs, OK (city) Tulsa County	107	0.58
Chippewa Falls, WI (city) Chippewa County	79	0.58
Durant, OK (city) Bryan County	82	0.53
Zachary, LA (city) East Baton Rouge Parish	75	0.53
Lighthouse Point, FL (city) Broward County	55	0.53
Addison, TX (town) Dallas County	68	0.52
Pampa, TX (city) Gray County	91	0.51
Del City, OK (city) Oklahoma County	106	0.50
Mustang, OK (city) Canadian County	82	0.50
Duncan, OK (city) Stephens County	111	0.48
Soddy-Daisy, TN (city) Hamilton County	58	0.47
Bixby, OK (city) Tulsa County	90	0.46
Forney, TX (city) Kaufman County	61	0.46
Mamakating, NY (town) Sullivan County	55	0.46
Westbury, NY (village) Nassau County	65	0.44
Country Club, CA (cdp) San Joaquin County	39	0.44
Midlothian, TX (city) Ellis County	71	0.43
Lenoir City, TN (city) Loudon County	36	0.43
Big Spring, TX (city) Howard County	111	0.42
Sweetwater, TX (city) Nolan County	45	0.42
Oklahoma City, OK (city) Oklahoma County	2,248	0.40
Midwest City, OK (city) Oklahoma County	210	0.39
Alice, TX (city) Jim Wells County	72	0.38
Pleasanton, TX (city) Atascosa County	34	0.38
Converse, TX (city) Bexar County	62	0.37
Sulphur Springs, TX (city) Hopkins County	56	0.37
Cushing, OK (city) Payne County	29	0.37
Guymon, OK (city) Texas County	38	0.35
Euless, TX (city) Tarrant County	170	0.34
Coweta, OK (city) Wagoner County	32	0.34
Brownfield, TX (city) Terry County	31	0.33
Muskogee, OK (city) Muskogee County	125	0.32
Hawaiian Paradise Park, HI (cdp) Hawaii County	25	0.32
Saks, AL (cdp) Calhoun County	35	0.31
Paris, TN (city) Henry County	31	0.31
Breaux Bridge, LA (city) St. Martin Parish	25	0.31
Saginaw, TX (city) Tarrant County	55	0.30
Guthrie, OK (city) Logan County	30	0.30
Lansing, NY (town) Tompkins County	32	0.29
Pine Ridge, FL (cdp) Citrus County	26	0.29
Jacksonville, AR (city) Pulaski County	79	0.28
Denison, TX (city) Grayson County	64	0.28
McKinleyville, CA (cdp) Humboldt County	48	0.28
Cordele, GA (city) Crisp County	31	0.28
Shawnee, OK (city) Pottawatomie County	80	0.27
West Odessa, TX (cdp) Ector County	59	0.27
Susanville, CA (city) Lassen County	48	0.27
Russellville, AR (city) Pope County	70	0.26
Universal City, TX (city) Bexar County	46	0.26
Jenks, OK (city) Tulsa County	40	0.26
Port Lavaca, TX (city) Calhoun County	32	0.26
Sallisaw, OK (city) Sequoyah County	23	0.26
Bartlesville, OK (city) Washington County	89	0.25
Ardmore, OK (city) Carter County	60	0.25
Ensley, FL (cdp) Escambia County	45	0.25
Seagoville, TX (city) Dallas County	35	0.25
Tulsa, OK (city) Tulsa County	944	0.24
Rosamond, CA (cdp) Kern County	41	0.24
The Village, OK (city) Oklahoma County	22	0.24
White City, OR (cdp) Jackson County	19	0.24
Norman, OK (city) Cleveland County	251	0.23
Broken Arrow, OK (city) Tulsa County	221	0.23
Bergenfield, NJ (borough) Bergen County	61	0.23
Mineral Wells, TX (city) Palo Pinto County	39	0.23
Miami Springs, FL (city) Miami-Dade County	32	0.23
Wells Branch, TX (cdp) Travis County	27	0.23
Bellmead, TX (city) McLennan County	22	0.23
Carthage, MO (city) Jasper County	31	0.22
White House, TN (city) Sumner County	21	0.22
Socorro, NM (city) Socorro County	20	0.22
Porterville, CA (city) Tulare County	109	0.21
Cabot, AR (city) Lonoke County	46	0.21
Van Buren, AR (city) Crawford County	46	0.21
Coventry, CT (town) Tolland County	26	0.21
Beachwood, NJ (borough) Ocean County	23	0.21
Coffeyville, KS (city) Montgomery County	22	0.21
Robinson, TX (city) McLennan County	21	0.21
Lawton, OK (city) Comanche County	192	0.20
Santa Paula, CA (city) Ventura County	57	0.20
Austin, MN (city) Mower County	50	0.20
Rockport, TX (city) Aransas County	17	0.20
Odessa, TX (city) Ector County	189	0.19
Cleburne, TX (city) Johnson County	54	0.19
Vernon, TX (city) Wilbarger County	21	0.19
Show Low, AZ (city) Navajo County	20	0.19
Amarillo, TX (city) Potter County	332	0.18
Fort Smith, AR (city) Sebastian County	156	0.18
Edmond, OK (city) Oklahoma County	139	0.18
Stillwater, OK (city) Payne County	80	0.18
Fort Hood, TX (cdp) Bell County	63	0.18
Hobbs, NM (city) Lea County	59	0.18
Carlsbad, NM (city) Eddy County	46	0.18
Benbrook, TX (city) Tarrant County	37	0.18
Brenham, TX (city) Washington County	28	0.18
Rosedale, CA (cdp) Kern County	26	0.18
Fruitville, FL (cdp) Sarasota County	25	0.18
Lindsay, CA (city) Tulare County	21	0.18
Parker, SC (cdp) Greenville County	19	0.18
Chelsea, AL (city) Shelby County	17	0.18
Independence, KS (city) Montgomery County	17	0.18
Edgewater, MD (cdp) Anne Arundel County	16	0.18
Landover, MD (cdp) Prince George's County	40	0.17
Claremore, OK (city) Rogers County	31	0.17
Dickinson, TX (city) Galveston County	31	0.17
Myrtle Grove, FL (cdp) Escambia County	27	0.17
West University Place, TX (city) Harris County	25	0.17
Red Oak, TX (city) Ellis County	17	0.17
Greenwood, AR (city) Sebastian County	15	0.17
Vinings, GA (cdp) Cobb County	15	0.17
Deptford, NJ (township) Gloucester County	48	0.16
Post Falls, ID (city) Kootenai County	41	0.16
Little Elm, TX (city) Denton County	36	0.16
Palestine, TX (city) Anderson County	30	0.16
Chowchilla, CA (city) Madera County	29	0.16
Center Point, AL (city) Jefferson County	27	0.16
Bonham, TX (city) Fannin County	16	0.16
Lopatcong, NJ (township) Warren County	12	0.16
Wichita Falls, TX (city) Wichita County	152	0.15
Clovis, NM (city) Curry County	54	0.15
Benton, AR (city) Saline County	44	0.15
Sunny Isles Beach, FL (city) Miami-Dade County	30	0.15

SECTION THREE

Ancestry

West Indian: Haitian, excluding Hispanic

U.S. and 50 States Sorted by Population and Percent of Total Population

Place	Population	%
United States	**813,186**	**0.27**
Florida	380,005	2.05
New York	179,024	0.93
Massachusetts	63,915	0.99
New Jersey	54,761	0.63
Georgia	22,360	0.24
Pennsylvania	19,433	0.15
Connecticut	18,345	0.52
Maryland	10,695	0.19
Illinois	7,639	0.06
California	7,538	0.02
Texas	5,240	0.02
Virginia	5,229	0.07
North Carolina	4,878	0.05
Ohio	2,912	0.03
Delaware	2,555	0.29
Rhode Island	2,477	0.23
Michigan	2,376	0.02
Tennessee	1,733	0.03
Indiana	1,721	0.03
Louisiana	1,719	0.04
Washington	1,652	0.03
New Hampshire	1,591	0.12
South Carolina	1,548	0.03
Missouri	1,278	0.02
Kentucky	1,121	0.03
Alabama	1,121	0.02
District of Columbia	1,095	0.19
Nevada	983	0.04
Arizona	792	0.01
Colorado	754	0.02
Minnesota	710	0.01
Kansas	664	0.02
Wisconsin	613	0.01
Oregon	601	0.02
Hawaii	482	0.04
Mississippi	453	0.02
Utah	444	0.02
Arkansas	423	0.01
Maine	364	0.03
Alaska	335	0.05
Nebraska	309	0.02
Oklahoma	306	0.01
Iowa	276	0.01
Idaho	245	0.02
New Mexico	218	0.01
Vermont	91	0.01
North Dakota	55	0.01
Montana	47	<0.01
South Dakota	36	<0.01
West Virginia	21	<0.01
Wyoming	3	<0.01

Place	Population	%
Florida	380,005	2.05
Massachusetts	63,915	0.99
New York	179,024	0.93
New Jersey	54,761	0.63
Connecticut	18,345	0.52
Delaware	2,555	0.29
United States	**813,186**	**0.27**
Georgia	22,360	0.24
Rhode Island	2,477	0.23
Maryland	10,695	0.19
District of Columbia	1,095	0.19
Pennsylvania	19,433	0.15
New Hampshire	1,591	0.12
Virginia	5,229	0.07
Illinois	7,639	0.06
North Carolina	4,878	0.05
Alaska	335	0.05
Louisiana	1,719	0.04
Nevada	983	0.04
Hawaii	482	0.04
Ohio	2,912	0.03
Tennessee	1,733	0.03
Indiana	1,721	0.03
Washington	1,652	0.03
South Carolina	1,548	0.03
Kentucky	1,121	0.03
Maine	364	0.03
California	7,538	0.02
Texas	5,240	0.02
Michigan	2,376	0.02
Missouri	1,278	0.02
Alabama	1,121	0.02
Colorado	754	0.02
Kansas	664	0.02
Oregon	601	0.02
Mississippi	453	0.02
Utah	444	0.02
Nebraska	309	0.02
Idaho	245	0.02
Arizona	792	0.01
Minnesota	710	0.01
Wisconsin	613	0.01
Arkansas	423	0.01
Oklahoma	306	0.01
Iowa	276	0.01
New Mexico	218	0.01
Vermont	91	0.01
North Dakota	55	0.01
Montana	47	<0.01
South Dakota	36	<0.01
West Virginia	21	<0.01
Wyoming	3	<0.01

Please refer to the Explanation of Data in the front of the book for more detailed information.

Ancestry

West Indian: Haitian, excluding Hispanic

Top 150 Places Sorted by Population

Based on all places, regardless of total population

Place	Population	%
New York, NY (city) Kings County	120,252	1.49
Brooklyn, NY (borough) Kings County	69,941	2.84
Queens, NY (borough) Queens County	38,368	1.74
North Miami, FL (city) Miami-Dade County	22,944	39.01
Boston, MA (city) Suffolk County	19,850	3.29
Miami, FL (city) Miami-Dade County	17,451	4.46
Hempstead, NY (town) Nassau County	17,422	2.31
Golden Glades, FL (cdp) Miami-Dade County	13,085	39.69
Fort Lauderdale, FL (city) Broward County	10,769	6.44
Miramar, FL (city) Broward County	10,494	9.23
Pine Hills, FL (cdp) Orange County	10,217	15.43
Brockton, MA (city) Plymouth County	9,939	10.59
North Miami Beach, FL (city) Miami-Dade County	9,807	23.71
Pompano Beach, FL (city) Broward County	9,316	9.28
Miami Gardens, FL (city) Miami-Dade County	9,122	8.63
Philadelphia, PA (city) Philadelphia County	9,026	0.60
Ramapo, NY (town) Rockland County	8,948	7.29
Boynton Beach, FL (city) Palm Beach County	8,900	13.17
Lauderhill, FL (city) Broward County	8,629	12.85
North Lauderdale, FL (city) Broward County	7,642	18.72
Irvington, NJ (township) Essex County	7,341	13.39
Delray Beach, FL (city) Palm Beach County	7,178	11.75
Orlando, FL (city) Orange County	7,164	3.07
Deerfield Beach, FL (city) Broward County	6,931	9.21
Spring Valley, NY (village) Rockland County	6,665	21.98
Pembroke Pines, FL (city) Broward County	6,591	4.33
Lauderdale Lakes, FL (city) Broward County	6,503	19.98
Manhattan, NY (borough) New York County	6,500	0.41
Islip, NY (town) Suffolk County	5,636	1.69
Elmont, NY (cdp) Nassau County	5,587	16.20
Sunrise, FL (city) Broward County	5,128	6.03
Stamford, CT (city/town) Fairfield County	5,112	4.23
Port St. Lucie, FL (city) St. Lucie County	4,942	3.19
Coral Springs, FL (city) Broward County	4,916	4.06
Bronx, NY (borough) Bronx County	4,652	0.34
Jacksonville, FL (city) Duval County	4,568	0.56
Hollywood, FL (city) Broward County	4,542	3.22
Randolph, MA (cdp/town) Norfolk County	4,214	13.31
Bridgeport, CT (city/town) Fairfield County	4,076	2.86
West Palm Beach, FL (city) Palm Beach County	3,930	4.02
Elizabeth, NJ (city) Union County	3,811	3.09
Babylon, NY (town) Suffolk County	3,789	1.77
East Orange, NJ (city) Essex County	3,699	5.70
Pinewood, FL (cdp) Miami-Dade County	3,655	22.90
Lake Worth, FL (city) Palm Beach County	3,598	10.16
Oakland Park, FL (city) Broward County	3,572	8.56
Fort Myers, FL (city) Lee County	3,519	5.64
Ives Estates, FL (cdp) Miami-Dade County	3,433	19.51
Lehigh Acres, FL (cdp) Lee County	3,428	4.06
Plantation, FL (city) Broward County	3,353	3.94
Margate, FL (city) Broward County	3,141	5.86
Newark, NJ (city) Essex County	3,138	1.14
City of Orange, NJ (township) Essex County	3,013	9.91
Tampa, FL (city) Hillsborough County	2,943	0.88
Malden, MA (city) Middlesex County	2,927	5.03
Everett, MA (city) Middlesex County	2,888	7.12
Cambridge, MA (city) Middlesex County	2,816	2.72
Chicago, IL (city) Cook County	2,734	0.10
Oak Ridge, FL (cdp) Orange County	2,725	13.59
West Little River, FL (cdp) Miami-Dade County	2,707	8.31
Palm Bay, FL (city) Brevard County	2,670	2.65
Immokalee, FL (cdp) Collier County	2,594	13.70
Union, NJ (township) Union County	2,530	4.54
Poinciana, FL (cdp) Osceola County	2,520	5.03
North Hempstead, NY (town) Nassau County	2,394	1.07
Jersey City, NJ (city) Hudson County	2,371	0.97
Roselle, NJ (borough) Union County	2,264	10.80
Fort Pierce, FL (city) St. Lucie County	2,187	5.15
Brentwood, NY (cdp) Suffolk County	2,162	3.94
Lake Park, FL (town) Palm Beach County	2,150	26.19
Tamarac, FL (city) Broward County	2,124	3.55
Hempstead, NY (village) Nassau County	2,104	3.94
Clarkstown, NY (town) Rockland County	2,077	2.49
Brookhaven, NY (town) Suffolk County	2,077	0.43
Norwich, CT (city/town) New London County	1,976	4.96
Uniondale, NY (cdp) Nassau County	1,927	7.87
Greenacres, FL (city) Palm Beach County	1,896	5.23
Belle Glade, FL (city) Palm Beach County	1,829	10.36
North Valley Stream, NY (cdp) Nassau County	1,827	11.07
Riviera Beach, FL (city) Palm Beach County	1,785	5.49
Tallahassee, FL (city) Leon County	1,735	0.98
Valley Stream, NY (village) Nassau County	1,727	4.67
Medford, MA (city) Middlesex County	1,690	3.05
Linden, NJ (city) Union County	1,682	4.21
Columbus, OH (city) Franklin County	1,655	0.21
Lynn, MA (city) Essex County	1,623	1.81
Coconut Creek, FL (city) Broward County	1,620	3.14
Central Islip, NY (cdp) Suffolk County	1,538	4.28
Los Angeles, CA (city) Los Angeles County	1,526	0.04
Hamilton, NJ (township) Mercer County	1,494	1.69
Golden Gate, FL (cdp) Collier County	1,469	6.09
Houston, TX (city) Harris County	1,438	0.07
Norwalk, CT (city/town) Fairfield County	1,377	1.63
Westview, FL (cdp) Miami-Dade County	1,341	14.34
Stratford, CT (cdp/town) Fairfield County	1,328	2.61
West Orange, NJ (township) Essex County	1,327	2.90
Baldwin, NY (cdp) Nassau County	1,323	5.58
Hillcrest, NY (cdp) Rockland County	1,310	15.98
Winter Haven, FL (city) Polk County	1,307	3.95
Huntington, NY (town) Suffolk County	1,277	0.63
South Miami Heights, FL (cdp) Miami-Dade County	1,272	3.47
Lantana, FL (town) Palm Beach County	1,270	12.27
Asbury Park, NJ (city) Monmouth County	1,265	7.77
Boca Raton, FL (city) Palm Beach County	1,265	1.49
Providence, RI (city) Providence County	1,254	0.70
Cape Coral, FL (city) Lee County	1,244	0.83
Homestead, FL (city) Miami-Dade County	1,236	2.24
Haverstraw, NY (town) Rockland County	1,200	3.34
Leisure City, FL (cdp) Miami-Dade County	1,177	5.45
University, FL (cdp) Hillsborough County	1,162	2.87
Washington, DC (city) District of Columbia	1,095	0.19
Somerville, MA (city) Middlesex County	1,094	1.45
Hillside, NJ (township) Union County	1,090	5.12
Maplewood, NJ (township) Essex County	1,070	4.51
Hallandale Beach, FL (city) Broward County	1,069	2.91
Trenton, NJ (city) Mercer County	1,054	1.24
Davie, FL (town) Broward County	1,054	1.16
New Cassel, NY (cdp) Nassau County	1,053	8.38
Florida City, FL (city) Miami-Dade County	1,052	9.92
San Castle, FL (cdp) Palm Beach County	1,050	33.81
Westbury, NY (village) Nassau County	1,042	6.99
Pleasantville, NJ (city) Atlantic County	1,026	5.08
Yonkers, NY (city) Westchester County	1,026	0.53
Nanuet, NY (cdp) Rockland County	1,014	5.70
Lely Resort, FL (cdp) Collier County	1,002	20.14
Willingboro, NJ (township) Burlington County	979	3.04
Salisbury, MD (city) Wicomico County	963	3.28
Royal Palm Beach, FL (village) Palm Beach County	961	2.98
Worcester, MA (city) Worcester County	957	0.53
Milton, MA (cdp/town) Norfolk County	956	3.58
Baltimore, MD (city) Baltimore city County	953	0.15
New Rochelle, NY (city) Westchester County	951	1.25
Wilton Manors, FL (city) Broward County	924	7.78
Deltona, FL (city) Volusia County	920	1.09
Palmetto Estates, FL (cdp) Miami-Dade County	898	6.59
Skokie, IL (village) Cook County	891	1.40
Pine Castle, FL (cdp) Orange County	886	8.11
Lowell, MA (city) Middlesex County	881	0.84
Daytona Beach, FL (city) Volusia County	872	1.39
Country Walk, FL (cdp) Miami-Dade County	858	5.39
Wellington, FL (village) Palm Beach County	858	1.60
Port Charlotte, FL (cdp) Charlotte County	834	1.48
North Bay Shore, NY (cdp) Suffolk County	831	4.26
Westgate, FL (cdp) Palm Beach County	820	11.09
Freeport, NY (village) Nassau County	818	1.92
Oyster Bay, NY (town) Nassau County	813	0.28
Bloomfield, NJ (township) Essex County	797	1.69
Staten Island, NY (borough) Richmond County	791	0.17
Orangetown, NY (town) Rockland County	782	1.61
Evanston, IL (city) Cook County	781	1.06

Ancestry

West Indian: Haitian, excluding Hispanic

Top 150 Places Sorted by Percent of Total Population

Based on all places, regardless of total population

Place	Population	%
Golden Glades, FL (cdp) Miami-Dade County	13,085	39.69
North Miami, FL (city) Miami-Dade County	22,944	39.01
Juntura, OR (cdp) Malheur County	16	34.78
San Castle, FL (cdp) Palm Beach County	1,050	33.81
Lake Park, FL (town) Palm Beach County	2,150	26.19
Bradley Junction, FL (cdp) Polk County	45	25.42
North Miami Beach, FL (city) Miami-Dade County	9,807	23.71
Pinewood, FL (cdp) Miami-Dade County	3,655	22.90
Spring Valley, NY (village) Rockland County	6,665	21.98
Stacey Street, FL (cdp) Palm Beach County	255	20.99
Lely Resort, FL (cdp) Collier County	1,002	20.14
Lauderdale Lakes, FL (city) Broward County	6,503	19.98
Ives Estates, FL (cdp) Miami-Dade County	3,433	19.51
North Lauderdale, FL (city) Broward County	7,642	18.72
Parker, MN (township) Marshall County	6	17.65
Elmont, NY (cdp) Nassau County	5,587	16.20
Hillcrest, NY (cdp) Rockland County	1,310	15.98
Pine Hills, FL (cdp) Orange County	10,217	15.43
El Portal, FL (village) Miami-Dade County	366	15.29
Washington Park, FL (cdp) Broward County	212	14.45
Westview, FL (cdp) Miami-Dade County	1,341	14.34
Immokalee, FL (cdp) Collier County	2,594	13.70
Oak Ridge, FL (cdp) Orange County	2,725	13.59
Irvington, NJ (township) Essex County	7,341	13.39
Randolph, MA (cdp/town) Norfolk County	4,214	13.31
Boynton Beach, FL (city) Palm Beach County	8,900	13.17
Lauderhill, FL (city) Broward County	8,629	12.85
Seminole Manor, FL (cdp) Palm Beach County	332	12.70
Lantana, FL (town) Palm Beach County	1,270	12.27
Delray Beach, FL (city) Palm Beach County	7,178	11.75
Westgate, FL (cdp) Palm Beach County	820	11.09
North Valley Stream, NY (cdp) Nassau County	1,827	11.07
Roselle, NJ (borough) Union County	2,264	10.80
Limestone Creek, FL (cdp) Palm Beach County	86	10.72
Lakewood Gardens, FL (cdp) Palm Beach County	87	10.69
Brockton, MA (city) Plymouth County	9,939	10.59
Belle Glade, FL (city) Palm Beach County	1,829	10.36
Lake Worth, FL (city) Palm Beach County	3,598	10.16
Florida City, FL (city) Miami-Dade County	1,052	9.92
City of Orange, NJ (township) Essex County	3,013	9.91
Stock Island, FL (cdp) Monroe County	354	9.86
Naples Manor, FL (cdp) Collier County	511	9.69
Pompano Beach, FL (city) Broward County	9,316	9.28
Hillburn, NY (village) Rockland County	88	9.27
Miramar, FL (city) Broward County	10,494	9.23
Deerfield Beach, FL (city) Broward County	6,931	9.21
Mangonia Park, FL (town) Palm Beach County	149	8.88
Wheatley Heights, NY (cdp) Suffolk County	545	8.80
Lake Belvedere Estates, FL (cdp) Palm Beach County	280	8.68
Miami Gardens, FL (city) Miami-Dade County	9,122	8.63
Delmar, DE (town) Sussex County	137	8.62
Oakland Park, FL (city) Broward County	3,572	8.56
Samoset, FL (cdp) Manatee County	355	8.43
New Cassel, NY (cdp) Nassau County	1,053	8.38
Seaford, DE (city) Sussex County	582	8.38
West Little River, FL (cdp) Miami-Dade County	2,707	8.31
Nyack, NY (village) Rockland County	577	8.29
Storden, MN (township) Cottonwood County	15	8.20
Pine Castle, FL (cdp) Orange County	886	8.11
Deferiet, NY (village) Jefferson County	38	8.09
Uniondale, NY (cdp) Nassau County	1,927	7.87
Blades, DE (town) Sussex County	97	7.85
Wilton Manors, FL (city) Broward County	924	7.78
Asbury Park, NJ (city) Monmouth County	1,265	7.77
South Dennis, MA (cdp) Barnstable County	295	7.76
Ruthville, ND (cdp) Ward County	17	7.59
Coats, NC (town) Harnett County	160	7.55
Monticello, FL (city) Jefferson County	188	7.39
Ramapo, NY (town) Rockland County	8,948	7.29
Chestnut Ridge, NY (village) Rockland County	570	7.26
Miami Shores, FL (village) Miami-Dade County	751	7.14
Hassell, NC (town) Martin County	4	7.14
Everett, MA (city) Middlesex County	2,888	7.12
Westbury, NY (village) Nassau County	1,042	6.99
Yatesville, PA (borough) Luzerne County	48	6.92
Fort Pierce South, FL (cdp) St. Lucie County	393	6.90
Walton Park, NY (cdp) Orange County	172	6.76
Palmetto Estates, FL (cdp) Miami-Dade County	898	6.59
Fort Lauderdale, FL (city) Broward County	10,769	6.44
East Lansdowne, PA (borough) Delaware County	170	6.43
New Holland, PA (borough) Lancaster County	343	6.42
Pomona, NY (village) Rockland County	227	6.42
Rodney Village, DE (cdp) Kent County	113	6.37
Locust Grove, GA (city) Henry County	318	6.36
New Hempstead, NY (village) Rockland County	314	6.26
Golden Gate, FL (cdp) Collier County	1,469	6.09
Sunrise, FL (city) Broward County	5,128	6.03
Holden Heights, FL (cdp) Orange County	297	5.98
Avon, MA (town) Norfolk County	257	5.93
Margate, FL (city) Broward County	3,141	5.86
Eagle Lake, FL (city) Polk County	95	5.80
East Orange, NJ (city) Essex County	3,699	5.70
Nanuet, NY (cdp) Rockland County	1,014	5.70
Fort Myers, FL (city) Lee County	3,519	5.64
Baldwin, NY (cdp) Nassau County	1,323	5.58
Golf, IL (village) Cook County	33	5.56
Riviera Beach, FL (city) Palm Beach County	1,785	5.49
Leisure City, FL (cdp) Miami-Dade County	1,177	5.45
Country Walk, FL (cdp) Miami-Dade County	858	5.39
Baldwin Harbor, NY (cdp) Nassau County	468	5.38
Voorhees, NJ (cdp) Somerset County	55	5.37
Dresden, NY (town) Washington County	44	5.36
Greenacres, FL (city) Palm Beach County	1,896	5.23
Pembroke Park, FL (town) Broward County	307	5.21
Reiffton, PA (cdp) Berks County	211	5.20
Fort Pierce, FL (city) St. Lucie County	2,187	5.15
Sky Lake, FL (cdp) Orange County	253	5.15
Hillside, NJ (township) Union County	1,090	5.12
North Pembroke, MA (cdp) Plymouth County	140	5.10
Pleasantville, NJ (city) Atlantic County	1,026	5.08
Malden, MA (city) Middlesex County	2,927	5.03
Poinciana, FL (cdp) Osceola County	2,520	5.03
Norwich, CT (city/town) New London County	1,976	4.96
Fairview, NY (cdp) Westchester County	118	4.95
Jefferson, PA (township) Berks County	100	4.95
Hyde Park, NY (cdp) Dutchess County	104	4.92
Wyandanch, NY (cdp) Suffolk County	521	4.77
Sanford, TX (town) Hutchinson County	9	4.69
Valley Stream, NY (village) Nassau County	1,727	4.67
Piermont, NY (village) Rockland County	115	4.58
Haverhill, FL (town) Palm Beach County	93	4.55
Micanopy, FL (town) Alachua County	32	4.55
Union, NJ (township) Union County	2,530	4.54
Maplewood, NJ (township) Essex County	1,070	4.51
Oak Bluffs, MA (town) Dukes County	197	4.51
Miami, FL (city) Miami-Dade County	17,451	4.46
East Farmingdale, NY (cdp) Suffolk County	273	4.46
Naranja, FL (cdp) Miami-Dade County	279	4.37
Southchase, FL (cdp) Orange County	715	4.34
West Haverstraw, NY (village) Rockland County	437	4.34
Pembroke Pines, FL (city) Broward County	6,591	4.33
Central Islip, NY (cdp) Suffolk County	1,538	4.28
North Bay Shore, NY (cdp) Suffolk County	831	4.26
Stamford, CT (city/town) Fairfield County	5,112	4.23
Woods, MN (township) Chippewa County	11	4.23
Linden, NJ (city) Union County	1,682	4.21
West Samoset, FL (cdp) Manatee County	235	4.10
Coral Springs, FL (city) Broward County	4,916	4.06
Lehigh Acres, FL (cdp) Lee County	3,428	4.06
Chester, NY (village) Orange County	161	4.06
South Bay, FL (city) Palm Beach County	193	4.04
West Palm Beach, FL (city) Palm Beach County	3,930	4.02
Bellerose Terrace, NY (cdp) Nassau County	76	3.99
Winter Haven, FL (city) Polk County	1,307	3.95
Plantation, FL (city) Broward County	3,353	3.94
Brentwood, NY (cdp) Suffolk County	2,162	3.94
Hempstead, NY (village) Nassau County	2,104	3.94
South Ashburnham, MA (cdp) Worcester County	46	3.93
Tangelo Park, FL (cdp) Orange County	86	3.92
Wauchula, FL (city) Hardee County	189	3.84

Please refer to the Explanation of Data in the front of the book for more detailed information.

Ancestry

West Indian: Haitian, excluding Hispanic

Top 150 Places Sorted by Percent of Total Population

Based on places with total population of 7,500 or more

Place	Population	%
Golden Glades, FL (cdp) Miami-Dade County	13,085	39.69
North Miami, FL (city) Miami-Dade County	22,944	39.01
Lake Park, FL (town) Palm Beach County	2,150	26.19
North Miami Beach, FL (city) Miami-Dade County	9,807	23.71
Pinewood, FL (cdp) Miami-Dade County	3,655	22.90
Spring Valley, NY (village) Rockland County	6,665	21.98
Lauderdale Lakes, FL (city) Broward County	6,503	19.98
Ives Estates, FL (cdp) Miami-Dade County	3,433	19.51
North Lauderdale, FL (city) Broward County	7,642	18.72
Elmont, NY (cdp) Nassau County	5,587	16.20
Hillcrest, NY (cdp) Rockland County	1,310	15.98
Pine Hills, FL (cdp) Orange County	10,217	15.43
Westview, FL (cdp) Miami-Dade County	1,341	14.34
Immokalee, FL (cdp) Collier County	2,594	13.70
Oak Ridge, FL (cdp) Orange County	2,725	13.59
Irvington, NJ (township) Essex County	7,341	13.39
Randolph, MA (cdp/town) Norfolk County	4,214	13.31
Boynton Beach, FL (city) Palm Beach County	8,900	13.17
Lauderhill, FL (city) Broward County	8,629	12.85
Lantana, FL (town) Palm Beach County	1,270	12.27
Delray Beach, FL (city) Palm Beach County	7,178	11.75
North Valley Stream, NY (cdp) Nassau County	1,827	11.07
Roselle, NJ (borough) Union County	2,264	10.80
Brockton, MA (city) Plymouth County	9,939	10.59
Belle Glade, FL (city) Palm Beach County	1,829	10.36
Lake Worth, FL (city) Palm Beach County	3,598	10.16
Florida City, FL (city) Miami-Dade County	1,052	9.92
City of Orange, NJ (township) Essex County	3,013	9.91
Pompano Beach, FL (city) Broward County	9,316	9.28
Miramar, FL (city) Broward County	10,494	9.23
Deerfield Beach, FL (city) Broward County	6,931	9.21
Miami Gardens, FL (city) Miami-Dade County	9,122	8.63
Oakland Park, FL (city) Broward County	3,572	8.56
New Cassel, NY (cdp) Nassau County	1,053	8.38
West Little River, FL (cdp) Miami-Dade County	2,707	8.31
Pine Castle, FL (cdp) Orange County	886	8.11
Uniondale, NY (cdp) Nassau County	1,927	7.87
Wilton Manors, FL (city) Broward County	924	7.78
Asbury Park, NJ (city) Monmouth County	1,265	7.77
Ramapo, NY (town) Rockland County	8,948	7.29
Chestnut Ridge, NY (village) Rockland County	570	7.26
Miami Shores, FL (village) Miami-Dade County	751	7.14
Everett, MA (city) Middlesex County	2,888	7.12
Westbury, NY (village) Nassau County	1,042	6.99
Palmetto Estates, FL (cdp) Miami-Dade County	898	6.59
Fort Lauderdale, FL (city) Broward County	10,769	6.44
Golden Gate, FL (cdp) Collier County	1,469	6.09
Sunrise, FL (city) Broward County	5,128	6.03
Margate, FL (city) Broward County	3,141	5.86
East Orange, NJ (city) Essex County	3,699	5.70
Nanuet, NY (cdp) Rockland County	1,014	5.70
Fort Myers, FL (city) Lee County	3,519	5.64
Baldwin, NY (cdp) Nassau County	1,323	5.58
Riviera Beach, FL (city) Palm Beach County	1,785	5.49
Leisure City, FL (cdp) Miami-Dade County	1,177	5.45
Country Walk, FL (cdp) Miami-Dade County	858	5.39
Baldwin Harbor, NY (cdp) Nassau County	468	5.38
Greenacres, FL (city) Palm Beach County	1,896	5.23
Fort Pierce, FL (city) St. Lucie County	2,187	5.15
Hillside, NJ (township) Union County	1,090	5.12
Pleasantville, NJ (city) Atlantic County	1,026	5.08
Malden, MA (city) Middlesex County	2,927	5.03
Poinciana, FL (cdp) Osceola County	2,520	5.03
Norwich, CT (city/town) New London County	1,976	4.96
Wyandanch, NY (cdp) Suffolk County	521	4.77
Valley Stream, NY (village) Nassau County	1,727	4.67
Union, NJ (township) Union County	2,530	4.54
Maplewood, NJ (township) Essex County	1,070	4.51
Miami, FL (city) Miami-Dade County	17,451	4.46
Southchase, FL (cdp) Orange County	715	4.34
West Haverstraw, NY (village) Rockland County	437	4.34
Pembroke Pines, FL (city) Broward County	6,591	4.33
Central Islip, NY (cdp) Suffolk County	1,538	4.28
North Bay Shore, NY (cdp) Suffolk County	831	4.26
Stamford, CT (city/town) Fairfield County	5,112	4.23

Place	Population	%
Linden, NJ (city) Union County	1,682	4.21
Coral Springs, FL (city) Broward County	4,916	4.06
Lehigh Acres, FL (cdp) Lee County	3,428	4.06
West Palm Beach, FL (city) Palm Beach County	3,930	4.02
Winter Haven, FL (city) Polk County	1,307	3.95
Plantation, FL (city) Broward County	3,353	3.94
Brentwood, NY (cdp) Suffolk County	2,162	3.94
Hempstead, NY (village) Nassau County	2,104	3.94
Lansdowne, PA (borough) Delaware County	402	3.77
North Amityville, NY (cdp) Suffolk County	655	3.68
Haverstraw, NY (village) Rockland County	419	3.64
Palm Springs, FL (village) Palm Beach County	678	3.63
Opa-locka, FL (city) Miami-Dade County	547	3.62
West Park, FL (city) Broward County	513	3.60
Milton, MA (cdp/town) Norfolk County	956	3.58
Tamarac, FL (city) Broward County	2,124	3.55
Ojus, FL (cdp) Miami-Dade County	595	3.50
South Miami Heights, FL (cdp) Miami-Dade County	1,272	3.47
Auburndale, FL (city) Polk County	459	3.43
Haverstraw, NY (town) Rockland County	1,200	3.34
Boston, MA (city) Suffolk County	19,850	3.29
Salisbury, MD (city) Wicomico County	963	3.28
Haines City, FL (city) Polk County	650	3.28
Bayshore Gardens, FL (cdp) Manatee County	548	3.28
Hollywood, FL (city) Broward County	4,542	3.22
Port St. Lucie, FL (city) St. Lucie County	4,942	3.19
Coconut Creek, FL (city) Broward County	1,620	3.14
The Crossings, FL (cdp) Miami-Dade County	741	3.12
Elizabeth, NJ (city) Union County	3,811	3.09
Orlando, FL (city) Orange County	7,164	3.07
Medford, MA (city) Middlesex County	1,690	3.05
Willingboro, NJ (township) Burlington County	979	3.04
Royal Palm Beach, FL (village) Palm Beach County	961	2.98
Hallandale Beach, FL (city) Broward County	1,069	2.91
North Lindenhurst, NY (cdp) Suffolk County	338	2.91
West Orange, NJ (township) Essex County	1,327	2.90
University, FL (cdp) Hillsborough County	1,162	2.87
Lancaster, MA (town) Worcester County	223	2.87
Bridgeport, CT (city/town) Fairfield County	4,076	2.86
Brooklyn, NY (borough) Kings County	69,941	2.84
Stoughton, MA (town) Norfolk County	761	2.84
Holbrook, MA (cdp/town) Norfolk County	302	2.82
Brownsville, FL (cdp) Miami-Dade County	356	2.73
Cambridge, MA (city) Middlesex County	2,816	2.72
East Lake-Orient Park, FL (cdp) Hillsborough County	649	2.71
East Massapequa, NY (cdp) Nassau County	481	2.70
Villa Rica, GA (city) Carroll County	337	2.69
Chester, NY (town) Orange County	324	2.67
Palm Bay, FL (city) Brevard County	2,670	2.65
Ocean, NJ (township) Monmouth County	714	2.62
Stratford, CT (cdp/town) Fairfield County	1,328	2.61
Melville, NY (cdp) Suffolk County	492	2.58
Dania Beach, FL (city) Broward County	754	2.56
Clarkstown, NY (town) Rockland County	2,077	2.49
Dennis, MA (town) Barnstable County	363	2.49
Gifford, FL (cdp) Indian River County	252	2.42
Hempstead, NY (town) Nassau County	17,422	2.31
West Perrine, FL (cdp) Miami-Dade County	231	2.31
Oronoko, MI (charter township) Berrien County	213	2.31
Triangle, VA (cdp) Prince William County	178	2.31
Acworth, GA (city) Cobb County	442	2.29
White Oak, MD (cdp) Montgomery County	378	2.27
Homestead, FL (city) Miami-Dade County	1,236	2.24
Stockbridge, GA (city) Henry County	531	2.24
Calverton, MD (cdp) Montgomery County	397	2.23
McDonough, GA (city) Henry County	440	2.18
Scotchtown, NY (cdp) Orange County	210	2.16
Middle Smithfield, PA (township) Monroe County	335	2.15
Mercerville, NJ (cdp) Mercer County	261	2.06
Baywood, NY (cdp) Suffolk County	160	2.03
San Carlos Park, FL (cdp) Lee County	358	2.02
Lakewood Park, FL (cdp) St. Lucie County	237	2.00
Woodbury, NY (village) Orange County	209	2.00
South Orange Village, NJ (township) Essex County	321	1.98
Deer Park, NY (cdp) Suffolk County	558	1.97

Please refer to the Explanation of Data in the front of the book for more detailed information.

Ancestry

West Indian: Jamaican, excluding Hispanic

U.S. and 50 States Sorted by Population and Percent of Total Population

Place	Population	%
United States	**941,339**	**0.31**
New York	300,094	1.56
Florida	246,902	1.33
New Jersey	55,938	0.64
Georgia	49,026	0.52
Connecticut	48,937	1.38
Maryland	32,252	0.57
California	25,882	0.07
Pennsylvania	25,515	0.20
Massachusetts	23,772	0.37
Texas	18,540	0.08
Virginia	15,574	0.20
North Carolina	12,897	0.14
Illinois	11,721	0.09
Ohio	8,744	0.08
Michigan	7,188	0.07
South Carolina	4,323	0.10
Delaware	4,136	0.47
Washington	3,920	0.06
District of Columbia	3,576	0.61
Alabama	3,378	0.07
Colorado	3,327	0.07
Arizona	3,184	0.05
Nevada	2,950	0.11
Wisconsin	2,747	0.05
Missouri	2,537	0.04
Indiana	2,228	0.03
Minnesota	2,177	0.04
Louisiana	2,140	0.05
Tennessee	2,092	0.03
Kentucky	1,708	0.04
New Hampshire	1,338	0.10
Oregon	1,234	0.03
Oklahoma	1,188	0.03
Rhode Island	1,144	0.11
West Virginia	963	0.05
Mississippi	962	0.03
Maine	846	0.06
Arkansas	840	0.03
Kansas	812	0.03
Hawaii	771	0.06
Iowa	760	0.03
New Mexico	645	0.03
Nebraska	546	0.03
Utah	433	0.02
Idaho	315	0.02
Vermont	290	0.05
Alaska	245	0.04
Montana	244	0.03
South Dakota	202	0.03
North Dakota	95	0.01
Wyoming	61	0.01

Place	Population	%
New York	300,094	1.56
Connecticut	48,937	1.38
Florida	246,902	1.33
New Jersey	55,938	0.64
District of Columbia	3,576	0.61
Maryland	32,252	0.57
Georgia	49,026	0.52
Delaware	4,136	0.47
Massachusetts	23,772	0.37
United States	**941,339**	**0.31**
Pennsylvania	25,515	0.20
Virginia	15,574	0.20
North Carolina	12,897	0.14
Nevada	2,950	0.11
Rhode Island	1,144	0.11
South Carolina	4,323	0.10
New Hampshire	1,338	0.10
Illinois	11,721	0.09
Texas	18,540	0.08
Ohio	8,744	0.08
California	25,882	0.07
Michigan	7,188	0.07
Alabama	3,378	0.07
Colorado	3,327	0.07
Washington	3,920	0.06
Maine	846	0.06
Hawaii	771	0.06
Arizona	3,184	0.05
Wisconsin	2,747	0.05
Louisiana	2,140	0.05
West Virginia	963	0.05
Vermont	290	0.05
Missouri	2,537	0.04
Minnesota	2,177	0.04
Kentucky	1,708	0.04
Alaska	245	0.04
Indiana	2,228	0.03
Tennessee	2,092	0.03
Oregon	1,234	0.03
Oklahoma	1,188	0.03
Mississippi	962	0.03
Arkansas	840	0.03
Kansas	812	0.03
Iowa	760	0.03
New Mexico	645	0.03
Nebraska	546	0.03
Montana	244	0.03
South Dakota	202	0.03
Utah	433	0.02
Idaho	315	0.02
North Dakota	95	0.01
Wyoming	61	0.01

Please refer to the Explanation of Data in the front of the book for more detailed information.

Ancestry

West Indian: Jamaican, excluding Hispanic

Top 150 Places Sorted by Population

Based on all places, regardless of total population

Place	Population	%
New York, NY (city) Kings County	216,495	2.68
Brooklyn, NY (borough) Kings County	80,999	3.28
Bronx, NY (borough) Bronx County	64,222	4.70
Queens, NY (borough) Queens County	59,999	2.73
Hempstead, NY (town) Nassau County	17,690	2.35
Miramar, FL (city) Broward County	14,117	12.42
Lauderhill, FL (city) Broward County	13,451	20.04
Hartford, CT (city/town) Hartford County	11,200	8.98
Sunrise, FL (city) Broward County	10,844	12.75
Mount Vernon, NY (city) Westchester County	10,445	15.57
Philadelphia, PA (city) Philadelphia County	10,082	0.67
Miami Gardens, FL (city) Miami-Dade County	9,447	8.94
Manhattan, NY (borough) New York County	9,242	0.58
Bridgeport, CT (city/town) Fairfield County	8,429	5.91
Pembroke Pines, FL (city) Broward County	8,136	5.34
Boston, MA (city) Suffolk County	7,904	1.31
Lauderdale Lakes, FL (city) Broward County	7,173	22.04
Plantation, FL (city) Broward County	5,589	6.57
Pine Hills, FL (cdp) Orange County	5,236	7.91
Yonkers, NY (city) Westchester County	5,051	2.59
Coral Springs, FL (city) Broward County	4,883	4.03
Babylon, NY (town) Suffolk County	4,758	2.23
Paterson, NJ (city) Passaic County	4,741	3.25
North Lauderdale, FL (city) Broward County	4,709	11.54
Port St. Lucie, FL (city) St. Lucie County	4,629	2.99
Chicago, IL (city) Cook County	4,601	0.17
Los Angeles, CA (city) Los Angeles County	4,559	0.12
Fort Lauderdale, FL (city) Broward County	4,265	2.55
Hollywood, FL (city) Broward County	4,072	2.88
Baltimore, MD (city) Baltimore city County	4,029	0.65
Palm Bay, FL (city) Brevard County	3,984	3.96
Tamarac, FL (city) Broward County	3,828	6.40
Jacksonville, FL (city) Duval County	3,825	0.47
Springfield, MA (city) Hampden County	3,692	2.41
Washington, DC (city) District of Columbia	3,576	0.61
Newark, NJ (city) Essex County	3,448	1.26
Bloomfield, CT (town) Hartford County	3,181	15.64
East Orange, NJ (city) Essex County	3,176	4.89
West Palm Beach, FL (city) Palm Beach County	3,173	3.24
Lehigh Acres, FL (cdp) Lee County	3,168	3.75
Poughkeepsie, NY (city) Dutchess County	3,093	9.53
Orlando, FL (city) Orange County	3,028	1.30
Elmont, NY (cdp) Nassau County	2,968	8.61
Stamford, CT (city/town) Fairfield County	2,945	2.44
Windsor, CT (town) Hartford County	2,923	10.10
Houston, TX (city) Harris County	2,897	0.14
North Miami, FL (city) Miami-Dade County	2,862	4.87
Rochester, NY (city) Monroe County	2,834	1.34
Hempstead, NY (village) Nassau County	2,809	5.26
Islip, NY (town) Suffolk County	2,690	0.81
New Rochelle, NY (city) Westchester County	2,635	3.48
Margate, FL (city) Broward County	2,558	4.77
Ramapo, NY (town) Rockland County	2,509	2.04
Irvington, NJ (township) Essex County	2,472	4.51
Poinciana, FL (cdp) Osceola County	2,471	4.94
City of Orange, NJ (township) Essex County	2,334	7.68
Charlotte, NC (city) Mecklenburg County	2,278	0.32
North Amityville, NY (cdp) Suffolk County	2,248	12.62
East Hartford, CT (cdp/town) Hartford County	2,176	4.27
Waterbury, CT (city/town) New Haven County	2,171	1.97
Tampa, FL (city) Hillsborough County	2,151	0.65
Greenburgh, NY (town) Westchester County	2,150	2.45
Staten Island, NY (borough) Richmond County	2,033	0.44
New Haven, CT (city/town) New Haven County	1,979	1.54
Detroit, MI (city) Wayne County	1,946	0.26
Uniondale, NY (cdp) Nassau County	1,905	7.78
Virginia Beach, VA (ind. city) Virginia Beach independent city	1,895	0.43
North Miami Beach, FL (city) Miami-Dade County	1,880	4.55
Freeport, NY (village) Nassau County	1,840	4.31
The Acreage, FL (cdp) Palm Beach County	1,809	4.78
Miami, FL (city) Miami-Dade County	1,770	0.45
Plainfield, NJ (city) Union County	1,690	3.45
Coconut Creek, FL (city) Broward County	1,685	3.27
Teaneck, NJ (township) Bergen County	1,680	4.26
Jersey City, NJ (city) Hudson County	1,670	0.69
Riviera Beach, FL (city) Palm Beach County	1,645	5.06
Tallahassee, FL (city) Leon County	1,644	0.93
Albany, NY (city) Albany County	1,636	1.67
Cutler Bay, FL (town) Miami-Dade County	1,608	4.19
Royal Palm Beach, FL (village) Palm Beach County	1,589	4.93
Port Charlotte, FL (cdp) Charlotte County	1,575	2.79
Trenton, NJ (city) Mercer County	1,571	1.84
Brookhaven, NY (town) Suffolk County	1,546	0.32
Baldwin, NY (cdp) Nassau County	1,531	6.46
Atlanta, GA (city) Fulton County	1,519	0.37
Wellington, FL (village) Palm Beach County	1,514	2.82
South Miami Heights, FL (cdp) Miami-Dade County	1,488	4.06
Davie, FL (town) Broward County	1,431	1.58
Brockton, MA (city) Plymouth County	1,424	1.52
Buffalo, NY (city) Erie County	1,420	0.53
Ives Estates, FL (cdp) Miami-Dade County	1,347	7.65
Boynton Beach, FL (city) Palm Beach County	1,347	1.99
Columbus, OH (city) Franklin County	1,305	0.17
Randolph, MA (cdp/town) Norfolk County	1,304	4.12
Palm Coast, FL (city) Flagler County	1,285	1.81
Cleveland, OH (city) Cuyahoga County	1,281	0.31
North Valley Stream, NY (cdp) Nassau County	1,257	7.62
Alafaya, FL (cdp) Orange County	1,252	1.62
Valley Stream, NY (village) Nassau County	1,248	3.37
Brandon, FL (cdp) Hillsborough County	1,222	1.23
Chillum, MD (cdp) Prince George's County	1,220	3.48
Milwaukee, WI (city) Milwaukee County	1,209	0.21
Norwalk, CT (city/town) Fairfield County	1,207	1.43
Weston, FL (city) Broward County	1,191	1.90
Evanston, IL (city) Cook County	1,181	1.60
Syracuse, NY (city) Onondaga County	1,181	0.82
West Haven, CT (city/town) New Haven County	1,150	2.09
Willingboro, NJ (township) Burlington County	1,130	3.51
Dania Beach, FL (city) Broward County	1,093	3.72
Pembroke Park, FL (town) Broward County	1,090	18.51
Norfolk, VA (ind. city) Norfolk independent city	1,082	0.45
Town 'n' Country, FL (cdp) Hillsborough County	1,077	1.40
Country Club, FL (cdp) Miami-Dade County	1,053	2.65
Englewood, NJ (city) Bergen County	1,046	3.90
Montgomery Village, MD (cdp) Montgomery County	1,045	3.30
Blue Hills, CT (cdp) Hartford County	1,037	35.86
San Diego, CA (city) San Diego County	1,036	0.08
Franklin, NJ (township) Somerset County	1,022	1.69
Lakeland, FL (city) Polk County	1,016	1.05
West Park, FL (city) Broward County	987	6.92
Daytona Beach, FL (city) Volusia County	984	1.56
Hamden, CT (town) New Haven County	979	1.62
Kendall, FL (cdp) Miami-Dade County	978	1.28
St. Petersburg, FL (city) Pinellas County	976	0.40
Oyster Bay, NY (town) Nassau County	972	0.33
Bloomfield, NJ (township) Essex County	969	2.06
Deerfield Beach, FL (city) Broward County	960	1.28
San Antonio, TX (city) Medina County	951	0.07
Winchester, VA (ind. city) Winchester independent city	934	3.60
Colorado Springs, CO (city) El Paso County	919	0.23
Country Walk, FL (cdp) Miami-Dade County	914	5.75
Raleigh, NC (city) Wake County	914	0.24
Roosevelt, NY (cdp) Nassau County	910	6.05
Riverview, FL (cdp) Hillsborough County	910	1.39
Phoenix, AZ (city) Maricopa County	910	0.06
Huntington, NY (town) Suffolk County	893	0.44
Durham, NC (city) Durham County	885	0.40
Toledo, OH (city) Lucas County	879	0.30
Hampton, VA (ind. city) Hampton independent city	873	0.63
North Hempstead, NY (town) Nassau County	868	0.39
Spring Valley, NY (village) Rockland County	866	2.86
Hallandale Beach, FL (city) Broward County	862	2.35
Greensboro, NC (city) Guilford County	860	0.33
Hillcrest, NY (cdp) Rockland County	854	10.42
University, FL (cdp) Hillsborough County	853	2.11
West Perrine, FL (cdp) Miami-Dade County	831	8.30
Bowie, MD (city) Prince George's County	828	1.52
Pompano Beach, FL (city) Broward County	827	0.82
Redan, GA (cdp) DeKalb County	826	2.41
Peekskill, NY (city) Westchester County	821	3.54

Please refer to the Explanation of Data in the front of the book for more detailed information.

Ancestry

West Indian: Jamaican, excluding Hispanic

Top 150 Places Sorted by Percent of Total Population

Based on all places, regardless of total population

Place	Population	%
Blue Hills, CT (cdp) Hartford County	1,037	35.86
Albrightsville, PA (cdp) Carbon County	54	27.69
Lauderdale Lakes, FL (city) Broward County	7,173	22.04
Slaughter Beach, DE (town) Sussex County	22	21.15
Lauderhill, FL (city) Broward County	13,451	20.04
Pembroke Park, FL (town) Broward County	1,090	18.51
Portage, MI (township) Mackinac County	155	18.07
Bloomfield, CT (town) Hartford County	3,181	15.64
Mount Vernon, NY (city) Westchester County	10,445	15.57
Harlem Heights, FL (cdp) Lee County	226	14.26
Lakeview, NY (cdp) Nassau County	791	14.20
Sunrise, FL (city) Broward County	10,844	12.75
North Amityville, NY (cdp) Suffolk County	2,248	12.62
Stacey Street, FL (cdp) Palm Beach County	153	12.59
Miramar, FL (city) Broward County	14,117	12.42
North Lauderdale, FL (city) Broward County	4,709	11.54
Keller, VA (town) Accomack County	25	11.36
Saxapahaw, NC (cdp) Alamance County	124	10.99
Hillcrest, NY (cdp) Rockland County	854	10.42
Madison, FL (city) Madison County	300	10.24
Windsor, CT (town) Hartford County	2,923	10.10
Poughkeepsie, NY (city) Dutchess County	3,093	9.53
Limestone Creek, FL (cdp) Palm Beach County	73	9.10
Mangonia Park, FL (town) Palm Beach County	152	9.06
South Floral Park, NY (village) Nassau County	141	9.03
Hartford, CT (city/town) Hartford County	11,200	8.98
Miami Gardens, FL (city) Miami-Dade County	9,447	8.94
Bonanza, GA (cdp) Clayton County	226	8.72
Elmont, NY (cdp) Nassau County	2,968	8.61
Royal Palm Estates, FL (cdp) Palm Beach County	309	8.44
West Perrine, FL (cdp) Miami-Dade County	831	8.30
Winter Beach, FL (cdp) Indian River County	121	8.23
Pine Hills, FL (cdp) Orange County	5,236	7.91
Uniondale, NY (cdp) Nassau County	1,905	7.78
City of Orange, NJ (township) Essex County	2,334	7.68
Ives Estates, FL (cdp) Miami-Dade County	1,347	7.65
Taft, FL (cdp) Orange County	141	7.64
North Valley Stream, NY (cdp) Nassau County	1,257	7.62
Pahokee, FL (city) Palm Beach County	416	7.16
Loon Lake, WA (cdp) Stevens County	53	7.08
Westview, FL (cdp) Miami-Dade County	652	6.97
Nantucket, MA (cdp) Nantucket County	553	6.96
West Park, FL (city) Broward County	987	6.92
Morrisville, NY (village) Madison County	173	6.83
Haverhill, FL (town) Palm Beach County	138	6.75
Clintondale, NY (cdp) Ulster County	71	6.71
Plantation, FL (city) Broward County	5,589	6.57
Brooklawn, NJ (borough) Camden County	111	6.54
Boonton, NJ (town) Morris County	549	6.53
Baldwin, NY (cdp) Nassau County	1,531	6.46
Kenwood Estates, FL (cdp) Palm Beach County	71	6.42
Tamarac, FL (city) Broward County	3,828	6.40
El Portal, FL (village) Miami-Dade County	150	6.27
Mount Healthy Heights, OH (cdp) Hamilton County	214	6.15
Kingston, GA (city) Bartow County	49	6.11
Roosevelt, NY (cdp) Nassau County	910	6.05
Bridgeport, CT (city/town) Fairfield County	8,429	5.91
Crystal River, FL (city) Citrus County	192	5.86
Dundee, FL (town) Polk County	210	5.79
Country Walk, FL (cdp) Miami-Dade County	914	5.75
Harvey, MI (cdp) Marquette County	83	5.58
East Lansdowne, PA (borough) Delaware County	146	5.52
Nantucket, MA (town) Nantucket County	553	5.49
Birch Hill, WI (cdp) Ashland County	23	5.39
Pembroke Pines, FL (city) Broward County	8,136	5.34
Broad Brook, CT (cdp) Hartford County	243	5.27
Hempstead, NY (village) Nassau County	2,809	5.26
Green Cove Springs, FL (city) Clay County	355	5.24
South Bay, FL (city) Palm Beach County	248	5.20
Wheatley Heights, NY (cdp) Suffolk County	319	5.15
Spencerville, MD (cdp) Montgomery County	77	5.15
Minneola, FL (city) Lake County	463	5.14
Riviera Beach, FL (city) Palm Beach County	1,645	5.06
Islandia, NY (village) Suffolk County	167	5.06
Gates, NY (cdp) Monroe County	271	5.04
Amityville, NY (village) Suffolk County	480	5.03
Yeadon, PA (borough) Delaware County	571	4.98
Naranja, FL (cdp) Miami-Dade County	318	4.98
Poinciana, FL (cdp) Osceola County	2,471	4.94
Royal Palm Beach, FL (village) Palm Beach County	1,589	4.93
Silver Springs Shores, FL (cdp) Marion County	338	4.92
North Key Largo, FL (cdp) Monroe County	65	4.91
East Orange, NJ (city) Essex County	3,176	4.89
North Miami, FL (city) Miami-Dade County	2,862	4.87
The Acreage, FL (cdp) Palm Beach County	1,809	4.78
Franklin, NY (village) Delaware County	16	4.78
Margate, FL (city) Broward County	2,558	4.77
Bronx, NY (borough) Bronx County	64,222	4.70
Fort White, FL (town) Columbia County	33	4.68
Glen Ridge, NJ (borough) Essex County	347	4.66
Brinckerhoff, NY (cdp) Dutchess County	150	4.64
Prairie View, TX (city) Waller County	243	4.63
Holden, ME (town) Penobscot County	140	4.59
Berrien Springs, MI (village) Berrien County	113	4.58
North Miami Beach, FL (city) Miami-Dade County	1,880	4.55
Irvington, NJ (township) Essex County	2,472	4.51
Boulevard Gardens, FL (cdp) Broward County	75	4.39
French Lick, IN (town) Orange County	84	4.37
Woodmere, OH (village) Cuyahoga County	40	4.34
Freeport, NY (village) Nassau County	1,840	4.31
Elmsford, NY (village) Westchester County	198	4.29
Houston Lake, MO (city) Platte County	9	4.29
Harlem, FL (cdp) Hendry County	133	4.28
East Hartford, CT (cdp/town) Hartford County	2,176	4.27
Teaneck, NJ (township) Bergen County	1,680	4.26
Waretown, NJ (cdp) Ocean County	56	4.25
Loganville, GA (city) Walton County	409	4.24
Palmetto Estates, FL (cdp) Miami-Dade County	576	4.23
Cedarville, MD (cdp) Prince George's County	37	4.22
Cutler Bay, FL (town) Miami-Dade County	1,608	4.19
Camden, DE (town) Kent County	135	4.16
Lake Wilderness, VA (cdp) Spotsylvania County	97	4.15
Randolph, MA (cdp/town) Norfolk County	1,304	4.12
Clarkston, GA (city) DeKalb County	310	4.10
Avon Park, FL (city) Highlands County	365	4.07
South Miami Heights, FL (cdp) Miami-Dade County	1,488	4.06
Washingtonville, NY (village) Orange County	240	4.04
Coral Springs, FL (city) Broward County	4,883	4.03
Maryland City, MD (cdp) Anne Arundel County	622	4.03
Palm Bay, FL (city) Brevard County	3,984	3.96
Wild Rice, MN (township) Norman County	10	3.94
Penn Estates, PA (cdp) Monroe County	165	3.93
Englewood, NJ (city) Bergen County	1,046	3.90
Quinby, SC (town) Florence County	45	3.88
Suffern, NY (village) Rockland County	413	3.86
Seminole Manor, FL (cdp) Palm Beach County	100	3.83
Princeton, FL (cdp) Miami-Dade County	787	3.82
Rockville, CT (cdp) Tolland County	292	3.79
Ovid, NY (village) Seneca County	18	3.77
Alden, MI (cdp) Antrim County	5	3.76
Lehigh Acres, FL (cdp) Lee County	3,168	3.75
Dania Beach, FL (city) Broward County	1,093	3.72
Edgemoor, DE (cdp) New Castle County	200	3.72
Parishville, NY (cdp) St. Lawrence County	25	3.71
Bithlo, FL (cdp) Orange County	282	3.69
Fairfield, NJ (township) Cumberland County	234	3.68
South Valley Stream, NY (cdp) Nassau County	193	3.67
Otego, NY (village) Otsego County	47	3.61
Winchester, VA (ind. city) Winchester independent city	934	3.60
Yosemite Valley, CA (cdp) Mariposa County	13	3.60
Wedgefield, FL (cdp) Orange County	231	3.56
Kidder, PA (township) Carbon County	65	3.56
Peekskill, NY (city) Westchester County	821	3.54
Belle Glade, FL (city) Palm Beach County	626	3.54
Wappingers Falls, NY (village) Dutchess County	193	3.53
North Laurel, MD (cdp) Howard County	144	3.53
Willingboro, NJ (township) Burlington County	1,130	3.51
Three Lakes, FL (cdp) Miami-Dade County	507	3.51
Cliffwood Beach, NJ (cdp) Monmouth County	107	3.50
Thomaston, AL (town) Marengo County	14	3.50

Please refer to the Explanation of Data in the front of the book for more detailed information.

Ancestry

West Indian: Jamaican, excluding Hispanic

Top 150 Places Sorted by Percent of Total Population

Based on places with total population of 7,500 or more

Place	Population	%
Lauderdale Lakes, FL (city) Broward County	7,173	22.04
Lauderhill, FL (city) Broward County	13,451	20.04
Bloomfield, CT (town) Hartford County	3,181	15.64
Mount Vernon, NY (city) Westchester County	10,445	15.57
Sunrise, FL (city) Broward County	10,844	12.75
North Amityville, NY (cdp) Suffolk County	2,248	12.62
Miramar, FL (city) Broward County	14,117	12.42
North Lauderdale, FL (city) Broward County	4,709	11.54
Hillcrest, NY (cdp) Rockland County	854	10.42
Windsor, CT (town) Hartford County	2,923	10.10
Poughkeepsie, NY (city) Dutchess County	3,093	9.53
Hartford, CT (city/town) Hartford County	11,200	8.98
Miami Gardens, FL (city) Miami-Dade County	9,447	8.94
Elmont, NY (cdp) Nassau County	2,968	8.61
West Perrine, FL (cdp) Miami-Dade County	831	8.30
Pine Hills, FL (cdp) Orange County	5,236	7.91
Uniondale, NY (cdp) Nassau County	1,905	7.78
City of Orange, NJ (township) Essex County	2,334	7.68
Ives Estates, FL (cdp) Miami-Dade County	1,347	7.65
North Valley Stream, NY (cdp) Nassau County	1,257	7.62
Westview, FL (cdp) Miami-Dade County	652	6.97
Nantucket, MA (cdp) Nantucket County	553	6.96
West Park, FL (city) Broward County	987	6.92
Plantation, FL (city) Broward County	5,589	6.57
Boonton, NJ (town) Morris County	549	6.53
Baldwin, NY (cdp) Nassau County	1,531	6.46
Tamarac, FL (city) Broward County	3,828	6.40
Roosevelt, NY (cdp) Nassau County	910	6.05
Bridgeport, CT (city/town) Fairfield County	8,429	5.91
Country Walk, FL (cdp) Miami-Dade County	914	5.75
Nantucket, MA (town) Nantucket County	553	5.49
Pembroke Pines, FL (city) Broward County	8,136	5.34
Hempstead, NY (village) Nassau County	2,809	5.26
Minneola, FL (city) Lake County	463	5.14
Riviera Beach, FL (city) Palm Beach County	1,645	5.06
Amityville, NY (village) Suffolk County	480	5.03
Yeadon, PA (borough) Delaware County	571	4.98
Poinciana, FL (cdp) Osceola County	2,471	4.94
Royal Palm Beach, FL (village) Palm Beach County	1,589	4.93
East Orange, NJ (city) Essex County	3,176	4.89
North Miami, FL (city) Miami-Dade County	2,862	4.87
The Acreage, FL (cdp) Palm Beach County	1,809	4.78
Margate, FL (city) Broward County	2,558	4.77
Bronx, NY (borough) Bronx County	64,222	4.70
North Miami Beach, FL (city) Miami-Dade County	1,880	4.55
Irvington, NJ (township) Essex County	2,472	4.51
Freeport, NY (village) Nassau County	1,840	4.31
East Hartford, CT (cdp/town) Hartford County	2,176	4.27
Teaneck, NJ (township) Bergen County	1,680	4.26
Loganville, GA (city) Walton County	409	4.24
Palmetto Estates, FL (cdp) Miami-Dade County	576	4.23
Cutler Bay, FL (town) Miami-Dade County	1,608	4.19
Randolph, MA (cdp/town) Norfolk County	1,304	4.12
Clarkston, GA (city) DeKalb County	310	4.10
Avon Park, FL (city) Highlands County	365	4.07
South Miami Heights, FL (cdp) Miami-Dade County	1,488	4.06
Coral Springs, FL (city) Broward County	4,883	4.03
Maryland City, MD (cdp) Anne Arundel County	622	4.03
Palm Bay, FL (city) Brevard County	3,984	3.96
Englewood, NJ (city) Bergen County	1,046	3.90
Suffern, NY (village) Rockland County	413	3.86
Princeton, FL (cdp) Miami-Dade County	787	3.82
Rockville, CT (cdp) Tolland County	292	3.79
Lehigh Acres, FL (cdp) Lee County	3,168	3.75
Dania Beach, FL (city) Broward County	1,093	3.72
Bithlo, FL (cdp) Orange County	282	3.69
Winchester, VA (ind. city) Winchester independent city	934	3.60
Peekskill, NY (city) Westchester County	821	3.54
Belle Glade, FL (city) Palm Beach County	626	3.54
Willingboro, NJ (township) Burlington County	1,130	3.51
Three Lakes, FL (cdp) Miami-Dade County	507	3.51
New Rochelle, NY (city) Westchester County	2,635	3.48
Chillum, MD (cdp) Prince George's County	1,220	3.48
Plainfield, NJ (city) Union County	1,690	3.45
Conyers, GA (city) Rockdale County	503	3.45
Valley Stream, NY (village) Nassau County	1,248	3.37
East Massapequa, NY (cdp) Nassau County	600	3.36
Montgomery Village, MD (cdp) Montgomery County	1,045	3.30
Brooklyn, NY (borough) Kings County	80,999	3.28
Coconut Creek, FL (city) Broward County	1,685	3.27
Paterson, NJ (city) Passaic County	4,741	3.25
West Palm Beach, FL (city) Palm Beach County	3,173	3.24
Morris, NJ (town) Morris County	587	3.18
Maplewood, NJ (township) Essex County	744	3.13
East Windsor, CT (town) Hartford County	335	3.07
Mount Rainier, MD (city) Prince George's County	248	3.04
Palmetto Bay, FL (village) Miami-Dade County	707	3.02
Temple Hills, MD (cdp) Prince George's County	231	3.02
Franklin, VA (ind. city) Franklin independent city	257	3.01
Port St. Lucie, FL (city) St. Lucie County	4,629	2.99
Adelphi, MD (cdp) Prince George's County	435	2.89
Hollywood, FL (city) Broward County	4,072	2.88
Spring Valley, NY (village) Rockland County	866	2.86
The Crossings, FL (cdp) Miami-Dade County	678	2.86
Lake Park, FL (town) Palm Beach County	234	2.85
Wellington, FL (village) Palm Beach County	1,514	2.82
Port Charlotte, FL (cdp) Charlotte County	1,575	2.79
Pinewood, FL (cdp) Miami-Dade County	446	2.79
East Franklin, NJ (cdp) Somerset County	212	2.75
Oronoko, MI (charter township) Berrien County	253	2.74
Queens, NY (borough) Queens County	59,999	2.73
Fairview Shores, FL (cdp) Orange County	281	2.73
New Cassel, NY (cdp) Nassau County	341	2.71
New York, NY (city) Kings County	216,495	2.68
Burtonsville, MD (cdp) Montgomery County	246	2.66
Country Club, FL (cdp) Miami-Dade County	1,053	2.65
Palm Springs, FL (village) Palm Beach County	495	2.65
East Riverdale, MD (cdp) Prince George's County	416	2.65
Takoma Park, MD (city) Montgomery County	443	2.63
Milford Mill, MD (cdp) Baltimore County	753	2.62
Wappinger, NY (town) Dutchess County	708	2.62
Neptune, NJ (township) Monmouth County	727	2.60
Yonkers, NY (city) Westchester County	5,051	2.59
Somerset, NJ (cdp) Somerset County	580	2.59
Fort Lauderdale, FL (city) Broward County	4,265	2.55
Lanham, MD (cdp) Prince George's County	227	2.54
New Carrollton, MD (city) Prince George's County	303	2.50
Beacon Square, FL (cdp) Pasco County	188	2.47
Greenburgh, NY (town) Westchester County	2,150	2.45
Sangaree, SC (cdp) Berkeley County	221	2.45
Stamford, CT (city/town) Fairfield County	2,945	2.44
Ossining, NY (village) Westchester County	605	2.44
Springfield, MA (city) Hampden County	3,692	2.41
Redan, GA (cdp) DeKalb County	826	2.41
McDonough, GA (city) Henry County	477	2.36
Hempstead, NY (town) Nassau County	17,690	2.35
Hallandale Beach, FL (city) Broward County	862	2.35
Leisure World, MD (cdp) Montgomery County	202	2.33
Buenaventura Lakes, FL (cdp) Osceola County	622	2.32
Golden Glades, FL (cdp) Miami-Dade County	759	2.30
Pebble Creek, FL (cdp) Hillsborough County	173	2.29
Miami Shores, FL (village) Miami-Dade County	235	2.24
Babylon, NY (town) Suffolk County	4,758	2.23
Stroud, PA (township) Monroe County	418	2.23
Wyandanch, NY (cdp) Suffolk County	242	2.21
Plattekill, NY (town) Ulster County	226	2.16
South Laurel, MD (cdp) Prince George's County	548	2.13
Baywood, NY (cdp) Suffolk County	167	2.12
University, FL (cdp) Hillsborough County	853	2.11
Parkland, FL (city) Broward County	474	2.11
West Haven, CT (city/town) New Haven County	1,150	2.09
Neabsco, VA (cdp) Prince William County	196	2.08
Laurel, MD (city) Prince George's County	505	2.07
Roselle, NJ (borough) Union County	433	2.07
Round Lake, IL (village) Lake County	334	2.07
New Windsor, NY (cdp) Orange County	188	2.07
Bloomfield, NJ (township) Essex County	969	2.06
Haines City, FL (city) Polk County	405	2.05
Ramapo, NY (town) Rockland County	2,509	2.04
Lochearn, MD (cdp) Baltimore County	525	2.04

SECTION THREE

Ancestry

West Indian: Trinidadian and Tobagonian, excluding Hispanic

U.S. and 50 States Sorted by Population and Percent of Total Population

Place	Population	%
United States	**189,059**	**0.06**
New York	89,490	0.47
Florida	29,267	0.16
New Jersey	11,749	0.13
Maryland	9,483	0.17
Georgia	6,991	0.07
Massachusetts	5,458	0.08
Pennsylvania	5,362	0.04
Texas	5,278	0.02
California	4,439	0.01
Virginia	3,765	0.05
Connecticut	2,823	0.08
North Carolina	2,499	0.03
District of Columbia	1,288	0.22
South Carolina	1,111	0.02
Illinois	1,069	0.01
Michigan	980	0.01
Ohio	938	0.01
Louisiana	806	0.02
Arizona	680	0.01
Washington	567	0.01
Delaware	541	0.06
Alabama	504	0.01
Tennessee	345	0.01
Nevada	343	0.01
Rhode Island	327	0.03
Kentucky	283	0.01
Minnesota	260	<0.01
Kansas	239	0.01
Indiana	233	<0.01
Missouri	229	<0.01
Colorado	208	<0.01
Utah	161	0.01
Iowa	156	0.01
Maine	150	0.01
Oklahoma	150	<0.01
Arkansas	140	<0.01
New Hampshire	123	0.01
Alaska	91	0.01
Nebraska	86	<0.01
New Mexico	77	<0.01
North Dakota	71	0.01
Mississippi	69	<0.01
West Virginia	63	<0.01
Wisconsin	45	<0.01
Hawaii	43	<0.01
Oregon	41	<0.01
Vermont	20	<0.01
South Dakota	17	<0.01
Idaho	1	<0.01
Montana	0	0.00
Wyoming	0	0.00

Place	Population	%
New York	89,490	0.47
District of Columbia	1,288	0.22
Maryland	9,483	0.17
Florida	29,267	0.16
New Jersey	11,749	0.13
Massachusetts	5,458	0.08
Connecticut	2,823	0.08
Georgia	6,991	0.07
United States	**189,059**	**0.06**
Delaware	541	0.06
Virginia	3,765	0.05
Pennsylvania	5,362	0.04
North Carolina	2,499	0.03
Rhode Island	327	0.03
Texas	5,278	0.02
South Carolina	1,111	0.02
Louisiana	806	0.02
California	4,439	0.01
Illinois	1,069	0.01
Michigan	980	0.01
Ohio	938	0.01
Arizona	680	0.01
Washington	567	0.01
Alabama	504	0.01
Tennessee	345	0.01
Nevada	343	0.01
Kentucky	283	0.01
Kansas	239	0.01
Utah	161	0.01
Iowa	156	0.01
Maine	150	0.01
New Hampshire	123	0.01
Alaska	91	0.01
North Dakota	71	0.01
Minnesota	260	<0.01
Indiana	233	<0.01
Missouri	229	<0.01
Colorado	208	<0.01
Oklahoma	150	<0.01
Arkansas	140	<0.01
Nebraska	86	<0.01
New Mexico	77	<0.01
Mississippi	69	<0.01
West Virginia	63	<0.01
Wisconsin	45	<0.01
Hawaii	43	<0.01
Oregon	41	<0.01
Vermont	20	<0.01
South Dakota	17	<0.01
Idaho	1	<0.01
Montana	0	0.00
Wyoming	0	0.00

Please refer to the Explanation of Data in the front of the book for more detailed information.

Ancestry

West Indian: Trinidadian and Tobagonian, excluding Hispanic

Top 150 Places Sorted by Population

Based on all places, regardless of total population

Place	Population	%
New York, NY (city) Kings County	76,240	0.94
Brooklyn, NY (borough) Kings County	46,490	1.88
Queens, NY (borough) Queens County	19,255	0.88
Bronx, NY (borough) Bronx County	4,811	0.35
Manhattan, NY (borough) New York County	3,877	0.24
Hempstead, NY (town) Nassau County	3,155	0.42
Boston, MA (city) Suffolk County	2,928	0.49
Philadelphia, PA (city) Philadelphia County	2,407	0.16
Staten Island, NY (borough) Richmond County	1,807	0.39
Baltimore, MD (city) Baltimore city County	1,502	0.24
Newark, NJ (city) Essex County	1,399	0.51
Washington, DC (city) District of Columbia	1,288	0.22
Brookhaven, NY (town) Suffolk County	1,200	0.25
Jersey City, NJ (city) Hudson County	1,140	0.47
East Orange, NJ (city) Essex County	1,131	1.74
Houston, TX (city) Harris County	1,106	0.05
Miramar, FL (city) Broward County	1,024	0.90
Port St. Lucie, FL (city) St. Lucie County	1,013	0.65
Babylon, NY (town) Suffolk County	854	0.40
Pembroke Pines, FL (city) Broward County	836	0.55
Sunrise, FL (city) Broward County	828	0.97
Virginia Beach, VA (ind. city) Virginia Beach independent city	809	0.19
Pine Hills, FL (cdp) Orange County	720	1.09
Yonkers, NY (city) Westchester County	689	0.35
Islip, NY (town) Suffolk County	665	0.20
Hollywood, FL (city) Broward County	664	0.47
Lauderhill, FL (city) Broward County	643	0.96
Irvington, NJ (township) Essex County	635	1.16
Los Angeles, CA (city) Los Angeles County	631	0.02
Orlando, FL (city) Orange County	613	0.26
Ramapo, NY (town) Rockland County	604	0.49
Pembroke Park, FL (town) Broward County	557	9.46
North Valley Stream, NY (cdp) Nassau County	551	3.34
Chicago, IL (city) Cook County	533	0.02
Brockton, MA (city) Plymouth County	487	0.52
Coral Springs, FL (city) Broward County	486	0.40
Palm Bay, FL (city) Brevard County	475	0.47
Elmont, NY (cdp) Nassau County	474	1.37
Norfolk, VA (ind. city) Norfolk independent city	459	0.19
Uniondale, NY (cdp) Nassau County	458	1.87
Tampa, FL (city) Hillsborough County	437	0.13
Tamarac, FL (city) Broward County	422	0.71
Palmetto Estates, FL (cdp) Miami-Dade County	421	3.09
South Miami Heights, FL (cdp) Miami-Dade County	419	1.14
Upper Darby, PA (township) Delaware County	411	0.50
Mount Vernon, NY (city) Westchester County	397	0.59
Oakland, CA (city) Alameda County	387	0.10
Palm Coast, FL (city) Flagler County	381	0.54
Jacksonville, FL (city) Duval County	381	0.05
North Lauderdale, FL (city) Broward County	377	0.92
Poinciana, FL (cdp) Osceola County	376	0.75
West Palm Beach, FL (city) Palm Beach County	375	0.38
Hillcrest, NY (cdp) Rockland County	367	4.48
Miami, FL (city) Miami-Dade County	352	0.09
Hackensack, NJ (city) Bergen County	349	0.82
Montgomery Village, MD (cdp) Montgomery County	348	1.10
Milford Mill, MD (cdp) Baltimore County	342	1.19
Cutler Bay, FL (town) Miami-Dade County	340	0.89
Cape Coral, FL (city) Lee County	339	0.23
Freeport, NY (village) Nassau County	333	0.78
Hempstead, NY (village) Nassau County	322	0.60
Homestead, FL (city) Miami-Dade County	320	0.58
New Rochelle, NY (city) Westchester County	317	0.42
Ives Estates, FL (cdp) Miami-Dade County	307	1.74
Dania Beach, FL (city) Broward County	298	1.01
Clermont, FL (city) Lake County	297	1.14
Margate, FL (city) Broward County	293	0.55
Conway, FL (cdp) Orange County	290	2.03
Central Islip, NY (cdp) Suffolk County	289	0.80
Rochester, NY (city) Monroe County	288	0.14
Plainfield, NJ (city) Union County	287	0.59
Alafaya, FL (cdp) Orange County	286	0.37
Town 'n' Country, FL (cdp) Hillsborough County	285	0.37
City of Orange, NJ (township) Essex County	283	0.93
The Acreage, FL (cdp) Palm Beach County	283	0.75
Lindenhurst, NY (village) Suffolk County	268	0.98
Pensacola, FL (city) Escambia County	264	0.50
Humboldt Hill, CA (cdp) Humboldt County	259	6.87
Bowie, MD (city) Prince George's County	255	0.47
Poughkeepsie, NY (city) Dutchess County	253	0.78
Montclair, NJ (township) Essex County	252	0.67
Fort Lauderdale, FL (city) Broward County	251	0.15
Marrero, LA (cdp) Jefferson Parish	250	0.76
Atlanta, GA (city) Fulton County	250	0.06
Miami Gardens, FL (city) Miami-Dade County	247	0.23
Hartford, CT (city/town) Hartford County	244	0.20
Hillcrest Heights, MD (cdp) Prince George's County	243	1.53
Troy, NY (city) Rensselaer County	243	0.49
Charlotte, NC (city) Mecklenburg County	241	0.03
Easton, PA (city) Northampton County	237	0.88
Seabrook, MD (cdp) Prince George's County	235	1.50
North Amityville, NY (cdp) Suffolk County	235	1.32
Scaggsville, MD (cdp) Howard County	235	1.02
Bridgeport, CT (city/town) Fairfield County	233	0.16
Sayreville, NJ (borough) Middlesex County	232	0.55
Lauderdale Lakes, FL (city) Broward County	226	0.69
Plantation, FL (city) Broward County	226	0.27
Lochearn, MD (cdp) Baltimore County	223	0.87
Kendall, FL (cdp) Miami-Dade County	221	0.29
Medford, NY (cdp) Suffolk County	219	0.89
Albany, NY (city) Albany County	219	0.22
Spring Valley, NY (village) Rockland County	217	0.72
College Park, MD (city) Prince George's County	215	0.73
West Orange, NJ (township) Essex County	215	0.47
Bloomfield, CT (town) Hartford County	213	1.05
Rockville, CT (cdp) Tolland County	211	2.74
Vernon, CT (town) Tolland County	211	0.72
Silver Spring, MD (cdp) Montgomery County	211	0.30
Waterbury, CT (city/town) New Haven County	210	0.19
Maplewood, NJ (township) Essex County	207	0.87
New Haven, CT (city/town) New Haven County	203	0.16
Oakland Park, FL (city) Broward County	202	0.48
Greenburgh, NY (town) Westchester County	201	0.23
Columbia, MD (cdp) Howard County	201	0.20
Union, NJ (township) Union County	200	0.36
Buffalo, NY (city) Erie County	200	0.08
Dallas, TX (city) Dallas County	200	0.02
Tallahassee, FL (city) Leon County	196	0.11
Baldwin, NY (cdp) Nassau County	195	0.82
Greenville, NC (city) Pitt County	195	0.24
West Deptford, NJ (township) Gloucester County	193	0.90
Concord, NC (city) Cabarrus County	193	0.26
San Antonio, TX (city) Medina County	192	0.01
Bloomfield, NJ (township) Essex County	187	0.40
High Point, NC (city) Guilford County	186	0.18
Baytown, TX (city) Harris County	184	0.26
Wallkill, NY (town) Orange County	183	0.67
Beverly, MA (city) Essex County	183	0.47
Richmond, VA (ind. city) Richmond independent city	182	0.09
Phoenix, AZ (city) Maricopa County	181	0.01
St. Petersburg, FL (city) Pinellas County	180	0.07
Glenn Dale, MD (cdp) Prince George's County	177	1.25
Takoma Park, MD (city) Montgomery County	177	1.05
Valley Stream, NY (village) Nassau County	177	0.48
Providence, RI (city) Providence County	177	0.10
North Bellport, NY (cdp) Suffolk County	176	1.56
Englewood, NJ (city) Bergen County	176	0.66
Kissimmee, FL (city) Osceola County	175	0.29
Madison, AL (city) Madison County	173	0.43
Riverview, FL (cdp) Hillsborough County	173	0.26
Coconut Creek, FL (city) Broward County	171	0.33
Huntington, NY (town) Suffolk County	170	0.08
Norwalk, CT (city/town) Fairfield County	169	0.20
Long Beach, CA (city) Los Angeles County	168	0.04
Fairland, MD (cdp) Montgomery County	167	0.72
North Miami Beach, FL (city) Miami-Dade County	167	0.40
Hialeah, FL (city) Miami-Dade County	167	0.07
Melbourne, FL (city) Brevard County	166	0.22
Leesburg, VA (town) Loudoun County	164	0.40
Garland, TX (city) Dallas County	163	0.07

SECTION THREE

Please refer to the Explanation of Data in the front of the book for more detailed information.

Ancestry

West Indian: Trinidadian and Tobagonian, excluding Hispanic

Top 150 Places Sorted by Percent of Total Population

Based on all places, regardless of total population

Place	Population	%
Oceola, OH (cdp) Crawford County	22	10.05
Pembroke Park, FL (town) Broward County	557	9.46
Greenevers, NC (town) Duplin County	68	7.17
Humboldt Hill, CA (cdp) Humboldt County	259	6.87
Brewster, NY (village) Putnam County	131	6.53
Seminole Manor, FL (cdp) Palm Beach County	125	4.78
Hillcrest, NY (cdp) Rockland County	367	4.48
Cedarville, MD (cdp) Prince George's County	37	4.22
East Marion, NY (cdp) Suffolk County	54	4.04
South Floral Park, NY (village) Nassau County	53	3.39
North Valley Stream, NY (cdp) Nassau County	551	3.34
Milford, ME (town) Penobscot County	99	3.24
Millville, DE (town) Sussex County	16	3.21
Palmetto Estates, FL (cdp) Miami-Dade County	421	3.09
Rockland, NY (town) Sullivan County	106	2.75
Rockville, CT (cdp) Tolland County	211	2.74
Garrett, WA (cdp) Walla Walla County	35	2.60
Pemberton Heights, NJ (cdp) Burlington County	67	2.51
Social Circle, GA (city) Walton County	105	2.49
Kenansville, NC (town) Duplin County	25	2.31
Rio Pinar, FL (cdp) Orange County	119	2.27
Iron Belt, WI (cdp) Iron County	6	2.25
Monaca, PA (borough) Beaver County	130	2.24
Spencerville, MD (cdp) Montgomery County	33	2.21
South Valley Stream, NY (cdp) Nassau County	110	2.09
Greenwood Lake, NY (village) Orange County	67	2.07
Conway, FL (cdp) Orange County	290	2.03
Goshen, NY (village) Orange County	111	2.00
Knight, WI (town) Iron County	6	1.98
Louisburg, NC (town) Franklin County	65	1.95
Old Orchard, PA (cdp) Northampton County	48	1.91
Brooklyn, NY (borough) Kings County	46,490	1.88
Uniondale, NY (cdp) Nassau County	458	1.87
Salem, NJ (city) Salem County	99	1.87
Ocean City, FL (cdp) Okaloosa County	98	1.86
East Arcadia, NC (town) Bladen County	9	1.80
Stuart, NE (village) Holt County	10	1.79
Barrett, TX (cdp) Harris County	40	1.75
Palm Shores, FL (town) Brevard County	14	1.75
East Orange, NJ (city) Essex County	1,131	1.74
Ives Estates, FL (cdp) Miami-Dade County	307	1.74
Oakland, FL (town) Orange County	39	1.71
Aristocrat Ranchettes, CO (cdp) Weld County	27	1.66
North Bellport, NY (cdp) Suffolk County	176	1.56
Hillcrest Heights, MD (cdp) Prince George's County	243	1.53
Seabrook, MD (cdp) Prince George's County	235	1.50
Gordon Heights, NY (cdp) Suffolk County	49	1.50
Bergen, NY (village) Genesee County	16	1.47
Eglin AFB, FL (cdp) Okaloosa County	73	1.43
Poestenkill, NY (town) Rensselaer County	64	1.43
Le Mars, IA (city) Plymouth County	136	1.40
Gilberts, IL (village) Kane County	82	1.40
Watertown, MN (township) Carver County	15	1.40
Elmont, NY (cdp) Nassau County	474	1.37
Dover Base Housing, DE (cdp) Kent County	35	1.37
Linglestown, PA (cdp) Dauphin County	91	1.33
North Amityville, NY (cdp) Suffolk County	235	1.32
Holden Heights, FL (cdp) Orange County	65	1.31
Crompond, NY (cdp) Westchester County	26	1.27
Berwyn Heights, MD (town) Prince George's County	39	1.26
Morrisville, NY (village) Madison County	32	1.26
Genoa, NY (town) Cayuga County	25	1.26
Glenn Dale, MD (cdp) Prince George's County	177	1.25
Henderson, GA (cdp) Chatham County	22	1.25
Pebble Creek, FL (cdp) Hillsborough County	94	1.24
Orangetree, FL (cdp) Collier County	53	1.24
Grimsley, TN (cdp) Fentress County	13	1.21
Hamilton, PA (township) Monroe County	110	1.20
Lanham, MD (cdp) Prince George's County	107	1.20
Milford Mill, MD (cdp) Baltimore County	342	1.19
Wheatley Heights, NY (cdp) Suffolk County	73	1.18
Magnolia, NJ (borough) Camden County	51	1.17
Irvington, NJ (township) Essex County	635	1.16
Greenville, NY (town) Orange County	52	1.15
Otego, NY (village) Otsego County	15	1.15
Dean, PA (township) Cambria County	4	1.15
South Miami Heights, FL (cdp) Miami-Dade County	419	1.14
Clermont, FL (city) Lake County	297	1.14
Mechanicstown, NY (cdp) Orange County	85	1.14
Marcus Hook, PA (borough) Delaware County	26	1.13
East Freehold, NJ (cdp) Monmouth County	57	1.12
Montgomery Village, MD (cdp) Montgomery County	348	1.10
Marlboro, NY (cdp) Ulster County	44	1.10
Fort Kent, ME (cdp) Aroostook County	32	1.10
Pine Hills, FL (cdp) Orange County	720	1.09
Woodmere, LA (cdp) Jefferson Parish	127	1.09
Dumfries, VA (town) Prince William County	54	1.09
Carrollton, MI (township) Saginaw County	67	1.08
Cottage City, MD (town) Prince George's County	12	1.08
Between, GA (town) Walton County	5	1.08
Brookhaven, NY (cdp) Suffolk County	29	1.07
Forestville, MD (cdp) Prince George's County	130	1.06
Bloomfield, CT (town) Hartford County	213	1.05
Takoma Park, MD (city) Montgomery County	177	1.05
Tavares, FL (city) Lake County	142	1.04
Scaggsville, MD (cdp) Howard County	235	1.02
Mastic, NY (cdp) Suffolk County	148	1.02
Dania Beach, FL (city) Broward County	298	1.01
Scotchtown, NY (cdp) Orange County	98	1.01
West Park, FL (city) Broward County	143	1.00
Wayne, PA (township) Clinton County	17	1.00
Ladera Heights, CA (cdp) Los Angeles County	66	0.99
Lindenhurst, NY (village) Suffolk County	268	0.98
Thompson, NY (town) Sullivan County	150	0.98
Stony Brook University, NY (cdp) Suffolk County	82	0.98
Hillandale, MD (cdp) Montgomery County	63	0.98
Ballville, OH (cdp) Sandusky County	31	0.98
Sunrise, FL (city) Broward County	828	0.97
Lauderhill, FL (city) Broward County	643	0.96
Somerville, NJ (borough) Somerset County	117	0.96
Odessa, FL (cdp) Pasco County	67	0.96
Valley Cottage, NY (cdp) Rockland County	90	0.95
New York, NY (city) Kings County	76,240	0.94
City of Orange, NJ (township) Essex County	283	0.93
Inwood, NY (cdp) Nassau County	97	0.93
Monticello, NY (village) Sullivan County	63	0.93
Howe, TX (town) Grayson County	24	0.93
North Lauderdale, FL (city) Broward County	377	0.92
Three Lakes, FL (cdp) Miami-Dade County	133	0.92
Monument, CO (town) El Paso County	45	0.92
Colwyn, PA (borough) Delaware County	23	0.92
Miramar, FL (city) Broward County	1,024	0.90
West Deptford, NJ (township) Gloucester County	193	0.90
Edmonston, MD (town) Prince George's County	12	0.90
Ames, TX (city) Liberty County	8	0.90
Cutler Bay, FL (town) Miami-Dade County	340	0.89
Medford, NY (cdp) Suffolk County	219	0.89
Maitland, FL (city) Orange County	140	0.89
Springdale, OH (city) Hamilton County	98	0.89
Queens, NY (borough) Queens County	19,255	0.88
Easton, PA (city) Northampton County	237	0.88
Bamberg, SC (town) Bamberg County	32	0.88
Lincoln University, PA (cdp) Chester County	17	0.88
Lochearn, MD (cdp) Baltimore County	223	0.87
Maplewood, NJ (township) Essex County	207	0.87
Spotswood, NJ (borough) Middlesex County	71	0.87
Orlovista, FL (cdp) Orange County	63	0.86
Highland Falls, NY (village) Orange County	19	0.86
Clear Spring, MD (town) Washington County	4	0.86
Stockport, NY (town) Columbia County	24	0.85
Rumney, NH (town) Grafton County	14	0.85
Fairwood, MD (cdp) Prince George's County	39	0.84
Hackensack, NJ (city) Bergen County	349	0.82
Baldwin, NY (cdp) Nassau County	195	0.82
Southeast, NY (town) Putnam County	150	0.82
Goshen, NY (town) Orange County	111	0.81
Century, FL (town) Escambia County	14	0.81
Central Islip, NY (cdp) Suffolk County	289	0.80
Dranesville, VA (cdp) Fairfax County	101	0.80
Nyack, NY (village) Rockland County	55	0.79

Please refer to the Explanation of Data in the front of the book for more detailed information.

Ancestry

West Indian: Trinidadian and Tobagonian, excluding Hispanic

Top 150 Places Sorted by Percent of Total Population

Based on places with total population of 7,500 or more

Place	Population	%
Hillcrest, NY (cdp) Rockland County	367	4.48
North Valley Stream, NY (cdp) Nassau County	551	3.34
Palmetto Estates, FL (cdp) Miami-Dade County	421	3.09
Rockville, CT (cdp) Tolland County	211	2.74
Conway, FL (cdp) Orange County	290	2.03
Brooklyn, NY (borough) Kings County	46,490	1.88
Uniondale, NY (cdp) Nassau County	458	1.87
East Orange, NJ (city) Essex County	1,131	1.74
Ives Estates, FL (cdp) Miami-Dade County	307	1.74
North Bellport, NY (cdp) Suffolk County	176	1.56
Hillcrest Heights, MD (cdp) Prince George's County	243	1.53
Seabrook, MD (cdp) Prince George's County	235	1.50
Le Mars, IA (city) Plymouth County	136	1.40
Elmont, NY (cdp) Nassau County	474	1.37
North Amityville, NY (cdp) Suffolk County	235	1.32
Glenn Dale, MD (cdp) Prince George's County	177	1.25
Pebble Creek, FL (cdp) Hillsborough County	94	1.24
Hamilton, PA (township) Monroe County	110	1.20
Lanham, MD (cdp) Prince George's County	107	1.20
Milford Mill, MD (cdp) Baltimore County	342	1.19
Irvington, NJ (township) Essex County	635	1.16
South Miami Heights, FL (cdp) Miami-Dade County	419	1.14
Clermont, FL (city) Lake County	297	1.14
Montgomery Village, MD (cdp) Montgomery County	348	1.10
Pine Hills, FL (cdp) Orange County	720	1.09
Woodmere, LA (cdp) Jefferson Parish	127	1.09
Forestville, MD (cdp) Prince George's County	130	1.06
Bloomfield, CT (town) Hartford County	213	1.05
Takoma Park, MD (city) Montgomery County	177	1.05
Tavares, FL (city) Lake County	142	1.04
Scaggsville, MD (cdp) Howard County	235	1.02
Mastic, NY (cdp) Suffolk County	148	1.02
Dania Beach, FL (city) Broward County	298	1.01
Scotchtown, NY (cdp) Orange County	98	1.01
West Park, FL (city) Broward County	143	1.00
Lindenhurst, NY (village) Suffolk County	268	0.98
Thompson, NY (town) Sullivan County	150	0.98
Stony Brook University, NY (cdp) Suffolk County	82	0.98
Sunrise, FL (city) Broward County	828	0.97
Lauderhill, FL (city) Broward County	643	0.96
Somerville, NJ (borough) Somerset County	117	0.96
Valley Cottage, NY (cdp) Rockland County	90	0.95
New York, NY (city) Kings County	76,240	0.94
City of Orange, NJ (township) Essex County	283	0.93
Inwood, NY (cdp) Nassau County	97	0.93
North Lauderdale, FL (city) Broward County	377	0.92
Three Lakes, FL (cdp) Miami-Dade County	133	0.92
Miramar, FL (city) Broward County	1,024	0.90
West Deptford, NJ (township) Gloucester County	193	0.90
Cutler Bay, FL (town) Miami-Dade County	340	0.89
Medford, NY (cdp) Suffolk County	219	0.89
Maitland, FL (city) Orange County	140	0.89
Springdale, OH (city) Hamilton County	98	0.89
Queens, NY (borough) Queens County	19,255	0.88
Easton, PA (city) Northampton County	237	0.88
Lochearn, MD (cdp) Baltimore County	223	0.87
Maplewood, NJ (township) Essex County	207	0.87
Spotswood, NJ (borough) Middlesex County	71	0.87
Hackensack, NJ (city) Bergen County	349	0.82
Baldwin, NY (cdp) Nassau County	195	0.82
Southeast, NY (town) Putnam County	150	0.82
Goshen, NY (town) Orange County	111	0.81
Central Islip, NY (cdp) Suffolk County	289	0.80
Dranesville, VA (cdp) Fairfax County	101	0.80
Freeport, NY (village) Nassau County	333	0.78
Poughkeepsie, NY (city) Dutchess County	253	0.78
East Riverdale, MD (cdp) Prince George's County	121	0.77
Marrero, LA (cdp) Jefferson Parish	250	0.76
Poinciana, FL (cdp) Osceola County	376	0.75
The Acreage, FL (cdp) Palm Beach County	283	0.75
Skippack, PA (township) Montgomery County	96	0.74
Bluffton, SC (town) Beaufort County	79	0.74
College Park, MD (city) Prince George's County	215	0.73
Spring Valley, NY (village) Rockland County	217	0.72
Vernon, CT (town) Tolland County	211	0.72

Place	Population	%
Fairland, MD (cdp) Montgomery County	167	0.72
Richmond Heights, FL (cdp) Miami-Dade County	65	0.72
Tamarac, FL (city) Broward County	422	0.71
Calverton, MD (cdp) Montgomery County	127	0.71
West Perrine, FL (cdp) Miami-Dade County	71	0.71
Beltsville, MD (cdp) Prince George's County	108	0.70
Clarksburg, MD (cdp) Montgomery County	74	0.70
Lauderdale Lakes, FL (city) Broward County	226	0.69
Montclair, NJ (township) Essex County	252	0.67
Wallkill, NY (town) Orange County	183	0.67
Englewood, NJ (city) Bergen County	176	0.66
Roosevelt, NY (cdp) Nassau County	99	0.66
Minneola, FL (city) Lake County	59	0.66
Port St. Lucie, FL (city) St. Lucie County	1,013	0.65
Meadow Woods, FL (cdp) Orange County	151	0.64
Laurel, MD (city) Prince George's County	155	0.63
Glasgow, DE (cdp) New Castle County	99	0.63
Azalea Park, FL (cdp) Orange County	83	0.63
Chatham, NJ (township) Morris County	66	0.63
Fresno, TX (cdp) Fort Bend County	103	0.62
Oronoko, MI (charter township) Berrien County	57	0.62
Hempstead, NY (village) Nassau County	322	0.60
Mount Vernon, NY (city) Westchester County	397	0.59
Plainfield, NJ (city) Union County	287	0.59
Guttenberg, NJ (town) Hudson County	65	0.59
Homestead, FL (city) Miami-Dade County	320	0.58
East Lake-Orient Park, FL (cdp) Hillsborough County	140	0.58
Palm River-Clair Mel, FL (cdp) Hillsborough County	119	0.57
Pembroke Pines, FL (city) Broward County	836	0.55
Margate, FL (city) Broward County	293	0.55
Sayreville, NJ (borough) Middlesex County	232	0.55
West Hempstead, NY (cdp) Nassau County	102	0.55
Palm Coast, FL (city) Flagler County	381	0.54
Deer Park, NY (cdp) Suffolk County	154	0.54
Farmingville, NY (cdp) Suffolk County	87	0.54
Stockbridge, GA (city) Henry County	125	0.53
McDonough, GA (city) Henry County	107	0.53
Avenel, NJ (cdp) Middlesex County	90	0.53
Maryland City, MD (cdp) Anne Arundel County	82	0.53
Brandermill, VA (cdp) Chesterfield County	66	0.53
Brockton, MA (city) Plymouth County	487	0.52
Glenmont, MD (cdp) Montgomery County	70	0.52
Newark, NJ (city) Essex County	1,399	0.51
The Crossings, FL (cdp) Miami-Dade County	121	0.51
Eustis, FL (city) Lake County	95	0.51
Rosaryville, MD (cdp) Prince George's County	58	0.51
Summerfield, MD (cdp) Prince George's County	57	0.51
East Stroudsburg, PA (borough) Monroe County	51	0.51
Leisure World, MD (cdp) Montgomery County	44	0.51
Upper Darby, PA (township) Delaware County	411	0.50
Pensacola, FL (city) Escambia County	264	0.50
Woodbury, CT (town) Litchfield County	50	0.50
Marlborough, NY (town) Ulster County	44	0.50
Boston, MA (city) Suffolk County	2,928	0.49
Ramapo, NY (town) Rockland County	604	0.49
Troy, NY (city) Rensselaer County	243	0.49
Woodstock, GA (city) Cherokee County	108	0.49
Easthampton Town, MA (city) Hampshire County	79	0.49
Adelphi, MD (cdp) Prince George's County	74	0.49
Oakland Park, FL (city) Broward County	202	0.48
Valley Stream, NY (village) Nassau County	177	0.48
Jersey City, NJ (city) Hudson County	1,140	0.47
Hollywood, FL (city) Broward County	664	0.47
Palm Bay, FL (city) Brevard County	475	0.47
Bowie, MD (city) Prince George's County	255	0.47
West Orange, NJ (township) Essex County	215	0.47
Beverly, MA (city) Essex County	183	0.47
New Carrollton, MD (city) Prince George's County	57	0.47
Bordentown, NJ (township) Burlington County	51	0.47
Redan, GA (cdp) DeKalb County	156	0.46
Maryland Heights, MO (city) St. Louis County	125	0.46
Eatontown, NJ (borough) Monmouth County	59	0.46
Randallstown, MD (cdp) Baltimore County	148	0.45
Pleasantville, NJ (city) Atlantic County	91	0.45
Sudley, VA (cdp) Prince William County	69	0.45

Ancestry

West Indian: U.S. Virgin Islander, excluding Hispanic

U.S. and 50 States Sorted by Population and Percent of Total Population

Place	Population	%
United States	**14,760**	**<0.01**
Florida	4,333	0.02
New York	2,873	0.01
Georgia	1,725	0.02
Pennsylvania	835	0.01
Virginia	682	0.01
Maryland	534	0.01
California	450	<0.01
Texas	436	<0.01
Massachusetts	433	0.01
New Jersey	392	<0.01
Connecticut	213	0.01
North Carolina	177	<0.01
District of Columbia	171	0.03
Illinois	157	<0.01
Alabama	141	<0.01
Washington	139	<0.01
Michigan	108	<0.01
Arizona	88	<0.01
Rhode Island	86	0.01
Tennessee	81	<0.01
Nebraska	66	<0.01
Oklahoma	59	<0.01
Ohio	56	<0.01
Louisiana	55	<0.01
Wisconsin	51	<0.01
Minnesota	43	<0.01
Delaware	42	<0.01
South Carolina	38	<0.01
Alaska	37	0.01
West Virginia	35	<0.01
Nevada	32	<0.01
Hawaii	28	<0.01
Iowa	26	<0.01
Colorado	21	<0.01
Maine	19	<0.01
Oregon	18	<0.01
Utah	18	<0.01
Mississippi	12	<0.01
North Dakota	12	<0.01
Kansas	9	<0.01
Kentucky	9	<0.01
Indiana	8	<0.01
New Hampshire	7	<0.01
Missouri	3	<0.01
South Dakota	2	<0.01
Arkansas	0	0.00
Idaho	0	0.00
Montana	0	0.00
New Mexico	0	0.00
Vermont	0	0.00
Wyoming	0	0.00

Place	Population	%
District of Columbia	171	0.03
Florida	4,333	0.02
Georgia	1,725	0.02
New York	2,873	0.01
Pennsylvania	835	0.01
Virginia	682	0.01
Maryland	534	0.01
Massachusetts	433	0.01
Connecticut	213	0.01
Rhode Island	86	0.01
Alaska	37	0.01
United States	**14,760**	**<0.01**
California	450	<0.01
Texas	436	<0.01
New Jersey	392	<0.01
North Carolina	177	<0.01
Illinois	157	<0.01
Alabama	141	<0.01
Washington	139	<0.01
Michigan	108	<0.01
Arizona	88	<0.01
Tennessee	81	<0.01
Nebraska	66	<0.01
Oklahoma	59	<0.01
Ohio	56	<0.01
Louisiana	55	<0.01
Wisconsin	51	<0.01
Minnesota	43	<0.01
Delaware	42	<0.01
South Carolina	38	<0.01
West Virginia	35	<0.01
Nevada	32	<0.01
Hawaii	28	<0.01
Iowa	26	<0.01
Colorado	21	<0.01
Maine	19	<0.01
Oregon	18	<0.01
Utah	18	<0.01
Mississippi	12	<0.01
North Dakota	12	<0.01
Kansas	9	<0.01
Kentucky	9	<0.01
Indiana	8	<0.01
New Hampshire	7	<0.01
Missouri	3	<0.01
South Dakota	2	<0.01
Arkansas	0	0.00
Idaho	0	0.00
Montana	0	0.00
New Mexico	0	0.00
Vermont	0	0.00
Wyoming	0	0.00

Please refer to the Explanation of Data in the front of the book for more detailed information.

Ancestry

West Indian: U.S. Virgin Islander, excluding Hispanic

Top 150 Places Sorted by Population

Based on all places, regardless of total population

Place	Population	%
New York, NY (city) Kings County	2,383	0.03
Bronx, NY (borough) Bronx County	952	0.07
Brooklyn, NY (borough) Kings County	558	0.02
Manhattan, NY (borough) New York County	487	0.03
Pine Hills, FL (cdp) Orange County	435	0.66
Queens, NY (borough) Queens County	364	0.02
Reading, PA (city) Berks County	289	0.33
Miami Gardens, FL (city) Miami-Dade County	252	0.24
Polk, PA (township) Monroe County	225	2.88
Sandy Springs, GA (city) Fulton County	219	0.24
Tampa, FL (city) Hillsborough County	209	0.06
Tallahassee, FL (city) Leon County	203	0.11
Brandon, FL (cdp) Hillsborough County	188	0.19
Washington, DC (city) District of Columbia	171	0.03
North Lauderdale, FL (city) Broward County	161	0.39
South Huntington, NY (cdp) Suffolk County	147	1.49
Huntington, NY (town) Suffolk County	147	0.07
Springfield, MA (city) Hampden County	143	0.09
Sunrise, FL (city) Broward County	141	0.17
Tacoma, WA (city) Pierce County	139	0.07
Alpharetta, GA (city) Fulton County	136	0.25
Hampton, VA (ind. city) Hampton independent city	118	0.08
Goldenrod, FL (cdp) Orange County	116	0.81
Bridgeport, CT (city/town) Fairfield County	116	0.08
Sayreville, NJ (borough) Middlesex County	108	0.26
Miramar, FL (city) Broward County	105	0.09
Orlando, FL (city) Orange County	105	0.04
Jacksonville, FL (city) Duval County	103	0.01
Philadelphia, PA (city) Philadelphia County	100	0.01
Palm River-Clair Mel, FL (cdp) Hillsborough County	97	0.46
Hollywood, FL (city) Broward County	93	0.07
Hoover, AL (city) Jefferson County	87	0.11
Providence, RI (city) Providence County	86	0.05
Yonkers, NY (city) Westchester County	83	0.04
Champaign, IL (city) Champaign County	81	0.10
Port St. Lucie, FL (city) St. Lucie County	81	0.05
Severn, MD (cdp) Anne Arundel County	79	0.19
Los Angeles, CA (city) Los Angeles County	77	<0.01
Virginia Beach, VA (ind. city) Virginia Beach independent city	76	0.02
Gainesville, FL (city) Alachua County	74	0.06
Columbus, GA (city) Muscogee County	71	0.04
Boston, MA (city) Suffolk County	68	0.01
Andover, MA (cdp) Essex County	66	0.77
Andover, MA (town) Essex County	66	0.20
Richmond, VA (ind. city) Richmond independent city	66	0.03
Chillum, MD (cdp) Prince George's County	65	0.19
Bellevue, NE (city) Sarpy County	61	0.12
Fayetteville, NC (city) Cumberland County	61	0.03
Alexandria, VA (ind. city) Alexandria independent city	60	0.04
Upper Darby, PA (township) Delaware County	59	0.07
Milton, MA (cdp/town) Norfolk County	58	0.22
Pasadena, TX (city) Harris County	57	0.04
Norfolk, VA (ind. city) Norfolk independent city	56	0.02
North Miami, FL (city) Miami-Dade County	55	0.09
Boca Raton, FL (city) Palm Beach County	55	0.06
Killeen, TX (city) Bell County	54	0.04
Forest Heights, MD (town) Prince George's County	53	2.46
Lutz, FL (cdp) Hillsborough County	51	0.26
Casa Grande, AZ (city) Pinal County	51	0.12
Johns Creek, GA (city) Fulton County	51	0.07
Elizabeth, NJ (city) Union County	49	0.04
Atlanta, GA (city) Fulton County	49	0.01
Yorkshire, VA (cdp) Prince William County	47	0.69
Seminole, FL (city) Pinellas County	47	0.27
Lauderhill, FL (city) Broward County	47	0.07
Inglewood, CA (city) Los Angeles County	46	0.04
Waterbury, CT (city/town) New Haven County	44	0.04
Candler-McAfee, GA (cdp) DeKalb County	43	0.18
Winter Garden, FL (city) Orange County	43	0.14
Woodbridge, NJ (township) Middlesex County	43	0.04
Satellite Beach, FL (city) Brevard County	42	0.40
Poughkeepsie, NY (city) Dutchess County	42	0.13
Lake Worth, FL (city) Palm Beach County	42	0.12
Baltimore, MD (city) Baltimore city County	42	0.01
Milwaukee, WI (city) Milwaukee County	42	0.01
Clarcona, FL (cdp) Orange County	41	1.59
East Lansdowne, PA (borough) Delaware County	41	1.55
Glen Burnie, MD (cdp) Anne Arundel County	41	0.06
Birmingham, AL (city) Jefferson County	41	0.02
Peachtree City, GA (city) Fayette County	40	0.12
Homestead, FL (city) Miami-Dade County	40	0.07
Miami, FL (city) Miami-Dade County	40	0.01
Hartford, CT (city/town) Hartford County	39	0.03
Conyers, GA (city) Rockdale County	38	0.26
McDonough, GA (city) Henry County	38	0.19
Linthicum, MD (cdp) Anne Arundel County	37	0.35
Anchorage, AK (municipality) Anchorage Municipality	37	0.01
Long Beach, CA (city) Los Angeles County	37	0.01
Greenacres, FL (city) Palm Beach County	36	0.10
Neabsco, VA (cdp) Prince William County	35	0.37
New Brunswick, NJ (city) Middlesex County	35	0.06
Miami Shores, FL (village) Miami-Dade County	34	0.32
Missouri City, TX (city) Fort Bend County	34	0.05
Middletown, NY (city) Orange County	33	0.12
Richmond West, FL (cdp) Miami-Dade County	33	0.10
Tamarac, FL (city) Broward County	33	0.06
Alafaya, FL (cdp) Orange County	33	0.04
St. Paul, MN (city) Ramsey County	33	0.01
Chicago, IL (city) Cook County	32	<0.01
Memphis, TN (city) Shelby County	32	<0.01
Azalea Park, FL (cdp) Orange County	31	0.24
Temple Terrace, FL (city) Hillsborough County	31	0.13
Lochearn, MD (cdp) Baltimore County	31	0.12
Lawton, OK (city) Comanche County	31	0.03
New Hyde Park, NY (village) Nassau County	30	0.31
Hempstead, NY (town) Nassau County	30	<0.01
Dale City, VA (cdp) Prince William County	29	0.05
West Palm Beach, FL (city) Palm Beach County	29	0.03
Roxbury, NY (town) Delaware County	28	1.12
Urban Honolulu, HI (cdp) Honolulu County	28	0.01
Nashville-Davidson, TN (metro govt) Davidson County	28	<0.01
Conway, FL (cdp) Orange County	27	0.19
Columbus, OH (city) Franklin County	27	<0.01
San Diego, CA (city) San Diego County	27	<0.01
Sewaren, NJ (cdp) Middlesex County	26	1.00
Muscatine, IA (city) Muscatine County	26	0.11
Paradise, NV (cdp) Clark County	26	0.01
Stoughton, MA (town) Norfolk County	24	0.09
Southfield, MI (city) Oakland County	24	0.03
Fontana, CA (city) San Bernardino County	24	0.01
Marion, VA (town) Smyth County	23	0.38
White Plains, NY (city) Westchester County	23	0.04
San Antonio, TX (city) Medina County	23	<0.01
Pompton Lakes, NJ (borough) Passaic County	22	0.20
Bartow, FL (city) Polk County	22	0.13
Lynn, MA (city) Essex County	22	0.02
Staten Island, NY (borough) Richmond County	22	<0.01
Gordon, GA (city) Wilkinson County	21	0.98
Colorado Springs, CO (city) El Paso County	21	0.01
Newark, NJ (city) Essex County	21	0.01
Elkridge, MD (cdp) Howard County	20	0.15
Pontiac, MI (city) Oakland County	20	0.03
Deltona, FL (city) Volusia County	20	0.02
Spring Hill, FL (cdp) Hernando County	20	0.02
Tucson, AZ (city) Pima County	20	<0.01
Bath, ME (city) Sagadahoc County	19	0.22
Spring Valley, NY (village) Rockland County	19	0.06
University, FL (cdp) Hillsborough County	19	0.05
Ramapo, NY (town) Rockland County	19	0.02
Augusta-Richmond County, GA (cons. govt) Richmond County	19	0.01
Glenolden, PA (borough) Delaware County	18	0.25
Countryside, VA (cdp) Loudoun County	18	0.19
Horsham, PA (cdp) Montgomery County	18	0.12
Horsham, PA (township) Montgomery County	18	0.07
Taylorsville, UT (city) Salt Lake County	18	0.03
Sugar Land, TX (city) Fort Bend County	18	0.02
Pembroke Pines, FL (city) Broward County	18	0.01
Winston-Salem, NC (city) Forsyth County	18	0.01
Portland, OR (city) Multnomah County	18	<0.01
Avenel, NJ (cdp) Middlesex County	17	0.10

SECTION THREE

Please refer to the Explanation of Data in the front of the book for more detailed information.

Ancestry

West Indian: U.S. Virgin Islander, excluding Hispanic

Top 150 Places Sorted by Percent of Total Population

Based on all places, regardless of total population

Place	Population	%
Polk, PA (township) Monroe County	225	2.88
Forest Heights, MD (town) Prince George's County	53	2.46
Eden, SD (town) Marshall County	2	2.06
Clarcona, FL (cdp) Orange County	41	1.59
East Lansdowne, PA (borough) Delaware County	41	1.55
South Huntington, NY (cdp) Suffolk County	147	1.49
Roxbury, NY (town) Delaware County	28	1.12
Sewaren, NJ (cdp) Middlesex County	26	1.00
Gordon, GA (city) Wilkinson County	21	0.98
Pollocksville, NC (town) Jones County	3	0.83
Goldenrod, FL (cdp) Orange County	116	0.81
Wysox, PA (township) Bradford County	14	0.80
Andover, MA (cdp) Essex County	66	0.77
Yorkshire, VA (cdp) Prince William County	47	0.69
Brownville, NY (village) Jefferson County	7	0.67
Pine Hills, FL (cdp) Orange County	435	0.66
Spring Arbor, MI (cdp) Jackson County	13	0.59
Mount Zion, GA (city) Carroll County	10	0.57
Norton Center, MA (cdp) Bristol County	14	0.54
Bessemer, PA (borough) Lawrence County	6	0.51
Palm River-Clair Mel, FL (cdp) Hillsborough County	97	0.46
Brookville, NY (village) Nassau County	15	0.43
Satellite Beach, FL (city) Brevard County	42	0.40
North Lauderdale, FL (city) Broward County	161	0.39
Marion, VA (town) Smyth County	23	0.38
Neabsco, VA (cdp) Prince William County	35	0.37
Otisville, NY (village) Orange County	4	0.36
Linthicum, MD (cdp) Anne Arundel County	37	0.35
Lancaster, MO (city) Schuyler County	3	0.34
Reading, PA (city) Berks County	289	0.33
Miami Shores, FL (village) Miami-Dade County	34	0.32
New Hyde Park, NY (village) Nassau County	30	0.31
Seminole, FL (city) Pinellas County	47	0.27
Custer, MI (township) Antrim County	3	0.27
Sayreville, NJ (borough) Middlesex County	108	0.26
Lutz, FL (cdp) Hillsborough County	51	0.26
Conyers, GA (city) Rockdale County	38	0.26
Turnersville, NJ (cdp) Gloucester County	9	0.26
Alpharetta, GA (city) Fulton County	136	0.25
Glenolden, PA (borough) Delaware County	18	0.25
Gregg, PA (township) Union County	13	0.25
Miami Gardens, FL (city) Miami-Dade County	252	0.24
Sandy Springs, GA (city) Fulton County	219	0.24
Azalea Park, FL (cdp) Orange County	31	0.24
Stroudsburg, PA (borough) Monroe County	14	0.24
Milton, MA (cdp/town) Norfolk County	58	0.22
Bath, ME (city) Sagadahoc County	19	0.22
Andover, MA (town) Essex County	66	0.20
Pompton Lakes, NJ (borough) Passaic County	22	0.20
Brandon, FL (cdp) Hillsborough County	188	0.19
Severn, MD (cdp) Anne Arundel County	79	0.19
Chillum, MD (cdp) Prince George's County	65	0.19
McDonough, GA (city) Henry County	38	0.19
Conway, FL (cdp) Orange County	27	0.19
Countryside, VA (cdp) Loudoun County	18	0.19
Jackson, SC (town) Aiken County	3	0.19
Candler-McAfee, GA (cdp) DeKalb County	43	0.18
Washingtonville, NY (village) Orange County	11	0.18
Sunrise, FL (city) Broward County	141	0.17
Spring Arbor, MI (township) Jackson County	13	0.16
Elkridge, MD (cdp) Howard County	20	0.15
Galena Park, TX (city) Harris County	16	0.15
Silver Springs Shores, FL (cdp) Marion County	10	0.15
Winter Garden, FL (city) Orange County	43	0.14
Poughkeepsie, NY (city) Dutchess County	42	0.13
Temple Terrace, FL (city) Hillsborough County	31	0.13
Bartow, FL (city) Polk County	22	0.13
Wallington, NJ (borough) Bergen County	15	0.13
Holly Springs, GA (city) Cherokee County	11	0.13
Attica, NY (town) Wyoming County	10	0.13
Oakdale, LA (city) Allen Parish	10	0.13
Montrose, PA (borough) Susquehanna County	3	0.13
Bellevue, NE (city) Sarpy County	61	0.12
Casa Grande, AZ (city) Pinal County	51	0.12
Lake Worth, FL (city) Palm Beach County	42	0.12
Peachtree City, GA (city) Fayette County	40	0.12
Middletown, NY (city) Orange County	33	0.12
Lochearn, MD (cdp) Baltimore County	31	0.12
Horsham, PA (cdp) Montgomery County	18	0.12
St. Gabriel, LA (city) Iberville Parish	8	0.12
Tallahassee, FL (city) Leon County	203	0.11
Hoover, AL (city) Jefferson County	87	0.11
Muscatine, IA (city) Muscatine County	26	0.11
College Park, GA (city) Fulton County	15	0.11
East Hampton, CT (town) Middlesex County	14	0.11
Brownville, NY (town) Jefferson County	7	0.11
Calverton, NY (cdp) Suffolk County	7	0.11
West Concord, MA (cdp) Middlesex County	7	0.11
Champaign, IL (city) Champaign County	81	0.10
Greenacres, FL (city) Palm Beach County	36	0.10
Richmond West, FL (cdp) Miami-Dade County	33	0.10
Avenel, NJ (cdp) Middlesex County	17	0.10
Groveton, VA (cdp) Fairfax County	14	0.10
Palatka, FL (city) Putnam County	11	0.10
Port Royal, SC (town) Beaufort County	10	0.10
Marcy, NY (town) Oneida County	9	0.10
Springfield, MA (city) Hampden County	143	0.09
Miramar, FL (city) Broward County	105	0.09
North Miami, FL (city) Miami-Dade County	55	0.09
Stoughton, MA (town) Norfolk County	24	0.09
Tavares, FL (city) Lake County	12	0.09
Scottdale, GA (cdp) DeKalb County	9	0.09
Hampton, VA (ind. city) Hampton independent city	118	0.08
Bridgeport, CT (city/town) Fairfield County	116	0.08
Four Corners, TX (cdp) Fort Bend County	10	0.08
Bronx, NY (borough) Bronx County	952	0.07
Huntington, NY (town) Suffolk County	147	0.07
Tacoma, WA (city) Pierce County	139	0.07
Hollywood, FL (city) Broward County	93	0.07
Upper Darby, PA (township) Delaware County	59	0.07
Johns Creek, GA (city) Fulton County	51	0.07
Lauderhill, FL (city) Broward County	47	0.07
Homestead, FL (city) Miami-Dade County	40	0.07
Horsham, PA (township) Montgomery County	18	0.07
Norton, MA (town) Bristol County	14	0.07
Dickinson, ND (city) Stark County	12	0.07
Hopatcong, NJ (borough) Sussex County	11	0.07
Stanford, CA (cdp) Santa Clara County	10	0.07
Jefferson, LA (cdp) Jefferson Parish	9	0.07
Fairview, TN (city) Williamson County	5	0.07
Tampa, FL (city) Hillsborough County	209	0.06
Gainesville, FL (city) Alachua County	74	0.06
Boca Raton, FL (city) Palm Beach County	55	0.06
Glen Burnie, MD (cdp) Anne Arundel County	41	0.06
New Brunswick, NJ (city) Middlesex County	35	0.06
Tamarac, FL (city) Broward County	33	0.06
Spring Valley, NY (village) Rockland County	19	0.06
Perry Hall, MD (cdp) Baltimore County	16	0.06
Leander, TX (city) Williamson County	14	0.06
Blooming Grove, NY (town) Orange County	11	0.06
Lindenwold, NJ (borough) Camden County	10	0.06
Longwood, FL (city) Seminole County	9	0.06
Moreau, NY (town) Saratoga County	9	0.06
Mount Hope, NY (town) Orange County	4	0.06
Providence, RI (city) Providence County	86	0.05
Port St. Lucie, FL (city) St. Lucie County	81	0.05
Missouri City, TX (city) Fort Bend County	34	0.05
Dale City, VA (cdp) Prince William County	29	0.05
University, FL (cdp) Hillsborough County	19	0.05
Kennesaw, GA (city) Cobb County	14	0.05
Fairland, MD (cdp) Montgomery County	11	0.05
West St. Paul, MN (city) Dakota County	10	0.05
Beacon, NY (city) Dutchess County	7	0.05
Fairburn, GA (city) Fulton County	6	0.05
Orlando, FL (city) Orange County	105	0.04
Yonkers, NY (city) Westchester County	83	0.04
Columbus, GA (city) Muscogee County	71	0.04
Alexandria, VA (ind. city) Alexandria independent city	60	0.04
Pasadena, TX (city) Harris County	57	0.04
Killeen, TX (city) Bell County	54	0.04

Please refer to the Explanation of Data in the front of the book for more detailed information.

Ancestry

West Indian: U.S. Virgin Islander, excluding Hispanic

Top 150 Places Sorted by Percent of Total Population

Based on places with total population of 7,500 or more

Place	Population	%
Polk, PA (township) Monroe County	225	2.88
South Huntington, NY (cdp) Suffolk County	147	1.49
Goldenrod, FL (cdp) Orange County	116	0.81
Andover, MA (cdp) Essex County	66	0.77
Pine Hills, FL (cdp) Orange County	435	0.66
Palm River-Clair Mel, FL (cdp) Hillsborough County	97	0.46
Satellite Beach, FL (city) Brevard County	42	0.40
North Lauderdale, FL (city) Broward County	161	0.39
Neabsco, VA (cdp) Prince William County	35	0.37
Linthicum, MD (cdp) Anne Arundel County	37	0.35
Reading, PA (city) Berks County	289	0.33
Miami Shores, FL (village) Miami-Dade County	34	0.32
New Hyde Park, NY (village) Nassau County	30	0.31
Seminole, FL (city) Pinellas County	47	0.27
Sayreville, NJ (borough) Middlesex County	108	0.26
Lutz, FL (cdp) Hillsborough County	51	0.26
Conyers, GA (city) Rockdale County	38	0.26
Alpharetta, GA (city) Fulton County	136	0.25
Miami Gardens, FL (city) Miami-Dade County	252	0.24
Sandy Springs, GA (city) Fulton County	219	0.24
Azalea Park, FL (cdp) Orange County	31	0.24
Milton, MA (cdp/town) Norfolk County	58	0.22
Bath, ME (city) Sagadahoc County	19	0.22
Andover, MA (town) Essex County	66	0.20
Pompton Lakes, NJ (borough) Passaic County	22	0.20
Brandon, FL (cdp) Hillsborough County	188	0.19
Severn, MD (cdp) Anne Arundel County	79	0.19
Chillum, MD (cdp) Prince George's County	65	0.19
McDonough, GA (city) Henry County	38	0.19
Conway, FL (cdp) Orange County	27	0.19
Countryside, VA (cdp) Loudoun County	18	0.19
Candler-McAfee, GA (cdp) DeKalb County	43	0.18
Sunrise, FL (city) Broward County	141	0.17
Spring Arbor, MI (township) Jackson County	13	0.16
Elkridge, MD (cdp) Howard County	20	0.15
Galena Park, TX (city) Harris County	16	0.15
Winter Garden, FL (city) Orange County	43	0.14
Poughkeepsie, NY (city) Dutchess County	42	0.13
Temple Terrace, FL (city) Hillsborough County	31	0.13
Bartow, FL (city) Polk County	22	0.13
Wallington, NJ (borough) Bergen County	15	0.13
Holly Springs, GA (city) Cherokee County	11	0.13
Attica, NY (town) Wyoming County	10	0.13
Oakdale, LA (city) Allen Parish	10	0.13
Bellevue, NE (city) Sarpy County	61	0.12
Casa Grande, AZ (city) Pinal County	51	0.12
Lake Worth, FL (city) Palm Beach County	42	0.12
Peachtree City, GA (city) Fayette County	40	0.12
Middletown, NY (city) Orange County	33	0.12
Lochearn, MD (cdp) Baltimore County	31	0.12
Horsham, PA (cdp) Montgomery County	18	0.12
Tallahassee, FL (city) Leon County	203	0.11
Hoover, AL (city) Jefferson County	87	0.11
Muscatine, IA (city) Muscatine County	26	0.11
College Park, GA (city) Fulton County	15	0.11
East Hampton, CT (town) Middlesex County	14	0.11
Champaign, IL (city) Champaign County	81	0.10
Greenacres, FL (city) Palm Beach County	36	0.10
Richmond West, FL (cdp) Miami-Dade County	33	0.10
Avenel, NJ (cdp) Middlesex County	17	0.10
Groveton, VA (cdp) Fairfax County	14	0.10
Palatka, FL (city) Putnam County	11	0.10
Port Royal, SC (town) Beaufort County	10	0.10
Marcy, NY (town) Oneida County	9	0.10
Springfield, MA (city) Hampden County	143	0.09
Miramar, FL (city) Broward County	105	0.09
North Miami, FL (city) Miami-Dade County	55	0.09
Stoughton, MA (town) Norfolk County	24	0.09
Tavares, FL (city) Lake County	12	0.09
Scottdale, GA (cdp) DeKalb County	9	0.09
Hampton, VA (ind. city) Hampton independent city	118	0.08
Bridgeport, CT (city/town) Fairfield County	116	0.08
Four Corners, TX (cdp) Fort Bend County	10	0.08
Bronx, NY (borough) Bronx County	952	0.07
Huntington, NY (town) Suffolk County	147	0.07
Tacoma, WA (city) Pierce County	139	0.07
Hollywood, FL (city) Broward County	93	0.07
Upper Darby, PA (township) Delaware County	59	0.07
Johns Creek, GA (city) Fulton County	51	0.07
Lauderhill, FL (city) Broward County	47	0.07
Homestead, FL (city) Miami-Dade County	40	0.07
Horsham, PA (township) Montgomery County	18	0.07
Norton, MA (town) Bristol County	14	0.07
Dickinson, ND (city) Stark County	12	0.07
Hopatcong, NJ (borough) Sussex County	11	0.07
Stanford, CA (cdp) Santa Clara County	10	0.07
Jefferson, LA (cdp) Jefferson Parish	9	0.07
Fairview, TN (city) Williamson County	5	0.07
Tampa, FL (city) Hillsborough County	209	0.06
Gainesville, FL (city) Alachua County	74	0.06
Boca Raton, FL (city) Palm Beach County	55	0.06
Glen Burnie, MD (cdp) Anne Arundel County	41	0.06
New Brunswick, NJ (city) Middlesex County	35	0.06
Tamarac, FL (city) Broward County	33	0.06
Spring Valley, NY (village) Rockland County	19	0.06
Perry Hall, MD (cdp) Baltimore County	16	0.06
Leander, TX (city) Williamson County	14	0.06
Blooming Grove, NY (town) Orange County	11	0.06
Lindenwold, NJ (borough) Camden County	10	0.06
Longwood, FL (city) Seminole County	9	0.06
Moreau, NY (town) Saratoga County	9	0.06
Providence, RI (city) Providence County	86	0.05
Port St. Lucie, FL (city) St. Lucie County	81	0.05
Missouri City, TX (city) Fort Bend County	34	0.05
Dale City, VA (cdp) Prince William County	29	0.05
University, FL (cdp) Hillsborough County	19	0.05
Kennesaw, GA (city) Cobb County	14	0.05
Fairland, MD (cdp) Montgomery County	11	0.05
West St. Paul, MN (city) Dakota County	10	0.05
Beacon, NY (city) Dutchess County	7	0.05
Fairburn, GA (city) Fulton County	6	0.05
Orlando, FL (city) Orange County	105	0.04
Yonkers, NY (city) Westchester County	83	0.04
Columbus, GA (city) Muscogee County	71	0.04
Alexandria, VA (ind. city) Alexandria independent city	60	0.04
Pasadena, TX (city) Harris County	57	0.04
Killeen, TX (city) Bell County	54	0.04
Elizabeth, NJ (city) Union County	49	0.04
Inglewood, CA (city) Los Angeles County	46	0.04
Waterbury, CT (city/town) New Haven County	44	0.04
Woodbridge, NJ (township) Middlesex County	43	0.04
Alafaya, FL (cdp) Orange County	33	0.04
White Plains, NY (city) Westchester County	23	0.04
Manassas, VA (ind. city) Manassas independent city	16	0.04
Brentwood, TN (city) Williamson County	14	0.04
Golden Glades, FL (cdp) Miami-Dade County	14	0.04
Winter Park, FL (city) Orange County	12	0.04
Shaler, PA (township) Allegheny County	11	0.04
Shawnee, OK (city) Pottawatomie County	11	0.04
Radcliff, KY (city) Hardin County	9	0.04
Somerset, NJ (cdp) Somerset County	8	0.04
South Milwaukee, WI (city) Milwaukee County	8	0.04
Concord, MA (town) Middlesex County	7	0.04
Niles, MI (township) Berrien County	5	0.04
New York, NY (city) Kings County	2,383	0.03
Manhattan, NY (borough) New York County	487	0.03
Washington, DC (city) District of Columbia	171	0.03
Richmond, VA (ind. city) Richmond independent city	66	0.03
Fayetteville, NC (city) Cumberland County	61	0.03
Hartford, CT (city/town) Hartford County	39	0.03
Lawton, OK (city) Comanche County	31	0.03
West Palm Beach, FL (city) Palm Beach County	29	0.03
Southfield, MI (city) Oakland County	24	0.03
Pontiac, MI (city) Oakland County	20	0.03
Taylorsville, UT (city) Salt Lake County	18	0.03
Bensalem, PA (township) Bucks County	17	0.03
Chicopee, MA (city) Hampden County	16	0.03
Irvington, NJ (township) Essex County	16	0.03
Margate, FL (city) Broward County	14	0.03
Charleston, WV (city) Kanawha County	13	0.03

Please refer to the Explanation of Data in the front of the book for more detailed information.

Ancestry

West Indian: West Indian, excluding Hispanic

U.S. and 50 States Sorted by Population and Percent of Total Population

Place	Population	%
United States	**276,827**	**0.09**
New York	128,763	0.67
Florida	38,779	0.21
New Jersey	12,560	0.14
Georgia	11,849	0.13
Maryland	8,974	0.16
Massachusetts	8,779	0.14
California	8,589	0.02
Pennsylvania	7,115	0.06
Texas	6,883	0.03
North Carolina	6,660	0.07
Connecticut	6,104	0.17
Virginia	5,880	0.07
Ohio	2,428	0.02
Illinois	2,142	0.02
South Carolina	1,884	0.04
Michigan	1,380	0.01
Tennessee	1,262	0.02
Washington	1,238	0.02
District of Columbia	1,217	0.21
Alabama	1,178	0.02
Colorado	1,049	0.02
Nevada	1,022	0.04
Arizona	997	0.02
Rhode Island	946	0.09
Delaware	878	0.10
Minnesota	878	0.02
Missouri	860	0.01
Indiana	804	0.01
Kentucky	750	0.02
Louisiana	648	0.01
Oregon	568	0.02
Wisconsin	511	0.01
Oklahoma	466	0.01
Hawaii	343	0.03
Utah	333	0.01
Kansas	287	0.01
West Virginia	204	0.01
New Mexico	201	0.01
New Hampshire	199	0.02
Alaska	185	0.03
Arkansas	162	0.01
Iowa	161	0.01
Maine	136	0.01
Vermont	118	0.02
North Dakota	113	0.02
Idaho	102	0.01
Mississippi	101	<0.01
Nebraska	76	<0.01
Wyoming	37	0.01
South Dakota	15	<0.01
Montana	13	<0.01

Place	Population	%
New York	128,763	0.67
Florida	38,779	0.21
District of Columbia	1,217	0.21
Connecticut	6,104	0.17
Maryland	8,974	0.16
New Jersey	12,560	0.14
Massachusetts	8,779	0.14
Georgia	11,849	0.13
Delaware	878	0.10
United States	**276,827**	**0.09**
Rhode Island	946	0.09
North Carolina	6,660	0.07
Virginia	5,880	0.07
Pennsylvania	7,115	0.06
South Carolina	1,884	0.04
Nevada	1,022	0.04
Texas	6,883	0.03
Hawaii	343	0.03
Alaska	185	0.03
California	8,589	0.02
Ohio	2,428	0.02
Illinois	2,142	0.02
Tennessee	1,262	0.02
Washington	1,238	0.02
Alabama	1,178	0.02
Colorado	1,049	0.02
Arizona	997	0.02
Minnesota	878	0.02
Kentucky	750	0.02
Oregon	568	0.02
New Hampshire	199	0.02
Vermont	118	0.02
North Dakota	113	0.02
Michigan	1,380	0.01
Missouri	860	0.01
Indiana	804	0.01
Louisiana	648	0.01
Wisconsin	511	0.01
Oklahoma	466	0.01
Utah	333	0.01
Kansas	287	0.01
West Virginia	204	0.01
New Mexico	201	0.01
Arkansas	162	0.01
Iowa	161	0.01
Maine	136	0.01
Idaho	102	0.01
Wyoming	37	0.01
Mississippi	101	<0.01
Nebraska	76	<0.01
South Dakota	15	<0.01
Montana	13	<0.01

Please refer to the Explanation of Data in the front of the book for more detailed information.

Ancestry

West Indian: West Indian, excluding Hispanic

Top 150 Places Sorted by Population

Based on all places, regardless of total population

Place	Population	%
New York, NY (city) Kings County	106,548	1.32
Brooklyn, NY (borough) Kings County	59,844	2.43
Bronx, NY (borough) Bronx County	21,941	1.61
Queens, NY (borough) Queens County	17,400	0.79
Manhattan, NY (borough) New York County	5,618	0.35
Hempstead, NY (town) Nassau County	4,748	0.63
Tampa, FL (city) Hillsborough County	3,326	1.00
Boston, MA (city) Suffolk County	3,307	0.55
Philadelphia, PA (city) Philadelphia County	2,445	0.16
Staten Island, NY (borough) Richmond County	1,745	0.38
Los Angeles, CA (city) Los Angeles County	1,476	0.04
Houston, TX (city) Harris County	1,453	0.07
Babylon, NY (town) Suffolk County	1,378	0.64
Brookhaven, NY (town) Suffolk County	1,323	0.28
Mount Vernon, NY (city) Westchester County	1,287	1.92
Washington, DC (city) District of Columbia	1,217	0.21
Orlando, FL (city) Orange County	1,216	0.52
Hartford, CT (city/town) Hartford County	1,211	0.97
Yonkers, NY (city) Westchester County	1,072	0.55
Jacksonville, FL (city) Duval County	1,067	0.13
Baltimore, MD (city) Baltimore city County	1,033	0.17
Pine Hills, FL (cdp) Orange County	977	1.48
Jersey City, NJ (city) Hudson County	975	0.40
Pembroke Pines, FL (city) Broward County	953	0.63
Rochester, NY (city) Monroe County	870	0.41
Newark, NJ (city) Essex County	865	0.31
Charlotte, NC (city) Mecklenburg County	855	0.12
Coral Springs, FL (city) Broward County	832	0.69
Lauderhill, FL (city) Broward County	830	1.24
Hempstead, NY (village) Nassau County	785	1.47
Durham, NC (city) Durham County	732	0.33
Miramar, FL (city) Broward County	712	0.63
Chicago, IL (city) Cook County	698	0.03
Islip, NY (town) Suffolk County	677	0.20
Coram, NY (cdp) Suffolk County	641	1.66
Egypt Lake-Leto, FL (cdp) Hillsborough County	634	1.81
Miami Gardens, FL (city) Miami-Dade County	633	0.60
Virginia Beach, VA (ind. city) Virginia Beach independent city	625	0.14
Raleigh, NC (city) Wake County	620	0.16
Atlanta, GA (city) Fulton County	618	0.15
Fayetteville, NC (city) Cumberland County	615	0.31
Chesapeake, VA (ind. city) Chesapeake independent city	605	0.28
Wellington, FL (village) Palm Beach County	603	1.12
Norfolk, VA (ind. city) Norfolk independent city	591	0.24
Albany, NY (city) Albany County	576	0.59
Uniondale, NY (cdp) Nassau County	557	2.27
Providence, RI (city) Providence County	554	0.31
Wesley Chapel, FL (cdp) Pasco County	541	1.38
University, FL (cdp) Hillsborough County	539	1.33
Chelsea, MA (city) Suffolk County	535	1.55
Poinciana, FL (cdp) Osceola County	510	1.02
Sunrise, FL (city) Broward County	506	0.59
East Orange, NJ (city) Essex County	504	0.78
Augusta-Richmond County, GA (cons. govt) Richmond County	501	0.26
Bridgeport, CT (city/town) Fairfield County	500	0.35
Silver Spring, MD (cdp) Montgomery County	491	0.70
New Haven, CT (city/town) New Haven County	490	0.38
San Diego, CA (city) San Diego County	474	0.04
North Lauderdale, FL (city) Broward County	468	1.15
Baldwin, NY (cdp) Nassau County	449	1.89
Schenectady, NY (city) Schenectady County	446	0.68
Greenburgh, NY (town) Westchester County	445	0.51
Palm Bay, FL (city) Brevard County	437	0.43
Oakland, CA (city) Alameda County	426	0.11
Bloomfield, CT (town) Hartford County	424	2.09
Fort Lauderdale, FL (city) Broward County	424	0.25
North Valley Stream, NY (cdp) Nassau County	422	2.56
Tallahassee, FL (city) Leon County	420	0.24
Valley Stream, NY (village) Nassau County	414	1.12
Lynn, MA (city) Essex County	412	0.46
Palm River-Clair Mel, FL (cdp) Hillsborough County	411	1.96
Freeport, NY (village) Nassau County	411	0.96
Long Beach, CA (city) Los Angeles County	407	0.09
Irvington, NJ (township) Essex County	397	0.72
Cary, NC (town) Wake County	386	0.30
Riverview, FL (cdp) Hillsborough County	385	0.59
Port Charlotte, FL (cdp) Charlotte County	379	0.67
Miami, FL (city) Miami-Dade County	372	0.10
North Amityville, NY (cdp) Suffolk County	370	2.08
Seattle, WA (city) King County	366	0.06
Syracuse, NY (city) Onondaga County	364	0.25
Cleveland, OH (city) Cuyahoga County	364	0.09
North Hempstead, NY (town) Nassau County	363	0.16
Town 'n' Country, FL (cdp) Hillsborough County	358	0.46
Columbus, OH (city) Franklin County	357	0.05
Plantation, FL (city) Broward County	352	0.41
Elmont, NY (cdp) Nassau County	351	1.02
Las Vegas, NV (city) Clark County	351	0.06
Roosevelt, NY (cdp) Nassau County	350	2.33
Englewood, NJ (city) Bergen County	339	1.26
Springfield, MA (city) Hampden County	338	0.22
Buffalo, NY (city) Erie County	338	0.13
West Babylon, NY (cdp) Suffolk County	336	0.75
Indianapolis, IN (city) Marion County	335	0.04
Lauderdale Lakes, FL (city) Broward County	334	1.03
Chillum, MD (cdp) Prince George's County	334	0.95
Killeen, TX (city) Bell County	334	0.28
Huntington, NY (town) Suffolk County	332	0.16
Deltona, FL (city) Volusia County	329	0.39
Winter Garden, FL (city) Orange County	328	1.04
Brentwood, NY (cdp) Suffolk County	324	0.59
Land O' Lakes, FL (cdp) Pasco County	323	1.00
Worcester, MA (city) Worcester County	323	0.18
Plainfield, NJ (city) Union County	321	0.65
Hillside, NJ (township) Union County	312	1.47
Piscataway, NJ (township) Middlesex County	310	0.56
Hollywood, FL (city) Broward County	310	0.22
Manchester, CT (town) Hartford County	309	0.54
Ramapo, NY (town) Rockland County	308	0.25
Waldorf, MD (cdp) Charles County	302	0.45
Davie, FL (town) Broward County	302	0.33
Franklin, NJ (township) Somerset County	301	0.50
Baytown, TX (city) Harris County	299	0.42
Kansas City, MO (city) Jackson County	298	0.07
San Antonio, TX (city) Medina County	298	0.02
Windsor, CT (town) Hartford County	297	1.03
Fairland, MD (cdp) Montgomery County	293	1.27
Stamford, CT (city/town) Fairfield County	287	0.24
Owings Mills, MD (cdp) Baltimore County	285	0.96
Newport News, VA (ind. city) Newport News independent city	280	0.15
Port Chester, NY (village) Westchester County	278	0.97
Rye, NY (town) Westchester County	278	0.61
Gainesville, FL (city) Alachua County	276	0.22
Poughkeepsie, NY (city) Dutchess County	269	0.83
Middle River, MD (cdp) Baltimore County	268	1.13
Manchester, CT (cdp) Hartford County	267	0.89
Port St. Lucie, FL (city) St. Lucie County	267	0.17
Columbus, GA (city) Muscogee County	267	0.14
Minneapolis, MN (city) Hennepin County	265	0.07
Framingham, MA (cdp/town) Middlesex County	264	0.39
Alafaya, FL (cdp) Orange County	257	0.33
West Hartford, CT (cdp/town) Hartford County	256	0.41
Mastic, NY (cdp) Suffolk County	254	1.75
Middletown, NJ (township) Monmouth County	252	0.38
Cambridge, MA (city) Middlesex County	252	0.24
Mobile, AL (city) Mobile County	252	0.13
Pittsburgh, PA (city) Allegheny County	248	0.08
Woodbridge, NJ (township) Middlesex County	246	0.25
Kendall, FL (cdp) Miami-Dade County	244	0.32
St. Petersburg, FL (city) Pinellas County	244	0.10
Nashville-Davidson, TN (metro govt) Davidson County	244	0.04
Randolph, MA (cdp/town) Norfolk County	243	0.77
City of Orange, NJ (township) Essex County	240	0.79
Meadow Woods, FL (cdp) Orange County	239	1.01
Montgomery, AL (city) Montgomery County	239	0.12
Lawton, OK (city) Comanche County	235	0.25
Elizabeth, NJ (city) Union County	231	0.19
Altamonte Springs, FL (city) Seminole County	229	0.54
Blooming Grove, NY (town) Orange County	228	1.26
Hackensack, NJ (city) Bergen County	225	0.53

Ancestry

West Indian: West Indian, excluding Hispanic

Top 150 Places Sorted by Percent of Total Population

Based on all places, regardless of total population

Place	Population	%
Belford, NJ (cdp) Monmouth County	121	8.67
Aurora, NY (village) Cayuga County	76	6.79
Rushville, NY (village) Yates County	44	6.48
Walton, NE (cdp) Lancaster County	12	6.00
Cranberry Isles, ME (town) Hancock County	6	5.94
Sheyenne, ND (city) Eddy County	16	5.82
Lublin, WI (village) Taylor County	10	5.65
Blue Hills, CT (cdp) Hartford County	154	5.33
Crenshaw, PA (cdp) Jefferson County	29	4.90
Fredericksburg, PA (cdp) Lebanon County	62	4.87
Chatham, LA (town) Jackson Parish	29	4.83
Fairview, NY (cdp) Westchester County	103	4.32
Pine Air, FL (cdp) Palm Beach County	86	4.04
Hillburn, NY (village) Rockland County	38	4.00
Metter, GA (city) Candler County	142	3.45
Ledyard, NY (town) Cayuga County	76	3.41
Macungie, PA (borough) Lehigh County	104	3.37
Salmon Brook, CT (cdp) Hartford County	75	3.25
South Blooming Grove, NY (village) Orange County	105	3.19
Bodfish, CA (cdp) Kern County	59	3.04
Lely, FL (cdp) Collier County	104	2.87
Oneida, KY (cdp) Clay County	12	2.85
South Hempstead, NY (cdp) Nassau County	90	2.82
Naranja, FL (cdp) Miami-Dade County	178	2.79
Moravia, NY (town) Cayuga County	102	2.75
Dover, FL (cdp) Hillsborough County	95	2.70
Rising Sun-Lebanon, DE (cdp) Kent County	73	2.59
Calcium, NY (cdp) Jefferson County	91	2.57
North Valley Stream, NY (cdp) Nassau County	422	2.56
Wamego, KS (city) Pottawatomie County	107	2.46
Brooklyn, NY (borough) Kings County	59,844	2.43
Richlands, NC (town) Onslow County	36	2.41
Roosevelt, NY (cdp) Nassau County	350	2.33
Cogan House, PA (township) Lycoming County	23	2.29
Uniondale, NY (cdp) Nassau County	557	2.27
Oak Bluffs, MA (town) Dukes County	98	2.25
Monmouth Junction, NJ (cdp) Middlesex County	62	2.24
Sweetwater, TN (city) Monroe County	129	2.22
East Farmingdale, NY (cdp) Suffolk County	129	2.11
Potter, NY (town) Yates County	44	2.11
St. Michaels, MD (town) Talbot County	23	2.10
Palisades, TX (village) Randall County	7	2.10
Bloomfield, CT (town) Hartford County	424	2.09
North Amityville, NY (cdp) Suffolk County	370	2.08
Country Lake Estates, NJ (cdp) Burlington County	78	2.08
Whitesboro, NJ (cdp) Cape May County	48	2.08
Bolton, NC (town) Columbus County	15	2.06
Hillcrest, NY (cdp) Rockland County	167	2.04
Hokendauqua, PA (cdp) Lehigh County	71	1.98
Palm River-Clair Mel, FL (cdp) Hillsborough County	411	1.96
Jonesboro, GA (city) Clayton County	147	1.96
Piney Mountain, VA (cdp) Albemarle County	26	1.94
Mount Vernon, NY (city) Westchester County	1,287	1.92
Washington Park, FL (cdp) Broward County	28	1.91
Baldwin, NY (cdp) Nassau County	449	1.89
Minneola, FL (city) Lake County	169	1.88
East Bank, WV (town) Kanawha County	19	1.87
La Fargeville, NY (cdp) Jefferson County	13	1.86
Somerdale, NJ (borough) Camden County	96	1.85
Lakeview, NY (cdp) Nassau County	102	1.83
Society Hill, NJ (cdp) Middlesex County	73	1.83
Egypt Lake-Leto, FL (cdp) Hillsborough County	634	1.81
George Mason, VA (cdp) Fairfax County	160	1.80
Alachua, FL (city) Alachua County	157	1.80
Wendell, NC (town) Wake County	100	1.80
Quiring, MN (township) Beltrami County	2	1.80
Silver Springs Shores, FL (cdp) Marion County	122	1.78
Boulevard Gardens, FL (cdp) Broward County	30	1.76
Mastic, NY (cdp) Suffolk County	254	1.75
Konterra, MD (cdp) Prince George's County	38	1.75
Lakeview Heights, KY (city) Rowan County	3	1.74
Brownville, NY (village) Jefferson County	18	1.72
Hallam, PA (borough) York County	42	1.69
Coram, NY (cdp) Suffolk County	641	1.66
Kennedale, TX (city) Tarrant County	109	1.65
Bronx, NY (borough) Bronx County	21,941	1.61
Bladensburg, MD (town) Prince George's County	143	1.60
San Jon, NM (village) Quay County	5	1.60
Watertown, FL (cdp) Columbia County	36	1.56
Chelsea, MA (city) Suffolk County	535	1.55
Orlovista, FL (cdp) Orange County	114	1.55
Waipio Acres, HI (cdp) Honolulu County	88	1.55
North Annville, PA (township) Lebanon County	40	1.55
Delanco, NJ (township) Burlington County	63	1.52
Harlem, FL (cdp) Hendry County	47	1.51
Weathersfield, VT (town) Windsor County	42	1.49
Pine Hills, FL (cdp) Orange County	977	1.48
Hempstead, NY (village) Nassau County	785	1.47
Hillside, NJ (township) Union County	312	1.47
El Valle de Arroyo Seco, NM (cdp) Santa Fe County	20	1.46
Dimondale, MI (village) Eaton County	18	1.45
Woodridge, NY (village) Sullivan County	13	1.45
Robbins, IL (village) Cook County	76	1.44
Kortright, NY (town) Delaware County	25	1.44
Prairie View, TX (city) Waller County	74	1.41
Peterborough, NH (cdp) Hillsborough County	40	1.41
South Floral Park, NY (village) Nassau County	22	1.41
Wheatley Heights, NY (cdp) Suffolk County	87	1.40
Manchester, VA (cdp) Chesterfield County	154	1.39
Wesley Chapel, FL (cdp) Pasco County	541	1.38
Shelburne, MA (town) Franklin County	28	1.38
Womelsdorf, PA (borough) Berks County	38	1.36
Gibraltar, PA (cdp) Berks County	8	1.35
Vonore, TN (town) Monroe County	19	1.34
Garrett, WA (cdp) Walla Walla County	18	1.34
University, FL (cdp) Hillsborough County	539	1.33
Stowe, PA (township) Allegheny County	85	1.33
Norco, LA (cdp) St. Charles Parish	45	1.33
New York, NY (city) Kings County	106,548	1.32
Clarcona, FL (cdp) Orange County	34	1.32
Piney Green, NC (cdp) Onslow County	182	1.31
Cornville, AZ (cdp) Yavapai County	37	1.31
Sartell, MN (city) Benton County	28	1.31
Warminster Heights, PA (cdp) Bucks County	59	1.30
Mayesville, SC (town) Sumter County	8	1.30
Lincoln University, PA (cdp) Chester County	25	1.29
Glenside, PA (cdp) Montgomery County	94	1.28
Cofield, NC (village) Hertford County	4	1.28
Fairland, MD (cdp) Montgomery County	293	1.27
Pocono, PA (township) Monroe County	141	1.27
Bethel, PA (township) Lebanon County	62	1.27
Brimfield, MA (town) Hampden County	45	1.27
Mountain City, GA (town) Rabun County	9	1.27
Englewood, NJ (city) Bergen County	339	1.26
Blooming Grove, NY (town) Orange County	228	1.26
Palo Alto, PA (borough) Schuylkill County	13	1.25
Elloree, SC (town) Orangeburg County	8	1.25
Lauderhill, FL (city) Broward County	830	1.24
Mount Kisco, NY (town/village) Westchester County	131	1.23
Rupert, VT (town) Bennington County	12	1.23
Roosevelt Gardens, FL (cdp) Broward County	28	1.22
Hope Mills, NC (town) Cumberland County	174	1.21
West Liberty, WV (town) Ohio County	16	1.20
Occoquan, VA (town) Prince William County	7	1.20
Cherry Hill, VA (cdp) Prince William County	183	1.18
Snyder, PA (township) Jefferson County	29	1.18
Ogunquit, ME (town) York County	13	1.18
Spring Lake, NC (town) Cumberland County	138	1.17
Flordell Hills, MO (city) St. Louis County	10	1.17
Inwood, NY (cdp) Nassau County	121	1.16
North Lauderdale, FL (city) Broward County	468	1.15
College Park, GA (city) Fulton County	160	1.14
Middle River, MD (cdp) Baltimore County	268	1.13
Weissport East, PA (cdp) Carbon County	16	1.13
Wilton Center, CT (cdp) Fairfield County	9	1.13
Wellington, FL (village) Palm Beach County	603	1.12
Valley Stream, NY (village) Nassau County	414	1.12
Pinewood, FL (cdp) Miami-Dade County	178	1.12
Eglin AFB, FL (cdp) Okaloosa County	57	1.12
Stewart Manor, NY (village) Nassau County	24	1.11

Please refer to the Explanation of Data in the front of the book for more detailed information.

Ancestry

West Indian: West Indian, excluding Hispanic

Top 150 Places Sorted by Percent of Total Population

Based on places with total population of 7,500 or more

Place	Population	%
North Valley Stream, NY (cdp) Nassau County	422	2.56
Brooklyn, NY (borough) Kings County	59,844	2.43
Roosevelt, NY (cdp) Nassau County	350	2.33
Uniondale, NY (cdp) Nassau County	557	2.27
Bloomfield, CT (town) Hartford County	424	2.09
North Amityville, NY (cdp) Suffolk County	370	2.08
Hillcrest, NY (cdp) Rockland County	167	2.04
Palm River-Clair Mel, FL (cdp) Hillsborough County	411	1.96
Jonesboro, GA (city) Clayton County	147	1.96
Mount Vernon, NY (city) Westchester County	1,287	1.92
Baldwin, NY (cdp) Nassau County	449	1.89
Minneola, FL (city) Lake County	169	1.88
Egypt Lake-Leto, FL (cdp) Hillsborough County	634	1.81
George Mason, VA (cdp) Fairfax County	160	1.80
Alachua, FL (city) Alachua County	157	1.80
Mastic, NY (cdp) Suffolk County	254	1.75
Coram, NY (cdp) Suffolk County	641	1.66
Bronx, NY (borough) Bronx County	21,941	1.61
Bladensburg, MD (town) Prince George's County	143	1.60
Chelsea, MA (city) Suffolk County	535	1.55
Pine Hills, FL (cdp) Orange County	977	1.48
Hempstead, NY (village) Nassau County	785	1.47
Hillside, NJ (township) Union County	312	1.47
Manchester, VA (cdp) Chesterfield County	154	1.39
Wesley Chapel, FL (cdp) Pasco County	541	1.38
University, FL (cdp) Hillsborough County	539	1.33
New York, NY (city) Kings County	106,548	1.32
Piney Green, NC (cdp) Onslow County	182	1.31
Fairland, MD (cdp) Montgomery County	293	1.27
Pocono, PA (township) Monroe County	141	1.27
Englewood, NJ (city) Bergen County	339	1.26
Blooming Grove, NY (town) Orange County	228	1.26
Lauderhill, FL (city) Broward County	830	1.24
Mount Kisco, NY (town/village) Westchester County	131	1.23
Hope Mills, NC (town) Cumberland County	174	1.21
Cherry Hill, VA (cdp) Prince William County	183	1.18
Spring Lake, NC (town) Cumberland County	138	1.17
Inwood, NY (cdp) Nassau County	121	1.16
North Lauderdale, FL (city) Broward County	468	1.15
College Park, GA (city) Fulton County	160	1.14
Middle River, MD (cdp) Baltimore County	268	1.13
Wellington, FL (village) Palm Beach County	603	1.12
Valley Stream, NY (village) Nassau County	414	1.12
Pinewood, FL (cdp) Miami-Dade County	178	1.12
Franklin, OH (city) Warren County	129	1.08
Beekman, NY (town) Dutchess County	156	1.07
Murphysboro, IL (city) Jackson County	90	1.07
Shiloh, IL (village) St. Clair County	126	1.05
Winter Garden, FL (city) Orange County	328	1.04
Lauderdale Lakes, FL (city) Broward County	334	1.03
Windsor, CT (town) Hartford County	297	1.03
Poinciana, FL (cdp) Osceola County	510	1.02
Elmont, NY (cdp) Nassau County	351	1.02
Meadow Woods, FL (cdp) Orange County	239	1.01
Zephyrhills, FL (city) Pasco County	134	1.01
Tampa, FL (city) Hillsborough County	3,326	1.00
Land O' Lakes, FL (cdp) Pasco County	323	1.00
Sharon, MA (town) Norfolk County	175	1.00
Hartford, CT (city/town) Hartford County	1,211	0.97
Port Chester, NY (village) Westchester County	278	0.97
Freeport, NY (village) Nassau County	411	0.96
Owings Mills, MD (cdp) Baltimore County	285	0.96
Chillum, MD (cdp) Prince George's County	334	0.95
Middle, DE (town) New Castle County	158	0.95
Asbury Park, NJ (city) Monmouth County	155	0.95
Fords, NJ (cdp) Middlesex County	142	0.94
Chevy Chase, MD (cdp) Montgomery County	89	0.91
University, FL (cdp) Orange County	190	0.90
Manchester, CT (cdp) Hartford County	267	0.89
Shawangunk, NY (town) Ulster County	125	0.89
Baywood, NY (cdp) Suffolk County	70	0.89
Polk, PA (township) Monroe County	69	0.88
East Greenbush, NY (town) Rensselaer County	142	0.87
Penn Forest, PA (township) Carbon County	77	0.87
Somerset, NJ (cdp) Somerset County	192	0.86
Coolbaugh, PA (township) Monroe County	173	0.86
Calverton, MD (cdp) Montgomery County	152	0.85
Westerly, RI (cdp) Washington County	147	0.84
Seven Oaks, SC (cdp) Lexington County	138	0.84
Poughkeepsie, NY (city) Dutchess County	269	0.83
Glenvar Heights, FL (cdp) Miami-Dade County	127	0.83
Lake City, FL (city) Columbia County	102	0.83
East Lake-Orient Park, FL (cdp) Hillsborough County	197	0.82
Miami Shores, FL (village) Miami-Dade County	86	0.82
Franklin Park, NJ (cdp) Somerset County	101	0.80
Absecon, NJ (city) Atlantic County	67	0.80
Queens, NY (borough) Queens County	17,400	0.79
City of Orange, NJ (township) Essex County	240	0.79
East Orange, NJ (city) Essex County	504	0.78
Takoma Park, MD (city) Montgomery County	131	0.78
Seabrook, MD (cdp) Prince George's County	122	0.78
Longwood, FL (city) Seminole County	110	0.78
Randolph, MA (cdp/town) Norfolk County	243	0.77
New Cassel, NY (cdp) Nassau County	97	0.77
Lantana, FL (town) Palm Beach County	79	0.76
West Babylon, NY (cdp) Suffolk County	336	0.75
Aberdeen, NJ (township) Monmouth County	136	0.75
Newburgh, NY (city) Orange County	214	0.74
Lansing, MI (charter township) Ingham County	61	0.74
Guttenberg, NJ (town) Hudson County	80	0.73
Wyandanch, NY (cdp) Suffolk County	80	0.73
Irvington, NJ (township) Essex County	397	0.72
Copiague, NY (cdp) Suffolk County	148	0.72
Wawarsing, NY (town) Ulster County	96	0.72
Needham, MA (cdp/town) Norfolk County	205	0.71
Ferry Pass, FL (cdp) Escambia County	195	0.71
Kingstowne, VA (cdp) Fairfax County	103	0.71
Mount Dora, FL (city) Lake County	88	0.71
Fort Meade, MD (cdp) Anne Arundel County	78	0.71
Silver Spring, MD (cdp) Montgomery County	491	0.70
South Bradenton, FL (cdp) Manatee County	153	0.70
South Park Township, PA (cdp) Allegheny County	94	0.70
South Park, PA (township) Allegheny County	94	0.70
Pine Castle, FL (cdp) Orange County	77	0.70
Coral Springs, FL (city) Broward County	832	0.69
Holly Springs, GA (city) Cherokee County	58	0.69
Schenectady, NY (city) Schenectady County	446	0.68
Greenbelt, MD (city) Prince George's County	155	0.68
Burlington, NJ (township) Burlington County	153	0.68
Laurel, VA (cdp) Henrico County	109	0.68
Watervliet, NY (city) Albany County	70	0.68
Dover, NY (town) Dutchess County	59	0.68
Port Charlotte, FL (cdp) Charlotte County	379	0.67
Granby, CT (town) Hartford County	75	0.67
Franklin Square, NY (cdp) Nassau County	196	0.66
Clermont, FL (city) Lake County	173	0.66
Rosamond, CA (cdp) Kern County	113	0.66
Plainfield, NJ (city) Union County	321	0.65
Rotterdam, NY (town) Schenectady County	187	0.65
Union Park, FL (cdp) Orange County	66	0.65
Babylon, NY (town) Suffolk County	1,378	0.64
Ocoee, FL (city) Orange County	219	0.64
Westerly, RI (town) Washington County	147	0.64
Fishkill, NY (town) Dutchess County	140	0.64
Fresno, TX (cdp) Fort Bend County	106	0.64
Scottdale, GA (cdp) DeKalb County	63	0.64
Ellisville, MO (city) St. Louis County	58	0.64
Chestnut Ridge, NY (village) Rockland County	50	0.64
Hempstead, NY (town) Nassau County	4,748	0.63
Pembroke Pines, FL (city) Broward County	953	0.63
Miramar, FL (city) Broward County	712	0.63
Buckingham, PA (township) Bucks County	122	0.63
West Hempstead, NY (cdp) Nassau County	117	0.63
Fairburn, GA (city) Fulton County	71	0.62
Rye, NY (town) Westchester County	278	0.61
Roselle, NJ (borough) Union County	128	0.61
Goshen, NY (town) Orange County	84	0.61
Lockhart, FL (cdp) Orange County	78	0.61
Riverhead, NY (cdp) Suffolk County	77	0.61
Marcy, NY (town) Oneida County	55	0.61

SECTION THREE

Ancestry

West Indian: Other, excluding Hispanic

U.S. and 50 States Sorted by Population and Percent of Total Population

Place	Population	%
United States	**5,350**	**<0.01**
New York	1,418	0.01
Florida	1,211	0.01
California	288	<0.01
New Jersey	277	<0.01
Texas	273	<0.01
Massachusetts	228	<0.01
Georgia	157	<0.01
Maryland	156	<0.01
Indiana	121	<0.01
Connecticut	116	<0.01
Alabama	111	<0.01
Arizona	104	<0.01
Pennsylvania	95	<0.01
Oregon	72	<0.01
Minnesota	68	<0.01
South Carolina	64	<0.01
Virginia	61	<0.01
Missouri	54	<0.01
Washington	54	<0.01
North Carolina	52	<0.01
Hawaii	50	<0.01
Ohio	44	<0.01
Michigan	42	<0.01
Mississippi	40	<0.01
Louisiana	29	<0.01
Tennessee	29	<0.01
Delaware	27	<0.01
Arkansas	17	<0.01
Colorado	17	<0.01
Montana	17	<0.01
New Hampshire	12	<0.01
Alaska	11	<0.01
Kentucky	11	<0.01
Illinois	9	<0.01
Oklahoma	6	<0.01
Iowa	4	<0.01
Vermont	4	<0.01
Nebraska	1	<0.01
District of Columbia	0	0.00
Idaho	0	0.00
Kansas	0	0.00
Maine	0	0.00
Nevada	0	0.00
New Mexico	0	0.00
North Dakota	0	0.00
Rhode Island	0	0.00
South Dakota	0	0.00
Utah	0	0.00
West Virginia	0	0.00
Wisconsin	0	0.00
Wyoming	0	0.00

Place	Population	%
New York	1,418	0.01
Florida	1,211	0.01
United States	**5,350**	**<0.01**
California	288	<0.01
New Jersey	277	<0.01
Texas	273	<0.01
Massachusetts	228	<0.01
Georgia	157	<0.01
Maryland	156	<0.01
Indiana	121	<0.01
Connecticut	116	<0.01
Alabama	111	<0.01
Arizona	104	<0.01
Pennsylvania	95	<0.01
Oregon	72	<0.01
Minnesota	68	<0.01
South Carolina	64	<0.01
Virginia	61	<0.01
Missouri	54	<0.01
Washington	54	<0.01
North Carolina	52	<0.01
Hawaii	50	<0.01
Ohio	44	<0.01
Michigan	42	<0.01
Mississippi	40	<0.01
Louisiana	29	<0.01
Tennessee	29	<0.01
Delaware	27	<0.01
Arkansas	17	<0.01
Colorado	17	<0.01
Montana	17	<0.01
New Hampshire	12	<0.01
Alaska	11	<0.01
Kentucky	11	<0.01
Illinois	9	<0.01
Oklahoma	6	<0.01
Iowa	4	<0.01
Vermont	4	<0.01
Nebraska	1	<0.01
District of Columbia	0	0.00
Idaho	0	0.00
Kansas	0	0.00
Maine	0	0.00
Nevada	0	0.00
New Mexico	0	0.00
North Dakota	0	0.00
Rhode Island	0	0.00
South Dakota	0	0.00
Utah	0	0.00
West Virginia	0	0.00
Wisconsin	0	0.00
Wyoming	0	0.00

Please refer to the Explanation of Data in the front of the book for more detailed information.

Ancestry

West Indian: Other, excluding Hispanic

Top 150 Places Sorted by Population

Based on all places, regardless of total population

Place	Population	%
New York, NY (city) Kings County	1,204	0.01
Brooklyn, NY (borough) Kings County	454	0.02
Queens, NY (borough) Queens County	452	0.02
Bronx, NY (borough) Bronx County	130	0.01
Manhattan, NY (borough) New York County	125	0.01
Somerville, MA (city) Middlesex County	120	0.16
Madison Park, NJ (cdp) Middlesex County	101	1.48
Old Bridge, NJ (township) Middlesex County	101	0.16
Milford Mill, MD (cdp) Baltimore County	98	0.34
Lakeland, FL (city) Polk County	97	0.10
Mesa, AZ (city) Maricopa County	94	0.02
North Miami, FL (city) Miami-Dade County	87	0.15
Houston, TX (city) Harris County	87	<0.01
Pace, FL (cdp) Santa Rosa County	82	0.42
Albany, NY (city) Albany County	67	0.07
Lehigh Acres, FL (cdp) Lee County	61	0.07
Braintree Town, MA (city) Norfolk County	59	0.17
St. Petersburg, FL (city) Pinellas County	58	0.02
Mobile, AL (city) Mobile County	54	0.03
Deerfield Beach, FL (city) Broward County	53	0.07
Hartford, CT (city/town) Hartford County	45	0.04
Poinciana, FL (cdp) Osceola County	44	0.09
Staten Island, NY (borough) Richmond County	43	0.01
Monroe, NY (village) Orange County	40	0.48
Monroe, NY (town) Orange County	40	0.10
San Jose, CA (city) Santa Clara County	38	<0.01
Philadelphia, PA (city) Philadelphia County	36	<0.01
Garfield, NJ (city) Bergen County	35	0.12
Columbia, MD (cdp) Howard County	35	0.04
Corpus Christi, TX (city) Nueces County	35	0.01
Lakeville, MN (city) Dakota County	34	0.06
San Diego, CA (city) San Diego County	34	<0.01
Makakilo, HI (cdp) Honolulu County	33	0.19
Los Angeles, CA (city) Los Angeles County	33	<0.01
The Hammocks, FL (cdp) Miami-Dade County	30	0.06
Marathon, FL (city) Monroe County	28	0.33
Riverview, FL (cdp) Hillsborough County	28	0.04
Anderson, IN (city) Madison County	27	0.05
Deltona, FL (city) Volusia County	27	0.03
Brookhaven, NY (town) Suffolk County	27	0.01
Cheltenham, PA (township) Montgomery County	26	0.07
Teaneck, NJ (township) Bergen County	26	0.07
Atlanta, GA (city) Fulton County	26	0.01
Jersey City, NJ (city) Hudson County	26	0.01
Gary, IN (city) Lake County	25	0.03
North Miami Beach, FL (city) Miami-Dade County	24	0.06
Lowell, MA (city) Middlesex County	23	0.02
Salem, OR (city) Marion County	23	0.02
Orlando, FL (city) Orange County	23	0.01
Rancho Cucamonga, CA (city) San Bernardino County	23	0.01
Tampa, FL (city) Hillsborough County	23	0.01
San Antonio, TX (city) Medina County	23	<0.01
Torrington, CT (city/town) Litchfield County	22	0.06
San Marcos, CA (city) San Diego County	22	0.03
Woodinville, WA (city) King County	21	0.20
Harvey, LA (cdp) Jefferson Parish	21	0.11
El Cerrito, CA (city) Contra Costa County	21	0.09
Marion, IN (city) Grant County	21	0.07
Grants Pass, OR (city) Josephine County	21	0.06
Stockton, CA (city) San Joaquin County	21	0.01
Charlotte, NC (city) Mecklenburg County	21	<0.01
Sun City Center, FL (cdp) Hillsborough County	20	0.10
New Milford, CT (town) Litchfield County	20	0.07
Pembroke Pines, FL (city) Broward County	20	0.01
McComb, MS (city) Pike County	19	0.15
Culpeper, VA (town) Culpeper County	19	0.12
Kennesaw, GA (city) Cobb County	19	0.07
Melbourne, FL (city) Brevard County	19	0.02
San Dimas, CA (city) Los Angeles County	18	0.05
Tallahassee, FL (city) Leon County	18	0.01
Austin, TX (city) Travis County	18	<0.01
Fort Stewart, GA (cdp) Liberty County	17	0.30
Ashland, OH (city) Ashland County	17	0.08
Culver City, CA (city) Los Angeles County	17	0.04
Freeport, NY (village) Nassau County	17	0.04
Missoula, MT (city) Missoula County	17	0.03
Boulder, CO (city) Boulder County	17	0.02
Hempstead, NY (town) Nassau County	17	<0.01
Newnan, GA (city) Coweta County	16	0.05
Country Club, FL (cdp) Miami-Dade County	16	0.04
Coral Gables, FL (city) Miami-Dade County	16	0.03
Fullerton, CA (city) Orange County	16	0.01
Lansing, MI (city) Ingham County	16	0.01
Lansing, MI (city) Ingham County	16	0.01
Fultondale, AL (city) Jefferson County	15	0.19
Springfield, TN (city) Robertson County	15	0.09
Massapequa, NY (cdp) Nassau County	15	0.07
Centereach, NY (cdp) Suffolk County	15	0.05
Lacey, NJ (township) Ocean County	15	0.05
Upper Merion, PA (township) Montgomery County	15	0.05
Egypt Lake-Leto, FL (cdp) Hillsborough County	15	0.04
Bloomfield, NJ (township) Essex County	15	0.03
Columbia, SC (city) Richland County	15	0.01
Oyster Bay, NY (town) Nassau County	15	0.01
Springfield, MA (city) Hampden County	15	0.01
Dallas, TX (city) Dallas County	15	<0.01
Tri-Lakes, IN (cdp) Whitley County	14	0.85
Purdue University, IN (cdp) Tippecanoe County	14	0.11
St. Louis Park, MN (city) Hennepin County	14	0.03
Daytona Beach, FL (city) Volusia County	14	0.02
Palm Coast, FL (city) Flagler County	14	0.02
Wilmington, DE (city) New Castle County	14	0.02
Nashville-Davidson, TN (metro govt) Davidson County	14	<0.01
Waikoloa Village, HI (cdp) Hawaii County	13	0.21
Somerset, NJ (cdp) Somerset County	13	0.06
Citrus Park, FL (cdp) Hillsborough County	13	0.05
Aspen Hill, MD (cdp) Montgomery County	13	0.03
Bedford, TX (city) Tarrant County	13	0.03
Linden, NJ (city) Union County	13	0.03
Troy, NY (city) Rensselaer County	13	0.03
Franklin, NJ (township) Somerset County	13	0.02
Suffolk, VA (ind. city) Suffolk independent city	13	0.02
Fresno, CA (city) Fresno County	13	<0.01
Southwest Ranches, FL (town) Broward County	12	0.16
Georgetown, GA (cdp) Chatham County	12	0.10
Claremont, NH (city) Sullivan County	12	0.09
Stony Brook, NY (cdp) Suffolk County	12	0.09
Princeton, FL (cdp) Miami-Dade County	12	0.06
Navarre, FL (cdp) Santa Rosa County	12	0.04
Walnut, CA (city) Los Angeles County	12	0.04
Alexandria, VA (ind. city) Alexandria independent city	12	0.01
Little Rock, AR (city) Pulaski County	12	0.01
Indianapolis, IN (city) Marion County	12	<0.01
Newark, NJ (city) Essex County	12	<0.01
Horseheads, NY (village) Chemung County	11	0.17
Calera, AL (city) Shelby County	11	0.11
Creve Coeur, MO (city) St. Louis County	11	0.06
Horseheads, NY (town) Chemung County	11	0.06
Frankfort, KY (city) Franklin County	11	0.04
Middletown, CT (city/town) Middlesex County	11	0.02
Bellingham, WA (city) Whatcom County	11	0.01
Brandon, FL (cdp) Hillsborough County	11	0.01
Anchorage, AK (municipality) Anchorage Municipality	11	<0.01
Boston, MA (city) Suffolk County	11	<0.01
Pascagoula, MS (city) Jackson County	10	0.04
Apache Junction, AZ (city) Pinal County	10	0.03
Cutler Bay, FL (town) Miami-Dade County	10	0.03
Lake Magdalene, FL (cdp) Hillsborough County	10	0.03
Cortlandt, NY (town) Westchester County	10	0.02
Greenville, SC (city) Greenville County	10	0.02
Baltimore, MD (city) Baltimore city County	10	<0.01
Cincinnati, OH (city) Hamilton County	10	<0.01
Irondale, GA (cdp) Clayton County	9	0.12
Oronoko, MI (charter township) Berrien County	9	0.10
Montgomery, OH (city) Hamilton County	9	0.09
Phoenixville, PA (borough) Chester County	9	0.06
Willmar, MN (city) Kandiyohi County	9	0.05
Springettsbury, PA (township) York County	9	0.03
University, FL (cdp) Hillsborough County	9	0.02
Brooklyn Park, MN (city) Hennepin County	9	0.01

Please refer to the Explanation of Data in the front of the book for more detailed information.

Ancestry

West Indian: Other, excluding Hispanic

Top 150 Places Sorted by Percent of Total Population

Based on all places, regardless of total population

Place	Population	%
Madison Park, NJ (cdp) Middlesex County	101	1.48
Burton, MN (township) Yellow Medicine County	2	1.23
Silverhill, AL (town) Baldwin County	6	0.95
Tri-Lakes, IN (cdp) Whitley County	14	0.85
Burton, TX (city) Washington County	3	0.75
Cammack Village, AR (city) Pulaski County	5	0.55
Unionville, NY (village) Orange County	2	0.52
Glendale, OR (city) Douglas County	4	0.50
Monroe, NY (village) Orange County	40	0.48
Pierson, FL (town) Volusia County	8	0.46
Pace, FL (cdp) Santa Rosa County	82	0.42
Milford Mill, MD (cdp) Baltimore County	98	0.34
Evart, MI (township) Osceola County	5	0.34
Marathon, FL (city) Monroe County	28	0.33
Fort Stewart, GA (cdp) Liberty County	17	0.30
New Haven, VT (town) Addison County	4	0.25
Waikoloa Village, HI (cdp) Hawaii County	13	0.21
Durant, IA (city) Cedar County	4	0.21
Woodinville, WA (city) King County	21	0.20
Makakilo, HI (cdp) Honolulu County	33	0.19
Fultondale, AL (city) Jefferson County	15	0.19
Brazoria, TX (city) Brazoria County	6	0.19
Braintree Town, MA (city) Norfolk County	59	0.17
Horseheads, NY (village) Chemung County	11	0.17
Somerville, MA (city) Middlesex County	120	0.16
Old Bridge, NJ (township) Middlesex County	101	0.16
Southwest Ranches, FL (town) Broward County	12	0.16
North Miami, FL (city) Miami-Dade County	87	0.15
McComb, MS (city) Pike County	19	0.15
St. Paul, MO (city) St. Charles County	3	0.15
St. Martinville, LA (city) St. Martin Parish	8	0.13
Garfield, NJ (city) Bergen County	35	0.12
Culpeper, VA (town) Culpeper County	19	0.12
Irondale, GA (cdp) Clayton County	9	0.12
Humboldt, NE (city) Richardson County	1	0.12
Harvey, LA (cdp) Jefferson Parish	21	0.11
Purdue University, IN (cdp) Tippecanoe County	14	0.11
Calera, AL (city) Shelby County	11	0.11
Lakeland, FL (city) Polk County	97	0.10
Monroe, NY (town) Orange County	40	0.10
Sun City Center, FL (cdp) Hillsborough County	20	0.10
Georgetown, GA (cdp) Chatham County	12	0.10
Oronoko, MI (charter township) Berrien County	9	0.10
Poinciana, FL (cdp) Osceola County	44	0.09
El Cerrito, CA (city) Contra Costa County	21	0.09
Springfield, TN (city) Robertson County	15	0.09
Claremont, NH (city) Sullivan County	12	0.09
Stony Brook, NY (cdp) Suffolk County	12	0.09
Montgomery, OH (city) Hamilton County	9	0.09
Ashland, OH (city) Ashland County	17	0.08
Albany, NY (city) Albany County	67	0.07
Lehigh Acres, FL (cdp) Lee County	61	0.07
Deerfield Beach, FL (city) Broward County	53	0.07
Cheltenham, PA (township) Montgomery County	26	0.07
Teaneck, NJ (township) Bergen County	26	0.07
Marion, IN (city) Grant County	21	0.07
New Milford, CT (town) Litchfield County	20	0.07
Kennesaw, GA (city) Cobb County	19	0.07
Massapequa, NY (cdp) Nassau County	15	0.07
Miami Shores, FL (village) Miami-Dade County	7	0.07
Williamson, NY (town) Wayne County	5	0.07
Lakeville, MN (city) Dakota County	34	0.06
The Hammocks, FL (cdp) Miami-Dade County	30	0.06
North Miami Beach, FL (city) Miami-Dade County	24	0.06
Torrington, CT (city/town) Litchfield County	22	0.06
Grants Pass, OR (city) Josephine County	21	0.06
Somerset, NJ (cdp) Somerset County	13	0.06
Princeton, FL (cdp) Miami-Dade County	12	0.06
Creve Coeur, MO (city) St. Louis County	11	0.06
Horseheads, NY (town) Chemung County	11	0.06
Phoenixville, PA (borough) Chester County	9	0.06
Anderson, IN (city) Madison County	27	0.05
San Dimas, CA (city) Los Angeles County	18	0.05
Newnan, GA (city) Coweta County	16	0.05
Centereach, NY (cdp) Suffolk County	15	0.05
Lacey, NJ (township) Ocean County	15	0.05
Upper Merion, PA (township) Montgomery County	15	0.05
Citrus Park, FL (cdp) Hillsborough County	13	0.05
Willmar, MN (city) Kandiyohi County	9	0.05
Minisink, NY (town) Orange County	2	0.05
Hartford, CT (city/town) Hartford County	45	0.04
Columbia, MD (cdp) Howard County	35	0.04
Riverview, FL (cdp) Hillsborough County	28	0.04
Culver City, CA (city) Los Angeles County	17	0.04
Freeport, NY (village) Nassau County	17	0.04
Country Club, FL (cdp) Miami-Dade County	16	0.04
Egypt Lake-Leto, FL (cdp) Hillsborough County	15	0.04
Navarre, FL (cdp) Santa Rosa County	12	0.04
Walnut, CA (city) Los Angeles County	12	0.04
Frankfort, KY (city) Franklin County	11	0.04
Pascagoula, MS (city) Jackson County	10	0.04
Mobile, AL (city) Mobile County	54	0.03
Deltona, FL (city) Volusia County	27	0.03
Gary, IN (city) Lake County	25	0.03
San Marcos, CA (city) San Diego County	22	0.03
Missoula, MT (city) Missoula County	17	0.03
Coral Gables, FL (city) Miami-Dade County	16	0.03
Bloomfield, NJ (township) Essex County	15	0.03
St. Louis Park, MN (city) Hennepin County	14	0.03
Aspen Hill, MD (cdp) Montgomery County	13	0.03
Bedford, TX (city) Tarrant County	13	0.03
Linden, NJ (city) Union County	13	0.03
Troy, NY (city) Rensselaer County	13	0.03
Apache Junction, AZ (city) Pinal County	10	0.03
Cutler Bay, FL (town) Miami-Dade County	10	0.03
Lake Magdalene, FL (cdp) Hillsborough County	10	0.03
Springettsbury, PA (township) York County	9	0.03
Brooklyn, NY (borough) Kings County	454	0.02
Queens, NY (borough) Queens County	452	0.02
Mesa, AZ (city) Maricopa County	94	0.02
St. Petersburg, FL (city) Pinellas County	58	0.02
Lowell, MA (city) Middlesex County	23	0.02
Salem, OR (city) Marion County	23	0.02
Melbourne, FL (city) Brevard County	19	0.02
Boulder, CO (city) Boulder County	17	0.02
Daytona Beach, FL (city) Volusia County	14	0.02
Palm Coast, FL (city) Flagler County	14	0.02
Wilmington, DE (city) New Castle County	14	0.02
Franklin, NJ (township) Somerset County	13	0.02
Suffolk, VA (ind. city) Suffolk independent city	13	0.02
Middletown, CT (city/town) Middlesex County	11	0.02
Cortlandt, NY (town) Westchester County	10	0.02
Greenville, SC (city) Greenville County	10	0.02
University, FL (cdp) Hillsborough County	9	0.02
Columbus, IN (city) Bartholomew County	8	0.02
Newark, OH (city) Licking County	8	0.02
Huntington Station, NY (cdp) Suffolk County	7	0.02
Ormond Beach, FL (city) Volusia County	7	0.02
Belmont, CA (city) San Mateo County	6	0.02
Seguin, TX (city) Guadalupe County	6	0.02
Granite Bay, CA (cdp) Placer County	5	0.02
Niles, MI (township) Berrien County	3	0.02
New York, NY (city) Kings County	1,204	0.01
Bronx, NY (borough) Bronx County	130	0.01
Manhattan, NY (borough) New York County	125	0.01
Staten Island, NY (borough) Richmond County	43	0.01
Corpus Christi, TX (city) Nueces County	35	0.01
Brookhaven, NY (town) Suffolk County	27	0.01
Atlanta, GA (city) Fulton County	26	0.01
Jersey City, NJ (city) Hudson County	26	0.01
Orlando, FL (city) Orange County	23	0.01
Rancho Cucamonga, CA (city) San Bernardino County	23	0.01
Tampa, FL (city) Hillsborough County	23	0.01
Stockton, CA (city) San Joaquin County	21	0.01
Pembroke Pines, FL (city) Broward County	20	0.01
Tallahassee, FL (city) Leon County	18	0.01
Fullerton, CA (city) Orange County	16	0.01
Lansing, MI (city) Ingham County	16	0.01
Lansing, MI (city) Ingham County	16	0.01
Columbia, SC (city) Richland County	15	0.01

Please refer to the Explanation of Data in the front of the book for more detailed information.

Ancestry

West Indian: Other, excluding Hispanic

Top 150 Places Sorted by Percent of Total Population

Based on places with total population of 7,500 or more

Place	Population	%
Monroe, NY (village) Orange County	40	0.48
Pace, FL (cdp) Santa Rosa County	82	0.42
Milford Mill, MD (cdp) Baltimore County	98	0.34
Marathon, FL (city) Monroe County	28	0.33
Woodinville, WA (city) King County	21	0.20
Makakilo, HI (cdp) Honolulu County	33	0.19
Fultondale, AL (city) Jefferson County	15	0.19
Braintree Town, MA (city) Norfolk County	59	0.17
Somerville, MA (city) Middlesex County	120	0.16
Old Bridge, NJ (township) Middlesex County	101	0.16
North Miami, FL (city) Miami-Dade County	87	0.15
McComb, MS (city) Pike County	19	0.15
Garfield, NJ (city) Bergen County	35	0.12
Culpeper, VA (town) Culpeper County	19	0.12
Harvey, LA (cdp) Jefferson Parish	21	0.11
Purdue University, IN (cdp) Tippecanoe County	14	0.11
Calera, AL (city) Shelby County	11	0.11
Lakeland, FL (city) Polk County	97	0.10
Monroe, NY (town) Orange County	40	0.10
Sun City Center, FL (cdp) Hillsborough County	20	0.10
Georgetown, GA (cdp) Chatham County	12	0.10
Oronoko, MI (charter township) Berrien County	9	0.10
Poinciana, FL (cdp) Osceola County	44	0.09
El Cerrito, CA (city) Contra Costa County	21	0.09
Springfield, TN (city) Robertson County	15	0.09
Claremont, NH (city) Sullivan County	12	0.09
Stony Brook, NY (cdp) Suffolk County	12	0.09
Montgomery, OH (city) Hamilton County	9	0.09
Ashland, OH (city) Ashland County	17	0.08
Albany, NY (city) Albany County	67	0.07
Lehigh Acres, FL (cdp) Lee County	61	0.07
Deerfield Beach, FL (city) Broward County	53	0.07
Cheltenham, PA (township) Montgomery County	26	0.07
Teaneck, NJ (township) Bergen County	26	0.07
Marion, IN (city) Grant County	21	0.07
New Milford, CT (town) Litchfield County	20	0.07
Kennesaw, GA (city) Cobb County	19	0.07
Massapequa, NY (cdp) Nassau County	15	0.07
Miami Shores, FL (village) Miami-Dade County	7	0.07
Lakeville, MN (city) Dakota County	34	0.06
The Hammocks, FL (cdp) Miami-Dade County	30	0.06
North Miami Beach, FL (city) Miami-Dade County	24	0.06
Torrington, CT (city/town) Litchfield County	22	0.06
Grants Pass, OR (city) Josephine County	21	0.06
Somerset, NJ (cdp) Somerset County	13	0.06
Princeton, FL (cdp) Miami-Dade County	12	0.06
Creve Coeur, MO (city) St. Louis County	11	0.06
Horseheads, NY (town) Chemung County	11	0.06
Phoenixville, PA (borough) Chester County	9	0.06
Anderson, IN (city) Madison County	27	0.05
San Dimas, CA (city) Los Angeles County	18	0.05
Newnan, GA (city) Coweta County	16	0.05
Centereach, NY (cdp) Suffolk County	15	0.05
Lacey, NJ (township) Ocean County	15	0.05
Upper Merion, PA (township) Montgomery County	15	0.05
Citrus Park, FL (cdp) Hillsborough County	13	0.05
Willmar, MN (city) Kandiyohi County	9	0.05
Hartford, CT (city/town) Hartford County	45	0.04
Columbia, MD (cdp) Howard County	35	0.04
Riverview, FL (cdp) Hillsborough County	28	0.04
Culver City, CA (city) Los Angeles County	17	0.04
Freeport, NY (village) Nassau County	17	0.04
Country Club, FL (cdp) Miami-Dade County	16	0.04
Egypt Lake-Leto, FL (cdp) Hillsborough County	15	0.04
Navarre, FL (cdp) Santa Rosa County	12	0.04
Walnut, CA (city) Los Angeles County	12	0.04
Frankfort, KY (city) Franklin County	11	0.04
Pascagoula, MS (city) Jackson County	10	0.04
Mobile, AL (city) Mobile County	54	0.03
Deltona, FL (city) Volusia County	27	0.03
Gary, IN (city) Lake County	25	0.03
San Marcos, CA (city) San Diego County	22	0.03
Missoula, MT (city) Missoula County	17	0.03
Coral Gables, FL (city) Miami-Dade County	16	0.03
Bloomfield, NJ (township) Essex County	15	0.03
St. Louis Park, MN (city) Hennepin County	14	0.03
Aspen Hill, MD (cdp) Montgomery County	13	0.03
Bedford, TX (city) Tarrant County	13	0.03
Linden, NJ (city) Union County	13	0.03
Troy, NY (city) Rensselaer County	13	0.03
Apache Junction, AZ (city) Pinal County	10	0.03
Cutler Bay, FL (town) Miami-Dade County	10	0.03
Lake Magdalene, FL (cdp) Hillsborough County	10	0.03
Springettsbury, PA (township) York County	9	0.03
Brooklyn, NY (borough) Kings County	454	0.02
Queens, NY (borough) Queens County	452	0.02
Mesa, AZ (city) Maricopa County	94	0.02
St. Petersburg, FL (city) Pinellas County	58	0.02
Lowell, MA (city) Middlesex County	23	0.02
Salem, OR (city) Marion County	23	0.02
Melbourne, FL (city) Brevard County	19	0.02
Boulder, CO (city) Boulder County	17	0.02
Daytona Beach, FL (city) Volusia County	14	0.02
Palm Coast, FL (city) Flagler County	14	0.02
Wilmington, DE (city) New Castle County	14	0.02
Franklin, NJ (township) Somerset County	13	0.02
Suffolk, VA (ind. city) Suffolk independent city	13	0.02
Middletown, CT (city/town) Middlesex County	11	0.02
Cortlandt, NY (town) Westchester County	10	0.02
Greenville, SC (city) Greenville County	10	0.02
University, FL (cdp) Hillsborough County	9	0.02
Columbus, IN (city) Bartholomew County	8	0.02
Newark, OH (city) Licking County	8	0.02
Huntington Station, NY (cdp) Suffolk County	7	0.02
Ormond Beach, FL (city) Volusia County	7	0.02
Belmont, CA (city) San Mateo County	6	0.02
Seguin, TX (city) Guadalupe County	6	0.02
Granite Bay, CA (cdp) Placer County	5	0.02
Niles, MI (township) Berrien County	3	0.02
New York, NY (city) Kings County	1,204	0.01
Bronx, NY (borough) Bronx County	130	0.01
Manhattan, NY (borough) New York County	125	0.01
Staten Island, NY (borough) Richmond County	43	0.01
Corpus Christi, TX (city) Nueces County	35	0.01
Brookhaven, NY (town) Suffolk County	27	0.01
Atlanta, GA (city) Fulton County	26	0.01
Jersey City, NJ (city) Hudson County	26	0.01
Orlando, FL (city) Orange County	23	0.01
Rancho Cucamonga, CA (city) San Bernardino County	23	0.01
Tampa, FL (city) Hillsborough County	23	0.01
Stockton, CA (city) San Joaquin County	21	0.01
Pembroke Pines, FL (city) Broward County	20	0.01
Tallahassee, FL (city) Leon County	18	0.01
Fullerton, CA (city) Orange County	16	0.01
Lansing, MI (city) Ingham County	16	0.01
Lansing, MI (city) Ingham County	16	0.01
Columbia, SC (city) Richland County	15	0.01
Oyster Bay, NY (town) Nassau County	15	0.01
Springfield, MA (city) Hampden County	15	0.01
Alexandria, VA (ind. city) Alexandria independent city	12	0.01
Little Rock, AR (city) Pulaski County	12	0.01
Bellingham, WA (city) Whatcom County	11	0.01
Brandon, FL (cdp) Hillsborough County	11	0.01
Brooklyn Park, MN (city) Hennepin County	9	0.01
West Hartford, CT (cdp/town) Hartford County	9	0.01
East Orange, NJ (city) Essex County	8	0.01
Port Arthur, TX (city) Jefferson County	8	0.01
Union, NJ (township) Union County	8	0.01
Everett, WA (city) Snohomish County	7	0.01
Dothan, AL (city) Houston County	6	0.01
Midwest City, OK (city) Oklahoma County	6	0.01
Portsmouth, VA (ind. city) Portsmouth independent city	6	0.01
Waterbury, CT (city/town) New Haven County	6	0.01
Trenton, NJ (city) Mercer County	5	0.01
Kailua, HI (cdp) Honolulu County	4	0.01
New London, CT (city/town) New London County	3	0.01
Houston, TX (city) Harris County	87	<0.01
San Jose, CA (city) Santa Clara County	38	<0.01
Philadelphia, PA (city) Philadelphia County	36	<0.01
San Diego, CA (city) San Diego County	34	<0.01

SECTION THREE

Please refer to the Explanation of Data in the front of the book for more detailed information.

Ancestry

Yugoslavian

U.S. and 50 States Sorted by Population and Percent of Total Population

Place	Population	%
United States	**330,705**	**0.11**
California	37,235	0.10
New York	28,253	0.15
Illinois	20,954	0.16
Michigan	20,532	0.21
Florida	20,414	0.11
Missouri	13,707	0.23
Washington	12,619	0.19
Pennsylvania	12,582	0.10
Ohio	12,485	0.11
Arizona	11,598	0.19
Texas	11,289	0.05
Georgia	9,408	0.10
New Jersey	9,241	0.11
Minnesota	8,826	0.17
Iowa	8,581	0.28
Colorado	8,233	0.17
Wisconsin	6,408	0.11
Indiana	6,328	0.10
Virginia	5,936	0.08
Utah	5,589	0.21
Connecticut	5,494	0.15
Kentucky	5,427	0.13
North Carolina	4,917	0.05
Oregon	4,596	0.12
Nevada	4,514	0.17
Massachusetts	4,342	0.07
Tennessee	3,465	0.06
Idaho	3,323	0.22
Montana	2,428	0.25
Maryland	2,087	0.04
Louisiana	1,909	0.04
Mississippi	1,687	0.06
New Hampshire	1,620	0.12
Vermont	1,354	0.22
New Mexico	1,166	0.06
Nebraska	1,161	0.06
West Virginia	1,103	0.06
Alabama	1,097	0.02
South Carolina	1,058	0.02
Kansas	1,035	0.04
Oklahoma	956	0.03
Wyoming	906	0.17
Alaska	895	0.13
North Dakota	883	0.13
South Dakota	860	0.11
Hawaii	589	0.04
Arkansas	480	0.02
Maine	368	0.03
Delaware	323	0.04
District of Columbia	243	0.04
Rhode Island	201	0.02

Place	Population	%
Iowa	8,581	0.28
Montana	2,428	0.25
Missouri	13,707	0.23
Idaho	3,323	0.22
Vermont	1,354	0.22
Michigan	20,532	0.21
Utah	5,589	0.21
Washington	12,619	0.19
Arizona	11,598	0.19
Minnesota	8,826	0.17
Colorado	8,233	0.17
Nevada	4,514	0.17
Wyoming	906	0.17
Illinois	20,954	0.16
New York	28,253	0.15
Connecticut	5,494	0.15
Kentucky	5,427	0.13
Alaska	895	0.13
North Dakota	883	0.13
Oregon	4,596	0.12
New Hampshire	1,620	0.12
United States	**330,705**	**0.11**
Florida	20,414	0.11
Ohio	12,485	0.11
New Jersey	9,241	0.11
Wisconsin	6,408	0.11
South Dakota	860	0.11
California	37,235	0.10
Pennsylvania	12,582	0.10
Georgia	9,408	0.10
Indiana	6,328	0.10
Virginia	5,936	0.08
Massachusetts	4,342	0.07
Tennessee	3,465	0.06
Mississippi	1,687	0.06
New Mexico	1,166	0.06
Nebraska	1,161	0.06
West Virginia	1,103	0.06
Texas	11,289	0.05
North Carolina	4,917	0.05
Maryland	2,087	0.04
Louisiana	1,909	0.04
Kansas	1,035	0.04
Hawaii	589	0.04
Delaware	323	0.04
District of Columbia	243	0.04
Oklahoma	956	0.03
Maine	368	0.03
Alabama	1,097	0.02
South Carolina	1,058	0.02
Arkansas	480	0.02
Rhode Island	201	0.02

Please refer to the Explanation of Data in the front of the book for more detailed information.

Ancestry

Yugoslavian

Top 150 Places Sorted by Population

Based on all places, regardless of total population

Place	Population	%
New York, NY (city) Kings County	12,410	0.15
Chicago, IL (city) Cook County	6,612	0.24
Phoenix, AZ (city) Maricopa County	5,305	0.37
Queens, NY (borough) Queens County	4,516	0.21
Jacksonville, FL (city) Duval County	3,786	0.47
Utica, NY (city) Oneida County	3,231	5.23
Brooklyn, NY (borough) Kings County	2,800	0.11
St. Louis, MO (city) St. Louis city County	2,707	0.85
Waterloo, IA (city) Black Hawk County	2,330	3.43
Los Angeles, CA (city) Los Angeles County	2,313	0.06
St. Petersburg, FL (city) Pinellas County	2,058	0.84
Louisville-Jefferson County, KY (metro govt) Jefferson County	2,040	0.35
Manhattan, NY (borough) New York County	1,876	0.12
Staten Island, NY (borough) Richmond County	1,738	0.38
Sterling Heights, MI (city) Macomb County	1,665	1.28
Lemay, MO (cdp) St. Louis County	1,654	10.39
San Jose, CA (city) Santa Clara County	1,585	0.17
Boise City, ID (city) Ada County	1,535	0.74
Bronx, NY (borough) Bronx County	1,480	0.11
Fort Wayne, IN (city) Allen County	1,443	0.57
Kentwood, MI (city) Kent County	1,378	2.86
Des Moines, IA (city) Polk County	1,347	0.67
Bowling Green, KY (city) Warren County	1,345	2.38
Houston, TX (city) Harris County	1,287	0.06
Charlotte, NC (city) Mecklenburg County	1,220	0.17
Mehlville, MO (cdp) St. Louis County	1,206	4.41
Hartford, CT (city/town) Hartford County	1,163	0.93
Hamtramck, MI (city) Wayne County	1,162	5.14
Affton, MO (cdp) St. Louis County	1,150	5.72
Akron, OH (city) Summit County	1,145	0.56
San Diego, CA (city) San Diego County	1,142	0.09
Portland, OR (city) Multnomah County	1,111	0.20
Salt Lake City, UT (city) Salt Lake County	1,086	0.59
Macomb, MI (township) Macomb County	1,041	1.39
Warren, MI (city) Macomb County	990	0.73
Manchester, NH (city) Hillsborough County	967	0.88
Nashville-Davidson, TN (metro govt) Davidson County	940	0.16
Urbandale, IA (city) Polk County	919	2.45
Seattle, WA (city) King County	919	0.15
Glendale, AZ (city) Maricopa County	901	0.39
Sacramento, CA (city) Sacramento County	900	0.20
Fort Worth, TX (city) Tarrant County	897	0.13
Columbus, OH (city) Franklin County	883	0.11
West Valley City, UT (city) Salt Lake County	861	0.69
Clinton, MI (charter township) Macomb County	850	0.87
Syracuse, NY (city) Onondaga County	774	0.53
Spring Valley, NV (cdp) Clark County	743	0.44
West Des Moines, IA (city) Polk County	716	1.31
Burlington, VT (city) Chittenden County	707	1.69
San Antonio, TX (city) Medina County	705	0.05
Colorado Springs, CO (city) El Paso County	702	0.17
Dallas, TX (city) Dallas County	702	0.06
Erie, PA (city) Erie County	697	0.69
East Ridge, TN (city) Hamilton County	692	3.33
Milwaukee, WI (city) Milwaukee County	674	0.11
Biloxi, MS (city) Harrison County	650	1.48
Hempstead, NY (town) Nassau County	649	0.09
Shelby, MI (charter township) Macomb County	638	0.88
Lawrenceville, GA (city) Gwinnett County	629	2.27
Spokane, WA (city) Spokane County	627	0.30
Aurora, CO (city) Arapahoe County	590	0.19
Sioux Falls, SD (city) Minnehaha County	582	0.39
Sandy Springs, GA (city) Fulton County	546	0.60
Las Vegas, NV (city) Clark County	545	0.09
Vancouver, WA (city) Clark County	544	0.34
Reno, NV (city) Washoe County	543	0.25
San Francisco, CA (city) San Francisco County	538	0.07
Fargo, ND (city) Cass County	535	0.52
Indianapolis, IN (city) Marion County	531	0.07
Pinellas Park, FL (city) Pinellas County	524	1.07
Mesa, AZ (city) Maricopa County	523	0.12
Pueblo West, CO (cdp) Pueblo County	522	1.87
New Britain, CT (city/town) Hartford County	522	0.72
Paradise, NV (cdp) Clark County	519	0.24
Brookhaven, NY (town) Suffolk County	518	0.11
South Bend, IN (city) St. Joseph County	514	0.50
Huntington Beach, CA (city) Orange County	514	0.27
Tucson, AZ (city) Pima County	514	0.10
Tukwila, WA (city) King County	513	2.76
Boston, MA (city) Suffolk County	507	0.08
Tuckahoe, VA (cdp) Henrico County	498	1.10
Enterprise, NV (cdp) Clark County	498	0.50
Grand Rapids, MI (city) Kent County	492	0.26
Rochester, MN (city) Olmsted County	490	0.47
Edina, MN (city) Hennepin County	485	1.02
Huntington, NY (town) Suffolk County	467	0.23
Citrus Heights, CA (city) Sacramento County	447	0.53
Mishawaka, IN (city) St. Joseph County	446	0.93
Kansas City, MO (city) Jackson County	445	0.10
Lakewood, CO (city) Jefferson County	444	0.31
Tempe, AZ (city) Maricopa County	440	0.27
Tampa, FL (city) Hillsborough County	438	0.13
Austin, TX (city) Travis County	433	0.06
Denver, CO (city) Denver County	420	0.07
Boulder, CO (city) Boulder County	408	0.42
Philadelphia, PA (city) Philadelphia County	406	0.03
East Lake, FL (cdp) Pinellas County	403	1.29
Tacoma, WA (city) Pierce County	402	0.20
Billings, MT (city) Yellowstone County	397	0.39
Gilbert, AZ (town) Maricopa County	390	0.20
Largo, FL (city) Pinellas County	387	0.50
Emmaus, PA (borough) Lehigh County	384	3.41
Scottsdale, AZ (city) Maricopa County	384	0.18
Des Plaines, IL (city) Cook County	381	0.66
Rockford, IL (city) Winnebago County	375	0.24
Farmington Hills, MI (city) Oakland County	374	0.47
Harrison, MI (charter township) Macomb County	373	1.51
Lower Paxton, PA (township) Dauphin County	371	0.79
Clive, IA (city) Polk County	366	2.45
Bakersfield, CA (city) Kern County	365	0.11
Clifton, NJ (city) Passaic County	364	0.44
Clearwater, FL (city) Pinellas County	363	0.34
Columbia, MO (city) Boone County	361	0.35
Elk Grove, CA (city) Sacramento County	358	0.25
Fort Collins, CO (city) Larimer County	354	0.25
Roseville, CA (city) Placer County	348	0.31
Wethersfield, CT (cdp/town) Hartford County	346	1.30
Livonia, MI (city) Wayne County	343	0.35
Anchorage, AK (municipality) Anchorage Municipality	343	0.12
Minneapolis, MN (city) Hennepin County	340	0.09
Troy, MI (city) Oakland County	338	0.42
Virginia Beach, VA (ind. city) Virginia Beach independent city	337	0.08
West Jordan, UT (city) Salt Lake County	335	0.34
Mason City, IA (city) Cerro Gordo County	334	1.19
Oyster Bay, NY (town) Nassau County	334	0.11
Butte-Silver Bow, MT (cons. govt) Silver Bow County	332	1.01
Parma, OH (city) Cuyahoga County	332	0.41
Niles, IL (village) Cook County	327	1.11
Lackawanna, NY (city) Erie County	326	1.79
Acworth, GA (city) Cobb County	326	1.69
Blaine, MN (city) Anoka County	323	0.58
Sunnyvale, CA (city) Santa Clara County	322	0.24
Peoria, AZ (city) Yavapai County	321	0.22
Torrance, CA (city) Los Angeles County	320	0.22
Mount Pleasant, NY (town) Westchester County	312	0.72
Santa Clarita, CA (city) Los Angeles County	311	0.18
Mansfield, OH (city) Richland County	307	0.63
Chandler, AZ (city) Maricopa County	305	0.13
Plano, TX (city) Collin County	305	0.12
Rock Springs, WY (city) Sweetwater County	302	1.37
Camarillo, CA (city) Ventura County	301	0.47
Rocklin, CA (city) Placer County	299	0.55
Wyoming, MI (city) Kent County	299	0.42
De Witt, NY (town) Onondaga County	298	1.17
Surprise, AZ (city) Maricopa County	294	0.28
Westland, MI (city) Wayne County	292	0.34
Kansas City, KS (city) Wyandotte County	290	0.20
Fridley, MN (city) Anoka County	289	1.05
Dix Hills, NY (cdp) Suffolk County	288	1.08
Cleveland, OH (city) Cuyahoga County	287	0.07

SECTION THREE

Please refer to the Explanation of Data in the front of the book for more detailed information.

Ancestry

Yugoslavian

Top 150 Places Sorted by Percent of Total Population

Based on all places, regardless of total population

Place	Population	%
Calpine, CA (cdp) Sierra County	41	33.61
Commodore, PA (cdp) Indiana County	56	31.64
Maryhill, WA (cdp) Klickitat County	16	30.19
Napeague, NY (cdp) Suffolk County	51	24.40
Inverness, MT (cdp) Hill County	9	20.00
Bella Villa, MO (city) St. Louis County	133	17.21
Wisconsin Dells, WI (city) Sauk County	40	17.17
Nesika Beach, OR (cdp) Curry County	70	16.91
Willow Creek, AK (cdp) Valdez-Cordova Census Area	14	16.47
Bearcreek, MT (town) Carbon County	12	15.79
Marblemount, WA (cdp) Skagit County	33	13.81
Eagleville, PA (cdp) Centre County	31	13.03
Ingram, WI (village) Rusk County	10	12.99
Maysville, CO (cdp) Chaffee County	17	11.97
Helvetia, WV (cdp) Randolph County	4	11.11
Lemay, MO (cdp) St. Louis County	1,654	10.39
Upper Pohatcong, NJ (cdp) Warren County	202	10.25
Wheeler, MN (township) Lake of the Woods County	45	10.14
Navajo Dam, NM (cdp) San Juan County	13	10.08
St. George, MO (city) St. Louis County	120	9.36
Brandonville, WV (town) Preston County	6	9.23
Wilbur Park, MO (village) St. Louis County	37	9.20
Mapletown, PA (cdp) Greene County	10	8.62
Royal, IA (city) Clay County	51	8.49
Marlborough, MO (village) St. Louis County	147	7.89
Leggett, CA (cdp) Mendocino County	5	7.35
Diamondhead Lake, IA (cdp) Guthrie County	12	7.23
Carnelian Bay, CA (cdp) Placer County	21	7.22
Ridott, IL (village) Stephenson County	8	7.21
Cooke City, MT (cdp) Park County	4	7.14
Salem, MN (township) Cass County	9	6.47
Pinckney, NY (town) Lewis County	15	6.33
Logan, MN (township) Aitkin County	10	6.10
Pohatcong, NJ (township) Warren County	202	5.95
Seymour, IA (city) Wayne County	53	5.76
Affton, MO (cdp) St. Louis County	1,150	5.72
Bovey, MN (city) Itasca County	43	5.60
Bonnieville, KY (city) Hart County	15	5.56
Pony, MT (cdp) Madison County	6	5.50
West Buechel, KY (city) Jefferson County	61	5.46
Lost Creek, WV (town) Harrison County	25	5.40
Highland, ME (plantation) Somerset County	3	5.36
Morcom, MN (township) St. Louis County	7	5.34
Waverly, MI (township) Cheboygan County	23	5.28
Utica, NY (city) Oneida County	3,231	5.23
Searchlight, NV (cdp) Clark County	15	5.21
Pick City, ND (city) Mercer County	8	5.16
Hamtramck, MI (city) Wayne County	1,162	5.14
Cedar Rapids, WI (town) Rusk County	2	5.00
Amsterdam, MT (cdp) Gallatin County	9	4.97
Lebanon, NY (town) Madison County	73	4.93
West Middletown, PA (borough) Washington County	6	4.84
Frankfort, OH (village) Ross County	53	4.83
Musselshell, MT (cdp) Musselshell County	4	4.76
Hawthorne, NY (cdp) Westchester County	211	4.66
Airport Drive, MO (village) Jasper County	30	4.57
Mason, WI (town) Bayfield County	11	4.53
Sherman, MI (township) Keweenaw County	4	4.49
Slater, MN (township) Cass County	9	4.48
North Lawrence, OH (cdp) Stark County	8	4.47
Mehlville, MO (cdp) St. Louis County	1,206	4.41
Cook, MN (city) St. Louis County	26	4.40
South Toledo Bend, TX (cdp) Newton County	33	4.17
Balkan, MN (township) St. Louis County	34	4.16
Richey, MT (town) Dawson County	8	4.15
Goodland, MN (township) Itasca County	19	4.07
Haysville, PA (borough) Allegheny County	3	4.00
Netarts, OR (cdp) Tillamook County	30	3.98
Schlusser, PA (cdp) Cumberland County	205	3.93
Angola on the Lake, NY (cdp) Erie County	55	3.92
West Belmar, NJ (cdp) Monmouth County	92	3.87
De Witt, IL (village) De Witt County	8	3.85
Alaska, MN (township) Beltrami County	6	3.85
Palmyra, UT (cdp) Utah County	23	3.84
Proctor, MN (city) St. Louis County	115	3.83
Columbia, NH (town) Coos County	28	3.83
Olinda, HI (cdp) Maui County	50	3.80
Thiensville, WI (village) Ozaukee County	123	3.79
Cornville, AZ (cdp) Yavapai County	106	3.75
Alborn, MN (township) St. Louis County	17	3.75
Green Park, MO (city) St. Louis County	98	3.74
Westlake, LA (city) Calcasieu Parish	169	3.72
Keewatin, MN (city) Itasca County	42	3.71
Twin Oaks, MO (village) St. Louis County	14	3.69
Crete, NE (city) Saline County	250	3.68
West Havre, MT (cdp) Hill County	7	3.66
Rice River, MN (township) Aitkin County	3	3.66
Ulm, MT (cdp) Cascade County	22	3.59
Washington, MA (town) Berkshire County	21	3.54
Spring Lake Park, MN (city) Anoka County	222	3.48
Alford, MA (town) Berkshire County	15	3.47
Dunfermline, IL (village) Fulton County	7	3.45
Waterloo, IA (city) Black Hawk County	2,330	3.43
Spring Creek, PA (township) Elk County	4	3.42
Emmaus, PA (borough) Lehigh County	384	3.41
Spring Lake Park, MN (city) Anoka County	222	3.40
Gaston, OR (city) Washington County	20	3.38
Arnot, PA (cdp) Tioga County	11	3.38
Waterbury, VT (village) Washington County	75	3.36
East Ridge, TN (city) Hamilton County	692	3.33
Piney Mountain, VA (cdp) Albemarle County	44	3.28
McArthur, CA (cdp) Shasta County	7	3.26
Meridian, CA (cdp) Sutter County	13	3.25
Aurora, MN (city) St. Louis County	48	3.24
Ness, MN (township) St. Louis County	2	3.23
Vicksburg, MI (village) Kalamazoo County	93	3.22
Stony River, MN (township) Lake County	7	3.21
Witt, IL (city) Montgomery County	31	3.18
Pelican Rapids, MN (city) Otter Tail County	85	3.17
Stony Point, MI (cdp) Monroe County	56	3.13
Exeter, NY (town) Otsego County	27	3.11
French, MN (township) St. Louis County	13	3.11
Medicine Park, OK (town) Comanche County	9	3.10
Bulger, PA (cdp) Washington County	15	3.08
Woodlawn Beach, FL (cdp) Santa Rosa County	60	3.07
Cle Elum, WA (city) Kittitas County	78	3.06
Diamondhead, MS (cdp) Hancock County	241	3.04
Bloss, PA (township) Tioga County	11	3.01
Lone Pine, MN (township) Itasca County	13	3.00
East Cook, MN (unorganized territory) Cook County	32	2.99
Johnsonburg, PA (borough) Elk County	81	2.98
Honaunau-Napoopoo, HI (cdp) Hawaii County	79	2.92
Columbia, CA (cdp) Tuolumne County	73	2.92
Whittlesey, WI (cdp) Taylor County	4	2.92
Fleischmanns, NY (village) Delaware County	6	2.91
Beckwourth, CA (cdp) Plumas County	12	2.89
Walstonburg, NC (town) Greene County	9	2.88
Kentwood, MI (city) Kent County	1,378	2.86
Rio, FL (cdp) Martin County	18	2.84
Paradise, CA (cdp) Mono County	8	2.83
Diamondville, WY (town) Lincoln County	22	2.82
Mead, CO (town) Weld County	91	2.81
Fayal, MN (township) St. Louis County	45	2.81
Masonville, NY (town) Delaware County	38	2.81
Milan, NY (town) Dutchess County	71	2.80
Johnstown, WY (cdp) Fremont County	7	2.78
Tukwila, WA (city) King County	513	2.76
Windham, NY (cdp) Greene County	12	2.76
Somo, WI (town) Lincoln County	3	2.73
Riverton, MN (city) Crow Wing County	3	2.70
Strathmore, NJ (cdp) Monmouth County	195	2.69
Collins, MN (township) McLeod County	14	2.69
Delleker, CA (cdp) Plumas County	15	2.68
Sheffield, MA (town) Berkshire County	87	2.67
Richland, WI (town) Rusk County	5	2.66
Shooks, MN (township) Beltrami County	6	2.65
Sunrise Lake, PA (cdp) Pike County	25	2.61
Antares, AZ (cdp) Mohave County	4	2.61
Fall Lake, MN (township) Lake County	16	2.60
Haworth, NJ (borough) Bergen County	87	2.58

Ancestry

Yugoslavian

Top 150 Places Sorted by Percent of Total Population

Based on places with total population of 7,500 or more

Place	Population	%
Lemay, MO (cdp) St. Louis County	1,654	10.39
Affton, MO (cdp) St. Louis County	1,150	5.72
Utica, NY (city) Oneida County	3,231	5.23
Hamtramck, MI (city) Wayne County	1,162	5.14
Mehlville, MO (cdp) St. Louis County	1,206	4.41
Waterloo, IA (city) Black Hawk County	2,330	3.43
Emmaus, PA (borough) Lehigh County	384	3.41
East Ridge, TN (city) Hamilton County	692	3.33
Diamondhead, MS (cdp) Hancock County	241	3.04
Kentwood, MI (city) Kent County	1,378	2.86
Tukwila, WA (city) King County	513	2.76
Urbandale, IA (city) Polk County	919	2.45
Clive, IA (city) Polk County	366	2.45
Bowling Green, KY (city) Warren County	1,345	2.38
Lawrenceville, GA (city) Gwinnett County	629	2.27
North Middleton, PA (township) Cumberland County	237	2.17
Wyoming, MN (city) Chisago County	151	1.97
Whitehall, PA (borough) Allegheny County	272	1.95
Pueblo West, CO (cdp) Pueblo County	522	1.87
Lackawanna, NY (city) Erie County	326	1.79
Camp Hill, PA (borough) Cumberland County	140	1.79
Lilburn, GA (city) Gwinnett County	207	1.77
Burlington, VT (city) Chittenden County	707	1.69
Acworth, GA (city) Cobb County	326	1.69
La Grange, NY (town) Dutchess County	261	1.66
Johnston, IA (city) Polk County	245	1.56
Hooksett, NH (town) Merrimack County	208	1.56
Port Jefferson Station, NY (cdp) Suffolk County	117	1.56
Harrison, MI (charter township) Macomb County	373	1.51
Ketchikan, AK (city) Ketchikan Gateway Borough	120	1.50
Biloxi, MS (city) Harrison County	650	1.48
Brookfield, IL (village) Cook County	279	1.48
Concord, MO (cdp) St. Louis County	233	1.47
Cromwell, CT (town) Middlesex County	200	1.44
Eastlake, OH (city) Lake County	265	1.40
Macomb, MI (township) Macomb County	1,041	1.39
Rock Springs, WY (city) Sweetwater County	302	1.37
Pleasant Valley, NY (town) Dutchess County	132	1.37
Grimes, IA (city) Polk County	104	1.36
West Des Moines, IA (city) Polk County	716	1.31
Wethersfield, CT (cdp/town) Hartford County	346	1.30
East Lake, FL (cdp) Pinellas County	403	1.29
Sterling Heights, MI (city) Macomb County	1,665	1.28
Canton, GA (city) Cherokee County	266	1.28
New Port Richey, FL (city) Pasco County	191	1.23
Gulf Hills, MS (cdp) Jackson County	97	1.23
Pequannock, NJ (township) Morris County	186	1.22
Mason City, IA (city) Cerro Gordo County	334	1.19
New Baltimore, MI (city) Macomb County	134	1.18
De Witt, NY (town) Onondaga County	298	1.17
Glen Allen, VA (cdp) Henrico County	183	1.17
Milford, NH (cdp) Hillsborough County	106	1.17
Willoughby Hills, OH (city) Lake County	107	1.14
Villa Park, IL (village) DuPage County	251	1.13
Derby, CT (city/town) New Haven County	144	1.12
Johnstown, NY (city) Fulton County	98	1.12
Niles, IL (village) Cook County	327	1.11
Tuckahoe, VA (cdp) Henrico County	498	1.10
Glen Rock, NJ (borough) Bergen County	127	1.10
Dix Hills, NY (cdp) Suffolk County	288	1.08
Aberdeen, NJ (township) Monmouth County	195	1.08
Lincolnwood, IL (village) Cook County	134	1.08
Upper Saddle River, NJ (borough) Bergen County	87	1.08
Mentor-on-the-Lake, OH (city) Lake County	82	1.08
Pinellas Park, FL (city) Pinellas County	524	1.07
Collegedale, TN (city) Hamilton County	85	1.07
Fridley, MN (city) Anoka County	289	1.05
Sugar Hill, GA (city) Gwinnett County	184	1.05
Center Line, MI (city) Macomb County	88	1.05
Medina, OH (city) Medina County	278	1.04
Edina, MN (city) Hennepin County	485	1.02
Wyndham, VA (cdp) Henrico County	95	1.02
Butte-Silver Bow, MT (cons. govt) Silver Bow County	332	1.01
Arnold, MO (city) Jefferson County	209	1.01
East Pennsboro, PA (township) Cumberland County	201	1.01
Morton Grove, IL (village) Cook County	227	0.99
Barre, VT (city) Washington County	90	0.99
Sappington, MO (cdp) St. Louis County	79	0.99
Chestnut Ridge, NY (village) Rockland County	78	0.99
Putnam, CT (cdp) Windham County	74	0.99
Belle Chasse, LA (cdp) Plaquemines Parish	146	0.98
Lower Allen, PA (township) Cumberland County	174	0.97
Hibbing, MN (city) St. Louis County	159	0.97
Glencoe, IL (village) Cook County	84	0.97
Oswego, IL (village) Kendall County	263	0.95
Norridge, IL (village) Cook County	137	0.95
Hartford, CT (city/town) Hartford County	1,163	0.93
Mishawaka, IN (city) St. Joseph County	446	0.93
Damascus, OR (city) Clackamas County	96	0.93
Gages Lake, IL (cdp) Lake County	95	0.93
Ingleside, TX (city) San Patricio County	87	0.92
Schoolcraft, MI (township) Kalamazoo County	74	0.92
Temescal Valley, CA (cdp) Riverside County	205	0.91
Shasta Lake, CA (city) Shasta County	92	0.91
Los Altos Hills, CA (town) Santa Clara County	70	0.89
Manchester, NH (city) Hillsborough County	967	0.88
Shelby, MI (charter township) Macomb County	638	0.88
Branford, CT (town) New Haven County	248	0.88
Lakeside, VA (cdp) Henrico County	106	0.88
Mounds View, MN (city) Ramsey County	106	0.88
Clinton, MI (charter township) Macomb County	850	0.87
Carlisle, PA (borough) Cumberland County	162	0.87
Southchase, FL (cdp) Orange County	144	0.87
Hollymead, VA (cdp) Albemarle County	69	0.86
St. Louis, MO (city) St. Louis city County	2,707	0.85
St. Petersburg, FL (city) Pinellas County	2,058	0.84
Asbury Lake, FL (cdp) Clay County	73	0.84
Ashland, NJ (cdp) Camden County	73	0.84
West Fargo, ND (city) Cass County	198	0.83
Channahon, IL (village) Will County	101	0.83
Clawson, MI (city) Oakland County	100	0.83
Tipp City, OH (city) Miami County	80	0.83
Deerpark, NY (town) Orange County	66	0.83
Bloomingdale, NJ (borough) Passaic County	62	0.82
Dalton, MI (township) Muskegon County	74	0.81
Mukwonago, WI (town) Waukesha County	63	0.81
Ramona, CA (cdp) San Diego County	171	0.80
Dyer, IN (town) Lake County	127	0.80
Lower Paxton, PA (township) Dauphin County	371	0.79
Malta, NY (town) Saratoga County	113	0.78
Scotts Valley, CA (city) Santa Cruz County	88	0.78
Wood-Ridge, NJ (borough) Bergen County	59	0.78
Onondaga, NY (town) Onondaga County	175	0.77
Putnam, CT (town) Windham County	74	0.77
Plymouth, MI (charter township) Wayne County	210	0.76
Ripon, CA (city) San Joaquin County	103	0.75
Mandeville, LA (city) St. Tammany Parish	86	0.75
Sonoma, CA (city) Sonoma County	77	0.75
Boise City, ID (city) Ada County	1,535	0.74
Jeffersontown, KY (city) Jefferson County	197	0.74
Keansburg, NJ (borough) Monmouth County	76	0.74
Summit, WA (cdp) Pierce County	59	0.74
Warren, MI (city) Macomb County	990	0.73
Independence, MI (charter township) Oakland County	250	0.73
Burien, WA (city) King County	238	0.73
Manchester, MO (city) St. Louis County	133	0.73
Mamakating, NY (town) Sullivan County	87	0.73
Artondale, WA (cdp) Pierce County	83	0.73
New Britain, CT (city/town) Hartford County	522	0.72
Mount Pleasant, NY (town) Westchester County	312	0.72
Norwalk, OH (city) Huron County	122	0.72
Waterford, CA (city) Stanislaus County	60	0.72
Mansfield, NJ (township) Warren County	57	0.72
Butler, NJ (borough) Morris County	54	0.72
Milford, NH (town) Hillsborough County	106	0.71
Hanover Park, IL (village) Cook County	265	0.70
Mount Olive, NJ (township) Morris County	193	0.70
West Valley City, UT (city) Salt Lake County	861	0.69
Erie, PA (city) Erie County	697	0.69
Germantown, WI (village) Washington County	135	0.69

SECTION THREE

Please refer to the Explanation of Data in the front of the book for more detailed information.

Hispanic Origin Rankings

Introduction

In this section of this book, each ethnicity contains four tables. The first table is split into two parts. Part one ranks the U.S. and all 50 states plus the District of Columbia by ethnic population. Part two ranks the same areas by percent of the total population. The second table shows the top 150 places sorted by ethnic population (based on all places, regardless of total population), the third table shows the top 150 places sorted by percent of the total population (based on all places, regardless of total population), the fourth table shows the top 150 places sorted by percent of the total population (based on places with total population of 7,500 or more).

Within each table, column one displays the place name, the state, and the county (if a place spans more than one county, the county that holds the majority of the population is shown). Column one in the first table displays the state only. Column two displays the number of people reporting each Hispanic origin. Column three is the percent of the total population reporting each Hispanic origin. The 100-percent population figure from Census 2010 Summary File 1 is used to calculate the value in the "%" column.

Alphabetical Hispanic Origin Cross-Reference Guide

Argentinean *see* Hispanic Origin–South American: Argentinean
Bolivian *see* Hispanic Origin–South American: Bolivian
Central American: Other *see* Hispanic Origin–Central American: Other Central American
Central American *see* Hispanic Origin–Central American, except Mexican
Chilean *see* Hispanic Origin–South American: Chilean
Colombian *see* Hispanic Origin–South American: Colombian
Costa Rican *see* Hispanic Origin–Central American: Costa Rican
Cuban *see* Hispanic Origin–Cuban
Dominican Republic *see* Hispanic Origin–Dominican Republic
Ecuadorian *see* Hispanic Origin–South American: Ecuadorian
Guatemalan *see* Hispanic Origin–Central American: Guatemalan
Hispanic or Latino: Other *see* Hispanic Origin–Other Hispanic or Latino
Hispanic or Latino: *see* Hispanic Origin–Hispanic or Latino (of any race)
Honduran *see* Hispanic Origin–Central American: Honduran
Mexican *see* Hispanic Origin–Mexican
Nicaraguan *see* Hispanic Origin–Central American: Nicaraguan
Panamanian *see* Hispanic Origin–Central American: Panamanian
Paraguayan *see* Hispanic Origin–South American: Paraguayan
Peruvian *see* Hispanic Origin–South American: Peruvian
Puerto Rican *see* Hispanic Origin–Puerto Rican
Salvadoran *see* Hispanic Origin–Central American: Salvadoran
South American: Other *see* Hispanic Origin–South American: Other South American
South American *see* Hispanic Origin–South American
Uruguayan *see* Hispanic Origin–South American: Uruguayan
Venezuelan *see* Hispanic Origin–South American: Venezuelan

Hispanic Origin

Hispanic or Latino (of any race)

U.S. and 50 States Sorted by Population and Percent of Total Population

Place	Population	%
United States	**50,477,594**	**16.35**
California	14,013,719	37.62
Texas	9,460,921	37.62
Florida	4,223,806	22.47
New York	3,416,922	17.63
Illinois	2,027,578	15.80
Arizona	1,895,149	29.65
New Jersey	1,555,144	17.69
Colorado	1,038,687	20.65
New Mexico	953,403	46.30
Georgia	853,689	8.81
North Carolina	800,120	8.39
Washington	755,790	11.24
Pennsylvania	719,660	5.67
Nevada	716,501	26.53
Virginia	631,825	7.90
Massachusetts	627,654	9.59
Connecticut	479,087	13.40
Maryland	470,632	8.15
Oregon	450,062	11.75
Michigan	436,358	4.41
Indiana	389,707	6.01
Utah	358,340	12.97
Ohio	354,674	3.07
Wisconsin	336,056	5.91
Oklahoma	332,007	8.85
Kansas	300,042	10.52
Tennessee	290,059	4.57
Minnesota	250,258	4.72
South Carolina	235,682	5.10
Missouri	212,470	3.55
Louisiana	192,560	4.25
Arkansas	186,050	6.38
Alabama	185,602	3.88
Idaho	175,901	11.22
Nebraska	167,405	9.17
Iowa	151,544	4.97
Kentucky	132,836	3.06
Rhode Island	130,655	12.41
Hawaii	120,842	8.88
Mississippi	81,481	2.75
Delaware	73,221	8.15
District of Columbia	54,749	9.10
Wyoming	50,231	8.91
Alaska	39,249	5.53
New Hampshire	36,704	2.79
Montana	28,565	2.89
West Virginia	22,268	1.20
South Dakota	22,119	2.72
Maine	16,935	1.27
North Dakota	13,467	2.00
Vermont	9,208	1.47

Place	Population	%
New Mexico	953,403	46.30
California	14,013,719	37.62
Texas	9,460,921	37.62
Arizona	1,895,149	29.65
Nevada	716,501	26.53
Florida	4,223,806	22.47
Colorado	1,038,687	20.65
New Jersey	1,555,144	17.69
New York	3,416,922	17.63
United States	**50,477,594**	**16.35**
Illinois	2,027,578	15.80
Connecticut	479,087	13.40
Utah	358,340	12.97
Rhode Island	130,655	12.41
Oregon	450,062	11.75
Washington	755,790	11.24
Idaho	175,901	11.22
Kansas	300,042	10.52
Massachusetts	627,654	9.59
Nebraska	167,405	9.17
District of Columbia	54,749	9.10
Wyoming	50,231	8.91
Hawaii	120,842	8.88
Oklahoma	332,007	8.85
Georgia	853,689	8.81
North Carolina	800,120	8.39
Maryland	470,632	8.15
Delaware	73,221	8.15
Virginia	631,825	7.90
Arkansas	186,050	6.38
Indiana	389,707	6.01
Wisconsin	336,056	5.91
Pennsylvania	719,660	5.67
Alaska	39,249	5.53
South Carolina	235,682	5.10
Iowa	151,544	4.97
Minnesota	250,258	4.72
Tennessee	290,059	4.57
Michigan	436,358	4.41
Louisiana	192,560	4.25
Alabama	185,602	3.88
Missouri	212,470	3.55
Ohio	354,674	3.07
Kentucky	132,836	3.06
Montana	28,565	2.89
New Hampshire	36,704	2.79
Mississippi	81,481	2.75
South Dakota	22,119	2.72
North Dakota	13,467	2.00
Vermont	9,208	1.47
Maine	16,935	1.27
West Virginia	22,268	1.20

Please refer to the Explanation of Data in the front of the book for more detailed information.

Hispanic Origin

Hispanic or Latino (of any race)

Top 150 Places Sorted by Population

Based on all places, regardless of total population

Place	Population	%
New York, NY (city) Kings County	2,336,076	28.58
Los Angeles, CA (city) Los Angeles County	1,838,822	48.48
Houston, TX (city) Harris County	919,668	43.81
San Antonio, TX (city) Medina County	838,952	63.20
Chicago, IL (city) Cook County	778,862	28.89
Bronx, NY (borough) Bronx County	741,413	53.53
Queens, NY (borough) Queens County	613,750	27.51
Phoenix, AZ (city) Maricopa County	589,877	40.80
El Paso, TX (city) El Paso County	523,721	80.68
Dallas, TX (city) Dallas County	507,309	42.35
Brooklyn, NY (borough) Kings County	496,285	19.81
Manhattan, NY (borough) New York County	403,577	25.45
San Diego, CA (city) San Diego County	376,020	28.76
San Jose, CA (city) Santa Clara County	313,636	33.16
Miami, FL (city) Miami-Dade County	279,456	69.96
Austin, TX (city) Travis County	277,707	35.14
Albuquerque, NM (city) Bernalillo County	255,055	46.73
Santa Ana, CA (city) Orange County	253,928	78.25
Fort Worth, TX (city) Tarrant County	252,468	34.06
Fresno, CA (city) Fresno County	232,055	46.91
Laredo, TX (city) Webb County	225,750	95.62
Tucson, AZ (city) Pima County	216,308	41.59
Hialeah, FL (city) Miami-Dade County	212,805	94.72
Denver, CO (city) Denver County	190,965	31.82
Long Beach, CA (city) Los Angeles County	188,412	40.76
Philadelphia, PA (city) Philadelphia County	187,611	12.29
Las Vegas, NV (city) Clark County	183,859	31.50
Corpus Christi, TX (city) Nueces County	182,181	59.69
Anaheim, CA (city) Orange County	177,467	52.78
Brownsville, TX (city) Cameron County	163,109	93.19
Bakersfield, CA (city) Kern County	158,205	45.53
Riverside, CA (city) Riverside County	148,953	49.02
Oxnard, CA (city) Ventura County	145,551	73.55
Chula Vista, CA (city) San Diego County	142,066	58.24
Hempstead, NY (town) Nassau County	132,154	17.39
Fontana, CA (city) San Bernardino County	130,957	66.79
San Bernardino, CA (city) San Bernardino County	125,994	60.02
Sacramento, CA (city) Sacramento County	125,276	26.86
East Los Angeles, CA (cdp) Los Angeles County	122,784	97.07
San Francisco, CA (city) San Francisco County	121,774	15.12
Stockton, CA (city) San Joaquin County	117,590	40.31
Mesa, AZ (city) Maricopa County	115,753	26.36
Ontario, CA (city) San Bernardino County	113,085	68.99
Salinas, CA (city) Monterey County	112,799	74.98
McAllen, TX (city) Hidalgo County	109,910	84.63
Boston, MA (city) Suffolk County	107,917	17.47
Moreno Valley, CA (city) Riverside County	105,169	54.39
Pomona, CA (city) Los Angeles County	105,135	70.53
Milwaukee, WI (city) Milwaukee County	103,007	17.32
Arlington, TX (city) Tarrant County	100,269	27.44
Oklahoma City, OK (city) Oklahoma County	100,038	17.25
Oakland, CA (city) Alameda County	99,068	25.35
Islip, NY (town) Suffolk County	97,371	29.02
Charlotte, NC (city) Mecklenburg County	95,688	13.08
Newark, NJ (city) Essex County	93,746	33.83
Aurora, CO (city) Arapahoe County	93,263	28.69
Pasadena, TX (city) Harris County	92,692	62.19
Sunrise Manor, NV (cdp) Clark County	91,764	48.46
South Gate, CA (city) Los Angeles County	89,442	94.75
Irving, TX (city) Dallas County	88,967	41.13
Garland, TX (city) Dallas County	85,784	37.81
Paterson, NJ (city) Passaic County	84,254	57.63
North Las Vegas, NV (city) Clark County	84,134	38.78
Palmdale, CA (city) Los Angeles County	83,097	54.40
Aurora, IL (city) Kane County	81,809	41.34
Staten Island, NY (borough) Richmond County	81,051	17.29
Glendale, AZ (city) Maricopa County	80,501	35.51
Downey, CA (city) Los Angeles County	78,996	70.68
El Monte, CA (city) Los Angeles County	78,317	69.02
Tampa, FL (city) Hillsborough County	77,472	23.08
Indianapolis, IN (city) Marion County	77,352	9.43
Grand Prairie, TX (city) Dallas County	74,893	42.70
Elizabeth, NJ (city) Union County	74,353	59.50
Norwalk, CA (city) Los Angeles County	74,041	70.15
Lubbock, TX (city) Lubbock County	73,625	32.07
Cicero, IL (town) Cook County	72,609	86.55
Modesto, CA (city) Stanislaus County	71,381	35.48
Escondido, CA (city) San Diego County	70,326	48.87
Santa Maria, CA (city) Santa Barbara County	70,114	70.43
Paradise, NV (cdp) Clark County	69,599	31.19
Jersey City, NJ (city) Hudson County	68,256	27.57
Edinburg, TX (city) Hidalgo County	67,989	88.18
Yonkers, NY (city) Westchester County	67,927	34.66
Providence, RI (city) Providence County	67,835	38.10
Rialto, CA (city) San Bernardino County	67,038	67.60
Colorado Springs, CO (city) El Paso County	66,866	16.06
Corona, CA (city) Riverside County	66,447	43.61
Mission, TX (city) Hidalgo County	65,812	85.41
Pharr, TX (city) Hidalgo County	65,496	93.03
Pembroke Pines, FL (city) Broward County	64,061	41.40
Jacksonville, FL (city) Duval County	63,485	7.73
Garden Grove, CA (city) Orange County	63,079	36.91
Compton, CA (city) Los Angeles County	62,669	64.97
Orlando, FL (city) Orange County	60,483	25.38
Lynwood, CA (city) Los Angeles County	60,452	86.64
Baldwin Park, CA (city) Los Angeles County	60,403	80.12
Nashville-Davidson, TN (metro govt) Davidson County	60,390	10.04
Brookhaven, NY (town) Suffolk County	60,270	12.40
Oceanside, CA (city) San Diego County	59,947	35.88
Lancaster, CA (city) Los Angeles County	59,596	38.05
Springfield, MA (city) Hampden County	59,451	38.84
Hayward, CA (city) Alameda County	58,730	40.73
Wichita, KS (city) Sedgwick County	58,348	15.26
Rancho Cucamonga, CA (city) San Bernardino County	57,688	34.91
Pico Rivera, CA (city) Los Angeles County	57,400	91.20
Visalia, CA (city) Tulare County	57,262	46.02
Florence-Graham, CA (cdp) Los Angeles County	57,066	90.03
West Covina, CA (city) Los Angeles County	56,471	53.23
Huntington Park, CA (city) Los Angeles County	56,445	97.13
Lawrence, MA (city) Essex County	56,363	73.80
Union City, NJ (city) Hudson County	56,291	84.71
Whittier, CA (city) Los Angeles County	56,081	65.72
Inglewood, CA (city) Los Angeles County	55,449	50.56
Las Cruces, NM (city) Doña Ana County	55,443	56.80
Victorville, CA (city) San Bernardino County	55,359	47.76
Tulsa, OK (city) Tulsa County	55,266	14.10
Bridgeport, CT (city/town) Fairfield County	55,100	38.20
Amarillo, TX (city) Potter County	54,881	28.78
Portland, OR (city) Multnomah County	54,840	9.39
Washington, DC (city) District of Columbia	54,749	9.10
Fountainebleau, FL (cdp) Miami-Dade County	54,727	91.57
Reno, NV (city) Washoe County	54,640	24.26
Hartford, CT (city/town) Hartford County	54,185	43.43
Omaha, NE (city) Douglas County	53,553	13.09
Pueblo, CO (city) Pueblo County	53,098	49.81
Orange, CA (city) Orange County	52,014	38.13
Santa Clarita, CA (city) Los Angeles County	51,941	29.46
Chandler, AZ (city) Maricopa County	51,808	21.94
Harlingen, TX (city) Cameron County	51,581	79.54
Indio, CA (city) Riverside County	51,540	67.78
Reading, PA (city) Berks County	51,230	58.16
Tamiami, FL (cdp) Miami-Dade County	51,217	92.67
Yuma, AZ (city) Yuma County	51,033	54.84
Odessa, TX (city) Ector County	50,601	50.63
Allentown, PA (city) Lehigh County	50,461	42.75
Montebello, CA (city) Los Angeles County	49,578	79.32
Passaic, NJ (city) Passaic County	49,557	71.02
Perris, CA (city) Riverside County	49,079	71.77
Detroit, MI (city) Wayne County	48,679	6.82
Kendale Lakes, FL (cdp) Miami-Dade County	48,584	86.53
Kendall, FL (cdp) Miami-Dade County	48,038	63.74
Santa Rosa, CA (city) Sonoma County	47,970	28.59
Waukegan, IL (city) Lake County	47,612	53.45
Elgin, IL (city) Kane County	47,121	43.55
Madera, CA (city) Madera County	47,103	76.69
Miami Beach, FL (city) Miami-Dade County	46,564	53.05
Fullerton, CA (city) Orange County	46,501	34.40
Pasadena, CA (city) Los Angeles County	46,174	33.67
Kansas City, MO (city) Jackson County	45,953	9.99
Raleigh, NC (city) Wake County	45,868	11.36

Please refer to the Explanation of Data in the front of the book for more detailed information.

Hispanic Origin

Hispanic or Latino (of any race)

Top 150 Places Sorted by Percent of Total Population

Based on all places, regardless of total population

Place	Population	%
Mikes, TX (cdp) Starr County	910	100.00
Garza-Salinas II, TX (cdp) Starr County	719	100.00
Valle Vista, TX (cdp) Starr County	469	100.00
Alto Bonito Heights, TX (cdp) Starr County	342	100.00
San Carlos I, TX (cdp) Webb County	316	100.00
Los Alvarez, TX (cdp) Starr County	303	100.00
Mi Ranchito Estate, TX (cdp) Starr County	281	100.00
Los Ebanos, TX (cdp) Starr County	280	100.00
El Rancho Vela, TX (cdp) Starr County	274	100.00
Olmito and Olmito, TX (cdp) Starr County	271	100.00
El Cenizo, TX (cdp) Starr County	249	100.00
Santa Rosa, TX (cdp) Starr County	241	100.00
La Paloma Ranchettes, TX (cdp) Starr County	239	100.00
Rancho Viejo, TX (cdp) Starr County	228	100.00
Ranchitos East, TX (cdp) Webb County	212	100.00
El Quiote, TX (cdp) Starr County	208	100.00
Lago, TX (cdp) Cameron County	204	100.00
El Castillo, TX (cdp) Starr County	188	100.00
Fronton, TX (cdp) Starr County	180	100.00
East Lopez, TX (cdp) Starr County	166	100.00
Loma Vista, TX (cdp) Starr County	160	100.00
Eugenio Saenz, TX (cdp) Starr County	159	100.00
La Escondida, TX (cdp) Starr County	153	100.00
Nina, TX (cdp) Starr County	141	100.00
Los Altos, TX (cdp) Webb County	140	100.00
Campo Verde, TX (cdp) Starr County	132	100.00
Falconaire, TX (cdp) Starr County	132	100.00
Villarreal, TX (cdp) Starr County	131	100.00
El Socio, TX (cdp) Starr County	130	100.00
La Casita, TX (cdp) Starr County	128	100.00
Miguel Barrera, TX (cdp) Starr County	128	100.00
Los Arcos, TX (cdp) Webb County	127	100.00
Flor del Rio, TX (cdp) Starr County	122	100.00
Los Angeles, TX (cdp) Willacy County	121	100.00
North Escobares, TX (cdp) Starr County	118	100.00
Ramos, TX (cdp) Starr County	116	100.00
Chaparrito, TX (cdp) Starr County	114	100.00
Loma Linda West, TX (cdp) Starr County	114	100.00
Ranchitos Del Norte, TX (cdp) Starr County	112	100.00
Sammy Martinez, TX (cdp) Starr County	110	100.00
Victoria Vera, TX (cdp) Starr County	110	100.00
Loma Grande, TX (cdp) Zavala County	107	100.00
Buena Vista, TX (cdp) Starr County	102	100.00
Old Escobares, TX (cdp) Starr County	97	100.00
Amaya, TX (cdp) Zavala County	93	100.00
Olivia Lopez de Gutierrez, TX (cdp) Starr County	93	100.00
Amada Acres, TX (cdp) Starr County	92	100.00
Longoria, TX (cdp) Starr County	92	100.00
Regino Ramirez, TX (cdp) Starr County	85	100.00
Gutierrez, TX (cdp) Starr County	79	100.00
Northridge, TX (cdp) Starr County	78	100.00
Hilltop, TX (cdp) Starr County	77	100.00
Manuel Garcia II, TX (cdp) Starr County	77	100.00
Evergreen, TX (cdp) Starr County	73	100.00
La Carla, TX (cdp) Starr County	70	100.00
Martinez, TX (cdp) Starr County	69	100.00
San Fernando, TX (cdp) Starr County	68	100.00
Pablo Pena, TX (cdp) Starr County	63	100.00
Concepcion, TX (cdp) Duval County	62	100.00
Rivereno, TX (cdp) Starr County	61	100.00
Zarate, TX (cdp) Starr County	59	100.00
Casa Blanca, TX (cdp) Starr County	54	100.00
Santa Cruz, TX (cdp) Starr County	54	100.00
Tanquecitos South Acres II, TX (cdp) Webb County	50	100.00
Grand Acres, TX (cdp) Cameron County	49	100.00
La Chuparosa, TX (cdp) Starr County	49	100.00
El Brazil, TX (cdp) Starr County	47	100.00
Sunset, TX (cdp) Starr County	47	100.00
Garciasville, TX (cdp) Starr County	46	100.00
Brazos, NM (cdp) Rio Arriba County	44	100.00
Cuevitas, TX (cdp) Hidalgo County	40	100.00
Casas, TX (cdp) Starr County	39	100.00
El Mesquite, TX (cdp) Starr County	38	100.00
Guadalupe-Guerra, TX (cdp) Starr County	37	100.00
Los Corralitos, TX (cdp) Webb County	35	100.00
Benjamin Perez, TX (cdp) Starr County	34	100.00
Sandoval, TX (cdp) Starr County	32	100.00
Netos, TX (cdp) Starr County	31	100.00
Elias-Fela Solis, TX (cdp) Starr County	30	100.00
Hillside Acres, TX (cdp) Webb County	30	100.00
Narciso Pena, TX (cdp) Starr County	30	100.00
Las Pilas, TX (cdp) Webb County	28	100.00
Tierra Dorada, TX (cdp) Starr County	28	100.00
Quesada, TX (cdp) Starr County	25	100.00
Los Veteranos I, TX (cdp) Webb County	24	100.00
Jardin de San Julian, TX (cdp) Starr County	22	100.00
Laredo Ranchettes, TX (cdp) Webb County	22	100.00
Los Minerales, TX (cdp) Webb County	20	100.00
Rafael Pena, TX (cdp) Starr County	17	100.00
Anacua, TX (cdp) Starr County	12	100.00
Las Haciendas, TX (cdp) Webb County	7	100.00
Brewster, FL (cdp) Polk County	3	100.00
East Alto Bonito, TX (cdp) Starr County	823	99.88
West Alto Bonito, TX (cdp) Starr County	695	99.86
Muniz, TX (cdp) Hidalgo County	1,367	99.78
Roma Creek, TX (cdp) Starr County	349	99.71
Granjeno, TX (city) Hidalgo County	292	99.66
Sullivan City, TX (city) Hidalgo County	3,986	99.60
Camargito, TX (cdp) Starr County	386	99.48
Santa Maria, TX (cdp) Cameron County	729	99.45
Airport Heights, TX (cdp) Starr County	160	99.38
La Presa, TX (cdp) Webb County	317	99.37
El Chaparral, TX (cdp) Starr County	461	99.35
Colorado Acres, TX (cdp) Webb County	294	99.32
Cameron Park, TX (cdp) Cameron County	6,913	99.28
Abram, TX (cdp) Hidalgo County	2,052	99.27
Siesta Acres, TX (cdp) Maverick County	1,871	99.26
Havana, TX (cdp) Hidalgo County	404	99.26
El Cenizo, TX (city) Webb County	3,248	99.24
Agua Dulce, TX (cdp) El Paso County	2,990	99.20
Tanquecitos South Acres, TX (cdp) Webb County	231	99.14
Sparks, TX (cdp) El Paso County	4,488	99.09
Barrera, TX (cdp) Starr County	107	99.07
South Alamo, TX (cdp) Hidalgo County	3,328	99.02
Eidson Road, TX (cdp) Maverick County	8,864	98.93
Cantua Creek, CA (cdp) Fresno County	461	98.93
Mila Doce, TX (cdp) Hidalgo County	6,153	98.89
Rio Bravo, TX (city) Webb County	4,741	98.89
Laguna Seca, TX (cdp) Hidalgo County	263	98.87
La Minita, TX (cdp) Starr County	169	98.83
Orange Grove Mobile Manor, AZ (cdp) Yuma County	587	98.82
La Rosita, TX (cdp) Starr County	84	98.82
La Puerta, TX (cdp) Starr County	624	98.73
Ramirez-Perez, TX (cdp) Starr County	77	98.72
San Elizario, TX (cdp) El Paso County	13,428	98.71
San Luis, AZ (city) Yuma County	25,171	98.69
Las Quintas Fronterizas, TX (cdp) Maverick County	3,247	98.69
Lopezville, TX (cdp) Hidalgo County	4,276	98.68
Mecca, CA (cdp) Riverside County	8,462	98.66
Tornillo, TX (cdp) El Paso County	1,547	98.66
Faysville, TX (cdp) Hidalgo County	433	98.63
Midway North, TX (cdp) Hidalgo County	4,684	98.57
Los Fresnos, TX (cdp) Webb County	66	98.51
San Carlos, TX (cdp) Hidalgo County	3,082	98.47
San Carlos II, TX (cdp) Webb County	257	98.47
New Falcon, TX (cdp) Zapata County	188	98.43
Berino, NM (cdp) Doña Ana County	1,418	98.40
Hidalgo, TX (city) Hidalgo County	11,015	98.37
Progreso, TX (city) Hidalgo County	5,417	98.37
North San Pedro, TX (cdp) Nueces County	880	98.32
Lopeño, TX (cdp) Zapata County	171	98.28
Los Barreras, TX (cdp) Starr County	283	98.26
Lago Vista, TX (cdp) Starr County	113	98.26
La Paloma, TX (cdp) Cameron County	2,852	98.24
Fronton Ranchettes, TX (cdp) Starr County	111	98.23
West Sharyland, TX (cdp) Hidalgo County	2,268	98.22
Chula Vista, TX (cdp) Zavala County	442	98.22
Los Ebanos, TX (cdp) Hidalgo County	329	98.21
Penitas, TX (city) Hidalgo County	4,323	98.18
Heber, CA (cdp) Imperial County	4,197	98.18

Please refer to the Explanation of Data in the front of the book for more detailed information.

Hispanic Origin

Hispanic or Latino (of any race)

Top 150 Places Sorted by Percent of Total Population

Based on places with total population of 7,500 or more

Place	Population	%
Eidson Road, TX (cdp) Maverick County	8,864	98.93
San Elizario, TX (cdp) El Paso County	13,428	98.71
San Luis, AZ (city) Yuma County	25,171	98.69
Mecca, CA (cdp) Riverside County	8,462	98.66
Hidalgo, TX (city) Hidalgo County	11,015	98.37
Parlier, CA (city) Fresno County	14,137	97.54
Maywood, CA (city) Los Angeles County	26,696	97.45
Anthony, NM (cdp) Doña Ana County	9,120	97.44
Walnut Park, CA (cdp) Los Angeles County	15,543	97.35
Huntington Park, CA (city) Los Angeles County	56,445	97.13
East Los Angeles, CA (cdp) Los Angeles County	122,784	97.07
La Homa, TX (cdp) Hidalgo County	11,632	97.05
Calexico, CA (city) Imperial County	37,354	96.84
Fabens, TX (cdp) El Paso County	7,993	96.80
Socorro, TX (city) El Paso County	30,964	96.72
San Juan, TX (city) Hidalgo County	32,734	96.69
Mendota, CA (city) Fresno County	10,643	96.63
Coachella, CA (city) Riverside County	39,254	96.44
Cudahy, CA (city) Los Angeles County	22,850	95.99
Somerton, AZ (city) Yuma County	13,708	95.95
Bell Gardens, CA (city) Los Angeles County	40,271	95.72
Laredo, TX (city) Webb County	225,750	95.62
Sweetwater, FL (city) Miami-Dade County	12,894	95.52
Eagle Pass, TX (city) Maverick County	25,065	95.49
Sunland Park, NM (city) Doña Ana County	13,434	95.24
Nogales, AZ (city) Santa Cruz County	19,793	94.99
Hialeah Gardens, FL (city) Miami-Dade County	20,630	94.88
Roma, TX (city) Starr County	9,261	94.84
South Gate, CA (city) Los Angeles County	89,442	94.75
Hialeah, FL (city) Miami-Dade County	212,805	94.72
Lamont, CA (cdp) Kern County	14,293	94.53
Commerce, CA (city) Los Angeles County	12,114	94.47
Rio Grande City, TX (city) Starr County	13,044	94.29
Alton, TX (city) Hidalgo County	11,554	93.62
Robstown, TX (city) Nueces County	10,752	93.60
Brownsville, TX (city) Cameron County	163,109	93.19
Bell, CA (city) Los Angeles County	33,028	93.10
Pharr, TX (city) Hidalgo County	65,496	93.03
Lennox, CA (cdp) Los Angeles County	21,162	93.01
Arvin, CA (city) Kern County	17,892	92.69
Tamiami, FL (cdp) Miami-Dade County	51,217	92.67
Orange Cove, CA (city) Fresno County	8,413	92.67
San Fernando, CA (city) Los Angeles County	21,867	92.48
Donna, TX (city) Hidalgo County	14,578	92.28
Mercedes, TX (city) Hidalgo County	14,302	91.86
Fountainebleau, FL (cdp) Miami-Dade County	54,727	91.57
McFarland, CA (city) Kern County	11,625	91.49
Earlimart, CA (cdp) Tulare County	7,805	91.43
Greenfield, CA (city) Monterey County	14,917	91.35
Firebaugh, CA (city) Fresno County	6,887	91.23
Pico Rivera, CA (city) Los Angeles County	57,400	91.20
Westchester, FL (cdp) Miami-Dade County	27,211	91.12
San Benito, TX (city) Cameron County	21,995	90.70
Florence-Graham, CA (cdp) Los Angeles County	57,066	90.03
Gonzales, CA (city) Monterey County	7,276	88.87
Coral Terrace, FL (cdp) Miami-Dade County	21,595	88.59
Kendall West, FL (cdp) Miami-Dade County	31,912	88.27
Edinburg, TX (city) Hidalgo County	67,989	88.18
South Houston, TX (city) Harris County	14,954	88.05
West Whittier-Los Nietos, CA (cdp) Los Angeles County	22,369	87.58
King City, CA (city) Monterey County	11,266	87.51
Espanola, NM (city) Rio Arriba County	8,910	87.15
Raymondville, TX (city) Willacy County	9,801	86.86
Orosi, CA (cdp) Tulare County	7,606	86.73
Lynwood, CA (city) Los Angeles County	60,452	86.64
Cicero, IL (town) Cook County	72,609	86.55
Kendale Lakes, FL (cdp) Miami-Dade County	48,584	86.53
South San Jose Hills, CA (cdp) Los Angeles County	17,713	86.19
Westwood Lakes, FL (cdp) Miami-Dade County	10,177	85.97
Horizon City, TX (city) El Paso County	14,373	85.89
Olympia Heights, FL (cdp) Miami-Dade County	11,573	85.80
West Puente Valley, CA (cdp) Los Angeles County	19,365	85.55
Lindsay, CA (city) Tulare County	10,056	85.45
Mission, TX (city) Hidalgo County	65,812	85.41
Rio Rico, AZ (cdp) Santa Cruz County	16,179	85.32
La Puente, CA (city) Los Angeles County	33,896	85.13
Alice, TX (city) Jim Wells County	16,259	85.11
Pearsall, TX (city) Frio County	7,784	85.11
Weslaco, TX (city) Hidalgo County	30,312	84.98
University Park, FL (cdp) Miami-Dade County	22,938	84.97
South El Monte, CA (city) Los Angeles County	17,079	84.90
Union City, NJ (city) Hudson County	56,291	84.71
McAllen, TX (city) Hidalgo County	109,910	84.63
Alamo, TX (city) Hidalgo County	15,528	84.61
Dinuba, CA (city) Tulare County	18,114	84.44
Del Rio, TX (city) Val Verde County	29,927	84.09
Chaparral, NM (cdp) Otero County	12,303	84.09
Jacinto City, TX (city) Harris County	8,856	83.92
Farmersville, CA (city) Tulare County	8,876	83.83
Pecos, TX (city) Reeves County	7,302	83.17
Muscoy, CA (cdp) San Bernardino County	8,824	82.90
Douglas, AZ (city) Cochise County	14,353	82.59
Toppenish, WA (city) Yakima County	7,388	82.56
Sunnyside, WA (city) Yakima County	13,043	82.25
Aldine, TX (cdp) Harris County	13,036	82.15
Avocado Heights, CA (cdp) Los Angeles County	12,648	82.07
East Rancho Dominguez, CA (cdp) Los Angeles County	12,407	81.98
El Centro, CA (city) Imperial County	34,751	81.58
Brawley, CA (city) Imperial County	20,344	81.53
Galena Park, TX (city) Harris County	8,860	81.38
Watsonville, CA (city) Santa Cruz County	41,656	81.36
Miami Lakes, FL (town) Miami-Dade County	23,826	81.15
Bloomington, CA (cdp) San Bernardino County	19,326	81.03
Santa Fe Springs, CA (city) Los Angeles County	13,137	80.98
El Paso, TX (city) El Paso County	523,721	80.68
Sanger, CA (city) Fresno County	19,537	80.50
Las Vegas, NM (city) San Miguel County	11,069	80.48
Sunset, FL (cdp) Miami-Dade County	13,164	80.32
Shafter, CA (city) Kern County	13,634	80.26
South Valley, NM (cdp) Bernalillo County	32,860	80.19
Baldwin Park, CA (city) Los Angeles County	60,403	80.12
Grandview, WA (city) Yakima County	8,655	79.68
Good Hope, CA (cdp) Riverside County	7,319	79.62
Harlingen, TX (city) Cameron County	51,581	79.54
Doral, FL (city) Miami-Dade County	36,344	79.52
Santa Paula, CA (city) Ventura County	23,299	79.46
Montebello, CA (city) Los Angeles County	49,578	79.32
Country Club, FL (cdp) Miami-Dade County	37,133	78.83
Valinda, CA (cdp) Los Angeles County	17,977	78.77
Paramount, CA (city) Los Angeles County	42,547	78.65
Richmond West, FL (cdp) Miami-Dade County	25,110	78.54
Uvalde, TX (city) Uvalde County	12,346	78.38
Santa Ana, CA (city) Orange County	253,928	78.25
Perth Amboy, NJ (city) Middlesex County	39,685	78.10
West New York, NJ (town) Hudson County	38,812	78.08
Selma, CA (city) Fresno County	18,014	77.58
Hawaiian Gardens, CA (city) Los Angeles County	11,010	77.24
South Whittier, CA (cdp) Los Angeles County	44,094	77.15
The Hammocks, FL (cdp) Miami-Dade County	39,244	76.94
Madera, CA (city) Madera County	47,103	76.69
Wasco, CA (city) Kern County	19,585	76.67
Langley Park, MD (cdp) Prince George's County	14,359	76.56
Reedley, CA (city) Fresno County	18,455	76.28
Immokalee, FL (cdp) Collier County	18,267	75.63
Salinas, CA (city) Monterey County	112,799	74.98
Leisure City, FL (cdp) Miami-Dade County	16,978	74.94
Vincent, CA (cdp) Los Angeles County	11,921	74.87
Imperial, CA (city) Imperial County	11,046	74.85
Fillmore, CA (city) Ventura County	11,212	74.74
Garnet, CA (cdp) Riverside County	5,580	73.98
Lawrence, MA (city) Essex County	56,363	73.80
Fort Stockton, TX (city) Pecos County	6,103	73.68
Home Gardens, CA (cdp) Riverside County	8,524	73.67
Oxnard, CA (city) Ventura County	145,551	73.55
Livingston, CA (city) Merced County	9,547	73.11
North Fair Oaks, CA (cdp) San Mateo County	10,731	73.06
Citrus, CA (cdp) Los Angeles County	7,911	72.81
Mead Valley, CA (cdp) Riverside County	13,395	72.37
Beeville, TX (city) Bee County	9,251	71.92
Avenal, CA (city) Kings County	11,130	71.78

SECTION THREE

Hispanic Origin

Central American, excluding Mexican

U.S. and 50 States Sorted by Population and Percent of Total Population

Place	Population	%
United States	**3,998,280**	**1.30**
California	1,132,520	3.04
Florida	432,665	2.30
Texas	420,683	1.67
New York	353,589	1.82
Virginia	206,568	2.58
Maryland	195,692	3.39
New Jersey	176,611	2.01
Georgia	106,987	1.10
North Carolina	105,066	1.10
Massachusetts	96,958	1.48
Illinois	70,000	0.55
Nevada	55,937	2.07
Louisiana	51,722	1.14
Tennessee	36,856	0.58
Arizona	36,642	0.57
Pennsylvania	35,453	0.28
Connecticut	35,023	0.98
Washington	33,661	0.50
Colorado	29,386	0.58
South Carolina	26,290	0.57
Rhode Island	23,817	2.26
District of Columbia	23,354	3.88
Arkansas	23,216	0.80
Alabama	22,800	0.48
Ohio	22,756	0.20
Indiana	22,093	0.34
Utah	20,442	0.74
Minnesota	19,908	0.38
Oregon	18,190	0.47
Michigan	17,785	0.18
Missouri	17,763	0.30
Nebraska	17,242	0.94
Oklahoma	15,641	0.42
Kansas	15,293	0.54
Iowa	13,289	0.44
Kentucky	11,479	0.26
Wisconsin	10,616	0.19
Mississippi	8,343	0.28
Delaware	8,112	0.90
New Mexico	6,621	0.32
Idaho	3,494	0.22
Hawaii	2,962	0.22
South Dakota	2,891	0.36
New Hampshire	2,731	0.21
Alaska	2,509	0.35
West Virginia	2,081	0.11
Maine	1,708	0.13
Wyoming	977	0.17
Montana	735	0.07
Vermont	671	0.11
North Dakota	452	0.07

Place	Population	%
District of Columbia	23,354	3.88
Maryland	195,692	3.39
California	1,132,520	3.04
Virginia	206,568	2.58
Florida	432,665	2.30
Rhode Island	23,817	2.26
Nevada	55,937	2.07
New Jersey	176,611	2.01
New York	353,589	1.82
Texas	420,683	1.67
Massachusetts	96,958	1.48
United States	**3,998,280**	**1.30**
Louisiana	51,722	1.14
Georgia	106,987	1.10
North Carolina	105,066	1.10
Connecticut	35,023	0.98
Nebraska	17,242	0.94
Delaware	8,112	0.90
Arkansas	23,216	0.80
Utah	20,442	0.74
Tennessee	36,856	0.58
Colorado	29,386	0.58
Arizona	36,642	0.57
South Carolina	26,290	0.57
Illinois	70,000	0.55
Kansas	15,293	0.54
Washington	33,661	0.50
Alabama	22,800	0.48
Oregon	18,190	0.47
Iowa	13,289	0.44
Oklahoma	15,641	0.42
Minnesota	19,908	0.38
South Dakota	2,891	0.36
Alaska	2,509	0.35
Indiana	22,093	0.34
New Mexico	6,621	0.32
Missouri	17,763	0.30
Pennsylvania	35,453	0.28
Mississippi	8,343	0.28
Kentucky	11,479	0.26
Idaho	3,494	0.22
Hawaii	2,962	0.22
New Hampshire	2,731	0.21
Ohio	22,756	0.20
Wisconsin	10,616	0.19
Michigan	17,785	0.18
Wyoming	977	0.17
Maine	1,708	0.13
West Virginia	2,081	0.11
Vermont	671	0.11
Montana	735	0.07
North Dakota	452	0.07

Please refer to the Explanation of Data in the front of the book for more detailed information.

Hispanic Origin

Central American, excluding Mexican

Top 150 Places Sorted by Population

Based on all places, regardless of total population

Place	Population	%
Los Angeles, CA (city) Los Angeles County	415,913	10.97
New York, NY (city) Kings County	151,378	1.85
Houston, TX (city) Harris County	140,815	6.71
Miami, FL (city) Miami-Dade County	62,995	15.77
Queens, NY (borough) Queens County	52,509	2.35
Hempstead, NY (town) Nassau County	49,236	6.48
Brooklyn, NY (borough) Kings County	46,119	1.84
Islip, NY (town) Suffolk County	38,530	11.48
Bronx, NY (borough) Bronx County	34,492	2.49
San Francisco, CA (city) San Francisco County	33,834	4.20
Chicago, IL (city) Cook County	31,263	1.16
Dallas, TX (city) Dallas County	28,798	2.40
Washington, DC (city) District of Columbia	23,354	3.88
Charlotte, NC (city) Mecklenburg County	22,359	3.06
Boston, MA (city) Suffolk County	21,286	3.45
Brentwood, NY (cdp) Suffolk County	19,957	32.90
Hialeah, FL (city) Miami-Dade County	17,305	7.70
Long Beach, CA (city) Los Angeles County	16,486	3.57
Hempstead, NY (village) Nassau County	16,171	30.01
Oakland, CA (city) Alameda County	15,387	3.94
Las Vegas, NV (city) Clark County	15,318	2.62
Irving, TX (city) Dallas County	15,203	7.03
Palmdale, CA (city) Los Angeles County	14,815	9.70
Phoenix, AZ (city) Maricopa County	14,788	1.02
San Jose, CA (city) Santa Clara County	14,697	1.55
Providence, RI (city) Providence County	14,630	8.22
Manhattan, NY (borough) New York County	13,948	0.88
Austin, TX (city) Travis County	13,423	1.70
Chelsea, MA (city) Suffolk County	12,682	36.05
Arlington, VA (cdp) Arlington County	12,171	5.86
Elizabeth, NJ (city) Union County	12,097	9.68
Wheaton, MD (cdp) Montgomery County	12,072	25.00
Silver Spring, MD (cdp) Montgomery County	11,474	16.06
North Hempstead, NY (town) Nassau County	11,455	5.06
Trenton, NJ (city) Mercer County	11,346	13.36
Nashville-Davidson, TN (metro govt) Davidson County	11,180	1.86
Babylon, NY (town) Suffolk County	11,096	5.19
Santa Ana, CA (city) Orange County	11,011	3.39
Alexandria, VA (ind. city) Alexandria independent city	10,963	7.83
San Antonio, TX (city) Medina County	10,735	0.81
Langley Park, MD (cdp) Prince George's County	10,197	54.37
Chillum, MD (cdp) Prince George's County	9,869	29.45
Stamford, CT (city/town) Fairfield County	9,866	8.04
Plainfield, NJ (city) Union County	9,822	19.72
Daly City, CA (city) San Mateo County	9,813	9.70
South Gate, CA (city) Los Angeles County	9,777	10.36
Huntington, NY (town) Suffolk County	9,599	4.72
Dale City, VA (cdp) Prince William County	9,389	14.23
Brookhaven, NY (town) Suffolk County	9,259	1.90
San Diego, CA (city) San Diego County	9,188	0.70
Union City, NJ (city) Hudson County	9,159	13.78
Fountainebleau, FL (cdp) Miami-Dade County	9,106	15.24
Metairie, LA (cdp) Jefferson Parish	9,085	6.56
Anaheim, CA (city) Orange County	9,074	2.70
Lynn, MA (city) Essex County	9,049	10.02
Fontana, CA (city) San Bernardino County	8,860	4.52
Inglewood, CA (city) Los Angeles County	8,697	7.93
Kenner, LA (city) Jefferson Parish	8,641	12.95
Hawthorne, CA (city) Los Angeles County	8,547	10.14
Downey, CA (city) Los Angeles County	8,546	7.65
Central Islip, NY (cdp) Suffolk County	8,487	24.64
Richmond, CA (city) Contra Costa County	8,329	8.03
Marumsco, VA (cdp) Prince William County	8,223	23.47
Lancaster, CA (city) Los Angeles County	8,114	5.18
Durham, NC (city) Durham County	8,052	3.53
Gaithersburg, MD (city) Montgomery County	7,812	13.03
Garland, TX (city) Dallas County	7,792	3.43
Riverside, CA (city) Riverside County	7,792	2.56
Indianapolis, IN (city) Marion County	7,746	0.94
San Rafael, CA (city) Marin County	7,740	13.41
Raleigh, NC (city) Wake County	7,519	1.86
Philadelphia, PA (city) Philadelphia County	7,511	0.49
Hayward, CA (city) Alameda County	7,505	5.21
Newark, NJ (city) Essex County	7,497	2.71
Bakersfield, CA (city) Kern County	7,497	2.16
Homestead, FL (city) Miami-Dade County	7,477	12.36
West New York, NJ (town) Hudson County	7,421	14.93
Huntington Station, NY (cdp) Suffolk County	7,370	22.31
New Orleans, LA (city) Orleans Parish	7,325	2.13
Aspen Hill, MD (cdp) Montgomery County	7,037	14.43
Baltimore, MD (city) Baltimore city County	6,921	1.11
Pomona, CA (city) Los Angeles County	6,907	4.63
Fort Worth, TX (city) Tarrant County	6,855	0.92
Jersey City, NJ (city) Hudson County	6,838	2.76
Sunrise Manor, NV (cdp) Clark County	6,672	3.52
Freeport, NY (village) Nassau County	6,668	15.56
Paradise, NV (cdp) Clark County	6,648	2.98
Jacksonville, FL (city) Duval County	6,594	0.80
San Mateo, CA (city) San Mateo County	6,575	6.76
Oklahoma City, OK (city) Oklahoma County	6,506	1.12
Huntington Park, CA (city) Los Angeles County	6,404	11.02
Glendale, CA (city) Los Angeles County	6,392	3.33
Lake Worth, FL (city) Palm Beach County	6,320	18.10
Uniondale, NY (cdp) Nassau County	6,264	25.30
Ontario, CA (city) San Bernardino County	6,264	3.82
Germantown, MD (cdp) Montgomery County	6,157	7.13
Aurora, CO (city) Arapahoe County	6,031	1.86
East Los Angeles, CA (cdp) Los Angeles County	5,994	4.74
North Bergen, NJ (township) Hudson County	5,991	9.86
Yonkers, NY (city) Westchester County	5,822	2.97
North Bay Shore, NY (cdp) Suffolk County	5,763	30.42
Lynwood, CA (city) Los Angeles County	5,761	8.26
Florence-Graham, CA (cdp) Los Angeles County	5,736	9.05
North Las Vegas, NV (city) Clark County	5,734	2.64
Pasadena, CA (city) Los Angeles County	5,724	4.17
Moreno Valley, CA (city) Riverside County	5,710	2.95
Santa Clarita, CA (city) Los Angeles County	5,657	3.21
San Bernardino, CA (city) San Bernardino County	5,616	2.68
Manassas, VA (ind. city) Manassas independent city	5,529	14.62
Norwalk, CA (city) Los Angeles County	5,460	5.17
West Palm Beach, FL (city) Palm Beach County	5,454	5.46
South San Francisco, CA (city) San Mateo County	5,381	8.46
Reno, NV (city) Washoe County	5,366	2.38
Ramapo, NY (town) Rockland County	5,319	4.20
Bailey's Crossroads, VA (cdp) Fairfax County	5,312	22.47
Tampa, FL (city) Hillsborough County	5,234	1.56
Sterling, VA (cdp) Loudoun County	5,227	18.79
Woodlawn, VA (cdp) Fairfax County	5,190	24.95
Norwalk, CT (city/town) Fairfield County	5,186	6.06
Sacramento, CA (city) Sacramento County	5,184	1.11
Herndon, VA (town) Fairfax County	5,149	22.11
Denver, CO (city) Denver County	5,114	0.85
West Little River, FL (cdp) Miami-Dade County	5,083	14.65
Kendale Lakes, FL (cdp) Miami-Dade County	5,076	9.04
Redwood City, CA (city) San Mateo County	5,032	6.55
Arlington, TX (city) Tarrant County	5,002	1.37
El Monte, CA (city) Los Angeles County	4,961	4.37
Oyster Bay, NY (town) Nassau County	4,958	1.69
Omaha, NE (city) Douglas County	4,943	1.21
Compton, CA (city) Los Angeles County	4,910	5.09
Hollywood, FL (city) Broward County	4,896	3.48
Memphis, TN (city) Shelby County	4,881	0.75
Tamiami, FL (cdp) Miami-Dade County	4,850	8.77
Concord, CA (city) Contra Costa County	4,761	3.90
Pasadena, TX (city) Harris County	4,703	3.16
Everett, MA (city) Middlesex County	4,673	11.22
Kendall, FL (cdp) Miami-Dade County	4,668	6.19
Miami Beach, FL (city) Miami-Dade County	4,661	5.31
Pembroke Pines, FL (city) Broward County	4,614	2.98
Annandale, VA (cdp) Fairfax County	4,487	10.94
Miramar, FL (city) Broward County	4,460	3.65
Revere, MA (city) Suffolk County	4,457	8.61
New Cassel, NY (cdp) Nassau County	4,455	31.69
Bridgeport, CT (city/town) Fairfield County	4,451	3.09
Fort Lauderdale, FL (city) Broward County	4,424	2.67
Rialto, CA (city) San Bernardino County	4,402	4.44
Richmond, VA (ind. city) Richmond independent city	4,382	2.15
Grand Prairie, TX (city) Dallas County	4,345	2.48
Miami Gardens, FL (city) Miami-Dade County	4,338	4.05
Burbank, CA (city) Los Angeles County	4,331	4.19

Please refer to the Explanation of Data in the front of the book for more detailed information.

Hispanic Origin

Central American, excluding Mexican

Top 150 Places Sorted by Percent of Total Population

Based on all places, regardless of total population

Place	Population	%
Islandia, FL (city) Miami-Dade County	15	83.33
Langley Park, MD (cdp) Prince George's County	10,197	54.37
Marydel, MD (town) Caroline County	60	42.55
Brewster, NY (village) Putnam County	967	40.46
Indiantown, FL (cdp) Martin County	2,331	38.32
Templeville, MD (town) Queen Anne's County	51	36.96
Chelsea, MA (city) Suffolk County	12,682	36.05
Chase Crossing, VA (cdp) Accomack County	135	35.81
Chamblee, GA (city) DeKalb County	3,521	35.59
Sargents, NH (purchase) Coos County	1	33.33
George, DE (town) Sussex County	2,120	33.01
Brentwood, NY (cdp) Suffolk County	19,957	32.90
New Cassel, NY (cdp) Nassau County	4,455	31.69
Colmar Manor, MD (town) Prince George's County	440	31.34
North Bay Shore, NY (cdp) Suffolk County	5,763	30.42
Hempstead, NY (village) Nassau County	16,171	30.01
Chillum, MD (cdp) Prince George's County	9,869	29.45
Henderson, MD (town) Caroline County	43	29.45
Brentwood, MD (town) Prince George's County	856	28.10
Adelphi, MD (cdp) Prince George's County	4,080	27.04
Sweetwater, FL (city) Miami-Dade County	3,538	26.21
Mendota, CA (city) Fresno County	2,885	26.19
Inwood, NY (cdp) Nassau County	2,509	25.62
Uniondale, NY (cdp) Nassau County	6,264	25.30
Wheaton, MD (cdp) Montgomery County	12,072	25.00
Edmonston, MD (town) Prince George's County	361	24.98
Woodlawn, VA (cdp) Fairfax County	5,190	24.95
Fairview, NJ (borough) Bergen County	3,433	24.81
Central Islip, NY (cdp) Suffolk County	8,487	24.64
Landover Hills, MD (town) Prince George's County	412	24.42
North Brentwood, MD (town) Prince George's County	125	24.18
Seven Corners, VA (cdp) Fairfax County	2,230	24.10
Woodlawn, MD (cdp) Prince George's County	1,510	23.84
Loch Lomond, VA (cdp) Prince William County	880	23.78
Marumsco, VA (cdp) Prince William County	8,223	23.47
Flanders, NY (cdp) Suffolk County	1,034	23.12
Roosevelt, NY (cdp) Nassau County	3,748	23.05
Bailey's Crossroads, VA (cdp) Fairfax County	5,312	22.47
Huntington Station, NY (cdp) Suffolk County	7,370	22.31
Herndon, VA (town) Fairfax County	5,149	22.11
Sudley, VA (cdp) Prince William County	3,551	21.92
Yorkshire, VA (cdp) Prince William County	1,645	21.81
Hyattsville, MD (city) Prince George's County	3,805	21.67
Mappsville, VA (cdp) Accomack County	95	21.59
East Riverdale, MD (cdp) Prince George's County	3,238	20.88
Broadview Park, FL (cdp) Broward County	1,486	20.86
Acacia Villas, FL (cdp) Palm Beach County	88	20.61
Tice, FL (cdp) Lee County	911	20.38
Cottage City, MD (town) Prince George's County	262	20.08
Bull Run, VA (cdp) Prince William County	2,964	19.78
Plainfield, NJ (city) Union County	9,822	19.72
Ellijay, GA (city) Gilmer County	319	19.70
Mount Rainier, MD (city) Prince George's County	1,591	19.69
Bound Brook, NJ (borough) Somerset County	2,035	19.56
Collinsville, AL (town) DeKalb County	383	19.31
Montalvin Manor, CA (cdp) Contra Costa County	553	19.23
Mount Kisco, NY (town/village) Westchester County	2,085	19.17
Sterling, VA (cdp) Loudoun County	5,227	18.79
South Fallsburg, NY (cdp) Sullivan County	537	18.71
Greenport, NY (village) Suffolk County	410	18.66
Alpena, SD (town) Jerauld County	53	18.53
East Ellijay, GA (city) Gilmer County	100	18.32
Schuyler, NE (city) Colfax County	1,130	18.19
Bensley, VA (cdp) Chesterfield County	1,056	18.15
Lake Worth, FL (city) Palm Beach County	6,320	18.10
Groveton, VA (cdp) Fairfax County	2,609	17.87
Glenmont, MD (cdp) Montgomery County	2,378	17.58
Riverdale Park, MD (town) Prince George's County	1,222	17.57
Wyandanch, NY (cdp) Suffolk County	2,024	17.38
Manassas Park, VA (ind. city) Manassas Park independent city	2,459	17.23
Beltsville, MD (cdp) Prince George's County	2,869	17.11
Morris, NJ (town) Morris County	3,067	16.66
Wallace, NC (town) Duplin County	639	16.47
Rollingwood, CA (cdp) Contra Costa County	478	16.10
Silver Spring, MD (cdp) Montgomery County	11,474	16.06
Central Falls, RI (city) Providence County	3,060	15.79
Miami, FL (city) Miami-Dade County	62,995	15.77
Hillandale, MD (cdp) Montgomery County	948	15.69
Freeport, NY (village) Nassau County	6,668	15.56
Sugarland Run, VA (cdp) Loudoun County	1,818	15.41
Fountainebleau, FL (cdp) Miami-Dade County	9,106	15.24
Stacey Street, FL (cdp) Palm Beach County	130	15.15
Lakewood Gardens, FL (cdp) Palm Beach County	191	15.00
West New York, NJ (town) Hudson County	7,421	14.93
Magnolia, NC (town) Duplin County	140	14.91
El Jebel, CO (cdp) Eagle County	565	14.86
North Richmond, CA (cdp) Contra Costa County	551	14.82
Lumpkin, GA (city) Stewart County	403	14.70
Monon, IN (town) White County	261	14.69
West Little River, FL (cdp) Miami-Dade County	5,083	14.65
West Falls Church, VA (cdp) Fairfax County	4,274	14.63
Manassas, VA (ind. city) Manassas independent city	5,529	14.62
Riverhead, NY (cdp) Suffolk County	1,944	14.62
North Amityville, NY (cdp) Suffolk County	2,597	14.54
Westgate, FL (cdp) Palm Beach County	1,154	14.47
Aspen Hill, MD (cdp) Montgomery County	7,037	14.43
Berwyn Heights, MD (town) Prince George's County	450	14.41
Carthage, MO (city) Jasper County	2,060	14.33
Dale City, VA (cdp) Prince William County	9,389	14.23
Colma, CA (town) San Mateo County	251	14.01
Saluda, SC (town) Saluda County	498	13.97
Kenwood Estates, FL (cdp) Palm Beach County	178	13.87
Union City, NJ (city) Hudson County	9,159	13.78
Redland, MD (cdp) Montgomery County	2,371	13.75
Quiogue, NY (cdp) Suffolk County	112	13.73
Springfield, VA (cdp) Fairfax County	4,125	13.53
Cudahy, CA (city) Los Angeles County	3,198	13.43
San Rafael, CA (city) Marin County	7,740	13.41
Lennox, CA (cdp) Los Angeles County	3,045	13.38
Trenton, NJ (city) Mercer County	11,346	13.36
Bedford Hills, NY (cdp) Westchester County	400	13.33
North Plainfield, NJ (borough) Somerset County	2,920	13.31
Hybla Valley, VA (cdp) Fairfax County	2,101	13.30
Cache, UT (cdp) Cache County	5	13.16
Cattaraugus Reservation, NY (reservation) Chautauqua County	5	13.16
Gaithersburg, MD (city) Montgomery County	7,812	13.03
Kenner, LA (city) Jefferson Parish	8,641	12.95
Huntington, VA (cdp) Fairfax County	1,453	12.90
Spring Valley, NY (village) Rockland County	4,034	12.87
New Carrollton, MD (city) Prince George's County	1,559	12.85
Doraville, GA (city) DeKalb County	1,059	12.71
Worthington, MN (city) Nobles County	1,619	12.68
Westmont, CA (cdp) Los Angeles County	4,034	12.66
Pine Air, FL (cdp) Palm Beach County	256	12.65
Woodridge, NY (village) Sullivan County	107	12.63
Siler City, NC (town) Chatham County	995	12.62
Homestead, FL (city) Miami-Dade County	7,477	12.36
Manorhaven, NY (village) Nassau County	810	12.36
Port Chester, NY (village) Westchester County	3,577	12.35
Lexington, NE (city) Dawson County	1,243	12.15
Northampton, NY (cdp) Suffolk County	69	12.11
Westbury, NY (village) Nassau County	1,831	12.09
Potomac Mills, VA (cdp) Prince William County	677	12.06
Guttenberg, NJ (town) Hudson County	1,340	11.99
Webster, TX (city) Harris County	1,247	11.99
Riverside, NY (cdp) Suffolk County	346	11.89
Westhampton Beach, NY (village) Suffolk County	204	11.85
Glen Cove, NY (city) Nassau County	3,158	11.71
Teachey, NC (town) Duplin County	44	11.70
Milan, MO (city) Sullivan County	226	11.53
Islip, NY (town) Suffolk County	38,530	11.48
Lincolnia, VA (cdp) Fairfax County	2,615	11.44
Montgomery Village, MD (cdp) Montgomery County	3,662	11.43
Modest Town, VA (cdp) Accomack County	17	11.41
Bladensburg, MD (town) Prince George's County	1,043	11.40
Russellville, AL (city) Franklin County	1,119	11.38
Dumfries, VA (town) Prince William County	562	11.33
Crete, NE (city) Saline County	788	11.32
Monterey, TN (town) Putnam County	322	11.30
Rose Hill, VA (cdp) Fairfax County	2,271	11.23

Please refer to the Explanation of Data in the front of the book for more detailed information.

Hispanic Origin

Central American, excluding Mexican

Top 150 Places Sorted by Percent of Total Population

Based on places with total population of 7,500 or more

Place	Population	%
Langley Park, MD (cdp) Prince George's County	10,197	54.37
Chelsea, MA (city) Suffolk County	12,682	36.05
Chamblee, GA (city) DeKalb County	3,521	35.59
Brentwood, NY (cdp) Suffolk County	19,957	32.90
New Cassel, NY (cdp) Nassau County	4,455	31.69
North Bay Shore, NY (cdp) Suffolk County	5,763	30.42
Hempstead, NY (village) Nassau County	16,171	30.01
Chillum, MD (cdp) Prince George's County	9,869	29.45
Adelphi, MD (cdp) Prince George's County	4,080	27.04
Sweetwater, FL (city) Miami-Dade County	3,538	26.21
Mendota, CA (city) Fresno County	2,885	26.19
Inwood, NY (cdp) Nassau County	2,509	25.62
Uniondale, NY (cdp) Nassau County	6,264	25.30
Wheaton, MD (cdp) Montgomery County	12,072	25.00
Woodlawn, VA (cdp) Fairfax County	5,190	24.95
Fairview, NJ (borough) Bergen County	3,433	24.81
Central Islip, NY (cdp) Suffolk County	8,487	24.64
Seven Corners, VA (cdp) Fairfax County	2,230	24.10
Marumsco, VA (cdp) Prince William County	8,223	23.47
Roosevelt, NY (cdp) Nassau County	3,748	23.05
Bailey's Crossroads, VA (cdp) Fairfax County	5,312	22.47
Huntington Station, NY (cdp) Suffolk County	7,370	22.31
Herndon, VA (town) Fairfax County	5,149	22.11
Sudley, VA (cdp) Prince William County	3,551	21.92
Yorkshire, VA (cdp) Prince William County	1,645	21.81
Hyattsville, MD (city) Prince George's County	3,805	21.67
East Riverdale, MD (cdp) Prince George's County	3,238	20.88
Bull Run, VA (cdp) Prince William County	2,964	19.78
Plainfield, NJ (city) Union County	9,822	19.72
Mount Rainier, MD (city) Prince George's County	1,591	19.69
Bound Brook, NJ (borough) Somerset County	2,035	19.56
Mount Kisco, NY (town/village) Westchester County	2,085	19.17
Sterling, VA (cdp) Loudoun County	5,227	18.79
Lake Worth, FL (city) Palm Beach County	6,320	18.10
Groveton, VA (cdp) Fairfax County	2,609	17.87
Glenmont, MD (cdp) Montgomery County	2,378	17.58
Wyandanch, NY (cdp) Suffolk County	2,024	17.38
Manassas Park, VA (ind. city) Manassas Park independent city	2,459	17.23
Beltsville, MD (cdp) Prince George's County	2,869	17.11
Morris, NJ (town) Morris County	3,067	16.66
Silver Spring, MD (cdp) Montgomery County	11,474	16.06
Central Falls, RI (city) Providence County	3,060	15.79
Miami, FL (city) Miami-Dade County	62,995	15.77
Freeport, NY (village) Nassau County	6,668	15.56
Sugarland Run, VA (cdp) Loudoun County	1,818	15.41
Fountainebleau, FL (cdp) Miami-Dade County	9,106	15.24
West New York, NJ (town) Hudson County	7,421	14.93
West Little River, FL (cdp) Miami-Dade County	5,083	14.65
West Falls Church, VA (cdp) Fairfax County	4,274	14.63
Manassas, VA (ind. city) Manassas independent city	5,529	14.62
Riverhead, NY (cdp) Suffolk County	1,944	14.62
North Amityville, NY (cdp) Suffolk County	2,597	14.54
Westgate, FL (cdp) Palm Beach County	1,154	14.47
Aspen Hill, MD (cdp) Montgomery County	7,037	14.43
Carthage, MO (city) Jasper County	2,060	14.33
Dale City, VA (cdp) Prince William County	9,389	14.23
Union City, NJ (city) Hudson County	9,159	13.78
Redland, MD (cdp) Montgomery County	2,371	13.75
Springfield, VA (cdp) Fairfax County	4,125	13.53
Cudahy, CA (city) Los Angeles County	3,198	13.43
San Rafael, CA (city) Marin County	7,740	13.41
Lennox, CA (cdp) Los Angeles County	3,045	13.38
Trenton, NJ (city) Mercer County	11,346	13.36
North Plainfield, NJ (borough) Somerset County	2,920	13.31
Hybla Valley, VA (cdp) Fairfax County	2,101	13.30
Gaithersburg, MD (city) Montgomery County	7,812	13.03
Kenner, LA (city) Jefferson Parish	8,641	12.95
Huntington, VA (cdp) Fairfax County	1,453	12.90
Spring Valley, NY (village) Rockland County	4,034	12.87
New Carrollton, MD (city) Prince George's County	1,559	12.85
Doraville, GA (city) DeKalb County	1,059	12.71
Worthington, MN (city) Nobles County	1,619	12.68
Westmont, CA (cdp) Los Angeles County	4,034	12.66
Siler City, NC (town) Chatham County	995	12.62
Homestead, FL (city) Miami-Dade County	7,477	12.36
Port Chester, NY (village) Westchester County	3,577	12.35
Lexington, NE (city) Dawson County	1,243	12.15
Westbury, NY (village) Nassau County	1,831	12.09
Guttenberg, NJ (town) Hudson County	1,340	11.99
Webster, TX (city) Harris County	1,247	11.99
Glen Cove, NY (city) Nassau County	3,158	11.71
Islip, NY (town) Suffolk County	38,530	11.48
Lincolnia, VA (cdp) Fairfax County	2,615	11.44
Montgomery Village, MD (cdp) Montgomery County	3,662	11.43
Bladensburg, MD (town) Prince George's County	1,043	11.40
Russellville, AL (city) Franklin County	1,119	11.38
Rose Hill, VA (cdp) Fairfax County	2,271	11.23
Everett, MA (city) Middlesex County	4,673	11.22
San Pablo, CA (city) Contra Costa County	3,235	11.10
Huntington Park, CA (city) Los Angeles County	6,404	11.02
Bell, CA (city) Los Angeles County	3,894	10.98
Los Angeles, CA (city) Los Angeles County	415,913	10.97
Annandale, VA (cdp) Fairfax County	4,487	10.94
North Kensington, MD (cdp) Montgomery County	1,040	10.93
Lawndale, CA (city) Los Angeles County	3,568	10.89
Leisure City, FL (cdp) Miami-Dade County	2,351	10.38
South Gate, CA (city) Los Angeles County	9,777	10.36
Richmond West, FL (cdp) Miami-Dade County	3,300	10.32
Mission Bend, TX (cdp) Fort Bend County	3,734	10.23
Hawthorne, CA (city) Los Angeles County	8,547	10.14
Lynn, MA (city) Essex County	9,049	10.02
North Bergen, NJ (township) Hudson County	5,991	9.86
Princeton, FL (cdp) Miami-Dade County	2,158	9.79
Lanham, MD (cdp) Prince George's County	991	9.76
White Oak, MD (cdp) Montgomery County	1,692	9.72
Palmdale, CA (city) Los Angeles County	14,815	9.70
Daly City, CA (city) San Mateo County	9,813	9.70
Elizabeth, NJ (city) Union County	12,097	9.68
South Miami Heights, FL (cdp) Miami-Dade County	3,456	9.68
Morganton, NC (city) Burke County	1,633	9.65
Brownsville, FL (cdp) Miami-Dade County	1,465	9.57
Copiague, NY (cdp) Suffolk County	2,199	9.56
Kendall West, FL (cdp) Miami-Dade County	3,435	9.50
Denison, IA (city) Crawford County	788	9.50
Hialeah Gardens, FL (city) Miami-Dade County	2,048	9.42
Gladeview, FL (cdp) Miami-Dade County	1,085	9.41
Perry, IA (city) Dallas County	722	9.37
Cedartown, GA (city) Polk County	910	9.33
Terrytown, LA (cdp) Jefferson Parish	2,174	9.32
Walnut Park, CA (cdp) Los Angeles County	1,461	9.15
Four Corners, MD (cdp) Montgomery County	721	9.07
Florence-Graham, CA (cdp) Los Angeles County	5,736	9.05
Kendale Lakes, FL (cdp) Miami-Dade County	5,076	9.04
Maywood, CA (city) Los Angeles County	2,460	8.98
Palmetto Estates, FL (cdp) Miami-Dade County	1,209	8.93
Kemp Mill, MD (cdp) Montgomery County	1,120	8.91
North Fair Oaks, CA (cdp) San Mateo County	1,296	8.82
Tamiami, FL (cdp) Miami-Dade County	4,850	8.77
Albertville, AL (city) Marshall County	1,856	8.77
Bell Gardens, CA (city) Los Angeles County	3,670	8.72
Idylwood, VA (cdp) Fairfax County	1,507	8.72
Dover, NJ (town) Morris County	1,568	8.64
Revere, MA (city) Suffolk County	4,457	8.61
Rye, NY (town) Westchester County	3,923	8.54
Cliffside Park, NJ (borough) Bergen County	2,011	8.52
South San Francisco, CA (city) San Mateo County	5,381	8.46
Annapolis, MD (city) Anne Arundel County	3,181	8.29
Lynwood, CA (city) Los Angeles County	5,761	8.26
Newburgh, NY (city) Orange County	2,381	8.25
Raymondville, TX (city) Willacy County	929	8.23
Providence, RI (city) Providence County	14,630	8.22
Laurel, MD (city) Prince George's County	2,029	8.08
Mamaroneck, NY (village) Westchester County	1,530	8.08
Stamford, CT (city/town) Fairfield County	9,866	8.04
Richmond, CA (city) Contra Costa County	8,329	8.03
Leesburg, VA (town) Loudoun County	3,419	8.02
The Hammocks, FL (cdp) Miami-Dade County	4,063	7.97
Inglewood, CA (city) Los Angeles County	8,697	7.93
Meadowbrook, VA (cdp) Chesterfield County	1,440	7.86
Alexandria, VA (ind. city) Alexandria independent city	10,963	7.83

Please refer to the Explanation of Data in the front of the book for more detailed information.

SECTION THREE

Hispanic Origin

Central American: Costa Rican

U.S. and 50 States Sorted by Population and Percent of Total Population

Place	Population	%
United States	**126,418**	**0.04**
California	22,469	0.06
Florida	20,761	0.11
New Jersey	19,933	0.23
New York	11,576	0.06
Texas	6,982	0.03
North Carolina	4,658	0.05
Georgia	3,114	0.03
Pennsylvania	3,048	0.02
Massachusetts	2,951	0.05
Connecticut	2,767	0.08
Virginia	2,630	0.03
Maryland	2,304	0.04
South Carolina	1,943	0.04
Illinois	1,874	0.01
Arizona	1,573	0.02
Washington	1,563	0.02
Nevada	1,433	0.05
Louisiana	1,212	0.03
Colorado	1,104	0.02
Ohio	1,093	0.01
Tennessee	1,045	0.02
Oregon	911	0.02
Michigan	903	0.01
Minnesota	785	0.01
Wisconsin	779	0.01
Utah	775	0.03
Indiana	592	0.01
Missouri	587	0.01
Alabama	504	0.01
Oklahoma	413	0.01
Kansas	385	0.01
New Mexico	342	0.02
Arkansas	333	0.01
Mississippi	317	0.01
Hawaii	289	0.02
District of Columbia	258	0.04
Iowa	255	0.01
Kentucky	253	0.01
Delaware	243	0.03
Rhode Island	242	0.02
New Hampshire	233	0.02
Idaho	230	0.01
Nebraska	166	0.01
Alaska	140	0.02
Maine	105	0.01
Vermont	73	0.01
Montana	71	0.01
West Virginia	68	<0.01
Wyoming	52	0.01
South Dakota	46	0.01
North Dakota	35	0.01

Place	Population	%
New Jersey	19,933	0.23
Florida	20,761	0.11
Connecticut	2,767	0.08
California	22,469	0.06
New York	11,576	0.06
North Carolina	4,658	0.05
Massachusetts	2,951	0.05
Nevada	1,433	0.05
United States	**126,418**	**0.04**
Maryland	2,304	0.04
South Carolina	1,943	0.04
District of Columbia	258	0.04
Texas	6,982	0.03
Georgia	3,114	0.03
Virginia	2,630	0.03
Louisiana	1,212	0.03
Utah	775	0.03
Delaware	243	0.03
Pennsylvania	3,048	0.02
Arizona	1,573	0.02
Washington	1,563	0.02
Colorado	1,104	0.02
Tennessee	1,045	0.02
Oregon	911	0.02
New Mexico	342	0.02
Hawaii	289	0.02
Rhode Island	242	0.02
New Hampshire	233	0.02
Alaska	140	0.02
Illinois	1,874	0.01
Ohio	1,093	0.01
Michigan	903	0.01
Minnesota	785	0.01
Wisconsin	779	0.01
Indiana	592	0.01
Missouri	587	0.01
Alabama	504	0.01
Oklahoma	413	0.01
Kansas	385	0.01
Arkansas	333	0.01
Mississippi	317	0.01
Iowa	255	0.01
Kentucky	253	0.01
Idaho	230	0.01
Nebraska	166	0.01
Maine	105	0.01
Vermont	73	0.01
Montana	71	0.01
Wyoming	52	0.01
South Dakota	46	0.01
North Dakota	35	0.01
West Virginia	68	<0.01

Please refer to the Explanation of Data in the front of the book for more detailed information.

Hispanic Origin

Central American: Costa Rican

Top 150 Places Sorted by Population

Based on all places, regardless of total population

Place	Population	%
New York, NY (city) Kings County	6,673	0.08
Los Angeles, CA (city) Los Angeles County	3,182	0.08
Brooklyn, NY (borough) Kings County	2,576	0.10
Queens, NY (borough) Queens County	1,749	0.08
Trenton, NJ (city) Mercer County	1,279	1.51
Paterson, NJ (city) Passaic County	1,241	0.85
Bound Brook, NJ (borough) Somerset County	1,229	11.82
Miami, FL (city) Miami-Dade County	1,197	0.30
Bronx, NY (borough) Bronx County	1,095	0.08
Norwalk, CT (city/town) Fairfield County	1,024	1.20
Summit, NJ (city) Union County	990	4.61
Manhattan, NY (borough) New York County	987	0.06
Houston, TX (city) Harris County	923	0.04
Philadelphia, PA (city) Philadelphia County	903	0.06
San Diego, CA (city) San Diego County	723	0.06
Chicago, IL (city) Cook County	681	0.03
Charlotte, NC (city) Mecklenburg County	673	0.09
Hempstead, NY (town) Nassau County	664	0.09
Elizabeth, NJ (city) Union County	660	0.53
Boston, MA (city) Suffolk County	652	0.11
Somerville, NJ (borough) Somerset County	627	5.18
Southampton, NY (town) Suffolk County	618	1.09
Manville, NJ (borough) Somerset County	576	5.57
Jacksonville, FL (city) Duval County	542	0.07
Bridgewater, NJ (township) Somerset County	497	1.12
San Francisco, CA (city) San Francisco County	487	0.06
Bridgeport, CT (city/town) Fairfield County	478	0.33
Hialeah, FL (city) Miami-Dade County	476	0.21
Long Beach, CA (city) Los Angeles County	467	0.10
Dallas, TX (city) Dallas County	462	0.04
Newark, NJ (city) Essex County	444	0.16
Lincolnton, NC (city) Lincoln County	431	4.11
Union, NJ (township) Union County	409	0.72
Pembroke Pines, FL (city) Broward County	407	0.26
Hampton Bays, NY (cdp) Suffolk County	406	2.98
Tampa, FL (city) Hillsborough County	374	0.11
San Antonio, TX (city) Medina County	364	0.03
Finderne, NJ (cdp) Somerset County	360	6.43
Hamilton, NJ (township) Mercer County	355	0.40
Hollywood, FL (city) Broward County	349	0.25
Phoenix, AZ (city) Maricopa County	348	0.02
Bloomfield, NJ (township) Essex County	319	0.67
Dover, NJ (town) Morris County	315	1.73
Miramar, FL (city) Broward County	315	0.26
Austin, TX (city) Travis County	312	0.04
Miami Beach, FL (city) Miami-Dade County	298	0.34
Islip, NY (town) Suffolk County	297	0.09
Anaheim, CA (city) Orange County	296	0.09
Las Vegas, NV (city) Clark County	292	0.05
Hillsborough, NJ (township) Somerset County	291	0.76
Raritan, NJ (borough) Somerset County	286	4.16
Staten Island, NY (borough) Richmond County	266	0.06
Downey, CA (city) Los Angeles County	263	0.24
Springfield, NJ (township) Union County	262	1.66
Kendall, FL (cdp) Miami-Dade County	260	0.34
Lakewood, NJ (township) Ocean County	258	0.28
Washington, DC (city) District of Columbia	258	0.04
San Jose, CA (city) Santa Clara County	258	0.03
Fountainebleau, FL (cdp) Miami-Dade County	255	0.43
Nashville-Davidson, TN (metro govt) Davidson County	252	0.04
Riverside, CA (city) Riverside County	249	0.08
Rancho Cucamonga, CA (city) San Bernardino County	245	0.15
Orlando, FL (city) Orange County	245	0.10
Jersey City, NJ (city) Hudson County	229	0.09
New Providence, NJ (borough) Union County	218	1.79
Torrance, CA (city) Los Angeles County	218	0.15
East Hampton, NY (town) Suffolk County	216	1.01
Milwaukee, WI (city) Milwaukee County	210	0.04
Cape Coral, FL (city) Lee County	207	0.13
Country Club, FL (cdp) Miami-Dade County	206	0.44
Davie, FL (town) Broward County	203	0.22
Metairie, LA (cdp) Jefferson Parish	200	0.14
Burbank, CA (city) Los Angeles County	199	0.19
Brookhaven, NY (town) Suffolk County	198	0.04
Irvington, NJ (township) Essex County	195	0.36
The Hammocks, FL (cdp) Miami-Dade County	190	0.37
Fontana, CA (city) San Bernardino County	187	0.10
Moreno Valley, CA (city) Riverside County	185	0.10
Santa Clarita, CA (city) Los Angeles County	185	0.10
Arlington, VA (cdp) Arlington County	185	0.09
Doral, FL (city) Miami-Dade County	184	0.40
Fort Worth, TX (city) Tarrant County	183	0.02
Homestead, FL (city) Miami-Dade County	181	0.30
Chula Vista, CA (city) San Diego County	181	0.07
Mesa, AZ (city) Maricopa County	180	0.04
Pasadena, CA (city) Los Angeles County	178	0.13
Town 'n' Country, FL (cdp) Hillsborough County	177	0.23
Palmdale, CA (city) Los Angeles County	176	0.12
Ontario, CA (city) San Bernardino County	175	0.11
Corona, CA (city) Riverside County	173	0.11
Irvine, CA (city) Orange County	172	0.08
Port St. Lucie, FL (city) St. Lucie County	170	0.10
Hawthorne, CA (city) Los Angeles County	169	0.20
West Palm Beach, FL (city) Palm Beach County	169	0.17
Reno, NV (city) Washoe County	168	0.07
North Bergen, NJ (township) Hudson County	167	0.27
Sunrise, FL (city) Broward County	166	0.20
Seattle, WA (city) King County	166	0.03
Coral Springs, FL (city) Broward County	165	0.14
Simi Valley, CA (city) Ventura County	164	0.13
Raleigh, NC (city) Wake County	164	0.04
Chelsea, MA (city) Suffolk County	163	0.46
Clifton, NJ (city) Passaic County	163	0.19
Frederick, MD (city) Frederick County	162	0.25
Sacramento, CA (city) Sacramento County	162	0.03
Middlesex, NJ (borough) Middlesex County	161	1.18
Plano, TX (city) Collin County	160	0.06
San Bernardino, CA (city) San Bernardino County	159	0.08
Kenner, LA (city) Jefferson Parish	158	0.24
Norwalk, CA (city) Los Angeles County	158	0.15
Lancaster, CA (city) Los Angeles County	156	0.10
Yonkers, NY (city) Westchester County	156	0.08
Hawthorne, NJ (borough) Passaic County	154	0.82
Kendale Lakes, FL (cdp) Miami-Dade County	153	0.27
Paradise, NV (cdp) Clark County	153	0.07
Whittier, CA (city) Los Angeles County	152	0.18
St. Petersburg, FL (city) Pinellas County	152	0.06
Spring Valley, NV (cdp) Clark County	150	0.08
Woodbridge, NJ (township) Middlesex County	148	0.15
Denver, CO (city) Denver County	147	0.02
Babylon, NY (town) Suffolk County	146	0.07
West Covina, CA (city) Los Angeles County	145	0.14
Glendale, CA (city) Los Angeles County	145	0.08
Oakland, CA (city) Alameda County	145	0.04
Tamiami, FL (cdp) Miami-Dade County	144	0.26
Portland, OR (city) Multnomah County	144	0.02
Fort Lauderdale, FL (city) Broward County	143	0.09
South Bound Brook, NJ (borough) Somerset County	141	3.09
Miami Gardens, FL (city) Miami-Dade County	140	0.13
Plantation, FL (city) Broward County	139	0.16
Bakersfield, CA (city) Kern County	139	0.04
Alafaya, FL (cdp) Orange County	136	0.17
Albuquerque, NM (city) Bernalillo County	136	0.02
Piscataway, NJ (township) Middlesex County	135	0.24
New Orleans, LA (city) Orleans Parish	135	0.04
Lakewood, NJ (cdp) Ocean County	134	0.25
Garland, TX (city) Dallas County	134	0.06
Arlington, TX (city) Tarrant County	134	0.04
Stamford, CT (city/town) Fairfield County	133	0.11
Westwood, NJ (borough) Bergen County	132	1.21
Greensboro, NC (city) Guilford County	132	0.05
Oceanside, CA (city) San Diego County	131	0.08
Virginia Beach, VA (ind. city) Virginia Beach independent city	131	0.03
Chandler, AZ (city) Maricopa County	129	0.05
Columbus, OH (city) Franklin County	129	0.02
Plainfield, NJ (city) Union County	128	0.26
Brandon, FL (cdp) Hillsborough County	128	0.12
Atlanta, GA (city) Fulton County	126	0.03
Gainesville, FL (city) Alachua County	125	0.10
Indianapolis, IN (city) Marion County	125	0.02

SECTION THREE

Please refer to the Explanation of Data in the front of the book for more detailed information.

Hispanic Origin

Central American: Costa Rican

Top 150 Places Sorted by Percent of Total Population

Based on all places, regardless of total population

Place	Population	%
Bound Brook, NJ (borough) Somerset County	1,229	11.82
North Central Cass, MN (unorganized territory) Cass County	2	7.14
Finderne, NJ (cdp) Somerset County	360	6.43
Manville, NJ (borough) Somerset County	576	5.57
Somerville, NJ (borough) Somerset County	627	5.18
Summit, NJ (city) Union County	990	4.61
Raritan, NJ (borough) Somerset County	286	4.16
Lincolnton, NC (city) Lincoln County	431	4.11
Sekiu, WA (cdp) Clallam County	1	3.70
South Bound Brook, NJ (borough) Somerset County	141	3.09
Hampton Bays, NY (cdp) Suffolk County	406	2.98
Victory Gardens, NJ (borough) Morris County	38	2.50
Blue Mountain, AR (town) Logan County	3	2.42
Love Valley, NC (town) Iredell County	2	2.22
Clinton, NJ (town) Hunterdon County	60	2.21
Delaware, NJ (cdp) Warren County	3	2.00
Hillcrest Heights, FL (town) Polk County	5	1.97
Belle Mead, NJ (cdp) Somerset County	4	1.85
Arcola, MO (village) Dade County	1	1.82
New Providence, NJ (borough) Union County	218	1.79
Caballo, NM (cdp) Sierra County	2	1.79
Dover, NJ (town) Morris County	315	1.73
Connelly, MN (township) Wilkin County	2	1.72
Black Hawk, CO (city) Gilpin County	2	1.69
Tuckahoe, NY (cdp) Suffolk County	23	1.68
Springfield, NJ (township) Union County	262	1.66
Prospect Park, NJ (borough) Passaic County	94	1.60
Springs, NY (cdp) Suffolk County	103	1.56
Flemington, NJ (borough) Hunterdon County	70	1.53
Keeler, CA (cdp) Inyo County	1	1.52
Trenton, NJ (city) Mercer County	1,279	1.51
Oakdale, TN (town) Morgan County	3	1.42
Maiden, NC (town) Catawba County	46	1.39
Sweden Valley, PA (cdp) Potter County	3	1.35
Redings Mill, MO (village) Newton County	2	1.32
Long Hill, NJ (township) Morris County	113	1.30
East Hampton North, NY (cdp) Suffolk County	53	1.28
Westwood, NJ (borough) Bergen County	132	1.21
Weston, NJ (cdp) Somerset County	15	1.21
Norwalk, CT (city/town) Fairfield County	1,024	1.20
Bridgehampton, NY (cdp) Suffolk County	21	1.20
Lake Como, NJ (borough) Monmouth County	21	1.19
Middlesex, NJ (borough) Middlesex County	161	1.18
Peconic, NY (cdp) Suffolk County	8	1.17
Haledon, NJ (borough) Passaic County	95	1.14
Cottage Grove, TN (town) Henry County	1	1.14
Bridgewater, NJ (township) Somerset County	497	1.12
Wharton, NJ (borough) Morris County	73	1.12
Altoona, FL (cdp) Lake County	1	1.12
Southampton, NY (town) Suffolk County	618	1.09
Spurr, MI (township) Baraga County	3	1.09
Crystal Beach, AZ (cdp) Mohave County	3	1.08
Hacketts, NJ (town) Warren County	104	1.07
Martinsburg, NE (village) Dixon County	1	1.06
Morrisville, PA (borough) Bucks County	92	1.05
Eddyville, NE (village) Dawson County	1	1.03
East Hampton, NY (town) Suffolk County	216	1.01
Shinnecock Hills, NY (cdp) Suffolk County	22	1.01
Mitchell, GA (town) Glascock County	2	1.01
Spillertown, IL (village) Williamson County	2	0.99
Slaughter Beach, DE (town) Sussex County	2	0.97
Georgetown, CT (cdp) Fairfield County	17	0.94
Woodridge, NY (village) Sullivan County	8	0.94
Upper Stewartsville, NJ (cdp) Warren County	2	0.94
Wainscott, NY (cdp) Suffolk County	6	0.92
Roberts, MN (township) Wilkin County	1	0.91
Gun Club Estates, FL (cdp) Palm Beach County	7	0.90
Silerton, TN (town) Hardeman County	1	0.90
Ferrelview, MO (village) Platte County	4	0.89
New Waverly, TX (city) Walker County	9	0.87
Allenwood, NJ (cdp) Monmouth County	8	0.86
Paterson, NJ (city) Passaic County	1,241	0.85
Caldwell, NJ (borough) Essex County	66	0.84
Berea, SC (cdp) Greenville County	119	0.83
Water Mill, NY (cdp) Suffolk County	13	0.83
Baneberry, TN (city) Jefferson County	4	0.83
Hawthorne, NJ (borough) Passaic County	154	0.82
Dunellen, NJ (borough) Middlesex County	59	0.82
Chewton, PA (cdp) Lawrence County	4	0.82
Virginia Gardens, FL (village) Miami-Dade County	19	0.80
Sweden, PA (township) Potter County	7	0.80
West Pelzer, SC (town) Anderson County	7	0.80
Blairstown, NJ (cdp) Warren County	4	0.78
Falcon, NC (town) Cumberland County	2	0.78
Glen Ellen, CA (cdp) Sonoma County	6	0.77
Hillsborough, NJ (township) Somerset County	291	0.76
Roslyn Harbor, NY (village) Nassau County	8	0.76
Oak Park, MN (township) Marshall County	1	0.76
Bird-in-Hand, PA (cdp) Lancaster County	3	0.75
Otter Creek, FL (town) Levy County	1	0.75
Berkeley Heights, NJ (township) Union County	98	0.74
Sans Souci, SC (cdp) Greenville County	58	0.74
Mine Hill, NJ (township) Morris County	27	0.74
Bodega Bay, CA (cdp) Sonoma County	8	0.74
East Hampton, NY (village) Suffolk County	8	0.74
Union, NJ (township) Union County	409	0.72
Schall Circle, FL (cdp) Palm Beach County	8	0.72
Voorhees, NJ (cdp) Somerset County	7	0.72
Big Falls, WI (town) Rusk County	1	0.71
Red Bank, NJ (borough) Monmouth County	85	0.70
East Quogue, NY (cdp) Suffolk County	33	0.69
Silver Lake, NJ (cdp) Essex County	29	0.68
Santa Susana, CA (cdp) Ventura County	7	0.68
Bloomfield, NJ (township) Essex County	319	0.67
Miami Springs, FL (city) Miami-Dade County	91	0.66
Jonesville, SC (town) Union County	6	0.66
Carbonado, WA (town) Pierce County	4	0.66
Cartwright, OK (cdp) Bryan County	4	0.66
Thornburg, PA (borough) Allegheny County	3	0.66
Sag Harbor, NY (village) Suffolk County	14	0.65
Paradise, CA (cdp) Mono County	1	0.65
Southampton, NY (village) Suffolk County	20	0.64
Wolfe City, TX (city) Hunt County	9	0.64
Girard, GA (town) Burke County	1	0.64
Shrewsbury, PA (township) Sullivan County	2	0.63
Millston, WI (town) Jackson County	1	0.63
Bluffton, SC (town) Beaufort County	77	0.61
Chester, NJ (borough) Morris County	10	0.61
Shrewsbury, NJ (township) Monmouth County	7	0.61
Midland Park, NJ (borough) Bergen County	43	0.60
Northwest Harbor, NY (cdp) Suffolk County	20	0.60
Cross Roads, PA (borough) York County	3	0.59
Waldo, OH (village) Marion County	2	0.59
White Oak, NC (cdp) Bladen County	2	0.59
Clark, MN (township) Aitkin County	1	0.59
Fernan Lake Village, ID (city) Kootenai County	1	0.59
Joseph, UT (town) Sevier County	2	0.58
Stewartsville, NJ (cdp) Warren County	2	0.57
Ramona, SD (town) Lake County	1	0.57
Fillmore, IN (town) Putnam County	3	0.56
Pittman, FL (cdp) Lake County	1	0.56
Amsterdam, NY (city) Montgomery County	102	0.55
Keyport, NJ (borough) Monmouth County	40	0.55
Beattystown, NJ (cdp) Warren County	25	0.55
South Hackensack, NJ (township) Bergen County	13	0.55
Millville, DE (town) Sussex County	3	0.55
North Plainfield, NJ (borough) Somerset County	119	0.54
Elizabeth, NJ (city) Union County	660	0.53
Washington, NJ (borough) Warren County	34	0.53
Caliente, NV (city) Lincoln County	6	0.53
Deal, NJ (borough) Monmouth County	4	0.53
Forks, PA (township) Sullivan County	2	0.53
Utica, PA (borough) Venango County	1	0.53
Madison, NJ (borough) Morris County	82	0.52
Austin, NV (cdp) Lander County	1	0.52
Chatham, NJ (borough) Morris County	46	0.51
East Bangor, PA (borough) Northampton County	6	0.51
Indio Hills, CA (cdp) Riverside County	5	0.51
Maiden Rock, WI (town) Pierce County	3	0.51
Rio Lucio, NM (cdp) Taos County	2	0.51

Please refer to the Explanation of Data in the front of the book for more detailed information.

Hispanic Origin

Central American: Costa Rican

Top 150 Places Sorted by Percent of Total Population

Based on places with total population of 7,500 or more

Place	Population	%
Bound Brook, NJ (borough) Somerset County	1,229	11.82
Manville, NJ (borough) Somerset County	576	5.57
Somerville, NJ (borough) Somerset County	627	5.18
Summit, NJ (city) Union County	990	4.61
Lincolnton, NC (city) Lincoln County	431	4.11
Hampton Bays, NY (cdp) Suffolk County	406	2.98
New Providence, NJ (borough) Union County	218	1.79
Dover, NJ (town) Morris County	315	1.73
Springfield, NJ (township) Union County	262	1.66
Trenton, NJ (city) Mercer County	1,279	1.51
Long Hill, NJ (township) Morris County	113	1.30
Westwood, NJ (borough) Bergen County	132	1.21
Norwalk, CT (city/town) Fairfield County	1,024	1.20
Middlesex, NJ (borough) Middlesex County	161	1.18
Haledon, NJ (borough) Passaic County	95	1.14
Bridgewater, NJ (township) Somerset County	497	1.12
Southampton, NY (town) Suffolk County	618	1.09
Hacketts, NJ (town) Warren County	104	1.07
Morrisville, PA (borough) Bucks County	92	1.05
East Hampton, NY (town) Suffolk County	216	1.01
Paterson, NJ (city) Passaic County	1,241	0.85
Caldwell, NJ (borough) Essex County	66	0.84
Berea, SC (cdp) Greenville County	119	0.83
Hawthorne, NJ (borough) Passaic County	154	0.82
Hillsborough, NJ (township) Somerset County	291	0.76
Berkeley Heights, NJ (township) Union County	98	0.74
Sans Souci, SC (cdp) Greenville County	58	0.74
Union, NJ (township) Union County	409	0.72
Red Bank, NJ (borough) Monmouth County	85	0.70
Bloomfield, NJ (township) Essex County	319	0.67
Miami Springs, FL (city) Miami-Dade County	91	0.66
Bluffton, SC (town) Beaufort County	77	0.61
Amsterdam, NY (city) Montgomery County	102	0.55
North Plainfield, NJ (borough) Somerset County	119	0.54
Elizabeth, NJ (city) Union County	660	0.53
Madison, NJ (borough) Morris County	82	0.52
Chatham, NJ (borough) Morris County	46	0.51
Del Aire, CA (cdp) Los Angeles County	47	0.47
Chelsea, MA (city) Suffolk County	163	0.46
Country Club, FL (cdp) Miami-Dade County	206	0.44
Ridgefield Park, NJ (village) Bergen County	56	0.44
Fountainebleau, FL (cdp) Miami-Dade County	255	0.43
Hamilton, NJ (township) Mercer County	355	0.40
Doral, FL (city) Miami-Dade County	184	0.40
Hillsdale, NJ (borough) Bergen County	40	0.39
Coral Terrace, FL (cdp) Miami-Dade County	92	0.38
Budd Lake, NJ (cdp) Morris County	34	0.38
Kenilworth, NJ (borough) Union County	30	0.38
The Hammocks, FL (cdp) Miami-Dade County	190	0.37
Ives Estates, FL (cdp) Miami-Dade County	73	0.37
Irvington, NJ (township) Essex County	195	0.36
Bradley Gardens, NJ (cdp) Somerset County	51	0.36
Roselle Park, NJ (borough) Union County	47	0.35
Martinsville, NJ (cdp) Somerset County	42	0.35
Parker, SC (cdp) Greenville County	40	0.35
Mansfield, NJ (township) Warren County	27	0.35
Miami Beach, FL (city) Miami-Dade County	298	0.34
Kendall, FL (cdp) Miami-Dade County	260	0.34
Westchester, FL (cdp) Miami-Dade County	103	0.34
Mount Olive, NJ (township) Morris County	97	0.34
Bergenfield, NJ (borough) Bergen County	92	0.34
The Crossings, FL (cdp) Miami-Dade County	77	0.34
Sunny Isles Beach, FL (city) Miami-Dade County	70	0.34
Three Lakes, FL (cdp) Miami-Dade County	51	0.34
St. Stephens, NC (cdp) Catawba County	30	0.34
Bridgeport, CT (city/town) Fairfield County	478	0.33
Richmond West, FL (cdp) Miami-Dade County	105	0.33
Miami Lakes, FL (town) Miami-Dade County	96	0.33
Raritan, NJ (township) Hunterdon County	74	0.33
Palm Springs, FL (village) Palm Beach County	63	0.33
Palmetto Estates, FL (cdp) Miami-Dade County	45	0.33
Totowa, NJ (borough) Passaic County	36	0.33
Bedminster, NJ (township) Somerset County	27	0.33
Palm River-Clair Mel, FL (cdp) Hillsborough County	67	0.32
Key Biscayne, FL (village) Miami-Dade County	40	0.32

Place	Population	%
Bethel, CT (cdp) Fairfield County	30	0.31
Miami, FL (city) Miami-Dade County	1,197	0.30
Homestead, FL (city) Miami-Dade County	181	0.30
Cutler Bay, FL (town) Miami-Dade County	122	0.30
Hallandale Beach, FL (city) Broward County	112	0.30
South Miami Heights, FL (cdp) Miami-Dade County	106	0.30
Lodi, NJ (borough) Bergen County	72	0.30
Inwood, NY (cdp) Nassau County	29	0.30
Hilton Head Island, SC (town) Beaufort County	108	0.29
Long Branch, NJ (city) Monmouth County	88	0.29
Ridgewood, NJ (village) Bergen County	73	0.29
Carteret, NJ (borough) Middlesex County	66	0.29
North Augusta, SC (city) Aiken County	61	0.29
Elmwood Park, NJ (borough) Bergen County	57	0.29
Ojus, FL (cdp) Miami-Dade County	53	0.29
Fords, NJ (cdp) Middlesex County	44	0.29
Phillipsburg, NJ (town) Warren County	43	0.29
Nantucket, MA (town) Nantucket County	30	0.29
Lakewood, NJ (township) Ocean County	258	0.28
North Miami Beach, FL (city) Miami-Dade County	115	0.28
Kendall West, FL (cdp) Miami-Dade County	100	0.28
Union Park, FL (cdp) Orange County	27	0.28
Alondra Park, CA (cdp) Los Angeles County	24	0.28
North Bergen, NJ (township) Hudson County	167	0.27
Kendale Lakes, FL (cdp) Miami-Dade County	153	0.27
Linden, NJ (city) Union County	109	0.27
Lawndale, CA (city) Los Angeles County	87	0.27
University Park, FL (cdp) Miami-Dade County	74	0.27
Meadow Woods, FL (cdp) Orange County	69	0.27
Palmetto Bay, FL (village) Miami-Dade County	63	0.27
Princeton, FL (cdp) Miami-Dade County	59	0.27
Glenvar Heights, FL (cdp) Miami-Dade County	45	0.27
South Miami, FL (city) Miami-Dade County	31	0.27
Pembroke Pines, FL (city) Broward County	407	0.26
Miramar, FL (city) Broward County	315	0.26
Tamiami, FL (cdp) Miami-Dade County	144	0.26
Plainfield, NJ (city) Union County	128	0.26
West Orange, NJ (township) Essex County	121	0.26
Hickory, NC (city) Catawba County	105	0.26
Montclair, NJ (township) Essex County	97	0.26
Egypt Lake-Leto, FL (cdp) Hillsborough County	90	0.26
City of Orange, NJ (township) Essex County	79	0.26
Glen Cove, NY (city) Nassau County	71	0.26
Southchase, FL (cdp) Orange County	41	0.26
Sweetwater, FL (city) Miami-Dade County	35	0.26
Dunn, NC (city) Harnett County	24	0.26
Hollywood, FL (city) Broward County	349	0.25
Frederick, MD (city) Frederick County	162	0.25
Lakewood, NJ (cdp) Ocean County	134	0.25
Freeport, NY (village) Nassau County	108	0.25
Belleville, NJ (township) Essex County	89	0.25
Woodbridge, NJ (cdp) Middlesex County	49	0.25
Country Walk, FL (cdp) Miami-Dade County	40	0.25
Downey, CA (city) Los Angeles County	263	0.24
Kenner, LA (city) Jefferson Parish	158	0.24
Piscataway, NJ (township) Middlesex County	135	0.24
Kearny, NJ (town) Hudson County	96	0.24
Cooper City, FL (city) Broward County	69	0.24
Randolph, NJ (township) Morris County	63	0.24
Maplewood, NJ (township) Essex County	58	0.24
Roosevelt, NY (cdp) Nassau County	39	0.24
Newton, NC (city) Catawba County	31	0.24
Wantage, NJ (township) Sussex County	27	0.24
White Meadow Lake, NJ (cdp) Morris County	21	0.24
Closter, NJ (borough) Bergen County	20	0.24
Town 'n' Country, FL (cdp) Hillsborough County	177	0.23
West New York, NJ (town) Hudson County	114	0.23
Greenacres, FL (city) Palm Beach County	86	0.23
Fair Lawn, NJ (borough) Bergen County	74	0.23
Bay Shore, NY (cdp) Suffolk County	60	0.23
Golden Gate, FL (cdp) Collier County	55	0.23
Leisure City, FL (cdp) Miami-Dade County	51	0.23
Millburn, NJ (township) Essex County	46	0.23
Laurel, VA (cdp) Henrico County	39	0.23
Branchburg, NJ (township) Somerset County	33	0.23

SECTION THREE

Please refer to the Explanation of Data in the front of the book for more detailed information.

Hispanic Origin

Central American: Guatemalan

U.S. and 50 States Sorted by Population and Percent of Total Population

Place	Population	%
United States	**1,044,209**	**0.34**
California	332,737	0.89
Florida	83,882	0.45
New York	73,806	0.38
Texas	66,244	0.26
New Jersey	48,869	0.56
Georgia	36,874	0.38
Illinois	35,321	0.28
Maryland	34,491	0.60
Virginia	33,556	0.42
Massachusetts	32,812	0.50
North Carolina	20,206	0.21
Rhode Island	18,852	1.79
Connecticut	16,715	0.47
Tennessee	14,323	0.23
Alabama	14,282	0.30
Arizona	13,426	0.21
Nevada	13,407	0.50
Pennsylvania	11,462	0.09
Washington	9,520	0.14
South Carolina	8,883	0.19
Ohio	8,680	0.08
Nebraska	8,616	0.47
Michigan	8,428	0.09
Oklahoma	7,960	0.21
Oregon	7,703	0.20
Colorado	7,488	0.15
Utah	6,877	0.25
Minnesota	6,754	0.13
Louisiana	6,660	0.15
Missouri	6,610	0.11
Indiana	5,933	0.09
Kansas	5,538	0.19
Kentucky	5,231	0.12
Delaware	5,202	0.58
Iowa	4,917	0.16
Arkansas	4,533	0.16
Wisconsin	3,037	0.05
Mississippi	2,978	0.10
District of Columbia	2,635	0.44
New Mexico	2,386	0.12
South Dakota	1,620	0.20
Idaho	1,168	0.07
New Hampshire	743	0.06
Hawaii	565	0.04
Alaska	508	0.07
Maine	457	0.03
Wyoming	418	0.07
West Virginia	347	0.02
Vermont	215	0.03
Montana	200	0.02
North Dakota	134	0.02

Place	Population	%
Rhode Island	18,852	1.79
California	332,737	0.89
Maryland	34,491	0.60
Delaware	5,202	0.58
New Jersey	48,869	0.56
Massachusetts	32,812	0.50
Nevada	13,407	0.50
Connecticut	16,715	0.47
Nebraska	8,616	0.47
Florida	83,882	0.45
District of Columbia	2,635	0.44
Virginia	33,556	0.42
New York	73,806	0.38
Georgia	36,874	0.38
United States	**1,044,209**	**0.34**
Alabama	14,282	0.30
Illinois	35,321	0.28
Texas	66,244	0.26
Utah	6,877	0.25
Tennessee	14,323	0.23
North Carolina	20,206	0.21
Arizona	13,426	0.21
Oklahoma	7,960	0.21
Oregon	7,703	0.20
South Dakota	1,620	0.20
South Carolina	8,883	0.19
Kansas	5,538	0.19
Iowa	4,917	0.16
Arkansas	4,533	0.16
Colorado	7,488	0.15
Louisiana	6,660	0.15
Washington	9,520	0.14
Minnesota	6,754	0.13
Kentucky	5,231	0.12
New Mexico	2,386	0.12
Missouri	6,610	0.11
Mississippi	2,978	0.10
Pennsylvania	11,462	0.09
Michigan	8,428	0.09
Indiana	5,933	0.09
Ohio	8,680	0.08
Idaho	1,168	0.07
Alaska	508	0.07
Wyoming	418	0.07
New Hampshire	743	0.06
Wisconsin	3,037	0.05
Hawaii	565	0.04
Maine	457	0.03
Vermont	215	0.03
West Virginia	347	0.02
Montana	200	0.02
North Dakota	134	0.02

Please refer to the Explanation of Data in the front of the book for more detailed information.

Hispanic Origin

Central American: Guatemalan

Top 150 Places Sorted by Population

Based on all places, regardless of total population

Place	Population	%
Los Angeles, CA (city) Los Angeles County	138,139	3.64
New York, NY (city) Kings County	30,420	0.37
Houston, TX (city) Harris County	25,205	1.20
Chicago, IL (city) Cook County	17,973	0.67
Queens, NY (borough) Queens County	13,700	0.61
Providence, RI (city) Providence County	11,930	6.70
Brooklyn, NY (borough) Kings County	9,160	0.37
Trenton, NJ (city) Mercer County	8,691	10.24
Stamford, CT (city/town) Fairfield County	7,707	6.28
Phoenix, AZ (city) Maricopa County	6,722	0.46
San Francisco, CA (city) San Francisco County	6,154	0.76
Hempstead, NY (town) Nassau County	5,948	0.78
San Rafael, CA (city) Marin County	5,895	10.21
Lynn, MA (city) Essex County	5,715	6.33
Oakland, CA (city) Alameda County	5,223	1.34
Long Beach, CA (city) Los Angeles County	5,134	1.11
Langley Park, MD (cdp) Prince George's County	5,029	26.81
Bronx, NY (borough) Bronx County	4,645	0.34
Boston, MA (city) Suffolk County	4,451	0.72
Lake Worth, FL (city) Palm Beach County	4,432	12.70
Plainfield, NJ (city) Union County	4,302	8.64
Oklahoma City, OK (city) Oklahoma County	4,256	0.73
Dallas, TX (city) Dallas County	4,238	0.35
Miami, FL (city) Miami-Dade County	4,135	1.04
Ramapo, NY (town) Rockland County	4,050	3.20
West Palm Beach, FL (city) Palm Beach County	3,897	3.90
Hawthorne, CA (city) Los Angeles County	3,669	4.35
Palmdale, CA (city) Los Angeles County	3,618	2.37
Inglewood, CA (city) Los Angeles County	3,593	3.28
Las Vegas, NV (city) Clark County	3,592	0.62
Anaheim, CA (city) Orange County	3,474	1.03
Grand Rapids, MI (city) Kent County	3,372	1.79
Riverside, CA (city) Riverside County	3,338	1.10
Santa Ana, CA (city) Orange County	3,300	1.02
Homestead, FL (city) Miami-Dade County	3,275	5.41
Spring Valley, NY (village) Rockland County	3,265	10.42
Islip, NY (town) Suffolk County	3,256	0.97
Waltham, MA (city) Middlesex County	3,252	5.36
Nashville-Davidson, TN (metro govt) Davidson County	3,140	0.52
Chamblee, GA (city) DeKalb County	3,056	30.89
Arlington, VA (cdp) Arlington County	3,017	1.45
Austin, TX (city) Travis County	3,007	0.38
San Mateo, CA (city) San Mateo County	2,755	2.83
San Diego, CA (city) San Diego County	2,696	0.21
Rye, NY (town) Westchester County	2,654	5.78
Washington, DC (city) District of Columbia	2,635	0.44
Chattanooga, TN (city) Hamilton County	2,633	1.57
South Gate, CA (city) Los Angeles County	2,629	2.79
Central Falls, RI (city) Providence County	2,574	13.28
Chelsea, MA (city) Suffolk County	2,553	7.26
Port Chester, NY (village) Westchester County	2,433	8.40
Charlotte, NC (city) Mecklenburg County	2,421	0.33
Santa Clarita, CA (city) Los Angeles County	2,410	1.37
Silver Spring, MD (cdp) Montgomery County	2,360	3.30
San Jose, CA (city) Santa Clara County	2,294	0.24
Lawrence, MA (city) Essex County	2,262	2.96
Philadelphia, PA (city) Philadelphia County	2,262	0.15
Indiantown, FL (cdp) Martin County	2,260	37.15
Rome, GA (city) Floyd County	2,234	6.15
Fontana, CA (city) San Bernardino County	2,230	1.14
Fairview, NJ (borough) Bergen County	2,191	15.84
Downey, CA (city) Los Angeles County	2,180	1.95
Southampton, NY (town) Suffolk County	2,081	3.66
Lancaster, CA (city) Los Angeles County	2,075	1.32
Manhattan, NY (borough) New York County	2,051	0.13
George, DE (town) Sussex County	2,046	31.86
Jupiter, FL (town) Palm Beach County	1,987	3.60
Lawndale, CA (city) Los Angeles County	1,953	5.96
Richmond, VA (ind. city) Richmond independent city	1,936	0.95
Portland, OR (city) Multnomah County	1,894	0.32
Pomona, CA (city) Los Angeles County	1,885	1.26
Omaha, NE (city) Douglas County	1,853	0.45
San Antonio, TX (city) Medina County	1,848	0.14
Carthage, MO (city) Jasper County	1,840	12.80
East Los Angeles, CA (cdp) Los Angeles County	1,825	1.44
Reno, NV (city) Washoe County	1,825	0.81
Huntington Park, CA (city) Los Angeles County	1,822	3.14
Bakersfield, CA (city) Kern County	1,804	0.52
Mount Kisco, NY (town/village) Westchester County	1,782	16.38
Fort Myers, FL (city) Lee County	1,757	2.82
Redwood City, CA (city) San Mateo County	1,756	2.29
Bailey's Crossroads, VA (cdp) Fairfax County	1,754	7.42
Lynwood, CA (city) Los Angeles County	1,754	2.51
Albertville, AL (city) Marshall County	1,740	8.22
Glendale, CA (city) Los Angeles County	1,723	0.90
Richmond, CA (city) Contra Costa County	1,717	1.66
Florence-Graham, CA (cdp) Los Angeles County	1,685	2.66
Memphis, TN (city) Shelby County	1,680	0.26
Ontario, CA (city) San Bernardino County	1,676	1.02
Paradise, NV (cdp) Clark County	1,669	0.75
Grand Island, NE (city) Hall County	1,665	3.43
Garland, TX (city) Dallas County	1,656	0.73
Norwalk, CT (city/town) Fairfield County	1,619	1.89
Indianapolis, IN (city) Marion County	1,616	0.20
North Bergen, NJ (township) Hudson County	1,596	2.63
West New York, NJ (town) Hudson County	1,594	3.21
Alexandria, VA (ind. city) Alexandria independent city	1,587	1.13
Chillum, MD (cdp) Prince George's County	1,569	4.68
Moreno Valley, CA (city) Riverside County	1,562	0.81
Brentwood, NY (cdp) Suffolk County	1,553	2.56
Hamilton, NJ (township) Mercer County	1,547	1.75
Bonita Springs, FL (city) Lee County	1,539	3.50
New Bedford, MA (city) Bristol County	1,532	1.61
Sunrise Manor, NV (cdp) Clark County	1,532	0.81
San Bernardino, CA (city) San Bernardino County	1,509	0.72
Morganton, NC (city) Burke County	1,507	8.91
Hayward, CA (city) Alameda County	1,504	1.04
Riverhead, NY (town) Suffolk County	1,491	4.45
Lennox, CA (cdp) Los Angeles County	1,474	6.48
Compton, CA (city) Los Angeles County	1,471	1.53
Mesa, AZ (city) Maricopa County	1,446	0.33
Westmont, CA (cdp) Los Angeles County	1,440	4.52
Immokalee, FL (cdp) Collier County	1,436	5.95
Miami Beach, FL (city) Miami-Dade County	1,432	1.63
Fort Lauderdale, FL (city) Broward County	1,413	0.85
Novato, CA (city) Marin County	1,412	2.72
Norwalk, CA (city) Los Angeles County	1,411	1.34
Brookhaven, NY (town) Suffolk County	1,411	0.29
Hempstead, NY (village) Nassau County	1,402	2.60
El Monte, CA (city) Los Angeles County	1,393	1.23
Canton, GA (city) Cherokee County	1,385	6.03
Newark, NJ (city) Essex County	1,375	0.50
Pasadena, CA (city) Los Angeles County	1,367	1.00
Daly City, CA (city) San Mateo County	1,363	1.35
Wheaton, MD (cdp) Montgomery County	1,354	2.80
Tulsa, OK (city) Tulsa County	1,352	0.34
Denver, CO (city) Denver County	1,324	0.22
Durham, NC (city) Durham County	1,323	0.58
Bridgeport, CT (city/town) Fairfield County	1,310	0.91
Pawtucket, RI (city) Providence County	1,301	1.83
Aurora, CO (city) Arapahoe County	1,300	0.40
Fort Worth, TX (city) Tarrant County	1,280	0.17
Lake Elsinore, CA (city) Riverside County	1,268	2.45
Cincinnati, OH (city) Hamilton County	1,257	0.42
Framingham, MA (cdp/town) Middlesex County	1,247	1.83
Baltimore, MD (city) Baltimore city County	1,246	0.20
Sioux City, IA (city) Woodbury County	1,244	1.50
Burbank, CA (city) Los Angeles County	1,238	1.20
New Rochelle, NY (city) Westchester County	1,232	1.60
North Hempstead, NY (town) Nassau County	1,193	0.53
Southeast, NY (town) Putnam County	1,192	6.48
Riverhead, NY (cdp) Suffolk County	1,181	8.88
Thousand Oaks, CA (city) Ventura County	1,173	0.93
Palisades Park, NJ (borough) Bergen County	1,159	5.91
Marietta, GA (city) Cobb County	1,152	2.04
Jersey City, NJ (city) Hudson County	1,148	0.46
Mamaroneck, NY (village) Westchester County	1,145	6.05
North Las Vegas, NV (city) Clark County	1,137	0.52
Costa Mesa, CA (city) Orange County	1,134	1.03
Elizabeth, NJ (city) Union County	1,131	0.91

SECTION THREE

Please refer to the Explanation of Data in the front of the book for more detailed information.

Hispanic Origin

Central American: Guatemalan

Top 150 Places Sorted by Percent of Total Population

Based on all places, regardless of total population

Place	Population	%
Marydel, MD (town) Caroline County	60	42.55
Brewster, NY (village) Putnam County	912	38.16
Indiantown, FL (cdp) Martin County	2,260	37.15
Chase Crossing, VA (cdp) Accomack County	135	35.81
Sargents, NH (purchase) Coos County	1	33.33
Templeville, MD (town) Queen Anne's County	44	31.88
George, DE (town) Sussex County	2,046	31.86
Chamblee, GA (city) DeKalb County	3,056	30.89
Henderson, MD (town) Caroline County	43	29.45
Langley Park, MD (cdp) Prince George's County	5,029	26.81
Mappsville, VA (cdp) Accomack County	94	21.36
Ellijay, GA (city) Gilmer County	314	19.39
Tice, FL (cdp) Lee County	834	18.66
Collinsville, AL (town) DeKalb County	367	18.51
East Ellijay, GA (city) Gilmer County	100	18.32
Alpena, SD (town) Jerauld County	49	17.13
Mount Kisco, NY (town/village) Westchester County	1,782	16.38
Fairview, NJ (borough) Bergen County	2,191	15.84
Flanders, NY (cdp) Suffolk County	678	15.16
Schuyler, NE (city) Colfax County	869	13.99
Saluda, SC (town) Saluda County	490	13.74
Central Falls, RI (city) Providence County	2,574	13.28
Cache, UT (cdp) Cache County	5	13.16
Cattaraugus Reservation, NY (reservation) Chautauqua County	5	13.16
Greenport, NY (village) Suffolk County	287	13.06
Carthage, MO (city) Jasper County	1,840	12.80
Lake Worth, FL (city) Palm Beach County	4,432	12.70
Quiogue, NY (cdp) Suffolk County	103	12.62
Stacey Street, FL (cdp) Palm Beach County	108	12.59
Modest Town, VA (cdp) Accomack County	17	11.41
Trion, GA (town) Chattooga County	198	10.84
Monterey, TN (town) Putnam County	307	10.77
Bedford Hills, NY (cdp) Westchester County	317	10.56
Spring Valley, NY (village) Rockland County	3,265	10.42
Westhampton Beach, NY (village) Suffolk County	178	10.34
Trenton, NJ (city) Mercer County	8,691	10.24
San Rafael, CA (city) Marin County	5,895	10.21
Russellville, AL (city) Franklin County	969	9.86
Westgate, FL (cdp) Palm Beach County	775	9.72
Riverside, NY (cdp) Suffolk County	273	9.38
Cedartown, GA (city) Polk County	895	9.18
Green Forest, AR (city) Carroll County	253	9.16
Morganton, NC (city) Burke County	1,507	8.91
Riverhead, NY (cdp) Suffolk County	1,181	8.88
Dover Plains, NY (cdp) Dutchess County	117	8.84
Juno Ridge, FL (cdp) Palm Beach County	63	8.77
Lexington, NE (city) Dawson County	891	8.71
Plainfield, NJ (city) Union County	4,302	8.64
Northampton, NY (cdp) Suffolk County	49	8.60
Port Chester, NY (village) Westchester County	2,433	8.40
Inglewood, NE (village) Dodge County	27	8.31
Eddyville, NE (village) Dawson County	8	8.25
Albertville, AL (city) Marshall County	1,740	8.22
Dawson, ND (city) Kidder County	5	8.20
Lakewood Gardens, FL (cdp) Palm Beach County	103	8.09
Postville, IA (city) Allamakee County	180	8.08
Crete, NE (city) Saline County	534	7.67
Inwood, NY (cdp) Nassau County	740	7.56
Bailey's Crossroads, VA (cdp) Fairfax County	1,754	7.42
Seven Springs, NC (town) Wayne County	8	7.27
Chelsea, MA (city) Suffolk County	2,553	7.26
Southwest City, MO (town) McDonald County	69	7.11
Worthington, MN (city) Nobles County	906	7.10
Fort Payne, AL (city) DeKalb County	980	6.99
Faison, NC (town) Duplin County	67	6.97
Doraville, GA (city) DeKalb County	580	6.96
Forks, WA (city) Clallam County	242	6.85
Grattan, MN (township) Itasca County	3	6.82
Broadview Park, FL (cdp) Broward County	482	6.76
Bensley, VA (cdp) Chesterfield County	393	6.75
Providence, RI (city) Providence County	11,930	6.70
Frankford, DE (town) Sussex County	55	6.49
Lennox, CA (cdp) Los Angeles County	1,474	6.48
Southeast, NY (town) Putnam County	1,192	6.48
Eton, GA (city) Murray County	58	6.37
Siler City, NC (town) Chatham County	502	6.36
Lynn, MA (city) Essex County	5,715	6.33
Palmer, KS (city) Washington County	7	6.31
Stamford, CT (city/town) Fairfield County	7,707	6.28
Limestone Creek, FL (cdp) Palm Beach County	63	6.21
Rome, GA (city) Floyd County	2,234	6.15
Guymon, OK (city) Texas County	704	6.15
Pine Air, FL (cdp) Palm Beach County	123	6.08
Kenwood Estates, FL (cdp) Palm Beach County	78	6.08
Wakefield, NE (city) Dixon County	88	6.06
Mamaroneck, NY (village) Westchester County	1,145	6.05
Canton, GA (city) Cherokee County	1,385	6.03
Barneston, NE (village) Gage County	7	6.03
Westhampton, NY (cdp) Suffolk County	185	6.01
Lawndale, CA (city) Los Angeles County	1,953	5.96
Immokalee, FL (cdp) Collier County	1,436	5.95
Cornelia, GA (city) Habersham County	247	5.94
Palisades Park, NJ (borough) Bergen County	1,159	5.91
Rye, NY (town) Westchester County	2,654	5.78
Boaz, AL (city) Marshall County	544	5.70
Carthage, MS (city) Leake County	285	5.62
Webster, TX (city) Harris County	578	5.56
Kenton Vale, KY (city) Kenton County	6	5.45
Homestead, FL (city) Miami-Dade County	3,275	5.41
Waltham, MA (city) Middlesex County	3,252	5.36
Nelsonia, VA (cdp) Accomack County	28	5.35
Tasley, VA (cdp) Accomack County	16	5.33
Bensenville, IL (village) DuPage County	969	5.28
Adelphi, MD (cdp) Prince George's County	761	5.04
Calhoun, GA (city) Gordon County	784	5.01
Springdale, OH (city) Hamilton County	562	5.01
Seven Corners, VA (cdp) Fairfax County	462	4.99
Greensboro, FL (town) Gadsden County	30	4.98
Noel, MO (city) McDonald County	91	4.97
North Plainfield, NJ (borough) Somerset County	1,089	4.96
Aquebogue, NY (cdp) Suffolk County	120	4.92
Tibbie, AL (cdp) Washington County	2	4.88
Riverdale Park, MD (town) Prince George's County	339	4.87
Hillcrest, NY (cdp) Rockland County	365	4.83
Atlantic Beach, SC (town) Horry County	16	4.79
Bull Run, VA (cdp) Prince William County	703	4.69
Peconic, NY (cdp) Suffolk County	32	4.69
Chillum, MD (cdp) Prince George's County	1,569	4.68
Belfair, WA (cdp) Mason County	184	4.68
Shelton, WA (city) Mason County	454	4.62
Forest, MS (city) Scott County	262	4.61
Watts Mills, SC (cdp) Laurens County	74	4.53
Westmont, CA (cdp) Los Angeles County	1,440	4.52
Greenport West, NY (cdp) Suffolk County	96	4.52
Flemington, NJ (borough) Hunterdon County	206	4.50
Everglades, FL (city) Collier County	18	4.50
Ellendale, DE (town) Sussex County	17	4.46
Riverhead, NY (town) Suffolk County	1,491	4.45
Chatsworth, GA (city) Murray County	191	4.44
North Richmond, CA (cdp) Contra Costa County	165	4.44
Cliffside Park, NJ (borough) Bergen County	1,044	4.42
Morris, NJ (town) Morris County	809	4.39
Hawthorne, CA (city) Los Angeles County	3,669	4.35
Elkton, SD (city) Brookings County	32	4.35
Loxahatchee Groves, FL (town) Palm Beach County	138	4.34
Venice, NY (town) Cayuga County	58	4.24
City View, SC (cdp) Greenville County	57	4.24
Sans Souci, SC (cdp) Greenville County	328	4.17
Katonah, NY (cdp) Westchester County	70	4.17
Hitchcock, OK (town) Blaine County	5	4.13
Windsor, SC (town) Aiken County	5	4.13
Pontoosuc, IL (village) Hancock County	6	4.11
Jennings, FL (town) Hamilton County	36	4.10
Pawling, NY (village) Dutchess County	95	4.05
Gorst, WA (cdp) Kitsap County	24	4.05
Booker, TX (town) Lipscomb County	61	4.02
Laurel, NY (cdp) Suffolk County	56	4.02
Manorhaven, NY (village) Nassau County	263	4.01
Avilla, MO (town) Jasper County	5	4.00
Eastport, NY (cdp) Suffolk County	73	3.99

Please refer to the Explanation of Data in the front of the book for more detailed information.

Hispanic Origin

Central American: Guatemalan

Top 150 Places Sorted by Percent of Total Population

Based on places with total population of 7,500 or more

Place	Population	%
Chamblee, GA (city) DeKalb County	3,056	30.89
Langley Park, MD (cdp) Prince George's County	5,029	26.81
Mount Kisco, NY (town/village) Westchester County	1,782	16.38
Fairview, NJ (borough) Bergen County	2,191	15.84
Central Falls, RI (city) Providence County	2,574	13.28
Carthage, MO (city) Jasper County	1,840	12.80
Lake Worth, FL (city) Palm Beach County	4,432	12.70
Spring Valley, NY (village) Rockland County	3,265	10.42
Trenton, NJ (city) Mercer County	8,691	10.24
San Rafael, CA (city) Marin County	5,895	10.21
Russellville, AL (city) Franklin County	969	9.86
Westgate, FL (cdp) Palm Beach County	775	9.72
Cedartown, GA (city) Polk County	895	9.18
Morganton, NC (city) Burke County	1,507	8.91
Riverhead, NY (cdp) Suffolk County	1,181	8.88
Lexington, NE (city) Dawson County	891	8.71
Plainfield, NJ (city) Union County	4,302	8.64
Port Chester, NY (village) Westchester County	2,433	8.40
Albertville, AL (city) Marshall County	1,740	8.22
Inwood, NY (cdp) Nassau County	740	7.56
Bailey's Crossroads, VA (cdp) Fairfax County	1,754	7.42
Chelsea, MA (city) Suffolk County	2,553	7.26
Worthington, MN (city) Nobles County	906	7.10
Fort Payne, AL (city) DeKalb County	980	6.99
Doraville, GA (city) DeKalb County	580	6.96
Providence, RI (city) Providence County	11,930	6.70
Lennox, CA (cdp) Los Angeles County	1,474	6.48
Southeast, NY (town) Putnam County	1,192	6.48
Siler City, NC (town) Chatham County	502	6.36
Lynn, MA (city) Essex County	5,715	6.33
Stamford, CT (city/town) Fairfield County	7,707	6.28
Rome, GA (city) Floyd County	2,234	6.15
Guymon, OK (city) Texas County	704	6.15
Mamaroneck, NY (village) Westchester County	1,145	6.05
Canton, GA (city) Cherokee County	1,385	6.03
Lawndale, CA (city) Los Angeles County	1,953	5.96
Immokalee, FL (cdp) Collier County	1,436	5.95
Palisades Park, NJ (borough) Bergen County	1,159	5.91
Rye, NY (town) Westchester County	2,654	5.78
Boaz, AL (city) Marshall County	544	5.70
Webster, TX (city) Harris County	578	5.56
Homestead, FL (city) Miami-Dade County	3,275	5.41
Waltham, MA (city) Middlesex County	3,252	5.36
Bensenville, IL (village) DuPage County	969	5.28
Adelphi, MD (cdp) Prince George's County	761	5.04
Calhoun, GA (city) Gordon County	784	5.01
Springdale, OH (city) Hamilton County	562	5.01
Seven Corners, VA (cdp) Fairfax County	462	4.99
North Plainfield, NJ (borough) Somerset County	1,089	4.96
Hillcrest, NY (cdp) Rockland County	365	4.83
Bull Run, VA (cdp) Prince William County	703	4.69
Chillum, MD (cdp) Prince George's County	1,569	4.68
Shelton, WA (city) Mason County	454	4.62
Westmont, CA (cdp) Los Angeles County	1,440	4.52
Riverhead, NY (town) Suffolk County	1,491	4.45
Cliffside Park, NJ (borough) Bergen County	1,044	4.42
Morris, NJ (town) Morris County	809	4.39
Hawthorne, CA (city) Los Angeles County	3,669	4.35
Sans Souci, SC (cdp) Greenville County	328	4.17
West Palm Beach, FL (city) Palm Beach County	3,897	3.90
Dodge City, KS (city) Ford County	1,043	3.81
Liberal, KS (city) Seward County	781	3.81
Cudahy, CA (city) Los Angeles County	902	3.79
North Fair Oaks, CA (cdp) San Mateo County	552	3.76
Peekskill, NY (city) Westchester County	882	3.74
Guttenberg, NJ (town) Hudson County	410	3.67
Alondra Park, CA (cdp) Los Angeles County	315	3.67
Southampton, NY (town) Suffolk County	2,081	3.66
Los Angeles, CA (city) Los Angeles County	138,139	3.64
Jupiter, FL (town) Palm Beach County	1,987	3.60
Mamaroneck, NY (town) Westchester County	1,036	3.55
Bonita Springs, FL (city) Lee County	1,539	3.50
Southold, NY (town) Suffolk County	769	3.50
Grand Island, NE (city) Hall County	1,665	3.43
East Riverdale, MD (cdp) Prince George's County	530	3.42
Norcross, GA (city) Gwinnett County	306	3.36
Sudley, VA (cdp) Prince William County	543	3.35
Perry, IA (city) Dallas County	257	3.34
Yorkshire, VA (cdp) Prince William County	251	3.33
Silver Spring, MD (cdp) Montgomery County	2,360	3.30
Inglewood, CA (city) Los Angeles County	3,593	3.28
Dover, NY (town) Dutchess County	283	3.25
West New York, NJ (town) Hudson County	1,594	3.21
Ramapo, NY (town) Rockland County	4,050	3.20
Shelbyville, KY (city) Shelby County	450	3.20
Huntington Park, CA (city) Los Angeles County	1,822	3.14
Hyattsville, MD (city) Prince George's County	541	3.08
Chambersburg, PA (borough) Franklin County	621	3.06
North Bay Shore, NY (cdp) Suffolk County	576	3.04
Cairo, GA (city) Grady County	292	3.04
Cocoa, FL (city) Brevard County	514	3.00
Manassas Park, VA (ind. city) Manassas Park independent city	428	3.00
Lawrence, MA (city) Essex County	2,262	2.96
Bell, CA (city) Los Angeles County	1,041	2.93
Princeton, NJ (borough) Mercer County	361	2.93
Port Salerno, FL (cdp) Martin County	295	2.92
West Falls Church, VA (cdp) Fairfax County	845	2.89
Garnet, CA (cdp) Riverside County	217	2.88
Milford, DE (city) Sussex County	273	2.86
San Mateo, CA (city) San Mateo County	2,755	2.83
Bedford, NY (town) Westchester County	491	2.83
Fort Myers, FL (city) Lee County	1,757	2.82
Wheaton, MD (cdp) Montgomery County	1,354	2.80
South Gate, CA (city) Los Angeles County	2,629	2.79
Beltsville, MD (cdp) Prince George's County	467	2.78
Batesville, AR (city) Independence County	284	2.77
Greenbriar, VA (cdp) Fairfax County	226	2.77
Marlborough, MA (city) Middlesex County	1,060	2.75
Dalton, GA (city) Whitfield County	909	2.74
Novato, CA (city) Marin County	1,412	2.72
West Athens, CA (cdp) Los Angeles County	235	2.69
Fallbrook, CA (cdp) San Diego County	815	2.67
Florence-Graham, CA (cdp) Los Angeles County	1,685	2.66
North Bergen, NJ (township) Hudson County	1,596	2.63
Golden Gate, FL (cdp) Collier County	631	2.63
Hempstead, NY (village) Nassau County	1,402	2.60
Brentwood, NY (cdp) Suffolk County	1,553	2.56
Neosho, MO (city) Newton County	298	2.52
Lynwood, CA (city) Los Angeles County	1,754	2.51
Freeport, NY (village) Nassau County	1,070	2.50
Fort Morgan, CO (city) Morgan County	282	2.49
Bound Brook, NJ (borough) Somerset County	258	2.48
Denison, IA (city) Crawford County	205	2.47
Lenoir City, TN (city) Loudon County	213	2.46
Lake Elsinore, CA (city) Riverside County	1,268	2.45
Easton, MD (town) Talbot County	389	2.44
Fair Oaks, GA (cdp) Cobb County	201	2.44
Home Gardens, CA (cdp) Riverside County	281	2.43
Walnut Park, CA (cdp) Los Angeles County	385	2.41
Palmdale, CA (city) Los Angeles County	3,618	2.37
Mount Rainier, MD (city) Prince George's County	190	2.35
Laurel, MD (city) Prince George's County	582	2.32
Stuart, FL (city) Martin County	360	2.31
Northlake, IL (city) Cook County	285	2.31
Redwood City, CA (city) San Mateo County	1,756	2.29
San Pablo, CA (city) Contra Costa County	667	2.29
South Sioux City, NE (city) Dakota County	306	2.29
Alamosa, CO (city) Alamosa County	200	2.28
Lincolnia, VA (cdp) Fairfax County	517	2.26
Huntington Station, NY (cdp) Suffolk County	739	2.24
Logansport, IN (city) Cass County	412	2.24
Bell Gardens, CA (city) Los Angeles County	934	2.22
Maywood, CA (city) Los Angeles County	609	2.22
Del Aire, CA (cdp) Los Angeles County	222	2.22
East Windsor, NJ (township) Mercer County	600	2.21
Leisure City, FL (cdp) Miami-Dade County	501	2.21
Raymondville, TX (city) Willacy County	247	2.19
Phoenixville, PA (borough) Chester County	355	2.16
Parker, SC (cdp) Greenville County	245	2.14
Dover, OH (city) Tuscarawas County	273	2.13

Please refer to the Explanation of Data in the front of the book for more detailed information.

Hispanic Origin

Central American: Honduran

U.S. and 50 States Sorted by Population and Percent of Total Population

Place	Population	%
United States	**633,401**	**0.21**
Florida	107,302	0.57
Texas	88,389	0.35
California	72,795	0.20
New York	71,919	0.37
New Jersey	36,556	0.42
North Carolina	30,900	0.32
Louisiana	30,617	0.68
Virginia	30,583	0.38
Georgia	20,577	0.21
Maryland	20,576	0.36
Massachusetts	12,533	0.19
Illinois	12,023	0.09
Tennessee	9,455	0.15
South Carolina	8,091	0.17
Pennsylvania	7,055	0.06
Connecticut	6,242	0.17
Indiana	5,345	0.08
Nevada	4,481	0.17
Washington	4,381	0.07
Colorado	4,356	0.09
Arizona	3,968	0.06
Ohio	3,699	0.03
Missouri	3,657	0.06
Alabama	3,280	0.07
Minnesota	3,186	0.06
Oklahoma	2,711	0.07
Michigan	2,694	0.03
Kansas	2,689	0.09
Mississippi	2,448	0.08
Wisconsin	2,402	0.04
District of Columbia	2,139	0.36
Utah	2,087	0.08
Arkansas	2,076	0.07
Kentucky	2,012	0.05
Oregon	1,644	0.04
Nebraska	1,547	0.08
Iowa	1,539	0.05
Rhode Island	1,250	0.12
Delaware	675	0.08
New Mexico	657	0.03
New Hampshire	506	0.04
Idaho	461	0.03
Hawaii	390	0.03
West Virginia	333	0.02
Maine	280	0.02
Alaska	272	0.04
South Dakota	221	0.03
Wyoming	145	0.03
Vermont	109	0.02
Montana	98	0.01
North Dakota	50	0.01

Place	Population	%
Louisiana	30,617	0.68
Florida	107,302	0.57
New Jersey	36,556	0.42
Virginia	30,583	0.38
New York	71,919	0.37
Maryland	20,576	0.36
District of Columbia	2,139	0.36
Texas	88,389	0.35
North Carolina	30,900	0.32
United States	**633,401**	**0.21**
Georgia	20,577	0.21
California	72,795	0.20
Massachusetts	12,533	0.19
South Carolina	8,091	0.17
Connecticut	6,242	0.17
Nevada	4,481	0.17
Tennessee	9,455	0.15
Rhode Island	1,250	0.12
Illinois	12,023	0.09
Colorado	4,356	0.09
Kansas	2,689	0.09
Indiana	5,345	0.08
Mississippi	2,448	0.08
Utah	2,087	0.08
Nebraska	1,547	0.08
Delaware	675	0.08
Washington	4,381	0.07
Alabama	3,280	0.07
Oklahoma	2,711	0.07
Arkansas	2,076	0.07
Pennsylvania	7,055	0.06
Arizona	3,968	0.06
Missouri	3,657	0.06
Minnesota	3,186	0.06
Kentucky	2,012	0.05
Iowa	1,539	0.05
Wisconsin	2,402	0.04
Oregon	1,644	0.04
New Hampshire	506	0.04
Alaska	272	0.04
Ohio	3,699	0.03
Michigan	2,694	0.03
New Mexico	657	0.03
Idaho	461	0.03
Hawaii	390	0.03
South Dakota	221	0.03
Wyoming	145	0.03
West Virginia	333	0.02
Maine	280	0.02
Vermont	109	0.02
Montana	98	0.01
North Dakota	50	0.01

Please refer to the Explanation of Data in the front of the book for more detailed information.

Hispanic Origin

Central American: Honduran

Top 150 Places Sorted by Population

Based on all places, regardless of total population

Place	Population	%
New York, NY (city) Kings County	42,400	0.52
Houston, TX (city) Harris County	32,807	1.56
Los Angeles, CA (city) Los Angeles County	23,919	0.63
Miami, FL (city) Miami-Dade County	23,209	5.81
Bronx, NY (borough) Bronx County	17,990	1.30
Brooklyn, NY (borough) Kings County	10,071	0.40
Queens, NY (borough) Queens County	8,546	0.38
Hempstead, NY (town) Nassau County	7,842	1.03
Charlotte, NC (city) Mecklenburg County	7,557	1.03
Dallas, TX (city) Dallas County	6,890	0.58
Metairie, LA (cdp) Jefferson Parish	5,611	4.05
Kenner, LA (city) Jefferson Parish	5,556	8.33
Chicago, IL (city) Cook County	5,021	0.19
New Orleans, LA (city) Orleans Parish	4,572	1.33
Austin, TX (city) Travis County	4,503	0.57
Islip, NY (town) Suffolk County	4,232	1.26
Manhattan, NY (borough) New York County	4,058	0.26
Boston, MA (city) Suffolk County	4,017	0.65
Hempstead, NY (village) Nassau County	3,758	6.97
Hialeah, FL (city) Miami-Dade County	3,744	1.67
Durham, NC (city) Durham County	3,451	1.51
Jersey City, NJ (city) Hudson County	3,041	1.23
Nashville-Davidson, TN (metro govt) Davidson County	3,018	0.50
Chelsea, MA (city) Suffolk County	2,938	8.35
San Antonio, TX (city) Medina County	2,776	0.21
New Brunswick, NJ (city) Middlesex County	2,772	5.02
Long Beach, CA (city) Los Angeles County	2,696	0.58
San Francisco, CA (city) San Francisco County	2,611	0.32
Union City, NJ (city) Hudson County	2,533	3.81
Baltimore, MD (city) Baltimore city County	2,386	0.38
Raleigh, NC (city) Wake County	2,345	0.58
Elizabeth, NJ (city) Union County	2,338	1.87
Waukegan, IL (city) Lake County	2,311	2.59
Indianapolis, IN (city) Marion County	2,302	0.28
Alexandria, VA (ind. city) Alexandria independent city	2,243	1.60
Washington, DC (city) District of Columbia	2,139	0.36
Newark, NJ (city) Essex County	2,126	0.77
Brentwood, NY (cdp) Suffolk County	2,062	3.40
Tampa, FL (city) Hillsborough County	2,004	0.60
Jacksonville, FL (city) Duval County	1,983	0.24
West Little River, FL (cdp) Miami-Dade County	1,902	5.48
Memphis, TN (city) Shelby County	1,895	0.29
San Jose, CA (city) Santa Clara County	1,890	0.20
Morris, NJ (town) Morris County	1,840	9.99
Fort Worth, TX (city) Tarrant County	1,820	0.25
Conroe, TX (city) Montgomery County	1,766	3.14
Springfield, VA (cdp) Fairfax County	1,759	5.77
Babylon, NY (town) Suffolk County	1,756	0.82
Staten Island, NY (borough) Richmond County	1,735	0.37
Huntington, NY (town) Suffolk County	1,651	0.81
Philadelphia, PA (city) Philadelphia County	1,642	0.11
North Hempstead, NY (town) Nassau County	1,572	0.69
Irving, TX (city) Dallas County	1,547	0.72
Newburgh, NY (city) Orange County	1,545	5.35
Phoenix, AZ (city) Maricopa County	1,535	0.11
Terrytown, LA (cdp) Jefferson Parish	1,528	6.55
Norwalk, CT (city/town) Fairfield County	1,506	1.76
Plainfield, NJ (city) Union County	1,493	3.00
Miami Beach, FL (city) Miami-Dade County	1,483	1.69
Yonkers, NY (city) Westchester County	1,451	0.74
Las Vegas, NV (city) Clark County	1,360	0.23
North Miami, FL (city) Miami-Dade County	1,342	2.28
Pasadena, TX (city) Harris County	1,335	0.90
San Diego, CA (city) San Diego County	1,293	0.10
Hollywood, FL (city) Broward County	1,283	0.91
Stamford, CT (city/town) Fairfield County	1,279	1.04
Huntington Station, NY (cdp) Suffolk County	1,260	3.81
Gaithersburg, MD (city) Montgomery County	1,211	2.02
Brookhaven, NY (town) Suffolk County	1,195	0.25
Silver Spring, MD (cdp) Montgomery County	1,166	1.63
Oakland, CA (city) Alameda County	1,160	0.30
Herndon, VA (town) Fairfax County	1,159	4.98
Central Islip, NY (cdp) Suffolk County	1,118	3.25
Fountainebleau, FL (cdp) Miami-Dade County	1,117	1.87
Wheaton, MD (cdp) Montgomery County	1,101	2.28
North Miami Beach, FL (city) Miami-Dade County	1,088	2.62
North Bergen, NJ (township) Hudson County	1,081	1.78
Miami Gardens, FL (city) Miami-Dade County	1,068	1.00
Garland, TX (city) Dallas County	1,058	0.47
Pompano Beach, FL (city) Broward County	1,036	1.04
Miramar, FL (city) Broward County	1,011	0.83
Fort Lauderdale, FL (city) Broward County	1,002	0.61
Bridgeport, CT (city/town) Fairfield County	999	0.69
Pembroke Pines, FL (city) Broward County	996	0.64
Harrisonburg, VA (ind. city) Harrisonburg independent city	978	2.00
Marumsco, VA (cdp) Prince William County	973	2.78
West New York, NJ (town) Hudson County	970	1.95
Aurora, CO (city) Arapahoe County	970	0.30
Port St. Lucie, FL (city) St. Lucie County	967	0.59
Orlando, FL (city) Orange County	956	0.40
Oyster Bay, NY (town) Nassau County	952	0.32
Oklahoma City, OK (city) Oklahoma County	944	0.16
Homestead, FL (city) Miami-Dade County	936	1.55
Roanoke, VA (ind. city) Roanoke independent city	936	0.96
Woodlawn, VA (cdp) Fairfax County	925	4.45
Dale City, VA (cdp) Prince William County	925	1.40
University, FL (cdp) Hillsborough County	922	2.24
Lake Worth, FL (city) Palm Beach County	906	2.60
Lehigh Acres, FL (cdp) Lee County	901	1.04
Pasadena, CA (city) Los Angeles County	897	0.65
Kansas City, MO (city) Jackson County	884	0.19
Arlington, VA (cdp) Arlington County	881	0.42
Harvey, LA (cdp) Jefferson Parish	862	4.24
Dover, NJ (town) Morris County	860	4.74
Atlantic City, NJ (city) Atlantic County	857	2.17
Norfolk, VA (ind. city) Norfolk independent city	856	0.35
South Miami Heights, FL (cdp) Miami-Dade County	839	2.35
Greenacres, FL (city) Palm Beach County	836	2.23
Arlington, TX (city) Tarrant County	835	0.23
Trenton, NJ (city) Mercer County	820	0.97
New Cassel, NY (cdp) Nassau County	812	5.78
Uniondale, NY (cdp) Nassau County	806	3.26
Tulsa, OK (city) Tulsa County	803	0.20
Denver, CO (city) Denver County	799	0.13
Ontario, CA (city) San Bernardino County	793	0.48
Freeport, NY (village) Nassau County	785	1.83
Columbus, OH (city) Franklin County	784	0.10
Sterling, VA (cdp) Loudoun County	779	2.80
Kansas City, KS (city) Wyandotte County	778	0.53
Gretna, LA (city) Jefferson Parish	762	4.30
Aspen Hill, MD (cdp) Montgomery County	755	1.55
Allentown, PA (city) Lehigh County	749	0.63
Country Club, FL (cdp) Miami-Dade County	748	1.59
Golden Gate, FL (cdp) Collier County	741	3.09
Sunrise Manor, NV (cdp) Clark County	741	0.39
Providence, RI (city) Providence County	731	0.41
Baton Rouge, LA (city) East Baton Rouge Parish	730	0.32
Langley Park, MD (cdp) Prince George's County	706	3.76
Kendall, FL (cdp) Miami-Dade County	705	0.94
Santa Ana, CA (city) Orange County	663	0.20
Carrollton, GA (city) Carroll County	660	2.71
Manassas, VA (ind. city) Manassas independent city	657	1.74
Palmdale, CA (city) Los Angeles County	656	0.43
Inglewood, CA (city) Los Angeles County	649	0.59
Richmond, VA (ind. city) Richmond independent city	640	0.31
Fontana, CA (city) San Bernardino County	636	0.32
Anaheim, CA (city) Orange County	636	0.19
Plano, TX (city) Collin County	635	0.24
Seattle, WA (city) King County	633	0.10
Pomona, CA (city) Los Angeles County	632	0.42
Cape Coral, FL (city) Lee County	625	0.41
Chillum, MD (cdp) Prince George's County	620	1.85
Davie, FL (town) Broward County	612	0.67
Annandale, VA (cdp) Fairfax County	611	1.49
Wallace, NC (town) Duplin County	605	15.59
Broadview Park, FL (cdp) Broward County	603	8.46
Pleasantville, NJ (city) Atlantic County	598	2.95
Bailey's Crossroads, VA (cdp) Fairfax County	594	2.51
The Hammocks, FL (cdp) Miami-Dade County	588	1.15
Hawthorne, CA (city) Los Angeles County	584	0.69

SECTION THREE

Please refer to the Explanation of Data in the front of the book for more detailed information.

Hispanic Origin

Central American: Honduran

Top 150 Places Sorted by Percent of Total Population

Based on all places, regardless of total population

Place	Population	%
Islandia, FL (city) Miami-Dade County	7	38.89
Wallace, NC (town) Duplin County	605	15.59
Acacia Villas, FL (cdp) Palm Beach County	63	14.75
Magnolia, NC (town) Duplin County	113	12.03
Teachey, NC (town) Duplin County	43	11.44
Morris, NJ (town) Morris County	1,840	9.99
Rose Hill, NC (town) Duplin County	160	9.84
Broadview Park, FL (cdp) Broward County	603	8.46
Chelsea, MA (city) Suffolk County	2,938	8.35
Gatlinburg, TN (city) Sevier County	329	8.34
Kenner, LA (city) Jefferson Parish	5,556	8.33
Bonnetsville, NC (cdp) Sampson County	35	7.90
Woodridge, NY (village) Sullivan County	60	7.08
Hempstead, NY (village) Nassau County	3,758	6.97
South Fallsburg, NY (cdp) Sullivan County	200	6.97
Selma, NC (town) Johnston County	416	6.85
Terrytown, LA (cdp) Jefferson Parish	1,528	6.55
Rogers, NE (village) Colfax County	6	6.32
Pigeon Forge, TN (city) Sevier County	352	5.99
Lumpkin, GA (city) Stewart County	161	5.87
Miami, FL (city) Miami-Dade County	23,209	5.81
New Cassel, NY (cdp) Nassau County	812	5.78
Springfield, VA (cdp) Fairfax County	1,759	5.77
West Little River, FL (cdp) Miami-Dade County	1,902	5.48
Newburgh, NY (city) Orange County	1,545	5.35
Lakewood Gardens, FL (cdp) Palm Beach County	68	5.34
Amherst, CO (cdp) Phillips County	3	5.17
New Brunswick, NJ (city) Middlesex County	2,772	5.02
Herndon, VA (town) Fairfax County	1,159	4.98
Chandler, MN (city) Murray County	13	4.81
Lemington, VT (town) Essex County	5	4.81
Kenwood Estates, FL (cdp) Palm Beach County	61	4.75
Dover, NJ (town) Morris County	860	4.74
Seven Corners, VA (cdp) Fairfax County	438	4.73
Pine Manor, FL (cdp) Lee County	155	4.52
Amelia, LA (cdp) St. Mary Parish	111	4.51
Woodlawn, VA (cdp) Fairfax County	925	4.45
Gardere, LA (cdp) East Baton Rouge Parish	467	4.41
East Franklin, NJ (cdp) Somerset County	377	4.35
North Springfield, VA (cdp) Fairfax County	314	4.32
Gretna, LA (city) Jefferson Parish	762	4.30
Harvey, LA (cdp) Jefferson Parish	862	4.24
Metompkin, VA (cdp) Accomack County	23	4.17
Metairie, LA (cdp) Jefferson Parish	5,611	4.05
Union City, NJ (city) Hudson County	2,533	3.81
Huntington Station, NY (cdp) Suffolk County	1,260	3.81
Mendota, CA (city) Fresno County	416	3.78
Langley Park, MD (cdp) Prince George's County	706	3.76
Gray Court, SC (town) Laurens County	29	3.65
Pearsall, TX (city) Frio County	333	3.64
Alton, IN (town) Crawford County	2	3.64
St. Rose, LA (cdp) St. Charles Parish	291	3.58
Las Pilas, TX (cdp) Webb County	1	3.57
Groveton, VA (cdp) Fairfax County	511	3.50
Avon, CO (town) Eagle County	225	3.49
Greenevers, NC (town) Duplin County	22	3.47
Gladeview, FL (cdp) Miami-Dade County	397	3.44
Victory Gardens, NJ (borough) Morris County	52	3.42
Pine Air, FL (cdp) Palm Beach County	69	3.41
Brentwood, NY (cdp) Suffolk County	2,062	3.40
Timberlane, LA (cdp) Jefferson Parish	347	3.39
Page Park, FL (cdp) Lee County	17	3.31
Uniondale, NY (cdp) Nassau County	806	3.26
Stockton, MD (cdp) Worcester County	3	3.26
Central Islip, NY (cdp) Suffolk County	1,118	3.25
West Samoset, FL (cdp) Manatee County	180	3.22
Berea, SC (cdp) Greenville County	455	3.18
Oyster Bay, NY (cdp) Nassau County	212	3.16
Los Arcos, TX (cdp) Webb County	4	3.15
Conroe, TX (city) Montgomery County	1,766	3.14
Golden Gate, FL (cdp) Collier County	741	3.09
Doraville, GA (city) DeKalb County	256	3.07
Plainfield, NJ (city) Union County	1,493	3.00
Wyandanch, NY (cdp) Suffolk County	349	3.00
Pleasantville, NJ (city) Atlantic County	598	2.95
Estelle, LA (cdp) Jefferson Parish	477	2.91
Laceyville, PA (borough) Wyoming County	11	2.90
Pinewood, FL (cdp) Miami-Dade County	477	2.89
North Bay Shore, NY (cdp) Suffolk County	539	2.85
Liberty, NY (village) Sullivan County	125	2.85
Chandler, MI (township) Charlevoix County	7	2.82
Sterling, VA (cdp) Loudoun County	779	2.80
Marumsco, VA (cdp) Prince William County	973	2.78
Edgewater Park, NJ (township) Burlington County	246	2.77
Brownsville, FL (cdp) Miami-Dade County	423	2.76
Mildred, TX (town) Navarro County	10	2.72
Carrollton, GA (city) Carroll County	660	2.71
Opa-locka, FL (city) Miami-Dade County	413	2.71
Miller's Cove, TX (town) Titus County	4	2.68
Brush Creek, MN (township) Faribault County	6	2.67
Spencer, NC (town) Rowan County	87	2.66
Wadley, AL (town) Randolph County	20	2.66
Milan, MO (city) Sullivan County	52	2.65
Laguna Seca, TX (cdp) Hidalgo County	7	2.63
Watha, NC (town) Pender County	5	2.63
Dennis Acres, MO (village) Newton County	2	2.63
North Miami Beach, FL (city) Miami-Dade County	1,088	2.62
El Portal, FL (village) Miami-Dade County	61	2.62
Lake Worth, FL (city) Palm Beach County	906	2.60
Waukegan, IL (city) Lake County	2,311	2.59
Aldine, TX (cdp) Harris County	402	2.53
City View, SC (cdp) Greenville County	34	2.53
Bailey's Crossroads, VA (cdp) Fairfax County	594	2.51
Edmundson Acres, CA (cdp) Kern County	7	2.51
Smithfield, NC (town) Johnston County	274	2.50
Huntington, VA (cdp) Fairfax County	280	2.49
Delway, NC (cdp) Sampson County	5	2.46
Jefferson, LA (cdp) Jefferson Parish	274	2.45
Freistatt, MO (village) Lawrence County	4	2.45
North Amityville, NY (cdp) Suffolk County	436	2.44
Raymondville, TX (city) Willacy County	275	2.44
Hallwood, VA (town) Accomack County	5	2.43
Roosevelt, NY (cdp) Nassau County	394	2.42
Rangerville, TX (village) Cameron County	7	2.42
Stock Island, FL (cdp) Monroe County	94	2.40
Fallsburg, NY (town) Sullivan County	305	2.37
South Miami Heights, FL (cdp) Miami-Dade County	839	2.35
Bloxom, VA (town) Accomack County	9	2.33
West Miami, FL (city) Miami-Dade County	137	2.30
Loch Lomond, VA (cdp) Prince William County	85	2.30
Sevierville, TN (city) Sevier County	339	2.29
North Miami, FL (city) Miami-Dade County	1,342	2.28
Wheaton, MD (cdp) Montgomery County	1,101	2.28
Westview, FL (cdp) Miami-Dade County	220	2.28
Martinez Lake, AZ (cdp) Yuma County	18	2.26
University, FL (cdp) Hillsborough County	922	2.24
Chalmette, LA (cdp) St. Bernard Parish	376	2.24
Greenacres, FL (city) Palm Beach County	836	2.23
Limestone, MN (township) Lincoln County	3	2.21
Flemington, NJ (borough) Hunterdon County	101	2.20
Virginia Gardens, FL (village) Miami-Dade County	52	2.19
Atlantic City, NJ (city) Atlantic County	857	2.17
Leisure City, FL (cdp) Miami-Dade County	489	2.16
Clinton, NC (city) Sampson County	186	2.15
Troy, SC (town) Greenwood County	2	2.15
Palm Springs, FL (village) Palm Beach County	405	2.14
Sugarland Run, VA (cdp) Loudoun County	253	2.14
Palmetto Estates, FL (cdp) Miami-Dade County	288	2.13
Wilson's Mills, NC (town) Johnston County	48	2.11
Wolford, MN (township) Crow Wing County	8	2.11
Chamblee, GA (city) DeKalb County	208	2.10
Galax, VA (ind. city) Galax independent city	148	2.10
Wharton, NJ (borough) Morris County	137	2.10
Hybla Valley, VA (cdp) Fairfax County	331	2.09
Guttenberg, NJ (town) Hudson County	233	2.08
Vails Gate, NY (cdp) Orange County	70	2.08
Bridge City, LA (cdp) Jefferson Parish	157	2.04
Avondale, LA (cdp) Jefferson Parish	101	2.04
North Plainfield, NJ (borough) Somerset County	446	2.03
Gaithersburg, MD (city) Montgomery County	1,211	2.02

Please refer to the Explanation of Data in the front of the book for more detailed information.

Hispanic Origin

Central American: Honduran

Top 150 Places Sorted by Percent of Total Population

Based on places with total population of 7,500 or more

Place	Population	%
Morris, NJ (town) Morris County	1,840	9.99
Chelsea, MA (city) Suffolk County	2,938	8.35
Kenner, LA (city) Jefferson Parish	5,556	8.33
Hempstead, NY (village) Nassau County	3,758	6.97
Terrytown, LA (cdp) Jefferson Parish	1,528	6.55
Miami, FL (city) Miami-Dade County	23,209	5.81
New Cassel, NY (cdp) Nassau County	812	5.78
Springfield, VA (cdp) Fairfax County	1,759	5.77
West Little River, FL (cdp) Miami-Dade County	1,902	5.48
Newburgh, NY (city) Orange County	1,545	5.35
New Brunswick, NJ (city) Middlesex County	2,772	5.02
Herndon, VA (town) Fairfax County	1,159	4.98
Dover, NJ (town) Morris County	860	4.74
Seven Corners, VA (cdp) Fairfax County	438	4.73
Woodlawn, VA (cdp) Fairfax County	925	4.45
Gardere, LA (cdp) East Baton Rouge Parish	467	4.41
East Franklin, NJ (cdp) Somerset County	377	4.35
Gretna, LA (city) Jefferson Parish	762	4.30
Harvey, LA (cdp) Jefferson Parish	862	4.24
Metairie, LA (cdp) Jefferson Parish	5,611	4.05
Union City, NJ (city) Hudson County	2,533	3.81
Huntington Station, NY (cdp) Suffolk County	1,260	3.81
Mendota, CA (city) Fresno County	416	3.78
Langley Park, MD (cdp) Prince George's County	706	3.76
Pearsall, TX (city) Frio County	333	3.64
St. Rose, LA (cdp) St. Charles Parish	291	3.58
Groveton, VA (cdp) Fairfax County	511	3.50
Gladeview, FL (cdp) Miami-Dade County	397	3.44
Brentwood, NY (cdp) Suffolk County	2,062	3.40
Timberlane, LA (cdp) Jefferson Parish	347	3.39
Uniondale, NY (cdp) Nassau County	806	3.26
Central Islip, NY (cdp) Suffolk County	1,118	3.25
Berea, SC (cdp) Greenville County	455	3.18
Conroe, TX (city) Montgomery County	1,766	3.14
Golden Gate, FL (cdp) Collier County	741	3.09
Doraville, GA (city) DeKalb County	256	3.07
Plainfield, NJ (city) Union County	1,493	3.00
Wyandanch, NY (cdp) Suffolk County	349	3.00
Pleasantville, NJ (city) Atlantic County	598	2.95
Estelle, LA (cdp) Jefferson Parish	477	2.91
Pinewood, FL (cdp) Miami-Dade County	477	2.89
North Bay Shore, NY (cdp) Suffolk County	539	2.85
Sterling, VA (cdp) Loudoun County	779	2.80
Marumsco, VA (cdp) Prince William County	973	2.78
Edgewater Park, NJ (township) Burlington County	246	2.77
Brownsville, FL (cdp) Miami-Dade County	423	2.76
Carrollton, GA (city) Carroll County	660	2.71
Opa-locka, FL (city) Miami-Dade County	413	2.71
North Miami Beach, FL (city) Miami-Dade County	1,088	2.62
Lake Worth, FL (city) Palm Beach County	906	2.60
Waukegan, IL (city) Lake County	2,311	2.59
Aldine, TX (cdp) Harris County	402	2.53
Bailey's Crossroads, VA (cdp) Fairfax County	594	2.51
Smithfield, NC (town) Johnston County	274	2.50
Huntington, VA (cdp) Fairfax County	280	2.49
Jefferson, LA (cdp) Jefferson Parish	274	2.45
North Amityville, NY (cdp) Suffolk County	436	2.44
Raymondville, TX (city) Willacy County	275	2.44
Roosevelt, NY (cdp) Nassau County	394	2.42
Fallsburg, NY (town) Sullivan County	305	2.37
South Miami Heights, FL (cdp) Miami-Dade County	839	2.35
Sevierville, TN (city) Sevier County	339	2.29
North Miami, FL (city) Miami-Dade County	1,342	2.28
Wheaton, MD (cdp) Montgomery County	1,101	2.28
Westview, FL (cdp) Miami-Dade County	220	2.28
University, FL (cdp) Hillsborough County	922	2.24
Chalmette, LA (cdp) St. Bernard Parish	376	2.24
Greenacres, FL (city) Palm Beach County	836	2.23
Atlantic City, NJ (city) Atlantic County	857	2.17
Leisure City, FL (cdp) Miami-Dade County	489	2.16
Clinton, NC (city) Sampson County	186	2.15
Palm Springs, FL (village) Palm Beach County	405	2.14
Sugarland Run, VA (cdp) Loudoun County	253	2.14
Palmetto Estates, FL (cdp) Miami-Dade County	288	2.13
Chamblee, GA (city) DeKalb County	208	2.10
Hybla Valley, VA (cdp) Fairfax County	331	2.09
Guttenberg, NJ (town) Hudson County	233	2.08
Bridge City, LA (cdp) Jefferson Parish	157	2.04
North Plainfield, NJ (borough) Somerset County	446	2.03
Gaithersburg, MD (city) Montgomery County	1,211	2.02
Harrisonburg, VA (ind. city) Harrisonburg independent city	978	2.00
Plymouth, IN (city) Marshall County	199	1.98
Farmingdale, NY (village) Nassau County	161	1.97
West New York, NJ (town) Hudson County	970	1.95
Oak Ridge, FL (cdp) Orange County	443	1.95
Princeton, FL (cdp) Miami-Dade County	415	1.88
Lenoir, NC (city) Caldwell County	343	1.88
Elizabeth, NJ (city) Union County	2,338	1.87
Fountainebleau, FL (cdp) Miami-Dade County	1,117	1.87
West Park, FL (city) Broward County	265	1.87
Chillum, MD (cdp) Prince George's County	620	1.85
Hialeah Gardens, FL (city) Miami-Dade County	402	1.85
Riverhead, NY (cdp) Suffolk County	245	1.84
Freeport, NY (village) Nassau County	785	1.83
Sweetwater, FL (city) Miami-Dade County	247	1.83
Copiague, NY (cdp) Suffolk County	412	1.79
North Bergen, NJ (township) Hudson County	1,081	1.78
Norwalk, CT (city/town) Fairfield County	1,506	1.76
Manassas, VA (ind. city) Manassas independent city	657	1.74
Westbury, NY (village) Nassau County	263	1.74
Willmar, MN (city) Kandiyohi County	337	1.72
Lindenwold, NJ (borough) Camden County	302	1.71
Mount Rainier, MD (city) Prince George's County	137	1.70
Miami Beach, FL (city) Miami-Dade County	1,483	1.69
Richmond West, FL (cdp) Miami-Dade County	540	1.69
Bluffton, SC (town) Beaufort County	210	1.68
Hialeah, FL (city) Miami-Dade County	3,744	1.67
Bull Run, VA (cdp) Prince William County	249	1.66
Rose Hill, VA (cdp) Fairfax County	331	1.64
Adelphi, MD (cdp) Prince George's County	248	1.64
Silver Spring, MD (cdp) Montgomery County	1,166	1.63
Lincolnia, VA (cdp) Fairfax County	371	1.62
Westgate, FL (cdp) Palm Beach County	129	1.62
Vienna, VA (town) Fairfax County	253	1.61
Glenmont, MD (cdp) Montgomery County	218	1.61
Destrehan, LA (cdp) St. Charles Parish	186	1.61
Alexandria, VA (ind. city) Alexandria independent city	2,243	1.60
Country Club, FL (cdp) Miami-Dade County	748	1.59
Coral Terrace, FL (cdp) Miami-Dade County	388	1.59
Garden City, GA (city) Chatham County	138	1.57
Houston, TX (city) Harris County	32,807	1.56
Homestead, FL (city) Miami-Dade County	936	1.55
Aspen Hill, MD (cdp) Montgomery County	755	1.55
East Riverdale, MD (cdp) Prince George's County	238	1.53
Durham, NC (city) Durham County	3,451	1.51
West Falls Church, VA (cdp) Fairfax County	441	1.51
Sudley, VA (cdp) Prince William County	243	1.50
Annandale, VA (cdp) Fairfax County	611	1.49
Golden Glades, FL (cdp) Miami-Dade County	489	1.48
Wright, FL (cdp) Okaloosa County	343	1.48
Mount Kisco, NY (town/village) Westchester County	161	1.48
Naranja, FL (cdp) Miami-Dade County	123	1.48
Liberty, NY (town) Sullivan County	145	1.47
Boonton, NJ (town) Morris County	123	1.47
Salisbury, NC (city) Rowan County	488	1.45
Laplace, LA (cdp) St. John the Baptist Parish	427	1.43
Azalea Park, FL (cdp) Orange County	179	1.43
Woodmere, LA (cdp) Jefferson Parish	173	1.43
Yorkshire, VA (cdp) Prince William County	107	1.42
Goulds, FL (cdp) Miami-Dade County	142	1.41
Dale City, VA (cdp) Prince William County	925	1.40
Webster, TX (city) Harris County	146	1.40
North Kensington, MD (cdp) Montgomery County	133	1.40
Manassas Park, VA (ind. city) Manassas Park independent city	198	1.39
Glenvar Heights, FL (cdp) Miami-Dade County	233	1.38
North Lauderdale, FL (city) Broward County	560	1.37
Waggaman, LA (cdp) Jefferson Parish	137	1.37
Redland, MD (cdp) Montgomery County	235	1.36
Glen Cove, NY (city) Nassau County	364	1.35
New Orleans, LA (city) Orleans Parish	4,572	1.33

SECTION THREE

Please refer to the Explanation of Data in the front of the book for more detailed information.

Hispanic Origin

Central American: Nicaraguan

U.S. and 50 States Sorted by Population and Percent of Total Population

Place	Population	%
United States	**348,202**	**0.11**
Florida	135,143	0.72
California	100,790	0.27
Texas	19,817	0.08
New York	13,006	0.07
New Jersey	8,222	0.09
Maryland	8,196	0.14
Virginia	7,388	0.09
Louisiana	6,390	0.14
North Carolina	4,964	0.05
Georgia	4,787	0.05
Nevada	4,475	0.17
Illinois	3,078	0.02
Arizona	2,813	0.04
Pennsylvania	2,400	0.02
Washington	2,313	0.03
Massachusetts	1,722	0.03
Wisconsin	1,624	0.03
Connecticut	1,538	0.04
Indiana	1,431	0.02
Ohio	1,383	0.01
Colorado	1,364	0.03
Tennessee	1,339	0.02
South Carolina	1,303	0.03
Oregon	1,104	0.03
Utah	1,043	0.04
Minnesota	970	0.02
Michigan	870	0.01
District of Columbia	859	0.14
Missouri	843	0.01
Alabama	739	0.02
Arkansas	704	0.02
Mississippi	700	0.02
Kansas	537	0.02
Kentucky	526	0.01
New Mexico	493	0.02
Iowa	472	0.02
Oklahoma	470	0.01
Nebraska	347	0.02
Hawaii	336	0.02
Rhode Island	267	0.03
Delaware	225	0.03
Idaho	222	0.01
Alaska	176	0.02
New Hampshire	174	0.01
West Virginia	162	0.01
South Dakota	99	0.01
Montana	91	0.01
Maine	89	0.01
Wyoming	73	0.01
Vermont	66	0.01
North Dakota	59	0.01

Place	Population	%
Florida	135,143	0.72
California	100,790	0.27
Nevada	4,475	0.17
Maryland	8,196	0.14
Louisiana	6,390	0.14
District of Columbia	859	0.14
United States	**348,202**	**0.11**
New Jersey	8,222	0.09
Virginia	7,388	0.09
Texas	19,817	0.08
New York	13,006	0.07
North Carolina	4,964	0.05
Georgia	4,787	0.05
Arizona	2,813	0.04
Connecticut	1,538	0.04
Utah	1,043	0.04
Washington	2,313	0.03
Massachusetts	1,722	0.03
Wisconsin	1,624	0.03
Colorado	1,364	0.03
South Carolina	1,303	0.03
Oregon	1,104	0.03
Rhode Island	267	0.03
Delaware	225	0.03
Illinois	3,078	0.02
Pennsylvania	2,400	0.02
Indiana	1,431	0.02
Tennessee	1,339	0.02
Minnesota	970	0.02
Alabama	739	0.02
Arkansas	704	0.02
Mississippi	700	0.02
Kansas	537	0.02
New Mexico	493	0.02
Iowa	472	0.02
Nebraska	347	0.02
Hawaii	336	0.02
Alaska	176	0.02
Ohio	1,383	0.01
Michigan	870	0.01
Missouri	843	0.01
Kentucky	526	0.01
Oklahoma	470	0.01
Idaho	222	0.01
New Hampshire	174	0.01
West Virginia	162	0.01
South Dakota	99	0.01
Montana	91	0.01
Maine	89	0.01
Wyoming	73	0.01
Vermont	66	0.01
North Dakota	59	0.01

Please refer to the Explanation of Data in the front of the book for more detailed information.

Hispanic Origin

Central American: Nicaraguan

Top 150 Places Sorted by Population

Based on all places, regardless of total population

Place	Population	%
Miami, FL (city) Miami-Dade County	28,618	7.16
Los Angeles, CA (city) Los Angeles County	15,572	0.41
Hialeah, FL (city) Miami-Dade County	10,410	4.63
New York, NY (city) Kings County	9,346	0.11
San Francisco, CA (city) San Francisco County	7,604	0.94
Fountainebleau, FL (cdp) Miami-Dade County	6,738	11.27
Houston, TX (city) Harris County	4,226	0.20
Kendale Lakes, FL (cdp) Miami-Dade County	3,560	6.34
Tamiami, FL (cdp) Miami-Dade County	3,476	6.29
Sweetwater, FL (city) Miami-Dade County	3,102	22.98
San Jose, CA (city) Santa Clara County	2,917	0.31
Queens, NY (borough) Queens County	2,842	0.13
Daly City, CA (city) San Mateo County	2,764	2.73
Kendall, FL (cdp) Miami-Dade County	2,629	3.49
Brooklyn, NY (borough) Kings County	2,407	0.10
The Hammocks, FL (cdp) Miami-Dade County	2,391	4.69
Bronx, NY (borough) Bronx County	2,342	0.17
Kendall West, FL (cdp) Miami-Dade County	2,265	6.26
Miami Gardens, FL (city) Miami-Dade County	2,134	1.99
West Little River, FL (cdp) Miami-Dade County	2,112	6.09
Richmond West, FL (cdp) Miami-Dade County	2,039	6.38
Country Club, FL (cdp) Miami-Dade County	1,772	3.76
Hayward, CA (city) Alameda County	1,745	1.21
Miramar, FL (city) Broward County	1,691	1.39
South San Francisco, CA (city) San Mateo County	1,639	2.58
South Miami Heights, FL (cdp) Miami-Dade County	1,585	4.44
Manhattan, NY (borough) New York County	1,556	0.10
Metairie, LA (cdp) Jefferson Parish	1,462	1.06
Pembroke Pines, FL (city) Broward County	1,423	0.92
Homestead, FL (city) Miami-Dade County	1,354	2.24
Hialeah Gardens, FL (city) Miami-Dade County	1,321	6.08
Hollywood, FL (city) Broward County	1,321	0.94
Charlotte, NC (city) Mecklenburg County	1,320	0.18
Kenner, LA (city) Jefferson Parish	1,306	1.96
Antioch, CA (city) Contra Costa County	1,269	1.24
Cutler Bay, FL (town) Miami-Dade County	1,266	3.14
Chicago, IL (city) Cook County	1,239	0.05
Las Vegas, NV (city) Clark County	1,217	0.21
Richmond, CA (city) Contra Costa County	1,209	1.17
University Park, FL (cdp) Miami-Dade County	1,167	4.32
Oakland, CA (city) Alameda County	1,156	0.30
Fontana, CA (city) San Bernardino County	1,152	0.59
Downey, CA (city) Los Angeles County	1,092	0.98
Princeton, FL (cdp) Miami-Dade County	1,077	4.89
San Antonio, TX (city) Medina County	1,059	0.08
Austin, TX (city) Travis County	1,041	0.13
Westchester, FL (cdp) Miami-Dade County	1,013	3.39
Long Beach, CA (city) Los Angeles County	1,007	0.22
North Miami, FL (city) Miami-Dade County	999	1.70
South Gate, CA (city) Los Angeles County	983	1.04
New Orleans, LA (city) Orleans Parish	976	0.28
Miami Beach, FL (city) Miami-Dade County	912	1.04
San Mateo, CA (city) San Mateo County	910	0.94
Jacksonville, FL (city) Duval County	902	0.11
Sacramento, CA (city) Sacramento County	895	0.19
San Diego, CA (city) San Diego County	895	0.07
Phoenix, AZ (city) Maricopa County	888	0.06
Concord, CA (city) Contra Costa County	886	0.73
The Crossings, FL (cdp) Miami-Dade County	885	3.89
Camden, NJ (city) Camden County	880	1.14
Pittsburg, CA (city) Contra Costa County	879	1.39
Philadelphia, PA (city) Philadelphia County	874	0.06
Doral, FL (city) Miami-Dade County	871	1.91
Brownsville, FL (cdp) Miami-Dade County	867	5.66
Coral Terrace, FL (cdp) Miami-Dade County	861	3.53
Washington, DC (city) District of Columbia	859	0.14
San Bruno, CA (city) San Mateo County	824	2.00
Port Arthur, TX (city) Jefferson County	822	1.53
Dallas, TX (city) Dallas County	816	0.07
Stockton, CA (city) San Joaquin County	786	0.27
North Miami Beach, FL (city) Miami-Dade County	699	1.68
Indianapolis, IN (city) Marion County	668	0.08
Ontario, CA (city) San Bernardino County	658	0.40
Hempstead, NY (town) Nassau County	656	0.09
Coral Gables, FL (city) Miami-Dade County	651	1.39
Palmdale, CA (city) Los Angeles County	650	0.43
Fremont, CA (city) Alameda County	645	0.30
Vallejo, CA (city) Solano County	629	0.54
Pomona, CA (city) Los Angeles County	625	0.42
Country Walk, FL (cdp) Miami-Dade County	624	3.90
Arlington, VA (cdp) Arlington County	614	0.30
West Covina, CA (city) Los Angeles County	611	0.58
Silver Spring, MD (cdp) Montgomery County	610	0.85
Norwalk, CA (city) Los Angeles County	603	0.57
Riverside, CA (city) Riverside County	600	0.20
Rancho Cucamonga, CA (city) San Bernardino County	598	0.36
Key West, FL (city) Monroe County	585	2.37
Miami Lakes, FL (town) Miami-Dade County	574	1.95
Redwood City, CA (city) San Mateo County	565	0.74
Wheaton, MD (cdp) Montgomery County	561	1.16
Palmetto Estates, FL (cdp) Miami-Dade County	559	4.13
San Bernardino, CA (city) San Bernardino County	559	0.27
Gladeview, FL (cdp) Miami-Dade County	557	4.83
Hawthorne, CA (city) Los Angeles County	556	0.66
Sunset, FL (cdp) Miami-Dade County	549	3.35
Leisure City, FL (cdp) Miami-Dade County	547	2.41
Huntington Park, CA (city) Los Angeles County	546	0.94
Anaheim, CA (city) Orange County	543	0.16
Davie, FL (town) Broward County	542	0.59
Germantown, MD (cdp) Montgomery County	537	0.62
Port St. Lucie, FL (city) St. Lucie County	537	0.33
Tampa, FL (city) Hillsborough County	537	0.16
Yonkers, NY (city) Westchester County	534	0.27
Opa-locka, FL (city) Miami-Dade County	532	3.50
Golden Glades, FL (cdp) Miami-Dade County	528	1.59
Moreno Valley, CA (city) Riverside County	528	0.27
Jersey City, NJ (city) Hudson County	528	0.21
Glendale, CA (city) Los Angeles County	526	0.27
Paradise, NV (cdp) Clark County	520	0.23
Pacifica, CA (city) San Mateo County	519	1.39
San Pablo, CA (city) Contra Costa County	517	1.77
Three Lakes, FL (cdp) Miami-Dade County	513	3.41
Pinewood, FL (cdp) Miami-Dade County	510	3.09
Modesto, CA (city) Stanislaus County	510	0.25
Alhambra, CA (city) Los Angeles County	509	0.61
West Palm Beach, FL (city) Palm Beach County	501	0.50
Rialto, CA (city) San Bernardino County	482	0.49
Fairfield, CA (city) Solano County	478	0.45
Sunrise Manor, NV (cdp) Clark County	458	0.24
Glenvar Heights, FL (cdp) Miami-Dade County	454	2.69
Elk Grove, CA (city) Sacramento County	453	0.30
El Monte, CA (city) Los Angeles County	450	0.40
San Leandro, CA (city) Alameda County	444	0.52
Lancaster, CA (city) Los Angeles County	442	0.28
Westwood Lakes, FL (cdp) Miami-Dade County	440	3.72
Baldwin Park, CA (city) Los Angeles County	440	0.58
Tracy, CA (city) San Joaquin County	427	0.51
Lehigh Acres, FL (cdp) Lee County	424	0.49
Gaithersburg, MD (city) Montgomery County	415	0.69
Bell Gardens, CA (city) Los Angeles County	414	0.98
Cape Coral, FL (city) Lee County	410	0.27
Elizabeth, NJ (city) Union County	407	0.33
Burbank, CA (city) Los Angeles County	406	0.39
Milwaukee, WI (city) Milwaukee County	397	0.07
Boston, MA (city) Suffolk County	397	0.06
Miami Springs, FL (city) Miami-Dade County	395	2.86
Aspen Hill, MD (cdp) Montgomery County	384	0.79
Bell, CA (city) Los Angeles County	381	1.07
Orlando, FL (city) Orange County	377	0.16
North Las Vegas, NV (city) Clark County	375	0.17
Santa Ana, CA (city) Orange County	375	0.12
Nashville-Davidson, TN (metro govt) Davidson County	374	0.06
Olympia Heights, FL (cdp) Miami-Dade County	372	2.76
Fort Worth, TX (city) Tarrant County	372	0.05
Pinecrest, FL (village) Miami-Dade County	368	2.02
Santa Clara, CA (city) Santa Clara County	368	0.32
Alexandria, VA (ind. city) Alexandria independent city	368	0.26
Pasadena, CA (city) Los Angeles County	357	0.26
Fort Lauderdale, FL (city) Broward County	354	0.21
Cudahy, CA (city) Los Angeles County	349	1.47

Hispanic Origin

Central American: Nicaraguan

Top 150 Places Sorted by Percent of Total Population

Based on all places, regardless of total population

Place	Population	%
Sweetwater, FL (city) Miami-Dade County	3,102	22.98
Fountainebleau, FL (cdp) Miami-Dade County	6,738	11.27
Montezuma, CO (town) Summit County	5	7.69
Miami, FL (city) Miami-Dade County	28,618	7.16
De Lamere, ND (cdp) Sargent County	2	6.67
Andover, SD (town) Day County	6	6.59
Richmond West, FL (cdp) Miami-Dade County	2,039	6.38
Kendale Lakes, FL (cdp) Miami-Dade County	3,560	6.34
Tamiami, FL (cdp) Miami-Dade County	3,476	6.29
Kendall West, FL (cdp) Miami-Dade County	2,265	6.26
West Little River, FL (cdp) Miami-Dade County	2,112	6.09
Hialeah Gardens, FL (city) Miami-Dade County	1,321	6.08
Pekin, ND (city) Nelson County	4	5.71
Brownsville, FL (cdp) Miami-Dade County	867	5.66
Stock Island, FL (cdp) Monroe County	222	5.66
Templeville, MD (town) Queen Anne's County	7	5.07
Princeton, FL (cdp) Miami-Dade County	1,077	4.89
Medley, FL (town) Miami-Dade County	41	4.89
Gladeview, FL (cdp) Miami-Dade County	557	4.83
The Hammocks, FL (cdp) Miami-Dade County	2,391	4.69
Hialeah, FL (city) Miami-Dade County	10,410	4.63
Teterboro, NJ (borough) Bergen County	3	4.48
South Miami Heights, FL (cdp) Miami-Dade County	1,585	4.44
University Park, FL (cdp) Miami-Dade County	1,167	4.32
Rollingwood, CA (cdp) Contra Costa County	123	4.14
Palmetto Estates, FL (cdp) Miami-Dade County	559	4.13
Colma, CA (town) San Mateo County	72	4.02
Country Walk, FL (cdp) Miami-Dade County	624	3.90
The Crossings, FL (cdp) Miami-Dade County	885	3.89
Country Club, FL (cdp) Miami-Dade County	1,772	3.76
Westwood Lakes, FL (cdp) Miami-Dade County	440	3.72
Montalvin Manor, CA (cdp) Contra Costa County	104	3.62
Naranja, FL (cdp) Miami-Dade County	296	3.56
Coral Terrace, FL (cdp) Miami-Dade County	861	3.53
Opa-locka, FL (city) Miami-Dade County	532	3.50
Kendall, FL (cdp) Miami-Dade County	2,629	3.49
West Miami, FL (city) Miami-Dade County	208	3.49
Big Creek, CA (cdp) Fresno County	6	3.43
Three Lakes, FL (cdp) Miami-Dade County	513	3.41
Westchester, FL (cdp) Miami-Dade County	1,013	3.39
Sunset, FL (cdp) Miami-Dade County	549	3.35
Virginia Gardens, FL (village) Miami-Dade County	79	3.33
Richmond Heights, FL (cdp) Miami-Dade County	283	3.31
Westview, FL (cdp) Miami-Dade County	311	3.22
Goulds, FL (cdp) Miami-Dade County	323	3.20
Cutler Bay, FL (town) Miami-Dade County	1,266	3.14
Pinewood, FL (cdp) Miami-Dade County	510	3.09
Harrells, NC (town) Sampson County	6	2.97
Miami Springs, FL (city) Miami-Dade County	395	2.86
Olympia Heights, FL (cdp) Miami-Dade County	372	2.76
West Perrine, FL (cdp) Miami-Dade County	259	2.74
Daly City, CA (city) San Mateo County	2,764	2.73
Glenvar Heights, FL (cdp) Miami-Dade County	454	2.69
South San Francisco, CA (city) San Mateo County	1,639	2.58
Broadmoor, CA (cdp) San Mateo County	107	2.56
Leisure City, FL (cdp) Miami-Dade County	547	2.41
Key West, FL (city) Monroe County	585	2.37
Broadview Park, FL (cdp) Broward County	167	2.34
Darwin, CA (cdp) Inyo County	1	2.33
Glen Ridge, FL (town) Palm Beach County	5	2.28
Fisher Island, FL (cdp) Miami-Dade County	3	2.27
Monterey Park Tract, CA (cdp) Stanislaus County	3	2.26
Homestead, FL (city) Miami-Dade County	1,354	2.24
Acacia Villas, FL (cdp) Palm Beach County	9	2.11
Key Biscayne, FL (village) Miami-Dade County	251	2.03
Pinecrest, FL (village) Miami-Dade County	368	2.02
San Bruno, CA (city) San Mateo County	824	2.00
Miami Gardens, FL (city) Miami-Dade County	2,134	1.99
Kenner, LA (city) Jefferson Parish	1,306	1.96
Miami Lakes, FL (town) Miami-Dade County	574	1.95
Doral, FL (city) Miami-Dade County	871	1.91
Pine Air, FL (cdp) Palm Beach County	37	1.83
Tara Hills, CA (cdp) Contra Costa County	92	1.79
San Pablo, CA (city) Contra Costa County	517	1.77
El Portal, FL (village) Miami-Dade County	40	1.72

Place	Population	%
Bayview, CA (cdp) Contra Costa County	30	1.71
Lismore, MN (township) Nobles County	3	1.71
North Miami, FL (city) Miami-Dade County	999	1.70
Dustin Acres, CA (cdp) Kern County	11	1.69
North Miami Beach, FL (city) Miami-Dade County	699	1.68
South Miami, FL (city) Miami-Dade County	191	1.64
Golden Glades, FL (cdp) Miami-Dade County	528	1.59
Nord, CA (cdp) Butte County	5	1.56
Port Arthur, TX (city) Jefferson County	822	1.53
Miami Shores, FL (village) Miami-Dade County	161	1.53
Dawson, IA (city) Dallas County	2	1.53
Marathon, FL (city) Monroe County	125	1.51
Palm Springs North, FL (cdp) Miami-Dade County	79	1.50
Cloud Lake, FL (town) Palm Beach County	2	1.48
Cudahy, CA (city) Los Angeles County	349	1.47
Palmetto Bay, FL (village) Miami-Dade County	341	1.46
Oscar, MN (township) Otter Tail County	3	1.45
Voorhees, NJ (cdp) Somerset County	14	1.43
Kenwood Estates, FL (cdp) Palm Beach County	18	1.40
Miramar, FL (city) Broward County	1,691	1.39
Pittsburg, CA (city) Contra Costa County	879	1.39
Coral Gables, FL (city) Miami-Dade County	651	1.39
Pacifica, CA (city) San Mateo County	519	1.39
Scott, MN (township) Stevens County	2	1.39
North Richmond, CA (cdp) Contra Costa County	51	1.37
Ives Estates, FL (cdp) Miami-Dade County	266	1.36
Piltzville, MT (cdp) Missoula County	5	1.27
Antioch, CA (city) Contra Costa County	1,269	1.24
Volta, CA (cdp) Merced County	3	1.22
Hayward, CA (city) Alameda County	1,745	1.21
Bluffview, WI (cdp) Sauk County	9	1.21
Westgate, FL (cdp) Palm Beach County	96	1.20
Ojus, FL (cdp) Miami-Dade County	215	1.19
West Park, FL (city) Broward County	169	1.19
Richmond, CA (city) Contra Costa County	1,209	1.17
Wheaton, MD (cdp) Montgomery County	561	1.16
Camden, NJ (city) Camden County	880	1.14
El Sobrante, CA (cdp) Contra Costa County	144	1.14
Ardentown, DE (village) New Castle County	3	1.14
Irwindale, CA (city) Los Angeles County	16	1.13
Bonnetsville, NC (cdp) Sampson County	5	1.13
Altha, FL (town) Calhoun County	6	1.12
Plantation Mobile Home Park, FL (cdp) Palm Beach County	14	1.11
Birmingham, PA (borough) Huntingdon County	1	1.11
Orrum, NC (town) Robeson County	1	1.10
Langley Park, MD (cdp) Prince George's County	204	1.09
Glenmont, MD (cdp) Montgomery County	148	1.09
Canal Point, FL (cdp) Palm Beach County	4	1.09
Biscayne Park, FL (village) Miami-Dade County	33	1.08
Bell, CA (city) Los Angeles County	381	1.07
Macdona, TX (cdp) Bexar County	6	1.07
Metairie, LA (cdp) Jefferson Parish	1,462	1.06
South Gate, CA (city) Los Angeles County	983	1.04
Miami Beach, FL (city) Miami-Dade County	912	1.04
Pinole, CA (city) Contra Costa County	189	1.03
Turkey, NC (town) Sampson County	3	1.03
Terrytown, LA (cdp) Jefferson Parish	234	1.00
Florida City, FL (city) Miami-Dade County	113	1.00
Ashland, CA (cdp) Alameda County	218	0.99
Downey, CA (city) Los Angeles County	1,092	0.98
Bell Gardens, CA (city) Los Angeles County	414	0.98
Millbrae, CA (city) San Mateo County	211	0.98
Morton, MS (city) Scott County	34	0.98
Quiogue, NY (cdp) Suffolk County	8	0.98
Montura, FL (cdp) Hendry County	32	0.97
Maywood, CA (city) Los Angeles County	263	0.96
Vincent, CA (cdp) Los Angeles County	151	0.95
North Bay Village, FL (city) Miami-Dade County	68	0.95
Kensington, MD (town) Montgomery County	21	0.95
San Francisco, CA (city) San Francisco County	7,604	0.94
Hollywood, FL (city) Broward County	1,321	0.94
San Mateo, CA (city) San Mateo County	910	0.94
Huntington Park, CA (city) Los Angeles County	546	0.94
Pennsauken, NJ (township) Camden County	336	0.94
Patterson Heights, PA (borough) Beaver County	6	0.94

Please refer to the Explanation of Data in the front of the book for more detailed information.

Hispanic Origin

Central American: Nicaraguan

Top 150 Places Sorted by Percent of Total Population

Based on places with total population of 7,500 or more

Place	Population	%
Sweetwater, FL (city) Miami-Dade County	3,102	22.98
Fountainebleau, FL (cdp) Miami-Dade County	6,738	11.27
Miami, FL (city) Miami-Dade County	28,618	7.16
Richmond West, FL (cdp) Miami-Dade County	2,039	6.38
Kendale Lakes, FL (cdp) Miami-Dade County	3,560	6.34
Tamiami, FL (cdp) Miami-Dade County	3,476	6.29
Kendall West, FL (cdp) Miami-Dade County	2,265	6.26
West Little River, FL (cdp) Miami-Dade County	2,112	6.09
Hialeah Gardens, FL (city) Miami-Dade County	1,321	6.08
Brownsville, FL (cdp) Miami-Dade County	867	5.66
Princeton, FL (cdp) Miami-Dade County	1,077	4.89
Gladeview, FL (cdp) Miami-Dade County	557	4.83
The Hammocks, FL (cdp) Miami-Dade County	2,391	4.69
Hialeah, FL (city) Miami-Dade County	10,410	4.63
South Miami Heights, FL (cdp) Miami-Dade County	1,585	4.44
University Park, FL (cdp) Miami-Dade County	1,167	4.32
Palmetto Estates, FL (cdp) Miami-Dade County	559	4.13
Country Walk, FL (cdp) Miami-Dade County	624	3.90
The Crossings, FL (cdp) Miami-Dade County	885	3.89
Country Club, FL (cdp) Miami-Dade County	1,772	3.76
Westwood Lakes, FL (cdp) Miami-Dade County	440	3.72
Naranja, FL (cdp) Miami-Dade County	296	3.56
Coral Terrace, FL (cdp) Miami-Dade County	861	3.53
Opa-locka, FL (city) Miami-Dade County	532	3.50
Kendall, FL (cdp) Miami-Dade County	2,629	3.49
Three Lakes, FL (cdp) Miami-Dade County	513	3.41
Westchester, FL (cdp) Miami-Dade County	1,013	3.39
Sunset, FL (cdp) Miami-Dade County	549	3.35
Richmond Heights, FL (cdp) Miami-Dade County	283	3.31
Westview, FL (cdp) Miami-Dade County	311	3.22
Goulds, FL (cdp) Miami-Dade County	323	3.20
Cutler Bay, FL (town) Miami-Dade County	1,266	3.14
Pinewood, FL (cdp) Miami-Dade County	510	3.09
Miami Springs, FL (city) Miami-Dade County	395	2.86
Olympia Heights, FL (cdp) Miami-Dade County	372	2.76
West Perrine, FL (cdp) Miami-Dade County	259	2.74
Daly City, CA (city) San Mateo County	2,764	2.73
Glenvar Heights, FL (cdp) Miami-Dade County	454	2.69
South San Francisco, CA (city) San Mateo County	1,639	2.58
Leisure City, FL (cdp) Miami-Dade County	547	2.41
Key West, FL (city) Monroe County	585	2.37
Homestead, FL (city) Miami-Dade County	1,354	2.24
Key Biscayne, FL (village) Miami-Dade County	251	2.03
Pinecrest, FL (village) Miami-Dade County	368	2.02
San Bruno, CA (city) San Mateo County	824	2.00
Miami Gardens, FL (city) Miami-Dade County	2,134	1.99
Kenner, LA (city) Jefferson Parish	1,306	1.96
Miami Lakes, FL (town) Miami-Dade County	574	1.95
Doral, FL (city) Miami-Dade County	871	1.91
San Pablo, CA (city) Contra Costa County	517	1.77
North Miami, FL (city) Miami-Dade County	999	1.70
North Miami Beach, FL (city) Miami-Dade County	699	1.68
South Miami, FL (city) Miami-Dade County	191	1.64
Golden Glades, FL (cdp) Miami-Dade County	528	1.59
Port Arthur, TX (city) Jefferson County	822	1.53
Miami Shores, FL (village) Miami-Dade County	161	1.53
Marathon, FL (city) Monroe County	125	1.51
Cudahy, CA (city) Los Angeles County	349	1.47
Palmetto Bay, FL (village) Miami-Dade County	341	1.46
Miramar, FL (city) Broward County	1,691	1.39
Pittsburg, CA (city) Contra Costa County	879	1.39
Coral Gables, FL (city) Miami-Dade County	651	1.39
Pacifica, CA (city) San Mateo County	519	1.39
Ives Estates, FL (cdp) Miami-Dade County	266	1.36
Antioch, CA (city) Contra Costa County	1,269	1.24
Hayward, CA (city) Alameda County	1,745	1.21
Westgate, FL (cdp) Palm Beach County	96	1.20
Ojus, FL (cdp) Miami-Dade County	215	1.19
West Park, FL (city) Broward County	169	1.19
Richmond, CA (city) Contra Costa County	1,209	1.17
Wheaton, MD (cdp) Montgomery County	561	1.16
Camden, NJ (city) Camden County	880	1.14
El Sobrante, CA (cdp) Contra Costa County	144	1.14
Langley Park, MD (cdp) Prince George's County	204	1.09
Glenmont, MD (cdp) Montgomery County	148	1.09

Place	Population	%
Bell, CA (city) Los Angeles County	381	1.07
Metairie, LA (cdp) Jefferson Parish	1,462	1.06
South Gate, CA (city) Los Angeles County	983	1.04
Miami Beach, FL (city) Miami-Dade County	912	1.04
Pinole, CA (city) Contra Costa County	189	1.03
Terrytown, LA (cdp) Jefferson Parish	234	1.00
Florida City, FL (city) Miami-Dade County	113	1.00
Ashland, CA (cdp) Alameda County	218	0.99
Downey, CA (city) Los Angeles County	1,092	0.98
Bell Gardens, CA (city) Los Angeles County	414	0.98
Millbrae, CA (city) San Mateo County	211	0.98
Maywood, CA (city) Los Angeles County	263	0.96
Vincent, CA (cdp) Los Angeles County	151	0.95
San Francisco, CA (city) San Francisco County	7,604	0.94
Hollywood, FL (city) Broward County	1,321	0.94
San Mateo, CA (city) San Mateo County	910	0.94
Huntington Park, CA (city) Los Angeles County	546	0.94
Pennsauken, NJ (township) Camden County	336	0.94
San Lorenzo, CA (cdp) Alameda County	219	0.93
Pembroke Pines, FL (city) Broward County	1,423	0.92
Palm Springs, FL (village) Palm Beach County	171	0.90
Rodeo, CA (cdp) Contra Costa County	78	0.90
Bay Point, CA (cdp) Contra Costa County	186	0.87
Asbury Park, NJ (city) Monmouth County	138	0.86
Adelphi, MD (cdp) Prince George's County	129	0.86
Cherryland, CA (cdp) Alameda County	126	0.86
Silver Spring, MD (cdp) Montgomery County	610	0.85
Bailey's Crossroads, VA (cdp) Fairfax County	197	0.83
Montgomery Village, MD (cdp) Montgomery County	263	0.82
Charter Oak, CA (cdp) Los Angeles County	76	0.82
Lawndale, CA (city) Los Angeles County	264	0.81
Inwood, NY (cdp) Nassau County	79	0.81
Aspen Hill, MD (cdp) Montgomery County	384	0.79
Greenacres, FL (city) Palm Beach County	294	0.78
Chillum, MD (cdp) Prince George's County	261	0.78
North Kensington, MD (cdp) Montgomery County	74	0.78
Hercules, CA (city) Contra Costa County	182	0.76
Belle Glade, FL (city) Palm Beach County	132	0.76
Redwood City, CA (city) San Mateo County	565	0.74
Concord, CA (city) Contra Costa County	886	0.73
Marumsco, VA (cdp) Prince William County	255	0.73
Hallandale Beach, FL (city) Broward County	265	0.71
Woodlawn, VA (cdp) Fairfax County	145	0.70
Fairview, CA (cdp) Alameda County	70	0.70
Gaithersburg, MD (city) Montgomery County	415	0.69
Mount Rainier, MD (city) Prince George's County	55	0.68
Santa Fe Springs, CA (city) Los Angeles County	109	0.67
Hawthorne, CA (city) Los Angeles County	556	0.66
East Riverdale, MD (cdp) Prince George's County	103	0.66
Walnut Park, CA (cdp) Los Angeles County	103	0.65
Destrehan, LA (cdp) St. Charles Parish	75	0.65
Annandale, VA (cdp) Fairfax County	262	0.64
Burlingame, CA (city) San Mateo County	184	0.64
Lennox, CA (cdp) Los Angeles County	145	0.64
Beltsville, MD (cdp) Prince George's County	107	0.64
Jefferson, LA (cdp) Jefferson Parish	72	0.64
Dayton, NV (cdp) Lyon County	57	0.64
La Puente, CA (city) Los Angeles County	250	0.63
Calverton, MD (cdp) Montgomery County	112	0.63
Germantown, MD (cdp) Montgomery County	537	0.62
West Falls Church, VA (cdp) Fairfax County	180	0.62
Alhambra, CA (city) Los Angeles County	509	0.61
West Puente Valley, CA (cdp) Los Angeles County	139	0.61
Hyattsville, MD (city) Prince George's County	107	0.61
Lincolnia, VA (cdp) Fairfax County	138	0.60
White Oak, MD (cdp) Montgomery County	104	0.60
Fontana, CA (city) San Bernardino County	1,152	0.59
Davie, FL (town) Broward County	542	0.59
Carrollton, GA (city) Carroll County	143	0.59
Haines City, FL (city) Polk County	121	0.59
West Covina, CA (city) Los Angeles County	611	0.58
Baldwin Park, CA (city) Los Angeles County	440	0.58
Carson City, NV (ind. city) Carson City County	320	0.58
North Lauderdale, FL (city) Broward County	236	0.58
East Franklin, NJ (cdp) Somerset County	50	0.58

Hispanic Origin

Central American: Panamanian

U.S. and 50 States Sorted by Population and Percent of Total Population

Place	Population	%
United States	**165,456**	**0.05**
Florida	28,741	0.15
New York	28,200	0.15
California	17,768	0.05
Texas	13,994	0.06
Georgia	8,678	0.09
Virginia	7,180	0.09
North Carolina	5,708	0.06
New Jersey	5,431	0.06
Maryland	5,341	0.09
Pennsylvania	3,234	0.03
Washington	2,939	0.04
Illinois	2,843	0.02
Massachusetts	2,436	0.04
Colorado	2,414	0.05
Arizona	2,251	0.04
South Carolina	2,104	0.05
Ohio	2,055	0.02
Tennessee	1,915	0.03
Nevada	1,615	0.06
Alabama	1,450	0.03
Louisiana	1,434	0.03
Michigan	1,359	0.01
Missouri	1,349	0.02
Connecticut	1,304	0.04
Indiana	1,218	0.02
Oklahoma	1,122	0.03
Kentucky	1,019	0.02
Minnesota	906	0.02
Kansas	888	0.03
Wisconsin	822	0.01
District of Columbia	742	0.12
Oregon	725	0.02
Mississippi	670	0.02
New Mexico	625	0.03
Utah	531	0.02
Hawaii	527	0.04
Delaware	501	0.06
Arkansas	485	0.02
Alaska	446	0.06
Iowa	413	0.01
Nebraska	398	0.02
Rhode Island	359	0.03
West Virginia	261	0.01
Idaho	223	0.01
New Hampshire	214	0.02
Maine	141	0.01
Montana	131	0.01
North Dakota	100	0.01
Vermont	91	0.01
Wyoming	81	0.01
South Dakota	74	0.01

Place	Population	%
Florida	28,741	0.15
New York	28,200	0.15
District of Columbia	742	0.12
Georgia	8,678	0.09
Virginia	7,180	0.09
Maryland	5,341	0.09
Texas	13,994	0.06
North Carolina	5,708	0.06
New Jersey	5,431	0.06
Nevada	1,615	0.06
Delaware	501	0.06
Alaska	446	0.06
United States	**165,456**	**0.05**
California	17,768	0.05
Colorado	2,414	0.05
South Carolina	2,104	0.05
Washington	2,939	0.04
Massachusetts	2,436	0.04
Arizona	2,251	0.04
Connecticut	1,304	0.04
Hawaii	527	0.04
Pennsylvania	3,234	0.03
Tennessee	1,915	0.03
Alabama	1,450	0.03
Louisiana	1,434	0.03
Oklahoma	1,122	0.03
Kansas	888	0.03
New Mexico	625	0.03
Rhode Island	359	0.03
Illinois	2,843	0.02
Ohio	2,055	0.02
Missouri	1,349	0.02
Indiana	1,218	0.02
Kentucky	1,019	0.02
Minnesota	906	0.02
Oregon	725	0.02
Mississippi	670	0.02
Utah	531	0.02
Arkansas	485	0.02
Nebraska	398	0.02
New Hampshire	214	0.02
Michigan	1,359	0.01
Wisconsin	822	0.01
Iowa	413	0.01
West Virginia	261	0.01
Idaho	223	0.01
Maine	141	0.01
Montana	131	0.01
North Dakota	100	0.01
Vermont	91	0.01
Wyoming	81	0.01
South Dakota	74	0.01

Please refer to the Explanation of Data in the front of the book for more detailed information.

Hispanic Origin

Central American: Panamanian

Top 150 Places Sorted by Population

Based on all places, regardless of total population

Place	Population	%
New York, NY (city) Kings County	22,353	0.27
Brooklyn, NY (borough) Kings County	13,681	0.55
Queens, NY (borough) Queens County	3,977	0.18
Bronx, NY (borough) Bronx County	2,372	0.17
Los Angeles, CA (city) Los Angeles County	2,131	0.06
Manhattan, NY (borough) New York County	1,716	0.11
San Antonio, TX (city) Medina County	1,602	0.12
Jacksonville, FL (city) Duval County	1,165	0.14
Hempstead, NY (town) Nassau County	1,163	0.15
Fayetteville, NC (city) Cumberland County	1,154	0.58
Miami, FL (city) Miami-Dade County	1,113	0.28
Houston, TX (city) Harris County	1,076	0.05
San Diego, CA (city) San Diego County	1,018	0.08
Killeen, TX (city) Bell County	998	0.78
Chicago, IL (city) Cook County	883	0.03
Washington, DC (city) District of Columbia	742	0.12
Boston, MA (city) Suffolk County	737	0.12
Philadelphia, PA (city) Philadelphia County	737	0.05
Virginia Beach, VA (ind. city) Virginia Beach independent city	702	0.16
Miramar, FL (city) Broward County	700	0.57
Columbus, GA (city) Muscogee County	696	0.37
Pembroke Pines, FL (city) Broward County	676	0.44
Tampa, FL (city) Hillsborough County	656	0.20
Colorado Springs, CO (city) El Paso County	642	0.15
Newport News, VA (ind. city) Newport News independent city	615	0.34
Charlotte, NC (city) Mecklenburg County	608	0.08
Staten Island, NY (borough) Richmond County	607	0.13
Austin, TX (city) Travis County	607	0.08
Orlando, FL (city) Orange County	596	0.25
Clarksville, TN (city) Montgomery County	588	0.44
El Paso, TX (city) El Paso County	551	0.08
Islip, NY (town) Suffolk County	466	0.14
Dallas, TX (city) Dallas County	458	0.04
Phoenix, AZ (city) Maricopa County	444	0.03
Fort Worth, TX (city) Tarrant County	419	0.06
San Francisco, CA (city) San Francisco County	399	0.05
Hollywood, FL (city) Broward County	398	0.28
Hialeah, FL (city) Miami-Dade County	391	0.17
Augusta-Richmond County, GA (cons. govt) Richmond County	389	0.20
Doral, FL (city) Miami-Dade County	387	0.85
Jersey City, NJ (city) Hudson County	384	0.16
Atlanta, GA (city) Fulton County	376	0.09
San Jose, CA (city) Santa Clara County	371	0.04
Las Vegas, NV (city) Clark County	367	0.06
Miami Gardens, FL (city) Miami-Dade County	361	0.34
Kendall, FL (cdp) Miami-Dade County	336	0.45
Norfolk, VA (ind. city) Norfolk independent city	330	0.14
Sacramento, CA (city) Sacramento County	325	0.07
Aurora, CO (city) Arapahoe County	321	0.10
Hampton, VA (ind. city) Hampton independent city	319	0.23
Tucson, AZ (city) Pima County	319	0.06
Raleigh, NC (city) Wake County	313	0.08
Long Beach, CA (city) Los Angeles County	313	0.07
The Hammocks, FL (cdp) Miami-Dade County	310	0.61
Albuquerque, NM (city) Bernalillo County	306	0.06
Babylon, NY (town) Suffolk County	305	0.14
Oakland, CA (city) Alameda County	301	0.08
Brandon, FL (cdp) Hillsborough County	294	0.28
Columbus, OH (city) Franklin County	294	0.04
Brookhaven, NY (town) Suffolk County	291	0.06
Coral Springs, FL (city) Broward County	290	0.24
Indianapolis, IN (city) Marion County	274	0.03
Fountainebleau, FL (cdp) Miami-Dade County	272	0.46
Baltimore, MD (city) Baltimore city County	269	0.04
Chesapeake, VA (ind. city) Chesapeake independent city	267	0.12
Riverview, FL (cdp) Hillsborough County	264	0.37
Port St. Lucie, FL (city) St. Lucie County	263	0.16
Tacoma, WA (city) Pierce County	263	0.13
Tallahassee, FL (city) Leon County	255	0.14
Anchorage, AK (municipality) Anchorage Municipality	254	0.09
Country Club, FL (cdp) Miami-Dade County	249	0.53
Louisville-Jefferson County, KY (metro govt) Jefferson County	246	0.04
Sunrise, FL (city) Broward County	244	0.29
North Las Vegas, NV (city) Clark County	244	0.11
Lawton, OK (city) Comanche County	243	0.25
Miami Beach, FL (city) Miami-Dade County	240	0.27
Arlington, TX (city) Tarrant County	240	0.07
Palm Bay, FL (city) Brevard County	237	0.23
Davie, FL (town) Broward County	231	0.25
Seattle, WA (city) King County	231	0.04
Alafaya, FL (cdp) Orange County	230	0.29
Hinesville, GA (city) Liberty County	229	0.68
Oklahoma City, OK (city) Oklahoma County	228	0.04
St. Petersburg, FL (city) Pinellas County	221	0.09
Newark, NJ (city) Essex County	220	0.08
Arlington, VA (cdp) Arlington County	217	0.10
Tamiami, FL (cdp) Miami-Dade County	216	0.39
Denver, CO (city) Denver County	216	0.04
Town 'n' Country, FL (cdp) Hillsborough County	214	0.27
Deltona, FL (city) Volusia County	213	0.25
Nashville-Davidson, TN (metro govt) Davidson County	212	0.04
Poinciana, FL (cdp) Osceola County	208	0.39
Richmond West, FL (cdp) Miami-Dade County	207	0.65
Alexandria, VA (ind. city) Alexandria independent city	203	0.15
Chula Vista, CA (city) San Diego County	203	0.08
Kendale Lakes, FL (cdp) Miami-Dade County	201	0.36
Homestead, FL (city) Miami-Dade County	200	0.33
Fort Lauderdale, FL (city) Broward County	198	0.12
Greensboro, NC (city) Guilford County	191	0.07
Cutler Bay, FL (town) Miami-Dade County	187	0.46
Tamarac, FL (city) Broward County	186	0.31
Moreno Valley, CA (city) Riverside County	186	0.10
Harker Heights, TX (city) Bell County	185	0.69
Willingboro, NJ (township) Burlington County	185	0.58
Dale City, VA (cdp) Prince William County	185	0.28
Yonkers, NY (city) Westchester County	185	0.09
Fontana, CA (city) San Bernardino County	179	0.09
Plantation, FL (city) Broward County	176	0.21
Elk Grove, CA (city) Sacramento County	175	0.11
Oceanside, CA (city) San Diego County	175	0.10
Henderson, NV (city) Clark County	171	0.07
Pasadena, CA (city) Los Angeles County	170	0.12
Lancaster, CA (city) Los Angeles County	170	0.11
Lakewood, WA (city) Pierce County	169	0.29
Providence, RI (city) Providence County	169	0.09
Kissimmee, FL (city) Osceola County	167	0.28
Savannah, GA (city) Chatham County	166	0.12
Gainesville, FL (city) Alachua County	165	0.13
New Orleans, LA (city) Orleans Parish	165	0.05
Germantown, MD (cdp) Montgomery County	163	0.19
Kendall West, FL (cdp) Miami-Dade County	162	0.45
Huntsville, AL (city) Madison County	159	0.09
Durham, NC (city) Durham County	159	0.07
South Miami Heights, FL (cdp) Miami-Dade County	158	0.44
Copperas Cove, TX (city) Coryell County	157	0.49
Springfield, MA (city) Hampden County	157	0.10
Pemberton, NJ (township) Burlington County	156	0.56
Sanford, FL (city) Seminole County	154	0.29
North Miami, FL (city) Miami-Dade County	154	0.26
Columbia, MD (cdp) Howard County	153	0.15
Plano, TX (city) Collin County	153	0.06
San Bernardino, CA (city) San Bernardino County	152	0.07
Coral Gables, FL (city) Miami-Dade County	151	0.32
Silver Spring, MD (cdp) Montgomery County	151	0.21
Milwaukee, WI (city) Milwaukee County	150	0.03
Freeport, NY (village) Nassau County	149	0.35
Brentwood, NY (cdp) Suffolk County	148	0.24
Paradise, NV (cdp) Clark County	147	0.07
Memphis, TN (city) Shelby County	147	0.02
Sierra Vista, AZ (city) Cochise County	145	0.33
Riverside, CA (city) Riverside County	144	0.05
Elmont, NY (cdp) Nassau County	143	0.43
Allentown, PA (city) Lehigh County	143	0.12
Sunrise Manor, NV (cdp) Clark County	142	0.07
Spring Hill, FL (cdp) Hernando County	139	0.14
Hempstead, NY (village) Nassau County	138	0.26
Weston, FL (city) Broward County	137	0.21
Portland, OR (city) Multnomah County	137	0.02
Melbourne, FL (city) Brevard County	136	0.18
Fountain, CO (city) El Paso County	134	0.52

SECTION THREE

Please refer to the Explanation of Data in the front of the book for more detailed information.

Hispanic Origin

Central American: Panamanian

Top 150 Places Sorted by Percent of Total Population

Based on all places, regardless of total population

Place	Population	%
Indian Creek, FL (village) Miami-Dade County	4	4.65
Haysville, PA (borough) Allegheny County	2	2.86
Fenwood, WI (village) Marathon County	4	2.63
Sidney, IN (town) Kosciusko County	2	2.41
Middlebrook, VA (cdp) Augusta County	5	2.35
Grattan, MN (township) Itasca County	1	2.27
Cascadia, OR (cdp) Linn County	3	2.04
North Robinson, OH (village) Crawford County	4	1.95
Lisbon, FL (cdp) Lake County	5	1.92
Vernon, CA (city) Los Angeles County	2	1.79
Twin Lakes, CO (cdp) Lake County	3	1.75
Wilson, OH (village) Monroe County	2	1.60
Hillcrest Heights, FL (town) Polk County	4	1.57
Chunky, MS (town) Newton County	5	1.53
Newton Hamilton, PA (borough) Mifflin County	3	1.46
Middleburg, MD (cdp) Washington County	1	1.43
Pemberton Heights, NJ (cdp) Burlington County	34	1.40
Springdale, WA (town) Stevens County	4	1.40
Victor, CA (cdp) San Joaquin County	4	1.37
Hanging Rock, OH (village) Lawrence County	3	1.36
Ormsby, MN (city) Watonwan County	1	1.33
Toco, TX (city) Lamar County	1	1.33
Ferndale, FL (cdp) Lake County	6	1.27
Barnhill, OH (village) Tuscarawas County	5	1.26
Belgium, MN (township) Polk County	1	1.23
Anderson, AK (city) Denali Borough	3	1.22
Kapowsin, WA (cdp) Pierce County	4	1.20
Shipman, VA (cdp) Nelson County	6	1.18
Santee, NE (village) Knox County	4	1.16
Falcon, NC (town) Cumberland County	3	1.16
Minneota, MN (township) Jackson County	3	1.16
Mono City, CA (cdp) Mono County	2	1.16
Webster, IA (city) Keokuk County	1	1.14
Gruver, IA (city) Emmet County	1	1.06
Stoutland, MO (city) Camden County	2	1.04
Cedar Crest, PA (cdp) Mifflin County	2	1.03
Lincolnville, KS (city) Marion County	2	0.99
St. Anthony, IA (city) Marshall County	1	0.98
Groton Long Point, CT (borough) New London County	5	0.97
Lakeview, NY (cdp) Nassau County	53	0.94
Greenleaf, KS (city) Washington County	3	0.91
Moose Lake, MN (township) Cass County	1	0.90
Rockfish, NC (cdp) Hoke County	29	0.88
Northampton, NY (cdp) Suffolk County	5	0.88
Wrightstown, NJ (borough) Burlington County	7	0.87
Seltzer, PA (cdp) Schuylkill County	3	0.86
Doral, FL (city) Miami-Dade County	387	0.85
Osino, NV (cdp) Elko County	6	0.85
Reed, PA (township) Dauphin County	2	0.84
White Mesa, UT (cdp) San Juan County	2	0.83
Whiteash, IL (village) Williamson County	2	0.83
Miramiguoa Park, MO (village) Franklin County	1	0.83
New River, VA (cdp) Pulaski County	2	0.82
Indian Springs, NV (cdp) Clark County	8	0.81
Evans Mills, NY (village) Jefferson County	5	0.81
Chestnut, IL (cdp) Logan County	2	0.81
Westwood, KY (city) Jefferson County	5	0.79
Parc, NY (cdp) Clinton County	2	0.79
Killeen, TX (city) Bell County	998	0.78
Palm Shores, FL (town) Brevard County	7	0.78
Hulett, WY (town) Crook County	3	0.78
Hagarville, AR (cdp) Johnson County	1	0.78
Saddle Butte, MT (cdp) Hill County	1	0.78
Pinckard, AL (town) Dale County	5	0.77
Huachuca City, AZ (town) Cochise County	14	0.76
Aquadale, NC (cdp) Stanly County	3	0.76
Ormsby, MN (city) Watonwan County	1	0.76
Walthourville, GA (city) Liberty County	31	0.75
Wintersburg, AZ (cdp) Maricopa County	1	0.74
Naranja, FL (cdp) Miami-Dade County	58	0.70
Cochiti Lake, NM (cdp) Sandoval County	4	0.70
Evant, TX (town) Coryell County	3	0.70
Harker Heights, TX (city) Bell County	185	0.69
Poquonock Bridge, CT (cdp) New London County	12	0.69
Clearfield, WI (town) Juneau County	5	0.69
Hinesville, GA (city) Liberty County	229	0.68
Bombay Beach, CA (cdp) Imperial County	2	0.68
Strong, PA (cdp) Northumberland County	1	0.68
Spring Lake, NC (town) Cumberland County	80	0.67
North Topsail Beach, NC (town) Onslow County	5	0.67
Whitakers, NC (town) Edgecombe County	5	0.67
Kooskia, ID (city) Idaho County	4	0.66
Brunsville, IA (city) Plymouth County	1	0.66
Richmond West, FL (cdp) Miami-Dade County	207	0.65
Washington Heights, NY (cdp) Orange County	11	0.65
Richmond Hill, GA (city) Bryan County	59	0.64
North Bay Village, FL (city) Miami-Dade County	46	0.64
Pemberton, NJ (borough) Burlington County	9	0.64
Pumpkin Center, NC (cdp) Onslow County	14	0.63
Camden Point, MO (city) Platte County	3	0.63
Bronson, KS (city) Bourbon County	2	0.62
Kerrick, MN (township) Pine County	2	0.62
The Hammocks, FL (cdp) Miami-Dade County	310	0.61
Browns Mills, NJ (cdp) Burlington County	68	0.61
Country Lake Estates, NJ (cdp) Burlington County	24	0.61
Hagan, GA (city) Evans County	6	0.60
Rosser, TX (village) Kaufman County	2	0.60
Why, AZ (cdp) Pima County	1	0.60
Princeton, FL (cdp) Miami-Dade County	130	0.59
Three Lakes, FL (cdp) Miami-Dade County	89	0.59
Landover Hills, MD (town) Prince George's County	10	0.59
Otego, NY (village) Otsego County	6	0.59
Fayetteville, NC (city) Cumberland County	1,154	0.58
Willingboro, NJ (township) Burlington County	185	0.58
Hope Mills, NC (town) Cumberland County	88	0.58
West Park, FL (city) Broward County	82	0.58
Woodfield, SC (cdp) Richland County	54	0.58
Lovejoy, GA (city) Clayton County	37	0.58
St. Robert, MO (city) Pulaski County	25	0.58
Quail Ridge, FL (cdp) Pasco County	6	0.58
Windemere, TX (cdp) Travis County	6	0.58
Allenhurst, GA (city) Liberty County	4	0.58
Selma, OR (cdp) Josephine County	4	0.58
Thayer, IL (village) Sangamon County	4	0.58
Johannesburg, CA (cdp) Kern County	1	0.58
Miramar, FL (city) Broward County	700	0.57
Saw Creek, PA (cdp) Pike County	23	0.57
Central Valley, UT (town) Sevier County	3	0.57
Milford, KS (city) Geary County	3	0.57
De Smet, ID (cdp) Benewah County	1	0.57
Pemberton, NJ (township) Burlington County	156	0.56
North Valley Stream, NY (cdp) Nassau County	93	0.56
Ocean City, FL (cdp) Okaloosa County	31	0.56
Fort Lee, VA (cdp) Prince George County	19	0.56
Corfu, NY (village) Genesee County	4	0.56
Capon Bridge, WV (town) Hampshire County	2	0.56
Brooklyn, NY (borough) Kings County	13,681	0.55
Palmetto Estates, FL (cdp) Miami-Dade County	74	0.55
Courtdale, PA (borough) Luzerne County	4	0.55
Creal Springs, IL (city) Williamson County	3	0.55
Leipsic, DE (town) Kent County	1	0.55
Flemington, GA (city) Liberty County	4	0.54
McClellan Park, CA (cdp) Sacramento County	4	0.54
Madison, MO (city) Monroe County	3	0.54
Valley Head, AL (town) DeKalb County	3	0.54
Avon, UT (cdp) Cache County	2	0.54
Geuda Springs, KS (city) Sumner County	1	0.54
Country Club, FL (cdp) Miami-Dade County	249	0.53
Glenvar Heights, FL (cdp) Miami-Dade County	90	0.53
Penney Farms, FL (town) Clay County	4	0.53
Skyland, NV (cdp) Douglas County	2	0.53
Fountain, CO (city) El Paso County	134	0.52
Saluda, VA (cdp) Middlesex County	4	0.52
Wauneta, NE (village) Chase County	3	0.52
West Sunbury, PA (borough) Butler County	1	0.52
Woodlawn, MD (cdp) Prince George's County	32	0.51
Penn Estates, PA (cdp) Monroe County	23	0.51
Voorhees, NJ (cdp) Somerset County	5	0.51
Riceville, IA (city) Mitchell County	4	0.51
Scott AFB, IL (cdp) St. Clair County	18	0.50

Please refer to the Explanation of Data in the front of the book for more detailed information.

Hispanic Origin

Central American: Panamanian

Top 150 Places Sorted by Percent of Total Population

Based on places with total population of 7,500 or more

Place	Population	%
Doral, FL (city) Miami-Dade County	387	0.85
Killeen, TX (city) Bell County	998	0.78
Naranja, FL (cdp) Miami-Dade County	58	0.70
Harker Heights, TX (city) Bell County	185	0.69
Hinesville, GA (city) Liberty County	229	0.68
Spring Lake, NC (town) Cumberland County	80	0.67
Richmond West, FL (cdp) Miami-Dade County	207	0.65
Richmond Hill, GA (city) Bryan County	59	0.64
The Hammocks, FL (cdp) Miami-Dade County	310	0.61
Browns Mills, NJ (cdp) Burlington County	68	0.61
Princeton, FL (cdp) Miami-Dade County	130	0.59
Three Lakes, FL (cdp) Miami-Dade County	89	0.59
Fayetteville, NC (city) Cumberland County	1,154	0.58
Willingboro, NJ (township) Burlington County	185	0.58
Hope Mills, NC (town) Cumberland County	88	0.58
West Park, FL (city) Broward County	82	0.58
Woodfield, SC (cdp) Richland County	54	0.58
Miramar, FL (city) Broward County	700	0.57
Pemberton, NJ (township) Burlington County	156	0.56
North Valley Stream, NY (cdp) Nassau County	93	0.56
Brooklyn, NY (borough) Kings County	13,681	0.55
Palmetto Estates, FL (cdp) Miami-Dade County	74	0.55
Country Club, FL (cdp) Miami-Dade County	249	0.53
Glenvar Heights, FL (cdp) Miami-Dade County	90	0.53
Fountain, CO (city) El Paso County	134	0.52
Copperas Cove, TX (city) Coryell County	157	0.49
Wyandanch, NY (cdp) Suffolk County	57	0.49
Junction City, KS (city) Geary County	112	0.48
Fountainebleau, FL (cdp) Miami-Dade County	272	0.46
Cutler Bay, FL (town) Miami-Dade County	187	0.46
North Amityville, NY (cdp) Suffolk County	83	0.46
Country Walk, FL (cdp) Miami-Dade County	73	0.46
Lumberton, NJ (township) Burlington County	58	0.46
Kendall, FL (cdp) Miami-Dade County	336	0.45
Kendall West, FL (cdp) Miami-Dade County	162	0.45
Pembroke Pines, FL (city) Broward County	676	0.44
Clarksville, TN (city) Montgomery County	588	0.44
South Miami Heights, FL (cdp) Miami-Dade County	158	0.44
The Crossings, FL (cdp) Miami-Dade County	99	0.44
Radcliff, KY (city) Hardin County	96	0.44
Union Park, FL (cdp) Orange County	43	0.44
Elmont, NY (cdp) Nassau County	143	0.43
Baldwin, NY (cdp) Nassau County	104	0.43
Fort Polk South, LA (cdp) Vernon Parish	39	0.43
Fort Bliss, TX (cdp) El Paso County	37	0.43
DuPont, WA (city) Pierce County	35	0.43
Citrus Park, FL (cdp) Hillsborough County	96	0.40
Ojus, FL (cdp) Miami-Dade County	72	0.40
Roosevelt, NY (cdp) Nassau County	65	0.40
Grovetown, GA (city) Columbia County	45	0.40
Fort Knox, KY (cdp) Hardin County	41	0.40
Tamiami, FL (cdp) Miami-Dade County	216	0.39
Poinciana, FL (cdp) Osceola County	208	0.39
Central Islip, NY (cdp) Suffolk County	134	0.39
Miami Lakes, FL (town) Miami-Dade County	115	0.39
Meadow Woods, FL (cdp) Orange County	100	0.39
Southchase, FL (cdp) Orange County	61	0.38
Piney Green, NC (cdp) Onslow County	51	0.38
Rosaryville, MD (cdp) Prince George's County	41	0.38
Mount Holly, NJ (township) Burlington County	36	0.38
Pebble Creek, FL (cdp) Hillsborough County	29	0.38
Columbus, GA (city) Muscogee County	696	0.37
Riverview, FL (cdp) Hillsborough County	264	0.37
Security-Widefield, CO (cdp) El Paso County	123	0.37
Converse, TX (city) Bexar County	68	0.37
Westampton, NJ (township) Burlington County	33	0.37
Kendale Lakes, FL (cdp) Miami-Dade County	201	0.36
Coolbaugh, PA (township) Monroe County	75	0.36
Cherry Hill, VA (cdp) Prince William County	58	0.36
South Miami, FL (city) Miami-Dade County	42	0.36
Fort Meade, MD (cdp) Anne Arundel County	34	0.36
West Perrine, FL (cdp) Miami-Dade County	34	0.36
Freeport, NY (village) Nassau County	149	0.35
Wright, FL (cdp) Okaloosa County	82	0.35
Oakleaf Plantation, FL (cdp) Clay County	71	0.35
Cibolo, TX (city) Guadalupe County	53	0.35
View Park-Windsor Hills, CA (cdp) Los Angeles County	39	0.35
Lehman, PA (township) Pike County	37	0.35
Goulds, FL (cdp) Miami-Dade County	35	0.35
Westview, FL (cdp) Miami-Dade County	34	0.35
Newport News, VA (ind. city) Newport News independent city	615	0.34
Miami Gardens, FL (city) Miami-Dade County	361	0.34
Leesburg, FL (city) Lake County	69	0.34
Fort Drum, NY (cdp) Jefferson County	44	0.34
Homestead, FL (city) Miami-Dade County	200	0.33
Sierra Vista, AZ (city) Cochise County	145	0.33
Stockbridge, GA (city) Henry County	84	0.33
Northdale, FL (cdp) Hillsborough County	73	0.33
Montclair, VA (cdp) Prince William County	65	0.33
Laurel, MS (city) Jones County	61	0.33
Kingstowne, VA (cdp) Fairfax County	52	0.33
Coral Gables, FL (city) Miami-Dade County	151	0.32
Fort Hood, TX (cdp) Bell County	94	0.32
Bellair-Meadowbrook Terrace, FL (cdp) Clay County	43	0.32
Fort Irwin, CA (cdp) San Bernardino County	28	0.32
Mount Rainier, MD (city) Prince George's County	26	0.32
Tamarac, FL (city) Broward County	186	0.31
Fairland, MD (cdp) Montgomery County	73	0.31
Burlington, NJ (township) Burlington County	69	0.31
Universal City, TX (city) Bexar County	58	0.31
Pinecrest, FL (village) Miami-Dade County	57	0.31
Neabsco, VA (cdp) Prince William County	37	0.31
Cusseta-Chattahoochee County, GA (unified govt) Chattahoochee County	35	0.31
Brock Hall, MD (cdp) Prince George's County	30	0.31
Laurel, MD (city) Prince George's County	76	0.30
White Oak, MD (cdp) Montgomery County	52	0.30
Ozark, AL (city) Dale County	45	0.30
Hunters Creek, FL (cdp) Orange County	43	0.30
Miami Springs, FL (city) Miami-Dade County	41	0.30
Highlands, NY (town) Orange County	37	0.30
Richmond Heights, FL (cdp) Miami-Dade County	26	0.30
Half Moon, NC (cdp) Onslow County	25	0.30
Sunrise, FL (city) Broward County	244	0.29
Alafaya, FL (cdp) Orange County	230	0.29
Lakewood, WA (city) Pierce County	169	0.29
Sanford, FL (city) Seminole County	154	0.29
Valley Stream, NY (village) Nassau County	110	0.29
South Laurel, MD (cdp) Prince George's County	75	0.29
Fort Walton Beach, FL (city) Okaloosa County	56	0.29
North Bay Shore, NY (cdp) Suffolk County	55	0.29
Dentsville, SC (cdp) Richland County	41	0.29
Azalea Park, FL (cdp) Orange County	36	0.29
Georgetown, GA (cdp) Chatham County	34	0.29
Summerfield, MD (cdp) Prince George's County	32	0.29
Cheval, FL (cdp) Hillsborough County	31	0.29
Burlington, NJ (city) Burlington County	29	0.29
Miami, FL (city) Miami-Dade County	1,113	0.28
Hollywood, FL (city) Broward County	398	0.28
Brandon, FL (cdp) Hillsborough County	294	0.28
Dale City, VA (cdp) Prince William County	185	0.28
Kissimmee, FL (city) Osceola County	167	0.28
Lake Ridge, VA (cdp) Prince William County	114	0.28
Odenton, MD (cdp) Anne Arundel County	104	0.28
Seaside, CA (city) Monterey County	93	0.28
Schertz, TX (city) Guadalupe County	89	0.28
New London, CT (city/town) New London County	76	0.28
Palmetto Bay, FL (village) Miami-Dade County	66	0.28
Le Ray, NY (town) Jefferson County	60	0.28
Crestview, FL (city) Okaloosa County	58	0.28
Marlton, MD (cdp) Prince George's County	25	0.28
New York, NY (city) Kings County	22,353	0.27
Miami Beach, FL (city) Miami-Dade County	240	0.27
Town 'n' Country, FL (cdp) Hillsborough County	214	0.27
Altamonte Springs, FL (city) Seminole County	114	0.27
Palm River-Clair Mel, FL (cdp) Hillsborough County	56	0.27
Ives Estates, FL (cdp) Miami-Dade County	53	0.27
Adelphi, MD (cdp) Prince George's County	40	0.27
Lake Arbor, MD (cdp) Prince George's County	26	0.27
Holly Springs, GA (city) Cherokee County	25	0.27
North Miami, FL (city) Miami-Dade County	154	0.26

Please refer to the Explanation of Data in the front of the book for more detailed information.

Hispanic Origin

Central American: Salvadoran

U.S. and 50 States Sorted by Population and Percent of Total Population

Place	Population	%
United States	**1,648,968**	**0.53**
California	573,956	1.54
Texas	222,599	0.89
New York	152,130	0.79
Virginia	123,800	1.55
Maryland	123,789	2.14
New Jersey	56,532	0.64
Florida	55,144	0.29
Massachusetts	43,400	0.66
North Carolina	37,778	0.40
Georgia	32,107	0.33
Nevada	30,043	1.11
District of Columbia	16,611	2.76
Arkansas	14,980	0.51
Illinois	14,217	0.11
Washington	12,637	0.19
Colorado	12,329	0.25
Arizona	12,225	0.19
Utah	8,998	0.33
Tennessee	8,570	0.14
Pennsylvania	7,952	0.06
Indiana	7,401	0.11
Minnesota	7,175	0.14
Connecticut	6,223	0.17
Nebraska	6,016	0.33
Oregon	5,906	0.15
Ohio	5,627	0.05
Iowa	5,601	0.18
Louisiana	5,120	0.11
Kansas	5,108	0.18
Missouri	4,628	0.08
South Carolina	3,830	0.08
Michigan	3,401	0.03
Oklahoma	2,788	0.07
Rhode Island	2,715	0.26
Alabama	2,419	0.05
Kentucky	2,351	0.05
New Mexico	2,051	0.10
Wisconsin	1,867	0.03
Delaware	1,231	0.14
Mississippi	1,174	0.04
Idaho	1,159	0.07
Alaska	938	0.13
West Virginia	893	0.05
New Hampshire	823	0.06
Hawaii	801	0.06
South Dakota	780	0.10
Maine	618	0.05
Wyoming	198	0.04
Montana	140	0.01
Vermont	116	0.02
North Dakota	73	0.01

Place	Population	%
District of Columbia	16,611	2.76
Maryland	123,789	2.14
Virginia	123,800	1.55
California	573,956	1.54
Nevada	30,043	1.11
Texas	222,599	0.89
New York	152,130	0.79
Massachusetts	43,400	0.66
New Jersey	56,532	0.64
United States	**1,648,968**	**0.53**
Arkansas	14,980	0.51
North Carolina	37,778	0.40
Georgia	32,107	0.33
Utah	8,998	0.33
Nebraska	6,016	0.33
Florida	55,144	0.29
Rhode Island	2,715	0.26
Colorado	12,329	0.25
Washington	12,637	0.19
Arizona	12,225	0.19
Iowa	5,601	0.18
Kansas	5,108	0.18
Connecticut	6,223	0.17
Oregon	5,906	0.15
Tennessee	8,570	0.14
Minnesota	7,175	0.14
Delaware	1,231	0.14
Alaska	938	0.13
Illinois	14,217	0.11
Indiana	7,401	0.11
Louisiana	5,120	0.11
New Mexico	2,051	0.10
South Dakota	780	0.10
Missouri	4,628	0.08
South Carolina	3,830	0.08
Oklahoma	2,788	0.07
Idaho	1,159	0.07
Pennsylvania	7,952	0.06
New Hampshire	823	0.06
Hawaii	801	0.06
Ohio	5,627	0.05
Alabama	2,419	0.05
Kentucky	2,351	0.05
West Virginia	893	0.05
Maine	618	0.05
Mississippi	1,174	0.04
Wyoming	198	0.04
Michigan	3,401	0.03
Wisconsin	1,867	0.03
Vermont	116	0.02
Montana	140	0.01
North Dakota	73	0.01

Please refer to the Explanation of Data in the front of the book for more detailed information.

Hispanic Origin

Central American: Salvadoran

Top 150 Places Sorted by Population

Based on all places, regardless of total population

Place	Population	%
Los Angeles, CA (city) Los Angeles County	228,990	6.04
Houston, TX (city) Harris County	75,907	3.62
New York, NY (city) Kings County	38,559	0.47
Hempstead, NY (town) Nassau County	32,681	4.30
Islip, NY (town) Suffolk County	29,849	8.90
Queens, NY (borough) Queens County	21,342	0.96
Washington, DC (city) District of Columbia	16,611	2.76
San Francisco, CA (city) San Francisco County	16,165	2.01
Brentwood, NY (cdp) Suffolk County	15,946	26.29
Dallas, TX (city) Dallas County	15,696	1.31
Irving, TX (city) Dallas County	12,544	5.80
Boston, MA (city) Suffolk County	10,850	1.76
Hempstead, NY (village) Nassau County	10,707	19.87
Charlotte, NC (city) Mecklenburg County	9,516	1.30
Palmdale, CA (city) Los Angeles County	9,488	6.21
Wheaton, MD (cdp) Montgomery County	8,912	18.46
Las Vegas, NV (city) Clark County	8,392	1.44
North Hempstead, NY (town) Nassau County	8,262	3.65
Babylon, NY (town) Suffolk County	7,805	3.65
Brooklyn, NY (borough) Kings County	7,737	0.31
Elizabeth, NJ (city) Union County	7,364	5.89
Chillum, MD (cdp) Prince George's County	7,315	21.83
Oakland, CA (city) Alameda County	7,246	1.85
Silver Spring, MD (cdp) Montgomery County	7,103	9.94
Arlington, VA (cdp) Arlington County	7,088	3.41
Dale City, VA (cdp) Prince William County	7,036	10.67
San Jose, CA (city) Santa Clara County	6,829	0.72
Long Beach, CA (city) Los Angeles County	6,657	1.44
Huntington, NY (town) Suffolk County	6,563	3.23
Alexandria, VA (ind. city) Alexandria independent city	6,436	4.60
Chelsea, MA (city) Suffolk County	6,391	18.17
Santa Ana, CA (city) Orange County	6,389	1.97
Central Islip, NY (cdp) Suffolk County	6,381	18.52
Marumsco, VA (cdp) Prince William County	6,261	17.87
Brookhaven, NY (town) Suffolk County	5,899	1.21
Bronx, NY (borough) Bronx County	5,469	0.39
South Gate, CA (city) Los Angeles County	5,407	5.73
Huntington Station, NY (cdp) Suffolk County	5,233	15.84
Chicago, IL (city) Cook County	5,204	0.19
Union City, NJ (city) Hudson County	5,060	7.61
Aspen Hill, MD (cdp) Montgomery County	5,023	10.30
Daly City, CA (city) San Mateo County	5,000	4.94
Uniondale, NY (cdp) Nassau County	4,998	20.19
Gaithersburg, MD (city) Montgomery County	4,994	8.33
Richmond, CA (city) Contra Costa County	4,888	4.71
Lancaster, CA (city) Los Angeles County	4,713	3.01
Phoenix, AZ (city) Maricopa County	4,697	0.32
Bakersfield, CA (city) Kern County	4,654	1.34
Garland, TX (city) Dallas County	4,627	2.04
Miami, FL (city) Miami-Dade County	4,610	1.15
North Bay Shore, NY (cdp) Suffolk County	4,530	23.91
West New York, NJ (town) Hudson County	4,504	9.06
Freeport, NY (village) Nassau County	4,439	10.36
Fontana, CA (city) San Bernardino County	4,382	2.23
Downey, CA (city) Los Angeles County	4,356	3.90
Langley Park, MD (cdp) Prince George's County	4,217	22.48
Nashville-Davidson, TN (metro govt) Davidson County	4,121	0.69
Germantown, MD (cdp) Montgomery County	3,989	4.62
Anaheim, CA (city) Orange County	3,957	1.18
Sterling, VA (cdp) Loudoun County	3,903	14.03
Everett, MA (city) Middlesex County	3,895	9.35
Manassas, VA (ind. city) Manassas independent city	3,870	10.23
Inglewood, CA (city) Los Angeles County	3,869	3.53
Austin, TX (city) Travis County	3,811	0.48
Woodlawn, VA (cdp) Fairfax County	3,728	17.92
Plainfield, NJ (city) Union County	3,684	7.40
Hayward, CA (city) Alameda County	3,676	2.55
Sunrise Manor, NV (cdp) Clark County	3,655	1.93
Herndon, VA (town) Fairfax County	3,603	15.47
Paradise, NV (cdp) Clark County	3,578	1.60
Pomona, CA (city) Los Angeles County	3,518	2.36
Glendale, CA (city) Los Angeles County	3,481	1.82
New Cassel, NY (cdp) Nassau County	3,477	24.73
Raleigh, NC (city) Wake County	3,476	0.86
Manhattan, NY (borough) New York County	3,419	0.22
Huntington Park, CA (city) Los Angeles County	3,381	5.82
Hawthorne, CA (city) Los Angeles County	3,335	3.96
Springdale, AR (city) Washington County	3,316	4.75
Oyster Bay, NY (town) Nassau County	3,297	1.12
North Las Vegas, NV (city) Clark County	3,293	1.52
East Los Angeles, CA (cdp) Los Angeles County	3,274	2.59
Florence-Graham, CA (cdp) Los Angeles County	3,239	5.11
Somerville, MA (city) Middlesex County	3,211	4.24
Lynwood, CA (city) Los Angeles County	3,154	4.52
Aurora, CO (city) Arapahoe County	3,128	0.96
Grand Prairie, TX (city) Dallas County	3,043	1.73
Carrollton, TX (city) Denton County	3,034	2.55
Revere, MA (city) Suffolk County	3,024	5.84
Newark, NJ (city) Essex County	3,000	1.08
Riverside, CA (city) Riverside County	2,995	0.99
San Antonio, TX (city) Medina County	2,969	0.22
Rogers, AR (city) Benton County	2,951	5.27
Arlington, TX (city) Tarrant County	2,938	0.80
Durham, NC (city) Durham County	2,929	1.28
Concord, CA (city) Contra Costa County	2,904	2.38
South San Francisco, CA (city) San Mateo County	2,897	4.55
Roosevelt, NY (cdp) Nassau County	2,891	17.78
Adelphi, MD (cdp) Prince George's County	2,884	19.12
Hyattsville, MD (city) Prince George's County	2,876	16.38
Norwalk, CA (city) Los Angeles County	2,871	2.72
North Bergen, NJ (township) Hudson County	2,825	4.65
Baltimore, MD (city) Baltimore city County	2,796	0.45
Moreno Valley, CA (city) Riverside County	2,794	1.44
Ontario, CA (city) San Bernardino County	2,791	1.70
Reno, NV (city) Washoe County	2,783	1.24
Worcester, MA (city) Worcester County	2,776	1.53
Annandale, VA (cdp) Fairfax County	2,770	6.75
West Falls Church, VA (cdp) Fairfax County	2,748	9.41
Bailey's Crossroads, VA (cdp) Fairfax County	2,730	11.55
Fort Worth, TX (city) Tarrant County	2,729	0.37
Annapolis, MD (city) Anne Arundel County	2,708	7.05
Indianapolis, IN (city) Marion County	2,695	0.33
Yonkers, NY (city) Westchester County	2,691	1.37
Pasadena, CA (city) Los Angeles County	2,689	1.96
Sudley, VA (cdp) Prince William County	2,651	16.36
San Bernardino, CA (city) San Bernardino County	2,641	1.26
Mission Bend, TX (cdp) Fort Bend County	2,616	7.17
San Mateo, CA (city) San Mateo County	2,571	2.64
El Monte, CA (city) Los Angeles County	2,570	2.26
Glen Cove, NY (city) Nassau County	2,544	9.43
Montgomery Village, MD (cdp) Montgomery County	2,522	7.87
Lynn, MA (city) Essex County	2,509	2.78
Leesburg, VA (town) Loudoun County	2,500	5.87
Pasadena, TX (city) Harris County	2,500	1.68
Frederick, MD (city) Frederick County	2,494	3.82
Compton, CA (city) Los Angeles County	2,470	2.56
Redwood City, CA (city) San Mateo County	2,432	3.17
Sacramento, CA (city) Sacramento County	2,425	0.52
San Diego, CA (city) San Diego County	2,415	0.18
Mendota, CA (city) Fresno County	2,411	21.89
Denver, CO (city) Denver County	2,372	0.40
East Riverdale, MD (cdp) Prince George's County	2,352	15.17
Omaha, NE (city) Douglas County	2,276	0.56
Baldwin Park, CA (city) Los Angeles County	2,272	3.01
Santa Clarita, CA (city) Los Angeles County	2,272	1.29
Rialto, CA (city) San Bernardino County	2,246	2.26
Burbank, CA (city) Los Angeles County	2,231	2.16
Antioch, CA (city) Contra Costa County	2,212	2.16
Reston, VA (cdp) Fairfax County	2,194	3.76
Rockville, MD (city) Montgomery County	2,135	3.49
Vallejo, CA (city) Solano County	2,135	1.84
Bell, CA (city) Los Angeles County	2,082	5.87
Pittsburg, CA (city) Contra Costa County	2,076	3.28
Beltsville, MD (cdp) Prince George's County	2,067	12.32
Westmont, CA (cdp) Los Angeles County	2,044	6.42
West Covina, CA (city) Los Angeles County	2,019	1.90
Costa Mesa, CA (city) Orange County	1,983	1.80
Bell Gardens, CA (city) Los Angeles County	1,967	4.68
Springfield, VA (cdp) Fairfax County	1,961	6.43
Winston-Salem, NC (city) Forsyth County	1,954	0.85

Hispanic Origin

Central American: Salvadoran

Top 150 Places Sorted by Percent of Total Population

Based on all places, regardless of total population

Place	Population	%
Islandia, FL (city) Miami-Dade County	8	44.44
Brentwood, NY (cdp) Suffolk County	15,946	26.29
New Cassel, NY (cdp) Nassau County	3,477	24.73
Colmar Manor, MD (town) Prince George's County	347	24.72
North Bay Shore, NY (cdp) Suffolk County	4,530	23.91
Langley Park, MD (cdp) Prince George's County	4,217	22.48
Edmonston, MD (town) Prince George's County	318	22.01
Brentwood, MD (town) Prince George's County	670	22.00
Mendota, CA (city) Fresno County	2,411	21.89
Chillum, MD (cdp) Prince George's County	7,315	21.83
Uniondale, NY (cdp) Nassau County	4,998	20.19
Hempstead, NY (village) Nassau County	10,707	19.87
North Brentwood, MD (town) Prince George's County	99	19.15
Adelphi, MD (cdp) Prince George's County	2,884	19.12
Landover Hills, MD (town) Prince George's County	322	19.09
Central Islip, NY (cdp) Suffolk County	6,381	18.52
Wheaton, MD (cdp) Montgomery County	8,912	18.46
Cottage City, MD (town) Prince George's County	239	18.31
Woodlawn, MD (cdp) Prince George's County	1,158	18.28
Chelsea, MA (city) Suffolk County	6,391	18.17
Woodlawn, VA (cdp) Fairfax County	3,728	17.92
Marumsco, VA (cdp) Prince William County	6,261	17.87
Roosevelt, NY (cdp) Nassau County	2,891	17.78
Loch Lomond, VA (cdp) Prince William County	653	17.64
Hyattsville, MD (city) Prince George's County	2,876	16.38
Sudley, VA (cdp) Prince William County	2,651	16.36
Yorkshire, VA (cdp) Prince William County	1,229	16.30
Huntington Station, NY (cdp) Suffolk County	5,233	15.84
Inwood, NY (cdp) Nassau County	1,523	15.55
Herndon, VA (town) Fairfax County	3,603	15.47
East Riverdale, MD (cdp) Prince George's County	2,352	15.17
Mount Rainier, MD (city) Prince George's County	1,167	14.44
Sterling, VA (cdp) Loudoun County	3,903	14.03
Monon, IN (town) White County	248	13.96
El Jebel, CO (cdp) Eagle County	524	13.79
Seven Corners, VA (cdp) Fairfax County	1,255	13.56
Groveton, VA (cdp) Fairfax County	1,870	12.81
Wyandanch, NY (cdp) Suffolk County	1,485	12.75
Glenmont, MD (cdp) Montgomery County	1,718	12.70
Bull Run, VA (cdp) Prince William County	1,883	12.57
Hillandale, MD (cdp) Montgomery County	754	12.48
Beltsville, MD (cdp) Prince George's County	2,067	12.32
Manassas Park, VA (ind. city) Manassas Park independent city	1,724	12.08
Sugarland Run, VA (cdp) Loudoun County	1,364	11.56
Bailey's Crossroads, VA (cdp) Fairfax County	2,730	11.55
Montalvin Manor, CA (cdp) Contra Costa County	329	11.44
Riverdale Park, MD (town) Prince George's County	771	11.08
Berwyn Heights, MD (town) Prince George's County	339	10.85
Dale City, VA (cdp) Prince William County	7,036	10.67
North Amityville, NY (cdp) Suffolk County	1,899	10.63
Freeport, NY (village) Nassau County	4,439	10.36
Aspen Hill, MD (cdp) Montgomery County	5,023	10.30
Manassas, VA (ind. city) Manassas independent city	3,870	10.23
Redland, MD (cdp) Montgomery County	1,749	10.14
New Carrollton, MD (city) Prince George's County	1,224	10.09
Silver Spring, MD (cdp) Montgomery County	7,103	9.94
Bensley, VA (cdp) Chesterfield County	573	9.85
Westbury, NY (village) Nassau County	1,449	9.57
South Fallsburg, NY (cdp) Sullivan County	274	9.55
Hybla Valley, VA (cdp) Fairfax County	1,494	9.46
Glen Cove, NY (city) Nassau County	2,544	9.43
West Falls Church, VA (cdp) Fairfax County	2,748	9.41
Everett, MA (city) Middlesex County	3,895	9.35
Spring, AR (town) Benton County	8	9.20
West New York, NJ (town) Hudson County	4,504	9.06
Islip, NY (town) Suffolk County	29,849	8.90
Dumfries, VA (town) Prince William County	433	8.73
Deloit, IA (city) Crawford County	23	8.71
Rollingwood, CA (cdp) Contra Costa County	257	8.66
Huntington, VA (cdp) Fairfax County	958	8.50
North Richmond, CA (cdp) Contra Costa County	316	8.50
Bladensburg, MD (town) Prince George's County	775	8.47
Potomac Mills, VA (cdp) Prince William County	469	8.35
Gaithersburg, MD (city) Montgomery County	4,994	8.33
Huntingburg, IN (city) Dubois County	498	8.22
Rose Hill, VA (cdp) Fairfax County	1,639	8.10
Montgomery Village, MD (cdp) Montgomery County	2,522	7.87
Fairview, NJ (borough) Bergen County	1,063	7.68
Forest Glen, MD (cdp) Montgomery County	502	7.63
Union City, NJ (city) Hudson County	5,060	7.61
Locust Valley, NY (cdp) Nassau County	256	7.52
Plainfield, NJ (city) Union County	3,684	7.40
Baywood, NY (cdp) Suffolk County	538	7.32
Manorhaven, NY (village) Nassau County	478	7.29
Nantucket, MA (cdp) Nantucket County	541	7.27
Mission Bend, TX (cdp) Fort Bend County	2,616	7.17
Colma, CA (town) San Mateo County	128	7.14
Annapolis, MD (city) Anne Arundel County	2,708	7.05
Four Corners, MD (cdp) Montgomery County	554	6.97
Lanham, MD (cdp) Prince George's County	705	6.94
Malden-on-Hudson, NY (cdp) Ulster County	28	6.91
Cudahy, CA (city) Los Angeles County	1,634	6.86
Annandale, VA (cdp) Fairfax County	2,770	6.75
Lincolnia, VA (cdp) Fairfax County	1,538	6.73
Kemp Mill, MD (cdp) Montgomery County	846	6.73
Woodbridge, VA (cdp) Prince William County	266	6.56
San Pablo, CA (city) Contra Costa County	1,908	6.55
White Oak, MD (cdp) Montgomery County	1,121	6.44
Springfield, VA (cdp) Fairfax County	1,961	6.43
Idylwood, VA (cdp) Fairfax County	1,111	6.43
Westmont, CA (cdp) Los Angeles County	2,044	6.42
North Kensington, MD (cdp) Montgomery County	609	6.40
Denison, IA (city) Crawford County	531	6.40
Copiague, NY (cdp) Suffolk County	1,457	6.34
University Center, VA (cdp) Loudoun County	227	6.33
Kalaeloa, HI (cdp) Honolulu County	3	6.25
East Farmingdale, NY (cdp) Suffolk County	404	6.23
Palmdale, CA (city) Los Angeles County	9,488	6.21
North Bellport, NY (cdp) Suffolk County	710	6.15
Black River, MN (township) Pennington County	5	6.10
Los Angeles, CA (city) Los Angeles County	228,990	6.04
Bethel Heights, AR (city) Benton County	141	5.94
Elizabeth, NJ (city) Union County	7,364	5.89
Leesburg, VA (town) Loudoun County	2,500	5.87
Bell, CA (city) Los Angeles County	2,082	5.87
Lumpkin, GA (city) Stewart County	161	5.87
Desert View Highlands, CA (cdp) Los Angeles County	138	5.85
Revere, MA (city) Suffolk County	3,024	5.84
Huntington Park, CA (city) Los Angeles County	3,381	5.82
Irving, TX (city) Dallas County	12,544	5.80
Marshall, MO (city) Saline County	753	5.76
South Gate, CA (city) Los Angeles County	5,407	5.73
Corinth, AR (town) Yell County	4	5.71
North Springfield, VA (cdp) Fairfax County	409	5.62
Bay Shore, NY (cdp) Suffolk County	1,477	5.61
Mifflintown, PA (borough) Juniata County	52	5.56
Garden City, CO (town) Weld County	13	5.56
Guttenberg, NJ (town) Hudson County	618	5.53
Walnut Park, CA (cdp) Los Angeles County	879	5.51
Nantucket, MA (town) Nantucket County	559	5.50
Perry, IA (city) Dallas County	422	5.48
Layhill, MD (cdp) Montgomery County	283	5.47
Dardanelle, AR (city) Yell County	257	5.42
Dulles Town Center, VA (cdp) Loudoun County	249	5.41
Calverton, MD (cdp) Montgomery County	952	5.37
South Hempstead, NY (cdp) Nassau County	174	5.37
North Plainfield, NJ (borough) Somerset County	1,167	5.32
Seabrook, MD (cdp) Prince George's County	920	5.32
Siloam Springs, AR (city) Benton County	796	5.29
Rogers, AR (city) Benton County	2,951	5.27
Highland Beach, MD (town) Anne Arundel County	5	5.21
Meadowbrook, VA (cdp) Chesterfield County	951	5.19
Landover, MD (cdp) Prince George's County	1,194	5.17
Colesville, MD (cdp) Montgomery County	756	5.16
Tara Hills, CA (cdp) Contra Costa County	263	5.13
Flanders, NY (cdp) Suffolk County	229	5.12
Florence-Graham, CA (cdp) Los Angeles County	3,239	5.11
Milan, MO (city) Sullivan County	100	5.10
Lennox, CA (cdp) Los Angeles County	1,151	5.06
Danville, AR (city) Yell County	122	5.06

Please refer to the Explanation of Data in the front of the book for more detailed information.

Hispanic Origin

Central American: Salvadoran

Top 150 Places Sorted by Percent of Total Population

Based on places with total population of 7,500 or more

Place	Population	%
Brentwood, NY (cdp) Suffolk County	15,946	26.29
New Cassel, NY (cdp) Nassau County	3,477	24.73
North Bay Shore, NY (cdp) Suffolk County	4,530	23.91
Langley Park, MD (cdp) Prince George's County	4,217	22.48
Mendota, CA (city) Fresno County	2,411	21.89
Chillum, MD (cdp) Prince George's County	7,315	21.83
Uniondale, NY (cdp) Nassau County	4,998	20.19
Hempstead, NY (village) Nassau County	10,707	19.87
Adelphi, MD (cdp) Prince George's County	2,884	19.12
Central Islip, NY (cdp) Suffolk County	6,381	18.52
Wheaton, MD (cdp) Montgomery County	8,912	18.46
Chelsea, MA (city) Suffolk County	6,391	18.17
Woodlawn, VA (cdp) Fairfax County	3,728	17.92
Marumsco, VA (cdp) Prince William County	6,261	17.87
Roosevelt, NY (cdp) Nassau County	2,891	17.78
Hyattsville, MD (city) Prince George's County	2,876	16.38
Sudley, VA (cdp) Prince William County	2,651	16.36
Yorkshire, VA (cdp) Prince William County	1,229	16.30
Huntington Station, NY (cdp) Suffolk County	5,233	15.84
Inwood, NY (cdp) Nassau County	1,523	15.55
Herndon, VA (town) Fairfax County	3,603	15.47
East Riverdale, MD (cdp) Prince George's County	2,352	15.17
Mount Rainier, MD (city) Prince George's County	1,167	14.44
Sterling, VA (cdp) Loudoun County	3,903	14.03
Seven Corners, VA (cdp) Fairfax County	1,255	13.56
Groveton, VA (cdp) Fairfax County	1,870	12.81
Wyandanch, NY (cdp) Suffolk County	1,485	12.75
Glenmont, MD (cdp) Montgomery County	1,718	12.70
Bull Run, VA (cdp) Prince William County	1,883	12.57
Beltsville, MD (cdp) Prince George's County	2,067	12.32
Manassas Park, VA (ind. city) Manassas Park independent city	1,724	12.08
Sugarland Run, VA (cdp) Loudoun County	1,364	11.56
Bailey's Crossroads, VA (cdp) Fairfax County	2,730	11.55
Dale City, VA (cdp) Prince William County	7,036	10.67
North Amityville, NY (cdp) Suffolk County	1,899	10.63
Freeport, NY (village) Nassau County	4,439	10.36
Aspen Hill, MD (cdp) Montgomery County	5,023	10.30
Manassas, VA (ind. city) Manassas independent city	3,870	10.23
Redland, MD (cdp) Montgomery County	1,749	10.14
New Carrollton, MD (city) Prince George's County	1,224	10.09
Silver Spring, MD (cdp) Montgomery County	7,103	9.94
Westbury, NY (village) Nassau County	1,449	9.57
Hybla Valley, VA (cdp) Fairfax County	1,494	9.46
Glen Cove, NY (city) Nassau County	2,544	9.43
West Falls Church, VA (cdp) Fairfax County	2,748	9.41
Everett, MA (city) Middlesex County	3,895	9.35
West New York, NJ (town) Hudson County	4,504	9.06
Islip, NY (town) Suffolk County	29,849	8.90
Huntington, VA (cdp) Fairfax County	958	8.50
Bladensburg, MD (town) Prince George's County	775	8.47
Gaithersburg, MD (city) Montgomery County	4,994	8.33
Rose Hill, VA (cdp) Fairfax County	1,639	8.10
Montgomery Village, MD (cdp) Montgomery County	2,522	7.87
Fairview, NJ (borough) Bergen County	1,063	7.68
Union City, NJ (city) Hudson County	5,060	7.61
Plainfield, NJ (city) Union County	3,684	7.40
Mission Bend, TX (cdp) Fort Bend County	2,616	7.17
Annapolis, MD (city) Anne Arundel County	2,708	7.05
Four Corners, MD (cdp) Montgomery County	554	6.97
Lanham, MD (cdp) Prince George's County	705	6.94
Cudahy, CA (city) Los Angeles County	1,634	6.86
Annandale, VA (cdp) Fairfax County	2,770	6.75
Lincolnia, VA (cdp) Fairfax County	1,538	6.73
Kemp Mill, MD (cdp) Montgomery County	846	6.73
San Pablo, CA (city) Contra Costa County	1,908	6.55
White Oak, MD (cdp) Montgomery County	1,121	6.44
Springfield, VA (cdp) Fairfax County	1,961	6.43
Idylwood, VA (cdp) Fairfax County	1,111	6.43
Westmont, CA (cdp) Los Angeles County	2,044	6.42
North Kensington, MD (cdp) Montgomery County	609	6.40
Denison, IA (city) Crawford County	531	6.40
Copiague, NY (cdp) Suffolk County	1,457	6.34
Palmdale, CA (city) Los Angeles County	9,488	6.21
North Bellport, NY (cdp) Suffolk County	710	6.15
Los Angeles, CA (city) Los Angeles County	228,990	6.04
Elizabeth, NJ (city) Union County	7,364	5.89
Leesburg, VA (town) Loudoun County	2,500	5.87
Bell, CA (city) Los Angeles County	2,082	5.87
Revere, MA (city) Suffolk County	3,024	5.84
Huntington Park, CA (city) Los Angeles County	3,381	5.82
Irving, TX (city) Dallas County	12,544	5.80
Marshall, MO (city) Saline County	753	5.76
South Gate, CA (city) Los Angeles County	5,407	5.73
Bay Shore, NY (cdp) Suffolk County	1,477	5.61
Guttenberg, NJ (town) Hudson County	618	5.53
Walnut Park, CA (cdp) Los Angeles County	879	5.51
Nantucket, MA (town) Nantucket County	559	5.50
Perry, IA (city) Dallas County	422	5.48
Calverton, MD (cdp) Montgomery County	952	5.37
North Plainfield, NJ (borough) Somerset County	1,167	5.32
Seabrook, MD (cdp) Prince George's County	920	5.32
Siloam Springs, AR (city) Benton County	796	5.29
Rogers, AR (city) Benton County	2,951	5.27
Meadowbrook, VA (cdp) Chesterfield County	951	5.19
Landover, MD (cdp) Prince George's County	1,194	5.17
Colesville, MD (cdp) Montgomery County	756	5.16
Florence-Graham, CA (cdp) Los Angeles County	3,239	5.11
Lennox, CA (cdp) Los Angeles County	1,151	5.06
Daly City, CA (city) San Mateo County	5,000	4.94
Maywood, CA (city) Los Angeles County	1,354	4.94
Lorton, VA (cdp) Fairfax County	912	4.90
Lindenwold, NJ (borough) Camden County	849	4.82
Webster, TX (city) Harris County	499	4.80
Mineola, NY (village) Nassau County	896	4.77
Springdale, AR (city) Washington County	3,316	4.75
Oxon Hill, MD (cdp) Prince George's County	842	4.75
Richmond, CA (city) Contra Costa County	4,888	4.71
Farmers Branch, TX (city) Dallas County	1,347	4.71
Takoma Park, MD (city) Montgomery County	787	4.71
Greenbelt, MD (city) Prince George's County	1,081	4.69
Siler City, NC (town) Chatham County	370	4.69
Bell Gardens, CA (city) Los Angeles County	1,967	4.68
North Bergen, NJ (township) Hudson County	2,825	4.65
Cherry Hill, VA (cdp) Prince William County	740	4.63
Germantown, MD (cdp) Montgomery County	3,989	4.62
Mecca, CA (cdp) Riverside County	396	4.62
Bay Point, CA (cdp) Contra Costa County	984	4.61
Alexandria, VA (ind. city) Alexandria independent city	6,436	4.60
Laurel, MD (city) Prince George's County	1,150	4.58
North Fair Oaks, CA (cdp) San Mateo County	673	4.58
South San Francisco, CA (city) San Mateo County	2,897	4.55
Triangle, VA (cdp) Prince William County	372	4.54
Lynwood, CA (city) Los Angeles County	3,154	4.52
Hempstead, NY (town) Nassau County	32,681	4.30
East Palo Alto, CA (city) San Mateo County	1,202	4.27
Somerville, MA (city) Middlesex County	3,211	4.24
Fairfax, VA (ind. city) Fairfax independent city	939	4.16
Sun Village, CA (cdp) Los Angeles County	478	4.13
Hawthorne, CA (city) Los Angeles County	3,335	3.96
Van Buren, AR (city) Crawford County	903	3.96
South Laurel, MD (cdp) Prince George's County	1,030	3.94
Greenlawn, NY (cdp) Suffolk County	538	3.92
Worthington, MN (city) Nobles County	500	3.92
Downey, CA (city) Los Angeles County	4,356	3.90
Frederick, MD (city) Frederick County	2,494	3.82
Bound Brook, NJ (borough) Somerset County	396	3.81
College Park, MD (city) Prince George's County	1,151	3.78
North Lindenhurst, NY (cdp) Suffolk County	439	3.77
Reston, VA (cdp) Fairfax County	2,194	3.76
Aldine, TX (cdp) Harris County	597	3.76
South San Jose Hills, CA (cdp) Los Angeles County	770	3.75
Cloverly, MD (cdp) Montgomery County	567	3.75
Fairland, MD (cdp) Montgomery County	885	3.74
Riverhead, NY (cdp) Suffolk County	495	3.72
Willowbrook, CA (cdp) Los Angeles County	1,333	3.70
Edgewater, MD (cdp) Anne Arundel County	330	3.66
North Hempstead, NY (town) Nassau County	8,262	3.65
Babylon, NY (town) Suffolk County	7,805	3.65
Chantilly, VA (cdp) Fairfax County	840	3.65
Houston, TX (city) Harris County	75,907	3.62

Please refer to the Explanation of Data in the front of the book for more detailed information.

Hispanic Origin

Central American: Other Central American

U.S. and 50 States Sorted by Population and Percent of Total Population

Place	Population	%
United States	**31,626**	**0.01**
California	12,005	0.03
New York	2,952	0.02
Texas	2,658	0.01
Florida	1,692	0.01
Virginia	1,431	0.02
Massachusetts	1,104	0.02
New Jersey	1,068	0.01
Maryland	995	0.02
North Carolina	852	0.01
Georgia	850	0.01
Illinois	644	0.01
Nevada	483	0.02
Arizona	386	0.01
Colorado	331	0.01
Washington	308	<0.01
Pennsylvania	302	<0.01
Louisiana	289	0.01
Connecticut	234	0.01
Ohio	219	<0.01
Tennessee	209	<0.01
Oregon	197	0.01
Oklahoma	177	<0.01
Indiana	173	<0.01
Nebraska	152	0.01
Kansas	148	0.01
South Carolina	136	<0.01
Rhode Island	132	0.01
Minnesota	132	<0.01
Utah	131	<0.01
Michigan	130	<0.01
Alabama	126	<0.01
District of Columbia	110	0.02
Arkansas	105	<0.01
Iowa	92	<0.01
Missouri	89	<0.01
Kentucky	87	<0.01
Wisconsin	85	<0.01
New Mexico	67	<0.01
Mississippi	56	<0.01
Hawaii	54	<0.01
South Dakota	51	0.01
New Hampshire	38	<0.01
Delaware	35	<0.01
Idaho	31	<0.01
Alaska	29	<0.01
Maine	18	<0.01
West Virginia	17	<0.01
Wyoming	10	<0.01
Montana	4	<0.01
North Dakota	1	<0.01
Vermont	1	<0.01

Place	Population	%
California	12,005	0.03
New York	2,952	0.02
Virginia	1,431	0.02
Massachusetts	1,104	0.02
Maryland	995	0.02
Nevada	483	0.02
District of Columbia	110	0.02
United States	**31,626**	**0.01**
Texas	2,658	0.01
Florida	1,692	0.01
New Jersey	1,068	0.01
North Carolina	852	0.01
Georgia	850	0.01
Illinois	644	0.01
Arizona	386	0.01
Colorado	331	0.01
Louisiana	289	0.01
Connecticut	234	0.01
Oregon	197	0.01
Nebraska	152	0.01
Kansas	148	0.01
Rhode Island	132	0.01
South Dakota	51	0.01
Washington	308	<0.01
Pennsylvania	302	<0.01
Ohio	219	<0.01
Tennessee	209	<0.01
Oklahoma	177	<0.01
Indiana	173	<0.01
South Carolina	136	<0.01
Minnesota	132	<0.01
Utah	131	<0.01
Michigan	130	<0.01
Alabama	126	<0.01
Arkansas	105	<0.01
Iowa	92	<0.01
Missouri	89	<0.01
Kentucky	87	<0.01
Wisconsin	85	<0.01
New Mexico	67	<0.01
Mississippi	56	<0.01
Hawaii	54	<0.01
New Hampshire	38	<0.01
Delaware	35	<0.01
Idaho	31	<0.01
Alaska	29	<0.01
Maine	18	<0.01
West Virginia	17	<0.01
Wyoming	10	<0.01
Montana	4	<0.01
North Dakota	1	<0.01
Vermont	1	<0.01

Please refer to the Explanation of Data in the front of the book for more detailed information.

Hispanic Origin

Central American: Other Central American

Top 150 Places Sorted by Population

Based on all places, regardless of total population

Place	Population	%
Los Angeles, CA (city) Los Angeles County	3,980	0.10
New York, NY (city) Kings County	1,627	0.02
Houston, TX (city) Harris County	671	0.03
Bronx, NY (borough) Bronx County	579	0.04
Brooklyn, NY (borough) Kings County	487	0.02
Chelsea, MA (city) Suffolk County	475	1.35
San Francisco, CA (city) San Francisco County	414	0.05
Queens, NY (borough) Queens County	353	0.02
Hempstead, NY (town) Nassau County	282	0.04
Charlotte, NC (city) Mecklenburg County	264	0.04
Chicago, IL (city) Cook County	262	0.01
Dallas, TX (city) Dallas County	238	0.02
Long Beach, CA (city) Los Angeles County	212	0.05
Boston, MA (city) Suffolk County	182	0.03
Islip, NY (town) Suffolk County	177	0.05
Arlington, VA (cdp) Arlington County	169	0.08
Manhattan, NY (borough) New York County	161	0.01
Oakland, CA (city) Alameda County	156	0.04
Phoenix, AZ (city) Maricopa County	154	0.01
San Diego, CA (city) San Diego County	148	0.01
Austin, TX (city) Travis County	142	0.02
San Jose, CA (city) Santa Clara County	138	0.01
South Gate, CA (city) Los Angeles County	136	0.14
San Antonio, TX (city) Medina County	117	0.01
Compton, CA (city) Los Angeles County	114	0.12
Miami, FL (city) Miami-Dade County	113	0.03
Santa Ana, CA (city) Orange County	113	0.03
North Hempstead, NY (town) Nassau County	110	0.05
Washington, DC (city) District of Columbia	110	0.02
Santa Clarita, CA (city) Los Angeles County	108	0.06
Brookhaven, NY (town) Suffolk County	106	0.02
Hawthorne, CA (city) Los Angeles County	104	0.12
Palmdale, CA (city) Los Angeles County	103	0.07
Dale City, VA (cdp) Prince William County	102	0.15
Riverside, CA (city) Riverside County	99	0.03
Las Vegas, NV (city) Clark County	98	0.02
Florence-Graham, CA (cdp) Los Angeles County	96	0.15
Fontana, CA (city) San Bernardino County	94	0.05
Babylon, NY (town) Suffolk County	88	0.04
Pomona, CA (city) Los Angeles County	87	0.06
Lancaster, CA (city) Los Angeles County	84	0.05
Providence, RI (city) Providence County	81	0.05
Jersey City, NJ (city) Hudson County	81	0.03
Daly City, CA (city) San Mateo County	80	0.08
Downey, CA (city) Los Angeles County	79	0.07
Victorville, CA (city) San Bernardino County	79	0.07
Lynwood, CA (city) Los Angeles County	78	0.11
Glendale, CA (city) Los Angeles County	78	0.04
Brentwood, NY (cdp) Suffolk County	76	0.13
North Las Vegas, NV (city) Clark County	76	0.04
Sunrise Manor, NV (cdp) Clark County	76	0.04
Aurora, CO (city) Arapahoe County	75	0.02
Bell, CA (city) Los Angeles County	73	0.21
Richmond, CA (city) Contra Costa County	73	0.07
Paradise, NV (cdp) Clark County	73	0.03
Huntington Park, CA (city) Los Angeles County	71	0.12
Westmont, CA (cdp) Los Angeles County	70	0.22
Elizabeth, NJ (city) Union County	70	0.06
Chamblee, GA (city) DeKalb County	69	0.70
Moreno Valley, CA (city) Riverside County	69	0.04
Ontario, CA (city) San Bernardino County	69	0.04
Guymon, OK (city) Texas County	68	0.59
Frederick, MD (city) Frederick County	68	0.10
East Los Angeles, CA (cdp) Los Angeles County	68	0.05
San Bernardino, CA (city) San Bernardino County	68	0.03
Anaheim, CA (city) Orange County	68	0.02
Baldwin Park, CA (city) Los Angeles County	67	0.09
Lynn, MA (city) Essex County	67	0.07
Irving, TX (city) Dallas County	67	0.03
Hempstead, NY (village) Nassau County	66	0.12
Pasadena, CA (city) Los Angeles County	66	0.05
New Orleans, LA (city) Orleans Parish	66	0.02
Indianapolis, IN (city) Marion County	66	0.01
Central Islip, NY (cdp) Suffolk County	65	0.19
San Mateo, CA (city) San Mateo County	65	0.07
Plano, TX (city) Collin County	63	0.02
Nashville-Davidson, TN (metro govt) Davidson County	63	0.01
El Monte, CA (city) Los Angeles County	62	0.05
Inglewood, CA (city) Los Angeles County	60	0.05
Fullerton, CA (city) Orange County	60	0.04
New Bedford, MA (city) Bristol County	59	0.06
Raleigh, NC (city) Wake County	59	0.01
Bell Gardens, CA (city) Los Angeles County	58	0.14
Herndon, VA (town) Fairfax County	57	0.24
Denver, CO (city) Denver County	56	0.01
Hesperia, CA (city) San Bernardino County	55	0.06
Hayward, CA (city) Alameda County	55	0.04
Whittier, CA (city) Los Angeles County	54	0.06
Columbus, OH (city) Franklin County	54	0.01
Garland, TX (city) Dallas County	53	0.02
Huntington, NY (town) Suffolk County	52	0.03
Fort Worth, TX (city) Tarrant County	52	0.01
Marumsco, VA (cdp) Prince William County	51	0.15
San Bruno, CA (city) San Mateo County	51	0.12
Alhambra, CA (city) Los Angeles County	51	0.06
Rialto, CA (city) San Bernardino County	51	0.05
Pico Rivera, CA (city) Los Angeles County	50	0.08
South San Francisco, CA (city) San Mateo County	50	0.08
West Covina, CA (city) Los Angeles County	50	0.05
Simi Valley, CA (city) Ventura County	50	0.04
Bakersfield, CA (city) Kern County	50	0.01
Stamford, CT (city/town) Fairfield County	49	0.04
Durham, NC (city) Durham County	49	0.02
Jacksonville, FL (city) Duval County	49	0.01
Newark, NJ (city) Essex County	47	0.02
Staten Island, NY (borough) Richmond County	47	0.01
Annandale, VA (cdp) Fairfax County	46	0.11
Plainfield, NJ (city) Union County	46	0.09
Union City, NJ (city) Hudson County	46	0.07
Oklahoma City, OK (city) Oklahoma County	46	0.01
Redwood City, CA (city) San Mateo County	45	0.06
Bridgeport, CT (city/town) Fairfield County	45	0.03
Metairie, LA (cdp) Jefferson Parish	45	0.03
Oyster Bay, NY (town) Nassau County	45	0.02
Reston, VA (cdp) Fairfax County	44	0.08
San Rafael, CA (city) Marin County	44	0.08
Waukegan, IL (city) Lake County	44	0.05
Philadelphia, PA (city) Philadelphia County	44	<0.01
Lennox, CA (cdp) Los Angeles County	43	0.19
Novato, CA (city) Marin County	43	0.08
Montebello, CA (city) Los Angeles County	43	0.07
Sacramento, CA (city) Sacramento County	43	0.01
Chillum, MD (cdp) Prince George's County	42	0.13
Lake Worth, FL (city) Palm Beach County	42	0.12
Reno, NV (city) Washoe County	41	0.02
Huntington Station, NY (cdp) Suffolk County	40	0.12
Yonkers, NY (city) Westchester County	40	0.02
Maywood, CA (city) Los Angeles County	39	0.14
Springfield, VA (cdp) Fairfax County	39	0.13
Alexandria, VA (ind. city) Alexandria independent city	39	0.03
Corona, CA (city) Riverside County	39	0.03
Cudahy, CA (city) Los Angeles County	38	0.16
New Cassel, NY (cdp) Nassau County	37	0.26
Baltimore, MD (city) Baltimore city County	37	0.01
Wichita, KS (city) Sedgwick County	37	0.01
Willowbrook, CA (cdp) Los Angeles County	36	0.10
Gardena, CA (city) Los Angeles County	36	0.06
Kenner, LA (city) Jefferson Parish	36	0.05
Escondido, CA (city) San Diego County	36	0.03
Orange, CA (city) Orange County	36	0.03
Pasadena, TX (city) Harris County	36	0.02
Spring Valley, NV (cdp) Clark County	36	0.02
Omaha, NE (city) Douglas County	36	0.01
Silver Spring, MD (cdp) Montgomery County	35	0.05
Buena Park, CA (city) Orange County	35	0.04
Norwalk, CA (city) Los Angeles County	35	0.03
Colorado Springs, CO (city) El Paso County	35	0.01
Revere, MA (city) Suffolk County	34	0.07
Rockville, MD (city) Montgomery County	34	0.06
Lakewood, NJ (township) Ocean County	34	0.04

SECTION THREE

Please refer to the Explanation of Data in the front of the book for more detailed information.

Hispanic Origin

Central American: Other Central American

Top 150 Places Sorted by Percent of Total Population

Based on all places, regardless of total population

Place	Population	%
Daisy, AR (town) Pike County	2	1.74
Chelsea, MA (city) Suffolk County	475	1.35
Stonerstown, PA (cdp) Bedford County	4	1.06
Morningside, SD (cdp) Beadle County	1	0.95
Loma Mar, CA (cdp) San Mateo County	1	0.88
Wallace, NE (village) Lincoln County	3	0.82
White, GA (city) Bartow County	5	0.75
Soldier, KS (city) Jackson County	1	0.74
Maplesville, AL (town) Chilton County	5	0.71
Chamblee, GA (city) DeKalb County	69	0.70
Ravenna, KY (city) Estill County	4	0.66
Lake Norden, SD (city) Hamlin County	3	0.64
Parkway Village, KY (city) Jefferson County	4	0.62
Guymon, OK (city) Texas County	68	0.59
Drain, OR (city) Douglas County	6	0.52
Laupahoehoe, HI (cdp) Hawaii County	3	0.52
Pajarito Mesa, NM (cdp) Bernalillo County	3	0.52
Worden, IL (village) Madison County	5	0.48
East Hope, ID (city) Bonner County	1	0.48
Pulaski, WI (village) Shawano County	1	0.46
Osyka, MS (town) Pike County	2	0.45
North Abington, PA (township) Lackawanna County	3	0.43
Alta, IA (city) Buena Vista County	8	0.42
Owaneco, IL (village) Christian County	1	0.42
Crooks, SD (city) Minnehaha County	5	0.39
Boling, TX (cdp) Wharton County	4	0.36
Sugar Hill, NH (town) Grafton County	2	0.36
Layhill, MD (cdp) Montgomery County	18	0.35
Camanche Village, CA (cdp) Amador County	3	0.35
West Siloam Springs, OK (town) Delaware County	3	0.35
Haymarket, VA (town) Prince William County	6	0.34
Roosevelt, NJ (borough) Monmouth County	3	0.34
Dorchester, NE (village) Saline County	2	0.34
Downs, KS (city) Osborne County	3	0.33
Weyers Cave, VA (cdp) Augusta County	8	0.32
Dublin, PA (borough) Bucks County	7	0.32
Melville, RI (cdp) Newport County	4	0.30
Mountain Village, CO (town) San Miguel County	4	0.30
Independence, CA (cdp) Inyo County	2	0.30
Mount Kisco, NY (town/village) Westchester County	31	0.29
Liberty, PA (township) Bedford County	4	0.29
Fort Sumner, NM (village) De Baca County	3	0.29
Huntington, VA (cdp) Fairfax County	32	0.28
Idyllwild-Pine Cove, CA (cdp) Riverside County	11	0.28
Pocono Ranch Lands, PA (cdp) Pike County	3	0.28
Sycamore, GA (city) Turner County	2	0.28
Poplar Hills, KY (city) Jefferson County	1	0.28
Lagunitas-Forest Knolls, CA (cdp) Marin County	5	0.27
Buttonwillow, CA (cdp) Kern County	4	0.27
Fairmount Heights, MD (town) Prince George's County	4	0.27
Leland, MI (cdp) Leelanau County	1	0.27
New Cassel, NY (cdp) Nassau County	37	0.26
Moravian Falls, NC (cdp) Wilkes County	5	0.26
Greensburg, KS (city) Kiowa County	2	0.26
Fairview, MO (town) Newton County	1	0.26
Siler City, NC (town) Chatham County	20	0.25
Southern Gateway, VA (cdp) Stafford County	7	0.25
Forest Heights, MD (town) Prince George's County	6	0.25
Alcester, SD (city) Union County	2	0.25
Spring Grove, MN (township) Houston County	1	0.25
Herndon, VA (town) Fairfax County	57	0.24
Broadmoor, CA (cdp) San Mateo County	10	0.24
Stanfield, OR (city) Umatilla County	5	0.24
Covelo, CA (cdp) Mendocino County	3	0.24
Eatonton, GA (city) Putnam County	15	0.23
Westmont, CA (cdp) Los Angeles County	70	0.22
Flanders, NY (cdp) Suffolk County	10	0.22
Spring Brook, PA (township) Lackawanna County	6	0.22
Colma, CA (town) San Mateo County	4	0.22
Bell, CA (city) Los Angeles County	73	0.21
Montalvin Manor, CA (cdp) Contra Costa County	6	0.21
Montara, CA (cdp) San Mateo County	6	0.21
Pawling, NY (village) Dutchess County	5	0.21
Cornish, ME (town) York County	3	0.21
Vansant, VA (cdp) Buchanan County	1	0.21

Place	Population	%
Amityville, NY (village) Suffolk County	19	0.20
Pomona, NJ (cdp) Atlantic County	14	0.20
Potomac Mills, VA (cdp) Prince William County	11	0.20
West Nyack, NY (cdp) Rockland County	7	0.20
Brentwood, MD (town) Prince George's County	6	0.20
Des Allemands, LA (cdp) St. Charles Parish	5	0.20
Gordonsville, VA (town) Orange County	3	0.20
Central Islip, NY (cdp) Suffolk County	65	0.19
Lennox, CA (cdp) Los Angeles County	43	0.19
Mount Rainier, MD (city) Prince George's County	15	0.19
Yorkshire, VA (cdp) Prince William County	14	0.19
Crete, NE (city) Saline County	13	0.19
Gerber, CA (cdp) Tehama County	2	0.19
Canaan, NH (cdp) Grafton County	1	0.19
Cedarville, CA (cdp) Modoc County	1	0.19
Northport, MI (village) Leelanau County	1	0.19
Manassas Park, VA (ind. city) Manassas Park independent city	26	0.18
Sheridan, CO (city) Arapahoe County	10	0.18
Basalt, CO (town) Eagle County	7	0.18
Berne, NY (town) Albany County	5	0.18
Loxley, AL (town) Baldwin County	3	0.18
Ellicott, CO (cdp) El Paso County	2	0.18
Greenvale, NY (cdp) Nassau County	2	0.18
Ruckersville, VA (cdp) Greene County	2	0.18
Edgewater Park, NJ (township) Burlington County	15	0.17
West Athens, CA (cdp) Los Angeles County	15	0.17
Park City, IL (city) Lake County	13	0.17
Broadview Park, FL (cdp) Broward County	12	0.17
Homeland, CA (cdp) Riverside County	10	0.17
Cockrell Hill, TX (city) Dallas County	7	0.17
Mattituck, NY (cdp) Suffolk County	7	0.17
Lenwood, CA (cdp) San Bernardino County	6	0.17
Mangum, OK (city) Greer County	5	0.17
Brewster, NY (village) Putnam County	4	0.17
Citrus City, TX (cdp) Hidalgo County	4	0.17
Fowler, IN (town) Benton County	4	0.17
Lake Como, NJ (borough) Monmouth County	3	0.17
Otisco, MN (township) Waseca County	1	0.17
Cudahy, CA (city) Los Angeles County	38	0.16
Beltsville, MD (cdp) Prince George's County	27	0.16
North Bellport, NY (cdp) Suffolk County	18	0.16
Mary Esther, FL (city) Okaloosa County	6	0.16
Cabazon, CA (cdp) Riverside County	4	0.16
Val Verde, CA (cdp) Los Angeles County	4	0.16
Port Carbon, PA (borough) Schuylkill County	3	0.16
Plattekill, NY (cdp) Ulster County	2	0.16
Woodbranch, TX (city) Montgomery County	2	0.16
Navarre Beach, FL (cdp) Santa Rosa County	1	0.16
Dale City, VA (cdp) Prince William County	102	0.15
Florence-Graham, CA (cdp) Los Angeles County	96	0.15
Marumsco, VA (cdp) Prince William County	51	0.15
Bull Run, VA (cdp) Prince William County	23	0.15
Wyandanch, NY (cdp) Suffolk County	18	0.15
Great Neck, NY (village) Nassau County	15	0.15
East Foothills, CA (cdp) Santa Clara County	12	0.15
East Farmingdale, NY (cdp) Suffolk County	10	0.15
Montevideo, MN (city) Chippewa County	8	0.15
Orangeburg, NY (cdp) Rockland County	7	0.15
Hampstead, NC (cdp) Pender County	6	0.15
Kelseyville, CA (cdp) Lake County	5	0.15
Castroville, TX (city) Medina County	4	0.15
Old Saybrook Center, CT (cdp) Middlesex County	3	0.15
Summit, WI (town) Juneau County	1	0.15
South Gate, CA (city) Los Angeles County	136	0.14
Bell Gardens, CA (city) Los Angeles County	58	0.14
Maywood, CA (city) Los Angeles County	39	0.14
Inwood, NY (cdp) Nassau County	14	0.14
Forest, MS (city) Scott County	8	0.14
Eagle Grove, IA (city) Wright County	5	0.14
East Dundee, IL (village) Kane County	4	0.14
Southport, NC (city) Brunswick County	4	0.14
Bay Park, NY (cdp) Nassau County	3	0.14
Bellport, NY (village) Suffolk County	3	0.14
Imperial, NE (city) Chase County	3	0.14
Southworth, WA (cdp) Kitsap County	3	0.14

Please refer to the Explanation of Data in the front of the book for more detailed information.

Hispanic Origin

Central American: Other Central American

Top 150 Places Sorted by Percent of Total Population

Based on places with total population of 7,500 or more

Place	Population	%
Chelsea, MA (city) Suffolk County	475	1.35
Chamblee, GA (city) DeKalb County	69	0.70
Guymon, OK (city) Texas County	68	0.59
Mount Kisco, NY (town/village) Westchester County	31	0.29
Huntington, VA (cdp) Fairfax County	32	0.28
New Cassel, NY (cdp) Nassau County	37	0.26
Siler City, NC (town) Chatham County	20	0.25
Herndon, VA (town) Fairfax County	57	0.24
Westmont, CA (cdp) Los Angeles County	70	0.22
Bell, CA (city) Los Angeles County	73	0.21
Amityville, NY (village) Suffolk County	19	0.20
Central Islip, NY (cdp) Suffolk County	65	0.19
Lennox, CA (cdp) Los Angeles County	43	0.19
Mount Rainier, MD (city) Prince George's County	15	0.19
Yorkshire, VA (cdp) Prince William County	14	0.19
Manassas Park, VA (ind. city) Manassas Park independent city	26	0.18
Edgewater Park, NJ (township) Burlington County	15	0.17
West Athens, CA (cdp) Los Angeles County	15	0.17
Park City, IL (city) Lake County	13	0.17
Cudahy, CA (city) Los Angeles County	38	0.16
Beltsville, MD (cdp) Prince George's County	27	0.16
North Bellport, NY (cdp) Suffolk County	18	0.16
Dale City, VA (cdp) Prince William County	102	0.15
Florence-Graham, CA (cdp) Los Angeles County	96	0.15
Marumsco, VA (cdp) Prince William County	51	0.15
Bull Run, VA (cdp) Prince William County	23	0.15
Wyandanch, NY (cdp) Suffolk County	18	0.15
Great Neck, NY (village) Nassau County	15	0.15
East Foothills, CA (cdp) Santa Clara County	12	0.15
South Gate, CA (city) Los Angeles County	136	0.14
Bell Gardens, CA (city) Los Angeles County	58	0.14
Maywood, CA (city) Los Angeles County	39	0.14
Inwood, NY (cdp) Nassau County	14	0.14
Brentwood, NY (cdp) Suffolk County	76	0.13
Chillum, MD (cdp) Prince George's County	42	0.13
Springfield, VA (cdp) Fairfax County	39	0.13
North Plainfield, NJ (borough) Somerset County	28	0.13
Westbury, NY (village) Nassau County	20	0.13
Compton, CA (city) Los Angeles County	114	0.12
Hawthorne, CA (city) Los Angeles County	104	0.12
Huntington Park, CA (city) Los Angeles County	71	0.12
Hempstead, NY (village) Nassau County	66	0.12
San Bruno, CA (city) San Mateo County	51	0.12
Lake Worth, FL (city) Palm Beach County	42	0.12
Huntington Station, NY (cdp) Suffolk County	40	0.12
Roosevelt, NY (cdp) Nassau County	19	0.12
Home Gardens, CA (cdp) Riverside County	14	0.12
Lanham, MD (cdp) Prince George's County	12	0.12
Lynwood, CA (city) Los Angeles County	78	0.11
Annandale, VA (cdp) Fairfax County	46	0.11
Woodlawn, VA (cdp) Fairfax County	23	0.11
McNair, VA (cdp) Fairfax County	20	0.11
Ferndale, MD (cdp) Anne Arundel County	18	0.11
Groveton, VA (cdp) Fairfax County	16	0.11
Riverdale, GA (city) Clayton County	16	0.11
Los Angeles, CA (city) Los Angeles County	3,980	0.10
Frederick, MD (city) Frederick County	68	0.10
Willowbrook, CA (cdp) Los Angeles County	36	0.10
Morris, NJ (town) Morris County	18	0.10
Santa Fe Springs, CA (city) Los Angeles County	17	0.10
Commerce, CA (city) Los Angeles County	13	0.10
Crestline, CA (cdp) San Bernardino County	11	0.10
South Huntington, NY (cdp) Suffolk County	9	0.10
Lansdowne, MD (cdp) Baltimore County	8	0.10
South San Gabriel, CA (cdp) Los Angeles County	8	0.10
Baldwin Park, CA (city) Los Angeles County	67	0.09
Plainfield, NJ (city) Union County	46	0.09
Gainesville, GA (city) Hall County	29	0.09
Columbus, NE (city) Platte County	19	0.09
Langley Park, MD (cdp) Prince George's County	17	0.09
Hyattsville, MD (city) Prince George's County	16	0.09
Idylwood, VA (cdp) Fairfax County	16	0.09
Lindenwold, NJ (borough) Camden County	16	0.09
Mastic Beach, NY (cdp) Suffolk County	12	0.09
Worthington, MN (city) Nobles County	12	0.09
Huron, SD (city) Beadle County	11	0.09
Manchester, VA (cdp) Chesterfield County	10	0.09
North Lindenhurst, NY (cdp) Suffolk County	10	0.09
Bladensburg, MD (town) Prince George's County	8	0.09
Seven Corners, VA (cdp) Fairfax County	8	0.09
Arlington, VA (cdp) Arlington County	169	0.08
Daly City, CA (city) San Mateo County	80	0.08
Pico Rivera, CA (city) Los Angeles County	50	0.08
South San Francisco, CA (city) San Mateo County	50	0.08
Reston, VA (cdp) Fairfax County	44	0.08
San Rafael, CA (city) Marin County	44	0.08
Novato, CA (city) Marin County	43	0.08
Laurel, MD (city) Prince George's County	20	0.08
South Pasadena, CA (city) Los Angeles County	20	0.08
Uniondale, NY (cdp) Nassau County	19	0.08
Rosemont, CA (cdp) Sacramento County	18	0.08
Shelbyville, TN (city) Bedford County	17	0.08
South San Jose Hills, CA (cdp) Los Angeles County	17	0.08
Mineola, NY (village) Nassau County	15	0.08
Ballenger Creek, MD (cdp) Frederick County	14	0.08
Oxon Hill, MD (cdp) Prince George's County	14	0.08
Hybla Valley, VA (cdp) Fairfax County	13	0.08
Mastic, NY (cdp) Suffolk County	13	0.08
Schofield Barracks, HI (cdp) Honolulu County	13	0.08
Fullerton, PA (cdp) Lehigh County	12	0.08
Vincent, CA (cdp) Los Angeles County	12	0.08
Walnut Park, CA (cdp) Los Angeles County	12	0.08
Fairview, NJ (borough) Bergen County	11	0.08
Kailua, HI (cdp) Hawaii County	10	0.08
Lake Grove, NY (village) Suffolk County	9	0.08
Mendota, CA (city) Fresno County	9	0.08
Smithfield, NC (town) Johnston County	9	0.08
Del Aire, CA (cdp) Los Angeles County	8	0.08
Butler, NJ (borough) Morris County	6	0.08
Purcellville, VA (town) Loudoun County	6	0.08
Wilson, PA (borough) Northampton County	6	0.08
Palmdale, CA (city) Los Angeles County	103	0.07
Downey, CA (city) Los Angeles County	79	0.07
Victorville, CA (city) San Bernardino County	79	0.07
Richmond, CA (city) Contra Costa County	73	0.07
Lynn, MA (city) Essex County	67	0.07
San Mateo, CA (city) San Mateo County	65	0.07
Union City, NJ (city) Hudson County	46	0.07
Montebello, CA (city) Los Angeles County	43	0.07
Revere, MA (city) Suffolk County	34	0.07
Hicksville, NY (cdp) Nassau County	28	0.07
Galloway, NJ (township) Atlantic County	27	0.07
Manassas, VA (ind. city) Manassas independent city	26	0.07
Lawndale, CA (city) Los Angeles County	23	0.07
Englewood, NJ (city) Bergen County	20	0.07
Lawrenceville, GA (city) Gwinnett County	19	0.07
Baldwin, NY (cdp) Nassau County	18	0.07
Cloverleaf, TX (cdp) Harris County	17	0.07
Lincolnia, VA (cdp) Fairfax County	17	0.07
Peekskill, NY (city) Westchester County	17	0.07
Cliffside Park, NJ (borough) Bergen County	16	0.07
Lemoore, CA (city) Kings County	16	0.07
Terrytown, LA (cdp) Jefferson Parish	16	0.07
South El Monte, CA (city) Los Angeles County	14	0.07
Yucca Valley, CA (town) San Bernardino County	14	0.07
Meadowbrook, VA (cdp) Chesterfield County	12	0.07
North Amityville, NY (cdp) Suffolk County	12	0.07
Adelphi, MD (cdp) Prince George's County	11	0.07
East Rancho Dominguez, CA (cdp) Los Angeles County	11	0.07
Cherry Hill Mall, NJ (cdp) Camden County	10	0.07
Clarksburg, MD (cdp) Montgomery County	10	0.07
Ripon, CA (city) San Joaquin County	10	0.07
Sweetwater, FL (city) Miami-Dade County	10	0.07
Justice, IL (village) Cook County	9	0.07
Palmetto, FL (city) Manatee County	9	0.07
Salisbury, NY (cdp) Nassau County	9	0.07
Knightdale, NC (town) Wake County	8	0.07
North Merrick, NY (cdp) Nassau County	8	0.07
Groton, CT (city) New London County	7	0.07
Storm Lake, IA (city) Buena Vista County	7	0.07

SECTION THREE

Please refer to the Explanation of Data in the front of the book for more detailed information.

Hispanic Origin

Cuban

U.S. and 50 States Sorted by Population and Percent of Total Population

Place	Population	%	Place	Population	%
United States	**1,785,547**	**0.58**	Florida	1,213,438	6.45
Florida	1,213,438	6.45	New Jersey	83,362	0.95
California	88,607	0.24	Nevada	21,459	0.79
New Jersey	83,362	0.95	**United States**	**1,785,547**	**0.58**
New York	70,803	0.37	New York	70,803	0.37
Texas	46,541	0.19	District of Columbia	1,789	0.30
Georgia	25,048	0.26	Connecticut	9,490	0.27
Illinois	22,541	0.18	Georgia	25,048	0.26
Nevada	21,459	0.79	California	88,607	0.24
North Carolina	18,079	0.19	Louisiana	10,330	0.23
Pennsylvania	17,930	0.14	Kentucky	9,323	0.21
Virginia	15,229	0.19	New Mexico	4,298	0.21
Massachusetts	11,306	0.17	Texas	46,541	0.19
Arizona	10,692	0.17	North Carolina	18,079	0.19
Maryland	10,366	0.18	Virginia	15,229	0.19
Louisiana	10,330	0.23	Illinois	22,541	0.18
Michigan	9,922	0.10	Maryland	10,366	0.18
Connecticut	9,490	0.27	Massachusetts	11,306	0.17
Kentucky	9,323	0.21	Arizona	10,692	0.17
Tennessee	7,773	0.12	Rhode Island	1,640	0.16
Ohio	7,523	0.07	Delaware	1,443	0.16
Washington	6,744	0.10	Pennsylvania	17,930	0.14
Colorado	6,253	0.12	South Carolina	5,955	0.13
South Carolina	5,955	0.13	Oregon	4,923	0.13
Missouri	4,979	0.08	Alaska	927	0.13
Oregon	4,923	0.13	Tennessee	7,773	0.12
New Mexico	4,298	0.21	Colorado	6,253	0.12
Alabama	4,064	0.09	Nebraska	2,152	0.12
Indiana	4,042	0.06	Hawaii	1,544	0.11
Wisconsin	3,696	0.06	Michigan	9,922	0.10
Minnesota	3,661	0.07	Washington	6,744	0.10
Oklahoma	2,755	0.07	Kansas	2,723	0.10
Kansas	2,723	0.10	New Hampshire	1,349	0.10
Nebraska	2,152	0.12	Alabama	4,064	0.09
Mississippi	2,063	0.07	Missouri	4,979	0.08
Utah	1,963	0.07	Vermont	510	0.08
District of Columbia	1,789	0.30	Ohio	7,523	0.07
Rhode Island	1,640	0.16	Minnesota	3,661	0.07
Hawaii	1,544	0.11	Oklahoma	2,755	0.07
Arkansas	1,493	0.05	Mississippi	2,063	0.07
Delaware	1,443	0.16	Utah	1,963	0.07
New Hampshire	1,349	0.10	Indiana	4,042	0.06
Iowa	1,226	0.04	Wisconsin	3,696	0.06
Alaska	927	0.13	Maine	783	0.06
Idaho	825	0.05	Arkansas	1,493	0.05
Maine	783	0.06	Idaho	825	0.05
West Virginia	764	0.04	Wyoming	275	0.05
Vermont	510	0.08	Iowa	1,226	0.04
Montana	421	0.04	West Virginia	764	0.04
Wyoming	275	0.05	Montana	421	0.04
South Dakota	265	0.03	North Dakota	260	0.04
North Dakota	260	0.04	South Dakota	265	0.03

Please refer to the Explanation of Data in the front of the book for more detailed information.

Hispanic Origin

Cuban

Top 150 Places Sorted by Population

Based on all places, regardless of total population

Place	Population	%
Hialeah, FL (city) Miami-Dade County	164,717	73.32
Miami, FL (city) Miami-Dade County	137,301	34.37
New York, NY (city) Kings County	40,840	0.50
Tamiami, FL (cdp) Miami-Dade County	36,180	65.46
Kendale Lakes, FL (cdp) Miami-Dade County	29,095	51.82
Fountainebleau, FL (cdp) Miami-Dade County	27,798	46.51
Kendall, FL (cdp) Miami-Dade County	24,533	32.55
Westchester, FL (cdp) Miami-Dade County	21,391	71.63
Tampa, FL (city) Hillsborough County	21,295	6.34
Pembroke Pines, FL (city) Broward County	19,826	12.81
Miami Beach, FL (city) Miami-Dade County	17,599	20.05
University Park, FL (cdp) Miami-Dade County	17,155	63.55
Coral Terrace, FL (cdp) Miami-Dade County	16,780	68.84
Miami Lakes, FL (town) Miami-Dade County	16,752	57.06
Kendall West, FL (cdp) Miami-Dade County	16,109	44.56
Country Club, FL (cdp) Miami-Dade County	15,509	32.92
Coral Gables, FL (city) Miami-Dade County	14,657	31.33
Hialeah Gardens, FL (city) Miami-Dade County	14,314	65.83
The Hammocks, FL (cdp) Miami-Dade County	13,605	26.67
Los Angeles, CA (city) Los Angeles County	13,494	0.36
South Miami Heights, FL (cdp) Miami-Dade County	13,466	37.72
Miramar, FL (city) Broward County	12,924	10.59
Richmond West, FL (cdp) Miami-Dade County	12,818	40.09
Manhattan, NY (borough) New York County	11,623	0.73
Town 'n' Country, FL (cdp) Hillsborough County	11,570	14.75
Queens, NY (borough) Queens County	11,020	0.49
Cutler Bay, FL (town) Miami-Dade County	9,858	24.47
Cape Coral, FL (city) Lee County	9,843	6.38
Egypt Lake-Leto, FL (cdp) Hillsborough County	9,697	27.48
Miami Gardens, FL (city) Miami-Dade County	9,587	8.95
Sunset, FL (cdp) Miami-Dade County	9,552	58.28
Homestead, FL (city) Miami-Dade County	9,524	15.74
Hollywood, FL (city) Broward County	9,258	6.58
Olympia Heights, FL (cdp) Miami-Dade County	9,103	67.49
Bronx, NY (borough) Bronx County	8,785	0.63
Chicago, IL (city) Cook County	8,331	0.31
West Little River, FL (cdp) Miami-Dade County	8,014	23.10
Sweetwater, FL (city) Miami-Dade County	7,672	56.83
Houston, TX (city) Harris County	7,663	0.37
Brooklyn, NY (borough) Kings County	7,581	0.30
Westwood Lakes, FL (cdp) Miami-Dade County	7,539	63.68
West New York, NJ (town) Hudson County	7,514	15.12
Union City, NJ (city) Hudson County	7,510	11.30
North Bergen, NJ (township) Hudson County	7,248	11.93
The Crossings, FL (cdp) Miami-Dade County	7,065	31.04
Jacksonville, FL (city) Duval County	7,006	0.85
Louisville-Jefferson County, KY (metro govt) Jefferson County	6,575	1.10
Elizabeth, NJ (city) Union County	6,570	5.26
Lehigh Acres, FL (cdp) Lee County	6,506	7.50
Glenvar Heights, FL (cdp) Miami-Dade County	6,488	38.40
Miami Springs, FL (city) Miami-Dade County	6,185	44.79
Davie, FL (town) Broward County	6,071	6.60
Leisure City, FL (cdp) Miami-Dade County	5,934	26.19
Doral, FL (city) Miami-Dade County	5,806	12.70
Las Vegas, NV (city) Clark County	5,471	0.94
West Palm Beach, FL (city) Palm Beach County	5,337	5.34
Princeton, FL (cdp) Miami-Dade County	5,294	24.02
Country Walk, FL (cdp) Miami-Dade County	5,230	32.69
Paradise, NV (cdp) Clark County	4,405	1.97
Orlando, FL (city) Orange County	4,299	1.80
Palmetto Bay, FL (village) Miami-Dade County	4,206	17.97
West Miami, FL (city) Miami-Dade County	4,153	69.62
Port St. Lucie, FL (city) St. Lucie County	4,120	2.50
Fort Lauderdale, FL (city) Broward County	4,093	2.47
Phoenix, AZ (city) Maricopa County	3,975	0.27
Golden Gate, FL (cdp) Collier County	3,941	16.45
Philadelphia, PA (city) Philadelphia County	3,930	0.26
Pinecrest, FL (village) Miami-Dade County	3,923	21.53
North Miami, FL (city) Miami-Dade County	3,762	6.40
Hempstead, NY (town) Nassau County	3,597	0.47
Plantation, FL (city) Broward County	3,398	4.00
Palm Springs, FL (village) Palm Beach County	3,249	17.17
Three Lakes, FL (cdp) Miami-Dade County	3,186	21.17
Austin, TX (city) Travis County	3,163	0.40
Weston, FL (city) Broward County	3,134	4.80

Place	Population	%
Palm Springs North, FL (cdp) Miami-Dade County	3,111	59.22
South Miami, FL (city) Miami-Dade County	3,012	25.84
Sunrise, FL (city) Broward County	2,956	3.50
Albuquerque, NM (city) Bernalillo County	2,915	0.53
North Miami Beach, FL (city) Miami-Dade County	2,909	7.01
Charlotte, NC (city) Mecklenburg County	2,902	0.40
Gainesville, FL (city) Alachua County	2,886	2.32
Coral Springs, FL (city) Broward County	2,853	2.36
St. Petersburg, FL (city) Pinellas County	2,835	1.16
San Diego, CA (city) San Diego County	2,694	0.21
Brandon, FL (cdp) Hillsborough County	2,690	2.60
Sunrise Manor, NV (cdp) Clark County	2,604	1.38
Palm River-Clair Mel, FL (cdp) Hillsborough County	2,497	11.88
San Antonio, TX (city) Medina County	2,468	0.19
Key West, FL (city) Monroe County	2,422	9.83
Palmetto Estates, FL (cdp) Miami-Dade County	2,404	17.76
The Acreage, FL (cdp) Palm Beach County	2,364	6.11
Dallas, TX (city) Dallas County	2,322	0.19
Boston, MA (city) Suffolk County	2,319	0.38
Tallahassee, FL (city) Leon County	2,302	1.27
Downey, CA (city) Los Angeles County	2,283	2.04
Hallandale Beach, FL (city) Broward County	2,251	6.07
Opa-locka, FL (city) Miami-Dade County	2,248	14.77
Cooper City, FL (city) Broward County	2,246	7.87
Newark, NJ (city) Essex County	2,241	0.81
Wellington, FL (village) Palm Beach County	2,179	3.86
Portland, OR (city) Multnomah County	2,172	0.37
Carrollwood, FL (cdp) Hillsborough County	2,108	6.32
Citrus Park, FL (cdp) Hillsborough County	2,069	8.53
Key Biscayne, FL (village) Miami-Dade County	2,051	16.62
Goulds, FL (cdp) Miami-Dade County	2,014	19.93
Spring Valley, NV (cdp) Clark County	2,010	1.13
San Francisco, CA (city) San Francisco County	1,992	0.25
Sunny Isles Beach, FL (city) Miami-Dade County	1,990	9.55
Alafaya, FL (cdp) Orange County	1,861	2.38
Staten Island, NY (borough) Richmond County	1,831	0.39
Washington, DC (city) District of Columbia	1,789	0.30
Nashville-Davidson, TN (metro govt) Davidson County	1,716	0.29
Jersey City, NJ (city) Hudson County	1,641	0.66
Rochester, NY (city) Monroe County	1,616	0.77
Pompano Beach, FL (city) Broward County	1,601	1.60
Greenacres, FL (city) Palm Beach County	1,593	4.24
Lakeland, FL (city) Polk County	1,563	1.60
Henderson, NV (city) Clark County	1,550	0.60
Deltona, FL (city) Volusia County	1,548	1.82
Boca Raton, FL (city) Palm Beach County	1,538	1.82
Kissimmee, FL (city) Osceola County	1,524	2.55
Royal Palm Beach, FL (village) Palm Beach County	1,521	4.46
Glendale, CA (city) Los Angeles County	1,513	0.79
Tamarac, FL (city) Broward County	1,510	2.50
Yonkers, NY (city) Westchester County	1,501	0.77
Brookhaven, NY (town) Suffolk County	1,500	0.31
Fort Worth, TX (city) Tarrant County	1,495	0.20
Northdale, FL (cdp) Hillsborough County	1,477	6.69
Naranja, FL (cdp) Miami-Dade County	1,458	17.56
Riverview, FL (cdp) Hillsborough County	1,450	2.04
Ojus, FL (cdp) Miami-Dade County	1,439	7.98
Lake Worth, FL (city) Palm Beach County	1,438	4.12
Golden Glades, FL (cdp) Miami-Dade County	1,428	4.31
Aventura, FL (city) Miami-Dade County	1,408	3.94
Metairie, LA (cdp) Jefferson Parish	1,396	1.01
Key Largo, FL (cdp) Monroe County	1,380	13.23
Palm Bay, FL (city) Brevard County	1,373	1.33
West Perrine, FL (cdp) Miami-Dade County	1,351	14.28
Lake Magdalene, FL (cdp) Hillsborough County	1,344	4.71
Atlanta, GA (city) Fulton County	1,333	0.32
Spring Hill, FL (cdp) Hernando County	1,332	1.35
Kansas City, MO (city) Jackson County	1,327	0.29
Oakland Park, FL (city) Broward County	1,319	3.19
Stock Island, FL (cdp) Monroe County	1,314	33.53
Southwest Ranches, FL (town) Broward County	1,300	17.70
New Orleans, LA (city) Orleans Parish	1,285	0.37
Brownsville, FL (cdp) Miami-Dade County	1,268	8.28
North Bay Village, FL (city) Miami-Dade County	1,266	17.74
Long Beach, CA (city) Los Angeles County	1,264	0.27

SECTION THREE

Hispanic Origin

Cuban

Top 150 Places Sorted by Percent of Total Population

Based on all places, regardless of total population

Place	Population	%
Hialeah, FL (city) Miami-Dade County	164,717	73.32
Medley, FL (town) Miami-Dade County	607	72.43
Westchester, FL (cdp) Miami-Dade County	21,391	71.63
West Miami, FL (city) Miami-Dade County	4,153	69.62
Coral Terrace, FL (cdp) Miami-Dade County	16,780	68.84
Olympia Heights, FL (cdp) Miami-Dade County	9,103	67.49
Hialeah Gardens, FL (city) Miami-Dade County	14,314	65.83
Tamiami, FL (cdp) Miami-Dade County	36,180	65.46
Westwood Lakes, FL (cdp) Miami-Dade County	7,539	63.68
University Park, FL (cdp) Miami-Dade County	17,155	63.55
Palm Springs North, FL (cdp) Miami-Dade County	3,111	59.22
Sunset, FL (cdp) Miami-Dade County	9,552	58.28
Miami Lakes, FL (town) Miami-Dade County	16,752	57.06
Sweetwater, FL (city) Miami-Dade County	7,672	56.83
Kendale Lakes, FL (cdp) Miami-Dade County	29,095	51.82
Fountainebleau, FL (cdp) Miami-Dade County	27,798	46.51
Miami Springs, FL (city) Miami-Dade County	6,185	44.79
Kendall West, FL (cdp) Miami-Dade County	16,109	44.56
Virginia Gardens, FL (village) Miami-Dade County	954	40.17
Richmond West, FL (cdp) Miami-Dade County	12,818	40.09
Glenvar Heights, FL (cdp) Miami-Dade County	6,488	38.40
South Miami Heights, FL (cdp) Miami-Dade County	13,466	37.72
Miami, FL (city) Miami-Dade County	137,301	34.37
Stock Island, FL (cdp) Monroe County	1,314	33.53
Country Club, FL (cdp) Miami-Dade County	15,509	32.92
Country Walk, FL (cdp) Miami-Dade County	5,230	32.69
Kendall, FL (cdp) Miami-Dade County	24,533	32.55
Coral Gables, FL (city) Miami-Dade County	14,657	31.33
The Crossings, FL (cdp) Miami-Dade County	7,065	31.04
Montura, FL (cdp) Hendry County	998	30.40
Gun Club Estates, FL (cdp) Palm Beach County	229	29.51
Egypt Lake-Leto, FL (cdp) Hillsborough County	9,697	27.48
The Hammocks, FL (cdp) Miami-Dade County	13,605	26.67
Leisure City, FL (cdp) Miami-Dade County	5,934	26.19
South Miami, FL (city) Miami-Dade County	3,012	25.84
Cutler Bay, FL (town) Miami-Dade County	9,858	24.47
Princeton, FL (cdp) Miami-Dade County	5,294	24.02
West Little River, FL (cdp) Miami-Dade County	8,014	23.10
Tavernier, FL (cdp) Monroe County	462	21.63
Pinecrest, FL (village) Miami-Dade County	3,923	21.53
Three Lakes, FL (cdp) Miami-Dade County	3,186	21.17
Surfside, FL (town) Miami-Dade County	1,192	20.75
Miami Beach, FL (city) Miami-Dade County	17,599	20.05
Goulds, FL (cdp) Miami-Dade County	2,014	19.93
Flaxton, ND (city) Burke County	12	18.18
Palmetto Bay, FL (village) Miami-Dade County	4,206	17.97
Palmetto Estates, FL (cdp) Miami-Dade County	2,404	17.76
North Bay Village, FL (city) Miami-Dade County	1,266	17.74
Southwest Ranches, FL (town) Broward County	1,300	17.70
Naranja, FL (cdp) Miami-Dade County	1,458	17.56
Palm Springs, FL (village) Palm Beach County	3,249	17.17
Broadview Park, FL (cdp) Broward County	1,219	17.11
Key Biscayne, FL (village) Miami-Dade County	2,051	16.62
Golden Gate, FL (cdp) Collier County	3,941	16.45
Pine Air, FL (cdp) Palm Beach County	332	16.40
Pioneer, FL (cdp) Hendry County	113	16.21
Homestead, FL (city) Miami-Dade County	9,524	15.74
Big Coppitt Key, FL (cdp) Monroe County	375	15.26
Marathon, FL (city) Monroe County	1,256	15.14
West New York, NJ (town) Hudson County	7,514	15.12
Opa-locka, FL (city) Miami-Dade County	2,248	14.77
Town 'n' Country, FL (cdp) Hillsborough County	11,570	14.75
Royal Palm Estates, FL (cdp) Palm Beach County	446	14.74
Glen Ridge, FL (town) Palm Beach County	32	14.61
West Perrine, FL (cdp) Miami-Dade County	1,351	14.28
Lake Clarke Shores, FL (town) Palm Beach County	471	13.95
Key Largo, FL (cdp) Monroe County	1,380	13.23
Pembroke Pines, FL (city) Broward County	19,826	12.81
Doral, FL (city) Miami-Dade County	5,806	12.70
North Bergen, NJ (township) Hudson County	7,248	11.93
Palm River-Clair Mel, FL (cdp) Hillsborough County	2,497	11.88
Indian Creek, FL (village) Miami-Dade County	10	11.63
Clewiston, FL (city) Hendry County	831	11.61
Union City, NJ (city) Hudson County	7,510	11.30
Orrum, NC (town) Robeson County	10	10.99
Miramar, FL (city) Broward County	12,924	10.59
Miami Shores, FL (village) Miami-Dade County	1,074	10.24
Westview, FL (cdp) Miami-Dade County	980	10.16
Bay Harbor Islands, FL (town) Miami-Dade County	565	10.04
Kenwood Estates, FL (cdp) Palm Beach County	128	9.98
Key West, FL (city) Monroe County	2,422	9.83
Biscayne Park, FL (village) Miami-Dade County	294	9.62
Sunny Isles Beach, FL (city) Miami-Dade County	1,990	9.55
Homestead Base, FL (cdp) Miami-Dade County	90	9.34
Richmond Heights, FL (cdp) Miami-Dade County	788	9.23
Guttenberg, NJ (town) Hudson County	1,011	9.05
Teterboro, NJ (borough) Bergen County	6	8.96
Miami Gardens, FL (city) Miami-Dade County	9,587	8.95
Citrus Park, FL (cdp) Hillsborough County	2,069	8.53
Acacia Villas, FL (cdp) Palm Beach County	36	8.43
Haverhill, FL (town) Palm Beach County	157	8.38
Brownsville, FL (cdp) Miami-Dade County	1,268	8.28
Florida City, FL (city) Miami-Dade County	911	8.10
Ojus, FL (cdp) Miami-Dade County	1,439	7.98
Cooper City, FL (city) Broward County	2,246	7.87
Golden Beach, FL (town) Miami-Dade County	72	7.83
Weehawken, NJ (township) Hudson County	980	7.81
Naples Manor, FL (cdp) Collier County	423	7.61
Lake Alice, MN (township) Hubbard County	7	7.53
Lehigh Acres, FL (cdp) Lee County	6,506	7.50
Bal Harbour, FL (village) Miami-Dade County	188	7.48
Sky Lake, FL (cdp) Orange County	459	7.46
Plantation Mobile Home Park, FL (cdp) Palm Beach County	91	7.22
Lakewood Gardens, FL (cdp) Palm Beach County	91	7.15
North Miami Beach, FL (city) Miami-Dade County	2,909	7.01
Northdale, FL (cdp) Hillsborough County	1,477	6.69
Lake Harbor, FL (cdp) Palm Beach County	3	6.67
Davie, FL (town) Broward County	6,071	6.60
Hollywood, FL (city) Broward County	9,258	6.58
Gladeview, FL (cdp) Miami-Dade County	749	6.49
North Miami, FL (city) Miami-Dade County	3,762	6.40
Cape Coral, FL (city) Lee County	9,843	6.38
West Park, FL (city) Broward County	901	6.36
Tampa, FL (city) Hillsborough County	21,295	6.34
Carrollwood, FL (cdp) Hillsborough County	2,108	6.32
Iago, TX (cdp) Wharton County	10	6.21
Horn, OK (town) Hughes County	6	6.19
West Buechel, KY (city) Jefferson County	76	6.18
The Acreage, FL (cdp) Palm Beach County	2,364	6.11
Hallandale Beach, FL (city) Broward County	2,251	6.07
Pinewood, FL (cdp) Miami-Dade County	995	6.02
Pine Castle, FL (cdp) Orange County	646	5.98
El Portal, FL (village) Miami-Dade County	139	5.98
Belle Glade, FL (city) Palm Beach County	1,042	5.97
Whitestone Logging Camp, AK (cdp) Hoonah-Angoon Census Area	1	5.88
Azalea Park, FL (cdp) Orange County	716	5.70
Lake Lindsey, FL (cdp) Hernando County	4	5.63
Big Pine Key, FL (cdp) Monroe County	239	5.62
Dahlen, ND (cdp) Nelson County	1	5.56
Port LaBelle, FL (cdp) Hendry County	194	5.50
Quintana, TX (town) Brazoria County	3	5.36
West Palm Beach, FL (city) Palm Beach County	5,337	5.34
Elizabeth, NJ (city) Union County	6,570	5.26
Ridgefield, NJ (borough) Bergen County	575	5.21
Orangetree, FL (cdp) Collier County	229	5.20
Kensington Park, FL (cdp) Sarasota County	202	5.18
Fairview, NJ (borough) Bergen County	709	5.12
Rio Pinar, FL (cdp) Orange County	267	5.12
Forest City, FL (cdp) Seminole County	680	4.91
Ridgefield Park, NJ (village) Bergen County	612	4.81
Weston, FL (city) Broward County	3,134	4.80
Islamorada, FL (village) Monroe County	291	4.76
Attu Station, AK (cdp) Aleutians West Census Area	1	4.76
Lake Magdalene, FL (cdp) Hillsborough County	1,344	4.71
McKinley, MN (city) St. Louis County	6	4.69
Royal Palm Beach, FL (village) Palm Beach County	1,521	4.46
Del Mar Heights, TX (cdp) Cameron County	5	4.42
Westgate, FL (cdp) Palm Beach County	350	4.39
Golden Glades, FL (cdp) Miami-Dade County	1,428	4.31
Lely Resort, FL (cdp) Collier County	198	4.26

Please refer to the Explanation of Data in the front of the book for more detailed information.

Hispanic Origin

Cuban

Top 150 Places Sorted by Percent of Total Population

Based on places with total population of 7,500 or more

Place	Population	%
Hialeah, FL (city) Miami-Dade County	164,717	73.32
Westchester, FL (cdp) Miami-Dade County	21,391	71.63
Coral Terrace, FL (cdp) Miami-Dade County	16,780	68.84
Olympia Heights, FL (cdp) Miami-Dade County	9,103	67.49
Hialeah Gardens, FL (city) Miami-Dade County	14,314	65.83
Tamiami, FL (cdp) Miami-Dade County	36,180	65.46
Westwood Lakes, FL (cdp) Miami-Dade County	7,539	63.68
University Park, FL (cdp) Miami-Dade County	17,155	63.55
Sunset, FL (cdp) Miami-Dade County	9,552	58.28
Miami Lakes, FL (town) Miami-Dade County	16,752	57.06
Sweetwater, FL (city) Miami-Dade County	7,672	56.83
Kendale Lakes, FL (cdp) Miami-Dade County	29,095	51.82
Fountainebleau, FL (cdp) Miami-Dade County	27,798	46.51
Miami Springs, FL (city) Miami-Dade County	6,185	44.79
Kendall West, FL (cdp) Miami-Dade County	16,109	44.56
Richmond West, FL (cdp) Miami-Dade County	12,818	40.09
Glenvar Heights, FL (cdp) Miami-Dade County	6,488	38.40
South Miami Heights, FL (cdp) Miami-Dade County	13,466	37.72
Miami, FL (city) Miami-Dade County	137,301	34.37
Country Club, FL (cdp) Miami-Dade County	15,509	32.92
Country Walk, FL (cdp) Miami-Dade County	5,230	32.69
Kendall, FL (cdp) Miami-Dade County	24,533	32.55
Coral Gables, FL (city) Miami-Dade County	14,657	31.33
The Crossings, FL (cdp) Miami-Dade County	7,065	31.04
Egypt Lake-Leto, FL (cdp) Hillsborough County	9,697	27.48
The Hammocks, FL (cdp) Miami-Dade County	13,605	26.67
Leisure City, FL (cdp) Miami-Dade County	5,934	26.19
South Miami, FL (city) Miami-Dade County	3,012	25.84
Cutler Bay, FL (town) Miami-Dade County	9,858	24.47
Princeton, FL (cdp) Miami-Dade County	5,294	24.02
West Little River, FL (cdp) Miami-Dade County	8,014	23.10
Pinecrest, FL (village) Miami-Dade County	3,923	21.53
Three Lakes, FL (cdp) Miami-Dade County	3,186	21.17
Miami Beach, FL (city) Miami-Dade County	17,599	20.05
Goulds, FL (cdp) Miami-Dade County	2,014	19.93
Palmetto Bay, FL (village) Miami-Dade County	4,206	17.97
Palmetto Estates, FL (cdp) Miami-Dade County	2,404	17.76
Naranja, FL (cdp) Miami-Dade County	1,458	17.56
Palm Springs, FL (village) Palm Beach County	3,249	17.17
Key Biscayne, FL (village) Miami-Dade County	2,051	16.62
Golden Gate, FL (cdp) Collier County	3,941	16.45
Homestead, FL (city) Miami-Dade County	9,524	15.74
Marathon, FL (city) Monroe County	1,256	15.14
West New York, NJ (town) Hudson County	7,514	15.12
Opa-locka, FL (city) Miami-Dade County	2,248	14.77
Town 'n' Country, FL (cdp) Hillsborough County	11,570	14.75
West Perrine, FL (cdp) Miami-Dade County	1,351	14.28
Key Largo, FL (cdp) Monroe County	1,380	13.23
Pembroke Pines, FL (city) Broward County	19,826	12.81
Doral, FL (city) Miami-Dade County	5,806	12.70
North Bergen, NJ (township) Hudson County	7,248	11.93
Palm River-Clair Mel, FL (cdp) Hillsborough County	2,497	11.88
Union City, NJ (city) Hudson County	7,510	11.30
Miramar, FL (city) Broward County	12,924	10.59
Miami Shores, FL (village) Miami-Dade County	1,074	10.24
Westview, FL (cdp) Miami-Dade County	980	10.16
Key West, FL (city) Monroe County	2,422	9.83
Sunny Isles Beach, FL (city) Miami-Dade County	1,990	9.55
Richmond Heights, FL (cdp) Miami-Dade County	788	9.23
Guttenberg, NJ (town) Hudson County	1,011	9.05
Miami Gardens, FL (city) Miami-Dade County	9,587	8.95
Citrus Park, FL (cdp) Hillsborough County	2,069	8.53
Brownsville, FL (cdp) Miami-Dade County	1,268	8.28
Florida City, FL (city) Miami-Dade County	911	8.10
Ojus, FL (cdp) Miami-Dade County	1,439	7.98
Cooper City, FL (city) Broward County	2,246	7.87
Weehawken, NJ (township) Hudson County	980	7.81
Lehigh Acres, FL (cdp) Lee County	6,506	7.50
North Miami Beach, FL (city) Miami-Dade County	2,909	7.01
Northdale, FL (cdp) Hillsborough County	1,477	6.69
Davie, FL (town) Broward County	6,071	6.60
Hollywood, FL (city) Broward County	9,258	6.58
Gladeview, FL (cdp) Miami-Dade County	749	6.49
North Miami, FL (city) Miami-Dade County	3,762	6.40
Cape Coral, FL (city) Lee County	9,843	6.38
West Park, FL (city) Broward County	901	6.36
Tampa, FL (city) Hillsborough County	21,295	6.34
Carrollwood, FL (cdp) Hillsborough County	2,108	6.32
The Acreage, FL (cdp) Palm Beach County	2,364	6.11
Hallandale Beach, FL (city) Broward County	2,251	6.07
Pinewood, FL (cdp) Miami-Dade County	995	6.02
Pine Castle, FL (cdp) Orange County	646	5.98
Belle Glade, FL (city) Palm Beach County	1,042	5.97
Azalea Park, FL (cdp) Orange County	716	5.70
West Palm Beach, FL (city) Palm Beach County	5,337	5.34
Elizabeth, NJ (city) Union County	6,570	5.26
Ridgefield, NJ (borough) Bergen County	575	5.21
Fairview, NJ (borough) Bergen County	709	5.12
Forest City, FL (cdp) Seminole County	680	4.91
Ridgefield Park, NJ (village) Bergen County	612	4.81
Weston, FL (city) Broward County	3,134	4.80
Lake Magdalene, FL (cdp) Hillsborough County	1,344	4.71
Royal Palm Beach, FL (village) Palm Beach County	1,521	4.46
Westgate, FL (cdp) Palm Beach County	350	4.39
Golden Glades, FL (cdp) Miami-Dade County	1,428	4.31
Greenacres, FL (city) Palm Beach County	1,593	4.24
Lake Worth, FL (city) Palm Beach County	1,438	4.12
Plantation, FL (city) Broward County	3,398	4.00
Aventura, FL (city) Miami-Dade County	1,408	3.94
Dania Beach, FL (city) Broward County	1,160	3.91
Wellington, FL (village) Palm Beach County	2,179	3.86
Ives Estates, FL (cdp) Miami-Dade County	752	3.85
Westchase, FL (cdp) Hillsborough County	778	3.58
Winchester, NV (cdp) Clark County	985	3.52
Union Park, FL (cdp) Orange County	344	3.52
Sunrise, FL (city) Broward County	2,956	3.50
Lutz, FL (cdp) Hillsborough County	665	3.44
Secaucus, NJ (town) Hudson County	554	3.41
Cliffside Park, NJ (borough) Bergen County	765	3.24
Bogota, NJ (borough) Bergen County	262	3.20
Oakland Park, FL (city) Broward County	1,319	3.19
Oak Ridge, FL (cdp) Orange County	724	3.19
Cheval, FL (cdp) Hillsborough County	339	3.17
Moultrie, GA (city) Colquitt County	444	3.11
Buenaventura Lakes, FL (cdp) Osceola County	799	3.06
Land O' Lakes, FL (cdp) Pasco County	933	2.92
Keystone, FL (cdp) Hillsborough County	671	2.79
Pebble Creek, FL (cdp) Hillsborough County	213	2.79
East Lake-Orient Park, FL (cdp) Hillsborough County	619	2.72
Leonia, NJ (borough) Bergen County	240	2.69
Jupiter Farms, FL (cdp) Palm Beach County	322	2.68
Southchase, FL (cdp) Orange County	423	2.66
Brandon, FL (cdp) Hillsborough County	2,690	2.60
Hasbrouck Heights, NJ (borough) Bergen County	306	2.58
Meadow Woods, FL (cdp) Orange County	657	2.57
Kissimmee, FL (city) Osceola County	1,524	2.55
Port St. Lucie, FL (city) St. Lucie County	4,120	2.50
Tamarac, FL (city) Broward County	1,510	2.50
Whitney, NV (cdp) Clark County	965	2.50
Fort Lauderdale, FL (city) Broward County	4,093	2.47
Little Ferry, NJ (borough) Bergen County	258	2.43
Alafaya, FL (cdp) Orange County	1,861	2.38
Coral Springs, FL (city) Broward County	2,853	2.36
Seffner, FL (cdp) Hillsborough County	179	2.36
Valrico, FL (cdp) Hillsborough County	830	2.34
Rutherford, NJ (borough) Bergen County	422	2.34
Highland City, FL (cdp) Polk County	253	2.34
Fuller Heights, FL (cdp) Polk County	205	2.34
Gainesville, FL (city) Alachua County	2,886	2.32
Roselle Park, NJ (borough) Union County	309	2.32
University, FL (cdp) Orange County	702	2.26
Wilton Manors, FL (city) Broward County	263	2.26
Wood-Ridge, NJ (borough) Bergen County	172	2.26
Lyndhurst, NJ (township) Bergen County	461	2.24
Lockhart, FL (cdp) Orange County	288	2.21
Harrison, NJ (town) Hudson County	299	2.20
Mango, FL (cdp) Hillsborough County	249	2.20
Lakeland Highlands, FL (cdp) Polk County	242	2.19
Del Aire, CA (cdp) Los Angeles County	219	2.19
Bell, CA (city) Los Angeles County	774	2.18

Please refer to the Explanation of Data in the front of the book for more detailed information.

Hispanic Origin

Dominican Republic

U.S. and 50 States Sorted by Population and Percent of Total Population

Place	Population	%
United States	**1,414,703**	**0.46**
New York	674,787	3.48
New Jersey	197,922	2.25
Florida	172,451	0.92
Massachusetts	103,292	1.58
Pennsylvania	62,348	0.49
Rhode Island	35,008	3.33
Connecticut	26,093	0.73
North Carolina	15,225	0.16
Georgia	14,941	0.15
Maryland	14,873	0.26
Texas	13,353	0.05
California	11,455	0.03
Virginia	10,504	0.13
Ohio	6,453	0.06
Illinois	5,691	0.04
Michigan	5,012	0.05
New Hampshire	4,460	0.34
Louisiana	3,238	0.07
Arizona	3,103	0.05
South Carolina	3,018	0.07
District of Columbia	2,508	0.42
Nevada	2,446	0.09
Indiana	2,340	0.04
Tennessee	2,113	0.03
Delaware	2,035	0.23
Alaska	1,909	0.27
Washington	1,819	0.03
Wisconsin	1,786	0.03
Colorado	1,744	0.03
Missouri	1,503	0.03
Minnesota	1,294	0.02
Utah	1,252	0.05
Kentucky	1,065	0.02
Alabama	852	0.02
Kansas	764	0.03
Mississippi	733	0.02
Oklahoma	727	0.02
Maine	610	0.05
Hawaii	600	0.04
Oregon	574	0.01
New Mexico	492	0.02
Iowa	429	0.01
Arkansas	384	0.01
West Virginia	363	0.02
Nebraska	358	0.02
Vermont	282	0.05
Idaho	185	0.01
Montana	95	0.01
North Dakota	90	0.01
South Dakota	79	0.01
Wyoming	45	0.01

Place	Population	%
New York	674,787	3.48
Rhode Island	35,008	3.33
New Jersey	197,922	2.25
Massachusetts	103,292	1.58
Florida	172,451	0.92
Connecticut	26,093	0.73
Pennsylvania	62,348	0.49
United States	**1,414,703**	**0.46**
District of Columbia	2,508	0.42
New Hampshire	4,460	0.34
Alaska	1,909	0.27
Maryland	14,873	0.26
Delaware	2,035	0.23
North Carolina	15,225	0.16
Georgia	14,941	0.15
Virginia	10,504	0.13
Nevada	2,446	0.09
Louisiana	3,238	0.07
South Carolina	3,018	0.07
Ohio	6,453	0.06
Texas	13,353	0.05
Michigan	5,012	0.05
Arizona	3,103	0.05
Utah	1,252	0.05
Maine	610	0.05
Vermont	282	0.05
Illinois	5,691	0.04
Indiana	2,340	0.04
Hawaii	600	0.04
California	11,455	0.03
Tennessee	2,113	0.03
Washington	1,819	0.03
Wisconsin	1,786	0.03
Colorado	1,744	0.03
Missouri	1,503	0.03
Kansas	764	0.03
Minnesota	1,294	0.02
Kentucky	1,065	0.02
Alabama	852	0.02
Mississippi	733	0.02
Oklahoma	727	0.02
New Mexico	492	0.02
West Virginia	363	0.02
Nebraska	358	0.02
Oregon	574	0.01
Iowa	429	0.01
Arkansas	384	0.01
Idaho	185	0.01
Montana	95	0.01
North Dakota	90	0.01
South Dakota	79	0.01
Wyoming	45	0.01

Please refer to the Explanation of Data in the front of the book for more detailed information.

Hispanic Origin

Dominican Republic

Top 150 Places Sorted by Population

Based on all places, regardless of total population

Place	Population	%
New York, NY (city) Kings County	576,701	7.05
Bronx, NY (borough) Bronx County	240,987	17.40
Manhattan, NY (borough) New York County	155,971	9.84
Queens, NY (borough) Queens County	88,061	3.95
Brooklyn, NY (borough) Kings County	86,764	3.46
Lawrence, MA (city) Essex County	30,243	39.60
Paterson, NJ (city) Passaic County	27,426	18.76
Boston, MA (city) Suffolk County	25,648	4.15
Providence, RI (city) Providence County	25,267	14.19
Hempstead, NY (town) Nassau County	16,914	2.23
Philadelphia, PA (city) Philadelphia County	15,963	1.05
Yonkers, NY (city) Westchester County	15,903	8.11
Perth Amboy, NJ (city) Middlesex County	14,773	29.07
Jersey City, NJ (city) Hudson County	13,512	5.46
Newark, NJ (city) Essex County	12,527	4.52
Passaic, NJ (city) Passaic County	12,340	17.68
Union City, NJ (city) Hudson County	10,020	15.08
Miami, FL (city) Miami-Dade County	9,668	2.42
Lynn, MA (city) Essex County	9,528	10.55
Allentown, PA (city) Lehigh County	9,340	7.91
Reading, PA (city) Berks County	8,716	9.90
Islip, NY (town) Suffolk County	8,547	2.55
Elizabeth, NJ (city) Union County	7,073	5.66
Babylon, NY (town) Suffolk County	6,543	3.06
Haverstraw, NY (town) Rockland County	6,277	17.13
North Bergen, NJ (township) Hudson County	5,999	9.87
Freeport, NY (village) Nassau County	5,539	12.92
Hazleton, PA (city) Luzerne County	5,327	21.02
West New York, NJ (town) Hudson County	4,935	9.93
Staten Island, NY (borough) Richmond County	4,918	1.05
Pembroke Pines, FL (city) Broward County	4,804	3.10
Brookhaven, NY (town) Suffolk County	4,781	0.98
Clifton, NJ (city) Passaic County	4,561	5.42
Miramar, FL (city) Broward County	4,529	3.71
Orlando, FL (city) Orange County	4,278	1.80
Worcester, MA (city) Worcester County	4,221	2.33
Hialeah, FL (city) Miami-Dade County	4,206	1.87
Brentwood, NY (cdp) Suffolk County	4,205	6.93
New Brunswick, NJ (city) Middlesex County	4,139	7.50
Camden, NJ (city) Camden County	4,006	5.18
Methuen Town, MA (city) Essex County	3,953	8.37
Danbury, CT (city/town) Fairfield County	3,852	4.76
Haverstraw, NY (village) Rockland County	3,847	32.30
Salem, MA (city) Essex County	3,749	9.07
Waterbury, CT (city/town) New Haven County	3,743	3.39
Hollywood, FL (city) Broward County	3,481	2.47
Charlotte, NC (city) Mecklenburg County	3,280	0.45
Tampa, FL (city) Hillsborough County	3,110	0.93
Kissimmee, FL (city) Osceola County	3,061	5.13
Hackensack, NJ (city) Bergen County	3,021	7.02
Cranston, RI (city) Providence County	3,003	3.74
Country Club, FL (cdp) Miami-Dade County	2,999	6.37
Copiague, NY (cdp) Suffolk County	2,846	12.38
Haverhill, MA (city) Essex County	2,780	4.57
Chicago, IL (city) Cook County	2,737	0.10
Springfield, MA (city) Hampden County	2,649	1.73
Miami Gardens, FL (city) Miami-Dade County	2,521	2.35
Washington, DC (city) District of Columbia	2,508	0.42
Bayonne, NJ (city) Hudson County	2,464	3.91
Bridgeport, CT (city/town) Fairfield County	2,429	1.68
Woodbridge, NJ (township) Middlesex County	2,406	2.42
Raleigh, NC (city) Wake County	2,378	0.59
Town 'n' Country, FL (cdp) Hillsborough County	2,248	2.87
Hartford, CT (city/town) Hartford County	2,191	1.76
Jacksonville, FL (city) Duval County	2,172	0.26
Fountainebleau, FL (cdp) Miami-Dade County	2,063	3.45
Garfield, NJ (city) Bergen County	2,057	6.75
Mount Pleasant, NY (town) Westchester County	2,030	4.64
Lowell, MA (city) Middlesex County	2,008	1.89
Teaneck, NJ (township) Bergen County	1,981	4.98
Coral Springs, FL (city) Broward County	1,938	1.60
The Hammocks, FL (cdp) Miami-Dade County	1,907	3.74
Lancaster, PA (city) Lancaster County	1,905	3.21
Pawtucket, RI (city) Providence County	1,894	2.66
Alafaya, FL (cdp) Orange County	1,878	2.40

Place	Population	%
Houston, TX (city) Harris County	1,876	0.09
Poinciana, FL (cdp) Osceola County	1,833	3.45
Sleepy Hollow, NY (village) Westchester County	1,831	18.55
Bergenfield, NJ (borough) Bergen County	1,818	6.79
Doral, FL (city) Miami-Dade County	1,751	3.83
Trenton, NJ (city) Mercer County	1,707	2.01
Buenaventura Lakes, FL (cdp) Osceola County	1,687	6.47
Port St. Lucie, FL (city) St. Lucie County	1,686	1.02
West Haverstraw, NY (village) Rockland County	1,667	16.40
Meadow Woods, FL (cdp) Orange County	1,651	6.46
Nashua, NH (city) Hillsborough County	1,639	1.89
Cape Coral, FL (city) Lee County	1,631	1.06
Anchorage, AK (municipality) Anchorage Municipality	1,626	0.56
Mount Vernon, NY (city) Westchester County	1,611	2.39
Los Angeles, CA (city) Los Angeles County	1,602	0.04
Plainfield, NJ (city) Union County	1,601	3.21
Columbus, OH (city) Franklin County	1,553	0.20
Davie, FL (town) Broward County	1,479	1.61
Stamford, CT (city/town) Fairfield County	1,476	1.20
Pleasantville, NJ (city) Atlantic County	1,461	7.22
Franklin, NJ (township) Somerset County	1,456	2.34
Oyster Bay, NY (town) Nassau County	1,429	0.49
Atlantic City, NJ (city) Atlantic County	1,419	3.59
Peabody, MA (city) Essex County	1,405	2.74
Greenburgh, NY (town) Westchester County	1,400	1.58
Hempstead, NY (village) Nassau County	1,398	2.59
Lodi, NJ (borough) Bergen County	1,396	5.78
North Miami, FL (city) Miami-Dade County	1,391	2.37
Sunrise, FL (city) Broward County	1,387	1.64
Kendall, FL (cdp) Miami-Dade County	1,383	1.83
Rochester, NY (city) Monroe County	1,373	0.65
North Hempstead, NY (town) Nassau County	1,362	0.60
Belleville, NJ (township) Essex County	1,352	3.76
Pennsauken, NJ (township) Camden County	1,347	3.75
Grand Rapids, MI (city) Kent County	1,342	0.71
Bloomfield, NJ (township) Essex County	1,340	2.83
North Miami Beach, FL (city) Miami-Dade County	1,336	3.22
Brandon, FL (cdp) Hillsborough County	1,335	1.29
North Brunswick, NJ (township) Middlesex County	1,300	3.19
Valley Stream, NY (village) Nassau County	1,281	3.41
Central Islip, NY (cdp) Suffolk County	1,261	3.66
Homestead, FL (city) Miami-Dade County	1,259	2.08
Deltona, FL (city) Volusia County	1,240	1.46
Central Falls, RI (city) Providence County	1,237	6.38
New London, CT (city/town) New London County	1,230	4.45
Manchester, NH (city) Hillsborough County	1,215	1.11
York, PA (city) York County	1,212	2.77
East Orange, NJ (city) Essex County	1,212	1.89
Miami Beach, FL (city) Miami-Dade County	1,212	1.38
Kendale Lakes, FL (cdp) Miami-Dade County	1,197	2.13
Englewood, NJ (city) Bergen County	1,180	4.35
West Little River, FL (cdp) Miami-Dade County	1,179	3.40
White Plains, NY (city) Westchester County	1,177	2.07
Cleveland, OH (city) Cuyahoga County	1,140	0.29
Virginia Beach, VA (ind. city) Virginia Beach independent city	1,135	0.26
Indianapolis, IN (city) Marion County	1,124	0.14
Richmond West, FL (cdp) Miami-Dade County	1,112	3.48
Baltimore, MD (city) Baltimore city County	1,111	0.18
Ridgefield Park, NJ (village) Bergen County	1,105	8.68
New Haven, CT (city/town) New Haven County	1,097	0.85
Albany, NY (city) Albany County	1,095	1.12
North Bay Shore, NY (cdp) Suffolk County	1,089	5.75
Kendall West, FL (cdp) Miami-Dade County	1,064	2.94
Cutler Bay, FL (town) Miami-Dade County	1,057	2.62
New Britain, CT (city/town) Hartford County	1,055	1.44
Egypt Lake-Leto, FL (cdp) Hillsborough County	1,042	2.95
Baldwin, NY (cdp) Nassau County	1,032	4.29
Ramapo, NY (town) Rockland County	1,021	0.81
Plantation, FL (city) Broward County	1,016	1.20
Huntington, NY (town) Suffolk County	1,011	0.50
Bethlehem, PA (city) Northampton County	1,010	1.35
Kearny, NJ (town) Hudson County	1,009	2.48
North Amityville, NY (cdp) Suffolk County	1,008	5.64
Riverview, FL (cdp) Hillsborough County	1,004	1.41
South Miami Heights, FL (cdp) Miami-Dade County	988	2.77

Please refer to the Explanation of Data in the front of the book for more detailed information.

Hispanic Origin

Dominican Republic

Top 150 Places Sorted by Percent of Total Population

Based on all places, regardless of total population

Place	Population	%
Lawrence, MA (city) Essex County	30,243	39.60
Haverstraw, NY (village) Rockland County	3,847	32.30
Perth Amboy, NJ (city) Middlesex County	14,773	29.07
Hazleton, PA (city) Luzerne County	5,327	21.02
West Hazleton, PA (borough) Luzerne County	939	20.44
Paterson, NJ (city) Passaic County	27,426	18.76
Sleepy Hollow, NY (village) Westchester County	1,831	18.55
Passaic, NJ (city) Passaic County	12,340	17.68
Bronx, NY (borough) Bronx County	240,987	17.40
Haverstraw, NY (town) Rockland County	6,277	17.13
West Haverstraw, NY (village) Rockland County	1,667	16.40
Union City, NJ (city) Hudson County	10,020	15.08
Providence, RI (city) Providence County	25,267	14.19
Freeport, NY (village) Nassau County	5,539	12.92
Copiague, NY (cdp) Suffolk County	2,846	12.38
Prospect Park, NJ (borough) Passaic County	705	12.02
Bogota, NJ (borough) Bergen County	971	11.86
East Franklin, NJ (cdp) Somerset County	938	10.82
Lynn, MA (city) Essex County	9,528	10.55
West New York, NJ (town) Hudson County	4,935	9.93
Reading, PA (city) Berks County	8,716	9.90
North Bergen, NJ (township) Hudson County	5,999	9.87
Manhattan, NY (borough) New York County	155,971	9.84
Salem, MA (city) Essex County	3,749	9.07
Lake Harbor, FL (cdp) Palm Beach County	4	8.89
Ridgefield Park, NJ (village) Bergen County	1,105	8.68
Methuen Town, MA (city) Essex County	3,953	8.37
Yonkers, NY (city) Westchester County	15,903	8.11
Allentown, PA (city) Lehigh County	9,340	7.91
Guttenberg, NJ (town) Hudson County	878	7.86
Decatur, PA (township) Clearfield County	354	7.78
Haledon, NJ (borough) Passaic County	634	7.62
Weehawken, NJ (township) Hudson County	950	7.57
New Brunswick, NJ (city) Middlesex County	4,139	7.50
Pleasantville, NJ (city) Atlantic County	1,461	7.22
New York, NY (city) Kings County	576,701	7.05
Hackensack, NJ (city) Bergen County	3,021	7.02
Brentwood, NY (cdp) Suffolk County	4,205	6.93
Bergenfield, NJ (borough) Bergen County	1,818	6.79
Garfield, NJ (city) Bergen County	2,057	6.75
Manley Hot Springs, AK (cdp) Yukon-Koyukuk Census Area	6	6.74
South Hackensack, NJ (township) Bergen County	160	6.73
Buenaventura Lakes, FL (cdp) Osceola County	1,687	6.47
Meadow Woods, FL (cdp) Orange County	1,651	6.46
Central Falls, RI (city) Providence County	1,237	6.38
Country Club, FL (cdp) Miami-Dade County	2,999	6.37
Mount Ivy, NY (cdp) Rockland County	424	6.16
Voorhees, NJ (cdp) Somerset County	60	6.15
Terryville, NY (cdp) Suffolk County	694	5.86
Lodi, NJ (borough) Bergen County	1,396	5.78
North Bay Shore, NY (cdp) Suffolk County	1,089	5.75
Elizabeth, NJ (city) Union County	7,073	5.66
North Amityville, NY (cdp) Suffolk County	1,008	5.64
Thiells, NY (cdp) Rockland County	280	5.56
Jersey City, NJ (city) Hudson County	13,512	5.46
Clifton, NJ (city) Passaic County	4,561	5.42
Silver Lake, NJ (cdp) Essex County	229	5.40
Camden, NJ (city) Camden County	4,006	5.18
Kissimmee, FL (city) Osceola County	3,061	5.13
Southchase, FL (cdp) Orange County	798	5.01
Teaneck, NJ (township) Bergen County	1,981	4.98
Tarrytown, NY (village) Westchester County	556	4.93
Highland Falls, NY (village) Orange County	190	4.87
Port Jefferson Station, NY (cdp) Suffolk County	376	4.80
Danbury, CT (city/town) Fairfield County	3,852	4.76
Fairview, NJ (borough) Bergen County	647	4.68
Mount Pleasant, NY (town) Westchester County	2,030	4.64
Haverhill, MA (city) Essex County	2,780	4.57
Newark, NJ (city) Essex County	12,527	4.52
Hazle, PA (township) Luzerne County	430	4.50
New London, CT (city/town) New London County	1,230	4.45
Westview, FL (cdp) Miami-Dade County	429	4.45
Englewood, NJ (city) Bergen County	1,180	4.35
Baldwin, NY (cdp) Nassau County	1,032	4.29
Oak Ridge, FL (cdp) Orange County	960	4.23
Sky Lake, FL (cdp) Orange County	258	4.19
Boston, MA (city) Suffolk County	25,648	4.15
Lakeview, NY (cdp) Nassau County	232	4.13
Opa-locka, FL (city) Miami-Dade County	605	3.98
Cross Anchor, SC (cdp) Spartanburg County	5	3.97
Maywood, NJ (borough) Bergen County	378	3.96
Queens, NY (borough) Queens County	88,061	3.95
Little Ferry, NJ (borough) Bergen County	420	3.95
Bayonne, NJ (city) Hudson County	2,464	3.91
Doral, FL (city) Miami-Dade County	1,751	3.83
Belleville, NJ (township) Essex County	1,352	3.76
Pennsauken, NJ (township) Camden County	1,347	3.75
Carteret, NJ (borough) Middlesex County	856	3.75
Cranston, RI (city) Providence County	3,003	3.74
The Hammocks, FL (cdp) Miami-Dade County	1,907	3.74
West Park, FL (city) Broward County	528	3.73
Miramar, FL (city) Broward County	4,529	3.71
North Lindenhurst, NY (cdp) Suffolk County	428	3.67
Central Islip, NY (cdp) Suffolk County	1,261	3.66
Victory Gardens, NJ (borough) Morris County	55	3.62
Cliffside Park, NJ (borough) Bergen County	852	3.61
Elmwood Park, NJ (borough) Bergen County	701	3.61
Atlantic City, NJ (city) Atlantic County	1,419	3.59
Roosevelt, NY (cdp) Nassau County	584	3.59
Hyde Park, PA (cdp) Berks County	90	3.56
Moonachie, NJ (borough) Bergen County	96	3.55
Richmond West, FL (cdp) Miami-Dade County	1,112	3.48
Ridgefield, NJ (borough) Bergen County	383	3.47
Brooklyn, NY (borough) Kings County	86,764	3.46
Fountainebleau, FL (cdp) Miami-Dade County	2,063	3.45
Poinciana, FL (cdp) Osceola County	1,833	3.45
Valley Stream, NY (village) Nassau County	1,281	3.41
West Little River, FL (cdp) Miami-Dade County	1,179	3.40
Waterbury, CT (city/town) New Haven County	3,743	3.39
Hialeah Gardens, FL (city) Miami-Dade County	724	3.33
Woodland Park, NJ (borough) Passaic County	392	3.32
Azalea Park, FL (cdp) Orange County	408	3.25
Three Lakes, FL (cdp) Miami-Dade County	488	3.24
Gordon Heights, NY (cdp) Suffolk County	131	3.24
North Miami Beach, FL (city) Miami-Dade County	1,336	3.22
Lancaster, PA (city) Lancaster County	1,905	3.21
Plainfield, NJ (city) Union County	1,601	3.21
Baywood, NY (cdp) Suffolk County	236	3.21
North Brunswick, NJ (township) Middlesex County	1,300	3.19
Country Walk, FL (cdp) Miami-Dade County	506	3.16
Pembroke Pines, FL (city) Broward County	4,804	3.10
Rockville Centre, NY (village) Nassau County	743	3.09
Babylon, NY (town) Suffolk County	6,543	3.06
Bay Shore, NY (cdp) Suffolk County	806	3.06
Lake Belvedere Estates, FL (cdp) Palm Beach County	102	3.06
Lebanon, PA (city) Lebanon County	778	3.05
Amityville, NY (village) Suffolk County	290	3.05
Acacia Villas, FL (cdp) Palm Beach County	13	3.04
Princeton, FL (cdp) Miami-Dade County	667	3.03
South Hempstead, NY (cdp) Nassau County	98	3.02
Stony Point, NY (cdp) Rockland County	360	2.96
Scott, WI (town) Monroe County	4	2.96
Egypt Lake-Leto, FL (cdp) Hillsborough County	1,042	2.95
Fullerton, PA (cdp) Lehigh County	441	2.95
Hunters Creek, FL (cdp) Orange County	422	2.95
Kendall West, FL (cdp) Miami-Dade County	1,064	2.94
New Milford, NJ (borough) Bergen County	478	2.93
Rochelle Park, NJ (township) Bergen County	162	2.93
Taylors Island, MD (cdp) Dorchester County	5	2.89
Town 'n' Country, FL (cdp) Hillsborough County	2,248	2.87
Dumont, NJ (borough) Bergen County	501	2.87
Bloomfield, NJ (township) Essex County	1,340	2.83
Winsted, CT (cdp) Litchfield County	217	2.81
Shenandoah, PA (borough) Schuylkill County	142	2.80
Pine Castle, FL (cdp) Orange County	300	2.78
New Hanover, NJ (township) Burlington County	205	2.78
Virginia Gardens, FL (village) Miami-Dade County	66	2.78
York, PA (city) York County	1,212	2.77
South Miami Heights, FL (cdp) Miami-Dade County	988	2.77
Gregg, PA (township) Union County	138	2.77

Please refer to the Explanation of Data in the front of the book for more detailed information.

Hispanic Origin

Dominican Republic

Top 150 Places Sorted by Percent of Total Population

Based on places with total population of 7,500 or more

Place	Population	%
Lawrence, MA (city) Essex County	30,243	39.60
Haverstraw, NY (village) Rockland County	3,847	32.30
Perth Amboy, NJ (city) Middlesex County	14,773	29.07
Hazleton, PA (city) Luzerne County	5,327	21.02
Paterson, NJ (city) Passaic County	27,426	18.76
Sleepy Hollow, NY (village) Westchester County	1,831	18.55
Passaic, NJ (city) Passaic County	12,340	17.68
Bronx, NY (borough) Bronx County	240,987	17.40
Haverstraw, NY (town) Rockland County	6,277	17.13
West Haverstraw, NY (village) Rockland County	1,667	16.40
Union City, NJ (city) Hudson County	10,020	15.08
Providence, RI (city) Providence County	25,267	14.19
Freeport, NY (village) Nassau County	5,539	12.92
Copiague, NY (cdp) Suffolk County	2,846	12.38
Bogota, NJ (borough) Bergen County	971	11.86
East Franklin, NJ (cdp) Somerset County	938	10.82
Lynn, MA (city) Essex County	9,528	10.55
West New York, NJ (town) Hudson County	4,935	9.93
Reading, PA (city) Berks County	8,716	9.90
North Bergen, NJ (township) Hudson County	5,999	9.87
Manhattan, NY (borough) New York County	155,971	9.84
Salem, MA (city) Essex County	3,749	9.07
Ridgefield Park, NJ (village) Bergen County	1,105	8.68
Methuen Town, MA (city) Essex County	3,953	8.37
Yonkers, NY (city) Westchester County	15,903	8.11
Allentown, PA (city) Lehigh County	9,340	7.91
Guttenberg, NJ (town) Hudson County	878	7.86
Haledon, NJ (borough) Passaic County	634	7.62
Weehawken, NJ (township) Hudson County	950	7.57
New Brunswick, NJ (city) Middlesex County	4,139	7.50
Pleasantville, NJ (city) Atlantic County	1,461	7.22
New York, NY (city) Kings County	576,701	7.05
Hackensack, NJ (city) Bergen County	3,021	7.02
Brentwood, NY (cdp) Suffolk County	4,205	6.93
Bergenfield, NJ (borough) Bergen County	1,818	6.79
Garfield, NJ (city) Bergen County	2,057	6.75
Buenaventura Lakes, FL (cdp) Osceola County	1,687	6.47
Meadow Woods, FL (cdp) Orange County	1,651	6.46
Central Falls, RI (city) Providence County	1,237	6.38
Country Club, FL (cdp) Miami-Dade County	2,999	6.37
Terryville, NY (cdp) Suffolk County	694	5.86
Lodi, NJ (borough) Bergen County	1,396	5.78
North Bay Shore, NY (cdp) Suffolk County	1,089	5.75
Elizabeth, NJ (city) Union County	7,073	5.66
North Amityville, NY (cdp) Suffolk County	1,008	5.64
Jersey City, NJ (city) Hudson County	13,512	5.46
Clifton, NJ (city) Passaic County	4,561	5.42
Camden, NJ (city) Camden County	4,006	5.18
Kissimmee, FL (city) Osceola County	3,061	5.13
Southchase, FL (cdp) Orange County	798	5.01
Teaneck, NJ (township) Bergen County	1,981	4.98
Tarrytown, NY (village) Westchester County	556	4.93
Port Jefferson Station, NY (cdp) Suffolk County	376	4.80
Danbury, CT (city/town) Fairfield County	3,852	4.76
Fairview, NJ (borough) Bergen County	647	4.68
Mount Pleasant, NY (town) Westchester County	2,030	4.64
Haverhill, MA (city) Essex County	2,780	4.57
Newark, NJ (city) Essex County	12,527	4.52
Hazle, PA (township) Luzerne County	430	4.50
New London, CT (city/town) New London County	1,230	4.45
Westview, FL (cdp) Miami-Dade County	429	4.45
Englewood, NJ (city) Bergen County	1,180	4.35
Baldwin, NY (cdp) Nassau County	1,032	4.29
Oak Ridge, FL (cdp) Orange County	960	4.23
Boston, MA (city) Suffolk County	25,648	4.15
Opa-locka, FL (city) Miami-Dade County	605	3.98
Maywood, NJ (borough) Bergen County	378	3.96
Queens, NY (borough) Queens County	88,061	3.95
Little Ferry, NJ (borough) Bergen County	420	3.95
Bayonne, NJ (city) Hudson County	2,464	3.91
Doral, FL (city) Miami-Dade County	1,751	3.83
Belleville, NJ (township) Essex County	1,352	3.76
Pennsauken, NJ (township) Camden County	1,347	3.75
Carteret, NJ (borough) Middlesex County	856	3.75
Cranston, RI (city) Providence County	3,003	3.74
The Hammocks, FL (cdp) Miami-Dade County	1,907	3.74
West Park, FL (city) Broward County	528	3.73
Miramar, FL (city) Broward County	4,529	3.71
North Lindenhurst, NY (cdp) Suffolk County	428	3.67
Central Islip, NY (cdp) Suffolk County	1,261	3.66
Cliffside Park, NJ (borough) Bergen County	852	3.61
Elmwood Park, NJ (borough) Bergen County	701	3.61
Atlantic City, NJ (city) Atlantic County	1,419	3.59
Roosevelt, NY (cdp) Nassau County	584	3.59
Richmond West, FL (cdp) Miami-Dade County	1,112	3.48
Ridgefield, NJ (borough) Bergen County	383	3.47
Brooklyn, NY (borough) Kings County	86,764	3.46
Fountainebleau, FL (cdp) Miami-Dade County	2,063	3.45
Poinciana, FL (cdp) Osceola County	1,833	3.45
Valley Stream, NY (village) Nassau County	1,281	3.41
West Little River, FL (cdp) Miami-Dade County	1,179	3.40
Waterbury, CT (city/town) New Haven County	3,743	3.39
Hialeah Gardens, FL (city) Miami-Dade County	724	3.33
Woodland Park, NJ (borough) Passaic County	392	3.32
Azalea Park, FL (cdp) Orange County	408	3.25
Three Lakes, FL (cdp) Miami-Dade County	488	3.24
North Miami Beach, FL (city) Miami-Dade County	1,336	3.22
Lancaster, PA (city) Lancaster County	1,905	3.21
Plainfield, NJ (city) Union County	1,601	3.21
North Brunswick, NJ (township) Middlesex County	1,300	3.19
Country Walk, FL (cdp) Miami-Dade County	506	3.16
Pembroke Pines, FL (city) Broward County	4,804	3.10
Rockville Centre, NY (village) Nassau County	743	3.09
Babylon, NY (town) Suffolk County	6,543	3.06
Bay Shore, NY (cdp) Suffolk County	806	3.06
Lebanon, PA (city) Lebanon County	778	3.05
Amityville, NY (village) Suffolk County	290	3.05
Princeton, FL (cdp) Miami-Dade County	667	3.03
Stony Point, NY (cdp) Rockland County	360	2.96
Egypt Lake-Leto, FL (cdp) Hillsborough County	1,042	2.95
Fullerton, PA (cdp) Lehigh County	441	2.95
Hunters Creek, FL (cdp) Orange County	422	2.95
Kendall West, FL (cdp) Miami-Dade County	1,064	2.94
New Milford, NJ (borough) Bergen County	478	2.93
Town 'n' Country, FL (cdp) Hillsborough County	2,248	2.87
Dumont, NJ (borough) Bergen County	501	2.87
Bloomfield, NJ (township) Essex County	1,340	2.83
Winsted, CT (cdp) Litchfield County	217	2.81
Pine Castle, FL (cdp) Orange County	300	2.78
York, PA (city) York County	1,212	2.77
South Miami Heights, FL (cdp) Miami-Dade County	988	2.77
Peabody, MA (city) Essex County	1,405	2.74
Fort Lee, NJ (borough) Bergen County	968	2.74
Fort Dix, NJ (cdp) Burlington County	211	2.73
Stony Point, NY (town) Rockland County	405	2.69
Fords, NJ (cdp) Middlesex County	405	2.67
Pawtucket, RI (city) Providence County	1,894	2.66
Clinton, MA (town) Worcester County	362	2.66
Palisades Park, NJ (borough) Bergen County	518	2.64
Ojus, FL (cdp) Miami-Dade County	476	2.64
Cutler Bay, FL (town) Miami-Dade County	1,057	2.62
Pinewood, FL (cdp) Miami-Dade County	431	2.61
North Valley Stream, NY (cdp) Nassau County	432	2.60
Hempstead, NY (village) Nassau County	1,398	2.59
Islip, NY (town) Suffolk County	8,547	2.55
Harrison, NJ (town) Hudson County	339	2.49
Kearny, NJ (town) Hudson County	1,009	2.48
Leonia, NJ (borough) Bergen County	222	2.48
Hollywood, FL (city) Broward County	3,481	2.47
Naranja, FL (cdp) Miami-Dade County	204	2.46
Uniondale, NY (cdp) Nassau County	601	2.43
Union Park, FL (cdp) Orange County	237	2.43
Miami, FL (city) Miami-Dade County	9,668	2.42
Woodbridge, NJ (township) Middlesex County	2,406	2.42
Alafaya, FL (cdp) Orange County	1,878	2.40
Mount Vernon, NY (city) Westchester County	1,611	2.39
North Miami, FL (city) Miami-Dade County	1,391	2.37
Linden, NJ (city) Union County	957	2.36
Ives Estates, FL (cdp) Miami-Dade County	460	2.36
Miami Gardens, FL (city) Miami-Dade County	2,521	2.35

Please refer to the Explanation of Data in the front of the book for more detailed information.

Hispanic Origin

Mexican

U.S. and 50 States Sorted by Population and Percent of Total Population

Place	Population	%
United States	**31,798,258**	**10.30**
California	11,423,146	30.66
Texas	7,951,193	31.62
Arizona	1,657,668	25.93
Illinois	1,602,403	12.49
Colorado	757,181	15.06
Florida	629,718	3.35
Washington	601,768	8.95
New Mexico	590,890	28.70
Nevada	540,978	20.03
Georgia	519,502	5.36
North Carolina	486,960	5.11
New York	457,288	2.36
Oregon	369,817	9.65
Michigan	317,903	3.22
Indiana	295,373	4.56
Oklahoma	267,016	7.12
Utah	258,905	9.37
Kansas	247,297	8.67
Wisconsin	244,248	4.29
New Jersey	217,715	2.48
Tennessee	186,615	2.94
Minnesota	176,007	3.32
Ohio	172,029	1.49
Virginia	155,067	1.94
Idaho	148,923	9.50
Missouri	147,254	2.46
South Carolina	138,358	2.99
Arkansas	138,194	4.74
Pennsylvania	129,568	1.02
Nebraska	128,060	7.01
Alabama	122,911	2.57
Iowa	117,090	3.84
Maryland	88,004	1.52
Kentucky	82,110	1.89
Louisiana	78,643	1.73
Mississippi	52,459	1.77
Connecticut	50,658	1.42
Massachusetts	38,379	0.59
Wyoming	37,719	6.69
Hawaii	35,415	2.60
Delaware	30,283	3.37
Alaska	21,642	3.05
Montana	20,048	2.03
South Dakota	13,839	1.70
West Virginia	9,704	0.52
North Dakota	9,223	1.37
Rhode Island	9,090	0.86
District of Columbia	8,507	1.41
New Hampshire	7,822	0.59
Maine	5,134	0.39
Vermont	2,534	0.40

Place	Population	%
Texas	7,951,193	31.62
California	11,423,146	30.66
New Mexico	590,890	28.70
Arizona	1,657,668	25.93
Nevada	540,978	20.03
Colorado	757,181	15.06
Illinois	1,602,403	12.49
United States	**31,798,258**	**10.30**
Oregon	369,817	9.65
Idaho	148,923	9.50
Utah	258,905	9.37
Washington	601,768	8.95
Kansas	247,297	8.67
Oklahoma	267,016	7.12
Nebraska	128,060	7.01
Wyoming	37,719	6.69
Georgia	519,502	5.36
North Carolina	486,960	5.11
Arkansas	138,194	4.74
Indiana	295,373	4.56
Wisconsin	244,248	4.29
Iowa	117,090	3.84
Delaware	30,283	3.37
Florida	629,718	3.35
Minnesota	176,007	3.32
Michigan	317,903	3.22
Alaska	21,642	3.05
South Carolina	138,358	2.99
Tennessee	186,615	2.94
Hawaii	35,415	2.60
Alabama	122,911	2.57
New Jersey	217,715	2.48
Missouri	147,254	2.46
New York	457,288	2.36
Montana	20,048	2.03
Virginia	155,067	1.94
Kentucky	82,110	1.89
Mississippi	52,459	1.77
Louisiana	78,643	1.73
South Dakota	13,839	1.70
Maryland	88,004	1.52
Ohio	172,029	1.49
Connecticut	50,658	1.42
District of Columbia	8,507	1.41
North Dakota	9,223	1.37
Pennsylvania	129,568	1.02
Rhode Island	9,090	0.86
Massachusetts	38,379	0.59
New Hampshire	7,822	0.59
West Virginia	9,704	0.52
Vermont	2,534	0.40
Maine	5,134	0.39

Please refer to the Explanation of Data in the front of the book for more detailed information.

Hispanic Origin

Mexican

Top 150 Places Sorted by Population

Based on all places, regardless of total population

Place	Population	%
Los Angeles, CA (city) Los Angeles County	1,209,573	31.89
San Antonio, TX (city) Medina County	705,530	53.15
Houston, TX (city) Harris County	673,093	32.06
Chicago, IL (city) Cook County	578,100	21.45
Phoenix, AZ (city) Maricopa County	519,635	35.95
El Paso, TX (city) El Paso County	486,186	74.90
Dallas, TX (city) Dallas County	439,460	36.69
San Diego, CA (city) San Diego County	325,812	24.92
New York, NY (city) Kings County	319,263	3.91
San Jose, CA (city) Santa Clara County	268,538	28.39
Santa Ana, CA (city) Orange County	230,381	70.99
Austin, TX (city) Travis County	229,865	29.08
Fort Worth, TX (city) Tarrant County	219,653	29.63
Fresno, CA (city) Fresno County	211,431	42.74
Laredo, TX (city) Webb County	205,079	86.86
Tucson, AZ (city) Pima County	193,994	37.30
Anaheim, CA (city) Orange County	154,554	45.96
Long Beach, CA (city) Los Angeles County	151,983	32.88
Brownsville, TX (city) Cameron County	150,945	86.24
Denver, CO (city) Denver County	149,366	24.89
Corpus Christi, TX (city) Nueces County	148,800	48.75
Albuquerque, NM (city) Bernalillo County	146,035	26.75
Las Vegas, NV (city) Clark County	140,104	24.00
Bakersfield, CA (city) Kern County	137,102	39.46
Oxnard, CA (city) Ventura County	136,991	69.22
Chula Vista, CA (city) San Diego County	130,413	53.47
Riverside, CA (city) Riverside County	127,165	41.85
Fontana, CA (city) San Bernardino County	111,818	57.03
East Los Angeles, CA (cdp) Los Angeles County	111,441	88.10
San Bernardino, CA (city) San Bernardino County	109,448	52.14
Sacramento, CA (city) Sacramento County	105,467	22.61
Salinas, CA (city) Monterey County	104,237	69.29
Stockton, CA (city) San Joaquin County	104,172	35.71
McAllen, TX (city) Hidalgo County	100,963	77.74
Mesa, AZ (city) Maricopa County	99,666	22.70
Ontario, CA (city) San Bernardino County	98,596	60.15
Brooklyn, NY (borough) Kings County	94,585	3.78
Queens, NY (borough) Queens County	92,835	4.16
Pomona, CA (city) Los Angeles County	90,988	61.04
Moreno Valley, CA (city) Riverside County	90,054	46.57
Arlington, TX (city) Tarrant County	82,834	22.67
Oklahoma City, OK (city) Oklahoma County	82,318	14.19
Pasadena, TX (city) Harris County	80,575	54.06
Sunrise Manor, NV (cdp) Clark County	74,476	39.33
South Gate, CA (city) Los Angeles County	73,677	78.05
Aurora, IL (city) Kane County	72,924	36.85
Aurora, CO (city) Arapahoe County	71,225	21.91
Bronx, NY (borough) Bronx County	71,194	5.14
Oakland, CA (city) Alameda County	70,799	18.12
Garland, TX (city) Dallas County	70,016	30.86
Glendale, AZ (city) Maricopa County	69,929	30.84
Milwaukee, WI (city) Milwaukee County	69,680	11.71
El Monte, CA (city) Los Angeles County	69,053	60.85
North Las Vegas, NV (city) Clark County	68,610	31.62
Cicero, IL (town) Cook County	65,694	78.31
Santa Maria, CA (city) Santa Barbara County	65,188	65.48
Irving, TX (city) Dallas County	64,396	29.77
Escondido, CA (city) San Diego County	63,552	44.16
Norwalk, CA (city) Los Angeles County	63,299	59.97
Edinburg, TX (city) Hidalgo County	63,294	82.09
Grand Prairie, TX (city) Dallas County	63,100	35.98
Modesto, CA (city) Stanislaus County	62,010	30.83
Mission, TX (city) Hidalgo County	61,703	80.07
Pharr, TX (city) Hidalgo County	61,340	87.13
Lubbock, TX (city) Lubbock County	60,977	26.56
Downey, CA (city) Los Angeles County	60,331	53.98
San Francisco, CA (city) San Francisco County	59,675	7.41
Palmdale, CA (city) Los Angeles County	58,207	38.11
Rialto, CA (city) San Bernardino County	57,699	58.18
Corona, CA (city) Riverside County	56,979	37.39
Indianapolis, IN (city) Marion County	56,771	6.92
Garden Grove, CA (city) Orange County	54,565	31.93
Compton, CA (city) Los Angeles County	54,084	56.07
Baldwin Park, CA (city) Los Angeles County	52,803	70.04
Oceanside, CA (city) San Diego County	52,217	31.25

Place	Population	%
Visalia, CA (city) Tulare County	52,121	41.88
Pico Rivera, CA (city) Los Angeles County	51,337	81.56
Lynwood, CA (city) Los Angeles County	51,021	73.13
Wichita, KS (city) Sedgwick County	49,700	13.00
Whittier, CA (city) Los Angeles County	48,567	56.92
Indio, CA (city) Riverside County	48,095	63.25
Paradise, NV (cdp) Clark County	48,022	21.52
Florence-Graham, CA (cdp) Los Angeles County	47,862	75.51
Amarillo, TX (city) Potter County	47,195	24.75
Yuma, AZ (city) Yuma County	47,190	50.71
West Covina, CA (city) Los Angeles County	46,505	43.83
Huntington Park, CA (city) Los Angeles County	46,467	79.96
Odessa, TX (city) Ector County	46,042	46.07
Las Cruces, NM (city) Doña Ana County	45,747	46.86
Rancho Cucamonga, CA (city) San Bernardino County	45,369	27.45
Harlingen, TX (city) Cameron County	45,357	69.94
Victorville, CA (city) San Bernardino County	45,246	39.04
Orange, CA (city) Orange County	45,074	33.04
Tulsa, OK (city) Tulsa County	45,013	11.49
Madera, CA (city) Madera County	44,444	72.37
Colorado Springs, CO (city) El Paso County	44,135	10.60
Montebello, CA (city) Los Angeles County	43,662	69.86
Perris, CA (city) Riverside County	43,641	63.82
Hayward, CA (city) Alameda County	43,597	30.24
Chandler, AZ (city) Maricopa County	42,911	18.17
Omaha, NE (city) Douglas County	42,701	10.44
Reno, NV (city) Washoe County	42,271	18.77
Lancaster, CA (city) Los Angeles County	42,115	26.89
Inglewood, CA (city) Los Angeles County	41,983	38.28
Manhattan, NY (borough) New York County	41,965	2.65
Elgin, IL (city) Kane County	41,265	38.14
Santa Rosa, CA (city) Sonoma County	40,889	24.37
Vista, CA (city) San Diego County	40,799	43.48
Charlotte, NC (city) Mecklenburg County	40,601	5.55
Fullerton, CA (city) Orange County	39,718	29.39
Portland, OR (city) Multnomah County	39,181	6.71
Watsonville, CA (city) Santa Cruz County	39,083	76.34
South Whittier, CA (cdp) Los Angeles County	38,766	67.82
Waukegan, IL (city) Lake County	38,636	43.37
Mesquite, TX (city) Dallas County	37,430	26.77
Coachella, CA (city) Riverside County	37,265	91.55
Paramount, CA (city) Los Angeles County	37,077	68.54
Midland, TX (city) Midland County	36,996	33.29
Nashville-Davidson, TN (metro govt) Davidson County	36,877	6.13
Santa Clarita, CA (city) Los Angeles County	36,666	20.80
Joliet, IL (city) Will County	36,570	24.80
Hesperia, CA (city) San Bernardino County	36,486	40.46
Detroit, MI (city) Wayne County	36,452	5.11
Calexico, CA (city) Imperial County	36,443	94.48
Chino, CA (city) San Bernardino County	36,069	46.25
Kansas City, MO (city) Jackson County	35,930	7.81
Merced, CA (city) Merced County	35,593	45.08
Kansas City, KS (city) Wyandotte County	34,764	23.85
Yakima, WA (city) Yakima County	34,697	38.10
Delano, CA (city) Kern County	34,658	65.34
Bell Gardens, CA (city) Los Angeles County	34,509	82.02
National City, CA (city) San Diego County	34,473	58.85
Pasadena, CA (city) Los Angeles County	34,168	24.92
Avondale, AZ (city) Maricopa County	34,041	44.65
West Valley City, UT (city) Salt Lake County	33,620	25.97
El Centro, CA (city) Imperial County	33,206	77.95
Waco, TX (city) McLennan County	33,080	26.51
Colton, CA (city) San Bernardino County	32,985	63.25
Pueblo, CO (city) Pueblo County	32,847	30.81
Bellflower, CA (city) Los Angeles County	32,587	42.53
Salt Lake City, UT (city) Salt Lake County	32,094	17.21
San Angelo, TX (city) Tom Green County	31,960	34.29
Costa Mesa, CA (city) Orange County	31,646	28.78
Tulare, CA (city) Tulare County	31,539	53.21
Porterville, CA (city) Tulare County	31,421	58.01
San Juan, TX (city) Hidalgo County	31,279	92.39
Memphis, TN (city) Shelby County	30,799	4.76
La Habra, CA (city) Orange County	30,316	50.33
Pasco, WA (city) Franklin County	30,104	50.36
Carson, CA (city) Los Angeles County	29,896	32.60

SECTION THREE

Please refer to the Explanation of Data in the front of the book for more detailed information.

Hispanic Origin

Mexican

Top 150 Places Sorted by Percent of Total Population

Based on all places, regardless of total population

Place	Population	%
Alto Bonito Heights, TX (cdp) Starr County	342	100.00
Mi Ranchito Estate, TX (cdp) Starr County	281	100.00
Los Ebanos, TX (cdp) Starr County	280	100.00
El Rancho Vela, TX (cdp) Starr County	274	100.00
El Cenizo, TX (cdp) Starr County	249	100.00
Santa Rosa, TX (cdp) Starr County	241	100.00
Rancho Viejo, TX (cdp) Starr County	228	100.00
El Quiote, TX (cdp) Starr County	208	100.00
El Castillo, TX (cdp) Starr County	188	100.00
East Lopez, TX (cdp) Starr County	166	100.00
Loma Vista, TX (cdp) Starr County	160	100.00
La Escondida, TX (cdp) Starr County	153	100.00
Los Altos, TX (cdp) Webb County	140	100.00
Campo Verde, TX (cdp) Starr County	132	100.00
Villarreal, TX (cdp) Starr County	131	100.00
El Socio, TX (cdp) Starr County	130	100.00
Miguel Barrera, TX (cdp) Starr County	128	100.00
Flor del Rio, TX (cdp) Starr County	122	100.00
North Escobares, TX (cdp) Starr County	118	100.00
Chaparrito, TX (cdp) Starr County	114	100.00
Loma Linda West, TX (cdp) Starr County	114	100.00
Ranchitos Del Norte, TX (cdp) Starr County	112	100.00
Sammy Martinez, TX (cdp) Starr County	110	100.00
Loma Grande, TX (cdp) Zavala County	107	100.00
Old Escobares, TX (cdp) Starr County	97	100.00
Olivia Lopez de Gutierrez, TX (cdp) Starr County	93	100.00
Amada Acres, TX (cdp) Starr County	92	100.00
Longoria, TX (cdp) Starr County	92	100.00
Gutierrez, TX (cdp) Starr County	79	100.00
Northridge, TX (cdp) Starr County	78	100.00
Hilltop, TX (cdp) Starr County	77	100.00
San Fernando, TX (cdp) Starr County	68	100.00
Rivereno, TX (cdp) Starr County	61	100.00
Zarate, TX (cdp) Starr County	59	100.00
Casa Blanca, TX (cdp) Starr County	54	100.00
Santa Cruz, TX (cdp) Starr County	54	100.00
Tanquecitos South Acres II, TX (cdp) Webb County	50	100.00
Grand Acres, TX (cdp) Cameron County	49	100.00
La Chuparosa, TX (cdp) Starr County	49	100.00
El Brazil, TX (cdp) Starr County	47	100.00
Sunset, TX (cdp) Starr County	47	100.00
Casas, TX (cdp) Starr County	39	100.00
El Mesquite, TX (cdp) Starr County	38	100.00
Guadalupe-Guerra, TX (cdp) Starr County	37	100.00
Los Corralitos, TX (cdp) Webb County	35	100.00
Benjamin Perez, TX (cdp) Starr County	34	100.00
Sandoval, TX (cdp) Starr County	32	100.00
Netos, TX (cdp) Starr County	31	100.00
Elias-Fela Solis, TX (cdp) Starr County	30	100.00
Hillside Acres, TX (cdp) Webb County	30	100.00
Tierra Dorada, TX (cdp) Starr County	28	100.00
Quesada, TX (cdp) Starr County	25	100.00
Los Veteranos I, TX (cdp) Webb County	24	100.00
Jardin de San Julian, TX (cdp) Starr County	22	100.00
Laredo Ranchettes, TX (cdp) Webb County	22	100.00
Los Minerales, TX (cdp) Webb County	20	100.00
Anacua, TX (cdp) Starr County	12	100.00
Las Haciendas, TX (cdp) Webb County	7	100.00
Brewster, FL (cdp) Polk County	3	100.00
Mikes, TX (cdp) Starr County	909	99.89
Roma Creek, TX (cdp) Starr County	349	99.71
Airport Heights, TX (cdp) Starr County	160	99.38
Valle Vista, TX (cdp) Starr County	466	99.36
Muniz, TX (cdp) Hidalgo County	1,361	99.34
Garza-Salinas II, TX (cdp) Starr County	714	99.30
Nina, TX (cdp) Starr County	140	99.29
West Alto Bonito, TX (cdp) Starr County	691	99.28
Olmito and Olmito, TX (cdp) Starr County	269	99.26
Ramos, TX (cdp) Starr County	115	99.14
Barrera, TX (cdp) Starr County	107	99.07
La Rosita, TX (cdp) Starr County	84	98.82
Eidson Road, TX (cdp) Maverick County	8,849	98.76
Eugenio Saenz, TX (cdp) Starr County	157	98.74
San Carlos I, TX (cdp) Webb County	312	98.73
Camargito, TX (cdp) Starr County	383	98.71
Manuel Garcia II, TX (cdp) Starr County	76	98.70
Abram, TX (cdp) Hidalgo County	2,039	98.65
Ranchitos East, TX (cdp) Webb County	209	98.58
Tornillo, TX (cdp) El Paso County	1,545	98.53
San Carlos II, TX (cdp) Webb County	257	98.47
Los Alvarez, TX (cdp) Starr County	298	98.35
Granjeno, TX (city) Hidalgo County	288	98.29
Lago Vista, TX (cdp) Starr County	113	98.26
Fronton Ranchettes, TX (cdp) Starr County	111	98.23
JF Villarreal, TX (cdp) Starr County	102	98.08
Sparks, TX (cdp) El Paso County	4,441	98.06
Indio, TX (cdp) Starr County	49	98.00
La Coma, TX (cdp) Webb County	47	97.92
South Alamo, TX (cdp) Hidalgo County	3,289	97.86
Penitas, TX (city) Hidalgo County	4,301	97.68
Los Angeles, TX (cdp) Willacy County	118	97.52
Doolittle, TX (cdp) Hidalgo County	2,700	97.51
Orange Grove Mobile Manor, AZ (cdp) Yuma County	579	97.47
Mila Doce, TX (cdp) Hidalgo County	6,056	97.33
Chula Vista, TX (cdp) Maverick County	3,715	97.30
Martinez, TX (cdp) Starr County	67	97.10
La Paloma Ranchettes, TX (cdp) Starr County	232	97.07
La Puerta, TX (cdp) Starr County	613	96.99
El Chaparral, TX (cdp) Starr County	450	96.98
Las Quintas Fronterizas, TX (cdp) Maverick County	3,190	96.96
Chula Vista, TX (cdp) Cameron County	279	96.88
La Casita, TX (cdp) Starr County	124	96.88
Cantua Creek, CA (cdp) Fresno County	450	96.57
B and E, TX (cdp) Starr County	500	96.53
Los Barreras, TX (cdp) Starr County	278	96.53
La Victoria, TX (cdp) Starr County	165	96.49
Hidalgo, TX (city) Hidalgo County	10,804	96.48
Morning Glory, TX (cdp) El Paso County	628	96.47
La Joya, TX (city) Hidalgo County	3,842	96.41
Havana, TX (cdp) Hidalgo County	392	96.31
Westway, TX (cdp) El Paso County	4,033	96.30
San Luis, AZ (city) Yuma County	24,543	96.23
Siesta Acres, TX (cdp) Maverick County	1,813	96.18
Pueblo Nuevo, TX (cdp) Webb County	501	96.16
Seco Mines, TX (cdp) Maverick County	537	95.89
Los Veteranos II, TX (cdp) Webb County	23	95.83
La Loma de Falcon, TX (cdp) Starr County	91	95.79
Lost Hills, CA (cdp) Kern County	2,310	95.77
Chapeno, TX (cdp) Starr County	45	95.74
La Carla, TX (cdp) Starr County	67	95.71
Amaya, TX (cdp) Zavala County	89	95.70
Mesquite, TX (cdp) Starr County	483	95.64
Colorado Acres, TX (cdp) Webb County	283	95.61
Heber, CA (cdp) Imperial County	4,084	95.53
Fabrica, TX (cdp) Maverick County	881	95.45
Victoria Vera, TX (cdp) Starr County	105	95.45
Radar Base, TX (cdp) Maverick County	727	95.41
El Cenizo, TX (city) Webb County	3,122	95.39
Ranchette Estates, TX (cdp) Willacy County	145	95.39
Chualar, CA (cdp) Monterey County	1,135	95.38
Olivarez, TX (cdp) Hidalgo County	3,649	95.35
Regino Ramirez, TX (cdp) Starr County	81	95.29
Sullivan City, TX (city) Hidalgo County	3,810	95.20
Villa Pancho, TX (cdp) Cameron County	750	95.18
Progreso, TX (city) Hidalgo County	5,238	95.12
Scissors, TX (cdp) Hidalgo County	3,030	95.10
Santa Maria, TX (cdp) Cameron County	697	95.09
Flowella, TX (cdp) Brooks County	112	94.92
Ramirez-Perez, TX (cdp) Starr County	74	94.87
Faysville, TX (cdp) Hidalgo County	416	94.76
La Grulla, TX (city) Starr County	1,536	94.70
La Homa, TX (cdp) Hidalgo County	11,348	94.69
Lago, TX (cdp) Cameron County	193	94.61
Palo Blanco, TX (cdp) Starr County	193	94.61
Calexico, CA (city) Imperial County	36,443	94.48
Cameron Park, TX (cdp) Cameron County	6,578	94.47
Doffing, TX (cdp) Hidalgo County	4,809	94.46
Moraida, TX (cdp) Starr County	200	94.34
Los Ebanos, TX (cdp) Hidalgo County	316	94.33
Three Rocks, CA (cdp) Fresno County	232	94.31

Please refer to the Explanation of Data in the front of the book for more detailed information.

Hispanic Origin

Mexican

Top 150 Places Sorted by Percent of Total Population

Based on places with total population of 7,500 or more

Place	Population	%
Eidson Road, TX (cdp) Maverick County	8,849	98.76
Hidalgo, TX (city) Hidalgo County	10,804	96.48
San Luis, AZ (city) Yuma County	24,543	96.23
La Homa, TX (cdp) Hidalgo County	11,348	94.69
Calexico, CA (city) Imperial County	36,443	94.48
San Elizario, TX (cdp) El Paso County	12,785	93.99
Somerton, AZ (city) Yuma County	13,311	93.17
Parlier, CA (city) Fresno County	13,445	92.76
San Juan, TX (city) Hidalgo County	31,279	92.39
Anthony, NM (cdp) Doña Ana County	8,618	92.07
Alton, TX (city) Hidalgo County	11,325	91.77
Coachella, CA (city) Riverside County	37,265	91.55
Mecca, CA (cdp) Riverside County	7,815	91.12
Roma, TX (city) Starr County	8,870	90.83
Socorro, TX (city) El Paso County	29,019	90.65
Fabens, TX (cdp) El Paso County	7,485	90.65
Nogales, AZ (city) Santa Cruz County	18,778	90.12
Eagle Pass, TX (city) Maverick County	23,574	89.81
Arvin, CA (city) Kern County	17,133	88.75
Rio Grande City, TX (city) Starr County	12,195	88.15
East Los Angeles, CA (cdp) Los Angeles County	111,441	88.10
Sunland Park, NM (city) Doña Ana County	12,294	87.15
Pharr, TX (city) Hidalgo County	61,340	87.13
Lamont, CA (cdp) Kern County	13,154	87.00
Earlimart, CA (cdp) Tulare County	7,427	87.00
Laredo, TX (city) Webb County	205,079	86.86
Greenfield, CA (city) Monterey County	14,164	86.74
Brownsville, TX (city) Cameron County	150,945	86.24
McFarland, CA (city) Kern County	10,839	85.30
Firebaugh, CA (city) Fresno County	6,434	85.23
Donna, TX (city) Hidalgo County	13,366	84.61
Orange Cove, CA (city) Fresno County	7,669	84.48
Gonzales, CA (city) Monterey County	6,899	84.27
Commerce, CA (city) Los Angeles County	10,758	83.90
Mercedes, TX (city) Hidalgo County	12,934	83.07
Maywood, CA (city) Los Angeles County	22,719	82.93
San Benito, TX (city) Cameron County	20,062	82.73
Walnut Park, CA (cdp) Los Angeles County	13,139	82.29
Orosi, CA (cdp) Tulare County	7,209	82.20
King City, CA (city) Monterey County	10,573	82.13
Edinburg, TX (city) Hidalgo County	63,294	82.09
Bell Gardens, CA (city) Los Angeles County	34,509	82.02
San Fernando, CA (city) Los Angeles County	19,373	81.93
Pico Rivera, CA (city) Los Angeles County	51,337	81.56
Lindsay, CA (city) Tulare County	9,533	81.01
Dinuba, CA (city) Tulare County	17,316	80.72
Horizon City, TX (city) El Paso County	13,507	80.71
Rio Rico, AZ (cdp) Santa Cruz County	15,245	80.40
Mission, TX (city) Hidalgo County	61,703	80.07
Chaparral, NM (cdp) Otero County	11,703	79.99
Huntington Park, CA (city) Los Angeles County	46,467	79.96
Robstown, TX (city) Nueces County	9,123	79.42
Farmersville, CA (city) Tulare County	8,339	78.76
Cicero, IL (town) Cook County	65,694	78.31
Toppenish, WA (city) Yakima County	6,994	78.15
South Gate, CA (city) Los Angeles County	73,677	78.05
El Centro, CA (city) Imperial County	33,206	77.95
Weslaco, TX (city) Hidalgo County	27,801	77.94
McAllen, TX (city) Hidalgo County	100,963	77.74
South Houston, TX (city) Harris County	13,193	77.68
Del Rio, TX (city) Val Verde County	27,626	77.62
West Whittier-Los Nietos, CA (cdp) Los Angeles County	19,824	77.62
South El Monte, CA (city) Los Angeles County	15,606	77.58
Sunnyside, WA (city) Yakima County	12,296	77.54
Brawley, CA (city) Imperial County	19,317	77.41
Douglas, AZ (city) Cochise County	13,363	76.90
Alamo, TX (city) Hidalgo County	14,094	76.79
Jacinto City, TX (city) Harris County	8,086	76.62
Watsonville, CA (city) Santa Cruz County	39,083	76.34
Sanger, CA (city) Fresno County	18,469	76.10
Cudahy, CA (city) Los Angeles County	18,073	75.92
Muscoy, CA (cdp) San Bernardino County	8,076	75.87
Florence-Graham, CA (cdp) Los Angeles County	47,862	75.51
Santa Paula, CA (city) Ventura County	22,077	75.29
West Puente Valley, CA (cdp) Los Angeles County	17,034	75.25

Place	Population	%
Grandview, WA (city) Yakima County	8,172	75.23
South San Jose Hills, CA (cdp) Los Angeles County	15,436	75.11
Bell, CA (city) Los Angeles County	26,606	75.00
Galena Park, TX (city) Harris County	8,161	74.96
El Paso, TX (city) El Paso County	486,186	74.90
La Puente, CA (city) Los Angeles County	29,607	74.36
Lennox, CA (cdp) Los Angeles County	16,817	73.91
Shafter, CA (city) Kern County	12,553	73.89
Selma, CA (city) Fresno County	17,061	73.48
Lynwood, CA (city) Los Angeles County	51,021	73.13
Bloomington, CA (cdp) San Bernardino County	17,441	73.12
Avocado Heights, CA (cdp) Los Angeles County	11,245	72.97
Pecos, TX (city) Reeves County	6,381	72.68
Madera, CA (city) Madera County	44,444	72.37
Good Hope, CA (cdp) Riverside County	6,615	71.96
Reedley, CA (city) Fresno County	17,406	71.94
East Rancho Dominguez, CA (cdp) Los Angeles County	10,864	71.78
Imperial, CA (city) Imperial County	10,525	71.32
Santa Ana, CA (city) Orange County	230,381	70.99
Livingston, CA (city) Merced County	9,244	70.79
Fillmore, CA (city) Ventura County	10,565	70.42
Baldwin Park, CA (city) Los Angeles County	52,803	70.04
Harlingen, TX (city) Cameron County	45,357	69.94
Aldine, TX (cdp) Harris County	11,093	69.90
Montebello, CA (city) Los Angeles County	43,662	69.86
Hawaiian Gardens, CA (city) Los Angeles County	9,955	69.84
Wasco, CA (city) Kern County	17,814	69.74
Salinas, CA (city) Monterey County	104,237	69.29
Oxnard, CA (city) Ventura County	136,991	69.22
Pearsall, TX (city) Frio County	6,328	69.19
Santa Fe Springs, CA (city) Los Angeles County	11,217	69.14
Alice, TX (city) Jim Wells County	13,187	69.03
Paramount, CA (city) Los Angeles County	37,077	68.54
Delhi, CA (cdp) Merced County	7,369	68.52
Winton, CA (cdp) Merced County	7,261	68.42
Valinda, CA (cdp) Los Angeles County	15,513	67.97
South Whittier, CA (cdp) Los Angeles County	38,766	67.82
Uvalde, TX (city) Uvalde County	10,532	66.87
Kerman, CA (city) Fresno County	9,043	66.77
Home Gardens, CA (cdp) Riverside County	7,647	66.09
August, CA (cdp) San Joaquin County	5,531	65.92
Santa Maria, CA (city) Santa Barbara County	65,188	65.48
Delano, CA (city) Kern County	34,658	65.34
Mendota, CA (city) Fresno County	7,183	65.22
Immokalee, FL (cdp) Collier County	15,714	65.06
Garden Acres, CA (cdp) San Joaquin County	6,916	64.95
Drexel Heights, AZ (cdp) Pima County	17,992	64.84
Garnet, CA (cdp) Riverside County	4,891	64.84
Citrus, CA (cdp) Los Angeles County	7,030	64.70
Mead Valley, CA (cdp) Riverside County	11,958	64.60
Alum Rock, CA (cdp) Santa Clara County	10,024	64.52
Vincent, CA (cdp) Los Angeles County	10,185	63.97
Perris, CA (city) Riverside County	43,641	63.82
Indio, CA (city) Riverside County	48,095	63.25
Colton, CA (city) San Bernardino County	32,985	63.25
Fort Stockton, TX (city) Pecos County	5,235	63.20
Soledad, CA (city) Monterey County	16,261	63.18
Raymondville, TX (city) Willacy County	7,105	62.97
Calipatria, CA (city) Imperial County	4,828	62.66
Hereford, TX (city) Deaf Smith County	9,609	62.52
Valencia West, AZ (cdp) Pima County	5,784	61.83
Rubidoux, CA (cdp) Riverside County	21,173	61.76
Mira Loma, CA (cdp) Riverside County	13,503	61.57
Avenal, CA (city) Kings County	9,481	61.15
Pomona, CA (city) Los Angeles County	90,988	61.04
Hollister, CA (city) San Benito County	21,304	60.99
El Monte, CA (city) Los Angeles County	69,053	60.85
Glen Avon, CA (cdp) Riverside County	12,282	60.80
Deming, NM (city) Luna County	8,953	60.27
Ontario, CA (city) San Bernardino County	98,596	60.15
Norwalk, CA (city) Los Angeles County	63,299	59.97
Kingsville, TX (city) Kleberg County	15,711	59.94
Montclair, CA (city) San Bernardino County	21,893	59.71
Madera Acres, CA (cdp) Madera County	5,469	59.69
Melrose Park, IL (village) Cook County	15,141	59.58

Hispanic Origin

Puerto Rican

U.S. and 50 States Sorted by Population and Percent of Total Population

Place	Population	%
United States	**4,623,716**	**1.50**
New York	1,070,558	5.52
Florida	847,550	4.51
New Jersey	434,092	4.94
Pennsylvania	366,082	2.88
Massachusetts	266,125	4.06
Connecticut	252,972	7.08
California	189,945	0.51
Illinois	182,989	1.43
Texas	130,576	0.52
Ohio	94,965	0.82
Virginia	73,958	0.92
Georgia	71,987	0.74
North Carolina	71,800	0.75
Wisconsin	46,323	0.81
Hawaii	44,116	3.24
Maryland	42,572	0.74
Michigan	37,267	0.38
Rhode Island	34,979	3.32
Arizona	34,787	0.54
Indiana	30,304	0.47
South Carolina	26,493	0.57
Washington	25,838	0.38
Colorado	22,995	0.46
Delaware	22,533	2.51
Tennessee	21,060	0.33
Nevada	20,664	0.77
Missouri	12,236	0.20
Alabama	12,225	0.26
Oklahoma	12,223	0.33
New Hampshire	11,729	0.89
Louisiana	11,603	0.26
Kentucky	11,454	0.26
Minnesota	10,807	0.20
Kansas	9,247	0.32
Oregon	8,845	0.23
New Mexico	7,964	0.39
Utah	7,182	0.26
Mississippi	5,888	0.20
Iowa	4,885	0.16
Arkansas	4,789	0.16
Alaska	4,502	0.63
Maine	4,377	0.33
West Virginia	3,701	0.20
Nebraska	3,242	0.18
District of Columbia	3,129	0.52
Idaho	2,910	0.19
Vermont	2,261	0.36
Montana	1,491	0.15
South Dakota	1,483	0.18
Wyoming	1,026	0.18
North Dakota	987	0.15

Place	Population	%
Connecticut	252,972	7.08
New York	1,070,558	5.52
New Jersey	434,092	4.94
Florida	847,550	4.51
Massachusetts	266,125	4.06
Rhode Island	34,979	3.32
Hawaii	44,116	3.24
Pennsylvania	366,082	2.88
Delaware	22,533	2.51
United States	**4,623,716**	**1.50**
Illinois	182,989	1.43
Virginia	73,958	0.92
New Hampshire	11,729	0.89
Ohio	94,965	0.82
Wisconsin	46,323	0.81
Nevada	20,664	0.77
North Carolina	71,800	0.75
Georgia	71,987	0.74
Maryland	42,572	0.74
Alaska	4,502	0.63
South Carolina	26,493	0.57
Arizona	34,787	0.54
Texas	130,576	0.52
District of Columbia	3,129	0.52
California	189,945	0.51
Indiana	30,304	0.47
Colorado	22,995	0.46
New Mexico	7,964	0.39
Michigan	37,267	0.38
Washington	25,838	0.38
Vermont	2,261	0.36
Tennessee	21,060	0.33
Oklahoma	12,223	0.33
Maine	4,377	0.33
Kansas	9,247	0.32
Alabama	12,225	0.26
Louisiana	11,603	0.26
Kentucky	11,454	0.26
Utah	7,182	0.26
Oregon	8,845	0.23
Missouri	12,236	0.20
Minnesota	10,807	0.20
Mississippi	5,888	0.20
West Virginia	3,701	0.20
Idaho	2,910	0.19
Nebraska	3,242	0.18
South Dakota	1,483	0.18
Wyoming	1,026	0.18
Iowa	4,885	0.16
Arkansas	4,789	0.16
Montana	1,491	0.15
North Dakota	987	0.15

Please refer to the Explanation of Data in the front of the book for more detailed information.

Hispanic Origin

Puerto Rican

Top 150 Places Sorted by Population

Based on all places, regardless of total population

Place	Population	%
New York, NY (city) Kings County	723,621	8.85
Bronx, NY (borough) Bronx County	298,921	21.58
Brooklyn, NY (borough) Kings County	176,528	7.05
Philadelphia, PA (city) Philadelphia County	121,643	7.97
Manhattan, NY (borough) New York County	107,774	6.80
Queens, NY (borough) Queens County	102,881	4.61
Chicago, IL (city) Cook County	102,703	3.81
Springfield, MA (city) Hampden County	50,798	33.19
Hartford, CT (city/town) Hartford County	41,995	33.66
Staten Island, NY (borough) Richmond County	37,517	8.00
Newark, NJ (city) Essex County	35,993	12.99
Bridgeport, CT (city/town) Fairfield County	31,881	22.10
Orlando, FL (city) Orange County	31,201	13.09
Boston, MA (city) Suffolk County	30,506	4.94
Allentown, PA (city) Lehigh County	29,640	25.11
Cleveland, OH (city) Cuyahoga County	29,286	7.38
Reading, PA (city) Berks County	28,160	31.97
Rochester, NY (city) Monroe County	27,734	13.17
Jersey City, NJ (city) Hudson County	25,677	10.37
Waterbury, CT (city/town) New Haven County	24,947	22.60
Milwaukee, WI (city) Milwaukee County	24,672	4.15
Tampa, FL (city) Hillsborough County	24,057	7.17
Camden, NJ (city) Camden County	23,759	30.72
Worcester, MA (city) Worcester County	23,074	12.74
Buffalo, NY (city) Erie County	22,076	8.45
New Britain, CT (city/town) Hartford County	21,914	29.93
Islip, NY (town) Suffolk County	21,506	6.41
Brookhaven, NY (town) Suffolk County	21,429	4.41
Jacksonville, FL (city) Duval County	21,128	2.57
Paterson, NJ (city) Passaic County	21,015	14.37
Hempstead, NY (town) Nassau County	20,508	2.70
New Haven, CT (city/town) New Haven County	20,505	15.80
Yonkers, NY (city) Westchester County	19,875	10.14
Kissimmee, FL (city) Osceola County	19,728	33.06
Poinciana, FL (cdp) Osceola County	19,055	35.82
Holyoke, MA (city) Hampden County	17,825	44.70
Deltona, FL (city) Volusia County	17,661	20.73
Lancaster, PA (city) Lancaster County	17,341	29.23
Lawrence, MA (city) Essex County	16,953	22.20
Vineland, NJ (city) Cumberland County	16,236	26.74
Los Angeles, CA (city) Los Angeles County	15,565	0.41
Providence, RI (city) Providence County	14,847	8.34
Alafaya, FL (cdp) Orange County	14,044	17.98
Bethlehem, PA (city) Northampton County	13,722	18.30
Elizabeth, NJ (city) Union County	13,488	10.79
San Antonio, TX (city) Medina County	13,164	0.99
Miami, FL (city) Miami-Dade County	12,789	3.20
Meriden, CT (city/town) New Haven County	12,572	20.65
Lorain, OH (city) Lorain County	12,413	19.37
Perth Amboy, NJ (city) Middlesex County	12,090	23.79
Lowell, MA (city) Middlesex County	12,079	11.34
Bethlehem, PA (city) Northampton County	11,715	21.06
Buenaventura Lakes, FL (cdp) Osceola County	11,618	44.55
Town 'n' Country, FL (cdp) Hillsborough County	10,742	13.69
Pembroke Pines, FL (city) Broward County	10,490	6.78
Trenton, NJ (city) Mercer County	9,746	11.48
Port St. Lucie, FL (city) St. Lucie County	9,737	5.92
Brandon, FL (cdp) Hillsborough County	9,574	9.25
New Bedford, MA (city) Bristol County	9,554	10.05
Virginia Beach, VA (ind. city) Virginia Beach independent city	9,461	2.16
Houston, TX (city) Harris County	9,290	0.44
Meadow Woods, FL (cdp) Orange County	8,974	35.11
East Hartford, CT (cdp/town) Hartford County	8,903	17.37
Hollywood, FL (city) Broward County	8,818	6.26
York, PA (city) York County	8,440	19.31
San Diego, CA (city) San Diego County	8,220	0.63
Killeen, TX (city) Bell County	8,117	6.35
Phoenix, AZ (city) Maricopa County	8,103	0.56
Spring Hill, FL (cdp) Hernando County	8,072	8.18
Lehigh Acres, FL (cdp) Lee County	7,864	9.06
Syracuse, NY (city) Onondaga County	7,594	5.23
Babylon, NY (town) Suffolk County	7,562	3.54
Fayetteville, NC (city) Cumberland County	7,526	3.75
Charlotte, NC (city) Mecklenburg County	7,521	1.03
Palm Bay, FL (city) Brevard County	7,463	7.23

Place	Population	%
Passaic, NJ (city) Passaic County	7,368	10.56
Cape Coral, FL (city) Lee County	7,261	4.71
Chicopee, MA (city) Hampden County	7,097	12.83
Miramar, FL (city) Broward County	6,658	5.46
Union City, NJ (city) Hudson County	6,643	10.00
St. Cloud, FL (city) Osceola County	6,574	18.69
Bayonne, NJ (city) Hudson County	6,209	9.85
Brentwood, NY (cdp) Suffolk County	6,125	10.10
Lebanon, PA (city) Lebanon County	6,081	23.87
Woodbridge, NJ (township) Middlesex County	6,063	6.09
Windham, CT (town) Windham County	6,061	23.99
Pennsauken, NJ (township) Camden County	6,038	16.83
Riverview, FL (cdp) Hillsborough County	5,992	8.43
Clifton, NJ (city) Passaic County	5,969	7.09
Coral Springs, FL (city) Broward County	5,910	4.88
Fitchburg, MA (city) Worcester County	5,871	14.56
El Paso, TX (city) El Paso County	5,793	0.89
Detroit, MI (city) Wayne County	5,783	0.81
Harrisburg, PA (city) Dauphin County	5,685	11.48
Fort Worth, TX (city) Tarrant County	5,650	0.76
Sanford, FL (city) Seminole County	5,538	10.34
Urban Honolulu, HI (cdp) Honolulu County	5,397	1.60
St. Petersburg, FL (city) Pinellas County	5,272	2.15
Las Vegas, NV (city) Clark County	5,209	0.89
Homestead, FL (city) Miami-Dade County	5,186	8.57
Brockton, MA (city) Plymouth County	5,154	5.49
North Bergen, NJ (township) Hudson County	5,090	8.38
Columbus, OH (city) Franklin County	5,034	0.64
Hialeah, FL (city) Miami-Dade County	5,027	2.24
Davie, FL (town) Broward County	5,006	5.44
Belleville, NJ (township) Essex County	5,001	13.92
Egypt Lake-Leto, FL (cdp) Hillsborough County	4,902	13.89
Lynn, MA (city) Essex County	4,894	5.42
Lakeland, FL (city) Polk County	4,857	4.99
University, FL (cdp) Hillsborough County	4,854	11.79
Oyster Bay, NY (town) Nassau County	4,810	1.64
Manchester, CT (town) Hartford County	4,782	8.21
San Jose, CA (city) Santa Clara County	4,763	0.50
Colorado Springs, CO (city) El Paso County	4,759	1.14
Erie, PA (city) Erie County	4,752	4.67
Altamonte Springs, FL (city) Seminole County	4,738	11.42
Pawtucket, RI (city) Providence County	4,729	6.65
Willimantic, CT (cdp) Windham County	4,686	26.42
Schenectady, NY (city) Schenectady County	4,677	7.07
Albany, NY (city) Albany County	4,654	4.76
Azalea Park, FL (cdp) Orange County	4,583	36.50
Newport News, VA (ind. city) Newport News independent city	4,544	2.51
Middletown, NY (city) Orange County	4,533	16.14
Chelsea, MA (city) Suffolk County	4,458	12.67
Wilmington, DE (city) New Castle County	4,404	6.22
Fall River, MA (city) Bristol County	4,401	4.95
Norfolk, VA (ind. city) Norfolk independent city	4,387	1.81
Four Corners, FL (cdp) Lake County	4,375	16.75
Raleigh, NC (city) Wake County	4,340	1.07
West Haven, CT (city/town) New Haven County	4,282	7.71
New London, CT (city/town) New London County	4,264	15.44
Utica, NY (city) Oneida County	4,220	6.78
Sunrise, FL (city) Broward County	4,210	4.99
San Francisco, CA (city) San Francisco County	4,204	0.52
Huntington, NY (town) Suffolk County	4,187	2.06
Bloomfield, NJ (township) Essex County	4,156	8.78
Woonsocket, RI (city) Providence County	4,117	10.00
Pine Hills, FL (cdp) Orange County	4,115	6.85
Hoboken, NJ (city) Hudson County	4,110	8.22
Haverstraw, NY (town) Rockland County	4,061	11.09
Austin, TX (city) Travis County	4,055	0.51
Stratford, CT (cdp/town) Fairfield County	3,974	7.73
Clarksville, TN (city) Montgomery County	3,957	2.98
Amsterdam, NY (city) Montgomery County	3,923	21.07
Hamilton, NJ (township) Mercer County	3,902	4.41
Aurora, IL (city) Kane County	3,867	1.95
Southbridge Town, MA (city) Worcester County	3,858	23.08
Youngstown, OH (city) Mahoning County	3,836	5.73
Fort Lauderdale, FL (city) Broward County	3,821	2.31
Wesley Chapel, FL (cdp) Pasco County	3,818	8.66

Please refer to the Explanation of Data in the front of the book for more detailed information.

Hispanic Origin

Puerto Rican

Top 150 Places Sorted by Percent of Total Population

Based on all places, regardless of total population

Place	Population	%
Holyoke, MA (city) Hampden County	17,825	44.70
Buenaventura Lakes, FL (cdp) Osceola County	11,618	44.55
Azalea Park, FL (cdp) Orange County	4,583	36.50
Poinciana, FL (cdp) Osceola County	19,055	35.82
Meadow Woods, FL (cdp) Orange County	8,974	35.11
Hartford, CT (city/town) Hartford County	41,995	33.66
Springfield, MA (city) Hampden County	50,798	33.19
Kissimmee, FL (city) Osceola County	19,728	33.06
Reading, PA (city) Berks County	28,160	31.97
Elwood, NJ (cdp) Atlantic County	453	31.52
Camden, NJ (city) Camden County	23,759	30.72
New Britain, CT (city/town) Hartford County	21,914	29.93
Lancaster, PA (city) Lancaster County	17,341	29.23
Kaskaskia, IL (village) Randolph County	4	28.57
Vineland, NJ (city) Cumberland County	16,236	26.74
Willimantic, CT (cdp) Windham County	4,686	26.42
Plattekill, NY (cdp) Ulster County	328	26.03
Union Park, FL (cdp) Orange County	2,520	25.81
Allentown, PA (city) Lehigh County	29,640	25.11
Windham, CT (town) Windham County	6,061	23.99
Lebanon, PA (city) Lebanon County	6,081	23.87
Perth Amboy, NJ (city) Middlesex County	12,090	23.79
Southbridge Town, MA (city) Worcester County	3,858	23.08
Harlem Heights, FL (cdp) Lee County	447	22.63
Waterbury, CT (city/town) New Haven County	24,947	22.60
Lawrence, MA (city) Essex County	16,953	22.20
Dunkirk, NY (city) Chautauqua County	2,782	22.14
Bridgeport, CT (city/town) Fairfield County	31,881	22.10
Sky Lake, FL (cdp) Orange County	1,359	22.09
Southchase, FL (cdp) Orange County	3,497	21.96
Pine Castle, FL (cdp) Orange County	2,349	21.74
Bronx, NY (borough) Bronx County	298,921	21.58
Amsterdam, NY (city) Montgomery County	3,923	21.07
Bethlehem, PA (city) Northampton County	11,715	21.06
Woodlynne, NJ (borough) Camden County	624	20.95
Deltona, FL (city) Volusia County	17,661	20.73
Meriden, CT (city/town) New Haven County	12,572	20.65
Ellenville, NY (village) Ulster County	832	20.12
Buena, NJ (borough) Atlantic County	901	19.57
Lorain, OH (city) Lorain County	12,413	19.37
York, PA (city) York County	8,440	19.31
St. Cloud, FL (city) Osceola County	6,574	18.69
Woodbine, NJ (borough) Cape May County	455	18.41
Interlachen, FL (town) Putnam County	257	18.32
Bethlehem, PA (city) Northampton County	13,722	18.30
Alafaya, FL (cdp) Orange County	14,044	17.98
Egg Harbor City, NJ (city) Atlantic County	750	17.68
East Hartford, CT (cdp/town) Hartford County	8,903	17.37
Taft, FL (cdp) Orange County	376	17.05
Pennsauken, NJ (township) Camden County	6,038	16.83
Four Corners, FL (cdp) Lake County	4,375	16.75
Silver Lake, NJ (cdp) Essex County	707	16.66
Oak Ridge, FL (cdp) Orange County	3,704	16.33
Loughman, FL (cdp) Polk County	437	16.31
Linndale, OH (village) Cuyahoga County	29	16.20
Middletown, NY (city) Orange County	4,533	16.14
Wedgefield, FL (cdp) Orange County	1,082	16.14
Fountain Hill, PA (borough) Lehigh County	739	16.08
Monticello, NY (village) Sullivan County	1,073	15.95
Penn Estates, PA (cdp) Monroe County	715	15.91
New Haven, CT (city/town) New Haven County	20,505	15.80
Freemansburg, PA (borough) Northampton County	413	15.67
Pine Ridge, PA (cdp) Pike County	420	15.52
Washington Heights, NY (cdp) Orange County	261	15.45
New London, CT (city/town) New London County	4,264	15.44
Scotchtown, NY (cdp) Orange County	1,410	15.31
Penns Grove, NJ (borough) Salem County	773	15.02
Seabrook Farms, NJ (cdp) Cumberland County	222	14.96
Pleasant Hill, PA (cdp) Lebanon County	393	14.87
Central Falls, RI (city) Providence County	2,878	14.85
Hunters Creek, FL (cdp) Orange County	2,099	14.66
Fitchburg, MA (city) Worcester County	5,871	14.56
Mechanicstown, NY (cdp) Orange County	996	14.52
Wildwood, NJ (city) Cape May County	766	14.38
Paterson, NJ (city) Passaic County	21,015	14.37
Haledon, NJ (borough) Passaic County	1,185	14.25
West Haverstraw, NY (village) Rockland County	1,440	14.17
Lancaster, PA (township) Lancaster County	2,279	14.11
Belleville, NJ (township) Essex County	5,001	13.92
Egypt Lake-Leto, FL (cdp) Hillsborough County	4,902	13.89
Warminster Heights, PA (cdp) Bucks County	568	13.77
Prospect Park, NJ (borough) Passaic County	806	13.74
Palm River-Clair Mel, FL (cdp) Hillsborough County	2,886	13.73
Carteret, NJ (borough) Middlesex County	3,135	13.72
Emerald Lakes, PA (cdp) Monroe County	396	13.72
Town 'n' Country, FL (cdp) Hillsborough County	10,742	13.69
Coolbaugh, PA (township) Monroe County	2,757	13.41
Campbell, OH (city) Mahoning County	1,090	13.24
Woodridge, NY (village) Sullivan County	112	13.22
Rochester, NY (city) Monroe County	27,734	13.17
North Bay Shore, NY (cdp) Suffolk County	2,487	13.13
Orlando, FL (city) Orange County	31,201	13.09
Mullica, NJ (township) Atlantic County	804	13.08
Pleasantville, NJ (city) Atlantic County	2,637	13.02
Newark, NJ (city) Essex County	35,993	12.99
Pocono Ranch Lands, PA (cdp) Pike County	138	12.99
Chicopee, MA (city) Hampden County	7,097	12.83
Spivey, KS (city) Kingman County	10	12.82
Worcester, MA (city) Worcester County	23,074	12.74
Davenport, FL (city) Polk County	368	12.74
New Morgan, PA (borough) Berks County	9	12.68
Chelsea, MA (city) Suffolk County	4,458	12.67
Bithlo, FL (cdp) Orange County	1,035	12.52
Hyde Park, PA (cdp) Berks County	316	12.50
Millville, NJ (city) Cumberland County	3,538	12.46
Lehman, PA (township) Pike County	1,329	12.46
Rio Pinar, FL (cdp) Orange County	648	12.44
Wallkill, NY (town) Orange County	3,386	12.35
Wawarsing, NY (town) Ulster County	1,609	12.23
Hebron, PA (cdp) Lebanon County	159	12.18
Walden, NY (village) Orange County	848	12.15
Halaula, HI (cdp) Hawaii County	57	12.15
Casselberry, FL (city) Seminole County	3,159	12.04
Haverstraw, NY (village) Rockland County	1,427	11.98
Kapaau, HI (cdp) Hawaii County	207	11.94
Mountain View, HI (cdp) Hawaii County	466	11.88
Vails Gate, NY (cdp) Orange County	400	11.87
Liberty, NY (village) Sullivan County	521	11.86
Hawi, HI (cdp) Hawaii County	128	11.84
Maybrook, NY (village) Orange County	350	11.83
Washingtonville, NY (village) Orange County	697	11.82
University, FL (cdp) Hillsborough County	4,854	11.79
Saw Creek, PA (cdp) Pike County	473	11.78
Orange City, FL (city) Volusia County	1,246	11.76
Goldenrod, FL (cdp) Orange County	1,401	11.64
Makaha Valley, HI (cdp) Honolulu County	156	11.63
Trenton, NJ (city) Mercer County	9,746	11.48
Harrisburg, PA (city) Dauphin County	5,685	11.48
Altamonte Springs, FL (city) Seminole County	4,738	11.42
Lowell, MA (city) Middlesex County	12,079	11.34
Plattekill, NY (town) Ulster County	1,185	11.29
Bristol, PA (borough) Bucks County	1,098	11.29
Citrus Park, FL (cdp) Hillsborough County	2,712	11.18
Thompson, NY (town) Sullivan County	1,705	11.14
Beacon, NY (city) Dutchess County	1,726	11.11
Haverstraw, NY (town) Rockland County	4,061	11.09
Dover, NJ (town) Morris County	2,012	11.08
San Castle, FL (cdp) Palm Beach County	378	11.03
South Windham, CT (cdp) Windham County	156	10.98
Makaha, HI (cdp) Honolulu County	905	10.93
Paauilo, HI (cdp) Hawaii County	65	10.92
Fort Myers Shores, FL (cdp) Lee County	598	10.90
West Reading, PA (borough) Berks County	455	10.80
Elizabeth, NJ (city) Union County	13,488	10.79
Orange Lake, NY (cdp) Orange County	743	10.64
Ainaloa, HI (cdp) Hawaii County	315	10.62
Minneola, FL (city) Lake County	994	10.57
Passaic, NJ (city) Passaic County	7,368	10.56
Pine Air, FL (cdp) Palm Beach County	213	10.52
Bethlehem, PA (city) Lehigh County	2,007	10.38

Please refer to the Explanation of Data in the front of the book for more detailed information.

Hispanic Origin

Puerto Rican

Top 150 Places Sorted by Percent of Total Population

Based on places with total population of 7,500 or more

Place	Population	%
Holyoke, MA (city) Hampden County	17,825	44.70
Buenaventura Lakes, FL (cdp) Osceola County	11,618	44.55
Azalea Park, FL (cdp) Orange County	4,583	36.50
Poinciana, FL (cdp) Osceola County	19,055	35.82
Meadow Woods, FL (cdp) Orange County	8,974	35.11
Hartford, CT (city/town) Hartford County	41,995	33.66
Springfield, MA (city) Hampden County	50,798	33.19
Kissimmee, FL (city) Osceola County	19,728	33.06
Reading, PA (city) Berks County	28,160	31.97
Camden, NJ (city) Camden County	23,759	30.72
New Britain, CT (city/town) Hartford County	21,914	29.93
Lancaster, PA (city) Lancaster County	17,341	29.23
Vineland, NJ (city) Cumberland County	16,236	26.74
Willimantic, CT (cdp) Windham County	4,686	26.42
Union Park, FL (cdp) Orange County	2,520	25.81
Allentown, PA (city) Lehigh County	29,640	25.11
Windham, CT (town) Windham County	6,061	23.99
Lebanon, PA (city) Lebanon County	6,081	23.87
Perth Amboy, NJ (city) Middlesex County	12,090	23.79
Southbridge Town, MA (city) Worcester County	3,858	23.08
Waterbury, CT (city/town) New Haven County	24,947	22.60
Lawrence, MA (city) Essex County	16,953	22.20
Dunkirk, NY (city) Chautauqua County	2,782	22.14
Bridgeport, CT (city/town) Fairfield County	31,881	22.10
Southchase, FL (cdp) Orange County	3,497	21.96
Pine Castle, FL (cdp) Orange County	2,349	21.74
Bronx, NY (borough) Bronx County	298,921	21.58
Amsterdam, NY (city) Montgomery County	3,923	21.07
Bethlehem, PA (city) Northampton County	11,715	21.06
Deltona, FL (city) Volusia County	17,661	20.73
Meriden, CT (city/town) New Haven County	12,572	20.65
Lorain, OH (city) Lorain County	12,413	19.37
York, PA (city) York County	8,440	19.31
St. Cloud, FL (city) Osceola County	6,574	18.69
Bethlehem, PA (city) Northampton County	13,722	18.30
Alafaya, FL (cdp) Orange County	14,044	17.98
East Hartford, CT (cdp/town) Hartford County	8,903	17.37
Pennsauken, NJ (township) Camden County	6,038	16.83
Four Corners, FL (cdp) Lake County	4,375	16.75
Oak Ridge, FL (cdp) Orange County	3,704	16.33
Middletown, NY (city) Orange County	4,533	16.14
New Haven, CT (city/town) New Haven County	20,505	15.80
New London, CT (city/town) New London County	4,264	15.44
Scotchtown, NY (cdp) Orange County	1,410	15.31
Central Falls, RI (city) Providence County	2,878	14.85
Hunters Creek, FL (cdp) Orange County	2,099	14.66
Fitchburg, MA (city) Worcester County	5,871	14.56
Paterson, NJ (city) Passaic County	21,015	14.37
Haledon, NJ (borough) Passaic County	1,185	14.25
West Haverstraw, NY (village) Rockland County	1,440	14.17
Lancaster, PA (township) Lancaster County	2,279	14.11
Belleville, NJ (township) Essex County	5,001	13.92
Egypt Lake-Leto, FL (cdp) Hillsborough County	4,902	13.89
Palm River-Clair Mel, FL (cdp) Hillsborough County	2,886	13.73
Carteret, NJ (borough) Middlesex County	3,135	13.72
Town 'n' Country, FL (cdp) Hillsborough County	10,742	13.69
Coolbaugh, PA (township) Monroe County	2,757	13.41
Campbell, OH (city) Mahoning County	1,090	13.24
Rochester, NY (city) Monroe County	27,734	13.17
North Bay Shore, NY (cdp) Suffolk County	2,487	13.13
Orlando, FL (city) Orange County	31,201	13.09
Pleasantville, NJ (city) Atlantic County	2,637	13.02
Newark, NJ (city) Essex County	35,993	12.99
Chicopee, MA (city) Hampden County	7,097	12.83
Worcester, MA (city) Worcester County	23,074	12.74
Chelsea, MA (city) Suffolk County	4,458	12.67
Bithlo, FL (cdp) Orange County	1,035	12.52
Millville, NJ (city) Cumberland County	3,538	12.46
Lehman, PA (township) Pike County	1,329	12.46
Wallkill, NY (town) Orange County	3,386	12.35
Wawarsing, NY (town) Ulster County	1,609	12.23
Casselberry, FL (city) Seminole County	3,159	12.04
Haverstraw, NY (village) Rockland County	1,427	11.98
University, FL (cdp) Hillsborough County	4,854	11.79
Orange City, FL (city) Volusia County	1,246	11.76
Goldenrod, FL (cdp) Orange County	1,401	11.64
Trenton, NJ (city) Mercer County	9,746	11.48
Harrisburg, PA (city) Dauphin County	5,685	11.48
Altamonte Springs, FL (city) Seminole County	4,738	11.42
Lowell, MA (city) Middlesex County	12,079	11.34
Plattekill, NY (town) Ulster County	1,185	11.29
Bristol, PA (borough) Bucks County	1,098	11.29
Citrus Park, FL (cdp) Hillsborough County	2,712	11.18
Thompson, NY (town) Sullivan County	1,705	11.14
Beacon, NY (city) Dutchess County	1,726	11.11
Haverstraw, NY (town) Rockland County	4,061	11.09
Dover, NJ (town) Morris County	2,012	11.08
Makaha, HI (cdp) Honolulu County	905	10.93
Elizabeth, NJ (city) Union County	13,488	10.79
Minneola, FL (city) Lake County	994	10.57
Passaic, NJ (city) Passaic County	7,368	10.56
Bethlehem, PA (city) Lehigh County	2,007	10.38
Jersey City, NJ (city) Hudson County	25,677	10.37
Sanford, FL (city) Seminole County	5,538	10.34
Manchester, CT (cdp) Hartford County	3,146	10.29
Newburgh, NY (city) Orange County	2,962	10.26
Yonkers, NY (city) Westchester County	19,875	10.14
Brentwood, NY (cdp) Suffolk County	6,125	10.10
Lockhart, FL (cdp) Orange County	1,316	10.08
New Bedford, MA (city) Bristol County	9,554	10.05
Middle Smithfield, PA (township) Monroe County	1,606	10.04
Central Islip, NY (cdp) Suffolk County	3,452	10.02
Union City, NJ (city) Hudson County	6,643	10.00
Woonsocket, RI (city) Providence County	4,117	10.00
Bayonne, NJ (city) Hudson County	6,209	9.85
Ansonia, CT (city/town) New Haven County	1,871	9.72
New Windsor, NY (cdp) Orange County	864	9.68
New Windsor, NY (town) Orange County	2,429	9.62
University, FL (cdp) Orange County	2,980	9.59
Haines City, FL (city) Polk County	1,951	9.50
Forest City, FL (cdp) Seminole County	1,299	9.38
Fallsburg, NY (town) Sullivan County	1,200	9.32
Brandon, FL (cdp) Hillsborough County	9,574	9.25
Geneva, NY (city) Ontario County	1,214	9.15
North Bellport, NY (cdp) Suffolk County	1,055	9.14
Lehigh Acres, FL (cdp) Lee County	7,864	9.06
Leisure City, FL (cdp) Miami-Dade County	2,050	9.05
Waianae, HI (cdp) Honolulu County	1,188	9.02
Avon Park, FL (city) Highlands County	795	9.00
Maili, HI (cdp) Honolulu County	850	8.96
Atlantic City, NJ (city) Atlantic County	3,506	8.86
Blooming Grove, NY (town) Orange County	1,598	8.86
New York, NY (city) Kings County	723,621	8.85
Mastic, NY (cdp) Suffolk County	1,363	8.80
Bloomfield, NJ (township) Essex County	4,156	8.78
Clermont, FL (city) Lake County	2,517	8.76
Groton, CT (city) New London County	905	8.71
Groveland, FL (city) Lake County	759	8.70
Newburgh, NY (town) Orange County	2,584	8.67
Montgomery, NY (town) Orange County	1,960	8.67
Wesley Chapel, FL (cdp) Pasco County	3,818	8.66
Fort Dix, NJ (cdp) Burlington County	668	8.66
Liberty, NY (town) Sullivan County	855	8.65
Homestead, FL (city) Miami-Dade County	5,186	8.57
Bay Shore, NY (cdp) Suffolk County	2,245	8.52
Buena Vista, NJ (township) Atlantic County	645	8.52
East Chicago, IN (city) Lake County	2,528	8.51
Buffalo, NY (city) Erie County	22,076	8.45
Riverview, FL (cdp) Hillsborough County	5,992	8.43
Mastic Beach, NY (cdp) Suffolk County	1,088	8.41
North Bergen, NJ (township) Hudson County	5,090	8.38
Providence, RI (city) Providence County	14,847	8.34
Carrollwood, FL (cdp) Hillsborough County	2,782	8.34
Naranja, FL (cdp) Miami-Dade County	687	8.27
Hoboken, NJ (city) Hudson County	4,110	8.22
Stroud, PA (township) Monroe County	1,580	8.22
Manchester, CT (town) Hartford County	4,782	8.21
Spring Hill, FL (cdp) Hernando County	8,072	8.18
Apopka, FL (city) Orange County	3,400	8.18
Princeton, FL (cdp) Miami-Dade County	1,797	8.15

Please refer to the Explanation of Data in the front of the book for more detailed information.

Hispanic Origin

South American

U.S. and 50 States Sorted by Population and Percent of Total Population

Place	Population	%
United States	**2,769,434**	**0.90**
Florida	674,542	3.59
New York	513,417	2.65
New Jersey	325,179	3.70
California	293,880	0.79
Texas	133,808	0.53
Virginia	101,480	1.27
Connecticut	71,355	2.00
Illinois	67,862	0.53
Maryland	61,400	1.06
Georgia	57,707	0.60
Massachusetts	54,398	0.83
Pennsylvania	48,126	0.38
North Carolina	46,307	0.49
Utah	26,028	0.94
Arizona	21,895	0.34
Washington	20,742	0.31
Colorado	19,117	0.38
Nevada	19,056	0.71
Minnesota	18,075	0.34
South Carolina	17,856	0.39
Ohio	17,571	0.15
Rhode Island	14,013	1.33
Michigan	13,243	0.13
Tennessee	11,039	0.17
Indiana	10,032	0.15
Wisconsin	9,675	0.17
Oregon	9,648	0.25
Louisiana	8,871	0.20
Missouri	8,731	0.15
District of Columbia	7,639	1.27
Oklahoma	7,134	0.19
Alabama	5,938	0.12
Kansas	5,845	0.20
Kentucky	5,405	0.12
New Mexico	4,841	0.24
New Hampshire	4,266	0.32
Delaware	3,849	0.43
Iowa	3,754	0.12
Idaho	3,707	0.24
Hawaii	3,549	0.26
Arkansas	3,028	0.10
Mississippi	2,833	0.10
Nebraska	2,824	0.15
Alaska	2,345	0.33
West Virginia	1,700	0.09
Maine	1,515	0.11
Vermont	1,204	0.19
Montana	997	0.10
Wyoming	852	0.15
South Dakota	617	0.08
North Dakota	539	0.08

Place	Population	%
New Jersey	325,179	3.70
Florida	674,542	3.59
New York	513,417	2.65
Connecticut	71,355	2.00
Rhode Island	14,013	1.33
Virginia	101,480	1.27
District of Columbia	7,639	1.27
Maryland	61,400	1.06
Utah	26,028	0.94
United States	**2,769,434**	**0.90**
Massachusetts	54,398	0.83
California	293,880	0.79
Nevada	19,056	0.71
Georgia	57,707	0.60
Texas	133,808	0.53
Illinois	67,862	0.53
North Carolina	46,307	0.49
Delaware	3,849	0.43
South Carolina	17,856	0.39
Pennsylvania	48,126	0.38
Colorado	19,117	0.38
Arizona	21,895	0.34
Minnesota	18,075	0.34
Alaska	2,345	0.33
New Hampshire	4,266	0.32
Washington	20,742	0.31
Hawaii	3,549	0.26
Oregon	9,648	0.25
New Mexico	4,841	0.24
Idaho	3,707	0.24
Louisiana	8,871	0.20
Kansas	5,845	0.20
Oklahoma	7,134	0.19
Vermont	1,204	0.19
Tennessee	11,039	0.17
Wisconsin	9,675	0.17
Ohio	17,571	0.15
Indiana	10,032	0.15
Missouri	8,731	0.15
Nebraska	2,824	0.15
Wyoming	852	0.15
Michigan	13,243	0.13
Alabama	5,938	0.12
Kentucky	5,405	0.12
Iowa	3,754	0.12
Maine	1,515	0.11
Arkansas	3,028	0.10
Mississippi	2,833	0.10
Montana	997	0.10
West Virginia	1,700	0.09
South Dakota	617	0.08
North Dakota	539	0.08

Please refer to the Explanation of Data in the front of the book for more detailed information.

Hispanic Origin

South American

Top 150 Places Sorted by Population

Based on all places, regardless of total population

Place	Population	%
New York, NY (city) Kings County	343,468	4.20
Queens, NY (borough) Queens County	214,022	9.59
Los Angeles, CA (city) Los Angeles County	49,352	1.30
Brooklyn, NY (borough) Kings County	49,003	1.96
Manhattan, NY (borough) New York County	36,748	2.32
Bronx, NY (borough) Bronx County	35,463	2.56
Miami, FL (city) Miami-Dade County	34,718	8.69
Chicago, IL (city) Cook County	32,129	1.19
Elizabeth, NJ (city) Union County	25,649	20.52
Houston, TX (city) Harris County	24,040	1.15
Hempstead, NY (town) Nassau County	23,626	3.11
Newark, NJ (city) Essex County	22,413	8.09
Doral, FL (city) Miami-Dade County	21,078	46.12
Pembroke Pines, FL (city) Broward County	19,424	12.55
Weston, FL (city) Broward County	18,234	27.91
Paterson, NJ (city) Passaic County	17,383	11.89
Islip, NY (town) Suffolk County	16,012	4.77
Miami Beach, FL (city) Miami-Dade County	15,106	17.21
Hollywood, FL (city) Broward County	14,020	9.96
Union City, NJ (city) Hudson County	13,923	20.95
Hialeah, FL (city) Miami-Dade County	13,835	6.16
The Hammocks, FL (cdp) Miami-Dade County	13,807	27.07
North Bergen, NJ (township) Hudson County	13,026	21.43
Miramar, FL (city) Broward County	12,551	10.28
Brookhaven, NY (town) Suffolk County	12,182	2.51
Coral Springs, FL (city) Broward County	11,749	9.70
Kendall, FL (cdp) Miami-Dade County	11,514	15.28
Boston, MA (city) Suffolk County	11,184	1.81
Fountainebleau, FL (cdp) Miami-Dade County	11,183	18.71
Jersey City, NJ (city) Hudson County	11,034	4.46
Charlotte, NC (city) Mecklenburg County	10,729	1.47
Country Club, FL (cdp) Miami-Dade County	10,161	21.57
Orlando, FL (city) Orange County	9,977	4.19
Philadelphia, PA (city) Philadelphia County	9,969	0.65
Clifton, NJ (city) Passaic County	9,347	11.11
Sunrise, FL (city) Broward County	9,204	10.90
Arlington, VA (cdp) Arlington County	9,089	4.38
Stamford, CT (city/town) Fairfield County	8,807	7.18
West New York, NJ (town) Hudson County	8,700	17.50
Kendale Lakes, FL (cdp) Miami-Dade County	8,687	15.47
San Francisco, CA (city) San Francisco County	8,618	1.07
Davie, FL (town) Broward County	8,321	9.05
Staten Island, NY (borough) Richmond County	8,232	1.76
San Diego, CA (city) San Diego County	8,220	0.63
Aventura, FL (city) Miami-Dade County	8,112	22.68
Kendall West, FL (cdp) Miami-Dade County	7,715	21.34
Danbury, CT (city/town) Fairfield County	7,674	9.49
Washington, DC (city) District of Columbia	7,639	1.27
Jacksonville, FL (city) Duval County	7,152	0.87
Kearny, NJ (town) Hudson County	7,015	17.24
Hackensack, NJ (city) Bergen County	6,917	16.08
Ossining, NY (town) Westchester County	6,825	18.12
Yonkers, NY (city) Westchester County	6,622	3.38
Tamarac, FL (city) Broward County	6,607	10.93
Rye, NY (town) Westchester County	6,585	14.34
Ossining, NY (village) Westchester County	6,440	25.70
Plantation, FL (city) Broward County	6,394	7.53
Brentwood, NY (cdp) Suffolk County	6,350	10.47
North Hempstead, NY (town) Nassau County	6,333	2.80
Minneapolis, MN (city) Hennepin County	6,270	1.64
Tampa, FL (city) Hillsborough County	6,102	1.82
San Jose, CA (city) Santa Clara County	6,035	0.64
White Plains, NY (city) Westchester County	5,850	10.29
Norwalk, CT (city/town) Fairfield County	5,799	6.77
Port Chester, NY (village) Westchester County	5,769	19.92
Oyster Bay, NY (town) Nassau County	5,752	1.96
San Antonio, TX (city) Medina County	5,698	0.43
Dallas, TX (city) Dallas County	5,683	0.47
Tamiami, FL (cdp) Miami-Dade County	5,642	10.21
Babylon, NY (town) Suffolk County	5,576	2.61
Bridgeport, CT (city/town) Fairfield County	5,531	3.83
Sunny Isles Beach, FL (city) Miami-Dade County	5,237	25.14
Port St. Lucie, FL (city) St. Lucie County	5,157	3.13
Kissimmee, FL (city) Osceola County	5,135	8.60
Phoenix, AZ (city) Maricopa County	5,116	0.35
Belleville, NJ (township) Essex County	5,012	13.95
Austin, TX (city) Travis County	5,002	0.63
Dover, NJ (town) Morris County	4,978	27.42
Coral Gables, FL (city) Miami-Dade County	4,941	10.56
Fort Lauderdale, FL (city) Broward County	4,939	2.98
Hallandale Beach, FL (city) Broward County	4,912	13.24
Las Vegas, NV (city) Clark County	4,838	0.83
North Miami Beach, FL (city) Miami-Dade County	4,830	11.63
The Crossings, FL (cdp) Miami-Dade County	4,756	20.90
Passaic, NJ (city) Passaic County	4,723	6.77
Town 'n' Country, FL (cdp) Hillsborough County	4,669	5.95
Cape Coral, FL (city) Lee County	4,657	3.02
Annandale, VA (cdp) Fairfax County	4,473	10.91
Germantown, MD (cdp) Montgomery County	4,441	5.14
Richmond West, FL (cdp) Miami-Dade County	4,392	13.74
Alexandria, VA (ind. city) Alexandria independent city	4,202	3.00
Coconut Creek, FL (city) Broward County	4,166	7.87
Margate, FL (city) Broward County	4,158	7.80
Long Beach, CA (city) Los Angeles County	4,123	0.89
Alafaya, FL (cdp) Orange County	4,114	5.27
Ojus, FL (cdp) Miami-Dade County	4,059	22.50
Peekskill, NY (city) Westchester County	4,041	17.14
Greenburgh, NY (town) Westchester County	4,004	4.53
Meadow Woods, FL (cdp) Orange County	3,989	15.61
Cutler Bay, FL (town) Miami-Dade County	3,989	9.90
Hartford, CT (city/town) Hartford County	3,773	3.02
Anaheim, CA (city) Orange County	3,763	1.12
Ramapo, NY (town) Rockland County	3,759	2.97
New Rochelle, NY (city) Westchester County	3,697	4.80
North Plainfield, NJ (borough) Somerset County	3,653	16.65
Linden, NJ (city) Union County	3,608	8.91
Pawtucket, RI (city) Providence County	3,582	5.03
Raleigh, NC (city) Wake County	3,574	0.88
Pompano Beach, FL (city) Broward County	3,572	3.58
Homestead, FL (city) Miami-Dade County	3,564	5.89
North Miami, FL (city) Miami-Dade County	3,560	6.06
Providence, RI (city) Providence County	3,544	1.99
Boca Raton, FL (city) Palm Beach County	3,543	4.20
Perth Amboy, NJ (city) Middlesex County	3,538	6.96
East Hampton, NY (town) Suffolk County	3,513	16.37
Downey, CA (city) Los Angeles County	3,506	3.14
Wellington, FL (village) Palm Beach County	3,468	6.14
New Haven, CT (city/town) New Haven County	3,426	2.64
Key Biscayne, FL (village) Miami-Dade County	3,413	27.65
Plainfield, NJ (city) Union County	3,400	6.83
West Orange, NJ (township) Essex County	3,398	7.35
Three Lakes, FL (cdp) Miami-Dade County	3,392	22.54
Bloomfield, NJ (township) Essex County	3,347	7.07
Seattle, WA (city) King County	3,346	0.55
Garfield, NJ (city) Bergen County	3,338	10.95
Santa Clarita, CA (city) Los Angeles County	3,311	1.88
West Falls Church, VA (cdp) Fairfax County	3,296	11.28
Glendale, CA (city) Los Angeles County	3,287	1.71
West Palm Beach, FL (city) Palm Beach County	3,265	3.27
Centreville, VA (cdp) Fairfax County	3,253	4.57
Greenacres, FL (city) Palm Beach County	3,241	8.63
Harrison, NJ (town) Hudson County	3,193	23.44
Revere, MA (city) Suffolk County	3,184	6.15
Woodbridge, NJ (township) Middlesex County	3,127	3.14
Deerfield Beach, FL (city) Broward County	3,070	4.09
Allentown, PA (city) Lehigh County	3,048	2.58
Huntington, NY (town) Suffolk County	3,043	1.50
Aspen Hill, MD (cdp) Montgomery County	3,025	6.20
Fort Worth, TX (city) Tarrant County	3,014	0.41
Greenwich, CT (town) Fairfield County	3,008	4.92
Miami Lakes, FL (town) Miami-Dade County	2,968	10.11
Gainesville, FL (city) Alachua County	2,966	2.39
Mount Pleasant, NY (town) Westchester County	2,921	6.68
Gaithersburg, MD (city) Montgomery County	2,870	4.79
Spring Valley, NY (village) Rockland County	2,841	9.06
Lodi, NJ (borough) Bergen County	2,824	11.70
Rancho Cucamonga, CA (city) San Bernardino County	2,823	1.71
Wheaton, MD (cdp) Montgomery County	2,789	5.78
Englewood, NJ (city) Bergen County	2,767	10.19
Denver, CO (city) Denver County	2,739	0.46

SECTION THREE

Hispanic Origin

South American

Top 150 Places Sorted by Percent of Total Population

Based on all places, regardless of total population

Place	Population	%
Doral, FL (city) Miami-Dade County	21,078	46.12
East Newark, NJ (borough) Hudson County	947	39.36
Victory Gardens, NJ (borough) Morris County	477	31.38
Weston, FL (city) Broward County	18,234	27.91
Key Biscayne, FL (village) Miami-Dade County	3,413	27.65
Dover, NJ (town) Morris County	4,978	27.42
The Hammocks, FL (cdp) Miami-Dade County	13,807	27.07
East Hampton North, NY (cdp) Suffolk County	1,076	25.98
Ossining, NY (village) Westchester County	6,440	25.70
Sunny Isles Beach, FL (city) Miami-Dade County	5,237	25.14
Springs, NY (cdp) Suffolk County	1,623	24.62
Bay Harbor Islands, FL (town) Miami-Dade County	1,367	24.29
North Bay Village, FL (city) Miami-Dade County	1,725	24.17
Harrison, NJ (town) Hudson County	3,193	23.44
Biggs Junction, OR (cdp) Sherman County	5	22.73
Aventura, FL (city) Miami-Dade County	8,112	22.68
Three Lakes, FL (cdp) Miami-Dade County	3,392	22.54
Ojus, FL (cdp) Miami-Dade County	4,059	22.50
Country Club, FL (cdp) Miami-Dade County	10,161	21.57
North Bergen, NJ (township) Hudson County	13,026	21.43
Kendall West, FL (cdp) Miami-Dade County	7,715	21.34
Sleepy Hollow, NY (village) Westchester County	2,098	21.26
Union City, NJ (city) Hudson County	13,923	20.95
Guttenberg, NJ (town) Hudson County	2,340	20.94
The Crossings, FL (cdp) Miami-Dade County	4,756	20.90
Elizabeth, NJ (city) Union County	25,649	20.52
Wharton, NJ (borough) Morris County	1,331	20.41
Port Chester, NY (village) Westchester County	5,769	19.92
Fountainebleau, FL (cdp) Miami-Dade County	11,183	18.71
Ossining, NY (town) Westchester County	6,825	18.12
West New York, NJ (town) Hudson County	8,700	17.50
Elmsford, NY (village) Westchester County	812	17.41
Virginia Gardens, FL (village) Miami-Dade County	410	17.26
Kearny, NJ (town) Hudson County	7,015	17.24
Miami Beach, FL (city) Miami-Dade County	15,106	17.21
Peekskill, NY (city) Westchester County	4,041	17.14
Country Walk, FL (cdp) Miami-Dade County	2,721	17.01
Hightstown, NJ (borough) Mercer County	929	16.91
Surfside, FL (town) Miami-Dade County	967	16.83
North Plainfield, NJ (borough) Somerset County	3,653	16.65
Silver Lake, NJ (cdp) Essex County	702	16.54
East Hampton, NY (town) Suffolk County	3,513	16.37
Hackensack, NJ (city) Bergen County	6,917	16.08
Meadow Woods, FL (cdp) Orange County	3,989	15.61
Kendale Lakes, FL (cdp) Miami-Dade County	8,687	15.47
Twin Rivers, NJ (cdp) Mercer County	1,150	15.45
Kendall, FL (cdp) Miami-Dade County	11,514	15.28
Patchogue, NY (village) Suffolk County	1,777	15.06
South Hackensack, NJ (township) Bergen County	356	14.97
Prospect Park, NJ (borough) Passaic County	854	14.56
Rye, NY (town) Westchester County	6,585	14.34
Norrie, CO (cdp) Pitkin County	1	14.29
Bal Harbour, FL (village) Miami-Dade County	358	14.25
Byram, CT (cdp) Fairfield County	587	14.16
Fairview, NY (cdp) Westchester County	436	14.07
Belleville, NJ (township) Essex County	5,012	13.95
Richmond West, FL (cdp) Miami-Dade County	4,392	13.74
Sunwest, AZ (cdp) La Paz County	2	13.33
Hallandale Beach, FL (city) Broward County	4,912	13.24
Southchase, FL (cdp) Orange County	2,073	13.02
Glenvar Heights, FL (cdp) Miami-Dade County	2,154	12.75
Pembroke Pines, FL (city) Broward County	19,424	12.55
Golden Beach, FL (town) Miami-Dade County	112	12.19
Teterboro, NJ (borough) Bergen County	8	11.94
Paterson, NJ (city) Passaic County	17,383	11.89
Lodi, NJ (borough) Bergen County	2,824	11.70
North Miami Beach, FL (city) Miami-Dade County	4,830	11.63
Central Falls, RI (city) Providence County	2,233	11.52
Haledon, NJ (borough) Passaic County	952	11.45
Miami Springs, FL (city) Miami-Dade County	1,565	11.33
West Falls Church, VA (cdp) Fairfax County	3,296	11.28
Biscayne Park, FL (village) Miami-Dade County	343	11.23
Roselle Park, NJ (borough) Union County	1,488	11.19
Clifton, NJ (city) Passaic County	9,347	11.11
Hunters Creek, FL (cdp) Orange County	1,569	10.96
Bedford Hills, NY (cdp) Westchester County	329	10.96
Garfield, NJ (city) Bergen County	3,338	10.95
Morris, NJ (town) Morris County	2,015	10.94
Tamarac, FL (city) Broward County	6,607	10.93
Annandale, VA (cdp) Fairfax County	4,473	10.91
Sunrise, FL (city) Broward County	9,204	10.90
Weehawken, NJ (township) Hudson County	1,360	10.83
Ives Estates, FL (cdp) Miami-Dade County	2,104	10.78
Coral Gables, FL (city) Miami-Dade County	4,941	10.56
Brentwood, NY (cdp) Suffolk County	6,350	10.47
Seven Corners, VA (cdp) Fairfax County	962	10.39
Cloud Lake, FL (town) Palm Beach County	14	10.37
Fairview, NJ (borough) Bergen County	1,430	10.34
White Plains, NY (city) Westchester County	5,850	10.29
Miramar, FL (city) Broward County	12,551	10.28
Shinnecock Hills, NY (cdp) Suffolk County	225	10.28
Tamiami, FL (cdp) Miami-Dade County	5,642	10.21
Bogota, NJ (borough) Bergen County	836	10.21
Ridgefield Park, NJ (village) Bergen County	1,298	10.20
Englewood, NJ (city) Bergen County	2,767	10.19
Miami Lakes, FL (town) Miami-Dade County	2,968	10.11
Hollywood, FL (city) Broward County	14,020	9.96
Bellerose Terrace, NY (cdp) Nassau County	219	9.96
Cutler Bay, FL (town) Miami-Dade County	3,989	9.90
Moonachie, NJ (borough) Bergen County	267	9.86
Bound Brook, NJ (borough) Somerset County	1,021	9.82
Coral Springs, FL (city) Broward County	11,749	9.70
Dunellen, NJ (borough) Middlesex County	697	9.64
Queens, NY (borough) Queens County	214,022	9.59
Hialeah Gardens, FL (city) Miami-Dade County	2,070	9.52
Danbury, CT (city/town) Fairfield County	7,674	9.49
Manorhaven, NY (village) Nassau County	615	9.38
Pinecrest, FL (village) Miami-Dade County	1,675	9.19
Spring Valley, NY (village) Rockland County	2,841	9.06
Davie, FL (town) Broward County	8,321	9.05
Palmetto Bay, FL (village) Miami-Dade County	2,114	9.03
East Windsor, NJ (township) Mercer County	2,448	9.00
North Bay Shore, NY (cdp) Suffolk County	1,693	8.94
Montauk, NY (cdp) Suffolk County	297	8.93
Linden, NJ (city) Union County	3,608	8.91
Little America, WY (cdp) Sweetwater County	6	8.82
Northwest Harbor, NY (cdp) Suffolk County	292	8.80
Mine Hill, NJ (township) Morris County	320	8.76
Lake Belvedere Estates, FL (cdp) Palm Beach County	290	8.70
Miami, FL (city) Miami-Dade County	34,718	8.69
Elmwood Park, NJ (borough) Bergen County	1,677	8.64
Greenacres, FL (city) Palm Beach County	3,241	8.63
Sunset, FL (cdp) Miami-Dade County	1,414	8.63
Buchanan, NY (village) Westchester County	192	8.61
Kissimmee, FL (city) Osceola County	5,135	8.60
Islandia, NY (village) Suffolk County	286	8.58
North Springfield, VA (cdp) Fairfax County	623	8.56
Island Park, NY (village) Nassau County	396	8.51
Bay Lake, FL (city) Orange County	4	8.51
Dulles Town Center, VA (cdp) Loudoun County	388	8.43
Roselle, NJ (borough) Union County	1,771	8.40
North Patchogue, NY (cdp) Suffolk County	609	8.40
Indian Creek, FL (village) Miami-Dade County	7	8.14
Hampton Bays, NY (cdp) Suffolk County	1,106	8.13
Newark, NJ (city) Essex County	22,413	8.09
Buenaventura Lakes, FL (cdp) Osceola County	2,108	8.08
Bergenfield, NJ (borough) Bergen County	2,143	8.01
Palm Springs, FL (village) Palm Beach County	1,509	7.97
Miami Shores, FL (village) Miami-Dade County	835	7.96
City of Orange, NJ (township) Essex County	2,375	7.88
Coconut Creek, FL (city) Broward County	4,166	7.87
Margate, FL (city) Broward County	4,158	7.80
University Park, FL (cdp) Miami-Dade County	2,104	7.79
Peapack and Gladstone, NJ (borough) Somerset County	201	7.78
Bailey's Crossroads, VA (cdp) Fairfax County	1,823	7.71
Lake Barcroft, VA (cdp) Fairfax County	737	7.71
Baywood, NY (cdp) Suffolk County	565	7.69
Lincolnia, VA (cdp) Fairfax County	1,754	7.67
Southwest Ranches, FL (town) Broward County	563	7.67
Bay Shore, NY (cdp) Suffolk County	1,997	7.58

Please refer to the Explanation of Data in the front of the book for more detailed information.

Hispanic Origin

South American

Top 150 Places Sorted by Percent of Total Population

Based on places with total population of 7,500 or more

Place	Population	%
Doral, FL (city) Miami-Dade County	21,078	46.12
Weston, FL (city) Broward County	18,234	27.91
Key Biscayne, FL (village) Miami-Dade County	3,413	27.65
Dover, NJ (town) Morris County	4,978	27.42
The Hammocks, FL (cdp) Miami-Dade County	13,807	27.07
Ossining, NY (village) Westchester County	6,440	25.70
Sunny Isles Beach, FL (city) Miami-Dade County	5,237	25.14
Harrison, NJ (town) Hudson County	3,193	23.44
Aventura, FL (city) Miami-Dade County	8,112	22.68
Three Lakes, FL (cdp) Miami-Dade County	3,392	22.54
Ojus, FL (cdp) Miami-Dade County	4,059	22.50
Country Club, FL (cdp) Miami-Dade County	10,161	21.57
North Bergen, NJ (township) Hudson County	13,026	21.43
Kendall West, FL (cdp) Miami-Dade County	7,715	21.34
Sleepy Hollow, NY (village) Westchester County	2,098	21.26
Union City, NJ (city) Hudson County	13,923	20.95
Guttenberg, NJ (town) Hudson County	2,340	20.94
The Crossings, FL (cdp) Miami-Dade County	4,756	20.90
Elizabeth, NJ (city) Union County	25,649	20.52
Port Chester, NY (village) Westchester County	5,769	19.92
Fountainebleau, FL (cdp) Miami-Dade County	11,183	18.71
Ossining, NY (town) Westchester County	6,825	18.12
West New York, NJ (town) Hudson County	8,700	17.50
Kearny, NJ (town) Hudson County	7,015	17.24
Miami Beach, FL (city) Miami-Dade County	15,106	17.21
Peekskill, NY (city) Westchester County	4,041	17.14
Country Walk, FL (cdp) Miami-Dade County	2,721	17.01
North Plainfield, NJ (borough) Somerset County	3,653	16.65
East Hampton, NY (town) Suffolk County	3,513	16.37
Hackensack, NJ (city) Bergen County	6,917	16.08
Meadow Woods, FL (cdp) Orange County	3,989	15.61
Kendale Lakes, FL (cdp) Miami-Dade County	8,687	15.47
Kendall, FL (cdp) Miami-Dade County	11,514	15.28
Patchogue, NY (village) Suffolk County	1,777	15.06
Rye, NY (town) Westchester County	6,585	14.34
Belleville, NJ (township) Essex County	5,012	13.95
Richmond West, FL (cdp) Miami-Dade County	4,392	13.74
Hallandale Beach, FL (city) Broward County	4,912	13.24
Southchase, FL (cdp) Orange County	2,073	13.02
Glenvar Heights, FL (cdp) Miami-Dade County	2,154	12.75
Pembroke Pines, FL (city) Broward County	19,424	12.55
Paterson, NJ (city) Passaic County	17,383	11.89
Lodi, NJ (borough) Bergen County	2,824	11.70
North Miami Beach, FL (city) Miami-Dade County	4,830	11.63
Central Falls, RI (city) Providence County	2,233	11.52
Haledon, NJ (borough) Passaic County	952	11.45
Miami Springs, FL (city) Miami-Dade County	1,565	11.33
West Falls Church, VA (cdp) Fairfax County	3,296	11.28
Roselle Park, NJ (borough) Union County	1,488	11.19
Clifton, NJ (city) Passaic County	9,347	11.11
Hunters Creek, FL (cdp) Orange County	1,569	10.96
Garfield, NJ (city) Bergen County	3,338	10.95
Morris, NJ (town) Morris County	2,015	10.94
Tamarac, FL (city) Broward County	6,607	10.93
Annandale, VA (cdp) Fairfax County	4,473	10.91
Sunrise, FL (city) Broward County	9,204	10.90
Weehawken, NJ (township) Hudson County	1,360	10.83
Ives Estates, FL (cdp) Miami-Dade County	2,104	10.78
Coral Gables, FL (city) Miami-Dade County	4,941	10.56
Brentwood, NY (cdp) Suffolk County	6,350	10.47
Seven Corners, VA (cdp) Fairfax County	962	10.39
Fairview, NJ (borough) Bergen County	1,430	10.34
White Plains, NY (city) Westchester County	5,850	10.29
Miramar, FL (city) Broward County	12,551	10.28
Tamiami, FL (cdp) Miami-Dade County	5,642	10.21
Bogota, NJ (borough) Bergen County	836	10.21
Ridgefield Park, NJ (village) Bergen County	1,298	10.20
Englewood, NJ (city) Bergen County	2,767	10.19
Miami Lakes, FL (town) Miami-Dade County	2,968	10.11
Hollywood, FL (city) Broward County	14,020	9.96
Cutler Bay, FL (town) Miami-Dade County	3,989	9.90
Bound Brook, NJ (borough) Somerset County	1,021	9.82
Coral Springs, FL (city) Broward County	11,749	9.70
Queens, NY (borough) Queens County	214,022	9.59
Hialeah Gardens, FL (city) Miami-Dade County	2,070	9.52
Danbury, CT (city/town) Fairfield County	7,674	9.49
Pinecrest, FL (village) Miami-Dade County	1,675	9.19
Spring Valley, NY (village) Rockland County	2,841	9.06
Davie, FL (town) Broward County	8,321	9.05
Palmetto Bay, FL (village) Miami-Dade County	2,114	9.03
East Windsor, NJ (township) Mercer County	2,448	9.00
North Bay Shore, NY (cdp) Suffolk County	1,693	8.94
Linden, NJ (city) Union County	3,608	8.91
Miami, FL (city) Miami-Dade County	34,718	8.69
Elmwood Park, NJ (borough) Bergen County	1,677	8.64
Greenacres, FL (city) Palm Beach County	3,241	8.63
Sunset, FL (cdp) Miami-Dade County	1,414	8.63
Kissimmee, FL (city) Osceola County	5,135	8.60
Roselle, NJ (borough) Union County	1,771	8.40
Hampton Bays, NY (cdp) Suffolk County	1,106	8.13
Newark, NJ (city) Essex County	22,413	8.09
Buenaventura Lakes, FL (cdp) Osceola County	2,108	8.08
Bergenfield, NJ (borough) Bergen County	2,143	8.01
Palm Springs, FL (village) Palm Beach County	1,509	7.97
Miami Shores, FL (village) Miami-Dade County	835	7.96
City of Orange, NJ (township) Essex County	2,375	7.88
Coconut Creek, FL (city) Broward County	4,166	7.87
Margate, FL (city) Broward County	4,158	7.80
University Park, FL (cdp) Miami-Dade County	2,104	7.79
Bailey's Crossroads, VA (cdp) Fairfax County	1,823	7.71
Lake Barcroft, VA (cdp) Fairfax County	737	7.71
Lincolnia, VA (cdp) Fairfax County	1,754	7.67
Bay Shore, NY (cdp) Suffolk County	1,997	7.58
Little Ferry, NJ (borough) Bergen County	802	7.55
Plantation, FL (city) Broward County	6,394	7.53
Naranja, FL (cdp) Miami-Dade County	619	7.46
Greenwich, CT (cdp) Fairfield County	954	7.37
West Orange, NJ (township) Essex County	3,398	7.35
Princeton, FL (cdp) Miami-Dade County	1,589	7.21
Dania Beach, FL (city) Broward County	2,135	7.20
Stamford, CT (city/town) Fairfield County	8,807	7.18
Palmetto Estates, FL (cdp) Miami-Dade County	972	7.18
South Miami, FL (city) Miami-Dade County	837	7.18
Mount Kisco, NY (town/village) Westchester County	780	7.17
North Arlington, NJ (borough) Bergen County	1,100	7.15
Bloomfield, NJ (township) Essex County	3,347	7.07
Carteret, NJ (borough) Middlesex County	1,615	7.07
Perth Amboy, NJ (city) Middlesex County	3,538	6.96
Valley Stream, NY (village) Nassau County	2,609	6.96
Woodland Park, NJ (borough) Passaic County	819	6.93
Tarrytown, NY (village) Westchester County	774	6.86
Plainfield, NJ (city) Union County	3,400	6.83
Norwalk, CT (city/town) Fairfield County	5,799	6.77
Passaic, NJ (city) Passaic County	4,723	6.77
Central Islip, NY (cdp) Suffolk County	2,327	6.75
Mount Pleasant, NY (town) Westchester County	2,921	6.68
Cooper City, FL (city) Broward County	1,881	6.59
Montgomery Village, MD (cdp) Montgomery County	2,083	6.50
Middlesex, NJ (borough) Middlesex County	874	6.41
Glen Cove, NY (city) Nassau County	1,715	6.36
Westwood Lakes, FL (cdp) Miami-Dade County	753	6.36
Coral Terrace, FL (cdp) Miami-Dade County	1,533	6.29
North Lauderdale, FL (city) Broward County	2,572	6.27
Bernardsville, NJ (borough) Somerset County	482	6.25
Aspen Hill, MD (cdp) Montgomery County	3,025	6.20
Citrus Park, FL (cdp) Hillsborough County	1,501	6.19
Cliffside Park, NJ (borough) Bergen County	1,458	6.18
Hialeah, FL (city) Miami-Dade County	13,835	6.16
Revere, MA (city) Suffolk County	3,184	6.15
Wellington, FL (village) Palm Beach County	3,468	6.14
Springfield, VA (cdp) Fairfax County	1,868	6.13
North Miami, FL (city) Miami-Dade County	3,560	6.06
Westchester, FL (cdp) Miami-Dade County	1,805	6.04
Lyndhurst, NJ (township) Bergen County	1,238	6.02
Horizon West, FL (cdp) Orange County	834	5.96
Sweetwater, FL (city) Miami-Dade County	804	5.96
Town 'n' Country, FL (cdp) Hillsborough County	4,669	5.95
Homestead, FL (city) Miami-Dade County	3,564	5.89
Burke Centre, VA (cdp) Fairfax County	1,016	5.86
Elmont, NY (cdp) Nassau County	1,941	5.85

SECTION THREE

Please refer to the Explanation of Data in the front of the book for more detailed information.

Hispanic Origin

South American: Argentinean

U.S. and 50 States Sorted by Population and Percent of Total Population

Place	Population	%
United States	**224,952**	**0.07**
Florida	56,260	0.30
California	44,410	0.12
New York	24,969	0.13
New Jersey	14,272	0.16
Texas	13,831	0.06
Virginia	6,263	0.08
Illinois	5,294	0.04
Maryland	5,138	0.09
Utah	4,639	0.17
Pennsylvania	4,269	0.03
Massachusetts	4,022	0.06
Connecticut	3,609	0.10
Nevada	3,419	0.13
Georgia	3,230	0.03
North Carolina	3,210	0.03
Arizona	2,775	0.04
Washington	2,376	0.04
Colorado	2,165	0.04
Michigan	2,113	0.02
Ohio	1,921	0.02
South Carolina	1,439	0.03
Oregon	1,381	0.04
District of Columbia	1,134	0.19
Wisconsin	1,065	0.02
Tennessee	1,028	0.02
Indiana	1,027	0.02
Minnesota	1,008	0.02
Missouri	991	0.02
Louisiana	707	0.02
New Mexico	653	0.03
Oklahoma	590	0.02
Hawaii	588	0.04
Kansas	531	0.02
Alabama	496	0.01
Kentucky	481	0.01
Rhode Island	471	0.04
Idaho	366	0.02
Delaware	360	0.04
Iowa	344	0.01
Arkansas	338	0.01
New Hampshire	322	0.02
Mississippi	276	0.01
Nebraska	243	0.01
Vermont	185	0.03
West Virginia	165	0.01
Alaska	149	0.02
Maine	149	0.01
Montana	115	0.01
Wyoming	76	0.01
South Dakota	48	0.01
North Dakota	41	0.01

Place	Population	%
Florida	56,260	0.30
District of Columbia	1,134	0.19
Utah	4,639	0.17
New Jersey	14,272	0.16
New York	24,969	0.13
Nevada	3,419	0.13
California	44,410	0.12
Connecticut	3,609	0.10
Maryland	5,138	0.09
Virginia	6,263	0.08
United States	**224,952**	**0.07**
Texas	13,831	0.06
Massachusetts	4,022	0.06
Illinois	5,294	0.04
Arizona	2,775	0.04
Washington	2,376	0.04
Colorado	2,165	0.04
Oregon	1,381	0.04
Hawaii	588	0.04
Rhode Island	471	0.04
Delaware	360	0.04
Pennsylvania	4,269	0.03
Georgia	3,230	0.03
North Carolina	3,210	0.03
South Carolina	1,439	0.03
New Mexico	653	0.03
Vermont	185	0.03
Michigan	2,113	0.02
Ohio	1,921	0.02
Wisconsin	1,065	0.02
Tennessee	1,028	0.02
Indiana	1,027	0.02
Minnesota	1,008	0.02
Missouri	991	0.02
Louisiana	707	0.02
Oklahoma	590	0.02
Kansas	531	0.02
Idaho	366	0.02
New Hampshire	322	0.02
Alaska	149	0.02
Alabama	496	0.01
Kentucky	481	0.01
Iowa	344	0.01
Arkansas	338	0.01
Mississippi	276	0.01
Nebraska	243	0.01
West Virginia	165	0.01
Maine	149	0.01
Montana	115	0.01
Wyoming	76	0.01
South Dakota	48	0.01
North Dakota	41	0.01

Please refer to the Explanation of Data in the front of the book for more detailed information.

Hispanic Origin

South American: Argentinean

Top 150 Places Sorted by Population

Based on all places, regardless of total population

Place	Population	%
New York, NY (city) Kings County	15,169	0.19
Los Angeles, CA (city) Los Angeles County	8,570	0.23
Queens, NY (borough) Queens County	6,345	0.28
Miami, FL (city) Miami-Dade County	4,891	1.22
Manhattan, NY (borough) New York County	4,339	0.27
Miami Beach, FL (city) Miami-Dade County	4,030	4.59
Brooklyn, NY (borough) Kings County	2,760	0.11
Houston, TX (city) Harris County	2,440	0.12
Chicago, IL (city) Cook County	1,743	0.06
Hollywood, FL (city) Broward County	1,626	1.16
Aventura, FL (city) Miami-Dade County	1,579	4.42
Hempstead, NY (town) Nassau County	1,500	0.20
San Diego, CA (city) San Diego County	1,322	0.10
Pembroke Pines, FL (city) Broward County	1,147	0.74
Washington, DC (city) District of Columbia	1,134	0.19
Bronx, NY (borough) Bronx County	1,117	0.08
San Francisco, CA (city) San Francisco County	1,100	0.14
Hialeah, FL (city) Miami-Dade County	1,087	0.48
Doral, FL (city) Miami-Dade County	1,082	2.37
Sunny Isles Beach, FL (city) Miami-Dade County	1,032	4.95
Philadelphia, PA (city) Philadelphia County	1,006	0.07
Weston, FL (city) Broward County	946	1.45
Las Vegas, NV (city) Clark County	935	0.16
Kendall, FL (cdp) Miami-Dade County	840	1.11
Coral Springs, FL (city) Broward County	832	0.69
Irving, TX (city) Dallas County	803	0.37
Fountainebleau, FL (cdp) Miami-Dade County	780	1.31
Hallandale Beach, FL (city) Broward County	724	1.95
Ojus, FL (cdp) Miami-Dade County	720	3.99
Arlington, VA (cdp) Arlington County	719	0.35
Key Biscayne, FL (village) Miami-Dade County	708	5.74
North Miami Beach, FL (city) Miami-Dade County	704	1.70
The Hammocks, FL (cdp) Miami-Dade County	687	1.35
San Jose, CA (city) Santa Clara County	666	0.07
Brookhaven, NY (town) Suffolk County	653	0.13
Long Beach, CA (city) Los Angeles County	650	0.14
Provo, UT (city) Utah County	635	0.56
Boston, MA (city) Suffolk County	631	0.10
North Miami, FL (city) Miami-Dade County	627	1.07
Orem, UT (city) Utah County	623	0.71
Santa Clarita, CA (city) Los Angeles County	621	0.35
Fort Lauderdale, FL (city) Broward County	616	0.37
Islip, NY (town) Suffolk County	616	0.18
Staten Island, NY (borough) Richmond County	608	0.13
Phoenix, AZ (city) Maricopa County	608	0.04
Austin, TX (city) Travis County	600	0.08
Dallas, TX (city) Dallas County	599	0.05
Davie, FL (town) Broward County	566	0.62
Rancho Cucamonga, CA (city) San Bernardino County	561	0.34
Miramar, FL (city) Broward County	558	0.46
Jersey City, NJ (city) Hudson County	558	0.23
Coral Gables, FL (city) Miami-Dade County	557	1.19
Elizabeth, NJ (city) Union County	557	0.45
Glendale, CA (city) Los Angeles County	539	0.28
Anaheim, CA (city) Orange County	519	0.15
Charlotte, NC (city) Mecklenburg County	514	0.07
Kendale Lakes, FL (cdp) Miami-Dade County	509	0.91
Seattle, WA (city) King County	505	0.08
North Bergen, NJ (township) Hudson County	494	0.81
San Antonio, TX (city) Medina County	488	0.04
Wellington, FL (village) Palm Beach County	460	0.81
Plantation, FL (city) Broward County	458	0.54
Sunrise, FL (city) Broward County	451	0.53
Union City, NJ (city) Hudson County	448	0.67
Spring Valley, NV (cdp) Clark County	442	0.25
Paradise, NV (cdp) Clark County	442	0.20
Oyster Bay, NY (town) Nassau County	441	0.15
Irvine, CA (city) Orange County	440	0.21
Henderson, NV (city) Clark County	437	0.17
Bay Harbor Islands, FL (town) Miami-Dade County	436	7.75
Fort Worth, TX (city) Tarrant County	436	0.06
North Hempstead, NY (town) Nassau County	435	0.19
Kendall West, FL (cdp) Miami-Dade County	432	1.19
North Bay Village, FL (city) Miami-Dade County	429	6.01
Downey, CA (city) Los Angeles County	429	0.38
Perth Amboy, NJ (city) Middlesex County	427	0.84
Greenwich, CT (town) Fairfield County	426	0.70
Ives Estates, FL (cdp) Miami-Dade County	422	2.16
Orlando, FL (city) Orange County	421	0.18
Burbank, CA (city) Los Angeles County	406	0.39
Pasadena, CA (city) Los Angeles County	404	0.29
Huntington Beach, CA (city) Orange County	394	0.21
Jacksonville, FL (city) Duval County	387	0.05
Tampa, FL (city) Hillsborough County	386	0.11
Portland, OR (city) Multnomah County	381	0.07
Riverside, CA (city) Riverside County	379	0.12
Bethesda, MD (cdp) Montgomery County	376	0.62
The Crossings, FL (cdp) Miami-Dade County	374	1.64
The Woodlands, TX (cdp) Montgomery County	373	0.40
Torrance, CA (city) Los Angeles County	371	0.26
Tamarac, FL (city) Broward County	370	0.61
Port St. Lucie, FL (city) St. Lucie County	369	0.22
Country Club, FL (cdp) Miami-Dade County	366	0.78
Tamiami, FL (cdp) Miami-Dade County	356	0.64
Simi Valley, CA (city) Ventura County	351	0.28
Newark, NJ (city) Essex County	351	0.13
Boca Raton, FL (city) Palm Beach County	345	0.41
Cutler Bay, FL (town) Miami-Dade County	343	0.85
Babylon, NY (town) Suffolk County	336	0.16
Surfside, FL (town) Miami-Dade County	334	5.81
Oakland, CA (city) Alameda County	334	0.09
Huntington, NY (town) Suffolk County	329	0.16
Paterson, NJ (city) Passaic County	327	0.22
Fontana, CA (city) San Bernardino County	323	0.16
Potomac, MD (cdp) Montgomery County	321	0.71
Annandale, VA (cdp) Fairfax County	313	0.76
Mission Viejo, CA (city) Orange County	313	0.34
Cape Coral, FL (city) Lee County	313	0.20
Raleigh, NC (city) Wake County	313	0.08
West New York, NJ (town) Hudson County	312	0.63
Cambridge, MA (city) Middlesex County	310	0.29
Coconut Creek, FL (city) Broward County	309	0.58
Palmdale, CA (city) Los Angeles County	307	0.20
Alexandria, VA (ind. city) Alexandria independent city	303	0.22
West Palm Beach, FL (city) Palm Beach County	302	0.30
Salt Lake City, UT (city) Salt Lake County	298	0.16
North Bethesda, MD (cdp) Montgomery County	297	0.68
Pompano Beach, FL (city) Broward County	292	0.29
Kissimmee, FL (city) Osceola County	283	0.47
Deerfield Beach, FL (city) Broward County	282	0.38
Stamford, CT (city/town) Fairfield County	278	0.23
Thousand Oaks, CA (city) Ventura County	278	0.22
Santa Ana, CA (city) Orange County	276	0.09
Baltimore, MD (city) Baltimore city County	276	0.04
Yonkers, NY (city) Westchester County	273	0.14
Columbus, OH (city) Franklin County	273	0.03
Santa Monica, CA (city) Los Angeles County	271	0.30
Denver, CO (city) Denver County	269	0.04
Dania Beach, FL (city) Broward County	266	0.90
Palmetto Bay, FL (village) Miami-Dade County	265	1.13
Tucson, AZ (city) Pima County	265	0.05
Margate, FL (city) Broward County	263	0.49
Lake Forest, CA (city) Orange County	261	0.34
Orange, CA (city) Orange County	257	0.19
Atlanta, GA (city) Fulton County	256	0.06
Albuquerque, NM (city) Bernalillo County	250	0.05
Greenacres, FL (city) Palm Beach County	246	0.65
Fullerton, CA (city) Orange County	244	0.18
Corona, CA (city) Riverside County	244	0.16
Pittsburgh, PA (city) Allegheny County	244	0.08
Clifton, NJ (city) Passaic County	243	0.29
Ontario, CA (city) San Bernardino County	243	0.15
Mesa, AZ (city) Maricopa County	242	0.06
Plano, TX (city) Collin County	241	0.09
El Paso, TX (city) El Paso County	240	0.04
Costa Mesa, CA (city) Orange County	239	0.22
Moreno Valley, CA (city) Riverside County	233	0.12
Redondo Beach, CA (city) Los Angeles County	232	0.35
Berkeley, CA (city) Alameda County	232	0.21
Chino, CA (city) San Bernardino County	229	0.29

SECTION THREE

Hispanic Origin

South American: Argentinean

Top 150 Places Sorted by Percent of Total Population

Based on all places, regardless of total population

Place	Population	%
Bay Harbor Islands, FL (town) Miami-Dade County	436	7.75
North Bay Village, FL (city) Miami-Dade County	429	6.01
Surfside, FL (town) Miami-Dade County	334	5.81
Key Biscayne, FL (village) Miami-Dade County	708	5.74
Sunny Isles Beach, FL (city) Miami-Dade County	1,032	4.95
Miami Beach, FL (city) Miami-Dade County	4,030	4.59
Aventura, FL (city) Miami-Dade County	1,579	4.42
Lazy Lake, FL (village) Broward County	1	4.17
Ojus, FL (cdp) Miami-Dade County	720	3.99
Bal Harbour, FL (village) Miami-Dade County	94	3.74
Biscayne Park, FL (village) Miami-Dade County	112	3.67
Edna, CA (cdp) San Luis Obispo County	5	2.59
Golden Beach, FL (town) Miami-Dade County	22	2.39
Doral, FL (city) Miami-Dade County	1,082	2.37
Ives Estates, FL (cdp) Miami-Dade County	422	2.16
Rivergrove, OR (city) Clackamas County	6	2.08
Hallandale Beach, FL (city) Broward County	724	1.95
Riverside, CT (cdp) Fairfield County	164	1.95
Rutherford, CA (cdp) Napa County	3	1.83
El Portal, FL (village) Miami-Dade County	41	1.76
North Miami Beach, FL (city) Miami-Dade County	704	1.70
La Crosse, FL (town) Alachua County	6	1.67
The Crossings, FL (cdp) Miami-Dade County	374	1.64
Miami Shores, FL (village) Miami-Dade County	172	1.64
Weston, FL (city) Broward County	946	1.45
Westwood, MO (village) St. Louis County	4	1.44
Swan, IA (city) Marion County	1	1.39
The Hammocks, FL (cdp) Miami-Dade County	687	1.35
Peak Place, NM (cdp) Santa Fe County	5	1.33
Fountainebleau, FL (cdp) Miami-Dade County	780	1.31
Custer, MT (cdp) Yellowstone County	2	1.26
Lopatcong Overlook, NJ (cdp) Warren County	9	1.23
Soda Springs, CA (cdp) Nevada County	1	1.23
Miami, FL (city) Miami-Dade County	4,891	1.22
Coral Gables, FL (city) Miami-Dade County	557	1.19
Kendall West, FL (cdp) Miami-Dade County	432	1.19
Lakewood Gardens, FL (cdp) Palm Beach County	15	1.18
Hollywood, FL (city) Broward County	1,626	1.16
Three Lakes, FL (cdp) Miami-Dade County	173	1.15
Palmetto Bay, FL (village) Miami-Dade County	265	1.13
Guttenberg, NJ (town) Hudson County	125	1.12
Kendall, FL (cdp) Miami-Dade County	840	1.11
Deerfield, MA (cdp) Franklin County	7	1.09
North Miami, FL (city) Miami-Dade County	627	1.07
Mount Aetna, MD (cdp) Washington County	6	1.07
Dry Creek, AK (cdp) Southeast Fairbanks Census Area	1	1.06
Pinecrest, FL (village) Miami-Dade County	192	1.05
Vienna, LA (town) Lincoln Parish	4	1.04
Captiva, FL (cdp) Lee County	6	1.03
Greenwood, MN (city) Hennepin County	7	1.02
Eagle Rock, MO (cdp) Barry County	2	1.01
Miami Springs, FL (city) Miami-Dade County	138	1.00
Friendship Heights Village, MD (cdp) Montgomery County	46	0.98
Blairstown, NJ (cdp) Warren County	5	0.97
Alder, MT (cdp) Madison County	1	0.97
Bradbury, CA (city) Los Angeles County	10	0.95
Russell Gardens, NY (village) Nassau County	9	0.95
Country Walk, FL (cdp) Miami-Dade County	151	0.94
Oak Glen, CA (cdp) San Bernardino County	6	0.94
Acacia Villas, FL (cdp) Palm Beach County	4	0.94
Pleasanton, NM (cdp) Catron County	1	0.94
Los Cerrillos, NM (cdp) Santa Fe County	3	0.93
Kiryas Joel, NY (village) Orange County	186	0.92
Lake Ivanhoe, WI (cdp) Walworth County	4	0.92
Belleair Shore, FL (town) Pinellas County	1	0.92
Kendale Lakes, FL (cdp) Miami-Dade County	509	0.91
Hobart, NY (village) Delaware County	4	0.91
Dania Beach, FL (city) Broward County	266	0.90
Sea Ranch Lakes, FL (village) Broward County	6	0.90
Shiremanstown, PA (borough) Cumberland County	14	0.89
North Key Largo, FL (cdp) Monroe County	11	0.88
Kenilworth, NJ (borough) Union County	69	0.87
South Miami, FL (city) Miami-Dade County	100	0.86
Old Greenwich, CT (cdp) Fairfield County	57	0.86
Belvidere, VT (town) Lamoille County	3	0.86
Cutler Bay, FL (town) Miami-Dade County	343	0.85
Lemont Furnace, PA (cdp) Fayette County	7	0.85
Graball, TN (cdp) Sumner County	2	0.85
Perth Amboy, NJ (city) Middlesex County	427	0.84
Glenvar Heights, FL (cdp) Miami-Dade County	140	0.83
Skillman, NJ (cdp) Somerset County	2	0.83
Sinai, SD (town) Brookings County	1	0.83
Somerset, MD (town) Montgomery County	10	0.82
Wanamie, PA (cdp) Luzerne County	5	0.82
North Bergen, NJ (township) Hudson County	494	0.81
Wellington, FL (village) Palm Beach County	460	0.81
Schall Circle, FL (cdp) Palm Beach County	9	0.81
Sunset, FL (cdp) Miami-Dade County	131	0.80
Dorset, VT (cdp) Bennington County	2	0.80
Chevy Chase Section Three, MD (village) Montgomery County	6	0.79
Country Club, FL (cdp) Miami-Dade County	366	0.78
Richmond, NH (town) Cheshire County	9	0.78
McKinley, MN (city) St. Louis County	1	0.78
Wildwood, KY (city) Jefferson County	2	0.77
Annandale, VA (cdp) Fairfax County	313	0.76
Gulf Stream, FL (town) Palm Beach County	6	0.76
Chevy Chase Section Five, MD (village) Montgomery County	5	0.76
Marble, CO (town) Gunnison County	1	0.76
Miami Lakes, FL (town) Miami-Dade County	220	0.75
Morton, MS (city) Scott County	26	0.75
Pembroke Pines, FL (city) Broward County	1,147	0.74
Quincy, MI (township) Houghton County	2	0.74
Weybridge, VT (town) Addison County	6	0.72
Orem, UT (city) Utah County	623	0.71
Potomac, MD (cdp) Montgomery County	321	0.71
Haiku-Pauwela, HI (cdp) Maui County	58	0.71
Greenleaf, ID (city) Canyon County	6	0.71
Pocono Mountain Lake Estates, PA (cdp) Pike County	6	0.71
Greenwich, CT (town) Fairfield County	426	0.70
Richmond West, FL (cdp) Miami-Dade County	223	0.70
Garrett, WA (cdp) Walla Walla County	10	0.70
Whitewater, CA (cdp) Riverside County	6	0.70
Coral Springs, FL (city) Broward County	832	0.69
Naranja, FL (cdp) Miami-Dade County	57	0.69
Pacific Beach, WA (cdp) Grays Harbor County	2	0.69
North Bethesda, MD (cdp) Montgomery County	297	0.68
West Falls Church, VA (cdp) Fairfax County	198	0.68
University Park, FL (cdp) Miami-Dade County	183	0.68
Lauderdale-by-the-Sea, FL (town) Broward County	41	0.68
Union City, NJ (city) Hudson County	448	0.67
Virginia Gardens, FL (village) Miami-Dade County	16	0.67
Northville, NY (cdp) Suffolk County	9	0.67
North Springfield, VA (cdp) Fairfax County	48	0.66
Dillon, CO (town) Summit County	6	0.66
North Hartland, VT (cdp) Windsor County	2	0.66
Greenacres, FL (city) Palm Beach County	246	0.65
Far Hills, NJ (borough) Somerset County	6	0.65
Aripeka, FL (cdp) Pasco County	2	0.65
Tamiami, FL (cdp) Miami-Dade County	356	0.64
Roselle Park, NJ (borough) Union County	85	0.64
Cos Cob, CT (cdp) Fairfield County	43	0.64
West Miami, FL (city) Miami-Dade County	38	0.64
Fern Forest, HI (cdp) Hawaii County	6	0.64
Gun Club Estates, FL (cdp) Palm Beach County	5	0.64
Woodsburgh, NY (village) Nassau County	5	0.64
Fidelis, FL (cdp) Santa Rosa County	1	0.64
West New York, NJ (town) Hudson County	312	0.63
Arroyo Hondo, NM (cdp) Taos County	3	0.63
Kirkwood, CA (cdp) Alpine County	1	0.63
Davie, FL (town) Broward County	566	0.62
Bethesda, MD (cdp) Montgomery County	376	0.62
Pembroke Park, FL (town) Broward County	38	0.62
Homestead Base, FL (cdp) Miami-Dade County	6	0.62
Cooks Valley, WI (town) Chippewa County	5	0.62
Fort Smith, MT (cdp) Big Horn County	1	0.62
Tamarac, FL (city) Broward County	370	0.61
Southwest Ranches, FL (town) Broward County	45	0.61
Asharoken, NY (village) Suffolk County	4	0.61
Kirby, VT (town) Caledonia County	3	0.61
Alsea, OR (cdp) Benton County	1	0.61

Please refer to the Explanation of Data in the front of the book for more detailed information.

Hispanic Origin

South American: Argentinean

Top 150 Places Sorted by Percent of Total Population

Based on places with total population of 7,500 or more

Place	Population	%
Key Biscayne, FL (village) Miami-Dade County	708	5.74
Sunny Isles Beach, FL (city) Miami-Dade County	1,032	4.95
Miami Beach, FL (city) Miami-Dade County	4,030	4.59
Aventura, FL (city) Miami-Dade County	1,579	4.42
Ojus, FL (cdp) Miami-Dade County	720	3.99
Doral, FL (city) Miami-Dade County	1,082	2.37
Ives Estates, FL (cdp) Miami-Dade County	422	2.16
Hallandale Beach, FL (city) Broward County	724	1.95
Riverside, CT (cdp) Fairfield County	164	1.95
North Miami Beach, FL (city) Miami-Dade County	704	1.70
The Crossings, FL (cdp) Miami-Dade County	374	1.64
Miami Shores, FL (village) Miami-Dade County	172	1.64
Weston, FL (city) Broward County	946	1.45
The Hammocks, FL (cdp) Miami-Dade County	687	1.35
Fountainebleau, FL (cdp) Miami-Dade County	780	1.31
Miami, FL (city) Miami-Dade County	4,891	1.22
Coral Gables, FL (city) Miami-Dade County	557	1.19
Kendall West, FL (cdp) Miami-Dade County	432	1.19
Hollywood, FL (city) Broward County	1,626	1.16
Three Lakes, FL (cdp) Miami-Dade County	173	1.15
Palmetto Bay, FL (village) Miami-Dade County	265	1.13
Guttenberg, NJ (town) Hudson County	125	1.12
Kendall, FL (cdp) Miami-Dade County	840	1.11
North Miami, FL (city) Miami-Dade County	627	1.07
Pinecrest, FL (village) Miami-Dade County	192	1.05
Miami Springs, FL (city) Miami-Dade County	138	1.00
Country Walk, FL (cdp) Miami-Dade County	151	0.94
Kiryas Joel, NY (village) Orange County	186	0.92
Kendale Lakes, FL (cdp) Miami-Dade County	509	0.91
Dania Beach, FL (city) Broward County	266	0.90
Kenilworth, NJ (borough) Union County	69	0.87
South Miami, FL (city) Miami-Dade County	100	0.86
Cutler Bay, FL (town) Miami-Dade County	343	0.85
Perth Amboy, NJ (city) Middlesex County	427	0.84
Glenvar Heights, FL (cdp) Miami-Dade County	140	0.83
North Bergen, NJ (township) Hudson County	494	0.81
Wellington, FL (village) Palm Beach County	460	0.81
Sunset, FL (cdp) Miami-Dade County	131	0.80
Country Club, FL (cdp) Miami-Dade County	366	0.78
Annandale, VA (cdp) Fairfax County	313	0.76
Miami Lakes, FL (town) Miami-Dade County	220	0.75
Pembroke Pines, FL (city) Broward County	1,147	0.74
Orem, UT (city) Utah County	623	0.71
Potomac, MD (cdp) Montgomery County	321	0.71
Haiku-Pauwela, HI (cdp) Maui County	58	0.71
Greenwich, CT (town) Fairfield County	426	0.70
Richmond West, FL (cdp) Miami-Dade County	223	0.70
Coral Springs, FL (city) Broward County	832	0.69
Naranja, FL (cdp) Miami-Dade County	57	0.69
North Bethesda, MD (cdp) Montgomery County	297	0.68
West Falls Church, VA (cdp) Fairfax County	198	0.68
University Park, FL (cdp) Miami-Dade County	183	0.68
Union City, NJ (city) Hudson County	448	0.67
Greenacres, FL (city) Palm Beach County	246	0.65
Tamiami, FL (cdp) Miami-Dade County	356	0.64
Roselle Park, NJ (borough) Union County	85	0.64
West New York, NJ (town) Hudson County	312	0.63
Davie, FL (town) Broward County	566	0.62
Bethesda, MD (cdp) Montgomery County	376	0.62
Tamarac, FL (city) Broward County	370	0.61
Hilton Head Island, SC (town) Beaufort County	221	0.60
Palm Springs, FL (village) Palm Beach County	114	0.60
Buenaventura Lakes, FL (cdp) Osceola County	154	0.59
Coconut Creek, FL (city) Broward County	309	0.58
Westchester, FL (cdp) Miami-Dade County	174	0.58
Bailey's Crossroads, VA (cdp) Fairfax County	137	0.58
Lynbrook, NY (village) Nassau County	110	0.57
Provo, UT (city) Utah County	635	0.56
Spanish Fork, UT (city) Utah County	196	0.56
Coral Terrace, FL (cdp) Miami-Dade County	137	0.56
Whitehall, OH (city) Franklin County	100	0.55
Plantation, FL (city) Broward County	458	0.54
Monroe, NY (town) Orange County	217	0.54
Sunrise, FL (city) Broward County	451	0.53
Lodi, NJ (borough) Bergen County	128	0.53
Maywood, NJ (borough) Bergen County	51	0.53
Hialeah Gardens, FL (city) Miami-Dade County	112	0.52
Cooper City, FL (city) Broward County	145	0.51
Bluffton, SC (town) Beaufort County	64	0.51
Doctor Phillips, FL (cdp) Orange County	56	0.51
Garfield, NJ (city) Bergen County	151	0.50
Stevenson Ranch, CA (cdp) Los Angeles County	87	0.50
Olympia Heights, FL (cdp) Miami-Dade County	68	0.50
Marina del Rey, CA (cdp) Los Angeles County	44	0.50
South Amboy, NJ (city) Middlesex County	43	0.50
Margate, FL (city) Broward County	263	0.49
Culver City, CA (city) Los Angeles County	190	0.49
Agoura Hills, CA (city) Los Angeles County	99	0.49
Stanford, CA (cdp) Santa Clara County	68	0.49
Hialeah, FL (city) Miami-Dade County	1,087	0.48
Meadow Woods, FL (cdp) Orange County	122	0.48
Seven Corners, VA (cdp) Fairfax County	44	0.48
Williamsburg, FL (cdp) Orange County	37	0.48
Kissimmee, FL (city) Osceola County	283	0.47
Lake Barcroft, VA (cdp) Fairfax County	45	0.47
Miramar, FL (city) Broward County	558	0.46
Oakland Park, FL (city) Broward County	191	0.46
Sweetwater, FL (city) Miami-Dade County	62	0.46
Elizabeth, NJ (city) Union County	557	0.45
Cinco Ranch, TX (cdp) Fort Bend County	83	0.45
Saddle Brook, NJ (township) Bergen County	62	0.45
Weehawken, NJ (township) Hudson County	57	0.45
Kearny, NJ (town) Hudson County	177	0.44
North Kensington, MD (cdp) Montgomery County	42	0.44
Leonia, NJ (borough) Bergen County	39	0.44
Hunters Creek, FL (cdp) Orange County	62	0.43
Haledon, NJ (borough) Passaic County	36	0.43
Springville, UT (city) Utah County	125	0.42
Eagle Mountain, UT (city) Utah County	89	0.42
Scarsdale, NY (town/village) Westchester County	72	0.42
Ridgefield Park, NJ (village) Bergen County	54	0.42
Boca Raton, FL (city) Palm Beach County	345	0.41
Payson, UT (city) Utah County	75	0.41
Rutherford, NJ (borough) Bergen County	74	0.41
Del Aire, CA (cdp) Los Angeles County	41	0.41
The Woodlands, TX (cdp) Montgomery County	373	0.40
Rancho Santa Margarita, CA (city) Orange County	193	0.40
Springfield, VA (cdp) Fairfax County	121	0.40
Burbank, CA (city) Los Angeles County	406	0.39
Pleasant Grove, UT (city) Utah County	131	0.39
La Verne, CA (city) Los Angeles County	121	0.39
Harrison, NY (town/village) Westchester County	107	0.39
Golden Gate, FL (cdp) Collier County	93	0.39
South Salt Lake, UT (city) Salt Lake County	92	0.39
Dover, NJ (town) Morris County	70	0.39
San Carlos Park, FL (cdp) Lee County	66	0.39
Downey, CA (city) Los Angeles County	429	0.38
Deerfield Beach, FL (city) Broward County	282	0.38
Monrovia, CA (city) Los Angeles County	139	0.38
Parkland, FL (city) Broward County	90	0.38
Princeton, FL (cdp) Miami-Dade County	84	0.38
Duarte, CA (city) Los Angeles County	81	0.38
Fords, NJ (cdp) Middlesex County	58	0.38
Sierra Madre, CA (city) Los Angeles County	41	0.38
Woodburn, VA (cdp) Fairfax County	32	0.38
Bedminster, NJ (township) Somerset County	31	0.38
Irving, TX (city) Dallas County	803	0.37
Fort Lauderdale, FL (city) Broward County	616	0.37
Linden, NJ (city) Union County	149	0.37
Elmont, NY (cdp) Nassau County	122	0.37
El Segundo, CA (city) Los Angeles County	61	0.37
Rolling Hills Estates, CA (city) Los Angeles County	30	0.37
McLean, VA (cdp) Fairfax County	171	0.36
West Hollywood, CA (city) Los Angeles County	125	0.36
La Crescenta-Montrose, CA (cdp) Los Angeles County	71	0.36
Bellaire, TX (city) Harris County	61	0.36
Hopatcong, NJ (borough) Sussex County	54	0.36
Woodland Park, NJ (borough) Passaic County	43	0.36
Ridgefield, NJ (borough) Bergen County	40	0.36
Bound Brook, NJ (borough) Somerset County	37	0.36

SECTION THREE

Please refer to the Explanation of Data in the front of the book for more detailed information.

Hispanic Origin

South American: Bolivian

U.S. and 50 States Sorted by Population and Percent of Total Population

Place	Population	%
United States	**99,210**	**0.03**
Virginia	31,333	0.39
California	13,351	0.04
Florida	10,938	0.06
Maryland	7,496	0.13
New York	7,122	0.04
Texas	4,913	0.02
New Jersey	3,361	0.04
Illinois	2,304	0.02
Rhode Island	1,912	0.18
Massachusetts	1,401	0.02
Utah	969	0.04
Pennsylvania	895	0.01
North Carolina	878	0.01
Georgia	872	0.01
Washington	782	0.01
Connecticut	781	0.02
Colorado	775	0.02
Arizona	750	0.01
Ohio	649	0.01
District of Columbia	591	0.10
Michigan	512	0.01
South Carolina	493	0.01
Nevada	481	0.02
Missouri	471	0.01
Minnesota	430	0.01
Wisconsin	430	0.01
Indiana	425	0.01
Tennessee	351	0.01
Oregon	345	0.01
Kansas	332	0.01
Oklahoma	300	0.01
Louisiana	295	0.01
Alabama	292	0.01
Arkansas	260	0.01
New Mexico	229	0.01
Kentucky	227	0.01
Iowa	171	0.01
West Virginia	139	0.01
Hawaii	131	0.01
Idaho	122	0.01
Delaware	112	0.01
Alaska	94	0.01
Mississippi	87	<0.01
Nebraska	86	<0.01
New Hampshire	82	0.01
Maine	52	<0.01
Montana	49	<0.01
South Dakota	45	0.01
Wyoming	43	0.01
Vermont	34	0.01
North Dakota	17	<0.01

Place	Population	%
Virginia	31,333	0.39
Rhode Island	1,912	0.18
Maryland	7,496	0.13
District of Columbia	591	0.10
Florida	10,938	0.06
California	13,351	0.04
New York	7,122	0.04
New Jersey	3,361	0.04
Utah	969	0.04
United States	**99,210**	**0.03**
Texas	4,913	0.02
Illinois	2,304	0.02
Massachusetts	1,401	0.02
Connecticut	781	0.02
Colorado	775	0.02
Nevada	481	0.02
Pennsylvania	895	0.01
North Carolina	878	0.01
Georgia	872	0.01
Washington	782	0.01
Arizona	750	0.01
Ohio	649	0.01
Michigan	512	0.01
South Carolina	493	0.01
Missouri	471	0.01
Minnesota	430	0.01
Wisconsin	430	0.01
Indiana	425	0.01
Tennessee	351	0.01
Oregon	345	0.01
Kansas	332	0.01
Oklahoma	300	0.01
Louisiana	295	0.01
Alabama	292	0.01
Arkansas	260	0.01
New Mexico	229	0.01
Kentucky	227	0.01
Iowa	171	0.01
West Virginia	139	0.01
Hawaii	131	0.01
Idaho	122	0.01
Delaware	112	0.01
Alaska	94	0.01
New Hampshire	82	0.01
South Dakota	45	0.01
Wyoming	43	0.01
Vermont	34	0.01
Mississippi	87	<0.01
Nebraska	86	<0.01
Maine	52	<0.01
Montana	49	<0.01
North Dakota	17	<0.01

Please refer to the Explanation of Data in the front of the book for more detailed information.

Hispanic Origin

South American: Bolivian

Top 150 Places Sorted by Population

Based on all places, regardless of total population

Place	Population	%
New York, NY (city) Kings County	4,488	0.05
Arlington, VA (cdp) Arlington County	4,225	2.03
Queens, NY (borough) Queens County	3,268	0.15
Annandale, VA (cdp) Fairfax County	2,740	6.68
Los Angeles, CA (city) Los Angeles County	2,561	0.07
West Falls Church, VA (cdp) Fairfax County	2,226	7.62
Alexandria, VA (ind. city) Alexandria independent city	1,227	0.88
Bailey's Crossroads, VA (cdp) Fairfax County	1,052	4.45
Providence, RI (city) Providence County	1,046	0.59
Lincolnia, VA (cdp) Fairfax County	1,003	4.39
Houston, TX (city) Harris County	958	0.05
Burke, VA (cdp) Fairfax County	936	2.28
Springfield, VA (cdp) Fairfax County	855	2.80
Centreville, VA (cdp) Fairfax County	818	1.15
Miami, FL (city) Miami-Dade County	709	0.18
Dale City, VA (cdp) Prince William County	656	0.99
Chicago, IL (city) Cook County	626	0.02
Seven Corners, VA (cdp) Fairfax County	601	6.49
Washington, DC (city) District of Columbia	591	0.10
Germantown, MD (cdp) Montgomery County	545	0.63
Manhattan, NY (borough) New York County	522	0.03
Aspen Hill, MD (cdp) Montgomery County	521	1.07
Hempstead, NY (town) Nassau County	494	0.07
Sterling, VA (cdp) Loudoun County	483	1.74
Wheaton, MD (cdp) Montgomery County	476	0.99
Lake Barcroft, VA (cdp) Fairfax County	472	4.94
San Jose, CA (city) Santa Clara County	459	0.05
Rockville, MD (city) Montgomery County	446	0.73
Gaithersburg, MD (city) Montgomery County	443	0.74
San Francisco, CA (city) San Francisco County	416	0.05
Fairfax, VA (ind. city) Fairfax independent city	414	1.83
Santa Ana, CA (city) Orange County	398	0.12
Chantilly, VA (cdp) Fairfax County	396	1.72
Reston, VA (cdp) Fairfax County	387	0.66
Lake Ridge, VA (cdp) Prince William County	375	0.91
Rye, NY (town) Westchester County	375	0.82
West Springfield, VA (cdp) Fairfax County	372	1.66
Burke Centre, VA (cdp) Fairfax County	362	2.09
Idylwood, VA (cdp) Fairfax County	362	2.09
North Springfield, VA (cdp) Fairfax County	354	4.87
Port Chester, NY (village) Westchester County	350	1.21
Silver Spring, MD (cdp) Montgomery County	348	0.49
San Diego, CA (city) San Diego County	345	0.03
Rose Hill, VA (cdp) Fairfax County	341	1.69
Oakton, VA (cdp) Fairfax County	338	0.99
North Bethesda, MD (cdp) Montgomery County	337	0.77
Jersey City, NJ (city) Hudson County	337	0.14
Marumsco, VA (cdp) Prince William County	327	0.93
Merrifield, VA (cdp) Fairfax County	310	2.04
Brooklyn, NY (borough) Kings County	310	0.01
Dallas, TX (city) Dallas County	301	0.03
Golden Gate, FL (cdp) Collier County	290	1.21
Linton Hall, VA (cdp) Prince William County	289	0.81
Tustin, CA (city) Orange County	285	0.38
San Antonio, TX (city) Medina County	284	0.02
Cranston, RI (city) Providence County	278	0.35
Kings Park West, VA (cdp) Fairfax County	275	2.05
Kendall, FL (cdp) Miami-Dade County	274	0.36
Herndon, VA (town) Fairfax County	268	1.15
Lorton, VA (cdp) Fairfax County	263	1.41
Boston, MA (city) Suffolk County	263	0.04
Newington, VA (cdp) Fairfax County	260	2.01
Clifton, NJ (city) Passaic County	255	0.30
Austin, TX (city) Travis County	244	0.03
Leesburg, VA (town) Loudoun County	238	0.56
Newington Forest, VA (cdp) Fairfax County	235	1.89
Manassas, VA (ind. city) Manassas independent city	233	0.62
Jacksonville, FL (city) Duval County	231	0.03
Woodburn, VA (cdp) Fairfax County	230	2.71
Bronx, NY (borough) Bronx County	227	0.02
Islip, NY (town) Suffolk County	220	0.07
Montgomery Village, MD (cdp) Montgomery County	216	0.67
Fountainebleau, FL (cdp) Miami-Dade County	215	0.36
Sugarland Run, VA (cdp) Loudoun County	212	1.80
Miami Beach, FL (city) Miami-Dade County	211	0.24
Anaheim, CA (city) Orange County	211	0.06
Burbank, CA (city) Los Angeles County	208	0.20
Woodlawn, VA (cdp) Fairfax County	204	0.98
Fair Oaks, VA (cdp) Fairfax County	203	0.67
Pimmit Hills, VA (cdp) Fairfax County	195	3.20
Ashburn, VA (cdp) Loudoun County	195	0.45
Doral, FL (city) Miami-Dade County	192	0.42
Franconia, VA (cdp) Fairfax County	189	1.04
Tysons Corner, VA (cdp) Fairfax County	181	0.92
Manassas Park, VA (ind. city) Manassas Park independent city	180	1.26
Phoenix, AZ (city) Maricopa County	180	0.01
Olney, MD (cdp) Montgomery County	175	0.52
Kings Park, VA (cdp) Fairfax County	171	3.95
McLean, VA (cdp) Fairfax County	167	0.35
Kendale Lakes, FL (cdp) Miami-Dade County	167	0.30
Elizabeth, NJ (city) Union County	164	0.13
Tampa, FL (city) Hillsborough County	164	0.05
Staten Island, NY (borough) Richmond County	161	0.03
Orange, CA (city) Orange County	157	0.12
Vienna, VA (town) Fairfax County	156	0.99
The Hammocks, FL (cdp) Miami-Dade County	156	0.31
Pembroke Pines, FL (city) Broward County	153	0.10
Glendale, CA (city) Los Angeles County	150	0.08
Seattle, WA (city) King County	150	0.02
Redland, MD (cdp) Montgomery County	149	0.86
Wakefield, VA (cdp) Fairfax County	148	1.31
Brookhaven, NY (town) Suffolk County	148	0.03
Glenmont, MD (cdp) Montgomery County	146	1.08
Coral Springs, FL (city) Broward County	146	0.12
Union City, NJ (city) Hudson County	145	0.22
Falls Church, VA (ind. city) Falls Church independent city	139	1.13
Passaic, NJ (city) Passaic County	139	0.20
Charlotte, NC (city) Mecklenburg County	138	0.02
Groveton, VA (cdp) Fairfax County	137	0.94
Framingham, MA (cdp/town) Middlesex County	137	0.20
Downey, CA (city) Los Angeles County	134	0.12
Bethesda, MD (cdp) Montgomery County	133	0.22
Sudley, VA (cdp) Prince William County	132	0.81
San Mateo, CA (city) San Mateo County	131	0.13
Weston, FL (city) Broward County	130	0.20
Hollywood, FL (city) Broward County	130	0.09
Denver, CO (city) Denver County	130	0.02
North Providence, RI (town) Providence County	128	0.40
Long Beach, CA (city) Los Angeles County	125	0.03
Santa Clarita, CA (city) Los Angeles County	124	0.07
Irvine, CA (city) Orange County	123	0.06
Countryside, VA (cdp) Loudoun County	119	1.18
Johnston, RI (town) Providence County	118	0.41
Frederick, MD (city) Frederick County	118	0.18
South Riding, VA (cdp) Loudoun County	116	0.48
Miramar, FL (city) Broward County	116	0.10
Bull Run, VA (cdp) Prince William County	115	0.77
Boca Raton, FL (city) Palm Beach County	114	0.14
Chula Vista, CA (city) San Diego County	113	0.05
Stamford, CT (city/town) Fairfield County	112	0.09
Richmond, VA (ind. city) Richmond independent city	112	0.05
Philadelphia, PA (city) Philadelphia County	112	0.01
Garden Grove, CA (city) Orange County	110	0.06
Oyster Bay, NY (town) Nassau County	110	0.04
Orlando, FL (city) Orange County	108	0.05
Hybla Valley, VA (cdp) Fairfax County	107	0.68
Fayetteville, AR (city) Washington County	107	0.15
Provo, UT (city) Utah County	105	0.09
Santa Clara, CA (city) Santa Clara County	105	0.09
Newark, NJ (city) Essex County	105	0.04
Columbia, MD (cdp) Howard County	104	0.10
Tucson, AZ (city) Pima County	103	0.02
Garfield, NJ (city) Bergen County	102	0.33
Riverside, CA (city) Riverside County	102	0.03
Kingstowne, VA (cdp) Fairfax County	101	0.65
Pasadena, CA (city) Los Angeles County	101	0.07
Kendall West, FL (cdp) Miami-Dade County	100	0.28
Madison, WI (city) Dane County	100	0.04
Tamiami, FL (cdp) Miami-Dade County	99	0.18
Colesville, MD (cdp) Montgomery County	97	0.66

SECTION THREE

Hispanic Origin

South American: Bolivian

Top 150 Places Sorted by Percent of Total Population

Based on all places, regardless of total population

Place	Population	%
Sunwest, AZ (cdp) La Paz County	2	13.33
West Falls Church, VA (cdp) Fairfax County	2,226	7.62
Annandale, VA (cdp) Fairfax County	2,740	6.68
Seven Corners, VA (cdp) Fairfax County	601	6.49
Lake Barcroft, VA (cdp) Fairfax County	472	4.94
North Springfield, VA (cdp) Fairfax County	354	4.87
Bailey's Crossroads, VA (cdp) Fairfax County	1,052	4.45
Lincolnia, VA (cdp) Fairfax County	1,003	4.39
Kings Park, VA (cdp) Fairfax County	171	3.95
St. Joseph, IA (cdp) Kossuth County	2	3.28
Pimmit Hills, VA (cdp) Fairfax County	195	3.20
Springfield, VA (cdp) Fairfax County	855	2.80
Woodburn, VA (cdp) Fairfax County	230	2.71
Burke, VA (cdp) Fairfax County	936	2.28
Cloud Lake, FL (town) Palm Beach County	3	2.22
Ravensworth, VA (cdp) Fairfax County	52	2.11
Burke Centre, VA (cdp) Fairfax County	362	2.09
Idylwood, VA (cdp) Fairfax County	362	2.09
Kings Park West, VA (cdp) Fairfax County	275	2.05
Merrifield, VA (cdp) Fairfax County	310	2.04
Dulles Town Center, VA (cdp) Loudoun County	94	2.04
Excello, MO (cdp) Macon County	1	2.04
Arlington, VA (cdp) Arlington County	4,225	2.03
Newington, VA (cdp) Fairfax County	260	2.01
Tuttle, CA (cdp) Merced County	2	1.94
Newington Forest, VA (cdp) Fairfax County	235	1.89
Fairfax, VA (ind. city) Fairfax independent city	414	1.83
Pettisville, OH (cdp) Fulton County	9	1.81
Sugarland Run, VA (cdp) Loudoun County	212	1.80
Sterling, VA (cdp) Loudoun County	483	1.74
Chantilly, VA (cdp) Fairfax County	396	1.72
Rose Hill, VA (cdp) Fairfax County	341	1.69
West Springfield, VA (cdp) Fairfax County	372	1.66
Oak Grove, VA (cdp) Loudoun County	27	1.52
Lorton, VA (cdp) Fairfax County	263	1.41
Pajaro Dunes, CA (cdp) Santa Cruz County	2	1.39
Wakefield, VA (cdp) Fairfax County	148	1.31
Manassas Park, VA (ind. city) Manassas Park independent city	180	1.26
Poospatuck Reservation, NY (reservation) Suffolk County	4	1.23
Port Chester, NY (village) Westchester County	350	1.21
Golden Gate, FL (cdp) Collier County	290	1.21
Countryside, VA (cdp) Loudoun County	119	1.18
Centreville, VA (cdp) Fairfax County	818	1.15
Herndon, VA (town) Fairfax County	268	1.15
Falls Church, VA (ind. city) Falls Church independent city	139	1.13
Greenbriar, VA (cdp) Fairfax County	90	1.10
Glenmont, MD (cdp) Montgomery County	146	1.08
Aspen Hill, MD (cdp) Montgomery County	521	1.07
Long Branch, VA (cdp) Fairfax County	81	1.07
Hideout, UT (town) Wasatch County	7	1.07
Loch Lomond, VA (cdp) Prince William County	39	1.05
Franconia, VA (cdp) Fairfax County	189	1.04
Dale City, VA (cdp) Prince William County	656	0.99
Wheaton, MD (cdp) Montgomery County	476	0.99
Oakton, VA (cdp) Fairfax County	338	0.99
Vienna, VA (town) Fairfax County	156	0.99
Yorkshire, VA (cdp) Prince William County	75	0.99
Hatton, WA (town) Adams County	1	0.99
Woodlawn, VA (cdp) Fairfax County	204	0.98
Mantua, VA (cdp) Fairfax County	70	0.98
University Center, VA (cdp) Loudoun County	35	0.98
Haymarket, VA (town) Prince William County	17	0.95
Groveton, VA (cdp) Fairfax County	137	0.94
Marumsco, VA (cdp) Prince William County	327	0.93
Stanley, LA (village) De Soto Parish	1	0.93
Tysons Corner, VA (cdp) Fairfax County	181	0.92
Lake Ridge, VA (cdp) Prince William County	375	0.91
Dumfries, VA (town) Prince William County	44	0.89
Alexandria, VA (ind. city) Alexandria independent city	1,227	0.88
Potomac Mills, VA (cdp) Prince William County	49	0.87
Layhill, MD (cdp) Montgomery County	45	0.87
Redland, MD (cdp) Montgomery County	149	0.86
George Mason, VA (cdp) Fairfax County	81	0.85
Dunn Loring, VA (cdp) Fairfax County	75	0.85
Four Corners, MD (cdp) Montgomery County	67	0.84
Rye, NY (town) Westchester County	375	0.82
Lake Park, GA (city) Lowndes County	6	0.82
Linton Hall, VA (cdp) Prince William County	289	0.81
Sudley, VA (cdp) Prince William County	132	0.81
North Kensington, MD (cdp) Montgomery County	74	0.78
North Bethesda, MD (cdp) Montgomery County	337	0.77
Bull Run, VA (cdp) Prince William County	115	0.77
Freeman, SD (city) Hutchinson County	10	0.77
Cokato, MN (township) Wright County	10	0.76
Gaithersburg, MD (city) Montgomery County	443	0.74
Rockville, MD (city) Montgomery County	446	0.73
Urbana, MD (cdp) Frederick County	67	0.73
Fair Lakes, VA (cdp) Fairfax County	58	0.73
Hillandale, MD (cdp) Montgomery County	44	0.73
Huntington, VA (cdp) Fairfax County	80	0.71
Forest Glen, MD (cdp) Montgomery County	47	0.71
Laurel Hill, VA (cdp) Fairfax County	48	0.70
Crary, ND (city) Ramsey County	1	0.70
Hybla Valley, VA (cdp) Fairfax County	107	0.68
Launiupoko, HI (cdp) Maui County	4	0.68
Montgomery Village, MD (cdp) Montgomery County	216	0.67
Fair Oaks, VA (cdp) Fairfax County	203	0.67
Fairfax Station, VA (cdp) Fairfax County	80	0.67
Reston, VA (cdp) Fairfax County	387	0.66
Colesville, MD (cdp) Montgomery County	97	0.66
South Run, VA (cdp) Fairfax County	42	0.66
Kingstowne, VA (cdp) Fairfax County	101	0.65
Gainesville, VA (cdp) Prince William County	73	0.64
Bell Arthur, NC (cdp) Pitt County	3	0.64
Germantown, MD (cdp) Montgomery County	545	0.63
Cloverly, MD (cdp) Montgomery County	96	0.63
Big Water, UT (town) Kane County	3	0.63
Manassas, VA (ind. city) Manassas independent city	233	0.62
Gillis, LA (cdp) Calcasieu Parish	4	0.61
Kemp Mill, MD (cdp) Montgomery County	76	0.60
Haverford College, PA (cdp) Delaware County	8	0.60
Sand Lake, MI (village) Kent County	3	0.60
Providence, RI (city) Providence County	1,046	0.59
Woodbridge, VA (cdp) Prince William County	23	0.57
Callaghan, VA (cdp) Alleghany County	2	0.57
Leesburg, VA (town) Loudoun County	238	0.56
North Bay Village, FL (city) Miami-Dade County	39	0.55
Martin's Additions, MD (village) Montgomery County	5	0.54
Hilshire Village, TX (city) Harris County	4	0.54
Buckhall, VA (cdp) Prince William County	86	0.53
Olney, MD (cdp) Montgomery County	175	0.52
Cascades, VA (cdp) Loudoun County	62	0.52
Biscayne Park, FL (village) Miami-Dade County	16	0.52
Silver Spring, MD (cdp) Montgomery County	348	0.49
Wauseon, OH (city) Fulton County	36	0.49
Tinmouth, VT (town) Rutland County	3	0.49
South Riding, VA (cdp) Loudoun County	116	0.48
Berwyn Heights, MD (town) Prince George's County	15	0.48
Merritt Park, NY (cdp) Dutchess County	6	0.48
Naples Park, FL (cdp) Collier County	28	0.47
Chevy Chase Village, MD (town) Montgomery County	9	0.46
Cary, ME (plantation) Aroostook County	1	0.46
Ashburn, VA (cdp) Loudoun County	195	0.45
Key Biscayne, FL (village) Miami-Dade County	55	0.45
Clarksburg, MD (cdp) Montgomery County	61	0.44
Bluffton, SC (town) Beaufort County	55	0.44
Inwood, NY (cdp) Nassau County	43	0.44
Lake of the Woods, CA (cdp) Kern County	4	0.44
Clyde, CA (cdp) Contra Costa County	3	0.44
Burns, KS (city) Marion County	1	0.44
Douglassville, TX (town) Cass County	1	0.44
Greensburg, MD (cdp) Washington County	1	0.44
White Oak, MD (cdp) Montgomery County	74	0.43
Stone Ridge, VA (cdp) Loudoun County	31	0.43
Friendship Heights Village, MD (cdp) Montgomery County	20	0.43
Byram, CT (cdp) Fairfield County	18	0.43
Topeka, IN (town) LaGrange County	5	0.43
Genoa, NV (cdp) Douglas County	4	0.43
Meadville, MO (city) Linn County	2	0.43
Doral, FL (city) Miami-Dade County	192	0.42

Please refer to the Explanation of Data in the front of the book for more detailed information.

Hispanic Origin

South American: Bolivian

Top 150 Places Sorted by Percent of Total Population

Based on places with total population of 7,500 or more

Place	Population	%
West Falls Church, VA (cdp) Fairfax County	2,226	7.62
Annandale, VA (cdp) Fairfax County	2,740	6.68
Seven Corners, VA (cdp) Fairfax County	601	6.49
Lake Barcroft, VA (cdp) Fairfax County	472	4.94
Bailey's Crossroads, VA (cdp) Fairfax County	1,052	4.45
Lincolnia, VA (cdp) Fairfax County	1,003	4.39
Springfield, VA (cdp) Fairfax County	855	2.80
Woodburn, VA (cdp) Fairfax County	230	2.71
Burke, VA (cdp) Fairfax County	936	2.28
Burke Centre, VA (cdp) Fairfax County	362	2.09
Idylwood, VA (cdp) Fairfax County	362	2.09
Kings Park West, VA (cdp) Fairfax County	275	2.05
Merrifield, VA (cdp) Fairfax County	310	2.04
Arlington, VA (cdp) Arlington County	4,225	2.03
Newington, VA (cdp) Fairfax County	260	2.01
Newington Forest, VA (cdp) Fairfax County	235	1.89
Fairfax, VA (ind. city) Fairfax independent city	414	1.83
Sugarland Run, VA (cdp) Loudoun County	212	1.80
Sterling, VA (cdp) Loudoun County	483	1.74
Chantilly, VA (cdp) Fairfax County	396	1.72
Rose Hill, VA (cdp) Fairfax County	341	1.69
West Springfield, VA (cdp) Fairfax County	372	1.66
Lorton, VA (cdp) Fairfax County	263	1.41
Wakefield, VA (cdp) Fairfax County	148	1.31
Manassas Park, VA (ind. city) Manassas Park independent city	180	1.26
Port Chester, NY (village) Westchester County	350	1.21
Golden Gate, FL (cdp) Collier County	290	1.21
Countryside, VA (cdp) Loudoun County	119	1.18
Centreville, VA (cdp) Fairfax County	818	1.15
Herndon, VA (town) Fairfax County	268	1.15
Falls Church, VA (ind. city) Falls Church independent city	139	1.13
Greenbriar, VA (cdp) Fairfax County	90	1.10
Glenmont, MD (cdp) Montgomery County	146	1.08
Aspen Hill, MD (cdp) Montgomery County	521	1.07
Long Branch, VA (cdp) Fairfax County	81	1.07
Franconia, VA (cdp) Fairfax County	189	1.04
Dale City, VA (cdp) Prince William County	656	0.99
Wheaton, MD (cdp) Montgomery County	476	0.99
Oakton, VA (cdp) Fairfax County	338	0.99
Vienna, VA (town) Fairfax County	156	0.99
Yorkshire, VA (cdp) Prince William County	75	0.99
Woodlawn, VA (cdp) Fairfax County	204	0.98
Groveton, VA (cdp) Fairfax County	137	0.94
Marumsco, VA (cdp) Prince William County	327	0.93
Tysons Corner, VA (cdp) Fairfax County	181	0.92
Lake Ridge, VA (cdp) Prince William County	375	0.91
Alexandria, VA (ind. city) Alexandria independent city	1,227	0.88
Redland, MD (cdp) Montgomery County	149	0.86
George Mason, VA (cdp) Fairfax County	81	0.85
Dunn Loring, VA (cdp) Fairfax County	75	0.85
Four Corners, MD (cdp) Montgomery County	67	0.84
Rye, NY (town) Westchester County	375	0.82
Linton Hall, VA (cdp) Prince William County	289	0.81
Sudley, VA (cdp) Prince William County	132	0.81
North Kensington, MD (cdp) Montgomery County	74	0.78
North Bethesda, MD (cdp) Montgomery County	337	0.77
Bull Run, VA (cdp) Prince William County	115	0.77
Gaithersburg, MD (city) Montgomery County	443	0.74
Rockville, MD (city) Montgomery County	446	0.73
Urbana, MD (cdp) Frederick County	67	0.73
Fair Lakes, VA (cdp) Fairfax County	58	0.73
Huntington, VA (cdp) Fairfax County	80	0.71
Hybla Valley, VA (cdp) Fairfax County	107	0.68
Montgomery Village, MD (cdp) Montgomery County	216	0.67
Fair Oaks, VA (cdp) Fairfax County	203	0.67
Fairfax Station, VA (cdp) Fairfax County	80	0.67
Reston, VA (cdp) Fairfax County	387	0.66
Colesville, MD (cdp) Montgomery County	97	0.66
Kingstowne, VA (cdp) Fairfax County	101	0.65
Gainesville, VA (cdp) Prince William County	73	0.64
Germantown, MD (cdp) Montgomery County	545	0.63
Cloverly, MD (cdp) Montgomery County	96	0.63
Manassas, VA (ind. city) Manassas independent city	233	0.62
Kemp Mill, MD (cdp) Montgomery County	76	0.60
Providence, RI (city) Providence County	1,046	0.59
Leesburg, VA (town) Loudoun County	238	0.56
Buckhall, VA (cdp) Prince William County	86	0.53
Olney, MD (cdp) Montgomery County	175	0.52
Cascades, VA (cdp) Loudoun County	62	0.52
Silver Spring, MD (cdp) Montgomery County	348	0.49
South Riding, VA (cdp) Loudoun County	116	0.48
Ashburn, VA (cdp) Loudoun County	195	0.45
Key Biscayne, FL (village) Miami-Dade County	55	0.45
Clarksburg, MD (cdp) Montgomery County	61	0.44
Bluffton, SC (town) Beaufort County	55	0.44
Inwood, NY (cdp) Nassau County	43	0.44
White Oak, MD (cdp) Montgomery County	74	0.43
Doral, FL (city) Miami-Dade County	192	0.42
McNair, VA (cdp) Fairfax County	73	0.42
Three Lakes, FL (cdp) Miami-Dade County	63	0.42
Neabsco, VA (cdp) Prince William County	51	0.42
Johnston, RI (town) Providence County	118	0.41
North Providence, RI (town) Providence County	128	0.40
Dranesville, VA (cdp) Fairfax County	48	0.40
Ojus, FL (cdp) Miami-Dade County	71	0.39
Lowes Island, VA (cdp) Loudoun County	42	0.39
Tustin, CA (city) Orange County	285	0.38
Franklin Farm, VA (cdp) Fairfax County	71	0.37
Calverton, MD (cdp) Montgomery County	66	0.37
Kendall, FL (cdp) Miami-Dade County	274	0.36
Fountainebleau, FL (cdp) Miami-Dade County	215	0.36
Mount Vernon, VA (cdp) Fairfax County	45	0.36
Cranston, RI (city) Providence County	278	0.35
McLean, VA (cdp) Fairfax County	167	0.35
Montclair, VA (cdp) Prince William County	68	0.35
Adelphi, MD (cdp) Prince George's County	53	0.35
Brambleton, VA (cdp) Loudoun County	34	0.35
East Rutherford, NJ (borough) Bergen County	31	0.35
Guttenberg, NJ (town) Hudson County	38	0.34
South Amboy, NJ (city) Middlesex County	29	0.34
Garfield, NJ (city) Bergen County	102	0.33
Palmetto Bay, FL (village) Miami-Dade County	74	0.32
Broadlands, VA (cdp) Loudoun County	39	0.32
East Rockaway, NY (village) Nassau County	31	0.32
The Hammocks, FL (cdp) Miami-Dade County	156	0.31
Cherry Hill, VA (cdp) Prince William County	49	0.31
Clifton, NJ (city) Passaic County	255	0.30
Kendale Lakes, FL (cdp) Miami-Dade County	167	0.30
University Park, FL (cdp) Miami-Dade County	80	0.30
The Crossings, FL (cdp) Miami-Dade County	69	0.30
Pinecrest, FL (village) Miami-Dade County	54	0.30
Miami Springs, FL (city) Miami-Dade County	41	0.30
Glenvar Heights, FL (cdp) Miami-Dade County	49	0.29
Beltsville, MD (cdp) Prince George's County	48	0.29
Country Walk, FL (cdp) Miami-Dade County	46	0.29
Kendall West, FL (cdp) Miami-Dade County	100	0.28
Lansdowne, VA (cdp) Loudoun County	32	0.28
Palm Springs, FL (village) Palm Beach County	51	0.27
Incline Village, NV (cdp) Washoe County	24	0.27
Triangle, VA (cdp) Prince William County	22	0.27
Sunset, FL (cdp) Miami-Dade County	42	0.26
Leisure World, MD (cdp) Montgomery County	23	0.26
Takoma Park, MD (city) Montgomery County	41	0.25
Miami Beach, FL (city) Miami-Dade County	211	0.24
Aventura, FL (city) Miami-Dade County	85	0.24
City of Orange, NJ (township) Essex County	72	0.24
Sunny Isles Beach, FL (city) Miami-Dade County	50	0.24
Central Falls, RI (city) Providence County	46	0.24
Middleton, WI (city) Dane County	41	0.24
Wolf Trap, VA (cdp) Fairfax County	38	0.24
Damascus, MD (cdp) Montgomery County	36	0.24
Lynbrook, NY (village) Nassau County	44	0.23
Hyattsville, MD (city) Prince George's County	40	0.23
San Carlos Park, FL (cdp) Lee County	38	0.23
Great Falls, VA (cdp) Fairfax County	35	0.23
Port Jefferson Station, NY (cdp) Suffolk County	18	0.23
Purcellville, VA (town) Loudoun County	18	0.23
Union City, NJ (city) Hudson County	145	0.22
Bethesda, MD (cdp) Montgomery County	133	0.22
Richmond West, FL (cdp) Miami-Dade County	69	0.22

SECTION THREE

Please refer to the Explanation of Data in the front of the book for more detailed information.

Hispanic Origin

South American: Chilean

U.S. and 50 States Sorted by Population and Percent of Total Population

Place	Population	%
United States	**126,810**	**0.04**
California	24,006	0.06
Florida	23,549	0.13
New York	15,050	0.08
New Jersey	8,100	0.09
Texas	6,282	0.02
Virginia	4,195	0.05
Maryland	4,146	0.07
Utah	3,364	0.12
Massachusetts	3,045	0.05
Illinois	2,753	0.02
Washington	2,625	0.04
North Carolina	2,525	0.03
Pennsylvania	2,521	0.02
Connecticut	2,356	0.07
Georgia	2,249	0.02
Arizona	1,955	0.03
Nevada	1,683	0.06
Colorado	1,678	0.03
Oregon	1,274	0.03
Michigan	1,160	0.01
Ohio	1,065	0.01
Minnesota	1,057	0.02
Wisconsin	815	0.01
Tennessee	774	0.01
District of Columbia	697	0.12
Missouri	665	0.01
Indiana	647	0.01
New Mexico	569	0.03
South Carolina	567	0.01
Louisiana	548	0.01
Alabama	451	0.01
Hawaii	408	0.03
Kansas	346	0.01
Idaho	336	0.02
Delaware	335	0.04
Kentucky	332	0.01
Iowa	329	0.01
Rhode Island	312	0.03
Oklahoma	289	0.01
Nebraska	228	0.01
New Hampshire	224	0.02
Alaska	223	0.03
Arkansas	219	0.01
Maine	166	0.01
Mississippi	146	<0.01
Vermont	127	0.02
West Virginia	110	0.01
Montana	105	0.01
South Dakota	79	0.01
Wyoming	78	0.01
North Dakota	47	0.01

Place	Population	%
Florida	23,549	0.13
Utah	3,364	0.12
District of Columbia	697	0.12
New Jersey	8,100	0.09
New York	15,050	0.08
Maryland	4,146	0.07
Connecticut	2,356	0.07
California	24,006	0.06
Nevada	1,683	0.06
Virginia	4,195	0.05
Massachusetts	3,045	0.05
United States	**126,810**	**0.04**
Washington	2,625	0.04
Delaware	335	0.04
North Carolina	2,525	0.03
Arizona	1,955	0.03
Colorado	1,678	0.03
Oregon	1,274	0.03
New Mexico	569	0.03
Hawaii	408	0.03
Rhode Island	312	0.03
Alaska	223	0.03
Texas	6,282	0.02
Illinois	2,753	0.02
Pennsylvania	2,521	0.02
Georgia	2,249	0.02
Minnesota	1,057	0.02
Idaho	336	0.02
New Hampshire	224	0.02
Vermont	127	0.02
Michigan	1,160	0.01
Ohio	1,065	0.01
Wisconsin	815	0.01
Tennessee	774	0.01
Missouri	665	0.01
Indiana	647	0.01
South Carolina	567	0.01
Louisiana	548	0.01
Alabama	451	0.01
Kansas	346	0.01
Kentucky	332	0.01
Iowa	329	0.01
Oklahoma	289	0.01
Nebraska	228	0.01
Arkansas	219	0.01
Maine	166	0.01
West Virginia	110	0.01
Montana	105	0.01
South Dakota	79	0.01
Wyoming	78	0.01
North Dakota	47	0.01
Mississippi	146	<0.01

Please refer to the Explanation of Data in the front of the book for more detailed information.

Hispanic Origin

South American: Chilean

Top 150 Places Sorted by Population

Based on all places, regardless of total population

Place	Population	%
New York, NY (city) Kings County	7,026	0.09
Los Angeles, CA (city) Los Angeles County	4,112	0.11
Queens, NY (borough) Queens County	3,184	0.14
Manhattan, NY (borough) New York County	1,824	0.12
Miami, FL (city) Miami-Dade County	1,427	0.36
Hempstead, NY (town) Nassau County	1,415	0.19
Brooklyn, NY (borough) Kings County	1,026	0.04
Houston, TX (city) Harris County	934	0.04
San Diego, CA (city) San Diego County	876	0.07
Chicago, IL (city) Cook County	876	0.03
San Francisco, CA (city) San Francisco County	754	0.09
Miami Beach, FL (city) Miami-Dade County	739	0.84
Washington, DC (city) District of Columbia	697	0.12
North Hempstead, NY (town) Nassau County	664	0.29
Bronx, NY (borough) Bronx County	646	0.05
San Jose, CA (city) Santa Clara County	632	0.07
Doral, FL (city) Miami-Dade County	622	1.36
Kendall, FL (cdp) Miami-Dade County	613	0.81
Hialeah, FL (city) Miami-Dade County	602	0.27
Oyster Bay, NY (town) Nassau County	569	0.19
The Hammocks, FL (cdp) Miami-Dade County	564	1.11
Pembroke Pines, FL (city) Broward County	558	0.36
Fountainebleau, FL (cdp) Miami-Dade County	549	0.92
Hollywood, FL (city) Broward County	542	0.39
North Bergen, NJ (township) Hudson County	472	0.78
Kendale Lakes, FL (cdp) Miami-Dade County	469	0.84
Las Vegas, NV (city) Clark County	467	0.08
Islip, NY (town) Suffolk County	448	0.13
Seattle, WA (city) King County	438	0.07
Boston, MA (city) Suffolk County	405	0.07
San Antonio, TX (city) Medina County	374	0.03
Union City, NJ (city) Hudson County	372	0.56
Charlotte, NC (city) Mecklenburg County	368	0.05
Brookhaven, NY (town) Suffolk County	363	0.07
Philadelphia, PA (city) Philadelphia County	357	0.02
Staten Island, NY (borough) Richmond County	346	0.07
Coral Springs, FL (city) Broward County	342	0.28
Miramar, FL (city) Broward County	340	0.28
Austin, TX (city) Travis County	340	0.04
Phoenix, AZ (city) Maricopa County	320	0.02
Jersey City, NJ (city) Hudson County	316	0.13
Provo, UT (city) Utah County	314	0.28
Portland, OR (city) Multnomah County	307	0.05
Weston, FL (city) Broward County	306	0.47
Arlington, VA (cdp) Arlington County	302	0.15
Tamiami, FL (cdp) Miami-Dade County	301	0.54
Oakland, CA (city) Alameda County	297	0.08
Tucson, AZ (city) Pima County	293	0.06
Orem, UT (city) Utah County	292	0.33
Orlando, FL (city) Orange County	290	0.12
Long Beach, CA (city) Los Angeles County	288	0.06
Jacksonville, FL (city) Duval County	287	0.03
Santa Clarita, CA (city) Los Angeles County	284	0.16
Dallas, TX (city) Dallas County	283	0.02
Stamford, CT (city/town) Fairfield County	282	0.23
Albuquerque, NM (city) Bernalillo County	282	0.05
Dover, NJ (town) Morris County	281	1.55
West New York, NJ (town) Hudson County	279	0.56
Kendall West, FL (cdp) Miami-Dade County	276	0.76
Cambridge, MA (city) Middlesex County	275	0.26
Alexandria, VA (ind. city) Alexandria independent city	274	0.20
The Crossings, FL (cdp) Miami-Dade County	269	1.18
Davie, FL (town) Broward County	268	0.29
Allentown, PA (city) Lehigh County	259	0.22
San Mateo, CA (city) San Mateo County	258	0.27
Huntington, NY (town) Suffolk County	252	0.12
Denver, CO (city) Denver County	249	0.04
Salt Lake City, UT (city) Salt Lake County	240	0.13
Riverside, CA (city) Riverside County	236	0.08
Manorhaven, NY (village) Nassau County	234	3.57
Country Club, FL (cdp) Miami-Dade County	233	0.49
Coral Gables, FL (city) Miami-Dade County	230	0.49
Glendale, CA (city) Los Angeles County	230	0.12
Germantown, MD (cdp) Montgomery County	228	0.26
Babylon, NY (town) Suffolk County	226	0.11
Torrance, CA (city) Los Angeles County	221	0.15
West Valley City, UT (city) Salt Lake County	220	0.17
Glen Cove, NY (city) Nassau County	217	0.80
Yonkers, NY (city) Westchester County	215	0.11
Aspen Hill, MD (cdp) Montgomery County	212	0.43
Plantation, FL (city) Broward County	212	0.25
Elizabeth, NJ (city) Union County	212	0.17
Valley Stream, NY (village) Nassau County	211	0.56
Stockton, CA (city) San Joaquin County	207	0.07
Sacramento, CA (city) Sacramento County	205	0.04
Paradise, NV (cdp) Clark County	202	0.09
Berkeley, CA (city) Alameda County	201	0.18
Spring Valley, NV (cdp) Clark County	200	0.11
Rockville, MD (city) Montgomery County	198	0.32
Irvine, CA (city) Orange County	198	0.09
Greenwich, CT (town) Fairfield County	196	0.32
Raleigh, NC (city) Wake County	196	0.05
North Bethesda, MD (cdp) Montgomery County	195	0.44
Cutler Bay, FL (town) Miami-Dade County	194	0.48
Port St. Lucie, FL (city) St. Lucie County	193	0.12
Rye, NY (town) Westchester County	192	0.42
Greenburgh, NY (town) Westchester County	192	0.22
Ossining, NY (town) Westchester County	190	0.50
Key Biscayne, FL (village) Miami-Dade County	185	1.50
Palmetto Bay, FL (village) Miami-Dade County	183	0.78
Bethesda, MD (cdp) Montgomery County	183	0.30
Anaheim, CA (city) Orange County	181	0.05
Mount Pleasant, NY (town) Westchester County	180	0.41
Fort Lauderdale, FL (city) Broward County	180	0.11
Oyster Bay, NY (cdp) Nassau County	179	2.67
Aventura, FL (city) Miami-Dade County	176	0.49
West Jordan, UT (city) Salt Lake County	174	0.17
Henderson, NV (city) Clark County	173	0.07
Palmdale, CA (city) Los Angeles County	172	0.11
Sunrise, FL (city) Broward County	171	0.20
Gainesville, FL (city) Alachua County	171	0.14
Pasadena, CA (city) Los Angeles County	171	0.12
Aurora, CO (city) Arapahoe County	171	0.05
Ossining, NY (village) Westchester County	169	0.67
Chula Vista, CA (city) San Diego County	168	0.07
Bayonne, NJ (city) Hudson County	167	0.26
Madison, WI (city) Dane County	167	0.07
Richmond West, FL (cdp) Miami-Dade County	165	0.52
Burbank, CA (city) Los Angeles County	165	0.16
Tampa, FL (city) Hillsborough County	165	0.05
New Haven, CT (city/town) New Haven County	164	0.13
Lancaster, CA (city) Los Angeles County	162	0.10
Reno, NV (city) Washoe County	162	0.07
North Miami Beach, FL (city) Miami-Dade County	160	0.39
Nashville-Davidson, TN (metro govt) Davidson County	160	0.03
Huntington Beach, CA (city) Orange County	159	0.08
Minneapolis, MN (city) Hennepin County	155	0.04
Brentwood, NY (cdp) Suffolk County	153	0.25
Fort Worth, TX (city) Tarrant County	153	0.02
Wheaton, MD (cdp) Montgomery County	151	0.31
Plano, TX (city) Collin County	151	0.06
Virginia Beach, VA (ind. city) Virginia Beach independent city	151	0.03
Potomac, MD (cdp) Montgomery County	150	0.33
North Miami, FL (city) Miami-Dade County	150	0.26
Port Washington, NY (cdp) Nassau County	149	0.94
Clifton, NJ (city) Passaic County	149	0.18
Sleepy Hollow, NY (village) Westchester County	146	1.48
Pinecrest, FL (village) Miami-Dade County	146	0.80
Sunny Isles Beach, FL (city) Miami-Dade County	146	0.70
Rancho Cucamonga, CA (city) San Bernardino County	146	0.09
Boca Raton, FL (city) Palm Beach County	145	0.17
Gaithersburg, MD (city) Montgomery County	143	0.24
Mesa, AZ (city) Maricopa County	141	0.03
Hallandale Beach, FL (city) Broward County	140	0.38
Hamden, CT (town) New Haven County	140	0.23
Corona, CA (city) Riverside County	140	0.09
Durham, NC (city) Durham County	140	0.06
Anchorage, AK (municipality) Anchorage Municipality	140	0.05
Pittsburgh, PA (city) Allegheny County	139	0.05
Richmond, CA (city) Contra Costa County	136	0.13

Please refer to the Explanation of Data in the front of the book for more detailed information.

Hispanic Origin

South American: Chilean

Top 150 Places Sorted by Percent of Total Population

Based on all places, regardless of total population

Place	Population	%
Norrie, CO (cdp) Pitkin County	1	14.29
Indian Creek, FL (village) Miami-Dade County	4	4.65
Boykin, SC (cdp) Kershaw County	4	4.00
Brookeville, MD (town) Montgomery County	5	3.73
Manorhaven, NY (village) Nassau County	234	3.57
Lowndesville, SC (town) Abbeville County	4	3.13
Coffee Creek, CA (cdp) Trinity County	6	2.76
Oyster Bay, NY (cdp) Nassau County	179	2.67
Curlew, WA (cdp) Ferry County	3	2.54
Sawpit, CO (town) San Miguel County	1	2.50
Cloverdale, OH (village) Putnam County	4	2.38
Strawberry, CA (cdp) Tuolumne County	2	2.33
Tatitlek, AK (cdp) Valdez-Cordova Census Area	2	2.27
Allen, MD (cdp) Wicomico County	4	1.90
Lynnville, IL (village) Morgan County	2	1.71
Eagleville, CA (cdp) Modoc County	1	1.69
Great Meadows, NJ (cdp) Warren County	5	1.65
Windham, NY (cdp) Greene County	6	1.63
Warm Springs, VA (cdp) Bath County	2	1.63
Crisman, CO (cdp) Boulder County	3	1.61
Dover, NJ (town) Morris County	281	1.55
Woody Creek, CO (cdp) Pitkin County	4	1.52
Key Biscayne, FL (village) Miami-Dade County	185	1.50
Baileyville, PA (cdp) Centre County	3	1.49
Sleepy Hollow, NY (village) Westchester County	146	1.48
Manzano Springs, NM (cdp) Torrance County	2	1.46
Forest Home, NY (cdp) Tompkins County	8	1.40
Ames, NY (village) Montgomery County	2	1.38
Doral, FL (city) Miami-Dade County	622	1.36
Northwest Stanwood, WA (cdp) Snohomish County	2	1.34
Victory Gardens, NJ (borough) Morris County	20	1.32
Halibut Cove, AK (cdp) Kenai Peninsula Borough	1	1.32
Wharton, NJ (borough) Morris County	83	1.27
Woodlawn Heights, IN (town) Madison County	1	1.27
North Bay Village, FL (city) Miami-Dade County	87	1.22
St. Johns, MN (township) Kandiyohi County	5	1.22
Goshen, VT (town) Addison County	2	1.22
The Crossings, FL (cdp) Miami-Dade County	269	1.18
Lindsay, NE (village) Platte County	3	1.18
Baileys Harbor, WI (cdp) Door County	3	1.17
Sombrillo, NM (cdp) Santa Fe County	4	1.14
The Hammocks, FL (cdp) Miami-Dade County	564	1.11
Inwood, NY (cdp) Nassau County	108	1.10
Maurice, IA (city) Sioux County	3	1.09
North Lynbrook, NY (cdp) Nassau County	8	1.01
Cedarhurst, NY (village) Nassau County	65	0.99
Beverly Shores, IN (town) Porter County	6	0.98
Bay Harbor Islands, FL (town) Miami-Dade County	54	0.96
Port Washington, NY (cdp) Nassau County	149	0.94
Fountainebleau, FL (cdp) Miami-Dade County	549	0.92
Paradise Valley, NV (cdp) Humboldt County	1	0.92
Hana, HI (cdp) Maui County	11	0.89
Oak Shores, CA (cdp) San Luis Obispo County	3	0.89
Locust Valley, NY (cdp) Nassau County	30	0.88
Virginia Gardens, FL (village) Miami-Dade County	21	0.88
Gurley, AL (town) Madison County	7	0.87
Mifflintown, PA (borough) Juniata County	8	0.85
Madaket, MA (cdp) Nantucket County	2	0.85
Miami Beach, FL (city) Miami-Dade County	739	0.84
Kendale Lakes, FL (cdp) Miami-Dade County	469	0.84
Port Washington North, NY (village) Nassau County	26	0.82
Mount Ayr, IN (town) Newton County	1	0.82
Kendall, FL (cdp) Miami-Dade County	613	0.81
Glen Cove, NY (city) Nassau County	217	0.80
Pinecrest, FL (village) Miami-Dade County	146	0.80
East Hampton North, NY (cdp) Suffolk County	33	0.80
Baxter Estates, NY (village) Nassau County	8	0.80
North Bergen, NJ (township) Hudson County	472	0.78
Palmetto Bay, FL (village) Miami-Dade County	183	0.78
Guttenberg, NJ (town) Hudson County	87	0.78
Halden, MN (township) St. Louis County	1	0.78
Three Lakes, FL (cdp) Miami-Dade County	116	0.77
Netcong, NJ (borough) Morris County	25	0.77
Oppelo, AR (city) Conway County	6	0.77
Kendall West, FL (cdp) Miami-Dade County	276	0.76

Place	Population	%
James Town, WY (cdp) Sweetwater County	4	0.75
Ojus, FL (cdp) Miami-Dade County	134	0.74
Pemberwick, CT (cdp) Fairfield County	27	0.73
Jersey, GA (city) Walton County	1	0.73
Country Walk, FL (cdp) Miami-Dade County	115	0.72
Cascade, WI (village) Sheboygan County	5	0.71
Sunny Isles Beach, FL (city) Miami-Dade County	146	0.70
Iola, PA (cdp) Columbia County	1	0.69
Hopewell, PA (township) Huntingdon County	4	0.68
Ossining, NY (village) Westchester County	169	0.67
Morenci, AZ (cdp) Greenlee County	10	0.67
Glenvar Heights, FL (cdp) Miami-Dade County	111	0.66
Ellenville, NY (village) Ulster County	27	0.65
Golden Beach, FL (town) Miami-Dade County	6	0.65
Tiffany, WI (town) Dunn County	4	0.65
Valley Falls, NY (village) Rensselaer County	3	0.64
North Kensington, MD (cdp) Montgomery County	60	0.63
Albany, CA (city) Alameda County	112	0.60
Tarrytown, NY (village) Westchester County	68	0.60
Laurel Mountain, PA (borough) Westmoreland County	1	0.60
Stanford, CA (cdp) Santa Clara County	81	0.59
Scotia, CA (cdp) Humboldt County	5	0.59
Long Lake, MN (township) Watonwan County	2	0.59
Mine Hill, NJ (township) Morris County	21	0.58
Fieldbrook, CA (cdp) Humboldt County	5	0.58
Agency, MO (village) Buchanan County	4	0.58
Anderson, NJ (cdp) Warren County	2	0.58
Sunset, FL (cdp) Miami-Dade County	94	0.57
Weehawken, NJ (township) Hudson County	72	0.57
Union City, NJ (city) Hudson County	372	0.56
West New York, NJ (town) Hudson County	279	0.56
Valley Stream, NY (village) Nassau County	211	0.56
Hewlett, NY (cdp) Nassau County	38	0.56
Surfside, FL (town) Miami-Dade County	32	0.56
El Portal, FL (village) Miami-Dade County	13	0.56
Lake Telemark, NJ (cdp) Morris County	7	0.56
Batesville, TX (cdp) Zavala County	6	0.56
Bingen, WA (city) Klickitat County	4	0.56
Fenton, MN (township) Murray County	1	0.56
Pittman, FL (cdp) Lake County	1	0.56
Rocky Ridge, UT (town) Juab County	4	0.55
Richfield, PA (cdp) Juniata County	3	0.55
Sheldon, MO (city) Vernon County	3	0.55
Riverdale, NE (village) Buffalo County	1	0.55
Tamiami, FL (cdp) Miami-Dade County	301	0.54
University of California Davis, CA (cdp) Yolo County	31	0.54
Sea Cliff, NY (village) Nassau County	27	0.54
Pine Air, FL (cdp) Palm Beach County	11	0.54
Meadow Vale, KY (city) Jefferson County	4	0.54
Amador City, CA (city) Amador County	1	0.54
Byram, CT (cdp) Fairfield County	22	0.53
Landess, IN (cdp) Grant County	1	0.53
Richmond West, FL (cdp) Miami-Dade County	165	0.52
Miami Springs, FL (city) Miami-Dade County	72	0.52
Greensboro, VT (town) Orleans County	4	0.52
Copper Mountain, CO (cdp) Summit County	2	0.52
Centerville, CA (cdp) Fresno County	2	0.51
Gem Lake, MN (city) Ramsey County	2	0.51
Ossining, NY (town) Westchester County	190	0.50
Bay Park, NY (cdp) Nassau County	11	0.50
Dagsboro, DE (town) Sussex County	4	0.50
Country Club, FL (cdp) Miami-Dade County	233	0.49
Coral Gables, FL (city) Miami-Dade County	230	0.49
Aventura, FL (city) Miami-Dade County	176	0.49
Coral Terrace, FL (cdp) Miami-Dade County	119	0.49
Island Park, NY (village) Nassau County	23	0.49
La Fargeville, NY (cdp) Jefferson County	3	0.49
Cutler Bay, FL (town) Miami-Dade County	194	0.48
Beattystown, NJ (cdp) Warren County	22	0.48
Levan, UT (town) Juab County	4	0.48
St. Charles, MN (township) Winona County	3	0.48
Timnath, CO (town) Larimer County	3	0.48
Weston, FL (city) Broward County	306	0.47
Upper Brookville, NY (village) Nassau County	8	0.47
Verplanck, NY (cdp) Westchester County	8	0.46

Please refer to the Explanation of Data in the front of the book for more detailed information.

Hispanic Origin

South American: Chilean

Top 150 Places Sorted by Percent of Total Population

Based on places with total population of 7,500 or more

Place	Population	%
Dover, NJ (town) Morris County	281	1.55
Key Biscayne, FL (village) Miami-Dade County	185	1.50
Sleepy Hollow, NY (village) Westchester County	146	1.48
Doral, FL (city) Miami-Dade County	622	1.36
The Crossings, FL (cdp) Miami-Dade County	269	1.18
The Hammocks, FL (cdp) Miami-Dade County	564	1.11
Inwood, NY (cdp) Nassau County	108	1.10
Port Washington, NY (cdp) Nassau County	149	0.94
Fountainebleau, FL (cdp) Miami-Dade County	549	0.92
Miami Beach, FL (city) Miami-Dade County	739	0.84
Kendale Lakes, FL (cdp) Miami-Dade County	469	0.84
Kendall, FL (cdp) Miami-Dade County	613	0.81
Glen Cove, NY (city) Nassau County	217	0.80
Pinecrest, FL (village) Miami-Dade County	146	0.80
North Bergen, NJ (township) Hudson County	472	0.78
Palmetto Bay, FL (village) Miami-Dade County	183	0.78
Guttenberg, NJ (town) Hudson County	87	0.78
Three Lakes, FL (cdp) Miami-Dade County	116	0.77
Kendall West, FL (cdp) Miami-Dade County	276	0.76
Ojus, FL (cdp) Miami-Dade County	134	0.74
Country Walk, FL (cdp) Miami-Dade County	115	0.72
Sunny Isles Beach, FL (city) Miami-Dade County	146	0.70
Ossining, NY (village) Westchester County	169	0.67
Glenvar Heights, FL (cdp) Miami-Dade County	111	0.66
North Kensington, MD (cdp) Montgomery County	60	0.63
Albany, CA (city) Alameda County	112	0.60
Tarrytown, NY (village) Westchester County	68	0.60
Stanford, CA (cdp) Santa Clara County	81	0.59
Sunset, FL (cdp) Miami-Dade County	94	0.57
Weehawken, NJ (township) Hudson County	72	0.57
Union City, NJ (city) Hudson County	372	0.56
West New York, NJ (town) Hudson County	279	0.56
Valley Stream, NY (village) Nassau County	211	0.56
Tamiami, FL (cdp) Miami-Dade County	301	0.54
Richmond West, FL (cdp) Miami-Dade County	165	0.52
Miami Springs, FL (city) Miami-Dade County	72	0.52
Ossining, NY (town) Westchester County	190	0.50
Country Club, FL (cdp) Miami-Dade County	233	0.49
Coral Gables, FL (city) Miami-Dade County	230	0.49
Aventura, FL (city) Miami-Dade County	176	0.49
Coral Terrace, FL (cdp) Miami-Dade County	119	0.49
Cutler Bay, FL (town) Miami-Dade County	194	0.48
Weston, FL (city) Broward County	306	0.47
Damascus, MD (cdp) Montgomery County	69	0.45
Hopatcong, NJ (borough) Sussex County	68	0.45
Budd Lake, NJ (cdp) Morris County	40	0.45
North Bethesda, MD (cdp) Montgomery County	195	0.44
Lynbrook, NY (village) Nassau County	85	0.44
Aspen Hill, MD (cdp) Montgomery County	212	0.43
Wawarsing, NY (town) Ulster County	57	0.43
Rye, NY (town) Westchester County	192	0.42
Port Chester, NY (village) Westchester County	123	0.42
Fairview, NJ (borough) Bergen County	58	0.42
Woodburn, VA (cdp) Fairfax County	36	0.42
Riverside, CT (cdp) Fairfield County	35	0.42
Mount Pleasant, NY (town) Westchester County	180	0.41
Miami Lakes, FL (town) Miami-Dade County	120	0.41
Cliffside Park, NJ (borough) Bergen County	95	0.40
Hollywood, FL (city) Broward County	542	0.39
North Miami Beach, FL (city) Miami-Dade County	160	0.39
University Park, FL (cdp) Miami-Dade County	104	0.39
West Park, FL (city) Broward County	55	0.39
South Miami, FL (city) Miami-Dade County	45	0.39
Hallandale Beach, FL (city) Broward County	140	0.38
Westchester, FL (cdp) Miami-Dade County	112	0.38
Ives Estates, FL (cdp) Miami-Dade County	75	0.38
Mammoth Lakes, CA (town) Mono County	31	0.38
Lincolnia, VA (cdp) Fairfax County	84	0.37
Sweetwater, FL (city) Miami-Dade County	50	0.37
Miami, FL (city) Miami-Dade County	1,427	0.36
Pembroke Pines, FL (city) Broward County	558	0.36
Elmont, NY (cdp) Nassau County	119	0.36
Olympia Heights, FL (cdp) Miami-Dade County	49	0.36
Palmetto Estates, FL (cdp) Miami-Dade County	49	0.36
Hastings-on-Hudson, NY (village) Westchester County	28	0.36
Secaucus, NJ (town) Hudson County	57	0.35
Westwood Lakes, FL (cdp) Miami-Dade County	41	0.35
Montgomery Village, MD (cdp) Montgomery County	108	0.34
Oronoko, MI (charter township) Berrien County	31	0.34
Orem, UT (city) Utah County	292	0.33
Potomac, MD (cdp) Montgomery County	150	0.33
Elmwood Park, NJ (borough) Bergen County	65	0.33
Rockville, MD (city) Montgomery County	198	0.32
Greenwich, CT (town) Fairfield County	196	0.32
Woodmere, NY (cdp) Nassau County	54	0.32
Wheaton, MD (cdp) Montgomery County	151	0.31
Rockaway, NJ (township) Morris County	75	0.31
East Hampton, NY (town) Suffolk County	66	0.31
Lowes Island, VA (cdp) Loudoun County	33	0.31
Rye Brook, NY (village) Westchester County	29	0.31
Mansfield, NJ (township) Warren County	24	0.31
Bethesda, MD (cdp) Montgomery County	183	0.30
Mount Olive, NJ (township) Morris County	85	0.30
Roselle Park, NJ (borough) Union County	40	0.30
Salisbury, NY (cdp) Nassau County	36	0.30
Miami Shores, FL (village) Miami-Dade County	32	0.30
North Hempstead, NY (town) Nassau County	664	0.29
Davie, FL (town) Broward County	268	0.29
Burke, VA (cdp) Fairfax County	121	0.29
Central Islip, NY (cdp) Suffolk County	99	0.29
Southchase, FL (cdp) Orange County	46	0.29
Coral Springs, FL (city) Broward County	342	0.28
Miramar, FL (city) Broward County	340	0.28
Provo, UT (city) Utah County	314	0.28
Long Branch, NJ (city) Monmouth County	87	0.28
Chantilly, VA (cdp) Fairfax County	65	0.28
Mineola, NY (village) Nassau County	52	0.28
Harrison, NJ (town) Hudson County	38	0.28
Garden City Park, NY (cdp) Nassau County	22	0.28
Hillcrest, NY (cdp) Rockland County	21	0.28
Hialeah, FL (city) Miami-Dade County	602	0.27
San Mateo, CA (city) San Mateo County	258	0.27
Greenacres, FL (city) Palm Beach County	101	0.27
Springville, UT (city) Utah County	79	0.27
Ocean, NJ (township) Monmouth County	74	0.27
Hialeah Gardens, FL (city) Miami-Dade County	59	0.27
Mamaroneck, NY (village) Westchester County	52	0.27
Greenwich, CT (cdp) Fairfield County	35	0.27
Ridgefield Park, NJ (village) Bergen County	34	0.27
Wakefield, VA (cdp) Fairfax County	30	0.27
Cambridge, MA (city) Middlesex County	275	0.26
Germantown, MD (cdp) Montgomery County	228	0.26
Bayonne, NJ (city) Hudson County	167	0.26
North Miami, FL (city) Miami-Dade County	150	0.26
Olney, MD (cdp) Montgomery County	88	0.26
Cooper City, FL (city) Broward County	74	0.26
El Cerrito, CA (city) Contra Costa County	62	0.26
North Salt Lake, UT (city) Davis County	43	0.26
Newington Forest, VA (cdp) Fairfax County	32	0.26
Plantation, FL (city) Broward County	212	0.25
Brentwood, NY (cdp) Suffolk County	153	0.25
West Falls Church, VA (cdp) Fairfax County	72	0.25
Princeton, FL (cdp) Miami-Dade County	56	0.25
Seymour, CT (town) New Haven County	42	0.25
Glenmont, MD (cdp) Montgomery County	34	0.25
College Place, WA (city) Walla Walla County	22	0.25
North Logan, UT (city) Cache County	21	0.25
Williamsburg, FL (cdp) Orange County	19	0.25
Gaithersburg, MD (city) Montgomery County	143	0.24
Kearny, NJ (town) Hudson County	97	0.24
South Miami Heights, FL (cdp) Miami-Dade County	84	0.24
Long Beach, NY (city) Nassau County	80	0.24
Oceanside, NY (cdp) Nassau County	76	0.24
Fairfax, VA (ind. city) Fairfax independent city	55	0.24
Leisure City, FL (cdp) Miami-Dade County	54	0.24
East Rockaway, NY (village) Nassau County	24	0.24
Lindon, UT (city) Utah County	24	0.24
Bogota, NJ (borough) Bergen County	20	0.24
Bridgewater, MA (cdp) Plymouth County	19	0.24
Stamford, CT (city/town) Fairfield County	282	0.23

SECTION THREE

Please refer to the Explanation of Data in the front of the book for more detailed information.

Hispanic Origin

South American: Colombian

U.S. and 50 States Sorted by Population and Percent of Total Population

Place	Population	%
United States	**908,734**	**0.29**
Florida	300,414	1.60
New York	141,879	0.73
New Jersey	101,593	1.16
California	64,416	0.17
Texas	50,810	0.20
Georgia	26,013	0.27
Massachusetts	23,843	0.36
Connecticut	20,048	0.56
Illinois	19,345	0.15
North Carolina	17,648	0.19
Pennsylvania	16,525	0.13
Virginia	15,797	0.20
Maryland	12,990	0.22
South Carolina	9,436	0.20
Rhode Island	8,283	0.79
Arizona	6,706	0.10
Washington	5,560	0.08
Ohio	5,247	0.05
Nevada	5,230	0.19
Colorado	4,858	0.10
Minnesota	4,484	0.08
Michigan	3,991	0.04
Tennessee	3,695	0.06
Utah	3,467	0.13
Louisiana	3,167	0.07
Wisconsin	2,941	0.05
Indiana	2,854	0.04
Missouri	2,659	0.04
Oklahoma	2,122	0.06
Oregon	2,067	0.05
Alabama	2,052	0.04
District of Columbia	1,982	0.33
New Hampshire	1,899	0.14
Kansas	1,769	0.06
Kentucky	1,729	0.04
New Mexico	1,347	0.07
Delaware	1,248	0.14
Iowa	1,026	0.03
Mississippi	1,025	0.03
Nebraska	974	0.05
Hawaii	904	0.07
Arkansas	888	0.03
Alaska	867	0.12
Idaho	734	0.05
Maine	496	0.04
West Virginia	483	0.03
Vermont	327	0.05
Montana	288	0.03
North Dakota	244	0.04
South Dakota	186	0.02
Wyoming	178	0.03

Place	Population	%
Florida	300,414	1.60
New Jersey	101,593	1.16
Rhode Island	8,283	0.79
New York	141,879	0.73
Connecticut	20,048	0.56
Massachusetts	23,843	0.36
District of Columbia	1,982	0.33
United States	**908,734**	**0.29**
Georgia	26,013	0.27
Maryland	12,990	0.22
Texas	50,810	0.20
Virginia	15,797	0.20
South Carolina	9,436	0.20
North Carolina	17,648	0.19
Nevada	5,230	0.19
California	64,416	0.17
Illinois	19,345	0.15
New Hampshire	1,899	0.14
Delaware	1,248	0.14
Pennsylvania	16,525	0.13
Utah	3,467	0.13
Alaska	867	0.12
Arizona	6,706	0.10
Colorado	4,858	0.10
Washington	5,560	0.08
Minnesota	4,484	0.08
Louisiana	3,167	0.07
New Mexico	1,347	0.07
Hawaii	904	0.07
Tennessee	3,695	0.06
Oklahoma	2,122	0.06
Kansas	1,769	0.06
Ohio	5,247	0.05
Wisconsin	2,941	0.05
Oregon	2,067	0.05
Nebraska	974	0.05
Idaho	734	0.05
Vermont	327	0.05
Michigan	3,991	0.04
Indiana	2,854	0.04
Missouri	2,659	0.04
Alabama	2,052	0.04
Kentucky	1,729	0.04
Maine	496	0.04
North Dakota	244	0.04
Iowa	1,026	0.03
Mississippi	1,025	0.03
Arkansas	888	0.03
West Virginia	483	0.03
Montana	288	0.03
Wyoming	178	0.03
South Dakota	186	0.02

Please refer to the Explanation of Data in the front of the book for more detailed information.

Hispanic Origin

South American: Colombian

Top 150 Places Sorted by Population

Based on all places, regardless of total population

Place	Population	%
New York, NY (city) Kings County	94,723	1.16
Queens, NY (borough) Queens County	70,290	3.15
Miami, FL (city) Miami-Dade County	12,966	3.25
Elizabeth, NJ (city) Union County	10,692	8.56
Houston, TX (city) Harris County	10,226	0.49
Pembroke Pines, FL (city) Broward County	9,937	6.42
Los Angeles, CA (city) Los Angeles County	9,766	0.26
Brooklyn, NY (borough) Kings County	8,861	0.35
Hempstead, NY (town) Nassau County	8,522	1.12
Manhattan, NY (borough) New York County	8,411	0.53
Weston, FL (city) Broward County	7,637	11.69
Chicago, IL (city) Cook County	7,547	0.28
The Hammocks, FL (cdp) Miami-Dade County	6,896	13.52
Hialeah, FL (city) Miami-Dade County	6,800	3.03
Doral, FL (city) Miami-Dade County	6,731	14.73
Boston, MA (city) Suffolk County	6,649	1.08
Country Club, FL (cdp) Miami-Dade County	6,439	13.67
Miramar, FL (city) Broward County	6,230	5.10
Hollywood, FL (city) Broward County	5,583	3.97
Coral Springs, FL (city) Broward County	5,521	4.56
Paterson, NJ (city) Passaic County	5,204	3.56
Islip, NY (town) Suffolk County	5,156	1.54
Kendall, FL (cdp) Miami-Dade County	4,870	6.46
North Bergen, NJ (township) Hudson County	4,784	7.87
Fountainebleau, FL (cdp) Miami-Dade County	4,714	7.89
Orlando, FL (city) Orange County	4,688	1.97
Philadelphia, PA (city) Philadelphia County	4,675	0.31
Bronx, NY (borough) Bronx County	4,635	0.33
Sunrise, FL (city) Broward County	4,592	5.44
Miami Beach, FL (city) Miami-Dade County	4,327	4.93
Kendale Lakes, FL (cdp) Miami-Dade County	4,281	7.62
Kendall West, FL (cdp) Miami-Dade County	3,772	10.43
Tamarac, FL (city) Broward County	3,762	6.23
Davie, FL (town) Broward County	3,715	4.04
Charlotte, NC (city) Mecklenburg County	3,338	0.46
Aventura, FL (city) Miami-Dade County	3,285	9.19
Union City, NJ (city) Hudson County	3,224	4.85
Jacksonville, FL (city) Duval County	3,197	0.39
Norwalk, CT (city/town) Fairfield County	3,084	3.60
West New York, NJ (town) Hudson County	3,077	6.19
Pawtucket, RI (city) Providence County	3,056	4.30
Clifton, NJ (city) Passaic County	2,973	3.53
Brookhaven, NY (town) Suffolk County	2,970	0.61
Plantation, FL (city) Broward County	2,947	3.47
Tampa, FL (city) Hillsborough County	2,846	0.85
Dover, NJ (town) Morris County	2,767	15.24
Stamford, CT (city/town) Fairfield County	2,679	2.18
Town 'n' Country, FL (cdp) Hillsborough County	2,631	3.35
Tamiami, FL (cdp) Miami-Dade County	2,594	4.69
Staten Island, NY (borough) Richmond County	2,526	0.54
Revere, MA (city) Suffolk County	2,520	4.87
Port St. Lucie, FL (city) St. Lucie County	2,518	1.53
Kissimmee, FL (city) Osceola County	2,370	3.97
Cape Coral, FL (city) Lee County	2,313	1.50
Englewood, NJ (city) Bergen County	2,306	8.49
Alafaya, FL (cdp) Orange County	2,251	2.88
Jersey City, NJ (city) Hudson County	2,246	0.91
Meadow Woods, FL (cdp) Orange County	2,226	8.71
Margate, FL (city) Broward County	2,220	4.17
San Diego, CA (city) San Diego County	2,214	0.17
Sunny Isles Beach, FL (city) Miami-Dade County	2,175	10.44
San Antonio, TX (city) Medina County	2,139	0.16
Richmond West, FL (cdp) Miami-Dade County	2,117	6.62
The Crossings, FL (cdp) Miami-Dade County	2,106	9.25
Brentwood, NY (cdp) Suffolk County	2,083	3.43
Babylon, NY (town) Suffolk County	2,036	0.95
Oyster Bay, NY (town) Nassau County	2,035	0.69
Central Falls, RI (city) Providence County	2,018	10.41
Washington, DC (city) District of Columbia	1,982	0.33
Bridgeport, CT (city/town) Fairfield County	1,948	1.35
North Hempstead, NY (town) Nassau County	1,914	0.85
Hallandale Beach, FL (city) Broward County	1,874	5.05
Coconut Creek, FL (city) Broward County	1,857	3.51
White Plains, NY (city) Westchester County	1,838	3.23
Hackensack, NJ (city) Bergen County	1,835	4.27
Fort Lauderdale, FL (city) Broward County	1,768	1.07
Cutler Bay, FL (town) Miami-Dade County	1,731	4.30
San Francisco, CA (city) San Francisco County	1,717	0.21
Greenacres, FL (city) Palm Beach County	1,707	4.54
North Miami Beach, FL (city) Miami-Dade County	1,687	4.06
Phoenix, AZ (city) Maricopa County	1,687	0.12
Coral Gables, FL (city) Miami-Dade County	1,678	3.59
Linden, NJ (city) Union County	1,652	4.08
Three Lakes, FL (cdp) Miami-Dade County	1,619	10.76
Austin, TX (city) Travis County	1,619	0.20
Lowell, MA (city) Middlesex County	1,575	1.48
Bergenfield, NJ (borough) Bergen County	1,566	5.85
Dallas, TX (city) Dallas County	1,563	0.13
Miami Lakes, FL (town) Miami-Dade County	1,548	5.27
Homestead, FL (city) Miami-Dade County	1,540	2.54
West Palm Beach, FL (city) Palm Beach County	1,535	1.54
Yonkers, NY (city) Westchester County	1,493	0.76
North Lauderdale, FL (city) Broward County	1,481	3.61
Wellington, FL (village) Palm Beach County	1,479	2.62
New Rochelle, NY (city) Westchester County	1,451	1.88
Ojus, FL (cdp) Miami-Dade County	1,415	7.85
Boca Raton, FL (city) Palm Beach County	1,412	1.67
Newark, NJ (city) Essex County	1,393	0.50
North Miami, FL (city) Miami-Dade County	1,363	2.32
Country Walk, FL (cdp) Miami-Dade County	1,322	8.26
Las Vegas, NV (city) Clark County	1,297	0.22
Morris, NJ (town) Morris County	1,267	6.88
San Jose, CA (city) Santa Clara County	1,266	0.13
Raleigh, NC (city) Wake County	1,261	0.31
Passaic, NJ (city) Passaic County	1,251	1.79
Pompano Beach, FL (city) Broward County	1,209	1.21
Arlington, VA (cdp) Arlington County	1,204	0.58
Buenaventura Lakes, FL (cdp) Osceola County	1,198	4.59
Lodi, NJ (borough) Bergen County	1,197	4.96
Deerfield Beach, FL (city) Broward County	1,196	1.59
Southchase, FL (cdp) Orange County	1,184	7.44
Gainesville, FL (city) Alachua County	1,172	0.94
Hialeah Gardens, FL (city) Miami-Dade County	1,142	5.25
Brandon, FL (cdp) Hillsborough County	1,139	1.10
Miami Gardens, FL (city) Miami-Dade County	1,127	1.05
Fort Worth, TX (city) Tarrant County	1,093	0.15
Carrollwood, FL (cdp) Hillsborough County	1,090	3.27
Key Biscayne, FL (village) Miami-Dade County	1,083	8.77
Germantown, MD (cdp) Montgomery County	1,077	1.25
Hartford, CT (city/town) Hartford County	1,074	0.86
Greenwich, CT (town) Fairfield County	1,038	1.70
Long Beach, CA (city) Los Angeles County	1,037	0.22
Egypt Lake-Leto, FL (cdp) Hillsborough County	1,027	2.91
Southampton, NY (town) Suffolk County	1,024	1.80
South Miami Heights, FL (cdp) Miami-Dade County	1,007	2.82
Atlanta, GA (city) Fulton County	989	0.24
East Hampton, NY (town) Suffolk County	987	4.60
Union, NJ (township) Union County	972	1.72
Providence, RI (city) Providence County	969	0.54
Huntington, NY (town) Suffolk County	957	0.47
Valley Stream, NY (village) Nassau County	944	2.52
North Plainfield, NJ (borough) Somerset County	941	4.29
Piscataway, NJ (township) Middlesex County	933	1.66
Virginia Beach, VA (ind. city) Virginia Beach independent city	929	0.21
Cooper City, FL (city) Broward County	923	3.23
Guttenberg, NJ (town) Hudson County	921	8.24
Royal Palm Beach, FL (village) Palm Beach County	917	2.69
Altamonte Springs, FL (city) Seminole County	908	2.19
Riverview, FL (cdp) Hillsborough County	899	1.27
Rye, NY (town) Westchester County	891	1.94
Anaheim, CA (city) Orange County	884	0.26
Garfield, NJ (city) Bergen County	880	2.89
Dania Beach, FL (city) Broward County	877	2.96
Woodbridge, NJ (township) Middlesex County	873	0.88
Wesley Chapel, FL (cdp) Pasco County	869	1.97
University Park, FL (cdp) Miami-Dade County	865	3.20
Glenvar Heights, FL (cdp) Miami-Dade County	850	5.03
Citrus Park, FL (cdp) Hillsborough County	848	3.50
Greenburgh, NY (town) Westchester County	845	0.96
St. Petersburg, FL (city) Pinellas County	844	0.34

Please refer to the Explanation of Data in the front of the book for more detailed information.

Hispanic Origin

South American: Colombian

Top 150 Places Sorted by Percent of Total Population

Based on all places, regardless of total population

Place	Population	%
Biggs Junction, OR (cdp) Sherman County	5	22.73
Victory Gardens, NJ (borough) Morris County	330	21.71
Dover, NJ (town) Morris County	2,767	15.24
Doral, FL (city) Miami-Dade County	6,731	14.73
Country Club, FL (cdp) Miami-Dade County	6,439	13.67
The Hammocks, FL (cdp) Miami-Dade County	6,896	13.52
Weston, FL (city) Broward County	7,637	11.69
Three Lakes, FL (cdp) Miami-Dade County	1,619	10.76
Sunny Isles Beach, FL (city) Miami-Dade County	2,175	10.44
Kendall West, FL (cdp) Miami-Dade County	3,772	10.43
Central Falls, RI (city) Providence County	2,018	10.41
Wharton, NJ (borough) Morris County	672	10.30
North Bay Village, FL (city) Miami-Dade County	662	9.28
The Crossings, FL (cdp) Miami-Dade County	2,106	9.25
Aventura, FL (city) Miami-Dade County	3,285	9.19
Key Biscayne, FL (village) Miami-Dade County	1,083	8.77
Meadow Woods, FL (cdp) Orange County	2,226	8.71
Elizabeth, NJ (city) Union County	10,692	8.56
Bay Lake, FL (city) Orange County	4	8.51
Englewood, NJ (city) Bergen County	2,306	8.49
Country Walk, FL (cdp) Miami-Dade County	1,322	8.26
Guttenberg, NJ (town) Hudson County	921	8.24
Fountainebleau, FL (cdp) Miami-Dade County	4,714	7.89
North Bergen, NJ (township) Hudson County	4,784	7.87
Ojus, FL (cdp) Miami-Dade County	1,415	7.85
Kendale Lakes, FL (cdp) Miami-Dade County	4,281	7.62
Southchase, FL (cdp) Orange County	1,184	7.44
Paxton, CA (cdp) Plumas County	1	7.14
Morris, NJ (town) Morris County	1,267	6.88
East Hampton North, NY (cdp) Suffolk County	284	6.86
Virginia Gardens, FL (village) Miami-Dade County	158	6.65
Richmond West, FL (cdp) Miami-Dade County	2,117	6.62
Springs, NY (cdp) Suffolk County	430	6.52
Bay Harbor Islands, FL (town) Miami-Dade County	365	6.49
Kendall, FL (cdp) Miami-Dade County	4,870	6.46
Pembroke Pines, FL (city) Broward County	9,937	6.42
Tamarac, FL (city) Broward County	3,762	6.23
West New York, NJ (town) Hudson County	3,077	6.19
Teterboro, NJ (borough) Bergen County	4	5.97
Bergenfield, NJ (borough) Bergen County	1,566	5.85
McRae, GA (city) Telfair County	335	5.84
Hunters Creek, FL (cdp) Orange County	830	5.80
Bellerose Terrace, NY (cdp) Nassau County	124	5.64
Mine Hill, NJ (township) Morris County	203	5.56
Roselle Park, NJ (borough) Union County	726	5.46
Lake Belvedere Estates, FL (cdp) Palm Beach County	182	5.46
Sunrise, FL (city) Broward County	4,592	5.44
Miami Lakes, FL (town) Miami-Dade County	1,548	5.27
Hialeah Gardens, FL (city) Miami-Dade County	1,142	5.25
Bal Harbour, FL (village) Miami-Dade County	132	5.25
Great Pond, ME (town) Hancock County	3	5.17
Miramar, FL (city) Broward County	6,230	5.10
South Hackensack, NJ (township) Bergen County	121	5.09
Hallandale Beach, FL (city) Broward County	1,874	5.05
Glenvar Heights, FL (cdp) Miami-Dade County	850	5.03
Byram, CT (cdp) Fairfield County	206	4.97
Lodi, NJ (borough) Bergen County	1,197	4.96
Miami Beach, FL (city) Miami-Dade County	4,327	4.93
Revere, MA (city) Suffolk County	2,520	4.87
Union City, NJ (city) Hudson County	3,224	4.85
Tamiami, FL (cdp) Miami-Dade County	2,594	4.69
Ridgefield Park, NJ (village) Bergen County	587	4.61
East Hampton, NY (town) Suffolk County	987	4.60
Buenaventura Lakes, FL (cdp) Osceola County	1,198	4.59
Golden Beach, FL (town) Miami-Dade County	42	4.57
Coral Springs, FL (city) Broward County	5,521	4.56
Greenacres, FL (city) Palm Beach County	1,707	4.54
Hampton Bays, NY (cdp) Suffolk County	614	4.51
Prospect Park, NJ (borough) Passaic County	261	4.45
Fairview, NJ (borough) Bergen County	607	4.39
Bound Brook, NJ (borough) Somerset County	456	4.38
Moonachie, NJ (borough) Bergen County	117	4.32
Pawtucket, RI (city) Providence County	3,056	4.30
Cutler Bay, FL (town) Miami-Dade County	1,731	4.30
North Plainfield, NJ (borough) Somerset County	941	4.29
Hazard, NE (village) Sherman County	3	4.29
Hackensack, NJ (city) Bergen County	1,835	4.27
Bogota, NJ (borough) Bergen County	344	4.20
Margate, FL (city) Broward County	2,220	4.17
Whitestone, AK (cdp) Southeast Fairbanks Census Area	4	4.12
Miami Springs, FL (city) Miami-Dade County	568	4.11
Linden, NJ (city) Union County	1,652	4.08
Ives Estates, FL (cdp) Miami-Dade County	797	4.08
Madison, NJ (borough) Morris County	646	4.08
Southwest Ranches, FL (town) Broward County	300	4.08
North Miami Beach, FL (city) Miami-Dade County	1,687	4.06
Davie, FL (town) Broward County	3,715	4.04
Elmsford, NY (village) Westchester County	186	3.99
Hollywood, FL (city) Broward County	5,583	3.97
Kissimmee, FL (city) Osceola County	2,370	3.97
Weehawken, NJ (township) Hudson County	493	3.93
Surfside, FL (town) Miami-Dade County	225	3.92
Shinnecock Hills, NY (cdp) Suffolk County	84	3.84
Rockaway, NJ (borough) Morris County	244	3.79
Palm Springs, FL (village) Palm Beach County	704	3.72
Decatur, PA (township) Clearfield County	166	3.65
Roselle, NJ (borough) Union County	767	3.64
North Lauderdale, FL (city) Broward County	1,481	3.61
Norwalk, CT (city/town) Fairfield County	3,084	3.60
Coral Gables, FL (city) Miami-Dade County	1,678	3.59
Greenwich, CT (cdp) Fairfield County	464	3.59
Little Ferry, NJ (borough) Bergen County	380	3.58
Montauk, NY (cdp) Suffolk County	119	3.58
Paterson, NJ (city) Passaic County	5,204	3.56
Clifton, NJ (city) Passaic County	2,973	3.53
Coconut Creek, FL (city) Broward County	1,857	3.51
Citrus Park, FL (cdp) Hillsborough County	848	3.50
Sunset, FL (cdp) Miami-Dade County	572	3.49
Plantation, FL (city) Broward County	2,947	3.47
Brentwood, NY (cdp) Suffolk County	2,083	3.43
Biscayne Park, FL (village) Miami-Dade County	104	3.40
Dunellen, NJ (borough) Middlesex County	245	3.39
Bloomer, MN (township) Marshall County	3	3.37
Town 'n' Country, FL (cdp) Hillsborough County	2,631	3.35
Naranja, FL (cdp) Miami-Dade County	276	3.32
Elmwood Park, NJ (borough) Bergen County	637	3.28
Carrollwood, FL (cdp) Hillsborough County	1,090	3.27
Miami, FL (city) Miami-Dade County	12,966	3.25
White Plains, NY (city) Westchester County	1,838	3.23
Cooper City, FL (city) Broward County	923	3.23
Princeton, FL (cdp) Miami-Dade County	711	3.23
University Park, FL (cdp) Miami-Dade County	865	3.20
Queens, NY (borough) Queens County	70,290	3.15
Palmetto Estates, FL (cdp) Miami-Dade County	426	3.15
Northwest Harbor, NY (cdp) Suffolk County	103	3.11
South Bound Brook, NJ (borough) Somerset County	140	3.07
Palm Springs North, FL (cdp) Miami-Dade County	161	3.06
Netcong, NJ (borough) Morris County	99	3.06
Royal Palm Estates, FL (cdp) Palm Beach County	92	3.04
Haverhill, FL (town) Palm Beach County	57	3.04
Hialeah, FL (city) Miami-Dade County	6,800	3.03
Pinecrest, FL (village) Miami-Dade County	545	2.99
Lakewood Gardens, FL (cdp) Palm Beach County	38	2.99
Medley, FL (town) Miami-Dade County	25	2.98
Orangetree, FL (cdp) Collier County	131	2.97
Dania Beach, FL (city) Broward County	877	2.96
Egypt Lake-Leto, FL (cdp) Hillsborough County	1,027	2.91
Garfield, NJ (city) Bergen County	880	2.89
Canaan, CT (cdp) Litchfield County	35	2.89
Alafaya, FL (cdp) Orange County	2,251	2.88
Horizon West, FL (cdp) Orange County	400	2.86
Pleasanton, NM (cdp) Catron County	3	2.83
South Miami Heights, FL (cdp) Miami-Dade County	1,007	2.82
Palmetto Bay, FL (village) Miami-Dade County	661	2.82
Islandia, NY (village) Suffolk County	94	2.82
Ossining, NY (village) Westchester County	703	2.81
Albany, OK (cdp) Bryan County	4	2.80
Randolph, NJ (township) Morris County	716	2.78
Cliffside Park, NJ (borough) Bergen County	652	2.76
Greer, SC (city) Greenville County	695	2.72

Please refer to the Explanation of Data in the front of the book for more detailed information.

Hispanic Origin

South American: Colombian

Top 150 Places Sorted by Percent of Total Population

Based on places with total population of 7,500 or more

Place	Population	%
Dover, NJ (town) Morris County	2,767	15.24
Doral, FL (city) Miami-Dade County	6,731	14.73
Country Club, FL (cdp) Miami-Dade County	6,439	13.67
The Hammocks, FL (cdp) Miami-Dade County	6,896	13.52
Weston, FL (city) Broward County	7,637	11.69
Three Lakes, FL (cdp) Miami-Dade County	1,619	10.76
Sunny Isles Beach, FL (city) Miami-Dade County	2,175	10.44
Kendall West, FL (cdp) Miami-Dade County	3,772	10.43
Central Falls, RI (city) Providence County	2,018	10.41
The Crossings, FL (cdp) Miami-Dade County	2,106	9.25
Aventura, FL (city) Miami-Dade County	3,285	9.19
Key Biscayne, FL (village) Miami-Dade County	1,083	8.77
Meadow Woods, FL (cdp) Orange County	2,226	8.71
Elizabeth, NJ (city) Union County	10,692	8.56
Englewood, NJ (city) Bergen County	2,306	8.49
Country Walk, FL (cdp) Miami-Dade County	1,322	8.26
Guttenberg, NJ (town) Hudson County	921	8.24
Fountainebleau, FL (cdp) Miami-Dade County	4,714	7.89
North Bergen, NJ (township) Hudson County	4,784	7.87
Ojus, FL (cdp) Miami-Dade County	1,415	7.85
Kendale Lakes, FL (cdp) Miami-Dade County	4,281	7.62
Southchase, FL (cdp) Orange County	1,184	7.44
Morris, NJ (town) Morris County	1,267	6.88
Richmond West, FL (cdp) Miami-Dade County	2,117	6.62
Kendall, FL (cdp) Miami-Dade County	4,870	6.46
Pembroke Pines, FL (city) Broward County	9,937	6.42
Tamarac, FL (city) Broward County	3,762	6.23
West New York, NJ (town) Hudson County	3,077	6.19
Bergenfield, NJ (borough) Bergen County	1,566	5.85
Hunters Creek, FL (cdp) Orange County	830	5.80
Roselle Park, NJ (borough) Union County	726	5.46
Sunrise, FL (city) Broward County	4,592	5.44
Miami Lakes, FL (town) Miami-Dade County	1,548	5.27
Hialeah Gardens, FL (city) Miami-Dade County	1,142	5.25
Miramar, FL (city) Broward County	6,230	5.10
Hallandale Beach, FL (city) Broward County	1,874	5.05
Glenvar Heights, FL (cdp) Miami-Dade County	850	5.03
Lodi, NJ (borough) Bergen County	1,197	4.96
Miami Beach, FL (city) Miami-Dade County	4,327	4.93
Revere, MA (city) Suffolk County	2,520	4.87
Union City, NJ (city) Hudson County	3,224	4.85
Tamiami, FL (cdp) Miami-Dade County	2,594	4.69
Ridgefield Park, NJ (village) Bergen County	587	4.61
East Hampton, NY (town) Suffolk County	987	4.60
Buenaventura Lakes, FL (cdp) Osceola County	1,198	4.59
Coral Springs, FL (city) Broward County	5,521	4.56
Greenacres, FL (city) Palm Beach County	1,707	4.54
Hampton Bays, NY (cdp) Suffolk County	614	4.51
Fairview, NJ (borough) Bergen County	607	4.39
Bound Brook, NJ (borough) Somerset County	456	4.38
Pawtucket, RI (city) Providence County	3,056	4.30
Cutler Bay, FL (town) Miami-Dade County	1,731	4.30
North Plainfield, NJ (borough) Somerset County	941	4.29
Hackensack, NJ (city) Bergen County	1,835	4.27
Bogota, NJ (borough) Bergen County	344	4.20
Margate, FL (city) Broward County	2,220	4.17
Miami Springs, FL (city) Miami-Dade County	568	4.11
Linden, NJ (city) Union County	1,652	4.08
Ives Estates, FL (cdp) Miami-Dade County	797	4.08
Madison, NJ (borough) Morris County	646	4.08
North Miami Beach, FL (city) Miami-Dade County	1,687	4.06
Davie, FL (town) Broward County	3,715	4.04
Hollywood, FL (city) Broward County	5,583	3.97
Kissimmee, FL (city) Osceola County	2,370	3.97
Weehawken, NJ (township) Hudson County	493	3.93
Palm Springs, FL (village) Palm Beach County	704	3.72
Roselle, NJ (borough) Union County	767	3.64
North Lauderdale, FL (city) Broward County	1,481	3.61
Norwalk, CT (city/town) Fairfield County	3,084	3.60
Coral Gables, FL (city) Miami-Dade County	1,678	3.59
Greenwich, CT (cdp) Fairfield County	464	3.59
Little Ferry, NJ (borough) Bergen County	380	3.58
Paterson, NJ (city) Passaic County	5,204	3.56
Clifton, NJ (city) Passaic County	2,973	3.53
Coconut Creek, FL (city) Broward County	1,857	3.51

Place	Population	%
Citrus Park, FL (cdp) Hillsborough County	848	3.50
Sunset, FL (cdp) Miami-Dade County	572	3.49
Plantation, FL (city) Broward County	2,947	3.47
Brentwood, NY (cdp) Suffolk County	2,083	3.43
Town 'n' Country, FL (cdp) Hillsborough County	2,631	3.35
Naranja, FL (cdp) Miami-Dade County	276	3.32
Elmwood Park, NJ (borough) Bergen County	637	3.28
Carrollwood, FL (cdp) Hillsborough County	1,090	3.27
Miami, FL (city) Miami-Dade County	12,966	3.25
White Plains, NY (city) Westchester County	1,838	3.23
Cooper City, FL (city) Broward County	923	3.23
Princeton, FL (cdp) Miami-Dade County	711	3.23
University Park, FL (cdp) Miami-Dade County	865	3.20
Queens, NY (borough) Queens County	70,290	3.15
Palmetto Estates, FL (cdp) Miami-Dade County	426	3.15
Hialeah, FL (city) Miami-Dade County	6,800	3.03
Pinecrest, FL (village) Miami-Dade County	545	2.99
Dania Beach, FL (city) Broward County	877	2.96
Egypt Lake-Leto, FL (cdp) Hillsborough County	1,027	2.91
Garfield, NJ (city) Bergen County	880	2.89
Alafaya, FL (cdp) Orange County	2,251	2.88
Horizon West, FL (cdp) Orange County	400	2.86
South Miami Heights, FL (cdp) Miami-Dade County	1,007	2.82
Palmetto Bay, FL (village) Miami-Dade County	661	2.82
Ossining, NY (village) Westchester County	703	2.81
Randolph, NJ (township) Morris County	716	2.78
Cliffside Park, NJ (borough) Bergen County	652	2.76
Greer, SC (city) Greenville County	695	2.72
Royal Palm Beach, FL (village) Palm Beach County	917	2.69
Ventnor City, NJ (city) Atlantic County	284	2.67
North Bay Shore, NY (cdp) Suffolk County	504	2.66
Dumont, NJ (borough) Bergen County	465	2.66
Maywood, NJ (borough) Bergen County	251	2.63
Wellington, FL (village) Palm Beach County	1,479	2.62
Sweetwater, FL (city) Miami-Dade County	354	2.62
Haledon, NJ (borough) Passaic County	218	2.62
Miami Shores, FL (village) Miami-Dade County	270	2.57
Homestead, FL (city) Miami-Dade County	1,540	2.54
Valley Stream, NY (village) Nassau County	944	2.52
Middlesex, NJ (borough) Middlesex County	344	2.52
Port Chester, NY (village) Westchester County	724	2.50
Valley Falls, RI (cdp) Providence County	287	2.49
Olympia Heights, FL (cdp) Miami-Dade County	331	2.45
Azalea Park, FL (cdp) Orange County	308	2.45
Westwood Lakes, FL (cdp) Miami-Dade County	289	2.44
South Miami, FL (city) Miami-Dade County	283	2.43
Rockaway, NJ (township) Morris County	566	2.34
Palisades Park, NJ (borough) Bergen County	459	2.34
North Miami, FL (city) Miami-Dade County	1,363	2.32
Mauldin, SC (city) Greenville County	531	2.32
Westchester, FL (cdp) Miami-Dade County	665	2.23
Leonia, NJ (borough) Bergen County	199	2.23
Berea, SC (cdp) Greenville County	317	2.22
Woodland Park, NJ (borough) Passaic County	262	2.22
Budd Lake, NJ (cdp) Morris County	199	2.22
Boonton, NJ (town) Morris County	185	2.22
Altamonte Springs, FL (city) Seminole County	908	2.19
Stamford, CT (city/town) Fairfield County	2,679	2.18
Ridgefield, NJ (borough) Bergen County	241	2.18
Coral Terrace, FL (cdp) Miami-Dade County	528	2.17
Williamsburg, FL (cdp) Orange County	165	2.16
Ossining, NY (town) Westchester County	805	2.14
Mineola, NY (village) Nassau County	399	2.12
East Rutherford, NJ (borough) Bergen County	189	2.12
Elmont, NY (cdp) Nassau County	698	2.10
Four Corners, FL (cdp) Lake County	540	2.07
Central Islip, NY (cdp) Suffolk County	711	2.06
Parkland, FL (city) Broward County	492	2.05
Northdale, FL (cdp) Hillsborough County	452	2.05
Casselberry, FL (city) Seminole County	533	2.03
Mount Kisco, NY (town/village) Westchester County	221	2.03
Kenilworth, NJ (borough) Union County	158	2.00
Orlando, FL (city) Orange County	4,688	1.97
Wesley Chapel, FL (cdp) Pasco County	869	1.97
Rye, NY (town) Westchester County	891	1.94

SECTION THREE

Please refer to the Explanation of Data in the front of the book for more detailed information.

Hispanic Origin

South American: Ecuadorian

U.S. and 50 States Sorted by Population and Percent of Total Population

Place	Population	%
United States	**564,631**	**0.18**
New York	228,216	1.18
New Jersey	100,480	1.14
Florida	60,574	0.32
California	35,750	0.10
Connecticut	23,677	0.66
Illinois	22,816	0.18
Texas	10,793	0.04
Pennsylvania	10,680	0.08
North Carolina	8,110	0.09
Massachusetts	7,592	0.12
Minnesota	7,290	0.14
Maryland	7,076	0.12
Virginia	6,902	0.09
Georgia	4,886	0.05
Arizona	2,516	0.04
Ohio	2,090	0.02
Nevada	2,045	0.08
Utah	2,026	0.07
Washington	1,855	0.03
South Carolina	1,602	0.03
Colorado	1,375	0.03
Michigan	1,312	0.01
Tennessee	1,151	0.02
Rhode Island	1,128	0.11
Indiana	1,092	0.02
Louisiana	1,069	0.02
Missouri	937	0.02
Wisconsin	886	0.02
Oregon	851	0.02
Iowa	795	0.03
District of Columbia	707	0.12
Kansas	701	0.02
Kentucky	615	0.01
New Hampshire	595	0.05
New Mexico	548	0.03
Delaware	545	0.06
Oklahoma	474	0.01
Alabama	466	0.01
Hawaii	362	0.03
Arkansas	302	0.01
Mississippi	298	0.01
Idaho	274	0.02
Nebraska	233	0.01
Alaska	189	0.03
Maine	178	0.01
West Virginia	155	0.01
Vermont	125	0.02
Montana	97	0.01
Wyoming	81	0.01
South Dakota	59	0.01
North Dakota	55	0.01

Place	Population	%
New York	228,216	1.18
New Jersey	100,480	1.14
Connecticut	23,677	0.66
Florida	60,574	0.32
United States	**564,631**	**0.18**
Illinois	22,816	0.18
Minnesota	7,290	0.14
Massachusetts	7,592	0.12
Maryland	7,076	0.12
District of Columbia	707	0.12
Rhode Island	1,128	0.11
California	35,750	0.10
North Carolina	8,110	0.09
Virginia	6,902	0.09
Pennsylvania	10,680	0.08
Nevada	2,045	0.08
Utah	2,026	0.07
Delaware	545	0.06
Georgia	4,886	0.05
New Hampshire	595	0.05
Texas	10,793	0.04
Arizona	2,516	0.04
Washington	1,855	0.03
South Carolina	1,602	0.03
Colorado	1,375	0.03
Iowa	795	0.03
New Mexico	548	0.03
Hawaii	362	0.03
Alaska	189	0.03
Ohio	2,090	0.02
Tennessee	1,151	0.02
Indiana	1,092	0.02
Louisiana	1,069	0.02
Missouri	937	0.02
Wisconsin	886	0.02
Oregon	851	0.02
Kansas	701	0.02
Idaho	274	0.02
Vermont	125	0.02
Michigan	1,312	0.01
Kentucky	615	0.01
Oklahoma	474	0.01
Alabama	466	0.01
Arkansas	302	0.01
Mississippi	298	0.01
Nebraska	233	0.01
Maine	178	0.01
West Virginia	155	0.01
Montana	97	0.01
Wyoming	81	0.01
South Dakota	59	0.01
North Dakota	55	0.01

Please refer to the Explanation of Data in the front of the book for more detailed information.

Hispanic Origin

South American: Ecuadorian

Top 150 Places Sorted by Population

Based on all places, regardless of total population

Place	Population	%
New York, NY (city) Kings County	167,209	2.05
Queens, NY (borough) Queens County	98,512	4.42
Brooklyn, NY (borough) Kings County	28,684	1.15
Bronx, NY (borough) Bronx County	23,206	1.68
Newark, NJ (city) Essex County	16,847	6.08
Chicago, IL (city) Cook County	15,466	0.57
Manhattan, NY (borough) New York County	14,132	0.89
Los Angeles, CA (city) Los Angeles County	7,314	0.19
Brookhaven, NY (town) Suffolk County	6,437	1.32
Union City, NJ (city) Hudson County	6,135	9.23
Danbury, CT (city/town) Fairfield County	6,125	7.57
Hempstead, NY (town) Nassau County	5,881	0.77
Jersey City, NJ (city) Hudson County	5,754	2.32
Elizabeth, NJ (city) Union County	5,591	4.47
Islip, NY (town) Suffolk County	5,323	1.59
North Bergen, NJ (township) Hudson County	5,064	8.33
Ossining, NY (town) Westchester County	4,988	13.24
Ossining, NY (village) Westchester County	4,840	19.31
Minneapolis, MN (city) Hennepin County	4,792	1.25
Hackensack, NJ (city) Bergen County	4,291	9.98
Peekskill, NY (city) Westchester County	3,490	14.80
West New York, NJ (town) Hudson County	3,348	6.74
Yonkers, NY (city) Westchester County	3,271	1.67
Charlotte, NC (city) Mecklenburg County	3,008	0.41
Ramapo, NY (town) Rockland County	2,915	2.30
Rye, NY (town) Westchester County	2,901	6.32
Belleville, NJ (township) Essex County	2,824	7.86
Miami, FL (city) Miami-Dade County	2,777	0.70
Port Chester, NY (village) Westchester County	2,774	9.58
Spring Valley, NY (village) Rockland County	2,681	8.55
Staten Island, NY (borough) Richmond County	2,675	0.57
East Hampton, NY (town) Suffolk County	2,319	10.81
Stamford, CT (city/town) Fairfield County	2,313	1.89
Kearny, NJ (town) Hudson County	2,230	5.48
Mount Pleasant, NY (town) Westchester County	2,090	4.78
North Plainfield, NJ (borough) Somerset County	2,063	9.40
Plainfield, NJ (city) Union County	2,061	4.14
Brentwood, NY (cdp) Suffolk County	1,985	3.27
New Haven, CT (city/town) New Haven County	1,978	1.52
North Hempstead, NY (town) Nassau County	1,966	0.87
Bridgeport, CT (city/town) Fairfield County	1,950	1.35
East Windsor, NJ (township) Mercer County	1,780	6.55
Pembroke Pines, FL (city) Broward County	1,732	1.12
Sleepy Hollow, NY (village) Westchester County	1,731	17.54
Bloomfield, NJ (township) Essex County	1,635	3.46
Patchogue, NY (village) Suffolk County	1,616	13.70
Hialeah, FL (city) Miami-Dade County	1,606	0.71
Houston, TX (city) Harris County	1,557	0.07
Philadelphia, PA (city) Philadelphia County	1,542	0.10
Greenburgh, NY (town) Westchester County	1,434	1.62
Babylon, NY (town) Suffolk County	1,348	0.63
Doral, FL (city) Miami-Dade County	1,248	2.73
Paterson, NJ (city) Passaic County	1,243	0.85
Allentown, PA (city) Lehigh County	1,241	1.05
City of Orange, NJ (township) Essex County	1,210	4.02
Hollywood, FL (city) Broward County	1,203	0.85
Springs, NY (cdp) Suffolk County	1,137	17.25
Miramar, FL (city) Broward County	1,132	0.93
Southampton, NY (town) Suffolk County	1,102	1.94
Oyster Bay, NY (town) Nassau County	1,082	0.37
East Patchogue, NY (cdp) Suffolk County	1,057	4.70
Harrison, NJ (town) Hudson County	1,056	7.75
Clarkstown, NY (town) Rockland County	1,051	1.25
Orlando, FL (city) Orange County	1,039	0.44
Bay Shore, NY (cdp) Suffolk County	1,038	3.94
Norwalk, CT (city/town) Fairfield County	1,027	1.20
Dover, NJ (town) Morris County	1,016	5.60
White Plains, NY (city) Westchester County	1,001	1.76
Weston, FL (city) Broward County	1,000	1.53
Sunrise, FL (city) Broward County	995	1.18
Irvington, NJ (township) Essex County	993	1.84
Clifton, NJ (city) Passaic County	993	1.18
Waterbury, CT (city/town) New Haven County	972	0.88
Coral Springs, FL (city) Broward County	956	0.79
Worcester, MA (city) Worcester County	953	0.53
Fountainebleau, FL (cdp) Miami-Dade County	914	1.53
Cortlandt, NY (town) Westchester County	903	2.17
The Hammocks, FL (cdp) Miami-Dade County	868	1.70
Guttenberg, NJ (town) Hudson County	849	7.60
Union, NJ (township) Union County	846	1.49
Miami Beach, FL (city) Miami-Dade County	830	0.95
Twin Rivers, NJ (cdp) Mercer County	829	11.14
Tampa, FL (city) Hillsborough County	814	0.24
Jacksonville, FL (city) Duval County	808	0.10
Trenton, NJ (city) Mercer County	802	0.94
Upper Darby, PA (township) Delaware County	783	0.95
Hightstown, NJ (borough) Mercer County	775	14.11
Davie, FL (town) Broward County	774	0.84
Country Club, FL (cdp) Miami-Dade County	768	1.63
Kendall, FL (cdp) Miami-Dade County	766	1.02
Passaic, NJ (city) Passaic County	761	1.09
Baltimore, MD (city) Baltimore city County	755	0.12
San Diego, CA (city) San Diego County	737	0.06
Boston, MA (city) Suffolk County	732	0.12
Port St. Lucie, FL (city) St. Lucie County	718	0.44
East Hampton North, NY (cdp) Suffolk County	717	17.31
Bayonne, NJ (city) Hudson County	709	1.12
Washington, DC (city) District of Columbia	707	0.12
Lodi, NJ (borough) Bergen County	682	2.83
Long Beach, CA (city) Los Angeles County	679	0.15
Downey, CA (city) Los Angeles County	678	0.61
Central Islip, NY (cdp) Suffolk County	676	1.96
Haverstraw, NY (town) Rockland County	669	1.83
Valley Stream, NY (village) Nassau County	650	1.73
Hamilton, NJ (township) Mercer County	650	0.73
North Bay Shore, NY (cdp) Suffolk County	641	3.38
Hempstead, NY (village) Nassau County	641	1.19
Huntington, NY (town) Suffolk County	637	0.31
Torrington, CT (city/town) Litchfield County	633	1.74
Providence, RI (city) Providence County	629	0.35
Phoenix, AZ (city) Maricopa County	628	0.04
Plantation, FL (city) Broward County	624	0.73
West Haven, CT (city/town) New Haven County	621	1.12
Garfield, NJ (city) Bergen County	619	2.03
West Orange, NJ (township) Essex County	599	1.30
Woodbridge, NJ (township) Middlesex County	599	0.60
Lawrence, MA (city) Essex County	597	0.78
San Francisco, CA (city) San Francisco County	577	0.07
Linden, NJ (city) Union County	563	1.39
Glendale, CA (city) Los Angeles County	542	0.28
Cape Coral, FL (city) Lee County	540	0.35
North Patchogue, NY (cdp) Suffolk County	537	7.41
Morris, NJ (town) Morris County	537	2.92
Las Vegas, NV (city) Clark County	537	0.09
Kissimmee, FL (city) Osceola County	533	0.89
Kendale Lakes, FL (cdp) Miami-Dade County	527	0.94
Meadow Woods, FL (cdp) Orange County	526	2.06
East Haven, CT (cdp/town) New Haven County	518	1.77
Fairview, NJ (borough) Bergen County	517	3.74
Tamarac, FL (city) Broward County	516	0.85
Milford, MA (cdp) Worcester County	509	2.03
Milford, MA (town) Worcester County	509	1.82
Santa Clarita, CA (city) Los Angeles County	509	0.29
Columbus, OH (city) Franklin County	491	0.06
Alafaya, FL (cdp) Orange County	489	0.63
Kendall West, FL (cdp) Miami-Dade County	487	1.35
Medford, NY (cdp) Suffolk County	480	1.99
Tamiami, FL (cdp) Miami-Dade County	480	0.87
East Newark, NJ (borough) Hudson County	478	19.87
Haverstraw, NY (village) Rockland County	474	3.98
San Antonio, TX (city) Medina County	471	0.04
Meriden, CT (city/town) New Haven County	470	0.77
Hillside, NJ (township) Union County	461	2.15
Town 'n' Country, FL (cdp) Hillsborough County	454	0.58
Arlington, VA (cdp) Arlington County	452	0.22
North Bellport, NY (cdp) Suffolk County	443	3.84
Freeport, NY (village) Nassau County	432	1.01
Elmont, NY (cdp) Nassau County	426	1.28
Anaheim, CA (city) Orange County	417	0.12
Tarrytown, NY (village) Westchester County	416	3.69

Please refer to the Explanation of Data in the front of the book for more detailed information.

Hispanic Origin

South American: Ecuadorian

Top 150 Places Sorted by Percent of Total Population

Based on all places, regardless of total population

Place	Population	%
East Newark, NJ (borough) Hudson County	478	19.87
Ossining, NY (village) Westchester County	4,840	19.31
Sleepy Hollow, NY (village) Westchester County	1,731	17.54
East Hampton North, NY (cdp) Suffolk County	717	17.31
Springs, NY (cdp) Suffolk County	1,137	17.25
Peekskill, NY (city) Westchester County	3,490	14.80
Hightstown, NJ (borough) Mercer County	775	14.11
Patchogue, NY (village) Suffolk County	1,616	13.70
Ossining, NY (town) Westchester County	4,988	13.24
Twin Rivers, NJ (cdp) Mercer County	829	11.14
East Hampton, NY (town) Suffolk County	2,319	10.81
Hackensack, NJ (city) Bergen County	4,291	9.98
Silver Lake, NJ (cdp) Essex County	409	9.64
Port Chester, NY (village) Westchester County	2,774	9.58
North Plainfield, NJ (borough) Somerset County	2,063	9.40
Union City, NJ (city) Hudson County	6,135	9.23
Spring Valley, NY (village) Rockland County	2,681	8.55
North Bergen, NJ (township) Hudson County	5,064	8.33
Belleville, NJ (township) Essex County	2,824	7.86
Harrison, NJ (town) Hudson County	1,056	7.75
Guttenberg, NJ (town) Hudson County	849	7.60
Danbury, CT (city/town) Fairfield County	6,125	7.57
Elmsford, NY (village) Westchester County	350	7.50
Fairview, NY (cdp) Westchester County	232	7.49
North Patchogue, NY (cdp) Suffolk County	537	7.41
South Hackensack, NJ (township) Bergen County	162	6.81
West New York, NJ (town) Hudson County	3,348	6.74
East Windsor, NJ (township) Mercer County	1,780	6.55
Rye, NY (town) Westchester County	2,901	6.32
Newark, NJ (city) Essex County	16,847	6.08
Teterboro, NJ (borough) Bergen County	4	5.97
Wainscott, NY (cdp) Suffolk County	38	5.85
Buchanan, NY (village) Westchester County	128	5.74
Dover, NJ (town) Morris County	1,016	5.60
Kearny, NJ (town) Hudson County	2,230	5.48
Bedford Hills, NY (cdp) Westchester County	164	5.46
Shinnecock Hills, NY (cdp) Suffolk County	117	5.35
Danforth, MN (township) Pine County	4	5.13
Northwest Harbor, NY (cdp) Suffolk County	166	5.00
Mount Pleasant, NY (town) Westchester County	2,090	4.78
East Patchogue, NY (cdp) Suffolk County	1,057	4.70
Moonachie, NJ (borough) Bergen County	123	4.54
Elizabeth, NJ (city) Union County	5,591	4.47
Queens, NY (borough) Queens County	98,512	4.42
Baxter Estates, NY (village) Nassau County	43	4.30
Wappingers Falls, NY (village) Dutchess County	235	4.26
Montauk, NY (cdp) Suffolk County	140	4.21
Amagansett, NY (cdp) Suffolk County	49	4.21
Plainfield, NJ (city) Union County	2,061	4.14
City of Orange, NJ (township) Essex County	1,210	4.02
Haverstraw, NY (village) Rockland County	474	3.98
Victory Gardens, NJ (borough) Morris County	60	3.95
Bay Shore, NY (cdp) Suffolk County	1,038	3.94
Roslyn, NY (village) Nassau County	108	3.90
North Bellport, NY (cdp) Suffolk County	443	3.84
Bridgehampton, NY (cdp) Suffolk County	66	3.76
Fairview, NJ (borough) Bergen County	517	3.74
Wharton, NJ (borough) Morris County	243	3.73
Millbourne, PA (borough) Delaware County	43	3.71
Tarrytown, NY (village) Westchester County	416	3.69
Pleasant Valley, WI (town) St. Croix County	19	3.69
Mount Kisco, NY (town/village) Westchester County	397	3.65
Bogota, NJ (borough) Bergen County	298	3.64
Tuckahoe, NY (cdp) Suffolk County	49	3.57
Bloomfield, NJ (township) Essex County	1,635	3.46
North Bay Shore, NY (cdp) Suffolk County	641	3.38
Brentwood, NY (cdp) Suffolk County	1,985	3.27
Weehawken, NJ (township) Hudson County	410	3.27
Ridgefield Park, NJ (village) Bergen County	415	3.26
Manorhaven, NY (village) Nassau County	213	3.25
Croton-on-Hudson, NY (village) Westchester County	257	3.18
East Hampton, NY (village) Suffolk County	34	3.14
Montrose, NY (cdp) Westchester County	84	3.08
Greenvale, NY (cdp) Nassau County	33	3.02
Saybrook Manor, CT (cdp) Middlesex County	31	2.95
Morris, NJ (town) Morris County	537	2.92
Virginia Gardens, FL (village) Miami-Dade County	69	2.91
Hampton Bays, NY (cdp) Suffolk County	393	2.89
Southampton, NY (village) Suffolk County	90	2.89
Lodi, NJ (borough) Bergen County	682	2.83
Dunellen, NJ (borough) Middlesex County	203	2.81
Cherokee City, AR (cdp) Benton County	2	2.78
Flanders, NY (cdp) Suffolk County	124	2.77
Pleasantville, NY (village) Westchester County	193	2.75
Doral, FL (city) Miami-Dade County	1,248	2.73
Brewster, NY (village) Putnam County	65	2.72
Islandia, NY (village) Suffolk County	90	2.70
North Sea, NY (cdp) Suffolk County	113	2.53
Little Ferry, NJ (borough) Bergen County	268	2.52
North Lynbrook, NY (cdp) Nassau County	19	2.40
Bethel, CT (cdp) Fairfield County	226	2.37
Riverside, NJ (township) Burlington County	190	2.35
Jersey City, NJ (city) Hudson County	5,754	2.32
North Arlington, NJ (borough) Bergen County	357	2.32
Ramapo, NY (town) Rockland County	2,915	2.30
Finesville, NJ (cdp) Warren County	4	2.29
Byram, CT (cdp) Fairfield County	94	2.27
Sag Harbor, NY (village) Suffolk County	49	2.26
Brookeville, MD (town) Montgomery County	3	2.24
Roselle Park, NJ (borough) Union County	297	2.23
Cloud Lake, FL (town) Palm Beach County	3	2.22
Rifton, NY (cdp) Ulster County	10	2.19
Cross Creek, PA (cdp) Washington County	3	2.19
Cortlandt, NY (town) Westchester County	903	2.17
Hillside, NJ (township) Union County	461	2.15
Shrub Oak, NY (cdp) Westchester County	43	2.14
Carlstadt, NJ (borough) Bergen County	130	2.12
Branford Center, CT (cdp) New Haven County	122	2.10
Columbia Heights, MN (city) Anoka County	404	2.07
Meadow Woods, FL (cdp) Orange County	526	2.06
New York, NY (city) Kings County	167,209	2.05
Baywood, NY (cdp) Suffolk County	150	2.04
Garfield, NJ (city) Bergen County	619	2.03
Milford, MA (cdp) Worcester County	509	2.03
Flower Hill, NY (village) Nassau County	94	2.02
Verplanck, NY (cdp) Westchester County	35	2.02
Medford, NY (cdp) Suffolk County	480	1.99
Hacketts, NJ (town) Warren County	193	1.98
Central Islip, NY (cdp) Suffolk County	676	1.96
Lyndhurst, NJ (township) Bergen County	403	1.96
Ansonia, CT (city/town) New Haven County	376	1.95
Southampton, NY (town) Suffolk County	1,102	1.94
Stamford, CT (city/town) Fairfield County	2,313	1.89
Port Washington, NY (cdp) Nassau County	299	1.89
Kenvil, NJ (cdp) Morris County	57	1.89
Nanuet, NY (cdp) Rockland County	337	1.88
Chappaqua, NY (cdp) Westchester County	27	1.88
Irvington, NJ (township) Essex County	993	1.84
Haverstraw, NY (town) Rockland County	669	1.83
Gordon Heights, NY (cdp) Suffolk County	74	1.83
Corwin Springs, MT (cdp) Park County	2	1.83
Milford, MA (town) Worcester County	509	1.82
Westbrook Center, CT (cdp) Middlesex County	44	1.82
Ridgefield, NJ (borough) Bergen County	199	1.80
Bound Brook, NJ (borough) Somerset County	186	1.79
New Milford, CT (cdp) Litchfield County	117	1.79
Great Barrington, MA (cdp) Berkshire County	40	1.79
South Bound Brook, NJ (borough) Somerset County	81	1.78
Clinton, CT (cdp) Middlesex County	60	1.78
East Haven, CT (cdp/town) New Haven County	518	1.77
White Plains, NY (city) Westchester County	1,001	1.76
Bernardsville, NJ (borough) Somerset County	136	1.76
Cliffside Park, NJ (borough) Bergen County	414	1.75
Padre Ranchitos, AZ (cdp) Yuma County	3	1.75
Torrington, CT (city/town) Litchfield County	633	1.74
Secaucus, NJ (town) Hudson County	283	1.74
Dover Plains, NY (cdp) Dutchess County	23	1.74
Valley Stream, NY (village) Nassau County	650	1.73
Beattystown, NJ (cdp) Warren County	79	1.73
Derby, CT (city/town) New Haven County	221	1.71

Please refer to the Explanation of Data in the front of the book for more detailed information.

Hispanic Origin

South American: Ecuadorian

Top 150 Places Sorted by Percent of Total Population

Based on places with total population of 7,500 or more

Place	Population	%
Ossining, NY (village) Westchester County	4,840	19.31
Sleepy Hollow, NY (village) Westchester County	1,731	17.54
Peekskill, NY (city) Westchester County	3,490	14.80
Patchogue, NY (village) Suffolk County	1,616	13.70
Ossining, NY (town) Westchester County	4,988	13.24
East Hampton, NY (town) Suffolk County	2,319	10.81
Hackensack, NJ (city) Bergen County	4,291	9.98
Port Chester, NY (village) Westchester County	2,774	9.58
North Plainfield, NJ (borough) Somerset County	2,063	9.40
Union City, NJ (city) Hudson County	6,135	9.23
Spring Valley, NY (village) Rockland County	2,681	8.55
North Bergen, NJ (township) Hudson County	5,064	8.33
Belleville, NJ (township) Essex County	2,824	7.86
Harrison, NJ (town) Hudson County	1,056	7.75
Guttenberg, NJ (town) Hudson County	849	7.60
Danbury, CT (city/town) Fairfield County	6,125	7.57
West New York, NJ (town) Hudson County	3,348	6.74
East Windsor, NJ (township) Mercer County	1,780	6.55
Rye, NY (town) Westchester County	2,901	6.32
Newark, NJ (city) Essex County	16,847	6.08
Dover, NJ (town) Morris County	1,016	5.60
Kearny, NJ (town) Hudson County	2,230	5.48
Mount Pleasant, NY (town) Westchester County	2,090	4.78
East Patchogue, NY (cdp) Suffolk County	1,057	4.70
Elizabeth, NJ (city) Union County	5,591	4.47
Queens, NY (borough) Queens County	98,512	4.42
Plainfield, NJ (city) Union County	2,061	4.14
City of Orange, NJ (township) Essex County	1,210	4.02
Haverstraw, NY (village) Rockland County	474	3.98
Bay Shore, NY (cdp) Suffolk County	1,038	3.94
North Bellport, NY (cdp) Suffolk County	443	3.84
Fairview, NJ (borough) Bergen County	517	3.74
Tarrytown, NY (village) Westchester County	416	3.69
Mount Kisco, NY (town/village) Westchester County	397	3.65
Bogota, NJ (borough) Bergen County	298	3.64
Bloomfield, NJ (township) Essex County	1,635	3.46
North Bay Shore, NY (cdp) Suffolk County	641	3.38
Brentwood, NY (cdp) Suffolk County	1,985	3.27
Weehawken, NJ (township) Hudson County	410	3.27
Ridgefield Park, NJ (village) Bergen County	415	3.26
Croton-on-Hudson, NY (village) Westchester County	257	3.18
Morris, NJ (town) Morris County	537	2.92
Hampton Bays, NY (cdp) Suffolk County	393	2.89
Lodi, NJ (borough) Bergen County	682	2.83
Doral, FL (city) Miami-Dade County	1,248	2.73
Little Ferry, NJ (borough) Bergen County	268	2.52
Bethel, CT (cdp) Fairfield County	226	2.37
Riverside, NJ (township) Burlington County	190	2.35
Jersey City, NJ (city) Hudson County	5,754	2.32
North Arlington, NJ (borough) Bergen County	357	2.32
Ramapo, NY (town) Rockland County	2,915	2.30
Roselle Park, NJ (borough) Union County	297	2.23
Cortlandt, NY (town) Westchester County	903	2.17
Hillside, NJ (township) Union County	461	2.15
Columbia Heights, MN (city) Anoka County	404	2.07
Meadow Woods, FL (cdp) Orange County	526	2.06
New York, NY (city) Kings County	167,209	2.05
Garfield, NJ (city) Bergen County	619	2.03
Milford, MA (cdp) Worcester County	509	2.03
Medford, NY (cdp) Suffolk County	480	1.99
Hacketts, NJ (town) Warren County	193	1.98
Central Islip, NY (cdp) Suffolk County	676	1.96
Lyndhurst, NJ (township) Bergen County	403	1.96
Ansonia, CT (city/town) New Haven County	376	1.95
Southampton, NY (town) Suffolk County	1,102	1.94
Stamford, CT (city/town) Fairfield County	2,313	1.89
Port Washington, NY (cdp) Nassau County	299	1.89
Nanuet, NY (cdp) Rockland County	337	1.88
Irvington, NJ (township) Essex County	993	1.84
Haverstraw, NY (town) Rockland County	669	1.83
Milford, MA (town) Worcester County	509	1.82
Ridgefield, NJ (borough) Bergen County	199	1.80
Bound Brook, NJ (borough) Somerset County	186	1.79
East Haven, CT (cdp/town) New Haven County	518	1.77
White Plains, NY (city) Westchester County	1,001	1.76
Bernardsville, NJ (borough) Somerset County	136	1.76
Cliffside Park, NJ (borough) Bergen County	414	1.75
Torrington, CT (city/town) Litchfield County	633	1.74
Secaucus, NJ (town) Hudson County	283	1.74
Valley Stream, NY (village) Nassau County	650	1.73
Derby, CT (city/town) New Haven County	221	1.71
The Hammocks, FL (cdp) Miami-Dade County	868	1.70
Bronx, NY (borough) Bronx County	23,206	1.68
Yonkers, NY (city) Westchester County	3,271	1.67
Hillcrest, NY (cdp) Rockland County	125	1.65
Country Club, FL (cdp) Miami-Dade County	768	1.63
Greenburgh, NY (town) Westchester County	1,434	1.62
Islip, NY (town) Suffolk County	5,323	1.59
South River, NJ (borough) Middlesex County	253	1.58
Westbury, NY (village) Nassau County	240	1.58
Weston, FL (city) Broward County	1,000	1.53
Fountainebleau, FL (cdp) Miami-Dade County	914	1.53
New Haven, CT (city/town) New Haven County	1,978	1.52
Wappinger, NY (town) Dutchess County	411	1.52
Southchase, FL (cdp) Orange County	242	1.52
Mastic, NY (cdp) Suffolk County	232	1.50
Union, NJ (township) Union County	846	1.49
South Plainfield, NJ (borough) Middlesex County	346	1.48
Wallingford Center, CT (cdp) New Haven County	270	1.48
Maywood, NJ (borough) Bergen County	140	1.47
East Whiteland, PA (township) Chester County	152	1.43
Middlesex, NJ (borough) Middlesex County	193	1.42
Elmwood Park, NJ (borough) Bergen County	274	1.41
Linden, NJ (city) Union County	563	1.39
East Rutherford, NJ (borough) Bergen County	122	1.37
Bethel, CT (town) Fairfield County	253	1.36
Bridgeport, CT (city/town) Fairfield County	1,950	1.35
Kendall West, FL (cdp) Miami-Dade County	487	1.35
Franklin Square, NY (cdp) Nassau County	395	1.35
Nutley, NJ (township) Essex County	382	1.35
Chestnut Ridge, NY (village) Rockland County	105	1.33
Brookhaven, NY (town) Suffolk County	6,437	1.32
Bedford, NY (town) Westchester County	227	1.31
Three Lakes, FL (cdp) Miami-Dade County	197	1.31
West Orange, NJ (township) Essex County	599	1.30
Country Walk, FL (cdp) Miami-Dade County	208	1.30
Elmont, NY (cdp) Nassau County	426	1.28
Greenwich, CT (cdp) Fairfield County	166	1.28
Minneapolis, MN (city) Hennepin County	4,792	1.25
Clarkstown, NY (town) Rockland County	1,051	1.25
Uniondale, NY (cdp) Nassau County	304	1.23
West Haverstraw, NY (village) Rockland County	125	1.23
Norwalk, CT (city/town) Fairfield County	1,027	1.20
Hempstead, NY (village) Nassau County	641	1.19
Sunrise, FL (city) Broward County	995	1.18
Clifton, NJ (city) Passaic County	993	1.18
Sunny Isles Beach, FL (city) Miami-Dade County	246	1.18
North Valley Stream, NY (cdp) Nassau County	194	1.17
Hasbrouck Heights, NJ (borough) Bergen County	138	1.17
Islip, NY (cdp) Suffolk County	217	1.16
Brooklyn, NY (borough) Kings County	28,684	1.15
Roselle, NJ (borough) Union County	242	1.15
Lake Carmel, NY (cdp) Putnam County	95	1.15
Carteret, NJ (borough) Middlesex County	259	1.13
Leonia, NJ (borough) Bergen County	101	1.13
Pembroke Pines, FL (city) Broward County	1,732	1.12
Bayonne, NJ (city) Hudson County	709	1.12
West Haven, CT (city/town) New Haven County	621	1.12
Ojus, FL (cdp) Miami-Dade County	198	1.10
Passaic, NJ (city) Passaic County	761	1.09
Key Biscayne, FL (village) Miami-Dade County	134	1.09
Patterson, NY (town) Putnam County	131	1.09
Haledon, NJ (borough) Passaic County	91	1.09
Mansfield, NJ (township) Warren County	84	1.09
Miami Springs, FL (city) Miami-Dade County	149	1.08
Saddle Brook, NJ (township) Bergen County	147	1.08
Putnam Valley, NY (town) Putnam County	128	1.08
Dover, NY (town) Dutchess County	93	1.07
Shirley, NY (cdp) Suffolk County	296	1.06
Allentown, PA (city) Lehigh County	1,241	1.05

Please refer to the Explanation of Data in the front of the book for more detailed information.

Hispanic Origin

South American: Paraguayan

U.S. and 50 States Sorted by Population and Percent of Total Population

Place	Population	%
United States	**20,023**	**0.01**
New York	5,940	0.03
Florida	2,222	0.01
New Jersey	1,964	0.02
California	1,228	<0.01
Maryland	1,161	0.02
Virginia	924	0.01
Texas	763	<0.01
Pennsylvania	500	<0.01
Connecticut	494	0.01
Illinois	423	<0.01
Massachusetts	380	0.01
Georgia	360	<0.01
Minnesota	287	0.01
North Carolina	245	<0.01
Michigan	225	<0.01
Colorado	214	<0.01
Kansas	212	0.01
Ohio	205	<0.01
Wisconsin	176	<0.01
Arizona	175	<0.01
Washington	165	<0.01
District of Columbia	161	0.03
Utah	158	0.01
Missouri	128	<0.01
Alabama	121	<0.01
Nevada	116	<0.01
Oregon	112	<0.01
South Carolina	111	<0.01
Tennessee	108	<0.01
Indiana	88	<0.01
Iowa	69	<0.01
Louisiana	68	<0.01
New Mexico	53	<0.01
Kentucky	52	<0.01
Delaware	48	0.01
Oklahoma	44	<0.01
Nebraska	38	<0.01
Mississippi	37	<0.01
Vermont	34	0.01
Idaho	28	<0.01
New Hampshire	28	<0.01
Maine	25	<0.01
Arkansas	24	<0.01
Hawaii	24	<0.01
Alaska	18	<0.01
Rhode Island	18	<0.01
West Virginia	16	<0.01
South Dakota	14	<0.01
Montana	11	<0.01
North Dakota	5	<0.01
Wyoming	3	<0.01

Place	Population	%
New York	5,940	0.03
District of Columbia	161	0.03
New Jersey	1,964	0.02
Maryland	1,161	0.02
United States	**20,023**	**0.01**
Florida	2,222	0.01
Virginia	924	0.01
Connecticut	494	0.01
Massachusetts	380	0.01
Minnesota	287	0.01
Kansas	212	0.01
Utah	158	0.01
Delaware	48	0.01
Vermont	34	0.01
California	1,228	<0.01
Texas	763	<0.01
Pennsylvania	500	<0.01
Illinois	423	<0.01
Georgia	360	<0.01
North Carolina	245	<0.01
Michigan	225	<0.01
Colorado	214	<0.01
Ohio	205	<0.01
Wisconsin	176	<0.01
Arizona	175	<0.01
Washington	165	<0.01
Missouri	128	<0.01
Alabama	121	<0.01
Nevada	116	<0.01
Oregon	112	<0.01
South Carolina	111	<0.01
Tennessee	108	<0.01
Indiana	88	<0.01
Iowa	69	<0.01
Louisiana	68	<0.01
New Mexico	53	<0.01
Kentucky	52	<0.01
Oklahoma	44	<0.01
Nebraska	38	<0.01
Mississippi	37	<0.01
Idaho	28	<0.01
New Hampshire	28	<0.01
Maine	25	<0.01
Arkansas	24	<0.01
Hawaii	24	<0.01
Alaska	18	<0.01
Rhode Island	18	<0.01
West Virginia	16	<0.01
South Dakota	14	<0.01
Montana	11	<0.01
North Dakota	5	<0.01
Wyoming	3	<0.01

Please refer to the Explanation of Data in the front of the book for more detailed information.

Hispanic Origin

South American: Paraguayan

Top 150 Places Sorted by Population

Based on all places, regardless of total population

Place	Population	%
New York, NY (city) Kings County	3,534	0.04
Queens, NY (borough) Queens County	2,775	0.12
Manhattan, NY (borough) New York County	268	0.02
Bernardsville, NJ (borough) Somerset County	266	3.45
White Plains, NY (city) Westchester County	260	0.46
Harrison, NY (town/village) Westchester County	235	0.86
Brooklyn, NY (borough) Kings County	230	0.01
Bronx, NY (borough) Bronx County	223	0.02
Hempstead, NY (town) Nassau County	185	0.02
Los Angeles, CA (city) Los Angeles County	180	<0.01
Washington, DC (city) District of Columbia	161	0.03
Raritan, NJ (borough) Somerset County	147	2.14
Greenburgh, NY (town) Westchester County	144	0.16
Peapack and Gladstone, NJ (borough) Somerset County	142	5.50
North Hempstead, NY (town) Nassau County	140	0.06
Miami, FL (city) Miami-Dade County	131	0.03
Mamaroneck, NY (village) Westchester County	130	0.69
Houston, TX (city) Harris County	119	0.01
Somerville, NJ (borough) Somerset County	114	0.94
Arlington, VA (cdp) Arlington County	113	0.05
Rye, NY (town) Westchester County	102	0.22
Rockville, MD (city) Montgomery County	101	0.17
Chicago, IL (city) Cook County	101	<0.01
Huntington, NY (town) Suffolk County	91	0.04
Mamaroneck, NY (town) Westchester County	88	0.30
Miami Beach, FL (city) Miami-Dade County	87	0.10
Bridgewater, NJ (township) Somerset County	82	0.18
Bedminster, NJ (township) Somerset County	81	0.99
Yonkers, NY (city) Westchester County	79	0.04
North Bethesda, MD (cdp) Montgomery County	78	0.18
Aspen Hill, MD (cdp) Montgomery County	77	0.16
Dallas, TX (city) Dallas County	74	0.01
Philadelphia, PA (city) Philadelphia County	74	<0.01
Wheaton, MD (cdp) Montgomery County	71	0.15
Greenwich, CT (town) Fairfield County	71	0.12
Gaithersburg, MD (city) Montgomery County	69	0.12
Mount Vernon, NY (city) Westchester County	68	0.10
Oyster Bay, NY (town) Nassau County	64	0.02
Bedford, NY (town) Westchester County	63	0.36
Mineola, NY (village) Nassau County	60	0.32
Doral, FL (city) Miami-Dade County	59	0.13
Islip, NY (town) Suffolk County	58	0.02
Boston, MA (city) Suffolk County	58	0.01
Fountainebleau, FL (cdp) Miami-Dade County	56	0.09
Bridgeport, CT (city/town) Fairfield County	54	0.04
Far Hills, NJ (borough) Somerset County	53	5.77
Bethesda, MD (cdp) Montgomery County	53	0.09
San Diego, CA (city) San Diego County	52	<0.01
Key Biscayne, FL (village) Miami-Dade County	50	0.41
Austin, TX (city) Travis County	50	0.01
Brookhaven, NY (town) Suffolk County	50	0.01
Manville, NJ (borough) Somerset County	49	0.47
New Rochelle, NY (city) Westchester County	49	0.06
Phoenix, AZ (city) Maricopa County	45	<0.01
San Francisco, CA (city) San Francisco County	43	0.01
Norwalk, CT (city/town) Fairfield County	41	0.05
Long Hill, NJ (township) Morris County	40	0.46
Montgomery Village, MD (cdp) Montgomery County	40	0.12
Port Chester, NY (village) Westchester County	39	0.13
Germantown, MD (cdp) Montgomery County	39	0.05
Alexandria, VA (ind. city) Alexandria independent city	39	0.03
Hollywood, FL (city) Broward County	38	0.03
Staten Island, NY (borough) Richmond County	38	0.01
Wichita, KS (city) Sedgwick County	38	0.01
San Antonio, TX (city) Medina County	38	<0.01
Bernards, NJ (township) Somerset County	37	0.14
Stamford, CT (city/town) Fairfield County	37	0.03
Babylon, NY (town) Suffolk County	37	0.02
Coral Gables, FL (city) Miami-Dade County	36	0.08
Brentwood, NY (cdp) Suffolk County	36	0.06
Elmsford, NY (village) Westchester County	35	0.75
North Castle, NY (town) Westchester County	35	0.30
Coral Springs, FL (city) Broward County	35	0.03
Cortlandt, NY (town) Westchester County	34	0.08
Fairfield, CT (town) Fairfield County	34	0.06
Bradley Gardens, NJ (cdp) Somerset County	33	0.23
Huntington Station, NY (cdp) Suffolk County	33	0.10
Pembroke Pines, FL (city) Broward County	33	0.02
Minneapolis, MN (city) Hennepin County	33	0.01
Atlanta, GA (city) Fulton County	32	0.01
Seattle, WA (city) King County	31	0.01
St. Paul, MN (city) Ramsey County	31	0.01
San Jose, CA (city) Santa Clara County	31	<0.01
Cutler Bay, FL (town) Miami-Dade County	30	0.07
Reston, VA (cdp) Fairfax County	30	0.05
Las Vegas, NV (city) Clark County	30	0.01
Madison, WI (city) Dane County	30	0.01
Bound Brook, NJ (borough) Somerset County	29	0.28
Ossining, NY (town) Westchester County	29	0.08
Lawrence, KS (city) Douglas County	29	0.03
Bedford, NY (cdp) Westchester County	28	1.53
Fairview, NY (cdp) Westchester County	28	0.90
Ossining, NY (village) Westchester County	28	0.11
Weston, FL (city) Broward County	28	0.04
Charlotte, NC (city) Mecklenburg County	28	<0.01
Pittsburg, KS (city) Crawford County	27	0.13
Mount Olive, NJ (township) Morris County	27	0.10
Silver Spring, MD (cdp) Montgomery County	27	0.04
Overland Park, KS (city) Johnson County	27	0.02
Denver, CO (city) Denver County	27	<0.01
Southampton, NY (town) Suffolk County	26	0.05
Jersey City, NJ (city) Hudson County	26	0.01
Eastchester, NY (town) Westchester County	25	0.08
Gainesville, FL (city) Alachua County	25	0.02
Finderne, NJ (cdp) Somerset County	24	0.43
Warren, NJ (township) Somerset County	24	0.16
Haverford, PA (township) Delaware County	24	0.05
Potomac, MD (cdp) Montgomery County	24	0.05
Hialeah, FL (city) Miami-Dade County	24	0.01
Kansas City, MO (city) Jackson County	24	0.01
Plano, TX (city) Collin County	24	0.01
Sunrise Manor, NV (cdp) Clark County	24	0.01
Baltimore, MD (city) Baltimore city County	24	<0.01
Byram, CT (cdp) Fairfield County	23	0.55
Kemp Mill, MD (cdp) Montgomery County	23	0.18
Westbury, NY (village) Nassau County	23	0.15
Southeast, NY (town) Putnam County	23	0.12
Washington, NJ (township) Morris County	23	0.12
Plantation, FL (city) Broward County	23	0.03
Elizabeth, NJ (city) Union County	23	0.02
Redland, MD (cdp) Montgomery County	22	0.13
Aventura, FL (city) Miami-Dade County	22	0.06
Oakton, VA (cdp) Fairfax County	22	0.06
Yorktown, NY (town) Westchester County	22	0.06
Kendall, FL (cdp) Miami-Dade County	22	0.03
Eastchester, NY (cdp) Westchester County	21	0.11
Olney, MD (cdp) Montgomery County	21	0.06
Manhattan, KS (city) Riley County	21	0.04
Newark, NJ (city) Essex County	21	0.01
Tallahassee, FL (city) Leon County	21	0.01
Union, NJ (township) Union County	20	0.04
Miramar, FL (city) Broward County	20	0.02
Upper Darby, PA (township) Delaware County	20	0.02
West Palm Beach, FL (city) Palm Beach County	20	0.02
Glendale, CA (city) Los Angeles County	20	0.01
Pittsburgh, PA (city) Allegheny County	20	0.01
Milwaukee, WI (city) Milwaukee County	20	<0.01
Portland, OR (city) Multnomah County	20	<0.01
Franklin Square, NY (cdp) Nassau County	19	0.06
Freeport, NY (village) Nassau County	19	0.04
Levittown, NY (cdp) Nassau County	19	0.04
Tamarac, FL (city) Broward County	19	0.03
Cambridge, MA (city) Middlesex County	19	0.02
Columbia, MD (cdp) Howard County	19	0.02
Albuquerque, NM (city) Bernalillo County	19	<0.01
Louisville-Jefferson County, KY (metro govt) Jefferson County	19	<0.01
Virginia Beach, VA (ind. city) Virginia Beach independent city	19	<0.01
Harding, NJ (township) Morris County	18	0.47
Trumbull, CT (cdp/town) Fairfield County	18	0.05
Valley Stream, NY (village) Nassau County	18	0.05

Please refer to the Explanation of Data in the front of the book for more detailed information.

Hispanic Origin

South American: Paraguayan

Top 150 Places Sorted by Percent of Total Population

Based on all places, regardless of total population

Place	Population	%
Far Hills, NJ (borough) Somerset County	53	5.77
Peapack and Gladstone, NJ (borough) Somerset County	142	5.50
Bernardsville, NJ (borough) Somerset County	266	3.45
Raritan, NJ (borough) Somerset County	147	2.14
Ohiowa, NE (village) Fillmore County	2	1.74
St. Joseph, IA (cdp) Kossuth County	1	1.64
Bedford, NY (cdp) Westchester County	28	1.53
Scotts Corners, NY (cdp) Westchester County	10	1.41
Watch Hill, RI (cdp) Washington County	2	1.30
Cove Neck, NY (village) Nassau County	3	1.05
Bedminster, NJ (township) Somerset County	81	0.99
Somerville, NJ (borough) Somerset County	114	0.94
Fairview, NY (cdp) Westchester County	28	0.90
Harrison, NY (town/village) Westchester County	235	0.86
Elmsford, NY (village) Westchester County	35	0.75
New Hamilton, MS (cdp) Monroe County	4	0.72
Kenwood Estates, FL (cdp) Palm Beach County	9	0.70
Mamaroneck, NY (village) Westchester County	130	0.69
Morris, PA (township) Tioga County	4	0.66
Geiger, AL (town) Sumter County	1	0.59
Alpine, OR (cdp) Benton County	1	0.58
Byram, CT (cdp) Fairfield County	23	0.55
Josephville, MO (village) St. Charles County	2	0.53
Lebanon, NJ (borough) Hunterdon County	7	0.52
Hewlett Bay Park, NY (village) Nassau County	2	0.50
Manville, NJ (borough) Somerset County	49	0.47
Harding, NJ (township) Morris County	18	0.47
Bedford Hills, NY (cdp) Westchester County	14	0.47
Acacia Villas, FL (cdp) Palm Beach County	2	0.47
White Plains, NY (city) Westchester County	260	0.46
Long Hill, NJ (township) Morris County	40	0.46
Spencerville, MD (cdp) Montgomery County	7	0.44
Finderne, NJ (cdp) Somerset County	24	0.43
Forest View, IL (village) Cook County	3	0.43
Union, AL (town) Greene County	1	0.42
Key Biscayne, FL (village) Miami-Dade County	50	0.41
Bethany, PA (borough) Wayne County	1	0.41
Partridge, KS (city) Reno County	1	0.40
Silver Lake, MN (township) Martin County	2	0.39
Parc, NY (cdp) Clinton County	1	0.39
Deerwood, MN (city) Crow Wing County	2	0.38
Long Valley, NJ (cdp) Morris County	7	0.37
Vanduser, MO (village) Scott County	1	0.37
Bedford, NY (town) Westchester County	63	0.36
South Bound Brook, NJ (borough) Somerset County	16	0.35
Delmar, PA (township) Tioga County	10	0.35
Chappaqua, NY (cdp) Westchester County	5	0.35
Brewster Hill, NY (cdp) Putnam County	7	0.34
Marshall, VA (cdp) Fauquier County	5	0.34
Bloomsbury, NJ (borough) Hunterdon County	3	0.34
Onaway, MI (city) Presque Isle County	3	0.34
West Union, SC (town) Oconee County	1	0.34
Mineola, NY (village) Nassau County	60	0.32
Southport, CT (cdp) Fairfield County	5	0.32
Carthage, IL (city) Hancock County	8	0.31
Shell Ridge, CA (cdp) Contra Costa County	3	0.31
Deerfield, MA (cdp) Franklin County	2	0.31
Port Clinton, PA (borough) Schuylkill County	1	0.31
Mamaroneck, NY (town) Westchester County	88	0.30
North Castle, NY (town) Westchester County	35	0.30
Hartsdale, NY (cdp) Westchester County	16	0.30
Chester, NJ (borough) Morris County	5	0.30
Durham, OR (city) Washington County	4	0.30
Stratton, NE (village) Hitchcock County	1	0.29
Bound Brook, NJ (borough) Somerset County	29	0.28
Mendham, NJ (borough) Morris County	14	0.28
North Abington, PA (township) Lackawanna County	2	0.28
Bradford, NH (cdp) Merrimack County	1	0.28
Jordan, MN (township) Fillmore County	1	0.28
Oceanside, OR (cdp) Tillamook County	1	0.28
Bellerose Terrace, NY (cdp) Nassau County	6	0.27
Ocean View, DE (town) Sussex County	5	0.27
Richmond, MA (town) Berkshire County	4	0.27
West Point, GA (city) Troup County	9	0.26
Berwyn Heights, MD (town) Prince George's County	8	0.26
Southampton, NY (village) Suffolk County	8	0.26
Sands Point, NY (village) Nassau County	7	0.26
Pine Ridge, FL (cdp) Collier County	5	0.26
Pound Ridge, NY (town) Westchester County	13	0.25
Princeton, WI (city) Green Lake County	3	0.25
Braceville, IL (village) Grundy County	2	0.25
Woodstock, NY (cdp) Ulster County	5	0.24
Plantation Mobile Home Park, FL (cdp) Palm Beach County	3	0.24
Jupiter Island, FL (town) Martin County	2	0.24
Bradley Gardens, NJ (cdp) Somerset County	33	0.23
South Floral Park, NY (village) Nassau County	4	0.23
Shoreham, MI (village) Berrien County	2	0.23
Rye, NY (town) Westchester County	102	0.22
Golden Beach, FL (town) Miami-Dade County	2	0.22
Surfside, FL (town) Miami-Dade County	12	0.21
Glenville, CT (cdp) Fairfield County	5	0.21
Tolland, MA (town) Hampden County	1	0.21
Veyo, UT (cdp) Washington County	1	0.21
Baxter Estates, NY (village) Nassau County	2	0.20
Hill Country Village, TX (city) Bexar County	2	0.20
Westlake, TX (town) Tarrant County	2	0.20
Valhalla, NY (cdp) Westchester County	6	0.19
Lakehurst, NJ (borough) Ocean County	5	0.19
Shoreham, NY (village) Suffolk County	1	0.19
Bridgewater, NJ (township) Somerset County	82	0.18
North Bethesda, MD (cdp) Montgomery County	78	0.18
Kemp Mill, MD (cdp) Montgomery County	23	0.18
Green Knoll, NJ (cdp) Somerset County	11	0.18
North Salem, NY (town) Westchester County	9	0.18
Oyster Bay Cove, NY (village) Nassau County	4	0.18
Shinnecock Hills, NY (cdp) Suffolk County	4	0.18
Havana, MN (township) Steele County	1	0.18
Ivanhoe, VA (cdp) Wythe County	1	0.18
Phillipsburg, OH (village) Montgomery County	1	0.18
Truchas, NM (cdp) Rio Arriba County	1	0.18
Rockville, MD (city) Montgomery County	101	0.17
Saranap, CA (cdp) Contra Costa County	9	0.17
Enon, VA (cdp) Chesterfield County	6	0.17
Kenvil, NJ (cdp) Morris County	5	0.17
Crompond, NY (cdp) Westchester County	4	0.17
Milan, NY (town) Dutchess County	4	0.17
Pawling, NY (village) Dutchess County	4	0.17
Buena Vista, WI (town) Portage County	2	0.17
Arcadia University, PA (cdp) Montgomery County	1	0.17
Gillford, MN (township) Wabasha County	1	0.17
Greenburgh, NY (town) Westchester County	144	0.16
Aspen Hill, MD (cdp) Montgomery County	77	0.16
Warren, NJ (township) Somerset County	24	0.16
Mansfield, NJ (township) Warren County	12	0.16
Bal Harbour, FL (village) Miami-Dade County	4	0.16
Matamoras, PA (borough) Pike County	4	0.16
Stinson Beach, CA (cdp) Marin County	1	0.16
Waleska, GA (city) Cherokee County	1	0.16
Wheaton, MD (cdp) Montgomery County	71	0.15
Westbury, NY (village) Nassau County	23	0.15
Northville, MI (city) Oakland County	5	0.15
Maunawili, HI (cdp) Honolulu County	3	0.15
Red Hook, NY (village) Dutchess County	3	0.15
South Woodstock, CT (cdp) Windham County	2	0.15
Chevy Chase Section Five, MD (village) Montgomery County	1	0.15
Hot Sulphur Springs, CO (town) Grand County	1	0.15
Malta, OH (village) Morgan County	1	0.15
Wartrace, TN (town) Bedford County	1	0.15
Bernards, NJ (township) Somerset County	37	0.14
Mount Kisco, NY (town/village) Westchester County	15	0.14
North Kensington, MD (cdp) Montgomery County	13	0.14
South Kensington, MD (cdp) Montgomery County	12	0.14
East Farmingdale, NY (cdp) Suffolk County	9	0.14
Stanhope, NJ (borough) Sussex County	5	0.14
Yountville, CA (city) Napa County	4	0.14
Redington Beach, FL (town) Pinellas County	2	0.14
Bowdoinham, ME (cdp) Sagadahoc County	1	0.14
Doral, FL (city) Miami-Dade County	59	0.13
Port Chester, NY (village) Westchester County	39	0.13
Pittsburg, KS (city) Crawford County	27	0.13

Please refer to the Explanation of Data in the front of the book for more detailed information.

Hispanic Origin

South American: Paraguayan

Top 150 Places Sorted by Percent of Total Population

Based on places with total population of 7,500 or more

Place	Population	%
Bernardsville, NJ (borough) Somerset County	266	3.45
Bedminster, NJ (township) Somerset County	81	0.99
Somerville, NJ (borough) Somerset County	114	0.94
Harrison, NY (town/village) Westchester County	235	0.86
Mamaroneck, NY (village) Westchester County	130	0.69
Manville, NJ (borough) Somerset County	49	0.47
White Plains, NY (city) Westchester County	260	0.46
Long Hill, NJ (township) Morris County	40	0.46
Key Biscayne, FL (village) Miami-Dade County	50	0.41
Bedford, NY (town) Westchester County	63	0.36
Mineola, NY (village) Nassau County	60	0.32
Mamaroneck, NY (town) Westchester County	88	0.30
North Castle, NY (town) Westchester County	35	0.30
Bound Brook, NJ (borough) Somerset County	29	0.28
Bradley Gardens, NJ (cdp) Somerset County	33	0.23
Rye, NY (town) Westchester County	102	0.22
Bridgewater, NJ (township) Somerset County	82	0.18
North Bethesda, MD (cdp) Montgomery County	78	0.18
Kemp Mill, MD (cdp) Montgomery County	23	0.18
Rockville, MD (city) Montgomery County	101	0.17
Greenburgh, NY (town) Westchester County	144	0.16
Aspen Hill, MD (cdp) Montgomery County	77	0.16
Warren, NJ (township) Somerset County	24	0.16
Mansfield, NJ (township) Warren County	12	0.16
Wheaton, MD (cdp) Montgomery County	71	0.15
Westbury, NY (village) Nassau County	23	0.15
Bernards, NJ (township) Somerset County	37	0.14
Mount Kisco, NY (town/village) Westchester County	15	0.14
North Kensington, MD (cdp) Montgomery County	13	0.14
South Kensington, MD (cdp) Montgomery County	12	0.14
Doral, FL (city) Miami-Dade County	59	0.13
Port Chester, NY (village) Westchester County	39	0.13
Pittsburg, KS (city) Crawford County	27	0.13
Redland, MD (cdp) Montgomery County	22	0.13
Greenwich, CT (cdp) Fairfield County	17	0.13
Elwood, NY (cdp) Suffolk County	14	0.13
South Huntington, NY (cdp) Suffolk County	12	0.13
Queens, NY (borough) Queens County	2,775	0.12
Greenwich, CT (town) Fairfield County	71	0.12
Gaithersburg, MD (city) Montgomery County	69	0.12
Montgomery Village, MD (cdp) Montgomery County	40	0.12
Southeast, NY (town) Putnam County	23	0.12
Washington, NJ (township) Morris County	23	0.12
South Farmingdale, NY (cdp) Nassau County	17	0.12
Glenmont, MD (cdp) Montgomery County	16	0.12
Falls Church, VA (ind. city) Falls Church independent city	15	0.12
South Miami, FL (city) Miami-Dade County	14	0.12
Perkiomen, PA (township) Montgomery County	11	0.12
Ossining, NY (village) Westchester County	28	0.11
Eastchester, NY (cdp) Westchester County	21	0.11
Miami Beach, FL (city) Miami-Dade County	87	0.10
Mount Vernon, NY (city) Westchester County	68	0.10
Huntington Station, NY (cdp) Suffolk County	33	0.10
Mount Olive, NJ (township) Morris County	27	0.10
Colesville, MD (cdp) Montgomery County	15	0.10
Pacific Grove, CA (city) Monterey County	15	0.10
Branchburg, NJ (township) Somerset County	14	0.10
Philipstown, NY (town) Putnam County	10	0.10
Rye Brook, NY (village) Westchester County	9	0.10
Burtonsville, MD (cdp) Montgomery County	8	0.10
Mahopac, NY (cdp) Putnam County	8	0.10
Fountainebleau, FL (cdp) Miami-Dade County	56	0.09
Bethesda, MD (cdp) Montgomery County	53	0.09
Idylwood, VA (cdp) Fairfax County	16	0.09
Glenvar Heights, FL (cdp) Miami-Dade County	15	0.09
Greenlawn, NY (cdp) Suffolk County	13	0.09
Seven Corners, VA (cdp) Fairfax County	8	0.09
Center Moriches, NY (cdp) Suffolk County	7	0.09
Rhinebeck, NY (town) Dutchess County	7	0.09
Coral Gables, FL (city) Miami-Dade County	36	0.08
Cortlandt, NY (town) Westchester County	34	0.08
Ossining, NY (town) Westchester County	29	0.08
Eastchester, NY (town) Westchester County	25	0.08
Sunny Isles Beach, FL (city) Miami-Dade County	17	0.08
Madison, NJ (borough) Morris County	13	0.08
Newington Forest, VA (cdp) Fairfax County	10	0.08
Esopus, NY (town) Ulster County	7	0.08
Chester, NJ (township) Morris County	6	0.08
Hastings-on-Hudson, NY (village) Westchester County	6	0.08
Ridgefield, CT (cdp) Fairfield County	6	0.08
Cutler Bay, FL (town) Miami-Dade County	30	0.07
The Crossings, FL (cdp) Miami-Dade County	16	0.07
Brookfield, IL (village) Cook County	13	0.07
Scarsdale, NY (town/village) Westchester County	12	0.07
Brandermill, VA (cdp) Chesterfield County	9	0.07
Cornelius, OR (city) Washington County	8	0.07
Martinsville, NJ (cdp) Somerset County	8	0.07
Wallington, NJ (borough) Bergen County	8	0.07
New Hyde Park, NY (village) Nassau County	7	0.07
Timonium, MD (cdp) Baltimore County	7	0.07
Pawling, NY (town) Dutchess County	6	0.07
White Meadow Lake, NJ (cdp) Morris County	6	0.07
North Hempstead, NY (town) Nassau County	140	0.06
New Rochelle, NY (city) Westchester County	49	0.06
Brentwood, NY (cdp) Suffolk County	36	0.06
Fairfield, CT (town) Fairfield County	34	0.06
Aventura, FL (city) Miami-Dade County	22	0.06
Oakton, VA (cdp) Fairfax County	22	0.06
Yorktown, NY (town) Westchester County	22	0.06
Olney, MD (cdp) Montgomery County	21	0.06
Franklin Square, NY (cdp) Nassau County	19	0.06
Bailey's Crossroads, VA (cdp) Fairfax County	15	0.06
Coral Terrace, FL (cdp) Miami-Dade County	14	0.06
Fairland, MD (cdp) Montgomery County	14	0.06
New Castle, NY (town) Westchester County	11	0.06
Palm Springs, FL (village) Palm Beach County	11	0.06
Burke Centre, VA (cdp) Fairfax County	10	0.06
South River, NJ (borough) Middlesex County	10	0.06
Merrifield, VA (cdp) Fairfax County	9	0.06
Opa-locka, FL (city) Miami-Dade County	9	0.06
Fallsburg, NY (town) Sullivan County	8	0.06
Jefferson Valley-Yorktown, NY (cdp) Westchester County	8	0.06
Wayland, MA (town) Middlesex County	8	0.06
Hamilton, PA (township) Franklin County	7	0.06
Hobe Sound, FL (cdp) Martin County	7	0.06
New Providence, NJ (borough) Union County	7	0.06
Pine, PA (township) Allegheny County	7	0.06
Arden Hills, MN (city) Ramsey County	6	0.06
Broomall, PA (cdp) Delaware County	6	0.06
Walnut Grove, WA (cdp) Clark County	6	0.06
Carneys Point, NJ (township) Salem County	5	0.06
Commerce, TX (city) Hunt County	5	0.06
Erwin, NY (town) Steuben County	5	0.06
Four Corners, MD (cdp) Montgomery County	5	0.06
Malverne, NY (village) Nassau County	5	0.06
Park Ridge, NJ (borough) Bergen County	5	0.06
Rockwood, VA (cdp) Chesterfield County	5	0.06
Seneca, SC (city) Oconee County	5	0.06
Arlington, VA (cdp) Arlington County	113	0.05
Norwalk, CT (city/town) Fairfield County	41	0.05
Germantown, MD (cdp) Montgomery County	39	0.05
Reston, VA (cdp) Fairfax County	30	0.05
Southampton, NY (town) Suffolk County	26	0.05
Haverford, PA (township) Delaware County	24	0.05
Potomac, MD (cdp) Montgomery County	24	0.05
Trumbull, CT (cdp/town) Fairfield County	18	0.05
Valley Stream, NY (village) Nassau County	18	0.05
Glen Cove, NY (city) Nassau County	14	0.05
Ridgefield, CT (town) Fairfield County	13	0.05
Gladstone, MO (city) Clay County	12	0.05
Chantilly, VA (cdp) Fairfax County	11	0.05
Franconia, VA (cdp) Fairfax County	10	0.05
Morris, NJ (town) Morris County	10	0.05
New Canaan, CT (town) Fairfield County	10	0.05
Taylors, SC (cdp) Greenville County	10	0.05
Calverton, MD (cdp) Montgomery County	9	0.05
Ojus, FL (cdp) Miami-Dade County	9	0.05
Shenandoah, LA (cdp) East Baton Rouge Parish	9	0.05
Bon Air, VA (cdp) Chesterfield County	8	0.05
Fairview Park, OH (city) Cuyahoga County	8	0.05

Please refer to the Explanation of Data in the front of the book for more detailed information.

Hispanic Origin

South American: Peruvian

U.S. and 50 States Sorted by Population and Percent of Total Population

Place	Population	%
United States	**531,358**	**0.17**
Florida	100,965	0.54
California	91,511	0.25
New Jersey	75,869	0.86
New York	66,318	0.34
Virginia	29,096	0.36
Texas	22,605	0.09
Maryland	18,229	0.32
Connecticut	16,424	0.46
Georgia	10,570	0.11
Illinois	10,213	0.08
North Carolina	8,247	0.09
Pennsylvania	7,783	0.06
Utah	7,514	0.27
Massachusetts	7,360	0.11
Colorado	5,835	0.12
Washington	5,276	0.08
Arizona	4,658	0.07
Nevada	4,581	0.17
Ohio	3,741	0.03
Oregon	2,650	0.07
Indiana	2,225	0.03
Michigan	2,040	0.02
Wisconsin	2,029	0.04
Minnesota	2,028	0.04
Tennessee	1,918	0.03
South Carolina	1,908	0.04
Oklahoma	1,805	0.05
Missouri	1,687	0.03
Idaho	1,560	0.10
District of Columbia	1,482	0.25
Louisiana	1,229	0.03
Kentucky	1,174	0.03
Kansas	1,151	0.04
Alabama	1,116	0.02
Rhode Island	1,067	0.10
New Mexico	913	0.04
Hawaii	721	0.05
Delaware	704	0.08
Arkansas	650	0.02
Nebraska	628	0.03
Alaska	611	0.09
Iowa	607	0.02
Mississippi	473	0.02
New Hampshire	471	0.04
West Virginia	444	0.02
Wyoming	305	0.05
Maine	272	0.02
Vermont	242	0.04
Montana	237	0.02
South Dakota	138	0.02
North Dakota	78	0.01

Place	Population	%
New Jersey	75,869	0.86
Florida	100,965	0.54
Connecticut	16,424	0.46
Virginia	29,096	0.36
New York	66,318	0.34
Maryland	18,229	0.32
Utah	7,514	0.27
California	91,511	0.25
District of Columbia	1,482	0.25
United States	**531,358**	**0.17**
Nevada	4,581	0.17
Colorado	5,835	0.12
Georgia	10,570	0.11
Massachusetts	7,360	0.11
Idaho	1,560	0.10
Rhode Island	1,067	0.10
Texas	22,605	0.09
North Carolina	8,247	0.09
Alaska	611	0.09
Illinois	10,213	0.08
Washington	5,276	0.08
Delaware	704	0.08
Arizona	4,658	0.07
Oregon	2,650	0.07
Pennsylvania	7,783	0.06
Oklahoma	1,805	0.05
Hawaii	721	0.05
Wyoming	305	0.05
Wisconsin	2,029	0.04
Minnesota	2,028	0.04
South Carolina	1,908	0.04
Kansas	1,151	0.04
New Mexico	913	0.04
New Hampshire	471	0.04
Vermont	242	0.04
Ohio	3,741	0.03
Indiana	2,225	0.03
Tennessee	1,918	0.03
Missouri	1,687	0.03
Louisiana	1,229	0.03
Kentucky	1,174	0.03
Nebraska	628	0.03
Michigan	2,040	0.02
Alabama	1,116	0.02
Arkansas	650	0.02
Iowa	607	0.02
Mississippi	473	0.02
West Virginia	444	0.02
Maine	272	0.02
Montana	237	0.02
South Dakota	138	0.02
North Dakota	78	0.01

Please refer to the Explanation of Data in the front of the book for more detailed information.

Hispanic Origin

South American: Peruvian

Top 150 Places Sorted by Population

Based on all places, regardless of total population

Place	Population	%
New York, NY (city) Kings County	36,018	0.44
Queens, NY (borough) Queens County	22,886	1.03
Los Angeles, CA (city) Los Angeles County	14,033	0.37
Paterson, NJ (city) Passaic County	9,943	6.80
Elizabeth, NJ (city) Union County	5,419	4.34
Miami, FL (city) Miami-Dade County	4,946	1.24
Hempstead, NY (town) Nassau County	4,510	0.59
Clifton, NJ (city) Passaic County	4,473	5.32
Brooklyn, NY (borough) Kings County	4,222	0.17
Chicago, IL (city) Cook County	4,075	0.15
Manhattan, NY (borough) New York County	3,852	0.24
Islip, NY (town) Suffolk County	3,599	1.07
Bronx, NY (borough) Bronx County	3,596	0.26
Kearny, NJ (town) Hudson County	3,315	8.15
San Francisco, CA (city) San Francisco County	3,260	0.40
Houston, TX (city) Harris County	3,237	0.15
Union City, NJ (city) Hudson County	3,111	4.68
Hollywood, FL (city) Broward County	2,995	2.13
Pembroke Pines, FL (city) Broward County	2,638	1.70
Stamford, CT (city/town) Fairfield County	2,560	2.09
Newark, NJ (city) Essex County	2,448	0.88
The Hammocks, FL (cdp) Miami-Dade County	2,403	4.71
Kendall, FL (cdp) Miami-Dade County	2,280	3.03
White Plains, NY (city) Westchester County	2,260	3.98
Passaic, NJ (city) Passaic County	2,228	3.19
Coral Springs, FL (city) Broward County	2,226	1.84
Charlotte, NC (city) Mecklenburg County	2,177	0.30
San Jose, CA (city) Santa Clara County	2,128	0.22
Hartford, CT (city/town) Hartford County	2,119	1.70
Miami Beach, FL (city) Miami-Dade County	2,091	2.38
Perth Amboy, NJ (city) Middlesex County	1,979	3.89
Hialeah, FL (city) Miami-Dade County	1,920	0.85
San Diego, CA (city) San Diego County	1,901	0.15
Rye, NY (town) Westchester County	1,734	3.78
Dallas, TX (city) Dallas County	1,725	0.14
Weston, FL (city) Broward County	1,677	2.57
Germantown, MD (cdp) Montgomery County	1,672	1.94
Harrison, NJ (town) Hudson County	1,651	12.12
Brentwood, NY (cdp) Suffolk County	1,610	2.65
North Bergen, NJ (township) Hudson County	1,590	2.62
Doral, FL (city) Miami-Dade County	1,535	3.36
Davie, FL (town) Broward County	1,533	1.67
Arlington, VA (cdp) Arlington County	1,531	0.74
Sunrise, FL (city) Broward County	1,503	1.78
Port Chester, NY (village) Westchester County	1,485	5.13
Washington, DC (city) District of Columbia	1,482	0.25
Kendale Lakes, FL (cdp) Miami-Dade County	1,473	2.62
Garfield, NJ (city) Bergen County	1,462	4.80
Staten Island, NY (borough) Richmond County	1,462	0.31
Fountainebleau, FL (cdp) Miami-Dade County	1,408	2.36
Centreville, VA (cdp) Fairfax County	1,406	1.98
Miramar, FL (city) Broward County	1,401	1.15
West Orange, NJ (township) Essex County	1,382	2.99
Kendall West, FL (cdp) Miami-Dade County	1,369	3.79
Anaheim, CA (city) Orange County	1,365	0.41
North Miami Beach, FL (city) Miami-Dade County	1,325	3.19
Babylon, NY (town) Suffolk County	1,313	0.61
New Rochelle, NY (city) Westchester County	1,297	1.68
Boston, MA (city) Suffolk County	1,286	0.21
Jacksonville, FL (city) Duval County	1,282	0.16
Downey, CA (city) Los Angeles County	1,277	1.14
San Antonio, TX (city) Medina County	1,258	0.09
Belleville, NJ (township) Essex County	1,239	3.45
Jersey City, NJ (city) Hudson County	1,221	0.49
West New York, NJ (town) Hudson County	1,205	2.42
Alexandria, VA (ind. city) Alexandria independent city	1,174	0.84
San Mateo, CA (city) San Mateo County	1,163	1.20
Oyster Bay, NY (town) Nassau County	1,156	0.39
Gaithersburg, MD (city) Montgomery County	1,150	1.92
Aspen Hill, MD (cdp) Montgomery County	1,144	2.35
Orlando, FL (city) Orange County	1,144	0.48
Wheaton, MD (cdp) Montgomery County	1,130	2.34
Long Beach, CA (city) Los Angeles County	1,109	0.24
Philadelphia, PA (city) Philadelphia County	1,085	0.07
Brookhaven, NY (town) Suffolk County	1,074	0.22
Plantation, FL (city) Broward County	1,071	1.26
Las Vegas, NV (city) Clark County	1,068	0.18
Aurora, CO (city) Arapahoe County	1,058	0.33
Concord, CA (city) Contra Costa County	1,056	0.87
Hallandale Beach, FL (city) Broward County	1,053	2.84
Phoenix, AZ (city) Maricopa County	1,048	0.07
Woodbridge, NJ (township) Middlesex County	1,043	1.05
Country Club, FL (cdp) Miami-Dade County	1,033	2.19
Bridgeport, CT (city/town) Fairfield County	1,017	0.71
The Crossings, FL (cdp) Miami-Dade County	1,006	4.42
Tamarac, FL (city) Broward County	966	1.60
West Hartford, CT (cdp/town) Hartford County	964	1.52
East Hartford, CT (cdp/town) Hartford County	962	1.88
Greenburgh, NY (town) Westchester County	962	1.09
Fort Lauderdale, FL (city) Broward County	962	0.58
Torrance, CA (city) Los Angeles County	955	0.66
Richmond West, FL (cdp) Miami-Dade County	954	2.98
Yonkers, NY (city) Westchester County	946	0.48
North Hempstead, NY (town) Nassau County	925	0.41
Annandale, VA (cdp) Fairfax County	917	2.24
Linden, NJ (city) Union County	906	2.24
Ojus, FL (cdp) Miami-Dade County	897	4.97
Carteret, NJ (borough) Middlesex County	896	3.92
Glen Cove, NY (city) Nassau County	883	3.27
Coconut Creek, FL (city) Broward County	859	1.62
Norwalk, CT (city/town) Fairfield County	859	1.00
Rockville, MD (city) Montgomery County	850	1.39
Montgomery Village, MD (cdp) Montgomery County	842	2.63
Denver, CO (city) Denver County	835	0.14
Santa Clarita, CA (city) Los Angeles County	831	0.47
Bloomfield, NJ (township) Essex County	820	1.73
Austin, TX (city) Travis County	804	0.10
Glendale, CA (city) Los Angeles County	803	0.42
Town 'n' Country, FL (cdp) Hillsborough County	800	1.02
Rancho Cucamonga, CA (city) San Bernardino County	800	0.48
Tampa, FL (city) Hillsborough County	800	0.24
Burke, VA (cdp) Fairfax County	774	1.89
Seattle, WA (city) King County	774	0.13
Margate, FL (city) Broward County	772	1.45
Hawthorne, CA (city) Los Angeles County	768	0.91
Dale City, VA (cdp) Prince William County	766	1.16
Hayward, CA (city) Alameda County	761	0.53
Ashburn, VA (cdp) Loudoun County	751	1.73
Kissimmee, FL (city) Osceola County	750	1.26
Cape Coral, FL (city) Lee County	749	0.49
Antioch, CA (city) Contra Costa County	748	0.73
Daly City, CA (city) San Mateo County	738	0.73
Leesburg, VA (town) Loudoun County	736	1.73
West Valley City, UT (city) Salt Lake County	736	0.57
Raleigh, NC (city) Wake County	729	0.18
Paradise, NV (cdp) Clark County	719	0.32
Simi Valley, CA (city) Ventura County	716	0.58
Aventura, FL (city) Miami-Dade County	713	1.99
Lodi, NJ (borough) Bergen County	705	2.92
Riverside, CA (city) Riverside County	702	0.23
Port St. Lucie, FL (city) St. Lucie County	701	0.43
Tamiami, FL (cdp) Miami-Dade County	697	1.26
Sterling, VA (cdp) Loudoun County	694	2.49
Newburgh, NY (city) Orange County	691	2.39
Oakland, CA (city) Alameda County	690	0.18
Sunny Isles Beach, FL (city) Miami-Dade County	653	3.13
Coral Gables, FL (city) Miami-Dade County	651	1.39
Pompano Beach, FL (city) Broward County	651	0.65
Salt Lake City, UT (city) Salt Lake County	651	0.35
Santa Ana, CA (city) Orange County	651	0.20
Fontana, CA (city) San Bernardino County	646	0.33
Rahway, NJ (city) Union County	644	2.36
Provo, UT (city) Utah County	644	0.57
Cutler Bay, FL (town) Miami-Dade County	643	1.60
Lake Ridge, VA (cdp) Prince William County	642	1.56
Fremont, CA (city) Alameda County	616	0.29
Deerfield Beach, FL (city) Broward County	615	0.82
Sacramento, CA (city) Sacramento County	614	0.13
Indianapolis, IN (city) Marion County	611	0.07
Virginia Beach, VA (ind. city) Virginia Beach independent city	609	0.14

SECTION THREE

Please refer to the Explanation of Data in the front of the book for more detailed information.

Hispanic Origin

South American: Peruvian

Top 150 Places Sorted by Percent of Total Population

Based on all places, regardless of total population

Place	Population	%
East Newark, NJ (borough) Hudson County	410	17.04
Harrison, NJ (town) Hudson County	1,651	12.12
Little America, WY (cdp) Sweetwater County	6	8.82
Prospect Park, NJ (borough) Passaic County	485	8.27
Kearny, NJ (town) Hudson County	3,315	8.15
Bayport, FL (cdp) Hernando County	3	6.98
Paterson, NJ (city) Passaic County	9,943	6.80
Haledon, NJ (borough) Passaic County	557	6.70
Islandia, FL (city) Miami-Dade County	1	5.56
Clifton, NJ (city) Passaic County	4,473	5.32
Port Chester, NY (village) Westchester County	1,485	5.13
Island Park, NY (village) Nassau County	234	5.03
Ojus, FL (cdp) Miami-Dade County	897	4.97
Garfield, NJ (city) Bergen County	1,462	4.80
The Hammocks, FL (cdp) Miami-Dade County	2,403	4.71
Union City, NJ (city) Hudson County	3,111	4.68
The Crossings, FL (cdp) Miami-Dade County	1,006	4.42
Elizabeth, NJ (city) Union County	5,419	4.34
Byram, CT (cdp) Fairfield County	177	4.27
Elmsford, NY (village) Westchester County	189	4.05
Branson, CO (town) Las Animas County	3	4.05
Butte City, ID (city) Butte County	3	4.05
El Rancho, CA (cdp) Tulare County	5	4.03
Ketchum, ID (city) Blaine County	108	4.02
Virginia Gardens, FL (village) Miami-Dade County	95	4.00
Delaware, NJ (cdp) Warren County	6	4.00
White Plains, NY (city) Westchester County	2,260	3.98
Carteret, NJ (borough) Middlesex County	896	3.92
Perth Amboy, NJ (city) Middlesex County	1,979	3.89
Kendall West, FL (cdp) Miami-Dade County	1,369	3.79
Rye, NY (town) Westchester County	1,734	3.78
Three Lakes, FL (cdp) Miami-Dade County	538	3.58
Dulles Town Center, VA (cdp) Loudoun County	160	3.48
Bay Harbor Islands, FL (town) Miami-Dade County	195	3.46
Belleville, NJ (township) Essex County	1,239	3.45
Silver Lake, NJ (cdp) Essex County	146	3.44
Buttzville, NJ (cdp) Warren County	5	3.42
Doral, FL (city) Miami-Dade County	1,535	3.36
Woodland Park, NJ (borough) Passaic County	396	3.35
Glen Cove, NY (city) Nassau County	883	3.27
Key Biscayne, FL (village) Miami-Dade County	397	3.22
Passaic, NJ (city) Passaic County	2,228	3.19
North Miami Beach, FL (city) Miami-Dade County	1,325	3.19
Kemps Mill, MD (cdp) Washington County	4	3.17
Sunny Isles Beach, FL (city) Miami-Dade County	653	3.13
University Center, VA (cdp) Loudoun County	110	3.07
Kendall, FL (cdp) Miami-Dade County	2,280	3.03
Baywood, NY (cdp) Suffolk County	222	3.02
Barnum Island, NY (cdp) Nassau County	73	3.02
West Orange, NJ (township) Essex County	1,382	2.99
Richmond West, FL (cdp) Miami-Dade County	954	2.98
Western, NE (village) Saline County	7	2.98
Elmwood Park, NJ (borough) Bergen County	568	2.93
Oak Grove, VA (cdp) Loudoun County	52	2.93
Lodi, NJ (borough) Bergen County	705	2.92
Country Walk, FL (cdp) Miami-Dade County	467	2.92
Vineyard, UT (town) Utah County	4	2.88
Fairview, NY (cdp) Westchester County	89	2.87
Hallandale Beach, FL (city) Broward County	1,053	2.84
North Bay Village, FL (city) Miami-Dade County	201	2.82
Manteo, NC (town) Dare County	40	2.79
Dover, NJ (town) Morris County	505	2.78
Bellerose Terrace, NY (cdp) Nassau County	60	2.73
Totowa, NJ (borough) Passaic County	294	2.72
Countryside, VA (cdp) Loudoun County	273	2.71
Bound Brook, NJ (borough) Somerset County	279	2.68
Freehold, NJ (borough) Monmouth County	322	2.67
Brentwood, NY (cdp) Suffolk County	1,610	2.65
Wharton, NJ (borough) Morris County	173	2.65
Montgomery Village, MD (cdp) Montgomery County	842	2.63
Ophir, UT (town) Tooele County	1	2.63
North Bergen, NJ (township) Hudson County	1,590	2.62
Kendale Lakes, FL (cdp) Miami-Dade County	1,473	2.62
Weston, FL (city) Broward County	1,677	2.57
Dunellen, NJ (borough) Middlesex County	185	2.56

Place	Population	%
Glenvar Heights, FL (cdp) Miami-Dade County	426	2.52
South Hackensack, NJ (township) Bergen County	60	2.52
Sterling, VA (cdp) Loudoun County	694	2.49
Miami Springs, FL (city) Miami-Dade County	344	2.49
Jamesburg, NJ (borough) Middlesex County	145	2.45
Rutherford, CA (cdp) Napa County	4	2.44
West New York, NJ (town) Hudson County	1,205	2.42
Sunbury, NC (cdp) Gates County	7	2.42
Roselle, NJ (borough) Union County	506	2.40
North Arlington, NJ (borough) Bergen County	369	2.40
Newburgh, NY (city) Orange County	691	2.39
Miami Beach, FL (city) Miami-Dade County	2,091	2.38
Dayton, ID (city) Franklin County	11	2.38
Fountainebleau, FL (cdp) Miami-Dade County	1,408	2.36
Rahway, NJ (city) Union County	644	2.36
Aspen Hill, MD (cdp) Montgomery County	1,144	2.35
Sugarland Run, VA (cdp) Loudoun County	277	2.35
Wheaton, MD (cdp) Montgomery County	1,130	2.34
Tilden, TX (cdp) McMullen County	6	2.30
Fabius, NY (village) Onondaga County	8	2.27
Burke Centre, VA (cdp) Fairfax County	390	2.25
Hailey, ID (city) Blaine County	179	2.25
Annandale, VA (cdp) Fairfax County	917	2.24
Linden, NJ (city) Union County	906	2.24
Ives Estates, FL (cdp) Miami-Dade County	429	2.20
Country Club, FL (cdp) Miami-Dade County	1,033	2.19
North Plainfield, NJ (borough) Somerset County	474	2.16
Pavillion, WY (town) Fremont County	5	2.16
Hollywood, FL (city) Broward County	2,995	2.13
North Bay Shore, NY (cdp) Suffolk County	404	2.13
Finderne, NJ (cdp) Somerset County	119	2.13
Palmetto Estates, FL (cdp) Miami-Dade County	285	2.11
Victory Gardens, NJ (borough) Morris County	32	2.11
Stamford, CT (city/town) Fairfield County	2,560	2.09
Golden Beach, FL (town) Miami-Dade County	19	2.07
Plattekill, NY (cdp) Ulster County	26	2.06
Jackson, MN (township) Scott County	30	2.05
Hawthorne, NJ (borough) Passaic County	375	2.00
Merrifield, VA (cdp) Fairfax County	304	2.00
Guttenberg, NJ (town) Hudson County	224	2.00
Aventura, FL (city) Miami-Dade County	713	1.99
Centreville, VA (cdp) Fairfax County	1,406	1.98
Locust Valley, NY (cdp) Nassau County	67	1.97
Germantown, MD (cdp) Montgomery County	1,672	1.94
Redland, MD (cdp) Montgomery County	334	1.94
Seven Corners, VA (cdp) Fairfax County	179	1.93
Gaithersburg, MD (city) Montgomery County	1,150	1.92
Middlesex, NJ (borough) Middlesex County	262	1.92
Onondaga Nation Reservation, NY (reservation) Onondaga County	9	1.92
Roxbury, KS (cdp) McPherson County	2	1.92
Herndon, VA (town) Fairfax County	443	1.90
Burke, VA (cdp) Fairfax County	774	1.89
East Hartford, CT (cdp/town) Hartford County	962	1.88
Springfield, VA (cdp) Fairfax County	573	1.88
Franklin, ID (city) Franklin County	12	1.87
Acacia Villas, FL (cdp) Palm Beach County	8	1.87
New London, CT (city/town) New London County	513	1.86
Weehawken, NJ (township) Hudson County	232	1.85
Coral Springs, FL (city) Broward County	2,226	1.84
Mamaroneck, NY (village) Westchester County	349	1.84
West Springfield, VA (cdp) Fairfax County	410	1.83
Bedford Hills, NY (cdp) Westchester County	55	1.83
Highland Falls, NY (village) Orange County	71	1.82
Glenmont, MD (cdp) Montgomery County	242	1.79
Sunrise, FL (city) Broward County	1,503	1.78
Chantilly, VA (cdp) Fairfax County	408	1.77
Vails Gate, NY (cdp) Orange County	59	1.75
Island Park, ID (city) Fremont County	5	1.75
Pimmit Hills, VA (cdp) Fairfax County	106	1.74
Bloomfield, NJ (township) Essex County	820	1.73
Ashburn, VA (cdp) Loudoun County	751	1.73
Leesburg, VA (town) Loudoun County	736	1.73
Fort Bidwell, CA (cdp) Modoc County	3	1.73
Newington, VA (cdp) Fairfax County	221	1.71
County Center, VA (cdp) Prince William County	56	1.71

Please refer to the Explanation of Data in the front of the book for more detailed information.

Hispanic Origin

South American: Peruvian

Top 150 Places Sorted by Percent of Total Population

Based on places with total population of 7,500 or more

Place	Population	%
Harrison, NJ (town) Hudson County	1,651	12.12
Kearny, NJ (town) Hudson County	3,315	8.15
Paterson, NJ (city) Passaic County	9,943	6.80
Haledon, NJ (borough) Passaic County	557	6.70
Clifton, NJ (city) Passaic County	4,473	5.32
Port Chester, NY (village) Westchester County	1,485	5.13
Ojus, FL (cdp) Miami-Dade County	897	4.97
Garfield, NJ (city) Bergen County	1,462	4.80
The Hammocks, FL (cdp) Miami-Dade County	2,403	4.71
Union City, NJ (city) Hudson County	3,111	4.68
The Crossings, FL (cdp) Miami-Dade County	1,006	4.42
Elizabeth, NJ (city) Union County	5,419	4.34
White Plains, NY (city) Westchester County	2,260	3.98
Carteret, NJ (borough) Middlesex County	896	3.92
Perth Amboy, NJ (city) Middlesex County	1,979	3.89
Kendall West, FL (cdp) Miami-Dade County	1,369	3.79
Rye, NY (town) Westchester County	1,734	3.78
Three Lakes, FL (cdp) Miami-Dade County	538	3.58
Belleville, NJ (township) Essex County	1,239	3.45
Doral, FL (city) Miami-Dade County	1,535	3.36
Woodland Park, NJ (borough) Passaic County	396	3.35
Glen Cove, NY (city) Nassau County	883	3.27
Key Biscayne, FL (village) Miami-Dade County	397	3.22
Passaic, NJ (city) Passaic County	2,228	3.19
North Miami Beach, FL (city) Miami-Dade County	1,325	3.19
Sunny Isles Beach, FL (city) Miami-Dade County	653	3.13
Kendall, FL (cdp) Miami-Dade County	2,280	3.03
West Orange, NJ (township) Essex County	1,382	2.99
Richmond West, FL (cdp) Miami-Dade County	954	2.98
Elmwood Park, NJ (borough) Bergen County	568	2.93
Lodi, NJ (borough) Bergen County	705	2.92
Country Walk, FL (cdp) Miami-Dade County	467	2.92
Hallandale Beach, FL (city) Broward County	1,053	2.84
Dover, NJ (town) Morris County	505	2.78
Totowa, NJ (borough) Passaic County	294	2.72
Countryside, VA (cdp) Loudoun County	273	2.71
Bound Brook, NJ (borough) Somerset County	279	2.68
Freehold, NJ (borough) Monmouth County	322	2.67
Brentwood, NY (cdp) Suffolk County	1,610	2.65
Montgomery Village, MD (cdp) Montgomery County	842	2.63
North Bergen, NJ (township) Hudson County	1,590	2.62
Kendale Lakes, FL (cdp) Miami-Dade County	1,473	2.62
Weston, FL (city) Broward County	1,677	2.57
Glenvar Heights, FL (cdp) Miami-Dade County	426	2.52
Sterling, VA (cdp) Loudoun County	694	2.49
Miami Springs, FL (city) Miami-Dade County	344	2.49
West New York, NJ (town) Hudson County	1,205	2.42
Roselle, NJ (borough) Union County	506	2.40
North Arlington, NJ (borough) Bergen County	369	2.40
Newburgh, NY (city) Orange County	691	2.39
Miami Beach, FL (city) Miami-Dade County	2,091	2.38
Fountainebleau, FL (cdp) Miami-Dade County	1,408	2.36
Rahway, NJ (city) Union County	644	2.36
Aspen Hill, MD (cdp) Montgomery County	1,144	2.35
Sugarland Run, VA (cdp) Loudoun County	277	2.35
Wheaton, MD (cdp) Montgomery County	1,130	2.34
Burke Centre, VA (cdp) Fairfax County	390	2.25
Hailey, ID (city) Blaine County	179	2.25
Annandale, VA (cdp) Fairfax County	917	2.24
Linden, NJ (city) Union County	906	2.24
Ives Estates, FL (cdp) Miami-Dade County	429	2.20
Country Club, FL (cdp) Miami-Dade County	1,033	2.19
North Plainfield, NJ (borough) Somerset County	474	2.16
Hollywood, FL (city) Broward County	2,995	2.13
North Bay Shore, NY (cdp) Suffolk County	404	2.13
Palmetto Estates, FL (cdp) Miami-Dade County	285	2.11
Stamford, CT (city/town) Fairfield County	2,560	2.09
Hawthorne, NJ (borough) Passaic County	375	2.00
Merrifield, VA (cdp) Fairfax County	304	2.00
Guttenberg, NJ (town) Hudson County	224	2.00
Aventura, FL (city) Miami-Dade County	713	1.99
Centreville, VA (cdp) Fairfax County	1,406	1.98
Germantown, MD (cdp) Montgomery County	1,672	1.94
Redland, MD (cdp) Montgomery County	334	1.94
Seven Corners, VA (cdp) Fairfax County	179	1.93
Gaithersburg, MD (city) Montgomery County	1,150	1.92
Middlesex, NJ (borough) Middlesex County	262	1.92
Herndon, VA (town) Fairfax County	443	1.90
Burke, VA (cdp) Fairfax County	774	1.89
East Hartford, CT (cdp/town) Hartford County	962	1.88
Springfield, VA (cdp) Fairfax County	573	1.88
New London, CT (city/town) New London County	513	1.86
Weehawken, NJ (township) Hudson County	232	1.85
Coral Springs, FL (city) Broward County	2,226	1.84
Mamaroneck, NY (village) Westchester County	349	1.84
West Springfield, VA (cdp) Fairfax County	410	1.83
Glenmont, MD (cdp) Montgomery County	242	1.79
Sunrise, FL (city) Broward County	1,503	1.78
Chantilly, VA (cdp) Fairfax County	408	1.77
Bloomfield, NJ (township) Essex County	820	1.73
Ashburn, VA (cdp) Loudoun County	751	1.73
Leesburg, VA (town) Loudoun County	736	1.73
Newington, VA (cdp) Fairfax County	221	1.71
Pembroke Pines, FL (city) Broward County	2,638	1.70
Hartford, CT (city/town) Hartford County	2,119	1.70
New Rochelle, NY (city) Westchester County	1,297	1.68
Davie, FL (town) Broward County	1,533	1.67
Westwood Lakes, FL (cdp) Miami-Dade County	196	1.66
Lincolnia, VA (cdp) Fairfax County	376	1.65
West Falls Church, VA (cdp) Fairfax County	480	1.64
City of Orange, NJ (township) Essex County	491	1.63
Coconut Creek, FL (city) Broward County	859	1.62
Central Islip, NY (cdp) Suffolk County	558	1.62
Palmetto Bay, FL (village) Miami-Dade County	379	1.62
Lyndhurst, NJ (township) Bergen County	334	1.62
North Kensington, MD (cdp) Montgomery County	153	1.61
Tamarac, FL (city) Broward County	966	1.60
Cutler Bay, FL (town) Miami-Dade County	643	1.60
Lawndale, CA (city) Los Angeles County	525	1.60
Idylwood, VA (cdp) Fairfax County	277	1.60
Newington Forest, VA (cdp) Fairfax County	198	1.59
Lake Ridge, VA (cdp) Prince William County	642	1.56
Rye Brook, NY (village) Westchester County	145	1.55
Miami Shores, FL (village) Miami-Dade County	161	1.53
West Hartford, CT (cdp/town) Hartford County	964	1.52
Ossining, NY (village) Westchester County	381	1.52
Roselle Park, NJ (borough) Union County	201	1.51
Somerville, NJ (borough) Somerset County	183	1.51
Avenel, NJ (cdp) Middlesex County	252	1.48
Yorkshire, VA (cdp) Prince William County	110	1.46
Margate, FL (city) Broward County	772	1.45
Marumsco, VA (cdp) Prince William County	509	1.45
Sunset, FL (cdp) Miami-Dade County	236	1.44
Woodburn, VA (cdp) Fairfax County	122	1.44
Elmont, NY (cdp) Nassau County	465	1.40
Rockville, MD (city) Montgomery County	850	1.39
Coral Gables, FL (city) Miami-Dade County	651	1.39
Dania Beach, FL (city) Broward County	411	1.39
North Lindenhurst, NY (cdp) Suffolk County	162	1.39
Fairfax, VA (ind. city) Fairfax independent city	311	1.38
Lansdowne, VA (cdp) Loudoun County	155	1.38
North Bethesda, MD (cdp) Montgomery County	601	1.37
Valley Stream, NY (village) Nassau County	513	1.37
Meadow Woods, FL (cdp) Orange County	351	1.37
Pinecrest, FL (village) Miami-Dade County	247	1.36
University Park, FL (cdp) Miami-Dade County	353	1.31
Wallington, NJ (borough) Bergen County	149	1.31
Lorton, VA (cdp) Fairfax County	242	1.30
Plantation, FL (city) Broward County	1,071	1.26
Kissimmee, FL (city) Osceola County	750	1.26
Tamiami, FL (cdp) Miami-Dade County	697	1.26
Miami Lakes, FL (town) Miami-Dade County	371	1.26
Bull Run, VA (cdp) Prince William County	189	1.26
Manville, NJ (borough) Somerset County	130	1.26
East Rutherford, NJ (borough) Bergen County	112	1.26
Norwich, CT (city/town) New London County	507	1.25
Fairfax Station, VA (cdp) Fairfax County	150	1.25
Bogota, NJ (borough) Bergen County	102	1.25
Miami, FL (city) Miami-Dade County	4,946	1.24
Oakland Park, FL (city) Broward County	514	1.24

SECTION THREE

Please refer to the Explanation of Data in the front of the book for more detailed information.

Hispanic Origin

South American: Uruguayan

U.S. and 50 States Sorted by Population and Percent of Total Population

Place	Population	%
United States	**56,884**	**0.02**
Florida	14,542	0.08
New Jersey	10,902	0.12
New York	6,021	0.03
California	4,110	0.01
Georgia	2,708	0.03
Texas	2,566	0.01
Massachusetts	2,317	0.04
Virginia	1,594	0.02
Connecticut	1,294	0.04
Maryland	1,282	0.02
Pennsylvania	1,181	0.01
Utah	1,011	0.04
North Carolina	980	0.01
South Carolina	853	0.02
Illinois	737	0.01
Arizona	422	0.01
Nevada	407	0.02
New Hampshire	351	0.03
Wisconsin	338	0.01
Washington	301	<0.01
Ohio	291	<0.01
Colorado	224	<0.01
Michigan	224	<0.01
Minnesota	223	<0.01
District of Columbia	216	0.04
Tennessee	214	<0.01
Missouri	179	<0.01
Indiana	150	<0.01
Oregon	132	<0.01
Alabama	129	<0.01
Rhode Island	112	0.01
Louisiana	109	<0.01
Kentucky	93	<0.01
Kansas	83	<0.01
New Mexico	81	<0.01
Oklahoma	78	<0.01
Hawaii	63	<0.01
Iowa	61	<0.01
Delaware	50	0.01
Mississippi	49	<0.01
Idaho	35	<0.01
Vermont	28	<0.01
West Virginia	26	<0.01
Arkansas	25	<0.01
Alaska	24	<0.01
Nebraska	24	<0.01
South Dakota	12	<0.01
Maine	11	<0.01
Wyoming	9	<0.01
Montana	8	<0.01
North Dakota	4	<0.01

Place	Population	%
New Jersey	10,902	0.12
Florida	14,542	0.08
Massachusetts	2,317	0.04
Connecticut	1,294	0.04
Utah	1,011	0.04
District of Columbia	216	0.04
New York	6,021	0.03
Georgia	2,708	0.03
New Hampshire	351	0.03
United States	**56,884**	**0.02**
Virginia	1,594	0.02
Maryland	1,282	0.02
South Carolina	853	0.02
Nevada	407	0.02
California	4,110	0.01
Texas	2,566	0.01
Pennsylvania	1,181	0.01
North Carolina	980	0.01
Illinois	737	0.01
Arizona	422	0.01
Wisconsin	338	0.01
Rhode Island	112	0.01
Delaware	50	0.01
Washington	301	<0.01
Ohio	291	<0.01
Colorado	224	<0.01
Michigan	224	<0.01
Minnesota	223	<0.01
Tennessee	214	<0.01
Missouri	179	<0.01
Indiana	150	<0.01
Oregon	132	<0.01
Alabama	129	<0.01
Louisiana	109	<0.01
Kentucky	93	<0.01
Kansas	83	<0.01
New Mexico	81	<0.01
Oklahoma	78	<0.01
Hawaii	63	<0.01
Iowa	61	<0.01
Mississippi	49	<0.01
Idaho	35	<0.01
Vermont	28	<0.01
West Virginia	26	<0.01
Arkansas	25	<0.01
Alaska	24	<0.01
Nebraska	24	<0.01
South Dakota	12	<0.01
Maine	11	<0.01
Wyoming	9	<0.01
Montana	8	<0.01
North Dakota	4	<0.01

Please refer to the Explanation of Data in the front of the book for more detailed information.

Hispanic Origin

South American: Uruguayan

Top 150 Places Sorted by Population

Based on all places, regardless of total population

Place	Population	%
New York, NY (city) Kings County	3,004	0.04
Elizabeth, NJ (city) Union County	2,553	2.04
Queens, NY (borough) Queens County	1,743	0.08
Miami, FL (city) Miami-Dade County	1,040	0.26
Miami Beach, FL (city) Miami-Dade County	958	1.09
Leominster, MA (city) Worcester County	824	2.02
West Orange, NJ (township) Essex County	733	1.59
Los Angeles, CA (city) Los Angeles County	697	0.02
Fitchburg, MA (city) Worcester County	650	1.61
Houston, TX (city) Harris County	642	0.03
Newark, NJ (city) Essex County	634	0.23
Manhattan, NY (borough) New York County	549	0.03
Hollywood, FL (city) Broward County	498	0.35
Brooklyn, NY (borough) Kings County	488	0.02
City of Orange, NJ (township) Essex County	445	1.48
Kearny, NJ (town) Hudson County	418	1.03
Stamford, CT (city/town) Fairfield County	371	0.30
Hempstead, NY (town) Nassau County	359	0.05
Dover, NJ (town) Morris County	307	1.69
Hialeah, FL (city) Miami-Dade County	291	0.13
Ossining, NY (town) Westchester County	273	0.72
Chicago, IL (city) Cook County	267	0.01
Charlotte, NC (city) Mecklenburg County	262	0.04
Pembroke Pines, FL (city) Broward County	243	0.16
Philadelphia, PA (city) Philadelphia County	234	0.02
Ossining, NY (village) Westchester County	230	0.92
Coral Springs, FL (city) Broward County	224	0.18
Oakland Park, FL (city) Broward County	218	0.53
Fort Lauderdale, FL (city) Broward County	218	0.13
Islip, NY (town) Suffolk County	216	0.06
Washington, DC (city) District of Columbia	216	0.04
Hallandale Beach, FL (city) Broward County	213	0.57
Rye, NY (town) Westchester County	211	0.46
Manchester, NH (city) Hillsborough County	211	0.19
Linden, NJ (city) Union County	209	0.52
Fountainebleau, FL (cdp) Miami-Dade County	209	0.35
Paterson, NJ (city) Passaic County	204	0.14
North Bergen, NJ (township) Hudson County	201	0.33
Deerfield Beach, FL (city) Broward County	195	0.26
Pompano Beach, FL (city) Broward County	195	0.20
Hilton Head Island, SC (town) Beaufort County	189	0.51
Kendall, FL (cdp) Miami-Dade County	188	0.25
North Miami Beach, FL (city) Miami-Dade County	186	0.45
Union City, NJ (city) Hudson County	181	0.27
Doral, FL (city) Miami-Dade County	180	0.39
Sunny Isles Beach, FL (city) Miami-Dade County	170	0.82
Woodbridge, NJ (township) Middlesex County	166	0.17
Kissimmee, FL (city) Osceola County	164	0.27
Kendale Lakes, FL (cdp) Miami-Dade County	161	0.29
Port Chester, NY (village) Westchester County	159	0.55
Jersey City, NJ (city) Hudson County	149	0.06
Aventura, FL (city) Miami-Dade County	148	0.41
Bronx, NY (borough) Bronx County	148	0.01
Coral Gables, FL (city) Miami-Dade County	147	0.31
Greenwich, CT (town) Fairfield County	146	0.24
Raleigh, NC (city) Wake County	146	0.04
Kendall West, FL (cdp) Miami-Dade County	145	0.40
Miramar, FL (city) Broward County	142	0.12
San Diego, CA (city) San Diego County	141	0.01
Cortlandt, NY (town) Westchester County	140	0.34
Harrison, NJ (town) Hudson County	137	1.01
Sunrise, FL (city) Broward County	135	0.16
Oyster Bay, NY (town) Nassau County	134	0.05
Weston, FL (city) Broward County	133	0.20
Union, NJ (township) Union County	131	0.23
Greenacres, FL (city) Palm Beach County	130	0.35
The Hammocks, FL (cdp) Miami-Dade County	130	0.25
Arlington, VA (cdp) Arlington County	129	0.06
Orlando, FL (city) Orange County	129	0.05
Jacksonville, FL (city) Duval County	129	0.02
Norwalk, CT (city/town) Fairfield County	128	0.15
West Palm Beach, FL (city) Palm Beach County	128	0.13
West New York, NJ (town) Hudson County	127	0.26
Hillside, NJ (township) Union County	125	0.58
Tamarac, FL (city) Broward County	125	0.21
Roselle, NJ (borough) Union County	124	0.59
West Jordan, UT (city) Salt Lake County	123	0.12
North Miami, FL (city) Miami-Dade County	122	0.21
Davie, FL (town) Broward County	121	0.13
Cape Coral, FL (city) Lee County	121	0.08
Wellington, FL (village) Palm Beach County	120	0.21
Belleville, NJ (township) Essex County	119	0.33
San Francisco, CA (city) San Francisco County	118	0.01
Las Vegas, NV (city) Clark County	117	0.02
Wharton, NJ (borough) Morris County	116	1.78
Plantation, FL (city) Broward County	115	0.14
Ojus, FL (cdp) Miami-Dade County	114	0.63
Bridgeport, CT (city/town) Fairfield County	110	0.08
Bloomfield, NJ (township) Essex County	108	0.23
Roswell, GA (city) Fulton County	107	0.12
Phoenix, AZ (city) Maricopa County	106	0.01
Palm Springs, FL (village) Palm Beach County	104	0.55
Dallas, TX (city) Dallas County	103	0.01
Port St. Lucie, FL (city) St. Lucie County	102	0.06
Country Club, FL (cdp) Miami-Dade County	100	0.21
Bluffton, SC (town) Beaufort County	98	0.78
Key Biscayne, FL (village) Miami-Dade County	93	0.75
Boynton Beach, FL (city) Palm Beach County	93	0.14
Peekskill, NY (city) Westchester County	92	0.39
Palm Coast, FL (city) Flagler County	92	0.12
Tampa, FL (city) Hillsborough County	91	0.03
Mount Olive, NJ (township) Morris County	88	0.31
New Rochelle, NY (city) Westchester County	88	0.11
Boca Raton, FL (city) Palm Beach County	88	0.10
Salt Lake City, UT (city) Salt Lake County	87	0.05
Brookhaven, NY (town) Suffolk County	87	0.02
Roselle Park, NJ (borough) Union County	86	0.65
San Antonio, TX (city) Medina County	86	0.01
North Hempstead, NY (town) Nassau County	84	0.04
The Crossings, FL (cdp) Miami-Dade County	81	0.36
Margate, FL (city) Broward County	80	0.15
Brentwood, NY (cdp) Suffolk County	80	0.13
Tamiami, FL (cdp) Miami-Dade County	79	0.14
Bethesda, MD (cdp) Montgomery County	79	0.13
Clifton, NJ (city) Passaic County	78	0.09
Austin, TX (city) Travis County	77	0.01
Boston, MA (city) Suffolk County	77	0.01
Perth Amboy, NJ (city) Middlesex County	76	0.15
Staten Island, NY (borough) Richmond County	76	0.02
Egypt Lake-Leto, FL (cdp) Hillsborough County	75	0.21
East Orange, NJ (city) Essex County	75	0.12
North Lauderdale, FL (city) Broward County	74	0.18
Passaic, NJ (city) Passaic County	73	0.10
Orem, UT (city) Utah County	73	0.08
Madison, WI (city) Dane County	70	0.03
Carteret, NJ (borough) Middlesex County	69	0.30
Gaithersburg, MD (city) Montgomery County	69	0.12
Rock Hill, SC (city) York County	69	0.10
Scranton, PA (city) Lackawanna County	69	0.09
Randolph, NJ (township) Morris County	68	0.26
Westchester, FL (cdp) Miami-Dade County	66	0.22
Anaheim, CA (city) Orange County	66	0.02
Greenburgh, NY (town) Westchester County	65	0.07
North Bethesda, MD (cdp) Montgomery County	64	0.15
Parsippany-Troy Hills, NJ (township) Morris County	64	0.12
Babylon, NY (town) Suffolk County	64	0.03
White Plains, NY (city) Westchester County	63	0.11
Germantown, MD (cdp) Montgomery County	63	0.07
Brandon, FL (cdp) Hillsborough County	63	0.06
Worcester, MA (city) Worcester County	63	0.03
Lake Worth, FL (city) Palm Beach County	62	0.18
Bayonne, NJ (city) Hudson County	62	0.10
Old Bridge, NJ (township) Middlesex County	62	0.09
Doraville, GA (city) DeKalb County	61	0.73
Allentown, PA (city) Lehigh County	61	0.05
Cutler Bay, FL (town) Miami-Dade County	59	0.15
Potomac, MD (cdp) Montgomery County	59	0.13
Baltimore, MD (city) Baltimore city County	59	0.01
Greenwich, CT (cdp) Fairfield County	58	0.45
Rockville, MD (city) Montgomery County	58	0.09

Please refer to the Explanation of Data in the front of the book for more detailed information.

SECTION THREE

Hispanic Origin

South American: Uruguayan

Top 150 Places Sorted by Percent of Total Population

Based on all places, regardless of total population

Place	Population	%
Ridgeway, WI (village) Iowa County	18	2.76
Albrightsville, PA (cdp) Carbon County	5	2.48
New Harmony, UT (town) Washington County	5	2.42
Vineyard, UT (town) Utah County	3	2.16
Elizabeth, NJ (city) Union County	2,553	2.04
Leominster, MA (city) Worcester County	824	2.02
Glen Ridge, FL (town) Palm Beach County	4	1.83
Wharton, NJ (borough) Morris County	116	1.78
Victory Gardens, NJ (borough) Morris County	26	1.71
Dover, NJ (town) Morris County	307	1.69
Fitchburg, MA (city) Worcester County	650	1.61
West Orange, NJ (township) Essex County	733	1.59
City of Orange, NJ (township) Essex County	445	1.48
Blawenburg, NJ (cdp) Somerset County	4	1.43
Grover, NC (town) Cleveland County	8	1.13
Miami Beach, FL (city) Miami-Dade County	958	1.09
Kearny, NJ (town) Hudson County	418	1.03
Harrison, NJ (town) Hudson County	137	1.01
Surfside, FL (town) Miami-Dade County	56	0.97
Brick Center, CO (cdp) Arapahoe County	1	0.93
Ossining, NY (village) Westchester County	230	0.92
Middleburg, VA (town) Loudoun County	6	0.89
Wing River, MN (township) Wadena County	4	0.85
Sunny Isles Beach, FL (city) Miami-Dade County	170	0.82
Bay Harbor Islands, FL (town) Miami-Dade County	45	0.80
Idledale, CO (cdp) Jefferson County	2	0.79
Bluffton, SC (town) Beaufort County	98	0.78
Deerfield, MA (cdp) Franklin County	5	0.78
Williston, TN (city) Fayette County	3	0.76
Fisher Island, FL (cdp) Miami-Dade County	1	0.76
Key Biscayne, FL (village) Miami-Dade County	93	0.75
Mount Sidney, VA (cdp) Augusta County	5	0.75
Doraville, GA (city) DeKalb County	61	0.73
Ossining, NY (town) Westchester County	273	0.72
Blue Mounds, WI (town) Dane County	7	0.72
Haena, HI (cdp) Kauai County	3	0.70
Cove Neck, NY (village) Nassau County	2	0.70
Glenville, CT (cdp) Fairfield County	16	0.69
Beattystown, NJ (cdp) Warren County	31	0.68
Lunenburg, MA (cdp) Worcester County	12	0.68
Hilshire Village, TX (city) Harris County	5	0.67
Novi, MI (township) Oakland County	1	0.67
North Bay Village, FL (city) Miami-Dade County	47	0.66
Royal Palm Estates, FL (cdp) Palm Beach County	20	0.66
Roselle Park, NJ (borough) Union County	86	0.65
Plain, WI (village) Sauk County	5	0.65
Brooklyn, WI (village) Green County	3	0.65
Topaz Lake, NV (cdp) Douglas County	1	0.64
Ojus, FL (cdp) Miami-Dade County	114	0.63
Mine Hill, NJ (township) Morris County	22	0.60
Roselle, NJ (borough) Union County	124	0.59
Centralia, KS (city) Nemaha County	3	0.59
Hillside, NJ (township) Union County	125	0.58
East Newark, NJ (borough) Hudson County	14	0.58
Buchanan, NY (village) Westchester County	13	0.58
Barnesville, MD (town) Montgomery County	1	0.58
Hallandale Beach, FL (city) Broward County	213	0.57
Pembroke Park, FL (town) Broward County	35	0.57
Irondale, GA (cdp) Clayton County	42	0.56
Port Chester, NY (village) Westchester County	159	0.55
Palm Springs, FL (village) Palm Beach County	104	0.55
Hillside Lake, NY (cdp) Dutchess County	6	0.55
Friendship, WI (village) Adams County	4	0.55
Oakland Park, FL (city) Broward County	218	0.53
Woxhall, PA (cdp) Montgomery County	7	0.53
Linden, NJ (city) Union County	209	0.52
Old Forge, PA (borough) Lackawanna County	43	0.52
Silver Lake, NJ (cdp) Essex County	22	0.52
Crugers, NY (cdp) Westchester County	8	0.52
Hilton Head Island, SC (town) Beaufort County	189	0.51
Byram, CT (cdp) Fairfield County	21	0.51
Glenfield, PA (borough) Allegheny County	1	0.49
Mansfield, NJ (township) Warren County	37	0.48
Rye, NY (town) Westchester County	211	0.46
North Miami Beach, FL (city) Miami-Dade County	186	0.45
Greenwich, CT (cdp) Fairfield County	58	0.45
Budd Lake, NJ (cdp) Morris County	40	0.45
Islandia, NY (village) Suffolk County	15	0.45
Golden Beach, FL (town) Miami-Dade County	4	0.44
Duryea, PA (borough) Luzerne County	21	0.43
Alhambra Valley, CA (cdp) Contra Costa County	4	0.43
Napoleon, IN (town) Ripley County	1	0.43
Chappaqua, NY (cdp) Westchester County	6	0.42
Aventura, FL (city) Miami-Dade County	148	0.41
Roseland, NJ (borough) Essex County	24	0.41
Kendall West, FL (cdp) Miami-Dade County	145	0.40
Newton, NJ (town) Sussex County	32	0.40
Kenvil, NJ (cdp) Morris County	12	0.40
Kingston, NJ (cdp) Middlesex County	6	0.40
Doral, FL (city) Miami-Dade County	180	0.39
Peekskill, NY (city) Westchester County	92	0.39
Madison Park, NJ (cdp) Middlesex County	28	0.39
Biscayne Park, FL (village) Miami-Dade County	12	0.39
Byron, CA (cdp) Contra Costa County	5	0.39
New Berlin, TX (city) Guadalupe County	2	0.39
Seminole Manor, FL (cdp) Palm Beach County	10	0.38
Desert View Highlands, CA (cdp) Los Angeles County	9	0.38
The Crossings, FL (cdp) Miami-Dade County	81	0.36
Evansville, WI (city) Rock County	18	0.36
South Chicago Heights, IL (village) Cook County	15	0.36
Hollywood, FL (city) Broward County	498	0.35
Fountainebleau, FL (cdp) Miami-Dade County	209	0.35
Greenacres, FL (city) Palm Beach County	130	0.35
Emerald Lakes, PA (cdp) Monroe County	10	0.35
Ghent, NY (cdp) Columbia County	2	0.35
Cortlandt, NY (town) Westchester County	140	0.34
Netcong, NJ (borough) Morris County	11	0.34
Brewster, WA (city) Okanogan County	8	0.34
Kensington, NY (village) Nassau County	4	0.34
Plandome Manor, NY (village) Nassau County	3	0.34
North Bergen, NJ (township) Hudson County	201	0.33
Belleville, NJ (township) Essex County	119	0.33
Penn Estates, PA (cdp) Monroe County	15	0.33
Montrose, NY (cdp) Westchester County	9	0.33
Kenilworth, NJ (borough) Union County	25	0.32
Coral Gables, FL (city) Miami-Dade County	147	0.31
Mount Olive, NJ (township) Morris County	88	0.31
Country Walk, FL (cdp) Miami-Dade County	50	0.31
Lovettsville, VA (town) Loudoun County	5	0.31
Kenwood Estates, FL (cdp) Palm Beach County	4	0.31
Beauregard, MS (village) Copiah County	1	0.31
Stamford, CT (city/town) Fairfield County	371	0.30
Carteret, NJ (borough) Middlesex County	69	0.30
Hopatcong, NJ (borough) Sussex County	45	0.30
Guttenberg, NJ (town) Hudson County	33	0.30
Lunenburg, MA (town) Worcester County	30	0.30
Lake Belvedere Estates, FL (cdp) Palm Beach County	10	0.30
Pine Air, FL (cdp) Palm Beach County	6	0.30
Millbrook, IL (village) Kendall County	1	0.30
Kendale Lakes, FL (cdp) Miami-Dade County	161	0.29
Sleepy Hollow, NY (village) Westchester County	29	0.29
Croton-on-Hudson, NY (village) Westchester County	23	0.29
Dunellen, NJ (borough) Middlesex County	21	0.29
Southwest Ranches, FL (town) Broward County	21	0.29
Bonanza, GA (cdp) Clayton County	9	0.29
Union, WI (town) Rock County	6	0.29
Upper Nyack, NY (village) Rockland County	6	0.29
Nissequogue, NY (village) Suffolk County	5	0.29
Richland, WI (town) Richland County	4	0.29
Edinburg, VA (town) Shenandoah County	3	0.29
Pioneer, FL (cdp) Hendry County	2	0.29
Rocky Hill, NJ (borough) Somerset County	2	0.29
Dodgeville, WI (city) Iowa County	13	0.28
Muhlenberg Park, PA (cdp) Berks County	4	0.28
Union City, NJ (city) Hudson County	181	0.27
Kissimmee, FL (city) Osceola County	164	0.27
Lyndhurst, NJ (township) Bergen County	56	0.27
Cos Cob, CT (cdp) Fairfield County	18	0.27
Hillsboro Beach, FL (town) Broward County	5	0.27
Lyndhurst, VA (cdp) Augusta County	4	0.27

Please refer to the Explanation of Data in the front of the book for more detailed information.

Hispanic Origin

South American: Uruguayan

Top 150 Places Sorted by Percent of Total Population

Based on places with total population of 7,500 or more

Place	Population	%
Elizabeth, NJ (city) Union County	2,553	2.04
Leominster, MA (city) Worcester County	824	2.02
Dover, NJ (town) Morris County	307	1.69
Fitchburg, MA (city) Worcester County	650	1.61
West Orange, NJ (township) Essex County	733	1.59
City of Orange, NJ (township) Essex County	445	1.48
Miami Beach, FL (city) Miami-Dade County	958	1.09
Kearny, NJ (town) Hudson County	418	1.03
Harrison, NJ (town) Hudson County	137	1.01
Ossining, NY (village) Westchester County	230	0.92
Sunny Isles Beach, FL (city) Miami-Dade County	170	0.82
Bluffton, SC (town) Beaufort County	98	0.78
Key Biscayne, FL (village) Miami-Dade County	93	0.75
Doraville, GA (city) DeKalb County	61	0.73
Ossining, NY (town) Westchester County	273	0.72
Roselle Park, NJ (borough) Union County	86	0.65
Ojus, FL (cdp) Miami-Dade County	114	0.63
Roselle, NJ (borough) Union County	124	0.59
Hillside, NJ (township) Union County	125	0.58
Hallandale Beach, FL (city) Broward County	213	0.57
Port Chester, NY (village) Westchester County	159	0.55
Palm Springs, FL (village) Palm Beach County	104	0.55
Oakland Park, FL (city) Broward County	218	0.53
Linden, NJ (city) Union County	209	0.52
Old Forge, PA (borough) Lackawanna County	43	0.52
Hilton Head Island, SC (town) Beaufort County	189	0.51
Mansfield, NJ (township) Warren County	37	0.48
Rye, NY (town) Westchester County	211	0.46
North Miami Beach, FL (city) Miami-Dade County	186	0.45
Greenwich, CT (cdp) Fairfield County	58	0.45
Budd Lake, NJ (cdp) Morris County	40	0.45
Aventura, FL (city) Miami-Dade County	148	0.41
Kendall West, FL (cdp) Miami-Dade County	145	0.40
Newton, NJ (town) Sussex County	32	0.40
Doral, FL (city) Miami-Dade County	180	0.39
Peekskill, NY (city) Westchester County	92	0.39
The Crossings, FL (cdp) Miami-Dade County	81	0.36
Hollywood, FL (city) Broward County	498	0.35
Fountainebleau, FL (cdp) Miami-Dade County	209	0.35
Greenacres, FL (city) Palm Beach County	130	0.35
Cortlandt, NY (town) Westchester County	140	0.34
North Bergen, NJ (township) Hudson County	201	0.33
Belleville, NJ (township) Essex County	119	0.33
Kenilworth, NJ (borough) Union County	25	0.32
Coral Gables, FL (city) Miami-Dade County	147	0.31
Mount Olive, NJ (township) Morris County	88	0.31
Country Walk, FL (cdp) Miami-Dade County	50	0.31
Stamford, CT (city/town) Fairfield County	371	0.30
Carteret, NJ (borough) Middlesex County	69	0.30
Hopatcong, NJ (borough) Sussex County	45	0.30
Guttenberg, NJ (town) Hudson County	33	0.30
Lunenburg, MA (town) Worcester County	30	0.30
Kendale Lakes, FL (cdp) Miami-Dade County	161	0.29
Sleepy Hollow, NY (village) Westchester County	29	0.29
Croton-on-Hudson, NY (village) Westchester County	23	0.29
Union City, NJ (city) Hudson County	181	0.27
Kissimmee, FL (city) Osceola County	164	0.27
Lyndhurst, NJ (township) Bergen County	56	0.27
Miami, FL (city) Miami-Dade County	1,040	0.26
Deerfield Beach, FL (city) Broward County	195	0.26
West New York, NJ (town) Hudson County	127	0.26
Randolph, NJ (township) Morris County	68	0.26
Weehawken, NJ (township) Hudson County	33	0.26
Kendall, FL (cdp) Miami-Dade County	188	0.25
The Hammocks, FL (cdp) Miami-Dade County	130	0.25
North Arlington, NJ (borough) Bergen County	38	0.25
Rye Brook, NY (village) Westchester County	23	0.25
Greenwich, CT (town) Fairfield County	146	0.24
Fords, NJ (cdp) Middlesex County	37	0.24
Woodland Park, NJ (borough) Passaic County	28	0.24
Newark, NJ (city) Essex County	634	0.23
Union, NJ (township) Union County	131	0.23
Bloomfield, NJ (township) Essex County	108	0.23
Woodbridge, NJ (cdp) Middlesex County	45	0.23
Mamaroneck, NY (village) Westchester County	44	0.23
Country Club Estates, GA (cdp) Glynn County	20	0.23
Westchester, FL (cdp) Miami-Dade County	66	0.22
Boonton, NJ (town) Morris County	18	0.22
Tamarac, FL (city) Broward County	125	0.21
North Miami, FL (city) Miami-Dade County	122	0.21
Wellington, FL (village) Palm Beach County	120	0.21
Country Club, FL (cdp) Miami-Dade County	100	0.21
Egypt Lake-Leto, FL (cdp) Hillsborough County	75	0.21
University Park, FL (cdp) Miami-Dade County	57	0.21
Springfield, NJ (township) Union County	34	0.21
Clark, NJ (township) Union County	31	0.21
Edgewater, NJ (borough) Bergen County	24	0.21
Pompano Beach, FL (city) Broward County	195	0.20
Weston, FL (city) Broward County	133	0.20
Golden Gate, FL (cdp) Collier County	47	0.20
Pinecrest, FL (village) Miami-Dade County	36	0.20
Farmingdale, NY (village) Nassau County	16	0.20
Manchester, NH (city) Hillsborough County	211	0.19
Oak Ridge, FL (cdp) Orange County	42	0.19
Avenel, NJ (cdp) Middlesex County	33	0.19
Coral Springs, FL (city) Broward County	224	0.18
North Lauderdale, FL (city) Broward County	74	0.18
Lake Worth, FL (city) Palm Beach County	62	0.18
Fairview, NJ (borough) Bergen County	25	0.18
Brookdale, NJ (cdp) Essex County	17	0.18
Haledon, NJ (borough) Passaic County	15	0.18
Woodbridge, NJ (township) Middlesex County	166	0.17
Miami Lakes, FL (town) Miami-Dade County	50	0.17
Lawrenceville, GA (city) Gwinnett County	49	0.17
Rockaway, NJ (township) Morris County	42	0.17
Hialeah Gardens, FL (city) Miami-Dade County	37	0.17
Ives Estates, FL (cdp) Miami-Dade County	34	0.17
Ridgefield Park, NJ (village) Bergen County	22	0.17
Lighthouse Point, FL (city) Broward County	18	0.17
Hacketts, NJ (town) Warren County	17	0.17
Pembroke Pines, FL (city) Broward County	243	0.16
Sunrise, FL (city) Broward County	135	0.16
Royal Palm Beach, FL (village) Palm Beach County	56	0.16
North Bay Shore, NY (cdp) Suffolk County	31	0.16
Beacon, NY (city) Dutchess County	25	0.16
Fernandina Beach, FL (city) Nassau County	18	0.16
Tarrytown, NY (village) Westchester County	18	0.16
Little Ferry, NJ (borough) Bergen County	17	0.16
Bogota, NJ (borough) Bergen County	13	0.16
Westgate, FL (cdp) Palm Beach County	13	0.16
Norwalk, CT (city/town) Fairfield County	128	0.15
Margate, FL (city) Broward County	80	0.15
Perth Amboy, NJ (city) Middlesex County	76	0.15
North Bethesda, MD (cdp) Montgomery County	64	0.15
Cutler Bay, FL (town) Miami-Dade County	59	0.15
Dania Beach, FL (city) Broward County	43	0.15
Wappinger, NY (town) Dutchess County	41	0.15
Coral Terrace, FL (cdp) Miami-Dade County	37	0.15
Roxbury, NJ (township) Morris County	36	0.15
Princeton, FL (cdp) Miami-Dade County	34	0.15
Sunset, FL (cdp) Miami-Dade County	25	0.15
Southchase, FL (cdp) Orange County	24	0.15
Brunswick, GA (city) Glynn County	23	0.15
Rye, NY (city) Westchester County	23	0.15
Three Lakes, FL (cdp) Miami-Dade County	23	0.15
South Miami, FL (city) Miami-Dade County	18	0.15
Paterson, NJ (city) Passaic County	204	0.14
Plantation, FL (city) Broward County	115	0.14
Boynton Beach, FL (city) Palm Beach County	93	0.14
Tamiami, FL (cdp) Miami-Dade County	79	0.14
Yorktown, NY (town) Westchester County	49	0.14
Peachtree City, GA (city) Fayette County	47	0.14
Rahway, NJ (city) Union County	37	0.14
Maplewood, NJ (township) Essex County	33	0.14
Elmwood Park, NJ (borough) Bergen County	27	0.14
Glenvar Heights, FL (cdp) Miami-Dade County	24	0.14
New Milford, NJ (borough) Bergen County	23	0.14
West University Place, TX (city) Harris County	20	0.14
Berkeley Heights, NJ (township) Union County	18	0.14
Lantana, FL (town) Palm Beach County	15	0.14

SECTION THREE

Please refer to the Explanation of Data in the front of the book for more detailed information.

Hispanic Origin

South American: Venezuelan

U.S. and 50 States Sorted by Population and Percent of Total Population

Place	Population	%
United States	**215,023**	**0.07**
Florida	102,116	0.54
Texas	20,162	0.08
New York	13,910	0.07
California	11,100	0.03
New Jersey	6,950	0.08
Georgia	6,289	0.06
Virginia	4,429	0.06
North Carolina	4,070	0.04
Massachusetts	3,982	0.06
Maryland	3,328	0.06
Illinois	3,283	0.03
Pennsylvania	3,243	0.03
Utah	2,698	0.10
Ohio	2,190	0.02
Connecticut	2,129	0.06
Colorado	1,802	0.04
Arizona	1,707	0.03
Tennessee	1,667	0.03
Louisiana	1,591	0.04
Washington	1,556	0.02
Michigan	1,496	0.02
Indiana	1,440	0.02
Oklahoma	1,352	0.04
South Carolina	1,315	0.03
Minnesota	1,017	0.02
Missouri	901	0.02
Nevada	878	0.03
Wisconsin	868	0.02
Alabama	757	0.02
Oregon	712	0.02
Rhode Island	643	0.06
Kansas	639	0.02
Kentucky	637	0.01
District of Columbia	596	0.10
Mississippi	412	0.01
New Mexico	394	0.02
Delaware	389	0.04
Nebraska	319	0.02
Iowa	310	0.01
Arkansas	300	0.01
Hawaii	287	0.02
New Hampshire	243	0.02
Idaho	200	0.01
Maine	146	0.01
West Virginia	142	0.01
Alaska	140	0.02
Vermont	87	0.01
Montana	67	0.01
Wyoming	66	0.01
North Dakota	43	0.01
South Dakota	25	<0.01

Place	Population	%
Florida	102,116	0.54
Utah	2,698	0.10
District of Columbia	596	0.10
Texas	20,162	0.08
New Jersey	6,950	0.08
United States	**215,023**	**0.07**
New York	13,910	0.07
Georgia	6,289	0.06
Virginia	4,429	0.06
Massachusetts	3,982	0.06
Maryland	3,328	0.06
Connecticut	2,129	0.06
Rhode Island	643	0.06
North Carolina	4,070	0.04
Colorado	1,802	0.04
Louisiana	1,591	0.04
Oklahoma	1,352	0.04
Delaware	389	0.04
California	11,100	0.03
Illinois	3,283	0.03
Pennsylvania	3,243	0.03
Arizona	1,707	0.03
Tennessee	1,667	0.03
South Carolina	1,315	0.03
Nevada	878	0.03
Ohio	2,190	0.02
Washington	1,556	0.02
Michigan	1,496	0.02
Indiana	1,440	0.02
Minnesota	1,017	0.02
Missouri	901	0.02
Wisconsin	868	0.02
Alabama	757	0.02
Oregon	712	0.02
Kansas	639	0.02
New Mexico	394	0.02
Nebraska	319	0.02
Hawaii	287	0.02
New Hampshire	243	0.02
Alaska	140	0.02
Kentucky	637	0.01
Mississippi	412	0.01
Iowa	310	0.01
Arkansas	300	0.01
Idaho	200	0.01
Maine	146	0.01
West Virginia	142	0.01
Vermont	87	0.01
Montana	67	0.01
Wyoming	66	0.01
North Dakota	43	0.01
South Dakota	25	<0.01

Please refer to the Explanation of Data in the front of the book for more detailed information.

Hispanic Origin

South American: Venezuelan

Top 150 Places Sorted by Population

Based on all places, regardless of total population

Place	Population	%
New York, NY (city) Kings County	9,619	0.12
Doral, FL (city) Miami-Dade County	9,423	20.62
Weston, FL (city) Broward County	6,360	9.73
Miami, FL (city) Miami-Dade County	5,770	1.44
Houston, TX (city) Harris County	3,770	0.18
Queens, NY (borough) Queens County	3,580	0.16
Pembroke Pines, FL (city) Broward County	2,937	1.90
Miramar, FL (city) Broward County	2,594	2.13
Manhattan, NY (borough) New York County	2,573	0.16
Fountainebleau, FL (cdp) Miami-Dade County	2,334	3.91
Orlando, FL (city) Orange County	2,076	0.87
The Hammocks, FL (cdp) Miami-Dade County	2,065	4.05
Brooklyn, NY (borough) Kings County	1,916	0.08
Miami Beach, FL (city) Miami-Dade County	1,802	2.05
Aventura, FL (city) Miami-Dade County	1,765	4.94
Kendall, FL (cdp) Miami-Dade County	1,611	2.14
Los Angeles, CA (city) Los Angeles County	1,490	0.04
Coral Springs, FL (city) Broward County	1,414	1.17
Hialeah, FL (city) Miami-Dade County	1,405	0.63
Hollywood, FL (city) Broward County	1,334	0.95
Bronx, NY (borough) Bronx County	1,296	0.09
Sunrise, FL (city) Broward County	1,241	1.47
Davie, FL (town) Broward County	1,231	1.34
Coral Gables, FL (city) Miami-Dade County	1,201	2.57
Country Club, FL (cdp) Miami-Dade County	1,161	2.46
Chicago, IL (city) Cook County	1,121	0.04
Kendall West, FL (cdp) Miami-Dade County	1,118	3.09
Kendale Lakes, FL (cdp) Miami-Dade County	1,082	1.93
Boston, MA (city) Suffolk County	1,019	0.16
Tamiami, FL (cdp) Miami-Dade County	1,018	1.84
Kissimmee, FL (city) Osceola County	848	1.42
Plantation, FL (city) Broward County	836	0.98
Austin, TX (city) Travis County	823	0.10
Charlotte, NC (city) Mecklenburg County	818	0.11
Tampa, FL (city) Hillsborough County	785	0.23
Philadelphia, PA (city) Philadelphia County	773	0.05
Jacksonville, FL (city) Duval County	751	0.09
Sunny Isles Beach, FL (city) Miami-Dade County	734	3.52
Pompano Beach, FL (city) Broward County	719	0.72
Key Biscayne, FL (village) Miami-Dade County	706	5.72
Homestead, FL (city) Miami-Dade County	667	1.10
Fort Lauderdale, FL (city) Broward County	661	0.40
Meadow Woods, FL (cdp) Orange County	660	2.58
Three Lakes, FL (cdp) Miami-Dade County	654	4.35
Alafaya, FL (cdp) Orange County	653	0.84
Tamarac, FL (city) Broward County	643	1.06
Cutler Bay, FL (town) Miami-Dade County	597	1.48
Washington, DC (city) District of Columbia	596	0.10
The Crossings, FL (cdp) Miami-Dade County	591	2.60
Gainesville, FL (city) Alachua County	581	0.47
Boca Raton, FL (city) Palm Beach County	554	0.66
Dallas, TX (city) Dallas County	548	0.05
Richmond West, FL (cdp) Miami-Dade County	537	1.68
Coconut Creek, FL (city) Broward County	531	1.00
San Diego, CA (city) San Diego County	525	0.04
Hempstead, NY (town) Nassau County	517	0.07
The Woodlands, TX (cdp) Montgomery County	516	0.55
San Antonio, TX (city) Medina County	505	0.04
Hallandale Beach, FL (city) Broward County	500	1.35
San Francisco, CA (city) San Francisco County	496	0.06
Ojus, FL (cdp) Miami-Dade County	491	2.72
Raleigh, NC (city) Wake County	457	0.11
Port St. Lucie, FL (city) St. Lucie County	441	0.27
Wellington, FL (village) Palm Beach County	439	0.78
Phoenix, AZ (city) Maricopa County	434	0.03
St. Petersburg, FL (city) Pinellas County	413	0.17
Hunters Creek, FL (cdp) Orange County	412	2.88
Cape Coral, FL (city) Lee County	411	0.27
Town 'n' Country, FL (cdp) Hillsborough County	397	0.51
Glenvar Heights, FL (cdp) Miami-Dade County	391	2.31
North Miami, FL (city) Miami-Dade County	390	0.66
Elizabeth, NJ (city) Union County	389	0.31
Tulsa, OK (city) Tulsa County	388	0.10
North Miami Beach, FL (city) Miami-Dade County	377	0.91
Columbus, OH (city) Franklin County	355	0.05
Country Walk, FL (cdp) Miami-Dade County	353	2.21
Atlanta, GA (city) Fulton County	350	0.08
San Jose, CA (city) Santa Clara County	350	0.04
Nashville-Davidson, TN (metro govt) Davidson County	349	0.06
Pinecrest, FL (village) Miami-Dade County	348	1.91
Palmetto Bay, FL (village) Miami-Dade County	345	1.47
Margate, FL (city) Broward County	341	0.64
Fort Worth, TX (city) Tarrant County	339	0.05
Miami Lakes, FL (town) Miami-Dade County	337	1.15
West Jordan, UT (city) Salt Lake County	330	0.32
Deerfield Beach, FL (city) Broward County	328	0.44
Islip, NY (town) Suffolk County	322	0.10
West Valley City, UT (city) Salt Lake County	321	0.25
Norwalk, CT (city/town) Fairfield County	319	0.37
Southchase, FL (cdp) Orange County	317	1.99
Indianapolis, IN (city) Marion County	314	0.04
Wesley Chapel, FL (cdp) Pasco County	313	0.71
University Park, FL (cdp) Miami-Dade County	306	1.13
Jersey City, NJ (city) Hudson County	303	0.12
Brookhaven, NY (town) Suffolk County	302	0.06
Newark, NJ (city) Essex County	299	0.11
West Palm Beach, FL (city) Palm Beach County	297	0.30
Plano, TX (city) Collin County	289	0.11
Denver, CO (city) Denver County	284	0.05
Princeton, FL (cdp) Miami-Dade County	283	1.28
Arlington, VA (cdp) Arlington County	279	0.13
Paterson, NJ (city) Passaic County	273	0.19
Altamonte Springs, FL (city) Seminole County	269	0.65
North Bergen, NJ (township) Hudson County	267	0.44
Seattle, WA (city) King County	267	0.04
Greenacres, FL (city) Palm Beach County	266	0.71
Union City, NJ (city) Hudson County	266	0.40
Oakland Park, FL (city) Broward County	260	0.63
Bakersfield, CA (city) Kern County	259	0.07
Coral Terrace, FL (cdp) Miami-Dade County	258	1.06
Westchester, FL (cdp) Miami-Dade County	258	0.86
Oklahoma City, OK (city) Oklahoma County	257	0.04
Dania Beach, FL (city) Broward County	255	0.86
Staten Island, NY (borough) Richmond County	254	0.05
Parkland, FL (city) Broward County	253	1.06
Cinco Ranch, TX (cdp) Fort Bend County	250	1.37
Tallahassee, FL (city) Leon County	245	0.14
Irving, TX (city) Dallas County	245	0.11
Germantown, MD (cdp) Montgomery County	244	0.28
West New York, NJ (town) Hudson County	243	0.49
Miami Gardens, FL (city) Miami-Dade County	240	0.22
Horizon West, FL (cdp) Orange County	237	1.69
Egypt Lake-Leto, FL (cdp) Hillsborough County	236	0.67
Hialeah Gardens, FL (city) Miami-Dade County	235	1.08
Cambridge, MA (city) Middlesex County	232	0.22
Miami Springs, FL (city) Miami-Dade County	230	1.67
Las Vegas, NV (city) Clark County	230	0.04
Alexandria, VA (ind. city) Alexandria independent city	229	0.16
Riverview, FL (cdp) Hillsborough County	228	0.32
Bay Harbor Islands, FL (town) Miami-Dade County	220	3.91
Sandy Springs, GA (city) Fulton County	209	0.22
Boynton Beach, FL (city) Palm Beach County	208	0.30
Yonkers, NY (city) Westchester County	207	0.11
Memphis, TN (city) Shelby County	207	0.03
Greensboro, NC (city) Guilford County	203	0.08
Sunset, FL (cdp) Miami-Dade County	200	1.22
Citrus Park, FL (cdp) Hillsborough County	200	0.82
Providence, RI (city) Providence County	200	0.11
Frisco, TX (city) Collin County	199	0.17
Carrollwood, FL (cdp) Hillsborough County	197	0.59
Royal Palm Beach, FL (village) Palm Beach County	195	0.57
Winter Garden, FL (city) Orange County	195	0.56
Baltimore, MD (city) Baltimore city County	195	0.03
Taylorsville, UT (city) Salt Lake County	194	0.33
Clearwater, FL (city) Pinellas County	193	0.18
Brandon, FL (cdp) Hillsborough County	191	0.18
Salt Lake City, UT (city) Salt Lake County	190	0.10
South Miami, FL (city) Miami-Dade County	188	1.61
Alpharetta, GA (city) Fulton County	187	0.32
Roswell, GA (city) Fulton County	187	0.21

Please refer to the Explanation of Data in the front of the book for more detailed information.

Hispanic Origin

South American: Venezuelan

Top 150 Places Sorted by Percent of Total Population

Based on all places, regardless of total population

Place	Population	%
Doral, FL (city) Miami-Dade County	9,423	20.62
Weston, FL (city) Broward County	6,360	9.73
Los Huisaches, TX (cdp) Webb County	1	5.88
Key Biscayne, FL (village) Miami-Dade County	706	5.72
Aventura, FL (city) Miami-Dade County	1,765	4.94
Three Lakes, FL (cdp) Miami-Dade County	654	4.35
The Hammocks, FL (cdp) Miami-Dade County	2,065	4.05
Fountainebleau, FL (cdp) Miami-Dade County	2,334	3.91
Bay Harbor Islands, FL (town) Miami-Dade County	220	3.91
Sunny Isles Beach, FL (city) Miami-Dade County	734	3.52
Kendall West, FL (cdp) Miami-Dade County	1,118	3.09
Unity Village, MO (village) Jackson County	3	3.03
Surfside, FL (town) Miami-Dade County	167	2.91
Gallatin River Ranch, MT (cdp) Gallatin County	2	2.90
Hunters Creek, FL (cdp) Orange County	412	2.88
Ojus, FL (cdp) Miami-Dade County	491	2.72
Bronwood, GA (town) Terrell County	6	2.67
North Bay Village, FL (city) Miami-Dade County	186	2.61
The Crossings, FL (cdp) Miami-Dade County	591	2.60
Meadow Woods, FL (cdp) Orange County	660	2.58
Coral Gables, FL (city) Miami-Dade County	1,201	2.57
Country Club, FL (cdp) Miami-Dade County	1,161	2.46
Glenvar Heights, FL (cdp) Miami-Dade County	391	2.31
Bal Harbour, FL (village) Miami-Dade County	58	2.31
Cloud Lake, FL (town) Palm Beach County	3	2.22
Country Walk, FL (cdp) Miami-Dade County	353	2.21
Old Bennington, VT (village) Bennington County	3	2.16
Kendall, FL (cdp) Miami-Dade County	1,611	2.14
Miramar, FL (city) Broward County	2,594	2.13
Loch Arbour, NJ (village) Monmouth County	4	2.06
Miami Beach, FL (city) Miami-Dade County	1,802	2.05
Southchase, FL (cdp) Orange County	317	1.99
Concorde Hills, OH (cdp) Hamilton County	13	1.96
Kendale Lakes, FL (cdp) Miami-Dade County	1,082	1.93
Pinecrest, FL (village) Miami-Dade County	348	1.91
Pembroke Pines, FL (city) Broward County	2,937	1.90
Tamiami, FL (cdp) Miami-Dade County	1,018	1.84
Virginia Gardens, FL (village) Miami-Dade County	43	1.81
Horizon West, FL (cdp) Orange County	237	1.69
Richmond West, FL (cdp) Miami-Dade County	537	1.68
New Sweden, MN (township) Nicollet County	5	1.68
Miami Springs, FL (city) Miami-Dade County	230	1.67
El Portal, FL (village) Miami-Dade County	38	1.63
South Miami, FL (city) Miami-Dade County	188	1.61
Cutler Bay, FL (town) Miami-Dade County	597	1.48
Sunrise, FL (city) Broward County	1,241	1.47
Palmetto Bay, FL (village) Miami-Dade County	345	1.47
Miami, FL (city) Miami-Dade County	5,770	1.44
Kissimmee, FL (city) Osceola County	848	1.42
Cinco Ranch, TX (cdp) Fort Bend County	250	1.37
Barton Hills, MI (village) Washtenaw County	4	1.36
Hallandale Beach, FL (city) Broward County	500	1.35
Southwest Ranches, FL (town) Broward County	99	1.35
Davie, FL (town) Broward County	1,231	1.34
Valley Park, OK (town) Rogers County	1	1.30
Princeton, FL (cdp) Miami-Dade County	283	1.28
Biscayne Park, FL (village) Miami-Dade County	39	1.28
Sunset, FL (cdp) Miami-Dade County	200	1.22
Miami Shores, FL (village) Miami-Dade County	128	1.22
Sea Ranch Lakes, FL (village) Broward County	8	1.19
Coral Springs, FL (city) Broward County	1,414	1.17
Westport, NY (cdp) Essex County	6	1.16
Indian Creek, FL (village) Miami-Dade County	1	1.16
Miami Lakes, FL (town) Miami-Dade County	337	1.15
University Park, FL (cdp) Miami-Dade County	306	1.13
Hillsboro Pines, FL (cdp) Broward County	5	1.12
Homestead, FL (city) Miami-Dade County	667	1.10
Naranja, FL (cdp) Miami-Dade County	91	1.10
Hitchcock, SD (town) Beadle County	1	1.10
Golden Beach, FL (town) Miami-Dade County	10	1.09
Ward, NY (town) Allegany County	4	1.09
Hialeah Gardens, FL (city) Miami-Dade County	235	1.08
Tamarac, FL (city) Broward County	643	1.06
Coral Terrace, FL (cdp) Miami-Dade County	258	1.06
Parkland, FL (city) Broward County	253	1.06
Celebration, FL (cdp) Osceola County	78	1.05
West Miami, FL (city) Miami-Dade County	62	1.04
Lake Butler, FL (cdp) Orange County	157	1.02
Coconut Creek, FL (city) Broward County	531	1.00
Plantation, FL (city) Broward County	836	0.98
Doctor Phillips, FL (cdp) Orange County	106	0.97
Brisbin, PA (borough) Clearfield County	4	0.97
Hollywood, FL (city) Broward County	1,334	0.95
Ives Estates, FL (cdp) Miami-Dade County	186	0.95
Acacia Villas, FL (cdp) Palm Beach County	4	0.94
North Miami Beach, FL (city) Miami-Dade County	377	0.91
Offerman, GA (city) Pierce County	4	0.91
Rose Hill Acres, TX (city) Hardin County	4	0.91
Red Butte, WY (cdp) Natrona County	4	0.89
Sweetwater, FL (city) Miami-Dade County	119	0.88
Palm Springs North, FL (cdp) Miami-Dade County	46	0.88
Loma Mar, CA (cdp) San Mateo County	1	0.88
Orlando, FL (city) Orange County	2,076	0.87
Westchester, FL (cdp) Miami-Dade County	258	0.86
Dania Beach, FL (city) Broward County	255	0.86
Alafaya, FL (cdp) Orange County	653	0.84
Citrus Park, FL (cdp) Hillsborough County	200	0.82
Westwood Lakes, FL (cdp) Miami-Dade County	96	0.81
White City, KS (city) Morris County	5	0.81
Blue Mountain, AR (town) Logan County	1	0.81
Olympia Heights, FL (cdp) Miami-Dade County	106	0.79
Orchard, NE (village) Antelope County	3	0.79
Wellington, FL (village) Palm Beach County	439	0.78
Heathrow, FL (cdp) Seminole County	46	0.78
Cheval, FL (cdp) Hillsborough County	82	0.77
Fisher Island, FL (cdp) Miami-Dade County	1	0.76
Colony, OK (town) Washita County	1	0.74
Sky Lake, FL (cdp) Orange County	45	0.73
Pompano Beach, FL (city) Broward County	719	0.72
Pebble Creek, FL (cdp) Hillsborough County	55	0.72
Wesley Chapel, FL (cdp) Pasco County	313	0.71
Greenacres, FL (city) Palm Beach County	266	0.71
Wellington, KY (city) Jefferson County	4	0.71
Oakland City, IN (city) Gibson County	17	0.70
Wampum, PA (borough) Lawrence County	5	0.70
Buenaventura Lakes, FL (cdp) Osceola County	177	0.68
Lopatcong Overlook, NJ (cdp) Warren County	5	0.68
Wilton Center, CT (cdp) Fairfield County	5	0.68
Dawson, NE (village) Richardson County	1	0.68
Egypt Lake-Leto, FL (cdp) Hillsborough County	236	0.67
Four Corners, FL (cdp) Lake County	176	0.67
Pembroke Park, FL (town) Broward County	41	0.67
Boca Raton, FL (city) Palm Beach County	554	0.66
North Miami, FL (city) Miami-Dade County	390	0.66
Altamonte Springs, FL (city) Seminole County	269	0.65
Cooper City, FL (city) Broward County	185	0.65
Margate, FL (city) Broward County	341	0.64
Lauderdale-by-the-Sea, FL (town) Broward County	39	0.64
Hialeah, FL (city) Miami-Dade County	1,405	0.63
Oakland Park, FL (city) Broward County	260	0.63
Palmetto Estates, FL (cdp) Miami-Dade County	84	0.62
South Gate Ridge, FL (cdp) Sarasota County	35	0.62
Edmonston, MD (town) Prince George's County	9	0.62
Fishing Creek, MD (cdp) Dorchester County	1	0.61
San Simon, AZ (cdp) Cochise County	1	0.61
Shinnecock Reservation, NY (reservation) Suffolk County	4	0.60
Benzonia, MI (village) Benzie County	3	0.60
Karnak, IL (village) Pulaski County	3	0.60
Madison, CA (cdp) Yolo County	3	0.60
Carrollwood, FL (cdp) Hillsborough County	197	0.59
West Perrine, FL (cdp) Miami-Dade County	56	0.59
Richmond Heights, FL (cdp) Miami-Dade County	50	0.59
Bay Hill, FL (cdp) Orange County	29	0.59
Quail Ridge, FL (cdp) Pasco County	6	0.58
Groton Long Point, CT (borough) New London County	3	0.58
Royal Palm Beach, FL (village) Palm Beach County	195	0.57
Maitland, FL (city) Orange County	90	0.57
Pedricktown, NJ (cdp) Salem County	3	0.57
Winter Garden, FL (city) Orange County	195	0.56
Northdale, FL (cdp) Hillsborough County	124	0.56

Please refer to the Explanation of Data in the front of the book for more detailed information.

Hispanic Origin

South American: Venezuelan

Top 150 Places Sorted by Percent of Total Population

Based on places with total population of 7,500 or more

Place	Population	%
Doral, FL (city) Miami-Dade County	9,423	20.62
Weston, FL (city) Broward County	6,360	9.73
Key Biscayne, FL (village) Miami-Dade County	706	5.72
Aventura, FL (city) Miami-Dade County	1,765	4.94
Three Lakes, FL (cdp) Miami-Dade County	654	4.35
The Hammocks, FL (cdp) Miami-Dade County	2,065	4.05
Fountainebleau, FL (cdp) Miami-Dade County	2,334	3.91
Sunny Isles Beach, FL (city) Miami-Dade County	734	3.52
Kendall West, FL (cdp) Miami-Dade County	1,118	3.09
Hunters Creek, FL (cdp) Orange County	412	2.88
Ojus, FL (cdp) Miami-Dade County	491	2.72
The Crossings, FL (cdp) Miami-Dade County	591	2.60
Meadow Woods, FL (cdp) Orange County	660	2.58
Coral Gables, FL (city) Miami-Dade County	1,201	2.57
Country Club, FL (cdp) Miami-Dade County	1,161	2.46
Glenvar Heights, FL (cdp) Miami-Dade County	391	2.31
Country Walk, FL (cdp) Miami-Dade County	353	2.21
Kendall, FL (cdp) Miami-Dade County	1,611	2.14
Miramar, FL (city) Broward County	2,594	2.13
Miami Beach, FL (city) Miami-Dade County	1,802	2.05
Southchase, FL (cdp) Orange County	317	1.99
Kendale Lakes, FL (cdp) Miami-Dade County	1,082	1.93
Pinecrest, FL (village) Miami-Dade County	348	1.91
Pembroke Pines, FL (city) Broward County	2,937	1.90
Tamiami, FL (cdp) Miami-Dade County	1,018	1.84
Horizon West, FL (cdp) Orange County	237	1.69
Richmond West, FL (cdp) Miami-Dade County	537	1.68
Miami Springs, FL (city) Miami-Dade County	230	1.67
South Miami, FL (city) Miami-Dade County	188	1.61
Cutler Bay, FL (town) Miami-Dade County	597	1.48
Sunrise, FL (city) Broward County	1,241	1.47
Palmetto Bay, FL (village) Miami-Dade County	345	1.47
Miami, FL (city) Miami-Dade County	5,770	1.44
Kissimmee, FL (city) Osceola County	848	1.42
Cinco Ranch, TX (cdp) Fort Bend County	250	1.37
Hallandale Beach, FL (city) Broward County	500	1.35
Davie, FL (town) Broward County	1,231	1.34
Princeton, FL (cdp) Miami-Dade County	283	1.28
Sunset, FL (cdp) Miami-Dade County	200	1.22
Miami Shores, FL (village) Miami-Dade County	128	1.22
Coral Springs, FL (city) Broward County	1,414	1.17
Miami Lakes, FL (town) Miami-Dade County	337	1.15
University Park, FL (cdp) Miami-Dade County	306	1.13
Homestead, FL (city) Miami-Dade County	667	1.10
Naranja, FL (cdp) Miami-Dade County	91	1.10
Hialeah Gardens, FL (city) Miami-Dade County	235	1.08
Tamarac, FL (city) Broward County	643	1.06
Coral Terrace, FL (cdp) Miami-Dade County	258	1.06
Parkland, FL (city) Broward County	253	1.06
Lake Butler, FL (cdp) Orange County	157	1.02
Coconut Creek, FL (city) Broward County	531	1.00
Plantation, FL (city) Broward County	836	0.98
Doctor Phillips, FL (cdp) Orange County	106	0.97
Hollywood, FL (city) Broward County	1,334	0.95
Ives Estates, FL (cdp) Miami-Dade County	186	0.95
North Miami Beach, FL (city) Miami-Dade County	377	0.91
Sweetwater, FL (city) Miami-Dade County	119	0.88
Orlando, FL (city) Orange County	2,076	0.87
Westchester, FL (cdp) Miami-Dade County	258	0.86
Dania Beach, FL (city) Broward County	255	0.86
Alafaya, FL (cdp) Orange County	653	0.84
Citrus Park, FL (cdp) Hillsborough County	200	0.82
Westwood Lakes, FL (cdp) Miami-Dade County	96	0.81
Olympia Heights, FL (cdp) Miami-Dade County	106	0.79
Wellington, FL (village) Palm Beach County	439	0.78
Cheval, FL (cdp) Hillsborough County	82	0.77
Pompano Beach, FL (city) Broward County	719	0.72
Pebble Creek, FL (cdp) Hillsborough County	55	0.72
Wesley Chapel, FL (cdp) Pasco County	313	0.71
Greenacres, FL (city) Palm Beach County	266	0.71
Buenaventura Lakes, FL (cdp) Osceola County	177	0.68
Egypt Lake-Leto, FL (cdp) Hillsborough County	236	0.67
Four Corners, FL (cdp) Lake County	176	0.67
Boca Raton, FL (city) Palm Beach County	554	0.66
North Miami, FL (city) Miami-Dade County	390	0.66
Altamonte Springs, FL (city) Seminole County	269	0.65
Cooper City, FL (city) Broward County	185	0.65
Margate, FL (city) Broward County	341	0.64
Hialeah, FL (city) Miami-Dade County	1,405	0.63
Oakland Park, FL (city) Broward County	260	0.63
Palmetto Estates, FL (cdp) Miami-Dade County	84	0.62
Carrollwood, FL (cdp) Hillsborough County	197	0.59
West Perrine, FL (cdp) Miami-Dade County	56	0.59
Richmond Heights, FL (cdp) Miami-Dade County	50	0.59
Royal Palm Beach, FL (village) Palm Beach County	195	0.57
Maitland, FL (city) Orange County	90	0.57
Winter Garden, FL (city) Orange County	195	0.56
Northdale, FL (cdp) Hillsborough County	124	0.56
Goulds, FL (cdp) Miami-Dade County	57	0.56
The Woodlands, TX (cdp) Montgomery County	516	0.55
Clermont, FL (city) Lake County	152	0.53
Guttenberg, NJ (town) Hudson County	59	0.53
Forest City, FL (cdp) Seminole County	72	0.52
Town 'n' Country, FL (cdp) Hillsborough County	397	0.51
Westchase, FL (cdp) Hillsborough County	109	0.50
West New York, NJ (town) Hudson County	243	0.49
Palm Springs, FL (village) Palm Beach County	93	0.49
Azalea Park, FL (cdp) Orange County	62	0.49
Wilton Manors, FL (city) Broward County	57	0.49
South Miami Heights, FL (cdp) Miami-Dade County	170	0.48
Pine Castle, FL (cdp) Orange County	52	0.48
Union Park, FL (cdp) Orange County	47	0.48
Gainesville, FL (city) Alachua County	581	0.47
Oak Ridge, FL (cdp) Orange County	107	0.47
St. Cloud, FL (city) Osceola County	161	0.46
Oviedo, FL (city) Seminole County	150	0.45
Deerfield Beach, FL (city) Broward County	328	0.44
North Bergen, NJ (township) Hudson County	267	0.44
Lake Magdalene, FL (cdp) Hillsborough County	116	0.41
Dumbarton, VA (cdp) Henrico County	32	0.41
Fort Lauderdale, FL (city) Broward County	661	0.40
Union City, NJ (city) Hudson County	266	0.40
North Lauderdale, FL (city) Broward County	158	0.39
Winter Springs, FL (city) Seminole County	130	0.39
Duluth, GA (city) Gwinnett County	105	0.39
Lake Mary, FL (city) Seminole County	52	0.38
Fuller Heights, FL (cdp) Polk County	33	0.38
Norwalk, CT (city/town) Fairfield County	319	0.37
Casselberry, FL (city) Seminole County	94	0.36
Conway, FL (cdp) Orange County	48	0.36
Greatwood, TX (cdp) Fort Bend County	42	0.36
Marathon, FL (city) Monroe County	30	0.36
Apopka, FL (city) Orange County	144	0.35
University, FL (cdp) Orange County	109	0.35
Goldenrod, FL (cdp) Orange County	42	0.35
Gateway, FL (cdp) Lee County	29	0.35
Milton, GA (city) Fulton County	112	0.34
Leisure City, FL (cdp) Miami-Dade County	76	0.34
Williamsburg, FL (cdp) Orange County	26	0.34
Taylorsville, UT (city) Salt Lake County	194	0.33
West Jordan, UT (city) Salt Lake County	330	0.32
Riverview, FL (cdp) Hillsborough County	228	0.32
Alpharetta, GA (city) Fulton County	187	0.32
Wekiwa Springs, FL (cdp) Seminole County	71	0.32
Elizabeth, NJ (city) Union County	389	0.31
Florida City, FL (city) Miami-Dade County	35	0.31
West Palm Beach, FL (city) Palm Beach County	297	0.30
Boynton Beach, FL (city) Palm Beach County	208	0.30
Palm Beach Gardens, FL (city) Palm Beach County	146	0.30
Ocoee, FL (city) Orange County	105	0.30
Bluffton, SC (town) Beaufort County	37	0.30
Pasadena Hills, FL (cdp) Pasco County	23	0.30
Poinciana, FL (cdp) Osceola County	155	0.29
Sanford, FL (city) Seminole County	155	0.29
Woodstock, GA (city) Cherokee County	69	0.29
Sugar Hill, GA (city) Gwinnett County	53	0.29
Cypress Lake, FL (cdp) Lee County	34	0.29
Pike Creek Valley, DE (cdp) New Castle County	33	0.29
Lighthouse Point, FL (city) Broward County	30	0.29
Groveland, FL (city) Lake County	25	0.29

Please refer to the Explanation of Data in the front of the book for more detailed information.

Hispanic Origin

South American: Other South American

U.S. and 50 States Sorted by Population and Percent of Total Population

Place	Population	%
United States	**21,809**	**0.01**
California	3,998	0.01
New York	3,992	0.02
Florida	2,962	0.02
New Jersey	1,688	0.02
Texas	1,083	<0.01
Virginia	947	0.01
Illinois	694	0.01
Maryland	554	0.01
Connecticut	543	0.02
Georgia	530	0.01
Pennsylvania	529	<0.01
Massachusetts	456	0.01
North Carolina	394	<0.01
Minnesota	251	<0.01
Washington	246	<0.01
Arizona	231	<0.01
Nevada	216	0.01
Colorado	191	<0.01
Utah	182	0.01
Ohio	172	<0.01
Michigan	170	<0.01
Tennessee	133	<0.01
South Carolina	132	<0.01
Wisconsin	127	<0.01
Oregon	124	<0.01
Missouri	113	<0.01
Louisiana	88	<0.01
Indiana	84	<0.01
Kansas	81	<0.01
Oklahoma	80	<0.01
District of Columbia	73	0.01
Rhode Island	67	0.01
Kentucky	65	<0.01
Hawaii	61	<0.01
Delaware	58	0.01
Alabama	58	<0.01
New Mexico	54	<0.01
Idaho	52	<0.01
Nebraska	51	<0.01
New Hampshire	51	<0.01
Iowa	42	<0.01
Alaska	30	<0.01
Mississippi	30	<0.01
Arkansas	22	<0.01
Maine	20	<0.01
Montana	20	<0.01
West Virginia	20	<0.01
Vermont	15	<0.01
Wyoming	13	<0.01
South Dakota	11	<0.01
North Dakota	5	<0.01

Place	Population	%
New York	3,992	0.02
Florida	2,962	0.02
New Jersey	1,688	0.02
Connecticut	543	0.02
United States	**21,809**	**0.01**
California	3,998	0.01
Virginia	947	0.01
Illinois	694	0.01
Maryland	554	0.01
Georgia	530	0.01
Massachusetts	456	0.01
Nevada	216	0.01
Utah	182	0.01
District of Columbia	73	0.01
Rhode Island	67	0.01
Delaware	58	0.01
Texas	1,083	<0.01
Pennsylvania	529	<0.01
North Carolina	394	<0.01
Minnesota	251	<0.01
Washington	246	<0.01
Arizona	231	<0.01
Colorado	191	<0.01
Ohio	172	<0.01
Michigan	170	<0.01
Tennessee	133	<0.01
South Carolina	132	<0.01
Wisconsin	127	<0.01
Oregon	124	<0.01
Missouri	113	<0.01
Louisiana	88	<0.01
Indiana	84	<0.01
Kansas	81	<0.01
Oklahoma	80	<0.01
Kentucky	65	<0.01
Hawaii	61	<0.01
Alabama	58	<0.01
New Mexico	54	<0.01
Idaho	52	<0.01
Nebraska	51	<0.01
New Hampshire	51	<0.01
Iowa	42	<0.01
Alaska	30	<0.01
Mississippi	30	<0.01
Arkansas	22	<0.01
Maine	20	<0.01
Montana	20	<0.01
West Virginia	20	<0.01
Vermont	15	<0.01
Wyoming	13	<0.01
South Dakota	11	<0.01
North Dakota	5	<0.01

Please refer to the Explanation of Data in the front of the book for more detailed information.

Hispanic Origin

South American: Other South American

Top 150 Places Sorted by Population

Based on all places, regardless of total population

Place	Population	%
New York, NY (city) Kings County	2,678	0.03
Queens, NY (borough) Queens County	1,439	0.06
Los Angeles, CA (city) Los Angeles County	629	0.02
Brooklyn, NY (borough) Kings County	506	0.02
Bronx, NY (borough) Bronx County	369	0.03
Chicago, IL (city) Cook County	307	0.01
Manhattan, NY (borough) New York County	278	0.02
Hempstead, NY (town) Nassau County	243	0.03
Newark, NJ (city) Essex County	190	0.07
Houston, TX (city) Harris County	157	0.01
San Francisco, CA (city) San Francisco County	137	0.02
Arlington, VA (cdp) Arlington County	135	0.07
Jersey City, NJ (city) Hudson County	124	0.05
Philadelphia, PA (city) Philadelphia County	111	0.01
San Diego, CA (city) San Diego County	107	0.01
Brookhaven, NY (town) Suffolk County	98	0.02
San Jose, CA (city) Santa Clara County	90	0.01
Staten Island, NY (borough) Richmond County	86	0.02
Charlotte, NC (city) Mecklenburg County	78	0.01
Dallas, TX (city) Dallas County	75	0.01
Washington, DC (city) District of Columbia	73	0.01
Hollywood, FL (city) Broward County	71	0.05
Orlando, FL (city) Orange County	67	0.03
Hartford, CT (city/town) Hartford County	65	0.05
Boston, MA (city) Suffolk County	64	0.01
Jacksonville, FL (city) Duval County	64	0.01
Yonkers, NY (city) Westchester County	63	0.03
Las Vegas, NV (city) Clark County	62	0.01
Miami, FL (city) Miami-Dade County	61	0.02
Phoenix, AZ (city) Maricopa County	60	<0.01
Santa Clarita, CA (city) Los Angeles County	59	0.03
Danbury, CT (city/town) Fairfield County	58	0.07
Austin, TX (city) Travis County	55	0.01
San Antonio, TX (city) Medina County	55	<0.01
Islip, NY (town) Suffolk County	54	0.02
Coral Springs, FL (city) Broward County	53	0.04
Minneapolis, MN (city) Hennepin County	53	0.01
Centreville, VA (cdp) Fairfax County	50	0.07
Kendall, FL (cdp) Miami-Dade County	50	0.07
Elizabeth, NJ (city) Union County	49	0.04
Long Beach, CA (city) Los Angeles County	49	0.01
Rancho Cucamonga, CA (city) San Bernardino County	47	0.03
North Bergen, NJ (township) Hudson County	46	0.08
Pembroke Pines, FL (city) Broward County	46	0.03
North Hempstead, NY (town) Nassau County	46	0.02
Oakland, CA (city) Alameda County	44	0.01
Schenectady, NY (city) Schenectady County	43	0.07
Fort Lauderdale, FL (city) Broward County	43	0.03
Fullerton, CA (city) Orange County	43	0.03
St. Petersburg, FL (city) Pinellas County	43	0.02
Torrance, CA (city) Los Angeles County	42	0.03
Irvine, CA (city) Orange County	40	0.02
Sacramento, CA (city) Sacramento County	40	0.01
Coconut Creek, FL (city) Broward County	39	0.07
San Mateo, CA (city) San Mateo County	39	0.04
Paradise, NV (cdp) Clark County	39	0.02
Fort Worth, TX (city) Tarrant County	39	0.01
Dale City, VA (cdp) Prince William County	37	0.06
Reston, VA (cdp) Fairfax County	37	0.06
Sunrise, FL (city) Broward County	37	0.04
Seattle, WA (city) King County	37	0.01
Town 'n' Country, FL (cdp) Hillsborough County	36	0.05
Woodbridge, NJ (township) Middlesex County	36	0.04
Cape Coral, FL (city) Lee County	36	0.02
Providence, RI (city) Providence County	36	0.02
Plano, TX (city) Collin County	36	0.01
Pine Hills, FL (cdp) Orange County	35	0.06
Downey, CA (city) Los Angeles County	35	0.03
Huntington, NY (town) Suffolk County	35	0.02
Port St. Lucie, FL (city) St. Lucie County	35	0.02
Santa Ana, CA (city) Orange County	35	0.01
Gaithersburg, MD (city) Montgomery County	34	0.06
Babylon, NY (town) Suffolk County	34	0.02
Tampa, FL (city) Hillsborough County	34	0.01
East Hampton, NY (town) Suffolk County	33	0.15
Mount Vernon, NY (city) Westchester County	33	0.05
Daly City, CA (city) San Mateo County	33	0.03
Stamford, CT (city/town) Fairfield County	33	0.03
Clermont, FL (city) Lake County	32	0.11
Greenburgh, NY (town) Westchester County	32	0.04
Pompano Beach, FL (city) Broward County	32	0.03
Oyster Bay, NY (town) Nassau County	32	0.01
Portland, OR (city) Multnomah County	32	0.01
Belleville, NJ (township) Essex County	31	0.09
Miami Beach, FL (city) Miami-Dade County	31	0.04
Plantation, FL (city) Broward County	31	0.04
Burbank, CA (city) Los Angeles County	31	0.03
Anaheim, CA (city) Orange County	31	0.01
Skokie, IL (village) Cook County	30	0.05
Union City, NJ (city) Hudson County	30	0.05
Pasadena, CA (city) Los Angeles County	30	0.02
City of Orange, NJ (township) Essex County	29	0.10
Annandale, VA (cdp) Fairfax County	29	0.07
Palm Bay, FL (city) Brevard County	29	0.03
Waterbury, CT (city/town) New Haven County	29	0.03
Corona, CA (city) Riverside County	29	0.02
Lancaster, CA (city) Los Angeles County	28	0.02
Simi Valley, CA (city) Ventura County	28	0.02
Valley Stream, NY (village) Nassau County	27	0.07
Levittown, NY (cdp) Nassau County	27	0.05
Gainesville, FL (city) Alachua County	27	0.02
McKinney, TX (city) Collin County	27	0.02
Ontario, CA (city) San Bernardino County	27	0.02
Glendale, CA (city) Los Angeles County	27	0.01
Huntington Beach, CA (city) Orange County	27	0.01
Salt Lake City, UT (city) Salt Lake County	27	0.01
Denver, CO (city) Denver County	27	<0.01
Fontana, CA (city) San Bernardino County	26	0.01
Virginia Beach, VA (ind. city) Virginia Beach independent city	26	0.01
Springfield, VA (cdp) Fairfax County	25	0.08
Winter Garden, FL (city) Orange County	25	0.07
Aspen Hill, MD (cdp) Montgomery County	25	0.05
Pomona, CA (city) Los Angeles County	25	0.02
Cleveland, OH (city) Cuyahoga County	25	0.01
Riverside, CA (city) Riverside County	25	0.01
Baltimore, MD (city) Baltimore city County	25	<0.01
Davie, FL (town) Broward County	24	0.03
Berkeley, CA (city) Alameda County	24	0.02
Thousand Oaks, CA (city) Ventura County	24	0.02
Kansas City, MO (city) Jackson County	24	0.01
Mesa, AZ (city) Maricopa County	24	0.01
St. Paul, MN (city) Ramsey County	24	0.01
Albuquerque, NM (city) Bernalillo County	24	<0.01
South River, NJ (borough) Middlesex County	23	0.14
Cortlandt, NY (town) Westchester County	23	0.06
Hempstead, NY (village) Nassau County	23	0.04
North Miami, FL (city) Miami-Dade County	23	0.04
Union, NJ (township) Union County	23	0.04
White Plains, NY (city) Westchester County	23	0.04
Germantown, MD (cdp) Montgomery County	23	0.03
Santa Monica, CA (city) Los Angeles County	23	0.03
Bridgeport, CT (city/town) Fairfield County	23	0.02
Mission Viejo, CA (city) Orange County	23	0.02
Four Corners, FL (cdp) Lake County	22	0.08
Monrovia, CA (city) Los Angeles County	22	0.06
Redwood City, CA (city) San Mateo County	22	0.03
Whittier, CA (city) Los Angeles County	22	0.03
Carlsbad, CA (city) San Diego County	22	0.02
Sandy Springs, GA (city) Fulton County	22	0.02
Temecula, CA (city) Riverside County	22	0.02
Columbus, OH (city) Franklin County	22	<0.01
Olney, MD (cdp) Montgomery County	21	0.06
Cutler Bay, FL (town) Miami-Dade County	21	0.05
North Miami Beach, FL (city) Miami-Dade County	21	0.05
Teaneck, NJ (township) Bergen County	21	0.05
Deerfield Beach, FL (city) Broward County	21	0.03
Enterprise, NV (cdp) Clark County	21	0.02
West Palm Beach, FL (city) Palm Beach County	21	0.02
Atlanta, GA (city) Fulton County	21	0.01
Bakersfield, CA (city) Kern County	21	0.01

Please refer to the Explanation of Data in the front of the book for more detailed information.

Hispanic Origin

South American: Other South American

Top 150 Places Sorted by Percent of Total Population

Based on all places, regardless of total population

Place	Population	%
Woodsburgh, NY (village) Nassau County	8	1.03
Bluffton, MN (city) Otter Tail County	2	0.97
Moskowite Corner, CA (cdp) Napa County	2	0.95
Amanda Park, WA (cdp) Grays Harbor County	2	0.79
Chandler, MN (city) Murray County	2	0.74
Levan, UT (town) Juab County	6	0.71
Independence, UT (town) Wasatch County	1	0.61
Palisade, MN (city) Aitkin County	1	0.60
Houston Acres, KY (city) Jefferson County	3	0.59
Lincoln Park, PA (cdp) Berks County	8	0.50
Buckeystown, MD (cdp) Frederick County	5	0.49
Quiogue, NY (cdp) Suffolk County	4	0.49
Jugtown, MD (cdp) Washington County	1	0.49
Pocono Ranch Lands, PA (cdp) Pike County	5	0.47
East Hampton North, NY (cdp) Suffolk County	19	0.46
Paxico, KS (city) Wabaunsee County	1	0.45
Kootenai, ID (city) Bonner County	3	0.44
Darby, MT (town) Ravalli County	3	0.42
New Seabury, MA (cdp) Barnstable County	3	0.42
Grand Cane, LA (village) De Soto Parish	1	0.41
Plattekill, NY (cdp) Ulster County	5	0.40
Branchville, SC (town) Orangeburg County	4	0.39
Windemere, TX (cdp) Travis County	4	0.39
Page Park, FL (cdp) Lee County	2	0.39
Elberta, UT (cdp) Utah County	1	0.39
Fayetteville, TX (city) Fayette County	1	0.39
Reynolds, IN (town) White County	2	0.38
Fort Greely, AK (cdp) Southeast Fairbanks Census Area	2	0.37
Robins AFB, GA (cdp) Houston County	4	0.34
Burnham, IL (village) Cook County	14	0.33
South Heart, ND (city) Stark County	1	0.33
Castle Hill, CA (cdp) Contra Costa County	4	0.31
Rough and Ready, CA (cdp) Nevada County	3	0.31
Frankfort, WI (town) Pepin County	1	0.29
St. Regis Park, KY (city) Jefferson County	4	0.28
Peapack and Gladstone, NJ (borough) Somerset County	7	0.27
Scio, NY (town) Allegany County	5	0.27
Pine Lake, GA (city) DeKalb County	2	0.27
East Liberty, OH (cdp) Logan County	1	0.27
Hayes, LA (cdp) Calcasieu Parish	2	0.26
Bismarck, MI (township) Presque Isle County	1	0.26
Charlo, MT (cdp) Lake County	1	0.26
Iron Gate, VA (town) Alleghany County	1	0.26
Hanover, PA (township) Lehigh County	4	0.25
Escalante, UT (city) Garfield County	2	0.25
White Lake, NC (town) Bladen County	2	0.25
Tierra Grande, TX (cdp) Nueces County	1	0.25
Northwest Harbor, NY (cdp) Suffolk County	8	0.24
Clarksburg, CA (cdp) Yolo County	1	0.24
Marietta, PA (borough) Lancaster County	6	0.23
Dolgeville, NY (village) Herkimer County	5	0.23
Tariffville, CT (cdp) Hartford County	3	0.23
Boydton, VA (town) Mecklenburg County	1	0.23
Jerome, AZ (town) Yavapai County	1	0.23
North Springfield, VA (cdp) Fairfax County	16	0.22
Far Hills, NJ (borough) Somerset County	2	0.22
Pleasant Plains, NJ (cdp) Somerset County	2	0.22
East Rutherford, NJ (borough) Bergen County	19	0.21
Lakeview, NY (cdp) Nassau County	12	0.21
Lewisburg, PA (borough) Union County	12	0.21
Harriman, NY (village) Orange County	5	0.21
Genoa, NV (cdp) Douglas County	2	0.21
Cold Spring, NY (village) Putnam County	4	0.20
Mentone, IN (town) Kosciusko County	2	0.20
Corn, OK (town) Washita County	1	0.20
Elmsford, NY (village) Westchester County	9	0.19
Waterville, NY (village) Oneida County	3	0.19
McCullom Lake, IL (village) McHenry County	2	0.19
Otisville, NY (village) Orange County	2	0.19
Mount Lena, MD (cdp) Washington County	1	0.19
Richwood, WI (town) Richland County	1	0.19
Greenbriar, VA (cdp) Fairfax County	15	0.18
Naples Park, FL (cdp) Collier County	11	0.18
Bay Hill, FL (cdp) Orange County	9	0.18
Northwest Harwich, MA (cdp) Barnstable County	7	0.18
Port Monmouth, NJ (cdp) Monmouth County	7	0.18
Hokendauqua, PA (cdp) Lehigh County	6	0.18
Alturas, CA (city) Modoc County	5	0.18
Covington, PA (township) Lackawanna County	4	0.18
Jolivue, VA (cdp) Augusta County	2	0.18
Wiscasset, ME (cdp) Lincoln County	2	0.18
Circleville, UT (town) Piute County	1	0.18
Hickory Hills, PA (cdp) Luzerne County	1	0.18
Wainwright, AK (city) North Slope Borough	1	0.18
Manhasset Hills, NY (cdp) Nassau County	6	0.17
Mokuleia, HI (cdp) Honolulu County	3	0.17
Upper Pohatcong, NJ (cdp) Warren County	3	0.17
Bradenton Beach, FL (city) Manatee County	2	0.17
Mountain Lake, NJ (cdp) Warren County	1	0.17
Benton City, WA (city) Benton County	5	0.16
Bay City, OR (city) Tillamook County	2	0.16
Clark, PA (borough) Mercer County	1	0.16
White City, KS (city) Morris County	1	0.16
East Hampton, NY (town) Suffolk County	33	0.15
Roselle Park, NJ (borough) Union County	20	0.15
Pinehurst, TX (cdp) Montgomery County	7	0.15
Manheim, NY (town) Herkimer County	5	0.15
Indian Lake, NY (town) Hamilton County	2	0.15
Boyle, MS (town) Bolivar County	1	0.15
Cylon, WI (town) St. Croix County	1	0.15
Russell, WI (town) Lincoln County	1	0.15
Spreckels, CA (cdp) Monterey County	1	0.15
South River, NJ (borough) Middlesex County	23	0.14
Tappan, NY (cdp) Rockland County	9	0.14
Layhill, MD (cdp) Montgomery County	7	0.14
Pound Ridge, NY (town) Westchester County	7	0.14
Liberty, NJ (township) Warren County	4	0.14
Marshall, NY (town) Oneida County	3	0.14
Ossun, LA (cdp) Lafayette Parish	3	0.14
Sackets Harbor, NY (village) Jefferson County	2	0.14
Sutton-Alpine, AK (cdp) Matanuska-Susitna Borough	2	0.14
Carlton, MT (cdp) Missoula County	1	0.14
Gainesville, VA (cdp) Prince William County	15	0.13
Lake Barcroft, VA (cdp) Fairfax County	12	0.13
Lake Mohegan, NY (cdp) Westchester County	8	0.13
Orlovista, FL (cdp) Orange County	8	0.13
West Yarmouth, MA (cdp) Barnstable County	8	0.13
Oneida, WI (town) Outagamie County	6	0.13
East Rockingham, NC (cdp) Richmond County	5	0.13
Springdale, MD (cdp) Prince George's County	4	0.13
Derwood, MD (cdp) Montgomery County	3	0.13
Lofall, WA (cdp) Kitsap County	3	0.13
Rhome, TX (city) Wise County	2	0.13
Wilderness Rim, WA (cdp) King County	2	0.13
Drammen, WI (town) Eau Claire County	1	0.13
Fair Haven, NY (village) Cayuga County	1	0.13
Kaumakani, HI (cdp) Kauai County	1	0.13
Penney Farms, FL (town) Clay County	1	0.13
Monticello, NY (village) Sullivan County	8	0.12
June Park, FL (cdp) Brevard County	5	0.12
County Center, VA (cdp) Prince William County	4	0.12
Montauk, NY (cdp) Suffolk County	4	0.12
Ocean Grove, NJ (cdp) Monmouth County	4	0.12
Oakland, FL (town) Orange County	3	0.12
Ridgecrest, FL (cdp) Pinellas County	3	0.12
Whittingham, NJ (cdp) Middlesex County	3	0.12
Bridgewater, CT (town) Litchfield County	2	0.12
Graton, CA (cdp) Sonoma County	2	0.12
Kerhonkson, NY (cdp) Ulster County	2	0.12
Lancaster, NH (cdp) Coos County	2	0.12
Vernon Valley, NJ (cdp) Sussex County	2	0.12
Clermont, FL (city) Lake County	32	0.11
New Hyde Park, NY (village) Nassau County	11	0.11
Murrells Inlet, SC (cdp) Georgetown County	8	0.11
New Hanover, NJ (township) Burlington County	8	0.11
Twin Rivers, NJ (cdp) Mercer County	8	0.11
Big Flats, NY (cdp) Chemung County	6	0.11
Bremen, IN (town) Marshall County	5	0.11
Caernarvon, PA (township) Lancaster County	5	0.11
Hainesville, IL (village) Lake County	4	0.11

Please refer to the Explanation of Data in the front of the book for more detailed information.

Hispanic Origin

South American: Other South American

Top 150 Places Sorted by Percent of Total Population

Based on places with total population of 7,500 or more

Place	Population	%
East Rutherford, NJ (borough) Bergen County	19	0.21
Greenbriar, VA (cdp) Fairfax County	15	0.18
East Hampton, NY (town) Suffolk County	33	0.15
Roselle Park, NJ (borough) Union County	20	0.15
South River, NJ (borough) Middlesex County	23	0.14
Gainesville, VA (cdp) Prince William County	15	0.13
Lake Barcroft, VA (cdp) Fairfax County	12	0.13
Clermont, FL (city) Lake County	32	0.11
New Hyde Park, NY (village) Nassau County	11	0.11
Murrells Inlet, SC (cdp) Georgetown County	8	0.11
City of Orange, NJ (township) Essex County	29	0.10
Calverton, MD (cdp) Montgomery County	18	0.10
Weehawken, NJ (township) Hudson County	13	0.10
Sterling, MA (town) Worcester County	8	0.10
Belleville, NJ (township) Essex County	31	0.09
Fords, NJ (cdp) Middlesex County	14	0.09
Secaucus, NJ (town) Hudson County	14	0.09
North Lindenhurst, NY (cdp) Suffolk County	11	0.09
Fort Dix, NJ (cdp) Burlington County	7	0.09
Garden City Park, NY (cdp) Nassau County	7	0.09
Monona, WI (city) Dane County	7	0.09
Port Jefferson Station, NY (cdp) Suffolk County	7	0.09
Wilson, PA (borough) Northampton County	7	0.09
North Bergen, NJ (township) Hudson County	46	0.08
Springfield, VA (cdp) Fairfax County	25	0.08
Four Corners, FL (cdp) Lake County	22	0.08
Peekskill, NY (city) Westchester County	18	0.08
Mastic, NY (cdp) Suffolk County	13	0.08
Hasbrouck Heights, NJ (borough) Bergen County	9	0.08
Jupiter Farms, FL (cdp) Palm Beach County	9	0.08
Villas, FL (cdp) Lee County	9	0.08
Groveland, FL (city) Lake County	7	0.08
Big Flats, NY (town) Chemung County	6	0.08
Kenilworth, NJ (borough) Union County	6	0.08
Newark, NJ (city) Essex County	190	0.07
Arlington, VA (cdp) Arlington County	135	0.07
Danbury, CT (city/town) Fairfield County	58	0.07
Centreville, VA (cdp) Fairfax County	50	0.07
Kendall, FL (cdp) Miami-Dade County	50	0.07
Schenectady, NY (city) Schenectady County	43	0.07
Coconut Creek, FL (city) Broward County	39	0.07
Annandale, VA (cdp) Fairfax County	29	0.07
Valley Stream, NY (village) Nassau County	27	0.07
Winter Garden, FL (city) Orange County	25	0.07
Buenaventura Lakes, FL (cdp) Osceola County	17	0.07
Medford, NY (cdp) Suffolk County	16	0.07
Northdale, FL (cdp) Hillsborough County	16	0.07
Mamaroneck, NY (village) Westchester County	14	0.07
Sunny Isles Beach, FL (city) Miami-Dade County	14	0.07
Tysons Corner, VA (cdp) Fairfax County	14	0.07
Morris, NJ (town) Morris County	13	0.07
Southchase, FL (cdp) Orange County	11	0.07
Hawaiian Paradise Park, HI (cdp) Hawaii County	8	0.07
New Providence, NJ (borough) Union County	8	0.07
Pine Castle, FL (cdp) Orange County	8	0.07
Chamblee, GA (city) DeKalb County	7	0.07
Cheval, FL (cdp) Hillsborough County	7	0.07
Philipstown, NY (town) Putnam County	7	0.07
Plattekill, NY (town) Ulster County	7	0.07
South Huntington, NY (cdp) Suffolk County	7	0.07
Boonton, NJ (town) Morris County	6	0.07
Brentwood, MO (city) St. Louis County	6	0.07
Haledon, NJ (borough) Passaic County	6	0.07
Glen Ridge, NJ (borough) Essex County	5	0.07
Long Branch, VA (cdp) Fairfax County	5	0.07
Wood-Ridge, NJ (borough) Bergen County	5	0.07
Queens, NY (borough) Queens County	1,439	0.06
Dale City, VA (cdp) Prince William County	37	0.06
Reston, VA (cdp) Fairfax County	37	0.06
Pine Hills, FL (cdp) Orange County	35	0.06
Gaithersburg, MD (city) Montgomery County	34	0.06
Cortlandt, NY (town) Westchester County	23	0.06
Monrovia, CA (city) Los Angeles County	22	0.06
Olney, MD (cdp) Montgomery County	21	0.06
Elmont, NY (cdp) Nassau County	19	0.06
Garfield, NJ (city) Bergen County	18	0.06
Burlingame, CA (city) San Mateo County	16	0.06
South Riding, VA (cdp) Loudoun County	15	0.06
Roselle, NJ (borough) Union County	12	0.06
Burke Centre, VA (cdp) Fairfax County	11	0.06
Langley Park, MD (cdp) Prince George's County	11	0.06
Lorton, VA (cdp) Fairfax County	11	0.06
Rutherford, NJ (borough) Bergen County	11	0.06
Ojus, FL (cdp) Miami-Dade County	10	0.06
Bull Run, VA (cdp) Prince William County	9	0.06
Cloverly, MD (cdp) Montgomery County	9	0.06
Horizon West, FL (cdp) Orange County	9	0.06
Springfield, NJ (township) Union County	9	0.06
Mercerville, NJ (cdp) Mercer County	8	0.06
Big Bear City, CA (cdp) San Bernardino County	7	0.06
Citrus, CA (cdp) Los Angeles County	7	0.06
Forestville, MD (cdp) Prince George's County	7	0.06
Harwich, MA (town) Barnstable County	7	0.06
Huntington, VA (cdp) Fairfax County	7	0.06
River Edge, NJ (borough) Bergen County	7	0.06
Wilton Manors, FL (city) Broward County	7	0.06
Del Aire, CA (cdp) Los Angeles County	6	0.06
Lehman, PA (township) Pike County	6	0.06
Minneola, FL (city) Lake County	6	0.06
Plano, IL (city) Kendall County	6	0.06
Pleasant Valley, NY (town) Dutchess County	6	0.06
Westview, FL (cdp) Miami-Dade County	6	0.06
Bithlo, FL (cdp) Orange County	5	0.06
Bothell East, WA (cdp) Snohomish County	5	0.06
Croton-on-Hudson, NY (village) Westchester County	5	0.06
Lansing, MI (charter township) Ingham County	5	0.06
Park Hills, MO (city) St. Francois County	5	0.06
Jersey City, NJ (city) Hudson County	124	0.05
Hollywood, FL (city) Broward County	71	0.05
Hartford, CT (city/town) Hartford County	65	0.05
Town 'n' Country, FL (cdp) Hillsborough County	36	0.05
Mount Vernon, NY (city) Westchester County	33	0.05
Skokie, IL (village) Cook County	30	0.05
Union City, NJ (city) Hudson County	30	0.05
Levittown, NY (cdp) Nassau County	27	0.05
Aspen Hill, MD (cdp) Montgomery County	25	0.05
Cutler Bay, FL (town) Miami-Dade County	21	0.05
North Miami Beach, FL (city) Miami-Dade County	21	0.05
Teaneck, NJ (township) Bergen County	21	0.05
Kearny, NJ (town) Hudson County	20	0.05
Linden, NJ (city) Union County	20	0.05
San Bruno, CA (city) San Mateo County	19	0.05
St. Cloud, FL (city) Osceola County	18	0.05
Pacifica, CA (city) San Mateo County	17	0.05
Mamaroneck, NY (town) Westchester County	15	0.05
Oceanside, NY (cdp) Nassau County	15	0.05
Bay Shore, NY (cdp) Suffolk County	14	0.05
Brooklyn Center, MN (city) Hennepin County	14	0.05
East Windsor, NJ (township) Mercer County	14	0.05
Lake Magdalene, FL (cdp) Hillsborough County	14	0.05
New London, CT (city/town) New London County	14	0.05
Sterling, VA (cdp) Loudoun County	14	0.05
South Plainfield, NJ (borough) Middlesex County	12	0.05
The Crossings, FL (cdp) Miami-Dade County	12	0.05
Coolbaugh, PA (township) Monroe County	11	0.05
Lynbrook, NY (village) Nassau County	10	0.05
North Bellmore, NY (cdp) Nassau County	10	0.05
Palm Springs, FL (village) Palm Beach County	10	0.05
Chestnuthill, PA (township) Monroe County	9	0.05
Denville, NJ (township) Morris County	9	0.05
Franklin Farm, VA (cdp) Fairfax County	9	0.05
Idylwood, VA (cdp) Fairfax County	9	0.05
North Babylon, NY (cdp) Suffolk County	9	0.05
Redland, MD (cdp) Montgomery County	9	0.05
Stroud, PA (township) Monroe County	9	0.05
Hudson, MA (cdp) Middlesex County	8	0.05
La Grange, NY (town) Dutchess County	8	0.05
Merrifield, VA (cdp) Fairfax County	8	0.05
North New Hyde Park, NY (cdp) Nassau County	8	0.05
Santa Fe Springs, CA (city) Los Angeles County	8	0.05

Hispanic Origin

Other Hispanic or Latino

U.S. and 50 States Sorted by Population and Percent of Total Population

Place	Population	%
United States	**4,087,656**	**1.32**
California	874,166	2.35
Texas	764,767	3.04
New Mexico	338,297	16.43
New York	276,480	1.43
Florida	253,442	1.35
Colorado	202,011	4.02
Arizona	130,362	2.04
New Jersey	120,263	1.37
Illinois	76,092	0.59
Virginia	69,019	0.86
Washington	65,218	0.97
Pennsylvania	60,153	0.47
Maryland	57,725	1.00
Georgia	57,517	0.59
Massachusetts	57,196	0.87
North Carolina	56,683	0.59
Nevada	55,961	2.07
Utah	42,568	1.54
Oregon	38,065	0.99
Michigan	35,226	0.36
Connecticut	33,496	0.94
Ohio	33,377	0.29
Hawaii	32,656	2.40
Louisiana	28,153	0.62
Oklahoma	26,511	0.71
Indiana	25,523	0.39
Tennessee	24,603	0.39
Minnesota	20,506	0.39
Missouri	20,004	0.33
Wisconsin	19,712	0.35
Kansas	18,873	0.66
South Carolina	17,712	0.38
Alabama	16,812	0.35
Idaho	15,857	1.01
Arkansas	14,946	0.51
Nebraska	13,527	0.74
Rhode Island	12,108	1.15
Kentucky	12,000	0.28
Iowa	10,871	0.36
Wyoming	9,337	1.66
Mississippi	9,162	0.31
District of Columbia	7,823	1.30
Alaska	5,415	0.76
Delaware	4,966	0.55
Montana	4,778	0.48
New Hampshire	4,347	0.33
West Virginia	3,955	0.21
South Dakota	2,945	0.36
Maine	2,808	0.21
North Dakota	1,916	0.28
Vermont	1,746	0.28

Place	Population	%
New Mexico	338,297	16.43
Colorado	202,011	4.02
Texas	764,767	3.04
Hawaii	32,656	2.40
California	874,166	2.35
Nevada	55,961	2.07
Arizona	130,362	2.04
Wyoming	9,337	1.66
Utah	42,568	1.54
New York	276,480	1.43
New Jersey	120,263	1.37
Florida	253,442	1.35
United States	**4,087,656**	**1.32**
District of Columbia	7,823	1.30
Rhode Island	12,108	1.15
Idaho	15,857	1.01
Maryland	57,725	1.00
Oregon	38,065	0.99
Washington	65,218	0.97
Connecticut	33,496	0.94
Massachusetts	57,196	0.87
Virginia	69,019	0.86
Alaska	5,415	0.76
Nebraska	13,527	0.74
Oklahoma	26,511	0.71
Kansas	18,873	0.66
Louisiana	28,153	0.62
Illinois	76,092	0.59
Georgia	57,517	0.59
North Carolina	56,683	0.59
Delaware	4,966	0.55
Arkansas	14,946	0.51
Montana	4,778	0.48
Pennsylvania	60,153	0.47
Indiana	25,523	0.39
Tennessee	24,603	0.39
Minnesota	20,506	0.39
South Carolina	17,712	0.38
Michigan	35,226	0.36
Iowa	10,871	0.36
South Dakota	2,945	0.36
Wisconsin	19,712	0.35
Alabama	16,812	0.35
Missouri	20,004	0.33
New Hampshire	4,347	0.33
Mississippi	9,162	0.31
Ohio	33,377	0.29
Kentucky	12,000	0.28
North Dakota	1,916	0.28
Vermont	1,746	0.28
West Virginia	3,955	0.21
Maine	2,808	0.21

Please refer to the Explanation of Data in the front of the book for more detailed information.

Hispanic Origin

Other Hispanic or Latino

Top 150 Places Sorted by Population

Based on all places, regardless of total population

Place	Population	%
New York, NY (city) Kings County	180,805	2.21
Los Angeles, CA (city) Los Angeles County	133,323	3.52
San Antonio, TX (city) Medina County	100,622	7.58
Albuquerque, NM (city) Bernalillo County	98,590	18.06
Houston, TX (city) Harris County	62,891	3.00
Queens, NY (borough) Queens County	52,422	2.35
Bronx, NY (borough) Bronx County	51,571	3.72
Phoenix, AZ (city) Maricopa County	37,395	2.59
Brooklyn, NY (borough) Kings County	35,705	1.43
Manhattan, NY (borough) New York County	35,548	2.24
Denver, CO (city) Denver County	30,019	5.00
Corpus Christi, TX (city) Nueces County	29,753	9.75
Dallas, TX (city) Dallas County	26,873	2.24
El Paso, TX (city) El Paso County	26,631	4.10
Chicago, IL (city) Cook County	23,599	0.88
Austin, TX (city) Travis County	21,833	2.76
San Diego, CA (city) San Diego County	20,983	1.60
Pueblo, CO (city) Pueblo County	19,228	18.04
Laredo, TX (city) Webb County	18,262	7.74
San Jose, CA (city) Santa Clara County	18,174	1.92
Santa Fe, NM (city) Santa Fe County	17,093	25.16
Miami, FL (city) Miami-Dade County	16,155	4.04
Fort Worth, TX (city) Tarrant County	15,331	2.07
Rio Rancho, NM (city) Sandoval County	14,237	16.27
Fresno, CA (city) Fresno County	13,849	2.80
Hempstead, NY (town) Nassau County	13,273	1.75
Tucson, AZ (city) Pima County	13,240	2.55
San Francisco, CA (city) San Francisco County	13,162	1.63
Philadelphia, PA (city) Philadelphia County	13,064	0.86
Colorado Springs, CO (city) El Paso County	12,844	3.08
Las Vegas, NV (city) Clark County	12,219	2.09
Long Beach, CA (city) Los Angeles County	11,337	2.45
South Valley, NM (cdp) Bernalillo County	11,300	27.58
Lubbock, TX (city) Lubbock County	11,013	4.80
Boston, MA (city) Suffolk County	11,013	1.78
Aurora, CO (city) Arapahoe County	10,544	3.24
Brownsville, TX (city) Cameron County	10,324	5.90
Bakersfield, CA (city) Kern County	9,517	2.74
Santa Ana, CA (city) Orange County	9,024	2.78
Newark, NJ (city) Essex County	8,739	3.15
Sacramento, CA (city) Sacramento County	8,674	1.86
Islip, NY (town) Suffolk County	8,524	2.54
Las Cruces, NM (city) Doña Ana County	8,456	8.66
Riverside, CA (city) Riverside County	8,353	2.75
Charlotte, NC (city) Mecklenburg County	8,296	1.13
San Bernardino, CA (city) San Bernardino County	8,199	3.91
Tampa, FL (city) Hillsborough County	8,091	2.41
Mesa, AZ (city) Maricopa County	8,040	1.83
Thornton, CO (city) Adams County	7,848	6.61
Washington, DC (city) District of Columbia	7,823	1.30
Anaheim, CA (city) Orange County	7,578	2.25
Lakewood, CO (city) Jefferson County	7,458	5.22
Las Vegas, NM (city) San Miguel County	7,102	51.64
Stockton, CA (city) San Joaquin County	7,003	2.40
Oakland, CA (city) Alameda County	6,729	1.72
Oklahoma City, OK (city) Oklahoma County	6,541	1.13
McAllen, TX (city) Hidalgo County	6,428	4.95
Arlington, TX (city) Tarrant County	6,392	1.75
Lancaster, CA (city) Los Angeles County	6,340	4.05
Amarillo, TX (city) Potter County	6,335	3.32
Palmdale, CA (city) Los Angeles County	6,233	4.08
Brookhaven, NY (town) Suffolk County	6,193	1.27
Fontana, CA (city) San Bernardino County	6,031	3.08
Hialeah, FL (city) Miami-Dade County	5,890	2.62
Providence, RI (city) Providence County	5,821	3.27
Espanola, NM (city) Rio Arriba County	5,762	56.36
Glendale, AZ (city) Maricopa County	5,741	2.53
Jacksonville, FL (city) Duval County	5,595	0.68
Staten Island, NY (borough) Richmond County	5,559	1.19
Salinas, CA (city) Monterey County	5,512	3.66
Moreno Valley, CA (city) Riverside County	5,511	2.85
Pasadena, TX (city) Harris County	5,498	3.69
Indianapolis, IN (city) Marion County	5,473	0.67
Portland, OR (city) Multnomah County	5,464	0.94
Urban Honolulu, HI (cdp) Honolulu County	5,426	1.61
Paradise, NV (cdp) Clark County	5,392	2.42
Elizabeth, NJ (city) Union County	5,350	4.28
Chula Vista, CA (city) San Diego County	5,264	2.16
Irving, TX (city) Dallas County	5,249	2.43
Harlingen, TX (city) Cameron County	5,241	8.08
Paterson, NJ (city) Passaic County	5,230	3.58
Westminster, CO (city) Adams County	5,207	4.91
Sunrise Manor, NV (cdp) Clark County	5,127	2.71
Pomona, CA (city) Los Angeles County	5,081	3.41
Ontario, CA (city) San Bernardino County	5,057	3.08
Seattle, WA (city) King County	5,048	0.83
North Las Vegas, NV (city) Clark County	5,042	2.32
Jersey City, NJ (city) Hudson County	5,019	2.03
Nashville-Davidson, TN (metro govt) Davidson County	4,982	0.83
Garland, TX (city) Dallas County	4,980	2.20
Roswell, NM (city) Chaves County	4,856	10.04
Greeley, CO (city) Weld County	4,715	5.08
Oxnard, CA (city) Ventura County	4,703	2.38
Modesto, CA (city) Stanislaus County	4,620	2.30
Grand Prairie, TX (city) Dallas County	4,601	2.62
Reno, NV (city) Washoe County	4,506	2.00
Los Lunas, NM (village) Valencia County	4,502	30.35
East Los Angeles, CA (cdp) Los Angeles County	4,486	3.55
Abilene, TX (city) Taylor County	4,453	3.80
Yonkers, NY (city) Westchester County	4,443	2.27
Clovis, NM (city) Curry County	4,409	11.67
Henderson, NV (city) Clark County	4,406	1.71
Salt Lake City, UT (city) Salt Lake County	4,295	2.30
Victoria, TX (city) Victoria County	4,255	6.80
Santa Clarita, CA (city) Los Angeles County	4,190	2.38
Columbus, OH (city) Franklin County	4,130	0.52
Arvada, CO (city) Jefferson County	4,093	3.85
Chandler, AZ (city) Maricopa County	4,079	1.73
Odessa, TX (city) Ector County	4,035	4.04
Lawrence, MA (city) Essex County	4,010	5.25
Farmington, NM (city) San Juan County	3,996	8.71
Victorville, CA (city) San Bernardino County	3,991	3.44
West Valley City, UT (city) Salt Lake County	3,941	3.04
Rancho Cucamonga, CA (city) San Bernardino County	3,911	2.37
Commerce City, CO (city) Adams County	3,900	8.49
Midland, TX (city) Midland County	3,900	3.51
Union City, NJ (city) Hudson County	3,847	5.79
Hayward, CA (city) Alameda County	3,839	2.66
Arlington, VA (cdp) Arlington County	3,821	1.84
Milwaukee, WI (city) Milwaukee County	3,808	0.64
Edinburg, TX (city) Hidalgo County	3,727	4.83
Omaha, NE (city) Douglas County	3,713	0.91
Pharr, TX (city) Hidalgo County	3,635	5.16
Allentown, PA (city) Lehigh County	3,616	3.06
Baltimore, MD (city) Baltimore city County	3,558	0.57
Virginia Beach, VA (ind. city) Virginia Beach independent city	3,551	0.81
South Gate, CA (city) Los Angeles County	3,529	3.74
Downey, CA (city) Los Angeles County	3,515	3.14
Brentwood, NY (cdp) Suffolk County	3,476	5.73
North Valley, NM (cdp) Bernalillo County	3,428	30.25
Hesperia, CA (city) San Bernardino County	3,423	3.80
Hollywood, FL (city) Broward County	3,382	2.40
Tulsa, OK (city) Tulsa County	3,379	0.86
Wichita, KS (city) Sedgwick County	3,368	0.88
Santa Maria, CA (city) Santa Barbara County	3,351	3.37
Hawthorne, CA (city) Los Angeles County	3,332	3.95
Escondido, CA (city) San Diego County	3,330	2.31
Babylon, NY (town) Suffolk County	3,321	1.55
Spring Valley, NV (cdp) Clark County	3,320	1.86
Big Spring, TX (city) Howard County	3,313	12.14
Visalia, CA (city) Tulare County	3,267	2.63
Bernalillo, NM (town) Sandoval County	3,251	39.07
Inglewood, CA (city) Los Angeles County	3,250	2.96
Pembroke Pines, FL (city) Broward County	3,245	2.10
Memphis, TN (city) Shelby County	3,233	0.50
Mission, TX (city) Hidalgo County	3,217	4.17
Rialto, CA (city) San Bernardino County	3,213	3.24
West Covina, CA (city) Los Angeles County	3,208	3.02
Miami Beach, FL (city) Miami-Dade County	3,196	3.64
Garden Grove, CA (city) Orange County	3,172	1.86

Please refer to the Explanation of Data in the front of the book for more detailed information.

Hispanic Origin

Other Hispanic or Latino

Top 150 Places Sorted by Percent of Total Population

Based on all places, regardless of total population

Place	Population	%
Alcalde, NM (cdp) Rio Arriba County	250	87.72
San Jose, NM (cdp) Rio Arriba County	538	77.41
Brazos, NM (cdp) Rio Arriba County	34	77.27
Los Ojos, NM (cdp) Rio Arriba County	96	76.80
Cañones, NM (cdp) Rio Arriba County	90	76.27
San Luis, NM (cdp) Sandoval County	45	76.27
Soham, NM (cdp) San Miguel County	158	75.24
Tierra Amarilla, NM (cdp) Rio Arriba County	287	75.13
Youngsville, NM (cdp) Rio Arriba County	41	73.21
Chamita, NM (cdp) Rio Arriba County	634	72.87
Pueblo, NM (cdp) San Miguel County	91	72.80
Cordova, NM (cdp) Rio Arriba County	298	71.98
Hernandez, NM (cdp) Rio Arriba County	674	71.25
Cundiyo, NM (cdp) Santa Fe County	51	70.83
Vadito, NM (cdp) Taos County	190	70.37
Villanueva, NM (cdp) San Miguel County	156	68.12
Lyden, NM (cdp) Rio Arriba County	163	66.53
Chimayo, NM (cdp) Rio Arriba County	2,069	65.12
Tecolote, NM (cdp) San Miguel County	194	65.10
Lumberton, NM (cdp) Rio Arriba County	47	64.38
Cubero, NM (cdp) Cibola County	185	64.01
Truchas, NM (cdp) Rio Arriba County	356	63.57
Tajique, NM (cdp) Torrance County	82	63.08
Coyote, NM (cdp) Rio Arriba County	80	62.50
Cuyamungue, NM (cdp) Santa Fe County	299	62.42
Manzano, NM (cdp) Torrance County	18	62.07
Costilla, NM (cdp) Taos County	127	61.95
Ensenada, NM (cdp) Rio Arriba County	66	61.68
Cobre, NM (cdp) Grant County	24	61.54
Seboyeta, NM (cdp) Cibola County	110	61.45
La Mesilla, NM (cdp) Rio Arriba County	1,086	61.29
Velarde, NM (cdp) Rio Arriba County	307	61.16
El Rancho, NM (cdp) Santa Fe County	726	60.55
La Villita, NM (cdp) Rio Arriba County	578	60.40
El Duende, NM (cdp) Rio Arriba County	425	60.11
Mora, NM (cdp) Mora County	390	59.45
Abiquiu, NM (cdp) Rio Arriba County	137	59.31
Cuartelez, NM (cdp) Santa Fe County	274	58.42
Bibo, NM (cdp) Cibola County	81	57.86
Ribera, NM (cdp) San Miguel County	240	57.69
Peñasco, NM (cdp) Taos County	338	57.39
La Jara, NM (cdp) Sandoval County	118	57.00
San Ysidro, NM (village) Sandoval County	110	56.99
Sena, NM (cdp) San Miguel County	73	56.59
Capulin, CO (cdp) Conejos County	113	56.50
La Puebla, NM (cdp) Santa Fe County	670	56.49
Espanola, NM (city) Rio Arriba County	5,762	56.36
Questa, NM (village) Taos County	991	55.99
Rio Lucio, NM (cdp) Taos County	217	55.78
Jacona, NM (cdp) Santa Fe County	228	55.34
Gallina, NM (cdp) Rio Arriba County	158	55.24
Talpa, NM (cdp) Taos County	427	54.88
Santa Rosa, NM (city) Guadalupe County	1,558	54.71
Algodones, NM (cdp) Sandoval County	445	54.67
San Jose, NM (cdp) San Miguel County	74	54.01
Chili, NM (cdp) Rio Arriba County	353	53.98
Anton Chico, NM (cdp) Guadalupe County	101	53.72
Peña Blanca, NM (cdp) Sandoval County	378	53.31
San Fidel, NM (cdp) Cibola County	73	52.90
Canova, NM (cdp) Rio Arriba County	62	52.54
El Rito, NM (cdp) Rio Arriba County	419	51.86
Las Vegas, NM (city) San Miguel County	7,102	51.64
Moquino, NM (cdp) Cibola County	19	51.35
Los Luceros, NM (cdp) Rio Arriba County	465	51.32
Dixon, NM (cdp) Rio Arriba County	475	51.30
Chilili, NM (cdp) Bernalillo County	70	51.09
Starkville, CO (town) Las Animas County	30	50.85
Nambe, NM (cdp) Santa Fe County	924	50.83
Conejos, CO (cdp) Conejos County	29	50.00
Abeytas, NM (cdp) Socorro County	28	50.00
Lynn, CO (cdp) Las Animas County	6	50.00
Arroyo Hondo, NM (cdp) Taos County	236	49.79
Antonito, CO (town) Conejos County	388	49.68
Chamisal, NM (cdp) Taos County	153	49.35
Tecolotito, NM (cdp) San Miguel County	114	49.14
Torreon, NM (cdp) Torrance County	116	48.95
Chama, NM (village) Rio Arriba County	495	48.43
Rio en Medio, NM (cdp) Santa Fe County	69	48.25
Puerto de Luna, NM (cdp) Guadalupe County	68	48.23
El Valle de Arroyo Seco, NM (cdp) Santa Fe County	691	47.99
Pastura, NM (cdp) Guadalupe County	11	47.83
Jaconita, NM (cdp) Santa Fe County	158	47.59
Vaughn, NM (town) Guadalupe County	211	47.31
Pecos, NM (village) San Miguel County	654	46.98
Llano del Medio, NM (cdp) Guadalupe County	55	46.61
San Mateo, NM (cdp) Cibola County	75	46.58
San Luis, CO (town) Costilla County	291	46.26
East Pecos, NM (cdp) San Miguel County	350	46.24
Rowe, NM (cdp) San Miguel County	191	46.02
Ranchos de Taos, NM (cdp) Taos County	1,135	45.08
San Acacio, CO (cdp) Costilla County	18	45.00
San Rafael, NM (cdp) Cibola County	418	44.80
Ponderosa, NM (cdp) Sandoval County	172	44.44
Blanco, NM (cdp) San Juan County	172	44.33
Alfred, TX (cdp) Jim Wells County	40	43.96
Springer, NM (town) Colfax County	452	43.17
Romeo, CO (town) Conejos County	172	42.57
North San Ysidro, NM (cdp) San Miguel County	67	42.14
Watrous, NM (cdp) Mora County	55	40.74
Pojoaque, NM (cdp) Santa Fe County	776	40.69
Pueblito, NM (cdp) Rio Arriba County	37	40.66
Encino, NM (village) Torrance County	33	40.24
Sausal, NM (cdp) Valencia County	424	40.15
Canjilon, NM (cdp) Rio Arriba County	102	39.84
La Jara, CO (town) Conejos County	322	39.36
Wagon Mound, NM (village) Mora County	123	39.17
Bernalillo, NM (town) Sandoval County	3,251	39.07
La Cienega, NM (cdp) Santa Fe County	1,486	38.91
Alice Acres, TX (cdp) Jim Wells County	190	38.78
Tome, NM (cdp) Valencia County	718	38.46
Edith Endave, NM (cdp) Bernalillo County	79	37.44
Walsenburg, CO (city) Huerfano County	1,132	36.90
Jarales, NM (cdp) Valencia County	910	36.77
Adelino, NM (cdp) Valencia County	301	36.57
Mosquero, NM (village) Harding County	34	36.56
Raton, NM (city) Colfax County	2,506	36.40
Buena Vista, TX (cdp) Starr County	37	36.27
Aragon, NM (cdp) Catron County	34	36.17
Jansen, CO (cdp) Las Animas County	40	35.71
Willard, NM (village) Torrance County	89	35.18
Capulin, NM (cdp) Union County	23	34.85
Weston, CO (cdp) Las Animas County	19	34.55
Clayton, NM (town) Union County	1,029	34.53
Valdez, CO (cdp) Las Animas County	16	34.04
Agua Fria, NM (cdp) Santa Fe County	952	34.00
Belen, NM (city) Valencia County	2,436	33.51
Highland Meadows, NM (cdp) Valencia County	209	33.49
Junction City, WA (cdp) Grays Harbor County	6	33.33
Manassa, CO (town) Conejos County	330	33.30
Lemitar, NM (cdp) Socorro County	109	33.03
Ignacio, CO (town) La Plata County	230	33.00
Arroyo Seco, NM (cdp) Taos County	585	32.77
Manzanola, CO (town) Otero County	141	32.49
Freer, TX (city) Duval County	915	32.47
Casa Colorada, NM (cdp) Valencia County	87	31.99
Cimarron, NM (village) Colfax County	322	31.54
Roy, NM (village) Harding County	73	31.20
La Madera, NM (cdp) Rio Arriba County	48	31.17
Los Chaves, NM (cdp) Valencia County	1,687	30.98
Fort Sumner, NM (village) De Baca County	319	30.94
El Cerro, NM (cdp) Valencia County	913	30.92
Taos, NM (town) Taos County	1,766	30.90
Las Nutrias, NM (cdp) Socorro County	46	30.87
Luis Lopez, NM (cdp) Socorro County	33	30.84
Sombrillo, NM (cdp) Santa Fe County	108	30.77
Magdalena, NM (village) Socorro County	288	30.70
La Joya, NM (cdp) Socorro County	25	30.49
Fort Garland, CO (cdp) Costilla County	132	30.48
Los Lunas, NM (village) Valencia County	4,502	30.35
San Diego, TX (city) Duval County	1,361	30.33

Please refer to the Explanation of Data in the front of the book for more detailed information.

Hispanic Origin

Other Hispanic or Latino

Top 150 Places Sorted by Percent of Total Population

Based on places with total population of 7,500 or more

Place	Population	%
Espanola, NM (city) Rio Arriba County	5,762	56.36
Las Vegas, NM (city) San Miguel County	7,102	51.64
Bernalillo, NM (town) Sandoval County	3,251	39.07
Los Lunas, NM (village) Valencia County	4,502	30.35
North Valley, NM (cdp) Bernalillo County	3,428	30.25
South Valley, NM (cdp) Bernalillo County	11,300	27.58
Grants, NM (city) Cibola County	2,498	27.21
Trinidad, CO (city) Las Animas County	2,410	26.50
Santa Fe, NM (city) Santa Fe County	17,093	25.16
Socorro, NM (city) Socorro County	1,836	20.29
California City, CA (city) Kern County	2,790	19.76
Alamosa, CO (city) Alamosa County	1,732	19.73
Albuquerque, NM (city) Bernalillo County	98,590	18.06
Pueblo, CO (city) Pueblo County	19,228	18.04
Corrales, NM (village) Sandoval County	1,388	16.66
Rio Rancho, NM (city) Sandoval County	14,237	16.27
Alice, TX (city) Jim Wells County	2,978	15.59
Bloomfield, NM (city) San Juan County	1,207	14.88
Raymondville, TX (city) Willacy County	1,621	14.37
Robstown, TX (city) Nueces County	1,566	13.63
Beeville, TX (city) Bee County	1,740	13.53
Langley Park, MD (cdp) Prince George's County	2,455	13.09
Portales, NM (city) Roosevelt County	1,510	12.30
Big Spring, TX (city) Howard County	3,313	12.14
Clovis, NM (city) Curry County	4,409	11.67
Pleasanton, TX (city) Atascosa County	1,022	11.44
Uvalde, TX (city) Uvalde County	1,724	10.95
Berkley, CO (cdp) Adams County	1,208	10.78
Silver City, NM (town) Grant County	1,099	10.65
Kingsville, TX (city) Kleberg County	2,724	10.39
Gallup, NM (city) McKinley County	2,178	10.05
Roswell, NM (city) Chaves County	4,856	10.04
Fort Stockton, TX (city) Pecos County	831	10.03
Pecos, TX (city) Reeves County	880	10.02
Sherrelwood, CO (cdp) Adams County	1,809	9.89
Corpus Christi, TX (city) Nueces County	29,753	9.75
Avenal, CA (city) Kings County	1,486	9.58
Pearsall, TX (city) Frio County	864	9.45
Artesia, NM (city) Eddy County	1,031	9.12
Lamesa, TX (city) Dawson County	848	9.00
Welby, CO (cdp) Adams County	1,313	8.84
Farmington, NM (city) San Juan County	3,996	8.71
Las Cruces, NM (city) Doña Ana County	8,456	8.66
Commerce City, CO (city) Adams County	3,900	8.49
Port Lavaca, TX (city) Calhoun County	1,037	8.47
Mercedes, TX (city) Hidalgo County	1,310	8.41
Carlsbad, NM (city) Eddy County	2,195	8.40
Hereford, TX (city) Deaf Smith County	1,288	8.38
Hondo, TX (city) Medina County	718	8.16
Derby, CO (cdp) Adams County	627	8.16
Harlingen, TX (city) Cameron County	5,241	8.08
Susanville, CA (city) Lassen County	1,429	7.96
Plainview, TX (city) Hale County	1,745	7.86
Laredo, TX (city) Webb County	18,262	7.74
Brighton, CO (city) Adams County	2,567	7.70
Pueblo West, CO (cdp) Pueblo County	2,280	7.69
San Antonio, TX (city) Medina County	100,622	7.58
Sunland Park, NM (city) Doña Ana County	1,068	7.57
Snyder, TX (city) Scurry County	842	7.52
Adelphi, MD (cdp) Prince George's County	1,132	7.50
Deming, NM (city) Luna County	1,104	7.43
Northglenn, CO (city) Adams County	2,596	7.25
Alamo, TX (city) Hidalgo County	1,327	7.23
San Benito, TX (city) Cameron County	1,743	7.19
Donna, TX (city) Hidalgo County	1,131	7.16
Soledad, CA (city) Monterey County	1,831	7.11
Los Alamos, NM (cdp) Los Alamos County	849	7.06
Key Biscayne, FL (village) Miami-Dade County	867	7.02
Brownfield, TX (city) Terry County	678	7.02
Kearny, NJ (town) Hudson County	2,826	6.95
Corcoran, CA (city) Kings County	1,723	6.94
Victoria, TX (city) Victoria County	4,255	6.80
Thornton, CO (city) Adams County	7,848	6.61
Blythe, CA (city) Riverside County	1,372	6.59
Federal Heights, CO (city) Adams County	734	6.40
Rawlins, WY (city) Carbon County	593	6.40
Weslaco, TX (city) Hidalgo County	2,229	6.25
Hobbs, NM (city) Lea County	2,126	6.23
Freeport, TX (city) Brazoria County	737	6.12
Sterling, CO (city) Logan County	882	5.97
Evans, CO (city) Weld County	1,103	5.95
Alamogordo, NM (city) Otero County	1,805	5.94
Brownsville, TX (city) Cameron County	10,324	5.90
Seguin, TX (city) Guadalupe County	1,486	5.90
Levelland, TX (city) Hockley County	793	5.86
Chowchilla, CA (city) Madera County	1,086	5.80
Bonham, TX (city) Fannin County	587	5.80
Lamar, CO (city) Prowers County	453	5.80
Union City, NJ (city) Hudson County	3,847	5.79
Fabens, TX (cdp) El Paso County	478	5.79
Somers, CT (town) Tolland County	657	5.74
Dalhart, TX (city) Dallam County	455	5.74
Brentwood, NY (cdp) Suffolk County	3,476	5.73
Lovington, NM (city) Lea County	627	5.70
Cortez, CO (city) Montezuma County	482	5.68
Chillum, MD (cdp) Prince George's County	1,900	5.67
Norfolk, MA (town) Norfolk County	632	5.63
Barstow, CA (city) San Bernardino County	1,272	5.62
Socorro, TX (city) El Paso County	1,797	5.61
Rio Grande City, TX (city) Starr County	776	5.61
Coolidge, AZ (city) Pinal County	653	5.52
Eloy, AZ (city) Pinal County	906	5.45
Aransas Pass, TX (city) San Patricio County	446	5.44
Fort Morgan, CO (city) Morgan County	611	5.40
Wheaton, MD (cdp) Montgomery County	2,602	5.39
Chelsea, MA (city) Suffolk County	1,878	5.34
Del Rio, TX (city) Val Verde County	1,886	5.30
Wharton, TX (city) Wharton County	468	5.30
Good Hope, CA (cdp) Riverside County	484	5.27
Lawrence, MA (city) Essex County	4,010	5.25
Ingleside, TX (city) San Patricio County	493	5.25
McFarland, CA (city) Kern County	666	5.24
Lakewood, CO (city) Jefferson County	7,458	5.22
Wheat Ridge, CO (city) Jefferson County	1,576	5.22
Dover, NJ (town) Morris County	940	5.18
Pharr, TX (city) Hidalgo County	3,635	5.16
Wasco, CA (city) Kern County	1,307	5.12
East Riverdale, MD (cdp) Prince George's County	793	5.11
Mendota, CA (city) Fresno County	563	5.11
North Bay Shore, NY (cdp) Suffolk County	967	5.10
Greeley, CO (city) Weld County	4,715	5.08
Mineral Wells, TX (city) Palo Pinto County	853	5.08
Crescent City, CA (city) Del Norte County	388	5.08
Maurice River, NJ (township) Cumberland County	403	5.05
Harrison, NJ (town) Hudson County	686	5.04
Douglas, AZ (city) Cochise County	874	5.03
Andrews, TX (city) Andrews County	558	5.03
Delta, CO (city) Delta County	447	5.01
Denver, CO (city) Denver County	30,019	5.00
Florence-Graham, CA (cdp) Los Angeles County	3,154	4.98
New Cassel, NY (cdp) Nassau County	699	4.97
McAllen, TX (city) Hidalgo County	6,428	4.95
Guttenberg, NJ (town) Hudson County	552	4.94
West New York, NJ (town) Hudson County	2,449	4.93
Eagle Pass, TX (city) Maverick County	1,295	4.93
Westminster, CO (city) Adams County	5,207	4.91
Anthony, NM (cdp) Doña Ana County	460	4.91
Kirby, TX (city) Bexar County	390	4.88
Delano, CA (city) Kern County	2,583	4.87
Hempstead, NY (village) Nassau County	2,609	4.84
Central Islip, NY (cdp) Suffolk County	1,667	4.84
El Campo, TX (city) Wharton County	562	4.84
Edinburg, TX (city) Hidalgo County	3,727	4.83
Lubbock, TX (city) Lubbock County	11,013	4.80
Portland, TX (city) San Patricio County	722	4.78
Inwood, NY (cdp) Nassau County	467	4.77
Maili, HI (cdp) Honolulu County	453	4.77
Leon Valley, TX (city) Bexar County	482	4.75
Rosenberg, TX (city) Fort Bend County	1,451	4.74
Orange Cove, CA (city) Fresno County	427	4.70

Please refer to the Explanation of Data in the front of the book for more detailed information.

Racial Group Rankings

Introduction

In this section of this book, each ethnicity contains four tables. The first table is split into two parts. Part one ranks the U.S. and all 50 states plus the District of Columbia by ethnic population. Part two ranks the same areas by percent of the total population. The second table shows the top 150 places sorted by ethnic population (based on all places, regardless of total population), the third table shows the top 150 places sorted by percent of the total population (based on all places, regardless of total population), the fourth table shows the top 150 places sorted by percent of the total population (based on places with total population of 7,500 or more).

Within each table, column one displays the place name, the state, and the county (if a place spans more than one county, the county that holds the majority of the population is shown). Column one in the first table displays the state only. Column two displays the number of people reporting each race alone or in combination with any other race. Column three is the percent of the total population reporting each race alone or in combination with any other race. The 100-percent population figure from Census 2010 Summary File 1 is used to calculate the value in the "%" column.

Major Racial Groups

Alphabetical Racial Group Cross-Reference Guide

African-American: Hispanic *see* Race–African-American/Black: Hispanic
African-American: Not Hispanic *see* Race–African-American/Black: Not Hispanic
African-American *see* Race–African-American/Black
Alaska Athabascan *see* Race–Alaska Native: Alaska Athabascan
Alaska Native: Hispanic *see* Race–American Indian/Alaska Native: Hispanic
Alaska Native: Not Hispanic *see* Race–American Indian/Alaska Native: Not Hispanic
Alaska Native *see* Race–American Indian/Alaska Native
Aleut *see* Race–Alaska Native: Aleut
American Indian: Hispanic *see* Race–American Indian/Alaska Native: Hispanic
American Indian: Not Hispanic *see* Race–American Indian/Alaska Native: Not Hispanic
American Indian *see* Race–American Indian/Alaska Native
Apache *see* Race–American Indian: Apache
Arapaho *see* Race–American Indian: Arapaho
Asian Indian *see* Race–Asian: Indian
Asian: Hispanic *see* Race–Asian: Hispanic
Asian: Not Hispanic *see* Race–Asian: Not Hispanic
Asian *see* Race–Asian
Bangladeshi *see* Race–Asian: Bangladeshi
Bhutanese *see* Race–Asian: Bhutanese
Black: Hispanic *see* Race–African-American/Black: Hispanic
Black: Not Hispanic *see* Race–African-American/Black: Not Hispanic
Black *see* Race–African-American/Black
Blackfeet *see* Race–American Indian: Blackfeet
Burmese *see* Race–Asian: Burmese
Cambodian *see* Race–Asian: Cambodian
Canadian/French American Indian *see* Race–American Indian: Canadian/French American Indian
Central American Indian *see* Race–American Indian: Central American Indian
Chamorro *see* Race–Hawaii Native/Pacific Islander: Guamanian or Chamorro
Cherokee *see* Race–American Indian: Cherokee
Cheyenne *see* Race–American Indian: Cheyenne
Chickasaw *see* Race–American Indian: Chickasaw
Chinese (except Taiwanese) *see* Race–Asian: Chinese, except Taiwanese
Chippewa *see* Race–American Indian: Chippewa
Choctaw *see* Race–American Indian: Choctaw
Colville *see* Race–American Indian: Colville
Comanche *see* Race–American Indian: Comanche
Cree *see* Race–American Indian: Cree
Creek *see* Race–American Indian: Creek
Crow *see* Race–American Indian: Crow
Delaware *see* Race–American Indian: Delaware
Eskimo *see* Race–Alaska Native: Inupiat
Fijian *see* Race–Hawaii Native/Pacific Islander: Fijian
Filipino *see* Race–Asian: Filipino
Guamanian *see* Race–Hawaii Native/Pacific Islander: Guamanian or Chamorro
Hawaii Native: Hispanic *see* Race–Hawaii Native/Pacific Islander: Hispanic
Hawaii Native: Not Hispanic *see* Race–Hawaii Native/Pacific Islander: Not Hispanic
Hawaii Native *see* Race–Hawaii Native/Pacific Islander
Hmong *see* Race–Asian: Hmong
Hopi *see* Race–American Indian: Hopi
Houma *see* Race–American Indian: Houma
Indonesian *see* Race–Asian: Indonesian
Inupiat *see* Race–Alaska Native: Inupiat
Iroquois *see* Race–American Indian: Iroquois
Japanese *see* Race–Asian: Japanese
Kiowa *see* Race–American Indian: Kiowa
Korean *see* Race–Asian: Korean
Laotian *see* Race–Asian: Laotian
Lumbee *see* Race–American Indian: Lumbee
Malaysian *see* Race–Asian: Malaysian
Marshallese *see* Race–Hawaii Native/Pacific Islander: Marshallese
Menominee *see* Race–American Indian: Menominee
Mexican American Indian *see* Race–American Indian: Mexican American Indian
Native Hawaiian *see* Race–Hawaii Native/Pacific Islander: Native Hawaiian
Navajo *see* Race–American Indian: Navajo
Nepalese *see* Race–Asian: Nepalese
Osage *see* Race–American Indian: Osage
Ottawa *see* Race–American Indian: Ottawa
Pacific Islander: Hispanic *see* Race–Hawaii Native/Pacific Islander: Hispanic
Pacific Islander: Not Hispanic *see* Race–Hawaii Native/Pacific Islander: Not Hispanic
Pacific Islander *see* Race–Hawaii Native/Pacific Islander
Paiute *see* Race–American Indian: Paiute
Pakistani *see* Race–Asian: Pakistani
Pima *see* Race–American Indian: Pima
Potawatomi *see* Race–American Indian: Potawatomi
Pueblo *see* Race–American Indian: Pueblo
Puget Sound Salish *see* Race–American Indian: Puget Sound Salish
Samoan *see* Race–Hawaii Native/Pacific Islander: Samoan
Seminole *see* Race–American Indian: Seminole
Shoshone *see* Race–American Indian: Shoshone
Sioux *see* Race–American Indian: Sioux
South American Indian *see* Race–American Indian: South American Indian
Spanish American Indian *see* Race–American Indian: Spanish American Indian
Sri Lankan *see* Race–Asian: Sri Lankan
Taiwanese *see* Race–Asian: Taiwanese
Thai *see* Race–Asian: Thai
Tlingit-Haida *see* Race–Alaska Native: Tlingit-Haida
Tohono O'Odham *see* Race–American Indian: Tohono O'Odham
Tongan *see* Race–Hawaii Native/Pacific Islander: Tongan
Tsimshian *see* Race–Alaska Native: Tsimshian
Ute *see* Race–American Indian: Ute
Vietnamese *see* Race–Asian: Vietnamese
White: Hispanic *see* Race–White: Hispanic
White: Not Hispanic *see* Race–White: Not Hispanic
White *see* Race–White
Yakama *see* Race–American Indian: Yakama
Yaqui *see* Race–American Indian: Yaqui
Yuman *see* Race–American Indian: Yuman
Yup'ik *see* Race–Alaska Native: Yup'ik

Race

African-American/Black

U.S. and 50 States Sorted by Population and Percent of Total Population

Place	Population	%
United States	**42,020,743**	**13.61**
New York	3,334,550	17.21
Florida	3,200,663	17.02
Texas	3,168,469	12.60
Georgia	3,054,098	31.53
California	2,683,914	7.20
North Carolina	2,151,456	22.56
Illinois	1,974,113	15.39
Maryland	1,783,899	30.90
Virginia	1,653,563	20.67
Ohio	1,541,771	13.36
Pennsylvania	1,507,965	11.87
Michigan	1,505,514	15.23
Louisiana	1,486,885	32.80
South Carolina	1,332,188	28.80
New Jersey	1,300,363	14.79
Alabama	1,281,118	26.80
Mississippi	1,115,801	37.60
Tennessee	1,107,178	17.45
Missouri	747,474	12.48
Indiana	654,415	10.09
Massachusetts	508,413	7.76
Arkansas	468,710	16.07
Connecticut	405,600	11.35
Wisconsin	403,527	7.10
Kentucky	376,213	8.67
Oklahoma	327,621	8.73
Minnesota	327,548	6.18
Washington	325,004	4.83
Arizona	318,665	4.99
District of Columbia	314,352	52.24
Nevada	254,452	9.42
Colorado	249,812	4.97
Delaware	205,923	22.93
Kansas	202,149	7.09
Iowa	113,225	3.72
Nebraska	98,959	5.42
Oregon	98,479	2.57
Rhode Island	77,754	7.39
West Virginia	76,945	4.15
New Mexico	57,040	2.77
Utah	43,209	1.56
Hawaii	38,820	2.85
Alaska	33,150	4.67
Maine	21,764	1.64
New Hampshire	21,736	1.65
Idaho	15,940	1.02
South Dakota	14,705	1.81
North Dakota	11,086	1.65
Vermont	9,343	1.49
Montana	7,917	0.80
Wyoming	7,285	1.29

Place	Population	%
District of Columbia	314,352	52.24
Mississippi	1,115,801	37.60
Louisiana	1,486,885	32.80
Georgia	3,054,098	31.53
Maryland	1,783,899	30.90
South Carolina	1,332,188	28.80
Alabama	1,281,118	26.80
Delaware	205,923	22.93
North Carolina	2,151,456	22.56
Virginia	1,653,563	20.67
Tennessee	1,107,178	17.45
New York	3,334,550	17.21
Florida	3,200,663	17.02
Arkansas	468,710	16.07
Illinois	1,974,113	15.39
Michigan	1,505,514	15.23
New Jersey	1,300,363	14.79
United States	**42,020,743**	**13.61**
Ohio	1,541,771	13.36
Texas	3,168,469	12.60
Missouri	747,474	12.48
Pennsylvania	1,507,965	11.87
Connecticut	405,600	11.35
Indiana	654,415	10.09
Nevada	254,452	9.42
Oklahoma	327,621	8.73
Kentucky	376,213	8.67
Massachusetts	508,413	7.76
Rhode Island	77,754	7.39
California	2,683,914	7.20
Wisconsin	403,527	7.10
Kansas	202,149	7.09
Minnesota	327,548	6.18
Nebraska	98,959	5.42
Arizona	318,665	4.99
Colorado	249,812	4.97
Washington	325,004	4.83
Alaska	33,150	4.67
West Virginia	76,945	4.15
Iowa	113,225	3.72
Hawaii	38,820	2.85
New Mexico	57,040	2.77
Oregon	98,479	2.57
South Dakota	14,705	1.81
New Hampshire	21,736	1.65
North Dakota	11,086	1.65
Maine	21,764	1.64
Utah	43,209	1.56
Vermont	9,343	1.49
Wyoming	7,285	1.29
Idaho	15,940	1.02
Montana	7,917	0.80

Please refer to the Explanation of Data in the front of the book for more detailed information.

Race

African-American/Black

Top 150 Places Sorted by Population

Based on all places, regardless of total population

Place	Population	%
New York, NY (city) Kings County	2,228,145	27.26
Chicago, IL (city) Cook County	913,009	33.87
Brooklyn, NY (borough) Kings County	896,165	35.78
Philadelphia, PA (city) Philadelphia County	686,870	45.01
Detroit, MI (city) Wayne County	601,988	84.34
Bronx, NY (borough) Bronx County	541,622	39.10
Houston, TX (city) Harris County	514,217	24.49
Queens, NY (borough) Queens County	462,351	20.73
Memphis, TN (city) Shelby County	414,928	64.14
Baltimore, MD (city) Baltimore city County	403,998	65.06
Los Angeles, CA (city) Los Angeles County	402,448	10.61
Washington, DC (city) District of Columbia	314,352	52.24
Dallas, TX (city) Dallas County	308,087	25.72
Manhattan, NY (borough) New York County	272,993	17.21
Charlotte, NC (city) Mecklenburg County	266,822	36.48
Jacksonville, FL (city) Duval County	263,662	32.08
Milwaukee, WI (city) Milwaukee County	250,003	42.03
Indianapolis, IN (city) Marion County	239,354	29.17
Columbus, OH (city) Franklin County	237,077	30.12
Atlanta, GA (city) Fulton County	231,948	55.23
Cleveland, OH (city) Cuyahoga County	219,027	55.20
New Orleans, LA (city) Orleans Parish	210,447	61.21
Nashville-Davidson, TN (metro govt) Davidson County	177,894	29.59
Boston, MA (city) Suffolk County	163,629	26.49
St. Louis, MO (city) St. Louis city County	161,796	50.67
Birmingham, AL (city) Jefferson County	157,136	74.04
Newark, NJ (city) Essex County	149,512	53.95
Fort Worth, TX (city) Tarrant County	147,411	19.89
Kansas City, MO (city) Jackson County	145,396	31.62
Louisville-Jefferson County, KY (metro govt) Jefferson County	145,117	24.29
Jackson, MS (city) Hinds County	138,940	80.07
Cincinnati, OH (city) Hamilton County	138,296	46.57
Hempstead, NY (town) Nassau County	133,280	17.54
Baton Rouge, LA (city) East Baton Rouge Parish	126,742	55.23
Raleigh, NC (city) Wake County	124,035	30.71
Oakland, CA (city) Alameda County	119,122	30.49
Montgomery, AL (city) Montgomery County	118,129	57.41
Greensboro, NC (city) Guilford County	114,156	42.33
Shreveport, LA (city) Caddo Parish	110,693	55.54
Augusta-Richmond County, GA (cons. govt) Richmond County	110,481	56.41
Norfolk, VA (ind. city) Norfolk independent city	109,734	45.19
Phoenix, AZ (city) Maricopa County	109,544	7.58
Buffalo, NY (city) Erie County	106,107	40.61
Richmond, VA (ind. city) Richmond independent city	106,068	51.94
San Diego, CA (city) San Diego County	104,374	7.98
San Antonio, TX (city) Medina County	102,748	7.74
Mobile, AL (city) Mobile County	100,265	51.39
Oklahoma City, OK (city) Oklahoma County	98,344	16.96
Durham, NC (city) Durham County	96,706	42.35
Rochester, NY (city) Monroe County	94,587	44.92
Virginia Beach, VA (ind. city) Virginia Beach independent city	94,211	21.51
Tampa, FL (city) Hillsborough County	93,054	27.72
Fayetteville, NC (city) Cumberland County	89,916	44.83
Columbus, GA (city) Muscogee County	89,897	47.34
Toledo, OH (city) Lucas County	85,254	29.68
Pittsburgh, PA (city) Allegheny County	84,819	27.75
Little Rock, AR (city) Pulaski County	83,613	43.21
Miami Gardens, FL (city) Miami-Dade County	83,474	77.89
Winston-Salem, NC (city) Forsyth County	82,853	36.08
Miami, FL (city) Miami-Dade County	80,625	20.18
Sacramento, CA (city) Sacramento County	80,469	17.25
Minneapolis, MN (city) Hennepin County	79,967	20.90
Newport News, VA (ind. city) Newport News independent city	78,376	43.37
Savannah, GA (city) Chatham County	77,270	56.70
Las Vegas, NV (city) Clark County	74,093	12.69
Arlington, TX (city) Tarrant County	73,417	20.09
Hampton, VA (ind. city) Hampton independent city	71,569	52.07
Austin, TX (city) Travis County	71,130	9.00
Orlando, FL (city) Orange County	70,758	29.69
Tulsa, OK (city) Tulsa County	70,084	17.88
Denver, CO (city) Denver County	69,999	11.66
Long Beach, CA (city) Los Angeles County	69,744	15.09
Chesapeake, VA (ind. city) Chesapeake independent city	69,511	31.28
Gary, IN (city) Lake County	69,508	86.57
Jersey City, NJ (city) Hudson County	68,694	27.74
Akron, OH (city) Summit County	67,240	33.77
Tallahassee, FL (city) Leon County	65,685	36.21
Dayton, OH (city) Montgomery County	63,535	44.89
Macon, GA (city) Bibb County	62,977	68.94
Omaha, NE (city) Douglas County	62,321	15.24
St. Petersburg, FL (city) Pinellas County	61,640	25.18
Flint, MI (city) Genesee County	60,928	59.48
Chattanooga, TN (city) Hamilton County	60,205	35.91
Aurora, CO (city) Arapahoe County	59,260	18.23
Miramar, FL (city) Broward County	58,514	47.95
Huntsville, AL (city) Madison County	58,434	32.44
East Orange, NJ (city) Essex County	58,193	90.54
San Francisco, CA (city) San Francisco County	57,810	7.18
Seattle, WA (city) King County	57,716	9.48
Beaumont, TX (city) Jefferson County	57,126	48.29
Albany, GA (city) Dougherty County	56,081	72.42
Columbia, SC (city) Richland County	55,929	43.26
Staten Island, NY (borough) Richmond County	55,014	11.74
Bridgeport, CT (city/town) Fairfield County	53,115	36.83
Fort Lauderdale, FL (city) Broward County	53,024	32.03
Portsmouth, VA (ind. city) Portsmouth independent city	52,499	54.95
Lauderhill, FL (city) Broward County	52,065	77.84
Southfield, MI (city) Oakland County	51,817	72.23
Wichita, KS (city) Sedgwick County	51,470	13.46
St. Paul, MN (city) Ramsey County	51,296	17.99
Hartford, CT (city/town) Hartford County	51,253	41.08
Inglewood, CA (city) Los Angeles County	50,219	45.79
Paterson, NJ (city) Passaic County	49,340	33.75
New Haven, CT (city/town) New Haven County	48,799	37.60
Killeen, TX (city) Bell County	48,448	37.87
Syracuse, NY (city) Onondaga County	48,029	33.08
North Las Vegas, NV (city) Clark County	47,802	22.03
North Charleston, SC (city) Charleston County	47,316	48.54
Lexington-Fayette, KY (cons. govt) Fayette County	47,144	15.94
Irvington, NJ (township) Essex County	46,928	87.02
Fresno, CA (city) Fresno County	46,895	9.48
Trenton, NJ (city) Mercer County	45,846	53.99
Portland, OR (city) Multnomah County	45,545	7.80
Fort Wayne, IN (city) Allen County	44,499	17.54
Mount Vernon, NY (city) Westchester County	44,244	65.75
Grand Rapids, MI (city) Kent County	44,032	23.42
Wilmington, DE (city) New Castle County	42,426	59.88
Pine Hills, FL (cdp) Orange County	41,922	69.78
Kansas City, KS (city) Wyandotte County	41,889	28.73
Stockton, CA (city) San Joaquin County	41,432	14.20
Yonkers, NY (city) Westchester County	40,198	20.51
Moreno Valley, CA (city) Riverside County	39,019	20.18
Camden, NJ (city) Camden County	38,960	50.37
Lafayette, LA (city) Lafayette Parish	38,528	31.94
Springfield, MA (city) Hampden County	38,318	25.03
Waldorf, MD (cdp) Charles County	38,259	56.47
Tuscaloosa, AL (city) Tuscaloosa County	38,029	42.04
San Jose, CA (city) Santa Clara County	37,836	4.00
Pine Bluff, AR (city) Jefferson County	37,497	76.40
Grand Prairie, TX (city) Dallas County	37,433	21.34
Babylon, NY (town) Suffolk County	37,421	17.52
Suffolk, VA (ind. city) Suffolk independent city	37,278	44.07
Islip, NY (town) Suffolk County	35,995	10.73
Rocky Mount, NC (city) Nash County	35,854	62.38
North Miami, FL (city) Miami-Dade County	35,824	60.94
High Point, NC (city) Guilford County	35,767	34.27
Lancaster, CA (city) Los Angeles County	35,558	22.70
San Bernardino, CA (city) San Bernardino County	35,348	16.84
Lake Charles, LA (city) Calcasieu Parish	35,336	49.08
Garland, TX (city) Dallas County	35,068	15.46
Providence, RI (city) Providence County	34,496	19.38
Clarksville, TN (city) Montgomery County	34,448	25.91
Rockford, IL (city) Winnebago County	34,438	22.53
DeSoto, TX (city) Dallas County	34,276	69.88
Brockton, MA (city) Plymouth County	34,218	36.48
Colorado Springs, CO (city) El Paso County	34,114	8.19
Peoria, IL (city) Peoria County	33,877	29.46
West Palm Beach, FL (city) Palm Beach County	33,705	33.73
Pembroke Pines, FL (city) Broward County	33,182	21.44
Knoxville, TN (city) Knox County	33,167	18.54

SECTION THREE

Please refer to the Explanation of Data in the front of the book for more detailed information.

Race

African-American/Black

Top 150 Places Sorted by Percent of Total Population

Based on all places, regardless of total population

Place	Population	%
Jenkinsville, SC (town) Fairfield County	46	100.00
Memphis, AL (town) Pickens County	29	100.00
Winstonville, MS (town) Bolivar County	190	99.48
Yellow Bluff, AL (town) Wilcox County	187	99.47
Coahoma, MS (town) Coahoma County	374	99.20
Franklin Park, FL (cdp) Broward County	853	99.19
Velda Village Hills, MO (village) St. Louis County	1,046	99.15
Alorton, IL (village) St. Clair County	1,980	98.90
Brookdale, SC (cdp) Orangeburg County	4,812	98.75
East St. Louis, IL (city) St. Clair County	26,665	98.74
Mound Bayou, MS (city) Bolivar County	1,512	98.63
Killona, LA (cdp) St. Charles Parish	782	98.61
Hayti Heights, MO (city) Pemiscot County	617	98.56
Jones, MS (town) Coahoma County	1,275	98.23
White Oak, MS (cdp) Tunica County	679	98.12
Lincoln University, PA (cdp) Chester County	1,693	98.09
Fayette, MS (city) Jefferson County	1,583	98.08
Royal Oak, MI (charter township) Oakland County	2,372	98.06
Glendora, MS (village) Tallahatchie County	148	98.01
Mosses, AL (town) Lowndes County	1,008	97.96
Panola, AL (cdp) Sumter County	141	97.92
Salem, GA (cdp) Upson County	303	97.74
Pine Lawn, MO (city) St. Louis County	3,199	97.68
Grambling, LA (city) Lincoln Parish	4,831	97.62
Centreville, IL (city) St. Clair County	5,180	97.57
Tchula, MS (town) Holmes County	2,045	97.57
Panthersville, GA (cdp) DeKalb County	9,503	97.48
Jericho, AR (town) Crittenden County	116	97.48
Lincoln Heights, OH (village) Hamilton County	3,203	97.47
Hillsdale, MO (village) St. Louis County	1,440	97.43
Wilson City, MO (village) Mississippi County	112	97.39
Roosevelt Gardens, FL (cdp) Broward County	2,391	97.35
Wellston, MO (city) St. Louis County	2,246	97.10
White Hall, AL (town) Lowndes County	833	97.09
Brooklyn, IL (village) St. Clair County	727	97.06
Movico, AL (cdp) Mobile County	296	97.05
Tuskegee, AL (city) Macon County	9,567	96.98
Ford Heights, IL (village) Cook County	2,679	96.96
North Courtland, AL (town) Lawrence County	612	96.84
Unionville, GA (cdp) Tift County	1,786	96.80
Homestown, MO (city) Pemiscot County	146	96.69
Tollette, AR (town) Howard County	232	96.67
Pinhook, MO (village) Mississippi County	29	96.67
Garysburg, NC (town) Northampton County	1,021	96.59
Princeville, NC (town) Edgecombe County	2,010	96.54
Velda City, MO (city) St. Louis County	1,370	96.48
Walker Mill, MD (cdp) Prince George's County	10,896	96.41
Uplands Park, MO (village) St. Louis County	429	96.40
Harlem, FL (cdp) Hendry County	2,555	96.12
Siracusaville, LA (cdp) St. Mary Parish	405	95.97
Washington Park, FL (cdp) Broward County	1,604	95.93
Alcorn State University, MS (cdp) Claiborne County	975	95.87
Boulevard Gardens, FL (cdp) Broward County	1,221	95.84
Renova, MS (town) Bolivar County	640	95.81
Venice, IL (city) Madison County	1,810	95.77
Metcalfe, MS (town) Washington County	1,021	95.69
Highland Park, MI (city) Wayne County	11,258	95.60
Pagedale, MO (city) St. Louis County	3,158	95.58
North Tunica, MS (cdp) Tunica County	989	95.56
Gifford, SC (town) Hampton County	275	95.49
Redan, GA (cdp) DeKalb County	31,497	95.40
Union, AL (town) Greene County	226	95.36
Warrensville Heights, OH (city) Cuyahoga County	12,909	95.33
Norwood Court, MO (town) St. Louis County	914	95.31
Langston, OK (town) Logan County	1,643	95.30
Gadsden, SC (cdp) Richland County	1,555	95.28
Boykin, AL (cdp) Wilcox County	262	95.27
Falcon, MS (town) Quitman County	159	95.21
Cheyney University, PA (cdp) Delaware County	940	95.14
Welcome, LA (cdp) St. James Parish	761	95.13
Northwoods, MO (city) St. Louis County	4,018	95.06
Mitchellville, AR (city) Desha County	342	95.00
Bayside, VA (cdp) Accomack County	114	95.00
Fairfield, AL (city) Jefferson County	10,559	94.98
Shelby, MS (city) Bolivar County	2,117	94.98
Kinloch, MO (city) St. Louis County	283	94.97
Thynedale, VA (cdp) Mecklenburg County	187	94.92
Savage Town, VA (cdp) Accomack County	74	94.87
Riverdale, IL (village) Cook County	12,852	94.86
Edgard, LA (cdp) St. John the Baptist Parish	2,315	94.84
Gordonville, AL (town) Lowndes County	309	94.79
Castle Point, MO (cdp) St. Louis County	3,755	94.78
East Cleveland, OH (city) Cuyahoga County	16,901	94.72
Friars Point, MS (town) Coahoma County	1,136	94.67
Robbins, IL (village) Cook County	5,051	94.64
Eastover, SC (town) Richland County	769	94.59
Merrydale, LA (cdp) East Baton Rouge Parish	9,234	94.49
Phillipsburg, GA (cdp) Tift County	668	94.48
Lake Arbor, MD (cdp) Prince George's County	9,232	94.44
Hillcrest Heights, MD (cdp) Prince George's County	15,544	94.38
Lake View, AR (city) Phillips County	418	94.36
Selmont-West Selmont, AL (cdp) Dallas County	2,520	94.35
Emelle, AL (town) Sumter County	50	94.34
Sidon, MS (town) Leflore County	480	94.30
Beverly Hills, MO (city) St. Louis County	541	94.25
Hopkins Park, IL (village) Kankakee County	568	94.20
Promised Land, SC (cdp) Greenwood County	481	94.13
Jennette, AR (town) Crittenden County	108	93.91
Kettering, MD (cdp) Prince George's County	12,001	93.83
Peppermill Village, MD (cdp) Prince George's County	4,587	93.71
Haywood City, MO (village) Scott County	193	93.69
Glenarden, MD (city) Prince George's County	5,617	93.62
Summerfield, MD (cdp) Prince George's County	10,201	93.60
Suitland, MD (cdp) Prince George's County	24,160	93.55
Silver Hill, MD (cdp) Prince George's County	5,564	93.51
Phoenix, IL (village) Cook County	1,836	93.48
Bayou Goula, LA (cdp) Iberville Parish	572	93.46
Riceboro, GA (city) Liberty County	756	93.45
Largo, MD (cdp) Prince George's County	10,004	93.42
Mississippi Valley State University, MS (cdp) Leflore County	1,104	93.40
Wilkinson Heights, SC (cdp) Orangeburg County	2,328	93.38
Shaw, MS (city) Bolivar County	1,822	93.34
Lisman, AL (town) Choctaw County	502	93.14
Moline Acres, MO (city) St. Louis County	2,274	93.12
East Arcadia, NC (town) Bladen County	453	93.02
Howardville, MO (city) New Madrid County	356	92.95
Vredenburgh, AL (town) Monroe County	290	92.95
Capitol Heights, MD (town) Prince George's County	4,029	92.90
Arcola, MS (town) Washington County	335	92.80
Silver City, NC (cdp) Hoke County	818	92.74
Seat Pleasant, MD (city) Prince George's County	4,208	92.65
Candler-McAfee, GA (cdp) DeKalb County	21,301	92.51
Flordell Hills, MO (city) St. Louis County	758	92.21
Dolton, IL (village) Cook County	21,318	92.07
University Park, IL (village) Will County	6,564	92.07
Eagle Harbor, MD (town) Prince George's County	58	92.06
Tangipahoa, LA (village) Tangipahoa Parish	688	91.98
Sunset, AR (town) Crittenden County	182	91.92
Coral Hills, MD (cdp) Prince George's County	9,094	91.91
Glen Echo Park, MO (village) St. Louis County	147	91.88
Waterproof, LA (town) Tensas Parish	632	91.86
Lawnside, NJ (borough) Camden County	2,705	91.85
District Heights, MD (city) Prince George's County	5,356	91.76
Springdale, MD (cdp) Prince George's County	2,743	91.62
Country Club Hills, MO (city) St. Louis County	1,166	91.52
Parmele, NC (town) Martin County	254	91.37
Wallace, LA (cdp) St. John the Baptist Parish	613	91.36
Benton Harbor, MI (city) Berrien County	9,170	91.35
East Hodge, LA (village) Jackson Parish	264	91.35
Lane, SC (town) Williamsburg County	464	91.34
Anthonyville, AR (town) Crittenden County	147	91.30
Lincoln Park, GA (cdp) Upson County	760	91.24
Bucksport, SC (cdp) Horry County	799	91.21
College Station, AR (cdp) Pulaski County	547	91.17
Epes, AL (town) Sumter County	175	91.15
Macedonia, AL (cdp) Pickens County	266	91.10
Beulah, MS (town) Bolivar County	317	91.09
Glassmanor, MD (cdp) Prince George's County	15,752	91.08
Goodlow, TX (city) Navarro County	182	91.00
Brock Hall, MD (cdp) Prince George's County	8,691	90.99

Please refer to the Explanation of Data in the front of the book for more detailed information.

Race

African-American/Black

Top 150 Places Sorted by Percent of Total Population

Based on places with total population of 7,500 or more

Place	Population	%
East St. Louis, IL (city) St. Clair County	26,665	98.74
Panthersville, GA (cdp) DeKalb County	9,503	97.48
Tuskegee, AL (city) Macon County	9,567	96.98
Walker Mill, MD (cdp) Prince George's County	10,896	96.41
Highland Park, MI (city) Wayne County	11,258	95.60
Redan, GA (cdp) DeKalb County	31,497	95.40
Warrensville Heights, OH (city) Cuyahoga County	12,909	95.33
Fairfield, AL (city) Jefferson County	10,559	94.98
Riverdale, IL (village) Cook County	12,852	94.86
East Cleveland, OH (city) Cuyahoga County	16,901	94.72
Merrydale, LA (cdp) East Baton Rouge Parish	9,234	94.49
Lake Arbor, MD (cdp) Prince George's County	9,232	94.44
Hillcrest Heights, MD (cdp) Prince George's County	15,544	94.38
Kettering, MD (cdp) Prince George's County	12,001	93.83
Summerfield, MD (cdp) Prince George's County	10,201	93.60
Suitland, MD (cdp) Prince George's County	24,160	93.55
Largo, MD (cdp) Prince George's County	10,004	93.42
Candler-McAfee, GA (cdp) DeKalb County	21,301	92.51
Dolton, IL (village) Cook County	21,318	92.07
Coral Hills, MD (cdp) Prince George's County	9,094	91.91
Benton Harbor, MI (city) Berrien County	9,170	91.35
Glassmanor, MD (cdp) Prince George's County	15,752	91.08
Brock Hall, MD (cdp) Prince George's County	8,691	90.99
Jennings, MO (city) St. Louis County	13,363	90.83
Yeadon, PA (borough) Delaware County	10,367	90.60
East Orange, NJ (city) Essex County	58,193	90.54
Marlboro Village, MD (cdp) Prince George's County	8,460	89.64
Forestville, MD (cdp) Prince George's County	11,067	89.59
View Park-Windsor Hills, CA (cdp) Los Angeles County	9,907	89.45
Temple Hills, MD (cdp) Prince George's County	6,996	89.10
Calumet Park, IL (village) Cook County	6,968	88.93
Country Club Hills, IL (city) Cook County	14,648	88.56
Mitchellville, MD (cdp) Prince George's County	9,630	87.81
Irvington, NJ (township) Essex County	46,928	87.02
East Highland Park, VA (cdp) Henrico County	12,869	86.98
Hazel Crest, IL (village) Cook County	12,238	86.79
Milford Mill, MD (cdp) Baltimore County	25,172	86.67
Gary, IN (city) Lake County	69,508	86.57
Prichard, AL (city) Mobile County	19,603	86.51
Richton Park, IL (village) Cook County	11,548	84.63
Detroit, MI (city) Wayne County	601,988	84.34
Rosaryville, MD (cdp) Prince George's County	9,016	84.29
Union City, GA (city) Fulton County	16,350	84.04
Landover, MD (cdp) Prince George's County	19,279	83.54
Marlton, MD (cdp) Prince George's County	7,531	83.39
Berkeley, MO (city) St. Louis County	7,471	83.21
Yazoo City, MS (city) Yazoo County	9,456	82.93
Clinton, MD (cdp) Prince George's County	29,771	82.77
Fort Valley, GA (city) Peach County	8,124	82.77
Lauderdale Lakes, FL (city) Broward County	26,966	82.74
Randallstown, MD (cdp) Baltimore County	26,807	82.66
Markham, IL (city) Cook County	10,329	82.58
Lochearn, MD (cdp) Baltimore County	20,892	82.47
Darby, PA (borough) Delaware County	8,751	81.88
Woodmere, LA (cdp) Jefferson Parish	9,864	81.66
Riverdale, GA (city) Clayton County	12,355	81.64
Friendly, MD (cdp) Prince George's County	7,540	81.51
Muskegon Heights, MI (city) Muskegon County	8,828	81.32
College Park, GA (city) Fulton County	11,312	81.14
Selma, AL (city) Dallas County	16,799	80.94
Camp Springs, MD (cdp) Prince George's County	15,398	80.63
Petersburg, VA (ind. city) Petersburg independent city	26,106	80.52
Matteson, IL (village) Cook County	15,291	80.44
Jackson, MS (city) Hinds County	138,940	80.07
Indianola, MS (city) Sunflower County	8,512	79.68
Holly Springs, MS (city) Marshall County	6,133	79.66
Clarksdale, MS (city) Coahoma County	14,256	79.37
Spanish Lake, MO (cdp) St. Louis County	15,524	79.00
Bedford Heights, OH (city) Cuyahoga County	8,458	78.67
Greenville, MS (city) Washington County	26,986	78.45
Baker, LA (city) East Baton Rouge Parish	10,851	78.09
Miami Gardens, FL (city) Miami-Dade County	83,474	77.89
Lauderhill, FL (city) Broward County	52,065	77.84
Belvedere Park, GA (cdp) DeKalb County	11,785	77.78
Broadview, IL (village) Cook County	6,169	77.77
Oxon Hill, MD (cdp) Prince George's County	13,765	77.67
Chester, PA (city) Delaware County	26,257	77.29
Harvey, IL (city) Cook County	19,506	77.15
Pinewood, FL (cdp) Miami-Dade County	12,744	77.14
Willingboro, NJ (township) Burlington County	24,215	76.56
Bellwood, IL (village) Cook County	14,593	76.52
Gladeview, FL (cdp) Miami-Dade County	8,821	76.47
Pine Bluff, AR (city) Jefferson County	37,497	76.40
Inkster, MI (city) Wayne County	19,324	76.17
East Point, GA (city) Fulton County	25,673	76.15
Opelousas, LA (city) St. Landry Parish	12,647	76.03
Orangeburg, SC (city) Orangeburg County	10,590	75.84
Brownsville, FL (cdp) Miami-Dade County	11,601	75.76
Maywood, IL (village) Cook County	18,221	75.64
South Holland, IL (village) Cook County	16,625	75.47
Helena-West Helena, AR (city) Phillips County	9,217	75.04
Canton, MS (city) Madison County	9,895	75.02
Golden Glades, FL (cdp) Miami-Dade County	24,852	74.98
Moss Point, MS (city) Jackson County	10,196	74.40
Birmingham, AL (city) Jefferson County	157,136	74.04
Richmond Heights, FL (cdp) Miami-Dade County	6,308	73.86
City of Orange, NJ (township) Essex County	22,223	73.75
Bellefontaine Neighbors, MO (city) St. Louis County	8,001	73.67
Bastrop, LA (city) Morehouse Parish	8,320	73.21
Fort Washington, MD (cdp) Prince George's County	17,298	72.94
Albany, GA (city) Dougherty County	56,081	72.42
Southfield, MI (city) Oakland County	51,817	72.23
Forestdale, AL (cdp) Jefferson County	7,316	71.99
Calumet City, IL (city) Cook County	26,633	71.90
Beecher, MI (cdp) Genesee County	7,346	71.79
Bessemer, AL (city) Jefferson County	19,702	71.76
Fairburn, GA (city) Fulton County	9,236	71.32
Westview, FL (cdp) Miami-Dade County	6,874	71.23
Dentsville, SC (cdp) Richland County	9,980	70.97
Trotwood, OH (city) Montgomery County	17,195	70.38
Lancaster, TX (city) Dallas County	25,497	70.12
Maple Heights, OH (city) Cuyahoga County	16,216	70.08
DeSoto, TX (city) Dallas County	34,276	69.88
Pine Hills, FL (cdp) Orange County	41,922	69.78
Wilkinsburg, PA (borough) Allegheny County	11,047	69.35
Ferguson, MO (city) St. Louis County	14,631	69.00
Macon, GA (city) Bibb County	62,977	68.94
Kinston, NC (city) Lenoir County	14,944	68.94
Montrose, VA (cdp) Henrico County	5,480	68.56
Forrest City, AR (city) St. Francis County	10,511	68.38
Glenwood, IL (village) Cook County	6,128	68.32
Forest Park, OH (city) Hamilton County	12,711	67.90
Highland Springs, VA (cdp) Henrico County	10,659	67.84
Greenwood, MS (city) Leflore County	10,304	67.77
Seabrook, MD (cdp) Prince George's County	11,681	67.57
Lynwood, IL (village) Cook County	6,086	67.57
Wyandanch, NY (cdp) Suffolk County	7,865	67.53
Riviera Beach, FL (city) Palm Beach County	21,921	67.47
St. Andrews, SC (cdp) Richland County	13,821	67.44
Cordele, GA (city) Crisp County	7,502	67.30
Bladensburg, MD (town) Prince George's County	6,132	67.03
Lanham, MD (cdp) Prince George's County	6,801	66.96
Opa-locka, FL (city) Miami-Dade County	10,184	66.92
McComb, MS (city) Pike County	8,541	66.78
Accokeek, MD (cdp) Prince George's County	7,047	66.65
Vicksburg, MS (city) Warren County	15,876	66.55
Mount Vernon, NY (city) Westchester County	44,244	65.75
Roosevelt, NY (cdp) Nassau County	10,657	65.55
Sauk Village, IL (village) Cook County	6,884	65.52
Brownsville, TN (city) Haywood County	6,730	65.39
Quincy, FL (city) Gadsden County	5,187	65.07
Baltimore, MD (city) Baltimore city County	403,998	65.06
Henderson, NC (city) Vance County	9,996	65.04
Gardere, LA (cdp) East Baton Rouge Parish	6,860	64.84
Bennettsville, SC (city) Marlboro County	5,878	64.81
Monroe, LA (city) Ouachita Parish	31,574	64.68
Waggaman, LA (cdp) Jefferson Parish	6,443	64.33
West Perrine, FL (cdp) Miami-Dade County	6,074	64.21
West Memphis, AR (city) Crittenden County	16,850	64.20
Americus, GA (city) Sumter County	10,937	64.18

Please refer to the Explanation of Data in the front of the book for more detailed information.

Race

African-American/Black: Not Hispanic

U.S. and 50 States Sorted by Population and Percent of Total Population

Place	Population	%
United States	**40,123,525**	**13.00**
Texas	3,019,318	12.01
Georgia	2,997,627	30.94
Florida	2,997,371	15.94
New York	2,946,880	15.21
California	2,436,082	6.54
North Carolina	2,107,630	22.10
Illinois	1,919,384	14.96
Maryland	1,745,599	30.23
Virginia	1,611,361	20.14
Ohio	1,511,035	13.10
Michigan	1,477,071	14.94
Louisiana	1,472,789	32.49
Pennsylvania	1,432,537	11.28
South Carolina	1,316,691	28.47
Alabama	1,271,554	26.60
New Jersey	1,186,433	13.49
Mississippi	1,109,300	37.38
Tennessee	1,094,696	17.25
Missouri	736,574	12.30
Indiana	638,353	9.85
Arkansas	464,242	15.92
Massachusetts	446,991	6.83
Wisconsin	388,920	6.84
Kentucky	369,025	8.50
Connecticut	365,707	10.23
Oklahoma	316,902	8.45
Minnesota	316,870	5.97
District of Columbia	308,617	51.29
Washington	302,894	4.50
Arizona	283,083	4.43
Nevada	236,042	8.74
Colorado	225,218	4.48
Delaware	198,589	22.12
Kansas	192,089	6.73
Iowa	108,852	3.57
Nebraska	95,189	5.21
Oregon	89,808	2.34
West Virginia	75,277	4.06
Rhode Island	64,890	6.16
New Mexico	44,273	2.15
Utah	37,057	1.34
Hawaii	33,564	2.47
Alaska	30,367	4.28
Maine	20,645	1.55
New Hampshire	19,346	1.47
South Dakota	14,065	1.73
Idaho	13,927	0.89
North Dakota	10,542	1.57
Vermont	8,693	1.39
Montana	7,159	0.72
Wyoming	6,397	1.13

Place	Population	%
District of Columbia	308,617	51.29
Mississippi	1,109,300	37.38
Louisiana	1,472,789	32.49
Georgia	2,997,627	30.94
Maryland	1,745,599	30.23
South Carolina	1,316,691	28.47
Alabama	1,271,554	26.60
Delaware	198,589	22.12
North Carolina	2,107,630	22.10
Virginia	1,611,361	20.14
Tennessee	1,094,696	17.25
Florida	2,997,371	15.94
Arkansas	464,242	15.92
New York	2,946,880	15.21
Illinois	1,919,384	14.96
Michigan	1,477,071	14.94
New Jersey	1,186,433	13.49
Ohio	1,511,035	13.10
United States	**40,123,525**	**13.00**
Missouri	736,574	12.30
Texas	3,019,318	12.01
Pennsylvania	1,432,537	11.28
Connecticut	365,707	10.23
Indiana	638,353	9.85
Nevada	236,042	8.74
Kentucky	369,025	8.50
Oklahoma	316,902	8.45
Wisconsin	388,920	6.84
Massachusetts	446,991	6.83
Kansas	192,089	6.73
California	2,436,082	6.54
Rhode Island	64,890	6.16
Minnesota	316,870	5.97
Nebraska	95,189	5.21
Washington	302,894	4.50
Colorado	225,218	4.48
Arizona	283,083	4.43
Alaska	30,367	4.28
West Virginia	75,277	4.06
Iowa	108,852	3.57
Hawaii	33,564	2.47
Oregon	89,808	2.34
New Mexico	44,273	2.15
South Dakota	14,065	1.73
North Dakota	10,542	1.57
Maine	20,645	1.55
New Hampshire	19,346	1.47
Vermont	8,693	1.39
Utah	37,057	1.34
Wyoming	6,397	1.13
Idaho	13,927	0.89
Montana	7,159	0.72

Please refer to the Explanation of Data in the front of the book for more detailed information.

Race

African-American/Black: Not Hispanic

Top 150 Places Sorted by Population

Based on all places, regardless of total population

Place	Population	%
New York, NY (city) Kings County	1,931,889	23.63
Chicago, IL (city) Cook County	889,783	33.01
Brooklyn, NY (borough) Kings County	820,437	32.76
Philadelphia, PA (city) Philadelphia County	662,568	43.42
Detroit, MI (city) Wayne County	596,963	83.63
Houston, TX (city) Harris County	495,792	23.62
Bronx, NY (borough) Bronx County	427,134	30.84
Queens, NY (borough) Queens County	419,695	18.81
Memphis, TN (city) Shelby County	412,759	63.81
Baltimore, MD (city) Baltimore city County	400,138	64.44
Los Angeles, CA (city) Los Angeles County	372,821	9.83
Washington, DC (city) District of Columbia	308,617	51.29
Dallas, TX (city) Dallas County	300,502	25.09
Charlotte, NC (city) Mecklenburg County	260,726	35.65
Jacksonville, FL (city) Duval County	256,648	31.23
Milwaukee, WI (city) Milwaukee County	243,059	40.86
Indianapolis, IN (city) Marion County	235,521	28.71
Columbus, OH (city) Franklin County	233,108	29.62
Atlanta, GA (city) Fulton County	228,575	54.42
Manhattan, NY (borough) New York County	217,102	13.69
Cleveland, OH (city) Cuyahoga County	213,920	53.91
New Orleans, LA (city) Orleans Parish	207,691	60.41
Nashville-Davidson, TN (metro govt) Davidson County	175,416	29.18
St. Louis, MO (city) St. Louis city County	160,631	50.31
Birmingham, AL (city) Jefferson County	156,470	73.72
Boston, MA (city) Suffolk County	147,088	23.82
Louisville-Jefferson County, KY (metro govt) Jefferson County	142,817	23.91
Kansas City, MO (city) Jackson County	142,748	31.05
Fort Worth, TX (city) Tarrant County	142,352	19.21
Newark, NJ (city) Essex County	140,365	50.65
Jackson, MS (city) Hinds County	138,363	79.74
Cincinnati, OH (city) Hamilton County	137,223	46.21
Baton Rouge, LA (city) East Baton Rouge Parish	125,944	54.88
Hempstead, NY (town) Nassau County	124,525	16.39
Raleigh, NC (city) Wake County	120,403	29.81
Montgomery, AL (city) Montgomery County	117,426	57.07
Oakland, CA (city) Alameda County	114,212	29.23
Greensboro, NC (city) Guilford County	112,136	41.58
Shreveport, LA (city) Caddo Parish	110,057	55.22
Augusta-Richmond County, GA (cons. govt) Richmond County	108,666	55.49
Norfolk, VA (ind. city) Norfolk independent city	106,646	43.92
Richmond, VA (ind. city) Richmond independent city	104,588	51.21
Buffalo, NY (city) Erie County	101,817	38.96
Mobile, AL (city) Mobile County	99,638	51.07
Phoenix, AZ (city) Maricopa County	98,091	6.79
Oklahoma City, OK (city) Oklahoma County	95,377	16.44
Durham, NC (city) Durham County	94,986	41.60
San Diego, CA (city) San Diego County	94,818	7.25
Virginia Beach, VA (ind. city) Virginia Beach independent city	90,128	20.58
San Antonio, TX (city) Medina County	89,802	6.77
Rochester, NY (city) Monroe County	88,052	41.82
Columbus, GA (city) Muscogee County	87,921	46.30
Tampa, FL (city) Hillsborough County	86,662	25.81
Fayetteville, NC (city) Cumberland County	86,376	43.07
Pittsburgh, PA (city) Allegheny County	83,539	27.33
Little Rock, AR (city) Pulaski County	83,115	42.95
Toledo, OH (city) Lucas County	82,886	28.86
Winston-Salem, NC (city) Forsyth County	80,608	35.11
Miami Gardens, FL (city) Miami-Dade County	79,681	74.35
Minneapolis, MN (city) Hennepin County	77,889	20.36
Savannah, GA (city) Chatham County	76,271	55.96
Newport News, VA (ind. city) Newport News independent city	75,788	41.94
Sacramento, CA (city) Sacramento County	74,051	15.87
Arlington, TX (city) Tarrant County	70,620	19.32
Hampton, VA (ind. city) Hampton independent city	69,775	50.77
Las Vegas, NV (city) Clark County	69,157	11.85
Gary, IN (city) Lake County	68,449	85.25
Tulsa, OK (city) Tulsa County	68,332	17.44
Chesapeake, VA (ind. city) Chesapeake independent city	67,958	30.58
Miami, FL (city) Miami-Dade County	66,636	16.68
Akron, OH (city) Summit County	66,385	33.34
Orlando, FL (city) Orange County	66,175	27.77
Austin, TX (city) Travis County	65,227	8.25
Long Beach, CA (city) Los Angeles County	65,067	14.08
Denver, CO (city) Denver County	64,607	10.76
Tallahassee, FL (city) Leon County	64,409	35.51
Dayton, OH (city) Montgomery County	62,972	44.49
Macon, GA (city) Bibb County	62,572	68.50
Jersey City, NJ (city) Hudson County	61,622	24.89
Omaha, NE (city) Douglas County	60,775	14.86
Flint, MI (city) Genesee County	60,166	58.74
St. Petersburg, FL (city) Pinellas County	60,020	24.52
Chattanooga, TN (city) Hamilton County	59,817	35.67
Huntsville, AL (city) Madison County	57,523	31.94
East Orange, NJ (city) Essex County	56,704	88.23
Beaumont, TX (city) Jefferson County	56,478	47.74
Albany, GA (city) Dougherty County	55,753	72.00
Seattle, WA (city) King County	55,325	9.09
Aurora, CO (city) Arapahoe County	55,188	16.98
Columbia, SC (city) Richland County	55,158	42.67
Miramar, FL (city) Broward County	54,974	45.05
San Francisco, CA (city) San Francisco County	53,760	6.68
Portsmouth, VA (ind. city) Portsmouth independent city	51,758	54.18
Fort Lauderdale, FL (city) Broward County	51,645	31.20
Southfield, MI (city) Oakland County	51,445	71.71
Lauderhill, FL (city) Broward County	51,107	76.41
St. Paul, MN (city) Ramsey County	49,191	17.26
Wichita, KS (city) Sedgwick County	49,113	12.84
Inglewood, CA (city) Los Angeles County	48,512	44.23
Bridgeport, CT (city/town) Fairfield County	48,372	33.54
Staten Island, NY (borough) Richmond County	47,521	10.14
North Charleston, SC (city) Charleston County	46,648	47.86
Lexington-Fayette, KY (cons. govt) Fayette County	46,163	15.61
Irvington, NJ (township) Essex County	45,917	85.15
Hartford, CT (city/town) Hartford County	45,704	36.63
New Haven, CT (city/town) New Haven County	45,302	34.91
North Las Vegas, NV (city) Clark County	45,197	20.83
Syracuse, NY (city) Onondaga County	45,084	31.06
Killeen, TX (city) Bell County	44,874	35.08
Trenton, NJ (city) Mercer County	43,372	51.08
Fort Wayne, IN (city) Allen County	43,301	17.07
Portland, OR (city) Multnomah County	43,057	7.38
Mount Vernon, NY (city) Westchester County	42,361	62.95
Paterson, NJ (city) Passaic County	42,328	28.95
Grand Rapids, MI (city) Kent County	41,741	22.20
Fresno, CA (city) Fresno County	41,526	8.39
Wilmington, DE (city) New Castle County	41,144	58.07
Pine Hills, FL (cdp) Orange County	40,711	67.77
Kansas City, KS (city) Wyandotte County	40,711	27.93
Lafayette, LA (city) Lafayette Parish	38,148	31.63
Tuscaloosa, AL (city) Tuscaloosa County	37,869	41.86
Waldorf, MD (cdp) Charles County	37,454	55.28
Stockton, CA (city) San Joaquin County	37,389	12.82
Pine Bluff, AR (city) Jefferson County	37,337	76.07
Suffolk, VA (ind. city) Suffolk independent city	36,790	43.49
Moreno Valley, CA (city) Riverside County	36,134	18.69
Grand Prairie, TX (city) Dallas County	35,887	20.46
Rocky Mount, NC (city) Nash County	35,605	61.95
High Point, NC (city) Guilford County	35,168	33.70
Camden, NJ (city) Camden County	35,088	45.37
Lake Charles, LA (city) Calcasieu Parish	35,022	48.65
Babylon, NY (town) Suffolk County	34,993	16.38
North Miami, FL (city) Miami-Dade County	34,105	58.02
DeSoto, TX (city) Dallas County	33,823	68.96
Garland, TX (city) Dallas County	33,685	14.85
Lancaster, CA (city) Los Angeles County	33,469	21.37
Peoria, IL (city) Peoria County	33,328	28.98
Rockford, IL (city) Winnebago County	33,293	21.78
Yonkers, NY (city) Westchester County	32,873	16.77
Clarksville, TN (city) Montgomery County	32,869	24.73
Knoxville, TN (city) Knox County	32,665	18.26
San Jose, CA (city) Santa Clara County	32,533	3.44
West Palm Beach, FL (city) Palm Beach County	32,440	32.47
Brockton, MA (city) Plymouth County	32,364	34.50
Springfield, MA (city) Hampden County	32,328	21.12
San Bernardino, CA (city) San Bernardino County	32,292	15.38
Greenville, NC (city) Pitt County	31,978	37.82
Pontiac, MI (city) Oakland County	31,897	53.59
Compton, CA (city) Los Angeles County	31,687	32.85
Monroe, LA (city) Ouachita Parish	31,404	64.33

SECTION THREE

Please refer to the Explanation of Data in the front of the book for more detailed information.

Race

African-American/Black: Not Hispanic

Top 150 Places Sorted by Percent of Total Population

Based on all places, regardless of total population

Place	Population	%
Jenkinsville, SC (town) Fairfield County	46	100.00
Memphis, AL (town) Pickens County	29	100.00
Winstonville, MS (town) Bolivar County	190	99.48
Yellow Bluff, AL (town) Wilcox County	187	99.47
Coahoma, MS (town) Coahoma County	374	99.20
Velda Village Hills, MO (village) St. Louis County	1,046	99.15
Alorton, IL (village) St. Clair County	1,976	98.70
East St. Louis, IL (city) St. Clair County	26,574	98.40
Killona, LA (cdp) St. Charles Parish	780	98.36
Franklin Park, FL (cdp) Broward County	845	98.26
Hayti Heights, MO (city) Pemiscot County	615	98.24
Brookdale, SC (cdp) Orangeburg County	4,782	98.13
Mound Bayou, MS (city) Bolivar County	1,504	98.11
Jones, MS (town) Coahoma County	1,271	97.92
Panola, AL (cdp) Sumter County	141	97.92
Fayette, MS (city) Jefferson County	1,580	97.89
White Oak, MS (cdp) Tunica County	677	97.83
Jericho, AR (town) Crittenden County	116	97.48
Salem, GA (cdp) Upson County	302	97.42
Wilson City, MO (village) Mississippi County	112	97.39
Centreville, IL (city) St. Clair County	5,169	97.36
Grambling, LA (city) Lincoln Parish	4,818	97.35
Lincoln Heights, OH (village) Hamilton County	3,193	97.17
Movico, AL (cdp) Mobile County	296	97.05
Tchula, MS (town) Holmes County	2,034	97.04
Royal Oak, MI (charter township) Oakland County	2,346	96.98
Pine Lawn, MO (city) St. Louis County	3,175	96.95
Panthersville, GA (cdp) DeKalb County	9,442	96.85
North Courtland, AL (town) Lawrence County	612	96.84
Wellston, MO (city) St. Louis County	2,239	96.80
Mosses, AL (town) Lowndes County	995	96.70
Glendora, MS (village) Tallahatchie County	146	96.69
Homestown, MO (city) Pemiscot County	146	96.69
Tollette, AR (town) Howard County	232	96.67
Pinhook, MO (village) Mississippi County	29	96.67
Ford Heights, IL (village) Cook County	2,668	96.56
Princeville, NC (town) Edgecombe County	2,010	96.54
Roosevelt Gardens, FL (cdp) Broward County	2,370	96.50
Hillsdale, MO (village) St. Louis County	1,425	96.41
White Hall, AL (town) Lowndes County	827	96.39
Velda City, MO (city) St. Louis County	1,368	96.34
Unionville, GA (cdp) Tift County	1,777	96.31
Tuskegee, AL (city) Macon County	9,489	96.19
Garysburg, NC (town) Northampton County	1,015	96.03
Siracusaville, LA (cdp) St. Mary Parish	405	95.97
Brooklyn, IL (village) St. Clair County	718	95.86
Harlem, FL (cdp) Hendry County	2,546	95.79
Uplands Park, MO (village) St. Louis County	426	95.73
Washington Park, FL (cdp) Broward County	1,599	95.63
North Tunica, MS (cdp) Tunica County	989	95.56
Gifford, SC (town) Hampton County	275	95.49
Walker Mill, MD (cdp) Prince George's County	10,791	95.48
Metcalfe, MS (town) Washington County	1,018	95.41
Union, AL (town) Greene County	226	95.36
Boykin, AL (cdp) Wilcox County	262	95.27
Falcon, MS (town) Quitman County	159	95.21
Welcome, LA (cdp) St. James Parish	761	95.13
Norwood Court, MO (town) St. Louis County	912	95.10
Pagedale, MO (city) St. Louis County	3,139	95.01
Bayside, VA (cdp) Accomack County	114	95.00
Kinloch, MO (city) St. Louis County	283	94.97
Renova, MS (town) Bolivar County	634	94.91
Alcorn State University, MS (cdp) Claiborne County	965	94.89
Highland Park, MI (city) Wayne County	11,172	94.87
Northwoods, MO (city) St. Louis County	4,009	94.84
Boulevard Gardens, FL (cdp) Broward County	1,208	94.82
Venice, IL (city) Madison County	1,792	94.81
Gordonville, AL (town) Lowndes County	309	94.79
Fairfield, AL (city) Jefferson County	10,528	94.70
Friars Point, MS (town) Coahoma County	1,135	94.58
Shelby, MS (city) Bolivar County	2,107	94.53
Lincoln University, PA (cdp) Chester County	1,631	94.50
Edgard, LA (cdp) St. John the Baptist Parish	2,304	94.39
Gadsden, SC (cdp) Richland County	1,540	94.36
Emelle, AL (town) Sumter County	50	94.34
Castle Point, MO (cdp) St. Louis County	3,737	94.32
Warrensville Heights, OH (city) Cuyahoga County	12,764	94.25
Selmont-West Selmont, AL (cdp) Dallas County	2,516	94.20
Merrydale, LA (cdp) East Baton Rouge Parish	9,200	94.15
Promised Land, SC (cdp) Greenwood County	481	94.13
Robbins, IL (village) Cook County	5,023	94.12
Riverdale, IL (village) Cook County	12,749	94.10
Hopkins Park, IL (village) Kankakee County	567	94.03
Redan, GA (cdp) DeKalb County	31,031	93.99
East Cleveland, OH (city) Cuyahoga County	16,770	93.99
Langston, OK (town) Logan County	1,620	93.97
Lake View, AR (city) Phillips County	416	93.91
Jennette, AR (town) Crittenden County	108	93.91
Sidon, MS (town) Leflore County	477	93.71
Phillipsburg, GA (cdp) Tift County	662	93.64
Mitchellville, AR (city) Desha County	337	93.61
Eastover, SC (town) Richland County	761	93.60
Bayou Goula, LA (cdp) Iberville Parish	572	93.46
Hillcrest Heights, MD (cdp) Prince George's County	15,381	93.39
Shaw, MS (city) Bolivar County	1,820	93.24
Lake Arbor, MD (cdp) Prince George's County	9,092	93.00
Mississippi Valley State University, MS (cdp) Leflore County	1,099	92.98
Lisman, AL (town) Choctaw County	501	92.95
Kettering, MD (cdp) Prince George's County	11,883	92.91
Thynedale, VA (cdp) Mecklenburg County	183	92.89
Beverly Hills, MO (city) St. Louis County	533	92.86
Arcola, MS (town) Washington County	335	92.80
Peppermill Village, MD (cdp) Prince George's County	4,542	92.79
Wilkinson Heights, SC (cdp) Orangeburg County	2,313	92.78
Suitland, MD (cdp) Prince George's County	23,933	92.67
Moline Acres, MO (city) St. Louis County	2,263	92.67
Silver City, NC (cdp) Hoke County	817	92.63
Cheyney University, PA (cdp) Delaware County	915	92.61
Howardville, MO (city) New Madrid County	354	92.43
Glenarden, MD (city) Prince George's County	5,544	92.40
Savage Town, VA (cdp) Accomack County	72	92.31
Haywood City, MO (village) Scott County	190	92.23
Silver Hill, MD (cdp) Prince George's County	5,487	92.22
Phoenix, IL (village) Cook County	1,811	92.21
Riceboro, GA (city) Liberty County	746	92.21
Seat Pleasant, MD (city) Prince George's County	4,185	92.14
Largo, MD (cdp) Prince George's County	9,861	92.08
Eagle Harbor, MD (town) Prince George's County	58	92.06
Summerfield, MD (cdp) Prince George's County	10,031	92.04
East Arcadia, NC (town) Bladen County	448	91.99
Flordell Hills, MO (city) St. Louis County	756	91.97
Candler-McAfee, GA (cdp) DeKalb County	21,164	91.92
Sunset, AR (town) Crittenden County	182	91.92
Tangipahoa, LA (village) Tangipahoa Parish	687	91.84
Capitol Heights, MD (town) Prince George's County	3,981	91.79
Waterproof, LA (town) Tensas Parish	631	91.72
Vredenburgh, AL (town) Monroe County	286	91.67
Country Club Hills, MO (city) St. Louis County	1,166	91.52
Dolton, IL (village) Cook County	21,164	91.41
Parmele, NC (town) Martin County	254	91.37
Anthonyville, AR (town) Crittenden County	147	91.30
College Station, AR (cdp) Pulaski County	547	91.17
Epes, AL (town) Sumter County	175	91.15
Lane, SC (town) Williamsburg County	463	91.14
Lincoln Park, GA (cdp) Upson County	759	91.12
Macedonia, AL (cdp) Pickens County	266	91.10
Beulah, MS (town) Bolivar County	317	91.09
District Heights, MD (city) Prince George's County	5,315	91.06
Wallace, LA (cdp) St. John the Baptist Parish	611	91.06
University Park, IL (village) Will County	6,486	90.98
Pointe a la Hache, LA (cdp) Plaquemines Parish	170	90.91
Coral Hills, MD (cdp) Prince George's County	8,989	90.84
Doddsville, MS (town) Sunflower County	89	90.82
Springdale, MD (cdp) Prince George's County	2,719	90.81
Benton Harbor, MI (city) Berrien County	9,101	90.67
Glen Echo Park, MO (village) St. Louis County	145	90.63
Carlisle, SC (town) Union County	395	90.60
Boligee, AL (town) Greene County	297	90.55
Bucksport, SC (cdp) Horry County	793	90.53
Union, AL (town) Perry County	1,606	90.48

Please refer to the Explanation of Data in the front of the book for more detailed information.

Race

African-American/Black: Not Hispanic

Top 150 Places Sorted by Percent of Total Population

Based on places with total population of 7,500 or more

Place	Population	%
East St. Louis, IL (city) St. Clair County	26,574	98.40
Panthersville, GA (cdp) DeKalb County	9,442	96.85
Tuskegee, AL (city) Macon County	9,489	96.19
Walker Mill, MD (cdp) Prince George's County	10,791	95.48
Highland Park, MI (city) Wayne County	11,172	94.87
Fairfield, AL (city) Jefferson County	10,528	94.70
Warrensville Heights, OH (city) Cuyahoga County	12,764	94.25
Merrydale, LA (cdp) East Baton Rouge Parish	9,200	94.15
Riverdale, IL (village) Cook County	12,749	94.10
Redan, GA (cdp) DeKalb County	31,031	93.99
East Cleveland, OH (city) Cuyahoga County	16,770	93.99
Hillcrest Heights, MD (cdp) Prince George's County	15,381	93.39
Lake Arbor, MD (cdp) Prince George's County	9,092	93.00
Kettering, MD (cdp) Prince George's County	11,883	92.91
Suitland, MD (cdp) Prince George's County	23,933	92.67
Largo, MD (cdp) Prince George's County	9,861	92.08
Summerfield, MD (cdp) Prince George's County	10,031	92.04
Candler-McAfee, GA (cdp) DeKalb County	21,164	91.92
Dolton, IL (village) Cook County	21,164	91.41
Coral Hills, MD (cdp) Prince George's County	8,989	90.84
Benton Harbor, MI (city) Berrien County	9,101	90.67
Jennings, MO (city) St. Louis County	13,310	90.47
Brock Hall, MD (cdp) Prince George's County	8,600	90.03
Glassmanor, MD (cdp) Prince George's County	15,513	89.70
Yeadon, PA (borough) Delaware County	10,244	89.52
Calumet Park, IL (village) Cook County	6,931	88.46
Forestville, MD (cdp) Prince George's County	10,917	88.38
Marlboro Village, MD (cdp) Prince George's County	8,333	88.29
East Orange, NJ (city) Essex County	56,704	88.23
Temple Hills, MD (cdp) Prince George's County	6,892	87.77
Country Club Hills, IL (city) Cook County	14,491	87.61
View Park-Windsor Hills, CA (cdp) Los Angeles County	9,650	87.13
Mitchellville, MD (cdp) Prince George's County	9,510	86.71
Prichard, AL (city) Mobile County	19,525	86.17
Hazel Crest, IL (village) Cook County	12,131	86.04
East Highland Park, VA (cdp) Henrico County	12,710	85.90
Milford Mill, MD (cdp) Baltimore County	24,840	85.53
Gary, IN (city) Lake County	68,449	85.25
Irvington, NJ (township) Essex County	45,917	85.15
Richton Park, IL (village) Cook County	11,429	83.75
Detroit, MI (city) Wayne County	596,963	83.63
Rosaryville, MD (cdp) Prince George's County	8,899	83.19
Union City, GA (city) Fulton County	16,134	82.93
Berkeley, MO (city) St. Louis County	7,423	82.68
Yazoo City, MS (city) Yazoo County	9,402	82.45
Marlton, MD (cdp) Prince George's County	7,434	82.32
Landover, MD (cdp) Prince George's County	18,986	82.27
Fort Valley, GA (city) Peach County	8,062	82.14
Markham, IL (city) Cook County	10,253	81.97
Clinton, MD (cdp) Prince George's County	29,417	81.78
Lochearn, MD (cdp) Baltimore County	20,708	81.74
Randallstown, MD (cdp) Baltimore County	26,491	81.69
Lauderdale Lakes, FL (city) Broward County	26,511	81.34
Darby, PA (borough) Delaware County	8,616	80.62
Friendly, MD (cdp) Prince George's County	7,454	80.58
Selma, AL (city) Dallas County	16,718	80.55
Woodmere, LA (cdp) Jefferson Parish	9,720	80.46
Muskegon Heights, MI (city) Muskegon County	8,731	80.43
Riverdale, GA (city) Clayton County	12,163	80.37
College Park, GA (city) Fulton County	11,149	79.97
Jackson, MS (city) Hinds County	138,363	79.74
Petersburg, VA (ind. city) Petersburg independent city	25,827	79.66
Matteson, IL (village) Cook County	15,119	79.54
Camp Springs, MD (cdp) Prince George's County	15,184	79.51
Holly Springs, MS (city) Marshall County	6,097	79.19
Indianola, MS (city) Sunflower County	8,446	79.06
Clarksdale, MS (city) Coahoma County	14,198	79.04
Spanish Lake, MO (cdp) St. Louis County	15,412	78.43
Greenville, MS (city) Washington County	26,875	78.13
Bedford Heights, OH (city) Cuyahoga County	8,383	77.97
Baker, LA (city) East Baton Rouge Parish	10,813	77.82
Belvedere Park, GA (cdp) DeKalb County	11,643	76.84
Broadview, IL (village) Cook County	6,091	76.79
Oxon Hill, MD (cdp) Prince George's County	13,570	76.57
Lauderhill, FL (city) Broward County	51,107	76.41
Harvey, IL (city) Cook County	19,293	76.31
Pine Bluff, AR (city) Jefferson County	37,337	76.07
Opelousas, LA (city) St. Landry Parish	12,598	75.74
Bellwood, IL (village) Cook County	14,391	75.46
Inkster, MI (city) Wayne County	19,106	75.31
Orangeburg, SC (city) Orangeburg County	10,504	75.22
East Point, GA (city) Fulton County	25,350	75.20
South Holland, IL (village) Cook County	16,497	74.88
Chester, PA (city) Delaware County	25,408	74.79
Maywood, IL (village) Cook County	18,018	74.79
Canton, MS (city) Madison County	9,858	74.74
Helena-West Helena, AR (city) Phillips County	9,155	74.54
Miami Gardens, FL (city) Miami-Dade County	79,681	74.35
Moss Point, MS (city) Jackson County	10,152	74.08
Gladeview, FL (cdp) Miami-Dade County	8,534	73.98
Pinewood, FL (cdp) Miami-Dade County	12,210	73.91
Birmingham, AL (city) Jefferson County	156,470	73.72
Willingboro, NJ (township) Burlington County	23,262	73.55
Bellefontaine Neighbors, MO (city) St. Louis County	7,977	73.45
Brownsville, FL (cdp) Miami-Dade County	11,156	72.85
Bastrop, LA (city) Morehouse Parish	8,276	72.82
Golden Glades, FL (cdp) Miami-Dade County	23,917	72.16
Albany, GA (city) Dougherty County	55,753	72.00
Fort Washington, MD (cdp) Prince George's County	17,045	71.87
Forestdale, AL (cdp) Jefferson County	7,299	71.83
Southfield, MI (city) Oakland County	51,445	71.71
Bessemer, AL (city) Jefferson County	19,649	71.57
City of Orange, NJ (township) Essex County	21,461	71.22
Beecher, MI (cdp) Genesee County	7,264	70.99
Calumet City, IL (city) Cook County	26,282	70.95
Richmond Heights, FL (cdp) Miami-Dade County	6,057	70.92
Fairburn, GA (city) Fulton County	9,102	70.29
Trotwood, OH (city) Montgomery County	17,113	70.05
Dentsville, SC (cdp) Richland County	9,807	69.74
Maple Heights, OH (city) Cuyahoga County	16,072	69.46
Lancaster, TX (city) Dallas County	25,217	69.35
DeSoto, TX (city) Dallas County	33,823	68.96
Ferguson, MO (city) St. Louis County	14,567	68.70
Kinston, NC (city) Lenoir County	14,851	68.51
Macon, GA (city) Bibb County	62,572	68.50
Wilkinsburg, PA (borough) Allegheny County	10,901	68.43
Pine Hills, FL (cdp) Orange County	40,711	67.77
Montrose, VA (cdp) Henrico County	5,410	67.68
Forrest City, AR (city) St. Francis County	10,399	67.65
Westview, FL (cdp) Miami-Dade County	6,515	67.51
Forest Park, OH (city) Hamilton County	12,617	67.40
Greenwood, MS (city) Leflore County	10,244	67.37
Glenwood, IL (village) Cook County	6,031	67.24
Highland Springs, VA (cdp) Henrico County	10,549	67.14
Cordele, GA (city) Crisp County	7,469	67.00
Lynwood, IL (village) Cook County	6,006	66.68
St. Andrews, SC (cdp) Richland County	13,649	66.60
Seabrook, MD (cdp) Prince George's County	11,476	66.39
McComb, MS (city) Pike County	8,491	66.39
Riviera Beach, FL (city) Palm Beach County	21,549	66.33
Vicksburg, MS (city) Warren County	15,812	66.28
Lanham, MD (cdp) Prince George's County	6,684	65.81
Bladensburg, MD (town) Prince George's County	5,989	65.47
Accokeek, MD (cdp) Prince George's County	6,912	65.37
Brownsville, TN (city) Haywood County	6,699	65.09
Wyandanch, NY (cdp) Suffolk County	7,550	64.82
Quincy, FL (city) Gadsden County	5,158	64.70
Bennettsville, SC (city) Marlboro County	5,849	64.49
Baltimore, MD (city) Baltimore city County	400,138	64.44
Gardere, LA (cdp) East Baton Rouge Parish	6,813	64.40
Monroe, LA (city) Ouachita Parish	31,404	64.33
Henderson, NC (city) Vance County	9,875	64.26
Sauk Village, IL (village) Cook County	6,748	64.23
West Memphis, AR (city) Crittenden County	16,775	63.92
Waggaman, LA (cdp) Jefferson Parish	6,401	63.91
Memphis, TN (city) Shelby County	412,759	63.81
Americus, GA (city) Sumter County	10,841	63.62
Cahokia, IL (village) St. Clair County	9,685	63.55
Center Point, AL (city) Jefferson County	10,695	63.21
Mount Vernon, NY (city) Westchester County	42,361	62.95

SECTION THREE

Please refer to the Explanation of Data in the front of the book for more detailed information.

Race

African-American/Black: Hispanic

U.S. and 50 States Sorted by Population and Percent of Total Population

Place	Population	%
United States	**1,897,218**	**0.61**
New York	387,670	2.00
California	247,832	0.67
Florida	203,292	1.08
Texas	149,151	0.59
New Jersey	113,930	1.30
Pennsylvania	75,428	0.59
Massachusetts	61,422	0.94
Georgia	56,471	0.58
Illinois	54,729	0.43
North Carolina	43,826	0.46
Virginia	42,202	0.53
Connecticut	39,893	1.12
Maryland	38,300	0.66
Arizona	35,582	0.56
Ohio	30,736	0.27
Michigan	28,443	0.29
Colorado	24,594	0.49
Washington	22,110	0.33
Nevada	18,410	0.68
Indiana	16,062	0.25
South Carolina	15,497	0.34
Wisconsin	14,607	0.26
Louisiana	14,096	0.31
Rhode Island	12,864	1.22
New Mexico	12,767	0.62
Tennessee	12,482	0.20
Missouri	10,900	0.18
Oklahoma	10,719	0.29
Minnesota	10,678	0.20
Kansas	10,060	0.35
Alabama	9,564	0.20
Oregon	8,671	0.23
Delaware	7,334	0.82
Kentucky	7,188	0.17
Mississippi	6,501	0.22
Utah	6,152	0.22
District of Columbia	5,735	0.95
Hawaii	5,256	0.39
Arkansas	4,468	0.15
Iowa	4,373	0.14
Nebraska	3,770	0.21
Alaska	2,783	0.39
New Hampshire	2,390	0.18
Idaho	2,013	0.13
West Virginia	1,668	0.09
Maine	1,119	0.08
Wyoming	888	0.16
Montana	758	0.08
Vermont	650	0.10
South Dakota	640	0.08
North Dakota	544	0.08

Place	Population	%
New York	387,670	2.00
New Jersey	113,930	1.30
Rhode Island	12,864	1.22
Connecticut	39,893	1.12
Florida	203,292	1.08
District of Columbia	5,735	0.95
Massachusetts	61,422	0.94
Delaware	7,334	0.82
Nevada	18,410	0.68
California	247,832	0.67
Maryland	38,300	0.66
New Mexico	12,767	0.62
United States	**1,897,218**	**0.61**
Texas	149,151	0.59
Pennsylvania	75,428	0.59
Georgia	56,471	0.58
Arizona	35,582	0.56
Virginia	42,202	0.53
Colorado	24,594	0.49
North Carolina	43,826	0.46
Illinois	54,729	0.43
Hawaii	5,256	0.39
Alaska	2,783	0.39
Kansas	10,060	0.35
South Carolina	15,497	0.34
Washington	22,110	0.33
Louisiana	14,096	0.31
Michigan	28,443	0.29
Oklahoma	10,719	0.29
Ohio	30,736	0.27
Wisconsin	14,607	0.26
Indiana	16,062	0.25
Oregon	8,671	0.23
Mississippi	6,501	0.22
Utah	6,152	0.22
Nebraska	3,770	0.21
Tennessee	12,482	0.20
Minnesota	10,678	0.20
Alabama	9,564	0.20
Missouri	10,900	0.18
New Hampshire	2,390	0.18
Kentucky	7,188	0.17
Wyoming	888	0.16
Arkansas	4,468	0.15
Iowa	4,373	0.14
Idaho	2,013	0.13
Vermont	650	0.10
West Virginia	1,668	0.09
Maine	1,119	0.08
Montana	758	0.08
South Dakota	640	0.08
North Dakota	544	0.08

Please refer to the Explanation of Data in the front of the book for more detailed information.

Race

African-American/Black: Hispanic

Top 150 Places Sorted by Population

Based on all places, regardless of total population

Place	Population	%
New York, NY (city) Kings County	296,256	3.62
Bronx, NY (borough) Bronx County	114,488	8.27
Brooklyn, NY (borough) Kings County	75,728	3.02
Manhattan, NY (borough) New York County	55,891	3.52
Queens, NY (borough) Queens County	42,656	1.91
Los Angeles, CA (city) Los Angeles County	29,627	0.78
Philadelphia, PA (city) Philadelphia County	24,302	1.59
Chicago, IL (city) Cook County	23,226	0.86
Houston, TX (city) Harris County	18,425	0.88
Boston, MA (city) Suffolk County	16,541	2.68
Miami, FL (city) Miami-Dade County	13,989	3.50
San Antonio, TX (city) Medina County	12,946	0.98
Phoenix, AZ (city) Maricopa County	11,453	0.79
San Diego, CA (city) San Diego County	9,556	0.73
Newark, NJ (city) Essex County	9,147	3.30
Hempstead, NY (town) Nassau County	8,755	1.15
Dallas, TX (city) Dallas County	7,585	0.63
Staten Island, NY (borough) Richmond County	7,493	1.60
Providence, RI (city) Providence County	7,449	4.18
Yonkers, NY (city) Westchester County	7,325	3.74
Jersey City, NJ (city) Hudson County	7,072	2.86
Jacksonville, FL (city) Duval County	7,014	0.85
Paterson, NJ (city) Passaic County	7,012	4.80
Milwaukee, WI (city) Milwaukee County	6,944	1.17
Rochester, NY (city) Monroe County	6,535	3.10
Sacramento, CA (city) Sacramento County	6,418	1.38
Tampa, FL (city) Hillsborough County	6,392	1.90
Charlotte, NC (city) Mecklenburg County	6,096	0.83
Springfield, MA (city) Hampden County	5,990	3.91
El Paso, TX (city) El Paso County	5,929	0.91
Austin, TX (city) Travis County	5,903	0.75
Lawrence, MA (city) Essex County	5,872	7.69
Washington, DC (city) District of Columbia	5,735	0.95
Islip, NY (town) Suffolk County	5,700	1.70
Hartford, CT (city/town) Hartford County	5,549	4.45
Hialeah, FL (city) Miami-Dade County	5,479	2.44
Albuquerque, NM (city) Bernalillo County	5,448	1.00
Denver, CO (city) Denver County	5,392	0.90
Fresno, CA (city) Fresno County	5,369	1.09
San Jose, CA (city) Santa Clara County	5,303	0.56
Cleveland, OH (city) Cuyahoga County	5,107	1.29
Fort Worth, TX (city) Tarrant County	5,059	0.68
Detroit, MI (city) Wayne County	5,025	0.70
Allentown, PA (city) Lehigh County	4,940	4.19
Las Vegas, NV (city) Clark County	4,936	0.85
Oakland, CA (city) Alameda County	4,910	1.26
Bridgeport, CT (city/town) Fairfield County	4,743	3.29
Tucson, AZ (city) Pima County	4,718	0.91
Long Beach, CA (city) Los Angeles County	4,677	1.01
Orlando, FL (city) Orange County	4,583	1.92
Reading, PA (city) Berks County	4,303	4.89
Elizabeth, NJ (city) Union County	4,298	3.44
Buffalo, NY (city) Erie County	4,290	1.64
Virginia Beach, VA (ind. city) Virginia Beach independent city	4,083	0.93
Aurora, CO (city) Arapahoe County	4,072	1.25
San Francisco, CA (city) San Francisco County	4,050	0.50
Stockton, CA (city) San Joaquin County	4,043	1.39
Columbus, OH (city) Franklin County	3,969	0.50
Camden, NJ (city) Camden County	3,872	5.01
Baltimore, MD (city) Baltimore city County	3,860	0.62
Indianapolis, IN (city) Marion County	3,833	0.47
Miami Gardens, FL (city) Miami-Dade County	3,793	3.54
Worcester, MA (city) Worcester County	3,758	2.08
Raleigh, NC (city) Wake County	3,632	0.90
Colorado Springs, CO (city) El Paso County	3,600	0.86
Waterbury, CT (city/town) New Haven County	3,593	3.26
Killeen, TX (city) Bell County	3,574	2.79
Miramar, FL (city) Broward County	3,540	2.90
Fayetteville, NC (city) Cumberland County	3,540	1.77
Brookhaven, NY (town) Suffolk County	3,517	0.72
New Haven, CT (city/town) New Haven County	3,497	2.69
Atlanta, GA (city) Fulton County	3,373	0.80
Union City, NJ (city) Hudson County	3,233	4.86
Passaic, NJ (city) Passaic County	3,121	4.47
Norfolk, VA (ind. city) Norfolk independent city	3,088	1.27

Place	Population	%
San Bernardino, CA (city) San Bernardino County	3,056	1.46
Bakersfield, CA (city) Kern County	3,047	0.88
Pembroke Pines, FL (city) Broward County	3,043	1.97
Lynn, MA (city) Essex County	2,976	3.29
Oklahoma City, OK (city) Oklahoma County	2,967	0.51
Syracuse, NY (city) Onondaga County	2,945	2.03
Moreno Valley, CA (city) Riverside County	2,885	1.49
Arlington, TX (city) Tarrant County	2,797	0.77
Riverside, CA (city) Riverside County	2,773	0.91
New Orleans, LA (city) Orleans Parish	2,756	0.80
Hollywood, FL (city) Broward County	2,740	1.95
Lancaster, PA (city) Lancaster County	2,721	4.59
Kansas City, MO (city) Jackson County	2,648	0.58
North Las Vegas, NV (city) Clark County	2,605	1.20
Newport News, VA (ind. city) Newport News independent city	2,588	1.43
Santa Ana, CA (city) Orange County	2,503	0.77
Portland, OR (city) Multnomah County	2,488	0.43
Nashville-Davidson, TN (metro govt) Davidson County	2,478	0.41
Trenton, NJ (city) Mercer County	2,474	2.91
Babylon, NY (town) Suffolk County	2,428	1.14
Perth Amboy, NJ (city) Middlesex County	2,403	4.73
Seattle, WA (city) King County	2,391	0.39
Fontana, CA (city) San Bernardino County	2,374	1.21
Toledo, OH (city) Lucas County	2,368	0.82
Wichita, KS (city) Sedgwick County	2,357	0.62
Kissimmee, FL (city) Osceola County	2,348	3.93
New Britain, CT (city/town) Hartford County	2,334	3.19
Poinciana, FL (cdp) Osceola County	2,306	4.34
Chula Vista, CA (city) San Diego County	2,303	0.94
Louisville-Jefferson County, KY (metro govt) Jefferson County	2,300	0.39
Grand Rapids, MI (city) Kent County	2,291	1.22
Winston-Salem, NC (city) Forsyth County	2,245	0.98
Albany, NY (city) Albany County	2,193	2.24
Memphis, TN (city) Shelby County	2,169	0.34
Mesa, AZ (city) Maricopa County	2,160	0.49
Brentwood, NY (cdp) Suffolk County	2,138	3.52
Sunrise Manor, NV (cdp) Clark County	2,131	1.13
Corpus Christi, TX (city) Nueces County	2,117	0.69
St. Paul, MN (city) Ramsey County	2,105	0.74
Lancaster, CA (city) Los Angeles County	2,089	1.33
Paradise, NV (cdp) Clark County	2,083	0.93
Minneapolis, MN (city) Hennepin County	2,078	0.54
Greensboro, NC (city) Guilford County	2,020	0.75
West New York, NJ (town) Hudson County	2,018	4.06
Town 'n' Country, FL (cdp) Hillsborough County	1,981	2.53
Columbus, GA (city) Muscogee County	1,976	1.04
Palmdale, CA (city) Los Angeles County	1,970	1.29
Tacoma, WA (city) Pierce County	1,965	0.99
Anaheim, CA (city) Orange County	1,918	0.57
North Bergen, NJ (township) Hudson County	1,917	3.15
Anchorage, AK (municipality) Anchorage Municipality	1,907	0.65
Deltona, FL (city) Volusia County	1,906	2.24
Port St. Lucie, FL (city) St. Lucie County	1,904	1.16
Mount Vernon, NY (city) Westchester County	1,883	2.80
Brockton, MA (city) Plymouth County	1,854	1.98
York, PA (city) York County	1,832	4.19
Augusta-Richmond County, GA (cons. govt) Richmond County	1,815	0.93
Harrisburg, PA (city) Dauphin County	1,796	3.63
Hampton, VA (ind. city) Hampton independent city	1,794	1.31
Lansing, MI (city) Ingham County	1,772	1.55
Tulsa, OK (city) Tulsa County	1,752	0.45
Oxnard, CA (city) Ventura County	1,733	0.88
Durham, NC (city) Durham County	1,720	0.75
North Miami, FL (city) Miami-Dade County	1,719	2.92
Lorain, OH (city) Lorain County	1,709	2.67
Inglewood, CA (city) Los Angeles County	1,707	1.56
Bethlehem, PA (city) Northampton County	1,704	2.27
Modesto, CA (city) Stanislaus County	1,696	0.84
Hempstead, NY (village) Nassau County	1,688	3.13
Vineland, NJ (city) Cumberland County	1,688	2.78
Lansing, MI (city) Ingham County	1,687	1.54
Brandon, FL (cdp) Hillsborough County	1,684	1.63
Victorville, CA (city) San Bernardino County	1,664	1.44
Glendale, AZ (city) Maricopa County	1,649	0.73
Stamford, CT (city/town) Fairfield County	1,640	1.34

Please refer to the Explanation of Data in the front of the book for more detailed information.

Race

African-American/Black: Hispanic

Top 150 Places Sorted by Percent of Total Population

Based on all places, regardless of total population

Place	Population	%
Los Huisaches, TX (cdp) Webb County	2	11.76
Los Angeles, TX (cdp) Willacy County	11	9.09
Biggs Junction, OR (cdp) Sherman County	2	9.09
Lake Harbor, FL (cdp) Palm Beach County	4	8.89
Plano, IA (city) Appanoose County	6	8.57
Bronx, NY (borough) Bronx County	114,488	8.27
Lawrence, MA (city) Essex County	5,872	7.69
Harper, OR (cdp) Malheur County	7	6.42
Cañones, NM (cdp) Rio Arriba County	7	5.93
Gordon Heights, NY (cdp) Suffolk County	221	5.47
Camden, NJ (city) Camden County	3,872	5.01
Opa-locka, FL (city) Miami-Dade County	746	4.90
Reading, PA (city) Berks County	4,303	4.89
Buenaventura Lakes, FL (cdp) Osceola County	1,272	4.88
St. Cloud, MO (village) Crawford County	2	4.88
Union City, NJ (city) Hudson County	3,233	4.86
Rest Haven, GA (town) Gwinnett County	3	4.84
Haverstraw, NY (village) Rockland County	574	4.82
Florissant, CO (cdp) Teller County	5	4.81
Paterson, NJ (city) Passaic County	7,012	4.80
Perth Amboy, NJ (city) Middlesex County	2,403	4.73
Ebro, MN (cdp) Clearwater County	3	4.69
Pleasantville, NJ (city) Atlantic County	933	4.61
Lancaster, PA (city) Lancaster County	2,721	4.59
Sky Lake, FL (cdp) Orange County	276	4.49
Passaic, NJ (city) Passaic County	3,121	4.47
Homestead Base, FL (cdp) Miami-Dade County	43	4.46
Hartford, CT (city/town) Hartford County	5,549	4.45
Del Mar Heights, TX (cdp) Cameron County	5	4.42
Poinciana, FL (cdp) Osceola County	2,306	4.34
Middletown, NY (city) Orange County	1,209	4.30
Cuney, TX (town) Cherokee County	6	4.29
Norcross, MN (city) Grant County	3	4.29
Decatur, PA (township) Clearfield County	194	4.27
Tierra Bonita, TX (cdp) Cameron County	6	4.26
Monticello, NY (village) Sullivan County	283	4.21
Allentown, PA (city) Lehigh County	4,940	4.19
York, PA (city) York County	1,832	4.19
Providence, RI (city) Providence County	7,449	4.18
Edgewater Estates, TX (cdp) San Patricio County	3	4.17
Prospect Park, NJ (borough) Passaic County	243	4.14
Gregg, PA (township) Union County	204	4.09
West New York, NJ (town) Hudson County	2,018	4.06
Azalea Park, FL (cdp) Orange County	510	4.06
Campo Bonito, AZ (cdp) Pinal County	3	4.05
Penn Estates, PA (cdp) Monroe County	181	4.03
Saw Creek, PA (cdp) Pike County	162	4.03
Washington Heights, NY (cdp) Orange County	68	4.03
Elmira, MO (village) Ray County	2	4.00
Girard, TX (cdp) Kent County	2	4.00
North Bay Shore, NY (cdp) Suffolk County	756	3.99
Seabrook Farms, NJ (cdp) Cumberland County	59	3.98
Lakeview, NY (cdp) Nassau County	223	3.97
Pleasant Hill, PA (cdp) Lebanon County	105	3.97
Parc, NY (cdp) Clinton County	10	3.94
Kissimmee, FL (city) Osceola County	2,348	3.93
Springfield, MA (city) Hampden County	5,990	3.91
Oak Ridge, FL (cdp) Orange County	884	3.90
Naranja, FL (cdp) Miami-Dade County	321	3.87
North Brentwood, MD (town) Prince George's County	20	3.87
West Little River, FL (cdp) Miami-Dade County	1,341	3.86
Harlem Heights, FL (cdp) Lee County	76	3.85
Elwood, NJ (cdp) Atlantic County	55	3.83
Meadow Woods, FL (cdp) Orange County	971	3.80
Voorhees, NJ (cdp) Somerset County	37	3.79
McClellan Park, CA (cdp) Sacramento County	28	3.77
Grayson, OK (town) Okmulgee County	6	3.77
McRae, GA (city) Telfair County	216	3.76
Yonkers, NY (city) Westchester County	7,325	3.74
Westview, FL (cdp) Miami-Dade County	359	3.72
Central Falls, RI (city) Providence County	717	3.70
Manzano Springs, NM (cdp) Torrance County	5	3.65
Harrisburg, PA (city) Dauphin County	1,796	3.63
New York, NY (city) Kings County	296,256	3.62
Dannemora, NY (village) Clinton County	142	3.61
Beacon, NY (city) Dutchess County	559	3.60
Lincoln University, PA (cdp) Chester County	62	3.59
Penns Grove, NJ (borough) Salem County	184	3.57
Lanare, CA (cdp) Fresno County	21	3.57
Quintana, TX (town) Brazoria County	2	3.57
Miami Gardens, FL (city) Miami-Dade County	3,793	3.54
Coolbaugh, PA (township) Monroe County	728	3.54
Manhattan, NY (borough) New York County	55,891	3.52
Brentwood, NY (cdp) Suffolk County	2,138	3.52
Scotchtown, NY (cdp) Orange County	324	3.52
Miami, FL (city) Miami-Dade County	13,989	3.50
Goodlow, TX (city) Navarro County	7	3.50
Victory Gardens, NJ (borough) Morris County	53	3.49
Central Islip, NY (cdp) Suffolk County	1,195	3.47
Palmetto Estates, FL (cdp) Miami-Dade County	468	3.46
Fort Dix, NJ (cdp) Burlington County	267	3.46
Atlantic City, NJ (city) Atlantic County	1,365	3.45
Elizabeth, NJ (city) Union County	4,298	3.44
Princeton, FL (cdp) Miami-Dade County	746	3.39
Country Club, FL (cdp) Miami-Dade County	1,594	3.38
New London, CT (city/town) New London County	932	3.37
West Park, FL (city) Broward County	475	3.36
Whiteface, TX (town) Cochran County	15	3.34
Fort Lee, VA (cdp) Prince George County	113	3.33
Newburgh, NY (city) Orange County	958	3.32
Newark, NJ (city) Essex County	9,147	3.30
Peekskill, NY (city) Westchester County	779	3.30
Pemberton Heights, NJ (cdp) Burlington County	80	3.30
Bridgeport, CT (city/town) Fairfield County	4,743	3.29
Lynn, MA (city) Essex County	2,976	3.29
Egypt Lake-Leto, FL (cdp) Hillsborough County	1,156	3.28
Woodbine, NJ (borough) Cape May County	81	3.28
Waterbury, CT (city/town) New Haven County	3,593	3.26
Freeport, NY (village) Nassau County	1,390	3.24
Willimantic, CT (cdp) Windham County	575	3.24
West Hazleton, PA (borough) Luzerne County	149	3.24
Pinewood, FL (cdp) Miami-Dade County	534	3.23
Chesterfield, NJ (township) Burlington County	248	3.22
Haverstraw, NY (town) Rockland County	1,177	3.21
Bogota, NJ (borough) Bergen County	263	3.21
Church Creek, MD (town) Dorchester County	4	3.20
New Britain, CT (city/town) Hartford County	2,334	3.19
Roosevelt, NY (cdp) Nassau County	519	3.19
West Haverstraw, NY (village) Rockland County	324	3.19
Ellenville, NY (village) Ulster County	132	3.19
Woodlynne, NJ (borough) Camden County	95	3.19
Holyoke, MA (city) Hampden County	1,267	3.18
Greenbush, VA (cdp) Accomack County	7	3.18
New Hanover, NJ (township) Burlington County	234	3.17
Egg Harbor City, NJ (city) Atlantic County	134	3.16
North Bergen, NJ (township) Hudson County	1,917	3.15
Welch, TX (cdp) Dawson County	7	3.15
Hempstead, NY (village) Nassau County	1,688	3.13
East Franklin, NJ (cdp) Somerset County	271	3.13
Schall Circle, FL (cdp) Palm Beach County	35	3.13
Hazleton, PA (city) Luzerne County	791	3.12
Pocono Ranch Lands, PA (cdp) Pike County	33	3.11
Rochester, NY (city) Monroe County	6,535	3.10
South Fallsburg, NY (cdp) Sullivan County	89	3.10
El Portal, FL (village) Miami-Dade County	72	3.10
Dixon, WY (town) Carbon County	3	3.09
Dover, FL (cdp) Hillsborough County	114	3.08
Randall, KS (city) Jewell County	2	3.08
Fairview, NY (cdp) Westchester County	95	3.07
Guttenberg, NJ (town) Hudson County	342	3.06
South Miami Heights, FL (cdp) Miami-Dade County	1,082	3.03
Liberty, NY (village) Sullivan County	133	3.03
Brooklyn, NY (borough) Kings County	75,728	3.02
Herlong, CA (cdp) Lassen County	9	3.02
Willingboro, NJ (township) Burlington County	953	3.01
North Amityville, NY (cdp) Suffolk County	537	3.01
Salem, NJ (city) Salem County	155	3.01
Mashantucket, CT (cdp) New London County	9	3.01
Daykin, NE (village) Jefferson County	5	3.01
Dannemora, NY (town) Clinton County	147	3.00

Please refer to the Explanation of Data in the front of the book for more detailed information.

Race

African-American/Black: Hispanic

Top 150 Places Sorted by Percent of Total Population

Based on places with total population of 7,500 or more

Place	Population	%
Bronx, NY (borough) Bronx County	114,488	8.27
Lawrence, MA (city) Essex County	5,872	7.69
Camden, NJ (city) Camden County	3,872	5.01
Opa-locka, FL (city) Miami-Dade County	746	4.90
Reading, PA (city) Berks County	4,303	4.89
Buenaventura Lakes, FL (cdp) Osceola County	1,272	4.88
Union City, NJ (city) Hudson County	3,233	4.86
Haverstraw, NY (village) Rockland County	574	4.82
Paterson, NJ (city) Passaic County	7,012	4.80
Perth Amboy, NJ (city) Middlesex County	2,403	4.73
Pleasantville, NJ (city) Atlantic County	933	4.61
Lancaster, PA (city) Lancaster County	2,721	4.59
Passaic, NJ (city) Passaic County	3,121	4.47
Hartford, CT (city/town) Hartford County	5,549	4.45
Poinciana, FL (cdp) Osceola County	2,306	4.34
Middletown, NY (city) Orange County	1,209	4.30
Allentown, PA (city) Lehigh County	4,940	4.19
York, PA (city) York County	1,832	4.19
Providence, RI (city) Providence County	7,449	4.18
West New York, NJ (town) Hudson County	2,018	4.06
Azalea Park, FL (cdp) Orange County	510	4.06
North Bay Shore, NY (cdp) Suffolk County	756	3.99
Kissimmee, FL (city) Osceola County	2,348	3.93
Springfield, MA (city) Hampden County	5,990	3.91
Oak Ridge, FL (cdp) Orange County	884	3.90
Naranja, FL (cdp) Miami-Dade County	321	3.87
West Little River, FL (cdp) Miami-Dade County	1,341	3.86
Meadow Woods, FL (cdp) Orange County	971	3.80
Yonkers, NY (city) Westchester County	7,325	3.74
Westview, FL (cdp) Miami-Dade County	359	3.72
Central Falls, RI (city) Providence County	717	3.70
Harrisburg, PA (city) Dauphin County	1,796	3.63
New York, NY (city) Kings County	296,256	3.62
Beacon, NY (city) Dutchess County	559	3.60
Miami Gardens, FL (city) Miami-Dade County	3,793	3.54
Coolbaugh, PA (township) Monroe County	728	3.54
Manhattan, NY (borough) New York County	55,891	3.52
Brentwood, NY (cdp) Suffolk County	2,138	3.52
Scotchtown, NY (cdp) Orange County	324	3.52
Miami, FL (city) Miami-Dade County	13,989	3.50
Central Islip, NY (cdp) Suffolk County	1,195	3.47
Palmetto Estates, FL (cdp) Miami-Dade County	468	3.46
Fort Dix, NJ (cdp) Burlington County	267	3.46
Atlantic City, NJ (city) Atlantic County	1,365	3.45
Elizabeth, NJ (city) Union County	4,298	3.44
Princeton, FL (cdp) Miami-Dade County	746	3.39
Country Club, FL (cdp) Miami-Dade County	1,594	3.38
New London, CT (city/town) New London County	932	3.37
West Park, FL (city) Broward County	475	3.36
Newburgh, NY (city) Orange County	958	3.32
Newark, NJ (city) Essex County	9,147	3.30
Peekskill, NY (city) Westchester County	779	3.30
Bridgeport, CT (city/town) Fairfield County	4,743	3.29
Lynn, MA (city) Essex County	2,976	3.29
Egypt Lake-Leto, FL (cdp) Hillsborough County	1,156	3.28
Waterbury, CT (city/town) New Haven County	3,593	3.26
Freeport, NY (village) Nassau County	1,390	3.24
Willimantic, CT (cdp) Windham County	575	3.24
Pinewood, FL (cdp) Miami-Dade County	534	3.23
Chesterfield, NJ (township) Burlington County	248	3.22
Haverstraw, NY (town) Rockland County	1,177	3.21
Bogota, NJ (borough) Bergen County	263	3.21
New Britain, CT (city/town) Hartford County	2,334	3.19
Roosevelt, NY (cdp) Nassau County	519	3.19
West Haverstraw, NY (village) Rockland County	324	3.19
Holyoke, MA (city) Hampden County	1,267	3.18
North Bergen, NJ (township) Hudson County	1,917	3.15
Hempstead, NY (village) Nassau County	1,688	3.13
East Franklin, NJ (cdp) Somerset County	271	3.13
Hazleton, PA (city) Luzerne County	791	3.12
Rochester, NY (city) Monroe County	6,535	3.10
Guttenberg, NJ (town) Hudson County	342	3.06
South Miami Heights, FL (cdp) Miami-Dade County	1,082	3.03
Brooklyn, NY (borough) Kings County	75,728	3.02
Willingboro, NJ (township) Burlington County	953	3.01
North Amityville, NY (cdp) Suffolk County	537	3.01
Bay Shore, NY (cdp) Suffolk County	779	2.96
Lebanon, PA (city) Lebanon County	754	2.96
Pine Castle, FL (cdp) Orange County	318	2.94
Goulds, FL (cdp) Miami-Dade County	297	2.94
Richmond Heights, FL (cdp) Miami-Dade County	251	2.94
Union Park, FL (cdp) Orange County	286	2.93
North Miami, FL (city) Miami-Dade County	1,719	2.92
Trenton, NJ (city) Mercer County	2,474	2.91
Brownsville, FL (cdp) Miami-Dade County	445	2.91
Miramar, FL (city) Broward County	3,540	2.90
New Brunswick, NJ (city) Middlesex County	1,598	2.90
Lehman, PA (township) Pike County	308	2.89
Haledon, NJ (borough) Passaic County	239	2.87
Jersey City, NJ (city) Hudson County	7,072	2.86
West Perrine, FL (cdp) Miami-Dade County	268	2.83
University, FL (cdp) Hillsborough County	1,160	2.82
Golden Glades, FL (cdp) Miami-Dade County	935	2.82
Mount Vernon, NY (city) Westchester County	1,883	2.80
Spring Lake, NC (town) Cumberland County	335	2.80
Killeen, TX (city) Bell County	3,574	2.79
Vineland, NJ (city) Cumberland County	1,688	2.78
North Miami Beach, FL (city) Miami-Dade County	1,154	2.78
Ridgefield Park, NJ (village) Bergen County	354	2.78
Windham, CT (town) Windham County	701	2.77
Roselle, NJ (borough) Union County	584	2.77
Southchase, FL (cdp) Orange County	438	2.75
Coatesville, PA (city) Chester County	360	2.75
Sleepy Hollow, NY (village) Westchester County	270	2.74
Palm River-Clair Mel, FL (cdp) Hillsborough County	571	2.72
North Bellport, NY (cdp) Suffolk County	314	2.72
East Chicago, IN (city) Lake County	805	2.71
Wyandanch, NY (cdp) Suffolk County	315	2.70
New Haven, CT (city/town) New Haven County	3,497	2.69
Hackensack, NJ (city) Bergen County	1,157	2.69
Teaneck, NJ (township) Bergen County	1,068	2.69
Boston, MA (city) Suffolk County	16,541	2.68
Lorain, OH (city) Lorain County	1,709	2.67
Thompson, NY (town) Sullivan County	406	2.65
Asbury Park, NJ (city) Monmouth County	425	2.64
East Hartford, CT (cdp/town) Hartford County	1,345	2.62
Pennsauken, NJ (township) Camden County	941	2.62
Bethlehem, PA (city) Northampton County	1,449	2.60
Chelsea, MA (city) Suffolk County	905	2.57
Englewood, NJ (city) Bergen County	698	2.57
Leisure City, FL (cdp) Miami-Dade County	580	2.56
Homestead, FL (city) Miami-Dade County	1,542	2.55
Ives Estates, FL (cdp) Miami-Dade County	497	2.55
Town 'n' Country, FL (cdp) Hillsborough County	1,981	2.53
City of Orange, NJ (township) Essex County	762	2.53
Plainfield, NJ (city) Union County	1,257	2.52
Wallkill, NY (town) Orange County	688	2.51
Chester, PA (city) Delaware County	849	2.50
Baldwin, NY (cdp) Nassau County	600	2.50
Gladeview, FL (cdp) Miami-Dade County	287	2.49
Hillcrest, NY (cdp) Rockland County	188	2.49
Chillum, MD (cdp) Prince George's County	828	2.47
Mount Rainier, MD (city) Prince George's County	198	2.45
Hialeah, FL (city) Miami-Dade County	5,479	2.44
Poughkeepsie, NY (city) Dutchess County	794	2.43
Mount Holly, NJ (township) Burlington County	231	2.42
East Lake-Orient Park, FL (cdp) Hillsborough County	548	2.41
Hinesville, GA (city) Liberty County	804	2.40
Uniondale, NY (cdp) Nassau County	593	2.40
Groton, CT (city) New London County	246	2.37
Wawarsing, NY (town) Ulster County	311	2.36
Schenectady, NY (city) Schenectady County	1,547	2.34
Dover, NJ (town) Morris County	424	2.34
Lancaster, PA (township) Lancaster County	377	2.33
Weehawken, NJ (township) Hudson County	293	2.33
East Orange, NJ (city) Essex County	1,489	2.32
View Park-Windsor Hills, CA (cdp) Los Angeles County	257	2.32
Hialeah Gardens, FL (city) Miami-Dade County	500	2.30
Bethlehem, PA (city) Northampton County	1,704	2.27
Florida City, FL (city) Miami-Dade County	255	2.27

Please refer to the Explanation of Data in the front of the book for more detailed information.

Race

American Indian/Alaska Native

U.S. and 50 States Sorted by Population and Percent of Total Population

Place	Population	%
United States	**5,220,579**	**1.69**
California	723,225	1.94
Oklahoma	482,760	12.87
Arizona	353,386	5.53
Texas	315,264	1.25
New York	221,058	1.14
New Mexico	219,512	10.66
Washington	198,998	2.96
North Carolina	184,082	1.93
Florida	162,562	0.86
Michigan	139,095	1.41
Alaska	138,312	19.47
Oregon	109,223	2.85
Colorado	107,832	2.14
Minnesota	101,900	1.92
Illinois	101,451	0.79
Ohio	90,124	0.78
Wisconsin	86,228	1.52
Georgia	84,024	0.87
South Dakota	82,073	10.08
Pennsylvania	81,092	0.64
Virginia	80,924	1.01
Montana	78,601	7.94
Missouri	72,376	1.21
New Jersey	70,716	0.80
Kansas	59,130	2.07
Maryland	58,657	1.02
Alabama	57,118	1.20
Nevada	55,945	2.07
Louisiana	55,079	1.21
Tennessee	54,874	0.86
Massachusetts	50,705	0.77
Utah	50,064	1.81
Indiana	49,738	0.77
Arkansas	47,588	1.63
North Dakota	42,996	6.39
South Carolina	42,171	0.91
Idaho	36,385	2.32
Hawaii	33,470	2.46
Kentucky	31,355	0.72
Connecticut	31,140	0.87
Nebraska	29,816	1.63
Mississippi	25,910	0.87
Iowa	24,511	0.80
Wyoming	18,596	3.30
Maine	18,482	1.39
Rhode Island	14,394	1.37
West Virginia	13,314	0.72
New Hampshire	10,524	0.80
Delaware	9,899	1.10
Vermont	7,379	1.18
District of Columbia	6,521	1.08

Place	Population	%
Alaska	138,312	19.47
Oklahoma	482,760	12.87
New Mexico	219,512	10.66
South Dakota	82,073	10.08
Montana	78,601	7.94
North Dakota	42,996	6.39
Arizona	353,386	5.53
Wyoming	18,596	3.30
Washington	198,998	2.96
Oregon	109,223	2.85
Hawaii	33,470	2.46
Idaho	36,385	2.32
Colorado	107,832	2.14
Kansas	59,130	2.07
Nevada	55,945	2.07
California	723,225	1.94
North Carolina	184,082	1.93
Minnesota	101,900	1.92
Utah	50,064	1.81
United States	**5,220,579**	**1.69**
Arkansas	47,588	1.63
Nebraska	29,816	1.63
Wisconsin	86,228	1.52
Michigan	139,095	1.41
Maine	18,482	1.39
Rhode Island	14,394	1.37
Texas	315,264	1.25
Missouri	72,376	1.21
Louisiana	55,079	1.21
Alabama	57,118	1.20
Vermont	7,379	1.18
New York	221,058	1.14
Delaware	9,899	1.10
District of Columbia	6,521	1.08
Maryland	58,657	1.02
Virginia	80,924	1.01
South Carolina	42,171	0.91
Georgia	84,024	0.87
Connecticut	31,140	0.87
Mississippi	25,910	0.87
Florida	162,562	0.86
Tennessee	54,874	0.86
New Jersey	70,716	0.80
Iowa	24,511	0.80
New Hampshire	10,524	0.80
Illinois	101,451	0.79
Ohio	90,124	0.78
Massachusetts	50,705	0.77
Indiana	49,738	0.77
Kentucky	31,355	0.72
West Virginia	13,314	0.72
Pennsylvania	81,092	0.64

Please refer to the Explanation of Data in the front of the book for more detailed information.

Race

American Indian/Alaska Native

Top 150 Places Sorted by Population

Based on all places, regardless of total population

Place	Population	%
New York, NY (city) Kings County	111,749	1.37
Los Angeles, CA (city) Los Angeles County	54,236	1.43
Phoenix, AZ (city) Maricopa County	43,724	3.02
Oklahoma City, OK (city) Oklahoma County	36,572	6.31
Anchorage, AK (municipality) Anchorage Municipality	36,062	12.36
Tulsa, OK (city) Tulsa County	35,990	9.18
Albuquerque, NM (city) Bernalillo County	32,571	5.97
Bronx, NY (borough) Bronx County	32,011	2.31
Queens, NY (borough) Queens County	30,033	1.35
Chicago, IL (city) Cook County	26,933	1.00
Brooklyn, NY (borough) Kings County	26,571	1.06
Houston, TX (city) Harris County	25,521	1.22
San Antonio, TX (city) Medina County	20,137	1.52
Tucson, AZ (city) Pima County	19,903	3.83
Manhattan, NY (borough) New York County	19,415	1.22
San Diego, CA (city) San Diego County	17,865	1.37
Philadelphia, PA (city) Philadelphia County	17,495	1.15
San Jose, CA (city) Santa Clara County	16,064	1.70
Denver, CO (city) Denver County	14,995	2.50
Portland, OR (city) Multnomah County	14,262	2.44
Fresno, CA (city) Fresno County	14,161	2.86
Dallas, TX (city) Dallas County	14,114	1.18
Mesa, AZ (city) Maricopa County	14,041	3.20
Minneapolis, MN (city) Hennepin County	13,381	3.50
Sacramento, CA (city) Sacramento County	13,242	2.84
Austin, TX (city) Travis County	12,725	1.61
Seattle, WA (city) King County	12,549	2.06
Farmington, NM (city) San Juan County	11,230	24.48
San Francisco, CA (city) San Francisco County	10,873	1.35
Gallup, NM (city) McKinley County	10,343	47.71
Rapid City, SD (city) Pennington County	10,337	15.21
Wichita, KS (city) Sedgwick County	10,084	2.64
Milwaukee, WI (city) Milwaukee County	9,678	1.63
Colorado Springs, CO (city) El Paso County	9,632	2.31
Fort Worth, TX (city) Tarrant County	9,188	1.24
Bakersfield, CA (city) Kern County	9,097	2.62
Norman, OK (city) Cleveland County	8,972	8.09
Las Vegas, NV (city) Clark County	8,917	1.53
Broken Arrow, OK (city) Tulsa County	8,786	8.89
Flagstaff, AZ (city) Coconino County	8,642	13.12
Muskogee, OK (city) Muskogee County	8,610	21.95
Detroit, MI (city) Wayne County	8,448	1.18
Charlotte, NC (city) Mecklenburg County	8,397	1.15
Columbus, OH (city) Franklin County	8,353	1.06
Oakland, CA (city) Alameda County	8,322	2.13
Jacksonville, FL (city) Duval County	8,319	1.01
Shiprock, NM (cdp) San Juan County	8,131	98.02
Tuba City, AZ (cdp) Coconino County	8,089	93.94
Long Beach, CA (city) Los Angeles County	7,958	1.72
Spokane, WA (city) Spokane County	7,880	3.77
Tacoma, WA (city) Pierce County	7,863	3.96
Indianapolis, IN (city) Marion County	7,323	0.89
Stockton, CA (city) San Joaquin County	7,284	2.50
El Paso, TX (city) El Paso County	7,204	1.11
Aurora, CO (city) Arapahoe County	7,040	2.17
Lawton, OK (city) Comanche County	7,008	7.23
Kansas City, MO (city) Jackson County	6,745	1.47
St. Paul, MN (city) Ramsey County	6,725	2.36
Omaha, NE (city) Douglas County	6,649	1.63
Boston, MA (city) Suffolk County	6,529	1.06
Washington, DC (city) District of Columbia	6,521	1.08
Riverside, CA (city) Riverside County	6,447	2.12
Baltimore, MD (city) Baltimore city County	6,441	1.04
Tempe, AZ (city) Maricopa County	6,238	3.86
Billings, MT (city) Yellowstone County	6,222	5.97
Zuni Pueblo, NM (cdp) McKinley County	6,180	98.06
Juneau, AK (borough) Juneau City and Borough	6,005	19.20
Tahlequah, OK (city) Cherokee County	5,971	37.90
Shawnee, OK (city) Pottawatomie County	5,732	19.20
Lower Red Lake, MN (unorganized territory) Beltrami County	5,712	98.65
Urban Honolulu, HI (cdp) Honolulu County	5,691	1.69
Glendale, AZ (city) Maricopa County	5,640	2.49
Green Bay, WI (city) Brown County	5,599	5.38
Santa Rosa, CA (city) Sonoma County	5,575	3.32
Modesto, CA (city) Stanislaus County	5,569	2.77
Sioux Falls, SD (city) Minnehaha County	5,539	3.60
Nashville-Davidson, TN (metro govt) Davidson County	5,520	0.92
Hempstead, NY (town) Nassau County	5,363	0.71
Chandler, AZ (city) Maricopa County	5,339	2.26
Virginia Beach, VA (ind. city) Virginia Beach independent city	5,331	1.22
Providence, RI (city) Providence County	5,234	2.94
Arlington, TX (city) Tarrant County	5,218	1.43
San Bernardino, CA (city) San Bernardino County	4,997	2.38
Reno, NV (city) Washoe County	4,938	2.19
Santa Ana, CA (city) Orange County	4,916	1.51
Kayenta, AZ (cdp) Navajo County	4,904	94.51
Fayetteville, NC (city) Cumberland County	4,901	2.44
Louisville-Jefferson County, KY (metro govt) Jefferson County	4,772	0.80
Anaheim, CA (city) Orange County	4,684	1.39
Bartlesville, OK (city) Washington County	4,649	13.00
Moore, OK (city) Cleveland County	4,642	8.43
Raleigh, NC (city) Wake County	4,541	1.12
Salem, OR (city) Marion County	4,503	2.91
Oxnard, CA (city) Ventura County	4,494	2.27
Fairbanks, AK (city) Fairbanks North Star Borough	4,415	14.00
Kirtland, NM (cdp) San Juan County	4,369	55.48
Eugene, OR (city) Lane County	4,346	2.78
Bethel, AK (city) Bethel Census Area	4,334	71.28
Claremore, OK (city) Rogers County	4,334	23.32
Great Falls, MT (city) Cascade County	4,326	7.39
Chinle, AZ (cdp) Apache County	4,190	92.74
Edmond, OK (city) Oklahoma County	4,095	5.03
Rio Rancho, NM (city) Sandoval County	4,066	4.65
Lincoln, NE (city) Lancaster County	4,061	1.57
Redding, CA (city) Shasta County	4,059	4.52
Midwest City, OK (city) Oklahoma County	4,057	7.46
Lawrence, KS (city) Douglas County	4,036	4.61
Whiteriver, AZ (cdp) Navajo County	4,022	98.00
Buffalo, NY (city) Erie County	4,019	1.54
Vancouver, WA (city) Clark County	4,013	2.48
Pueblo, CO (city) Pueblo County	4,012	3.76
Cleveland, OH (city) Cuyahoga County	4,008	1.01
Memphis, TN (city) Shelby County	3,991	0.62
San Carlos, AZ (cdp) Gila County	3,957	97.99
Topeka, KS (city) Shawnee County	3,938	3.09
Ada, OK (city) Pontotoc County	3,925	23.35
Florence, AZ (town) Pinal County	3,875	15.17
Anadarko, OK (city) Caddo County	3,860	57.08
Brookhaven, NY (town) Suffolk County	3,782	0.78
Salt Lake City, UT (city) Salt Lake County	3,760	2.02
Menominee, WI (town) Menominee County	3,754	88.71
Henderson, NV (city) Clark County	3,737	1.45
Staten Island, NY (borough) Richmond County	3,719	0.79
Paradise, NV (cdp) Clark County	3,652	1.64
Moreno Valley, CA (city) Riverside County	3,611	1.87
Norfolk, VA (ind. city) Norfolk independent city	3,594	1.48
Syracuse, NY (city) Onondaga County	3,537	2.44
Lakewood, CO (city) Jefferson County	3,523	2.46
Duluth, MN (city) St. Louis County	3,512	4.07
Ardmore, OK (city) Carter County	3,508	14.45
Corpus Christi, TX (city) Nueces County	3,499	1.15
Fort Defiance, AZ (cdp) Apache County	3,482	96.08
Fontana, CA (city) San Bernardino County	3,482	1.78
North Las Vegas, NV (city) Clark County	3,476	1.60
Greensboro, NC (city) Guilford County	3,454	1.28
Chula Vista, CA (city) San Diego County	3,421	1.40
Islip, NY (town) Suffolk County	3,396	1.01
Atlanta, GA (city) Fulton County	3,363	0.80
Toledo, OH (city) Lucas County	3,359	1.17
McAlester, OK (city) Pittsburg County	3,355	18.25
Bismarck, ND (city) Burleigh County	3,329	5.43
Grand Rapids, MI (city) Kent County	3,327	1.77
Sapulpa, OK (city) Creek County	3,318	16.15
Lancaster, CA (city) Los Angeles County	3,310	2.11
Owasso, OK (city) Tulsa County	3,291	11.38
Garland, TX (city) Dallas County	3,288	1.45
Ponca City, OK (city) Kay County	3,271	12.88
Newark, NJ (city) Essex County	3,258	1.18
Irving, TX (city) Dallas County	3,254	1.50
Pine Ridge, SD (cdp) Shannon County	3,251	98.28

SECTION THREE

Please refer to the Explanation of Data in the front of the book for more detailed information.

Race

American Indian/Alaska Native

Top 150 Places Sorted by Percent of Total Population

Based on all places, regardless of total population

Place	Population	%
Bitter Springs, AZ (cdp) Coconino County	452	100.00
Wounded Knee, SD (cdp) Shannon County	382	100.00
Del Muerto, AZ (cdp) Apache County	329	100.00
Turkey Creek, AZ (cdp) Navajo County	294	100.00
Nageezi, NM (cdp) San Juan County	286	100.00
Brimhall Nizhoni, NM (cdp) McKinley County	199	100.00
Gu Oidak, AZ (cdp) Pima County	188	100.00
Anegam, AZ (cdp) Pima County	151	100.00
Porcupine, ND (cdp) Sioux County	146	100.00
Cowlic, AZ (cdp) Pima County	135	100.00
Sehili, AZ (cdp) Apache County	135	100.00
Ali Chukson, AZ (cdp) Pima County	132	100.00
South Komelik, AZ (cdp) Pima County	111	100.00
Tselakai Dezza, UT (cdp) San Juan County	109	100.00
Corn Creek, SD (cdp) Mellette County	105	100.00
Haivana Nakya, AZ (cdp) Pima County	96	100.00
Pinehill, NM (cdp) Cibola County	88	100.00
Chiawuli Tak, AZ (cdp) Pima County	78	100.00
New Allakaket, AK (cdp) Yukon-Koyukuk Census Area	66	100.00
Oak Springs, AZ (cdp) Apache County	63	100.00
Ventana, AZ (cdp) Pima County	49	100.00
Tonawanda Reservation, NY (reservation) Erie County	34	100.00
Birch Creek, AK (cdp) Yukon-Koyukuk Census Area	33	100.00
Ak Chin, AZ (cdp) Pima County	30	100.00
Kohatk, AZ (cdp) Pinal County	27	100.00
Lupton, AZ (cdp) Apache County	25	100.00
Odanah, WI (cdp) Ashland County	13	100.00
Toyei, AZ (cdp) Apache County	13	100.00
Comobabi, AZ (cdp) Pima County	8	100.00
Ivanof Bay, AK (cdp) Lake and Peninsula Borough	7	100.00
Hoot Owl, OK (town) Mayes County	4	100.00
Criehaven, ME (unorganized territory) Knox County	1	100.00
Hobart Bay, AK (cdp) Hoonah-Angoon Census Area	1	100.00
Niles, MI (city) Cass County	1	100.00
Oil Springs Reservation, NY (reservation) Allegany County	1	100.00
Round Rock, AZ (cdp) Apache County	788	99.87
Low Mountain, AZ (cdp) Navajo County	756	99.87
Zia Pueblo, NM (cdp) Sandoval County	736	99.86
East Fork, AZ (cdp) Navajo County	698	99.86
Canyon Day, AZ (cdp) Gila County	1,207	99.83
Tonalea, AZ (cdp) Coconino County	548	99.82
Nazlini, AZ (cdp) Apache County	488	99.80
Dennehotso, AZ (cdp) Apache County	744	99.73
Sanostee, NM (cdp) San Juan County	370	99.73
Bullhead, SD (cdp) Corson County	347	99.71
Shongopovi, AZ (cdp) Navajo County	828	99.64
Bylas, AZ (cdp) Graham County	1,954	99.59
Lukachukai, AZ (cdp) Apache County	1,694	99.59
Little Rock, MN (cdp) Beltrami County	1,203	99.59
Sheep Springs, NM (cdp) San Juan County	244	99.59
San Felipe Pueblo, NM (cdp) Sandoval County	2,394	99.58
Seven Mile, AZ (cdp) Navajo County	704	99.58
Scammon Bay, AK (city) Wade Hampton Census Area	472	99.58
Cottonwood, AZ (cdp) Apache County	225	99.56
Kaibito, AZ (cdp) Coconino County	1,515	99.54
Twin Lakes, NM (cdp) McKinley County	1,047	99.52
Santo Domingo Pueblo, NM (cdp) Sandoval County	2,444	99.51
Rock Springs, NM (cdp) McKinley County	564	99.47
Napi Headquarters, NM (cdp) San Juan County	723	99.45
Chilchinbito, AZ (cdp) Navajo County	503	99.41
Parker School, MT (cdp) Hill County	338	99.41
Pisinemo, AZ (cdp) Pima County	319	99.38
Maish Vaya, AZ (cdp) Pima County	157	99.37
Oljato-Monument Valley, AZ (cdp) Navajo County	153	99.35
Naschitti, NM (cdp) San Juan County	299	99.34
Topawa, AZ (cdp) Pima County	297	99.33
Dilkon, AZ (cdp) Navajo County	1,176	99.32
Steamboat, AZ (cdp) Apache County	282	99.30
Tolani Lake, AZ (cdp) Coconino County	278	99.29
Kaka, AZ (cdp) Maricopa County	140	99.29
Rainbow City, AZ (cdp) Navajo County	961	99.28
Halchita, UT (cdp) San Juan County	264	99.25
Church Rock, NM (cdp) McKinley County	1,119	99.20
Sawmill, AZ (cdp) Apache County	742	99.20
Teec Nos Pos, AZ (cdp) Apache County	724	99.18
Soldier Creek, SD (cdp) Todd County	225	99.12
Peridot, AZ (cdp) Graham County	1,338	99.11
LeChee, AZ (cdp) Coconino County	1,430	99.10
Ojo Amarillo, NM (cdp) San Juan County	759	99.09
Moenkopi, AZ (cdp) Coconino County	955	99.07
Little Eagle, SD (cdp) Corson County	316	99.06
Jemez Pueblo, NM (cdp) Sandoval County	1,771	99.05
Allakaket, AK (city) Yukon-Koyukuk Census Area	104	99.05
South Acomita Village, NM (cdp) Cibola County	104	99.05
Crystal, NM (cdp) San Juan County	308	99.04
Supai, AZ (cdp) Coconino County	206	99.04
Ponemah, MN (cdp) Beltrami County	717	99.03
Zoar, WI (cdp) Menominee County	97	98.98
Porcupine, SD (cdp) Shannon County	1,051	98.96
Koyukuk, AK (city) Yukon-Koyukuk Census Area	95	98.96
Leupp, AZ (cdp) Coconino County	941	98.95
Nakaibito, NM (cdp) McKinley County	461	98.93
Middle Village, WI (cdp) Shawano County	278	98.93
Fort Totten, ND (cdp) Benson County	1,229	98.87
Red Rock, AZ (cdp) Apache County	167	98.82
Beaver, AK (cdp) Yukon-Koyukuk Census Area	83	98.81
Sweet Water Village, AZ (cdp) Pinal County	82	98.80
Whitecone, AZ (cdp) Navajo County	807	98.78
Skyline-Ganipa, NM (cdp) Cibola County	1,209	98.77
Klagetoh, AZ (cdp) Apache County	239	98.76
Tees Toh, AZ (cdp) Navajo County	442	98.66
Lower Red Lake, MN (unorganized territory) Beltrami County	5,712	98.65
South Browning, MT (cdp) Glacier County	1,760	98.60
East Dunseith, ND (cdp) Rolette County	493	98.60
Navajo Mountain, UT (cdp) San Juan County	349	98.59
St. Pierre, MT (cdp) Hill County	345	98.57
Diaperville, WI (cdp) Ashland County	69	98.57
Sacaton Flats Village, AZ (cdp) Pinal County	533	98.52
Red Lake, MN (cdp) Beltrami County	1,705	98.50
Laguna, NM (cdp) Cibola County	1,222	98.47
Heart Butte, MT (cdp) Pondera County	573	98.45
Vaiva Vo, AZ (cdp) Pinal County	126	98.44
Carrizo, AZ (cdp) Gila County	125	98.43
Komatke, AZ (cdp) Maricopa County	808	98.42
Boneau, MT (cdp) Chouteau County	374	98.42
Parmelee, SD (cdp) Todd County	553	98.40
Upper Fruitland, NM (cdp) San Juan County	1,635	98.38
Oglala, SD (cdp) Shannon County	1,269	98.37
Sangrey, MT (cdp) Hill County	301	98.37
Houck, AZ (cdp) Apache County	1,007	98.34
Macy, NE (cdp) Thurston County	1,006	98.34
Rocky Boy West, MT (cdp) Chouteau County	875	98.31
Pine Ridge, SD (cdp) Shannon County	3,251	98.28
Redby, MN (cdp) Beltrami County	1,311	98.28
Manderson-White Horse Creek, SD (cdp) Shannon County	615	98.24
Pilot Station, AK (city) Wade Hampton Census Area	558	98.24
First Mesa, AZ (cdp) Navajo County	1,527	98.20
Pitkas Point, AK (cdp) Wade Hampton Census Area	107	98.17
Shell Valley, ND (cdp) Rolette County	1,175	98.16
Chuichu, AZ (cdp) Pinal County	264	98.14
Ali Chuk, AZ (cdp) Pima County	158	98.14
Rock Point, AZ (cdp) Apache County	630	98.13
Lower Santan Village, AZ (cdp) Pinal County	367	98.13
Spring Creek, SD (cdp) Todd County	263	98.13
Charco, AZ (cdp) Pima County	51	98.08
Wanblee, SD (cdp) Jackson County	711	98.07
Zuni Pueblo, NM (cdp) McKinley County	6,180	98.06
Cornfields, AZ (cdp) Apache County	250	98.04
Shiprock, NM (cdp) San Juan County	8,131	98.02
Starr School, MT (cdp) Glacier County	247	98.02
Whiteriver, AZ (cdp) Navajo County	4,022	98.00
Aneth, UT (cdp) San Juan County	491	98.00
San Carlos, AZ (cdp) Gila County	3,957	97.99
Kipnuk, AK (cdp) Bethel Census Area	626	97.97
Crow Agency, MT (cdp) Big Horn County	1,583	97.96
Northway Village, AK (cdp) Southeast Fairbanks Census Area	96	97.96
Kongiganak, AK (cdp) Bethel Census Area	430	97.95
Fort McDermitt, NV (cdp) Humboldt County	334	97.95
Antelope, SD (cdp) Todd County	809	97.94
McCartys Village, NM (cdp) Cibola County	47	97.92

Please refer to the Explanation of Data in the front of the book for more detailed information.

Race

American Indian/Alaska Native

Top 150 Places Sorted by Percent of Total Population

Based on places with total population of 7,500 or more

Place	Population	%
Shiprock, NM (cdp) San Juan County	8,131	98.02
Tuba City, AZ (cdp) Coconino County	8,089	93.94
Kirtland, NM (cdp) San Juan County	4,369	55.48
Gallup, NM (city) McKinley County	10,343	47.71
Tahlequah, OK (city) Cherokee County	5,971	37.90
Sallisaw, OK (city) Sequoyah County	2,804	31.58
Winslow, AZ (city) Navajo County	2,788	28.88
Okmulgee, OK (city) Okmulgee County	3,142	25.50
Sitka, AK (borough) Sitka City and Borough	2,184	24.59
Ketchikan, AK (city) Ketchikan Gateway Borough	1,977	24.56
Farmington, NM (city) San Juan County	11,230	24.48
Miami, OK (city) Ottawa County	3,246	23.92
Pryor Creek, OK (city) Mayes County	2,275	23.85
Wagoner, OK (city) Wagoner County	1,955	23.49
Ada, OK (city) Pontotoc County	3,925	23.35
Claremore, OK (city) Rogers County	4,334	23.32
Sault Ste. Marie, MI (city) Chippewa County	3,167	22.39
Muskogee, OK (city) Muskogee County	8,610	21.95
Glenpool, OK (city) Tulsa County	2,210	20.45
Bloomfield, NM (city) San Juan County	1,644	20.27
Juneau, AK (borough) Juneau City and Borough	6,005	19.20
Shawnee, OK (city) Pottawatomie County	5,732	19.20
Durant, OK (city) Bryan County	2,975	18.76
Grants, NM (city) Cibola County	1,710	18.62
McAlester, OK (city) Pittsburg County	3,355	18.25
Coweta, OK (city) Wagoner County	1,788	17.98
Poteau, OK (city) Le Flore County	1,401	16.44
Sapulpa, OK (city) Creek County	3,318	16.15
Havre, MT (city) Hill County	1,489	15.99
Rapid City, SD (city) Pennington County	10,337	15.21
Florence, AZ (town) Pinal County	3,875	15.17
Shawano, WI (city) Shawano County	1,376	14.79
Bemidji, MN (city) Beltrami County	1,983	14.76
Lumberton, NC (city) Robeson County	3,178	14.75
Ardmore, OK (city) Carter County	3,508	14.45
El Reno, OK (city) Canadian County	2,385	14.24
Kinross, MI (charter township) Chippewa County	1,077	14.24
College, AK (cdp) Fairbanks North Star Borough	1,838	14.18
Fairbanks, AK (city) Fairbanks North Star Borough	4,415	14.00
Cortez, CO (city) Montezuma County	1,157	13.64
Cloquet, MN (city) Carlton County	1,649	13.60
Sand Springs, OK (city) Tulsa County	2,512	13.29
Flagstaff, AZ (city) Coconino County	8,642	13.12
Bartlesville, OK (city) Washington County	4,649	13.00
Ponca City, OK (city) Kay County	3,271	12.88
Riverton, WY (city) Fremont County	1,362	12.83
Pierre, SD (city) Hughes County	1,737	12.73
Cushing, OK (city) Payne County	968	12.37
Anchorage, AK (municipality) Anchorage Municipality	36,062	12.36
Owasso, OK (city) Tulsa County	3,291	11.38
Ashland, WI (city) Ashland County	898	10.93
Newcastle, OK (city) McClain County	833	10.84
Yreka, CA (city) Siskiyou County	813	10.47
Knik-Fairview, AK (cdp) Matanuska-Susitna Borough	1,541	10.33
Meadow Lakes, AK (cdp) Matanuska-Susitna Borough	777	10.26
Lakes, AK (cdp) Matanuska-Susitna Borough	837	10.01
Camp Verde, AZ (town) Yavapai County	1,059	9.74
Toppenish, WA (city) Yakima County	859	9.60
Wasilla, AK (city) Matanuska-Susitna Borough	752	9.60
Bixby, OK (city) Tulsa County	1,988	9.52
Clinton, OK (city) Custer County	857	9.49
Coffeyville, KS (city) Montgomery County	975	9.47
Tulsa, OK (city) Tulsa County	35,990	9.18
Jenks, OK (city) Tulsa County	1,522	8.99
Kalifornsky, AK (cdp) Kenai Peninsula Borough	703	8.96
Choctaw, OK (city) Oklahoma County	994	8.92
Broken Arrow, OK (city) Tulsa County	8,786	8.89
Tanaina, AK (cdp) Matanuska-Susitna Borough	722	8.81
Blanchard, OK (city) McClain County	664	8.66
Chickasha, OK (city) Grady County	1,382	8.62
Del City, OK (city) Oklahoma County	1,824	8.55
Moore, OK (city) Cleveland County	4,642	8.43
Badger, AK (cdp) Fairbanks North Star Borough	1,628	8.36
Oroville East, CA (cdp) Butte County	689	8.32
Weatherford, OK (city) Custer County	891	8.22
Norman, OK (city) Cleveland County	8,972	8.09
Duncan, OK (city) Stephens County	1,873	7.99
Siloam Springs, AR (city) Benton County	1,200	7.98
Durango, CO (city) La Plata County	1,324	7.84
Anderson, CA (city) Shasta County	775	7.80
McKinleyville, CA (cdp) Humboldt County	1,162	7.66
Coolidge, AZ (city) Pinal County	887	7.50
Laurinburg, NC (city) Scotland County	1,195	7.49
Midwest City, OK (city) Oklahoma County	4,057	7.46
Great Falls, MT (city) Cascade County	4,326	7.39
Lawton, OK (city) Comanche County	7,008	7.23
Shasta Lake, CA (city) Shasta County	728	7.16
Galliano, LA (cdp) Lafourche Parish	549	7.15
Klamath Falls, OR (city) Klamath County	1,486	7.13
Stillwater, OK (city) Payne County	3,213	7.03
Eureka, CA (city) Humboldt County	1,904	7.00
Bayou Blue, LA (cdp) Lafourche Parish	860	6.96
Globe, AZ (city) Gila County	519	6.89
Drexel Heights, AZ (cdp) Pima County	1,890	6.81
Box Elder, SD (city) Pennington County	531	6.81
Lake Worth, FL (city) Palm Beach County	2,346	6.72
Oroville, CA (city) Butte County	1,041	6.70
Crescent City, CA (city) Del Norte County	509	6.66
Mustang, OK (city) Canadian County	1,145	6.58
Guthrie, OK (city) Logan County	670	6.57
Detroit Lakes, MN (city) Becker County	562	6.56
Rapid Valley, SD (cdp) Pennington County	542	6.56
Hoquiam, WA (city) Grays Harbor County	568	6.51
Fortuna, CA (city) Humboldt County	770	6.46
Ukiah, CA (city) Mendocino County	1,028	6.40
Casa Grande, AZ (city) Pinal County	3,077	6.34
Oklahoma City, OK (city) Oklahoma County	36,572	6.31
The Village, OK (city) Oklahoma County	557	6.24
Mandan, ND (city) Morton County	1,123	6.13
Alliance, NE (city) Box Butte County	518	6.10
Shelton, WA (city) Mason County	599	6.09
Altamont, OR (cdp) Klamath County	1,170	6.08
Greenfield, CA (city) Monterey County	989	6.06
Clearlake, CA (city) Lake County	923	6.05
Olivehurst, CA (cdp) Yuba County	824	6.03
Yukon, OK (city) Canadian County	1,362	6.00
Aberdeen, WA (city) Grays Harbor County	1,010	5.98
Albuquerque, NM (city) Bernalillo County	32,571	5.97
Billings, MT (city) Yellowstone County	6,222	5.97
Bernalillo, NM (town) Sandoval County	486	5.84
Port Angeles, WA (city) Clallam County	1,096	5.76
Warr Acres, OK (city) Oklahoma County	577	5.75
Bethany, OK (city) Oklahoma County	1,079	5.66
Lincoln City, OR (city) Lincoln County	448	5.65
Coos Bay, OR (city) Coos County	899	5.63
Elk City, OK (city) Beckham County	658	5.63
Red Bluff, CA (city) Tehama County	788	5.60
Williston, ND (city) Williams County	817	5.55
Show Low, AZ (city) Navajo County	589	5.53
Bismarck, ND (city) Burleigh County	3,329	5.43
Green Bay, WI (city) Brown County	5,599	5.38
Valencia West, AZ (cdp) Pima County	501	5.36
Marysville, CA (city) Yuba County	643	5.33
North Bend, OR (city) Coos County	516	5.32
Arcata, CA (city) Humboldt County	889	5.16
Massena, NY (town) St. Lawrence County	664	5.15
Helena Valley Southeast, MT (cdp) Lewis and Clark County	421	5.12
Linda, CA (cdp) Yuba County	903	5.08
Alamosa, CO (city) Alamosa County	446	5.08
Arkansas City, KS (city) Cowley County	630	5.07
Socorro, NM (city) Socorro County	456	5.04
Edmond, OK (city) Oklahoma County	4,095	5.03
Pendleton, OR (city) Umatilla County	833	5.01
Houma, LA (city) Terrebonne Parish	1,663	4.93
Fallon, NV (city) Churchill County	424	4.93
Arizona City, AZ (cdp) Pinal County	510	4.87
Hawaiian Paradise Park, HI (cdp) Hawaii County	554	4.86
Fife, WA (city) Pierce County	442	4.82
Midland, WA (cdp) Pierce County	432	4.82
Vermillion, SD (city) Clay County	507	4.80

Please refer to the Explanation of Data in the front of the book for more detailed information.

Race

American Indian/Alaska Native: Not Hispanic

U.S. and 50 States Sorted by Population and Percent of Total Population

Place	Population	%
United States	**4,029,675**	**1.31**
Oklahoma	459,178	12.24
California	383,957	1.03
Arizona	294,027	4.60
New Mexico	190,050	9.23
Texas	178,127	0.71
Washington	168,849	2.51
North Carolina	162,311	1.70
Alaska	133,387	18.78
New York	128,049	0.66
Michigan	123,267	1.25
Florida	118,469	0.63
Minnesota	90,505	1.71
Oregon	89,776	2.34
Ohio	79,872	0.69
South Dakota	78,770	9.67
Wisconsin	75,495	1.33
Montana	74,452	7.52
Missouri	65,131	1.09
Georgia	64,925	0.67
Colorado	63,963	1.27
Virginia	62,978	0.79
Pennsylvania	62,066	0.49
Illinois	60,948	0.48
Alabama	52,863	1.11
Kansas	49,659	1.74
Louisiana	49,593	1.09
Tennessee	47,888	0.75
Maryland	45,047	0.78
Arkansas	43,527	1.49
North Dakota	41,470	6.17
Indiana	41,469	0.64
Nevada	40,994	1.52
New Jersey	40,487	0.46
Utah	39,575	1.43
South Carolina	36,942	0.80
Massachusetts	35,635	0.54
Idaho	29,445	1.88
Kentucky	28,170	0.65
Nebraska	23,945	1.31
Mississippi	23,657	0.80
Hawaii	22,895	1.68
Connecticut	22,203	0.62
Iowa	19,863	0.65
Maine	17,654	1.33
Wyoming	15,988	2.84
West Virginia	12,539	0.68
Rhode Island	10,580	1.01
New Hampshire	9,527	0.72
Delaware	7,679	0.86
Vermont	6,897	1.10
District of Columbia	4,932	0.82

Place	Population	%
Alaska	133,387	18.78
Oklahoma	459,178	12.24
South Dakota	78,770	9.67
New Mexico	190,050	9.23
Montana	74,452	7.52
North Dakota	41,470	6.17
Arizona	294,027	4.60
Wyoming	15,988	2.84
Washington	168,849	2.51
Oregon	89,776	2.34
Idaho	29,445	1.88
Kansas	49,659	1.74
Minnesota	90,505	1.71
North Carolina	162,311	1.70
Hawaii	22,895	1.68
Nevada	40,994	1.52
Arkansas	43,527	1.49
Utah	39,575	1.43
Wisconsin	75,495	1.33
Maine	17,654	1.33
United States	**4,029,675**	**1.31**
Nebraska	23,945	1.31
Colorado	63,963	1.27
Michigan	123,267	1.25
Alabama	52,863	1.11
Vermont	6,897	1.10
Missouri	65,131	1.09
Louisiana	49,593	1.09
California	383,957	1.03
Rhode Island	10,580	1.01
Delaware	7,679	0.86
District of Columbia	4,932	0.82
South Carolina	36,942	0.80
Mississippi	23,657	0.80
Virginia	62,978	0.79
Maryland	45,047	0.78
Tennessee	47,888	0.75
New Hampshire	9,527	0.72
Texas	178,127	0.71
Ohio	79,872	0.69
West Virginia	12,539	0.68
Georgia	64,925	0.67
New York	128,049	0.66
Kentucky	28,170	0.65
Iowa	19,863	0.65
Indiana	41,469	0.64
Florida	118,469	0.63
Connecticut	22,203	0.62
Massachusetts	35,635	0.54
Pennsylvania	62,066	0.49
Illinois	60,948	0.48
New Jersey	40,487	0.46

Please refer to the Explanation of Data in the front of the book for more detailed information.

Race

American Indian/Alaska Native: Not Hispanic

Top 150 Places Sorted by Population

Based on all places, regardless of total population

Place	Population	%
New York, NY (city) Kings County	44,541	0.54
Anchorage, AK (municipality) Anchorage Municipality	33,633	11.53
Tulsa, OK (city) Tulsa County	33,420	8.53
Oklahoma City, OK (city) Oklahoma County	32,292	5.57
Phoenix, AZ (city) Maricopa County	30,204	2.09
Albuquerque, NM (city) Bernalillo County	24,591	4.51
Los Angeles, CA (city) Los Angeles County	19,510	0.51
Queens, NY (borough) Queens County	15,412	0.69
Chicago, IL (city) Cook County	12,449	0.46
Brooklyn, NY (borough) Kings County	12,062	0.48
Tucson, AZ (city) Pima County	11,821	2.27
Philadelphia, PA (city) Philadelphia County	11,409	0.75
Portland, OR (city) Multnomah County	11,163	1.91
Mesa, AZ (city) Maricopa County	10,820	2.46
Minneapolis, MN (city) Hennepin County	10,662	2.79
Farmington, NM (city) San Juan County	10,561	23.02
Seattle, WA (city) King County	10,346	1.70
San Diego, CA (city) San Diego County	10,117	0.77
Rapid City, SD (city) Pennington County	9,470	13.94
Gallup, NM (city) McKinley County	9,235	42.60
Houston, TX (city) Harris County	8,735	0.42
Norman, OK (city) Cleveland County	8,455	7.62
Broken Arrow, OK (city) Tulsa County	8,336	8.43
Muskogee, OK (city) Muskogee County	8,314	21.20
Shiprock, NM (cdp) San Juan County	8,018	96.66
Wichita, KS (city) Sedgwick County	7,993	2.09
Flagstaff, AZ (city) Coconino County	7,922	12.03
Tuba City, AZ (cdp) Coconino County	7,889	91.62
Sacramento, CA (city) Sacramento County	7,885	1.69
Bronx, NY (borough) Bronx County	7,638	0.55
Denver, CO (city) Denver County	7,399	1.23
Manhattan, NY (borough) New York County	7,395	0.47
Columbus, OH (city) Franklin County	7,286	0.93
Milwaukee, WI (city) Milwaukee County	7,226	1.21
Dallas, TX (city) Dallas County	7,020	0.59
Jacksonville, FL (city) Duval County	7,014	0.85
Detroit, MI (city) Wayne County	6,965	0.98
Spokane, WA (city) Spokane County	6,894	3.30
San Antonio, TX (city) Medina County	6,483	0.49
Tacoma, WA (city) Pierce County	6,404	3.23
Colorado Springs, CO (city) El Paso County	6,248	1.50
Fresno, CA (city) Fresno County	6,241	1.26
San Francisco, CA (city) San Francisco County	6,241	0.78
San Jose, CA (city) Santa Clara County	6,164	0.65
Charlotte, NC (city) Mecklenburg County	6,096	0.83
Zuni Pueblo, NM (cdp) McKinley County	6,056	96.10
Lawton, OK (city) Comanche County	6,037	6.23
Indianapolis, IN (city) Marion County	5,844	0.71
Fort Worth, TX (city) Tarrant County	5,723	0.77
Las Vegas, NV (city) Clark County	5,708	0.98
Tahlequah, OK (city) Cherokee County	5,707	36.23
Juneau, AK (borough) Juneau City and Borough	5,656	18.08
Lower Red Lake, MN (unorganized territory) Beltrami County	5,644	97.48
Kansas City, MO (city) Jackson County	5,584	1.21
Billings, MT (city) Yellowstone County	5,562	5.34
Austin, TX (city) Travis County	5,512	0.70
Shawnee, OK (city) Pottawatomie County	5,373	18.00
Baltimore, MD (city) Baltimore city County	5,370	0.86
St. Paul, MN (city) Ramsey County	5,276	1.85
Sioux Falls, SD (city) Minnehaha County	5,118	3.33
Washington, DC (city) District of Columbia	4,932	0.82
Tempe, AZ (city) Maricopa County	4,865	3.01
Green Bay, WI (city) Brown County	4,837	4.65
Kayenta, AZ (cdp) Navajo County	4,830	93.08
Omaha, NE (city) Douglas County	4,830	1.18
Oakland, CA (city) Alameda County	4,795	1.23
Bakersfield, CA (city) Kern County	4,742	1.36
Virginia Beach, VA (ind. city) Virginia Beach independent city	4,456	1.02
Bartlesville, OK (city) Washington County	4,422	12.37
Bethel, AK (city) Bethel Census Area	4,286	70.49
Moore, OK (city) Cleveland County	4,265	7.74
Louisville-Jefferson County, KY (metro govt) Jefferson County	4,242	0.71
Claremore, OK (city) Rogers County	4,241	22.82
Fairbanks, AK (city) Fairbanks North Star Borough	4,228	13.41
Nashville-Davidson, TN (metro govt) Davidson County	4,219	0.70
Kirtland, NM (cdp) San Juan County	4,181	53.09
Fayetteville, NC (city) Cumberland County	4,180	2.08
Urban Honolulu, HI (cdp) Honolulu County	4,154	1.23
Boston, MA (city) Suffolk County	4,135	0.67
Aurora, CO (city) Arapahoe County	4,127	1.27
Chinle, AZ (cdp) Apache County	4,111	90.99
Long Beach, CA (city) Los Angeles County	4,002	0.87
Great Falls, MT (city) Cascade County	3,999	6.84
Whiteriver, AZ (cdp) Navajo County	3,968	96.69
Glendale, AZ (city) Maricopa County	3,928	1.73
Edmond, OK (city) Oklahoma County	3,879	4.77
San Carlos, AZ (cdp) Gila County	3,855	95.47
Stockton, CA (city) San Joaquin County	3,819	1.31
Chandler, AZ (city) Maricopa County	3,806	1.61
Ada, OK (city) Pontotoc County	3,771	22.43
Midwest City, OK (city) Oklahoma County	3,767	6.93
Florence, AZ (town) Pinal County	3,717	14.56
Reno, NV (city) Washoe County	3,593	1.60
Menominee, WI (town) Menominee County	3,586	84.74
Lawrence, KS (city) Douglas County	3,562	4.06
Eugene, OR (city) Lane County	3,517	2.25
Salem, OR (city) Marion County	3,487	2.25
Anadarko, OK (city) Caddo County	3,417	50.53
Fort Defiance, AZ (cdp) Apache County	3,413	94.18
Redding, CA (city) Shasta County	3,383	3.76
Memphis, TN (city) Shelby County	3,357	0.52
Ardmore, OK (city) Carter County	3,323	13.68
Duluth, MN (city) St. Louis County	3,301	3.83
Arlington, TX (city) Tarrant County	3,262	0.89
Vancouver, WA (city) Clark County	3,236	2.00
Buffalo, NY (city) Erie County	3,229	1.24
Santa Rosa, CA (city) Sonoma County	3,221	1.92
Lincoln, NE (city) Lancaster County	3,215	1.24
Sapulpa, OK (city) Creek County	3,210	15.63
Cleveland, OH (city) Cuyahoga County	3,202	0.81
Bismarck, ND (city) Burleigh County	3,195	5.21
Pine Ridge, SD (cdp) Shannon County	3,190	96.43
Owasso, OK (city) Tulsa County	3,164	10.94
Miami, OK (city) Ottawa County	3,163	23.31
McAlester, OK (city) Pittsburg County	3,159	17.18
Sault Ste. Marie, MI (city) Chippewa County	3,137	22.18
St. Regis Mohawk Reservation, NY (reservation) Franklin County	3,116	96.53
Topeka, KS (city) Shawnee County	3,082	2.42
Modesto, CA (city) Stanislaus County	3,080	1.53
Lumberton, NC (city) Robeson County	3,076	14.28
Stillwater, OK (city) Payne County	3,068	6.72
Syracuse, NY (city) Onondaga County	3,067	2.11
Providence, RI (city) Providence County	3,066	1.72
Ponca City, OK (city) Kay County	3,037	11.96
Okmulgee, OK (city) Okmulgee County	3,027	24.57
Pearl River, MS (cdp) Neshoba County	3,017	83.78
Raleigh, NC (city) Wake County	3,015	0.75
Norfolk, VA (ind. city) Norfolk independent city	2,967	1.22
Rio Rancho, NM (city) Sandoval County	2,935	3.35
Greensboro, NC (city) Guilford County	2,892	1.07
Riverside, CA (city) Riverside County	2,862	0.94
Durant, OK (city) Bryan County	2,860	18.04
Barrow, AK (city) North Slope Borough	2,840	67.43
Hempstead, NY (town) Nassau County	2,835	0.37
Springfield, MO (city) Christian County	2,817	1.77
Atlanta, GA (city) Fulton County	2,814	0.67
St. Louis, MO (city) St. Louis city County	2,760	0.86
Fort Smith, AR (city) Sebastian County	2,727	3.16
Henderson, NV (city) Clark County	2,708	1.05
Sallisaw, OK (city) Sequoyah County	2,705	30.46
El Paso, TX (city) El Paso County	2,702	0.42
Toledo, OH (city) Lucas County	2,675	0.93
Page, AZ (city) Coconino County	2,658	36.68
Warm Springs, OR (cdp) Jefferson County	2,617	88.86
Brookhaven, NY (town) Suffolk County	2,586	0.53
Window Rock, AZ (cdp) Apache County	2,575	94.95
Kotzebue, AK (city) Northwest Arctic Borough	2,571	80.32
Missoula, MT (city) Missoula County	2,533	3.79
Salt Lake City, UT (city) Salt Lake County	2,529	1.36
Boise City, ID (city) Ada County	2,502	1.22

SECTION THREE

Please refer to the Explanation of Data in the front of the book for more detailed information.

Race

American Indian/Alaska Native: Not Hispanic

Top 150 Places Sorted by Percent of Total Population

Based on all places, regardless of total population

Place	Population	%
Cowlic, AZ (cdp) Pima County	135	100.00
Corn Creek, SD (cdp) Mellette County	105	100.00
New Allakaket, AK (cdp) Yukon-Koyukuk Census Area	66	100.00
Tonawanda Reservation, NY (reservation) Erie County	34	100.00
Birch Creek, AK (cdp) Yukon-Koyukuk Census Area	33	100.00
Lupton, AZ (cdp) Apache County	25	100.00
Toyei, AZ (cdp) Apache County	13	100.00
Comobabi, AZ (cdp) Pima County	8	100.00
Ivanof Bay, AK (cdp) Lake and Peninsula Borough	7	100.00
Hoot Owl, OK (town) Mayes County	4	100.00
Criehaven, ME (unorganized territory) Knox County	1	100.00
Hobart Bay, AK (cdp) Hoonah-Angoon Census Area	1	100.00
Niles, MI (city) Cass County	1	100.00
Oil Springs Reservation, NY (reservation) Allegany County	1	100.00
Scammon Bay, AK (city) Wade Hampton Census Area	472	99.58
Cottonwood, AZ (cdp) Apache County	225	99.56
Parker School, MT (cdp) Hill County	338	99.41
Maish Vaya, AZ (cdp) Pima County	157	99.37
Ali Chukson, AZ (cdp) Pima County	131	99.24
Low Mountain, AZ (cdp) Navajo County	751	99.21
Sanostee, NM (cdp) San Juan County	368	99.19
Bitter Springs, AZ (cdp) Coconino County	448	99.12
Allakaket, AK (city) Yukon-Koyukuk Census Area	104	99.05
San Felipe Pueblo, NM (cdp) Sandoval County	2,380	99.00
Nazlini, AZ (cdp) Apache County	484	98.98
Zoar, WI (cdp) Menominee County	97	98.98
Haivana Nakya, AZ (cdp) Pima County	95	98.96
Koyukuk, AK (city) Yukon-Koyukuk Census Area	95	98.96
Rainbow City, AZ (cdp) Navajo County	957	98.86
Del Muerto, AZ (cdp) Apache County	325	98.78
Sheep Springs, NM (cdp) San Juan County	242	98.78
Ponemah, MN (cdp) Beltrami County	715	98.76
Tonalea, AZ (cdp) Coconino County	542	98.72
Crystal, NM (cdp) San Juan County	307	98.71
Santo Domingo Pueblo, NM (cdp) Sandoval County	2,424	98.70
Canyon Day, AZ (cdp) Gila County	1,193	98.68
Turkey Creek, AZ (cdp) Navajo County	290	98.64
Navajo Mountain, UT (cdp) San Juan County	349	98.59
Twin Lakes, NM (cdp) McKinley County	1,037	98.57
Jemez Pueblo, NM (cdp) Sandoval County	1,762	98.55
Peridot, AZ (cdp) Graham County	1,330	98.52
Sehili, AZ (cdp) Apache County	133	98.52
Round Rock, AZ (cdp) Apache County	777	98.48
Shongopovi, AZ (cdp) Navajo County	818	98.44
Vaiva Vo, AZ (cdp) Pinal County	126	98.44
Rock Springs, NM (cdp) McKinley County	558	98.41
Sawmill, AZ (cdp) Apache County	735	98.26
Pilot Station, AK (city) Wade Hampton Census Area	558	98.24
Chilchinbito, AZ (cdp) Navajo County	497	98.22
Red Rock, AZ (cdp) Apache County	166	98.22
Wounded Knee, SD (cdp) Shannon County	375	98.17
Pitkas Point, AK (cdp) Wade Hampton Census Area	107	98.17
Tselakai Dezza, UT (cdp) San Juan County	107	98.17
Kaibito, AZ (cdp) Coconino County	1,494	98.16
Fort Totten, ND (cdp) Benson County	1,220	98.15
Dilkon, AZ (cdp) Navajo County	1,162	98.14
Halchita, UT (cdp) San Juan County	261	98.12
Parmelee, SD (cdp) Todd County	551	98.04
Shell Valley, ND (cdp) Rolette County	1,173	97.99
Kipnuk, AK (cdp) Bethel Census Area	626	97.97
Northway Village, AK (cdp) Southeast Fairbanks Census Area	96	97.96
Little Rock, MN (cdp) Beltrami County	1,183	97.93
Klagetoh, AZ (cdp) Apache County	237	97.93
Hooper Bay, AK (city) Wade Hampton Census Area	1,070	97.90
Seven Mile, AZ (cdp) Navajo County	692	97.88
Kivalina, AK (city) Northwest Arctic Borough	366	97.86
Zia Pueblo, NM (cdp) Sandoval County	721	97.83
Atmautluak, AK (cdp) Bethel Census Area	271	97.83
Lukachukai, AZ (cdp) Apache County	1,664	97.82
Moenkopi, AZ (cdp) Coconino County	943	97.82
Teec Nos Pos, AZ (cdp) Apache County	714	97.81
Beclabito, NM (cdp) San Juan County	310	97.79
Bullhead, SD (cdp) Corson County	340	97.70
Cornfields, AZ (cdp) Apache County	249	97.65
Carrizo, AZ (cdp) Gila County	124	97.64
Red Lake, MN (cdp) Beltrami County	1,690	97.63
Nunapitchuk, AK (city) Bethel Census Area	484	97.58
Kotlik, AK (city) Wade Hampton Census Area	563	97.57
Kwethluk, AK (city) Bethel Census Area	703	97.50
Alakanuk, AK (city) Wade Hampton Census Area	660	97.49
Brimhall Nizhoni, NM (cdp) McKinley County	194	97.49
Lower Red Lake, MN (unorganized territory) Beltrami County	5,644	97.48
Chiawuli Tak, AZ (cdp) Pima County	76	97.44
First Mesa, AZ (cdp) Navajo County	1,515	97.43
St. Pierre, MT (cdp) Hill County	341	97.43
Aneth, UT (cdp) San Juan County	488	97.41
Skyline-Ganipa, NM (cdp) Cibola County	1,192	97.39
LeChee, AZ (cdp) Coconino County	1,405	97.37
Buckland, AK (city) Northwest Arctic Borough	405	97.36
Soldier Creek, SD (cdp) Todd County	221	97.36
Dennehotso, AZ (cdp) Apache County	726	97.32
Topawa, AZ (cdp) Pima County	291	97.32
Twin Hills, AK (cdp) Dillingham Census Area	72	97.30
Alatna, AK (cdp) Yukon-Koyukuk Census Area	36	97.30
East Fork, AZ (cdp) Navajo County	680	97.28
Antelope, SD (cdp) Todd County	803	97.22
East Dunseith, ND (cdp) Rolette County	486	97.20
Porcupine, SD (cdp) Shannon County	1,032	97.18
Napakiak, AK (city) Bethel Census Area	344	97.18
Lower Kalskag, AK (city) Bethel Census Area	274	97.16
South Acomita Village, NM (cdp) Cibola County	102	97.14
Chevak, AK (city) Wade Hampton Census Area	911	97.12
Marshall, AK (city) Wade Hampton Census Area	402	97.10
Noatak, AK (cdp) Northwest Arctic Borough	499	97.08
Birney, MT (cdp) Rosebud County	133	97.08
Tuntutuliak, AK (cdp) Bethel Census Area	396	97.06
Napaskiak, AK (city) Bethel Census Area	393	97.04
Naschitti, NM (cdp) San Juan County	292	97.01
Crow Agency, MT (cdp) Big Horn County	1,567	96.97
Napi Headquarters, NM (cdp) San Juan County	705	96.97
Leupp, AZ (cdp) Coconino County	922	96.95
Quinhagak, AK (city) Bethel Census Area	648	96.86
Mekoryuk, AK (city) Bethel Census Area	185	96.86
Redby, MN (cdp) Beltrami County	1,292	96.85
Bylas, AZ (cdp) Graham County	1,900	96.84
Oak Springs, AZ (cdp) Apache County	61	96.83
Russian Mission, AK (city) Wade Hampton Census Area	302	96.79
Tolani Lake, AZ (cdp) Coconino County	271	96.79
Houck, AZ (cdp) Apache County	991	96.78
South Browning, MT (cdp) Glacier County	1,727	96.75
Rock Point, AZ (cdp) Apache County	621	96.73
Emmonak, AK (city) Wade Hampton Census Area	737	96.72
Whiteriver, AZ (cdp) Navajo County	3,968	96.69
Ak Chin, AZ (cdp) Pima County	29	96.67
Shiprock, NM (cdp) San Juan County	8,018	96.66
Kasigluk, AK (cdp) Bethel Census Area	550	96.66
Koliganek, AK (cdp) Dillingham Census Area	202	96.65
Eek, AK (city) Bethel Census Area	286	96.62
Newtok, AK (cdp) Bethel Census Area	342	96.61
Porcupine, ND (cdp) Sioux County	141	96.58
Kwigillingok, AK (cdp) Bethel Census Area	310	96.57
Lime Village, AK (cdp) Bethel Census Area	28	96.55
St. Regis Mohawk Reservation, NY (reservation) Franklin County	3,116	96.53
Oglala, SD (cdp) Shannon County	1,245	96.51
Macy, NE (cdp) Thurston County	987	96.48
Anvik, AK (city) Yukon-Koyukuk Census Area	82	96.47
Pine Ridge, SD (cdp) Shannon County	3,190	96.43
Tees Toh, AZ (cdp) Navajo County	432	96.43
Starr School, MT (cdp) Glacier County	243	96.43
Chefornak, AK (city) Bethel Census Area	403	96.41
Shaktoolik, AK (city) Nome Census Area	242	96.41
Shageluk, AK (city) Yukon-Koyukuk Census Area	80	96.39
Nakaibito, NM (cdp) McKinley County	449	96.35
Anzac Village, NM (cdp) Cibola County	52	96.30
Gu Oidak, AZ (cdp) Pima County	181	96.28
Marty, SD (cdp) Charles Mix County	387	96.27
Spring Creek, SD (cdp) Todd County	258	96.27
St. Mary's, AK (city) Wade Hampton Census Area	488	96.25
Little Eagle, SD (cdp) Corson County	307	96.24
Manokotak, AK (city) Dillingham Census Area	425	96.15

Please refer to the Explanation of Data in the front of the book for more detailed information.

Race

American Indian/Alaska Native: Not Hispanic

Top 150 Places Sorted by Percent of Total Population

Based on places with total population of 7,500 or more

Place	Population	%
Shiprock, NM (cdp) San Juan County	8,018	96.66
Tuba City, AZ (cdp) Coconino County	7,889	91.62
Kirtland, NM (cdp) San Juan County	4,181	53.09
Gallup, NM (city) McKinley County	9,235	42.60
Tahlequah, OK (city) Cherokee County	5,707	36.23
Sallisaw, OK (city) Sequoyah County	2,705	30.46
Winslow, AZ (city) Navajo County	2,499	25.88
Okmulgee, OK (city) Okmulgee County	3,027	24.57
Miami, OK (city) Ottawa County	3,163	23.31
Sitka, AK (borough) Sitka City and Borough	2,070	23.31
Ketchikan, AK (city) Ketchikan Gateway Borough	1,872	23.25
Pryor Creek, OK (city) Mayes County	2,207	23.14
Wagoner, OK (city) Wagoner County	1,919	23.06
Farmington, NM (city) San Juan County	10,561	23.02
Claremore, OK (city) Rogers County	4,241	22.82
Ada, OK (city) Pontotoc County	3,771	22.43
Sault Ste. Marie, MI (city) Chippewa County	3,137	22.18
Muskogee, OK (city) Muskogee County	8,314	21.20
Glenpool, OK (city) Tulsa County	2,137	19.77
Bloomfield, NM (city) San Juan County	1,522	18.76
Juneau, AK (borough) Juneau City and Borough	5,656	18.08
Durant, OK (city) Bryan County	2,860	18.04
Shawnee, OK (city) Pottawatomie County	5,373	18.00
Coweta, OK (city) Wagoner County	1,744	17.54
McAlester, OK (city) Pittsburg County	3,159	17.18
Grants, NM (city) Cibola County	1,497	16.30
Poteau, OK (city) Le Flore County	1,354	15.89
Sapulpa, OK (city) Creek County	3,210	15.63
Havre, MT (city) Hill County	1,401	15.05
Florence, AZ (town) Pinal County	3,717	14.56
Lumberton, NC (city) Robeson County	3,076	14.28
Bemidji, MN (city) Beltrami County	1,895	14.11
Rapid City, SD (city) Pennington County	9,470	13.94
Shawano, WI (city) Shawano County	1,291	13.87
Kinross, MI (charter township) Chippewa County	1,044	13.81
Ardmore, OK (city) Carter County	3,323	13.68
College, AK (cdp) Fairbanks North Star Borough	1,766	13.62
Fairbanks, AK (city) Fairbanks North Star Borough	4,228	13.41
Cloquet, MN (city) Carlton County	1,592	13.13
El Reno, OK (city) Canadian County	2,162	12.91
Sand Springs, OK (city) Tulsa County	2,420	12.80
Bartlesville, OK (city) Washington County	4,422	12.37
Pierre, SD (city) Hughes County	1,656	12.14
Flagstaff, AZ (city) Coconino County	7,922	12.03
Ponca City, OK (city) Kay County	3,037	11.96
Cortez, CO (city) Montezuma County	1,014	11.95
Anchorage, AK (municipality) Anchorage Municipality	33,633	11.53
Cushing, OK (city) Payne County	895	11.44
Riverton, WY (city) Fremont County	1,167	10.99
Owasso, OK (city) Tulsa County	3,164	10.94
Newcastle, OK (city) McClain County	811	10.55
Ashland, WI (city) Ashland County	866	10.54
Meadow Lakes, AK (cdp) Matanuska-Susitna Borough	749	9.89
Knik-Fairview, AK (cdp) Matanuska-Susitna Borough	1,441	9.66
Lakes, AK (cdp) Matanuska-Susitna Borough	804	9.61
Bixby, OK (city) Tulsa County	1,924	9.21
Coffeyville, KS (city) Montgomery County	922	8.96
Wasilla, AK (city) Matanuska-Susitna Borough	702	8.96
Yreka, CA (city) Siskiyou County	693	8.92
Jenks, OK (city) Tulsa County	1,483	8.76
Kalifornsky, AK (cdp) Kenai Peninsula Borough	684	8.71
Choctaw, OK (city) Oklahoma County	959	8.60
Tulsa, OK (city) Tulsa County	33,420	8.53
Broken Arrow, OK (city) Tulsa County	8,336	8.43
Clinton, OK (city) Custer County	761	8.42
Blanchard, OK (city) McClain County	637	8.31
Tanaina, AK (cdp) Matanuska-Susitna Borough	680	8.30
Del City, OK (city) Oklahoma County	1,692	7.93
Badger, AK (cdp) Fairbanks North Star Borough	1,543	7.92
Camp Verde, AZ (town) Yavapai County	858	7.89
Toppenish, WA (city) Yakima County	704	7.87
Chickasha, OK (city) Grady County	1,242	7.75
Moore, OK (city) Cleveland County	4,265	7.74
Norman, OK (city) Cleveland County	8,455	7.62
Weatherford, OK (city) Custer County	823	7.60
Siloam Springs, AR (city) Benton County	1,122	7.46
Duncan, OK (city) Stephens County	1,728	7.37
Laurinburg, NC (city) Scotland County	1,170	7.33
Oroville East, CA (cdp) Butte County	601	7.26
Midwest City, OK (city) Oklahoma County	3,767	6.93
Durango, CO (city) La Plata County	1,162	6.88
Great Falls, MT (city) Cascade County	3,999	6.84
Galliano, LA (cdp) Lafourche Parish	524	6.83
Bayou Blue, LA (cdp) Lafourche Parish	835	6.76
Stillwater, OK (city) Payne County	3,068	6.72
McKinleyville, CA (cdp) Humboldt County	992	6.54
Anderson, CA (city) Shasta County	641	6.45
Mustang, OK (city) Canadian County	1,096	6.30
Guthrie, OK (city) Logan County	640	6.28
Detroit Lakes, MN (city) Becker County	536	6.26
Lawton, OK (city) Comanche County	6,037	6.23
Eureka, CA (city) Humboldt County	1,679	6.17
Shasta Lake, CA (city) Shasta County	605	5.95
Klamath Falls, OR (city) Klamath County	1,233	5.92
Rapid Valley, SD (cdp) Pennington County	489	5.92
Box Elder, SD (city) Pennington County	462	5.92
The Village, OK (city) Oklahoma County	522	5.85
Mandan, ND (city) Morton County	1,070	5.84
Hoquiam, WA (city) Grays Harbor County	508	5.82
Yukon, OK (city) Canadian County	1,279	5.63
Globe, AZ (city) Gila County	424	5.63
Oklahoma City, OK (city) Oklahoma County	32,292	5.57
Fortuna, CA (city) Humboldt County	655	5.49
Oroville, CA (city) Butte County	850	5.47
Crescent City, CA (city) Del Norte County	412	5.39
Port Angeles, WA (city) Clallam County	1,022	5.37
Billings, MT (city) Yellowstone County	5,562	5.34
Altamont, OR (cdp) Klamath County	1,021	5.30
Williston, ND (city) Williams County	778	5.29
Bethany, OK (city) Oklahoma County	997	5.23
Elk City, OK (city) Beckham County	612	5.23
Bismarck, ND (city) Burleigh County	3,195	5.21
Coos Bay, OR (city) Coos County	817	5.12
Aberdeen, WA (city) Grays Harbor County	864	5.11
Bernalillo, NM (town) Sandoval County	409	4.92
Warr Acres, OK (city) Oklahoma County	492	4.90
Coolidge, AZ (city) Pinal County	578	4.89
Massena, NY (town) St. Lawrence County	629	4.88
Alliance, NE (city) Box Butte County	414	4.88
Lincoln City, OR (city) Lincoln County	387	4.88
Show Low, AZ (city) Navajo County	517	4.85
Houma, LA (city) Terrebonne Parish	1,619	4.80
Helena Valley Southeast, MT (cdp) Lewis and Clark County	393	4.78
Edmond, OK (city) Oklahoma County	3,879	4.77
North Bend, OR (city) Coos County	458	4.72
Green Bay, WI (city) Brown County	4,837	4.65
Olivehurst, CA (cdp) Yuba County	628	4.60
Shelton, WA (city) Mason County	447	4.55
Clearlake, CA (city) Lake County	691	4.53
Albuquerque, NM (city) Bernalillo County	24,591	4.51
Aberdeen, SD (city) Brown County	1,176	4.51
Pendleton, OR (city) Umatilla County	749	4.51
Arkansas City, KS (city) Cowley County	557	4.49
Virginia, MN (city) St. Louis County	389	4.47
Vermillion, SD (city) Clay County	470	4.45
Escanaba, MI (city) Delta County	557	4.42
Ukiah, CA (city) Mendocino County	707	4.40
Superior, WI (city) Douglas County	1,152	4.23
Arcata, CA (city) Humboldt County	727	4.22
Anaconda-Deer Lodge County, MT (special city) Deer Lodge County	389	4.18
Minot, ND (city) Ward County	1,699	4.16
Casa Grande, AZ (city) Pinal County	2,004	4.13
Lawrence, KS (city) Douglas County	3,562	4.06
Ledyard, CT (town) New London County	611	4.06
Red Bluff, CA (city) Tehama County	571	4.06
Midland, WA (cdp) Pierce County	358	3.99
Mashpee, MA (town) Barnstable County	557	3.98
Union, MI (charter township) Isabella County	512	3.96
Marysville, CA (city) Yuba County	474	3.93
Fallon, NV (city) Churchill County	337	3.92

SECTION THREE

Please refer to the Explanation of Data in the front of the book for more detailed information.

Race

American Indian/Alaska Native: Hispanic

U.S. and 50 States Sorted by Population and Percent of Total Population

Place	Population	%
United States	**1,190,904**	**0.39**
California	339,268	0.91
Texas	137,137	0.55
New York	93,009	0.48
Arizona	59,359	0.93
Florida	44,093	0.23
Colorado	43,869	0.87
Illinois	40,503	0.32
New Jersey	30,229	0.34
Washington	30,149	0.45
New Mexico	29,462	1.43
Oklahoma	23,582	0.63
North Carolina	21,771	0.23
Oregon	19,447	0.51
Georgia	19,099	0.20
Pennsylvania	19,026	0.15
Virginia	17,946	0.22
Michigan	15,828	0.16
Massachusetts	15,070	0.23
Nevada	14,951	0.55
Maryland	13,610	0.24
Minnesota	11,395	0.21
Wisconsin	10,733	0.19
Hawaii	10,575	0.78
Utah	10,489	0.38
Ohio	10,252	0.09
Kansas	9,471	0.33
Connecticut	8,937	0.25
Indiana	8,269	0.13
Missouri	7,245	0.12
Tennessee	6,986	0.11
Idaho	6,940	0.44
Nebraska	5,871	0.32
Louisiana	5,486	0.12
South Carolina	5,229	0.11
Alaska	4,925	0.69
Iowa	4,648	0.15
Alabama	4,255	0.09
Montana	4,149	0.42
Arkansas	4,061	0.14
Rhode Island	3,814	0.36
South Dakota	3,303	0.41
Kentucky	3,185	0.07
Wyoming	2,608	0.46
Mississippi	2,253	0.08
Delaware	2,220	0.25
District of Columbia	1,589	0.26
North Dakota	1,526	0.23
New Hampshire	997	0.08
Maine	828	0.06
West Virginia	775	0.04
Vermont	482	0.08

Place	Population	%
New Mexico	29,462	1.43
Arizona	59,359	0.93
California	339,268	0.91
Colorado	43,869	0.87
Hawaii	10,575	0.78
Alaska	4,925	0.69
Oklahoma	23,582	0.63
Texas	137,137	0.55
Nevada	14,951	0.55
Oregon	19,447	0.51
New York	93,009	0.48
Wyoming	2,608	0.46
Washington	30,149	0.45
Idaho	6,940	0.44
Montana	4,149	0.42
South Dakota	3,303	0.41
United States	**1,190,904**	**0.39**
Utah	10,489	0.38
Rhode Island	3,814	0.36
New Jersey	30,229	0.34
Kansas	9,471	0.33
Illinois	40,503	0.32
Nebraska	5,871	0.32
District of Columbia	1,589	0.26
Connecticut	8,937	0.25
Delaware	2,220	0.25
Maryland	13,610	0.24
Florida	44,093	0.23
North Carolina	21,771	0.23
Massachusetts	15,070	0.23
North Dakota	1,526	0.23
Virginia	17,946	0.22
Minnesota	11,395	0.21
Georgia	19,099	0.20
Wisconsin	10,733	0.19
Michigan	15,828	0.16
Pennsylvania	19,026	0.15
Iowa	4,648	0.15
Arkansas	4,061	0.14
Indiana	8,269	0.13
Missouri	7,245	0.12
Louisiana	5,486	0.12
Tennessee	6,986	0.11
South Carolina	5,229	0.11
Ohio	10,252	0.09
Alabama	4,255	0.09
Mississippi	2,253	0.08
New Hampshire	997	0.08
Vermont	482	0.08
Kentucky	3,185	0.07
Maine	828	0.06
West Virginia	775	0.04

Please refer to the Explanation of Data in the front of the book for more detailed information.

Race

American Indian/Alaska Native: Hispanic

Top 150 Places Sorted by Population

Based on all places, regardless of total population

Place	Population	%
New York, NY (city) Kings County	67,208	0.82
Los Angeles, CA (city) Los Angeles County	34,726	0.92
Bronx, NY (borough) Bronx County	24,373	1.76
Houston, TX (city) Harris County	16,786	0.80
Queens, NY (borough) Queens County	14,621	0.66
Brooklyn, NY (borough) Kings County	14,509	0.58
Chicago, IL (city) Cook County	14,484	0.54
San Antonio, TX (city) Medina County	13,654	1.03
Phoenix, AZ (city) Maricopa County	13,520	0.94
Manhattan, NY (borough) New York County	12,020	0.76
San Jose, CA (city) Santa Clara County	9,900	1.05
Tucson, AZ (city) Pima County	8,082	1.55
Albuquerque, NM (city) Bernalillo County	7,980	1.46
Fresno, CA (city) Fresno County	7,920	1.60
San Diego, CA (city) San Diego County	7,748	0.59
Denver, CO (city) Denver County	7,596	1.27
Austin, TX (city) Travis County	7,213	0.91
Dallas, TX (city) Dallas County	7,094	0.59
Philadelphia, PA (city) Philadelphia County	6,086	0.40
Sacramento, CA (city) Sacramento County	5,357	1.15
San Francisco, CA (city) San Francisco County	4,632	0.58
El Paso, TX (city) El Paso County	4,502	0.69
Bakersfield, CA (city) Kern County	4,355	1.25
Oklahoma City, OK (city) Oklahoma County	4,280	0.74
Santa Ana, CA (city) Orange County	3,956	1.22
Long Beach, CA (city) Los Angeles County	3,956	0.86
Riverside, CA (city) Riverside County	3,585	1.18
Oakland, CA (city) Alameda County	3,527	0.90
Oxnard, CA (city) Ventura County	3,471	1.75
Stockton, CA (city) San Joaquin County	3,465	1.19
Fort Worth, TX (city) Tarrant County	3,465	0.47
Colorado Springs, CO (city) El Paso County	3,384	0.81
Mesa, AZ (city) Maricopa County	3,221	0.73
Las Vegas, NV (city) Clark County	3,209	0.55
Portland, OR (city) Multnomah County	3,099	0.53
San Bernardino, CA (city) San Bernardino County	3,004	1.43
Aurora, CO (city) Arapahoe County	2,913	0.90
Anaheim, CA (city) Orange County	2,911	0.87
Minneapolis, MN (city) Hennepin County	2,719	0.71
Pueblo, CO (city) Pueblo County	2,701	2.53
Tulsa, OK (city) Tulsa County	2,570	0.66
Hempstead, NY (town) Nassau County	2,528	0.33
Modesto, CA (city) Stanislaus County	2,489	1.24
Milwaukee, WI (city) Milwaukee County	2,452	0.41
Anchorage, AK (municipality) Anchorage Municipality	2,429	0.83
Fontana, CA (city) San Bernardino County	2,398	1.22
Boston, MA (city) Suffolk County	2,394	0.39
Santa Rosa, CA (city) Sonoma County	2,354	1.40
Charlotte, NC (city) Mecklenburg County	2,301	0.31
Salinas, CA (city) Monterey County	2,233	1.48
Seattle, WA (city) King County	2,203	0.36
Pomona, CA (city) Los Angeles County	2,180	1.46
Paterson, NJ (city) Passaic County	2,171	1.48
Providence, RI (city) Providence County	2,168	1.22
Santa Maria, CA (city) Santa Barbara County	2,139	2.15
Ontario, CA (city) San Bernardino County	2,101	1.28
Wichita, KS (city) Sedgwick County	2,091	0.55
Chula Vista, CA (city) San Diego County	2,001	0.82
Arlington, TX (city) Tarrant County	1,956	0.54
Moreno Valley, CA (city) Riverside County	1,930	1.00
Lake Worth, FL (city) Palm Beach County	1,926	5.52
Madera, CA (city) Madera County	1,904	3.10
East Los Angeles, CA (cdp) Los Angeles County	1,869	1.48
Islip, NY (town) Suffolk County	1,831	0.55
Corpus Christi, TX (city) Nueces County	1,829	0.60
Omaha, NE (city) Douglas County	1,819	0.44
Elgin, IL (city) Kane County	1,815	1.68
Yonkers, NY (city) Westchester County	1,806	0.92
Glendale, AZ (city) Maricopa County	1,712	0.76
Staten Island, NY (borough) Richmond County	1,685	0.36
Lakewood, CO (city) Jefferson County	1,682	1.18
Newark, NJ (city) Essex County	1,635	0.59
Washington, DC (city) District of Columbia	1,589	0.26
Escondido, CA (city) San Diego County	1,587	1.10
Hayward, CA (city) Alameda County	1,559	1.08
Garland, TX (city) Dallas County	1,550	0.68
Urban Honolulu, HI (cdp) Honolulu County	1,537	0.46
Chandler, AZ (city) Maricopa County	1,533	0.65
Irving, TX (city) Dallas County	1,532	0.71
Raleigh, NC (city) Wake County	1,526	0.38
Visalia, CA (city) Tulare County	1,496	1.20
Detroit, MI (city) Wayne County	1,483	0.21
Victorville, CA (city) San Bernardino County	1,482	1.28
Indianapolis, IN (city) Marion County	1,479	0.18
Lancaster, CA (city) Los Angeles County	1,467	0.94
Tacoma, WA (city) Pierce County	1,459	0.74
St. Paul, MN (city) Ramsey County	1,449	0.51
Palmdale, CA (city) Los Angeles County	1,439	0.94
Oceanside, CA (city) San Diego County	1,435	0.86
Miami, FL (city) Miami-Dade County	1,430	0.36
Lawrence, MA (city) Essex County	1,407	1.84
Las Cruces, NM (city) Doña Ana County	1,391	1.42
Elizabeth, NJ (city) Union County	1,386	1.11
Thornton, CO (city) Adams County	1,381	1.16
Rancho Cucamonga, CA (city) San Bernardino County	1,376	0.83
Tempe, AZ (city) Maricopa County	1,373	0.85
Norwalk, CA (city) Los Angeles County	1,346	1.28
San Buenaventura (Ventura), CA (city) Ventura County	1,346	1.26
Reno, NV (city) Washoe County	1,345	0.60
Whittier, CA (city) Los Angeles County	1,339	1.57
Springfield, MA (city) Hampden County	1,333	0.87
Paradise, NV (cdp) Clark County	1,309	0.59
Jacksonville, FL (city) Duval County	1,305	0.16
Nashville-Davidson, TN (metro govt) Davidson County	1,301	0.22
El Monte, CA (city) Los Angeles County	1,297	1.14
North Las Vegas, NV (city) Clark County	1,297	0.60
Lubbock, TX (city) Lubbock County	1,297	0.56
Corona, CA (city) Riverside County	1,264	0.83
West Covina, CA (city) Los Angeles County	1,257	1.18
Jersey City, NJ (city) Hudson County	1,257	0.51
Sunrise Manor, NV (cdp) Clark County	1,249	0.66
Salt Lake City, UT (city) Salt Lake County	1,231	0.66
Rialto, CA (city) San Bernardino County	1,215	1.23
Brookhaven, NY (town) Suffolk County	1,196	0.25
Arlington, VA (cdp) Arlington County	1,174	0.57
Guadalupe, AZ (town) Maricopa County	1,167	21.13
Union City, NJ (city) Hudson County	1,163	1.75
Kansas City, MO (city) Jackson County	1,161	0.25
Vista, CA (city) San Diego County	1,159	1.24
Pasadena, CA (city) Los Angeles County	1,159	0.85
Waukegan, IL (city) Lake County	1,158	1.30
Grand Prairie, TX (city) Dallas County	1,149	0.66
Allentown, PA (city) Lehigh County	1,147	0.97
Pasadena, TX (city) Harris County	1,144	0.77
Laredo, TX (city) Webb County	1,138	0.48
Rio Rancho, NM (city) Sandoval County	1,131	1.29
Aurora, IL (city) Kane County	1,130	0.57
Buena Park, CA (city) Orange County	1,129	1.40
Hesperia, CA (city) San Bernardino County	1,127	1.25
Merced, CA (city) Merced County	1,125	1.42
Greeley, CO (city) Weld County	1,123	1.21
Passaic, NJ (city) Passaic County	1,120	1.61
Gallup, NM (city) McKinley County	1,108	5.11
South Gate, CA (city) Los Angeles County	1,108	1.17
Garden Grove, CA (city) Orange County	1,102	0.64
Casa Grande, AZ (city) Pinal County	1,073	2.21
Baltimore, MD (city) Baltimore city County	1,071	0.17
Orange, CA (city) Orange County	1,070	0.78
Santa Clarita, CA (city) Los Angeles County	1,067	0.61
Columbus, OH (city) Franklin County	1,067	0.14
Fullerton, CA (city) Orange County	1,063	0.79
Hemet, CA (city) Riverside County	1,061	1.35
Yuma, AZ (city) Yuma County	1,053	1.13
Tampa, FL (city) Hillsborough County	1,040	0.31
New Bedford, MA (city) Bristol County	1,038	1.09
Pico Rivera, CA (city) Los Angeles County	1,037	1.65
Elk Grove, CA (city) Sacramento County	1,034	0.68
Downey, CA (city) Los Angeles County	1,031	0.92
Henderson, NV (city) Clark County	1,029	0.40
Fremont, CA (city) Alameda County	1,027	0.48

Race

American Indian/Alaska Native: Hispanic

Top 150 Places Sorted by Percent of Total Population

Based on all places, regardless of total population

Place	Population	%
Mojave Ranch Estates, AZ (cdp) Mohave County	13	25.00
Loveland, OK (town) Tillman County	3	23.08
Sacate Village, AZ (cdp) Pinal County	36	21.30
Guadalupe, AZ (town) Maricopa County	1,167	21.13
Ak-Chin Village, AZ (cdp) Pinal County	178	20.65
Goodyear Village, AZ (cdp) Pinal County	92	20.13
Posey, CA (cdp) Tulare County	2	20.00
Sweet Water Village, AZ (cdp) Pinal County	16	19.28
Midway, MN (cdp) Mahnomen County	5	19.23
Blackwater, AZ (cdp) Pinal County	189	17.80
Komatke, AZ (cdp) Maricopa County	146	17.78
Oak Grove, OK (town) Pawnee County	3	16.67
Cutter, AZ (cdp) Gila County	12	16.22
Lower Santan Village, AZ (cdp) Pinal County	55	14.71
Weston, CO (cdp) Las Animas County	8	14.55
Grattan, MN (township) Itasca County	6	13.64
Fort Apache, AZ (cdp) Navajo County	19	13.29
Cattaraugus Reservation, NY (reservation) Chautauqua County	5	13.16
East Globe, AZ (cdp) Gila County	29	12.83
Stevens Village, AK (cdp) Yukon-Koyukuk Census Area	10	12.82
Wet Camp Village, AZ (cdp) Pinal County	29	12.66
Gila Crossing, AZ (cdp) Maricopa County	77	12.40
Sorrento, FL (cdp) Lake County	106	12.31
Arizona Village, AZ (cdp) Mohave County	114	12.05
Abiquiu, NM (cdp) Rio Arriba County	27	11.69
Sun Valley, TX (city) Lamar County	8	11.59
Casa Blanca, AZ (cdp) Pinal County	157	11.31
Akhiok, AK (city) Kodiak Island Borough	8	11.27
Ali Chuk, AZ (cdp) Pima County	18	11.18
McNary, AZ (cdp) Apache County	58	10.98
Stotonic Village, AZ (cdp) Pinal County	72	10.93
Sacaton Flats Village, AZ (cdp) Pinal County	59	10.91
Poston, AZ (cdp) La Paz County	31	10.88
Moquino, NM (cdp) Cibola County	4	10.81
Sacaton, AZ (cdp) Pinal County	284	10.63
Los Ybanez, TX (city) Dawson County	2	10.53
Maricopa Colony, AZ (cdp) Maricopa County	74	10.44
Picuris Pueblo, NM (cdp) Taos County	7	10.29
Seboyeta, NM (cdp) Cibola County	18	10.06
Chuichu, AZ (cdp) Pinal County	27	10.04
South Komelik, AZ (cdp) Pima County	11	9.91
Chamizal, NM (cdp) Socorro County	10	9.90
Charco, AZ (cdp) Pima County	5	9.62
Hooper, CO (town) Alamosa County	9	8.74
Villanueva, NM (cdp) San Miguel County	20	8.73
San Fidel, NM (cdp) Cibola County	12	8.70
Mescalero, NM (cdp) Otero County	116	8.67
La Garde, MN (township) Mahnomen County	14	8.64
Ohkay Owingeh, NM (cdp) Rio Arriba County	97	8.49
Pueblo of Sandia Village, NM (cdp) Sandoval County	31	8.40
Vantage, WA (cdp) Kittitas County	6	8.11
Nolic, AZ (cdp) Pima County	3	8.11
Fort Bidwell, CA (cdp) Modoc County	14	8.09
Nubieber, CA (cdp) Lassen County	4	8.00
Pinehill, NM (cdp) Cibola County	7	7.95
Raisin City, CA (cdp) Fresno County	30	7.89
Redford, TX (cdp) Presidio County	7	7.78
Sena, NM (cdp) San Miguel County	10	7.75
Odanah, WI (cdp) Ashland County	1	7.69
Warm Springs, OR (cdp) Jefferson County	223	7.57
Owl Ranch, TX (cdp) Jim Wells County	17	7.56
Big Lagoon, CA (cdp) Humboldt County	7	7.53
Dulce, NM (cdp) Rio Arriba County	204	7.44
San Ildefonso Pueblo, NM (cdp) Santa Fe County	39	7.44
Kohatk, AZ (cdp) Pinal County	2	7.41
Mashantucket, CT (cdp) New London County	22	7.36
Marmarth, ND (city) Slope County	10	7.35
Rennert, NC (town) Robeson County	28	7.31
Fort Hall, ID (cdp) Bannock County	231	7.22
Santiago, WA (cdp) Grays Harbor County	3	7.14
Piedra, CO (cdp) Hinsdale County	2	7.14
Muddy, MT (cdp) Big Horn County	44	7.13
Padre Ranchitos, AZ (cdp) Yuma County	12	7.02
Wahak Hotrontk, AZ (cdp) Pima County	8	7.02
Schurz, NV (cdp) Mineral County	46	6.99
Angoon, AK (city) Hoonah-Angoon Census Area	32	6.97
Santee, NE (village) Knox County	24	6.94
Ignacio, CO (town) La Plata County	48	6.89
Mandaree, ND (cdp) McKenzie County	41	6.88
Klamath, CA (cdp) Del Norte County	53	6.80
Narciso Pena, TX (cdp) Starr County	2	6.67
Nageezi, NM (cdp) San Juan County	19	6.64
Anadarko, OK (city) Caddo County	443	6.55
Kilgore, NE (village) Cherry County	5	6.49
Canyondam, CA (cdp) Plumas County	2	6.45
North Omak, WA (cdp) Okanogan County	44	6.40
Pueblo, NM (cdp) San Miguel County	8	6.40
Hard Rock, AZ (cdp) Navajo County	6	6.38
Neah Bay, WA (cdp) Clallam County	55	6.36
Isleta Village Proper, NM (cdp) Bernalillo County	31	6.31
Bryce, AZ (cdp) Graham County	11	6.29
Keshena, WI (cdp) Menominee County	79	6.26
Morrison Bluff, AR (town) Logan County	4	6.25
New Odanah, WI (cdp) Ashland County	29	6.14
Cornish, OK (town) Jefferson County	10	6.13
Kickapoo Site 7, KS (cdp) Brown County	4	6.06
Pojoaque, NM (cdp) Santa Fe County	113	5.93
Pisinemo, AZ (cdp) Pima County	19	5.92
Nisqually Indian Community, WA (cdp) Thurston County	34	5.91
Tooleville, CA (cdp) Tulare County	20	5.90
Kickapoo Site 2, KS (cdp) Brown County	2	5.88
Upper Santan Village, AZ (cdp) Pinal County	29	5.86
Garfield, NM (cdp) Doña Ana County	8	5.84
Walsenburg, CO (city) Huerfano County	179	5.83
Santa Clara Pueblo, NM (cdp) Rio Arriba County	59	5.80
Taholah, WA (cdp) Grays Harbor County	48	5.71
Encinal, NM (cdp) Cibola County	12	5.71
Norcross, MN (city) Grant County	4	5.71
Duran, NM (cdp) Torrance County	2	5.71
Mission, OR (cdp) Umatilla County	59	5.69
Sheridan Lake, CO (town) Kiowa County	5	5.68
Kaka, AZ (cdp) Maricopa County	8	5.67
Southern Ute, CO (cdp) La Plata County	10	5.65
Ririe, ID (city) Jefferson County	37	5.64
Atlanta, KS (city) Cowley County	11	5.64
Chical, NM (cdp) Valencia County	6	5.61
Vineland, CO (cdp) Pueblo County	14	5.58
Tesuque Pueblo, NM (cdp) Santa Fe County	13	5.58
Greenfield, CA (city) Monterey County	907	5.55
Parshall, ND (city) Mountrail County	50	5.54
Lake Worth, FL (city) Palm Beach County	1,926	5.52
Lumberton, NM (cdp) Rio Arriba County	4	5.48
Cherry Tree, OK (cdp) Adair County	48	5.44
Santa Cruz, AZ (cdp) Pinal County	2	5.41
Valmy, NV (cdp) Humboldt County	2	5.41
Nambe, NM (cdp) Santa Fe County	97	5.34
North Hurley, NM (cdp) Grant County	16	5.33
Concho, AZ (cdp) Apache County	2	5.26
Moskowite Corner, CA (cdp) Napa County	11	5.21
Noble, LA (village) Sabine Parish	13	5.16
Horn, OK (town) Hughes County	5	5.15
San Lorenzo, NM (cdp) Grant County	5	5.15
Lake Leelanau, MI (cdp) Leelanau County	13	5.14
Gallup, NM (city) McKinley County	1,108	5.11
Baxter Estates, NY (village) Nassau County	51	5.11
San Jose, NM (cdp) San Miguel County	7	5.11
Nespelem, WA (town) Okanogan County	12	5.08
Llano del Medio, NM (cdp) Guadalupe County	6	5.08
Mulberry, OK (cdp) Adair County	7	5.07
Johnstown, WY (cdp) Fremont County	12	4.96
Seama, NM (cdp) Cibola County	23	4.95
Indiahoma, OK (town) Comanche County	17	4.94
Sisquoc, CA (cdp) Santa Barbara County	9	4.92
Platinum, AK (city) Bethel Census Area	3	4.92
Ravinia, SD (town) Charles Mix County	3	4.92
St. Joseph, IA (cdp) Kossuth County	3	4.92
Winston, NM (cdp) Sierra County	3	4.92
Magdalena, NM (village) Socorro County	46	4.90
Sells, AZ (cdp) Pima County	122	4.89
Sanborn, WI (town) Ashland County	65	4.88

Please refer to the Explanation of Data in the front of the book for more detailed information.

Race

American Indian/Alaska Native: Hispanic

Top 150 Places Sorted by Percent of Total Population

Based on places with total population of 7,500 or more

Place	Population	%
Greenfield, CA (city) Monterey County	907	5.55
Lake Worth, FL (city) Palm Beach County	1,926	5.52
Gallup, NM (city) McKinley County	1,108	5.11
Alamosa, CO (city) Alamosa County	304	3.46
Drexel Heights, AZ (cdp) Pima County	933	3.36
Langley Park, MD (cdp) Prince George's County	597	3.18
King City, CA (city) Monterey County	401	3.11
Madera, CA (city) Madera County	1,904	3.10
Woodburn, OR (city) Marion County	740	3.07
Winslow, AZ (city) Navajo County	289	2.99
Livingston, CA (city) Merced County	385	2.95
Valencia West, AZ (cdp) Pima County	266	2.84
Trinidad, CO (city) Las Animas County	255	2.80
Coolidge, AZ (city) Pinal County	309	2.61
Chamblee, GA (city) DeKalb County	257	2.60
Pueblo, CO (city) Pueblo County	2,701	2.53
Kirtland, NM (cdp) San Juan County	188	2.39
Welby, CO (cdp) Adams County	353	2.38
Grants, NM (city) Cibola County	213	2.32
Tuba City, AZ (cdp) Coconino County	200	2.32
Hollister, CA (city) San Benito County	782	2.24
Alum Rock, CA (cdp) Santa Clara County	346	2.23
Casa Grande, AZ (city) Pinal County	1,073	2.21
Santa Maria, CA (city) Santa Barbara County	2,139	2.15
Selma, CA (city) Fresno County	492	2.12
Berkley, CO (cdp) Adams County	236	2.11
Gonzales, CA (city) Monterey County	172	2.10
Country Club, CA (cdp) San Joaquin County	196	2.09
Gilroy, CA (city) Santa Clara County	1,014	2.08
Siler City, NC (town) Chatham County	162	2.05
West New York, NJ (town) Hudson County	1,005	2.02
Sherrelwood, CO (cdp) Adams County	370	2.02
Waianae, HI (cdp) Honolulu County	266	2.02
North Atlanta, GA (cdp) DeKalb County	812	2.01
Ukiah, CA (city) Mendocino County	321	2.00
Arizona City, AZ (cdp) Pinal County	210	2.00
Walnut Park, CA (cdp) Los Angeles County	318	1.99
Farmersville, CA (city) Tulare County	209	1.97
Commerce City, CO (city) Adams County	861	1.88
Windsor, CA (town) Sonoma County	505	1.88
Makaha, HI (cdp) Honolulu County	156	1.88
Lemon Hill, CA (cdp) Sacramento County	256	1.86
Camp Verde, AZ (town) Yavapai County	201	1.85
Lawrence, MA (city) Essex County	1,407	1.84
McFarland, CA (city) Kern County	234	1.84
Healdsburg, CA (city) Sonoma County	207	1.84
Riverton, WY (city) Fremont County	195	1.84
Barstow, CA (city) San Bernardino County	406	1.79
Bronx, NY (borough) Bronx County	24,373	1.76
Lompoc, CA (city) Santa Barbara County	745	1.76
Oxnard, CA (city) Ventura County	3,471	1.75
Union City, NJ (city) Hudson County	1,163	1.75
Hawaiian Paradise Park, HI (cdp) Hawaii County	199	1.75
August, CA (cdp) San Joaquin County	146	1.74
San Rafael, CA (city) Marin County	996	1.73
Toppenish, WA (city) Yakima County	155	1.73
Las Vegas, NM (city) San Miguel County	234	1.70
Cortez, CO (city) Montezuma County	143	1.69
Elgin, IL (city) Kane County	1,815	1.68
Newburgh, NY (city) Orange County	486	1.68
West Whittier-Los Nietos, CA (cdp) Los Angeles County	430	1.68
Tahlequah, OK (city) Cherokee County	264	1.68
Derby, CO (cdp) Adams County	129	1.68
Round Lake Park, IL (village) Lake County	126	1.68
Pico Rivera, CA (city) Los Angeles County	1,037	1.65
Huntington Park, CA (city) Los Angeles County	954	1.64
South Valley, NM (cdp) Bernalillo County	673	1.64
Red Bank, NJ (borough) Monmouth County	200	1.64
South Whittier, CA (cdp) Los Angeles County	933	1.63
Galt, CA (city) Sacramento County	384	1.62
Passaic, NJ (city) Passaic County	1,120	1.61
Santa Fe Springs, CA (city) Los Angeles County	262	1.61
Fresno, CA (city) Fresno County	7,920	1.60
Adelphi, MD (cdp) Prince George's County	242	1.60
Los Lunas, NM (village) Valencia County	238	1.60
Parkway, CA (cdp) Sacramento County	234	1.60
Grover Beach, CA (city) San Luis Obispo County	211	1.60
Kapaa, HI (cdp) Kauai County	171	1.60
Lamont, CA (cdp) Kern County	241	1.59
Garden Acres, CA (cdp) San Joaquin County	169	1.59
Santa Paula, CA (city) Ventura County	462	1.58
Whittier, CA (city) Los Angeles County	1,339	1.57
Porterville, CA (city) Tulare County	851	1.57
Los Banos, CA (city) Merced County	564	1.57
Orange Cove, CA (city) Fresno County	142	1.56
Firebaugh, CA (city) Fresno County	118	1.56
Tucson, AZ (city) Pima County	8,082	1.55
Shelton, WA (city) Mason County	152	1.55
Yreka, CA (city) Siskiyou County	120	1.55
Perth Amboy, NJ (city) Middlesex County	780	1.54
San Fernando, CA (city) Los Angeles County	363	1.54
Arvin, CA (city) Kern County	297	1.54
Wahiawa, HI (cdp) Honolulu County	274	1.54
Red Bluff, CA (city) Tehama County	217	1.54
Carpinteria, CA (city) Santa Barbara County	199	1.53
Mendota, CA (city) Fresno County	169	1.53
Banning, CA (city) Riverside County	450	1.52
Eloy, AZ (city) Pinal County	252	1.52
Clearlake, CA (city) Lake County	232	1.52
Colton, CA (city) San Bernardino County	788	1.51
East Hemet, CA (cdp) Riverside County	263	1.51
Scottsbluff, NE (city) Scotts Bluff County	227	1.51
Bloomfield, NM (city) San Juan County	122	1.50
West Sacramento, CA (city) Yolo County	728	1.49
Azusa, CA (city) Los Angeles County	689	1.49
Nipomo, CA (cdp) San Luis Obispo County	249	1.49
Espanola, NM (city) Rio Arriba County	152	1.49
Salinas, CA (city) Monterey County	2,233	1.48
Paterson, NJ (city) Passaic County	2,171	1.48
East Los Angeles, CA (cdp) Los Angeles County	1,869	1.48
New Brunswick, NJ (city) Middlesex County	816	1.48
Muscoy, CA (cdp) San Bernardino County	158	1.48
Adelanto, CA (city) San Bernardino County	468	1.47
Commerce, CA (city) Los Angeles County	189	1.47
Albuquerque, NM (city) Bernalillo County	7,980	1.46
Pomona, CA (city) Los Angeles County	2,180	1.46
Farmington, NM (city) San Juan County	669	1.46
San Jacinto, CA (city) Riverside County	644	1.46
Winton, CA (cdp) Merced County	155	1.46
Socorro, NM (city) Socorro County	132	1.46
El Centro, CA (city) Imperial County	618	1.45
Madera Acres, CA (cdp) Madera County	133	1.45
Watsonville, CA (city) Santa Cruz County	736	1.44
Parlier, CA (city) Fresno County	209	1.44
Olivehurst, CA (cdp) Yuba County	196	1.44
Maili, HI (cdp) Honolulu County	137	1.44
San Bernardino, CA (city) San Bernardino County	3,004	1.43
Bloomington, CA (cdp) San Bernardino County	341	1.43
West Puente Valley, CA (cdp) Los Angeles County	323	1.43
South El Monte, CA (city) Los Angeles County	287	1.43
Las Cruces, NM (city) Doña Ana County	1,391	1.42
Merced, CA (city) Merced County	1,125	1.42
Port Hueneme, CA (city) Ventura County	309	1.42
Woodlawn, VA (cdp) Fairfax County	295	1.42
Lake Los Angeles, CA (cdp) Los Angeles County	175	1.42
Fillmore, CA (city) Ventura County	212	1.41
Cherryland, CA (cdp) Alameda County	208	1.41
Sun Village, CA (cdp) Los Angeles County	163	1.41
Artesia, NM (city) Eddy County	159	1.41
Santa Rosa, CA (city) Sonoma County	2,354	1.40
Buena Park, CA (city) Orange County	1,129	1.40
Chelsea, MA (city) Suffolk County	493	1.40
Brighton, CO (city) Adams County	468	1.40
Marysville, CA (city) Yuba County	169	1.40
Flowing Wells, AZ (cdp) Pima County	228	1.39
Valle Vista, CA (cdp) Riverside County	203	1.39
Sans Souci, SC (cdp) Greenville County	109	1.39
Santa Fe, NM (city) Santa Fe County	926	1.36
Montclair, CA (city) San Bernardino County	497	1.36
Round Lake Beach, IL (village) Lake County	384	1.36

Please refer to the Explanation of Data in the front of the book for more detailed information.

Race

Alaska Native: Alaska Athabascan

U.S. and 50 States Sorted by Population and Percent of Total Population

Place	Population	%
United States	**22,484**	**0.01**
Alaska	16,665	2.35
Washington	1,222	0.02
California	697	<0.01
Oregon	445	0.01
Texas	296	<0.01
Arizona	222	<0.01
Florida	195	<0.01
Colorado	175	<0.01
Idaho	144	0.01
Nevada	119	<0.01
New York	116	<0.01
Michigan	113	<0.01
Oklahoma	103	<0.01
Ohio	100	<0.01
Missouri	98	<0.01
New Mexico	95	<0.01
Virginia	95	<0.01
Georgia	94	<0.01
Wisconsin	93	<0.01
Pennsylvania	92	<0.01
Montana	87	0.01
Illinois	86	<0.01
Minnesota	80	<0.01
North Carolina	78	<0.01
Hawaii	77	0.01
Arkansas	67	<0.01
Louisiana	66	<0.01
Utah	64	<0.01
New Jersey	53	<0.01
Kansas	50	<0.01
South Carolina	50	<0.01
Maryland	47	<0.01
South Dakota	45	0.01
Tennessee	43	<0.01
Kentucky	41	<0.01
Nebraska	41	<0.01
Alabama	40	<0.01
Connecticut	39	<0.01
Indiana	36	<0.01
Wyoming	34	0.01
Iowa	34	<0.01
Mississippi	32	<0.01
Massachusetts	31	<0.01
Maine	20	<0.01
North Dakota	18	<0.01
New Hampshire	10	<0.01
District of Columbia	9	<0.01
Vermont	8	<0.01
Rhode Island	7	<0.01
West Virginia	7	<0.01
Delaware	5	<0.01

Place	Population	%
Alaska	16,665	2.35
Washington	1,222	0.02
United States	**22,484**	**0.01**
Oregon	445	0.01
Idaho	144	0.01
Montana	87	0.01
Hawaii	77	0.01
South Dakota	45	0.01
Wyoming	34	0.01
California	697	<0.01
Texas	296	<0.01
Arizona	222	<0.01
Florida	195	<0.01
Colorado	175	<0.01
Nevada	119	<0.01
New York	116	<0.01
Michigan	113	<0.01
Oklahoma	103	<0.01
Ohio	100	<0.01
Missouri	98	<0.01
New Mexico	95	<0.01
Virginia	95	<0.01
Georgia	94	<0.01
Wisconsin	93	<0.01
Pennsylvania	92	<0.01
Illinois	86	<0.01
Minnesota	80	<0.01
North Carolina	78	<0.01
Arkansas	67	<0.01
Louisiana	66	<0.01
Utah	64	<0.01
New Jersey	53	<0.01
Kansas	50	<0.01
South Carolina	50	<0.01
Maryland	47	<0.01
Tennessee	43	<0.01
Kentucky	41	<0.01
Nebraska	41	<0.01
Alabama	40	<0.01
Connecticut	39	<0.01
Indiana	36	<0.01
Iowa	34	<0.01
Mississippi	32	<0.01
Massachusetts	31	<0.01
Maine	20	<0.01
North Dakota	18	<0.01
New Hampshire	10	<0.01
District of Columbia	9	<0.01
Vermont	8	<0.01
Rhode Island	7	<0.01
West Virginia	7	<0.01
Delaware	5	<0.01

Please refer to the Explanation of Data in the front of the book for more detailed information.

Race

Alaska Native: Alaska Athabascan

Top 150 Places Sorted by Population

Based on all places, regardless of total population

Place	Population	%
Anchorage, AK (municipality) Anchorage Municipality	4,333	1.48
Fairbanks, AK (city) Fairbanks North Star Borough	1,631	5.17
College, AK (cdp) Fairbanks North Star Borough	667	5.15
Fort Yukon, AK (city) Yukon-Koyukuk Census Area	496	85.08
Badger, AK (cdp) Fairbanks North Star Borough	426	2.19
Galena, AK (city) Yukon-Koyukuk Census Area	290	61.70
Kenai, AK (city) Kenai Peninsula Borough	282	3.97
Chena Ridge, AK (cdp) Fairbanks North Star Borough	262	4.52
Huslia, AK (city) Yukon-Koyukuk Census Area	254	92.36
Nulato, AK (city) Yukon-Koyukuk Census Area	246	93.18
Tanana, AK (city) Yukon-Koyukuk Census Area	202	82.11
Knik-Fairview, AK (cdp) Matanuska-Susitna Borough	200	1.34
Minto, AK (cdp) Yukon-Koyukuk Census Area	184	87.62
Tok, AK (cdp) Southeast Fairbanks Census Area	178	14.15
Kaltag, AK (city) Yukon-Koyukuk Census Area	176	92.63
Grayling, AK (city) Yukon-Koyukuk Census Area	169	87.11
Nikiski, AK (cdp) Kenai Peninsula Borough	168	3.74
Kalifornsky, AK (cdp) Kenai Peninsula Borough	168	2.14
Farmers Loop, AK (cdp) Fairbanks North Star Borough	167	3.44
Holy Cross, AK (city) Yukon-Koyukuk Census Area	162	91.01
Tyonek, AK (cdp) Kenai Peninsula Borough	150	87.72
Venetie, AK (cdp) Yukon-Koyukuk Census Area	149	89.76
Steele Creek, AK (cdp) Fairbanks North Star Borough	149	2.24
Ruby, AK (city) Yukon-Koyukuk Census Area	142	85.54
McGrath, AK (city) Yukon-Koyukuk Census Area	137	39.60
Nenana, AK (city) Yukon-Koyukuk Census Area	130	34.39
Copper Center, AK (cdp) Valdez-Cordova Census Area	128	39.02
Juneau, AK (borough) Juneau City and Borough	119	0.38
Tanacross, AK (cdp) Southeast Fairbanks Census Area	113	83.09
Nondalton, AK (city) Lake and Peninsula Borough	109	66.46
Arctic Village, AK (cdp) Yukon-Koyukuk Census Area	106	69.74
Tetlin, AK (cdp) Southeast Fairbanks Census Area	105	82.68
Meadow Lakes, AK (cdp) Matanuska-Susitna Borough	103	1.36
Allakaket, AK (city) Yukon-Koyukuk Census Area	96	91.43
Koyukuk, AK (city) Yukon-Koyukuk Census Area	94	97.92
Tazlina, AK (cdp) Valdez-Cordova Census Area	93	31.31
Tanaina, AK (cdp) Matanuska-Susitna Borough	93	1.13
Bethel, AK (city) Bethel Census Area	90	1.48
Seattle, WA (city) King County	90	0.01
Northway Village, AK (cdp) Southeast Fairbanks Census Area	89	90.82
Ester, AK (cdp) Fairbanks North Star Borough	83	3.43
Beaver, AK (cdp) Yukon-Koyukuk Census Area	81	96.43
Soldotna, AK (city) Kenai Peninsula Borough	80	1.92
Lakes, AK (cdp) Matanuska-Susitna Borough	80	0.96
Mentasta Lake, AK (cdp) Valdez-Cordova Census Area	79	70.54
Palmer, AK (city) Matanuska-Susitna Borough	79	1.33
Ninilchik, AK (cdp) Kenai Peninsula Borough	78	8.83
Sutton-Alpine, AK (cdp) Matanuska-Susitna Borough	76	5.25
Wasilla, AK (city) Matanuska-Susitna Borough	76	0.97
Shageluk, AK (city) Yukon-Koyukuk Census Area	75	90.36
Circle, AK (cdp) Yukon-Koyukuk Census Area	75	72.12
Tacoma, WA (city) Pierce County	74	0.04
Anvik, AK (city) Yukon-Koyukuk Census Area	69	81.18
Valdez, AK (city) Valdez-Cordova Census Area	69	1.74
Hughes, AK (city) Yukon-Koyukuk Census Area	68	88.31
Stevens Village, AK (cdp) Yukon-Koyukuk Census Area	66	84.62
Fishhook, AK (cdp) Matanuska-Susitna Borough	66	1.41
New Allakaket, AK (cdp) Yukon-Koyukuk Census Area	65	98.48
Gulkana, AK (cdp) Valdez-Cordova Census Area	65	54.62
Sterling, AK (cdp) Kenai Peninsula Borough	62	1.10
Northway, AK (cdp) Southeast Fairbanks Census Area	57	80.28
Salamatof, AK (cdp) Kenai Peninsula Borough	57	5.82
Gateway, AK (cdp) Matanuska-Susitna Borough	57	1.03
Portland, OR (city) Multnomah County	57	0.01
Nikolai, AK (city) Yukon-Koyukuk Census Area	56	59.57
Glennallen, AK (cdp) Valdez-Cordova Census Area	55	11.39
Albuquerque, NM (city) Bernalillo County	53	0.01
Goldstream, AK (cdp) Fairbanks North Star Borough	52	1.46
Dot Lake Village, AK (cdp) Southeast Fairbanks Census Area	51	82.26
Ketchikan, AK (city) Ketchikan Gateway Borough	49	0.61
Los Angeles, CA (city) Los Angeles County	49	<0.01
Homer, AK (city) Kenai Peninsula Borough	47	0.94
Sitka, AK (borough) Sitka City and Borough	45	0.51
Nome, AK (city) Nome Census Area	44	1.22
Seward, AK (city) Kenai Peninsula Borough	42	1.56
Big Lake, AK (cdp) Matanuska-Susitna Borough	42	1.25
Iliamna, AK (cdp) Lake and Peninsula Borough	41	37.61
North Pole, AK (city) Fairbanks North Star Borough	41	1.94
Chalkyitsik, AK (cdp) Yukon-Koyukuk Census Area	40	57.97
Seldovia Village, AK (cdp) Kenai Peninsula Borough	39	23.64
San Diego, CA (city) San Diego County	39	<0.01
Bear Creek, AK (cdp) Kenai Peninsula Borough	37	1.89
Salem, OR (city) Marion County	37	0.02
New York, NY (city) Kings County	37	<0.01
Northway Junction, AK (cdp) Southeast Fairbanks Census Area	36	66.67
Gakona, AK (cdp) Valdez-Cordova Census Area	36	16.51
Phoenix, AZ (city) Maricopa County	35	<0.01
Butte, AK (cdp) Matanuska-Susitna Borough	33	1.02
Birch Creek, AK (cdp) Yukon-Koyukuk Census Area	31	93.94
Alatna, AK (cdp) Yukon-Koyukuk Census Area	31	83.78
Chitina, AK (cdp) Valdez-Cordova Census Area	31	24.60
Spokane, WA (city) Spokane County	31	0.01
Houston, AK (city) Matanuska-Susitna Borough	30	1.57
Anchor Point, AK (cdp) Kenai Peninsula Borough	30	1.55
Dillingham, AK (city) Dillingham Census Area	30	1.29
Chistochina, AK (cdp) Valdez-Cordova Census Area	29	31.18
Stony River, AK (cdp) Bethel Census Area	26	48.15
Mesa, AZ (city) Maricopa County	26	0.01
Reno, NV (city) Washoe County	26	0.01
Kenny Lake, AK (cdp) Valdez-Cordova Census Area	25	7.04
Kent, WA (city) King County	25	0.03
Everett, WA (city) Snohomish County	25	0.02
Cantwell, AK (cdp) Denali Borough	24	10.96
Susitna North, AK (cdp) Matanuska-Susitna Borough	24	1.90
Rampart, AK (cdp) Yukon-Koyukuk Census Area	23	95.83
Eagle Village, AK (cdp) Southeast Fairbanks Census Area	23	34.33
Seldovia, AK (city) Kenai Peninsula Borough	23	9.02
Ridgeway, AK (cdp) Kenai Peninsula Borough	23	1.14
Manley Hot Springs, AK (cdp) Yukon-Koyukuk Census Area	22	24.72
Aniak, AK (city) Bethel Census Area	22	4.39
Happy Valley, AK (cdp) Kenai Peninsula Borough	22	3.71
Willow, AK (cdp) Matanuska-Susitna Borough	22	1.05
Auburn, WA (city) King County	22	0.03
Newhalen, AK (city) Lake and Peninsula Borough	21	11.05
Vancouver, WA (city) Clark County	21	0.01
Pedro Bay, AK (cdp) Lake and Peninsula Borough	20	47.62
Cohoe, AK (cdp) Kenai Peninsula Borough	20	1.47
Deltana, AK (cdp) Southeast Fairbanks Census Area	20	0.89
Kotzebue, AK (city) Northwest Arctic Borough	20	0.62
Lime Village, AK (cdp) Bethel Census Area	19	65.52
South Van Horn, AK (cdp) Fairbanks North Star Borough	19	3.41
Yakutat, AK (cdp) Yakutat City and Borough	19	2.87
Federal Way, WA (city) King County	19	0.02
Colorado Springs, CO (city) El Paso County	19	<0.01
Denver, CO (city) Denver County	19	<0.01
Edmonds, WA (city) Snohomish County	18	0.05
Lynnwood, WA (city) Snohomish County	18	0.05
Spokane Valley, WA (city) Spokane County	18	0.02
Fort Worth, TX (city) Tarrant County	18	<0.01
Las Vegas, NV (city) Clark County	18	<0.01
Manhattan, NY (borough) New York County	18	<0.01
Delta Junction, AK (city) Southeast Fairbanks Census Area	17	1.77
Eugene, OR (city) Lane County	17	0.01
Urban Honolulu, HI (cdp) Honolulu County	17	0.01
Fritz Creek, AK (cdp) Kenai Peninsula Borough	16	0.83
Kodiak, AK (city) Kodiak Island Borough	16	0.26
Kirkland, WA (city) King County	16	0.03
Modesto, CA (city) Stanislaus County	16	0.01
Fox, AK (cdp) Fairbanks North Star Borough	15	3.60
Bellingham, WA (city) Whatcom County	15	0.02
Redding, CA (city) Shasta County	15	0.02
Boise City, ID (city) Ada County	15	0.01
San Antonio, TX (city) Medina County	15	<0.01
Pleasant Valley, AK (cdp) Fairbanks North Star Borough	14	1.93
Barrow, AK (city) North Slope Borough	14	0.33
Parkland, WA (cdp) Pierce County	14	0.04
Tucson, AZ (city) Pima County	14	<0.01
Kasilof, AK (cdp) Kenai Peninsula Borough	13	2.37
Hudson, CO (town) Weld County	13	0.55
Graham, WA (cdp) Pierce County	13	0.06

Please refer to the Explanation of Data in the front of the book for more detailed information.

Race

Alaska Native: Alaska Athabascan

Top 150 Places Sorted by Percent of Total Population

Based on all places, regardless of total population

Place	Population	%
New Allakaket, AK (cdp) Yukon-Koyukuk Census Area	65	98.48
Koyukuk, AK (city) Yukon-Koyukuk Census Area	94	97.92
Beaver, AK (cdp) Yukon-Koyukuk Census Area	81	96.43
Rampart, AK (cdp) Yukon-Koyukuk Census Area	23	95.83
Birch Creek, AK (cdp) Yukon-Koyukuk Census Area	31	93.94
Nulato, AK (city) Yukon-Koyukuk Census Area	246	93.18
Kaltag, AK (city) Yukon-Koyukuk Census Area	176	92.63
Huslia, AK (city) Yukon-Koyukuk Census Area	254	92.36
Allakaket, AK (city) Yukon-Koyukuk Census Area	96	91.43
Holy Cross, AK (city) Yukon-Koyukuk Census Area	162	91.01
Northway Village, AK (cdp) Southeast Fairbanks Census Area	89	90.82
Shageluk, AK (city) Yukon-Koyukuk Census Area	75	90.36
Venetie, AK (cdp) Yukon-Koyukuk Census Area	149	89.76
Hughes, AK (city) Yukon-Koyukuk Census Area	68	88.31
Tyonek, AK (cdp) Kenai Peninsula Borough	150	87.72
Minto, AK (cdp) Yukon-Koyukuk Census Area	184	87.62
Grayling, AK (city) Yukon-Koyukuk Census Area	169	87.11
Ruby, AK (city) Yukon-Koyukuk Census Area	142	85.54
Fort Yukon, AK (city) Yukon-Koyukuk Census Area	496	85.08
Stevens Village, AK (cdp) Yukon-Koyukuk Census Area	66	84.62
Alatna, AK (cdp) Yukon-Koyukuk Census Area	31	83.78
Tanacross, AK (cdp) Southeast Fairbanks Census Area	113	83.09
Tetlin, AK (cdp) Southeast Fairbanks Census Area	105	82.68
Dot Lake Village, AK (cdp) Southeast Fairbanks Census Area	51	82.26
Tanana, AK (city) Yukon-Koyukuk Census Area	202	82.11
Anvik, AK (city) Yukon-Koyukuk Census Area	69	81.18
Northway, AK (cdp) Southeast Fairbanks Census Area	57	80.28
Healy Lake, AK (cdp) Southeast Fairbanks Census Area	10	76.92
Circle, AK (cdp) Yukon-Koyukuk Census Area	75	72.12
Mentasta Lake, AK (cdp) Valdez-Cordova Census Area	79	70.54
Arctic Village, AK (cdp) Yukon-Koyukuk Census Area	106	69.74
Northway Junction, AK (cdp) Southeast Fairbanks Census Area	36	66.67
Nondalton, AK (city) Lake and Peninsula Borough	109	66.46
Lime Village, AK (cdp) Bethel Census Area	19	65.52
Galena, AK (city) Yukon-Koyukuk Census Area	290	61.70
Nikolai, AK (city) Yukon-Koyukuk Census Area	56	59.57
Chalkyitsik, AK (cdp) Yukon-Koyukuk Census Area	40	57.97
Gulkana, AK (cdp) Valdez-Cordova Census Area	65	54.62
Loring, AK (cdp) Ketchikan Gateway Borough	2	50.00
Stony River, AK (cdp) Bethel Census Area	26	48.15
Pedro Bay, AK (cdp) Lake and Peninsula Borough	20	47.62
Evansville, AK (cdp) Yukon-Koyukuk Census Area	6	40.00
McGrath, AK (city) Yukon-Koyukuk Census Area	137	39.60
Copper Center, AK (cdp) Valdez-Cordova Census Area	128	39.02
Iliamna, AK (cdp) Lake and Peninsula Borough	41	37.61
Nenana, AK (city) Yukon-Koyukuk Census Area	130	34.39
Eagle Village, AK (cdp) Southeast Fairbanks Census Area	23	34.33
Tazlina, AK (cdp) Valdez-Cordova Census Area	93	31.31
Chistochina, AK (cdp) Valdez-Cordova Census Area	29	31.18
Lake Minchumina, AK (cdp) Yukon-Koyukuk Census Area	4	30.77
Manley Hot Springs, AK (cdp) Yukon-Koyukuk Census Area	22	24.72
Chitina, AK (cdp) Valdez-Cordova Census Area	31	24.60
Seldovia Village, AK (cdp) Kenai Peninsula Borough	39	23.64
Dot Lake, AK (cdp) Southeast Fairbanks Census Area	3	23.08
Red Devil, AK (cdp) Bethel Census Area	5	21.74
Four Mile Road, AK (cdp) Yukon-Koyukuk Census Area	9	20.93
Gakona, AK (cdp) Valdez-Cordova Census Area	36	16.51
Tok, AK (cdp) Southeast Fairbanks Census Area	178	14.15
Takotna, AK (cdp) Yukon-Koyukuk Census Area	7	13.46
Glennallen, AK (cdp) Valdez-Cordova Census Area	55	11.39
Newhalen, AK (city) Lake and Peninsula Borough	21	11.05
Cantwell, AK (cdp) Denali Borough	24	10.96
Coldfoot, AK (cdp) Yukon-Koyukuk Census Area	1	10.00
Chenega, AK (cdp) Valdez-Cordova Census Area	7	9.21
Seldovia, AK (city) Kenai Peninsula Borough	23	9.02
Ninilchik, AK (cdp) Kenai Peninsula Borough	78	8.83
Nelchina, AK (cdp) Valdez-Cordova Census Area	5	8.47
Bettles, AK (city) Yukon-Koyukuk Census Area	1	8.33
Ugashik, AK (cdp) Lake and Peninsula Borough	1	8.33
Silver Springs, AK (cdp) Valdez-Cordova Census Area	9	7.89
Kenny Lake, AK (cdp) Valdez-Cordova Census Area	25	7.04
Sleetmute, AK (cdp) Bethel Census Area	6	6.98
Salamatof, AK (cdp) Kenai Peninsula Borough	57	5.82
Eagle, AK (city) Southeast Fairbanks Census Area	5	5.81
Clam Gulch, AK (cdp) Kenai Peninsula Borough	10	5.68
Klukwan, AK (cdp) Hoonah-Angoon Census Area	5	5.26
Sutton-Alpine, AK (cdp) Matanuska-Susitna Borough	76	5.25
Fairbanks, AK (city) Fairbanks North Star Borough	1,631	5.17
College, AK (cdp) Fairbanks North Star Borough	667	5.15
Beluga, AK (cdp) Kenai Peninsula Borough	1	5.00
Slana, AK (cdp) Valdez-Cordova Census Area	7	4.76
Crooked Creek, AK (cdp) Bethel Census Area	5	4.76
Whittier, AK (city) Valdez-Cordova Census Area	10	4.55
Chena Ridge, AK (cdp) Fairbanks North Star Borough	262	4.52
Port Alsworth, AK (cdp) Lake and Peninsula Borough	7	4.40
Aniak, AK (city) Bethel Census Area	22	4.39
Crown Point, AK (cdp) Kenai Peninsula Borough	3	4.05
Chickaloon, AK (cdp) Matanuska-Susitna Borough	11	4.04
Kenai, AK (city) Kenai Peninsula Borough	282	3.97
Nikiski, AK (cdp) Kenai Peninsula Borough	168	3.74
Happy Valley, AK (cdp) Kenai Peninsula Borough	22	3.71
Willow Creek, AK (cdp) Valdez-Cordova Census Area	7	3.66
Fox, AK (cdp) Fairbanks North Star Borough	15	3.60
Farmers Loop, AK (cdp) Fairbanks North Star Borough	167	3.44
Ester, AK (cdp) Fairbanks North Star Borough	83	3.43
South Van Horn, AK (cdp) Fairbanks North Star Borough	19	3.41
Tatitlek, AK (cdp) Valdez-Cordova Census Area	3	3.41
Port Graham, AK (cdp) Kenai Peninsula Borough	6	3.39
Central, AK (cdp) Yukon-Koyukuk Census Area	3	3.13
St. George, AK (city) Aleutians West Census Area	3	2.94
Pilot Point, AK (city) Lake and Peninsula Borough	2	2.94
Levelock, AK (cdp) Lake and Peninsula Borough	2	2.90
Yakutat, AK (cdp) Yakutat City and Borough	19	2.87
Kobuk, AK (city) Northwest Arctic Borough	4	2.65
Ekwok, AK (city) Dillingham Census Area	3	2.61
Saxman, AK (city) Ketchikan Gateway Borough	10	2.43
Kasilof, AK (cdp) Kenai Peninsula Borough	13	2.37
Steele Creek, AK (cdp) Fairbanks North Star Borough	149	2.24
Badger, AK (cdp) Fairbanks North Star Borough	426	2.19
Kalifornsky, AK (cdp) Kenai Peninsula Borough	168	2.14
Trapper Creek, AK (cdp) Matanuska-Susitna Borough	10	2.08
North Pole, AK (city) Fairbanks North Star Borough	41	1.94
Pleasant Valley, AK (cdp) Fairbanks North Star Borough	14	1.93
Soldotna, AK (city) Kenai Peninsula Borough	80	1.92
Susitna North, AK (cdp) Matanuska-Susitna Borough	24	1.90
Bear Creek, AK (cdp) Kenai Peninsula Borough	37	1.89
Ouzinkie, AK (city) Kodiak Island Borough	3	1.86
Delta Junction, AK (city) Southeast Fairbanks Census Area	17	1.77
Kokhanok, AK (cdp) Lake and Peninsula Borough	3	1.76
Valdez, AK (city) Valdez-Cordova Census Area	69	1.74
Point MacKenzie, AK (cdp) Matanuska-Susitna Borough	9	1.70
Goodnews Bay, AK (city) Bethel Census Area	4	1.65
Unalakleet, AK (city) Nome Census Area	11	1.60
Houston, AK (city) Matanuska-Susitna Borough	30	1.57
Seward, AK (city) Kenai Peninsula Borough	42	1.56
Anchor Point, AK (cdp) Kenai Peninsula Borough	30	1.55
Anchorage, AK (municipality) Anchorage Municipality	4,333	1.48
Bethel, AK (city) Bethel Census Area	90	1.48
Cohoe, AK (cdp) Kenai Peninsula Borough	20	1.47
Naknek, AK (cdp) Bristol Bay Borough	8	1.47
Goldstream, AK (cdp) Fairbanks North Star Borough	52	1.46
St. Paul, AK (city) Aleutians West Census Area	7	1.46
Zortman, MT (cdp) Phillips County	1	1.45
Willapa, WA (cdp) Pacific County	3	1.43
Fishhook, AK (cdp) Matanuska-Susitna Borough	66	1.41
Unity, OR (city) Baker County	1	1.41
St. Mary's, AK (city) Wade Hampton Census Area	7	1.38
Meadow Lakes, AK (cdp) Matanuska-Susitna Borough	103	1.36
Knik-Fairview, AK (cdp) Matanuska-Susitna Borough	200	1.34
Moose Creek, AK (cdp) Fairbanks North Star Borough	10	1.34
Palmer, AK (city) Matanuska-Susitna Borough	79	1.33
Angoon, AK (city) Hoonah-Angoon Census Area	6	1.31
Dillingham, AK (city) Dillingham Census Area	30	1.29
Buffalo Soapstone, AK (cdp) Matanuska-Susitna Borough	11	1.29
Atqasuk, AK (city) North Slope Borough	3	1.29
Tonsina, AK (cdp) Valdez-Cordova Census Area	1	1.28
Kachemak, AK (city) Kenai Peninsula Borough	6	1.27
Big Lake, AK (cdp) Matanuska-Susitna Borough	42	1.25
St. Michael, AK (city) Nome Census Area	5	1.25
Anaktuvuk Pass, AK (city) North Slope Borough	4	1.23

Please refer to the Explanation of Data in the front of the book for more detailed information.

Race

Alaska Native: Alaska Athabascan

Top 150 Places Sorted by Percent of Total Population

Based on places with total population of 7,500 or more

Place	Population	%
Fairbanks, AK (city) Fairbanks North Star Borough	1,631	5.17
College, AK (cdp) Fairbanks North Star Borough	667	5.15
Badger, AK (cdp) Fairbanks North Star Borough	426	2.19
Kalifornsky, AK (cdp) Kenai Peninsula Borough	168	2.14
Anchorage, AK (municipality) Anchorage Municipality	4,333	1.48
Meadow Lakes, AK (cdp) Matanuska-Susitna Borough	103	1.36
Knik-Fairview, AK (cdp) Matanuska-Susitna Borough	200	1.34
Tanaina, AK (cdp) Matanuska-Susitna Borough	93	1.13
Wasilla, AK (city) Matanuska-Susitna Borough	76	0.97
Lakes, AK (cdp) Matanuska-Susitna Borough	80	0.96
Ketchikan, AK (city) Ketchikan Gateway Borough	49	0.61
Sitka, AK (borough) Sitka City and Borough	45	0.51
Juneau, AK (borough) Juneau City and Borough	119	0.38
Lincoln City, OR (city) Lincoln County	9	0.11
Stayton, OR (city) Marion County	8	0.10
Fallon, NV (city) Churchill County	8	0.09
Hoquiam, WA (city) Grays Harbor County	8	0.09
North Bend, OR (city) Coos County	8	0.08
Picnic Point, WA (cdp) Snohomish County	7	0.08
Ephrata, WA (city) Grant County	6	0.08
Port Townsend, WA (city) Jefferson County	6	0.07
Graham, WA (cdp) Pierce County	13	0.06
Port Angeles, WA (city) Clallam County	11	0.06
Colchester, CT (town) New London County	9	0.06
Lake Forest Park, WA (city) King County	7	0.06
Fort Meade, MD (cdp) Anne Arundel County	6	0.06
Shasta Lake, CA (city) Shasta County	6	0.06
Pennfield, MI (charter township) Calhoun County	5	0.06
Sweet Home, OR (city) Linn County	5	0.06
Edmonds, WA (city) Snohomish County	18	0.05
Lynnwood, WA (city) Snohomish County	18	0.05
Kingsgate, WA (cdp) King County	6	0.05
Grandview, WA (city) Yakima County	5	0.05
Kalaoa, HI (cdp) Hawaii County	5	0.05
Sedro-Woolley, WA (city) Skagit County	5	0.05
Blair, NE (city) Washington County	4	0.05
Haiku-Pauwela, HI (cdp) Maui County	4	0.05
Liberty Lake, WA (city) Spokane County	4	0.05
Summit, WA (cdp) Pierce County	4	0.05
Tacoma, WA (city) Pierce County	74	0.04
Parkland, WA (cdp) Pierce County	14	0.04
Security-Widefield, CO (cdp) El Paso County	13	0.04
Fort Hood, TX (cdp) Bell County	12	0.04
Lake Stevens, WA (city) Snohomish County	12	0.04
Bainbridge Island, WA (city) Kitsap County	10	0.04
SeaTac, WA (city) King County	10	0.04
Eagle, ID (city) Ada County	8	0.04
Durango, CO (city) La Plata County	7	0.04
Cedar Lake, IN (town) Lake County	5	0.04
Lakeland North, WA (cdp) King County	5	0.04
Richmond, TX (city) Fort Bend County	5	0.04
West Richland, WA (city) Benton County	5	0.04
Ferndale, WA (city) Whatcom County	4	0.04
Prineville, OR (city) Crook County	4	0.04
Sandy, OR (city) Clackamas County	4	0.04
Vashon, WA (cdp) King County	4	0.04
Abingdon, VA (town) Washington County	3	0.04
Cortez, CO (city) Montezuma County	3	0.04
Florence, OR (city) Lane County	3	0.04
Hollymead, VA (cdp) Albemarle County	3	0.04
Northridge, OH (cdp) Clark County	3	0.04
Thousand Palms, CA (cdp) Riverside County	3	0.04
Kent, WA (city) King County	25	0.03
Auburn, WA (city) King County	22	0.03
Kirkland, WA (city) King County	16	0.03
Lewiston, ID (city) Nez Perce County	11	0.03
Longview, WA (city) Cowlitz County	11	0.03
Bremerton, WA (city) Kitsap County	10	0.03
Keizer, OR (city) Marion County	10	0.03
Mount Vernon, WA (city) Skagit County	9	0.03
Issaquah, WA (city) King County	8	0.03
Watertown, NY (city) Jefferson County	8	0.03
Spanaway, WA (cdp) Pierce County	7	0.03
Mountlake Terrace, WA (city) Snohomish County	6	0.03
Newberg, OR (city) Yamhill County	6	0.03
Watertown, SD (city) Codington County	6	0.03
Dixon, CA (city) Solano County	5	0.03
Orchards, WA (cdp) Clark County	5	0.03
Clearlake, CA (city) Lake County	4	0.03
Clemson, SC (city) Pickens County	4	0.03
Elk Plain, WA (cdp) Pierce County	4	0.03
Forestville, MD (cdp) Prince George's County	4	0.03
Fortuna, CA (city) Humboldt County	4	0.03
Horizon West, FL (cdp) Orange County	4	0.03
Kerman, CA (city) Fresno County	4	0.03
Maitland, FL (city) Orange County	4	0.03
Ozark, AL (city) Dale County	4	0.03
Plymouth, CT (town) Litchfield County	4	0.03
Rio Linda, CA (cdp) Sacramento County	4	0.03
Astoria, OR (city) Clatsop County	3	0.03
Dalton, MI (township) Muskegon County	3	0.03
Kaneohe Station, HI (cdp) Honolulu County	3	0.03
Kapaa, HI (cdp) Kauai County	3	0.03
Valley Falls, RI (cdp) Providence County	3	0.03
Vermillion, SD (city) Clay County	3	0.03
Lake Stickney, WA (cdp) Snohomish County	2	0.03
Mount Vista, WA (cdp) Clark County	2	0.03
Waller, WA (cdp) Pierce County	2	0.03
Salem, OR (city) Marion County	37	0.02
Everett, WA (city) Snohomish County	25	0.02
Federal Way, WA (city) King County	19	0.02
Spokane Valley, WA (city) Spokane County	18	0.02
Bellingham, WA (city) Whatcom County	15	0.02
Redding, CA (city) Shasta County	15	0.02
Marysville, WA (city) Snohomish County	13	0.02
Kennewick, WA (city) Benton County	12	0.02
Lakewood, WA (city) Pierce County	12	0.02
Tigard, OR (city) Washington County	12	0.02
Corvallis, OR (city) Benton County	11	0.02
Olympia, WA (city) Thurston County	11	0.02
Cheyenne, WY (city) Laramie County	10	0.02
Coeur d'Alene, ID (city) Kootenai County	10	0.02
Idaho Falls, ID (city) Bonneville County	10	0.02
Springfield, OR (city) Lane County	10	0.02
Middletown, CT (city/town) Middlesex County	9	0.02
Bothell, WA (city) King County	8	0.02
Lacey, WA (city) Thurston County	7	0.02
Roy, UT (city) Weber County	7	0.02
Des Moines, WA (city) King County	6	0.02
Grants Pass, OR (city) Josephine County	6	0.02
Kailua, HI (cdp) Honolulu County	6	0.02
Madison, MS (city) Madison County	6	0.02
Burien, WA (city) King County	5	0.02
Corsicana, TX (city) Navarro County	5	0.02
Eureka, CA (city) Humboldt County	5	0.02
Moses Lake, WA (city) Grant County	5	0.02
Oak Harbor, WA (city) Island County	5	0.02
Oakdale, MN (city) Washington County	5	0.02
Post Falls, ID (city) Kootenai County	5	0.02
Pullman, WA (city) Whitman County	5	0.02
Roseburg, OR (city) Douglas County	5	0.02
Bay Point, CA (cdp) Contra Costa County	4	0.02
Brent, FL (cdp) Escambia County	4	0.02
Cañon City, CO (city) Fremont County	4	0.02
Chester, VA (cdp) Chesterfield County	4	0.02
Cottage Lake, WA (cdp) King County	4	0.02
Ellensburg, WA (city) Kittitas County	4	0.02
Fortuna Foothills, AZ (cdp) Yuma County	4	0.02
French Valley, CA (cdp) Riverside County	4	0.02
Hudson, OH (city) Summit County	4	0.02
Inglewood-Finn Hill, WA (cdp) King County	4	0.02
Lomita, CA (city) Los Angeles County	4	0.02
Maple Valley, WA (city) King County	4	0.02
Mill Creek, WA (city) Snohomish County	4	0.02
Mukilteo, WA (city) Snohomish County	4	0.02
North Lynnwood, WA (cdp) Snohomish County	4	0.02
Redmond, OR (city) Deschutes County	4	0.02
Salmon Creek, WA (cdp) Clark County	4	0.02
Silver Firs, WA (cdp) Snohomish County	4	0.02
Sun Valley, NV (cdp) Washoe County	4	0.02

SECTION THREE

Please refer to the Explanation of Data in the front of the book for more detailed information.

Race

Alaska Native: Aleut

U.S. and 50 States Sorted by Population and Percent of Total Population

Place	Population	%
United States	**19,282**	**0.01**
Alaska	11,216	1.58
Washington	2,870	0.04
California	1,107	<0.01
Oregon	631	0.02
Texas	259	<0.01
Colorado	241	<0.01
Arizona	218	<0.01
Oklahoma	168	<0.01
Florida	154	<0.01
Nevada	127	<0.01
Idaho	121	0.01
North Carolina	111	<0.01
Pennsylvania	108	<0.01
Hawaii	107	0.01
Michigan	107	<0.01
Minnesota	99	<0.01
Virginia	99	<0.01
Illinois	97	<0.01
Missouri	92	<0.01
Montana	88	0.01
Kansas	88	<0.01
Ohio	88	<0.01
Georgia	84	<0.01
New York	82	<0.01
Utah	79	<0.01
Wisconsin	73	<0.01
Tennessee	70	<0.01
New Mexico	69	<0.01
Alabama	61	<0.01
Indiana	55	<0.01
Maryland	49	<0.01
Arkansas	41	<0.01
Massachusetts	40	<0.01
South Carolina	40	<0.01
Kentucky	39	<0.01
South Dakota	37	<0.01
Maine	34	<0.01
Iowa	33	<0.01
Louisiana	32	<0.01
New Jersey	31	<0.01
Wyoming	29	0.01
Mississippi	26	<0.01
New Hampshire	20	<0.01
Nebraska	15	<0.01
Connecticut	14	<0.01
North Dakota	9	<0.01
Vermont	9	<0.01
West Virginia	6	<0.01
Delaware	3	<0.01
District of Columbia	3	<0.01
Rhode Island	3	<0.01

Place	Population	%
Alaska	11,216	1.58
Washington	2,870	0.04
Oregon	631	0.02
United States	**19,282**	**0.01**
Idaho	121	0.01
Hawaii	107	0.01
Montana	88	0.01
Wyoming	29	0.01
California	1,107	<0.01
Texas	259	<0.01
Colorado	241	<0.01
Arizona	218	<0.01
Oklahoma	168	<0.01
Florida	154	<0.01
Nevada	127	<0.01
North Carolina	111	<0.01
Pennsylvania	108	<0.01
Michigan	107	<0.01
Minnesota	99	<0.01
Virginia	99	<0.01
Illinois	97	<0.01
Missouri	92	<0.01
Kansas	88	<0.01
Ohio	88	<0.01
Georgia	84	<0.01
New York	82	<0.01
Utah	79	<0.01
Wisconsin	73	<0.01
Tennessee	70	<0.01
New Mexico	69	<0.01
Alabama	61	<0.01
Indiana	55	<0.01
Maryland	49	<0.01
Arkansas	41	<0.01
Massachusetts	40	<0.01
South Carolina	40	<0.01
Kentucky	39	<0.01
South Dakota	37	<0.01
Maine	34	<0.01
Iowa	33	<0.01
Louisiana	32	<0.01
New Jersey	31	<0.01
Mississippi	26	<0.01
New Hampshire	20	<0.01
Nebraska	15	<0.01
Connecticut	14	<0.01
North Dakota	9	<0.01
Vermont	9	<0.01
West Virginia	6	<0.01
Delaware	3	<0.01
District of Columbia	3	<0.01
Rhode Island	3	<0.01

Please refer to the Explanation of Data in the front of the book for more detailed information.

Race

Alaska Native: Aleut

Top 150 Places Sorted by Population

Based on all places, regardless of total population

Place	Population	%
Anchorage, AK (municipality) Anchorage Municipality	3,982	1.36
Kodiak, AK (city) Kodiak Island Borough	478	7.80
St. Paul, AK (city) Aleutians West Census Area	375	78.29
King Cove, AK (city) Aleutians East Borough	309	32.94
Sand Point, AK (city) Aleutians East Borough	309	31.66
Seattle, WA (city) King County	224	0.04
Cordova, AK (city) Valdez-Cordova Census Area	206	9.20
Unalaska, AK (city) Aleutians West Census Area	206	4.71
Juneau, AK (borough) Juneau City and Borough	186	0.59
Old Harbor, AK (city) Kodiak Island Borough	176	80.73
Nanwalek, AK (cdp) Kenai Peninsula Borough	167	65.75
Knik-Fairview, AK (cdp) Matanuska-Susitna Borough	162	1.09
Ouzinkie, AK (city) Kodiak Island Borough	133	82.61
Valdez, AK (city) Valdez-Cordova Census Area	128	3.22
Kokhanok, AK (cdp) Lake and Peninsula Borough	127	74.71
Port Lions, AK (city) Kodiak Island Borough	105	54.12
Tanaina, AK (cdp) Matanuska-Susitna Borough	105	1.28
Perryville, AK (cdp) Lake and Peninsula Borough	103	91.15
Dillingham, AK (city) Dillingham Census Area	101	4.34
Meadow Lakes, AK (cdp) Matanuska-Susitna Borough	101	1.33
Palmer, AK (city) Matanuska-Susitna Borough	99	1.67
Kenai, AK (city) Kenai Peninsula Borough	94	1.32
Lakes, AK (cdp) Matanuska-Susitna Borough	92	1.10
Tacoma, WA (city) Pierce County	88	0.04
Ketchikan, AK (city) Ketchikan Gateway Borough	85	1.06
St. George, AK (city) Aleutians West Census Area	83	81.37
Seward, AK (city) Kenai Peninsula Borough	78	2.90
Sitka, AK (borough) Sitka City and Borough	77	0.87
Portland, OR (city) Multnomah County	74	0.01
Port Heiden, AK (city) Lake and Peninsula Borough	73	71.57
Akutan, AK (city) Aleutians East Borough	69	6.72
Homer, AK (city) Kenai Peninsula Borough	69	1.38
Bellingham, WA (city) Whatcom County	69	0.09
Gateway, AK (cdp) Matanuska-Susitna Borough	67	1.21
Port Graham, AK (cdp) Kenai Peninsula Borough	66	37.29
King Salmon, AK (cdp) Bristol Bay Borough	66	17.65
Chignik Lake, AK (cdp) Lake and Peninsula Borough	65	89.04
Wasilla, AK (city) Matanuska-Susitna Borough	65	0.83
Larsen Bay, AK (city) Kodiak Island Borough	60	68.97
Everett, WA (city) Snohomish County	60	0.06
Akhiok, AK (city) Kodiak Island Borough	59	83.10
Fairbanks, AK (city) Fairbanks North Star Borough	57	0.18
Marysville, WA (city) Snohomish County	57	0.09
Chignik Lagoon, AK (cdp) Lake and Peninsula Borough	56	71.79
Atka, AK (city) Aleutians West Census Area	55	90.16
Kalifornsky, AK (cdp) Kenai Peninsula Borough	54	0.69
Naknek, AK (cdp) Bristol Bay Borough	52	9.56
Bear Creek, AK (cdp) Kenai Peninsula Borough	52	2.66
Vancouver, WA (city) Clark County	52	0.03
Tatitlek, AK (cdp) Valdez-Cordova Census Area	51	57.95
San Diego, CA (city) San Diego County	51	<0.01
Soldotna, AK (city) Kenai Peninsula Borough	50	1.20
Chignik, AK (city) Lake and Peninsula Borough	46	50.55
College, AK (cdp) Fairbanks North Star Borough	46	0.35
South Naknek, AK (cdp) Bristol Bay Borough	45	56.96
Shoreline, WA (city) King County	45	0.08
Womens Bay, AK (cdp) Kodiak Island Borough	44	6.12
Auburn, WA (city) King County	44	0.06
Renton, WA (city) King County	44	0.05
Big Lake, AK (cdp) Matanuska-Susitna Borough	43	1.28
Edmonds, WA (city) Snohomish County	40	0.10
Pilot Point, AK (city) Lake and Peninsula Borough	39	57.35
Sutton-Alpine, AK (cdp) Matanuska-Susitna Borough	39	2.70
Wrangell, AK (borough) Wrangell City and Borough	38	1.60
Sterling, AK (cdp) Kenai Peninsula Borough	38	0.68
Spokane, WA (city) Spokane County	38	0.02
Butte, AK (cdp) Matanuska-Susitna Borough	37	1.14
Fishhook, AK (cdp) Matanuska-Susitna Borough	36	0.77
Puyallup, WA (city) Pierce County	36	0.10
Los Angeles, CA (city) Los Angeles County	35	<0.01
Phoenix, AZ (city) Maricopa County	34	<0.01
Lake Stevens, WA (city) Snohomish County	33	0.12
San Jose, CA (city) Santa Clara County	33	<0.01
Nelson Lagoon, AK (cdp) Aleutians East Borough	32	61.54
Houston, AK (city) Matanuska-Susitna Borough	32	1.67
Ridgeway, AK (cdp) Kenai Peninsula Borough	32	1.58
Nikiski, AK (cdp) Kenai Peninsula Borough	32	0.71
Federal Way, WA (city) King County	32	0.04
Egegik, AK (city) Lake and Peninsula Borough	31	28.44
Badger, AK (cdp) Fairbanks North Star Borough	31	0.16
Lynnwood, WA (city) Snohomish County	31	0.09
Karluk, AK (cdp) Kodiak Island Borough	30	81.08
San Francisco, CA (city) San Francisco County	30	<0.01
Bethel, AK (city) Bethel Census Area	29	0.48
South Hill, WA (cdp) Pierce County	29	0.06
Chenega, AK (cdp) Valdez-Cordova Census Area	28	36.84
Port Angeles, WA (city) Clallam County	28	0.15
Salamatof, AK (cdp) Kenai Peninsula Borough	26	2.65
Eugene, OR (city) Lane County	26	0.02
Boise City, ID (city) Ada County	26	0.01
New York, NY (city) Kings County	26	<0.01
Adak, AK (city) Aleutians West Census Area	25	7.67
False Pass, AK (city) Aleutians East Borough	24	68.57
Bremerton, WA (city) Kitsap County	24	0.06
Wichita, KS (city) Sedgwick County	24	0.01
Port Alsworth, AK (cdp) Lake and Peninsula Borough	23	14.47
Parkland, WA (cdp) Pierce County	23	0.06
Kent, WA (city) King County	23	0.02
Colorado Springs, CO (city) El Paso County	23	0.01
Igiugig, AK (cdp) Lake and Peninsula Borough	22	44.00
Hudson, CO (town) Weld County	22	0.93
Anacortes, WA (city) Skagit County	22	0.14
Albuquerque, NM (city) Bernalillo County	22	<0.01
Denver, CO (city) Denver County	22	<0.01
Bend, OR (city) Deschutes County	21	0.03
Santa Rosa, CA (city) Sonoma County	21	0.01
Vacaville, CA (city) Solano County	20	0.02
Aurora, CO (city) Arapahoe County	20	0.01
Sacramento, CA (city) Sacramento County	20	<0.01
Ninilchik, AK (cdp) Kenai Peninsula Borough	19	2.15
Des Moines, WA (city) King County	19	0.06
Olympia, WA (city) Thurston County	18	0.04
Bellevue, WA (city) King County	18	0.01
Las Vegas, NV (city) Clark County	18	<0.01
Tucson, AZ (city) Pima County	18	<0.01
Nikolski, AK (cdp) Aleutians West Census Area	17	94.44
Pilot Station, AK (city) Wade Hampton Census Area	17	2.99
Lazy Mountain, AK (cdp) Matanuska-Susitna Borough	17	1.15
Fritz Creek, AK (cdp) Kenai Peninsula Borough	17	0.88
Lakewood, WA (city) Pierce County	17	0.03
Salem, OR (city) Marion County	17	0.01
Stockton, CA (city) San Joaquin County	17	0.01
Oklahoma City, OK (city) Oklahoma County	17	<0.01
Petersburg, AK (city) Petersburg Census Area	16	0.54
Kenmore, WA (city) King County	16	0.08
Tukwila, WA (city) King County	16	0.08
Hillsboro, OR (city) Washington County	16	0.02
Chandler, AZ (city) Maricopa County	16	0.01
Modesto, CA (city) Stanislaus County	16	0.01
San Antonio, TX (city) Medina County	16	<0.01
Point MacKenzie, AK (cdp) Matanuska-Susitna Borough	15	2.84
Craig, AK (city) Prince of Wales-Hyder Census Area	15	1.25
Cohoe, AK (cdp) Kenai Peninsula Borough	15	1.10
Steele Creek, AK (cdp) Fairbanks North Star Borough	15	0.23
East Renton Highlands, WA (cdp) King County	15	0.13
Spokane Valley, WA (city) Spokane County	15	0.02
Willow, AK (cdp) Matanuska-Susitna Borough	14	0.67
Farmers Loop, AK (cdp) Fairbanks North Star Borough	14	0.29
Birch Bay, WA (cdp) Whatcom County	14	0.17
Ellensburg, WA (city) Kittitas County	14	0.08
Lacey, WA (city) Thurston County	14	0.03
Paradise, NV (cdp) Clark County	14	0.01
Indianapolis, IN (city) Marion County	14	<0.01
Urban Honolulu, HI (cdp) Honolulu County	14	<0.01
Cold Bay, AK (city) Aleutians East Borough	13	12.04
Snohomish, WA (city) Snohomish County	13	0.14
Shelton, WA (city) Mason County	13	0.13
Ferndale, WA (city) Whatcom County	13	0.11
Red Wing, MN (city) Goodhue County	13	0.08
Arlington, WA (city) Snohomish County	13	0.07

SECTION THREE

Race

Alaska Native: Aleut

Top 150 Places Sorted by Percent of Total Population

Based on all places, regardless of total population

Place	Population	%
Ivanof Bay, AK (cdp) Lake and Peninsula Borough	7	100.00
Nikolski, AK (cdp) Aleutians West Census Area	17	94.44
Perryville, AK (cdp) Lake and Peninsula Borough	103	91.15
Atka, AK (city) Aleutians West Census Area	55	90.16
Chignik Lake, AK (cdp) Lake and Peninsula Borough	65	89.04
Akhiok, AK (city) Kodiak Island Borough	59	83.10
Ouzinkie, AK (city) Kodiak Island Borough	133	82.61
St. George, AK (city) Aleutians West Census Area	83	81.37
Karluk, AK (cdp) Kodiak Island Borough	30	81.08
Old Harbor, AK (city) Kodiak Island Borough	176	80.73
St. Paul, AK (city) Aleutians West Census Area	375	78.29
Kokhanok, AK (cdp) Lake and Peninsula Borough	127	74.71
Chignik Lagoon, AK (cdp) Lake and Peninsula Borough	56	71.79
Port Heiden, AK (city) Lake and Peninsula Borough	73	71.57
Larsen Bay, AK (city) Kodiak Island Borough	60	68.97
False Pass, AK (city) Aleutians East Borough	24	68.57
Nanwalek, AK (cdp) Kenai Peninsula Borough	167	65.75
Nelson Lagoon, AK (cdp) Aleutians East Borough	32	61.54
Tatitlek, AK (cdp) Valdez-Cordova Census Area	51	57.95
Pilot Point, AK (city) Lake and Peninsula Borough	39	57.35
South Naknek, AK (cdp) Bristol Bay Borough	45	56.96
Port Lions, AK (city) Kodiak Island Borough	105	54.12
Chignik, AK (city) Lake and Peninsula Borough	46	50.55
Pope-Vannoy Landing, AK (cdp) Lake and Peninsula Borough	3	50.00
Igiugig, AK (cdp) Lake and Peninsula Borough	22	44.00
Port Graham, AK (cdp) Kenai Peninsula Borough	66	37.29
Chenega, AK (cdp) Valdez-Cordova Census Area	28	36.84
King Cove, AK (city) Aleutians East Borough	309	32.94
Sand Point, AK (city) Aleutians East Borough	309	31.66
Egegik, AK (city) Lake and Peninsula Borough	31	28.44
Ugashik, AK (cdp) Lake and Peninsula Borough	3	25.00
King Salmon, AK (cdp) Bristol Bay Borough	66	17.65
Port Alsworth, AK (cdp) Lake and Peninsula Borough	23	14.47
Cold Bay, AK (city) Aleutians East Borough	13	12.04
Naknek, AK (cdp) Bristol Bay Borough	52	9.56
Pedro Bay, AK (cdp) Lake and Peninsula Borough	4	9.52
Cordova, AK (city) Valdez-Cordova Census Area	206	9.20
Levelock, AK (cdp) Lake and Peninsula Borough	6	8.70
Kodiak, AK (city) Kodiak Island Borough	478	7.80
Adak, AK (city) Aleutians West Census Area	25	7.67
Akutan, AK (city) Aleutians East Borough	69	6.72
Clark's Point, AK (city) Dillingham Census Area	4	6.45
Tonsina, AK (cdp) Valdez-Cordova Census Area	5	6.41
Chiniak, AK (cdp) Kodiak Island Borough	3	6.38
Womens Bay, AK (cdp) Kodiak Island Borough	44	6.12
Stony River, AK (cdp) Bethel Census Area	3	5.56
Seldovia Village, AK (cdp) Kenai Peninsula Borough	9	5.45
Beluga, AK (cdp) Kenai Peninsula Borough	1	5.00
Platinum, AK (city) Bethel Census Area	3	4.92
Unalaska, AK (city) Aleutians West Census Area	206	4.71
Willow Creek, AK (cdp) Valdez-Cordova Census Area	9	4.71
Dillingham, AK (city) Dillingham Census Area	101	4.34
Newhalen, AK (city) Lake and Peninsula Borough	7	3.68
Lime Village, AK (cdp) Bethel Census Area	1	3.45
Valdez, AK (city) Valdez-Cordova Census Area	128	3.22
Whittier, AK (city) Valdez-Cordova Census Area	7	3.18
Seldovia, AK (city) Kenai Peninsula Borough	8	3.14
Pilot Station, AK (city) Wade Hampton Census Area	17	2.99
Seward, AK (city) Kenai Peninsula Borough	78	2.90
Point MacKenzie, AK (cdp) Matanuska-Susitna Borough	15	2.84
Aleknagik, AK (city) Dillingham Census Area	6	2.74
Sutton-Alpine, AK (cdp) Matanuska-Susitna Borough	39	2.70
Bear Creek, AK (cdp) Kenai Peninsula Borough	52	2.66
Salamatof, AK (cdp) Kenai Peninsula Borough	26	2.65
Pelican, AK (city) Hoonah-Angoon Census Area	2	2.27
Ninilchik, AK (cdp) Kenai Peninsula Borough	19	2.15
Copper Center, AK (cdp) Valdez-Cordova Census Area	7	2.13
Kasaan, AK (city) Prince of Wales-Hyder Census Area	1	2.04
Lutak, AK (cdp) Haines Borough	1	2.04
Kenny Lake, AK (cdp) Valdez-Cordova Census Area	7	1.97
Naukati Bay, AK (cdp) Prince of Wales-Hyder Census Area	2	1.77
Magnet, NE (village) Cedar County	1	1.75
Camas, MT (cdp) Sanders County	1	1.72
Clam Gulch, AK (cdp) Kenai Peninsula Borough	3	1.70
Chuathbaluk, AK (city) Bethel Census Area	2	1.69
Palmer, AK (city) Matanuska-Susitna Borough	99	1.67
Houston, AK (city) Matanuska-Susitna Borough	32	1.67
South Van Horn, AK (cdp) Fairbanks North Star Borough	9	1.61
Wrangell, AK (borough) Wrangell City and Borough	38	1.60
Ridgeway, AK (cdp) Kenai Peninsula Borough	32	1.58
Yakutat, AK (cdp) Yakutat City and Borough	10	1.51
Addy, WA (cdp) Stevens County	4	1.49
Unalakleet, AK (city) Nome Census Area	10	1.45
Huslia, AK (city) Yukon-Koyukuk Census Area	4	1.45
Homer, AK (city) Kenai Peninsula Borough	69	1.38
Anchorage, AK (municipality) Anchorage Municipality	3,982	1.36
Tazlina, AK (cdp) Valdez-Cordova Census Area	4	1.35
Branson, CO (town) Las Animas County	1	1.35
Crown Point, AK (cdp) Kenai Peninsula Borough	1	1.35
Meadow Lakes, AK (cdp) Matanuska-Susitna Borough	101	1.33
Kenai, AK (city) Kenai Peninsula Borough	94	1.32
Lincoln, WI (town) Burnett County	4	1.29
Snoqualmie Pass, WA (cdp) Kittitas County	4	1.29
Tanaina, AK (cdp) Matanuska-Susitna Borough	105	1.28
Big Lake, AK (cdp) Matanuska-Susitna Borough	43	1.28
Craig, AK (city) Prince of Wales-Hyder Census Area	15	1.25
Alsea, OR (cdp) Benton County	2	1.22
Gateway, AK (cdp) Matanuska-Susitna Borough	67	1.21
Soldotna, AK (city) Kenai Peninsula Borough	50	1.20
Fox, AK (cdp) Fairbanks North Star Borough	5	1.20
Anvik, AK (city) Yukon-Koyukuk Census Area	1	1.18
Anderson, NJ (cdp) Warren County	4	1.17
Lazy Mountain, AK (cdp) Matanuska-Susitna Borough	17	1.15
Butte, AK (cdp) Matanuska-Susitna Borough	37	1.14
Grays River, WA (cdp) Wahkiakum County	3	1.14
Lakes, AK (cdp) Matanuska-Susitna Borough	92	1.10
Cohoe, AK (cdp) Kenai Peninsula Borough	15	1.10
Knik-Fairview, AK (cdp) Matanuska-Susitna Borough	162	1.09
Ketchikan, AK (city) Ketchikan Gateway Borough	85	1.06
Garrison, MT (cdp) Powell County	1	1.04
Long Creek, OR (city) Grant County	2	1.02
Knik River, AK (cdp) Matanuska-Susitna Borough	7	0.94
Hudson, CO (town) Weld County	22	0.93
Gakona, AK (cdp) Valdez-Cordova Census Area	2	0.92
Iliamna, AK (cdp) Lake and Peninsula Borough	1	0.92
Manokotak, AK (city) Dillingham Census Area	4	0.90
Fritz Creek, AK (cdp) Kenai Peninsula Borough	17	0.88
Sitka, AK (borough) Sitka City and Borough	77	0.87
Diamond Ridge, AK (cdp) Kenai Peninsula Borough	10	0.87
Ekwok, AK (city) Dillingham Census Area	1	0.87
Fallon Station, NV (cdp) Churchill County	6	0.85
Halaula, HI (cdp) Hawaii County	4	0.85
Selawik, AK (city) Northwest Arctic Borough	7	0.84
Gulkana, AK (cdp) Valdez-Cordova Census Area	1	0.84
Wasilla, AK (city) Matanuska-Susitna Borough	65	0.83
Siletz, OR (city) Lincoln County	10	0.83
Trapper Creek, AK (cdp) Matanuska-Susitna Borough	4	0.83
Baltimore, VT (town) Windsor County	2	0.82
Goodnews Bay, AK (city) Bethel Census Area	2	0.82
Talkeetna, AK (cdp) Matanuska-Susitna Borough	7	0.80
Hydaburg, AK (city) Prince of Wales-Hyder Census Area	3	0.80
Fishhook, AK (cdp) Matanuska-Susitna Borough	36	0.77
Skagway, AK (cdp) Skagway Municipality	7	0.76
Tenakee Springs, AK (city) Hoonah-Angoon Census Area	1	0.76
Fine Lakes, MN (township) St. Louis County	1	0.75
Pomme de Terre, MN (township) Grant County	1	0.75
Nikiski, AK (cdp) Kenai Peninsula Borough	32	0.71
Kalifornsky, AK (cdp) Kenai Peninsula Borough	54	0.69
Sterling, AK (cdp) Kenai Peninsula Borough	38	0.68
Gustavus, AK (city) Hoonah-Angoon Census Area	3	0.68
Slana, AK (cdp) Valdez-Cordova Census Area	1	0.68
Willow, AK (cdp) Matanuska-Susitna Borough	14	0.67
Keswick, CA (cdp) Shasta County	3	0.67
Klawock, AK (city) Prince of Wales-Hyder Census Area	5	0.66
Blaine, ME (cdp) Aroostook County	2	0.66
Angoon, AK (city) Hoonah-Angoon Census Area	3	0.65
Red Dog Mine, AK (cdp) Northwest Arctic Borough	2	0.65
Klamath, CA (cdp) Del Norte County	5	0.64
Nikolaevsk, AK (cdp) Kenai Peninsula Borough	2	0.63
Crawfordsville, OR (cdp) Linn County	2	0.60

Please refer to the Explanation of Data in the front of the book for more detailed information.

Race

Alaska Native: Aleut

Top 150 Places Sorted by Percent of Total Population

Based on places with total population of 7,500 or more

Place	Population	%
Anchorage, AK (municipality) Anchorage Municipality	3,982	1.36
Meadow Lakes, AK (cdp) Matanuska-Susitna Borough	101	1.33
Tanaina, AK (cdp) Matanuska-Susitna Borough	105	1.28
Lakes, AK (cdp) Matanuska-Susitna Borough	92	1.10
Knik-Fairview, AK (cdp) Matanuska-Susitna Borough	162	1.09
Ketchikan, AK (city) Ketchikan Gateway Borough	85	1.06
Sitka, AK (borough) Sitka City and Borough	77	0.87
Wasilla, AK (city) Matanuska-Susitna Borough	65	0.83
Kalifornsky, AK (cdp) Kenai Peninsula Borough	54	0.69
Juneau, AK (borough) Juneau City and Borough	186	0.59
College, AK (cdp) Fairbanks North Star Borough	46	0.35
Fairbanks, AK (city) Fairbanks North Star Borough	57	0.18
Birch Bay, WA (cdp) Whatcom County	14	0.17
Badger, AK (cdp) Fairbanks North Star Borough	31	0.16
Port Angeles, WA (city) Clallam County	28	0.15
Anacortes, WA (city) Skagit County	22	0.14
Snohomish, WA (city) Snohomish County	13	0.14
East Renton Highlands, WA (cdp) King County	15	0.13
Shelton, WA (city) Mason County	13	0.13
Lake Stevens, WA (city) Snohomish County	33	0.12
Burlington, WA (city) Skagit County	10	0.12
Ferndale, WA (city) Whatcom County	13	0.11
Edmonds, WA (city) Snohomish County	40	0.10
Puyallup, WA (city) Pierce County	36	0.10
Sedro-Woolley, WA (city) Skagit County	11	0.10
Washington Terrace, UT (city) Weber County	9	0.10
Bellingham, WA (city) Whatcom County	69	0.09
Marysville, WA (city) Snohomish County	57	0.09
Lynnwood, WA (city) Snohomish County	31	0.09
Lynden, WA (city) Whatcom County	11	0.09
Newport, OR (city) Lincoln County	9	0.09
Alderwood Manor, WA (cdp) Snohomish County	8	0.09
Fife, WA (city) Pierce County	8	0.09
Hoquiam, WA (city) Grays Harbor County	8	0.09
Midland, WA (cdp) Pierce County	8	0.09
Mount Vista, WA (cdp) Clark County	7	0.09
Shoreline, WA (city) King County	45	0.08
Kenmore, WA (city) King County	16	0.08
Tukwila, WA (city) King County	16	0.08
Ellensburg, WA (city) Kittitas County	14	0.08
Red Wing, MN (city) Goodhue County	13	0.08
Lakeland South, WA (cdp) King County	9	0.08
Vashon, WA (cdp) King County	8	0.08
Arlington, WA (city) Snohomish County	13	0.07
Centralia, WA (city) Lewis County	11	0.07
Kelso, WA (city) Cowlitz County	8	0.07
Snoqualmie, WA (city) King County	8	0.07
Sumner, WA (city) Pierce County	7	0.07
Everett, WA (city) Snohomish County	60	0.06
Auburn, WA (city) King County	44	0.06
South Hill, WA (cdp) Pierce County	29	0.06
Bremerton, WA (city) Kitsap County	24	0.06
Parkland, WA (cdp) Pierce County	23	0.06
Des Moines, WA (city) King County	19	0.06
Mountlake Terrace, WA (city) Snohomish County	12	0.06
Monroe, WA (city) Snohomish County	11	0.06
Rosamond, CA (cdp) Kern County	11	0.06
Clearlake, CA (city) Lake County	9	0.06
Martha Lake, WA (cdp) Snohomish County	9	0.06
Troutdale, OR (city) Multnomah County	9	0.06
White Center, WA (cdp) King County	8	0.06
Lake Forest Park, WA (city) King County	7	0.06
Lyndon, KY (city) Jefferson County	7	0.06
Anderson, CA (city) Shasta County	6	0.06
Cody, WY (city) Park County	6	0.06
Coweta, OK (city) Wagoner County	6	0.06
Grandview, WA (city) Yakima County	6	0.06
Newman, CA (city) Stanislaus County	6	0.06
Lewistown, PA (borough) Mifflin County	5	0.06
Mansfield, NJ (township) Warren County	5	0.06
Picnic Point, WA (cdp) Snohomish County	5	0.06
Sweet Home, OR (city) Linn County	5	0.06
Renton, WA (city) King County	44	0.05
Bainbridge Island, WA (city) Kitsap County	12	0.05
Oak Harbor, WA (city) Island County	11	0.05
Silver Firs, WA (cdp) Snohomish County	11	0.05
Durango, CO (city) La Plata County	9	0.05
Mill Creek, WA (city) Snohomish County	9	0.05
North Lynnwood, WA (cdp) Snohomish County	9	0.05
Aberdeen, WA (city) Grays Harbor County	8	0.05
Coos Bay, OR (city) Coos County	8	0.05
Kingsgate, WA (cdp) King County	6	0.05
Prairie Ridge, WA (cdp) Pierce County	6	0.05
Cheney, WA (city) Spokane County	5	0.05
Cottage Grove, OR (city) Lane County	5	0.05
Lake Morton-Berrydale, WA (cdp) King County	5	0.05
Prineville, OR (city) Crook County	5	0.05
Larkfield-Wikiup, CA (cdp) Sonoma County	4	0.05
Liberty Lake, WA (city) Spokane County	4	0.05
New Richmond, WI (city) St. Croix County	4	0.05
Poteau, OK (city) Le Flore County	4	0.05
Sutherlin, OR (city) Douglas County	4	0.05
Seattle, WA (city) King County	224	0.04
Tacoma, WA (city) Pierce County	88	0.04
Federal Way, WA (city) King County	32	0.04
Olympia, WA (city) Thurston County	18	0.04
Longview, WA (city) Cowlitz County	13	0.04
McMinnville, OR (city) Yamhill County	12	0.04
East Hill-Meridian, WA (cdp) King County	11	0.04
Spanaway, WA (cdp) Pierce County	11	0.04
Windsor, CA (town) Sonoma County	11	0.04
Graham, WA (cdp) Pierce County	10	0.04
SeaTac, WA (city) King County	10	0.04
Hazel Dell, WA (cdp) Clark County	8	0.04
Maple Valley, WA (city) King County	8	0.04
Newberg, OR (city) Yamhill County	8	0.04
Orchards, WA (cdp) Clark County	8	0.04
Bonney Lake, WA (city) Pierce County	7	0.04
Susanville, CA (city) Lassen County	7	0.04
Elk Plain, WA (cdp) Pierce County	6	0.04
Hueytown, AL (city) Jefferson County	6	0.04
Oak Grove, OR (cdp) Clackamas County	6	0.04
Oatfield, OR (cdp) Clackamas County	6	0.04
Washougal, WA (city) Clark County	6	0.04
Happy Valley, OR (city) Clackamas County	5	0.04
Astoria, OR (city) Clatsop County	4	0.04
Edgewood, WA (city) Pierce County	4	0.04
Enumclaw, WA (city) King County	4	0.04
Grand Rapids, MN (city) Itasca County	4	0.04
Jennings, LA (city) Jefferson Davis Parish	4	0.04
Maltby, WA (cdp) Snohomish County	4	0.04
Port Townsend, WA (city) Jefferson County	4	0.04
Poulsbo, WA (city) Kitsap County	4	0.04
Vermillion, SD (city) Clay County	4	0.04
Woodinville, WA (city) King County	4	0.04
Box Elder, SD (city) Pennington County	3	0.04
Lake Stickney, WA (cdp) Snohomish County	3	0.04
Ocean Pointe, HI (cdp) Honolulu County	3	0.04
Waller, WA (cdp) Pierce County	3	0.04
Webster City, IA (city) Hamilton County	3	0.04
Vancouver, WA (city) Clark County	52	0.03
Bend, OR (city) Deschutes County	21	0.03
Lakewood, WA (city) Pierce County	17	0.03
Lacey, WA (city) Thurston County	14	0.03
Coeur d'Alene, ID (city) Kootenai County	13	0.03
Mount Vernon, WA (city) Skagit County	11	0.03
Burien, WA (city) King County	9	0.03
University Place, WA (city) Pierce County	9	0.03
Walla Walla, WA (city) Walla Walla County	9	0.03
American Fork, UT (city) Utah County	7	0.03
Columbus, MS (city) Lowndes County	7	0.03
Eastmont, WA (cdp) Snohomish County	7	0.03
Eureka, CA (city) Humboldt County	7	0.03
Forest Grove, OR (city) Washington County	7	0.03
Granite Bay, CA (cdp) Placer County	7	0.03
Redmond, OR (city) Deschutes County	7	0.03
Rockledge, FL (city) Brevard County	7	0.03
Sapulpa, OK (city) Creek County	7	0.03
Frederickson, WA (cdp) Pierce County	6	0.03
Inglewood-Finn Hill, WA (cdp) King County	6	0.03

Please refer to the Explanation of Data in the front of the book for more detailed information.

Race

American Indian: Apache

U.S. and 50 States Sorted by Population and Percent of Total Population

Place	Population	%
United States	**111,810**	**0.04**
Arizona	28,149	0.44
California	24,799	0.07
New Mexico	9,926	0.48
Texas	9,529	0.04
Colorado	5,829	0.12
Oklahoma	3,576	0.10
Washington	2,234	0.03
Florida	1,912	0.01
Oregon	1,811	0.05
Illinois	1,521	0.01
Nevada	1,409	0.05
Ohio	1,325	0.01
Michigan	1,246	0.01
Missouri	1,183	0.02
New York	1,080	0.01
Hawaii	1,068	0.08
Kansas	1,048	0.04
Utah	976	0.04
North Carolina	927	0.01
Pennsylvania	911	0.01
Georgia	897	0.01
Virginia	860	0.01
Indiana	824	0.01
Tennessee	752	0.01
Arkansas	627	0.02
Idaho	622	0.04
Wisconsin	593	0.01
Maryland	495	0.01
Louisiana	486	0.01
Alabama	440	0.01
Kentucky	417	0.01
New Jersey	404	<0.01
Alaska	367	0.05
South Carolina	366	0.01
Montana	360	0.04
Iowa	346	0.01
Minnesota	337	0.01
Massachusetts	334	0.01
Nebraska	293	0.02
Mississippi	266	0.01
Wyoming	246	0.04
Connecticut	194	0.01
West Virginia	157	0.01
Maine	113	0.01
New Hampshire	111	0.01
South Dakota	103	0.01
Vermont	81	0.01
Delaware	76	0.01
North Dakota	67	0.01
Rhode Island	66	0.01
District of Columbia	51	0.01

Place	Population	%
New Mexico	9,926	0.48
Arizona	28,149	0.44
Colorado	5,829	0.12
Oklahoma	3,576	0.10
Hawaii	1,068	0.08
California	24,799	0.07
Oregon	1,811	0.05
Nevada	1,409	0.05
Alaska	367	0.05
United States	**111,810**	**0.04**
Texas	9,529	0.04
Kansas	1,048	0.04
Utah	976	0.04
Idaho	622	0.04
Montana	360	0.04
Wyoming	246	0.04
Washington	2,234	0.03
Missouri	1,183	0.02
Arkansas	627	0.02
Nebraska	293	0.02
Florida	1,912	0.01
Illinois	1,521	0.01
Ohio	1,325	0.01
Michigan	1,246	0.01
New York	1,080	0.01
North Carolina	927	0.01
Pennsylvania	911	0.01
Georgia	897	0.01
Virginia	860	0.01
Indiana	824	0.01
Tennessee	752	0.01
Wisconsin	593	0.01
Maryland	495	0.01
Louisiana	486	0.01
Alabama	440	0.01
Kentucky	417	0.01
South Carolina	366	0.01
Iowa	346	0.01
Minnesota	337	0.01
Massachusetts	334	0.01
Mississippi	266	0.01
Connecticut	194	0.01
West Virginia	157	0.01
Maine	113	0.01
New Hampshire	111	0.01
South Dakota	103	0.01
Vermont	81	0.01
Delaware	76	0.01
North Dakota	67	0.01
Rhode Island	66	0.01
District of Columbia	51	0.01
New Jersey	404	<0.01

Please refer to the Explanation of Data in the front of the book for more detailed information.

Race

American Indian: Apache

Top 150 Places Sorted by Population

Based on all places, regardless of total population

Place	Population	%
Whiteriver, AZ (cdp) Navajo County	3,528	85.96
San Carlos, AZ (cdp) Gila County	3,264	80.83
Dulce, NM (cdp) Rio Arriba County	1,989	72.51
Phoenix, AZ (city) Maricopa County	1,905	0.13
Bylas, AZ (cdp) Graham County	1,551	79.05
Cibecue, AZ (cdp) Navajo County	1,549	90.43
Los Angeles, CA (city) Los Angeles County	1,531	0.04
Canyon Day, AZ (cdp) Gila County	1,135	93.88
Peridot, AZ (cdp) Graham County	1,121	83.04
Mescalero, NM (cdp) Otero County	1,107	82.74
Albuquerque, NM (city) Bernalillo County	1,095	0.20
North Fork, AZ (cdp) Navajo County	1,075	75.86
San Antonio, TX (city) Medina County	1,050	0.08
San Jose, CA (city) Santa Clara County	959	0.10
Rainbow City, AZ (cdp) Navajo County	884	91.32
Denver, CO (city) Denver County	849	0.14
Tucson, AZ (city) Pima County	744	0.14
Hondah, AZ (cdp) Navajo County	659	81.16
Mesa, AZ (city) Maricopa County	659	0.15
Fresno, CA (city) Fresno County	648	0.13
East Fork, AZ (cdp) Navajo County	618	88.41
San Diego, CA (city) San Diego County	616	0.05
Seven Mile, AZ (cdp) Navajo County	613	86.70
Anadarko, OK (city) Caddo County	528	7.81
Sacramento, CA (city) Sacramento County	476	0.10
Colorado Springs, CO (city) El Paso County	444	0.11
Pueblo, CO (city) Pueblo County	440	0.41
El Paso, TX (city) El Paso County	431	0.07
Oklahoma City, OK (city) Oklahoma County	412	0.07
New York, NY (city) Kings County	401	<0.01
Stockton, CA (city) San Joaquin County	384	0.13
McNary, AZ (cdp) Apache County	379	71.78
Chicago, IL (city) Cook County	350	0.01
Bakersfield, CA (city) Kern County	336	0.10
Austin, TX (city) Travis County	329	0.04
Houston, TX (city) Harris County	319	0.02
Tempe, AZ (city) Maricopa County	302	0.19
Portland, OR (city) Multnomah County	299	0.05
Cedar Creek, AZ (cdp) Gila County	282	88.68
Aurora, CO (city) Arapahoe County	277	0.09
San Francisco, CA (city) San Francisco County	271	0.03
Las Cruces, NM (city) Doña Ana County	270	0.28
Glendale, AZ (city) Maricopa County	267	0.12
Modesto, CA (city) Stanislaus County	266	0.13
Las Vegas, NV (city) Clark County	264	0.05
Turkey Creek, AZ (cdp) Navajo County	262	89.12
Riverside, CA (city) Riverside County	256	0.08
San Bernardino, CA (city) San Bernardino County	254	0.12
Long Beach, CA (city) Los Angeles County	244	0.05
Lakewood, CO (city) Jefferson County	240	0.17
Corpus Christi, TX (city) Nueces County	239	0.08
Anaheim, CA (city) Orange County	228	0.07
Fort Worth, TX (city) Tarrant County	225	0.03
Dallas, TX (city) Dallas County	225	0.02
Globe, AZ (city) Gila County	223	2.96
Lawton, OK (city) Comanche County	218	0.23
Wichita, KS (city) Sedgwick County	206	0.05
East Globe, AZ (cdp) Gila County	190	84.07
Farmington, NM (city) San Juan County	189	0.41
Thornton, CO (city) Adams County	184	0.15
Santa Rosa, CA (city) Sonoma County	184	0.11
Chandler, AZ (city) Maricopa County	184	0.08
Tulsa, OK (city) Tulsa County	182	0.05
Victorville, CA (city) San Bernardino County	174	0.15
Lubbock, TX (city) Lubbock County	174	0.08
Oakland, CA (city) Alameda County	174	0.04
Urban Honolulu, HI (cdp) Honolulu County	165	0.05
Fontana, CA (city) San Bernardino County	162	0.08
Visalia, CA (city) Tulare County	152	0.12
Alamogordo, NM (city) Otero County	151	0.50
Lancaster, CA (city) Los Angeles County	151	0.10
Seattle, WA (city) King County	151	0.02
Oxnard, CA (city) Ventura County	146	0.07
Santa Ana, CA (city) Orange County	143	0.04
Paradise, NV (cdp) Clark County	139	0.06
Anchorage, AK (municipality) Anchorage Municipality	139	0.05
Whittier, CA (city) Los Angeles County	138	0.16
Huntington Beach, CA (city) Orange County	138	0.07
Rio Rancho, NM (city) Sandoval County	136	0.16
Payson, AZ (town) Gila County	134	0.88
Tularosa, NM (village) Otero County	133	4.68
North Las Vegas, NV (city) Clark County	133	0.06
Henderson, NV (city) Clark County	133	0.05
Arvada, CO (city) Jefferson County	131	0.12
San Buenaventura (Ventura), CA (city) Ventura County	131	0.12
Flagstaff, AZ (city) Coconino County	130	0.20
Pomona, CA (city) Los Angeles County	129	0.09
Chula Vista, CA (city) San Diego County	128	0.05
Hesperia, CA (city) San Bernardino County	126	0.14
Amarillo, TX (city) Potter County	125	0.07
Moreno Valley, CA (city) Riverside County	125	0.06
Oceanside, CA (city) San Diego County	124	0.07
Sunrise Manor, NV (cdp) Clark County	124	0.07
Reno, NV (city) Washoe County	124	0.06
Arlington, TX (city) Tarrant County	124	0.03
Gilbert, AZ (town) Maricopa County	122	0.06
Brooklyn, NY (borough) Kings County	122	<0.01
Palmdale, CA (city) Los Angeles County	121	0.08
Greeley, CO (city) Weld County	120	0.13
Westminster, CO (city) Adams County	119	0.11
Hayward, CA (city) Alameda County	118	0.08
Philadelphia, PA (city) Philadelphia County	118	0.01
Rancho Cucamonga, CA (city) San Bernardino County	113	0.07
Carrizo, AZ (cdp) Gila County	112	88.19
Jacksonville, FL (city) Duval County	110	0.01
Hemet, CA (city) Riverside County	109	0.14
Columbus, OH (city) Franklin County	109	0.01
Orange, CA (city) Orange County	106	0.08
Roswell, NM (city) Chaves County	105	0.22
Santa Clarita, CA (city) Los Angeles County	105	0.06
Scottsdale, AZ (city) Maricopa County	105	0.05
Fort Apache, AZ (cdp) Navajo County	103	72.03
Salem, OR (city) Marion County	102	0.07
Norwalk, CA (city) Los Angeles County	100	0.09
Peoria, AZ (city) Yavapai County	100	0.06
Apache, OK (town) Caddo County	99	6.86
Bronx, NY (borough) Bronx County	99	0.01
Gilroy, CA (city) Santa Clara County	98	0.20
Ontario, CA (city) San Bernardino County	98	0.06
Fremont, CA (city) Alameda County	98	0.05
Indianapolis, IN (city) Marion County	98	0.01
Santa Fe, NM (city) Santa Fe County	97	0.14
Odessa, TX (city) Ector County	97	0.10
Elk Grove, CA (city) Sacramento County	96	0.06
Grand Prairie, TX (city) Dallas County	96	0.05
Clovis, CA (city) Fresno County	95	0.10
Concord, CA (city) Contra Costa County	95	0.08
Vallejo, CA (city) Solano County	95	0.08
Abilene, TX (city) Taylor County	93	0.08
Salinas, CA (city) Monterey County	93	0.06
Tacoma, WA (city) Pierce County	92	0.05
Manhattan, NY (borough) New York County	92	0.01
South Whittier, CA (cdp) Los Angeles County	91	0.16
Fort Collins, CO (city) Larimer County	91	0.06
Boise City, ID (city) Ada County	91	0.04
Spokane, WA (city) Spokane County	91	0.04
Milwaukee, WI (city) Milwaukee County	91	0.02
Pico Rivera, CA (city) Los Angeles County	90	0.14
Kansas City, MO (city) Jackson County	89	0.02
Longmont, CO (city) Boulder County	88	0.10
Garden Grove, CA (city) Orange County	88	0.05
Manteca, CA (city) San Joaquin County	87	0.13
West Covina, CA (city) Los Angeles County	86	0.08
Corona, CA (city) Riverside County	86	0.06
Commerce City, CO (city) Adams County	85	0.19
Apple Valley, CA (town) San Bernardino County	84	0.12
Fairfield, CA (city) Solano County	84	0.08
South Valley, NM (cdp) Bernalillo County	82	0.20
Roseville, CA (city) Placer County	82	0.07
Ruidoso, NM (village) Lincoln County	81	1.01

Please refer to the Explanation of Data in the front of the book for more detailed information.

Race

American Indian: Apache

Top 150 Places Sorted by Percent of Total Population

Based on all places, regardless of total population

Place	Population	%
Canyon Day, AZ (cdp) Gila County	1,135	93.88
Rainbow City, AZ (cdp) Navajo County	884	91.32
Cibecue, AZ (cdp) Navajo County	1,549	90.43
Turkey Creek, AZ (cdp) Navajo County	262	89.12
Cedar Creek, AZ (cdp) Gila County	282	88.68
East Fork, AZ (cdp) Navajo County	618	88.41
Carrizo, AZ (cdp) Gila County	112	88.19
Seven Mile, AZ (cdp) Navajo County	613	86.70
Whiteriver, AZ (cdp) Navajo County	3,528	85.96
East Globe, AZ (cdp) Gila County	190	84.07
Peridot, AZ (cdp) Graham County	1,121	83.04
Mescalero, NM (cdp) Otero County	1,107	82.74
Hondah, AZ (cdp) Navajo County	659	81.16
San Carlos, AZ (cdp) Gila County	3,264	80.83
Bylas, AZ (cdp) Graham County	1,551	79.05
North Fork, AZ (cdp) Navajo County	1,075	75.86
Dulce, NM (cdp) Rio Arriba County	1,989	72.51
Fort Apache, AZ (cdp) Navajo County	103	72.03
McNary, AZ (cdp) Apache County	379	71.78
Cutter, AZ (cdp) Gila County	34	45.95
Picuris Pueblo, NM (cdp) Taos County	8	11.76
Valentine, AZ (cdp) Mohave County	3	7.89
Anadarko, OK (city) Caddo County	528	7.81
Fredericksburg, IN (town) Washington County	6	7.06
Apache, OK (town) Caddo County	99	6.86
Johnsonville, IL (village) Wayne County	5	6.49
Morrison Bluff, AR (town) Logan County	4	6.25
Mojave Ranch Estates, AZ (cdp) Mohave County	3	5.77
Duran, NM (cdp) Torrance County	2	5.71
Weston, CO (cdp) Las Animas County	3	5.45
Quail, TX (cdp) Collingsworth County	1	5.26
San Lorenzo, NM (cdp) Grant County	5	5.15
Garfield, NM (cdp) Doña Ana County	7	5.11
Pinal, AZ (cdp) Gila County	22	5.01
Lake Hattie, MN (township) Hubbard County	10	4.95
Owl Ranch, TX (cdp) Jim Wells County	11	4.89
Tularosa, NM (village) Otero County	133	4.68
Bryce, AZ (cdp) Graham County	8	4.57
Canaan, IN (cdp) Jefferson County	4	4.44
Gotebo, OK (town) Kiowa County	10	4.42
Mazie, OK (cdp) Mayes County	4	4.40
Lost Springs, KS (city) Marion County	3	4.29
Gulkana, AK (cdp) Valdez-Cordova Census Area	5	4.20
Edith Endave, NM (cdp) Bernalillo County	8	3.79
North Hurley, NM (cdp) Grant County	11	3.67
Preston, NE (village) Richardson County	1	3.57
Vernon, AZ (cdp) Apache County	4	3.28
Fort Thomas, AZ (cdp) Graham County	12	3.21
Macdoel, CA (cdp) Siskiyou County	4	3.01
Globe, AZ (city) Gila County	223	2.96
Carnegie, OK (town) Caddo County	50	2.90
Whitecone, AZ (cdp) Navajo County	23	2.82
St. Johns, AZ (cdp) Maricopa County	13	2.73
Randlett, UT (cdp) Uintah County	6	2.73
Valmy, NV (cdp) Humboldt County	1	2.70
Normanna, TX (cdp) Bee County	3	2.65
Pyote, TX (town) Ward County	3	2.63
Steamboat, AZ (cdp) Apache County	7	2.46
Acequia, ID (city) Minidoka County	3	2.42
Clear Creek, CA (cdp) Lassen County	4	2.37
Sugden, OK (town) Jefferson County	1	2.33
Smartsville, CA (cdp) Yuba County	4	2.26
Truxton, AZ (cdp) Mohave County	3	2.24
Sisquoc, CA (cdp) Santa Barbara County	4	2.19
Sams Corner, OK (cdp) Mayes County	3	2.19
Wet Camp Village, AZ (cdp) Pinal County	5	2.18
Del Muerto, AZ (cdp) Apache County	7	2.13
Leupp, AZ (cdp) Coconino County	20	2.10
Des Moines, NM (village) Union County	3	2.10
Santa Rosa, AZ (cdp) Pima County	13	2.07
Fort Cobb, OK (town) Caddo County	13	2.05
Lemon Cove, CA (cdp) Tulare County	6	1.95
Alton, KS (city) Osborne County	2	1.94
Topaz Lake, NV (cdp) Douglas County	3	1.91
Willow Creek, MT (cdp) Gallatin County	4	1.90
Greasewood, AZ (cdp) Navajo County	10	1.83
Springerton, IL (village) White County	2	1.82
Venetie, AK (cdp) Yukon-Koyukuk Census Area	3	1.81
Eakly, OK (town) Caddo County	6	1.78
Sacate Village, AZ (cdp) Pinal County	3	1.78
Six Shooter Canyon, AZ (cdp) Gila County	18	1.77
Anchor Bay, CA (cdp) Mendocino County	6	1.76
Veguita, NM (cdp) Socorro County	4	1.72
Kirk, CO (cdp) Yuma County	1	1.69
Aguilar, CO (town) Las Animas County	9	1.67
Menlo, KS (city) Thomas County	1	1.64
Winston, NM (cdp) Sierra County	1	1.64
Walsenburg, CO (city) Huerfano County	50	1.63
Pettus, TX (cdp) Bee County	9	1.61
Kaibab, AZ (cdp) Mohave County	2	1.61
Rest Haven, GA (town) Gwinnett County	1	1.61
Nisqually Indian Community, WA (cdp) Thurston County	9	1.57
Olney, MT (cdp) Flathead County	3	1.57
Williamsburg, NM (village) Sierra County	7	1.56
Crescent Mills, CA (cdp) Plumas County	3	1.53
Shonto, AZ (cdp) Navajo County	9	1.52
Pinos Altos, NM (cdp) Grant County	3	1.52
Capulin, NM (cdp) Union County	1	1.52
Radersburg, MT (cdp) Broadwater County	1	1.52
Mountain View, OK (town) Kiowa County	12	1.51
Tetonia, ID (city) Teton County	4	1.49
Boone, CO (town) Pueblo County	5	1.47
Red Mesa, AZ (cdp) Apache County	7	1.46
Steely Hollow, OK (cdp) Cherokee County	3	1.46
St. Ignatius, MT (town) Lake County	12	1.43
Courtland, CA (cdp) Sacramento County	5	1.41
Rancho Grande, NM (cdp) Catron County	2	1.41
Claypool, AZ (cdp) Gila County	21	1.37
Chama, NM (village) Rio Arriba County	14	1.37
Dodd City, TX (town) Fannin County	5	1.36
Morse, TX (cdp) Hansford County	2	1.36
California Pines, CA (cdp) Modoc County	7	1.35
Eldorado, OK (town) Jackson County	6	1.35
Tazlina, AK (cdp) Valdez-Cordova Census Area	4	1.35
Branson, CO (town) Las Animas County	1	1.35
Kim, CO (town) Las Animas County	1	1.35
Tees Toh, AZ (cdp) Navajo County	6	1.34
Herlong, CA (cdp) Lassen County	4	1.34
Whites Landing, OH (cdp) Erie County	5	1.33
Oasis, UT (cdp) Millard County	1	1.33
Sandia, TX (cdp) Jim Wells County	5	1.32
Nordheim, TX (city) DeWitt County	4	1.30
Sanders, AZ (cdp) Apache County	8	1.27
Elmer, MO (city) Macon County	1	1.25
Riverdale Park, CA (cdp) Stanislaus County	14	1.24
Central, AZ (cdp) Graham County	8	1.24
Glennallen, AK (cdp) Valdez-Cordova Census Area	6	1.24
Macks Creek, MO (city) Camden County	3	1.23
Ohkay Owingeh, NM (cdp) Rio Arriba County	14	1.22
Caryville, FL (town) Washington County	5	1.22
Three Rocks, CA (cdp) Fresno County	3	1.22
Morenci, AZ (cdp) Greenlee County	18	1.21
Ringwood, OK (town) Major County	6	1.21
Lake City, MI (city) Missaukee County	10	1.20
Bennington, OK (town) Bryan County	4	1.20
Lookeba, OK (town) Caddo County	2	1.20
Clifton, AZ (town) Greenlee County	39	1.18
Icehouse Canyon, AZ (cdp) Gila County	8	1.18
Antonito, CO (town) Conejos County	9	1.15
Mertzon, TX (city) Irion County	9	1.15
Ignacio, CO (town) La Plata County	8	1.15
Round Rock, AZ (cdp) Apache County	9	1.14
Cambridge, KY (city) Jefferson County	2	1.14
Wide Ruins, AZ (cdp) Apache County	2	1.14
Cyril, OK (town) Caddo County	12	1.13
Verden, OK (town) Grady County	6	1.13
Alexandria, NE (village) Thayer County	2	1.13
Bayard, NM (city) Grant County	26	1.12
Hood, CA (cdp) Sacramento County	3	1.11
Love Valley, NC (town) Iredell County	1	1.11

Race

American Indian: Apache

Top 150 Places Sorted by Percent of Total Population

Based on places with total population of 7,500 or more

Place	Population	%
Globe, AZ (city) Gila County	223	2.96
Ruidoso, NM (village) Lincoln County	81	1.01
Payson, AZ (town) Gila County	134	0.88
Show Low, AZ (city) Navajo County	65	0.61
Camp Verde, AZ (town) Yavapai County	61	0.56
Safford, AZ (city) Graham County	53	0.55
Alamogordo, NM (city) Otero County	151	0.50
Tuba City, AZ (cdp) Coconino County	43	0.50
Trinidad, CO (city) Las Animas County	44	0.48
Winslow, AZ (city) Navajo County	42	0.44
Pueblo, CO (city) Pueblo County	440	0.41
Farmington, NM (city) San Juan County	189	0.41
Kirtland, NM (cdp) San Juan County	31	0.39
Silver City, NM (town) Grant County	39	0.38
Alamosa, CO (city) Alamosa County	33	0.38
Bloomfield, NM (city) San Juan County	29	0.36
Welby, CO (cdp) Adams County	52	0.35
Artesia, NM (city) Eddy County	38	0.34
Sherrelwood, CO (cdp) Adams County	58	0.32
Holualoa, HI (cdp) Hawaii County	25	0.29
Las Cruces, NM (city) Doña Ana County	270	0.28
Durango, CO (city) La Plata County	48	0.28
Alum Rock, CA (cdp) Santa Clara County	44	0.28
Chickasha, OK (city) Grady County	41	0.26
Garden Acres, CA (cdp) San Joaquin County	27	0.25
Country Club, CA (cdp) San Joaquin County	23	0.25
Valencia West, AZ (cdp) Pima County	23	0.25
Alice, TX (city) Jim Wells County	46	0.24
East Hemet, CA (cdp) Riverside County	42	0.24
Kapaa, HI (cdp) Kauai County	26	0.24
Lawton, OK (city) Comanche County	218	0.23
Roswell, NM (city) Chaves County	105	0.22
West Whittier-Los Nietos, CA (cdp) Los Angeles County	55	0.22
Cimarron Hills, CO (cdp) El Paso County	36	0.22
Berkley, CO (cdp) Adams County	25	0.22
Cortez, CO (city) Montezuma County	19	0.22
Cushing, OK (city) Payne County	17	0.22
Yreka, CA (city) Siskiyou County	17	0.22
Fountain, CO (city) El Paso County	55	0.21
Gallup, NM (city) McKinley County	46	0.21
August, CA (cdp) San Joaquin County	18	0.21
Catalina, AZ (cdp) Pima County	16	0.21
Albuquerque, NM (city) Bernalillo County	1,095	0.20
Flagstaff, AZ (city) Coconino County	130	0.20
Gilroy, CA (city) Santa Clara County	98	0.20
South Valley, NM (cdp) Bernalillo County	82	0.20
Brighton, CO (city) Adams County	67	0.20
Drexel Heights, AZ (cdp) Pima County	56	0.20
Olivehurst, CA (cdp) Yuba County	27	0.20
Socorro, NM (city) Socorro County	18	0.20
Eagle Point, OR (city) Jackson County	17	0.20
Tempe, AZ (city) Maricopa County	302	0.19
Commerce City, CO (city) Adams County	85	0.19
Los Banos, CA (city) Merced County	69	0.19
Barstow, CA (city) San Bernardino County	44	0.19
Wahiawa, HI (cdp) Honolulu County	33	0.19
Big Bear City, CA (cdp) San Bernardino County	23	0.19
Shiprock, NM (cdp) San Juan County	16	0.19
Security-Widefield, CO (cdp) El Paso County	58	0.18
Port Hueneme, CA (city) Ventura County	40	0.18
Cañon City, CO (city) Fremont County	30	0.18
Grand Terrace, CA (city) San Bernardino County	22	0.18
Verde Village, AZ (cdp) Yavapai County	21	0.18
Fort Morgan, CO (city) Morgan County	20	0.18
Maili, HI (cdp) Honolulu County	17	0.18
Orange Cove, CA (city) Fresno County	16	0.18
Fruitvale, CO (cdp) Mesa County	14	0.18
Lakewood, CO (city) Jefferson County	240	0.17
Clovis, NM (city) Curry County	63	0.17
Adelanto, CA (city) San Bernardino County	53	0.17
Pueblo West, CO (cdp) Pueblo County	50	0.17
Duncan, OK (city) Stephens County	39	0.17
Santa Fe Springs, CA (city) Los Angeles County	28	0.17
Schofield Barracks, HI (cdp) Honolulu County	28	0.17
Clearlake, CA (city) Lake County	26	0.17
Las Vegas, NM (city) San Miguel County	23	0.17
Livingston, CA (city) Merced County	22	0.17
Waianae, HI (cdp) Honolulu County	22	0.17
Fort Lewis, WA (cdp) Pierce County	19	0.17
Hawaiian Paradise Park, HI (cdp) Hawaii County	19	0.17
Ingleside, TX (city) San Patricio County	16	0.17
Golden Hills, CA (cdp) Kern County	15	0.17
Whittier, CA (city) Los Angeles County	138	0.16
Rio Rancho, NM (city) Sandoval County	136	0.16
South Whittier, CA (cdp) Los Angeles County	91	0.16
Englewood, CO (city) Arapahoe County	47	0.16
Florence, AZ (town) Pinal County	40	0.16
California City, CA (city) Kern County	23	0.16
Muscoy, CA (cdp) San Bernardino County	17	0.16
Grants, NM (city) Cibola County	15	0.16
Bernalillo, NM (town) Sandoval County	13	0.16
Mesa, AZ (city) Maricopa County	659	0.15
Thornton, CO (city) Adams County	184	0.15
Victorville, CA (city) San Bernardino County	174	0.15
Enid, OK (city) Garfield County	73	0.15
Northglenn, CO (city) Adams County	55	0.15
Carlsbad, NM (city) Eddy County	38	0.15
Clifton, CO (cdp) Mesa County	29	0.15
Deming, NM (city) Luna County	23	0.15
Lemon Hill, CA (cdp) Sacramento County	20	0.15
Lake Los Angeles, CA (cdp) Los Angeles County	18	0.15
Marysville, CA (city) Yuba County	18	0.15
Newport, OR (city) Lincoln County	15	0.15
Delta, CO (city) Delta County	13	0.15
Ione, CA (city) Amador County	12	0.15
Ketchikan, AK (city) Ketchikan Gateway Borough	12	0.15
Lansing, MI (charter township) Ingham County	12	0.15
Pukalani, HI (cdp) Maui County	11	0.15
Denver, CO (city) Denver County	849	0.14
Tucson, AZ (city) Pima County	744	0.14
Hesperia, CA (city) San Bernardino County	126	0.14
Hemet, CA (city) Riverside County	109	0.14
Santa Fe, NM (city) Santa Fe County	97	0.14
Pico Rivera, CA (city) Los Angeles County	90	0.14
Foothill Farms, CA (cdp) Sacramento County	48	0.14
Oildale, CA (cdp) Kern County	47	0.14
Ken Caryl, CO (cdp) Jefferson County	44	0.14
Lomita, CA (city) Los Angeles County	29	0.14
Oroville, CA (city) Butte County	21	0.14
Parkway, CA (cdp) Sacramento County	21	0.14
Borger, TX (city) Hutchinson County	18	0.14
Pedley, CA (cdp) Riverside County	18	0.14
Okmulgee, OK (city) Okmulgee County	17	0.14
Portales, NM (city) Roosevelt County	17	0.14
Federal Heights, CO (city) Adams County	16	0.14
Los Alamitos, CA (city) Orange County	16	0.14
Scotts Valley, CA (city) Santa Cruz County	16	0.14
Capitola, CA (city) Santa Cruz County	14	0.14
Espanola, NM (city) Rio Arriba County	14	0.14
Warr Acres, OK (city) Oklahoma County	14	0.14
Hondo, TX (city) Medina County	12	0.14
Makaha, HI (cdp) Honolulu County	12	0.14
Derby, CO (cdp) Adams County	11	0.14
Phoenix, AZ (city) Maricopa County	1,905	0.13
Fresno, CA (city) Fresno County	648	0.13
Stockton, CA (city) San Joaquin County	384	0.13
Modesto, CA (city) Stanislaus County	266	0.13
Greeley, CO (city) Weld County	120	0.13
Manteca, CA (city) San Joaquin County	87	0.13
Grand Junction, CO (city) Mesa County	78	0.13
Covina, CA (city) Los Angeles County	61	0.13
Azusa, CA (city) Los Angeles County	59	0.13
Sierra Vista, AZ (city) Cochise County	59	0.13
Morgan Hill, CA (city) Santa Clara County	48	0.13
Wheat Ridge, CO (city) Jefferson County	39	0.13
Paradise, CA (town) Butte County	33	0.13
Lafayette, CO (city) Boulder County	31	0.13
Douglas, AZ (city) Cochise County	23	0.13
Arcata, CA (city) Humboldt County	22	0.13
Flowing Wells, AZ (cdp) Pima County	21	0.13

SECTION THREE

Please refer to the Explanation of Data in the front of the book for more detailed information.

Race

American Indian: Arapaho

U.S. and 50 States Sorted by Population and Percent of Total Population

Place	Population	%
United States	**10,861**	**<0.01**
Wyoming	5,224	0.93
Oklahoma	961	0.03
California	727	<0.01
Colorado	459	0.01
Montana	381	0.04
Washington	326	<0.01
Texas	283	<0.01
Utah	199	0.01
Arizona	185	<0.01
South Dakota	180	0.02
Kansas	173	0.01
New Mexico	141	0.01
Idaho	135	0.01
Missouri	120	<0.01
Oregon	106	<0.01
Florida	96	<0.01
Ohio	95	<0.01
Illinois	93	<0.01
Nevada	84	<0.01
Michigan	67	<0.01
New York	65	<0.01
Alaska	61	0.01
Virginia	55	<0.01
Nebraska	52	<0.01
North Carolina	50	<0.01
Hawaii	44	<0.01
Indiana	43	<0.01
Maryland	42	<0.01
Pennsylvania	41	<0.01
Minnesota	36	<0.01
Wisconsin	35	<0.01
Tennessee	34	<0.01
Iowa	30	<0.01
New Jersey	28	<0.01
Arkansas	27	<0.01
Georgia	26	<0.01
Alabama	25	<0.01
Louisiana	23	<0.01
North Dakota	18	<0.01
Massachusetts	15	<0.01
Kentucky	14	<0.01
Connecticut	13	<0.01
West Virginia	12	<0.01
New Hampshire	11	<0.01
Maine	9	<0.01
South Carolina	8	<0.01
Mississippi	5	<0.01
Delaware	2	<0.01
District of Columbia	1	<0.01
Vermont	1	<0.01
Rhode Island	0	0.00

Place	Population	%
Wyoming	5,224	0.93
Montana	381	0.04
Oklahoma	961	0.03
South Dakota	180	0.02
Colorado	459	0.01
Utah	199	0.01
Kansas	173	0.01
New Mexico	141	0.01
Idaho	135	0.01
Alaska	61	0.01
United States	**10,861**	**<0.01**
California	727	<0.01
Washington	326	<0.01
Texas	283	<0.01
Arizona	185	<0.01
Missouri	120	<0.01
Oregon	106	<0.01
Florida	96	<0.01
Ohio	95	<0.01
Illinois	93	<0.01
Nevada	84	<0.01
Michigan	67	<0.01
New York	65	<0.01
Virginia	55	<0.01
Nebraska	52	<0.01
North Carolina	50	<0.01
Hawaii	44	<0.01
Indiana	43	<0.01
Maryland	42	<0.01
Pennsylvania	41	<0.01
Minnesota	36	<0.01
Wisconsin	35	<0.01
Tennessee	34	<0.01
Iowa	30	<0.01
New Jersey	28	<0.01
Arkansas	27	<0.01
Georgia	26	<0.01
Alabama	25	<0.01
Louisiana	23	<0.01
North Dakota	18	<0.01
Massachusetts	15	<0.01
Kentucky	14	<0.01
Connecticut	13	<0.01
West Virginia	12	<0.01
New Hampshire	11	<0.01
Maine	9	<0.01
South Carolina	8	<0.01
Mississippi	5	<0.01
Delaware	2	<0.01
District of Columbia	1	<0.01
Vermont	1	<0.01
Rhode Island	0	0.00

Please refer to the Explanation of Data in the front of the book for more detailed information.

Race

American Indian: Arapaho

Top 150 Places Sorted by Population

Based on all places, regardless of total population

Place	Population	%
Arapahoe, WY (cdp) Fremont County	1,169	70.59
Ethete, WY (cdp) Fremont County	1,104	71.09
Riverton, WY (city) Fremont County	666	6.27
Fort Washakie, WY (cdp) Fremont County	317	18.02
Lander, WY (city) Fremont County	217	2.90
Oklahoma City, OK (city) Oklahoma County	132	0.02
Casper, WY (city) Natrona County	113	0.20
El Reno, OK (city) Canadian County	93	0.56
Boulder Flats, WY (cdp) Fremont County	77	18.87
Billings, MT (city) Yellowstone County	72	0.07
Denver, CO (city) Denver County	67	0.01
Johnstown, WY (cdp) Fremont County	62	25.62
Cheyenne, WY (city) Laramie County	52	0.09
Wichita, KS (city) Sedgwick County	50	0.01
Albuquerque, NM (city) Bernalillo County	49	0.01
Lawrence, KS (city) Douglas County	44	0.05
Phoenix, AZ (city) Maricopa County	42	<0.01
Laramie, WY (city) Albany County	41	0.13
Rapid City, SD (city) Pennington County	41	0.06
Geary, OK (city) Blaine County	40	3.13
Lawton, OK (city) Comanche County	39	0.04
Aurora, CO (city) Arapahoe County	37	0.01
Idaho Falls, ID (city) Bonneville County	36	0.06
West Valley City, UT (city) Salt Lake County	36	0.03
Colorado Springs, CO (city) El Paso County	33	0.01
Watonga, OK (city) Blaine County	32	0.63
Weatherford, OK (city) Custer County	32	0.30
Anchorage, AK (municipality) Anchorage Municipality	28	0.01
Clinton, OK (city) Custer County	27	0.30
Rawlins, WY (city) Carbon County	27	0.29
Pueblo, CO (city) Pueblo County	26	0.02
Pacifica, CA (city) San Mateo County	25	0.07
Salt Lake City, UT (city) Salt Lake County	25	0.01
Thornton, CO (city) Adams County	24	0.02
Los Angeles, CA (city) Los Angeles County	24	<0.01
Rio Rancho, NM (city) Sandoval County	23	0.03
Hudson, WY (town) Fremont County	22	4.80
Tulsa, OK (city) Tulsa County	22	0.01
Seattle, WA (city) King County	22	<0.01
Pocatello, ID (city) Bannock County	21	0.04
New York, NY (city) Kings County	21	<0.01
Buffalo, WY (city) Johnson County	20	0.44
Chicago, IL (city) Cook County	20	<0.01
Arlington, TX (city) Tarrant County	19	0.01
Spokane, WA (city) Spokane County	19	0.01
Hardin, MT (city) Big Horn County	18	0.51
Great Falls, MT (city) Cascade County	18	0.03
Tacoma, WA (city) Pierce County	18	0.01
Pine Ridge, SD (cdp) Shannon County	17	0.51
Mills, WY (town) Natrona County	17	0.49
Reno, NV (city) Washoe County	17	0.01
Nashville-Davidson, TN (metro govt) Davidson County	17	<0.01
San Francisco, CA (city) San Francisco County	17	<0.01
Wolf Point, MT (city) Roosevelt County	16	0.61
Juneau, AK (borough) Juneau City and Borough	16	0.05
Norman, OK (city) Cleveland County	16	0.01
Oakland, CA (city) Alameda County	16	<0.01
Omaha, NE (city) Douglas County	16	<0.01
San Diego, CA (city) San Diego County	16	<0.01
Canton, OK (town) Blaine County	15	2.40
Douglas, WY (city) Converse County	15	0.25
Gillette, WY (city) Campbell County	15	0.05
Enid, OK (city) Garfield County	15	0.03
Moore, OK (city) Cleveland County	15	0.03
Provo, UT (city) Utah County	15	0.01
Lakewood, CO (city) Jefferson County	14	0.01
Sioux Falls, SD (city) Minnehaha County	14	0.01
Dallas, TX (city) Dallas County	14	<0.01
Mesa, AZ (city) Maricopa County	14	<0.01
Airway Heights, WA (city) Spokane County	13	0.21
Miami, OK (city) Ottawa County	13	0.10
Rock Springs, WY (city) Sweetwater County	13	0.06
Ponca City, OK (city) Kay County	13	0.05
Loveland, CO (city) Larimer County	13	0.02
Midwest City, OK (city) Oklahoma County	13	0.02
Yakima, WA (city) Yakima County	13	0.01
Bakersfield, CA (city) Kern County	13	<0.01
Las Vegas, NV (city) Clark County	13	<0.01
Tucson, AZ (city) Pima County	13	<0.01
White Mesa, UT (cdp) San Juan County	12	4.96
Lame Deer, MT (cdp) Rosebud County	12	0.58
North Browning, MT (cdp) Glacier County	12	0.50
Thermopolis, WY (town) Hot Springs County	12	0.40
Missoula, MT (city) Missoula County	12	0.02
Killeen, TX (city) Bell County	12	0.01
Lancaster, CA (city) Los Angeles County	12	0.01
Topeka, KS (city) Shawnee County	12	0.01
Birney, MT (cdp) Rosebud County	11	8.03
Muddy, MT (cdp) Big Horn County	11	1.78
Oglala, SD (cdp) Shannon County	11	0.85
Kent, WA (city) King County	11	0.01
Norfolk, VA (ind. city) Norfolk independent city	11	<0.01
Portland, OR (city) Multnomah County	11	<0.01
Urban Honolulu, HI (cdp) Honolulu County	11	<0.01
Boneau, MT (cdp) Chouteau County	10	2.63
Anadarko, OK (city) Caddo County	10	0.15
Parsons, KS (city) Labette County	10	0.10
Sheridan, WY (city) Sheridan County	10	0.06
Columbine, CO (cdp) Jefferson County	10	0.04
Kearns, UT (cdp) Salt Lake County	10	0.03
Dayton, OH (city) Montgomery County	10	0.01
Hayward, CA (city) Alameda County	10	0.01
Salem, OR (city) Marion County	10	0.01
Brooklyn, NY (borough) Kings County	10	<0.01
Houston, TX (city) Harris County	10	<0.01
Sacramento, CA (city) Sacramento County	10	<0.01
Busby, MT (cdp) Big Horn County	9	1.21
East Hill-Meridian, WA (cdp) King County	9	0.03
Midvale, UT (city) Salt Lake County	9	0.03
Apple Valley, CA (town) San Bernardino County	9	0.01
Auburn, WA (city) King County	9	0.01
Fort Collins, CO (city) Larimer County	9	0.01
Pasadena, CA (city) Los Angeles County	9	0.01
Roseville, CA (city) Placer County	9	0.01
West Jordan, UT (city) Salt Lake County	9	0.01
Fort Worth, TX (city) Tarrant County	9	<0.01
Riverside, CA (city) Riverside County	9	<0.01
San Antonio, TX (city) Medina County	9	<0.01
San Jose, CA (city) Santa Clara County	9	<0.01
Stockton, CA (city) San Joaquin County	9	<0.01
Manderson-White Horse Creek, SD (cdp) Shannon County	8	1.28
Harbor Springs, MI (city) Emmet County	8	0.67
Crow Agency, MT (cdp) Big Horn County	8	0.50
Ronan, MT (city) Lake County	8	0.43
Calera, OK (town) Bryan County	8	0.37
Fort Hall, ID (cdp) Bannock County	8	0.25
Stratmoor, CO (cdp) El Paso County	8	0.12
Tecumseh, OK (city) Pottawatomie County	8	0.12
Cody, WY (city) Park County	8	0.08
Fort Carson, CO (cdp) El Paso County	8	0.06
Commerce City, CO (city) Adams County	8	0.02
Covina, CA (city) Los Angeles County	8	0.02
Littleton, CO (city) Arapahoe County	8	0.02
Willowbrook, CA (cdp) Los Angeles County	8	0.02
Arvada, CO (city) Jefferson County	8	0.01
Carson, CA (city) Los Angeles County	8	0.01
Concord, CA (city) Contra Costa County	8	0.01
El Cajon, CA (city) San Diego County	8	0.01
Hemet, CA (city) Riverside County	8	0.01
Olathe, KS (city) Johnson County	8	0.01
Taylorsville, UT (city) Salt Lake County	8	0.01
Amarillo, TX (city) Potter County	8	<0.01
Boise City, ID (city) Ada County	8	<0.01
Memphis, TN (city) Shelby County	8	<0.01
Hays, MT (cdp) Blaine County	7	0.83
Basin, WY (town) Big Horn County	7	0.54
Eagle Butte, SD (city) Ziebach County	7	0.53
Pawhuska, OK (city) Osage County	7	0.20
South Greeley, WY (cdp) Laramie County	7	0.17
Polson, MT (city) Lake County	7	0.16

Please refer to the Explanation of Data in the front of the book for more detailed information.

Race

American Indian: Arapaho

Top 150 Places Sorted by Percent of Total Population

Based on all places, regardless of total population

Place	Population	%
Ethete, WY (cdp) Fremont County	1,104	71.09
Arapahoe, WY (cdp) Fremont County	1,169	70.59
Johnstown, WY (cdp) Fremont County	62	25.62
Boulder Flats, WY (cdp) Fremont County	77	18.87
Fort Washakie, WY (cdp) Fremont County	317	18.02
Birney, MT (cdp) Rosebud County	11	8.03
Riverton, WY (city) Fremont County	666	6.27
White Mesa, UT (cdp) San Juan County	12	4.96
Hudson, WY (town) Fremont County	22	4.80
Geary, OK (city) Blaine County	40	3.13
Lander, WY (city) Fremont County	217	2.90
Crowheart, WY (cdp) Fremont County	4	2.84
Texola, OK (town) Beckham County	1	2.78
Sula, MT (cdp) Ravalli County	1	2.70
Boneau, MT (cdp) Chouteau County	10	2.63
Canton, OK (town) Blaine County	15	2.40
Colony, OK (town) Washita County	3	2.21
Silesia, MT (cdp) Carbon County	2	2.08
Lodge Pole, MT (cdp) Blaine County	5	1.89
Hunter, OK (town) Garfield County	3	1.82
Muddy, MT (cdp) Big Horn County	11	1.78
Kit Carson, CO (town) Cheyenne County	4	1.72
Whiterocks, UT (cdp) Uintah County	4	1.38
Manderson-White Horse Creek, SD (cdp) Shannon County	8	1.28
Busby, MT (cdp) Big Horn County	9	1.21
Lookeba, OK (town) Caddo County	2	1.20
Calumet, OK (town) Canadian County	6	1.18
Santee, NE (village) Knox County	4	1.16
Otway, OH (village) Scioto County	1	1.15
Wamsutter, WY (town) Sweetwater County	5	1.11
Kicking Horse, MT (cdp) Lake County	3	1.05
Oktaha, OK (town) Muskogee County	4	1.03
Lane, OK (cdp) Atoka County	4	0.97
Evaro, MT (cdp) Missoula County	3	0.93
Tselakai Dezza, UT (cdp) San Juan County	1	0.92
Pleasant Valley, TX (town) Wichita County	3	0.89
Indiahoma, OK (town) Comanche County	3	0.87
Pavillion, WY (town) Fremont County	2	0.87
Oglala, SD (cdp) Shannon County	11	0.85
Hays, MT (cdp) Blaine County	7	0.83
Jamestown, WA (cdp) Clallam County	3	0.83
Dodson, MT (town) Phillips County	1	0.81
Kyle, SD (cdp) Shannon County	6	0.71
Lodge Grass, MT (town) Big Horn County	3	0.70
Harbor Springs, MI (city) Emmet County	8	0.67
Pryor, MT (cdp) Big Horn County	4	0.65
Watonga, OK (city) Blaine County	32	0.63
Arapaho, OK (town) Custer County	5	0.63
Shoshoni, WY (town) Fremont County	4	0.62
Wolf Point, MT (city) Roosevelt County	16	0.61
Lame Deer, MT (cdp) Rosebud County	12	0.58
Haviland, KS (city) Kiowa County	4	0.57
El Reno, OK (city) Canadian County	93	0.56
Kenilworth, UT (cdp) Carbon County	1	0.56
Basin, WY (town) Big Horn County	7	0.54
Layton, FL (city) Monroe County	1	0.54
Eagle Butte, SD (city) Ziebach County	7	0.53
Wounded Knee, SD (cdp) Shannon County	2	0.52
Long Hollow, SD (cdp) Roberts County	1	0.52
Hardin, MT (city) Big Horn County	18	0.51
Pine Ridge, SD (cdp) Shannon County	17	0.51
North Browning, MT (cdp) Glacier County	12	0.50
Crow Agency, MT (cdp) Big Horn County	8	0.50
Casper Mountain, WY (cdp) Natrona County	2	0.50
Mills, WY (town) Natrona County	17	0.49
Ashland, MT (cdp) Rosebud County	4	0.49
Clinton, MT (cdp) Missoula County	5	0.48
Porcupine, SD (cdp) Shannon County	5	0.47
Fort Belknap Agency, MT (cdp) Blaine County	6	0.46
Rushville, NE (city) Sheridan County	4	0.45
Randlett, UT (cdp) Uintah County	1	0.45
Whittier, AK (city) Valdez-Cordova Census Area	1	0.45
Buffalo, WY (city) Johnson County	20	0.44
Leawood, MO (village) Newton County	3	0.44
Ronan, MT (city) Lake County	8	0.43

Place	Population	%
Kemp, TX (city) Kaufman County	5	0.43
Waynoka, OK (city) Woods County	4	0.43
Delleker, CA (cdp) Plumas County	3	0.43
Chester, NE (village) Thayer County	1	0.43
Fort Duchesne, UT (cdp) Uintah County	3	0.42
Wheatland, IN (town) Knox County	2	0.42
Thermopolis, WY (town) Hot Springs County	12	0.40
Vineland, CO (cdp) Pueblo County	1	0.40
Geronimo, OK (town) Comanche County	5	0.39
Clearview Acres, WY (cdp) Sweetwater County	3	0.38
White Oak, OK (cdp) Craig County	1	0.38
Calera, OK (town) Bryan County	8	0.37
Redby, MN (cdp) Beltrami County	5	0.37
Poplar, MT (city) Roosevelt County	3	0.37
Rodessa, LA (village) Caddo Parish	1	0.37
Union City, OK (town) Canadian County	6	0.36
Simsboro, LA (village) Lincoln Parish	3	0.36
St. Ignatius, MT (town) Lake County	3	0.36
Story, WY (cdp) Sheridan County	3	0.36
Akeley, MN (township) Hubbard County	2	0.36
Cole, OK (town) McClain County	2	0.36
Seiling, OK (city) Dewey County	3	0.35
Freedom, OK (town) Woods County	1	0.35
Black Eagle, MT (cdp) Cascade County	3	0.33
Dodge, NE (village) Dodge County	2	0.33
First Mesa, AZ (cdp) Navajo County	5	0.32
Simla, CO (town) Elbert County	2	0.32
Francis, OK (town) Pontotoc County	1	0.32
Hotevilla-Bacavi, AZ (cdp) Navajo County	3	0.31
Chilhowee, MO (town) Johnson County	1	0.31
Weatherford, OK (city) Custer County	32	0.30
Clinton, OK (city) Custer County	27	0.30
Bertram, TX (city) Burnet County	4	0.30
Bennington, OK (town) Bryan County	1	0.30
Montezuma Creek, UT (cdp) San Juan County	1	0.30
Rawlins, WY (city) Carbon County	27	0.29
Coal Creek, CO (town) Fremont County	1	0.29
St. Pierre, MT (cdp) Hill County	1	0.29
Fairmead, CA (cdp) Madera County	4	0.28
Titanic, OK (cdp) Adair County	1	0.28
Blanca, CO (town) Costilla County	1	0.26
Douglas, WY (city) Converse County	15	0.25
Fort Hall, ID (cdp) Bannock County	8	0.25
Mooreland, OK (town) Woodward County	3	0.25
Harlem, MT (city) Blaine County	2	0.25
Mountain View, OK (town) Kiowa County	2	0.25
New Deal, TX (town) Lubbock County	2	0.25
Purcell, MO (city) Jasper County	1	0.25
Antelope Valley-Crestview, WY (cdp) Campbell County	4	0.24
String, OK (town) Atoka County	1	0.24
Big Pine, CA (cdp) Inyo County	4	0.23
Watford City, ND (city) McKenzie County	4	0.23
Beale AFB, CA (cdp) Yuba County	3	0.23
Cameron, AZ (cdp) Coconino County	2	0.23
Almond, WI (village) Portage County	1	0.22
Rifton, NY (cdp) Ulster County	1	0.22
Airway Heights, WA (city) Spokane County	13	0.21
Cut Bank, MT (city) Glacier County	6	0.21
Flandreau, SD (city) Moody County	5	0.21
Cave City, AR (city) Sharp County	4	0.21
Shamrock, TX (city) Wheeler County	4	0.21
Apache, OK (town) Caddo County	3	0.21
Elephant Butte, NM (city) Sierra County	3	0.21
Montrose, SD (city) McCook County	1	0.21
North Washington, CO (cdp) Adams County	1	0.21
St. Johns, AZ (cdp) Maricopa County	1	0.21
Casper, WY (city) Natrona County	113	0.20
Pawhuska, OK (city) Osage County	7	0.20
Corvallis, MT (cdp) Ravalli County	2	0.20
Santa Clara Pueblo, NM (cdp) Rio Arriba County	2	0.20
Craigmont, ID (city) Lewis County	1	0.20
Valier, MT (town) Pondera County	1	0.20
Lusk, WY (town) Niobrara County	3	0.19
New Cuyama, CA (cdp) Santa Barbara County	1	0.19
Cache, OK (city) Comanche County	5	0.18

Please refer to the Explanation of Data in the front of the book for more detailed information.

Race

American Indian: Arapaho

Top 150 Places Sorted by Percent of Total Population

Based on places with total population of 7,500 or more

Place	Population	%
Riverton, WY (city) Fremont County	666	6.27
El Reno, OK (city) Canadian County	93	0.56
Weatherford, OK (city) Custer County	32	0.30
Clinton, OK (city) Custer County	27	0.30
Rawlins, WY (city) Carbon County	27	0.29
Casper, WY (city) Natrona County	113	0.20
Laramie, WY (city) Albany County	41	0.13
Miami, OK (city) Ottawa County	13	0.10
Parsons, KS (city) Labette County	10	0.10
Cheyenne, WY (city) Laramie County	52	0.09
Cody, WY (city) Park County	8	0.08
Toppenish, WA (city) Yakima County	7	0.08
Billings, MT (city) Yellowstone County	72	0.07
Pacifica, CA (city) San Mateo County	25	0.07
Jackson, WY (town) Teton County	7	0.07
Rapid City, SD (city) Pennington County	41	0.06
Idaho Falls, ID (city) Bonneville County	36	0.06
Rock Springs, WY (city) Sweetwater County	13	0.06
Sheridan, WY (city) Sheridan County	10	0.06
Fort Carson, CO (cdp) El Paso County	8	0.06
Woodward, OK (city) Woodward County	7	0.06
Cushing, OK (city) Payne County	5	0.06
Harwood Heights, IL (village) Cook County	5	0.06
Tuba City, AZ (cdp) Coconino County	5	0.06
Lawrence, KS (city) Douglas County	44	0.05
Juneau, AK (borough) Juneau City and Borough	16	0.05
Gillette, WY (city) Campbell County	15	0.05
Ponca City, OK (city) Kay County	13	0.05
Aurora, MO (city) Lawrence County	4	0.05
Cold Springs, NV (cdp) Washoe County	4	0.05
Conning Towers Nautilus Park, CT (cdp) New London County	4	0.05
Gering, NE (city) Scotts Bluff County	4	0.05
Shiprock, NM (cdp) San Juan County	4	0.05
Lawton, OK (city) Comanche County	39	0.04
Pocatello, ID (city) Bannock County	21	0.04
Columbine, CO (cdp) Jefferson County	10	0.04
Claremore, OK (city) Rogers County	7	0.04
Manchester, MO (city) St. Louis County	7	0.04
Chubbuck, ID (city) Bannock County	6	0.04
Durango, CO (city) La Plata County	6	0.04
Evanston, WY (city) Uinta County	5	0.04
Okmulgee, OK (city) Okmulgee County	5	0.04
St. Helens, OR (city) Columbia County	5	0.04
Independence, KS (city) Montgomery County	4	0.04
Shawano, WI (city) Shawano County	4	0.04
Fairwood, WA (cdp) Spokane County	3	0.04
Miles City, MT (city) Custer County	3	0.04
Pleasant View, UT (city) Weber County	3	0.04
West Valley City, UT (city) Salt Lake County	36	0.03
Rio Rancho, NM (city) Sandoval County	23	0.03
Great Falls, MT (city) Cascade County	18	0.03
Enid, OK (city) Garfield County	15	0.03
Moore, OK (city) Cleveland County	15	0.03
Kearns, UT (cdp) Salt Lake County	10	0.03
East Hill-Meridian, WA (cdp) King County	9	0.03
Midvale, UT (city) Salt Lake County	9	0.03
South Salt Lake, UT (city) Salt Lake County	7	0.03
Bethany, OK (city) Oklahoma County	6	0.03
Corsicana, TX (city) Navarro County	6	0.03
Badger, AK (cdp) Fairbanks North Star Borough	5	0.03
Cimarron Hills, CO (cdp) El Paso County	5	0.03
Welby, CO (cdp) Adams County	5	0.03
Elk City, OK (city) Beckham County	4	0.03
Kapolei, HI (cdp) Honolulu County	4	0.03
Yankton, SD (city) Yankton County	4	0.03
Blackfoot, ID (city) Bingham County	3	0.03
Burley, ID (city) Cassia County	3	0.03
Damascus, OR (city) Clackamas County	3	0.03
Festus, MO (city) Jefferson County	3	0.03
Fort Lewis, WA (cdp) Pierce County	3	0.03
Glenwood Springs, CO (city) Garfield County	3	0.03
Gunbarrel, CO (cdp) Boulder County	3	0.03
La Riviera, CA (cdp) Sacramento County	3	0.03
Montgomery, OH (city) Hamilton County	3	0.03
Waseca, MN (city) Waseca County	3	0.03
Westwood, MI (cdp) Kalamazoo County	3	0.03
Globe, AZ (city) Gila County	2	0.03
Lamar, CO (city) Prowers County	2	0.03
Mansfield, NJ (township) Warren County	2	0.03
Meadow Lakes, AK (cdp) Matanuska-Susitna Borough	2	0.03
Sutherlin, OR (city) Douglas County	2	0.03
Waterloo, NY (town) Seneca County	2	0.03
Oklahoma City, OK (city) Oklahoma County	132	0.02
Pueblo, CO (city) Pueblo County	26	0.02
Thornton, CO (city) Adams County	24	0.02
Loveland, CO (city) Larimer County	13	0.02
Midwest City, OK (city) Oklahoma County	13	0.02
Missoula, MT (city) Missoula County	12	0.02
Commerce City, CO (city) Adams County	8	0.02
Covina, CA (city) Los Angeles County	8	0.02
Littleton, CO (city) Arapahoe County	8	0.02
Willowbrook, CA (cdp) Los Angeles County	8	0.02
Foothill Farms, CA (cdp) Sacramento County	7	0.02
Muskogee, OK (city) Muskogee County	7	0.02
Stillwater, OK (city) Payne County	7	0.02
Calexico, CA (city) Imperial County	6	0.02
Clovis, NM (city) Curry County	6	0.02
Del City, OK (city) Oklahoma County	5	0.02
Dodge City, KS (city) Ford County	5	0.02
Duncan, OK (city) Stephens County	5	0.02
Holly Springs, NC (town) Wake County	5	0.02
Ken Caryl, CO (cdp) Jefferson County	5	0.02
Shawnee, OK (city) Pottawatomie County	5	0.02
Yukon, OK (city) Canadian County	5	0.02
Barstow, CA (city) San Bernardino County	4	0.02
Clifton, CO (cdp) Mesa County	4	0.02
Collinsville, IL (city) Madison County	4	0.02
Derry, PA (township) Dauphin County	4	0.02
Garfield, MI (charter township) Grand Traverse County	4	0.02
Makakilo, HI (cdp) Honolulu County	4	0.02
Mineral Wells, TX (city) Palo Pinto County	4	0.02
Overland, MO (city) St. Louis County	4	0.02
Park Forest, IL (village) Cook County	4	0.02
Sand Springs, OK (city) Tulsa County	4	0.02
South San Jose Hills, CA (cdp) Los Angeles County	4	0.02
Altamont, OR (cdp) Klamath County	3	0.02
Boulder City, NV (city) Clark County	3	0.02
Eustis, FL (city) Lake County	3	0.02
Gatesville, TX (city) Coryell County	3	0.02
Great Bend, KS (city) Barton County	3	0.02
Happy Valley, OR (city) Clackamas County	3	0.02
Jasper, IN (city) Dubois County	3	0.02
Levelland, TX (city) Hockley County	3	0.02
Live Oak, TX (city) Bexar County	3	0.02
Los Lunas, NM (village) Valencia County	3	0.02
Malta, NY (town) Saratoga County	3	0.02
Mandan, ND (city) Morton County	3	0.02
McKinleyville, CA (cdp) Humboldt County	3	0.02
North Salt Lake, UT (city) Davis County	3	0.02
Waterville, ME (city) Kennebec County	3	0.02
Baker City, OR (city) Baker County	2	0.02
Bay St. Louis, MS (city) Hancock County	2	0.02
Delta, CO (city) Delta County	2	0.02
Fife, WA (city) Pierce County	2	0.02
Garden City, ID (city) Ada County	2	0.02
Gardnerville Ranchos, NV (cdp) Douglas County	2	0.02
Holualoa, HI (cdp) Hawaii County	2	0.02
Lahaina, HI (cdp) Maui County	2	0.02
Lake Arrowhead, CA (cdp) San Bernardino County	2	0.02
Lakeland South, WA (cdp) King County	2	0.02
Lindon, UT (city) Utah County	2	0.02
London, OH (city) Madison County	2	0.02
Merriam, KS (city) Johnson County	2	0.02
Pell City, AL (city) St. Clair County	2	0.02
Philipstown, NY (town) Putnam County	2	0.02
Rifle, CO (city) Garfield County	2	0.02
Roxboro, NC (city) Person County	2	0.02
Scotts Valley, CA (city) Santa Cruz County	2	0.02
Vermillion, SD (city) Clay County	2	0.02
Webb City, MO (city) Jasper County	2	0.02

SECTION THREE

Please refer to the Explanation of Data in the front of the book for more detailed information.

Race

American Indian: Blackfeet

U.S. and 50 States Sorted by Population and Percent of Total Population

Place	Population	%
United States	**105,304**	**0.03**
California	15,420	0.04
Montana	12,831	1.30
Washington	6,573	0.10
Ohio	4,916	0.04
New York	4,496	0.02
Florida	4,377	0.02
Michigan	3,911	0.04
Texas	3,744	0.01
Pennsylvania	3,347	0.03
Oregon	2,943	0.08
Illinois	2,752	0.02
Missouri	2,473	0.04
North Carolina	2,231	0.02
Virginia	2,209	0.03
Maryland	2,099	0.04
Indiana	2,065	0.03
New Jersey	1,987	0.02
Colorado	1,969	0.04
Georgia	1,952	0.02
Massachusetts	1,645	0.03
Arizona	1,536	0.02
Oklahoma	1,325	0.04
Hawaii	1,309	0.10
Tennessee	1,251	0.02
Nevada	1,161	0.04
Kansas	1,123	0.04
Connecticut	1,071	0.03
Kentucky	986	0.02
Wisconsin	942	0.02
South Carolina	937	0.02
Arkansas	799	0.03
Minnesota	742	0.01
Alabama	738	0.02
Idaho	671	0.04
Louisiana	650	0.01
West Virginia	636	0.03
Alaska	609	0.09
Iowa	583	0.02
New Hampshire	555	0.04
Utah	489	0.02
New Mexico	463	0.02
Vermont	406	0.06
Maine	370	0.03
Rhode Island	351	0.03
Delaware	336	0.04
Mississippi	305	0.01
Nebraska	302	0.02
Wyoming	262	0.05
District of Columbia	236	0.04
South Dakota	136	0.02
North Dakota	84	0.01

Place	Population	%
Montana	12,831	1.30
Washington	6,573	0.10
Hawaii	1,309	0.10
Alaska	609	0.09
Oregon	2,943	0.08
Vermont	406	0.06
Wyoming	262	0.05
California	15,420	0.04
Ohio	4,916	0.04
Michigan	3,911	0.04
Missouri	2,473	0.04
Maryland	2,099	0.04
Colorado	1,969	0.04
Oklahoma	1,325	0.04
Nevada	1,161	0.04
Kansas	1,123	0.04
Idaho	671	0.04
New Hampshire	555	0.04
Delaware	336	0.04
District of Columbia	236	0.04
United States	**105,304**	**0.03**
Pennsylvania	3,347	0.03
Virginia	2,209	0.03
Indiana	2,065	0.03
Massachusetts	1,645	0.03
Connecticut	1,071	0.03
Arkansas	799	0.03
West Virginia	636	0.03
Maine	370	0.03
Rhode Island	351	0.03
New York	4,496	0.02
Florida	4,377	0.02
Illinois	2,752	0.02
North Carolina	2,231	0.02
New Jersey	1,987	0.02
Georgia	1,952	0.02
Arizona	1,536	0.02
Tennessee	1,251	0.02
Kentucky	986	0.02
Wisconsin	942	0.02
South Carolina	937	0.02
Alabama	738	0.02
Iowa	583	0.02
Utah	489	0.02
New Mexico	463	0.02
Nebraska	302	0.02
South Dakota	136	0.02
Texas	3,744	0.01
Minnesota	742	0.01
Louisiana	650	0.01
Mississippi	305	0.01
North Dakota	84	0.01

Please refer to the Explanation of Data in the front of the book for more detailed information.

Race

American Indian: Blackfeet

Top 150 Places Sorted by Population

Based on all places, regardless of total population

Place	Population	%
North Browning, MT (cdp) Glacier County	2,198	91.28
South Browning, MT (cdp) Glacier County	1,641	91.93
New York, NY (city) Kings County	1,627	0.02
Los Angeles, CA (city) Los Angeles County	966	0.03
Browning, MT (town) Glacier County	819	80.61
Great Falls, MT (city) Cascade County	784	1.34
Philadelphia, PA (city) Philadelphia County	679	0.04
Missoula, MT (city) Missoula County	597	0.89
Chicago, IL (city) Cook County	590	0.02
Seattle, WA (city) King County	567	0.09
Columbus, OH (city) Franklin County	539	0.07
Brooklyn, NY (borough) Kings County	531	0.02
Portland, OR (city) Multnomah County	515	0.09
Heart Butte, MT (cdp) Pondera County	502	86.25
Sacramento, CA (city) Sacramento County	485	0.10
Cut Bank, MT (city) Glacier County	448	15.62
Spokane, WA (city) Spokane County	441	0.21
Detroit, MI (city) Wayne County	441	0.06
San Diego, CA (city) San Diego County	426	0.03
Tacoma, WA (city) Pierce County	378	0.19
Manhattan, NY (borough) New York County	356	0.02
Indianapolis, IN (city) Marion County	354	0.04
Queens, NY (borough) Queens County	342	0.02
Oakland, CA (city) Alameda County	328	0.08
Bronx, NY (borough) Bronx County	310	0.02
Phoenix, AZ (city) Maricopa County	306	0.02
Kansas City, MO (city) Jackson County	284	0.06
San Francisco, CA (city) San Francisco County	284	0.04
Denver, CO (city) Denver County	282	0.05
Anchorage, AK (municipality) Anchorage Municipality	278	0.10
San Jose, CA (city) Santa Clara County	267	0.03
Las Vegas, NV (city) Clark County	263	0.05
Jacksonville, FL (city) Duval County	263	0.03
Billings, MT (city) Yellowstone County	249	0.24
Baltimore, MD (city) Baltimore city County	248	0.04
Cleveland, OH (city) Cuyahoga County	240	0.06
Washington, DC (city) District of Columbia	236	0.04
Starr School, MT (cdp) Glacier County	229	90.87
Stockton, CA (city) San Joaquin County	229	0.08
Colorado Springs, CO (city) El Paso County	229	0.05
Urban Honolulu, HI (cdp) Honolulu County	222	0.07
Fresno, CA (city) Fresno County	216	0.04
Long Beach, CA (city) Los Angeles County	214	0.05
Milwaukee, WI (city) Milwaukee County	213	0.04
Boston, MA (city) Suffolk County	212	0.03
Virginia Beach, VA (ind. city) Virginia Beach independent city	211	0.05
Aurora, CO (city) Arapahoe County	210	0.06
San Antonio, TX (city) Medina County	210	0.02
Oklahoma City, OK (city) Oklahoma County	200	0.03
Pittsburgh, PA (city) Allegheny County	199	0.07
Tulsa, OK (city) Tulsa County	189	0.05
Bakersfield, CA (city) Kern County	186	0.05
Charlotte, NC (city) Mecklenburg County	186	0.03
East Glacier Park Village, MT (cdp) Glacier County	182	50.14
Wichita, KS (city) Sedgwick County	182	0.05
Houston, TX (city) Harris County	179	0.01
Little Browning, MT (cdp) Glacier County	173	83.98
Lancaster, CA (city) Los Angeles County	168	0.11
Yakima, WA (city) Yakima County	167	0.18
Brookhaven, NY (town) Suffolk County	164	0.03
Louisville-Jefferson County, KY (metro govt) Jefferson County	162	0.03
St. Louis, MO (city) St. Louis city County	161	0.05
Cincinnati, OH (city) Hamilton County	160	0.05
Salem, OR (city) Marion County	158	0.10
Toledo, OH (city) Lucas County	158	0.06
Tucson, AZ (city) Pima County	154	0.03
Lansing, MI (city) Ingham County	147	0.13
Austin, TX (city) Travis County	147	0.02
Fayetteville, NC (city) Cumberland County	143	0.07
Lansing, MI (city) Ingham County	142	0.13
Flint, MI (city) Genesee County	141	0.14
Minneapolis, MN (city) Hennepin County	141	0.04
Albuquerque, NM (city) Bernalillo County	141	0.03
Pablo, MT (cdp) Lake County	139	6.17
Riverside, CA (city) Riverside County	139	0.05
Vancouver, WA (city) Clark County	137	0.08
Norfolk, VA (ind. city) Norfolk independent city	137	0.06
Rochester, NY (city) Monroe County	134	0.06
Dallas, TX (city) Dallas County	134	0.01
Modesto, CA (city) Stanislaus County	129	0.06
Nashville-Davidson, TN (metro govt) Davidson County	126	0.02
Federal Way, WA (city) King County	124	0.14
Omaha, NE (city) Douglas County	124	0.03
Greensboro, NC (city) Guilford County	123	0.05
Helena, MT (city) Lewis and Clark County	121	0.43
Babb, MT (cdp) Glacier County	120	68.97
Fort Worth, TX (city) Tarrant County	119	0.02
Hempstead, NY (town) Nassau County	117	0.02
Akron, OH (city) Summit County	115	0.06
Spokane Valley, WA (city) Spokane County	114	0.13
Victorville, CA (city) San Bernardino County	114	0.10
Newport News, VA (ind. city) Newport News independent city	113	0.06
San Bernardino, CA (city) San Bernardino County	112	0.05
Syracuse, NY (city) Onondaga County	111	0.08
Fort Wayne, IN (city) Allen County	110	0.04
Kent, WA (city) King County	109	0.12
Eugene, OR (city) Lane County	107	0.07
Palmdale, CA (city) Los Angeles County	107	0.07
Atlanta, GA (city) Fulton County	106	0.03
Hampton, VA (ind. city) Hampton independent city	105	0.08
Henderson, NV (city) Clark County	105	0.04
Auburn, WA (city) King County	104	0.15
Kansas City, KS (city) Wyandotte County	104	0.07
Grand Rapids, MI (city) Kent County	104	0.06
Buffalo, NY (city) Erie County	104	0.04
Gresham, OR (city) Multnomah County	101	0.10
Raleigh, NC (city) Wake County	101	0.03
Memphis, TN (city) Shelby County	101	0.02
Bozeman, MT (city) Gallatin County	100	0.27
Canton, OH (city) Stark County	100	0.14
Dayton, OH (city) Montgomery County	100	0.07
Providence, RI (city) Providence County	99	0.06
Havre, MT (city) Hill County	98	1.05
Butte-Silver Bow, MT (cons. govt) Silver Bow County	98	0.29
Santa Rosa, CA (city) Sonoma County	97	0.06
Tampa, FL (city) Hillsborough County	97	0.03
Sunrise Manor, NV (cdp) Clark County	96	0.05
North Las Vegas, NV (city) Clark County	96	0.04
Elk Grove, CA (city) Sacramento County	95	0.06
Springfield, MA (city) Hampden County	95	0.06
Kalispell, MT (city) Flathead County	94	0.47
Redding, CA (city) Shasta County	94	0.10
Springfield, MO (city) Christian County	90	0.06
Arlington, TX (city) Tarrant County	90	0.02
Antioch, CA (city) Contra Costa County	89	0.09
Paradise, NV (cdp) Clark County	89	0.04
St. Petersburg, FL (city) Pinellas County	89	0.04
Staten Island, NY (borough) Richmond County	88	0.02
Bremerton, WA (city) Kitsap County	86	0.23
Reno, NV (city) Washoe County	86	0.04
St. Paul, MN (city) Ramsey County	86	0.03
Independence, MO (city) Jackson County	85	0.07
Richmond, VA (ind. city) Richmond independent city	85	0.04
Marysville, WA (city) Snohomish County	84	0.14
Chesapeake, VA (ind. city) Chesapeake independent city	84	0.04
Fontana, CA (city) San Bernardino County	84	0.04
Polson, MT (city) Lake County	83	1.85
Pueblo, CO (city) Pueblo County	83	0.08
Mesa, AZ (city) Maricopa County	83	0.02
Lakewood, WA (city) Pierce County	81	0.14
Chico, CA (city) Butte County	81	0.09
Vallejo, CA (city) Solano County	81	0.07
Rancho Cucamonga, CA (city) San Bernardino County	80	0.05
Des Moines, IA (city) Polk County	80	0.04
Concord, CA (city) Contra Costa County	79	0.06
Hayward, CA (city) Alameda County	79	0.05
Huntington Beach, CA (city) Orange County	79	0.04
Rancho Cordova, CA (city) Sacramento County	77	0.12
Arden-Arcade, CA (cdp) Sacramento County	77	0.08
Everett, WA (city) Snohomish County	77	0.07

Please refer to the Explanation of Data in the front of the book for more detailed information.

Race

American Indian: Blackfeet

Top 150 Places Sorted by Percent of Total Population

Based on all places, regardless of total population

Place	Population	%
South Browning, MT (cdp) Glacier County	1,641	91.93
North Browning, MT (cdp) Glacier County	2,198	91.28
Starr School, MT (cdp) Glacier County	229	90.87
Heart Butte, MT (cdp) Pondera County	502	86.25
Little Browning, MT (cdp) Glacier County	173	83.98
Browning, MT (town) Glacier County	819	80.61
Babb, MT (cdp) Glacier County	120	68.97
East Glacier Park Village, MT (cdp) Glacier County	182	50.14
Royalton, MN (city) Benton County	1	33.33
Cut Bank, MT (city) Glacier County	448	15.62
Santa Rita, MT (cdp) Glacier County	14	12.39
Elkhorn, MT (cdp) Jefferson County	1	10.00
Turtle Lake, MT (cdp) Lake County	20	9.57
Ugashik, AK (cdp) Lake and Peninsula Borough	1	8.33
Valier, MT (town) Pondera County	36	7.07
Dupuyer, MT (cdp) Pondera County	6	6.98
Osgood, MO (village) Sullivan County	3	6.25
Pablo, MT (cdp) Lake County	139	6.17
Pilot Point, AK (city) Lake and Peninsula Borough	4	5.88
Dodson, MT (town) Phillips County	7	5.65
Beluga, AK (cdp) Kenai Peninsula Borough	1	5.00
Turner, MT (cdp) Blaine County	3	4.92
Vanceboro, ME (town) Washington County	6	4.29
Arlee, MT (cdp) Lake County	27	4.25
Silesia, MT (cdp) Carbon County	4	4.17
Beaulieu, MN (cdp) Mahnomen County	2	4.17
Scottsville, KS (city) Mitchell County	1	4.00
Spivey, KS (city) Kingman County	3	3.85
Old Agency, MT (cdp) Sanders County	4	3.74
Evaro, MT (cdp) Missoula County	12	3.73
Gunn City, MO (village) Cass County	4	3.39
Darlington, MO (village) Gentry County	4	3.31
New, MO (town) Sullivan County	6	3.28
Lake City, CA (cdp) Modoc County	2	3.28
St. Ignatius, MT (town) Lake County	26	3.09
Mitchell, OR (city) Wheeler County	4	3.08
Bushnell, SD (town) Brookings County	2	3.08
Seldovia Village, AK (cdp) Kenai Peninsula Borough	5	3.03
Forbestown, CA (cdp) Butte County	9	2.81
Shaniko, OR (city) Wasco County	1	2.78
Rickreall, OR (cdp) Polk County	2	2.60
Herron, MT (cdp) Hill County	3	2.59
Florence, MN (city) Lyon County	1	2.56
Cliff Village, MO (village) Newton County	1	2.50
Ellisburg, NY (village) Jefferson County	6	2.46
White Swan, WA (cdp) Yakima County	19	2.40
Boneau, MT (cdp) Chouteau County	9	2.37
Box Elder, MT (cdp) Hill County	2	2.30
Spring, AR (town) Benton County	2	2.30
Highwood, MT (cdp) Chouteau County	4	2.27
Elmo, MT (cdp) Lake County	4	2.22
Hollister, ID (city) Twin Falls County	6	2.21
Fort Shaw, MT (cdp) Cascade County	6	2.14
Harlem, MT (city) Blaine County	17	2.10
Ronan, MT (city) Lake County	39	2.08
Chief, MN (township) Mahnomen County	2	2.08
Reevesville, SC (town) Dorchester County	4	2.04
Kasaan, AK (city) Prince of Wales-Hyder Census Area	1	2.04
Frenchtown-Rumbly, MD (cdp) Somerset County	2	2.00
Lake Annette, MO (city) Cass County	2	2.00
Rocky Boy's Agency, MT (cdp) Hill County	7	1.97
Blenheim, SC (town) Marlboro County	3	1.95
Hancock, VT (town) Addison County	6	1.86
Polson, MT (city) Lake County	83	1.85
Walnut Hill, IL (village) Marion County	2	1.85
Datil, NM (cdp) Catron County	1	1.85
Backus, MI (township) Roscommon County	6	1.82
Cascade, MT (town) Cascade County	12	1.75
Plush, OR (cdp) Lake County	1	1.75
Daisy, AR (town) Pike County	2	1.74
St. Pierre, MT (cdp) Hill County	6	1.71
Grand River, IA (city) Decatur County	4	1.69
Alexandria, NE (village) Thayer County	3	1.69
Starkville, CO (town) Las Animas County	1	1.69
Higden, AR (town) Cleburne County	2	1.67
Hyampom, CA (cdp) Trinity County	4	1.66
Manitou, OK (town) Tillman County	3	1.66
Cal-Nev-Ari, NV (cdp) Clark County	4	1.64
Port Colden, NJ (cdp) Warren County	2	1.64
Aurora, IA (city) Buchanan County	3	1.62
Sun River, MT (cdp) Cascade County	2	1.61
Jette, MT (cdp) Lake County	4	1.58
Whitewater, MT (cdp) Phillips County	1	1.56
Havre North, MT (cdp) Hill County	11	1.54
Aaronsburg, PA (cdp) Washington County	4	1.54
Smoot, WY (cdp) Lincoln County	3	1.54
Mercersville, MD (cdp) Washington County	2	1.54
Jameson, MO (town) Daviess County	2	1.50
Bivalve, MD (cdp) Wicomico County	3	1.49
Inchelium, WA (cdp) Ferry County	6	1.47
Faxon, OK (town) Comanche County	2	1.47
Jenner, CA (cdp) Sonoma County	2	1.47
Brandywine, WV (cdp) Pendleton County	3	1.38
Gray, PA (township) Greene County	3	1.37
Great Falls, MT (city) Cascade County	784	1.34
Maple, MN (township) Cass County	5	1.33
Williford, AR (town) Sharp County	1	1.33
Hollansburg, OH (village) Darke County	3	1.32
Tuskahoma, OK (cdp) Pushmataha County	2	1.32
Ravalli, MT (cdp) Lake County	1	1.32
Coram, MT (cdp) Flathead County	7	1.30
Davey, NE (village) Lancaster County	2	1.30
Brandon, IA (city) Buchanan County	4	1.29
Tesuque Pueblo, NM (cdp) Santa Fe County	3	1.29
Midland, CO (cdp) Teller County	2	1.28
Disautel, WA (cdp) Okanogan County	1	1.28
Nespelem, WA (town) Okanogan County	3	1.27
Bonner-West Riverside, MT (cdp) Missoula County	21	1.26
Gove City, KS (city) Gove County	1	1.25
Olowalu, HI (cdp) Maui County	1	1.25
Rose Hill, IL (village) Jasper County	1	1.25
Tupman, CA (cdp) Kern County	2	1.24
Conrad, MT (city) Pondera County	31	1.21
Busby, MT (cdp) Big Horn County	9	1.21
Bronaugh, MO (city) Vernon County	3	1.20
Kerr, MT (cdp) Lake County	3	1.20
Weeksville, MT (cdp) Sanders County	1	1.20
Adeline, IL (village) Ogle County	1	1.18
Oyehut, WA (cdp) Grays Harbor County	1	1.18
Ball Club, MN (cdp) Itasca County	4	1.17
Millfield, OH (cdp) Athens County	4	1.17
Baileys Harbor, WI (cdp) Door County	3	1.17
Little Elbow, MN (township) Mahnomen County	3	1.16
Rudyard, MT (cdp) Hill County	3	1.16
California Pines, CA (cdp) Modoc County	6	1.15
Prescott, KS (city) Linn County	3	1.14
Simms, MT (cdp) Cascade County	4	1.13
Cabery, IL (village) Ford County	3	1.13
Big Arm, MT (cdp) Lake County	2	1.13
Darby, MT (town) Ravalli County	8	1.11
Shelby, MT (city) Toole County	37	1.10
Harveysburg, OH (village) Warren County	6	1.10
Hot Springs, MT (town) Sanders County	6	1.10
Rader Creek, MT (cdp) Jefferson County	4	1.10
Chignik, AK (city) Lake and Peninsula Borough	1	1.10
Daphnedale Park, CA (cdp) Modoc County	2	1.09
Dodd City, TX (town) Fannin County	4	1.08
Ramah, NM (cdp) McKinley County	4	1.08
Coulee City, WA (town) Grant County	6	1.07
Camp Dennison, OH (cdp) Hamilton County	4	1.07
Nixon, NV (cdp) Washoe County	4	1.07
Lindisfarne, MT (cdp) Lake County	3	1.06
Havre, MT (city) Hill County	98	1.05
Azure, MT (cdp) Hill County	3	1.05
Allen, MI (village) Hillsdale County	2	1.05
Olney, MT (cdp) Flathead County	2	1.05
Blairstown, MO (city) Henry County	1	1.03
New Pine Creek, CA (cdp) Modoc County	1	1.02
Godley, IL (village) Will County	6	1.00
Albright, WV (town) Preston County	3	1.00

Please refer to the Explanation of Data in the front of the book for more detailed information.

Race

American Indian: Blackfeet

Top 150 Places Sorted by Percent of Total Population

Based on places with total population of 7,500 or more

Place	Population	%
Great Falls, MT (city) Cascade County	784	1.34
Havre, MT (city) Hill County	98	1.05
Missoula, MT (city) Missoula County	597	0.89
Helena Valley Southeast, MT (cdp) Lewis and Clark County	51	0.62
Kalispell, MT (city) Flathead County	94	0.47
Helena, MT (city) Lewis and Clark County	121	0.43
Helena Valley West Central, MT (cdp) Lewis and Clark County	30	0.38
Butte-Silver Bow, MT (cons. govt) Silver Bow County	98	0.29
Evergreen, MT (cdp) Flathead County	22	0.29
Bryn Mawr-Skyway, WA (cdp) King County	44	0.28
White Center, WA (cdp) King County	38	0.28
Bozeman, MT (city) Gallatin County	100	0.27
Kalaoa, HI (cdp) Hawaii County	26	0.27
Holualoa, HI (cdp) Hawaii County	23	0.27
Graham, WA (cdp) Pierce County	60	0.26
Hawaiian Paradise Park, HI (cdp) Hawaii County	30	0.26
Billings, MT (city) Yellowstone County	249	0.24
Fort Lewis, WA (cdp) Pierce County	27	0.24
Shelton, WA (city) Mason County	24	0.24
Waimea, HI (cdp) Hawaii County	22	0.24
Bremerton, WA (city) Kitsap County	86	0.23
Wahiawa, HI (cdp) Honolulu County	41	0.23
Makakilo, HI (cdp) Honolulu County	40	0.22
Parkway, CA (cdp) Sacramento County	32	0.22
Spokane, WA (city) Spokane County	441	0.21
Kelso, WA (city) Cowlitz County	25	0.21
Crestline, CA (cdp) San Bernardino County	23	0.21
Montague, MA (town) Franklin County	18	0.21
Oberlin, OH (city) Lorain County	17	0.21
Parkland, WA (cdp) Pierce County	70	0.20
Magalia, CA (cdp) Butte County	23	0.20
North Bellport, NY (cdp) Suffolk County	23	0.20
Tacoma, WA (city) Pierce County	378	0.19
Burien, WA (city) King County	62	0.19
Eureka, CA (city) Humboldt County	52	0.19
SeaTac, WA (city) King County	50	0.19
Olivehurst, CA (cdp) Yuba County	26	0.19
Grass Valley, CA (city) Nevada County	24	0.19
Lakes, AK (cdp) Matanuska-Susitna Borough	16	0.19
Yreka, CA (city) Siskiyou County	15	0.19
Yakima, WA (city) Yakima County	167	0.18
Longview, WA (city) Cowlitz County	67	0.18
Foothill Farms, CA (cdp) Sacramento County	58	0.18
Frederickson, WA (cdp) Pierce County	33	0.18
Clearlake, CA (city) Lake County	27	0.18
Kailua, HI (cdp) Hawaii County	21	0.18
East Renton Highlands, WA (cdp) King County	20	0.18
Ahuimanu, HI (cdp) Honolulu County	16	0.18
Golden Hills, CA (cdp) Kern County	16	0.18
Lincoln City, OR (city) Lincoln County	14	0.18
Thousand Palms, CA (cdp) Riverside County	14	0.18
Wasilla, AK (city) Matanuska-Susitna Borough	14	0.18
Washougal, WA (city) Clark County	24	0.17
Port Orchard, WA (city) Kitsap County	19	0.17
Kapaa, HI (cdp) Kauai County	18	0.17
Vermilion, OH (city) Lorain County	18	0.17
Shasta Lake, CA (city) Shasta County	17	0.17
Cottage Grove, OR (city) Lane County	16	0.17
Thompsonville, CT (cdp) Hartford County	15	0.17
Haiku-Pauwela, HI (cdp) Maui County	14	0.17
Willingboro, NJ (township) Burlington County	51	0.16
Tukwila, WA (city) King County	31	0.16
Lebanon, OR (city) Linn County	25	0.16
Oroville, CA (city) Butte County	25	0.16
Berlin, NH (city) Coos County	16	0.16
Acton, CA (cdp) Los Angeles County	12	0.16
North Hanover, NJ (township) Burlington County	12	0.16
Auburn, WA (city) King County	104	0.15
North Highlands, CA (cdp) Sacramento County	64	0.15
Oildale, CA (cdp) Kern County	48	0.15
Mountlake Terrace, WA (city) Snohomish County	29	0.15
Linda, CA (cdp) Yuba County	27	0.15
Ewa Beach, HI (cdp) Honolulu County	22	0.15
Big Bear City, CA (cdp) San Bernardino County	18	0.15
Palmer Town, MA (city) Hampden County	18	0.15
Walker Mill, MD (cdp) Prince George's County	17	0.15
Emeryville, CA (city) Alameda County	15	0.15
Fife, WA (city) Pierce County	14	0.15
Fallon, NV (city) Churchill County	13	0.15
Florence, OR (city) Lane County	13	0.15
Springfield, FL (city) Bay County	13	0.15
Bellevue, OH (city) Sandusky County	12	0.15
Summit, WA (cdp) Pierce County	12	0.15
Meadow Lakes, AK (cdp) Matanuska-Susitna Borough	11	0.15
Flint, MI (city) Genesee County	141	0.14
Federal Way, WA (city) King County	124	0.14
Canton, OH (city) Stark County	100	0.14
Marysville, WA (city) Snohomish County	84	0.14
Lakewood, WA (city) Pierce County	81	0.14
Grandview, MO (city) Jackson County	35	0.14
Junction City, KS (city) Geary County	33	0.14
Covington, WA (city) King County	24	0.14
Waianae, HI (cdp) Honolulu County	19	0.14
Bedford, OH (city) Cuyahoga County	18	0.14
Marysville, CA (city) Yuba County	17	0.14
Lakeland South, WA (cdp) King County	16	0.14
Rosaryville, MD (cdp) Prince George's County	15	0.14
Anaconda-Deer Lodge County, MT (special city) Deer Lodge County	13	0.14
Madison, MI (charter township) Lenawee County	12	0.14
Park Hills, MO (city) St. Francois County	12	0.14
Princeton, IN (city) Gibson County	12	0.14
Lansing, MI (city) Ingham County	147	0.13
Lansing, MI (city) Ingham County	142	0.13
Spokane Valley, WA (city) Spokane County	114	0.13
Rock Island, IL (city) Rock Island County	50	0.13
Des Moines, WA (city) King County	39	0.13
Ewa Gentry, HI (cdp) Honolulu County	30	0.13
Hayesville, OR (cdp) Marion County	26	0.13
Orchards, WA (cdp) Clark County	25	0.13
Pinole, CA (city) Contra Costa County	24	0.13
Arcata, CA (city) Humboldt County	22	0.13
Greenfield Town, MA (city) Franklin County	22	0.13
Mountain Home, ID (city) Elmore County	19	0.13
Red Bluff, CA (city) Tehama County	19	0.13
Rio Linda, CA (cdp) Sacramento County	19	0.13
Elk Plain, WA (cdp) Pierce County	18	0.13
North Adams, MA (city) Berkshire County	18	0.13
Nanakuli, HI (cdp) Honolulu County	17	0.13
Lake Arrowhead, CA (cdp) San Bernardino County	16	0.13
Gardnerville Ranchos, NV (cdp) Douglas County	15	0.13
Pontiac, IL (city) Livingston County	15	0.13
Spring Lake, NC (town) Cumberland County	15	0.13
Coldwater, MI (city) Branch County	14	0.13
Summerfield, MD (cdp) Prince George's County	14	0.13
View Park-Windsor Hills, CA (cdp) Los Angeles County	14	0.13
Coral Hills, MD (cdp) Prince George's County	13	0.13
Ecorse, MI (city) Wayne County	12	0.13
Fort Polk South, LA (cdp) Vernon Parish	12	0.13
Lincoln Village, OH (cdp) Franklin County	12	0.13
Ocean Pointe, HI (cdp) Honolulu County	11	0.13
Center, PA (township) Butler County	10	0.13
Pleasant View, UT (city) Weber County	10	0.13
Kent, WA (city) King County	109	0.12
Rancho Cordova, CA (city) Sacramento County	77	0.12
Highland, CA (city) San Bernardino County	62	0.12
Grants Pass, OR (city) Josephine County	43	0.12
University Place, WA (city) Pierce County	36	0.12
Englewood, NJ (city) Bergen County	32	0.12
Paradise, CA (town) Butte County	31	0.12
Rosemont, CA (cdp) Sacramento County	28	0.12
Yucca Valley, CA (town) San Bernardino County	25	0.12
Ypsilanti, MI (city) Washtenaw County	24	0.12
Ashtabula, OH (city) Ashtabula County	22	0.12
Bonney Lake, WA (city) Pierce County	20	0.12
Huron, MI (charter township) Wayne County	19	0.12
Cherryland, CA (cdp) Alameda County	17	0.12
Dryden, NY (town) Tompkins County	17	0.12
Ladson, SC (cdp) Berkeley County	16	0.12
The Dalles, OR (city) Wasco County	16	0.12
Fort Drum, NY (cdp) Jefferson County	15	0.12

Please refer to the Explanation of Data in the front of the book for more detailed information.

Race

American Indian: Canadian/French American Indian

U.S. and 50 States Sorted by Population and Percent of Total Population

Place	Population	%
United States	**14,822**	**<0.01**
Washington	2,079	0.03
California	1,645	<0.01
Michigan	1,366	0.01
New York	1,022	0.01
Florida	684	<0.01
Texas	658	<0.01
Minnesota	470	0.01
Massachusetts	458	0.01
Oregon	376	0.01
Ohio	338	<0.01
Maine	307	0.02
Arizona	298	<0.01
Pennsylvania	288	<0.01
Illinois	279	<0.01
Wisconsin	255	<0.01
Virginia	251	<0.01
Connecticut	250	0.01
Indiana	248	<0.01
Colorado	234	<0.01
Montana	207	0.02
Louisiana	187	<0.01
North Carolina	179	<0.01
Alaska	173	0.02
New Jersey	173	<0.01
New Hampshire	155	0.01
Georgia	145	<0.01
Vermont	144	0.02
Nevada	143	0.01
Tennessee	143	<0.01
Idaho	133	0.01
Missouri	127	<0.01
Maryland	126	<0.01
Hawaii	101	0.01
New Mexico	99	<0.01
Oklahoma	99	<0.01
Kansas	95	<0.01
Rhode Island	94	0.01
South Carolina	88	<0.01
Alabama	80	<0.01
Utah	80	<0.01
Kentucky	78	<0.01
North Dakota	74	0.01
Nebraska	64	<0.01
Iowa	61	<0.01
Mississippi	60	<0.01
South Dakota	51	0.01
Arkansas	49	<0.01
West Virginia	35	<0.01
Wyoming	32	0.01
Delaware	28	<0.01
District of Columbia	13	<0.01

Place	Population	%
Washington	2,079	0.03
Maine	307	0.02
Montana	207	0.02
Alaska	173	0.02
Vermont	144	0.02
Michigan	1,366	0.01
New York	1,022	0.01
Minnesota	470	0.01
Massachusetts	458	0.01
Oregon	376	0.01
Connecticut	250	0.01
New Hampshire	155	0.01
Nevada	143	0.01
Idaho	133	0.01
Hawaii	101	0.01
Rhode Island	94	0.01
North Dakota	74	0.01
South Dakota	51	0.01
Wyoming	32	0.01
United States	**14,822**	**<0.01**
California	1,645	<0.01
Florida	684	<0.01
Texas	658	<0.01
Ohio	338	<0.01
Arizona	298	<0.01
Pennsylvania	288	<0.01
Illinois	279	<0.01
Wisconsin	255	<0.01
Virginia	251	<0.01
Indiana	248	<0.01
Colorado	234	<0.01
Louisiana	187	<0.01
North Carolina	179	<0.01
New Jersey	173	<0.01
Georgia	145	<0.01
Tennessee	143	<0.01
Missouri	127	<0.01
Maryland	126	<0.01
New Mexico	99	<0.01
Oklahoma	99	<0.01
Kansas	95	<0.01
South Carolina	88	<0.01
Alabama	80	<0.01
Utah	80	<0.01
Kentucky	78	<0.01
Nebraska	64	<0.01
Iowa	61	<0.01
Mississippi	60	<0.01
Arkansas	49	<0.01
West Virginia	35	<0.01
Delaware	28	<0.01
District of Columbia	13	<0.01

Please refer to the Explanation of Data in the front of the book for more detailed information.

Race

American Indian: Canadian/French American Indian

Top 150 Places Sorted by Population

Based on all places, regardless of total population

Place	Population	%
Seattle, WA (city) King County	198	0.03
New York, NY (city) Kings County	197	<0.01
Los Angeles, CA (city) Los Angeles County	119	<0.01
Tacoma, WA (city) Pierce County	104	0.05
Portland, OR (city) Multnomah County	67	0.01
San Antonio, TX (city) Medina County	64	<0.01
Brooklyn, NY (borough) Kings County	62	<0.01
Manhattan, NY (borough) New York County	62	<0.01
Buffalo, NY (city) Erie County	57	0.02
Chicago, IL (city) Cook County	55	<0.01
San Diego, CA (city) San Diego County	53	<0.01
Bellingham, WA (city) Whatcom County	52	0.06
Syracuse, NY (city) Onondaga County	51	0.04
Spokane, WA (city) Spokane County	49	0.02
Houston, TX (city) Harris County	49	<0.01
Kent, WA (city) King County	48	0.05
Detroit, MI (city) Wayne County	45	0.01
San Jose, CA (city) Santa Clara County	45	<0.01
Renton, WA (city) King County	44	0.05
Anchorage, AK (municipality) Anchorage Municipality	44	0.02
Minneapolis, MN (city) Hennepin County	42	0.01
San Francisco, CA (city) San Francisco County	42	0.01
Sault Ste. Marie, MI (city) Chippewa County	40	0.28
Federal Way, WA (city) King County	38	0.04
Warren, MI (city) Macomb County	38	0.03
Tucson, AZ (city) Pima County	38	0.01
Phoenix, AZ (city) Maricopa County	38	<0.01
Queens, NY (borough) Queens County	38	<0.01
Burien, WA (city) King County	36	0.11
St. Paul, MN (city) Ramsey County	36	0.01
Philadelphia, PA (city) Philadelphia County	34	<0.01
Everett, WA (city) Snohomish County	33	0.03
Colorado Springs, CO (city) El Paso County	33	0.01
Albuquerque, NM (city) Bernalillo County	30	0.01
Long Beach, CA (city) Los Angeles County	30	0.01
Lansing, MI (city) Ingham County	29	0.03
Lansing, MI (city) Ingham County	29	0.03
Boston, MA (city) Suffolk County	29	<0.01
Milwaukee, WI (city) Milwaukee County	29	<0.01
Duluth, MN (city) St. Louis County	28	0.03
Mesa, AZ (city) Maricopa County	27	0.01
Oakland, CA (city) Alameda County	27	0.01
Las Vegas, NV (city) Clark County	27	<0.01
Missoula, MT (city) Missoula County	26	0.04
Nampa, ID (city) Canyon County	26	0.03
Bronx, NY (borough) Bronx County	25	<0.01
Denver, CO (city) Denver County	25	<0.01
Fort Worth, TX (city) Tarrant County	25	<0.01
Austin, TX (city) Travis County	24	<0.01
International Falls, MN (city) Koochiching County	23	0.36
Port Huron, MI (city) St. Clair County	23	0.08
Springfield, MA (city) Hampden County	23	0.02
Toledo, OH (city) Lucas County	23	0.01
Nashville-Davidson, TN (metro govt) Davidson County	23	<0.01
Bremerton, WA (city) Kitsap County	22	0.06
Marysville, WA (city) Snohomish County	22	0.04
Indianapolis, IN (city) Marion County	22	<0.01
Jacksonville, FL (city) Duval County	22	<0.01
Bainbridge Island, WA (city) Kitsap County	21	0.09
Auburn, WA (city) King County	21	0.03
Worcester, MA (city) Worcester County	21	0.01
Columbus, OH (city) Franklin County	21	<0.01
Fresno, CA (city) Fresno County	21	<0.01
Sacramento, CA (city) Sacramento County	21	<0.01
Suquamish, WA (cdp) Kitsap County	20	0.48
SeaTac, WA (city) King County	20	0.07
Niagara Falls, NY (city) Niagara County	20	0.04
Redmond, WA (city) King County	20	0.04
Chandler, AZ (city) Maricopa County	20	0.01
Vancouver, WA (city) Clark County	20	0.01
Dallas, TX (city) Dallas County	20	<0.01
Lynnwood, WA (city) Snohomish County	19	0.05
Victorville, CA (city) San Bernardino County	19	0.02
Wichita, KS (city) Sedgwick County	19	<0.01
Cloquet, MN (city) Carlton County	18	0.15
Port Angeles, WA (city) Clallam County	18	0.09
Tukwila, WA (city) King County	18	0.09
Des Moines, WA (city) King County	18	0.06
Lincoln Park, MI (city) Wayne County	18	0.05
Palm Bay, FL (city) Brevard County	18	0.02
Akron, OH (city) Summit County	18	0.01
New Orleans, LA (city) Orleans Parish	18	0.01
Omaha, NE (city) Douglas County	18	<0.01
Bryn Mawr-Skyway, WA (cdp) King County	17	0.11
Grand Rapids, MI (city) Kent County	17	0.01
Stockton, CA (city) San Joaquin County	17	0.01
Buenaventura Lakes, FL (cdp) Osceola County	16	0.06
Clay, NY (town) Onondaga County	16	0.03
Redford, MI (charter township) Wayne County	16	0.03
South Hill, WA (cdp) Pierce County	16	0.03
Spokane Valley, WA (city) Spokane County	16	0.02
Ann Arbor, MI (city) Washtenaw County	16	0.01
Arlington, TX (city) Tarrant County	16	<0.01
Urban Honolulu, HI (cdp) Honolulu County	16	<0.01
Virginia Beach, VA (ind. city) Virginia Beach independent city	16	<0.01
Aberdeen, WA (city) Grays Harbor County	15	0.09
Grand Island, NY (town) Erie County	15	0.07
Minot, ND (city) Ward County	15	0.04
Olympia, WA (city) Thurston County	15	0.03
Shoreline, WA (city) King County	15	0.03
Kennewick, WA (city) Benton County	15	0.02
Bellevue, WA (city) King County	15	0.01
Reno, NV (city) Washoe County	15	0.01
Brookhaven, NY (town) Suffolk County	15	<0.01
Charlotte, NC (city) Mecklenburg County	15	<0.01
Pittsburgh, PA (city) Allegheny County	15	<0.01
Omak, WA (city) Okanogan County	14	0.29
Potsdam, NY (town) St. Lawrence County	14	0.09
Badger, AK (cdp) Fairbanks North Star Borough	14	0.07
De Witt, NY (town) Onondaga County	14	0.05
Lewiston, ME (city) Androscoggin County	14	0.04
Billings, MT (city) Yellowstone County	14	0.01
Greece, NY (town) Monroe County	14	0.01
Manchester, NH (city) Hillsborough County	14	0.01
Anaheim, CA (city) Orange County	14	<0.01
Baltimore, MD (city) Baltimore city County	14	<0.01
Bay Mills, MI (township) Chippewa County	13	0.88
East Wenatchee, WA (city) Douglas County	13	0.10
Union, MI (charter township) Isabella County	13	0.10
Auburn, ME (city) Androscoggin County	13	0.06
Mukilteo, WA (city) Snohomish County	13	0.06
Medford, MA (city) Middlesex County	13	0.02
New Britain, CT (city/town) Hartford County	13	0.02
Pawtucket, RI (city) Providence County	13	0.02
Taylor, MI (city) Wayne County	13	0.02
Boulder, CO (city) Boulder County	13	0.01
Cambridge, MA (city) Middlesex County	13	0.01
Compton, CA (city) Los Angeles County	13	0.01
El Cajon, CA (city) San Diego County	13	0.01
Huntington Beach, CA (city) Orange County	13	0.01
Newport News, VA (ind. city) Newport News independent city	13	0.01
Paradise, NV (cdp) Clark County	13	0.01
El Paso, TX (city) El Paso County	13	<0.01
Washington, DC (city) District of Columbia	13	<0.01
Avalon, PA (borough) Allegheny County	12	0.26
Graham, WA (cdp) Pierce County	12	0.05
Eastpointe, MI (city) Macomb County	12	0.04
Granger, IN (cdp) St. Joseph County	12	0.04
Juneau, AK (borough) Juneau City and Borough	12	0.04
Madison Heights, MI (city) Oakland County	12	0.04
Wenatchee, WA (city) Chelan County	12	0.04
Great Falls, MT (city) Cascade County	12	0.02
Hamburg, NY (town) Erie County	12	0.02
Richland, WA (city) Benton County	12	0.02
Santa Fe, NM (city) Santa Fe County	12	0.02
Boise City, ID (city) Ada County	12	0.01
Cape Coral, FL (city) Lee County	12	0.01
Clinton, MI (charter township) Macomb County	12	0.01
Eugene, OR (city) Lane County	12	0.01
Lancaster, CA (city) Los Angeles County	12	0.01

Race

American Indian: Canadian/French American Indian

Top 150 Places Sorted by Percent of Total Population

Based on all places, regardless of total population

Place	Population	%
Victory, VT (town) Essex County	2	3.23
Nett Lake, MN (unorganized territory) Koochiching County	3	2.97
Rice Lake, MN (cdp) Clearwater County	6	2.55
La Prairie, MN (township) Clearwater County	6	1.69
King William, VA (cdp) King William County	4	1.59
Rogers, MN (township) Cass County	1	1.59
Diaperville, WI (cdp) Ashland County	1	1.43
McConnico, AZ (cdp) Mohave County	1	1.43
Northway, AK (cdp) Southeast Fairbanks Census Area	1	1.41
Rushville, OH (village) Fairfield County	4	1.32
Ellsworth, NH (town) Grafton County	1	1.20
Eastbrook, ME (town) Hancock County	5	1.18
McIntosh, SD (city) Corson County	2	1.16
Camden, IL (village) Schuyler County	1	1.16
Bullhead, SD (cdp) Corson County	4	1.15
Dodge, ND (city) Dunn County	1	1.15
North Clearwater, MN (unorganized territory) Clearwater County	1	1.15
White Swan, WA (cdp) Yakima County	9	1.13
Shaokatan, MN (township) Lincoln County	2	1.12
Tonawanda Reservation, NY (reservation) Genesee County	5	1.04
Central, AK (cdp) Yukon-Koyukuk Census Area	1	1.04
Northway Village, AK (cdp) Southeast Fairbanks Census Area	1	1.02
Clare, NY (town) St. Lawrence County	1	0.95
Reserve, WI (cdp) Sawyer County	4	0.93
Squaw Lake, MN (city) Itasca County	1	0.93
Truchas, NM (cdp) Rio Arriba County	5	0.89
Ponderosa Pines, MT (cdp) Gallatin County	3	0.89
Bay Mills, MI (township) Chippewa County	13	0.88
Sumner, MN (township) Fillmore County	4	0.87
Curlew, WA (cdp) Ferry County	1	0.85
Ames, OK (town) Major County	2	0.84
Porter, PA (township) Pike County	4	0.82
Comfrey, MN (city) Brown County	3	0.82
Comfrey, MN (city) Brown County	3	0.79
Farnham, NY (village) Erie County	3	0.79
Nehalem, OR (city) Tillamook County	2	0.74
Island Pond, VT (cdp) Essex County	6	0.73
Oakville, WA (city) Grays Harbor County	5	0.73
Jackson, ME (town) Waldo County	4	0.73
North Roseau, MN (unorganized territory) Roseau County	1	0.72
Azure, MT (cdp) Hill County	2	0.70
Nett Lake, MN (cdp) St. Louis County	2	0.70
Verlot, WA (cdp) Snohomish County	2	0.70
Chief Lake, WI (cdp) Sawyer County	4	0.69
Fort Snelling, MN (unorganized territory) Hennepin County	1	0.67
Reedsville, WI (village) Manitowoc County	8	0.66
Devol, OK (town) Cotton County	1	0.66
Oroville, WA (city) Okanogan County	11	0.65
Drowning Creek, OK (cdp) Delaware County	1	0.65
Hendricks, MI (township) Mackinac County	1	0.65
Ona, FL (cdp) Hardee County	2	0.64
Zeba, MI (cdp) Baraga County	3	0.63
Mansfield, WA (town) Douglas County	2	0.63
Nett Lake, MN (unorganized territory) St. Louis County	2	0.63
Norton, VT (town) Essex County	1	0.59
Neah Bay, WA (cdp) Clallam County	5	0.58
South Hills, MT (cdp) Jefferson County	3	0.58
Nectar, AL (town) Blount County	2	0.58
Babb, MT (cdp) Glacier County	1	0.57
Rocky Boy's Agency, MT (cdp) Hill County	2	0.56
Carpenter, MN (township) Itasca County	1	0.56
Elmo, MT (cdp) Lake County	1	0.56
Navarino, WI (cdp) Shawano County	1	0.56
Hudson, MI (township) Mackinac County	1	0.55
Enosburg Falls, VT (village) Franklin County	7	0.53
Rapid River, MI (township) Kalkaska County	6	0.52
Green Acres, ND (cdp) Rolette County	3	0.52
Port Sulphur, LA (cdp) Plaquemines Parish	9	0.51
Orwell, NY (town) Oswego County	6	0.51
Loleta, CA (cdp) Humboldt County	4	0.51
Cerro Gordo, MN (township) Lac qui Parle County	1	0.51
Finland, MN (cdp) Lake County	1	0.51
Hamlet, IN (town) Starke County	4	0.50
Eldred, IL (village) Greene County	1	0.50
Brighton, VT (town) Essex County	6	0.49
Browning, MT (town) Glacier County	5	0.49
Gateway, AR (town) Benton County	2	0.49
Marblemount, WA (cdp) Skagit County	1	0.49
Suquamish, WA (cdp) Kitsap County	20	0.48
Stacy, MN (city) Chisago County	7	0.48
Hungry Horse, MT (cdp) Flathead County	4	0.48
Chester, MA (cdp) Hampden County	3	0.48
Cusick, WA (town) Pend Oreille County	1	0.48
Dragoon, AZ (cdp) Cochise County	1	0.48
Moclips, WA (cdp) Grays Harbor County	1	0.48
Walkerton, IN (town) St. Joseph County	10	0.47
West Perry, PA (township) Snyder County	5	0.47
Clyman, WI (village) Dodge County	2	0.47
Dougherty, OK (town) Murray County	1	0.47
Wiscasset, ME (cdp) Lincoln County	5	0.46
Eastport, MI (cdp) Antrim County	1	0.46
Hamlin, ME (town) Aroostook County	1	0.46
Koontz Lake, IN (cdp) Starke County	7	0.45
Occidental, CA (cdp) Sonoma County	5	0.45
Louisville, IL (village) Clay County	5	0.44
Maple Grove, MN (township) Becker County	2	0.44
Rifton, NY (cdp) Ulster County	2	0.44
Winterfield, MI (township) Clare County	2	0.44
East Globe, AZ (cdp) Gila County	1	0.44
Schley, WI (town) Lincoln County	4	0.43
Armenia, WI (town) Juneau County	3	0.43
Viburnum, MO (city) Iron County	3	0.43
Garfield, MN (township) Polk County	2	0.43
Cypress, IL (village) Johnson County	1	0.43
Pavillion, WY (town) Fremont County	1	0.43
Southeast Roseau, MN (unorganized territory) Roseau County	1	0.43
Owyhee, NV (cdp) Elko County	4	0.42
Beaver Bay, MN (township) Lake County	2	0.42
Hanover, ME (town) Oxford County	1	0.42
Liberty, MN (township) Beltrami County	3	0.41
Richmond, VT (cdp) Chittenden County	3	0.41
Lake Viking, MO (cdp) Daviess County	2	0.41
Hay Brook, MN (township) Kanabec County	1	0.41
Lynch, NE (village) Boyd County	1	0.41
Priest River, ID (city) Bonner County	7	0.40
McGuffey, OH (village) Hardin County	2	0.40
O'Brien, OR (cdp) Josephine County	2	0.40
Tonasket, WA (city) Okanogan County	4	0.39
Parma, MI (village) Jackson County	3	0.39
Winhall, VT (town) Bennington County	3	0.39
Worley, ID (city) Kootenai County	1	0.39
Sumas, WA (city) Whatcom County	5	0.38
Canaan, NH (cdp) Grafton County	2	0.38
North Cass, MN (unorganized territory) Cass County	1	0.38
Chester, MA (town) Hampden County	5	0.37
Peach Springs, AZ (cdp) Mohave County	4	0.37
Kinston, AL (town) Coffee County	2	0.37
Marshfield, VT (village) Washington County	1	0.37
Paint Rock, TX (town) Concho County	1	0.37
Proberta, CA (cdp) Tehama County	1	0.37
International Falls, MN (city) Koochiching County	23	0.36
Skandia, MI (township) Marquette County	3	0.36
Norfolk, CT (cdp) Litchfield County	2	0.36
Paxton, MN (township) Redwood County	2	0.36
South Van Horn, AK (cdp) Fairbanks North Star Borough	2	0.36
Crystal Beach, AZ (cdp) Mohave County	1	0.36
Hodges, MN (township) Stevens County	1	0.36
Haines, AK (cdp) Haines Borough	6	0.35
Springvale, MN (township) Isanti County	5	0.35
Au Train, MI (township) Alger County	4	0.35
Boothville, LA (cdp) Plaquemines Parish	3	0.35
Verona, NY (cdp) Oneida County	3	0.35
Butlerville, IN (cdp) Jennings County	1	0.35
Beaugrand, MI (township) Cheboygan County	4	0.34
White Oak, MI (township) Ingham County	4	0.34
Oxford, MN (township) Isanti County	3	0.34
Pembina, ND (city) Pembina County	2	0.34
Sinclairville, NY (village) Chautauqua County	2	0.34
East Haven, VT (town) Essex County	1	0.34
Pakala Village, HI (cdp) Kauai County	1	0.34

Please refer to the Explanation of Data in the front of the book for more detailed information.

Race

American Indian: Canadian/French American Indian

Top 150 Places Sorted by Percent of Total Population

Based on places with total population of 7,500 or more

Place	Population	%
Sault Ste. Marie, MI (city) Chippewa County	40	0.28
Cloquet, MN (city) Carlton County	18	0.15
Ketchikan, AK (city) Ketchikan Gateway Borough	11	0.14
Meadow Lakes, AK (cdp) Matanuska-Susitna Borough	10	0.13
Burien, WA (city) King County	36	0.11
Bryn Mawr-Skyway, WA (cdp) King County	17	0.11
Waller, WA (cdp) Pierce County	9	0.11
East Wenatchee, WA (city) Douglas County	13	0.10
Union, MI (charter township) Isabella County	13	0.10
Clay, MI (township) St. Clair County	9	0.10
Midland, WA (cdp) Pierce County	9	0.10
Birch Bay, WA (cdp) Whatcom County	8	0.10
Bainbridge Island, WA (city) Kitsap County	21	0.09
Port Angeles, WA (city) Clallam County	18	0.09
Tukwila, WA (city) King County	18	0.09
Aberdeen, WA (city) Grays Harbor County	15	0.09
Potsdam, NY (town) St. Lawrence County	14	0.09
Massena, NY (town) St. Lawrence County	11	0.09
Ferndale, WA (city) Whatcom County	10	0.09
Kinross, MI (charter township) Chippewa County	7	0.09
Port Huron, MI (city) St. Clair County	23	0.08
Lake Los Angeles, CA (cdp) Los Angeles County	10	0.08
Sanford, ME (cdp) York County	8	0.08
Old Orchard Beach, ME (cdp/town) York County	7	0.08
Virginia, MN (city) St. Louis County	7	0.08
Farmington, ME (town) Franklin County	6	0.08
Orange, MA (town) Franklin County	6	0.08
SeaTac, WA (city) King County	20	0.07
Grand Island, NY (town) Erie County	15	0.07
Badger, AK (cdp) Fairbanks North Star Borough	14	0.07
Clinton, MA (town) Worcester County	10	0.07
Middleburg, FL (cdp) Clay County	9	0.07
White Center, WA (cdp) King County	9	0.07
Port Orchard, WA (city) Kitsap County	8	0.07
Spencer, MA (town) Worcester County	8	0.07
West Richland, WA (city) Benton County	8	0.07
Rensselaer, NY (city) Rensselaer County	7	0.07
Orange Cove, CA (city) Fresno County	6	0.07
Port Townsend, WA (city) Jefferson County	6	0.07
Ephrata, WA (city) Grant County	5	0.07
Bellingham, WA (city) Whatcom County	52	0.06
Bremerton, WA (city) Kitsap County	22	0.06
Des Moines, WA (city) King County	18	0.06
Buenaventura Lakes, FL (cdp) Osceola County	16	0.06
Auburn, ME (city) Androscoggin County	13	0.06
Mukilteo, WA (city) Snohomish County	13	0.06
Covington, WA (city) King County	10	0.06
Schofield Barracks, HI (cdp) Honolulu County	10	0.06
DeWitt, MI (charter township) Clinton County	9	0.06
Fraser, MI (city) Macomb County	8	0.06
Traverse City, MI (city) Grand Traverse County	8	0.06
East Renton Highlands, WA (cdp) King County	7	0.06
Massena, NY (village) St. Lawrence County	7	0.06
North Bellport, NY (cdp) Suffolk County	7	0.06
East Bay, MI (township) Grand Traverse County	6	0.06
Ecorse, MI (city) Wayne County	6	0.06
Grand Haven, MI (city) Ottawa County	6	0.06
Blair, MI (township) Grand Traverse County	5	0.06
Fairview, OR (city) Multnomah County	5	0.06
Greenville, RI (cdp) Providence County	5	0.06
Helena Valley West Central, MT (cdp) Lewis and Clark County	5	0.06
Hoquiam, WA (city) Grays Harbor County	5	0.06
Lake Carmel, NY (cdp) Putnam County	5	0.06
Littleton, MA (town) Middlesex County	5	0.06
Rhinelander, WI (city) Oneida County	5	0.06
Sitka, AK (borough) Sitka City and Borough	5	0.06
South Kensington, MD (cdp) Montgomery County	5	0.06
Springfield, FL (city) Bay County	5	0.06
Tacoma, WA (city) Pierce County	104	0.05
Kent, WA (city) King County	48	0.05
Renton, WA (city) King County	44	0.05
Lynnwood, WA (city) Snohomish County	19	0.05
Lincoln Park, MI (city) Wayne County	18	0.05
De Witt, NY (town) Onondaga County	14	0.05
Graham, WA (cdp) Pierce County	12	0.05
Sanford, ME (town) York County	11	0.05
Kenmore, WA (city) King County	10	0.05
Augusta, ME (city) Kennebec County	9	0.05
Grand Haven, MI (charter township) Ottawa County	8	0.05
Traverse City, MI (city) Grand Traverse County	8	0.05
Bangor, MI (charter township) Bay County	7	0.05
McKinleyville, CA (cdp) Humboldt County	7	0.05
Salem, OH (city) Columbiana County	6	0.05
Yeadon, PA (borough) Delaware County	6	0.05
Camp Pendleton South, CA (cdp) San Diego County	5	0.05
DeRidder, LA (city) Beauregard Parish	5	0.05
Lake Morton-Berrydale, WA (cdp) King County	5	0.05
Port Huron, MI (charter township) St. Clair County	5	0.05
Boxford, MA (town) Essex County	4	0.05
Brockport, NY (village) Monroe County	4	0.05
Brooksville, FL (city) Hernando County	4	0.05
Burlington, WA (city) Skagit County	4	0.05
Chesterfield, NJ (township) Burlington County	4	0.05
Detroit Lakes, MN (city) Becker County	4	0.05
Eagle Point, OR (city) Jackson County	4	0.05
Fountain Inn, SC (city) Greenville County	4	0.05
Freeport, ME (town) Cumberland County	4	0.05
Halifax, MA (town) Plymouth County	4	0.05
Lacombe, LA (cdp) St. Tammany Parish	4	0.05
Picnic Point, WA (cdp) Snohomish County	4	0.05
Princeton, IN (city) Gibson County	4	0.05
Syracuse, NY (city) Onondaga County	51	0.04
Federal Way, WA (city) King County	38	0.04
Missoula, MT (city) Missoula County	26	0.04
Marysville, WA (city) Snohomish County	22	0.04
Niagara Falls, NY (city) Niagara County	20	0.04
Redmond, WA (city) King County	20	0.04
Minot, ND (city) Ward County	15	0.04
Lewiston, ME (city) Androscoggin County	14	0.04
Eastpointe, MI (city) Macomb County	12	0.04
Granger, IN (cdp) St. Joseph County	12	0.04
Juneau, AK (borough) Juneau City and Borough	12	0.04
Madison Heights, MI (city) Oakland County	12	0.04
Wenatchee, WA (city) Chelan County	12	0.04
Emporia, KS (city) Lyon County	11	0.04
Lake Stevens, WA (city) Snohomish County	11	0.04
Mount Pleasant, MI (city) Isabella County	11	0.04
Wyandotte, MI (city) Wayne County	11	0.04
Post Falls, ID (city) Kootenai County	10	0.04
Superior, WI (city) Douglas County	10	0.04
Brunswick, ME (town) Cumberland County	9	0.04
Tarpon Springs, FL (city) Pinellas County	9	0.04
Edgewater, FL (city) Volusia County	8	0.04
Mountlake Terrace, WA (city) Snohomish County	8	0.04
Plattsburgh, NY (city) Clinton County	8	0.04
Trenton, MI (city) Wayne County	8	0.04
Ferndale, MI (city) Oakland County	7	0.04
Four Corners, OR (cdp) Marion County	7	0.04
Haslett, MI (cdp) Ingham County	7	0.04
La Vista, NE (city) Sarpy County	7	0.04
Monroe, CT (town) Fairfield County	7	0.04
North Lynnwood, WA (cdp) Snohomish County	7	0.04
Red Wing, MN (city) Goodhue County	7	0.04
Rutland, VT (city) Rutland County	7	0.04
Towamencin, PA (township) Montgomery County	7	0.04
Anoka, MN (city) Anoka County	6	0.04
Mountain Home, ID (city) Elmore County	6	0.04
North Mankato, MN (city) Nicollet County	6	0.04
Amherst, OH (city) Lorain County	5	0.04
Bemidji, MN (city) Beltrami County	5	0.04
Borger, TX (city) Hutchinson County	5	0.04
Chippewa Falls, WI (city) Chippewa County	5	0.04
El Campo, TX (city) Wharton County	5	0.04
Kent, NY (town) Putnam County	5	0.04
Lake Forest Park, WA (city) King County	5	0.04
Lake Tapps, WA (cdp) Pierce County	5	0.04
Lakewood Park, FL (cdp) St. Lucie County	5	0.04
Lebanon, NH (city) Grafton County	5	0.04
Middlesex, NJ (borough) Middlesex County	5	0.04
North Smithfield, RI (town) Providence County	5	0.04

SECTION THREE

Please refer to the Explanation of Data in the front of the book for more detailed information.

Race

American Indian: Central American Indian

U.S. and 50 States Sorted by Population and Percent of Total Population

Place	Population	%
United States	**27,844**	**0.01**
New York	8,602	0.04
California	4,329	0.01
Florida	2,454	0.01
Texas	2,072	0.01
New Jersey	1,247	0.01
Massachusetts	967	0.01
Maryland	728	0.01
Virginia	669	0.01
Georgia	558	0.01
North Carolina	523	0.01
Ohio	458	<0.01
Pennsylvania	443	<0.01
Illinois	424	<0.01
Washington	386	0.01
Louisiana	296	0.01
Tennessee	242	<0.01
Connecticut	241	0.01
Arizona	233	<0.01
Rhode Island	211	0.02
Oregon	210	0.01
Michigan	194	<0.01
Alabama	182	<0.01
Colorado	181	<0.01
South Carolina	166	<0.01
Nevada	160	0.01
Nebraska	154	0.01
Indiana	152	<0.01
Minnesota	131	<0.01
Oklahoma	116	<0.01
New Mexico	103	0.01
Utah	100	<0.01
District of Columbia	96	0.02
Missouri	91	<0.01
Mississippi	83	<0.01
Wisconsin	80	<0.01
Kentucky	70	<0.01
Arkansas	67	<0.01
Iowa	67	<0.01
Hawaii	65	<0.01
Kansas	65	<0.01
Delaware	64	0.01
New Hampshire	31	<0.01
Alaska	29	<0.01
Maine	22	<0.01
Idaho	17	<0.01
Vermont	16	<0.01
West Virginia	15	<0.01
Montana	10	<0.01
Wyoming	10	<0.01
South Dakota	9	<0.01
North Dakota	5	<0.01

Place	Population	%
New York	8,602	0.04
Rhode Island	211	0.02
District of Columbia	96	0.02
United States	**27,844**	**0.01**
California	4,329	0.01
Florida	2,454	0.01
Texas	2,072	0.01
New Jersey	1,247	0.01
Massachusetts	967	0.01
Maryland	728	0.01
Virginia	669	0.01
Georgia	558	0.01
North Carolina	523	0.01
Washington	386	0.01
Louisiana	296	0.01
Connecticut	241	0.01
Oregon	210	0.01
Nevada	160	0.01
Nebraska	154	0.01
New Mexico	103	0.01
Delaware	64	0.01
Ohio	458	<0.01
Pennsylvania	443	<0.01
Illinois	424	<0.01
Tennessee	242	<0.01
Arizona	233	<0.01
Michigan	194	<0.01
Alabama	182	<0.01
Colorado	181	<0.01
South Carolina	166	<0.01
Indiana	152	<0.01
Minnesota	131	<0.01
Oklahoma	116	<0.01
Utah	100	<0.01
Missouri	91	<0.01
Mississippi	83	<0.01
Wisconsin	80	<0.01
Kentucky	70	<0.01
Arkansas	67	<0.01
Iowa	67	<0.01
Hawaii	65	<0.01
Kansas	65	<0.01
New Hampshire	31	<0.01
Alaska	29	<0.01
Maine	22	<0.01
Idaho	17	<0.01
Vermont	16	<0.01
West Virginia	15	<0.01
Montana	10	<0.01
Wyoming	10	<0.01
South Dakota	9	<0.01
North Dakota	5	<0.01

Please refer to the Explanation of Data in the front of the book for more detailed information.

Race

American Indian: Central American Indian

Top 150 Places Sorted by Population

Based on all places, regardless of total population

Place	Population	%
New York, NY (city) Kings County	7,662	0.09
Bronx, NY (borough) Bronx County	4,520	0.33
Los Angeles, CA (city) Los Angeles County	1,602	0.04
Brooklyn, NY (borough) Kings County	1,263	0.05
Manhattan, NY (borough) New York County	1,090	0.07
Houston, TX (city) Harris County	876	0.04
Queens, NY (borough) Queens County	733	0.03
New Bedford, MA (city) Bristol County	265	0.28
Lake Worth, FL (city) Palm Beach County	255	0.73
Miami, FL (city) Miami-Dade County	222	0.06
Boston, MA (city) Suffolk County	207	0.03
Chicago, IL (city) Cook County	203	0.01
Oakland, CA (city) Alameda County	199	0.05
Providence, RI (city) Providence County	168	0.09
San Francisco, CA (city) San Francisco County	144	0.02
New Orleans, LA (city) Orleans Parish	131	0.04
Philadelphia, PA (city) Philadelphia County	111	0.01
Yonkers, NY (city) Westchester County	103	0.05
Paterson, NJ (city) Passaic County	100	0.07
Cincinnati, OH (city) Hamilton County	98	0.03
Washington, DC (city) District of Columbia	96	0.02
Austin, TX (city) Travis County	92	0.01
Port Arthur, TX (city) Jefferson County	90	0.17
Hempstead, NY (town) Nassau County	87	0.01
Dallas, TX (city) Dallas County	83	0.01
Lawrence, MA (city) Essex County	80	0.10
Long Beach, CA (city) Los Angeles County	78	0.02
Grand Rapids, MI (city) Kent County	77	0.04
Newark, NJ (city) Essex County	74	0.03
Islip, NY (town) Suffolk County	73	0.02
Charlotte, NC (city) Mecklenburg County	67	0.01
Jacksonville, FL (city) Duval County	65	0.01
Seattle, WA (city) King County	64	0.01
Phoenix, AZ (city) Maricopa County	63	<0.01
Perth Amboy, NJ (city) Middlesex County	61	0.12
Passaic, NJ (city) Passaic County	61	0.09
Arlington, VA (cdp) Arlington County	61	0.03
West New York, NJ (town) Hudson County	60	0.12
Langley Park, MD (cdp) Prince George's County	59	0.31
Silver Spring, MD (cdp) Montgomery County	59	0.08
Portland, OR (city) Multnomah County	59	0.01
San Diego, CA (city) San Diego County	59	<0.01
Jersey City, NJ (city) Hudson County	58	0.02
Chamblee, GA (city) DeKalb County	57	0.58
Jupiter, FL (town) Palm Beach County	56	0.10
San Rafael, CA (city) Marin County	56	0.10
Omaha, NE (city) Douglas County	56	0.01
Staten Island, NY (borough) Richmond County	56	0.01
San Antonio, TX (city) Medina County	56	<0.01
Union City, NJ (city) Hudson County	55	0.08
Tampa, FL (city) Hillsborough County	54	0.02
Brookhaven, NY (town) Suffolk County	53	0.01
San Jose, CA (city) Santa Clara County	51	0.01
Elizabeth, NJ (city) Union County	47	0.04
Chattanooga, TN (city) Hamilton County	46	0.03
Canton, OH (city) Stark County	45	0.06
Trenton, NJ (city) Mercer County	44	0.05
Mount Kisco, NY (town/village) Westchester County	43	0.40
Metairie, LA (cdp) Jefferson Parish	42	0.03
Eufaula, AL (city) Barbour County	41	0.31
West Palm Beach, FL (city) Palm Beach County	41	0.04
Plainfield, NJ (city) Union County	40	0.08
Allentown, PA (city) Lehigh County	40	0.03
North Las Vegas, NV (city) Clark County	40	0.02
Las Vegas, NV (city) Clark County	39	0.01
Nashville-Davidson, TN (metro govt) Davidson County	39	0.01
Tucson, AZ (city) Pima County	39	0.01
Tulsa, OK (city) Tulsa County	39	0.01
Grand Island, NE (city) Hall County	36	0.07
Brentwood, NY (cdp) Suffolk County	36	0.06
Fort Myers, FL (city) Lee County	36	0.06
New Philadelphia, OH (city) Tuscarawas County	35	0.20
Miami Beach, FL (city) Miami-Dade County	35	0.04
Minneapolis, MN (city) Hennepin County	35	0.01
Fresno, CA (city) Fresno County	34	0.01
Fort Worth, TX (city) Tarrant County	34	<0.01
Dover, OH (city) Tuscarawas County	33	0.26
Chelsea, MA (city) Suffolk County	33	0.09
North Miami, FL (city) Miami-Dade County	33	0.06
Inglewood, CA (city) Los Angeles County	33	0.03
North Bergen, NJ (township) Hudson County	32	0.05
Columbia, MD (cdp) Howard County	32	0.03
Alexandria, VA (ind. city) Alexandria independent city	32	0.02
Cleveland, OH (city) Cuyahoga County	32	0.01
Riverside, CA (city) Riverside County	32	0.01
Morganton, NC (city) Burke County	31	0.18
Central Islip, NY (cdp) Suffolk County	31	0.09
Richmond, CA (city) Contra Costa County	31	0.03
Bremerton, WA (city) Kitsap County	30	0.08
Wheaton, MD (cdp) Montgomery County	30	0.06
Germantown, MD (cdp) Montgomery County	30	0.03
Waterbury, CT (city/town) New Haven County	30	0.03
Worcester, MA (city) Worcester County	30	0.02
Albuquerque, NM (city) Bernalillo County	30	0.01
El Monte, CA (city) Los Angeles County	29	0.03
Lynn, MA (city) Essex County	29	0.03
Bakersfield, CA (city) Kern County	29	0.01
Durham, NC (city) Durham County	29	0.01
Rochester, NY (city) Monroe County	29	0.01
Homestead, FL (city) Miami-Dade County	28	0.05
Pomona, CA (city) Los Angeles County	28	0.02
Orlando, FL (city) Orange County	28	0.01
Baltimore, MD (city) Baltimore city County	28	<0.01
Denver, CO (city) Denver County	28	<0.01
Logansport, IN (city) Cass County	27	0.15
Bailey's Crossroads, VA (cdp) Fairfax County	27	0.11
Massillon, OH (city) Stark County	27	0.08
Davie, FL (town) Broward County	27	0.03
Rialto, CA (city) San Bernardino County	27	0.03
Port St. Lucie, FL (city) St. Lucie County	27	0.02
Canton, GA (city) Cherokee County	26	0.11
North Lauderdale, FL (city) Broward County	26	0.06
Dale City, VA (cdp) Prince William County	26	0.04
Florence-Graham, CA (cdp) Los Angeles County	26	0.04
Escondido, CA (city) San Diego County	26	0.02
Aurora, CO (city) Arapahoe County	26	0.01
Chesapeake, VA (ind. city) Chesapeake independent city	26	0.01
Oklahoma City, OK (city) Oklahoma County	26	<0.01
Schuyler, NE (city) Colfax County	25	0.40
Chillum, MD (cdp) Prince George's County	25	0.07
Redwood City, CA (city) San Mateo County	25	0.03
Wilmington, NC (city) New Hanover County	25	0.02
Winston-Salem, NC (city) Forsyth County	25	0.01
Milwaukee, WI (city) Milwaukee County	25	<0.01
Lincolnia, VA (cdp) Fairfax County	24	0.11
Fallbrook, CA (cdp) San Diego County	24	0.08
West Falls Church, VA (cdp) Fairfax County	24	0.08
Camden, NJ (city) Camden County	24	0.03
Hartford, CT (city/town) Hartford County	24	0.02
Hialeah, FL (city) Miami-Dade County	24	0.01
Forest, MS (city) Scott County	23	0.40
Kenner, LA (city) Jefferson Parish	23	0.03
Waukegan, IL (city) Lake County	23	0.03
Fontana, CA (city) San Bernardino County	23	0.01
Raleigh, NC (city) Wake County	23	0.01
Sacramento, CA (city) Sacramento County	23	<0.01
Morris, NJ (town) Morris County	22	0.12
Berkeley, CA (city) Alameda County	22	0.02
Ramapo, NY (town) Rockland County	22	0.02
San Mateo, CA (city) San Mateo County	22	0.02
Babylon, NY (town) Suffolk County	22	0.01
Irving, TX (city) Dallas County	22	0.01
Lancaster, CA (city) Los Angeles County	22	0.01
Springfield, MA (city) Hampden County	22	0.01
Adelphi, MD (cdp) Prince George's County	21	0.14
Woodlawn, VA (cdp) Fairfax County	21	0.10
Huntington Park, CA (city) Los Angeles County	21	0.04
Atascocita, TX (cdp) Harris County	21	0.03
Concord, CA (city) Contra Costa County	21	0.02
East Los Angeles, CA (cdp) Los Angeles County	21	0.02

Race

American Indian: Central American Indian

Top 150 Places Sorted by Percent of Total Population

Based on all places, regardless of total population

Place	Population	%
Resaca, GA (town) Gordon County	6	1.10
Texico, NM (city) Curry County	12	1.06
Shelter Island, NY (cdp) Suffolk County	14	1.05
Pickrell, NE (village) Gage County	2	1.01
Pioneer, FL (cdp) Hendry County	6	0.86
White Mesa, UT (cdp) San Juan County	2	0.83
Wallace, NE (village) Lincoln County	3	0.82
Smoaks, SC (town) Colleton County	1	0.79
Lake Worth, FL (city) Palm Beach County	255	0.73
Shelter Island, NY (town) Suffolk County	16	0.67
Beaver, PA (township) Columbia County	6	0.65
Bluewater Village, NM (cdp) Cibola County	4	0.64
Chamblee, GA (city) DeKalb County	57	0.58
Sumas, WA (city) Whatcom County	7	0.54
Macdona, TX (cdp) Bexar County	3	0.54
North Star, MN (township) St. Louis County	1	0.53
Nelliston, NY (village) Montgomery County	3	0.50
Cornelia, GA (city) Habersham County	20	0.48
Moclips, WA (cdp) Grays Harbor County	1	0.48
Lakewood Gardens, FL (cdp) Palm Beach County	6	0.47
Levering, MI (cdp) Emmet County	1	0.47
Hinckley, UT (town) Millard County	3	0.43
Mount Kisco, NY (town/village) Westchester County	43	0.40
Schuyler, NE (city) Colfax County	25	0.40
Forest, MS (city) Scott County	23	0.40
Lewisville, MN (city) Watonwan County	1	0.40
McNary, AZ (cdp) Apache County	2	0.38
Wildwood, KY (city) Jefferson County	1	0.38
Hardeeville, SC (city) Jasper County	11	0.37
East Ellijay, GA (city) Gilmer County	2	0.37
Hunterstown, PA (cdp) Adams County	2	0.37
Washington Heights, NY (cdp) Orange County	6	0.36
Snead, AL (town) Blount County	3	0.36
Woodside, MN (township) Otter Tail County	1	0.36
Tunnel Hill, GA (city) Whitfield County	3	0.35
Bronx, NY (borough) Bronx County	4,520	0.33
Victory Gardens, NJ (borough) Morris County	5	0.33
Langley Park, MD (cdp) Prince George's County	59	0.31
Eufaula, AL (city) Barbour County	41	0.31
Casnovia, MI (village) Kent County	1	0.31
Hawley, MA (town) Franklin County	1	0.30
Kawela Bay, HI (cdp) Honolulu County	1	0.30
Long Prairie, MN (city) Todd County	10	0.29
Lee, MA (cdp) Berkshire County	6	0.29
Stafford, KS (city) Stafford County	3	0.29
New Bedford, MA (city) Bristol County	265	0.28
Carthage, MS (city) Leake County	14	0.28
North Haven, ME (town) Knox County	1	0.28
Mahtowa, MN (cdp) Carlton County	1	0.27
Dover, OH (city) Tuscarawas County	33	0.26
Indiantown, FL (cdp) Martin County	16	0.26
Maddock, ND (city) Benson County	1	0.26
Copenhagen, NY (village) Lewis County	2	0.25
Alger, WA (cdp) Skagit County	1	0.25
Spring Grove, MN (township) Houston County	1	0.25
Aurora, WI (town) Taylor County	1	0.24
Grasonville, MD (cdp) Queen Anne's County	8	0.23
Shell Rock, IA (city) Butler County	3	0.23
Rural Valley, PA (borough) Armstrong County	2	0.23
Stacey Street, FL (cdp) Palm Beach County	2	0.23
Glendon, PA (borough) Northampton County	1	0.23
El Lago, TX (city) Harris County	6	0.22
Holden, MO (city) Johnson County	5	0.22
Weir, TX (city) Williamson County	1	0.22
Columbus, NY (town) Chenango County	2	0.21
Tutuilla, OR (cdp) Umatilla County	1	0.21
New Philadelphia, OH (city) Tuscarawas County	35	0.20
Cleveland, WI (town) Marathon County	3	0.20
Farmersville, PA (cdp) Lancaster County	2	0.20
Hollywood, AL (town) Jackson County	2	0.20
Elkhorn, CA (cdp) Monterey County	3	0.19
Shelter Island Heights, NY (cdp) Suffolk County	2	0.19
Bolton Landing, NY (cdp) Warren County	1	0.19
Laurel Hill, FL (city) Okaloosa County	1	0.19
Lovilia, IA (city) Monroe County	1	0.19
Mount Vernon, OR (city) Grant County	1	0.19
Red Creek, NY (village) Wayne County	1	0.19
Searchlight, NV (cdp) Clark County	1	0.19
Morganton, NC (city) Burke County	31	0.18
Dupont, PA (borough) Luzerne County	5	0.18
Monterey, TN (town) Putnam County	5	0.18
Apalachicola, FL (city) Franklin County	4	0.18
Orland, ME (town) Hancock County	4	0.18
Saugerties South, NY (cdp) Ulster County	4	0.18
Orange, WI (town) Juneau County	1	0.18
Valley Head, AL (town) DeKalb County	1	0.18
Vienna, ME (town) Kennebec County	1	0.18
Port Arthur, TX (city) Jefferson County	90	0.17
Guymon, OK (city) Texas County	20	0.17
Shelton, WA (city) Mason County	17	0.17
Woodlawn, MD (cdp) Prince George's County	11	0.17
Royal Palm Estates, FL (cdp) Palm Beach County	5	0.17
Bourbon, IN (town) Marshall County	3	0.17
Rocky Ripple, IN (town) Marion County	1	0.17
Alamosa, CO (city) Alamosa County	14	0.16
Zebulon, NC (town) Wake County	7	0.16
Eau Claire, MI (village) Berrien County	1	0.16
Mahtowa, MN (township) Carlton County	1	0.16
Nelsonville, NY (village) Putnam County	1	0.16
Pine Lake, MN (township) Otter Tail County	1	0.16
Logansport, IN (city) Cass County	27	0.15
Orangeburg, NY (cdp) Rockland County	7	0.15
Baldwin, GA (city) Habersham County	5	0.15
Cleves, OH (village) Hamilton County	5	0.15
Beaver Dam, AZ (cdp) Mohave County	3	0.15
Asharoken, NY (village) Suffolk County	1	0.15
Littlefork, MN (city) Koochiching County	1	0.15
Spreckels, CA (cdp) Monterey County	1	0.15
Wartrace, TN (town) Bedford County	1	0.15
Adelphi, MD (cdp) Prince George's County	21	0.14
Sans Souci, SC (cdp) Greenville County	11	0.14
Trooper, PA (cdp) Montgomery County	8	0.14
Pittsboro, IN (town) Hendricks County	4	0.14
Spring, PA (township) Perry County	3	0.14
Hughestown, PA (borough) Luzerne County	2	0.14
Irwindale, CA (city) Los Angeles County	2	0.14
Wymore, NE (city) Gage County	2	0.14
Horseshoe Bend, ID (city) Boise County	1	0.14
Crestline, OH (city) Crawford County	6	0.13
Jacksboro, TX (city) Jack County	6	0.13
Rolesville, NC (town) Wake County	5	0.13
Crockett, CA (cdp) Contra Costa County	4	0.13
North East, NY (town) Dutchess County	4	0.13
Clyman, WI (town) Dodge County	1	0.13
Maple Grove, MN (township) Crow Wing County	1	0.13
Perth Amboy, NJ (city) Middlesex County	61	0.12
West New York, NJ (town) Hudson County	60	0.12
Morris, NJ (town) Morris County	22	0.12
Springdale, OH (city) Hamilton County	14	0.12
Okeechobee, FL (city) Okeechobee County	7	0.12
Canterbury, CT (town) Windham County	6	0.12
Manor, TX (city) Travis County	6	0.12
Tara Hills, CA (cdp) Contra Costa County	6	0.12
Caruthers, CA (cdp) Fresno County	3	0.12
East Newark, NJ (borough) Hudson County	3	0.12
Everson, WA (city) Whatcom County	3	0.12
Parish, NY (town) Oswego County	3	0.12
Sky Valley, CA (cdp) Riverside County	3	0.12
Bolinas, CA (cdp) Marin County	2	0.12
Channel Lake, IL (cdp) Lake County	2	0.12
Shamokin Dam, PA (borough) Snyder County	2	0.12
Arbo, MN (township) Itasca County	1	0.12
Blue River, CO (town) Summit County	1	0.12
Branchville, NJ (borough) Sussex County	1	0.12
Camanche Village, CA (cdp) Amador County	1	0.12
Woodridge, NY (village) Sullivan County	1	0.12
Bailey's Crossroads, VA (cdp) Fairfax County	27	0.11
Canton, GA (city) Cherokee County	26	0.11
Lincolnia, VA (cdp) Fairfax County	24	0.11
Fairview, NJ (borough) Bergen County	15	0.11

Please refer to the Explanation of Data in the front of the book for more detailed information.

Race

American Indian: Central American Indian

Top 150 Places Sorted by Percent of Total Population

Based on places with total population of 7,500 or more

Place	Population	%
Lake Worth, FL (city) Palm Beach County	255	0.73
Chamblee, GA (city) DeKalb County	57	0.58
Mount Kisco, NY (town/village) Westchester County	43	0.40
Bronx, NY (borough) Bronx County	4,520	0.33
Langley Park, MD (cdp) Prince George's County	59	0.31
Eufaula, AL (city) Barbour County	41	0.31
New Bedford, MA (city) Bristol County	265	0.28
Dover, OH (city) Tuscarawas County	33	0.26
New Philadelphia, OH (city) Tuscarawas County	35	0.20
Morganton, NC (city) Burke County	31	0.18
Port Arthur, TX (city) Jefferson County	90	0.17
Guymon, OK (city) Texas County	20	0.17
Shelton, WA (city) Mason County	17	0.17
Alamosa, CO (city) Alamosa County	14	0.16
Logansport, IN (city) Cass County	27	0.15
Adelphi, MD (cdp) Prince George's County	21	0.14
Sans Souci, SC (cdp) Greenville County	11	0.14
Perth Amboy, NJ (city) Middlesex County	61	0.12
West New York, NJ (town) Hudson County	60	0.12
Morris, NJ (town) Morris County	22	0.12
Springdale, OH (city) Hamilton County	14	0.12
Bailey's Crossroads, VA (cdp) Fairfax County	27	0.11
Canton, GA (city) Cherokee County	26	0.11
Lincolnia, VA (cdp) Fairfax County	24	0.11
Fairview, NJ (borough) Bergen County	15	0.11
Lawrence, MA (city) Essex County	80	0.10
Jupiter, FL (town) Palm Beach County	56	0.10
San Rafael, CA (city) Marin County	56	0.10
Woodlawn, VA (cdp) Fairfax County	21	0.10
Guttenberg, NJ (town) Hudson County	11	0.10
Home Gardens, CA (cdp) Riverside County	11	0.10
Webster, TX (city) Harris County	10	0.10
Arcadia, FL (city) DeSoto County	8	0.10
Riverside, NJ (township) Burlington County	8	0.10
New York, NY (city) Kings County	7,662	0.09
Providence, RI (city) Providence County	168	0.09
Passaic, NJ (city) Passaic County	61	0.09
Chelsea, MA (city) Suffolk County	33	0.09
Central Islip, NY (cdp) Suffolk County	31	0.09
East Ridge, TN (city) Hamilton County	19	0.09
Northbrook, OH (cdp) Hamilton County	10	0.09
Russellville, AL (city) Franklin County	9	0.09
Silver Spring, MD (cdp) Montgomery County	59	0.08
Union City, NJ (city) Hudson County	55	0.08
Plainfield, NJ (city) Union County	40	0.08
Bremerton, WA (city) Kitsap County	30	0.08
Massillon, OH (city) Stark County	27	0.08
Fallbrook, CA (cdp) San Diego County	24	0.08
West Falls Church, VA (cdp) Fairfax County	24	0.08
Shelbyville, TN (city) Bedford County	17	0.08
Beltsville, MD (cdp) Prince George's County	13	0.08
Chalmette, LA (cdp) St. Bernard Parish	13	0.08
Cornelius, OR (city) Washington County	10	0.08
Haverstraw, NY (village) Rockland County	10	0.08
Garrison, MD (cdp) Baltimore County	7	0.08
Center Moriches, NY (cdp) Suffolk County	6	0.08
Manhattan, NY (borough) New York County	1,090	0.07
Paterson, NJ (city) Passaic County	100	0.07
Grand Island, NE (city) Hall County	36	0.07
Chillum, MD (cdp) Prince George's County	25	0.07
Buenaventura Lakes, FL (cdp) Osceola County	17	0.07
Buckhall, VA (cdp) Prince William County	11	0.07
New Cassel, NY (cdp) Nassau County	10	0.07
Palmetto Estates, FL (cdp) Miami-Dade County	10	0.07
Booneville, MS (city) Prentiss County	6	0.07
Fort Irwin, CA (cdp) San Bernardino County	6	0.07
Mahopac, NY (cdp) Putnam County	6	0.07
Halifax, MA (town) Plymouth County	5	0.07
Miami, FL (city) Miami-Dade County	222	0.06
Canton, OH (city) Stark County	45	0.06
Brentwood, NY (cdp) Suffolk County	36	0.06
Fort Myers, FL (city) Lee County	36	0.06
North Miami, FL (city) Miami-Dade County	33	0.06
Wheaton, MD (cdp) Montgomery County	30	0.06
North Lauderdale, FL (city) Broward County	26	0.06
Burien, WA (city) King County	19	0.06
Westmont, CA (cdp) Los Angeles County	19	0.06
Middle River, MD (cdp) Baltimore County	16	0.06
Carrollton, GA (city) Carroll County	14	0.06
Lumberton, NC (city) Robeson County	14	0.06
Central Falls, RI (city) Providence County	12	0.06
South El Monte, CA (city) Los Angeles County	12	0.06
East Riverdale, MD (cdp) Prince George's County	10	0.06
Ojus, FL (cdp) Miami-Dade County	10	0.06
Aldine, TX (cdp) Harris County	9	0.06
Roosevelt, NY (cdp) Nassau County	9	0.06
Lansdowne, VA (cdp) Loudoun County	7	0.06
Mendota, CA (city) Fresno County	7	0.06
North Lindenhurst, NY (cdp) Suffolk County	7	0.06
Northlake, IL (city) Cook County	7	0.06
Milford, DE (city) Sussex County	6	0.06
Seven Corners, VA (cdp) Fairfax County	6	0.06
Sleepy Hollow, NY (village) Westchester County	6	0.06
Denison, IA (city) Crawford County	5	0.06
Gonzales, CA (city) Monterey County	5	0.06
Hamilton, PA (township) Monroe County	5	0.06
Lake Stickney, WA (cdp) Snohomish County	5	0.06
Triangle, VA (cdp) Prince William County	5	0.06
Brooklyn, NY (borough) Kings County	1,263	0.05
Oakland, CA (city) Alameda County	199	0.05
Yonkers, NY (city) Westchester County	103	0.05
Trenton, NJ (city) Mercer County	44	0.05
North Bergen, NJ (township) Hudson County	32	0.05
Homestead, FL (city) Miami-Dade County	28	0.05
Greenacres, FL (city) Palm Beach County	20	0.05
San Pablo, CA (city) Contra Costa County	16	0.05
Sanford, NC (city) Lee County	14	0.05
Bridgeton, NJ (city) Cumberland County	13	0.05
Uniondale, NY (cdp) Nassau County	13	0.05
East Lake-Orient Park, FL (cdp) Hillsborough County	11	0.05
Leisure City, FL (cdp) Miami-Dade County	11	0.05
Palm River-Clair Mel, FL (cdp) Hillsborough County	11	0.05
Camp Springs, MD (cdp) Prince George's County	10	0.05
Calverton, MD (cdp) Montgomery County	9	0.05
Laurel, VA (cdp) Henrico County	9	0.05
Addison, TX (town) Dallas County	7	0.05
Berea, SC (cdp) Greenville County	7	0.05
Olean, NY (city) Cattaraugus County	7	0.05
Somerton, AZ (city) Yuma County	7	0.05
Huntington, VA (cdp) Fairfax County	6	0.05
Jefferson, LA (cdp) Jefferson Parish	6	0.05
Mastic Beach, NY (cdp) Suffolk County	6	0.05
Worthington, MN (city) Nobles County	6	0.05
Cedartown, GA (city) Polk County	5	0.05
George Mason, VA (cdp) Fairfax County	5	0.05
Lake Barcroft, VA (cdp) Fairfax County	5	0.05
Maili, HI (cdp) Honolulu County	5	0.05
Port Salerno, FL (cdp) Martin County	5	0.05
Wrentham, MA (town) Norfolk County	5	0.05
Aransas Pass, TX (city) San Patricio County	4	0.05
Bernardsville, NJ (borough) Somerset County	4	0.05
Black Mountain, NC (town) Buncombe County	4	0.05
Garden City, GA (city) Chatham County	4	0.05
Liberty Lake, WA (city) Spokane County	4	0.05
Meadow Lakes, AK (cdp) Matanuska-Susitna Borough	4	0.05
West Athens, CA (cdp) Los Angeles County	4	0.05
Los Angeles, CA (city) Los Angeles County	1,602	0.04
Houston, TX (city) Harris County	876	0.04
New Orleans, LA (city) Orleans Parish	131	0.04
Grand Rapids, MI (city) Kent County	77	0.04
Elizabeth, NJ (city) Union County	47	0.04
West Palm Beach, FL (city) Palm Beach County	41	0.04
Miami Beach, FL (city) Miami-Dade County	35	0.04
Dale City, VA (cdp) Prince William County	26	0.04
Florence-Graham, CA (cdp) Los Angeles County	26	0.04
Huntington Park, CA (city) Los Angeles County	21	0.04
Bloomfield, NJ (township) Essex County	19	0.04
Freeport, NY (village) Nassau County	18	0.04
Covington, KY (city) Kenton County	15	0.04
Kearny, NJ (town) Hudson County	15	0.04

Please refer to the Explanation of Data in the front of the book for more detailed information.

Race

American Indian: Cherokee

U.S. and 50 States Sorted by Population and Percent of Total Population

Place	Population	%
United States	**819,105**	**0.27**
Oklahoma	185,850	4.95
California	92,246	0.25
Texas	50,954	0.20
Florida	32,342	0.17
North Carolina	32,030	0.34
Ohio	26,584	0.23
Missouri	25,373	0.42
Georgia	21,525	0.22
Alabama	21,144	0.44
Arkansas	20,330	0.70
Washington	20,257	0.30
Tennessee	19,938	0.31
Michigan	17,821	0.18
Virginia	17,433	0.22
Illinois	17,033	0.13
New York	16,947	0.09
Oregon	16,203	0.42
Kansas	15,772	0.55
Pennsylvania	14,552	0.11
Colorado	14,310	0.28
Indiana	12,583	0.19
Arizona	11,178	0.17
Maryland	11,055	0.19
Kentucky	10,731	0.25
South Carolina	10,675	0.23
Hawaii	8,024	0.59
New Jersey	7,716	0.09
Louisiana	7,631	0.17
Nevada	6,200	0.23
West Virginia	4,600	0.25
Massachusetts	4,539	0.07
New Mexico	4,358	0.21
Wisconsin	4,226	0.07
Idaho	4,089	0.26
Alaska	3,563	0.50
Mississippi	3,431	0.12
Utah	3,351	0.12
Iowa	3,338	0.11
Connecticut	3,168	0.09
Minnesota	3,147	0.06
Nebraska	1,989	0.11
Montana	1,860	0.19
Delaware	1,669	0.19
Wyoming	1,282	0.23
Maine	1,230	0.09
New Hampshire	1,229	0.09
District of Columbia	1,036	0.17
Rhode Island	987	0.09
Vermont	672	0.11
South Dakota	543	0.07
North Dakota	361	0.05

Place	Population	%
Oklahoma	185,850	4.95
Arkansas	20,330	0.70
Hawaii	8,024	0.59
Kansas	15,772	0.55
Alaska	3,563	0.50
Alabama	21,144	0.44
Missouri	25,373	0.42
Oregon	16,203	0.42
North Carolina	32,030	0.34
Tennessee	19,938	0.31
Washington	20,257	0.30
Colorado	14,310	0.28
United States	**819,105**	**0.27**
Idaho	4,089	0.26
California	92,246	0.25
Kentucky	10,731	0.25
West Virginia	4,600	0.25
Ohio	26,584	0.23
South Carolina	10,675	0.23
Nevada	6,200	0.23
Wyoming	1,282	0.23
Georgia	21,525	0.22
Virginia	17,433	0.22
New Mexico	4,358	0.21
Texas	50,954	0.20
Indiana	12,583	0.19
Maryland	11,055	0.19
Montana	1,860	0.19
Delaware	1,669	0.19
Michigan	17,821	0.18
Florida	32,342	0.17
Arizona	11,178	0.17
Louisiana	7,631	0.17
District of Columbia	1,036	0.17
Illinois	17,033	0.13
Mississippi	3,431	0.12
Utah	3,351	0.12
Pennsylvania	14,552	0.11
Iowa	3,338	0.11
Nebraska	1,989	0.11
Vermont	672	0.11
New York	16,947	0.09
New Jersey	7,716	0.09
Connecticut	3,168	0.09
Maine	1,230	0.09
New Hampshire	1,229	0.09
Rhode Island	987	0.09
Massachusetts	4,539	0.07
Wisconsin	4,226	0.07
South Dakota	543	0.07
Minnesota	3,147	0.06
North Dakota	361	0.05

Please refer to the Explanation of Data in the front of the book for more detailed information.

Race

American Indian: Cherokee

Top 150 Places Sorted by Population

Based on all places, regardless of total population

Place	Population	%
Tulsa, OK (city) Tulsa County	16,720	4.27
Oklahoma City, OK (city) Oklahoma County	7,210	1.24
New York, NY (city) Kings County	6,952	0.09
Muskogee, OK (city) Muskogee County	5,163	13.16
Los Angeles, CA (city) Los Angeles County	4,661	0.12
Broken Arrow, OK (city) Tulsa County	4,505	4.56
Tahlequah, OK (city) Cherokee County	4,490	28.50
Claremore, OK (city) Rogers County	3,042	16.37
Wichita, KS (city) Sedgwick County	2,696	0.71
Chicago, IL (city) Cook County	2,639	0.10
Bartlesville, OK (city) Washington County	2,549	7.13
Philadelphia, PA (city) Philadelphia County	2,484	0.16
San Diego, CA (city) San Diego County	2,342	0.18
Sallisaw, OK (city) Sequoyah County	2,267	25.53
San Antonio, TX (city) Medina County	2,136	0.16
Houston, TX (city) Harris County	2,120	0.10
Columbus, OH (city) Franklin County	2,100	0.27
Owasso, OK (city) Tulsa County	2,030	7.02
Sacramento, CA (city) Sacramento County	2,019	0.43
Jacksonville, FL (city) Duval County	2,004	0.24
Stilwell, OK (city) Adair County	1,992	50.44
Norman, OK (city) Cleveland County	1,952	1.76
Brooklyn, NY (borough) Kings County	1,903	0.08
Phoenix, AZ (city) Maricopa County	1,881	0.13
Portland, OR (city) Multnomah County	1,874	0.32
Manhattan, NY (borough) New York County	1,845	0.12
Kansas City, MO (city) Jackson County	1,693	0.37
Austin, TX (city) Travis County	1,686	0.21
Dallas, TX (city) Dallas County	1,684	0.14
Indianapolis, IN (city) Marion County	1,682	0.21
Fort Worth, TX (city) Tarrant County	1,675	0.23
San Jose, CA (city) Santa Clara County	1,622	0.17
Cherokee, NC (cdp) Jackson County	1,593	74.51
Park Hill, OK (cdp) Cherokee County	1,542	39.45
Pryor Creek, OK (city) Mayes County	1,525	15.99
Denver, CO (city) Denver County	1,522	0.25
Colorado Springs, CO (city) El Paso County	1,484	0.36
Nashville-Davidson, TN (metro govt) Davidson County	1,467	0.24
Louisville-Jefferson County, KY (metro govt) Jefferson County	1,455	0.24
Bakersfield, CA (city) Kern County	1,444	0.42
Anchorage, AK (municipality) Anchorage Municipality	1,443	0.49
San Francisco, CA (city) San Francisco County	1,441	0.18
Queens, NY (borough) Queens County	1,425	0.06
Fresno, CA (city) Fresno County	1,408	0.28
Miami, OK (city) Ottawa County	1,399	10.31
Fort Smith, AR (city) Sebastian County	1,370	1.59
Seattle, WA (city) King County	1,364	0.22
Wagoner, OK (city) Wagoner County	1,357	16.30
Urban Honolulu, HI (cdp) Honolulu County	1,321	0.39
Detroit, MI (city) Wayne County	1,321	0.19
Bronx, NY (borough) Bronx County	1,312	0.09
Charlotte, NC (city) Mecklenburg County	1,294	0.18
Sand Springs, OK (city) Tulsa County	1,268	6.71
Vinita, OK (city) Craig County	1,245	21.68
Moore, OK (city) Cleveland County	1,235	2.24
Virginia Beach, VA (ind. city) Virginia Beach independent city	1,222	0.28
Las Vegas, NV (city) Clark County	1,213	0.21
Sapulpa, OK (city) Creek County	1,202	5.85
Stockton, CA (city) San Joaquin County	1,176	0.40
Baltimore, MD (city) Baltimore city County	1,131	0.18
Albuquerque, NM (city) Bernalillo County	1,113	0.20
Edmond, OK (city) Oklahoma County	1,098	1.35
Huntsville, AL (city) Madison County	1,078	0.60
Springfield, MO (city) Christian County	1,076	0.67
Catoosa, OK (city) Rogers County	1,066	14.91
Washington, DC (city) District of Columbia	1,036	0.17
Stillwater, OK (city) Payne County	1,033	2.26
Tucson, AZ (city) Pima County	1,019	0.20
Fort Gibson, OK (town) Muskogee County	1,012	24.36
Modesto, CA (city) Stanislaus County	1,004	0.50
Jay, OK (city) Delaware County	990	40.44
Arlington, TX (city) Tarrant County	974	0.27
Oakland, CA (city) Alameda County	971	0.25
Aurora, CO (city) Arapahoe County	969	0.30
Skiatook, OK (town) Osage County	967	13.07

Place	Population	%
Bixby, OK (city) Tulsa County	965	4.62
Long Beach, CA (city) Los Angeles County	947	0.20
Memphis, TN (city) Shelby County	931	0.14
Midwest City, OK (city) Oklahoma County	905	1.66
Coweta, OK (city) Wagoner County	873	8.78
Siloam Springs, AR (city) Benton County	873	5.80
Cleveland, OH (city) Cuyahoga County	865	0.22
Grove, OK (city) Delaware County	855	12.91
Atlanta, GA (city) Fulton County	836	0.20
St. Louis, MO (city) St. Louis city County	826	0.26
Nowata, OK (city) Nowata County	822	22.03
Norfolk, VA (ind. city) Norfolk independent city	818	0.34
Fayetteville, NC (city) Cumberland County	815	0.41
Greensboro, NC (city) Guilford County	789	0.29
Toledo, OH (city) Lucas County	784	0.27
Raleigh, NC (city) Wake County	775	0.19
Tacoma, WA (city) Pierce County	765	0.39
Glenpool, OK (city) Tulsa County	758	7.01
Fayetteville, AR (city) Washington County	750	1.02
Milwaukee, WI (city) Milwaukee County	738	0.12
Eugene, OR (city) Lane County	732	0.47
Collinsville, OK (city) Tulsa County	731	13.04
Kenwood, OK (cdp) Delaware County	718	58.66
Knoxville, TN (city) Knox County	717	0.40
Mesa, AZ (city) Maricopa County	695	0.16
Riverside, CA (city) Riverside County	693	0.23
Joplin, MO (city) Jasper County	689	1.37
Shawnee, OK (city) Pottawatomie County	682	2.28
Lawton, OK (city) Comanche County	679	0.70
Cherry Tree, OK (cdp) Adair County	678	76.78
Independence, MO (city) Jackson County	674	0.58
Topeka, KS (city) Shawnee County	672	0.53
Jenks, OK (city) Tulsa County	670	3.96
Tampa, FL (city) Hillsborough County	669	0.20
Lexington-Fayette, KY (cons. govt) Fayette County	662	0.22
Muldrow, OK (town) Sequoyah County	661	19.07
Cincinnati, OH (city) Hamilton County	652	0.22
Boston, MA (city) Suffolk County	645	0.10
Ponca City, OK (city) Kay County	644	2.54
Spokane, WA (city) Spokane County	637	0.30
Clarksville, TN (city) Montgomery County	633	0.48
Enid, OK (city) Garfield County	621	1.26
Newport News, VA (ind. city) Newport News independent city	620	0.34
Redding, CA (city) Shasta County	599	0.67
Vancouver, WA (city) Clark County	598	0.37
Chesapeake, VA (ind. city) Chesapeake independent city	585	0.26
Locust Grove, OK (town) Mayes County	580	40.76
Westville, OK (town) Adair County	576	35.14
Kansas City, KS (city) Wyandotte County	573	0.39
Amarillo, TX (city) Potter County	573	0.30
Hempstead, NY (town) Nassau County	572	0.08
Henderson, NV (city) Clark County	571	0.22
McAlester, OK (city) Pittsburg County	567	3.08
Springdale, AR (city) Washington County	567	0.81
Elk Grove, CA (city) Sacramento County	555	0.36
Verdigris, OK (town) Rogers County	546	13.67
Brookhaven, NY (town) Suffolk County	546	0.11
Coffeyville, KS (city) Montgomery County	544	5.28
Salem, OR (city) Marion County	542	0.35
El Paso, TX (city) El Paso County	542	0.08
Hampton, VA (ind. city) Hampton independent city	541	0.39
Chelsea, OK (town) Rogers County	536	27.29
San Buenaventura (Ventura), CA (city) Ventura County	536	0.50
Boise City, ID (city) Ada County	536	0.26
Akron, OH (city) Summit County	534	0.27
Pittsburgh, PA (city) Allegheny County	533	0.17
Omaha, NE (city) Douglas County	528	0.13
Visalia, CA (city) Tulare County	526	0.42
Plano, TX (city) Collin County	523	0.20
Salina, OK (town) Mayes County	521	37.32
San Bernardino, CA (city) San Bernardino County	512	0.24
Santa Rosa, CA (city) Sonoma County	511	0.30
Reno, NV (city) Washoe County	510	0.23
Corpus Christi, TX (city) Nueces County	502	0.16
Augusta-Richmond County, GA (cons. govt) Richmond County	499	0.25

Please refer to the Explanation of Data in the front of the book for more detailed information.

Race

American Indian: Cherokee

Top 150 Places Sorted by Percent of Total Population

Based on all places, regardless of total population

Place	Population	%
Hoot Owl, OK (town) Mayes County	4	100.00
Old Eucha, OK (cdp) Delaware County	42	80.77
Bull Hollow, OK (cdp) Delaware County	54	80.60
Cherry Tree, OK (cdp) Adair County	678	76.78
Cherokee, NC (cdp) Jackson County	1,593	74.51
Oaks, OK (town) Delaware County	203	70.49
Zion, OK (cdp) Adair County	28	68.29
Chewey, OK (cdp) Adair County	89	65.93
Wauhillau, OK (cdp) Adair County	222	64.35
Flute Springs, OK (cdp) Sequoyah County	82	63.08
Mulberry, OK (cdp) Adair County	87	63.04
Bell, OK (cdp) Adair County	321	60.00
Greasy, OK (cdp) Adair County	220	59.14
Rocky Mountain, OK (cdp) Adair County	248	59.05
Kenwood, OK (cdp) Delaware County	718	58.66
Dripping Springs, OK (cdp) Delaware County	27	54.00
Grandview, OK (cdp) Cherokee County	204	51.78
Leach, OK (cdp) Delaware County	122	51.48
Marble City, OK (town) Sequoyah County	134	50.95
Pinhook Corner, OK (cdp) Sequoyah County	87	50.88
Hulbert, OK (town) Cherokee County	298	50.51
Stilwell, OK (city) Adair County	1,992	50.44
Fairfield, OK (cdp) Adair County	294	50.34
Titanic, OK (cdp) Adair County	179	50.28
Lotsee, OK (town) Tulsa County	1	50.00
West Peavine, OK (cdp) Adair County	108	49.54
Marietta, OK (cdp) Adair County	52	49.06
Peavine, OK (cdp) Adair County	207	48.94
Twin Oaks, OK (cdp) Delaware County	96	48.48
Kansas, OK (town) Delaware County	370	46.13
Nicut, OK (cdp) Sequoyah County	164	45.56
Elm Grove, OK (cdp) Adair County	90	45.45
Lost City, OK (cdp) Cherokee County	349	45.32
Sycamore, OK (cdp) Delaware County	80	45.20
Blackgum, OK (cdp) Sequoyah County	23	45.10
Lyons Switch, OK (cdp) Adair County	128	44.44
Welling, OK (cdp) Cherokee County	338	43.84
New Eucha, OK (cdp) Delaware County	175	43.21
Tenkiller, OK (cdp) Cherokee County	271	42.81
Rocky Ford, OK (cdp) Delaware County	26	42.62
Salem, OK (cdp) Adair County	47	41.96
Butler, OK (cdp) Delaware County	48	41.03
Woodall, OK (cdp) Cherokee County	336	40.83
Locust Grove, OK (town) Mayes County	580	40.76
Eldon, OK (cdp) Cherokee County	150	40.76
Jay, OK (city) Delaware County	990	40.44
Keys, OK (cdp) Cherokee County	228	40.35
Shady Grove, OK (cdp) Cherokee County	223	40.11
Wickliffe, OK (cdp) Mayes County	30	40.00
Park Hill, OK (cdp) Cherokee County	1,542	39.45
Piney, OK (cdp) Adair County	45	39.13
Box, OK (cdp) Sequoyah County	87	38.84
Belfonte, OK (cdp) Sequoyah County	152	38.58
Peggs, OK (cdp) Cherokee County	311	38.25
Old Green, OK (cdp) Adair County	120	38.10
Briggs, OK (cdp) Cherokee County	115	37.95
Notchietown, OK (cdp) Sequoyah County	140	37.53
Salina, OK (town) Mayes County	521	37.32
Zeb, OK (cdp) Cherokee County	185	37.22
Dry Creek, OK (cdp) Cherokee County	82	36.12
New Alluwe, OK (town) Nowata County	32	35.56
Brushy, OK (cdp) Sequoyah County	319	35.44
Westville, OK (town) Adair County	576	35.14
Proctor, OK (cdp) Adair County	81	35.06
Sour John, OK (cdp) Muskogee County	21	35.00
Christie, OK (cdp) Adair County	74	33.94
Sams Corner, OK (cdp) Mayes County	45	32.85
Deer Lick, OK (cdp) Delaware County	15	32.61
Watts, OK (town) Adair County	105	32.41
White Oak, OK (cdp) Craig County	85	32.32
Cloud Creek, OK (cdp) Delaware County	39	32.23
Steely Hollow, OK (cdp) Cherokee County	65	31.55
Spavinaw, OK (town) Mayes County	136	31.12
Tagg Flats, OK (cdp) Delaware County	4	30.77
Vian, OK (town) Sequoyah County	450	30.70

Place	Population	%
Carlisle, OK (cdp) Sequoyah County	180	29.70
Strang, OK (town) Mayes County	26	29.21
Indianola, OK (cdp) Delaware County	14	29.17
Rose, OK (cdp) Mayes County	83	29.12
Porum, OK (town) Muskogee County	210	28.89
Tahlequah, OK (city) Cherokee County	4,490	28.50
Teresita, OK (cdp) Cherokee County	45	28.30
Duchess Landing, OK (cdp) McIntosh County	32	28.07
Stidham, OK (town) McIntosh County	5	27.78
Evening Shade, OK (cdp) Sequoyah County	99	27.58
Chelsea, OK (town) Rogers County	536	27.29
Ballou, OK (cdp) Mayes County	48	27.27
Zena, OK (cdp) Delaware County	33	27.05
Braggs, OK (town) Muskogee County	70	27.03
Pettit, OK (cdp) Cherokee County	257	26.94
Colcord, OK (town) Delaware County	216	26.50
Simms, OK (cdp) Muskogee County	86	26.46
Gore, OK (town) Sequoyah County	258	26.41
Scraper, OK (cdp) Cherokee County	50	26.18
Dodge, OK (cdp) Delaware County	30	26.09
Lenapah, OK (town) Nowata County	75	25.60
Sallisaw, OK (city) Sequoyah County	2,267	25.53
Petersville, AK (cdp) Matanuska-Susitna Borough	1	25.00
Murphy, OK (cdp) Mayes County	54	24.66
Fort Gibson, OK (town) Muskogee County	1,012	24.36
Cedar Crest, OK (cdp) Mayes County	76	24.36
Long, OK (cdp) Sequoyah County	90	24.32
Webbers Falls, OK (town) Muskogee County	147	23.86
White Water, OK (cdp) Delaware County	19	23.75
Sand Hill, OK (cdp) Muskogee County	93	23.54
Disney, OK (town) Mayes County	73	23.47
Akins, OK (cdp) Sequoyah County	114	23.12
Sportsmen Acres, OK (town) Mayes County	74	22.98
Wann, OK (town) Nowata County	28	22.40
Bushyhead, OK (cdp) Rogers County	292	22.22
Nowata, OK (city) Nowata County	822	22.03
Oktaha, OK (town) Muskogee County	85	21.79
Vinita, OK (city) Craig County	1,245	21.68
Foyil, OK (town) Rogers County	74	21.51
Adair, OK (town) Mayes County	167	21.14
Okay, OK (town) Wagoner County	131	21.13
Valley Park, OK (town) Rogers County	16	20.78
Flint Creek, OK (cdp) Delaware County	151	20.63
Stoney Point, OK (cdp) Sequoyah County	49	20.59
Afton, OK (town) Ottawa County	213	20.31
Welch, OK (town) Craig County	125	20.19
Gans, OK (town) Sequoyah County	63	20.19
Short, OK (cdp) Sequoyah County	59	20.14
Brush Creek, OK (cdp) Delaware County	7	20.00
Picher, OK (city) Ottawa County	4	20.00
Warner, OK (town) Muskogee County	327	19.93
Fairland, OK (town) Ottawa County	210	19.87
West Siloam Springs, OK (town) Delaware County	166	19.62
Shady Grove, OK (cdp) McIntosh County	38	19.59
Pump Back, OK (cdp) Mayes County	34	19.43
Talala, OK (town) Rogers County	53	19.41
Langley, OK (town) Mayes County	157	19.17
Muldrow, OK (town) Sequoyah County	661	19.07
Delaware, OK (town) Nowata County	78	18.71
Big Cabin, OK (town) Craig County	49	18.49
Iron Post, OK (cdp) Mayes County	17	18.48
Snake Creek, OK (cdp) Mayes County	47	18.29
Liberty, OK (cdp) Sequoyah County	40	18.18
Dwight Mission, OK (cdp) Sequoyah County	10	18.18
Chouteau, OK (town) Mayes County	379	18.07
Blackburn, OK (town) Pawnee County	19	17.59
Grand Lake Towne, OK (town) Mayes County	13	17.57
Bartlett, KS (city) Labette County	14	17.50
Justice, OK (cdp) Rogers County	227	17.15
Badger Lee, OK (cdp) Sequoyah County	13	17.11
Brent, OK (cdp) Sequoyah County	120	16.76
Oak Grove, OK (town) Pawnee County	3	16.67
Fair Oaks, OK (town) Wagoner County	17	16.50
South Coffeyville, OK (town) Nowata County	129	16.43
Claremore, OK (city) Rogers County	3,042	16.37

Please refer to the Explanation of Data in the front of the book for more detailed information.

Race

American Indian: Cherokee

Top 150 Places Sorted by Percent of Total Population
Based on places with total population of 7,500 or more

Place	Population	%
Tahlequah, OK (city) Cherokee County	4,490	28.50
Sallisaw, OK (city) Sequoyah County	2,267	25.53
Claremore, OK (city) Rogers County	3,042	16.37
Wagoner, OK (city) Wagoner County	1,357	16.30
Pryor Creek, OK (city) Mayes County	1,525	15.99
Muskogee, OK (city) Muskogee County	5,163	13.16
Miami, OK (city) Ottawa County	1,399	10.31
Coweta, OK (city) Wagoner County	873	8.78
Bartlesville, OK (city) Washington County	2,549	7.13
Owasso, OK (city) Tulsa County	2,030	7.02
Glenpool, OK (city) Tulsa County	758	7.01
Sand Springs, OK (city) Tulsa County	1,268	6.71
Sapulpa, OK (city) Creek County	1,202	5.85
Siloam Springs, AR (city) Benton County	873	5.80
Coffeyville, KS (city) Montgomery County	544	5.28
Bixby, OK (city) Tulsa County	965	4.62
Broken Arrow, OK (city) Tulsa County	4,505	4.56
Tulsa, OK (city) Tulsa County	16,720	4.27
Jenks, OK (city) Tulsa County	670	3.96
Okmulgee, OK (city) Okmulgee County	481	3.90
Cushing, OK (city) Payne County	291	3.72
Poteau, OK (city) Le Flore County	281	3.30
McAlester, OK (city) Pittsburg County	567	3.08
Choctaw, OK (city) Oklahoma County	303	2.72
Ponca City, OK (city) Kay County	644	2.54
Newcastle, OK (city) McClain County	188	2.45
Shawnee, OK (city) Pottawatomie County	682	2.28
Blanchard, OK (city) McClain County	175	2.28
Stillwater, OK (city) Payne County	1,033	2.26
Guthrie, OK (city) Logan County	230	2.26
Moore, OK (city) Cleveland County	1,235	2.24
Ada, OK (city) Pontotoc County	372	2.21
Van Buren, AR (city) Crawford County	494	2.17
Olivehurst, CA (cdp) Yuba County	253	1.85
Independence, KS (city) Montgomery County	175	1.85
Greenwood, AR (city) Sebastian County	162	1.81
Norman, OK (city) Cleveland County	1,952	1.76
Midwest City, OK (city) Oklahoma County	905	1.66
Durant, OK (city) Bryan County	263	1.66
Mustang, OK (city) Canadian County	286	1.64
Fort Smith, AR (city) Sebastian County	1,370	1.59
Del City, OK (city) Oklahoma County	339	1.59
Duncan, OK (city) Stephens County	359	1.53
The Village, OK (city) Oklahoma County	136	1.52
Chickasha, OK (city) Grady County	235	1.47
Makaha, HI (cdp) Honolulu County	121	1.46
Yukon, OK (city) Canadian County	325	1.43
Joplin, MO (city) Jasper County	689	1.37
Parsons, KS (city) Labette County	144	1.37
Edmond, OK (city) Oklahoma County	1,098	1.35
Linda, CA (cdp) Yuba County	234	1.32
Warr Acres, OK (city) Oklahoma County	133	1.32
Arkansas City, KS (city) Cowley County	163	1.31
Marysville, CA (city) Yuba County	158	1.31
Weatherford, OK (city) Custer County	140	1.29
Clearlake, CA (city) Lake County	195	1.28
Enid, OK (city) Garfield County	621	1.26
Webb City, MO (city) Jasper County	139	1.26
Oklahoma City, OK (city) Oklahoma County	7,210	1.24
Woodward, OK (city) Woodward County	147	1.22
Neosho, MO (city) Newton County	144	1.22
El Reno, OK (city) Canadian County	203	1.21
Shasta Lake, CA (city) Shasta County	123	1.21
Oildale, CA (cdp) Kern County	381	1.17
Oroville, CA (city) Butte County	179	1.15
Wellington, KS (city) Sumner County	94	1.15
Hawaiian Paradise Park, HI (cdp) Hawaii County	127	1.11
Bethany, OK (city) Oklahoma County	210	1.10
Coos Bay, OR (city) Coos County	174	1.09
Ardmore, OK (city) Carter County	263	1.08
Waianae, HI (cdp) Honolulu County	138	1.05
Kapaa, HI (cdp) Kauai County	110	1.03
Fayetteville, AR (city) Washington County	750	1.02
Elk City, OK (city) Beckham County	117	1.00
Scottsboro, AL (city) Jackson County	143	0.97
Kelso, WA (city) Cowlitz County	114	0.96
Anderson, CA (city) Shasta County	95	0.96
Chanute, KS (city) Neosho County	87	0.95
Wasilla, AK (city) Matanuska-Susitna Borough	74	0.94
Wahiawa, HI (cdp) Honolulu County	166	0.93
Carthage, MO (city) Jasper County	133	0.93
Baker City, OR (city) Baker County	91	0.93
Magalia, CA (cdp) Butte County	104	0.92
Bentonville, AR (city) Benton County	322	0.91
Fort Lewis, WA (cdp) Pierce County	101	0.91
Bella Vista, AR (town) Benton County	237	0.90
Knik-Fairview, AK (cdp) Matanuska-Susitna Borough	134	0.90
Placerville, CA (city) El Dorado County	94	0.90
Clinton, OK (city) Custer County	81	0.90
Red Bluff, CA (city) Tehama County	125	0.89
Garden Acres, CA (cdp) San Joaquin County	95	0.89
Borger, TX (city) Hutchinson County	117	0.88
Diamond Springs, CA (cdp) El Dorado County	97	0.88
Crestline, CA (cdp) San Bernardino County	95	0.88
Sutherlin, OR (city) Douglas County	69	0.88
North Bend, OR (city) Coos County	84	0.87
Augusta, KS (city) Butler County	81	0.87
Hartselle, AL (city) Morgan County	123	0.86
Fortuna, CA (city) Humboldt County	103	0.86
Oroville East, CA (cdp) Butte County	71	0.86
Kalaoa, HI (cdp) Hawaii County	82	0.85
Kaneohe, HI (cdp) Honolulu County	291	0.84
El Dorado, KS (city) Butler County	110	0.84
Winfield, KS (city) Cowley County	103	0.84
Cottage Grove, OR (city) Lane County	81	0.84
Big Bear City, CA (cdp) San Bernardino County	102	0.83
Kapolei, HI (cdp) Honolulu County	125	0.82
Fort Payne, AL (city) DeKalb County	115	0.82
Grass Valley, CA (city) Nevada County	105	0.82
Oakdale, LA (city) Allen Parish	64	0.82
Springdale, AR (city) Washington County	567	0.81
Nanakuli, HI (cdp) Honolulu County	102	0.81
Centerton, AR (city) Benton County	77	0.81
Monett, MO (city) Barry County	72	0.81
Meadow Lakes, AK (cdp) Matanuska-Susitna Borough	61	0.81
Hilo, HI (cdp) Hawaii County	346	0.80
Altus, OK (city) Jackson County	158	0.80
Haysville, KS (city) Sedgwick County	87	0.80
Eureka, CA (city) Humboldt County	216	0.79
Ocean Pointe, HI (cdp) Honolulu County	66	0.79
Pittsburg, KS (city) Crawford County	157	0.78
Kailua, HI (cdp) Hawaii County	93	0.78
Ahuimanu, HI (cdp) Honolulu County	69	0.78
Kalifornsky, AK (cdp) Kenai Peninsula Borough	61	0.78
Paradise, CA (town) Butte County	202	0.77
Green, OR (cdp) Douglas County	57	0.76
Yuba City, CA (city) Sutter County	490	0.75
Paris, TX (city) Lamar County	188	0.75
Arcata, CA (city) Humboldt County	129	0.75
Auburn, CA (city) Placer County	100	0.75
Klamath Falls, OR (city) Klamath County	154	0.74
Harrison, AR (city) Boone County	96	0.74
Waimea, HI (cdp) Hawaii County	68	0.74
Rosedale, CA (cdp) Kern County	103	0.73
Excelsior Springs, MO (city) Clay County	81	0.73
Makakilo, HI (cdp) Honolulu County	131	0.72
St. Helens, OR (city) Columbia County	93	0.72
Ottawa, KS (city) Franklin County	91	0.72
Fort Scott, KS (city) Bourbon County	58	0.72
Wichita, KS (city) Sedgwick County	2,696	0.71
Longview, WA (city) Cowlitz County	262	0.71
Grants Pass, OR (city) Josephine County	245	0.71
Mililani Town, HI (cdp) Honolulu County	196	0.71
Oakdale, CA (city) Stanislaus County	146	0.71
Conning Towers Nautilus Park, CT (cdp) New London County	63	0.71
Lawton, OK (city) Comanche County	679	0.70
Rogers, AR (city) Benton County	392	0.70
Chowchilla, CA (city) Madera County	131	0.70
East Milton, FL (cdp) Santa Rosa County	77	0.70
North Highlands, CA (cdp) Sacramento County	294	0.69

Please refer to the Explanation of Data in the front of the book for more detailed information.

Race

American Indian: Cheyenne

U.S. and 50 States Sorted by Population and Percent of Total Population

Place	Population	%
United States	**19,051**	**0.01**
Montana	5,912	0.60
Oklahoma	3,157	0.08
California	1,546	<0.01
Washington	764	0.01
Colorado	676	0.01
Texas	628	<0.01
Oregon	453	0.01
South Dakota	417	0.05
New Mexico	354	0.02
Arizona	328	0.01
Kansas	324	0.01
Florida	263	<0.01
Ohio	236	<0.01
Wyoming	233	0.04
Illinois	224	<0.01
Utah	213	0.01
Missouri	212	<0.01
Pennsylvania	185	<0.01
Idaho	182	0.01
Michigan	175	<0.01
New York	163	<0.01
North Carolina	158	<0.01
Indiana	157	<0.01
Nevada	148	0.01
Virginia	145	<0.01
Minnesota	131	<0.01
Tennessee	127	<0.01
Arkansas	121	<0.01
Hawaii	120	0.01
Nebraska	118	0.01
Iowa	116	<0.01
Georgia	108	<0.01
Maryland	108	<0.01
Kentucky	105	<0.01
North Dakota	98	0.01
Wisconsin	98	<0.01
Alaska	78	0.01
New Jersey	73	<0.01
Louisiana	65	<0.01
Alabama	51	<0.01
Massachusetts	51	<0.01
South Carolina	47	<0.01
Connecticut	42	<0.01
Mississippi	37	<0.01
West Virginia	34	<0.01
New Hampshire	18	<0.01
Vermont	17	<0.01
Maine	15	<0.01
Delaware	8	<0.01
Rhode Island	8	<0.01
District of Columbia	4	<0.01

Place	Population	%
Montana	5,912	0.60
Oklahoma	3,157	0.08
South Dakota	417	0.05
Wyoming	233	0.04
New Mexico	354	0.02
United States	**19,051**	**0.01**
Washington	764	0.01
Colorado	676	0.01
Oregon	453	0.01
Arizona	328	0.01
Kansas	324	0.01
Utah	213	0.01
Idaho	182	0.01
Nevada	148	0.01
Hawaii	120	0.01
Nebraska	118	0.01
North Dakota	98	0.01
Alaska	78	0.01
California	1,546	<0.01
Texas	628	<0.01
Florida	263	<0.01
Ohio	236	<0.01
Illinois	224	<0.01
Missouri	212	<0.01
Pennsylvania	185	<0.01
Michigan	175	<0.01
New York	163	<0.01
North Carolina	158	<0.01
Indiana	157	<0.01
Virginia	145	<0.01
Minnesota	131	<0.01
Tennessee	127	<0.01
Arkansas	121	<0.01
Iowa	116	<0.01
Georgia	108	<0.01
Maryland	108	<0.01
Kentucky	105	<0.01
Wisconsin	98	<0.01
New Jersey	73	<0.01
Louisiana	65	<0.01
Alabama	51	<0.01
Massachusetts	51	<0.01
South Carolina	47	<0.01
Connecticut	42	<0.01
Mississippi	37	<0.01
West Virginia	34	<0.01
New Hampshire	18	<0.01
Vermont	17	<0.01
Maine	15	<0.01
Delaware	8	<0.01
Rhode Island	8	<0.01
District of Columbia	4	<0.01

Please refer to the Explanation of Data in the front of the book for more detailed information.

Race

American Indian: Cheyenne

Top 150 Places Sorted by Population

Based on all places, regardless of total population

Place	Population	%
Lame Deer, MT (cdp) Rosebud County	1,634	79.63
Billings, MT (city) Yellowstone County	782	0.75
Busby, MT (cdp) Big Horn County	538	72.21
Muddy, MT (cdp) Big Horn County	486	78.77
Oklahoma City, OK (city) Oklahoma County	444	0.08
Ashland, MT (cdp) Rosebud County	427	51.82
El Reno, OK (city) Canadian County	244	1.46
Clinton, OK (city) Custer County	202	2.24
Colstrip, MT (city) Rosebud County	174	7.86
Tulsa, OK (city) Tulsa County	125	0.03
Albuquerque, NM (city) Bernalillo County	120	0.02
Weatherford, OK (city) Custer County	113	1.04
Birney, MT (cdp) Rosebud County	106	77.37
Hammon, OK (town) Roger Mills County	102	17.96
Rapid City, SD (city) Pennington County	95	0.14
Denver, CO (city) Denver County	87	0.01
Elk City, OK (city) Beckham County	85	0.73
Phoenix, AZ (city) Maricopa County	81	0.01
Lawton, OK (city) Comanche County	79	0.08
Los Angeles, CA (city) Los Angeles County	77	<0.01
Spokane, WA (city) Spokane County	76	0.04
Lockwood, MT (cdp) Yellowstone County	74	1.09
Woodward, OK (city) Woodward County	69	0.57
Wichita, KS (city) Sedgwick County	68	0.02
Colorado Springs, CO (city) El Paso County	66	0.02
Portland, OR (city) Multnomah County	66	0.01
Missoula, MT (city) Missoula County	65	0.10
Kingfisher, OK (city) Kingfisher County	64	1.38
Watonga, OK (city) Blaine County	64	1.25
Norman, OK (city) Cleveland County	61	0.05
Tacoma, WA (city) Pierce County	60	0.03
Hardin, MT (city) Big Horn County	58	1.65
Enid, OK (city) Garfield County	49	0.10
Bozeman, MT (city) Gallatin County	48	0.13
Sacramento, CA (city) Sacramento County	46	0.01
New York, NY (city) Kings County	46	<0.01
Great Falls, MT (city) Cascade County	44	0.08
Aurora, CO (city) Arapahoe County	44	0.01
Seattle, WA (city) King County	43	0.01
Geary, OK (city) Blaine County	39	3.05
Shawnee, OK (city) Pottawatomie County	39	0.13
San Antonio, TX (city) Medina County	39	<0.01
Seiling, OK (city) Dewey County	37	4.30
Miles City, MT (city) Custer County	37	0.44
Lawrence, KS (city) Douglas County	37	0.04
Pueblo, CO (city) Pueblo County	37	0.03
Salt Lake City, UT (city) Salt Lake County	37	0.02
Sioux Falls, SD (city) Minnehaha County	36	0.02
Anchorage, AK (municipality) Anchorage Municipality	35	0.01
Helena, MT (city) Lewis and Clark County	34	0.12
Anadarko, OK (city) Caddo County	32	0.47
Butte-Silver Bow, MT (cons. govt) Silver Bow County	31	0.09
San Diego, CA (city) San Diego County	31	<0.01
Del City, OK (city) Oklahoma County	30	0.14
Gresham, OR (city) Multnomah County	29	0.03
Boise City, ID (city) Ada County	29	0.01
Midwest City, OK (city) Oklahoma County	28	0.05
Oakland, CA (city) Alameda County	28	0.01
Mesa, AZ (city) Maricopa County	27	0.01
Urban Honolulu, HI (cdp) Honolulu County	27	0.01
Chicago, IL (city) Cook County	27	<0.01
Canton, OK (town) Blaine County	26	4.16
Ponca City, OK (city) Kay County	26	0.10
Crow Agency, MT (cdp) Big Horn County	25	1.55
Vancouver, WA (city) Clark County	25	0.02
Sheridan, WY (city) Sheridan County	24	0.14
Minneapolis, MN (city) Hennepin County	24	0.01
Las Vegas, NV (city) Clark County	24	<0.01
Moore, OK (city) Cleveland County	22	0.04
Amarillo, TX (city) Potter County	22	0.01
Dallas, TX (city) Dallas County	22	<0.01
Fresno, CA (city) Fresno County	22	<0.01
Houston, TX (city) Harris County	22	<0.01
Kansas City, MO (city) Jackson County	22	<0.01
Long Beach, CA (city) Los Angeles County	22	<0.01
Tahlequah, OK (city) Cherokee County	21	0.13
Stillwater, OK (city) Payne County	21	0.05
Eugene, OR (city) Lane County	21	0.01
Bethany, OK (city) Oklahoma County	20	0.10
Gillette, WY (city) Campbell County	20	0.07
Spokane Valley, WA (city) Spokane County	20	0.02
Lakewood, CO (city) Jefferson County	20	0.01
Queens, NY (borough) Queens County	20	<0.01
Tucson, AZ (city) Pima County	20	<0.01
Miami, OK (city) Ottawa County	19	0.14
Broken Arrow, OK (city) Tulsa County	19	0.02
Kent, WA (city) King County	19	0.02
Austin, TX (city) Travis County	19	<0.01
Bismarck, ND (city) Burleigh County	18	0.03
Indianapolis, IN (city) Marion County	18	<0.01
Ronan, MT (city) Lake County	17	0.91
Anaconda-Deer Lodge County, MT (special city) Deer Lodge County	17	0.18
Havre, MT (city) Hill County	17	0.18
Bartlesville, OK (city) Washington County	17	0.05
Edmond, OK (city) Oklahoma County	17	0.02
Lincoln, NE (city) Lancaster County	17	0.01
Reno, NV (city) Washoe County	17	0.01
West Valley City, UT (city) Salt Lake County	17	0.01
Longdale, OK (town) Blaine County	16	6.11
Spearfish, SD (city) Lawrence County	16	0.15
Yukon, OK (city) Canadian County	16	0.07
Auburn, WA (city) King County	16	0.02
Fargo, ND (city) Cass County	16	0.02
Fort Collins, CO (city) Larimer County	16	0.01
Palmdale, CA (city) Los Angeles County	16	0.01
Salem, OR (city) Marion County	16	0.01
Stockton, CA (city) San Joaquin County	16	0.01
Torrance, CA (city) Los Angeles County	16	0.01
Nashville-Davidson, TN (metro govt) Davidson County	16	<0.01
San Jose, CA (city) Santa Clara County	16	<0.01
Farmington, NM (city) San Juan County	15	0.03
Apple Valley, CA (town) San Bernardino County	15	0.02
Nampa, ID (city) Canyon County	15	0.02
Paradise, NV (cdp) Clark County	15	0.01
Bakersfield, CA (city) Kern County	15	<0.01
Columbus, OH (city) Franklin County	15	<0.01
Louisville-Jefferson County, KY (metro govt) Jefferson County	15	<0.01
Helena Valley Southeast, MT (cdp) Lewis and Clark County	14	0.17
Trinidad, CO (city) Las Animas County	14	0.15
Riverton, WY (city) Fremont County	14	0.13
Pierre, SD (city) Hughes County	14	0.10
Fort Smith, AR (city) Sebastian County	14	0.02
Akron, OH (city) Summit County	14	0.01
North Las Vegas, NV (city) Clark County	14	0.01
San Bernardino, CA (city) San Bernardino County	14	0.01
Santa Rosa, CA (city) Sonoma County	14	0.01
West Covina, CA (city) Los Angeles County	14	0.01
El Paso, TX (city) El Paso County	14	<0.01
San Francisco, CA (city) San Francisco County	14	<0.01
Ethete, WY (cdp) Fremont County	13	0.84
Laurel, MT (city) Yellowstone County	13	0.19
Lander, WY (city) Fremont County	13	0.17
Eagle Mountain, UT (city) Utah County	13	0.06
Gallup, NM (city) McKinley County	13	0.06
Keizer, OR (city) Marion County	13	0.04
Santa Fe, NM (city) Santa Fe County	13	0.02
Arden-Arcade, CA (cdp) Sacramento County	13	0.01
Tempe, AZ (city) Maricopa County	13	0.01
Thornton, CO (city) Adams County	13	0.01
Fort Worth, TX (city) Tarrant County	13	<0.01
Lexington-Fayette, KY (cons. govt) Fayette County	13	<0.01
Milwaukee, WI (city) Milwaukee County	13	<0.01
Omaha, NE (city) Douglas County	13	<0.01
Riverside, CA (city) Riverside County	13	<0.01
Arapaho, OK (town) Custer County	12	1.51
South Browning, MT (cdp) Glacier County	12	0.67
Lolo, MT (cdp) Missoula County	12	0.31
Blackwell, OK (city) Kay County	12	0.17
Box Elder, SD (city) Pennington County	12	0.15
Warr Acres, OK (city) Oklahoma County	12	0.12

Race

American Indian: Cheyenne

Top 150 Places Sorted by Percent of Total Population

Based on all places, regardless of total population

Place	Population	%
Lame Deer, MT (cdp) Rosebud County	1,634	79.63
Muddy, MT (cdp) Big Horn County	486	78.77
Birney, MT (cdp) Rosebud County	106	77.37
Busby, MT (cdp) Big Horn County	538	72.21
Ashland, MT (cdp) Rosebud County	427	51.82
Hammon, OK (town) Roger Mills County	102	17.96
Colstrip, MT (city) Rosebud County	174	7.86
Longdale, OK (town) Blaine County	16	6.11
Qui-nai-elt Village, WA (cdp) Grays Harbor County	3	5.56
Seiling, OK (city) Dewey County	37	4.30
Lebanon, SD (town) Potter County	2	4.26
Gulkana, AK (cdp) Valdez-Cordova Census Area	5	4.20
Canton, OK (town) Blaine County	26	4.16
Hitchcock, OK (town) Blaine County	5	4.13
Winston, MT (cdp) Broadwater County	6	4.08
Babb, MT (cdp) Glacier County	7	4.02
Albany, OK (cdp) Bryan County	5	3.50
Box Elder, MT (cdp) Hill County	3	3.45
Canova, NM (cdp) Rio Arriba County	4	3.39
Mutual, OK (town) Woodward County	2	3.28
Geary, OK (city) Blaine County	39	3.05
Little Browning, MT (cdp) Glacier County	6	2.91
Custer City, OK (town) Custer County	9	2.40
Clinton, OK (city) Custer County	202	2.24
Frazer, MT (cdp) Valley County	8	2.21
Colony, OK (town) Washita County	3	2.21
Haworth, OK (town) McCurtain County	6	2.02
Calumet, OK (town) Canadian County	10	1.97
Boulder Flats, WY (cdp) Fremont County	8	1.96
Sumpter, OR (city) Baker County	4	1.96
Antelope, MT (cdp) Sheridan County	1	1.96
Broadus, MT (town) Powder River County	9	1.92
Frannie, WY (town) Big Horn County	3	1.91
Crystal Mountain, MI (cdp) Benzie County	1	1.85
Marland, OK (town) Noble County	4	1.78
Red Rock, OK (town) Noble County	5	1.77
Heart Butte, MT (cdp) Pondera County	10	1.72
Pacific Beach, WA (cdp) Grays Harbor County	5	1.72
Hardin, MT (city) Big Horn County	58	1.65
Crow Agency, MT (cdp) Big Horn County	25	1.55
Maple Grove, MN (township) Becker County	7	1.54
Arapaho, OK (town) Custer County	12	1.51
Picuris Pueblo, NM (cdp) Taos County	1	1.47
El Reno, OK (city) Canadian County	244	1.46
Horace, KS (city) Greeley County	1	1.43
College Springs, IA (city) Page County	3	1.40
Kingfisher, OK (city) Kingfisher County	64	1.38
Old Harbor, AK (city) Kodiak Island Borough	3	1.38
Ravalli, MT (cdp) Lake County	1	1.32
Kyle, SD (cdp) Shannon County	11	1.30
Canute, OK (town) Washita County	7	1.29
Otter Lake, MI (village) Lapeer County	5	1.29
Farson, WY (cdp) Sweetwater County	4	1.28
Hysham, MT (town) Treasure County	4	1.28
Loyal, OK (town) Kingfisher County	1	1.27
Watonga, OK (city) Blaine County	64	1.25
St. Xavier, MT (cdp) Big Horn County	1	1.20
Starr School, MT (cdp) Glacier County	3	1.19
Four Bears Village, ND (cdp) McKenzie County	6	1.16
Shepherd, MT (cdp) Yellowstone County	6	1.16
Rulo, NE (village) Richardson County	2	1.16
Zeeland, ND (city) McIntosh County	1	1.16
Gage, OK (town) Ellis County	5	1.13
Alexandria, NE (village) Thayer County	2	1.13
Power, MT (cdp) Teton County	2	1.12
Lockwood, MT (cdp) Yellowstone County	74	1.09
Tuppers Plains, OH (cdp) Meigs County	5	1.08
Greenfield, OK (town) Blaine County	1	1.08
Lavina, MT (town) Golden Valley County	2	1.07
Okabena, MN (city) Jackson County	2	1.06
Kendall, WA (cdp) Whatcom County	2	1.05
Virginia City, MT (town) Madison County	2	1.05
Weatherford, OK (city) Custer County	113	1.04
Oaks, OK (town) Delaware County	3	1.04
Mountain View, WY (cdp) Natrona County	1	1.04

Place	Population	%
Kelso, MN (township) Sibley County	3	1.03
Cochiti, NM (cdp) Sandoval County	5	0.95
Sand Coulee, MT (cdp) Cascade County	2	0.94
Lodge Grass, MT (town) Big Horn County	4	0.93
Wyola, MT (cdp) Big Horn County	2	0.93
Batesland, SD (town) Shannon County	1	0.93
Toston, MT (cdp) Broadwater County	1	0.93
Leedey, OK (town) Dewey County	4	0.92
Midland, AR (town) Sebastian County	3	0.92
Ronan, MT (city) Lake County	17	0.91
Williamsburg, NM (village) Sierra County	4	0.89
Altamont, UT (town) Duchesne County	2	0.89
Worcester, VT (cdp) Washington County	1	0.89
Gotebo, OK (town) Kiowa County	2	0.88
Santee, NE (village) Knox County	3	0.87
Ignacio, CO (town) La Plata County	6	0.86
Fort Peck, MT (town) Valley County	2	0.86
Ethete, WY (cdp) Fremont County	13	0.84
Orick, CA (cdp) Humboldt County	3	0.84
Bethune, CO (town) Kit Carson County	2	0.84
Manderson-White Horse Creek, SD (cdp) Shannon County	5	0.80
Nixon, NV (cdp) Washoe County	3	0.80
Wounded Knee, SD (cdp) Shannon County	3	0.79
Wye, MT (cdp) Missoula County	4	0.78
Fort Belknap Agency, MT (cdp) Blaine County	10	0.77
Bangor, CA (cdp) Butte County	5	0.77
Billings, MT (city) Yellowstone County	782	0.75
Lodge Pole, MT (cdp) Blaine County	2	0.75
Everton, AR (town) Boone County	1	0.75
Elk City, OK (city) Beckham County	85	0.73
Nichols, WI (village) Outagamie County	2	0.73
Shady Grove, OK (cdp) Cherokee County	4	0.72
Mulberry, OK (cdp) Adair County	1	0.72
St. Ignatius, MT (town) Lake County	6	0.71
Azure, MT (cdp) Hill County	2	0.70
Nageezi, NM (cdp) San Juan County	2	0.70
Kingvale, CA (cdp) Nevada County	1	0.70
Mound City, MO (city) Holt County	8	0.69
Thomas, OK (city) Custer County	8	0.68
South Browning, MT (cdp) Glacier County	12	0.67
Huntley, MT (cdp) Yellowstone County	3	0.67
Seymour, WI (town) Lafayette County	3	0.67
Cimarron City, OK (town) Logan County	1	0.67
Foss, OK (town) Washita County	1	0.66
Augusta, MT (cdp) Lewis and Clark County	2	0.65
Sangrey, MT (cdp) Hill County	2	0.65
Towaoc, CO (cdp) Montezuma County	7	0.64
Richland, OR (city) Baker County	1	0.64
Rosebud, SD (cdp) Todd County	10	0.63
Fort Cobb, OK (town) Caddo County	4	0.63
Evaro, MT (cdp) Missoula County	2	0.62
Reeder, ND (city) Adams County	1	0.62
Tryon, OK (town) Lincoln County	3	0.61
Lura, MN (township) Faribault County	1	0.61
Montgomery Creek, CA (cdp) Shasta County	1	0.61
Palmetto, LA (village) St. Landry Parish	1	0.61
Corn, OK (town) Washita County	3	0.60
Randolph, IA (city) Fremont County	1	0.60
Mission, SD (city) Todd County	7	0.59
Beemer, NE (village) Cuming County	4	0.59
North La Junta, CO (cdp) Otero County	3	0.59
Elcho, WI (cdp) Langlade County	2	0.59
Parker School, MT (cdp) Hill County	2	0.59
Kindred, ND (city) Cass County	4	0.58
Granada, CO (town) Prowers County	3	0.58
Johannesburg, CA (cdp) Kern County	1	0.58
Woodward, OK (city) Woodward County	69	0.57
Fort Washakie, WY (cdp) Fremont County	10	0.57
White Cloud, KS (city) Doniphan County	1	0.57
West Kootenai, MT (cdp) Lincoln County	2	0.55
Johnson City, KS (city) Stanton County	8	0.54
Fern Forest, HI (cdp) Hawaii County	5	0.54
Victor, MT (cdp) Ravalli County	4	0.54
Boneau, MT (cdp) Chouteau County	2	0.53
Seventh Mountain, OR (cdp) Deschutes County	1	0.53

Please refer to the Explanation of Data in the front of the book for more detailed information.

Race

American Indian: Cheyenne

Top 150 Places Sorted by Percent of Total Population

Based on places with total population of 7,500 or more

Place	Population	%
Clinton, OK (city) Custer County	202	2.24
El Reno, OK (city) Canadian County	244	1.46
Weatherford, OK (city) Custer County	113	1.04
Billings, MT (city) Yellowstone County	782	0.75
Elk City, OK (city) Beckham County	85	0.73
Woodward, OK (city) Woodward County	69	0.57
Miles City, MT (city) Custer County	37	0.44
Anaconda-Deer Lodge County, MT (special city) Deer Lodge County	17	0.18
Havre, MT (city) Hill County	17	0.18
Helena Valley Southeast, MT (cdp) Lewis and Clark County	14	0.17
Spearfish, SD (city) Lawrence County	16	0.15
Trinidad, CO (city) Las Animas County	14	0.15
Box Elder, SD (city) Pennington County	12	0.15
Rapid City, SD (city) Pennington County	95	0.14
Del City, OK (city) Oklahoma County	30	0.14
Sheridan, WY (city) Sheridan County	24	0.14
Miami, OK (city) Ottawa County	19	0.14
Bozeman, MT (city) Gallatin County	48	0.13
Shawnee, OK (city) Pottawatomie County	39	0.13
Tahlequah, OK (city) Cherokee County	21	0.13
Riverton, WY (city) Fremont County	14	0.13
Helena, MT (city) Lewis and Clark County	34	0.12
Warr Acres, OK (city) Oklahoma County	12	0.12
Midland, WA (cdp) Pierce County	11	0.12
Pryor Creek, OK (city) Mayes County	11	0.12
Missoula, MT (city) Missoula County	65	0.10
Enid, OK (city) Garfield County	49	0.10
Ponca City, OK (city) Kay County	26	0.10
Bethany, OK (city) Oklahoma County	20	0.10
Pierre, SD (city) Hughes County	14	0.10
Guymon, OK (city) Texas County	11	0.10
Crookston, MN (city) Polk County	8	0.10
Butte-Silver Bow, MT (cons. govt) Silver Bow County	31	0.09
Delta, CO (city) Delta County	8	0.09
The Village, OK (city) Oklahoma County	8	0.09
Oklahoma City, OK (city) Oklahoma County	444	0.08
Lawton, OK (city) Comanche County	79	0.08
Great Falls, MT (city) Cascade County	44	0.08
Vermillion, SD (city) Clay County	8	0.08
Bernalillo, NM (town) Sandoval County	7	0.08
Lakes, AK (cdp) Matanuska-Susitna Borough	7	0.08
Rawlins, WY (city) Carbon County	7	0.08
Gillette, WY (city) Campbell County	20	0.07
Yukon, OK (city) Canadian County	16	0.07
Hawaiian Paradise Park, HI (cdp) Hawaii County	8	0.07
Greenwood, AR (city) Sebastian County	6	0.07
Eagle Mountain, UT (city) Utah County	13	0.06
Gallup, NM (city) McKinley County	13	0.06
Mustang, OK (city) Canadian County	11	0.06
Franklin, OH (city) Warren County	7	0.06
Seabrook, TX (city) Harris County	7	0.06
Kimball, MI (township) St. Clair County	6	0.06
Malvern, AR (city) Hot Spring County	6	0.06
Elwood, IN (city) Madison County	5	0.06
Mount Vista, WA (cdp) Clark County	5	0.06
Riverside, IL (village) Cook County	5	0.06
Shiprock, NM (cdp) San Juan County	5	0.06
Norman, OK (city) Cleveland County	61	0.05
Midwest City, OK (city) Oklahoma County	28	0.05
Stillwater, OK (city) Payne County	21	0.05
Bartlesville, OK (city) Washington County	17	0.05
Fountain, CO (city) El Paso County	12	0.05
Sapulpa, OK (city) Creek County	10	0.05
Ada, OK (city) Pontotoc County	9	0.05
St. Helens, OR (city) Columbia County	7	0.05
Waianae, HI (cdp) Honolulu County	7	0.05
Arkansas City, KS (city) Cowley County	6	0.05
Blackfoot, ID (city) Bingham County	6	0.05
Cottonwood, AZ (city) Yavapai County	6	0.05
McPherson, KS (city) McPherson County	6	0.05
Rochester, MI (city) Oakland County	6	0.05
Accokeek, MD (cdp) Prince George's County	5	0.05
Camp Pendleton South, CA (cdp) San Diego County	5	0.05
Glenpool, OK (city) Tulsa County	5	0.05
Merriam, KS (city) Johnson County	5	0.05
Rifle, CO (city) Garfield County	5	0.05
Sedro-Woolley, WA (city) Skagit County	5	0.05
Waimea, HI (cdp) Hawaii County	5	0.05
Cortez, CO (city) Montezuma County	4	0.05
Hardyston, NJ (township) Sussex County	4	0.05
Murphysboro, IL (city) Jackson County	4	0.05
Poteau, OK (city) Le Flore County	4	0.05
Rapid Valley, SD (cdp) Pennington County	4	0.05
Tuba City, AZ (cdp) Coconino County	4	0.05
Spokane, WA (city) Spokane County	76	0.04
Lawrence, KS (city) Douglas County	37	0.04
Moore, OK (city) Cleveland County	22	0.04
Keizer, OR (city) Marion County	13	0.04
Paris, TX (city) Lamar County	11	0.04
Altamont, OR (cdp) Klamath County	8	0.04
Hazel Dell, WA (cdp) Clark County	8	0.04
McAlester, OK (city) Pittsburg County	8	0.04
Shelbyville, TN (city) Bedford County	8	0.04
Altus, OK (city) Jackson County	7	0.04
Kalispell, MT (city) Flathead County	7	0.04
Sherrelwood, CO (cdp) Adams County	7	0.04
Durango, CO (city) La Plata County	6	0.04
Kent, NY (town) Putnam County	6	0.04
Upper Grand Lagoon, FL (cdp) Bay County	6	0.04
Escanaba, MI (city) Delta County	5	0.04
Fort Carson, CO (cdp) El Paso County	5	0.04
Los Osos, CA (cdp) San Luis Obispo County	5	0.04
Sharon, PA (city) Mercer County	5	0.04
Washougal, WA (city) Clark County	5	0.04
Lackland AFB, TX (cdp) Bexar County	4	0.04
Ontario, OR (city) Malheur County	4	0.04
Sandy, OR (city) Clackamas County	4	0.04
Uniontown, PA (city) Fayette County	4	0.04
Vashon, WA (cdp) King County	4	0.04
Elgin, TX (city) Bastrop County	3	0.04
Four Corners, MD (cdp) Montgomery County	3	0.04
Kirtland, NM (cdp) San Juan County	3	0.04
Southampton, PA (township) Franklin County	3	0.04
Temple Hills, MD (cdp) Prince George's County	3	0.04
Tuscumbia, AL (city) Colbert County	3	0.04
Westgate, FL (cdp) Palm Beach County	3	0.04
White City, OR (cdp) Jackson County	3	0.04
Tulsa, OK (city) Tulsa County	125	0.03
Tacoma, WA (city) Pierce County	60	0.03
Pueblo, CO (city) Pueblo County	37	0.03
Gresham, OR (city) Multnomah County	29	0.03
Bismarck, ND (city) Burleigh County	18	0.03
Farmington, NM (city) San Juan County	15	0.03
Brighton, CO (city) Adams County	11	0.03
Fort Hood, TX (cdp) Bell County	10	0.03
Muskogee, OK (city) Muskogee County	10	0.03
Sherman, TX (city) Grayson County	10	0.03
Pueblo West, CO (cdp) Pueblo County	9	0.03
West Whittier-Los Nietos, CA (cdp) Los Angeles County	8	0.03
Windsor, CA (town) Sonoma County	8	0.03
Imperial Beach, CA (city) San Diego County	7	0.03
Klamath Falls, OR (city) Klamath County	7	0.03
Twentynine Palms, CA (city) San Bernardino County	7	0.03
Berlin, CT (town) Hartford County	6	0.03
Covington, WA (city) King County	6	0.03
Frederickson, WA (cdp) Pierce County	6	0.03
Mandan, ND (city) Morton County	6	0.03
Oak Harbor, WA (city) Island County	6	0.03
Port Hueneme, CA (city) Ventura County	6	0.03
Wahiawa, HI (cdp) Honolulu County	6	0.03
Arcata, CA (city) Humboldt County	5	0.03
Dumas, TX (city) Moore County	5	0.03
Four Corners, OR (cdp) Marion County	5	0.03
Hayesville, OR (cdp) Marion County	5	0.03
Middleton, WI (city) Dane County	5	0.03
Mitchell, SD (city) Davison County	5	0.03
Ocean Acres, NJ (cdp) Ocean County	5	0.03
Pendleton, OR (city) Umatilla County	5	0.03
Vincennes, IN (city) Knox County	5	0.03
Wailuku, HI (cdp) Maui County	5	0.03

SECTION THREE

Please refer to the Explanation of Data in the front of the book for more detailed information.

Race

American Indian: Chickasaw

U.S. and 50 States Sorted by Population and Percent of Total Population

Place	Population	%
United States	**52,278**	**0.02**
Oklahoma	27,538	0.73
Texas	6,836	0.03
California	4,827	0.01
Washington	945	0.01
Arizona	848	0.01
Missouri	789	0.01
Oregon	774	0.02
Colorado	760	0.02
Florida	685	<0.01
Kansas	643	0.02
Arkansas	613	0.02
New Mexico	498	0.02
Tennessee	437	0.01
Nevada	387	0.01
Virginia	361	<0.01
Illinois	351	<0.01
Louisiana	335	0.01
Georgia	314	<0.01
North Carolina	298	<0.01
Ohio	289	<0.01
Alabama	276	0.01
Mississippi	272	0.01
Michigan	261	<0.01
New York	215	<0.01
South Carolina	201	<0.01
Indiana	195	<0.01
Pennsylvania	186	<0.01
Idaho	185	0.01
Utah	179	0.01
Maryland	170	<0.01
Hawaii	161	0.01
Kentucky	149	<0.01
Alaska	147	0.02
Wisconsin	127	<0.01
New Jersey	118	<0.01
Massachusetts	116	<0.01
Minnesota	109	<0.01
Iowa	107	<0.01
Montana	99	0.01
Nebraska	96	0.01
Connecticut	72	<0.01
Wyoming	67	0.01
Maine	50	<0.01
West Virginia	44	<0.01
District of Columbia	36	0.01
New Hampshire	28	<0.01
Rhode Island	24	<0.01
South Dakota	19	<0.01
North Dakota	18	<0.01
Vermont	13	<0.01
Delaware	10	<0.01

Place	Population	%
Oklahoma	27,538	0.73
Texas	6,836	0.03
United States	**52,278**	**0.02**
Oregon	774	0.02
Colorado	760	0.02
Kansas	643	0.02
Arkansas	613	0.02
New Mexico	498	0.02
Alaska	147	0.02
California	4,827	0.01
Washington	945	0.01
Arizona	848	0.01
Missouri	789	0.01
Tennessee	437	0.01
Nevada	387	0.01
Louisiana	335	0.01
Alabama	276	0.01
Mississippi	272	0.01
Idaho	185	0.01
Utah	179	0.01
Hawaii	161	0.01
Montana	99	0.01
Nebraska	96	0.01
Wyoming	67	0.01
District of Columbia	36	0.01
Florida	685	<0.01
Virginia	361	<0.01
Illinois	351	<0.01
Georgia	314	<0.01
North Carolina	298	<0.01
Ohio	289	<0.01
Michigan	261	<0.01
New York	215	<0.01
South Carolina	201	<0.01
Indiana	195	<0.01
Pennsylvania	186	<0.01
Maryland	170	<0.01
Kentucky	149	<0.01
Wisconsin	127	<0.01
New Jersey	118	<0.01
Massachusetts	116	<0.01
Minnesota	109	<0.01
Iowa	107	<0.01
Connecticut	72	<0.01
Maine	50	<0.01
West Virginia	44	<0.01
New Hampshire	28	<0.01
Rhode Island	24	<0.01
South Dakota	19	<0.01
North Dakota	18	<0.01
Vermont	13	<0.01
Delaware	10	<0.01

Please refer to the Explanation of Data in the front of the book for more detailed information.

Race

American Indian: Chickasaw

Top 150 Places Sorted by Population

Based on all places, regardless of total population

Place	Population	%
Oklahoma City, OK (city) Oklahoma County	2,766	0.48
Ada, OK (city) Pontotoc County	1,568	9.33
Ardmore, OK (city) Carter County	1,324	5.45
Norman, OK (city) Cleveland County	911	0.82
Tulsa, OK (city) Tulsa County	705	0.18
Moore, OK (city) Cleveland County	500	0.91
Edmond, OK (city) Oklahoma County	395	0.49
Midwest City, OK (city) Oklahoma County	379	0.70
Tishomingo, OK (city) Johnston County	369	12.16
Sulphur, OK (city) Murray County	339	6.88
Durant, OK (city) Bryan County	326	2.06
Lone Grove, OK (city) Carter County	321	6.35
Dallas, TX (city) Dallas County	284	0.02
Shawnee, OK (city) Pottawatomie County	278	0.93
Fort Worth, TX (city) Tarrant County	277	0.04
Duncan, OK (city) Stephens County	276	1.18
Lawton, OK (city) Comanche County	255	0.26
Broken Arrow, OK (city) Tulsa County	212	0.21
Los Angeles, CA (city) Los Angeles County	207	0.01
Davis, OK (city) Murray County	199	7.42
Phoenix, AZ (city) Maricopa County	198	0.01
Austin, TX (city) Travis County	191	0.02
Byng, OK (town) Pontotoc County	186	15.83
Newcastle, OK (city) McClain County	182	2.37
Houston, TX (city) Harris County	168	0.01
Pauls Valley, OK (city) Garvin County	164	2.65
Purcell, OK (city) McClain County	159	2.70
Stillwater, OK (city) Payne County	154	0.34
Wichita, KS (city) Sedgwick County	149	0.04
San Antonio, TX (city) Medina County	145	0.01
Albuquerque, NM (city) Bernalillo County	142	0.03
San Diego, CA (city) San Diego County	141	0.01
McAlester, OK (city) Pittsburg County	136	0.74
Madill, OK (city) Marshall County	134	3.55
Muskogee, OK (city) Muskogee County	131	0.33
Arlington, TX (city) Tarrant County	130	0.04
Kingston, OK (town) Marshall County	126	7.87
Chickasha, OK (city) Grady County	123	0.77
Mustang, OK (city) Canadian County	117	0.67
Del City, OK (city) Oklahoma County	114	0.53
New York, NY (city) Kings County	113	<0.01
Bakersfield, CA (city) Kern County	112	0.03
Sherman, TX (city) Grayson County	111	0.29
Tuttle, OK (city) Grady County	109	1.81
Seminole, OK (city) Seminole County	105	1.40
Enid, OK (city) Garfield County	104	0.21
Stratford, OK (town) Garvin County	102	6.69
McKinney, TX (city) Collin County	102	0.08
Yukon, OK (city) Canadian County	100	0.44
Healdton, OK (city) Carter County	99	3.55
Kansas City, MO (city) Jackson County	97	0.02
Choctaw, OK (city) Oklahoma County	96	0.86
Plano, TX (city) Collin County	96	0.04
Sacramento, CA (city) Sacramento County	96	0.02
Denison, TX (city) Grayson County	95	0.42
Blanchard, OK (city) McClain County	90	1.17
Garland, TX (city) Dallas County	90	0.04
Lubbock, TX (city) Lubbock County	89	0.04
Amarillo, TX (city) Potter County	88	0.05
Marietta, OK (city) Love County	87	3.31
Colorado Springs, CO (city) El Paso County	87	0.02
Wichita Falls, TX (city) Wichita County	83	0.08
Coalgate, OK (city) Coal County	80	4.07
San Francisco, CA (city) San Francisco County	80	0.01
Noble, OK (city) Cleveland County	79	1.22
Denton, TX (city) Denton County	79	0.07
Denver, CO (city) Denver County	79	0.01
Mannsville, OK (town) Johnston County	76	8.81
Modesto, CA (city) Stanislaus County	76	0.04
Tucson, AZ (city) Pima County	75	0.01
Portland, OR (city) Multnomah County	74	0.01
Springer, OK (town) Carter County	73	10.43
Bethany, OK (city) Oklahoma County	73	0.38
Marlow, OK (city) Stephens County	72	1.54
Fresno, CA (city) Fresno County	71	0.01
Seattle, WA (city) King County	70	0.01
Slaughterville, OK (town) Cleveland County	69	1.67
Allen, OK (town) Pontotoc County	68	7.30
Wilson, OK (city) Carter County	68	3.94
Oakland, OK (town) Marshall County	67	6.34
Frisco, TX (city) Collin County	67	0.06
Calera, OK (town) Bryan County	66	3.05
Okmulgee, OK (city) Okmulgee County	66	0.54
Ravia, OK (town) Johnston County	65	12.31
Dickson, OK (town) Carter County	64	5.30
Nashville-Davidson, TN (metro govt) Davidson County	64	0.01
Anchorage, AK (municipality) Anchorage Municipality	63	0.02
Allen, TX (city) Collin County	62	0.07
Lewisville, TX (city) Denton County	61	0.06
Mill Creek, OK (town) Johnston County	60	18.81
Guthrie, OK (city) Logan County	60	0.59
Jenks, OK (city) Tulsa County	58	0.34
Bartlesville, OK (city) Washington County	58	0.16
Visalia, CA (city) Tulare County	58	0.05
Mesquite, TX (city) Dallas County	58	0.04
Ponca City, OK (city) Kay County	57	0.22
Chicago, IL (city) Cook County	56	<0.01
El Reno, OK (city) Canadian County	54	0.32
Owasso, OK (city) Tulsa County	54	0.19
San Jose, CA (city) Santa Clara County	53	0.01
Altus, OK (city) Jackson County	51	0.26
Sapulpa, OK (city) Creek County	51	0.25
Odessa, TX (city) Ector County	51	0.05
Las Vegas, NV (city) Clark County	51	0.01
Henderson, NV (city) Clark County	50	0.02
Sand Springs, OK (city) Tulsa County	49	0.26
Roff, OK (town) Pontotoc County	48	6.62
Claremore, OK (city) Rogers County	48	0.26
Wewoka, OK (city) Seminole County	47	1.37
Tecumseh, OK (city) Pottawatomie County	47	0.73
Carrollton, TX (city) Denton County	47	0.04
Maysville, OK (town) Garvin County	46	3.73
Wynnewood, OK (city) Garvin County	46	2.08
Warr Acres, OK (city) Oklahoma County	46	0.46
Irving, TX (city) Dallas County	46	0.02
Stonewall, OK (town) Pontotoc County	45	9.57
Cushing, OK (city) Payne County	45	0.58
North Richland Hills, TX (city) Tarrant County	45	0.07
Memphis, TN (city) Shelby County	45	0.01
Oakland, CA (city) Alameda County	45	0.01
Wayne, OK (town) McClain County	44	6.40
Harrah, OK (city) Oklahoma County	44	0.86
Salem, OR (city) Marion County	44	0.03
El Paso, TX (city) El Paso County	44	0.01
Richardson, TX (city) Dallas County	43	0.04
Grand Prairie, TX (city) Dallas County	43	0.02
Long Beach, CA (city) Los Angeles County	43	0.01
Manhattan, NY (borough) New York County	43	<0.01
Konawa, OK (city) Seminole County	40	3.08
Comanche, OK (city) Stephens County	40	2.41
Weatherford, OK (city) Custer County	40	0.37
Achille, OK (town) Bryan County	39	7.93
Lexington, OK (city) Cleveland County	39	1.81
Holdenville, OK (city) Hughes County	39	0.68
The Village, OK (city) Oklahoma County	39	0.44
Pryor Creek, OK (city) Mayes County	39	0.41
Bixby, OK (city) Tulsa County	39	0.19
Oildale, CA (cdp) Kern County	39	0.12
Mansfield, TX (city) Tarrant County	39	0.07
Fort Smith, AR (city) Sebastian County	39	0.05
Midland, TX (city) Midland County	39	0.04
Glenpool, OK (city) Tulsa County	38	0.35
Reno, NV (city) Washoe County	38	0.02
Goldsby, OK (town) McClain County	37	2.05
Anadarko, OK (city) Caddo County	37	0.55
Paradise, NV (cdp) Clark County	37	0.02
Santa Clarita, CA (city) Los Angeles County	37	0.02
Mesa, AZ (city) Maricopa County	37	0.01
Stockton, CA (city) San Joaquin County	37	0.01
Tahlequah, OK (city) Cherokee County	36	0.23

SECTION THREE

Race

American Indian: Chickasaw

Top 150 Places Sorted by Percent of Total Population

Based on all places, regardless of total population

Place	Population	%
Loveland, OK (town) Tillman County	3	23.08
Mill Creek, OK (town) Johnston County	60	18.81
Byng, OK (town) Pontotoc County	186	15.83
Norrie, CO (cdp) Pitkin County	1	14.29
Blue Sky, CO (cdp) Morgan County	3	12.50
Ravia, OK (town) Johnston County	65	12.31
Tishomingo, OK (city) Johnston County	369	12.16
Malo, WA (cdp) Ferry County	3	10.71
Piedra, CO (cdp) Hinsdale County	3	10.71
Dougherty, OK (town) Murray County	23	10.70
Springer, OK (town) Carter County	73	10.43
Stonewall, OK (town) Pontotoc County	45	9.57
Lebanon, OK (cdp) Marshall County	29	9.57
Ada, OK (city) Pontotoc County	1,568	9.33
Waldron, KS (city) Harper County	1	9.09
Kemp, OK (town) Bryan County	12	9.02
Mannsville, OK (town) Johnston County	76	8.81
Fitzhugh, OK (town) Pontotoc County	19	8.26
Achille, OK (town) Bryan County	39	7.93
Kingston, OK (town) Marshall County	126	7.87
Davis, OK (city) Murray County	199	7.42
Allen, OK (town) Pontotoc County	68	7.30
Hickory, OK (town) Murray County	5	7.04
Sulphur, OK (city) Murray County	339	6.88
Stratford, OK (town) Garvin County	102	6.69
Tribbey, OK (town) Pottawatomie County	26	6.65
Roff, OK (town) Pontotoc County	48	6.62
Mead, OK (town) Bryan County	8	6.56
Wayne, OK (town) McClain County	44	6.40
Tupelo, OK (city) Coal County	21	6.38
Lone Grove, OK (city) Carter County	321	6.35
Oakland, OK (town) Marshall County	67	6.34
Byars, OK (town) McClain County	16	6.27
Bromide, OK (town) Johnston County	10	6.06
Ashland, OK (town) Pittsburg County	4	6.06
Pittsburg, OK (town) Pittsburg County	12	5.80
Ardmore, OK (city) Carter County	1,324	5.45
Dickson, OK (town) Carter County	64	5.30
Francis, OK (town) Pontotoc County	16	5.08
Wainwright, OK (town) Muskogee County	8	4.85
New Woodville, OK (town) Marshall County	6	4.55
Phillips, OK (town) Coal County	6	4.44
Milburn, OK (town) Johnston County	14	4.42
Cornish, OK (town) Jefferson County	7	4.29
Centrahoma, OK (city) Coal County	4	4.12
Benedict, KS (city) Wilson County	3	4.11
Coalgate, OK (city) Coal County	80	4.07
Katie, OK (town) Garvin County	14	4.02
Sasakwa, OK (town) Seminole County	6	4.00
Tatums, OK (town) Carter County	6	3.97
Wilson, OK (city) Carter County	68	3.94
Wapanucka, OK (town) Johnston County	17	3.88
Maysville, OK (town) Garvin County	46	3.73
Silo, OK (town) Bryan County	12	3.63
Gilbert, AR (town) Searcy County	1	3.57
Madill, OK (city) Marshall County	134	3.55
Healdton, OK (city) Carter County	99	3.55
Erin Springs, OK (town) Garvin County	3	3.45
Pump Back, OK (cdp) Mayes County	6	3.43
Velma, OK (town) Stephens County	21	3.39
Gerty, OK (town) Hughes County	4	3.39
Thackerville, OK (town) Love County	15	3.37
Ratliff City, OK (town) Carter County	4	3.33
New Alluwe, OK (town) Nowata County	3	3.33
Marietta, OK (city) Love County	87	3.31
Shoshone, CA (cdp) Inyo County	1	3.23
Grayson, OK (town) Okmulgee County	5	3.14
Rentiesville, OK (town) McIntosh County	4	3.13
Marland, OK (town) Noble County	7	3.11
Konawa, OK (city) Seminole County	40	3.08
Calera, OK (town) Bryan County	66	3.05
Garfield, NM (cdp) Doña Ana County	4	2.92
Amber, OK (town) Grady County	12	2.86
Bee, OK (cdp) Johnston County	4	2.86
Armstrong, OK (town) Bryan County	3	2.86
Gould, OK (town) Harmon County	4	2.84
Asher, OK (town) Pottawatomie County	11	2.80
Purcell, OK (city) McClain County	159	2.70
Pauls Valley, OK (city) Garvin County	164	2.65
Lehigh, OK (city) Coal County	9	2.53
Gene Autry, OK (town) Carter County	4	2.53
Ringling, OK (town) Jefferson County	26	2.51
Paoli, OK (town) Garvin County	15	2.46
Comanche, OK (city) Stephens County	40	2.41
Newcastle, OK (city) McClain County	182	2.37
Colbert, OK (town) Bryan County	26	2.28
Manitou, OK (town) Tillman County	4	2.21
Mulberry, OK (cdp) Adair County	3	2.17
Wynnewood, OK (city) Garvin County	46	2.08
Durant, OK (city) Bryan County	326	2.06
Goldsby, OK (town) McClain County	37	2.05
Savanna, OK (town) Pittsburg County	14	2.04
Kenefic, OK (town) Bryan County	4	2.04
Wanette, OK (town) Pottawatomie County	7	2.00
Tuskahoma, OK (cdp) Pushmataha County	3	1.99
Haileyville, OK (city) Pittsburg County	16	1.97
Lamar, OK (town) Hughes County	3	1.90
Stella, MO (town) Newton County	3	1.90
Yale, OK (city) Payne County	23	1.87
Tuttle, OK (city) Grady County	109	1.81
Lexington, OK (city) Cleveland County	39	1.81
Cartwright, OK (cdp) Bryan County	11	1.81
Washington, OK (town) McClain County	11	1.78
Hammon, OK (town) Roger Mills County	10	1.76
Pinhook Corner, OK (cdp) Sequoyah County	3	1.75
Meridian, OK (cdp) Stephens County	26	1.74
Mountain Park, OK (town) Kiowa County	7	1.71
Slaughterville, OK (town) Cleveland County	69	1.67
Rodney, IA (city) Monona County	1	1.67
Bray, OK (town) Stephens County	20	1.65
Kiowa, OK (town) Pittsburg County	12	1.64
Alex, OK (town) Grady County	9	1.64
Elmore City, OK (town) Garvin County	11	1.58
Empire City, OK (town) Stephens County	15	1.57
Hoffman, OK (town) Okmulgee County	2	1.57
Marlow, OK (city) Stephens County	72	1.54
Maysville, AR (cdp) Benton County	2	1.54
Grandview, OK (cdp) Cherokee County	6	1.52
Pink, OK (town) Pottawatomie County	31	1.51
Porum, OK (town) Muskogee County	11	1.51
Verden, OK (town) Grady County	8	1.51
Arpelar, OK (cdp) Pittsburg County	4	1.47
Rosedale, OK (town) McClain County	1	1.47
String, OK (town) Atoka County	6	1.46
Caney, OK (town) Atoka County	3	1.46
Cherokee, CA (cdp) Butte County	1	1.45
Cole, OK (town) McClain County	8	1.44
Pin Oak Acres, OK (cdp) Mayes County	6	1.43
Ralston, WY (cdp) Park County	4	1.43
Nescatunga, OK (cdp) Alfalfa County	1	1.43
Jacksonport, AR (town) Jackson County	3	1.42
Seminole, OK (city) Seminole County	105	1.40
Wewoka, OK (city) Seminole County	47	1.37
Warwick, OK (town) Lincoln County	2	1.35
Vantage, WA (cdp) Kittitas County	1	1.35
Notchietown, OK (cdp) Sequoyah County	5	1.34
Mulhall, OK (town) Logan County	3	1.33
Yeager, OK (town) Hughes County	1	1.33
Valley Brook, OK (town) Oklahoma County	10	1.31
Wright City, OK (town) McCurtain County	10	1.31
Middle Frisco, NM (cdp) Catron County	1	1.30
Redbird Smith, OK (cdp) Sequoyah County	6	1.29
Boswell, OK (town) Choctaw County	9	1.27
Waurika, OK (city) Jefferson County	26	1.26
Gracemont, OK (town) Caddo County	4	1.26
Grandfield, OK (city) Tillman County	13	1.25
Dibble, OK (town) McClain County	11	1.25
Morrison, OK (town) Noble County	9	1.23
Bowlegs, OK (town) Seminole County	5	1.23
Noble, OK (city) Cleveland County	79	1.22

Please refer to the Explanation of Data in the front of the book for more detailed information.

Race

American Indian: Chickasaw

Top 150 Places Sorted by Percent of Total Population

Based on places with total population of 7,500 or more

Place	Population	%
Ada, OK (city) Pontotoc County	1,568	9.33
Ardmore, OK (city) Carter County	1,324	5.45
Newcastle, OK (city) McClain County	182	2.37
Durant, OK (city) Bryan County	326	2.06
Duncan, OK (city) Stephens County	276	1.18
Blanchard, OK (city) McClain County	90	1.17
Shawnee, OK (city) Pottawatomie County	278	0.93
Moore, OK (city) Cleveland County	500	0.91
Choctaw, OK (city) Oklahoma County	96	0.86
Norman, OK (city) Cleveland County	911	0.82
Chickasha, OK (city) Grady County	123	0.77
McAlester, OK (city) Pittsburg County	136	0.74
Midwest City, OK (city) Oklahoma County	379	0.70
Mustang, OK (city) Canadian County	117	0.67
Guthrie, OK (city) Logan County	60	0.59
Cushing, OK (city) Payne County	45	0.58
Okmulgee, OK (city) Okmulgee County	66	0.54
Del City, OK (city) Oklahoma County	114	0.53
Edmond, OK (city) Oklahoma County	395	0.49
Oklahoma City, OK (city) Oklahoma County	2,766	0.48
Warr Acres, OK (city) Oklahoma County	46	0.46
Yukon, OK (city) Canadian County	100	0.44
The Village, OK (city) Oklahoma County	39	0.44
Denison, TX (city) Grayson County	95	0.42
Pryor Creek, OK (city) Mayes County	39	0.41
Bethany, OK (city) Oklahoma County	73	0.38
Weatherford, OK (city) Custer County	40	0.37
Wagoner, OK (city) Wagoner County	31	0.37
Glenpool, OK (city) Tulsa County	38	0.35
Stillwater, OK (city) Payne County	154	0.34
Jenks, OK (city) Tulsa County	58	0.34
Muskogee, OK (city) Muskogee County	131	0.33
El Reno, OK (city) Canadian County	54	0.32
Sherman, TX (city) Grayson County	111	0.29
Lawton, OK (city) Comanche County	255	0.26
Altus, OK (city) Jackson County	51	0.26
Sand Springs, OK (city) Tulsa County	49	0.26
Claremore, OK (city) Rogers County	48	0.26
Sapulpa, OK (city) Creek County	51	0.25
Poteau, OK (city) Le Flore County	21	0.25
Tahlequah, OK (city) Cherokee County	36	0.23
Sallisaw, OK (city) Sequoyah County	20	0.23
Ponca City, OK (city) Kay County	57	0.22
Gainesville, TX (city) Cooke County	35	0.22
Broken Arrow, OK (city) Tulsa County	212	0.21
Enid, OK (city) Garfield County	104	0.21
Owasso, OK (city) Tulsa County	54	0.19
Bixby, OK (city) Tulsa County	39	0.19
Burkburnett, TX (city) Wichita County	21	0.19
Tulsa, OK (city) Tulsa County	705	0.18
Woodward, OK (city) Woodward County	22	0.18
Bartlesville, OK (city) Washington County	58	0.16
Miami, OK (city) Ottawa County	20	0.15
Elk City, OK (city) Beckham County	16	0.14
Coweta, OK (city) Wagoner County	14	0.14
Clay, MI (township) St. Clair County	13	0.14
Clinton, OK (city) Custer County	13	0.14
Borger, TX (city) Hutchinson County	17	0.13
Arkansas City, KS (city) Cowley County	16	0.13
Azle, TX (city) Tarrant County	14	0.13
Anna, TX (city) Collin County	11	0.13
Oildale, CA (cdp) Kern County	39	0.12
Mineral Wells, TX (city) Palo Pinto County	19	0.11
Crete, IL (village) Will County	9	0.11
Highland Village, TX (city) Denton County	15	0.10
Lovington, NM (city) Lea County	11	0.10
Southlake, TX (city) Tarrant County	23	0.09
Corinth, TX (city) Denton County	18	0.09
Pampa, TX (city) Gray County	17	0.09
Alpine, CA (cdp) San Diego County	13	0.09
Rosedale, CA (cdp) Kern County	12	0.09
Coolidge, AZ (city) Pinal County	11	0.09
Crowley, TX (city) Tarrant County	11	0.09
Newport, OR (city) Lincoln County	9	0.09
Greenwood, AR (city) Sebastian County	8	0.09
Napoleon, OH (city) Henry County	8	0.09
Green, OR (cdp) Douglas County	7	0.09
Haiku-Pauwela, HI (cdp) Maui County	7	0.09
McKinney, TX (city) Collin County	102	0.08
Wichita Falls, TX (city) Wichita County	83	0.08
Fort Mohave, AZ (cdp) Mohave County	12	0.08
Sulphur Springs, TX (city) Hopkins County	12	0.08
Ripon, CA (city) San Joaquin County	11	0.08
Big Bear City, CA (cdp) San Bernardino County	10	0.08
Fortuna, CA (city) Humboldt County	10	0.08
Grover Beach, CA (city) San Luis Obispo County	10	0.08
Rendon, TX (cdp) Tarrant County	10	0.08
Tomball, TX (city) Harris County	9	0.08
Lamesa, TX (city) Dawson County	8	0.08
Fallon, NV (city) Churchill County	7	0.08
Holualoa, HI (cdp) Hawaii County	7	0.08
Calimesa, CA (city) Riverside County	6	0.08
Olivette, MO (city) St. Louis County	6	0.08
Denton, TX (city) Denton County	79	0.07
Allen, TX (city) Collin County	62	0.07
North Richland Hills, TX (city) Tarrant County	45	0.07
Mansfield, TX (city) Tarrant County	39	0.07
Keller, TX (city) Tarrant County	27	0.07
Little Elm, TX (city) Denton County	19	0.07
Paris, TX (city) Lamar County	17	0.07
Blythe, CA (city) Riverside County	15	0.07
Colleyville, TX (city) Tarrant County	15	0.07
Patterson, CA (city) Stanislaus County	15	0.07
Seagoville, TX (city) Dallas County	11	0.07
Hutto, TX (city) Williamson County	10	0.07
El Sobrante, CA (cdp) Contra Costa County	9	0.07
The Dalles, OR (city) Wasco County	9	0.07
Webb City, MO (city) Jasper County	8	0.07
Flossmoor, IL (village) Cook County	7	0.07
Cold Springs, NV (cdp) Washoe County	6	0.07
Golden Hills, CA (cdp) Kern County	6	0.07
Tanaina, AK (cdp) Matanuska-Susitna Borough	6	0.07
Frisco, TX (city) Collin County	67	0.06
Lewisville, TX (city) Denton County	61	0.06
New Braunfels, TX (city) Comal County	32	0.06
Joplin, MO (city) Jasper County	30	0.06
Grapevine, TX (city) Tarrant County	28	0.06
Farmington, NM (city) San Juan County	26	0.06
Hurst, TX (city) Tarrant County	24	0.06
Wylie, TX (city) Collin County	23	0.06
Carlsbad, NM (city) Eddy County	16	0.06
Russellville, AR (city) Pope County	16	0.06
Brushy Creek, TX (cdp) Williamson County	14	0.06
Barstow, CA (city) San Bernardino County	13	0.06
Watauga, TX (city) Tarrant County	13	0.06
Sachse, TX (city) Dallas County	12	0.06
Arcata, CA (city) Humboldt County	11	0.06
Great Bend, KS (city) Barton County	10	0.06
Forney, TX (city) Kaufman County	9	0.06
McKinleyville, CA (cdp) Humboldt County	9	0.06
Marshall, MN (city) Lyon County	8	0.06
Mountain Home, ID (city) Elmore County	8	0.06
Campton Hills, IL (village) Kane County	7	0.06
Guymon, OK (city) Texas County	7	0.06
Richmond, TX (city) Fort Bend County	7	0.06
Anderson, CA (city) Shasta County	6	0.06
Farmersville, CA (city) Tulare County	6	0.06
Gulf Shores, AL (city) Baldwin County	6	0.06
Prineville, OR (city) Crook County	6	0.06
Red Oak, TX (city) Ellis County	6	0.06
Asbury Lake, FL (cdp) Clay County	5	0.06
Gold River, CA (cdp) Sacramento County	5	0.06
Oroville East, CA (cdp) Butte County	5	0.06
Waterford, CA (city) Stanislaus County	5	0.06
Amarillo, TX (city) Potter County	88	0.05
Visalia, CA (city) Tulare County	58	0.05
Odessa, TX (city) Ector County	51	0.05
Fort Smith, AR (city) Sebastian County	39	0.05
Fayetteville, AR (city) Washington County	36	0.05
Flower Mound, TX (town) Denton County	32	0.05

SECTION THREE

Race

American Indian: Chippewa

U.S. and 50 States Sorted by Population and Percent of Total Population

Place	Population	%	Place	Population	%
United States	**170,742**	**0.06**	North Dakota	16,994	2.53
Minnesota	44,213	0.83	Minnesota	44,213	0.83
Michigan	36,296	0.37	Montana	4,284	0.43
Wisconsin	19,326	0.34	Michigan	36,296	0.37
North Dakota	16,994	2.53	Wisconsin	19,326	0.34
California	7,250	0.02	Alaska	872	0.12
Washington	6,519	0.10	Washington	6,519	0.10
Montana	4,284	0.43	South Dakota	825	0.10
Oregon	3,023	0.08	Oregon	3,023	0.08
Illinois	2,740	0.02	Wyoming	457	0.08
Florida	2,689	0.01	**United States**	**170,742**	**0.06**
Texas	2,098	0.01	Idaho	847	0.05
Arizona	1,930	0.03	Colorado	1,805	0.04
Colorado	1,805	0.04	Arizona	1,930	0.03
Ohio	1,599	0.01	Oklahoma	984	0.03
Indiana	1,208	0.02	Nevada	832	0.03
New York	1,125	0.01	Kansas	726	0.03
North Carolina	1,032	0.01	New Mexico	696	0.03
Oklahoma	984	0.03	Hawaii	389	0.03
Missouri	945	0.02	California	7,250	0.02
Virginia	902	0.01	Illinois	2,740	0.02
Alaska	872	0.12	Indiana	1,208	0.02
Idaho	847	0.05	Missouri	945	0.02
Nevada	832	0.03	Iowa	710	0.02
South Dakota	825	0.10	Utah	486	0.02
Tennessee	780	0.01	Nebraska	412	0.02
Pennsylvania	770	0.01	Florida	2,689	0.01
Georgia	734	0.01	Texas	2,098	0.01
Kansas	726	0.03	Ohio	1,599	0.01
Iowa	710	0.02	New York	1,125	0.01
New Mexico	696	0.03	North Carolina	1,032	0.01
Maryland	509	0.01	Virginia	902	0.01
Utah	486	0.02	Tennessee	780	0.01
Wyoming	457	0.08	Pennsylvania	770	0.01
Massachusetts	450	0.01	Georgia	734	0.01
Nebraska	412	0.02	Maryland	509	0.01
Kentucky	406	0.01	Massachusetts	450	0.01
Hawaii	389	0.03	Kentucky	406	0.01
South Carolina	388	0.01	South Carolina	388	0.01
Arkansas	374	0.01	Arkansas	374	0.01
Alabama	368	0.01	Alabama	368	0.01
New Jersey	354	<0.01	Connecticut	281	0.01
Connecticut	281	0.01	Louisiana	232	0.01
Louisiana	232	0.01	Maine	179	0.01
Maine	179	0.01	Mississippi	171	0.01
Mississippi	171	0.01	New Hampshire	169	0.01
New Hampshire	169	0.01	West Virginia	119	0.01
West Virginia	119	0.01	Vermont	77	0.01
Vermont	77	0.01	Rhode Island	71	0.01
Rhode Island	71	0.01	Delaware	61	0.01
Delaware	61	0.01	District of Columbia	35	0.01
District of Columbia	35	0.01	New Jersey	354	<0.01

Please refer to the Explanation of Data in the front of the book for more detailed information.

Race

American Indian: Chippewa

Top 150 Places Sorted by Population

Based on all places, regardless of total population

Place	Population	%
Lower Red Lake, MN (unorganized territory) Beltrami County	4,598	79.41
Minneapolis, MN (city) Hennepin County	4,363	1.14
Sault Ste. Marie, MI (city) Chippewa County	2,558	18.09
Belcourt, ND (cdp) Rolette County	1,864	89.70
Lac du Flambeau, WI (town) Vilas County	1,717	49.90
Duluth, MN (city) St. Louis County	1,661	1.93
St. Paul, MN (city) Ramsey County	1,584	0.56
Red Lake, MN (cdp) Beltrami County	1,433	82.78
Lac du Flambeau, WI (cdp) Vilas County	1,418	72.02
Milwaukee, WI (city) Milwaukee County	1,301	0.22
Cloquet, MN (city) Carlton County	1,289	10.63
Bemidji, MN (city) Beltrami County	1,166	8.68
Shell Valley, ND (cdp) Rolette County	1,116	93.23
Sanborn, WI (town) Ashland County	1,049	78.81
Grand Forks, ND (city) Grand Forks County	1,008	1.91
Redby, MN (cdp) Beltrami County	986	73.91
Pike Bay, MN (township) Cass County	986	61.24
Little Rock, MN (cdp) Beltrami County	915	75.75
Russell, WI (town) Bayfield County	911	71.23
Kathio, MN (township) Mille Lacs County	911	55.99
Little Round Lake, WI (cdp) Sawyer County	857	79.28
Bass Lake, WI (town) Sawyer County	839	35.30
Kinross, MI (charter township) Chippewa County	826	10.92
Fargo, ND (city) Cass County	810	0.77
Vineland, MN (cdp) Mille Lacs County	798	79.72
Chippewa, MI (township) Isabella County	782	16.80
Hayward, WI (town) Sawyer County	757	21.22
Bay Mills, MI (township) Chippewa County	749	50.71
Minot, ND (city) Ward County	698	1.71
Ashland, WI (city) Ashland County	688	8.37
Baraga, MI (township) Baraga County	685	17.96
Twin Lakes, MN (township) Mahnomen County	684	83.62
St. Ignace, MI (city) Mackinac County	681	27.77
Chicago, IL (city) Cook County	659	0.02
Soo, MI (township) Chippewa County	645	20.53
Ponemah, MN (cdp) Beltrami County	621	85.77
Bowstring Lake, MN (unorganized territory) Itasca County	618	53.00
Portland, OR (city) Multnomah County	588	0.10
Superior, WI (city) Douglas County	586	2.15
Dunseith, ND (city) Rolette County	581	75.16
Great Falls, MT (city) Cascade County	557	0.95
Ten Lake, MN (township) Beltrami County	546	53.22
White Earth, MN (township) Becker County	529	63.89
Bismarck, ND (city) Burleigh County	523	0.85
Spokane, WA (city) Spokane County	523	0.25
Naytahwaush, MN (cdp) Mahnomen County	522	90.31
Green Acres, ND (cdp) Rolette County	504	87.65
Rolla, ND (city) Rolette County	489	38.20
East Dunseith, ND (cdp) Rolette County	474	94.80
White Earth, MN (cdp) Becker County	464	80.00
Suttons Bay, MI (township) Leelanau County	453	15.19
L'Anse, MI (township) Baraga County	448	11.66
Cass Lake, MN (city) Cass County	446	57.92
Baraga, MI (village) Baraga County	446	21.72
Grand Rapids, MI (city) Kent County	436	0.23
New Odanah, WI (cdp) Ashland County	426	90.25
Seattle, WA (city) King County	399	0.07
Chief Lake, WI (cdp) Sawyer County	391	67.07
Phoenix, AZ (city) Maricopa County	391	0.03
Green Bay, WI (city) Brown County	388	0.37
Billings, MT (city) Yellowstone County	386	0.37
Coon Rapids, MN (city) Anoka County	383	0.62
Williston, ND (city) Williams County	382	2.60
Lansing, MI (city) Ingham County	381	0.33
Mount Pleasant, MI (city) Isabella County	380	1.46
Lansing, MI (city) Ingham County	376	0.34
Grand Portage, MN (unorganized territory) Cook County	371	65.66
Moorhead, MN (city) Clay County	345	0.91
Union, MI (charter township) Isabella County	337	2.61
Anchorage, AK (municipality) Anchorage Municipality	334	0.11
Reserve, WI (cdp) Sawyer County	333	77.62
Los Angeles, CA (city) Los Angeles County	331	0.01
Detroit Lakes, MN (city) Becker County	330	3.85
Mahnomen, MN (city) Mahnomen County	327	26.94
Manistique, MI (city) Schoolcraft County	326	10.53
Pine Point, MN (cdp) Becker County	318	94.08
Pine Point, MN (township) Becker County	318	79.50
Blaine, MN (city) Anoka County	316	0.55
Tacoma, WA (city) Pierce County	306	0.15
Superior, MI (township) Chippewa County	303	22.66
Pembina, MN (township) Mahnomen County	302	42.72
Nashville, WI (town) Forest County	293	27.54
Marquette, MI (city) Marquette County	292	1.37
Bruce, MI (township) Chippewa County	288	13.53
Detroit, MI (city) Wayne County	285	0.04
Mole Lake, WI (cdp) Forest County	277	63.68
Brooklyn Park, MN (city) Hennepin County	275	0.36
St. Ignace, MI (township) Mackinac County	274	29.18
Madison, WI (city) Dane County	270	0.12
Nett Lake, MN (unorganized territory) St. Louis County	266	83.39
Devils Lake, ND (city) Ramsey County	258	3.61
Maple Grove, MN (township) Becker County	254	55.82
Birch Hill, WI (cdp) Ashland County	253	86.35
Albuquerque, NM (city) Bernalillo County	253	0.05
New York, NY (city) Kings County	252	<0.01
Perch Lake, MN (township) Carlton County	251	24.00
Hayward, WI (city) Sawyer County	245	10.57
West Allis, WI (city) Milwaukee County	244	0.40
Escanaba, MI (city) Delta County	243	1.93
Nett Lake, MN (cdp) St. Louis County	240	84.51
Ball Club, MN (cdp) Itasca County	240	70.18
Brevator, MN (township) St. Louis County	239	18.83
Clark, MI (township) Mackinac County	239	11.62
Mandan, ND (city) Morton County	239	1.30
San Diego, CA (city) San Diego County	238	0.02
Greenwood, MN (township) St. Louis County	235	25.03
Virginia, MN (city) St. Louis County	235	2.70
Flint, MI (city) Genesee County	231	0.23
Fridley, MN (city) Anoka County	230	0.85
Hunter, WI (town) Sawyer County	229	33.78
Bloomington, MN (city) Hennepin County	228	0.28
Turtle Lake, MN (township) Cass County	225	32.94
La Prairie, MN (township) Clearwater County	222	62.36
Riverland, MN (cdp) Mahnomen County	220	79.71
Moran, MI (township) Mackinac County	219	22.03
Rolette, ND (city) Rolette County	216	36.36
St. Cloud, MN (city) Stearns County	215	0.33
Bay City, MI (city) Bay County	212	0.61
Cheboygan, MI (city) Cheboygan County	210	4.31
Denver, CO (city) Denver County	208	0.03
Watersmeet, MI (township) Gogebic County	206	14.54
St. John, ND (city) Rolette County	204	59.82
Brainerd, MN (city) Crow Wing County	203	1.49
Couderay, WI (town) Sawyer County	202	50.37
Columbia Heights, MN (city) Anoka County	202	1.04
Chocolay, MI (charter township) Marquette County	199	3.37
Colorado Springs, CO (city) El Paso County	199	0.05
Tucson, AZ (city) Pima County	197	0.04
Shingobee, MN (township) Cass County	194	12.81
New Post, WI (cdp) Sawyer County	193	63.28
Bemidji, MN (township) Beltrami County	189	6.03
Northern, MN (township) Beltrami County	187	4.02
Little Elbow, MN (township) Mahnomen County	186	71.81
Zeba, MI (cdp) Baraga County	185	38.54
Eau Claire, WI (city) Eau Claire County	185	0.28
Spokane Valley, WA (city) Spokane County	184	0.21
Eau Claire, WI (city) Eau Claire County	182	0.28
San Jose, CA (city) Santa Clara County	181	0.02
Dafter, MI (township) Chippewa County	180	14.25
Kenosha, WI (city) Kenosha County	180	0.18
Westland, MI (city) Wayne County	179	0.21
Munising, MI (township) Alger County	176	5.90
Inger, MN (cdp) Itasca County	175	82.55
Manistique, MI (township) Schoolcraft County	173	15.80
Mahnomen, MN (cdp) St. Louis County	171	71.55
Waubun, MN (city) Mahnomen County	171	42.75
Sugar Island, MI (township) Chippewa County	171	26.23
Warren, MI (city) Macomb County	171	0.13
Garfield, MI (charter township) Grand Traverse County	169	1.04
Salem, OR (city) Marion County	169	0.11

Please refer to the Explanation of Data in the front of the book for more detailed information.

Race

American Indian: Chippewa

Top 150 Places Sorted by Percent of Total Population

Based on all places, regardless of total population

Place	Population	%
Odanah, WI (cdp) Ashland County	13	100.00
East Dunseith, ND (cdp) Rolette County	474	94.80
Pine Point, MN (cdp) Becker County	318	94.08
Shell Valley, ND (cdp) Rolette County	1,116	93.23
Naytahwaush, MN (cdp) Mahnomen County	522	90.31
New Odanah, WI (cdp) Ashland County	426	90.25
Belcourt, ND (cdp) Rolette County	1,864	89.70
Diaperville, WI (cdp) Ashland County	62	88.57
Green Acres, ND (cdp) Rolette County	504	87.65
Franks Field, WI (cdp) Ashland County	133	86.36
Birch Hill, WI (cdp) Ashland County	253	86.35
Ponemah, MN (cdp) Beltrami County	621	85.77
Nett Lake, MN (cdp) St. Louis County	240	84.51
Twin Lakes, MN (township) Mahnomen County	684	83.62
Nett Lake, MN (unorganized territory) St. Louis County	266	83.39
Red Lake, MN (cdp) Beltrami County	1,433	82.78
Inger, MN (cdp) Itasca County	175	82.55
White Earth, MN (cdp) Becker County	464	80.00
South End, MN (cdp) Clearwater County	20	80.00
Vineland, MN (cdp) Mille Lacs County	798	79.72
Riverland, MN (cdp) Mahnomen County	220	79.71
Pine Point, MN (township) Becker County	318	79.50
Lower Red Lake, MN (unorganized territory) Beltrami County	4,598	79.41
Little Round Lake, WI (cdp) Sawyer County	857	79.28
Sanborn, WI (town) Ashland County	1,049	78.81
The Ranch, MN (cdp) Mahnomen County	7	77.78
Reserve, WI (cdp) Sawyer County	333	77.62
North Clearwater, MN (unorganized territory) Clearwater County	66	75.86
Little Rock, MN (cdp) Beltrami County	915	75.75
Dunseith, ND (city) Rolette County	581	75.16
Redby, MN (cdp) Beltrami County	986	73.91
Lac du Flambeau, WI (cdp) Vilas County	1,418	72.02
Little Elbow, MN (township) Mahnomen County	186	71.81
Mahnomen, MN (cdp) St. Louis County	171	71.55
Nett Lake, MN (unorganized territory) Koochiching County	72	71.29
Russell, WI (town) Bayfield County	911	71.23
Ball Club, MN (cdp) Itasca County	240	70.18
Rice Lake, MN (cdp) Clearwater County	164	69.79
Bena, MN (city) Cass County	80	68.97
Twin Lakes, MN (cdp) Mahnomen County	100	67.11
Chief Lake, WI (cdp) Sawyer County	391	67.07
Grand Portage, MN (unorganized territory) Cook County	371	65.66
Pine Bend, MN (cdp) Mahnomen County	18	64.29
White Earth, MN (township) Becker County	529	63.89
Mole Lake, WI (cdp) Forest County	277	63.68
New Post, WI (cdp) Sawyer County	193	63.28
Elbow Lake, MN (cdp) Becker County	60	63.16
La Prairie, MN (township) Clearwater County	222	62.36
West Roy Lake, MN (cdp) Mahnomen County	46	62.16
Pike Bay, MN (township) Cass County	986	61.24
St. John, ND (city) Rolette County	204	59.82
Cass Lake, MN (city) Cass County	446	57.92
Ebro, MN (cdp) Clearwater County	37	57.81
Upper Red Lake, MN (unorganized territory) Beltrami County	8	57.14
Clover, MN (township) Mahnomen County	69	57.02
Kathio, MN (township) Mille Lacs County	911	55.99
Maple Grove, MN (township) Becker County	254	55.82
North Cass, MN (unorganized territory) Cass County	147	55.68
Ten Lake, MN (township) Beltrami County	546	53.22
Bowstring Lake, MN (unorganized territory) Itasca County	618	53.00
Bay Mills, MI (township) Chippewa County	749	50.71
Couderay, WI (town) Sawyer County	202	50.37
Midway, MN (cdp) Mahnomen County	13	50.00
Lac du Flambeau, WI (town) Vilas County	1,717	49.90
Gould, MN (township) Cass County	110	49.11
Eagle View, MN (township) Becker County	62	47.33
Round Lake, MN (township) Becker County	86	46.99
Ogema, MN (township) Pine County	159	45.17
Ogema, MN (city) Becker County	83	45.11
Squaw Lake, MN (city) Itasca County	47	43.93
Boy Lake, MN (township) Cass County	112	43.75
Waubun, MN (city) Mahnomen County	171	42.75
Pembina, MN (township) Mahnomen County	302	42.72
Callaway, MN (city) Becker County	98	41.88
Wilkinson, MN (township) Cass County	167	41.65
Hangaard, MN (township) Clearwater County	2	40.00
Beaulieu, MN (cdp) Mahnomen County	19	39.58
Zeba, MI (cdp) Baraga County	185	38.54
Rolla, ND (city) Rolette County	489	38.20
Oakland, MN (township) Mahnomen County	111	37.63
Rolette, ND (city) Rolette County	216	36.36
Bass Lake, WI (town) Sawyer County	839	35.30
Beaulieu, MN (township) Mahnomen County	38	35.19
Hunter, WI (town) Sawyer County	229	33.78
Falk, MN (township) Clearwater County	95	33.45
Turtle Lake, MN (township) Cass County	225	32.94
La Garde, MN (township) Mahnomen County	50	30.86
Spalding, MN (township) Aitkin County	99	30.09
Federal Dam, MN (city) Cass County	33	30.00
Sugar Bush, MN (township) Becker County	150	29.76
Hudson, MI (township) Mackinac County	53	29.28
St. Ignace, MI (township) Mackinac County	274	29.18
Big Lake, MN (cdp) Carlton County	127	28.67
St. Ignace, MI (city) Mackinac County	681	27.77
Nashville, WI (town) Forest County	293	27.54
Brook Lake, MN (unorganized territory) Beltrami County	64	27.47
Mahnomen, MN (city) Mahnomen County	327	26.94
Stoney Brook, MN (township) St. Louis County	89	26.81
Sugar Island, MI (township) Chippewa County	171	26.23
Lake Grove, MN (township) Mahnomen County	48	25.40
Greenwood, MN (township) St. Louis County	235	25.03
Roy Lake, MN (cdp) Clearwater County	3	25.00
Perch Lake, MN (township) Carlton County	251	24.00
Callaway, MN (township) Becker County	67	23.34
Superior, MI (township) Chippewa County	303	22.66
Bejou, MN (city) Mahnomen County	20	22.47
Moran, MI (township) Mackinac County	219	22.03
Max, MN (township) Itasca County	31	21.83
Watersmeet, MI (cdp) Gogebic County	93	21.73
Baraga, MI (village) Baraga County	446	21.72
Hayward, WI (town) Sawyer County	757	21.22
Soo, MI (township) Chippewa County	645	20.53
Popple Grove, MN (township) Mahnomen County	28	20.14
Freeport, KS (city) Harper County	1	20.00
Funkley, MN (city) Beltrami County	1	20.00
Sugar Bush, MN (township) Beltrami County	49	19.84
Island Lake, MN (township) Mahnomen County	46	19.74
Marsh Creek, MN (township) Mahnomen County	30	19.74
Couderay, WI (village) Sawyer County	17	19.32
Mackinac Island, MI (city) Mackinac County	95	19.31
Bayfield, WI (town) Bayfield County	130	19.12
Hendricks, MI (township) Mackinac County	29	18.95
Brevator, MN (township) St. Louis County	239	18.83
Long Lost Lake, MN (township) Clearwater County	8	18.60
Swiss, WI (town) Burnett County	146	18.48
Sault Ste. Marie, MI (city) Chippewa County	2,558	18.09
Baraga, MI (township) Baraga County	685	17.96
Ormsby, MN (city) Martin County	10	17.86
Spring Creek, MN (township) Becker County	20	17.54
Sand Lake, WI (town) Burnett County	92	17.33
La Follette, WI (town) Burnett County	92	17.16
Sand Lake, WI (town) Sawyer County	138	16.97
Johnstown, WI (town) Polk County	90	16.85
Chippewa, MI (township) Isabella County	782	16.80
Leech Lake, MN (township) Cass County	73	16.74
Chief, MN (township) Mahnomen County	16	16.67
Rice, MN (township) Clearwater County	25	15.82
Manistique, MI (township) Schoolcraft County	173	15.80
Orr, MN (city) St. Louis County	41	15.36
Suttons Bay, MI (township) Leelanau County	453	15.19
Brookston, MN (city) St. Louis County	21	14.89
Grand Island, MI (township) Alger County	7	14.89
Watersmeet, MI (township) Gogebic County	206	14.54
Leiding, MN (township) St. Louis County	58	14.50
Farden, MN (township) Hubbard County	164	14.42
Dafter, MI (township) Chippewa County	180	14.25
Isle, MN (city) Mille Lacs County	107	14.25
Barry, MN (township) Pine County	81	13.85
Garfield, MI (township) Mackinac County	158	13.79
Brevort, MI (township) Mackinac County	81	13.64

Please refer to the Explanation of Data in the front of the book for more detailed information.

Race

American Indian: Chippewa

Top 150 Places Sorted by Percent of Total Population

Based on places with total population of 7,500 or more

Place	Population	%
Sault Ste. Marie, MI (city) Chippewa County	2,558	18.09
Kinross, MI (charter township) Chippewa County	826	10.92
Cloquet, MN (city) Carlton County	1,289	10.63
Bemidji, MN (city) Beltrami County	1,166	8.68
Ashland, WI (city) Ashland County	688	8.37
Detroit Lakes, MN (city) Becker County	330	3.85
Virginia, MN (city) St. Louis County	235	2.70
Union, MI (charter township) Isabella County	337	2.61
Williston, ND (city) Williams County	382	2.60
Superior, WI (city) Douglas County	586	2.15
Duluth, MN (city) St. Louis County	1,661	1.93
Escanaba, MI (city) Delta County	243	1.93
Grand Forks, ND (city) Grand Forks County	1,008	1.91
Blair, MI (township) Grand Traverse County	143	1.74
Minot, ND (city) Ward County	698	1.71
Havre, MT (city) Hill County	151	1.62
Brainerd, MN (city) Crow Wing County	203	1.49
Mount Pleasant, MI (city) Isabella County	380	1.46
Grand Rapids, MN (city) Itasca County	157	1.44
Marquette, MI (city) Marquette County	292	1.37
Mandan, ND (city) Morton County	239	1.30
East Grand Forks, MN (city) Polk County	109	1.27
Wahpeton, ND (city) Richland County	99	1.27
Minneapolis, MN (city) Hennepin County	4,363	1.14
Traverse City, MI (city) Grand Traverse County	166	1.13
Thief River Falls, MN (city) Pennington County	97	1.13
Traverse City, MI (city) Grand Traverse County	162	1.12
Helena Valley Southeast, MT (cdp) Lewis and Clark County	86	1.05
Columbia Heights, MN (city) Anoka County	202	1.04
Garfield, MI (charter township) Grand Traverse County	169	1.04
Shawano, WI (city) Shawano County	95	1.02
Great Falls, MT (city) Cascade County	557	0.95
Moorhead, MN (city) Clay County	345	0.91
Crookston, MN (city) Polk County	68	0.86
Bismarck, ND (city) Burleigh County	523	0.85
Fridley, MN (city) Anoka County	230	0.85
Hermantown, MN (city) St. Louis County	77	0.82
Fargo, ND (city) Cass County	810	0.77
East Bay, MI (township) Grand Traverse County	79	0.74
Hibbing, MN (city) St. Louis County	115	0.70
Jamestown, ND (city) Stutsman County	99	0.64
Coon Rapids, MN (city) Anoka County	383	0.62
Long Lake, MI (township) Grand Traverse County	54	0.62
Bay City, MI (city) Bay County	212	0.61
West Fargo, ND (city) Cass County	149	0.58
Anoka, MN (city) Anoka County	100	0.58
Little Falls, MN (city) Morrison County	48	0.58
Mounds View, MN (city) Ramsey County	69	0.57
St. Paul, MN (city) Ramsey County	1,584	0.56
Blaine, MN (city) Anoka County	316	0.55
Rice Lake, WI (city) Barron County	46	0.55
Helena, MT (city) Lewis and Clark County	152	0.54
Rhinelander, WI (city) Oneida County	42	0.54
North St. Paul, MN (city) Ramsey County	61	0.53
Alpena, MI (township) Alpena County	45	0.50
Fergus Falls, MN (city) Otter Tail County	64	0.49
Crystal, MN (city) Hennepin County	107	0.48
New Hope, MN (city) Hennepin County	97	0.48
Bridgeport, MI (charter township) Saginaw County	50	0.48
Little Canada, MN (city) Ramsey County	47	0.48
Hazel Park, MI (city) Oakland County	77	0.47
St. Anthony, MN (city) Hennepin and Ramsey Counties	39	0.47
Richfield, MN (city) Hennepin County	158	0.45
Brooklyn Center, MN (city) Hennepin County	136	0.45
Lapeer, MI (city) Lapeer County	40	0.45
St. Johns, MI (city) Clinton County	35	0.45
Ramsey, MN (city) Anoka County	103	0.44
Vadnais Heights, MN (city) Ramsey County	53	0.43
Vienna, MI (charter township) Genesee County	56	0.42
Hampton, MI (charter township) Bay County	41	0.42
Ludington, MI (city) Mason County	34	0.42
Aberdeen, SD (city) Brown County	106	0.41
South St. Paul, MN (city) Dakota County	82	0.41
Hopkins, MN (city) Hennepin County	73	0.41
Buffalo, MN (city) Wright County	63	0.41
Robbinsdale, MN (city) Hennepin County	57	0.41
Mason, MI (city) Ingham County	34	0.41
West Allis, WI (city) Milwaukee County	244	0.40
Roseville, MN (city) Ramsey County	134	0.40
Champlin, MN (city) Hennepin County	93	0.40
East Bethel, MN (city) Anoka County	47	0.40
Egelston, MI (township) Muskegon County	40	0.40
Buena Vista, MI (charter township) Saginaw County	35	0.40
Andover, MN (city) Anoka County	119	0.39
Prior Lake, MN (city) Scott County	90	0.39
New Brighton, MN (city) Ramsey County	83	0.39
Evergreen, MT (cdp) Flathead County	30	0.39
Iron Mountain, MI (city) Dickinson County	30	0.39
Cudahy, WI (city) Milwaukee County	69	0.38
Port Huron, MI (charter township) St. Clair County	41	0.38
Marion, MI (township) Livingston County	38	0.38
Anaconda-Deer Lodge County, MT (special city) Deer Lodge County	35	0.38
Cambridge, MN (city) Isanti County	31	0.38
Green Bay, WI (city) Brown County	388	0.37
Billings, MT (city) Yellowstone County	386	0.37
Burton, MI (city) Genesee County	111	0.37
DeWitt, MI (charter township) Clinton County	53	0.37
Fenton, MI (city) Genesee County	43	0.37
Fenton, MI (city) Genesee County	43	0.37
Wyoming, MN (city) Chisago County	29	0.37
Brooklyn Park, MN (city) Hennepin County	275	0.36
Tyrone, MI (township) Livingston County	36	0.36
St. Francis, WI (city) Milwaukee County	34	0.36
Sitka, AK (borough) Sitka City and Borough	32	0.36
West St. Paul, MN (city) Dakota County	68	0.35
Otsego, MN (city) Wright County	48	0.35
Lansing, MI (city) Ingham County	376	0.34
Butte-Silver Bow, MT (cons. govt) Silver Bow County	113	0.34
Elk River, MN (city) Sherburne County	78	0.34
South Milwaukee, WI (city) Milwaukee County	71	0.34
Golden Valley, MN (city) Hennepin County	69	0.34
Ashwaubenon, WI (village) Brown County	58	0.34
Chippewa Falls, WI (city) Chippewa County	46	0.34
Pierre, SD (city) Hughes County	46	0.34
Flushing, MI (charter township) Genesee County	36	0.34
Waseca, MN (city) Waseca County	32	0.34
Menominee, MI (city) Menominee County	29	0.34
Antigo, WI (city) Langlade County	28	0.34
Lansing, MI (city) Ingham County	381	0.33
St. Cloud, MN (city) Stearns County	215	0.33
Inver Grove Heights, MN (city) Dakota County	113	0.33
Red Wing, MN (city) Goodhue County	55	0.33
Bangor, MI (charter township) Bay County	48	0.33
Tittabawassee, MI (township) Saginaw County	32	0.33
Alma, MI (city) Gratiot County	31	0.33
Richfield, MI (township) Genesee County	29	0.33
Port Huron, MI (city) St. Clair County	98	0.32
Hastings, MN (city) Dakota County	72	0.32
Monticello, MN (city) Wright County	41	0.32
Monitor, MI (charter township) Bay County	34	0.32
Cadillac, MI (city) Wexford County	33	0.32
Big Lake, MN (city) Sherburne County	32	0.32
Dalton, MI (township) Muskegon County	30	0.32
Miles City, MT (city) Custer County	27	0.32
Handy, MI (township) Livingston County	26	0.32
Grand Ledge, MI (city) Eaton County	25	0.32
Grand Ledge, MI (city) Eaton County	25	0.32
Helena Valley West Central, MT (cdp) Lewis and Clark County	25	0.32
Genesee, MI (charter township) Genesee County	67	0.31
Mount Morris, MI (township) Genesee County	66	0.31
Davison, MI (township) Genesee County	60	0.31
Brandon, MI (charter township) Oakland County	47	0.31
Cutlerville, MI (cdp) Kent County	45	0.31
Alexandria, MN (city) Douglas County	34	0.31
Grand Haven, MI (city) Ottawa County	32	0.31
Houghton, MI (city) Houghton County	24	0.31
St. Louis Park, MN (city) Hennepin County	134	0.30
Savage, MN (city) Scott County	82	0.30
White Bear Lake, MN (city) Ramsey County	71	0.30
White Bear Lake, MN (city) Ramsey County	71	0.30

Please refer to the Explanation of Data in the front of the book for more detailed information.

Race

American Indian: Choctaw

U.S. and 50 States Sorted by Population and Percent of Total Population

Place	Population	%
United States	**195,764**	**0.06**
Oklahoma	79,006	2.11
Texas	24,024	0.10
California	23,403	0.06
Mississippi	9,260	0.31
Arkansas	4,840	0.17
Alabama	4,513	0.09
Washington	3,886	0.06
Louisiana	3,736	0.08
Oregon	3,637	0.09
Arizona	3,516	0.06
Florida	2,829	0.02
Missouri	2,793	0.05
Colorado	2,659	0.05
Kansas	2,604	0.09
Illinois	1,934	0.02
New Mexico	1,679	0.08
Tennessee	1,659	0.03
Nevada	1,469	0.05
Michigan	1,463	0.01
Georgia	1,419	0.01
Virginia	1,386	0.02
Ohio	1,194	0.01
North Carolina	1,130	0.01
New York	1,052	0.01
Indiana	852	0.01
Hawaii	842	0.06
Idaho	841	0.05
Pennsylvania	787	0.01
Alaska	778	0.11
Maryland	701	0.01
Utah	603	0.02
Minnesota	587	0.01
Wisconsin	548	0.01
Kentucky	487	0.01
South Carolina	481	0.01
Massachusetts	412	0.01
New Jersey	363	<0.01
Nebraska	351	0.02
Iowa	349	0.01
Montana	303	0.03
Wyoming	277	0.05
Connecticut	245	0.01
South Dakota	151	0.02
New Hampshire	128	0.01
West Virginia	120	0.01
District of Columbia	105	0.02
Maine	102	0.01
North Dakota	89	0.01
Delaware	63	0.01
Vermont	58	0.01
Rhode Island	50	<0.01

Place	Population	%
Oklahoma	79,006	2.11
Mississippi	9,260	0.31
Arkansas	4,840	0.17
Alaska	778	0.11
Texas	24,024	0.10
Alabama	4,513	0.09
Oregon	3,637	0.09
Kansas	2,604	0.09
Louisiana	3,736	0.08
New Mexico	1,679	0.08
United States	**195,764**	**0.06**
California	23,403	0.06
Washington	3,886	0.06
Arizona	3,516	0.06
Hawaii	842	0.06
Missouri	2,793	0.05
Colorado	2,659	0.05
Nevada	1,469	0.05
Idaho	841	0.05
Wyoming	277	0.05
Tennessee	1,659	0.03
Montana	303	0.03
Florida	2,829	0.02
Illinois	1,934	0.02
Virginia	1,386	0.02
Utah	603	0.02
Nebraska	351	0.02
South Dakota	151	0.02
District of Columbia	105	0.02
Michigan	1,463	0.01
Georgia	1,419	0.01
Ohio	1,194	0.01
North Carolina	1,130	0.01
New York	1,052	0.01
Indiana	852	0.01
Pennsylvania	787	0.01
Maryland	701	0.01
Minnesota	587	0.01
Wisconsin	548	0.01
Kentucky	487	0.01
South Carolina	481	0.01
Massachusetts	412	0.01
Iowa	349	0.01
Connecticut	245	0.01
New Hampshire	128	0.01
West Virginia	120	0.01
Maine	102	0.01
North Dakota	89	0.01
Delaware	63	0.01
Vermont	58	0.01
New Jersey	363	<0.01
Rhode Island	50	<0.01

Please refer to the Explanation of Data in the front of the book for more detailed information.

Race

American Indian: Choctaw

Top 150 Places Sorted by Population

Based on all places, regardless of total population

Place	Population	%
Oklahoma City, OK (city) Oklahoma County	6,527	1.13
Tulsa, OK (city) Tulsa County	3,043	0.78
Pearl River, MS (cdp) Neshoba County	2,719	75.51
Durant, OK (city) Bryan County	1,961	12.37
McAlester, OK (city) Pittsburg County	1,853	10.08
Norman, OK (city) Cleveland County	1,807	1.63
Ardmore, OK (city) Carter County	1,330	5.48
Los Angeles, CA (city) Los Angeles County	1,133	0.03
Moore, OK (city) Cleveland County	1,057	1.92
Ada, OK (city) Pontotoc County	1,053	6.26
Dallas, TX (city) Dallas County	1,030	0.09
Conehatta, MS (cdp) Newton County	845	62.97
Poteau, OK (city) Le Flore County	811	9.52
Broken Arrow, OK (city) Tulsa County	804	0.81
Idabel, OK (city) McCurtain County	767	10.94
Broken Bow, OK (city) McCurtain County	757	18.37
Bogue Chitto, MS (cdp) Kemper and Neshoba Counties	755	85.12
Edmond, OK (city) Oklahoma County	723	0.89
Fort Worth, TX (city) Tarrant County	717	0.10
Hugo, OK (city) Choctaw County	715	13.47
Muskogee, OK (city) Muskogee County	714	1.82
Houston, TX (city) Harris County	697	0.03
Midwest City, OK (city) Oklahoma County	695	1.28
Phoenix, AZ (city) Maricopa County	682	0.05
Duncan, OK (city) Stephens County	615	2.62
Austin, TX (city) Travis County	559	0.07
Lawton, OK (city) Comanche County	544	0.56
Shawnee, OK (city) Pottawatomie County	537	1.80
Fort Smith, AR (city) Sebastian County	535	0.62
San Antonio, TX (city) Medina County	514	0.04
Chicago, IL (city) Cook County	513	0.02
Wichita, KS (city) Sedgwick County	488	0.13
San Diego, CA (city) San Diego County	487	0.04
Tucker, MS (cdp) Neshoba County	469	70.85
Bakersfield, CA (city) Kern County	467	0.13
Arlington, TX (city) Tarrant County	462	0.13
Albuquerque, NM (city) Bernalillo County	442	0.08
Talihina, OK (town) Le Flore County	437	39.23
Redwater, MS (cdp) Leake County	429	67.77
Sacramento, CA (city) Sacramento County	426	0.09
Wilburton, OK (city) Latimer County	417	14.67
Stillwater, OK (city) Payne County	413	0.90
Fresno, CA (city) Fresno County	411	0.08
Hartshorne, OK (city) Pittsburg County	405	19.06
New York, NY (city) Kings County	405	<0.01
Atoka, OK (city) Atoka County	403	12.97
Portland, OR (city) Multnomah County	401	0.07
Standing Pine, MS (cdp) Leake County	395	78.37
Modesto, CA (city) Stanislaus County	385	0.19
San Jose, CA (city) Santa Clara County	371	0.04
Antlers, OK (city) Pushmataha County	351	14.31
Calera, OK (town) Bryan County	341	15.76
Anchorage, AK (municipality) Anchorage Municipality	341	0.12
Chickasha, OK (city) Grady County	332	2.07
Amarillo, TX (city) Potter County	327	0.17
Plano, TX (city) Collin County	326	0.13
Kansas City, MO (city) Jackson County	325	0.07
Lone Grove, OK (city) Carter County	324	6.41
Wright City, OK (town) McCurtain County	319	41.86
San Francisco, CA (city) San Francisco County	318	0.04
Del City, OK (city) Oklahoma County	313	1.47
Sherman, TX (city) Grayson County	313	0.81
Mustang, OK (city) Canadian County	310	1.78
Coalgate, OK (city) Coal County	307	15.61
Garland, TX (city) Dallas County	293	0.13
Heavener, OK (city) Le Flore County	290	8.49
Seattle, WA (city) King County	287	0.05
Wichita Falls, TX (city) Wichita County	283	0.27
Oakland, CA (city) Alameda County	282	0.07
Yukon, OK (city) Canadian County	279	1.23
Sand Springs, OK (city) Tulsa County	277	1.47
Colorado Springs, CO (city) El Paso County	277	0.07
Stockton, CA (city) San Joaquin County	276	0.09
Stigler, OK (city) Haskell County	275	10.24
Paris, TX (city) Lamar County	275	1.09
Denver, CO (city) Denver County	275	0.05
Denison, TX (city) Grayson County	271	1.19
Sulphur, OK (city) Murray County	270	5.48
Tahlequah, OK (city) Cherokee County	261	1.66
Lubbock, TX (city) Lubbock County	261	0.11
Irving, TX (city) Dallas County	258	0.12
Owasso, OK (city) Tulsa County	254	0.88
Krebs, OK (city) Pittsburg County	251	12.23
Mesquite, TX (city) Dallas County	249	0.18
Tucson, AZ (city) Pima County	246	0.05
Las Vegas, NV (city) Clark County	241	0.04
Long Beach, CA (city) Los Angeles County	240	0.05
McKinney, TX (city) Collin County	238	0.18
Choctaw, OK (city) Oklahoma County	228	2.05
Pauls Valley, OK (city) Garvin County	227	3.67
Pocola, OK (town) Le Flore County	224	5.52
Claremore, OK (city) Rogers County	222	1.19
Enid, OK (city) Garfield County	222	0.45
Lawrence, KS (city) Douglas County	217	0.25
Grand Prairie, TX (city) Dallas County	215	0.12
Mesa, AZ (city) Maricopa County	214	0.05
Sapulpa, OK (city) Creek County	212	1.03
Bixby, OK (city) Tulsa County	206	0.99
Memphis, TN (city) Shelby County	205	0.03
Newcastle, OK (city) McClain County	202	2.63
Bethany, OK (city) Oklahoma County	200	1.05
Frisco, TX (city) Collin County	199	0.17
Okmulgee, OK (city) Okmulgee County	196	1.59
Caddo, OK (town) Bryan County	193	19.36
Denton, TX (city) Denton County	193	0.17
Detroit, MI (city) Wayne County	193	0.03
Bartlesville, OK (city) Washington County	190	0.53
Corpus Christi, TX (city) Nueces County	190	0.06
Marlow, OK (city) Stephens County	188	4.03
Blanchard, OK (city) McClain County	188	2.45
Aurora, CO (city) Arapahoe County	188	0.06
Eugene, OR (city) Lane County	187	0.12
Purcell, OK (city) McClain County	184	3.13
Glenpool, OK (city) Tulsa County	182	1.68
Riverside, CA (city) Riverside County	182	0.06
Panama, OK (town) Le Flore County	179	12.67
Manhattan, NY (borough) New York County	179	0.01
Jacksonville, FL (city) Duval County	178	0.02
Redding, CA (city) Shasta County	175	0.19
Noble, OK (city) Cleveland County	174	2.68
Ponca City, OK (city) Kay County	174	0.69
Wister, OK (town) Le Flore County	170	15.43
Visalia, CA (city) Tulare County	168	0.14
Spiro, OK (town) Le Flore County	167	7.72
Tishomingo, OK (city) Johnston County	165	5.44
Henderson, NV (city) Clark County	164	0.06
Seminole, OK (city) Seminole County	163	2.18
Jenks, OK (city) Tulsa County	162	0.96
New Orleans, LA (city) Orleans Parish	161	0.05
Allen, TX (city) Collin County	160	0.19
Philadelphia, MS (city) Neshoba County	157	2.10
Spokane, WA (city) Spokane County	156	0.07
Quinton, OK (town) Pittsburg County	155	14.75
San Buenaventura (Ventura), CA (city) Ventura County	155	0.15
Nashville-Davidson, TN (metro govt) Davidson County	155	0.03
Tacoma, WA (city) Pierce County	154	0.08
Fayetteville, AR (city) Washington County	152	0.21
Haileyville, OK (city) Pittsburg County	151	18.57
Clovis, CA (city) Fresno County	150	0.16
Sallisaw, OK (city) Sequoyah County	148	1.67
Kansas City, KS (city) Wyandotte County	148	0.10
San Bernardino, CA (city) San Bernardino County	146	0.07
Glendale, AZ (city) Maricopa County	146	0.06
Oildale, CA (cdp) Kern County	145	0.44
El Reno, OK (city) Canadian County	144	0.86
Santa Rosa, CA (city) Sonoma County	143	0.09
Mobile, AL (city) Mobile County	142	0.07
Coweta, OK (city) Wagoner County	140	1.41
Tecumseh, OK (city) Pottawatomie County	139	2.15
Killeen, TX (city) Bell County	139	0.11

Race

American Indian: Choctaw

Top 150 Places Sorted by Percent of Total Population

Based on all places, regardless of total population

Place	Population	%
Bogue Chitto, MS (cdp) Kemper and Neshoba Counties	755	85.12
Standing Pine, MS (cdp) Leake County	395	78.37
Pearl River, MS (cdp) Neshoba County	2,719	75.51
Tucker, MS (cdp) Neshoba County	469	70.85
Redwater, MS (cdp) Leake County	429	67.77
Conehatta, MS (cdp) Newton County	845	62.97
Wright City, OK (town) McCurtain County	319	41.86
Talihina, OK (town) Le Flore County	437	39.23
Albion, OK (town) Pushmataha County	37	34.91
Le Flore, OK (town) Le Flore County	59	31.05
Tuskahoma, OK (cdp) Pushmataha County	40	26.49
Ashland, OK (town) Pittsburg County	17	25.76
Smithville, OK (town) McCurtain County	29	25.66
Phillips, OK (town) Coal County	33	24.44
Red Oak, OK (town) Latimer County	133	24.23
Bennington, OK (town) Bryan County	80	23.95
Sims Chapel, AL (cdp) Washington County	36	23.53
Soper, OK (town) Choctaw County	54	20.69
Whitesboro, OK (cdp) Le Flore County	51	20.40
Caddo, OK (town) Bryan County	193	19.36
Fairford, AL (cdp) Washington County	36	19.35
Tupelo, OK (city) Coal County	63	19.15
Hartshorne, OK (city) Pittsburg County	405	19.06
McCurtain, OK (town) Haskell County	98	18.99
Tushka, OK (town) Atoka County	58	18.59
Haileyville, OK (city) Pittsburg County	151	18.57
Broken Bow, OK (city) McCurtain County	757	18.37
Pittsburg, OK (town) Pittsburg County	38	18.36
Rattan, OK (town) Pushmataha County	56	18.06
Lane, OK (cdp) Atoka County	74	17.87
Millerton, OK (town) McCurtain County	56	17.50
Boswell, OK (town) Choctaw County	118	16.64
Bokoshe, OK (town) Le Flore County	85	16.60
String, OK (town) Atoka County	65	15.85
Kenefic, OK (town) Bryan County	31	15.82
Calera, OK (town) Bryan County	341	15.76
Silo, OK (town) Bryan County	52	15.71
Achille, OK (town) Bryan County	77	15.65
Coalgate, OK (city) Coal County	307	15.61
Cameron, OK (town) Le Flore County	47	15.56
Fanshawe, OK (town) Le Flore County	65	15.51
Alderson, OK (town) Pittsburg County	47	15.46
Wister, OK (town) Le Flore County	170	15.43
Clayton, OK (town) Pushmataha County	126	15.35
Sawyer, OK (town) Choctaw County	49	15.26
Armstrong, OK (town) Bryan County	16	15.24
Caney, OK (town) Atoka County	31	15.12
Elfin Cove, AK (cdp) Hoonah-Angoon Census Area	3	15.00
Quinton, OK (town) Pittsburg County	155	14.75
Keota, OK (town) Haskell County	83	14.72
Wilburton, OK (city) Latimer County	417	14.67
Blue, OK (cdp) Bryan County	28	14.36
Antlers, OK (city) Pushmataha County	351	14.31
Kemp, OK (town) Bryan County	18	13.53
Lehigh, OK (city) Coal County	48	13.48
Hugo, OK (city) Choctaw County	715	13.47
Atoka, OK (city) Atoka County	403	12.97
Savanna, OK (town) Pittsburg County	89	12.97
Panama, OK (town) Le Flore County	179	12.67
Hendrix, OK (town) Bryan County	10	12.66
Valliant, OK (town) McCurtain County	95	12.60
Durant, OK (city) Bryan County	1,961	12.37
Krebs, OK (city) Pittsburg County	251	12.23
Haworth, OK (town) McCurtain County	35	11.78
Kiowa, OK (town) Pittsburg County	86	11.76
Arpelar, OK (cdp) Pittsburg County	32	11.76
Bokchito, OK (town) Bryan County	73	11.55
Grant, OK (cdp) Choctaw County	33	11.42
Idabel, OK (city) McCurtain County	767	10.94
Stigler, OK (city) Haskell County	275	10.24
McAlester, OK (city) Pittsburg County	1,853	10.08
Stuart, OK (town) Hughes County	18	10.00
Hickory, OK (town) Murray County	7	9.86
Bromide, OK (town) Johnston County	16	9.70
Poteau, OK (city) Le Flore County	811	9.52

Place	Population	%
Sugden, OK (town) Jefferson County	4	9.30
Bradley, OK (town) Grady County	12	9.23
Gene Autry, OK (town) Carter County	14	8.86
Fort Towson, OK (town) Choctaw County	45	8.67
Stonewall, OK (town) Pontotoc County	40	8.51
Heavener, OK (city) Le Flore County	290	8.49
Texola, OK (town) Beckham County	3	8.33
Byars, OK (town) McClain County	21	8.24
Wapanucka, OK (town) Johnston County	36	8.22
Mead, OK (town) Bryan County	10	8.20
Whitefield, OK (town) Haskell County	32	8.18
Howe, OK (town) Le Flore County	63	7.86
Spiro, OK (town) Le Flore County	167	7.72
Cartwright, OK (cdp) Bryan County	47	7.72
Gerty, OK (town) Hughes County	9	7.63
Shady Point, OK (town) Le Flore County	78	7.60
Smith Village, OK (town) Oklahoma County	5	7.58
Tibbie, AL (cdp) Washington County	3	7.32
Allen, OK (town) Pontotoc County	68	7.30
Hanna, OK (town) McIntosh County	10	7.25
Eagletown, OK (cdp) McCurtain County	38	7.20
Bee, OK (cdp) Johnston County	10	7.14
Kinta, OK (town) Haskell County	21	7.07
Byng, OK (town) Pontotoc County	83	7.06
Duchess Landing, OK (cdp) McIntosh County	8	7.02
Rock Island, OK (town) Le Flore County	45	6.97
Athol, KS (city) Smith County	3	6.82
Lone Grove, OK (city) Carter County	324	6.41
Vining, MN (city) Otter Tail County	5	6.41
Stratford, OK (town) Garvin County	97	6.36
Albany, OK (cdp) Bryan County	9	6.29
Ada, OK (city) Pontotoc County	1,053	6.26
Tamaha, OK (town) Haskell County	11	6.25
Osgood, MO (village) Sullivan County	3	6.25
Colbert, OK (town) Bryan County	71	6.23
Centrahoma, OK (city) Coal County	6	6.19
Cornish, OK (town) Jefferson County	10	6.13
Rush Springs, OK (town) Grady County	75	6.09
Foss, OK (town) Washita County	9	5.96
Lebanon, OK (cdp) Marshall County	18	5.94
Vera, OK (town) Washington County	14	5.81
Cowlington, OK (town) Le Flore County	9	5.81
Erin Springs, OK (town) Garvin County	5	5.75
Francis, OK (town) Pontotoc County	18	5.71
Oakland, OK (town) Marshall County	60	5.68
Mannsville, OK (town) Johnston County	49	5.68
Hitchita, OK (town) McIntosh County	5	5.68
Fort Coffee, OK (town) Le Flore County	24	5.66
Grayson, OK (town) Okmulgee County	9	5.66
Mill Creek, OK (town) Johnston County	18	5.64
Foster, OK (town) Garvin County	9	5.59
Gulfcrest, AL (cdp) Mobile County	9	5.59
Crowder, OK (town) Pittsburg County	24	5.58
Township 158-30, MN (township) Lake of the Woods County	2	5.56
Pocola, OK (town) Le Flore County	224	5.52
Kingston, OK (town) Marshall County	88	5.50
Ardmore, OK (city) Carter County	1,330	5.48
Sulphur, OK (city) Murray County	270	5.48
Tishomingo, OK (city) Johnston County	165	5.44
Asher, OK (town) Pottawatomie County	21	5.34
Klukwan, AK (cdp) Hoonah-Angoon Census Area	5	5.26
Mentone, TX (cdp) Loving County	1	5.26
Pocasset, OK (town) Grady County	8	5.13
Amagon, AR (town) Jackson County	5	5.10
Indianola, OK (town) Pittsburg County	8	4.94
Dickson, OK (town) Carter County	59	4.89
Paoli, OK (town) Garvin County	29	4.75
Milburn, OK (town) Johnston County	15	4.73
Rentiesville, OK (town) McIntosh County	6	4.69
Swink, OK (cdp) Choctaw County	3	4.55
Ringling, OK (town) Jefferson County	47	4.53
Maysville, OK (town) Garvin County	55	4.46
Springer, OK (town) Carter County	31	4.43
Davis, OK (city) Murray County	117	4.36
Velma, OK (town) Stephens County	27	4.35

Please refer to the Explanation of Data in the front of the book for more detailed information.

Race

American Indian: Choctaw

Top 150 Places Sorted by Percent of Total Population

Based on places with total population of 7,500 or more

Place	Population	%
Durant, OK (city) Bryan County	1,961	12.37
McAlester, OK (city) Pittsburg County	1,853	10.08
Poteau, OK (city) Le Flore County	811	9.52
Ada, OK (city) Pontotoc County	1,053	6.26
Ardmore, OK (city) Carter County	1,330	5.48
Newcastle, OK (city) McClain County	202	2.63
Duncan, OK (city) Stephens County	615	2.62
Blanchard, OK (city) McClain County	188	2.45
Chickasha, OK (city) Grady County	332	2.07
Choctaw, OK (city) Oklahoma County	228	2.05
Moore, OK (city) Cleveland County	1,057	1.92
Muskogee, OK (city) Muskogee County	714	1.82
Shawnee, OK (city) Pottawatomie County	537	1.80
Mustang, OK (city) Canadian County	310	1.78
Glenpool, OK (city) Tulsa County	182	1.68
Sallisaw, OK (city) Sequoyah County	148	1.67
Tahlequah, OK (city) Cherokee County	261	1.66
Norman, OK (city) Cleveland County	1,807	1.63
Okmulgee, OK (city) Okmulgee County	196	1.59
Del City, OK (city) Oklahoma County	313	1.47
Sand Springs, OK (city) Tulsa County	277	1.47
Coweta, OK (city) Wagoner County	140	1.41
Wagoner, OK (city) Wagoner County	114	1.37
Midwest City, OK (city) Oklahoma County	695	1.28
Yukon, OK (city) Canadian County	279	1.23
Denison, TX (city) Grayson County	271	1.19
Claremore, OK (city) Rogers County	222	1.19
Cushing, OK (city) Payne County	91	1.16
Oklahoma City, OK (city) Oklahoma County	6,527	1.13
Paris, TX (city) Lamar County	275	1.09
Bethany, OK (city) Oklahoma County	200	1.05
Sapulpa, OK (city) Creek County	212	1.03
Elk City, OK (city) Beckham County	117	1.00
The Village, OK (city) Oklahoma County	89	1.00
Bixby, OK (city) Tulsa County	206	0.99
Jenks, OK (city) Tulsa County	162	0.96
Guthrie, OK (city) Logan County	97	0.95
Stillwater, OK (city) Payne County	413	0.90
Edmond, OK (city) Oklahoma County	723	0.89
Warr Acres, OK (city) Oklahoma County	89	0.89
Owasso, OK (city) Tulsa County	254	0.88
El Reno, OK (city) Canadian County	144	0.86
Pryor Creek, OK (city) Mayes County	81	0.85
Weatherford, OK (city) Custer County	90	0.83
Broken Arrow, OK (city) Tulsa County	804	0.81
Sherman, TX (city) Grayson County	313	0.81
Greenwood, AR (city) Sebastian County	71	0.79
Tulsa, OK (city) Tulsa County	3,043	0.78
Ponca City, OK (city) Kay County	174	0.69
Fort Smith, AR (city) Sebastian County	535	0.62
Borger, TX (city) Hutchinson County	82	0.62
Vernon, TX (city) Wilbarger County	68	0.62
Clinton, OK (city) Custer County	52	0.58
Van Buren, AR (city) Crawford County	131	0.57
Lawton, OK (city) Comanche County	544	0.56
Miami, OK (city) Ottawa County	74	0.55
Bartlesville, OK (city) Washington County	190	0.53
Saraland, AL (city) Mobile County	70	0.52
Burkburnett, TX (city) Wichita County	54	0.50
Woodward, OK (city) Woodward County	58	0.48
Enid, OK (city) Garfield County	222	0.45
Altus, OK (city) Jackson County	89	0.45
Oildale, CA (cdp) Kern County	145	0.44
Olivehurst, CA (cdp) Yuba County	60	0.44
Bonham, TX (city) Fannin County	40	0.39
Anderson, CA (city) Shasta County	37	0.37
Marysville, CA (city) Yuba County	44	0.36
Siloam Springs, AR (city) Benton County	52	0.35
Sachse, TX (city) Dallas County	66	0.32
Centerton, AR (city) Benton County	30	0.32
Midland, WA (cdp) Pierce County	29	0.32
The Colony, TX (city) Denton County	113	0.31
Clearlake, CA (city) Lake County	47	0.31
Gautier, MS (city) Jackson County	56	0.30
Rosedale, CA (cdp) Kern County	42	0.30
Anna, TX (city) Collin County	25	0.30
Sweet Home, OR (city) Linn County	26	0.29
Green, OR (cdp) Douglas County	22	0.29
Sulphur Springs, TX (city) Hopkins County	44	0.28
Crowley, TX (city) Tarrant County	36	0.28
Coffeyville, KS (city) Montgomery County	29	0.28
Kalifornsky, AK (cdp) Kenai Peninsula Borough	22	0.28
Wichita Falls, TX (city) Wichita County	283	0.27
Bentonville, AR (city) Benton County	96	0.27
Fortuna, CA (city) Humboldt County	32	0.27
Lacombe, LA (cdp) St. Tammany Parish	23	0.27
Pampa, TX (city) Gray County	46	0.26
Gainesville, TX (city) Cooke County	42	0.26
Lebanon, OR (city) Linn County	41	0.26
Knik-Fairview, AK (cdp) Matanuska-Susitna Borough	39	0.26
Hawaiian Paradise Park, HI (cdp) Hawaii County	30	0.26
Lawrence, KS (city) Douglas County	217	0.25
Corinth, TX (city) Denton County	49	0.25
Rendon, TX (cdp) Tarrant County	32	0.25
Spring Creek, NV (cdp) Elko County	31	0.25
Camp Verde, AZ (town) Yavapai County	27	0.25
Wylie, TX (city) Collin County	101	0.24
Rockwall, TX (city) Rockwall County	89	0.24
Shasta Lake, CA (city) Shasta County	24	0.24
Cloverdale, CA (city) Sonoma County	21	0.24
Kirtland, NM (cdp) San Juan County	19	0.24
Richland Hills, TX (city) Tarrant County	19	0.24
Greenville, TX (city) Hunt County	58	0.23
Balch Springs, TX (city) Dallas County	55	0.23
Bayou Blue, LA (cdp) Lafourche Parish	28	0.23
Parsons, KS (city) Labette County	24	0.23
Placerville, CA (city) El Dorado County	24	0.23
Little Elm, TX (city) Denton County	56	0.22
Long Beach, MS (city) Harrison County	32	0.22
Canyon, TX (city) Randall County	29	0.22
Kilgore, TX (city) Gregg County	28	0.22
Diamond Springs, CA (cdp) El Dorado County	24	0.22
Augusta, KS (city) Butler County	20	0.22
Westwego, LA (city) Jefferson Parish	19	0.22
Bloomfield, NM (city) San Juan County	18	0.22
Oroville East, CA (cdp) Butte County	18	0.22
Fayetteville, AR (city) Washington County	152	0.21
Texarkana, AR (city) Miller County	62	0.21
Ridgecrest, CA (city) Kern County	59	0.21
Paradise, CA (town) Butte County	55	0.21
Weatherford, TX (city) Parker County	53	0.21
Mount Pleasant, TX (city) Titus County	32	0.21
Forney, TX (city) Kaufman County	31	0.21
Petal, MS (city) Forrest County	22	0.21
Royse City, TX (city) Rockwall County	20	0.21
Winslow, AZ (city) Navajo County	20	0.21
Golden Hills, CA (cdp) Kern County	18	0.21
Rowlett, TX (city) Dallas County	115	0.20
Hurst, TX (city) Tarrant County	74	0.20
Orcutt, CA (cdp) Santa Barbara County	57	0.20
Lemoore, CA (city) Kings County	48	0.20
Galt, CA (city) Sacramento County	47	0.20
Parkway, CA (cdp) Sacramento County	29	0.20
Glenn Heights, TX (city) Dallas County	23	0.20
Crestline, CA (cdp) San Bernardino County	22	0.20
Farmersville, CA (city) Tulare County	21	0.20
Fort Polk South, LA (cdp) Vernon Parish	18	0.20
Bridge City, TX (city) Orange County	16	0.20
Commerce, TX (city) Hunt County	16	0.20
Ruidoso, NM (village) Lincoln County	16	0.20
Wellington, KS (city) Sumner County	16	0.20
Corning, CA (city) Tehama County	15	0.20
Modesto, CA (city) Stanislaus County	385	0.19
Redding, CA (city) Shasta County	175	0.19
Allen, TX (city) Collin County	160	0.19
Eureka, CA (city) Humboldt County	51	0.19
Benbrook, TX (city) Tarrant County	40	0.19
Saginaw, TX (city) Tarrant County	38	0.19
White Settlement, TX (city) Tarrant County	31	0.19
Dumas, TX (city) Moore County	28	0.19

SECTION THREE

Race

American Indian: Colville

U.S. and 50 States Sorted by Population and Percent of Total Population

Place	Population	%
United States	**10,549**	**<0.01**
Washington	8,645	0.13
California	368	<0.01
Oregon	328	0.01
Idaho	263	0.02
Montana	122	0.01
Arizona	98	<0.01
Oklahoma	89	<0.01
Texas	76	<0.01
Alaska	50	0.01
Colorado	42	<0.01
Nevada	36	<0.01
New Mexico	36	<0.01
Georgia	26	<0.01
North Carolina	24	<0.01
New York	22	<0.01
Missouri	20	<0.01
Virginia	20	<0.01
Florida	19	<0.01
Alabama	18	<0.01
Kansas	17	<0.01
Wisconsin	17	<0.01
Illinois	16	<0.01
Minnesota	16	<0.01
Utah	16	<0.01
Arkansas	15	<0.01
Michigan	15	<0.01
Pennsylvania	15	<0.01
Hawaii	14	<0.01
Indiana	14	<0.01
Ohio	11	<0.01
South Dakota	8	<0.01
Tennessee	8	<0.01
Kentucky	7	<0.01
Maryland	7	<0.01
Iowa	6	<0.01
Mississippi	6	<0.01
Nebraska	6	<0.01
Connecticut	5	<0.01
Louisiana	5	<0.01
District of Columbia	4	<0.01
Massachusetts	4	<0.01
Wyoming	4	<0.01
North Dakota	3	<0.01
New Hampshire	2	<0.01
South Carolina	2	<0.01
Maine	1	<0.01
New Jersey	1	<0.01
Rhode Island	1	<0.01
West Virginia	1	<0.01
Delaware	0	0.00
Vermont	0	0.00

Place	Population	%
Washington	8,645	0.13
Idaho	263	0.02
Oregon	328	0.01
Montana	122	0.01
Alaska	50	0.01
United States	**10,549**	**<0.01**
California	368	<0.01
Arizona	98	<0.01
Oklahoma	89	<0.01
Texas	76	<0.01
Colorado	42	<0.01
Nevada	36	<0.01
New Mexico	36	<0.01
Georgia	26	<0.01
North Carolina	24	<0.01
New York	22	<0.01
Missouri	20	<0.01
Virginia	20	<0.01
Florida	19	<0.01
Alabama	18	<0.01
Kansas	17	<0.01
Wisconsin	17	<0.01
Illinois	16	<0.01
Minnesota	16	<0.01
Utah	16	<0.01
Arkansas	15	<0.01
Michigan	15	<0.01
Pennsylvania	15	<0.01
Hawaii	14	<0.01
Indiana	14	<0.01
Ohio	11	<0.01
South Dakota	8	<0.01
Tennessee	8	<0.01
Kentucky	7	<0.01
Maryland	7	<0.01
Iowa	6	<0.01
Mississippi	6	<0.01
Nebraska	6	<0.01
Connecticut	5	<0.01
Louisiana	5	<0.01
District of Columbia	4	<0.01
Massachusetts	4	<0.01
Wyoming	4	<0.01
North Dakota	3	<0.01
New Hampshire	2	<0.01
South Carolina	2	<0.01
Maine	1	<0.01
New Jersey	1	<0.01
Rhode Island	1	<0.01
West Virginia	1	<0.01
Delaware	0	0.00
Vermont	0	0.00

Please refer to the Explanation of Data in the front of the book for more detailed information.

Race

American Indian: Colville

Top 150 Places Sorted by Population

Based on all places, regardless of total population

Place	Population	%
Omak, WA (city) Okanogan County	645	13.31
Spokane, WA (city) Spokane County	599	0.29
North Omak, WA (cdp) Okanogan County	461	67.01
Coulee Dam, WA (town) Okanogan County	350	31.88
Inchelium, WA (cdp) Ferry County	281	68.70
Nespelem Community, WA (cdp) Okanogan County	199	78.66
Keller, WA (cdp) Ferry County	167	71.37
Nespelem, WA (town) Okanogan County	149	63.14
Spokane Valley, WA (city) Spokane County	140	0.16
Okanogan, WA (city) Okanogan County	135	5.29
Seattle, WA (city) King County	129	0.02
Tacoma, WA (city) Pierce County	112	0.06
Yakima, WA (city) Yakima County	103	0.11
Grand Coulee, WA (city) Grant County	90	9.11
Elmer City, WA (town) Okanogan County	82	34.45
Wenatchee, WA (city) Chelan County	76	0.24
Portland, OR (city) Multnomah County	61	0.01
Disautel, WA (cdp) Okanogan County	55	70.51
Electric City, WA (city) Grant County	44	4.55
Colville, WA (city) Stevens County	42	0.90
Plummer, ID (city) Benewah County	39	3.74
Auburn, WA (city) King County	39	0.06
Cheney, WA (city) Spokane County	38	0.36
Fairwood, WA (cdp) Spokane County	37	0.47
Vancouver, WA (city) Clark County	34	0.02
Everett, WA (city) Snohomish County	32	0.03
East Wenatchee, WA (city) Douglas County	30	0.23
Twin Lakes, WA (cdp) Ferry County	29	49.15
Phoenix, AZ (city) Maricopa County	29	<0.01
Moses Lake, WA (city) Grant County	28	0.14
Los Angeles, CA (city) Los Angeles County	27	<0.01
Kennewick, WA (city) Benton County	26	0.04
Oroville, WA (city) Okanogan County	25	1.48
Kettle Falls, WA (city) Stevens County	23	1.44
Wilbur, WA (town) Lincoln County	22	2.49
Lynnwood, WA (city) Snohomish County	22	0.06
Federal Way, WA (city) King County	22	0.02
Olympia, WA (city) Thurston County	21	0.05
Pasco, WA (city) Franklin County	21	0.04
Kent, WA (city) King County	21	0.02
Lapwai, ID (city) Nez Perce County	20	1.76
Aberdeen, WA (city) Grays Harbor County	20	0.12
Coeur d'Alene, ID (city) Kootenai County	20	0.05
Toppenish, WA (city) Yakima County	19	0.21
Missoula, MT (city) Missoula County	19	0.03
SeaTac, WA (city) King County	18	0.07
Pullman, WA (city) Whitman County	18	0.06
Marysville, WA (city) Snohomish County	18	0.03
Bellingham, WA (city) Whatcom County	17	0.02
Anchorage, AK (municipality) Anchorage Municipality	17	0.01
Riverside, WA (town) Okanogan County	16	5.71
Post Falls, ID (city) Kootenai County	16	0.06
Lacey, WA (city) Thurston County	16	0.04
Albuquerque, NM (city) Bernalillo County	16	<0.01
Fife, WA (city) Pierce County	15	0.16
Mead, WA (cdp) Spokane County	14	0.19
Richland, WA (city) Benton County	14	0.03
Warm Springs, OR (cdp) Jefferson County	13	0.44
Airway Heights, WA (city) Spokane County	13	0.21
Shelton, WA (city) Mason County	13	0.13
Taholah, WA (cdp) Grays Harbor County	12	1.43
Brewster, WA (city) Okanogan County	12	0.51
Deer Park, WA (city) Spokane County	12	0.33
Country Homes, WA (cdp) Spokane County	12	0.21
Hoquiam, WA (city) Grays Harbor County	12	0.14
Mountlake Terrace, WA (city) Snohomish County	12	0.06
Silverdale, WA (cdp) Kitsap County	12	0.06
Spanaway, WA (cdp) Pierce County	12	0.04
Longview, WA (city) Cowlitz County	12	0.03
Bellevue, WA (city) King County	12	0.01
Sacramento, CA (city) Sacramento County	12	<0.01
De Smet, ID (cdp) Benewah County	11	6.29
Malott, WA (cdp) Okanogan County	11	2.26
Harrah, WA (town) Yakima County	11	1.76
Loon Lake, WA (cdp) Stevens County	11	1.40
Polson, MT (city) Lake County	11	0.25
Ellensburg, WA (city) Kittitas County	11	0.06
Puyallup, WA (city) Pierce County	11	0.03
Skokomish, WA (cdp) Mason County	10	1.62
Tonasket, WA (city) Okanogan County	10	0.97
Moses Lake North, WA (cdp) Grant County	10	0.23
Clarkston, WA (city) Asotin County	10	0.14
Liberty Lake, WA (city) Spokane County	10	0.13
Renton, WA (city) King County	10	0.01
Boise City, ID (city) Ada County	10	<0.01
Oklahoma City, OK (city) Oklahoma County	10	<0.01
Pateros, WA (city) Okanogan County	9	1.35
Mission, OR (cdp) Umatilla County	9	0.87
Hines, OR (city) Harney County	9	0.58
Chewelah, WA (city) Stevens County	9	0.35
Chelan, WA (city) Chelan County	9	0.23
Town and Country, WA (cdp) Spokane County	9	0.19
Sutherlin, OR (city) Douglas County	9	0.12
White Center, WA (cdp) King County	9	0.07
East Hill-Meridian, WA (cdp) King County	9	0.03
Corvallis, OR (city) Benton County	9	0.02
Shoreline, WA (city) King County	9	0.02
Eugene, OR (city) Lane County	9	0.01
Norwalk, CA (city) Los Angeles County	9	0.01
Mesa, AZ (city) Maricopa County	9	<0.01
New York, NY (city) Kings County	9	<0.01
Worley, ID (city) Kootenai County	8	3.11
North Bend, WA (city) King County	8	0.14
Ephrata, WA (city) Grant County	8	0.10
North Lynnwood, WA (cdp) Snohomish County	8	0.05
Pendleton, OR (city) Umatilla County	8	0.05
Badger, AK (cdp) Fairbanks North Star Borough	8	0.04
Frederickson, WA (cdp) Pierce County	8	0.04
Tukwila, WA (city) King County	8	0.04
Lake Stevens, WA (city) Snohomish County	8	0.03
Killeen, TX (city) Bell County	8	0.01
Lakewood, WA (city) Pierce County	8	0.01
El Paso, TX (city) El Paso County	8	<0.01
Rancho Cucamonga, CA (city) San Bernardino County	8	<0.01
San Francisco, CA (city) San Francisco County	8	<0.01
Mexican Colony, CA (cdp) Kern County	7	2.49
Harrington, WA (city) Lincoln County	7	1.65
Cherokee, NC (cdp) Jackson County	7	0.33
Pablo, MT (cdp) Lake County	7	0.31
Burns, OR (city) Harney County	7	0.25
Fort Hall, ID (cdp) Bannock County	7	0.22
Union Gap, WA (city) Yakima County	7	0.12
Prairie Ridge, WA (cdp) Pierce County	7	0.06
Maple Valley, WA (city) King County	7	0.03
Redmond, OR (city) Deschutes County	7	0.03
Bothell, WA (city) King County	7	0.02
University Place, WA (city) Pierce County	7	0.02
Glendale, AZ (city) Maricopa County	7	<0.01
San Jose, CA (city) Santa Clara County	7	<0.01
Tucson, AZ (city) Pima County	7	<0.01
Hunter, OK (town) Garfield County	6	3.64
Reardan, WA (town) Lincoln County	6	1.05
Nisqually Indian Community, WA (cdp) Thurston County	6	1.04
Republic, WA (city) Ferry County	6	0.56
Bridgeport, WA (city) Douglas County	6	0.25
Suquamish, WA (cdp) Kitsap County	6	0.14
Hugo, OK (city) Choctaw County	6	0.11
Bangor Base, WA (cdp) Kitsap County	6	0.10
Pacific, WA (city) King County	6	0.09
Parkwood, WA (cdp) Kitsap County	6	0.08
Jerome, ID (city) Jerome County	6	0.06
Newport, OR (city) Lincoln County	6	0.06
Sumner, WA (city) Pierce County	6	0.06
Elk City, OK (city) Beckham County	6	0.05
Centralia, WA (city) Lewis County	6	0.04
Coos Bay, OR (city) Coos County	6	0.04
Washougal, WA (city) Clark County	6	0.04
Bonney Lake, WA (city) Pierce County	6	0.03
Covington, WA (city) King County	6	0.03
Fernley, NV (city) Lyon County	6	0.03

Please refer to the Explanation of Data in the front of the book for more detailed information.

Race

American Indian: Colville

Top 150 Places Sorted by Percent of Total Population

Based on all places, regardless of total population

Place	Population	%
Nespelem Community, WA (cdp) Okanogan County	199	78.66
Keller, WA (cdp) Ferry County	167	71.37
Disautel, WA (cdp) Okanogan County	55	70.51
Inchelium, WA (cdp) Ferry County	281	68.70
North Omak, WA (cdp) Okanogan County	461	67.01
Nespelem, WA (town) Okanogan County	149	63.14
Twin Lakes, WA (cdp) Ferry County	29	49.15
Elmer City, WA (town) Okanogan County	82	34.45
Coulee Dam, WA (town) Okanogan County	350	31.88
Boyds, WA (cdp) Ferry County	5	14.71
Omak, WA (city) Okanogan County	645	13.31
Grand Coulee, WA (city) Grant County	90	9.11
De Smet, ID (cdp) Benewah County	11	6.29
Riverside, WA (town) Okanogan County	16	5.71
Okanogan, WA (city) Okanogan County	135	5.29
Electric City, WA (city) Grant County	44	4.55
Veteran, WY (cdp) Goshen County	1	4.35
Plummer, ID (city) Benewah County	39	3.74
Hunter, OK (town) Garfield County	6	3.64
Worley, ID (city) Kootenai County	8	3.11
Danville, WA (cdp) Ferry County	1	2.94
Wilbur, WA (town) Lincoln County	22	2.49
Mexican Colony, CA (cdp) Kern County	7	2.49
Malott, WA (cdp) Okanogan County	11	2.26
Creston, WA (town) Lincoln County	5	2.12
Torboy, WA (cdp) Ferry County	1	2.04
Marblemount, WA (cdp) Skagit County	4	1.97
Lapwai, ID (city) Nez Perce County	20	1.76
Harrah, WA (town) Yakima County	11	1.76
Juntura, OR (cdp) Malheur County	1	1.75
Barstow, WA (cdp) Ferry County	1	1.69
Harrington, WA (city) Lincoln County	7	1.65
Skokomish, WA (cdp) Mason County	10	1.62
Oroville, WA (city) Okanogan County	25	1.48
Kettle Falls, WA (city) Stevens County	23	1.44
Taholah, WA (cdp) Grays Harbor County	12	1.43
Loon Lake, WA (cdp) Stevens County	11	1.40
Pateros, WA (city) Okanogan County	9	1.35
Hoodsport, WA (cdp) Mason County	4	1.06
Reardan, WA (town) Lincoln County	6	1.05
Nisqually Indian Community, WA (cdp) Thurston County	6	1.04
Tonasket, WA (city) Okanogan County	10	0.97
Conconully, WA (town) Okanogan County	2	0.95
Waverly, WA (town) Spokane County	1	0.94
Colville, WA (city) Stevens County	42	0.90
Mission, OR (cdp) Umatilla County	9	0.87
Orient, WA (cdp) Ferry County	1	0.87
Clallam Bay, WA (cdp) Clallam County	3	0.83
Pine Grove, WA (cdp) Ferry County	1	0.69
Hines, OR (city) Harney County	9	0.58
Banks Lake South, WA (cdp) Grant County	1	0.57
Republic, WA (city) Ferry County	6	0.56
Notus, ID (city) Canyon County	3	0.56
Elmo, MT (cdp) Lake County	1	0.56
Latah, WA (town) Spokane County	1	0.55
Marcus, WA (town) Stevens County	1	0.55
Rockford Bay, ID (cdp) Kootenai County	1	0.54
Gisela, AZ (cdp) Gila County	3	0.53
Culdesac, ID (city) Nez Perce County	2	0.53
Brewster, WA (city) Okanogan County	12	0.51
Loda, IL (village) Iroquois County	2	0.49
Malden, WA (town) Whitman County	1	0.49
Moclips, WA (cdp) Grays Harbor County	1	0.48
Fairwood, WA (cdp) Spokane County	37	0.47
Clayton, WA (cdp) Stevens County	2	0.45
Warm Springs, OR (cdp) Jefferson County	13	0.44
Hauser, ID (city) Kootenai County	3	0.44
Curlew Lake, WA (cdp) Ferry County	2	0.43
Bingen, WA (city) Klickitat County	3	0.42
Fossil, OR (city) Wheeler County	2	0.42
Starr School, MT (cdp) Glacier County	1	0.40
Tekoa, WA (city) Whitman County	3	0.39
Cheney, WA (city) Spokane County	38	0.36
St. Ignatius, MT (town) Lake County	3	0.36
Fort Shaw, MT (cdp) Cascade County	1	0.36
Chewelah, WA (city) Stevens County	9	0.35
Kicking Horse, MT (cdp) Lake County	1	0.35
Lindisfarne, MT (cdp) Lake County	1	0.35
Deer Park, WA (city) Spokane County	12	0.33
Cherokee, NC (cdp) Jackson County	7	0.33
Fairfield, WA (town) Spokane County	2	0.33
Union, WA (cdp) Mason County	2	0.32
Pablo, MT (cdp) Lake County	7	0.31
Arlee, MT (cdp) Lake County	2	0.31
Elim, AK (city) Nome Census Area	1	0.30
Spokane, WA (city) Spokane County	599	0.29
Santa Clara Pueblo, NM (cdp) Rio Arriba County	3	0.29
Ball Club, MN (cdp) Itasca County	1	0.29
Winchester, ID (city) Lewis County	1	0.29
Millwood, WA (town) Spokane County	5	0.28
Nixon, NV (cdp) Washoe County	1	0.27
Polson, MT (city) Lake County	11	0.25
Burns, OR (city) Harney County	7	0.25
Bridgeport, WA (city) Douglas County	6	0.25
White Swan, WA (cdp) Yakima County	2	0.25
Wenatchee, WA (city) Chelan County	76	0.24
Hungry Horse, MT (cdp) Flathead County	2	0.24
East Wenatchee, WA (city) Douglas County	30	0.23
Moses Lake North, WA (cdp) Grant County	10	0.23
Chelan, WA (city) Chelan County	9	0.23
Tekamah, NE (city) Burt County	4	0.23
Dibble, OK (town) McClain County	2	0.23
Neah Bay, WA (cdp) Clallam County	2	0.23
Fort Hall, ID (cdp) Bannock County	7	0.22
Lakeview, WA (cdp) Grant County	2	0.22
Odessa, WA (town) Lincoln County	2	0.22
Port Gamble Tribal Comunity, WA (cdp) Kitsap County	2	0.22
Twisp, WA (town) Okanogan County	2	0.22
River Road, WA (cdp) Clallam County	1	0.22
Toppenish, WA (city) Yakima County	19	0.21
Airway Heights, WA (city) Spokane County	13	0.21
Country Homes, WA (cdp) Spokane County	12	0.21
Parkside, PA (borough) Delaware County	5	0.21
Ames Lake, WA (cdp) King County	3	0.20
Bouse, AZ (cdp) La Paz County	2	0.20
Mead, WA (cdp) Spokane County	14	0.19
Town and Country, WA (cdp) Spokane County	9	0.19
Warden, WA (city) Grant County	5	0.19
Lexington, OK (city) Cleveland County	4	0.19
St. Croix Falls, WI (city) Polk County	4	0.19
Tyrone, PA (township) Perry County	4	0.19
McMillin, WA (cdp) Pierce County	3	0.19
Covington, OK (town) Garfield County	1	0.19
Fort Towson, OK (town) Choctaw County	1	0.19
Cascade Valley, WA (cdp) Grant County	4	0.18
Waterville, WA (town) Douglas County	2	0.18
Fairchild, WI (village) Eau Claire County	1	0.18
Casco, WI (village) Kewaunee County	1	0.17
White Haven, MT (cdp) Lincoln County	1	0.17
Spokane Valley, WA (city) Spokane County	140	0.16
Fife, WA (city) Pierce County	15	0.16
North Eagle Butte, SD (cdp) Dewey County	3	0.15
Home, WA (cdp) Pierce County	2	0.15
Nooksack, WA (city) Whatcom County	2	0.15
Condon, OR (city) Gilliam County	1	0.15
Powers, OR (city) Coos County	1	0.15
Schurz, NV (cdp) Mineral County	1	0.15
Moses Lake, WA (city) Grant County	28	0.14
Hoquiam, WA (city) Grays Harbor County	12	0.14
Clarkston, WA (city) Asotin County	10	0.14
North Bend, WA (city) King County	8	0.14
Suquamish, WA (cdp) Kitsap County	6	0.14
Raymond, WA (city) Pacific County	4	0.14
Brundidge, AL (city) Pike County	3	0.14
Fife Heights, WA (cdp) Pierce County	3	0.14
Lake Waccamaw, NC (town) Columbus County	2	0.14
Concrete, WA (town) Skagit County	1	0.14
Fort Duchesne, UT (cdp) Uintah County	1	0.14
Shelton, WA (city) Mason County	13	0.13
Liberty Lake, WA (city) Spokane County	10	0.13

Please refer to the Explanation of Data in the front of the book for more detailed information.

Race

American Indian: Colville

Top 150 Places Sorted by Percent of Total Population

Based on places with total population of 7,500 or more

Place	Population	%
Fairwood, WA (cdp) Spokane County	37	0.47
Cheney, WA (city) Spokane County	38	0.36
Spokane, WA (city) Spokane County	599	0.29
Wenatchee, WA (city) Chelan County	76	0.24
East Wenatchee, WA (city) Douglas County	30	0.23
Toppenish, WA (city) Yakima County	19	0.21
Spokane Valley, WA (city) Spokane County	140	0.16
Fife, WA (city) Pierce County	15	0.16
Moses Lake, WA (city) Grant County	28	0.14
Hoquiam, WA (city) Grays Harbor County	12	0.14
Shelton, WA (city) Mason County	13	0.13
Liberty Lake, WA (city) Spokane County	10	0.13
Aberdeen, WA (city) Grays Harbor County	20	0.12
Sutherlin, OR (city) Douglas County	9	0.12
Yakima, WA (city) Yakima County	103	0.11
Ephrata, WA (city) Grant County	8	0.10
SeaTac, WA (city) King County	18	0.07
White Center, WA (cdp) King County	9	0.07
Tacoma, WA (city) Pierce County	112	0.06
Auburn, WA (city) King County	39	0.06
Lynnwood, WA (city) Snohomish County	22	0.06
Pullman, WA (city) Whitman County	18	0.06
Post Falls, ID (city) Kootenai County	16	0.06
Mountlake Terrace, WA (city) Snohomish County	12	0.06
Silverdale, WA (cdp) Kitsap County	12	0.06
Ellensburg, WA (city) Kittitas County	11	0.06
Prairie Ridge, WA (cdp) Pierce County	7	0.06
Jerome, ID (city) Jerome County	6	0.06
Newport, OR (city) Lincoln County	6	0.06
Sumner, WA (city) Pierce County	6	0.06
Olympia, WA (city) Thurston County	21	0.05
Coeur d'Alene, ID (city) Kootenai County	20	0.05
North Lynnwood, WA (cdp) Snohomish County	8	0.05
Pendleton, OR (city) Umatilla County	8	0.05
Elk City, OK (city) Beckham County	6	0.05
Poulsbo, WA (city) Kitsap County	5	0.05
Sedro-Woolley, WA (city) Skagit County	5	0.05
College Place, WA (city) Walla Walla County	4	0.05
Picnic Point, WA (cdp) Snohomish County	4	0.05
Kennewick, WA (city) Benton County	26	0.04
Pasco, WA (city) Franklin County	21	0.04
Lacey, WA (city) Thurston County	16	0.04
Spanaway, WA (cdp) Pierce County	12	0.04
Badger, AK (cdp) Fairbanks North Star Borough	8	0.04
Frederickson, WA (cdp) Pierce County	8	0.04
Tukwila, WA (city) King County	8	0.04
Centralia, WA (city) Lewis County	6	0.04
Coos Bay, OR (city) Coos County	6	0.04
Washougal, WA (city) Clark County	6	0.04
Elk Plain, WA (cdp) Pierce County	5	0.04
Astoria, OR (city) Clatsop County	4	0.04
East Renton Highlands, WA (cdp) King County	4	0.04
Maltby, WA (cdp) Snohomish County	4	0.04
Silverton, OR (city) Marion County	4	0.04
Snoqualmie, WA (city) King County	4	0.04
Fort Riley, KS (cdp) Riley County	3	0.04
Meadow Lakes, AK (cdp) Matanuska-Susitna Borough	3	0.04
Summit, WA (cdp) Pierce County	3	0.04
Everett, WA (city) Snohomish County	32	0.03
Missoula, MT (city) Missoula County	19	0.03
Marysville, WA (city) Snohomish County	18	0.03
Richland, WA (city) Benton County	14	0.03
Longview, WA (city) Cowlitz County	12	0.03
Puyallup, WA (city) Pierce County	11	0.03
East Hill-Meridian, WA (cdp) King County	9	0.03
Lake Stevens, WA (city) Snohomish County	8	0.03
Maple Valley, WA (city) King County	7	0.03
Redmond, OR (city) Deschutes County	7	0.03
Bonney Lake, WA (city) Pierce County	6	0.03
Covington, WA (city) King County	6	0.03
Fernley, NV (city) Lyon County	6	0.03
Moscow, ID (city) Latah County	6	0.03
Tumwater, WA (city) Thurston County	6	0.03
Arlington, WA (city) Snohomish County	5	0.03
Bothell West, WA (cdp) Snohomish County	5	0.03

Place	Population	%
Hartland, MI (township) Livingston County	5	0.03
Mill Creek East, WA (cdp) Snohomish County	5	0.03
Artondale, WA (cdp) Pierce County	4	0.03
Bryn Mawr-Skyway, WA (cdp) King County	4	0.03
Hayden, ID (city) Kootenai County	4	0.03
Kelso, WA (city) Cowlitz County	4	0.03
Martha Lake, WA (cdp) Snohomish County	4	0.03
Speedway, IN (town) Marion County	4	0.03
Damascus, OR (city) Clackamas County	3	0.03
Dent, OH (cdp) Hamilton County	3	0.03
Edgewood, WA (city) Pierce County	3	0.03
Fairview, CA (cdp) Alameda County	3	0.03
Lake Tapps, WA (cdp) Pierce County	3	0.03
Lakeland South, WA (cdp) King County	3	0.03
Midland, WA (cdp) Pierce County	3	0.03
Newcastle, WA (city) King County	3	0.03
Sandy, OR (city) Clackamas County	3	0.03
Sitka, AK (borough) Sitka City and Borough	3	0.03
Seattle, WA (city) King County	129	0.02
Vancouver, WA (city) Clark County	34	0.02
Federal Way, WA (city) King County	22	0.02
Kent, WA (city) King County	21	0.02
Bellingham, WA (city) Whatcom County	17	0.02
Corvallis, OR (city) Benton County	9	0.02
Shoreline, WA (city) King County	9	0.02
Bothell, WA (city) King County	7	0.02
University Place, WA (city) Pierce County	7	0.02
Des Moines, WA (city) King County	6	0.02
Fairbanks, AK (city) Fairbanks North Star Borough	6	0.02
Lewiston, ID (city) Nez Perce County	6	0.02
Griffin, GA (city) Spalding County	5	0.02
Silver Firs, WA (cdp) Snohomish County	5	0.02
Kihei, HI (cdp) Maui County	4	0.02
Oak Grove, OR (cdp) Clackamas County	4	0.02
Orchards, WA (cdp) Clark County	4	0.02
Salmon Creek, WA (cdp) Clark County	4	0.02
Commerce, CA (city) Los Angeles County	3	0.02
Dickinson, ND (city) Stark County	3	0.02
Hazel Dell, WA (cdp) Clark County	3	0.02
Kalispell, MT (city) Flathead County	3	0.02
Pacific Grove, CA (city) Monterey County	3	0.02
Port Angeles, WA (city) Clallam County	3	0.02
Sunnyside, WA (city) Yakima County	3	0.02
Alderwood Manor, WA (cdp) Snohomish County	2	0.02
Clayton, CA (city) Contra Costa County	2	0.02
El Dorado, KS (city) Butler County	2	0.02
Enumclaw, WA (city) King County	2	0.02
Guthrie, OK (city) Logan County	2	0.02
Kingsgate, WA (cdp) King County	2	0.02
Klahanie, WA (cdp) King County	2	0.02
Lake Forest Park, WA (city) King County	2	0.02
Lindsay, CA (city) Tulare County	2	0.02
Los Alamitos, CA (city) Orange County	2	0.02
Tanaina, AK (cdp) Matanuska-Susitna Borough	2	0.02
Warr Acres, OK (city) Oklahoma County	2	0.02
West Richland, WA (city) Benton County	2	0.02
Woodinville, WA (city) King County	2	0.02
Portland, OR (city) Multnomah County	61	0.01
Anchorage, AK (municipality) Anchorage Municipality	17	0.01
Bellevue, WA (city) King County	12	0.01
Renton, WA (city) King County	10	0.01
Eugene, OR (city) Lane County	9	0.01
Norwalk, CA (city) Los Angeles County	9	0.01
Killeen, TX (city) Bell County	8	0.01
Lakewood, WA (city) Pierce County	8	0.01
Arvada, CO (city) Jefferson County	6	0.01
Bend, OR (city) Deschutes County	6	0.01
Camarillo, CA (city) Ventura County	6	0.01
Gresham, OR (city) Multnomah County	6	0.01
South Hill, WA (cdp) Pierce County	6	0.01
Bremerton, WA (city) Kitsap County	5	0.01
Clovis, CA (city) Fresno County	5	0.01
Great Falls, MT (city) Cascade County	5	0.01
Parkland, WA (cdp) Pierce County	5	0.01
Rocklin, CA (city) Placer County	5	0.01

Please refer to the Explanation of Data in the front of the book for more detailed information.

Race

American Indian: Comanche

U.S. and 50 States Sorted by Population and Percent of Total Population

Place	Population	%
United States	**23,330**	**0.01**
Oklahoma	8,741	0.23
Texas	3,989	0.02
California	2,920	0.01
Colorado	576	0.01
Washington	488	0.01
Arizona	469	0.01
New Mexico	454	0.02
Kansas	445	0.02
Florida	385	<0.01
Missouri	304	0.01
Oregon	301	0.01
Virginia	275	<0.01
Illinois	251	<0.01
Ohio	237	<0.01
Michigan	214	<0.01
Arkansas	203	0.01
New York	199	<0.01
North Carolina	199	<0.01
Nevada	197	0.01
Georgia	170	<0.01
Wisconsin	148	<0.01
Louisiana	143	<0.01
Indiana	142	<0.01
Tennessee	135	<0.01
Pennsylvania	133	<0.01
Utah	127	<0.01
Maryland	125	<0.01
Hawaii	124	0.01
Minnesota	116	<0.01
Alabama	101	<0.01
South Carolina	99	<0.01
Alaska	98	0.01
New Jersey	98	<0.01
Idaho	95	0.01
Iowa	84	<0.01
Kentucky	74	<0.01
Massachusetts	72	<0.01
Montana	67	0.01
Wyoming	59	0.01
Mississippi	50	<0.01
Connecticut	32	<0.01
West Virginia	32	<0.01
Nebraska	31	<0.01
South Dakota	31	<0.01
New Hampshire	20	<0.01
Maine	17	<0.01
District of Columbia	15	<0.01
North Dakota	14	<0.01
Vermont	14	<0.01
Rhode Island	10	<0.01
Delaware	7	<0.01

Place	Population	%
Oklahoma	8,741	0.23
Texas	3,989	0.02
New Mexico	454	0.02
Kansas	445	0.02
United States	**23,330**	**0.01**
California	2,920	0.01
Colorado	576	0.01
Washington	488	0.01
Arizona	469	0.01
Missouri	304	0.01
Oregon	301	0.01
Arkansas	203	0.01
Nevada	197	0.01
Hawaii	124	0.01
Alaska	98	0.01
Idaho	95	0.01
Montana	67	0.01
Wyoming	59	0.01
Florida	385	<0.01
Virginia	275	<0.01
Illinois	251	<0.01
Ohio	237	<0.01
Michigan	214	<0.01
New York	199	<0.01
North Carolina	199	<0.01
Georgia	170	<0.01
Wisconsin	148	<0.01
Louisiana	143	<0.01
Indiana	142	<0.01
Tennessee	135	<0.01
Pennsylvania	133	<0.01
Utah	127	<0.01
Maryland	125	<0.01
Minnesota	116	<0.01
Alabama	101	<0.01
South Carolina	99	<0.01
New Jersey	98	<0.01
Iowa	84	<0.01
Kentucky	74	<0.01
Massachusetts	72	<0.01
Mississippi	50	<0.01
Connecticut	32	<0.01
West Virginia	32	<0.01
Nebraska	31	<0.01
South Dakota	31	<0.01
New Hampshire	20	<0.01
Maine	17	<0.01
District of Columbia	15	<0.01
North Dakota	14	<0.01
Vermont	14	<0.01
Rhode Island	10	<0.01
Delaware	7	<0.01

Please refer to the Explanation of Data in the front of the book for more detailed information.

Race

American Indian: Comanche

Top 150 Places Sorted by Population

Based on all places, regardless of total population

Place	Population	%
Lawton, OK (city) Comanche County	1,874	1.93
Oklahoma City, OK (city) Oklahoma County	672	0.12
Cache, OK (city) Comanche County	435	15.56
Anadarko, OK (city) Caddo County	357	5.28
Walters, OK (city) Cotton County	315	12.35
Norman, OK (city) Cleveland County	280	0.25
San Antonio, TX (city) Medina County	200	0.02
Tulsa, OK (city) Tulsa County	186	0.05
Dallas, TX (city) Dallas County	178	0.01
Fort Worth, TX (city) Tarrant County	163	0.02
Apache, OK (town) Caddo County	159	11.01
Houston, TX (city) Harris County	151	0.01
Los Angeles, CA (city) Los Angeles County	145	<0.01
Wichita, KS (city) Sedgwick County	138	0.04
Geronimo, OK (town) Comanche County	134	10.57
Albuquerque, NM (city) Bernalillo County	128	0.02
Austin, TX (city) Travis County	123	0.02
Duncan, OK (city) Stephens County	107	0.46
Phoenix, AZ (city) Maricopa County	107	0.01
Elgin, OK (city) Comanche County	95	4.41
Indiahoma, OK (town) Comanche County	92	26.74
San Jose, CA (city) Santa Clara County	91	0.01
Chickasha, OK (city) Grady County	88	0.55
Moore, OK (city) Cleveland County	82	0.15
San Diego, CA (city) San Diego County	79	0.01
Fresno, CA (city) Fresno County	77	0.02
New York, NY (city) Kings County	76	<0.01
Lubbock, TX (city) Lubbock County	73	0.03
Wichita Falls, TX (city) Wichita County	68	0.07
Cyril, OK (town) Caddo County	64	6.04
Amarillo, TX (city) Potter County	63	0.03
Arlington, TX (city) Tarrant County	62	0.02
Shawnee, OK (city) Pottawatomie County	61	0.20
Colorado Springs, CO (city) El Paso County	61	0.01
Bakersfield, CA (city) Kern County	57	0.02
Midwest City, OK (city) Oklahoma County	54	0.10
Denver, CO (city) Denver County	53	0.01
Irving, TX (city) Dallas County	52	0.02
San Francisco, CA (city) San Francisco County	47	0.01
Chicago, IL (city) Cook County	47	<0.01
Edmond, OK (city) Oklahoma County	46	0.06
Las Vegas, NV (city) Clark County	45	0.01
Broken Arrow, OK (city) Tulsa County	44	0.04
Sacramento, CA (city) Sacramento County	44	0.01
Odessa, TX (city) Ector County	43	0.04
Springfield, MO (city) Christian County	43	0.03
Fletcher, OK (town) Comanche County	42	3.57
Temple, OK (town) Cotton County	41	4.09
Ponca City, OK (city) Kay County	41	0.16
Yukon, OK (city) Canadian County	40	0.18
Seattle, WA (city) King County	40	0.01
Lawrence, KS (city) Douglas County	39	0.04
Santa Rosa, CA (city) Sonoma County	39	0.02
Aurora, CO (city) Arapahoe County	39	0.01
El Paso, TX (city) El Paso County	39	0.01
Denton, TX (city) Denton County	38	0.03
Grand Prairie, TX (city) Dallas County	38	0.02
Mesa, AZ (city) Maricopa County	38	0.01
Corpus Christi, TX (city) Nueces County	37	0.01
Portland, OR (city) Multnomah County	36	0.01
Tucson, AZ (city) Pima County	32	0.01
Rio Rancho, NM (city) Sandoval County	30	0.03
Garland, TX (city) Dallas County	29	0.01
Urban Honolulu, HI (cdp) Honolulu County	29	0.01
Visalia, CA (city) Tulare County	28	0.02
Anchorage, AK (municipality) Anchorage Municipality	28	0.01
Indianapolis, IN (city) Marion County	28	<0.01
Bethany, OK (city) Oklahoma County	27	0.14
Carrollton, TX (city) Denton County	27	0.02
Fort Collins, CO (city) Larimer County	27	0.02
San Bernardino, CA (city) San Bernardino County	27	0.01
Sterling, OK (town) Comanche County	26	3.28
Marlow, OK (city) Stephens County	26	0.56
Mesquite, TX (city) Dallas County	26	0.02
Riverside, CA (city) Riverside County	26	0.01
Bronx, NY (borough) Bronx County	26	<0.01
Citrus Heights, CA (city) Sacramento County	25	0.03
Pueblo, CO (city) Pueblo County	25	0.02
Chula Vista, CA (city) San Diego County	25	0.01
McLoud, OK (town) Pottawatomie County	24	0.59
North Richland Hills, TX (city) Tarrant County	24	0.04
Yuma, AZ (city) Yuma County	24	0.03
Killeen, TX (city) Bell County	24	0.02
Modesto, CA (city) Stanislaus County	24	0.01
Oakland, CA (city) Alameda County	24	0.01
Plano, TX (city) Collin County	24	0.01
Chattanooga, OK (town) Comanche County	23	4.99
Ada, OK (city) Pontotoc County	23	0.14
El Reno, OK (city) Canadian County	23	0.14
Enid, OK (city) Garfield County	23	0.05
Stillwater, OK (city) Payne County	23	0.05
McKinney, TX (city) Collin County	23	0.02
Midland, TX (city) Midland County	23	0.02
McAlester, OK (city) Pittsburg County	22	0.12
Cedar Park, TX (city) Williamson County	22	0.04
Minneapolis, MN (city) Hennepin County	22	0.01
Manhattan, NY (borough) New York County	22	<0.01
Muskogee, OK (city) Muskogee County	21	0.05
Euless, TX (city) Tarrant County	21	0.04
San Buenaventura (Ventura), CA (city) Ventura County	21	0.02
Thornton, CO (city) Adams County	21	0.02
Huntington Beach, CA (city) Orange County	21	0.01
Weatherford, OK (city) Custer County	20	0.18
Tahlequah, OK (city) Cherokee County	20	0.13
Claremore, OK (city) Rogers County	20	0.11
Farmington, NM (city) San Juan County	20	0.04
Abilene, TX (city) Taylor County	20	0.02
Lewisville, TX (city) Denton County	20	0.02
Round Rock, TX (city) Williamson County	20	0.02
Eugene, OR (city) Lane County	20	0.01
Oxnard, CA (city) Ventura County	20	0.01
Spokane, WA (city) Spokane County	20	0.01
Sunrise Manor, NV (cdp) Clark County	20	0.01
Virginia Beach, VA (ind. city) Virginia Beach independent city	20	<0.01
Mansfield, TX (city) Tarrant County	19	0.03
Victoria, TX (city) Victoria County	19	0.03
Brooklyn, NY (borough) Kings County	19	<0.01
Jacksonville, FL (city) Duval County	19	<0.01
Nashville-Davidson, TN (metro govt) Davidson County	19	<0.01
Haysville, KS (city) Sedgwick County	18	0.17
Flagstaff, AZ (city) Coconino County	18	0.03
Temple, TX (city) Bell County	18	0.03
Clovis, CA (city) Fresno County	18	0.02
Santa Barbara, CA (city) Santa Barbara County	18	0.02
Paradise, NV (cdp) Clark County	18	0.01
Salem, OR (city) Marion County	18	0.01
Spring Valley, NV (cdp) Clark County	18	0.01
Topeka, KS (city) Shawnee County	18	0.01
Carnegie, OK (town) Caddo County	17	0.99
Corona, CA (city) Riverside County	17	0.01
Gilbert, AZ (town) Maricopa County	17	0.01
Reno, NV (city) Washoe County	17	0.01
Tacoma, WA (city) Pierce County	17	0.01
Columbus, OH (city) Franklin County	17	<0.01
Pawnee, OK (city) Pawnee County	16	0.73
Tecumseh, OK (city) Pottawatomie County	16	0.25
Guthrie, OK (city) Logan County	16	0.16
Del City, OK (city) Oklahoma County	16	0.08
Federal Way, WA (city) King County	16	0.02
Boise City, ID (city) Ada County	16	0.01
Clarksville, TN (city) Montgomery County	16	0.01
Fremont, CA (city) Alameda County	16	0.01
Rancho Cucamonga, CA (city) San Bernardino County	16	0.01
Salinas, CA (city) Monterey County	16	0.01
Anaheim, CA (city) Orange County	16	<0.01
Detroit, MI (city) Wayne County	16	<0.01
Fort Cobb, OK (town) Caddo County	15	2.37
Blanchard, OK (city) McClain County	15	0.20
Allen, TX (city) Collin County	15	0.02
Redding, CA (city) Shasta County	15	0.02

SECTION THREE

Please refer to the Explanation of Data in the front of the book for more detailed information.

Race

American Indian: Comanche

Top 150 Places Sorted by Percent of Total Population

Based on all places, regardless of total population

Place	Population	%
Indiahoma, OK (town) Comanche County	92	26.74
Cache, OK (city) Comanche County	435	15.56
Walters, OK (city) Cotton County	315	12.35
Apache, OK (town) Caddo County	159	11.01
Geronimo, OK (town) Comanche County	134	10.57
Cyril, OK (town) Caddo County	64	6.04
Texola, OK (town) Beckham County	2	5.56
Anadarko, OK (city) Caddo County	357	5.28
Chattanooga, OK (town) Comanche County	23	4.99
Braddock, ND (city) Emmons County	1	4.76
Elgin, OK (city) Comanche County	95	4.41
Temple, OK (town) Cotton County	41	4.09
Medicine Park, OK (town) Comanche County	14	3.66
Fletcher, OK (town) Comanche County	42	3.57
Sterling, OK (town) Comanche County	26	3.28
Fort Cobb, OK (town) Caddo County	15	2.37
Faxon, OK (town) Comanche County	3	2.21
Escondida, NM (cdp) Socorro County	1	2.13
Beaulieu, MN (cdp) Mahnomen County	1	2.08
Yoder, KS (cdp) Reno County	4	2.06
Milton, KS (cdp) Sumner County	3	1.94
Lawton, OK (city) Comanche County	1,874	1.93
Olustee, OK (town) Jackson County	11	1.81
Sparks, OK (town) Lincoln County	3	1.78
Pyote, TX (town) Ward County	2	1.75
Linden, NC (town) Cumberland County	2	1.54
Hunnewell, KS (city) Sumner County	1	1.49
Olivet, KS (city) Osage County	1	1.49
Mountain Park, OK (town) Kiowa County	6	1.47
Colony, OK (town) Washita County	2	1.47
Cherokee, CA (cdp) Butte County	1	1.45
Red Rock, OK (town) Noble County	4	1.41
South Haven, KS (city) Sumner County	5	1.38
Kekoskee, WI (village) Dodge County	2	1.24
String, OK (town) Atoka County	5	1.22
Partridge, KS (city) Reno County	3	1.21
Roosevelt, OK (town) Kiowa County	3	1.21
Cement, OK (town) Caddo County	6	1.20
Old Monroe, MO (city) Lincoln County	3	1.13
Polvadera, NM (cdp) Socorro County	3	1.12
Pelzer, SC (town) Anderson County	1	1.12
Bokchito, OK (town) Bryan County	7	1.11
Elmo, MT (cdp) Lake County	2	1.11
Central High, OK (town) Stephens County	13	1.08
Sunizona, AZ (cdp) Cochise County	3	1.07
Richville, MN (city) Otter Tail County	1	1.04
Bear Creek, CA (cdp) Merced County	3	1.03
Haworth, OK (town) McCurtain County	3	1.01
Carnegie, OK (town) Caddo County	17	0.99
Steely Hollow, OK (cdp) Cherokee County	2	0.97
Sedalia, NC (town) Guilford County	6	0.96
Ravia, OK (town) Johnston County	5	0.95
Vona, CO (town) Kit Carson County	1	0.94
Beaulieu, MN (township) Mahnomen County	1	0.93
Todd Mission, TX (city) Grimes County	1	0.93
Whittier, AK (city) Valdez-Cordova Census Area	2	0.91
Ketchum, OK (town) Craig County	4	0.90
Anderson, TX (city) Grimes County	2	0.90
Soldier Creek, SD (cdp) Todd County	2	0.88
Snyder, OK (city) Kiowa County	12	0.86
Redbird Smith, OK (cdp) Sequoyah County	4	0.86
Forest, WI (town) Richland County	3	0.85
Morrison, OK (town) Noble County	6	0.82
Talihina, OK (town) Le Flore County	9	0.81
Runnells, IA (city) Polk County	4	0.79
Snook, TX (city) Burleson County	4	0.78
Oktaha, OK (town) Muskogee County	3	0.77
Asher, OK (town) Pottawatomie County	3	0.76
North Sultan, WA (cdp) Snohomish County	2	0.76
Pawnee, OK (city) Pawnee County	16	0.73
Golinda, TX (city) Falls County	4	0.72
Crowheart, WY (cdp) Fremont County	1	0.71
Puerto de Luna, NM (cdp) Guadalupe County	1	0.71
Geary, OK (city) Blaine County	9	0.70
Malcom, IA (city) Poweshiek County	2	0.70
Rolling Hills, WY (town) Converse County	3	0.68
Meridian, OK (cdp) Stephens County	10	0.67
Maud, OK (city) Pottawatomie County	7	0.67
Newell, CA (cdp) Modoc County	3	0.67
Spencer, NE (village) Boyd County	3	0.66
Devol, OK (town) Cotton County	1	0.66
Magdalena, NM (village) Socorro County	6	0.64
Gracemont, OK (town) Caddo County	2	0.63
Rice, MN (township) Clearwater County	1	0.63
Buckhorn, KY (city) Perry County	1	0.62
Comanche, OK (city) Stephens County	10	0.60
Adrian, TX (city) Oldham County	1	0.60
Cranmoor, WI (town) Wood County	1	0.60
Lookeba, OK (town) Caddo County	1	0.60
McLoud, OK (town) Pottawatomie County	24	0.59
Bransford, TN (cdp) Sumner County	1	0.59
Shady Point, OK (town) Le Flore County	6	0.58
Westport, NY (cdp) Essex County	3	0.58
Metaline, WA (town) Pend Oreille County	1	0.58
Sausal, NM (cdp) Valencia County	6	0.57
Deming, WA (cdp) Whatcom County	2	0.57
Marlow, OK (city) Stephens County	26	0.56
Cato, NY (village) Cayuga County	3	0.56
Jayton, TX (city) Kent County	3	0.56
Mud Lake, ID (city) Jefferson County	2	0.56
Camargo, OK (town) Dewey County	1	0.56
Elderon, WI (village) Marathon County	1	0.56
Ogden, AR (city) Little River County	1	0.56
Chickasha, OK (city) Grady County	88	0.55
Cole, OK (town) McClain County	3	0.54
Kenefick, TX (town) Liberty County	3	0.53
Empire City, OK (town) Stephens County	5	0.52
Turon, KS (city) Reno County	2	0.52
Adair, OK (town) Mayes County	4	0.51
Lodoga, CA (cdp) Colusa County	1	0.51
Kansas, OK (town) Delaware County	4	0.50
Mountain View, OK (town) Kiowa County	4	0.50
Buckhorn, NM (cdp) Grant County	1	0.50
Coultervillle, CA (cdp) Mariposa County	1	0.50
Lee, MI (township) Calhoun County	6	0.49
Cameron, LA (cdp) Cameron Parish	2	0.49
Hanston, KS (city) Hodgeman County	1	0.49
Mount Hermon, CA (cdp) Santa Cruz County	5	0.48
Hosmer, SD (city) Edmunds County	1	0.48
Seiling, OK (city) Dewey County	4	0.47
Evant, TX (town) Coryell County	2	0.47
Duncan, OK (city) Stephens County	107	0.46
Randlett, OK (town) Cotton County	2	0.46
Gasquet, CA (cdp) Del Norte County	3	0.45
Thackerville, OK (town) Love County	2	0.45
South Mills, NC (cdp) Camden County	2	0.44
Hillsdale, KS (cdp) Miami County	1	0.44
Newkirk, OK (city) Kay County	10	0.43
Delleker, CA (cdp) Plumas County	3	0.43
Brazos Country, TX (city) Austin County	2	0.43
Nisland, SD (town) Butte County	1	0.43
Study Butte, TX (cdp) Brewster County	1	0.43
Leach, OK (cdp) Delaware County	1	0.42
Aurora, TX (city) Wise County	5	0.41
Wolverine, MI (village) Cheboygan County	1	0.41
Rose, PA (township) Jefferson County	5	0.40
Caddo, OK (town) Bryan County	4	0.40
Ninnekah, OK (town) Grady County	4	0.40
Alburg, VT (village) Grand Isle County	2	0.40
Galisteo, NM (cdp) Santa Fe County	1	0.40
Hornbrook, CA (cdp) Siskiyou County	1	0.40
Vineland, CO (cdp) Pueblo County	1	0.40
Hollis, OK (city) Harmon County	8	0.39
Grandfield, OK (city) Tillman County	4	0.39
Gainesville, MO (city) Ozark County	3	0.39
Huntsville, AR (city) Madison County	9	0.38
Dennard, AR (cdp) Van Buren County	2	0.38
Jamesport, MO (city) Daviess County	2	0.38
Wellington, TX (city) Collingsworth County	8	0.37
Kingston, OK (town) Marshall County	6	0.37

Please refer to the Explanation of Data in the front of the book for more detailed information.

Race

American Indian: Comanche

Top 150 Places Sorted by Percent of Total Population

Based on places with total population of 7,500 or more

Place	Population	%
Lawton, OK (city) Comanche County	1,874	1.93
Chickasha, OK (city) Grady County	88	0.55
Duncan, OK (city) Stephens County	107	0.46
Norman, OK (city) Cleveland County	280	0.25
Shawnee, OK (city) Pottawatomie County	61	0.20
Blanchard, OK (city) McClain County	15	0.20
Yukon, OK (city) Canadian County	40	0.18
Weatherford, OK (city) Custer County	20	0.18
Haysville, KS (city) Sedgwick County	18	0.17
Ponca City, OK (city) Kay County	41	0.16
Guthrie, OK (city) Logan County	16	0.16
Moore, OK (city) Cleveland County	82	0.15
Bethany, OK (city) Oklahoma County	27	0.14
Ada, OK (city) Pontotoc County	23	0.14
El Reno, OK (city) Canadian County	23	0.14
Clinton, OK (city) Custer County	13	0.14
Cushing, OK (city) Payne County	11	0.14
Tahlequah, OK (city) Cherokee County	20	0.13
Richland Hills, TX (city) Tarrant County	10	0.13
Oklahoma City, OK (city) Oklahoma County	672	0.12
McAlester, OK (city) Pittsburg County	22	0.12
Newcastle, OK (city) McClain County	9	0.12
Claremore, OK (city) Rogers County	20	0.11
Warr Acres, OK (city) Oklahoma County	11	0.11
Graham, TX (city) Young County	10	0.11
Midwest City, OK (city) Oklahoma County	54	0.10
Enumclaw, WA (city) King County	10	0.09
Del City, OK (city) Oklahoma County	16	0.08
Stephenville, TX (city) Erath County	14	0.08
Andrews, TX (city) Andrews County	9	0.08
Pryor Creek, OK (city) Mayes County	8	0.08
Corrales, NM (village) Sandoval County	7	0.08
Wichita Falls, TX (city) Wichita County	68	0.07
Burkburnett, TX (city) Wichita County	8	0.07
Minnehaha, WA (cdp) Clark County	7	0.07
The Village, OK (city) Oklahoma County	6	0.07
Templeton, CA (cdp) San Luis Obispo County	5	0.07
Edmond, OK (city) Oklahoma County	46	0.06
Sapulpa, OK (city) Creek County	13	0.06
Saginaw, TX (city) Tarrant County	11	0.06
Forney, TX (city) Kaufman County	9	0.06
Fruita, CO (city) Mesa County	8	0.06
Kilgore, TX (city) Gregg County	8	0.06
Okmulgee, OK (city) Okmulgee County	8	0.06
Port Orchard, WA (city) Kitsap County	7	0.06
Spring Creek, NV (cdp) Elko County	7	0.06
Woodward, OK (city) Woodward County	7	0.06
Sedro-Woolley, WA (city) Skagit County	6	0.06
Ione, CA (city) Amador County	5	0.06
Tulsa, OK (city) Tulsa County	186	0.05
Enid, OK (city) Garfield County	23	0.05
Stillwater, OK (city) Payne County	23	0.05
Muskogee, OK (city) Muskogee County	21	0.05
Kingsville, TX (city) Kleberg County	13	0.05
Lake Jackson, TX (city) Brazoria County	13	0.05
Alvin, TX (city) Brazoria County	12	0.05
Junction City, KS (city) Geary County	12	0.05
Ardmore, OK (city) Carter County	11	0.05
Bixby, OK (city) Tulsa County	10	0.05
Castaic, CA (cdp) Los Angeles County	9	0.05
Mustang, OK (city) Canadian County	9	0.05
Alum Rock, CA (cdp) Santa Clara County	8	0.05
Coolidge, AZ (city) Pinal County	6	0.05
Lockhart, TX (city) Caldwell County	6	0.05
San Anselmo, CA (town) Marin County	6	0.05
Fort Lewis, WA (cdp) Pierce County	5	0.05
Glenpool, OK (city) Tulsa County	5	0.05
Royse City, TX (city) Rockwall County	5	0.05
San Diego Country Estates, CA (cdp) San Diego County	5	0.05
Aurora, MO (city) Lawrence County	4	0.05
Dalhart, TX (city) Dallam County	4	0.05
Fort Riley, KS (cdp) Riley County	4	0.05
Golden Hills, CA (cdp) Kern County	4	0.05
Kirby, TX (city) Bexar County	4	0.05
London, KY (city) Laurel County	4	0.05
Shiprock, NM (cdp) San Juan County	4	0.05
Wichita, KS (city) Sedgwick County	138	0.04
Broken Arrow, OK (city) Tulsa County	44	0.04
Odessa, TX (city) Ector County	43	0.04
Lawrence, KS (city) Douglas County	39	0.04
North Richland Hills, TX (city) Tarrant County	24	0.04
Cedar Park, TX (city) Williamson County	22	0.04
Euless, TX (city) Tarrant County	21	0.04
Farmington, NM (city) San Juan County	20	0.04
The Colony, TX (city) Denton County	14	0.04
Owasso, OK (city) Tulsa County	13	0.04
Eureka, CA (city) Humboldt County	12	0.04
Paris, TX (city) Lamar County	11	0.04
Pueblo West, CO (cdp) Pueblo County	11	0.04
Kyle, TX (city) Hays County	10	0.04
Watauga, TX (city) Tarrant County	10	0.04
Rosemont, CA (cdp) Sacramento County	9	0.04
Altus, OK (city) Jackson County	8	0.04
Clifton, CO (cdp) Mesa County	8	0.04
Port Hueneme, CA (city) Ventura County	8	0.04
Wadsworth, OH (city) Medina County	8	0.04
Badger, AK (cdp) Fairbanks North Star Borough	7	0.04
Gainesville, TX (city) Cooke County	7	0.04
Menasha, WI (town) Winnebago County	7	0.04
White Settlement, TX (city) Tarrant County	7	0.04
East Lampeter, PA (township) Lancaster County	6	0.04
Lemon Hill, CA (cdp) Sacramento County	6	0.04
Ripon, CA (city) San Joaquin County	6	0.04
Borger, TX (city) Hutchinson County	5	0.04
Carpinteria, CA (city) Santa Barbara County	5	0.04
Cornelius, OR (city) Washington County	5	0.04
Discovery Bay, CA (cdp) Contra Costa County	5	0.04
Evanston, WY (city) Uinta County	5	0.04
Freeport, TX (city) Brazoria County	5	0.04
Gainesville, VA (cdp) Prince William County	5	0.04
Greenlawn, NY (cdp) Suffolk County	5	0.04
Niles, MI (city) Berrien County	5	0.04
Niles, MI (city) Berrien County	5	0.04
Timberwood Park, TX (cdp) Bexar County	5	0.04
Waukee, IA (city) Dallas County	5	0.04
Alpena, MI (city) Alpena County	4	0.04
Atchison, KS (city) Atchison County	4	0.04
Berkley, CO (cdp) Adams County	4	0.04
Bonham, TX (city) Fannin County	4	0.04
Celina, OH (city) Mercer County	4	0.04
Crestline, CA (cdp) San Bernardino County	4	0.04
Half Moon Bay, CA (city) San Mateo County	4	0.04
Hawaiian Paradise Park, HI (cdp) Hawaii County	4	0.04
Heath, OH (city) Licking County	4	0.04
Jacinto City, TX (city) Harris County	4	0.04
Milford, PA (township) Bucks County	4	0.04
Monmouth, IL (city) Warren County	4	0.04
Mooresville, IN (town) Morgan County	4	0.04
Riverton, WY (city) Fremont County	4	0.04
Socorro, NM (city) Socorro County	4	0.04
Valencia West, AZ (cdp) Pima County	4	0.04
View Park-Windsor Hills, CA (cdp) Los Angeles County	4	0.04
Warren, RI (town) Bristol County	4	0.04
Aransas Pass, TX (city) San Patricio County	3	0.04
Bridge City, TX (city) Orange County	3	0.04
Butner, NC (town) Granville County	3	0.04
Catalina, AZ (cdp) Pima County	3	0.04
Fort Stockton, TX (city) Pecos County	3	0.04
Four Corners, MD (cdp) Montgomery County	3	0.04
Granbury, TX (city) Hood County	3	0.04
Kalifornsky, AK (cdp) Kenai Peninsula Borough	3	0.04
Kirtland, NM (cdp) San Juan County	3	0.04
New Richmond, WI (city) St. Croix County	3	0.04
Pleasant Hill, MO (city) Cass County	3	0.04
Pukalani, HI (cdp) Maui County	3	0.04
Smithfield, VA (town) Isle of Wight County	3	0.04
Wasilla, AK (city) Matanuska-Susitna Borough	3	0.04
Yreka, CA (city) Siskiyou County	3	0.04
Lubbock, TX (city) Lubbock County	73	0.03
Amarillo, TX (city) Potter County	63	0.03

Please refer to the Explanation of Data in the front of the book for more detailed information.

Race

American Indian: Cree

U.S. and 50 States Sorted by Population and Percent of Total Population

Place	Population	%
United States	**7,983**	**<0.01**
California	1,053	<0.01
Washington	736	0.01
Montana	661	0.07
Florida	433	<0.01
Michigan	358	<0.01
Texas	303	<0.01
Oregon	274	0.01
New York	263	<0.01
Minnesota	245	<0.01
Pennsylvania	217	<0.01
Illinois	197	<0.01
Arizona	194	<0.01
Ohio	194	<0.01
Colorado	180	<0.01
Massachusetts	145	<0.01
Oklahoma	132	<0.01
Virginia	131	<0.01
Nevada	123	<0.01
New Jersey	120	<0.01
Idaho	119	0.01
Indiana	115	<0.01
Missouri	106	<0.01
Wisconsin	105	<0.01
Hawaii	104	0.01
North Carolina	104	<0.01
Tennessee	100	<0.01
Alaska	99	0.01
Maryland	93	<0.01
Georgia	87	<0.01
Utah	87	<0.01
New Mexico	83	<0.01
Connecticut	73	<0.01
Kansas	72	<0.01
Alabama	65	<0.01
Rhode Island	58	0.01
New Hampshire	58	<0.01
Kentucky	54	<0.01
South Carolina	50	<0.01
Maine	47	<0.01
Arkansas	44	<0.01
Vermont	43	0.01
Iowa	42	<0.01
Louisiana	41	<0.01
North Dakota	38	0.01
Nebraska	36	<0.01
South Dakota	24	<0.01
West Virginia	23	<0.01
Wyoming	21	<0.01
Mississippi	18	<0.01
District of Columbia	10	<0.01
Delaware	5	<0.01

Place	Population	%
Montana	661	0.07
Washington	736	0.01
Oregon	274	0.01
Idaho	119	0.01
Hawaii	104	0.01
Alaska	99	0.01
Rhode Island	58	0.01
Vermont	43	0.01
North Dakota	38	0.01
United States	**7,983**	**<0.01**
California	1,053	<0.01
Florida	433	<0.01
Michigan	358	<0.01
Texas	303	<0.01
New York	263	<0.01
Minnesota	245	<0.01
Pennsylvania	217	<0.01
Illinois	197	<0.01
Arizona	194	<0.01
Ohio	194	<0.01
Colorado	180	<0.01
Massachusetts	145	<0.01
Oklahoma	132	<0.01
Virginia	131	<0.01
Nevada	123	<0.01
New Jersey	120	<0.01
Indiana	115	<0.01
Missouri	106	<0.01
Wisconsin	105	<0.01
North Carolina	104	<0.01
Tennessee	100	<0.01
Maryland	93	<0.01
Georgia	87	<0.01
Utah	87	<0.01
New Mexico	83	<0.01
Connecticut	73	<0.01
Kansas	72	<0.01
Alabama	65	<0.01
New Hampshire	58	<0.01
Kentucky	54	<0.01
South Carolina	50	<0.01
Maine	47	<0.01
Arkansas	44	<0.01
Iowa	42	<0.01
Louisiana	41	<0.01
Nebraska	36	<0.01
South Dakota	24	<0.01
West Virginia	23	<0.01
Wyoming	21	<0.01
Mississippi	18	<0.01
District of Columbia	10	<0.01
Delaware	5	<0.01

Please refer to the Explanation of Data in the front of the book for more detailed information.

Race

American Indian: Cree

Top 150 Places Sorted by Population

Based on all places, regardless of total population

Place	Population	%
Great Falls, MT (city) Cascade County	85	0.15
New York, NY (city) Kings County	81	<0.01
Los Angeles, CA (city) Los Angeles County	66	<0.01
Seattle, WA (city) King County	61	0.01
Chicago, IL (city) Cook County	54	<0.01
Spokane, WA (city) Spokane County	51	0.02
Portland, OR (city) Multnomah County	48	0.01
San Diego, CA (city) San Diego County	40	<0.01
Sacramento, CA (city) Sacramento County	39	0.01
Phoenix, AZ (city) Maricopa County	37	<0.01
Minneapolis, MN (city) Hennepin County	36	0.01
San Francisco, CA (city) San Francisco County	35	<0.01
Missoula, MT (city) Missoula County	32	0.05
Detroit, MI (city) Wayne County	32	<0.01
Urban Honolulu, HI (cdp) Honolulu County	27	0.01
Anchorage, AK (municipality) Anchorage Municipality	25	0.01
Albuquerque, NM (city) Bernalillo County	25	<0.01
Jacksonville, FL (city) Duval County	25	<0.01
Milwaukee, WI (city) Milwaukee County	25	<0.01
Philadelphia, PA (city) Philadelphia County	25	<0.01
Spokane Valley, WA (city) Spokane County	24	0.03
Billings, MT (city) Yellowstone County	24	0.02
Boise City, ID (city) Ada County	24	0.01
Queens, NY (borough) Queens County	24	<0.01
Las Vegas, NV (city) Clark County	22	<0.01
Manhattan, NY (borough) New York County	22	<0.01
Oklahoma City, OK (city) Oklahoma County	22	<0.01
Denver, CO (city) Denver County	21	<0.01
Browning, MT (town) Glacier County	20	1.97
Salem, OR (city) Marion County	20	0.01
Colorado Springs, CO (city) El Paso County	20	<0.01
Nashville-Davidson, TN (metro govt) Davidson County	20	<0.01
South Browning, MT (cdp) Glacier County	18	1.01
Austin, TX (city) Travis County	18	<0.01
San Jose, CA (city) Santa Clara County	18	<0.01
Tucson, AZ (city) Pima County	18	<0.01
Pablo, MT (cdp) Lake County	17	0.75
Cut Bank, MT (city) Glacier County	17	0.59
Havre, MT (city) Hill County	17	0.18
St. Paul, MN (city) Ramsey County	17	0.01
Columbus, OH (city) Franklin County	17	<0.01
Houston, TX (city) Harris County	17	<0.01
Kent, WA (city) King County	16	0.02
Manchester, NH (city) Hillsborough County	16	0.01
Sunrise Manor, NV (cdp) Clark County	16	0.01
Bronx, NY (borough) Bronx County	16	<0.01
Kansas City, MO (city) Jackson County	16	<0.01
Tempe, AZ (city) Maricopa County	15	0.01
Brooklyn, NY (borough) Kings County	15	<0.01
Fresno, CA (city) Fresno County	15	<0.01
Tulsa, OK (city) Tulsa County	15	<0.01
Chistochina, AK (cdp) Valdez-Cordova Census Area	14	15.05
Fayette, PA (township) Juniata County	14	0.40
Butte-Silver Bow, MT (cons. govt) Silver Bow County	14	0.04
Ann Arbor, MI (city) Washtenaw County	14	0.01
Oakland, CA (city) Alameda County	14	<0.01
Tampa, FL (city) Hillsborough County	14	<0.01
Wichita, KS (city) Sedgwick County	14	<0.01
Eugene, OR (city) Lane County	13	0.01
Santa Rosa, CA (city) Sonoma County	13	0.01
Tacoma, WA (city) Pierce County	13	0.01
Fort Worth, TX (city) Tarrant County	13	<0.01
Indianapolis, IN (city) Marion County	13	<0.01
Long Beach, CA (city) Los Angeles County	13	<0.01
Mesa, AZ (city) Maricopa County	13	<0.01
Bellingham, WA (city) Whatcom County	12	0.01
North Las Vegas, NV (city) Clark County	12	0.01
Paradise, NV (cdp) Clark County	12	0.01
Omaha, NE (city) Douglas County	12	<0.01
San Antonio, TX (city) Medina County	12	<0.01
Lincoln, RI (town) Providence County	11	0.05
Longview, WA (city) Cowlitz County	11	0.03
Moorhead, MN (city) Clay County	11	0.03
Everett, WA (city) Snohomish County	11	0.01
Fayetteville, NC (city) Cumberland County	11	0.01
Provo, UT (city) Utah County	11	0.01
Vancouver, WA (city) Clark County	11	0.01
Auburn Hills, MI (city) Oakland County	10	0.05
Kalispell, MT (city) Flathead County	10	0.05
Helena, MT (city) Lewis and Clark County	10	0.04
Altadena, CA (cdp) Los Angeles County	10	0.02
Carson City, NV (ind. city) Carson City County	10	0.02
Clarksville, TN (city) Montgomery County	10	0.01
Baltimore, MD (city) Baltimore city County	10	<0.01
Boston, MA (city) Suffolk County	10	<0.01
Charlotte, NC (city) Mecklenburg County	10	<0.01
Chesapeake, VA (ind. city) Chesapeake independent city	10	<0.01
Washington, DC (city) District of Columbia	10	<0.01
Heart Butte, MT (cdp) Pondera County	9	1.55
Hays, MT (cdp) Blaine County	9	1.07
Bryn Mawr-Skyway, WA (cdp) King County	9	0.06
Pocatello, ID (city) Bannock County	9	0.02
Gresham, OR (city) Multnomah County	9	0.01
Marysville, WA (city) Snohomish County	9	0.01
Terre Haute, IN (city) Vigo County	9	0.01
Fort Wayne, IN (city) Allen County	9	<0.01
St. Louis, MO (city) St. Louis city County	9	<0.01
North Browning, MT (cdp) Glacier County	8	0.33
Helena Valley Southeast, MT (cdp) Lewis and Clark County	8	0.10
Magalia, CA (cdp) Butte County	8	0.07
Carlsbad, NM (city) Eddy County	8	0.03
Flint, MI (charter township) Genesee County	8	0.03
Bellevue, WA (city) King County	8	0.01
Berkeley, CA (city) Alameda County	8	0.01
El Cajon, CA (city) San Diego County	8	0.01
Elk Grove, CA (city) Sacramento County	8	0.01
Lakewood, CO (city) Jefferson County	8	0.01
Pasadena, CA (city) Los Angeles County	8	0.01
Redmond, WA (city) King County	8	0.01
Santa Cruz, CA (city) Santa Cruz County	8	0.01
Springfield, MA (city) Hampden County	8	0.01
Stamford, CT (city/town) Fairfield County	8	0.01
The Woodlands, TX (cdp) Montgomery County	8	0.01
Vacaville, CA (city) Solano County	8	0.01
Vallejo, CA (city) Solano County	8	0.01
Akron, OH (city) Summit County	8	<0.01
Modesto, CA (city) Stanislaus County	8	<0.01
Salt Lake City, UT (city) Salt Lake County	8	<0.01
Chinook, MT (city) Blaine County	7	0.58
Fort Hall, ID (cdp) Bannock County	7	0.22
Cheney, WA (city) Spokane County	7	0.07
Clearlake, CA (city) Lake County	7	0.05
Red Wing, MN (city) Goodhue County	7	0.04
Oak Harbor, WA (city) Island County	7	0.03
Spanaway, WA (cdp) Pierce County	7	0.03
Claremont, CA (city) Los Angeles County	7	0.02
Danville, IL (city) Vermilion County	7	0.02
Gloucester, MA (city) Essex County	7	0.02
Hilo, HI (cdp) Hawaii County	7	0.02
North Highlands, CA (cdp) Sacramento County	7	0.02
Blaine, MN (city) Anoka County	7	0.01
Duluth, MN (city) St. Louis County	7	0.01
Gary, IN (city) Lake County	7	0.01
Lakewood, CA (city) Los Angeles County	7	0.01
Lodi, CA (city) San Joaquin County	7	0.01
Richland, WA (city) Benton County	7	0.01
Richmond, CA (city) Contra Costa County	7	0.01
Sarasota, FL (city) Sarasota County	7	0.01
Shelby, MI (charter township) Macomb County	7	0.01
Visalia, CA (city) Tulare County	7	0.01
West Valley City, UT (city) Salt Lake County	7	0.01
Arlington, TX (city) Tarrant County	7	<0.01
Aurora, CO (city) Arapahoe County	7	<0.01
Moreno Valley, CA (city) Riverside County	7	<0.01
New Orleans, LA (city) Orleans Parish	7	<0.01
Oceanside, CA (city) San Diego County	7	<0.01
San Bernardino, CA (city) San Bernardino County	7	<0.01
Torrance, CA (city) Los Angeles County	7	<0.01
Hardin, MT (city) Big Horn County	6	0.17
West DeLand, FL (cdp) Volusia County	6	0.17

Race

American Indian: Cree

Top 150 Places Sorted by Percent of Total Population

Based on all places, regardless of total population

Place	Population	%
Chistochina, AK (cdp) Valdez-Cordova Census Area	14	15.05
Furnace Creek, CA (cdp) Inyo County	2	8.33
Rapid River, MN (township) Lake of the Woods County	1	8.33
Niarada, MT (cdp) Flathead County	1	3.70
Rexford, MT (town) Lincoln County	3	2.86
Floriston, CA (cdp) Nevada County	2	2.74
Rollis, MN (township) Marshall County	3	2.61
Lincoln, MN (township) Marshall County	3	2.56
Byram Center, NJ (cdp) Sussex County	2	2.22
Starr School, MT (cdp) Glacier County	5	1.98
Browning, MT (town) Glacier County	20	1.97
Nelson Lagoon, AK (cdp) Aleutians East Borough	1	1.92
Otter Tail Peninsula, MN (township) Cass County	1	1.85
Clover, MN (township) Clearwater County	2	1.77
Babb, MT (cdp) Glacier County	3	1.72
Fairbanks, MN (township) St. Louis County	1	1.59
Heart Butte, MT (cdp) Pondera County	9	1.55
Dixon, MT (cdp) Sanders County	3	1.48
Packwood, WA (cdp) Lewis County	5	1.46
St. Pierre, MT (cdp) Hill County	5	1.43
East Glacier Park Village, MT (cdp) Glacier County	5	1.38
Ravalli, MT (cdp) Lake County	1	1.32
Gurney, WI (town) Iron County	2	1.26
Millbrook, IL (village) Kendall County	4	1.19
Dupuyer, MT (cdp) Pondera County	1	1.16
Pelican, AK (city) Hoonah-Angoon Census Area	1	1.14
Rader Creek, MT (cdp) Jefferson County	4	1.10
Hays, MT (cdp) Blaine County	9	1.07
Azure, MT (cdp) Hill County	3	1.05
South Browning, MT (cdp) Glacier County	18	1.01
Toston, MT (cdp) Broadwater County	1	0.93
McDermott, OH (cdp) Scioto County	4	0.92
Federal Dam, MN (city) Cass County	1	0.91
Geneva, MN (city) Freeborn County	5	0.90
Rocky Boy's Agency, MT (cdp) Hill County	3	0.85
Dodson, MT (town) Phillips County	1	0.81
King Salmon, AK (cdp) Bristol Bay Borough	3	0.80
Pablo, MT (cdp) Lake County	17	0.75
Lodge Pole, MT (cdp) Blaine County	2	0.75
Hazel, KY (city) Calloway County	3	0.73
Emerado, ND (city) Grand Forks County	3	0.72
Vineyard, UT (town) Utah County	1	0.72
Summit Lake, WI (cdp) Langlade County	1	0.69
Elizabethtown, NY (cdp) Essex County	5	0.66
Henry, TN (town) Henry County	3	0.65
Loomis, WA (cdp) Okanogan County	1	0.63
Wainwright, OK (town) Muskogee County	1	0.61
Cut Bank, MT (city) Glacier County	17	0.59
Wye, MT (cdp) Missoula County	3	0.59
Chinook, MT (city) Blaine County	7	0.58
South Hills, MT (cdp) Jefferson County	3	0.58
Havre North, MT (cdp) Hill County	4	0.56
Elmo, MT (cdp) Lake County	1	0.56
Frazer, MT (cdp) Valley County	2	0.55
Gilchrist, MN (township) Pope County	1	0.52
Willow Creek, AK (cdp) Valdez-Cordova Census Area	1	0.52
Greenleaf, MI (township) Sanilac County	4	0.51
Finland, MN (cdp) Lake County	1	0.51
Minden City, MI (village) Sanilac County	1	0.51
Ruth, CA (cdp) Trinity County	1	0.51
Belgium, IL (village) Vermilion County	2	0.50
Tenstrike, MN (city) Beltrami County	1	0.50
Arlee, MT (cdp) Lake County	3	0.47
Wadena, MN (township) Wadena County	4	0.46
Tucker, MS (cdp) Neshoba County	3	0.45
Lee Vining, CA (cdp) Mono County	1	0.45
Lewellen, NE (village) Garden County	1	0.45
Viola, WI (village) Vernon County	1	0.45
Rocky Hill, NJ (borough) Somerset County	3	0.44
Elizabethtown, NY (town) Essex County	5	0.43
Boulder, MT (city) Jefferson County	5	0.42
Fieldon, IL (village) Jersey County	1	0.42
Lexington, OR (town) Morrow County	1	0.42
Losantville, IN (town) Randolph County	1	0.42
Graeagle, CA (cdp) Plumas County	3	0.41
Ryegate, MT (town) Golden Valley County	1	0.41
Fayette, PA (township) Juniata County	14	0.40
Basye, VA (cdp) Shenandoah County	5	0.40
Matagorda, TX (cdp) Matagorda County	2	0.40
Fort Belknap Agency, MT (cdp) Blaine County	5	0.39
McCurtain, OK (town) Haskell County	2	0.39
Little Elbow, MN (township) Mahnomen County	1	0.39
Marenisco, MI (cdp) Gogebic County	1	0.39
Brookville, KS (city) Saline County	1	0.38
Fairview, KS (city) Brown County	1	0.38
Harlem, MT (city) Blaine County	3	0.37
Toad Lake, MN (township) Becker County	2	0.37
St. Ignatius, MT (town) Lake County	3	0.36
Stateline, NV (cdp) Douglas County	3	0.36
Homer, NE (village) Dakota County	2	0.36
Jones, MN (township) Beltrami County	1	0.36
Augusta, KY (city) Bracken County	4	0.34
Rocky Boy West, MT (cdp) Chouteau County	3	0.34
Darnen, MN (township) Stevens County	1	0.34
North Browning, MT (cdp) Glacier County	8	0.33
Harriston, VA (cdp) Augusta County	3	0.33
Briggs, OK (cdp) Cherokee County	1	0.33
Pe Ell, WA (town) Lewis County	2	0.32
Electric City, WA (city) Grant County	3	0.31
Benbow, CA (cdp) Humboldt County	1	0.31
Evaro, MT (cdp) Missoula County	1	0.31
Lake Bosworth, WA (cdp) Snohomish County	2	0.30
Panton, VT (town) Addison County	2	0.30
Schurz, NV (cdp) Mineral County	2	0.30
Quonochontaug, RI (cdp) Washington County	1	0.30
Cascade, MT (town) Cascade County	2	0.29
Parker School, MT (cdp) Hill County	1	0.29
Clear Lake, WA (cdp) Pierce County	4	0.28
Simms, MT (cdp) Cascade County	1	0.28
Ronan, MT (city) Lake County	5	0.27
Bellevue, MN (township) Morrison County	3	0.27
Cedar Fort, UT (town) Utah County	1	0.27
Twin Bridges, MT (town) Madison County	1	0.27
Mounds, OK (town) Creek County	3	0.26
Gopher Flats, OR (cdp) Umatilla County	1	0.26
Norman, AR (town) Montgomery County	1	0.26
Fonda, NY (village) Montgomery County	2	0.25
Bertha, MN (township) Todd County	1	0.25
Lewistown Heights, MT (cdp) Fergus County	1	0.25
Osmond, WY (cdp) Lincoln County	1	0.25
Stanford, MT (town) Judith Basin County	1	0.25
Wilkinson, MN (township) Cass County	1	0.25
Choteau, MT (city) Teton County	4	0.24
Ashland, MT (cdp) Rosebud County	2	0.24
Germantown, NY (cdp) Columbia County	2	0.24
Garden Valley, WI (town) Jackson County	1	0.24
New Auburn, MN (township) Sibley County	1	0.24
Willow River, MN (city) Pine County	1	0.24
Lower Lake, CA (cdp) Lake County	3	0.23
Kenansville, NC (town) Duplin County	2	0.23
Naalehu, HI (cdp) Hawaii County	2	0.23
Clinton, MI (township) Oscoda County	1	0.23
Forestville, WI (village) Door County	1	0.23
Hill Lake, MN (township) Aitkin County	1	0.23
Fort Hall, ID (cdp) Bannock County	7	0.22
Allentown, NJ (borough) Monmouth County	4	0.22
Byron, WI (town) Monroe County	3	0.22
Bowie, AZ (cdp) Cochise County	1	0.22
Finleyville, PA (borough) Washington County	1	0.22
Port Gibson, NY (cdp) Ontario County	1	0.22
Springbrook, WI (town) Washburn County	1	0.22
Melrose, MI (township) Charlevoix County	3	0.21
Ortonville, MI (village) Oakland County	3	0.21
Bridgewater, VT (town) Windsor County	2	0.21
Coolidge, TX (town) Limestone County	2	0.21
Discovery Harbour, HI (cdp) Hawaii County	2	0.21
White Sulphur Springs, MT (city) Meagher County	2	0.21
Woodruff, WI (cdp) Oneida County	2	0.21
Beaver Bay, MN (township) Lake County	1	0.21
Isle La Motte, VT (town) Grand Isle County	1	0.21

Please refer to the Explanation of Data in the front of the book for more detailed information.

Race

American Indian: Cree

Top 150 Places Sorted by Percent of Total Population

Based on places with total population of 7,500 or more

Place	Population	%
Havre, MT (city) Hill County	17	0.18
Great Falls, MT (city) Cascade County	85	0.15
Helena Valley Southeast, MT (cdp) Lewis and Clark County	8	0.10
Grand Ledge, MI (city) Eaton County	6	0.08
Grand Ledge, MI (city) Eaton County	6	0.08
Magalia, CA (cdp) Butte County	8	0.07
Cheney, WA (city) Spokane County	7	0.07
Bryn Mawr-Skyway, WA (cdp) King County	9	0.06
Birch Bay, WA (cdp) Whatcom County	5	0.06
Richmond, RI (town) Washington County	5	0.06
Missoula, MT (city) Missoula County	32	0.05
Lincoln, RI (town) Providence County	11	0.05
Auburn Hills, MI (city) Oakland County	10	0.05
Kalispell, MT (city) Flathead County	10	0.05
Clearlake, CA (city) Lake County	7	0.05
Minooka, IL (village) Grundy County	5	0.05
Conning Towers Nautilus Park, CT (cdp) New London County	4	0.05
Lansdowne, MD (cdp) Baltimore County	4	0.05
Newton, NJ (town) Sussex County	4	0.05
Ocean Pointe, HI (cdp) Honolulu County	4	0.05
Stayton, OR (city) Marion County	4	0.05
Virginia, MN (city) St. Louis County	4	0.05
Butte-Silver Bow, MT (cons. govt) Silver Bow County	14	0.04
Helena, MT (city) Lewis and Clark County	10	0.04
Red Wing, MN (city) Goodhue County	7	0.04
Anacortes, WA (city) Skagit County	6	0.04
Amherst, NH (town) Hillsborough County	5	0.04
Hayden, ID (city) Kootenai County	5	0.04
Olivehurst, CA (cdp) Yuba County	5	0.04
Valley Falls, RI (cdp) Providence County	5	0.04
Anaconda-Deer Lodge County, MT (special city) Deer Lodge County	4	0.04
Berlin, NH (city) Coos County	4	0.04
Diamond Springs, CA (cdp) El Dorado County	4	0.04
Fort Meade, MD (cdp) Anne Arundel County	4	0.04
Reserve, LA (cdp) St. John the Baptist Parish	4	0.04
Sedro-Woolley, WA (city) Skagit County	4	0.04
Vernal, UT (city) Uintah County	4	0.04
Waimea, HI (cdp) Hawaii County	4	0.04
Winslow, AZ (city) Navajo County	4	0.04
Corning, CA (city) Tehama County	3	0.04
Eaton, OH (city) Preble County	3	0.04
Glenside, PA (cdp) Montgomery County	3	0.04
Haiku-Pauwela, HI (cdp) Maui County	3	0.04
Hastings-on-Hudson, NY (village) Westchester County	3	0.04
Pulaski, TN (city) Giles County	3	0.04
Smithfield, VA (town) Isle of Wight County	3	0.04
South Kensington, MD (cdp) Montgomery County	3	0.04
Wagoner, OK (city) Wagoner County	3	0.04
Wellington, KS (city) Sumner County	3	0.04
Spokane Valley, WA (city) Spokane County	24	0.03
Longview, WA (city) Cowlitz County	11	0.03
Moorhead, MN (city) Clay County	11	0.03
Carlsbad, NM (city) Eddy County	8	0.03
Flint, MI (charter township) Genesee County	8	0.03
Oak Harbor, WA (city) Island County	7	0.03
Spanaway, WA (cdp) Pierce County	7	0.03
Brigham City, UT (city) Box Elder County	6	0.03
Graham, WA (cdp) Pierce County	6	0.03
Monroe, WA (city) Snohomish County	6	0.03
Valinda, CA (cdp) Los Angeles County	6	0.03
Asbury Park, NJ (city) Monmouth County	5	0.03
Pendleton, OR (city) Umatilla County	5	0.03
Stuart, FL (city) Martin County	5	0.03
Tahlequah, OK (city) Cherokee County	5	0.03
Wailuku, HI (cdp) Maui County	5	0.03
Waterford, CT (town) New London County	5	0.03
Ada, MI (township) Kent County	4	0.03
Arcadia, NY (town) Wayne County	4	0.03
Blackfoot, ID (city) Bingham County	4	0.03
Brandon, MI (charter township) Oakland County	4	0.03
Elkridge, MD (cdp) Howard County	4	0.03
Festus, MO (city) Jefferson County	4	0.03
Lakeland South, WA (cdp) King County	4	0.03
Mercerville, NJ (cdp) Mercer County	4	0.03
Mesquite, NV (city) Clark County	4	0.03
Warren, NJ (township) Somerset County	4	0.03
White Center, WA (cdp) King County	4	0.03
Williston, ND (city) Williams County	4	0.03
Baker City, OR (city) Baker County	3	0.03
Beecher, MI (cdp) Genesee County	3	0.03
Coweta, OK (city) Wagoner County	3	0.03
Essex Junction, VT (village) Chittenden County	3	0.03
Grovetown, GA (city) Columbia County	3	0.03
Hamlin, NY (town) Monroe County	3	0.03
Heath, OH (city) Licking County	3	0.03
Holly Hill, FL (city) Volusia County	3	0.03
Lake Tapps, WA (cdp) Pierce County	3	0.03
Little River, SC (cdp) Horry County	3	0.03
New Port Richey East, FL (cdp) Pasco County	3	0.03
Newark, NY (village) Wayne County	3	0.03
Plymouth, IN (city) Marshall County	3	0.03
Quartz Hill, CA (cdp) Los Angeles County	3	0.03
Toppenish, WA (city) Yakima County	3	0.03
Valencia West, AZ (cdp) Pima County	3	0.03
Caldwell, NJ (borough) Essex County	2	0.03
Cushing, OK (city) Payne County	2	0.03
Evergreen, MT (cdp) Flathead County	2	0.03
Glen Ridge, NJ (borough) Essex County	2	0.03
Helena Valley West Central, MT (cdp) Lewis and Clark County	2	0.03
Kalifornsky, AK (cdp) Kenai Peninsula Borough	2	0.03
Liberty Lake, WA (city) Spokane County	2	0.03
Rhinelander, WI (city) Oneida County	2	0.03
Sutherlin, OR (city) Douglas County	2	0.03
West Earl, PA (township) Lancaster County	2	0.03
Woodstock, CT (town) Windham County	2	0.03
Spokane, WA (city) Spokane County	51	0.02
Billings, MT (city) Yellowstone County	24	0.02
Kent, WA (city) King County	16	0.02
Altadena, CA (cdp) Los Angeles County	10	0.02
Carson City, NV (ind. city) Carson City County	10	0.02
Pocatello, ID (city) Bannock County	9	0.02
Claremont, CA (city) Los Angeles County	7	0.02
Danville, IL (city) Vermilion County	7	0.02
Gloucester, MA (city) Essex County	7	0.02
Hilo, HI (cdp) Hawaii County	7	0.02
North Highlands, CA (cdp) Sacramento County	7	0.02
Brighton, CO (city) Adams County	6	0.02
Carrollwood, FL (cdp) Hillsborough County	6	0.02
Cottage Grove, MN (city) Washington County	6	0.02
Juneau, AK (borough) Juneau City and Borough	6	0.02
Leavenworth, KS (city) Leavenworth County	6	0.02
Romeoville, IL (village) Will County	6	0.02
Wenatchee, WA (city) Chelan County	6	0.02
Zanesville, OH (city) Muskingum County	6	0.02
Cottage Lake, WA (cdp) King County	5	0.02
Des Moines, WA (city) King County	5	0.02
Eastmont, WA (cdp) Snohomish County	5	0.02
Eastpointe, MI (city) Macomb County	5	0.02
Ewa Gentry, HI (cdp) Honolulu County	5	0.02
Gallup, NM (city) McKinley County	5	0.02
Land O' Lakes, FL (cdp) Pasco County	5	0.02
West Warwick, RI (town) Kent County	5	0.02
Badger, AK (cdp) Fairbanks North Star Borough	4	0.02
Battle Ground, WA (city) Clark County	4	0.02
Blythe, CA (city) Riverside County	4	0.02
Casselberry, FL (city) Seminole County	4	0.02
Essex, VT (town) Chittenden County	4	0.02
Forest Hills, MI (cdp) Kent County	4	0.02
Hammond, LA (city) Tangipahoa Parish	4	0.02
Hastings, NE (city) Adams County	4	0.02
Hazelwood, MO (city) St. Louis County	4	0.02
Marshfield, MA (town) Plymouth County	4	0.02
Murphy, TX (city) Collin County	4	0.02
Port Angeles, WA (city) Clallam County	4	0.02
Rosemont, CA (cdp) Sacramento County	4	0.02
Silverdale, WA (cdp) Kitsap County	4	0.02
Somerset, MA (cdp/town) Bristol County	4	0.02
South St. Paul, MN (city) Dakota County	4	0.02
Wasco, CA (city) Kern County	4	0.02
Belchertown, MA (town) Hampshire County	3	0.02

Please refer to the Explanation of Data in the front of the book for more detailed information.

Race

American Indian: Creek

U.S. and 50 States Sorted by Population and Percent of Total Population

Place	Population	%
United States	**88,332**	**0.03**
Oklahoma	44,170	1.18
Florida	6,779	0.04
California	6,195	0.02
Alabama	5,905	0.12
Texas	4,823	0.02
Georgia	2,370	0.02
Kansas	1,777	0.06
Arkansas	1,059	0.04
Arizona	1,022	0.02
Washington	1,008	0.01
Missouri	998	0.02
Oregon	837	0.02
Colorado	813	0.02
Virginia	715	0.01
Tennessee	709	0.01
North Carolina	671	0.01
New York	624	<0.01
Michigan	620	0.01
Illinois	599	<0.01
Louisiana	598	0.01
Ohio	579	0.01
New Mexico	475	0.02
South Carolina	415	0.01
Nevada	395	0.01
Pennsylvania	393	<0.01
Indiana	375	0.01
Mississippi	359	0.01
Maryland	349	0.01
Kentucky	247	0.01
New Jersey	243	<0.01
Wisconsin	209	<0.01
Hawaii	204	0.01
Minnesota	202	<0.01
Utah	195	0.01
Alaska	185	0.03
Idaho	152	0.01
Massachusetts	152	<0.01
Nebraska	149	0.01
Iowa	137	<0.01
Connecticut	111	<0.01
Montana	98	0.01
District of Columbia	62	0.01
Maine	61	<0.01
Wyoming	57	0.01
West Virginia	54	<0.01
South Dakota	51	0.01
New Hampshire	46	<0.01
Delaware	29	<0.01
Rhode Island	23	<0.01
North Dakota	20	<0.01
Vermont	13	<0.01

Place	Population	%
Oklahoma	44,170	1.18
Alabama	5,905	0.12
Kansas	1,777	0.06
Florida	6,779	0.04
Arkansas	1,059	0.04
United States	**88,332**	**0.03**
Alaska	185	0.03
California	6,195	0.02
Texas	4,823	0.02
Georgia	2,370	0.02
Arizona	1,022	0.02
Missouri	998	0.02
Oregon	837	0.02
Colorado	813	0.02
New Mexico	475	0.02
Washington	1,008	0.01
Virginia	715	0.01
Tennessee	709	0.01
North Carolina	671	0.01
Michigan	620	0.01
Louisiana	598	0.01
Ohio	579	0.01
South Carolina	415	0.01
Nevada	395	0.01
Indiana	375	0.01
Mississippi	359	0.01
Maryland	349	0.01
Kentucky	247	0.01
Hawaii	204	0.01
Utah	195	0.01
Idaho	152	0.01
Nebraska	149	0.01
Montana	98	0.01
District of Columbia	62	0.01
Wyoming	57	0.01
South Dakota	51	0.01
New York	624	<0.01
Illinois	599	<0.01
Pennsylvania	393	<0.01
New Jersey	243	<0.01
Wisconsin	209	<0.01
Minnesota	202	<0.01
Massachusetts	152	<0.01
Iowa	137	<0.01
Connecticut	111	<0.01
Maine	61	<0.01
West Virginia	54	<0.01
New Hampshire	46	<0.01
Delaware	29	<0.01
Rhode Island	23	<0.01
North Dakota	20	<0.01
Vermont	13	<0.01

Please refer to the Explanation of Data in the front of the book for more detailed information.

Race

American Indian: Creek

Top 150 Places Sorted by Population

Based on all places, regardless of total population

Place	Population	%
Tulsa, OK (city) Tulsa County	5,849	1.49
Oklahoma City, OK (city) Oklahoma County	2,905	0.50
Okmulgee, OK (city) Okmulgee County	1,882	15.27
Muskogee, OK (city) Muskogee County	1,317	3.36
Broken Arrow, OK (city) Tulsa County	1,259	1.27
Sapulpa, OK (city) Creek County	1,143	5.56
Glenpool, OK (city) Tulsa County	893	8.26
Henryetta, OK (city) Okmulgee County	765	12.91
Okemah, OK (city) Okfuskee County	723	22.43
Shawnee, OK (city) Pottawatomie County	586	1.96
Norman, OK (city) Cleveland County	580	0.52
Wichita, KS (city) Sedgwick County	557	0.15
Holdenville, OK (city) Hughes County	544	9.43
Coweta, OK (city) Wagoner County	490	4.93
Wetumka, OK (city) Hughes County	420	32.76
Sand Springs, OK (city) Tulsa County	390	2.06
Bixby, OK (city) Tulsa County	386	1.85
Bristow, OK (city) Creek County	369	8.74
Eufaula, OK (city) McIntosh County	357	12.69
Jenks, OK (city) Tulsa County	356	2.10
Midwest City, OK (city) Oklahoma County	347	0.64
Edmond, OK (city) Oklahoma County	341	0.42
Checotah, OK (city) McIntosh County	340	10.19
Los Angeles, CA (city) Los Angeles County	334	0.01
Moore, OK (city) Cleveland County	330	0.60
New York, NY (city) Kings County	291	<0.01
Morris, OK (city) Okmulgee County	289	19.54
Weleetka, OK (town) Okfuskee County	271	27.15
Seminole, OK (city) Seminole County	265	3.54
Claremore, OK (city) Rogers County	262	1.41
Stillwater, OK (city) Payne County	254	0.56
Dallas, TX (city) Dallas County	251	0.02
Del City, OK (city) Oklahoma County	247	1.16
Jacksonville, FL (city) Duval County	241	0.03
Tahlequah, OK (city) Cherokee County	232	1.47
Owasso, OK (city) Tulsa County	232	0.80
Ada, OK (city) Pontotoc County	227	1.35
Wagoner, OK (city) Wagoner County	222	2.67
Phoenix, AZ (city) Maricopa County	216	0.01
Lawrence, KS (city) Douglas County	197	0.22
Houston, TX (city) Harris County	192	0.01
Fort Worth, TX (city) Tarrant County	189	0.03
Wewoka, OK (city) Seminole County	184	5.36
Dewar, OK (town) Okmulgee County	170	19.14
Austin, TX (city) Travis County	168	0.02
San Diego, CA (city) San Diego County	163	0.01
Fresno, CA (city) Fresno County	162	0.03
Mobile, AL (city) Mobile County	159	0.08
Atmore, AL (city) Escambia County	156	1.53
Dustin, OK (town) Hughes County	155	39.24
Portland, OR (city) Multnomah County	152	0.03
Kansas City, MO (city) Jackson County	150	0.03
Bartlesville, OK (city) Washington County	149	0.42
Lawton, OK (city) Comanche County	148	0.15
Tecumseh, OK (city) Pottawatomie County	147	2.28
Bakersfield, CA (city) Kern County	143	0.04
McAlester, OK (city) Pittsburg County	139	0.76
Denver, CO (city) Denver County	139	0.02
Chicago, IL (city) Cook County	139	0.01
Pensacola, FL (city) Escambia County	138	0.27
Montgomery, AL (city) Montgomery County	138	0.07
Arlington, TX (city) Tarrant County	136	0.04
Catoosa, OK (city) Rogers County	133	1.86
Haskell, OK (town) Muskogee County	131	6.53
Albuquerque, NM (city) Bernalillo County	131	0.02
San Antonio, TX (city) Medina County	130	0.01
Bellview, FL (cdp) Escambia County	129	0.55
Beggs, OK (city) Okmulgee County	125	9.46
Ensley, FL (cdp) Escambia County	116	0.56
San Jose, CA (city) Santa Clara County	115	0.01
Kiefer, OK (town) Creek County	114	6.77
Sacramento, CA (city) Sacramento County	114	0.02
Skiatook, OK (town) Osage County	112	1.51
Pace, FL (cdp) Santa Rosa County	109	0.54
San Francisco, CA (city) San Francisco County	108	0.01
West Pensacola, FL (cdp) Escambia County	100	0.47
Long Beach, CA (city) Los Angeles County	98	0.02
Texanna, OK (cdp) McIntosh County	97	4.29
Oakland, CA (city) Alameda County	97	0.02
Mounds, OK (town) Creek County	96	8.22
Yukon, OK (city) Canadian County	96	0.42
Ferry Pass, FL (cdp) Escambia County	96	0.33
Mesa, AZ (city) Maricopa County	95	0.02
Fort Gibson, OK (town) Muskogee County	91	2.19
Columbus, GA (city) Muscogee County	91	0.05
Modesto, CA (city) Stanislaus County	85	0.04
Cushing, OK (city) Payne County	84	1.07
Tallahassee, FL (city) Leon County	83	0.05
Enid, OK (city) Garfield County	82	0.17
Ponca City, OK (city) Kay County	81	0.32
Plano, TX (city) Collin County	81	0.03
Brooklyn, NY (borough) Kings County	81	<0.01
Pryor Creek, OK (city) Mayes County	80	0.84
Colorado Springs, CO (city) El Paso County	80	0.02
Mustang, OK (city) Canadian County	78	0.45
Las Vegas, NV (city) Clark County	78	0.01
Seattle, WA (city) King County	78	0.01
Gonzalez, FL (cdp) Escambia County	77	0.58
Kellyville, OK (town) Creek County	76	6.61
San Bernardino, CA (city) San Bernardino County	76	0.04
Mannford, OK (town) Creek County	73	2.37
Choctaw, OK (city) Oklahoma County	73	0.65
Nashville-Davidson, TN (metro govt) Davidson County	73	0.01
Queens, NY (borough) Queens County	73	<0.01
Kansas City, KS (city) Wyandotte County	72	0.05
Warrington, FL (cdp) Escambia County	71	0.49
Atlanta, GA (city) Fulton County	71	0.02
Aurora, CO (city) Arapahoe County	71	0.02
Detroit, MI (city) Wayne County	71	0.01
Prague, OK (city) Lincoln County	70	2.93
Drumright, OK (city) Creek County	70	2.41
McLoud, OK (town) Pottawatomie County	70	1.73
Anchorage, AK (municipality) Anchorage Municipality	70	0.02
Oakhurst, OK (cdp) Tulsa County	69	3.16
Clinton, OK (city) Custer County	67	0.74
Harrah, OK (city) Oklahoma County	65	1.28
Spencer, OK (city) Oklahoma County	64	1.64
Ardmore, OK (city) Carter County	64	0.26
Virginia Beach, VA (ind. city) Virginia Beach independent city	64	0.01
El Reno, OK (city) Canadian County	63	0.38
Brent, FL (cdp) Escambia County	63	0.29
Fort Smith, AR (city) Sebastian County	63	0.07
Collinsville, OK (city) Tulsa County	62	1.11
Miami, OK (city) Ottawa County	62	0.46
Bethany, OK (city) Oklahoma County	62	0.33
Washington, DC (city) District of Columbia	62	0.01
Pawhuska, OK (city) Osage County	61	1.70
Dothan, AL (city) Houston County	61	0.09
Manhattan, NY (borough) New York County	61	<0.01
Amarillo, TX (city) Potter County	60	0.03
Paden, OK (town) Okfuskee County	59	12.80
Myrtle Grove, FL (cdp) Escambia County	59	0.37
Philadelphia, PA (city) Philadelphia County	59	<0.01
Bay Minette, AL (city) Baldwin County	58	0.72
Tucson, AZ (city) Pima County	58	0.01
Schulter, OK (town) Okmulgee County	57	11.20
Turley, OK (cdp) Tulsa County	57	2.07
Enterprise, AL (city) Coffee County	57	0.21
Birmingham, AL (city) Jefferson County	56	0.03
Blanchard, OK (city) McClain County	55	0.72
East Milton, FL (cdp) Santa Rosa County	55	0.50
McKinney, TX (city) Collin County	55	0.04
Panama City, FL (city) Bay County	54	0.15
Huntsville, AL (city) Madison County	54	0.03
Tampa, FL (city) Hillsborough County	54	0.02
Elk City, OK (city) Beckham County	53	0.45
Topeka, KS (city) Shawnee County	53	0.04
El Paso, TX (city) El Paso County	53	0.01
Vacaville, CA (city) Solano County	52	0.06
Garland, TX (city) Dallas County	51	0.02

Race

American Indian: Creek

Top 150 Places Sorted by Percent of Total Population

Based on all places, regardless of total population

Place	Population	%
Dustin, OK (town) Hughes County	155	39.24
Wetumka, OK (city) Hughes County	420	32.76
Yeager, OK (town) Hughes County	22	29.33
Hanna, OK (town) McIntosh County	40	28.99
Weleetka, OK (town) Okfuskee County	271	27.15
Okemah, OK (city) Okfuskee County	723	22.43
Morris, OK (city) Okmulgee County	289	19.54
Dewar, OK (town) Okmulgee County	170	19.14
Brooksville, OK (town) Pottawatomie County	11	17.46
Stidham, OK (town) McIntosh County	3	16.67
Grayson, OK (town) Okmulgee County	25	15.72
IXL, OK (town) Okfuskee County	8	15.69
Okmulgee, OK (city) Okmulgee County	1,882	15.27
Henryetta, OK (city) Okmulgee County	765	12.91
Paden, OK (town) Okfuskee County	59	12.80
Eufaula, OK (city) McIntosh County	357	12.69
Hitchita, OK (town) McIntosh County	11	12.50
Cromwell, OK (town) Seminole County	34	11.89
Schulter, OK (town) Okmulgee County	57	11.20
Slick, OK (town) Creek County	14	10.69
Arcadia, OK (town) Oklahoma County	26	10.53
Checotah, OK (city) McIntosh County	340	10.19
Ebro, FL (town) Washington County	26	9.63
Beggs, OK (city) Okmulgee County	125	9.46
Holdenville, OK (city) Hughes County	544	9.43
Bristow, OK (city) Creek County	369	8.74
Glenpool, OK (city) Tulsa County	893	8.26
Mounds, OK (town) Creek County	96	8.22
Depew, OK (town) Creek County	39	8.19
Castle, OK (town) Okfuskee County	8	7.55
Lamar, OK (town) Hughes County	11	6.96
Athol, KS (city) Smith County	3	6.82
Kiefer, OK (town) Creek County	114	6.77
Okay, OK (town) Wagoner County	42	6.77
Bearden, OK (town) Okfuskee County	9	6.77
Kellyville, OK (town) Creek County	76	6.61
Haskell, OK (town) Muskogee County	131	6.53
Fidelis, FL (cdp) Santa Rosa County	10	6.41
Spaulding, OK (town) Hughes County	11	6.18
Boynton, OK (town) Muskogee County	15	6.05
Liberty, OK (town) Tulsa County	13	5.91
Uriah, AL (cdp) Monroe County	17	5.78
Sapulpa, OK (city) Creek County	1,143	5.56
Grand Lake Towne, OK (town) Mayes County	4	5.41
Oktaha, OK (town) Muskogee County	21	5.38
Wewoka, OK (city) Seminole County	184	5.36
Libertyville, AL (town) Covington County	6	5.13
Council Hill, OK (town) Muskogee County	8	5.06
Coweta, OK (city) Wagoner County	490	4.93
Wainwright, OK (town) Muskogee County	8	4.85
Murphy, OK (cdp) Mayes County	10	4.57
Duchess Landing, OK (cdp) McIntosh County	5	4.39
Texanna, OK (cdp) McIntosh County	97	4.29
Notchietown, OK (cdp) Sequoyah County	16	4.29
Snake Creek, OK (cdp) Mayes County	11	4.28
New Brockton, AL (town) Coffee County	47	4.10
Sasakwa, OK (town) Seminole County	6	4.00
Shamrock, OK (town) Creek County	4	3.96
Hoffman, OK (town) Okmulgee County	5	3.94
Agra, OK (town) Lincoln County	13	3.83
Luna, NM (cdp) Catron County	6	3.80
Springhill, FL (cdp) Santa Rosa County	6	3.75
Dwight Mission, OK (cdp) Sequoyah County	2	3.64
Mulberry, OK (cdp) Adair County	5	3.62
Seminole, OK (city) Seminole County	265	3.54
Butler, OK (cdp) Delaware County	4	3.42
Muskogee, OK (city) Muskogee County	1,317	3.36
Rodney, IA (city) Monona County	2	3.33
Iron Post, OK (cdp) Mayes County	3	3.26
Megargel, AL (cdp) Monroe County	2	3.23
Oakhurst, OK (cdp) Tulsa County	69	3.16
Rentiesville, OK (town) McIntosh County	4	3.13
Macomb, OK (town) Pottawatomie County	1	3.13
Konawa, OK (city) Seminole County	40	3.08
Peggs, OK (cdp) Cherokee County	25	3.08

Place	Population	%
Breedsville, MI (village) Van Buren County	6	3.02
Sperry, OK (town) Tulsa County	36	2.99
Oilton, OK (city) Creek County	30	2.96
Rosedale, OK (town) McClain County	2	2.94
Prague, OK (city) Lincoln County	70	2.93
Winchester, OK (town) Okmulgee County	15	2.91
Brush Creek, OK (cdp) Delaware County	1	2.86
Floriston, CA (cdp) Nevada County	2	2.74
Wagoner, OK (city) Wagoner County	222	2.67
River Bottom, OK (cdp) Muskogee County	4	2.60
Cedar Crest, OK (cdp) Mayes County	8	2.56
Teresita, OK (cdp) Cherokee County	4	2.52
Fargo, GA (city) Clinch County	8	2.49
Mead, OK (town) Bryan County	3	2.46
Oologah, OK (town) Rogers County	28	2.44
Drumright, OK (city) Creek County	70	2.41
Kinston, AL (town) Coffee County	13	2.41
Mannford, OK (town) Creek County	73	2.37
Tecumseh, OK (city) Pottawatomie County	147	2.28
Quinton, OK (town) Pittsburg County	24	2.28
Sand Hill, OK (cdp) Muskogee County	9	2.28
Canadian, OK (town) Pittsburg County	5	2.27
Pine Level, FL (cdp) Santa Rosa County	5	2.20
Fort Gibson, OK (town) Muskogee County	91	2.19
Warner, OK (town) Muskogee County	36	2.19
Redbird, OK (town) Wagoner County	3	2.19
San Fidel, NM (cdp) Cibola County	3	2.17
Treece, KS (city) Cherokee County	3	2.17
Peru, KS (city) Chautauqua County	3	2.16
Summit, OK (town) Muskogee County	3	2.16
Jenks, OK (city) Tulsa County	356	2.10
Clearview, OK (town) Okfuskee County	1	2.08
Turley, OK (cdp) Tulsa County	57	2.07
Sand Springs, OK (city) Tulsa County	390	2.06
Shady Grove, OK (cdp) McIntosh County	4	2.06
Johnson, OK (town) Pottawatomie County	5	2.02
Twin Oaks, OK (cdp) Delaware County	4	2.02
Pettit, OK (cdp) Cherokee County	19	1.99
Lehigh, OK (city) Coal County	7	1.97
Shawnee, OK (city) Pottawatomie County	586	1.96
Shedd, OR (cdp) Linn County	4	1.96
Drowning Creek, OK (cdp) Delaware County	3	1.94
Jakin, GA (city) Early County	3	1.94
Jennings, OK (town) Pawnee County	7	1.93
Cattaraugus Reservation, NY (reservation) Cattaraugus County	6	1.91
Ochelata, OK (town) Washington County	8	1.89
Tullahassee, OK (town) Wagoner County	2	1.89
Chumuckla, FL (cdp) Santa Rosa County	16	1.88
Catoosa, OK (city) Rogers County	133	1.86
Boley, OK (town) Okfuskee County	22	1.86
Bixby, OK (city) Tulsa County	386	1.85
Fall River, KS (city) Greenwood County	3	1.85
Lake Mystic, FL (cdp) Liberty County	9	1.80
Centerville, WA (cdp) Klickitat County	2	1.79
Morrison, OK (town) Noble County	13	1.77
Mount Carmel, FL (cdp) Santa Rosa County	4	1.76
Horn Hill, AL (town) Covington County	4	1.75
McLoud, OK (town) Pottawatomie County	70	1.73
Pump Back, OK (cdp) Mayes County	3	1.71
Pawhuska, OK (city) Osage County	61	1.70
Calvin, OK (town) Hughes County	5	1.70
Spencer, OK (city) Oklahoma County	64	1.64
Webbers Falls, OK (town) Muskogee County	10	1.62
Dearing, KS (city) Montgomery County	7	1.62
Vernon, FL (city) Washington County	11	1.60
Berrydale, FL (cdp) Santa Rosa County	7	1.59
Old Green, OK (cdp) Adair County	5	1.59
Meeker, OK (town) Lincoln County	18	1.57
Avant, OK (town) Osage County	5	1.56
Sentinel, OK (town) Washita County	14	1.55
Atmore, AL (city) Escambia County	156	1.53
Ali Chukson, AZ (cdp) Pima County	2	1.52
Swink, OK (cdp) Choctaw County	1	1.52
Skiatook, OK (town) Osage County	112	1.51
Tulsa, OK (city) Tulsa County	5,849	1.49

Please refer to the Explanation of Data in the front of the book for more detailed information.

Race

American Indian: Creek

Top 150 Places Sorted by Percent of Total Population

Based on places with total population of 7,500 or more

Place	Population	%
Okmulgee, OK (city) Okmulgee County	1,882	15.27
Glenpool, OK (city) Tulsa County	893	8.26
Sapulpa, OK (city) Creek County	1,143	5.56
Coweta, OK (city) Wagoner County	490	4.93
Muskogee, OK (city) Muskogee County	1,317	3.36
Wagoner, OK (city) Wagoner County	222	2.67
Jenks, OK (city) Tulsa County	356	2.10
Sand Springs, OK (city) Tulsa County	390	2.06
Shawnee, OK (city) Pottawatomie County	586	1.96
Bixby, OK (city) Tulsa County	386	1.85
Atmore, AL (city) Escambia County	156	1.53
Tulsa, OK (city) Tulsa County	5,849	1.49
Tahlequah, OK (city) Cherokee County	232	1.47
Claremore, OK (city) Rogers County	262	1.41
Ada, OK (city) Pontotoc County	227	1.35
Broken Arrow, OK (city) Tulsa County	1,259	1.27
Del City, OK (city) Oklahoma County	247	1.16
Cushing, OK (city) Payne County	84	1.07
Pryor Creek, OK (city) Mayes County	80	0.84
Owasso, OK (city) Tulsa County	232	0.80
McAlester, OK (city) Pittsburg County	139	0.76
Clinton, OK (city) Custer County	67	0.74
Bay Minette, AL (city) Baldwin County	58	0.72
Blanchard, OK (city) McClain County	55	0.72
Choctaw, OK (city) Oklahoma County	73	0.65
Midwest City, OK (city) Oklahoma County	347	0.64
Newcastle, OK (city) McClain County	49	0.64
Moore, OK (city) Cleveland County	330	0.60
Gonzalez, FL (cdp) Escambia County	77	0.58
Stillwater, OK (city) Payne County	254	0.56
Ensley, FL (cdp) Escambia County	116	0.56
Bellview, FL (cdp) Escambia County	129	0.55
Pace, FL (cdp) Santa Rosa County	109	0.54
Norman, OK (city) Cleveland County	580	0.52
Oklahoma City, OK (city) Oklahoma County	2,905	0.50
East Milton, FL (cdp) Santa Rosa County	55	0.50
Warrington, FL (cdp) Escambia County	71	0.49
West Pensacola, FL (cdp) Escambia County	100	0.47
Miami, OK (city) Ottawa County	62	0.46
Sallisaw, OK (city) Sequoyah County	41	0.46
Mustang, OK (city) Canadian County	78	0.45
Elk City, OK (city) Beckham County	53	0.45
The Village, OK (city) Oklahoma County	40	0.45
Edmond, OK (city) Oklahoma County	341	0.42
Bartlesville, OK (city) Washington County	149	0.42
Yukon, OK (city) Canadian County	96	0.42
Guthrie, OK (city) Logan County	43	0.42
El Reno, OK (city) Canadian County	63	0.38
Myrtle Grove, FL (cdp) Escambia County	59	0.37
Ferry Pass, FL (cdp) Escambia County	96	0.33
Bethany, OK (city) Oklahoma County	62	0.33
Ponca City, OK (city) Kay County	81	0.32
Durant, OK (city) Bryan County	50	0.32
Gulf Shores, AL (city) Baldwin County	31	0.32
Weatherford, OK (city) Custer County	33	0.30
Warr Acres, OK (city) Oklahoma County	30	0.30
Brent, FL (cdp) Escambia County	63	0.29
Saraland, AL (city) Mobile County	38	0.28
Pensacola, FL (city) Escambia County	138	0.27
Siloam Springs, AR (city) Benton County	40	0.27
Milton, FL (city) Santa Rosa County	24	0.27
Ardmore, OK (city) Carter County	64	0.26
Coffeyville, KS (city) Montgomery County	26	0.25
Chickasha, OK (city) Grady County	39	0.24
Cairo, GA (city) Grady County	22	0.23
Lawrence, KS (city) Douglas County	197	0.22
Springfield, FL (city) Bay County	20	0.22
Enterprise, AL (city) Coffee County	57	0.21
Duncan, OK (city) Stephens County	46	0.20
Daphne, AL (city) Baldwin County	42	0.19
Lynn Haven, FL (city) Bay County	35	0.19
Arkansas City, KS (city) Cowley County	23	0.19
Altus, OK (city) Jackson County	35	0.18
Ozark, AL (city) Dale County	27	0.18
Poteau, OK (city) Le Flore County	15	0.18
Enid, OK (city) Garfield County	82	0.17
Crestview, FL (city) Okaloosa County	35	0.17
Andalusia, AL (city) Covington County	15	0.17
Troy, AL (city) Pike County	29	0.16
Linda, CA (cdp) Yuba County	28	0.16
Tillmans Corner, AL (cdp) Mobile County	28	0.16
Midway, FL (cdp) Santa Rosa County	26	0.16
Anna, TX (city) Collin County	13	0.16
Aurora, MO (city) Lawrence County	12	0.16
Meadow Lakes, AK (cdp) Matanuska-Susitna Borough	12	0.16
Stayton, OR (city) Marion County	12	0.16
Wichita, KS (city) Sedgwick County	557	0.15
Lawton, OK (city) Comanche County	148	0.15
Panama City, FL (city) Bay County	54	0.15
Winfield, KS (city) Cowley County	19	0.15
New Kingman-Butler, AZ (cdp) Mohave County	18	0.15
Greenwood, AR (city) Sebastian County	13	0.15
Niceville, FL (city) Okaloosa County	18	0.14
Ottawa, KS (city) Franklin County	18	0.14
Thonotosassa, FL (cdp) Hillsborough County	18	0.14
Augusta, KS (city) Butler County	13	0.14
Oildale, CA (cdp) Kern County	42	0.13
Denison, TX (city) Grayson County	29	0.13
Callaway, FL (city) Bay County	19	0.13
Kingsburg, CA (city) Fresno County	15	0.13
Haysville, KS (city) Sedgwick County	14	0.13
Van Buren, AR (city) Crawford County	28	0.12
Wright, FL (cdp) Okaloosa County	28	0.12
Derby, KS (city) Sedgwick County	27	0.12
Fort Walton Beach, FL (city) Okaloosa County	23	0.12
Fairhope, AL (city) Baldwin County	19	0.12
Millbrook, AL (city) Elmore County	18	0.12
Woodward, OK (city) Woodward County	15	0.12
Vernon, TX (city) Wilbarger County	13	0.12
Forestdale, AL (cdp) Jefferson County	12	0.12
Independence, KS (city) Montgomery County	11	0.12
Fultondale, AL (city) Jefferson County	10	0.12
Ocean Pointe, HI (cdp) Honolulu County	10	0.12
Foley, AL (city) Baldwin County	16	0.11
Upper Grand Lagoon, FL (cdp) Bay County	15	0.11
Bainbridge, GA (city) Decatur County	14	0.11
Destin, FL (city) Okaloosa County	13	0.11
Kaneohe Station, HI (cdp) Honolulu County	10	0.11
Orange Park, FL (town) Clay County	9	0.11
Green, OR (cdp) Douglas County	8	0.11
Joplin, MO (city) Jasper County	48	0.10
Haltom City, TX (city) Tarrant County	43	0.10
Jasper, AL (city) Walker County	15	0.10
Jacksonville, AL (city) Calhoun County	13	0.10
St. Helens, OR (city) Columbia County	13	0.10
Fort Valley, GA (city) Peach County	10	0.10
Royse City, TX (city) Rockwall County	9	0.10
Lamar, CO (city) Prowers County	8	0.10
Shiprock, NM (cdp) San Juan County	8	0.10
Dothan, AL (city) Houston County	61	0.09
Ceres, CA (city) Stanislaus County	43	0.09
Navarre, FL (cdp) Santa Rosa County	29	0.09
Prichard, AL (city) Mobile County	20	0.09
Blythe, CA (city) Riverside County	18	0.09
Alexander City, AL (city) Tallapoosa County	14	0.09
Fort Payne, AL (city) DeKalb County	13	0.09
Sylacauga, AL (city) Talladega County	12	0.09
Moody, AL (city) St. Clair County	10	0.09
Harrisonville, MO (city) Cass County	9	0.09
Shasta Lake, CA (city) Shasta County	9	0.09
Clanton, AL (city) Chilton County	8	0.09
Lacombe, LA (cdp) St. Tammany Parish	8	0.09
Mobile, AL (city) Mobile County	159	0.08
Rogers, AR (city) Benton County	44	0.08
Bentonville, AR (city) Benton County	30	0.08
Sherman, TX (city) Grayson County	29	0.08
Imperial Beach, CA (city) San Diego County	21	0.08
Saginaw, TX (city) Tarrant County	15	0.08
Thomasville, GA (city) Thomas County	14	0.08
Wilkinsburg, PA (borough) Allegheny County	13	0.08

SECTION THREE

Race

American Indian: Crow

U.S. and 50 States Sorted by Population and Percent of Total Population

Place	Population	%
United States	**15,203**	**<0.01**
Montana	8,680	0.88
California	866	<0.01
Washington	484	0.01
Texas	312	<0.01
Wyoming	239	0.04
Oregon	238	0.01
Arizona	235	<0.01
Florida	228	<0.01
Oklahoma	210	0.01
Colorado	208	<0.01
Ohio	204	<0.01
New York	181	<0.01
Michigan	169	<0.01
Kansas	165	0.01
Missouri	154	<0.01
Pennsylvania	150	<0.01
Illinois	147	<0.01
North Carolina	145	<0.01
New Mexico	135	0.01
Virginia	134	<0.01
Indiana	122	<0.01
Maryland	110	<0.01
South Dakota	109	0.01
Utah	109	<0.01
Idaho	99	0.01
Minnesota	98	<0.01
North Dakota	96	0.01
Tennessee	91	<0.01
Georgia	82	<0.01
Alaska	81	0.01
Nevada	79	<0.01
Alabama	74	<0.01
Hawaii	71	0.01
Arkansas	68	<0.01
Wisconsin	67	<0.01
Kentucky	66	<0.01
Massachusetts	64	<0.01
South Carolina	63	<0.01
Iowa	56	<0.01
New Jersey	53	<0.01
Louisiana	45	<0.01
Nebraska	40	<0.01
Connecticut	35	<0.01
West Virginia	31	<0.01
Maine	27	<0.01
Vermont	23	<0.01
Mississippi	20	<0.01
New Hampshire	15	<0.01
District of Columbia	9	<0.01
Delaware	8	<0.01
Rhode Island	8	<0.01

Place	Population	%
Montana	8,680	0.88
Wyoming	239	0.04
Washington	484	0.01
Oregon	238	0.01
Oklahoma	210	0.01
Kansas	165	0.01
New Mexico	135	0.01
South Dakota	109	0.01
Idaho	99	0.01
North Dakota	96	0.01
Alaska	81	0.01
Hawaii	71	0.01
United States	**15,203**	**<0.01**
California	866	<0.01
Texas	312	<0.01
Arizona	235	<0.01
Florida	228	<0.01
Colorado	208	<0.01
Ohio	204	<0.01
New York	181	<0.01
Michigan	169	<0.01
Missouri	154	<0.01
Pennsylvania	150	<0.01
Illinois	147	<0.01
North Carolina	145	<0.01
Virginia	134	<0.01
Indiana	122	<0.01
Maryland	110	<0.01
Utah	109	<0.01
Minnesota	98	<0.01
Tennessee	91	<0.01
Georgia	82	<0.01
Nevada	79	<0.01
Alabama	74	<0.01
Arkansas	68	<0.01
Wisconsin	67	<0.01
Kentucky	66	<0.01
Massachusetts	64	<0.01
South Carolina	63	<0.01
Iowa	56	<0.01
New Jersey	53	<0.01
Louisiana	45	<0.01
Nebraska	40	<0.01
Connecticut	35	<0.01
West Virginia	31	<0.01
Maine	27	<0.01
Vermont	23	<0.01
Mississippi	20	<0.01
New Hampshire	15	<0.01
District of Columbia	9	<0.01
Delaware	8	<0.01
Rhode Island	8	<0.01

Please refer to the Explanation of Data in the front of the book for more detailed information.

Race

American Indian: Crow

Top 150 Places Sorted by Population

Based on all places, regardless of total population

Place	Population	%
Crow Agency, MT (cdp) Big Horn County	1,409	87.19
Billings, MT (city) Yellowstone County	1,383	1.33
Hardin, MT (city) Big Horn County	1,133	32.33
Pryor, MT (cdp) Big Horn County	396	64.08
Lodge Grass, MT (town) Big Horn County	339	79.21
Wyola, MT (cdp) Big Horn County	150	69.77
Lockwood, MT (cdp) Yellowstone County	136	2.00
Lame Deer, MT (cdp) Rosebud County	118	5.75
Missoula, MT (city) Missoula County	96	0.14
Bozeman, MT (city) Gallatin County	84	0.23
Ashland, MT (cdp) Rosebud County	62	7.52
Albuquerque, NM (city) Bernalillo County	51	0.01
Busby, MT (cdp) Big Horn County	50	6.71
New York, NY (city) Kings County	50	<0.01
Ranchester, WY (town) Sheridan County	48	5.61
Los Angeles, CA (city) Los Angeles County	44	<0.01
Sheridan, WY (city) Sheridan County	43	0.25
Butte-Silver Bow, MT (cons. govt) Silver Bow County	40	0.12
St. Xavier, MT (cdp) Big Horn County	39	46.99
Lawrence, KS (city) Douglas County	38	0.04
Seattle, WA (city) King County	38	0.01
Fort Belknap Agency, MT (cdp) Blaine County	37	2.86
Sacramento, CA (city) Sacramento County	37	0.01
Anchorage, AK (municipality) Anchorage Municipality	36	0.01
Portland, OR (city) Multnomah County	35	0.01
Tulsa, OK (city) Tulsa County	34	0.01
Great Falls, MT (city) Cascade County	33	0.06
Rapid City, SD (city) Pennington County	33	0.05
Pablo, MT (cdp) Lake County	32	1.42
Muddy, MT (cdp) Big Horn County	30	4.86
Phoenix, AZ (city) Maricopa County	30	<0.01
Spokane, WA (city) Spokane County	28	0.01
Kansas City, MO (city) Jackson County	27	0.01
Fort Smith, MT (cdp) Big Horn County	26	16.15
Laurel, MT (city) Yellowstone County	25	0.37
Anaconda-Deer Lodge County, MT (special city) Deer Lodge County	24	0.26
San Francisco, CA (city) San Francisco County	23	<0.01
Oakland, CA (city) Alameda County	22	0.01
Oklahoma City, OK (city) Oklahoma County	22	<0.01
San Antonio, TX (city) Medina County	20	<0.01
San Diego, CA (city) San Diego County	20	<0.01
Brooklyn, NY (borough) Kings County	19	<0.01
Minneapolis, MN (city) Hennepin County	19	<0.01
Ronan, MT (city) Lake County	18	0.96
Colstrip, MT (city) Rosebud County	18	0.81
Bismarck, ND (city) Burleigh County	18	0.03
Colorado Springs, CO (city) El Paso County	18	<0.01
Fresno, CA (city) Fresno County	18	<0.01
Polson, MT (city) Lake County	17	0.38
Chicago, IL (city) Cook County	17	<0.01
Detroit, MI (city) Wayne County	17	<0.01
Fort Worth, TX (city) Tarrant County	17	<0.01
Louisville-Jefferson County, KY (metro govt) Jefferson County	17	<0.01
Turtle Lake, MT (cdp) Lake County	16	7.66
Dayton, WY (town) Sheridan County	16	2.11
Bronx, NY (borough) Bronx County	16	<0.01
Islip, NY (town) Suffolk County	16	<0.01
Mesa, AZ (city) Maricopa County	16	<0.01
Tucson, AZ (city) Pima County	16	<0.01
Wolf Point, MT (city) Roosevelt County	15	0.57
Austin, TX (city) Travis County	15	<0.01
Philadelphia, PA (city) Philadelphia County	15	<0.01
Reno, NV (city) Washoe County	14	0.01
Denver, CO (city) Denver County	14	<0.01
Fort Washakie, WY (cdp) Fremont County	13	0.74
Omak, WA (city) Okanogan County	13	0.27
Toppenish, WA (city) Yakima County	13	0.15
Helena, MT (city) Lewis and Clark County	13	0.05
Chula Vista, CA (city) San Diego County	13	0.01
Eugene, OR (city) Lane County	13	0.01
Fort Collins, CO (city) Larimer County	13	0.01
Gresham, OR (city) Multnomah County	13	0.01
Lawton, OK (city) Comanche County	13	0.01
Charlotte, NC (city) Mecklenburg County	13	<0.01
Ethete, WY (cdp) Fremont County	12	0.77
Boise City, ID (city) Ada County	12	0.01
Federal Way, WA (city) King County	12	0.01
Hillsboro, OR (city) Washington County	12	0.01
Sioux Falls, SD (city) Minnehaha County	12	0.01
Tacoma, WA (city) Pierce County	12	0.01
West Jordan, UT (city) Salt Lake County	12	0.01
Columbus, OH (city) Franklin County	12	<0.01
Dallas, TX (city) Dallas County	12	<0.01
Fort Wayne, IN (city) Allen County	12	<0.01
Stockton, CA (city) San Joaquin County	12	<0.01
Wichita, KS (city) Sedgwick County	12	<0.01
Havre, MT (city) Hill County	11	0.12
Brentwood, NY (cdp) Suffolk County	11	0.02
Burbank, CA (city) Los Angeles County	11	0.01
Chesapeake, VA (ind. city) Chesapeake independent city	11	<0.01
Indianapolis, IN (city) Marion County	11	<0.01
Jacksonville, FL (city) Duval County	11	<0.01
Manhattan, NY (borough) New York County	11	<0.01
Milwaukee, WI (city) Milwaukee County	11	<0.01
St. Petersburg, FL (city) Pinellas County	11	<0.01
Heart Butte, MT (cdp) Pondera County	10	1.72
Harlem, MT (city) Blaine County	10	1.24
New Town, ND (city) Mountrail County	10	0.52
Dillon, MT (city) Beaverhead County	10	0.24
West Sacramento, CA (city) Yolo County	10	0.02
Auburn, WA (city) King County	10	0.01
Lakewood, CO (city) Jefferson County	10	0.01
O'Fallon, MO (city) St. Charles County	10	0.01
Ogden, UT (city) Weber County	10	0.01
Overland Park, KS (city) Johnson County	10	0.01
Renton, WA (city) King County	10	0.01
Rockford, IL (city) Winnebago County	10	0.01
Santa Rosa, CA (city) Sonoma County	10	0.01
Topeka, KS (city) Shawnee County	10	0.01
Cleveland, OH (city) Cuyahoga County	10	<0.01
Virginia Beach, VA (ind. city) Virginia Beach independent city	10	<0.01
St. Ignatius, MT (town) Lake County	9	1.07
Arden-Arcade, CA (cdp) Sacramento County	9	0.01
Corona, CA (city) Riverside County	9	0.01
Kent, WA (city) King County	9	0.01
Napa, CA (city) Napa County	9	0.01
Spokane Valley, WA (city) Spokane County	9	0.01
Houston, TX (city) Harris County	9	<0.01
Madison, WI (city) Dane County	9	<0.01
North Las Vegas, NV (city) Clark County	9	<0.01
Washington, DC (city) District of Columbia	9	<0.01
Poplar, MT (city) Roosevelt County	8	0.99
Rocky Boy West, MT (cdp) Chouteau County	8	0.90
Browning, MT (town) Glacier County	8	0.79
Ellendale, ND (city) Dickey County	8	0.57
Cut Bank, MT (city) Glacier County	8	0.28
Mountain View Acres, CA (cdp) San Bernardino County	8	0.26
Fort Defiance, AZ (cdp) Apache County	8	0.22
Lewistown, MT (city) Fergus County	8	0.14
Anadarko, OK (city) Caddo County	8	0.12
Wheat Ridge, CO (city) Jefferson County	8	0.03
Gilroy, CA (city) Santa Clara County	8	0.02
Grants Pass, OR (city) Josephine County	8	0.02
Bellevue, WA (city) King County	8	0.01
Broken Arrow, OK (city) Tulsa County	8	0.01
Peoria, AZ (city) Yavapai County	8	0.01
Salem, OR (city) Marion County	8	0.01
St. Joseph, MO (city) Buchanan County	8	0.01
Arlington, VA (cdp) Arlington County	8	<0.01
Huntington Beach, CA (city) Orange County	8	<0.01
Pittsburgh, PA (city) Allegheny County	8	<0.01
Riverside, CA (city) Riverside County	8	<0.01
Scottsdale, AZ (city) Maricopa County	8	<0.01
St. Louis, MO (city) St. Louis city County	8	<0.01
Leupp, AZ (cdp) Coconino County	7	0.74
Glendive, MT (city) Dawson County	7	0.14
Townsend, MA (town) Middlesex County	7	0.08
Shasta Lake, CA (city) Shasta County	7	0.07
California, MD (cdp) St. Mary's County	7	0.06
Lake Arrowhead, CA (cdp) San Bernardino County	7	0.06

SECTION THREE

Please refer to the Explanation of Data in the front of the book for more detailed information.

Race

American Indian: Crow

Top 150 Places Sorted by Percent of Total Population

Based on all places, regardless of total population

Place	Population	%
Crow Agency, MT (cdp) Big Horn County	1,409	87.19
Lodge Grass, MT (town) Big Horn County	339	79.21
Wyola, MT (cdp) Big Horn County	150	69.77
Pryor, MT (cdp) Big Horn County	396	64.08
St. Xavier, MT (cdp) Big Horn County	39	46.99
Hardin, MT (city) Big Horn County	1,133	32.33
Fort Smith, MT (cdp) Big Horn County	26	16.15
Turtle Lake, MT (cdp) Lake County	16	7.66
Ashland, MT (cdp) Rosebud County	62	7.52
Busby, MT (cdp) Big Horn County	50	6.71
Lame Deer, MT (cdp) Rosebud County	118	5.75
Ranchester, WY (town) Sheridan County	48	5.61
Muddy, MT (cdp) Big Horn County	30	4.86
Old Agency, MT (cdp) Sanders County	4	3.74
Boulder, WY (cdp) Sublette County	5	2.94
Fort Belknap Agency, MT (cdp) Blaine County	37	2.86
Lance Creek, WY (cdp) Niobrara County	1	2.33
Dayton, WY (town) Sheridan County	16	2.11
Azure, MT (cdp) Hill County	6	2.10
Lockwood, MT (cdp) Yellowstone County	136	2.00
Heart Butte, MT (cdp) Pondera County	10	1.72
Sussex, VA (cdp) Sussex County	4	1.56
Latty, OH (village) Paulding County	3	1.55
Gibson Flats, MT (cdp) Cascade County	3	1.51
St. Pierre, MT (cdp) Hill County	5	1.43
Encinal, NM (cdp) Cibola County	3	1.43
Pablo, MT (cdp) Lake County	32	1.42
Green Bank, WV (cdp) Pocahontas County	2	1.40
Stirling City, CA (cdp) Butte County	4	1.36
Nixon, NV (cdp) Washoe County	5	1.34
Billings, MT (city) Yellowstone County	1,383	1.33
Mecosta, MI (village) Mecosta County	6	1.31
Ballantine, MT (cdp) Yellowstone County	4	1.25
Harlem, MT (city) Blaine County	10	1.24
Shepherd, MT (cdp) Yellowstone County	6	1.16
Lodge Pole, MT (cdp) Blaine County	3	1.13
Frazer, MT (cdp) Valley County	4	1.10
Chistochina, AK (cdp) Valdez-Cordova Census Area	1	1.08
St. Ignatius, MT (town) Lake County	9	1.07
Reed Point, MT (cdp) Stillwater County	2	1.04
Poplar, MT (city) Roosevelt County	8	0.99
Ronan, MT (city) Lake County	18	0.96
Rocky Boy West, MT (cdp) Chouteau County	8	0.90
Emington, IL (village) Livingston County	1	0.85
Firth, ID (city) Bingham County	4	0.84
Cal-Nev-Ari, NV (cdp) Clark County	2	0.82
Colstrip, MT (city) Rosebud County	18	0.81
Dodson, MT (town) Phillips County	1	0.81
Browning, MT (town) Glacier County	8	0.79
Willard, NM (village) Torrance County	2	0.79
Ethete, WY (cdp) Fremont County	12	0.77
Superior, IA (city) Dickinson County	1	0.77
Fort Washakie, WY (cdp) Fremont County	13	0.74
Leupp, AZ (cdp) Coconino County	7	0.74
New Salem, IL (village) Pike County	1	0.73
Puerto de Luna, NM (cdp) Guadalupe County	1	0.71
Kicking Horse, MT (cdp) Lake County	2	0.70
Killdeer, ND (city) Dunn County	5	0.67
Birmingham, IA (city) Van Buren County	3	0.67
Hysham, MT (town) Treasure County	2	0.64
New Salem, ND (city) Morton County	6	0.63
Winchester, AR (town) Drew County	1	0.60
Kyle, SD (cdp) Shannon County	5	0.59
Valier, MT (town) Pondera County	3	0.59
Wolf Point, MT (city) Roosevelt County	15	0.57
Ellendale, ND (city) Dickey County	8	0.57
Townsend, MA (cdp) Middlesex County	6	0.53
Boneau, MT (cdp) Chouteau County	2	0.53
Roseville, PA (borough) Tioga County	1	0.53
New Town, ND (city) Mountrail County	10	0.52
Benson, NY (town) Hamilton County	1	0.52
Kickapoo Tribal Center, KS (cdp) Brown County	1	0.52
Lyons, MN (township) Wadena County	1	0.52
Everglades, FL (city) Collier County	2	0.50
Fredericktown, PA (cdp) Washington County	2	0.50

Place	Population	%
Carolina, WV (cdp) Marion County	2	0.49
Little Browning, MT (cdp) Glacier County	1	0.49
Wadsworth, NV (cdp) Washoe County	4	0.48
Fort Thompson, SD (cdp) Buffalo County	6	0.47
Hays, MT (cdp) Blaine County	4	0.47
Arlee, MT (cdp) Lake County	3	0.47
Minnesota Falls, MN (township) Yellow Medicine County	2	0.47
Mayview, MO (city) Lafayette County	1	0.47
Ordway, CO (town) Crowley County	5	0.46
Autaugaville, AL (town) Autauga County	4	0.46
Belfry, MT (cdp) Carbon County	1	0.46
Moose Pass, AK (cdp) Kenai Peninsula Borough	1	0.46
Huntley, MT (cdp) Yellowstone County	2	0.45
Leslie, AR (city) Searcy County	2	0.45
Pecos, NM (village) San Miguel County	6	0.43
East Fork, AZ (cdp) Navajo County	3	0.43
Sharpsburg, MD (town) Washington County	3	0.43
Cabot, VT (village) Washington County	1	0.43
Robinson, KS (city) Brown County	1	0.43
Seven Mile, AZ (cdp) Navajo County	3	0.42
Ridgeway, VA (town) Henry County	3	0.40
Vineland, CO (cdp) Pueblo County	1	0.40
Four Bears Village, ND (cdp) McKenzie County	2	0.39
Brockton, MT (town) Roosevelt County	1	0.39
New Effington, SD (town) Roberts County	1	0.39
Winston, MO (village) Daviess County	1	0.39
Polson, MT (city) Lake County	17	0.38
Laurel, MT (city) Yellowstone County	25	0.37
Bombay, NY (town) Franklin County	5	0.37
Edgerton, KS (city) Johnson County	6	0.36
Story, WY (cdp) Sheridan County	3	0.36
Bear Dance, MT (cdp) Lake County	1	0.36
Ralston, WY (cdp) Park County	1	0.36
White Horse, SD (cdp) Todd County	1	0.36
Huntland, TN (town) Franklin County	3	0.34
Chinook, MT (city) Blaine County	4	0.33
Hopkins Park, IL (village) Kankakee County	2	0.33
Coalton, IL (village) Montgomery County	1	0.33
Keams Canyon, AZ (cdp) Navajo County	1	0.33
Sangrey, MT (cdp) Hill County	1	0.33
Tse Bonito, NM (cdp) McKinley County	1	0.33
Geronimo, OK (town) Comanche County	4	0.32
Sun Prairie, MT (cdp) Cascade County	5	0.31
Galveston, IN (town) Cass County	4	0.31
Sweet, MN (township) Pipestone County	1	0.31
Arapahoe, WY (cdp) Fremont County	5	0.30
Pine Point, MN (cdp) Becker County	1	0.30
Ponderosa Pines, MT (cdp) Gallatin County	1	0.30
White Shield, ND (cdp) McLean County	1	0.30
Tanner, WA (cdp) King County	3	0.29
Lakeside, WI (town) Douglas County	2	0.29
Parker School, MT (cdp) Hill County	1	0.29
Santa Clara, NY (town) Franklin County	1	0.29
Cut Bank, MT (city) Glacier County	8	0.28
Fairmead, CA (cdp) Madera County	4	0.28
South Windham, CT (cdp) Windham County	4	0.28
Delleker, CA (cdp) Plumas County	2	0.28
Fort Duchesne, UT (cdp) Uintah County	2	0.28
Belle Rive, IL (village) Jefferson County	1	0.28
Rocky Boy's Agency, MT (cdp) Hill County	1	0.28
Stark, WI (town) Vernon County	1	0.28
Omak, WA (city) Okanogan County	13	0.27
Desert Shores, CA (cdp) Imperial County	3	0.27
Mountainaire, AZ (cdp) Coconino County	3	0.27
King Arthur Park, MT (cdp) Gallatin County	2	0.27
Kevil, KY (city) Ballard County	1	0.27
Kivalina, AK (city) Northwest Arctic Borough	1	0.27
Anaconda-Deer Lodge County, MT (special city) Deer Lodge County	24	0.26
Mountain View Acres, CA (cdp) San Bernardino County	8	0.26
Glasgow, VA (town) Rockbridge County	3	0.26
Lapwai, ID (city) Nez Perce County	3	0.26
Sheridan, WY (city) Sheridan County	43	0.25
Comfort, TX (cdp) Kendall County	6	0.25
Mission, SD (city) Todd County	3	0.25
Caswell Beach, NC (town) Brunswick County	1	0.25

Race

American Indian: Crow

Top 150 Places Sorted by Percent of Total Population

Based on places with total population of 7,500 or more

Place	Population	%
Billings, MT (city) Yellowstone County	1,383	1.33
Anaconda-Deer Lodge County, MT (special city) Deer Lodge County	24	0.26
Sheridan, WY (city) Sheridan County	43	0.25
Bozeman, MT (city) Gallatin County	84	0.23
Toppenish, WA (city) Yakima County	13	0.15
Missoula, MT (city) Missoula County	96	0.14
Butte-Silver Bow, MT (cons. govt) Silver Bow County	40	0.12
Havre, MT (city) Hill County	11	0.12
Townsend, MA (town) Middlesex County	7	0.08
Shasta Lake, CA (city) Shasta County	7	0.07
Great Falls, MT (city) Cascade County	33	0.06
California, MD (cdp) St. Mary's County	7	0.06
Lake Arrowhead, CA (cdp) San Bernardino County	7	0.06
Camp Verde, AZ (town) Yavapai County	6	0.06
Maili, HI (cdp) Honolulu County	6	0.06
Tuba City, AZ (cdp) Coconino County	5	0.06
Rapid City, SD (city) Pennington County	33	0.05
Helena, MT (city) Lewis and Clark County	13	0.05
Kilgore, TX (city) Gregg County	6	0.05
Riverton, WY (city) Fremont County	5	0.05
Cortez, CO (city) Montezuma County	4	0.05
Lacombe, LA (cdp) St. Tammany Parish	4	0.05
Orange Park, FL (town) Clay County	4	0.05
Lawrence, KS (city) Douglas County	38	0.04
Coos Bay, OR (city) Coos County	6	0.04
Red Wing, MN (city) Goodhue County	6	0.04
Royal Kunia, HI (cdp) Honolulu County	6	0.04
Welby, CO (cdp) Adams County	6	0.04
Cairo, GA (city) Grady County	4	0.04
Tyrone, MI (township) Livingston County	4	0.04
Erwin, NY (town) Steuben County	3	0.04
Helena Valley West Central, MT (cdp) Lewis and Clark County	3	0.04
Kinross, MI (charter township) Chippewa County	3	0.04
Richland Hills, TX (city) Tarrant County	3	0.04
Riverdale, UT (city) Weber County	3	0.04
Templeton, MA (town) Worcester County	3	0.04
Bismarck, ND (city) Burleigh County	18	0.03
Wheat Ridge, CO (city) Jefferson County	8	0.03
Alliance, OH (city) Stark County	7	0.03
Junction City, KS (city) Geary County	7	0.03
Brigham City, UT (city) Box Elder County	6	0.03
Franklin, IN (city) Johnson County	6	0.03
Kalispell, MT (city) Flathead County	6	0.03
Mililani Mauka, HI (cdp) Honolulu County	6	0.03
Pottstown, PA (borough) Montgomery County	6	0.03
Rock Springs, WY (city) Sweetwater County	6	0.03
Ada, OK (city) Pontotoc County	5	0.03
American Canyon, CA (city) Napa County	5	0.03
Camas, WA (city) Clark County	5	0.03
Cameron Park, CA (cdp) El Dorado County	5	0.03
North Salt Lake, UT (city) Davis County	5	0.03
Seagoville, TX (city) Dallas County	5	0.03
Somerton, AZ (city) Yuma County	5	0.03
Tahlequah, OK (city) Cherokee County	5	0.03
Beatrice, NE (city) Gage County	4	0.03
Evanston, WY (city) Uinta County	4	0.03
Geneva, NY (city) Ontario County	4	0.03
Knik-Fairview, AK (cdp) Matanuska-Susitna Borough	4	0.03
Loveland, OH (city) Hamilton County	4	0.03
McKinleyville, CA (cdp) Humboldt County	4	0.03
Piney Green, NC (cdp) Onslow County	4	0.03
Waimalu, HI (cdp) Honolulu County	4	0.03
Artesia, NM (city) Eddy County	3	0.03
Atchison, KS (city) Atchison County	3	0.03
Fort Salonga, NY (cdp) Suffolk County	3	0.03
Lake Morton-Berrydale, WA (cdp) King County	3	0.03
Liberty, NY (town) Sullivan County	3	0.03
Lyons, IL (village) Cook County	3	0.03
Middleton, MA (town) Essex County	3	0.03
Minneola, FL (city) Lake County	3	0.03
Mount Washington, KY (city) Bullitt County	3	0.03
Muskegon Heights, MI (city) Muskegon County	3	0.03
Oakwood, OH (city) Montgomery County	3	0.03
Ontario, OR (city) Malheur County	3	0.03
Paris, IL (city) Edgar County	3	0.03
Picnic Point, WA (cdp) Snohomish County	3	0.03
Poulsbo, WA (city) Kitsap County	3	0.03
Richland, PA (township) Allegheny County	3	0.03
Sedro-Woolley, WA (city) Skagit County	3	0.03
Shawano, WI (city) Shawano County	3	0.03
Dunbar, WV (city) Kanawha County	2	0.03
Evergreen, MT (cdp) Flathead County	2	0.03
Four Corners, MD (cdp) Montgomery County	2	0.03
Jefferson, WI (city) Jefferson County	2	0.03
Kalifornsky, AK (cdp) Kenai Peninsula Borough	2	0.03
London, KY (city) Laurel County	2	0.03
Wahpeton, ND (city) Richland County	2	0.03
Brentwood, NY (cdp) Suffolk County	11	0.02
West Sacramento, CA (city) Yolo County	10	0.02
Gilroy, CA (city) Santa Clara County	8	0.02
Grants Pass, OR (city) Josephine County	8	0.02
Fort Hood, TX (cdp) Bell County	7	0.02
Ballwin, MO (city) St. Louis County	6	0.02
Flint, MI (charter township) Genesee County	6	0.02
Foothill Farms, CA (cdp) Sacramento County	6	0.02
Tualatin, OR (city) Washington County	6	0.02
Wake Forest, NC (town) Wake County	6	0.02
Centerville, OH (city) Montgomery County	5	0.02
East Hill-Meridian, WA (cdp) King County	5	0.02
Fairbanks, AK (city) Fairbanks North Star Borough	5	0.02
Laramie, WY (city) Albany County	5	0.02
Paradise, CA (town) Butte County	5	0.02
Port Hueneme, CA (city) Ventura County	5	0.02
Security-Widefield, CO (cdp) El Paso County	5	0.02
Vernon, CT (town) Tolland County	5	0.02
Cudahy, CA (city) Los Angeles County	4	0.02
Dickinson, ND (city) Stark County	4	0.02
Dixon, CA (city) Solano County	4	0.02
Duarte, CA (city) Los Angeles County	4	0.02
Five Corners, WA (cdp) Clark County	4	0.02
Greenfield, IN (city) Hancock County	4	0.02
Hueytown, AL (city) Jefferson County	4	0.02
Norfolk, NE (city) Madison County	4	0.02
North Bay Shore, NY (cdp) Suffolk County	4	0.02
Rolla, MO (city) Phelps County	4	0.02
West Fargo, ND (city) Cass County	4	0.02
Windham, CT (town) Windham County	4	0.02
Ashtabula, OH (city) Ashtabula County	3	0.02
Auburn, CA (city) Placer County	3	0.02
Bemidji, MN (city) Beltrami County	3	0.02
Central Point, OR (city) Jackson County	3	0.02
Covington, WA (city) King County	3	0.02
Eastlake, OH (city) Lake County	3	0.02
Falls Church, VA (ind. city) Falls Church independent city	3	0.02
Fort Carson, CO (cdp) El Paso County	3	0.02
Hollins, VA (cdp) Roanoke County	3	0.02
Jasmine Estates, FL (cdp) Pasco County	3	0.02
Lake Forest, IL (city) Lake County	3	0.02
Laurinburg, NC (city) Scotland County	3	0.02
Mattoon, IL (city) Coles County	3	0.02
Montville, CT (town) New London County	3	0.02
Newport, KY (city) Campbell County	3	0.02
Port St. John, FL (cdp) Brevard County	3	0.02
Sterling, IL (city) Whiteside County	3	0.02
Westbrook, ME (city) Cumberland County	3	0.02
Westminster, MD (city) Carroll County	3	0.02
Alachua, FL (city) Alachua County	2	0.02
Avon Park, FL (city) Highlands County	2	0.02
Bogalusa, LA (city) Washington Parish	2	0.02
Brattleboro, VT (town) Windham County	2	0.02
Brentwood, MO (city) St. Louis County	2	0.02
Cheney, WA (city) Spokane County	2	0.02
Claiborne, LA (cdp) Ouachita Parish	2	0.02
Collingdale, PA (borough) Delaware County	2	0.02
Coshocton, OH (city) Coshocton County	2	0.02
Diamond Springs, CA (cdp) El Dorado County	2	0.02
Edgewood, WA (city) Pierce County	2	0.02
Fallon, NV (city) Churchill County	2	0.02
Federal Heights, CO (city) Adams County	2	0.02
Fort Madison, IA (city) Lee County	2	0.02

Please refer to the Explanation of Data in the front of the book for more detailed information.

Race

American Indian: Delaware

U.S. and 50 States Sorted by Population and Percent of Total Population

Place	Population	%
United States	**18,264**	**0.01**
Oklahoma	3,100	0.08
New Jersey	2,509	0.03
Pennsylvania	1,680	0.01
New York	1,384	0.01
California	1,289	<0.01
Texas	849	<0.01
Kansas	657	0.02
Florida	647	<0.01
Ohio	608	0.01
Missouri	394	0.01
Washington	383	0.01
Delaware	360	0.04
Michigan	308	<0.01
Virginia	301	<0.01
Oregon	290	0.01
Colorado	281	0.01
North Carolina	249	<0.01
Maryland	239	<0.01
Arizona	226	<0.01
Georgia	196	<0.01
Indiana	196	<0.01
Illinois	186	<0.01
Idaho	185	0.01
Tennessee	150	<0.01
Arkansas	140	<0.01
New Mexico	127	0.01
West Virginia	123	0.01
Hawaii	102	0.01
Massachusetts	98	<0.01
Kentucky	97	<0.01
Connecticut	84	<0.01
Minnesota	82	<0.01
Nevada	78	<0.01
South Carolina	76	<0.01
Louisiana	69	<0.01
Alabama	66	<0.01
Utah	66	<0.01
Wisconsin	61	<0.01
Alaska	47	0.01
Wyoming	40	0.01
Maine	35	<0.01
Nebraska	34	<0.01
Iowa	30	<0.01
Montana	28	<0.01
New Hampshire	24	<0.01
Mississippi	21	<0.01
Vermont	21	<0.01
Rhode Island	18	<0.01
South Dakota	15	<0.01
District of Columbia	12	<0.01
North Dakota	3	<0.01

Place	Population	%
Oklahoma	3,100	0.08
Delaware	360	0.04
New Jersey	2,509	0.03
Kansas	657	0.02
United States	**18,264**	**0.01**
Pennsylvania	1,680	0.01
New York	1,384	0.01
Ohio	608	0.01
Missouri	394	0.01
Washington	383	0.01
Oregon	290	0.01
Colorado	281	0.01
Idaho	185	0.01
New Mexico	127	0.01
West Virginia	123	0.01
Hawaii	102	0.01
Alaska	47	0.01
Wyoming	40	0.01
California	1,289	<0.01
Texas	849	<0.01
Florida	647	<0.01
Michigan	308	<0.01
Virginia	301	<0.01
North Carolina	249	<0.01
Maryland	239	<0.01
Arizona	226	<0.01
Georgia	196	<0.01
Indiana	196	<0.01
Illinois	186	<0.01
Tennessee	150	<0.01
Arkansas	140	<0.01
Massachusetts	98	<0.01
Kentucky	97	<0.01
Connecticut	84	<0.01
Minnesota	82	<0.01
Nevada	78	<0.01
South Carolina	76	<0.01
Louisiana	69	<0.01
Alabama	66	<0.01
Utah	66	<0.01
Wisconsin	61	<0.01
Maine	35	<0.01
Nebraska	34	<0.01
Iowa	30	<0.01
Montana	28	<0.01
New Hampshire	24	<0.01
Mississippi	21	<0.01
Vermont	21	<0.01
Rhode Island	18	<0.01
South Dakota	15	<0.01
District of Columbia	12	<0.01
North Dakota	3	<0.01

Please refer to the Explanation of Data in the front of the book for more detailed information.

Race

American Indian: Delaware

Top 150 Places Sorted by Population

Based on all places, regardless of total population

Place	Population	%
Oklahoma City, OK (city) Oklahoma County	280	0.05
Bartlesville, OK (city) Washington County	255	0.71
Philadelphia, PA (city) Philadelphia County	239	0.02
Tulsa, OK (city) Tulsa County	232	0.06
New York, NY (city) Kings County	177	<0.01
Ramapo, NY (town) Rockland County	167	0.13
Ringwood, NJ (borough) Passaic County	155	1.27
Anadarko, OK (city) Caddo County	125	1.85
Mahwah, NJ (township) Bergen County	121	0.47
Hillburn, NY (village) Rockland County	120	12.62
Fairfield, NJ (township) Cumberland County	95	1.51
Norman, OK (city) Cleveland County	95	0.09
Millville, NJ (city) Cumberland County	93	0.33
Nowata, OK (city) Nowata County	92	2.47
Wichita, KS (city) Sedgwick County	90	0.02
Los Angeles, CA (city) Los Angeles County	80	<0.01
Bridgeton, NJ (city) Cumberland County	77	0.30
Dewey, OK (city) Washington County	62	1.81
Vineland, NJ (city) Cumberland County	60	0.10
Warwick, NY (town) Orange County	58	0.18
Wallkill, NY (town) Orange County	57	0.21
Canton, OH (city) Stark County	57	0.08
West Milford, NJ (township) Passaic County	56	0.22
Paterson, NJ (city) Passaic County	54	0.04
Manhattan, NY (borough) New York County	54	<0.01
Chelsea, OK (town) Rogers County	52	2.65
Claremore, OK (city) Rogers County	52	0.28
Blooming Grove, NY (town) Orange County	51	0.28
Broken Arrow, OK (city) Tulsa County	51	0.05
Houston, TX (city) Harris County	49	<0.01
Edmond, OK (city) Oklahoma County	46	0.06
Wanaque, NJ (borough) Passaic County	44	0.40
Middletown, NY (city) Orange County	43	0.15
Staten Island, NY (borough) Richmond County	43	0.01
Phoenix, AZ (city) Maricopa County	42	<0.01
Moore, OK (city) Cleveland County	41	0.07
Columbus, OH (city) Franklin County	40	0.01
Portland, OR (city) Multnomah County	40	0.01
Port Jervis, NY (city) Orange County	39	0.44
Albuquerque, NM (city) Bernalillo County	39	0.01
Jacksonville, FL (city) Duval County	39	<0.01
Vinita, OK (city) Craig County	38	0.66
San Francisco, CA (city) San Francisco County	38	<0.01
Copan, OK (town) Washington County	37	5.05
Kansas City, MO (city) Jackson County	37	0.01
Seattle, WA (city) King County	37	0.01
Miami, OK (city) Ottawa County	36	0.27
Lawrence, KS (city) Douglas County	35	0.04
Brooklyn, NY (borough) Kings County	35	<0.01
Queens, NY (borough) Queens County	35	<0.01
Chickasha, OK (city) Grady County	34	0.21
Dover, DE (city) Kent County	34	0.09
Overland Park, KS (city) Johnson County	33	0.02
Haverstraw, NY (town) Rockland County	32	0.09
Mamakating, NY (town) Sullivan County	31	0.26
Boise City, ID (city) Ada County	30	0.01
San Antonio, TX (city) Medina County	30	<0.01
Joplin, MO (city) Jasper County	29	0.06
Lawton, OK (city) Comanche County	29	0.03
Toms River, NJ (cdp) Ocean County	29	0.03
Toms River, NJ (township) Ocean County	29	0.03
Owasso, OK (city) Tulsa County	28	0.10
Shawnee, OK (city) Pottawatomie County	28	0.09
Gloucester, NJ (township) Camden County	28	0.04
Dallas, TX (city) Dallas County	28	<0.01
Detroit, MI (city) Wayne County	28	<0.01
Pittsgrove, NJ (township) Salem County	27	0.29
Hamilton, NJ (township) Atlantic County	27	0.10
Indianapolis, IN (city) Marion County	27	<0.01
Fairton, NJ (cdp) Cumberland County	26	2.06
Goshen, NY (town) Orange County	26	0.19
Enid, OK (city) Garfield County	26	0.05
Independence, MO (city) Jackson County	26	0.02
Kansas City, KS (city) Wyandotte County	26	0.02
Virginia Beach, VA (ind. city) Virginia Beach independent city	26	0.01

Place	Population	%
Charlotte, NC (city) Mecklenburg County	26	<0.01
San Diego, CA (city) San Diego County	26	<0.01
Mountain Lodge Park, NY (cdp) Orange County	25	1.57
Midwest City, OK (city) Oklahoma County	25	0.05
Washington, NJ (township) Gloucester County	25	0.05
Chicago, IL (city) Cook County	25	<0.01
Las Vegas, NV (city) Clark County	25	<0.01
San Jose, CA (city) Santa Clara County	25	<0.01
Sand Springs, OK (city) Tulsa County	24	0.13
Linden, NJ (city) Union County	24	0.06
Lawrence, NJ (township) Cumberland County	23	0.70
Coffeyville, KS (city) Montgomery County	23	0.22
Springdale, AR (city) Washington County	23	0.03
Dingman, PA (township) Pike County	22	0.18
Newburgh, NY (city) Orange County	22	0.08
Bethlehem, PA (city) Northampton County	22	0.03
Nampa, ID (city) Canyon County	22	0.03
Passaic, NJ (city) Passaic County	22	0.03
Upper Darby, PA (township) Delaware County	22	0.03
Austin, TX (city) Travis County	22	<0.01
Hopewell, NJ (township) Cumberland County	21	0.46
Wawarsing, NY (town) Ulster County	21	0.16
Neptune, NJ (township) Monmouth County	21	0.08
Allentown, PA (city) Lehigh County	21	0.02
Colorado Springs, CO (city) El Paso County	21	0.01
Urban Honolulu, HI (cdp) Honolulu County	21	0.01
Denver, CO (city) Denver County	21	<0.01
Philippi, WV (city) Barbour County	20	0.67
Collinsville, OK (city) Tulsa County	20	0.36
Pennsauken, NJ (township) Camden County	20	0.06
Middletown, NJ (township) Monmouth County	20	0.03
Sacramento, CA (city) Sacramento County	20	<0.01
Caney, KS (city) Montgomery County	19	0.86
Deptford, NJ (township) Gloucester County	19	0.06
Jackson, NJ (township) Ocean County	19	0.03
Camden, NJ (city) Camden County	19	0.02
Olathe, KS (city) Johnson County	19	0.02
Stockton, CA (city) San Joaquin County	19	0.01
Fort Worth, TX (city) Tarrant County	19	<0.01
Scotchtown, NY (cdp) Orange County	18	0.20
Pemberton, NJ (township) Burlington County	18	0.06
Monroe, NJ (township) Gloucester County	18	0.05
Taylor, MI (city) Wayne County	18	0.03
Anchorage, AK (municipality) Anchorage Municipality	18	0.01
Oakland, CA (city) Alameda County	18	<0.01
Chester, NY (village) Orange County	17	0.43
Catoosa, OK (city) Rogers County	17	0.24
Chester, NY (town) Orange County	17	0.14
Wilmington, DE (city) New Castle County	17	0.02
Akron, OH (city) Summit County	17	0.01
Newark, NJ (city) Essex County	17	0.01
Springfield, MO (city) Christian County	17	0.01
Tucson, AZ (city) Pima County	17	<0.01
Chestnuthill, PA (township) Monroe County	16	0.09
Montgomery, NY (town) Orange County	16	0.07
Englewood, NJ (city) Bergen County	16	0.06
Clarkstown, NY (town) Rockland County	16	0.02
Fresno, CA (city) Fresno County	16	<0.01
Mesa, AZ (city) Maricopa County	16	<0.01
Greenwood Lake, NY (village) Orange County	15	0.48
Commercial, NJ (township) Cumberland County	15	0.29
Airmont, NY (village) Rockland County	15	0.17
Woodbury, NJ (city) Gloucester County	15	0.15
New Windsor, NY (town) Orange County	15	0.06
Galloway, NJ (township) Atlantic County	15	0.04
Albany, OR (city) Linn County	15	0.03
Bethlehem, PA (city) Northampton County	15	0.03
Levittown, PA (cdp) Bucks County	15	0.03
Reading, PA (city) Berks County	15	0.02
Westland, MI (city) Wayne County	15	0.02
Arlington, TX (city) Tarrant County	15	<0.01
Downe, NJ (township) Cumberland County	14	0.88
West Pleasant View, CO (cdp) Jefferson County	14	0.36
Goshen, NY (village) Orange County	14	0.26
Upper Deerfield, NJ (township) Cumberland County	14	0.18

Race

American Indian: Delaware

Top 150 Places Sorted by Percent of Total Population

Based on all places, regardless of total population

Place	Population	%
Hillburn, NY (village) Rockland County	120	12.62
Coyville, KS (city) Wilson County	3	6.52
Copan, OK (town) Washington County	37	5.05
New Alluwe, OK (town) Nowata County	4	4.44
Randsburg, CA (cdp) Kern County	3	4.35
Lazy Lake, FL (village) Broward County	1	4.17
Niotaze, KS (city) Chautauqua County	3	3.66
Asherville, KS (cdp) Mitchell County	1	3.57
La Due, MO (village) Henry County	1	3.57
Mutual, OK (town) Woodward County	2	3.28
Grainola, OK (town) Osage County	1	3.23
Hutchinson, NJ (cdp) Warren County	4	2.96
Castle, OK (town) Okfuskee County	3	2.83
White Oak, OK (cdp) Craig County	7	2.66
Chelsea, OK (town) Rogers County	52	2.65
Bridgeport, OK (city) Caddo County	3	2.59
Pocasset, OK (town) Grady County	4	2.56
Nowata, OK (city) Nowata County	92	2.47
Guys Mills, PA (cdp) Crawford County	3	2.42
Callaway, MN (city) Becker County	5	2.14
Fairton, NJ (cdp) Cumberland County	26	2.06
Corning, KS (city) Nemaha County	3	1.91
Alston, GA (town) Montgomery County	3	1.89
Anadarko, OK (city) Caddo County	125	1.85
Dewey, OK (city) Washington County	62	1.81
Binger, OK (town) Caddo County	12	1.79
Ochelata, OK (town) Washington County	7	1.65
Mountain Lodge Park, NY (cdp) Orange County	25	1.57
Foundryville, PA (cdp) Columbia County	4	1.56
Fairfield, NJ (township) Cumberland County	95	1.51
Barnett, MO (city) Morgan County	3	1.48
Ekron, KY (city) Meade County	2	1.48
Schoenchen, KS (city) Ellis County	3	1.45
Hartly, DE (town) Kent County	1	1.35
River Bottom, OK (cdp) Muskogee County	2	1.30
Ringwood, NJ (borough) Passaic County	155	1.27
Vera, OK (town) Washington County	3	1.24
Ramona, OK (town) Washington County	6	1.12
Talala, OK (town) Rogers County	3	1.10
Bailey Lakes, OH (village) Ashland County	4	1.08
Alton, MO (city) Oregon County	9	1.03
Quinton, NJ (cdp) Salem County	6	1.02
Harding-Birch Lakes, AK (cdp) Fairbanks North Star Borough	3	1.00
Milroy, IN (cdp) Rush County	6	0.99
North Branch, PA (township) Wyoming County	2	0.97
Keensburg, IL (village) Wabash County	2	0.95
Waverly, WA (town) Spokane County	1	0.94
Del Muerto, AZ (cdp) Apache County	3	0.91
Robertsville, OH (cdp) Stark County	3	0.91
Chautauqua, KS (city) Chautauqua County	1	0.90
Downe, NJ (township) Cumberland County	14	0.88
Ironton, MN (city) Crow Wing County	5	0.87
Dodge, OK (cdp) Delaware County	1	0.87
Caney, KS (city) Montgomery County	19	0.86
Butler, OK (cdp) Delaware County	1	0.85
Pomona, KS (city) Franklin County	7	0.84
Brushton, NY (village) Franklin County	4	0.84
Meridian, CA (cdp) Sutter County	3	0.84
Abbott, PA (township) Potter County	2	0.83
Vienna, NJ (cdp) Warren County	8	0.82
La Fargeville, NY (cdp) Jefferson County	5	0.82
Zena, OK (cdp) Delaware County	1	0.82
Ogle, PA (township) Somerset County	4	0.80
Dexter City, OH (village) Noble County	1	0.78
Hobucken, NC (cdp) Pamlico County	1	0.78
Centennial, WY (cdp) Albany County	2	0.74
Wayne, OK (town) McClain County	5	0.73
Cheswold, DE (town) Kent County	10	0.72
Norfolk, CT (cdp) Litchfield County	4	0.72
Delaware, OK (town) Nowata County	3	0.72
Bartlesville, OK (city) Washington County	255	0.71
Arboles, CO (cdp) Archuleta County	2	0.71
Lawrence, NJ (township) Cumberland County	23	0.70
Cromwell, OK (town) Seminole County	2	0.70
Cubero, NM (cdp) Cibola County	2	0.69
Kimbolton, OH (cdp) Guernsey County	1	0.69
Delta, MO (city) Cape Girardeau County	3	0.68
Ketchum, OK (town) Craig County	3	0.68
Philippi, WV (city) Barbour County	20	0.67
Vinita, OK (city) Craig County	38	0.66
Sherrodsville, OH (village) Carroll County	2	0.66
Clover, MN (township) Hubbard County	1	0.65
Wurtsboro, NY (village) Sullivan County	8	0.64
Cedarville, NJ (cdp) Cumberland County	5	0.64
South Coffeyville, OK (town) Nowata County	5	0.64
Cedar Crest, OK (cdp) Mayes County	2	0.64
Fort Cobb, OK (town) Caddo County	4	0.63
Gracemont, OK (town) Caddo County	2	0.63
Rose Bud, AR (town) White County	3	0.62
Langley, OK (town) Mayes County	5	0.61
Webster, WI (village) Burnett County	4	0.61
Happys Inn, MT (cdp) Lincoln County	1	0.61
Cement, OK (town) Caddo County	3	0.60
Silo, OK (town) Bryan County	2	0.60
Deary, ID (city) Latah County	3	0.59
Pershing, WI (town) Taylor County	1	0.56
Woodside, DE (town) Kent County	1	0.55
Monroe, PA (borough) Bradford County	3	0.54
Chetopa, KS (city) Labette County	6	0.53
Leeton, MO (city) Johnson County	3	0.53
Meshoppen, PA (borough) Wyoming County	3	0.53
Brandon, NY (town) Franklin County	3	0.52
Cedar Vale, KS (city) Chautauqua County	3	0.52
Scraper, OK (cdp) Cherokee County	1	0.52
Decatur City, IA (city) Decatur County	1	0.51
Sun Valley, PA (cdp) Monroe County	12	0.50
La Plume, PA (township) Lackawanna County	3	0.50
Forkston, PA (township) Wyoming County	2	0.50
Washington, OK (town) McClain County	3	0.49
Sumpter, OR (city) Baker County	1	0.49
Greenwood Lake, NY (village) Orange County	15	0.48
Cleora, OK (cdp) Delaware County	7	0.48
Morgantown, PA (cdp) Berks County	4	0.48
Welch, OK (town) Craig County	3	0.48
Asbury, MO (city) Jasper County	1	0.48
Mahwah, NJ (township) Bergen County	121	0.47
Mays Landing, NJ (cdp) Atlantic County	10	0.47
Sheldon, IL (village) Iroquois County	5	0.47
Hopewell, NJ (township) Cumberland County	21	0.46
Rosenhayn, NJ (cdp) Cumberland County	5	0.46
Dearing, KS (city) Montgomery County	2	0.46
Mehoopany, PA (township) Wyoming County	4	0.45
Belle Valley, OH (village) Noble County	1	0.45
Tyro, KS (city) Montgomery County	1	0.45
Port Jervis, NY (city) Orange County	39	0.44
Port Norris, NJ (cdp) Cumberland County	6	0.44
Cascade, MT (town) Cascade County	3	0.44
Nanticoke, MD (cdp) Wicomico County	1	0.44
Rockland, MI (township) Ontonagon County	1	0.44
Valley Home, CA (cdp) Stanislaus County	1	0.44
Chester, NY (village) Orange County	17	0.43
Elmer, NJ (borough) Salem County	6	0.43
Prue, OK (town) Osage County	2	0.43
Fairmount, GA (city) Gordon County	3	0.42
Roseboom, NY (town) Otsego County	3	0.42
Rupert, VT (town) Bennington County	3	0.42
Lausanne, PA (township) Carbon County	1	0.42
Eaton Estates, OH (cdp) Lorain County	5	0.41
East Freedom, PA (cdp) Blair County	4	0.41
Wanaque, NJ (borough) Passaic County	44	0.40
Watson, IL (village) Effingham County	3	0.40
Dripping Springs, TX (city) Hays County	7	0.39
Meigs, GA (city) Thomas County	4	0.39
Quinton, NJ (township) Salem County	10	0.38
Burlington, PA (township) Bradford County	3	0.38
South Blooming Grove, NY (village) Orange County	12	0.37
Maybrook, NY (village) Orange County	11	0.37
Eaglewood, NJ (township) Ocean County	6	0.37
Ascutney, VT (cdp) Windsor County	2	0.37
Clarksdale, MO (city) DeKalb County	1	0.37

Please refer to the Explanation of Data in the front of the book for more detailed information.

Race

American Indian: Delaware

Top 150 Places Sorted by Percent of Total Population

Based on places with total population of 7,500 or more

Place	Population	%
Ringwood, NJ (borough) Passaic County	155	1.27
Bartlesville, OK (city) Washington County	255	0.71
Mahwah, NJ (township) Bergen County	121	0.47
Port Jervis, NY (city) Orange County	39	0.44
Wanaque, NJ (borough) Passaic County	44	0.40
Millville, NJ (city) Cumberland County	93	0.33
Bridgeton, NJ (city) Cumberland County	77	0.30
Pittsgrove, NJ (township) Salem County	27	0.29
Claremore, OK (city) Rogers County	52	0.28
Blooming Grove, NY (town) Orange County	51	0.28
Miami, OK (city) Ottawa County	36	0.27
Mamakating, NY (town) Sullivan County	31	0.26
West Milford, NJ (township) Passaic County	56	0.22
Coffeyville, KS (city) Montgomery County	23	0.22
Wallkill, NY (town) Orange County	57	0.21
Chickasha, OK (city) Grady County	34	0.21
Scotchtown, NY (cdp) Orange County	18	0.20
Goshen, NY (town) Orange County	26	0.19
Warwick, NY (town) Orange County	58	0.18
Dingman, PA (township) Pike County	22	0.18
Upper Deerfield, NJ (township) Cumberland County	14	0.18
Airmont, NY (village) Rockland County	15	0.17
Wawarsing, NY (town) Ulster County	21	0.16
Deerpark, NY (town) Orange County	13	0.16
Middletown, NY (city) Orange County	43	0.15
Woodbury, NJ (city) Gloucester County	15	0.15
Chester, NY (town) Orange County	17	0.14
Liberty, NY (town) Sullivan County	14	0.14
Ramapo, NY (town) Rockland County	167	0.13
Sand Springs, OK (city) Tulsa County	24	0.13
Parsons, KS (city) Labette County	14	0.13
West Haverstraw, NY (village) Rockland County	13	0.13
Florence, OR (city) Lane County	11	0.13
Millstone, NJ (township) Monmouth County	13	0.12
Carneys Point, NJ (township) Salem County	9	0.11
Vineland, NJ (city) Cumberland County	60	0.10
Owasso, OK (city) Tulsa County	28	0.10
Hamilton, NJ (township) Atlantic County	27	0.10
Richland, PA (township) Bucks County	13	0.10
Highlands, NY (town) Orange County	12	0.10
Augusta, KS (city) Butler County	9	0.10
Monroe, NY (village) Orange County	8	0.10
Wilson, PA (borough) Northampton County	8	0.10
Norman, OK (city) Cleveland County	95	0.09
Dover, DE (city) Kent County	34	0.09
Haverstraw, NY (town) Rockland County	32	0.09
Shawnee, OK (city) Pottawatomie County	28	0.09
Chestnuthill, PA (township) Monroe County	16	0.09
Ocean City, NJ (city) Cape May County	11	0.09
Woodbury, NY (village) Orange County	10	0.09
Woodbury, NY (town) Orange County	10	0.09
Esopus, NY (town) Ulster County	8	0.09
Bushkill, PA (township) Northampton County	7	0.09
Maurice River, NJ (township) Cumberland County	7	0.09
Canton, OH (city) Stark County	57	0.08
Newburgh, NY (city) Orange County	22	0.08
Neptune, NJ (township) Monmouth County	21	0.08
El Dorado, KS (city) Butler County	11	0.08
Cornwall, NY (town) Orange County	10	0.08
Haverstraw, NY (village) Rockland County	10	0.08
Oakland, NJ (borough) Bergen County	10	0.08
Choctaw, OK (city) Oklahoma County	9	0.08
Matawan, NJ (borough) Monmouth County	7	0.08
West Caln, PA (township) Chester County	7	0.08
Crestwood Village, NJ (cdp) Ocean County	6	0.08
Moore, OK (city) Cleveland County	41	0.07
Montgomery, NY (town) Orange County	16	0.07
Bethany, OK (city) Oklahoma County	14	0.07
Coolbaugh, PA (township) Monroe County	14	0.07
El Reno, OK (city) Canadian County	12	0.07
Browns Mills, NJ (cdp) Burlington County	8	0.07
Lehigh, PA (township) Northampton County	7	0.07
Mount Holly, NJ (township) Burlington County	7	0.07
Warr Acres, OK (city) Oklahoma County	7	0.07
Congers, NY (cdp) Rockland County	6	0.07

Place	Population	%
Hardyston, NJ (township) Sussex County	6	0.07
Riverside, NJ (township) Burlington County	6	0.07
The Village, OK (city) Oklahoma County	6	0.07
White Meadow Lake, NJ (cdp) Morris County	6	0.07
Bloomingdale, NJ (borough) Passaic County	5	0.07
Tulsa, OK (city) Tulsa County	232	0.06
Edmond, OK (city) Oklahoma County	46	0.06
Joplin, MO (city) Jasper County	29	0.06
Linden, NJ (city) Union County	24	0.06
Pennsauken, NJ (township) Camden County	20	0.06
Deptford, NJ (township) Gloucester County	19	0.06
Pemberton, NJ (township) Burlington County	18	0.06
Englewood, NJ (city) Bergen County	16	0.06
New Windsor, NY (town) Orange County	15	0.06
Palmer, PA (township) Northampton County	13	0.06
South Plainfield, NJ (borough) Middlesex County	13	0.06
Buckingham, PA (township) Bucks County	12	0.06
Chowchilla, CA (city) Madera County	12	0.06
Franklin, NJ (township) Gloucester County	10	0.06
Mustang, OK (city) Canadian County	10	0.06
Tahlequah, OK (city) Cherokee County	10	0.06
Mantua, NJ (township) Gloucester County	9	0.06
North Whitehall, PA (township) Lehigh County	9	0.06
Massena, NY (town) St. Lawrence County	8	0.06
Annapolis Neck, MD (cdp) Anne Arundel County	7	0.06
Glenpool, OK (city) Tulsa County	7	0.06
Gloucester City, NJ (city) Camden County	7	0.06
Stony Point, NY (cdp) Rockland County	7	0.06
Weatherford, OK (city) Custer County	7	0.06
Hacketts, NJ (town) Warren County	6	0.06
Independence, KS (city) Montgomery County	6	0.06
Lansdowne, PA (borough) Delaware County	6	0.06
Suffern, NY (village) Rockland County	6	0.06
August, CA (cdp) San Joaquin County	5	0.06
Bithlo, FL (cdp) Orange County	5	0.06
Boonton, NJ (town) Morris County	5	0.06
Clinton, OK (city) Custer County	5	0.06
Conning Towers Nautilus Park, CT (cdp) New London County	5	0.06
Doylestown, PA (borough) Bucks County	5	0.06
Kirby, TX (city) Bexar County	5	0.06
Plumsted, NJ (township) Ocean County	5	0.06
Wagoner, OK (city) Wagoner County	5	0.06
White Oak, PA (borough) Allegheny County	5	0.06
Oklahoma City, OK (city) Oklahoma County	280	0.05
Broken Arrow, OK (city) Tulsa County	51	0.05
Enid, OK (city) Garfield County	26	0.05
Midwest City, OK (city) Oklahoma County	25	0.05
Washington, NJ (township) Gloucester County	25	0.05
Monroe, NJ (township) Gloucester County	18	0.05
Easton, PA (city) Northampton County	13	0.05
Lacey, NJ (township) Ocean County	13	0.05
Rockaway, NJ (township) Morris County	12	0.05
Zanesville, OH (city) Muskingum County	12	0.05
Del City, OK (city) Oklahoma County	11	0.05
Yukon, OK (city) Canadian County	11	0.05
Aberdeen, NJ (township) Monmouth County	10	0.05
Newton, KS (city) Harvey County	10	0.05
Ithaca, NY (town) Tompkins County	9	0.05
Saugerties, NY (town) Ulster County	9	0.05
Kuna, ID (city) Ada County	8	0.05
New Philadelphia, OH (city) Tuscarawas County	8	0.05
Lyon, MI (charter township) Oakland County	7	0.05
Pequannock, NJ (township) Morris County	7	0.05
Phillipsburg, NJ (town) Warren County	7	0.05
Siloam Springs, AR (city) Benton County	7	0.05
Stony Point, NY (town) Rockland County	7	0.05
Atchison, KS (city) Atchison County	6	0.05
Eatontown, NJ (borough) Monmouth County	6	0.05
Logan, PA (township) Blair County	6	0.05
Waianae, HI (cdp) Honolulu County	6	0.05
Bolivar, MO (city) Polk County	5	0.05
Cedartown, GA (city) Polk County	5	0.05
Diamond Springs, CA (cdp) El Dorado County	5	0.05
Kalaoa, HI (cdp) Hawaii County	5	0.05
Kendall Park, NJ (cdp) Middlesex County	5	0.05

Please refer to the Explanation of Data in the front of the book for more detailed information.

Race

American Indian: Hopi

U.S. and 50 States Sorted by Population and Percent of Total Population

Place	Population	%
United States	**18,327**	**0.01**
Arizona	11,612	0.18
California	2,238	0.01
New Mexico	891	0.04
Colorado	401	0.01
Texas	359	<0.01
Utah	327	0.01
Washington	260	<0.01
Nevada	239	0.01
Oregon	160	<0.01
Oklahoma	137	<0.01
New York	115	<0.01
Ohio	105	<0.01
Florida	99	<0.01
Illinois	99	<0.01
Missouri	92	<0.01
Pennsylvania	82	<0.01
North Carolina	68	<0.01
Michigan	66	<0.01
Kansas	64	<0.01
New Jersey	64	<0.01
Indiana	60	<0.01
Wisconsin	58	<0.01
Virginia	56	<0.01
Georgia	54	<0.01
Hawaii	46	<0.01
Idaho	46	<0.01
Kentucky	45	<0.01
Tennessee	42	<0.01
Connecticut	36	<0.01
Massachusetts	35	<0.01
Iowa	33	<0.01
Minnesota	32	<0.01
Maryland	31	<0.01
Arkansas	29	<0.01
Montana	29	<0.01
South Dakota	29	<0.01
Alaska	25	<0.01
Alabama	24	<0.01
Louisiana	18	<0.01
South Carolina	18	<0.01
Wyoming	17	<0.01
Maine	16	<0.01
Delaware	14	<0.01
North Dakota	12	<0.01
West Virginia	12	<0.01
Rhode Island	8	<0.01
New Hampshire	7	<0.01
Nebraska	6	<0.01
Vermont	6	<0.01
Mississippi	3	<0.01
District of Columbia	2	<0.01

Place	Population	%
Arizona	11,612	0.18
New Mexico	891	0.04
United States	**18,327**	**0.01**
California	2,238	0.01
Colorado	401	0.01
Utah	327	0.01
Nevada	239	0.01
Texas	359	<0.01
Washington	260	<0.01
Oregon	160	<0.01
Oklahoma	137	<0.01
New York	115	<0.01
Ohio	105	<0.01
Florida	99	<0.01
Illinois	99	<0.01
Missouri	92	<0.01
Pennsylvania	82	<0.01
North Carolina	68	<0.01
Michigan	66	<0.01
Kansas	64	<0.01
New Jersey	64	<0.01
Indiana	60	<0.01
Wisconsin	58	<0.01
Virginia	56	<0.01
Georgia	54	<0.01
Hawaii	46	<0.01
Idaho	46	<0.01
Kentucky	45	<0.01
Tennessee	42	<0.01
Connecticut	36	<0.01
Massachusetts	35	<0.01
Iowa	33	<0.01
Minnesota	32	<0.01
Maryland	31	<0.01
Arkansas	29	<0.01
Montana	29	<0.01
South Dakota	29	<0.01
Alaska	25	<0.01
Alabama	24	<0.01
Louisiana	18	<0.01
South Carolina	18	<0.01
Wyoming	17	<0.01
Maine	16	<0.01
Delaware	14	<0.01
North Dakota	12	<0.01
West Virginia	12	<0.01
Rhode Island	8	<0.01
New Hampshire	7	<0.01
Nebraska	6	<0.01
Vermont	6	<0.01
Mississippi	3	<0.01
District of Columbia	2	<0.01

Please refer to the Explanation of Data in the front of the book for more detailed information.

Race

American Indian: Hopi

Top 150 Places Sorted by Population

Based on all places, regardless of total population

Place	Population	%
Phoenix, AZ (city) Maricopa County	1,648	0.11
First Mesa, AZ (cdp) Navajo County	1,145	73.63
Hotevilla-Bacavi, AZ (cdp) Navajo County	791	82.65
Second Mesa, AZ (cdp) Navajo County	758	78.79
Moenkopi, AZ (cdp) Coconino County	743	77.07
Shongopovi, AZ (cdp) Navajo County	730	87.85
Flagstaff, AZ (city) Coconino County	625	0.95
Kykotsmovi Village, AZ (cdp) Navajo County	612	82.04
Tuba City, AZ (cdp) Coconino County	403	4.68
Mesa, AZ (city) Maricopa County	352	0.08
Albuquerque, NM (city) Bernalillo County	276	0.05
Winslow, AZ (city) Navajo County	244	2.53
Tucson, AZ (city) Pima County	219	0.04
Keams Canyon, AZ (cdp) Navajo County	184	60.53
Glendale, AZ (city) Maricopa County	179	0.08
Los Angeles, CA (city) Los Angeles County	163	<0.01
Tempe, AZ (city) Maricopa County	161	0.10
Chandler, AZ (city) Maricopa County	108	0.05
Denver, CO (city) Denver County	81	0.01
Scottsdale, AZ (city) Maricopa County	80	0.04
Winslow West, AZ (cdp) Navajo County	74	16.89
Gallup, NM (city) McKinley County	63	0.29
Holbrook, AZ (city) Navajo County	62	1.23
Farmington, NM (city) San Juan County	61	0.13
Riverside, CA (city) Riverside County	59	0.02
San Jose, CA (city) Santa Clara County	58	0.01
San Diego, CA (city) San Diego County	57	<0.01
Camp Verde, AZ (town) Yavapai County	56	0.52
New York, NY (city) Kings County	49	<0.01
Doney Park, AZ (cdp) Coconino County	48	0.89
Fresno, CA (city) Fresno County	45	0.01
Jeddito, AZ (cdp) Navajo County	44	15.02
Grand Canyon Village, AZ (cdp) Coconino County	44	2.20
Gilbert, AZ (town) Maricopa County	41	0.02
Peoria, AZ (city) Yavapai County	40	0.03
Parker, AZ (town) La Paz County	39	1.27
Kayenta, AZ (cdp) Navajo County	38	0.73
Page, AZ (city) Coconino County	37	0.51
Casa Grande, AZ (city) Pinal County	36	0.07
Surprise, AZ (city) Maricopa County	34	0.03
Rio Rancho, NM (city) Sandoval County	31	0.04
Salt Lake City, UT (city) Salt Lake County	30	0.02
Zuni Pueblo, NM (cdp) McKinley County	29	0.46
Prescott, AZ (city) Yavapai County	29	0.07
Carson City, NV (ind. city) Carson City County	29	0.05
Goodyear, AZ (city) Maricopa County	29	0.04
Aurora, CO (city) Arapahoe County	28	0.01
Sacramento, CA (city) Sacramento County	28	0.01
Portland, OR (city) Multnomah County	28	<0.01
Snowflake, AZ (town) Navajo County	27	0.48
Drexel Heights, AZ (cdp) Pima County	27	0.10
Bakersfield, CA (city) Kern County	27	0.01
San Bernardino, CA (city) San Bernardino County	27	0.01
Oklahoma City, OK (city) Oklahoma County	27	<0.01
Kingman, AZ (city) Mohave County	26	0.09
Avondale, AZ (city) Maricopa County	26	0.03
Oakland, CA (city) Alameda County	26	0.01
Chicago, IL (city) Cook County	26	<0.01
Las Vegas, NV (city) Clark County	26	<0.01
Anaheim, CA (city) Orange County	25	0.01
Greasewood, AZ (cdp) Navajo County	24	4.39
Shiprock, NM (cdp) San Juan County	24	0.29
West Valley City, UT (city) Salt Lake County	24	0.02
Palmdale, CA (city) Los Angeles County	23	0.02
Dallas, TX (city) Dallas County	23	<0.01
San Antonio, TX (city) Medina County	23	<0.01
San Francisco, CA (city) San Francisco County	23	<0.01
Buckeye, AZ (town) Maricopa County	22	0.04
Sparks, NV (city) Washoe County	22	0.02
Sunrise Manor, NV (cdp) Clark County	22	0.01
El Paso, TX (city) El Paso County	22	<0.01
Long Beach, CA (city) Los Angeles County	22	<0.01
Lakewood, CO (city) Jefferson County	21	0.01
Roosevelt, UT (city) Duchesne County	20	0.33
Brigham City, UT (city) Box Elder County	20	0.11
Prescott Valley, AZ (town) Yavapai County	20	0.05
Glendale, CA (city) Los Angeles County	20	0.01
Hayward, CA (city) Alameda County	20	0.01
Colorado Springs, CO (city) El Paso County	20	<0.01
Seattle, WA (city) King County	20	<0.01
Antioch, CA (city) Contra Costa County	19	0.02
Ogden, UT (city) Weber County	19	0.02
Orem, UT (city) Utah County	19	0.02
San Tan Valley, AZ (cdp) Pinal County	19	0.02
Payson, AZ (town) Gila County	18	0.12
Santa Fe, NM (city) Santa Fe County	18	0.03
Norwalk, CA (city) Los Angeles County	18	0.02
Eugene, OR (city) Lane County	18	0.01
Tacoma, WA (city) Pierce County	18	0.01
Black Rock, NM (cdp) McKinley County	17	1.28
Fort Defiance, AZ (cdp) Apache County	17	0.47
Show Low, AZ (city) Navajo County	17	0.16
Florence, AZ (town) Pinal County	17	0.07
Pleasant Grove, UT (city) Utah County	17	0.05
Alhambra, CA (city) Los Angeles County	17	0.02
Downey, CA (city) Los Angeles County	17	0.02
Hesperia, CA (city) San Bernardino County	17	0.02
San Buenaventura (Ventura), CA (city) Ventura County	17	0.02
West Covina, CA (city) Los Angeles County	17	0.02
Yuma, AZ (city) Yuma County	17	0.02
St. Louis, MO (city) St. Louis city County	17	0.01
Thornton, CO (city) Adams County	17	0.01
Sells, AZ (cdp) Pima County	16	0.64
South Tucson, AZ (city) Pima County	16	0.28
Maricopa, AZ (city) Pinal County	16	0.04
Henderson, NV (city) Clark County	16	0.01
Stockton, CA (city) San Joaquin County	16	0.01
Austin, TX (city) Travis County	16	<0.01
Houston, TX (city) Harris County	16	<0.01
Cameron, AZ (cdp) Coconino County	15	1.69
Durango, CO (city) La Plata County	15	0.09
Eloy, AZ (city) Pinal County	15	0.09
Oxnard, CA (city) Ventura County	15	0.01
Pomona, CA (city) Los Angeles County	15	0.01
Manhattan, NY (borough) New York County	15	<0.01
Queens, NY (borough) Queens County	15	<0.01
Leupp, AZ (cdp) Coconino County	14	1.47
Lake Montezuma, AZ (cdp) Yavapai County	14	0.30
Grants, NM (city) Cibola County	14	0.15
Commerce City, CO (city) Adams County	14	0.03
Apple Valley, CA (town) San Bernardino County	14	0.02
Lawrence, KS (city) Douglas County	14	0.02
Aurora, IL (city) Kane County	14	0.01
Corona, CA (city) Riverside County	14	0.01
Huntington Beach, CA (city) Orange County	14	0.01
North Las Vegas, NV (city) Clark County	14	0.01
Oceanside, CA (city) San Diego County	14	0.01
Anchorage, AK (municipality) Anchorage Municipality	14	<0.01
Santa Ana, CA (city) Orange County	14	<0.01
Wichita, KS (city) Sedgwick County	14	<0.01
Low Mountain, AZ (cdp) Navajo County	13	1.72
Sacaton, AZ (cdp) Pinal County	13	0.49
Clifton, AZ (town) Greenlee County	13	0.39
Guadalupe, AZ (town) Maricopa County	13	0.24
Fountain Hills, AZ (town) Maricopa County	13	0.06
Marana, AZ (town) Pima County	13	0.04
Casas Adobes, AZ (cdp) Pima County	13	0.02
Lancaster, CA (city) Los Angeles County	13	0.01
Paradise, NV (cdp) Clark County	13	0.01
Provo, UT (city) Utah County	13	0.01
Reno, NV (city) Washoe County	13	0.01
Spring Valley, NV (cdp) Clark County	13	0.01
Vallejo, CA (city) Solano County	13	0.01
Indianapolis, IN (city) Marion County	13	<0.01
Cottonwood, AZ (city) Yavapai County	12	0.11
Kearns, UT (cdp) Salt Lake County	12	0.03
South Valley, NM (cdp) Bernalillo County	12	0.03
Watsonville, CA (city) Santa Cruz County	12	0.02
Buena Park, CA (city) Orange County	12	0.01
Ontario, CA (city) San Bernardino County	12	0.01

Please refer to the Explanation of Data in the front of the book for more detailed information.

Race

American Indian: Hopi

Top 150 Places Sorted by Percent of Total Population

Based on all places, regardless of total population

Place	Population	%
Shongopovi, AZ (cdp) Navajo County	730	87.85
Hotevilla-Bacavi, AZ (cdp) Navajo County	791	82.65
Kykotsmovi Village, AZ (cdp) Navajo County	612	82.04
Second Mesa, AZ (cdp) Navajo County	758	78.79
Moenkopi, AZ (cdp) Coconino County	743	77.07
First Mesa, AZ (cdp) Navajo County	1,145	73.63
Keams Canyon, AZ (cdp) Navajo County	184	60.53
Winslow West, AZ (cdp) Navajo County	74	16.89
Jeddito, AZ (cdp) Navajo County	44	15.02
Seba Dalkai, AZ (cdp) Navajo County	11	8.09
Mojave Ranch Estates, AZ (cdp) Mohave County	3	5.77
Tuba City, AZ (cdp) Coconino County	403	4.68
Greasewood, AZ (cdp) Navajo County	24	4.39
Cherokee, CA (cdp) Butte County	3	4.35
McCartys Village, NM (cdp) Cibola County	2	4.17
Sun Valley, AZ (cdp) Navajo County	11	3.48
Helix, OR (city) Umatilla County	6	3.26
Latty, OH (village) Paulding County	5	2.59
Winslow, AZ (city) Navajo County	244	2.53
Tolani Lake, AZ (cdp) Coconino County	7	2.50
Supai, AZ (cdp) Coconino County	5	2.40
Truxton, AZ (cdp) Mohave County	3	2.24
Grand Canyon Village, AZ (cdp) Coconino County	44	2.20
Tees Toh, AZ (cdp) Navajo County	9	2.01
Chilchinbito, AZ (cdp) Navajo County	9	1.78
Low Mountain, AZ (cdp) Navajo County	13	1.72
Cameron, AZ (cdp) Coconino County	15	1.69
Santa Rosa, AZ (cdp) Pima County	10	1.59
Leupp, AZ (cdp) Coconino County	14	1.47
Picuris Pueblo, NM (cdp) Taos County	1	1.47
Inger, MN (cdp) Itasca County	3	1.42
Branson, CO (town) Las Animas County	1	1.35
Anegam, AZ (cdp) Pima County	2	1.32
Wet Camp Village, AZ (cdp) Pinal County	3	1.31
Black Rock, NM (cdp) McKinley County	17	1.28
Parker, AZ (town) La Paz County	39	1.27
Holbrook, AZ (city) Navajo County	62	1.23
Etna, WY (cdp) Lincoln County	2	1.22
St. Johns, AZ (cdp) Maricopa County	5	1.05
Paraje, NM (cdp) Cibola County	8	1.03
Isleta Village Proper, NM (cdp) Bernalillo County	5	1.02
Northwood, PA (cdp) Blair County	3	1.01
Topawa, AZ (cdp) Pima County	3	1.00
Flagstaff, AZ (city) Coconino County	625	0.95
Ak-Chin Village, AZ (cdp) Pinal County	8	0.93
Peach Springs, AZ (cdp) Mohave County	10	0.92
Doney Park, AZ (cdp) Coconino County	48	0.89
Cottonwood, AZ (cdp) Apache County	2	0.88
Shonto, AZ (cdp) Navajo County	5	0.85
Navajo Mountain, UT (cdp) San Juan County	3	0.85
Ganado, AZ (cdp) Apache County	10	0.83
Santa Clara Pueblo, NM (cdp) Rio Arriba County	8	0.79
North Salem, IN (town) Hendricks County	4	0.77
Rodey, NM (cdp) Doña Ana County	3	0.77
Kayenta, AZ (cdp) Navajo County	38	0.73
Paguate, NM (cdp) Cibola County	3	0.71
Concow, CA (cdp) Butte County	5	0.70
Cochiti Lake, NM (cdp) Sandoval County	4	0.70
Steamboat, AZ (cdp) Apache County	2	0.70
Fort Apache, AZ (cdp) Navajo County	1	0.70
Rio en Medio, NM (cdp) Santa Fe County	1	0.70
Dutch John, UT (cdp) Daggett County	1	0.69
Teec Nos Pos, AZ (cdp) Apache County	5	0.68
Many Farms, AZ (cdp) Apache County	9	0.67
Bowie, AZ (cdp) Cochise County	3	0.67
Ojo Amarillo, NM (cdp) San Juan County	5	0.65
Sells, AZ (cdp) Pima County	16	0.64
Ali Chuk, AZ (cdp) Pima County	1	0.62
Sacate Village, AZ (cdp) Pinal County	1	0.59
Joseph City, AZ (cdp) Navajo County	8	0.58
Duncan, AZ (town) Greenlee County	4	0.57
Blackwater, AZ (cdp) Pinal County	6	0.56
Sacaton Flats Village, AZ (cdp) Pinal County	3	0.55
Pueblo of Sandia Village, NM (cdp) Sandoval County	2	0.54
Bay View Gardens, IL (village) Woodford County	2	0.53
Camp Verde, AZ (town) Yavapai County	56	0.52
Page, AZ (city) Coconino County	37	0.51
Mesita, NM (cdp) Cibola County	4	0.50
Sacaton, AZ (cdp) Pinal County	13	0.49
LeChee, AZ (cdp) Coconino County	7	0.49
Komatke, AZ (cdp) Maricopa County	4	0.49
Elephant Head, AZ (cdp) Pima County	3	0.49
Snowflake, AZ (town) Navajo County	27	0.48
Laguna, NM (cdp) Cibola County	6	0.48
Valle, AZ (cdp) Coconino County	4	0.48
Encinal, NM (cdp) Cibola County	1	0.48
Fort Defiance, AZ (cdp) Apache County	17	0.47
Zuni Pueblo, NM (cdp) McKinley County	29	0.46
West Peavine, OK (cdp) Adair County	1	0.46
East Globe, AZ (cdp) Gila County	1	0.44
Seama, NM (cdp) Cibola County	2	0.43
North Fork, AZ (cdp) Navajo County	6	0.42
Liberal, MO (city) Barton County	3	0.40
Upper Santan Village, AZ (cdp) Pinal County	2	0.40
Galisteo, NM (cdp) Santa Fe County	1	0.40
Clifton, AZ (town) Greenlee County	13	0.39
Braggs, OK (town) Muskogee County	1	0.39
Wild Rice, MN (township) Norman County	1	0.39
Naturita, CO (town) Montrose County	2	0.37
Kerby, OR (cdp) Josephine County	2	0.34
Arrowsmith, IL (village) McLean County	1	0.34
Turkey Creek, AZ (cdp) Navajo County	1	0.34
Roosevelt, UT (city) Duchesne County	20	0.33
Dulce, NM (cdp) Rio Arriba County	9	0.33
Nambe, NM (cdp) Santa Fe County	6	0.33
Kaibito, AZ (cdp) Coconino County	5	0.33
Pinon, AZ (cdp) Navajo County	3	0.33
North Acomita Village, NM (cdp) Cibola County	1	0.33
Munds Park, AZ (cdp) Coconino County	2	0.32
Kachina Village, AZ (cdp) Coconino County	8	0.31
Bylas, AZ (cdp) Graham County	6	0.31
Oak Leaf, TX (city) Ellis County	4	0.31
Mayville, WI (town) Clark County	3	0.31
Shell Ridge, CA (cdp) Contra Costa County	3	0.31
Cedar Creek, AZ (cdp) Gila County	1	0.31
Lake Montezuma, AZ (cdp) Yavapai County	14	0.30
Williams, AZ (city) Coconino County	9	0.30
Chester, NJ (borough) Morris County	5	0.30
Gallup, NM (city) McKinley County	63	0.29
Shiprock, NM (cdp) San Juan County	24	0.29
Santo Domingo Pueblo, NM (cdp) Sandoval County	7	0.29
LaGrange, OH (village) Lorain County	6	0.29
Pirtleville, AZ (cdp) Cochise County	5	0.29
Casa Blanca, AZ (cdp) Pinal County	4	0.29
South Tucson, AZ (city) Pima County	16	0.28
St. Michaels, AZ (cdp) Apache County	4	0.28
Fort Duchesne, UT (cdp) Uintah County	2	0.28
Maricopa Colony, AZ (cdp) Maricopa County	2	0.28
Peña Blanca, NM (cdp) Sandoval County	2	0.28
Lower Santan Village, AZ (cdp) Pinal County	1	0.27
Nixon, NV (cdp) Washoe County	1	0.27
Remer, MN (city) Cass County	1	0.27
Clearlake Riviera, CA (cdp) Lake County	8	0.26
Taft Mosswood, CA (cdp) San Joaquin County	4	0.26
Bowstring Lake, MN (unorganized territory) Itasca County	3	0.26
Ship Bottom, NJ (borough) Ocean County	3	0.26
Taos Pueblo, NM (cdp) Taos County	3	0.26
Mamre, MN (township) Kandiyohi County	1	0.26
San Carlos, AZ (cdp) Gila County	10	0.25
Canton Valley, CT (cdp) Hartford County	4	0.25
El Rancho, NM (cdp) Santa Fe County	3	0.25
Herald, CA (cdp) Sacramento County	3	0.25
Mission, SD (city) Todd County	3	0.25
Mountain View, OK (town) Kiowa County	2	0.25
Clay Springs, AZ (cdp) Navajo County	1	0.25
Couderay, WI (town) Sawyer County	1	0.25
Guadalupe, AZ (town) Maricopa County	13	0.24
Lukachukai, AZ (cdp) Apache County	4	0.24
Valle Vista, AZ (cdp) Mohave County	4	0.24
Covelo, CA (cdp) Mendocino County	3	0.24

Please refer to the Explanation of Data in the front of the book for more detailed information.

Race

American Indian: Hopi

Top 150 Places Sorted by Percent of Total Population

Based on places with total population of 7,500 or more

Place	Population	%
Tuba City, AZ (cdp) Coconino County	403	4.68
Winslow, AZ (city) Navajo County	244	2.53
Flagstaff, AZ (city) Coconino County	625	0.95
Camp Verde, AZ (town) Yavapai County	56	0.52
Gallup, NM (city) McKinley County	63	0.29
Shiprock, NM (cdp) San Juan County	24	0.29
Show Low, AZ (city) Navajo County	17	0.16
Grants, NM (city) Cibola County	14	0.15
Farmington, NM (city) San Juan County	61	0.13
Payson, AZ (town) Gila County	18	0.12
Phoenix, AZ (city) Maricopa County	1,648	0.11
Brigham City, UT (city) Box Elder County	20	0.11
Cottonwood, AZ (city) Yavapai County	12	0.11
Tempe, AZ (city) Maricopa County	161	0.10
Drexel Heights, AZ (cdp) Pima County	27	0.10
North Valley, NM (cdp) Bernalillo County	11	0.10
Kingman, AZ (city) Mohave County	26	0.09
Durango, CO (city) La Plata County	15	0.09
Eloy, AZ (city) Pinal County	15	0.09
Mesa, AZ (city) Maricopa County	352	0.08
Glendale, AZ (city) Maricopa County	179	0.08
Sun Village, CA (cdp) Los Angeles County	9	0.08
Catalina, AZ (cdp) Pima County	6	0.08
Casa Grande, AZ (city) Pinal County	36	0.07
Prescott, AZ (city) Yavapai County	29	0.07
Florence, AZ (town) Pinal County	17	0.07
Richfield, UT (city) Sevier County	5	0.07
Tremonton, UT (city) Box Elder County	5	0.07
Fountain Hills, AZ (town) Maricopa County	13	0.06
Fort Lewis, WA (cdp) Pierce County	7	0.06
Verde Village, AZ (cdp) Yavapai County	7	0.06
Cortez, CO (city) Montezuma County	5	0.06
Doylestown, PA (borough) Bucks County	5	0.06
DuPont, WA (city) Pierce County	5	0.06
Gonzales, CA (city) Monterey County	5	0.06
Albuquerque, NM (city) Bernalillo County	276	0.05
Chandler, AZ (city) Maricopa County	108	0.05
Carson City, NV (ind. city) Carson City County	29	0.05
Prescott Valley, AZ (town) Yavapai County	20	0.05
Pleasant Grove, UT (city) Utah County	17	0.05
Prunedale, CA (cdp) Monterey County	9	0.05
Arizona City, AZ (cdp) Pinal County	5	0.05
Garden Acres, CA (cdp) San Joaquin County	5	0.05
Pella, IA (city) Marion County	5	0.05
Riverton, WY (city) Fremont County	5	0.05
Mammoth Lakes, CA (town) Mono County	4	0.05
Wilmington Manor, DE (cdp) New Castle County	4	0.05
Tucson, AZ (city) Pima County	219	0.04
Scottsdale, AZ (city) Maricopa County	80	0.04
Rio Rancho, NM (city) Sandoval County	31	0.04
Goodyear, AZ (city) Maricopa County	29	0.04
Buckeye, AZ (town) Maricopa County	22	0.04
Maricopa, AZ (city) Pinal County	16	0.04
Marana, AZ (town) Pima County	13	0.04
Fallbrook, CA (cdp) San Diego County	11	0.04
Fernley, NV (city) Lyon County	8	0.04
Gibsonton, FL (cdp) Hillsborough County	6	0.04
Kuna, ID (city) Ada County	6	0.04
Alpine, CA (cdp) San Diego County	5	0.04
Spring Creek, NV (cdp) Elko County	5	0.04
Canton, CT (town) Hartford County	4	0.04
Chino Valley, AZ (town) Yavapai County	4	0.04
Country Club, CA (cdp) San Joaquin County	4	0.04
Hawaiian Paradise Park, HI (cdp) Hawaii County	4	0.04
Johns, CO (town) Weld County	4	0.04
Muscoy, CA (cdp) San Bernardino County	4	0.04
Norwalk, IA (city) Warren County	4	0.04
Sedro-Woolley, WA (city) Skagit County	4	0.04
Somers Point, NJ (city) Atlantic County	4	0.04
Spearfish, SD (city) Lawrence County	4	0.04
East Foothills, CA (cdp) Santa Clara County	3	0.04
Gettysburg, PA (borough) Adams County	3	0.04
Globe, AZ (city) Gila County	3	0.04
Golden Valley, AZ (cdp) Mohave County	3	0.04
Kirtland, NM (cdp) San Juan County	3	0.04
Ocean Pointe, HI (cdp) Honolulu County	3	0.04
Peoria, AZ (city) Yavapai County	40	0.03
Surprise, AZ (city) Maricopa County	34	0.03
Avondale, AZ (city) Maricopa County	26	0.03
Santa Fe, NM (city) Santa Fe County	18	0.03
Commerce City, CO (city) Adams County	14	0.03
Kearns, UT (cdp) Salt Lake County	12	0.03
South Valley, NM (cdp) Bernalillo County	12	0.03
Apache Junction, AZ (city) Pinal County	10	0.03
Hollister, CA (city) San Benito County	10	0.03
Rubidoux, CA (cdp) Riverside County	10	0.03
La Verne, CA (city) Los Angeles County	9	0.03
Maywood, CA (city) Los Angeles County	8	0.03
Anthem, AZ (cdp) Maricopa County	7	0.03
Port Hueneme, CA (city) Ventura County	7	0.03
Sahuarita, AZ (town) Pima County	7	0.03
South Pasadena, CA (city) Los Angeles County	7	0.03
Ashland, CA (cdp) Alameda County	6	0.03
Cherryland, CA (cdp) Alameda County	5	0.03
Deming, NM (city) Luna County	5	0.03
Gatesville, TX (city) Coryell County	5	0.03
Green Oak, MI (township) Livingston County	5	0.03
Mill Creek, WA (city) Snohomish County	5	0.03
Raymore, MO (city) Cass County	5	0.03
Stafford, TX (city) Fort Bend County	5	0.03
Tanque Verde, AZ (cdp) Pima County	5	0.03
Artondale, WA (cdp) Pierce County	4	0.03
Boulder City, NV (city) Clark County	4	0.03
Ledyard, CT (town) New London County	4	0.03
Levelland, TX (city) Hockley County	4	0.03
Livingston, CA (city) Merced County	4	0.03
Los Alamos, NM (cdp) Los Alamos County	4	0.03
Mesquite, NV (city) Clark County	4	0.03
Sierra Vista Southeast, AZ (cdp) Cochise County	4	0.03
Whitewater, WI (city) Walworth County	4	0.03
Coffeyville, KS (city) Montgomery County	3	0.03
Frankfort Square, IL (cdp) Will County	3	0.03
Gold Canyon, AZ (cdp) Pinal County	3	0.03
Grantsville, UT (city) Tooele County	3	0.03
Kapaa, HI (cdp) Kauai County	3	0.03
Massena, NY (village) St. Lawrence County	3	0.03
Mentone, CA (cdp) San Bernardino County	3	0.03
Piedmont, CA (city) Alameda County	3	0.03
Rossmoor, CA (cdp) Orange County	3	0.03
Sierra Madre, CA (city) Los Angeles County	3	0.03
Smyrna, DE (town) Kent County	3	0.03
Sturgeon Bay, WI (city) Door County	3	0.03
The Village, OK (city) Oklahoma County	3	0.03
Valley Center, CA (cdp) San Diego County	3	0.03
View Park-Windsor Hills, CA (cdp) Los Angeles County	3	0.03
Whitewater, WI (city) Walworth County	3	0.03
Cleveland, TX (city) Liberty County	2	0.03
Crescent City, CA (city) Del Norte County	2	0.03
Lincoln City, OR (city) Lincoln County	2	0.03
Riverside, CA (city) Riverside County	59	0.02
Gilbert, AZ (town) Maricopa County	41	0.02
Salt Lake City, UT (city) Salt Lake County	30	0.02
West Valley City, UT (city) Salt Lake County	24	0.02
Palmdale, CA (city) Los Angeles County	23	0.02
Sparks, NV (city) Washoe County	22	0.02
Antioch, CA (city) Contra Costa County	19	0.02
Ogden, UT (city) Weber County	19	0.02
Orem, UT (city) Utah County	19	0.02
San Tan Valley, AZ (cdp) Pinal County	19	0.02
Norwalk, CA (city) Los Angeles County	18	0.02
Alhambra, CA (city) Los Angeles County	17	0.02
Downey, CA (city) Los Angeles County	17	0.02
Hesperia, CA (city) San Bernardino County	17	0.02
San Buenaventura (Ventura), CA (city) Ventura County	17	0.02
West Covina, CA (city) Los Angeles County	17	0.02
Yuma, AZ (city) Yuma County	17	0.02
Apple Valley, CA (town) San Bernardino County	14	0.02
Lawrence, KS (city) Douglas County	14	0.02
Casas Adobes, AZ (cdp) Pima County	13	0.02
Watsonville, CA (city) Santa Cruz County	12	0.02

SECTION THREE

Race

American Indian: Houma

U.S. and 50 States Sorted by Population and Percent of Total Population

Place	Population	%
United States	**10,768**	**<0.01**
Louisiana	8,666	0.19
Mississippi	393	0.01
Texas	377	<0.01
Florida	175	<0.01
California	137	<0.01
Georgia	104	<0.01
Alabama	89	<0.01
Tennessee	72	<0.01
North Carolina	61	<0.01
Arkansas	49	<0.01
New York	48	<0.01
Oklahoma	44	<0.01
Indiana	43	<0.01
Colorado	42	<0.01
Virginia	35	<0.01
Oregon	34	<0.01
Washington	34	<0.01
Missouri	31	<0.01
Illinois	28	<0.01
Pennsylvania	28	<0.01
South Carolina	26	<0.01
Ohio	22	<0.01
Arizona	21	<0.01
Massachusetts	20	<0.01
New Jersey	20	<0.01
Maryland	19	<0.01
Kansas	15	<0.01
Michigan	15	<0.01
Minnesota	14	<0.01
Wisconsin	14	<0.01
Connecticut	12	<0.01
New Mexico	11	<0.01
Kentucky	10	<0.01
Nevada	9	<0.01
Utah	9	<0.01
Iowa	8	<0.01
Alaska	6	<0.01
Delaware	5	<0.01
Hawaii	4	<0.01
Rhode Island	4	<0.01
District of Columbia	2	<0.01
Montana	2	<0.01
Vermont	2	<0.01
West Virginia	2	<0.01
Idaho	1	<0.01
Maine	1	<0.01
Nebraska	1	<0.01
New Hampshire	1	<0.01
North Dakota	1	<0.01
Wyoming	1	<0.01
South Dakota	0	0.00

Place	Population	%
Louisiana	8,666	0.19
Mississippi	393	0.01
United States	**10,768**	**<0.01**
Texas	377	<0.01
Florida	175	<0.01
California	137	<0.01
Georgia	104	<0.01
Alabama	89	<0.01
Tennessee	72	<0.01
North Carolina	61	<0.01
Arkansas	49	<0.01
New York	48	<0.01
Oklahoma	44	<0.01
Indiana	43	<0.01
Colorado	42	<0.01
Virginia	35	<0.01
Oregon	34	<0.01
Washington	34	<0.01
Missouri	31	<0.01
Illinois	28	<0.01
Pennsylvania	28	<0.01
South Carolina	26	<0.01
Ohio	22	<0.01
Arizona	21	<0.01
Massachusetts	20	<0.01
New Jersey	20	<0.01
Maryland	19	<0.01
Kansas	15	<0.01
Michigan	15	<0.01
Minnesota	14	<0.01
Wisconsin	14	<0.01
Connecticut	12	<0.01
New Mexico	11	<0.01
Kentucky	10	<0.01
Nevada	9	<0.01
Utah	9	<0.01
Iowa	8	<0.01
Alaska	6	<0.01
Delaware	5	<0.01
Hawaii	4	<0.01
Rhode Island	4	<0.01
District of Columbia	2	<0.01
Montana	2	<0.01
Vermont	2	<0.01
West Virginia	2	<0.01
Idaho	1	<0.01
Maine	1	<0.01
Nebraska	1	<0.01
New Hampshire	1	<0.01
North Dakota	1	<0.01
Wyoming	1	<0.01
South Dakota	0	0.00

Please refer to the Explanation of Data in the front of the book for more detailed information.

Race

American Indian: Houma

Top 150 Places Sorted by Population

Based on all places, regardless of total population

Place	Population	%
Houma, LA (city) Terrebonne Parish	885	2.62
Dulac, LA (cdp) Terrebonne Parish	423	28.91
Bayou Blue, LA (cdp) Lafourche Parish	326	2.64
Galliano, LA (cdp) Lafourche Parish	320	4.17
Bayou Cane, LA (cdp) Terrebonne Parish	307	1.59
Cut Off, LA (cdp) Lafourche Parish	214	3.58
Larose, LA (cdp) Lafourche Parish	162	2.19
Marrero, LA (cdp) Jefferson Parish	119	0.36
Golden Meadow, LA (town) Lafourche Parish	107	5.09
Morgan City, LA (city) St. Mary Parish	90	0.73
Estelle, LA (cdp) Jefferson Parish	85	0.52
Gray, LA (cdp) Terrebonne Parish	82	1.47
Lafayette, LA (city) Lafayette Parish	79	0.07
Bourg, LA (cdp) Terrebonne Parish	76	2.95
Raceland, LA (cdp) Lafourche Parish	73	0.72
Metairie, LA (cdp) Jefferson Parish	72	0.05
Jean Lafitte, LA (town) Jefferson Parish	66	3.47
New Orleans, LA (city) Orleans Parish	66	0.02
Montegut, LA (cdp) Terrebonne Parish	64	4.16
Westwego, LA (city) Jefferson Parish	57	0.67
Bayou Vista, LA (cdp) St. Mary Parish	54	1.16
Chauvin, LA (cdp) Terrebonne Parish	51	1.75
Lockport, LA (town) Lafourche Parish	48	1.86
Schriever, LA (cdp) Terrebonne Parish	48	0.70
Belle Chasse, LA (cdp) Plaquemines Parish	47	0.37
Thibodaux, LA (city) Lafourche Parish	47	0.32
Franklin, LA (city) St. Mary Parish	45	0.59
Slidell, LA (city) St. Tammany Parish	44	0.16
Boothville, LA (cdp) Plaquemines Parish	42	4.92
Baton Rouge, LA (city) East Baton Rouge Parish	41	0.02
Berwick, LA (town) St. Mary Parish	38	0.77
Kenner, LA (city) Jefferson Parish	38	0.06
Terrytown, LA (cdp) Jefferson Parish	36	0.15
Laplace, LA (cdp) St. John the Baptist Parish	35	0.12
Harvey, LA (cdp) Jefferson Parish	34	0.17
Chalmette, LA (cdp) St. Bernard Parish	33	0.20
Patterson, LA (city) St. Mary Parish	31	0.51
Gretna, LA (city) Jefferson Parish	31	0.17
Meraux, LA (cdp) St. Bernard Parish	30	0.52
Jacksonville, FL (city) Duval County	27	<0.01
Des Allemands, LA (cdp) St. Charles Parish	26	1.04
Harahan, LA (city) Jefferson Parish	26	0.28
Bayou L'Ourse, LA (cdp) Assumption Parish	24	1.21
Chackbay, LA (cdp) Lafourche Parish	24	0.46
Shreveport, LA (city) Caddo Parish	24	0.01
New York, NY (city) Kings County	23	<0.01
Violet, LA (cdp) St. Bernard Parish	21	0.42
Presquille, LA (cdp) Terrebonne Parish	20	1.11
Poydras, LA (cdp) St. Bernard Parish	20	0.85
Picayune, MS (city) Pearl River County	19	0.17
Luling, LA (cdp) St. Charles Parish	19	0.16
Arlington, TX (city) Tarrant County	19	0.01
Lockport Heights, LA (cdp) Lafourche Parish	18	1.40
Baldwin, LA (town) St. Mary Parish	18	0.74
Prairieville, LA (cdp) Ascension Parish	18	0.07
Fort Worth, TX (city) Tarrant County	18	<0.01
Lafitte, LA (cdp) Jefferson Parish	17	1.75
Avondale, LA (cdp) Jefferson Parish	17	0.34
Waggaman, LA (cdp) Jefferson Parish	17	0.17
Woodmere, LA (cdp) Jefferson Parish	17	0.14
Central, LA (city) East Baton Rouge Parish	17	0.06
Barataria, LA (cdp) Jefferson Parish	16	1.44
Grand Isle, LA (town) Jefferson Parish	16	1.23
Port Sulphur, LA (cdp) Plaquemines Parish	16	0.91
Mathews, LA (cdp) Lafourche Parish	16	0.72
Houston, TX (city) Harris County	16	<0.01
Mobile, AL (city) Mobile County	15	0.01
Bridge City, LA (cdp) Jefferson Parish	14	0.18
New Iberia, LA (city) Iberia Parish	14	0.05
Eden Isle, LA (cdp) St. Tammany Parish	13	0.18
Broussard, LA (city) Lafayette Parish	13	0.16
Timberlane, LA (cdp) Jefferson Parish	13	0.13
Jefferson, LA (cdp) Jefferson Parish	13	0.12
Abbeville, LA (city) Vermilion Parish	13	0.11
Sulphur, LA (city) Calcasieu Parish	13	0.06
Portland, OR (city) Multnomah County	13	<0.01
Ensley, FL (cdp) Escambia County	12	0.06
Bronx, NY (borough) Bronx County	12	<0.01
San Diego, CA (city) San Diego County	12	<0.01
Alexandria, LA (city) Rapides Parish	11	0.02
Aurora, CO (city) Arapahoe County	11	<0.01
Amelia, LA (cdp) St. Mary Parish	10	0.41
Arabi, LA (cdp) St. Bernard Parish	10	0.28
Pineville, LA (city) Rapides Parish	10	0.07
River Ridge, LA (cdp) Jefferson Parish	10	0.07
Biloxi, MS (city) Harrison County	10	0.02
Lake Charles, LA (city) Calcasieu Parish	10	0.01
Missouri City, TX (city) Fort Bend County	10	0.01
Los Angeles, CA (city) Los Angeles County	10	<0.01
Oakley, CA (city) Contra Costa County	9	0.03
Murfreesboro, TN (city) Rutherford County	9	0.01
Paradis, LA (cdp) St. Charles Parish	8	0.62
Charenton, LA (cdp) St. Mary Parish	8	0.42
Bayou Gauche, LA (cdp) St. Charles Parish	8	0.39
Natalbany, LA (cdp) Tangipahoa Parish	8	0.27
Pierre Part, LA (cdp) Assumption Parish	8	0.25
Gulf Hills, MS (cdp) Jackson County	8	0.11
Breaux Bridge, LA (city) St. Martin Parish	8	0.10
Youngsville, LA (city) Lafayette Parish	8	0.10
Destrehan, LA (cdp) St. Charles Parish	8	0.07
Austin, TX (city) Travis County	8	<0.01
Venice, LA (cdp) Plaquemines Parish	7	3.47
Sherman, MS (town) Pontotoc County	7	1.08
Sunset, LA (town) St. Landry Parish	7	0.24
Salem, PA (township) Luzerne County	7	0.16
Linwood, MN (township) Anoka County	7	0.14
Marksville, LA (city) Avoyelles Parish	7	0.12
Waveland, MS (city) Hancock County	7	0.11
Old Jefferson, LA (cdp) East Baton Rouge Parish	7	0.10
Scott, LA (city) Lafayette Parish	7	0.08
Long Beach, MS (city) Harrison County	7	0.05
Bellview, FL (cdp) Escambia County	7	0.03
Haltom City, TX (city) Tarrant County	7	0.02
Beaumont, TX (city) Jefferson County	7	0.01
Cañada de los Alamos, NM (cdp) Santa Fe County	6	1.38
Choctaw, LA (cdp) Lafourche Parish	6	0.68
Delcambre, LA (town) Vermilion Parish	6	0.32
Kinder, LA (town) Allen Parish	6	0.24
Springfield, GA (city) Effingham County	6	0.21
Iowa, LA (town) Calcasieu Parish	6	0.20
Gramercy, LA (town) St. James Parish	6	0.17
Escatawpa, MS (cdp) Jackson County	6	0.16
Jeanerette, LA (city) Iberia Parish	6	0.11
Gonzales, LA (city) Ascension Parish	6	0.06
Paradise, CA (town) Butte County	6	0.02
Ponca City, OK (city) Kay County	6	0.02
Waxahachie, TX (city) Ellis County	6	0.02
Lafayette, IN (city) Tippecanoe County	6	0.01
Medford, OR (city) Jackson County	6	0.01
Monroe, LA (city) Ouachita Parish	6	0.01
Clarksville, TN (city) Montgomery County	6	<0.01
Knoxville, TN (city) Knox County	6	<0.01
Pembroke Pines, FL (city) Broward County	6	<0.01
Tulsa, OK (city) Tulsa County	6	<0.01
Noble, LA (village) Sabine Parish	5	1.98
Gillis, LA (cdp) Calcasieu Parish	5	0.76
Kraemer, LA (cdp) Lafourche Parish	5	0.54
Conehatta, MS (cdp) Newton County	5	0.37
Ossun, LA (cdp) Lafayette Parish	5	0.23
Amite City, LA (town) Tangipahoa Parish	5	0.12
Diamondhead, MS (cdp) Hancock County	5	0.06
St. Rose, LA (cdp) St. Charles Parish	5	0.06
Bay St. Louis, MS (city) Hancock County	5	0.05
Mandeville, LA (city) St. Tammany Parish	5	0.04
Moss Bluff, LA (cdp) Calcasieu Parish	5	0.04
Fort Mohave, AZ (cdp) Mohave County	5	0.03
Ledyard, CT (town) New London County	5	0.03
Shenandoah, LA (cdp) East Baton Rouge Parish	5	0.03
Hammond, LA (city) Tangipahoa Parish	5	0.02
Ken Caryl, CO (cdp) Jefferson County	5	0.02

SECTION THREE

Please refer to the Explanation of Data in the front of the book for more detailed information.

Race

American Indian: Houma

Top 150 Places Sorted by Percent of Total Population

Based on all places, regardless of total population

Place	Population	%
Dulac, LA (cdp) Terrebonne Parish	423	28.91
Golden Meadow, LA (town) Lafourche Parish	107	5.09
Boothville, LA (cdp) Plaquemines Parish	42	4.92
Galliano, LA (cdp) Lafourche Parish	320	4.17
Montegut, LA (cdp) Terrebonne Parish	64	4.16
Cut Off, LA (cdp) Lafourche Parish	214	3.58
Jean Lafitte, LA (town) Jefferson Parish	66	3.47
Venice, LA (cdp) Plaquemines Parish	7	3.47
Blue Mountain, AR (town) Logan County	4	3.23
Bourg, LA (cdp) Terrebonne Parish	76	2.95
Bear Bluff, WI (town) Jackson County	4	2.90
Bayou Blue, LA (cdp) Lafourche Parish	326	2.64
Houma, LA (city) Terrebonne Parish	885	2.62
Larose, LA (cdp) Lafourche Parish	162	2.19
Noble, LA (village) Sabine Parish	5	1.98
Lockport, LA (town) Lafourche Parish	48	1.86
Chauvin, LA (cdp) Terrebonne Parish	51	1.75
Lafitte, LA (cdp) Jefferson Parish	17	1.75
Bayou Cane, LA (cdp) Terrebonne Parish	307	1.59
Gray, LA (cdp) Terrebonne Parish	82	1.47
Barataria, LA (cdp) Jefferson Parish	16	1.44
Lockport Heights, LA (cdp) Lafourche Parish	18	1.40
Cañada de los Alamos, NM (cdp) Santa Fe County	6	1.38
Grand Isle, LA (town) Jefferson Parish	16	1.23
Bayou L'Ourse, LA (cdp) Assumption Parish	24	1.21
Bayou Vista, LA (cdp) St. Mary Parish	54	1.16
Presquille, LA (cdp) Terrebonne Parish	20	1.11
Sherman, MS (town) Pontotoc County	7	1.08
Des Allemands, LA (cdp) St. Charles Parish	26	1.04
Port Sulphur, LA (cdp) Plaquemines Parish	16	0.91
Rose Hill Acres, TX (city) Hardin County	4	0.91
Poydras, LA (cdp) St. Bernard Parish	20	0.85
Plaucheville, LA (village) Avoyelles Parish	2	0.81
Berwick, LA (town) St. Mary Parish	38	0.77
Gillis, LA (cdp) Calcasieu Parish	5	0.76
Baldwin, LA (town) St. Mary Parish	18	0.74
Morgan City, LA (city) St. Mary Parish	90	0.73
Raceland, LA (cdp) Lafourche Parish	73	0.72
Mathews, LA (cdp) Lafourche Parish	16	0.72
Schriever, LA (cdp) Terrebonne Parish	48	0.70
Choctaw, LA (cdp) Lafourche Parish	6	0.68
Westwego, LA (city) Jefferson Parish	57	0.67
Florien, LA (village) Sabine Parish	4	0.63
Paradis, LA (cdp) St. Charles Parish	8	0.62
Franklin, LA (city) St. Mary Parish	45	0.59
Yonah, GA (cdp) White County	3	0.59
Kraemer, LA (cdp) Lafourche Parish	5	0.54
Estelle, LA (cdp) Jefferson Parish	85	0.52
Meraux, LA (cdp) St. Bernard Parish	30	0.52
Marion, LA (town) Union Parish	4	0.52
Patterson, LA (city) St. Mary Parish	31	0.51
Chackbay, LA (cdp) Lafourche Parish	24	0.46
Bogue Chitto, MS (cdp) Kemper and Neshoba Counties	4	0.45
Reeves, LA (village) Allen Parish	1	0.43
Violet, LA (cdp) St. Bernard Parish	21	0.42
Charenton, LA (cdp) St. Mary Parish	8	0.42
Lydia, LA (cdp) Iberia Parish	4	0.42
Folsom, LA (village) St. Tammany Parish	3	0.42
Amelia, LA (cdp) St. Mary Parish	10	0.41
Warren, TX (cdp) Tyler County	3	0.40
Athens, LA (village) Claiborne Parish	1	0.40
Pleasure Bend, LA (cdp) St. John the Baptist Parish	1	0.40
Bayou Gauche, LA (cdp) St. Charles Parish	8	0.39
Belle Chasse, LA (cdp) Plaquemines Parish	47	0.37
Conehatta, MS (cdp) Newton County	5	0.37
Woodland, NC (town) Northampton County	3	0.37
Marrero, LA (cdp) Jefferson Parish	119	0.36
Rock Hill, LA (cdp) Grant Parish	1	0.36
Avondale, LA (cdp) Jefferson Parish	17	0.34
La Fontaine, IN (town) Wabash County	3	0.34
Vergennes, IL (village) Jackson County	1	0.34
Big Point, MS (cdp) Jackson County	2	0.33
Thibodaux, LA (city) Lafourche Parish	47	0.32
Delcambre, LA (town) Vermilion Parish	6	0.32
Buras, LA (cdp) Plaquemines Parish	3	0.32
Midway, LA (cdp) La Salle Parish	4	0.31
Watson, LA (cdp) Livingston Parish	3	0.29
Mize, MS (town) Smith County	1	0.29
Harahan, LA (city) Jefferson Parish	26	0.28
Arabi, LA (cdp) St. Bernard Parish	10	0.28
Natalbany, LA (cdp) Tangipahoa Parish	8	0.27
Meridian, TX (city) Bosque County	4	0.27
Roseland, LA (town) Tangipahoa Parish	3	0.27
Kiowa, OK (town) Pittsburg County	2	0.27
Colfax, LA (town) Grant Parish	4	0.26
Pierre Part, LA (cdp) Assumption Parish	8	0.25
Robinhood, MS (cdp) Rankin County	4	0.25
Fifth Ward, LA (cdp) Avoyelles Parish	2	0.25
Hessmer, LA (village) Avoyelles Parish	2	0.25
Point Place, LA (cdp) Natchitoches Parish	1	0.25
Sunset, LA (town) St. Landry Parish	7	0.24
Kinder, LA (town) Allen Parish	6	0.24
Elkader, IA (city) Clayton County	3	0.24
Ossun, LA (cdp) Lafayette Parish	5	0.23
Labadieville, LA (cdp) Assumption Parish	4	0.22
Long Branch, PA (borough) Washington County	1	0.22
Springfield, GA (city) Effingham County	6	0.21
Sorrento, LA (town) Ascension Parish	3	0.21
Toluca, IL (city) Marshall County	3	0.21
Chalmette, LA (cdp) St. Bernard Parish	33	0.20
Iowa, LA (town) Calcasieu Parish	6	0.20
Lafourche Crossing, LA (cdp) Lafourche Parish	4	0.20
Newton, AL (town) Dale County	3	0.20
Lumberton, MS (city) Lamar County	4	0.19
Bridge City, LA (cdp) Jefferson Parish	14	0.18
Eden Isle, LA (cdp) St. Tammany Parish	13	0.18
Elton, LA (town) Jefferson Davis Parish	2	0.18
Chatham, LA (town) Jackson Parish	1	0.18
Grannis, AR (city) Polk County	1	0.18
Harvey, LA (cdp) Jefferson Parish	34	0.17
Gretna, LA (city) Jefferson Parish	31	0.17
Picayune, MS (city) Pearl River County	19	0.17
Waggaman, LA (cdp) Jefferson Parish	17	0.17
Gramercy, LA (town) St. James Parish	6	0.17
Abita Springs, LA (town) St. Tammany Parish	4	0.17
Risingsun, OH (village) Wood County	1	0.17
Slidell, LA (city) St. Tammany Parish	44	0.16
Luling, LA (cdp) St. Charles Parish	19	0.16
Broussard, LA (city) Lafayette Parish	13	0.16
Salem, PA (township) Luzerne County	7	0.16
Escatawpa, MS (cdp) Jackson County	6	0.16
New Augusta, MS (town) Perry County	1	0.16
New Houlka, MS (town) Chickasaw County	1	0.16
Terrytown, LA (cdp) Jefferson Parish	36	0.15
Cecilia, LA (cdp) St. Martin Parish	3	0.15
Ama, LA (cdp) St. Charles Parish	2	0.15
Pearlington, MS (cdp) Hancock County	2	0.15
Roscoe, TX (city) Nolan County	2	0.15
Cotton Plant, AR (city) Woodruff County	1	0.15
Woodmere, LA (cdp) Jefferson Parish	17	0.14
Linwood, MN (township) Anoka County	7	0.14
Poplarville, MS (city) Pearl River County	4	0.14
Erath, LA (town) Vermilion Parish	3	0.14
Montgomery, LA (town) Grant Parish	1	0.14
Tickfaw, LA (village) Tangipahoa Parish	1	0.14
Timberlane, LA (cdp) Jefferson Parish	13	0.13
Nicholson, MS (cdp) Pearl River County	4	0.13
Norco, LA (cdp) St. Charles Parish	4	0.13
Reno, TX (city) Lamar County	4	0.13
Good Hope, AL (town) Cullman County	3	0.13
Sorrel, LA (cdp) St. Mary Parish	1	0.13
Sparta, MN (township) Chippewa County	1	0.13
Laplace, LA (cdp) St. John the Baptist Parish	35	0.12
Jefferson, LA (cdp) Jefferson Parish	13	0.12
Marksville, LA (city) Avoyelles Parish	7	0.12
Amite City, LA (town) Tangipahoa Parish	5	0.12
DeQuincy, LA (city) Calcasieu Parish	4	0.12
Hahnville, LA (cdp) St. Charles Parish	4	0.12
West Orange, TX (city) Orange County	4	0.12
Brusly, LA (town) West Baton Rouge Parish	3	0.12

Please refer to the Explanation of Data in the front of the book for more detailed information.

Race

American Indian: Houma

Top 150 Places Sorted by Percent of Total Population

Based on places with total population of 7,500 or more

Place	Population	%
Galliano, LA (cdp) Lafourche Parish	320	4.17
Bayou Blue, LA (cdp) Lafourche Parish	326	2.64
Houma, LA (city) Terrebonne Parish	885	2.62
Bayou Cane, LA (cdp) Terrebonne Parish	307	1.59
Morgan City, LA (city) St. Mary Parish	90	0.73
Raceland, LA (cdp) Lafourche Parish	73	0.72
Westwego, LA (city) Jefferson Parish	57	0.67
Franklin, LA (city) St. Mary Parish	45	0.59
Estelle, LA (cdp) Jefferson Parish	85	0.52
Belle Chasse, LA (cdp) Plaquemines Parish	47	0.37
Marrero, LA (cdp) Jefferson Parish	119	0.36
Thibodaux, LA (city) Lafourche Parish	47	0.32
Harahan, LA (city) Jefferson Parish	26	0.28
Chalmette, LA (cdp) St. Bernard Parish	33	0.20
Bridge City, LA (cdp) Jefferson Parish	14	0.18
Harvey, LA (cdp) Jefferson Parish	34	0.17
Gretna, LA (city) Jefferson Parish	31	0.17
Picayune, MS (city) Pearl River County	19	0.17
Waggaman, LA (cdp) Jefferson Parish	17	0.17
Slidell, LA (city) St. Tammany Parish	44	0.16
Luling, LA (cdp) St. Charles Parish	19	0.16
Broussard, LA (city) Lafayette Parish	13	0.16
Terrytown, LA (cdp) Jefferson Parish	36	0.15
Woodmere, LA (cdp) Jefferson Parish	17	0.14
Timberlane, LA (cdp) Jefferson Parish	13	0.13
Laplace, LA (cdp) St. John the Baptist Parish	35	0.12
Jefferson, LA (cdp) Jefferson Parish	13	0.12
Abbeville, LA (city) Vermilion Parish	13	0.11
Breaux Bridge, LA (city) St. Martin Parish	8	0.10
Youngsville, LA (city) Lafayette Parish	8	0.10
Scott, LA (city) Lafayette Parish	7	0.08
Lafayette, LA (city) Lafayette Parish	79	0.07
Prairieville, LA (cdp) Ascension Parish	18	0.07
Pineville, LA (city) Rapides Parish	10	0.07
River Ridge, LA (cdp) Jefferson Parish	10	0.07
Destrehan, LA (cdp) St. Charles Parish	8	0.07
Kenner, LA (city) Jefferson Parish	38	0.06
Central, LA (city) East Baton Rouge Parish	17	0.06
Sulphur, LA (city) Calcasieu Parish	13	0.06
Ensley, FL (cdp) Escambia County	12	0.06
Gonzales, LA (city) Ascension Parish	6	0.06
Diamondhead, MS (cdp) Hancock County	5	0.06
St. Rose, LA (cdp) St. Charles Parish	5	0.06
Metairie, LA (cdp) Jefferson Parish	72	0.05
New Iberia, LA (city) Iberia Parish	14	0.05
Long Beach, MS (city) Harrison County	7	0.05
Bay St. Louis, MS (city) Hancock County	5	0.05
Charlestown, IN (city) Clark County	4	0.05
Covington, LA (city) St. Tammany Parish	4	0.05
East York, PA (cdp) York County	4	0.05
Lacombe, LA (cdp) St. Tammany Parish	4	0.05
Mandeville, LA (city) St. Tammany Parish	5	0.04
Moss Bluff, LA (cdp) Calcasieu Parish	5	0.04
Oakley, CA (city) Contra Costa County	9	0.03
Bellview, FL (cdp) Escambia County	7	0.03
Fort Mohave, AZ (cdp) Mohave County	5	0.03
Ledyard, CT (town) New London County	5	0.03
Shenandoah, LA (cdp) East Baton Rouge Parish	5	0.03
Baker, LA (city) East Baton Rouge Parish	4	0.03
Hutto, TX (city) Williamson County	4	0.03
Kilgore, TX (city) Gregg County	4	0.03
McComb, MS (city) Pike County	4	0.03
Brentwood, PA (borough) Allegheny County	3	0.03
Coweta, OK (city) Wagoner County	3	0.03
Eunice, LA (city) St. Landry Parish	3	0.03
Grantsville, UT (city) Tooele County	3	0.03
Jennings, LA (city) Jefferson Davis Parish	3	0.03
Lexington Park, MD (cdp) St. Mary's County	3	0.03
Little Ferry, NJ (borough) Bergen County	3	0.03
Martinsville, IN (city) Morgan County	3	0.03
Sutton, MA (town) Worcester County	3	0.03
Vermilion, OH (city) Lorain County	3	0.03
Carencro, LA (city) Lafayette Parish	2	0.03
Cushing, OK (city) Payne County	2	0.03
Lexington, TN (city) Henderson County	2	0.03

Place	Population	%
New Orleans, LA (city) Orleans Parish	66	0.02
Baton Rouge, LA (city) East Baton Rouge Parish	41	0.02
Alexandria, LA (city) Rapides Parish	11	0.02
Biloxi, MS (city) Harrison County	10	0.02
Haltom City, TX (city) Tarrant County	7	0.02
Paradise, CA (town) Butte County	6	0.02
Ponca City, OK (city) Kay County	6	0.02
Waxahachie, TX (city) Ellis County	6	0.02
Hammond, LA (city) Tangipahoa Parish	5	0.02
Ken Caryl, CO (cdp) Jefferson County	5	0.02
Cranford, NJ (township) Union County	4	0.02
Murphy, TX (city) Collin County	4	0.02
Ruston, LA (city) Lincoln Parish	4	0.02
Bogalusa, LA (city) Washington Parish	3	0.02
Canton, MS (city) Madison County	3	0.02
College Park, GA (city) Fulton County	3	0.02
Franklin, NJ (township) Gloucester County	3	0.02
Groves, TX (city) Jefferson County	3	0.02
Lake Shore, MD (cdp) Anne Arundel County	3	0.02
Lithia Springs, GA (cdp) Douglas County	3	0.02
Midway, FL (cdp) Santa Rosa County	3	0.02
Opelousas, LA (city) St. Landry Parish	3	0.02
Saginaw, TX (city) Tarrant County	3	0.02
Sugar Hill, GA (city) Gwinnett County	3	0.02
Trussville, AL (city) Jefferson County	3	0.02
Union City, GA (city) Fulton County	3	0.02
Zachary, LA (city) East Baton Rouge Parish	3	0.02
Atlantic Beach, FL (city) Duval County	2	0.02
Azle, TX (city) Tarrant County	2	0.02
Cornwall, NY (town) Orange County	2	0.02
Crowley, LA (city) Acadia Parish	2	0.02
Denham Springs, LA (city) Livingston Parish	2	0.02
DuPont, WA (city) Pierce County	2	0.02
Gardere, LA (cdp) East Baton Rouge Parish	2	0.02
Golden Hills, CA (cdp) Kern County	2	0.02
Lansdowne, PA (borough) Delaware County	2	0.02
Liberty, NY (town) Sullivan County	2	0.02
Penn Forest, PA (township) Carbon County	2	0.02
Pine Ridge, FL (cdp) Citrus County	2	0.02
Spring Lake, NC (town) Cumberland County	2	0.02
West Monroe, LA (city) Ouachita Parish	2	0.02
Shreveport, LA (city) Caddo Parish	24	0.01
Arlington, TX (city) Tarrant County	19	0.01
Mobile, AL (city) Mobile County	15	0.01
Lake Charles, LA (city) Calcasieu Parish	10	0.01
Missouri City, TX (city) Fort Bend County	10	0.01
Murfreesboro, TN (city) Rutherford County	9	0.01
Beaumont, TX (city) Jefferson County	7	0.01
Lafayette, IN (city) Tippecanoe County	6	0.01
Medford, OR (city) Jackson County	6	0.01
Monroe, LA (city) Ouachita Parish	6	0.01
Gulfport, MS (city) Harrison County	5	0.01
Lauderhill, FL (city) Broward County	5	0.01
Manteca, CA (city) San Joaquin County	5	0.01
San Angelo, TX (city) Tom Green County	5	0.01
Coconut Creek, FL (city) Broward County	4	0.01
Nacogdoches, TX (city) Nacogdoches County	4	0.01
North Richland Hills, TX (city) Tarrant County	4	0.01
O'Fallon, MO (city) St. Charles County	4	0.01
Pflugerville, TX (city) Travis County	4	0.01
Royal Palm Beach, FL (village) Palm Beach County	4	0.01
Springettsbury, PA (township) York County	4	0.01
Temple, TX (city) Bell County	4	0.01
Texas City, TX (city) Galveston County	4	0.01
University City, MO (city) St. Louis County	4	0.01
Aloha, OR (cdp) Washington County	3	0.01
Cabot, AR (city) Lonoke County	3	0.01
Canton, GA (city) Cherokee County	3	0.01
Egg Harbor, NJ (township) Atlantic County	3	0.01
Evans, GA (cdp) Columbia County	3	0.01
Fairbanks, AK (city) Fairbanks North Star Borough	3	0.01
Gardena, CA (city) Los Angeles County	3	0.01
Goldsboro, NC (city) Wayne County	3	0.01
Goose Creek, SC (city) Berkeley County	3	0.01
Hattiesburg, MS (city) Forrest County	3	0.01

SECTION THREE

Please refer to the Explanation of Data in the front of the book for more detailed information.

Race

Alaska Native: Inupiat (Eskimo)

U.S. and 50 States Sorted by Population and Percent of Total Population

Place	Population	%
United States	**33,360**	**0.01**
Alaska	25,687	3.62
Washington	1,365	0.02
California	1,019	<0.01
Oregon	487	0.01
Arizona	358	0.01
Texas	317	<0.01
Colorado	297	0.01
Florida	289	<0.01
Oklahoma	196	0.01
Illinois	173	<0.01
Virginia	170	<0.01
New York	169	<0.01
Michigan	150	<0.01
Nevada	144	0.01
Minnesota	137	<0.01
Montana	135	0.01
North Carolina	130	<0.01
Wisconsin	129	<0.01
Georgia	124	<0.01
New Mexico	123	0.01
Hawaii	118	0.01
Ohio	115	<0.01
Missouri	113	<0.01
Idaho	112	0.01
Indiana	95	<0.01
Utah	94	<0.01
Pennsylvania	91	<0.01
Maryland	88	<0.01
Tennessee	74	<0.01
Alabama	72	<0.01
Arkansas	64	<0.01
Iowa	64	<0.01
Kansas	63	<0.01
South Carolina	63	<0.01
Massachusetts	61	<0.01
New Hampshire	50	<0.01
Maine	46	<0.01
Kentucky	44	<0.01
New Jersey	40	<0.01
Nebraska	37	<0.01
North Dakota	35	0.01
Louisiana	35	<0.01
West Virginia	34	<0.01
South Dakota	31	<0.01
Wyoming	29	0.01
Connecticut	29	<0.01
Mississippi	23	<0.01
Delaware	12	<0.01
Vermont	12	<0.01
Rhode Island	11	<0.01
District of Columbia	6	<0.01

Place	Population	%
Alaska	25,687	3.62
Washington	1,365	0.02
United States	**33,360**	**0.01**
Oregon	487	0.01
Arizona	358	0.01
Colorado	297	0.01
Oklahoma	196	0.01
Nevada	144	0.01
Montana	135	0.01
New Mexico	123	0.01
Hawaii	118	0.01
Idaho	112	0.01
North Dakota	35	0.01
Wyoming	29	0.01
California	1,019	<0.01
Texas	317	<0.01
Florida	289	<0.01
Illinois	173	<0.01
Virginia	170	<0.01
New York	169	<0.01
Michigan	150	<0.01
Minnesota	137	<0.01
North Carolina	130	<0.01
Wisconsin	129	<0.01
Georgia	124	<0.01
Ohio	115	<0.01
Missouri	113	<0.01
Indiana	95	<0.01
Utah	94	<0.01
Pennsylvania	91	<0.01
Maryland	88	<0.01
Tennessee	74	<0.01
Alabama	72	<0.01
Arkansas	64	<0.01
Iowa	64	<0.01
Kansas	63	<0.01
South Carolina	63	<0.01
Massachusetts	61	<0.01
New Hampshire	50	<0.01
Maine	46	<0.01
Kentucky	44	<0.01
New Jersey	40	<0.01
Nebraska	37	<0.01
Louisiana	35	<0.01
West Virginia	34	<0.01
South Dakota	31	<0.01
Connecticut	29	<0.01
Mississippi	23	<0.01
Delaware	12	<0.01
Vermont	12	<0.01
Rhode Island	11	<0.01
District of Columbia	6	<0.01

Please refer to the Explanation of Data in the front of the book for more detailed information.

Race

Alaska Native: Inupiat (Eskimo)

Top 150 Places Sorted by Population

Based on all places, regardless of total population

Place	Population	%
Anchorage, AK (municipality) Anchorage Municipality	6,103	2.09
Barrow, AK (city) North Slope Borough	2,223	52.78
Kotzebue, AK (city) Northwest Arctic Borough	1,946	60.79
Nome, AK (city) Nome Census Area	1,519	42.22
Chevak, AK (city) Wade Hampton Census Area	803	85.61
Selawik, AK (city) Northwest Arctic Borough	734	88.54
Noorvik, AK (city) Northwest Arctic Borough	619	92.66
Point Hope, AK (city) North Slope Borough	616	91.39
Shishmaref, AK (city) Nome Census Area	525	93.25
Wainwright, AK (city) North Slope Borough	501	90.11
Unalakleet, AK (city) Nome Census Area	496	72.09
Noatak, AK (cdp) Northwest Arctic Borough	467	90.86
Fairbanks, AK (city) Fairbanks North Star Borough	447	1.42
Kivalina, AK (city) Northwest Arctic Borough	364	97.33
Buckland, AK (city) Northwest Arctic Borough	364	87.50
Brevig Mission, AK (city) Nome Census Area	352	90.72
Kiana, AK (city) Northwest Arctic Borough	318	88.09
Koyuk, AK (city) Nome Census Area	292	87.95
College, AK (cdp) Fairbanks North Star Borough	289	2.23
Elim, AK (city) Nome Census Area	280	84.85
Anaktuvuk Pass, AK (city) North Slope Borough	257	79.32
Shungnak, AK (city) Northwest Arctic Borough	243	92.75
Nuiqsut, AK (city) North Slope Borough	225	55.97
Shaktoolik, AK (city) Nome Census Area	222	88.45
Ambler, AK (city) Northwest Arctic Borough	218	84.50
Bethel, AK (city) Bethel Census Area	213	3.50
Knik-Fairview, AK (cdp) Matanuska-Susitna Borough	212	1.42
Badger, AK (cdp) Fairbanks North Star Borough	203	1.04
Juneau, AK (borough) Juneau City and Borough	174	0.56
Teller, AK (city) Nome Census Area	168	73.36
Mekoryuk, AK (city) Bethel Census Area	164	85.86
White Mountain, AK (city) Nome Census Area	160	84.21
Kaktovik, AK (city) North Slope Borough	151	63.18
Point Lay, AK (cdp) North Slope Borough	150	79.37
Atqasuk, AK (city) North Slope Borough	143	61.37
Palmer, AK (city) Matanuska-Susitna Borough	136	2.29
Golovin, AK (city) Nome Census Area	135	86.54
Wales, AK (city) Nome Census Area	132	91.03
Kenai, AK (city) Kenai Peninsula Borough	130	1.83
Kobuk, AK (city) Northwest Arctic Borough	129	85.43
Lakes, AK (cdp) Matanuska-Susitna Borough	112	1.34
Seattle, WA (city) King County	112	0.02
Diomede, AK (city) Nome Census Area	110	95.65
Deering, AK (city) Northwest Arctic Borough	105	86.07
Wasilla, AK (city) Matanuska-Susitna Borough	101	1.29
Red Dog Mine, AK (cdp) Northwest Arctic Borough	96	31.07
Tanaina, AK (cdp) Matanuska-Susitna Borough	95	1.16
Kalifornsky, AK (cdp) Kenai Peninsula Borough	94	1.20
Gateway, AK (cdp) Matanuska-Susitna Borough	91	1.64
Dillingham, AK (city) Dillingham Census Area	85	3.65
Meadow Lakes, AK (cdp) Matanuska-Susitna Borough	84	1.11
Seward, AK (city) Kenai Peninsula Borough	79	2.93
Steele Creek, AK (cdp) Fairbanks North Star Borough	77	1.16
Sitka, AK (borough) Sitka City and Borough	71	0.80
Tacoma, WA (city) Pierce County	69	0.03
Farmers Loop, AK (cdp) Fairbanks North Star Borough	65	1.34
Chena Ridge, AK (cdp) Fairbanks North Star Borough	65	1.12
Portland, OR (city) Multnomah County	64	0.01
Sutton-Alpine, AK (cdp) Matanuska-Susitna Borough	60	4.15
New York, NY (city) Kings County	58	<0.01
Nikiski, AK (cdp) Kenai Peninsula Borough	56	1.25
Los Angeles, CA (city) Los Angeles County	56	<0.01
Hudson, CO (town) Weld County	51	2.16
Phoenix, AZ (city) Maricopa County	51	<0.01
Fishhook, AK (cdp) Matanuska-Susitna Borough	49	1.05
Homer, AK (city) Kenai Peninsula Borough	47	0.94
Valdez, AK (city) Valdez-Cordova Census Area	42	1.06
San Diego, CA (city) San Diego County	41	<0.01
Salamatof, AK (cdp) Kenai Peninsula Borough	39	3.98
Soldotna, AK (city) Kenai Peninsula Borough	39	0.94
Everett, WA (city) Snohomish County	39	0.04
Bear Creek, AK (cdp) Kenai Peninsula Borough	38	1.94
Willow, AK (cdp) Matanuska-Susitna Borough	36	1.71
Spokane, WA (city) Spokane County	34	0.02
Colorado Springs, CO (city) El Paso County	34	0.01
Salem, OR (city) Marion County	33	0.02
Albuquerque, NM (city) Bernalillo County	33	0.01
Goldstream, AK (cdp) Fairbanks North Star Borough	31	0.87
Eugene, OR (city) Lane County	31	0.02
Vancouver, WA (city) Clark County	30	0.02
Chicago, IL (city) Cook County	30	<0.01
Big Lake, AK (cdp) Matanuska-Susitna Borough	29	0.87
Bellingham, WA (city) Whatcom County	29	0.04
Houston, AK (city) Matanuska-Susitna Borough	28	1.46
Sacramento, CA (city) Sacramento County	27	0.01
Mesa, AZ (city) Maricopa County	26	0.01
Oakland, CA (city) Alameda County	26	0.01
San Jose, CA (city) Santa Clara County	26	<0.01
Federal Way, WA (city) King County	25	0.03
Glendale, AZ (city) Maricopa County	24	0.01
Denver, CO (city) Denver County	24	<0.01
Butte, AK (cdp) Matanuska-Susitna Borough	23	0.71
Sterling, AK (cdp) Kenai Peninsula Borough	23	0.41
Ketchikan, AK (city) Ketchikan Gateway Borough	23	0.29
Urban Honolulu, HI (cdp) Honolulu County	23	0.01
Point MacKenzie, AK (cdp) Matanuska-Susitna Borough	22	4.16
San Francisco, CA (city) San Francisco County	22	<0.01
Tucson, AZ (city) Pima County	22	<0.01
Ester, AK (cdp) Fairbanks North Star Borough	21	0.87
Brooklyn, NY (borough) Kings County	21	<0.01
Las Vegas, NV (city) Clark County	21	<0.01
Oklahoma City, OK (city) Oklahoma County	21	<0.01
Ridgeway, AK (cdp) Kenai Peninsula Borough	20	0.99
Redding, CA (city) Shasta County	20	0.02
Santa Rosa, CA (city) Sonoma County	20	0.01
Indianapolis, IN (city) Marion County	20	<0.01
Farm Loop, AK (cdp) Matanuska-Susitna Borough	19	1.85
Billings, MT (city) Yellowstone County	19	0.02
Yakutat, AK (cdp) Yakutat City and Borough	18	2.72
Lynnwood, WA (city) Snohomish County	18	0.05
Auburn, WA (city) King County	18	0.03
Lakewood, WA (city) Pierce County	18	0.03
Beaverton, OR (city) Washington County	18	0.02
Longmont, CO (city) Boulder County	18	0.02
Austin, TX (city) Travis County	18	<0.01
Hoonah, AK (city) Hoonah-Angoon Census Area	17	2.24
Bellevue, WA (city) King County	17	0.01
North Las Vegas, NV (city) Clark County	17	0.01
Sunrise Manor, NV (cdp) Clark County	17	0.01
Tulsa, OK (city) Tulsa County	17	<0.01
Deltana, AK (cdp) Southeast Fairbanks Census Area	16	0.71
Reno, NV (city) Washoe County	16	0.01
Metlakatla, AK (cdp) Prince of Wales-Hyder Census Area	15	1.07
Lazy Mountain, AK (cdp) Matanuska-Susitna Borough	15	1.01
Bylas, AZ (cdp) Graham County	15	0.76
Flagstaff, AZ (city) Coconino County	15	0.02
Marysville, WA (city) Snohomish County	15	0.02
Gilbert, AZ (town) Maricopa County	15	0.01
Bronx, NY (borough) Bronx County	15	<0.01
San Antonio, TX (city) Medina County	15	<0.01
Funny River, AK (cdp) Kenai Peninsula Borough	14	1.60
North Pole, AK (city) Fairbanks North Star Borough	14	0.66
Unalaska, AK (city) Aleutians West Census Area	14	0.32
Parkland, WA (cdp) Pierce County	14	0.04
Albany, OR (city) Linn County	14	0.03
Caldwell, ID (city) Canyon County	14	0.03
Lawrence, KS (city) Douglas County	14	0.02
Killeen, TX (city) Bell County	14	0.01
El Paso, TX (city) El Paso County	14	<0.01
Houston, TX (city) Harris County	14	<0.01
Minneapolis, MN (city) Hennepin County	14	<0.01
Kasigluk, AK (cdp) Bethel Census Area	13	2.28
Ninilchik, AK (cdp) Kenai Peninsula Borough	13	1.47
Clearlake, CA (city) Lake County	13	0.09
Longview, WA (city) Cowlitz County	13	0.04
Bremerton, WA (city) Kitsap County	13	0.03
Shoreline, WA (city) King County	13	0.02
Spokane Valley, WA (city) Spokane County	13	0.01
Springfield, MO (city) Christian County	13	0.01
Arlington, TX (city) Tarrant County	13	<0.01

Please refer to the Explanation of Data in the front of the book for more detailed information.

Race

Alaska Native: Inupiat (Eskimo)

Top 150 Places Sorted by Percent of Total Population

Based on all places, regardless of total population

Place	Population	%
Kivalina, AK (city) Northwest Arctic Borough	364	97.33
Diomede, AK (city) Nome Census Area	110	95.65
Shishmaref, AK (city) Nome Census Area	525	93.25
Shungnak, AK (city) Northwest Arctic Borough	243	92.75
Noorvik, AK (city) Northwest Arctic Borough	619	92.66
Point Hope, AK (city) North Slope Borough	616	91.39
Wales, AK (city) Nome Census Area	132	91.03
Noatak, AK (cdp) Northwest Arctic Borough	467	90.86
Brevig Mission, AK (city) Nome Census Area	352	90.72
Wainwright, AK (city) North Slope Borough	501	90.11
Selawik, AK (city) Northwest Arctic Borough	734	88.54
Shaktoolik, AK (city) Nome Census Area	222	88.45
Kiana, AK (city) Northwest Arctic Borough	318	88.09
Koyuk, AK (city) Nome Census Area	292	87.95
Buckland, AK (city) Northwest Arctic Borough	364	87.50
Golovin, AK (city) Nome Census Area	135	86.54
Deering, AK (city) Northwest Arctic Borough	105	86.07
Mekoryuk, AK (city) Bethel Census Area	164	85.86
Chevak, AK (city) Wade Hampton Census Area	803	85.61
Kobuk, AK (city) Northwest Arctic Borough	129	85.43
Elim, AK (city) Nome Census Area	280	84.85
Ambler, AK (city) Northwest Arctic Borough	218	84.50
White Mountain, AK (city) Nome Census Area	160	84.21
Point Lay, AK (cdp) North Slope Borough	150	79.37
Anaktuvuk Pass, AK (city) North Slope Borough	257	79.32
Teller, AK (city) Nome Census Area	168	73.36
Unalakleet, AK (city) Nome Census Area	496	72.09
Kaktovik, AK (city) North Slope Borough	151	63.18
Atqasuk, AK (city) North Slope Borough	143	61.37
Kotzebue, AK (city) Northwest Arctic Borough	1,946	60.79
Nuiqsut, AK (city) North Slope Borough	225	55.97
Barrow, AK (city) North Slope Borough	2,223	52.78
Nome, AK (city) Nome Census Area	1,519	42.22
Red Dog Mine, AK (cdp) Northwest Arctic Borough	96	31.07
Takotna, AK (cdp) Yukon-Koyukuk Census Area	8	15.38
Pedro Bay, AK (cdp) Lake and Peninsula Borough	6	14.29
Northway Junction, AK (cdp) Southeast Fairbanks Census Area	6	11.11
Chenega, AK (cdp) Valdez-Cordova Census Area	7	9.21
Excursion Inlet, AK (cdp) Haines Borough	1	8.33
Four Mile Road, AK (cdp) Yukon-Koyukuk Census Area	3	6.98
Pelican, AK (city) Hoonah-Angoon Census Area	6	6.82
Hughes, AK (city) Yukon-Koyukuk Census Area	5	6.49
Birch Creek, AK (cdp) Yukon-Koyukuk Census Area	2	6.06
Mendeltna, AK (cdp) Valdez-Cordova Census Area	2	5.13
Atka, AK (city) Aleutians West Census Area	3	4.92
Dot Lake Village, AK (cdp) Southeast Fairbanks Census Area	3	4.84
Tatitlek, AK (cdp) Valdez-Cordova Census Area	4	4.55
Eagle Village, AK (cdp) Southeast Fairbanks Census Area	3	4.48
Cotesfield, NE (village) Howard County	2	4.35
Point MacKenzie, AK (cdp) Matanuska-Susitna Borough	22	4.16
Sutton-Alpine, AK (cdp) Matanuska-Susitna Borough	60	4.15
Salamatof, AK (cdp) Kenai Peninsula Borough	39	3.98
St. George, AK (city) Aleutians West Census Area	4	3.92
Dillingham, AK (city) Dillingham Census Area	85	3.65
Perryville, AK (cdp) Lake and Peninsula Borough	4	3.54
Bethel, AK (city) Bethel Census Area	213	3.50
Arctic Village, AK (cdp) Yukon-Koyukuk Census Area	5	3.29
Nenana, AK (city) Yukon-Koyukuk Census Area	12	3.17
Tetlin, AK (cdp) Southeast Fairbanks Census Area	4	3.15
Copper Center, AK (cdp) Valdez-Cordova Census Area	10	3.05
Harding-Birch Lakes, AK (cdp) Fairbanks North Star Borough	9	3.01
Seward, AK (city) Kenai Peninsula Borough	79	2.93
Oscarville, AK (cdp) Bethel Census Area	2	2.86
Akhiok, AK (city) Kodiak Island Borough	2	2.82
Conner, MT (cdp) Ravalli County	6	2.78
Seldovia, AK (city) Kenai Peninsula Borough	7	2.75
St. Michael, AK (city) Nome Census Area	11	2.74
Yakutat, AK (cdp) Yakutat City and Borough	18	2.72
Palmer, AK (city) Matanuska-Susitna Borough	136	2.29
Kasigluk, AK (cdp) Bethel Census Area	13	2.28
Aleknagik, AK (city) Dillingham Census Area	5	2.28
Hoonah, AK (city) Hoonah-Angoon Census Area	17	2.24
Wealthwood, MN (township) Aitkin County	6	2.24
College, AK (cdp) Fairbanks North Star Borough	289	2.23
Tanacross, AK (cdp) Southeast Fairbanks Census Area	3	2.21

Place	Population	%
Hudson, CO (town) Weld County	51	2.16
Hydaburg, AK (city) Prince of Wales-Hyder Census Area	8	2.13
Nikolai, AK (city) Yukon-Koyukuk Census Area	2	2.13
Kaltag, AK (city) Yukon-Koyukuk Census Area	4	2.11
Anchorage, AK (municipality) Anchorage Municipality	6,103	2.09
Northway Village, AK (cdp) Southeast Fairbanks Census Area	2	2.04
Igiugig, AK (cdp) Lake and Peninsula Borough	1	2.00
Stebbins, AK (city) Nome Census Area	11	1.98
Nanwalek, AK (cdp) Kenai Peninsula Borough	5	1.97
Bear Creek, AK (cdp) Kenai Peninsula Borough	38	1.94
Galena, AK (city) Yukon-Koyukuk Census Area	9	1.91
Farm Loop, AK (cdp) Matanuska-Susitna Borough	19	1.85
Kenai, AK (city) Kenai Peninsula Borough	130	1.83
Egegik, AK (city) Lake and Peninsula Borough	2	1.83
Venetie, AK (cdp) Yukon-Koyukuk Census Area	3	1.81
Willow, AK (cdp) Matanuska-Susitna Borough	36	1.71
Cochiti, NM (cdp) Sandoval County	9	1.70
Gunn City, MO (village) Cass County	2	1.69
Nelchina, AK (cdp) Valdez-Cordova Census Area	1	1.69
Fox, AK (cdp) Fairbanks North Star Borough	7	1.68
Trapper Creek, AK (cdp) Matanuska-Susitna Borough	8	1.66
Gateway, AK (cdp) Matanuska-Susitna Borough	91	1.64
Funny River, AK (cdp) Kenai Peninsula Borough	14	1.60
Klawock, AK (city) Prince of Wales-Hyder Census Area	12	1.59
Newhalen, AK (city) Lake and Peninsula Borough	3	1.58
New Allakaket, AK (cdp) Yukon-Koyukuk Census Area	1	1.52
Ninilchik, AK (cdp) Kenai Peninsula Borough	13	1.47
Houston, AK (city) Matanuska-Susitna Borough	28	1.46
Huslia, AK (city) Yukon-Koyukuk Census Area	4	1.45
Chalkyitsik, AK (cdp) Yukon-Koyukuk Census Area	1	1.45
Levelock, AK (cdp) Lake and Peninsula Borough	1	1.45
South Van Horn, AK (cdp) Fairbanks North Star Borough	8	1.43
Fairbanks, AK (city) Fairbanks North Star Borough	447	1.42
Knik-Fairview, AK (cdp) Matanuska-Susitna Borough	212	1.42
Buffalo Soapstone, AK (cdp) Matanuska-Susitna Borough	12	1.40
Two Rivers, AK (cdp) Fairbanks North Star Borough	10	1.39
St. Mary's, AK (city) Wade Hampton Census Area	7	1.38
Lakes, AK (cdp) Matanuska-Susitna Borough	112	1.34
Farmers Loop, AK (cdp) Fairbanks North Star Borough	65	1.34
Alakanuk, AK (city) Wade Hampton Census Area	9	1.33
Angoon, AK (city) Hoonah-Angoon Census Area	6	1.31
Wasilla, AK (city) Matanuska-Susitna Borough	101	1.29
South Naknek, AK (cdp) Bristol Bay Borough	1	1.27
Cedar Creek, AZ (cdp) Gila County	4	1.26
Nikiski, AK (cdp) Kenai Peninsula Borough	56	1.25
Saxman, AK (city) Ketchikan Gateway Borough	5	1.22
Naytahwaush, MN (cdp) Mahnomen County	7	1.21
Seldovia Village, AK (cdp) Kenai Peninsula Borough	2	1.21
Sutherland, UT (cdp) Millard County	2	1.21
Kalifornsky, AK (cdp) Kenai Peninsula Borough	94	1.20
Ruby, AK (city) Yukon-Koyukuk Census Area	2	1.20
Tyonek, AK (cdp) Kenai Peninsula Borough	2	1.17
Tanaina, AK (cdp) Matanuska-Susitna Borough	95	1.16
Steele Creek, AK (cdp) Fairbanks North Star Borough	77	1.16
Minerva, MN (township) Clearwater County	3	1.15
Chena Ridge, AK (cdp) Fairbanks North Star Borough	65	1.12
Meadow Lakes, AK (cdp) Matanuska-Susitna Borough	84	1.11
Pleasant Valley, AK (cdp) Fairbanks North Star Borough	8	1.10
Metlakatla, AK (cdp) Prince of Wales-Hyder Census Area	15	1.07
King Salmon, AK (cdp) Bristol Bay Borough	4	1.07
Valdez, AK (city) Valdez-Cordova Census Area	42	1.06
Churchtown, PA (cdp) Lancaster County	5	1.06
Fishhook, AK (cdp) Matanuska-Susitna Borough	49	1.05
Klukwan, AK (cdp) Hoonah-Angoon Census Area	1	1.05
Badger, AK (cdp) Fairbanks North Star Borough	203	1.04
Kotlik, AK (city) Wade Hampton Census Area	6	1.04
Hope, AK (cdp) Kenai Peninsula Borough	2	1.04
Koyukuk, AK (city) Yukon-Koyukuk Census Area	1	1.04
Gambell, AK (city) Nome Census Area	7	1.03
Lazy Mountain, AK (cdp) Matanuska-Susitna Borough	15	1.01
Tazlina, AK (cdp) Valdez-Cordova Census Area	3	1.01
Colebrook, PA (township) Clinton County	2	1.01
Aniak, AK (city) Bethel Census Area	5	1.00
Huetter, ID (city) Kootenai County	1	1.00
Ridgeway, AK (cdp) Kenai Peninsula Borough	20	0.99

Please refer to the Explanation of Data in the front of the book for more detailed information.

Race

Alaska Native: Inupiat (Eskimo)

Top 150 Places Sorted by Percent of Total Population

Based on places with total population of 7,500 or more

Place	Population	%
College, AK (cdp) Fairbanks North Star Borough	289	2.23
Anchorage, AK (municipality) Anchorage Municipality	6,103	2.09
Fairbanks, AK (city) Fairbanks North Star Borough	447	1.42
Knik-Fairview, AK (cdp) Matanuska-Susitna Borough	212	1.42
Lakes, AK (cdp) Matanuska-Susitna Borough	112	1.34
Wasilla, AK (city) Matanuska-Susitna Borough	101	1.29
Kalifornsky, AK (cdp) Kenai Peninsula Borough	94	1.20
Tanaina, AK (cdp) Matanuska-Susitna Borough	95	1.16
Meadow Lakes, AK (cdp) Matanuska-Susitna Borough	84	1.11
Badger, AK (cdp) Fairbanks North Star Borough	203	1.04
Sitka, AK (borough) Sitka City and Borough	71	0.80
Juneau, AK (borough) Juneau City and Borough	174	0.56
Ketchikan, AK (city) Ketchikan Gateway Borough	23	0.29
Tuba City, AZ (cdp) Coconino County	9	0.10
Clearlake, CA (city) Lake County	13	0.09
Sumner, WA (city) Pierce County	8	0.08
Fallon, NV (city) Churchill County	7	0.08
Picnic Point, WA (cdp) Snohomish County	7	0.08
Durango, CO (city) La Plata County	11	0.07
Hanover, NH (cdp) Grafton County	6	0.07
Kalispell, MT (city) Flathead County	12	0.06
Arlington, WA (city) Snohomish County	10	0.06
Bemidji, MN (city) Beltrami County	8	0.06
Shelton, WA (city) Mason County	6	0.06
Waller, WA (cdp) Pierce County	5	0.06
Lynnwood, WA (city) Snohomish County	18	0.05
Del City, OK (city) Oklahoma County	11	0.05
Mira Loma, CA (cdp) Riverside County	11	0.05
Willowick, OH (city) Lake County	7	0.05
Cloquet, MN (city) Carlton County	6	0.05
Hanover, NH (town) Grafton County	6	0.05
Marlton, NJ (cdp) Burlington County	5	0.05
Waimea, HI (cdp) Hawaii County	5	0.05
Cedar Hills, OR (cdp) Washington County	4	0.05
Cushing, OK (city) Payne County	4	0.05
Globe, AZ (city) Gila County	4	0.05
Hoquiam, WA (city) Grays Harbor County	4	0.05
Lake Wylie, SC (cdp) York County	4	0.05
Molalla, OR (city) Clackamas County	4	0.05
Everett, WA (city) Snohomish County	39	0.04
Bellingham, WA (city) Whatcom County	29	0.04
Parkland, WA (cdp) Pierce County	14	0.04
Longview, WA (city) Cowlitz County	13	0.04
Mount Vernon, WA (city) Skagit County	12	0.04
Ponca City, OK (city) Kay County	10	0.04
SeaTac, WA (city) King County	10	0.04
Ellensburg, WA (city) Kittitas County	8	0.04
Frederickson, WA (cdp) Pierce County	8	0.04
Fremont, OH (city) Sandusky County	6	0.04
North Lynnwood, WA (cdp) Snohomish County	6	0.04
Schofield Barracks, HI (cdp) Honolulu County	6	0.04
Holliston, MA (town) Middlesex County	5	0.04
Washougal, WA (city) Clark County	5	0.04
Alpena, MI (township) Alpena County	4	0.04
Cottage Grove, OR (city) Lane County	4	0.04
DeForest, WI (village) Dane County	4	0.04
Ferndale, WA (city) Whatcom County	4	0.04
Kapaa, HI (cdp) Kauai County	4	0.04
Midland, WA (cdp) Pierce County	4	0.04
Sanford, ME (cdp) York County	4	0.04
Shasta Lake, CA (city) Shasta County	4	0.04
Vashon, WA (cdp) King County	4	0.04
Weddington, NC (town) Union County	4	0.04
Erwin, NY (town) Steuben County	3	0.04
Guntersville, AL (city) Marshall County	3	0.04
Makaha, HI (cdp) Honolulu County	3	0.04
Rapid Valley, SD (cdp) Pennington County	3	0.04
Triangle, VA (cdp) Prince William County	3	0.04
Tacoma, WA (city) Pierce County	69	0.03
Federal Way, WA (city) King County	25	0.03
Auburn, WA (city) King County	18	0.03
Lakewood, WA (city) Pierce County	18	0.03
Albany, OR (city) Linn County	14	0.03
Caldwell, ID (city) Canyon County	14	0.03
Bremerton, WA (city) Kitsap County	13	0.03
Keizer, OR (city) Marion County	12	0.03
Puyallup, WA (city) Pierce County	12	0.03
Edmonds, WA (city) Snohomish County	11	0.03
Walla Walla, WA (city) Walla Walla County	10	0.03
East Hill-Meridian, WA (cdp) King County	9	0.03
Issaquah, WA (city) King County	9	0.03
Post Falls, ID (city) Kootenai County	8	0.03
Spanaway, WA (cdp) Pierce County	8	0.03
University Place, WA (city) Pierce County	8	0.03
Greenville, TX (city) Hunt County	7	0.03
Twentynine Palms, CA (city) San Bernardino County	7	0.03
Anthem, AZ (cdp) Maricopa County	6	0.03
Hyattsville, MD (city) Prince George's County	6	0.03
Klamath Falls, OR (city) Klamath County	6	0.03
Marina, CA (city) Monterey County	6	0.03
Mukilteo, WA (city) Snohomish County	6	0.03
South Lake Tahoe, CA (city) El Dorado County	6	0.03
Arcata, CA (city) Humboldt County	5	0.03
Bonney Lake, WA (city) Pierce County	5	0.03
Centralia, WA (city) Lewis County	5	0.03
Lealman, FL (cdp) Pinellas County	5	0.03
Mill Creek, WA (city) Snohomish County	5	0.03
Mountlake Terrace, WA (city) Snohomish County	5	0.03
Port Angeles, WA (city) Clallam County	5	0.03
Salmon Creek, WA (cdp) Clark County	5	0.03
Wahiawa, HI (cdp) Honolulu County	5	0.03
Wailuku, HI (cdp) Maui County	5	0.03
Broadlands, VA (cdp) Loudoun County	4	0.03
Evanston, WY (city) Uinta County	4	0.03
Fort Drum, NY (cdp) Jefferson County	4	0.03
Fortuna, CA (city) Humboldt County	4	0.03
Kapolei, HI (cdp) Honolulu County	4	0.03
Lincoln, IL (city) Logan County	4	0.03
Oatfield, OR (cdp) Clackamas County	4	0.03
Prairie Ridge, WA (cdp) Pierce County	4	0.03
Ripon, CA (city) San Joaquin County	4	0.03
Spring Creek, NV (cdp) Elko County	4	0.03
Algoma, MI (township) Kent County	3	0.03
Branson, MO (city) Taney County	3	0.03
Camp Verde, AZ (town) Yavapai County	3	0.03
Cody, WY (city) Park County	3	0.03
Crestline, CA (cdp) San Bernardino County	3	0.03
Dayton, NV (cdp) Lyon County	3	0.03
Diamond Springs, CA (cdp) El Dorado County	3	0.03
Edgewood, WA (city) Pierce County	3	0.03
Egelston, MI (township) Muskegon County	3	0.03
Federal Heights, CO (city) Adams County	3	0.03
Fife, WA (city) Pierce County	3	0.03
Fort Bliss, TX (cdp) El Paso County	3	0.03
Groton, MA (town) Middlesex County	3	0.03
Kailua, HI (cdp) Hawaii County	3	0.03
Lynden, WA (city) Whatcom County	3	0.03
Madison, IN (city) Jefferson County	3	0.03
Marion, MI (township) Livingston County	3	0.03
Old Orchard Beach, ME (cdp/town) York County	3	0.03
Poulsbo, WA (city) Kitsap County	3	0.03
Snohomish, WA (city) Snohomish County	3	0.03
St. Albans, WV (city) Kanawha County	3	0.03
St. Pete Beach, FL (city) Pinellas County	3	0.03
Union Park, FL (cdp) Orange County	3	0.03
Fruitvale, CO (cdp) Mesa County	2	0.03
Garden City Park, NY (cdp) Nassau County	2	0.03
Green, OR (cdp) Douglas County	2	0.03
McFarland, WI (village) Dane County	2	0.03
Summit, WA (cdp) Pierce County	2	0.03
Seattle, WA (city) King County	112	0.02
Spokane, WA (city) Spokane County	34	0.02
Salem, OR (city) Marion County	33	0.02
Eugene, OR (city) Lane County	31	0.02
Vancouver, WA (city) Clark County	30	0.02
Redding, CA (city) Shasta County	20	0.02
Billings, MT (city) Yellowstone County	19	0.02
Beaverton, OR (city) Washington County	18	0.02
Longmont, CO (city) Boulder County	18	0.02
Flagstaff, AZ (city) Coconino County	15	0.02

Please refer to the Explanation of Data in the front of the book for more detailed information.

Race

American Indian: Iroquois

U.S. and 50 States Sorted by Population and Percent of Total Population

Place	Population	%
United States	**81,002**	**0.03**
New York	26,567	0.14
Wisconsin	6,677	0.12
California	5,443	0.01
Oklahoma	3,548	0.09
Florida	3,312	0.02
Pennsylvania	2,816	0.02
Michigan	2,803	0.03
North Carolina	2,507	0.03
Ohio	1,807	0.02
Texas	1,764	0.01
Washington	1,542	0.02
Massachusetts	1,441	0.02
Virginia	1,410	0.02
Illinois	1,336	0.01
Arizona	1,275	0.02
Missouri	1,261	0.02
New Jersey	1,221	0.01
Oregon	1,039	0.03
Colorado	999	0.02
Connecticut	870	0.02
Maryland	818	0.01
Georgia	792	0.01
Kansas	788	0.03
Tennessee	683	0.01
Indiana	640	0.01
Minnesota	625	0.01
South Carolina	575	0.01
Vermont	524	0.08
New Hampshire	512	0.04
Nevada	511	0.02
Hawaii	493	0.04
New Mexico	448	0.02
Kentucky	369	0.01
Utah	355	0.01
Arkansas	310	0.01
Alaska	309	0.04
Maine	282	0.02
Rhode Island	278	0.03
Alabama	276	0.01
West Virginia	267	0.01
Idaho	230	0.01
Louisiana	202	<0.01
Iowa	200	0.01
Montana	187	0.02
Nebraska	146	0.01
Mississippi	119	<0.01
Delaware	104	0.01
Wyoming	102	0.02
South Dakota	101	0.01
District of Columbia	82	0.01
North Dakota	36	0.01

Place	Population	%
New York	26,567	0.14
Wisconsin	6,677	0.12
Oklahoma	3,548	0.09
Vermont	524	0.08
New Hampshire	512	0.04
Hawaii	493	0.04
Alaska	309	0.04
United States	**81,002**	**0.03**
Michigan	2,803	0.03
North Carolina	2,507	0.03
Oregon	1,039	0.03
Kansas	788	0.03
Rhode Island	278	0.03
Florida	3,312	0.02
Pennsylvania	2,816	0.02
Ohio	1,807	0.02
Washington	1,542	0.02
Massachusetts	1,441	0.02
Virginia	1,410	0.02
Arizona	1,275	0.02
Missouri	1,261	0.02
Colorado	999	0.02
Connecticut	870	0.02
Nevada	511	0.02
New Mexico	448	0.02
Maine	282	0.02
Montana	187	0.02
Wyoming	102	0.02
California	5,443	0.01
Texas	1,764	0.01
Illinois	1,336	0.01
New Jersey	1,221	0.01
Maryland	818	0.01
Georgia	792	0.01
Tennessee	683	0.01
Indiana	640	0.01
Minnesota	625	0.01
South Carolina	575	0.01
Kentucky	369	0.01
Utah	355	0.01
Arkansas	310	0.01
Alabama	276	0.01
West Virginia	267	0.01
Idaho	230	0.01
Iowa	200	0.01
Nebraska	146	0.01
Delaware	104	0.01
South Dakota	101	0.01
District of Columbia	82	0.01
North Dakota	36	0.01
Louisiana	202	<0.01
Mississippi	119	<0.01

Please refer to the Explanation of Data in the front of the book for more detailed information.

Race

American Indian: Iroquois

Top 150 Places Sorted by Population

Based on all places, regardless of total population

Place	Population	%
St. Regis Mohawk Reservation, NY (reservation) Franklin County	2,493	77.23
Green Bay, WI (city) Brown County	1,426	1.37
Syracuse, NY (city) Onondaga County	1,373	0.95
Buffalo, NY (city) Erie County	1,316	0.50
Cattaraugus Reservation, NY (reservation) Erie County	1,295	70.65
New York, NY (city) Kings County	1,276	0.02
Salamanca, NY (city) Cattaraugus County	951	16.35
Milwaukee, WI (city) Milwaukee County	938	0.16
Niagara Falls, NY (city) Niagara County	801	1.60
Allegany Reservation, NY (reservation) Cattaraugus County	610	59.80
Rochester, NY (city) Monroe County	483	0.23
Massena, NY (town) St. Lawrence County	442	3.43
Brooklyn, NY (borough) Kings County	381	0.02
Chicago, IL (city) Cook County	359	0.01
Miami, OK (city) Ottawa County	334	2.46
Los Angeles, CA (city) Los Angeles County	321	0.01
Queens, NY (borough) Queens County	308	0.01
Onondaga, NY (town) Onondaga County	293	1.27
Tulsa, OK (city) Tulsa County	272	0.07
Manhattan, NY (borough) New York County	265	0.02
Massena, NY (village) St. Lawrence County	257	2.35
Tonawanda, NY (town) Erie County	256	0.35
Clay, NY (town) Onondaga County	252	0.43
Phoenix, AZ (city) Maricopa County	250	0.02
Cattaraugus Reservation, NY (reservation) Cattaraugus County	227	72.29
Philadelphia, PA (city) Philadelphia County	216	0.01
Bombay, NY (town) Franklin County	206	15.18
Fort Covington, NY (town) Franklin County	197	11.75
Oklahoma City, OK (city) Oklahoma County	195	0.03
Cheektowaga, NY (town) Erie County	194	0.22
Fort Covington Hamlet, NY (cdp) Franklin County	190	14.53
Salina, NY (town) Onondaga County	189	0.56
Evans, NY (town) Erie County	184	1.12
San Diego, CA (city) San Diego County	183	0.01
Greece, NY (town) Monroe County	181	0.19
Oneida, NY (city) Madison County	180	1.58
Cheektowaga, NY (cdp) Erie County	179	0.24
Jamestown, NY (city) Chautauqua County	175	0.56
Bronx, NY (borough) Bronx County	170	0.01
Tonawanda Reservation, NY (reservation) Genesee County	168	34.78
Nedrow, NY (cdp) Onondaga County	166	7.40
Tonawanda, NY (cdp) Erie County	165	0.28
Hamburg, NY (town) Erie County	159	0.28
Albuquerque, NM (city) Bernalillo County	156	0.03
Ashwaubenon, WI (village) Brown County	155	0.91
Amherst, NY (town) Erie County	155	0.13
Portland, OR (city) Multnomah County	152	0.03
Staten Island, NY (borough) Richmond County	152	0.03
De Pere, WI (city) Brown County	151	0.63
Appleton, WI (city) Outagamie County	150	0.21
De Witt, NY (town) Onondaga County	149	0.58
Hempstead, NY (town) Nassau County	145	0.02
Geddes, NY (town) Onondaga County	143	0.84
Collins, NY (town) Erie County	141	2.14
Detroit, MI (city) Wayne County	140	0.02
Jacksonville, FL (city) Duval County	139	0.02
San Francisco, CA (city) San Francisco County	133	0.02
Niagara, NY (town) Niagara County	132	1.58
Appleton, WI (city) Outagamie County	129	0.21
Lewiston, NY (town) Niagara County	128	0.79
West Allis, WI (city) Milwaukee County	127	0.21
Columbus, OH (city) Franklin County	126	0.02
Gowanda, NY (village) Cattaraugus County	123	4.54
North Tonawanda, NY (city) Niagara County	122	0.39
Camillus, NY (town) Onondaga County	121	0.50
Hanover, NY (town) Chautauqua County	119	1.67
Cicero, NY (town) Onondaga County	119	0.38
Tucson, AZ (city) Pima County	117	0.02
San Jose, CA (city) Santa Clara County	117	0.01
Brookhaven, NY (town) Suffolk County	116	0.02
Charlotte, NC (city) Mecklenburg County	116	0.02
Virginia Beach, VA (ind. city) Virginia Beach independent city	112	0.03
Menominee, WI (town) Menominee County	111	2.62
Seattle, WA (city) King County	110	0.02
Anchorage, AK (municipality) Anchorage Municipality	109	0.04
LaFayette, NY (town) Onondaga County	108	2.18
Houston, TX (city) Harris County	107	0.01
Manlius, NY (town) Onondaga County	106	0.33
Minneapolis, MN (city) Hennepin County	106	0.03
Erie, PA (city) Erie County	105	0.10
Colorado Springs, CO (city) El Paso County	103	0.02
Howard, WI (village) Brown County	102	0.59
Lockport, NY (city) Niagara County	102	0.48
Albany, NY (city) Albany County	102	0.10
Boston, MA (city) Suffolk County	99	0.02
Denver, CO (city) Denver County	99	0.02
Pawhuska, OK (city) Osage County	98	2.73
Lysander, NY (town) Onondaga County	98	0.45
Irondequoit, NY (cdp/town) Monroe County	98	0.19
Las Vegas, NV (city) Clark County	97	0.02
Olean, NY (city) Cattaraugus County	96	0.66
Indianapolis, IN (city) Marion County	96	0.01
Madison, WI (city) Dane County	95	0.04
Oakland, CA (city) Alameda County	95	0.02
Utica, NY (city) Oneida County	94	0.15
Onondaga Nation Reservation, NY (reservation) Onondaga County	93	19.87
Tuscarora Nation Reservation, NY (reservation) Niagara County	92	7.99
Islip, NY (town) Suffolk County	92	0.03
Sacramento, CA (city) Sacramento County	92	0.02
Kenmore, NY (village) Erie County	91	0.59
Oshkosh, WI (city) Winnebago County	91	0.14
Wichita, KS (city) Sedgwick County	89	0.02
Austin, TX (city) Travis County	89	0.01
Schenectady, NY (city) Schenectady County	88	0.13
Springfield, MA (city) Hampden County	88	0.06
Solvay, NY (village) Onondaga County	87	1.32
Ogdensburg, NY (city) St. Lawrence County	87	0.78
Mesa, AZ (city) Maricopa County	86	0.02
Broken Arrow, OK (city) Tulsa County	85	0.09
San Antonio, TX (city) Medina County	85	0.01
Auburn, NY (city) Cayuga County	84	0.30
Urban Honolulu, HI (cdp) Honolulu County	83	0.02
Sullivan, NY (town) Madison County	82	0.53
Watertown, NY (city) Jefferson County	82	0.30
Washington, DC (city) District of Columbia	82	0.01
Shawano, WI (city) Shawano County	80	0.86
Grove, OK (city) Delaware County	79	1.19
Newstead, NY (town) Erie County	79	0.92
Binghamton, NY (city) Broome County	79	0.17
Long Beach, CA (city) Los Angeles County	79	0.02
Van Buren, NY (town) Onondaga County	78	0.59
Henrietta, NY (town) Monroe County	78	0.18
St. Petersburg, FL (city) Pinellas County	77	0.03
Fairmount, NY (cdp) Onondaga County	73	0.71
Manitowoc, WI (city) Manitowoc County	73	0.22
Kansas City, MO (city) Jackson County	72	0.02
Greenfield, WI (city) Milwaukee County	71	0.19
Seneca, MO (city) Newton County	70	3.00
Dunkirk, NY (city) Chautauqua County	70	0.56
Lockport, NY (town) Niagara County	70	0.34
Tampa, FL (city) Hillsborough County	68	0.02
Lancaster, NY (town) Erie County	67	0.16
Aurora, CO (city) Arapahoe County	67	0.02
Grand Island, NY (town) Erie County	66	0.32
Rome, NY (city) Oneida County	66	0.20
Norman, OK (city) Cleveland County	66	0.06
Perrysburg, NY (town) Cattaraugus County	65	4.00
Brant, NY (town) Erie County	65	3.15
Persia, NY (town) Cattaraugus County	65	2.70
Babylon, NY (town) Suffolk County	65	0.03
Kaukauna, WI (city) Outagamie County	64	0.41
Potsdam, NY (town) St. Lawrence County	64	0.40
Elmira, NY (city) Chemung County	64	0.22
West Seneca, NY (cdp/town) Erie County	64	0.14
Baltimore, MD (city) Baltimore city County	63	0.01
Wheatfield, NY (town) Niagara County	62	0.34
Gates, NY (town) Monroe County	62	0.22
Orchard Park, NY (town) Erie County	62	0.21
Cleveland, OH (city) Cuyahoga County	62	0.02
Hastings, NY (town) Oswego County	61	0.65

Please refer to the Explanation of Data in the front of the book for more detailed information.

Race

American Indian: Iroquois

Top 150 Places Sorted by Percent of Total Population

Based on all places, regardless of total population

Place	Population	%
St. Regis Mohawk Reservation, NY (reservation) Franklin County	2,493	77.23
Tonawanda Reservation, NY (reservation) Erie County	26	76.47
Cattaraugus Reservation, NY (reservation) Cattaraugus County	227	72.29
Cattaraugus Reservation, NY (reservation) Erie County	1,295	70.65
Allegany Reservation, NY (reservation) Cattaraugus County	610	59.80
Cattaraugus Reservation, NY (reservation) Chautauqua County	20	52.63
Tonawanda Reservation, NY (reservation) Genesee County	168	34.78
Onondaga Nation Reservation, NY (reservation) Onondaga County	93	19.87
Salamanca, NY (city) Cattaraugus County	951	16.35
Bombay, NY (town) Franklin County	206	15.18
Fort Covington Hamlet, NY (cdp) Franklin County	190	14.53
Wyandotte, OK (town) Ottawa County	45	13.51
Fort Covington, NY (town) Franklin County	197	11.75
Bowmore, NC (cdp) Hoke County	10	9.71
Tuscarora Nation Reservation, NY (reservation) Niagara County	92	7.99
Nedrow, NY (cdp) Onondaga County	166	7.40
Kirkpatrick, OR (cdp) Umatilla County	13	7.26
Farnham, NY (village) Erie County	24	6.28
Butler, OK (cdp) Delaware County	6	5.13
Perrysburg, NY (village) Cattaraugus County	20	4.99
Kickapoo Site 1, KS (cdp) Brown County	5	4.95
Spring, AR (town) Benton County	4	4.60
Gowanda, NY (village) Cattaraugus County	123	4.54
Reeds, MO (town) Jasper County	4	4.21
Perrysburg, NY (town) Cattaraugus County	65	4.00
Stryker, MT (cdp) Lincoln County	1	3.85
Salamanca, NY (town) Cattaraugus County	17	3.53
Keshena, WI (cdp) Menominee County	44	3.49
North Miami, OK (town) Ottawa County	13	3.48
Massena, NY (town) St. Lawrence County	442	3.43
Middle Village, WI (cdp) Shawano County	9	3.20
Brant, NY (town) Erie County	65	3.15
Freistatt, MO (village) Lawrence County	5	3.07
Bartelme, WI (town) Shawano County	25	3.05
Neopit, WI (cdp) Menominee County	21	3.04
Seneca, MO (city) Newton County	70	3.00
Quapaw, OK (town) Ottawa County	27	2.98
Navarino, WI (cdp) Shawano County	5	2.82
Sand Lake, MN (township) Itasca County	4	2.74
Pawhuska, OK (city) Osage County	98	2.73
Persia, NY (town) Cattaraugus County	65	2.70
Magnolia, DE (town) Kent County	6	2.67
Red House, NY (town) Cattaraugus County	1	2.63
Menominee, WI (town) Menominee County	111	2.62
Orient, WA (cdp) Ferry County	3	2.61
Tustin, WI (cdp) Waushara County	3	2.56
White Water, OK (cdp) Delaware County	2	2.50
Miami, OK (city) Ottawa County	334	2.46
North Collins, NY (village) Erie County	30	2.44
Elmo, MO (city) Nodaway County	4	2.38
Fairland, OK (town) Ottawa County	25	2.37
Massena, NY (village) St. Lawrence County	257	2.35
Lance Creek, WY (cdp) Niobrara County	1	2.33
Brasher, NY (town) St. Lawrence County	58	2.31
Oneida Castle, NY (village) Oneida County	14	2.24
Pulcifer, WI (cdp) Shawano County	3	2.24
Durhamville, NY (cdp) Oneida County	13	2.23
Bridgewater, IA (city) Adair County	4	2.20
LaFayette, NY (town) Onondaga County	108	2.18
Cataract, WI (cdp) Monroe County	4	2.15
Collins, NY (town) Erie County	141	2.14
Angola, NY (village) Erie County	45	2.12
Sunset Bay, NY (cdp) Chautauqua County	14	2.12
Silver Creek, NY (village) Chautauqua County	56	2.11
Coldspring, NY (town) Cattaraugus County	14	2.11
Falls Creek, PA (borough) Clearfield County	1	2.08
Rillito, AZ (cdp) Pima County	2	2.06
Pine River, WI (cdp) Waushara County	3	2.04
Elm Grove, OK (cdp) Adair County	4	2.02
Esbon, KS (city) Jewell County	2	2.02
Narcissa, OK (cdp) Ottawa County	2	2.02
Harmonsburg, PA (cdp) Crawford County	8	2.00
Dotyville, OK (cdp) Ottawa County	2	1.98
Grugan, PA (township) Clinton County	1	1.96
Commerce, OK (city) Ottawa County	47	1.90
Legend Lake, WI (cdp) Menominee County	29	1.90
Beaver, MN (township) Aitkin County	1	1.89
Gresham, WI (village) Shawano County	11	1.88
Little Round Lake, WI (cdp) Sawyer County	20	1.85
Pulaski, WI (village) Shawano County	4	1.83
Gilliam, LA (village) Caddo Parish	3	1.83
Sanford, TX (town) Hutchinson County	3	1.83
Shinnecock Reservation, NY (reservation) Suffolk County	12	1.81
Hammond, NY (village) St. Lawrence County	5	1.79
Barnesville, MD (town) Montgomery County	3	1.74
Peck, WI (town) Langlade County	6	1.72
Hanover, NY (town) Chautauqua County	119	1.67
Pin Oak Acres, OK (cdp) Mayes County	7	1.66
Frenchboro, ME (town) Hancock County	1	1.64
Helix, OR (city) Umatilla County	3	1.63
Dresden, NY (village) Yates County	5	1.62
Overton, PA (township) Bradford County	4	1.62
Angola on the Lake, NY (cdp) Erie County	27	1.61
Niagara Falls, NY (city) Niagara County	801	1.60
Seymour, WI (town) Outagamie County	19	1.59
Chitina, AK (cdp) Valdez-Cordova Census Area	2	1.59
Oneida, NY (city) Madison County	180	1.58
Niagara, NY (town) Niagara County	132	1.58
Le Flore, OK (town) Le Flore County	3	1.58
Diamond, MO (town) Newton County	14	1.55
Little Elbow, MN (township) Mahnomen County	4	1.54
Akron, NY (village) Erie County	44	1.53
Napoli, NY (town) Cattaraugus County	19	1.52
Shannon, NC (cdp) Robeson County	4	1.52
Red Springs, WI (town) Shawano County	14	1.51
Malden, WA (town) Whitman County	3	1.48
Bluejacket, OK (town) Craig County	5	1.47
Draper, WI (town) Sawyer County	3	1.47
Little Sturgeon, WI (cdp) Door County	2	1.47
Sanborn, NY (cdp) Niagara County	24	1.46
Mission, OR (cdp) Umatilla County	15	1.45
Canaseraga, NY (village) Allegany County	8	1.45
Treece, KS (city) Cherokee County	2	1.45
Stark City, MO (town) Newton County	2	1.44
Nicholson, PA (borough) Wyoming County	11	1.43
Sanders, AZ (cdp) Apache County	9	1.43
Sawyerville, IL (village) Macoupin County	4	1.43
Diaperville, WI (cdp) Ashland County	1	1.43
Alburg, VT (village) Grand Isle County	7	1.41
Lake Lindsey, FL (cdp) Hernando County	1	1.41
Green Bay, WI (city) Brown County	1,426	1.37
Lac du Flambeau, WI (cdp) Vilas County	27	1.37
Westville, NY (town) Franklin County	25	1.37
Wynona, OK (town) Osage County	6	1.37
Townsend, WI (cdp) Oconto County	2	1.37
East Syracuse, NY (village) Onondaga County	42	1.36
Piffard, NY (cdp) Livingston County	3	1.36
Villenova, NY (town) Chautauqua County	15	1.35
Navarino, WI (town) Shawano County	6	1.35
Ellicottville, NY (village) Cattaraugus County	5	1.33
Hopewell Junction, NY (cdp) Dutchess County	5	1.33
Solvay, NY (village) Onondaga County	87	1.32
Morris, WI (town) Shawano County	6	1.32
Bowler, WI (village) Shawano County	4	1.32
Lac du Flambeau, WI (town) Vilas County	45	1.31
Suring, WI (village) Oconto County	7	1.29
Almond, NY (village) Allegany County	6	1.29
Alabama, NY (town) Genesee County	24	1.28
Busti, NY (cdp) Chautauqua County	5	1.28
Millport, NY (village) Chemung County	4	1.28
Onondaga, NY (town) Onondaga County	293	1.27
Louisville, NY (town) St. Lawrence County	40	1.27
Longford, KS (city) Clay County	1	1.27
New Witten, SD (town) Tripp County	1	1.27
South Naknek, AK (cdp) Bristol Bay Borough	1	1.27
Parkline, ID (cdp) Benewah County	1	1.25
Stockbridge, NY (town) Madison County	26	1.24
Seneca Knolls, NY (cdp) Onondaga County	25	1.24
Montgomery Creek, CA (cdp) Shasta County	2	1.23
Stafford, OH (village) Monroe County	1	1.23

Please refer to the Explanation of Data in the front of the book for more detailed information.

Race

American Indian: Iroquois

Top 150 Places Sorted by Percent of Total Population

Based on places with total population of 7,500 or more

Place	Population	%
Massena, NY (town) St. Lawrence County	442	3.43
Miami, OK (city) Ottawa County	334	2.46
Massena, NY (village) St. Lawrence County	257	2.35
Niagara Falls, NY (city) Niagara County	801	1.60
Oneida, NY (city) Madison County	180	1.58
Niagara, NY (town) Niagara County	132	1.58
Green Bay, WI (city) Brown County	1,426	1.37
Onondaga, NY (town) Onondaga County	293	1.27
Evans, NY (town) Erie County	184	1.12
Syracuse, NY (city) Onondaga County	1,373	0.95
Newstead, NY (town) Erie County	79	0.92
Ashwaubenon, WI (village) Brown County	155	0.91
Shawano, WI (city) Shawano County	80	0.86
Geddes, NY (town) Onondaga County	143	0.84
Lewiston, NY (town) Niagara County	128	0.79
Ogdensburg, NY (city) St. Lawrence County	87	0.78
Fairmount, NY (cdp) Onondaga County	73	0.71
Schroeppel, NY (town) Oswego County	57	0.67
Olean, NY (city) Cattaraugus County	96	0.66
Hastings, NY (town) Oswego County	61	0.65
De Pere, WI (city) Brown County	151	0.63
Howard, WI (village) Brown County	102	0.59
Kenmore, NY (village) Erie County	91	0.59
Van Buren, NY (town) Onondaga County	78	0.59
De Witt, NY (town) Onondaga County	149	0.58
Newfane, NY (town) Niagara County	56	0.58
Salina, NY (town) Onondaga County	189	0.56
Jamestown, NY (city) Chautauqua County	175	0.56
Dunkirk, NY (city) Chautauqua County	70	0.56
South Lockport, NY (cdp) Niagara County	45	0.54
Sullivan, NY (town) Madison County	82	0.53
Buffalo, NY (city) Erie County	1,316	0.50
Camillus, NY (town) Onondaga County	121	0.50
Lockport, NY (city) Niagara County	102	0.48
Sturgeon Bay, WI (city) Door County	44	0.48
Lysander, NY (town) Onondaga County	98	0.45
Clay, NY (town) Onondaga County	252	0.43
Kaukauna, WI (city) Outagamie County	64	0.41
Lenox, NY (town) Madison County	37	0.41
Concord, NY (town) Erie County	35	0.41
Potsdam, NY (town) St. Lawrence County	64	0.40
North Tonawanda, NY (city) Niagara County	122	0.39
Allouez, WI (village) Brown County	55	0.39
Cicero, NY (town) Onondaga County	119	0.38
Royalton, NY (town) Niagara County	28	0.37
Bellevue, WI (village) Brown County	53	0.36
Tonawanda, NY (town) Erie County	256	0.35
Lockport, NY (town) Niagara County	70	0.34
Wheatfield, NY (town) Niagara County	62	0.34
Allegany, NY (town) Cattaraugus County	27	0.34
Manlius, NY (town) Onondaga County	106	0.33
Antigo, WI (city) Langlade County	27	0.33
Grand Island, NY (town) Erie County	66	0.32
Batavia, NY (city) Genesee County	50	0.32
Malone, NY (town) Franklin County	45	0.31
Fulton, NY (city) Oswego County	37	0.31
Auburn, NY (city) Cayuga County	84	0.30
Watertown, NY (city) Jefferson County	82	0.30
Lackawanna, NY (city) Erie County	54	0.30
Canton, NY (town) St. Lawrence County	33	0.30
Manchester, NY (town) Ontario County	28	0.30
Eden, NY (town) Erie County	23	0.30
Tonawanda, NY (city) Erie County	44	0.29
Potsdam, NY (village) St. Lawrence County	27	0.29
Tonawanda, NY (cdp) Erie County	165	0.28
Hamburg, NY (town) Erie County	159	0.28
Canandaigua, NY (city) Ontario County	30	0.28
Sodus, NY (town) Wayne County	23	0.27
Livonia, NY (town) Livingston County	21	0.27
Pomfret, NY (town) Chautauqua County	39	0.26
Little Chute, WI (village) Outagamie County	27	0.26
Boston, NY (town) Erie County	21	0.26
Sweden, NY (town) Monroe County	35	0.25
Victor, NY (town) Ontario County	35	0.25
Seneca Falls, NY (town) Seneca County	23	0.25
Cheektowaga, NY (cdp) Erie County	179	0.24
Fredonia, NY (village) Chautauqua County	27	0.24
Suamico, WI (village) Brown County	27	0.24
Rochester, NY (city) Monroe County	483	0.23
Cortland, NY (city) Cortland County	44	0.23
Amsterdam, NY (city) Montgomery County	43	0.23
Neosho, MO (city) Newton County	27	0.23
Cheektowaga, NY (town) Erie County	194	0.22
Manitowoc, WI (city) Manitowoc County	73	0.22
Elmira, NY (city) Chemung County	64	0.22
Gates, NY (town) Monroe County	62	0.22
Plattsburgh, NY (city) Clinton County	44	0.22
Lancaster, NY (village) Erie County	23	0.22
North Gates, NY (cdp) Monroe County	21	0.22
Marcy, NY (town) Oneida County	20	0.22
Cortlandville, NY (town) Cortland County	19	0.22
Le Roy, NY (town) Genesee County	17	0.22
Appleton, WI (city) Outagamie County	150	0.21
Appleton, WI (city) Outagamie County	129	0.21
West Allis, WI (city) Milwaukee County	127	0.21
Orchard Park, NY (town) Erie County	62	0.21
Chili, NY (town) Monroe County	61	0.21
St. Francis, WI (city) Milwaukee County	20	0.21
Albion, NY (town) Orleans County	18	0.21
Bradford, PA (city) McKean County	18	0.21
Rhinelander, WI (city) Oneida County	16	0.21
Rome, NY (city) Oneida County	66	0.20
Claremore, OK (city) Rogers County	37	0.20
Cudahy, WI (city) Milwaukee County	36	0.20
Schodack, NY (town) Rensselaer County	26	0.20
Alden, NY (town) Erie County	22	0.20
Hamburg, NY (village) Erie County	19	0.20
Greece, NY (town) Monroe County	181	0.19
Irondequoit, NY (cdp/town) Monroe County	98	0.19
Greenfield, WI (city) Milwaukee County	71	0.19
Ponca City, OK (city) Kay County	47	0.19
Ogden, NY (town) Monroe County	38	0.19
Gloversville, NY (city) Fulton County	29	0.19
Parma, NY (town) Monroe County	29	0.19
Ballston, NY (town) Saratoga County	19	0.19
Canandaigua, NY (town) Ontario County	19	0.19
Pryor Creek, OK (city) Mayes County	18	0.19
Barton, NY (town) Tioga County	17	0.19
Henrietta, NY (town) Monroe County	78	0.18
Le Ray, NY (town) Jefferson County	40	0.18
Menasha, WI (city) Winnebago County	28	0.18
Arcadia, NY (town) Wayne County	25	0.18
German Flatts, NY (town) Herkimer County	24	0.18
Sun Village, CA (cdp) Los Angeles County	21	0.18
Lisbon, WI (town) Waukesha County	18	0.18
Hornell, NY (city) Steuben County	15	0.18
Binghamton, NY (city) Broome County	79	0.17
South Milwaukee, WI (city) Milwaukee County	37	0.17
Menasha, WI (city) Winnebago County	30	0.17
Dryden, NY (town) Tompkins County	24	0.17
Appleton, WI (city) Calumet County	19	0.17
Southport, NY (town) Chemung County	19	0.17
Newark, NY (village) Wayne County	16	0.17
Brockport, NY (village) Monroe County	14	0.17
Milwaukee, WI (city) Milwaukee County	938	0.16
Lancaster, NY (town) Erie County	67	0.16
Plattsburgh, NY (town) Clinton County	19	0.16
Grosse Ile, MI (township) Wayne County	17	0.16
North Elba, NY (town) Essex County	14	0.16
Port Jervis, NY (city) Orange County	14	0.16
Norway, WI (town) Racine County	13	0.16
Palmyra, NY (town) Wayne County	13	0.16
Big Flats, NY (town) Chemung County	12	0.16
Waterloo, NY (town) Seneca County	12	0.16
Utica, NY (city) Oneida County	94	0.15
Bartlesville, OK (city) Washington County	52	0.15
Neenah, WI (city) Winnebago County	39	0.15
Malta, NY (town) Saratoga County	22	0.15
Brunswick, NY (town) Rensselaer County	18	0.15
Chester, NY (town) Orange County	18	0.15

SECTION THREE

Please refer to the Explanation of Data in the front of the book for more detailed information.

Race

American Indian: Kiowa

U.S. and 50 States Sorted by Population and Percent of Total Population

Place	Population	%
United States	**13,787**	**<0.01**
Oklahoma	7,711	0.21
New Mexico	1,343	0.07
Texas	895	<0.01
California	784	<0.01
Kansas	365	0.01
Arizona	348	0.01
Colorado	244	<0.01
Washington	203	<0.01
Missouri	143	<0.01
Florida	137	<0.01
Oregon	116	<0.01
Arkansas	106	<0.01
Pennsylvania	98	<0.01
Illinois	95	<0.01
Virginia	81	<0.01
Iowa	80	<0.01
Ohio	70	<0.01
North Carolina	68	<0.01
Nevada	67	<0.01
Wisconsin	58	<0.01
Georgia	55	<0.01
Tennessee	54	<0.01
Utah	53	<0.01
Minnesota	51	<0.01
Louisiana	49	<0.01
Maryland	44	<0.01
Michigan	44	<0.01
New York	44	<0.01
Hawaii	35	<0.01
Indiana	35	<0.01
Kentucky	32	<0.01
Montana	30	<0.01
Alaska	29	<0.01
Idaho	26	<0.01
Nebraska	23	<0.01
South Carolina	23	<0.01
Alabama	21	<0.01
Massachusetts	21	<0.01
New Jersey	21	<0.01
South Dakota	18	<0.01
Mississippi	14	<0.01
Wyoming	10	<0.01
Maine	9	<0.01
Connecticut	7	<0.01
New Hampshire	7	<0.01
Delaware	5	<0.01
Rhode Island	4	<0.01
Vermont	4	<0.01
North Dakota	3	<0.01
District of Columbia	2	<0.01
West Virginia	2	<0.01

Place	Population	%
Oklahoma	7,711	0.21
New Mexico	1,343	0.07
Kansas	365	0.01
Arizona	348	0.01
United States	**13,787**	**<0.01**
Texas	895	<0.01
California	784	<0.01
Colorado	244	<0.01
Washington	203	<0.01
Missouri	143	<0.01
Florida	137	<0.01
Oregon	116	<0.01
Arkansas	106	<0.01
Pennsylvania	98	<0.01
Illinois	95	<0.01
Virginia	81	<0.01
Iowa	80	<0.01
Ohio	70	<0.01
North Carolina	68	<0.01
Nevada	67	<0.01
Wisconsin	58	<0.01
Georgia	55	<0.01
Tennessee	54	<0.01
Utah	53	<0.01
Minnesota	51	<0.01
Louisiana	49	<0.01
Maryland	44	<0.01
Michigan	44	<0.01
New York	44	<0.01
Hawaii	35	<0.01
Indiana	35	<0.01
Kentucky	32	<0.01
Montana	30	<0.01
Alaska	29	<0.01
Idaho	26	<0.01
Nebraska	23	<0.01
South Carolina	23	<0.01
Alabama	21	<0.01
Massachusetts	21	<0.01
New Jersey	21	<0.01
South Dakota	18	<0.01
Mississippi	14	<0.01
Wyoming	10	<0.01
Maine	9	<0.01
Connecticut	7	<0.01
New Hampshire	7	<0.01
Delaware	5	<0.01
Rhode Island	4	<0.01
Vermont	4	<0.01
North Dakota	3	<0.01
District of Columbia	2	<0.01
West Virginia	2	<0.01

Please refer to the Explanation of Data in the front of the book for more detailed information.

Race

American Indian: Kiowa

Top 150 Places Sorted by Population

Based on all places, regardless of total population

Place	Population	%
Anadarko, OK (city) Caddo County	1,298	19.20
Oklahoma City, OK (city) Oklahoma County	950	0.16
Lawton, OK (city) Comanche County	757	0.78
Santo Domingo Pueblo, NM (cdp) Sandoval County	707	28.79
Carnegie, OK (town) Caddo County	298	17.30
Tulsa, OK (city) Tulsa County	276	0.07
Norman, OK (city) Cleveland County	212	0.19
Wichita, KS (city) Sedgwick County	174	0.05
Albuquerque, NM (city) Bernalillo County	141	0.03
Chickasha, OK (city) Grady County	100	0.62
Moore, OK (city) Cleveland County	100	0.18
Hobart, OK (city) Kiowa County	99	2.64
Phoenix, AZ (city) Maricopa County	90	0.01
Midwest City, OK (city) Oklahoma County	84	0.15
El Reno, OK (city) Canadian County	76	0.45
Mountain View, OK (town) Kiowa County	72	9.06
Shawnee, OK (city) Pottawatomie County	72	0.24
Dallas, TX (city) Dallas County	72	0.01
Apache, OK (town) Caddo County	69	4.78
Fort Worth, TX (city) Tarrant County	61	0.01
Lawrence, KS (city) Douglas County	56	0.06
Los Angeles, CA (city) Los Angeles County	49	<0.01
Edmond, OK (city) Oklahoma County	48	0.06
Weatherford, OK (city) Custer County	44	0.41
Del City, OK (city) Oklahoma County	42	0.20
Grand Prairie, TX (city) Dallas County	38	0.02
Claremore, OK (city) Rogers County	37	0.20
Duncan, OK (city) Stephens County	35	0.15
Bartlesville, OK (city) Washington County	35	0.10
Tahlequah, OK (city) Cherokee County	34	0.22
Yukon, OK (city) Canadian County	34	0.15
Arlington, TX (city) Tarrant County	33	0.01
Colorado Springs, CO (city) El Paso County	33	0.01
Denver, CO (city) Denver County	33	0.01
Ada, OK (city) Pontotoc County	31	0.18
Davenport, IA (city) Scott County	31	0.03
Wichita Falls, TX (city) Wichita County	30	0.03
Fort Cobb, OK (town) Caddo County	29	4.57
Muskogee, OK (city) Muskogee County	29	0.07
Ponca City, OK (city) Kay County	28	0.11
Kansas City, MO (city) Jackson County	28	0.01
Altus, OK (city) Jackson County	27	0.14
Portland, OR (city) Multnomah County	27	<0.01
Elgin, OK (city) Comanche County	26	1.21
Bethany, OK (city) Oklahoma County	26	0.14
San Antonio, TX (city) Medina County	26	<0.01
San Jose, CA (city) Santa Clara County	25	<0.01
Cache, OK (city) Comanche County	24	0.86
Bernalillo, NM (town) Sandoval County	24	0.29
Clinton, OK (city) Custer County	24	0.27
Ardmore, OK (city) Carter County	24	0.10
Houston, TX (city) Harris County	24	<0.01
Stillwater, OK (city) Payne County	23	0.05
Denton, TX (city) Denton County	23	0.02
Amarillo, TX (city) Potter County	23	0.01
Chicago, IL (city) Cook County	23	<0.01
Walters, OK (city) Cotton County	22	0.86
Seattle, WA (city) King County	22	<0.01
Santa Fe, NM (city) Santa Fe County	21	0.03
Fresno, CA (city) Fresno County	21	<0.01
Broken Arrow, OK (city) Tulsa County	20	0.02
Porterville, CA (city) Tulare County	19	0.04
Bakersfield, CA (city) Kern County	19	0.01
Irving, TX (city) Dallas County	19	0.01
Cushing, OK (city) Payne County	18	0.23
Okmulgee, OK (city) Okmulgee County	18	0.15
Flagstaff, AZ (city) Coconino County	18	0.03
Tecumseh, OK (city) Pottawatomie County	17	0.26
Mesa, AZ (city) Maricopa County	17	<0.01
Cyril, OK (town) Caddo County	16	1.51
Mesquite, TX (city) Dallas County	16	0.01
Austin, TX (city) Travis County	16	<0.01
San Diego, CA (city) San Diego County	16	<0.01
Warr Acres, OK (city) Oklahoma County	15	0.15
Farmington, NM (city) San Juan County	15	0.03
Chandler, AZ (city) Maricopa County	15	0.01
Chesapeake, VA (ind. city) Chesapeake independent city	15	0.01
Scottsdale, AZ (city) Maricopa County	15	0.01
Tempe, AZ (city) Maricopa County	15	0.01
New York, NY (city) Kings County	15	<0.01
Sacramento, CA (city) Sacramento County	15	<0.01
Burkburnett, TX (city) Wichita County	14	0.13
McAlester, OK (city) Pittsburg County	14	0.08
Owasso, OK (city) Tulsa County	14	0.05
Plano, TX (city) Collin County	14	0.01
Hominy, OK (city) Osage County	13	0.36
Coweta, OK (city) Wagoner County	13	0.13
Mustang, OK (city) Canadian County	13	0.07
Eugene, OR (city) Lane County	13	0.01
Gracemont, OK (town) Caddo County	12	3.77
Hulbert, OK (town) Cherokee County	12	2.03
Kingfisher, OK (city) Kingfisher County	12	0.26
Holbrook, AZ (city) Navajo County	12	0.24
Kayenta, AZ (cdp) Navajo County	12	0.23
Sand Springs, OK (city) Tulsa County	12	0.06
Aurora, CO (city) Arapahoe County	12	<0.01
Geary, OK (city) Blaine County	11	0.86
Park Hill, OK (cdp) Cherokee County	11	0.28
McLoud, OK (town) Pottawatomie County	11	0.27
The Village, OK (city) Oklahoma County	11	0.12
Sapulpa, OK (city) Creek County	11	0.05
Vineyard, CA (cdp) Sacramento County	11	0.04
North Richland Hills, TX (city) Tarrant County	11	0.02
McKinney, TX (city) Collin County	11	0.01
Rio Rancho, NM (city) Sandoval County	11	0.01
Thornton, CO (city) Adams County	11	0.01
Whittier, CA (city) Los Angeles County	11	0.01
Cleveland, OH (city) Cuyahoga County	11	<0.01
Manhattan, NY (borough) New York County	11	<0.01
Oakland, CA (city) Alameda County	11	<0.01
Stratmoor, CO (cdp) El Paso County	10	0.14
Pryor Creek, OK (city) Mayes County	10	0.10
Bixby, OK (city) Tulsa County	10	0.05
Gallup, NM (city) McKinley County	10	0.05
Clovis, NM (city) Curry County	10	0.03
Casa Grande, AZ (city) Pinal County	10	0.02
Rogers, AR (city) Benton County	10	0.02
Boulder, CO (city) Boulder County	10	0.01
Fort Smith, AR (city) Sebastian County	10	0.01
Oxnard, CA (city) Ventura County	10	0.01
West Valley City, UT (city) Salt Lake County	10	0.01
San Francisco, CA (city) San Francisco County	10	<0.01
Thomas, OK (city) Custer County	9	0.76
Pawnee, OK (city) Pawnee County	9	0.41
Oaklawn-Sunview, KS (cdp) Sedgwick County	9	0.27
Verdigris, OK (town) Rogers County	9	0.23
Holdenville, OK (city) Hughes County	9	0.16
Tuttle, OK (city) Grady County	9	0.15
Elk City, OK (city) Beckham County	9	0.08
Radcliff, KY (city) Hardin County	9	0.04
Pico Rivera, CA (city) Los Angeles County	9	0.01
Rancho Cucamonga, CA (city) San Bernardino County	9	0.01
Fremont, CA (city) Alameda County	9	<0.01
Las Vegas, NV (city) Clark County	9	<0.01
Omaha, NE (city) Douglas County	9	<0.01
Philadelphia, PA (city) Philadelphia County	9	<0.01
Virginia Beach, VA (ind. city) Virginia Beach independent city	9	<0.01
Commerce, OK (city) Ottawa County	8	0.32
Harrah, OK (city) Oklahoma County	8	0.16
Seminole, OK (city) Seminole County	8	0.11
Glenpool, OK (city) Tulsa County	8	0.07
Jenks, OK (city) Tulsa County	8	0.05
Tukwila, WA (city) King County	8	0.04
Brentwood, CA (city) Contra Costa County	8	0.02
Bowie, MD (city) Prince George's County	8	0.01
Greeley, CO (city) Weld County	8	0.01
Lewisville, TX (city) Denton County	8	0.01
Rancho Cordova, CA (city) Sacramento County	8	0.01
Salem, OR (city) Marion County	8	0.01
Springdale, AR (city) Washington County	8	0.01

SECTION THREE

Please refer to the Explanation of Data in the front of the book for more detailed information.

Race

American Indian: Kiowa

Top 150 Places Sorted by Percent of Total Population

Based on all places, regardless of total population

Place	Population	%
Santo Domingo Pueblo, NM (cdp) Sandoval County	707	28.79
Anadarko, OK (city) Caddo County	1,298	19.20
Carnegie, OK (town) Caddo County	298	17.30
Mountain View, OK (town) Kiowa County	72	9.06
Horn, OK (town) Hughes County	5	5.15
Apache, OK (town) Caddo County	69	4.78
Fort Cobb, OK (town) Caddo County	29	4.57
Gracemont, OK (town) Caddo County	12	3.77
Hobart, OK (city) Kiowa County	99	2.64
Red Rock, OK (town) Noble County	7	2.47
Hulbert, OK (town) Cherokee County	12	2.03
Ranchette Estates, TX (cdp) Willacy County	3	1.97
Fair Oaks, OK (town) Wagoner County	2	1.94
Asher, OK (town) Pottawatomie County	7	1.78
Gotebo, OK (town) Kiowa County	4	1.77
Cyril, OK (town) Caddo County	16	1.51
Peavine, OK (cdp) Adair County	6	1.42
Sombrillo, NM (cdp) Santa Fe County	5	1.42
McCord Bend, MO (village) Stone County	4	1.35
West Roy Lake, MN (cdp) Mahnomen County	1	1.35
Verden, OK (town) Grady County	7	1.32
Proctor, OK (cdp) Adair County	3	1.30
Westphalia, KS (city) Anderson County	2	1.23
Tupelo, OK (city) Coal County	4	1.22
Elgin, OK (city) Comanche County	26	1.21
Pinehill, NM (cdp) Cibola County	1	1.14
Iron Post, OK (cdp) Mayes County	1	1.09
Medicine Park, OK (town) Comanche County	4	1.05
Klukwan, AK (cdp) Hoonah-Angoon Census Area	1	1.05
Centrahoma, OK (city) Coal County	1	1.03
Spring Hill, IN (town) Marion County	1	1.02
Peña Blanca, NM (cdp) Sandoval County	7	0.99
Alex, OK (town) Grady County	5	0.91
Cache, OK (city) Comanche County	24	0.86
Walters, OK (city) Cotton County	22	0.86
Geary, OK (city) Blaine County	11	0.86
Elmore City, OK (town) Garvin County	6	0.86
Bridgeport, OK (city) Caddo County	1	0.86
Red Mesa, AZ (cdp) Apache County	4	0.83
Eldon, OK (cdp) Cherokee County	3	0.82
Roosevelt, OK (town) Kiowa County	2	0.81
Cement, OK (town) Caddo County	4	0.80
Lawton, OK (city) Comanche County	757	0.78
Mulberry, KS (city) Crawford County	4	0.77
Thomas, OK (city) Custer County	9	0.76
Bentley, KS (city) Sedgwick County	4	0.75
Hammon, OK (town) Roger Mills County	4	0.70
Fort Apache, AZ (cdp) Navajo County	1	0.70
Kingvale, CA (cdp) Nevada County	1	0.70
Mill Creek, OK (town) Johnston County	2	0.63
Port Alsworth, AK (cdp) Lake and Peninsula Borough	1	0.63
Chickasha, OK (city) Grady County	100	0.62
Bromide, OK (town) Johnston County	1	0.61
Byers, TX (city) Clay County	3	0.60
Ringwood, OK (town) Major County	3	0.60
Indiahoma, OK (town) Comanche County	2	0.58
Kenwood, OK (cdp) Delaware County	7	0.57
Walker, PA (township) Schuylkill County	6	0.57
Cochiti, NM (cdp) Sandoval County	3	0.57
Camargo, OK (town) Dewey County	1	0.56
Dale, OK (cdp) Pottawatomie County	1	0.55
Hurtsboro, AL (town) Russell County	3	0.54
Welling, OK (cdp) Cherokee County	4	0.52
Broughton, IL (village) Hamilton County	1	0.52
Oktaha, OK (town) Muskogee County	2	0.51
Medford, OK (city) Grant County	5	0.50
Arapaho, OK (town) Custer County	4	0.50
Creedmoor, TX (city) Travis County	1	0.50
Greenview, CA (cdp) Siskiyou County	1	0.50
Peggs, OK (cdp) Cherokee County	4	0.49
Custer, MN (township) Lyon County	1	0.49
East Duke, OK (town) Jackson County	2	0.47
Dougherty, OK (town) Murray County	1	0.47
El Reno, OK (city) Canadian County	76	0.45
Beggs, OK (city) Okmulgee County	6	0.45
Cherry Tree, OK (cdp) Adair County	4	0.45
Taos Pueblo, NM (cdp) Taos County	5	0.44
Sentinel, OK (town) Washita County	4	0.44
Cuyamungue, NM (cdp) Santa Fe County	2	0.42
St. Johns, AZ (cdp) Maricopa County	2	0.42
Weatherford, OK (city) Custer County	44	0.41
Pawnee, OK (city) Pawnee County	9	0.41
Roff, OK (town) Pontotoc County	3	0.41
Johnson, OK (town) Pottawatomie County	1	0.40
Calumet, OK (town) Canadian County	2	0.39
Schulter, OK (town) Okmulgee County	2	0.39
Carter, OK (town) Beckham County	1	0.39
Doyle, TX (cdp) San Patricio County	1	0.39
Springdale, UT (town) Washington County	2	0.38
Longdale, OK (town) Blaine County	1	0.38
Laverne, OK (town) Harper County	5	0.37
Cashion, OK (town) Kingfisher County	3	0.37
Centennial, WY (cdp) Albany County	1	0.37
Chickaloon, AK (cdp) Matanuska-Susitna Borough	1	0.37
Hominy, OK (city) Osage County	13	0.36
Greenwood, MI (township) Oscoda County	4	0.36
Dill City, OK (town) Washita County	2	0.36
Bogata, TX (city) Red River County	4	0.35
Rock Springs, NM (cdp) McKinley County	2	0.35
Almira, WA (town) Lincoln County	1	0.35
Butler, OK (town) Custer County	1	0.35
Pink, OK (town) Pottawatomie County	7	0.34
Boley, OK (town) Okfuskee County	4	0.34
Bray, OK (town) Stephens County	4	0.33
Mashantucket, CT (cdp) New London County	1	0.33
Commerce, OK (city) Ottawa County	8	0.32
Geronimo, OK (town) Comanche County	4	0.32
Keystone, IA (city) Benton County	2	0.32
Welch, OK (town) Craig County	2	0.32
Davidson, OK (town) Tillman County	1	0.32
Pike Bay, MN (township) Cass County	5	0.31
Berryville, TX (town) Henderson County	3	0.31
Empire City, OK (town) Stephens County	3	0.31
Marine, IL (village) Madison County	3	0.31
Binger, OK (town) Caddo County	2	0.30
Eakly, OK (town) Caddo County	1	0.30
Vicco, KY (city) Perry County	1	0.30
Bernalillo, NM (town) Sandoval County	24	0.29
Granite, OK (town) Greer County	6	0.29
Holstein, IA (city) Ida County	4	0.29
Wauhillau, OK (cdp) Adair County	1	0.29
Park Hill, OK (cdp) Cherokee County	11	0.28
Turtle River, MN (township) Beltrami County	3	0.28
Jennings, OK (town) Pawnee County	1	0.28
St. Mary, MO (city) Ste. Genevieve County	1	0.28
Clinton, OK (city) Custer County	24	0.27
McLoud, OK (town) Pottawatomie County	11	0.27
Oaklawn-Sunview, KS (cdp) Sedgwick County	9	0.27
Meridian, OK (cdp) Stephens County	4	0.27
Chiloquin, OR (city) Klamath County	2	0.27
Lower Santan Village, AZ (cdp) Pinal County	1	0.27
Tecumseh, OK (city) Pottawatomie County	17	0.26
Kingfisher, OK (city) Kingfisher County	12	0.26
Byng, OK (town) Pontotoc County	3	0.26
Columbia, LA (town) Caldwell Parish	1	0.26
Mill Hall, PA (borough) Clinton County	4	0.25
Minco, OK (city) Grady County	4	0.25
Central High, OK (town) Stephens County	3	0.25
Williamsburg, KS (city) Franklin County	1	0.25
Shawnee, OK (city) Pottawatomie County	72	0.24
Holbrook, AZ (city) Navajo County	12	0.24
Spencerville, NM (cdp) San Juan County	3	0.24
Adelino, NM (cdp) Valencia County	2	0.24
Wadsworth, NV (cdp) Washoe County	2	0.24
Cushing, OK (city) Payne County	18	0.23
Kayenta, AZ (cdp) Navajo County	12	0.23
Verdigris, OK (town) Rogers County	9	0.23
Buffalo, OK (town) Harper County	3	0.23
Wetumka, OK (city) Hughes County	3	0.23
Virginia City, NV (cdp) Storey County	2	0.23

Please refer to the Explanation of Data in the front of the book for more detailed information.

Race

American Indian: Kiowa

Top 150 Places Sorted by Percent of Total Population

Based on places with total population of 7,500 or more

Place	Population	%
Lawton, OK (city) Comanche County	757	0.78
Chickasha, OK (city) Grady County	100	0.62
El Reno, OK (city) Canadian County	76	0.45
Weatherford, OK (city) Custer County	44	0.41
Bernalillo, NM (town) Sandoval County	24	0.29
Clinton, OK (city) Custer County	24	0.27
Shawnee, OK (city) Pottawatomie County	72	0.24
Cushing, OK (city) Payne County	18	0.23
Tahlequah, OK (city) Cherokee County	34	0.22
Del City, OK (city) Oklahoma County	42	0.20
Claremore, OK (city) Rogers County	37	0.20
Norman, OK (city) Cleveland County	212	0.19
Moore, OK (city) Cleveland County	100	0.18
Ada, OK (city) Pontotoc County	31	0.18
Oklahoma City, OK (city) Oklahoma County	950	0.16
Midwest City, OK (city) Oklahoma County	84	0.15
Duncan, OK (city) Stephens County	35	0.15
Yukon, OK (city) Canadian County	34	0.15
Okmulgee, OK (city) Okmulgee County	18	0.15
Warr Acres, OK (city) Oklahoma County	15	0.15
Altus, OK (city) Jackson County	27	0.14
Bethany, OK (city) Oklahoma County	26	0.14
Burkburnett, TX (city) Wichita County	14	0.13
Coweta, OK (city) Wagoner County	13	0.13
The Village, OK (city) Oklahoma County	11	0.12
Ponca City, OK (city) Kay County	28	0.11
Bartlesville, OK (city) Washington County	35	0.10
Ardmore, OK (city) Carter County	24	0.10
Pryor Creek, OK (city) Mayes County	10	0.10
Newcastle, OK (city) McClain County	7	0.09
McAlester, OK (city) Pittsburg County	14	0.08
Elk City, OK (city) Beckham County	9	0.08
Poteau, OK (city) Le Flore County	7	0.08
Crookston, MN (city) Polk County	6	0.08
Tulsa, OK (city) Tulsa County	276	0.07
Muskogee, OK (city) Muskogee County	29	0.07
Mustang, OK (city) Canadian County	13	0.07
Glenpool, OK (city) Tulsa County	8	0.07
Ocean Pointe, HI (cdp) Honolulu County	6	0.07
Lawrence, KS (city) Douglas County	56	0.06
Edmond, OK (city) Oklahoma County	48	0.06
Sand Springs, OK (city) Tulsa County	12	0.06
Augusta, KS (city) Butler County	6	0.06
Lansdowne, PA (borough) Delaware County	6	0.06
Summit, WA (cdp) Pierce County	5	0.06
Wichita, KS (city) Sedgwick County	174	0.05
Stillwater, OK (city) Payne County	23	0.05
Owasso, OK (city) Tulsa County	14	0.05
Sapulpa, OK (city) Creek County	11	0.05
Bixby, OK (city) Tulsa County	10	0.05
Gallup, NM (city) McKinley County	10	0.05
Jenks, OK (city) Tulsa County	8	0.05
Guthrie, OK (city) Logan County	5	0.05
Blanchard, OK (city) McClain County	4	0.05
Flowood, MS (city) Rankin County	4	0.05
Ketchikan, AK (city) Ketchikan Gateway Borough	4	0.05
Liberty Lake, WA (city) Spokane County	4	0.05
Ruidoso, NM (village) Lincoln County	4	0.05
St. Johns, MI (city) Clinton County	4	0.05
St. Marys, OH (city) Auglaize County	4	0.05
Wellington, KS (city) Sumner County	4	0.05
Porterville, CA (city) Tulare County	19	0.04
Vineyard, CA (cdp) Sacramento County	11	0.04
Radcliff, KY (city) Hardin County	9	0.04
Tukwila, WA (city) King County	8	0.04
Mill Creek East, WA (cdp) Snohomish County	6	0.04
Grovetown, GA (city) Columbia County	5	0.04
Miami, OK (city) Ottawa County	5	0.04
Excelsior Springs, MO (city) Clay County	4	0.04
Show Low, AZ (city) Navajo County	4	0.04
West Hanover, PA (township) Dauphin County	4	0.04
Cortez, CO (city) Montezuma County	3	0.04
Fairwood, WA (cdp) Spokane County	3	0.04
Smithfield, VA (town) Isle of Wight County	3	0.04
Temperance, MI (cdp) Monroe County	3	0.04
Albuquerque, NM (city) Bernalillo County	141	0.03
Davenport, IA (city) Scott County	31	0.03
Wichita Falls, TX (city) Wichita County	30	0.03
Santa Fe, NM (city) Santa Fe County	21	0.03
Flagstaff, AZ (city) Coconino County	18	0.03
Farmington, NM (city) San Juan County	15	0.03
Clovis, NM (city) Curry County	10	0.03
Bonney Lake, WA (city) Pierce County	6	0.03
Derby, KS (city) Sedgwick County	6	0.03
Saginaw, TX (city) Tarrant County	6	0.03
West Puente Valley, CA (cdp) Los Angeles County	6	0.03
Knik-Fairview, AK (cdp) Matanuska-Susitna Borough	5	0.03
Menasha, WI (town) Winnebago County	5	0.03
Sherrelwood, CO (cdp) Adams County	5	0.03
Arkansas City, KS (city) Cowley County	4	0.03
Bangor, MI (charter township) Bay County	4	0.03
Clive, IA (city) Polk County	4	0.03
Forney, TX (city) Kaufman County	4	0.03
Fort Carson, CO (cdp) El Paso County	4	0.03
Lakeland Village, CA (cdp) Riverside County	4	0.03
Phelan, CA (cdp) San Bernardino County	4	0.03
Diamond Springs, CA (cdp) El Dorado County	3	0.03
Espanola, NM (city) Rio Arriba County	3	0.03
Ironton, OH (city) Lawrence County	3	0.03
Mandeville, LA (city) St. Tammany Parish	3	0.03
Mountain Top, PA (cdp) Luzerne County	3	0.03
North Valley, NM (cdp) Bernalillo County	3	0.03
Redlands, CO (cdp) Mesa County	3	0.03
Silverton, OR (city) Marion County	3	0.03
Union, MO (city) Franklin County	3	0.03
Vernal, UT (city) Uintah County	3	0.03
Webster, TX (city) Harris County	3	0.03
Winslow, AZ (city) Navajo County	3	0.03
Dalhart, TX (city) Dallam County	2	0.03
Harrison, TN (cdp) Hamilton County	2	0.03
Honey Brook, PA (township) Chester County	2	0.03
Wasilla, AK (city) Matanuska-Susitna Borough	2	0.03
Grand Prairie, TX (city) Dallas County	38	0.02
Denton, TX (city) Denton County	23	0.02
Broken Arrow, OK (city) Tulsa County	20	0.02
North Richland Hills, TX (city) Tarrant County	11	0.02
Casa Grande, AZ (city) Pinal County	10	0.02
Rogers, AR (city) Benton County	10	0.02
Brentwood, CA (city) Contra Costa County	8	0.02
Fort Hood, TX (cdp) Bell County	7	0.02
Bell, CA (city) Los Angeles County	6	0.02
Gurnee, IL (village) Lake County	6	0.02
Kyle, TX (city) Hays County	6	0.02
Sherman, TX (city) Grayson County	6	0.02
Bella Vista, AR (town) Benton County	5	0.02
Denison, TX (city) Grayson County	5	0.02
Harker Heights, TX (city) Bell County	5	0.02
McCandless, PA (township) Allegheny County	5	0.02
Mililani Mauka, HI (cdp) Honolulu County	5	0.02
Carlsbad, NM (city) Eddy County	4	0.02
Coralville, IA (city) Johnson County	4	0.02
Derry, NH (cdp) Rockingham County	4	0.02
Mint Hill, NC (town) Mecklenburg County	4	0.02
San Fernando, CA (city) Los Angeles County	4	0.02
San Lorenzo, CA (cdp) Alameda County	4	0.02
White Settlement, TX (city) Tarrant County	4	0.02
Cañon City, CO (city) Fremont County	3	0.02
Dumas, TX (city) Moore County	3	0.02
Effingham, IL (city) Effingham County	3	0.02
Happy Valley, OR (city) Clackamas County	3	0.02
Herrin, IL (city) Williamson County	3	0.02
Kingston, PA (borough) Luzerne County	3	0.02
Lemon Hill, CA (cdp) Sacramento County	3	0.02
Ottawa, KS (city) Franklin County	3	0.02
Plumstead, PA (township) Bucks County	3	0.02
Wells Branch, TX (cdp) Travis County	3	0.02
Azalea Park, FL (cdp) Orange County	2	0.02
Canyon, TX (city) Randall County	2	0.02
Chamblee, GA (city) DeKalb County	2	0.02
Choctaw, OK (city) Oklahoma County	2	0.02

SECTION THREE

Please refer to the Explanation of Data in the front of the book for more detailed information.

Race

American Indian: Lumbee

U.S. and 50 States Sorted by Population and Percent of Total Population

Place	Population	%
United States	**73,691**	**0.02**
North Carolina	58,306	0.61
South Carolina	2,212	0.05
Maryland	1,715	0.03
Florida	1,459	0.01
Virginia	1,302	0.02
Michigan	1,130	0.01
California	855	<0.01
Georgia	765	0.01
Texas	642	<0.01
Pennsylvania	505	<0.01
Tennessee	409	0.01
Ohio	406	<0.01
New York	304	<0.01
Washington	293	<0.01
Alabama	239	0.01
Arizona	215	<0.01
Illinois	205	<0.01
New Jersey	200	<0.01
Indiana	189	<0.01
Colorado	186	<0.01
Missouri	171	<0.01
Kentucky	147	<0.01
Oregon	139	<0.01
Oklahoma	137	<0.01
Kansas	118	<0.01
Connecticut	112	<0.01
Massachusetts	103	<0.01
Arkansas	100	<0.01
Wisconsin	98	<0.01
Louisiana	88	<0.01
Nevada	80	<0.01
West Virginia	76	<0.01
New Mexico	74	<0.01
Alaska	73	0.01
Hawaii	61	<0.01
Utah	61	<0.01
Idaho	60	<0.01
Iowa	57	<0.01
Delaware	54	0.01
Minnesota	54	<0.01
Mississippi	54	<0.01
New Hampshire	49	<0.01
District of Columbia	35	0.01
Maine	30	<0.01
Nebraska	24	<0.01
Rhode Island	23	<0.01
Montana	21	<0.01
North Dakota	18	<0.01
Wyoming	13	<0.01
South Dakota	12	<0.01
Vermont	12	<0.01

Place	Population	%
North Carolina	58,306	0.61
South Carolina	2,212	0.05
Maryland	1,715	0.03
United States	**73,691**	**0.02**
Virginia	1,302	0.02
Florida	1,459	0.01
Michigan	1,130	0.01
Georgia	765	0.01
Tennessee	409	0.01
Alabama	239	0.01
Alaska	73	0.01
Delaware	54	0.01
District of Columbia	35	0.01
California	855	<0.01
Texas	642	<0.01
Pennsylvania	505	<0.01
Ohio	406	<0.01
New York	304	<0.01
Washington	293	<0.01
Arizona	215	<0.01
Illinois	205	<0.01
New Jersey	200	<0.01
Indiana	189	<0.01
Colorado	186	<0.01
Missouri	171	<0.01
Kentucky	147	<0.01
Oregon	139	<0.01
Oklahoma	137	<0.01
Kansas	118	<0.01
Connecticut	112	<0.01
Massachusetts	103	<0.01
Arkansas	100	<0.01
Wisconsin	98	<0.01
Louisiana	88	<0.01
Nevada	80	<0.01
West Virginia	76	<0.01
New Mexico	74	<0.01
Hawaii	61	<0.01
Utah	61	<0.01
Idaho	60	<0.01
Iowa	57	<0.01
Minnesota	54	<0.01
Mississippi	54	<0.01
New Hampshire	49	<0.01
Maine	30	<0.01
Nebraska	24	<0.01
Rhode Island	23	<0.01
Montana	21	<0.01
North Dakota	18	<0.01
Wyoming	13	<0.01
South Dakota	12	<0.01
Vermont	12	<0.01

Please refer to the Explanation of Data in the front of the book for more detailed information.

Race

American Indian: Lumbee

Top 150 Places Sorted by Population

Based on all places, regardless of total population

Place	Population	%
Lumberton, NC (city) Robeson County	1,952	9.06
Pembroke, NC (town) Robeson County	1,599	53.78
Fayetteville, NC (city) Cumberland County	893	0.45
Charlotte, NC (city) Mecklenburg County	763	0.10
Prospect, NC (cdp) Robeson County	754	76.86
Laurinburg, NC (city) Scotland County	662	4.15
Greensboro, NC (city) Guilford County	488	0.18
Raleigh, NC (city) Wake County	392	0.10
Baltimore, MD (city) Baltimore city County	335	0.05
Red Springs, NC (town) Robeson County	301	8.78
Fairmont, NC (town) Robeson County	274	10.29
Dundalk, MD (cdp) Baltimore County	232	0.36
Elrod, NC (cdp) Robeson County	217	52.04
Maxton, NC (town) Robeson County	215	8.86
Winston-Salem, NC (city) Forsyth County	180	0.08
Hope Mills, NC (town) Cumberland County	177	1.17
Raemon, NC (cdp) Robeson County	163	57.80
High Point, NC (city) Guilford County	161	0.15
Durham, NC (city) Durham County	155	0.07
Rennert, NC (town) Robeson County	127	33.16
Jacksonville, FL (city) Duval County	127	0.02
Cary, NC (town) Wake County	124	0.09
Philadelphia, PA (city) Philadelphia County	121	0.01
Wilmington, NC (city) New Hanover County	120	0.11
Virginia Beach, VA (ind. city) Virginia Beach independent city	120	0.03
Raeford, NC (city) Hoke County	114	2.47
Barker Ten Mile, NC (cdp) Robeson County	110	11.55
Chesapeake, VA (ind. city) Chesapeake independent city	99	0.04
Laurel Hill, NC (cdp) Scotland County	90	7.18
Rockingham, NC (city) Richmond County	89	0.93
New York, NY (city) Kings County	89	<0.01
Shannon, NC (cdp) Robeson County	87	33.08
Concord, NC (city) Cabarrus County	87	0.11
Indian Trail, NC (town) Union County	86	0.26
Jacksonville, NC (city) Onslow County	77	0.11
Warren, MI (city) Macomb County	77	0.06
Greenville, NC (city) Pitt County	72	0.09
St. Pauls, NC (town) Robeson County	70	3.44
Thomasville, NC (city) Davidson County	70	0.26
Norfolk, VA (ind. city) Norfolk independent city	69	0.03
Wakulla, NC (cdp) Robeson County	68	64.76
Essex, MD (cdp) Baltimore County	66	0.17
Chapel Hill, NC (town) Orange County	65	0.11
Los Angeles, CA (city) Los Angeles County	59	<0.01
Mint Hill, NC (town) Mecklenburg County	58	0.26
Tampa, FL (city) Hillsborough County	57	0.02
McColl, SC (town) Marlboro County	56	2.58
Columbus, OH (city) Franklin County	56	0.01
Hampton, VA (ind. city) Hampton independent city	53	0.04
Aberdeen, NC (town) Moore County	52	0.82
Rockfish, NC (cdp) Hoke County	51	1.55
Middle River, MD (cdp) Baltimore County	49	0.19
Wagram, NC (town) Scotland County	48	5.71
Detroit, MI (city) Wayne County	48	0.01
Monroe, NC (city) Union County	47	0.14
East Rockingham, NC (cdp) Richmond County	46	1.23
Hamlet, NC (city) Richmond County	46	0.71
Gibson, NC (town) Scotland County	45	8.33
Glen Burnie, MD (cdp) Anne Arundel County	45	0.07
Newport News, VA (ind. city) Newport News independent city	45	0.02
San Diego, CA (city) San Diego County	45	<0.01
Gastonia, NC (city) Gaston County	44	0.06
Taylor, MI (city) Wayne County	43	0.07
Archdale, NC (city) Randolph County	42	0.37
Huntersville, NC (town) Mecklenburg County	42	0.09
Sanford, NC (city) Lee County	41	0.15
Kannapolis, NC (city) Cabarrus County	40	0.09
Eastover, NC (town) Cumberland County	38	1.05
Matthews, NC (town) Mecklenburg County	38	0.14
Burlington, NC (city) Alamance County	38	0.08
North Charleston, SC (city) Charleston County	38	0.04
El Paso, TX (city) El Paso County	38	0.01
Phoenix, AZ (city) Maricopa County	38	<0.01
Ashley Heights, NC (cdp) Hoke County	37	9.74
Southern Pines, NC (town) Moore County	37	0.30

Place	Population	%
Stallings, NC (town) Union County	37	0.27
Asheville, NC (city) Buncombe County	37	0.04
Kernersville, NC (town) Forsyth County	35	0.15
Mooresville, NC (town) Iredell County	35	0.11
Washington, DC (city) District of Columbia	35	0.01
Pinehurst, NC (village) Moore County	34	0.26
Holly Springs, NC (town) Wake County	33	0.13
Colorado Springs, CO (city) El Paso County	33	0.01
Lincoln Park, MI (city) Wayne County	32	0.08
East Laurinburg, NC (town) Scotland County	31	10.33
Rowland, NC (town) Robeson County	31	2.99
Chadbourn, NC (town) Columbus County	31	1.67
Garner, NC (town) Wake County	31	0.12
Dillon, SC (city) Dillon County	30	0.44
Asheboro, NC (city) Randolph County	30	0.12
Albuquerque, NM (city) Bernalillo County	30	0.01
Queens, NY (borough) Queens County	30	<0.01
Eden, NC (city) Rockingham County	29	0.19
Florence, SC (city) Florence County	29	0.08
Atlanta, GA (city) Fulton County	29	0.01
Fort Worth, TX (city) Tarrant County	29	<0.01
Morrisville, NC (town) Wake County	28	0.15
Sumter, SC (city) Sumter County	28	0.07
St. Clair Shores, MI (city) Macomb County	28	0.05
Anchorage, AK (municipality) Anchorage Municipality	28	0.01
Richmond, VA (ind. city) Richmond independent city	28	0.01
Austin, TX (city) Travis County	28	<0.01
Nashville-Davidson, TN (metro govt) Davidson County	28	<0.01
Clarksville, TN (city) Montgomery County	27	0.02
Whiteville, NC (city) Columbus County	26	0.48
Columbia, SC (city) Richland County	26	0.02
Huntsville, AL (city) Madison County	26	0.01
Oklahoma City, OK (city) Oklahoma County	26	<0.01
McDonald, NC (town) Robeson County	25	22.12
Clio, SC (town) Marlboro County	25	3.44
Apex, NC (town) Wake County	25	0.07
Shelby, MI (charter township) Macomb County	25	0.03
Chicago, IL (city) Cook County	25	<0.01
Bennettsville, SC (city) Marlboro County	24	0.26
Fuquay-Varina, NC (town) Wake County	24	0.13
Goldsboro, NC (city) Wayne County	24	0.07
Rocky Mount, NC (city) Nash County	24	0.04
Knoxville, TN (city) Knox County	24	0.01
Tulsa, OK (city) Tulsa County	24	0.01
Brooklyn, NY (borough) Kings County	24	<0.01
Old Hundred, NC (cdp) Scotland County	23	8.01
Hazel Park, MI (city) Oakland County	23	0.14
Salisbury, NC (city) Rowan County	23	0.07
Wilson, NC (city) Wilson County	23	0.05
Augusta-Richmond County, GA (cons. govt) Richmond County	23	0.01
Denver, CO (city) Denver County	23	<0.01
Red Hill, SC (cdp) Horry County	22	0.17
Leland, NC (town) Brunswick County	22	0.16
Mount Holly, NC (city) Gaston County	22	0.16
Navarre, FL (cdp) Santa Rosa County	22	0.07
New Bern, NC (city) Craven County	22	0.07
Longview, WA (city) Cowlitz County	22	0.06
Hempstead, NY (town) Nassau County	22	<0.01
Manhattan, NY (borough) New York County	21	<0.01
Five Points, NC (cdp) Hoke County	20	2.90
Hickory, NC (city) Catawba County	20	0.05
Roseville, MI (city) Macomb County	20	0.04
Killeen, TX (city) Bell County	20	0.02
Livonia, MI (city) Wayne County	20	0.02
Portsmouth, VA (ind. city) Portsmouth independent city	20	0.02
Sterling Heights, MI (city) Macomb County	20	0.02
Westland, MI (city) Wayne County	20	0.02
Louisville-Jefferson County, KY (metro govt) Jefferson County	20	<0.01
Seattle, WA (city) King County	20	<0.01
Tucson, AZ (city) Pima County	20	<0.01
Clayton, NC (town) Johnston County	19	0.12
Pasadena, MD (cdp) Anne Arundel County	19	0.08
Carney, MD (cdp) Baltimore County	19	0.06
Eastpointe, MI (city) Macomb County	19	0.06
Goose Creek, SC (city) Berkeley County	19	0.05

Race

American Indian: Lumbee

Top 150 Places Sorted by Percent of Total Population

Based on all places, regardless of total population

Place	Population	%
Prospect, NC (cdp) Robeson County	754	76.86
Wakulla, NC (cdp) Robeson County	68	64.76
Raemon, NC (cdp) Robeson County	163	57.80
Pembroke, NC (town) Robeson County	1,599	53.78
Elrod, NC (cdp) Robeson County	217	52.04
Rennert, NC (town) Robeson County	127	33.16
Shannon, NC (cdp) Robeson County	87	33.08
McDonald, NC (town) Robeson County	25	22.12
Rex, NC (cdp) Robeson County	11	20.00
Bowmore, NC (cdp) Hoke County	12	11.65
Barker Ten Mile, NC (cdp) Robeson County	110	11.55
East Laurinburg, NC (town) Scotland County	31	10.33
Fairmont, NC (town) Robeson County	274	10.29
Ashley Heights, NC (cdp) Hoke County	37	9.74
Raynham, NC (town) Robeson County	7	9.72
Lumberton, NC (city) Robeson County	1,952	9.06
Maxton, NC (town) Robeson County	215	8.86
Red Springs, NC (town) Robeson County	301	8.78
Gibson, NC (town) Scotland County	45	8.33
Old Hundred, NC (cdp) Scotland County	23	8.01
Dundarrach, NC (cdp) Hoke County	3	7.32
Laurel Hill, NC (cdp) Scotland County	90	7.18
West Denton, MD (cdp) Caroline County	3	5.77
Wagram, NC (town) Scotland County	48	5.71
Proctorville, NC (town) Robeson County	6	5.13
Pantego, NC (town) Beaufort County	9	5.03
Orrum, NC (town) Robeson County	4	4.40
Lumber Bridge, NC (town) Robeson County	4	4.26
Laurinburg, NC (city) Scotland County	662	4.15
Parkton, NC (town) Robeson County	16	3.67
St. Pauls, NC (town) Robeson County	70	3.44
Clio, SC (town) Marlboro County	25	3.44
Wing, ND (city) Burleigh County	5	3.29
Rowland, NC (town) Robeson County	31	2.99
Five Points, NC (cdp) Hoke County	20	2.90
Hoffman, NC (town) Richmond County	17	2.89
McColl, SC (town) Marlboro County	56	2.58
Raeford, NC (city) Hoke County	114	2.47
Cerro Gordo, NC (town) Columbus County	5	2.42
Port Protection, AK (cdp) Prince of Wales-Hyder Census Area	1	2.08
Scotch Meadows, NC (cdp) Scotland County	12	2.07
Dublin, NC (town) Bladen County	7	2.07
Kinde, MI (village) Huron County	8	1.79
High Shoals, NC (town) Gaston County	12	1.72
Deercroft, NC (cdp) Scotland County	7	1.70
Chadbourn, NC (town) Columbus County	31	1.67
Rockfish, NC (cdp) Hoke County	51	1.55
Bennett, NC (cdp) Chatham County	4	1.42
Tatum, SC (town) Marlboro County	1	1.33
Staley, NC (town) Randolph County	5	1.27
Sand Fork, WV (town) Gilmer County	2	1.26
East Rockingham, NC (cdp) Richmond County	46	1.23
Port Deposit, MD (town) Cecil County	8	1.23
Vander, NC (cdp) Cumberland County	14	1.22
Port Wing, WI (cdp) Bayfield County	2	1.22
Hope Mills, NC (town) Cumberland County	177	1.17
Patrick, SC (town) Chesterfield County	4	1.14
Addy, WA (cdp) Stevens County	3	1.12
Medon, TN (city) Madison County	2	1.12
Vass, NC (town) Moore County	8	1.11
Ruffin, NC (cdp) Rockingham County	4	1.09
Bakersville, NC (town) Mitchell County	5	1.08
Eastover, NC (town) Cumberland County	38	1.05
Lincoln, MI (township) Huron County	8	0.99
Spivey's Corner, NC (cdp) Sampson County	5	0.99
Rodeo, NM (cdp) Hidalgo County	1	0.99
Clarkton, NC (town) Bladen County	8	0.96
Rockingham, NC (city) Richmond County	89	0.93
Bunnlevel, NC (cdp) Harnett County	5	0.91
Wallace, SC (cdp) Marlboro County	8	0.90
Bonnetsville, NC (cdp) Sampson County	4	0.90
Bethune, SC (town) Kershaw County	3	0.90
Marseilles, OH (village) Wyandot County	1	0.89
Hemingway, SC (town) Williamsburg County	4	0.87
Riegelwood, NC (cdp) Columbus County	5	0.86
Allisonia, VA (cdp) Pulaski County	1	0.85
Charlos Heights, MT (cdp) Ravalli County	1	0.83
Aberdeen, NC (town) Moore County	52	0.82
East Arcadia, NC (town) Bladen County	4	0.82
Cherokee, NC (cdp) Jackson County	17	0.80
Garland, NC (town) Sampson County	5	0.80
Lake Mystic, FL (cdp) Liberty County	4	0.80
Cordova, NC (cdp) Richmond County	14	0.79
Morven, NC (town) Anson County	4	0.78
Carthage, NC (town) Moore County	17	0.77
Limestone, NY (village) Cattaraugus County	3	0.77
Rodanthe, NC (cdp) Dare County	2	0.77
Monroe, NH (town) Grafton County	6	0.76
Chevy Chase Section Five, MD (village) Montgomery County	5	0.76
Garwin, IA (city) Tama County	4	0.76
Lake Waccamaw, NC (town) Columbus County	11	0.74
Opal, VA (cdp) Fauquier County	5	0.72
Bakerhill, AL (town) Barbour County	2	0.72
Hamlet, NC (city) Richmond County	46	0.71
Quinby, VA (cdp) Accomack County	2	0.71
Bear Lake, MI (village) Manistee County	2	0.70
Stedman, NC (town) Cumberland County	7	0.68
Hemby Bridge, NC (town) Union County	10	0.66
Stem, NC (town) Granville County	3	0.65
Blenheim, SC (town) Marlboro County	1	0.65
Buckshot, AZ (cdp) Yuma County	1	0.65
Round Mountain, CA (cdp) Shasta County	1	0.65
Ingold, NC (cdp) Sampson County	3	0.64
Wellston, MI (cdp) Manistee County	2	0.64
Grass Lake, MI (village) Jackson County	7	0.60
Hackett, WI (town) Price County	1	0.59
Midland, NC (town) Cabarrus County	17	0.55
Point Comfort, TX (city) Calhoun County	4	0.54
Port Wing, WI (town) Bayfield County	2	0.54
Dairyland, WI (town) Douglas County	1	0.54
Ponderay, ID (city) Bonner County	6	0.53
Dortches, NC (town) Nash County	5	0.53
Metamora, MI (village) Lapeer County	3	0.53
Legend Lake, WI (cdp) Menominee County	8	0.52
Pinebluff, NC (town) Moore County	7	0.52
Winton, NC (town) Hertford County	4	0.52
Crossnore, NC (town) Avery County	1	0.52
Mesick, MI (village) Wexford County	2	0.51
Wagener, SC (town) Aiken County	4	0.50
Camden, NC (cdp) Camden County	3	0.50
Lake View, TX (cdp) Val Verde County	1	0.50
Pine Harbor, TX (cdp) Marion County	4	0.49
Sheyenne, ND (city) Eddy County	1	0.49
Whiteville, NC (city) Columbus County	26	0.48
Candor, NC (town) Montgomery County	4	0.48
Hoopers Creek, NC (cdp) Henderson County	5	0.47
Wallburg, NC (town) Davidson County	14	0.46
Star, NC (town) Montgomery County	4	0.46
North Powder, OR (city) Union County	2	0.46
Salemburg, NC (town) Sampson County	2	0.46
Fayetteville, NC (city) Cumberland County	893	0.45
Silver City, NC (cdp) Hoke County	4	0.45
Shinnecock Reservation, NY (reservation) Suffolk County	3	0.45
Dillon, SC (city) Dillon County	30	0.44
Valley Home, CA (cdp) Stanislaus County	1	0.44
Hallsboro, NC (cdp) Columbus County	2	0.43
Mount Vernon, SD (city) Davison County	2	0.43
Norwood, NC (town) Stanly County	10	0.42
Princeton, NC (town) Johnston County	5	0.42
Taylor, NC (town) Moore County	3	0.42
Liberty, NC (town) Randolph County	11	0.41
Plain View, NC (cdp) Sampson County	8	0.41
Harrison, IL (cdp) Jackson County	4	0.41
Tabor City, NC (town) Columbus County	10	0.40
Bladenboro, NC (town) Bladen County	7	0.40
Newark, IL (village) Kendall County	4	0.40
Argyle, MI (township) Sanilac County	3	0.40
Newfield Hamlet, NY (cdp) Tompkins County	3	0.40
Lakewood Club, MI (village) Muskegon County	5	0.39
Sonora, KY (city) Hardin County	2	0.39

Race

American Indian: Lumbee

Top 150 Places Sorted by Percent of Total Population

Based on places with total population of 7,500 or more

Place	Population	%
Lumberton, NC (city) Robeson County	1,952	9.06
Laurinburg, NC (city) Scotland County	662	4.15
Hope Mills, NC (town) Cumberland County	177	1.17
Rockingham, NC (city) Richmond County	89	0.93
Fayetteville, NC (city) Cumberland County	893	0.45
Archdale, NC (city) Randolph County	42	0.37
Dundalk, MD (cdp) Baltimore County	232	0.36
Southern Pines, NC (town) Moore County	37	0.30
Stallings, NC (town) Union County	37	0.27
Indian Trail, NC (town) Union County	86	0.26
Thomasville, NC (city) Davidson County	70	0.26
Mint Hill, NC (town) Mecklenburg County	58	0.26
Pinehurst, NC (village) Moore County	34	0.26
Bennettsville, SC (city) Marlboro County	24	0.26
Clinton, NC (city) Sampson County	18	0.21
Middle River, MD (cdp) Baltimore County	49	0.19
Eden, NC (city) Rockingham County	29	0.19
Greensboro, NC (city) Guilford County	488	0.18
Dunn, NC (city) Harnett County	17	0.18
Essex, MD (cdp) Baltimore County	66	0.17
Red Hill, SC (cdp) Horry County	22	0.17
Morehead City, NC (town) Carteret County	15	0.17
Leland, NC (town) Brunswick County	22	0.16
Mount Holly, NC (city) Gaston County	22	0.16
Sebring, FL (city) Highlands County	17	0.16
Belmont, NC (city) Gaston County	16	0.16
Summerfield, NC (town) Guilford County	16	0.16
High Point, NC (city) Guilford County	161	0.15
Sanford, NC (city) Lee County	41	0.15
Kernersville, NC (town) Forsyth County	35	0.15
Morrisville, NC (town) Wake County	28	0.15
Siler City, NC (town) Chatham County	12	0.15
Monroe, NC (city) Union County	47	0.14
Matthews, NC (town) Mecklenburg County	38	0.14
Hazel Park, MI (city) Oakland County	23	0.14
Myrtle Grove, NC (cdp) New Hanover County	12	0.14
Holly Springs, NC (town) Wake County	33	0.13
Fuquay-Varina, NC (town) Wake County	24	0.13
Graham, NC (city) Alamance County	18	0.13
Harrisburg, NC (town) Cabarrus County	15	0.13
Spring Lake, NC (town) Cumberland County	15	0.13
Garner, NC (town) Wake County	31	0.12
Asheboro, NC (city) Randolph County	30	0.12
Clayton, NC (town) Johnston County	19	0.12
Cayce, SC (city) Lexington County	15	0.12
Riviera Beach, MD (cdp) Anne Arundel County	15	0.12
Half Moon, NC (cdp) Onslow County	10	0.12
Butner, NC (town) Granville County	9	0.12
Wilmington, NC (city) New Hanover County	120	0.11
Concord, NC (city) Cabarrus County	87	0.11
Jacksonville, NC (city) Onslow County	77	0.11
Chapel Hill, NC (town) Orange County	65	0.11
Mooresville, NC (town) Iredell County	35	0.11
Waxhaw, NC (town) Union County	11	0.11
Kings Grant, NC (cdp) New Hanover County	9	0.11
Sangaree, SC (cdp) Berkeley County	9	0.11
Charlotte, NC (city) Mecklenburg County	763	0.10
Raleigh, NC (city) Wake County	392	0.10
Lexington, NC (city) Davidson County	18	0.10
Fort Mill, SC (town) York County	11	0.10
Flat Rock, MI (city) Wayne County	10	0.10
Edgemere, MD (cdp) Baltimore County	9	0.10
Fort Bliss, TX (cdp) El Paso County	9	0.10
Franklin, VA (ind. city) Franklin independent city	9	0.10
Little River, SC (cdp) Horry County	9	0.10
St. Stephens, NC (cdp) Catawba County	9	0.10
Jefferson City, TN (city) Jefferson County	8	0.10
Mapleton, UT (city) Utah County	8	0.10
Mayo, MD (cdp) Anne Arundel County	8	0.10
Roxboro, NC (city) Person County	8	0.10
Cary, NC (town) Wake County	124	0.09
Greenville, NC (city) Pitt County	72	0.09
Huntersville, NC (town) Mecklenburg County	42	0.09
Kannapolis, NC (city) Cabarrus County	40	0.09
Carrboro, NC (town) Orange County	18	0.09
Rosedale, MD (cdp) Baltimore County	17	0.09
Conway, SC (city) Horry County	15	0.09
Lewisville, NC (town) Forsyth County	12	0.09
Piney Green, NC (cdp) Onslow County	12	0.09
Kelso, WA (city) Cowlitz County	11	0.09
Mansfield, NJ (township) Burlington County	8	0.09
Pasadena Hills, FL (cdp) Pasco County	7	0.09
Winston-Salem, NC (city) Forsyth County	180	0.08
Burlington, NC (city) Alamance County	38	0.08
Lincoln Park, MI (city) Wayne County	32	0.08
Florence, SC (city) Florence County	29	0.08
Pasadena, MD (cdp) Anne Arundel County	19	0.08
Montclair, VA (cdp) Prince William County	16	0.08
Boone, NC (town) Watauga County	13	0.08
Ferndale, MD (cdp) Anne Arundel County	13	0.08
Albemarle, NC (city) Stanly County	12	0.08
Fraser, MI (city) Macomb County	12	0.08
Murraysville, NC (cdp) New Hanover County	12	0.08
Reidsville, NC (city) Rockingham County	11	0.08
New Baltimore, MI (city) Macomb County	10	0.08
Newton, NC (city) Catawba County	10	0.08
Mount Airy, NC (city) Surry County	8	0.08
Fort Meade, MD (cdp) Anne Arundel County	7	0.08
Hartsville, SC (city) Darlington County	6	0.08
Moncks Corner, SC (town) Berkeley County	6	0.08
Durham, NC (city) Durham County	155	0.07
Glen Burnie, MD (cdp) Anne Arundel County	45	0.07
Taylor, MI (city) Wayne County	43	0.07
Sumter, SC (city) Sumter County	28	0.07
Apex, NC (town) Wake County	25	0.07
Goldsboro, NC (city) Wayne County	24	0.07
Salisbury, NC (city) Rowan County	23	0.07
Navarre, FL (cdp) Santa Rosa County	22	0.07
New Bern, NC (city) Craven County	22	0.07
Cornelius, NC (town) Mecklenburg County	17	0.07
Statesville, NC (city) Iredell County	17	0.07
Lake Shore, MD (cdp) Anne Arundel County	14	0.07
Simpsonville, SC (city) Greenville County	12	0.07
Bedford, IN (city) Lawrence County	10	0.07
Brooklyn Park, MD (cdp) Anne Arundel County	10	0.07
North Myrtle Beach, SC (city) Horry County	10	0.07
Rossville, MD (cdp) Baltimore County	10	0.07
Mebane, NC (city) Alamance County	8	0.07
Overlea, MD (cdp) Baltimore County	8	0.07
Weddington, NC (town) Union County	7	0.07
Garden City, SC (cdp) Horry County	6	0.07
Smithfield, VA (town) Isle of Wight County	6	0.07
Union, SC (city) Union County	6	0.07
Urbana, MD (cdp) Frederick County	6	0.07
York, MI (charter township) Washtenaw County	6	0.07
Williamsburg, FL (cdp) Orange County	5	0.07
Warren, MI (city) Macomb County	77	0.06
Gastonia, NC (city) Gaston County	44	0.06
Longview, WA (city) Cowlitz County	22	0.06
Carney, MD (cdp) Baltimore County	19	0.06
Eastpointe, MI (city) Macomb County	19	0.06
Bel Air North, MD (cdp) Harford County	17	0.06
Parkville, MD (cdp) Baltimore County	17	0.06
Myrtle Beach, SC (city) Horry County	16	0.06
Washington, MI (township) Macomb County	15	0.06
Havelock, NC (city) Craven County	13	0.06
Socastee, SC (cdp) Horry County	12	0.06
Colonial Heights, VA (ind. city) Colonial Heights independent city	10	0.06
Sudley, VA (cdp) Prince William County	10	0.06
Henderson, NC (city) Vance County	9	0.06
Manassas Park, VA (ind. city) Manassas Park independent city	8	0.06
Mount Vernon, VA (cdp) Fairfax County	8	0.06
Davidson, NC (town) Mecklenburg County	7	0.06
Georgetown, GA (cdp) Chatham County	7	0.06
Fort Knox, KY (cdp) Hardin County	6	0.06
Howell, MI (city) Livingston County	6	0.06
London, OH (city) Madison County	6	0.06
White Marsh, MD (cdp) Baltimore County	6	0.06
Clay, MI (township) St. Clair County	5	0.06
Seneca, SC (city) Oconee County	5	0.06

SECTION THREE

Please refer to the Explanation of Data in the front of the book for more detailed information.

Race

American Indian: Menominee

U.S. and 50 States Sorted by Population and Percent of Total Population

Place	Population	%
United States	**11,133**	**<0.01**
Wisconsin	8,388	0.15
Illinois	390	<0.01
California	316	<0.01
Michigan	212	<0.01
Minnesota	176	<0.01
Florida	121	<0.01
Texas	109	<0.01
Oregon	106	<0.01
Washington	95	<0.01
Arizona	90	<0.01
Colorado	82	<0.01
Kansas	72	<0.01
Indiana	71	<0.01
Ohio	66	<0.01
Alaska	54	0.01
Georgia	51	<0.01
Oklahoma	51	<0.01
New Mexico	49	<0.01
North Carolina	49	<0.01
Maryland	47	<0.01
Missouri	43	<0.01
Iowa	42	<0.01
New York	41	<0.01
Virginia	39	<0.01
Hawaii	35	<0.01
Nevada	33	<0.01
Nebraska	28	<0.01
Pennsylvania	27	<0.01
Tennessee	27	<0.01
South Dakota	24	<0.01
Idaho	21	<0.01
Massachusetts	20	<0.01
Utah	18	<0.01
North Dakota	16	<0.01
Montana	15	<0.01
South Carolina	15	<0.01
Arkansas	13	<0.01
Kentucky	13	<0.01
Louisiana	10	<0.01
Mississippi	10	<0.01
New Jersey	9	<0.01
Connecticut	7	<0.01
New Hampshire	6	<0.01
Rhode Island	6	<0.01
Alabama	5	<0.01
Delaware	5	<0.01
West Virginia	4	<0.01
Wyoming	3	<0.01
Maine	2	<0.01
District of Columbia	1	<0.01
Vermont	0	0.00

Place	Population	%
Wisconsin	8,388	0.15
Alaska	54	0.01
United States	**11,133**	**<0.01**
Illinois	390	<0.01
California	316	<0.01
Michigan	212	<0.01
Minnesota	176	<0.01
Florida	121	<0.01
Texas	109	<0.01
Oregon	106	<0.01
Washington	95	<0.01
Arizona	90	<0.01
Colorado	82	<0.01
Kansas	72	<0.01
Indiana	71	<0.01
Ohio	66	<0.01
Georgia	51	<0.01
Oklahoma	51	<0.01
New Mexico	49	<0.01
North Carolina	49	<0.01
Maryland	47	<0.01
Missouri	43	<0.01
Iowa	42	<0.01
New York	41	<0.01
Virginia	39	<0.01
Hawaii	35	<0.01
Nevada	33	<0.01
Nebraska	28	<0.01
Pennsylvania	27	<0.01
Tennessee	27	<0.01
South Dakota	24	<0.01
Idaho	21	<0.01
Massachusetts	20	<0.01
Utah	18	<0.01
North Dakota	16	<0.01
Montana	15	<0.01
South Carolina	15	<0.01
Arkansas	13	<0.01
Kentucky	13	<0.01
Louisiana	10	<0.01
Mississippi	10	<0.01
New Jersey	9	<0.01
Connecticut	7	<0.01
New Hampshire	6	<0.01
Rhode Island	6	<0.01
Alabama	5	<0.01
Delaware	5	<0.01
West Virginia	4	<0.01
Wyoming	3	<0.01
Maine	2	<0.01
District of Columbia	1	<0.01
Vermont	0	0.00

Please refer to the Explanation of Data in the front of the book for more detailed information.

Race

American Indian: Menominee

Top 150 Places Sorted by Population

Based on all places, regardless of total population

Place	Population	%
Menominee, WI (town) Menominee County	3,085	72.90
Keshena, WI (cdp) Menominee County	1,049	83.12
Legend Lake, WI (cdp) Menominee County	909	59.61
Shawano, WI (city) Shawano County	826	8.88
Green Bay, WI (city) Brown County	757	0.73
Neopit, WI (cdp) Menominee County	539	78.12
Milwaukee, WI (city) Milwaukee County	504	0.08
Red Springs, WI (town) Shawano County	219	23.68
Middle Village, WI (cdp) Shawano County	209	74.38
Chicago, IL (city) Cook County	117	<0.01
Zoar, WI (cdp) Menominee County	97	98.98
Appleton, WI (city) Outagamie County	89	0.12
West Allis, WI (city) Milwaukee County	83	0.14
Wescott, WI (town) Shawano County	81	2.54
Oshkosh, WI (city) Winnebago County	79	0.12
Appleton, WI (city) Outagamie County	77	0.13
Gresham, WI (village) Shawano County	69	11.77
Bartelme, WI (town) Shawano County	67	8.18
Madison, WI (city) Dane County	62	0.03
Sheboygan, WI (city) Sheboygan County	52	0.11
Kenosha, WI (city) Kenosha County	52	0.05
Wausau, WI (city) Marathon County	51	0.13
Ashwaubenon, WI (village) Brown County	48	0.28
Minneapolis, MN (city) Hennepin County	46	0.01
Oneida, WI (town) Outagamie County	42	0.90
Richmond, WI (town) Shawano County	40	2.15
Anchorage, AK (municipality) Anchorage Municipality	39	0.01
Hobart, WI (village) Brown County	37	0.60
De Pere, WI (city) Brown County	37	0.16
Howard, WI (village) Brown County	34	0.20
Gillett, WI (city) Oconto County	31	2.24
Kaukauna, WI (city) Outagamie County	31	0.20
Bellevue, WI (village) Brown County	30	0.21
Manitowoc, WI (city) Manitowoc County	30	0.09
Lawrence, KS (city) Douglas County	28	0.03
Underhill, WI (town) Oconto County	27	3.06
Brockway, WI (town) Jackson County	27	0.95
Albuquerque, NM (city) Bernalillo County	27	<0.01
Beloit, WI (city) Rock County	26	0.07
Fond du Lac, WI (city) Fond du Lac County	26	0.06
Herman, WI (town) Shawano County	25	3.22
South Milwaukee, WI (city) Milwaukee County	25	0.12
How, WI (town) Oconto County	24	4.65
Neenah, WI (city) Winnebago County	24	0.09
Two Rivers, WI (city) Manitowoc County	23	0.20
Franklin, WI (city) Milwaukee County	23	0.06
Phoenix, AZ (city) Maricopa County	23	<0.01
Bowler, WI (village) Shawano County	22	7.28
Menasha, WI (town) Winnebago County	22	0.12
Greenfield, WI (city) Milwaukee County	22	0.06
Tigerton, WI (village) Shawano County	21	2.83
Allouez, WI (village) Brown County	20	0.14
San Diego, CA (city) San Diego County	19	<0.01
Belle Plaine, WI (town) Shawano County	18	0.97
Cudahy, WI (city) Milwaukee County	18	0.10
Menomonee Falls, WI (village) Waukesha County	18	0.05
Los Angeles, CA (city) Los Angeles County	18	<0.01
Cecil, WI (village) Shawano County	17	2.98
Crandon, WI (city) Forest County	17	0.89
Lac du Flambeau, WI (town) Vilas County	17	0.49
Washington, WI (town) Shawano County	16	0.84
Wauwatosa, WI (city) Milwaukee County	16	0.03
Komensky, WI (town) Jackson County	15	2.95
Hutchins, WI (town) Shawano County	15	2.50
Oconto Falls, WI (city) Oconto County	15	0.52
Menasha, WI (city) Winnebago County	15	0.10
Menasha, WI (city) Winnebago County	15	0.09
Grand Chute, WI (town) Outagamie County	15	0.07
Oak Creek, WI (city) Milwaukee County	15	0.04
Detroit, MI (city) Wayne County	15	<0.01
Wabeno, WI (town) Forest County	14	1.20
Duluth, MN (city) St. Louis County	14	0.02
Suring, WI (village) Oconto County	13	2.39
Clintonville, WI (city) Waupaca County	13	0.29
Rhinelander, WI (city) Oneida County	13	0.17

Place	Population	%
Little Chute, WI (village) Outagamie County	13	0.12
Stevens Point, WI (city) Portage County	13	0.05
Janesville, WI (city) Rock County	13	0.02
Portland, OR (city) Multnomah County	13	<0.01
Delton, WI (town) Sauk County	12	0.50
Pulaski, WI (village) Brown County	12	0.36
Pulaski, WI (village) Brown County	12	0.34
Appleton, WI (city) Calumet County	12	0.11
Woodburn, OR (city) Marion County	12	0.05
La Crosse, WI (city) La Crosse County	12	0.02
Springfield, IL (city) Sangamon County	12	0.01
Bonduel, WI (village) Shawano County	11	0.74
Lac du Flambeau, WI (cdp) Vilas County	11	0.56
Bass Lake, WI (town) Sawyer County	11	0.46
Black River Falls, WI (city) Jackson County	11	0.30
Waupaca, WI (city) Waupaca County	11	0.18
Kronenwetter, WI (village) Marathon County	11	0.15
Richfield, WI (village) Washington County	11	0.10
Suamico, WI (village) Brown County	11	0.10
Greendale, WI (village) Milwaukee County	11	0.08
West Bend, WI (city) Washington County	11	0.04
Eau Claire, WI (city) Eau Claire County	11	0.02
Eau Claire, WI (city) Eau Claire County	11	0.02
Omaha, NE (city) Douglas County	11	<0.01
St. Paul, MN (city) Ramsey County	11	<0.01
Toledo, OH (city) Lucas County	11	<0.01
Tucson, AZ (city) Pima County	11	<0.01
Mountain, WI (town) Oconto County	10	1.22
Hazelhurst, WI (town) Oneida County	10	0.79
Oconto, WI (city) Oconto County	10	0.22
Kimberly, WI (village) Outagamie County	10	0.15
North Bend, OR (city) Coos County	10	0.10
Weston, WI (village) Marathon County	10	0.07
Wisconsin Rapids, WI (city) Wood County	10	0.05
Mount Pleasant, WI (village) Racine County	10	0.04
Crystal Lake, IL (city) McHenry County	10	0.02
Racine, WI (city) Racine County	10	0.01
Anaheim, CA (city) Orange County	10	<0.01
Henderson, NV (city) Clark County	10	<0.01
New York, NY (city) Kings County	10	<0.01
Maple Valley, WI (town) Oconto County	9	1.36
Larrabee, WI (town) Waupaca County	9	0.65
Freedom, WI (town) Outagamie County	9	0.15
Maili, HI (cdp) Honolulu County	9	0.09
Camp Pendleton South, CA (cdp) San Diego County	9	0.08
Plover, WI (village) Portage County	9	0.07
Trenton, MI (city) Wayne County	9	0.05
Caledonia, WI (village) Racine County	9	0.04
Brookfield, WI (city) Waukesha County	9	0.02
Fargo, ND (city) Cass County	9	0.01
Vancouver, WA (city) Clark County	9	0.01
Waukesha, WI (city) Waukesha County	9	0.01
San Jose, CA (city) Santa Clara County	9	<0.01
Seattle, WA (city) King County	9	<0.01
Levis, WI (town) Clark County	8	1.63
Pella, WI (town) Shawano County	8	0.92
Angelica, WI (town) Shawano County	8	0.45
Bristol, WI (town) Kenosha County	8	0.34
Seymour, WI (city) Outagamie County	8	0.23
Hayward, WI (town) Sawyer County	8	0.22
New London, WI (city) Waupaca County	8	0.11
Antigo, WI (city) Langlade County	8	0.10
Oconomowoc, WI (city) Waukesha County	8	0.05
Elmhurst, IL (city) DuPage County	8	0.02
New Berlin, WI (city) Waukesha County	8	0.02
Burnsville, MN (city) Dakota County	8	0.01
Cedar Rapids, IA (city) Linn County	8	0.01
Davenport, IA (city) Scott County	8	0.01
Riverview, FL (cdp) Hillsborough County	8	0.01
Plano, TX (city) Collin County	8	<0.01
Wichita, KS (city) Sedgwick County	8	<0.01
Seneca, WI (town) Shawano County	7	1.25
Marion, WI (city) Waupaca County	7	0.57
Marion, WI (city) Waupaca County	7	0.56
Byron, WI (town) Monroe County	7	0.52

Race

American Indian: Menominee

Top 150 Places Sorted by Percent of Total Population

Based on all places, regardless of total population

Place	Population	%
Zoar, WI (cdp) Menominee County	97	98.98
Keshena, WI (cdp) Menominee County	1,049	83.12
Neopit, WI (cdp) Menominee County	539	78.12
Middle Village, WI (cdp) Shawano County	209	74.38
Menominee, WI (town) Menominee County	3,085	72.90
Legend Lake, WI (cdp) Menominee County	909	59.61
Red Springs, WI (town) Shawano County	219	23.68
Gresham, WI (village) Shawano County	69	11.77
Shawano, WI (city) Shawano County	826	8.88
Bartelme, WI (town) Shawano County	67	8.18
Bowler, WI (village) Shawano County	22	7.28
How, WI (town) Oconto County	24	4.65
Herman, WI (town) Shawano County	25	3.22
Underhill, WI (town) Oconto County	27	3.06
Cecil, WI (village) Shawano County	17	2.98
Komensky, WI (town) Jackson County	15	2.95
Tigerton, WI (village) Shawano County	21	2.83
Wescott, WI (town) Shawano County	81	2.54
Hutchins, WI (town) Shawano County	15	2.50
Suring, WI (village) Oconto County	13	2.39
Gillett, WI (city) Oconto County	31	2.24
Tilleda, WI (cdp) Shawano County	2	2.20
Cotesfield, NE (village) Howard County	1	2.17
Richmond, WI (town) Shawano County	40	2.15
Levis, WI (town) Clark County	8	1.63
Thornton, WI (cdp) Shawano County	1	1.54
Mountain, WI (cdp) Oconto County	5	1.38
Townsend, WI (cdp) Oconto County	2	1.37
Maple Valley, WI (town) Oconto County	9	1.36
New Post, WI (cdp) Sawyer County	4	1.31
Seneca, WI (town) Shawano County	7	1.25
Mountain, WI (town) Oconto County	10	1.22
Wabeno, WI (town) Forest County	14	1.20
Millville, WI (town) Grant County	2	1.20
Reserve, WI (cdp) Sawyer County	5	1.17
Krakow, WI (cdp) Shawano County	4	1.13
Harrison, WI (town) Marathon County	4	1.07
Belle Plaine, WI (town) Shawano County	18	0.97
Brockway, WI (town) Jackson County	27	0.95
Pella, WI (town) Shawano County	8	0.92
Oneida, WI (town) Outagamie County	42	0.90
Washington, WI (town) La Crosse County	5	0.90
Crandon, WI (city) Forest County	17	0.89
Weir, TX (city) Williamson County	4	0.89
Posen, MI (village) Presque Isle County	2	0.85
Washington, WI (town) Shawano County	16	0.84
Bayview, WI (town) Bayfield County	4	0.82
Millston, WI (cdp) Jackson County	1	0.80
Hazelhurst, WI (town) Oneida County	10	0.79
Weston, WI (town) Marathon County	5	0.78
Brockton, MT (town) Roosevelt County	2	0.78
Bonduel, WI (village) Shawano County	11	0.74
Aniwa, WI (town) Shawano County	4	0.74
Green Bay, WI (city) Brown County	757	0.73
White Horse, SD (cdp) Todd County	2	0.72
Coleman, WI (village) Marinette County	5	0.69
Neshkoro, WI (village) Marquette County	3	0.69
Bagley, WI (town) Oconto County	2	0.69
Whitelaw, WI (village) Manitowoc County	5	0.66
Princeton, CA (cdp) Colusa County	2	0.66
Larrabee, WI (town) Waupaca County	9	0.65
Lincoln, WI (town) Forest County	6	0.63
Deer Creek, WI (town) Outagamie County	4	0.63
Millston, WI (town) Jackson County	1	0.63
Crandon, WI (town) Forest County	4	0.62
Fargo, GA (city) Clinch County	2	0.62
Hobart, WI (village) Brown County	37	0.60
Hunter, WI (town) Sawyer County	4	0.59
Westfield, WI (town) Marquette County	5	0.58
Danbury, WI (cdp) Burnett County	1	0.58
Marion, WI (city) Waupaca County	7	0.57
Lac du Flambeau, WI (cdp) Vilas County	11	0.56
Marion, WI (city) Waupaca County	7	0.56
Little Round Lake, WI (cdp) Sawyer County	6	0.56
Wittenberg, WI (village) Shawano County	6	0.56
Breed, WI (town) Oconto County	4	0.56
Navarino, WI (cdp) Shawano County	1	0.56
Stone Lake, WI (cdp) Sawyer County	1	0.56
Necedah, WI (village) Juneau County	5	0.55
Hanover, WI (cdp) Rock County	1	0.55
Pella, WI (cdp) Shawano County	1	0.54
Flora, MN (township) Renville County	1	0.53
Oconto Falls, WI (city) Oconto County	15	0.52
Byron, WI (town) Monroe County	7	0.52
Birnamwood, WI (town) Shawano County	4	0.52
Hatley, WI (village) Marathon County	3	0.52
Clay Banks, WI (town) Door County	2	0.52
Fence, WI (town) Florence County	1	0.52
Kickapoo Tribal Center, KS (cdp) Brown County	1	0.52
Almon, WI (town) Shawano County	3	0.51
Delton, WI (town) Sauk County	12	0.50
Lowville, WI (town) Columbia County	5	0.50
Couderay, WI (town) Sawyer County	2	0.50
Lac du Flambeau, WI (town) Vilas County	17	0.49
Eden, WI (town) Fond du Lac County	5	0.49
Lakewood, WI (town) Oconto County	4	0.49
Radisson, WI (town) Sawyer County	2	0.49
Lessor, WI (town) Shawano County	6	0.48
Bliss, MI (township) Emmet County	3	0.48
Charleston, UT (town) Wasatch County	2	0.48
Marion, WI (town) Juneau County	2	0.47
Bass Lake, WI (town) Sawyer County	11	0.46
Humboldt, WI (town) Brown County	6	0.46
Halsey, WI (town) Marathon County	3	0.46
Hixton, WI (town) Jackson County	3	0.46
Angelica, WI (town) Shawano County	8	0.45
Cicero, WI (town) Outagamie County	5	0.45
Hartland, WI (town) Shawano County	4	0.44
Plover, WI (town) Marathon County	3	0.44
Wagner, WI (town) Marinette County	3	0.44
Price, WI (town) Langlade County	1	0.44
Rutledge, MN (city) Pine County	1	0.44
Kelly, WI (town) Bayfield County	2	0.43
Beaver Brook, WI (town) Washburn County	3	0.42
Buffalo, WI (town) Marquette County	5	0.41
Laona, WI (town) Forest County	5	0.41
Bloomington, WI (village) Grant County	3	0.41
Cloverland, WI (town) Vilas County	4	0.39
Doty, WI (town) Oconto County	1	0.38
Minerva, MN (township) Clearwater County	1	0.38
Port Washington, WI (town) Ozaukee County	6	0.37
Sand Lake, WI (town) Sawyer County	3	0.37
Sturgeon Bay, WI (town) Door County	3	0.37
Caroline, WI (cdp) Shawano County	1	0.37
Nehalem, OR (city) Tillamook County	1	0.37
Pulaski, WI (village) Brown County	12	0.36
Spruce, WI (town) Oconto County	3	0.36
Neshkoro, WI (town) Marquette County	2	0.36
Fieldbrook, CA (cdp) Humboldt County	3	0.35
Wausaukee, WI (village) Marinette County	2	0.35
Pulaski, WI (village) Brown County	12	0.34
Bristol, WI (town) Kenosha County	8	0.34
Osborn, WI (town) Outagamie County	4	0.34
New Knoxville, OH (village) Auglaize County	3	0.34
Elderon, WI (town) Marathon County	2	0.33
Belmont, WI (town) Portage County	2	0.32
Fairbanks, WI (town) Shawano County	2	0.32
Wellington, WI (town) Monroe County	2	0.32
Leola, WI (town) Adams County	1	0.32
New Chester, WI (town) Adams County	7	0.31
Schleswig, WI (town) Manitowoc County	6	0.31
Rietbrock, WI (town) Marathon County	3	0.31
Centerville, WI (town) Manitowoc County	2	0.31
Cutler, WI (town) Juneau County	1	0.31
Lakewood, WI (cdp) Oconto County	1	0.31
Polk, NE (village) Polk County	1	0.31
Black River Falls, WI (city) Jackson County	11	0.30
Cassian, WI (town) Oneida County	3	0.30
Ekalaka, MT (town) Carter County	1	0.30
Germania, WI (town) Shawano County	1	0.30

Please refer to the Explanation of Data in the front of the book for more detailed information.

Race

American Indian: Menominee

Top 150 Places Sorted by Percent of Total Population

Based on places with total population of 7,500 or more

Place	Population	%
Shawano, WI (city) Shawano County	826	8.88
Green Bay, WI (city) Brown County	757	0.73
Ashwaubenon, WI (village) Brown County	48	0.28
Bellevue, WI (village) Brown County	30	0.21
Howard, WI (village) Brown County	34	0.20
Kaukauna, WI (city) Outagamie County	31	0.20
Two Rivers, WI (city) Manitowoc County	23	0.20
Rhinelander, WI (city) Oneida County	13	0.17
De Pere, WI (city) Brown County	37	0.16
West Allis, WI (city) Milwaukee County	83	0.14
Allouez, WI (village) Brown County	20	0.14
Appleton, WI (city) Outagamie County	77	0.13
Wausau, WI (city) Marathon County	51	0.13
Appleton, WI (city) Outagamie County	89	0.12
Oshkosh, WI (city) Winnebago County	79	0.12
South Milwaukee, WI (city) Milwaukee County	25	0.12
Menasha, WI (town) Winnebago County	22	0.12
Little Chute, WI (village) Outagamie County	13	0.12
Sheboygan, WI (city) Sheboygan County	52	0.11
Appleton, WI (city) Calumet County	12	0.11
Cudahy, WI (city) Milwaukee County	18	0.10
Menasha, WI (city) Winnebago County	15	0.10
Richfield, WI (village) Washington County	11	0.10
Suamico, WI (village) Brown County	11	0.10
North Bend, OR (city) Coos County	10	0.10
Antigo, WI (city) Langlade County	8	0.10
Manitowoc, WI (city) Manitowoc County	30	0.09
Neenah, WI (city) Winnebago County	24	0.09
Menasha, WI (city) Winnebago County	15	0.09
Maili, HI (cdp) Honolulu County	9	0.09
Ashland, WI (city) Ashland County	7	0.09
Mukwonago, WI (town) Waukesha County	7	0.09
Milwaukee, WI (city) Milwaukee County	504	0.08
Greendale, WI (village) Milwaukee County	11	0.08
Camp Pendleton South, CA (cdp) San Diego County	9	0.08
Menominee, MI (city) Menominee County	7	0.08
Northfield, MI (township) Washtenaw County	7	0.08
Beloit, WI (city) Rock County	26	0.07
Grand Chute, WI (town) Outagamie County	15	0.07
Weston, WI (village) Marathon County	10	0.07
Plover, WI (village) Portage County	9	0.07
Monmouth, IL (city) Warren County	7	0.07
Portage, WI (city) Columbia County	7	0.07
St. Francis, WI (city) Milwaukee County	7	0.07
Sturgeon Bay, WI (city) Door County	6	0.07
Clayton, MI (charter township) Genesee County	5	0.07
Fond du Lac, WI (city) Fond du Lac County	26	0.06
Franklin, WI (city) Milwaukee County	23	0.06
Greenfield, WI (city) Milwaukee County	22	0.06
Salem, WI (town) Kenosha County	7	0.06
Kenosha, WI (city) Kenosha County	52	0.05
Menomonee Falls, WI (village) Waukesha County	18	0.05
Stevens Point, WI (city) Portage County	13	0.05
Woodburn, OR (city) Marion County	12	0.05
Wisconsin Rapids, WI (city) Wood County	10	0.05
Trenton, MI (city) Wayne County	9	0.05
Oconomowoc, WI (city) Waukesha County	8	0.05
Chippewa Falls, WI (city) Chippewa County	7	0.05
Pewaukee, WI (city) Waukesha County	6	0.05
Chalco, NE (cdp) Sarpy County	5	0.05
Somers, WI (town) Kenosha County	5	0.05
Tomah, WI (city) Monroe County	5	0.05
McFarland, WI (village) Dane County	4	0.05
Ripon, WI (city) Fond du Lac County	4	0.05
Oak Creek, WI (city) Milwaukee County	15	0.04
West Bend, WI (city) Washington County	11	0.04
Mount Pleasant, WI (village) Racine County	10	0.04
Caledonia, WI (village) Racine County	9	0.04
Coos Bay, OR (city) Coos County	6	0.04
Whitefish Bay, WI (village) Milwaukee County	5	0.04
Bethalto, IL (village) Madison County	4	0.04
Holly, MI (township) Oakland County	4	0.04
Madison Heights, VA (cdp) Amherst County	4	0.04
River Grove, IL (village) Cook County	4	0.04
Waukesha, WI (town) Waukesha County	4	0.04
Delafield, WI (town) Waukesha County	3	0.04
Delavan, WI (city) Walworth County	3	0.04
Jefferson, WI (city) Jefferson County	3	0.04
Kearney, MO (city) Clay County	3	0.04
Meadow Lakes, AK (cdp) Matanuska-Susitna Borough	3	0.04
Norway, WI (town) Racine County	3	0.04
Plymouth, WI (city) Sheboygan County	3	0.04
Watertown, WI (city) Dodge County	3	0.04
West Frankfort, IL (city) Franklin County	3	0.04
Madison, WI (city) Dane County	62	0.03
Lawrence, KS (city) Douglas County	28	0.03
Wauwatosa, WI (city) Milwaukee County	16	0.03
Frenchtown, MI (township) Monroe County	7	0.03
Germantown, WI (village) Washington County	5	0.03
Marshfield, WI (city) Wood County	5	0.03
Marshfield, WI (city) Wood County	5	0.03
Middleton, WI (city) Dane County	5	0.03
Pleasant Prairie, WI (village) Kenosha County	5	0.03
Baraboo, WI (city) Sauk County	4	0.03
Glendale, WI (city) Milwaukee County	4	0.03
Kuna, ID (city) Ada County	4	0.03
Lahaina, HI (cdp) Maui County	4	0.03
Lindenhurst, IL (village) Lake County	4	0.03
Shorewood, WI (village) Milwaukee County	4	0.03
Coffeyville, KS (city) Montgomery County	3	0.03
Elkhorn, WI (city) Walworth County	3	0.03
Fairview, OR (city) Multnomah County	3	0.03
Fort Irwin, CA (cdp) San Bernardino County	3	0.03
Harrison, WI (town) Calumet County	3	0.03
Harvard, IL (city) McHenry County	3	0.03
Lyons, IL (village) Cook County	3	0.03
Melvindale, MI (city) Wayne County	3	0.03
Schiller Park, IL (village) Cook County	3	0.03
Verde Village, AZ (cdp) Yavapai County	3	0.03
Virginia, MN (city) St. Louis County	3	0.03
Waseca, MN (city) Waseca County	3	0.03
Waxhaw, NC (town) Union County	3	0.03
Winfield, IL (village) DuPage County	3	0.03
Fern Park, FL (cdp) Seminole County	2	0.03
Marengo, IL (city) McHenry County	2	0.03
Round Lake Park, IL (village) Lake County	2	0.03
Sheboygan Falls, WI (city) Sheboygan County	2	0.03
Waupun, WI (city) Dodge County	2	0.03
Duluth, MN (city) St. Louis County	14	0.02
Janesville, WI (city) Rock County	13	0.02
La Crosse, WI (city) La Crosse County	12	0.02
Eau Claire, WI (city) Eau Claire County	11	0.02
Eau Claire, WI (city) Eau Claire County	11	0.02
Crystal Lake, IL (city) McHenry County	10	0.02
Brookfield, WI (city) Waukesha County	9	0.02
Elmhurst, IL (city) DuPage County	8	0.02
New Berlin, WI (city) Waukesha County	8	0.02
Carpentersville, IL (village) Kane County	7	0.02
Delta, MI (charter township) Eaton County	7	0.02
Pekin, IL (city) Tazewell County	7	0.02
Southgate, MI (city) Wayne County	7	0.02
Fitchburg, WI (city) Dane County	6	0.02
Ken Caryl, CO (cdp) Jefferson County	6	0.02
Marshalltown, IA (city) Marshall County	5	0.02
Beaver Dam, WI (city) Dodge County	4	0.02
Brookings, SD (city) Brookings County	4	0.02
Menomonie, WI (city) Dunn County	4	0.02
Mount Pleasant, MI (city) Isabella County	4	0.02
Onalaska, WI (city) La Crosse County	4	0.02
Rockledge, FL (city) Brevard County	4	0.02
Sapulpa, OK (city) Creek County	4	0.02
Watertown, WI (city) Jefferson County	4	0.02
Zion, IL (city) Lake County	4	0.02
Auburndale, FL (city) Polk County	3	0.02
Fairview Heights, IL (city) St. Clair County	3	0.02
Glens Falls, NY (city) Warren County	3	0.02
Hope Mills, NC (town) Cumberland County	3	0.02
La Grande, OR (city) Union County	3	0.02
Lake Zurich, IL (village) Lake County	3	0.02
Maitland, FL (city) Orange County	3	0.02

SECTION THREE

Please refer to the Explanation of Data in the front of the book for more detailed information.

Race

American Indian: Mexican American Indian

U.S. and 50 States Sorted by Population and Percent of Total Population

Place	Population	%
United States	**175,494**	**0.06**
California	66,424	0.18
Texas	20,349	0.08
Florida	7,967	0.04
New York	7,439	0.04
Illinois	7,421	0.06
Arizona	5,796	0.09
Washington	5,060	0.08
Oregon	4,397	0.11
Colorado	4,184	0.08
North Carolina	3,826	0.04
Georgia	3,796	0.04
New Jersey	2,931	0.03
Michigan	2,219	0.02
Virginia	1,979	0.02
Nevada	1,930	0.07
New Mexico	1,757	0.09
Massachusetts	1,580	0.02
Utah	1,571	0.06
Wisconsin	1,559	0.03
Pennsylvania	1,520	0.01
Maryland	1,495	0.03
Minnesota	1,481	0.03
Ohio	1,472	0.01
Oklahoma	1,470	0.04
Tennessee	1,448	0.02
Indiana	1,441	0.02
Kansas	1,274	0.04
South Carolina	1,248	0.03
Missouri	1,147	0.02
Alabama	970	0.02
Nebraska	913	0.05
Idaho	865	0.06
Iowa	751	0.02
Arkansas	727	0.02
Connecticut	699	0.02
Kentucky	681	0.02
Louisiana	675	0.01
Mississippi	448	0.02
Rhode Island	447	0.04
Hawaii	424	0.03
Delaware	368	0.04
District of Columbia	220	0.04
Wyoming	186	0.03
Alaska	155	0.02
Montana	155	0.02
West Virginia	140	0.01
New Hampshire	133	0.01
Maine	116	0.01
South Dakota	102	0.01
Vermont	82	0.01
North Dakota	56	0.01

Place	Population	%
California	66,424	0.18
Oregon	4,397	0.11
Arizona	5,796	0.09
New Mexico	1,757	0.09
Texas	20,349	0.08
Washington	5,060	0.08
Colorado	4,184	0.08
Nevada	1,930	0.07
United States	**175,494**	**0.06**
Illinois	7,421	0.06
Utah	1,571	0.06
Idaho	865	0.06
Nebraska	913	0.05
Florida	7,967	0.04
New York	7,439	0.04
North Carolina	3,826	0.04
Georgia	3,796	0.04
Oklahoma	1,470	0.04
Kansas	1,274	0.04
Rhode Island	447	0.04
Delaware	368	0.04
District of Columbia	220	0.04
New Jersey	2,931	0.03
Wisconsin	1,559	0.03
Maryland	1,495	0.03
Minnesota	1,481	0.03
South Carolina	1,248	0.03
Hawaii	424	0.03
Wyoming	186	0.03
Michigan	2,219	0.02
Virginia	1,979	0.02
Massachusetts	1,580	0.02
Tennessee	1,448	0.02
Indiana	1,441	0.02
Missouri	1,147	0.02
Alabama	970	0.02
Iowa	751	0.02
Arkansas	727	0.02
Connecticut	699	0.02
Kentucky	681	0.02
Mississippi	448	0.02
Alaska	155	0.02
Montana	155	0.02
Pennsylvania	1,520	0.01
Ohio	1,472	0.01
Louisiana	675	0.01
West Virginia	140	0.01
New Hampshire	133	0.01
Maine	116	0.01
South Dakota	102	0.01
Vermont	82	0.01
North Dakota	56	0.01

Please refer to the Explanation of Data in the front of the book for more detailed information.

Race

American Indian: Mexican American Indian

Top 150 Places Sorted by Population

Based on all places, regardless of total population

Place	Population	%
Los Angeles, CA (city) Los Angeles County	9,589	0.25
New York, NY (city) Kings County	4,922	0.06
Houston, TX (city) Harris County	3,570	0.17
Chicago, IL (city) Cook County	2,810	0.10
Phoenix, AZ (city) Maricopa County	1,725	0.12
San Jose, CA (city) Santa Clara County	1,697	0.18
Fresno, CA (city) Fresno County	1,666	0.34
Queens, NY (borough) Queens County	1,640	0.07
Lake Worth, FL (city) Palm Beach County	1,624	4.65
San Diego, CA (city) San Diego County	1,561	0.12
San Antonio, TX (city) Medina County	1,546	0.12
Dallas, TX (city) Dallas County	1,495	0.12
Oxnard, CA (city) Ventura County	1,377	0.70
Brooklyn, NY (borough) Kings County	1,363	0.05
San Francisco, CA (city) San Francisco County	1,209	0.15
Austin, TX (city) Travis County	1,006	0.13
Santa Ana, CA (city) Orange County	974	0.30
Bronx, NY (borough) Bronx County	963	0.07
Oakland, CA (city) Alameda County	945	0.24
Madera, CA (city) Madera County	891	1.45
Santa Maria, CA (city) Santa Barbara County	868	0.87
Long Beach, CA (city) Los Angeles County	840	0.18
Tucson, AZ (city) Pima County	831	0.16
Portland, OR (city) Multnomah County	786	0.13
Greenfield, CA (city) Monterey County	765	4.68
Manhattan, NY (borough) New York County	752	0.05
Sacramento, CA (city) Sacramento County	746	0.16
Denver, CO (city) Denver County	733	0.12
Fort Worth, TX (city) Tarrant County	715	0.10
Riverside, CA (city) Riverside County	633	0.21
Anaheim, CA (city) Orange County	592	0.18
San Bernardino, CA (city) San Bernardino County	540	0.26
Woodburn, OR (city) Marion County	532	2.21
North Atlanta, GA (cdp) DeKalb County	508	1.26
Salinas, CA (city) Monterey County	508	0.34
El Paso, TX (city) El Paso County	497	0.08
Albuquerque, NM (city) Bernalillo County	495	0.09
East Los Angeles, CA (cdp) Los Angeles County	487	0.38
Stockton, CA (city) San Joaquin County	485	0.17
Bakersfield, CA (city) Kern County	474	0.14
Chula Vista, CA (city) San Diego County	451	0.18
Las Vegas, NV (city) Clark County	450	0.08
New Bedford, MA (city) Bristol County	430	0.45
Ontario, CA (city) San Bernardino County	417	0.25
Mesa, AZ (city) Maricopa County	413	0.09
Santa Rosa, CA (city) Sonoma County	410	0.24
Oklahoma City, OK (city) Oklahoma County	402	0.07
Escondido, CA (city) San Diego County	374	0.26
Fontana, CA (city) San Bernardino County	374	0.19
Seattle, WA (city) King County	372	0.06
Minneapolis, MN (city) Hennepin County	365	0.10
Omaha, NE (city) Douglas County	362	0.09
Pomona, CA (city) Los Angeles County	355	0.24
Aurora, CO (city) Arapahoe County	346	0.11
Oceanside, CA (city) San Diego County	338	0.20
Moreno Valley, CA (city) Riverside County	338	0.17
Charlotte, NC (city) Mecklenburg County	331	0.05
Modesto, CA (city) Stanislaus County	323	0.16
Wichita, KS (city) Sedgwick County	323	0.08
Gresham, OR (city) Multnomah County	319	0.30
Hayward, CA (city) Alameda County	309	0.21
Vista, CA (city) San Diego County	308	0.33
Providence, RI (city) Providence County	293	0.16
Elgin, IL (city) Kane County	292	0.27
Milwaukee, WI (city) Milwaukee County	291	0.05
South Gate, CA (city) Los Angeles County	290	0.31
Huntington Park, CA (city) Los Angeles County	286	0.49
Tulsa, OK (city) Tulsa County	279	0.07
El Monte, CA (city) Los Angeles County	277	0.24
Arlington, TX (city) Tarrant County	276	0.08
Colorado Springs, CO (city) El Paso County	273	0.07
Hollister, CA (city) San Benito County	268	0.77
Inglewood, CA (city) Los Angeles County	268	0.24
Indianapolis, IN (city) Marion County	263	0.03
Cicero, IL (town) Cook County	256	0.31
Pasadena, CA (city) Los Angeles County	249	0.18
San Rafael, CA (city) Marin County	248	0.43
Lancaster, CA (city) Los Angeles County	245	0.16
Corpus Christi, TX (city) Nueces County	242	0.08
Raleigh, NC (city) Wake County	242	0.06
Detroit, MI (city) Wayne County	238	0.03
Pasadena, TX (city) Harris County	236	0.16
Watsonville, CA (city) Santa Cruz County	233	0.46
Norwalk, CA (city) Los Angeles County	232	0.22
Whittier, CA (city) Los Angeles County	229	0.27
Antioch, CA (city) Contra Costa County	224	0.22
Nashville-Davidson, TN (metro govt) Davidson County	224	0.04
Aurora, IL (city) Kane County	222	0.11
Victorville, CA (city) San Bernardino County	221	0.19
Washington, DC (city) District of Columbia	220	0.04
North Las Vegas, NV (city) Clark County	219	0.10
Visalia, CA (city) Tulare County	215	0.17
West Covina, CA (city) Los Angeles County	214	0.20
Florence-Graham, CA (cdp) Los Angeles County	213	0.34
Palmdale, CA (city) Los Angeles County	212	0.14
West Palm Beach, FL (city) Palm Beach County	206	0.21
Tacoma, WA (city) Pierce County	206	0.10
Staten Island, NY (borough) Richmond County	204	0.04
Hawthorne, CA (city) Los Angeles County	203	0.24
Columbus, OH (city) Franklin County	203	0.03
Rialto, CA (city) San Bernardino County	198	0.20
St. Paul, MN (city) Ramsey County	198	0.07
Costa Mesa, CA (city) Orange County	197	0.18
Salt Lake City, UT (city) Salt Lake County	197	0.11
Sunrise Manor, NV (cdp) Clark County	196	0.10
West Valley City, UT (city) Salt Lake County	193	0.15
Waukegan, IL (city) Lake County	192	0.22
Lynwood, CA (city) Los Angeles County	190	0.27
Pico Rivera, CA (city) Los Angeles County	189	0.30
Boston, MA (city) Suffolk County	189	0.03
Pueblo, CO (city) Pueblo County	188	0.18
Glendale, AZ (city) Maricopa County	188	0.08
Garland, TX (city) Dallas County	187	0.08
Compton, CA (city) Los Angeles County	185	0.19
Philadelphia, PA (city) Philadelphia County	185	0.01
Salem, OR (city) Marion County	182	0.12
Indio, CA (city) Riverside County	179	0.24
Orange, CA (city) Orange County	179	0.13
Santa Clarita, CA (city) Los Angeles County	179	0.10
Fremont, CA (city) Alameda County	179	0.08
Reno, NV (city) Washoe County	179	0.08
San Buenaventura (Ventura), CA (city) Ventura County	178	0.17
Merced, CA (city) Merced County	176	0.22
Rancho Cucamonga, CA (city) San Bernardino County	176	0.11
Paradise, NV (cdp) Clark County	176	0.08
Jupiter, FL (town) Palm Beach County	175	0.32
Baldwin Park, CA (city) Los Angeles County	175	0.23
Garden Grove, CA (city) Orange County	175	0.10
Irving, TX (city) Dallas County	175	0.08
Gilroy, CA (city) Santa Clara County	174	0.36
Richmond, CA (city) Contra Costa County	173	0.17
Kansas City, MO (city) Jackson County	173	0.04
Fullerton, CA (city) Orange County	172	0.13
Corona, CA (city) Riverside County	171	0.11
Yonkers, NY (city) Westchester County	171	0.09
San Leandro, CA (city) Alameda County	170	0.20
Redwood City, CA (city) San Mateo County	169	0.22
Chandler, AZ (city) Maricopa County	167	0.07
Laredo, TX (city) Webb County	167	0.07
West New York, NJ (town) Hudson County	166	0.33
Grand Rapids, MI (city) Kent County	166	0.09
Hesperia, CA (city) San Bernardino County	164	0.18
Hillsboro, OR (city) Washington County	164	0.18
Berkeley, CA (city) Alameda County	164	0.15
White Plains, NY (city) Westchester County	162	0.28
Montebello, CA (city) Los Angeles County	162	0.26
Passaic, NJ (city) Passaic County	162	0.23
Poughkeepsie, NY (city) Dutchess County	160	0.49
Concord, CA (city) Contra Costa County	160	0.13
Lakewood, CO (city) Jefferson County	160	0.11

SECTION THREE

Please refer to the Explanation of Data in the front of the book for more detailed information.

Race

American Indian: Mexican American Indian

Top 150 Places Sorted by Percent of Total Population

Based on all places, regardless of total population

Place	Population	%
Cattaraugus Reservation, NY (reservation) Chautauqua County	5	13.16
Sun Valley, TX (city) Lamar County	8	11.59
Raisin City, CA (cdp) Fresno County	27	7.11
Tooleville, CA (cdp) Tulare County	17	5.01
McGee Creek, CA (cdp) Mono County	2	4.88
Greenfield, CA (city) Monterey County	765	4.68
Lake Worth, FL (city) Palm Beach County	1,624	4.65
Campo Bonito, AZ (cdp) Pinal County	3	4.05
Mobeetie, TX (city) Wheeler County	4	3.96
Moskowite Corner, CA (cdp) Napa County	8	3.79
Cartago, CA (cdp) Inyo County	3	3.26
No Name, CO (cdp) Garfield County	4	3.25
Orovada, NV (cdp) Humboldt County	5	3.23
Blomkest, MN (city) Kandiyohi County	5	3.18
Mahnomen, MN (cdp) St. Louis County	7	2.93
Nolic, AZ (cdp) Pima County	1	2.70
Santa Cruz, AZ (cdp) Pinal County	1	2.70
Ford City, CA (cdp) Kern County	112	2.62
Y-O Ranch, WY (cdp) Platte County	5	2.56
Lebam, WA (cdp) Pacific County	4	2.50
Coloma, CA (cdp) El Dorado County	13	2.46
Belfair, WA (cdp) Mason County	95	2.42
Parkdale, OR (cdp) Hood River County	7	2.25
Lee Vining, CA (cdp) Mono County	5	2.25
Woodburn, OR (city) Marion County	532	2.21
Neahkahnie, OR (cdp) Tillamook County	4	2.08
Rillito, AZ (cdp) Pima County	2	2.06
Indiantown, FL (cdp) Martin County	125	2.05
New Pine Creek, CA (cdp) Modoc County	2	2.04
Pajaro, CA (cdp) Monterey County	62	2.02
Rufus, OR (city) Sherman County	5	2.01
Newell, CA (cdp) Modoc County	9	2.00
Dunbar, WI (cdp) Marinette County	1	2.00
Paradise, CA (cdp) Mono County	3	1.96
Blackgum, OK (cdp) Sequoyah County	1	1.96
Klickitat, WA (cdp) Klickitat County	7	1.93
Weedpatch, CA (cdp) Kern County	51	1.92
Cherokee Strip, CA (cdp) Kern County	4	1.76
Poston, AZ (cdp) La Paz County	5	1.75
Ducor, CA (cdp) Tulare County	10	1.63
Acme, WA (cdp) Whatcom County	4	1.63
Gunnison, CO (city) Gunnison County	95	1.62
Princeton, SC (cdp) Laurens County	1	1.61
Ruth, NV (cdp) White Pine County	7	1.59
Chase Crossing, VA (cdp) Accomack County	6	1.59
Mountain Center, CA (cdp) Riverside County	1	1.59
Hermitage, AR (town) Bradley County	13	1.57
Mission, OR (cdp) Umatilla County	16	1.54
Mitchell, OR (city) Wheeler County	2	1.54
Viola, KS (city) Sedgwick County	2	1.54
Dixie, WA (cdp) Walla Walla County	3	1.52
Chelsea, IA (city) Tama County	4	1.50
Othello, WA (city) Adams County	109	1.48
McArthur, CA (cdp) Shasta County	5	1.48
Madera, CA (city) Madera County	891	1.45
Farmington, CA (cdp) San Joaquin County	3	1.45
Harrah, WA (town) Yakima County	9	1.44
Cedar Point, IL (village) LaSalle County	4	1.44
Lamont, WA (town) Whitman County	1	1.43
Paw Paw, WV (town) Morgan County	7	1.38
Lumberton, NM (cdp) Rio Arriba County	1	1.37
Alpaugh, CA (cdp) Tulare County	14	1.36
Stonyford, CA (cdp) Colusa County	2	1.34
Hornitos, CA (cdp) Mariposa County	1	1.33
Blue Springs, MS (village) Union County	3	1.32
Sans Souci, SC (cdp) Greenville County	102	1.30
Gervais, OR (city) Marion County	32	1.30
Platte Woods, MO (city) Platte County	5	1.30
Cuartelez, NM (cdp) Santa Fe County	6	1.28
Alto Pass, IL (village) Union County	5	1.28
Bieber, CA (cdp) Lassen County	4	1.28
Keller, WA (cdp) Ferry County	3	1.28
North Atlanta, GA (cdp) DeKalb County	508	1.26
Higgins, TX (city) Lipscomb County	5	1.26
Shinnecock Hills, NY (cdp) Suffolk County	27	1.23
McCune, KS (city) Crawford County	5	1.23
Enchanted Oaks, TX (town) Henderson County	4	1.23
Menan, ID (city) Jefferson County	9	1.21
Pateros, WA (city) Okanogan County	8	1.20
Charleston, UT (town) Wasatch County	5	1.20
Ojibwa, WI (town) Sawyer County	3	1.20
Las Lomas, CA (cdp) Monterey County	36	1.19
Salt Creek, CO (cdp) Pueblo County	7	1.19
Lawrence, MN (township) Grant County	1	1.19
Mudgett, MN (township) Mille Lacs County	1	1.19
Fort Jesup, LA (cdp) Sabine Parish	6	1.18
Doyle, TX (cdp) San Patricio County	3	1.18
Highland, OH (village) Highland County	3	1.18
Wixon Valley, TX (city) Brazos County	3	1.18
Hubbard, OR (city) Marion County	37	1.17
Biola, CA (cdp) Fresno County	19	1.17
Klamath, CA (cdp) Del Norte County	9	1.16
El Rio, CA (cdp) Ventura County	83	1.15
Smith River, CA (cdp) Del Norte County	10	1.15
Skokomish, WA (cdp) Mason County	7	1.13
Bradford, NH (cdp) Merrimack County	4	1.12
Berlin, IL (village) Sangamon County	2	1.11
La Hacienda, NM (cdp) Luna County	8	1.10
Fertile, IA (city) Worth County	4	1.08
Bradley, CA (cdp) Monterey County	1	1.08
Chamblee, GA (city) DeKalb County	106	1.07
Saxon, SC (cdp) Spartanburg County	36	1.05
Fall River Mills, CA (cdp) Shasta County	6	1.05
Cobden, IL (village) Union County	12	1.04
Ak-Chin Village, AZ (cdp) Pinal County	9	1.04
Rennert, NC (town) Robeson County	4	1.04
Bertsch-Oceanview, CA (cdp) Del Norte County	25	1.03
Cotton City, NM (cdp) Hidalgo County	4	1.03
Arlington, AZ (cdp) Maricopa County	2	1.03
Anderson, MO (city) McDonald County	20	1.02
Blanchard, ME (unorganized territory) Piscataquis County	1	1.02
Downieville-Lawson-Dumont, CO (cdp) Clear Creek County	6	1.01
Good Hope, IL (village) McDonough County	4	1.01
Brimhall Nizhoni, NM (cdp) McKinley County	2	1.01
Farmersville, CA (city) Tulare County	106	1.00
Heron Lake, MN (city) Jackson County	7	1.00
Mashantucket, CT (cdp) New London County	3	1.00
Coulterville, CA (cdp) Mariposa County	2	1.00
Surrency, GA (town) Appling County	2	1.00
Stonewall, TX (cdp) Gillespie County	5	0.99
Romeo, CO (town) Conejos County	4	0.99
Flournoy, CA (cdp) Tehama County	1	0.99
Moapa Town, NV (cdp) Clark County	10	0.98
Belvoir, NC (cdp) Pitt County	3	0.98
Tice, FL (cdp) Lee County	43	0.96
Delmar, WI (town) Chippewa County	9	0.96
Crystal, NM (cdp) San Juan County	3	0.96
Esmont, VA (cdp) Albemarle County	5	0.95
Neilton, WA (cdp) Grays Harbor County	3	0.95
Hantho, MN (township) Lac qui Parle County	1	0.95
Dudleyville, AZ (cdp) Pinal County	9	0.94
Bliss, ID (city) Gooding County	3	0.94
Mud Bay, AK (cdp) Haines Borough	2	0.94
O'Brien, TX (city) Haskell County	1	0.94
Fowler, CA (city) Fresno County	51	0.92
Fairlea, WV (cdp) Greenbrier County	16	0.92
Voorhees, NJ (cdp) Somerset County	9	0.92
Dustin Acres, CA (cdp) Kern County	6	0.92
Alamosa, CO (city) Alamosa County	80	0.91
London, CA (cdp) Tulare County	17	0.91
Berlin, GA (city) Colquitt County	5	0.91
Greenbush, VA (cdp) Accomack County	2	0.91
Wildrose, ND (city) Williams County	1	0.91
Chautauqua, KS (city) Chautauqua County	1	0.90
Spreckels, CA (cdp) Monterey County	6	0.89
Almond, WI (village) Portage County	4	0.89
Gould, MN (township) Cass County	2	0.89
Marietta, IL (village) Fulton County	1	0.89
Salem, NE (village) Richardson County	1	0.89
Patagonia, AZ (town) Santa Cruz County	8	0.88

Please refer to the Explanation of Data in the front of the book for more detailed information.

Race

American Indian: Mexican American Indian

Top 150 Places Sorted by Percent of Total Population

Based on places with total population of 7,500 or more

Place	Population	%
Greenfield, CA (city) Monterey County	765	4.68
Lake Worth, FL (city) Palm Beach County	1,624	4.65
Woodburn, OR (city) Marion County	532	2.21
Madera, CA (city) Madera County	891	1.45
Sans Souci, SC (cdp) Greenville County	102	1.30
North Atlanta, GA (cdp) DeKalb County	508	1.26
Chamblee, GA (city) DeKalb County	106	1.07
Farmersville, CA (city) Tulare County	106	1.00
Alamosa, CO (city) Alamosa County	80	0.91
Santa Maria, CA (city) Santa Barbara County	868	0.87
King City, CA (city) Monterey County	112	0.87
McFarland, CA (city) Kern County	106	0.83
Arvin, CA (city) Kern County	156	0.81
Hollister, CA (city) San Benito County	268	0.77
Langley Park, MD (cdp) Prince George's County	144	0.77
Shelton, WA (city) Mason County	75	0.76
Walnut Park, CA (cdp) Los Angeles County	116	0.73
Doraville, GA (city) DeKalb County	61	0.73
Healdsburg, CA (city) Sonoma County	81	0.72
Oxnard, CA (city) Ventura County	1,377	0.70
Burlington, WA (city) Skagit County	59	0.70
Siler City, NC (town) Chatham County	50	0.63
Lamont, CA (cdp) Kern County	90	0.60
Westgate, FL (cdp) Palm Beach County	48	0.60
Livingston, CA (city) Merced County	70	0.54
Alum Rock, CA (cdp) Santa Clara County	79	0.51
Lemon Hill, CA (cdp) Sacramento County	69	0.50
Fife, WA (city) Pierce County	46	0.50
Huntington Park, CA (city) Los Angeles County	286	0.49
Poughkeepsie, NY (city) Dutchess County	160	0.49
Gonzales, CA (city) Monterey County	39	0.48
Morganton, NC (city) Burke County	80	0.47
Watsonville, CA (city) Santa Cruz County	233	0.46
Selma, CA (city) Fresno County	107	0.46
Jacksonville, TX (city) Cherokee County	67	0.46
New Bedford, MA (city) Bristol County	430	0.45
Mount Vernon, WA (city) Skagit County	142	0.45
Muscoy, CA (cdp) San Bernardino County	47	0.44
Lexington, NE (city) Dawson County	45	0.44
San Rafael, CA (city) Marin County	248	0.43
Nipomo, CA (cdp) San Luis Obispo County	72	0.43
Orange Cove, CA (city) Fresno County	37	0.41
August, CA (cdp) San Joaquin County	34	0.41
Windsor, CA (town) Sonoma County	108	0.40
South El Monte, CA (city) Los Angeles County	81	0.40
Lake Los Angeles, CA (cdp) Los Angeles County	49	0.40
Cudahy, CA (city) Los Angeles County	94	0.39
Welby, CO (cdp) Adams County	58	0.39
Grover Beach, CA (city) San Luis Obispo County	51	0.39
Russellville, AL (city) Franklin County	38	0.39
East Los Angeles, CA (cdp) Los Angeles County	487	0.38
Parlier, CA (city) Fresno County	55	0.38
Fairview, NJ (borough) Bergen County	52	0.38
Country Club, CA (cdp) San Joaquin County	36	0.38
New Garden, PA (township) Chester County	44	0.37
Corning, CA (city) Tehama County	28	0.37
Gilroy, CA (city) Santa Clara County	174	0.36
Sanger, CA (city) Fresno County	87	0.36
Commerce, CA (city) Los Angeles County	46	0.36
Madera Acres, CA (cdp) Madera County	33	0.36
Santa Fe Springs, CA (city) Los Angeles County	56	0.35
Red Bank, NJ (borough) Monmouth County	43	0.35
Independence, OR (city) Polk County	30	0.35
Fresno, CA (city) Fresno County	1,666	0.34
Salinas, CA (city) Monterey County	508	0.34
Florence-Graham, CA (cdp) Los Angeles County	213	0.34
Graham, NC (city) Alamance County	48	0.34
Citrus, CA (cdp) Los Angeles County	37	0.34
Fair Oaks, GA (cdp) Cobb County	28	0.34
Vista, CA (city) San Diego County	308	0.33
West New York, NJ (town) Hudson County	166	0.33
Commerce City, CO (city) Adams County	152	0.33
Canton, GA (city) Cherokee County	76	0.33
West Puente Valley, CA (cdp) Los Angeles County	75	0.33
Lennox, CA (cdp) Los Angeles County	74	0.33
Ukiah, CA (city) Mendocino County	53	0.33
West Columbia, SC (city) Lexington County	49	0.33
Garden Acres, CA (cdp) San Joaquin County	35	0.33
Jupiter, FL (town) Palm Beach County	175	0.32
Montclair, CA (city) San Bernardino County	117	0.32
Los Banos, CA (city) Merced County	116	0.32
San Fernando, CA (city) Los Angeles County	75	0.32
Forest Grove, OR (city) Washington County	67	0.32
Home Gardens, CA (cdp) Riverside County	37	0.32
South Gate, CA (city) Los Angeles County	290	0.31
Cicero, IL (town) Cook County	256	0.31
Lompoc, CA (city) Santa Barbara County	130	0.31
Burien, WA (city) King County	102	0.31
Reedley, CA (city) Fresno County	74	0.31
Albertville, AL (city) Marshall County	66	0.31
Kerman, CA (city) Fresno County	42	0.31
Ontario, OR (city) Malheur County	35	0.31
Quartz Hill, CA (cdp) Los Angeles County	34	0.31
Valencia West, AZ (cdp) Pima County	29	0.31
Orosi, CA (cdp) Tulare County	27	0.31
Round Lake Park, IL (village) Lake County	23	0.31
Santa Ana, CA (city) Orange County	974	0.30
Gresham, OR (city) Multnomah County	319	0.30
Pico Rivera, CA (city) Los Angeles County	189	0.30
Fallbrook, CA (cdp) San Diego County	93	0.30
Cornelius, OR (city) Washington County	36	0.30
Toppenish, WA (city) Yakima County	27	0.30
Firebaugh, CA (city) Fresno County	23	0.30
Paramount, CA (city) Los Angeles County	159	0.29
Bloomington, CA (cdp) San Bernardino County	70	0.29
Bay Point, CA (cdp) Contra Costa County	62	0.29
Heber, UT (city) Wasatch County	33	0.29
White Plains, NY (city) Westchester County	162	0.28
Sherrelwood, CO (cdp) Adams County	51	0.28
Manchester, VA (cdp) Chesterfield County	30	0.28
Mount Kisco, NY (town/village) Westchester County	30	0.28
Northbrook, OH (cdp) Hamilton County	30	0.28
Larkfield-Wikiup, CA (cdp) Sonoma County	25	0.28
Elgin, IL (city) Kane County	292	0.27
Whittier, CA (city) Los Angeles County	229	0.27
Lynwood, CA (city) Los Angeles County	190	0.27
La Puente, CA (city) Los Angeles County	109	0.27
Stanton, CA (city) Orange County	103	0.27
Bell, CA (city) Los Angeles County	95	0.27
Maywood, CA (city) Los Angeles County	75	0.27
Soledad, CA (city) Monterey County	69	0.27
Hermiston, OR (city) Umatilla County	46	0.27
Taft, CA (city) Kern County	25	0.27
San Bernardino, CA (city) San Bernardino County	540	0.26
Escondido, CA (city) San Diego County	374	0.26
Montebello, CA (city) Los Angeles County	162	0.26
Fort Myers, FL (city) Lee County	159	0.26
Colton, CA (city) San Bernardino County	134	0.26
West Sacramento, CA (city) Yolo County	129	0.26
Moorpark, CA (city) Ventura County	90	0.26
Lawndale, CA (city) Los Angeles County	86	0.26
Santa Paula, CA (city) Ventura County	77	0.26
Hayesville, OR (cdp) Marion County	52	0.26
Rio Linda, CA (cdp) Sacramento County	40	0.26
North Fair Oaks, CA (cdp) San Mateo County	38	0.26
Monmouth, OR (city) Polk County	25	0.26
Los Angeles, CA (city) Los Angeles County	9,589	0.25
Ontario, CA (city) San Bernardino County	417	0.25
Azusa, CA (city) Los Angeles County	114	0.25
Greenacres, FL (city) Palm Beach County	95	0.25
Seaside, CA (city) Monterey County	84	0.25
Valinda, CA (cdp) Los Angeles County	57	0.25
South Lake Tahoe, CA (city) El Dorado County	53	0.25
Bensenville, IL (village) DuPage County	45	0.25
Douglas, AZ (city) Cochise County	43	0.25
Fillmore, CA (city) Ventura County	38	0.25
Cherryland, CA (cdp) Alameda County	37	0.25
Imperial, CA (city) Imperial County	37	0.25
Somerton, AZ (city) Yuma County	36	0.25
Carpinteria, CA (city) Santa Barbara County	33	0.25

SECTION THREE

Race

American Indian: Navajo

U.S. and 50 States Sorted by Population and Percent of Total Population

Place	Population	%
United States	**332,129**	**0.11**
Arizona	140,263	2.19
New Mexico	116,157	5.64
Utah	17,703	0.64
California	17,080	0.05
Colorado	9,235	0.18
Texas	4,269	0.02
Nevada	2,597	0.10
Washington	2,372	0.04
Oklahoma	1,954	0.05
Oregon	1,533	0.04
Idaho	1,321	0.08
Kansas	1,192	0.04
Illinois	1,063	0.01
Florida	1,043	0.01
Ohio	809	0.01
Missouri	798	0.01
New York	788	<0.01
North Carolina	774	0.01
Virginia	753	0.01
Hawaii	656	0.05
Georgia	653	0.01
Michigan	646	0.01
Montana	621	0.06
Pennsylvania	619	<0.01
Indiana	547	0.01
Maryland	520	0.01
Wyoming	506	0.09
Alaska	475	0.07
Tennessee	415	0.01
Wisconsin	411	0.01
Minnesota	388	0.01
Arkansas	331	0.01
Massachusetts	321	<0.01
Nebraska	314	0.02
Kentucky	307	0.01
South Dakota	300	0.04
South Carolina	297	0.01
New Jersey	294	<0.01
Louisiana	277	0.01
Iowa	272	0.01
Alabama	251	0.01
Connecticut	164	<0.01
Mississippi	163	0.01
North Dakota	144	0.02
West Virginia	111	0.01
Maine	106	0.01
New Hampshire	96	0.01
Rhode Island	73	0.01
District of Columbia	62	0.01
Delaware	46	0.01
Vermont	39	0.01

Place	Population	%
New Mexico	116,157	5.64
Arizona	140,263	2.19
Utah	17,703	0.64
Colorado	9,235	0.18
United States	**332,129**	**0.11**
Nevada	2,597	0.10
Wyoming	506	0.09
Idaho	1,321	0.08
Alaska	475	0.07
Montana	621	0.06
California	17,080	0.05
Oklahoma	1,954	0.05
Hawaii	656	0.05
Washington	2,372	0.04
Oregon	1,533	0.04
Kansas	1,192	0.04
South Dakota	300	0.04
Texas	4,269	0.02
Nebraska	314	0.02
North Dakota	144	0.02
Illinois	1,063	0.01
Florida	1,043	0.01
Ohio	809	0.01
Missouri	798	0.01
North Carolina	774	0.01
Virginia	753	0.01
Georgia	653	0.01
Michigan	646	0.01
Indiana	547	0.01
Maryland	520	0.01
Tennessee	415	0.01
Wisconsin	411	0.01
Minnesota	388	0.01
Arkansas	331	0.01
Kentucky	307	0.01
South Carolina	297	0.01
Louisiana	277	0.01
Iowa	272	0.01
Alabama	251	0.01
Mississippi	163	0.01
West Virginia	111	0.01
Maine	106	0.01
New Hampshire	96	0.01
Rhode Island	73	0.01
District of Columbia	62	0.01
Delaware	46	0.01
Vermont	39	0.01
New York	788	<0.01
Pennsylvania	619	<0.01
Massachusetts	321	<0.01
New Jersey	294	<0.01
Connecticut	164	<0.01

Please refer to the Explanation of Data in the front of the book for more detailed information.

Race

American Indian: Navajo

Top 150 Places Sorted by Population

Based on all places, regardless of total population

Place	Population	%
Albuquerque, NM (city) Bernalillo County	12,768	2.34
Phoenix, AZ (city) Maricopa County	12,260	0.85
Farmington, NM (city) San Juan County	9,522	20.76
Gallup, NM (city) McKinley County	8,119	37.45
Shiprock, NM (cdp) San Juan County	7,603	91.66
Tuba City, AZ (cdp) Coconino County	7,050	81.87
Flagstaff, AZ (city) Coconino County	5,504	8.36
Kayenta, AZ (cdp) Navajo County	4,450	85.76
Mesa, AZ (city) Maricopa County	4,243	0.97
Kirtland, NM (cdp) San Juan County	3,975	50.48
Chinle, AZ (cdp) Apache County	3,967	87.80
Fort Defiance, AZ (cdp) Apache County	3,187	87.94
Page, AZ (city) Coconino County	2,356	32.51
Window Rock, AZ (cdp) Apache County	2,295	84.62
Tempe, AZ (city) Maricopa County	2,234	1.38
Crownpoint, NM (cdp) McKinley County	1,913	83.98
Winslow, AZ (city) Navajo County	1,845	19.11
Tucson, AZ (city) Pima County	1,840	0.35
Lukachukai, AZ (cdp) Apache County	1,651	97.06
Glendale, AZ (city) Maricopa County	1,570	0.69
Upper Fruitland, NM (cdp) San Juan County	1,521	91.52
Kaibito, AZ (cdp) Coconino County	1,456	95.66
Navajo, NM (cdp) McKinley County	1,431	86.99
Thoreau, NM (cdp) McKinley County	1,385	74.26
LeChee, AZ (cdp) Coconino County	1,379	95.56
Bloomfield, NM (city) San Juan County	1,346	16.59
Los Angeles, CA (city) Los Angeles County	1,260	0.03
Rio Rancho, NM (city) Sandoval County	1,234	1.41
Many Farms, AZ (cdp) Apache County	1,188	88.13
Chandler, AZ (city) Maricopa County	1,180	0.50
St. Michaels, AZ (cdp) Apache County	1,144	79.28
Holbrook, AZ (city) Navajo County	1,143	22.62
Salt Lake City, UT (city) Salt Lake County	1,137	0.61
Denver, CO (city) Denver County	1,118	0.19
Dilkon, AZ (cdp) Navajo County	1,103	93.16
Tsaile, AZ (cdp) Apache County	1,056	87.63
Church Rock, NM (cdp) McKinley County	1,032	91.49
Ganado, AZ (cdp) Apache County	1,029	85.04
Alamo, NM (cdp) Socorro County	1,019	93.92
Houck, AZ (cdp) Apache County	977	95.41
Twin Lakes, NM (cdp) McKinley County	931	88.50
Lee Acres, NM (cdp) San Juan County	893	15.24
Leupp, AZ (cdp) Coconino County	877	92.22
Grants, NM (city) Cibola County	861	9.38
Blanding, UT (city) San Juan County	860	25.48
West Valley City, UT (city) Salt Lake County	818	0.63
Cameron, AZ (cdp) Coconino County	801	90.51
Pinon, AZ (cdp) Navajo County	776	85.84
Whitecone, AZ (cdp) Navajo County	769	94.12
Round Rock, AZ (cdp) Apache County	752	95.31
Ojo Amarillo, NM (cdp) San Juan County	727	94.91
Cortez, CO (city) Montezuma County	718	8.46
Gilbert, AZ (town) Maricopa County	714	0.34
Dennehotso, AZ (cdp) Apache County	713	95.58
Low Mountain, AZ (cdp) Navajo County	707	93.39
Napi Headquarters, NM (cdp) San Juan County	702	96.56
Teec Nos Pos, AZ (cdp) Apache County	700	95.89
Waterflow, NM (cdp) San Juan County	700	41.92
Sawmill, AZ (cdp) Apache County	694	92.78
Colorado Springs, CO (city) El Paso County	674	0.16
Tohatchi, NM (cdp) McKinley County	671	83.04
St. George, UT (city) Washington County	642	0.88
Nenahnezad, NM (cdp) San Juan County	627	91.13
Rock Point, AZ (cdp) Apache County	611	95.17
Scottsdale, AZ (city) Maricopa County	610	0.28
Oljato-Monument Valley, UT (cdp) San Juan County	604	89.61
Doney Park, AZ (cdp) Coconino County	595	11.03
Las Vegas, NV (city) Clark County	582	0.10
Durango, CO (city) La Plata County	561	3.32
Aztec, NM (city) San Juan County	535	7.91
Rock Springs, NM (cdp) McKinley County	532	93.83
San Diego, CA (city) San Diego County	532	0.04
Tonalea, AZ (cdp) Coconino County	522	95.08
Shonto, AZ (cdp) Navajo County	520	87.99
Peoria, AZ (city) Yavapai County	499	0.32
Burnside, AZ (cdp) Apache County	477	88.83
Greasewood, AZ (cdp) Navajo County	477	87.20
San Jose, CA (city) Santa Clara County	476	0.05
Aneth, UT (cdp) San Juan County	472	94.21
Chilchinbito, AZ (cdp) Navajo County	463	91.50
Nazlini, AZ (cdp) Apache County	444	90.80
Bitter Springs, AZ (cdp) Coconino County	442	97.79
Sanders, AZ (cdp) Apache County	434	68.89
Provo, UT (city) Utah County	428	0.38
Tees Toh, AZ (cdp) Navajo County	426	95.09
Yah-ta-hey, NM (cdp) McKinley County	422	71.53
Nakaibito, NM (cdp) McKinley County	420	90.13
Ogden, UT (city) Weber County	402	0.49
Orem, UT (city) Utah County	395	0.45
Avondale, AZ (city) Maricopa County	385	0.50
Rough Rock, AZ (cdp) Apache County	384	92.75
Red Mesa, AZ (cdp) Apache County	367	76.46
Las Cruces, NM (city) Doña Ana County	365	0.37
West Jordan, UT (city) Salt Lake County	365	0.35
Sanostee, NM (cdp) San Juan County	358	96.50
Sacramento, CA (city) Sacramento County	355	0.08
Pueblo, CO (city) Pueblo County	340	0.32
Lawrence, KS (city) Douglas County	336	0.38
Aurora, CO (city) Arapahoe County	334	0.10
Millcreek, UT (cdp) Salt Lake County	332	0.53
Navajo Mountain, UT (cdp) San Juan County	325	91.81
South Salt Lake, UT (city) Salt Lake County	321	1.36
Long Beach, CA (city) Los Angeles County	320	0.07
Milan, NM (village) Cibola County	317	9.77
Lakewood, CO (city) Jefferson County	315	0.22
San Tan Valley, AZ (cdp) Pinal County	314	0.39
Del Muerto, AZ (cdp) Apache County	313	95.14
Cedar City, UT (city) Iron County	310	1.07
Henderson, NV (city) Clark County	307	0.12
Logan, UT (city) Cache County	305	0.63
West Hammond, NM (cdp) San Juan County	301	10.79
Beclabito, NM (cdp) San Juan County	294	92.74
Fresno, CA (city) Fresno County	294	0.06
Santa Fe, NM (city) Santa Fe County	292	0.43
Naschitti, NM (cdp) San Juan County	291	96.68
Taylorsville, UT (city) Salt Lake County	289	0.49
Snowflake, AZ (town) Navajo County	286	5.12
Montezuma Creek, UT (cdp) San Juan County	285	85.07
Newcomb, NM (cdp) San Juan County	280	82.60
Nageezi, NM (cdp) San Juan County	279	97.55
Torreon, NM (cdp) Sandoval County	278	85.28
San Antonio, TX (city) Medina County	278	0.02
New York, NY (city) Kings County	272	<0.01
Grand Canyon Village, AZ (cdp) Coconino County	271	13.52
Maricopa, AZ (city) Pinal County	270	0.62
Anchorage, AK (municipality) Anchorage Municipality	261	0.09
Chicago, IL (city) Cook County	261	0.01
Halchita, UT (cdp) San Juan County	258	96.99
Crystal, NM (cdp) San Juan County	258	82.96
Socorro, NM (city) Socorro County	258	2.85
Steamboat, AZ (cdp) Apache County	256	90.14
Tolani Lake, AZ (cdp) Coconino County	252	90.00
South Valley, NM (cdp) Bernalillo County	249	0.61
Portland, OR (city) Multnomah County	245	0.04
Oklahoma City, OK (city) Oklahoma County	244	0.04
Sheep Springs, NM (cdp) San Juan County	243	99.18
San Francisco, CA (city) San Francisco County	242	0.03
Kearns, UT (cdp) Salt Lake County	240	0.67
El Paso, TX (city) El Paso County	239	0.04
Stockton, CA (city) San Joaquin County	233	0.08
Klagetoh, AZ (cdp) Apache County	230	95.04
Indian Wells, AZ (cdp) Navajo County	227	89.02
Paradise, NV (cdp) Clark County	224	0.10
Cornfields, AZ (cdp) Apache County	218	85.49
Murray, UT (city) Salt Lake County	218	0.47
Tse Bonito, NM (cdp) McKinley County	211	70.57
Sunrise Manor, NV (cdp) Clark County	210	0.11
Seattle, WA (city) King County	208	0.03
Show Low, AZ (city) Navajo County	207	1.94
Riverside, CA (city) Riverside County	201	0.07

SECTION THREE

Please refer to the Explanation of Data in the front of the book for more detailed information.

Race

American Indian: Navajo

Top 150 Places Sorted by Percent of Total Population

Based on all places, regardless of total population

Place	Population	%
Sheep Springs, NM (cdp) San Juan County	243	99.18
Bitter Springs, AZ (cdp) Coconino County	442	97.79
Nageezi, NM (cdp) San Juan County	279	97.55
Lukachukai, AZ (cdp) Apache County	1,651	97.06
Halchita, UT (cdp) San Juan County	258	96.99
Naschitti, NM (cdp) San Juan County	291	96.68
Napi Headquarters, NM (cdp) San Juan County	702	96.56
Sanostee, NM (cdp) San Juan County	358	96.50
Sehili, AZ (cdp) Apache County	130	96.30
Wide Ruins, AZ (cdp) Apache County	169	96.02
Teec Nos Pos, AZ (cdp) Apache County	700	95.89
Kaibito, AZ (cdp) Coconino County	1,456	95.66
Dennehotso, AZ (cdp) Apache County	713	95.58
LeChee, AZ (cdp) Coconino County	1,379	95.56
Houck, AZ (cdp) Apache County	977	95.41
Tselakai Dezza, UT (cdp) San Juan County	104	95.41
Round Rock, AZ (cdp) Apache County	752	95.31
Rock Point, AZ (cdp) Apache County	611	95.17
Del Muerto, AZ (cdp) Apache County	313	95.14
Tees Toh, AZ (cdp) Navajo County	426	95.09
Tonalea, AZ (cdp) Coconino County	522	95.08
Klagetoh, AZ (cdp) Apache County	230	95.04
Ojo Amarillo, NM (cdp) San Juan County	727	94.91
Aneth, UT (cdp) San Juan County	472	94.21
Whitecone, AZ (cdp) Navajo County	769	94.12
Alamo, NM (cdp) Socorro County	1,019	93.92
Rock Springs, NM (cdp) McKinley County	532	93.83
Brimhall Nizhoni, NM (cdp) McKinley County	186	93.47
Low Mountain, AZ (cdp) Navajo County	707	93.39
Dilkon, AZ (cdp) Navajo County	1,103	93.16
Sawmill, AZ (cdp) Apache County	694	92.78
Rough Rock, AZ (cdp) Apache County	384	92.75
Beclabito, NM (cdp) San Juan County	294	92.74
Red Rock, AZ (cdp) Apache County	156	92.31
Toyei, AZ (cdp) Apache County	12	92.31
Leupp, AZ (cdp) Coconino County	877	92.22
Navajo Mountain, UT (cdp) San Juan County	325	91.81
Shiprock, NM (cdp) San Juan County	7,603	91.66
Upper Fruitland, NM (cdp) San Juan County	1,521	91.52
Chilchinbito, AZ (cdp) Navajo County	463	91.50
Church Rock, NM (cdp) McKinley County	1,032	91.49
Nenahnezad, NM (cdp) San Juan County	627	91.13
Nazlini, AZ (cdp) Apache County	444	90.80
Cameron, AZ (cdp) Coconino County	801	90.51
Oak Springs, AZ (cdp) Apache County	57	90.48
Steamboat, AZ (cdp) Apache County	256	90.14
Nakaibito, NM (cdp) McKinley County	420	90.13
Tolani Lake, AZ (cdp) Coconino County	252	90.00
Oljato-Monument Valley, UT (cdp) San Juan County	604	89.61
Indian Wells, AZ (cdp) Navajo County	227	89.02
Burnside, AZ (cdp) Apache County	477	88.83
Twin Lakes, NM (cdp) McKinley County	931	88.50
Many Farms, AZ (cdp) Apache County	1,188	88.13
Pueblo Pintado, NM (cdp) McKinley County	169	88.02
Lupton, AZ (cdp) Apache County	22	88.00
Shonto, AZ (cdp) Navajo County	520	87.99
Fort Defiance, AZ (cdp) Apache County	3,187	87.94
Chinle, AZ (cdp) Apache County	3,967	87.80
Tsaile, AZ (cdp) Apache County	1,056	87.63
Greasewood, AZ (cdp) Navajo County	477	87.20
Navajo, NM (cdp) McKinley County	1,431	86.99
Pinon, AZ (cdp) Navajo County	776	85.84
Kayenta, AZ (cdp) Navajo County	4,450	85.76
Cornfields, AZ (cdp) Apache County	218	85.49
Torreon, NM (cdp) Sandoval County	278	85.28
Montezuma Creek, UT (cdp) San Juan County	285	85.07
Ganado, AZ (cdp) Apache County	1,029	85.04
Window Rock, AZ (cdp) Apache County	2,295	84.62
Crownpoint, NM (cdp) McKinley County	1,913	83.98
Oljato-Monument Valley, AZ (cdp) Navajo County	129	83.77
Tohatchi, NM (cdp) McKinley County	671	83.04
Crystal, NM (cdp) San Juan County	258	82.96
Newcomb, NM (cdp) San Juan County	280	82.60
Tuba City, AZ (cdp) Coconino County	7,050	81.87
St. Michaels, AZ (cdp) Apache County	1,144	79.28

Place	Population	%
Pinehill, NM (cdp) Cibola County	69	78.41
Red Mesa, AZ (cdp) Apache County	367	76.46
Cottonwood, AZ (cdp) Apache County	172	76.11
Thoreau, NM (cdp) McKinley County	1,385	74.26
Seba Dalkai, AZ (cdp) Navajo County	99	72.79
Hard Rock, AZ (cdp) Navajo County	68	72.34
Lake Valley, NM (cdp) San Juan County	46	71.88
Yah-ta-hey, NM (cdp) McKinley County	422	71.53
Tse Bonito, NM (cdp) McKinley County	211	70.57
Sanders, AZ (cdp) Apache County	434	68.89
Jeddito, AZ (cdp) Navajo County	197	67.24
Kirtland, NM (cdp) San Juan County	3,975	50.48
Waterflow, NM (cdp) San Juan County	700	41.92
Gallup, NM (city) McKinley County	8,119	37.45
Page, AZ (city) Coconino County	2,356	32.51
Winslow West, AZ (cdp) Navajo County	122	27.85
Blanding, UT (city) San Juan County	860	25.48
Bluff, UT (cdp) San Juan County	63	24.42
Holbrook, AZ (city) Navajo County	1,143	22.62
White Mesa, UT (cdp) San Juan County	53	21.90
Farmington, NM (city) San Juan County	9,522	20.76
Cuba, NM (village) Sandoval County	149	20.38
Cutter, AZ (cdp) Gila County	15	20.27
Winslow, AZ (city) Navajo County	1,845	19.11
Ramah, NM (cdp) McKinley County	65	17.57
Quemado, NM (cdp) Catron County	38	16.67
Bloomfield, NM (city) San Juan County	1,346	16.59
Lee Acres, NM (cdp) San Juan County	893	15.24
Keams Canyon, AZ (cdp) Navajo County	43	14.14
Grand Canyon Village, AZ (cdp) Coconino County	271	13.52
Valentine, AZ (cdp) Mohave County	5	13.16
McCartys Village, NM (cdp) Cibola County	6	12.50
First Mesa, AZ (cdp) Navajo County	192	12.35
Moenkopi, AZ (cdp) Coconino County	114	11.83
Towaoc, CO (cdp) Montezuma County	128	11.78
Sun Valley, AZ (cdp) Navajo County	37	11.71
Doney Park, AZ (cdp) Coconino County	595	11.03
West Hammond, NM (cdp) San Juan County	301	10.79
Highland Meadows, NM (cdp) Valencia County	67	10.74
Anegam, AZ (cdp) Pima County	16	10.60
Manzano, NM (cdp) Torrance County	3	10.34
Bluewater Village, NM (cdp) Cibola County	64	10.19
Milan, NM (village) Cibola County	317	9.77
Magdalena, NM (village) Socorro County	91	9.70
Cowlic, AZ (cdp) Pima County	13	9.63
Grants, NM (city) Cibola County	861	9.38
Anzac Village, NM (cdp) Cibola County	5	9.26
Tusayan, AZ (cdp) Coconino County	50	8.96
Chamizal, NM (cdp) Socorro County	9	8.91
Kaka, AZ (cdp) Maricopa County	12	8.51
Cortez, CO (city) Montezuma County	718	8.46
Flagstaff, AZ (city) Coconino County	5,504	8.36
Aztec, NM (city) San Juan County	535	7.91
Joseph City, AZ (cdp) Navajo County	108	7.79
Old Eucha, OK (cdp) Delaware County	4	7.69
Chical, NM (cdp) Valencia County	8	7.48
Montgomery Creek, CA (cdp) Shasta County	12	7.36
Dulce, NM (cdp) Rio Arriba County	198	7.22
Edith Endave, NM (cdp) Bernalillo County	15	7.11
Fort Apache, AZ (cdp) Navajo County	10	6.99
Lumberton, NM (cdp) Rio Arriba County	5	6.85
McNary, AZ (cdp) Apache County	36	6.82
Young Place, NM (cdp) San Juan County	12	6.42
Carrizo, AZ (cdp) Gila County	8	6.30
Valle, AZ (cdp) Coconino County	52	6.25
Fredonia, AZ (town) Coconino County	82	6.24
Second Mesa, AZ (cdp) Navajo County	59	6.13
Turkey Creek, AZ (cdp) Navajo County	18	6.12
Hondah, AZ (cdp) Navajo County	49	6.03
North Acomita Village, NM (cdp) Cibola County	18	5.94
Bent, NM (cdp) Otero County	7	5.88
Picuris Pueblo, NM (cdp) Taos County	4	5.88
Bluewater Acres, NM (cdp) Cibola County	12	5.83
Seama, NM (cdp) Cibola County	27	5.81
Kykotsmovi Village, AZ (cdp) Navajo County	42	5.63

Please refer to the Explanation of Data in the front of the book for more detailed information.

Race

American Indian: Navajo

Top 150 Places Sorted by Percent of Total Population

Based on places with total population of 7,500 or more

Place	Population	%
Shiprock, NM (cdp) San Juan County	7,603	91.66
Tuba City, AZ (cdp) Coconino County	7,050	81.87
Kirtland, NM (cdp) San Juan County	3,975	50.48
Gallup, NM (city) McKinley County	8,119	37.45
Farmington, NM (city) San Juan County	9,522	20.76
Winslow, AZ (city) Navajo County	1,845	19.11
Bloomfield, NM (city) San Juan County	1,346	16.59
Grants, NM (city) Cibola County	861	9.38
Cortez, CO (city) Montezuma County	718	8.46
Flagstaff, AZ (city) Coconino County	5,504	8.36
Durango, CO (city) La Plata County	561	3.32
Socorro, NM (city) Socorro County	258	2.85
Albuquerque, NM (city) Bernalillo County	12,768	2.34
Show Low, AZ (city) Navajo County	207	1.94
North Valley, NM (cdp) Bernalillo County	178	1.57
Rio Rancho, NM (city) Sandoval County	1,234	1.41
Tempe, AZ (city) Maricopa County	2,234	1.38
South Salt Lake, UT (city) Salt Lake County	321	1.36
Cedar City, UT (city) Iron County	310	1.07
Richfield, UT (city) Sevier County	81	1.07
Mesa, AZ (city) Maricopa County	4,243	0.97
Bernalillo, NM (town) Sandoval County	77	0.93
Portales, NM (city) Roosevelt County	112	0.91
Price, UT (city) Carbon County	79	0.91
Camp Verde, AZ (town) Yavapai County	97	0.89
St. George, UT (city) Washington County	642	0.88
Phoenix, AZ (city) Maricopa County	12,260	0.85
Brigham City, UT (city) Box Elder County	149	0.83
Payson, AZ (town) Gila County	120	0.78
Hurricane, UT (city) Washington County	104	0.76
Glendale, AZ (city) Maricopa County	1,570	0.69
Los Lunas, NM (village) Valencia County	101	0.68
Corrales, NM (village) Sandoval County	57	0.68
Kearns, UT (cdp) Salt Lake County	240	0.67
West Valley City, UT (city) Salt Lake County	818	0.63
Logan, UT (city) Cache County	305	0.63
Maricopa, AZ (city) Pinal County	270	0.62
Salt Lake City, UT (city) Salt Lake County	1,137	0.61
South Valley, NM (cdp) Bernalillo County	249	0.61
Alamosa, CO (city) Alamosa County	50	0.57
Kingman, AZ (city) Mohave County	156	0.56
Barstow, CA (city) San Bernardino County	127	0.56
Las Vegas, NM (city) San Miguel County	74	0.54
Millcreek, UT (cdp) Salt Lake County	332	0.53
El Mirage, AZ (city) Maricopa County	169	0.53
Florence, AZ (town) Pinal County	136	0.53
Midvale, UT (city) Salt Lake County	146	0.52
Ruidoso, NM (village) Lincoln County	42	0.52
Tooele, UT (city) Tooele County	162	0.51
Chandler, AZ (city) Maricopa County	1,180	0.50
Avondale, AZ (city) Maricopa County	385	0.50
Ogden, UT (city) Weber County	402	0.49
Taylorsville, UT (city) Salt Lake County	289	0.49
Murray, UT (city) Salt Lake County	218	0.47
Magna, UT (cdp) Salt Lake County	124	0.47
Blackfoot, ID (city) Bingham County	56	0.47
Verde Village, AZ (cdp) Yavapai County	55	0.47
Trinidad, CO (city) Las Animas County	43	0.47
Washington, UT (city) Washington County	87	0.46
Artesia, NM (city) Eddy County	52	0.46
Orem, UT (city) Utah County	395	0.45
Santa Fe, NM (city) Santa Fe County	292	0.43
Burley, ID (city) Cassia County	43	0.42
Safford, AZ (city) Graham County	40	0.42
Cottonwood, AZ (city) Yavapai County	45	0.40
San Tan Valley, AZ (cdp) Pinal County	314	0.39
Welby, CO (cdp) Adams County	58	0.39
Chino Valley, AZ (town) Yavapai County	42	0.39
Provo, UT (city) Utah County	428	0.38
Lawrence, KS (city) Douglas County	336	0.38
Las Cruces, NM (city) Doña Ana County	365	0.37
Casa Grande, AZ (city) Pinal County	178	0.37
Sherrelwood, CO (cdp) Adams County	68	0.37
New Kingman-Butler, AZ (cdp) Mohave County	45	0.37
Camp Pendleton South, CA (cdp) San Diego County	39	0.37
Santaquin, UT (city) Utah County	34	0.37
Globe, AZ (city) Gila County	28	0.37
Prescott, AZ (city) Yavapai County	144	0.36
Mesquite, NV (city) Clark County	55	0.36
Silver City, NM (town) Grant County	37	0.36
Tucson, AZ (city) Pima County	1,840	0.35
West Jordan, UT (city) Salt Lake County	365	0.35
Buckeye, AZ (town) Maricopa County	176	0.35
Mapleton, UT (city) Utah County	28	0.35
Gilbert, AZ (town) Maricopa County	714	0.34
North Salt Lake, UT (city) Davis County	55	0.34
Espanola, NM (city) Rio Arriba County	35	0.34
Woods Cross, UT (city) Davis County	33	0.34
Fountain, CO (city) El Paso County	86	0.33
Eagle Mountain, UT (city) Utah County	70	0.33
Flowing Wells, AZ (cdp) Pima County	55	0.33
Riverdale, UT (city) Weber County	28	0.33
Peoria, AZ (city) Yavapai County	499	0.32
Pueblo, CO (city) Pueblo County	340	0.32
Douglas, AZ (city) Cochise County	56	0.32
Alamogordo, NM (city) Otero County	95	0.31
Tanque Verde, AZ (cdp) Pima County	52	0.31
Federal Heights, CO (city) Adams County	36	0.31
Prescott Valley, AZ (town) Yavapai County	115	0.30
Springville, UT (city) Utah County	89	0.30
Payson, UT (city) Utah County	54	0.30
Coolidge, AZ (city) Pinal County	35	0.30
Hyrum, UT (city) Cache County	23	0.30
Schofield Barracks, HI (cdp) Honolulu County	48	0.29
West Haven, UT (city) Weber County	30	0.29
Scottsdale, AZ (city) Maricopa County	610	0.28
Goodyear, AZ (city) Maricopa County	184	0.28
Spanish Fork, UT (city) Utah County	98	0.28
Hobbs, NM (city) Lea County	97	0.28
Evanston, WY (city) Uinta County	34	0.28
Picture Rocks, AZ (cdp) Pima County	27	0.28
Valencia West, AZ (cdp) Pima County	26	0.28
Vernal, UT (city) Uintah County	25	0.28
Washington Terrace, UT (city) Weber County	25	0.28
Northglenn, CO (city) Adams County	95	0.27
Clearfield, UT (city) Davis County	81	0.27
North Logan, UT (city) Cache County	22	0.27
Lehi, UT (city) Utah County	122	0.26
Englewood, CO (city) Arapahoe County	79	0.26
Gold Canyon, AZ (cdp) Pinal County	26	0.26
West Point, UT (city) Davis County	25	0.26
Commerce City, CO (city) Adams County	114	0.25
Wheat Ridge, CO (city) Jefferson County	76	0.25
North Ogden, UT (city) Weber County	44	0.25
South Ogden, UT (city) Weber County	41	0.25
Drexel Heights, AZ (cdp) Pima County	66	0.24
Riverton, WY (city) Fremont County	26	0.24
Arizona City, AZ (cdp) Pinal County	25	0.24
Casas Adobes, AZ (cdp) Pima County	155	0.23
Grand Junction, CO (city) Mesa County	132	0.23
Apache Junction, AZ (city) Pinal County	84	0.23
Security-Widefield, CO (cdp) El Paso County	75	0.23
Carlsbad, NM (city) Eddy County	60	0.23
Green River, WY (city) Sweetwater County	29	0.23
Fort Lewis, WA (cdp) Pierce County	25	0.23
Lovington, NM (city) Lea County	25	0.23
Clinton, OK (city) Custer County	21	0.23
Lakewood, CO (city) Jefferson County	315	0.22
Sierra Vista, AZ (city) Cochise County	98	0.22
Roy, UT (city) Weber County	81	0.22
Twentynine Palms, CA (city) San Bernardino County	55	0.22
Elko, NV (city) Elko County	41	0.22
Tucson Estates, AZ (cdp) Pima County	27	0.22
Berkley, CO (cdp) Adams County	25	0.22
Sedona, AZ (city) Yavapai County	22	0.22
Delta, CO (city) Delta County	20	0.22
Grantsville, UT (city) Tooele County	20	0.22
Fallon, NV (city) Churchill County	19	0.22
Golden Valley, AZ (cdp) Mohave County	18	0.22
Fruitvale, CO (cdp) Mesa County	17	0.22

SECTION THREE

Please refer to the Explanation of Data in the front of the book for more detailed information.

Race

American Indian: Osage

U.S. and 50 States Sorted by Population and Percent of Total Population

Place	Population	%
United States	**18,576**	**0.01**
Oklahoma	7,586	0.20
California	2,168	0.01
Texas	1,535	0.01
Kansas	898	0.03
Missouri	799	0.01
Oregon	580	0.02
Colorado	541	0.01
Washington	518	0.01
Arkansas	379	0.01
Arizona	312	<0.01
Florida	308	<0.01
Illinois	238	<0.01
New Mexico	234	0.01
Virginia	153	<0.01
Georgia	137	<0.01
Nevada	131	<0.01
North Carolina	131	<0.01
Idaho	129	0.01
Ohio	125	<0.01
Tennessee	123	<0.01
Indiana	114	<0.01
Michigan	110	<0.01
Louisiana	103	<0.01
Utah	95	<0.01
New York	86	<0.01
Hawaii	83	0.01
Pennsylvania	80	<0.01
Maryland	77	<0.01
Kentucky	76	<0.01
Alaska	75	0.01
Montana	70	0.01
Wisconsin	70	<0.01
Minnesota	62	<0.01
Massachusetts	60	<0.01
Iowa	52	<0.01
South Carolina	45	<0.01
New Jersey	41	<0.01
Mississippi	38	<0.01
Alabama	33	<0.01
Wyoming	30	0.01
South Dakota	28	<0.01
Nebraska	25	<0.01
New Hampshire	19	<0.01
District of Columbia	17	<0.01
Connecticut	16	<0.01
Maine	13	<0.01
Vermont	13	<0.01
Rhode Island	7	<0.01
West Virginia	7	<0.01
Delaware	4	<0.01
North Dakota	2	<0.01

Place	Population	%
Oklahoma	7,586	0.20
Kansas	898	0.03
Oregon	580	0.02
United States	**18,576**	**0.01**
California	2,168	0.01
Texas	1,535	0.01
Missouri	799	0.01
Colorado	541	0.01
Washington	518	0.01
Arkansas	379	0.01
New Mexico	234	0.01
Idaho	129	0.01
Hawaii	83	0.01
Alaska	75	0.01
Montana	70	0.01
Wyoming	30	0.01
Arizona	312	<0.01
Florida	308	<0.01
Illinois	238	<0.01
Virginia	153	<0.01
Georgia	137	<0.01
Nevada	131	<0.01
North Carolina	131	<0.01
Ohio	125	<0.01
Tennessee	123	<0.01
Indiana	114	<0.01
Michigan	110	<0.01
Louisiana	103	<0.01
Utah	95	<0.01
New York	86	<0.01
Pennsylvania	80	<0.01
Maryland	77	<0.01
Kentucky	76	<0.01
Wisconsin	70	<0.01
Minnesota	62	<0.01
Massachusetts	60	<0.01
Iowa	52	<0.01
South Carolina	45	<0.01
New Jersey	41	<0.01
Mississippi	38	<0.01
Alabama	33	<0.01
South Dakota	28	<0.01
Nebraska	25	<0.01
New Hampshire	19	<0.01
District of Columbia	17	<0.01
Connecticut	16	<0.01
Maine	13	<0.01
Vermont	13	<0.01
Rhode Island	7	<0.01
West Virginia	7	<0.01
Delaware	4	<0.01
North Dakota	2	<0.01

Please refer to the Explanation of Data in the front of the book for more detailed information.

Race

American Indian: Osage

Top 150 Places Sorted by Population

Based on all places, regardless of total population

Place	Population	%
Tulsa, OK (city) Tulsa County	855	0.22
Pawhuska, OK (city) Osage County	567	15.82
Bartlesville, OK (city) Washington County	358	1.00
Oklahoma City, OK (city) Oklahoma County	308	0.05
Hominy, OK (city) Osage County	304	8.53
Skiatook, OK (town) Osage County	276	3.73
Fairfax, OK (town) Osage County	263	19.06
Broken Arrow, OK (city) Tulsa County	205	0.21
Wichita, KS (city) Sedgwick County	189	0.05
Ponca City, OK (city) Kay County	179	0.71
Norman, OK (city) Cleveland County	135	0.12
Stillwater, OK (city) Payne County	133	0.29
Los Angeles, CA (city) Los Angeles County	107	<0.01
Owasso, OK (city) Tulsa County	86	0.30
Barnsdall, OK (city) Osage County	84	6.76
Houston, TX (city) Harris County	84	<0.01
Sand Springs, OK (city) Tulsa County	76	0.40
San Diego, CA (city) San Diego County	70	0.01
Colorado Springs, CO (city) El Paso County	67	0.02
Phoenix, AZ (city) Maricopa County	64	<0.01
Denver, CO (city) Denver County	62	0.01
Claremore, OK (city) Rogers County	61	0.33
San Antonio, TX (city) Medina County	60	<0.01
Edmond, OK (city) Oklahoma County	58	0.07
Portland, OR (city) Multnomah County	58	0.01
Albuquerque, NM (city) Bernalillo County	56	0.01
Dallas, TX (city) Dallas County	55	<0.01
Fort Worth, TX (city) Tarrant County	54	0.01
Kansas City, MO (city) Jackson County	51	0.01
Muskogee, OK (city) Muskogee County	46	0.12
Austin, TX (city) Travis County	45	0.01
Dewey, OK (city) Washington County	44	1.28
Jenks, OK (city) Tulsa County	43	0.25
Enid, OK (city) Garfield County	43	0.09
Lawrence, KS (city) Douglas County	43	0.05
Tahlequah, OK (city) Cherokee County	42	0.27
Bixby, OK (city) Tulsa County	41	0.20
Fayetteville, AR (city) Washington County	40	0.05
Overland Park, KS (city) Johnson County	37	0.02
San Jose, CA (city) Santa Clara County	35	<0.01
Cleveland, OK (city) Pawnee County	33	1.02
Moore, OK (city) Cleveland County	33	0.06
Seattle, WA (city) King County	33	0.01
Independence, MO (city) Jackson County	32	0.03
Topeka, KS (city) Shawnee County	32	0.03
Salem, OR (city) Marion County	32	0.02
Nowata, OK (city) Nowata County	31	0.83
Sapulpa, OK (city) Creek County	31	0.15
Eugene, OR (city) Lane County	31	0.02
Chicago, IL (city) Cook County	31	<0.01
McCord, OK (cdp) Osage County	30	2.08
Collinsville, OK (city) Tulsa County	30	0.54
Midwest City, OK (city) Oklahoma County	30	0.06
Sacramento, CA (city) Sacramento County	30	0.01
Anchorage, AK (municipality) Anchorage Municipality	29	0.01
Long Beach, CA (city) Los Angeles County	29	0.01
Las Vegas, NV (city) Clark County	29	<0.01
Pawnee, OK (city) Pawnee County	28	1.28
Coffeyville, KS (city) Montgomery County	28	0.27
Fort Collins, CO (city) Larimer County	28	0.02
Arkansas City, KS (city) Cowley County	27	0.22
Joplin, MO (city) Jasper County	27	0.05
Springfield, OR (city) Lane County	27	0.05
Spokane, WA (city) Spokane County	27	0.01
Allen, TX (city) Collin County	26	0.03
San Francisco, CA (city) San Francisco County	26	<0.01
Tucson, AZ (city) Pima County	26	<0.01
Coweta, OK (city) Wagoner County	25	0.25
Aurora, CO (city) Arapahoe County	25	0.01
Blackwell, OK (city) Kay County	24	0.34
Glenpool, OK (city) Tulsa County	24	0.22
Fresno, CA (city) Fresno County	24	<0.01
Mustang, OK (city) Canadian County	23	0.13
Mesa, AZ (city) Maricopa County	23	0.01
New York, NY (city) Kings County	23	<0.01
Turley, OK (cdp) Tulsa County	22	0.80
Catoosa, OK (city) Rogers County	22	0.31
Lawton, OK (city) Comanche County	22	0.02
Olathe, KS (city) Johnson County	22	0.02
Ardmore, OK (city) Carter County	21	0.09
Huntington Beach, CA (city) Orange County	21	0.01
Kansas City, KS (city) Wyandotte County	21	0.01
Stockton, CA (city) San Joaquin County	21	0.01
Jacksonville, FL (city) Duval County	21	<0.01
Miami, OK (city) Ottawa County	20	0.15
McAlester, OK (city) Pittsburg County	20	0.11
Lake Forest, CA (city) Orange County	20	0.03
Plano, TX (city) Collin County	20	0.01
Riverside, CA (city) Riverside County	20	0.01
Ralston, OK (town) Pawnee County	19	5.76
Bakersfield, CA (city) Kern County	19	0.01
Corpus Christi, TX (city) Nueces County	19	0.01
Henderson, NV (city) Clark County	19	0.01
Tacoma, WA (city) Pierce County	19	0.01
Chico, CA (city) Butte County	18	0.02
Independence, KS (city) Montgomery County	17	0.18
Pryor Creek, OK (city) Mayes County	17	0.18
Beaumont, CA (city) Riverside County	17	0.05
Coeur d'Alene, ID (city) Kootenai County	17	0.04
Vacaville, CA (city) Solano County	17	0.02
Irvine, CA (city) Orange County	17	0.01
Scottsdale, AZ (city) Maricopa County	17	0.01
Springfield, MO (city) Christian County	17	0.01
Washington, DC (city) District of Columbia	17	<0.01
Sperry, OK (town) Tulsa County	16	1.33
Caney, KS (city) Montgomery County	16	0.73
Cushing, OK (city) Payne County	16	0.20
Bethany, OK (city) Oklahoma County	16	0.08
Shawnee, OK (city) Pottawatomie County	16	0.05
Round Rock, TX (city) Williamson County	16	0.02
Urban Honolulu, HI (cdp) Honolulu County	16	<0.01
Wagoner, OK (city) Wagoner County	15	0.18
Yukon, OK (city) Canadian County	15	0.07
Amarillo, TX (city) Potter County	15	0.01
Modesto, CA (city) Stanislaus County	15	0.01
Oxnard, CA (city) Ventura County	15	0.01
Simi Valley, CA (city) Ventura County	15	0.01
Indianapolis, IN (city) Marion County	15	<0.01
Avant, OK (town) Osage County	14	4.38
Wynona, OK (town) Osage County	14	3.20
Morrison, OK (town) Noble County	14	1.91
Grove, OK (city) Delaware County	14	0.21
Manhattan, KS (city) Riley County	14	0.03
Springdale, AR (city) Washington County	14	0.02
Odessa, TX (city) Ector County	14	0.01
San Bernardino, CA (city) San Bernardino County	14	0.01
San Buenaventura (Ventura), CA (city) Ventura County	14	0.01
Santa Rosa, CA (city) Sonoma County	14	0.01
Burbank, OK (town) Osage County	13	9.22
Wellington, KS (city) Sumner County	13	0.16
Haysville, KS (city) Sedgwick County	13	0.12
Dallas, OR (city) Polk County	13	0.09
Duncan, OK (city) Stephens County	13	0.06
La Porte, TX (city) Harris County	13	0.04
Leavenworth, KS (city) Leavenworth County	13	0.04
Castle Rock, CO (town) Douglas County	13	0.03
Conway, AR (city) Faulkner County	13	0.02
Fontana, CA (city) San Bernardino County	13	0.01
Garland, TX (city) Dallas County	13	0.01
Lancaster, CA (city) Los Angeles County	13	0.01
Las Cruces, NM (city) Doña Ana County	13	0.01
Lubbock, TX (city) Lubbock County	13	0.01
Torrance, CA (city) Los Angeles County	13	0.01
Oakland, CA (city) Alameda County	13	<0.01
Jennings, OK (town) Pawnee County	12	3.31
Shidler, OK (city) Osage County	12	2.72
Tonkawa, OK (city) Kay County	12	0.37
Park Hill, OK (cdp) Cherokee County	12	0.31
Verdigris, OK (town) Rogers County	12	0.30
Durango, CO (city) La Plata County	12	0.07

Please refer to the Explanation of Data in the front of the book for more detailed information.

Race

American Indian: Osage

Top 150 Places Sorted by Percent of Total Population

Based on all places, regardless of total population

Place	Population	%
Fairfax, OK (town) Osage County	263	19.06
Grainola, OK (town) Osage County	5	16.13
Pawhuska, OK (city) Osage County	567	15.82
Burbank, OK (town) Osage County	13	9.22
Hominy, OK (city) Osage County	304	8.53
Barnsdall, OK (city) Osage County	84	6.76
Ralston, OK (town) Pawnee County	19	5.76
Avant, OK (town) Osage County	14	4.38
Talmage, KS (cdp) Dickinson County	4	4.04
Old Eucha, OK (cdp) Delaware County	2	3.85
Skiatook, OK (town) Osage County	276	3.73
Jennings, OK (town) Pawnee County	12	3.31
Wynona, OK (town) Osage County	14	3.20
Fairmont, OK (town) Garfield County	4	2.99
Garey, CA (cdp) Santa Barbara County	2	2.94
Terlton, OK (town) Pawnee County	3	2.83
Blackburn, OK (town) Pawnee County	3	2.78
Barney's Junction, WA (cdp) Ferry County	4	2.74
Shidler, OK (city) Osage County	12	2.72
Red Rock, OK (town) Noble County	7	2.47
McCord, OK (cdp) Osage County	30	2.08
Vera, OK (town) Washington County	5	2.07
Morrison, OK (town) Noble County	14	1.91
Ochelata, OK (town) Washington County	8	1.89
Qui-nai-elt Village, WA (cdp) Grays Harbor County	1	1.85
Talala, OK (town) Rogers County	5	1.83
Ballou, OK (cdp) Mayes County	3	1.70
Wann, OK (town) Nowata County	2	1.60
Green, KS (city) Clay County	2	1.56
Delaware, OK (town) Nowata County	6	1.44
Latham, KS (city) Butler County	2	1.44
Sperry, OK (town) Tulsa County	16	1.33
Boneau, MT (cdp) Chouteau County	5	1.32
Sodaville, OR (city) Linn County	4	1.30
Dewey, OK (city) Washington County	44	1.28
Pawnee, OK (city) Pawnee County	28	1.28
Osage, OK (town) Osage County	2	1.28
Maish Vaya, AZ (cdp) Pima County	2	1.27
Summit, OR (cdp) Benton County	1	1.22
Arcadia, OK (town) Oklahoma County	3	1.21
Elgin, KS (city) Chautauqua County	1	1.12
Bessie, OK (town) Washita County	2	1.10
Como, NC (town) Hertford County	1	1.10
Maramec, OK (town) Pawnee County	1	1.10
Copan, OK (town) Washington County	8	1.09
Bagnell, MO (town) Miller County	1	1.08
Cedar Vale, KS (city) Chautauqua County	6	1.04
Cleveland, OK (city) Pawnee County	33	1.02
Lenapah, OK (town) Nowata County	3	1.02
Brooks, OR (cdp) Marion County	4	1.01
Bartlesville, OK (city) Washington County	358	1.00
Beaver, AR (town) Carroll County	1	1.00
Lake Annette, MO (city) Cass County	1	1.00
Champion, NE (cdp) Chase County	1	0.97
Parkdale, OR (cdp) Hood River County	3	0.96
Fort Supply, OK (town) Woodward County	3	0.91
Chautauqua, KS (city) Chautauqua County	1	0.90
Knapp, WI (village) Dunn County	4	0.86
Nowata, OK (city) Nowata County	31	0.83
Paoli, OK (town) Garvin County	5	0.82
Turley, OK (cdp) Tulsa County	22	0.80
Tamms, IL (village) Alexander County	5	0.79
Gordonville, PA (cdp) Lancaster County	4	0.79
Fairview, MO (town) Newton County	3	0.78
James, MO (town) Moniteau County	3	0.78
Kremlin, OK (town) Garfield County	2	0.78
Ten Sleep, WY (town) Washakie County	2	0.77
Spang, MN (township) Itasca County	2	0.76
Gateway, AR (town) Benton County	3	0.74
Caney, KS (city) Montgomery County	16	0.73
Peru, KS (city) Chautauqua County	1	0.72
Raritan, IL (village) Henderson County	1	0.72
Ponca City, OK (city) Kay County	179	0.71
Peavine, OK (cdp) Adair County	3	0.71
North Enid, OK (town) Garfield County	6	0.70
Hulbert, OK (town) Cherokee County	4	0.68
Warwick, OK (town) Lincoln County	1	0.68
Minocqua, WI (cdp) Oneida County	3	0.67
Kinta, OK (town) Haskell County	2	0.67
Gardners, PA (cdp) Adams County	1	0.67
Lebanon, OK (cdp) Marshall County	2	0.66
Lahoma, OK (town) Garfield County	4	0.65
Argyle, MN (city) Marshall County	4	0.63
Arlington, KS (city) Reno County	3	0.63
Sedan, KS (city) Chautauqua County	7	0.62
Carney, OK (town) Lincoln County	4	0.62
Hancock, VT (town) Addison County	2	0.62
Big Spring, MO (cdp) Montgomery County	1	0.60
Huey, IL (village) Clinton County	1	0.59
Pilot Mound, IA (city) Boone County	1	0.58
Airport Drive, MO (village) Jasper County	4	0.57
Ramona, OK (town) Washington County	3	0.56
Hurley, MO (city) Stone County	1	0.56
Collinsville, OK (city) Tulsa County	30	0.54
Country Acres, TX (cdp) San Patricio County	1	0.54
Reardan, WA (town) Lincoln County	3	0.53
Orion, MN (township) Olmsted County	3	0.51
Royal Lakes, IL (village) Macoupin County	1	0.51
Swan Valley, ID (city) Bonneville County	1	0.49
Tygh Valley, OR (cdp) Wasco County	1	0.49
Lamont, OK (town) Grant County	2	0.48
Buffalo Soapstone, AK (cdp) Matanuska-Susitna Borough	4	0.47
Redwater, MS (cdp) Leake County	3	0.47
Jet, OK (town) Alfalfa County	1	0.47
Hinsdale, MT (cdp) Valley County	1	0.46
Norwood, MO (city) Wright County	3	0.45
Rolla, KS (city) Morton County	2	0.45
Big Rock, IL (village) Kane County	5	0.44
McRae, AR (city) White County	3	0.44
Keswick, CA (cdp) Shasta County	2	0.44
Marland, OK (town) Noble County	1	0.44
Hermitage, MO (city) Hickory County	2	0.43
Prue, OK (town) Osage County	2	0.43
Emma, MO (city) Saline County	1	0.43
Proctor, OK (cdp) Adair County	1	0.43
Okeene, OK (town) Blaine County	5	0.42
Loma Linda, MO (town) Newton County	3	0.41
Porum, OK (town) Muskogee County	3	0.41
Cal-Nev-Ari, NV (cdp) Clark County	1	0.41
Hyampom, CA (cdp) Trinity County	1	0.41
Sand Springs, OK (city) Tulsa County	76	0.40
Hilshire Village, TX (city) Harris County	3	0.40
Bardolph, IL (village) McDonough County	1	0.40
Bison, KS (city) Rush County	1	0.39
Drumright, OK (city) Creek County	11	0.38
Adair, OK (town) Mayes County	3	0.38
Tonkawa, OK (city) Kay County	12	0.37
Howe, OK (town) Le Flore County	3	0.37
Langley, OK (town) Mayes County	3	0.37
Effingham, KS (city) Atchison County	2	0.37
Brashear, MO (city) Adair County	1	0.37
Pierce, CO (town) Weld County	3	0.36
Alba, MO (city) Jasper County	2	0.36
Holland, AR (city) Faulkner County	2	0.36
King Lake, NE (cdp) Douglas County	1	0.36
Princeton, KS (city) Franklin County	1	0.36
Haskell, OK (town) Muskogee County	7	0.35
Panama, OK (town) Le Flore County	5	0.35
Fulshear, TX (city) Fort Bend County	4	0.35
Oregon, MO (city) Holt County	3	0.35
Cromwell, OK (town) Seminole County	1	0.35
Pukwana, SD (town) Brule County	1	0.35
Blackwell, OK (city) Kay County	24	0.34
Sparta, MO (city) Christian County	6	0.34
Cleora, OK (cdp) Delaware County	5	0.34
Marble Hill, MO (city) Bollinger County	5	0.34
Galva, KS (city) McPherson County	3	0.34
Stronghurst, IL (village) Henderson County	3	0.34
New Haven, OH (cdp) Hamilton County	2	0.34
Bombay Beach, CA (cdp) Imperial County	1	0.34

Please refer to the Explanation of Data in the front of the book for more detailed information.

Race

American Indian: Osage

Top 150 Places Sorted by Percent of Total Population

Based on places with total population of 7,500 or more

Place	Population	%
Bartlesville, OK (city) Washington County	358	1.00
Ponca City, OK (city) Kay County	179	0.71
Sand Springs, OK (city) Tulsa County	76	0.40
Claremore, OK (city) Rogers County	61	0.33
Owasso, OK (city) Tulsa County	86	0.30
Stillwater, OK (city) Payne County	133	0.29
Tahlequah, OK (city) Cherokee County	42	0.27
Coffeyville, KS (city) Montgomery County	28	0.27
Jenks, OK (city) Tulsa County	43	0.25
Coweta, OK (city) Wagoner County	25	0.25
Tulsa, OK (city) Tulsa County	855	0.22
Arkansas City, KS (city) Cowley County	27	0.22
Glenpool, OK (city) Tulsa County	24	0.22
Broken Arrow, OK (city) Tulsa County	205	0.21
Bixby, OK (city) Tulsa County	41	0.20
Cushing, OK (city) Payne County	16	0.20
Independence, KS (city) Montgomery County	17	0.18
Pryor Creek, OK (city) Mayes County	17	0.18
Wagoner, OK (city) Wagoner County	15	0.18
Wellington, KS (city) Sumner County	13	0.16
Sapulpa, OK (city) Creek County	31	0.15
Miami, OK (city) Ottawa County	20	0.15
Mustang, OK (city) Canadian County	23	0.13
Newcastle, OK (city) McClain County	10	0.13
Norman, OK (city) Cleveland County	135	0.12
Muskogee, OK (city) Muskogee County	46	0.12
Haysville, KS (city) Sedgwick County	13	0.12
McAlester, OK (city) Pittsburg County	20	0.11
Warr Acres, OK (city) Oklahoma County	10	0.10
Enid, OK (city) Garfield County	43	0.09
Ardmore, OK (city) Carter County	21	0.09
Dallas, OR (city) Polk County	13	0.09
Andover, KS (city) Butler County	11	0.09
Elk City, OK (city) Beckham County	11	0.09
Winfield, KS (city) Cowley County	11	0.09
Guthrie, OK (city) Logan County	9	0.09
Newport, OR (city) Lincoln County	9	0.09
Ruidoso, NM (village) Lincoln County	7	0.09
Yreka, CA (city) Siskiyou County	7	0.09
Bethany, OK (city) Oklahoma County	16	0.08
El Dorado, KS (city) Butler County	11	0.08
Larkfield-Wikiup, CA (cdp) Sonoma County	7	0.08
Edmond, OK (city) Oklahoma County	58	0.07
Yukon, OK (city) Canadian County	15	0.07
Durango, CO (city) La Plata County	12	0.07
Siloam Springs, AR (city) Benton County	11	0.07
Artondale, WA (cdp) Pierce County	9	0.07
Guymon, OK (city) Texas County	8	0.07
Weatherford, OK (city) Custer County	8	0.07
Chanute, KS (city) Neosho County	6	0.07
Hanover, NH (cdp) Grafton County	6	0.07
Marina del Rey, CA (cdp) Los Angeles County	6	0.07
The Village, OK (city) Oklahoma County	6	0.07
Hyrum, UT (city) Cache County	5	0.07
Moore, OK (city) Cleveland County	33	0.06
Midwest City, OK (city) Oklahoma County	30	0.06
Duncan, OK (city) Stephens County	13	0.06
Nixa, MO (city) Christian County	12	0.06
Borger, TX (city) Hutchinson County	8	0.06
Webb City, MO (city) Jasper County	7	0.06
Clinton, OK (city) Custer County	5	0.06
Itasca, IL (village) DuPage County	5	0.06
Ketchikan, AK (city) Ketchikan Gateway Borough	5	0.06
Lakes, AK (cdp) Matanuska-Susitna Borough	5	0.06
Pleasant View, UT (city) Weber County	5	0.06
Rolling Hills Estates, CA (city) Los Angeles County	5	0.06
Oklahoma City, OK (city) Oklahoma County	308	0.05
Wichita, KS (city) Sedgwick County	189	0.05
Lawrence, KS (city) Douglas County	43	0.05
Fayetteville, AR (city) Washington County	40	0.05
Joplin, MO (city) Jasper County	27	0.05
Springfield, OR (city) Lane County	27	0.05
Beaumont, CA (city) Riverside County	17	0.05
Shawnee, OK (city) Pottawatomie County	16	0.05
Canyon Lake, TX (cdp) Comal County	11	0.05
Del City, OK (city) Oklahoma County	11	0.05
Gallup, NM (city) McKinley County	10	0.05
Bryant, AR (city) Saline County	9	0.05
Durant, OK (city) Bryan County	8	0.05
El Reno, OK (city) Canadian County	8	0.05
Wailuku, HI (cdp) Maui County	8	0.05
Clearlake, CA (city) Lake County	7	0.05
Auburn, CA (city) Placer County	6	0.05
Choctaw, OK (city) Oklahoma County	6	0.05
Hanover, NH (town) Grafton County	6	0.05
Lake Los Angeles, CA (cdp) Los Angeles County	6	0.05
Lakeway, TX (city) Travis County	6	0.05
Niceville, FL (city) Okaloosa County	6	0.05
Centerton, AR (city) Benton County	5	0.05
Fife, WA (city) Pierce County	5	0.05
Harrisonville, MO (city) Cass County	5	0.05
Lovington, NM (city) Lea County	5	0.05
Maltby, WA (cdp) Snohomish County	5	0.05
Morro Bay, CA (city) San Luis Obispo County	5	0.05
Sauk Village, IL (village) Cook County	5	0.05
Trinidad, CO (city) Las Animas County	5	0.05
Waukesha, WI (town) Waukesha County	5	0.05
Acton, CA (cdp) Los Angeles County	4	0.05
Fruitvale, CO (cdp) Mesa County	4	0.05
Nevada, MO (city) Vernon County	4	0.05
Richland Hills, TX (city) Tarrant County	4	0.05
Sallisaw, OK (city) Sequoyah County	4	0.05
Sunset Hills, MO (city) St. Louis County	4	0.05
Waterford, CA (city) Stanislaus County	4	0.05
Coeur d'Alene, ID (city) Kootenai County	17	0.04
La Porte, TX (city) Harris County	13	0.04
Leavenworth, KS (city) Leavenworth County	13	0.04
McMinnville, OR (city) Yamhill County	12	0.04
Hayesville, OR (cdp) Marion County	8	0.04
Sachse, TX (city) Dallas County	8	0.04
Ada, OK (city) Pontotoc County	7	0.04
Corinth, TX (city) Denton County	7	0.04
Prunedale, CA (cdp) Monterey County	7	0.04
Raymore, MO (city) Cass County	7	0.04
Tanque Verde, AZ (cdp) Pima County	7	0.04
Alamo, CA (cdp) Contra Costa County	6	0.04
Concord, MO (cdp) St. Louis County	6	0.04
Four Corners, OR (cdp) Marion County	6	0.04
Lebanon, OR (city) Linn County	6	0.04
Athens, TX (city) Henderson County	5	0.04
Anderson, CA (city) Shasta County	4	0.04
Berkley, CO (cdp) Adams County	4	0.04
Canyon Lake, CA (city) Riverside County	4	0.04
Cottonwood, AZ (city) Yavapai County	4	0.04
Craig, CO (city) Moffat County	4	0.04
Diamond Springs, CA (cdp) El Dorado County	4	0.04
Hawaiian Paradise Park, HI (cdp) Hawaii County	4	0.04
Jerome, ID (city) Jerome County	4	0.04
Kalaoa, HI (cdp) Hawaii County	4	0.04
Show Low, AZ (city) Navajo County	4	0.04
Valley Center, CA (cdp) San Diego County	4	0.04
Anna, TX (city) Collin County	3	0.04
Bonadelle Ranchos-Madera Ranchos, CA (cdp) Madera County	3	0.04
Camp Hill, PA (borough) Cumberland County	3	0.04
Cold Springs, NV (cdp) Washoe County	3	0.04
Florence, OR (city) Lane County	3	0.04
Fort Scott, KS (city) Bourbon County	3	0.04
Freeport, ME (town) Cumberland County	3	0.04
Highlands, TX (cdp) Harris County	3	0.04
Lincoln City, OR (city) Lincoln County	3	0.04
Sangaree, SC (cdp) Berkeley County	3	0.04
Independence, MO (city) Jackson County	32	0.03
Topeka, KS (city) Shawnee County	32	0.03
Allen, TX (city) Collin County	26	0.03
Lake Forest, CA (city) Orange County	20	0.03
Manhattan, KS (city) Riley County	14	0.03
Castle Rock, CO (town) Douglas County	13	0.03
Bentonville, AR (city) Benton County	11	0.03
Grants Pass, OR (city) Josephine County	11	0.03
University Place, WA (city) Pierce County	8	0.03

Race

American Indian: Ottawa

U.S. and 50 States Sorted by Population and Percent of Total Population

Place	Population	%
United States	**13,033**	**<0.01**
Michigan	7,499	0.08
California	651	<0.01
Oklahoma	637	0.02
Wisconsin	543	0.01
Texas	415	<0.01
Florida	264	<0.01
Missouri	240	<0.01
Ohio	229	<0.01
Illinois	222	<0.01
Washington	191	<0.01
Oregon	179	<0.01
Arizona	164	<0.01
Indiana	164	<0.01
Kansas	119	<0.01
Virginia	110	<0.01
Colorado	104	<0.01
Tennessee	100	<0.01
Minnesota	93	<0.01
North Carolina	87	<0.01
Nevada	82	<0.01
Arkansas	77	<0.01
Georgia	75	<0.01
Idaho	65	<0.01
Kentucky	65	<0.01
Louisiana	56	<0.01
Maryland	52	<0.01
New York	52	<0.01
Alabama	45	<0.01
New Mexico	40	<0.01
Alaska	39	0.01
Pennsylvania	36	<0.01
New Jersey	31	<0.01
Iowa	29	<0.01
Utah	29	<0.01
Hawaii	27	<0.01
Mississippi	26	<0.01
South Carolina	25	<0.01
Nebraska	23	<0.01
Montana	21	<0.01
Wyoming	20	<0.01
Connecticut	16	<0.01
Delaware	16	<0.01
Massachusetts	15	<0.01
South Dakota	14	<0.01
New Hampshire	12	<0.01
North Dakota	9	<0.01
West Virginia	9	<0.01
Vermont	7	<0.01
Maine	6	<0.01
District of Columbia	2	<0.01
Rhode Island	1	<0.01

Place	Population	%
Michigan	7,499	0.08
Oklahoma	637	0.02
Wisconsin	543	0.01
Alaska	39	0.01
United States	**13,033**	**<0.01**
California	651	<0.01
Texas	415	<0.01
Florida	264	<0.01
Missouri	240	<0.01
Ohio	229	<0.01
Illinois	222	<0.01
Washington	191	<0.01
Oregon	179	<0.01
Arizona	164	<0.01
Indiana	164	<0.01
Kansas	119	<0.01
Virginia	110	<0.01
Colorado	104	<0.01
Tennessee	100	<0.01
Minnesota	93	<0.01
North Carolina	87	<0.01
Nevada	82	<0.01
Arkansas	77	<0.01
Georgia	75	<0.01
Idaho	65	<0.01
Kentucky	65	<0.01
Louisiana	56	<0.01
Maryland	52	<0.01
New York	52	<0.01
Alabama	45	<0.01
New Mexico	40	<0.01
Pennsylvania	36	<0.01
New Jersey	31	<0.01
Iowa	29	<0.01
Utah	29	<0.01
Hawaii	27	<0.01
Mississippi	26	<0.01
South Carolina	25	<0.01
Nebraska	23	<0.01
Montana	21	<0.01
Wyoming	20	<0.01
Connecticut	16	<0.01
Delaware	16	<0.01
Massachusetts	15	<0.01
South Dakota	14	<0.01
New Hampshire	12	<0.01
North Dakota	9	<0.01
West Virginia	9	<0.01
Vermont	7	<0.01
Maine	6	<0.01
District of Columbia	2	<0.01
Rhode Island	1	<0.01

Please refer to the Explanation of Data in the front of the book for more detailed information.

Race

American Indian: Ottawa

Top 150 Places Sorted by Population

Based on all places, regardless of total population

Place	Population	%
Grand Rapids, MI (city) Kent County	286	0.15
Lansing, MI (city) Ingham County	191	0.17
Muskegon, MI (city) Muskegon County	181	0.47
Lansing, MI (city) Ingham County	181	0.17
Petoskey, MI (city) Emmet County	178	3.14
Manistee, MI (city) Manistee County	154	2.47
Bear Creek, MI (township) Emmet County	140	2.26
Muskegon, MI (charter township) Muskegon County	137	0.77
Wyoming, MI (city) Kent County	122	0.17
Norton Shores, MI (city) Muskegon County	101	0.42
Manistee, MI (township) Manistee County	85	2.08
Miami, OK (city) Ottawa County	73	0.54
Tulsa, OK (city) Tulsa County	73	0.02
Suttons Bay, MI (township) Leelanau County	70	2.35
Littlefield, MI (township) Emmet County	67	2.25
Garfield, MI (charter township) Grand Traverse County	67	0.41
Egelston, MI (township) Muskegon County	64	0.65
Ludington, MI (city) Mason County	62	0.77
Detroit, MI (city) Wayne County	59	0.01
Fruitland, MI (township) Muskegon County	52	0.94
Dalton, MI (township) Muskegon County	51	0.55
Fruitport, MI (charter township) Muskegon County	51	0.38
West Traverse, MI (township) Emmet County	49	3.05
McKinley, MI (township) Emmet County	48	3.70
Delta, MI (charter township) Eaton County	47	0.15
Pellston, MI (village) Emmet County	45	5.47
Traverse City, MI (city) Grand Traverse County	45	0.31
Traverse City, MI (city) Grand Traverse County	44	0.30
Mount Pleasant, MI (city) Isabella County	44	0.17
Harbor Springs, MI (city) Emmet County	42	3.52
Battle Creek, MI (city) Calhoun County	42	0.08
Flint, MI (city) Genesee County	41	0.04
Toledo, OH (city) Lucas County	41	0.01
Chicago, IL (city) Cook County	41	<0.01
East Bay, MI (township) Grand Traverse County	40	0.38
Milwaukee, WI (city) Milwaukee County	40	0.01
Resort, MI (township) Emmet County	39	1.45
Chippewa, MI (township) Isabella County	36	0.77
Kentwood, MI (city) Kent County	36	0.07
Gaines, MI (charter township) Kent County	35	0.14
Springvale, MI (township) Emmet County	34	1.59
Warren, MI (city) Macomb County	34	0.03
Cheboygan, MI (city) Cheboygan County	33	0.68
Holland, MI (city) Ottawa County	32	0.10
Holland, MI (charter township) Ottawa County	32	0.09
Racine, WI (city) Racine County	32	0.04
Blair, MI (township) Grand Traverse County	31	0.38
Grand Haven, MI (city) Ottawa County	31	0.30
Walker, MI (city) Kent County	31	0.13
Broken Arrow, OK (city) Tulsa County	31	0.03
Cross Village, MI (township) Emmet County	30	10.68
Maple River, MI (township) Emmet County	30	2.23
Blue Lake, MI (township) Muskegon County	30	1.25
Bay Shore, MI (cdp) Charlevoix County	29	3.85
Escanaba, MI (city) Delta County	29	0.23
Spring Lake, MI (township) Ottawa County	29	0.20
Little Traverse, MI (township) Emmet County	28	1.18
Waverly, MI (cdp) Eaton County	28	0.12
East Lansing, MI (city) Ingham County	28	0.06
Friendship, MI (township) Emmet County	27	3.04
Alpine, MI (township) Kent County	27	0.20
Sault Ste. Marie, MI (city) Chippewa County	27	0.19
East Lansing, MI (city) Ingham County	27	0.06
Georgetown, MI (charter township) Ottawa County	27	0.06
Oklahoma City, OK (city) Oklahoma County	27	<0.01
Hayes, MI (township) Charlevoix County	26	1.35
Wolf Lake, MI (cdp) Muskegon County	26	0.63
Portage, MI (city) Kalamazoo County	26	0.06
Boyne City, MI (city) Charlevoix County	25	0.67
Mancelona, MI (township) Antrim County	25	0.57
Comstock Park, MI (cdp) Kent County	25	0.25
Muskegon Heights, MI (city) Muskegon County	25	0.23
Holland, MI (city) Ottawa County	25	0.10
Bay City, MI (city) Bay County	25	0.07
Kalamazoo, MI (charter township) Kalamazoo County	24	0.11
Los Angeles, CA (city) Los Angeles County	24	<0.01
Phoenix, AZ (city) Maricopa County	24	<0.01
Quapaw, OK (town) Ottawa County	23	2.54
Denver, MI (township) Newaygo County	23	1.19
Filer, MI (charter township) Manistee County	23	0.99
DeWitt, MI (charter township) Clinton County	23	0.16
Royal Oak, MI (city) Oakland County	23	0.04
Kalamazoo, MI (city) Kalamazoo County	23	0.03
Green Bay, WI (city) Brown County	23	0.02
Center, MI (township) Emmet County	22	3.87
Delhi, MI (charter township) Ingham County	22	0.09
Holt, MI (cdp) Ingham County	22	0.09
Port Huron, MI (city) St. Clair County	22	0.07
Joplin, MO (city) Jasper County	22	0.04
Waterford, MI (charter township) Oakland County	22	0.03
Canton, MI (charter township) Wayne County	22	0.02
San Diego, CA (city) San Diego County	22	<0.01
Eveline, MI (township) Charlevoix County	21	1.42
Tuscarora, MI (township) Cheboygan County	21	0.69
Fort Atkinson, WI (city) Jefferson County	21	0.17
Plainfield, MI (charter township) Kent County	21	0.07
Mesa, AZ (city) Maricopa County	21	<0.01
Portland, OR (city) Multnomah County	21	<0.01
Wilson, MI (township) Charlevoix County	20	1.02
Charlevoix, MI (city) Charlevoix County	20	0.80
Kinross, MI (charter township) Chippewa County	20	0.26
Eastlake, MI (village) Manistee County	19	3.71
McMillan, MI (township) Luce County	19	0.71
Roosevelt Park, MI (city) Muskegon County	19	0.50
Pittsfield, MI (charter township) Washtenaw County	19	0.05
Anchorage, AK (municipality) Anchorage Municipality	19	0.01
Sterling Heights, MI (city) Macomb County	19	0.01
Bliss, MI (township) Emmet County	18	2.90
Norman, MI (township) Manistee County	18	1.16
Benzonia, MI (township) Benzie County	18	0.66
Coopersville, MI (city) Ottawa County	18	0.42
Cadillac, MI (city) Wexford County	18	0.17
Cutlerville, MI (cdp) Kent County	18	0.13
Midland, MI (city) Midland County	18	0.04
Midland, MI (city) Midland County	18	0.04
Ann Arbor, MI (city) Washtenaw County	18	0.02
Livonia, MI (city) Wayne County	18	0.02
Shelby, MI (township) Oceana County	17	0.42
Flint, MI (charter township) Genesee County	17	0.05
Norman, OK (city) Cleveland County	17	0.02
Colorado Springs, CO (city) El Paso County	17	<0.01
Alanson, MI (village) Emmet County	16	2.17
Harris, MI (township) Menominee County	16	0.81
Newfield, MI (township) Oceana County	16	0.67
L'Anse, MI (township) Baraga County	16	0.42
Grand Haven, MI (charter township) Ottawa County	16	0.11
Byron, MI (township) Kent County	16	0.08
Pontiac, MI (city) Oakland County	16	0.03
Taylor, MI (city) Wayne County	16	0.03
Clinton, MI (charter township) Macomb County	16	0.02
Henderson, NV (city) Clark County	16	0.01
Stronach, MI (township) Manistee County	15	1.83
Crystal, MI (township) Oceana County	15	1.79
Maple Grove, MI (township) Manistee County	15	1.14
Indian River, MI (cdp) Cheboygan County	15	0.77
Holton, MI (township) Muskegon County	15	0.60
Reynolds, MI (township) Montcalm County	15	0.28
Laketon, MI (township) Muskegon County	15	0.20
Sparta, MI (township) Kent County	15	0.16
Marquette, MI (city) Marquette County	15	0.07
Dearborn Heights, MI (city) Wayne County	15	0.03
Hemet, CA (city) Riverside County	15	0.02
Macomb, MI (township) Macomb County	15	0.02
Fort Wayne, IN (city) Allen County	15	0.01
Springfield, MO (city) Christian County	15	0.01
Indianapolis, IN (city) Marion County	15	<0.01
Las Vegas, NV (city) Clark County	15	<0.01
East Jordan, MI (city) Charlevoix County	14	0.60
Seneca, MO (city) Newton County	14	0.60
North Muskegon, MI (city) Muskegon County	14	0.37

Race

American Indian: Ottawa

Top 150 Places Sorted by Percent of Total Population

Based on all places, regardless of total population

Place	Population	%
Cross Village, MI (township) Emmet County	30	10.68
Cross Village, MI (cdp) Emmet County	6	6.45
Pellston, MI (village) Emmet County	45	5.47
Conway, MI (cdp) Emmet County	9	4.41
Center, MI (township) Emmet County	22	3.87
Meade, MI (township) Mason County	7	3.87
Bay Shore, MI (cdp) Charlevoix County	29	3.85
Eastlake, MI (village) Manistee County	19	3.71
McKinley, MI (township) Emmet County	48	3.70
Harbor Springs, MI (city) Emmet County	42	3.52
Oden, MI (cdp) Emmet County	12	3.31
Garden, MI (village) Delta County	7	3.17
Petoskey, MI (city) Emmet County	178	3.14
Long Hollow, SD (cdp) Roberts County	6	3.13
West Traverse, MI (township) Emmet County	49	3.05
Friendship, MI (township) Emmet County	27	3.04
Bliss, MI (township) Emmet County	18	2.90
Quapaw, OK (town) Ottawa County	23	2.54
Manistee, MI (city) Manistee County	154	2.47
Walkerville, MI (village) Oceana County	6	2.43
Suttons Bay, MI (township) Leelanau County	70	2.35
Zeba, MI (cdp) Baraga County	11	2.29
Bear Creek, MI (township) Emmet County	140	2.26
Littlefield, MI (township) Emmet County	67	2.25
Omena, MI (cdp) Leelanau County	6	2.25
Readmond, MI (township) Emmet County	13	2.24
Maple River, MI (township) Emmet County	30	2.23
Milo, MO (village) Vernon County	2	2.22
Alanson, MI (village) Emmet County	16	2.17
Manistee, MI (township) Manistee County	85	2.08
Free Soil, MI (village) Mason County	3	2.08
Cogswell, ND (city) Sargent County	2	2.02
Dotyville, OK (cdp) Ottawa County	2	1.98
Burt, MI (township) Cheboygan County	13	1.91
Levering, MI (cdp) Emmet County	4	1.86
Stronach, MI (township) Manistee County	15	1.83
Crystal, MI (township) Oceana County	15	1.79
Springvale, MI (township) Emmet County	34	1.59
Thompsonville, MI (village) Benzie County	7	1.59
Horton Bay, MI (cdp) Charlevoix County	8	1.56
Fountain, MI (village) Mason County	3	1.55
Wyandotte, OK (town) Ottawa County	5	1.50
Suttons Bay, MI (village) Leelanau County	9	1.46
Resort, MI (township) Emmet County	39	1.45
Eveline, MI (township) Charlevoix County	21	1.42
Rothbury, MI (village) Oceana County	6	1.39
Hayes, MI (township) Charlevoix County	26	1.35
Pleasantview, MI (township) Emmet County	11	1.34
Garden, MI (township) Delta County	10	1.33
Hendricks, MI (township) Mackinac County	2	1.31
Weldon, MI (township) Benzie County	7	1.29
Posen, MI (village) Presque Isle County	3	1.28
Hesperia, MI (village) Oceana County	12	1.26
Mahnomen, MN (cdp) St. Louis County	3	1.26
Blue Lake, MI (township) Muskegon County	30	1.25
Honor, MI (village) Benzie County	4	1.22
Denver, MI (township) Newaygo County	23	1.19
Little Traverse, MI (township) Emmet County	28	1.18
Norman, MI (township) Manistee County	18	1.16
Nunda, MI (township) Cheboygan County	12	1.15
Maple Grove, MI (township) Manistee County	15	1.14
Leavitt, MI (township) Oceana County	10	1.12
Pound, WI (village) Marinette County	4	1.06
Custer, MI (village) Mason County	3	1.06
Oak Hill, MI (cdp) Manistee County	6	1.05
Bois Blanc, MI (township) Mackinac County	1	1.05
Newald, WI (cdp) Forest County	1	1.05
Custer, MI (township) Mason County	13	1.04
Peaine, MI (township) Charlevoix County	3	1.03
Copemish, MI (village) Manistee County	2	1.03
Nessen City, MI (cdp) Benzie County	1	1.03
Wilson, MI (township) Charlevoix County	20	1.02
Calvin, OK (town) Hughes County	3	1.02
Brevort, MI (township) Mackinac County	6	1.01
Filer, MI (charter township) Manistee County	23	0.99
Wellston, MI (cdp) Manistee County	3	0.96
Circle, AK (cdp) Yukon-Koyukuk Census Area	1	0.96
Fruitland, MI (township) Muskegon County	52	0.94
Melrose, MI (township) Charlevoix County	13	0.93
Copper Harbor, MI (cdp) Keweenaw County	1	0.93
De Tour Village, MI (village) Chippewa County	3	0.92
Walker, MI (township) Cheboygan County	3	0.92
Brutus, MI (cdp) Emmet County	2	0.92
Mullett, MI (township) Cheboygan County	12	0.91
McDougald, MN (township) Lake of the Woods County	2	0.89
Grant, MI (township) Mason County	8	0.88
Whitefish, MI (township) Chippewa County	5	0.87
Filer City, MI (cdp) Manistee County	1	0.86
Ferry, MI (township) Oceana County	11	0.85
Lakewood Club, MI (village) Muskegon County	11	0.85
Free Soil, MI (township) Mason County	7	0.85
Skandia, MI (township) Marquette County	7	0.85
Parkdale, MI (cdp) Manistee County	6	0.85
Ellis, MI (township) Cheboygan County	5	0.84
Norwood, MI (township) Charlevoix County	6	0.83
Harris, MI (township) Menominee County	16	0.81
Charlevoix, MI (city) Charlevoix County	20	0.80
Bay, MI (township) Charlevoix County	9	0.80
Empire, MI (village) Leelanau County	3	0.80
Newkirk, MI (township) Lake County	5	0.79
Schoepke, WI (town) Oneida County	3	0.78
Cokedale, CO (town) Las Animas County	1	0.78
Muskegon, MI (charter township) Muskegon County	137	0.77
Ludington, MI (city) Mason County	62	0.77
Chippewa, MI (township) Isabella County	36	0.77
Indian River, MI (cdp) Cheboygan County	15	0.77
Star, MI (township) Antrim County	7	0.76
Wawatam, MI (township) Emmet County	5	0.76
Boyne Valley, MI (township) Charlevoix County	9	0.75
Phelps, WI (town) Vilas County	9	0.75
Merrill, MI (township) Newaygo County	5	0.75
Green Valley, WI (cdp) Shawano County	1	0.75
Ross, WI (town) Forest County	1	0.74
Brethren, MI (cdp) Manistee County	3	0.73
Sheridan, MI (township) Mecosta County	10	0.72
McMillan, MI (township) Luce County	19	0.71
Oliver, MI (township) Kalkaska County	2	0.71
Marion, MI (township) Charlevoix County	12	0.70
Tuscarora, MI (township) Cheboygan County	21	0.69
Cheboygan, MI (city) Cheboygan County	33	0.68
Onekama, MI (township) Manistee County	9	0.68
Cleveland, MI (township) Leelanau County	7	0.68
Boyne Falls, MI (village) Charlevoix County	2	0.68
Boyne City, MI (city) Charlevoix County	25	0.67
Newfield, MI (township) Oceana County	16	0.67
Charlevoix, MI (township) Charlevoix County	11	0.67
Brampton, MI (township) Delta County	7	0.67
Brown, MI (township) Manistee County	5	0.67
Benzonia, MI (township) Benzie County	18	0.66
Carp Lake, MI (township) Emmet County	5	0.66
Vandalia, MI (village) Cass County	2	0.66
Egelston, MI (township) Muskegon County	64	0.65
Sheridan, MI (township) Mason County	7	0.65
Grawn, MI (cdp) Grand Traverse County	5	0.65
Coldwater, MI (township) Isabella County	5	0.64
Kaleva, MI (village) Manistee County	3	0.64
Wolf Lake, MI (cdp) Muskegon County	26	0.63
Joyfield, MI (township) Benzie County	5	0.63
Lodgepole, NE (village) Cheyenne County	2	0.63
Utica, KS (city) Ness County	1	0.63
Mackinaw City, MI (village) Emmet County	5	0.62
Advance, MI (cdp) Charlevoix County	2	0.61
Holton, MI (township) Muskegon County	15	0.60
East Jordan, MI (city) Charlevoix County	14	0.60
Seneca, MO (city) Newton County	14	0.60
Superior, MI (township) Chippewa County	8	0.60
Dickson, MI (township) Manistee County	6	0.60
Sauble, MI (township) Lake County	2	0.60
Newberry, MI (village) Luce County	9	0.59
Beaver, MI (township) Newaygo County	3	0.59

Please refer to the Explanation of Data in the front of the book for more detailed information.

Race

American Indian: Ottawa

Top 150 Places Sorted by Percent of Total Population

Based on places with total population of 7,500 or more

Place	Population	%
Muskegon, MI (charter township) Muskegon County	137	0.77
Ludington, MI (city) Mason County	62	0.77
Egelston, MI (township) Muskegon County	64	0.65
Dalton, MI (township) Muskegon County	51	0.55
Miami, OK (city) Ottawa County	73	0.54
Muskegon, MI (city) Muskegon County	181	0.47
Norton Shores, MI (city) Muskegon County	101	0.42
Garfield, MI (charter township) Grand Traverse County	67	0.41
Fruitport, MI (charter township) Muskegon County	51	0.38
East Bay, MI (township) Grand Traverse County	40	0.38
Blair, MI (township) Grand Traverse County	31	0.38
Traverse City, MI (city) Grand Traverse County	45	0.31
Traverse City, MI (city) Grand Traverse County	44	0.30
Grand Haven, MI (city) Ottawa County	31	0.30
Kinross, MI (charter township) Chippewa County	20	0.26
Comstock Park, MI (cdp) Kent County	25	0.25
Escanaba, MI (city) Delta County	29	0.23
Muskegon Heights, MI (city) Muskegon County	25	0.23
Spring Lake, MI (township) Ottawa County	29	0.20
Alpine, MI (township) Kent County	27	0.20
Laketon, MI (township) Muskegon County	15	0.20
Sault Ste. Marie, MI (city) Chippewa County	27	0.19
St. Johns, MI (city) Clinton County	14	0.18
Lansing, MI (city) Ingham County	191	0.17
Lansing, MI (city) Ingham County	181	0.17
Wyoming, MI (city) Kent County	122	0.17
Mount Pleasant, MI (city) Isabella County	44	0.17
Fort Atkinson, WI (city) Jefferson County	21	0.17
Cadillac, MI (city) Wexford County	18	0.17
Greenville, MI (city) Montcalm County	14	0.17
DeWitt, MI (charter township) Clinton County	23	0.16
Sparta, MI (township) Kent County	15	0.16
Grand Rapids, MI (city) Kent County	286	0.15
Delta, MI (charter township) Eaton County	47	0.15
Gaines, MI (charter township) Kent County	35	0.14
Flushing, MI (city) Genesee County	12	0.14
Walker, MI (city) Kent County	31	0.13
Cutlerville, MI (cdp) Kent County	18	0.13
Grand Ledge, MI (city) Eaton County	10	0.13
Grand Ledge, MI (city) Eaton County	10	0.13
Waverly, MI (cdp) Eaton County	28	0.12
Big Rapids, MI (city) Mecosta County	13	0.12
Kalamazoo, MI (charter township) Kalamazoo County	24	0.11
Grand Haven, MI (charter township) Ottawa County	16	0.11
Union, MI (charter township) Isabella County	14	0.11
Bath, MI (charter township) Clinton County	13	0.11
Lansing, MI (charter township) Ingham County	9	0.11
Thornapple, MI (township) Barry County	9	0.11
Holland, MI (city) Ottawa County	32	0.10
Holland, MI (city) Ottawa County	25	0.10
Holland, MI (charter township) Ottawa County	32	0.09
Delhi, MI (charter township) Ingham County	22	0.09
Holt, MI (cdp) Ingham County	22	0.09
Owosso, MI (city) Shiawassee County	14	0.09
Bangor, MI (charter township) Bay County	13	0.09
Northview, MI (cdp) Kent County	13	0.09
Emmett, MI (charter township) Calhoun County	11	0.09
Glenpool, OK (city) Tulsa County	10	0.09
Alpena, MI (township) Alpena County	8	0.09
Charlotte, MI (city) Eaton County	8	0.09
Long Lake, MI (township) Grand Traverse County	8	0.09
Mayfield, MI (township) Lapeer County	7	0.09
Tallmadge, MI (charter township) Ottawa County	7	0.09
Battle Creek, MI (city) Calhoun County	42	0.08
Byron, MI (township) Kent County	16	0.08
Grandville, MI (city) Kent County	13	0.08
Caledonia, MI (township) Kent County	10	0.08
Spring Creek, NV (cdp) Elko County	10	0.08
Alpena, MI (city) Alpena County	8	0.08
Cottage Grove, OR (city) Lane County	8	0.08
Zeeland, MI (charter township) Ottawa County	8	0.08
Iron Mountain, MI (city) Dickinson County	6	0.08
Kentwood, MI (city) Kent County	36	0.07
Bay City, MI (city) Bay County	25	0.07
Port Huron, MI (city) St. Clair County	22	0.07
Plainfield, MI (charter township) Kent County	21	0.07
Marquette, MI (city) Marquette County	15	0.07
Hamburg, MI (township) Livingston County	14	0.07
Mount Morris, MI (township) Genesee County	14	0.07
Ferndale, MI (city) Oakland County	13	0.07
Grand Rapids, MI (charter township) Kent County	12	0.07
Ottawa, KS (city) Franklin County	9	0.07
Fenton, MI (city) Genesee County	8	0.07
Fenton, MI (city) Genesee County	8	0.07
Marion, MI (township) Livingston County	7	0.07
Groveland, FL (city) Lake County	6	0.07
East Lansing, MI (city) Ingham County	28	0.06
East Lansing, MI (city) Ingham County	27	0.06
Georgetown, MI (charter township) Ottawa County	27	0.06
Portage, MI (city) Kalamazoo County	26	0.06
Allendale, MI (charter township) Ottawa County	13	0.06
Davison, MI (township) Genesee County	12	0.06
Allendale, MI (cdp) Ottawa County	11	0.06
Antwerp, MI (township) Van Buren County	7	0.06
Oceola, MI (township) Livingston County	7	0.06
Beecher, MI (cdp) Genesee County	6	0.06
Buena Vista, MI (charter township) Saginaw County	5	0.06
Crete, IL (village) Will County	5	0.06
Jefferson, WI (city) Jefferson County	5	0.06
Menominee, MI (city) Menominee County	5	0.06
Three Rivers, MI (city) St. Joseph County	5	0.06
Pittsfield, MI (charter township) Washtenaw County	19	0.05
Flint, MI (charter township) Genesee County	17	0.05
Frenchtown, MI (township) Monroe County	11	0.05
Genesee, MI (charter township) Genesee County	11	0.05
Summit, MI (township) Jackson County	11	0.05
Badger, AK (cdp) Fairbanks North Star Borough	9	0.05
Jenison, MI (cdp) Ottawa County	9	0.05
Wayne, MI (city) Wayne County	9	0.05
Cannon, MI (township) Kent County	7	0.05
Comstock, MI (charter township) Kalamazoo County	7	0.05
Harper Woods, MI (city) Wayne County	7	0.05
Phelan, CA (cdp) San Bernardino County	7	0.05
Azle, TX (city) Tarrant County	6	0.05
Fort Madison, IA (city) Lee County	6	0.05
Woodhaven, MI (city) Wayne County	6	0.05
Cooper, MI (charter township) Kalamazoo County	5	0.05
Flat Rock, MI (city) Wayne County	5	0.05
Melvindale, MI (city) Wayne County	5	0.05
Oronoko, MI (charter township) Berrien County	5	0.05
Rossmoor, CA (cdp) Orange County	5	0.05
Albion, MI (city) Calhoun County	4	0.05
Bacliff, TX (cdp) Galveston County	4	0.05
Courtland, MI (township) Kent County	4	0.05
Handy, MI (township) Livingston County	4	0.05
Lapeer, MI (city) Lapeer County	4	0.05
Makaha, HI (cdp) Honolulu County	4	0.05
Mason, MI (city) Ingham County	4	0.05
Newton, NJ (town) Sussex County	4	0.05
Rodeo, CA (cdp) Contra Costa County	4	0.05
St. Joseph, MI (city) Berrien County	4	0.05
Flint, MI (city) Genesee County	41	0.04
Racine, WI (city) Racine County	32	0.04
Royal Oak, MI (city) Oakland County	23	0.04
Joplin, MO (city) Jasper County	22	0.04
Midland, MI (city) Midland County	18	0.04
Midland, MI (city) Midland County	18	0.04
Eastpointe, MI (city) Macomb County	12	0.04
West Bend, WI (city) Washington County	12	0.04
Owasso, OK (city) Tulsa County	11	0.04
Desert Hot Springs, CA (city) Riverside County	10	0.04
Monroe, MI (city) Monroe County	9	0.04
Romulus, MI (city) Wayne County	9	0.04
Claremore, OK (city) Rogers County	8	0.04
Oshtemo, MI (charter township) Kalamazoo County	8	0.04
Oxford, MI (charter township) Oakland County	8	0.04
South Holland, IL (village) Cook County	8	0.04
Pinole, CA (city) Contra Costa County	7	0.04
Beaver Dam, WI (city) Dodge County	6	0.04
Fenton, MI (charter township) Genesee County	6	0.04

Please refer to the Explanation of Data in the front of the book for more detailed information.

SECTION THREE

Race

American Indian: Paiute

U.S. and 50 States Sorted by Population and Percent of Total Population

Place	Population	%
United States	**13,767**	**<0.01**
Nevada	4,859	0.18
California	4,153	0.01
Utah	1,059	0.04
Oregon	732	0.02
Arizona	667	0.01
Washington	363	0.01
Texas	216	<0.01
Idaho	188	0.01
Colorado	150	<0.01
New Mexico	127	0.01
Oklahoma	94	<0.01
Florida	86	<0.01
Kansas	80	<0.01
Montana	61	0.01
Illinois	55	<0.01
Tennessee	55	<0.01
New York	49	<0.01
Alaska	45	0.01
Hawaii	43	<0.01
Michigan	41	<0.01
Missouri	41	<0.01
New Jersey	41	<0.01
Wisconsin	40	<0.01
North Carolina	39	<0.01
Ohio	39	<0.01
Indiana	36	<0.01
Pennsylvania	36	<0.01
Louisiana	34	<0.01
Virginia	34	<0.01
Georgia	33	<0.01
Arkansas	30	<0.01
Minnesota	26	<0.01
Wyoming	26	<0.01
Iowa	25	<0.01
Kentucky	20	<0.01
Nebraska	17	<0.01
Maryland	15	<0.01
Maine	14	<0.01
Massachusetts	14	<0.01
Alabama	12	<0.01
Connecticut	10	<0.01
South Carolina	10	<0.01
South Dakota	10	<0.01
West Virginia	10	<0.01
North Dakota	9	<0.01
Mississippi	7	<0.01
New Hampshire	7	<0.01
District of Columbia	3	<0.01
Delaware	2	<0.01
Rhode Island	2	<0.01
Vermont	2	<0.01

Place	Population	%
Nevada	4,859	0.18
Utah	1,059	0.04
Oregon	732	0.02
California	4,153	0.01
Arizona	667	0.01
Washington	363	0.01
Idaho	188	0.01
New Mexico	127	0.01
Montana	61	0.01
Alaska	45	0.01
United States	**13,767**	**<0.01**
Texas	216	<0.01
Colorado	150	<0.01
Oklahoma	94	<0.01
Florida	86	<0.01
Kansas	80	<0.01
Illinois	55	<0.01
Tennessee	55	<0.01
New York	49	<0.01
Hawaii	43	<0.01
Michigan	41	<0.01
Missouri	41	<0.01
New Jersey	41	<0.01
Wisconsin	40	<0.01
North Carolina	39	<0.01
Ohio	39	<0.01
Indiana	36	<0.01
Pennsylvania	36	<0.01
Louisiana	34	<0.01
Virginia	34	<0.01
Georgia	33	<0.01
Arkansas	30	<0.01
Minnesota	26	<0.01
Wyoming	26	<0.01
Iowa	25	<0.01
Kentucky	20	<0.01
Nebraska	17	<0.01
Maryland	15	<0.01
Maine	14	<0.01
Massachusetts	14	<0.01
Alabama	12	<0.01
Connecticut	10	<0.01
South Carolina	10	<0.01
South Dakota	10	<0.01
West Virginia	10	<0.01
North Dakota	9	<0.01
Mississippi	7	<0.01
New Hampshire	7	<0.01
District of Columbia	3	<0.01
Delaware	2	<0.01
Rhode Island	2	<0.01
Vermont	2	<0.01

Please refer to the Explanation of Data in the front of the book for more detailed information.

Race

American Indian: Paiute

Top 150 Places Sorted by Population

Based on all places, regardless of total population

Place	Population	%
Reno, NV (city) Washoe County	509	0.23
Schurz, NV (cdp) Mineral County	458	69.60
Wadsworth, NV (cdp) Washoe County	434	52.04
Nixon, NV (cdp) Washoe County	251	67.11
Cedar City, UT (city) Iron County	247	0.86
Sparks, NV (city) Washoe County	238	0.26
Carson City, NV (ind. city) Carson City County	234	0.42
Bakersfield, CA (city) Kern County	214	0.06
Susanville, CA (city) Lassen County	156	0.87
Yerington, NV (city) Lyon County	155	5.09
St. George, UT (city) Washington County	149	0.20
Las Vegas, NV (city) Clark County	141	0.02
Fernley, NV (city) Lyon County	121	0.62
Sutcliffe, NV (cdp) Washoe County	120	47.43
Sun Valley, NV (cdp) Washoe County	109	0.56
Sacramento, CA (city) Sacramento County	107	0.02
Lovelock, NV (city) Pershing County	99	5.23
Phoenix, AZ (city) Maricopa County	91	0.01
Los Angeles, CA (city) Los Angeles County	86	<0.01
Sunrise Manor, NV (cdp) Clark County	84	0.04
Kaibab, AZ (cdp) Mohave County	82	66.13
Henderson, NV (city) Clark County	70	0.03
Modesto, CA (city) Stanislaus County	70	0.03
Portland, OR (city) Multnomah County	69	0.01
Fresno, CA (city) Fresno County	67	0.01
San Diego, CA (city) San Diego County	62	<0.01
Fort Bidwell, CA (cdp) Modoc County	59	34.10
San Jose, CA (city) Santa Clara County	58	0.01
Klamath Falls, OR (city) Klamath County	55	0.26
Winnemucca, NV (city) Humboldt County	54	0.73
North Las Vegas, NV (city) Clark County	48	0.02
Salt Lake City, UT (city) Salt Lake County	47	0.03
Independence, CA (cdp) Inyo County	46	6.88
Pahrump, NV (cdp) Nye County	46	0.13
San Francisco, CA (city) San Francisco County	44	0.01
Oildale, CA (cdp) Kern County	43	0.13
Hawthorne, NV (cdp) Mineral County	41	1.25
Elko, NV (city) Elko County	41	0.22
Benton, CA (cdp) Mono County	39	13.93
Albuquerque, NM (city) Bernalillo County	38	0.01
Spanish Springs, NV (cdp) Washoe County	35	0.23
Tuba City, AZ (cdp) Coconino County	34	0.39
Manteca, CA (city) San Joaquin County	33	0.05
Redding, CA (city) Shasta County	33	0.04
Visalia, CA (city) Tulare County	33	0.03
Merced, CA (city) Merced County	32	0.04
Tracy, CA (city) San Joaquin County	32	0.04
Fallon, NV (city) Churchill County	31	0.36
Spring Valley, NV (cdp) Clark County	31	0.02
Oakland, CA (city) Alameda County	31	0.01
Bridgeport, CA (cdp) Mono County	30	5.22
Bishop, CA (city) Inyo County	30	0.77
Ivins, UT (city) Washington County	30	0.44
Mesa, AZ (city) Maricopa County	30	0.01
Spokane, WA (city) Spokane County	30	0.01
Tucson, AZ (city) Pima County	30	0.01
Warm Springs, OR (cdp) Jefferson County	29	0.98
Antioch, CA (city) Contra Costa County	27	0.03
Big Pine, CA (cdp) Inyo County	26	1.48
Enoch, UT (city) Iron County	26	0.45
Dayton, NV (cdp) Lyon County	25	0.28
Gardnerville Ranchos, NV (cdp) Douglas County	25	0.22
Ridgecrest, CA (city) Kern County	25	0.09
Lawrence, KS (city) Douglas County	25	0.03
Eugene, OR (city) Lane County	25	0.02
Salinas, CA (city) Monterey County	25	0.02
Glendale, AZ (city) Maricopa County	25	0.01
Walker, CA (cdp) Mono County	24	3.33
Weldon, CA (cdp) Kern County	24	0.91
Washington, UT (city) Washington County	24	0.13
Stockton, CA (city) San Joaquin County	24	0.01
Seattle, WA (city) King County	24	<0.01
Owyhee, NV (cdp) Elko County	23	2.41
Burns, OR (city) Harney County	23	0.82
West Valley City, UT (city) Salt Lake County	23	0.02
Paradise, NV (cdp) Clark County	22	0.01
Richfield, UT (city) Sevier County	21	0.28
Hayward, CA (city) Alameda County	21	0.01
Lemmon Valley, NV (cdp) Washoe County	20	0.40
Chandler, AZ (city) Maricopa County	20	0.01
Moreno Valley, CA (city) Riverside County	20	0.01
Salem, OR (city) Marion County	20	0.01
San Bernardino, CA (city) San Bernardino County	20	0.01
San Antonio, TX (city) Medina County	20	<0.01
Silver Springs, NV (cdp) Lyon County	19	0.36
Mammoth Lakes, CA (town) Mono County	19	0.23
Caldwell, ID (city) Canyon County	19	0.04
Rancho Cordova, CA (city) Sacramento County	19	0.03
Rialto, CA (city) San Bernardino County	19	0.02
Tempe, AZ (city) Maricopa County	19	0.01
Fort McDermitt, NV (cdp) Humboldt County	18	5.28
Woodland, CA (city) Yolo County	18	0.03
Citrus Heights, CA (city) Sacramento County	18	0.02
Clovis, CA (city) Fresno County	18	0.02
Fairfield, CA (city) Solano County	18	0.02
Lancaster, CA (city) Los Angeles County	18	0.01
Colorado Springs, CO (city) El Paso County	18	<0.01
New York, NY (city) Kings County	18	<0.01
Navajo Mountain, UT (cdp) San Juan County	17	4.80
Ontario, OR (city) Malheur County	17	0.15
Missoula, MT (city) Missoula County	17	0.03
Chico, CA (city) Butte County	17	0.02
Vacaville, CA (city) Solano County	17	0.02
Anaheim, CA (city) Orange County	17	0.01
Anchorage, AK (municipality) Anchorage Municipality	17	0.01
Elk Grove, CA (city) Sacramento County	17	0.01
Riverside, CA (city) Riverside County	17	0.01
Houston, TX (city) Harris County	17	<0.01
Spring Creek, NV (cdp) Elko County	16	0.13
Apple Valley, CA (town) San Bernardino County	16	0.02
Roseville, CA (city) Placer County	16	0.01
Smith Valley, NV (cdp) Lyon County	15	0.94
Lake Isabella, CA (cdp) Kern County	15	0.43
Moapa Valley, NV (cdp) Clark County	15	0.22
North Highlands, CA (cdp) Sacramento County	15	0.04
Hillsboro, OR (city) Washington County	15	0.02
Concord, CA (city) Contra Costa County	15	0.01
Caliente, NV (city) Lincoln County	14	1.24
Indian Hills, NV (cdp) Douglas County	14	0.25
Truckee, CA (town) Nevada County	14	0.09
Hemet, CA (city) Riverside County	14	0.02
San Leandro, CA (city) Alameda County	14	0.02
Boise City, ID (city) Ada County	14	0.01
Oxnard, CA (city) Ventura County	14	0.01
Palmdale, CA (city) Los Angeles County	14	0.01
Pueblo, CO (city) Pueblo County	14	0.01
Rancho Cucamonga, CA (city) San Bernardino County	14	0.01
Oklahoma City, OK (city) Oklahoma County	14	<0.01
Chiloquin, OR (city) Klamath County	13	1.77
Moapa Town, NV (cdp) Clark County	13	1.27
Lone Pine, CA (cdp) Inyo County	13	0.64
Dixon Lane-Meadow Creek, CA (cdp) Inyo County	13	0.49
Wanamassa, NJ (cdp) Monmouth County	13	0.29
Altamont, OR (cdp) Klamath County	13	0.07
Ocean, NJ (township) Monmouth County	13	0.05
Prescott, AZ (city) Yavapai County	13	0.03
Riverton, UT (city) Salt Lake County	13	0.03
Madera, CA (city) Madera County	13	0.02
Vancouver, WA (city) Clark County	13	0.01
Gardnerville, NV (cdp) Douglas County	12	0.21
Shiprock, NM (cdp) San Juan County	12	0.14
Grass Valley, CA (city) Nevada County	12	0.09
South Salt Lake, UT (city) Salt Lake County	12	0.05
Bend, OR (city) Deschutes County	12	0.02
Goodyear, AZ (city) Maricopa County	12	0.02
Provo, UT (city) Utah County	12	0.01
Santa Rosa, CA (city) Sonoma County	12	0.01
Tacoma, WA (city) Pierce County	12	0.01
Lee Vining, CA (cdp) Mono County	11	4.95
Madras, OR (city) Jefferson County	11	0.18

Race

American Indian: Paiute

Top 150 Places Sorted by Percent of Total Population

Based on all places, regardless of total population

Place	Population	%
Schurz, NV (cdp) Mineral County	458	69.60
Nixon, NV (cdp) Washoe County	251	67.11
Kaibab, AZ (cdp) Mohave County	82	66.13
Wadsworth, NV (cdp) Washoe County	434	52.04
Sutcliffe, NV (cdp) Washoe County	120	47.43
Fort Bidwell, CA (cdp) Modoc County	59	34.10
Benton, CA (cdp) Mono County	39	13.93
Valmy, NV (cdp) Humboldt County	4	10.81
Independence, CA (cdp) Inyo County	46	6.88
Fort McDermitt, NV (cdp) Humboldt County	18	5.28
Lovelock, NV (city) Pershing County	99	5.23
Bridgeport, CA (cdp) Mono County	30	5.22
Yerington, NV (city) Lyon County	155	5.09
Lee Vining, CA (cdp) Mono County	11	4.95
Navajo Mountain, UT (cdp) San Juan County	17	4.80
Atlanta, KS (city) Cowley County	7	3.59
Walker, CA (cdp) Mono County	24	3.33
Tupman, CA (cdp) Kern County	5	3.11
McDermitt, NV (cdp) Humboldt County	5	2.91
Nespelem Community, WA (cdp) Okanogan County	7	2.77
Tecopa, CA (cdp) Inyo County	4	2.67
New Pine Creek, OR (cdp) Lake County	3	2.50
Driscoll, ND (cdp) Burleigh County	2	2.44
Owyhee, NV (cdp) Elko County	23	2.41
Cartago, CA (cdp) Inyo County	2	2.17
White Mesa, UT (cdp) San Juan County	5	2.07
Cedarville, CA (cdp) Modoc County	10	1.95
Gabbs, NV (cdp) Nye County	5	1.86
Chiloquin, OR (city) Klamath County	13	1.77
Honcut, CA (cdp) Butte County	6	1.62
Round Valley, CA (cdp) Inyo County	7	1.61
Teasdale, UT (cdp) Wayne County	3	1.57
Mesa Vista, CA (cdp) Alpine County	3	1.50
Truxton, AZ (cdp) Mohave County	2	1.49
Big Pine, CA (cdp) Inyo County	26	1.48
Walker Lake, NV (cdp) Mineral County	4	1.45
Empire, NV (cdp) Washoe County	3	1.38
Mina, NV (cdp) Mineral County	2	1.29
Moapa Town, NV (cdp) Clark County	13	1.27
Hawthorne, NV (cdp) Mineral County	41	1.25
Caliente, NV (city) Lincoln County	14	1.24
Scipio, UT (town) Millard County	4	1.22
Montello, NV (cdp) Elko County	1	1.19
Beryl Junction, UT (cdp) Iron County	2	1.02
Herlong, CA (cdp) Lassen County	3	1.01
Warm Springs, OR (cdp) Jefferson County	29	0.98
Hazleton, IA (city) Buchanan County	8	0.97
Smith Valley, NV (cdp) Lyon County	15	0.94
Forbestown, CA (cdp) Butte County	3	0.94
Elsie, NE (village) Perkins County	1	0.94
Weldon, CA (cdp) Kern County	24	0.91
Greasewood, AZ (cdp) Navajo County	5	0.91
Ruth, NV (cdp) White Pine County	4	0.91
Susanville, CA (city) Lassen County	156	0.87
Cedar City, UT (city) Iron County	247	0.86
Onyx, CA (cdp) Kern County	4	0.84
Humboldt River Ranch, NV (cdp) Pershing County	1	0.84
Burns, OR (city) Harney County	23	0.82
La Mesa, NM (cdp) Doña Ana County	6	0.82
Amalga, UT (town) Cache County	4	0.82
Coleville, CA (cdp) Mono County	4	0.81
Bishop, CA (city) Inyo County	30	0.77
Fredonia, AZ (town) Coconino County	10	0.76
Seba Dalkai, AZ (cdp) Navajo County	1	0.74
Winnemucca, NV (city) Humboldt County	54	0.73
Carter Springs, NV (cdp) Douglas County	4	0.72
Tehama, CA (city) Tehama County	3	0.72
Wilkerson, CA (cdp) Inyo County	4	0.71
McGill, NV (cdp) White Pine County	8	0.70
Virginia City, NV (cdp) Storey County	6	0.70
Pine Grove, WA (cdp) Ferry County	1	0.69
Orlando, OK (town) Logan County	1	0.68
Kinta, OK (town) Haskell County	2	0.67
Lone Pine, CA (cdp) Inyo County	13	0.64
Newton, UT (town) Cache County	5	0.63

Place	Population	%
Fernley, NV (city) Lyon County	121	0.62
Dustin Acres, CA (cdp) Kern County	4	0.61
Del Muerto, AZ (cdp) Apache County	2	0.61
Kernville, CA (cdp) Kern County	8	0.57
De Smet, ID (cdp) Benewah County	1	0.57
Sun Valley, NV (cdp) Washoe County	109	0.56
Fountain Green, UT (city) Sanpete County	6	0.56
Beaver Brook, WI (town) Washburn County	4	0.56
Marcus, WA (town) Stevens County	1	0.55
Bunkerville, NV (cdp) Clark County	7	0.54
Leupp, AZ (cdp) Coconino County	5	0.53
Gu Oidak, AZ (cdp) Pima County	1	0.53
Grass Valley, NV (cdp) Pershing County	6	0.52
Kickapoo Tribal Center, KS (cdp) Brown County	1	0.52
Olancha, CA (cdp) Inyo County	1	0.52
Golden Valley, NV (cdp) Washoe County	8	0.51
Portage Lake, ME (town) Aroostook County	2	0.51
Escalante, UT (city) Garfield County	4	0.50
Dixon Lane-Meadow Creek, CA (cdp) Inyo County	13	0.49
Monroe, OR (city) Benton County	3	0.49
Gerlach, NV (cdp) Washoe County	1	0.49
Stagecoach, NV (cdp) Lyon County	9	0.48
Bend, CA (cdp) Tehama County	3	0.48
June Lake, CA (cdp) Mono County	3	0.48
New Harmony, UT (town) Washington County	1	0.48
Holstein, NE (village) Adams County	1	0.47
Bodega Bay, CA (cdp) Sonoma County	5	0.46
Enoch, UT (city) Iron County	26	0.45
Inyokern, CA (cdp) Kern County	5	0.45
Oljato-Monument Valley, UT (cdp) San Juan County	3	0.45
Randlett, UT (cdp) Uintah County	1	0.45
Whittier, AK (city) Valdez-Cordova Census Area	1	0.45
Ivins, UT (city) Washington County	30	0.44
Greenville, CA (cdp) Plumas County	5	0.44
Doyle, CA (cdp) Lassen County	3	0.44
Lake Isabella, CA (cdp) Kern County	15	0.43
Westwood, CA (cdp) Lassen County	7	0.43
Patton Village, CA (cdp) Lassen County	3	0.43
Nisland, SD (town) Butte County	1	0.43
Carson City, NV (ind. city) Carson City County	234	0.42
Canyon Day, AZ (cdp) Gila County	5	0.41
Nazlini, AZ (cdp) Apache County	2	0.41
Tutuilla, OR (cdp) Umatilla County	2	0.41
Lemmon Valley, NV (cdp) Washoe County	20	0.40
Topaz Ranch Estates, NV (cdp) Douglas County	6	0.40
McClellan Park, CA (cdp) Sacramento County	3	0.40
Mesa, CA (cdp) Inyo County	1	0.40
Tuba City, AZ (cdp) Coconino County	34	0.39
Perrysburg, NY (town) Cattaraugus County	6	0.37
Hooper Bay, AK (city) Wade Hampton Census Area	4	0.37
Detour, MI (township) Chippewa County	3	0.37
Hollister, ID (city) Twin Falls County	1	0.37
Fallon, NV (city) Churchill County	31	0.36
Silver Springs, NV (cdp) Lyon County	19	0.36
Toquerville, UT (town) Washington County	5	0.36
Drain, OR (city) Douglas County	4	0.35
John Day, OR (city) Grant County	6	0.34
Artois, CA (cdp) Glenn County	1	0.34
Chester, CA (cdp) Plumas County	7	0.33
Cattaraugus Reservation, NY (reservation) Erie County	6	0.33
Midpines, CA (cdp) Mariposa County	4	0.33
Redway, CA (cdp) Humboldt County	4	0.33
Lake of the Woods, CA (cdp) Kern County	3	0.33
Crystal Bay, NV (cdp) Washoe County	1	0.33
China Lake Acres, CA (cdp) Kern County	6	0.32
Hines, OR (city) Harney County	5	0.32
Coulterville, IL (village) Randolph County	3	0.32
Lockport Heights, LA (cdp) Lafourche Parish	4	0.31
Mogul, NV (cdp) Washoe County	4	0.31
Oak Glen, CA (cdp) San Bernardino County	2	0.31
Beatty, NV (cdp) Nye County	3	0.30
Indian Springs, NV (cdp) Clark County	3	0.30
Crawfordsville, OR (cdp) Linn County	1	0.30
Superior, WY (town) Sweetwater County	1	0.30
Wanamassa, NJ (cdp) Monmouth County	13	0.29

Please refer to the Explanation of Data in the front of the book for more detailed information.

Race

American Indian: Paiute

Top 150 Places Sorted by Percent of Total Population

Based on places with total population of 7,500 or more

Place	Population	%
Susanville, CA (city) Lassen County	156	0.87
Cedar City, UT (city) Iron County	247	0.86
Fernley, NV (city) Lyon County	121	0.62
Sun Valley, NV (cdp) Washoe County	109	0.56
Carson City, NV (ind. city) Carson City County	234	0.42
Tuba City, AZ (cdp) Coconino County	34	0.39
Fallon, NV (city) Churchill County	31	0.36
Dayton, NV (cdp) Lyon County	25	0.28
Richfield, UT (city) Sevier County	21	0.28
Sparks, NV (city) Washoe County	238	0.26
Klamath Falls, OR (city) Klamath County	55	0.26
Reno, NV (city) Washoe County	509	0.23
Spanish Springs, NV (cdp) Washoe County	35	0.23
Mammoth Lakes, CA (town) Mono County	19	0.23
Elko, NV (city) Elko County	41	0.22
Gardnerville Ranchos, NV (cdp) Douglas County	25	0.22
St. George, UT (city) Washington County	149	0.20
Ontario, OR (city) Malheur County	17	0.15
Shiprock, NM (cdp) San Juan County	12	0.14
Pahrump, NV (cdp) Nye County	46	0.13
Oildale, CA (cdp) Kern County	43	0.13
Washington, UT (city) Washington County	24	0.13
Spring Creek, NV (cdp) Elko County	16	0.13
Oroville East, CA (cdp) Butte County	8	0.10
Ridgecrest, CA (city) Kern County	25	0.09
Truckee, CA (town) Nevada County	14	0.09
Grass Valley, CA (city) Nevada County	12	0.09
Quartz Hill, CA (cdp) Los Angeles County	10	0.09
Calipatria, CA (city) Imperial County	7	0.09
Cold Springs, NV (cdp) Washoe County	7	0.08
Altamont, OR (cdp) Klamath County	13	0.07
Clearlake, CA (city) Lake County	11	0.07
Tehachapi, CA (city) Kern County	10	0.07
Anderson, CA (city) Shasta County	7	0.07
Crescent City, CA (city) Del Norte County	5	0.07
Bakersfield, CA (city) Kern County	214	0.06
Rosamond, CA (cdp) Kern County	11	0.06
Exeter, CA (city) Tulare County	6	0.06
Guthrie, OK (city) Logan County	6	0.06
Golden Hills, CA (cdp) Kern County	5	0.06
Golden Valley, AZ (cdp) Mohave County	5	0.06
Manteca, CA (city) San Joaquin County	33	0.05
Ocean, NJ (township) Monmouth County	13	0.05
South Salt Lake, UT (city) Salt Lake County	12	0.05
South Lake Tahoe, CA (city) El Dorado County	11	0.05
Arvin, CA (city) Kern County	10	0.05
Patterson, CA (city) Stanislaus County	10	0.05
Brigham City, UT (city) Box Elder County	9	0.05
East Hemet, CA (cdp) Riverside County	8	0.05
Mesquite, NV (city) Clark County	8	0.05
Los Osos, CA (cdp) San Luis Obispo County	7	0.05
Oroville, CA (city) Butte County	7	0.05
Fortuna, CA (city) Humboldt County	6	0.05
Hillsborough, CA (town) San Mateo County	5	0.05
Shasta Lake, CA (city) Shasta County	5	0.05
Kennedy, PA (township) Allegheny County	4	0.05
Lakes, AK (cdp) Matanuska-Susitna Borough	4	0.05
Ruidoso, NM (village) Lincoln County	4	0.05
Waterford, CA (city) Stanislaus County	4	0.05
Sunrise Manor, NV (cdp) Clark County	84	0.04
Redding, CA (city) Shasta County	33	0.04
Merced, CA (city) Merced County	32	0.04
Tracy, CA (city) San Joaquin County	32	0.04
Caldwell, ID (city) Canyon County	19	0.04
North Highlands, CA (cdp) Sacramento County	15	0.04
Ashland, CA (cdp) Alameda County	9	0.04
Hayesville, OR (cdp) Marion County	8	0.04
California City, CA (city) Kern County	6	0.04
Oatfield, OR (cdp) Clackamas County	6	0.04
Red Bluff, CA (city) Tehama County	6	0.04
Kerman, CA (city) Fresno County	5	0.04
Magalia, CA (cdp) Butte County	5	0.04
Mountain Home, ID (city) Elmore County	5	0.04
North Auburn, CA (cdp) Placer County	5	0.04
West Richland, WA (city) Benton County	5	0.04
Garden City, ID (city) Ada County	4	0.04
Monmouth, IL (city) Warren County	4	0.04
Newmarket, NH (town) Rockingham County	4	0.04
Prineville, OR (city) Crook County	4	0.04
Silverton, OR (city) Marion County	4	0.04
Molalla, OR (city) Clackamas County	3	0.04
Henderson, NV (city) Clark County	70	0.03
Modesto, CA (city) Stanislaus County	70	0.03
Salt Lake City, UT (city) Salt Lake County	47	0.03
Visalia, CA (city) Tulare County	33	0.03
Antioch, CA (city) Contra Costa County	27	0.03
Lawrence, KS (city) Douglas County	25	0.03
Rancho Cordova, CA (city) Sacramento County	19	0.03
Woodland, CA (city) Yolo County	18	0.03
Missoula, MT (city) Missoula County	17	0.03
Prescott, AZ (city) Yavapai County	13	0.03
Riverton, UT (city) Salt Lake County	13	0.03
Oakley, CA (city) Contra Costa County	11	0.03
Foothill Farms, CA (cdp) Sacramento County	9	0.03
Clinton, UT (city) Davis County	7	0.03
Eureka, CA (city) Humboldt County	7	0.03
Galt, CA (city) Sacramento County	7	0.03
Rosemont, CA (cdp) Sacramento County	7	0.03
San Fernando, CA (city) Los Angeles County	7	0.03
French Valley, CA (cdp) Riverside County	6	0.03
Lathrop, CA (city) San Joaquin County	6	0.03
Durant, OK (city) Bryan County	5	0.03
Four Corners, OR (cdp) Marion County	5	0.03
Linda, CA (cdp) Yuba County	5	0.03
Pinole, CA (city) Contra Costa County	5	0.03
Ukiah, CA (city) Mendocino County	5	0.03
Carpinteria, CA (city) Santa Barbara County	4	0.03
Knik-Fairview, AK (cdp) Matanuska-Susitna Borough	4	0.03
Lebanon, IN (city) Boone County	4	0.03
Lemon Hill, CA (cdp) Sacramento County	4	0.03
Martha Lake, WA (cdp) Snohomish County	4	0.03
Marysville, CA (city) Yuba County	4	0.03
Milford, MI (charter township) Oakland County	4	0.03
Mill Creek East, WA (cdp) Snohomish County	4	0.03
Olivehurst, CA (cdp) Yuba County	4	0.03
Parkway, CA (cdp) Sacramento County	4	0.03
Rio Linda, CA (cdp) Sacramento County	4	0.03
Sun Village, CA (cdp) Los Angeles County	4	0.03
The Dalles, OR (city) Wasco County	4	0.03
Beachwood, NJ (borough) Ocean County	3	0.03
Capitola, CA (city) Santa Cruz County	3	0.03
Cloverdale, CA (city) Sonoma County	3	0.03
Cornelius, OR (city) Washington County	3	0.03
Coweta, OK (city) Wagoner County	3	0.03
Crestline, CA (cdp) San Bernardino County	3	0.03
Delhi, CA (cdp) Merced County	3	0.03
Garden Acres, CA (cdp) San Joaquin County	3	0.03
Jerome, ID (city) Jerome County	3	0.03
Kingsburg, CA (city) Fresno County	3	0.03
Lake Tapps, WA (cdp) Pierce County	3	0.03
Sandy, OR (city) Clackamas County	3	0.03
Silver City, NM (town) Grant County	3	0.03
Soquel, CA (cdp) Santa Cruz County	3	0.03
Kirtland, NM (cdp) San Juan County	2	0.03
Mapleton, UT (city) Utah County	2	0.03
Mount Vista, WA (cdp) Clark County	2	0.03
Pukalani, HI (cdp) Maui County	2	0.03
Yreka, CA (city) Siskiyou County	2	0.03
Las Vegas, NV (city) Clark County	141	0.02
Sacramento, CA (city) Sacramento County	107	0.02
North Las Vegas, NV (city) Clark County	48	0.02
Spring Valley, NV (cdp) Clark County	31	0.02
Eugene, OR (city) Lane County	25	0.02
Salinas, CA (city) Monterey County	25	0.02
West Valley City, UT (city) Salt Lake County	23	0.02
Rialto, CA (city) San Bernardino County	19	0.02
Citrus Heights, CA (city) Sacramento County	18	0.02
Clovis, CA (city) Fresno County	18	0.02
Fairfield, CA (city) Solano County	18	0.02
Chico, CA (city) Butte County	17	0.02

SECTION THREE

Please refer to the Explanation of Data in the front of the book for more detailed information.

Race

American Indian: Pima

U.S. and 50 States Sorted by Population and Percent of Total Population

Place	Population	%
United States	**26,655**	**0.01**
Arizona	22,119	0.35
California	2,127	0.01
Texas	250	<0.01
New Mexico	218	0.01
Oregon	202	0.01
Washington	175	<0.01
Nevada	125	<0.01
Colorado	124	<0.01
Oklahoma	122	<0.01
Utah	100	<0.01
Illinois	85	<0.01
Wisconsin	71	<0.01
Idaho	62	<0.01
North Carolina	58	<0.01
Kansas	55	<0.01
Florida	53	<0.01
Georgia	50	<0.01
New York	40	<0.01
Virginia	40	<0.01
Hawaii	39	<0.01
Michigan	36	<0.01
Pennsylvania	36	<0.01
Alaska	35	<0.01
Missouri	33	<0.01
Minnesota	28	<0.01
Tennessee	28	<0.01
Ohio	27	<0.01
Nebraska	25	<0.01
Indiana	24	<0.01
Iowa	23	<0.01
Montana	23	<0.01
New Jersey	22	<0.01
Kentucky	21	<0.01
Massachusetts	20	<0.01
Arkansas	18	<0.01
South Dakota	17	<0.01
Alabama	16	<0.01
West Virginia	15	<0.01
Louisiana	13	<0.01
Maryland	13	<0.01
South Carolina	11	<0.01
Connecticut	10	<0.01
North Dakota	10	<0.01
Wyoming	10	<0.01
Mississippi	9	<0.01
Delaware	6	<0.01
Maine	4	<0.01
Vermont	4	<0.01
District of Columbia	1	<0.01
New Hampshire	1	<0.01
Rhode Island	1	<0.01

Place	Population	%
Arizona	22,119	0.35
United States	**26,655**	**0.01**
California	2,127	0.01
New Mexico	218	0.01
Oregon	202	0.01
Texas	250	<0.01
Washington	175	<0.01
Nevada	125	<0.01
Colorado	124	<0.01
Oklahoma	122	<0.01
Utah	100	<0.01
Illinois	85	<0.01
Wisconsin	71	<0.01
Idaho	62	<0.01
North Carolina	58	<0.01
Kansas	55	<0.01
Florida	53	<0.01
Georgia	50	<0.01
New York	40	<0.01
Virginia	40	<0.01
Hawaii	39	<0.01
Michigan	36	<0.01
Pennsylvania	36	<0.01
Alaska	35	<0.01
Missouri	33	<0.01
Minnesota	28	<0.01
Tennessee	28	<0.01
Ohio	27	<0.01
Nebraska	25	<0.01
Indiana	24	<0.01
Iowa	23	<0.01
Montana	23	<0.01
New Jersey	22	<0.01
Kentucky	21	<0.01
Massachusetts	20	<0.01
Arkansas	18	<0.01
South Dakota	17	<0.01
Alabama	16	<0.01
West Virginia	15	<0.01
Louisiana	13	<0.01
Maryland	13	<0.01
South Carolina	11	<0.01
Connecticut	10	<0.01
North Dakota	10	<0.01
Wyoming	10	<0.01
Mississippi	9	<0.01
Delaware	6	<0.01
Maine	4	<0.01
Vermont	4	<0.01
District of Columbia	1	<0.01
New Hampshire	1	<0.01
Rhode Island	1	<0.01

Please refer to the Explanation of Data in the front of the book for more detailed information.

Race

American Indian: Pima

Top 150 Places Sorted by Population

Based on all places, regardless of total population

Place	Population	%
Phoenix, AZ (city) Maricopa County	2,614	0.18
Sacaton, AZ (cdp) Pinal County	2,219	83.05
Mesa, AZ (city) Maricopa County	1,378	0.31
Casa Blanca, AZ (cdp) Pinal County	1,169	84.22
Blackwater, AZ (cdp) Pinal County	876	82.49
Komatke, AZ (cdp) Maricopa County	699	85.14
Maricopa Colony, AZ (cdp) Maricopa County	594	83.78
Stotonic Village, AZ (cdp) Pinal County	538	81.64
Gila Crossing, AZ (cdp) Maricopa County	531	85.51
Chandler, AZ (city) Maricopa County	529	0.22
Casa Grande, AZ (city) Pinal County	475	0.98
Sacaton Flats Village, AZ (cdp) Pinal County	473	87.43
Upper Santan Village, AZ (cdp) Pinal County	416	84.04
St. Johns, AZ (cdp) Maricopa County	380	79.83
Goodyear Village, AZ (cdp) Pinal County	355	77.68
Lower Santan Village, AZ (cdp) Pinal County	336	89.84
Tucson, AZ (city) Pima County	266	0.05
Tempe, AZ (city) Maricopa County	234	0.14
Glendale, AZ (city) Maricopa County	199	0.09
Wet Camp Village, AZ (cdp) Pinal County	190	82.97
Coolidge, AZ (city) Pinal County	160	1.35
Los Angeles, CA (city) Los Angeles County	152	<0.01
Gilbert, AZ (town) Maricopa County	150	0.07
Scottsdale, AZ (city) Maricopa County	144	0.07
Maricopa, AZ (city) Pinal County	135	0.31
Sacate Village, AZ (cdp) Pinal County	134	79.29
Sweet Water Village, AZ (cdp) Pinal County	82	98.80
Yuma, AZ (city) Yuma County	81	0.09
Florence, AZ (town) Pinal County	79	0.31
San Tan Valley, AZ (cdp) Pinal County	71	0.09
Eloy, AZ (city) Pinal County	68	0.41
Avondale, AZ (city) Maricopa County	67	0.09
Guadalupe, AZ (town) Maricopa County	63	1.14
Ak-Chin Village, AZ (cdp) Pinal County	62	7.19
Albuquerque, NM (city) Bernalillo County	62	0.01
Arizona City, AZ (cdp) Pinal County	55	0.53
Riverside, CA (city) Riverside County	51	0.02
Surprise, AZ (city) Maricopa County	45	0.04
San Diego, CA (city) San Diego County	44	<0.01
Peoria, AZ (city) Yavapai County	41	0.03
Bakersfield, CA (city) Kern County	41	0.01
Fresno, CA (city) Fresno County	41	0.01
Buckeye, AZ (town) Maricopa County	40	0.08
San Jose, CA (city) Santa Clara County	38	<0.01
San Francisco, CA (city) San Francisco County	36	<0.01
Portland, OR (city) Multnomah County	34	0.01
Santa Cruz, AZ (cdp) Pinal County	33	89.19
Sacramento, CA (city) Sacramento County	33	0.01
Las Vegas, NV (city) Clark County	32	0.01
Sells, AZ (cdp) Pima County	31	1.24
San Carlos, AZ (cdp) Gila County	31	0.77
Stockton, CA (city) San Joaquin County	31	0.01
Victorville, CA (city) San Bernardino County	30	0.03
Oklahoma City, OK (city) Oklahoma County	30	0.01
Queen Creek, AZ (town) Maricopa County	29	0.11
San Bernardino, CA (city) San Bernardino County	27	0.01
Whiteriver, AZ (cdp) Navajo County	26	0.63
Hanford, CA (city) Kings County	25	0.05
Long Beach, CA (city) Los Angeles County	25	0.01
Oakland, CA (city) Alameda County	25	0.01
Porterville, CA (city) Tulare County	23	0.04
Denver, CO (city) Denver County	23	<0.01
Shongopovi, AZ (cdp) Navajo County	22	2.65
South Tucson, AZ (city) Pima County	22	0.39
Tuba City, AZ (cdp) Coconino County	22	0.26
Flagstaff, AZ (city) Coconino County	22	0.03
West Covina, CA (city) Los Angeles County	22	0.02
Colorado Springs, CO (city) El Paso County	22	0.01
Chuichu, AZ (cdp) Pinal County	21	7.81
Holbrook, AZ (city) Navajo County	21	0.42
Dallas, TX (city) Dallas County	21	<0.01
Douglas, AZ (city) Cochise County	20	0.12
Hesperia, CA (city) San Bernardino County	20	0.02
Temecula, CA (city) Riverside County	20	0.02
Modesto, CA (city) Stanislaus County	20	0.01
Hondah, AZ (cdp) Navajo County	19	2.34
Lawrence, KS (city) Douglas County	19	0.02
Mammoth, AZ (town) Pinal County	18	1.26
Kayenta, AZ (cdp) Navajo County	18	0.35
Gresham, OR (city) Multnomah County	18	0.02
Norwalk, CA (city) Los Angeles County	18	0.02
Anaheim, CA (city) Orange County	18	0.01
Anchorage, AK (municipality) Anchorage Municipality	18	0.01
Kaka, AZ (cdp) Maricopa County	17	12.06
Goodyear, AZ (city) Maricopa County	17	0.03
Paradise, NV (cdp) Clark County	17	0.01
Pasadena, CA (city) Los Angeles County	17	0.01
Reno, NV (city) Washoe County	17	0.01
Houston, TX (city) Harris County	17	<0.01
Drexel Heights, AZ (cdp) Pima County	16	0.06
Apache Junction, AZ (city) Pinal County	16	0.04
Chicago, IL (city) Cook County	16	<0.01
El Paso, TX (city) El Paso County	16	<0.01
Moenkopi, AZ (cdp) Coconino County	15	1.56
Indio, CA (city) Riverside County	15	0.02
South Gate, CA (city) Los Angeles County	15	0.02
Wichita, KS (city) Sedgwick County	15	<0.01
Parker, AZ (town) La Paz County	14	0.45
Lompoc, CA (city) Santa Barbara County	14	0.03
Boise City, ID (city) Ada County	14	0.01
Chula Vista, CA (city) San Diego County	14	0.01
Eugene, OR (city) Lane County	14	0.01
Santa Ana, CA (city) Orange County	14	<0.01
Seattle, WA (city) King County	14	<0.01
Camp Verde, AZ (town) Yavapai County	13	0.12
Milwaukee, WI (city) Milwaukee County	13	<0.01
Needles, CA (city) San Bernardino County	12	0.25
East Los Angeles, CA (cdp) Los Angeles County	12	0.01
Lawton, OK (city) Comanche County	12	0.01
Murrieta, CA (city) Riverside County	12	0.01
Ontario, CA (city) San Bernardino County	12	0.01
Pomona, CA (city) Los Angeles County	12	0.01
Salt Lake City, UT (city) Salt Lake County	12	0.01
Vancouver, WA (city) Clark County	12	0.01
San Antonio, TX (city) Medina County	12	<0.01
McNary, AZ (cdp) Apache County	11	2.08
North Fork, AZ (cdp) Navajo County	11	0.78
Gila Bend, AZ (town) Maricopa County	11	0.57
New Kingman-Butler, AZ (cdp) Mohave County	11	0.09
Shafter, CA (city) Kern County	11	0.06
Arden-Arcade, CA (cdp) Sacramento County	11	0.01
Downey, CA (city) Los Angeles County	11	0.01
Orange, CA (city) Orange County	11	0.01
Salem, OR (city) Marion County	11	0.01
Rainbow City, AZ (cdp) Navajo County	10	1.03
Peridot, AZ (cdp) Graham County	10	0.74
Waynesville, MO (city) Pulaski County	10	0.21
Lomita, CA (city) Los Angeles County	10	0.05
Hollister, CA (city) San Benito County	10	0.03
San Gabriel, CA (city) Los Angeles County	10	0.03
Coachella, CA (city) Riverside County	10	0.02
La Habra, CA (city) Orange County	10	0.02
Chino Hills, CA (city) San Bernardino County	10	0.01
Clarksville, TN (city) Montgomery County	10	0.01
Garden Grove, CA (city) Orange County	10	0.01
San Buenaventura (Ventura), CA (city) Ventura County	10	0.01
St. George, UT (city) Washington County	10	0.01
Fort Worth, TX (city) Tarrant County	10	<0.01
Vaiva Vo, AZ (cdp) Pinal County	9	7.03
Nazlini, AZ (cdp) Apache County	9	1.84
Peach Springs, AZ (cdp) Mohave County	9	0.83
First Mesa, AZ (cdp) Navajo County	9	0.58
Pinetop Country Club, AZ (cdp) Navajo County	9	0.50
Oracle, AZ (cdp) Pinal County	9	0.24
Tanque Verde, AZ (cdp) Pima County	9	0.05
Sahuarita, AZ (town) Pima County	9	0.04
West Puente Valley, CA (cdp) Los Angeles County	9	0.04
Oakley, CA (city) Contra Costa County	9	0.03
Lake Havasu City, AZ (city) Mohave County	9	0.02
Olympia, WA (city) Thurston County	9	0.02

Please refer to the Explanation of Data in the front of the book for more detailed information.

Race

American Indian: Pima

Top 150 Places Sorted by Percent of Total Population

Based on all places, regardless of total population

Place	Population	%
Sweet Water Village, AZ (cdp) Pinal County	82	98.80
Lower Santan Village, AZ (cdp) Pinal County	336	89.84
Santa Cruz, AZ (cdp) Pinal County	33	89.19
Sacaton Flats Village, AZ (cdp) Pinal County	473	87.43
Gila Crossing, AZ (cdp) Maricopa County	531	85.51
Komatke, AZ (cdp) Maricopa County	699	85.14
Casa Blanca, AZ (cdp) Pinal County	1,169	84.22
Upper Santan Village, AZ (cdp) Pinal County	416	84.04
Maricopa Colony, AZ (cdp) Maricopa County	594	83.78
Sacaton, AZ (cdp) Pinal County	2,219	83.05
Wet Camp Village, AZ (cdp) Pinal County	190	82.97
Blackwater, AZ (cdp) Pinal County	876	82.49
Stotonic Village, AZ (cdp) Pinal County	538	81.64
St. Johns, AZ (cdp) Maricopa County	380	79.83
Sacate Village, AZ (cdp) Pinal County	134	79.29
Goodyear Village, AZ (cdp) Pinal County	355	77.68
Kohatk, AZ (cdp) Pinal County	6	22.22
Kaka, AZ (cdp) Maricopa County	17	12.06
Chuichu, AZ (cdp) Pinal County	21	7.81
Hard Rock, AZ (cdp) Navajo County	7	7.45
Ak-Chin Village, AZ (cdp) Pinal County	62	7.19
Vaiva Vo, AZ (cdp) Pinal County	9	7.03
Ak Chin, AZ (cdp) Pima County	2	6.67
Kaibab, AZ (cdp) Mohave County	8	6.45
Seba Dalkai, AZ (cdp) Navajo County	6	4.41
Antares, AZ (cdp) Mohave County	5	3.97
Mojave Ranch Estates, AZ (cdp) Mohave County	2	3.85
Kickapoo Site 1, KS (cdp) Brown County	3	2.97
Shongopovi, AZ (cdp) Navajo County	22	2.65
East Globe, AZ (cdp) Gila County	6	2.65
Valentine, AZ (cdp) Mohave County	1	2.63
Maish Vaya, AZ (cdp) Pima County	4	2.53
Hondah, AZ (cdp) Navajo County	19	2.34
McNary, AZ (cdp) Apache County	11	2.08
Amado, AZ (cdp) Santa Cruz County	6	2.03
Nazlini, AZ (cdp) Apache County	9	1.84
Jeddito, AZ (cdp) Navajo County	5	1.71
Indian Wells, AZ (cdp) Navajo County	4	1.57
Moenkopi, AZ (cdp) Coconino County	15	1.56
Beryl Junction, UT (cdp) Iron County	3	1.52
Crystal Beach, AZ (cdp) Mohave County	4	1.43
Weott, CA (cdp) Humboldt County	4	1.39
Randlett, UT (cdp) Uintah County	3	1.36
Coolidge, AZ (city) Pinal County	160	1.35
Cutter, AZ (cdp) Gila County	1	1.35
Keams Canyon, AZ (cdp) Navajo County	4	1.32
Mammoth, AZ (town) Pinal County	18	1.26
Sells, AZ (cdp) Pima County	31	1.24
Why, AZ (cdp) Pima County	2	1.20
Guadalupe, AZ (town) Maricopa County	63	1.14
Santa Rosa, AZ (cdp) Pima County	7	1.11
Stanfield, AZ (cdp) Pinal County	8	1.08
Nixon, NV (cdp) Washoe County	4	1.07
Steamboat, AZ (cdp) Apache County	3	1.06
Peters, CA (cdp) San Joaquin County	7	1.04
Haivana Nakya, AZ (cdp) Pima County	1	1.04
Rainbow City, AZ (cdp) Navajo County	10	1.03
Topawa, AZ (cdp) Pima County	3	1.00
Chamizal, NM (cdp) Socorro County	1	0.99
Casa Grande, AZ (city) Pinal County	475	0.98
Two Strike, SD (cdp) Todd County	2	0.96
Kykotsmovi Village, AZ (cdp) Navajo County	7	0.94
Tees Toh, AZ (cdp) Navajo County	4	0.89
Leupp, AZ (cdp) Coconino County	8	0.84
Peach Springs, AZ (cdp) Mohave County	9	0.83
Second Mesa, AZ (cdp) Navajo County	8	0.83
Pueblo of Sandia Village, NM (cdp) Sandoval County	3	0.81
Joppa, AL (cdp) Cullman County	4	0.80
North Fork, AZ (cdp) Navajo County	11	0.78
San Carlos, AZ (cdp) Gila County	31	0.77
Ali Chukson, AZ (cdp) Pima County	1	0.76
Peridot, AZ (cdp) Graham County	10	0.74
Santa Clara Pueblo, NM (cdp) Rio Arriba County	7	0.69
Turkey Creek, AZ (cdp) Navajo County	2	0.68
Anegam, AZ (cdp) Pima County	1	0.66
Devol, OK (town) Cotton County	1	0.66
Whiteriver, AZ (cdp) Navajo County	26	0.63
Dudleyville, AZ (cdp) Pinal County	6	0.63
Pisinemo, AZ (cdp) Pima County	2	0.62
Wadsworth, NV (cdp) Washoe County	5	0.60
Fort McDermitt, NV (cdp) Humboldt County	2	0.59
First Mesa, AZ (cdp) Navajo County	9	0.58
Gila Bend, AZ (town) Maricopa County	11	0.57
Arizona City, AZ (cdp) Pinal County	55	0.53
Olancha, CA (cdp) Inyo County	1	0.52
Walthill, NE (village) Thurston County	4	0.51
Pinetop Country Club, AZ (cdp) Navajo County	9	0.50
Whitecone, AZ (cdp) Navajo County	4	0.49
Supai, AZ (cdp) Coconino County	1	0.48
Pinal, AZ (cdp) Gila County	2	0.46
Parker, AZ (town) La Paz County	14	0.45
Cameron, AZ (cdp) Coconino County	4	0.45
Neola, UT (cdp) Duchesne County	2	0.43
Seama, NM (cdp) Cibola County	2	0.43
Holbrook, AZ (city) Navajo County	21	0.42
Moroni, UT (city) Sanpete County	6	0.42
Dilkon, AZ (cdp) Navajo County	5	0.42
Seven Mile, AZ (cdp) Navajo County	3	0.42
Eloy, AZ (city) Pinal County	68	0.41
Cibecue, AZ (cdp) Navajo County	7	0.41
Cibola, AZ (cdp) La Paz County	1	0.40
South Tucson, AZ (city) Pima County	22	0.39
Pillsbury, MN (township) Swift County	1	0.39
Hood, CA (cdp) Sacramento County	1	0.37
Kayenta, AZ (cdp) Navajo County	18	0.35
Cubero, NM (cdp) Cibola County	1	0.35
Poston, AZ (cdp) La Paz County	1	0.35
Shonto, AZ (cdp) Navajo County	2	0.34
Yah-ta-hey, NM (cdp) McKinley County	2	0.34
Bombay Beach, CA (cdp) Imperial County	1	0.34
Cameron, OK (town) Le Flore County	1	0.33
North Hurley, NM (cdp) Grant County	1	0.33
Beaverdale, IA (cdp) Des Moines County	3	0.32
Sanders, AZ (cdp) Apache County	2	0.32
Mesa, AZ (city) Maricopa County	1,378	0.31
Maricopa, AZ (city) Pinal County	135	0.31
Florence, AZ (town) Pinal County	79	0.31
Bylas, AZ (cdp) Graham County	6	0.31
Felton, DE (town) Kent County	4	0.31
Cedar Creek, AZ (cdp) Gila County	1	0.31
Niland, CA (cdp) Imperial County	3	0.30
Fremont, MI (township) Saginaw County	6	0.29
Six Shooter Canyon, AZ (cdp) Gila County	3	0.29
Olton, TX (city) Lamb County	6	0.27
Forestville, WI (town) Door County	3	0.27
Peak Place, NM (cdp) Santa Fe County	1	0.27
Scandia, KS (city) Republic County	1	0.27
Tuba City, AZ (cdp) Coconino County	22	0.26
Crownpoint, NM (cdp) McKinley County	6	0.26
Kearny, AZ (town) Pinal County	5	0.26
Taos Pueblo, NM (cdp) Taos County	3	0.26
Needles, CA (city) San Bernardino County	12	0.25
Mission, SD (city) Todd County	3	0.25
Davenport, CA (cdp) Santa Cruz County	1	0.25
Ludlow, ME (town) Aroostook County	1	0.25
Oracle, AZ (cdp) Pinal County	9	0.24
Val Verde, CA (cdp) Los Angeles County	6	0.24
Scenic, AZ (cdp) Mohave County	4	0.24
Granby, MO (city) Newton County	5	0.23
Stratford, CA (cdp) Kings County	3	0.23
Dyer, AR (city) Crawford County	2	0.23
Beckwourth, CA (cdp) Plumas County	1	0.23
Keene, CA (cdp) Kern County	1	0.23
Watersmeet, MI (cdp) Gogebic County	1	0.23
Chandler, AZ (city) Maricopa County	529	0.22
Window Rock, AZ (cdp) Apache County	6	0.22
Desert Hills, AZ (cdp) Mohave County	5	0.22
Tombstone, AZ (city) Cochise County	3	0.22
Chilcoot-Vinton, CA (cdp) Plumas County	1	0.22
Paden, OK (town) Okfuskee County	1	0.22

Please refer to the Explanation of Data in the front of the book for more detailed information.

Race

American Indian: Pima

Top 150 Places Sorted by Percent of Total Population

Based on places with total population of 7,500 or more

Place	Population	%
Coolidge, AZ (city) Pinal County	160	1.35
Casa Grande, AZ (city) Pinal County	475	0.98
Arizona City, AZ (cdp) Pinal County	55	0.53
Eloy, AZ (city) Pinal County	68	0.41
Mesa, AZ (city) Maricopa County	1,378	0.31
Maricopa, AZ (city) Pinal County	135	0.31
Florence, AZ (town) Pinal County	79	0.31
Tuba City, AZ (cdp) Coconino County	22	0.26
Chandler, AZ (city) Maricopa County	529	0.22
Phoenix, AZ (city) Maricopa County	2,614	0.18
Tempe, AZ (city) Maricopa County	234	0.14
Douglas, AZ (city) Cochise County	20	0.12
Camp Verde, AZ (town) Yavapai County	13	0.12
Queen Creek, AZ (town) Maricopa County	29	0.11
Glendale, AZ (city) Maricopa County	199	0.09
Yuma, AZ (city) Yuma County	81	0.09
San Tan Valley, AZ (cdp) Pinal County	71	0.09
Avondale, AZ (city) Maricopa County	67	0.09
New Kingman-Butler, AZ (cdp) Mohave County	11	0.09
Buckeye, AZ (town) Maricopa County	40	0.08
Ocean Pointe, HI (cdp) Honolulu County	7	0.08
Globe, AZ (city) Gila County	6	0.08
Gilbert, AZ (town) Maricopa County	150	0.07
Scottsdale, AZ (city) Maricopa County	144	0.07
North Valley, NM (cdp) Bernalillo County	8	0.07
Golden Valley, AZ (cdp) Mohave County	6	0.07
Makaha, HI (cdp) Honolulu County	6	0.07
Drexel Heights, AZ (cdp) Pima County	16	0.06
Shafter, CA (city) Kern County	11	0.06
Crestline, CA (cdp) San Bernardino County	7	0.06
Sweet Home, OR (city) Linn County	5	0.06
Tucson, AZ (city) Pima County	266	0.05
Hanford, CA (city) Kings County	25	0.05
Lomita, CA (city) Los Angeles County	10	0.05
Tanque Verde, AZ (cdp) Pima County	9	0.05
Payson, AZ (town) Gila County	8	0.05
Clearlake, CA (city) Lake County	7	0.05
Grants, NM (city) Cibola County	5	0.05
Lexington, NE (city) Dawson County	5	0.05
Sallisaw, OK (city) Sequoyah County	4	0.05
Surprise, AZ (city) Maricopa County	45	0.04
Porterville, CA (city) Tulare County	23	0.04
Apache Junction, AZ (city) Pinal County	16	0.04
Sahuarita, AZ (town) Pima County	9	0.04
West Puente Valley, CA (cdp) Los Angeles County	9	0.04
Barstow, CA (city) San Bernardino County	8	0.04
Vincent, CA (cdp) Los Angeles County	6	0.04
Verde Village, AZ (cdp) Yavapai County	5	0.04
Canyon Lake, CA (city) Riverside County	4	0.04
Cottonwood, AZ (city) Yavapai County	4	0.04
Minnehaha, WA (cdp) Clark County	4	0.04
Shasta Lake, CA (city) Shasta County	4	0.04
Shawano, WI (city) Shawano County	4	0.04
Soquel, CA (cdp) Santa Cruz County	4	0.04
Winslow, AZ (city) Navajo County	4	0.04
Hamilton, MA (town) Essex County	3	0.04
South San Gabriel, CA (cdp) Los Angeles County	3	0.04
Peoria, AZ (city) Yavapai County	41	0.03
Victorville, CA (city) San Bernardino County	30	0.03
Flagstaff, AZ (city) Coconino County	22	0.03
Goodyear, AZ (city) Maricopa County	17	0.03
Lompoc, CA (city) Santa Barbara County	14	0.03
Hollister, CA (city) San Benito County	10	0.03
San Gabriel, CA (city) Los Angeles County	10	0.03
Oakley, CA (city) Contra Costa County	9	0.03
El Mirage, AZ (city) Maricopa County	8	0.03
De Pere, WI (city) Brown County	7	0.03
Post Falls, ID (city) Kootenai County	7	0.03
Wasco, CA (city) Kern County	7	0.03
Gallup, NM (city) McKinley County	6	0.03
Nogales, AZ (city) Santa Cruz County	6	0.03
Sand Springs, OK (city) Tulsa County	5	0.03
Somerton, AZ (city) Yuma County	5	0.03
Willmar, MN (city) Kandiyohi County	5	0.03
Big Bear City, CA (cdp) San Bernardino County	4	0.03
El Sobrante, CA (cdp) Riverside County	4	0.03
Sun Lakes, AZ (cdp) Maricopa County	4	0.03
Anaconda-Deer Lodge County, MT (special city) Deer Lodge County	3	0.03
Cedar Lake, IN (town) Lake County	3	0.03
Chino Valley, AZ (town) Yavapai County	3	0.03
Citrus, CA (cdp) Los Angeles County	3	0.03
Diamond Springs, CA (cdp) El Dorado County	3	0.03
Gold Canyon, AZ (cdp) Pinal County	3	0.03
Parsons, KS (city) Labette County	3	0.03
Toppenish, WA (city) Yakima County	3	0.03
Valencia West, AZ (cdp) Pima County	3	0.03
Calimesa, CA (city) Riverside County	2	0.03
Riverside, CA (city) Riverside County	51	0.02
West Covina, CA (city) Los Angeles County	22	0.02
Hesperia, CA (city) San Bernardino County	20	0.02
Temecula, CA (city) Riverside County	20	0.02
Lawrence, KS (city) Douglas County	19	0.02
Gresham, OR (city) Multnomah County	18	0.02
Norwalk, CA (city) Los Angeles County	18	0.02
Indio, CA (city) Riverside County	15	0.02
South Gate, CA (city) Los Angeles County	15	0.02
Coachella, CA (city) Riverside County	10	0.02
La Habra, CA (city) Orange County	10	0.02
Lake Havasu City, AZ (city) Mohave County	9	0.02
Olympia, WA (city) Thurston County	9	0.02
Prescott Valley, AZ (town) Yavapai County	9	0.02
Rowland Heights, CA (cdp) Los Angeles County	9	0.02
Monrovia, CA (city) Los Angeles County	7	0.02
North Highlands, CA (cdp) Sacramento County	7	0.02
Pleasant Grove, UT (city) Utah County	7	0.02
Adelanto, CA (city) San Bernardino County	6	0.02
Bremerton, WA (city) Kitsap County	6	0.02
Fortuna Foothills, AZ (cdp) Yuma County	6	0.02
Kingman, AZ (city) Mohave County	6	0.02
La Puente, CA (city) Los Angeles County	6	0.02
Lafayette, CO (city) Boulder County	6	0.02
Lemoore, CA (city) Kings County	6	0.02
Los Banos, CA (city) Merced County	6	0.02
Rubidoux, CA (cdp) Riverside County	6	0.02
Santa Paula, CA (city) Ventura County	6	0.02
West Whittier-Los Nietos, CA (cdp) Los Angeles County	6	0.02
Fountain Hills, AZ (town) Maricopa County	5	0.02
Lansing, IL (village) Cook County	5	0.02
Paradise, CA (town) Butte County	5	0.02
Blythe, CA (city) Riverside County	4	0.02
Burlington, NJ (township) Burlington County	4	0.02
Casa de Oro-Mount Helix, CA (cdp) San Diego County	4	0.02
Corcoran, CA (city) Kings County	4	0.02
Jasmine Estates, FL (cdp) Pasco County	4	0.02
Kerrville, TX (city) Kerr County	4	0.02
Magna, UT (cdp) Salt Lake County	4	0.02
Makakilo, HI (cdp) Honolulu County	4	0.02
South Pasadena, CA (city) Los Angeles County	4	0.02
Winter Gardens, CA (cdp) San Diego County	4	0.02
Albany, CA (city) Alameda County	3	0.02
Arvin, CA (city) Kern County	3	0.02
Auburn, CA (city) Placer County	3	0.02
Camas, WA (city) Clark County	3	0.02
Cameron Park, CA (cdp) El Dorado County	3	0.02
Clifton, CO (cdp) Mesa County	3	0.02
Covington, WA (city) King County	3	0.02
Elko, NV (city) Elko County	3	0.02
Evans, CO (city) Weld County	3	0.02
Frederickson, WA (cdp) Pierce County	3	0.02
Highlands, NY (town) Orange County	3	0.02
Malibu, CA (city) Los Angeles County	3	0.02
Rio Rico, AZ (cdp) Santa Cruz County	3	0.02
Schofield Barracks, HI (cdp) Honolulu County	3	0.02
Shelbyville, KY (city) Shelby County	3	0.02
Silverdale, WA (cdp) Kitsap County	3	0.02
California, MD (cdp) St. Mary's County	2	0.02
Cloverdale, CA (city) Sonoma County	2	0.02
Corte Madera, CA (town) Marin County	2	0.02
Edgewater Park, NJ (township) Burlington County	2	0.02
Essex Junction, VT (village) Chittenden County	2	0.02

SECTION THREE

Please refer to the Explanation of Data in the front of the book for more detailed information.

Race

American Indian: Potawatomi

U.S. and 50 States Sorted by Population and Percent of Total Population

Place	Population	%
United States	**33,771**	**0.01**
Oklahoma	8,078	0.22
Michigan	4,901	0.05
Kansas	3,852	0.14
California	2,962	0.01
Texas	2,099	0.01
Wisconsin	1,874	0.03
Washington	801	0.01
Indiana	724	0.01
Missouri	723	0.01
Colorado	709	0.01
Illinois	625	<0.01
Arizona	574	0.01
Florida	565	<0.01
Oregon	546	0.01
Arkansas	325	0.01
Nevada	290	0.01
Ohio	276	<0.01
Minnesota	263	<0.01
New Mexico	246	0.01
Virginia	230	<0.01
Tennessee	227	<0.01
North Carolina	210	<0.01
Georgia	208	<0.01
Montana	202	0.02
Idaho	182	0.01
New York	166	<0.01
Nebraska	162	0.01
Utah	162	0.01
Pennsylvania	157	<0.01
Iowa	135	<0.01
Alaska	131	0.02
Louisiana	115	<0.01
Maryland	107	<0.01
Massachusetts	98	<0.01
New Jersey	93	<0.01
Alabama	90	<0.01
Kentucky	87	<0.01
South Carolina	83	<0.01
Mississippi	76	<0.01
Hawaii	71	0.01
South Dakota	56	0.01
Wyoming	46	0.01
Connecticut	41	<0.01
West Virginia	36	<0.01
Delaware	34	<0.01
Maine	28	<0.01
Vermont	27	<0.01
North Dakota	26	<0.01
New Hampshire	24	<0.01
District of Columbia	15	<0.01
Rhode Island	13	<0.01

Place	Population	%
Oklahoma	8,078	0.22
Kansas	3,852	0.14
Michigan	4,901	0.05
Wisconsin	1,874	0.03
Montana	202	0.02
Alaska	131	0.02
United States	**33,771**	**0.01**
California	2,962	0.01
Texas	2,099	0.01
Washington	801	0.01
Indiana	724	0.01
Missouri	723	0.01
Colorado	709	0.01
Arizona	574	0.01
Oregon	546	0.01
Arkansas	325	0.01
Nevada	290	0.01
New Mexico	246	0.01
Idaho	182	0.01
Nebraska	162	0.01
Utah	162	0.01
Hawaii	71	0.01
South Dakota	56	0.01
Wyoming	46	0.01
Illinois	625	<0.01
Florida	565	<0.01
Ohio	276	<0.01
Minnesota	263	<0.01
Virginia	230	<0.01
Tennessee	227	<0.01
North Carolina	210	<0.01
Georgia	208	<0.01
New York	166	<0.01
Pennsylvania	157	<0.01
Iowa	135	<0.01
Louisiana	115	<0.01
Maryland	107	<0.01
Massachusetts	98	<0.01
New Jersey	93	<0.01
Alabama	90	<0.01
Kentucky	87	<0.01
South Carolina	83	<0.01
Mississippi	76	<0.01
Connecticut	41	<0.01
West Virginia	36	<0.01
Delaware	34	<0.01
Maine	28	<0.01
Vermont	27	<0.01
North Dakota	26	<0.01
New Hampshire	24	<0.01
District of Columbia	15	<0.01
Rhode Island	13	<0.01

Please refer to the Explanation of Data in the front of the book for more detailed information.

Race

American Indian: Potawatomi

Top 150 Places Sorted by Population

Based on all places, regardless of total population

Place	Population	%
Oklahoma City, OK (city) Oklahoma County	982	0.17
Topeka, KS (city) Shawnee County	873	0.68
Shawnee, OK (city) Pottawatomie County	559	1.87
Norman, OK (city) Cleveland County	439	0.40
Harris, MI (township) Menominee County	335	17.02
Tecumseh, OK (city) Pottawatomie County	311	4.82
Tulsa, OK (city) Tulsa County	306	0.08
Lincoln, WI (town) Forest County	254	26.60
Wabeno, WI (town) Forest County	196	16.81
Wichita, KS (city) Sedgwick County	184	0.05
Moore, OK (city) Cleveland County	182	0.33
Lawrence, KS (city) Douglas County	179	0.20
Grand Rapids, MI (city) Kent County	166	0.09
Milwaukee, WI (city) Milwaukee County	161	0.03
Dowagiac, MI (city) Cass County	140	2.38
Phoenix, AZ (city) Maricopa County	137	0.01
Kansas City, MO (city) Jackson County	135	0.03
Edmond, OK (city) Oklahoma County	126	0.15
Chicago, IL (city) Cook County	115	<0.01
Los Angeles, CA (city) Los Angeles County	115	<0.01
Midwest City, OK (city) Oklahoma County	111	0.20
Dallas, TX (city) Dallas County	104	0.01
Purcell, OK (city) McClain County	92	1.56
Broken Arrow, OK (city) Tulsa County	89	0.09
Indianapolis, IN (city) Marion County	88	0.01
Wyoming, MI (city) Kent County	86	0.12
Green Bay, WI (city) Brown County	85	0.08
Escanaba, MI (city) Delta County	84	0.67
Holton, KS (city) Jackson County	81	2.43
Battle Creek, MI (city) Calhoun County	81	0.15
Kalamazoo, MI (city) Kalamazoo County	81	0.11
San Diego, CA (city) San Diego County	80	0.01
Bethel Acres, OK (town) Pottawatomie County	78	2.69
LaGrange, MI (township) Cass County	75	2.14
South Bend, IN (city) St. Joseph County	74	0.07
Choctaw, OK (city) Oklahoma County	72	0.65
Denver, CO (city) Denver County	70	0.01
Noble, OK (city) Cleveland County	68	1.05
Kansas City, KS (city) Wyandotte County	67	0.05
Crandon, WI (city) Forest County	66	3.44
Austin, TX (city) Travis County	66	0.01
Yukon, OK (city) Canadian County	65	0.29
Houston, TX (city) Harris County	63	<0.01
Mustang, OK (city) Canadian County	62	0.36
Minneapolis, MN (city) Hennepin County	62	0.02
Detroit, MI (city) Wayne County	61	0.01
Manhattan, KS (city) Riley County	60	0.11
Niles, MI (township) Berrien County	58	0.41
Mishawaka, IN (city) St. Joseph County	58	0.12
Fort Worth, TX (city) Tarrant County	58	0.01
Las Vegas, NV (city) Clark County	58	0.01
Colorado Springs, CO (city) El Paso County	57	0.01
Lawton, OK (city) Comanche County	56	0.06
Stillwater, OK (city) Payne County	55	0.12
Sacramento, CA (city) Sacramento County	54	0.01
Seattle, WA (city) King County	54	0.01
Bartlesville, OK (city) Washington County	53	0.15
Bakersfield, CA (city) Kern County	52	0.01
San Jose, CA (city) Santa Clara County	52	0.01
Slaughterville, OK (town) Cleveland County	51	1.23
Lansing, MI (city) Ingham County	51	0.04
Hartford, MI (city) Van Buren County	50	1.86
Niles, MI (city) Berrien County	50	0.43
Niles, MI (city) Berrien County	50	0.43
Lansing, MI (city) Ingham County	50	0.05
Lubbock, TX (city) Lubbock County	50	0.02
Hoyt, KS (city) Jackson County	49	7.32
Portage, MI (city) Kalamazoo County	49	0.11
Omaha, NE (city) Douglas County	49	0.01
Anchorage, AK (municipality) Anchorage Municipality	48	0.02
McLoud, OK (town) Pottawatomie County	47	1.16
Fresno, CA (city) Fresno County	47	0.01
Pawhuska, OK (city) Osage County	46	1.28
Overland Park, KS (city) Johnson County	46	0.03
Albuquerque, NM (city) Bernalillo County	46	0.01
San Antonio, TX (city) Medina County	46	<0.01
Portland, OR (city) Multnomah County	45	0.01
Horton, KS (city) Brown County	44	2.48
Newcastle, OK (city) McClain County	44	0.57
Benton, MI (charter township) Berrien County	42	0.28
Wausau, WI (city) Marathon County	42	0.11
Georgetown, MI (charter township) Ottawa County	42	0.09
Rossville, KS (city) Shawnee County	41	3.56
Hartford, MI (township) Van Buren County	41	1.25
Lac du Flambeau, WI (town) Vilas County	40	1.16
Harrah, OK (city) Oklahoma County	40	0.79
Grand Haven, MI (charter township) Ottawa County	40	0.26
New York, NY (city) Kings County	40	<0.01
Hominy, OK (city) Osage County	39	1.09
Ponca City, OK (city) Kay County	39	0.15
Muskogee, OK (city) Muskogee County	39	0.10
Tucson, AZ (city) Pima County	39	0.01
Athens, MI (township) Calhoun County	38	1.49
Cutlerville, MI (cdp) Kent County	38	0.26
Ada, OK (city) Pontotoc County	38	0.23
Eugene, OR (city) Lane County	38	0.02
Plano, TX (city) Collin County	38	0.01
Silver Creek, MI (township) Cass County	37	1.15
Emmett, MI (charter township) Calhoun County	37	0.31
Mesa, AZ (city) Maricopa County	37	0.01
Wabeno, WI (cdp) Forest County	36	6.26
Corpus Christi, TX (city) Nueces County	36	0.01
Wayne, MI (township) Cass County	35	1.32
Stockton, CA (city) San Joaquin County	35	0.01
Mayetta, KS (city) Jackson County	34	9.97
Springfield, MO (city) Christian County	34	0.02
San Francisco, CA (city) San Francisco County	34	<0.01
Sulphur, OK (city) Murray County	33	0.67
Jenks, OK (city) Tulsa County	33	0.19
Del City, OK (city) Oklahoma County	33	0.15
Oshtemo, MI (charter township) Kalamazoo County	33	0.15
Neenah, WI (city) Winnebago County	33	0.13
Enid, OK (city) Garfield County	33	0.07
Kentwood, MI (city) Kent County	33	0.07
Toledo, OH (city) Lucas County	33	0.01
Skiatook, OK (town) Osage County	32	0.43
Amarillo, TX (city) Potter County	32	0.02
Arlington, TX (city) Tarrant County	32	0.01
Seminole, OK (city) Seminole County	31	0.41
Jackson, MI (city) Jackson County	31	0.09
McKinney, TX (city) Collin County	31	0.02
Olathe, KS (city) Johnson County	31	0.02
Visalia, CA (city) Tulare County	31	0.02
Henderson, NV (city) Clark County	31	0.01
Riverside, CA (city) Riverside County	31	0.01
Blackwell, OK (city) Kay County	30	0.42
Lakewood, CO (city) Jefferson County	30	0.02
Tacoma, WA (city) Pierce County	30	0.02
Pauls Valley, OK (city) Garvin County	29	0.47
El Reno, OK (city) Canadian County	29	0.17
West Allis, WI (city) Milwaukee County	29	0.05
Redding, CA (city) Shasta County	29	0.03
Boise City, ID (city) Ada County	29	0.01
Chickasha, OK (city) Grady County	28	0.17
Bethany, OK (city) Oklahoma County	28	0.15
Gaines, MI (charter township) Kent County	28	0.11
Owasso, OK (city) Tulsa County	28	0.10
Elkhart, IN (city) Elkhart County	28	0.05
Tempe, AZ (city) Maricopa County	28	0.02
Earlsboro, OK (town) Pottawatomie County	27	4.30
Rhinelander, WI (city) Oneida County	27	0.35
Bixby, OK (city) Tulsa County	27	0.13
Muskegon, MI (city) Muskegon County	27	0.07
Long Beach, CA (city) Los Angeles County	27	0.01
Lac du Flambeau, WI (cdp) Vilas County	26	1.32
Lexington, OK (city) Cleveland County	26	1.21
Claremore, OK (city) Rogers County	26	0.14
Sand Springs, OK (city) Tulsa County	26	0.14
Appleton, WI (city) Outagamie County	26	0.04
Aurora, CO (city) Arapahoe County	26	0.01

Race

American Indian: Potawatomi

Top 150 Places Sorted by Percent of Total Population

Based on all places, regardless of total population

Place	Population	%
Lincoln, WI (town) Forest County	254	26.60
Harris, MI (township) Menominee County	335	17.02
Wabeno, WI (town) Forest County	196	16.81
Kickapoo Site 5, KS (cdp) Brown County	10	15.15
Kickapoo Site 1, KS (cdp) Brown County	15	14.85
Kickapoo Site 7, KS (cdp) Brown County	9	13.64
Mayetta, KS (city) Jackson County	34	9.97
Delia, KS (city) Jackson County	14	8.28
Marion, WI (city) Shawano County	2	8.00
Hoyt, KS (city) Jackson County	49	7.32
Grainola, OK (town) Osage County	2	6.45
Wabeno, WI (cdp) Forest County	36	6.26
Metz, MO (town) Vernon County	3	6.12
Willard, KS (city) Shawnee County	5	5.43
Kickapoo Tribal Center, KS (cdp) Brown County	10	5.15
Dotyville, OK (cdp) Ottawa County	5	4.95
Tecumseh, OK (city) Pottawatomie County	311	4.82
Earlsboro, OK (town) Pottawatomie County	27	4.30
Horn, OK (town) Hughes County	4	4.12
Goff, KS (city) Nemaha County	5	3.97
St. Louis, OK (town) Pottawatomie County	6	3.80
Revere, MO (town) Clark County	3	3.80
Rossville, KS (city) Shawnee County	41	3.56
Yale, IL (village) Jasper County	3	3.49
Crandon, WI (city) Forest County	66	3.44
Caswell, WI (town) Forest County	3	3.30
Crandon, WI (town) Forest County	21	3.23
Mole Lake, WI (cdp) Forest County	14	3.22
Wanette, OK (town) Pottawatomie County	11	3.14
Butler, WI (town) Clark County	3	3.13
Yellow Pine, ID (cdp) Valley County	1	3.13
Asher, OK (town) Pottawatomie County	12	3.05
Waukena, CA (cdp) Tulare County	3	2.78
Lipscomb, TX (cdp) Lipscomb County	1	2.70
Bethel Acres, OK (town) Pottawatomie County	78	2.69
Amesville, OH (village) Athens County	4	2.60
Milburn, OK (town) Johnston County	8	2.52
Bushton, KS (city) Rice County	7	2.51
Zeba, MI (cdp) Baraga County	12	2.50
Horton, KS (city) Brown County	44	2.48
Lakewood, WI (cdp) Oconto County	8	2.48
Cornish, OK (town) Jefferson County	4	2.45
Summit, WI (town) Langlade County	4	2.45
Holton, KS (city) Jackson County	81	2.43
Maud, OK (city) Pottawatomie County	25	2.39
Dowagiac, MI (city) Cass County	140	2.38
Kirwin, KS (city) Phillips County	4	2.34
Freedom, WI (town) Forest County	8	2.32
Wynona, OK (town) Osage County	10	2.29
Soldier, KS (city) Jackson County	3	2.21
Parrish, WI (town) Langlade County	2	2.20
LaGrange, MI (township) Cass County	75	2.14
Hard Rock, AZ (cdp) Navajo County	2	2.13
Emmett, KS (city) Pottawatomie County	4	2.09
Belvidere, NE (village) Thayer County	1	2.08
Townsend, WI (cdp) Oconto County	3	2.05
Nashville, WI (town) Forest County	21	1.97
Pocasset, OK (town) Grady County	3	1.92
Havana, KS (city) Montgomery County	2	1.92
Gourley, MI (township) Menominee County	8	1.90
Shawnee, OK (city) Pottawatomie County	559	1.87
Hartford, MI (city) Van Buren County	50	1.86
Dougherty, OK (town) Murray County	4	1.86
Foster, OK (town) Garvin County	3	1.86
Kiowa, OK (town) Pittsburg County	13	1.78
Willow Hill, IL (village) Jasper County	4	1.74
Wisconsin Dells, WI (city) Sauk County	3	1.71
Rice Lake, MN (cdp) Clearwater County	4	1.70
Iron Horse, CA (cdp) Plumas County	5	1.68
Grantville, KS (cdp) Jefferson County	3	1.67
Whiting, KS (city) Jackson County	3	1.60
Shidler, OK (city) Osage County	7	1.59
Brooksville, OK (town) Pottawatomie County	1	1.59
Purcell, OK (city) McClain County	92	1.56
Fairfield, TN (cdp) Sumner County	2	1.53
Slick, OK (town) Creek County	2	1.53
Pitkin, CO (town) Gunnison County	1	1.52
Smith Village, OK (town) Oklahoma County	1	1.52
Williamsburg, KS (city) Franklin County	6	1.51
Bearden, OK (town) Okfuskee County	2	1.50
Athens, MI (township) Calhoun County	38	1.49
Hamilton, KS (city) Greenwood County	4	1.49
Pittsburg, OK (town) Pittsburg County	3	1.45
Breen, MI (township) Dickinson County	7	1.40
Levering, MI (cdp) Emmet County	3	1.40
Deer Island, OR (cdp) Columbia County	4	1.36
Paxico, KS (city) Wabaunsee County	3	1.36
Atwood, OK (town) Hughes County	1	1.35
Wayne, MI (township) Cass County	35	1.32
Lac du Flambeau, WI (cdp) Vilas County	26	1.32
Bowler, WI (village) Shawano County	4	1.32
Devol, OK (town) Cotton County	2	1.32
Powhattan, KS (city) Brown County	1	1.30
Moscow, KS (city) Stevens County	4	1.29
Pawhuska, OK (city) Osage County	46	1.28
Tribbey, OK (town) Pottawatomie County	5	1.28
Struble, IA (city) Plymouth County	1	1.28
Leach, OK (cdp) Delaware County	3	1.27
Hartford, MI (township) Van Buren County	41	1.25
Laona, WI (town) Forest County	15	1.24
Slaughterville, OK (town) Cleveland County	51	1.23
Moro, OR (city) Sherman County	4	1.23
String, OK (town) Atoka County	5	1.22
Lexington, OK (city) Cleveland County	26	1.21
Nadeau, MI (township) Menominee County	14	1.21
Partridge, KS (city) Reno County	3	1.21
Cedarville, MI (township) Menominee County	3	1.19
Silver Lake, KS (city) Shawnee County	17	1.18
Agra, OK (town) Lincoln County	4	1.18
Union, WI (town) Burnett County	4	1.18
Byars, OK (town) McClain County	3	1.18
Circleville, KS (city) Jackson County	2	1.18
Rush Center, KS (city) Rush County	2	1.18
Sparks, OK (town) Lincoln County	2	1.18
Oyehut, WA (cdp) Grays Harbor County	1	1.18
Argonne, WI (town) Forest County	6	1.17
Watersmeet, MI (cdp) Gogebic County	5	1.17
McLoud, OK (town) Pottawatomie County	47	1.16
Lac du Flambeau, WI (town) Vilas County	40	1.16
Rulo, NE (village) Richardson County	2	1.16
Silver Creek, MI (township) Cass County	37	1.15
Bark River, MI (township) Delta County	18	1.14
White Cloud, KS (city) Doniphan County	2	1.14
Lake Aluma, OK (town) Oklahoma County	1	1.14
Crescent, OK (city) Logan County	16	1.13
Verden, OK (town) Grady County	6	1.13
La Prairie, MN (township) Clearwater County	4	1.12
Stone Lake, WI (cdp) Sawyer County	2	1.12
Suring, WI (village) Oconto County	6	1.10
Paint Rock, TX (town) Concho County	3	1.10
Hominy, OK (city) Osage County	39	1.09
Cartago, CA (cdp) Inyo County	1	1.09
Newkirk, OK (city) Kay County	25	1.08
Konawa, OK (city) Seminole County	14	1.08
Jones, MN (township) Beltrami County	3	1.08
Noble, OK (city) Cleveland County	68	1.05
Meeker, OK (town) Lincoln County	12	1.05
Cedar Valley, OK (city) Logan County	3	1.04
Cubero, NM (cdp) Cibola County	3	1.04
Wayne, OK (town) McClain County	7	1.02
New Strawn, KS (city) Coffey County	4	1.02
Montier, MO (cdp) Shannon County	1	1.02
Kinta, OK (town) Haskell County	3	1.01
Haviland, KS (city) Kiowa County	7	1.00
Lakewood, WI (town) Oconto County	8	0.98
Cameron, WI (town) Wood County	5	0.98
Goodwill, SD (cdp) Roberts County	5	0.97
Cedar Crest, OK (cdp) Mayes County	3	0.96
Hiles, WI (town) Forest County	3	0.96
Amber, OK (town) Grady County	4	0.95

Please refer to the Explanation of Data in the front of the book for more detailed information.

Race

American Indian: Potawatomi

Top 150 Places Sorted by Percent of Total Population

Based on places with total population of 7,500 or more

Place	Population	%
Shawnee, OK (city) Pottawatomie County	559	1.87
Topeka, KS (city) Shawnee County	873	0.68
Escanaba, MI (city) Delta County	84	0.67
Choctaw, OK (city) Oklahoma County	72	0.65
Newcastle, OK (city) McClain County	44	0.57
Niles, MI (city) Berrien County	50	0.43
Niles, MI (city) Berrien County	50	0.43
Niles, MI (township) Berrien County	58	0.41
Norman, OK (city) Cleveland County	439	0.40
Mustang, OK (city) Canadian County	62	0.36
Rhinelander, WI (city) Oneida County	27	0.35
Moore, OK (city) Cleveland County	182	0.33
Emmett, MI (charter township) Calhoun County	37	0.31
Yukon, OK (city) Canadian County	65	0.29
Benton, MI (charter township) Berrien County	42	0.28
Thornapple, MI (township) Barry County	21	0.27
Grand Haven, MI (charter township) Ottawa County	40	0.26
Cutlerville, MI (cdp) Kent County	38	0.26
Coffeyville, KS (city) Montgomery County	25	0.24
Kinross, MI (charter township) Chippewa County	18	0.24
Ada, OK (city) Pontotoc County	38	0.23
Guthrie, OK (city) Logan County	23	0.23
Egelston, MI (township) Muskegon County	22	0.22
Wagoner, OK (city) Wagoner County	18	0.22
Kirtland, NM (cdp) San Juan County	17	0.22
Antwerp, MI (township) Van Buren County	25	0.21
Lawrence, KS (city) Douglas County	179	0.20
Midwest City, OK (city) Oklahoma County	111	0.20
The Village, OK (city) Oklahoma County	18	0.20
Jenks, OK (city) Tulsa County	33	0.19
Shawano, WI (city) Shawano County	18	0.19
Grand Haven, MI (city) Ottawa County	19	0.18
Weatherford, OK (city) Custer County	19	0.18
Coweta, OK (city) Wagoner County	18	0.18
Blanchard, OK (city) McClain County	14	0.18
Oklahoma City, OK (city) Oklahoma County	982	0.17
El Reno, OK (city) Canadian County	29	0.17
Chickasha, OK (city) Grady County	28	0.17
St. Joseph, MI (charter township) Berrien County	17	0.17
Antigo, WI (city) Langlade County	14	0.17
Richland, MI (township) Kalamazoo County	13	0.17
Sault Ste. Marie, MI (city) Chippewa County	22	0.16
Pryor Creek, OK (city) Mayes County	15	0.16
Poteau, OK (city) Le Flore County	14	0.16
Schoolcraft, MI (township) Kalamazoo County	13	0.16
Edmond, OK (city) Oklahoma County	126	0.15
Battle Creek, MI (city) Calhoun County	81	0.15
Bartlesville, OK (city) Washington County	53	0.15
Ponca City, OK (city) Kay County	39	0.15
Del City, OK (city) Oklahoma County	33	0.15
Oshtemo, MI (charter township) Kalamazoo County	33	0.15
Bethany, OK (city) Oklahoma County	28	0.15
Prosper, TX (town) Collin County	14	0.15
Wellington, KS (city) Sumner County	12	0.15
Claremore, OK (city) Rogers County	26	0.14
Sand Springs, OK (city) Tulsa County	26	0.14
Glenpool, OK (city) Tulsa County	15	0.14
Benton Harbor, MI (city) Berrien County	14	0.14
St. Joseph, MI (city) Berrien County	12	0.14
Neenah, WI (city) Winnebago County	33	0.13
Bixby, OK (city) Tulsa County	27	0.13
Fair Plain, MI (cdp) Berrien County	10	0.13
Wyoming, MI (city) Kent County	86	0.12
Mishawaka, IN (city) St. Joseph County	58	0.12
Stillwater, OK (city) Payne County	55	0.12
Muskegon, MI (charter township) Muskegon County	22	0.12
Lincoln, MI (charter township) Berrien County	18	0.12
Spring Lake, MI (township) Ottawa County	17	0.12
Alpine, MI (township) Kent County	16	0.12
Union, MI (charter township) Isabella County	16	0.12
Independence, KS (city) Montgomery County	11	0.12
Menominee, MI (city) Menominee County	10	0.12
Westwood, MI (cdp) Kalamazoo County	10	0.12
Kalamazoo, MI (city) Kalamazoo County	81	0.11
Manhattan, KS (city) Riley County	60	0.11
Portage, MI (city) Kalamazoo County	49	0.11
Wausau, WI (city) Marathon County	42	0.11
Gaines, MI (charter township) Kent County	28	0.11
Jenison, MI (cdp) Ottawa County	19	0.11
Durant, OK (city) Bryan County	18	0.11
Menasha, WI (city) Winnebago County	16	0.11
Ottawa, KS (city) Franklin County	14	0.11
Woodward, OK (city) Woodward County	13	0.11
Comstock Park, MI (cdp) Kent County	11	0.11
Warr Acres, OK (city) Oklahoma County	11	0.11
Bedford, MI (charter township) Calhoun County	10	0.11
Clinton, OK (city) Custer County	10	0.11
Oronoko, MI (charter township) Berrien County	10	0.11
Ocean Pointe, HI (cdp) Honolulu County	9	0.11
Laketon, MI (township) Muskegon County	8	0.11
Muskogee, OK (city) Muskogee County	39	0.10
Owasso, OK (city) Tulsa County	28	0.10
Norton Shores, MI (city) Muskegon County	25	0.10
Duncan, OK (city) Stephens County	23	0.10
Sun Valley, NV (cdp) Washoe County	20	0.10
McAlester, OK (city) Pittsburg County	19	0.10
Wisconsin Rapids, WI (city) Wood County	19	0.10
Arkansas City, KS (city) Cowley County	13	0.10
Fruitport, MI (charter township) Muskegon County	13	0.10
Lake Arrowhead, CA (cdp) San Bernardino County	12	0.10
Shasta Lake, CA (city) Shasta County	10	0.10
Chanute, KS (city) Neosho County	9	0.10
Greenwood, AR (city) Sebastian County	9	0.10
Harvard, IL (city) McHenry County	9	0.10
Pennfield, MI (charter township) Calhoun County	9	0.10
Sallisaw, OK (city) Sequoyah County	9	0.10
Lakes, AK (cdp) Matanuska-Susitna Borough	8	0.10
Grand Rapids, MI (city) Kent County	166	0.09
Broken Arrow, OK (city) Tulsa County	89	0.09
Georgetown, MI (charter township) Ottawa County	42	0.09
Jackson, MI (city) Jackson County	31	0.09
Byron, MI (township) Kent County	19	0.09
Menasha, WI (city) Winnebago County	16	0.09
Harrisonville, MO (city) Cass County	9	0.09
Alpena, MI (township) Alpena County	8	0.09
Valley Center, CA (cdp) San Diego County	8	0.09
Cushing, OK (city) Payne County	7	0.09
Lansing, MI (charter township) Ingham County	7	0.09
Tulsa, OK (city) Tulsa County	306	0.08
Green Bay, WI (city) Brown County	85	0.08
Mount Pleasant, MI (city) Isabella County	22	0.08
Kalamazoo, MI (charter township) Kalamazoo County	18	0.08
Derby, KS (city) Sedgwick County	17	0.08
Pittsburg, KS (city) Crawford County	17	0.08
Hazel Park, MI (city) Oakland County	13	0.08
Comstock, MI (charter township) Kalamazoo County	12	0.08
Grandville, MI (city) Kent County	12	0.08
Miami, OK (city) Ottawa County	11	0.08
Borger, TX (city) Hutchinson County	10	0.08
Flushing, MI (charter township) Genesee County	9	0.08
Marinette, WI (city) Marinette County	9	0.08
East Bay, MI (township) Grand Traverse County	8	0.08
Augusta, KS (city) Butler County	7	0.08
Mission, KS (city) Johnson County	7	0.08
Taft, CA (city) Kern County	7	0.08
South Bend, IN (city) St. Joseph County	74	0.07
Enid, OK (city) Garfield County	33	0.07
Kentwood, MI (city) Kent County	33	0.07
Muskegon, MI (city) Muskegon County	27	0.07
Bella Vista, AR (town) Benton County	18	0.07
Palm Springs, FL (village) Palm Beach County	14	0.07
Siloam Springs, AR (city) Benton County	11	0.07
Spanish Springs, NV (cdp) Washoe County	11	0.07
Tahlequah, OK (city) Cherokee County	11	0.07
Crowley, TX (city) Tarrant County	9	0.07
McPherson, KS (city) McPherson County	9	0.07
Atchison, KS (city) Atchison County	8	0.07
Citrus, CA (cdp) Los Angeles County	8	0.07
Grand Rapids, MN (city) Itasca County	8	0.07
Kingsburg, CA (city) Fresno County	8	0.07

SECTION THREE

Race

American Indian: Pueblo

U.S. and 50 States Sorted by Population and Percent of Total Population

Place	Population	%
United States	**62,540**	**0.02**
New Mexico	42,481	2.06
California	5,569	0.01
Texas	2,599	0.01
Arizona	2,270	0.04
Colorado	1,620	0.03
New York	1,096	0.01
Washington	592	0.01
Nevada	481	0.02
Utah	463	0.02
Oklahoma	436	0.01
Florida	375	<0.01
Oregon	365	0.01
New Jersey	302	<0.01
Virginia	237	<0.01
Illinois	230	<0.01
North Carolina	210	<0.01
Pennsylvania	204	<0.01
Massachusetts	191	<0.01
Kansas	189	0.01
Missouri	187	<0.01
Hawaii	178	0.01
Ohio	163	<0.01
Alaska	159	0.02
Georgia	157	<0.01
Michigan	150	<0.01
Maryland	142	<0.01
Indiana	132	<0.01
Idaho	124	0.01
Tennessee	105	<0.01
Connecticut	98	<0.01
Arkansas	96	<0.01
Minnesota	95	<0.01
Wisconsin	85	<0.01
Montana	77	0.01
Louisiana	73	<0.01
Alabama	72	<0.01
South Carolina	72	<0.01
Kentucky	68	<0.01
Wyoming	58	0.01
Nebraska	49	<0.01
South Dakota	41	0.01
New Hampshire	38	<0.01
Rhode Island	36	<0.01
Mississippi	32	<0.01
District of Columbia	29	<0.01
North Dakota	29	<0.01
Iowa	28	<0.01
Maine	23	<0.01
West Virginia	18	<0.01
Delaware	10	<0.01
Vermont	6	<0.01

Place	Population	%
New Mexico	42,481	2.06
Arizona	2,270	0.04
Colorado	1,620	0.03
United States	**62,540**	**0.02**
Nevada	481	0.02
Utah	463	0.02
Alaska	159	0.02
California	5,569	0.01
Texas	2,599	0.01
New York	1,096	0.01
Washington	592	0.01
Oklahoma	436	0.01
Oregon	365	0.01
Kansas	189	0.01
Hawaii	178	0.01
Idaho	124	0.01
Montana	77	0.01
Wyoming	58	0.01
South Dakota	41	0.01
Florida	375	<0.01
New Jersey	302	<0.01
Virginia	237	<0.01
Illinois	230	<0.01
North Carolina	210	<0.01
Pennsylvania	204	<0.01
Massachusetts	191	<0.01
Missouri	187	<0.01
Ohio	163	<0.01
Georgia	157	<0.01
Michigan	150	<0.01
Maryland	142	<0.01
Indiana	132	<0.01
Tennessee	105	<0.01
Connecticut	98	<0.01
Arkansas	96	<0.01
Minnesota	95	<0.01
Wisconsin	85	<0.01
Louisiana	73	<0.01
Alabama	72	<0.01
South Carolina	72	<0.01
Kentucky	68	<0.01
Nebraska	49	<0.01
New Hampshire	38	<0.01
Rhode Island	36	<0.01
Mississippi	32	<0.01
District of Columbia	29	<0.01
North Dakota	29	<0.01
Iowa	28	<0.01
Maine	23	<0.01
West Virginia	18	<0.01
Delaware	10	<0.01
Vermont	6	<0.01

Please refer to the Explanation of Data in the front of the book for more detailed information.

Race

American Indian: Pueblo

Top 150 Places Sorted by Population

Based on all places, regardless of total population

Place	Population	%
Albuquerque, NM (city) Bernalillo County	6,137	1.12
Zuni Pueblo, NM (cdp) McKinley County	5,883	93.35
Jemez Pueblo, NM (cdp) Sandoval County	1,603	89.65
San Felipe Pueblo, NM (cdp) Sandoval County	1,509	62.77
Santo Domingo Pueblo, NM (cdp) Sandoval County	1,474	60.02
Skyline-Ganipa, NM (cdp) Cibola County	1,122	91.67
Laguna, NM (cdp) Cibola County	1,119	90.17
Black Rock, NM (cdp) McKinley County	1,048	79.21
Taos Pueblo, NM (cdp) Taos County	935	82.38
New York, NY (city) Kings County	892	0.01
Ohkay Owingeh, NM (cdp) Rio Arriba County	879	76.90
El Paso, TX (city) El Paso County	861	0.13
Rio Rancho, NM (city) Sandoval County	800	0.91
Mesita, NM (cdp) Cibola County	716	89.05
Zia Pueblo, NM (cdp) Sandoval County	708	96.07
Gallup, NM (city) McKinley County	675	3.11
Paraje, NM (cdp) Cibola County	666	85.71
Santa Clara Pueblo, NM (cdp) Rio Arriba County	591	58.06
Santa Ana Pueblo, NM (cdp) Sandoval County	554	90.82
Phoenix, AZ (city) Maricopa County	501	0.03
Los Angeles, CA (city) Los Angeles County	493	0.01
Grants, NM (city) Cibola County	462	5.03
Santa Fe, NM (city) Santa Fe County	462	0.68
Cochiti, NM (cdp) Sandoval County	437	82.77
Nambe, NM (cdp) Santa Fe County	437	24.04
Isleta Village Proper, NM (cdp) Bernalillo County	430	87.58
Las Cruces, NM (city) Doña Ana County	413	0.42
Seama, NM (cdp) Cibola County	397	85.38
Bronx, NY (borough) Bronx County	382	0.03
Paguate, NM (cdp) Cibola County	378	89.79
Acomita Lake, NM (cdp) Cibola County	355	85.34
Socorro, TX (city) El Paso County	350	1.09
Pueblo of Sandia Village, NM (cdp) Sandoval County	327	88.62
South Valley, NM (cdp) Bernalillo County	276	0.67
San Ildefonso Pueblo, NM (cdp) Santa Fe County	264	50.38
Pojoaque, NM (cdp) Santa Fe County	260	13.63
North Acomita Village, NM (cdp) Cibola County	259	85.48
Denver, CO (city) Denver County	257	0.04
Tesuque Pueblo, NM (cdp) Santa Fe County	203	87.12
Encinal, NM (cdp) Cibola County	187	89.05
Taos, NM (town) Taos County	183	3.20
Bernalillo, NM (town) Sandoval County	175	2.10
Manhattan, NY (borough) New York County	175	0.01
Mesa, AZ (city) Maricopa County	174	0.04
Brooklyn, NY (borough) Kings County	169	0.01
Farmington, NM (city) San Juan County	165	0.36
Queens, NY (borough) Queens County	161	0.01
Los Lunas, NM (village) Valencia County	160	1.08
Tucson, AZ (city) Pima County	156	0.03
San Diego, CA (city) San Diego County	150	0.01
Espanola, NM (city) Rio Arriba County	132	1.29
Barstow, CA (city) San Bernardino County	131	0.58
Colorado Springs, CO (city) El Paso County	126	0.03
San Jose, CA (city) Santa Clara County	114	0.01
San Antonio, TX (city) Medina County	113	0.01
Las Vegas, NV (city) Clark County	112	0.02
South Acomita Village, NM (cdp) Cibola County	95	90.48
Houston, TX (city) Harris County	93	<0.01
Long Beach, CA (city) Los Angeles County	83	0.02
Oakland, CA (city) Alameda County	83	0.02
San Francisco, CA (city) San Francisco County	83	0.01
Aurora, CO (city) Arapahoe County	82	0.03
Chical, NM (cdp) Valencia County	81	75.70
Sacramento, CA (city) Sacramento County	81	0.02
Anchorage, AK (municipality) Anchorage Municipality	80	0.03
Glendale, AZ (city) Maricopa County	79	0.03
Chandler, AZ (city) Maricopa County	76	0.03
Lakewood, CO (city) Jefferson County	75	0.05
Dallas, TX (city) Dallas County	71	0.01
Chicago, IL (city) Cook County	71	<0.01
Fresno, CA (city) Fresno County	68	0.01
University Park, NM (cdp) Doña Ana County	67	1.60
Flagstaff, AZ (city) Coconino County	67	0.10
Dulce, NM (cdp) Rio Arriba County	66	2.41
Winslow, AZ (city) Navajo County	66	0.68
Tempe, AZ (city) Maricopa County	66	0.04
Riverside, CA (city) Riverside County	66	0.02
Boston, MA (city) Suffolk County	66	0.01
Oklahoma City, OK (city) Oklahoma County	66	0.01
Milan, NM (village) Cibola County	65	2.00
Stockton, CA (city) San Joaquin County	65	0.02
Portland, OR (city) Multnomah County	65	0.01
Seattle, WA (city) King County	64	0.01
Paradise Hills, NM (cdp) Bernalillo County	62	1.46
Pueblo, CO (city) Pueblo County	62	0.06
North Valley, NM (cdp) Bernalillo County	61	0.54
San Bernardino, CA (city) San Bernardino County	61	0.03
Alamogordo, NM (city) Otero County	59	0.19
Apple Valley, CA (town) San Bernardino County	58	0.08
Bakersfield, CA (city) Kern County	58	0.02
Chamita, NM (cdp) Rio Arriba County	56	6.44
Fontana, CA (city) San Bernardino County	56	0.03
Roswell, NM (city) Chaves County	55	0.11
Henderson, NV (city) Clark County	53	0.02
Anzac Village, NM (cdp) Cibola County	51	94.44
Cochiti Lake, NM (cdp) Sandoval County	50	8.79
Austin, TX (city) Travis County	48	0.01
Peña Blanca, NM (cdp) Sandoval County	47	6.63
Thornton, CO (city) Adams County	47	0.04
Peoria, AZ (city) Yavapai County	47	0.03
Chimayo, NM (cdp) Rio Arriba County	46	1.45
Fort Defiance, AZ (cdp) Apache County	45	1.24
Whittier, CA (city) Los Angeles County	45	0.05
Victorville, CA (city) San Bernardino County	45	0.04
McCartys Village, NM (cdp) Cibola County	44	91.67
Algodones, NM (cdp) Sandoval County	44	5.41
El Cerro Mission, NM (cdp) Valencia County	44	0.94
Picuris Pueblo, NM (cdp) Taos County	43	63.24
Meadow Lake, NM (cdp) Valencia County	43	0.91
Salt Lake City, UT (city) Salt Lake County	43	0.02
Crownpoint, NM (cdp) McKinley County	42	1.84
North Las Vegas, NV (city) Clark County	42	0.02
Philadelphia, PA (city) Philadelphia County	42	<0.01
Newark, NJ (city) Essex County	40	0.01
Durango, CO (city) La Plata County	39	0.23
Tulsa, OK (city) Tulsa County	39	0.01
Kirtland, NM (cdp) San Juan County	38	0.48
Greeley, CO (city) Weld County	38	0.04
Fort Worth, TX (city) Tarrant County	38	0.01
Shiprock, NM (cdp) San Juan County	37	0.45
El Cajon, CA (city) San Diego County	37	0.04
Arvada, CO (city) Jefferson County	37	0.03
Modesto, CA (city) Stanislaus County	37	0.02
Sunrise Manor, NV (cdp) Clark County	37	0.02
Ranchos de Taos, NM (cdp) Taos County	36	1.43
San Elizario, TX (cdp) El Paso County	36	0.26
Horizon City, TX (city) El Paso County	36	0.22
Lawrence, KS (city) Douglas County	36	0.04
Rialto, CA (city) San Bernardino County	36	0.04
Murrieta, CA (city) Riverside County	36	0.03
Westminster, CO (city) Adams County	36	0.03
Gilbert, AZ (town) Maricopa County	36	0.02
Oxnard, CA (city) Ventura County	36	0.02
Scottsdale, AZ (city) Maricopa County	35	0.02
Chula Vista, CA (city) San Diego County	35	0.01
Socorro, NM (city) Socorro County	34	0.38
Los Alamos, NM (cdp) Los Alamos County	34	0.28
Hayward, CA (city) Alameda County	34	0.02
Anaheim, CA (city) Orange County	34	0.01
Oceanside, CA (city) San Diego County	33	0.02
Palmdale, CA (city) Los Angeles County	33	0.02
Urban Honolulu, HI (cdp) Honolulu County	33	0.01
Pueblito, NM (cdp) Rio Arriba County	32	35.16
San Ysidro, NM (village) Sandoval County	32	16.58
Las Vegas, NM (city) San Miguel County	32	0.23
Tracy, CA (city) San Joaquin County	32	0.04
First Mesa, AZ (cdp) Navajo County	31	1.99
Gilroy, CA (city) Santa Clara County	31	0.06
Santa Clarita, CA (city) Los Angeles County	31	0.02
Clovis, NM (city) Curry County	30	0.08

SECTION THREE

Please refer to the Explanation of Data in the front of the book for more detailed information.

Race

American Indian: Pueblo

Top 150 Places Sorted by Percent of Total Population

Based on all places, regardless of total population

Place	Population	%
Zia Pueblo, NM (cdp) Sandoval County	708	96.07
Anzac Village, NM (cdp) Cibola County	51	94.44
Zuni Pueblo, NM (cdp) McKinley County	5,883	93.35
Skyline-Ganipa, NM (cdp) Cibola County	1,122	91.67
McCartys Village, NM (cdp) Cibola County	44	91.67
Santa Ana Pueblo, NM (cdp) Sandoval County	554	90.82
South Acomita Village, NM (cdp) Cibola County	95	90.48
Laguna, NM (cdp) Cibola County	1,119	90.17
Paguate, NM (cdp) Cibola County	378	89.79
Jemez Pueblo, NM (cdp) Sandoval County	1,603	89.65
Mesita, NM (cdp) Cibola County	716	89.05
Encinal, NM (cdp) Cibola County	187	89.05
Pueblo of Sandia Village, NM (cdp) Sandoval County	327	88.62
Isleta Village Proper, NM (cdp) Bernalillo County	430	87.58
Tesuque Pueblo, NM (cdp) Santa Fe County	203	87.12
Paraje, NM (cdp) Cibola County	666	85.71
North Acomita Village, NM (cdp) Cibola County	259	85.48
Seama, NM (cdp) Cibola County	397	85.38
Acomita Lake, NM (cdp) Cibola County	355	85.34
Cochiti, NM (cdp) Sandoval County	437	82.77
Taos Pueblo, NM (cdp) Taos County	935	82.38
Black Rock, NM (cdp) McKinley County	1,048	79.21
Ohkay Owingeh, NM (cdp) Rio Arriba County	879	76.90
Chical, NM (cdp) Valencia County	81	75.70
Picuris Pueblo, NM (cdp) Taos County	43	63.24
San Felipe Pueblo, NM (cdp) Sandoval County	1,509	62.77
Santo Domingo Pueblo, NM (cdp) Sandoval County	1,474	60.02
Santa Clara Pueblo, NM (cdp) Rio Arriba County	591	58.06
San Ildefonso Pueblo, NM (cdp) Santa Fe County	264	50.38
Pueblito, NM (cdp) Rio Arriba County	32	35.16
Nambe, NM (cdp) Santa Fe County	437	24.04
Moquino, NM (cdp) Cibola County	7	18.92
San Ysidro, NM (village) Sandoval County	32	16.58
San Fidel, NM (cdp) Cibola County	22	15.94
Seboyeta, NM (cdp) Cibola County	25	13.97
Pojoaque, NM (cdp) Santa Fe County	260	13.63
Fence Lake, NM (cdp) Cibola County	5	11.90
Manzano, NM (cdp) Torrance County	3	10.34
Cochiti Lake, NM (cdp) Sandoval County	50	8.79
Pinehill, NM (cdp) Cibola County	7	7.95
Peña Blanca, NM (cdp) Sandoval County	47	6.63
Cubero, NM (cdp) Cibola County	19	6.57
Chamita, NM (cdp) Rio Arriba County	56	6.44
Cañon, NM (cdp) Sandoval County	20	6.12
Edith Endave, NM (cdp) Bernalillo County	12	5.69
Ponderosa, NM (cdp) Sandoval County	21	5.43
Algodones, NM (cdp) Sandoval County	44	5.41
Grants, NM (city) Cibola County	462	5.03
Pueblo Pintado, NM (cdp) McKinley County	9	4.69
Richvale, CA (cdp) Butte County	10	4.10
Santa Cruz, NM (cdp) Santa Fe County	15	4.08
Yah-ta-hey, NM (cdp) McKinley County	24	4.07
Chamizal, NM (cdp) Socorro County	4	3.96
Cuyamungue, NM (cdp) Santa Fe County	17	3.55
Highland Meadows, NM (cdp) Valencia County	22	3.53
Taos, NM (town) Taos County	183	3.20
Alcalde, NM (cdp) Rio Arriba County	9	3.16
Gallup, NM (city) McKinley County	675	3.11
Marble, CO (town) Gunnison County	4	3.05
Brimhall Nizhoni, NM (cdp) McKinley County	6	3.02
La Villita, NM (cdp) Rio Arriba County	28	2.93
Bibo, NM (cdp) Cibola County	4	2.86
Valentine, AZ (cdp) Mohave County	1	2.63
Cañones, NM (cdp) Rio Arriba County	3	2.54
Martha, OK (town) Jackson County	4	2.47
Dulce, NM (cdp) Rio Arriba County	66	2.41
Ruby, AK (city) Yukon-Koyukuk Census Area	4	2.41
Peak Place, NM (cdp) Santa Fe County	9	2.39
Sugden, OK (town) Jefferson County	1	2.33
Steamboat, AZ (cdp) Apache County	6	2.11
Bernalillo, NM (town) Sandoval County	175	2.10
Milan, NM (village) Cibola County	65	2.00
Capulin, CO (cdp) Conejos County	4	2.00
First Mesa, AZ (cdp) Navajo County	31	1.99
Velarde, NM (cdp) Rio Arriba County	10	1.99
Naschitti, NM (cdp) San Juan County	6	1.99
Keams Canyon, AZ (cdp) Navajo County	6	1.97
Arroyo Hondo, NM (cdp) Taos County	9	1.90
Sun Valley, AZ (cdp) Navajo County	6	1.90
San Jose, NM (cdp) Rio Arriba County	13	1.87
Ensenada, NM (cdp) Rio Arriba County	2	1.87
Crownpoint, NM (cdp) McKinley County	42	1.84
Rockford, ID (cdp) Bingham County	5	1.81
Youngsville, NM (cdp) Rio Arriba County	1	1.79
Canova, NM (cdp) Rio Arriba County	2	1.69
San Luis, NM (cdp) Sandoval County	1	1.69
Gildford, MT (cdp) Hill County	3	1.68
Bent, NM (cdp) Otero County	2	1.68
Chupadero, NM (cdp) Santa Fe County	6	1.66
Haynesville, ME (town) Aroostook County	2	1.65
Crystal, NM (cdp) San Juan County	5	1.61
University Park, NM (cdp) Doña Ana County	67	1.60
El Rancho, NM (cdp) Santa Fe County	19	1.58
Lake Valley, NM (cdp) San Juan County	1	1.56
Rio Lucio, NM (cdp) Taos County	6	1.54
Cuartelez, NM (cdp) Santa Fe County	7	1.49
Paradise Hills, NM (cdp) Bernalillo County	62	1.46
Jacona, NM (cdp) Santa Fe County	6	1.46
Chimayo, NM (cdp) Rio Arriba County	46	1.45
Ranchos de Taos, NM (cdp) Taos County	36	1.43
Mescalero, NM (cdp) Otero County	19	1.42
Fort Apache, AZ (cdp) Navajo County	2	1.40
Cuba, NM (village) Sandoval County	10	1.37
Randlett, UT (cdp) Uintah County	3	1.36
Ramah, NM (cdp) McKinley County	5	1.35
Cutter, AZ (cdp) Gila County	1	1.35
Cuyamungue Grant, NM (cdp) Santa Fe County	3	1.33
Yeager, OK (town) Hughes County	1	1.33
Los Luceros, NM (cdp) Rio Arriba County	12	1.32
Abiquiu, NM (cdp) Rio Arriba County	3	1.30
Kilgore, NE (village) Cherry County	1	1.30
Espanola, NM (city) Rio Arriba County	132	1.29
Trenton, UT (town) Cache County	6	1.29
Rodey, NM (cdp) Doña Ana County	5	1.29
Luna, NM (cdp) Catron County	2	1.27
Fort Defiance, AZ (cdp) Apache County	45	1.24
Tohatchi, NM (cdp) McKinley County	10	1.24
Klagetoh, AZ (cdp) Apache County	3	1.24
Encino, NM (village) Torrance County	1	1.22
Fairacres, NM (cdp) Doña Ana County	10	1.21
Jaconita, NM (cdp) Santa Fe County	4	1.20
Aurora, WI (town) Taylor County	5	1.18
Vandervoort, AR (town) Polk County	1	1.15
Albuquerque, NM (city) Bernalillo County	6,137	1.12
Vadito, NM (cdp) Taos County	3	1.11
South Greenfield, MO (village) Dade County	1	1.11
Socorro, TX (city) El Paso County	350	1.09
Tonalea, AZ (cdp) Coconino County	6	1.09
Tordenskjold, MN (township) Otter Tail County	6	1.09
Los Lunas, NM (village) Valencia County	160	1.08
Chili, NM (cdp) Rio Arriba County	7	1.07
Gu Oidak, AZ (cdp) Pima County	2	1.06
Moriarty, NM (city) Torrance County	20	1.05
New Cuyama, CA (cdp) Santa Barbara County	5	0.97
Bluewater Acres, NM (cdp) Cibola County	2	0.97
La Mesilla, NM (cdp) Rio Arriba County	17	0.96
Rowe, NM (cdp) San Miguel County	4	0.96
Spencerville, NM (cdp) San Juan County	12	0.95
McNary, AZ (cdp) Apache County	5	0.95
Francis, OK (town) Pontotoc County	3	0.95
El Cerro Mission, NM (cdp) Valencia County	44	0.94
Moenkopi, AZ (cdp) Coconino County	9	0.93
Lamy, NM (cdp) Santa Fe County	2	0.92
Rio Rancho, NM (city) Sandoval County	800	0.91
Meadow Lake, NM (cdp) Valencia County	43	0.91
Talpa, NM (cdp) Taos County	7	0.90
Monterey Park, NM (cdp) Valencia County	14	0.89
Castleford, ID (city) Twin Falls County	2	0.88
Nenahnezad, NM (cdp) San Juan County	6	0.87
Tome, NM (cdp) Valencia County	16	0.86

Please refer to the Explanation of Data in the front of the book for more detailed information.

Race

American Indian: Pueblo

Top 150 Places Sorted by Percent of Total Population

Based on places with total population of 7,500 or more

Place	Population	%
Grants, NM (city) Cibola County	462	5.03
Gallup, NM (city) McKinley County	675	3.11
Bernalillo, NM (town) Sandoval County	175	2.10
Espanola, NM (city) Rio Arriba County	132	1.29
Albuquerque, NM (city) Bernalillo County	6,137	1.12
Socorro, TX (city) El Paso County	350	1.09
Los Lunas, NM (village) Valencia County	160	1.08
Rio Rancho, NM (city) Sandoval County	800	0.91
Santa Fe, NM (city) Santa Fe County	462	0.68
Winslow, AZ (city) Navajo County	66	0.68
South Valley, NM (cdp) Bernalillo County	276	0.67
Barstow, CA (city) San Bernardino County	131	0.58
North Valley, NM (cdp) Bernalillo County	61	0.54
Kirtland, NM (cdp) San Juan County	38	0.48
Shiprock, NM (cdp) San Juan County	37	0.45
Las Cruces, NM (city) Doña Ana County	413	0.42
Socorro, NM (city) Socorro County	34	0.38
Farmington, NM (city) San Juan County	165	0.36
Corrales, NM (village) Sandoval County	28	0.34
Los Alamos, NM (cdp) Los Alamos County	34	0.28
San Elizario, TX (cdp) El Paso County	36	0.26
Durango, CO (city) La Plata County	39	0.23
Las Vegas, NM (city) San Miguel County	32	0.23
Horizon City, TX (city) El Paso County	36	0.22
Tuba City, AZ (cdp) Coconino County	17	0.20
Alamogordo, NM (city) Otero County	59	0.19
Deming, NM (city) Luna County	28	0.19
Artesia, NM (city) Eddy County	20	0.18
Ruidoso, NM (village) Lincoln County	13	0.16
Portales, NM (city) Roosevelt County	18	0.15
El Paso, TX (city) El Paso County	861	0.13
Trinidad, CO (city) Las Animas County	12	0.13
Cortez, CO (city) Montezuma County	11	0.13
Alpine, UT (city) Utah County	11	0.12
Roswell, NM (city) Chaves County	55	0.11
Carlsbad, NM (city) Eddy County	29	0.11
Fort Knox, KY (cdp) Hardin County	11	0.11
Clinton, OK (city) Custer County	10	0.11
Delta, CO (city) Delta County	10	0.11
Kaneohe Station, HI (cdp) Honolulu County	10	0.11
Flagstaff, AZ (city) Coconino County	67	0.10
Gardnerville Ranchos, NV (cdp) Douglas County	11	0.10
Silver City, NM (town) Grant County	10	0.10
Alamosa, CO (city) Alamosa County	9	0.10
Havre, MT (city) Hill County	9	0.10
Bloomfield, NM (city) San Juan County	8	0.10
Larkfield-Wikiup, CA (cdp) Sonoma County	8	0.09
Garnet, CA (cdp) Riverside County	7	0.09
Apple Valley, CA (town) San Bernardino County	58	0.08
Clovis, NM (city) Curry County	30	0.08
Hobbs, NM (city) Lea County	28	0.08
Chaparral, NM (cdp) Otero County	11	0.08
El Sobrante, CA (cdp) Contra Costa County	10	0.08
Fort Drum, NY (cdp) Jefferson County	10	0.08
Tucson Estates, AZ (cdp) Pima County	10	0.08
Arizona City, AZ (cdp) Pinal County	8	0.08
East La Mirada, CA (cdp) Los Angeles County	8	0.08
Firestone, CO (town) Weld County	8	0.08
Fabens, TX (cdp) El Paso County	7	0.08
Fallon, NV (city) Churchill County	7	0.08
Live Oak, CA (city) Sutter County	7	0.08
Tooele, UT (city) Tooele County	22	0.07
Wheat Ridge, CO (city) Jefferson County	22	0.07
Fountain, CO (city) El Paso County	19	0.07
Marina, CA (city) Monterey County	13	0.07
Fort Mohave, AZ (cdp) Mohave County	10	0.07
Fort Carson, CO (cdp) El Paso County	9	0.07
Cottonwood, AZ (city) Yavapai County	8	0.07
Canyon Lake, CA (city) Riverside County	7	0.07
Enumclaw, WA (city) King County	7	0.07
Alondra Park, CA (cdp) Los Angeles County	6	0.07
Fort Bliss, TX (cdp) El Paso County	6	0.07
Mount Rainier, MD (city) Prince George's County	6	0.07
Blanchard, OK (city) McClain County	5	0.07
Crescent City, CA (city) Del Norte County	5	0.07
Fruitvale, CO (cdp) Mesa County	5	0.07
Pueblo, CO (city) Pueblo County	62	0.06
Gilroy, CA (city) Santa Clara County	31	0.06
Littleton, CO (city) Arapahoe County	24	0.06
Northglenn, CO (city) Adams County	20	0.06
Sahuarita, AZ (town) Pima County	16	0.06
Evans, CO (city) Weld County	12	0.06
Badger, AK (cdp) Fairbanks North Star Borough	11	0.06
Brigham City, UT (city) Box Elder County	11	0.06
Castaic, CA (cdp) Los Angeles County	11	0.06
Pedley, CA (cdp) Riverside County	8	0.06
Los Alamitos, CA (city) Orange County	7	0.06
Spring Creek, NV (cdp) Elko County	7	0.06
Verde Village, AZ (cdp) Yavapai County	7	0.06
Soquel, CA (cdp) Santa Cruz County	6	0.06
Bogota, NJ (borough) Bergen County	5	0.06
Carbondale, PA (city) Lackawanna County	5	0.06
Hanover, NH (cdp) Grafton County	5	0.06
Independence, OR (city) Polk County	5	0.06
North Madison, OH (cdp) Lake County	5	0.06
Waterford, CA (city) Stanislaus County	5	0.06
Lakewood, CO (city) Jefferson County	75	0.05
Whittier, CA (city) Los Angeles County	45	0.05
La Mirada, CA (city) Los Angeles County	23	0.05
Dakota Ridge, CO (cdp) Jefferson County	15	0.05
American Fork, UT (city) Utah County	14	0.05
Ridgecrest, CA (city) Kern County	14	0.05
Twentynine Palms, CA (city) San Bernardino County	13	0.05
Le Ray, NY (town) Jefferson County	11	0.05
Lomita, CA (city) Los Angeles County	11	0.05
Makakilo, HI (cdp) Honolulu County	10	0.05
Pinole, CA (city) Contra Costa County	10	0.05
Universal City, TX (city) Bexar County	10	0.05
North Amityville, NY (cdp) Suffolk County	9	0.05
Dumas, TX (city) Moore County	8	0.05
Sierra Vista Southeast, AZ (cdp) Cochise County	8	0.05
Tahlequah, OK (city) Cherokee County	8	0.05
Glenmont, MD (cdp) Montgomery County	7	0.05
Sterling, CO (city) Logan County	7	0.05
Glenn Heights, TX (city) Dallas County	6	0.05
Grass Valley, CA (city) Nevada County	6	0.05
Guymon, OK (city) Texas County	6	0.05
Sun Village, CA (cdp) Los Angeles County	6	0.05
Garden Acres, CA (cdp) San Joaquin County	5	0.05
Show Low, AZ (city) Navajo County	5	0.05
Sleepy Hollow, NY (village) Westchester County	5	0.05
Vail, AZ (cdp) Pima County	5	0.05
Winton, CA (cdp) Merced County	5	0.05
Derby, CO (cdp) Adams County	4	0.05
Fort Irwin, CA (cdp) San Bernardino County	4	0.05
Spring Valley Lake, CA (cdp) San Bernardino County	4	0.05
Denver, CO (city) Denver County	257	0.04
Mesa, AZ (city) Maricopa County	174	0.04
Tempe, AZ (city) Maricopa County	66	0.04
Thornton, CO (city) Adams County	47	0.04
Victorville, CA (city) San Bernardino County	45	0.04
Greeley, CO (city) Weld County	38	0.04
El Cajon, CA (city) San Diego County	37	0.04
Lawrence, KS (city) Douglas County	36	0.04
Rialto, CA (city) San Bernardino County	36	0.04
Tracy, CA (city) San Joaquin County	32	0.04
New Britain, CT (city/town) Hartford County	30	0.04
Taylorsville, UT (city) Salt Lake County	23	0.04
Castle Rock, CO (town) Douglas County	20	0.04
Antelope, CA (cdp) Sacramento County	19	0.04
Morgan Hill, CA (city) Santa Clara County	17	0.04
Copperas Cove, TX (city) Coryell County	14	0.04
Prescott, AZ (city) Yavapai County	14	0.04
San Dimas, CA (city) Los Angeles County	14	0.04
Juneau, AK (borough) Juneau City and Borough	13	0.04
Oakley, CA (city) Contra Costa County	13	0.04
Fairbanks, AK (city) Fairbanks North Star Borough	12	0.04
Midvale, UT (city) Salt Lake County	12	0.04
Englewood, CO (city) Arapahoe County	11	0.04
Imperial Beach, CA (city) San Diego County	10	0.04

SECTION THREE

Please refer to the Explanation of Data in the front of the book for more detailed information.

Race

American Indian: Puget Sound Salish

U.S. and 50 States Sorted by Population and Percent of Total Population

Place	Population	%
United States	**20,260**	**0.01**
Washington	16,964	0.25
California	749	<0.01
Oregon	507	0.01
Idaho	185	0.01
Arizona	161	<0.01
Alaska	158	0.02
Montana	125	0.01
Texas	121	<0.01
Colorado	94	<0.01
Nevada	85	<0.01
New Mexico	73	<0.01
Florida	71	<0.01
Utah	63	<0.01
Hawaii	58	<0.01
Illinois	56	<0.01
Oklahoma	52	<0.01
Tennessee	52	<0.01
Michigan	46	<0.01
Pennsylvania	41	<0.01
North Carolina	40	<0.01
Virginia	39	<0.01
Minnesota	35	<0.01
Mississippi	35	<0.01
Missouri	35	<0.01
New York	33	<0.01
Ohio	32	<0.01
Maryland	30	<0.01
Kansas	28	<0.01
Wisconsin	28	<0.01
South Carolina	25	<0.01
Georgia	24	<0.01
Arkansas	20	<0.01
Indiana	19	<0.01
Massachusetts	19	<0.01
New Jersey	19	<0.01
Iowa	17	<0.01
Wyoming	17	<0.01
South Dakota	16	<0.01
Alabama	14	<0.01
Connecticut	14	<0.01
Kentucky	13	<0.01
Nebraska	11	<0.01
Louisiana	9	<0.01
Maine	7	<0.01
Rhode Island	5	<0.01
West Virginia	5	<0.01
New Hampshire	4	<0.01
North Dakota	4	<0.01
Delaware	1	<0.01
Vermont	1	<0.01
District of Columbia	0	0.00

Place	Population	%
Washington	16,964	0.25
Alaska	158	0.02
United States	**20,260**	**0.01**
Oregon	507	0.01
Idaho	185	0.01
Montana	125	0.01
California	749	<0.01
Arizona	161	<0.01
Texas	121	<0.01
Colorado	94	<0.01
Nevada	85	<0.01
New Mexico	73	<0.01
Florida	71	<0.01
Utah	63	<0.01
Hawaii	58	<0.01
Illinois	56	<0.01
Oklahoma	52	<0.01
Tennessee	52	<0.01
Michigan	46	<0.01
Pennsylvania	41	<0.01
North Carolina	40	<0.01
Virginia	39	<0.01
Minnesota	35	<0.01
Mississippi	35	<0.01
Missouri	35	<0.01
New York	33	<0.01
Ohio	32	<0.01
Maryland	30	<0.01
Kansas	28	<0.01
Wisconsin	28	<0.01
South Carolina	25	<0.01
Georgia	24	<0.01
Arkansas	20	<0.01
Indiana	19	<0.01
Massachusetts	19	<0.01
New Jersey	19	<0.01
Iowa	17	<0.01
Wyoming	17	<0.01
South Dakota	16	<0.01
Alabama	14	<0.01
Connecticut	14	<0.01
Kentucky	13	<0.01
Nebraska	11	<0.01
Louisiana	9	<0.01
Maine	7	<0.01
Rhode Island	5	<0.01
West Virginia	5	<0.01
New Hampshire	4	<0.01
North Dakota	4	<0.01
Delaware	1	<0.01
Vermont	1	<0.01
District of Columbia	0	0.00

Please refer to the Explanation of Data in the front of the book for more detailed information.

Race

American Indian: Puget Sound Salish

Top 150 Places Sorted by Population

Based on all places, regardless of total population

Place	Population	%
Tacoma, WA (city) Pierce County	1,014	0.51
Auburn, WA (city) King County	772	1.10
Marysville, WA (city) Snohomish County	568	0.95
Seattle, WA (city) King County	394	0.06
Suquamish, WA (cdp) Kitsap County	368	8.89
Skokomish, WA (cdp) Mason County	366	59.32
Nisqually Indian Community, WA (cdp) Thurston County	290	50.43
Everett, WA (city) Snohomish County	286	0.28
South Hill, WA (cdp) Pierce County	152	0.29
Bellingham, WA (city) Whatcom County	149	0.18
Puyallup, WA (city) Pierce County	144	0.39
Spokane, WA (city) Spokane County	136	0.07
Shelton, WA (city) Mason County	130	1.32
Arlington, WA (city) Snohomish County	115	0.64
Federal Way, WA (city) King County	115	0.13
Waller, WA (cdp) Pierce County	111	1.40
Fife, WA (city) Pierce County	111	1.21
Indianola, WA (cdp) Kitsap County	104	2.97
Lakewood, WA (city) Pierce County	104	0.18
Mount Vernon, WA (city) Skagit County	99	0.31
Parkland, WA (cdp) Pierce County	98	0.27
Lacey, WA (city) Thurston County	88	0.21
Midland, WA (cdp) Pierce County	82	0.91
Yakima, WA (city) Yakima County	82	0.09
Bremerton, WA (city) Kitsap County	81	0.21
Olympia, WA (city) Thurston County	79	0.17
Kent, WA (city) King County	77	0.08
Lake Stevens, WA (city) Snohomish County	74	0.26
Sedro-Woolley, WA (city) Skagit County	69	0.65
Portland, OR (city) Multnomah County	68	0.01
Summit, WA (cdp) Pierce County	60	0.75
University Place, WA (city) Pierce County	60	0.19
Renton, WA (city) King County	58	0.06
Anacortes, WA (city) Skagit County	57	0.36
Frederickson, WA (cdp) Pierce County	57	0.30
Bainbridge Island, WA (city) Kitsap County	55	0.24
Spanaway, WA (cdp) Pierce County	54	0.20
Tanglewilde, WA (cdp) Thurston County	51	0.87
Elk Plain, WA (cdp) Pierce County	50	0.35
Aberdeen, WA (city) Grays Harbor County	50	0.30
Des Moines, WA (city) King County	50	0.17
Peaceful Valley, WA (cdp) Whatcom County	49	1.47
Graham, WA (cdp) Pierce County	46	0.20
Anchorage, AK (municipality) Anchorage Municipality	46	0.02
Spokane Valley, WA (city) Spokane County	45	0.05
Burlington, WA (city) Skagit County	44	0.52
Taholah, WA (cdp) Grays Harbor County	43	5.12
Ferndale, WA (city) Whatcom County	42	0.37
La Conner, WA (town) Skagit County	37	4.15
Yelm, WA (city) Thurston County	37	0.54
Bonney Lake, WA (city) Pierce County	36	0.21
Tumwater, WA (city) Thurston County	35	0.20
SeaTac, WA (city) King County	33	0.12
Poulsbo, WA (city) Kitsap County	32	0.35
Port Angeles, WA (city) Clallam County	32	0.17
San Diego, CA (city) San Diego County	32	<0.01
Summit View, WA (cdp) Pierce County	31	0.43
Edgewood, WA (city) Pierce County	29	0.31
Centralia, WA (city) Lewis County	29	0.18
Burien, WA (city) King County	29	0.09
Shoreline, WA (city) King County	29	0.05
Woods Creek, WA (cdp) Snohomish County	28	0.50
Prairie Ridge, WA (cdp) Pierce County	28	0.24
Maple Valley, WA (city) King County	28	0.12
East Hill-Meridian, WA (cdp) King County	28	0.09
Stanwood, WA (city) Snohomish County	27	0.43
Lynnwood, WA (city) Snohomish County	27	0.08
North Yelm, WA (cdp) Thurston County	26	0.89
White Center, WA (cdp) King County	26	0.19
Bothell West, WA (cdp) Snohomish County	26	0.16
Silverdale, WA (cdp) Kitsap County	26	0.14
Sammamish, WA (city) King County	26	0.06
Vancouver, WA (city) Clark County	26	0.02
Clover Creek, WA (cdp) Pierce County	25	0.38
Enumclaw, WA (city) King County	25	0.23
Bellevue, WA (city) King County	25	0.02
Orting, WA (city) Pierce County	24	0.36
Port Orchard, WA (city) Kitsap County	24	0.22
Kennewick, WA (city) Benton County	24	0.03
Warm Beach, WA (cdp) Snohomish County	23	0.94
Granite Falls, WA (city) Snohomish County	23	0.68
Prairie Heights, WA (cdp) Pierce County	22	0.50
Milton, WA (city) Pierce County	22	0.32
Hoquiam, WA (city) Grays Harbor County	22	0.25
Snohomish, WA (city) Snohomish County	22	0.24
Eastmont, WA (cdp) Snohomish County	22	0.11
Klamath Falls, OR (city) Klamath County	22	0.11
Edmonds, WA (city) Snohomish County	22	0.06
Albuquerque, NM (city) Bernalillo County	22	<0.01
Los Angeles, CA (city) Los Angeles County	22	<0.01
Raymond, WA (city) Pacific County	21	0.73
Omak, WA (city) Okanogan County	21	0.43
Lakeland South, WA (cdp) King County	21	0.18
Tigard, OR (city) Washington County	21	0.04
Nampa, ID (city) Canyon County	21	0.03
Urban Honolulu, HI (cdp) Honolulu County	21	0.01
Sacramento, CA (city) Sacramento County	21	<0.01
Snoqualmie, WA (city) King County	20	0.19
Artondale, WA (cdp) Pierce County	20	0.16
Mountlake Terrace, WA (city) Snohomish County	20	0.10
Longview, WA (city) Cowlitz County	20	0.05
Port Gamble Tribal Comunity, WA (cdp) Kitsap County	19	2.07
North Bend, WA (city) King County	19	0.33
Pacific, WA (city) King County	19	0.29
Bothell, WA (city) King County	19	0.06
Richland, WA (city) Benton County	19	0.04
Queets, WA (cdp) Jefferson County	18	10.34
Lake Morton-Berrydale, WA (cdp) King County	18	0.18
Lake Tapps, WA (cdp) Pierce County	18	0.15
North Lynnwood, WA (cdp) Snohomish County	18	0.11
Tukwila, WA (city) King County	18	0.09
Port Hadlock-Irondale, WA (cdp) Jefferson County	17	0.47
Lake Stickney, WA (cdp) Snohomish County	17	0.22
Sumner, WA (city) Pierce County	17	0.18
Ellensburg, WA (city) Kittitas County	17	0.09
Silver Firs, WA (cdp) Snohomish County	17	0.08
Aloha, OR (cdp) Washington County	17	0.03
Las Vegas, NV (city) Clark County	17	<0.01
Phoenix, AZ (city) Maricopa County	17	<0.01
Darrington, WA (town) Snohomish County	16	1.19
North Puyallup, WA (cdp) Pierce County	16	0.92
Everson, WA (city) Whatcom County	16	0.64
Lakeland North, WA (cdp) King County	16	0.12
Wenatchee, WA (city) Chelan County	16	0.05
Tucson, AZ (city) Pima County	16	<0.01
Union, WA (cdp) Mason County	15	2.38
White Swan, WA (cdp) Yakima County	15	1.89
Longbranch, WA (cdp) Pierce County	15	0.40
Boulevard Park, WA (cdp) King County	15	0.28
Birch Bay, WA (cdp) Whatcom County	15	0.18
Port Townsend, WA (city) Jefferson County	15	0.16
Covington, WA (city) King County	15	0.09
Boise City, ID (city) Ada County	15	0.01
South Bend, WA (city) Pacific County	14	0.86
Parkwood, WA (cdp) Kitsap County	14	0.20
Toppenish, WA (city) Yakima County	14	0.16
Monroe, WA (city) Snohomish County	14	0.08
Cottage Lake, WA (cdp) King County	14	0.06
Hillsboro, OR (city) Washington County	14	0.02
Gilbert, AZ (town) Maricopa County	14	0.01
Bakersfield, CA (city) Kern County	14	<0.01
Fife Heights, WA (cdp) Pierce County	13	0.61
Rochester, WA (cdp) Thurston County	13	0.54
Sultan, WA (city) Snohomish County	13	0.28
Wapato, WA (city) Yakima County	13	0.26
East Renton Highlands, WA (cdp) King County	13	0.12
Oak Harbor, WA (city) Island County	13	0.06
Lakewood, CO (city) Jefferson County	13	0.01
Salem, OR (city) Marion County	13	0.01
Torrance, CA (city) Los Angeles County	13	0.01

Please refer to the Explanation of Data in the front of the book for more detailed information.

Race

American Indian: Puget Sound Salish

Top 150 Places Sorted by Percent of Total Population

Based on all places, regardless of total population

Place	Population	%
Skokomish, WA (cdp) Mason County	366	59.32
Nisqually Indian Community, WA (cdp) Thurston County	290	50.43
Queets, WA (cdp) Jefferson County	18	10.34
Suquamish, WA (cdp) Kitsap County	368	8.89
Taholah, WA (cdp) Grays Harbor County	43	5.12
Santiago, WA (cdp) Grays Harbor County	2	4.76
La Conner, WA (town) Skagit County	37	4.15
Qui-nai-elt Village, WA (cdp) Grays Harbor County	2	3.70
Kupreanof, AK (city) Petersburg Census Area	1	3.70
Moclips, WA (cdp) Grays Harbor County	7	3.38
Indianola, WA (cdp) Kitsap County	104	2.97
Marblemount, WA (cdp) Skagit County	6	2.96
Union, WA (cdp) Mason County	15	2.38
Nespelem, WA (town) Okanogan County	5	2.12
Port Gamble Tribal Comunity, WA (cdp) Kitsap County	19	2.07
Port Alexander, AK (city) Petersburg Census Area	1	1.92
White Swan, WA (cdp) Yakima County	15	1.89
McDermitt, NV (cdp) Humboldt County	3	1.74
Clallam Bay, WA (cdp) Clallam County	6	1.65
Peaceful Valley, WA (cdp) Whatcom County	49	1.47
Waller, WA (cdp) Pierce County	111	1.40
Valley, WA (cdp) Stevens County	2	1.37
Shelton, WA (city) Mason County	130	1.32
Belmont, OH (village) Belmont County	6	1.32
Tokeland, WA (cdp) Pacific County	2	1.32
Fort Washington, CA (cdp) Fresno County	3	1.29
Keller, WA (cdp) Ferry County	3	1.28
Maple Falls, WA (cdp) Whatcom County	4	1.23
Crouch, ID (city) Boise County	2	1.23
Acme, WA (cdp) Whatcom County	3	1.22
Anderson, AK (city) Denali Borough	3	1.22
Fife, WA (city) Pierce County	111	1.21
Darrington, WA (town) Snohomish County	16	1.19
Swede Heaven, WA (cdp) Snohomish County	9	1.17
Camp Three, MT (cdp) Musselshell County	2	1.16
South Prairie, WA (town) Pierce County	5	1.15
Auburn, WA (city) King County	772	1.10
Gate, OK (town) Beaver County	1	1.08
Quilcene, WA (cdp) Jefferson County	6	1.01
Hamilton, WA (town) Skagit County	3	1.00
Concrete, WA (town) Skagit County	7	0.99
Mosquito Lake, AK (cdp) Haines Borough	3	0.97
Washtucna, WA (town) Adams County	2	0.96
Marysville, WA (city) Snohomish County	568	0.95
Warm Beach, WA (cdp) Snohomish County	23	0.94
North Puyallup, WA (cdp) Pierce County	16	0.92
Neah Bay, WA (cdp) Clallam County	8	0.92
Midland, WA (cdp) Pierce County	82	0.91
North Yelm, WA (cdp) Thurston County	26	0.89
Oakville, WA (city) Grays Harbor County	6	0.88
Tanglewilde, WA (cdp) Thurston County	51	0.87
South Bend, WA (city) Pacific County	14	0.86
Gates, OR (city) Marion County	4	0.85
Spokane Creek, MT (cdp) Broadwater County	3	0.85
Glacier View, AK (cdp) Matanuska-Susitna Borough	2	0.85
Hydaburg, AK (city) Prince of Wales-Hyder Census Area	3	0.80
Nespelem Community, WA (cdp) Okanogan County	2	0.79
Yucca, AZ (cdp) Mohave County	1	0.79
Sunday Lake, WA (cdp) Snohomish County	5	0.78
Summit, WA (cdp) Pierce County	60	0.75
Dash Point, WA (cdp) Pierce County	7	0.75
Brinnon, WA (cdp) Jefferson County	6	0.75
Lake Bosworth, WA (cdp) Snohomish County	5	0.75
Startup, WA (cdp) Snohomish County	5	0.74
Raymond, WA (city) Pacific County	21	0.73
Saxman, AK (city) Ketchikan Gateway Borough	3	0.73
Aberdeen Gardens, WA (cdp) Grays Harbor County	2	0.72
Springdale, WA (town) Stevens County	2	0.70
Verlot, WA (cdp) Snohomish County	2	0.70
Granite Falls, WA (city) Snohomish County	23	0.68
Chiloquin, OR (city) Klamath County	5	0.68
Nooksack, WA (city) Whatcom County	9	0.67
Browns Point, WA (cdp) Pierce County	8	0.67
Moose Creek, AK (cdp) Fairbanks North Star Borough	5	0.67
Ruston, WA (town) Pierce County	5	0.67
River Road, WA (cdp) Clallam County	3	0.66
Hartline, WA (town) Grant County	1	0.66
Sedro-Woolley, WA (city) Skagit County	69	0.65
Clinton, WA (cdp) Island County	6	0.65
Arlington, WA (city) Snohomish County	115	0.64
Everson, WA (city) Whatcom County	16	0.64
Roosevelt, WA (cdp) Klickitat County	1	0.64
Arlee, MT (cdp) Lake County	4	0.63
Easton, WA (cdp) Kittitas County	3	0.63
Franklin, ID (city) Franklin County	4	0.62
Fife Heights, WA (cdp) Pierce County	13	0.61
Bryant, WA (cdp) Snohomish County	11	0.59
St. Ignatius, MT (town) Lake County	5	0.59
West Point, CA (cdp) Calaveras County	4	0.59
Clear Creek, CA (cdp) Lassen County	1	0.59
Mission, OR (cdp) Umatilla County	6	0.58
Wishram, WA (cdp) Klickitat County	2	0.58
Deming, WA (cdp) Whatcom County	2	0.57
Kirkpatrick, OR (cdp) Umatilla County	1	0.56
Jamestown, WA (cdp) Clallam County	2	0.55
Yelm, WA (city) Thurston County	37	0.54
Rochester, WA (cdp) Thurston County	13	0.54
Arlington Heights, WA (cdp) Snohomish County	12	0.53
Burlington, WA (city) Skagit County	44	0.52
Tacoma, WA (city) Pierce County	1,014	0.51
Newton, UT (town) Cache County	4	0.51
Skykomish, WA (town) King County	1	0.51
Woods Creek, WA (cdp) Snohomish County	28	0.50
Prairie Heights, WA (cdp) Pierce County	22	0.50
Alger, WA (cdp) Skagit County	2	0.50
Pelham, TN (cdp) Grundy County	2	0.50
Onalaska, WA (cdp) Lewis County	3	0.48
Cusick, WA (town) Pend Oreille County	1	0.48
Port Hadlock-Irondale, WA (cdp) Jefferson County	17	0.47
Lake Marcel-Stillwater, WA (cdp) King County	6	0.47
Sumas, WA (city) Whatcom County	6	0.46
Coffee Creek, CA (cdp) Trinity County	1	0.46
Angoon, AK (city) Hoonah-Angoon Census Area	2	0.44
Summit View, WA (cdp) Pierce County	31	0.43
Stanwood, WA (city) Snohomish County	27	0.43
Omak, WA (city) Okanogan County	21	0.43
Sacramento, KY (city) McLean County	2	0.43
Fort Peck, MT (town) Valley County	1	0.43
Malone, WA (cdp) Grays Harbor County	2	0.42
Thorne Bay, AK (city) Prince of Wales-Hyder Census Area	2	0.42
Faulkton, SD (city) Faulk County	3	0.41
Longbranch, WA (cdp) Pierce County	15	0.40
Amanda Park, WA (cdp) Grays Harbor County	1	0.40
Puyallup, WA (city) Pierce County	144	0.39
Meadowdale, WA (cdp) Snohomish County	11	0.39
Burley, WA (cdp) Kitsap County	8	0.39
Tanner, WA (cdp) King County	4	0.39
Four Lakes, WA (cdp) Spokane County	2	0.39
Clover Creek, WA (cdp) Pierce County	25	0.38
South Cle Elum, WA (town) Kittitas County	2	0.38
St. Marie, MT (cdp) Valley County	1	0.38
Ferndale, WA (city) Whatcom County	42	0.37
Erlands Point-Kitsap Lake, WA (cdp) Kitsap County	11	0.37
Biola, CA (cdp) Fresno County	6	0.37
Harlem, MT (city) Blaine County	3	0.37
Henry, SD (town) Codington County	1	0.37
Polvadera, NM (cdp) Socorro County	1	0.37
Anacortes, WA (city) Skagit County	57	0.36
Orting, WA (city) Pierce County	24	0.36
Bucoda, WA (town) Thurston County	2	0.36
Keyport, WA (cdp) Kitsap County	2	0.36
Bay Center, WA (cdp) Pacific County	1	0.36
Elk Plain, WA (cdp) Pierce County	50	0.35
Poulsbo, WA (city) Kitsap County	32	0.35
Ak-Chin Village, AZ (cdp) Pinal County	3	0.35
Troy, ID (city) Latah County	3	0.35
Almira, WA (town) Lincoln County	1	0.35
Whitley Gardens, CA (cdp) San Luis Obispo County	1	0.35
Carnation, WA (city) King County	6	0.34
Rocky Boy West, MT (cdp) Chouteau County	3	0.34

Please refer to the Explanation of Data in the front of the book for more detailed information.

Race

American Indian: Puget Sound Salish

Top 150 Places Sorted by Percent of Total Population

Based on places with total population of 7,500 or more

Place	Population	%
Waller, WA (cdp) Pierce County	111	1.40
Shelton, WA (city) Mason County	130	1.32
Fife, WA (city) Pierce County	111	1.21
Auburn, WA (city) King County	772	1.10
Marysville, WA (city) Snohomish County	568	0.95
Midland, WA (cdp) Pierce County	82	0.91
Summit, WA (cdp) Pierce County	60	0.75
Sedro-Woolley, WA (city) Skagit County	69	0.65
Arlington, WA (city) Snohomish County	115	0.64
Burlington, WA (city) Skagit County	44	0.52
Tacoma, WA (city) Pierce County	1,014	0.51
Puyallup, WA (city) Pierce County	144	0.39
Ferndale, WA (city) Whatcom County	42	0.37
Anacortes, WA (city) Skagit County	57	0.36
Elk Plain, WA (cdp) Pierce County	50	0.35
Poulsbo, WA (city) Kitsap County	32	0.35
Mount Vernon, WA (city) Skagit County	99	0.31
Edgewood, WA (city) Pierce County	29	0.31
Frederickson, WA (cdp) Pierce County	57	0.30
Aberdeen, WA (city) Grays Harbor County	50	0.30
South Hill, WA (cdp) Pierce County	152	0.29
Everett, WA (city) Snohomish County	286	0.28
Parkland, WA (cdp) Pierce County	98	0.27
Lake Stevens, WA (city) Snohomish County	74	0.26
Hoquiam, WA (city) Grays Harbor County	22	0.25
Bainbridge Island, WA (city) Kitsap County	55	0.24
Prairie Ridge, WA (cdp) Pierce County	28	0.24
Snohomish, WA (city) Snohomish County	22	0.24
Enumclaw, WA (city) King County	25	0.23
Port Orchard, WA (city) Kitsap County	24	0.22
Lake Stickney, WA (cdp) Snohomish County	17	0.22
Lacey, WA (city) Thurston County	88	0.21
Bremerton, WA (city) Kitsap County	81	0.21
Bonney Lake, WA (city) Pierce County	36	0.21
Spanaway, WA (cdp) Pierce County	54	0.20
Graham, WA (cdp) Pierce County	46	0.20
Tumwater, WA (city) Thurston County	35	0.20
University Place, WA (city) Pierce County	60	0.19
White Center, WA (cdp) King County	26	0.19
Snoqualmie, WA (city) King County	20	0.19
Bellingham, WA (city) Whatcom County	149	0.18
Lakewood, WA (city) Pierce County	104	0.18
Centralia, WA (city) Lewis County	29	0.18
Lakeland South, WA (cdp) King County	21	0.18
Lake Morton-Berrydale, WA (cdp) King County	18	0.18
Sumner, WA (city) Pierce County	17	0.18
Birch Bay, WA (cdp) Whatcom County	15	0.18
Olympia, WA (city) Thurston County	79	0.17
Des Moines, WA (city) King County	50	0.17
Port Angeles, WA (city) Clallam County	32	0.17
Bothell West, WA (cdp) Snohomish County	26	0.16
Artondale, WA (cdp) Pierce County	20	0.16
Port Townsend, WA (city) Jefferson County	15	0.16
Toppenish, WA (city) Yakima County	14	0.16
Lake Tapps, WA (cdp) Pierce County	18	0.15
Silverdale, WA (cdp) Kitsap County	26	0.14
Federal Way, WA (city) King County	115	0.13
SeaTac, WA (city) King County	33	0.12
Maple Valley, WA (city) King County	28	0.12
Lakeland North, WA (cdp) King County	16	0.12
East Renton Highlands, WA (cdp) King County	13	0.12
Eastmont, WA (cdp) Snohomish County	22	0.11
Klamath Falls, OR (city) Klamath County	22	0.11
North Lynnwood, WA (cdp) Snohomish County	18	0.11
Fort Lewis, WA (cdp) Pierce County	12	0.11
Picnic Point, WA (cdp) Snohomish County	10	0.11
Helena Valley Southeast, MT (cdp) Lewis and Clark County	9	0.11
Mountlake Terrace, WA (city) Snohomish County	20	0.10
Yakima, WA (city) Yakima County	82	0.09
Burien, WA (city) King County	29	0.09
East Hill-Meridian, WA (cdp) King County	28	0.09
Tukwila, WA (city) King County	18	0.09
Ellensburg, WA (city) Kittitas County	17	0.09
Covington, WA (city) King County	15	0.09
Lake Forest Park, WA (city) King County	11	0.09
Garden Acres, CA (cdp) San Joaquin County	10	0.09
Silverton, OR (city) Marion County	8	0.09
Evergreen, MT (cdp) Flathead County	7	0.09
Kent, WA (city) King County	77	0.08
Lynnwood, WA (city) Snohomish County	27	0.08
Silver Firs, WA (cdp) Snohomish County	17	0.08
Monroe, WA (city) Snohomish County	14	0.08
Bryn Mawr-Skyway, WA (cdp) King County	12	0.08
Mill Creek East, WA (cdp) Snohomish County	12	0.08
Kelso, WA (city) Cowlitz County	10	0.08
Lynden, WA (city) Whatcom County	9	0.08
Maltby, WA (cdp) Snohomish County	9	0.08
Spokane, WA (city) Spokane County	136	0.07
East Wenatchee, WA (city) Douglas County	9	0.07
Grass Valley, CA (city) Nevada County	9	0.07
Vashon, WA (cdp) King County	7	0.07
Seattle, WA (city) King County	394	0.06
Renton, WA (city) King County	58	0.06
Sammamish, WA (city) King County	26	0.06
Edmonds, WA (city) Snohomish County	22	0.06
Bothell, WA (city) King County	19	0.06
Cottage Lake, WA (cdp) King County	14	0.06
Oak Harbor, WA (city) Island County	13	0.06
Salmon Creek, WA (cdp) Clark County	12	0.06
Mill Creek, WA (city) Snohomish County	11	0.06
Union Hill-Novelty Hill, WA (cdp) King County	11	0.06
Coos Bay, OR (city) Coos County	9	0.06
Cheney, WA (city) Spokane County	6	0.06
Spokane Valley, WA (city) Spokane County	45	0.05
Shoreline, WA (city) King County	29	0.05
Longview, WA (city) Cowlitz County	20	0.05
Wenatchee, WA (city) Chelan County	16	0.05
Orchards, WA (cdp) Clark County	10	0.05
Cimarron Hills, CO (cdp) El Paso County	8	0.05
Dallas, OR (city) Polk County	8	0.05
Martha Lake, WA (cdp) Snohomish County	8	0.05
Washougal, WA (city) Clark County	7	0.05
Kingsgate, WA (cdp) King County	6	0.05
Centerton, AR (city) Benton County	5	0.05
Catalina, AZ (cdp) Pima County	4	0.05
Molalla, OR (city) Clackamas County	4	0.05
Pleasant View, UT (city) Weber County	4	0.05
Shiprock, NM (cdp) San Juan County	4	0.05
Sitka, AK (borough) Sitka City and Borough	4	0.05
Tobyhanna, PA (township) Monroe County	4	0.05
Woodway, TX (city) McLennan County	4	0.05
Tigard, OR (city) Washington County	21	0.04
Richland, WA (city) Benton County	19	0.04
Inglewood-Finn Hill, WA (cdp) King County	10	0.04
Knik-Fairview, AK (cdp) Matanuska-Susitna Borough	6	0.04
Glen Carbon, IL (village) Madison County	5	0.04
Mountain Home, ID (city) Elmore County	5	0.04
Cusseta-Chattahoochee County, GA (unified govt) Chattahoochee County	4	0.04
Grandview, WA (city) Yakima County	4	0.04
Kapaa, HI (cdp) Kauai County	4	0.04
Newcastle, WA (city) King County	4	0.04
North Bend, OR (city) Coos County	4	0.04
Rockcreek, OR (cdp) Washington County	4	0.04
Alderwood Manor, WA (cdp) Snohomish County	3	0.04
Bothell East, WA (cdp) Snohomish County	3	0.04
Lakes, AK (cdp) Matanuska-Susitna Borough	3	0.04
Milan, TN (city) Gibson County	3	0.04
Richland Hills, TX (city) Tarrant County	3	0.04
Kennewick, WA (city) Benton County	24	0.03
Nampa, ID (city) Canyon County	21	0.03
Aloha, OR (cdp) Washington County	17	0.03
Juneau, AK (borough) Juneau City and Borough	9	0.03
Clearfield, UT (city) Davis County	8	0.03
Issaquah, WA (city) King County	8	0.03
Pullman, WA (city) Whitman County	8	0.03
Imperial Beach, CA (city) San Diego County	7	0.03
Moses Lake, WA (city) Grant County	7	0.03
Redmond, OR (city) Deschutes County	7	0.03
Battle Ground, WA (city) Clark County	6	0.03
Kalispell, MT (city) Flathead County	6	0.03

Please refer to the Explanation of Data in the front of the book for more detailed information.

SECTION THREE

Race

American Indian: Seminole

U.S. and 50 States Sorted by Population and Percent of Total Population

Place	Population	%
United States	**31,971**	**0.01**
Oklahoma	11,493	0.31
Florida	4,816	0.03
California	2,992	0.01
Texas	1,496	0.01
New York	848	<0.01
Georgia	664	0.01
Pennsylvania	660	0.01
Washington	596	0.01
Kansas	468	0.02
North Carolina	466	<0.01
Ohio	460	<0.01
Virginia	439	0.01
Colorado	424	0.01
New Jersey	419	<0.01
Missouri	400	0.01
Michigan	375	<0.01
Arizona	358	0.01
Oregon	354	0.01
Maryland	340	0.01
Illinois	316	<0.01
South Carolina	230	<0.01
Nevada	228	0.01
Massachusetts	227	<0.01
Tennessee	217	<0.01
Arkansas	216	0.01
New Mexico	213	0.01
Alabama	196	<0.01
Hawaii	191	0.01
Kentucky	160	<0.01
Minnesota	153	<0.01
Louisiana	150	<0.01
Indiana	149	<0.01
Wisconsin	130	<0.01
Mississippi	123	<0.01
Utah	120	<0.01
Connecticut	116	<0.01
Alaska	112	0.02
Iowa	91	<0.01
Idaho	80	0.01
South Dakota	58	0.01
Montana	57	0.01
Maine	50	<0.01
Delaware	49	0.01
West Virginia	44	<0.01
Rhode Island	43	<0.01
New Hampshire	41	<0.01
District of Columbia	40	0.01
Nebraska	38	<0.01
Wyoming	28	<0.01
North Dakota	19	<0.01
Vermont	18	<0.01

Place	Population	%
Oklahoma	11,493	0.31
Florida	4,816	0.03
Kansas	468	0.02
Alaska	112	0.02
United States	**31,971**	**0.01**
California	2,992	0.01
Texas	1,496	0.01
Georgia	664	0.01
Pennsylvania	660	0.01
Washington	596	0.01
Virginia	439	0.01
Colorado	424	0.01
Missouri	400	0.01
Arizona	358	0.01
Oregon	354	0.01
Maryland	340	0.01
Nevada	228	0.01
Arkansas	216	0.01
New Mexico	213	0.01
Hawaii	191	0.01
Idaho	80	0.01
South Dakota	58	0.01
Montana	57	0.01
Delaware	49	0.01
District of Columbia	40	0.01
New York	848	<0.01
North Carolina	466	<0.01
Ohio	460	<0.01
New Jersey	419	<0.01
Michigan	375	<0.01
Illinois	316	<0.01
South Carolina	230	<0.01
Massachusetts	227	<0.01
Tennessee	217	<0.01
Alabama	196	<0.01
Kentucky	160	<0.01
Minnesota	153	<0.01
Louisiana	150	<0.01
Indiana	149	<0.01
Wisconsin	130	<0.01
Mississippi	123	<0.01
Utah	120	<0.01
Connecticut	116	<0.01
Iowa	91	<0.01
Maine	50	<0.01
West Virginia	44	<0.01
Rhode Island	43	<0.01
New Hampshire	41	<0.01
Nebraska	38	<0.01
Wyoming	28	<0.01
North Dakota	19	<0.01
Vermont	18	<0.01

Please refer to the Explanation of Data in the front of the book for more detailed information.

Race

American Indian: Seminole

Top 150 Places Sorted by Population

Based on all places, regardless of total population

Place	Population	%
Oklahoma City, OK (city) Oklahoma County	1,745	0.30
Seminole, OK (city) Seminole County	883	11.79
Shawnee, OK (city) Pottawatomie County	738	2.47
Tulsa, OK (city) Tulsa County	554	0.14
Wewoka, OK (city) Seminole County	488	14.23
New York, NY (city) Kings County	357	<0.01
Norman, OK (city) Cleveland County	255	0.23
Holdenville, OK (city) Hughes County	254	4.40
Los Angeles, CA (city) Los Angeles County	234	0.01
Ada, OK (city) Pontotoc County	210	1.25
Konawa, OK (city) Seminole County	205	15.79
Midwest City, OK (city) Oklahoma County	203	0.37
Tecumseh, OK (city) Pottawatomie County	191	2.96
Philadelphia, PA (city) Philadelphia County	189	0.01
Moore, OK (city) Cleveland County	175	0.32
Jacksonville, FL (city) Duval County	165	0.02
Wichita, KS (city) Sedgwick County	147	0.04
Immokalee, FL (cdp) Collier County	119	0.49
San Diego, CA (city) San Diego County	114	0.01
Lawton, OK (city) Comanche County	112	0.12
Maud, OK (city) Pottawatomie County	110	10.50
Del City, OK (city) Oklahoma County	110	0.52
Manhattan, NY (borough) New York County	110	0.01
Edmond, OK (city) Oklahoma County	108	0.13
Dallas, TX (city) Dallas County	104	0.01
San Antonio, TX (city) Medina County	92	0.01
Brooklyn, NY (borough) Kings County	92	<0.01
Oakland, CA (city) Alameda County	86	0.02
Davie, FL (town) Broward County	84	0.09
Denver, CO (city) Denver County	82	0.01
Okmulgee, OK (city) Okmulgee County	81	0.66
Lawrence, KS (city) Douglas County	81	0.09
Chicago, IL (city) Cook County	80	<0.01
Queens, NY (borough) Queens County	79	<0.01
Muskogee, OK (city) Muskogee County	78	0.20
Broken Arrow, OK (city) Tulsa County	72	0.07
Phoenix, AZ (city) Maricopa County	72	<0.01
Kansas City, MO (city) Jackson County	69	0.02
Portland, OR (city) Multnomah County	68	0.01
San Francisco, CA (city) San Francisco County	68	0.01
Fort Worth, TX (city) Tarrant County	67	0.01
Houston, TX (city) Harris County	67	<0.01
Tampa, FL (city) Hillsborough County	66	0.02
Pembroke Pines, FL (city) Broward County	65	0.04
Albuquerque, NM (city) Bernalillo County	64	0.01
Sapulpa, OK (city) Creek County	63	0.31
Detroit, MI (city) Wayne County	63	0.01
Las Vegas, NV (city) Clark County	63	0.01
Sacramento, CA (city) Sacramento County	63	0.01
Seattle, WA (city) King County	63	0.01
Stillwater, OK (city) Payne County	61	0.13
Hollywood, FL (city) Broward County	60	0.04
Port St. Lucie, FL (city) St. Lucie County	60	0.04
Glenpool, OK (city) Tulsa County	58	0.54
Brandon, FL (cdp) Hillsborough County	57	0.06
Ardmore, OK (city) Carter County	54	0.22
San Jose, CA (city) Santa Clara County	54	0.01
Wetumka, OK (city) Hughes County	51	3.98
Okeechobee, FL (city) Okeechobee County	50	0.89
Bronx, NY (borough) Bronx County	50	<0.01
Fresno, CA (city) Fresno County	49	0.01
Long Beach, CA (city) Los Angeles County	48	0.01
Stockton, CA (city) San Joaquin County	46	0.02
Lehigh Acres, FL (cdp) Lee County	44	0.05
Rochester, NY (city) Monroe County	44	0.02
Anchorage, AK (municipality) Anchorage Municipality	43	0.01
Riverside, CA (city) Riverside County	43	0.01
Henryetta, OK (city) Okmulgee County	42	0.71
Bakersfield, CA (city) Kern County	42	0.01
Columbus, OH (city) Franklin County	42	0.01
Claremore, OK (city) Rogers County	41	0.22
Boston, MA (city) Suffolk County	41	0.01
Bethany, OK (city) Oklahoma County	40	0.21
Aurora, CO (city) Arapahoe County	40	0.01
Washington, DC (city) District of Columbia	40	0.01
McLoud, OK (town) Pottawatomie County	39	0.96
Choctaw, OK (city) Oklahoma County	39	0.35
St. Petersburg, FL (city) Pinellas County	39	0.02
El Reno, OK (city) Canadian County	38	0.23
Tallahassee, FL (city) Leon County	38	0.02
Colorado Springs, CO (city) El Paso County	38	0.01
Moreno Valley, CA (city) Riverside County	36	0.02
Newark, NJ (city) Essex County	36	0.01
Tahlequah, OK (city) Cherokee County	35	0.22
Baltimore, MD (city) Baltimore city County	35	0.01
Sasakwa, OK (town) Seminole County	34	22.67
Anadarko, OK (city) Caddo County	34	0.50
Owasso, OK (city) Tulsa County	34	0.12
Tucson, AZ (city) Pima County	34	0.01
Virginia Beach, VA (ind. city) Virginia Beach independent city	34	0.01
Charlotte, NC (city) Mecklenburg County	34	<0.01
Bowlegs, OK (town) Seminole County	33	8.15
Brookhaven, NY (town) Suffolk County	33	0.01
Nashville-Davidson, TN (metro govt) Davidson County	33	0.01
Yukon, OK (city) Canadian County	32	0.14
Eugene, OR (city) Lane County	31	0.02
Pittsburgh, PA (city) Allegheny County	31	0.01
Bartlesville, OK (city) Washington County	30	0.08
Plantation, FL (city) Broward County	30	0.04
Tacoma, WA (city) Pierce County	30	0.02
Cleveland, OH (city) Cuyahoga County	30	0.01
Atlanta, GA (city) Fulton County	29	0.01
Blackwell, OK (city) Kay County	28	0.39
Mesa, AZ (city) Maricopa County	28	0.01
Minneapolis, MN (city) Hennepin County	28	0.01
Austin, TX (city) Travis County	28	<0.01
Hempstead, NY (town) Nassau County	28	<0.01
Okemah, OK (city) Okfuskee County	27	0.84
Modesto, CA (city) Stanislaus County	27	0.01
Vallejo, CA (city) Solano County	26	0.02
Staten Island, NY (borough) Richmond County	26	0.01
Urban Honolulu, HI (cdp) Honolulu County	26	0.01
Ponca City, OK (city) Kay County	25	0.10
Valrico, FL (cdp) Hillsborough County	25	0.07
Lancaster, CA (city) Los Angeles County	25	0.02
Springfield, MO (city) Christian County	25	0.02
Visalia, CA (city) Tulare County	25	0.02
McAlester, OK (city) Pittsburg County	24	0.13
Vacaville, CA (city) Solano County	24	0.03
Columbus, GA (city) Muscogee County	24	0.01
Fayetteville, NC (city) Cumberland County	24	0.01
Fort Lauderdale, FL (city) Broward County	24	0.01
North Las Vegas, NV (city) Clark County	24	0.01
Santa Rosa, CA (city) Sonoma County	24	0.01
Louisville-Jefferson County, KY (metro govt) Jefferson County	24	<0.01
Montura, FL (cdp) Hendry County	23	0.70
Miramar, FL (city) Broward County	23	0.02
Palm Bay, FL (city) Brevard County	23	0.02
Buffalo, NY (city) Erie County	23	0.01
Chesapeake, VA (ind. city) Chesapeake independent city	23	0.01
Orlando, FL (city) Orange County	23	0.01
Paradise, NV (cdp) Clark County	23	0.01
Byng, OK (town) Pontotoc County	22	1.87
Weatherford, OK (city) Custer County	22	0.20
Gainesville, FL (city) Alachua County	22	0.02
Killeen, TX (city) Bell County	22	0.02
Allen, OK (town) Pontotoc County	21	2.25
Park Hill, OK (cdp) Cherokee County	21	0.54
Stilwell, OK (city) Adair County	21	0.53
Warr Acres, OK (city) Oklahoma County	21	0.21
Mustang, OK (city) Canadian County	21	0.12
Bixby, OK (city) Tulsa County	21	0.10
Victorville, CA (city) San Bernardino County	21	0.02
Anaheim, CA (city) Orange County	21	0.01
Garland, TX (city) Dallas County	21	0.01
Lakewood, CO (city) Jefferson County	21	0.01
Oceanside, CA (city) San Diego County	21	0.01
St. Paul, MN (city) Ramsey County	21	0.01
Portsmouth, VA (ind. city) Portsmouth independent city	20	0.02
Cincinnati, OH (city) Hamilton County	20	0.01

SECTION THREE

Please refer to the Explanation of Data in the front of the book for more detailed information.

Race

American Indian: Seminole

Top 150 Places Sorted by Percent of Total Population

Based on all places, regardless of total population

Place	Population	%
Sasakwa, OK (town) Seminole County	34	22.67
Hangaard, MN (township) Clearwater County	1	20.00
Dwight Mission, OK (cdp) Sequoyah County	9	16.36
Konawa, OK (city) Seminole County	205	15.79
Brooksville, OK (town) Pottawatomie County	9	14.29
Wewoka, OK (city) Seminole County	488	14.23
Seminole, OK (city) Seminole County	883	11.79
Maud, OK (city) Pottawatomie County	110	10.50
Bowlegs, OK (town) Seminole County	33	8.15
Holdenville, OK (city) Hughes County	254	4.40
Cromwell, OK (town) Seminole County	12	4.20
Wetumka, OK (city) Hughes County	51	3.98
Tecumseh, OK (city) Pottawatomie County	191	2.96
Sams Corner, OK (cdp) Mayes County	4	2.92
Earlsboro, OK (town) Pottawatomie County	18	2.87
Castle, OK (town) Okfuskee County	3	2.83
Cantwell, AK (cdp) Denali Borough	6	2.74
Valmy, NV (cdp) Humboldt County	1	2.70
Yeager, OK (town) Hughes County	2	2.67
Scraper, OK (cdp) Cherokee County	5	2.62
Gerty, OK (town) Hughes County	3	2.54
Lamar, OK (town) Hughes County	4	2.53
St. Louis, OK (town) Pottawatomie County	4	2.53
Shawnee, OK (city) Pottawatomie County	738	2.47
Johnson, OK (town) Pottawatomie County	6	2.43
Steely Hollow, OK (cdp) Cherokee County	5	2.43
Allen, OK (town) Pontotoc County	21	2.25
Stoney Point, OK (cdp) Sequoyah County	5	2.10
Elmer, OK (town) Jackson County	2	2.08
Horn, OK (town) Hughes County	2	2.06
Ona, FL (cdp) Hardee County	6	1.91
Lima, OK (town) Seminole County	1	1.89
Byng, OK (town) Pontotoc County	22	1.87
Valley Brook, OK (town) Oklahoma County	13	1.70
Loco, OK (town) Stephens County	2	1.64
La Tour, MO (cdp) Johnson County	1	1.61
Oak Springs, AZ (cdp) Apache County	1	1.59
Mercersville, MD (cdp) Washington County	2	1.54
Slick, OK (town) Creek County	2	1.53
Paden, OK (town) Okfuskee County	7	1.52
Goodyears Bar, CA (cdp) Sierra County	1	1.47
Atwood, OK (town) Hughes County	1	1.35
Lawrence Creek, OK (town) Creek County	2	1.34
Veguita, NM (cdp) Socorro County	3	1.29
Francis, OK (town) Pontotoc County	4	1.27
Ada, OK (city) Pontotoc County	210	1.25
Yorktown, IA (city) Page County	1	1.18
Garvin, OK (town) McCurtain County	3	1.17
Sperry, OK (town) Tulsa County	14	1.16
Antioch, OH (village) Monroe County	1	1.16
Sycamore, OK (cdp) Delaware County	2	1.13
Traver, CA (cdp) Tulare County	8	1.12
Weleetka, OK (town) Okfuskee County	11	1.10
Askov, MN (city) Pine County	4	1.10
Fort Yates, ND (city) Sioux County	2	1.09
Peru, VT (town) Bennington County	4	1.07
Stonewall, OK (town) Pontotoc County	5	1.06
Deering, ND (city) McHenry County	1	1.02
Everglades, FL (city) Collier County	4	1.00
Hatton, WA (town) Adams County	1	0.99
Roff, OK (town) Pontotoc County	7	0.97
McLoud, OK (town) Pottawatomie County	39	0.96
Oto, IA (city) Woodbury County	1	0.93
Okeechobee, FL (city) Okeechobee County	50	0.89
Conehatta, MS (cdp) Newton County	12	0.89
Marland, OK (town) Noble County	2	0.89
Centerville, WA (cdp) Klickitat County	1	0.89
Pink, OK (town) Pottawatomie County	18	0.87
Warfield, VA (cdp) Brunswick County	1	0.87
Katie, OK (town) Garvin County	3	0.86
Wanette, OK (town) Pottawatomie County	3	0.86
Williams, SC (town) Colleton County	1	0.85
Okemah, OK (city) Okfuskee County	27	0.84
Nicut, OK (cdp) Sequoyah County	3	0.83
New Pine Creek, OR (cdp) Lake County	1	0.83

Place	Population	%
Tutuilla, OR (cdp) Umatilla County	4	0.82
Munson, FL (cdp) Santa Rosa County	3	0.81
Boynton, OK (town) Muskogee County	2	0.81
Forest Park, OK (town) Oklahoma County	8	0.80
Dewar, OK (town) Okmulgee County	7	0.79
Fort Cobb, OK (town) Caddo County	5	0.79
Chinese Camp, CA (cdp) Tuolumne County	1	0.79
Oelrichs, SD (town) Fall River County	1	0.79
Trenton, KY (city) Todd County	3	0.78
Eolia, MO (village) Pike County	4	0.77
Conway, MO (city) Laclede County	6	0.76
Asher, OK (town) Pottawatomie County	3	0.76
Dustin, OK (town) Hughes County	3	0.76
Grandview, OK (cdp) Cherokee County	3	0.76
Ali Chukson, AZ (cdp) Pima County	1	0.76
Riverton, KS (cdp) Cherokee County	7	0.75
Morris, OK (city) Okmulgee County	11	0.74
Wayne, OK (town) McClain County	5	0.73
Mountain Park, OK (town) Kiowa County	3	0.73
Henryetta, OK (city) Okmulgee County	42	0.71
Prague, OK (city) Lincoln County	17	0.71
Springer, OK (town) Carter County	5	0.71
Bee, OK (cdp) Johnston County	1	0.71
Montura, FL (cdp) Hendry County	23	0.70
Watersmeet, MI (cdp) Gogebic County	3	0.70
Trenton, NC (town) Jones County	2	0.70
Hastings, OK (town) Jefferson County	1	0.70
Kingston, OK (town) Marshall County	11	0.69
Alpine, AZ (cdp) Apache County	1	0.69
Lone Wolf, OK (town) Kiowa County	3	0.68
Calvin, OK (town) Hughes County	2	0.68
Princeton, ID (cdp) Latah County	1	0.68
Camden, NC (cdp) Camden County	4	0.67
Okmulgee, OK (city) Okmulgee County	81	0.66
Quapaw, OK (town) Ottawa County	6	0.66
Briggs, OK (cdp) Cherokee County	2	0.66
Tuskahoma, OK (cdp) Pushmataha County	1	0.66
Antlers, OK (city) Pushmataha County	16	0.65
Rattan, OK (town) Pushmataha County	2	0.65
Midland, CO (cdp) Teller County	1	0.64
Gracemont, OK (town) Caddo County	2	0.63
Springhill, FL (cdp) Santa Rosa County	1	0.63
Summertown, GA (city) Emanuel County	1	0.63
Ballard, UT (town) Uintah County	5	0.62
Cheyenne, OK (town) Roger Mills County	5	0.62
Roseland, FL (cdp) Indian River County	9	0.61
Meeker, OK (town) Lincoln County	7	0.61
Panacea, FL (cdp) Wakulla County	5	0.61
Mounds, OK (town) Creek County	7	0.60
Bethel Acres, OK (town) Pottawatomie County	17	0.59
Strathmoor Manor, KY (city) Jefferson County	2	0.59
Cypress Quarters, FL (cdp) Okeechobee County	7	0.58
Corona, NM (village) Lincoln County	1	0.58
Hardtner, KS (city) Barber County	1	0.58
Quinton, OK (town) Pittsburg County	6	0.57
Cherry Tree, OK (cdp) Adair County	5	0.57
Locust Grove, OK (town) Mayes County	8	0.56
Elmo, MT (cdp) Lake County	1	0.56
Kettle River, MN (city) Carlton County	1	0.56
Slayden, TN (town) Dickson County	1	0.56
Glenpool, OK (city) Tulsa County	58	0.54
Park Hill, OK (cdp) Cherokee County	21	0.54
Cole, OK (town) McClain County	3	0.54
Stark, NH (town) Coos County	3	0.54
Ramah, NM (cdp) McKinley County	2	0.54
Stilwell, OK (city) Adair County	21	0.53
Dill City, OK (town) Washita County	3	0.53
Porter, OK (town) Wagoner County	3	0.53
Del City, OK (city) Oklahoma County	110	0.52
Payne Springs, TX (town) Henderson County	4	0.52
Long Hollow, SD (cdp) Roberts County	1	0.52
Checotah, OK (city) McIntosh County	17	0.51
Boley, OK (town) Okfuskee County	6	0.51
Oklahoma, PA (cdp) Clearfield County	4	0.51
White Springs, FL (town) Hamilton County	4	0.51

Please refer to the Explanation of Data in the front of the book for more detailed information.

Race

American Indian: Seminole

Top 150 Places Sorted by Percent of Total Population

Based on places with total population of 7,500 or more

Place	Population	%
Shawnee, OK (city) Pottawatomie County	738	2.47
Ada, OK (city) Pontotoc County	210	1.25
Okmulgee, OK (city) Okmulgee County	81	0.66
Glenpool, OK (city) Tulsa County	58	0.54
Del City, OK (city) Oklahoma County	110	0.52
Immokalee, FL (cdp) Collier County	119	0.49
Midwest City, OK (city) Oklahoma County	203	0.37
Choctaw, OK (city) Oklahoma County	39	0.35
Moore, OK (city) Cleveland County	175	0.32
Sapulpa, OK (city) Creek County	63	0.31
Oklahoma City, OK (city) Oklahoma County	1,745	0.30
Norman, OK (city) Cleveland County	255	0.23
El Reno, OK (city) Canadian County	38	0.23
Ardmore, OK (city) Carter County	54	0.22
Claremore, OK (city) Rogers County	41	0.22
Tahlequah, OK (city) Cherokee County	35	0.22
Bethany, OK (city) Oklahoma County	40	0.21
Warr Acres, OK (city) Oklahoma County	21	0.21
Newcastle, OK (city) McClain County	16	0.21
Muskogee, OK (city) Muskogee County	78	0.20
Weatherford, OK (city) Custer County	22	0.20
The Village, OK (city) Oklahoma County	17	0.19
Coweta, OK (city) Wagoner County	18	0.18
Tulsa, OK (city) Tulsa County	554	0.14
Yukon, OK (city) Canadian County	32	0.14
Shiprock, NM (cdp) San Juan County	12	0.14
Edmond, OK (city) Oklahoma County	108	0.13
Stillwater, OK (city) Payne County	61	0.13
McAlester, OK (city) Pittsburg County	24	0.13
Poteau, OK (city) Le Flore County	11	0.13
Lawton, OK (city) Comanche County	112	0.12
Owasso, OK (city) Tulsa County	34	0.12
Mustang, OK (city) Canadian County	21	0.12
Clinton, OK (city) Custer County	11	0.12
Arkansas City, KS (city) Cowley County	14	0.11
Ponca City, OK (city) Kay County	25	0.10
Bixby, OK (city) Tulsa County	21	0.10
East La Mirada, CA (cdp) Los Angeles County	10	0.10
Guthrie, OK (city) Logan County	10	0.10
Pryor Creek, OK (city) Mayes County	10	0.10
Blanchard, OK (city) McClain County	8	0.10
Corning, CA (city) Tehama County	8	0.10
Davie, FL (town) Broward County	84	0.09
Lawrence, KS (city) Douglas County	81	0.09
Chickasha, OK (city) Grady County	15	0.09
View Park-Windsor Hills, CA (cdp) Los Angeles County	10	0.09
Bartlesville, OK (city) Washington County	30	0.08
Durant, OK (city) Bryan County	12	0.08
Ahuimanu, HI (cdp) Honolulu County	7	0.08
Bernalillo, NM (town) Sandoval County	7	0.08
Burlington, WA (city) Skagit County	7	0.08
Perryton, TX (city) Ochiltree County	7	0.08
Sheffield Lake, OH (city) Lorain County	7	0.08
Broken Arrow, OK (city) Tulsa County	72	0.07
Valrico, FL (cdp) Hillsborough County	25	0.07
McKeesport, PA (city) Allegheny County	13	0.07
Chesapeake Ranch Estates, MD (cdp) Calvert County	7	0.07
North Kensington, MD (cdp) Montgomery County	7	0.07
Corrales, NM (village) Sandoval County	6	0.07
Brandon, FL (cdp) Hillsborough County	57	0.06
Spring Valley, CA (cdp) San Diego County	17	0.06
Duncan, OK (city) Stephens County	14	0.06
Blythe, CA (city) Riverside County	13	0.06
Batavia, NY (city) Genesee County	10	0.06
Jenks, OK (city) Tulsa County	10	0.06
Callaway, FL (city) Bay County	9	0.06
Ukiah, CA (city) Mendocino County	9	0.06
Cambridge, MD (city) Dorchester County	8	0.06
Homosassa Springs, FL (cdp) Citrus County	8	0.06
Lake City, FL (city) Columbia County	7	0.06
New Kingman-Butler, AZ (cdp) Mohave County	7	0.06
Canyon Lake, CA (city) Riverside County	6	0.06
Largo, MD (cdp) Prince George's County	6	0.06
Croton-on-Hudson, NY (village) Westchester County	5	0.06
Tanaina, AK (cdp) Matanuska-Susitna Borough	5	0.06
Wahpeton, ND (city) Richland County	5	0.06
Wasilla, AK (city) Matanuska-Susitna Borough	5	0.06
Lehigh Acres, FL (cdp) Lee County	44	0.05
Cooper City, FL (city) Broward County	15	0.05
Four Corners, FL (cdp) Lake County	12	0.05
Greenville, TX (city) Hunt County	12	0.05
El Cerrito, CA (city) Contra Costa County	11	0.05
Pace, FL (cdp) Santa Rosa County	11	0.05
Palm River-Clair Mel, FL (cdp) Hillsborough County	11	0.05
Sand Springs, OK (city) Tulsa County	9	0.05
Parkway, CA (cdp) Sacramento County	8	0.05
Clearlake, CA (city) Lake County	7	0.05
Katy, TX (city) Harris County	7	0.05
Miami, OK (city) Ottawa County	7	0.05
Upper Grand Lagoon, FL (cdp) Bay County	7	0.05
Vero Beach, FL (city) Indian River County	7	0.05
Doctor Phillips, FL (cdp) Orange County	6	0.05
Guymon, OK (city) Texas County	6	0.05
Lakeland Village, CA (cdp) Riverside County	6	0.05
Mango, FL (cdp) Hillsborough County	6	0.05
South Daytona, FL (city) Volusia County	6	0.05
Thonotosassa, FL (cdp) Hillsborough County	6	0.05
Winfield, KS (city) Cowley County	6	0.05
Augusta, KS (city) Butler County	5	0.05
Fairview Shores, FL (cdp) Orange County	5	0.05
Harrisonville, MO (city) Cass County	5	0.05
Lititz, PA (borough) Lancaster County	5	0.05
Oak Grove, SC (cdp) Lexington County	5	0.05
Scottdale, GA (cdp) DeKalb County	5	0.05
Shasta Lake, CA (city) Shasta County	5	0.05
Anna, TX (city) Collin County	4	0.05
Fairview, TN (city) Williamson County	4	0.05
Gold River, CA (cdp) Sacramento County	4	0.05
Greenbriar, VA (cdp) Fairfax County	4	0.05
Orange Park, FL (town) Clay County	4	0.05
Purcellville, VA (town) Loudoun County	4	0.05
Quincy, FL (city) Gadsden County	4	0.05
South San Gabriel, CA (cdp) Los Angeles County	4	0.05
Wichita, KS (city) Sedgwick County	147	0.04
Pembroke Pines, FL (city) Broward County	65	0.04
Hollywood, FL (city) Broward County	60	0.04
Port St. Lucie, FL (city) St. Lucie County	60	0.04
Plantation, FL (city) Broward County	30	0.04
Enid, OK (city) Garfield County	19	0.04
Hilo, HI (cdp) Hawaii County	19	0.04
Del Rio, TX (city) Val Verde County	14	0.04
Oviedo, FL (city) Seminole County	13	0.04
Hinesville, GA (city) Liberty County	12	0.04
Lakeside, FL (cdp) Clay County	12	0.04
Fountain, CO (city) El Paso County	11	0.04
Fleming Island, FL (cdp) Clay County	10	0.04
Monroeville, PA (municipality) Allegheny County	10	0.04
East Peoria, IL (city) Tazewell County	9	0.04
Franklin Park, IL (village) Cook County	7	0.04
Lynn Haven, FL (city) Bay County	7	0.04
Rosamond, CA (cdp) Kern County	7	0.04
Country Club Hills, IL (city) Cook County	6	0.04
Foley, AL (city) Baldwin County	6	0.04
Fort Leonard Wood, MO (cdp) Pulaski County	6	0.04
Foxborough, MA (town) Norfolk County	6	0.04
Gibsonton, FL (cdp) Hillsborough County	6	0.04
Hurricane, UT (city) Washington County	6	0.04
Lake Wales, FL (city) Polk County	6	0.04
Rio Linda, CA (cdp) Sacramento County	6	0.04
Rosedale, CA (cdp) Kern County	6	0.04
Uvalde, TX (city) Uvalde County	6	0.04
Wilkinsburg, PA (borough) Allegheny County	6	0.04
Ardmore, PA (cdp) Montgomery County	5	0.04
Artesia, NM (city) Eddy County	5	0.04
Berkley, CO (cdp) Adams County	5	0.04
El Sobrante, CA (cdp) Riverside County	5	0.04
Fairburn, GA (city) Fulton County	5	0.04
Fernway, PA (cdp) Butler County	5	0.04
Highlands, NY (town) Orange County	5	0.04
Kingsburg, CA (city) Fresno County	5	0.04

Please refer to the Explanation of Data in the front of the book for more detailed information.

Race

American Indian: Shoshone

U.S. and 50 States Sorted by Population and Percent of Total Population

Place	Population	%	Place	Population	%
United States	**13,002**	**<0.01**	Wyoming	2,818	0.50
Wyoming	2,818	0.50	Nevada	1,788	0.07
California	2,217	0.01	Idaho	812	0.05
Nevada	1,788	0.07	Utah	960	0.03
Utah	960	0.03	Montana	176	0.02
Idaho	812	0.05	California	2,217	0.01
Washington	499	0.01	Washington	499	0.01
Arizona	378	0.01	Arizona	378	0.01
Colorado	362	0.01	Colorado	362	0.01
Oregon	294	0.01	Oregon	294	0.01
Texas	267	<0.01	Oklahoma	198	0.01
Oklahoma	198	0.01	New Mexico	182	0.01
New Mexico	182	0.01	Hawaii	118	0.01
Montana	176	0.02	Alaska	82	0.01
Florida	165	<0.01	South Dakota	48	0.01
Hawaii	118	0.01	North Dakota	38	0.01
Illinois	107	<0.01	**United States**	**13,002**	**<0.01**
Missouri	107	<0.01	Texas	267	<0.01
Ohio	99	<0.01	Florida	165	<0.01
Pennsylvania	98	<0.01	Illinois	107	<0.01
New York	96	<0.01	Missouri	107	<0.01
North Carolina	95	<0.01	Ohio	99	<0.01
Alaska	82	0.01	Pennsylvania	98	<0.01
Kansas	77	<0.01	New York	96	<0.01
Michigan	77	<0.01	North Carolina	95	<0.01
Indiana	75	<0.01	Kansas	77	<0.01
New Jersey	62	<0.01	Michigan	77	<0.01
Virginia	60	<0.01	Indiana	75	<0.01
Minnesota	52	<0.01	New Jersey	62	<0.01
Massachusetts	50	<0.01	Virginia	60	<0.01
Georgia	49	<0.01	Minnesota	52	<0.01
South Dakota	48	0.01	Massachusetts	50	<0.01
Arkansas	47	<0.01	Georgia	49	<0.01
Maryland	47	<0.01	Arkansas	47	<0.01
Wisconsin	44	<0.01	Maryland	47	<0.01
Louisiana	42	<0.01	Wisconsin	44	<0.01
North Dakota	38	0.01	Louisiana	42	<0.01
Tennessee	38	<0.01	Tennessee	38	<0.01
Nebraska	36	<0.01	Nebraska	36	<0.01
Connecticut	33	<0.01	Connecticut	33	<0.01
South Carolina	32	<0.01	South Carolina	32	<0.01
Kentucky	29	<0.01	Kentucky	29	<0.01
West Virginia	29	<0.01	West Virginia	29	<0.01
New Hampshire	20	<0.01	New Hampshire	20	<0.01
Alabama	19	<0.01	Alabama	19	<0.01
Iowa	16	<0.01	Iowa	16	<0.01
Vermont	16	<0.01	Vermont	16	<0.01
Maine	15	<0.01	Maine	15	<0.01
Rhode Island	12	<0.01	Rhode Island	12	<0.01
Mississippi	9	<0.01	Mississippi	9	<0.01
Delaware	8	<0.01	Delaware	8	<0.01
District of Columbia	4	<0.01	District of Columbia	4	<0.01

Please refer to the Explanation of Data in the front of the book for more detailed information.

Race

American Indian: Shoshone

Top 150 Places Sorted by Population

Based on all places, regardless of total population

Place	Population	%
Fort Washakie, WY (cdp) Fremont County	1,061	60.32
Lander, WY (city) Fremont County	202	2.70
Riverton, WY (city) Fremont County	173	1.63
Reno, NV (city) Washoe County	169	0.08
Boulder Flats, WY (cdp) Fremont County	162	39.71
Ethete, WY (cdp) Fremont County	133	8.56
Fort Hall, ID (cdp) Bannock County	129	4.03
Elko, NV (city) Elko County	118	0.64
Los Angeles, CA (city) Los Angeles County	116	<0.01
Pocatello, ID (city) Bannock County	89	0.16
Ely, NV (city) White Pine County	85	2.00
Las Vegas, NV (city) Clark County	79	0.01
Salt Lake City, UT (city) Salt Lake County	72	0.04
Phoenix, AZ (city) Maricopa County	71	<0.01
Carson City, NV (ind. city) Carson City County	70	0.13
Ogden, UT (city) Weber County	70	0.08
Sparks, NV (city) Washoe County	70	0.08
West Valley City, UT (city) Salt Lake County	59	0.05
Denver, CO (city) Denver County	56	0.01
Boise City, ID (city) Ada County	53	0.03
San Diego, CA (city) San Diego County	51	<0.01
Johnstown, WY (cdp) Fremont County	49	20.25
Sacramento, CA (city) Sacramento County	49	0.01
Crowheart, WY (cdp) Fremont County	48	34.04
Casper, WY (city) Natrona County	48	0.09
New York, NY (city) Kings County	46	<0.01
San Jose, CA (city) Santa Clara County	46	<0.01
Bakersfield, CA (city) Kern County	45	0.01
Colorado Springs, CO (city) El Paso County	44	0.01
Portland, OR (city) Multnomah County	44	0.01
Albuquerque, NM (city) Bernalillo County	43	0.01
Arapahoe, WY (cdp) Fremont County	42	2.54
North Las Vegas, NV (city) Clark County	42	0.02
Cheyenne, WY (city) Laramie County	41	0.07
Seattle, WA (city) King County	41	0.01
Chubbuck, ID (city) Bannock County	40	0.29
Blackfoot, ID (city) Bingham County	39	0.33
Brigham City, UT (city) Box Elder County	39	0.22
Fallon, NV (city) Churchill County	37	0.43
Spring Creek, NV (cdp) Elko County	37	0.30
Anchorage, AK (municipality) Anchorage Municipality	36	0.01
Fresno, CA (city) Fresno County	36	0.01
Spokane, WA (city) Spokane County	35	0.02
Tucson, AZ (city) Pima County	35	0.01
Tooele, UT (city) Tooele County	34	0.11
Sunrise Manor, NV (cdp) Clark County	30	0.02
Anaheim, CA (city) Orange County	30	0.01
Battle Mountain, NV (cdp) Lander County	29	0.80
West Wendover, NV (city) Elko County	29	0.66
Twin Falls, ID (city) Twin Falls County	29	0.07
Long Beach, CA (city) Los Angeles County	29	0.01
Oakland, CA (city) Alameda County	29	0.01
Paradise, NV (cdp) Clark County	29	0.01
Idaho Falls, ID (city) Bonneville County	27	0.05
Nampa, ID (city) Canyon County	26	0.03
Spring Valley, NV (cdp) Clark County	26	0.01
Wells, NV (city) Elko County	25	1.93
Sun Valley, NV (cdp) Washoe County	25	0.13
Gillette, WY (city) Campbell County	25	0.09
Lancaster, CA (city) Los Angeles County	25	0.02
Henderson, NV (city) Clark County	25	0.01
Huntington Beach, CA (city) Orange County	25	0.01
Oklahoma City, OK (city) Oklahoma County	25	<0.01
San Francisco, CA (city) San Francisco County	25	<0.01
Vancouver, WA (city) Clark County	24	0.01
Chico, CA (city) Butte County	23	0.03
Provo, UT (city) Utah County	23	0.02
Mesa, AZ (city) Maricopa County	23	0.01
Brooklyn, NY (borough) Kings County	23	<0.01
Grantsville, UT (city) Tooele County	22	0.25
South Salt Lake, UT (city) Salt Lake County	22	0.09
Laramie, WY (city) Albany County	22	0.07
Pahrump, NV (cdp) Nye County	21	0.06
Billings, MT (city) Yellowstone County	20	0.02
Lemmon Valley, NV (cdp) Washoe County	19	0.38
Great Falls, MT (city) Cascade County	19	0.03
Aurora, CO (city) Arapahoe County	19	0.01
Eugene, OR (city) Lane County	19	0.01
Jerome, ID (city) Jerome County	18	0.17
Midvale, UT (city) Salt Lake County	18	0.06
Kearns, UT (cdp) Salt Lake County	18	0.05
Sandy, UT (city) Salt Lake County	18	0.02
West Jordan, UT (city) Salt Lake County	18	0.02
Wichita, KS (city) Sedgwick County	18	<0.01
Vernal, UT (city) Uintah County	17	0.19
Evanston, WY (city) Uinta County	17	0.14
Lawrence, KS (city) Douglas County	17	0.02
Stockton, CA (city) San Joaquin County	17	0.01
Chicago, IL (city) Cook County	17	<0.01
Murray, UT (city) Salt Lake County	16	0.03
Salinas, CA (city) Monterey County	16	0.01
Jacksonville, FL (city) Duval County	16	<0.01
San Antonio, TX (city) Medina County	16	<0.01
Furnace Creek, CA (cdp) Inyo County	15	62.50
Gardnerville Ranchos, NV (cdp) Douglas County	15	0.13
Green River, WY (city) Sweetwater County	15	0.12
North Highlands, CA (cdp) Sacramento County	15	0.04
Apple Valley, CA (town) San Bernardino County	15	0.02
Citrus Heights, CA (city) Sacramento County	15	0.02
Medford, OR (city) Jackson County	15	0.02
Whittier, CA (city) Los Angeles County	15	0.02
Lakewood, CO (city) Jefferson County	15	0.01
Roseville, CA (city) Placer County	15	0.01
Riverside, CA (city) Riverside County	15	<0.01
Roosevelt, UT (city) Duchesne County	14	0.23
Fernley, NV (city) Lyon County	14	0.07
Woodland, CA (city) Yolo County	14	0.03
Arden-Arcade, CA (cdp) Sacramento County	14	0.02
Carmichael, CA (cdp) Sacramento County	14	0.02
Downey, CA (city) Los Angeles County	14	0.01
Escondido, CA (city) San Diego County	14	0.01
Oceanside, CA (city) San Diego County	14	0.01
Austin, TX (city) Travis County	14	<0.01
Santa Ana, CA (city) Orange County	14	<0.01
Carlin, NV (city) Elko County	13	0.55
Bishop, CA (city) Inyo County	13	0.34
Foothill Farms, CA (cdp) Sacramento County	13	0.04
Meridian, ID (city) Ada County	13	0.02
Millcreek, UT (cdp) Salt Lake County	13	0.02
Rapid City, SD (city) Pennington County	13	0.02
Fontana, CA (city) San Bernardino County	13	0.01
Lawton, OK (city) Comanche County	13	0.01
Modesto, CA (city) Stanislaus County	13	0.01
Orange, CA (city) Orange County	13	0.01
Schurz, NV (cdp) Mineral County	12	1.82
Clearfield, UT (city) Davis County	12	0.04
Moorpark, CA (city) Ventura County	12	0.03
Morgan Hill, CA (city) Santa Clara County	12	0.03
Whitney, NV (cdp) Clark County	12	0.03
Lakewood, WA (city) Pierce County	12	0.02
Thornton, CO (city) Adams County	12	0.01
Victorville, CA (city) San Bernardino County	12	0.01
Dyer, NV (cdp) Esmeralda County	11	4.25
Ruth, NV (cdp) White Pine County	11	2.50
Panaca, NV (cdp) Lincoln County	11	1.14
Valle Vista, CA (cdp) Riverside County	11	0.08
Spanish Springs, NV (cdp) Washoe County	11	0.07
Rock Springs, WY (city) Sweetwater County	11	0.05
Englewood, CO (city) Arapahoe County	11	0.04
Roy, UT (city) Weber County	11	0.03
Bismarck, ND (city) Burleigh County	11	0.02
Logan, UT (city) Cache County	11	0.02
Santa Fe, NM (city) Santa Fe County	11	0.02
Fayetteville, NC (city) Cumberland County	11	0.01
Pomona, CA (city) Los Angeles County	11	0.01
Tacoma, WA (city) Pierce County	11	0.01
Philadelphia, PA (city) Philadelphia County	11	<0.01
Urban Honolulu, HI (cdp) Honolulu County	11	<0.01
Owyhee, NV (cdp) Elko County	10	1.05
McGill, NV (cdp) White Pine County	10	0.87

SECTION THREE

Please refer to the Explanation of Data in the front of the book for more detailed information.

Race

American Indian: Shoshone

Top 150 Places Sorted by Percent of Total Population

Based on all places, regardless of total population

Place	Population	%
Furnace Creek, CA (cdp) Inyo County	15	62.50
Fort Washakie, WY (cdp) Fremont County	1,061	60.32
Boulder Flats, WY (cdp) Fremont County	162	39.71
Crowheart, WY (cdp) Fremont County	48	34.04
Johnstown, WY (cdp) Fremont County	49	20.25
Ethete, WY (cdp) Fremont County	133	8.56
Valmy, NV (cdp) Humboldt County	3	8.11
Tecopa, CA (cdp) Inyo County	7	4.67
Dyer, NV (cdp) Esmeralda County	11	4.25
Fort Hall, ID (cdp) Bannock County	129	4.03
Truxton, AZ (cdp) Mohave County	5	3.73
Paradise, CA (cdp) Mono County	5	3.27
Lund, NV (cdp) White Pine County	9	3.19
Lander, WY (city) Fremont County	202	2.70
Arapahoe, WY (cdp) Fremont County	42	2.54
Ruth, NV (cdp) White Pine County	11	2.50
Bloomington, ID (city) Bear Lake County	5	2.43
Cartago, CA (cdp) Inyo County	2	2.17
Nixon, NV (cdp) Washoe County	8	2.14
Ely, NV (city) White Pine County	85	2.00
Wells, NV (city) Elko County	25	1.93
Schurz, NV (cdp) Mineral County	12	1.82
Jeffrey City, WY (cdp) Fremont County	1	1.72
Metaline Falls, WA (town) Pend Oreille County	4	1.68
Riverton, WY (city) Fremont County	173	1.63
Anton Chico, NM (cdp) Guadalupe County	3	1.60
Gabbs, NV (cdp) Nye County	4	1.49
Shoshoni, WY (town) Fremont County	9	1.39
Cutter, AZ (cdp) Gila County	1	1.35
Pavillion, WY (town) Fremont County	3	1.30
Oljato-Monument Valley, AZ (cdp) Navajo County	2	1.30
Fort Duchesne, UT (cdp) Uintah County	9	1.26
Panaca, NV (cdp) Lincoln County	11	1.14
Polvadera, NM (cdp) Socorro County	3	1.12
Frank, WV (cdp) Pocahontas County	1	1.11
Hudson, WY (town) Fremont County	5	1.09
Owyhee, NV (cdp) Elko County	10	1.05
Liberal, MO (city) Barton County	8	1.05
Mountain View, WY (cdp) Natrona County	1	1.04
Lodge Grass, MT (town) Big Horn County	4	0.93
Chalfant, CA (cdp) Mono County	6	0.92
Wamsutter, WY (town) Sweetwater County	4	0.89
Dinosaur, CO (town) Moffat County	3	0.88
Wahak Hotrontk, AZ (cdp) Pima County	1	0.88
McGill, NV (cdp) White Pine County	10	0.87
Fort Bridger, WY (cdp) Uinta County	3	0.87
Wadsworth, NV (cdp) Washoe County	7	0.84
White Mesa, UT (cdp) San Juan County	2	0.83
Dubois, WY (town) Fremont County	8	0.82
Battle Mountain, NV (cdp) Lander County	29	0.80
East Thermopolis, WY (town) Hot Springs County	2	0.79
Hulett, WY (town) Crook County	3	0.78
Crescent Valley, NV (cdp) Eureka County	3	0.77
Point MacKenzie, AK (cdp) Matanuska-Susitna Borough	4	0.76
Woodland, NC (town) Northampton County	6	0.74
Wendover, UT (city) Tooele County	10	0.71
Coleman, FL (city) Sumter County	5	0.71
Lindisfarne, MT (cdp) Lake County	2	0.70
Springdale, WA (town) Stevens County	2	0.70
Mission, OR (cdp) Umatilla County	7	0.68
Lanare, CA (cdp) Fresno County	4	0.68
Twin Lakes, MN (cdp) Mahnomen County	1	0.67
West Wendover, NV (city) Elko County	29	0.66
Mina, NV (cdp) Mineral County	1	0.65
Parker, WA (cdp) Yakima County	1	0.65
Elko, NV (city) Elko County	118	0.64
Camptonville, CA (cdp) Yuba County	1	0.63
Del Muerto, AZ (cdp) Apache County	2	0.61
Happys Inn, MT (cdp) Lincoln County	1	0.61
Willow City, ND (city) Bottineau County	1	0.61
Texline, TX (town) Dallam County	3	0.59
Boulder, WY (cdp) Sublette County	1	0.59
Farnam, NE (village) Dawson County	1	0.58
Fort Bidwell, CA (cdp) Modoc County	1	0.58
McDermitt, NV (cdp) Humboldt County	1	0.58
Fallon Station, NV (cdp) Churchill County	4	0.57
St. Pierre, MT (cdp) Hill County	2	0.57
Notus, ID (city) Canyon County	3	0.56
Mount Charleston, NV (cdp) Clark County	2	0.56
Carlin, NV (city) Elko County	13	0.55
Ellis Grove, IL (village) Randolph County	2	0.55
Bruno, MN (township) Pine County	1	0.54
Tyhee, ID (cdp) Bannock County	6	0.53
Ashland Heights, SD (cdp) Pennington County	4	0.53
Hoonah, AK (city) Hoonah-Angoon Census Area	4	0.53
Kickapoo Tribal Center, KS (cdp) Brown County	1	0.52
Meadow Acres, WY (cdp) Natrona County	1	0.51
Lone Pine, CA (cdp) Inyo County	10	0.49
Ballico, CA (cdp) Merced County	2	0.49
Bluewater Acres, NM (cdp) Cibola County	1	0.49
Little Browning, MT (cdp) Glacier County	1	0.49
Lovelock, NV (city) Pershing County	9	0.48
Onalaska, WA (cdp) Lewis County	3	0.48
Castalia, OH (village) Erie County	4	0.47
Rhinecliff, NY (cdp) Dutchess County	2	0.47
Independence, CA (cdp) Inyo County	3	0.45
Hobart, NY (village) Delaware County	2	0.45
Randlett, UT (cdp) Uintah County	1	0.45
Greenville, CA (cdp) Plumas County	5	0.44
Hanalei, HI (cdp) Kauai County	2	0.44
Fallon, NV (city) Churchill County	37	0.43
Sequoyah, OK (cdp) Rogers County	3	0.43
Shelter Cove, CA (cdp) Humboldt County	3	0.43
Nisland, SD (town) Butte County	1	0.43
Rupert, VT (town) Bennington County	3	0.42
McCrea, MN (township) Marshall County	1	0.41
Big Pine, CA (cdp) Inyo County	7	0.40
Sutcliffe, NV (cdp) Washoe County	1	0.40
Pomfret, MD (cdp) Charles County	2	0.39
Dix, NE (village) Kimball County	1	0.39
Lemmon Valley, NV (cdp) Washoe County	19	0.38
Deerwood, MN (township) Crow Wing County	5	0.38
Purple Sage, WY (cdp) Sweetwater County	2	0.37
Goldfield, NV (cdp) Esmeralda County	1	0.37
St. Ignatius, MT (town) Lake County	3	0.36
Trout Lake, WA (cdp) Klickitat County	2	0.36
Lanesville, IN (town) Harrison County	2	0.35
Myton, UT (city) Duchesne County	2	0.35
Williamsfield, IL (village) Knox County	2	0.35
Azure, MT (cdp) Hill County	1	0.35
Poston, AZ (cdp) La Paz County	1	0.35
Bishop, CA (city) Inyo County	13	0.34
Lame Deer, MT (cdp) Rosebud County	7	0.34
Iowa Colony, TX (village) Brazoria County	4	0.34
East Haven, VT (town) Essex County	1	0.34
Mehama, OR (cdp) Marion County	1	0.34
Blackfoot, ID (city) Bingham County	39	0.33
Jackpot, NV (cdp) Elko County	4	0.33
Arbon Valley, ID (cdp) Power County	2	0.33
Lawrence, NE (village) Nuckolls County	1	0.33
Muddy, MT (cdp) Big Horn County	2	0.32
Rosburg, WA (cdp) Wahkiakum County	1	0.32
Sun Valley, AZ (cdp) Navajo County	1	0.32
West Bishop, CA (cdp) Inyo County	8	0.31
Yates, NY (town) Orleans County	8	0.31
Crownpoint, NM (cdp) McKinley County	7	0.31
Second Mesa, AZ (cdp) Navajo County	3	0.31
Cañon, NM (cdp) Sandoval County	1	0.31
Evaro, MT (cdp) Missoula County	1	0.31
Spring Creek, NV (cdp) Elko County	37	0.30
Plymouth, CA (city) Amador County	3	0.30
Slaughter, LA (town) East Feliciana Parish	3	0.30
Eureka, UT (city) Juab County	2	0.30
Oljato-Monument Valley, UT (cdp) San Juan County	2	0.30
Newry, ME (town) Oxford County	1	0.30
Teton Village, WY (cdp) Teton County	1	0.30
Chubbuck, ID (city) Bannock County	40	0.29
Fort McDermitt, NV (cdp) Humboldt County	1	0.29
Parker School, MT (cdp) Hill County	1	0.29
Tonopah, NV (cdp) Nye County	7	0.28

Race

American Indian: Shoshone

Top 150 Places Sorted by Percent of Total Population

Based on places with total population of 7,500 or more

Place	Population	%
Riverton, WY (city) Fremont County	173	1.63
Elko, NV (city) Elko County	118	0.64
Fallon, NV (city) Churchill County	37	0.43
Blackfoot, ID (city) Bingham County	39	0.33
Spring Creek, NV (cdp) Elko County	37	0.30
Chubbuck, ID (city) Bannock County	40	0.29
Grantsville, UT (city) Tooele County	22	0.25
Brigham City, UT (city) Box Elder County	39	0.22
Vernal, UT (city) Uintah County	17	0.19
Jerome, ID (city) Jerome County	18	0.17
Pocatello, ID (city) Bannock County	89	0.16
Evanston, WY (city) Uinta County	17	0.14
Carson City, NV (ind. city) Carson City County	70	0.13
Sun Valley, NV (cdp) Washoe County	25	0.13
Gardnerville Ranchos, NV (cdp) Douglas County	15	0.13
Tremonton, UT (city) Box Elder County	10	0.13
Green River, WY (city) Sweetwater County	15	0.12
Tooele, UT (city) Tooele County	34	0.11
West Point, UT (city) Davis County	10	0.11
Dayton, NV (cdp) Lyon County	9	0.10
Casper, WY (city) Natrona County	48	0.09
Gillette, WY (city) Campbell County	25	0.09
South Salt Lake, UT (city) Salt Lake County	22	0.09
Reno, NV (city) Washoe County	169	0.08
Ogden, UT (city) Weber County	70	0.08
Sparks, NV (city) Washoe County	70	0.08
Valle Vista, CA (cdp) Riverside County	11	0.08
Coweta, OK (city) Wagoner County	8	0.08
West Haven, UT (city) Weber County	8	0.08
Yreka, CA (city) Siskiyou County	6	0.08
Cheyenne, WY (city) Laramie County	41	0.07
Twin Falls, ID (city) Twin Falls County	29	0.07
Laramie, WY (city) Albany County	22	0.07
Fernley, NV (city) Lyon County	14	0.07
Spanish Springs, NV (cdp) Washoe County	11	0.07
Burley, ID (city) Cassia County	7	0.07
Cold Springs, NV (cdp) Washoe County	6	0.07
Price, UT (city) Carbon County	6	0.07
Tuba City, AZ (cdp) Coconino County	6	0.07
Pahrump, NV (cdp) Nye County	21	0.06
Midvale, UT (city) Salt Lake County	18	0.06
New Kingman-Butler, AZ (cdp) Mohave County	7	0.06
Cloverdale, CA (city) Sonoma County	5	0.06
Makaha, HI (cdp) Honolulu County	5	0.06
West Valley City, UT (city) Salt Lake County	59	0.05
Idaho Falls, ID (city) Bonneville County	27	0.05
Kearns, UT (cdp) Salt Lake County	18	0.05
Rock Springs, WY (city) Sweetwater County	11	0.05
South Lake Tahoe, CA (city) El Dorado County	10	0.05
Clearlake, CA (city) Lake County	8	0.05
Kapolei, HI (cdp) Honolulu County	8	0.05
Fortuna, CA (city) Humboldt County	6	0.05
Grass Valley, CA (city) Nevada County	6	0.05
Columbia, PA (borough) Lancaster County	5	0.05
Firestone, CO (town) Weld County	5	0.05
Garden City, ID (city) Ada County	5	0.05
Weatherford, OK (city) Custer County	5	0.05
Woods Cross, UT (city) Davis County	5	0.05
Eagle Point, OR (city) Jackson County	4	0.05
Haiku-Pauwela, HI (cdp) Maui County	4	0.05
Rapid Valley, SD (cdp) Pennington County	4	0.05
Rodeo, CA (cdp) Contra Costa County	4	0.05
Salt Lake City, UT (city) Salt Lake County	72	0.04
North Highlands, CA (cdp) Sacramento County	15	0.04
Foothill Farms, CA (cdp) Sacramento County	13	0.04
Clearfield, UT (city) Davis County	12	0.04
Englewood, CO (city) Arapahoe County	11	0.04
Fortuna Foothills, AZ (cdp) Yuma County	10	0.04
Magna, UT (cdp) Salt Lake County	10	0.04
Ridgecrest, CA (city) Kern County	10	0.04
Gallup, NM (city) McKinley County	8	0.04
Rosemont, CA (cdp) Sacramento County	8	0.04
Ada, OK (city) Pontotoc County	6	0.04
Kerman, CA (city) Fresno County	6	0.04
Mountain Home, ID (city) Elmore County	6	0.04
Welby, CO (cdp) Adams County	6	0.04
Freeport, TX (city) Brazoria County	5	0.04
Halawa, HI (cdp) Honolulu County	5	0.04
Lemon Hill, CA (cdp) Sacramento County	5	0.04
Washington, PA (township) Franklin County	5	0.04
Camp Verde, AZ (town) Yavapai County	4	0.04
Cody, WY (city) Park County	4	0.04
East Renton Highlands, WA (cdp) King County	4	0.04
Exeter, NH (cdp) Rockingham County	4	0.04
Rawlins, WY (city) Carbon County	4	0.04
Snohomish, WA (city) Snohomish County	4	0.04
Fairwood, WA (cdp) Spokane County	3	0.04
Half Moon, NC (cdp) Onslow County	3	0.04
Live Oak, CA (city) Sutter County	3	0.04
Perryville, MO (city) Perry County	3	0.04
Poteau, OK (city) Le Flore County	3	0.04
Wasilla, AK (city) Matanuska-Susitna Borough	3	0.04
Boise City, ID (city) Ada County	53	0.03
Nampa, ID (city) Canyon County	26	0.03
Chico, CA (city) Butte County	23	0.03
Great Falls, MT (city) Cascade County	19	0.03
Murray, UT (city) Salt Lake County	16	0.03
Woodland, CA (city) Yolo County	14	0.03
Moorpark, CA (city) Ventura County	12	0.03
Morgan Hill, CA (city) Santa Clara County	12	0.03
Whitney, NV (cdp) Clark County	12	0.03
Roy, UT (city) Weber County	11	0.03
Santa Paula, CA (city) Ventura County	10	0.03
Hobbs, NM (city) Lea County	9	0.03
San Dimas, CA (city) Los Angeles County	9	0.03
Cedar City, UT (city) Iron County	8	0.03
Duncan, OK (city) Stephens County	8	0.03
Fountain, CO (city) El Paso County	8	0.03
Paradise, CA (town) Butte County	8	0.03
Imperial Beach, CA (city) San Diego County	7	0.03
Kihei, HI (cdp) Maui County	7	0.03
Post Falls, ID (city) Kootenai County	7	0.03
Cameron Park, CA (cdp) El Dorado County	6	0.03
Badger, AK (cdp) Fairbanks North Star Borough	5	0.03
Lebanon, OR (city) Linn County	5	0.03
Sheridan, WY (city) Sheridan County	5	0.03
Vincent, CA (cdp) Los Angeles County	5	0.03
Big Bear City, CA (cdp) San Bernardino County	4	0.03
East Greenwich, RI (town) Kent County	4	0.03
Exeter, NH (town) Rockingham County	4	0.03
Hayden, ID (city) Kootenai County	4	0.03
Pataskala, OH (city) Licking County	4	0.03
Waipio, HI (cdp) Honolulu County	4	0.03
Anderson, CA (city) Shasta County	3	0.03
Camp Pendleton South, CA (cdp) San Diego County	3	0.03
Cornelius, OR (city) Washington County	3	0.03
Grants, NM (city) Cibola County	3	0.03
Kalaoa, HI (cdp) Hawaii County	3	0.03
Larkfield-Wikiup, CA (cdp) Sonoma County	3	0.03
Pryor Creek, OK (city) Mayes County	3	0.03
Redlands, CO (cdp) Mesa County	3	0.03
Shasta Lake, CA (city) Shasta County	3	0.03
Silver City, NM (town) Grant County	3	0.03
Smithfield, UT (city) Cache County	3	0.03
Sweet Home, OR (city) Linn County	3	0.03
Warr Acres, OK (city) Oklahoma County	3	0.03
Garnet, CA (cdp) Riverside County	2	0.03
Kirtland, NM (cdp) San Juan County	2	0.03
Rhinebeck, NY (town) Dutchess County	2	0.03
North Las Vegas, NV (city) Clark County	42	0.02
Spokane, WA (city) Spokane County	35	0.02
Sunrise Manor, NV (cdp) Clark County	30	0.02
Lancaster, CA (city) Los Angeles County	25	0.02
Provo, UT (city) Utah County	23	0.02
Billings, MT (city) Yellowstone County	20	0.02
Sandy, UT (city) Salt Lake County	18	0.02
West Jordan, UT (city) Salt Lake County	18	0.02
Lawrence, KS (city) Douglas County	17	0.02
Apple Valley, CA (town) San Bernardino County	15	0.02
Citrus Heights, CA (city) Sacramento County	15	0.02

Please refer to the Explanation of Data in the front of the book for more detailed information.

Race

American Indian: Sioux

U.S. and 50 States Sorted by Population and Percent of Total Population

Place	Population	%
United States	**170,110**	**0.06**
South Dakota	61,582	7.56
California	12,439	0.03
North Dakota	11,210	1.67
Minnesota	8,691	0.16
Nebraska	6,259	0.34
Colorado	6,041	0.12
Washington	5,702	0.08
Texas	3,951	0.02
Oregon	3,823	0.10
Arizona	3,478	0.05
Iowa	2,725	0.09
Montana	2,698	0.27
Florida	2,480	0.01
Oklahoma	2,352	0.06
Illinois	2,270	0.02
Missouri	2,159	0.04
Ohio	2,069	0.02
New Mexico	1,885	0.09
Michigan	1,856	0.02
New York	1,758	0.01
Kansas	1,703	0.06
Pennsylvania	1,695	0.01
Wisconsin	1,615	0.03
Wyoming	1,408	0.25
Utah	1,384	0.05
Virginia	1,356	0.02
Indiana	1,340	0.02
Nevada	1,328	0.05
North Carolina	1,283	0.01
Idaho	1,093	0.07
Georgia	1,027	0.01
Tennessee	837	0.01
Maryland	819	0.01
Hawaii	777	0.06
New Jersey	769	0.01
Alaska	714	0.10
South Carolina	688	0.01
Massachusetts	649	0.01
Kentucky	625	0.01
Arkansas	609	0.02
Alabama	540	0.01
Louisiana	469	0.01
Connecticut	400	0.01
New Hampshire	294	0.02
Mississippi	287	0.01
West Virginia	262	0.01
Maine	239	0.02
Rhode Island	133	0.01
Delaware	131	0.01
Vermont	125	0.02
District of Columbia	83	0.01

Place	Population	%
South Dakota	61,582	7.56
North Dakota	11,210	1.67
Nebraska	6,259	0.34
Montana	2,698	0.27
Wyoming	1,408	0.25
Minnesota	8,691	0.16
Colorado	6,041	0.12
Oregon	3,823	0.10
Alaska	714	0.10
Iowa	2,725	0.09
New Mexico	1,885	0.09
Washington	5,702	0.08
Idaho	1,093	0.07
United States	**170,110**	**0.06**
Oklahoma	2,352	0.06
Kansas	1,703	0.06
Hawaii	777	0.06
Arizona	3,478	0.05
Utah	1,384	0.05
Nevada	1,328	0.05
Missouri	2,159	0.04
California	12,439	0.03
Wisconsin	1,615	0.03
Texas	3,951	0.02
Illinois	2,270	0.02
Ohio	2,069	0.02
Michigan	1,856	0.02
Virginia	1,356	0.02
Indiana	1,340	0.02
Arkansas	609	0.02
New Hampshire	294	0.02
Maine	239	0.02
Vermont	125	0.02
Florida	2,480	0.01
New York	1,758	0.01
Pennsylvania	1,695	0.01
North Carolina	1,283	0.01
Georgia	1,027	0.01
Tennessee	837	0.01
Maryland	819	0.01
New Jersey	769	0.01
South Carolina	688	0.01
Massachusetts	649	0.01
Kentucky	625	0.01
Alabama	540	0.01
Louisiana	469	0.01
Connecticut	400	0.01
Mississippi	287	0.01
West Virginia	262	0.01
Rhode Island	133	0.01
Delaware	131	0.01
District of Columbia	83	0.01

Please refer to the Explanation of Data in the front of the book for more detailed information.

Race

American Indian: Sioux

Top 150 Places Sorted by Population

Based on all places, regardless of total population

Place	Population	%
Rapid City, SD (city) Pennington County	6,605	9.72
Sioux Falls, SD (city) Minnehaha County	2,830	1.84
Pine Ridge, SD (cdp) Shannon County	2,802	84.70
North Eagle Butte, SD (cdp) Dewey County	1,713	87.67
Rosebud, SD (cdp) Todd County	1,438	90.61
Minneapolis, MN (city) Hennepin County	1,306	0.34
Bismarck, ND (city) Burleigh County	1,273	2.08
Denver, CO (city) Denver County	1,213	0.20
Oglala, SD (cdp) Shannon County	1,146	88.84
Eagle Butte, SD (city) Ziebach County	1,106	83.92
Fort Totten, ND (cdp) Benson County	1,092	87.85
Fort Thompson, SD (cdp) Buffalo County	1,029	80.27
Pierre, SD (city) Hughes County	1,001	7.34
Porcupine, SD (cdp) Shannon County	977	92.00
Mission, SD (city) Todd County	915	77.41
Sisseton, SD (city) Roberts County	898	36.36
Sioux City, IA (city) Woodbury County	887	1.07
St. Paul, MN (city) Ramsey County	807	0.28
Omaha, NE (city) Douglas County	793	0.19
Lincoln, NE (city) Lancaster County	790	0.31
Portland, OR (city) Multnomah County	786	0.13
Antelope, SD (cdp) Todd County	769	93.10
Cannon Ball, ND (cdp) Sioux County	746	85.26
Kyle, SD (cdp) Shannon County	737	87.12
Albuquerque, NM (city) Bernalillo County	726	0.13
Phoenix, AZ (city) Maricopa County	669	0.05
Wanblee, SD (cdp) Jackson County	662	91.31
Los Angeles, CA (city) Los Angeles County	661	0.02
Aberdeen, SD (city) Brown County	635	2.43
St. Francis, SD (town) Todd County	630	88.86
Wagner, SD (city) Charles Mix County	602	38.44
Devils Lake, ND (city) Ramsey County	600	8.40
Manderson-White Horse Creek, SD (cdp) Shannon County	553	88.34
Mobridge, SD (city) Walworth County	551	15.90
Martin, SD (city) Bennett County	543	50.70
Parmelee, SD (cdp) Todd County	528	93.95
Flandreau, SD (city) Moody County	519	22.17
New York, NY (city) Kings County	464	0.01
Seattle, WA (city) King County	462	0.08
Aurora, CO (city) Arapahoe County	454	0.14
Watertown, SD (city) Codington County	428	1.99
Goodwill, SD (cdp) Roberts County	416	81.09
Mandan, ND (city) Morton County	416	2.27
McLaughlin, SD (city) Corson County	408	61.54
Lower Brule, SD (cdp) Lyman County	396	64.60
Lake Andes, SD (city) Charles Mix County	386	43.91
Chicago, IL (city) Cook County	385	0.01
Allen, SD (cdp) Bennett County	384	91.43
Rapid Valley, SD (cdp) Pennington County	368	4.46
Fargo, ND (city) Cass County	361	0.34
Wounded Knee, SD (cdp) Shannon County	360	94.24
Marty, SD (cdp) Charles Mix County	354	88.06
Dupree, SD (city) Ziebach County	353	67.24
Prior Lake, MN (city) Scott County	350	1.54
Scottsbluff, NE (city) Scotts Bluff County	340	2.26
Billings, MT (city) Yellowstone County	340	0.33
Bullhead, SD (cdp) Corson County	335	96.26
Winner, SD (city) Tripp County	335	11.56
San Diego, CA (city) San Diego County	335	0.03
Colorado Springs, CO (city) El Paso County	330	0.08
Redwood Falls, MN (city) Redwood County	327	6.22
Hot Springs, SD (city) Fall River County	322	8.68
Alliance, NE (city) Box Butte County	319	3.76
Tucson, AZ (city) Pima County	318	0.06
Mitchell, SD (city) Davison County	313	2.05
San Jose, CA (city) Santa Clara County	313	0.03
Lakewood, CO (city) Jefferson County	312	0.22
Wichita, KS (city) Sedgwick County	312	0.08
Sacramento, CA (city) Sacramento County	302	0.06
Chamberlain, SD (city) Brule County	296	12.40
Vermillion, SD (city) Clay County	296	2.80
Spokane, WA (city) Spokane County	293	0.14
Little Eagle, SD (cdp) Corson County	292	91.54
Yankton, SD (city) Yankton County	289	2.00
Lawrence, KS (city) Douglas County	284	0.32
Santee, NE (village) Knox County	282	81.50
Box Elder, SD (city) Pennington County	279	3.58
Anchorage, AK (municipality) Anchorage Municipality	276	0.09
Oklahoma City, OK (city) Oklahoma County	271	0.05
Red Wing, MN (city) Goodhue County	270	1.64
Tulsa, OK (city) Tulsa County	266	0.07
Grand Forks, ND (city) Grand Forks County	262	0.50
Spring Creek, SD (cdp) Todd County	258	96.27
Chadron, NE (city) Dawes County	256	4.38
White River, SD (city) Mellette County	252	43.37
Gordon, NE (city) Sheridan County	252	15.63
San Francisco, CA (city) San Francisco County	251	0.03
White Horse, SD (cdp) Todd County	244	88.41
Tacoma, WA (city) Pierce County	240	0.12
Okreek, SD (cdp) Todd County	239	88.85
San Antonio, TX (city) Medina County	222	0.02
Soldier Creek, SD (cdp) Todd County	219	96.48
Salem, OR (city) Marion County	219	0.14
Kansas City, MO (city) Jackson County	218	0.05
Mesa, AZ (city) Maricopa County	218	0.05
Oakland, CA (city) Alameda County	213	0.05
Spearfish, SD (city) Lawrence County	212	2.02
Las Vegas, NV (city) Clark County	202	0.03
Valentine, NE (city) Cherry County	201	7.34
Indianapolis, IN (city) Marion County	201	0.02
Philadelphia, PA (city) Philadelphia County	199	0.01
Des Moines, IA (city) Polk County	195	0.10
Springfield, SD (city) Bon Homme County	194	9.75
Thornton, CO (city) Adams County	188	0.16
Brookings, SD (city) Brookings County	187	0.85
Timber Lake, SD (city) Dewey County	186	41.99
Stockton, CA (city) San Joaquin County	185	0.06
Two Strike, SD (cdp) Todd County	184	88.04
Houston, TX (city) Harris County	184	0.01
Shakopee, MN (city) Scott County	182	0.49
Columbus, OH (city) Franklin County	182	0.02
Sherman, MN (township) Redwood County	175	47.30
Dallas, TX (city) Dallas County	175	0.01
Eugene, OR (city) Lane County	173	0.11
Paxton, MN (township) Redwood County	172	30.99
Long Beach, CA (city) Los Angeles County	166	0.04
Milwaukee, WI (city) Milwaukee County	166	0.03
Fort Worth, TX (city) Tarrant County	165	0.02
Cheyenne, WY (city) Laramie County	163	0.27
Arvada, CO (city) Jefferson County	160	0.15
Fort Collins, CO (city) Larimer County	158	0.11
Westminster, CO (city) Adams County	156	0.15
Waubay, SD (city) Day County	153	26.56
Gillette, WY (city) Campbell County	153	0.53
Fort Yates, ND (city) Sioux County	152	82.61
Rushville, NE (city) Sheridan County	152	17.08
Minot, ND (city) Ward County	151	0.37
Wolf Point, MT (city) Roosevelt County	150	5.72
La Plant, SD (cdp) Dewey County	149	87.13
Agency Village, SD (cdp) Roberts County	149	82.32
Fresno, CA (city) Fresno County	149	0.03
Vancouver, WA (city) Clark County	148	0.09
Grand Island, NE (city) Hall County	147	0.30
Pueblo, CO (city) Pueblo County	147	0.14
Jacksonville, FL (city) Duval County	146	0.02
Norfolk, NE (city) Madison County	143	0.59
Boise City, ID (city) Ada County	143	0.07
Urban Honolulu, HI (cdp) Honolulu County	142	0.04
Minnesota Falls, MN (township) Yellow Medicine County	141	32.87
Fort Pierre, SD (city) Stanley County	140	6.74
Greeley, CO (city) Weld County	140	0.15
Reno, NV (city) Washoe County	134	0.06
Porcupine, ND (cdp) Sioux County	133	91.10
Manhattan, NY (borough) New York County	133	0.01
Everett, WA (city) Snohomish County	132	0.13
Tempe, AZ (city) Maricopa County	130	0.08
Whitehorse, SD (cdp) Dewey County	129	91.49
Moorhead, MN (city) Clay County	124	0.33
Austin, TX (city) Travis County	124	0.02
Belle Fourche, SD (city) Butte County	122	2.18

SECTION THREE

Please refer to the Explanation of Data in the front of the book for more detailed information.

Race

American Indian: Sioux

Top 150 Places Sorted by Percent of Total Population

Based on all places, regardless of total population

Place	Population	%
Soldier Creek, SD (cdp) Todd County	219	96.48
Spring Creek, SD (cdp) Todd County	258	96.27
Bullhead, SD (cdp) Corson County	335	96.26
Batesland, SD (town) Shannon County	102	94.44
Corn Creek, SD (cdp) Mellette County	99	94.29
Wounded Knee, SD (cdp) Shannon County	360	94.24
Parmelee, SD (cdp) Todd County	528	93.95
Antelope, SD (cdp) Todd County	769	93.10
Porcupine, SD (cdp) Shannon County	977	92.00
Little Eagle, SD (cdp) Corson County	292	91.54
Whitehorse, SD (cdp) Dewey County	129	91.49
Allen, SD (cdp) Bennett County	384	91.43
Green Grass, SD (cdp) Dewey County	32	91.43
Wanblee, SD (cdp) Jackson County	662	91.31
Porcupine, ND (cdp) Sioux County	133	91.10
Rosebud, SD (cdp) Todd County	1,438	90.61
St. Francis, SD (town) Todd County	630	88.86
Okreek, SD (cdp) Todd County	239	88.85
Oglala, SD (cdp) Shannon County	1,146	88.84
White Horse, SD (cdp) Todd County	244	88.41
Manderson-White Horse Creek, SD (cdp) Shannon County	553	88.34
Marty, SD (cdp) Charles Mix County	354	88.06
Two Strike, SD (cdp) Todd County	184	88.04
Fort Totten, ND (cdp) Benson County	1,092	87.85
North Eagle Butte, SD (cdp) Dewey County	1,713	87.67
La Plant, SD (cdp) Dewey County	149	87.13
Kyle, SD (cdp) Shannon County	737	87.12
Cannon Ball, ND (cdp) Sioux County	746	85.26
Pine Ridge, SD (cdp) Shannon County	2,802	84.70
Eagle Butte, SD (city) Ziebach County	1,106	83.92
Fort Yates, ND (city) Sioux County	152	82.61
Agency Village, SD (cdp) Roberts County	149	82.32
Santee, NE (village) Knox County	282	81.50
Goodwill, SD (cdp) Roberts County	416	81.09
Fort Thompson, SD (cdp) Buffalo County	1,029	80.27
Mission, SD (city) Todd County	915	77.41
Norris, SD (cdp) Mellette County	107	70.39
Dupree, SD (city) Ziebach County	353	67.24
Lower Brule, SD (cdp) Lyman County	396	64.60
Ravinia, SD (town) Charles Mix County	38	62.30
McLaughlin, SD (city) Corson County	408	61.54
Selfridge, ND (city) Sioux County	90	56.25
Martin, SD (city) Bennett County	543	50.70
Long Hollow, SD (cdp) Roberts County	91	47.40
Sherman, MN (township) Redwood County	175	47.30
Solen, ND (city) Sioux County	37	44.58
Lake Andes, SD (city) Charles Mix County	386	43.91
White River, SD (city) Mellette County	252	43.37
Timber Lake, SD (city) Dewey County	186	41.99
Peever, SD (town) Roberts County	69	41.07
Wagner, SD (city) Charles Mix County	602	38.44
Sisseton, SD (city) Roberts County	898	36.36
Minnesota Falls, MN (township) Yellow Medicine County	141	32.87
Paxton, MN (township) Redwood County	172	30.99
Warwick, ND (city) Benson County	19	29.23
New Effington, SD (town) Roberts County	74	28.91
Oberon, ND (city) Benson County	28	26.67
Waubay, SD (city) Day County	153	26.56
Isabel, SD (town) Dewey County	32	23.70
Midway, MN (cdp) Mahnomen County	6	23.08
Wood, SD (town) Mellette County	14	22.58
Flandreau, SD (city) Moody County	519	22.17
Bonesteel, SD (city) Gregory County	55	20.00
Summit, SD (town) Roberts County	55	19.10
McIntosh, SD (city) Corson County	32	18.50
St. Charles, SD (cdp) Gregory County	2	18.18
Interior, SD (town) Jackson County	17	18.09
Reliance, SD (town) Lyman County	34	17.80
Rushville, NE (city) Sheridan County	152	17.08
Oelrichs, SD (town) Fall River County	21	16.67
Lowry, SD (town) Walworth County	1	16.67
Mobridge, SD (city) Walworth County	551	15.90
Gordon, NE (city) Sheridan County	252	15.63
Belvidere, SD (town) Jackson County	7	14.29
Pukwana, SD (town) Brule County	39	13.68
Kadoka, SD (city) Jackson County	86	13.15
Dante, SD (town) Charles Mix County	11	13.10
York, ND (city) Benson County	3	13.04
Kilgore, NE (village) Cherry County	10	12.99
Browns Valley, MN (city) Traverse County	74	12.56
Chamberlain, SD (city) Brule County	296	12.40
Claire City, SD (town) Roberts County	9	11.84
Winner, SD (city) Tripp County	335	11.56
Nutrioso, AZ (cdp) Apache County	3	11.54
Cottonwood, SD (town) Jackson County	1	11.11
Ortley, SD (town) Roberts County	7	10.77
Veblen, SD (city) Marshall County	56	10.55
Minnewaukan, ND (city) Benson County	23	10.27
Delmont, SD (city) Douglas County	24	10.26
Springfield, SD (city) Bon Homme County	194	9.75
Rapid City, SD (city) Pennington County	6,605	9.72
Picks, SD (town) Charles Mix County	19	9.45
Wall, SD (town) Pennington County	71	9.27
Kennebec, SD (town) Lyman County	21	8.75
Hot Springs, SD (city) Fall River County	322	8.68
Marsh Creek, MN (township) Mahnomen County	13	8.55
St. Xavier, MT (cdp) Big Horn County	7	8.43
Devils Lake, ND (city) Ramsey County	600	8.40
Raleigh, ND (cdp) Grant County	1	8.33
White Shield, ND (cdp) McLean County	27	8.04
Wilmot, SD (city) Roberts County	39	7.93
Kicking Horse, MT (cdp) Lake County	22	7.69
Lindy, NE (cdp) Knox County	1	7.69
Niobrara, NE (village) Knox County	28	7.57
Hermosa, SD (town) Custer County	30	7.54
Otranto, IA (cdp) Mitchell County	2	7.41
Pierre, SD (city) Hughes County	1,001	7.34
Valentine, NE (city) Cherry County	201	7.34
Gann Valley, SD (cdp) Buffalo County	1	7.14
Mandaree, ND (cdp) McKenzie County	41	6.88
Gregory, SD (city) Gregory County	88	6.80
Fort Pierre, SD (city) Stanley County	140	6.74
New Underwood, SD (city) Pennington County	43	6.52
Oacoma, SD (town) Lyman County	29	6.43
Sheyenne, ND (city) Eddy County	13	6.37
Buffalo Gap, SD (town) Custer County	8	6.35
Winnebago, NE (village) Thurston County	49	6.33
Merriman, NE (village) Cherry County	8	6.25
Mantador, ND (city) Richland County	4	6.25
Ward, SD (town) Moody County	3	6.25
Redwood Falls, MN (city) Redwood County	327	6.22
Java, SD (town) Walworth County	8	6.20
Hunnewell, KS (city) Sumner County	4	5.97
Kickapoo Site 2, KS (cdp) Brown County	2	5.88
Marvin, SD (town) Grant County	2	5.88
Welch, MN (township) Goodhue County	44	5.84
Crookston, NE (village) Cherry County	4	5.80
Wolf Point, MT (city) Roosevelt County	150	5.72
Green Valley, SD (cdp) Pennington County	52	5.60
Stockholm, SD (town) Grant County	6	5.56
Granite Falls, MN (city) Chippewa County	46	5.39
Johnstown, WY (cdp) Fremont County	13	5.37
Center, NE (village) Knox County	5	5.32
Willis, KS (city) Brown County	2	5.26
Ashland Heights, SD (cdp) Pennington County	39	5.17
Brook Lake, MN (unorganized territory) Beltrami County	12	5.15
Morton, MN (city) Renville County	21	5.11
Hay Springs, NE (village) Sheridan County	29	5.09
Egan, SD (city) Moody County	14	5.04
Walthill, NE (village) Thurston County	39	5.00
Dallas, SD (town) Gregory County	6	5.00
Burke, SD (city) Gregory County	29	4.80
Herrick, SD (town) Gregory County	5	4.76
Colome, SD (city) Tripp County	14	4.73
Squaw Lake, MN (city) Itasca County	5	4.67
Darwin, CA (cdp) Inyo County	2	4.65
Long Lost Lake, MN (township) Clearwater County	2	4.65
Richfield, NE (cdp) Sarpy County	2	4.65
Poplar, MT (city) Roosevelt County	37	4.57
Beaverdam, NV (cdp) Lincoln County	2	4.55

Please refer to the Explanation of Data in the front of the book for more detailed information.

Race

American Indian: Sioux

Top 150 Places Sorted by Percent of Total Population

Based on places with total population of 7,500 or more

Place	Population	%
Rapid City, SD (city) Pennington County	6,605	9.72
Pierre, SD (city) Hughes County	1,001	7.34
Rapid Valley, SD (cdp) Pennington County	368	4.46
Alliance, NE (city) Box Butte County	319	3.76
Box Elder, SD (city) Pennington County	279	3.58
Vermillion, SD (city) Clay County	296	2.80
Aberdeen, SD (city) Brown County	635	2.43
Mandan, ND (city) Morton County	416	2.27
Scottsbluff, NE (city) Scotts Bluff County	340	2.26
Bismarck, ND (city) Burleigh County	1,273	2.08
Mitchell, SD (city) Davison County	313	2.05
Spearfish, SD (city) Lawrence County	212	2.02
Yankton, SD (city) Yankton County	289	2.00
Watertown, SD (city) Codington County	428	1.99
Sioux Falls, SD (city) Minnehaha County	2,830	1.84
Red Wing, MN (city) Goodhue County	270	1.64
Prior Lake, MN (city) Scott County	350	1.54
Gering, NE (city) Scotts Bluff County	96	1.13
Sioux City, IA (city) Woodbury County	887	1.07
Huron, SD (city) Beadle County	117	0.93
Wahpeton, ND (city) Richland County	70	0.90
Brookings, SD (city) Brookings County	187	0.85
South Sioux City, NE (city) Dakota County	113	0.85
Norfolk, NE (city) Madison County	143	0.59
Jamestown, ND (city) Stutsman County	90	0.58
Riverton, WY (city) Fremont County	57	0.54
Gillette, WY (city) Campbell County	153	0.53
Grand Forks, ND (city) Grand Forks County	262	0.50
Shakopee, MN (city) Scott County	182	0.49
Williston, ND (city) Williams County	71	0.48
Brandon, SD (city) Minnehaha County	42	0.48
Bemidji, MN (city) Beltrami County	62	0.46
Havre, MT (city) Hill County	37	0.40
Minot, ND (city) Ward County	151	0.37
Berkley, CO (cdp) Adams County	40	0.36
Minneapolis, MN (city) Hennepin County	1,306	0.34
Fargo, ND (city) Cass County	361	0.34
East Grand Forks, MN (city) Polk County	29	0.34
Billings, MT (city) Yellowstone County	340	0.33
Moorhead, MN (city) Clay County	124	0.33
West St. Paul, MN (city) Dakota County	64	0.33
Dickinson, ND (city) Stark County	58	0.33
Lawrence, KS (city) Douglas County	284	0.32
Welby, CO (cdp) Adams County	48	0.32
Kirtland, NM (cdp) San Juan County	25	0.32
Lincoln, NE (city) Lancaster County	790	0.31
Cimarron Hills, CO (cdp) El Paso County	50	0.31
Grand Island, NE (city) Hall County	147	0.30
Helena, MT (city) Lewis and Clark County	82	0.29
Miles City, MT (city) Custer County	24	0.29
McCook, NE (city) Red Willow County	22	0.29
St. Paul, MN (city) Ramsey County	807	0.28
North Platte, NE (city) Lincoln County	69	0.28
Waller, WA (cdp) Pierce County	22	0.28
Cheyenne, WY (city) Laramie County	163	0.27
West Fargo, ND (city) Cass County	68	0.26
Sherrelwood, CO (cdp) Adams County	48	0.26
Beatrice, NE (city) Gage County	32	0.26
Waseca, MN (city) Waseca County	24	0.26
Sheridan, WY (city) Sheridan County	44	0.25
Kelso, WA (city) Cowlitz County	30	0.25
Sitka, AK (borough) Sitka City and Borough	22	0.25
Shiprock, NM (cdp) San Juan County	21	0.25
Crookston, MN (city) Polk County	20	0.25
Chubbuck, ID (city) Bannock County	33	0.24
Cushing, OK (city) Payne County	19	0.24
Fremont, NE (city) Dodge County	61	0.23
Lakewood, CO (city) Jefferson County	312	0.22
Fernley, NV (city) Lyon County	43	0.22
Vadnais Heights, MN (city) Ramsey County	27	0.22
Rawlins, WY (city) Carbon County	20	0.22
Detroit Lakes, MN (city) Becker County	19	0.22
Wasilla, AK (city) Matanuska-Susitna Borough	17	0.22
Shasta Lake, CA (city) Shasta County	21	0.21
Cody, WY (city) Park County	20	0.21
Santaquin, UT (city) Utah County	19	0.21
Denver, CO (city) Denver County	1,213	0.20
Bremerton, WA (city) Kitsap County	74	0.20
Brighton, CO (city) Adams County	68	0.20
Kearney, NE (city) Buffalo County	61	0.20
St. Helens, OR (city) Columbia County	26	0.20
Lexington, NE (city) Dawson County	20	0.20
Omaha, NE (city) Douglas County	793	0.19
Bellevue, NE (city) Sarpy County	96	0.19
Cottage Grove, MN (city) Washington County	65	0.19
Roseville, MN (city) Ramsey County	65	0.19
Evans, CO (city) Weld County	36	0.19
Sterling, CO (city) Logan County	28	0.19
Harrison, AR (city) Boone County	24	0.19
Fort Morgan, CO (city) Morgan County	22	0.19
Le Mars, IA (city) Plymouth County	19	0.19
Hermantown, MN (city) St. Louis County	18	0.19
Florence, OR (city) Lane County	16	0.19
Missoula, MT (city) Missoula County	120	0.18
Great Falls, MT (city) Cascade County	105	0.18
Wheat Ridge, CO (city) Jefferson County	54	0.18
Hastings, NE (city) Adams County	45	0.18
Durango, CO (city) La Plata County	31	0.18
El Reno, OK (city) Canadian County	30	0.18
Pendleton, OR (city) Umatilla County	30	0.18
Spring Lake, NC (town) Cumberland County	22	0.18
White Bear, MN (township) Ramsey County	20	0.18
Fox Lake, IL (village) Lake County	19	0.18
Prineville, OR (city) Crook County	17	0.18
Winslow, AZ (city) Navajo County	17	0.18
Bloomfield, NM (city) San Juan County	15	0.18
Makaha, HI (cdp) Honolulu County	15	0.18
Casper, WY (city) Natrona County	92	0.17
Maplewood, MN (city) Ramsey County	64	0.17
Englewood, CO (city) Arapahoe County	52	0.17
Kalispell, MT (city) Flathead County	33	0.17
Escanaba, MI (city) Delta County	21	0.17
Federal Heights, CO (city) Adams County	19	0.17
Anaconda-Deer Lodge County, MT (special city) Deer Lodge County	16	0.17
Fallon, NV (city) Churchill County	15	0.17
Tuba City, AZ (cdp) Coconino County	15	0.17
Thornton, CO (city) Adams County	188	0.16
Commerce City, CO (city) Adams County	75	0.16
Farmington, NM (city) San Juan County	73	0.16
Bozeman, MT (city) Gallatin County	61	0.16
Keizer, OR (city) Marion County	57	0.16
Gallup, NM (city) McKinley County	34	0.16
Moses Lake, WA (city) Grant County	32	0.16
Mountlake Terrace, WA (city) Snohomish County	31	0.16
Willmar, MN (city) Kandiyohi County	31	0.16
Golden, CO (city) Jefferson County	30	0.16
Dallas, OR (city) Polk County	23	0.16
Mountain Home, ID (city) Elmore County	23	0.16
Waianae, HI (cdp) Honolulu County	21	0.16
Chalco, NE (cdp) Sarpy County	18	0.16
Fort Lewis, WA (cdp) Pierce County	18	0.16
Gardnerville Ranchos, NV (cdp) Douglas County	18	0.16
North St. Paul, MN (city) Ramsey County	18	0.16
Show Low, AZ (city) Navajo County	17	0.16
Thief River Falls, MN (city) Pennington County	14	0.16
Arvada, CO (city) Jefferson County	160	0.15
Westminster, CO (city) Adams County	156	0.15
Greeley, CO (city) Weld County	140	0.15
Council Bluffs, IA (city) Pottawattamie County	93	0.15
St. Louis Park, MN (city) Hennepin County	68	0.15
Northglenn, CO (city) Adams County	52	0.15
Eureka, CA (city) Humboldt County	41	0.15
Fridley, MN (city) Anoka County	41	0.15
Ponca City, OK (city) Kay County	38	0.15
Oak Harbor, WA (city) Island County	33	0.15
Farmington, MN (city) Dakota County	32	0.15
Roseburg, OR (city) Douglas County	32	0.15
Hayesville, OR (cdp) Marion County	30	0.15
Claremore, OK (city) Rogers County	27	0.15
Evanston, WY (city) Uinta County	18	0.15

SECTION THREE

Race

American Indian: South American Indian

U.S. and 50 States Sorted by Population and Percent of Total Population

Place	Population	%
United States	**47,233**	**0.02**
New York	13,078	0.07
Florida	5,238	0.03
New Jersey	4,232	0.05
California	4,121	0.01
Pennsylvania	2,122	0.02
Massachusetts	1,747	0.03
Connecticut	1,666	0.05
Texas	1,644	0.01
Virginia	1,526	0.02
Illinois	1,402	0.01
Maryland	1,325	0.02
Georgia	872	0.01
North Carolina	783	0.01
Ohio	650	0.01
Washington	489	0.01
Colorado	437	0.01
Arizona	411	0.01
Wisconsin	406	0.01
Minnesota	390	0.01
Rhode Island	378	0.04
Michigan	348	<0.01
Utah	340	0.01
Oregon	310	0.01
Indiana	257	<0.01
Hawaii	240	0.02
Tennessee	238	<0.01
Nevada	233	0.01
Missouri	226	<0.01
South Carolina	186	<0.01
Oklahoma	167	<0.01
Delaware	162	0.02
District of Columbia	154	0.03
New Mexico	151	0.01
Kansas	136	<0.01
Alabama	125	<0.01
Louisiana	122	<0.01
Kentucky	115	<0.01
Iowa	100	<0.01
Idaho	97	0.01
Alaska	93	0.01
New Hampshire	84	0.01
Nebraska	80	<0.01
Arkansas	61	<0.01
Vermont	56	0.01
Maine	56	<0.01
West Virginia	48	<0.01
Mississippi	47	<0.01
Wyoming	31	0.01
Montana	28	<0.01
South Dakota	19	<0.01
North Dakota	6	<0.01

Place	Population	%
New York	13,078	0.07
New Jersey	4,232	0.05
Connecticut	1,666	0.05
Rhode Island	378	0.04
Florida	5,238	0.03
Massachusetts	1,747	0.03
District of Columbia	154	0.03
United States	**47,233**	**0.02**
Pennsylvania	2,122	0.02
Virginia	1,526	0.02
Maryland	1,325	0.02
Hawaii	240	0.02
Delaware	162	0.02
California	4,121	0.01
Texas	1,644	0.01
Illinois	1,402	0.01
Georgia	872	0.01
North Carolina	783	0.01
Ohio	650	0.01
Washington	489	0.01
Colorado	437	0.01
Arizona	411	0.01
Wisconsin	406	0.01
Minnesota	390	0.01
Utah	340	0.01
Oregon	310	0.01
Nevada	233	0.01
New Mexico	151	0.01
Idaho	97	0.01
Alaska	93	0.01
New Hampshire	84	0.01
Vermont	56	0.01
Wyoming	31	0.01
Michigan	348	<0.01
Indiana	257	<0.01
Tennessee	238	<0.01
Missouri	226	<0.01
South Carolina	186	<0.01
Oklahoma	167	<0.01
Kansas	136	<0.01
Alabama	125	<0.01
Louisiana	122	<0.01
Kentucky	115	<0.01
Iowa	100	<0.01
Nebraska	80	<0.01
Arkansas	61	<0.01
Maine	56	<0.01
West Virginia	48	<0.01
Mississippi	47	<0.01
Montana	28	<0.01
South Dakota	19	<0.01
North Dakota	6	<0.01

Please refer to the Explanation of Data in the front of the book for more detailed information.

Race

American Indian: South American Indian

Top 150 Places Sorted by Population

Based on all places, regardless of total population

Place	Population	%
New York, NY (city) Kings County	9,464	0.12
Bronx, NY (borough) Bronx County	2,938	0.21
Queens, NY (borough) Queens County	2,448	0.11
Manhattan, NY (borough) New York County	1,935	0.12
Brooklyn, NY (borough) Kings County	1,855	0.07
Chicago, IL (city) Cook County	743	0.03
Philadelphia, PA (city) Philadelphia County	657	0.04
Los Angeles, CA (city) Los Angeles County	595	0.02
Boston, MA (city) Suffolk County	301	0.05
Hempstead, NY (town) Nassau County	294	0.04
Staten Island, NY (borough) Richmond County	288	0.06
Yonkers, NY (city) Westchester County	270	0.14
Islip, NY (town) Suffolk County	249	0.07
Newark, NJ (city) Essex County	230	0.08
Jersey City, NJ (city) Hudson County	228	0.09
Providence, RI (city) Providence County	225	0.13
Paterson, NJ (city) Passaic County	208	0.14
Houston, TX (city) Harris County	206	0.01
San Francisco, CA (city) San Francisco County	198	0.02
Elizabeth, NJ (city) Union County	197	0.16
Springfield, MA (city) Hampden County	196	0.13
Hartford, CT (city/town) Hartford County	194	0.16
Orlando, FL (city) Orange County	166	0.07
Tampa, FL (city) Hillsborough County	166	0.05
Arlington, VA (cdp) Arlington County	156	0.08
Washington, DC (city) District of Columbia	154	0.03
Miami, FL (city) Miami-Dade County	147	0.04
Bridgeport, CT (city/town) Fairfield County	146	0.10
Rochester, NY (city) Monroe County	144	0.07
Jacksonville, FL (city) Duval County	144	0.02
Milwaukee, WI (city) Milwaukee County	141	0.02
Brookhaven, NY (town) Suffolk County	136	0.03
Allentown, PA (city) Lehigh County	135	0.11
Oakland, CA (city) Alameda County	134	0.03
San Jose, CA (city) Santa Clara County	133	0.01
Union City, NJ (city) Hudson County	129	0.19
San Antonio, TX (city) Medina County	122	0.01
White Plains, NY (city) Westchester County	116	0.20
Austin, TX (city) Travis County	114	0.01
Passaic, NJ (city) Passaic County	113	0.16
Lawrence, MA (city) Essex County	113	0.15
Perth Amboy, NJ (city) Middlesex County	112	0.22
Kearny, NJ (town) Hudson County	111	0.27
New Haven, CT (city/town) New Haven County	108	0.08
San Diego, CA (city) San Diego County	106	0.01
Cleveland, OH (city) Cuyahoga County	105	0.03
Seattle, WA (city) King County	103	0.02
Poinciana, FL (cdp) Osceola County	94	0.18
Fayetteville, NC (city) Cumberland County	94	0.05
Minneapolis, MN (city) Hennepin County	92	0.02
Waterbury, CT (city/town) New Haven County	88	0.08
Charlotte, NC (city) Mecklenburg County	88	0.01
Brentwood, NY (cdp) Suffolk County	87	0.14
Trenton, NJ (city) Mercer County	86	0.10
Dallas, TX (city) Dallas County	86	0.01
Clifton, NJ (city) Passaic County	83	0.10
Babylon, NY (town) Suffolk County	82	0.04
West New York, NJ (town) Hudson County	80	0.16
Lorain, OH (city) Lorain County	79	0.12
North Hempstead, NY (town) Nassau County	79	0.03
Aurora, CO (city) Arapahoe County	79	0.02
Stamford, CT (city/town) Fairfield County	78	0.06
Lancaster, PA (city) Lancaster County	77	0.13
Long Beach, CA (city) Los Angeles County	77	0.02
Kissimmee, FL (city) Osceola County	76	0.13
Germantown, MD (cdp) Montgomery County	76	0.09
Virginia Beach, VA (ind. city) Virginia Beach independent city	76	0.02
Baltimore, MD (city) Baltimore city County	76	0.01
Deltona, FL (city) Volusia County	75	0.09
Hollywood, FL (city) Broward County	75	0.05
Pembroke Pines, FL (city) Broward County	75	0.05
Camden, NJ (city) Camden County	74	0.10
Reading, PA (city) Berks County	74	0.08
North Bergen, NJ (township) Hudson County	73	0.12
Bethlehem, PA (city) Northampton County	73	0.10
Greenburgh, NY (town) Westchester County	72	0.08
Denver, CO (city) Denver County	72	0.01
Portland, OR (city) Multnomah County	72	0.01
Haverstraw, NY (town) Rockland County	71	0.19
Silver Spring, MD (cdp) Montgomery County	69	0.10
Port St. Lucie, FL (city) St. Lucie County	69	0.04
Huntington, NY (town) Suffolk County	69	0.03
Ramapo, NY (town) Rockland County	68	0.05
Holyoke, MA (city) Hampden County	67	0.17
Vineland, NJ (city) Cumberland County	67	0.11
West Hartford, CT (cdp/town) Hartford County	67	0.11
New Britain, CT (city/town) Hartford County	67	0.09
Worcester, MA (city) Worcester County	67	0.04
Albuquerque, NM (city) Bernalillo County	67	0.01
Phoenix, AZ (city) Maricopa County	67	<0.01
Woodbridge, NJ (township) Middlesex County	66	0.07
Alafaya, FL (cdp) Orange County	63	0.08
Miami Beach, FL (city) Miami-Dade County	62	0.07
Buffalo, NY (city) Erie County	60	0.02
Nashville-Davidson, TN (metro govt) Davidson County	60	0.01
Sunrise, FL (city) Broward County	59	0.07
New London, CT (city/town) New London County	58	0.21
Hackensack, NJ (city) Bergen County	58	0.13
Town 'n' Country, FL (cdp) Hillsborough County	58	0.07
Miramar, FL (city) Broward County	58	0.05
Gaithersburg, MD (city) Montgomery County	57	0.10
Killeen, TX (city) Bell County	57	0.04
Oyster Bay, NY (town) Nassau County	57	0.02
Aspen Hill, MD (cdp) Montgomery County	56	0.11
New Rochelle, NY (city) Westchester County	56	0.07
Bethlehem, PA (city) Northampton County	54	0.10
Cape Coral, FL (city) Lee County	52	0.03
Madison, WI (city) Dane County	52	0.02
Fort Worth, TX (city) Tarrant County	52	0.01
Rye, NY (town) Westchester County	51	0.11
Columbus, OH (city) Franklin County	51	0.01
Newburgh, NY (city) Orange County	50	0.17
Lowell, MA (city) Middlesex County	50	0.05
Urban Honolulu, HI (cdp) Honolulu County	50	0.01
Central Islip, NY (cdp) Suffolk County	49	0.14
Bayonne, NJ (city) Hudson County	49	0.08
Albany, NY (city) Albany County	49	0.05
Syracuse, NY (city) Onondaga County	49	0.03
Tucson, AZ (city) Pima County	49	0.01
Ossining, NY (town) Westchester County	48	0.13
Hialeah, FL (city) Miami-Dade County	48	0.02
Altamonte Springs, FL (city) Seminole County	47	0.11
Annandale, VA (cdp) Fairfax County	47	0.11
Davie, FL (town) Broward County	47	0.05
Berkeley, CA (city) Alameda County	47	0.04
New Brunswick, NJ (city) Middlesex County	46	0.08
Dale City, VA (cdp) Prince William County	46	0.07
Brandon, FL (cdp) Hillsborough County	46	0.04
Cambridge, MA (city) Middlesex County	46	0.04
Gainesville, FL (city) Alachua County	46	0.04
Raleigh, NC (city) Wake County	46	0.01
Wheaton, MD (cdp) Montgomery County	45	0.09
Greenwich, CT (town) Fairfield County	45	0.07
Rockville, MD (city) Montgomery County	45	0.07
Atlanta, GA (city) Fulton County	45	0.01
Riverside, CA (city) Riverside County	45	0.01
Danbury, CT (city/town) Fairfield County	44	0.05
Coral Springs, FL (city) Broward County	44	0.04
Palm Bay, FL (city) Brevard County	44	0.04
Newport News, VA (ind. city) Newport News independent city	44	0.02
Las Vegas, NV (city) Clark County	44	0.01
Port Chester, NY (village) Westchester County	43	0.15
Groton, CT (town) New London County	43	0.11
Franklin, NJ (township) Somerset County	43	0.07
Sacramento, CA (city) Sacramento County	43	0.01
Middletown, NY (city) Orange County	42	0.15
Anchorage, AK (municipality) Anchorage Municipality	42	0.01
Lehigh Acres, FL (cdp) Lee County	41	0.05
Columbia, MD (cdp) Howard County	41	0.04
Norfolk, VA (ind. city) Norfolk independent city	41	0.02

Race

American Indian: South American Indian

Top 150 Places Sorted by Percent of Total Population

Based on all places, regardless of total population

Place	Population	%
St. Joseph, IA (cdp) Kossuth County	3	4.92
Aniak, AK (city) Bethel Census Area	16	3.19
Kickapoo Site 7, KS (cdp) Brown County	2	3.03
Onondaga Nation Reservation, NY (reservation) Onondaga County	9	1.92
El Nido, CA (cdp) Merced County	6	1.82
Cattaraugus Reservation, NY (reservation) Cattaraugus County	5	1.59
Kickapoo Site 5, KS (cdp) Brown County	1	1.52
Plainfield, WI (town) Waushara County	7	1.27
Blyn, WA (cdp) Clallam County	1	0.99
Agency, IA (city) Wapello County	6	0.94
Castle, OK (town) Okfuskee County	1	0.94
Siletz, OR (city) Lincoln County	11	0.91
Jeromesville, OH (village) Ashland County	5	0.89
Allegany Reservation, NY (reservation) Cattaraugus County	9	0.88
Fort McDermitt, NV (cdp) Humboldt County	3	0.88
Quinton, NJ (cdp) Salem County	5	0.85
Shinnecock Hills, NY (cdp) Suffolk County	18	0.82
Popple Grove, MN (township) Mahnomen County	1	0.72
Crary, ND (city) Ramsey County	1	0.70
Sunbury, NC (cdp) Gates County	2	0.69
Ridgway, CO (town) Ouray County	6	0.65
Poospatuck Reservation, NY (reservation) Suffolk County	2	0.62
Alburg, VT (village) Grand Isle County	3	0.60
Josephville, MO (village) St. Charles County	2	0.53
Saw Creek, PA (cdp) Pike County	21	0.52
Paradise Park, CA (cdp) Santa Cruz County	2	0.51
Coulterville, CA (cdp) Mariposa County	1	0.50
South Waverly, PA (borough) Bradford County	5	0.49
Ackermanville, PA (cdp) Northampton County	3	0.49
Tinmouth, VT (town) Rutland County	3	0.49
Melfa, VA (town) Accomack County	2	0.49
Chippewa, MI (township) Chippewa County	1	0.47
Edith Endave, NM (cdp) Bernalillo County	1	0.47
Pemberwick, CT (cdp) Fairfield County	17	0.46
Central Garage, VA (cdp) King William County	6	0.46
Hawi, HI (cdp) Hawaii County	5	0.46
Lake Don Pedro, CA (cdp) Mariposa County	5	0.46
Rio Vista, TX (city) Johnson County	4	0.46
San Jon, NM (village) Quay County	1	0.46
Palm Shores, FL (town) Brevard County	4	0.44
Chevak, AK (city) Wade Hampton Census Area	4	0.43
Hopewell, PA (borough) Bedford County	1	0.43
Blue Hills, CT (cdp) Hartford County	12	0.41
Balm, FL (cdp) Hillsborough County	6	0.41
Cottonwood, MN (city) Lyon County	5	0.41
Ellington, MO (city) Reynolds County	4	0.41
Cuba, NM (village) Sandoval County	3	0.41
Avoca, NE (village) Cass County	1	0.41
Bethany, PA (borough) Wayne County	1	0.41
Nespelem Community, WA (cdp) Okanogan County	1	0.40
Pocono Ranch Lands, PA (cdp) Pike County	4	0.38
Quail Ridge, FL (cdp) Pasco County	4	0.38
Roslyn Harbor, NY (village) Nassau County	4	0.38
Deerwood, MN (city) Crow Wing County	2	0.38
Floodwood, MN (city) St. Louis County	2	0.38
Garrett, TX (town) Ellis County	3	0.37
Orleans, VT (village) Orleans County	3	0.37
Greenville, VA (cdp) Augusta County	3	0.36
Websterville, VT (cdp) Washington County	2	0.36
Benton, CA (cdp) Mono County	1	0.36
Fairview, NY (cdp) Westchester County	11	0.35
North Enid, OK (town) Garfield County	3	0.35
Adamstown, PA (borough) Lancaster County	6	0.34
Adamstown, PA (borough) Lancaster County	6	0.34
Lake Como, NJ (borough) Monmouth County	6	0.34
Mill Creek, PA (township) Lycoming County	2	0.33
Dummer, NH (town) Coos County	1	0.33
Lehman, PA (township) Pike County	34	0.32
Birch Run, MI (village) Saginaw County	5	0.32
Brooklyn Heights, OH (village) Cuyahoga County	5	0.32
Otto, PA (township) McKean County	5	0.32
Baltic, CT (cdp) New London County	4	0.32
Wagon Mound, NM (village) Mora County	1	0.32
East Hampton North, NY (cdp) Suffolk County	13	0.31
St. Regis Mohawk Reservation, NY (reservation) Franklin County	10	0.31
Conashaugh Lakes, PA (cdp) Pike County	4	0.31
Bryantown, MD (cdp) Charles County	2	0.31
Franklin, ID (city) Franklin County	2	0.31
Castle Valley, UT (town) Grand County	1	0.31
Weston, NE (village) Saunders County	1	0.31
Concord, PA (township) Erie County	4	0.30
Spreckels, CA (cdp) Monterey County	2	0.30
Bison, SD (town) Perkins County	1	0.30
Kaaawa, HI (cdp) Honolulu County	4	0.29
Littlerock, CA (cdp) Los Angeles County	4	0.29
Mount Pleasant, PA (township) Wayne County	4	0.29
Brampton, MI (township) Delta County	3	0.29
Milford, PA (borough) Pike County	3	0.29
Anderson, NJ (cdp) Warren County	1	0.29
Cliffwood Beach, NJ (cdp) Monmouth County	9	0.28
Emerald Lakes, PA (cdp) Monroe County	8	0.28
Honaker, VA (town) Russell County	4	0.28
Matherville, IL (village) Mercer County	2	0.28
Fremont, MN (township) Winona County	1	0.28
Kearny, NJ (town) Hudson County	111	0.27
Haverstraw, NY (village) Rockland County	32	0.27
North El Monte, CA (cdp) Los Angeles County	10	0.27
Fort Lee, VA (cdp) Prince George County	9	0.27
Montura, FL (cdp) Hendry County	9	0.27
Maybrook, NY (village) Orange County	8	0.27
Lake Helen, FL (city) Volusia County	7	0.27
Trainer, PA (borough) Delaware County	5	0.27
Hooper Bay, AK (city) Wade Hampton Census Area	3	0.27
Tivoli, NY (village) Dutchess County	3	0.27
White Haven, PA (borough) Luzerne County	3	0.27
Fort Thomas, AZ (cdp) Graham County	1	0.27
Sky Lake, FL (cdp) Orange County	16	0.26
Deerfield, WI (village) Dane County	6	0.26
Crugers, NY (cdp) Westchester County	4	0.26
Dixon, MO (city) Pulaski County	4	0.26
Hemby Bridge, NC (town) Union County	4	0.26
Victory Gardens, NJ (borough) Morris County	4	0.26
Pine River, MN (township) Cass County	3	0.26
Sidney, IA (city) Fremont County	3	0.26
Blue Ridge Manor, KY (city) Jefferson County	2	0.26
Davenport, CA (cdp) Santa Cruz County	1	0.25
McCune, KS (city) Crawford County	1	0.25
Radisson, WI (town) Sawyer County	1	0.25
West Haverstraw, NY (village) Rockland County	24	0.24
Seven Corners, VA (cdp) Fairfax County	22	0.24
Hightstown, NJ (borough) Mercer County	13	0.24
Elmsford, NY (village) Westchester County	11	0.24
Northwest Harbor, NY (cdp) Suffolk County	8	0.24
Apison, TN (cdp) Hamilton County	6	0.24
Fairton, NJ (cdp) Cumberland County	3	0.24
Royalton, MN (city) Morrison County	3	0.24
Royalton, MN (city) Morrison County	3	0.24
Fox, AK (cdp) Fairbanks North Star Borough	1	0.24
Oneida, KY (cdp) Clay County	1	0.24
Rayland, OH (village) Jefferson County	1	0.24
South Philipsburg, PA (cdp) Centre County	1	0.24
North Valley Stream, NY (cdp) Nassau County	38	0.23
Lansing, NY (village) Tompkins County	8	0.23
Old Mystic, CT (cdp) New London County	8	0.23
Sloatsburg, NY (village) Rockland County	7	0.23
Quinton, NJ (township) Salem County	6	0.23
Bellerose Terrace, NY (cdp) Nassau County	5	0.23
Bakerstown, PA (cdp) Allegheny County	4	0.23
Nissequogue, NY (village) Suffolk County	4	0.23
Cleveland, AL (town) Blount County	3	0.23
Molino, FL (cdp) Escambia County	3	0.23
West Stockbridge, MA (town) Berkshire County	3	0.23
Brantleyville, AL (cdp) Shelby County	2	0.23
Bedias, TX (city) Grimes County	1	0.23
Fort Garland, CO (cdp) Costilla County	1	0.23
Groton, VT (cdp) Caledonia County	1	0.23
Perth Amboy, NJ (city) Middlesex County	112	0.22
Harrison, NJ (town) Hudson County	30	0.22
Gregg, PA (township) Union County	11	0.22
Logan, WV (city) Logan County	4	0.22

Please refer to the Explanation of Data in the front of the book for more detailed information.

Race

American Indian: South American Indian

Top 150 Places Sorted by Percent of Total Population

Based on places with total population of 7,500 or more

Place	Population	%
Lehman, PA (township) Pike County	34	0.32
Kearny, NJ (town) Hudson County	111	0.27
Haverstraw, NY (village) Rockland County	32	0.27
West Haverstraw, NY (village) Rockland County	24	0.24
Seven Corners, VA (cdp) Fairfax County	22	0.24
North Valley Stream, NY (cdp) Nassau County	38	0.23
Perth Amboy, NJ (city) Middlesex County	112	0.22
Harrison, NJ (town) Hudson County	30	0.22
Bronx, NY (borough) Bronx County	2,938	0.21
New London, CT (city/town) New London County	58	0.21
White Plains, NY (city) Westchester County	116	0.20
Union City, NJ (city) Hudson County	129	0.19
Haverstraw, NY (town) Rockland County	71	0.19
Groton, CT (city) New London County	20	0.19
Poinciana, FL (cdp) Osceola County	94	0.18
Holyoke, MA (city) Hampden County	67	0.17
Newburgh, NY (city) Orange County	50	0.17
Weehawken, NJ (township) Hudson County	21	0.17
Elizabeth, NJ (city) Union County	197	0.16
Hartford, CT (city/town) Hartford County	194	0.16
Passaic, NJ (city) Passaic County	113	0.16
West New York, NJ (town) Hudson County	80	0.16
Ossining, NY (village) Westchester County	39	0.16
Avenel, NJ (cdp) Middlesex County	28	0.16
North Kensington, MD (cdp) Montgomery County	15	0.16
Scotchtown, NY (cdp) Orange County	15	0.16
Lawrence, MA (city) Essex County	113	0.15
Port Chester, NY (village) Westchester County	43	0.15
Middletown, NY (city) Orange County	42	0.15
North Amityville, NY (cdp) Suffolk County	27	0.15
Willimantic, CT (cdp) Windham County	26	0.15
Bound Brook, NJ (borough) Somerset County	16	0.15
East Franklin, NJ (cdp) Somerset County	13	0.15
Yonkers, NY (city) Westchester County	270	0.14
Paterson, NJ (city) Passaic County	208	0.14
Brentwood, NY (cdp) Suffolk County	87	0.14
Central Islip, NY (cdp) Suffolk County	49	0.14
East Hampton, NY (town) Suffolk County	30	0.14
Coolbaugh, PA (township) Monroe County	28	0.14
La Grange, NY (town) Dutchess County	22	0.14
Tobyhanna, PA (township) Monroe County	12	0.14
Bernardsville, NJ (borough) Somerset County	11	0.14
Chesterfield, NJ (township) Burlington County	11	0.14
Providence, RI (city) Providence County	225	0.13
Springfield, MA (city) Hampden County	196	0.13
Lancaster, PA (city) Lancaster County	77	0.13
Kissimmee, FL (city) Osceola County	76	0.13
Hackensack, NJ (city) Bergen County	58	0.13
Ossining, NY (town) Westchester County	48	0.13
Bay Shore, NY (cdp) Suffolk County	33	0.13
Casselberry, FL (city) Seminole County	33	0.13
Windham, CT (town) Windham County	33	0.13
Morris, NJ (town) Morris County	24	0.13
Ridgefield Park, NJ (village) Bergen County	16	0.13
Upper Montclair, NJ (cdp) Essex County	15	0.13
Penn Forest, PA (township) Carbon County	12	0.13
New York, NY (city) Kings County	9,464	0.12
Manhattan, NY (borough) New York County	1,935	0.12
Lorain, OH (city) Lorain County	79	0.12
North Bergen, NJ (township) Hudson County	73	0.12
Milford, MA (cdp) Worcester County	30	0.12
Elmwood Park, NJ (borough) Bergen County	24	0.12
Blooming Grove, NY (town) Orange County	22	0.12
Aberdeen, NJ (township) Monmouth County	21	0.12
Southchase, FL (cdp) Orange County	19	0.12
Greenlawn, NY (cdp) Suffolk County	17	0.12
Somerville, NJ (borough) Somerset County	14	0.12
Conning Towers Nautilus Park, CT (cdp) New London County	11	0.12
Fort Meade, MD (cdp) Anne Arundel County	11	0.12
George Mason, VA (cdp) Fairfax County	11	0.12
Medulla, FL (cdp) Polk County	11	0.12
Braselton, GA (town) Gwinnett County	9	0.12
Lake Geneva, WI (city) Walworth County	9	0.12
Queens, NY (borough) Queens County	2,448	0.11
Allentown, PA (city) Lehigh County	135	0.11
Vineland, NJ (city) Cumberland County	67	0.11
West Hartford, CT (cdp/town) Hartford County	67	0.11
Aspen Hill, MD (cdp) Montgomery County	56	0.11
Rye, NY (town) Westchester County	51	0.11
Altamonte Springs, FL (city) Seminole County	47	0.11
Annandale, VA (cdp) Fairfax County	47	0.11
Groton, CT (town) New London County	43	0.11
Garfield, NJ (city) Bergen County	33	0.11
Franklin Square, NY (cdp) Nassau County	32	0.11
Milford, MA (town) Worcester County	30	0.11
Meadow Woods, FL (cdp) Orange County	29	0.11
Citrus Park, FL (cdp) Hillsborough County	27	0.11
Herndon, VA (town) Fairfax County	25	0.11
Bloomfield, CT (town) Hartford County	22	0.11
West Hempstead, NY (cdp) Nassau County	21	0.11
Dover, NJ (town) Morris County	20	0.11
Country Walk, FL (cdp) Miami-Dade County	17	0.11
Manassas Park, VA (ind. city) Manassas Park independent city	15	0.11
Bridgeport, CT (city/town) Fairfield County	146	0.10
Trenton, NJ (city) Mercer County	86	0.10
Clifton, NJ (city) Passaic County	83	0.10
Camden, NJ (city) Camden County	74	0.10
Bethlehem, PA (city) Northampton County	73	0.10
Silver Spring, MD (cdp) Montgomery County	69	0.10
Gaithersburg, MD (city) Montgomery County	57	0.10
Bethlehem, PA (city) Northampton County	54	0.10
Montclair, NJ (township) Essex County	36	0.10
Valley Stream, NY (village) Nassau County	36	0.10
Huntington Station, NY (cdp) Suffolk County	32	0.10
Wallkill, NY (town) Orange County	28	0.10
Rahway, NJ (city) Union County	26	0.10
Lebanon, PA (city) Lebanon County	25	0.10
Peekskill, NY (city) Westchester County	24	0.10
Lodi, NJ (borough) Bergen County	23	0.10
Bethlehem, PA (city) Lehigh County	19	0.10
Islip, NY (cdp) Suffolk County	19	0.10
Beacon, NY (city) Dutchess County	15	0.10
Groveton, VA (cdp) Fairfax County	14	0.10
Mastic Beach, NY (cdp) Suffolk County	13	0.10
Huntington, VA (cdp) Fairfax County	11	0.10
Lowes Island, VA (cdp) Loudoun County	11	0.10
Plattekill, NY (town) Ulster County	11	0.10
East Stroudsburg, PA (borough) Monroe County	10	0.10
Avon Park, FL (city) Highlands County	9	0.10
Farmingdale, NY (village) Nassau County	8	0.10
Jersey City, NJ (city) Hudson County	228	0.09
Germantown, MD (cdp) Montgomery County	76	0.09
Deltona, FL (city) Volusia County	75	0.09
New Britain, CT (city/town) Hartford County	67	0.09
Wheaton, MD (cdp) Montgomery County	45	0.09
Norwich, CT (city/town) New London County	35	0.09
Amherst, MA (town) Hampshire County	33	0.09
St. Cloud, FL (city) Osceola County	33	0.09
Spring Valley, NY (village) Rockland County	28	0.09
Newburgh, NY (town) Orange County	26	0.09
Cliffside Park, NJ (borough) Bergen County	22	0.09
Hazleton, PA (city) Luzerne County	22	0.09
Montgomery, NY (town) Orange County	21	0.09
Montville, CT (town) New London County	18	0.09
Amsterdam, NY (city) Montgomery County	16	0.09
Colchester, CT (town) New London County	15	0.09
Cherry Hill, VA (cdp) Prince William County	14	0.09
Colesville, MD (cdp) Montgomery County	13	0.09
Lake Mary, FL (city) Seminole County	13	0.09
Westbury, NY (village) Nassau County	13	0.09
Bedford, MA (town) Middlesex County	12	0.09
Richland, PA (township) Bucks County	12	0.09
Guttenberg, NJ (town) Hudson County	10	0.09
Highland City, FL (cdp) Polk County	10	0.09
Wanaque, NJ (borough) Passaic County	10	0.09
Airmont, NY (village) Rockland County	8	0.09
Alondra Park, CA (cdp) Los Angeles County	8	0.09
East Rutherford, NJ (borough) Bergen County	8	0.09
White Meadow Lake, NJ (cdp) Morris County	8	0.09
Woodburn, VA (cdp) Fairfax County	8	0.09

SECTION THREE

Please refer to the Explanation of Data in the front of the book for more detailed information.

Race

American Indian: Spanish American Indian

U.S. and 50 States Sorted by Population and Percent of Total Population

Place	Population	%
United States	**19,951**	**0.01**
California	4,271	0.01
New York	3,506	0.02
Texas	1,845	0.01
Florida	1,358	0.01
New Jersey	1,073	0.01
Colorado	765	0.02
North Carolina	543	0.01
New Mexico	540	0.03
Illinois	535	<0.01
Arizona	465	0.01
Massachusetts	459	0.01
Virginia	418	0.01
Pennsylvania	383	<0.01
Georgia	316	<0.01
Maryland	303	0.01
Washington	257	<0.01
Nevada	217	0.01
Connecticut	201	0.01
Oregon	195	0.01
Tennessee	195	<0.01
Minnesota	177	<0.01
Utah	153	0.01
Michigan	143	<0.01
Indiana	137	<0.01
Louisiana	131	<0.01
Ohio	124	<0.01
Oklahoma	109	<0.01
Missouri	104	<0.01
South Carolina	97	<0.01
Rhode Island	94	0.01
Wisconsin	93	<0.01
Nebraska	90	<0.01
Alabama	84	<0.01
Arkansas	62	<0.01
Kansas	56	<0.01
Iowa	55	<0.01
Idaho	52	<0.01
District of Columbia	51	0.01
Mississippi	48	<0.01
Hawaii	43	<0.01
Kentucky	39	<0.01
Delaware	38	<0.01
Wyoming	35	0.01
Montana	18	<0.01
Alaska	16	<0.01
New Hampshire	15	<0.01
Maine	13	<0.01
Vermont	11	<0.01
West Virginia	9	<0.01
South Dakota	6	<0.01
North Dakota	3	<0.01

Place	Population	%
New Mexico	540	0.03
New York	3,506	0.02
Colorado	765	0.02
United States	**19,951**	**0.01**
California	4,271	0.01
Texas	1,845	0.01
Florida	1,358	0.01
New Jersey	1,073	0.01
North Carolina	543	0.01
Arizona	465	0.01
Massachusetts	459	0.01
Virginia	418	0.01
Maryland	303	0.01
Nevada	217	0.01
Connecticut	201	0.01
Oregon	195	0.01
Utah	153	0.01
Rhode Island	94	0.01
District of Columbia	51	0.01
Wyoming	35	0.01
Illinois	535	<0.01
Pennsylvania	383	<0.01
Georgia	316	<0.01
Washington	257	<0.01
Tennessee	195	<0.01
Minnesota	177	<0.01
Michigan	143	<0.01
Indiana	137	<0.01
Louisiana	131	<0.01
Ohio	124	<0.01
Oklahoma	109	<0.01
Missouri	104	<0.01
South Carolina	97	<0.01
Wisconsin	93	<0.01
Nebraska	90	<0.01
Alabama	84	<0.01
Arkansas	62	<0.01
Kansas	56	<0.01
Iowa	55	<0.01
Idaho	52	<0.01
Mississippi	48	<0.01
Hawaii	43	<0.01
Kentucky	39	<0.01
Delaware	38	<0.01
Montana	18	<0.01
Alaska	16	<0.01
New Hampshire	15	<0.01
Maine	13	<0.01
Vermont	11	<0.01
West Virginia	9	<0.01
South Dakota	6	<0.01
North Dakota	3	<0.01

Please refer to the Explanation of Data in the front of the book for more detailed information.

Race

American Indian: Spanish American Indian

Top 150 Places Sorted by Population

Based on all places, regardless of total population

Place	Population	%
New York, NY (city) Kings County	2,594	0.03
Bronx, NY (borough) Bronx County	992	0.07
Queens, NY (borough) Queens County	659	0.03
Los Angeles, CA (city) Los Angeles County	564	0.01
Manhattan, NY (borough) New York County	514	0.03
Houston, TX (city) Harris County	421	0.02
Brooklyn, NY (borough) Kings County	382	0.02
Chicago, IL (city) Cook County	225	0.01
Santa Ana, CA (city) Orange County	170	0.05
Philadelphia, PA (city) Philadelphia County	156	0.01
Denver, CO (city) Denver County	148	0.02
Lawrence, MA (city) Essex County	141	0.18
Phoenix, AZ (city) Maricopa County	141	0.01
Hempstead, NY (town) Nassau County	137	0.02
Albuquerque, NM (city) Bernalillo County	136	0.02
Yonkers, NY (city) Westchester County	132	0.07
Dallas, TX (city) Dallas County	127	0.01
Elizabeth, NJ (city) Union County	124	0.10
San Antonio, TX (city) Medina County	117	0.01
Paterson, NJ (city) Passaic County	111	0.08
Miami, FL (city) Miami-Dade County	105	0.03
Austin, TX (city) Travis County	103	0.01
Charlotte, NC (city) Mecklenburg County	101	0.01
Newburgh, NY (city) Orange County	92	0.32
Islip, NY (town) Suffolk County	91	0.03
Livingston, CA (city) Merced County	87	0.67
San Jose, CA (city) Santa Clara County	82	0.01
Boston, MA (city) Suffolk County	80	0.01
Minneapolis, MN (city) Hennepin County	73	0.02
Union City, NJ (city) Hudson County	72	0.11
Colorado Springs, CO (city) El Paso County	71	0.02
Winton, CA (cdp) Merced County	69	0.65
Providence, RI (city) Providence County	69	0.04
Sorrento, FL (cdp) Lake County	68	7.90
Smyrna, TN (town) Rutherford County	65	0.16
Sacramento, CA (city) Sacramento County	65	0.01
Pueblo, CO (city) Pueblo County	63	0.06
Long Beach, CA (city) Los Angeles County	62	0.01
Las Vegas, NV (city) Clark County	60	0.01
Newark, NJ (city) Essex County	59	0.02
Fresno, CA (city) Fresno County	58	0.01
Brentwood, NY (cdp) Suffolk County	52	0.09
Riverside, CA (city) Riverside County	52	0.02
Washington, DC (city) District of Columbia	51	0.01
San Diego, CA (city) San Diego County	51	<0.01
El Paso, TX (city) El Paso County	50	0.01
Hempstead, NY (village) Nassau County	47	0.09
Passaic, NJ (city) Passaic County	47	0.07
Staten Island, NY (borough) Richmond County	47	0.01
Delhi, CA (cdp) Merced County	46	0.43
Anaheim, CA (city) Orange County	46	0.01
Raleigh, NC (city) Wake County	44	0.01
San Francisco, CA (city) San Francisco County	41	0.01
Tucson, AZ (city) Pima County	41	0.01
Bailey's Crossroads, VA (cdp) Fairfax County	40	0.17
Santa Maria, CA (city) Santa Barbara County	40	0.04
Lakewood, CO (city) Jefferson County	40	0.03
North Hempstead, NY (town) Nassau County	40	0.02
Fontana, CA (city) San Bernardino County	37	0.02
Waukegan, IL (city) Lake County	36	0.04
Corona, CA (city) Riverside County	35	0.02
Grand Prairie, TX (city) Dallas County	35	0.02
Hialeah, FL (city) Miami-Dade County	35	0.02
Omaha, NE (city) Douglas County	35	0.01
Florence-Graham, CA (cdp) Los Angeles County	34	0.05
Brookhaven, NY (town) Suffolk County	34	0.01
Plainfield, NJ (city) Union County	33	0.07
East Los Angeles, CA (cdp) Los Angeles County	33	0.03
Pomona, CA (city) Los Angeles County	33	0.02
Jersey City, NJ (city) Hudson County	33	0.01
Orlando, FL (city) Orange County	33	0.01
Lindenwold, NJ (borough) Camden County	32	0.18
Wheaton, MD (cdp) Montgomery County	32	0.07
Trenton, NJ (city) Mercer County	32	0.04
Vista, CA (city) San Diego County	32	0.03
Oxnard, CA (city) Ventura County	32	0.02
Oakland, CA (city) Alameda County	32	0.01
Compton, CA (city) Los Angeles County	31	0.03
Arlington, VA (cdp) Arlington County	31	0.01
North Las Vegas, NV (city) Clark County	31	0.01
Woodburn, OR (city) Marion County	30	0.12
Moreno Valley, CA (city) Riverside County	30	0.02
Oklahoma City, OK (city) Oklahoma County	30	0.01
Portland, OR (city) Multnomah County	30	0.01
Seattle, WA (city) King County	30	<0.01
Ontario, CA (city) San Bernardino County	29	0.02
Alhambra, CA (city) Los Angeles County	28	0.03
Aurora, IL (city) Kane County	28	0.01
Azusa, CA (city) Los Angeles County	27	0.06
Perth Amboy, NJ (city) Middlesex County	27	0.05
Allentown, PA (city) Lehigh County	27	0.02
El Monte, CA (city) Los Angeles County	27	0.02
Thornton, CO (city) Adams County	27	0.02
Modesto, CA (city) Stanislaus County	27	0.01
Dale City, VA (cdp) Prince William County	26	0.04
Merced, CA (city) Merced County	26	0.03
Rio Rancho, NM (city) Sandoval County	26	0.03
Bridgeport, CT (city/town) Fairfield County	26	0.02
Pasadena, CA (city) Los Angeles County	26	0.02
Santa Rosa, CA (city) Sonoma County	26	0.02
Springfield, MA (city) Hampden County	26	0.02
Waterbury, CT (city/town) New Haven County	26	0.02
Jacksonville, FL (city) Duval County	26	<0.01
Milwaukee, WI (city) Milwaukee County	26	<0.01
Freeport, NY (village) Nassau County	25	0.06
Burlington, NC (city) Alamance County	25	0.05
Arlington, TX (city) Tarrant County	25	0.01
Irving, TX (city) Dallas County	25	0.01
Mesa, AZ (city) Maricopa County	25	0.01
Oyster Bay, NY (town) Nassau County	25	0.01
San Bernardino, CA (city) San Bernardino County	25	0.01
Fort Worth, TX (city) Tarrant County	25	<0.01
Clifton, NJ (city) Passaic County	24	0.03
Bakersfield, CA (city) Kern County	24	0.01
Garland, TX (city) Dallas County	24	0.01
Central Islip, NY (cdp) Suffolk County	23	0.07
La Puente, CA (city) Los Angeles County	23	0.06
West New York, NJ (town) Hudson County	23	0.05
Greenburgh, NY (town) Westchester County	23	0.03
Kenner, LA (city) Jefferson Parish	23	0.03
Daly City, CA (city) San Mateo County	23	0.02
Garden Grove, CA (city) Orange County	23	0.01
Glendale, AZ (city) Maricopa County	23	0.01
Oceanside, CA (city) San Diego County	23	0.01
Paradise, NV (cdp) Clark County	23	0.01
Indianapolis, IN (city) Marion County	23	<0.01
West Orange, NJ (township) Essex County	22	0.05
Miami Beach, FL (city) Miami-Dade County	22	0.03
Durham, NC (city) Durham County	22	0.01
Baltimore, MD (city) Baltimore city County	22	<0.01
Mineola, NY (village) Nassau County	21	0.11
Hollister, CA (city) San Benito County	21	0.06
La Vergne, TN (city) Rutherford County	21	0.06
Bloomington, IN (city) Monroe County	21	0.03
North Bergen, NJ (township) Hudson County	21	0.03
Aurora, CO (city) Arapahoe County	21	0.01
Stockton, CA (city) San Joaquin County	21	0.01
Wichita, KS (city) Sedgwick County	21	0.01
Northglenn, CO (city) Adams County	20	0.06
Camden, NJ (city) Camden County	20	0.03
Las Cruces, NM (city) Doña Ana County	20	0.02
Chandler, AZ (city) Maricopa County	20	0.01
Fremont, CA (city) Alameda County	20	0.01
Henderson, NV (city) Clark County	20	0.01
Palmdale, CA (city) Los Angeles County	20	0.01
Worcester, MA (city) Worcester County	20	0.01
Nashville-Davidson, TN (metro govt) Davidson County	20	<0.01
Lennox, CA (cdp) Los Angeles County	19	0.08
La Verne, CA (city) Los Angeles County	19	0.06
Aspen Hill, MD (cdp) Montgomery County	19	0.04

Please refer to the Explanation of Data in the front of the book for more detailed information.

Race

American Indian: Spanish American Indian

Top 150 Places Sorted by Percent of Total Population

Based on all places, regardless of total population

Place	Population	%
Sorrento, FL (cdp) Lake County	68	7.90
Pueblo, NM (cdp) San Miguel County	7	5.60
Bern, KS (city) Nemaha County	5	3.01
Ophir, UT (town) Tooele County	1	2.63
Hallie, WI (town) Chippewa County	3	1.86
Osborne, MN (township) Pipestone County	5	1.75
Romeo, CO (town) Conejos County	6	1.49
Picuris Pueblo, NM (cdp) Taos County	1	1.47
Chilili, NM (cdp) Bernalillo County	2	1.46
Mashantucket, CT (cdp) New London County	4	1.34
Rennert, NC (town) Robeson County	5	1.31
Ak-Chin Village, AZ (cdp) Pinal County	11	1.28
Oak Ridge, MO (town) Cape Girardeau County	3	1.23
Young Place, NM (cdp) San Juan County	2	1.07
West Union, SC (town) Oconee County	3	1.03
Pomeroy, PA (cdp) Chester County	4	1.00
Ensenada, NM (cdp) Rio Arriba County	1	0.93
Mole Lake, WI (cdp) Forest County	4	0.92
Boonville, CA (cdp) Mendocino County	9	0.87
Fredonia, IA (city) Louisa County	2	0.82
Monument Hills, CA (cdp) Yolo County	12	0.78
Tansem, MN (township) Clay County	2	0.77
Truxton, AZ (cdp) Mohave County	1	0.75
Inchelium, WA (cdp) Ferry County	3	0.73
Waveland, IN (town) Montgomery County	3	0.71
La Mesa, NM (cdp) Doña Ana County	5	0.69
Livingston, CA (city) Merced County	87	0.67
Las Nutrias, NM (cdp) Socorro County	1	0.67
Winton, CA (cdp) Merced County	69	0.65
Shinnecock Reservation, NY (reservation) Suffolk County	4	0.60
Moapa Town, NV (cdp) Clark County	6	0.59
Hollister, NC (cdp) Halifax County	4	0.59
Corona, NM (village) Lincoln County	1	0.58
Fort Covington Hamlet, NY (cdp) Franklin County	7	0.54
Garden Valley, ID (cdp) Boise County	2	0.51
Encinal, NM (cdp) Cibola County	1	0.48
Lexington, MN (city) Anoka County	9	0.44
Aurora, OR (city) Marion County	4	0.44
Delhi, CA (cdp) Merced County	46	0.43
Long Island, ME (town) Cumberland County	1	0.43
Fort Covington, NY (town) Franklin County	7	0.42
Voorhees, NJ (cdp) Somerset County	4	0.41
Rockvale, CO (town) Fremont County	2	0.41
Mount Plymouth, FL (cdp) Lake County	16	0.40
Vandling, PA (borough) Lackawanna County	3	0.40
Dixon, IA (city) Scott County	1	0.40
Willard, NM (village) Torrance County	1	0.40
Chama, NM (village) Rio Arriba County	4	0.39
Port William, OH (village) Clinton County	1	0.39
Nashville, WI (town) Forest County	4	0.38
West Haven, VT (town) Rutland County	1	0.38
Hood, CA (cdp) Sacramento County	1	0.37
Hughestown, PA (borough) Luzerne County	5	0.36
Pecos, NM (village) San Miguel County	5	0.36
Truchas, NM (cdp) Rio Arriba County	2	0.36
Cubero, NM (cdp) Cibola County	1	0.35
Oberlin, PA (cdp) Dauphin County	2	0.34
Salt Creek, CO (cdp) Pueblo County	2	0.34
New Hampton, MO (city) Harrison County	1	0.34
Washburn, WI (town) Clark County	1	0.34
Los Luceros, NM (cdp) Rio Arriba County	3	0.33
Newburgh, NY (city) Orange County	92	0.32
Lavonia, GA (city) Franklin County	7	0.32
Wautoma, WI (city) Waushara County	7	0.32
Highland Meadows, NM (cdp) Valencia County	2	0.32
Avery, CA (cdp) Calaveras County	2	0.31
Parkway Village, KY (city) Jefferson County	2	0.31
Palisades, TX (village) Randall County	1	0.31
Lebanon, NY (town) Madison County	4	0.30
Hawk Point, MO (city) Lincoln County	2	0.30
Richland Springs, TX (town) San Saba County	1	0.30
Mono Vista, CA (cdp) Tuolumne County	9	0.29
Westhampton Beach, NY (village) Suffolk County	5	0.29
Hampton, NJ (borough) Hunterdon County	4	0.29
Hillman, MI (village) Montmorency County	2	0.29
Longton, KS (city) Elk County	1	0.29
South La Paloma, TX (cdp) Jim Wells County	1	0.29
South Mansfield, LA (village) De Soto Parish	1	0.29
Greenport West, NY (cdp) Suffolk County	6	0.28
Questa, NM (village) Taos County	5	0.28
Bellevue, TX (city) Clay County	1	0.28
Potomac Mills, VA (cdp) Prince William County	15	0.27
Jeffers Gardens, OR (cdp) Clatsop County	1	0.27
Absarokee, MT (cdp) Stillwater County	3	0.26
Batavia, MT (cdp) Flathead County	1	0.26
Lewistown Heights, MT (cdp) Fergus County	1	0.25
Wells, VT (cdp) Rutland County	1	0.25
Fulton, MD (cdp) Howard County	5	0.24
Judson, SC (cdp) Greenville County	5	0.24
Liberty, UT (cdp) Weber County	3	0.24
Meadow Lake, NM (cdp) Valencia County	11	0.23
Leadville, CO (city) Lake County	6	0.23
Liberty, NC (town) Randolph County	6	0.23
Boronda, CA (cdp) Monterey County	4	0.23
South Floral Park, NY (village) Nassau County	4	0.23
Breckenridge, MI (village) Gratiot County	3	0.23
Geary, OK (city) Blaine County	3	0.23
Cameron, AZ (cdp) Coconino County	2	0.23
Villa Verde, TX (cdp) Hidalgo County	2	0.23
Keene, CA (cdp) Kern County	1	0.23
Manzanola, CO (town) Otero County	1	0.23
Ropesville, TX (city) Hockley County	1	0.23
Ruth, NV (cdp) White Pine County	1	0.23
Ingram, TX (city) Kerr County	4	0.22
Summerfield, IL (village) St. Clair County	1	0.22
El Valle de Arroyo Seco, NM (cdp) Santa Fe County	3	0.21
Skelly, TX (town) Carson County	1	0.21
Dumfries, VA (town) Prince William County	10	0.20
Primera, TX (town) Cameron County	8	0.20
Central City, AR (town) Sebastian County	1	0.20
Latimer, IA (city) Franklin County	1	0.20
Pinehurst, TX (city) Orange County	4	0.19
Woodstock, NY (cdp) Ulster County	4	0.19
Washington, VT (town) Orange County	2	0.19
Lawrence, MA (city) Essex County	141	0.18
Lindenwold, NJ (borough) Camden County	32	0.18
Shaw Heights, CO (cdp) Adams County	9	0.18
Dimmitt, TX (city) Castro County	8	0.18
Agua Fria, NM (cdp) Santa Fe County	5	0.18
Canisteo, NY (village) Steuben County	4	0.18
Moundville, WI (town) Marquette County	1	0.18
Somerville, ME (town) Lincoln County	1	0.18
Stewart, MN (city) McLeod County	1	0.18
Bailey's Crossroads, VA (cdp) Fairfax County	40	0.17
Farmingdale, NY (village) Nassau County	14	0.17
Willington, CT (town) Tolland County	10	0.17
Sunset Beach, NC (town) Brunswick County	6	0.17
El Cerro, NM (cdp) Valencia County	5	0.17
Fruitdale, OR (cdp) Josephine County	2	0.17
Corsica, SD (city) Douglas County	1	0.17
Pajarito Mesa, NM (cdp) Bernalillo County	1	0.17
Whitsett, NC (town) Guilford County	1	0.17
Smyrna, TN (town) Rutherford County	65	0.16
St. Anthony, MN (city) Hennepin County	8	0.16
Dade City North, FL (cdp) Pasco County	5	0.16
Lagunitas-Forest Knolls, CA (cdp) Marin County	3	0.16
Carnuel, NM (cdp) Bernalillo County	2	0.16
Lake Luzerne, NY (cdp) Warren County	2	0.16
Hardin, KY (city) Marshall County	1	0.16
Greenbriar, VA (cdp) Fairfax County	12	0.15
Islandia, NY (village) Suffolk County	5	0.15
Campo, CA (cdp) San Diego County	4	0.15
Mora, NM (cdp) Mora County	1	0.15
Petrolia, TX (city) Clay County	1	0.15
Walkerville, MT (town) Silver Bow County	1	0.15
Wimauma, FL (cdp) Hillsborough County	9	0.14
Monte Vista, CO (city) Rio Grande County	6	0.14
Bono, AR (city) Craighead County	3	0.14
Merrimac, VA (cdp) Montgomery County	3	0.14
Kettleman City, CA (cdp) Kings County	2	0.14

Please refer to the Explanation of Data in the front of the book for more detailed information.

Race

American Indian: Spanish American Indian

Top 150 Places Sorted by Percent of Total Population

Based on places with total population of 7,500 or more

Place	Population	%
Livingston, CA (city) Merced County	87	0.67
Winton, CA (cdp) Merced County	69	0.65
Delhi, CA (cdp) Merced County	46	0.43
Newburgh, NY (city) Orange County	92	0.32
Lawrence, MA (city) Essex County	141	0.18
Lindenwold, NJ (borough) Camden County	32	0.18
Bailey's Crossroads, VA (cdp) Fairfax County	40	0.17
Farmingdale, NY (village) Nassau County	14	0.17
Smyrna, TN (town) Rutherford County	65	0.16
Greenbriar, VA (cdp) Fairfax County	12	0.15
Inwood, NY (cdp) Nassau County	13	0.13
Trinidad, CO (city) Las Animas County	12	0.13
Siler City, NC (town) Chatham County	10	0.13
Woodburn, OR (city) Marion County	30	0.12
Union City, NJ (city) Hudson County	72	0.11
Mineola, NY (village) Nassau County	21	0.11
Gering, NE (city) Scotts Bluff County	9	0.11
Elizabeth, NJ (city) Union County	124	0.10
Langley Park, MD (cdp) Prince George's County	18	0.10
St. Anthony, MN (city) Hennepin and Ramsey Counties	8	0.10
Brentwood, NY (cdp) Suffolk County	52	0.09
Hempstead, NY (village) Nassau County	47	0.09
Graham, NC (city) Alamance County	13	0.09
Tarrytown, NY (village) Westchester County	10	0.09
Paterson, NJ (city) Passaic County	111	0.08
Lennox, CA (cdp) Los Angeles County	19	0.08
Groveton, VA (cdp) Fairfax County	11	0.08
New Cassel, NY (cdp) Nassau County	11	0.08
Sleepy Hollow, NY (village) Westchester County	8	0.08
Mecca, CA (cdp) Riverside County	7	0.08
Seven Corners, VA (cdp) Fairfax County	7	0.08
Acton, CA (cdp) Los Angeles County	6	0.08
Bronx, NY (borough) Bronx County	992	0.07
Yonkers, NY (city) Westchester County	132	0.07
Passaic, NJ (city) Passaic County	47	0.07
Plainfield, NJ (city) Union County	33	0.07
Wheaton, MD (cdp) Montgomery County	32	0.07
Central Islip, NY (cdp) Suffolk County	23	0.07
Fuquay-Varina, NC (town) Wake County	12	0.07
Damascus, MD (cdp) Montgomery County	11	0.07
Las Vegas, NM (city) San Miguel County	10	0.07
Welby, CO (cdp) Adams County	10	0.07
Berkley, CO (cdp) Adams County	8	0.07
North Lindenhurst, NY (cdp) Suffolk County	8	0.07
Tomball, TX (city) Harris County	7	0.07
Corning, CA (city) Tehama County	5	0.07
Pueblo, CO (city) Pueblo County	63	0.06
Azusa, CA (city) Los Angeles County	27	0.06
Freeport, NY (village) Nassau County	25	0.06
La Puente, CA (city) Los Angeles County	23	0.06
Hollister, CA (city) San Benito County	21	0.06
La Vergne, TN (city) Rutherford County	21	0.06
Northglenn, CO (city) Adams County	20	0.06
La Verne, CA (city) Los Angeles County	19	0.06
Morristown, TN (city) Hamblen County	17	0.06
Round Lake Beach, IL (village) Lake County	17	0.06
Citrus Park, FL (cdp) Hillsborough County	15	0.06
Carteret, NJ (borough) Middlesex County	14	0.06
Pleasantville, NJ (city) Atlantic County	13	0.06
Pinole, CA (city) Contra Costa County	11	0.06
Santa Fe Springs, CA (city) Los Angeles County	10	0.06
Dentsville, SC (cdp) Richland County	8	0.06
Haverstraw, NY (village) Rockland County	7	0.06
Healdsburg, CA (city) Sonoma County	7	0.06
Portales, NM (city) Roosevelt County	7	0.06
Chamblee, GA (city) DeKalb County	6	0.06
Delta, CO (city) Delta County	5	0.06
Larkfield-Wikiup, CA (cdp) Sonoma County	5	0.06
Montvale, NJ (borough) Bergen County	5	0.06
Santa Ana, CA (city) Orange County	170	0.05
Florence-Graham, CA (cdp) Los Angeles County	34	0.05
Perth Amboy, NJ (city) Middlesex County	27	0.05
Burlington, NC (city) Alamance County	25	0.05
West New York, NJ (town) Hudson County	23	0.05
West Orange, NJ (township) Essex County	22	0.05
Lake Worth, FL (city) Palm Beach County	18	0.05
El Mirage, AZ (city) Maricopa County	17	0.05
Norristown, PA (borough) Montgomery County	17	0.05
West Little River, FL (cdp) Miami-Dade County	16	0.05
Long Branch, NJ (city) Monmouth County	14	0.05
Magna, UT (cdp) Salt Lake County	12	0.05
Valinda, CA (cdp) Los Angeles County	12	0.05
Bear, DE (cdp) New Castle County	9	0.05
Central Falls, RI (city) Providence County	9	0.05
Willimantic, CT (cdp) Windham County	9	0.05
Beltsville, MD (cdp) Prince George's County	8	0.05
Ledyard, CT (town) New London County	8	0.05
Prunedale, CA (cdp) Monterey County	8	0.05
Springfield, TN (city) Robertson County	8	0.05
Adelphi, MD (cdp) Prince George's County	7	0.05
Thompson, NY (town) Sullivan County	7	0.05
King City, CA (city) Monterey County	6	0.05
Lexington Park, MD (cdp) St. Mary's County	6	0.05
North Auburn, CA (cdp) Placer County	6	0.05
North Bellport, NY (cdp) Suffolk County	6	0.05
Bardmoor, FL (cdp) Pinellas County	5	0.05
Newman, CA (city) Stanislaus County	5	0.05
North Kensington, MD (cdp) Montgomery County	5	0.05
Port Royal, SC (town) Beaufort County	5	0.05
Silver City, NM (town) Grant County	5	0.05
Summerfield, MD (cdp) Prince George's County	5	0.05
Zeeland, MI (charter township) Ottawa County	5	0.05
Alamosa, CO (city) Alamosa County	4	0.05
August, CA (cdp) San Joaquin County	4	0.05
Bogota, NJ (borough) Bergen County	4	0.05
Bryan, OH (city) Williams County	4	0.05
Moncks Corner, SC (town) Berkeley County	4	0.05
Woodstock, CT (town) Windham County	4	0.05
Providence, RI (city) Providence County	69	0.04
Santa Maria, CA (city) Santa Barbara County	40	0.04
Waukegan, IL (city) Lake County	36	0.04
Trenton, NJ (city) Mercer County	32	0.04
Dale City, VA (cdp) Prince William County	26	0.04
Aspen Hill, MD (cdp) Montgomery County	19	0.04
Ashburn, VA (cdp) Loudoun County	18	0.04
Bell Gardens, CA (city) Los Angeles County	17	0.04
Hackensack, NJ (city) Bergen County	17	0.04
San Bruno, CA (city) San Mateo County	17	0.04
Clovis, NM (city) Curry County	16	0.04
South Valley, NM (cdp) Bernalillo County	16	0.04
Chelsea, MA (city) Suffolk County	15	0.04
Carol Stream, IL (village) DuPage County	14	0.04
Glen Cove, NY (city) Nassau County	12	0.04
Englewood, NJ (city) Bergen County	11	0.04
Westchester, FL (cdp) Miami-Dade County	11	0.04
Columbus, NE (city) Platte County	9	0.04
North Plainfield, NJ (borough) Somerset County	9	0.04
South Bradenton, FL (cdp) Manatee County	9	0.04
Windham, CT (town) Windham County	9	0.04
East Patchogue, NY (cdp) Suffolk County	8	0.04
Evans, CO (city) Weld County	8	0.04
Sherrelwood, CO (cdp) Adams County	8	0.04
Estelle, LA (cdp) Jefferson Parish	7	0.04
Pinecrest, FL (village) Miami-Dade County	7	0.04
Southchase, FL (cdp) Orange County	7	0.04
Greenfield, CA (city) Monterey County	6	0.04
Hartford, WI (city) Washington County	6	0.04
Kingstowne, VA (cdp) Fairfax County	6	0.04
Ukiah, CA (city) Mendocino County	6	0.04
Borger, TX (city) Hutchinson County	5	0.04
Brandermill, VA (cdp) Chesterfield County	5	0.04
El Sobrante, CA (cdp) Contra Costa County	5	0.04
Fairburn, GA (city) Fulton County	5	0.04
Fort Payne, AL (city) DeKalb County	5	0.04
Guymon, OK (city) Texas County	5	0.04
Hendersonville, NC (city) Henderson County	5	0.04
Moody, AL (city) St. Clair County	5	0.04
Olivehurst, CA (cdp) Yuba County	5	0.04
Ontario, OR (city) Malheur County	5	0.04
Palmetto Estates, FL (cdp) Miami-Dade County	5	0.04

SECTION THREE

Race

Alaska Native: Tlingit-Haida

U.S. and 50 States Sorted by Population and Percent of Total Population

Place	Population	%
United States	**26,080**	**0.01**
Alaska	13,186	1.86
Washington	5,733	0.09
California	1,571	<0.01
Oregon	1,225	0.03
Florida	374	<0.01
Arizona	325	0.01
Texas	290	<0.01
Colorado	289	0.01
Idaho	256	0.02
Nevada	201	0.01
New York	169	<0.01
New Mexico	152	0.01
Montana	135	0.01
Missouri	125	<0.01
Michigan	123	<0.01
Oklahoma	122	<0.01
Hawaii	116	0.01
Virginia	107	<0.01
Pennsylvania	95	<0.01
Utah	88	<0.01
Illinois	86	<0.01
Minnesota	86	<0.01
Wisconsin	86	<0.01
Georgia	80	<0.01
Ohio	77	<0.01
Kansas	74	<0.01
New Jersey	73	<0.01
North Carolina	73	<0.01
Massachusetts	70	<0.01
Tennessee	68	<0.01
Indiana	65	<0.01
South Carolina	62	<0.01
Maryland	53	<0.01
Arkansas	47	<0.01
Connecticut	43	<0.01
Wyoming	40	0.01
Alabama	38	<0.01
Iowa	34	<0.01
Louisiana	33	<0.01
Maine	31	<0.01
West Virginia	29	<0.01
Kentucky	28	<0.01
South Dakota	27	<0.01
Nebraska	20	<0.01
Mississippi	19	<0.01
North Dakota	16	<0.01
New Hampshire	14	<0.01
District of Columbia	10	<0.01
Rhode Island	9	<0.01
Delaware	4	<0.01
Vermont	3	<0.01

Place	Population	%
Alaska	13,186	1.86
Washington	5,733	0.09
Oregon	1,225	0.03
Idaho	256	0.02
United States	**26,080**	**0.01**
Arizona	325	0.01
Colorado	289	0.01
Nevada	201	0.01
New Mexico	152	0.01
Montana	135	0.01
Hawaii	116	0.01
Wyoming	40	0.01
California	1,571	<0.01
Florida	374	<0.01
Texas	290	<0.01
New York	169	<0.01
Missouri	125	<0.01
Michigan	123	<0.01
Oklahoma	122	<0.01
Virginia	107	<0.01
Pennsylvania	95	<0.01
Utah	88	<0.01
Illinois	86	<0.01
Minnesota	86	<0.01
Wisconsin	86	<0.01
Georgia	80	<0.01
Ohio	77	<0.01
Kansas	74	<0.01
New Jersey	73	<0.01
North Carolina	73	<0.01
Massachusetts	70	<0.01
Tennessee	68	<0.01
Indiana	65	<0.01
South Carolina	62	<0.01
Maryland	53	<0.01
Arkansas	47	<0.01
Connecticut	43	<0.01
Alabama	38	<0.01
Iowa	34	<0.01
Louisiana	33	<0.01
Maine	31	<0.01
West Virginia	29	<0.01
Kentucky	28	<0.01
South Dakota	27	<0.01
Nebraska	20	<0.01
Mississippi	19	<0.01
North Dakota	16	<0.01
New Hampshire	14	<0.01
District of Columbia	10	<0.01
Rhode Island	9	<0.01
Delaware	4	<0.01
Vermont	3	<0.01

Please refer to the Explanation of Data in the front of the book for more detailed information.

Race

Alaska Native: Tlingit-Haida

Top 150 Places Sorted by Population

Based on all places, regardless of total population

Place	Population	%
Juneau, AK (borough) Juneau City and Borough	3,825	12.23
Anchorage, AK (municipality) Anchorage Municipality	2,241	0.77
Sitka, AK (borough) Sitka City and Borough	1,394	15.70
Ketchikan, AK (city) Ketchikan Gateway Borough	988	12.27
Seattle, WA (city) King County	729	0.12
Hoonah, AK (city) Hoonah-Angoon Census Area	388	51.05
Wrangell, AK (borough) Wrangell City and Borough	351	14.82
Klawock, AK (city) Prince of Wales-Hyder Census Area	322	42.65
Kake, AK (city) Petersburg Census Area	316	56.73
Angoon, AK (city) Hoonah-Angoon Census Area	300	65.36
Hydaburg, AK (city) Prince of Wales-Hyder Census Area	263	69.95
Petersburg, AK (city) Petersburg Census Area	252	8.55
Craig, AK (city) Prince of Wales-Hyder Census Area	237	19.73
Saxman, AK (city) Ketchikan Gateway Borough	225	54.74
Yakutat, AK (cdp) Yakutat City and Borough	223	33.69
Tacoma, WA (city) Pierce County	201	0.10
Portland, OR (city) Multnomah County	188	0.03
Haines, AK (cdp) Haines Borough	187	10.92
Everett, WA (city) Snohomish County	148	0.14
Bellingham, WA (city) Whatcom County	111	0.14
Auburn, WA (city) King County	102	0.15
Marysville, WA (city) Snohomish County	98	0.16
Federal Way, WA (city) King County	97	0.11
Kent, WA (city) King County	95	0.10
Renton, WA (city) King County	95	0.10
Spokane, WA (city) Spokane County	95	0.05
Vancouver, WA (city) Clark County	88	0.05
Knik-Fairview, AK (cdp) Matanuska-Susitna Borough	87	0.58
Fairbanks, AK (city) Fairbanks North Star Borough	77	0.24
Edmonds, WA (city) Snohomish County	75	0.19
New York, NY (city) Kings County	75	<0.01
Shoreline, WA (city) King County	74	0.14
Phoenix, AZ (city) Maricopa County	74	0.01
San Diego, CA (city) San Diego County	70	0.01
Los Angeles, CA (city) Los Angeles County	69	<0.01
Klukwan, AK (cdp) Hoonah-Angoon Census Area	67	70.53
Port Angeles, WA (city) Clallam County	61	0.32
Salem, OR (city) Marion County	60	0.04
Mountlake Terrace, WA (city) Snohomish County	56	0.28
Sacramento, CA (city) Sacramento County	55	0.01
Tanaina, AK (cdp) Matanuska-Susitna Borough	54	0.66
Bellevue, WA (city) King County	54	0.04
Badger, AK (cdp) Fairbanks North Star Borough	53	0.27
Burien, WA (city) King County	53	0.16
Mount Vernon, WA (city) Skagit County	52	0.16
Eugene, OR (city) Lane County	51	0.03
Wasilla, AK (city) Matanuska-Susitna Borough	49	0.63
Kenai, AK (city) Kenai Peninsula Borough	48	0.68
Lakewood, WA (city) Pierce County	47	0.08
Yakima, WA (city) Yakima County	47	0.05
Metlakatla, AK (cdp) Prince of Wales-Hyder Census Area	46	3.27
Bothell, WA (city) King County	46	0.14
Lakes, AK (cdp) Matanuska-Susitna Borough	45	0.54
Puyallup, WA (city) Pierce County	45	0.12
Bremerton, WA (city) Kitsap County	42	0.11
SeaTac, WA (city) King County	41	0.15
Valdez, AK (city) Valdez-Cordova Census Area	40	1.01
Parkland, WA (cdp) Pierce County	40	0.11
San Jose, CA (city) Santa Clara County	40	<0.01
South Hill, WA (cdp) Pierce County	39	0.07
Lynnwood, WA (city) Snohomish County	38	0.11
Gresham, OR (city) Multnomah County	38	0.04
Martha Lake, WA (cdp) Snohomish County	37	0.24
Des Moines, WA (city) King County	37	0.12
Albuquerque, NM (city) Bernalillo County	37	0.01
Boise City, ID (city) Ada County	36	0.02
Colorado Springs, CO (city) El Paso County	36	0.01
Meadow Lakes, AK (cdp) Matanuska-Susitna Borough	35	0.46
College, AK (cdp) Fairbanks North Star Borough	35	0.27
Lake Stevens, WA (city) Snohomish County	35	0.12
Springfield, OR (city) Lane County	35	0.06
East Hill-Meridian, WA (cdp) King County	34	0.11
Gateway, AK (cdp) Matanuska-Susitna Borough	33	0.59
Palmer, AK (city) Matanuska-Susitna Borough	32	0.54
Keizer, OR (city) Marion County	32	0.09

Place	Population	%
Tucson, AZ (city) Pima County	32	0.01
Anacortes, WA (city) Skagit County	30	0.19
Bothell West, WA (cdp) Snohomish County	30	0.18
Hudson, CO (town) Weld County	29	1.23
Graham, WA (cdp) Pierce County	29	0.12
Las Vegas, NV (city) Clark County	29	<0.01
San Francisco, CA (city) San Francisco County	29	<0.01
Kodiak, AK (city) Kodiak Island Borough	28	0.46
McMinnville, OR (city) Yamhill County	28	0.09
Spokane Valley, WA (city) Spokane County	28	0.03
Brooklyn, NY (borough) Kings County	28	<0.01
Pacific, WA (city) King County	27	0.41
Fairwood, WA (cdp) King County	27	0.14
Lacey, WA (city) Thurston County	27	0.06
Nikiski, AK (cdp) Kenai Peninsula Borough	26	0.58
Covington, WA (city) King County	26	0.15
Reno, NV (city) Washoe County	26	0.01
Urban Honolulu, HI (cdp) Honolulu County	26	0.01
Seward, AK (city) Kenai Peninsula Borough	25	0.93
Soldotna, AK (city) Kenai Peninsula Borough	25	0.60
Lake Stickney, WA (cdp) Snohomish County	25	0.32
Longview, WA (city) Cowlitz County	25	0.07
Bryn Mawr-Skyway, WA (cdp) King County	24	0.15
University Place, WA (city) Pierce County	24	0.08
Prairie Ridge, WA (cdp) Pierce County	23	0.20
Bonney Lake, WA (city) Pierce County	23	0.13
Sammamish, WA (city) King County	23	0.05
Redmond, WA (city) King County	23	0.04
Skagway, AK (cdp) Skagway Municipality	22	2.39
Suquamish, WA (cdp) Kitsap County	22	0.53
White Center, WA (cdp) King County	22	0.16
Durango, CO (city) La Plata County	22	0.13
Corvallis, OR (city) Benton County	22	0.04
Goldstream, AK (cdp) Fairbanks North Star Borough	21	0.59
Sterling, AK (cdp) Kenai Peninsula Borough	21	0.37
Bethany, OR (cdp) Washington County	21	0.10
Kenmore, WA (city) King County	21	0.10
Kirkland, WA (city) King County	21	0.04
North Miami, FL (city) Miami-Dade County	21	0.04
Pocatello, ID (city) Bannock County	21	0.04
Kennewick, WA (city) Benton County	21	0.03
Henderson, NV (city) Clark County	21	0.01
Paradise, NV (cdp) Clark County	21	0.01
Mesa, AZ (city) Maricopa County	21	<0.01
Bear Creek, AK (cdp) Kenai Peninsula Borough	20	1.02
Kalifornsky, AK (cdp) Kenai Peninsula Borough	20	0.25
Maple Valley, WA (city) King County	20	0.09
Issaquah, WA (city) King County	20	0.07
Fremont, CA (city) Alameda County	20	0.01
Queens, NY (borough) Queens County	20	<0.01
Nome, AK (city) Nome Census Area	19	0.53
Ferndale, WA (city) Whatcom County	19	0.17
Lake Forest Park, WA (city) King County	19	0.15
Bainbridge Island, WA (city) Kitsap County	19	0.08
Hillsboro, OR (city) Washington County	19	0.02
Redding, CA (city) Shasta County	19	0.02
Virginia Beach, VA (ind. city) Virginia Beach independent city	19	<0.01
Pelican, AK (city) Hoonah-Angoon Census Area	18	20.45
Bethel, AK (city) Bethel Census Area	18	0.30
Aberdeen, WA (city) Grays Harbor County	18	0.11
Coos Bay, OR (city) Coos County	18	0.11
Five Corners, WA (cdp) Clark County	18	0.10
Stockton, CA (city) San Joaquin County	18	0.01
Austin, TX (city) Travis County	18	<0.01
El Paso, TX (city) El Paso County	18	<0.01
Philadelphia, PA (city) Philadelphia County	18	<0.01
Kotzebue, AK (city) Northwest Arctic Borough	17	0.53
Unalaska, AK (city) Aleutians West Census Area	17	0.39
Vashon, WA (cdp) King County	17	0.16
North Lynnwood, WA (cdp) Snohomish County	17	0.10
Mill Creek, WA (city) Snohomish County	17	0.09
Eastmont, WA (cdp) Snohomish County	17	0.08
Mukilteo, WA (city) Snohomish County	17	0.08
Spanaway, WA (cdp) Pierce County	17	0.06
Tigard, OR (city) Washington County	17	0.04

Please refer to the Explanation of Data in the front of the book for more detailed information.

Race

Alaska Native: Tlingit-Haida

Top 150 Places Sorted by Percent of Total Population

Based on all places, regardless of total population

Place	Population	%
Hobart Bay, AK (cdp) Hoonah-Angoon Census Area	1	100.00
Klukwan, AK (cdp) Hoonah-Angoon Census Area	67	70.53
Hydaburg, AK (city) Prince of Wales-Hyder Census Area	263	69.95
Angoon, AK (city) Hoonah-Angoon Census Area	300	65.36
Kake, AK (city) Petersburg Census Area	316	56.73
Saxman, AK (city) Ketchikan Gateway Borough	225	54.74
Hoonah, AK (city) Hoonah-Angoon Census Area	388	51.05
Klawock, AK (city) Prince of Wales-Hyder Census Area	322	42.65
Yakutat, AK (cdp) Yakutat City and Borough	223	33.69
Kasaan, AK (city) Prince of Wales-Hyder Census Area	12	24.49
Port Protection, AK (cdp) Prince of Wales-Hyder Census Area	10	20.83
Pelican, AK (city) Hoonah-Angoon Census Area	18	20.45
Craig, AK (city) Prince of Wales-Hyder Census Area	237	19.73
Whitestone Logging Camp, AK (cdp) Hoonah-Angoon Census Area	3	17.65
Ugashik, AK (cdp) Lake and Peninsula Borough	2	16.67
Sitka, AK (borough) Sitka City and Borough	1,394	15.70
Wrangell, AK (borough) Wrangell City and Borough	351	14.82
Ketchikan, AK (city) Ketchikan Gateway Borough	988	12.27
Juneau, AK (borough) Juneau City and Borough	3,825	12.23
Haines, AK (cdp) Haines Borough	187	10.92
Elfin Cove, AK (cdp) Hoonah-Angoon Census Area	2	10.00
Perryville, AK (cdp) Lake and Peninsula Borough	11	9.73
Petersburg, AK (city) Petersburg Census Area	252	8.55
Excursion Inlet, AK (cdp) Haines Borough	1	8.33
Point Baker, AK (cdp) Prince of Wales-Hyder Census Area	1	6.67
Covenant Life, AK (cdp) Haines Borough	5	5.81
Hollis, AK (cdp) Prince of Wales-Hyder Census Area	6	5.36
Hyder, AK (cdp) Prince of Wales-Hyder Census Area	4	4.60
Red Devil, AK (cdp) Bethel Census Area	1	4.35
Chitina, AK (cdp) Valdez-Cordova Census Area	5	3.97
Sleetmute, AK (cdp) Bethel Census Area	3	3.49
Metlakatla, AK (cdp) Prince of Wales-Hyder Census Area	46	3.27
Gustavus, AK (city) Hoonah-Angoon Census Area	14	3.17
Mosquito Lake, AK (cdp) Haines Borough	9	2.91
Coffman Cove, AK (city) Prince of Wales-Hyder Census Area	5	2.84
Naukati Bay, AK (cdp) Prince of Wales-Hyder Census Area	3	2.65
Primrose, AK (cdp) Kenai Peninsula Borough	2	2.56
Skagway, AK (cdp) Skagway Municipality	22	2.39
Eagle, AK (city) Southeast Fairbanks Census Area	2	2.33
Tenakee Springs, AK (city) Hoonah-Angoon Census Area	3	2.29
Idanha, OR (city) Marion County	3	2.24
Tetherow, OR (cdp) Deschutes County	1	2.22
Glacier View, AK (cdp) Matanuska-Susitna Borough	5	2.14
Spooner, MN (township) Lake of the Woods County	4	2.11
Lutak, AK (cdp) Haines Borough	1	2.04
Port Alexander, AK (city) Petersburg Census Area	1	1.92
Mud Bay, AK (cdp) Haines Borough	4	1.89
Egegik, AK (city) Lake and Peninsula Borough	2	1.83
Skamokawa Valley, WA (cdp) Wahkiakum County	7	1.75
Bessie, OK (town) Washita County	3	1.66
Clover, MN (township) Mahnomen County	2	1.65
Amanda Park, WA (cdp) Grays Harbor County	4	1.59
Jacksonport, AR (town) Jackson County	3	1.42
Sprague, WA (city) Lincoln County	6	1.35
Olivet, SD (town) Hutchinson County	1	1.35
Hudson, CO (town) Weld County	29	1.23
Nondalton, AK (city) Lake and Peninsula Borough	2	1.22
Cambridge, KS (city) Cowley County	1	1.22
Nanwalek, AK (cdp) Kenai Peninsula Borough	3	1.18
Ravenna, KY (city) Estill County	7	1.16
French Gulch, CA (cdp) Shasta County	4	1.16
Port Graham, AK (cdp) Kenai Peninsula Borough	2	1.13
Salamatof, AK (cdp) Kenai Peninsula Borough	11	1.12
Whiting, KS (city) Jackson County	2	1.07
Nipinnawasee, CA (cdp) Madera County	5	1.05
Central, AK (cdp) Yukon-Koyukuk Census Area	1	1.04
Bear Creek, AK (cdp) Kenai Peninsula Borough	20	1.02
Valdez, AK (city) Valdez-Cordova Census Area	40	1.01
Pawleys Island, SC (town) Georgetown County	1	0.97
Seward, AK (city) Kenai Peninsula Borough	25	0.93
Sutton-Alpine, AK (cdp) Matanuska-Susitna Borough	13	0.90
Hingham, MT (town) Hill County	1	0.85
Crystal Lakes, MO (city) Ray County	3	0.84
Knik River, AK (cdp) Matanuska-Susitna Borough	6	0.81
Holley, OR (cdp) Linn County	3	0.79
Anchorage, AK (municipality) Anchorage Municipality	2,241	0.77
Clark Fork, ID (city) Bonner County	4	0.75
Addy, WA (cdp) Stevens County	2	0.75
Henry, SD (town) Codington County	2	0.75
Alger, WA (cdp) Skagit County	3	0.74
Fox, AK (cdp) Fairbanks North Star Borough	3	0.72
Harrington, WA (city) Lincoln County	3	0.71
Orange, WI (town) Juneau County	4	0.70
Kenai, AK (city) Kenai Peninsula Borough	48	0.68
Farm Loop, AK (cdp) Matanuska-Susitna Borough	7	0.68
Tanaina, AK (cdp) Matanuska-Susitna Borough	54	0.66
Raft Island, WA (cdp) Pierce County	3	0.65
Long Barn, CA (cdp) Tuolumne County	1	0.65
Ridgeway, AK (cdp) Kenai Peninsula Borough	13	0.64
Wasilla, AK (city) Matanuska-Susitna Borough	49	0.63
Soldotna, AK (city) Kenai Peninsula Borough	25	0.60
Gateway, AK (cdp) Matanuska-Susitna Borough	33	0.59
Goldstream, AK (cdp) Fairbanks North Star Borough	21	0.59
Wimer, OR (cdp) Jackson County	4	0.59
Norway, SC (town) Orangeburg County	2	0.59
Kokhanok, AK (cdp) Lake and Peninsula Borough	1	0.59
Knik-Fairview, AK (cdp) Matanuska-Susitna Borough	87	0.58
Nikiski, AK (cdp) Kenai Peninsula Borough	26	0.58
Cordova, AK (city) Valdez-Cordova Census Area	13	0.58
Savanna, OK (town) Pittsburg County	4	0.58
McIntosh, SD (city) Corson County	1	0.58
Babb, MT (cdp) Glacier County	1	0.57
De Smet, ID (cdp) Benewah County	1	0.57
Two Rivers, AK (cdp) Fairbanks North Star Borough	4	0.56
Evening Shade, OK (cdp) Sequoyah County	2	0.56
Kenny Lake, AK (cdp) Valdez-Cordova Census Area	2	0.56
Orick, CA (cdp) Humboldt County	2	0.56
Hot Springs, MT (town) Sanders County	3	0.55
Lakes, AK (cdp) Matanuska-Susitna Borough	45	0.54
Palmer, AK (city) Matanuska-Susitna Borough	32	0.54
Dover, ID (city) Bonner County	3	0.54
Suquamish, WA (cdp) Kitsap County	22	0.53
Nome, AK (city) Nome Census Area	19	0.53
Kotzebue, AK (city) Northwest Arctic Borough	17	0.53
Lake Belt, MN (township) Martin County	1	0.53
Lake Grove, MN (township) Mahnomen County	1	0.53
Robie Creek, ID (cdp) Boise County	6	0.52
Bancroft, WV (town) Putnam County	3	0.51
Edgerton, WY (town) Natrona County	1	0.51
Ruth, CA (cdp) Trinity County	1	0.51
Meadowdale, WA (cdp) Snohomish County	14	0.50
Quilcene, WA (cdp) Jefferson County	3	0.50
Freeland, WA (cdp) Island County	10	0.49
Bowlegs, OK (town) Seminole County	2	0.49
Wilson Creek, WA (town) Grant County	1	0.49
Stansberry Lake, WA (cdp) Pierce County	10	0.48
Tok, AK (cdp) Southeast Fairbanks Census Area	6	0.48
Adair Village, OR (city) Benton County	4	0.48
Onalaska, WA (cdp) Lewis County	3	0.48
Fairfield, ID (city) Camas County	2	0.48
Cusick, WA (town) Pend Oreille County	1	0.48
Peavine, OK (cdp) Adair County	2	0.47
Meadow Lakes, AK (cdp) Matanuska-Susitna Borough	35	0.46
Kodiak, AK (city) Kodiak Island Borough	28	0.46
Butte, AK (cdp) Matanuska-Susitna Borough	15	0.46
North Powder, OR (city) Union County	2	0.46
Williamsburg, NM (village) Sierra County	2	0.45
Baring, WA (cdp) King County	1	0.45
Troy, MT (city) Lincoln County	4	0.43
Metolius, OR (city) Jefferson County	3	0.42
Womens Bay, AK (cdp) Kodiak Island Borough	3	0.42
Pacific, WA (city) King County	27	0.41
Ester, AK (cdp) Fairbanks North Star Borough	10	0.41
Moose Creek, AK (cdp) Fairbanks North Star Borough	3	0.40
Coleville, CA (cdp) Mono County	2	0.40
Hornbrook, CA (cdp) Siskiyou County	1	0.40
Unalaska, AK (city) Aleutians West Census Area	17	0.39
Big Lake, AK (cdp) Matanuska-Susitna Borough	13	0.39
Browning, MT (town) Glacier County	4	0.39
Garibaldi, OR (city) Tillamook County	3	0.39

Race

Alaska Native: Tlingit-Haida

Top 150 Places Sorted by Percent of Total Population

Based on places with total population of 7,500 or more

Place	Population	%
Sitka, AK (borough) Sitka City and Borough	1,394	15.70
Ketchikan, AK (city) Ketchikan Gateway Borough	988	12.27
Juneau, AK (borough) Juneau City and Borough	3,825	12.23
Anchorage, AK (municipality) Anchorage Municipality	2,241	0.77
Tanaina, AK (cdp) Matanuska-Susitna Borough	54	0.66
Wasilla, AK (city) Matanuska-Susitna Borough	49	0.63
Knik-Fairview, AK (cdp) Matanuska-Susitna Borough	87	0.58
Lakes, AK (cdp) Matanuska-Susitna Borough	45	0.54
Meadow Lakes, AK (cdp) Matanuska-Susitna Borough	35	0.46
Port Angeles, WA (city) Clallam County	61	0.32
Lake Stickney, WA (cdp) Snohomish County	25	0.32
Mountlake Terrace, WA (city) Snohomish County	56	0.28
Badger, AK (cdp) Fairbanks North Star Borough	53	0.27
College, AK (cdp) Fairbanks North Star Borough	35	0.27
Kalifornsky, AK (cdp) Kenai Peninsula Borough	20	0.25
Fairbanks, AK (city) Fairbanks North Star Borough	77	0.24
Martha Lake, WA (cdp) Snohomish County	37	0.24
Prairie Ridge, WA (cdp) Pierce County	23	0.20
Edmonds, WA (city) Snohomish County	75	0.19
Anacortes, WA (city) Skagit County	30	0.19
Bothell West, WA (cdp) Snohomish County	30	0.18
Alderwood Manor, WA (cdp) Snohomish County	15	0.18
Ferndale, WA (city) Whatcom County	19	0.17
Marysville, WA (city) Snohomish County	98	0.16
Burien, WA (city) King County	53	0.16
Mount Vernon, WA (city) Skagit County	52	0.16
White Center, WA (cdp) King County	22	0.16
Vashon, WA (cdp) King County	17	0.16
Poulsbo, WA (city) Kitsap County	15	0.16
Midland, WA (cdp) Pierce County	14	0.16
Auburn, WA (city) King County	102	0.15
SeaTac, WA (city) King County	41	0.15
Covington, WA (city) King County	26	0.15
Bryn Mawr-Skyway, WA (cdp) King County	24	0.15
Lake Forest Park, WA (city) King County	19	0.15
Sedro-Woolley, WA (city) Skagit County	16	0.15
Picnic Point, WA (cdp) Snohomish County	13	0.15
Everett, WA (city) Snohomish County	148	0.14
Bellingham, WA (city) Whatcom County	111	0.14
Shoreline, WA (city) King County	74	0.14
Bothell, WA (city) King County	46	0.14
Fairwood, WA (cdp) King County	27	0.14
Lakeland South, WA (cdp) King County	16	0.14
Shelton, WA (city) Mason County	14	0.14
Bonney Lake, WA (city) Pierce County	23	0.13
Durango, CO (city) La Plata County	22	0.13
Lake Tapps, WA (cdp) Pierce County	16	0.13
Edgewood, WA (city) Pierce County	12	0.13
Fife, WA (city) Pierce County	12	0.13
Seattle, WA (city) King County	729	0.12
Puyallup, WA (city) Pierce County	45	0.12
Des Moines, WA (city) King County	37	0.12
Lake Stevens, WA (city) Snohomish County	35	0.12
Graham, WA (cdp) Pierce County	29	0.12
Newport, OR (city) Lincoln County	12	0.12
Federal Way, WA (city) King County	97	0.11
Bremerton, WA (city) Kitsap County	42	0.11
Parkland, WA (cdp) Pierce County	40	0.11
Lynnwood, WA (city) Snohomish County	38	0.11
East Hill-Meridian, WA (cdp) King County	34	0.11
Aberdeen, WA (city) Grays Harbor County	18	0.11
Coos Bay, OR (city) Coos County	18	0.11
Bothell East, WA (cdp) Snohomish County	9	0.11
Summit, WA (cdp) Pierce County	9	0.11
Tacoma, WA (city) Pierce County	201	0.10
Kent, WA (city) King County	95	0.10
Renton, WA (city) King County	95	0.10
Bethany, OR (cdp) Washington County	21	0.10
Kenmore, WA (city) King County	21	0.10
Five Corners, WA (cdp) Clark County	18	0.10
North Lynnwood, WA (cdp) Snohomish County	17	0.10
Lakeland North, WA (cdp) King County	13	0.10
Port Townsend, WA (city) Jefferson County	9	0.10
Sumner, WA (city) Pierce County	9	0.10
Burlington, WA (city) Skagit County	8	0.10

Place	Population	%
Lincoln City, OR (city) Lincoln County	8	0.10
Keizer, OR (city) Marion County	32	0.09
McMinnville, OR (city) Yamhill County	28	0.09
Maple Valley, WA (city) King County	20	0.09
Mill Creek, WA (city) Snohomish County	17	0.09
Monroe, WA (city) Snohomish County	15	0.09
Centralia, WA (city) Lewis County	14	0.09
Astoria, OR (city) Clatsop County	9	0.09
Miami Shores, FL (village) Miami-Dade County	9	0.09
Shasta Lake, CA (city) Shasta County	9	0.09
Country Club, CA (cdp) San Joaquin County	8	0.09
Lakewood, WA (city) Pierce County	47	0.08
University Place, WA (city) Pierce County	24	0.08
Bainbridge Island, WA (city) Kitsap County	19	0.08
Eastmont, WA (cdp) Snohomish County	17	0.08
Mukilteo, WA (city) Snohomish County	17	0.08
Tukwila, WA (city) King County	15	0.08
Canby, OR (city) Clackamas County	13	0.08
Dallas, OR (city) Polk County	12	0.08
Elk Plain, WA (cdp) Pierce County	11	0.08
Washougal, WA (city) Clark County	11	0.08
East Wenatchee, WA (city) Douglas County	10	0.08
St. Helens, OR (city) Columbia County	10	0.08
Cheney, WA (city) Spokane County	9	0.08
Port Orchard, WA (city) Kitsap County	9	0.08
College Place, WA (city) Walla Walla County	7	0.08
Stayton, OR (city) Marion County	6	0.08
Sutherlin, OR (city) Douglas County	6	0.08
White City, OR (cdp) Jackson County	6	0.08
South Hill, WA (cdp) Pierce County	39	0.07
Longview, WA (city) Cowlitz County	25	0.07
Issaquah, WA (city) King County	20	0.07
Moses Lake, WA (city) Grant County	15	0.07
Silver Firs, WA (cdp) Snohomish County	15	0.07
Arlington, WA (city) Snohomish County	13	0.07
Ellensburg, WA (city) Kittitas County	13	0.07
Salmon Creek, WA (cdp) Clark County	13	0.07
Pendleton, OR (city) Umatilla County	12	0.07
West Richland, WA (city) Benton County	8	0.07
Woodinville, WA (city) King County	8	0.07
Birch Bay, WA (cdp) Whatcom County	6	0.07
Springfield, OR (city) Lane County	35	0.06
Lacey, WA (city) Thurston County	27	0.06
Spanaway, WA (cdp) Pierce County	17	0.06
Moscow, ID (city) Latah County	15	0.06
Redmond, OR (city) Deschutes County	15	0.06
Lebanon, OR (city) Linn County	10	0.06
Tumwater, WA (city) Thurston County	10	0.06
Artondale, WA (cdp) Pierce County	7	0.06
East Renton Highlands, WA (cdp) King County	7	0.06
Newcastle, WA (city) King County	6	0.06
Molalla, OR (city) Clackamas County	5	0.06
Waihee-Waiehu, HI (cdp) Maui County	5	0.06
Waller, WA (cdp) Pierce County	5	0.06
Spokane, WA (city) Spokane County	95	0.05
Vancouver, WA (city) Clark County	88	0.05
Yakima, WA (city) Yakima County	47	0.05
Sammamish, WA (city) King County	23	0.05
Oak Harbor, WA (city) Island County	10	0.05
Silverdale, WA (cdp) Kitsap County	9	0.05
Boulder City, NV (city) Clark County	7	0.05
Gladstone, OR (city) Clackamas County	6	0.05
Enumclaw, WA (city) King County	5	0.05
Havre, MT (city) Hill County	5	0.05
Maltby, WA (cdp) Snohomish County	5	0.05
Valley Center, CA (cdp) San Diego County	5	0.05
Walnut Grove, WA (cdp) Clark County	5	0.05
August, CA (cdp) San Joaquin County	4	0.05
Aurora, MO (city) Lawrence County	4	0.05
Cold Springs, NV (cdp) Washoe County	4	0.05
Hoquiam, WA (city) Grays Harbor County	4	0.05
Hornell, NY (city) Steuben County	4	0.05
Ione, CA (city) Amador County	4	0.05
Liberty Lake, WA (city) Spokane County	4	0.05
Sallisaw, OK (city) Sequoyah County	4	0.05

SECTION THREE

Please refer to the Explanation of Data in the front of the book for more detailed information.

Race

American Indian: Tohono O'Odham

U.S. and 50 States Sorted by Population and Percent of Total Population

Place	Population	%
United States	**23,478**	**0.01**
Arizona	19,001	0.30
California	2,359	0.01
Texas	252	<0.01
New Mexico	207	0.01
Nevada	120	<0.01
Washington	113	<0.01
Colorado	111	<0.01
New York	103	<0.01
Oregon	103	<0.01
Oklahoma	86	<0.01
Florida	71	<0.01
Idaho	69	<0.01
Pennsylvania	63	<0.01
Virginia	61	<0.01
Illinois	47	<0.01
North Carolina	47	<0.01
Utah	46	<0.01
Georgia	45	<0.01
Ohio	41	<0.01
Kansas	37	<0.01
Minnesota	29	<0.01
Missouri	29	<0.01
Alaska	28	<0.01
Hawaii	28	<0.01
Montana	27	<0.01
Tennessee	27	<0.01
Indiana	26	<0.01
Maryland	26	<0.01
Arkansas	25	<0.01
Kentucky	23	<0.01
New Jersey	23	<0.01
Michigan	22	<0.01
Massachusetts	21	<0.01
Iowa	20	<0.01
South Carolina	20	<0.01
Alabama	18	<0.01
Wisconsin	18	<0.01
Connecticut	15	<0.01
Wyoming	14	<0.01
Louisiana	8	<0.01
Maine	8	<0.01
Rhode Island	8	<0.01
South Dakota	8	<0.01
Mississippi	6	<0.01
New Hampshire	6	<0.01
Nebraska	5	<0.01
District of Columbia	3	<0.01
Delaware	2	<0.01
West Virginia	2	<0.01
North Dakota	1	<0.01
Vermont	0	0.00

Place	Population	%
Arizona	19,001	0.30
United States	**23,478**	**0.01**
California	2,359	0.01
New Mexico	207	0.01
Texas	252	<0.01
Nevada	120	<0.01
Washington	113	<0.01
Colorado	111	<0.01
New York	103	<0.01
Oregon	103	<0.01
Oklahoma	86	<0.01
Florida	71	<0.01
Idaho	69	<0.01
Pennsylvania	63	<0.01
Virginia	61	<0.01
Illinois	47	<0.01
North Carolina	47	<0.01
Utah	46	<0.01
Georgia	45	<0.01
Ohio	41	<0.01
Kansas	37	<0.01
Minnesota	29	<0.01
Missouri	29	<0.01
Alaska	28	<0.01
Hawaii	28	<0.01
Montana	27	<0.01
Tennessee	27	<0.01
Indiana	26	<0.01
Maryland	26	<0.01
Arkansas	25	<0.01
Kentucky	23	<0.01
New Jersey	23	<0.01
Michigan	22	<0.01
Massachusetts	21	<0.01
Iowa	20	<0.01
South Carolina	20	<0.01
Alabama	18	<0.01
Wisconsin	18	<0.01
Connecticut	15	<0.01
Wyoming	14	<0.01
Louisiana	8	<0.01
Maine	8	<0.01
Rhode Island	8	<0.01
South Dakota	8	<0.01
Mississippi	6	<0.01
New Hampshire	6	<0.01
Nebraska	5	<0.01
District of Columbia	3	<0.01
Delaware	2	<0.01
West Virginia	2	<0.01
North Dakota	1	<0.01
Vermont	0	0.00

Please refer to the Explanation of Data in the front of the book for more detailed information.

Race

American Indian: Tohono O'Odham

Top 150 Places Sorted by Population

Based on all places, regardless of total population

Place	Population	%
Tucson, AZ (city) Pima County	3,636	0.70
Sells, AZ (cdp) Pima County	2,076	83.21
Phoenix, AZ (city) Maricopa County	1,448	0.10
Casa Grande, AZ (city) Pinal County	873	1.80
Santa Rosa, AZ (cdp) Pima County	548	87.26
Drexel Heights, AZ (cdp) Pima County	407	1.47
Pisinemo, AZ (cdp) Pima County	300	93.46
Topawa, AZ (cdp) Pima County	287	95.99
Mesa, AZ (city) Maricopa County	252	0.06
Ajo, AZ (cdp) Pima County	248	7.51
Eloy, AZ (city) Pinal County	221	1.33
Los Angeles, CA (city) Los Angeles County	220	0.01
South Tucson, AZ (city) Pima County	213	3.77
Chuichu, AZ (cdp) Pinal County	191	71.00
San Miguel, AZ (cdp) Pima County	177	89.85
Gu Oidak, AZ (cdp) Pima County	160	85.11
Glendale, AZ (city) Maricopa County	157	0.07
Ali Chuk, AZ (cdp) Pima County	148	91.93
Chandler, AZ (city) Maricopa County	143	0.06
Maish Vaya, AZ (cdp) Pima County	141	89.24
Coolidge, AZ (city) Pinal County	121	1.02
Ali Chukson, AZ (cdp) Pima County	119	90.15
Arizona City, AZ (cdp) Pinal County	119	1.14
Florence, AZ (town) Pinal County	117	0.46
Cowlic, AZ (cdp) Pima County	116	85.93
Vaiva Vo, AZ (cdp) Pinal County	110	85.94
Wahak Hotrontk, AZ (cdp) Pima County	109	95.61
South Komelik, AZ (cdp) Pima County	108	97.30
Sacaton, AZ (cdp) Pinal County	108	4.04
Tempe, AZ (city) Maricopa County	101	0.06
Kaka, AZ (cdp) Maricopa County	97	68.79
Haivana Nakya, AZ (cdp) Pima County	92	95.83
Valencia West, AZ (cdp) Pima County	91	0.97
Yuma, AZ (city) Yuma County	84	0.09
Casas Adobes, AZ (cdp) Pima County	80	0.12
Chiawuli Tak, AZ (cdp) Pima County	78	100.00
Anegam, AZ (cdp) Pima County	78	51.66
Gila Bend, AZ (town) Maricopa County	78	4.06
Avondale, AZ (city) Maricopa County	71	0.09
San Diego, CA (city) San Diego County	69	0.01
Sahuarita, AZ (town) Pima County	68	0.27
San Jose, CA (city) Santa Clara County	68	0.01
Ali Molina, AZ (cdp) Pima County	67	94.37
Guadalupe, AZ (town) Maricopa County	66	1.20
Marana, AZ (town) Pima County	65	0.19
Albuquerque, NM (city) Bernalillo County	64	0.01
Fresno, CA (city) Fresno County	62	0.01
Three Points, AZ (cdp) Pima County	59	1.06
Maricopa, AZ (city) Pinal County	58	0.13
Flowing Wells, AZ (cdp) Pima County	57	0.35
San Tan Valley, AZ (cdp) Pinal County	50	0.06
Gilbert, AZ (town) Maricopa County	50	0.02
New York, NY (city) Kings County	48	<0.01
Ventana, AZ (cdp) Pima County	47	95.92
Tucson Estates, AZ (cdp) Pima County	47	0.39
Charco, AZ (cdp) Pima County	46	88.46
Ak-Chin Village, AZ (cdp) Pinal County	44	5.10
Surprise, AZ (city) Maricopa County	42	0.04
Peoria, AZ (city) Yavapai County	42	0.03
Scottsdale, AZ (city) Maricopa County	41	0.02
Winslow, AZ (city) Navajo County	37	0.38
Dallas, TX (city) Dallas County	37	<0.01
Blackwater, AZ (cdp) Pinal County	35	3.30
Buckeye, AZ (town) Maricopa County	35	0.07
Victorville, CA (city) San Bernardino County	35	0.03
Casa Blanca, AZ (cdp) Pinal County	33	2.38
Nolic, AZ (cdp) Pima County	32	86.49
Ko Vaya, AZ (cdp) Pima County	32	69.57
Bakersfield, CA (city) Kern County	32	0.01
Stanfield, AZ (cdp) Pinal County	31	4.19
Komatke, AZ (cdp) Maricopa County	30	3.65
Oakland, CA (city) Alameda County	29	0.01
Riverside, CA (city) Riverside County	29	0.01
San Antonio, TX (city) Medina County	29	<0.01
Chula Vista, CA (city) San Diego County	28	0.01

Place	Population	%
Colorado Springs, CO (city) El Paso County	28	0.01
Fort Worth, TX (city) Tarrant County	28	<0.01
Banning, CA (city) Riverside County	27	0.09
Moreno Valley, CA (city) Riverside County	27	0.01
Las Vegas, NV (city) Clark County	27	<0.01
San Francisco, CA (city) San Francisco County	27	<0.01
Upper Santan Village, AZ (cdp) Pinal County	26	5.25
Sacramento, CA (city) Sacramento County	26	0.01
Second Mesa, AZ (cdp) Navajo County	24	2.49
Summit, AZ (cdp) Pima County	24	0.45
Kohatk, AZ (cdp) Pinal County	23	85.19
Ak Chin, AZ (cdp) Pima County	23	76.67
Sacate Village, AZ (cdp) Pinal County	23	13.61
Sacaton Flats Village, AZ (cdp) Pinal County	23	4.25
Anaheim, CA (city) Orange County	23	0.01
Fort Defiance, AZ (cdp) Apache County	22	0.61
Avra Valley, AZ (cdp) Pima County	22	0.36
South Whittier, CA (cdp) Los Angeles County	22	0.04
Flagstaff, AZ (city) Coconino County	22	0.03
Goodyear, AZ (city) Maricopa County	21	0.03
Fontana, CA (city) San Bernardino County	21	0.01
Modesto, CA (city) Stanislaus County	21	0.01
Maricopa Colony, AZ (cdp) Maricopa County	20	2.82
First Mesa, AZ (cdp) Navajo County	20	1.29
Oxnard, CA (city) Ventura County	20	0.01
Goodyear Village, AZ (cdp) Pinal County	19	4.16
Hotevilla-Bacavi, AZ (cdp) Navajo County	19	1.99
Picture Rocks, AZ (cdp) Pima County	19	0.20
Catalina Foothills, AZ (cdp) Pima County	19	0.04
Hesperia, CA (city) San Bernardino County	19	0.02
Anchorage, AK (municipality) Anchorage Municipality	19	0.01
Palmdale, CA (city) Los Angeles County	19	0.01
Paradise, NV (cdp) Clark County	19	0.01
Lower Santan Village, AZ (cdp) Pinal County	18	4.81
Stotonic Village, AZ (cdp) Pinal County	18	2.73
Dublin, CA (city) Alameda County	18	0.04
Denver, CO (city) Denver County	18	<0.01
Long Beach, CA (city) Los Angeles County	18	<0.01
Oklahoma City, OK (city) Oklahoma County	18	<0.01
Portland, OR (city) Multnomah County	18	<0.01
Holbrook, AZ (city) Navajo County	17	0.34
Rio Rico, AZ (cdp) Santa Cruz County	17	0.09
Apache Junction, AZ (city) Pinal County	17	0.05
San Buenaventura (Ventura), CA (city) Ventura County	17	0.02
West Covina, CA (city) Los Angeles County	17	0.02
Santa Clara, CA (city) Santa Clara County	17	0.01
Moenkopi, AZ (cdp) Coconino County	16	1.66
Whiteriver, AZ (cdp) Navajo County	16	0.39
Gallup, NM (city) McKinley County	16	0.07
Oro Valley, AZ (town) Pima County	16	0.04
Montebello, CA (city) Los Angeles County	16	0.03
East Los Angeles, CA (cdp) Los Angeles County	16	0.01
Santa Ana, CA (city) Orange County	16	<0.01
Kayenta, AZ (cdp) Navajo County	15	0.29
Desert Hot Springs, CA (city) Riverside County	15	0.06
Citrus Heights, CA (city) Sacramento County	15	0.02
Simi Valley, CA (city) Ventura County	15	0.01
Stockton, CA (city) San Joaquin County	15	0.01
Manhattan, NY (borough) New York County	15	<0.01
Inglewood, CA (city) Los Angeles County	14	0.01
San Bernardino, CA (city) San Bernardino County	14	0.01
St. Johns, AZ (cdp) Maricopa County	13	2.73
San Carlos, AZ (cdp) Gila County	13	0.32
Somerton, AZ (city) Yuma County	13	0.09
Whittier, CA (city) Los Angeles County	13	0.02
Escondido, CA (city) San Diego County	13	0.01
Gila Crossing, AZ (cdp) Maricopa County	12	1.93
Prescott Valley, AZ (town) Yavapai County	12	0.03
Sierra Vista, AZ (city) Cochise County	12	0.03
Glendora, CA (city) Los Angeles County	12	0.02
Huntington Park, CA (city) Los Angeles County	12	0.02
Deltona, FL (city) Volusia County	12	0.01
North Las Vegas, NV (city) Clark County	12	0.01
Norwalk, CA (city) Los Angeles County	12	0.01
Lompoc, CA (city) Santa Barbara County	11	0.03

Please refer to the Explanation of Data in the front of the book for more detailed information.

Race

American Indian: Tohono O'Odham

Top 150 Places Sorted by Percent of Total Population

Based on all places, regardless of total population

Place	Population	%
Chiawuli Tak, AZ (cdp) Pima County	78	100.00
Comobabi, AZ (cdp) Pima County	8	100.00
South Komelik, AZ (cdp) Pima County	108	97.30
Topawa, AZ (cdp) Pima County	287	95.99
Ventana, AZ (cdp) Pima County	47	95.92
Haivana Nakya, AZ (cdp) Pima County	92	95.83
Wahak Hotrontk, AZ (cdp) Pima County	109	95.61
Ali Molina, AZ (cdp) Pima County	67	94.37
Pisinemo, AZ (cdp) Pima County	300	93.46
Ali Chuk, AZ (cdp) Pima County	148	91.93
Ali Chukson, AZ (cdp) Pima County	119	90.15
San Miguel, AZ (cdp) Pima County	177	89.85
Maish Vaya, AZ (cdp) Pima County	141	89.24
Charco, AZ (cdp) Pima County	46	88.46
Santa Rosa, AZ (cdp) Pima County	548	87.26
Nolic, AZ (cdp) Pima County	32	86.49
Vaiva Vo, AZ (cdp) Pinal County	110	85.94
Cowlic, AZ (cdp) Pima County	116	85.93
Kohatk, AZ (cdp) Pinal County	23	85.19
Gu Oidak, AZ (cdp) Pima County	160	85.11
Sells, AZ (cdp) Pima County	2,076	83.21
Ak Chin, AZ (cdp) Pima County	23	76.67
Chuichu, AZ (cdp) Pinal County	191	71.00
Ko Vaya, AZ (cdp) Pima County	32	69.57
Kaka, AZ (cdp) Maricopa County	97	68.79
Tat Momoli, AZ (cdp) Pinal County	6	60.00
Anegam, AZ (cdp) Pima County	78	51.66
Sacate Village, AZ (cdp) Pinal County	23	13.61
Hard Rock, AZ (cdp) Navajo County	9	9.57
Ajo, AZ (cdp) Pima County	248	7.51
Upper Santan Village, AZ (cdp) Pinal County	26	5.25
Ak-Chin Village, AZ (cdp) Pinal County	44	5.10
Lower Santan Village, AZ (cdp) Pinal County	18	4.81
Sacaton Flats Village, AZ (cdp) Pinal County	23	4.25
Stanfield, AZ (cdp) Pinal County	31	4.19
Goodyear Village, AZ (cdp) Pinal County	19	4.16
Gila Bend, AZ (town) Maricopa County	78	4.06
Sacaton, AZ (cdp) Pinal County	108	4.04
South Tucson, AZ (city) Pima County	213	3.77
Komatke, AZ (cdp) Maricopa County	30	3.65
Blackwater, AZ (cdp) Pinal County	35	3.30
Maricopa Colony, AZ (cdp) Maricopa County	20	2.82
Stotonic Village, AZ (cdp) Pinal County	18	2.73
St. Johns, AZ (cdp) Maricopa County	13	2.73
Second Mesa, AZ (cdp) Navajo County	24	2.49
Jeddito, AZ (cdp) Navajo County	7	2.39
Casa Blanca, AZ (cdp) Pinal County	33	2.38
Wide Ruins, AZ (cdp) Apache County	4	2.27
Hotevilla-Bacavi, AZ (cdp) Navajo County	19	1.99
Gila Crossing, AZ (cdp) Maricopa County	12	1.93
Bald Head Island, NC (village) Brunswick County	3	1.90
Grayson, OK (town) Okmulgee County	3	1.89
Old Agency, MT (cdp) Sanders County	2	1.87
Casa Grande, AZ (city) Pinal County	873	1.80
Moenkopi, AZ (cdp) Coconino County	16	1.66
Winston, NM (cdp) Sierra County	1	1.64
Carrizo, AZ (cdp) Gila County	2	1.57
Drexel Heights, AZ (cdp) Pima County	407	1.47
Kicking Horse, MT (cdp) Lake County	4	1.40
Whiterocks, UT (cdp) Uintah County	4	1.38
Eloy, AZ (city) Pinal County	221	1.33
Keams Canyon, AZ (cdp) Navajo County	4	1.32
Wet Camp Village, AZ (cdp) Pinal County	3	1.31
First Mesa, AZ (cdp) Navajo County	20	1.29
Guadalupe, AZ (town) Maricopa County	66	1.20
Why, AZ (cdp) Pima County	2	1.20
Arizona City, AZ (cdp) Pinal County	119	1.14
St. Pierre, MT (cdp) Hill County	4	1.14
Three Points, AZ (cdp) Pima County	59	1.06
Picacho, AZ (cdp) Pinal County	5	1.06
Coolidge, AZ (city) Pinal County	121	1.02
Valencia West, AZ (cdp) Pima County	91	0.97
Schurz, NV (cdp) Mineral County	6	0.91
Seama, NM (cdp) Cibola County	4	0.86
Frazer, MT (cdp) Valley County	3	0.83
Garden Farms, CA (cdp) San Luis Obispo County	3	0.78
Ash Fork, AZ (cdp) Yavapai County	3	0.76
Tucson, AZ (city) Pima County	3,636	0.70
Littletown, AZ (cdp) Pima County	6	0.69
Wenden, AZ (cdp) La Paz County	5	0.69
North Acomita Village, NM (cdp) Cibola County	2	0.66
Elephant Head, AZ (cdp) Pima County	4	0.65
Fort Defiance, AZ (cdp) Apache County	22	0.61
Isleta Village Proper, NM (cdp) Bernalillo County	3	0.61
Arivaca, AZ (cdp) Pima County	4	0.58
Fort Bidwell, CA (cdp) Modoc County	1	0.58
Goessel, KS (city) Marion County	3	0.56
Sheldon, MO (city) Vernon County	3	0.55
Glencoe, OK (town) Payne County	3	0.50
Buckhorn, NM (cdp) Grant County	1	0.50
Shongopovi, AZ (cdp) Navajo County	4	0.48
Florence, AZ (town) Pinal County	117	0.46
Summit, AZ (cdp) Pima County	24	0.45
Icehouse Canyon, AZ (cdp) Gila County	3	0.44
Hillburn, NY (village) Rockland County	4	0.42
St. David, AZ (cdp) Cochise County	7	0.41
Knoxville, AR (town) Johnson County	3	0.41
Sawmill, AZ (cdp) Apache County	3	0.40
Tucson Estates, AZ (cdp) Pima County	47	0.39
Whiteriver, AZ (cdp) Navajo County	16	0.39
Indian Wells, AZ (cdp) Navajo County	1	0.39
Winslow, AZ (city) Navajo County	37	0.38
Halchita, UT (cdp) San Juan County	1	0.38
Avra Valley, AZ (cdp) Pima County	22	0.36
Miles, TX (city) Runnels County	3	0.36
York, AZ (cdp) Greenlee County	2	0.36
Flowing Wells, AZ (cdp) Pima County	57	0.35
Heber-Overgaard, AZ (cdp) Navajo County	10	0.35
Crownpoint, NM (cdp) McKinley County	8	0.35
Mammoth, AZ (town) Pinal County	5	0.35
North Fork, AZ (cdp) Navajo County	5	0.35
Holbrook, AZ (city) Navajo County	17	0.34
Dilkon, AZ (cdp) Navajo County	4	0.34
Boyne Falls, MI (village) Charlevoix County	1	0.34
Waconia, MN (township) Carver County	4	0.33
Groveland, CA (cdp) Tuolumne County	2	0.33
San Carlos, AZ (cdp) Gila County	13	0.32
Parker, AZ (town) La Paz County	10	0.32
Kayenta, AZ (cdp) Navajo County	15	0.29
Toquerville, UT (town) Washington County	4	0.29
San Manuel, AZ (cdp) Pinal County	10	0.28
St. Michaels, AZ (cdp) Apache County	4	0.28
Fort Duchesne, UT (cdp) Uintah County	2	0.28
Sahuarita, AZ (town) Pima County	68	0.27
Kykotsmovi Village, AZ (cdp) Navajo County	2	0.27
Grenada, CA (cdp) Siskiyou County	1	0.27
Talty, TX (town) Kaufman County	4	0.26
Boneau, MT (cdp) Chouteau County	1	0.26
Superior, AZ (town) Pinal County	7	0.25
Bylas, AZ (cdp) Graham County	5	0.25
Canyon Day, AZ (cdp) Gila County	3	0.25
Happy Camp, CA (cdp) Siskiyou County	3	0.25
Tumacacori-Carmen, AZ (cdp) Santa Cruz County	1	0.25
Winterhaven, CA (cdp) Imperial County	1	0.25
Swift Trail Junction, AZ (cdp) Graham County	7	0.24
Covington, NY (town) Wyoming County	3	0.24
Laguna, NM (cdp) Cibola County	3	0.24
Mariposa, CA (cdp) Mariposa County	5	0.23
Hallstead, PA (borough) Susquehanna County	3	0.23
Keene, CA (cdp) Kern County	1	0.23
Manzanola, CO (town) Otero County	1	0.23
Los Luceros, NM (cdp) Rio Arriba County	2	0.22
Seligman, AZ (cdp) Yavapai County	1	0.22
Monterey, TN (town) Putnam County	6	0.21
Wellton, AZ (town) Yuma County	6	0.21
Moriarty, NM (city) Torrance County	4	0.21
Empire City, OK (town) Stephens County	2	0.21
Picture Rocks, AZ (cdp) Pima County	19	0.20
Cactus Flats, AZ (cdp) Graham County	3	0.20
Morenci, AZ (cdp) Greenlee County	3	0.20

Please refer to the Explanation of Data in the front of the book for more detailed information.

Race

American Indian: Tohono O'Odham

Top 150 Places Sorted by Percent of Total Population

Based on places with total population of 7,500 or more

Place	Population	%
Casa Grande, AZ (city) Pinal County	873	1.80
Drexel Heights, AZ (cdp) Pima County	407	1.47
Eloy, AZ (city) Pinal County	221	1.33
Arizona City, AZ (cdp) Pinal County	119	1.14
Coolidge, AZ (city) Pinal County	121	1.02
Valencia West, AZ (cdp) Pima County	91	0.97
Tucson, AZ (city) Pima County	3,636	0.70
Florence, AZ (town) Pinal County	117	0.46
Tucson Estates, AZ (cdp) Pima County	47	0.39
Winslow, AZ (city) Navajo County	37	0.38
Flowing Wells, AZ (cdp) Pima County	57	0.35
Sahuarita, AZ (town) Pima County	68	0.27
Picture Rocks, AZ (cdp) Pima County	19	0.20
Marana, AZ (town) Pima County	65	0.19
Maricopa, AZ (city) Pinal County	58	0.13
Casas Adobes, AZ (cdp) Pima County	80	0.12
Earlimart, CA (cdp) Tulare County	9	0.11
Phoenix, AZ (city) Maricopa County	1,448	0.10
Yuma, AZ (city) Yuma County	84	0.09
Avondale, AZ (city) Maricopa County	71	0.09
Banning, CA (city) Riverside County	27	0.09
Rio Rico, AZ (cdp) Santa Cruz County	17	0.09
Somerton, AZ (city) Yuma County	13	0.09
Grants, NM (city) Cibola County	8	0.09
Derby, CO (cdp) Adams County	6	0.08
Glendale, AZ (city) Maricopa County	157	0.07
Buckeye, AZ (town) Maricopa County	35	0.07
Gallup, NM (city) McKinley County	16	0.07
Muscoy, CA (cdp) San Bernardino County	7	0.07
Mesa, AZ (city) Maricopa County	252	0.06
Chandler, AZ (city) Maricopa County	143	0.06
Tempe, AZ (city) Maricopa County	101	0.06
San Tan Valley, AZ (cdp) Pinal County	50	0.06
Desert Hot Springs, CA (city) Riverside County	15	0.06
Douglas, AZ (city) Cochise County	10	0.06
Charter Oak, CA (cdp) Los Angeles County	6	0.06
Safford, AZ (city) Graham County	6	0.06
Vail, AZ (cdp) Pima County	6	0.06
Waseca, MN (city) Waseca County	6	0.06
Thousand Palms, CA (cdp) Riverside County	5	0.06
Apache Junction, AZ (city) Pinal County	17	0.05
Sun Village, CA (cdp) Los Angeles County	6	0.05
Anaconda-Deer Lodge County, MT (special city) Deer Lodge County	5	0.05
Silver City, NM (town) Grant County	5	0.05
Cortez, CO (city) Montezuma County	4	0.05
Globe, AZ (city) Gila County	4	0.05
Oak Hills, CA (cdp) San Bernardino County	4	0.05
Surprise, AZ (city) Maricopa County	42	0.04
South Whittier, CA (cdp) Los Angeles County	22	0.04
Catalina Foothills, AZ (cdp) Pima County	19	0.04
Dublin, CA (city) Alameda County	18	0.04
Oro Valley, AZ (town) Pima County	16	0.04
Blythe, CA (city) Riverside County	8	0.04
Salida, CA (cdp) Stanislaus County	6	0.04
Santa Fe Springs, CA (city) Los Angeles County	6	0.04
Valle Vista, CA (cdp) Riverside County	6	0.04
Lake City, FL (city) Columbia County	5	0.04
Lake Los Angeles, CA (cdp) Los Angeles County	5	0.04
Verde Village, AZ (cdp) Yavapai County	5	0.04
Artesia, NM (city) Eddy County	4	0.04
Chino Valley, AZ (town) Yavapai County	4	0.04
College, PA (township) Centre County	4	0.04
Forest Acres, SC (city) Richland County	4	0.04
Summit, IL (village) Cook County	4	0.04
Wells, ME (town) York County	4	0.04
White House, TN (city) Sumner County	4	0.04
Calimesa, CA (city) Riverside County	3	0.04
Catalina, AZ (cdp) Pima County	3	0.04
White City, OR (cdp) Jackson County	3	0.04
Peoria, AZ (city) Yavapai County	42	0.03
Victorville, CA (city) San Bernardino County	35	0.03
Flagstaff, AZ (city) Coconino County	22	0.03
Goodyear, AZ (city) Maricopa County	21	0.03
Montebello, CA (city) Los Angeles County	16	0.03
Prescott Valley, AZ (town) Yavapai County	12	0.03
Sierra Vista, AZ (city) Cochise County	12	0.03
Lompoc, CA (city) Santa Barbara County	11	0.03
Bell, CA (city) Los Angeles County	10	0.03
Fortuna Foothills, AZ (cdp) Yuma County	8	0.03
Corsicana, TX (city) Navarro County	7	0.03
Fountain, CO (city) El Paso County	7	0.03
Maywood, CA (city) Los Angeles County	7	0.03
San Luis, AZ (city) Yuma County	7	0.03
Valinda, CA (cdp) Los Angeles County	7	0.03
Winter Gardens, CA (cdp) San Diego County	7	0.03
Meadowbrook, VA (cdp) Chesterfield County	6	0.03
Arcata, CA (city) Humboldt County	5	0.03
Dyersburg, TN (city) Dyer County	5	0.03
Fernley, NV (city) Lyon County	5	0.03
Four Corners, OR (cdp) Marion County	5	0.03
Lathrop, CA (city) San Joaquin County	5	0.03
Tanque Verde, AZ (cdp) Pima County	5	0.03
Addison, TX (town) Dallas County	4	0.03
Graham, NC (city) Alamance County	4	0.03
Lebanon, OR (city) Linn County	4	0.03
Soddy-Daisy, TN (city) Hamilton County	4	0.03
Chester, NY (town) Orange County	3	0.03
Country Club, CA (cdp) San Joaquin County	3	0.03
Federal Heights, CO (city) Adams County	3	0.03
Knightdale, NC (town) Wake County	3	0.03
Largo, MD (cdp) Prince George's County	3	0.03
Mitchellville, MD (cdp) Prince George's County	3	0.03
Silverton, OR (city) Marion County	3	0.03
View Park-Windsor Hills, CA (cdp) Los Angeles County	3	0.03
Center, PA (township) Butler County	2	0.03
Mount Vista, WA (cdp) Clark County	2	0.03
Gilbert, AZ (town) Maricopa County	50	0.02
Scottsdale, AZ (city) Maricopa County	41	0.02
Hesperia, CA (city) San Bernardino County	19	0.02
San Buenaventura (Ventura), CA (city) Ventura County	17	0.02
West Covina, CA (city) Los Angeles County	17	0.02
Citrus Heights, CA (city) Sacramento County	15	0.02
Whittier, CA (city) Los Angeles County	13	0.02
Glendora, CA (city) Los Angeles County	12	0.02
Huntington Park, CA (city) Los Angeles County	12	0.02
Gardena, CA (city) Los Angeles County	10	0.02
Hacienda Heights, CA (cdp) Los Angeles County	10	0.02
Santa Cruz, CA (city) Santa Cruz County	10	0.02
Twin Falls, ID (city) Twin Falls County	10	0.02
La Mirada, CA (city) Los Angeles County	9	0.02
San Bruno, CA (city) San Mateo County	9	0.02
Highland, CA (city) San Bernardino County	8	0.02
La Presa, CA (cdp) San Diego County	8	0.02
Novato, CA (city) Marin County	8	0.02
Azusa, CA (city) Los Angeles County	7	0.02
La Puente, CA (city) Los Angeles County	7	0.02
Moorpark, CA (city) Ventura County	7	0.02
Atwater, CA (city) Merced County	6	0.02
Middletown, NY (city) Orange County	6	0.02
Mount Vernon, WA (city) Skagit County	6	0.02
New Windsor, NY (town) Orange County	6	0.02
Twentynine Palms, CA (city) San Bernardino County	6	0.02
Uniondale, NY (cdp) Nassau County	6	0.02
Wildomar, CA (city) Riverside County	6	0.02
Atascadero, CA (city) San Luis Obispo County	5	0.02
Bay Point, CA (cdp) Contra Costa County	5	0.02
El Mirage, AZ (city) Maricopa County	5	0.02
Kingman, AZ (city) Mohave County	5	0.02
San Fernando, CA (city) Los Angeles County	5	0.02
Tualatin, OR (city) Washington County	5	0.02
University Place, WA (city) Pierce County	5	0.02
Vineyard, CA (cdp) Sacramento County	5	0.02
Cameron Park, CA (cdp) El Dorado County	4	0.02
Hercules, CA (city) Contra Costa County	4	0.02
Lakeside, CA (cdp) San Diego County	4	0.02
Nogales, AZ (city) Santa Cruz County	4	0.02
Oak Harbor, WA (city) Island County	4	0.02
Oakdale, CA (city) Stanislaus County	4	0.02
Rosamond, CA (cdp) Kern County	4	0.02
Roselle, NJ (borough) Union County	4	0.02

SECTION THREE

Please refer to the Explanation of Data in the front of the book for more detailed information.

Race

Alaska Native: Tsimshian

U.S. and 50 States Sorted by Population and Percent of Total Population

Place	Population	%
United States	**3,755**	**<0.01**
Alaska	1,939	0.27
Washington	956	0.01
California	190	<0.01
Oregon	153	<0.01
Idaho	43	<0.01
Arizona	37	<0.01
Texas	35	<0.01
Colorado	33	<0.01
Ohio	28	<0.01
Florida	24	<0.01
Michigan	22	<0.01
Oklahoma	20	<0.01
Georgia	18	<0.01
Nevada	18	<0.01
Montana	17	<0.01
New Mexico	16	<0.01
Hawaii	15	<0.01
Maine	15	<0.01
Tennessee	14	<0.01
Kentucky	13	<0.01
Pennsylvania	13	<0.01
Wisconsin	13	<0.01
Maryland	12	<0.01
Utah	12	<0.01
Kansas	11	<0.01
Virginia	11	<0.01
Iowa	9	<0.01
Minnesota	9	<0.01
South Carolina	8	<0.01
Illinois	7	<0.01
Missouri	7	<0.01
Indiana	5	<0.01
New York	5	<0.01
North Carolina	5	<0.01
Alabama	4	<0.01
Connecticut	4	<0.01
Massachusetts	3	<0.01
North Dakota	3	<0.01
Arkansas	2	<0.01
Mississippi	2	<0.01
Nebraska	1	<0.01
New Jersey	1	<0.01
Rhode Island	1	<0.01
Vermont	1	<0.01
Delaware	0	0.00
District of Columbia	0	0.00
Louisiana	0	0.00
New Hampshire	0	0.00
South Dakota	0	0.00
West Virginia	0	0.00
Wyoming	0	0.00

Place	Population	%
Alaska	1,939	0.27
Washington	956	0.01
United States	**3,755**	**<0.01**
California	190	<0.01
Oregon	153	<0.01
Idaho	43	<0.01
Arizona	37	<0.01
Texas	35	<0.01
Colorado	33	<0.01
Ohio	28	<0.01
Florida	24	<0.01
Michigan	22	<0.01
Oklahoma	20	<0.01
Georgia	18	<0.01
Nevada	18	<0.01
Montana	17	<0.01
New Mexico	16	<0.01
Hawaii	15	<0.01
Maine	15	<0.01
Tennessee	14	<0.01
Kentucky	13	<0.01
Pennsylvania	13	<0.01
Wisconsin	13	<0.01
Maryland	12	<0.01
Utah	12	<0.01
Kansas	11	<0.01
Virginia	11	<0.01
Iowa	9	<0.01
Minnesota	9	<0.01
South Carolina	8	<0.01
Illinois	7	<0.01
Missouri	7	<0.01
Indiana	5	<0.01
New York	5	<0.01
North Carolina	5	<0.01
Alabama	4	<0.01
Connecticut	4	<0.01
Massachusetts	3	<0.01
North Dakota	3	<0.01
Arkansas	2	<0.01
Mississippi	2	<0.01
Nebraska	1	<0.01
New Jersey	1	<0.01
Rhode Island	1	<0.01
Vermont	1	<0.01
Delaware	0	0.00
District of Columbia	0	0.00
Louisiana	0	0.00
New Hampshire	0	0.00
South Dakota	0	0.00
West Virginia	0	0.00
Wyoming	0	0.00

Please refer to the Explanation of Data in the front of the book for more detailed information.

Race

Alaska Native: Tsimshian

Top 150 Places Sorted by Population

Based on all places, regardless of total population

Place	Population	%
Metlakatla, AK (cdp) Prince of Wales-Hyder Census Area	1,019	72.53
Ketchikan, AK (city) Ketchikan Gateway Borough	254	3.16
Anchorage, AK (municipality) Anchorage Municipality	221	0.08
Juneau, AK (borough) Juneau City and Borough	114	0.36
Seattle, WA (city) King County	108	0.02
Sitka, AK (borough) Sitka City and Borough	65	0.73
Portland, OR (city) Multnomah County	32	0.01
Auburn, WA (city) King County	30	0.04
Everett, WA (city) Snohomish County	26	0.03
Tacoma, WA (city) Pierce County	24	0.01
Shoreline, WA (city) King County	22	0.04
Vancouver, WA (city) Clark County	21	0.01
Wrangell, AK (borough) Wrangell City and Borough	20	0.84
Kent, WA (city) King County	20	0.02
Burien, WA (city) King County	19	0.06
Eugene, OR (city) Lane County	19	0.01
Federal Way, WA (city) King County	18	0.02
Bellingham, WA (city) Whatcom County	17	0.02
Marysville, WA (city) Snohomish County	16	0.03
Kenai, AK (city) Kenai Peninsula Borough	15	0.21
Renton, WA (city) King County	15	0.02
Los Angeles, CA (city) Los Angeles County	14	<0.01
Bellevue, WA (city) King County	13	0.01
Unalaska, AK (city) Aleutians West Census Area	12	0.27
Edmonds, WA (city) Snohomish County	12	0.03
Valdez, AK (city) Valdez-Cordova Census Area	11	0.28
Phoenix, AZ (city) Maricopa County	11	<0.01
Saxman, AK (city) Ketchikan Gateway Borough	10	2.43
Lakes, AK (cdp) Matanuska-Susitna Borough	10	0.12
Inglewood-Finn Hill, WA (cdp) King County	10	0.04
Lakewood, WA (city) Pierce County	10	0.02
Yakima, WA (city) Yakima County	10	0.01
Des Moines, WA (city) King County	9	0.03
Sammamish, WA (city) King County	9	0.02
Salem, OR (city) Marion County	9	0.01
Kotzebue, AK (city) Northwest Arctic Borough	8	0.25
Port Angeles, WA (city) Clallam County	8	0.04
Parkland, WA (cdp) Pierce County	8	0.02
Kennewick, WA (city) Benton County	8	0.01
Westminster, CA (city) Orange County	8	0.01
Colorado Springs, CO (city) El Paso County	8	<0.01
Mesa, AZ (city) Maricopa County	8	<0.01
San Francisco, CA (city) San Francisco County	8	<0.01
Bothell, WA (city) King County	7	0.02
Lewiston, ID (city) Nez Perce County	7	0.02
Lynnwood, WA (city) Snohomish County	7	0.02
Chico, CA (city) Butte County	7	0.01
Lenexa, KS (city) Johnson County	7	0.01
Thornton, CO (city) Adams County	7	0.01
San Diego, CA (city) San Diego County	7	<0.01
Spokane, WA (city) Spokane County	7	<0.01
Skagway, AK (cdp) Skagway Municipality	6	0.65
Ocean Shores, WA (city) Grays Harbor County	6	0.11
Hoquiam, WA (city) Grays Harbor County	6	0.07
Independence, OR (city) Polk County	6	0.07
Lakeland South, WA (cdp) King County	6	0.05
Centralia, WA (city) Lewis County	6	0.04
Waterville, ME (city) Kennebec County	6	0.04
Covington, WA (city) King County	6	0.03
Frederickson, WA (cdp) Pierce County	6	0.03
Longview, WA (city) Cowlitz County	6	0.02
Puyallup, WA (city) Pierce County	6	0.02
SeaTac, WA (city) King County	6	0.02
El Paso, TX (city) El Paso County	6	<0.01
Durand, WI (town) Pepin County	5	0.67
Craig, AK (city) Prince of Wales-Hyder Census Area	5	0.42
Westport, WA (city) Grays Harbor County	5	0.24
Oakfield, MI (township) Kent County	5	0.09
Pacific, WA (city) King County	5	0.08
Palmer, AK (city) Matanuska-Susitna Borough	5	0.08
Steilacoom, WA (town) Pierce County	5	0.08
Terrace Heights, WA (cdp) Yakima County	5	0.07
Bothell West, WA (cdp) Snohomish County	5	0.03
Brownwood, TX (city) Brown County	5	0.03
Mountlake Terrace, WA (city) Snohomish County	5	0.03
Silverdale, WA (cdp) Kitsap County	5	0.03
Bainbridge Island, WA (city) Kitsap County	5	0.02
East Hill-Meridian, WA (cdp) King County	5	0.02
Antelope, CA (cdp) Sacramento County	5	0.01
Idaho Falls, ID (city) Bonneville County	5	0.01
Redding, CA (city) Shasta County	5	0.01
Baltimore, MD (city) Baltimore city County	5	<0.01
Sacramento, CA (city) Sacramento County	5	<0.01
Brule, WI (cdp) Douglas County	4	1.57
Petersburg, KY (cdp) Boone County	4	0.65
Brule, WI (town) Douglas County	4	0.61
Puget Island, WA (cdp) Wahkiakum County	4	0.48
Coupeville, WA (town) Island County	4	0.22
Oakland, PA (township) Butler County	4	0.13
Creswell, OR (city) Lane County	4	0.08
Brier, WA (city) Snohomish County	4	0.07
Woods Creek, WA (cdp) Snohomish County	4	0.07
Normandy Park, WA (city) King County	4	0.06
Larkfield-Wikiup, CA (cdp) Sonoma County	4	0.05
Minnehaha, WA (cdp) Clark County	4	0.04
Poulsbo, WA (city) Kitsap County	4	0.04
Sedro-Woolley, WA (city) Skagit County	4	0.04
Sumner, WA (city) Pierce County	4	0.04
Bryn Mawr-Skyway, WA (cdp) King County	4	0.03
Lakeland North, WA (cdp) King County	4	0.03
Payson, AZ (town) Gila County	4	0.03
Cottage Lake, WA (cdp) King County	4	0.02
Fairwood, WA (cdp) King County	4	0.02
Five Corners, WA (cdp) Clark County	4	0.02
Graham, WA (cdp) Pierce County	4	0.02
Hermiston, OR (city) Umatilla County	4	0.02
Kenmore, WA (city) King County	4	0.02
Mukilteo, WA (city) Snohomish County	4	0.02
Tukwila, WA (city) King County	4	0.02
Collierville, TN (town) Shelby County	4	0.01
Logan, UT (city) Cache County	4	0.01
Montebello, CA (city) Los Angeles County	4	0.01
Mount Vernon, WA (city) Skagit County	4	0.01
Arden-Arcade, CA (cdp) Sacramento County	4	<0.01
Broken Arrow, OK (city) Tulsa County	4	<0.01
Davenport, IA (city) Scott County	4	<0.01
Elk Grove, CA (city) Sacramento County	4	<0.01
Gresham, OR (city) Multnomah County	4	<0.01
Hayward, CA (city) Alameda County	4	<0.01
Houston, TX (city) Harris County	4	<0.01
Las Vegas, NV (city) Clark County	4	<0.01
New York, NY (city) Kings County	4	<0.01
Oklahoma City, OK (city) Oklahoma County	4	<0.01
Tallahassee, FL (city) Leon County	4	<0.01
Westminster, CO (city) Adams County	4	<0.01
Hydaburg, AK (city) Prince of Wales-Hyder Census Area	3	0.80
Quilcene, WA (cdp) Jefferson County	3	0.50
Klawock, AK (city) Prince of Wales-Hyder Census Area	3	0.40
Redway, CA (cdp) Humboldt County	3	0.24
Fords Prairie, WA (cdp) Lewis County	3	0.15
Cascade Valley, WA (cdp) Grant County	3	0.13
Pine City, MN (city) Pine County	3	0.10
Port Angeles East, WA (cdp) Clallam County	3	0.10
Clearview, WA (cdp) Snohomish County	3	0.09
Elkland, MI (township) Tuscola County	3	0.09
Marietta-Alderwood, WA (cdp) Whatcom County	3	0.08
Nome, AK (city) Nome Census Area	3	0.08
Scappoose, OR (city) Columbia County	3	0.05
Sudden Valley, WA (cdp) Whatcom County	3	0.05
Kirtland, NM (cdp) San Juan County	3	0.04
Milton, WA (city) Pierce County	3	0.04
Tanaina, AK (cdp) Matanuska-Susitna Borough	3	0.04
Wasilla, AK (city) Matanuska-Susitna Borough	3	0.04
Fairview, CA (cdp) Alameda County	3	0.03
Fairview, OR (city) Multnomah County	3	0.03
Port Orchard, WA (city) Kitsap County	3	0.03
Kingsgate, WA (cdp) King County	3	0.02
Salmon Creek, WA (cdp) Clark County	3	0.02
Carson City, NV (ind. city) Carson City County	3	0.01
Corvallis, OR (city) Benton County	3	0.01

SECTION THREE

Please refer to the Explanation of Data in the front of the book for more detailed information.

Race

Alaska Native: Tsimshian

Top 150 Places Sorted by Percent of Total Population

Based on all places, regardless of total population

Place	Population	%
Metlakatla, AK (cdp) Prince of Wales-Hyder Census Area	1,019	72.53
Loring, AK (cdp) Ketchikan Gateway Borough	2	50.00
Ketchikan, AK (city) Ketchikan Gateway Borough	254	3.16
Saxman, AK (city) Ketchikan Gateway Borough	10	2.43
Brule, WI (cdp) Douglas County	4	1.57
Nondalton, AK (city) Lake and Peninsula Borough	2	1.22
Wrangell, AK (borough) Wrangell City and Borough	20	0.84
Hydaburg, AK (city) Prince of Wales-Hyder Census Area	3	0.80
Sitka, AK (borough) Sitka City and Borough	65	0.73
Durand, WI (town) Pepin County	5	0.67
Herron Island, WA (cdp) Pierce County	1	0.66
Skagway, AK (cdp) Skagway Municipality	6	0.65
Petersburg, KY (cdp) Boone County	4	0.65
Loomis, WA (cdp) Okanogan County	1	0.63
Brule, WI (town) Douglas County	4	0.61
Quilcene, WA (cdp) Jefferson County	3	0.50
Puget Island, WA (cdp) Wahkiakum County	4	0.48
Craig, AK (city) Prince of Wales-Hyder Census Area	5	0.42
Klawock, AK (city) Prince of Wales-Hyder Census Area	3	0.40
Lyle, WA (cdp) Klickitat County	2	0.40
Juneau, AK (borough) Juneau City and Borough	114	0.36
Kake, AK (city) Petersburg Census Area	2	0.36
Neilton, WA (cdp) Grays Harbor County	1	0.32
Valdez, AK (city) Valdez-Cordova Census Area	11	0.28
Toledo, WA (city) Lewis County	2	0.28
Clallam Bay, WA (cdp) Clallam County	1	0.28
Unalaska, AK (city) Aleutians West Census Area	12	0.27
Oakview, MO (village) Clay County	1	0.27
Kotzebue, AK (city) Northwest Arctic Borough	8	0.25
Westport, WA (city) Grays Harbor County	5	0.24
Redway, CA (cdp) Humboldt County	3	0.24
Copalis Beach, WA (cdp) Grays Harbor County	1	0.24
Neah Bay, WA (cdp) Clallam County	2	0.23
Coupeville, WA (town) Island County	4	0.22
Kenai, AK (city) Kenai Peninsula Borough	15	0.21
West Manchester, OH (village) Preble County	1	0.21
Craigmont, ID (city) Lewis County	1	0.20
Tijeras, NM (village) Bernalillo County	1	0.18
Diamond Ridge, AK (cdp) Kenai Peninsula Borough	2	0.17
Happy Valley, AK (cdp) Kenai Peninsula Borough	1	0.17
Smelterville, ID (city) Shoshone County	1	0.16
Westwood, KY (city) Jefferson County	1	0.16
Fords Prairie, WA (cdp) Lewis County	3	0.15
Hampton, MN (city) Dakota County	1	0.15
Oakland, PA (township) Butler County	4	0.13
Cascade Valley, WA (cdp) Grant County	3	0.13
Waldo, ME (town) Waldo County	1	0.13
Lakes, AK (cdp) Matanuska-Susitna Borough	10	0.12
Bell Hill, WA (cdp) Clallam County	1	0.12
Fort Jones, CA (city) Siskiyou County	1	0.12
Ocean Shores, WA (city) Grays Harbor County	6	0.11
Blue Hill, ME (cdp) Hancock County	1	0.11
Pine City, MN (city) Pine County	3	0.10
Port Angeles East, WA (cdp) Clallam County	3	0.10
Burley, WA (cdp) Kitsap County	2	0.10
Freeland, WA (cdp) Island County	2	0.10
Langley, WA (city) Island County	1	0.10
Oakfield, MI (township) Kent County	5	0.09
Clearview, WA (cdp) Snohomish County	3	0.09
Elkland, MI (township) Tuscola County	3	0.09
Ohkay Owingeh, NM (cdp) Rio Arriba County	1	0.09
Anchorage, AK (municipality) Anchorage Municipality	221	0.08
Pacific, WA (city) King County	5	0.08
Palmer, AK (city) Matanuska-Susitna Borough	5	0.08
Steilacoom, WA (town) Pierce County	5	0.08
Creswell, OR (city) Lane County	4	0.08
Marietta-Alderwood, WA (cdp) Whatcom County	3	0.08
Nome, AK (city) Nome Census Area	3	0.08
Hudson, CO (town) Weld County	2	0.08
Lochsloy, WA (cdp) Snohomish County	2	0.08
Hoquiam, WA (city) Grays Harbor County	6	0.07
Independence, OR (city) Polk County	6	0.07
Terrace Heights, WA (cdp) Yakima County	5	0.07
Brier, WA (city) Snohomish County	4	0.07
Woods Creek, WA (cdp) Snohomish County	4	0.07
Jacksonville, OR (city) Jackson County	2	0.07
Cohoe, AK (cdp) Kenai Peninsula Borough	1	0.07
Lazy Mountain, AK (cdp) Matanuska-Susitna Borough	1	0.07
Perryville, AR (city) Perry County	1	0.07
Sangerville, ME (town) Piscataquis County	1	0.07
Todd, PA (township) Fulton County	1	0.07
Burien, WA (city) King County	19	0.06
Normandy Park, WA (city) King County	4	0.06
Glide, OR (cdp) Douglas County	1	0.06
Haines, AK (cdp) Haines Borough	1	0.06
Sebago, ME (town) Cumberland County	1	0.06
Waterflow, NM (cdp) San Juan County	1	0.06
Lakeland South, WA (cdp) King County	6	0.05
Larkfield-Wikiup, CA (cdp) Sonoma County	4	0.05
Scappoose, OR (city) Columbia County	3	0.05
Sudden Valley, WA (cdp) Whatcom County	3	0.05
Belfair, WA (cdp) Mason County	2	0.05
Dexter, MI (village) Washtenaw County	2	0.05
Suquamish, WA (cdp) Kitsap County	2	0.05
Wayland, MI (city) Allegan County	2	0.05
Anchor Point, AK (cdp) Kenai Peninsula Borough	1	0.05
Bridgton, ME (cdp) Cumberland County	1	0.05
Frenchtown, MT (cdp) Missoula County	1	0.05
Friday Harbor, WA (town) San Juan County	1	0.05
Golden Shores, AZ (cdp) Mohave County	1	0.05
Leesport, PA (borough) Berks County	1	0.05
Auburn, WA (city) King County	30	0.04
Shoreline, WA (city) King County	22	0.04
Inglewood-Finn Hill, WA (cdp) King County	10	0.04
Port Angeles, WA (city) Clallam County	8	0.04
Centralia, WA (city) Lewis County	6	0.04
Waterville, ME (city) Kennebec County	6	0.04
Minnehaha, WA (cdp) Clark County	4	0.04
Poulsbo, WA (city) Kitsap County	4	0.04
Sedro-Woolley, WA (city) Skagit County	4	0.04
Sumner, WA (city) Pierce County	4	0.04
Kirtland, NM (cdp) San Juan County	3	0.04
Milton, WA (city) Pierce County	3	0.04
Tanaina, AK (cdp) Matanuska-Susitna Borough	3	0.04
Wasilla, AK (city) Matanuska-Susitna Borough	3	0.04
Boulevard Park, WA (cdp) King County	2	0.04
Cicero, IN (town) Hamilton County	2	0.04
Creve Coeur, IL (village) Tazewell County	2	0.04
Daleville, AL (city) Dale County	2	0.04
Gateway, AK (cdp) Matanuska-Susitna Borough	2	0.04
Kawkawlin, MI (township) Bay County	2	0.04
Manchester, WA (cdp) Kitsap County	2	0.04
Omak, WA (city) Okanogan County	2	0.04
Sterling, AK (cdp) Kenai Peninsula Borough	2	0.04
Sunset, UT (city) Davis County	2	0.04
Blue Hill, ME (town) Hancock County	1	0.04
Bonners Ferry, ID (city) Boundary County	1	0.04
Brewster, WA (city) Okanogan County	1	0.04
Dalton Gardens, ID (city) Kootenai County	1	0.04
Dunkirk, MD (cdp) Calvert County	1	0.04
Navy Yard City, WA (cdp) Kitsap County	1	0.04
Warm Beach, WA (cdp) Snohomish County	1	0.04
Window Rock, AZ (cdp) Apache County	1	0.04
Everett, WA (city) Snohomish County	26	0.03
Marysville, WA (city) Snohomish County	16	0.03
Edmonds, WA (city) Snohomish County	12	0.03
Des Moines, WA (city) King County	9	0.03
Covington, WA (city) King County	6	0.03
Frederickson, WA (cdp) Pierce County	6	0.03
Bothell West, WA (cdp) Snohomish County	5	0.03
Brownwood, TX (city) Brown County	5	0.03
Mountlake Terrace, WA (city) Snohomish County	5	0.03
Silverdale, WA (cdp) Kitsap County	5	0.03
Bryn Mawr-Skyway, WA (cdp) King County	4	0.03
Lakeland North, WA (cdp) King County	4	0.03
Payson, AZ (town) Gila County	4	0.03
Fairview, CA (cdp) Alameda County	3	0.03
Fairview, OR (city) Multnomah County	3	0.03
Port Orchard, WA (city) Kitsap County	3	0.03
Brookville, OH (city) Montgomery County	2	0.03

Please refer to the Explanation of Data in the front of the book for more detailed information.

Race

Alaska Native: Tsimshian

Top 150 Places Sorted by Percent of Total Population

Based on places with total population of 7,500 or more

Place	Population	%
Ketchikan, AK (city) Ketchikan Gateway Borough	254	3.16
Sitka, AK (borough) Sitka City and Borough	65	0.73
Juneau, AK (borough) Juneau City and Borough	114	0.36
Lakes, AK (cdp) Matanuska-Susitna Borough	10	0.12
Anchorage, AK (municipality) Anchorage Municipality	221	0.08
Hoquiam, WA (city) Grays Harbor County	6	0.07
Independence, OR (city) Polk County	6	0.07
Burien, WA (city) King County	19	0.06
Lakeland South, WA (cdp) King County	6	0.05
Larkfield-Wikiup, CA (cdp) Sonoma County	4	0.05
Auburn, WA (city) King County	30	0.04
Shoreline, WA (city) King County	22	0.04
Inglewood-Finn Hill, WA (cdp) King County	10	0.04
Port Angeles, WA (city) Clallam County	8	0.04
Centralia, WA (city) Lewis County	6	0.04
Waterville, ME (city) Kennebec County	6	0.04
Minnehaha, WA (cdp) Clark County	4	0.04
Poulsbo, WA (city) Kitsap County	4	0.04
Sedro-Woolley, WA (city) Skagit County	4	0.04
Sumner, WA (city) Pierce County	4	0.04
Kirtland, NM (cdp) San Juan County	3	0.04
Tanaina, AK (cdp) Matanuska-Susitna Borough	3	0.04
Wasilla, AK (city) Matanuska-Susitna Borough	3	0.04
Everett, WA (city) Snohomish County	26	0.03
Marysville, WA (city) Snohomish County	16	0.03
Edmonds, WA (city) Snohomish County	12	0.03
Des Moines, WA (city) King County	9	0.03
Covington, WA (city) King County	6	0.03
Frederickson, WA (cdp) Pierce County	6	0.03
Bothell West, WA (cdp) Snohomish County	5	0.03
Brownwood, TX (city) Brown County	5	0.03
Mountlake Terrace, WA (city) Snohomish County	5	0.03
Silverdale, WA (cdp) Kitsap County	5	0.03
Bryn Mawr-Skyway, WA (cdp) King County	4	0.03
Lakeland North, WA (cdp) King County	4	0.03
Payson, AZ (town) Gila County	4	0.03
Fairview, CA (cdp) Alameda County	3	0.03
Fairview, OR (city) Multnomah County	3	0.03
Port Orchard, WA (city) Kitsap County	3	0.03
Kalifornsky, AK (cdp) Kenai Peninsula Borough	2	0.03
Seattle, WA (city) King County	108	0.02
Kent, WA (city) King County	20	0.02
Federal Way, WA (city) King County	18	0.02
Bellingham, WA (city) Whatcom County	17	0.02
Renton, WA (city) King County	15	0.02
Lakewood, WA (city) Pierce County	10	0.02
Sammamish, WA (city) King County	9	0.02
Parkland, WA (cdp) Pierce County	8	0.02
Bothell, WA (city) King County	7	0.02
Lewiston, ID (city) Nez Perce County	7	0.02
Lynnwood, WA (city) Snohomish County	7	0.02
Longview, WA (city) Cowlitz County	6	0.02
Puyallup, WA (city) Pierce County	6	0.02
SeaTac, WA (city) King County	6	0.02
Bainbridge Island, WA (city) Kitsap County	5	0.02
East Hill-Meridian, WA (cdp) King County	5	0.02
Cottage Lake, WA (cdp) King County	4	0.02
Fairwood, WA (cdp) King County	4	0.02
Five Corners, WA (cdp) Clark County	4	0.02
Graham, WA (cdp) Pierce County	4	0.02
Hermiston, OR (city) Umatilla County	4	0.02
Kenmore, WA (city) King County	4	0.02
Mukilteo, WA (city) Snohomish County	4	0.02
Tukwila, WA (city) King County	4	0.02
Kingsgate, WA (cdp) King County	3	0.02
Salmon Creek, WA (cdp) Clark County	3	0.02
College, AK (cdp) Fairbanks North Star Borough	2	0.02
East Wenatchee, WA (city) Douglas County	2	0.02
Fife, WA (city) Pierce County	2	0.02
Grass Valley, CA (city) Nevada County	2	0.02
Independence, KS (city) Montgomery County	2	0.02
Laurens, SC (city) Laurens County	2	0.02
Newcastle, WA (city) King County	2	0.02
Newport, OR (city) Lincoln County	2	0.02
St. Helens, OR (city) Columbia County	2	0.02
Thompson, CT (town) Windham County	2	0.02
Waihee-Waiehu, HI (cdp) Maui County	2	0.02
Portland, OR (city) Multnomah County	32	0.01
Tacoma, WA (city) Pierce County	24	0.01
Vancouver, WA (city) Clark County	21	0.01
Eugene, OR (city) Lane County	19	0.01
Bellevue, WA (city) King County	13	0.01
Yakima, WA (city) Yakima County	10	0.01
Salem, OR (city) Marion County	9	0.01
Kennewick, WA (city) Benton County	8	0.01
Westminster, CA (city) Orange County	8	0.01
Chico, CA (city) Butte County	7	0.01
Lenexa, KS (city) Johnson County	7	0.01
Thornton, CO (city) Adams County	7	0.01
Antelope, CA (cdp) Sacramento County	5	0.01
Idaho Falls, ID (city) Bonneville County	5	0.01
Redding, CA (city) Shasta County	5	0.01
Collierville, TN (town) Shelby County	4	0.01
Logan, UT (city) Cache County	4	0.01
Montebello, CA (city) Los Angeles County	4	0.01
Mount Vernon, WA (city) Skagit County	4	0.01
Carson City, NV (ind. city) Carson City County	3	0.01
Corvallis, OR (city) Benton County	3	0.01
Fairbanks, AK (city) Fairbanks North Star Borough	3	0.01
Farmington, NM (city) San Juan County	3	0.01
Fort Dodge, IA (city) Webster County	3	0.01
Great Falls, MT (city) Cascade County	3	0.01
Hopkinsville, KY (city) Christian County	3	0.01
Kahului, HI (cdp) Maui County	3	0.01
Kihei, HI (cdp) Maui County	3	0.01
Klamath Falls, OR (city) Klamath County	3	0.01
Lacey, WA (city) Thurston County	3	0.01
Lower Merion, PA (township) Montgomery County	3	0.01
Manhattan Beach, CA (city) Los Angeles County	3	0.01
Olney, MD (cdp) Montgomery County	3	0.01
Pleasant Hill, CA (city) Contra Costa County	3	0.01
Rohnert Park, CA (city) Sonoma County	3	0.01
Rosemont, CA (cdp) Sacramento County	3	0.01
South Jordan, UT (city) Salt Lake County	3	0.01
University Place, WA (city) Pierce County	3	0.01
Bremerton, WA (city) Kitsap County	2	0.01
Dallas, OR (city) Polk County	2	0.01
Durango, CO (city) La Plata County	2	0.01
Fraser, MI (city) Macomb County	2	0.01
Gahanna, OH (city) Franklin County	2	0.01
Gorham, ME (town) Cumberland County	2	0.01
Green, OH (city) Summit County	2	0.01
Kalispell, MT (city) Flathead County	2	0.01
Knik-Fairview, AK (cdp) Matanuska-Susitna Borough	2	0.01
Lake Stevens, WA (city) Snohomish County	2	0.01
Las Vegas, NM (city) San Miguel County	2	0.01
Martha Lake, WA (cdp) Snohomish County	2	0.01
Mercer Island, WA (city) King County	2	0.01
Mill Creek, WA (city) Snohomish County	2	0.01
Norton Shores, MI (city) Muskegon County	2	0.01
Orchards, WA (cdp) Clark County	2	0.01
Oroville, CA (city) Butte County	2	0.01
Ponca City, OK (city) Kay County	2	0.01
Scio, MI (township) Washtenaw County	2	0.01
Takoma Park, MD (city) Montgomery County	2	0.01
Troutdale, OR (city) Multnomah County	2	0.01
Tumwater, WA (city) Thurston County	2	0.01
Walla Walla, WA (city) Walla Walla County	2	0.01
Wenatchee, WA (city) Chelan County	2	0.01
West Pensacola, FL (cdp) Escambia County	2	0.01
White Center, WA (cdp) King County	2	0.01
Aberdeen, WA (city) Grays Harbor County	1	0.01
Ammon, ID (city) Bonneville County	1	0.01
Artondale, WA (cdp) Pierce County	1	0.01
Badger, AK (cdp) Fairbanks North Star Borough	1	0.01
Birch Bay, WA (cdp) Whatcom County	1	0.01
Bonney Lake, WA (city) Pierce County	1	0.01
Bothell East, WA (cdp) Snohomish County	1	0.01
Cheney, WA (city) Spokane County	1	0.01
Chowchilla, CA (city) Madera County	1	0.01

SECTION THREE

Please refer to the Explanation of Data in the front of the book for more detailed information.

Race

American Indian: Ute

U.S. and 50 States Sorted by Population and Percent of Total Population

Place	Population	%
United States	**11,491**	**<0.01**
Utah	3,914	0.14
Colorado	3,404	0.07
California	1,111	<0.01
New Mexico	546	0.03
Arizona	338	0.01
Texas	216	<0.01
Washington	182	<0.01
Nevada	166	0.01
Oregon	155	<0.01
Idaho	125	0.01
Florida	83	<0.01
Missouri	81	<0.01
Illinois	72	<0.01
Wyoming	71	0.01
Kansas	71	<0.01
Oklahoma	66	<0.01
Virginia	60	<0.01
Indiana	56	<0.01
Montana	54	0.01
Tennessee	47	<0.01
Minnesota	45	<0.01
Michigan	43	<0.01
Hawaii	42	<0.01
Georgia	41	<0.01
Maryland	41	<0.01
Alaska	39	0.01
North Carolina	37	<0.01
New York	36	<0.01
Pennsylvania	33	<0.01
Wisconsin	33	<0.01
Ohio	32	<0.01
Arkansas	31	<0.01
Massachusetts	26	<0.01
Iowa	25	<0.01
Kentucky	25	<0.01
New Jersey	24	<0.01
South Dakota	24	<0.01
North Dakota	21	<0.01
South Carolina	18	<0.01
Alabama	13	<0.01
Connecticut	12	<0.01
Louisiana	12	<0.01
Nebraska	7	<0.01
New Hampshire	3	<0.01
Rhode Island	3	<0.01
Maine	2	<0.01
Mississippi	2	<0.01
Vermont	2	<0.01
District of Columbia	1	<0.01
Delaware	0	0.00
West Virginia	0	0.00

Place	Population	%
Utah	3,914	0.14
Colorado	3,404	0.07
New Mexico	546	0.03
Arizona	338	0.01
Nevada	166	0.01
Idaho	125	0.01
Wyoming	71	0.01
Montana	54	0.01
Alaska	39	0.01
United States	**11,491**	**<0.01**
California	1,111	<0.01
Texas	216	<0.01
Washington	182	<0.01
Oregon	155	<0.01
Florida	83	<0.01
Missouri	81	<0.01
Illinois	72	<0.01
Kansas	71	<0.01
Oklahoma	66	<0.01
Virginia	60	<0.01
Indiana	56	<0.01
Tennessee	47	<0.01
Minnesota	45	<0.01
Michigan	43	<0.01
Hawaii	42	<0.01
Georgia	41	<0.01
Maryland	41	<0.01
North Carolina	37	<0.01
New York	36	<0.01
Pennsylvania	33	<0.01
Wisconsin	33	<0.01
Ohio	32	<0.01
Arkansas	31	<0.01
Massachusetts	26	<0.01
Iowa	25	<0.01
Kentucky	25	<0.01
New Jersey	24	<0.01
South Dakota	24	<0.01
North Dakota	21	<0.01
South Carolina	18	<0.01
Alabama	13	<0.01
Connecticut	12	<0.01
Louisiana	12	<0.01
Nebraska	7	<0.01
New Hampshire	3	<0.01
Rhode Island	3	<0.01
Maine	2	<0.01
Mississippi	2	<0.01
Vermont	2	<0.01
District of Columbia	1	<0.01
Delaware	0	0.00
West Virginia	0	0.00

Please refer to the Explanation of Data in the front of the book for more detailed information.

Race

American Indian: Ute

Top 150 Places Sorted by Population

Based on all places, regardless of total population

Place	Population	%
Towaoc, CO (cdp) Montezuma County	675	62.10
Fort Duchesne, UT (cdp) Uintah County	578	80.95
Roosevelt, UT (city) Duchesne County	388	6.42
Whiterocks, UT (cdp) Uintah County	215	74.39
Salt Lake City, UT (city) Salt Lake County	188	0.10
Denver, CO (city) Denver County	160	0.03
White Mesa, UT (cdp) San Juan County	148	61.16
Randlett, UT (cdp) Uintah County	141	64.09
Cortez, CO (city) Montezuma County	119	1.40
Vernal, UT (city) Uintah County	111	1.22
West Valley City, UT (city) Salt Lake County	104	0.08
Albuquerque, NM (city) Bernalillo County	102	0.02
Colorado Springs, CO (city) El Paso County	102	0.02
Farmington, NM (city) San Juan County	84	0.18
Ogden, UT (city) Weber County	77	0.09
Aurora, CO (city) Arapahoe County	75	0.02
Ignacio, CO (town) La Plata County	72	10.33
Durango, CO (city) La Plata County	72	0.43
West Jordan, UT (city) Salt Lake County	62	0.06
Pueblo, CO (city) Pueblo County	55	0.05
Phoenix, AZ (city) Maricopa County	49	<0.01
Los Angeles, CA (city) Los Angeles County	48	<0.01
Lakewood, CO (city) Jefferson County	46	0.03
Southern Ute, CO (cdp) La Plata County	43	24.29
Provo, UT (city) Utah County	42	0.04
Myton, UT (city) Duchesne County	41	7.21
Arvada, CO (city) Jefferson County	40	0.04
Tucson, AZ (city) Pima County	39	0.01
Taylorsville, UT (city) Salt Lake County	37	0.06
Orem, UT (city) Utah County	36	0.04
Ballard, UT (town) Uintah County	35	4.37
Kirtland, NM (cdp) San Juan County	34	0.43
Grand Junction, CO (city) Mesa County	32	0.05
South Salt Lake, UT (city) Salt Lake County	31	0.13
Longmont, CO (city) Boulder County	31	0.04
Rio Rancho, NM (city) Sandoval County	30	0.03
Mesa, AZ (city) Maricopa County	30	0.01
Neola, UT (cdp) Duchesne County	29	6.29
Westminster, CO (city) Adams County	28	0.03
Kearns, UT (cdp) Salt Lake County	27	0.08
Murray, UT (city) Salt Lake County	27	0.06
Bayfield, CO (town) La Plata County	26	1.11
Las Vegas, NV (city) Clark County	26	<0.01
Layton, UT (city) Davis County	25	0.04
Millcreek, UT (cdp) Salt Lake County	25	0.04
Fort Collins, CO (city) Larimer County	23	0.02
Cedar City, UT (city) Iron County	22	0.08
San Diego, CA (city) San Diego County	22	<0.01
Clifton, CO (cdp) Mesa County	21	0.11
Lawrence, KS (city) Douglas County	21	0.02
Portland, OR (city) Multnomah County	21	<0.01
Sacramento, CA (city) Sacramento County	21	<0.01
Las Cruces, NM (city) Doña Ana County	20	0.02
Thornton, CO (city) Adams County	20	0.02
Fresno, CA (city) Fresno County	20	<0.01
Seattle, WA (city) King County	20	<0.01
St. George, UT (city) Washington County	19	0.03
Centennial, CO (city) Arapahoe County	19	0.02
Long Beach, CA (city) Los Angeles County	19	<0.01
Manteca, CA (city) San Joaquin County	18	0.03
San Francisco, CA (city) San Francisco County	18	<0.01
Alamosa, CO (city) Alamosa County	17	0.19
Sandy, UT (city) Salt Lake County	17	0.02
Glendale, AZ (city) Maricopa County	17	0.01
New York, NY (city) Kings County	17	<0.01
San Jose, CA (city) Santa Clara County	17	<0.01
Montrose, CO (city) Montrose County	16	0.08
Security-Widefield, CO (cdp) El Paso County	16	0.05
Concord, CA (city) Contra Costa County	16	0.01
Riverside, CA (city) Riverside County	16	0.01
Blanding, UT (city) San Juan County	15	0.44
Gallup, NM (city) McKinley County	15	0.07
Northglenn, CO (city) Adams County	15	0.04
Roy, UT (city) Weber County	15	0.04
Stockton, CA (city) San Joaquin County	15	0.01
Shiprock, NM (cdp) San Juan County	14	0.17
Price, UT (city) Carbon County	14	0.16
Santaquin, UT (city) Utah County	14	0.15
Tooele, UT (city) Tooele County	14	0.04
Reno, NV (city) Washoe County	14	0.01
Virginia Beach, VA (ind. city) Virginia Beach independent city	14	<0.01
Holladay, UT (city) Salt Lake County	13	0.05
Lehi, UT (city) Utah County	13	0.03
Broomfield, CO (city) Broomfield County	13	0.02
Billings, MT (city) Yellowstone County	13	0.01
Henderson, NV (city) Clark County	13	0.01
Orchard Mesa, CO (cdp) Mesa County	12	0.18
Magna, UT (cdp) Salt Lake County	12	0.05
Brighton, CO (city) Adams County	12	0.04
Draper, UT (city) Salt Lake County	12	0.03
Logan, UT (city) Cache County	12	0.02
Corona, CA (city) Riverside County	12	0.01
Greeley, CO (city) Weld County	12	0.01
Wichita, KS (city) Sedgwick County	12	<0.01
Brigham City, UT (city) Box Elder County	11	0.06
American Fork, UT (city) Utah County	11	0.04
South Valley, NM (cdp) Bernalillo County	11	0.03
Spanish Fork, UT (city) Utah County	11	0.03
Castle Rock, CO (town) Douglas County	11	0.02
Livermore, CA (city) Alameda County	11	0.01
Nampa, ID (city) Canyon County	11	0.01
Peoria, AZ (city) Yavapai County	11	0.01
Salem, OR (city) Marion County	11	0.01
Santa Clarita, CA (city) Los Angeles County	11	0.01
Spring Valley, NV (cdp) Clark County	11	0.01
Tempe, AZ (city) Maricopa County	11	0.01
Austin, TX (city) Travis County	11	<0.01
Gillette, WY (city) Campbell County	10	0.03
Wheat Ridge, CO (city) Jefferson County	10	0.03
Amarillo, TX (city) Potter County	10	0.01
Santa Rosa, CA (city) Sonoma County	10	0.01
Sunrise Manor, NV (cdp) Clark County	10	0.01
Chandler, AZ (city) Maricopa County	10	<0.01
Fort Worth, TX (city) Tarrant County	10	<0.01
Houston, TX (city) Harris County	10	<0.01
San Bernardino, CA (city) San Bernardino County	10	<0.01
Tulsa, OK (city) Tulsa County	10	<0.01
Fort Hall, ID (cdp) Bannock County	9	0.28
Maeser, UT (cdp) Uintah County	9	0.25
Moab, UT (city) Grand County	9	0.18
Aztec, NM (city) San Juan County	9	0.13
Syracuse, UT (city) Davis County	9	0.04
Laramie, WY (city) Albany County	9	0.03
Pueblo West, CO (cdp) Pueblo County	9	0.03
Commerce City, CO (city) Adams County	9	0.02
Riverton, UT (city) Salt Lake County	9	0.02
Antioch, CA (city) Contra Costa County	9	0.01
Flagstaff, AZ (city) Coconino County	9	0.01
Rancho Cucamonga, CA (city) San Bernardino County	9	0.01
Union City, CA (city) Alameda County	9	0.01
Vacaville, CA (city) Solano County	9	0.01
Spokane, WA (city) Spokane County	9	<0.01
West Wendover, NV (city) Elko County	8	0.18
Ivins, UT (city) Washington County	8	0.12
Bloomfield, NM (city) San Juan County	8	0.10
Woods Cross, UT (city) Davis County	8	0.08
Black Forest, CO (cdp) El Paso County	8	0.06
Sterling, CO (city) Logan County	8	0.05
Sherrelwood, CO (cdp) Adams County	8	0.04
Midvale, UT (city) Salt Lake County	8	0.03
Spring Hill, TN (city) Williamson County	8	0.03
South Jordan, UT (city) Salt Lake County	8	0.02
Buena Park, CA (city) Orange County	8	0.01
Independence, MO (city) Jackson County	8	0.01
Simi Valley, CA (city) Ventura County	8	0.01
Anchorage, AK (municipality) Anchorage Municipality	8	<0.01
Boise City, ID (city) Ada County	8	<0.01
Chicago, IL (city) Cook County	8	<0.01
Louisville-Jefferson County, KY (metro govt) Jefferson County	8	<0.01
North Las Vegas, NV (city) Clark County	8	<0.01

Race

American Indian: Ute

Top 150 Places Sorted by Percent of Total Population

Based on all places, regardless of total population

Place	Population	%
Fort Duchesne, UT (cdp) Uintah County	578	80.95
Whiterocks, UT (cdp) Uintah County	215	74.39
Randlett, UT (cdp) Uintah County	141	64.09
Towaoc, CO (cdp) Montezuma County	675	62.10
White Mesa, UT (cdp) San Juan County	148	61.16
Southern Ute, CO (cdp) La Plata County	43	24.29
Ignacio, CO (town) La Plata County	72	10.33
Myton, UT (city) Duchesne County	41	7.21
Roosevelt, UT (city) Duchesne County	388	6.42
Neola, UT (cdp) Duchesne County	29	6.29
Sheridan Lake, CO (town) Kiowa County	4	4.55
Ballard, UT (town) Uintah County	35	4.37
Marion, WI (city) Shawano County	1	4.00
Florissant, CO (cdp) Teller County	4	3.85
Young Place, NM (cdp) San Juan County	4	2.14
Arboles, CO (cdp) Archuleta County	5	1.79
Bluff, UT (cdp) San Juan County	4	1.55
Copper Center, AK (cdp) Valdez-Cordova Census Area	5	1.52
Capulin, CO (cdp) Conejos County	3	1.50
Picuris Pueblo, NM (cdp) Taos County	1	1.47
Nightmute, AK (city) Bethel Census Area	4	1.43
Cortez, CO (city) Montezuma County	119	1.40
Kim, CO (town) Las Animas County	1	1.35
Rye, AZ (cdp) Gila County	1	1.30
Vernal, UT (city) Uintah County	111	1.22
Johnson Village, CO (cdp) Chaffee County	3	1.22
Etna, WY (cdp) Lincoln County	2	1.22
Bayfield, CO (town) La Plata County	26	1.11
Hood, CA (cdp) Sacramento County	3	1.11
Scottsville, TX (city) Harrison County	4	1.06
Beclabito, NM (cdp) San Juan County	3	0.95
Browns Valley, MN (city) Traverse County	5	0.85
Coaldale, CO (cdp) Fremont County	2	0.78
Tropic, UT (town) Garfield County	4	0.75
Centerview, MO (city) Johnson County	2	0.75
Halchita, UT (cdp) San Juan County	2	0.75
Atwood, CO (cdp) Logan County	1	0.75
Truxton, AZ (cdp) Mohave County	1	0.75
Gerrard, CO (cdp) Rio Grande County	2	0.72
Crowheart, WY (cdp) Fremont County	1	0.71
Pecan Hill, TX (city) Ellis County	4	0.64
Aquinnah, MA (town) Dukes County	2	0.64
Saguache, CO (town) Saguache County	3	0.62
Amalga, UT (town) Cache County	3	0.61
East Dunseith, ND (cdp) Rolette County	3	0.60
Montezuma Creek, UT (cdp) San Juan County	2	0.60
Why, AZ (cdp) Pima County	1	0.60
Parker School, MT (cdp) Hill County	2	0.59
Fort Bidwell, CA (cdp) Modoc County	1	0.58
Hawk Run, PA (cdp) Clearfield County	3	0.56
Crisman, CO (cdp) Boulder County	1	0.54
Sandy Hook, MD (cdp) Washington County	1	0.53
Antonito, CO (town) Conejos County	4	0.51
Salt Creek, CO (cdp) Pueblo County	3	0.51
New England, ND (city) Hettinger County	3	0.50
Muddy, MT (cdp) Big Horn County	3	0.49
Shongopovi, AZ (cdp) Navajo County	4	0.48
Stotonic Village, AZ (cdp) Pinal County	3	0.46
Crawford, CO (town) Delta County	2	0.46
Mancos, CO (town) Montezuma County	6	0.45
Blanding, UT (city) San Juan County	15	0.44
Lapwai, ID (city) Nez Perce County	5	0.44
Altamont, UT (town) Duchesne County	1	0.44
Durango, CO (city) La Plata County	72	0.43
Kirtland, NM (cdp) San Juan County	34	0.43
Dolores, CO (town) Montezuma County	4	0.43
Garden City, CO (town) Weld County	1	0.43
Proctor, OK (cdp) Adair County	1	0.43
Cedar Crest, NM (cdp) Bernalillo County	4	0.42
Green River, UT (city) Emery County	4	0.42
Redvale, CO (cdp) Montrose County	1	0.42
Fort Washakie, WY (cdp) Fremont County	7	0.40
Naples, UT (city) Uintah County	7	0.40
Ambler, AK (city) Northwest Arctic Borough	1	0.39
Seldovia, AK (city) Kenai Peninsula Borough	1	0.39
Newton, UT (town) Cache County	3	0.38
Hollister, ID (city) Twin Falls County	1	0.37
Paul, ID (city) Minidoka County	4	0.34
Bluebell, UT (cdp) Duchesne County	1	0.34
Huntsville, UT (town) Weber County	2	0.33
Naschitti, NM (cdp) San Juan County	1	0.33
Canby, CA (cdp) Modoc County	1	0.32
Meadow, UT (town) Millard County	1	0.32
Miracle Valley, AZ (cdp) Cochise County	2	0.31
Rock Point, AZ (cdp) Apache County	2	0.31
Mescalero, NM (cdp) Otero County	4	0.30
Aurora, UT (city) Sevier County	3	0.30
Oljato-Monument Valley, UT (cdp) San Juan County	2	0.30
Stratton, CO (town) Kit Carson County	2	0.30
Deweyville, UT (town) Box Elder County	1	0.30
Pagosa Springs, CO (town) Archuleta County	5	0.29
Cascade, MT (town) Cascade County	2	0.29
Corinne, UT (city) Box Elder County	2	0.29
Springer, OK (town) Carter County	2	0.29
Dinosaur, CO (town) Moffat County	1	0.29
Fort Hall, ID (cdp) Bannock County	9	0.28
Meeker, CO (town) Rio Blanco County	7	0.28
Delleker, CA (cdp) Plumas County	2	0.28
Lima, WI (town) Pepin County	2	0.28
Lebec, CA (cdp) Kern County	4	0.27
Nixon, NV (cdp) Washoe County	1	0.27
Afton, WY (town) Lincoln County	5	0.26
Ojo Amarillo, NM (cdp) San Juan County	2	0.26
Maeser, UT (cdp) Uintah County	9	0.25
Skyline-Ganipa, NM (cdp) Cibola County	3	0.25
Skamokawa Valley, WA (cdp) Wahkiakum County	1	0.25
Pierce, CO (town) Weld County	2	0.24
Loma, CO (cdp) Mesa County	3	0.23
Sanford, CO (town) Conejos County	2	0.23
Lodge Grass, MT (town) Big Horn County	1	0.23
Dillon, CO (town) Summit County	2	0.22
Cold Springs, CA (cdp) El Dorado County	1	0.22
Canyonville, OR (city) Douglas County	4	0.21
El Valle de Arroyo Seco, NM (cdp) Santa Fe County	3	0.21
Second Mesa, AZ (cdp) Navajo County	2	0.21
Walsenburg, CO (city) Huerfano County	6	0.20
Bayview, CA (cdp) Humboldt County	5	0.20
Lazy Mountain, AK (cdp) Matanuska-Susitna Borough	3	0.20
Alamosa, CO (city) Alamosa County	17	0.19
Crockett, CA (cdp) Contra Costa County	6	0.19
Volcano, HI (cdp) Hawaii County	5	0.19
Ethete, WY (cdp) Fremont County	3	0.19
First Mesa, AZ (cdp) Navajo County	3	0.19
Norwood, CO (town) San Miguel County	1	0.19
Farmington, NM (city) San Juan County	84	0.18
Orchard Mesa, CO (cdp) Mesa County	12	0.18
Moab, UT (city) Grand County	9	0.18
West Wendover, NV (city) Elko County	8	0.18
Twain Harte, CA (cdp) Tuolumne County	4	0.18
Castle Dale, UT (city) Emery County	3	0.18
Spring Glen, UT (cdp) Carbon County	2	0.18
Taos Pueblo, NM (cdp) Taos County	2	0.18
Alba, MO (city) Jasper County	1	0.18
La Barge, WY (town) Lincoln County	1	0.18
Waterloo, WI (town) Grant County	1	0.18
Shiprock, NM (cdp) San Juan County	14	0.17
Rangely, CO (town) Rio Blanco County	4	0.17
Jemez Pueblo, NM (cdp) Sandoval County	3	0.17
Groveland, CA (cdp) Tuolumne County	1	0.17
Pine Lake, MN (township) Pine County	1	0.17
Yah-ta-hey, NM (cdp) McKinley County	1	0.17
Price, UT (city) Carbon County	14	0.16
Laporte, CO (cdp) Larimer County	4	0.16
Richmond, UT (city) Cache County	4	0.16
Salina, UT (city) Sevier County	4	0.16
Strasburg, CO (cdp) Adams County	4	0.16
Winamac, IN (town) Pulaski County	4	0.16
Coarsegold, CA (cdp) Madera County	3	0.16
Doe Valley, KY (cdp) Meade County	3	0.16
Olathe, CO (town) Montrose County	3	0.16

Please refer to the Explanation of Data in the front of the book for more detailed information.

Race

American Indian: Ute

Top 150 Places Sorted by Percent of Total Population

Based on places with total population of 7,500 or more

Place	Population	%
Cortez, CO (city) Montezuma County	119	1.40
Vernal, UT (city) Uintah County	111	1.22
Durango, CO (city) La Plata County	72	0.43
Kirtland, NM (cdp) San Juan County	34	0.43
Alamosa, CO (city) Alamosa County	17	0.19
Farmington, NM (city) San Juan County	84	0.18
Shiprock, NM (cdp) San Juan County	14	0.17
Price, UT (city) Carbon County	14	0.16
Santaquin, UT (city) Utah County	14	0.15
South Salt Lake, UT (city) Salt Lake County	31	0.13
Clifton, CO (cdp) Mesa County	21	0.11
Salt Lake City, UT (city) Salt Lake County	188	0.10
Bloomfield, NM (city) San Juan County	8	0.10
Ogden, UT (city) Weber County	77	0.09
Richfield, UT (city) Sevier County	7	0.09
West Valley City, UT (city) Salt Lake County	104	0.08
Kearns, UT (cdp) Salt Lake County	27	0.08
Cedar City, UT (city) Iron County	22	0.08
Montrose, CO (city) Montrose County	16	0.08
Woods Cross, UT (city) Davis County	8	0.08
Delta, CO (city) Delta County	7	0.08
Gallup, NM (city) McKinley County	15	0.07
Tremonton, UT (city) Box Elder County	5	0.07
West Jordan, UT (city) Salt Lake County	62	0.06
Taylorsville, UT (city) Salt Lake County	37	0.06
Murray, UT (city) Salt Lake County	27	0.06
Brigham City, UT (city) Box Elder County	11	0.06
Black Forest, CO (cdp) El Paso County	8	0.06
Grantsville, UT (city) Tooele County	5	0.06
Saline, MI (city) Washtenaw County	5	0.06
Pueblo, CO (city) Pueblo County	55	0.05
Grand Junction, CO (city) Mesa County	32	0.05
Security-Widefield, CO (cdp) El Paso County	16	0.05
Holladay, UT (city) Salt Lake County	13	0.05
Magna, UT (cdp) Salt Lake County	12	0.05
Sterling, CO (city) Logan County	8	0.05
Lakeland Village, CA (cdp) Riverside County	6	0.05
Firestone, CO (town) Weld County	5	0.05
Grants, NM (city) Cibola County	5	0.05
Trinidad, CO (city) Las Animas County	5	0.05
Bernalillo, NM (town) Sandoval County	4	0.05
Fairmount, CO (cdp) Jefferson County	4	0.05
Fallon, NV (city) Churchill County	4	0.05
Putnam, MI (township) Livingston County	4	0.05
Provo, UT (city) Utah County	42	0.04
Arvada, CO (city) Jefferson County	40	0.04
Orem, UT (city) Utah County	36	0.04
Longmont, CO (city) Boulder County	31	0.04
Layton, UT (city) Davis County	25	0.04
Millcreek, UT (cdp) Salt Lake County	25	0.04
Northglenn, CO (city) Adams County	15	0.04
Roy, UT (city) Weber County	15	0.04
Tooele, UT (city) Tooele County	14	0.04
Brighton, CO (city) Adams County	12	0.04
American Fork, UT (city) Utah County	11	0.04
Syracuse, UT (city) Davis County	9	0.04
Sherrelwood, CO (cdp) Adams County	8	0.04
Cañon City, CO (city) Fremont County	7	0.04
Makakilo, HI (cdp) Honolulu County	7	0.04
Washington, UT (city) Washington County	7	0.04
Elk Plain, WA (cdp) Pierce County	6	0.04
North Salt Lake, UT (city) Davis County	6	0.04
Rio Linda, CA (cdp) Sacramento County	6	0.04
Berkley, CO (cdp) Adams County	5	0.04
Fruita, CO (city) Mesa County	5	0.04
North Valley, NM (cdp) Bernalillo County	4	0.04
Sonoma, CA (city) Sonoma County	4	0.04
Washington Terrace, UT (city) Weber County	4	0.04
Acton, CA (cdp) Los Angeles County	3	0.04
Burlington, WA (city) Skagit County	3	0.04
Derby, CO (cdp) Adams County	3	0.04
Upton, MA (town) Worcester County	3	0.04
White City, OR (cdp) Jackson County	3	0.04
Denver, CO (city) Denver County	160	0.03
Lakewood, CO (city) Jefferson County	46	0.03
Rio Rancho, NM (city) Sandoval County	30	0.03
Westminster, CO (city) Adams County	28	0.03
St. George, UT (city) Washington County	19	0.03
Manteca, CA (city) San Joaquin County	18	0.03
Lehi, UT (city) Utah County	13	0.03
Draper, UT (city) Salt Lake County	12	0.03
South Valley, NM (cdp) Bernalillo County	11	0.03
Spanish Fork, UT (city) Utah County	11	0.03
Gillette, WY (city) Campbell County	10	0.03
Wheat Ridge, CO (city) Jefferson County	10	0.03
Laramie, WY (city) Albany County	9	0.03
Pueblo West, CO (cdp) Pueblo County	9	0.03
Midvale, UT (city) Salt Lake County	8	0.03
Spring Hill, TN (city) Williamson County	8	0.03
Lafayette, CO (city) Boulder County	7	0.03
Moscow, ID (city) Latah County	7	0.03
Patterson, CA (city) Stanislaus County	7	0.03
Broadlands, VA (cdp) Loudoun County	4	0.03
Calhoun, GA (city) Gordon County	4	0.03
Chubbuck, ID (city) Bannock County	4	0.03
Evanston, WY (city) Uinta County	4	0.03
Franklin, OH (city) Warren County	4	0.03
Mesquite, NV (city) Clark County	4	0.03
Welby, CO (cdp) Adams County	4	0.03
Dranesville, VA (cdp) Fairfax County	3	0.03
Edgewood, WA (city) Pierce County	3	0.03
Federal Heights, CO (city) Adams County	3	0.03
Heber, UT (city) Wasatch County	3	0.03
Johns, CO (town) Weld County	3	0.03
La Plata, MD (town) Charles County	3	0.03
Lansing, KS (city) Leavenworth County	3	0.03
Redlands, CO (cdp) Mesa County	3	0.03
Reedsburg, WI (city) Sauk County	3	0.03
Verde Village, AZ (cdp) Yavapai County	3	0.03
Vernon, TX (city) Wilbarger County	3	0.03
Winslow, AZ (city) Navajo County	3	0.03
Woodmoor, CO (cdp) El Paso County	3	0.03
Catalina, AZ (cdp) Pima County	2	0.03
Corning, CA (city) Tehama County	2	0.03
Fruitvale, CO (cdp) Mesa County	2	0.03
Albuquerque, NM (city) Bernalillo County	102	0.02
Colorado Springs, CO (city) El Paso County	102	0.02
Aurora, CO (city) Arapahoe County	75	0.02
Fort Collins, CO (city) Larimer County	23	0.02
Lawrence, KS (city) Douglas County	21	0.02
Las Cruces, NM (city) Doña Ana County	20	0.02
Thornton, CO (city) Adams County	20	0.02
Centennial, CO (city) Arapahoe County	19	0.02
Sandy, UT (city) Salt Lake County	17	0.02
Broomfield, CO (city) Broomfield County	13	0.02
Logan, UT (city) Cache County	12	0.02
Castle Rock, CO (town) Douglas County	11	0.02
Commerce City, CO (city) Adams County	9	0.02
Riverton, UT (city) Salt Lake County	9	0.02
South Jordan, UT (city) Salt Lake County	8	0.02
Dublin, CA (city) Alameda County	7	0.02
Twin Falls, ID (city) Twin Falls County	7	0.02
Belleville, NJ (township) Essex County	6	0.02
Cottage Grove, MN (city) Washington County	6	0.02
Cottonwood Heights, UT (city) Salt Lake County	6	0.02
Oakley, CA (city) Contra Costa County	6	0.02
Oildale, CA (cdp) Kern County	6	0.02
Springville, UT (city) Utah County	6	0.02
Winchester, NV (cdp) Clark County	6	0.02
Barstow, CA (city) San Bernardino County	5	0.02
Clearfield, UT (city) Davis County	5	0.02
Clinton, UT (city) Davis County	5	0.02
Lewiston, ID (city) Nez Perce County	5	0.02
Villa Park, IL (village) DuPage County	5	0.02
Columbine, CO (cdp) Jefferson County	4	0.02
Derby, KS (city) Sedgwick County	4	0.02
El Reno, OK (city) Canadian County	4	0.02
Fountain, CO (city) El Paso County	4	0.02
Grayslake, IL (village) Lake County	4	0.02
Klamath Falls, OR (city) Klamath County	4	0.02

SECTION THREE

Please refer to the Explanation of Data in the front of the book for more detailed information.

Race

American Indian: Yakama

U.S. and 50 States Sorted by Population and Percent of Total Population

Place	Population	%
United States	**11,527**	**<0.01**
Washington	8,974	0.13
Oregon	1,025	0.03
California	385	<0.01
Idaho	160	0.01
Arizona	97	<0.01
Texas	83	<0.01
Montana	74	0.01
Alaska	73	0.01
Oklahoma	46	<0.01
New Mexico	44	<0.01
Hawaii	41	<0.01
Colorado	39	<0.01
Florida	34	<0.01
Nevada	33	<0.01
Kansas	32	<0.01
Minnesota	31	<0.01
North Carolina	29	<0.01
Georgia	25	<0.01
Ohio	19	<0.01
New York	18	<0.01
Utah	18	<0.01
Illinois	17	<0.01
Michigan	17	<0.01
Missouri	17	<0.01
Arkansas	16	<0.01
Virginia	16	<0.01
Nebraska	13	<0.01
Alabama	12	<0.01
South Dakota	11	<0.01
Tennessee	11	<0.01
Pennsylvania	10	<0.01
Wyoming	10	<0.01
Iowa	9	<0.01
South Carolina	9	<0.01
Wisconsin	9	<0.01
New Jersey	8	<0.01
Indiana	7	<0.01
Maryland	7	<0.01
Massachusetts	7	<0.01
Louisiana	6	<0.01
Maine	6	<0.01
Mississippi	6	<0.01
Vermont	5	<0.01
North Dakota	4	<0.01
Kentucky	3	<0.01
West Virginia	3	<0.01
Delaware	2	<0.01
District of Columbia	2	<0.01
New Hampshire	2	<0.01
Connecticut	1	<0.01
Rhode Island	1	<0.01

Place	Population	%
Washington	8,974	0.13
Oregon	1,025	0.03
Idaho	160	0.01
Montana	74	0.01
Alaska	73	0.01
United States	**11,527**	**<0.01**
California	385	<0.01
Arizona	97	<0.01
Texas	83	<0.01
Oklahoma	46	<0.01
New Mexico	44	<0.01
Hawaii	41	<0.01
Colorado	39	<0.01
Florida	34	<0.01
Nevada	33	<0.01
Kansas	32	<0.01
Minnesota	31	<0.01
North Carolina	29	<0.01
Georgia	25	<0.01
Ohio	19	<0.01
New York	18	<0.01
Utah	18	<0.01
Illinois	17	<0.01
Michigan	17	<0.01
Missouri	17	<0.01
Arkansas	16	<0.01
Virginia	16	<0.01
Nebraska	13	<0.01
Alabama	12	<0.01
South Dakota	11	<0.01
Tennessee	11	<0.01
Pennsylvania	10	<0.01
Wyoming	10	<0.01
Iowa	9	<0.01
South Carolina	9	<0.01
Wisconsin	9	<0.01
New Jersey	8	<0.01
Indiana	7	<0.01
Maryland	7	<0.01
Massachusetts	7	<0.01
Louisiana	6	<0.01
Maine	6	<0.01
Mississippi	6	<0.01
Vermont	5	<0.01
North Dakota	4	<0.01
Kentucky	3	<0.01
West Virginia	3	<0.01
Delaware	2	<0.01
District of Columbia	2	<0.01
New Hampshire	2	<0.01
Connecticut	1	<0.01
Rhode Island	1	<0.01

Please refer to the Explanation of Data in the front of the book for more detailed information.

Race

American Indian: Yakama

Top 150 Places Sorted by Population

Based on all places, regardless of total population

Place	Population	%
Yakima, WA (city) Yakima County	657	0.72
White Swan, WA (cdp) Yakima County	524	66.08
Toppenish, WA (city) Yakima County	492	5.50
Wapato, WA (city) Yakima County	199	3.98
Portland, OR (city) Multnomah County	166	0.03
Tacoma, WA (city) Pierce County	138	0.07
Seattle, WA (city) King County	111	0.02
Spokane, WA (city) Spokane County	91	0.04
Harrah, WA (town) Yakima County	85	13.60
Warm Springs, OR (cdp) Jefferson County	84	2.85
Mission, OR (cdp) Umatilla County	67	6.46
Union Gap, WA (city) Yakima County	67	1.11
Zillah, WA (city) Yakima County	65	2.19
Auburn, WA (city) King County	59	0.08
Vancouver, WA (city) Clark County	55	0.03
Terrace Heights, WA (cdp) Yakima County	52	0.75
Everett, WA (city) Snohomish County	45	0.04
Goldendale, WA (city) Klickitat County	44	1.29
Granger, WA (city) Yakima County	37	1.14
Pendleton, OR (city) Umatilla County	37	0.22
Lapwai, ID (city) Nez Perce County	34	2.99
Kent, WA (city) King County	33	0.04
Lakewood, WA (city) Pierce County	32	0.06
The Dalles, OR (city) Wasco County	31	0.23
Sunnyside, WA (city) Yakima County	28	0.18
Madras, OR (city) Jefferson County	25	0.41
Richland, WA (city) Benton County	25	0.05
Carson, WA (cdp) Skamania County	23	1.01
Kennewick, WA (city) Benton County	23	0.03
Gresham, OR (city) Multnomah County	23	0.02
Anchorage, AK (municipality) Anchorage Municipality	23	0.01
Ellensburg, WA (city) Kittitas County	22	0.12
Marysville, WA (city) Snohomish County	21	0.03
Burien, WA (city) King County	20	0.06
Federal Way, WA (city) King County	20	0.02
Moxee, WA (city) Yakima County	19	0.57
Spokane Valley, WA (city) Spokane County	19	0.02
Springfield, OR (city) Lane County	18	0.03
Tutuilla, OR (cdp) Umatilla County	17	3.49
Dallesport, WA (cdp) Klickitat County	17	1.41
Olympia, WA (city) Thurston County	17	0.04
Selah, WA (city) Yakima County	16	0.22
Salem, OR (city) Marion County	16	0.01
Longview, WA (city) Cowlitz County	15	0.04
Los Angeles, CA (city) Los Angeles County	15	<0.01
Phoenix, AZ (city) Maricopa County	15	<0.01
Ahtanum, WA (cdp) Yakima County	14	0.39
Grandview, WA (city) Yakima County	14	0.13
Bonney Lake, WA (city) Pierce County	14	0.08
Lawrence, KS (city) Douglas County	14	0.02
Buena, WA (cdp) Yakima County	13	1.31
Cornelius, OR (city) Washington County	13	0.11
Lewiston, ID (city) Nez Perce County	13	0.04
Renton, WA (city) King County	13	0.01
Frederickson, WA (cdp) Pierce County	12	0.06
Albuquerque, NM (city) Bernalillo County	12	<0.01
San Diego, CA (city) San Diego County	12	<0.01
Suquamish, WA (cdp) Kitsap County	11	0.27
Cheney, WA (city) Spokane County	11	0.10
Pullman, WA (city) Whitman County	11	0.04
Bremerton, WA (city) Kitsap County	11	0.03
Puyallup, WA (city) Pierce County	11	0.03
Lodi, CA (city) San Joaquin County	11	0.02
Eugene, OR (city) Lane County	11	0.01
Inchelium, WA (cdp) Ferry County	10	2.44
Grand Mound, WA (cdp) Thurston County	10	0.34
North Lynnwood, WA (cdp) Snohomish County	10	0.06
Lacey, WA (city) Thurston County	10	0.02
Pasco, WA (city) Franklin County	10	0.02
Shoreline, WA (city) King County	10	0.02
Bend, OR (city) Deschutes County	10	0.01
Minneapolis, MN (city) Hennepin County	10	<0.01
San Antonio, TX (city) Medina County	10	<0.01
Tampico, WA (cdp) Yakima County	9	2.88
Omak, WA (city) Okanogan County	9	0.19
Kelso, WA (city) Cowlitz County	9	0.08
Orchards, WA (cdp) Clark County	9	0.05
Beaverton, OR (city) Washington County	9	0.01
Mesa, AZ (city) Maricopa County	9	<0.01
Oklahoma City, OK (city) Oklahoma County	9	<0.01
Kirkpatrick, OR (cdp) Umatilla County	8	4.47
Klickitat, WA (cdp) Klickitat County	8	2.21
Nisqually Indian Community, WA (cdp) Thurston County	8	1.39
Taholah, WA (cdp) Grays Harbor County	8	0.95
Coulee Dam, WA (town) Okanogan County	8	0.73
Athena, OR (city) Umatilla County	8	0.71
Gleed, WA (cdp) Yakima County	8	0.28
Forks, WA (city) Clallam County	8	0.23
Orting, WA (city) Pierce County	8	0.12
St. Helens, OR (city) Columbia County	8	0.06
Aberdeen, WA (city) Grays Harbor County	8	0.05
Anacortes, WA (city) Skagit County	8	0.05
Klamath Falls, OR (city) Klamath County	8	0.04
Oregon City, OR (city) Clackamas County	8	0.03
Albany, OR (city) Linn County	8	0.02
Lynnwood, WA (city) Snohomish County	8	0.02
South Hill, WA (cdp) Pierce County	8	0.02
Bellingham, WA (city) Whatcom County	8	0.01
Round Rock, TX (city) Williamson County	8	0.01
Henderson, NV (city) Clark County	8	<0.01
New York, NY (city) Kings County	8	<0.01
Nespelem Community, WA (cdp) Okanogan County	7	2.77
Skokomish, WA (cdp) Mason County	7	1.13
North Bonneville, WA (city) Skamania County	7	0.73
Plummer, ID (city) Benewah County	7	0.67
White Salmon, WA (city) Klickitat County	7	0.31
Lake Stickney, WA (cdp) Snohomish County	7	0.09
Edgewood, WA (city) Pierce County	7	0.07
Durango, CO (city) La Plata County	7	0.04
El Paso de Robles (Paso Robles), CA (city) San Luis Obispo County	7	0.02
Walla Walla, WA (city) Walla Walla County	7	0.02
Billings, MT (city) Yellowstone County	7	0.01
Hillsboro, OR (city) Washington County	7	0.01
Las Vegas, NV (city) Clark County	7	<0.01
Long Beach, CA (city) Los Angeles County	7	<0.01
Oakland, CA (city) Alameda County	7	<0.01
Omaha, NE (city) Douglas County	7	<0.01
San Francisco, CA (city) San Francisco County	7	<0.01
San Jose, CA (city) Santa Clara County	7	<0.01
Urban Honolulu, HI (cdp) Honolulu County	7	<0.01
Parker, WA (cdp) Yakima County	6	3.90
Hamilton, WA (town) Skagit County	6	1.99
Summitview, WA (cdp) Yakima County	6	0.62
Kamiah, ID (city) Lewis County	6	0.46
Houston, AK (city) Matanuska-Susitna Borough	6	0.31
Pawnee, OK (city) Pawnee County	6	0.27
Whitesboro, NJ (cdp) Cape May County	6	0.27
Connell, WA (city) Franklin County	6	0.14
Fruitland, ID (city) Payette County	6	0.13
Mead, WA (cdp) Spokane County	6	0.08
Hoquiam, WA (city) Grays Harbor County	6	0.07
Midland, WA (cdp) Pierce County	6	0.07
Graham, WA (cdp) Pierce County	6	0.03
Hayesville, OR (cdp) Marion County	6	0.03
Middle, NJ (township) Cape May County	6	0.03
Parkland, WA (cdp) Pierce County	6	0.02
Kirkland, WA (city) King County	6	0.01
Lake Havasu City, AZ (city) Mohave County	6	0.01
Madera, CA (city) Madera County	6	0.01
Medford, OR (city) Jackson County	6	0.01
Redondo Beach, CA (city) Los Angeles County	6	0.01
Rio Rancho, NM (city) Sandoval County	6	0.01
Smyrna, GA (city) Cobb County	6	0.01
Yuma, AZ (city) Yuma County	6	0.01
Anaheim, CA (city) Orange County	6	<0.01
Dallas, TX (city) Dallas County	6	<0.01
El Paso, TX (city) El Paso County	6	<0.01
Paradise, NV (cdp) Clark County	6	<0.01
Rancho Cucamonga, CA (city) San Bernardino County	6	<0.01
Sacramento, CA (city) Sacramento County	6	<0.01

SECTION THREE

Race

American Indian: Yakama

Top 150 Places Sorted by Percent of Total Population

Based on all places, regardless of total population

Place	Population	%
White Swan, WA (cdp) Yakima County	524	66.08
Loring, AK (cdp) Ketchikan Gateway Borough	1	25.00
Harrah, WA (town) Yakima County	85	13.60
Mission, OR (cdp) Umatilla County	67	6.46
Toppenish, WA (city) Yakima County	492	5.50
Donald, WA (cdp) Yakima County	5	5.49
Kirkpatrick, OR (cdp) Umatilla County	8	4.47
Wapato, WA (city) Yakima County	199	3.98
Parker, WA (cdp) Yakima County	6	3.90
Tutuilla, OR (cdp) Umatilla County	17	3.49
Lapwai, ID (city) Nez Perce County	34	2.99
Tampico, WA (cdp) Yakima County	9	2.88
Warm Springs, OR (cdp) Jefferson County	84	2.85
Nespelem Community, WA (cdp) Okanogan County	7	2.77
Augsburg, MN (township) Marshall County	2	2.70
Dayville, OR (town) Grant County	4	2.68
Inchelium, WA (cdp) Ferry County	10	2.44
Klickitat, WA (cdp) Klickitat County	8	2.21
Zillah, WA (city) Yakima County	65	2.19
Hamilton, WA (town) Skagit County	6	1.99
Port Alexander, AK (city) Petersburg Census Area	1	1.92
Qui-nai-elt Village, WA (cdp) Grays Harbor County	1	1.85
Keeler, CA (cdp) Inyo County	1	1.52
Dallesport, WA (cdp) Klickitat County	17	1.41
Nisqually Indian Community, WA (cdp) Thurston County	8	1.39
Buena, WA (cdp) Yakima County	13	1.31
Goldendale, WA (city) Klickitat County	44	1.29
Disautel, WA (cdp) Okanogan County	1	1.28
Metaline Falls, WA (town) Pend Oreille County	3	1.26
Adak, AK (city) Aleutians West Census Area	4	1.23
Granger, WA (city) Yakima County	37	1.14
Pelican, AK (city) Hoonah-Angoon Census Area	1	1.14
Skokomish, WA (cdp) Mason County	7	1.13
Addy, WA (cdp) Stevens County	3	1.12
Union Gap, WA (city) Yakima County	67	1.11
Gopher Flats, OR (cdp) Umatilla County	4	1.06
Moore, MT (town) Fergus County	2	1.04
Carson, WA (cdp) Skamania County	23	1.01
Riverside, OR (cdp) Umatilla County	2	1.01
Taholah, WA (cdp) Grays Harbor County	8	0.95
Nespelem, WA (town) Okanogan County	2	0.85
Elmer City, WA (town) Okanogan County	2	0.84
Gardiner, OR (cdp) Douglas County	2	0.81
Holly, MN (township) Murray County	1	0.79
Terrace Heights, WA (cdp) Yakima County	52	0.75
Coulee Dam, WA (town) Okanogan County	8	0.73
North Bonneville, WA (city) Skamania County	7	0.73
Yakima, WA (city) Yakima County	657	0.72
Colton, WA (town) Whitman County	3	0.72
Spangle, WA (city) Spokane County	2	0.72
Athena, OR (city) Umatilla County	8	0.71
Plummer, ID (city) Benewah County	7	0.67
Prescott, WA (city) Walla Walla County	2	0.63
Umapine, OR (cdp) Umatilla County	2	0.63
Summitview, WA (cdp) Yakima County	6	0.62
Mayetta, KS (city) Jackson County	2	0.59
Moxee, WA (city) Yakima County	19	0.57
Ballou, OK (cdp) Mayes County	1	0.57
Kickapoo Tribal Center, KS (cdp) Brown County	1	0.52
Ocean City, WA (cdp) Grays Harbor County	1	0.50
Tygh Valley, OR (cdp) Wasco County	1	0.49
Turtle Lake, MT (cdp) Lake County	1	0.48
Pe Ell, WA (town) Lewis County	3	0.47
Kamiah, ID (city) Lewis County	6	0.46
Ashford, WA (cdp) Pierce County	1	0.46
Echo, OR (city) Umatilla County	3	0.43
Keller, WA (cdp) Ferry County	1	0.43
Fort Duchesne, UT (cdp) Uintah County	3	0.42
Metolius, OR (city) Jefferson County	3	0.42
Kaktovik, AK (city) North Slope Borough	1	0.42
Madras, OR (city) Jefferson County	25	0.41
Glennallen, AK (cdp) Valdez-Cordova Census Area	2	0.41
Grand Coulee, WA (city) Grant County	4	0.40
Lyle, WA (cdp) Klickitat County	2	0.40
Ahtanum, WA (cdp) Yakima County	14	0.39
Brevator, MN (township) St. Louis County	5	0.39
Eagle Butte, SD (city) Ziebach County	5	0.38
Neah Bay, WA (cdp) Clallam County	3	0.35
Endicott, WA (town) Whitman County	1	0.35
Grand Mound, WA (cdp) Thurston County	10	0.34
Tieton, WA (town) Yakima County	4	0.34
Woodstock, VT (village) Windsor County	3	0.33
Terrebonne, OR (cdp) Deschutes County	4	0.32
Hat Creek, CA (cdp) Shasta County	1	0.32
Sodaville, OR (city) Linn County	1	0.32
White Salmon, WA (city) Klickitat County	7	0.31
Houston, AK (city) Matanuska-Susitna Borough	6	0.31
Desert Aire, WA (cdp) Grant County	5	0.31
Grand Ronde, OR (cdp) Polk County	5	0.30
Weston, OR (city) Umatilla County	2	0.30
Idaville, OR (cdp) Tillamook County	1	0.30
Kittitas, WA (city) Kittitas County	4	0.29
North Omak, WA (cdp) Okanogan County	2	0.29
Packwood, WA (cdp) Lewis County	1	0.29
St. Pierre, MT (cdp) Hill County	1	0.29
Wishram, WA (cdp) Klickitat County	1	0.29
Gleed, WA (cdp) Yakima County	8	0.28
Suquamish, WA (cdp) Kitsap County	11	0.27
Pawnee, OK (city) Pawnee County	6	0.27
Whitesboro, NJ (cdp) Cape May County	6	0.27
McMillin, WA (cdp) Pierce County	4	0.26
Cascade Locks, OR (city) Hood River County	3	0.26
Sandia, TX (cdp) Jim Wells County	1	0.26
Kettle Falls, WA (city) Stevens County	4	0.25
Maupin, OR (city) Wasco County	1	0.24
The Dalles, OR (city) Wasco County	31	0.23
Forks, WA (city) Clallam County	8	0.23
North Powder, OR (city) Union County	1	0.23
South Prairie, WA (town) Pierce County	1	0.23
Pendleton, OR (city) Umatilla County	37	0.22
Selah, WA (city) Yakima County	16	0.22
Chenoweth, OR (cdp) Wasco County	4	0.22
South Browning, MT (cdp) Glacier County	4	0.22
Home, WA (cdp) Pierce County	3	0.22
San Geronimo, CA (cdp) Marin County	1	0.22
Cave Junction, OR (city) Josephine County	4	0.21
Fossil, OR (city) Wheeler County	1	0.21
Rail Road Flat, CA (cdp) Calaveras County	1	0.21
Thorne Bay, AK (city) Prince of Wales-Hyder Census Area	1	0.21
Manson, WA (cdp) Chelan County	3	0.20
Stevenson, WA (city) Skamania County	3	0.20
Palouse, WA (city) Whitman County	2	0.20
Omak, WA (city) Okanogan County	9	0.19
Amboy, WA (cdp) Clark County	3	0.19
Ellsworth, IA (city) Hamilton County	1	0.19
Sunnyside, WA (city) Yakima County	28	0.18
Saratoga, WY (town) Carbon County	3	0.18
Talihina, OK (town) Le Flore County	2	0.18
Grand Portage, MN (unorganized territory) Cook County	1	0.18
Kake, AK (city) Petersburg Census Area	1	0.18
Jemez Pueblo, NM (cdp) Sandoval County	3	0.17
Linden, CA (cdp) San Joaquin County	3	0.17
Fort Hall, ID (cdp) Bannock County	5	0.16
Crocker, WA (cdp) Pierce County	2	0.16
Kooskia, ID (city) Idaho County	1	0.16
Chewelah, WA (city) Stevens County	4	0.15
Black Rock, NM (cdp) McKinley County	2	0.15
Heppner, OR (city) Morrow County	2	0.15
Loma, CO (cdp) Mesa County	2	0.15
Tioga, PA (borough) Tioga County	1	0.15
Connell, WA (city) Franklin County	6	0.14
Fife Heights, WA (cdp) Pierce County	3	0.14
Gold Bar, WA (city) Snohomish County	3	0.14
Kingston, WA (cdp) Kitsap County	3	0.14
Bunker Hill, OR (cdp) Coos County	2	0.14
Cohassett Beach, WA (cdp) Grays Harbor County	1	0.14
Darby, MT (town) Ravalli County	1	0.14
Etna, CA (city) Siskiyou County	1	0.14
Ignacio, CO (town) La Plata County	1	0.14
Zayante, CA (cdp) Santa Cruz County	1	0.14

Please refer to the Explanation of Data in the front of the book for more detailed information.

Race

American Indian: Yakama

Top 150 Places Sorted by Percent of Total Population

Based on places with total population of 7,500 or more

Place	Population	%
Toppenish, WA (city) Yakima County	492	5.50
Yakima, WA (city) Yakima County	657	0.72
The Dalles, OR (city) Wasco County	31	0.23
Pendleton, OR (city) Umatilla County	37	0.22
Sunnyside, WA (city) Yakima County	28	0.18
Grandview, WA (city) Yakima County	14	0.13
Ellensburg, WA (city) Kittitas County	22	0.12
Cornelius, OR (city) Washington County	13	0.11
Cheney, WA (city) Spokane County	11	0.10
Lake Stickney, WA (cdp) Snohomish County	7	0.09
Auburn, WA (city) King County	59	0.08
Bonney Lake, WA (city) Pierce County	14	0.08
Kelso, WA (city) Cowlitz County	9	0.08
Tacoma, WA (city) Pierce County	138	0.07
Edgewood, WA (city) Pierce County	7	0.07
Hoquiam, WA (city) Grays Harbor County	6	0.07
Midland, WA (cdp) Pierce County	6	0.07
Lakewood, WA (city) Pierce County	32	0.06
Burien, WA (city) King County	20	0.06
Frederickson, WA (cdp) Pierce County	12	0.06
North Lynnwood, WA (cdp) Snohomish County	10	0.06
St. Helens, OR (city) Columbia County	8	0.06
Waller, WA (cdp) Pierce County	5	0.06
Richland, WA (city) Benton County	25	0.05
Orchards, WA (cdp) Clark County	9	0.05
Aberdeen, WA (city) Grays Harbor County	8	0.05
Anacortes, WA (city) Skagit County	8	0.05
Enumclaw, WA (city) King County	5	0.05
Lincoln City, OR (city) Lincoln County	4	0.05
Summit, WA (cdp) Pierce County	4	0.05
Spokane, WA (city) Spokane County	91	0.04
Everett, WA (city) Snohomish County	45	0.04
Kent, WA (city) King County	33	0.04
Olympia, WA (city) Thurston County	17	0.04
Longview, WA (city) Cowlitz County	15	0.04
Lewiston, ID (city) Nez Perce County	13	0.04
Pullman, WA (city) Whitman County	11	0.04
Klamath Falls, OR (city) Klamath County	8	0.04
Durango, CO (city) La Plata County	7	0.04
Artondale, WA (cdp) Pierce County	5	0.04
Oak Hills, OR (cdp) Washington County	5	0.04
Cedar Hills, UT (city) Utah County	4	0.04
Fife, WA (city) Pierce County	4	0.04
Alderwood Manor, WA (cdp) Snohomish County	3	0.04
Cedar Hills, OR (cdp) Washington County	3	0.04
Ketchikan, AK (city) Ketchikan Gateway Borough	3	0.04
Kirtland, NM (cdp) San Juan County	3	0.04
Wasilla, AK (city) Matanuska-Susitna Borough	3	0.04
Portland, OR (city) Multnomah County	166	0.03
Vancouver, WA (city) Clark County	55	0.03
Kennewick, WA (city) Benton County	23	0.03
Marysville, WA (city) Snohomish County	21	0.03
Springfield, OR (city) Lane County	18	0.03
Bremerton, WA (city) Kitsap County	11	0.03
Puyallup, WA (city) Pierce County	11	0.03
Oregon City, OR (city) Clackamas County	8	0.03
Graham, WA (cdp) Pierce County	6	0.03
Hayesville, OR (cdp) Marion County	6	0.03
Middle, NJ (township) Cape May County	6	0.03
Bryn Mawr-Skyway, WA (cdp) King County	5	0.03
Camas, WA (city) Clark County	5	0.03
Fairwood, WA (cdp) King County	5	0.03
Kalispell, MT (city) Flathead County	5	0.03
Salmon Creek, WA (cdp) Clark County	5	0.03
Dallas, OR (city) Polk County	4	0.03
Gladstone, OR (city) Clackamas County	4	0.03
Knik-Fairview, AK (cdp) Matanuska-Susitna Borough	4	0.03
Millbrook, AL (city) Elmore County	4	0.03
Parkway, CA (cdp) Sacramento County	4	0.03
Waianae, HI (cdp) Honolulu County	4	0.03
College Place, WA (city) Walla Walla County	3	0.03
DeRidder, LA (city) Beauregard Parish	3	0.03
Minnehaha, WA (cdp) Clark County	3	0.03
Prairie Ridge, WA (cdp) Pierce County	3	0.03
Scotts Valley, CA (city) Santa Cruz County	3	0.03
Vashon, WA (cdp) King County	3	0.03
West Richland, WA (city) Benton County	3	0.03
Green, OR (cdp) Douglas County	2	0.03
Pasadena Hills, FL (cdp) Pasco County	2	0.03
Seattle, WA (city) King County	111	0.02
Gresham, OR (city) Multnomah County	23	0.02
Federal Way, WA (city) King County	20	0.02
Spokane Valley, WA (city) Spokane County	19	0.02
Lawrence, KS (city) Douglas County	14	0.02
Lodi, CA (city) San Joaquin County	11	0.02
Lacey, WA (city) Thurston County	10	0.02
Pasco, WA (city) Franklin County	10	0.02
Shoreline, WA (city) King County	10	0.02
Albany, OR (city) Linn County	8	0.02
Lynnwood, WA (city) Snohomish County	8	0.02
South Hill, WA (cdp) Pierce County	8	0.02
El Paso de Robles (Paso Robles), CA (city) San Luis Obispo County	7	0.02
Walla Walla, WA (city) Walla Walla County	7	0.02
Parkland, WA (cdp) Pierce County	6	0.02
Des Moines, WA (city) King County	5	0.02
Juneau, AK (borough) Juneau City and Borough	5	0.02
Kihei, HI (cdp) Maui County	5	0.02
Redmond, OR (city) Deschutes County	5	0.02
Bethany, OR (cdp) Washington County	4	0.02
Covington, WA (city) King County	4	0.02
Hazel Dell, WA (cdp) Clark County	4	0.02
Hermiston, OR (city) Umatilla County	4	0.02
Kahului, HI (cdp) Maui County	4	0.02
La Cañada Flintridge, CA (city) Los Angeles County	4	0.02
Monroe, WA (city) Snohomish County	4	0.02
Moses Lake, WA (city) Grant County	4	0.02
Mountlake Terrace, WA (city) Snohomish County	4	0.02
Oak Grove, OR (cdp) Clackamas County	4	0.02
Port Angeles, WA (city) Clallam County	4	0.02
Radford, VA (ind. city) Radford independent city	4	0.02
Schofield Barracks, HI (cdp) Honolulu County	4	0.02
Battle Ground, WA (city) Clark County	3	0.02
El Segundo, CA (city) Los Angeles County	3	0.02
Ewa Beach, HI (cdp) Honolulu County	3	0.02
Martha Lake, WA (cdp) Snohomish County	3	0.02
Mill Creek, WA (city) Snohomish County	3	0.02
Mountain Home, ID (city) Elmore County	3	0.02
Seagoville, TX (city) Dallas County	3	0.02
Tumwater, WA (city) Thurston County	3	0.02
White Center, WA (cdp) King County	3	0.02
Birch Bay, WA (cdp) Whatcom County	2	0.02
Colonial Park, PA (cdp) Dauphin County	2	0.02
Damascus, OR (city) Clackamas County	2	0.02
East Wenatchee, WA (city) Douglas County	2	0.02
Fairview, OR (city) Multnomah County	2	0.02
Ferndale, WA (city) Whatcom County	2	0.02
La Grande, OR (city) Union County	2	0.02
Lakeville, MA (town) Plymouth County	2	0.02
Larkspur, CA (city) Marin County	2	0.02
Maltby, WA (cdp) Snohomish County	2	0.02
Miles City, MT (city) Custer County	2	0.02
Parsons, KS (city) Labette County	2	0.02
Port Orchard, WA (city) Kitsap County	2	0.02
Sedro-Woolley, WA (city) Skagit County	2	0.02
Snoqualmie, WA (city) King County	2	0.02
Woodinville, WA (city) King County	2	0.02
Anchorage, AK (municipality) Anchorage Municipality	23	0.01
Salem, OR (city) Marion County	16	0.01
Renton, WA (city) King County	13	0.01
Eugene, OR (city) Lane County	11	0.01
Bend, OR (city) Deschutes County	10	0.01
Beaverton, OR (city) Washington County	9	0.01
Bellingham, WA (city) Whatcom County	8	0.01
Round Rock, TX (city) Williamson County	8	0.01
Billings, MT (city) Yellowstone County	7	0.01
Hillsboro, OR (city) Washington County	7	0.01
Kirkland, WA (city) King County	6	0.01
Lake Havasu City, AZ (city) Mohave County	6	0.01
Madera, CA (city) Madera County	6	0.01
Medford, OR (city) Jackson County	6	0.01

Race

American Indian: Yaqui

U.S. and 50 States Sorted by Population and Percent of Total Population

Place	Population	%
United States	**32,595**	**0.01**
Arizona	17,362	0.27
California	10,375	0.03
Texas	736	<0.01
Washington	387	0.01
Colorado	379	0.01
Oregon	351	0.01
Nevada	266	0.01
New Mexico	238	0.01
Illinois	193	<0.01
Florida	157	<0.01
Hawaii	146	0.01
Utah	124	<0.01
Michigan	119	<0.01
Oklahoma	108	<0.01
New York	104	<0.01
Missouri	95	<0.01
Idaho	85	0.01
Virginia	83	<0.01
Georgia	82	<0.01
Kansas	81	<0.01
North Carolina	76	<0.01
Wisconsin	74	<0.01
Arkansas	73	<0.01
Ohio	73	<0.01
Maryland	64	<0.01
Pennsylvania	61	<0.01
Alabama	55	<0.01
Minnesota	55	<0.01
Massachusetts	51	<0.01
Indiana	50	<0.01
Tennessee	45	<0.01
Iowa	43	<0.01
Alaska	42	0.01
Nebraska	37	<0.01
Wyoming	33	0.01
New Jersey	32	<0.01
South Carolina	32	<0.01
Montana	27	<0.01
Connecticut	26	<0.01
Mississippi	24	<0.01
Louisiana	23	<0.01
Kentucky	22	<0.01
Maine	18	<0.01
New Hampshire	17	<0.01
District of Columbia	15	<0.01
South Dakota	15	<0.01
North Dakota	13	<0.01
West Virginia	13	<0.01
Rhode Island	7	<0.01
Vermont	7	<0.01
Delaware	1	<0.01

Place	Population	%
Arizona	17,362	0.27
California	10,375	0.03
United States	**32,595**	**0.01**
Washington	387	0.01
Colorado	379	0.01
Oregon	351	0.01
Nevada	266	0.01
New Mexico	238	0.01
Hawaii	146	0.01
Idaho	85	0.01
Alaska	42	0.01
Wyoming	33	0.01
Texas	736	<0.01
Illinois	193	<0.01
Florida	157	<0.01
Utah	124	<0.01
Michigan	119	<0.01
Oklahoma	108	<0.01
New York	104	<0.01
Missouri	95	<0.01
Virginia	83	<0.01
Georgia	82	<0.01
Kansas	81	<0.01
North Carolina	76	<0.01
Wisconsin	74	<0.01
Arkansas	73	<0.01
Ohio	73	<0.01
Maryland	64	<0.01
Pennsylvania	61	<0.01
Alabama	55	<0.01
Minnesota	55	<0.01
Massachusetts	51	<0.01
Indiana	50	<0.01
Tennessee	45	<0.01
Iowa	43	<0.01
Nebraska	37	<0.01
New Jersey	32	<0.01
South Carolina	32	<0.01
Montana	27	<0.01
Connecticut	26	<0.01
Mississippi	24	<0.01
Louisiana	23	<0.01
Kentucky	22	<0.01
Maine	18	<0.01
New Hampshire	17	<0.01
District of Columbia	15	<0.01
South Dakota	15	<0.01
North Dakota	13	<0.01
West Virginia	13	<0.01
Rhode Island	7	<0.01
Vermont	7	<0.01
Delaware	1	<0.01

Please refer to the Explanation of Data in the front of the book for more detailed information.

Race

American Indian: Yaqui

Top 150 Places Sorted by Population

Based on all places, regardless of total population

Place	Population	%
Tucson, AZ (city) Pima County	3,852	0.74
Guadalupe, AZ (town) Maricopa County	2,542	46.03
Phoenix, AZ (city) Maricopa County	1,945	0.13
Drexel Heights, AZ (cdp) Pima County	725	2.61
Tempe, AZ (city) Maricopa County	670	0.41
Los Angeles, CA (city) Los Angeles County	647	0.02
Mesa, AZ (city) Maricopa County	564	0.13
Fresno, CA (city) Fresno County	522	0.11
San Jose, CA (city) Santa Clara County	354	0.04
Chandler, AZ (city) Maricopa County	350	0.15
San Diego, CA (city) San Diego County	310	0.02
South Tucson, AZ (city) Pima County	242	4.28
Sacramento, CA (city) Sacramento County	207	0.04
Scottsdale, AZ (city) Maricopa County	192	0.09
Coolidge, AZ (city) Pinal County	188	1.59
Yuma, AZ (city) Yuma County	183	0.20
Stockton, CA (city) San Joaquin County	166	0.06
Valencia West, AZ (cdp) Pima County	155	1.66
Bakersfield, CA (city) Kern County	154	0.04
Casa Grande, AZ (city) Pinal County	140	0.29
Marana, AZ (town) Pima County	134	0.38
Long Beach, CA (city) Los Angeles County	130	0.03
Glendale, AZ (city) Maricopa County	128	0.06
San Bernardino, CA (city) San Bernardino County	108	0.05
Riverside, CA (city) Riverside County	103	0.03
Avondale, AZ (city) Maricopa County	100	0.13
Modesto, CA (city) Stanislaus County	100	0.05
Oxnard, CA (city) Ventura County	91	0.05
San Francisco, CA (city) San Francisco County	90	0.01
Casas Adobes, AZ (cdp) Pima County	86	0.13
Fontana, CA (city) San Bernardino County	86	0.04
Ontario, CA (city) San Bernardino County	84	0.05
Anaheim, CA (city) Orange County	84	0.02
El Paso, TX (city) El Paso County	79	0.01
Chula Vista, CA (city) San Diego County	77	0.03
San Antonio, TX (city) Medina County	77	0.01
Rancho Cucamonga, CA (city) San Bernardino County	73	0.04
Denver, CO (city) Denver County	73	0.01
Tucson Estates, AZ (cdp) Pima County	68	0.56
Gilbert, AZ (town) Maricopa County	67	0.03
Oakland, CA (city) Alameda County	67	0.02
East Los Angeles, CA (cdp) Los Angeles County	66	0.05
Rialto, CA (city) San Bernardino County	63	0.06
Albuquerque, NM (city) Bernalillo County	63	0.01
Las Vegas, NV (city) Clark County	63	0.01
Lancaster, CA (city) Los Angeles County	62	0.04
Flowing Wells, AZ (cdp) Pima County	59	0.36
Hesperia, CA (city) San Bernardino County	59	0.07
Moreno Valley, CA (city) Riverside County	59	0.03
Chicago, IL (city) Cook County	58	<0.01
Pico Rivera, CA (city) Los Angeles County	56	0.09
Visalia, CA (city) Tulare County	56	0.05
Corona, CA (city) Riverside County	56	0.04
El Monte, CA (city) Los Angeles County	55	0.05
Santa Rosa, CA (city) Sonoma County	55	0.03
New York, NY (city) Kings County	54	<0.01
Fullerton, CA (city) Orange County	53	0.04
Seattle, WA (city) King County	53	0.01
San Buenaventura (Ventura), CA (city) Ventura County	52	0.05
Maricopa, AZ (city) Pinal County	51	0.12
Palmdale, CA (city) Los Angeles County	51	0.03
Whittier, CA (city) Los Angeles County	50	0.06
Sahuarita, AZ (town) Pima County	49	0.19
Three Points, AZ (cdp) Pima County	48	0.86
Victorville, CA (city) San Bernardino County	48	0.04
Redlands, CA (city) San Bernardino County	47	0.07
Huntington Beach, CA (city) Orange County	46	0.02
Eloy, AZ (city) Pinal County	45	0.27
El Cajon, CA (city) San Diego County	45	0.05
Escondido, CA (city) San Diego County	44	0.03
Santa Clarita, CA (city) Los Angeles County	43	0.02
Portland, OR (city) Multnomah County	43	0.01
South Whittier, CA (cdp) Los Angeles County	42	0.07
Apache Junction, AZ (city) Pinal County	41	0.11
El Centro, CA (city) Imperial County	41	0.10
Salinas, CA (city) Monterey County	41	0.03
Santa Maria, CA (city) Santa Barbara County	40	0.04
Peoria, AZ (city) Yavapai County	40	0.03
Calexico, CA (city) Imperial County	39	0.10
Buckeye, AZ (town) Maricopa County	39	0.08
West Covina, CA (city) Los Angeles County	39	0.04
Avra Valley, AZ (cdp) Pima County	38	0.63
Goodyear, AZ (city) Maricopa County	38	0.06
Santa Ana, CA (city) Orange County	38	0.01
Manteca, CA (city) San Joaquin County	37	0.06
Chino, CA (city) San Bernardino County	37	0.05
Hemet, CA (city) Riverside County	37	0.05
Antioch, CA (city) Contra Costa County	37	0.04
Fremont, CA (city) Alameda County	37	0.02
El Mirage, AZ (city) Maricopa County	36	0.11
Gilroy, CA (city) Santa Clara County	36	0.07
Alhambra, CA (city) Los Angeles County	36	0.04
La Mirada, CA (city) Los Angeles County	35	0.07
Merced, CA (city) Merced County	35	0.04
Covina, CA (city) Los Angeles County	34	0.07
Montebello, CA (city) Los Angeles County	34	0.05
Austin, TX (city) Travis County	34	<0.01
Florence, AZ (town) Pinal County	33	0.13
Delano, CA (city) Kern County	33	0.06
Santa Barbara, CA (city) Santa Barbara County	33	0.04
Houston, TX (city) Harris County	33	<0.01
Picture Rocks, AZ (cdp) Pima County	32	0.33
San Tan Valley, AZ (cdp) Pinal County	32	0.04
Santa Clara, CA (city) Santa Clara County	32	0.03
Elk Grove, CA (city) Sacramento County	32	0.02
Sunrise Manor, NV (cdp) Clark County	32	0.02
Yucaipa, CA (city) San Bernardino County	31	0.06
Chico, CA (city) Butte County	31	0.04
Clovis, CA (city) Fresno County	31	0.03
Colorado Springs, CO (city) El Paso County	31	0.01
Douglas, AZ (city) Cochise County	30	0.17
Highland, CA (city) San Bernardino County	30	0.06
Apple Valley, CA (town) San Bernardino County	30	0.04
Upland, CA (city) San Bernardino County	30	0.04
Orange, CA (city) Orange County	30	0.02
Sacaton, AZ (cdp) Pinal County	29	1.09
Ajo, AZ (cdp) Pima County	29	0.88
Summit, AZ (cdp) Pima County	29	0.54
Colton, CA (city) San Bernardino County	29	0.06
La Mesa, CA (city) San Diego County	29	0.05
Berkeley, CA (city) Alameda County	29	0.03
Oceanside, CA (city) San Diego County	29	0.02
West Whittier-Los Nietos, CA (cdp) Los Angeles County	28	0.11
Woodland, CA (city) Yolo County	28	0.05
Arden-Arcade, CA (cdp) Sacramento County	28	0.03
Buena Park, CA (city) Orange County	28	0.03
Downey, CA (city) Los Angeles County	28	0.03
Ogden, UT (city) Weber County	28	0.03
Dallas, TX (city) Dallas County	28	<0.01
Imperial Beach, CA (city) San Diego County	27	0.10
Tulare, CA (city) Tulare County	27	0.05
Madera, CA (city) Madera County	27	0.04
Carson, CA (city) Los Angeles County	27	0.03
Urban Honolulu, HI (cdp) Honolulu County	27	0.01
Banning, CA (city) Riverside County	26	0.09
Oro Valley, AZ (town) Pima County	26	0.06
Vista, CA (city) San Diego County	26	0.03
Hayward, CA (city) Alameda County	26	0.02
Pasadena, CA (city) Los Angeles County	26	0.02
Torrance, CA (city) Los Angeles County	26	0.02
Winslow, AZ (city) Navajo County	25	0.26
Alum Rock, CA (cdp) Santa Clara County	25	0.16
Brawley, CA (city) Imperial County	25	0.10
Lompoc, CA (city) Santa Barbara County	25	0.06
Porterville, CA (city) Tulare County	25	0.05
Santee, CA (city) San Diego County	25	0.05
Indio, CA (city) Riverside County	25	0.03
Norwalk, CA (city) Los Angeles County	25	0.02
Richmond, CA (city) Contra Costa County	25	0.02
Arizona City, AZ (cdp) Pinal County	24	0.23

Please refer to the Explanation of Data in the front of the book for more detailed information.

Race

American Indian: Yaqui

Top 150 Places Sorted by Percent of Total Population

Based on all places, regardless of total population

Place	Population	%
Guadalupe, AZ (town) Maricopa County	2,542	46.03
Charco, AZ (cdp) Pima County	5	9.62
Swiftwater, MN (township) Lake of the Woods County	4	6.67
Oxford, ID (city) Franklin County	3	6.25
Nolic, AZ (cdp) Pima County	2	5.41
San Miguel, AZ (cdp) Pima County	10	5.08
South Tucson, AZ (city) Pima County	242	4.28
Ak Chin, AZ (cdp) Pima County	1	3.33
Goodyear Village, AZ (cdp) Pinal County	13	2.84
Drexel Heights, AZ (cdp) Pima County	725	2.61
Clear Creek, CA (cdp) Lassen County	4	2.37
Winterhaven, CA (cdp) Imperial County	9	2.28
Rillito, AZ (cdp) Pima County	2	2.06
Nazlini, AZ (cdp) Apache County	9	1.84
Tonopah, AZ (cdp) Maricopa County	1	1.67
Valencia West, AZ (cdp) Pima County	155	1.66
Arivaca Junction, AZ (cdp) Pima County	18	1.65
Gu Oidak, AZ (cdp) Pima County	3	1.60
Coolidge, AZ (city) Pinal County	188	1.59
Gazelle, CA (cdp) Siskiyou County	1	1.43
Ali Molina, AZ (cdp) Pima County	1	1.41
Littlefield, AZ (cdp) Mohave County	4	1.30
Maish Vaya, AZ (cdp) Pima County	2	1.27
Soda Springs, CA (cdp) Nevada County	1	1.23
San Simon, AZ (cdp) Cochise County	2	1.21
Cromberg, CA (cdp) Plumas County	3	1.15
Sacaton, AZ (cdp) Pinal County	29	1.09
Nakaibito, NM (cdp) McKinley County	5	1.07
Hotevilla-Bacavi, AZ (cdp) Navajo County	10	1.04
Littletown, AZ (cdp) Pima County	9	1.03
Lemon Cove, CA (cdp) Tulare County	3	0.97
Tehama, CA (city) Tehama County	4	0.96
Ajo, AZ (cdp) Pima County	29	0.88
Sells, AZ (cdp) Pima County	22	0.88
Centennial Park, AZ (cdp) Mohave County	11	0.87
Three Points, AZ (cdp) Pima County	48	0.86
East Pleasant View, CO (cdp) Jefferson County	3	0.84
Linnell Camp, CA (cdp) Tulare County	7	0.82
Raisin City, CA (cdp) Fresno County	3	0.79
West Park, CA (cdp) Fresno County	9	0.78
Patagonia, AZ (town) Santa Cruz County	7	0.77
Tucson, AZ (city) Pima County	3,852	0.74
Indio Hills, CA (cdp) Riverside County	7	0.72
Keene, CA (cdp) Kern County	3	0.70
Eldora, CO (cdp) Boulder County	1	0.70
Fort Apache, AZ (cdp) Navajo County	1	0.70
Placitas, NM (cdp) Doña Ana County	4	0.69
Kerby, OR (cdp) Josephine County	4	0.67
Haworth, OK (town) McCurtain County	2	0.67
Topawa, AZ (cdp) Pima County	2	0.67
Tecopa, CA (cdp) Inyo County	1	0.67
Blackwater, AZ (cdp) Pinal County	7	0.66
Casa Blanca, AZ (cdp) Pinal County	9	0.65
Avra Valley, AZ (cdp) Pima County	38	0.63
Mammoth, AZ (town) Pinal County	9	0.63
Baudette, MN (city) Lake of the Woods County	7	0.63
Moore, TX (cdp) Frio County	3	0.63
Red Mesa, AZ (cdp) Apache County	3	0.63
Pleasant Valley, TX (town) Wichita County	2	0.60
Happy, TX (town) Swisher County	4	0.59
Bryce, AZ (cdp) Graham County	1	0.57
Mulford, CO (cdp) Garfield County	1	0.57
Tucson Estates, AZ (cdp) Pima County	68	0.56
Sycamore, OK (cdp) Delaware County	1	0.56
Sacaton Flats Village, AZ (cdp) Pinal County	3	0.55
Summit, AZ (cdp) Pima County	29	0.54
Walnut Creek, AZ (cdp) Mohave County	3	0.53
Crestmore Heights, CA (cdp) Riverside County	2	0.52
Winchester Bay, OR (cdp) Douglas County	2	0.52
Austin, NV (cdp) Lander County	1	0.52
Goshen, CA (cdp) Tulare County	15	0.50
Whitecone, AZ (cdp) Navajo County	4	0.49
Hubbard, WI (town) Rusk County	1	0.49
Bark Ranch, CO (cdp) Boulder County	1	0.47
Moskowite Corner, CA (cdp) Napa County	1	0.47
Mud Bay, AK (cdp) Haines Borough	1	0.47
Heber-Overgaard, AZ (cdp) Navajo County	13	0.46
Cactus Flats, AZ (cdp) Graham County	7	0.46
Peach Springs, AZ (cdp) Mohave County	5	0.46
Ak-Chin Village, AZ (cdp) Pinal County	4	0.46
Potrero, CA (cdp) San Diego County	3	0.46
Lamy, NM (cdp) Santa Fe County	1	0.46
Bodega, CA (cdp) Sonoma County	1	0.45
Parshall, ND (city) Mountrail County	4	0.44
Pinon, AZ (cdp) Navajo County	4	0.44
Descanso, CA (cdp) San Diego County	6	0.42
Picacho, AZ (cdp) Pinal County	2	0.42
Tempe, AZ (city) Maricopa County	670	0.41
Minkler, CA (cdp) Fresno County	4	0.40
Schubert, PA (cdp) Berks County	1	0.40
Junction, TX (city) Kimble County	10	0.39
Florence, MT (cdp) Ravalli County	3	0.39
Greenview, IL (village) Menard County	3	0.39
Nelson, AZ (cdp) Pima County	1	0.39
Marana, AZ (town) Pima County	134	0.38
North Edwards, CA (cdp) Kern County	4	0.38
Centennial, WY (cdp) Albany County	1	0.37
Flowing Wells, AZ (cdp) Pima County	59	0.36
Spring Valley, CA (cdp) Lake County	3	0.36
Trout Lake, WA (cdp) Klickitat County	2	0.36
Halfway, OR (city) Baker County	1	0.35
Morenci, AZ (cdp) Greenlee County	5	0.34
Jeddito, AZ (cdp) Navajo County	1	0.34
Picture Rocks, AZ (cdp) Pima County	32	0.33
Barview, OR (cdp) Coos County	6	0.33
Burns, WY (town) Laramie County	1	0.33
Rembert, SC (cdp) Sumter County	1	0.33
Strathmore, CA (cdp) Tulare County	9	0.32
Fern Forest, HI (cdp) Hawaii County	3	0.32
Gila Crossing, AZ (cdp) Maricopa County	2	0.32
Tampico, WA (cdp) Yakima County	1	0.32
Gila Bend, AZ (town) Maricopa County	6	0.31
Cedar Creek, AZ (cdp) Gila County	1	0.31
Pisinemo, AZ (cdp) Pima County	1	0.31
Kawela Bay, HI (cdp) Honolulu County	1	0.30
Lemitar, NM (cdp) Socorro County	1	0.30
Casa Grande, AZ (city) Pinal County	140	0.29
Sonora, CA (city) Tuolumne County	14	0.29
Freedom, CA (cdp) Santa Cruz County	9	0.29
Joseph City, AZ (cdp) Navajo County	4	0.29
Saticoy, CA (cdp) Ventura County	3	0.29
Winchester, ID (city) Lewis County	1	0.29
Atoka, NM (cdp) Eddy County	3	0.28
Olinda, HI (cdp) Maui County	3	0.28
Evening Shade, OK (cdp) Sequoyah County	1	0.28
Eloy, AZ (city) Pinal County	45	0.27
Stagecoach, NV (cdp) Lyon County	5	0.27
Pine Bluffs, WY (town) Laramie County	3	0.27
Kaumakani, HI (cdp) Kauai County	2	0.27
Netarts, OR (cdp) Tillamook County	2	0.27
Skyland, NV (cdp) Douglas County	1	0.27
Trinidad, CA (city) Humboldt County	1	0.27
Winslow, AZ (city) Navajo County	25	0.26
Tolleson, AZ (city) Maricopa County	17	0.26
South Wenatchee, WA (cdp) Chelan County	4	0.26
Taft Mosswood, CA (cdp) San Joaquin County	4	0.26
Alta, UT (town) Salt Lake County	1	0.26
River Pines, CA (cdp) Amador County	1	0.26
Linn, WI (town) Walworth County	6	0.25
Dell Prairie, WI (town) Adams County	4	0.25
South Dos Palos, CA (cdp) Merced County	4	0.25
Westhaven-Moonstone, CA (cdp) Humboldt County	3	0.25
Osmond, WY (cdp) Lincoln County	1	0.25
Rosedale, NM (cdp) Grant County	1	0.25
Skamokawa Valley, WA (cdp) Wahkiakum County	1	0.25
Wagon Wheel, AZ (cdp) Navajo County	4	0.24
Centerville, MI (township) Leelanau County	3	0.24
Redway, CA (cdp) Humboldt County	3	0.24
Komatke, AZ (cdp) Maricopa County	2	0.24
Copalis Beach, WA (cdp) Grays Harbor County	1	0.24

Please refer to the Explanation of Data in the front of the book for more detailed information.

Race

American Indian: Yaqui

Top 150 Places Sorted by Percent of Total Population

Based on places with total population of 7,500 or more

Place	Population	%
Drexel Heights, AZ (cdp) Pima County	725	2.61
Valencia West, AZ (cdp) Pima County	155	1.66
Coolidge, AZ (city) Pinal County	188	1.59
Tucson, AZ (city) Pima County	3,852	0.74
Tucson Estates, AZ (cdp) Pima County	68	0.56
Tempe, AZ (city) Maricopa County	670	0.41
Marana, AZ (town) Pima County	134	0.38
Flowing Wells, AZ (cdp) Pima County	59	0.36
Picture Rocks, AZ (cdp) Pima County	32	0.33
Casa Grande, AZ (city) Pinal County	140	0.29
Eloy, AZ (city) Pinal County	45	0.27
Winslow, AZ (city) Navajo County	25	0.26
Arizona City, AZ (cdp) Pinal County	24	0.23
Tuba City, AZ (cdp) Coconino County	20	0.23
Yuma, AZ (city) Yuma County	183	0.20
Sahuarita, AZ (town) Pima County	49	0.19
Calipatria, CA (city) Imperial County	15	0.19
Douglas, AZ (city) Cochise County	30	0.17
Alum Rock, CA (cdp) Santa Clara County	25	0.16
Chandler, AZ (city) Maricopa County	350	0.15
Imperial, CA (city) Imperial County	22	0.15
Coalinga, CA (city) Fresno County	20	0.15
Safford, AZ (city) Graham County	13	0.14
Phoenix, AZ (city) Maricopa County	1,945	0.13
Mesa, AZ (city) Maricopa County	564	0.13
Avondale, AZ (city) Maricopa County	100	0.13
Casas Adobes, AZ (cdp) Pima County	86	0.13
Florence, AZ (town) Pinal County	33	0.13
Golden Valley, AZ (cdp) Mohave County	11	0.13
Maricopa, AZ (city) Pinal County	51	0.12
Garnet, CA (cdp) Riverside County	9	0.12
Fresno, CA (city) Fresno County	522	0.11
Apache Junction, AZ (city) Pinal County	41	0.11
El Mirage, AZ (city) Maricopa County	36	0.11
West Whittier-Los Nietos, CA (cdp) Los Angeles County	28	0.11
Yucca Valley, CA (town) San Bernardino County	23	0.11
Catalina, AZ (cdp) Pima County	8	0.11
El Centro, CA (city) Imperial County	41	0.10
Calexico, CA (city) Imperial County	39	0.10
Imperial Beach, CA (city) San Diego County	27	0.10
Brawley, CA (city) Imperial County	25	0.10
East Hemet, CA (cdp) Riverside County	17	0.10
Olivehurst, CA (cdp) Yuba County	13	0.10
Grand Terrace, CA (city) San Bernardino County	12	0.10
Chino Valley, AZ (town) Yavapai County	11	0.10
East La Mirada, CA (cdp) Los Angeles County	10	0.10
Vail, AZ (cdp) Pima County	10	0.10
East Foothills, CA (cdp) Santa Clara County	8	0.10
Scottsdale, AZ (city) Maricopa County	192	0.09
Pico Rivera, CA (city) Los Angeles County	56	0.09
Banning, CA (city) Riverside County	26	0.09
Desert Hot Springs, CA (city) Riverside County	24	0.09
Selma, CA (city) Fresno County	20	0.09
Nogales, AZ (city) Santa Cruz County	18	0.09
Kerman, CA (city) Fresno County	12	0.09
Salida, CA (cdp) Stanislaus County	12	0.09
Country Club, CA (cdp) San Joaquin County	8	0.09
Mentone, CA (cdp) San Bernardino County	8	0.09
Buckeye, AZ (town) Maricopa County	39	0.08
Blythe, CA (city) Riverside County	17	0.08
Grover Beach, CA (city) San Luis Obispo County	11	0.08
Live Oak, TX (city) Bexar County	10	0.08
Verde Village, AZ (cdp) Yavapai County	9	0.08
Soquel, CA (cdp) Santa Cruz County	8	0.08
August, CA (cdp) San Joaquin County	7	0.08
Thousand Palms, CA (cdp) Riverside County	6	0.08
Hesperia, CA (city) San Bernardino County	59	0.07
Redlands, CA (city) San Bernardino County	47	0.07
South Whittier, CA (cdp) Los Angeles County	42	0.07
Gilroy, CA (city) Santa Clara County	36	0.07
La Mirada, CA (city) Los Angeles County	35	0.07
Covina, CA (city) Los Angeles County	34	0.07
Atascadero, CA (city) San Luis Obispo County	19	0.07
Orcutt, CA (cdp) Santa Barbara County	19	0.07
San Fernando, CA (city) Los Angeles County	16	0.07
Barstow, CA (city) San Bernardino County	15	0.07
Lakeside, CA (cdp) San Diego County	14	0.07
Rio Rico, AZ (cdp) Santa Cruz County	14	0.07
Live Oak, CA (cdp) Santa Cruz County	12	0.07
Santa Fe Springs, CA (city) Los Angeles County	11	0.07
El Sobrante, CA (cdp) Riverside County	9	0.07
Delhi, CA (cdp) Merced County	7	0.07
Kapaa, HI (cdp) Kauai County	7	0.07
Morro Bay, CA (city) San Luis Obispo County	7	0.07
Show Low, AZ (city) Navajo County	7	0.07
Larkfield-Wikiup, CA (cdp) Sonoma County	6	0.07
Stockton, CA (city) San Joaquin County	166	0.06
Glendale, AZ (city) Maricopa County	128	0.06
Rialto, CA (city) San Bernardino County	63	0.06
Whittier, CA (city) Los Angeles County	50	0.06
Goodyear, AZ (city) Maricopa County	38	0.06
Manteca, CA (city) San Joaquin County	37	0.06
Delano, CA (city) Kern County	33	0.06
Yucaipa, CA (city) San Bernardino County	31	0.06
Highland, CA (city) San Bernardino County	30	0.06
Colton, CA (city) San Bernardino County	29	0.06
Oro Valley, AZ (town) Pima County	26	0.06
Lompoc, CA (city) Santa Barbara County	25	0.06
Kingman, AZ (city) Mohave County	17	0.06
Santa Paula, CA (city) Ventura County	17	0.06
Corcoran, CA (city) Kings County	16	0.06
Lemon Grove, CA (city) San Diego County	14	0.06
Castaic, CA (cdp) Los Angeles County	12	0.06
Arroyo Grande, CA (city) San Luis Obispo County	11	0.06
Chowchilla, CA (city) Madera County	11	0.06
Arcata, CA (city) Humboldt County	10	0.06
Nipomo, CA (cdp) San Luis Obispo County	10	0.06
Prunedale, CA (cdp) Monterey County	10	0.06
Ukiah, CA (city) Mendocino County	10	0.06
Lamont, CA (cdp) Kern County	9	0.06
Red Bluff, CA (city) Tehama County	8	0.06
Marysville, CA (city) Yuba County	7	0.06
Camp Verde, AZ (town) Yavapai County	6	0.06
Citrus, CA (cdp) Los Angeles County	6	0.06
Winton, CA (cdp) Merced County	6	0.06
Alliance, NE (city) Box Butte County	5	0.06
San Bernardino, CA (city) San Bernardino County	108	0.05
Modesto, CA (city) Stanislaus County	100	0.05
Oxnard, CA (city) Ventura County	91	0.05
Ontario, CA (city) San Bernardino County	84	0.05
East Los Angeles, CA (cdp) Los Angeles County	66	0.05
Visalia, CA (city) Tulare County	56	0.05
El Monte, CA (city) Los Angeles County	55	0.05
San Buenaventura (Ventura), CA (city) Ventura County	52	0.05
El Cajon, CA (city) San Diego County	45	0.05
Chino, CA (city) San Bernardino County	37	0.05
Hemet, CA (city) Riverside County	37	0.05
Montebello, CA (city) Los Angeles County	34	0.05
La Mesa, CA (city) San Diego County	29	0.05
Woodland, CA (city) Yolo County	28	0.05
Tulare, CA (city) Tulare County	27	0.05
Porterville, CA (city) Tulare County	25	0.05
Santee, CA (city) San Diego County	25	0.05
Azusa, CA (city) Los Angeles County	22	0.05
West Sacramento, CA (city) Yolo County	22	0.05
Ceres, CA (city) Stanislaus County	21	0.05
Hollister, CA (city) San Benito County	18	0.05
La Quinta, CA (city) Riverside County	17	0.05
Montclair, CA (city) San Bernardino County	17	0.05
Wildomar, CA (city) Riverside County	17	0.05
Dakota Ridge, CO (cdp) Jefferson County	16	0.05
Rubidoux, CA (cdp) Riverside County	16	0.05
Fallbrook, CA (cdp) San Diego County	14	0.05
Ridgecrest, CA (city) Kern County	13	0.05
Spring Valley, CA (cdp) San Diego County	13	0.05
Sanger, CA (city) Fresno County	12	0.05
Ashland, CA (cdp) Alameda County	11	0.05
Klamath Falls, OR (city) Klamath County	11	0.05
Port Hueneme, CA (city) Ventura County	10	0.05
Papillion, NE (city) Sarpy County	9	0.05

SECTION THREE

Race

American Indian: Yuman

U.S. and 50 States Sorted by Population and Percent of Total Population

Place	Population	%
United States	**10,089**	**<0.01**
Arizona	5,490	0.09
California	2,988	0.01
Nevada	190	0.01
Texas	160	<0.01
New Mexico	138	0.01
Oklahoma	112	<0.01
Washington	106	<0.01
Colorado	76	<0.01
Oregon	76	<0.01
Hawaii	57	<0.01
Utah	53	<0.01
Montana	48	<0.01
New York	45	<0.01
Minnesota	37	<0.01
Florida	35	<0.01
Virginia	34	<0.01
Illinois	33	<0.01
Ohio	31	<0.01
Missouri	30	<0.01
Kansas	29	<0.01
North Carolina	26	<0.01
Michigan	22	<0.01
Alaska	21	<0.01
Idaho	21	<0.01
Pennsylvania	18	<0.01
South Dakota	17	<0.01
Georgia	14	<0.01
Maryland	14	<0.01
Massachusetts	14	<0.01
Alabama	13	<0.01
Indiana	13	<0.01
New Jersey	11	<0.01
Louisiana	10	<0.01
Wisconsin	10	<0.01
North Dakota	9	<0.01
Arkansas	8	<0.01
Connecticut	8	<0.01
Nebraska	8	<0.01
Rhode Island	8	<0.01
South Carolina	8	<0.01
Tennessee	8	<0.01
Kentucky	7	<0.01
Mississippi	7	<0.01
New Hampshire	6	<0.01
Wyoming	6	<0.01
District of Columbia	5	<0.01
Iowa	5	<0.01
West Virginia	2	<0.01
Delaware	1	<0.01
Vermont	1	<0.01
Maine	0	0.00

Place	Population	%
Arizona	5,490	0.09
California	2,988	0.01
Nevada	190	0.01
New Mexico	138	0.01
United States	**10,089**	**<0.01**
Texas	160	<0.01
Oklahoma	112	<0.01
Washington	106	<0.01
Colorado	76	<0.01
Oregon	76	<0.01
Hawaii	57	<0.01
Utah	53	<0.01
Montana	48	<0.01
New York	45	<0.01
Minnesota	37	<0.01
Florida	35	<0.01
Virginia	34	<0.01
Illinois	33	<0.01
Ohio	31	<0.01
Missouri	30	<0.01
Kansas	29	<0.01
North Carolina	26	<0.01
Michigan	22	<0.01
Alaska	21	<0.01
Idaho	21	<0.01
Pennsylvania	18	<0.01
South Dakota	17	<0.01
Georgia	14	<0.01
Maryland	14	<0.01
Massachusetts	14	<0.01
Alabama	13	<0.01
Indiana	13	<0.01
New Jersey	11	<0.01
Louisiana	10	<0.01
Wisconsin	10	<0.01
North Dakota	9	<0.01
Arkansas	8	<0.01
Connecticut	8	<0.01
Nebraska	8	<0.01
Rhode Island	8	<0.01
South Carolina	8	<0.01
Tennessee	8	<0.01
Kentucky	7	<0.01
Mississippi	7	<0.01
New Hampshire	6	<0.01
Wyoming	6	<0.01
District of Columbia	5	<0.01
Iowa	5	<0.01
West Virginia	2	<0.01
Delaware	1	<0.01
Vermont	1	<0.01
Maine	0	0.00

Please refer to the Explanation of Data in the front of the book for more detailed information.

Race

American Indian: Yuman

Top 150 Places Sorted by Population

Based on all places, regardless of total population

Place	Population	%
Peach Springs, AZ (cdp) Mohave County	891	81.74
Phoenix, AZ (city) Maricopa County	494	0.03
Yuma, AZ (city) Yuma County	407	0.44
Arizona Village, AZ (cdp) Mohave County	299	31.61
Supai, AZ (cdp) Coconino County	191	91.83
Parker, AZ (town) La Paz County	172	5.58
Needles, CA (city) San Bernardino County	153	3.16
Mesa, AZ (city) Maricopa County	138	0.03
Los Angeles, CA (city) Los Angeles County	105	<0.01
Tucson, AZ (city) Pima County	101	0.02
Kingman, AZ (city) Mohave County	94	0.33
Flagstaff, AZ (city) Coconino County	77	0.12
Mohave Valley, AZ (cdp) Mohave County	66	2.52
Albuquerque, NM (city) Bernalillo County	51	0.01
Riverside, CA (city) Riverside County	48	0.02
San Diego, CA (city) San Diego County	48	<0.01
Glendale, AZ (city) Maricopa County	47	0.02
Tempe, AZ (city) Maricopa County	44	0.03
Avenue B and C, AZ (cdp) Yuma County	43	1.03
Chandler, AZ (city) Maricopa County	43	0.02
Bullhead City, AZ (city) Mohave County	42	0.11
San Jose, CA (city) Santa Clara County	41	<0.01
Willow Valley, AZ (cdp) Mohave County	37	3.48
Camp Verde, AZ (town) Yavapai County	37	0.34
Prescott Valley, AZ (town) Yavapai County	37	0.10
Long Beach, CA (city) Los Angeles County	37	0.01
Fortuna Foothills, AZ (cdp) Yuma County	34	0.13
Casa Grande, AZ (city) Pinal County	34	0.07
New Kingman-Butler, AZ (cdp) Mohave County	33	0.27
Prescott, AZ (city) Yavapai County	32	0.08
Gilbert, AZ (town) Maricopa County	32	0.02
Mojave Ranch Estates, AZ (cdp) Mohave County	31	59.62
Victorville, CA (city) San Bernardino County	30	0.03
Sunrise Manor, NV (cdp) Clark County	30	0.02
Bluewater, AZ (cdp) La Paz County	27	3.72
San Bernardino, CA (city) San Bernardino County	27	0.01
Fort Mohave, AZ (cdp) Mohave County	26	0.18
Anaheim, CA (city) Orange County	26	0.01
Fresno, CA (city) Fresno County	26	0.01
Las Vegas, NV (city) Clark County	24	<0.01
Somerton, AZ (city) Yuma County	23	0.16
Lake Havasu City, AZ (city) Mohave County	22	0.04
Avondale, AZ (city) Maricopa County	22	0.03
Peoria, AZ (city) Yavapai County	22	0.01
New York, NY (city) Kings County	22	<0.01
Winterhaven, CA (cdp) Imperial County	21	5.33
Paradise, NV (cdp) Clark County	20	0.01
Pomona, CA (city) Los Angeles County	19	0.01
Mesquite Creek, AZ (cdp) Mohave County	18	4.33
Buckeye, AZ (town) Maricopa County	18	0.04
Lawrence, KS (city) Douglas County	18	0.02
Kapaa, HI (cdp) Kauai County	17	0.16
Porterville, CA (city) Tulare County	17	0.03
Fontana, CA (city) San Bernardino County	17	0.01
Valentine, AZ (cdp) Mohave County	16	42.11
Grand Canyon Village, AZ (cdp) Coconino County	16	0.80
Ontario, CA (city) San Bernardino County	16	0.01
Oklahoma City, OK (city) Oklahoma County	16	<0.01
Clarkdale, AZ (town) Yavapai County	15	0.37
Anchorage, AK (municipality) Anchorage Municipality	15	0.01
Chicago, IL (city) Cook County	15	<0.01
Oakland, CA (city) Alameda County	15	<0.01
Portland, OR (city) Multnomah County	15	<0.01
Sacramento, CA (city) Sacramento County	15	<0.01
Colton, CA (city) San Bernardino County	14	0.03
Hemet, CA (city) Riverside County	14	0.02
Surprise, AZ (city) Maricopa County	14	0.01
Houston, TX (city) Harris County	14	<0.01
San Antonio, TX (city) Medina County	14	<0.01
Fountain Hills, AZ (town) Maricopa County	13	0.06
Florence, AZ (town) Pinal County	13	0.05
Banning, CA (city) Riverside County	13	0.04
Henderson, NV (city) Clark County	13	0.01
Reno, NV (city) Washoe County	13	0.01
Scottsdale, AZ (city) Maricopa County	13	0.01
Urban Honolulu, HI (cdp) Honolulu County	13	<0.01
Komatke, AZ (cdp) Maricopa County	12	1.46
Sells, AZ (cdp) Pima County	12	0.48
San Carlos, AZ (cdp) Gila County	12	0.30
Anadarko, OK (city) Caddo County	12	0.18
Verde Village, AZ (cdp) Yavapai County	12	0.10
El Centro, CA (city) Imperial County	12	0.03
Spring Valley, NV (cdp) Clark County	12	0.01
Stockton, CA (city) San Joaquin County	12	<0.01
Moenkopi, AZ (cdp) Coconino County	11	1.14
Valle Vista, AZ (cdp) Mohave County	11	0.66
Sacaton, AZ (cdp) Pinal County	11	0.41
Coolidge, AZ (city) Pinal County	11	0.09
Adelanto, CA (city) San Bernardino County	11	0.03
Apple Valley, CA (town) San Bernardino County	11	0.02
Chino, CA (city) San Bernardino County	11	0.01
Corona, CA (city) Riverside County	11	0.01
Huntington Beach, CA (city) Orange County	11	0.01
Moreno Valley, CA (city) Riverside County	11	0.01
Rancho Cucamonga, CA (city) San Bernardino County	11	0.01
San Tan Valley, AZ (cdp) Pinal County	11	0.01
Calexico, CA (city) Imperial County	10	0.03
Baldwin Park, CA (city) Los Angeles County	10	0.01
El Monte, CA (city) Los Angeles County	10	0.01
Kent, WA (city) King County	10	0.01
Roseville, CA (city) Placer County	10	0.01
Chula Vista, CA (city) San Diego County	10	<0.01
Colorado Springs, CO (city) El Paso County	10	<0.01
Denver, CO (city) Denver County	10	<0.01
North Las Vegas, NV (city) Clark County	10	<0.01
San Francisco, CA (city) San Francisco County	10	<0.01
Seligman, AZ (cdp) Yavapai County	9	2.02
First Mesa, AZ (cdp) Navajo County	9	0.58
West Bishop, CA (cdp) Inyo County	9	0.35
King City, CA (city) Monterey County	9	0.07
Great Falls, MT (city) Cascade County	9	0.02
Maricopa, AZ (city) Pinal County	9	0.02
Enterprise, NV (cdp) Clark County	9	0.01
Goodyear, AZ (city) Maricopa County	9	0.01
Oceanside, CA (city) San Diego County	9	0.01
Simi Valley, CA (city) Ventura County	9	0.01
Austin, TX (city) Travis County	9	<0.01
New Prague, MN (city) Scott County	8	0.19
Globe, AZ (city) Gila County	8	0.11
New Prague, MN (city) Scott County	8	0.11
Gardnerville Ranchos, NV (cdp) Douglas County	8	0.07
Kalispell, MT (city) Flathead County	8	0.04
Drexel Heights, AZ (cdp) Pima County	8	0.03
Bell, CA (city) Los Angeles County	8	0.02
Delano, CA (city) Kern County	8	0.02
Billings, MT (city) Yellowstone County	8	0.01
El Cajon, CA (city) San Diego County	8	0.01
Lakewood, CO (city) Jefferson County	8	0.01
Palmdale, CA (city) Los Angeles County	8	0.01
Pasadena, CA (city) Los Angeles County	8	0.01
Vista, CA (city) San Diego County	8	0.01
Arlington, TX (city) Tarrant County	8	<0.01
Brooklyn, NY (borough) Kings County	8	<0.01
Philadelphia, PA (city) Philadelphia County	8	<0.01
Goodyear Village, AZ (cdp) Pinal County	7	1.53
Maricopa Colony, AZ (cdp) Maricopa County	7	0.99
Desert Shores, CA (cdp) Imperial County	7	0.63
Peridot, AZ (cdp) Graham County	7	0.52
Lucerne Valley, CA (cdp) San Bernardino County	7	0.12
Thermalito, CA (cdp) Butte County	7	0.11
Winslow, AZ (city) Navajo County	7	0.07
West Plains, MO (city) Howell County	7	0.06
Douglas, AZ (city) Cochise County	7	0.04
Barstow, CA (city) San Bernardino County	7	0.03
Ceres, CA (city) Stanislaus County	7	0.02
Lompoc, CA (city) Santa Barbara County	7	0.02
Carson City, NV (ind. city) Carson City County	7	0.01
Casas Adobes, AZ (cdp) Pima County	7	0.01
La Mirada, CA (city) Los Angeles County	7	0.01
Madera, CA (city) Madera County	7	0.01

Race

American Indian: Yuman

Top 150 Places Sorted by Percent of Total Population

Based on all places, regardless of total population

Place	Population	%
Supai, AZ (cdp) Coconino County	191	91.83
Peach Springs, AZ (cdp) Mohave County	891	81.74
Mojave Ranch Estates, AZ (cdp) Mohave County	31	59.62
Valentine, AZ (cdp) Mohave County	16	42.11
Arizona Village, AZ (cdp) Mohave County	299	31.61
Parker, AZ (town) La Paz County	172	5.58
Winterhaven, CA (cdp) Imperial County	21	5.33
Mesquite Creek, AZ (cdp) Mohave County	18	4.33
Bluewater, AZ (cdp) La Paz County	27	3.72
Willow Valley, AZ (cdp) Mohave County	37	3.48
Needles, CA (city) San Bernardino County	153	3.16
Truxton, AZ (cdp) Mohave County	4	2.99
Alderpoint, CA (cdp) Humboldt County	5	2.69
Mohave Valley, AZ (cdp) Mohave County	66	2.52
Antares, AZ (cdp) Mohave County	3	2.38
Seligman, AZ (cdp) Yavapai County	9	2.02
Drysdale, AZ (cdp) Yuma County	5	1.84
Goodyear Village, AZ (cdp) Pinal County	7	1.53
Crescent Mills, CA (cdp) Plumas County	3	1.53
Komatke, AZ (cdp) Maricopa County	12	1.46
Kelsey, MN (township) St. Louis County	2	1.43
Bern, KS (city) Nemaha County	2	1.20
Moenkopi, AZ (cdp) Coconino County	11	1.14
Seama, NM (cdp) Cibola County	5	1.08
Poston, AZ (cdp) La Paz County	3	1.05
Avenue B and C, AZ (cdp) Yuma County	43	1.03
Jeddito, AZ (cdp) Navajo County	3	1.02
Maricopa Colony, AZ (cdp) Maricopa County	7	0.99
Miranda, CA (cdp) Humboldt County	5	0.96
Rock Point, MD (cdp) Charles County	1	0.93
El Rancho, CA (cdp) Tulare County	1	0.81
Grand Canyon Village, AZ (cdp) Coconino County	16	0.80
Wikieup, AZ (cdp) Mohave County	1	0.75
Kaka, AZ (cdp) Maricopa County	1	0.71
Blue Diamond, NV (cdp) Clark County	2	0.69
Topawa, AZ (cdp) Pima County	2	0.67
Valle Vista, AZ (cdp) Mohave County	11	0.66
Keams Canyon, AZ (cdp) Navajo County	2	0.66
Gila Crossing, AZ (cdp) Maricopa County	4	0.64
Desert Shores, CA (cdp) Imperial County	7	0.63
Red Mesa, AZ (cdp) Apache County	3	0.63
Second Mesa, AZ (cdp) Navajo County	6	0.62
First Mesa, AZ (cdp) Navajo County	9	0.58
Bluewater, CA (cdp) San Bernardino County	1	0.58
Peridot, AZ (cdp) Graham County	7	0.52
Amo, IN (town) Hendricks County	2	0.50
Sells, AZ (cdp) Pima County	12	0.48
Santa Rosa, AZ (cdp) Pima County	3	0.48
Cusick, WA (town) Pend Oreille County	1	0.48
Wyola, MT (cdp) Big Horn County	1	0.47
Yuma, AZ (city) Yuma County	407	0.44
Ohkay Owingeh, NM (cdp) Rio Arriba County	5	0.44
Prospect, OR (cdp) Jackson County	2	0.44
West Park, CA (cdp) Fresno County	5	0.43
Decatur, NE (village) Burt County	2	0.42
Sacaton, AZ (cdp) Pinal County	11	0.41
Cibola, AZ (cdp) La Paz County	1	0.40
Big River, CA (cdp) San Bernardino County	5	0.38
Clarkdale, AZ (town) Yavapai County	15	0.37
Chloride, AZ (cdp) Mohave County	1	0.37
West Bishop, CA (cdp) Inyo County	9	0.35
Myton, UT (city) Duchesne County	2	0.35
Camp Verde, AZ (town) Yavapai County	37	0.34
Happy Camp, CA (cdp) Siskiyou County	4	0.34
White River, SD (city) Mellette County	2	0.34
Turkey Creek, AZ (cdp) Navajo County	1	0.34
Kingman, AZ (city) Mohave County	94	0.33
Beaver Dam, AZ (cdp) Mohave County	6	0.31
Biola, CA (cdp) Fresno County	5	0.31
White Hills, AZ (cdp) Mohave County	1	0.31
San Carlos, AZ (cdp) Gila County	12	0.30
Golden Shores, AZ (cdp) Mohave County	6	0.29
Blackwater, AZ (cdp) Pinal County	3	0.28
Towaoc, CO (cdp) Montezuma County	3	0.28
New Kingman-Butler, AZ (cdp) Mohave County	33	0.27
White Mountain Lake, AZ (cdp) Navajo County	6	0.27
Gila Bend, AZ (town) Maricopa County	5	0.26
Canyon Day, AZ (cdp) Gila County	3	0.25
Boulder Flats, WY (cdp) Fremont County	1	0.25
Whitecone, AZ (cdp) Navajo County	2	0.24
Paguate, NM (cdp) Cibola County	1	0.24
Winslow West, AZ (cdp) Navajo County	1	0.23
Cienega Springs, AZ (cdp) La Paz County	4	0.22
Funks, MD (town) Washington County	2	0.22
Leupp, AZ (cdp) Coconino County	2	0.21
Congress, AZ (cdp) Yavapai County	4	0.20
Donovan Estates, AZ (cdp) Yuma County	3	0.20
Morris, OK (city) Okmulgee County	3	0.20
El Prado Estates, AZ (cdp) Yuma County	1	0.20
Upper Santan Village, AZ (cdp) Pinal County	1	0.20
New Prague, MN (city) Scott County	8	0.19
Kotzebue, AK (city) Northwest Arctic Borough	6	0.19
Calwa, CA (cdp) Fresno County	4	0.19
Lakeview, CA (cdp) Riverside County	4	0.19
Mission, OR (cdp) Umatilla County	2	0.19
Fort Mohave, AZ (cdp) Mohave County	26	0.18
Anadarko, OK (city) Caddo County	12	0.18
Sacaton Flats Village, AZ (cdp) Pinal County	1	0.18
Mescal, AZ (cdp) Cochise County	3	0.17
Waubay, SD (city) Day County	1	0.17
Somerton, AZ (city) Yuma County	23	0.16
Kapaa, HI (cdp) Kauai County	17	0.16
Sanders, AZ (cdp) Apache County	1	0.16
Dixon Lane-Meadow Creek, CA (cdp) Inyo County	4	0.15
Easton, CA (cdp) Fresno County	3	0.14
Varnville, SC (town) Hampton County	3	0.14
Baker, CA (cdp) San Bernardino County	1	0.14
Duncan, AZ (town) Greenlee County	1	0.14
Fort Duchesne, UT (cdp) Uintah County	1	0.14
Parma, MO (city) New Madrid County	1	0.14
Fortuna Foothills, AZ (cdp) Yuma County	34	0.13
Lake Montezuma, AZ (cdp) Yavapai County	6	0.13
Salton City, CA (cdp) Imperial County	5	0.13
Anahola, HI (cdp) Kauai County	3	0.13
Crownpoint, NM (cdp) McKinley County	3	0.13
Leilani Estates, HI (cdp) Hawaii County	2	0.13
Flagstaff, AZ (city) Coconino County	77	0.12
Lucerne Valley, CA (cdp) San Bernardino County	7	0.12
Sunnyside, CA (cdp) Fresno County	5	0.12
Caledonia, WI (town) Waupaca County	2	0.12
Crow Agency, MT (cdp) Big Horn County	2	0.12
Colcord, OK (town) Delaware County	1	0.12
Shongopovi, AZ (cdp) Navajo County	1	0.12
Woodall, OK (cdp) Cherokee County	1	0.12
Bullhead City, AZ (city) Mohave County	42	0.11
Globe, AZ (city) Gila County	8	0.11
New Prague, MN (city) Scott County	8	0.11
Thermalito, CA (cdp) Butte County	7	0.11
Dewar, OK (town) Okmulgee County	1	0.11
Prescott Valley, AZ (town) Yavapai County	37	0.10
Verde Village, AZ (cdp) Yavapai County	12	0.10
Bishop, CA (city) Inyo County	4	0.10
Park Hill, OK (cdp) Cherokee County	4	0.10
Homestead Valley, CA (cdp) San Bernardino County	3	0.10
Wellton, AZ (town) Yuma County	3	0.10
Bylas, AZ (cdp) Graham County	2	0.10
Chelsea, OK (town) Rogers County	2	0.10
Dolan Springs, AZ (cdp) Mohave County	2	0.10
Hotevilla-Bacavi, AZ (cdp) Navajo County	1	0.10
Coolidge, AZ (city) Pinal County	11	0.09
Tolleson, AZ (city) Maricopa County	6	0.09
Mayfair, CA (cdp) Fresno County	4	0.09
Fort Hall, ID (cdp) Bannock County	3	0.09
Okemah, OK (city) Okfuskee County	3	0.09
Lapwai, ID (city) Nez Perce County	1	0.09
Prescott, AZ (city) Yavapai County	32	0.08
Belen, NM (city) Valencia County	6	0.08
Lenwood, CA (cdp) San Bernardino County	3	0.08
Mission Hills, CA (cdp) Santa Barbara County	3	0.08
Mogadore, OH (village) Summit County	3	0.08

Please refer to the Explanation of Data in the front of the book for more detailed information.

Race

American Indian: Yuman

Top 150 Places Sorted by Percent of Total Population

Based on places with total population of 7,500 or more

Place	Population	%
Yuma, AZ (city) Yuma County	407	0.44
Camp Verde, AZ (town) Yavapai County	37	0.34
Kingman, AZ (city) Mohave County	94	0.33
New Kingman-Butler, AZ (cdp) Mohave County	33	0.27
Fort Mohave, AZ (cdp) Mohave County	26	0.18
Somerton, AZ (city) Yuma County	23	0.16
Kapaa, HI (cdp) Kauai County	17	0.16
Fortuna Foothills, AZ (cdp) Yuma County	34	0.13
Flagstaff, AZ (city) Coconino County	77	0.12
Bullhead City, AZ (city) Mohave County	42	0.11
Globe, AZ (city) Gila County	8	0.11
Prescott Valley, AZ (town) Yavapai County	37	0.10
Verde Village, AZ (cdp) Yavapai County	12	0.10
Coolidge, AZ (city) Pinal County	11	0.09
Prescott, AZ (city) Yavapai County	32	0.08
Casa Grande, AZ (city) Pinal County	34	0.07
King City, CA (city) Monterey County	9	0.07
Gardnerville Ranchos, NV (cdp) Douglas County	8	0.07
Winslow, AZ (city) Navajo County	7	0.07
Tuba City, AZ (cdp) Coconino County	6	0.07
Fountain Hills, AZ (town) Maricopa County	13	0.06
West Plains, MO (city) Howell County	7	0.06
Florence, AZ (town) Pinal County	13	0.05
Galena Park, TX (city) Harris County	5	0.05
Deerpark, NY (town) Orange County	4	0.05
Golden Valley, AZ (cdp) Mohave County	4	0.05
Kirtland, NM (cdp) San Juan County	4	0.05
Lake Havasu City, AZ (city) Mohave County	22	0.04
Buckeye, AZ (town) Maricopa County	18	0.04
Banning, CA (city) Riverside County	13	0.04
Kalispell, MT (city) Flathead County	8	0.04
Douglas, AZ (city) Cochise County	7	0.04
Payson, AZ (town) Gila County	6	0.04
Pierre, SD (city) Hughes County	6	0.04
Valle Vista, CA (cdp) Riverside County	6	0.04
Lake Arrowhead, CA (cdp) San Bernardino County	5	0.04
Okmulgee, OK (city) Okmulgee County	5	0.04
Cottonwood, AZ (city) Yavapai County	4	0.04
Hawaiian Paradise Park, HI (cdp) Hawaii County	4	0.04
Mountain House, CA (cdp) San Joaquin County	4	0.04
North Valley, NM (cdp) Bernalillo County	4	0.04
Shasta Lake, CA (city) Shasta County	4	0.04
Bloomfield, NM (city) San Juan County	3	0.04
Richfield, UT (city) Sevier County	3	0.04
Phoenix, AZ (city) Maricopa County	494	0.03
Mesa, AZ (city) Maricopa County	138	0.03
Tempe, AZ (city) Maricopa County	44	0.03
Victorville, CA (city) San Bernardino County	30	0.03
Avondale, AZ (city) Maricopa County	22	0.03
Porterville, CA (city) Tulare County	17	0.03
Colton, CA (city) San Bernardino County	14	0.03
El Centro, CA (city) Imperial County	12	0.03
Adelanto, CA (city) San Bernardino County	11	0.03
Calexico, CA (city) Imperial County	10	0.03
Drexel Heights, AZ (cdp) Pima County	8	0.03
Barstow, CA (city) San Bernardino County	7	0.03
Arcata, CA (city) Humboldt County	6	0.03
Bainbridge Island, WA (city) Kitsap County	6	0.03
Lakeside, CA (cdp) San Diego County	6	0.03
Sun Valley, NV (cdp) Washoe County	6	0.03
Casa de Oro-Mount Helix, CA (cdp) San Diego County	5	0.03
Elko, NV (city) Elko County	5	0.03
Imperial, CA (city) Imperial County	5	0.03
Port Angeles, WA (city) Clallam County	5	0.03
Irondale, AL (city) Jefferson County	4	0.03
Fallon, NV (city) Churchill County	3	0.03
Parsons, KS (city) Labette County	3	0.03
Redding, CT (town) Fairfield County	3	0.03
Sedona, AZ (city) Yavapai County	3	0.03
Valencia West, AZ (cdp) Pima County	3	0.03
Park City, UT (city) Summit County	2	0.03
Richland Hills, TX (city) Tarrant County	2	0.03
Williamsburg, FL (cdp) Orange County	2	0.03
Yreka, CA (city) Siskiyou County	2	0.03
Tucson, AZ (city) Pima County	101	0.02
Riverside, CA (city) Riverside County	48	0.02
Glendale, AZ (city) Maricopa County	47	0.02
Chandler, AZ (city) Maricopa County	43	0.02
Gilbert, AZ (town) Maricopa County	32	0.02
Sunrise Manor, NV (cdp) Clark County	30	0.02
Lawrence, KS (city) Douglas County	18	0.02
Hemet, CA (city) Riverside County	14	0.02
Apple Valley, CA (town) San Bernardino County	11	0.02
Great Falls, MT (city) Cascade County	9	0.02
Maricopa, AZ (city) Pinal County	9	0.02
Bell, CA (city) Los Angeles County	8	0.02
Delano, CA (city) Kern County	8	0.02
Ceres, CA (city) Stanislaus County	7	0.02
Lompoc, CA (city) Santa Barbara County	7	0.02
Claremont, CA (city) Los Angeles County	6	0.02
San Luis, AZ (city) Yuma County	6	0.02
Wildwood, MO (city) St. Louis County	6	0.02
Bloomington, CA (cdp) San Bernardino County	5	0.02
Cudahy, CA (city) Los Angeles County	5	0.02
El Mirage, AZ (city) Maricopa County	5	0.02
Gallup, NM (city) McKinley County	5	0.02
Redmond, OR (city) Deschutes County	5	0.02
Twentynine Palms, CA (city) San Bernardino County	5	0.02
Belmont, CA (city) San Mateo County	4	0.02
Brawley, CA (city) Imperial County	4	0.02
Chickasha, OK (city) Grady County	4	0.02
De Witt, NY (town) Onondaga County	4	0.02
Keene, NH (city) Cheshire County	4	0.02
Sahuarita, AZ (town) Pima County	4	0.02
Wadsworth, OH (city) Medina County	4	0.02
Arvin, CA (city) Kern County	3	0.02
Big Bear City, CA (cdp) San Bernardino County	3	0.02
Central Point, OR (city) Jackson County	3	0.02
Commerce, CA (city) Los Angeles County	3	0.02
East Hemet, CA (cdp) Riverside County	3	0.02
Frederickson, WA (cdp) Pierce County	3	0.02
Pendleton, OR (city) Umatilla County	3	0.02
Phelan, CA (cdp) San Bernardino County	3	0.02
Ripon, CA (city) San Joaquin County	3	0.02
Rosamond, CA (cdp) Kern County	3	0.02
Washington, UT (city) Washington County	3	0.02
Willmar, MN (city) Kandiyohi County	3	0.02
August, CA (cdp) San Joaquin County	2	0.02
Corrales, NM (village) Sandoval County	2	0.02
Firestone, CO (town) Weld County	2	0.02
Lahaina, HI (cdp) Maui County	2	0.02
Signal Hill, CA (city) Los Angeles County	2	0.02
Solana Beach, CA (city) San Diego County	2	0.02
Spearfish, SD (city) Lawrence County	2	0.02
Taft, CA (city) Kern County	2	0.02
Thornbury, PA (township) Delaware County	2	0.02
Tucson Estates, AZ (cdp) Pima County	2	0.02
Wabash, IN (city) Wabash County	2	0.02
Albuquerque, NM (city) Bernalillo County	51	0.01
Long Beach, CA (city) Los Angeles County	37	0.01
San Bernardino, CA (city) San Bernardino County	27	0.01
Anaheim, CA (city) Orange County	26	0.01
Fresno, CA (city) Fresno County	26	0.01
Peoria, AZ (city) Yavapai County	22	0.01
Paradise, NV (cdp) Clark County	20	0.01
Pomona, CA (city) Los Angeles County	19	0.01
Fontana, CA (city) San Bernardino County	17	0.01
Ontario, CA (city) San Bernardino County	16	0.01
Anchorage, AK (municipality) Anchorage Municipality	15	0.01
Surprise, AZ (city) Maricopa County	14	0.01
Henderson, NV (city) Clark County	13	0.01
Reno, NV (city) Washoe County	13	0.01
Scottsdale, AZ (city) Maricopa County	13	0.01
Spring Valley, NV (cdp) Clark County	12	0.01
Chino, CA (city) San Bernardino County	11	0.01
Corona, CA (city) Riverside County	11	0.01
Huntington Beach, CA (city) Orange County	11	0.01
Moreno Valley, CA (city) Riverside County	11	0.01
Rancho Cucamonga, CA (city) San Bernardino County	11	0.01
San Tan Valley, AZ (cdp) Pinal County	11	0.01

SECTION THREE

Please refer to the Explanation of Data in the front of the book for more detailed information.

Race

Alaska Native: Yup'ik

U.S. and 50 States Sorted by Population and Percent of Total Population

Place	Population	%
United States	**33,889**	**0.01**
Alaska	30,868	4.35
Washington	584	0.01
California	323	<0.01
Oregon	300	0.01
Arizona	131	<0.01
Colorado	131	<0.01
Texas	120	<0.01
Hawaii	93	0.01
Florida	86	<0.01
Minnesota	82	<0.01
Arkansas	69	<0.01
Montana	67	0.01
Oklahoma	63	<0.01
Michigan	62	<0.01
Utah	58	<0.01
Nevada	57	<0.01
New Mexico	51	<0.01
Illinois	49	<0.01
Ohio	47	<0.01
Missouri	45	<0.01
North Carolina	45	<0.01
Idaho	43	<0.01
Tennessee	41	<0.01
New York	39	<0.01
Virginia	36	<0.01
Wisconsin	35	<0.01
Kansas	32	<0.01
Indiana	29	<0.01
Alabama	27	<0.01
Georgia	25	<0.01
Pennsylvania	25	<0.01
Massachusetts	24	<0.01
New Jersey	22	<0.01
Wyoming	21	<0.01
Maryland	18	<0.01
Kentucky	17	<0.01
Nebraska	15	<0.01
Iowa	12	<0.01
Maine	12	<0.01
Rhode Island	12	<0.01
South Carolina	12	<0.01
West Virginia	11	<0.01
South Dakota	9	<0.01
New Hampshire	8	<0.01
North Dakota	8	<0.01
Vermont	8	<0.01
Louisiana	6	<0.01
Mississippi	5	<0.01
District of Columbia	3	<0.01
Connecticut	2	<0.01
Delaware	1	<0.01

Place	Population	%
Alaska	30,868	4.35
United States	**33,889**	**0.01**
Washington	584	0.01
Oregon	300	0.01
Hawaii	93	0.01
Montana	67	0.01
California	323	<0.01
Arizona	131	<0.01
Colorado	131	<0.01
Texas	120	<0.01
Florida	86	<0.01
Minnesota	82	<0.01
Arkansas	69	<0.01
Oklahoma	63	<0.01
Michigan	62	<0.01
Utah	58	<0.01
Nevada	57	<0.01
New Mexico	51	<0.01
Illinois	49	<0.01
Ohio	47	<0.01
Missouri	45	<0.01
North Carolina	45	<0.01
Idaho	43	<0.01
Tennessee	41	<0.01
New York	39	<0.01
Virginia	36	<0.01
Wisconsin	35	<0.01
Kansas	32	<0.01
Indiana	29	<0.01
Alabama	27	<0.01
Georgia	25	<0.01
Pennsylvania	25	<0.01
Massachusetts	24	<0.01
New Jersey	22	<0.01
Wyoming	21	<0.01
Maryland	18	<0.01
Kentucky	17	<0.01
Nebraska	15	<0.01
Iowa	12	<0.01
Maine	12	<0.01
Rhode Island	12	<0.01
South Carolina	12	<0.01
West Virginia	11	<0.01
South Dakota	9	<0.01
New Hampshire	8	<0.01
North Dakota	8	<0.01
Vermont	8	<0.01
Louisiana	6	<0.01
Mississippi	5	<0.01
District of Columbia	3	<0.01
Connecticut	2	<0.01
Delaware	1	<0.01

Please refer to the Explanation of Data in the front of the book for more detailed information.

Race

Alaska Native: Yup'ik

Top 150 Places Sorted by Population

Based on all places, regardless of total population

Place	Population	%
Anchorage, AK (municipality) Anchorage Municipality	4,835	1.66
Bethel, AK (city) Bethel Census Area	2,837	46.66
Dillingham, AK (city) Dillingham Census Area	1,078	46.29
Hooper Bay, AK (city) Wade Hampton Census Area	729	66.70
Togiak, AK (city) Dillingham Census Area	716	87.64
Mountain Village, AK (city) Wade Hampton Census Area	709	87.21
Emmonak, AK (city) Wade Hampton Census Area	694	91.08
Kwethluk, AK (city) Bethel Census Area	661	91.68
Gambell, AK (city) Nome Census Area	632	92.80
Quinhagak, AK (city) Bethel Census Area	628	93.87
Kipnuk, AK (cdp) Bethel Census Area	599	93.74
Savoonga, AK (city) Nome Census Area	596	88.82
Alakanuk, AK (city) Wade Hampton Census Area	582	85.97
Akiachak, AK (cdp) Bethel Census Area	577	92.03
Pilot Station, AK (city) Wade Hampton Census Area	549	96.65
Toksook Bay, AK (city) Bethel Census Area	523	88.64
Kasigluk, AK (cdp) Bethel Census Area	516	90.69
Stebbins, AK (city) Nome Census Area	498	89.57
New Stuyahok, AK (city) Dillingham Census Area	482	94.51
Kotlik, AK (city) Wade Hampton Census Area	472	81.80
Scammon Bay, AK (city) Wade Hampton Census Area	458	96.62
St. Mary's, AK (city) Wade Hampton Census Area	447	88.17
Manokotak, AK (city) Dillingham Census Area	403	91.18
Chefornak, AK (city) Bethel Census Area	390	93.30
Nunapitchuk, AK (city) Bethel Census Area	386	77.82
Napaskiak, AK (city) Bethel Census Area	380	93.83
Kongiganak, AK (cdp) Bethel Census Area	375	85.42
Tuntutuliak, AK (cdp) Bethel Census Area	369	90.44
Tuluksak, AK (cdp) Bethel Census Area	352	94.37
Newtok, AK (cdp) Bethel Census Area	337	95.20
Napakiak, AK (city) Bethel Census Area	336	94.92
Akiak, AK (city) Bethel Census Area	310	89.60
Tununak, AK (cdp) Bethel Census Area	304	92.97
Aniak, AK (city) Bethel Census Area	296	59.08
Kwigillingok, AK (cdp) Bethel Census Area	289	90.03
Marshall, AK (city) Wade Hampton Census Area	275	66.43
Lower Kalskag, AK (city) Bethel Census Area	258	91.49
Atmautluak, AK (cdp) Bethel Census Area	251	90.61
Eek, AK (city) Bethel Census Area	251	84.80
Russian Mission, AK (city) Wade Hampton Census Area	220	70.51
Nightmute, AK (city) Bethel Census Area	218	77.86
Goodnews Bay, AK (city) Bethel Census Area	216	88.89
Koliganek, AK (cdp) Dillingham Census Area	185	88.52
Upper Kalskag, AK (city) Bethel Census Area	178	84.76
Naknek, AK (cdp) Bristol Bay Borough	175	32.17
Nunam Iqua, AK (city) Wade Hampton Census Area	174	93.05
Aleknagik, AK (city) Dillingham Census Area	172	78.54
College, AK (cdp) Fairbanks North Star Borough	149	1.15
Newhalen, AK (city) Lake and Peninsula Borough	132	69.47
Fairbanks, AK (city) Fairbanks North Star Borough	132	0.42
Lakes, AK (cdp) Matanuska-Susitna Borough	115	1.37
Seward, AK (city) Kenai Peninsula Borough	113	4.20
Juneau, AK (borough) Juneau City and Borough	113	0.36
Knik-Fairview, AK (cdp) Matanuska-Susitna Borough	106	0.71
Kenai, AK (city) Kenai Peninsula Borough	100	1.41
Pitkas Point, AK (cdp) Wade Hampton Census Area	99	90.83
Nome, AK (city) Nome Census Area	99	2.75
Ekwok, AK (city) Dillingham Census Area	93	80.87
Wasilla, AK (city) Matanuska-Susitna Borough	90	1.15
Crooked Creek, AK (cdp) Bethel Census Area	89	84.76
Chuathbaluk, AK (city) Bethel Census Area	85	72.03
St. Michael, AK (city) Nome Census Area	81	20.20
Palmer, AK (city) Matanuska-Susitna Borough	81	1.36
Badger, AK (cdp) Fairbanks North Star Borough	79	0.41
Meadow Lakes, AK (cdp) Matanuska-Susitna Borough	76	1.00
Tanaina, AK (cdp) Matanuska-Susitna Borough	76	0.93
Twin Hills, AK (cdp) Dillingham Census Area	66	89.19
Oscarville, AK (cdp) Bethel Census Area	62	88.57
Chevak, AK (city) Wade Hampton Census Area	62	6.61
Sitka, AK (borough) Sitka City and Borough	60	0.68
Kalifornsky, AK (cdp) Kenai Peninsula Borough	56	0.71
King Salmon, AK (cdp) Bristol Bay Borough	55	14.71
Sleetmute, AK (cdp) Bethel Census Area	54	62.79
Sutton-Alpine, AK (cdp) Matanuska-Susitna Borough	54	3.73
Clark's Point, AK (city) Dillingham Census Area	51	82.26
Levelock, AK (cdp) Lake and Peninsula Borough	51	73.91
Kodiak, AK (city) Kodiak Island Borough	48	0.78
Kotzebue, AK (city) Northwest Arctic Borough	45	1.41
Portland, OR (city) Multnomah County	45	0.01
Platinum, AK (city) Bethel Census Area	42	68.85
Springdale, AR (city) Washington County	42	0.06
Hudson, CO (town) Weld County	41	1.74
Farmers Loop, AK (cdp) Fairbanks North Star Borough	41	0.84
Seattle, WA (city) King County	41	0.01
Urban Honolulu, HI (cdp) Honolulu County	38	0.01
Sterling, AK (cdp) Kenai Peninsula Borough	37	0.66
Salamatof, AK (cdp) Kenai Peninsula Borough	35	3.57
Big Lake, AK (cdp) Matanuska-Susitna Borough	33	0.99
Barrow, AK (city) North Slope Borough	32	0.76
Nikiski, AK (cdp) Kenai Peninsula Borough	30	0.67
Bear Creek, AK (cdp) Kenai Peninsula Borough	29	1.48
Point MacKenzie, AK (cdp) Matanuska-Susitna Borough	28	5.29
Spokane, WA (city) Spokane County	28	0.01
Houston, AK (city) Matanuska-Susitna Borough	27	1.41
Gateway, AK (cdp) Matanuska-Susitna Borough	27	0.49
Auburn, WA (city) King County	25	0.04
Tucson, AZ (city) Pima County	25	<0.01
Valdez, AK (city) Valdez-Cordova Census Area	24	0.60
Homer, AK (city) Kenai Peninsula Borough	23	0.46
Tacoma, WA (city) Pierce County	23	0.01
Albuquerque, NM (city) Bernalillo County	23	<0.01
Phoenix, AZ (city) Maricopa County	23	<0.01
Ester, AK (cdp) Fairbanks North Star Borough	22	0.91
Soldotna, AK (city) Kenai Peninsula Borough	22	0.53
Salem, OR (city) Marion County	22	0.01
Stony River, AK (cdp) Bethel Census Area	21	38.89
Fishhook, AK (cdp) Matanuska-Susitna Borough	21	0.45
Unalakleet, AK (city) Nome Census Area	20	2.91
San Diego, CA (city) San Diego County	20	<0.01
South Naknek, AK (cdp) Bristol Bay Borough	19	24.05
Two Rivers, AK (cdp) Fairbanks North Star Borough	19	2.64
Steele Creek, AK (cdp) Fairbanks North Star Borough	19	0.29
Ketchikan, AK (city) Ketchikan Gateway Borough	18	0.22
Iliamna, AK (cdp) Lake and Peninsula Borough	17	15.60
Butte, AK (cdp) Matanuska-Susitna Borough	17	0.52
Goldstream, AK (cdp) Fairbanks North Star Borough	17	0.48
Eugene, OR (city) Lane County	17	0.01
Los Angeles, CA (city) Los Angeles County	17	<0.01
Kaktovik, AK (city) North Slope Borough	16	6.69
West Valley City, UT (city) Salt Lake County	16	0.01
Aurora, CO (city) Arapahoe County	16	<0.01
Willow, AK (cdp) Matanuska-Susitna Borough	15	0.71
St. Paul, AK (city) Aleutians West Census Area	14	2.92
Susitna North, AK (cdp) Matanuska-Susitna Borough	14	1.11
Hayesville, OR (cdp) Marion County	14	0.07
Spokane Valley, WA (city) Spokane County	13	0.01
Vancouver, WA (city) Clark County	13	0.01
Colorado Springs, CO (city) El Paso County	13	<0.01
Denver, CO (city) Denver County	13	<0.01
Buffalo Soapstone, AK (cdp) Matanuska-Susitna Borough	12	1.40
Igiugig, AK (cdp) Lake and Peninsula Borough	11	22.00
Cohoe, AK (cdp) Kenai Peninsula Borough	11	0.81
Keizer, OR (city) Marion County	11	0.03
San Antonio, TX (city) Medina County	11	<0.01
McGrath, AK (city) Yukon-Koyukuk Census Area	10	2.89
Kasilof, AK (cdp) Kenai Peninsula Borough	10	1.82
Chena Ridge, AK (cdp) Fairbanks North Star Borough	10	0.17
SeaTac, WA (city) King County	10	0.04
Everett, WA (city) Snohomish County	10	0.01
Federal Way, WA (city) King County	10	0.01
Chicago, IL (city) Cook County	10	<0.01
Glendale, AZ (city) Maricopa County	10	<0.01
Kansas City, MO (city) Jackson County	10	<0.01
New York, NY (city) Kings County	10	<0.01
Kokhanok, AK (cdp) Lake and Peninsula Borough	9	5.29
Teller, AK (city) Nome Census Area	9	3.93
Nanwalek, AK (cdp) Kenai Peninsula Borough	9	3.54
Adak, AK (city) Aleutians West Census Area	9	2.76
Moose Creek, AK (cdp) Fairbanks North Star Borough	9	1.20
Metlakatla, AK (cdp) Prince of Wales-Hyder Census Area	9	0.64

Please refer to the Explanation of Data in the front of the book for more detailed information.

Race

Alaska Native: Yup'ik

Top 150 Places Sorted by Percent of Total Population

Based on all places, regardless of total population

Place	Population	%
Pilot Station, AK (city) Wade Hampton Census Area	549	96.65
Scammon Bay, AK (city) Wade Hampton Census Area	458	96.62
Newtok, AK (cdp) Bethel Census Area	337	95.20
Napakiak, AK (city) Bethel Census Area	336	94.92
New Stuyahok, AK (city) Dillingham Census Area	482	94.51
Tuluksak, AK (cdp) Bethel Census Area	352	94.37
Quinhagak, AK (city) Bethel Census Area	628	93.87
Napaskiak, AK (city) Bethel Census Area	380	93.83
Kipnuk, AK (cdp) Bethel Census Area	599	93.74
Chefornak, AK (city) Bethel Census Area	390	93.30
Nunam Iqua, AK (city) Wade Hampton Census Area	174	93.05
Tununak, AK (cdp) Bethel Census Area	304	92.97
Gambell, AK (city) Nome Census Area	632	92.80
Akiachak, AK (cdp) Bethel Census Area	577	92.03
Kwethluk, AK (city) Bethel Census Area	661	91.68
Lower Kalskag, AK (city) Bethel Census Area	258	91.49
Manokotak, AK (city) Dillingham Census Area	403	91.18
Emmonak, AK (city) Wade Hampton Census Area	694	91.08
Pitkas Point, AK (cdp) Wade Hampton Census Area	99	90.83
Kasigluk, AK (cdp) Bethel Census Area	516	90.69
Atmautluak, AK (cdp) Bethel Census Area	251	90.61
Tuntutuliak, AK (cdp) Bethel Census Area	369	90.44
Kwigillingok, AK (cdp) Bethel Census Area	289	90.03
Akiak, AK (city) Bethel Census Area	310	89.60
Stebbins, AK (city) Nome Census Area	498	89.57
Twin Hills, AK (cdp) Dillingham Census Area	66	89.19
Goodnews Bay, AK (city) Bethel Census Area	216	88.89
Savoonga, AK (city) Nome Census Area	596	88.82
Toksook Bay, AK (city) Bethel Census Area	523	88.64
Oscarville, AK (cdp) Bethel Census Area	62	88.57
Koliganek, AK (cdp) Dillingham Census Area	185	88.52
St. Mary's, AK (city) Wade Hampton Census Area	447	88.17
Togiak, AK (city) Dillingham Census Area	716	87.64
Mountain Village, AK (city) Wade Hampton Census Area	709	87.21
Alakanuk, AK (city) Wade Hampton Census Area	582	85.97
Kongiganak, AK (cdp) Bethel Census Area	375	85.42
Eek, AK (city) Bethel Census Area	251	84.80
Upper Kalskag, AK (city) Bethel Census Area	178	84.76
Crooked Creek, AK (cdp) Bethel Census Area	89	84.76
Clark's Point, AK (city) Dillingham Census Area	51	82.26
Kotlik, AK (city) Wade Hampton Census Area	472	81.80
Ekwok, AK (city) Dillingham Census Area	93	80.87
Aleknagik, AK (city) Dillingham Census Area	172	78.54
Nightmute, AK (city) Bethel Census Area	218	77.86
Nunapitchuk, AK (city) Bethel Census Area	386	77.82
Levelock, AK (cdp) Lake and Peninsula Borough	51	73.91
Chuathbaluk, AK (city) Bethel Census Area	85	72.03
Russian Mission, AK (city) Wade Hampton Census Area	220	70.51
Newhalen, AK (city) Lake and Peninsula Borough	132	69.47
Platinum, AK (city) Bethel Census Area	42	68.85
Hooper Bay, AK (city) Wade Hampton Census Area	729	66.70
Marshall, AK (city) Wade Hampton Census Area	275	66.43
Sleetmute, AK (cdp) Bethel Census Area	54	62.79
Aniak, AK (city) Bethel Census Area	296	59.08
Portage Creek, AK (cdp) Dillingham Census Area	1	50.00
Bethel, AK (city) Bethel Census Area	2,837	46.66
Dillingham, AK (city) Dillingham Census Area	1,078	46.29
Stony River, AK (cdp) Bethel Census Area	21	38.89
Naknek, AK (cdp) Bristol Bay Borough	175	32.17
South Naknek, AK (cdp) Bristol Bay Borough	19	24.05
Igiugig, AK (cdp) Lake and Peninsula Borough	11	22.00
Red Devil, AK (cdp) Bethel Census Area	5	21.74
St. Michael, AK (city) Nome Census Area	81	20.20
Iliamna, AK (cdp) Lake and Peninsula Borough	17	15.60
King Salmon, AK (cdp) Bristol Bay Borough	55	14.71
Lime Village, AK (cdp) Bethel Census Area	4	13.79
Alatna, AK (cdp) Yukon-Koyukuk Census Area	5	13.51
False Pass, AK (city) Aleutians East Borough	4	11.43
Kings Valley, OR (cdp) Benton County	6	9.23
Pilot Point, AK (city) Lake and Peninsula Borough	6	8.82
Eureka Roadhouse, AK (cdp) Matanuska-Susitna Borough	2	6.90
Chignik Lake, AK (cdp) Lake and Peninsula Borough	5	6.85
Kaktovik, AK (city) North Slope Borough	16	6.69
Chevak, AK (city) Wade Hampton Census Area	62	6.61
Kasaan, AK (city) Prince of Wales-Hyder Census Area	3	6.12
Point MacKenzie, AK (cdp) Matanuska-Susitna Borough	28	5.29
Kokhanok, AK (cdp) Lake and Peninsula Borough	9	5.29
Tetlin, AK (cdp) Southeast Fairbanks Census Area	6	4.72
Tyonek, AK (cdp) Kenai Peninsula Borough	8	4.68
Tatitlek, AK (cdp) Valdez-Cordova Census Area	4	4.55
Nikolai, AK (city) Yukon-Koyukuk Census Area	4	4.26
Seward, AK (city) Kenai Peninsula Borough	113	4.20
Northway Village, AK (cdp) Southeast Fairbanks Census Area	4	4.08
Teller, AK (city) Nome Census Area	9	3.93
Sutton-Alpine, AK (cdp) Matanuska-Susitna Borough	54	3.73
Old Harbor, AK (city) Kodiak Island Borough	8	3.67
Mekoryuk, AK (city) Bethel Census Area	7	3.66
Salamatof, AK (cdp) Kenai Peninsula Borough	35	3.57
Nanwalek, AK (cdp) Kenai Peninsula Borough	9	3.54
Nondalton, AK (city) Lake and Peninsula Borough	5	3.05
St. Paul, AK (city) Aleutians West Census Area	14	2.92
Unalakleet, AK (city) Nome Census Area	20	2.91
McGrath, AK (city) Yukon-Koyukuk Census Area	10	2.89
Adak, AK (city) Aleutians West Census Area	9	2.76
Nome, AK (city) Nome Census Area	99	2.75
Slana, AK (cdp) Valdez-Cordova Census Area	4	2.72
Karluk, AK (cdp) Kodiak Island Borough	1	2.70
Two Rivers, AK (cdp) Fairbanks North Star Borough	19	2.64
Willow Creek, AK (cdp) Valdez-Cordova Census Area	5	2.62
Chignik, AK (city) Lake and Peninsula Borough	2	2.20
Wales, AK (city) Nome Census Area	3	2.07
Port Lions, AK (city) Kodiak Island Borough	4	2.06
Lutak, AK (cdp) Haines Borough	1	2.04
Tazlina, AK (cdp) Valdez-Cordova Census Area	6	2.02
Kenny Lake, AK (cdp) Valdez-Cordova Census Area	7	1.97
Custer, MT (cdp) Yellowstone County	3	1.89
Anaktuvuk Pass, AK (city) North Slope Borough	6	1.85
Kasilof, AK (cdp) Kenai Peninsula Borough	10	1.82
Hudson, CO (town) Weld County	41	1.74
Nelchina, AK (cdp) Valdez-Cordova Census Area	1	1.69
Anchorage, AK (municipality) Anchorage Municipality	4,835	1.66
White Mountain, AK (city) Nome Census Area	3	1.58
Grayling, AK (city) Yukon-Koyukuk Census Area	3	1.55
Galena, AK (city) Yukon-Koyukuk Census Area	7	1.49
Bear Creek, AK (cdp) Kenai Peninsula Borough	29	1.48
Minto, AK (cdp) Yukon-Koyukuk Census Area	3	1.43
Kenai, AK (city) Kenai Peninsula Borough	100	1.41
Kotzebue, AK (city) Northwest Arctic Borough	45	1.41
Houston, AK (city) Matanuska-Susitna Borough	27	1.41
Buffalo Soapstone, AK (cdp) Matanuska-Susitna Borough	12	1.40
Lakes, AK (cdp) Matanuska-Susitna Borough	115	1.37
Palmer, AK (city) Matanuska-Susitna Borough	81	1.36
Tokeland, WA (cdp) Pacific County	2	1.32
Chenega, AK (cdp) Valdez-Cordova Census Area	1	1.32
Halibut Cove, AK (cdp) Kenai Peninsula Borough	1	1.32
Chignik Lagoon, AK (cdp) Lake and Peninsula Borough	1	1.28
Port Alsworth, AK (cdp) Lake and Peninsula Borough	2	1.26
Copper Center, AK (cdp) Valdez-Cordova Census Area	4	1.22
Anderson, AK (city) Denali Borough	3	1.22
Moose Creek, AK (cdp) Fairbanks North Star Borough	9	1.20
Koyuk, AK (city) Nome Census Area	4	1.20
Venetie, AK (cdp) Yukon-Koyukuk Census Area	2	1.20
Shageluk, AK (city) Yukon-Koyukuk Census Area	1	1.20
College, AK (cdp) Fairbanks North Star Borough	149	1.15
Wasilla, AK (city) Matanuska-Susitna Borough	90	1.15
Susitna North, AK (cdp) Matanuska-Susitna Borough	14	1.11
Yakutat, AK (cdp) Yakutat City and Borough	7	1.06
Hoonah, AK (city) Hoonah-Angoon Census Area	8	1.05
Brevig Mission, AK (city) Nome Census Area	4	1.03
Meadow Lakes, AK (cdp) Matanuska-Susitna Borough	76	1.00
Big Lake, AK (cdp) Matanuska-Susitna Borough	33	0.99
Noatak, AK (cdp) Northwest Arctic Borough	5	0.97
Fox, AK (cdp) Fairbanks North Star Borough	4	0.96
Tanaina, AK (cdp) Matanuska-Susitna Borough	76	0.93
Egegik, AK (city) Lake and Peninsula Borough	1	0.92
Ester, AK (cdp) Fairbanks North Star Borough	22	0.91
Cantwell, AK (cdp) Denali Borough	2	0.91
Noorvik, AK (city) Northwest Arctic Borough	6	0.90
Stoney Brook, MN (township) St. Louis County	3	0.90
Naukati Bay, AK (cdp) Prince of Wales-Hyder Census Area	1	0.88

Please refer to the Explanation of Data in the front of the book for more detailed information.

Race

Alaska Native: Yup'ik

Top 150 Places Sorted by Percent of Total Population

Based on places with total population of 7,500 or more

Place	Population	%
Anchorage, AK (municipality) Anchorage Municipality	4,835	1.66
Lakes, AK (cdp) Matanuska-Susitna Borough	115	1.37
College, AK (cdp) Fairbanks North Star Borough	149	1.15
Wasilla, AK (city) Matanuska-Susitna Borough	90	1.15
Meadow Lakes, AK (cdp) Matanuska-Susitna Borough	76	1.00
Tanaina, AK (cdp) Matanuska-Susitna Borough	76	0.93
Knik-Fairview, AK (cdp) Matanuska-Susitna Borough	106	0.71
Kalifornsky, AK (cdp) Kenai Peninsula Borough	56	0.71
Sitka, AK (borough) Sitka City and Borough	60	0.68
Fairbanks, AK (city) Fairbanks North Star Borough	132	0.42
Badger, AK (cdp) Fairbanks North Star Borough	79	0.41
Juneau, AK (borough) Juneau City and Borough	113	0.36
Ketchikan, AK (city) Ketchikan Gateway Borough	18	0.22
Fort Irwin, CA (cdp) San Bernardino County	9	0.10
Hayesville, OR (cdp) Marion County	14	0.07
Springdale, AR (city) Washington County	42	0.06
Ferndale, WA (city) Whatcom County	7	0.06
Lynden, WA (city) Whatcom County	7	0.06
Bruce, MI (township) Macomb County	5	0.06
Durango, CO (city) La Plata County	9	0.05
Four Corners, OR (cdp) Marion County	8	0.05
Havre, MT (city) Hill County	5	0.05
Maili, HI (cdp) Honolulu County	5	0.05
Troy, MO (city) Lincoln County	5	0.05
Boulder Hill, IL (cdp) Kendall County	4	0.05
Lincoln City, OR (city) Lincoln County	4	0.05
Auburn, WA (city) King County	25	0.04
SeaTac, WA (city) King County	10	0.04
Oroville, CA (city) Butte County	6	0.04
Sault Ste. Marie, MI (city) Chippewa County	6	0.04
Fort Campbell North, KY (cdp) Christian County	5	0.04
Prairie Ridge, WA (cdp) Pierce County	5	0.04
Washougal, WA (city) Clark County	5	0.04
Alderwood Manor, WA (cdp) Snohomish County	3	0.04
Flushing, MI (city) Genesee County	3	0.04
North Hanover, NJ (township) Burlington County	3	0.04
Yreka, CA (city) Siskiyou County	3	0.04
Keizer, OR (city) Marion County	11	0.03
Mount Vernon, WA (city) Skagit County	9	0.03
Oswego, IL (village) Kendall County	8	0.03
Tualatin, OR (city) Washington County	8	0.03
Bainbridge Island, WA (city) Kitsap County	6	0.03
Tumwater, WA (city) Thurston County	6	0.03
Bryn Mawr-Skyway, WA (cdp) King County	5	0.03
Lebanon, OR (city) Linn County	5	0.03
Canby, OR (city) Clackamas County	4	0.03
Elk Plain, WA (cdp) Pierce County	4	0.03
Green River, WY (city) Sweetwater County	4	0.03
Kelso, WA (city) Cowlitz County	4	0.03
La Grande, OR (city) Union County	4	0.03
Martha Lake, WA (cdp) Snohomish County	4	0.03
Worthington, MN (city) Nobles County	4	0.03
Astoria, OR (city) Clatsop County	3	0.03
Burley, ID (city) Cassia County	3	0.03
Canton, NY (town) St. Lawrence County	3	0.03
Pennsville, NJ (cdp) Salem County	3	0.03
Sallisaw, OK (city) Sequoyah County	3	0.03
Sonoma, CA (city) Sonoma County	3	0.03
Washington, IN (city) Daviess County	3	0.03
Hyrum, UT (city) Cache County	2	0.03
Waller, WA (cdp) Pierce County	2	0.03
Albany, OR (city) Linn County	9	0.02
Springfield, OR (city) Lane County	9	0.02
McMinnville, OR (city) Yamhill County	8	0.02
Shoreline, WA (city) King County	8	0.02
Tigard, OR (city) Washington County	8	0.02
Burien, WA (city) King County	7	0.02
Parkland, WA (cdp) Pierce County	7	0.02
Oak Harbor, WA (city) Island County	5	0.02
Pittsburg, KS (city) Crawford County	5	0.02
Webster Groves, MO (city) St. Louis County	5	0.02
Bonney Lake, WA (city) Pierce County	4	0.02
Kahului, HI (cdp) Maui County	4	0.02
Magna, UT (cdp) Salt Lake County	4	0.02
Newberg, OR (city) Yamhill County	4	0.02
Ponca City, OK (city) Kay County	4	0.02
Salmon Creek, WA (cdp) Clark County	4	0.02
Union Hill-Novelty Hill, WA (cdp) King County	4	0.02
Woodburn, OR (city) Marion County	4	0.02
Albany, CA (city) Alameda County	3	0.02
Altamont, OR (cdp) Klamath County	3	0.02
Chickasha, OK (city) Grady County	3	0.02
Covington, WA (city) King County	3	0.02
Ellensburg, WA (city) Kittitas County	3	0.02
Fort Drum, NY (cdp) Jefferson County	3	0.02
Maumelle, AR (city) Pulaski County	3	0.02
Ottawa, IL (city) LaSalle County	3	0.02
Pennsville, NJ (township) Salem County	3	0.02
Schofield Barracks, HI (cdp) Honolulu County	3	0.02
Birch Bay, WA (cdp) Whatcom County	2	0.02
Centerton, AR (city) Benton County	2	0.02
Cottonwood, AZ (city) Yavapai County	2	0.02
Maltby, WA (cdp) Snohomish County	2	0.02
Mexico, MO (city) Audrain County	2	0.02
Midland, WA (cdp) Pierce County	2	0.02
Monmouth, OR (city) Polk County	2	0.02
North Bend, OR (city) Coos County	2	0.02
Riverton, WY (city) Fremont County	2	0.02
Sedro-Woolley, WA (city) Skagit County	2	0.02
Snoqualmie, WA (city) King County	2	0.02
Portland, OR (city) Multnomah County	45	0.01
Seattle, WA (city) King County	41	0.01
Urban Honolulu, HI (cdp) Honolulu County	38	0.01
Spokane, WA (city) Spokane County	28	0.01
Tacoma, WA (city) Pierce County	23	0.01
Salem, OR (city) Marion County	22	0.01
Eugene, OR (city) Lane County	17	0.01
West Valley City, UT (city) Salt Lake County	16	0.01
Spokane Valley, WA (city) Spokane County	13	0.01
Vancouver, WA (city) Clark County	13	0.01
Everett, WA (city) Snohomish County	10	0.01
Federal Way, WA (city) King County	10	0.01
Rancho Cucamonga, CA (city) San Bernardino County	9	0.01
Bellingham, WA (city) Whatcom County	8	0.01
Lakewood, WA (city) Pierce County	8	0.01
Bellevue, WA (city) King County	7	0.01
Bend, OR (city) Deschutes County	7	0.01
Enid, OK (city) Garfield County	7	0.01
Renton, WA (city) King County	7	0.01
Rogers, AR (city) Benton County	7	0.01
Flagstaff, AZ (city) Coconino County	6	0.01
Lawrence, KS (city) Douglas County	6	0.01
Lompoc, CA (city) Santa Barbara County	6	0.01
Corvallis, OR (city) Benton County	5	0.01
Fountain Valley, CA (city) Orange County	5	0.01
Hacienda Heights, CA (cdp) Los Angeles County	5	0.01
Hillsboro, OR (city) Washington County	5	0.01
Huber Heights, OH (city) Montgomery County	5	0.01
Kent, WA (city) King County	5	0.01
Kirkland, WA (city) King County	5	0.01
Lakeville, MN (city) Dakota County	5	0.01
Missoula, MT (city) Missoula County	5	0.01
Sammamish, WA (city) King County	5	0.01
Bullhead City, AZ (city) Mohave County	4	0.01
Cookeville, TN (city) Putnam County	4	0.01
Florence, KY (city) Boone County	4	0.01
Gardena, CA (city) Los Angeles County	4	0.01
Lacey, WA (city) Thurston County	4	0.01
Laramie, WY (city) Albany County	4	0.01
Macomb, MI (township) Macomb County	4	0.01
Mankato, MN (city) Blue Earth County	4	0.01
Mankato, MN (city) Blue Earth County	4	0.01
Millcreek, UT (cdp) Salt Lake County	4	0.01
Odenton, MD (cdp) Anne Arundel County	4	0.01
Oregon City, OR (city) Clackamas County	4	0.01
Parker, CO (town) Douglas County	4	0.01
Prattville, AL (city) Autauga County	4	0.01
Rohnert Park, CA (city) Sonoma County	4	0.01
San Juan, TX (city) Hidalgo County	4	0.01
Walla Walla, WA (city) Walla Walla County	4	0.01

Race

Asian

U.S. and 50 States Sorted by Population and Percent of Total Population

Place	Population	%
United States	**17,320,856**	**5.61**
California	5,556,592	14.92
New York	1,579,494	8.15
Texas	1,110,666	4.42
New Jersey	795,163	9.04
Hawaii	780,968	57.41
Illinois	668,694	5.21
Washington	604,251	8.99
Florida	573,083	3.05
Virginia	522,199	6.53
Pennsylvania	402,587	3.17
Massachusetts	394,211	6.02
Maryland	370,044	6.41
Georgia	365,497	3.77
Michigan	289,607	2.93
North Carolina	252,585	2.65
Minnesota	247,132	4.66
Nevada	242,916	9.00
Ohio	238,292	2.07
Arizona	230,907	3.61
Oregon	186,281	4.86
Colorado	185,589	3.69
Connecticut	157,088	4.40
Wisconsin	151,513	2.66
Indiana	126,750	1.95
Missouri	123,571	2.06
Tennessee	113,398	1.79
Louisiana	84,335	1.86
Oklahoma	84,170	2.24
Kansas	83,930	2.94
Utah	77,748	2.81
South Carolina	75,674	1.64
Alabama	67,036	1.40
Iowa	64,512	2.12
Kentucky	62,029	1.43
Alaska	50,402	7.10
Arkansas	44,943	1.54
Nebraska	40,561	2.22
New Mexico	40,456	1.96
Rhode Island	36,763	3.49
New Hampshire	34,522	2.62
Delaware	33,701	3.75
Mississippi	32,560	1.10
Idaho	29,698	1.89
District of Columbia	26,857	4.46
Maine	18,333	1.38
West Virginia	16,465	0.89
Montana	10,482	1.06
Vermont	10,463	1.67
South Dakota	10,216	1.25
North Dakota	9,193	1.37
Wyoming	6,729	1.19

Place	Population	%
Hawaii	780,968	57.41
California	5,556,592	14.92
New Jersey	795,163	9.04
Nevada	242,916	9.00
Washington	604,251	8.99
New York	1,579,494	8.15
Alaska	50,402	7.10
Virginia	522,199	6.53
Maryland	370,044	6.41
Massachusetts	394,211	6.02
United States	**17,320,856**	**5.61**
Illinois	668,694	5.21
Oregon	186,281	4.86
Minnesota	247,132	4.66
District of Columbia	26,857	4.46
Texas	1,110,666	4.42
Connecticut	157,088	4.40
Georgia	365,497	3.77
Delaware	33,701	3.75
Colorado	185,589	3.69
Arizona	230,907	3.61
Rhode Island	36,763	3.49
Pennsylvania	402,587	3.17
Florida	573,083	3.05
Kansas	83,930	2.94
Michigan	289,607	2.93
Utah	77,748	2.81
Wisconsin	151,513	2.66
North Carolina	252,585	2.65
New Hampshire	34,522	2.62
Oklahoma	84,170	2.24
Nebraska	40,561	2.22
Iowa	64,512	2.12
Ohio	238,292	2.07
Missouri	123,571	2.06
New Mexico	40,456	1.96
Indiana	126,750	1.95
Idaho	29,698	1.89
Louisiana	84,335	1.86
Tennessee	113,398	1.79
Vermont	10,463	1.67
South Carolina	75,674	1.64
Arkansas	44,943	1.54
Kentucky	62,029	1.43
Alabama	67,036	1.40
Maine	18,333	1.38
North Dakota	9,193	1.37
South Dakota	10,216	1.25
Wyoming	6,729	1.19
Mississippi	32,560	1.10
Montana	10,482	1.06
West Virginia	16,465	0.89

Please refer to the Explanation of Data in the front of the book for more detailed information.

Race

Asian

Top 150 Places Sorted by Population

Based on all places, regardless of total population

Place	Population	%
New York, NY (city) Kings County	1,134,919	13.88
Queens, NY (borough) Queens County	552,867	24.78
Los Angeles, CA (city) Los Angeles County	483,585	12.75
San Jose, CA (city) Santa Clara County	326,627	34.53
San Francisco, CA (city) San Francisco County	288,529	35.83
Brooklyn, NY (borough) Kings County	284,489	11.36
San Diego, CA (city) San Diego County	241,293	18.46
Urban Honolulu, HI (cdp) Honolulu County	230,071	68.22
Manhattan, NY (borough) New York County	199,722	12.59
Chicago, IL (city) Cook County	166,770	6.19
Houston, TX (city) Harris County	139,960	6.67
Fremont, CA (city) Alameda County	116,755	54.54
Philadelphia, PA (city) Philadelphia County	106,720	6.99
Seattle, WA (city) King County	100,727	16.55
Sacramento, CA (city) Sacramento County	98,705	21.16
Irvine, CA (city) Orange County	91,896	43.27
Oakland, CA (city) Alameda County	73,775	18.88
Stockton, CA (city) San Joaquin County	71,852	24.63
Fresno, CA (city) Fresno County	69,765	14.10
Long Beach, CA (city) Los Angeles County	67,961	14.70
Garden Grove, CA (city) Orange County	65,923	38.58
Jersey City, NJ (city) Hudson County	62,449	25.22
Sunnyvale, CA (city) Santa Clara County	61,253	43.73
Boston, MA (city) Suffolk County	60,712	9.83
Daly City, CA (city) San Mateo County	59,093	58.44
Bronx, NY (borough) Bronx County	59,085	4.27
Austin, TX (city) Travis County	57,893	7.32
Phoenix, AZ (city) Maricopa County	57,619	3.99
Torrance, CA (city) Los Angeles County	55,499	38.16
Anaheim, CA (city) Orange County	55,024	16.36
Portland, OR (city) Multnomah County	51,854	8.88
Plano, TX (city) Collin County	47,565	18.31
Santa Clara, CA (city) Santa Clara County	47,564	40.84
Elk Grove, CA (city) Sacramento County	46,861	30.63
Las Vegas, NV (city) Clark County	45,537	7.80
St. Paul, MN (city) Ramsey County	45,480	15.95
Alhambra, CA (city) Los Angeles County	45,395	54.63
Hempstead, NY (town) Nassau County	45,112	5.94
Edison, NJ (township) Middlesex County	44,924	44.94
Westminster, CA (city) Orange County	44,192	49.27
Milpitas, CA (city) Santa Clara County	43,466	65.08
Jacksonville, FL (city) Duval County	43,100	5.24
San Antonio, TX (city) Medina County	42,623	3.21
Chula Vista, CA (city) San Diego County	41,840	17.15
Monterey Park, CA (city) Los Angeles County	41,284	68.50
Charlotte, NC (city) Mecklenburg County	40,918	5.59
Dallas, TX (city) Dallas County	39,508	3.30
Staten Island, NY (borough) Richmond County	38,756	8.27
Cupertino, CA (city) Santa Clara County	38,503	66.04
Union City, CA (city) Alameda County	38,427	55.28
Columbus, OH (city) Franklin County	37,743	4.80
North Hempstead, NY (town) Nassau County	36,973	16.34
Bellevue, WA (city) King County	36,899	30.16
Glendale, CA (city) Los Angeles County	36,832	19.21
Hayward, CA (city) Alameda County	36,334	25.20
Santa Ana, CA (city) Orange County	36,324	11.19
Spring Valley, NV (cdp) Clark County	35,247	19.76
Arcadia, CA (city) Los Angeles County	34,416	61.06
Pearl City, HI (cdp) Honolulu County	34,051	71.39
Virginia Beach, VA (ind. city) Virginia Beach independent city	33,906	7.74
Fullerton, CA (city) Orange County	33,256	24.60
Rosemead, CA (city) Los Angeles County	33,107	61.58
Vallejo, CA (city) Solano County	32,761	28.26
East Honolulu, HI (cdp) Honolulu County	32,752	65.62
Fort Worth, TX (city) Tarrant County	32,411	4.37
Irving, TX (city) Dallas County	32,212	14.89
Cerritos, CA (city) Los Angeles County	31,691	64.62
Diamond Bar, CA (city) Los Angeles County	30,478	54.87
Waipahu, HI (cdp) Honolulu County	30,298	79.28
Rowland Heights, CA (cdp) Los Angeles County	30,088	61.41
Anchorage, AK (municipality) Anchorage Municipality	30,047	10.30
Sugar Land, TX (city) Fort Bend County	29,224	37.08
Oyster Bay, NY (town) Nassau County	29,203	9.96
El Monte, CA (city) Los Angeles County	29,188	25.72
West Covina, CA (city) Los Angeles County	29,177	27.50
San Ramon, CA (city) Contra Costa County	28,406	39.37
Arlington, TX (city) Tarrant County	27,745	7.59
Oklahoma City, OK (city) Oklahoma County	27,716	4.78
San Leandro, CA (city) Alameda County	27,280	32.11
Washington, DC (city) District of Columbia	26,857	4.46
Riverside, CA (city) Riverside County	26,675	8.78
Enterprise, NV (cdp) Clark County	26,600	24.52
Hilo, HI (cdp) Hawaii County	26,420	61.07
Alameda, CA (city) Alameda County	26,240	35.55
Denver, CO (city) Denver County	26,139	4.36
Paradise, NV (cdp) Clark County	25,826	11.57
Bakersfield, CA (city) Kern County	25,815	7.43
Berkeley, CA (city) Alameda County	25,707	22.83
Huntington Beach, CA (city) Orange County	25,619	13.48
South San Francisco, CA (city) San Mateo County	25,409	39.93
Carson, CA (city) Los Angeles County	25,296	27.58
Minneapolis, MN (city) Hennepin County	25,227	6.59
San Gabriel, CA (city) Los Angeles County	24,672	62.12
Chino Hills, CA (city) San Bernardino County	24,637	32.94
Henderson, NV (city) Clark County	24,315	9.43
Milwaukee, WI (city) Milwaukee County	23,685	3.98
Arlington, VA (cdp) Arlington County	23,678	11.40
Woodbridge, NJ (township) Middlesex County	23,571	23.67
Buena Park, CA (city) Orange County	23,063	28.64
Naperville, IL (city) DuPage County	23,042	16.24
Garland, TX (city) Dallas County	23,007	10.14
Quincy, MA (city) Norfolk County	22,968	24.89
Lowell, MA (city) Middlesex County	22,764	21.37
Nashville-Davidson, TN (metro govt) Davidson County	22,739	3.78
Chandler, AZ (city) Maricopa County	22,619	9.58
Pasadena, CA (city) Los Angeles County	22,513	16.42
Kaneohe, HI (cdp) Honolulu County	21,959	63.47
Tacoma, WA (city) Pierce County	21,903	11.04
Brookhaven, NY (town) Suffolk County	21,849	4.50
Renton, WA (city) King County	21,646	23.81
Wichita, KS (city) Sedgwick County	21,541	5.63
Mountain View, CA (city) Santa Clara County	21,527	29.06
San Mateo, CA (city) San Mateo County	21,349	21.96
Indianapolis, IN (city) Marion County	21,294	2.60
Hacienda Heights, CA (cdp) Los Angeles County	20,891	38.66
Rancho Cucamonga, CA (city) San Bernardino County	20,512	12.41
Tucson, AZ (city) Pima County	20,448	3.93
Temple City, CA (city) Los Angeles County	20,412	57.40
Raleigh, NC (city) Wake County	20,389	5.05
Aurora, CO (city) Arapahoe County	20,109	6.19
Fairfield, CA (city) Solano County	20,062	19.05
Centreville, VA (cdp) Fairfax County	19,925	28.01
Fountain Valley, CA (city) Orange County	19,755	35.71
Piscataway, NJ (township) Middlesex County	19,733	35.21
Albuquerque, NM (city) Bernalillo County	19,631	3.60
Mililani Town, HI (cdp) Honolulu County	19,609	70.97
Madison, WI (city) Dane County	19,548	8.38
Palo Alto, CA (city) Santa Clara County	19,492	30.27
Cary, NC (town) Wake County	19,370	14.32
Colorado Springs, CO (city) El Paso County	19,260	4.63
Walnut, CA (city) Los Angeles County	19,258	66.02
Johns Creek, GA (city) Fulton County	18,977	24.73
Kahului, HI (cdp) Maui County	18,830	71.50
Germantown, MD (cdp) Montgomery County	18,684	21.63
Pleasanton, CA (city) Alameda County	18,484	26.30
Santa Clarita, CA (city) Los Angeles County	18,381	10.42
Ann Arbor, MI (city) Washtenaw County	18,345	16.10
Cambridge, MA (city) Middlesex County	18,124	17.23
North Las Vegas, NV (city) Clark County	18,046	8.32
Skokie, IL (village) Cook County	17,996	27.78
Corona, CA (city) Riverside County	17,899	11.75
Baltimore, MD (city) Baltimore city County	17,769	2.86
Reno, NV (city) Washoe County	17,700	7.86
Modesto, CA (city) Stanislaus County	17,695	8.80
Orange, CA (city) Orange County	17,473	12.81
Carrollton, TX (city) Denton County	17,278	14.51
Oxnard, CA (city) Ventura County	17,273	8.73
Concord, CA (city) Contra Costa County	17,105	14.01
Tustin, CA (city) Orange County	16,973	22.47
Gardena, CA (city) Los Angeles County	16,602	28.22

SECTION THREE

Race

Asian

Top 150 Places Sorted by Percent of Total Population

Based on all places, regardless of total population

Place	Population	%
Greens, NH (grant) Coos County	1	100.00
Laurier, WA (cdp) Ferry County	1	100.00
Kaumakani, HI (cdp) Kauai County	658	87.85
Whitmore Village, HI (cdp) Honolulu County	3,815	84.80
Ewa Villages, HI (cdp) Honolulu County	4,998	81.83
Waipahu, HI (cdp) Honolulu County	30,298	79.28
Hanamaulu, HI (cdp) Kauai County	3,010	78.49
Eleele, HI (cdp) Kauai County	1,871	78.28
Waipio, HI (cdp) Honolulu County	9,058	77.59
Lanai City, HI (cdp) Maui County	2,360	76.08
Keaau, HI (cdp) Hawaii County	1,705	75.68
Pahala, HI (cdp) Hawaii County	1,026	75.66
Aiea, HI (cdp) Honolulu County	7,061	75.62
Royal Kunia, HI (cdp) Honolulu County	10,949	75.38
West Loch Estate, HI (cdp) Honolulu County	4,089	74.55
Paauilo, HI (cdp) Hawaii County	441	74.12
Waikele, HI (cdp) Honolulu County	5,530	73.94
Mililani Mauka, HI (cdp) Honolulu County	15,389	73.15
Puhi, HI (cdp) Kauai County	2,114	72.75
Ewa Beach, HI (cdp) Honolulu County	10,867	72.66
Kahului, HI (cdp) Maui County	18,830	71.50
Pearl City, HI (cdp) Honolulu County	34,051	71.39
Mililani Town, HI (cdp) Honolulu County	19,609	70.97
Halawa, HI (cdp) Honolulu County	9,772	69.73
Halaula, HI (cdp) Hawaii County	324	69.08
Hanapepe, HI (cdp) Kauai County	1,817	68.88
Monterey Park, CA (city) Los Angeles County	41,284	68.50
Urban Honolulu, HI (cdp) Honolulu County	230,071	68.22
Waimalu, HI (cdp) Honolulu County	9,332	67.97
Wahiawa, HI (cdp) Honolulu County	12,085	67.81
Pepeekeo, HI (cdp) Hawaii County	1,207	67.47
Naalehu, HI (cdp) Hawaii County	584	67.44
Ewa Gentry, HI (cdp) Honolulu County	15,205	67.01
Waialua, HI (cdp) Honolulu County	2,585	66.97
Cupertino, CA (city) Santa Clara County	38,503	66.04
Walnut, CA (city) Los Angeles County	19,258	66.02
East Honolulu, HI (cdp) Honolulu County	32,752	65.62
Milpitas, CA (city) Santa Clara County	43,466	65.08
Honokaa, HI (cdp) Hawaii County	1,469	65.06
Lihue, HI (cdp) Kauai County	4,174	64.66
Cerritos, CA (city) Los Angeles County	31,691	64.62
Kapaau, HI (cdp) Hawaii County	1,117	64.42
Loudoun Valley Estates, VA (cdp) Loudoun County	2,343	64.09
Pahoa, HI (cdp) Hawaii County	604	63.92
Waimea, HI (cdp) Kauai County	1,184	63.83
Kaneohe, HI (cdp) Honolulu County	21,959	63.47
Heeia, HI (cdp) Honolulu County	3,149	63.45
Papaikou, HI (cdp) Hawaii County	833	63.39
Kurtistown, HI (cdp) Hawaii County	820	63.17
Wainaku, HI (cdp) Hawaii County	771	62.99
Waihee-Waiehu, HI (cdp) Maui County	5,555	62.83
Kapolei, HI (cdp) Honolulu County	9,540	62.82
San Gabriel, CA (city) Los Angeles County	24,672	62.12
Waikapu, HI (cdp) Maui County	1,827	61.62
Rosemead, CA (city) Los Angeles County	33,107	61.58
Rowland Heights, CA (cdp) Los Angeles County	30,088	61.41
Waipio Acres, HI (cdp) Honolulu County	3,203	61.17
Ahuimanu, HI (cdp) Honolulu County	5,381	61.08
Hilo, HI (cdp) Hawaii County	26,420	61.07
Arcadia, CA (city) Los Angeles County	34,416	61.06
Wailuku, HI (cdp) Maui County	9,327	60.91
Koloa, HI (cdp) Kauai County	1,293	60.31
Millbourne, PA (borough) Delaware County	687	59.28
Haliimaile, HI (cdp) Maui County	568	58.92
Palisades Park, NJ (borough) Bergen County	11,498	58.60
Daly City, CA (city) San Mateo County	59,093	58.44
Haleiwa, HI (cdp) Honolulu County	2,314	58.29
Kekaha, HI (cdp) Kauai County	2,045	57.82
Makakilo, HI (cdp) Honolulu County	10,511	57.60
Temple City, CA (city) Los Angeles County	20,412	57.40
Hawi, HI (cdp) Hawaii County	619	57.26
San Marino, CA (city) Los Angeles County	7,349	55.90
Maunaloa, HI (cdp) Maui County	208	55.32
Union City, CA (city) Alameda County	38,427	55.28
Camino Tassajara, CA (cdp) Contra Costa County	1,209	55.03
Diamond Bar, CA (city) Los Angeles County	30,478	54.87
Alhambra, CA (city) Los Angeles County	45,395	54.63
Adak, AK (city) Aleutians West Census Area	178	54.60
Fremont, CA (city) Alameda County	116,755	54.54
Lahaina, HI (cdp) Maui County	6,342	54.19
Honomu, HI (cdp) Hawaii County	274	53.83
Waimanalo, HI (cdp) Honolulu County	2,929	53.73
Kaunakakai, HI (cdp) Maui County	1,813	52.93
Ten Mile Run, NJ (cdp) Somerset County	1,034	52.78
Kukuihaele, HI (cdp) Hawaii County	176	52.38
Pakala Village, HI (cdp) Kauai County	154	52.38
Wailua, HI (cdp) Kauai County	1,178	52.26
Mountain View, HI (cdp) Hawaii County	2,049	52.22
Kahaluu, HI (cdp) Honolulu County	2,471	52.15
East San Gabriel, CA (cdp) Los Angeles County	7,739	52.03
Waiohinu, HI (cdp) Hawaii County	110	51.64
South San Gabriel, CA (cdp) Los Angeles County	4,159	51.54
Kealakekua, HI (cdp) Hawaii County	1,037	51.36
Maunawili, HI (cdp) Honolulu County	1,039	50.93
La Palma, CA (city) Orange County	7,896	50.72
Maili, HI (cdp) Honolulu County	4,766	50.23
Swanville, MN (city) Todd County	1	50.00
Plainsboro Center, NJ (cdp) Middlesex County	1,348	49.71
Kualapuu, HI (cdp) Maui County	1,006	49.63
Waianae, HI (cdp) Honolulu County	6,497	49.31
Kapaa, HI (cdp) Kauai County	5,274	49.29
Westminster, CA (city) Orange County	44,192	49.27
Oak Grove, VA (cdp) Loudoun County	873	49.13
Hercules, CA (city) Contra Costa County	11,815	49.11
Captain Cook, HI (cdp) Hawaii County	1,682	49.05
Foster City, CA (city) San Mateo County	14,910	48.78
Midway City, CA (cdp) Orange County	4,110	48.44
Kahuku, HI (cdp) Honolulu County	1,263	48.32
Iselin, NJ (cdp) Middlesex County	9,018	48.24
Waikane, HI (cdp) Honolulu County	375	48.20
Plainsboro, NJ (township) Middlesex County	11,001	47.83
Pukalani, HI (cdp) Maui County	3,618	47.77
Princeton Meadows, NJ (cdp) Middlesex County	6,576	47.54
Ocean Pointe, HI (cdp) Honolulu County	3,973	47.52
Dayton, NJ (cdp) Middlesex County	3,343	47.33
University of California Davis, CA (cdp) Yolo County	2,712	46.87
Laupahoehoe, HI (cdp) Hawaii County	269	46.30
Lawai, HI (cdp) Kauai County	1,092	46.21
Society Hill, NJ (cdp) Middlesex County	1,759	45.94
Millbrae, CA (city) San Mateo County	9,866	45.82
Herricks, NY (cdp) Nassau County	1,943	45.24
Akutan, AK (city) Aleutians East Borough	462	44.99
Edison, NJ (township) Middlesex County	44,924	44.94
Paukaa, HI (cdp) Hawaii County	191	44.94
Kalaheo, HI (cdp) Kauai County	2,053	44.68
Makaha, HI (cdp) Honolulu County	3,671	44.35
Mountain House, CA (cdp) San Joaquin County	4,289	44.33
Saratoga, CA (city) Santa Clara County	13,230	44.21
Orchidlands Estates, HI (cdp) Hawaii County	1,243	44.16
Sunnyvale, CA (city) Santa Clara County	61,253	43.73
Makawao, HI (cdp) Maui County	3,136	43.65
Broadmoor, CA (cdp) San Mateo County	1,823	43.65
New Territory, TX (cdp) Fort Bend County	6,627	43.64
Hawaiian Paradise Park, HI (cdp) Hawaii County	4,965	43.54
Ainaloa, HI (cdp) Hawaii County	1,286	43.37
Irvine, CA (city) Orange County	91,896	43.27
Omao, HI (cdp) Kauai County	563	43.27
Waimea, HI (cdp) Hawaii County	3,965	43.04
Paia, HI (cdp) Maui County	1,137	42.62
McNair, VA (cdp) Fairfax County	7,460	42.60
Norris Canyon, CA (cdp) Contra Costa County	405	42.32
Manhasset Hills, NY (cdp) Nassau County	1,483	41.29
Kailua, HI (cdp) Honolulu County	15,851	41.03
Nanakuli, HI (cdp) Honolulu County	5,197	41.03
Searingtown, NY (cdp) Nassau County	2,008	40.85
Santa Clara, CA (city) Santa Clara County	47,564	40.84
Wailua Homesteads, HI (cdp) Kauai County	2,090	40.29
North El Monte, CA (cdp) Los Angeles County	1,496	40.18
Englewood Cliffs, NJ (borough) Bergen County	2,118	40.11
South San Francisco, CA (city) San Mateo County	25,409	39.93

Please refer to the Explanation of Data in the front of the book for more detailed information.

Race

Asian

Top 150 Places Sorted by Percent of Total Population

Based on places with total population of 7,500 or more

Place	Population	%
Waipahu, HI (cdp) Honolulu County	30,298	79.28
Waipio, HI (cdp) Honolulu County	9,058	77.59
Aiea, HI (cdp) Honolulu County	7,061	75.62
Royal Kunia, HI (cdp) Honolulu County	10,949	75.38
Mililani Mauka, HI (cdp) Honolulu County	15,389	73.15
Ewa Beach, HI (cdp) Honolulu County	10,867	72.66
Kahului, HI (cdp) Maui County	18,830	71.50
Pearl City, HI (cdp) Honolulu County	34,051	71.39
Mililani Town, HI (cdp) Honolulu County	19,609	70.97
Halawa, HI (cdp) Honolulu County	9,772	69.73
Monterey Park, CA (city) Los Angeles County	41,284	68.50
Urban Honolulu, HI (cdp) Honolulu County	230,071	68.22
Waimalu, HI (cdp) Honolulu County	9,332	67.97
Wahiawa, HI (cdp) Honolulu County	12,085	67.81
Ewa Gentry, HI (cdp) Honolulu County	15,205	67.01
Cupertino, CA (city) Santa Clara County	38,503	66.04
Walnut, CA (city) Los Angeles County	19,258	66.02
East Honolulu, HI (cdp) Honolulu County	32,752	65.62
Milpitas, CA (city) Santa Clara County	43,466	65.08
Cerritos, CA (city) Los Angeles County	31,691	64.62
Kaneohe, HI (cdp) Honolulu County	21,959	63.47
Waihee-Waiehu, HI (cdp) Maui County	5,555	62.83
Kapolei, HI (cdp) Honolulu County	9,540	62.82
San Gabriel, CA (city) Los Angeles County	24,672	62.12
Rosemead, CA (city) Los Angeles County	33,107	61.58
Rowland Heights, CA (cdp) Los Angeles County	30,088	61.41
Ahuimanu, HI (cdp) Honolulu County	5,381	61.08
Hilo, HI (cdp) Hawaii County	26,420	61.07
Arcadia, CA (city) Los Angeles County	34,416	61.06
Wailuku, HI (cdp) Maui County	9,327	60.91
Palisades Park, NJ (borough) Bergen County	11,498	58.60
Daly City, CA (city) San Mateo County	59,093	58.44
Makakilo, HI (cdp) Honolulu County	10,511	57.60
Temple City, CA (city) Los Angeles County	20,412	57.40
San Marino, CA (city) Los Angeles County	7,349	55.90
Union City, CA (city) Alameda County	38,427	55.28
Diamond Bar, CA (city) Los Angeles County	30,478	54.87
Alhambra, CA (city) Los Angeles County	45,395	54.63
Fremont, CA (city) Alameda County	116,755	54.54
Lahaina, HI (cdp) Maui County	6,342	54.19
East San Gabriel, CA (cdp) Los Angeles County	7,739	52.03
South San Gabriel, CA (cdp) Los Angeles County	4,159	51.54
La Palma, CA (city) Orange County	7,896	50.72
Maili, HI (cdp) Honolulu County	4,766	50.23
Waianae, HI (cdp) Honolulu County	6,497	49.31
Kapaa, HI (cdp) Kauai County	5,274	49.29
Westminster, CA (city) Orange County	44,192	49.27
Hercules, CA (city) Contra Costa County	11,815	49.11
Foster City, CA (city) San Mateo County	14,910	48.78
Midway City, CA (cdp) Orange County	4,110	48.44
Iselin, NJ (cdp) Middlesex County	9,018	48.24
Plainsboro, NJ (township) Middlesex County	11,001	47.83
Pukalani, HI (cdp) Maui County	3,618	47.77
Princeton Meadows, NJ (cdp) Middlesex County	6,576	47.54
Ocean Pointe, HI (cdp) Honolulu County	3,973	47.52
Millbrae, CA (city) San Mateo County	9,866	45.82
Edison, NJ (township) Middlesex County	44,924	44.94
Makaha, HI (cdp) Honolulu County	3,671	44.35
Mountain House, CA (cdp) San Joaquin County	4,289	44.33
Saratoga, CA (city) Santa Clara County	13,230	44.21
Sunnyvale, CA (city) Santa Clara County	61,253	43.73
New Territory, TX (cdp) Fort Bend County	6,627	43.64
Hawaiian Paradise Park, HI (cdp) Hawaii County	4,965	43.54
Irvine, CA (city) Orange County	91,896	43.27
Waimea, HI (cdp) Hawaii County	3,965	43.04
McNair, VA (cdp) Fairfax County	7,460	42.60
Kailua, HI (cdp) Honolulu County	15,851	41.03
Nanakuli, HI (cdp) Honolulu County	5,197	41.03
Santa Clara, CA (city) Santa Clara County	47,564	40.84
South San Francisco, CA (city) San Mateo County	25,409	39.93
West Windsor, NJ (township) Mercer County	10,743	39.55
Fort Lee, NJ (borough) Bergen County	13,964	39.51
San Ramon, CA (city) Contra Costa County	28,406	39.37
Artesia, CA (city) Los Angeles County	6,408	38.78
Hacienda Heights, CA (cdp) Los Angeles County	20,891	38.66
Garden Grove, CA (city) Orange County	65,923	38.58
Torrance, CA (city) Los Angeles County	55,499	38.16
Merrifield, VA (cdp) Fairfax County	5,718	37.59
South Brunswick, NJ (township) Middlesex County	16,194	37.30
Sugar Land, TX (city) Fort Bend County	29,224	37.08
Edgewater, NJ (borough) Bergen County	4,247	36.89
American Canyon, CA (city) Napa County	7,145	36.73
Leonia, NJ (borough) Bergen County	3,273	36.62
Franklin Park, NJ (cdp) Somerset County	4,867	36.61
Kailua, HI (cdp) Hawaii County	4,364	36.44
Four Corners, TX (cdp) Fort Bend County	4,495	36.30
Floris, VA (cdp) Fairfax County	3,027	36.14
North Potomac, MD (cdp) Montgomery County	8,779	35.96
San Francisco, CA (city) San Francisco County	288,529	35.83
Clarksburg, MD (cdp) Montgomery County	4,923	35.76
Fountain Valley, CA (city) Orange County	19,755	35.71
Fair Lakes, VA (cdp) Fairfax County	2,836	35.71
Alameda, CA (city) Alameda County	26,240	35.55
Albany, CA (city) Alameda County	6,568	35.43
Piscataway, NJ (township) Middlesex County	19,733	35.21
Garden City Park, NY (cdp) Nassau County	2,698	34.56
San Jose, CA (city) Santa Clara County	326,627	34.53
South Pasadena, CA (city) Los Angeles County	8,844	34.52
Kalaoa, HI (cdp) Hawaii County	3,310	34.32
Bethany, OR (cdp) Washington County	7,061	34.20
Cypress, CA (city) Orange County	16,239	33.97
West Carson, CA (cdp) Los Angeles County	7,304	33.66
Vineyard, CA (cdp) Sacramento County	8,262	33.27
Kihei, HI (cdp) Maui County	6,913	33.11
Chino Hills, CA (city) San Bernardino County	24,637	32.94
Bradley Gardens, NJ (cdp) Somerset County	4,638	32.65
Closter, NJ (borough) Bergen County	2,731	32.62
Rancho Palos Verdes, CA (city) Los Angeles County	13,481	32.37
Stanford, CA (cdp) Santa Clara County	4,446	32.20
San Leandro, CA (city) Alameda County	27,280	32.11
Travilah, MD (cdp) Montgomery County	3,875	31.87
South Riding, VA (cdp) Loudoun County	7,661	31.58
Florin, CA (cdp) Sacramento County	14,937	31.44
El Cerrito, CA (city) Contra Costa County	7,357	31.24
Hillsborough, CA (town) San Mateo County	3,382	31.24
Emeryville, CA (city) Alameda County	3,144	31.19
Loma Linda, CA (city) San Bernardino County	7,231	31.09
Parsippany-Troy Hills, NJ (township) Morris County	16,491	30.98
Newark, CA (city) Alameda County	13,163	30.92
Tysons Corner, VA (cdp) Fairfax County	6,054	30.85
North New Hyde Park, NY (cdp) Nassau County	4,585	30.77
Elk Grove, CA (city) Sacramento County	46,861	30.63
Dublin, CA (city) Alameda County	14,050	30.52
Bothell East, WA (cdp) Snohomish County	2,443	30.47
Palo Alto, CA (city) Santa Clara County	19,492	30.27
Holualoa, HI (cdp) Hawaii County	2,583	30.25
Bellevue, WA (city) King County	36,899	30.16
Bryn Mawr-Skyway, WA (cdp) King County	4,711	30.11
Ridgefield, NJ (borough) Bergen County	3,313	30.03
Morton Grove, IL (village) Cook County	6,933	29.79
Los Altos Hills, CA (town) Santa Clara County	2,360	29.79
La Crescenta-Montrose, CA (cdp) Los Angeles County	5,830	29.66
Brambleton, VA (cdp) Loudoun County	2,879	29.24
Mountain View, CA (city) Santa Clara County	21,527	29.06
Morrisville, NC (town) Wake County	5,378	28.95
Lincolnwood, IL (village) Cook County	3,639	28.90
San Bruno, CA (city) San Mateo County	11,867	28.86
Cresskill, NJ (borough) Bergen County	2,471	28.82
Buena Park, CA (city) Orange County	23,063	28.64
Fair Oaks, VA (cdp) Fairfax County	8,625	28.54
Vallejo, CA (city) Solano County	32,761	28.26
Gardena, CA (city) Los Angeles County	16,602	28.22
La Cañada Flintridge, CA (city) Los Angeles County	5,711	28.21
Rolling Hills Estates, CA (city) Los Angeles County	2,262	28.04
Newcastle, WA (city) King County	2,909	28.03
Centreville, VA (cdp) Fairfax County	19,925	28.01
Tenafly, NJ (borough) Bergen County	4,048	27.94
Skokie, IL (village) Cook County	17,996	27.78
Redmond, WA (city) King County	15,037	27.77
Chantilly, VA (cdp) Fairfax County	6,366	27.63

Race

Asian: Not Hispanic

U.S. and 50 States Sorted by Population and Percent of Total Population

Place	Population	%
United States	**16,722,710**	**5.42**
California	5,324,591	14.29
New York	1,545,106	7.97
Texas	1,063,715	4.23
New Jersey	780,769	8.88
Hawaii	725,913	53.36
Illinois	652,951	5.09
Washington	587,411	8.74
Florida	546,075	2.90
Virginia	512,103	6.40
Pennsylvania	394,941	3.11
Massachusetts	388,293	5.93
Maryland	363,580	6.30
Georgia	357,791	3.69
Michigan	284,695	2.88
North Carolina	245,810	2.58
Minnesota	243,897	4.60
Ohio	234,053	2.03
Nevada	230,685	8.54
Arizona	212,889	3.33
Oregon	180,139	4.70
Colorado	174,577	3.47
Connecticut	153,269	4.29
Wisconsin	148,605	2.61
Indiana	123,750	1.91
Missouri	121,013	2.02
Tennessee	110,618	1.74
Louisiana	82,002	1.81
Kansas	81,491	2.86
Oklahoma	81,353	2.17
Utah	74,064	2.68
South Carolina	73,426	1.59
Alabama	65,311	1.37
Iowa	63,185	2.07
Kentucky	60,537	1.40
Alaska	48,530	6.83
Arkansas	43,589	1.49
Nebraska	39,398	2.16
Rhode Island	35,535	3.38
New Mexico	34,771	1.69
New Hampshire	34,018	2.58
Delaware	33,042	3.68
Mississippi	31,595	1.06
Idaho	27,926	1.78
District of Columbia	26,126	4.34
Maine	17,975	1.35
West Virginia	16,096	0.87
Vermont	10,278	1.64
Montana	9,992	1.01
South Dakota	9,958	1.22
North Dakota	8,987	1.34
Wyoming	6,286	1.12

Place	Population	%
Hawaii	725,913	53.36
California	5,324,591	14.29
New Jersey	780,769	8.88
Washington	587,411	8.74
Nevada	230,685	8.54
New York	1,545,106	7.97
Alaska	48,530	6.83
Virginia	512,103	6.40
Maryland	363,580	6.30
Massachusetts	388,293	5.93
United States	**16,722,710**	**5.42**
Illinois	652,951	5.09
Oregon	180,139	4.70
Minnesota	243,897	4.60
District of Columbia	26,126	4.34
Connecticut	153,269	4.29
Texas	1,063,715	4.23
Georgia	357,791	3.69
Delaware	33,042	3.68
Colorado	174,577	3.47
Rhode Island	35,535	3.38
Arizona	212,889	3.33
Pennsylvania	394,941	3.11
Florida	546,075	2.90
Michigan	284,695	2.88
Kansas	81,491	2.86
Utah	74,064	2.68
Wisconsin	148,605	2.61
North Carolina	245,810	2.58
New Hampshire	34,018	2.58
Oklahoma	81,353	2.17
Nebraska	39,398	2.16
Iowa	63,185	2.07
Ohio	234,053	2.03
Missouri	121,013	2.02
Indiana	123,750	1.91
Louisiana	82,002	1.81
Idaho	27,926	1.78
Tennessee	110,618	1.74
New Mexico	34,771	1.69
Vermont	10,278	1.64
South Carolina	73,426	1.59
Arkansas	43,589	1.49
Kentucky	60,537	1.40
Alabama	65,311	1.37
Maine	17,975	1.35
North Dakota	8,987	1.34
South Dakota	9,958	1.22
Wyoming	6,286	1.12
Mississippi	31,595	1.06
Montana	9,992	1.01
West Virginia	16,096	0.87

Please refer to the Explanation of Data in the front of the book for more detailed information.

Race

Asian: Not Hispanic

Top 150 Places Sorted by Population

Based on all places, regardless of total population

Place	Population	%
New York, NY (city) Kings County	1,110,964	13.59
Queens, NY (borough) Queens County	545,389	24.45
Los Angeles, CA (city) Los Angeles County	465,942	12.29
San Jose, CA (city) Santa Clara County	318,607	33.68
San Francisco, CA (city) San Francisco County	283,435	35.20
Brooklyn, NY (borough) Kings County	279,499	11.16
San Diego, CA (city) San Diego County	232,029	17.75
Urban Honolulu, HI (cdp) Honolulu County	222,126	65.86
Manhattan, NY (borough) New York County	194,929	12.29
Chicago, IL (city) Cook County	161,439	5.99
Houston, TX (city) Harris County	135,594	6.46
Fremont, CA (city) Alameda County	115,097	53.76
Philadelphia, PA (city) Philadelphia County	104,551	6.85
Seattle, WA (city) King County	98,921	16.25
Sacramento, CA (city) Sacramento County	94,141	20.18
Irvine, CA (city) Orange County	90,762	42.74
Oakland, CA (city) Alameda County	71,892	18.40
Stockton, CA (city) San Joaquin County	65,993	22.62
Fresno, CA (city) Fresno County	65,854	13.31
Garden Grove, CA (city) Orange County	65,071	38.08
Long Beach, CA (city) Los Angeles County	64,834	14.03
Jersey City, NJ (city) Hudson County	61,418	24.81
Sunnyvale, CA (city) Santa Clara County	60,435	43.14
Boston, MA (city) Suffolk County	59,745	9.67
Daly City, CA (city) San Mateo County	57,841	57.20
Austin, TX (city) Travis County	55,842	7.07
Torrance, CA (city) Los Angeles County	54,136	37.22
Bronx, NY (borough) Bronx County	53,458	3.86
Anaheim, CA (city) Orange County	53,269	15.84
Phoenix, AZ (city) Maricopa County	53,095	3.67
Portland, OR (city) Multnomah County	50,635	8.67
Plano, TX (city) Collin County	47,116	18.13
Santa Clara, CA (city) Santa Clara County	46,702	40.10
St. Paul, MN (city) Ramsey County	45,032	15.80
Elk Grove, CA (city) Sacramento County	44,901	29.34
Edison, NJ (township) Middlesex County	44,748	44.76
Alhambra, CA (city) Los Angeles County	44,579	53.65
Hempstead, NY (town) Nassau County	43,880	5.78
Westminster, CA (city) Orange County	43,687	48.70
Milpitas, CA (city) Santa Clara County	42,929	64.27
Las Vegas, NV (city) Clark County	42,871	7.34
Jacksonville, FL (city) Duval County	41,726	5.08
Monterey Park, CA (city) Los Angeles County	40,660	67.46
Charlotte, NC (city) Mecklenburg County	40,149	5.49
Cupertino, CA (city) Santa Clara County	38,342	65.76
Chula Vista, CA (city) San Diego County	38,101	15.62
Dallas, TX (city) Dallas County	37,744	3.15
Union City, CA (city) Alameda County	37,720	54.26
Staten Island, NY (borough) Richmond County	37,689	8.04
San Antonio, TX (city) Medina County	37,486	2.82
Columbus, OH (city) Franklin County	37,170	4.72
Bellevue, WA (city) King County	36,656	29.96
North Hempstead, NY (town) Nassau County	36,641	16.19
Glendale, CA (city) Los Angeles County	35,949	18.75
Santa Ana, CA (city) Orange County	34,961	10.77
Hayward, CA (city) Alameda County	34,827	24.15
Spring Valley, NV (cdp) Clark County	34,201	19.17
Arcadia, CA (city) Los Angeles County	34,096	60.49
Rosemead, CA (city) Los Angeles County	32,749	60.91
Virginia Beach, VA (ind. city) Virginia Beach independent city	32,681	7.46
Fullerton, CA (city) Orange County	32,479	24.03
Pearl City, HI (cdp) Honolulu County	32,040	67.17
East Honolulu, HI (cdp) Honolulu County	31,841	63.79
Irving, TX (city) Dallas County	31,808	14.71
Vallejo, CA (city) Solano County	31,408	27.09
Cerritos, CA (city) Los Angeles County	31,229	63.68
Fort Worth, TX (city) Tarrant County	30,971	4.18
Diamond Bar, CA (city) Los Angeles County	29,892	53.82
Rowland Heights, CA (cdp) Los Angeles County	29,752	60.73
Anchorage, AK (municipality) Anchorage Municipality	28,994	9.94
Sugar Land, TX (city) Fort Bend County	28,966	36.75
Oyster Bay, NY (town) Nassau County	28,910	9.86
Waipahu, HI (cdp) Honolulu County	28,838	75.46
El Monte, CA (city) Los Angeles County	28,605	25.21
West Covina, CA (city) Los Angeles County	27,998	26.39
San Ramon, CA (city) Contra Costa County	27,937	38.72
Arlington, TX (city) Tarrant County	27,092	7.41
Oklahoma City, OK (city) Oklahoma County	26,942	4.65
San Leandro, CA (city) Alameda County	26,490	31.18
Washington, DC (city) District of Columbia	26,126	4.34
Enterprise, NV (cdp) Clark County	25,795	23.78
Alameda, CA (city) Alameda County	25,552	34.62
Berkeley, CA (city) Alameda County	25,158	22.35
Riverside, CA (city) Riverside County	24,912	8.20
Minneapolis, MN (city) Hennepin County	24,848	6.49
Huntington Beach, CA (city) Orange County	24,694	13.00
Paradise, NV (cdp) Clark County	24,583	11.02
Denver, CO (city) Denver County	24,571	4.09
South San Francisco, CA (city) San Mateo County	24,507	38.51
San Gabriel, CA (city) Los Angeles County	24,430	61.51
Carson, CA (city) Los Angeles County	24,363	26.56
Hilo, HI (cdp) Hawaii County	23,823	55.07
Chino Hills, CA (city) San Bernardino County	23,813	31.84
Bakersfield, CA (city) Kern County	23,435	6.74
Woodbridge, NJ (township) Middlesex County	23,312	23.41
Arlington, VA (cdp) Arlington County	23,197	11.17
Henderson, NV (city) Clark County	23,003	8.93
Milwaukee, WI (city) Milwaukee County	22,970	3.86
Quincy, MA (city) Norfolk County	22,870	24.79
Naperville, IL (city) DuPage County	22,868	16.12
Garland, TX (city) Dallas County	22,492	9.91
Lowell, MA (city) Middlesex County	22,459	21.08
Buena Park, CA (city) Orange County	22,417	27.84
Nashville-Davidson, TN (metro govt) Davidson County	22,251	3.70
Chandler, AZ (city) Maricopa County	21,753	9.21
Pasadena, CA (city) Los Angeles County	21,709	15.83
Renton, WA (city) King County	21,275	23.40
Brookhaven, NY (town) Suffolk County	21,257	4.37
Mountain View, CA (city) Santa Clara County	21,116	28.51
Tacoma, WA (city) Pierce County	21,087	10.63
Wichita, KS (city) Sedgwick County	20,978	5.49
Indianapolis, IN (city) Marion County	20,777	2.53
San Mateo, CA (city) San Mateo County	20,645	21.24
Hacienda Heights, CA (cdp) Los Angeles County	20,414	37.78
Kaneohe, HI (cdp) Honolulu County	20,385	58.92
Temple City, CA (city) Los Angeles County	20,154	56.68
Raleigh, NC (city) Wake County	20,006	4.95
Centreville, VA (cdp) Fairfax County	19,744	27.76
Piscataway, NJ (township) Middlesex County	19,583	34.94
Fountain Valley, CA (city) Orange County	19,481	35.22
Palo Alto, CA (city) Santa Clara County	19,336	30.02
Madison, WI (city) Dane County	19,326	8.29
Cary, NC (town) Wake County	19,231	14.22
Rancho Cucamonga, CA (city) San Bernardino County	19,216	11.63
Aurora, CO (city) Arapahoe County	19,053	5.86
Walnut, CA (city) Los Angeles County	18,976	65.05
Johns Creek, GA (city) Fulton County	18,899	24.63
Fairfield, CA (city) Solano County	18,804	17.85
Germantown, MD (cdp) Montgomery County	18,470	21.38
Tucson, AZ (city) Pima County	18,307	3.52
Ann Arbor, MI (city) Washtenaw County	18,205	15.98
Pleasanton, CA (city) Alameda County	18,108	25.76
Mililani Town, HI (cdp) Honolulu County	18,075	65.42
Cambridge, MA (city) Middlesex County	17,944	17.06
Colorado Springs, CO (city) El Paso County	17,806	4.28
Skokie, IL (village) Cook County	17,752	27.40
Kahului, HI (cdp) Maui County	17,524	66.54
Santa Clarita, CA (city) Los Angeles County	17,448	9.90
Albuquerque, NM (city) Bernalillo County	17,372	3.18
Baltimore, MD (city) Baltimore city County	17,372	2.80
Carrollton, TX (city) Denton County	16,994	14.27
Corona, CA (city) Riverside County	16,857	11.06
Reno, NV (city) Washoe County	16,838	7.48
North Las Vegas, NV (city) Clark County	16,822	7.75
Orange, CA (city) Orange County	16,795	12.31
Tustin, CA (city) Orange County	16,578	21.95
Parsippany-Troy Hills, NJ (township) Morris County	16,392	30.79
Troy, MI (city) Oakland County	16,356	20.20
Davis, CA (city) Yolo County	16,170	24.64
Concord, CA (city) Contra Costa County	16,144	13.23

Please refer to the Explanation of Data in the front of the book for more detailed information.

Race

Asian: Not Hispanic

Top 150 Places Sorted by Percent of Total Population

Based on all places, regardless of total population

Place	Population	%
Greens, NH (grant) Coos County	1	100.00
Laurier, WA (cdp) Ferry County	1	100.00
Kaumakani, HI (cdp) Kauai County	630	84.11
Whitmore Village, HI (cdp) Honolulu County	3,561	79.15
Waipahu, HI (cdp) Honolulu County	28,838	75.46
Ewa Villages, HI (cdp) Honolulu County	4,525	74.08
Eleele, HI (cdp) Kauai County	1,738	72.72
Hanamaulu, HI (cdp) Kauai County	2,787	72.67
Waipio, HI (cdp) Honolulu County	8,424	72.16
Aiea, HI (cdp) Honolulu County	6,679	71.52
Royal Kunia, HI (cdp) Honolulu County	10,356	71.30
Waikele, HI (cdp) Honolulu County	5,235	70.00
West Loch Estate, HI (cdp) Honolulu County	3,833	69.88
Keaau, HI (cdp) Hawaii County	1,573	69.82
Lanai City, HI (cdp) Maui County	2,162	69.70
Mililani Mauka, HI (cdp) Honolulu County	14,506	68.95
Puhi, HI (cdp) Kauai County	1,993	68.58
Pahala, HI (cdp) Hawaii County	924	68.14
Monterey Park, CA (city) Los Angeles County	40,660	67.46
Pearl City, HI (cdp) Honolulu County	32,040	67.17
Kahului, HI (cdp) Maui County	17,524	66.54
Urban Honolulu, HI (cdp) Honolulu County	222,126	65.86
Cupertino, CA (city) Santa Clara County	38,342	65.76
Halawa, HI (cdp) Honolulu County	9,201	65.66
Ewa Beach, HI (cdp) Honolulu County	9,790	65.46
Mililani Town, HI (cdp) Honolulu County	18,075	65.42
Walnut, CA (city) Los Angeles County	18,976	65.05
Milpitas, CA (city) Santa Clara County	42,929	64.27
Loudoun Valley Estates, VA (cdp) Loudoun County	2,339	63.98
East Honolulu, HI (cdp) Honolulu County	31,841	63.79
Cerritos, CA (city) Los Angeles County	31,229	63.68
Naalehu, HI (cdp) Hawaii County	550	63.51
Hanapepe, HI (cdp) Kauai County	1,672	63.38
Waimalu, HI (cdp) Honolulu County	8,689	63.28
Paauilo, HI (cdp) Hawaii County	369	62.02
San Gabriel, CA (city) Los Angeles County	24,430	61.51
Waialua, HI (cdp) Honolulu County	2,357	61.06
Rosemead, CA (city) Los Angeles County	32,749	60.91
Rowland Heights, CA (cdp) Los Angeles County	29,752	60.73
Pahoa, HI (cdp) Hawaii County	572	60.53
Arcadia, CA (city) Los Angeles County	34,096	60.49
Ewa Gentry, HI (cdp) Honolulu County	13,668	60.24
Wahiawa, HI (cdp) Honolulu County	10,727	60.19
Lihue, HI (cdp) Kauai County	3,882	60.14
Heeia, HI (cdp) Honolulu County	2,984	60.12
Pepeekeo, HI (cdp) Hawaii County	1,072	59.92
Kaneohe, HI (cdp) Honolulu County	20,385	58.92
Millbourne, PA (borough) Delaware County	682	58.84
Waimea, HI (cdp) Kauai County	1,085	58.49
Palisades Park, NJ (borough) Bergen County	11,445	58.33
Waihee-Waiehu, HI (cdp) Maui County	5,116	57.87
Wainaku, HI (cdp) Hawaii County	707	57.76
Kurtistown, HI (cdp) Hawaii County	746	57.47
Honokaa, HI (cdp) Hawaii County	1,296	57.40
Daly City, CA (city) San Mateo County	57,841	57.20
Papaikou, HI (cdp) Hawaii County	745	56.70
Temple City, CA (city) Los Angeles County	20,154	56.68
Kapolei, HI (cdp) Honolulu County	8,567	56.41
Wailuku, HI (cdp) Maui County	8,571	55.97
Waikapu, HI (cdp) Maui County	1,654	55.78
San Marino, CA (city) Los Angeles County	7,293	55.47
Ahuimanu, HI (cdp) Honolulu County	4,866	55.23
Hilo, HI (cdp) Hawaii County	23,823	55.07
Koloa, HI (cdp) Kauai County	1,178	54.94
Adak, AK (city) Aleutians West Census Area	178	54.60
Kapaau, HI (cdp) Hawaii County	946	54.56
Camino Tassajara, CA (cdp) Contra Costa County	1,196	54.44
Halaula, HI (cdp) Hawaii County	255	54.37
Union City, CA (city) Alameda County	37,720	54.26
Waipio Acres, HI (cdp) Honolulu County	2,839	54.22
Diamond Bar, CA (city) Los Angeles County	29,892	53.82
Fremont, CA (city) Alameda County	115,097	53.76
Alhambra, CA (city) Los Angeles County	44,579	53.65
Haliimaile, HI (cdp) Maui County	513	53.22
Haleiwa, HI (cdp) Honolulu County	2,084	52.49

Place	Population	%
Ten Mile Run, NJ (cdp) Somerset County	1,028	52.48
Lahaina, HI (cdp) Maui County	6,062	51.79
Kekaha, HI (cdp) Kauai County	1,829	51.71
East San Gabriel, CA (cdp) Los Angeles County	7,610	51.16
South San Gabriel, CA (cdp) Los Angeles County	4,069	50.42
Makakilo, HI (cdp) Honolulu County	9,150	50.14
Swanville, MN (city) Todd County	1	50.00
La Palma, CA (city) Orange County	7,771	49.92
Plainsboro Center, NJ (cdp) Middlesex County	1,341	49.45
Maunawili, HI (cdp) Honolulu County	1,008	49.41
Kaunakakai, HI (cdp) Maui County	1,684	49.17
Waiohinu, HI (cdp) Hawaii County	104	48.83
Westminster, CA (city) Orange County	43,687	48.70
Oak Grove, VA (cdp) Loudoun County	864	48.62
Wailua, HI (cdp) Kauai County	1,091	48.40
Kealakekua, HI (cdp) Hawaii County	973	48.19
Foster City, CA (city) San Mateo County	14,701	48.09
Iselin, NJ (cdp) Middlesex County	8,969	47.98
Midway City, CA (cdp) Orange County	4,068	47.94
Hercules, CA (city) Contra Costa County	11,490	47.76
Plainsboro, NJ (township) Middlesex County	10,949	47.61
Honomu, HI (cdp) Hawaii County	241	47.35
Kukuihaele, HI (cdp) Hawaii County	159	47.32
Dayton, NJ (cdp) Middlesex County	3,341	47.30
Princeton Meadows, NJ (cdp) Middlesex County	6,540	47.27
Waimanalo, HI (cdp) Honolulu County	2,565	47.06
Pakala Village, HI (cdp) Kauai County	137	46.60
Captain Cook, HI (cdp) Hawaii County	1,586	46.25
Kahaluu, HI (cdp) Honolulu County	2,186	46.14
University of California Davis, CA (cdp) Yolo County	2,669	46.13
Hawi, HI (cdp) Hawaii County	495	45.79
Society Hill, NJ (cdp) Middlesex County	1,746	45.60
Kualapuu, HI (cdp) Maui County	924	45.58
Maunaloa, HI (cdp) Maui County	171	45.48
Waikane, HI (cdp) Honolulu County	352	45.24
Millbrae, CA (city) San Mateo County	9,708	45.09
Herricks, NY (cdp) Nassau County	1,931	44.96
Edison, NJ (township) Middlesex County	44,748	44.76
Kapaa, HI (cdp) Kauai County	4,755	44.44
Akutan, AK (city) Aleutians East Borough	451	43.91
Saratoga, CA (city) Santa Clara County	13,135	43.89
Kahuku, HI (cdp) Honolulu County	1,136	43.46
New Territory, TX (cdp) Fort Bend County	6,585	43.36
Mountain House, CA (cdp) San Joaquin County	4,178	43.18
Ocean Pointe, HI (cdp) Honolulu County	3,609	43.16
Sunnyvale, CA (city) Santa Clara County	60,435	43.14
Paukaa, HI (cdp) Hawaii County	183	43.06
Irvine, CA (city) Orange County	90,762	42.74
McNair, VA (cdp) Fairfax County	7,433	42.44
Norris Canyon, CA (cdp) Contra Costa County	404	42.22
Pukalani, HI (cdp) Maui County	3,189	42.10
Broadmoor, CA (cdp) San Mateo County	1,736	41.57
Manhasset Hills, NY (cdp) Nassau County	1,476	41.09
Searingtown, NY (cdp) Nassau County	2,000	40.69
Lawai, HI (cdp) Kauai County	956	40.46
Kalaheo, HI (cdp) Kauai County	1,853	40.33
Maili, HI (cdp) Honolulu County	3,824	40.30
Waianae, HI (cdp) Honolulu County	5,308	40.28
Santa Clara, CA (city) Santa Clara County	46,702	40.10
Englewood Cliffs, NJ (borough) Bergen County	2,108	39.92
Mountain View, HI (cdp) Hawaii County	1,560	39.76
North El Monte, CA (cdp) Los Angeles County	1,477	39.67
Laupahoehoe, HI (cdp) Hawaii County	229	39.41
West Windsor, NJ (township) Mercer County	10,702	39.40
Fort Lee, NJ (borough) Bergen County	13,893	39.31
Moorefield Station, VA (cdp) Loudoun County	30	38.96
Waimea, HI (cdp) Hawaii County	3,582	38.88
Heathcote, NJ (cdp) Middlesex County	2,263	38.88
Kodiak, AK (city) Kodiak Island Borough	2,380	38.83
San Ramon, CA (city) Contra Costa County	27,937	38.72
South San Francisco, CA (city) San Mateo County	24,507	38.51
Kailua, HI (cdp) Honolulu County	14,868	38.48
Artesia, CA (city) Los Angeles County	6,322	38.26
Garden Grove, CA (city) Orange County	65,071	38.08
Paia, HI (cdp) Maui County	1,014	38.01

Please refer to the Explanation of Data in the front of the book for more detailed information.

Race

Asian: Not Hispanic

Top 150 Places Sorted by Percent of Total Population

Based on places with total population of 7,500 or more

Place	Population	%
Waipahu, HI (cdp) Honolulu County	28,838	75.46
Waipio, HI (cdp) Honolulu County	8,424	72.16
Aiea, HI (cdp) Honolulu County	6,679	71.52
Royal Kunia, HI (cdp) Honolulu County	10,356	71.30
Mililani Mauka, HI (cdp) Honolulu County	14,506	68.95
Monterey Park, CA (city) Los Angeles County	40,660	67.46
Pearl City, HI (cdp) Honolulu County	32,040	67.17
Kahului, HI (cdp) Maui County	17,524	66.54
Urban Honolulu, HI (cdp) Honolulu County	222,126	65.86
Cupertino, CA (city) Santa Clara County	38,342	65.76
Halawa, HI (cdp) Honolulu County	9,201	65.66
Ewa Beach, HI (cdp) Honolulu County	9,790	65.46
Mililani Town, HI (cdp) Honolulu County	18,075	65.42
Walnut, CA (city) Los Angeles County	18,976	65.05
Milpitas, CA (city) Santa Clara County	42,929	64.27
East Honolulu, HI (cdp) Honolulu County	31,841	63.79
Cerritos, CA (city) Los Angeles County	31,229	63.68
Waimalu, HI (cdp) Honolulu County	8,689	63.28
San Gabriel, CA (city) Los Angeles County	24,430	61.51
Rosemead, CA (city) Los Angeles County	32,749	60.91
Rowland Heights, CA (cdp) Los Angeles County	29,752	60.73
Arcadia, CA (city) Los Angeles County	34,096	60.49
Ewa Gentry, HI (cdp) Honolulu County	13,668	60.24
Wahiawa, HI (cdp) Honolulu County	10,727	60.19
Kaneohe, HI (cdp) Honolulu County	20,385	58.92
Palisades Park, NJ (borough) Bergen County	11,445	58.33
Waihee-Waiehu, HI (cdp) Maui County	5,116	57.87
Daly City, CA (city) San Mateo County	57,841	57.20
Temple City, CA (city) Los Angeles County	20,154	56.68
Kapolei, HI (cdp) Honolulu County	8,567	56.41
Wailuku, HI (cdp) Maui County	8,571	55.97
San Marino, CA (city) Los Angeles County	7,293	55.47
Ahuimanu, HI (cdp) Honolulu County	4,866	55.23
Hilo, HI (cdp) Hawaii County	23,823	55.07
Union City, CA (city) Alameda County	37,720	54.26
Diamond Bar, CA (city) Los Angeles County	29,892	53.82
Fremont, CA (city) Alameda County	115,097	53.76
Alhambra, CA (city) Los Angeles County	44,579	53.65
Lahaina, HI (cdp) Maui County	6,062	51.79
East San Gabriel, CA (cdp) Los Angeles County	7,610	51.16
South San Gabriel, CA (cdp) Los Angeles County	4,069	50.42
Makakilo, HI (cdp) Honolulu County	9,150	50.14
La Palma, CA (city) Orange County	7,771	49.92
Westminster, CA (city) Orange County	43,687	48.70
Foster City, CA (city) San Mateo County	14,701	48.09
Iselin, NJ (cdp) Middlesex County	8,969	47.98
Midway City, CA (cdp) Orange County	4,068	47.94
Hercules, CA (city) Contra Costa County	11,490	47.76
Plainsboro, NJ (township) Middlesex County	10,949	47.61
Princeton Meadows, NJ (cdp) Middlesex County	6,540	47.27
Millbrae, CA (city) San Mateo County	9,708	45.09
Edison, NJ (township) Middlesex County	44,748	44.76
Kapaa, HI (cdp) Kauai County	4,755	44.44
Saratoga, CA (city) Santa Clara County	13,135	43.89
New Territory, TX (cdp) Fort Bend County	6,585	43.36
Mountain House, CA (cdp) San Joaquin County	4,178	43.18
Ocean Pointe, HI (cdp) Honolulu County	3,609	43.16
Sunnyvale, CA (city) Santa Clara County	60,435	43.14
Irvine, CA (city) Orange County	90,762	42.74
McNair, VA (cdp) Fairfax County	7,433	42.44
Pukalani, HI (cdp) Maui County	3,189	42.10
Maili, HI (cdp) Honolulu County	3,824	40.30
Waianae, HI (cdp) Honolulu County	5,308	40.28
Santa Clara, CA (city) Santa Clara County	46,702	40.10
West Windsor, NJ (township) Mercer County	10,702	39.40
Fort Lee, NJ (borough) Bergen County	13,893	39.31
Waimea, HI (cdp) Hawaii County	3,582	38.88
San Ramon, CA (city) Contra Costa County	27,937	38.72
South San Francisco, CA (city) San Mateo County	24,507	38.51
Kailua, HI (cdp) Honolulu County	14,868	38.48
Artesia, CA (city) Los Angeles County	6,322	38.26
Garden Grove, CA (city) Orange County	65,071	38.08
Hacienda Heights, CA (cdp) Los Angeles County	20,414	37.78
Merrifield, VA (cdp) Fairfax County	5,695	37.44
Torrance, CA (city) Los Angeles County	54,136	37.22
South Brunswick, NJ (township) Middlesex County	16,135	37.16
Sugar Land, TX (city) Fort Bend County	28,966	36.75
Edgewater, NJ (borough) Bergen County	4,226	36.71
Franklin Park, NJ (cdp) Somerset County	4,829	36.32
Leonia, NJ (borough) Bergen County	3,241	36.26
Four Corners, TX (cdp) Fort Bend County	4,457	36.00
Floris, VA (cdp) Fairfax County	3,013	35.98
North Potomac, MD (cdp) Montgomery County	8,741	35.81
Hawaiian Paradise Park, HI (cdp) Hawaii County	4,059	35.59
Clarksburg, MD (cdp) Montgomery County	4,881	35.46
Fair Lakes, VA (cdp) Fairfax County	2,811	35.39
Fountain Valley, CA (city) Orange County	19,481	35.22
American Canyon, CA (city) Napa County	6,849	35.21
San Francisco, CA (city) San Francisco County	283,435	35.20
Piscataway, NJ (township) Middlesex County	19,583	34.94
Makaha, HI (cdp) Honolulu County	2,884	34.84
Nanakuli, HI (cdp) Honolulu County	4,408	34.80
Albany, CA (city) Alameda County	6,431	34.69
Alameda, CA (city) Alameda County	25,552	34.62
Garden City Park, NY (cdp) Nassau County	2,670	34.20
Bethany, OR (cdp) Washington County	7,019	34.00
San Jose, CA (city) Santa Clara County	318,607	33.68
South Pasadena, CA (city) Los Angeles County	8,605	33.59
Cypress, CA (city) Orange County	15,864	33.19
West Carson, CA (cdp) Los Angeles County	7,083	32.64
Closter, NJ (borough) Bergen County	2,725	32.55
Bradley Gardens, NJ (cdp) Somerset County	4,622	32.54
Kailua, HI (cdp) Hawaii County	3,886	32.45
Vineyard, CA (cdp) Sacramento County	7,918	31.88
Chino Hills, CA (city) San Bernardino County	23,813	31.84
Rancho Palos Verdes, CA (city) Los Angeles County	13,259	31.84
Travilah, MD (cdp) Montgomery County	3,872	31.84
Stanford, CA (cdp) Santa Clara County	4,377	31.70
South Riding, VA (cdp) Loudoun County	7,607	31.36
San Leandro, CA (city) Alameda County	26,490	31.18
Hillsborough, CA (town) San Mateo County	3,339	30.85
Parsippany-Troy Hills, NJ (township) Morris County	16,392	30.79
Kihei, HI (cdp) Maui County	6,404	30.67
Emeryville, CA (city) Alameda County	3,090	30.65
Tysons Corner, VA (cdp) Fairfax County	6,013	30.64
North New Hyde Park, NY (cdp) Nassau County	4,558	30.59
El Cerrito, CA (city) Contra Costa County	7,198	30.57
Florin, CA (cdp) Sacramento County	14,420	30.35
Kalaoa, HI (cdp) Hawaii County	2,921	30.29
Loma Linda, CA (city) San Bernardino County	7,040	30.27
Bothell East, WA (cdp) Snohomish County	2,417	30.14
Palo Alto, CA (city) Santa Clara County	19,336	30.02
Bellevue, WA (city) King County	36,656	29.96
Newark, CA (city) Alameda County	12,711	29.86
Ridgefield, NJ (borough) Bergen County	3,285	29.78
Los Altos Hills, CA (town) Santa Clara County	2,356	29.74
Dublin, CA (city) Alameda County	13,683	29.72
Morton Grove, IL (village) Cook County	6,884	29.58
Bryn Mawr-Skyway, WA (cdp) King County	4,602	29.42
Elk Grove, CA (city) Sacramento County	44,901	29.34
La Crescenta-Montrose, CA (cdp) Los Angeles County	5,726	29.14
Brambleton, VA (cdp) Loudoun County	2,866	29.11
Morrisville, NC (town) Wake County	5,354	28.82
Cresskill, NJ (borough) Bergen County	2,454	28.62
Lincolnwood, IL (village) Cook County	3,596	28.56
Mountain View, CA (city) Santa Clara County	21,116	28.51
Fair Oaks, VA (cdp) Fairfax County	8,557	28.31
Holualoa, HI (cdp) Hawaii County	2,380	27.88
Buena Park, CA (city) Orange County	22,417	27.84
Tenafly, NJ (borough) Bergen County	4,026	27.79
La Cañada Flintridge, CA (city) Los Angeles County	5,623	27.77
Centreville, VA (cdp) Fairfax County	19,744	27.76
Newcastle, WA (city) King County	2,879	27.74
Rolling Hills Estates, CA (city) Los Angeles County	2,227	27.61
San Bruno, CA (city) San Mateo County	11,349	27.60
Redmond, WA (city) King County	14,931	27.58
Skokie, IL (village) Cook County	17,752	27.40
Chantilly, VA (cdp) Fairfax County	6,307	27.38
Gardena, CA (city) Los Angeles County	16,023	27.24
New Hyde Park, NY (village) Nassau County	2,643	27.21

Please refer to the Explanation of Data in the front of the book for more detailed information.

Race

Asian: Hispanic

U.S. and 50 States Sorted by Population and Percent of Total Population

Place	Population	%
United States	**598,146**	**0.19**
California	232,001	0.62
Hawaii	55,055	4.05
Texas	46,951	0.19
New York	34,388	0.18
Florida	27,008	0.14
Arizona	18,018	0.28
Washington	16,840	0.25
Illinois	15,743	0.12
New Jersey	14,394	0.16
Nevada	12,231	0.45
Colorado	11,012	0.22
Virginia	10,096	0.13
Georgia	7,706	0.08
Pennsylvania	7,646	0.06
North Carolina	6,775	0.07
Maryland	6,464	0.11
Oregon	6,142	0.16
Massachusetts	5,918	0.09
New Mexico	5,685	0.28
Michigan	4,912	0.05
Ohio	4,239	0.04
Connecticut	3,819	0.11
Utah	3,684	0.13
Minnesota	3,235	0.06
Indiana	3,000	0.05
Wisconsin	2,908	0.05
Oklahoma	2,817	0.08
Tennessee	2,780	0.04
Missouri	2,558	0.04
Kansas	2,439	0.09
Louisiana	2,333	0.05
South Carolina	2,248	0.05
Alaska	1,872	0.26
Idaho	1,772	0.11
Alabama	1,725	0.04
Kentucky	1,492	0.03
Arkansas	1,354	0.05
Iowa	1,327	0.04
Rhode Island	1,228	0.12
Nebraska	1,163	0.06
Mississippi	965	0.03
District of Columbia	731	0.12
Delaware	659	0.07
New Hampshire	504	0.04
Montana	490	0.05
Wyoming	443	0.08
West Virginia	369	0.02
Maine	358	0.03
South Dakota	258	0.03
North Dakota	206	0.03
Vermont	185	0.03

Place	Population	%
Hawaii	55,055	4.05
California	232,001	0.62
Nevada	12,231	0.45
Arizona	18,018	0.28
New Mexico	5,685	0.28
Alaska	1,872	0.26
Washington	16,840	0.25
Colorado	11,012	0.22
United States	**598,146**	**0.19**
Texas	46,951	0.19
New York	34,388	0.18
New Jersey	14,394	0.16
Oregon	6,142	0.16
Florida	27,008	0.14
Virginia	10,096	0.13
Utah	3,684	0.13
Illinois	15,743	0.12
Rhode Island	1,228	0.12
District of Columbia	731	0.12
Maryland	6,464	0.11
Connecticut	3,819	0.11
Idaho	1,772	0.11
Massachusetts	5,918	0.09
Kansas	2,439	0.09
Georgia	7,706	0.08
Oklahoma	2,817	0.08
Wyoming	443	0.08
North Carolina	6,775	0.07
Delaware	659	0.07
Pennsylvania	7,646	0.06
Minnesota	3,235	0.06
Nebraska	1,163	0.06
Michigan	4,912	0.05
Indiana	3,000	0.05
Wisconsin	2,908	0.05
Louisiana	2,333	0.05
South Carolina	2,248	0.05
Arkansas	1,354	0.05
Montana	490	0.05
Ohio	4,239	0.04
Tennessee	2,780	0.04
Missouri	2,558	0.04
Alabama	1,725	0.04
Iowa	1,327	0.04
New Hampshire	504	0.04
Kentucky	1,492	0.03
Mississippi	965	0.03
Maine	358	0.03
South Dakota	258	0.03
North Dakota	206	0.03
Vermont	185	0.03
West Virginia	369	0.02

Please refer to the Explanation of Data in the front of the book for more detailed information.

Race

Asian: Hispanic

Top 150 Places Sorted by Population

Based on all places, regardless of total population

Place	Population	%
New York, NY (city) Kings County	23,955	0.29
Los Angeles, CA (city) Los Angeles County	17,643	0.47
San Diego, CA (city) San Diego County	9,264	0.71
San Jose, CA (city) Santa Clara County	8,020	0.85
Urban Honolulu, HI (cdp) Honolulu County	7,945	2.36
Queens, NY (borough) Queens County	7,478	0.34
Stockton, CA (city) San Joaquin County	5,859	2.01
Bronx, NY (borough) Bronx County	5,627	0.41
Chicago, IL (city) Cook County	5,331	0.20
San Antonio, TX (city) Medina County	5,137	0.39
San Francisco, CA (city) San Francisco County	5,094	0.63
Brooklyn, NY (borough) Kings County	4,990	0.20
Manhattan, NY (borough) New York County	4,793	0.30
Sacramento, CA (city) Sacramento County	4,564	0.98
Phoenix, AZ (city) Maricopa County	4,524	0.31
Houston, TX (city) Harris County	4,366	0.21
Fresno, CA (city) Fresno County	3,911	0.79
Chula Vista, CA (city) San Diego County	3,739	1.53
Long Beach, CA (city) Los Angeles County	3,127	0.68
Las Vegas, NV (city) Clark County	2,666	0.46
Hilo, HI (cdp) Hawaii County	2,597	6.00
Bakersfield, CA (city) Kern County	2,380	0.68
Albuquerque, NM (city) Bernalillo County	2,259	0.41
El Paso, TX (city) El Paso County	2,234	0.34
Philadelphia, PA (city) Philadelphia County	2,169	0.14
Tucson, AZ (city) Pima County	2,141	0.41
Austin, TX (city) Travis County	2,051	0.26
Pearl City, HI (cdp) Honolulu County	2,011	4.22
Elk Grove, CA (city) Sacramento County	1,960	1.28
Salinas, CA (city) Monterey County	1,935	1.29
Oakland, CA (city) Alameda County	1,883	0.48
Seattle, WA (city) King County	1,806	0.30
Dallas, TX (city) Dallas County	1,764	0.15
Riverside, CA (city) Riverside County	1,763	0.58
Anaheim, CA (city) Orange County	1,755	0.52
Modesto, CA (city) Stanislaus County	1,717	0.85
Fremont, CA (city) Alameda County	1,658	0.77
Kaneohe, HI (cdp) Honolulu County	1,574	4.55
Denver, CO (city) Denver County	1,568	0.26
Ewa Gentry, HI (cdp) Honolulu County	1,537	6.77
Mililani Town, HI (cdp) Honolulu County	1,534	5.55
Hayward, CA (city) Alameda County	1,507	1.05
Oxnard, CA (city) Ventura County	1,468	0.74
Waipahu, HI (cdp) Honolulu County	1,460	3.82
Colorado Springs, CO (city) El Paso County	1,454	0.35
Fort Worth, TX (city) Tarrant County	1,440	0.19
Jacksonville, FL (city) Duval County	1,374	0.17
Torrance, CA (city) Los Angeles County	1,363	0.94
Santa Ana, CA (city) Orange County	1,363	0.42
Makakilo, HI (cdp) Honolulu County	1,361	7.46
Wahiawa, HI (cdp) Honolulu County	1,358	7.62
Vallejo, CA (city) Solano County	1,353	1.17
Henderson, NV (city) Clark County	1,312	0.51
Kahului, HI (cdp) Maui County	1,306	4.96
Moreno Valley, CA (city) Riverside County	1,305	0.67
Rancho Cucamonga, CA (city) San Bernardino County	1,296	0.78
Oceanside, CA (city) San Diego County	1,285	0.77
Fairfield, CA (city) Solano County	1,258	1.19
Fontana, CA (city) San Bernardino County	1,258	0.64
Daly City, CA (city) San Mateo County	1,252	1.24
Paradise, NV (cdp) Clark County	1,243	0.56
Hempstead, NY (town) Nassau County	1,232	0.16
Virginia Beach, VA (ind. city) Virginia Beach independent city	1,225	0.28
North Las Vegas, NV (city) Clark County	1,224	0.56
Portland, OR (city) Multnomah County	1,219	0.21
Waianae, HI (cdp) Honolulu County	1,189	9.02
West Covina, CA (city) Los Angeles County	1,179	1.11
Irvine, CA (city) Orange County	1,134	0.53
San Bernardino, CA (city) San Bernardino County	1,114	0.53
Antioch, CA (city) Contra Costa County	1,096	1.07
Ewa Beach, HI (cdp) Honolulu County	1,077	7.20
Staten Island, NY (borough) Richmond County	1,067	0.23
Tracy, CA (city) San Joaquin County	1,064	1.28
Santa Maria, CA (city) Santa Barbara County	1,064	1.07
Aurora, CO (city) Arapahoe County	1,056	0.32
Anchorage, AK (municipality) Anchorage Municipality	1,053	0.36
Spring Valley, NV (cdp) Clark County	1,046	0.59
Ontario, CA (city) San Bernardino County	1,044	0.64
Corona, CA (city) Riverside County	1,042	0.68
Jersey City, NJ (city) Hudson County	1,031	0.42
Sunrise Manor, NV (cdp) Clark County	1,004	0.53
Kailua, HI (cdp) Honolulu County	983	2.54
Kapolei, HI (cdp) Honolulu County	973	6.41
Boston, MA (city) Suffolk County	967	0.16
Mesa, AZ (city) Maricopa County	966	0.22
Concord, CA (city) Contra Costa County	961	0.79
Murrieta, CA (city) Riverside County	959	0.93
Palmdale, CA (city) Los Angeles County	951	0.62
Maili, HI (cdp) Honolulu County	942	9.93
Pomona, CA (city) Los Angeles County	938	0.63
Carson, CA (city) Los Angeles County	933	1.02
Santa Clarita, CA (city) Los Angeles County	933	0.53
Huntington Beach, CA (city) Orange County	925	0.49
Lancaster, CA (city) Los Angeles County	914	0.58
East Honolulu, HI (cdp) Honolulu County	911	1.83
Hawaiian Paradise Park, HI (cdp) Hawaii County	906	7.94
South San Francisco, CA (city) San Mateo County	902	1.42
Victorville, CA (city) San Bernardino County	885	0.76
Mililani Mauka, HI (cdp) Honolulu County	883	4.20
Visalia, CA (city) Tulare County	883	0.71
Glendale, CA (city) Los Angeles County	883	0.46
Chandler, AZ (city) Maricopa County	866	0.37
Santa Clara, CA (city) Santa Clara County	862	0.74
Reno, NV (city) Washoe County	862	0.38
Garden Grove, CA (city) Orange County	852	0.50
Temecula, CA (city) Riverside County	847	0.85
Chino Hills, CA (city) San Bernardino County	824	1.10
Sunnyvale, CA (city) Santa Clara County	818	0.58
Alhambra, CA (city) Los Angeles County	816	0.98
Tacoma, WA (city) Pierce County	816	0.41
Killeen, TX (city) Bell County	812	0.63
Downey, CA (city) Los Angeles County	810	0.72
Enterprise, NV (cdp) Clark County	805	0.74
Pasadena, CA (city) Los Angeles County	804	0.59
Glendale, AZ (city) Maricopa County	801	0.35
Vacaville, CA (city) Solano County	795	0.86
San Leandro, CA (city) Alameda County	790	0.93
Nanakuli, HI (cdp) Honolulu County	789	6.23
Makaha, HI (cdp) Honolulu County	787	9.51
Lakewood, CA (city) Los Angeles County	784	0.98
Fullerton, CA (city) Orange County	777	0.57
Manteca, CA (city) San Joaquin County	775	1.16
Oklahoma City, OK (city) Oklahoma County	774	0.13
Charlotte, NC (city) Mecklenburg County	769	0.11
Wailuku, HI (cdp) Maui County	756	4.94
Norwalk, CA (city) Los Angeles County	755	0.72
Miami, FL (city) Miami-Dade County	754	0.19
Whittier, CA (city) Los Angeles County	749	0.88
Roseville, CA (city) Placer County	736	0.62
Washington, DC (city) District of Columbia	731	0.12
Corpus Christi, TX (city) Nueces County	728	0.24
Pittsburg, CA (city) Contra Costa County	726	1.15
Milwaukee, WI (city) Milwaukee County	715	0.12
Santa Rosa, CA (city) Sonoma County	713	0.42
Escondido, CA (city) San Diego County	709	0.49
Union City, CA (city) Alameda County	707	1.02
Clovis, CA (city) Fresno County	707	0.74
San Mateo, CA (city) San Mateo County	704	0.72
Delano, CA (city) Kern County	698	1.32
Alameda, CA (city) Alameda County	688	0.93
Orange, CA (city) Orange County	678	0.50
Gilbert, AZ (town) Maricopa County	655	0.31
Arlington, TX (city) Tarrant County	653	0.18
Chino, CA (city) San Bernardino County	647	0.83
Buena Park, CA (city) Orange County	646	0.80
Waimalu, HI (cdp) Honolulu County	643	4.68
Waipio, HI (cdp) Honolulu County	634	5.43
Simi Valley, CA (city) Ventura County	628	0.51
Monterey Park, CA (city) Los Angeles County	624	1.04
National City, CA (city) San Diego County	623	1.06

SECTION THREE

Please refer to the Explanation of Data in the front of the book for more detailed information.

Race

Asian: Hispanic

Top 150 Places Sorted by Percent of Total Population

Based on all places, regardless of total population

Place	Population	%
Bucks Lake, CA (cdp) Plumas County	3	30.00
Halaula, HI (cdp) Hawaii County	69	14.71
Oasis, NV (cdp) Elko County	4	13.79
Mountain View, HI (cdp) Hawaii County	489	12.46
Paauilo, HI (cdp) Hawaii County	72	12.10
Hawi, HI (cdp) Hawaii County	124	11.47
Posey, CA (cdp) Tulare County	1	10.00
Maili, HI (cdp) Honolulu County	942	9.93
Kapaau, HI (cdp) Hawaii County	171	9.86
Maunaloa, HI (cdp) Maui County	37	9.84
Makaha, HI (cdp) Honolulu County	787	9.51
Waianae, HI (cdp) Honolulu County	1,189	9.02
Ainaloa, HI (cdp) Hawaii County	266	8.97
Eden Roc, HI (cdp) Hawaii County	82	8.70
Fern Acres, HI (cdp) Hawaii County	127	8.44
Makaha Valley, HI (cdp) Honolulu County	112	8.35
Hawaiian Paradise Park, HI (cdp) Hawaii County	906	7.94
Ewa Villages, HI (cdp) Honolulu County	473	7.74
Hawaiian Beaches, HI (cdp) Hawaii County	328	7.66
Honokaa, HI (cdp) Hawaii County	173	7.66
Wahiawa, HI (cdp) Honolulu County	1,358	7.62
Pepeekeo, HI (cdp) Hawaii County	135	7.55
Pahala, HI (cdp) Hawaii County	102	7.52
Makakilo, HI (cdp) Honolulu County	1,361	7.46
Makawao, HI (cdp) Maui County	520	7.24
Ewa Beach, HI (cdp) Honolulu County	1,077	7.20
Orchidlands Estates, HI (cdp) Hawaii County	197	7.00
Waipio Acres, HI (cdp) Honolulu County	364	6.95
Laupahoehoe, HI (cdp) Hawaii County	40	6.88
Ewa Gentry, HI (cdp) Honolulu County	1,537	6.77
Papaikou, HI (cdp) Hawaii County	88	6.70
Waimanalo, HI (cdp) Honolulu County	364	6.68
Point Baker, AK (cdp) Prince of Wales-Hyder Census Area	1	6.67
Nanawale Estates, HI (cdp) Hawaii County	93	6.52
Honomu, HI (cdp) Hawaii County	33	6.48
Kapolei, HI (cdp) Honolulu County	973	6.41
Lanai City, HI (cdp) Maui County	198	6.38
Nanakuli, HI (cdp) Honolulu County	789	6.23
Svea, MN (township) Kittson County	3	6.12
Kekaha, HI (cdp) Kauai County	216	6.11
Kahaluu, HI (cdp) Honolulu County	285	6.02
Hilo, HI (cdp) Hawaii County	2,597	6.00
Waialua, HI (cdp) Honolulu County	228	5.91
Hana, HI (cdp) Maui County	73	5.91
Keaau, HI (cdp) Hawaii County	132	5.86
Ahuimanu, HI (cdp) Honolulu County	515	5.85
Waikapu, HI (cdp) Maui County	173	5.83
Hanamaulu, HI (cdp) Kauai County	223	5.81
Haleiwa, HI (cdp) Honolulu County	230	5.79
Pakala Village, HI (cdp) Kauai County	17	5.78
Lawai, HI (cdp) Kauai County	136	5.76
Haliimaile, HI (cdp) Maui County	55	5.71
Pekin, ND (city) Nelson County	4	5.71
Kurtistown, HI (cdp) Hawaii County	74	5.70
Pukalani, HI (cdp) Maui County	429	5.66
Whitmore Village, HI (cdp) Honolulu County	254	5.65
Eleele, HI (cdp) Kauai County	133	5.56
Mililani Town, HI (cdp) Honolulu County	1,534	5.55
Hawaiian Acres, HI (cdp) Hawaii County	149	5.52
Hanapepe, HI (cdp) Kauai County	145	5.50
Waipio, HI (cdp) Honolulu County	634	5.43
Omao, HI (cdp) Kauai County	70	5.38
Kaaawa, HI (cdp) Honolulu County	74	5.37
Koloa, HI (cdp) Kauai County	115	5.36
Waimea, HI (cdp) Kauai County	99	5.34
Wainaku, HI (cdp) Hawaii County	64	5.23
Barneston, NE (village) Gage County	6	5.17
Kukuihaele, HI (cdp) Hawaii County	17	5.06
Waihee-Waiehu, HI (cdp) Maui County	439	4.97
Kahului, HI (cdp) Maui County	1,306	4.96
Wailuku, HI (cdp) Maui County	756	4.94
Ualapu'e, HI (cdp) Maui County	21	4.94
Kahuku, HI (cdp) Honolulu County	127	4.86
Kapaa, HI (cdp) Kauai County	519	4.85
Iroquois Point, HI (cdp) Honolulu County	160	4.74

Place	Population	%
Fern Forest, HI (cdp) Hawaii County	44	4.73
Waimalu, HI (cdp) Honolulu County	643	4.68
West Loch Estate, HI (cdp) Honolulu County	256	4.67
Paia, HI (cdp) Maui County	123	4.61
Anahola, HI (cdp) Kauai County	102	4.59
Kaneohe, HI (cdp) Honolulu County	1,574	4.55
Lihue, HI (cdp) Kauai County	292	4.52
Ocean Pointe, HI (cdp) Honolulu County	364	4.35
Kalaheo, HI (cdp) Kauai County	200	4.35
Pearl City, HI (cdp) Honolulu County	2,011	4.22
Mililani Mauka, HI (cdp) Honolulu County	883	4.20
Waimea, HI (cdp) Hawaii County	383	4.16
Puhi, HI (cdp) Kauai County	121	4.16
Aiea, HI (cdp) Honolulu County	382	4.09
Royal Kunia, HI (cdp) Honolulu County	593	4.08
Hawaiian Ocean View, HI (cdp) Hawaii County	181	4.08
Halawa, HI (cdp) Honolulu County	571	4.07
Wailua Homesteads, HI (cdp) Kauai County	210	4.05
Kualapuu, HI (cdp) Maui County	82	4.05
Kalaoa, HI (cdp) Hawaii County	389	4.03
Martinez Lake, AZ (cdp) Yuma County	32	4.01
Big Creek, CA (cdp) Fresno County	7	4.00
C-Road, CA (cdp) Plumas County	6	4.00
Kailua, HI (cdp) Hawaii County	478	3.99
Volcano, HI (cdp) Hawaii County	102	3.96
Waikele, HI (cdp) Honolulu County	295	3.94
Naalehu, HI (cdp) Hawaii County	34	3.93
Haiku-Pauwela, HI (cdp) Maui County	315	3.88
Wailua, HI (cdp) Kauai County	87	3.86
Mojave Ranch Estates, AZ (cdp) Mohave County	2	3.85
Dripping Springs, AZ (cdp) Gila County	9	3.83
Waipahu, HI (cdp) Honolulu County	1,460	3.82
Niland, CA (cdp) Imperial County	38	3.78
Waimanalo Beach, HI (cdp) Honolulu County	169	3.77
Kaunakakai, HI (cdp) Maui County	129	3.77
Kaumakani, HI (cdp) Kauai County	28	3.74
Lasana, TX (cdp) Cameron County	3	3.57
Keokea, HI (cdp) Maui County	56	3.47
Hauula, HI (cdp) Honolulu County	141	3.40
Pahoa, HI (cdp) Hawaii County	32	3.39
Honalo, HI (cdp) Hawaii County	82	3.38
Discovery Harbour, HI (cdp) Hawaii County	32	3.37
Heeia, HI (cdp) Honolulu County	165	3.32
Lake Alice, MN (township) Hubbard County	3	3.23
Waikoloa Village, HI (cdp) Hawaii County	203	3.19
Davenport, CA (cdp) Santa Cruz County	13	3.19
Hard Rock, AZ (cdp) Navajo County	3	3.19
Kealakekua, HI (cdp) Hawaii County	64	3.17
Kula, HI (cdp) Maui County	193	2.99
Drytown, CA (cdp) Amador County	5	2.99
Poipu, HI (cdp) Kauai County	29	2.96
Waikane, HI (cdp) Honolulu County	23	2.96
Mokuleia, HI (cdp) Honolulu County	52	2.87
Bairoil, WY (town) Sweetwater County	3	2.83
Guadalupe, CA (city) Santa Barbara County	200	2.82
Waiohinu, HI (cdp) Hawaii County	6	2.82
Country Club, CA (cdp) San Joaquin County	263	2.80
Captain Cook, HI (cdp) Hawaii County	96	2.80
Rio en Medio, NM (cdp) Santa Fe County	4	2.80
Shaniko, OR (city) Wasco County	1	2.78
Tolstoy, SD (town) Potter County	1	2.78
Latah, WA (town) Spokane County	5	2.73
Honaunau-Napoopoo, HI (cdp) Hawaii County	68	2.65
Lincoln Village, CA (cdp) San Joaquin County	114	2.60
Launiupoko, HI (cdp) Maui County	15	2.55
Kailua, HI (cdp) Honolulu County	983	2.54
Echo, MN (city) Yellow Medicine County	7	2.52
Edmundson Acres, CA (cdp) Kern County	7	2.51
Olinda, HI (cdp) Maui County	27	2.49
Shumway, IL (village) Effingham County	5	2.48
Kihei, HI (cdp) Maui County	509	2.44
Fallon Station, NV (cdp) Churchill County	17	2.41
Wall Lane, AZ (cdp) Yuma County	10	2.41
Lahaina, HI (cdp) Maui County	280	2.39
Holualoa, HI (cdp) Hawaii County	203	2.38

Please refer to the Explanation of Data in the front of the book for more detailed information.

Race

Asian: Hispanic

Top 150 Places Sorted by Percent of Total Population

Based on places with total population of 7,500 or more

Place	Population	%
Maili, HI (cdp) Honolulu County	942	9.93
Makaha, HI (cdp) Honolulu County	787	9.51
Waianae, HI (cdp) Honolulu County	1,189	9.02
Hawaiian Paradise Park, HI (cdp) Hawaii County	906	7.94
Wahiawa, HI (cdp) Honolulu County	1,358	7.62
Makakilo, HI (cdp) Honolulu County	1,361	7.46
Ewa Beach, HI (cdp) Honolulu County	1,077	7.20
Ewa Gentry, HI (cdp) Honolulu County	1,537	6.77
Kapolei, HI (cdp) Honolulu County	973	6.41
Nanakuli, HI (cdp) Honolulu County	789	6.23
Hilo, HI (cdp) Hawaii County	2,597	6.00
Ahuimanu, HI (cdp) Honolulu County	515	5.85
Pukalani, HI (cdp) Maui County	429	5.66
Mililani Town, HI (cdp) Honolulu County	1,534	5.55
Waipio, HI (cdp) Honolulu County	634	5.43
Waihee-Waiehu, HI (cdp) Maui County	439	4.97
Kahului, HI (cdp) Maui County	1,306	4.96
Wailuku, HI (cdp) Maui County	756	4.94
Kapaa, HI (cdp) Kauai County	519	4.85
Waimalu, HI (cdp) Honolulu County	643	4.68
Kaneohe, HI (cdp) Honolulu County	1,574	4.55
Ocean Pointe, HI (cdp) Honolulu County	364	4.35
Pearl City, HI (cdp) Honolulu County	2,011	4.22
Mililani Mauka, HI (cdp) Honolulu County	883	4.20
Waimea, HI (cdp) Hawaii County	383	4.16
Aiea, HI (cdp) Honolulu County	382	4.09
Royal Kunia, HI (cdp) Honolulu County	593	4.08
Halawa, HI (cdp) Honolulu County	571	4.07
Kalaoa, HI (cdp) Hawaii County	389	4.03
Kailua, HI (cdp) Hawaii County	478	3.99
Haiku-Pauwela, HI (cdp) Maui County	315	3.88
Waipahu, HI (cdp) Honolulu County	1,460	3.82
Country Club, CA (cdp) San Joaquin County	263	2.80
Kailua, HI (cdp) Honolulu County	983	2.54
Kihei, HI (cdp) Maui County	509	2.44
Lahaina, HI (cdp) Maui County	280	2.39
Holualoa, HI (cdp) Hawaii County	203	2.38
Urban Honolulu, HI (cdp) Honolulu County	7,945	2.36
Stockton, CA (city) San Joaquin County	5,859	2.01
East Honolulu, HI (cdp) Honolulu County	911	1.83
Marina, CA (city) Monterey County	309	1.57
Chula Vista, CA (city) San Diego County	3,739	1.53
American Canyon, CA (city) Napa County	296	1.52
Gonzales, CA (city) Monterey County	120	1.47
Lathrop, CA (city) San Joaquin County	263	1.46
Salida, CA (cdp) Stanislaus County	201	1.46
South San Francisco, CA (city) San Mateo County	902	1.42
Suisun City, CA (city) Solano County	400	1.42
Vineyard, CA (cdp) Sacramento County	344	1.39
August, CA (cdp) San Joaquin County	114	1.36
Hercules, CA (city) Contra Costa County	325	1.35
Delano, CA (city) Kern County	698	1.32
Charter Oak, CA (cdp) Los Angeles County	123	1.32
Imperial Beach, CA (city) San Diego County	346	1.31
Salinas, CA (city) Monterey County	1,935	1.29
East Foothills, CA (cdp) Santa Clara County	107	1.29
Elk Grove, CA (city) Sacramento County	1,960	1.28
Tracy, CA (city) San Joaquin County	1,064	1.28
Pacifica, CA (city) San Mateo County	477	1.28
Imperial, CA (city) Imperial County	188	1.27
San Bruno, CA (city) San Mateo County	518	1.26
Daly City, CA (city) San Mateo County	1,252	1.24
La Presa, CA (cdp) San Diego County	421	1.23
Bonita, CA (cdp) San Diego County	153	1.22
Fairfield, CA (city) Solano County	1,258	1.19
Lemon Grove, CA (city) San Diego County	300	1.18
Vallejo, CA (city) Solano County	1,353	1.17
Oakley, CA (city) Contra Costa County	416	1.17
Manteca, CA (city) San Joaquin County	775	1.16
Brawley, CA (city) Imperial County	289	1.16
Pittsburg, CA (city) Contra Costa County	726	1.15
Parkway, CA (cdp) Sacramento County	169	1.15
Garden Acres, CA (cdp) San Joaquin County	122	1.15
Mountain House, CA (cdp) San Joaquin County	111	1.15
San Lorenzo, CA (cdp) Alameda County	264	1.13
Nipomo, CA (cdp) San Luis Obispo County	189	1.13
South San Gabriel, CA (cdp) Los Angeles County	90	1.12
West Covina, CA (city) Los Angeles County	1,179	1.11
Morgan Hill, CA (city) Santa Clara County	422	1.11
Chino Hills, CA (city) San Bernardino County	824	1.10
Prunedale, CA (cdp) Monterey County	193	1.10
Earlimart, CA (cdp) Tulare County	94	1.10
Florin, CA (cdp) Sacramento County	517	1.09
Alum Rock, CA (cdp) Santa Clara County	169	1.09
Antioch, CA (city) Contra Costa County	1,096	1.07
Santa Maria, CA (city) Santa Barbara County	1,064	1.07
Fairview, CA (cdp) Alameda County	107	1.07
National City, CA (city) San Diego County	623	1.06
Diamond Bar, CA (city) Los Angeles County	586	1.06
Newark, CA (city) Alameda County	452	1.06
Hayward, CA (city) Alameda County	1,507	1.05
Rodeo, CA (cdp) Contra Costa County	91	1.05
Monterey Park, CA (city) Los Angeles County	624	1.04
Gilroy, CA (city) Santa Clara County	501	1.03
Lomita, CA (city) Los Angeles County	209	1.03
Kaneohe Station, HI (cdp) Honolulu County	98	1.03
Calipatria, CA (city) Imperial County	79	1.03
Carson, CA (city) Los Angeles County	933	1.02
Union City, CA (city) Alameda County	707	1.02
Covina, CA (city) Los Angeles County	488	1.02
West Carson, CA (cdp) Los Angeles County	221	1.02
Los Banos, CA (city) Merced County	362	1.01
Port Hueneme, CA (city) Ventura County	217	1.00
Schofield Barracks, HI (cdp) Honolulu County	164	1.00
Orcutt, CA (cdp) Santa Barbara County	287	0.99
Pinole, CA (city) Contra Costa County	182	0.99
Alondra Park, CA (cdp) Los Angeles County	85	0.99
Sacramento, CA (city) Sacramento County	4,564	0.98
Alhambra, CA (city) Los Angeles County	816	0.98
Lakewood, CA (city) Los Angeles County	784	0.98
Gardena, CA (city) Los Angeles County	579	0.98
Eastvale, CA (cdp) Riverside County	525	0.98
Walnut, CA (city) Los Angeles County	282	0.97
El Sobrante, CA (cdp) Riverside County	122	0.96
Hollister, CA (city) San Benito County	332	0.95
Torrance, CA (city) Los Angeles County	1,363	0.94
Cerritos, CA (city) Los Angeles County	462	0.94
Murrieta, CA (city) Riverside County	959	0.93
San Leandro, CA (city) Alameda County	790	0.93
Alameda, CA (city) Alameda County	688	0.93
Brentwood, CA (city) Contra Costa County	479	0.93
West Sacramento, CA (city) Yolo County	454	0.93
San Dimas, CA (city) Los Angeles County	310	0.93
South Pasadena, CA (city) Los Angeles County	239	0.93
Lemoore, CA (city) Kings County	227	0.93
Cherryland, CA (cdp) Alameda County	137	0.93
Azusa, CA (city) Los Angeles County	425	0.92
Rosemont, CA (cdp) Sacramento County	208	0.92
Seaside, CA (city) Monterey County	299	0.91
Galt, CA (city) Sacramento County	215	0.91
El Centro, CA (city) Imperial County	379	0.89
Benicia, CA (city) Solano County	240	0.89
Whittier, CA (city) Los Angeles County	749	0.88
Hacienda Heights, CA (cdp) Los Angeles County	477	0.88
French Valley, CA (cdp) Riverside County	200	0.87
East San Gabriel, CA (cdp) Los Angeles County	129	0.87
Vacaville, CA (city) Solano County	795	0.86
Lawndale, CA (city) Los Angeles County	283	0.86
San Jose, CA (city) Santa Clara County	8,020	0.85
Modesto, CA (city) Stanislaus County	1,717	0.85
Temecula, CA (city) Riverside County	847	0.85
Lompoc, CA (city) Santa Barbara County	359	0.85
Valinda, CA (cdp) Los Angeles County	195	0.85
Duarte, CA (city) Los Angeles County	182	0.85
Santa Fe Springs, CA (city) Los Angeles County	138	0.85
El Sobrante, CA (cdp) Contra Costa County	108	0.85
Fort Irwin, CA (cdp) San Bernardino County	75	0.85
Castro Valley, CA (cdp) Alameda County	513	0.84
Camp Pendleton South, CA (cdp) San Diego County	89	0.84
Chino, CA (city) San Bernardino County	647	0.83

Please refer to the Explanation of Data in the front of the book for more detailed information.

Race

Asian: Bangladeshi

U.S. and 50 States Sorted by Population and Percent of Total Population

Place	Population	%
United States	**147,300**	**0.05**
New York	67,063	0.35
California	10,494	0.03
Texas	8,930	0.04
Michigan	8,730	0.09
New Jersey	8,680	0.10
Virginia	6,552	0.08
Florida	6,115	0.03
Pennsylvania	4,262	0.03
Georgia	3,966	0.04
Maryland	3,585	0.06
Massachusetts	2,387	0.04
Connecticut	2,287	0.06
Illinois	2,088	0.02
Arizona	1,161	0.02
Ohio	1,052	0.01
North Carolina	945	0.01
Minnesota	858	0.02
Washington	666	0.01
Oklahoma	630	0.02
Indiana	539	0.01
Kansas	531	0.02
Missouri	530	0.01
Tennessee	521	0.01
Nevada	482	0.02
Louisiana	403	0.01
Alabama	395	0.01
Delaware	383	0.04
Oregon	378	0.01
Colorado	308	0.01
Wisconsin	283	<0.01
District of Columbia	266	0.04
South Carolina	234	0.01
Arkansas	210	0.01
Kentucky	196	<0.01
Iowa	163	0.01
New Hampshire	137	0.01
Mississippi	126	<0.01
Rhode Island	83	0.01
New Mexico	83	<0.01
West Virginia	82	<0.01
Hawaii	74	0.01
Nebraska	70	<0.01
Utah	68	<0.01
North Dakota	67	0.01
Vermont	47	0.01
Maine	45	<0.01
South Dakota	41	0.01
Alaska	39	0.01
Idaho	39	<0.01
Wyoming	15	<0.01
Montana	11	<0.01

Place	Population	%
New York	67,063	0.35
New Jersey	8,680	0.10
Michigan	8,730	0.09
Virginia	6,552	0.08
Maryland	3,585	0.06
Connecticut	2,287	0.06
United States	**147,300**	**0.05**
Texas	8,930	0.04
Georgia	3,966	0.04
Massachusetts	2,387	0.04
Delaware	383	0.04
District of Columbia	266	0.04
California	10,494	0.03
Florida	6,115	0.03
Pennsylvania	4,262	0.03
Illinois	2,088	0.02
Arizona	1,161	0.02
Minnesota	858	0.02
Oklahoma	630	0.02
Kansas	531	0.02
Nevada	482	0.02
Ohio	1,052	0.01
North Carolina	945	0.01
Washington	666	0.01
Indiana	539	0.01
Missouri	530	0.01
Tennessee	521	0.01
Louisiana	403	0.01
Alabama	395	0.01
Oregon	378	0.01
Colorado	308	0.01
South Carolina	234	0.01
Arkansas	210	0.01
Iowa	163	0.01
New Hampshire	137	0.01
Rhode Island	83	0.01
Hawaii	74	0.01
North Dakota	67	0.01
Vermont	47	0.01
South Dakota	41	0.01
Alaska	39	0.01
Wisconsin	283	<0.01
Kentucky	196	<0.01
Mississippi	126	<0.01
New Mexico	83	<0.01
West Virginia	82	<0.01
Nebraska	70	<0.01
Utah	68	<0.01
Maine	45	<0.01
Idaho	39	<0.01
Wyoming	15	<0.01
Montana	11	<0.01

Please refer to the Explanation of Data in the front of the book for more detailed information.

Race

Asian: Bangladeshi

Top 150 Places Sorted by Population

Based on all places, regardless of total population

Place	Population	%
New York, NY (city) Kings County	61,788	0.76
Queens, NY (borough) Queens County	38,341	1.72
Brooklyn, NY (borough) Kings County	12,408	0.50
Bronx, NY (borough) Bronx County	8,623	0.62
Los Angeles, CA (city) Los Angeles County	3,483	0.09
Hamtramck, MI (city) Wayne County	3,083	13.75
Detroit, MI (city) Wayne County	2,825	0.40
Paterson, NJ (city) Passaic County	2,119	1.45
Manhattan, NY (borough) New York County	2,029	0.13
Warren, MI (city) Macomb County	1,061	0.79
Atlantic City, NJ (city) Atlantic County	1,042	2.63
Philadelphia, PA (city) Philadelphia County	978	0.06
Houston, TX (city) Harris County	847	0.04
Arlington, VA (cdp) Arlington County	802	0.39
Chicago, IL (city) Cook County	679	0.03
Brookhaven, NY (town) Suffolk County	621	0.13
Upper Darby, PA (township) Delaware County	605	0.73
Irving, TX (city) Dallas County	605	0.28
Plano, TX (city) Collin County	604	0.23
Hempstead, NY (town) Nassau County	582	0.08
San Jose, CA (city) Santa Clara County	576	0.06
Lansdale, PA (borough) Montgomery County	564	3.47
Austin, TX (city) Travis County	521	0.07
Cambridge, MA (city) Middlesex County	455	0.43
North Hempstead, NY (town) Nassau County	441	0.19
Allen, TX (city) Collin County	395	0.47
Staten Island, NY (borough) Richmond County	387	0.08
Dallas, TX (city) Dallas County	373	0.03
Columbus, OH (city) Franklin County	366	0.05
Oyster Bay, NY (town) Nassau County	365	0.12
Islip, NY (town) Suffolk County	356	0.11
Alexandria, VA (ind. city) Alexandria independent city	351	0.25
Arlington, TX (city) Tarrant County	351	0.10
Boston, MA (city) Suffolk County	343	0.06
Babylon, NY (town) Suffolk County	341	0.16
Jersey City, NJ (city) Hudson County	332	0.13
Phoenix, AZ (city) Maricopa County	322	0.02
Richardson, TX (city) Dallas County	309	0.31
Manchester, CT (town) Hartford County	305	0.52
Fort Worth, TX (city) Tarrant County	302	0.04
Reno, NV (city) Washoe County	290	0.13
Silver Spring, MD (cdp) Montgomery County	273	0.38
Hudson, NY (city) Columbia County	271	4.04
Washington, DC (city) District of Columbia	266	0.04
Egg Harbor, NJ (township) Atlantic County	254	0.59
San Diego, CA (city) San Diego County	254	0.02
Stamford, CT (city/town) Fairfield County	249	0.20
Oklahoma City, OK (city) Oklahoma County	247	0.04
Springfield, VA (cdp) Fairfax County	240	0.79
Anaheim, CA (city) Orange County	240	0.07
Wichita, KS (city) Sedgwick County	236	0.06
Troy, MI (city) Oakland County	232	0.29
Fremont, CA (city) Alameda County	231	0.11
Deer Park, NY (cdp) Suffolk County	224	0.81
Sterling Heights, MI (city) Macomb County	223	0.17
Hatfield, PA (borough) Montgomery County	219	6.66
North Atlanta, GA (cdp) DeKalb County	214	0.53
Chandler, AZ (city) Maricopa County	210	0.09
Germantown, MD (cdp) Montgomery County	209	0.24
Buffalo, NY (city) Erie County	206	0.08
Doraville, GA (city) DeKalb County	202	2.42
Manchester, CT (cdp) Hartford County	194	0.63
Hatfield, PA (township) Montgomery County	192	1.11
Gilbert, AZ (town) Maricopa County	188	0.09
Glendale, CA (city) Los Angeles County	182	0.09
Ventnor City, NJ (city) Atlantic County	180	1.69
Long Beach, CA (city) Los Angeles County	180	0.04
Santa Clara, CA (city) Santa Clara County	177	0.15
Raleigh, NC (city) Wake County	177	0.04
Lincolnia, VA (cdp) Fairfax County	176	0.77
Clifton, NJ (city) Passaic County	173	0.21
San Antonio, TX (city) Medina County	172	0.01
Millbourne, PA (borough) Delaware County	171	14.75
Marumsco, VA (cdp) Prince William County	171	0.49
Albany, NY (city) Albany County	171	0.17
Yonkers, NY (city) Westchester County	167	0.09
Hicksville, NY (cdp) Nassau County	165	0.40
Bridgeport, CT (city/town) Fairfield County	163	0.11
Edison, NJ (township) Middlesex County	162	0.16
Nashville-Davidson, TN (metro govt) Davidson County	159	0.03
Kissimmee, FL (city) Osceola County	155	0.26
Rockville, MD (city) Montgomery County	154	0.25
Haledon, NJ (borough) Passaic County	149	1.79
Woodbridge, NJ (township) Middlesex County	146	0.15
Rancho Cucamonga, CA (city) San Bernardino County	144	0.09
Atlanta, GA (city) Fulton County	142	0.03
Ashburn, VA (cdp) Loudoun County	141	0.32
Garland, TX (city) Dallas County	138	0.06
McKinney, TX (city) Collin County	137	0.10
Irvine, CA (city) Orange County	136	0.06
Piscataway, NJ (township) Middlesex County	135	0.24
Bethany, OR (cdp) Washington County	132	0.64
Danbury, CT (city/town) Fairfield County	132	0.16
Gaithersburg, MD (city) Montgomery County	131	0.22
Centreville, VA (cdp) Fairfax County	129	0.18
Herndon, VA (town) Fairfax County	128	0.55
Columbia, MD (cdp) Howard County	128	0.13
Carrollton, TX (city) Denton County	128	0.11
Indianapolis, IN (city) Marion County	128	0.02
Chamblee, GA (city) DeKalb County	127	1.28
Ellicott City, MD (cdp) Howard County	127	0.19
Canton, MI (charter township) Wayne County	125	0.14
Woodlawn, MD (cdp) Baltimore County	124	0.33
Norwalk, CT (city/town) Fairfield County	124	0.14
Cary, NC (town) Wake County	124	0.09
Elizabeth, NJ (city) Union County	123	0.10
Gloucester, NJ (township) Camden County	122	0.19
Dale City, VA (cdp) Prince William County	121	0.18
Baltimore, MD (city) Baltimore city County	121	0.02
Lynn, MA (city) Essex County	120	0.13
Huntington, NY (town) Suffolk County	120	0.06
South Brunswick, NJ (township) Middlesex County	116	0.27
Moreno Valley, CA (city) Riverside County	115	0.06
Greenacres, FL (city) Palm Beach County	114	0.30
Frisco, TX (city) Collin County	114	0.10
San Bernardino, CA (city) San Bernardino County	114	0.05
Montgomery Village, MD (cdp) Montgomery County	113	0.35
Newark, NJ (city) Essex County	113	0.04
San Francisco, CA (city) San Francisco County	113	0.01
Davie, FL (town) Broward County	112	0.12
Woodlawn, VA (cdp) Fairfax County	109	0.52
Lake Ridge, VA (cdp) Prince William County	109	0.27
Somerville, MA (city) Middlesex County	109	0.14
Boynton Beach, FL (city) Palm Beach County	107	0.16
Gainesville, FL (city) Alachua County	107	0.09
St. Petersburg, FL (city) Pinellas County	105	0.04
Bailey's Crossroads, VA (cdp) Fairfax County	103	0.44
Ann Arbor, MI (city) Washtenaw County	102	0.09
North Bethesda, MD (cdp) Montgomery County	101	0.23
North Miami Beach, FL (city) Miami-Dade County	100	0.24
Folsom, CA (city) Sacramento County	99	0.14
Sugar Land, TX (city) Fort Bend County	99	0.13
Hollywood, FL (city) Broward County	99	0.07
Skokie, IL (village) Cook County	98	0.15
Burke, VA (cdp) Fairfax County	97	0.24
Tampa, FL (city) Hillsborough County	97	0.03
South Riding, VA (cdp) Loudoun County	96	0.40
Sterling, VA (cdp) Loudoun County	96	0.35
Durham, NC (city) Durham County	96	0.04
Tulsa, OK (city) Tulsa County	96	0.02
Madison Heights, MI (city) Oakland County	95	0.32
Fort Lauderdale, FL (city) Broward County	95	0.06
Aurora, IL (city) Kane County	95	0.05
Loma Linda, CA (city) San Bernardino County	93	0.40
Lilburn, GA (city) Gwinnett County	90	0.78
Linton Hall, VA (cdp) Prince William County	88	0.25
Poughkeepsie, NY (town) Dutchess County	88	0.20
Pembroke Pines, FL (city) Broward County	88	0.06
Florence, NJ (township) Burlington County	87	0.72
Jericho, NY (cdp) Nassau County	87	0.64

SECTION THREE

Please refer to the Explanation of Data in the front of the book for more detailed information.

Race

Asian: Bangladeshi

Top 150 Places Sorted by Percent of Total Population

Based on all places, regardless of total population

Place	Population	%
Millbourne, PA (borough) Delaware County	171	14.75
Hamtramck, MI (city) Wayne County	3,083	13.75
Hatfield, PA (borough) Montgomery County	219	6.66
Hudson, NY (city) Columbia County	271	4.04
Lansdale, PA (borough) Montgomery County	564	3.47
East Rocky Hill, NJ (cdp) Somerset County	16	3.41
Atlantic City, NJ (city) Atlantic County	1,042	2.63
Doraville, GA (city) DeKalb County	202	2.42
Oak Grove, VA (cdp) Loudoun County	41	2.31
Bellerose Terrace, NY (cdp) Nassau County	44	2.00
Roebling, NJ (cdp) Burlington County	73	1.97
Haledon, NJ (borough) Passaic County	149	1.79
Queens, NY (borough) Queens County	38,341	1.72
Barton Hills, MI (village) Washtenaw County	5	1.70
Ventnor City, NJ (city) Atlantic County	180	1.69
Harriman, NY (village) Orange County	40	1.65
Clintondale, NY (cdp) Ulster County	22	1.52
Paterson, NJ (city) Passaic County	2,119	1.45
Kenwood Estates, FL (cdp) Palm Beach County	18	1.40
Douglassville, PA (cdp) Berks County	6	1.34
East Lansdowne, PA (borough) Delaware County	35	1.31
Chamblee, GA (city) DeKalb County	127	1.28
Albion, CA (cdp) Mendocino County	2	1.19
Hatfield, PA (township) Montgomery County	192	1.11
Prospect Park, NJ (borough) Passaic County	64	1.09
Laurel Hill, VA (cdp) Fairfax County	74	1.08
Berlin, NJ (township) Camden County	56	1.05
Manhasset Hills, NY (cdp) Nassau County	33	0.92
Pomona, NJ (cdp) Atlantic County	63	0.88
Newport, DE (town) New Castle County	9	0.85
Bordentown, NJ (city) Burlington County	32	0.82
Greenvale, NY (cdp) Nassau County	9	0.82
Deer Park, NY (cdp) Suffolk County	224	0.81
Norcross, GA (city) Gwinnett County	74	0.81
Absecon, NJ (city) Atlantic County	68	0.81
Herricks, NY (cdp) Nassau County	35	0.81
Warren, MI (city) Macomb County	1,061	0.79
Springfield, VA (cdp) Fairfax County	240	0.79
Lime Ridge, PA (cdp) Columbia County	7	0.79
Lilburn, GA (city) Gwinnett County	90	0.78
Lincolnia, VA (cdp) Fairfax County	176	0.77
Loudoun Valley Estates, VA (cdp) Loudoun County	28	0.77
New York, NY (city) Kings County	61,788	0.76
Claymont, DE (cdp) New Castle County	63	0.76
Upper Darby, PA (township) Delaware County	605	0.73
Sugarland Run, VA (cdp) Loudoun County	86	0.73
Stony Brook University, NY (cdp) Suffolk County	67	0.73
Florence, NJ (township) Burlington County	87	0.72
Blawenburg, NJ (cdp) Somerset County	2	0.71
Garden City Park, NY (cdp) Nassau County	55	0.70
Garrison, TX (city) Nacogdoches County	6	0.67
Totowa, NJ (borough) Passaic County	70	0.65
Muir Beach, CA (cdp) Marin County	2	0.65
Bethany, OR (cdp) Washington County	132	0.64
Jericho, NY (cdp) Nassau County	87	0.64
Carle Place, NY (cdp) Nassau County	32	0.64
Manchester, CT (cdp) Hartford County	194	0.63
Southport, CT (cdp) Fairfield County	10	0.63
Clermont, IA (city) Fayette County	4	0.63
Bronx, NY (borough) Bronx County	8,623	0.62
Brooklawn, NJ (borough) Camden County	12	0.61
Cuyler, NY (town) Cortland County	6	0.61
Egg Harbor, NJ (township) Atlantic County	254	0.59
Dayton, NJ (cdp) Middlesex County	42	0.59
Berwyn Heights, MD (town) Prince George's County	18	0.58
Woodbridge, VA (cdp) Prince William County	23	0.57
Hillside, NY (cdp) Ulster County	5	0.57
Dunkirk, MD (cdp) Calvert County	14	0.56
Herndon, VA (town) Fairfax County	128	0.55
Rose Valley, PA (borough) Delaware County	5	0.55
Northfield, NJ (city) Atlantic County	47	0.54
North Atlanta, GA (cdp) DeKalb County	214	0.53
North New Hyde Park, NY (cdp) Nassau County	79	0.53
Westgate, FL (cdp) Palm Beach County	42	0.53
Peninsula, OH (village) Summit County	3	0.53
Manchester, CT (town) Hartford County	305	0.52
Woodlawn, VA (cdp) Fairfax County	109	0.52
Neabsco, VA (cdp) Prince William County	61	0.51
Center Line, MI (city) Macomb County	42	0.51
Wappingers Falls, NY (village) Dutchess County	28	0.51
Breinigsville, PA (cdp) Lehigh County	21	0.51
Brooklyn, NY (borough) Kings County	12,408	0.50
Woodburn, VA (cdp) Fairfax County	42	0.50
Banks Springs, LA (cdp) Caldwell Parish	6	0.50
Hewlett Bay Park, NY (village) Nassau County	2	0.50
Marumsco, VA (cdp) Prince William County	171	0.49
Hybla Valley, VA (cdp) Fairfax County	78	0.49
Floris, VA (cdp) Fairfax County	41	0.49
Manorhaven, NY (village) Nassau County	32	0.49
Spackenkill, NY (cdp) Dutchess County	20	0.49
Morton, PA (borough) Delaware County	13	0.49
Merritt Park, NY (cdp) Dutchess County	6	0.48
Allen, TX (city) Collin County	395	0.47
Lorton, VA (cdp) Fairfax County	87	0.47
Arlington, NY (cdp) Dutchess County	19	0.47
Forest Glen, MD (cdp) Montgomery County	30	0.46
Franconia, VA (cdp) Fairfax County	82	0.45
Concorde Hills, OH (cdp) Hamilton County	3	0.45
Bailey's Crossroads, VA (cdp) Fairfax County	103	0.44
Cherry Hill, VA (cdp) Prince William County	70	0.44
Kingstowne, VA (cdp) Fairfax County	69	0.44
Glenmont, MD (cdp) Montgomery County	59	0.44
Dumbarton, VA (cdp) Henrico County	35	0.44
Marshfield, WI (city) Marathon County	4	0.44
Cambridge, MA (city) Middlesex County	455	0.43
Iowa Colony, TX (village) Brazoria County	5	0.43
Ronkonkoma, NY (cdp) Suffolk County	81	0.42
Palm Springs, FL (village) Palm Beach County	79	0.42
Baywood, NY (cdp) Suffolk County	31	0.42
Clarksburg, MD (cdp) Montgomery County	56	0.41
Innsbrook, VA (cdp) Henrico County	32	0.41
Bel Aire, KS (city) Sedgwick County	28	0.41
Detroit, MI (city) Wayne County	2,825	0.40
Hicksville, NY (cdp) Nassau County	165	0.40
South Riding, VA (cdp) Loudoun County	96	0.40
Loma Linda, CA (city) San Bernardino County	93	0.40
Bull Run, VA (cdp) Prince William County	60	0.40
Four Corners, TX (cdp) Fort Bend County	49	0.40
County Center, VA (cdp) Prince William County	13	0.40
Arlington, VA (cdp) Arlington County	802	0.39
Iselin, NJ (cdp) Middlesex County	72	0.39
Searingtown, NY (cdp) Nassau County	19	0.39
Ellenville, NY (village) Ulster County	16	0.39
Society Hill, NJ (cdp) Middlesex County	15	0.39
Silver Spring, MD (cdp) Montgomery County	273	0.38
Lowes Island, VA (cdp) Loudoun County	41	0.38
Burtonsville, MD (cdp) Montgomery County	32	0.38
Round Lake Heights, IL (village) Lake County	10	0.37
Walton Park, NY (cdp) Orange County	10	0.37
Roscoe, NY (cdp) Sullivan County	2	0.37
Lake Belvedere Estates, FL (cdp) Palm Beach County	12	0.36
Vails Gate, NY (cdp) Orange County	12	0.36
South Centre, PA (township) Columbia County	7	0.36
Walnut Creek, NC (village) Wayne County	3	0.36
Montgomery Village, MD (cdp) Montgomery County	113	0.35
Sterling, VA (cdp) Loudoun County	96	0.35
Lake Ronkonkoma, NY (cdp) Suffolk County	71	0.35
Belmont, VA (cdp) Loudoun County	21	0.35
Forest Home, NY (cdp) Tompkins County	2	0.35
Higbee, MO (city) Randolph County	2	0.35
Madison Park, NJ (cdp) Middlesex County	24	0.34
Jellico, TN (city) Campbell County	8	0.34
Laflin, PA (borough) Luzerne County	5	0.34
Washington Mills, NY (cdp) Oneida County	4	0.34
Pigeon Creek, OH (cdp) Summit County	3	0.34
Woodlawn, MD (cdp) Baltimore County	124	0.33
Chantilly, VA (cdp) Fairfax County	75	0.33
Calverton, MD (cdp) Montgomery County	58	0.33
Woodbury, NY (town) Orange County	37	0.33
Clifton Heights, PA (borough) Delaware County	22	0.33

Please refer to the Explanation of Data in the front of the book for more detailed information.

Race

Asian: Bangladeshi

Top 150 Places Sorted by Percent of Total Population

Based on places with total population of 7,500 or more

Place	Population	%
Hamtramck, MI (city) Wayne County	3,083	13.75
Lansdale, PA (borough) Montgomery County	564	3.47
Atlantic City, NJ (city) Atlantic County	1,042	2.63
Doraville, GA (city) DeKalb County	202	2.42
Haledon, NJ (borough) Passaic County	149	1.79
Queens, NY (borough) Queens County	38,341	1.72
Ventnor City, NJ (city) Atlantic County	180	1.69
Paterson, NJ (city) Passaic County	2,119	1.45
Chamblee, GA (city) DeKalb County	127	1.28
Hatfield, PA (township) Montgomery County	192	1.11
Deer Park, NY (cdp) Suffolk County	224	0.81
Norcross, GA (city) Gwinnett County	74	0.81
Absecon, NJ (city) Atlantic County	68	0.81
Warren, MI (city) Macomb County	1,061	0.79
Springfield, VA (cdp) Fairfax County	240	0.79
Lilburn, GA (city) Gwinnett County	90	0.78
Lincolnia, VA (cdp) Fairfax County	176	0.77
New York, NY (city) Kings County	61,788	0.76
Claymont, DE (cdp) New Castle County	63	0.76
Upper Darby, PA (township) Delaware County	605	0.73
Sugarland Run, VA (cdp) Loudoun County	86	0.73
Stony Brook University, NY (cdp) Suffolk County	67	0.73
Florence, NJ (township) Burlington County	87	0.72
Garden City Park, NY (cdp) Nassau County	55	0.70
Totowa, NJ (borough) Passaic County	70	0.65
Bethany, OR (cdp) Washington County	132	0.64
Jericho, NY (cdp) Nassau County	87	0.64
Manchester, CT (cdp) Hartford County	194	0.63
Bronx, NY (borough) Bronx County	8,623	0.62
Egg Harbor, NJ (township) Atlantic County	254	0.59
Herndon, VA (town) Fairfax County	128	0.55
Northfield, NJ (city) Atlantic County	47	0.54
North Atlanta, GA (cdp) DeKalb County	214	0.53
North New Hyde Park, NY (cdp) Nassau County	79	0.53
Westgate, FL (cdp) Palm Beach County	42	0.53
Manchester, CT (town) Hartford County	305	0.52
Woodlawn, VA (cdp) Fairfax County	109	0.52
Neabsco, VA (cdp) Prince William County	61	0.51
Center Line, MI (city) Macomb County	42	0.51
Brooklyn, NY (borough) Kings County	12,408	0.50
Woodburn, VA (cdp) Fairfax County	42	0.50
Marumsco, VA (cdp) Prince William County	171	0.49
Hybla Valley, VA (cdp) Fairfax County	78	0.49
Floris, VA (cdp) Fairfax County	41	0.49
Allen, TX (city) Collin County	395	0.47
Lorton, VA (cdp) Fairfax County	87	0.47
Franconia, VA (cdp) Fairfax County	82	0.45
Bailey's Crossroads, VA (cdp) Fairfax County	103	0.44
Cherry Hill, VA (cdp) Prince William County	70	0.44
Kingstowne, VA (cdp) Fairfax County	69	0.44
Glenmont, MD (cdp) Montgomery County	59	0.44
Dumbarton, VA (cdp) Henrico County	35	0.44
Cambridge, MA (city) Middlesex County	455	0.43
Ronkonkoma, NY (cdp) Suffolk County	81	0.42
Palm Springs, FL (village) Palm Beach County	79	0.42
Clarksburg, MD (cdp) Montgomery County	56	0.41
Innsbrook, VA (cdp) Henrico County	32	0.41
Detroit, MI (city) Wayne County	2,825	0.40
Hicksville, NY (cdp) Nassau County	165	0.40
South Riding, VA (cdp) Loudoun County	96	0.40
Loma Linda, CA (city) San Bernardino County	93	0.40
Bull Run, VA (cdp) Prince William County	60	0.40
Four Corners, TX (cdp) Fort Bend County	49	0.40
Arlington, VA (cdp) Arlington County	802	0.39
Iselin, NJ (cdp) Middlesex County	72	0.39
Silver Spring, MD (cdp) Montgomery County	273	0.38
Lowes Island, VA (cdp) Loudoun County	41	0.38
Burtonsville, MD (cdp) Montgomery County	32	0.38
Montgomery Village, MD (cdp) Montgomery County	113	0.35
Sterling, VA (cdp) Loudoun County	96	0.35
Lake Ronkonkoma, NY (cdp) Suffolk County	71	0.35
Woodlawn, MD (cdp) Baltimore County	124	0.33
Chantilly, VA (cdp) Fairfax County	75	0.33
Calverton, MD (cdp) Montgomery County	58	0.33
Woodbury, NY (town) Orange County	37	0.33
Ashburn, VA (cdp) Loudoun County	141	0.32
Madison Heights, MI (city) Oakland County	95	0.32
North Potomac, MD (cdp) Montgomery County	79	0.32
Southchase, FL (cdp) Orange County	51	0.32
Richardson, TX (city) Dallas County	309	0.31
Brushy Creek, TX (cdp) Williamson County	67	0.31
Murphy, TX (city) Collin County	55	0.31
Greenacres, FL (city) Palm Beach County	114	0.30
Tucker, GA (cdp) DeKalb County	83	0.30
Countryside, VA (cdp) Loudoun County	30	0.30
Troy, MI (city) Oakland County	232	0.29
North Bay Shore, NY (cdp) Suffolk County	54	0.29
McNair, VA (cdp) Fairfax County	51	0.29
Cloverly, MD (cdp) Montgomery County	44	0.29
Salisbury, NY (cdp) Nassau County	35	0.29
Irving, TX (city) Dallas County	605	0.28
Bay Shore, NY (cdp) Suffolk County	74	0.28
Dix Hills, NY (cdp) Suffolk County	74	0.28
Farmingville, NY (cdp) Suffolk County	43	0.28
Princeton Meadows, NJ (cdp) Middlesex County	39	0.28
Brigantine, NJ (city) Atlantic County	26	0.28
Seven Corners, VA (cdp) Fairfax County	26	0.28
Kulpsville, PA (cdp) Montgomery County	23	0.28
South Brunswick, NJ (township) Middlesex County	116	0.27
Lake Ridge, VA (cdp) Prince William County	109	0.27
Fairland, MD (cdp) Montgomery County	63	0.27
Colesville, MD (cdp) Montgomery County	39	0.27
Lincolnwood, IL (village) Cook County	34	0.27
Dranesville, VA (cdp) Fairfax County	32	0.27
Lansdowne, VA (cdp) Loudoun County	30	0.27
Oronoko, MI (charter township) Berrien County	25	0.27
Greenbriar, VA (cdp) Fairfax County	22	0.27
Kissimmee, FL (city) Osceola County	155	0.26
Centereach, NY (cdp) Suffolk County	82	0.26
Plainsboro, NJ (township) Middlesex County	60	0.26
Redland, MD (cdp) Montgomery County	45	0.26
Beltsville, MD (cdp) Prince George's County	44	0.26
Newington Forest, VA (cdp) Fairfax County	32	0.26
Burlington, NJ (city) Burlington County	26	0.26
Port Jefferson Station, NY (cdp) Suffolk County	20	0.26
Alexandria, VA (ind. city) Alexandria independent city	351	0.25
Rockville, MD (city) Montgomery County	154	0.25
Linton Hall, VA (cdp) Prince William County	88	0.25
North Druid Hills, GA (cdp) DeKalb County	48	0.25
Mount Vernon, VA (cdp) Fairfax County	31	0.25
Purdue University, IN (cdp) Tippecanoe County	31	0.25
Travilah, MD (cdp) Montgomery County	30	0.25
Lake Grove, NY (village) Suffolk County	28	0.25
Lloyd, NY (town) Ulster County	27	0.25
Pine Castle, FL (cdp) Orange County	27	0.25
Germantown, MD (cdp) Montgomery County	209	0.24
Piscataway, NJ (township) Middlesex County	135	0.24
North Miami Beach, FL (city) Miami-Dade County	100	0.24
Burke, VA (cdp) Fairfax County	97	0.24
Cromwell, CT (town) Middlesex County	34	0.24
Cascades, VA (cdp) Loudoun County	28	0.24
Scottdale, GA (cdp) DeKalb County	25	0.24
Urbana, MD (cdp) Frederick County	22	0.24
Lake Stickney, WA (cdp) Snohomish County	19	0.24
Plano, TX (city) Collin County	604	0.23
North Bethesda, MD (cdp) Montgomery County	101	0.23
Wappinger, NY (town) Dutchess County	63	0.23
Upper Macungie, PA (township) Lehigh County	47	0.23
Elmwood Park, NJ (borough) Bergen County	44	0.23
Idylwood, VA (cdp) Fairfax County	40	0.23
Newington, VA (cdp) Fairfax County	30	0.23
New Hyde Park, NY (village) Nassau County	22	0.23
Yorkshire, VA (cdp) Prince William County	17	0.23
Gaithersburg, MD (city) Montgomery County	131	0.22
Galloway, NJ (township) Atlantic County	81	0.22
Lexington, MA (cdp/town) Middlesex County	70	0.22
DeLand, FL (city) Volusia County	60	0.22
Selden, NY (cdp) Suffolk County	44	0.22
Morrisville, NC (town) Wake County	41	0.22
Artesia, CA (city) Los Angeles County	36	0.22

Race

Asian: Bhutanese

U.S. and 50 States Sorted by Population and Percent of Total Population

Place	Population	%
United States	**19,439**	**0.01**
Texas	2,275	0.01
New York	1,824	0.01
Georgia	1,703	0.02
Arizona	1,210	0.02
Pennsylvania	1,198	0.01
Washington	977	0.01
Ohio	865	0.01
New Hampshire	764	0.06
California	750	<0.01
North Carolina	614	0.01
Colorado	592	0.01
Illinois	559	<0.01
Massachusetts	544	0.01
Virginia	514	0.01
Tennessee	498	0.01
Michigan	443	<0.01
Idaho	423	0.03
Utah	399	0.01
North Dakota	354	0.05
Kentucky	336	0.01
Missouri	309	0.01
Maryland	288	<0.01
Minnesota	284	0.01
Oregon	281	0.01
Vermont	276	0.04
Florida	232	<0.01
Nevada	165	0.01
Kansas	163	0.01
New Jersey	126	<0.01
South Dakota	107	0.01
Iowa	80	<0.01
Rhode Island	72	0.01
New Mexico	49	<0.01
Alaska	42	0.01
Nebraska	38	<0.01
Connecticut	30	<0.01
Hawaii	13	<0.01
Louisiana	12	<0.01
Wyoming	10	<0.01
South Carolina	5	<0.01
Montana	4	<0.01
District of Columbia	3	<0.01
Indiana	3	<0.01
Wisconsin	2	<0.01
Alabama	1	<0.01
Delaware	1	<0.01
Maine	1	<0.01
Arkansas	0	0.00
Mississippi	0	0.00
Oklahoma	0	0.00
West Virginia	0	0.00

Place	Population	%
New Hampshire	764	0.06
North Dakota	354	0.05
Vermont	276	0.04
Idaho	423	0.03
Georgia	1,703	0.02
Arizona	1,210	0.02
United States	**19,439**	**0.01**
Texas	2,275	0.01
New York	1,824	0.01
Pennsylvania	1,198	0.01
Washington	977	0.01
Ohio	865	0.01
North Carolina	614	0.01
Colorado	592	0.01
Massachusetts	544	0.01
Virginia	514	0.01
Tennessee	498	0.01
Utah	399	0.01
Kentucky	336	0.01
Missouri	309	0.01
Minnesota	284	0.01
Oregon	281	0.01
Nevada	165	0.01
Kansas	163	0.01
South Dakota	107	0.01
Rhode Island	72	0.01
Alaska	42	0.01
California	750	<0.01
Illinois	559	<0.01
Michigan	443	<0.01
Maryland	288	<0.01
Florida	232	<0.01
New Jersey	126	<0.01
Iowa	80	<0.01
New Mexico	49	<0.01
Nebraska	38	<0.01
Connecticut	30	<0.01
Hawaii	13	<0.01
Louisiana	12	<0.01
Wyoming	10	<0.01
South Carolina	5	<0.01
Montana	4	<0.01
District of Columbia	3	<0.01
Indiana	3	<0.01
Wisconsin	2	<0.01
Alabama	1	<0.01
Delaware	1	<0.01
Maine	1	<0.01
Arkansas	0	0.00
Mississippi	0	0.00
Oklahoma	0	0.00
West Virginia	0	0.00

Please refer to the Explanation of Data in the front of the book for more detailed information.

Race

Asian: Bhutanese

Top 150 Places Sorted by Population

Based on all places, regardless of total population

Place	Population	%
Houston, TX (city) Harris County	788	0.04
Dallas, TX (city) Dallas County	614	0.05
Phoenix, AZ (city) Maricopa County	609	0.04
Tucson, AZ (city) Pima County	571	0.11
Clarkston, GA (city) DeKalb County	530	7.02
Syracuse, NY (city) Onondaga County	516	0.36
Nashville-Davidson, TN (metro govt) Davidson County	462	0.08
Rochester, NY (city) Monroe County	411	0.20
Erie, PA (city) Erie County	395	0.39
New York, NY (city) Kings County	388	<0.01
Buffalo, NY (city) Erie County	370	0.14
Scottdale, GA (cdp) DeKalb County	354	3.33
Fort Worth, TX (city) Tarrant County	343	0.05
Chicago, IL (city) Cook County	339	0.01
Akron, OH (city) Summit County	318	0.16
Manchester, NH (city) Hillsborough County	316	0.29
St. Louis, MO (city) St. Louis city County	306	0.10
Concord, NH (city) Merrimack County	288	0.67
Lansing, MI (city) Ingham County	281	0.26
Lansing, MI (city) Ingham County	281	0.25
Charlotte, NC (city) Mecklenburg County	277	0.04
Denver, CO (city) Denver County	273	0.05
Oakland, CA (city) Alameda County	272	0.07
Aurora, CO (city) Arapahoe County	266	0.08
Twin Falls, ID (city) Twin Falls County	256	0.58
Queens, NY (borough) Queens County	250	0.01
Jacksonville, FL (city) Duval County	231	0.03
Louisville-Jefferson County, KY (metro govt) Jefferson County	228	0.04
Worcester, MA (city) Worcester County	222	0.12
Tukwila, WA (city) King County	221	1.16
Lancaster, PA (city) Lancaster County	209	0.35
San Antonio, TX (city) Medina County	209	0.02
Fargo, ND (city) Cass County	204	0.19
Spokane, WA (city) Spokane County	198	0.09
Burlington, VT (city) Chittenden County	175	0.41
Greensboro, NC (city) Guilford County	173	0.06
Portland, OR (city) Multnomah County	168	0.03
St. Paul, MN (city) Ramsey County	167	0.06
Baltimore, MD (city) Baltimore city County	165	0.03
Paradise, NV (cdp) Clark County	160	0.07
Abilene, TX (city) Taylor County	158	0.13
Boise City, ID (city) Ada County	155	0.08
Kansas City, KS (city) Wyandotte County	144	0.10
Kent, WA (city) King County	143	0.15
Arden-Arcade, CA (cdp) Sacramento County	142	0.15
Millcreek, UT (cdp) Salt Lake County	139	0.22
South Salt Lake, UT (city) Salt Lake County	138	0.58
Roanoke, VA (ind. city) Roanoke independent city	132	0.14
Laconia, NH (city) Belknap County	128	0.80
Grand Forks, ND (city) Grand Forks County	115	0.22
Austin, TX (city) Travis County	107	0.01
Everett, WA (city) Snohomish County	106	0.10
Sioux Falls, SD (city) Minnehaha County	106	0.07
Whitehall, PA (borough) Allegheny County	105	0.75
Dunwoody, GA (city) DeKalb County	104	0.22
Bronx, NY (borough) Bronx County	104	0.01
Harrisburg, PA (city) Dauphin County	101	0.20
Scranton, PA (city) Lackawanna County	101	0.13
Grand Rapids, MI (city) Kent County	98	0.05
Columbus, OH (city) Franklin County	96	0.01
Cleveland, OH (city) Cuyahoga County	94	0.02
Seattle, WA (city) King County	94	0.02
Salt Lake City, UT (city) Salt Lake County	92	0.05
Winooski, VT (city) Chittenden County	84	1.16
Lexington-Fayette, KY (cons. govt) Fayette County	82	0.03
Aurora, IL (city) Kane County	81	0.04
San Diego, CA (city) San Diego County	81	0.01
Des Moines, IA (city) Polk County	79	0.04
Tuckahoe, VA (cdp) Henrico County	77	0.17
Elizabeth, NJ (city) Union County	74	0.06
Cincinnati, OH (city) Hamilton County	74	0.02
SeaTac, WA (city) King County	72	0.27
Providence, RI (city) Providence County	72	0.04
Alameda, CA (city) Alameda County	71	0.10
Wheaton, IL (city) DuPage County	68	0.13
Raleigh, NC (city) Wake County	68	0.02
Lynn, MA (city) Essex County	66	0.07
Springfield, MA (city) Hampden County	66	0.04
Lowell, MA (city) Middlesex County	65	0.06
Albany, NY (city) Albany County	62	0.06
High Point, NC (city) Guilford County	61	0.06
Beaverton, OR (city) Washington County	60	0.07
Charlottesville, VA (ind. city) Charlottesville independent city	59	0.14
Stone Mountain, GA (city) DeKalb County	58	1.00
Lauderdale, MN (city) Ramsey County	56	2.35
Pittsburgh, PA (city) Allegheny County	56	0.02
South Euclid, OH (city) Cuyahoga County	55	0.25
Cuyahoga Falls, OH (city) Summit County	54	0.11
Castle Shannon, PA (borough) Allegheny County	51	0.61
East Riverdale, MD (cdp) Prince George's County	51	0.33
Philadelphia, PA (city) Philadelphia County	51	<0.01
North Decatur, GA (cdp) DeKalb County	50	0.30
Newport News, VA (ind. city) Newport News independent city	50	0.03
Lakewood, OH (city) Cuyahoga County	49	0.09
West Springfield Town, MA (city) Hampden County	48	0.17
Cleveland Heights, OH (city) Cuyahoga County	48	0.10
Albuquerque, NM (city) Bernalillo County	46	0.01
Anchorage, AK (municipality) Anchorage Municipality	42	0.01
Fredericksburg, VA (ind. city) Fredericksburg independent city	41	0.17
East Hill-Meridian, WA (cdp) King County	36	0.12
Utica, NY (city) Oneida County	36	0.06
Memphis, TN (city) Shelby County	36	0.01
Los Angeles, CA (city) Los Angeles County	36	<0.01
Burien, WA (city) King County	35	0.11
Lower Paxton, PA (township) Dauphin County	34	0.07
Minneapolis, MN (city) Hennepin County	32	0.01
Hyattsville, MD (city) Prince George's County	31	0.18
West Fargo, ND (city) Cass County	30	0.12
Rock Island, IL (city) Rock Island County	29	0.07
Trenton, NJ (city) Mercer County	29	0.03
Durham, NC (city) Durham County	29	0.01
Haltom City, TX (city) Tarrant County	26	0.06
Hampton, VA (ind. city) Hampton independent city	26	0.02
Manhattan, NY (borough) New York County	26	<0.01
Finneytown, OH (cdp) Hamilton County	25	0.20
Glendale, AZ (city) Maricopa County	25	0.01
Carmichael, CA (cdp) Sacramento County	24	0.04
Dale City, VA (cdp) Prince William County	24	0.04
Omaha, NE (city) Douglas County	24	0.01
Boston, MA (city) Suffolk County	24	<0.01
Westfield, MA (city) Hampden County	23	0.06
Boardman, OR (city) Morrow County	22	0.68
Gresham, OR (city) Multnomah County	22	0.02
Santa Clara, CA (city) Santa Clara County	22	0.02
Penn Hills, PA (township) Allegheny County	20	0.05
Holladay, UT (city) Salt Lake County	19	0.07
Bowling Green, KY (city) Warren County	19	0.03
Grand Haven, MI (city) Ottawa County	18	0.17
Roseville, MN (city) Ramsey County	18	0.05
Glendale, CO (city) Arapahoe County	17	0.41
Country Homes, WA (cdp) Spokane County	17	0.29
Glenmont, MD (cdp) Montgomery County	17	0.13
Hartford, CT (city/town) Hartford County	17	0.01
White Oak, OH (cdp) Hamilton County	16	0.08
Kent, OH (city) Portage County	15	0.05
Colonial Park, PA (cdp) Dauphin County	14	0.11
Glendale Heights, IL (village) DuPage County	14	0.04
Overland Park, KS (city) Johnson County	13	0.01
Kentwood, MI (city) Kent County	12	0.02
Baton Rouge, LA (city) East Baton Rouge Parish	12	0.01
Colorado Springs, CO (city) El Paso County	12	<0.01
Mount Oliver, PA (borough) Allegheny County	11	0.32
Murray, UT (city) Salt Lake County	11	0.02
Lincoln, NE (city) Lancaster County	11	<0.01
Carnegie, PA (borough) Allegheny County	10	0.13
Stanford, CA (cdp) Santa Clara County	10	0.07
Moline, IL (city) Rock Island County	10	0.02
Santa Barbara, CA (city) Santa Barbara County	10	0.01
Bellevue, PA (borough) Allegheny County	9	0.11
Garden City, ID (city) Ada County	9	0.08

Race

Asian: Bhutanese

Top 150 Places Sorted by Percent of Total Population

Based on all places, regardless of total population

Place	Population	%
Clarkston, GA (city) DeKalb County	530	7.02
Scottdale, GA (cdp) DeKalb County	354	3.33
Lauderdale, MN (city) Ramsey County	56	2.35
Tukwila, WA (city) King County	221	1.16
Winooski, VT (city) Chittenden County	84	1.16
Stone Mountain, GA (city) DeKalb County	58	1.00
Laconia, NH (city) Belknap County	128	0.80
Whitehall, PA (borough) Allegheny County	105	0.75
Boardman, OR (city) Morrow County	22	0.68
Blue Ball, PA (cdp) Lancaster County	7	0.68
Concord, NH (city) Merrimack County	288	0.67
Castle Shannon, PA (borough) Allegheny County	51	0.61
Twin Falls, ID (city) Twin Falls County	256	0.58
South Salt Lake, UT (city) Salt Lake County	138	0.58
Burlington, VT (city) Chittenden County	175	0.41
Glendale, CO (city) Arapahoe County	17	0.41
Erie, PA (city) Erie County	395	0.39
Syracuse, NY (city) Onondaga County	516	0.36
Lancaster, PA (city) Lancaster County	209	0.35
East Riverdale, MD (cdp) Prince George's County	51	0.33
Leetsdale, PA (borough) Allegheny County	4	0.33
Mount Oliver, PA (borough) Allegheny County	11	0.32
North Decatur, GA (cdp) DeKalb County	50	0.30
Manchester, NH (city) Hillsborough County	316	0.29
Country Homes, WA (cdp) Spokane County	17	0.29
SeaTac, WA (city) King County	72	0.27
Lansing, MI (city) Ingham County	281	0.26
Lansing, MI (city) Ingham County	281	0.25
South Euclid, OH (city) Cuyahoga County	55	0.25
Millcreek, UT (cdp) Salt Lake County	139	0.22
Grand Forks, ND (city) Grand Forks County	115	0.22
Dunwoody, GA (city) DeKalb County	104	0.22
Swanton, VT (village) Franklin County	5	0.21
Rochester, NY (city) Monroe County	411	0.20
Harrisburg, PA (city) Dauphin County	101	0.20
Finneytown, OH (cdp) Hamilton County	25	0.20
Meredith, NY (town) Delaware County	3	0.20
Fargo, ND (city) Cass County	204	0.19
Hyattsville, MD (city) Prince George's County	31	0.18
Akron, PA (borough) Lancaster County	7	0.18
Tuckahoe, VA (cdp) Henrico County	77	0.17
West Springfield Town, MA (city) Hampden County	48	0.17
Fredericksburg, VA (ind. city) Fredericksburg independent city	41	0.17
Grand Haven, MI (city) Ottawa County	18	0.17
Oconomowoc Lake, WI (village) Waukesha County	1	0.17
Akron, OH (city) Summit County	318	0.16
Wakefield, NH (town) Carroll County	8	0.16
Emsworth, PA (borough) Allegheny County	4	0.16
Kent, WA (city) King County	143	0.15
Arden-Arcade, CA (cdp) Sacramento County	142	0.15
Marin City, CA (cdp) Marin County	4	0.15
Buffalo, NY (city) Erie County	370	0.14
Roanoke, VA (ind. city) Roanoke independent city	132	0.14
Charlottesville, VA (ind. city) Charlottesville independent city	59	0.14
Abilene, TX (city) Taylor County	158	0.13
Scranton, PA (city) Lackawanna County	101	0.13
Wheaton, IL (city) DuPage County	68	0.13
Glenmont, MD (cdp) Montgomery County	17	0.13
Carnegie, PA (borough) Allegheny County	10	0.13
Worcester, MA (city) Worcester County	222	0.12
East Hill-Meridian, WA (cdp) King County	36	0.12
West Fargo, ND (city) Cass County	30	0.12
Crafton, PA (borough) Allegheny County	7	0.12
Fremont, MI (city) Newaygo County	5	0.12
Tucson, AZ (city) Pima County	571	0.11
Cuyahoga Falls, OH (city) Summit County	54	0.11
Burien, WA (city) King County	35	0.11
Colonial Park, PA (cdp) Dauphin County	14	0.11
Bellevue, PA (borough) Allegheny County	9	0.11
Greenville, NY (cdp) Westchester County	8	0.11
East Earl, PA (township) Lancaster County	7	0.11
Norton Center, MA (cdp) Bristol County	3	0.11
St. Louis, MO (city) St. Louis city County	306	0.10
Kansas City, KS (city) Wyandotte County	144	0.10
Everett, WA (city) Snohomish County	106	0.10
Alameda, CA (city) Alameda County	71	0.10
Cleveland Heights, OH (city) Cuyahoga County	48	0.10
Spokane, WA (city) Spokane County	198	0.09
Lakewood, OH (city) Cuyahoga County	49	0.09
Lansing, MI (charter township) Ingham County	7	0.09
Honesdale, PA (borough) Wayne County	4	0.09
Cactus, TX (city) Moore County	3	0.09
Nashville-Davidson, TN (metro govt) Davidson County	462	0.08
Aurora, CO (city) Arapahoe County	266	0.08
Boise City, ID (city) Ada County	155	0.08
White Oak, OH (cdp) Hamilton County	16	0.08
Garden City, ID (city) Ada County	9	0.08
Pimmit Hills, VA (cdp) Fairfax County	5	0.08
Swanton, VT (town) Franklin County	5	0.08
Boscawen, NH (town) Merrimack County	3	0.08
Oakland, CA (city) Alameda County	272	0.07
Paradise, NV (cdp) Clark County	160	0.07
Sioux Falls, SD (city) Minnehaha County	106	0.07
Lynn, MA (city) Essex County	66	0.07
Beaverton, OR (city) Washington County	60	0.07
Lower Paxton, PA (township) Dauphin County	34	0.07
Rock Island, IL (city) Rock Island County	29	0.07
Holladay, UT (city) Salt Lake County	19	0.07
Stanford, CA (cdp) Santa Clara County	10	0.07
Hanover, NH (cdp) Grafton County	6	0.07
Hiram, OH (village) Portage County	1	0.07
Greensboro, NC (city) Guilford County	173	0.06
St. Paul, MN (city) Ramsey County	167	0.06
Elizabeth, NJ (city) Union County	74	0.06
Lowell, MA (city) Middlesex County	65	0.06
Albany, NY (city) Albany County	62	0.06
High Point, NC (city) Guilford County	61	0.06
Utica, NY (city) Oneida County	36	0.06
Haltom City, TX (city) Tarrant County	26	0.06
Westfield, MA (city) Hampden County	23	0.06
Lebanon, NH (city) Grafton County	8	0.06
Fruitland, ID (city) Payette County	3	0.06
Town and Country, WA (cdp) Spokane County	3	0.06
Kerhonkson, NY (cdp) Ulster County	1	0.06
Dallas, TX (city) Dallas County	614	0.05
Fort Worth, TX (city) Tarrant County	343	0.05
Denver, CO (city) Denver County	273	0.05
Grand Rapids, MI (city) Kent County	98	0.05
Salt Lake City, UT (city) Salt Lake County	92	0.05
Penn Hills, PA (township) Allegheny County	20	0.05
Roseville, MN (city) Ramsey County	18	0.05
Kent, OH (city) Portage County	15	0.05
South Burlington, VT (city) Chittenden County	9	0.05
Grandville, MI (city) Kent County	7	0.05
Sullivan, NY (town) Madison County	7	0.05
Hanover, NH (town) Grafton County	6	0.05
Monfort Heights, OH (cdp) Hamilton County	6	0.05
Walnut Grove, WA (cdp) Clark County	5	0.05
Westport, WA (city) Grays Harbor County	1	0.05
Houston, TX (city) Harris County	788	0.04
Phoenix, AZ (city) Maricopa County	609	0.04
Charlotte, NC (city) Mecklenburg County	277	0.04
Louisville-Jefferson County, KY (metro govt) Jefferson County	228	0.04
Aurora, IL (city) Kane County	81	0.04
Des Moines, IA (city) Polk County	79	0.04
Providence, RI (city) Providence County	72	0.04
Springfield, MA (city) Hampden County	66	0.04
Carmichael, CA (cdp) Sacramento County	24	0.04
Dale City, VA (cdp) Prince William County	24	0.04
Glendale Heights, IL (village) DuPage County	14	0.04
Jackson, WY (town) Teton County	4	0.04
Morganville, NJ (cdp) Monmouth County	2	0.04
Harmony, NJ (township) Warren County	1	0.04
Jacksonville, FL (city) Duval County	231	0.03
Portland, OR (city) Multnomah County	168	0.03
Baltimore, MD (city) Baltimore city County	165	0.03
Lexington-Fayette, KY (cons. govt) Fayette County	82	0.03
Newport News, VA (ind. city) Newport News independent city	50	0.03
Trenton, NJ (city) Mercer County	29	0.03
Bowling Green, KY (city) Warren County	19	0.03

Please refer to the Explanation of Data in the front of the book for more detailed information.

Race

Asian: Bhutanese

Top 150 Places Sorted by Percent of Total Population

Based on places with total population of 7,500 or more

Place	Population	%
Clarkston, GA (city) DeKalb County	530	7.02
Scottdale, GA (cdp) DeKalb County	354	3.33
Tukwila, WA (city) King County	221	1.16
Laconia, NH (city) Belknap County	128	0.80
Whitehall, PA (borough) Allegheny County	105	0.75
Concord, NH (city) Merrimack County	288	0.67
Castle Shannon, PA (borough) Allegheny County	51	0.61
Twin Falls, ID (city) Twin Falls County	256	0.58
South Salt Lake, UT (city) Salt Lake County	138	0.58
Burlington, VT (city) Chittenden County	175	0.41
Erie, PA (city) Erie County	395	0.39
Syracuse, NY (city) Onondaga County	516	0.36
Lancaster, PA (city) Lancaster County	209	0.35
East Riverdale, MD (cdp) Prince George's County	51	0.33
North Decatur, GA (cdp) DeKalb County	50	0.30
Manchester, NH (city) Hillsborough County	316	0.29
SeaTac, WA (city) King County	72	0.27
Lansing, MI (city) Ingham County	281	0.26
Lansing, MI (city) Ingham County	281	0.25
South Euclid, OH (city) Cuyahoga County	55	0.25
Millcreek, UT (cdp) Salt Lake County	139	0.22
Grand Forks, ND (city) Grand Forks County	115	0.22
Dunwoody, GA (city) DeKalb County	104	0.22
Rochester, NY (city) Monroe County	411	0.20
Harrisburg, PA (city) Dauphin County	101	0.20
Finneytown, OH (cdp) Hamilton County	25	0.20
Fargo, ND (city) Cass County	204	0.19
Hyattsville, MD (city) Prince George's County	31	0.18
Tuckahoe, VA (cdp) Henrico County	77	0.17
West Springfield Town, MA (city) Hampden County	48	0.17
Fredericksburg, VA (ind. city) Fredericksburg independent city	41	0.17
Grand Haven, MI (city) Ottawa County	18	0.17
Akron, OH (city) Summit County	318	0.16
Kent, WA (city) King County	143	0.15
Arden-Arcade, CA (cdp) Sacramento County	142	0.15
Buffalo, NY (city) Erie County	370	0.14
Roanoke, VA (ind. city) Roanoke independent city	132	0.14
Charlottesville, VA (ind. city) Charlottesville independent city	59	0.14
Abilene, TX (city) Taylor County	158	0.13
Scranton, PA (city) Lackawanna County	101	0.13
Wheaton, IL (city) DuPage County	68	0.13
Glenmont, MD (cdp) Montgomery County	17	0.13
Carnegie, PA (borough) Allegheny County	10	0.13
Worcester, MA (city) Worcester County	222	0.12
East Hill-Meridian, WA (cdp) King County	36	0.12
West Fargo, ND (city) Cass County	30	0.12
Tucson, AZ (city) Pima County	571	0.11
Cuyahoga Falls, OH (city) Summit County	54	0.11
Burien, WA (city) King County	35	0.11
Colonial Park, PA (cdp) Dauphin County	14	0.11
Bellevue, PA (borough) Allegheny County	9	0.11
St. Louis, MO (city) St. Louis city County	306	0.10
Kansas City, KS (city) Wyandotte County	144	0.10
Everett, WA (city) Snohomish County	106	0.10
Alameda, CA (city) Alameda County	71	0.10
Cleveland Heights, OH (city) Cuyahoga County	48	0.10
Spokane, WA (city) Spokane County	198	0.09
Lakewood, OH (city) Cuyahoga County	49	0.09
Lansing, MI (charter township) Ingham County	7	0.09
Nashville-Davidson, TN (metro govt) Davidson County	462	0.08
Aurora, CO (city) Arapahoe County	266	0.08
Boise City, ID (city) Ada County	155	0.08
White Oak, OH (cdp) Hamilton County	16	0.08
Garden City, ID (city) Ada County	9	0.08
Oakland, CA (city) Alameda County	272	0.07
Paradise, NV (cdp) Clark County	160	0.07
Sioux Falls, SD (city) Minnehaha County	106	0.07
Lynn, MA (city) Essex County	66	0.07
Beaverton, OR (city) Washington County	60	0.07
Lower Paxton, PA (township) Dauphin County	34	0.07
Rock Island, IL (city) Rock Island County	29	0.07
Holladay, UT (city) Salt Lake County	19	0.07
Stanford, CA (cdp) Santa Clara County	10	0.07
Hanover, NH (cdp) Grafton County	6	0.07
Greensboro, NC (city) Guilford County	173	0.06
St. Paul, MN (city) Ramsey County	167	0.06
Elizabeth, NJ (city) Union County	74	0.06
Lowell, MA (city) Middlesex County	65	0.06
Albany, NY (city) Albany County	62	0.06
High Point, NC (city) Guilford County	61	0.06
Utica, NY (city) Oneida County	36	0.06
Haltom City, TX (city) Tarrant County	26	0.06
Westfield, MA (city) Hampden County	23	0.06
Lebanon, NH (city) Grafton County	8	0.06
Dallas, TX (city) Dallas County	614	0.05
Fort Worth, TX (city) Tarrant County	343	0.05
Denver, CO (city) Denver County	273	0.05
Grand Rapids, MI (city) Kent County	98	0.05
Salt Lake City, UT (city) Salt Lake County	92	0.05
Penn Hills, PA (township) Allegheny County	20	0.05
Roseville, MN (city) Ramsey County	18	0.05
Kent, OH (city) Portage County	15	0.05
South Burlington, VT (city) Chittenden County	9	0.05
Grandville, MI (city) Kent County	7	0.05
Sullivan, NY (town) Madison County	7	0.05
Hanover, NH (town) Grafton County	6	0.05
Monfort Heights, OH (cdp) Hamilton County	6	0.05
Walnut Grove, WA (cdp) Clark County	5	0.05
Houston, TX (city) Harris County	788	0.04
Phoenix, AZ (city) Maricopa County	609	0.04
Charlotte, NC (city) Mecklenburg County	277	0.04
Louisville-Jefferson County, KY (metro govt) Jefferson County	228	0.04
Aurora, IL (city) Kane County	81	0.04
Des Moines, IA (city) Polk County	79	0.04
Providence, RI (city) Providence County	72	0.04
Springfield, MA (city) Hampden County	66	0.04
Carmichael, CA (cdp) Sacramento County	24	0.04
Dale City, VA (cdp) Prince William County	24	0.04
Glendale Heights, IL (village) DuPage County	14	0.04
Jackson, WY (town) Teton County	4	0.04
Jacksonville, FL (city) Duval County	231	0.03
Portland, OR (city) Multnomah County	168	0.03
Baltimore, MD (city) Baltimore city County	165	0.03
Lexington-Fayette, KY (cons. govt) Fayette County	82	0.03
Newport News, VA (ind. city) Newport News independent city	50	0.03
Trenton, NJ (city) Mercer County	29	0.03
Bowling Green, KY (city) Warren County	19	0.03
Northglenn, CO (city) Adams County	9	0.03
Springfield, VA (cdp) Fairfax County	9	0.03
Harrison, NY (town/village) Westchester County	8	0.03
Lincolnia, VA (cdp) Fairfax County	6	0.03
Tumwater, WA (city) Thurston County	6	0.03
Ansonia, CT (city/town) New Haven County	5	0.03
Baldwin, PA (borough) Allegheny County	5	0.03
Dumas, TX (city) Moore County	5	0.03
Spring Lake, MI (township) Ottawa County	5	0.03
Greatwood, TX (cdp) Fort Bend County	4	0.03
Perry, GA (city) Houston County	4	0.03
San Anselmo, CA (town) Marin County	4	0.03
San Antonio, TX (city) Medina County	209	0.02
Cleveland, OH (city) Cuyahoga County	94	0.02
Seattle, WA (city) King County	94	0.02
Cincinnati, OH (city) Hamilton County	74	0.02
Raleigh, NC (city) Wake County	68	0.02
Pittsburgh, PA (city) Allegheny County	56	0.02
Hampton, VA (ind. city) Hampton independent city	26	0.02
Gresham, OR (city) Multnomah County	22	0.02
Santa Clara, CA (city) Santa Clara County	22	0.02
Kentwood, MI (city) Kent County	12	0.02
Murray, UT (city) Salt Lake County	11	0.02
Moline, IL (city) Rock Island County	10	0.02
Georgetown, MI (charter township) Ottawa County	9	0.02
Edina, MN (city) Hennepin County	8	0.02
Wheaton, MD (cdp) Montgomery County	8	0.02
San Pablo, CA (city) Contra Costa County	7	0.02
Amherst Center, MA (cdp) Hampshire County	4	0.02
Norton, MA (town) Bristol County	4	0.02
South Hadley, MA (town) Hampshire County	4	0.02
St. Andrews, SC (cdp) Richland County	4	0.02
Colchester, VT (town) Chittenden County	3	0.02

Please refer to the Explanation of Data in the front of the book for more detailed information.

Race

Asian: Burmese

U.S. and 50 States Sorted by Population and Percent of Total Population

Place	Population	%
United States	**100,200**	**0.03**
California	17,978	0.05
New York	12,174	0.06
Texas	10,451	0.04
Indiana	7,868	0.12
North Carolina	3,779	0.04
Minnesota	3,763	0.07
Maryland	3,450	0.06
Illinois	2,950	0.02
Arizona	2,675	0.04
Georgia	2,646	0.03
Florida	2,578	0.01
Nebraska	2,250	0.12
Washington	2,058	0.03
Michigan	1,856	0.02
Colorado	1,822	0.04
Pennsylvania	1,822	0.01
Virginia	1,668	0.02
Kentucky	1,524	0.04
Ohio	1,356	0.01
Tennessee	1,324	0.02
Iowa	1,260	0.04
Kansas	1,204	0.04
Wisconsin	1,197	0.02
New Jersey	1,197	0.01
Oklahoma	1,146	0.03
Utah	1,090	0.04
Massachusetts	1,072	0.02
Oregon	977	0.03
Missouri	842	0.01
Connecticut	763	0.02
South Dakota	669	0.08
South Carolina	425	0.01
Idaho	399	0.03
Nevada	349	0.01
Hawaii	281	0.02
Louisiana	270	0.01
Alabama	146	<0.01
District of Columbia	134	0.02
Vermont	126	0.02
West Virginia	109	0.01
Rhode Island	108	0.01
New Mexico	89	<0.01
New Hampshire	67	0.01
Maine	65	<0.01
Arkansas	53	<0.01
Delaware	51	0.01
Mississippi	37	<0.01
Alaska	30	<0.01
North Dakota	28	<0.01
Montana	14	<0.01
Wyoming	10	<0.01

Place	Population	%
Indiana	7,868	0.12
Nebraska	2,250	0.12
South Dakota	669	0.08
Minnesota	3,763	0.07
New York	12,174	0.06
Maryland	3,450	0.06
California	17,978	0.05
Texas	10,451	0.04
North Carolina	3,779	0.04
Arizona	2,675	0.04
Colorado	1,822	0.04
Kentucky	1,524	0.04
Iowa	1,260	0.04
Kansas	1,204	0.04
Utah	1,090	0.04
United States	**100,200**	**0.03**
Georgia	2,646	0.03
Washington	2,058	0.03
Oklahoma	1,146	0.03
Oregon	977	0.03
Idaho	399	0.03
Illinois	2,950	0.02
Michigan	1,856	0.02
Virginia	1,668	0.02
Tennessee	1,324	0.02
Wisconsin	1,197	0.02
Massachusetts	1,072	0.02
Connecticut	763	0.02
Hawaii	281	0.02
District of Columbia	134	0.02
Vermont	126	0.02
Florida	2,578	0.01
Pennsylvania	1,822	0.01
Ohio	1,356	0.01
New Jersey	1,197	0.01
Missouri	842	0.01
South Carolina	425	0.01
Nevada	349	0.01
Louisiana	270	0.01
West Virginia	109	0.01
Rhode Island	108	0.01
New Hampshire	67	0.01
Delaware	51	0.01
Alabama	146	<0.01
New Mexico	89	<0.01
Maine	65	<0.01
Arkansas	53	<0.01
Mississippi	37	<0.01
Alaska	30	<0.01
North Dakota	28	<0.01
Montana	14	<0.01
Wyoming	10	<0.01

Please refer to the Explanation of Data in the front of the book for more detailed information.

Race

Asian: Burmese

Top 150 Places Sorted by Population

Based on all places, regardless of total population

Place	Population	%
New York, NY (city) Kings County	4,132	0.05
Fort Wayne, IN (city) Allen County	3,819	1.51
Indianapolis, IN (city) Marion County	3,622	0.44
St. Paul, MN (city) Ramsey County	2,587	0.91
Buffalo, NY (city) Erie County	2,361	0.90
Queens, NY (borough) Queens County	2,344	0.11
Utica, NY (city) Oneida County	2,317	3.72
Phoenix, AZ (city) Maricopa County	2,184	0.15
Dallas, TX (city) Dallas County	2,127	0.18
Daly City, CA (city) San Mateo County	2,023	2.00
Omaha, NE (city) Douglas County	1,779	0.44
Amarillo, TX (city) Potter County	1,679	0.88
San Francisco, CA (city) San Francisco County	1,579	0.20
Houston, TX (city) Harris County	1,460	0.07
Fremont, CA (city) Alameda County	1,450	0.68
Brooklyn, NY (borough) Kings County	1,260	0.05
Syracuse, NY (city) Onondaga County	1,218	0.84
Lewisville, TX (city) Denton County	942	0.99
Jacksonville, FL (city) Duval County	910	0.11
Nashville-Davidson, TN (metro govt) Davidson County	883	0.15
Milwaukee, WI (city) Milwaukee County	882	0.15
Los Angeles, CA (city) Los Angeles County	842	0.02
San Diego, CA (city) San Diego County	824	0.06
Des Moines, IA (city) Polk County	810	0.40
Denver, CO (city) Denver County	800	0.13
Fort Worth, TX (city) Tarrant County	791	0.11
Portland, OR (city) Multnomah County	747	0.13
Chicago, IL (city) Cook County	711	0.03
Bowling Green, KY (city) Warren County	694	1.20
Tulsa, OK (city) Tulsa County	659	0.17
New Bern, NC (city) Craven County	623	2.11
Frederick, MD (city) Frederick County	621	0.95
Akron, OH (city) Summit County	603	0.30
San Jose, CA (city) Santa Clara County	602	0.06
Kansas City, KS (city) Wyandotte County	578	0.40
Rochester, NY (city) Monroe County	565	0.27
Hartford, CT (city/town) Hartford County	553	0.44
Charlotte, NC (city) Mecklenburg County	542	0.07
San Antonio, TX (city) Medina County	535	0.04
Alhambra, CA (city) Los Angeles County	528	0.64
Louisville-Jefferson County, KY (metro govt) Jefferson County	528	0.09
Cactus, TX (city) Moore County	521	16.39
Huron, SD (city) Beadle County	515	4.09
Dumas, TX (city) Moore County	507	3.45
Clarkston, GA (city) DeKalb County	501	6.63
Austin, TX (city) Travis County	492	0.06
Garden City, KS (city) Finney County	465	1.74
Aurora, CO (city) Arapahoe County	452	0.14
Grand Rapids, MI (city) Kent County	424	0.23
Arbutus, MD (cdp) Baltimore County	423	2.07
Scottdale, GA (cdp) DeKalb County	412	3.88
High Point, NC (city) Guilford County	406	0.39
Rockford, IL (city) Winnebago County	403	0.26
Raleigh, NC (city) Wake County	397	0.10
Lincoln, NE (city) Lancaster County	395	0.15
Chapel Hill, NC (town) Orange County	393	0.69
Philadelphia, PA (city) Philadelphia County	388	0.03
Salt Lake City, UT (city) Salt Lake County	385	0.21
Kent, WA (city) King County	384	0.42
Lansing, MI (city) Ingham County	383	0.34
Oakland, CA (city) Alameda County	377	0.10
Rosemead, CA (city) Los Angeles County	376	0.70
Arcadia, CA (city) Los Angeles County	376	0.67
Lansing, MI (city) Ingham County	373	0.34
Springfield, MI (city) Calhoun County	349	6.63
Spokane, WA (city) Spokane County	343	0.16
Carrboro, NC (town) Orange County	339	1.73
Albany, NY (city) Albany County	322	0.33
Manhattan, NY (borough) New York County	317	0.02
Rensselaer, NY (city) Rensselaer County	316	3.36
Union City, CA (city) Alameda County	314	0.45
Savage, MD (cdp) Howard County	313	4.44
Battle Creek, MI (city) Calhoun County	301	0.58
Worthington, MN (city) Nobles County	296	2.32
Bakersfield, CA (city) Kern County	294	0.08
Boise City, ID (city) Ada County	292	0.14
Rock Island, IL (city) Rock Island County	282	0.72
Monterey Park, CA (city) Los Angeles County	279	0.46
Roseville, MN (city) Ramsey County	275	0.82
Greensboro, NC (city) Guilford County	272	0.10
Tukwila, WA (city) King County	269	1.41
Kansas City, MO (city) Jackson County	262	0.06
San Gabriel, CA (city) Los Angeles County	261	0.66
Greeley, CO (city) Weld County	248	0.27
Wheaton, IL (city) DuPage County	245	0.46
Port Lavaca, TX (city) Calhoun County	244	1.99
Smyrna, TN (town) Rutherford County	241	0.60
El Monte, CA (city) Los Angeles County	241	0.21
St. Louis, MO (city) St. Louis city County	241	0.08
South Salt Lake, UT (city) Salt Lake County	228	0.97
Glen Ellyn, IL (village) DuPage County	226	0.82
Maplewood, MN (city) Ramsey County	224	0.59
Oklahoma City, OK (city) Oklahoma County	222	0.04
Aurora, IL (city) Kane County	206	0.10
Trenton, NJ (city) Mercer County	205	0.24
Columbus, OH (city) Franklin County	204	0.03
Charlottesville, VA (ind. city) Charlottesville independent city	183	0.42
Seattle, WA (city) King County	182	0.03
West Covina, CA (city) Los Angeles County	178	0.17
Worcester, MA (city) Worcester County	171	0.09
South San Francisco, CA (city) San Mateo County	168	0.26
Diamond Bar, CA (city) Los Angeles County	166	0.30
Rockville, MD (city) Montgomery County	165	0.27
Kennewick, WA (city) Benton County	157	0.21
Winston-Salem, NC (city) Forsyth County	154	0.07
Guymon, OK (city) Texas County	153	1.34
Whitehall, PA (borough) Allegheny County	151	1.08
Marshalltown, IA (city) Marshall County	151	0.55
Lakewood, OH (city) Cuyahoga County	146	0.28
Temple City, CA (city) Los Angeles County	145	0.41
Newark, CA (city) Alameda County	145	0.34
Pittsburgh, PA (city) Allegheny County	145	0.05
Logansport, IN (city) Cass County	144	0.78
Rowland Heights, CA (cdp) Los Angeles County	143	0.29
St. Andrews, SC (cdp) Richland County	141	0.69
Lancaster, PA (city) Lancaster County	135	0.23
Milpitas, CA (city) Santa Clara County	135	0.20
Lumberton, NC (city) Robeson County	134	0.62
Washington, DC (city) District of Columbia	134	0.02
Sioux Falls, SD (city) Minnehaha County	132	0.09
Staten Island, NY (borough) Richmond County	130	0.03
Logan, UT (city) Cache County	128	0.27
Irvine, CA (city) Orange County	127	0.06
Midland, TX (city) Midland County	125	0.11
Sunnyvale, CA (city) Santa Clara County	125	0.09
El Cajon, CA (city) San Diego County	124	0.12
Boston, MA (city) Suffolk County	124	0.02
Millcreek, UT (cdp) Salt Lake County	123	0.20
Erie, PA (city) Erie County	121	0.12
Allentown, PA (city) Lehigh County	121	0.10
Hayward, CA (city) Alameda County	120	0.08
Walnut, CA (city) Los Angeles County	119	0.41
Santa Clara, CA (city) Santa Clara County	115	0.10
Glendale, AZ (city) Maricopa County	115	0.05
Culver City, CA (city) Los Angeles County	114	0.29
Lowell, MA (city) Middlesex County	114	0.11
Tampa, FL (city) Hillsborough County	114	0.03
Crescent Springs, KY (city) Kenton County	108	2.84
Urban Honolulu, HI (cdp) Honolulu County	107	0.03
Garden Grove, CA (city) Orange County	104	0.06
Torrance, CA (city) Los Angeles County	103	0.07
Quincy, MA (city) Norfolk County	100	0.11
Columbia, MD (cdp) Howard County	99	0.10
Baldwin Park, CA (city) Los Angeles County	97	0.13
Columbia, MO (city) Boone County	97	0.09
Anaheim, CA (city) Orange County	97	0.03
Concord, CA (city) Contra Costa County	96	0.08
North Bethesda, MD (cdp) Montgomery County	95	0.22
Aspen Hill, MD (cdp) Montgomery County	95	0.19
Moline, IL (city) Rock Island County	94	0.22

SECTION THREE

Please refer to the Explanation of Data in the front of the book for more detailed information.

Race

Asian: Burmese

Top 150 Places Sorted by Percent of Total Population

Based on all places, regardless of total population

Place	Population	%
Cactus, TX (city) Moore County	521	16.39
Clarkston, GA (city) DeKalb County	501	6.63
Springfield, MI (city) Calhoun County	349	6.63
Savage, MD (cdp) Howard County	313	4.44
Huron, SD (city) Beadle County	515	4.09
Scottdale, GA (cdp) DeKalb County	412	3.88
Utica, NY (city) Oneida County	2,317	3.72
Dumas, TX (city) Moore County	507	3.45
Fenton, MN (township) Murray County	6	3.39
Columbus Junction, IA (city) Louisa County	64	3.37
Rensselaer, NY (city) Rensselaer County	316	3.36
Fulda, MN (city) Murray County	44	3.34
Liscomb, IA (city) Marshall County	9	2.99
Crescent Springs, KY (city) Kenton County	108	2.84
Marienthal, KS (cdp) Wichita County	2	2.82
Moorefield, WV (town) Hardy County	61	2.40
Worthington, MN (city) Nobles County	296	2.32
Westport, MN (township) Pope County	6	2.16
New Bern, NC (city) Craven County	623	2.11
Arbutus, MD (cdp) Baltimore County	423	2.07
East Ithaca, NY (cdp) Tompkins County	46	2.06
Daly City, CA (city) San Mateo County	2,023	2.00
Port Lavaca, TX (city) Calhoun County	244	1.99
White Lake, SD (city) Aurora County	7	1.88
Columbus City, IA (city) Louisa County	7	1.79
Garden City, KS (city) Finney County	465	1.74
Carrboro, NC (town) Orange County	339	1.73
Fredonia, IA (city) Louisa County	4	1.64
Fort Wayne, IN (city) Allen County	3,819	1.51
Muir, MI (village) Ionia County	9	1.49
Tukwila, WA (city) King County	269	1.41
Somerdale, NJ (borough) Camden County	70	1.36
Guymon, OK (city) Texas County	153	1.34
Worthington, MN (township) Nobles County	4	1.22
Bowling Green, KY (city) Warren County	694	1.20
Whitehall, PA (borough) Allegheny County	151	1.08
Comer, GA (city) Madison County	12	1.07
Glendale, CO (city) Arapahoe County	43	1.03
Oronoco, MN (city) Olmsted County	13	1.00
Hall Summit, LA (village) Red River Parish	3	1.00
Lewisville, TX (city) Denton County	942	0.99
Sadieville, KY (city) Scott County	3	0.99
South Salt Lake, UT (city) Salt Lake County	228	0.97
Frederick, MD (city) Frederick County	621	0.95
Arcadia Lakes, SC (town) Richland County	8	0.93
St. Paul, MN (city) Ramsey County	2,587	0.91
Buffalo, NY (city) Erie County	2,361	0.90
Amarillo, TX (city) Potter County	1,679	0.88
Rushmore, MN (city) Nobles County	3	0.88
Syracuse, NY (city) Onondaga County	1,218	0.84
Roseville, MN (city) Ramsey County	275	0.82
Glen Ellyn, IL (village) DuPage County	226	0.82
Embarrass, MN (township) St. Louis County	5	0.82
South San Gabriel, CA (cdp) Los Angeles County	65	0.81
Logansport, IN (city) Cass County	144	0.78
Storm Lake, IA (city) Buena Vista County	82	0.77
Oaklyn, NJ (borough) Camden County	31	0.77
Archer, IA (city) O'Brien County	1	0.76
Rock Island, IL (city) Rock Island County	282	0.72
Talmage, CA (cdp) Mendocino County	8	0.71
Rosemead, CA (city) Los Angeles County	376	0.70
Washington, IN (city) Daviess County	80	0.70
Chapel Hill, NC (town) Orange County	393	0.69
St. Andrews, SC (cdp) Richland County	141	0.69
Broadmoor, CA (cdp) San Mateo County	29	0.69
Fremont, CA (city) Alameda County	1,450	0.68
Arcadia, CA (city) Los Angeles County	376	0.67
Lakeside, IA (city) Buena Vista County	4	0.67
San Gabriel, CA (city) Los Angeles County	261	0.66
Welch, MN (township) Goodhue County	5	0.66
Richland, WI (town) Richland County	9	0.65
Franks Field, WI (cdp) Ashland County	1	0.65
Alhambra, CA (city) Los Angeles County	528	0.64
Grangeville, CA (cdp) Kings County	3	0.64
Tonyville, CA (cdp) Tulare County	2	0.63
Lumberton, NC (city) Robeson County	134	0.62
Smyrna, TN (town) Rutherford County	241	0.60
Maplewood, MN (city) Ramsey County	224	0.59
Wormleysburg, PA (borough) Cumberland County	18	0.59
Battle Creek, MI (city) Calhoun County	301	0.58
Baudette, MN (township) Lake of the Woods County	2	0.58
Princeville, HI (cdp) Kauai County	12	0.56
Martin, SD (city) Bennett County	6	0.56
Marshalltown, IA (city) Marshall County	151	0.55
Eckford, MI (township) Calhoun County	7	0.54
Grandview, IA (city) Louisa County	3	0.54
Lakeville, NY (cdp) Livingston County	4	0.53
Pine Castle, FL (cdp) Orange County	56	0.52
Stone Mountain, GA (city) DeKalb County	30	0.52
Topeka, IN (town) LaGrange County	6	0.52
Norris Canyon, CA (cdp) Contra Costa County	5	0.52
Brooklawn, NJ (borough) Camden County	10	0.51
Union Springs, NY (village) Cayuga County	6	0.50
Winooski, VT (city) Chittenden County	35	0.48
Monterey Park, CA (city) Los Angeles County	279	0.46
Wheaton, IL (city) DuPage County	245	0.46
Ballenger Creek, MD (cdp) Frederick County	84	0.46
Elkridge, MD (cdp) Howard County	72	0.46
Rockingham, NC (city) Richmond County	44	0.46
North El Monte, CA (cdp) Los Angeles County	17	0.46
Howe, TX (town) Grayson County	12	0.46
Union City, CA (city) Alameda County	314	0.45
Northeast Ithaca, NY (cdp) Tompkins County	12	0.45
Colma, CA (town) San Mateo County	8	0.45
Indianapolis, IN (city) Marion County	3,622	0.44
Omaha, NE (city) Douglas County	1,779	0.44
Hartford, CT (city/town) Hartford County	553	0.44
Hampton, MN (city) Dakota County	3	0.44
Boardman, OR (city) Morrow County	14	0.43
Kent, WA (city) King County	384	0.42
Charlottesville, VA (ind. city) Charlottesville independent city	183	0.42
Green Island, NY (town/village) Albany County	11	0.42
Temple City, CA (city) Los Angeles County	145	0.41
Walnut, CA (city) Los Angeles County	119	0.41
Southport, IN (city) Marion County	7	0.41
Des Moines, IA (city) Polk County	810	0.40
Kansas City, KS (city) Wyandotte County	578	0.40
High Point, NC (city) Guilford County	406	0.39
Woodland, NC (town) Northampton County	3	0.37
Speedway, IN (town) Marion County	42	0.36
Lewiston Woodville, NC (town) Bertie County	2	0.36
Lansing, MI (city) Ingham County	383	0.34
Lansing, MI (city) Ingham County	373	0.34
Newark, CA (city) Alameda County	145	0.34
Albany, NY (city) Albany County	322	0.33
Guntersville, AL (city) Marshall County	27	0.33
North Kansas City, MO (city) Clay County	14	0.33
Hiouchi, CA (cdp) Del Norte County	1	0.33
Ithaca, NY (town) Tompkins County	63	0.32
Lititz, PA (borough) Lancaster County	30	0.32
Konterra, MD (cdp) Prince George's County	8	0.32
Bellerose Terrace, NY (cdp) Nassau County	7	0.32
Jamestown, PA (borough) Mercer County	2	0.32
Rosburg, WA (cdp) Wahkiakum County	1	0.32
Burlington, WI (city) Racine County	32	0.31
Sebree, KY (city) Webster County	5	0.31
Akron, OH (city) Summit County	603	0.30
Diamond Bar, CA (city) Los Angeles County	166	0.30
Castle Shannon, PA (borough) Allegheny County	25	0.30
Herricks, NY (cdp) Nassau County	13	0.30
Rowland Heights, CA (cdp) Los Angeles County	143	0.29
Culver City, CA (city) Los Angeles County	114	0.29
West Springfield Town, MA (city) Hampden County	83	0.29
Taylors, SC (cdp) Greenville County	63	0.29
Albert Lea, MN (city) Freeborn County	52	0.29
Redland, MD (cdp) Montgomery County	50	0.29
Lima, PA (cdp) Delaware County	8	0.29
Cairo, NY (cdp) Greene County	4	0.29
Quincy, MN (township) Olmsted County	1	0.29
Lakewood, OH (city) Cuyahoga County	146	0.28

Please refer to the Explanation of Data in the front of the book for more detailed information.

Race

Asian: Burmese

Top 150 Places Sorted by Percent of Total Population

Based on places with total population of 7,500 or more

Place	Population	%
Clarkston, GA (city) DeKalb County	501	6.63
Huron, SD (city) Beadle County	515	4.09
Scottdale, GA (cdp) DeKalb County	412	3.88
Utica, NY (city) Oneida County	2,317	3.72
Dumas, TX (city) Moore County	507	3.45
Rensselaer, NY (city) Rensselaer County	316	3.36
Worthington, MN (city) Nobles County	296	2.32
New Bern, NC (city) Craven County	623	2.11
Arbutus, MD (cdp) Baltimore County	423	2.07
Daly City, CA (city) San Mateo County	2,023	2.00
Port Lavaca, TX (city) Calhoun County	244	1.99
Garden City, KS (city) Finney County	465	1.74
Carrboro, NC (town) Orange County	339	1.73
Fort Wayne, IN (city) Allen County	3,819	1.51
Tukwila, WA (city) King County	269	1.41
Guymon, OK (city) Texas County	153	1.34
Bowling Green, KY (city) Warren County	694	1.20
Whitehall, PA (borough) Allegheny County	151	1.08
Lewisville, TX (city) Denton County	942	0.99
South Salt Lake, UT (city) Salt Lake County	228	0.97
Frederick, MD (city) Frederick County	621	0.95
St. Paul, MN (city) Ramsey County	2,587	0.91
Buffalo, NY (city) Erie County	2,361	0.90
Amarillo, TX (city) Potter County	1,679	0.88
Syracuse, NY (city) Onondaga County	1,218	0.84
Roseville, MN (city) Ramsey County	275	0.82
Glen Ellyn, IL (village) DuPage County	226	0.82
South San Gabriel, CA (cdp) Los Angeles County	65	0.81
Logansport, IN (city) Cass County	144	0.78
Storm Lake, IA (city) Buena Vista County	82	0.77
Rock Island, IL (city) Rock Island County	282	0.72
Rosemead, CA (city) Los Angeles County	376	0.70
Washington, IN (city) Daviess County	80	0.70
Chapel Hill, NC (town) Orange County	393	0.69
St. Andrews, SC (cdp) Richland County	141	0.69
Fremont, CA (city) Alameda County	1,450	0.68
Arcadia, CA (city) Los Angeles County	376	0.67
San Gabriel, CA (city) Los Angeles County	261	0.66
Alhambra, CA (city) Los Angeles County	528	0.64
Lumberton, NC (city) Robeson County	134	0.62
Smyrna, TN (town) Rutherford County	241	0.60
Maplewood, MN (city) Ramsey County	224	0.59
Battle Creek, MI (city) Calhoun County	301	0.58
Marshalltown, IA (city) Marshall County	151	0.55
Pine Castle, FL (cdp) Orange County	56	0.52
Monterey Park, CA (city) Los Angeles County	279	0.46
Wheaton, IL (city) DuPage County	245	0.46
Ballenger Creek, MD (cdp) Frederick County	84	0.46
Elkridge, MD (cdp) Howard County	72	0.46
Rockingham, NC (city) Richmond County	44	0.46
Union City, CA (city) Alameda County	314	0.45
Indianapolis, IN (city) Marion County	3,622	0.44
Omaha, NE (city) Douglas County	1,779	0.44
Hartford, CT (city/town) Hartford County	553	0.44
Kent, WA (city) King County	384	0.42
Charlottesville, VA (ind. city) Charlottesville independent city	183	0.42
Temple City, CA (city) Los Angeles County	145	0.41
Walnut, CA (city) Los Angeles County	119	0.41
Des Moines, IA (city) Polk County	810	0.40
Kansas City, KS (city) Wyandotte County	578	0.40
High Point, NC (city) Guilford County	406	0.39
Speedway, IN (town) Marion County	42	0.36
Lansing, MI (city) Ingham County	383	0.34
Lansing, MI (city) Ingham County	373	0.34
Newark, CA (city) Alameda County	145	0.34
Albany, NY (city) Albany County	322	0.33
Guntersville, AL (city) Marshall County	27	0.33
Ithaca, NY (town) Tompkins County	63	0.32
Lititz, PA (borough) Lancaster County	30	0.32
Burlington, WI (city) Racine County	32	0.31
Akron, OH (city) Summit County	603	0.30
Diamond Bar, CA (city) Los Angeles County	166	0.30
Castle Shannon, PA (borough) Allegheny County	25	0.30
Rowland Heights, CA (cdp) Los Angeles County	143	0.29
Culver City, CA (city) Los Angeles County	114	0.29
West Springfield Town, MA (city) Hampden County	83	0.29
Taylors, SC (cdp) Greenville County	63	0.29
Albert Lea, MN (city) Freeborn County	52	0.29
Redland, MD (cdp) Montgomery County	50	0.29
Lakewood, OH (city) Cuyahoga County	146	0.28
Rochester, NY (city) Monroe County	565	0.27
Greeley, CO (city) Weld County	248	0.27
Rockville, MD (city) Montgomery County	165	0.27
Logan, UT (city) Cache County	128	0.27
East San Gabriel, CA (cdp) Los Angeles County	40	0.27
San Marino, CA (city) Los Angeles County	35	0.27
Rockford, IL (city) Winnebago County	403	0.26
South San Francisco, CA (city) San Mateo County	168	0.26
Trenton, NJ (city) Mercer County	205	0.24
Jenks, OK (city) Tulsa County	40	0.24
Sault Ste. Marie, MI (city) Chippewa County	34	0.24
Grand Rapids, MI (city) Kent County	424	0.23
Lancaster, PA (city) Lancaster County	135	0.23
Audubon, NJ (borough) Camden County	20	0.23
North Bethesda, MD (cdp) Montgomery County	95	0.22
Moline, IL (city) Rock Island County	94	0.22
Morehead City, NC (town) Carteret County	19	0.22
Salt Lake City, UT (city) Salt Lake County	385	0.21
El Monte, CA (city) Los Angeles County	241	0.21
Kennewick, WA (city) Benton County	157	0.21
Blue Ash, OH (city) Hamilton County	26	0.21
San Francisco, CA (city) San Francisco County	1,579	0.20
Milpitas, CA (city) Santa Clara County	135	0.20
Millcreek, UT (cdp) Salt Lake County	123	0.20
Scaggsville, MD (cdp) Howard County	49	0.20
Millbrae, CA (city) San Mateo County	42	0.20
Glenside, PA (cdp) Montgomery County	17	0.20
Aspen Hill, MD (cdp) Montgomery County	95	0.19
Holladay, UT (city) Salt Lake County	50	0.19
Charter Oak, CA (cdp) Los Angeles County	18	0.19
Dallas, TX (city) Dallas County	2,127	0.18
Burlington, VT (city) Chittenden County	76	0.18
Ithaca, NY (city) Tompkins County	53	0.18
Clive, IA (city) Polk County	28	0.18
Rossville, MD (cdp) Baltimore County	28	0.18
Cayce, SC (city) Lexington County	22	0.18
Mandeville, LA (city) St. Tammany Parish	21	0.18
Gettysburg, PA (borough) Adams County	14	0.18
Tulsa, OK (city) Tulsa County	659	0.17
West Covina, CA (city) Los Angeles County	178	0.17
Atlantic City, NJ (city) Atlantic County	67	0.17
Burien, WA (city) King County	58	0.17
Franconia, VA (cdp) Fairfax County	31	0.17
Mays Chapel, MD (cdp) Baltimore County	19	0.17
Emeryville, CA (city) Alameda County	17	0.17
Montgomery, OH (city) Hamilton County	17	0.17
Boaz, AL (city) Marshall County	16	0.17
Alderwood Manor, WA (cdp) Snohomish County	14	0.17
Spokane, WA (city) Spokane County	343	0.16
Covina, CA (city) Los Angeles County	77	0.16
Hercules, CA (city) Contra Costa County	38	0.16
East Moline, IL (city) Rock Island County	34	0.16
Colesville, MD (cdp) Montgomery County	24	0.16
North New Hyde Park, NY (cdp) Nassau County	24	0.16
Crowley, TX (city) Tarrant County	21	0.16
Phoenix, AZ (city) Maricopa County	2,184	0.15
Nashville-Davidson, TN (metro govt) Davidson County	883	0.15
Milwaukee, WI (city) Milwaukee County	882	0.15
Lincoln, NE (city) Lancaster County	395	0.15
Wheaton, MD (cdp) Montgomery County	72	0.15
Montgomery Village, MD (cdp) Montgomery County	47	0.15
Fair Lakes, VA (cdp) Fairfax County	12	0.15
Aurora, CO (city) Arapahoe County	452	0.14
Boise City, ID (city) Ada County	292	0.14
Twin Falls, ID (city) Twin Falls County	61	0.14
Rome, NY (city) Oneida County	48	0.14
Northfield, NJ (city) Atlantic County	12	0.14
Denver, CO (city) Denver County	800	0.13
Portland, OR (city) Multnomah County	747	0.13
Baldwin Park, CA (city) Los Angeles County	97	0.13

Please refer to the Explanation of Data in the front of the book for more detailed information.

Race

Asian: Cambodian

U.S. and 50 States Sorted by Population and Percent of Total Population

Place	Population	%
United States	**276,667**	**0.09**
California	102,317	0.27
Massachusetts	28,424	0.43
Washington	22,934	0.34
Texas	14,347	0.06
Pennsylvania	14,118	0.11
Minnesota	9,543	0.18
Virginia	7,306	0.09
Florida	6,267	0.03
Rhode Island	5,961	0.57
Georgia	5,423	0.06
New York	5,114	0.03
Ohio	4,570	0.04
Illinois	4,366	0.03
North Carolina	4,345	0.05
Oregon	3,934	0.10
Connecticut	3,308	0.09
Maryland	3,137	0.05
Colorado	2,803	0.06
Arizona	2,635	0.04
Utah	2,328	0.08
Michigan	2,219	0.02
Tennessee	1,949	0.03
Maine	1,691	0.13
New Jersey	1,667	0.02
Nevada	1,630	0.06
South Carolina	1,617	0.03
Kansas	1,409	0.05
Missouri	1,328	0.02
Wisconsin	1,294	0.02
Iowa	1,057	0.03
Indiana	1,019	0.02
Kentucky	910	0.02
Alabama	827	0.02
New Hampshire	807	0.06
Louisiana	735	0.02
Hawaii	705	0.05
Oklahoma	504	0.01
Alaska	328	0.05
Mississippi	302	0.01
Nebraska	243	0.01
Arkansas	230	0.01
Idaho	199	0.01
New Mexico	154	0.01
South Dakota	125	0.02
Vermont	117	0.02
Delaware	113	0.01
District of Columbia	97	0.02
North Dakota	79	0.01
West Virginia	65	<0.01
Wyoming	39	0.01
Montana	28	<0.01

Place	Population	%
Rhode Island	5,961	0.57
Massachusetts	28,424	0.43
Washington	22,934	0.34
California	102,317	0.27
Minnesota	9,543	0.18
Maine	1,691	0.13
Pennsylvania	14,118	0.11
Oregon	3,934	0.10
United States	**276,667**	**0.09**
Virginia	7,306	0.09
Connecticut	3,308	0.09
Utah	2,328	0.08
Texas	14,347	0.06
Georgia	5,423	0.06
Colorado	2,803	0.06
Nevada	1,630	0.06
New Hampshire	807	0.06
North Carolina	4,345	0.05
Maryland	3,137	0.05
Kansas	1,409	0.05
Hawaii	705	0.05
Alaska	328	0.05
Ohio	4,570	0.04
Arizona	2,635	0.04
Florida	6,267	0.03
New York	5,114	0.03
Illinois	4,366	0.03
Tennessee	1,949	0.03
South Carolina	1,617	0.03
Iowa	1,057	0.03
Michigan	2,219	0.02
New Jersey	1,667	0.02
Missouri	1,328	0.02
Wisconsin	1,294	0.02
Indiana	1,019	0.02
Kentucky	910	0.02
Alabama	827	0.02
Louisiana	735	0.02
South Dakota	125	0.02
Vermont	117	0.02
District of Columbia	97	0.02
Oklahoma	504	0.01
Mississippi	302	0.01
Nebraska	243	0.01
Arkansas	230	0.01
Idaho	199	0.01
New Mexico	154	0.01
Delaware	113	0.01
North Dakota	79	0.01
Wyoming	39	0.01
West Virginia	65	<0.01
Montana	28	<0.01

Please refer to the Explanation of Data in the front of the book for more detailed information.

Race

Asian: Cambodian

Top 150 Places Sorted by Population

Based on all places, regardless of total population

Place	Population	%
Long Beach, CA (city) Los Angeles County	19,998	4.33
Lowell, MA (city) Middlesex County	14,470	13.58
Stockton, CA (city) San Joaquin County	11,429	3.92
Philadelphia, PA (city) Philadelphia County	9,912	0.65
San Jose, CA (city) Santa Clara County	4,934	0.52
Fresno, CA (city) Fresno County	4,798	0.97
San Diego, CA (city) San Diego County	4,650	0.36
Los Angeles, CA (city) Los Angeles County	4,280	0.11
Lynn, MA (city) Essex County	3,899	4.32
Tacoma, WA (city) Pierce County	3,562	1.80
Providence, RI (city) Providence County	3,339	1.88
Oakland, CA (city) Alameda County	3,175	0.81
Modesto, CA (city) Stanislaus County	2,752	1.37
New York, NY (city) Kings County	2,591	0.03
Seattle, WA (city) King County	2,185	0.36
Santa Ana, CA (city) Orange County	1,818	0.56
Columbus, OH (city) Franklin County	1,794	0.23
Jacksonville, FL (city) Duval County	1,683	0.20
Cranston, RI (city) Providence County	1,592	1.98
San Francisco, CA (city) San Francisco County	1,518	0.19
Rochester, MN (city) Olmsted County	1,512	1.42
Chicago, IL (city) Cook County	1,404	0.05
Lakewood, CA (city) Los Angeles County	1,317	1.65
Fall River, MA (city) Bristol County	1,241	1.40
Charlotte, NC (city) Mecklenburg County	1,236	0.17
Bronx, NY (borough) Bronx County	1,188	0.09
St. Paul, MN (city) Ramsey County	1,177	0.41
Sacramento, CA (city) Sacramento County	1,082	0.23
Houston, TX (city) Harris County	1,050	0.05
Portland, OR (city) Multnomah County	1,018	0.17
San Bernardino, CA (city) San Bernardino County	1,014	0.48
Kent, WA (city) King County	1,003	1.09
Rosemead, CA (city) Los Angeles County	994	1.85
Dallas, TX (city) Dallas County	992	0.08
Bellflower, CA (city) Los Angeles County	978	1.28
Revere, MA (city) Suffolk County	974	1.88
West Valley City, UT (city) Salt Lake County	971	0.75
Wichita, KS (city) Sedgwick County	936	0.24
Santa Rosa, CA (city) Sonoma County	931	0.55
Signal Hill, CA (city) Los Angeles County	927	8.42
Carrollton, TX (city) Denton County	906	0.76
Renton, WA (city) King County	837	0.92
Pomona, CA (city) Los Angeles County	836	0.56
Anaheim, CA (city) Orange County	831	0.25
Garden Grove, CA (city) Orange County	753	0.44
Brooklyn, NY (borough) Kings County	751	0.03
Holland, MI (charter township) Ottawa County	749	2.10
Boston, MA (city) Suffolk County	745	0.12
Danbury, CT (city/town) Fairfield County	744	0.92
Phoenix, AZ (city) Maricopa County	744	0.05
Norwalk, CA (city) Los Angeles County	743	0.70
Everett, WA (city) Snohomish County	709	0.69
Attleboro, MA (city) Bristol County	708	1.62
Denver, CO (city) Denver County	679	0.11
Fort Worth, TX (city) Tarrant County	679	0.09
Monterey Park, CA (city) Los Angeles County	676	1.12
Greensboro, NC (city) Guilford County	648	0.24
Portland, ME (city) Cumberland County	647	0.98
White Center, WA (cdp) King County	642	4.76
Nashville-Davidson, TN (metro govt) Davidson County	641	0.11
Lawrence, MA (city) Essex County	636	0.83
El Monte, CA (city) Los Angeles County	632	0.56
St. Petersburg, FL (city) Pinellas County	628	0.26
Garland, TX (city) Dallas County	615	0.27
Bloomington, MN (city) Hennepin County	585	0.71
Shakopee, MN (city) Scott County	580	1.56
Memphis, TN (city) Shelby County	548	0.08
Vancouver, WA (city) Clark County	538	0.33
Bakersfield, CA (city) Kern County	520	0.15
Aurora, CO (city) Arapahoe County	519	0.16
Alhambra, CA (city) Los Angeles County	497	0.60
Moreno Valley, CA (city) Riverside County	496	0.26
Federal Way, WA (city) King County	491	0.55
Des Moines, IA (city) Polk County	488	0.24
Utica, NY (city) Oneida County	480	0.77
East Hill-Meridian, WA (cdp) King County	476	1.59
SeaTac, WA (city) King County	467	1.74
Savage, MN (city) Scott County	447	1.66
Midland, WA (cdp) Pierce County	446	4.98
Worcester, MA (city) Worcester County	433	0.24
Burien, WA (city) King County	413	1.24
Dracut, MA (town) Middlesex County	409	1.39
Eagan, MN (city) Dakota County	404	0.63
Bridgeport, CT (city/town) Fairfield County	402	0.28
Aloha, OR (cdp) Washington County	400	0.81
Madison, WI (city) Dane County	390	0.17
Minneapolis, MN (city) Hennepin County	389	0.10
Elk Grove, CA (city) Sacramento County	384	0.25
Ceres, CA (city) Stanislaus County	383	0.84
San Gabriel, CA (city) Los Angeles County	382	0.96
Rochester, NY (city) Monroe County	381	0.18
Bellevue, WA (city) King County	374	0.31
Riverside, CA (city) Riverside County	373	0.12
Palm Coast, FL (city) Flagler County	370	0.49
Eastvale, CA (cdp) Riverside County	367	0.68
Burnsville, MN (city) Dakota County	367	0.61
Lexington, NC (city) Davidson County	365	1.93
Arlington, VA (cdp) Arlington County	362	0.17
Hillsboro, OR (city) Washington County	361	0.39
Parkland, WA (cdp) Pierce County	358	1.00
Fontana, CA (city) San Bernardino County	358	0.18
Florin, CA (cdp) Sacramento County	357	0.75
Orange, CA (city) Orange County	351	0.26
Baldwin Park, CA (city) Los Angeles County	350	0.46
Kansas City, MO (city) Jackson County	350	0.08
Cerritos, CA (city) Los Angeles County	349	0.71
Tustin, CA (city) Orange County	336	0.44
Irvine, CA (city) Orange County	336	0.16
San Leandro, CA (city) Alameda County	335	0.39
Tukwila, WA (city) King County	333	1.74
Corona, CA (city) Riverside County	332	0.22
Columbia, MO (city) Boone County	329	0.30
Cleveland, OH (city) Cuyahoga County	328	0.08
Lacey, WA (city) Thurston County	327	0.77
Hayward, CA (city) Alameda County	312	0.22
Rialto, CA (city) San Bernardino County	310	0.31
Ontario, CA (city) San Bernardino County	309	0.19
Las Vegas, NV (city) Clark County	307	0.05
Queens, NY (borough) Queens County	303	0.01
Camden, NJ (city) Camden County	300	0.39
Tracy, CA (city) San Joaquin County	299	0.36
Holland, MI (city) Ottawa County	295	0.89
Brooklyn Park, MN (city) Hennepin County	294	0.39
Upper Darby, PA (township) Delaware County	294	0.36
Janesville, WI (city) Rock County	293	0.46
Austin, TX (city) Travis County	291	0.04
Beaverton, OR (city) Washington County	290	0.32
Buena Park, CA (city) Orange County	282	0.35
Westminster, CA (city) Orange County	282	0.31
Chandler, AZ (city) Maricopa County	282	0.12
Urban Honolulu, HI (cdp) Honolulu County	277	0.08
Paramount, CA (city) Los Angeles County	275	0.51
Auburn, WA (city) King County	269	0.38
Murrieta, CA (city) Riverside County	268	0.26
Des Moines, WA (city) King County	265	0.89
Salem, OR (city) Marion County	265	0.17
Holland, MI (city) Ottawa County	264	1.01
Eastmont, WA (cdp) Snohomish County	262	1.30
Clovis, CA (city) Fresno County	254	0.27
Pennsauken, NJ (township) Camden County	249	0.69
Union City, CA (city) Alameda County	248	0.36
Malden, MA (city) Middlesex County	246	0.41
Lakeville, MN (city) Dakota County	244	0.44
Spring Valley, NV (cdp) Clark County	244	0.14
Anchorage, AK (municipality) Anchorage Municipality	239	0.08
Carson, CA (city) Los Angeles County	236	0.26
West Covina, CA (city) Los Angeles County	236	0.22
Lynnwood, WA (city) Snohomish County	232	0.65
Newport News, VA (ind. city) Newport News independent city	232	0.13
Lake Elsinore, CA (city) Riverside County	230	0.44

Please refer to the Explanation of Data in the front of the book for more detailed information.

SECTION THREE

Race

Asian: Cambodian

Top 150 Places Sorted by Percent of Total Population

Based on all places, regardless of total population

Place	Population	%
Swanville, MN (city) Todd County	1	50.00
Lowell, MA (city) Middlesex County	14,470	13.58
Buras, LA (cdp) Plaquemines Parish	100	10.58
Signal Hill, CA (city) Los Angeles County	927	8.42
Rouse, CA (cdp) Stanislaus County	152	7.58
Junction City, WA (cdp) Grays Harbor County	1	5.56
Iowa Colony, TX (village) Brazoria County	60	5.13
Midland, WA (cdp) Pierce County	446	4.98
White Center, WA (cdp) King County	642	4.76
Bayou La Batre, AL (city) Mobile County	120	4.69
Ocean City, WA (cdp) Grays Harbor County	9	4.50
Olivet, KS (city) Osage County	3	4.48
Sun Valley, TX (city) Lamar County	3	4.35
Larch Way, WA (cdp) Snohomish County	144	4.34
Long Beach, CA (city) Los Angeles County	19,998	4.33
Lynn, MA (city) Essex County	3,899	4.32
Stockton, CA (city) San Joaquin County	11,429	3.92
Cascade, MN (township) Olmsted County	98	3.48
South Bend, WA (city) Pacific County	52	3.18
Redstone, CO (cdp) Pitkin County	4	3.08
Riverton, WA (cdp) King County	179	2.79
Long Island, ME (town) Cumberland County	6	2.61
Soudersburg, PA (cdp) Lancaster County	14	2.59
West Modesto, CA (cdp) Stanislaus County	138	2.43
Wheatland, CA (city) Yuba County	84	2.43
Urbancrest, OH (village) Franklin County	23	2.40
Oyehut, WA (cdp) Grays Harbor County	2	2.35
Hardtner, KS (city) Barber County	4	2.33
Empire, LA (cdp) Plaquemines Parish	22	2.22
Campobello, SC (town) Spartanburg County	11	2.19
Holland, MI (charter township) Ottawa County	749	2.10
Cranston, RI (city) Providence County	1,592	1.98
Paradise, CA (cdp) Mono County	3	1.96
Fairforest, SC (cdp) Spartanburg County	33	1.95
Lexington, NC (city) Davidson County	365	1.93
La Motte, IA (city) Jackson County	5	1.92
Providence, RI (city) Providence County	3,339	1.88
Revere, MA (city) Suffolk County	974	1.88
Boulevard Park, WA (cdp) King County	99	1.87
Boothville, LA (cdp) Plaquemines Parish	16	1.87
Rosemead, CA (city) Los Angeles County	994	1.85
Tacoma, WA (city) Pierce County	3,562	1.80
South Amherst, MA (cdp) Hampshire County	90	1.80
SeaTac, WA (city) King County	467	1.74
Tukwila, WA (city) King County	333	1.74
Barnesville, MD (town) Montgomery County	3	1.74
Fife Heights, WA (cdp) Pierce County	37	1.73
Middlefield, MA (town) Hampshire County	9	1.73
Fife, WA (city) Pierce County	158	1.72
Beechwood, MI (cdp) Ottawa County	52	1.72
Ravensworth, VA (cdp) Fairfax County	42	1.70
Riverdale Park, CA (cdp) Stanislaus County	19	1.68
Savage, MN (city) Scott County	447	1.66
Lakewood, CA (city) Los Angeles County	1,317	1.65
Attleboro, MA (city) Bristol County	708	1.62
Banks, AR (town) Bradley County	2	1.61
East Hill-Meridian, WA (cdp) King County	476	1.59
Shakopee, MN (city) Scott County	580	1.56
Inman, SC (city) Spartanburg County	36	1.55
Oronoco, MN (city) Olmsted County	20	1.54
Coldspring, TX (city) San Jacinto County	13	1.52
Tanglewilde, WA (cdp) Thurston County	89	1.51
Brooks, OR (cdp) Marion County	6	1.51
Dennison, MN (city) Goodhue County	3	1.51
Haverhill, MN (township) Olmsted County	22	1.47
Martha Lake, WA (cdp) Snohomish County	224	1.45
Elma, WA (city) Grays Harbor County	45	1.45
Riverside, UT (cdp) Box Elder County	11	1.45
Rochester, MN (city) Olmsted County	1,512	1.42
Bellwood, VA (cdp) Chesterfield County	90	1.42
Dennison, MN (city) Goodhue County	3	1.42
Fall River, MA (city) Bristol County	1,241	1.40
Kingsgate, WA (cdp) King County	183	1.40
Sanford, ME (cdp) York County	137	1.40
Dracut, MA (town) Middlesex County	409	1.39

Place	Population	%
Modesto, CA (city) Stanislaus County	2,752	1.37
Taft Mosswood, CA (cdp) San Joaquin County	21	1.37
Lake Stickney, WA (cdp) Snohomish County	105	1.35
Weston, OR (city) Umatilla County	9	1.35
Warwick, OK (town) Lincoln County	2	1.35
Kenneth City, FL (town) Pinellas County	66	1.33
Sunnyside, CA (cdp) Fresno County	56	1.32
Reklaw, TX (city) Cherokee County	5	1.32
Monmouth, CA (cdp) Fresno County	2	1.32
Eastmont, WA (cdp) Snohomish County	262	1.30
Bellflower, CA (city) Los Angeles County	978	1.28
Danforth, MN (township) Pine County	1	1.28
Bensley, VA (cdp) Chesterfield County	74	1.27
Clover Creek, WA (cdp) Pierce County	82	1.26
Carver, MN (city) Carver County	47	1.26
Raymond, WA (city) Pacific County	36	1.25
Burien, WA (city) King County	413	1.24
Alger, WA (cdp) Skagit County	5	1.24
Artesia, CA (city) Los Angeles County	202	1.22
Highwater, MN (township) Cottonwood County	2	1.20
Corunna, IN (town) DeKalb County	3	1.18
Morrow, GA (city) Clayton County	75	1.16
Monterey Park, CA (city) Los Angeles County	676	1.12
Dresbach, MN (township) Winona County	5	1.10
Kent, WA (city) King County	1,003	1.09
Riverdale, GA (city) Clayton County	165	1.09
Pleasant Run, OH (cdp) Hamilton County	54	1.09
Sanford, ME (town) York County	223	1.07
Dash Point, WA (cdp) Pierce County	10	1.07
Summit View, WA (cdp) Pierce County	77	1.06
Algona, WA (city) King County	32	1.06
Meadowbrook, VA (cdp) Chesterfield County	193	1.05
Bystrom, CA (cdp) Stanislaus County	42	1.05
East Lansdowne, PA (borough) Delaware County	28	1.05
Gordon, TX (city) Palo Pinto County	5	1.05
Frederickson, WA (cdp) Pierce County	195	1.04
South San Gabriel, CA (cdp) Los Angeles County	84	1.04
Springvale, ME (cdp) York County	34	1.03
Ridgeside, TN (city) Hamilton County	4	1.03
West Elkton, OH (village) Preble County	2	1.02
Holland, MI (city) Ottawa County	264	1.01
Welcome, NC (cdp) Davidson County	42	1.01
Parkland, WA (cdp) Pierce County	358	1.00
Portland, ME (city) Cumberland County	647	0.98
Bothell West, WA (cdp) Snohomish County	163	0.98
Pelham, MA (town) Hampshire County	13	0.98
Fresno, CA (city) Fresno County	4,798	0.97
San Gabriel, CA (city) Los Angeles County	382	0.96
Tyngsborough, MA (town) Middlesex County	105	0.93
North Springfield, VA (cdp) Fairfax County	68	0.93
Renton, WA (city) King County	837	0.92
Danbury, CT (city/town) Fairfield County	744	0.92
Airport, CA (cdp) Stanislaus County	18	0.92
Shepherd, TX (city) San Jacinto County	21	0.91
Holland, MI (city) Ottawa County	295	0.89
Des Moines, WA (city) King County	265	0.89
Silver Firs, WA (cdp) Snohomish County	186	0.89
Hainesville, IL (village) Lake County	32	0.89
Hawaiian Gardens, CA (city) Los Angeles County	125	0.88
Catherine, CO (cdp) Garfield County	2	0.88
Fowlerville, NY (cdp) Livingston County	2	0.88
Mayfield, KS (city) Sumner County	1	0.88
Landfall, MN (city) Washington County	6	0.87
Summit, WA (cdp) Pierce County	69	0.86
Mayer, MN (city) Carver County	15	0.86
Millbourne, PA (borough) Delaware County	10	0.86
Roseland, CA (cdp) Sonoma County	54	0.85
Elko New Market, MN (city) Scott County	35	0.85
West Kennebunk, ME (cdp) York County	10	0.85
Madrone, NM (cdp) Valencia County	6	0.85
Emington, IL (village) Livingston County	1	0.85
Ceres, CA (city) Stanislaus County	383	0.84
South Sanford, ME (cdp) York County	38	0.84
Post Oak Bend City, TX (town) Kaufman County	5	0.84
Lawrence, MA (city) Essex County	636	0.83

Please refer to the Explanation of Data in the front of the book for more detailed information.

Race

Asian: Cambodian

Top 150 Places Sorted by Percent of Total Population

Based on places with total population of 7,500 or more

Place	Population	%
Lowell, MA (city) Middlesex County	14,470	13.58
Signal Hill, CA (city) Los Angeles County	927	8.42
Midland, WA (cdp) Pierce County	446	4.98
White Center, WA (cdp) King County	642	4.76
Long Beach, CA (city) Los Angeles County	19,998	4.33
Lynn, MA (city) Essex County	3,899	4.32
Stockton, CA (city) San Joaquin County	11,429	3.92
Holland, MI (charter township) Ottawa County	749	2.10
Cranston, RI (city) Providence County	1,592	1.98
Lexington, NC (city) Davidson County	365	1.93
Providence, RI (city) Providence County	3,339	1.88
Revere, MA (city) Suffolk County	974	1.88
Rosemead, CA (city) Los Angeles County	994	1.85
Tacoma, WA (city) Pierce County	3,562	1.80
SeaTac, WA (city) King County	467	1.74
Tukwila, WA (city) King County	333	1.74
Fife, WA (city) Pierce County	158	1.72
Savage, MN (city) Scott County	447	1.66
Lakewood, CA (city) Los Angeles County	1,317	1.65
Attleboro, MA (city) Bristol County	708	1.62
East Hill-Meridian, WA (cdp) King County	476	1.59
Shakopee, MN (city) Scott County	580	1.56
Martha Lake, WA (cdp) Snohomish County	224	1.45
Rochester, MN (city) Olmsted County	1,512	1.42
Fall River, MA (city) Bristol County	1,241	1.40
Kingsgate, WA (cdp) King County	183	1.40
Sanford, ME (cdp) York County	137	1.40
Dracut, MA (town) Middlesex County	409	1.39
Modesto, CA (city) Stanislaus County	2,752	1.37
Lake Stickney, WA (cdp) Snohomish County	105	1.35
Eastmont, WA (cdp) Snohomish County	262	1.30
Bellflower, CA (city) Los Angeles County	978	1.28
Burien, WA (city) King County	413	1.24
Artesia, CA (city) Los Angeles County	202	1.22
Monterey Park, CA (city) Los Angeles County	676	1.12
Kent, WA (city) King County	1,003	1.09
Riverdale, GA (city) Clayton County	165	1.09
Sanford, ME (town) York County	223	1.07
Meadowbrook, VA (cdp) Chesterfield County	193	1.05
Frederickson, WA (cdp) Pierce County	195	1.04
South San Gabriel, CA (cdp) Los Angeles County	84	1.04
Holland, MI (city) Ottawa County	264	1.01
Parkland, WA (cdp) Pierce County	358	1.00
Portland, ME (city) Cumberland County	647	0.98
Bothell West, WA (cdp) Snohomish County	163	0.98
Fresno, CA (city) Fresno County	4,798	0.97
San Gabriel, CA (city) Los Angeles County	382	0.96
Tyngsborough, MA (town) Middlesex County	105	0.93
Renton, WA (city) King County	837	0.92
Danbury, CT (city/town) Fairfield County	744	0.92
Holland, MI (city) Ottawa County	295	0.89
Des Moines, WA (city) King County	265	0.89
Silver Firs, WA (cdp) Snohomish County	186	0.89
Hawaiian Gardens, CA (city) Los Angeles County	125	0.88
Summit, WA (cdp) Pierce County	69	0.86
Ceres, CA (city) Stanislaus County	383	0.84
Lawrence, MA (city) Essex County	636	0.83
Oakland, CA (city) Alameda County	3,175	0.81
Aloha, OR (cdp) Washington County	400	0.81
Picnic Point, WA (cdp) Snohomish County	71	0.81
North Lynnwood, WA (cdp) Snohomish County	132	0.80
Mill Creek East, WA (cdp) Snohomish County	124	0.79
Orchards, WA (cdp) Clark County	152	0.78
Utica, NY (city) Oneida County	480	0.77
Lacey, WA (city) Thurston County	327	0.77
Lansdale, PA (borough) Montgomery County	125	0.77
Carrollton, TX (city) Denton County	906	0.76
West Valley City, UT (city) Salt Lake County	971	0.75
Florin, CA (cdp) Sacramento County	357	0.75
Bryn Mawr-Skyway, WA (cdp) King County	118	0.75
August, CA (cdp) San Joaquin County	63	0.75
Bothell East, WA (cdp) Snohomish County	60	0.75
Tremonton, UT (city) Box Elder County	57	0.75
Faribault, MN (city) Rice County	172	0.74
Zeeland, MI (charter township) Ottawa County	74	0.74
Bloomington, MN (city) Hennepin County	585	0.71
Cerritos, CA (city) Los Angeles County	349	0.71
Sterling, VA (cdp) Loudoun County	197	0.71
Easthampton Town, MA (city) Hampshire County	114	0.71
Lakeland North, WA (cdp) King County	92	0.71
Park City, IL (city) Lake County	54	0.71
Norwalk, CA (city) Los Angeles County	743	0.70
Everett, WA (city) Snohomish County	709	0.69
Pennsauken, NJ (township) Camden County	249	0.69
Lealman, FL (cdp) Pinellas County	138	0.69
Waller, WA (cdp) Pierce County	55	0.69
Eastvale, CA (cdp) Riverside County	367	0.68
Lilburn, GA (city) Gwinnett County	78	0.67
Dumbarton, VA (cdp) Henrico County	53	0.67
Five Corners, WA (cdp) Clark County	119	0.66
Philadelphia, PA (city) Philadelphia County	9,912	0.65
Lynnwood, WA (city) Snohomish County	232	0.65
Lathrop, CA (city) San Joaquin County	118	0.65
Country Club, CA (cdp) San Joaquin County	60	0.64
Eagan, MN (city) Dakota County	404	0.63
Bethel, CT (cdp) Fairfield County	60	0.63
Parkway, CA (cdp) Sacramento County	91	0.62
Burnsville, MN (city) Dakota County	367	0.61
Aberdeen, WA (city) Grays Harbor County	103	0.61
Alhambra, CA (city) Los Angeles County	497	0.60
Saugus, MA (cdp/town) Essex County	160	0.60
Mountain House, CA (cdp) San Joaquin County	58	0.60
New Carrollton, MD (city) Prince George's County	72	0.59
Westbrook, ME (city) Cumberland County	101	0.58
Santa Ana, CA (city) Orange County	1,818	0.56
Pomona, CA (city) Los Angeles County	836	0.56
El Monte, CA (city) Los Angeles County	632	0.56
Calverton, MD (cdp) Montgomery County	100	0.56
Alderwood Manor, WA (cdp) Snohomish County	47	0.56
Santa Rosa, CA (city) Sonoma County	931	0.55
Federal Way, WA (city) King County	491	0.55
Cloverly, MD (cdp) Montgomery County	83	0.55
Chelmsford, MA (town) Middlesex County	184	0.54
Spanaway, WA (cdp) Pierce County	147	0.54
Mill Creek, WA (city) Snohomish County	99	0.54
Kemp Mill, MD (cdp) Montgomery County	68	0.54
Annandale, VA (cdp) Fairfax County	218	0.53
San Lorenzo, CA (cdp) Alameda County	124	0.53
San Jose, CA (city) Santa Clara County	4,934	0.52
Paramount, CA (city) Los Angeles County	275	0.51
Springfield, VA (cdp) Fairfax County	156	0.51
South Portland, ME (city) Cumberland County	127	0.51
Fairwood, WA (cdp) King County	97	0.51
Bon Air, VA (cdp) Chesterfield County	84	0.51
Colesville, MD (cdp) Montgomery County	75	0.51
Amherst, MA (town) Hampshire County	188	0.50
Lemon Hill, CA (cdp) Sacramento County	68	0.50
El Sobrante, CA (cdp) Riverside County	63	0.50
Woodinville, WA (city) King County	55	0.50
Doraville, GA (city) DeKalb County	42	0.50
Palm Coast, FL (city) Flagler County	370	0.49
Woonsocket, RI (city) Providence County	202	0.49
La Palma, CA (city) Orange County	76	0.49
Belchertown, MA (town) Hampshire County	72	0.49
San Bernardino, CA (city) San Bernardino County	1,014	0.48
Farmington, MN (city) Dakota County	102	0.48
West Lealman, FL (cdp) Pinellas County	73	0.47
Baldwin Park, CA (city) Los Angeles County	350	0.46
Janesville, WI (city) Rock County	293	0.46
Hercules, CA (city) Contra Costa County	110	0.46
King of Prussia, PA (cdp) Montgomery County	92	0.46
Mountlake Terrace, WA (city) Snohomish County	91	0.46
Alum Rock, CA (cdp) Santa Clara County	71	0.46
Madeira, OH (city) Hamilton County	40	0.46
West Falls Church, VA (cdp) Fairfax County	130	0.45
Manassas Park, VA (ind. city) Manassas Park independent city	64	0.45
Happy Valley, OR (city) Clackamas County	62	0.45
Boiling Springs, SC (cdp) Spartanburg County	37	0.45
Garden Grove, CA (city) Orange County	753	0.44
Tustin, CA (city) Orange County	336	0.44

SECTION THREE

Please refer to the Explanation of Data in the front of the book for more detailed information.

Race

Asian: Chinese, except Taiwanese

U.S. and 50 States Sorted by Population and Percent of Total Population

Place	Population	%
United States	**3,794,673**	**1.23**
California	1,349,111	3.62
New York	598,597	3.09
Hawaii	198,711	14.61
Texas	166,837	0.66
New Jersey	139,699	1.59
Massachusetts	131,846	2.01
Washington	113,144	1.68
Illinois	112,951	0.88
Pennsylvania	92,970	0.73
Florida	90,381	0.48
Maryland	74,587	1.29
Virginia	68,707	0.86
Georgia	50,725	0.52
Michigan	48,302	0.49
Ohio	47,861	0.41
Arizona	40,507	0.63
Oregon	39,589	1.03
North Carolina	38,764	0.41
Nevada	38,108	1.41
Connecticut	35,350	0.99
Colorado	31,781	0.63
Minnesota	28,776	0.54
Indiana	24,468	0.38
Missouri	24,457	0.41
Wisconsin	20,056	0.35
Tennessee	17,422	0.27
Utah	15,597	0.56
Kansas	12,677	0.44
Louisiana	11,290	0.25
South Carolina	11,271	0.24
Oklahoma	11,104	0.30
Iowa	10,912	0.36
Alabama	10,637	0.22
Kentucky	10,024	0.23
Rhode Island	7,924	0.75
New Mexico	7,335	0.36
New Hampshire	7,327	0.56
Delaware	6,761	0.75
District of Columbia	6,204	1.03
Arkansas	5,936	0.20
Nebraska	5,527	0.30
Idaho	5,212	0.33
Mississippi	5,168	0.17
Maine	4,285	0.32
Alaska	3,639	0.51
West Virginia	3,044	0.16
Vermont	2,723	0.44
Montana	1,845	0.19
North Dakota	1,691	0.25
South Dakota	1,534	0.19
Wyoming	1,299	0.23

Place	Population	%
Hawaii	198,711	14.61
California	1,349,111	3.62
New York	598,597	3.09
Massachusetts	131,846	2.01
Washington	113,144	1.68
New Jersey	139,699	1.59
Nevada	38,108	1.41
Maryland	74,587	1.29
United States	**3,794,673**	**1.23**
Oregon	39,589	1.03
District of Columbia	6,204	1.03
Connecticut	35,350	0.99
Illinois	112,951	0.88
Virginia	68,707	0.86
Rhode Island	7,924	0.75
Delaware	6,761	0.75
Pennsylvania	92,970	0.73
Texas	166,837	0.66
Arizona	40,507	0.63
Colorado	31,781	0.63
Utah	15,597	0.56
New Hampshire	7,327	0.56
Minnesota	28,776	0.54
Georgia	50,725	0.52
Alaska	3,639	0.51
Michigan	48,302	0.49
Florida	90,381	0.48
Kansas	12,677	0.44
Vermont	2,723	0.44
Ohio	47,861	0.41
North Carolina	38,764	0.41
Missouri	24,457	0.41
Indiana	24,468	0.38
Iowa	10,912	0.36
New Mexico	7,335	0.36
Wisconsin	20,056	0.35
Idaho	5,212	0.33
Maine	4,285	0.32
Oklahoma	11,104	0.30
Nebraska	5,527	0.30
Tennessee	17,422	0.27
Louisiana	11,290	0.25
North Dakota	1,691	0.25
South Carolina	11,271	0.24
Kentucky	10,024	0.23
Wyoming	1,299	0.23
Alabama	10,637	0.22
Arkansas	5,936	0.20
Montana	1,845	0.19
South Dakota	1,534	0.19
Mississippi	5,168	0.17
West Virginia	3,044	0.16

Please refer to the Explanation of Data in the front of the book for more detailed information.

Race

Asian: Chinese, except Taiwanese

Top 150 Places Sorted by Population

Based on all places, regardless of total population

Place	Population	%
New York, NY (city) Kings County	500,434	6.12
Queens, NY (borough) Queens County	200,714	9.00
San Francisco, CA (city) San Francisco County	181,707	22.57
Brooklyn, NY (borough) Kings County	178,214	7.12
Manhattan, NY (borough) New York County	99,287	6.26
Los Angeles, CA (city) Los Angeles County	75,827	2.00
San Jose, CA (city) Santa Clara County	67,093	7.09
Urban Honolulu, HI (cdp) Honolulu County	63,881	18.94
Chicago, IL (city) Cook County	46,446	1.72
San Diego, CA (city) San Diego County	40,557	3.10
Oakland, CA (city) Alameda County	37,235	9.53
Fremont, CA (city) Alameda County	36,484	17.04
Philadelphia, PA (city) Philadelphia County	32,773	2.15
Alhambra, CA (city) Los Angeles County	31,493	37.90
Monterey Park, CA (city) Los Angeles County	29,537	49.01
Seattle, WA (city) King County	28,837	4.74
Houston, TX (city) Harris County	28,268	1.35
Boston, MA (city) Suffolk County	25,921	4.20
Irvine, CA (city) Orange County	25,177	11.85
Sacramento, CA (city) Sacramento County	23,350	5.01
Arcadia, CA (city) Los Angeles County	21,744	38.58
Rosemead, CA (city) Los Angeles County	20,548	38.22
Sunnyvale, CA (city) Santa Clara County	17,556	12.53
San Gabriel, CA (city) Los Angeles County	17,137	43.15
Daly City, CA (city) San Mateo County	16,992	16.80
Rowland Heights, CA (cdp) Los Angeles County	16,563	33.81
El Monte, CA (city) Los Angeles County	16,151	14.23
Quincy, MA (city) Norfolk County	14,979	16.23
Cupertino, CA (city) Santa Clara County	14,930	25.61
Staten Island, NY (borough) Richmond County	14,107	3.01
Temple City, CA (city) Los Angeles County	13,931	39.18
Plano, TX (city) Collin County	12,905	4.97
Diamond Bar, CA (city) Los Angeles County	12,547	22.59
Portland, OR (city) Multnomah County	12,434	2.13
San Leandro, CA (city) Alameda County	12,337	14.52
Austin, TX (city) Travis County	11,810	1.49
Alameda, CA (city) Alameda County	11,760	15.93
Bellevue, WA (city) King County	11,725	9.58
Hacienda Heights, CA (cdp) Los Angeles County	11,348	21.00
East Honolulu, HI (cdp) Honolulu County	10,863	21.76
Elk Grove, CA (city) Sacramento County	10,629	6.95
Berkeley, CA (city) Alameda County	10,374	9.21
North Hempstead, NY (town) Nassau County	10,292	4.55
Milpitas, CA (city) Santa Clara County	10,156	15.21
Palo Alto, CA (city) Santa Clara County	9,739	15.12
Spring Valley, NV (cdp) Clark County	9,578	5.37
San Ramon, CA (city) Contra Costa County	9,284	12.87
Walnut, CA (city) Los Angeles County	9,242	31.68
West Covina, CA (city) Los Angeles County	9,089	8.57
Phoenix, AZ (city) Maricopa County	8,958	0.62
San Mateo, CA (city) San Mateo County	8,674	8.92
Santa Clara, CA (city) Santa Clara County	8,652	7.43
Mountain View, CA (city) Santa Clara County	8,277	11.18
Sugar Land, TX (city) Fort Bend County	8,218	10.43
Bronx, NY (borough) Bronx County	8,112	0.59
Union City, CA (city) Alameda County	8,102	11.65
Torrance, CA (city) Los Angeles County	8,045	5.53
Hempstead, NY (town) Nassau County	7,849	1.03
Castro Valley, CA (cdp) Alameda County	7,718	12.57
South San Francisco, CA (city) San Mateo County	7,687	12.08
Kaneohe, HI (cdp) Honolulu County	7,527	21.76
Edison, NJ (township) Middlesex County	7,486	7.49
Pasadena, CA (city) Los Angeles County	7,316	5.34
Pearl City, HI (cdp) Honolulu County	7,245	15.19
Oyster Bay, NY (town) Nassau County	7,054	2.41
Davis, CA (city) Yolo County	7,009	10.68
Malden, MA (city) Middlesex County	6,926	11.65
Chino Hills, CA (city) San Bernardino County	6,895	9.22
Hilo, HI (cdp) Hawaii County	6,805	15.73
Columbus, OH (city) Franklin County	6,780	0.86
Foster City, CA (city) San Mateo County	6,701	21.92
Cambridge, MA (city) Middlesex County	6,693	6.36
Dallas, TX (city) Dallas County	6,608	0.55
Ann Arbor, MI (city) Washtenaw County	6,555	5.75
Hayward, CA (city) Alameda County	6,398	4.44
Stockton, CA (city) San Joaquin County	6,382	2.19
Millbrae, CA (city) San Mateo County	6,268	29.11
Cerritos, CA (city) Los Angeles County	6,267	12.78
Washington, DC (city) District of Columbia	6,204	1.03
Brookhaven, NY (town) Suffolk County	6,107	1.26
Saratoga, CA (city) Santa Clara County	6,049	20.21
Newton, MA (city) Middlesex County	6,040	7.09
Kailua, HI (cdp) Honolulu County	5,971	15.45
Pleasanton, CA (city) Alameda County	5,928	8.43
Jersey City, NJ (city) Hudson County	5,886	2.38
Las Vegas, NV (city) Clark County	5,877	1.01
Long Beach, CA (city) Los Angeles County	5,734	1.24
San Antonio, TX (city) Medina County	5,707	0.43
Naperville, IL (city) DuPage County	5,487	3.87
Riverside, CA (city) Riverside County	5,471	1.80
Madison, WI (city) Dane County	5,402	2.32
Anaheim, CA (city) Orange County	5,374	1.60
Rockville, MD (city) Montgomery County	5,173	8.45
East San Gabriel, CA (cdp) Los Angeles County	4,965	33.38
Charlotte, NC (city) Mecklenburg County	4,883	0.67
Pittsburgh, PA (city) Allegheny County	4,872	1.59
Enterprise, NV (cdp) Clark County	4,857	4.48
Fresno, CA (city) Fresno County	4,726	0.96
San Marino, CA (city) Los Angeles County	4,707	35.80
Chandler, AZ (city) Maricopa County	4,702	1.99
Mililani Town, HI (cdp) Honolulu County	4,658	16.86
Richmond, CA (city) Contra Costa County	4,581	4.42
Huntington Beach, CA (city) Orange County	4,507	2.37
Brookline, MA (cdp/town) Norfolk County	4,432	7.55
Germantown, MD (cdp) Montgomery County	4,431	5.13
Renton, WA (city) King County	4,414	4.85
Tucson, AZ (city) Pima County	4,413	0.85
East Brunswick, NJ (township) Middlesex County	4,378	9.21
Denver, CO (city) Denver County	4,333	0.72
Cary, NC (town) Wake County	4,330	3.20
North Potomac, MD (cdp) Montgomery County	4,236	17.35
Fullerton, CA (city) Orange County	4,235	3.13
Johns Creek, GA (city) Fulton County	4,227	5.51
South Pasadena, CA (city) Los Angeles County	4,132	16.13
Thousand Oaks, CA (city) Ventura County	4,113	3.25
Baldwin Park, CA (city) Los Angeles County	4,086	5.42
Arlington, VA (cdp) Arlington County	4,053	1.95
Dublin, CA (city) Alameda County	4,016	8.72
Baltimore, MD (city) Baltimore city County	3,904	0.63
Redmond, WA (city) King County	3,886	7.18
Minneapolis, MN (city) Hennepin County	3,819	1.00
Troy, MI (city) Oakland County	3,809	4.70
Rancho Cucamonga, CA (city) San Bernardino County	3,715	2.25
San Bruno, CA (city) San Mateo County	3,688	8.97
Mililani Mauka, HI (cdp) Honolulu County	3,677	17.48
Redwood City, CA (city) San Mateo County	3,628	4.72
Eastvale, CA (cdp) Riverside County	3,625	6.75
Raleigh, NC (city) Wake County	3,607	0.89
Concord, CA (city) Contra Costa County	3,601	2.95
Henderson, NV (city) Clark County	3,594	1.39
Los Altos, CA (city) Santa Clara County	3,576	12.34
Sammamish, WA (city) King County	3,574	7.81
Albuquerque, NM (city) Bernalillo County	3,566	0.65
Pomona, CA (city) Los Angeles County	3,460	2.32
Ellicott City, MD (cdp) Howard County	3,441	5.23
Walnut Creek, CA (city) Contra Costa County	3,426	5.34
Richardson, TX (city) Dallas County	3,426	3.45
Rancho Palos Verdes, CA (city) Los Angeles County	3,424	8.22
Atlanta, GA (city) Fulton County	3,417	0.81
El Cerrito, CA (city) Contra Costa County	3,309	14.05
Ewa Gentry, HI (cdp) Honolulu County	3,303	14.56
West Windsor, NJ (township) Mercer County	3,267	12.03
Paradise, NV (cdp) Clark County	3,266	1.46
Gaithersburg, MD (city) Montgomery County	3,245	5.41
Parsippany-Troy Hills, NJ (township) Morris County	3,205	6.02
Indianapolis, IN (city) Marion County	3,197	0.39
Jacksonville, FL (city) Duval County	3,152	0.38
Durham, NC (city) Durham County	3,150	1.38
Amherst, NY (town) Erie County	3,146	2.57
Burlingame, CA (city) San Mateo County	3,126	10.85

Race

Asian: Chinese, except Taiwanese

Top 150 Places Sorted by Percent of Total Population

Based on all places, regardless of total population

Place	Population	%
Monterey Park, CA (city) Los Angeles County	29,537	49.01
San Gabriel, CA (city) Los Angeles County	17,137	43.15
Temple City, CA (city) Los Angeles County	13,931	39.18
Arcadia, CA (city) Los Angeles County	21,744	38.58
Rosemead, CA (city) Los Angeles County	20,548	38.22
Alhambra, CA (city) Los Angeles County	31,493	37.90
San Marino, CA (city) Los Angeles County	4,707	35.80
Rowland Heights, CA (cdp) Los Angeles County	16,563	33.81
East San Gabriel, CA (cdp) Los Angeles County	4,965	33.38
Walnut, CA (city) Los Angeles County	9,242	31.68
South San Gabriel, CA (cdp) Los Angeles County	2,385	29.55
Millbrae, CA (city) San Mateo County	6,268	29.11
Cupertino, CA (city) Santa Clara County	14,930	25.61
Camino Tassajara, CA (cdp) Contra Costa County	518	23.58
Kahaluu, HI (cdp) Honolulu County	1,109	23.41
North El Monte, CA (cdp) Los Angeles County	869	23.34
Hawi, HI (cdp) Hawaii County	247	22.85
Ahuimanu, HI (cdp) Honolulu County	2,010	22.81
Diamond Bar, CA (city) Los Angeles County	12,547	22.59
San Francisco, CA (city) San Francisco County	181,707	22.57
Waimanalo Beach, HI (cdp) Honolulu County	998	22.27
Foster City, CA (city) San Mateo County	6,701	21.92
East Honolulu, HI (cdp) Honolulu County	10,863	21.76
Kaneohe, HI (cdp) Honolulu County	7,527	21.76
Maunaloa, HI (cdp) Maui County	81	21.54
University of California Davis, CA (cdp) Yolo County	1,245	21.52
Heeia, HI (cdp) Honolulu County	1,066	21.48
Kukuihaele, HI (cdp) Hawaii County	71	21.13
Hacienda Heights, CA (cdp) Los Angeles County	11,348	21.00
Ualapu'e, HI (cdp) Maui County	89	20.94
Waianae, HI (cdp) Honolulu County	2,682	20.35
Hana, HI (cdp) Maui County	251	20.32
Saratoga, CA (city) Santa Clara County	6,049	20.21
Waimanalo, HI (cdp) Honolulu County	1,092	20.03
New Auburn, WI (village) Barron County	4	20.00
Waikane, HI (cdp) Honolulu County	154	19.79
Mountain View, HI (cdp) Hawaii County	766	19.52
Kaaawa, HI (cdp) Honolulu County	269	19.51
Hillsborough, CA (town) San Mateo County	2,100	19.40
Nanakuli, HI (cdp) Honolulu County	2,446	19.31
Halaula, HI (cdp) Hawaii County	89	18.98
Urban Honolulu, HI (cdp) Honolulu County	63,881	18.94
Kapaau, HI (cdp) Hawaii County	328	18.92
Kapolei, HI (cdp) Honolulu County	2,833	18.66
Maunawili, HI (cdp) Honolulu County	371	18.19
Talmage, CA (cdp) Mendocino County	202	17.88
Maili, HI (cdp) Honolulu County	1,695	17.86
Makaha, HI (cdp) Honolulu County	1,467	17.72
Mililani Mauka, HI (cdp) Honolulu County	3,677	17.48
Kualapuu, HI (cdp) Maui County	354	17.46
North Potomac, MD (cdp) Montgomery County	4,236	17.35
Fremont, CA (city) Alameda County	36,484	17.04
Mililani Town, HI (cdp) Honolulu County	4,658	16.86
University Gardens, NY (cdp) Nassau County	711	16.82
Daly City, CA (city) San Mateo County	16,992	16.80
Waikele, HI (cdp) Honolulu County	1,254	16.77
Kalaeloa, HI (cdp) Honolulu County	8	16.67
Albany, CA (city) Alameda County	3,066	16.54
Mayflower Village, CA (cdp) Los Angeles County	903	16.37
Eden Roc, HI (cdp) Hawaii County	154	16.35
Waipio, HI (cdp) Honolulu County	1,902	16.29
Quincy, MA (city) Norfolk County	14,979	16.23
Makakilo, HI (cdp) Honolulu County	2,960	16.22
Halawa, HI (cdp) Honolulu County	2,263	16.15
South Pasadena, CA (city) Los Angeles County	4,132	16.13
Alameda, CA (city) Alameda County	11,760	15.93
Highlands-Baywood Park, CA (cdp) San Mateo County	640	15.89
Hilo, HI (cdp) Hawaii County	6,805	15.73
Pahala, HI (cdp) Hawaii County	212	15.63
Kaunakakai, HI (cdp) Maui County	533	15.56
Kailua, HI (cdp) Honolulu County	5,971	15.45
Keokea, HI (cdp) Maui County	248	15.38
Fern Acres, HI (cdp) Hawaii County	231	15.36
Aiea, HI (cdp) Honolulu County	1,432	15.34
Kahuku, HI (cdp) Honolulu County	398	15.23
Milpitas, CA (city) Santa Clara County	10,156	15.21
Hauula, HI (cdp) Honolulu County	631	15.21
Thomaston, NY (village) Nassau County	398	15.21
Pearl City, HI (cdp) Honolulu County	7,245	15.19
Palo Alto, CA (city) Santa Clara County	9,739	15.12
Kurtistown, HI (cdp) Hawaii County	196	15.10
Ainaloa, HI (cdp) Hawaii County	447	15.08
Waipio Acres, HI (cdp) Honolulu County	777	14.84
Waimea, HI (cdp) Kauai County	275	14.82
Wahiawa, HI (cdp) Honolulu County	2,631	14.76
Waimalu, HI (cdp) Honolulu County	2,020	14.71
Los Altos Hills, CA (town) Santa Clara County	1,158	14.62
Punaluu, HI (cdp) Honolulu County	170	14.60
Ewa Gentry, HI (cdp) Honolulu County	3,303	14.56
San Leandro, CA (city) Alameda County	12,337	14.52
Waimea, HI (cdp) Hawaii County	1,320	14.33
El Monte, CA (city) Los Angeles County	16,151	14.23
Hawaiian Beaches, HI (cdp) Hawaii County	607	14.18
Broadmoor, CA (cdp) San Mateo County	588	14.08
Laie, HI (cdp) Honolulu County	863	14.06
El Cerrito, CA (city) Contra Costa County	3,309	14.05
Norris Canyon, CA (cdp) Contra Costa County	133	13.90
Piedmont, CA (city) Alameda County	1,475	13.83
Makaha Valley, HI (cdp) Honolulu County	185	13.80
Manele, HI (cdp) Maui County	4	13.79
East Pasadena, CA (cdp) Los Angeles County	842	13.70
Makawao, HI (cdp) Maui County	982	13.67
Waiohinu, HI (cdp) Hawaii County	29	13.62
Stanford, CA (cdp) Santa Clara County	1,879	13.61
Haleiwa, HI (cdp) Honolulu County	540	13.60
Anahola, HI (cdp) Kauai County	302	13.59
West Loch Estate, HI (cdp) Honolulu County	743	13.55
Hawaiian Paradise Park, HI (cdp) Hawaii County	1,494	13.10
Ewa Villages, HI (cdp) Honolulu County	800	13.10
Travilah, MD (cdp) Montgomery County	1,586	13.04
Lake Success, NY (village) Nassau County	382	13.02
Waihee-Waiehu, HI (cdp) Maui County	1,148	12.98
San Ramon, CA (city) Contra Costa County	9,284	12.87
Honokaa, HI (cdp) Hawaii County	290	12.84
Wailuku, HI (cdp) Maui County	1,962	12.81
Cerritos, CA (city) Los Angeles County	6,267	12.78
Keaau, HI (cdp) Hawaii County	284	12.61
Paauilo, HI (cdp) Hawaii County	75	12.61
Russell Gardens, NY (village) Nassau County	119	12.59
Castro Valley, CA (cdp) Alameda County	7,718	12.57
Sunnyvale, CA (city) Santa Clara County	17,556	12.53
Waikapu, HI (cdp) Maui County	370	12.48
Loyola, CA (cdp) Santa Clara County	404	12.39
Pepeekeo, HI (cdp) Hawaii County	221	12.35
Los Altos, CA (city) Santa Clara County	3,576	12.34
Ewa Beach, HI (cdp) Honolulu County	1,812	12.12
Brisbane, CA (city) San Mateo County	519	12.12
South San Francisco, CA (city) San Mateo County	7,687	12.08
West Windsor, NJ (township) Mercer County	3,267	12.03
Derwood, MD (cdp) Montgomery County	284	11.93
Nanawale Estates, HI (cdp) Hawaii County	170	11.92
Hanapepe, HI (cdp) Kauai County	314	11.90
Forest Home, NY (cdp) Tompkins County	68	11.89
Irvine, CA (city) Orange County	25,177	11.85
Orchidlands Estates, HI (cdp) Hawaii County	330	11.72
Laupahoehoe, HI (cdp) Hawaii County	68	11.70
Union City, CA (city) Alameda County	8,102	11.65
Malden, MA (city) Middlesex County	6,926	11.65
Royal Kunia, HI (cdp) Honolulu County	1,686	11.61
Manhasset Hills, NY (cdp) Nassau County	417	11.61
Kalaoa, HI (cdp) Hawaii County	1,105	11.46
Naalehu, HI (cdp) Hawaii County	99	11.43
Pukalani, HI (cdp) Maui County	862	11.38
Binghamton University, NY (cdp) Broome County	694	11.24
Mountain View, CA (city) Santa Clara County	8,277	11.18
Pahoa, HI (cdp) Hawaii County	104	11.01
Plainsboro, NJ (township) Middlesex County	2,529	11.00
Honaunau-Napoopoo, HI (cdp) Hawaii County	280	10.91
Burlingame, CA (city) San Mateo County	3,126	10.85
Floris, VA (cdp) Fairfax County	909	10.85

Please refer to the Explanation of Data in the front of the book for more detailed information.

Race

Asian: Chinese, except Taiwanese

Top 150 Places Sorted by Percent of Total Population

Based on places with total population of 7,500 or more

Place	Population	%
Monterey Park, CA (city) Los Angeles County	29,537	49.01
San Gabriel, CA (city) Los Angeles County	17,137	43.15
Temple City, CA (city) Los Angeles County	13,931	39.18
Arcadia, CA (city) Los Angeles County	21,744	38.58
Rosemead, CA (city) Los Angeles County	20,548	38.22
Alhambra, CA (city) Los Angeles County	31,493	37.90
San Marino, CA (city) Los Angeles County	4,707	35.80
Rowland Heights, CA (cdp) Los Angeles County	16,563	33.81
East San Gabriel, CA (cdp) Los Angeles County	4,965	33.38
Walnut, CA (city) Los Angeles County	9,242	31.68
South San Gabriel, CA (cdp) Los Angeles County	2,385	29.55
Millbrae, CA (city) San Mateo County	6,268	29.11
Cupertino, CA (city) Santa Clara County	14,930	25.61
Ahuimanu, HI (cdp) Honolulu County	2,010	22.81
Diamond Bar, CA (city) Los Angeles County	12,547	22.59
San Francisco, CA (city) San Francisco County	181,707	22.57
Foster City, CA (city) San Mateo County	6,701	21.92
East Honolulu, HI (cdp) Honolulu County	10,863	21.76
Kaneohe, HI (cdp) Honolulu County	7,527	21.76
Hacienda Heights, CA (cdp) Los Angeles County	11,348	21.00
Waianae, HI (cdp) Honolulu County	2,682	20.35
Saratoga, CA (city) Santa Clara County	6,049	20.21
Hillsborough, CA (town) San Mateo County	2,100	19.40
Nanakuli, HI (cdp) Honolulu County	2,446	19.31
Urban Honolulu, HI (cdp) Honolulu County	63,881	18.94
Kapolei, HI (cdp) Honolulu County	2,833	18.66
Maili, HI (cdp) Honolulu County	1,695	17.86
Makaha, HI (cdp) Honolulu County	1,467	17.72
Mililani Mauka, HI (cdp) Honolulu County	3,677	17.48
North Potomac, MD (cdp) Montgomery County	4,236	17.35
Fremont, CA (city) Alameda County	36,484	17.04
Mililani Town, HI (cdp) Honolulu County	4,658	16.86
Daly City, CA (city) San Mateo County	16,992	16.80
Albany, CA (city) Alameda County	3,066	16.54
Waipio, HI (cdp) Honolulu County	1,902	16.29
Quincy, MA (city) Norfolk County	14,979	16.23
Makakilo, HI (cdp) Honolulu County	2,960	16.22
Halawa, HI (cdp) Honolulu County	2,263	16.15
South Pasadena, CA (city) Los Angeles County	4,132	16.13
Alameda, CA (city) Alameda County	11,760	15.93
Hilo, HI (cdp) Hawaii County	6,805	15.73
Kailua, HI (cdp) Honolulu County	5,971	15.45
Aiea, HI (cdp) Honolulu County	1,432	15.34
Milpitas, CA (city) Santa Clara County	10,156	15.21
Pearl City, HI (cdp) Honolulu County	7,245	15.19
Palo Alto, CA (city) Santa Clara County	9,739	15.12
Wahiawa, HI (cdp) Honolulu County	2,631	14.76
Waimalu, HI (cdp) Honolulu County	2,020	14.71
Los Altos Hills, CA (town) Santa Clara County	1,158	14.62
Ewa Gentry, HI (cdp) Honolulu County	3,303	14.56
San Leandro, CA (city) Alameda County	12,337	14.52
Waimea, HI (cdp) Hawaii County	1,320	14.33
El Monte, CA (city) Los Angeles County	16,151	14.23
El Cerrito, CA (city) Contra Costa County	3,309	14.05
Piedmont, CA (city) Alameda County	1,475	13.83
Stanford, CA (cdp) Santa Clara County	1,879	13.61
Hawaiian Paradise Park, HI (cdp) Hawaii County	1,494	13.10
Travilah, MD (cdp) Montgomery County	1,586	13.04
Waihee-Waiehu, HI (cdp) Maui County	1,148	12.98
San Ramon, CA (city) Contra Costa County	9,284	12.87
Wailuku, HI (cdp) Maui County	1,962	12.81
Cerritos, CA (city) Los Angeles County	6,267	12.78
Castro Valley, CA (cdp) Alameda County	7,718	12.57
Sunnyvale, CA (city) Santa Clara County	17,556	12.53
Los Altos, CA (city) Santa Clara County	3,576	12.34
Ewa Beach, HI (cdp) Honolulu County	1,812	12.12
South San Francisco, CA (city) San Mateo County	7,687	12.08
West Windsor, NJ (township) Mercer County	3,267	12.03
Irvine, CA (city) Orange County	25,177	11.85
Union City, CA (city) Alameda County	8,102	11.65
Malden, MA (city) Middlesex County	6,926	11.65
Royal Kunia, HI (cdp) Honolulu County	1,686	11.61
Kalaoa, HI (cdp) Hawaii County	1,105	11.46
Pukalani, HI (cdp) Maui County	862	11.38
Mountain View, CA (city) Santa Clara County	8,277	11.18

Place	Population	%
Plainsboro, NJ (township) Middlesex County	2,529	11.00
Burlingame, CA (city) San Mateo County	3,126	10.85
Floris, VA (cdp) Fairfax County	909	10.85
Montgomery, NJ (township) Somerset County	2,407	10.82
Clarksburg, MD (cdp) Montgomery County	1,481	10.76
Davis, CA (city) Yolo County	7,009	10.68
Purdue University, IN (cdp) Tippecanoe County	1,285	10.55
Sugar Land, TX (city) Fort Bend County	8,218	10.43
Kapaa, HI (cdp) Kauai County	1,101	10.29
Bradley Gardens, NJ (cdp) Somerset County	1,440	10.14
Belmont, CA (city) San Mateo County	2,614	10.12
Holmdel, NJ (township) Monmouth County	1,678	10.00
Newcastle, WA (city) King County	1,036	9.98
Emeryville, CA (city) Alameda County	1,006	9.98
Hercules, CA (city) Contra Costa County	2,363	9.82
Kailua, HI (cdp) Hawaii County	1,174	9.80
Klahanie, WA (cdp) King County	1,046	9.80
Ocean Pointe, HI (cdp) Honolulu County	806	9.64
Bellevue, WA (city) King County	11,725	9.58
Oakland, CA (city) Alameda County	37,235	9.53
Lexington, MA (cdp/town) Middlesex County	2,984	9.51
Acton, MA (town) Middlesex County	2,063	9.41
Stony Brook University, NY (cdp) Suffolk County	863	9.36
Kahului, HI (cdp) Maui County	2,456	9.33
Livingston, NJ (township) Essex County	2,722	9.27
Chino Hills, CA (city) San Bernardino County	6,895	9.22
Berkeley, CA (city) Alameda County	10,374	9.21
East Brunswick, NJ (township) Middlesex County	4,378	9.21
Moraga, CA (town) Contra Costa County	1,470	9.18
Princeton Meadows, NJ (cdp) Middlesex County	1,257	9.09
Queens, NY (borough) Queens County	200,714	9.00
San Bruno, CA (city) San Mateo County	3,688	8.97
San Mateo, CA (city) San Mateo County	8,674	8.92
Bethany, OR (cdp) Washington County	1,818	8.81
Dublin, CA (city) Alameda County	4,016	8.72
University of Virginia, VA (cdp) Albemarle County	663	8.61
West Covina, CA (city) Los Angeles County	9,089	8.57
Jericho, NY (cdp) Nassau County	1,160	8.55
Syosset, NY (cdp) Nassau County	1,608	8.54
Rockville, MD (city) Montgomery County	5,173	8.45
Pleasanton, CA (city) Alameda County	5,928	8.43
Rancho Palos Verdes, CA (city) Los Angeles County	3,424	8.22
Blackhawk, CA (cdp) Contra Costa County	750	8.02
Orinda, CA (city) Contra Costa County	1,406	7.97
Princeton, NJ (borough) Mercer County	980	7.96
San Lorenzo, CA (cdp) Alameda County	1,865	7.95
Harrison, NJ (town) Hudson County	1,076	7.90
Millburn, NJ (township) Essex County	1,584	7.86
Ithaca, NY (city) Tompkins County	2,354	7.84
Ashland, CA (cdp) Alameda County	1,720	7.84
Mercer Island, WA (city) King County	1,777	7.83
Haiku-Pauwela, HI (cdp) Maui County	636	7.83
Sammamish, WA (city) King County	3,574	7.81
North New Hyde Park, NY (cdp) Nassau County	1,131	7.59
Brookline, MA (cdp/town) Norfolk County	4,432	7.55
Edison, NJ (township) Middlesex County	7,486	7.49
Fort Lee, NJ (borough) Bergen County	2,633	7.45
Urbana, IL (city) Champaign County	3,067	7.44
Short Hills, NJ (cdp) Essex County	979	7.44
Santa Clara, CA (city) Santa Clara County	8,652	7.43
La Palma, CA (city) Orange County	1,146	7.36
Marlboro, NJ (township) Monmouth County	2,943	7.32
Waipahu, HI (cdp) Honolulu County	2,762	7.23
Redmond, WA (city) King County	3,886	7.18
Highland Park, NJ (borough) Middlesex County	1,003	7.17
Brooklyn, NY (borough) Kings County	178,214	7.12
San Jose, CA (city) Santa Clara County	67,093	7.09
Newton, MA (city) Middlesex County	6,040	7.09
Holualoa, HI (cdp) Hawaii County	604	7.07
Bellaire, TX (city) Harris County	1,189	7.05
Elk Grove, CA (city) Sacramento County	10,629	6.95
Princeton, NJ (township) Mercer County	1,119	6.88
Garden City Park, NY (cdp) Nassau County	530	6.79
Eastvale, CA (cdp) Riverside County	3,625	6.75
Newark, CA (city) Alameda County	2,852	6.70

Please refer to the Explanation of Data in the front of the book for more detailed information.

Race

Asian: Filipino

U.S. and 50 States Sorted by Population and Percent of Total Population

Place	Population	%
United States	**3,416,840**	**1.11**
California	1,474,707	3.96
Hawaii	342,095	25.15
Illinois	139,090	1.08
Texas	137,713	0.55
Washington	137,083	2.04
New Jersey	126,793	1.44
New York	126,129	0.65
Nevada	123,891	4.59
Florida	122,691	0.65
Virginia	90,493	1.13
Maryland	56,909	0.99
Arizona	53,067	0.83
Pennsylvania	33,021	0.26
Michigan	32,324	0.33
North Carolina	29,314	0.31
Oregon	29,101	0.76
Georgia	28,528	0.29
Ohio	27,661	0.24
Colorado	26,242	0.52
Alaska	25,424	3.58
Massachusetts	18,673	0.29
Missouri	17,706	0.30
Indiana	16,988	0.26
Connecticut	16,402	0.46
Minnesota	15,660	0.30
South Carolina	15,228	0.33
Tennessee	14,409	0.23
Wisconsin	13,158	0.23
Oklahoma	10,850	0.29
Utah	10,657	0.39
Louisiana	10,243	0.23
Kansas	9,399	0.33
New Mexico	8,535	0.41
Kentucky	8,402	0.19
Alabama	8,224	0.17
Arkansas	6,396	0.22
Idaho	6,211	0.40
Iowa	6,026	0.20
Mississippi	5,638	0.19
Nebraska	4,900	0.27
Delaware	4,637	0.52
Rhode Island	4,117	0.39
District of Columbia	3,670	0.61
New Hampshire	3,369	0.26
West Virginia	3,059	0.17
Maine	2,918	0.22
Montana	2,829	0.29
South Dakota	1,864	0.23
North Dakota	1,704	0.25
Wyoming	1,657	0.29
Vermont	1,035	0.17

Place	Population	%
Hawaii	342,095	25.15
Nevada	123,891	4.59
California	1,474,707	3.96
Alaska	25,424	3.58
Washington	137,083	2.04
New Jersey	126,793	1.44
Virginia	90,493	1.13
United States	**3,416,840**	**1.11**
Illinois	139,090	1.08
Maryland	56,909	0.99
Arizona	53,067	0.83
Oregon	29,101	0.76
New York	126,129	0.65
Florida	122,691	0.65
District of Columbia	3,670	0.61
Texas	137,713	0.55
Colorado	26,242	0.52
Delaware	4,637	0.52
Connecticut	16,402	0.46
New Mexico	8,535	0.41
Idaho	6,211	0.40
Utah	10,657	0.39
Rhode Island	4,117	0.39
Michigan	32,324	0.33
South Carolina	15,228	0.33
Kansas	9,399	0.33
North Carolina	29,314	0.31
Missouri	17,706	0.30
Minnesota	15,660	0.30
Georgia	28,528	0.29
Massachusetts	18,673	0.29
Oklahoma	10,850	0.29
Montana	2,829	0.29
Wyoming	1,657	0.29
Nebraska	4,900	0.27
Pennsylvania	33,021	0.26
Indiana	16,988	0.26
New Hampshire	3,369	0.26
North Dakota	1,704	0.25
Ohio	27,661	0.24
Tennessee	14,409	0.23
Wisconsin	13,158	0.23
Louisiana	10,243	0.23
South Dakota	1,864	0.23
Arkansas	6,396	0.22
Maine	2,918	0.22
Iowa	6,026	0.20
Kentucky	8,402	0.19
Mississippi	5,638	0.19
Alabama	8,224	0.17
West Virginia	3,059	0.17
Vermont	1,035	0.17

Please refer to the Explanation of Data in the front of the book for more detailed information.

Race

Asian: Filipino

Top 150 Places Sorted by Population

Based on all places, regardless of total population

Place	Population	%
Los Angeles, CA (city) Los Angeles County	139,859	3.69
San Diego, CA (city) San Diego County	92,828	7.10
New York, NY (city) Kings County	78,030	0.95
Urban Honolulu, HI (cdp) Honolulu County	64,964	19.26
San Jose, CA (city) Santa Clara County	62,549	6.61
San Francisco, CA (city) San Francisco County	43,646	5.42
Queens, NY (borough) Queens County	41,773	1.87
Daly City, CA (city) San Mateo County	36,028	35.63
Chicago, IL (city) Cook County	35,188	1.31
Chula Vista, CA (city) San Diego County	31,344	12.85
Vallejo, CA (city) Solano County	27,622	23.82
Stockton, CA (city) San Joaquin County	27,113	9.29
Waipahu, HI (cdp) Honolulu County	25,040	65.52
Long Beach, CA (city) Los Angeles County	24,963	5.40
Las Vegas, NV (city) Clark County	24,185	4.14
Virginia Beach, VA (ind. city) Virginia Beach independent city	22,092	5.04
Carson, CA (city) Los Angeles County	21,539	23.48
Seattle, WA (city) King County	21,003	3.45
Jacksonville, FL (city) Duval County	18,513	2.25
Sacramento, CA (city) Sacramento County	18,503	3.97
Jersey City, NJ (city) Hudson County	17,268	6.97
Hayward, CA (city) Alameda County	17,134	11.88
Fremont, CA (city) Alameda County	17,070	7.97
Union City, CA (city) Alameda County	15,289	21.99
Elk Grove, CA (city) Sacramento County	14,891	9.73
Glendale, CA (city) Los Angeles County	14,442	7.53
South San Francisco, CA (city) San Mateo County	14,358	22.56
Enterprise, NV (cdp) Clark County	14,074	12.97
Spring Valley, NV (cdp) Clark County	13,813	7.74
Anaheim, CA (city) Orange County	13,813	4.11
Paradise, NV (cdp) Clark County	13,769	6.17
Manhattan, NY (borough) New York County	13,388	0.84
Kahului, HI (cdp) Maui County	13,099	49.74
Anchorage, AK (municipality) Anchorage Municipality	12,768	4.38
Milpitas, CA (city) Santa Clara County	12,649	18.94
Fairfield, CA (city) Solano County	12,265	11.65
North Las Vegas, NV (city) Clark County	11,879	5.48
Oxnard, CA (city) Ventura County	11,788	5.96
West Covina, CA (city) Los Angeles County	11,726	11.05
Henderson, NV (city) Clark County	11,525	4.47
Phoenix, AZ (city) Maricopa County	11,428	0.79
Pearl City, HI (cdp) Honolulu County	11,421	23.94
Houston, TX (city) Harris County	11,140	0.53
National City, CA (city) San Diego County	10,695	18.26
Ewa Gentry, HI (cdp) Honolulu County	10,438	46.00
Brooklyn, NY (borough) Kings County	10,208	0.41
San Antonio, TX (city) Medina County	9,328	0.70
Bakersfield, CA (city) Kern County	9,074	2.61
San Leandro, CA (city) Alameda County	9,060	10.67
Hilo, HI (cdp) Hawaii County	8,928	20.64
Sunrise Manor, NV (cdp) Clark County	8,747	4.62
Fresno, CA (city) Fresno County	8,726	1.76
Oakland, CA (city) Alameda County	8,661	2.22
Ewa Beach, HI (cdp) Honolulu County	8,650	57.84
Santa Clara, CA (city) Santa Clara County	8,558	7.35
Irvine, CA (city) Orange County	8,085	3.81
Cerritos, CA (city) Los Angeles County	7,917	16.14
Oceanside, CA (city) San Diego County	7,853	4.70
Sunnyvale, CA (city) Santa Clara County	7,847	5.60
Reno, NV (city) Washoe County	7,769	3.45
Salinas, CA (city) Monterey County	7,740	5.14
Lakewood, CA (city) Los Angeles County	7,715	9.64
Royal Kunia, HI (cdp) Honolulu County	7,703	53.03
Antioch, CA (city) Contra Costa County	7,541	7.37
Buena Park, CA (city) Orange County	7,506	9.32
Santa Clarita, CA (city) Los Angeles County	7,378	4.18
Mililani Town, HI (cdp) Honolulu County	7,372	26.68
Pittsburg, CA (city) Contra Costa County	7,301	11.54
Chino Hills, CA (city) San Bernardino County	7,257	9.70
Hempstead, NY (town) Nassau County	7,212	0.95
Fontana, CA (city) San Bernardino County	7,014	3.58
Temecula, CA (city) Riverside County	6,969	6.96
Delano, CA (city) Kern County	6,927	13.06
Philadelphia, PA (city) Philadelphia County	6,849	0.45
Concord, CA (city) Contra Costa County	6,837	5.60
Wahiawa, HI (cdp) Honolulu County	6,821	38.28
Alameda, CA (city) Alameda County	6,809	9.22
Moreno Valley, CA (city) Riverside County	6,788	3.51
Rancho Cucamonga, CA (city) San Bernardino County	6,762	4.09
Riverside, CA (city) Riverside County	6,761	2.22
Torrance, CA (city) Los Angeles County	6,715	4.62
Hercules, CA (city) Contra Costa County	6,670	27.72
Tracy, CA (city) San Joaquin County	6,666	8.04
Bronx, NY (borough) Bronx County	6,456	0.47
Makakilo, HI (cdp) Honolulu County	6,454	35.37
Murrieta, CA (city) Riverside County	6,449	6.23
Norfolk, VA (ind. city) Norfolk independent city	6,326	2.61
Staten Island, NY (borough) Richmond County	6,205	1.32
Norwalk, CA (city) Los Angeles County	6,135	5.81
Portland, OR (city) Multnomah County	5,688	0.97
Kapolei, HI (cdp) Honolulu County	5,663	37.29
Corona, CA (city) Riverside County	5,660	3.71
Burbank, CA (city) Los Angeles County	5,612	5.43
San Mateo, CA (city) San Mateo County	5,611	5.77
Kaneohe, HI (cdp) Honolulu County	5,590	16.16
American Canyon, CA (city) Napa County	5,572	28.64
San Bruno, CA (city) San Mateo County	5,548	13.49
Renton, WA (city) King County	5,295	5.82
Mililani Mauka, HI (cdp) Honolulu County	5,230	24.86
Bellflower, CA (city) Los Angeles County	5,088	6.64
Kihei, HI (cdp) Maui County	4,927	23.60
Skokie, IL (village) Cook County	4,896	7.56
Pacifica, CA (city) San Mateo County	4,881	13.11
Roseville, CA (city) Placer County	4,791	4.03
Newark, CA (city) Alameda County	4,775	11.22
Escondido, CA (city) San Diego County	4,768	3.31
Bergenfield, NJ (borough) Bergen County	4,767	17.81
Lahaina, HI (cdp) Maui County	4,760	40.67
Colorado Springs, CO (city) El Paso County	4,655	1.12
Pasadena, CA (city) Los Angeles County	4,632	3.38
Modesto, CA (city) Stanislaus County	4,614	2.29
Chesapeake, VA (ind. city) Chesapeake independent city	4,583	2.06
Vacaville, CA (city) Solano County	4,581	4.96
Santa Maria, CA (city) Santa Barbara County	4,514	4.53
Tacoma, WA (city) Pierce County	4,507	2.27
Richmond, CA (city) Contra Costa County	4,500	4.34
Suisun City, CA (city) Solano County	4,493	15.98
Kent, WA (city) King County	4,431	4.79
San Ramon, CA (city) Contra Costa County	4,416	6.12
Lancaster, CA (city) Los Angeles County	4,399	2.81
Halawa, HI (cdp) Honolulu County	4,373	31.20
Waipio, HI (cdp) Honolulu County	4,318	36.99
Palmdale, CA (city) Los Angeles County	4,273	2.80
Fullerton, CA (city) Orange County	4,263	3.15
Ewa Villages, HI (cdp) Honolulu County	4,235	69.34
Walnut, CA (city) Los Angeles County	4,216	14.45
Austin, TX (city) Travis County	4,214	0.53
Wailuku, HI (cdp) Maui County	4,154	27.13
Tucson, AZ (city) Pima County	4,024	0.77
Eastvale, CA (cdp) Riverside County	3,973	7.40
Garden Grove, CA (city) Orange County	3,944	2.31
Waianae, HI (cdp) Honolulu County	3,933	29.85
Pomona, CA (city) Los Angeles County	3,879	2.60
Huntington Beach, CA (city) Orange County	3,863	2.03
Waihee-Waiehu, HI (cdp) Maui County	3,828	43.30
Diamond Bar, CA (city) Los Angeles County	3,767	6.78
Baldwin Park, CA (city) Los Angeles County	3,733	4.95
Fort Worth, TX (city) Tarrant County	3,715	0.50
Kailua, HI (cdp) Honolulu County	3,701	9.58
Washington, DC (city) District of Columbia	3,670	0.61
Chandler, AZ (city) Maricopa County	3,615	1.53
Simi Valley, CA (city) Ventura County	3,612	2.91
Orange, CA (city) Orange County	3,607	2.64
Union, NJ (township) Union County	3,602	6.36
East Honolulu, HI (cdp) Honolulu County	3,578	7.17
San Marcos, CA (city) San Diego County	3,575	4.27
Ontario, CA (city) San Bernardino County	3,566	2.18
West Carson, CA (cdp) Los Angeles County	3,564	16.42
Federal Way, WA (city) King County	3,552	3.98
Whitney, NV (cdp) Clark County	3,540	9.17

SECTION THREE

Please refer to the Explanation of Data in the front of the book for more detailed information.

Race

Asian: Filipino

Top 150 Places Sorted by Percent of Total Population

Based on all places, regardless of total population

Place	Population	%
Greens, NH (grant) Coos County	1	100.00
Laurier, WA (cdp) Ferry County	1	100.00
Kaumakani, HI (cdp) Kauai County	611	81.58
Whitmore Village, HI (cdp) Honolulu County	3,361	74.71
Ewa Villages, HI (cdp) Honolulu County	4,235	69.34
Hanamaulu, HI (cdp) Kauai County	2,558	66.70
Waipahu, HI (cdp) Honolulu County	25,040	65.52
Lanai City, HI (cdp) Maui County	1,999	64.44
Pahala, HI (cdp) Hawaii County	812	59.88
Paauilo, HI (cdp) Hawaii County	352	59.16
Puhi, HI (cdp) Kauai County	1,716	59.05
Eleele, HI (cdp) Kauai County	1,388	58.08
Ewa Beach, HI (cdp) Honolulu County	8,650	57.84
Halaula, HI (cdp) Hawaii County	251	53.52
Royal Kunia, HI (cdp) Honolulu County	7,703	53.03
Naalehu, HI (cdp) Hawaii County	450	51.96
Keaau, HI (cdp) Hawaii County	1,142	50.69
Adak, AK (city) Aleutians West Census Area	164	50.31
West Loch Estate, HI (cdp) Honolulu County	2,756	50.25
Kahului, HI (cdp) Maui County	13,099	49.74
Waialua, HI (cdp) Honolulu County	1,885	48.83
Honokaa, HI (cdp) Hawaii County	1,083	47.96
Ewa Gentry, HI (cdp) Honolulu County	10,438	46.00
Kapaau, HI (cdp) Hawaii County	797	45.96
Pahoa, HI (cdp) Hawaii County	426	45.08
Hanapepe, HI (cdp) Kauai County	1,175	44.54
Maunaloa, HI (cdp) Maui County	167	44.41
Waihee-Waiehu, HI (cdp) Maui County	3,828	43.30
Kekaha, HI (cdp) Kauai County	1,518	42.92
Koloa, HI (cdp) Kauai County	913	42.58
Pepeekeo, HI (cdp) Hawaii County	761	42.54
Wainaku, HI (cdp) Hawaii County	517	42.24
Akutan, AK (city) Aleutians East Borough	427	41.58
Haliimaile, HI (cdp) Maui County	400	41.49
Lahaina, HI (cdp) Maui County	4,760	40.67
Haleiwa, HI (cdp) Honolulu County	1,548	38.99
Wahiawa, HI (cdp) Honolulu County	6,821	38.28
Hawi, HI (cdp) Hawaii County	413	38.21
Pakala Village, HI (cdp) Kauai County	111	37.76
Kapolei, HI (cdp) Honolulu County	5,663	37.29
Waipio, HI (cdp) Honolulu County	4,318	36.99
Kodiak, AK (city) Kodiak Island Borough	2,222	36.25
King Cove, AK (city) Aleutians East Borough	336	35.82
Kukuihaele, HI (cdp) Hawaii County	120	35.71
Daly City, CA (city) San Mateo County	36,028	35.63
Papaikou, HI (cdp) Hawaii County	467	35.54
Makakilo, HI (cdp) Honolulu County	6,454	35.37
Kaunakakai, HI (cdp) Maui County	1,201	35.07
Waikapu, HI (cdp) Maui County	1,037	34.97
Kahuku, HI (cdp) Honolulu County	898	34.35
Maili, HI (cdp) Honolulu County	3,219	33.93
Waipio Acres, HI (cdp) Honolulu County	1,737	33.17
Sand Point, AK (city) Aleutians East Borough	323	33.09
Lihue, HI (cdp) Kauai County	2,059	31.90
Kualapuu, HI (cdp) Maui County	637	31.43
Halawa, HI (cdp) Honolulu County	4,373	31.20
Kapaa, HI (cdp) Kauai County	3,276	30.62
Waikele, HI (cdp) Honolulu County	2,280	30.49
Waimea, HI (cdp) Kauai County	562	30.30
Ocean Pointe, HI (cdp) Honolulu County	2,514	30.07
Bucks Lake, CA (cdp) Plumas County	3	30.00
Unalaska, AK (city) Aleutians West Census Area	1,307	29.87
Waianae, HI (cdp) Honolulu County	3,933	29.85
Orchidlands Estates, HI (cdp) Hawaii County	833	29.59
Waimanalo, HI (cdp) Honolulu County	1,608	29.50
Ainaloa, HI (cdp) Hawaii County	860	29.01
American Canyon, CA (city) Napa County	5,572	28.64
Paia, HI (cdp) Maui County	755	28.30
Hercules, CA (city) Contra Costa County	6,670	27.72
Aiea, HI (cdp) Honolulu County	2,578	27.61
Makaha, HI (cdp) Honolulu County	2,285	27.60
Hawaiian Paradise Park, HI (cdp) Hawaii County	3,135	27.49
Wailuku, HI (cdp) Maui County	4,154	27.13
Mountain View, HI (cdp) Hawaii County	1,060	27.01
Mililani Town, HI (cdp) Honolulu County	7,372	26.68
Nanawale Estates, HI (cdp) Hawaii County	378	26.51
Colma, CA (town) San Mateo County	473	26.40
Waimalu, HI (cdp) Honolulu County	3,538	25.77
Broadmoor, CA (cdp) San Mateo County	1,075	25.74
Laupahoehoe, HI (cdp) Hawaii County	148	25.47
Honomu, HI (cdp) Hawaii County	129	25.34
Kalaeloa, HI (cdp) Honolulu County	12	25.00
Omao, HI (cdp) Kauai County	325	24.98
Waiohinu, HI (cdp) Hawaii County	53	24.88
Mililani Mauka, HI (cdp) Honolulu County	5,230	24.86
Waikane, HI (cdp) Honolulu County	193	24.81
Hawaiian Beaches, HI (cdp) Hawaii County	1,033	24.14
Pearl City, HI (cdp) Honolulu County	11,421	23.94
Kalaheo, HI (cdp) Kauai County	1,095	23.83
Vallejo, CA (city) Solano County	27,622	23.82
Kihei, HI (cdp) Maui County	4,927	23.60
Carson, CA (city) Los Angeles County	21,539	23.48
Wailua, HI (cdp) Kauai County	528	23.43
Nanakuli, HI (cdp) Honolulu County	2,949	23.28
Kurtistown, HI (cdp) Hawaii County	301	23.19
Makawao, HI (cdp) Maui County	1,663	23.15
Kilauea, HI (cdp) Kauai County	633	22.58
South San Francisco, CA (city) San Mateo County	14,358	22.56
Lawai, HI (cdp) Kauai County	525	22.22
Union City, CA (city) Alameda County	15,289	21.99
Pukalani, HI (cdp) Maui County	1,645	21.72
Waimea, HI (cdp) Hawaii County	1,955	21.22
Kealakekua, HI (cdp) Hawaii County	428	21.20
Mountain House, CA (cdp) San Joaquin County	2,037	21.05
Kailua, HI (cdp) Hawaii County	2,512	20.98
Hilo, HI (cdp) Hawaii County	8,928	20.64
Ualapu'e, HI (cdp) Maui County	87	20.47
Wailua Homesteads, HI (cdp) Kauai County	1,061	20.45
Napili-Honokowai, HI (cdp) Maui County	1,481	20.40
Makaha Valley, HI (cdp) Honolulu County	266	19.84
Akhiok, AK (city) Kodiak Island Borough	14	19.72
Iroquois Point, HI (cdp) Honolulu County	656	19.44
Urban Honolulu, HI (cdp) Honolulu County	64,964	19.26
Milpitas, CA (city) Santa Clara County	12,649	18.94
Captain Cook, HI (cdp) Hawaii County	649	18.93
Fern Acres, HI (cdp) Hawaii County	283	18.82
National City, CA (city) San Diego County	10,695	18.26
Waikoloa Village, HI (cdp) Hawaii County	1,154	18.14
Hana, HI (cdp) Maui County	223	18.06
Bergenfield, NJ (borough) Bergen County	4,767	17.81
Kahaluu, HI (cdp) Honolulu County	807	17.03
Ahuimanu, HI (cdp) Honolulu County	1,455	16.52
Kalaoa, HI (cdp) Hawaii County	1,592	16.51
West Carson, CA (cdp) Los Angeles County	3,564	16.42
Eden Roc, HI (cdp) Hawaii County	153	16.24
Hawaiian Acres, HI (cdp) Hawaii County	437	16.19
Kaneohe, HI (cdp) Honolulu County	5,590	16.16
Cerritos, CA (city) Los Angeles County	7,917	16.14
Suisun City, CA (city) Solano County	4,493	15.98
Fern Forest, HI (cdp) Hawaii County	143	15.36
Honalo, HI (cdp) Hawaii County	371	15.31
Anahola, HI (cdp) Kauai County	339	15.25
Lathrop, CA (city) San Joaquin County	2,736	15.18
Olowalu, HI (cdp) Maui County	12	15.00
Honaunau-Napoopoo, HI (cdp) Hawaii County	379	14.76
Holualoa, HI (cdp) Hawaii County	1,258	14.73
Poplar-Cotton Center, CA (cdp) Tulare County	361	14.62
Walnut, CA (city) Los Angeles County	4,216	14.45
Mahinahina, HI (cdp) Maui County	124	14.09
Discovery Harbour, HI (cdp) Hawaii County	133	14.01
San Bruno, CA (city) San Mateo County	5,548	13.49
Pacifica, CA (city) San Mateo County	4,881	13.11
Delano, CA (city) Kern County	6,927	13.06
Artesia, CA (city) Los Angeles County	2,158	13.06
Enterprise, NV (cdp) Clark County	14,074	12.97
Paukaa, HI (cdp) Hawaii County	55	12.94
Chula Vista, CA (city) San Diego County	31,344	12.85
Rodeo, CA (cdp) Contra Costa County	1,093	12.59
Keokea, HI (cdp) Maui County	198	12.28
Hawaiian Ocean View, HI (cdp) Hawaii County	542	12.22

Please refer to the Explanation of Data in the front of the book for more detailed information.

Race

Asian: Filipino

Top 150 Places Sorted by Percent of Total Population

Based on places with total population of 7,500 or more

Place	Population	%
Waipahu, HI (cdp) Honolulu County	25,040	65.52
Ewa Beach, HI (cdp) Honolulu County	8,650	57.84
Royal Kunia, HI (cdp) Honolulu County	7,703	53.03
Kahului, HI (cdp) Maui County	13,099	49.74
Ewa Gentry, HI (cdp) Honolulu County	10,438	46.00
Waihee-Waiehu, HI (cdp) Maui County	3,828	43.30
Lahaina, HI (cdp) Maui County	4,760	40.67
Wahiawa, HI (cdp) Honolulu County	6,821	38.28
Kapolei, HI (cdp) Honolulu County	5,663	37.29
Waipio, HI (cdp) Honolulu County	4,318	36.99
Daly City, CA (city) San Mateo County	36,028	35.63
Makakilo, HI (cdp) Honolulu County	6,454	35.37
Maili, HI (cdp) Honolulu County	3,219	33.93
Halawa, HI (cdp) Honolulu County	4,373	31.20
Kapaa, HI (cdp) Kauai County	3,276	30.62
Ocean Pointe, HI (cdp) Honolulu County	2,514	30.07
Waianae, HI (cdp) Honolulu County	3,933	29.85
American Canyon, CA (city) Napa County	5,572	28.64
Hercules, CA (city) Contra Costa County	6,670	27.72
Aiea, HI (cdp) Honolulu County	2,578	27.61
Makaha, HI (cdp) Honolulu County	2,285	27.60
Hawaiian Paradise Park, HI (cdp) Hawaii County	3,135	27.49
Wailuku, HI (cdp) Maui County	4,154	27.13
Mililani Town, HI (cdp) Honolulu County	7,372	26.68
Waimalu, HI (cdp) Honolulu County	3,538	25.77
Mililani Mauka, HI (cdp) Honolulu County	5,230	24.86
Pearl City, HI (cdp) Honolulu County	11,421	23.94
Vallejo, CA (city) Solano County	27,622	23.82
Kihei, HI (cdp) Maui County	4,927	23.60
Carson, CA (city) Los Angeles County	21,539	23.48
Nanakuli, HI (cdp) Honolulu County	2,949	23.28
South San Francisco, CA (city) San Mateo County	14,358	22.56
Union City, CA (city) Alameda County	15,289	21.99
Pukalani, HI (cdp) Maui County	1,645	21.72
Waimea, HI (cdp) Hawaii County	1,955	21.22
Mountain House, CA (cdp) San Joaquin County	2,037	21.05
Kailua, HI (cdp) Hawaii County	2,512	20.98
Hilo, HI (cdp) Hawaii County	8,928	20.64
Urban Honolulu, HI (cdp) Honolulu County	64,964	19.26
Milpitas, CA (city) Santa Clara County	12,649	18.94
National City, CA (city) San Diego County	10,695	18.26
Bergenfield, NJ (borough) Bergen County	4,767	17.81
Ahuimanu, HI (cdp) Honolulu County	1,455	16.52
Kalaoa, HI (cdp) Hawaii County	1,592	16.51
West Carson, CA (cdp) Los Angeles County	3,564	16.42
Kaneohe, HI (cdp) Honolulu County	5,590	16.16
Cerritos, CA (city) Los Angeles County	7,917	16.14
Suisun City, CA (city) Solano County	4,493	15.98
Lathrop, CA (city) San Joaquin County	2,736	15.18
Holualoa, HI (cdp) Hawaii County	1,258	14.73
Walnut, CA (city) Los Angeles County	4,216	14.45
San Bruno, CA (city) San Mateo County	5,548	13.49
Pacifica, CA (city) San Mateo County	4,881	13.11
Delano, CA (city) Kern County	6,927	13.06
Artesia, CA (city) Los Angeles County	2,158	13.06
Enterprise, NV (cdp) Clark County	14,074	12.97
Chula Vista, CA (city) San Diego County	31,344	12.85
Rodeo, CA (cdp) Contra Costa County	1,093	12.59
Hayward, CA (city) Alameda County	17,134	11.88
Fairfield, CA (city) Solano County	12,265	11.65
Pittsburg, CA (city) Contra Costa County	7,301	11.54
Pinole, CA (city) Contra Costa County	2,101	11.42
Newark, CA (city) Alameda County	4,775	11.22
Ketchikan, AK (city) Ketchikan Gateway Borough	891	11.07
West Covina, CA (city) Los Angeles County	11,726	11.05
Haiku-Pauwela, HI (cdp) Maui County	884	10.89
La Palma, CA (city) Orange County	1,684	10.82
Loma Linda, CA (city) San Bernardino County	2,505	10.77
San Leandro, CA (city) Alameda County	9,060	10.67
Oak Harbor, WA (city) Island County	2,285	10.35
Silverdale, WA (cdp) Kitsap County	1,948	10.14
San Lorenzo, CA (cdp) Alameda County	2,375	10.13
New Milford, NJ (borough) Bergen County	1,594	9.75
Elk Grove, CA (city) Sacramento County	14,891	9.73
Chino Hills, CA (city) San Bernardino County	7,257	9.70
Lakewood, CA (city) Los Angeles County	7,715	9.64
La Presa, CA (cdp) San Diego County	3,280	9.60
Kailua, HI (cdp) Honolulu County	3,701	9.58
Marina, CA (city) Monterey County	1,849	9.38
French Valley, CA (cdp) Riverside County	2,159	9.36
Buena Park, CA (city) Orange County	7,506	9.32
Stockton, CA (city) San Joaquin County	27,113	9.29
Alameda, CA (city) Alameda County	6,809	9.22
Whitney, NV (cdp) Clark County	3,540	9.17
Lemoore, CA (city) Kings County	2,161	8.81
Bryn Mawr-Skyway, WA (cdp) King County	1,372	8.77
Benicia, CA (city) Solano County	2,255	8.35
Fort Washington, MD (cdp) Prince George's County	1,963	8.28
Duarte, CA (city) Los Angeles County	1,765	8.28
Bonita, CA (cdp) San Diego County	1,030	8.22
Orosi, CA (cdp) Tulare County	717	8.18
Tracy, CA (city) San Joaquin County	6,666	8.04
Fremont, CA (city) Alameda County	17,070	7.97
Ashland, CA (cdp) Alameda County	1,734	7.91
Morton Grove, IL (village) Cook County	1,835	7.89
Spring Valley, NV (cdp) Clark County	13,813	7.74
Skokie, IL (village) Cook County	4,896	7.56
Belleville, NJ (township) Essex County	2,708	7.54
Glendale, CA (city) Los Angeles County	14,442	7.53
Fairview, CA (cdp) Alameda County	747	7.47
Eastvale, CA (cdp) Riverside County	3,973	7.40
Antioch, CA (city) Contra Costa County	7,541	7.37
Santa Clara, CA (city) Santa Clara County	8,558	7.35
Imperial Beach, CA (city) San Diego County	1,930	7.33
El Sobrante, CA (cdp) Riverside County	926	7.28
East Honolulu, HI (cdp) Honolulu County	3,578	7.17
Vineyard, CA (cdp) Sacramento County	1,772	7.13
Dumont, NJ (borough) Bergen County	1,246	7.13
Rowland Heights, CA (cdp) Los Angeles County	3,487	7.12
San Diego, CA (city) San Diego County	92,828	7.10
Dublin, CA (city) Alameda County	3,251	7.06
Cypress, CA (city) Orange County	3,363	7.04
Jersey City, NJ (city) Hudson County	17,268	6.97
Temecula, CA (city) Riverside County	6,969	6.96
Millbrae, CA (city) San Mateo County	1,499	6.96
Valinda, CA (cdp) Los Angeles County	1,586	6.95
Castaic, CA (cdp) Los Angeles County	1,322	6.95
Stevenson Ranch, CA (cdp) Los Angeles County	1,216	6.93
Earlimart, CA (cdp) Tulare County	583	6.83
DuPont, WA (city) Pierce County	558	6.81
Diamond Bar, CA (city) Los Angeles County	3,767	6.78
Brookdale, NJ (cdp) Essex County	624	6.75
Bellflower, CA (city) Los Angeles County	5,088	6.64
East Hill-Meridian, WA (cdp) King County	1,977	6.62
San Jose, CA (city) Santa Clara County	62,549	6.61
Juneau, AK (borough) Juneau City and Borough	2,042	6.53
San Pablo, CA (city) Contra Costa County	1,864	6.40
Union, NJ (township) Union County	3,602	6.36
Fairwood, WA (cdp) King County	1,200	6.28
Murrieta, CA (city) Riverside County	6,449	6.23
Bay Point, CA (cdp) Contra Costa County	1,329	6.23
Oakleaf Plantation, FL (cdp) Clay County	1,259	6.20
Paradise, NV (cdp) Clark County	13,769	6.17
Seaside, CA (city) Monterey County	2,039	6.17
San Ramon, CA (city) Contra Costa County	4,416	6.12
Country Club, CA (cdp) San Joaquin County	574	6.12
Signal Hill, CA (city) Los Angeles County	669	6.07
Sitka, AK (borough) Sitka City and Borough	535	6.02
Lake Stickney, WA (cdp) Snohomish County	464	5.97
Oxnard, CA (city) Ventura County	11,788	5.96
Glendale Heights, IL (village) DuPage County	2,027	5.93
Summerlin South, NV (cdp) Clark County	1,413	5.87
Foster City, CA (city) San Mateo County	1,784	5.84
Hillcrest, NY (cdp) Rockland County	441	5.83
Renton, WA (city) King County	5,295	5.82
Norwalk, CA (city) Los Angeles County	6,135	5.81
San Mateo, CA (city) San Mateo County	5,611	5.77
Fife, WA (city) Pierce County	529	5.77
La Mirada, CA (city) Los Angeles County	2,797	5.76
Brentwood, CA (city) Contra Costa County	2,958	5.75

Please refer to the Explanation of Data in the front of the book for more detailed information.

Race

Asian: Hmong

U.S. and 50 States Sorted by Population and Percent of Total Population

Place	Population	%
United States	**260,073**	**0.08**
California	91,224	0.24
Minnesota	66,181	1.25
Wisconsin	49,240	0.87
North Carolina	10,864	0.11
Michigan	5,924	0.06
Colorado	3,859	0.08
Georgia	3,623	0.04
Alaska	3,534	0.50
Oklahoma	3,369	0.09
Oregon	2,920	0.08
Washington	2,404	0.04
Arkansas	2,143	0.07
Kansas	1,732	0.06
Missouri	1,329	0.02
South Carolina	1,218	0.03
Florida	1,208	0.01
Massachusetts	1,080	0.02
Pennsylvania	1,021	0.01
Rhode Island	1,015	0.10
Texas	920	<0.01
Illinois	651	0.01
Ohio	589	0.01
Iowa	534	0.02
Utah	426	0.02
Tennessee	400	0.01
New York	296	<0.01
Nevada	254	0.01
Montana	253	0.03
Arizona	229	<0.01
Connecticut	225	0.01
Indiana	218	<0.01
Nebraska	188	0.01
Virginia	188	<0.01
Alabama	122	<0.01
South Dakota	94	0.01
Hawaii	87	0.01
New Jersey	83	<0.01
Maryland	76	<0.01
Kentucky	71	<0.01
Mississippi	50	<0.01
Louisiana	49	<0.01
Idaho	44	<0.01
North Dakota	33	<0.01
New Mexico	28	<0.01
New Hampshire	27	<0.01
District of Columbia	26	<0.01
Wyoming	8	<0.01
Maine	7	<0.01
West Virginia	5	<0.01
Delaware	3	<0.01
Vermont	1	<0.01

Place	Population	%
Minnesota	66,181	1.25
Wisconsin	49,240	0.87
Alaska	3,534	0.50
California	91,224	0.24
North Carolina	10,864	0.11
Rhode Island	1,015	0.10
Oklahoma	3,369	0.09
United States	**260,073**	**0.08**
Colorado	3,859	0.08
Oregon	2,920	0.08
Arkansas	2,143	0.07
Michigan	5,924	0.06
Kansas	1,732	0.06
Georgia	3,623	0.04
Washington	2,404	0.04
South Carolina	1,218	0.03
Montana	253	0.03
Missouri	1,329	0.02
Massachusetts	1,080	0.02
Iowa	534	0.02
Utah	426	0.02
Florida	1,208	0.01
Pennsylvania	1,021	0.01
Illinois	651	0.01
Ohio	589	0.01
Tennessee	400	0.01
Nevada	254	0.01
Connecticut	225	0.01
Nebraska	188	0.01
South Dakota	94	0.01
Hawaii	87	0.01
Texas	920	<0.01
New York	296	<0.01
Arizona	229	<0.01
Indiana	218	<0.01
Virginia	188	<0.01
Alabama	122	<0.01
New Jersey	83	<0.01
Maryland	76	<0.01
Kentucky	71	<0.01
Mississippi	50	<0.01
Louisiana	49	<0.01
Idaho	44	<0.01
North Dakota	33	<0.01
New Mexico	28	<0.01
New Hampshire	27	<0.01
District of Columbia	26	<0.01
Wyoming	8	<0.01
Maine	7	<0.01
West Virginia	5	<0.01
Delaware	3	<0.01
Vermont	1	<0.01

Please refer to the Explanation of Data in the front of the book for more detailed information.

Race

Asian: Hmong

Top 150 Places Sorted by Population

Based on all places, regardless of total population

Place	Population	%
St. Paul, MN (city) Ramsey County	29,662	10.41
Fresno, CA (city) Fresno County	24,328	4.92
Sacramento, CA (city) Sacramento County	16,676	3.57
Milwaukee, WI (city) Milwaukee County	10,245	1.72
Minneapolis, MN (city) Hennepin County	7,512	1.96
Stockton, CA (city) San Joaquin County	6,073	2.08
Brooklyn Park, MN (city) Hennepin County	5,151	6.80
Merced, CA (city) Merced County	4,741	6.00
Wausau, WI (city) Marathon County	3,783	9.67
Sheboygan, WI (city) Sheboygan County	3,716	7.54
Anchorage, AK (municipality) Anchorage Municipality	3,408	1.17
Brooklyn Center, MN (city) Hennepin County	3,170	10.53
Appleton, WI (city) Outagamie County	3,156	4.35
Green Bay, WI (city) Brown County	3,020	2.90
Clovis, CA (city) Fresno County	3,001	3.14
Florin, CA (cdp) Sacramento County	2,933	6.17
Madison, WI (city) Dane County	2,728	1.17
Appleton, WI (city) Outagamie County	2,521	4.20
Maplewood, MN (city) Ramsey County	2,512	6.61
Eau Claire, WI (city) Eau Claire County	2,213	3.36
Eau Claire, WI (city) Eau Claire County	1,987	3.11
Elk Grove, CA (city) Sacramento County	1,789	1.17
Linda, CA (cdp) Yuba County	1,742	9.80
La Crosse, WI (city) La Crosse County	1,563	3.05
Oakdale, MN (city) Washington County	1,524	5.57
Oshkosh, WI (city) Winnebago County	1,469	2.22
Kansas City, KS (city) Wyandotte County	1,355	0.93
Charlotte, NC (city) Mecklenburg County	1,304	0.18
Manitowoc, WI (city) Manitowoc County	1,278	3.79
Chico, CA (city) Butte County	1,225	1.42
Warren, MI (city) Macomb County	1,218	0.91
San Diego, CA (city) San Diego County	1,166	0.09
Portland, OR (city) Multnomah County	1,115	0.19
Woodbury, MN (city) Washington County	1,103	1.78
Weston, WI (village) Marathon County	1,089	7.32
Lemon Hill, CA (cdp) Sacramento County	1,009	7.35
Tulsa, OK (city) Tulsa County	972	0.25
Thermalito, CA (cdp) Butte County	966	14.54
Blaine, MN (city) Anoka County	950	1.66
Westminster, CO (city) Adams County	895	0.84
Cottage Grove, MN (city) Washington County	890	2.57
Parkway, CA (cdp) Sacramento County	779	5.31
Oroville, CA (city) Butte County	773	4.97
Coon Rapids, MN (city) Anoka County	765	1.24
Thornton, CO (city) Adams County	760	0.64
Stevens Point, WI (city) Portage County	757	2.83
Franklin, CA (cdp) Merced County	744	12.10
South Oroville, CA (cdp) Butte County	726	12.64
Pontiac, MI (city) Oakland County	695	1.17
Onalaska, WI (city) La Crosse County	674	3.80
Providence, RI (city) Providence County	673	0.38
Little Canada, MN (city) Ramsey County	650	6.65
Lansing, MI (city) Ingham County	643	0.56
Visalia, CA (city) Tulare County	594	0.48
Banning, CA (city) Riverside County	591	2.00
Vadnais Heights, MN (city) Ramsey County	578	4.70
Detroit, MI (city) Wayne County	578	0.08
Wisconsin Rapids, WI (city) Wood County	562	3.06
Appleton, WI (city) Calumet County	553	4.99
Lansing, MI (city) Ingham County	549	0.50
North St. Paul, MN (city) Ramsey County	546	4.76
Holmen, WI (village) La Crosse County	538	5.97
Eureka, CA (city) Humboldt County	515	1.89
Atwater, CA (city) Merced County	489	1.74
Hickory, NC (city) Catawba County	479	1.20
Olivehurst, CA (cdp) Yuba County	466	3.41
White Bear Lake, MN (city) Ramsey County	454	1.94
White Bear Lake, MN (city) Ramsey County	454	1.91
Winton, CA (cdp) Merced County	453	4.27
Menomonie, WI (city) Dunn County	450	2.77
Gresham, OR (city) Multnomah County	450	0.43
Rancho Cordova, CA (city) Sacramento County	440	0.68
Sun Prairie, WI (city) Dane County	434	1.48
Fruitridge Pocket, CA (cdp) Sacramento County	422	7.28
Fridley, MN (city) Anoka County	419	1.54
Fond du Lac, WI (city) Fond du Lac County	419	0.97
Roseville, MN (city) Ramsey County	413	1.23
Fitchburg, MA (city) Worcester County	412	1.02
Bellevue, WI (village) Brown County	403	2.77
Akron, OH (city) Summit County	362	0.18
Santa Ana, CA (city) Orange County	361	0.11
Lino Lakes, MN (city) Anoka County	358	1.77
Plover, WI (village) Portage County	343	2.83
Vineyard, CA (cdp) Sacramento County	339	1.36
Grand Chute, WI (town) Outagamie County	338	1.62
Long Beach, CA (city) Los Angeles County	327	0.07
Broken Arrow, OK (city) Tulsa County	322	0.33
Mounds View, MN (city) Ramsey County	321	2.64
Lompoc, CA (city) Santa Barbara County	309	0.73
Inver Grove Heights, MN (city) Dakota County	303	0.89
Menasha, WI (town) Winnebago County	293	1.58
Arden-Arcade, CA (cdp) Sacramento County	292	0.32
Albemarle, NC (city) Stanly County	291	1.83
Brown Deer, WI (village) Milwaukee County	289	2.41
Modesto, CA (city) Stanislaus County	287	0.14
Broomfield, CO (city) Broomfield County	283	0.51
Menasha, WI (city) Winnebago County	265	1.53
Hugo, MN (city) Washington County	264	1.98
Commerce City, CO (city) Adams County	264	0.58
Newton, NC (city) Catawba County	262	2.02
Rio Linda, CA (cdp) Sacramento County	256	1.69
Rochester, MN (city) Olmsted County	256	0.24
Eagan, MN (city) Dakota County	255	0.40
St. Stephens, NC (cdp) Catawba County	250	2.85
Biola, CA (cdp) Fresno County	249	15.34
Fitchburg, WI (city) Dane County	249	0.99
Sunnyside, CA (cdp) Fresno County	245	5.79
Spokane, WA (city) Spokane County	238	0.11
Northglenn, CO (city) Adams County	236	0.66
Yuba City, CA (city) Sutter County	235	0.36
Menasha, WI (city) Winnebago County	231	1.53
Kronenwetter, WI (village) Marathon County	228	3.16
Crescent City, CA (city) Del Norte County	228	2.98
Eau Claire, WI (city) Chippewa County	226	11.41
Rib Mountain, WI (town) Marathon County	226	3.31
San Jose, CA (city) Santa Clara County	219	0.02
Ham Lake, MN (city) Anoka County	218	1.43
Winona, MN (city) Winona County	218	0.79
Waterford, MI (charter township) Oakland County	217	0.30
Ramsey, MN (city) Anoka County	216	0.91
Walnut Grove, MN (city) Redwood County	215	24.68
Sanger, CA (city) Fresno County	213	0.88
Two Rivers, WI (city) Manitowoc County	212	1.81
Garden Grove, CA (city) Orange County	212	0.12
Andover, MN (city) Anoka County	207	0.68
Tracy, MN (city) Lyon County	204	9.43
Owasso, OK (city) Tulsa County	204	0.71
Davis, CA (city) Yolo County	204	0.31
Porterville, CA (city) Tulare County	203	0.37
Champlin, MN (city) Hennepin County	201	0.87
Auburn, GA (city) Barrow County	199	2.89
West Sacramento, CA (city) Yolo County	196	0.40
Rib Mountain, WI (cdp) Marathon County	194	3.43
Kingsgate, WA (cdp) King County	193	1.48
Hillsboro, OR (city) Washington County	188	0.21
West Allis, WI (city) Milwaukee County	185	0.31
Des Moines, IA (city) Polk County	181	0.09
Crystal, MN (city) Hennepin County	180	0.81
Menomonie, WI (town) Dunn County	178	5.29
Sheboygan, WI (town) Sheboygan County	176	2.42
Robbinsdale, MN (city) Hennepin County	175	1.25
Sterling Heights, MI (city) Macomb County	175	0.13
Kennedy, CA (cdp) San Joaquin County	171	5.26
Tarpey Village, CA (cdp) Fresno County	170	4.37
Leominster, MA (city) Worcester County	170	0.42
Fairfield, CA (city) Solano County	170	0.16
Arvada, CO (city) Jefferson County	169	0.16
Columbia Heights, MN (city) Anoka County	168	0.86
North Highlands, CA (cdp) Sacramento County	166	0.39
Madison, WI (town) Dane County	165	2.63

SECTION THREE

Please refer to the Explanation of Data in the front of the book for more detailed information.

Race

Asian: Hmong

Top 150 Places Sorted by Percent of Total Population

Based on all places, regardless of total population

Place	Population	%
Walnut Grove, MN (city) Redwood County	215	24.68
Biola, CA (cdp) Fresno County	249	15.34
Thermalito, CA (cdp) Butte County	966	14.54
South Oroville, CA (cdp) Butte County	726	12.64
Springdale, MN (township) Redwood County	27	12.44
Franklin, CA (cdp) Merced County	744	12.10
Granite Rock, MN (township) Redwood County	26	11.56
Eau Claire, WI (city) Chippewa County	226	11.41
Brooklyn Center, MN (city) Hennepin County	3,170	10.53
St. Paul, MN (city) Ramsey County	29,662	10.41
Cherokee, CA (cdp) Butte County	7	10.14
Linda, CA (cdp) Yuba County	1,742	9.80
Wausau, WI (city) Marathon County	3,783	9.67
Tracy, MN (city) Lyon County	204	9.43
Trowbridge, CA (cdp) Sutter County	20	8.85
Gardner, FL (cdp) Hardee County	36	7.78
Underwood, MN (township) Redwood County	16	7.77
Sheboygan, WI (city) Sheboygan County	3,716	7.54
North Hero, MN (township) Redwood County	12	7.45
Lemon Hill, CA (cdp) Sacramento County	1,009	7.35
Weston, WI (village) Marathon County	1,089	7.32
Fruitridge Pocket, CA (cdp) Sacramento County	422	7.28
Raynham, NC (town) Robeson County	5	6.94
Brooklyn Park, MN (city) Hennepin County	5,151	6.80
Little Canada, MN (city) Ramsey County	650	6.65
Maplewood, MN (city) Ramsey County	2,512	6.61
White Water, OK (cdp) Delaware County	5	6.25
Florin, CA (cdp) Sacramento County	2,933	6.17
Merced, CA (city) Merced County	4,741	6.00
Connelly Springs, NC (town) Burke County	100	5.99
Holmen, WI (village) La Crosse County	538	5.97
Gregory, OK (cdp) Rogers County	10	5.85
Sunnyside, CA (cdp) Fresno County	245	5.79
Sletten, MN (township) Polk County	10	5.65
Shaokatan, MN (township) Lincoln County	10	5.62
Oakdale, MN (city) Washington County	1,524	5.57
Twin Oaks, OK (cdp) Delaware County	11	5.56
Appleton, WI (city) Winnebago County	82	5.50
Parkway, CA (cdp) Sacramento County	779	5.31
Menomonie, WI (town) Dunn County	178	5.29
Kennedy, CA (cdp) San Joaquin County	171	5.26
Clements, MN (city) Redwood County	8	5.23
New Cambria, MO (city) Macon County	10	5.13
Appleton, WI (city) Calumet County	553	4.99
Oroville, CA (city) Butte County	773	4.97
Fresno, CA (city) Fresno County	24,328	4.92
North St. Paul, MN (city) Ramsey County	546	4.76
Vadnais Heights, MN (city) Ramsey County	578	4.70
Nord, CA (cdp) Butte County	15	4.69
Bear Creek, CA (cdp) Merced County	13	4.48
Elk Mound, WI (village) Dunn County	39	4.44
Schofield, WI (city) Marathon County	95	4.38
Tarpey Village, CA (cdp) Fresno County	170	4.37
Appleton, WI (city) Outagamie County	3,156	4.35
Emerald, WI (cdp) St. Croix County	7	4.35
Winton, CA (cdp) Merced County	453	4.27
Rose, OK (cdp) Mayes County	12	4.21
Appleton, WI (city) Outagamie County	2,521	4.20
New Avon, MN (township) Redwood County	8	4.19
Limestone, OK (cdp) Rogers County	26	4.13
Richfield, NC (town) Stanly County	25	4.08
Westline, MN (township) Redwood County	7	3.93
Wausau, WI (town) Marathon County	86	3.86
Onalaska, WI (city) La Crosse County	674	3.80
Mosel, WI (town) Sheboygan County	30	3.80
Manitowoc, WI (city) Manitowoc County	1,278	3.79
Russell, GA (cdp) Barrow County	45	3.74
Taft Mosswood, CA (cdp) San Joaquin County	57	3.73
Eagle Grove, GA (cdp) Hart County	6	3.66
Vesta, MN (township) Redwood County	7	3.65
Junction City, WI (village) Portage County	16	3.64
Sacramento, CA (city) Sacramento County	16,676	3.57
Box, OK (cdp) Sequoyah County	8	3.57
Union, WI (town) Eau Claire County	94	3.53
Gentry, AR (city) Benton County	111	3.51
Maine, WI (town) Marathon County	81	3.47
Monroe, MN (township) Lyon County	7	3.47
Rib Mountain, WI (cdp) Marathon County	194	3.43
Olivehurst, CA (cdp) Yuba County	466	3.41
Tiffany, WI (town) Dunn County	21	3.40
Eau Claire, WI (city) Eau Claire County	2,213	3.36
Rib Mountain, WI (town) Marathon County	226	3.31
Gem Lake, MN (city) Ramsey County	13	3.31
Bertsch-Oceanview, CA (cdp) Del Norte County	80	3.28
Long View, NC (town) Catawba County	158	3.24
Clifton, MN (township) Lyon County	8	3.21
Fairforest, SC (cdp) Spartanburg County	54	3.19
Old Green, OK (cdp) Adair County	10	3.17
Kronenwetter, WI (village) Marathon County	228	3.16
Clovis, CA (city) Fresno County	3,001	3.14
Eau Claire, WI (city) Eau Claire County	1,987	3.11
East Nicolaus, CA (cdp) Sutter County	7	3.11
Welda, KS (cdp) Anderson County	4	3.10
Afton, MN (city) Washington County	89	3.08
Wisconsin Rapids, WI (city) Wood County	562	3.06
Vail, MN (township) Redwood County	7	3.06
La Crosse, WI (city) La Crosse County	1,563	3.05
Glen Alpine, NC (town) Burke County	46	3.03
Roosevelt, WI (town) Burnett County	6	3.02
Wheaton, WI (town) Chippewa County	81	3.00
Crescent City, CA (city) Del Norte County	228	2.98
Shaw Heights, CO (cdp) Adams County	152	2.97
Hildebran, NC (town) Burke County	60	2.97
New Eucha, OK (cdp) Delaware County	12	2.96
Green Bay, WI (city) Brown County	3,020	2.90
Auburn, GA (city) Barrow County	199	2.89
Palermo, CA (cdp) Butte County	155	2.88
Sun Prairie, WI (town) Dane County	67	2.88
St. Stephens, NC (cdp) Catawba County	250	2.85
Johnson, WI (town) Marathon County	28	2.84
Stevens Point, WI (city) Portage County	757	2.83
Plover, WI (village) Portage County	343	2.83
Mayfair, CA (cdp) Fresno County	129	2.81
Rio Oso, CA (cdp) Sutter County	10	2.81
Forbestown, CA (cdp) Butte County	9	2.81
Swartzville, PA (cdp) Lancaster County	64	2.80
Menomonie, WI (city) Dunn County	450	2.77
Bellevue, WI (village) Brown County	403	2.77
Mattoon, WI (village) Shawano County	12	2.74
Woodson, AR (cdp) Pulaski County	11	2.73
Rothschild, WI (village) Marathon County	142	2.70
Rockland, WI (village) La Crosse County	16	2.69
Columbus, MN (city) Anoka County	105	2.68
Park Ridge, WI (village) Portage County	13	2.65
Mounds View, MN (city) Ramsey County	321	2.64
Madison, WI (town) Dane County	165	2.63
Elk Mound, WI (town) Dunn County	47	2.62
McSwain, CA (cdp) Merced County	109	2.61
Remington, WI (town) Wood County	7	2.61
Adamstown, PA (borough) Lancaster County	46	2.60
Cottage Grove, MN (city) Washington County	890	2.57
Adamstown, PA (borough) Lancaster County	46	2.57
Shullsburg, WI (town) Lafayette County	9	2.54
Stella, MO (town) Newton County	4	2.53
Texas, WI (town) Marathon County	40	2.48
Farmington, WI (town) La Crosse County	51	2.47
Bertha, MN (township) Todd County	10	2.45
Pine Springs, MN (city) Washington County	10	2.45
Black Hammer, MN (township) Houston County	6	2.45
Rollingstone, MN (township) Winona County	17	2.43
Sheboygan, WI (town) Sheboygan County	176	2.42
Harding, WI (town) Lincoln County	9	2.42
Brown Deer, WI (village) Milwaukee County	289	2.41
Weston, WI (town) Dunn County	14	2.36
Drexel, NC (town) Burke County	43	2.31
Spring Brook, WI (town) Dunn County	36	2.31
Laketown, MN (township) Carver County	51	2.27
West Lakeland, MN (township) Washington County	91	2.25
Oshkosh, WI (city) Winnebago County	1,469	2.22
Oakdale, WI (town) Monroe County	17	2.20

Please refer to the Explanation of Data in the front of the book for more detailed information.

Race

Asian: Hmong

Top 150 Places Sorted by Percent of Total Population

Based on places with total population of 7,500 or more

Place	Population	%
Brooklyn Center, MN (city) Hennepin County	3,170	10.53
St. Paul, MN (city) Ramsey County	29,662	10.41
Linda, CA (cdp) Yuba County	1,742	9.80
Wausau, WI (city) Marathon County	3,783	9.67
Sheboygan, WI (city) Sheboygan County	3,716	7.54
Lemon Hill, CA (cdp) Sacramento County	1,009	7.35
Weston, WI (village) Marathon County	1,089	7.32
Brooklyn Park, MN (city) Hennepin County	5,151	6.80
Little Canada, MN (city) Ramsey County	650	6.65
Maplewood, MN (city) Ramsey County	2,512	6.61
Florin, CA (cdp) Sacramento County	2,933	6.17
Merced, CA (city) Merced County	4,741	6.00
Holmen, WI (village) La Crosse County	538	5.97
Oakdale, MN (city) Washington County	1,524	5.57
Parkway, CA (cdp) Sacramento County	779	5.31
Appleton, WI (city) Calumet County	553	4.99
Oroville, CA (city) Butte County	773	4.97
Fresno, CA (city) Fresno County	24,328	4.92
North St. Paul, MN (city) Ramsey County	546	4.76
Vadnais Heights, MN (city) Ramsey County	578	4.70
Appleton, WI (city) Outagamie County	3,156	4.35
Winton, CA (cdp) Merced County	453	4.27
Appleton, WI (city) Outagamie County	2,521	4.20
Onalaska, WI (city) La Crosse County	674	3.80
Manitowoc, WI (city) Manitowoc County	1,278	3.79
Sacramento, CA (city) Sacramento County	16,676	3.57
Olivehurst, CA (cdp) Yuba County	466	3.41
Eau Claire, WI (city) Eau Claire County	2,213	3.36
Clovis, CA (city) Fresno County	3,001	3.14
Eau Claire, WI (city) Eau Claire County	1,987	3.11
Wisconsin Rapids, WI (city) Wood County	562	3.06
La Crosse, WI (city) La Crosse County	1,563	3.05
Crescent City, CA (city) Del Norte County	228	2.98
Green Bay, WI (city) Brown County	3,020	2.90
St. Stephens, NC (cdp) Catawba County	250	2.85
Stevens Point, WI (city) Portage County	757	2.83
Plover, WI (village) Portage County	343	2.83
Menomonie, WI (city) Dunn County	450	2.77
Bellevue, WI (village) Brown County	403	2.77
Mounds View, MN (city) Ramsey County	321	2.64
Cottage Grove, MN (city) Washington County	890	2.57
Brown Deer, WI (village) Milwaukee County	289	2.41
Oshkosh, WI (city) Winnebago County	1,469	2.22
Stockton, CA (city) San Joaquin County	6,073	2.08
Newton, NC (city) Catawba County	262	2.02
Banning, CA (city) Riverside County	591	2.00
Hugo, MN (city) Washington County	264	1.98
Minneapolis, MN (city) Hennepin County	7,512	1.96
Conover, NC (city) Catawba County	160	1.96
White Bear Lake, MN (city) Ramsey County	454	1.94
White Bear Lake, MN (city) Ramsey County	454	1.91
Eureka, CA (city) Humboldt County	515	1.89
Lake Elmo, MN (city) Washington County	149	1.85
Albemarle, NC (city) Stanly County	291	1.83
Two Rivers, WI (city) Manitowoc County	212	1.81
Woodbury, MN (city) Washington County	1,103	1.78
Lino Lakes, MN (city) Anoka County	358	1.77
Atwater, CA (city) Merced County	489	1.74
Milwaukee, WI (city) Milwaukee County	10,245	1.72
Rio Linda, CA (cdp) Sacramento County	256	1.69
Oroville East, CA (cdp) Butte County	140	1.69
Blaine, MN (city) Anoka County	950	1.66
Grand Chute, WI (town) Outagamie County	338	1.62
Menasha, WI (town) Winnebago County	293	1.58
Fridley, MN (city) Anoka County	419	1.54
Menasha, WI (city) Winnebago County	265	1.53
Menasha, WI (city) Winnebago County	231	1.53
Sun Prairie, WI (city) Dane County	434	1.48
Kingsgate, WA (cdp) King County	193	1.48
Garden Acres, CA (cdp) San Joaquin County	158	1.48
Ham Lake, MN (city) Anoka County	218	1.43
Chico, CA (city) Butte County	1,225	1.42
Vineyard, CA (cdp) Sacramento County	339	1.36
Oak Grove, MN (city) Anoka County	103	1.28
Robbinsdale, MN (city) Hennepin County	175	1.25
Coon Rapids, MN (city) Anoka County	765	1.24
Roseville, MN (city) Ramsey County	413	1.23
Hickory, NC (city) Catawba County	479	1.20
Anchorage, AK (municipality) Anchorage Municipality	3,408	1.17
Madison, WI (city) Dane County	2,728	1.17
Elk Grove, CA (city) Sacramento County	1,789	1.17
Pontiac, MI (city) Oakland County	695	1.17
East Cocalico, PA (township) Lancaster County	120	1.16
Hudson, WI (town) St. Croix County	97	1.15
Winder, GA (city) Barrow County	159	1.13
Arden Hills, MN (city) Ramsey County	103	1.08
Kaukauna, WI (city) Outagamie County	162	1.05
Fitchburg, MA (city) Worcester County	412	1.02
Fitchburg, WI (city) Dane County	249	0.99
Fond du Lac, WI (city) Fond du Lac County	419	0.97
Morganton, NC (city) Burke County	163	0.96
East Bethel, MN (city) Anoka County	110	0.95
Ashwaubenon, WI (village) Brown County	160	0.94
Kansas City, KS (city) Wyandotte County	1,355	0.93
White Bear, MN (township) Ramsey County	102	0.93
Warren, MI (city) Macomb County	1,218	0.91
Ramsey, MN (city) Anoka County	216	0.91
Marysville, CA (city) Yuba County	109	0.90
Inver Grove Heights, MN (city) Dakota County	303	0.89
Sanger, CA (city) Fresno County	213	0.88
Champlin, MN (city) Hennepin County	201	0.87
Columbia Heights, MN (city) Anoka County	168	0.86
Westminster, CO (city) Adams County	895	0.84
Storm Lake, IA (city) Buena Vista County	88	0.83
Crystal, MN (city) Hennepin County	180	0.81
Winona, MN (city) Winona County	218	0.79
Allouez, WI (village) Brown County	107	0.77
Federal Heights, CO (city) Adams County	88	0.77
Harrison, WI (town) Calumet County	84	0.77
Howard, WI (village) Brown County	133	0.76
Lompoc, CA (city) Santa Barbara County	309	0.73
Marshall, MN (city) Lyon County	98	0.72
Braselton, GA (town) Gwinnett County	54	0.72
Owasso, OK (city) Tulsa County	204	0.71
Frederick, CO (town) Weld County	62	0.71
Berkley, CO (cdp) Adams County	79	0.70
Little Chute, WI (village) Outagamie County	73	0.70
West Earl, PA (township) Lancaster County	55	0.70
Ephrata, PA (township) Lancaster County	65	0.69
Rancho Cordova, CA (city) Sacramento County	440	0.68
Andover, MN (city) Anoka County	207	0.68
Upper Leacock, PA (township) Lancaster County	59	0.68
Northglenn, CO (city) Adams County	236	0.66
New Hope, MN (city) Hennepin County	135	0.66
Thornton, CO (city) Adams County	760	0.64
Forest Lake, MN (city) Washington County	116	0.63
Rogers, MN (city) Hennepin County	53	0.62
Shoreview, MN (city) Ramsey County	150	0.60
DeForest, WI (village) Dane County	54	0.60
August, CA (cdp) San Joaquin County	50	0.60
Live Oak, CA (city) Sutter County	50	0.60
Delhi, CA (cdp) Merced County	63	0.59
Greenville, WI (town) Outagamie County	61	0.59
Commerce City, CO (city) Adams County	264	0.58
Statesville, NC (city) Iredell County	140	0.57
Lansing, MI (city) Ingham County	643	0.56
Anoka, MN (city) Anoka County	94	0.55
Broomfield, CO (city) Broomfield County	283	0.51
St. Michael, MN (city) Wright County	83	0.51
Bonadelle Ranchos-Madera Ranchos, CA (cdp) Madera County	44	0.51
Lansing, MI (city) Ingham County	549	0.50
Center Line, MI (city) Macomb County	41	0.50
River Falls, WI (city) Pierce County	58	0.49
Country Club, CA (cdp) San Joaquin County	46	0.49
Visalia, CA (city) Tulare County	594	0.48
Platteville, WI (city) Grant County	54	0.48
Suisun City, CA (city) Solano County	133	0.47
Rosemont, CA (cdp) Sacramento County	107	0.47
River Falls, WI (city) Pierce County	69	0.46
St. Peter, MN (city) Nicollet County	51	0.46

Please refer to the Explanation of Data in the front of the book for more detailed information.

Race

Asian: Indian

U.S. and 50 States Sorted by Population and Percent of Total Population

Place	Population	%
United States	**3,183,063**	**1.03**
California	590,445	1.58
New York	368,767	1.90
New Jersey	311,310	3.54
Texas	269,327	1.07
Illinois	203,669	1.59
Florida	151,438	0.81
Virginia	114,471	1.43
Pennsylvania	113,389	0.89
Georgia	105,444	1.09
Maryland	88,709	1.54
Massachusetts	85,441	1.30
Michigan	84,750	0.86
Ohio	71,211	0.62
Washington	68,978	1.03
North Carolina	63,852	0.67
Connecticut	50,806	1.42
Arizona	40,510	0.63
Minnesota	38,097	0.72
Indiana	30,947	0.48
Tennessee	26,619	0.42
Missouri	26,263	0.44
Wisconsin	25,998	0.46
Colorado	24,135	0.48
Oregon	20,200	0.53
South Carolina	17,961	0.39
Kansas	15,644	0.55
Alabama	14,951	0.31
Nevada	14,290	0.53
Kentucky	14,253	0.33
Oklahoma	14,078	0.38
Louisiana	13,147	0.29
Iowa	12,525	0.41
Delaware	12,344	1.37
Arkansas	9,101	0.31
New Hampshire	9,075	0.69
Utah	7,598	0.27
Nebraska	6,708	0.37
Mississippi	6,458	0.22
District of Columbia	6,417	1.07
New Mexico	5,727	0.28
Rhode Island	5,645	0.54
Hawaii	4,737	0.35
West Virginia	3,969	0.21
Idaho	2,786	0.18
Maine	2,397	0.18
Alaska	1,911	0.27
North Dakota	1,740	0.26
Vermont	1,723	0.28
South Dakota	1,433	0.18
Montana	930	0.09
Wyoming	739	0.13

Place	Population	%
New Jersey	311,310	3.54
New York	368,767	1.90
Illinois	203,669	1.59
California	590,445	1.58
Maryland	88,709	1.54
Virginia	114,471	1.43
Connecticut	50,806	1.42
Delaware	12,344	1.37
Massachusetts	85,441	1.30
Georgia	105,444	1.09
Texas	269,327	1.07
District of Columbia	6,417	1.07
United States	**3,183,063**	**1.03**
Washington	68,978	1.03
Pennsylvania	113,389	0.89
Michigan	84,750	0.86
Florida	151,438	0.81
Minnesota	38,097	0.72
New Hampshire	9,075	0.69
North Carolina	63,852	0.67
Arizona	40,510	0.63
Ohio	71,211	0.62
Kansas	15,644	0.55
Rhode Island	5,645	0.54
Oregon	20,200	0.53
Nevada	14,290	0.53
Indiana	30,947	0.48
Colorado	24,135	0.48
Wisconsin	25,998	0.46
Missouri	26,263	0.44
Tennessee	26,619	0.42
Iowa	12,525	0.41
South Carolina	17,961	0.39
Oklahoma	14,078	0.38
Nebraska	6,708	0.37
Hawaii	4,737	0.35
Kentucky	14,253	0.33
Alabama	14,951	0.31
Arkansas	9,101	0.31
Louisiana	13,147	0.29
New Mexico	5,727	0.28
Vermont	1,723	0.28
Utah	7,598	0.27
Alaska	1,911	0.27
North Dakota	1,740	0.26
Mississippi	6,458	0.22
West Virginia	3,969	0.21
Idaho	2,786	0.18
Maine	2,397	0.18
South Dakota	1,433	0.18
Wyoming	739	0.13
Montana	930	0.09

Please refer to the Explanation of Data in the front of the book for more detailed information.

Race

Asian: Indian

Top 150 Places Sorted by Population

Based on all places, regardless of total population

Place	Population	%
New York, NY (city) Kings County	232,696	2.85
Queens, NY (borough) Queens County	141,147	6.33
San Jose, CA (city) Santa Clara County	46,410	4.91
Fremont, CA (city) Alameda County	40,010	18.69
Los Angeles, CA (city) Los Angeles County	38,574	1.02
Chicago, IL (city) Cook County	33,528	1.24
Brooklyn, NY (borough) Kings County	33,490	1.34
Manhattan, NY (borough) New York County	29,979	1.89
Edison, NJ (township) Middlesex County	29,277	29.29
Houston, TX (city) Harris County	29,128	1.39
Jersey City, NJ (city) Hudson County	28,688	11.59
Sunnyvale, CA (city) Santa Clara County	22,285	15.91
Philadelphia, PA (city) Philadelphia County	20,809	1.36
Bronx, NY (borough) Bronx County	20,357	1.47
San Diego, CA (city) San Diego County	19,096	1.46
Irving, TX (city) Dallas County	18,025	8.33
Hempstead, NY (town) Nassau County	17,802	2.34
Plano, TX (city) Collin County	17,723	6.82
Woodbridge, NJ (township) Middlesex County	16,495	16.56
Santa Clara, CA (city) Santa Clara County	16,412	14.09
Austin, TX (city) Travis County	16,162	2.04
Charlotte, NC (city) Mecklenburg County	14,258	1.95
North Hempstead, NY (town) Nassau County	13,427	5.93
Cupertino, CA (city) Santa Clara County	13,415	23.01
Phoenix, AZ (city) Maricopa County	13,308	0.92
San Francisco, CA (city) San Francisco County	11,583	1.44
Columbus, OH (city) Franklin County	11,364	1.44
South Brunswick, NJ (township) Middlesex County	11,344	26.13
Irvine, CA (city) Orange County	11,325	5.33
Oyster Bay, NY (town) Nassau County	11,289	3.85
Piscataway, NJ (township) Middlesex County	11,189	19.96
Naperville, IL (city) DuPage County	10,917	7.70
Sacramento, CA (city) Sacramento County	10,700	2.29
Fresno, CA (city) Fresno County	9,825	1.99
San Antonio, TX (city) Medina County	9,716	0.73
Parsippany-Troy Hills, NJ (township) Morris County	9,576	17.99
Yuba City, CA (city) Sutter County	9,352	14.40
Bellevue, WA (city) King County	9,343	7.64
Cary, NC (town) Wake County	9,217	6.82
Sugar Land, TX (city) Fort Bend County	8,856	11.24
Union City, CA (city) Alameda County	8,570	12.33
Boston, MA (city) Suffolk County	8,489	1.37
San Ramon, CA (city) Contra Costa County	8,468	11.74
Dallas, TX (city) Dallas County	8,314	0.69
Schaumburg, IL (village) Cook County	8,303	11.19
Franklin, NJ (township) Somerset County	7,998	12.84
Jacksonville, FL (city) Duval County	7,900	0.96
Bakersfield, CA (city) Kern County	7,896	2.27
Staten Island, NY (borough) Richmond County	7,723	1.65
Troy, MI (city) Oakland County	7,564	9.34
Canton, MI (charter township) Wayne County	7,546	8.37
Iselin, NJ (cdp) Middlesex County	7,273	38.90
North Brunswick, NJ (township) Middlesex County	7,197	17.66
Plainsboro, NJ (township) Middlesex County	6,957	30.25
Aurora, IL (city) Kane County	6,828	3.45
Johns Creek, GA (city) Fulton County	6,685	8.71
Milpitas, CA (city) Santa Clara County	6,602	9.88
Redmond, WA (city) King County	6,433	11.88
Washington, DC (city) District of Columbia	6,417	1.07
Germantown, MD (cdp) Montgomery County	6,003	6.95
Seattle, WA (city) King County	5,988	0.98
Hoffman Estates, IL (village) Cook County	5,985	11.53
Chandler, AZ (city) Maricopa County	5,925	2.51
Elk Grove, CA (city) Sacramento County	5,856	3.83
Yonkers, NY (city) Westchester County	5,818	2.97
Brookhaven, NY (town) Suffolk County	5,745	1.18
Stockton, CA (city) San Joaquin County	5,630	1.93
Pleasanton, CA (city) Alameda County	5,476	7.79
Fort Worth, TX (city) Tarrant County	5,467	0.74
Hayward, CA (city) Alameda County	5,409	3.75
Stamford, CT (city/town) Fairfield County	5,404	4.41
Indianapolis, IN (city) Marion County	5,358	0.65
West Windsor, NJ (township) Mercer County	5,280	19.44
Farmington Hills, MI (city) Oakland County	5,216	6.54
Raleigh, NC (city) Wake County	5,143	1.27
Atlanta, GA (city) Fulton County	5,141	1.22
McNair, VA (cdp) Fairfax County	5,125	29.26
Hicksville, NY (cdp) Nassau County	5,111	12.30
Old Bridge, NJ (township) Middlesex County	5,110	7.82
Overland Park, KS (city) Johnson County	4,998	2.88
Frisco, TX (city) Collin County	4,984	4.26
Carrollton, TX (city) Denton County	4,980	4.18
Anaheim, CA (city) Orange County	4,915	1.46
Arlington, VA (cdp) Arlington County	4,813	2.32
Oklahoma City, OK (city) Oklahoma County	4,765	0.82
Ellicott City, MD (cdp) Howard County	4,712	7.16
Nashville-Davidson, TN (metro govt) Davidson County	4,691	0.78
Missouri City, TX (city) Fort Bend County	4,684	6.95
Alpharetta, GA (city) Fulton County	4,630	8.05
Skokie, IL (village) Cook County	4,624	7.14
Mountain View, CA (city) Santa Clara County	4,612	6.23
Richardson, TX (city) Dallas County	4,601	4.64
Sayreville, NJ (borough) Middlesex County	4,483	10.50
Bensalem, PA (township) Bucks County	4,480	7.41
Princeton Meadows, NJ (cdp) Middlesex County	4,428	32.01
Tampa, FL (city) Hillsborough County	4,425	1.32
Garland, TX (city) Dallas County	4,358	1.92
Torrance, CA (city) Los Angeles County	4,290	2.95
Islip, NY (town) Suffolk County	4,276	1.27
Centreville, VA (cdp) Fairfax County	4,251	5.98
Ann Arbor, MI (city) Washtenaw County	4,216	3.70
Cambridge, MA (city) Middlesex County	4,129	3.93
Bloomington, IL (city) McLean County	4,090	5.34
Pittsburgh, PA (city) Allegheny County	4,025	1.32
Cerritos, CA (city) Los Angeles County	3,983	8.12
Folsom, CA (city) Sacramento County	3,981	5.51
Baltimore, MD (city) Baltimore city County	3,946	0.64
Allen, TX (city) Collin County	3,923	4.66
Bridgewater, NJ (township) Somerset County	3,917	8.81
Clifton, NJ (city) Passaic County	3,899	4.63
Clarkstown, NY (town) Rockland County	3,874	4.60
Madison, WI (city) Dane County	3,851	1.65
Morrisville, NC (town) Wake County	3,809	20.50
East Brunswick, NJ (township) Middlesex County	3,772	7.94
Arlington, TX (city) Tarrant County	3,749	1.03
Novi, MI (city) Oakland County	3,657	6.62
Louisville-Jefferson County, KY (metro govt) Jefferson County	3,649	0.61
Columbia, MD (cdp) Howard County	3,636	3.65
Simi Valley, CA (city) Ventura County	3,617	2.91
Foster City, CA (city) San Mateo County	3,593	11.75
Sterling Heights, MI (city) Macomb County	3,551	2.74
Minneapolis, MN (city) Hennepin County	3,539	0.93
Huntington, NY (town) Suffolk County	3,529	1.74
Franklin Park, NJ (cdp) Somerset County	3,528	26.54
Greenburgh, NY (town) Westchester County	3,518	3.98
Amherst, NY (town) Erie County	3,491	2.85
Rochester Hills, MI (city) Oakland County	3,470	4.89
Pembroke Pines, FL (city) Broward County	3,466	2.24
East Windsor, NJ (township) Mercer County	3,448	12.68
Modesto, CA (city) Stanislaus County	3,403	1.69
Tracy, CA (city) San Joaquin County	3,395	4.09
Denver, CO (city) Denver County	3,395	0.57
Ashburn, VA (cdp) Loudoun County	3,376	7.76
Sammamish, WA (city) King County	3,337	7.29
Dublin, CA (city) Alameda County	3,323	7.22
Mount Prospect, IL (village) Cook County	3,314	6.12
Durham, NC (city) Durham County	3,306	1.45
Gaithersburg, MD (city) Montgomery County	3,302	5.51
Nashua, NH (city) Hillsborough County	3,298	3.81
Carteret, NJ (borough) Middlesex County	3,284	14.38
Shrewsbury, MA (town) Worcester County	3,261	9.16
Glendale Heights, IL (village) DuPage County	3,215	9.40
Des Plaines, IL (city) Cook County	3,214	5.51
Upper Darby, PA (township) Delaware County	3,208	3.87
Berkeley, CA (city) Alameda County	3,197	2.84
Kent, WA (city) King County	3,182	3.44
Hanover Park, IL (village) Cook County	3,151	8.30
Coral Springs, FL (city) Broward County	3,141	2.59
Bartlett, IL (village) DuPage County	3,120	7.57
Palo Alto, CA (city) Santa Clara County	3,099	4.81

Please refer to the Explanation of Data in the front of the book for more detailed information.

Race

Asian: Indian

Top 150 Places Sorted by Percent of Total Population

Based on all places, regardless of total population

Place	Population	%
Loudoun Valley Estates, VA (cdp) Loudoun County	1,557	42.59
Iselin, NJ (cdp) Middlesex County	7,273	38.90
Ten Mile Run, NJ (cdp) Somerset County	711	36.29
Plainsboro Center, NJ (cdp) Middlesex County	973	35.88
Dayton, NJ (cdp) Middlesex County	2,528	35.79
Millbourne, PA (borough) Delaware County	398	34.34
Princeton Meadows, NJ (cdp) Middlesex County	4,428	32.01
Plainsboro, NJ (township) Middlesex County	6,957	30.25
Edison, NJ (township) Middlesex County	29,277	29.29
McNair, VA (cdp) Fairfax County	5,125	29.26
Moorefield Station, VA (cdp) Loudoun County	21	27.27
Franklin Park, NJ (cdp) Somerset County	3,528	26.54
South Brunswick, NJ (township) Middlesex County	11,344	26.13
Heathcote, NJ (cdp) Middlesex County	1,460	25.08
Monmouth Junction, NJ (cdp) Middlesex County	723	25.04
Dixville, NH (township) Coos County	3	25.00
Arcola, VA (cdp) Loudoun County	58	24.89
Pleasant Plains, NJ (cdp) Somerset County	227	24.62
Park, MN (township) Pine County	9	24.32
Society Hill, NJ (cdp) Middlesex County	926	24.18
Herricks, NY (cdp) Nassau County	1,036	24.12
Cupertino, CA (city) Santa Clara County	13,415	23.01
Morrisville, NC (town) Wake County	3,809	20.50
Oak Grove, VA (cdp) Loudoun County	363	20.43
Piscataway, NJ (township) Middlesex County	11,189	19.96
West Windsor, NJ (township) Mercer County	5,280	19.44
Manhasset Hills, NY (cdp) Nassau County	690	19.21
Garden City Park, NY (cdp) Nassau County	1,487	19.05
Searingtown, NY (cdp) Nassau County	935	19.02
Fremont, CA (city) Alameda County	40,010	18.69
New Territory, TX (cdp) Fort Bend County	2,829	18.63
Parsippany-Troy Hills, NJ (township) Morris County	9,576	17.99
North Brunswick, NJ (township) Middlesex County	7,197	17.66
Madison Park, NJ (cdp) Middlesex County	1,243	17.40
New Hyde Park, NY (village) Nassau County	1,682	17.32
Avenel, NJ (cdp) Middlesex County	2,912	17.12
North New Hyde Park, NY (cdp) Nassau County	2,547	17.10
Hurstbourne Acres, KY (city) Jefferson County	301	16.62
Woodbridge, NJ (township) Middlesex County	16,495	16.56
Bradley Gardens, NJ (cdp) Somerset County	2,353	16.56
Merritt Park, NY (cdp) Dutchess County	208	16.56
Muttontown, NY (village) Nassau County	569	16.27
Six Mile Run, NJ (cdp) Somerset County	511	16.05
Sunnyvale, CA (city) Santa Clara County	22,285	15.91
Sunnyvale, TX (town) Dallas County	814	15.87
Kendall Park, NJ (cdp) Middlesex County	1,460	15.63
Livingston, CA (city) Merced County	2,039	15.61
South Barrington, IL (village) Cook County	702	15.38
Floris, VA (cdp) Fairfax County	1,285	15.34
Woodbridge, NJ (cdp) Middlesex County	2,932	15.22
Brambleton, VA (cdp) Loudoun County	1,482	15.05
Robbinsville, NJ (cdp) Mercer County	439	14.44
Yuba City, CA (city) Sutter County	9,352	14.40
Carteret, NJ (borough) Middlesex County	3,284	14.38
Norris Canyon, CA (cdp) Contra Costa County	137	14.32
Oak Brook, IL (village) DuPage County	1,116	14.16
Santa Clara, CA (city) Santa Clara County	16,412	14.09
Scottdale, GA (cdp) DeKalb County	1,481	13.93
Innsbrook, VA (cdp) Henrico County	1,063	13.71
Stone Ridge, VA (cdp) Loudoun County	987	13.68
Albertson, NY (cdp) Nassau County	690	13.32
Middlebush, NJ (cdp) Somerset County	306	13.16
Hatfield, PA (borough) Montgomery County	430	13.07
Franklin, NJ (township) Somerset County	7,998	12.84
East Windsor, NJ (township) Mercer County	3,448	12.68
Bellerose Terrace, NY (cdp) Nassau County	277	12.60
Fords, NJ (cdp) Middlesex County	1,884	12.41
Union City, CA (city) Alameda County	8,570	12.33
Hicksville, NY (cdp) Nassau County	5,111	12.30
South Riding, VA (cdp) Loudoun County	2,982	12.29
Exton, PA (cdp) Chester County	592	12.23
Westborough, MA (town) Worcester County	2,229	12.20
Merrifield, VA (cdp) Fairfax County	1,851	12.17
Farmington, MI (city) Oakland County	1,240	11.96
Pomona, NJ (cdp) Atlantic County	850	11.93
Redmond, WA (city) King County	6,433	11.88
Bothell East, WA (cdp) Snohomish County	950	11.85
Foster City, CA (city) San Mateo County	3,593	11.75
San Ramon, CA (city) Contra Costa County	8,468	11.74
Blackwells Mills, NJ (cdp) Somerset County	94	11.71
East Caln, PA (township) Chester County	565	11.68
Dulles Town Center, VA (cdp) Loudoun County	534	11.61
Jersey City, NJ (city) Hudson County	28,688	11.59
Hoffman Estates, IL (village) Cook County	5,985	11.53
Bethany, OR (cdp) Washington County	2,380	11.53
Montgomery, NJ (township) Somerset County	2,519	11.32
Sugar Land, TX (city) Fort Bend County	8,856	11.24
Schaumburg, IL (village) Cook County	8,303	11.19
Echelon, NJ (cdp) Camden County	1,190	11.08
King of Prussia, PA (cdp) Montgomery County	2,198	11.03
Belmont, VA (cdp) Loudoun County	646	10.83
Sayreville, NJ (borough) Middlesex County	4,483	10.50
Mountain House, CA (cdp) San Joaquin County	1,015	10.49
Clarksburg, MD (cdp) Montgomery County	1,442	10.48
Menands, NY (village) Albany County	418	10.48
Burtonsville, MD (cdp) Montgomery County	867	10.42
Saratoga, CA (city) Santa Clara County	3,057	10.22
Secaucus, NJ (town) Hudson County	1,662	10.22
Four Corners, TX (cdp) Fort Bend County	1,248	10.08
Hurstbourne, KY (city) Jefferson County	422	10.01
Summerhaven, AZ (cdp) Pima County	4	10.00
Wormleysburg, PA (borough) Cumberland County	305	9.93
Morton Grove, IL (village) Cook County	2,309	9.92
Murphy, TX (city) Collin County	1,757	9.92
Milpitas, CA (city) Santa Clara County	6,602	9.88
Short Pump, VA (cdp) Henrico County	2,409	9.74
Broadlands, VA (cdp) Loudoun County	1,196	9.71
Camino Tassajara, CA (cdp) Contra Costa County	212	9.65
Somerset, NJ (cdp) Somerset County	2,106	9.54
Scott, PA (township) Allegheny County	1,620	9.52
Walnut Grove, MN (city) Redwood County	82	9.41
Glendale Heights, IL (village) DuPage County	3,215	9.40
Hatfield, PA (township) Montgomery County	1,619	9.39
Travilah, MD (cdp) Montgomery County	1,140	9.38
Tysons Corner, VA (cdp) Fairfax County	1,835	9.35
Troy, MI (city) Oakland County	7,564	9.34
Fair Lakes, VA (cdp) Fairfax County	740	9.32
Burlington, MA (cdp/town) Middlesex County	2,276	9.29
Burr Ridge, IL (village) DuPage County	968	9.17
Shrewsbury, MA (town) Worcester County	3,261	9.16
Lincolnwood, IL (village) Cook County	1,151	9.14
Upper Uwchlan, PA (township) Chester County	1,020	9.09
Herndon, VA (town) Fairfax County	2,082	8.94
Bridgewater, NJ (township) Somerset County	3,917	8.81
South Plainfield, NJ (borough) Middlesex County	2,048	8.76
Harlingen, NJ (cdp) Somerset County	26	8.75
Johns Creek, GA (city) Fulton County	6,685	8.71
Green Brook, NJ (township) Somerset County	626	8.69
Stafford, TX (city) Fort Bend County	1,527	8.63
Voorhees, NJ (township) Camden County	2,497	8.57
Artesia, CA (city) Los Angeles County	1,407	8.52
Canton, MI (charter township) Wayne County	7,546	8.37
Idylwood, VA (cdp) Fairfax County	1,445	8.36
Irving, TX (city) Dallas County	18,025	8.33
Hanover Park, IL (village) Cook County	3,151	8.30
Live Oak, CA (city) Sutter County	696	8.29
Upper Merion, PA (township) Montgomery County	2,352	8.28
Gregory, OK (cdp) Rogers County	14	8.19
Cerritos, CA (city) Los Angeles County	3,983	8.12
Alpharetta, GA (city) Fulton County	4,630	8.05
Lawrence, NJ (township) Mercer County	2,661	7.95
Hebron, TX (town) Denton County	33	7.95
East Brunswick, NJ (township) Middlesex County	3,772	7.94
Morganville, NJ (cdp) Monmouth County	399	7.92
Rocky Hill, CT (town) Hartford County	1,558	7.91
Audubon, PA (cdp) Montgomery County	663	7.86
Caruthers, CA (cdp) Fresno County	196	7.85
Old Bridge, NJ (township) Middlesex County	5,110	7.82
Hamtramck, MI (city) Wayne County	1,751	7.81
North Potomac, MD (cdp) Montgomery County	1,904	7.80

Please refer to the Explanation of Data in the front of the book for more detailed information.

Race

Asian: Indian

Top 150 Places Sorted by Percent of Total Population

Based on places with total population of 7,500 or more

Place	Population	%
Iselin, NJ (cdp) Middlesex County	7,273	38.90
Princeton Meadows, NJ (cdp) Middlesex County	4,428	32.01
Plainsboro, NJ (township) Middlesex County	6,957	30.25
Edison, NJ (township) Middlesex County	29,277	29.29
McNair, VA (cdp) Fairfax County	5,125	29.26
Franklin Park, NJ (cdp) Somerset County	3,528	26.54
South Brunswick, NJ (township) Middlesex County	11,344	26.13
Cupertino, CA (city) Santa Clara County	13,415	23.01
Morrisville, NC (town) Wake County	3,809	20.50
Piscataway, NJ (township) Middlesex County	11,189	19.96
West Windsor, NJ (township) Mercer County	5,280	19.44
Garden City Park, NY (cdp) Nassau County	1,487	19.05
Fremont, CA (city) Alameda County	40,010	18.69
New Territory, TX (cdp) Fort Bend County	2,829	18.63
Parsippany-Troy Hills, NJ (township) Morris County	9,576	17.99
North Brunswick, NJ (township) Middlesex County	7,197	17.66
New Hyde Park, NY (village) Nassau County	1,682	17.32
Avenel, NJ (cdp) Middlesex County	2,912	17.12
North New Hyde Park, NY (cdp) Nassau County	2,547	17.10
Woodbridge, NJ (township) Middlesex County	16,495	16.56
Bradley Gardens, NJ (cdp) Somerset County	2,353	16.56
Sunnyvale, CA (city) Santa Clara County	22,285	15.91
Kendall Park, NJ (cdp) Middlesex County	1,460	15.63
Livingston, CA (city) Merced County	2,039	15.61
Floris, VA (cdp) Fairfax County	1,285	15.34
Woodbridge, NJ (cdp) Middlesex County	2,932	15.22
Brambleton, VA (cdp) Loudoun County	1,482	15.05
Yuba City, CA (city) Sutter County	9,352	14.40
Carteret, NJ (borough) Middlesex County	3,284	14.38
Oak Brook, IL (village) DuPage County	1,116	14.16
Santa Clara, CA (city) Santa Clara County	16,412	14.09
Scottdale, GA (cdp) DeKalb County	1,481	13.93
Innsbrook, VA (cdp) Henrico County	1,063	13.71
Franklin, NJ (township) Somerset County	7,998	12.84
East Windsor, NJ (township) Mercer County	3,448	12.68
Fords, NJ (cdp) Middlesex County	1,884	12.41
Union City, CA (city) Alameda County	8,570	12.33
Hicksville, NY (cdp) Nassau County	5,111	12.30
South Riding, VA (cdp) Loudoun County	2,982	12.29
Westborough, MA (town) Worcester County	2,229	12.20
Merrifield, VA (cdp) Fairfax County	1,851	12.17
Farmington, MI (city) Oakland County	1,240	11.96
Redmond, WA (city) King County	6,433	11.88
Bothell East, WA (cdp) Snohomish County	950	11.85
Foster City, CA (city) San Mateo County	3,593	11.75
San Ramon, CA (city) Contra Costa County	8,468	11.74
Jersey City, NJ (city) Hudson County	28,688	11.59
Hoffman Estates, IL (village) Cook County	5,985	11.53
Bethany, OR (cdp) Washington County	2,380	11.53
Montgomery, NJ (township) Somerset County	2,519	11.32
Sugar Land, TX (city) Fort Bend County	8,856	11.24
Schaumburg, IL (village) Cook County	8,303	11.19
Echelon, NJ (cdp) Camden County	1,190	11.08
King of Prussia, PA (cdp) Montgomery County	2,198	11.03
Sayreville, NJ (borough) Middlesex County	4,483	10.50
Mountain House, CA (cdp) San Joaquin County	1,015	10.49
Clarksburg, MD (cdp) Montgomery County	1,442	10.48
Burtonsville, MD (cdp) Montgomery County	867	10.42
Saratoga, CA (city) Santa Clara County	3,057	10.22
Secaucus, NJ (town) Hudson County	1,662	10.22
Four Corners, TX (cdp) Fort Bend County	1,248	10.08
Morton Grove, IL (village) Cook County	2,309	9.92
Murphy, TX (city) Collin County	1,757	9.92
Milpitas, CA (city) Santa Clara County	6,602	9.88
Short Pump, VA (cdp) Henrico County	2,409	9.74
Broadlands, VA (cdp) Loudoun County	1,196	9.71
Somerset, NJ (cdp) Somerset County	2,106	9.54
Scott, PA (township) Allegheny County	1,620	9.52
Glendale Heights, IL (village) DuPage County	3,215	9.40
Hatfield, PA (township) Montgomery County	1,619	9.39
Travilah, MD (cdp) Montgomery County	1,140	9.38
Tysons Corner, VA (cdp) Fairfax County	1,835	9.35
Troy, MI (city) Oakland County	7,564	9.34
Fair Lakes, VA (cdp) Fairfax County	740	9.32
Burlington, MA (cdp/town) Middlesex County	2,276	9.29

Place	Population	%
Burr Ridge, IL (village) DuPage County	968	9.17
Shrewsbury, MA (town) Worcester County	3,261	9.16
Lincolnwood, IL (village) Cook County	1,151	9.14
Upper Uwchlan, PA (township) Chester County	1,020	9.09
Herndon, VA (town) Fairfax County	2,082	8.94
Bridgewater, NJ (township) Somerset County	3,917	8.81
South Plainfield, NJ (borough) Middlesex County	2,048	8.76
Johns Creek, GA (city) Fulton County	6,685	8.71
Stafford, TX (city) Fort Bend County	1,527	8.63
Voorhees, NJ (township) Camden County	2,497	8.57
Artesia, CA (city) Los Angeles County	1,407	8.52
Canton, MI (charter township) Wayne County	7,546	8.37
Idylwood, VA (cdp) Fairfax County	1,445	8.36
Irving, TX (city) Dallas County	18,025	8.33
Hanover Park, IL (village) Cook County	3,151	8.30
Live Oak, CA (city) Sutter County	696	8.29
Upper Merion, PA (township) Montgomery County	2,352	8.28
Cerritos, CA (city) Los Angeles County	3,983	8.12
Alpharetta, GA (city) Fulton County	4,630	8.05
Lawrence, NJ (township) Mercer County	2,661	7.95
East Brunswick, NJ (township) Middlesex County	3,772	7.94
Rocky Hill, CT (town) Hartford County	1,558	7.91
Audubon, PA (cdp) Montgomery County	663	7.86
Old Bridge, NJ (township) Middlesex County	5,110	7.82
Hamtramck, MI (city) Wayne County	1,751	7.81
North Potomac, MD (cdp) Montgomery County	1,904	7.80
Pleasanton, CA (city) Alameda County	5,476	7.79
Ashburn, VA (cdp) Loudoun County	3,376	7.76
Naperville, IL (city) DuPage County	10,917	7.70
Kerman, CA (city) Fresno County	1,037	7.66
Bellevue, WA (city) King County	9,343	7.64
Robbinsville, NJ (township) Mercer County	1,038	7.61
Bartlett, IL (village) DuPage County	3,120	7.57
Monroe, NJ (township) Middlesex County	2,952	7.54
Wyndham, VA (cdp) Henrico County	737	7.53
Streamwood, IL (village) Cook County	2,962	7.43
Bensalem, PA (township) Bucks County	4,480	7.41
Carol Stream, IL (village) DuPage County	2,929	7.38
Sammamish, WA (city) King County	3,337	7.29
Montville, NJ (township) Morris County	1,567	7.28
Dublin, CA (city) Alameda County	3,323	7.22
Marlboro, NJ (township) Monmouth County	2,903	7.22
Los Altos Hills, CA (town) Santa Clara County	571	7.21
Ellicott City, MD (cdp) Howard County	4,712	7.16
Dublin, OH (city) Franklin County	2,986	7.15
Skokie, IL (village) Cook County	4,624	7.14
Milton, GA (city) Fulton County	2,332	7.14
Elmont, NY (cdp) Nassau County	2,355	7.09
Paramus, NJ (borough) Bergen County	1,856	7.05
Pebble Creek, FL (cdp) Hillsborough County	536	7.03
Coppell, TX (city) Dallas County	2,709	7.01
Union Hill-Novelty Hill, WA (cdp) King County	1,318	7.01
Germantown, MD (cdp) Montgomery County	6,003	6.95
Missouri City, TX (city) Fort Bend County	4,684	6.95
Harrison, NJ (town) Hudson County	945	6.94
Oak Hills, OR (cdp) Washington County	780	6.88
Acton, MA (town) Middlesex County	1,501	6.85
West Whiteland, PA (township) Chester County	1,250	6.84
Jericho, NY (cdp) Nassau County	928	6.84
Klahanie, WA (cdp) King County	730	6.84
Plano, TX (city) Collin County	17,723	6.82
Cary, NC (town) Wake County	9,217	6.82
Bordentown, NJ (township) Burlington County	762	6.70
North Valley Stream, NY (cdp) Nassau County	1,113	6.69
Blue Ash, OH (city) Hamilton County	807	6.66
Novi, MI (city) Oakland County	3,657	6.62
Chantilly, VA (cdp) Fairfax County	1,520	6.60
Farmington Hills, MI (city) Oakland County	5,216	6.54
Cloverly, MD (cdp) Montgomery County	984	6.51
Congers, NY (cdp) Rockland County	543	6.49
Greenbriar, VA (cdp) Fairfax County	524	6.42
Roselle Park, NJ (borough) Union County	850	6.39
Newark, CA (city) Alameda County	2,716	6.38
Queens, NY (borough) Queens County	141,147	6.33
East Whiteland, PA (township) Chester County	672	6.31

SECTION THREE

Please refer to the Explanation of Data in the front of the book for more detailed information.

Race

Asian: Indonesian

U.S. and 50 States Sorted by Population and Percent of Total Population

Place	Population	%
United States	**95,270**	**0.03**
California	39,506	0.11
New York	6,122	0.03
Texas	5,244	0.02
Washington	4,081	0.06
Pennsylvania	3,926	0.03
Florida	2,874	0.02
Maryland	2,495	0.04
Virginia	2,351	0.03
New Jersey	2,224	0.03
Georgia	2,114	0.02
Colorado	2,037	0.04
Oregon	1,830	0.05
Illinois	1,665	0.01
Arizona	1,602	0.03
Massachusetts	1,379	0.02
Ohio	1,354	0.01
New Hampshire	1,257	0.10
Nevada	1,165	0.04
Michigan	1,148	0.01
North Carolina	1,121	0.01
Hawaii	990	0.07
Indiana	823	0.01
Minnesota	665	0.01
Connecticut	636	0.02
Wisconsin	629	0.01
Oklahoma	527	0.01
Tennessee	484	0.01
Missouri	475	0.01
Utah	472	0.02
Louisiana	394	0.01
Kansas	380	0.01
Alabama	362	0.01
Kentucky	341	0.01
Iowa	287	0.01
South Carolina	286	0.01
New Mexico	238	0.01
Arkansas	229	0.01
District of Columbia	226	0.04
Idaho	216	0.01
Nebraska	153	0.01
Alaska	133	0.02
Mississippi	129	<0.01
Delaware	123	0.01
Maine	109	0.01
Rhode Island	95	0.01
Montana	86	0.01
Wyoming	85	0.02
West Virginia	83	<0.01
South Dakota	46	0.01
Vermont	39	0.01
North Dakota	34	0.01

Place	Population	%
California	39,506	0.11
New Hampshire	1,257	0.10
Hawaii	990	0.07
Washington	4,081	0.06
Oregon	1,830	0.05
Maryland	2,495	0.04
Colorado	2,037	0.04
Nevada	1,165	0.04
District of Columbia	226	0.04
United States	**95,270**	**0.03**
New York	6,122	0.03
Pennsylvania	3,926	0.03
Virginia	2,351	0.03
New Jersey	2,224	0.03
Arizona	1,602	0.03
Texas	5,244	0.02
Florida	2,874	0.02
Georgia	2,114	0.02
Massachusetts	1,379	0.02
Connecticut	636	0.02
Utah	472	0.02
Alaska	133	0.02
Wyoming	85	0.02
Illinois	1,665	0.01
Ohio	1,354	0.01
Michigan	1,148	0.01
North Carolina	1,121	0.01
Indiana	823	0.01
Minnesota	665	0.01
Wisconsin	629	0.01
Oklahoma	527	0.01
Tennessee	484	0.01
Missouri	475	0.01
Louisiana	394	0.01
Kansas	380	0.01
Alabama	362	0.01
Kentucky	341	0.01
Iowa	287	0.01
South Carolina	286	0.01
New Mexico	238	0.01
Arkansas	229	0.01
Idaho	216	0.01
Nebraska	153	0.01
Delaware	123	0.01
Maine	109	0.01
Rhode Island	95	0.01
Montana	86	0.01
South Dakota	46	0.01
Vermont	39	0.01
North Dakota	34	0.01
Mississippi	129	<0.01
West Virginia	83	<0.01

Please refer to the Explanation of Data in the front of the book for more detailed information.

Race

Asian: Indonesian

Top 150 Places Sorted by Population

Based on all places, regardless of total population

Place	Population	%
New York, NY (city) Kings County	4,791	0.06
Los Angeles, CA (city) Los Angeles County	3,670	0.10
Queens, NY (borough) Queens County	3,386	0.15
Philadelphia, PA (city) Philadelphia County	2,222	0.15
San Francisco, CA (city) San Francisco County	1,349	0.17
San Jose, CA (city) Santa Clara County	948	0.10
Loma Linda, CA (city) San Bernardino County	929	3.99
Houston, TX (city) Harris County	888	0.04
San Diego, CA (city) San Diego County	879	0.07
Seattle, WA (city) King County	832	0.14
San Bernardino, CA (city) San Bernardino County	769	0.37
Rancho Cucamonga, CA (city) San Bernardino County	723	0.44
Manhattan, NY (borough) New York County	693	0.04
Alhambra, CA (city) Los Angeles County	647	0.78
Dover, NH (city) Strafford County	569	1.90
Brooklyn, NY (borough) Kings County	564	0.02
Fontana, CA (city) San Bernardino County	503	0.26
Irvine, CA (city) Orange County	498	0.23
Anaheim, CA (city) Orange County	462	0.14
Rowland Heights, CA (cdp) Los Angeles County	459	0.94
Aurora, CO (city) Arapahoe County	436	0.13
Redlands, CA (city) San Bernardino County	434	0.63
Chicago, IL (city) Cook County	430	0.02
Colton, CA (city) San Bernardino County	429	0.82
West Covina, CA (city) Los Angeles County	427	0.40
Arcadia, CA (city) Los Angeles County	422	0.75
Chino Hills, CA (city) San Bernardino County	389	0.52
Upland, CA (city) San Bernardino County	371	0.50
Riverside, CA (city) Riverside County	370	0.12
Portland, OR (city) Multnomah County	370	0.06
Fremont, CA (city) Alameda County	360	0.17
Austin, TX (city) Travis County	354	0.04
Diamond Bar, CA (city) Los Angeles County	350	0.63
Ontario, CA (city) San Bernardino County	344	0.21
Phoenix, AZ (city) Maricopa County	330	0.02
Columbus, OH (city) Franklin County	326	0.04
Pasadena, CA (city) Los Angeles County	325	0.24
Denver, CO (city) Denver County	322	0.05
Somersworth, NH (city) Strafford County	315	2.68
Long Beach, CA (city) Los Angeles County	304	0.07
Everett, WA (city) Snohomish County	291	0.28
Monterey Park, CA (city) Los Angeles County	284	0.47
Edison, NJ (township) Middlesex County	282	0.28
Daly City, CA (city) San Mateo County	281	0.28
Walnut, CA (city) Los Angeles County	280	0.96
San Gabriel, CA (city) Los Angeles County	280	0.70
Urban Honolulu, HI (cdp) Honolulu County	279	0.08
Fullerton, CA (city) Orange County	278	0.21
Sacramento, CA (city) Sacramento County	278	0.06
Lake Forest, CA (city) Orange County	266	0.34
Huntington Beach, CA (city) Orange County	263	0.14
Scranton, PA (city) Lackawanna County	260	0.34
Fresno, CA (city) Fresno County	253	0.05
Woodbridge, NJ (township) Middlesex County	250	0.25
Temple City, CA (city) Los Angeles County	240	0.67
Santa Clarita, CA (city) Los Angeles County	236	0.13
Corona, CA (city) Riverside County	227	0.15
Washington, DC (city) District of Columbia	226	0.04
Montclair, CA (city) San Bernardino County	224	0.61
Plano, TX (city) Collin County	224	0.09
Garden Grove, CA (city) Orange County	223	0.13
Torrance, CA (city) Los Angeles County	221	0.15
Simi Valley, CA (city) Ventura County	220	0.18
Las Vegas, NV (city) Clark County	220	0.04
Pomona, CA (city) Los Angeles County	219	0.15
Boston, MA (city) Suffolk County	218	0.04
Santa Clara, CA (city) Santa Clara County	209	0.18
Wheaton, MD (cdp) Montgomery County	208	0.43
Arlington, VA (cdp) Arlington County	208	0.10
Union City, CA (city) Alameda County	207	0.30
Highland, CA (city) San Bernardino County	206	0.39
Hacienda Heights, CA (cdp) Los Angeles County	205	0.38
Concord, CA (city) Contra Costa County	201	0.16
San Ramon, CA (city) Contra Costa County	199	0.28
Oakland, CA (city) Alameda County	196	0.05
Hayward, CA (city) Alameda County	195	0.14
Sugar Land, TX (city) Fort Bend County	191	0.24
Rockville, MD (city) Montgomery County	188	0.31
San Antonio, TX (city) Medina County	186	0.01
Berkeley, CA (city) Alameda County	179	0.16
Covina, CA (city) Los Angeles County	178	0.37
Sunnyvale, CA (city) Santa Clara County	178	0.13
Dallas, TX (city) Dallas County	178	0.01
Pleasant Hill, CA (city) Contra Costa County	177	0.53
Cerritos, CA (city) Los Angeles County	177	0.36
Chino, CA (city) San Bernardino County	177	0.23
Bellevue, WA (city) King County	176	0.14
Avenel, NJ (cdp) Middlesex County	174	1.02
Eastvale, CA (cdp) Riverside County	172	0.32
Mission Viejo, CA (city) Orange County	172	0.18
Bakersfield, CA (city) Kern County	167	0.05
Charlotte, NC (city) Mecklenburg County	163	0.02
Orange, CA (city) Orange County	162	0.12
Paradise, NV (cdp) Clark County	161	0.07
South San Francisco, CA (city) San Mateo County	160	0.25
Spring Valley, NV (cdp) Clark County	159	0.09
Yorba Linda, CA (city) Orange County	158	0.25
Glendora, CA (city) Los Angeles County	149	0.30
Moreno Valley, CA (city) Riverside County	149	0.08
Placentia, CA (city) Orange County	146	0.29
Madison, WI (city) Dane County	145	0.06
Indianapolis, IN (city) Marion County	142	0.02
Chandler, AZ (city) Maricopa County	139	0.06
Arlington, TX (city) Tarrant County	139	0.04
Gaithersburg, MD (city) Montgomery County	138	0.23
Lexington-Fayette, KY (cons. govt) Fayette County	138	0.05
Glendale, CA (city) Los Angeles County	137	0.07
North Bethesda, MD (cdp) Montgomery County	136	0.31
Mountain View, CA (city) Santa Clara County	136	0.18
Henderson, NV (city) Clark County	136	0.05
Oklahoma City, OK (city) Oklahoma County	136	0.02
El Monte, CA (city) Los Angeles County	135	0.12
Colorado Springs, CO (city) El Paso County	135	0.03
Roswell, GA (city) Fulton County	132	0.15
Costa Mesa, CA (city) Orange County	131	0.12
Monrovia, CA (city) Los Angeles County	130	0.36
Lakewood, CA (city) Los Angeles County	130	0.16
San Mateo, CA (city) San Mateo County	129	0.13
Thousand Oaks, CA (city) Ventura County	129	0.10
Fort Worth, TX (city) Tarrant County	128	0.02
Tempe, AZ (city) Maricopa County	127	0.08
Elk Grove, CA (city) Sacramento County	125	0.08
Buena Park, CA (city) Orange County	123	0.15
Irving, TX (city) Dallas County	123	0.06
Jacksonville, FL (city) Duval County	123	0.01
Aspen Hill, MD (cdp) Montgomery County	122	0.25
Raleigh, NC (city) Wake County	121	0.03
East San Gabriel, CA (cdp) Los Angeles County	118	0.79
Azusa, CA (city) Los Angeles County	116	0.25
Laguna Niguel, CA (city) Orange County	116	0.18
Germantown, MD (cdp) Montgomery County	116	0.13
Temecula, CA (city) Riverside County	116	0.12
Antioch, CA (city) Contra Costa County	116	0.11
Santa Ana, CA (city) Orange County	116	0.04
Redondo Beach, CA (city) Los Angeles County	114	0.17
Atlanta, GA (city) Fulton County	114	0.03
Westminster, CA (city) Orange County	113	0.13
Murrieta, CA (city) Riverside County	112	0.11
Johns Creek, GA (city) Fulton County	111	0.14
Cupertino, CA (city) Santa Clara County	110	0.19
Victorville, CA (city) San Bernardino County	110	0.09
Mesa, AZ (city) Maricopa County	110	0.03
Bellflower, CA (city) Los Angeles County	109	0.14
Laguna Hills, CA (city) Orange County	107	0.35
Pleasanton, CA (city) Alameda County	107	0.15
Rialto, CA (city) San Bernardino County	107	0.11
Aliso Viejo, CA (city) Orange County	106	0.22
Palmdale, CA (city) Los Angeles County	106	0.07
Norwalk, CA (city) Los Angeles County	105	0.10
Cypress, CA (city) Orange County	104	0.22

SECTION THREE

Race

Asian: Indonesian

Top 150 Places Sorted by Percent of Total Population

Based on all places, regardless of total population

Place	Population	%
Amesville, OH (village) Athens County	7	4.55
Loma Linda, CA (city) San Bernardino County	929	3.99
Oakhaven, AR (town) Hempstead County	2	3.17
Somersworth, NH (city) Strafford County	315	2.68
Wisconsin Dells, WI (city) Sauk County	4	2.29
Forest Home, NY (cdp) Tompkins County	11	1.92
Dover, NH (city) Strafford County	569	1.90
Rollis, MN (township) Marshall County	2	1.74
Paukaa, HI (cdp) Hawaii County	6	1.41
Danforth, MN (township) Pine County	1	1.28
Adamsburg, PA (borough) Westmoreland County	2	1.16
North El Monte, CA (cdp) Los Angeles County	43	1.15
Chloride, AZ (cdp) Mohave County	3	1.11
Burnt Ranch, CA (cdp) Trinity County	3	1.07
Norris Canyon, CA (cdp) Contra Costa County	10	1.04
Avenel, NJ (cdp) Middlesex County	174	1.02
Kensington, MD (town) Montgomery County	22	0.99
Wallace, CA (cdp) Calaveras County	4	0.99
Walnut, CA (city) Los Angeles County	280	0.96
Rowland Heights, CA (cdp) Los Angeles County	459	0.94
Middletown, IA (city) Des Moines County	3	0.94
Pleasant Valley, TX (town) Wichita County	3	0.89
Leshara, NE (village) Saunders County	1	0.89
Colton, CA (city) San Bernardino County	429	0.82
Forest Glen, MD (cdp) Montgomery County	54	0.82
Hillsboro, NM (cdp) Sierra County	1	0.81
East San Gabriel, CA (cdp) Los Angeles County	118	0.79
Alhambra, CA (city) Los Angeles County	647	0.78
Arcadia, CA (city) Los Angeles County	422	0.75
Bay View, MI (cdp) Emmet County	1	0.75
Davenport, CA (cdp) Santa Cruz County	3	0.74
Berrien Springs, MI (village) Berrien County	13	0.72
Grand Terrace, CA (city) San Bernardino County	85	0.71
San Gabriel, CA (city) Los Angeles County	280	0.70
Kalihiwai, HI (cdp) Kauai County	3	0.70
Grand View-on-Hudson, NY (village) Rockland County	2	0.70
Du Bois, NE (village) Pawnee County	1	0.68
Temple City, CA (city) Los Angeles County	240	0.67
Oronoko, MI (charter township) Berrien County	62	0.67
Kings Point, MT (cdp) Lake County	1	0.66
Redlands, CA (city) San Bernardino County	434	0.63
Diamond Bar, CA (city) Los Angeles County	350	0.63
Quantico, VA (town) Prince William County	3	0.63
Lake Hughes, CA (cdp) Los Angeles County	4	0.62
Montclair, CA (city) San Bernardino County	224	0.61
Glenmont, MD (cdp) Montgomery County	83	0.61
Diablo Grande, CA (cdp) Stanislaus County	5	0.61
Highwater, MN (township) Cottonwood County	1	0.60
Lake Stickney, WA (cdp) Snohomish County	46	0.59
Birch Lake, MN (unorganized territory) St. Louis County	3	0.59
Mentone, CA (cdp) San Bernardino County	51	0.58
Brady, PA (township) Lycoming County	3	0.58
California Pines, CA (cdp) Modoc County	3	0.58
Colton, NY (cdp) St. Lawrence County	2	0.58
Lake, MI (charter township) Berrien County	17	0.57
Lyndon, NY (town) Cattaraugus County	4	0.57
Jordan, MN (township) Fillmore County	2	0.57
San Marino, CA (city) Los Angeles County	73	0.56
Mayflower Village, CA (cdp) Los Angeles County	31	0.56
Summerland, CA (cdp) Santa Barbara County	8	0.55
Ford Cliff, PA (borough) Armstrong County	2	0.54
Lake Sherwood, WI (cdp) Adams County	2	0.54
Pleasant Hill, CA (city) Contra Costa County	177	0.53
Haverford College, PA (cdp) Delaware County	7	0.53
Acalanes Ridge, CA (cdp) Contra Costa County	6	0.53
Takilma, OR (cdp) Josephine County	2	0.53
Chino Hills, CA (city) San Bernardino County	389	0.52
Holly Hills, CO (cdp) Arapahoe County	13	0.52
Millbourne, PA (borough) Delaware County	6	0.52
Bucyrus, KS (cdp) Miami County	1	0.52
Willow Creek, AK (cdp) Valdez-Cordova Census Area	1	0.52
Clayhatchee, AL (town) Dale County	3	0.51
Newport, WI (town) Columbia County	3	0.51
Upland, CA (city) San Bernardino County	371	0.50
East Pasadena, CA (cdp) Los Angeles County	31	0.50

Place	Population	%
Griggstown, NJ (cdp) Somerset County	4	0.49
Union Deposit, PA (cdp) Dauphin County	2	0.49
Phippsburg, CO (cdp) Routt County	1	0.49
North Lynnwood, WA (cdp) Snohomish County	79	0.48
Metuchen, NJ (borough) Middlesex County	65	0.48
Citrus, CA (cdp) Los Angeles County	52	0.48
Copperton, UT (cdp) Salt Lake County	4	0.48
Monterey Park, CA (city) Los Angeles County	284	0.47
Brent, FL (cdp) Escambia County	101	0.46
Berwick, ME (cdp) York County	10	0.46
Coffee Creek, CA (cdp) Trinity County	1	0.46
Colma, CA (town) San Mateo County	8	0.45
Midland, MD (town) Allegany County	2	0.45
Rancho Cucamonga, CA (city) San Bernardino County	723	0.44
Waikapu, HI (cdp) Maui County	13	0.44
Wheaton, MD (cdp) Montgomery County	208	0.43
Portsmouth, NH (city) Rockingham County	89	0.43
Angwin, CA (cdp) Napa County	13	0.43
Avon, ME (town) Franklin County	2	0.43
Rutherford, PA (cdp) Dauphin County	18	0.42
Friday Harbor, WA (town) San Juan County	9	0.42
Nanawale Estates, HI (cdp) Hawaii County	6	0.42
Reeseville, WI (village) Dodge County	3	0.42
Neponset, IL (village) Bureau County	2	0.42
Rocheport, MO (city) Boone County	1	0.42
West Covina, CA (city) Los Angeles County	427	0.40
Garrett Park, MD (town) Montgomery County	4	0.40
Kennerdell, PA (cdp) Venango County	1	0.40
Highland, CA (city) San Bernardino County	206	0.39
North Kensington, MD (cdp) Montgomery County	37	0.39
Henry Clay, PA (township) Fayette County	8	0.39
San Pasqual, CA (cdp) Los Angeles County	8	0.39
Tanner, WA (cdp) King County	4	0.39
Windemere, TX (cdp) Travis County	4	0.39
Gingles, WI (town) Ashland County	3	0.39
Puako, HI (cdp) Hawaii County	3	0.39
Utica, IN (town) Clark County	3	0.39
Ranshaw, PA (cdp) Northumberland County	2	0.39
Nelson, AZ (cdp) Pima County	1	0.39
Hacienda Heights, CA (cdp) Los Angeles County	205	0.38
Derwood, MD (cdp) Montgomery County	9	0.38
Woodway, WA (city) Snohomish County	5	0.38
San Bernardino, CA (city) San Bernardino County	769	0.37
Covina, CA (city) Los Angeles County	178	0.37
Lawnton, PA (cdp) Dauphin County	14	0.37
Alvord, TX (town) Wise County	5	0.37
El Rito, NM (cdp) Rio Arriba County	3	0.37
Hackett, AR (city) Sebastian County	3	0.37
Cerritos, CA (city) Los Angeles County	177	0.36
Monrovia, CA (city) Los Angeles County	130	0.36
Bethany, OR (cdp) Washington County	74	0.36
Charleroi, PA (borough) Washington County	15	0.36
Larch Way, WA (cdp) Snohomish County	12	0.36
Dyberry, PA (township) Wayne County	5	0.36
Mountainaire, AZ (cdp) Coconino County	4	0.36
Washington, NH (town) Sullivan County	4	0.36
Laguna Hills, CA (city) Orange County	107	0.35
Artesia, CA (city) Los Angeles County	58	0.35
Island Park, ID (city) Fremont County	1	0.35
Siloam, GA (town) Greene County	1	0.35
Lake Forest, CA (city) Orange County	266	0.34
Scranton, PA (city) Lackawanna County	260	0.34
Kahaluu-Keauhou, HI (cdp) Hawaii County	12	0.34
New Chapel Hill, TX (city) Smith County	2	0.34
South San Gabriel, CA (cdp) Los Angeles County	27	0.33
Cherokee, NC (cdp) Jackson County	7	0.33
Arenas Valley, NM (cdp) Grant County	5	0.33
Glenwillow, OH (village) Cuyahoga County	3	0.33
Lake of the Woods, CA (cdp) Kern County	3	0.33
Strawberry, AR (town) Lawrence County	1	0.33
Eastvale, CA (cdp) Riverside County	172	0.32
Callender, CA (cdp) San Luis Obispo County	4	0.32
Dash Point, WA (cdp) Pierce County	3	0.32
Canby, CA (cdp) Modoc County	1	0.32
Rockville, MD (city) Montgomery County	188	0.31

Please refer to the Explanation of Data in the front of the book for more detailed information.

Race

Asian: Indonesian

Top 150 Places Sorted by Percent of Total Population

Based on places with total population of 7,500 or more

Place	Population	%
Loma Linda, CA (city) San Bernardino County	929	3.99
Somersworth, NH (city) Strafford County	315	2.68
Dover, NH (city) Strafford County	569	1.90
Avenel, NJ (cdp) Middlesex County	174	1.02
Walnut, CA (city) Los Angeles County	280	0.96
Rowland Heights, CA (cdp) Los Angeles County	459	0.94
Colton, CA (city) San Bernardino County	429	0.82
East San Gabriel, CA (cdp) Los Angeles County	118	0.79
Alhambra, CA (city) Los Angeles County	647	0.78
Arcadia, CA (city) Los Angeles County	422	0.75
Grand Terrace, CA (city) San Bernardino County	85	0.71
San Gabriel, CA (city) Los Angeles County	280	0.70
Temple City, CA (city) Los Angeles County	240	0.67
Oronoko, MI (charter township) Berrien County	62	0.67
Redlands, CA (city) San Bernardino County	434	0.63
Diamond Bar, CA (city) Los Angeles County	350	0.63
Montclair, CA (city) San Bernardino County	224	0.61
Glenmont, MD (cdp) Montgomery County	83	0.61
Lake Stickney, WA (cdp) Snohomish County	46	0.59
Mentone, CA (cdp) San Bernardino County	51	0.58
San Marino, CA (city) Los Angeles County	73	0.56
Pleasant Hill, CA (city) Contra Costa County	177	0.53
Chino Hills, CA (city) San Bernardino County	389	0.52
Upland, CA (city) San Bernardino County	371	0.50
North Lynnwood, WA (cdp) Snohomish County	79	0.48
Metuchen, NJ (borough) Middlesex County	65	0.48
Citrus, CA (cdp) Los Angeles County	52	0.48
Monterey Park, CA (city) Los Angeles County	284	0.47
Brent, FL (cdp) Escambia County	101	0.46
Rancho Cucamonga, CA (city) San Bernardino County	723	0.44
Wheaton, MD (cdp) Montgomery County	208	0.43
Portsmouth, NH (city) Rockingham County	89	0.43
West Covina, CA (city) Los Angeles County	427	0.40
Highland, CA (city) San Bernardino County	206	0.39
North Kensington, MD (cdp) Montgomery County	37	0.39
Hacienda Heights, CA (cdp) Los Angeles County	205	0.38
San Bernardino, CA (city) San Bernardino County	769	0.37
Covina, CA (city) Los Angeles County	178	0.37
Cerritos, CA (city) Los Angeles County	177	0.36
Monrovia, CA (city) Los Angeles County	130	0.36
Bethany, OR (cdp) Washington County	74	0.36
Laguna Hills, CA (city) Orange County	107	0.35
Artesia, CA (city) Los Angeles County	58	0.35
Lake Forest, CA (city) Orange County	266	0.34
Scranton, PA (city) Lackawanna County	260	0.34
South San Gabriel, CA (cdp) Los Angeles County	27	0.33
Eastvale, CA (cdp) Riverside County	172	0.32
Rockville, MD (city) Montgomery County	188	0.31
North Bethesda, MD (cdp) Montgomery County	136	0.31
Mukilteo, WA (city) Snohomish County	62	0.31
Merrifield, VA (cdp) Fairfax County	47	0.31
El Sobrante, CA (cdp) Riverside County	40	0.31
Union City, CA (city) Alameda County	207	0.30
Glendora, CA (city) Los Angeles County	149	0.30
La Verne, CA (city) Los Angeles County	92	0.30
Placentia, CA (city) Orange County	146	0.29
Claremont, CA (city) Los Angeles County	103	0.29
El Segundo, CA (city) Los Angeles County	48	0.29
Home Gardens, CA (cdp) Riverside County	34	0.29
Everett, WA (city) Snohomish County	291	0.28
Edison, NJ (township) Middlesex County	282	0.28
Daly City, CA (city) San Mateo County	281	0.28
San Ramon, CA (city) Contra Costa County	199	0.28
Emeryville, CA (city) Alameda County	28	0.28
Rochester, NH (city) Strafford County	81	0.27
Del Aire, CA (cdp) Los Angeles County	27	0.27
Fontana, CA (city) San Bernardino County	503	0.26
Lynnwood, WA (city) Snohomish County	94	0.26
Mountlake Terrace, WA (city) Snohomish County	51	0.26
Martha Lake, WA (cdp) Snohomish County	40	0.26
Woodbridge, NJ (township) Middlesex County	250	0.25
South San Francisco, CA (city) San Mateo County	160	0.25
Yorba Linda, CA (city) Orange County	158	0.25
Aspen Hill, MD (cdp) Montgomery County	122	0.25
Azusa, CA (city) Los Angeles County	116	0.25
Duarte, CA (city) Los Angeles County	53	0.25
Pasadena, CA (city) Los Angeles County	325	0.24
Sugar Land, TX (city) Fort Bend County	191	0.24
Beaumont, CA (city) Riverside County	88	0.24
New Territory, TX (cdp) Fort Bend County	37	0.24
Irvine, CA (city) Orange County	498	0.23
Chino, CA (city) San Bernardino County	177	0.23
Gaithersburg, MD (city) Montgomery County	138	0.23
Millbrae, CA (city) San Mateo County	50	0.23
Silver Firs, WA (cdp) Snohomish County	48	0.23
Chambersburg, PA (borough) Franklin County	46	0.23
Marina, CA (city) Monterey County	46	0.23
Idylwood, VA (cdp) Fairfax County	40	0.23
Aliso Viejo, CA (city) Orange County	106	0.22
Cypress, CA (city) Orange County	104	0.22
San Dimas, CA (city) Los Angeles County	72	0.22
Tysons Corner, VA (cdp) Fairfax County	44	0.22
Mill Creek East, WA (cdp) Snohomish County	35	0.22
Vincent, CA (cdp) Los Angeles County	35	0.22
Progress, PA (cdp) Dauphin County	21	0.22
Ontario, CA (city) San Bernardino County	344	0.21
Fullerton, CA (city) Orange County	278	0.21
West Carson, CA (cdp) Los Angeles County	46	0.21
Albany, CA (city) Alameda County	39	0.21
Pinole, CA (city) Contra Costa County	38	0.21
Laguna Woods, CA (city) Orange County	34	0.21
Sierra Madre, CA (city) Los Angeles County	23	0.21
Alondra Park, CA (cdp) Los Angeles County	18	0.21
Foster City, CA (city) San Mateo County	62	0.20
Swatara, PA (township) Dauphin County	47	0.20
Newcastle, WA (city) King County	21	0.20
Chamblee, GA (city) DeKalb County	20	0.20
Haiku-Pauwela, HI (cdp) Maui County	16	0.20
Cupertino, CA (city) Santa Clara County	110	0.19
Rosemead, CA (city) Los Angeles County	100	0.19
Urbana, IL (city) Champaign County	80	0.19
Fairfax, VA (ind. city) Fairfax independent city	44	0.19
Mill Creek, WA (city) Snohomish County	34	0.19
Fords, NJ (cdp) Middlesex County	29	0.19
Cedar Mill, OR (cdp) Washington County	27	0.19
Purdue University, IN (cdp) Tippecanoe County	23	0.19
Blackhawk, CA (cdp) Contra Costa County	18	0.19
Simi Valley, CA (city) Ventura County	220	0.18
Santa Clara, CA (city) Santa Clara County	209	0.18
Mission Viejo, CA (city) Orange County	172	0.18
Mountain View, CA (city) Santa Clara County	136	0.18
Laguna Niguel, CA (city) Orange County	116	0.18
Yucaipa, CA (city) San Bernardino County	91	0.18
Pacifica, CA (city) San Mateo County	67	0.18
South Pasadena, CA (city) Los Angeles County	47	0.18
Ladera Ranch, CA (cdp) Orange County	41	0.18
Burke Centre, VA (cdp) Fairfax County	32	0.18
Stevenson Ranch, CA (cdp) Los Angeles County	32	0.18
Capitola, CA (city) Santa Cruz County	18	0.18
Charter Oak, CA (cdp) Los Angeles County	17	0.18
Long Branch, VA (cdp) Fairfax County	14	0.18
San Francisco, CA (city) San Francisco County	1,349	0.17
Fremont, CA (city) Alameda County	360	0.17
Redondo Beach, CA (city) Los Angeles County	114	0.17
Bethesda, MD (cdp) Montgomery County	103	0.17
Shoreline, WA (city) King County	88	0.17
Dublin, CA (city) Alameda County	80	0.17
Brea, CA (city) Orange County	65	0.17
West Lafayette, IN (city) Tippecanoe County	49	0.17
Duluth, GA (city) Gwinnett County	46	0.17
Athens, OH (city) Athens County	41	0.17
El Cerrito, CA (city) Contra Costa County	39	0.17
Lake Forest Park, WA (city) King County	21	0.17
Lake Barcroft, VA (cdp) Fairfax County	16	0.17
Concord, CA (city) Contra Costa County	201	0.16
Berkeley, CA (city) Alameda County	179	0.16
Lakewood, CA (city) Los Angeles County	130	0.16
Rancho Cordova, CA (city) Sacramento County	102	0.16
Redmond, WA (city) King County	88	0.16
Fountain Valley, CA (city) Orange County	86	0.16

SECTION THREE

Please refer to the Explanation of Data in the front of the book for more detailed information.

Race

Asian: Japanese

U.S. and 50 States Sorted by Population and Percent of Total Population

Place	Population	%
United States	**1,304,286**	**0.42**
California	428,014	1.15
Hawaii	312,292	22.96
Washington	67,597	1.01
New York	51,781	0.27
Texas	37,715	0.15
Illinois	28,623	0.22
Florida	25,747	0.14
Oregon	24,535	0.64
Colorado	22,714	0.45
Nevada	21,364	0.79
Virginia	20,138	0.25
New Jersey	19,710	0.22
Arizona	19,611	0.31
Michigan	17,412	0.18
Ohio	16,995	0.15
Massachusetts	15,358	0.23
Georgia	14,247	0.15
North Carolina	12,878	0.14
Maryland	12,826	0.22
Utah	12,782	0.46
Pennsylvania	12,699	0.10
Indiana	8,437	0.13
Minnesota	7,995	0.15
Missouri	7,084	0.12
Tennessee	6,955	0.11
Connecticut	6,203	0.17
Kentucky	6,197	0.14
Wisconsin	5,967	0.10
Idaho	5,698	0.36
Oklahoma	5,580	0.15
New Mexico	4,889	0.24
South Carolina	4,745	0.10
Alabama	4,336	0.09
Kansas	4,178	0.15
Alaska	3,926	0.55
Louisiana	3,117	0.07
Nebraska	3,106	0.17
Iowa	2,854	0.09
Arkansas	2,384	0.08
District of Columbia	2,010	0.33
Montana	1,854	0.19
New Hampshire	1,842	0.14
Mississippi	1,752	0.06
Rhode Island	1,455	0.14
Delaware	1,196	0.13
Maine	1,181	0.09
West Virginia	1,159	0.06
Wyoming	982	0.17
Vermont	842	0.13
South Dakota	696	0.09
North Dakota	628	0.09

Place	Population	%
Hawaii	312,292	22.96
California	428,014	1.15
Washington	67,597	1.01
Nevada	21,364	0.79
Oregon	24,535	0.64
Alaska	3,926	0.55
Utah	12,782	0.46
Colorado	22,714	0.45
United States	**1,304,286**	**0.42**
Idaho	5,698	0.36
District of Columbia	2,010	0.33
Arizona	19,611	0.31
New York	51,781	0.27
Virginia	20,138	0.25
New Mexico	4,889	0.24
Massachusetts	15,358	0.23
Illinois	28,623	0.22
New Jersey	19,710	0.22
Maryland	12,826	0.22
Montana	1,854	0.19
Michigan	17,412	0.18
Connecticut	6,203	0.17
Nebraska	3,106	0.17
Wyoming	982	0.17
Texas	37,715	0.15
Ohio	16,995	0.15
Georgia	14,247	0.15
Minnesota	7,995	0.15
Oklahoma	5,580	0.15
Kansas	4,178	0.15
Florida	25,747	0.14
North Carolina	12,878	0.14
Kentucky	6,197	0.14
New Hampshire	1,842	0.14
Rhode Island	1,455	0.14
Indiana	8,437	0.13
Delaware	1,196	0.13
Vermont	842	0.13
Missouri	7,084	0.12
Tennessee	6,955	0.11
Pennsylvania	12,699	0.10
Wisconsin	5,967	0.10
South Carolina	4,745	0.10
Alabama	4,336	0.09
Iowa	2,854	0.09
Maine	1,181	0.09
South Dakota	696	0.09
North Dakota	628	0.09
Arkansas	2,384	0.08
Louisiana	3,117	0.07
Mississippi	1,752	0.06
West Virginia	1,159	0.06

Please refer to the Explanation of Data in the front of the book for more detailed information.

Race

Asian: Japanese

Top 150 Places Sorted by Population

Based on all places, regardless of total population

Place	Population	%
Urban Honolulu, HI (cdp) Honolulu County	95,201	28.23
Los Angeles, CA (city) Los Angeles County	43,978	1.16
New York, NY (city) Kings County	31,742	0.39
Pearl City, HI (cdp) Honolulu County	19,604	41.10
East Honolulu, HI (cdp) Honolulu County	19,536	39.14
Torrance, CA (city) Los Angeles County	18,532	12.74
San Diego, CA (city) San Diego County	16,815	1.29
Manhattan, NY (borough) New York County	16,600	1.05
San Jose, CA (city) Santa Clara County	16,322	1.73
Hilo, HI (cdp) Hawaii County	15,537	35.91
San Francisco, CA (city) San Francisco County	15,278	1.90
Seattle, WA (city) King County	13,064	2.15
Kaneohe, HI (cdp) Honolulu County	12,759	36.88
Mililani Town, HI (cdp) Honolulu County	10,648	38.54
Mililani Mauka, HI (cdp) Honolulu County	9,047	43.00
Irvine, CA (city) Orange County	8,797	4.14
Sacramento, CA (city) Sacramento County	8,759	1.88
Kailua, HI (cdp) Honolulu County	7,983	20.66
Queens, NY (borough) Queens County	7,790	0.35
Chicago, IL (city) Cook County	7,044	0.26
Gardena, CA (city) Los Angeles County	6,584	11.19
Brooklyn, NY (borough) Kings County	5,917	0.24
Portland, OR (city) Multnomah County	5,543	0.95
Kahului, HI (cdp) Maui County	5,197	19.73
Wahiawa, HI (cdp) Honolulu County	4,744	26.62
Las Vegas, NV (city) Clark County	4,685	0.80
Long Beach, CA (city) Los Angeles County	4,683	1.01
Waipahu, HI (cdp) Honolulu County	4,619	12.09
Huntington Beach, CA (city) Orange County	4,451	2.34
Wailuku, HI (cdp) Maui County	4,445	29.03
Waimalu, HI (cdp) Honolulu County	4,342	31.62
Waipio, HI (cdp) Honolulu County	4,150	35.55
Ewa Gentry, HI (cdp) Honolulu County	4,130	18.20
Halawa, HI (cdp) Honolulu County	4,059	28.96
Monterey Park, CA (city) Los Angeles County	4,034	6.69
Sunnyvale, CA (city) Santa Clara County	3,950	2.82
Fresno, CA (city) Fresno County	3,787	0.77
Bellevue, WA (city) King County	3,765	3.08
Phoenix, AZ (city) Maricopa County	3,731	0.26
Aiea, HI (cdp) Honolulu County	3,714	39.77
Oakland, CA (city) Alameda County	3,667	0.94
Rancho Palos Verdes, CA (city) Los Angeles County	3,577	8.59
Houston, TX (city) Harris County	3,463	0.16
Chula Vista, CA (city) San Diego County	3,369	1.38
Anaheim, CA (city) Orange County	3,145	0.94
Makakilo, HI (cdp) Honolulu County	3,110	17.04
Henderson, NV (city) Clark County	3,074	1.19
San Antonio, TX (city) Medina County	3,062	0.23
Ahuimanu, HI (cdp) Honolulu County	2,961	33.61
Berkeley, CA (city) Alameda County	2,948	2.62
Denver, CO (city) Denver County	2,925	0.49
Fremont, CA (city) Alameda County	2,852	1.33
San Mateo, CA (city) San Mateo County	2,835	2.92
Pasadena, CA (city) Los Angeles County	2,808	2.05
Elk Grove, CA (city) Sacramento County	2,725	1.78
Royal Kunia, HI (cdp) Honolulu County	2,709	18.65
Kapolei, HI (cdp) Honolulu County	2,706	17.82
Waikele, HI (cdp) Honolulu County	2,668	35.67
Redondo Beach, CA (city) Los Angeles County	2,658	3.98
Santa Clara, CA (city) Santa Clara County	2,617	2.25
Cupertino, CA (city) Santa Clara County	2,489	4.27
Austin, TX (city) Travis County	2,433	0.31
Oceanside, CA (city) San Diego County	2,376	1.42
Boston, MA (city) Suffolk County	2,376	0.38
Colorado Springs, CO (city) El Paso County	2,354	0.57
Stockton, CA (city) San Joaquin County	2,344	0.80
Columbus, OH (city) Franklin County	2,331	0.30
Tacoma, WA (city) Pierce County	2,242	1.13
Paradise, NV (cdp) Clark County	2,212	0.99
Spring Valley, NV (cdp) Clark County	2,171	1.22
Novi, MI (city) Oakland County	2,120	3.84
Mountain View, CA (city) Santa Clara County	2,091	2.82
Tucson, AZ (city) Pima County	2,085	0.40
Albuquerque, NM (city) Bernalillo County	2,085	0.38
Anchorage, AK (municipality) Anchorage Municipality	2,067	0.71
Lihue, HI (cdp) Kauai County	2,040	31.60
Heeia, HI (cdp) Honolulu County	2,037	41.04
Washington, DC (city) District of Columbia	2,010	0.33
Fullerton, CA (city) Orange County	1,966	1.45
Philadelphia, PA (city) Philadelphia County	1,956	0.13
Cerritos, CA (city) Los Angeles County	1,951	3.98
Santa Monica, CA (city) Los Angeles County	1,924	2.14
Riverside, CA (city) Riverside County	1,907	0.63
Costa Mesa, CA (city) Orange County	1,905	1.73
Culver City, CA (city) Los Angeles County	1,898	4.88
Santa Clarita, CA (city) Los Angeles County	1,892	1.07
Kapaa, HI (cdp) Kauai County	1,862	17.40
Ewa Beach, HI (cdp) Honolulu County	1,845	12.34
Pukalani, HI (cdp) Maui County	1,838	24.27
Palo Alto, CA (city) Santa Clara County	1,831	2.84
Fountain Valley, CA (city) Orange County	1,817	3.28
Glendale, CA (city) Los Angeles County	1,785	0.93
Orange, CA (city) Orange County	1,772	1.30
Waianae, HI (cdp) Honolulu County	1,696	12.87
Davis, CA (city) Yolo County	1,674	2.55
Montebello, CA (city) Los Angeles County	1,669	2.67
Enterprise, NV (cdp) Clark County	1,647	1.52
Alhambra, CA (city) Los Angeles County	1,642	1.98
Thousand Oaks, CA (city) Ventura County	1,640	1.29
Mission Viejo, CA (city) Orange County	1,639	1.76
Aurora, CO (city) Arapahoe County	1,634	0.50
Eugene, OR (city) Lane County	1,622	1.04
El Paso, TX (city) El Paso County	1,614	0.25
Virginia Beach, VA (ind. city) Virginia Beach independent city	1,609	0.37
Reno, NV (city) Washoe County	1,605	0.71
Foster City, CA (city) San Mateo County	1,588	5.20
Cypress, CA (city) Orange County	1,588	3.32
Arlington, VA (cdp) Arlington County	1,582	0.76
Hawaiian Paradise Park, HI (cdp) Hawaii County	1,533	13.44
Carlsbad, CA (city) San Diego County	1,528	1.45
Jacksonville, FL (city) Duval County	1,514	0.18
Alameda, CA (city) Alameda County	1,496	2.03
North Las Vegas, NV (city) Clark County	1,495	0.69
Waimea, HI (cdp) Hawaii County	1,488	16.15
Kihei, HI (cdp) Maui County	1,479	7.08
Fairfield, CA (city) Solano County	1,452	1.38
Renton, WA (city) King County	1,450	1.59
Hacienda Heights, CA (cdp) Los Angeles County	1,449	2.68
Ann Arbor, MI (city) Washtenaw County	1,428	1.25
Lexington-Fayette, KY (cons. govt) Fayette County	1,413	0.48
Oxnard, CA (city) Ventura County	1,411	0.71
Roseville, CA (city) Placer County	1,400	1.18
Fort Lee, NJ (borough) Bergen County	1,397	3.95
Concord, CA (city) Contra Costa County	1,382	1.13
Beaverton, OR (city) Washington County	1,364	1.52
Waihee-Waiehu, HI (cdp) Maui County	1,358	15.36
Aliso Viejo, CA (city) Orange County	1,357	2.84
Tustin, CA (city) Orange County	1,343	1.78
Salt Lake City, UT (city) Salt Lake County	1,340	0.72
Kailua, HI (cdp) Hawaii County	1,338	11.17
Dallas, TX (city) Dallas County	1,337	0.11
Kalaoa, HI (cdp) Hawaii County	1,329	13.78
Spokane, WA (city) Spokane County	1,308	0.63
Garden Grove, CA (city) Orange County	1,297	0.76
Makawao, HI (cdp) Maui County	1,296	18.04
Lahaina, HI (cdp) Maui County	1,296	11.07
Mesa, AZ (city) Maricopa County	1,295	0.29
Redmond, WA (city) King County	1,284	2.37
Hayward, CA (city) Alameda County	1,276	0.88
Lake Forest, CA (city) Orange County	1,267	1.64
Cambridge, MA (city) Middlesex County	1,267	1.20
Camarillo, CA (city) Ventura County	1,266	1.94
San Ramon, CA (city) Contra Costa County	1,266	1.75
North Hempstead, NY (town) Nassau County	1,266	0.56
El Cerrito, CA (city) Contra Costa County	1,247	5.30
Waipio Acres, HI (cdp) Honolulu County	1,245	23.78
Harrison, NY (town/village) Westchester County	1,239	4.51
Arcadia, CA (city) Los Angeles County	1,235	2.19
Newport Beach, CA (city) Orange County	1,230	1.44
Greenburgh, NY (town) Westchester County	1,230	1.39

SECTION THREE

Please refer to the Explanation of Data in the front of the book for more detailed information.

Race

Asian: Japanese

Top 150 Places Sorted by Percent of Total Population

Based on all places, regardless of total population

Place	Population	%
Greens, NH (grant) Coos County	1	100.00
Mililani Mauka, HI (cdp) Honolulu County	9,047	43.00
Pearl City, HI (cdp) Honolulu County	19,604	41.10
Heeia, HI (cdp) Honolulu County	2,037	41.04
Aiea, HI (cdp) Honolulu County	3,714	39.77
East Honolulu, HI (cdp) Honolulu County	19,536	39.14
Mililani Town, HI (cdp) Honolulu County	10,648	38.54
Kaneohe, HI (cdp) Honolulu County	12,759	36.88
Kurtistown, HI (cdp) Hawaii County	472	36.36
Hilo, HI (cdp) Hawaii County	15,537	35.91
Waikele, HI (cdp) Honolulu County	2,668	35.67
Waipio, HI (cdp) Honolulu County	4,150	35.55
Ahuimanu, HI (cdp) Honolulu County	2,961	33.61
Waimea, HI (cdp) Kauai County	623	33.58
Waimalu, HI (cdp) Honolulu County	4,342	31.62
Maunawili, HI (cdp) Honolulu County	645	31.62
Lihue, HI (cdp) Kauai County	2,040	31.60
Honomu, HI (cdp) Hawaii County	155	30.45
Wailuku, HI (cdp) Maui County	4,445	29.03
Halawa, HI (cdp) Honolulu County	4,059	28.96
Captain Cook, HI (cdp) Hawaii County	981	28.61
Paukaa, HI (cdp) Hawaii County	121	28.47
Urban Honolulu, HI (cdp) Honolulu County	95,201	28.23
Kealakekua, HI (cdp) Hawaii County	567	28.08
Wailua, HI (cdp) Kauai County	619	27.46
Waiohinu, HI (cdp) Hawaii County	57	26.76
Wahiawa, HI (cdp) Honolulu County	4,744	26.62
Hanapepe, HI (cdp) Kauai County	702	26.61
Waikapu, HI (cdp) Maui County	772	26.04
Keaau, HI (cdp) Hawaii County	567	25.17
Papaikou, HI (cdp) Hawaii County	325	24.73
Pukalani, HI (cdp) Maui County	1,838	24.27
Eleele, HI (cdp) Kauai County	578	24.18
Lawai, HI (cdp) Kauai County	570	24.12
Pepeekeo, HI (cdp) Hawaii County	430	24.04
Waipio Acres, HI (cdp) Honolulu County	1,245	23.78
Kahaluu, HI (cdp) Honolulu County	1,110	23.43
Wainaku, HI (cdp) Hawaii County	263	21.49
Mountain View, HI (cdp) Hawaii County	834	21.25
Hawi, HI (cdp) Hawaii County	225	20.81
Kailua, HI (cdp) Honolulu County	7,983	20.66
Honalo, HI (cdp) Hawaii County	495	20.43
Kalaheo, HI (cdp) Kauai County	938	20.41
Koloa, HI (cdp) Kauai County	430	20.06
Kahului, HI (cdp) Maui County	5,197	19.73
Omao, HI (cdp) Kauai County	250	19.22
Wailua Homesteads, HI (cdp) Kauai County	969	18.68
Royal Kunia, HI (cdp) Honolulu County	2,709	18.65
Kapaau, HI (cdp) Hawaii County	323	18.63
Pahala, HI (cdp) Hawaii County	251	18.51
Ewa Gentry, HI (cdp) Honolulu County	4,130	18.20
Honokaa, HI (cdp) Hawaii County	408	18.07
Makawao, HI (cdp) Maui County	1,296	18.04
Pahoa, HI (cdp) Hawaii County	170	17.99
Kapolei, HI (cdp) Honolulu County	2,706	17.82
Waialua, HI (cdp) Honolulu County	685	17.75
Kapaa, HI (cdp) Kauai County	1,862	17.40
Kukuihaele, HI (cdp) Hawaii County	58	17.26
West Loch Estate, HI (cdp) Honolulu County	942	17.17
Kekaha, HI (cdp) Kauai County	603	17.05
Makakilo, HI (cdp) Honolulu County	3,110	17.04
Kula, HI (cdp) Maui County	1,086	16.83
Puhi, HI (cdp) Kauai County	483	16.62
Haliimaile, HI (cdp) Maui County	160	16.60
Paauilo, HI (cdp) Hawaii County	98	16.47
Waimea, HI (cdp) Hawaii County	1,488	16.15
Laupahoehoe, HI (cdp) Hawaii County	93	16.01
Haleiwa, HI (cdp) Honolulu County	630	15.87
Honaunau-Napoopoo, HI (cdp) Hawaii County	404	15.74
Waikane, HI (cdp) Honolulu County	121	15.55
Waimanalo, HI (cdp) Honolulu County	841	15.43
Waihee-Waiehu, HI (cdp) Maui County	1,358	15.36
Halaula, HI (cdp) Hawaii County	70	14.93
Hanamaulu, HI (cdp) Kauai County	556	14.50
Naalehu, HI (cdp) Hawaii County	123	14.20
Kalaoa, HI (cdp) Hawaii County	1,329	13.78
Hawaiian Paradise Park, HI (cdp) Hawaii County	1,533	13.44
Ewa Villages, HI (cdp) Honolulu County	801	13.11
Hanalei, HI (cdp) Kauai County	59	13.11
Waianae, HI (cdp) Honolulu County	1,696	12.87
Ocean Pointe, HI (cdp) Honolulu County	1,076	12.87
Kaunakakai, HI (cdp) Maui County	440	12.85
Torrance, CA (city) Los Angeles County	18,532	12.74
Olowalu, HI (cdp) Maui County	10	12.50
Hamer, ID (city) Jefferson County	6	12.50
Ewa Beach, HI (cdp) Honolulu County	1,845	12.34
Waipahu, HI (cdp) Honolulu County	4,619	12.09
Volcano, HI (cdp) Hawaii County	310	12.04
Ainaloa, HI (cdp) Hawaii County	355	11.97
Poipu, HI (cdp) Kauai County	116	11.85
Kualapuu, HI (cdp) Maui County	240	11.84
Pakala Village, HI (cdp) Kauai County	34	11.56
Paia, HI (cdp) Maui County	308	11.54
Hawaiian Beaches, HI (cdp) Hawaii County	487	11.38
Makaha, HI (cdp) Honolulu County	940	11.36
Olinda, HI (cdp) Maui County	123	11.35
Holualoa, HI (cdp) Hawaii County	965	11.30
Gardena, CA (city) Los Angeles County	6,584	11.19
Kailua, HI (cdp) Hawaii County	1,338	11.17
Lahaina, HI (cdp) Maui County	1,296	11.07
Maili, HI (cdp) Honolulu County	1,046	11.02
Lanai City, HI (cdp) Maui County	338	10.90
Nanawale Estates, HI (cdp) Hawaii County	155	10.87
Kaaawa, HI (cdp) Honolulu County	149	10.80
Orchidlands Estates, HI (cdp) Hawaii County	300	10.66
Punaluu, HI (cdp) Honolulu County	124	10.65
Waimanalo Beach, HI (cdp) Honolulu County	477	10.64
Waikoloa Village, HI (cdp) Hawaii County	675	10.61
Whitmore Village, HI (cdp) Honolulu County	477	10.60
Fern Acres, HI (cdp) Hawaii County	158	10.51
Hana, HI (cdp) Maui County	129	10.45
Anahola, HI (cdp) Kauai County	232	10.44
Kalaeloa, HI (cdp) Honolulu County	5	10.42
Maunaloa, HI (cdp) Maui County	38	10.11
Ualapu'e, HI (cdp) Maui County	42	9.88
Haiku-Pauwela, HI (cdp) Maui County	789	9.72
Keokea, HI (cdp) Maui County	156	9.68
Hawaiian Acres, HI (cdp) Hawaii County	261	9.67
Eden Roc, HI (cdp) Hawaii County	88	9.34
Pupukea, HI (cdp) Honolulu County	424	9.32
Puako, HI (cdp) Hawaii County	70	9.07
Nanakuli, HI (cdp) Honolulu County	1,122	8.86
Kilauea, HI (cdp) Kauai County	244	8.70
Rancho Palos Verdes, CA (city) Los Angeles County	3,577	8.59
Kahaluu-Keauhou, HI (cdp) Hawaii County	303	8.54
Kahuku, HI (cdp) Honolulu County	220	8.42
Mokuleia, HI (cdp) Honolulu County	151	8.34
Discovery Harbour, HI (cdp) Hawaii County	78	8.22
Svea, MN (township) Kittson County	4	8.16
Hauula, HI (cdp) Honolulu County	338	8.15
Rolling Hills Estates, CA (city) Los Angeles County	645	8.00
Ko Olina, HI (cdp) Honolulu County	141	7.84
Fern Forest, HI (cdp) Hawaii County	72	7.73
Makaha Valley, HI (cdp) Honolulu County	102	7.61
South San Gabriel, CA (cdp) Los Angeles County	607	7.52
Kaumakani, HI (cdp) Kauai County	55	7.34
Laie, HI (cdp) Honolulu County	437	7.12
Kihei, HI (cdp) Maui County	1,479	7.08
Vernon, CO (cdp) Yuma County	2	6.90
Rose Hills, CA (cdp) Los Angeles County	190	6.78
Monterey Park, CA (city) Los Angeles County	4,034	6.69
Point Baker, AK (cdp) Prince of Wales-Hyder Census Area	1	6.67
Pella, WI (cdp) Shawano County	12	6.49
Buck Meadows, CA (cdp) Mariposa County	2	6.45
Napili-Honokowai, HI (cdp) Maui County	456	6.28
Spring Garden, CA (cdp) Plumas County	1	6.25
Iroquois Point, HI (cdp) Honolulu County	210	6.22
Makena, HI (cdp) Maui County	6	6.06
Hatton, WA (town) Adams County	6	5.94
Lewis, MN (township) Mille Lacs County	3	5.77

Please refer to the Explanation of Data in the front of the book for more detailed information.

Race

Asian: Japanese

Top 150 Places Sorted by Percent of Total Population

Based on places with total population of 7,500 or more

Place	Population	%
Mililani Mauka, HI (cdp) Honolulu County	9,047	43.00
Pearl City, HI (cdp) Honolulu County	19,604	41.10
Aiea, HI (cdp) Honolulu County	3,714	39.77
East Honolulu, HI (cdp) Honolulu County	19,536	39.14
Mililani Town, HI (cdp) Honolulu County	10,648	38.54
Kaneohe, HI (cdp) Honolulu County	12,759	36.88
Hilo, HI (cdp) Hawaii County	15,537	35.91
Waipio, HI (cdp) Honolulu County	4,150	35.55
Ahuimanu, HI (cdp) Honolulu County	2,961	33.61
Waimalu, HI (cdp) Honolulu County	4,342	31.62
Wailuku, HI (cdp) Maui County	4,445	29.03
Halawa, HI (cdp) Honolulu County	4,059	28.96
Urban Honolulu, HI (cdp) Honolulu County	95,201	28.23
Wahiawa, HI (cdp) Honolulu County	4,744	26.62
Pukalani, HI (cdp) Maui County	1,838	24.27
Kailua, HI (cdp) Honolulu County	7,983	20.66
Kahului, HI (cdp) Maui County	5,197	19.73
Royal Kunia, HI (cdp) Honolulu County	2,709	18.65
Ewa Gentry, HI (cdp) Honolulu County	4,130	18.20
Kapolei, HI (cdp) Honolulu County	2,706	17.82
Kapaa, HI (cdp) Kauai County	1,862	17.40
Makakilo, HI (cdp) Honolulu County	3,110	17.04
Waimea, HI (cdp) Hawaii County	1,488	16.15
Waihee-Waiehu, HI (cdp) Maui County	1,358	15.36
Kalaoa, HI (cdp) Hawaii County	1,329	13.78
Hawaiian Paradise Park, HI (cdp) Hawaii County	1,533	13.44
Waianae, HI (cdp) Honolulu County	1,696	12.87
Ocean Pointe, HI (cdp) Honolulu County	1,076	12.87
Torrance, CA (city) Los Angeles County	18,532	12.74
Ewa Beach, HI (cdp) Honolulu County	1,845	12.34
Waipahu, HI (cdp) Honolulu County	4,619	12.09
Makaha, HI (cdp) Honolulu County	940	11.36
Holualoa, HI (cdp) Hawaii County	965	11.30
Gardena, CA (city) Los Angeles County	6,584	11.19
Kailua, HI (cdp) Hawaii County	1,338	11.17
Lahaina, HI (cdp) Maui County	1,296	11.07
Maili, HI (cdp) Honolulu County	1,046	11.02
Haiku-Pauwela, HI (cdp) Maui County	789	9.72
Nanakuli, HI (cdp) Honolulu County	1,122	8.86
Rancho Palos Verdes, CA (city) Los Angeles County	3,577	8.59
Rolling Hills Estates, CA (city) Los Angeles County	645	8.00
South San Gabriel, CA (cdp) Los Angeles County	607	7.52
Kihei, HI (cdp) Maui County	1,479	7.08
Monterey Park, CA (city) Los Angeles County	4,034	6.69
La Palma, CA (city) Orange County	886	5.69
El Cerrito, CA (city) Contra Costa County	1,247	5.30
Edgewater, NJ (borough) Bergen County	608	5.28
Foster City, CA (city) San Mateo County	1,588	5.20
West Carson, CA (cdp) Los Angeles County	1,090	5.02
Culver City, CA (city) Los Angeles County	1,898	4.88
Palos Verdes Estates, CA (city) Los Angeles County	634	4.72
Lomita, CA (city) Los Angeles County	937	4.63
Albany, CA (city) Alameda County	853	4.60
South Pasadena, CA (city) Los Angeles County	1,164	4.54
Harrison, NY (town/village) Westchester County	1,239	4.51
Newcastle, WA (city) King County	459	4.42
Cupertino, CA (city) Santa Clara County	2,489	4.27
Irvine, CA (city) Orange County	8,797	4.14
Redondo Beach, CA (city) Los Angeles County	2,658	3.98
Cerritos, CA (city) Los Angeles County	1,951	3.98
Fort Lee, NJ (borough) Bergen County	1,397	3.95
Novi, MI (city) Oakland County	2,120	3.84
Klahanie, WA (cdp) King County	393	3.68
Mercer Island, WA (city) King County	772	3.40
Cypress, CA (city) Orange County	1,588	3.32
Fountain Valley, CA (city) Orange County	1,817	3.28
Los Altos, CA (city) Santa Clara County	938	3.24
Manhattan Beach, CA (city) Los Angeles County	1,111	3.16
Saratoga, CA (city) Santa Clara County	944	3.15
Eastchester, NY (cdp) Westchester County	610	3.12
Bellevue, WA (city) King County	3,765	3.08
Rye, NY (city) Westchester County	482	3.07
Marina, CA (city) Monterey County	600	3.04
East San Gabriel, CA (cdp) Los Angeles County	448	3.01
San Mateo, CA (city) San Mateo County	2,835	2.92
Rossmoor, CA (cdp) Orange County	296	2.89
Palo Alto, CA (city) Santa Clara County	1,831	2.84
Aliso Viejo, CA (city) Orange County	1,357	2.84
Sunnyvale, CA (city) Santa Clara County	3,950	2.82
Mountain View, CA (city) Santa Clara County	2,091	2.82
San Marino, CA (city) Los Angeles County	371	2.82
Eastchester, NY (town) Westchester County	903	2.79
Belmont, CA (city) San Mateo County	722	2.79
Riverside, CT (cdp) Fairfield County	233	2.77
Dublin, OH (city) Franklin County	1,154	2.76
Bryn Mawr-Skyway, WA (cdp) King County	431	2.75
Piedmont, CA (city) Alameda County	290	2.72
Campbell, CA (city) Santa Clara County	1,058	2.69
Hacienda Heights, CA (cdp) Los Angeles County	1,449	2.68
Montebello, CA (city) Los Angeles County	1,669	2.67
Berkeley, CA (city) Alameda County	2,948	2.62
Davis, CA (city) Yolo County	1,674	2.55
Fairwood, WA (cdp) King County	485	2.54
Marina del Rey, CA (cdp) Los Angeles County	224	2.53
La Cañada Flintridge, CA (city) Los Angeles County	508	2.51
El Segundo, CA (city) Los Angeles County	416	2.50
Scarsdale, NY (town/village) Westchester County	428	2.49
Seal Beach, CA (city) Orange County	597	2.47
Moraga, CA (town) Contra Costa County	396	2.47
Walnut, CA (city) Los Angeles County	709	2.43
Emeryville, CA (city) Alameda County	243	2.41
Redmond, WA (city) King County	1,284	2.37
Huntington Beach, CA (city) Orange County	4,451	2.34
Burlingame, CA (city) San Mateo County	675	2.34
Cresskill, NJ (borough) Bergen County	200	2.33
Hillsborough, CA (town) San Mateo County	250	2.31
Santa Clara, CA (city) Santa Clara County	2,617	2.25
Stanford, CA (cdp) Santa Clara County	305	2.21
Los Gatos, CA (town) Santa Clara County	648	2.20
Arcadia, CA (city) Los Angeles County	1,235	2.19
Los Alamitos, CA (city) Orange County	251	2.19
Kirkland, WA (city) King County	1,056	2.16
Tenafly, NJ (borough) Bergen County	313	2.16
Seattle, WA (city) King County	13,064	2.15
Diamond Bar, CA (city) Los Angeles County	1,194	2.15
Millbrae, CA (city) San Mateo County	463	2.15
Santa Monica, CA (city) Los Angeles County	1,924	2.14
Los Altos Hills, CA (town) Santa Clara County	164	2.07
Pasadena, CA (city) Los Angeles County	2,808	2.05
Brookline, MA (cdp/town) Norfolk County	1,203	2.05
Alameda, CA (city) Alameda County	1,496	2.03
Bethany, OR (cdp) Washington County	420	2.03
Alhambra, CA (city) Los Angeles County	1,642	1.98
Isla Vista, CA (cdp) Santa Barbara County	458	1.98
Alondra Park, CA (cdp) Los Angeles County	170	1.98
Temple City, CA (city) Los Angeles County	700	1.97
Lake Forest Park, WA (city) King County	248	1.97
Camarillo, CA (city) Ventura County	1,266	1.94
San Carlos, CA (city) San Mateo County	552	1.94
Ontario, OR (city) Malheur County	220	1.94
San Gabriel, CA (city) Los Angeles County	765	1.93
Oak Hills, OR (cdp) Washington County	219	1.93
Tamalpais-Homestead Valley, CA (cdp) Marin County	207	1.93
Greenwich, CT (town) Fairfield County	1,177	1.92
Pleasant Hill, CA (city) Contra Costa County	637	1.92
Monterey, CA (city) Monterey County	533	1.92
Issaquah, WA (city) King County	581	1.91
Sierra Madre, CA (city) Los Angeles County	209	1.91
San Francisco, CA (city) San Francisco County	15,278	1.90
Sacramento, CA (city) Sacramento County	8,759	1.88
Oak Harbor, WA (city) Island County	416	1.88
Sammamish, WA (city) King County	858	1.87
Woodinville, WA (city) King County	205	1.87
Hermosa Beach, CA (city) Los Angeles County	362	1.86
Corte Madera, CA (town) Marin County	172	1.86
Seaside, CA (city) Monterey County	610	1.85
Mill Creek, WA (city) Snohomish County	338	1.85
Shoreline, WA (city) King County	976	1.84
Laguna Niguel, CA (city) Orange County	1,151	1.83
Lafayette, CA (city) Contra Costa County	434	1.82

SECTION THREE

Please refer to the Explanation of Data in the front of the book for more detailed information.

Race

Asian: Korean

U.S. and 50 States Sorted by Population and Percent of Total Population

Place	Population	%
United States	**1,706,822**	**0.55**
California	505,225	1.36
New York	153,609	0.79
New Jersey	100,334	1.14
Texas	85,332	0.34
Virginia	82,006	1.02
Washington	80,049	1.19
Illinois	70,263	0.55
Georgia	60,836	0.63
Maryland	55,051	0.95
Hawaii	48,699	3.58
Pennsylvania	47,429	0.37
Florida	35,629	0.19
Michigan	30,292	0.31
Massachusetts	28,904	0.44
Colorado	28,177	0.56
North Carolina	25,420	0.27
Ohio	21,207	0.18
Arizona	21,125	0.33
Minnesota	20,995	0.40
Oregon	20,395	0.53
Nevada	18,518	0.69
Indiana	13,685	0.21
Tennessee	13,245	0.21
Missouri	12,689	0.21
Connecticut	11,760	0.33
Wisconsin	10,949	0.19
Alabama	10,624	0.22
Oklahoma	9,072	0.24
Utah	7,888	0.29
Kansas	7,756	0.27
Iowa	7,375	0.24
Kentucky	7,264	0.17
South Carolina	7,162	0.15
Alaska	6,542	0.92
Louisiana	4,752	0.10
Nebraska	3,815	0.21
New Mexico	3,760	0.18
Arkansas	3,247	0.11
Delaware	3,099	0.35
New Hampshire	3,021	0.23
District of Columbia	2,990	0.50
Idaho	2,806	0.18
Rhode Island	2,658	0.25
Mississippi	2,301	0.08
Maine	1,741	0.13
West Virginia	1,571	0.08
Montana	1,369	0.14
Vermont	1,271	0.20
South Dakota	1,179	0.14
North Dakota	933	0.14
Wyoming	803	0.14

Place	Population	%
Hawaii	48,699	3.58
California	505,225	1.36
Washington	80,049	1.19
New Jersey	100,334	1.14
Virginia	82,006	1.02
Maryland	55,051	0.95
Alaska	6,542	0.92
New York	153,609	0.79
Nevada	18,518	0.69
Georgia	60,836	0.63
Colorado	28,177	0.56
United States	**1,706,822**	**0.55**
Illinois	70,263	0.55
Oregon	20,395	0.53
District of Columbia	2,990	0.50
Massachusetts	28,904	0.44
Minnesota	20,995	0.40
Pennsylvania	47,429	0.37
Delaware	3,099	0.35
Texas	85,332	0.34
Arizona	21,125	0.33
Connecticut	11,760	0.33
Michigan	30,292	0.31
Utah	7,888	0.29
North Carolina	25,420	0.27
Kansas	7,756	0.27
Rhode Island	2,658	0.25
Oklahoma	9,072	0.24
Iowa	7,375	0.24
New Hampshire	3,021	0.23
Alabama	10,624	0.22
Indiana	13,685	0.21
Tennessee	13,245	0.21
Missouri	12,689	0.21
Nebraska	3,815	0.21
Vermont	1,271	0.20
Florida	35,629	0.19
Wisconsin	10,949	0.19
Ohio	21,207	0.18
New Mexico	3,760	0.18
Idaho	2,806	0.18
Kentucky	7,264	0.17
South Carolina	7,162	0.15
Montana	1,369	0.14
South Dakota	1,179	0.14
North Dakota	933	0.14
Wyoming	803	0.14
Maine	1,741	0.13
Arkansas	3,247	0.11
Louisiana	4,752	0.10
Mississippi	2,301	0.08
West Virginia	1,571	0.08

Please refer to the Explanation of Data in the front of the book for more detailed information.

Race

Asian: Korean

Top 150 Places Sorted by Population

Based on all places, regardless of total population

Place	Population	%
Los Angeles, CA (city) Los Angeles County	114,140	3.01
New York, NY (city) Kings County	102,820	1.26
Queens, NY (borough) Queens County	66,124	2.96
Manhattan, NY (borough) New York County	21,996	1.39
Urban Honolulu, HI (cdp) Honolulu County	20,716	6.14
Irvine, CA (city) Orange County	19,473	9.17
Fullerton, CA (city) Orange County	16,004	11.84
San Diego, CA (city) San Diego County	15,883	1.21
Chicago, IL (city) Cook County	13,418	0.50
San Jose, CA (city) Santa Clara County	12,929	1.37
Torrance, CA (city) Los Angeles County	12,779	8.79
San Francisco, CA (city) San Francisco County	11,558	1.44
Glendale, CA (city) Los Angeles County	10,650	5.56
Palisades Park, NJ (borough) Bergen County	10,259	52.28
Seattle, WA (city) King County	8,682	1.43
Fort Lee, NJ (borough) Bergen County	8,437	23.87
Brooklyn, NY (borough) Kings County	8,201	0.33
Buena Park, CA (city) Orange County	8,001	9.94
Centreville, VA (cdp) Fairfax County	7,747	10.89
Houston, TX (city) Harris County	7,578	0.36
Cerritos, CA (city) Los Angeles County	7,451	15.19
Philadelphia, PA (city) Philadelphia County	7,074	0.46
Anaheim, CA (city) Orange County	6,999	2.08
Austin, TX (city) Travis County	6,564	0.83
North Hempstead, NY (town) Nassau County	6,015	2.66
Diamond Bar, CA (city) Los Angeles County	5,961	10.73
Garden Grove, CA (city) Orange County	5,951	3.48
Cypress, CA (city) Orange County	5,878	12.30
Ellicott City, MD (cdp) Howard County	5,531	8.40
Federal Way, WA (city) King County	5,303	5.94
Johns Creek, GA (city) Fulton County	5,138	6.70
Colorado Springs, CO (city) El Paso County	5,103	1.23
Oyster Bay, NY (town) Nassau County	4,977	1.70
Bellevue, WA (city) King County	4,912	4.01
Anchorage, AK (municipality) Anchorage Municipality	4,667	1.60
Boston, MA (city) Suffolk County	4,540	0.74
San Antonio, TX (city) Medina County	4,337	0.33
Aurora, CO (city) Arapahoe County	4,110	1.26
La Crescenta-Montrose, CA (cdp) Los Angeles County	4,058	20.65
Phoenix, AZ (city) Maricopa County	4,028	0.28
Tacoma, WA (city) Pierce County	3,880	1.96
La Mirada, CA (city) Los Angeles County	3,791	7.81
Santa Clara, CA (city) Santa Clara County	3,789	3.25
Dallas, TX (city) Dallas County	3,760	0.31
Chino Hills, CA (city) San Bernardino County	3,662	4.90
Rowland Heights, CA (cdp) Los Angeles County	3,636	7.42
Gardena, CA (city) Los Angeles County	3,636	6.18
Las Vegas, NV (city) Clark County	3,624	0.62
Plano, TX (city) Collin County	3,586	1.38
Riverside, CA (city) Riverside County	3,557	1.17
Fremont, CA (city) Alameda County	3,459	1.62
Portland, OR (city) Multnomah County	3,438	0.59
Staten Island, NY (borough) Richmond County	3,398	0.72
Annandale, VA (cdp) Fairfax County	3,380	8.24
Spring Valley, NV (cdp) Clark County	3,343	1.87
Columbus, OH (city) Franklin County	3,330	0.42
Sunnyvale, CA (city) Santa Clara County	3,294	2.35
Irving, TX (city) Dallas County	3,261	1.51
Santa Clarita, CA (city) Los Angeles County	3,238	1.84
Charlotte, NC (city) Mecklenburg County	3,168	0.43
Ann Arbor, MI (city) Washtenaw County	3,159	2.77
East Honolulu, HI (cdp) Honolulu County	3,116	6.24
Bronx, NY (borough) Bronx County	3,101	0.22
Oakland, CA (city) Alameda County	3,096	0.79
Fair Oaks, VA (cdp) Fairfax County	3,075	10.17
Hempstead, NY (town) Nassau County	3,074	0.40
Rancho Palos Verdes, CA (city) Los Angeles County	3,066	7.36
La Cañada Flintridge, CA (city) Los Angeles County	3,030	14.97
Pasadena, CA (city) Los Angeles County	3,017	2.20
Washington, DC (city) District of Columbia	2,990	0.50
Columbia, MD (cdp) Howard County	2,986	3.00
Killeen, TX (city) Bell County	2,978	2.33
Ridgefield, NJ (borough) Bergen County	2,886	26.16
Cupertino, CA (city) Santa Clara County	2,876	4.93
Berkeley, CA (city) Alameda County	2,754	2.45
Minneapolis, MN (city) Hennepin County	2,700	0.71
Duluth, GA (city) Gwinnett County	2,683	10.09
Norwalk, CA (city) Los Angeles County	2,678	2.54
Brea, CA (city) Orange County	2,676	6.81
Carrollton, TX (city) Denton County	2,676	2.25
La Palma, CA (city) Orange County	2,656	17.06
Downey, CA (city) Los Angeles County	2,619	2.34
Hacienda Heights, CA (cdp) Los Angeles County	2,609	4.83
Cambridge, MA (city) Middlesex County	2,566	2.44
San Ramon, CA (city) Contra Costa County	2,548	3.53
Fort Worth, TX (city) Tarrant County	2,523	0.34
Burke, VA (cdp) Fairfax County	2,494	6.07
Atlanta, GA (city) Fulton County	2,493	0.59
Jersey City, NJ (city) Hudson County	2,482	1.00
El Paso, TX (city) El Paso County	2,461	0.38
Rancho Cucamonga, CA (city) San Bernardino County	2,443	1.48
Leonia, NJ (borough) Bergen County	2,426	27.15
Tustin, CA (city) Orange County	2,422	3.21
Denver, CO (city) Denver County	2,415	0.40
Lakewood, WA (city) Pierce County	2,412	4.15
Baltimore, MD (city) Baltimore city County	2,404	0.39
Chula Vista, CA (city) San Diego County	2,397	0.98
Long Beach, CA (city) Los Angeles County	2,385	0.52
La Habra, CA (city) Orange County	2,375	3.94
Raleigh, NC (city) Wake County	2,357	0.58
Henderson, NV (city) Clark County	2,338	0.91
Burbank, CA (city) Los Angeles County	2,324	2.25
Fayetteville, NC (city) Cumberland County	2,323	1.16
Glenview, IL (village) Cook County	2,321	5.19
Edgewater, NJ (borough) Bergen County	2,316	20.12
Tenafly, NJ (borough) Bergen County	2,308	15.93
Arlington, VA (cdp) Arlington County	2,270	1.09
Madison, WI (city) Dane County	2,261	0.97
Yorba Linda, CA (city) Orange County	2,132	3.32
Huntington, NY (town) Suffolk County	2,122	1.04
Chandler, AZ (city) Maricopa County	2,109	0.89
Arcadia, CA (city) Los Angeles County	2,094	3.72
Jacksonville, FL (city) Duval County	2,087	0.25
Germantown, MD (cdp) Montgomery County	2,067	2.39
Champaign, IL (city) Champaign County	2,060	2.54
McLean, VA (cdp) Fairfax County	2,057	4.28
Nashville-Davidson, TN (metro govt) Davidson County	2,052	0.34
Pleasanton, CA (city) Alameda County	2,046	2.91
Oakton, VA (cdp) Fairfax County	2,043	5.98
Orange, CA (city) Orange County	2,039	1.49
Enterprise, NV (cdp) Clark County	2,032	1.87
Brookhaven, NY (town) Suffolk County	2,025	0.42
Northbrook, IL (village) Cook County	2,005	6.04
Pittsburgh, PA (city) Allegheny County	2,002	0.65
Oklahoma City, OK (city) Oklahoma County	1,998	0.34
Schaumburg, IL (village) Cook County	1,994	2.69
Sacramento, CA (city) Sacramento County	1,994	0.43
Corona, CA (city) Riverside County	1,993	1.31
Huntington Beach, CA (city) Orange County	1,990	1.05
Palo Alto, CA (city) Santa Clara County	1,978	3.07
Clarksville, TN (city) Montgomery County	1,977	1.49
Pearl City, HI (cdp) Honolulu County	1,974	4.14
Tucson, AZ (city) Pima County	1,892	0.36
Skokie, IL (village) Cook County	1,880	2.90
Montgomery, AL (city) Montgomery County	1,870	0.91
Naperville, IL (city) DuPage County	1,864	1.31
Paramus, NJ (borough) Bergen County	1,859	7.06
Paradise, NV (cdp) Clark County	1,836	0.82
Cliffside Park, NJ (borough) Bergen County	1,828	7.75
Bloomington, IN (city) Monroe County	1,807	2.25
Virginia Beach, VA (ind. city) Virginia Beach independent city	1,802	0.41
Closter, NJ (borough) Bergen County	1,787	21.34
Buffalo Grove, IL (village) Lake County	1,780	4.29
Rockville, MD (city) Montgomery County	1,780	2.91
South Pasadena, CA (city) Los Angeles County	1,774	6.92
Davis, CA (city) Yolo County	1,766	2.69
Montgomery, PA (township) Montgomery County	1,765	7.12
Stevenson Ranch, CA (cdp) Los Angeles County	1,764	10.05
Alameda, CA (city) Alameda County	1,751	2.37
Mukilteo, WA (city) Snohomish County	1,698	8.38

Please refer to the Explanation of Data in the front of the book for more detailed information.

Race

Asian: Korean

Top 150 Places Sorted by Percent of Total Population

Based on all places, regardless of total population

Place	Population	%
Palisades Park, NJ (borough) Bergen County	10,259	52.28
Leonia, NJ (borough) Bergen County	2,426	27.15
Ridgefield, NJ (borough) Bergen County	2,886	26.16
Odell, NH (township) Coos County	1	25.00
Fort Lee, NJ (borough) Bergen County	8,437	23.87
Closter, NJ (borough) Bergen County	1,787	21.34
Englewood Cliffs, NJ (borough) Bergen County	1,106	20.94
La Crescenta-Montrose, CA (cdp) Los Angeles County	4,058	20.65
Norwood, NJ (borough) Bergen County	1,164	20.38
Edgewater, NJ (borough) Bergen County	2,316	20.12
Cresskill, NJ (borough) Bergen County	1,560	18.20
Demarest, NJ (borough) Bergen County	859	17.60
Old Tappan, NJ (borough) Bergen County	1,010	17.57
La Palma, CA (city) Orange County	2,656	17.06
Northvale, NJ (borough) Bergen County	760	16.38
Four Mile Road, AK (cdp) Yukon-Koyukuk Census Area	7	16.28
Tenafly, NJ (borough) Bergen County	2,308	15.93
Alpine, NJ (borough) Bergen County	292	15.79
Cerritos, CA (city) Los Angeles County	7,451	15.19
La Cañada Flintridge, CA (city) Los Angeles County	3,030	14.97
Harrington Park, NJ (borough) Bergen County	628	13.46
Little Ferry, NJ (borough) Bergen County	1,315	12.38
Cypress, CA (city) Orange County	5,878	12.30
Fullerton, CA (city) Orange County	16,004	11.84
River Edge, NJ (borough) Bergen County	1,313	11.58
Centreville, VA (cdp) Fairfax County	7,747	10.89
Fair Lakes, VA (cdp) Fairfax County	864	10.88
Laurel Hill, VA (cdp) Fairfax County	738	10.77
Diamond Bar, CA (city) Los Angeles County	5,961	10.73
Fair Oaks, VA (cdp) Fairfax County	3,075	10.17
Duluth, GA (city) Gwinnett County	2,683	10.09
Stevenson Ranch, CA (cdp) Los Angeles County	1,764	10.05
Buena Park, CA (city) Orange County	8,001	9.94
Lake Success, NY (village) Nassau County	290	9.88
Suwanee, GA (city) Gwinnett County	1,506	9.81
Forest Home, NY (cdp) Tompkins County	54	9.44
Long Branch, VA (cdp) Fairfax County	704	9.27
Irvine, CA (city) Orange County	19,473	9.17
University Gardens, NY (cdp) Nassau County	383	9.06
Torrance, CA (city) Los Angeles County	12,779	8.79
Mantua, VA (cdp) Fairfax County	616	8.63
Bannockburn, IL (village) Lake County	134	8.46
Ellicott City, MD (cdp) Howard County	5,531	8.40
Mukilteo, WA (city) Snohomish County	1,698	8.38
Fishkill, NY (village) Dutchess County	179	8.25
Annandale, VA (cdp) Fairfax County	3,380	8.24
Elliott, ND (city) Ransom County	2	8.00
Thomaston, NY (village) Nassau County	209	7.99
Jericho, NY (cdp) Nassau County	1,078	7.95
La Mirada, CA (city) Los Angeles County	3,791	7.81
Cliffside Park, NJ (borough) Bergen County	1,828	7.75
Camino Tassajara, CA (cdp) Contra Costa County	170	7.74
Searingtown, NY (cdp) Nassau County	380	7.73
Tysons Corner, VA (cdp) Fairfax County	1,513	7.71
Rolling Hills Estates, CA (city) Los Angeles County	622	7.71
North Hills, NY (village) Nassau County	383	7.55
Rowland Heights, CA (cdp) Los Angeles County	3,636	7.42
Rancho Palos Verdes, CA (city) Los Angeles County	3,066	7.36
Fulton, MD (cdp) Howard County	147	7.17
Montgomery, PA (township) Montgomery County	1,765	7.12
Paramus, NJ (borough) Bergen County	1,859	7.06
Manorhaven, NY (village) Nassau County	457	6.97
South Pasadena, CA (city) Los Angeles County	1,774	6.92
Burke Centre, VA (cdp) Fairfax County	1,182	6.82
Brea, CA (city) Orange County	2,676	6.81
Haworth, NJ (borough) Bergen County	229	6.77
Lansing, NY (village) Tompkins County	237	6.72
Johns Creek, GA (city) Fulton County	5,138	6.70
Merrifield, VA (cdp) Fairfax County	1,011	6.65
Mill Creek, WA (city) Snohomish County	1,183	6.48
Kings Park West, VA (cdp) Fairfax County	851	6.36
Mililani Mauka, HI (cdp) Honolulu County	1,332	6.33
Waimalu, HI (cdp) Honolulu County	866	6.31
Montgomeryville, PA (cdp) Montgomery County	792	6.27
Hillsboro, VA (town) Loudoun County	5	6.25
Walpack, NJ (township) Sussex County	1	6.25
East Honolulu, HI (cdp) Honolulu County	3,116	6.24
West Carson, CA (cdp) Los Angeles County	1,350	6.22
Gardena, CA (city) Los Angeles County	3,636	6.18
North Lynnwood, WA (cdp) Snohomish County	1,021	6.16
Urban Honolulu, HI (cdp) Honolulu County	20,716	6.14
Syosset, NY (cdp) Nassau County	1,144	6.08
Burke, VA (cdp) Fairfax County	2,494	6.07
Northbrook, IL (village) Cook County	2,005	6.04
Oakton, VA (cdp) Fairfax County	2,043	5.98
Albany, CA (city) Alameda County	1,105	5.96
Lake Stickney, WA (cdp) Snohomish County	463	5.95
Federal Way, WA (city) King County	5,303	5.94
University at Buffalo, NY (cdp) Erie County	359	5.92
Clarksburg, MD (cdp) Montgomery County	812	5.90
North Laurel, MD (cdp) Howard County	263	5.88
Fife, WA (city) Pierce County	537	5.85
Ridgewood, NJ (village) Bergen County	1,441	5.77
Subiaco, AR (town) Logan County	33	5.77
Manhasset Hills, NY (cdp) Nassau County	207	5.76
Vernon Hills, IL (village) Lake County	1,429	5.69
Larch Way, WA (cdp) Snohomish County	187	5.64
Quantico, VA (town) Prince William County	27	5.63
Whitpain, PA (township) Montgomery County	1,056	5.59
Glendale, CA (city) Los Angeles County	10,650	5.56
Wakefield, VA (cdp) Fairfax County	621	5.51
Northeast Ithaca, NY (cdp) Tompkins County	145	5.49
Donald, WA (cdp) Yakima County	5	5.49
California Hot Springs, CA (cdp) Tulare County	2	5.41
Ridgefield Park, NJ (village) Bergen County	686	5.39
South Riding, VA (cdp) Loudoun County	1,302	5.37
Marina, CA (city) Monterey County	1,058	5.37
Winchester, MN (township) Norman County	3	5.36
West Springfield, VA (cdp) Fairfax County	1,202	5.35
Picnic Point, WA (cdp) Snohomish County	469	5.32
Savoy, IL (village) Champaign County	386	5.30
Hawaiian Gardens, CA (city) Los Angeles County	754	5.29
Luverne, AL (city) Crenshaw County	148	5.29
Mililani Town, HI (cdp) Honolulu County	1,457	5.27
Herricks, NY (cdp) Nassau County	226	5.26
Angus, MN (township) Polk County	4	5.26
Ophir, UT (town) Tooele County	2	5.26
Bancroft, SD (town) Kingsbury County	1	5.26
Glenview, IL (village) Cook County	2,321	5.19
Indian Creek, IL (village) Lake County	24	5.19
Albertson, NY (cdp) Nassau County	266	5.13
Rutherford, NJ (borough) Bergen County	921	5.10
Deering, ND (city) McHenry County	5	5.10
Binghamton University, NY (cdp) Broome County	314	5.08
Waikele, HI (cdp) Honolulu County	379	5.07
Ilchester, MD (cdp) Howard County	1,187	5.06
Eastgate, WA (cdp) King County	250	5.04
North Potomac, MD (cdp) Montgomery County	1,226	5.02
Artesia, CA (city) Los Angeles County	830	5.02
Mill Creek East, WA (cdp) Snohomish County	787	5.01
Allendale, NJ (borough) Bergen County	324	4.98
Cupertino, CA (city) Santa Clara County	2,876	4.93
Bothell East, WA (cdp) Snohomish County	395	4.93
Chantilly, VA (cdp) Fairfax County	1,132	4.91
Gainesville, VA (cdp) Prince William County	564	4.91
Chino Hills, CA (city) San Bernardino County	3,662	4.90
Fairfax Station, VA (cdp) Fairfax County	582	4.84
Hacienda Heights, CA (cdp) Los Angeles County	2,609	4.83
Roslyn Heights, NY (cdp) Nassau County	317	4.82
Hedwig Village, TX (city) Harris County	122	4.77
Dante, SD (town) Charles Mix County	4	4.76
Maxbass, ND (city) Bottineau County	4	4.76
University Place, WA (city) Pierce County	1,469	4.72
Siglerville, PA (cdp) Mifflin County	5	4.72
East Rutherford, NJ (borough) Bergen County	412	4.62
Wahiawa, HI (cdp) Honolulu County	822	4.61
Stanford, CA (cdp) Santa Clara County	637	4.61
Oradell, NJ (borough) Bergen County	368	4.61
Blue Bell, PA (cdp) Montgomery County	279	4.60
Morton Grove, IL (village) Cook County	1,069	4.59

Please refer to the Explanation of Data in the front of the book for more detailed information.

Race

Asian: Korean

Top 150 Places Sorted by Percent of Total Population

Based on places with total population of 7,500 or more

Place	Population	%
Palisades Park, NJ (borough) Bergen County	10,259	52.28
Leonia, NJ (borough) Bergen County	2,426	27.15
Ridgefield, NJ (borough) Bergen County	2,886	26.16
Fort Lee, NJ (borough) Bergen County	8,437	23.87
Closter, NJ (borough) Bergen County	1,787	21.34
La Crescenta-Montrose, CA (cdp) Los Angeles County	4,058	20.65
Edgewater, NJ (borough) Bergen County	2,316	20.12
Cresskill, NJ (borough) Bergen County	1,560	18.20
La Palma, CA (city) Orange County	2,656	17.06
Tenafly, NJ (borough) Bergen County	2,308	15.93
Cerritos, CA (city) Los Angeles County	7,451	15.19
La Cañada Flintridge, CA (city) Los Angeles County	3,030	14.97
Little Ferry, NJ (borough) Bergen County	1,315	12.38
Cypress, CA (city) Orange County	5,878	12.30
Fullerton, CA (city) Orange County	16,004	11.84
River Edge, NJ (borough) Bergen County	1,313	11.58
Centreville, VA (cdp) Fairfax County	7,747	10.89
Fair Lakes, VA (cdp) Fairfax County	864	10.88
Diamond Bar, CA (city) Los Angeles County	5,961	10.73
Fair Oaks, VA (cdp) Fairfax County	3,075	10.17
Duluth, GA (city) Gwinnett County	2,683	10.09
Stevenson Ranch, CA (cdp) Los Angeles County	1,764	10.05
Buena Park, CA (city) Orange County	8,001	9.94
Suwanee, GA (city) Gwinnett County	1,506	9.81
Long Branch, VA (cdp) Fairfax County	704	9.27
Irvine, CA (city) Orange County	19,473	9.17
Torrance, CA (city) Los Angeles County	12,779	8.79
Ellicott City, MD (cdp) Howard County	5,531	8.40
Mukilteo, WA (city) Snohomish County	1,698	8.38
Annandale, VA (cdp) Fairfax County	3,380	8.24
Jericho, NY (cdp) Nassau County	1,078	7.95
La Mirada, CA (city) Los Angeles County	3,791	7.81
Cliffside Park, NJ (borough) Bergen County	1,828	7.75
Tysons Corner, VA (cdp) Fairfax County	1,513	7.71
Rolling Hills Estates, CA (city) Los Angeles County	622	7.71
Rowland Heights, CA (cdp) Los Angeles County	3,636	7.42
Rancho Palos Verdes, CA (city) Los Angeles County	3,066	7.36
Montgomery, PA (township) Montgomery County	1,765	7.12
Paramus, NJ (borough) Bergen County	1,859	7.06
South Pasadena, CA (city) Los Angeles County	1,774	6.92
Burke Centre, VA (cdp) Fairfax County	1,182	6.82
Brea, CA (city) Orange County	2,676	6.81
Johns Creek, GA (city) Fulton County	5,138	6.70
Merrifield, VA (cdp) Fairfax County	1,011	6.65
Mill Creek, WA (city) Snohomish County	1,183	6.48
Kings Park West, VA (cdp) Fairfax County	851	6.36
Mililani Mauka, HI (cdp) Honolulu County	1,332	6.33
Waimalu, HI (cdp) Honolulu County	866	6.31
Montgomeryville, PA (cdp) Montgomery County	792	6.27
East Honolulu, HI (cdp) Honolulu County	3,116	6.24
West Carson, CA (cdp) Los Angeles County	1,350	6.22
Gardena, CA (city) Los Angeles County	3,636	6.18
North Lynnwood, WA (cdp) Snohomish County	1,021	6.16
Urban Honolulu, HI (cdp) Honolulu County	20,716	6.14
Syosset, NY (cdp) Nassau County	1,144	6.08
Burke, VA (cdp) Fairfax County	2,494	6.07
Northbrook, IL (village) Cook County	2,005	6.04
Oakton, VA (cdp) Fairfax County	2,043	5.98
Albany, CA (city) Alameda County	1,105	5.96
Lake Stickney, WA (cdp) Snohomish County	463	5.95
Federal Way, WA (city) King County	5,303	5.94
Clarksburg, MD (cdp) Montgomery County	812	5.90
Fife, WA (city) Pierce County	537	5.85
Ridgewood, NJ (village) Bergen County	1,441	5.77
Vernon Hills, IL (village) Lake County	1,429	5.69
Whitpain, PA (township) Montgomery County	1,056	5.59
Glendale, CA (city) Los Angeles County	10,650	5.56
Wakefield, VA (cdp) Fairfax County	621	5.51
Ridgefield Park, NJ (village) Bergen County	686	5.39
South Riding, VA (cdp) Loudoun County	1,302	5.37
Marina, CA (city) Monterey County	1,058	5.37
West Springfield, VA (cdp) Fairfax County	1,202	5.35
Picnic Point, WA (cdp) Snohomish County	469	5.32
Hawaiian Gardens, CA (city) Los Angeles County	754	5.29
Mililani Town, HI (cdp) Honolulu County	1,457	5.27
Glenview, IL (village) Cook County	2,321	5.19
Rutherford, NJ (borough) Bergen County	921	5.10
Ilchester, MD (cdp) Howard County	1,187	5.06
North Potomac, MD (cdp) Montgomery County	1,226	5.02
Artesia, CA (city) Los Angeles County	830	5.02
Mill Creek East, WA (cdp) Snohomish County	787	5.01
Cupertino, CA (city) Santa Clara County	2,876	4.93
Bothell East, WA (cdp) Snohomish County	395	4.93
Chantilly, VA (cdp) Fairfax County	1,132	4.91
Gainesville, VA (cdp) Prince William County	564	4.91
Chino Hills, CA (city) San Bernardino County	3,662	4.90
Fairfax Station, VA (cdp) Fairfax County	582	4.84
Hacienda Heights, CA (cdp) Los Angeles County	2,609	4.83
University Place, WA (city) Pierce County	1,469	4.72
East Rutherford, NJ (borough) Bergen County	412	4.62
Wahiawa, HI (cdp) Honolulu County	822	4.61
Stanford, CA (cdp) Santa Clara County	637	4.61
Oradell, NJ (borough) Bergen County	368	4.61
Morton Grove, IL (village) Cook County	1,069	4.59
Waipio, HI (cdp) Honolulu County	535	4.58
University of Virginia, VA (cdp) Albemarle County	349	4.53
Los Alamitos, CA (city) Orange County	518	4.52
Newcastle, WA (city) King County	468	4.51
Emeryville, CA (city) Alameda County	455	4.51
Purdue University, IN (cdp) Tippecanoe County	542	4.45
Bethany, OR (cdp) Washington County	913	4.42
DuPont, WA (city) Pierce County	361	4.40
Lakeland South, WA (cdp) King County	507	4.38
River Vale, NJ (township) Bergen County	422	4.37
Cloverly, MD (cdp) Montgomery County	660	4.36
Gold River, CA (cdp) Sacramento County	345	4.36
Buffalo Grove, IL (village) Lake County	1,780	4.29
McLean, VA (cdp) Fairfax County	2,057	4.28
Parkland, WA (cdp) Pierce County	1,524	4.26
Dunn Loring, VA (cdp) Fairfax County	369	4.19
Lakewood, WA (city) Pierce County	2,412	4.15
Pearl City, HI (cdp) Honolulu County	1,974	4.14
Oronoko, MI (charter township) Berrien County	380	4.13
Beverly Hills, CA (city) Los Angeles County	1,399	4.10
Upper Dublin, PA (township) Montgomery County	1,047	4.09
Glen Rock, NJ (borough) Bergen County	471	4.06
Bellevue, WA (city) King County	4,912	4.01
Walnut, CA (city) Los Angeles County	1,171	4.01
Loma Linda, CA (city) San Bernardino County	931	4.00
Greenbriar, VA (cdp) Fairfax County	326	3.99
George Mason, VA (cdp) Fairfax County	378	3.98
Aiea, HI (cdp) Honolulu County	372	3.98
La Habra, CA (city) Orange County	2,375	3.94
Lynnwood, WA (city) Snohomish County	1,412	3.94
Plainview, NY (cdp) Nassau County	1,028	3.92
Urbana, IL (city) Champaign County	1,598	3.87
Worcester, PA (township) Montgomery County	376	3.86
Travilah, MD (cdp) Montgomery County	468	3.85
Lakeland North, WA (cdp) King County	493	3.81
Scaggsville, MD (cdp) Howard County	924	3.80
Lorton, VA (cdp) Fairfax County	705	3.79
Ahuimanu, HI (cdp) Honolulu County	334	3.79
Arcadia, CA (city) Los Angeles County	2,094	3.72
Makakilo, HI (cdp) Honolulu County	677	3.71
Mays Chapel, MD (cdp) Baltimore County	421	3.69
Fairfax, VA (ind. city) Fairfax independent city	828	3.67
Halawa, HI (cdp) Honolulu County	515	3.67
Kaneohe, HI (cdp) Honolulu County	1,266	3.66
Kapolei, HI (cdp) Honolulu County	556	3.66
Long Grove, IL (village) Lake County	294	3.66
Lincolnwood, IL (village) Cook County	456	3.62
Wailuku, HI (cdp) Maui County	548	3.58
Lower Moreland, PA (township) Montgomery County	462	3.56
San Ramon, CA (city) Contra Costa County	2,548	3.53
Palos Verdes Estates, CA (city) Los Angeles County	471	3.50
Hamilton, MA (town) Essex County	272	3.50
Garden Grove, CA (city) Orange County	5,951	3.48
Lexington, MA (cdp/town) Middlesex County	1,088	3.47
Lower Gwynedd, PA (township) Montgomery County	396	3.47
Upper Saddle River, NJ (borough) Bergen County	284	3.46

Please refer to the Explanation of Data in the front of the book for more detailed information.

Race

Asian: Laotian

U.S. and 50 States Sorted by Population and Percent of Total Population

Place	Population	%
United States	**232,130**	**0.08**
California	69,303	0.19
Texas	15,784	0.06
Minnesota	12,009	0.23
Washington	11,568	0.17
Tennessee	7,276	0.11
Illinois	7,102	0.06
Georgia	6,638	0.07
North Carolina	6,562	0.07
Florida	6,152	0.03
Oregon	5,792	0.15
Iowa	5,744	0.19
Kansas	5,406	0.19
Arkansas	4,614	0.16
Wisconsin	4,562	0.08
Massachusetts	4,530	0.07
New York	4,471	0.02
Ohio	4,183	0.04
Virginia	3,980	0.05
Connecticut	3,964	0.11
Rhode Island	3,380	0.32
Michigan	3,380	0.03
Pennsylvania	3,280	0.03
Utah	3,189	0.12
Hawaii	2,620	0.19
Nevada	2,581	0.10
Colorado	2,576	0.05
Arizona	2,388	0.04
Alaska	2,121	0.30
Louisiana	1,902	0.04
Alabama	1,551	0.03
Oklahoma	1,469	0.04
Indiana	1,466	0.02
South Carolina	1,432	0.03
Maryland	1,420	0.02
Missouri	1,180	0.02
Nebraska	1,130	0.06
New Jersey	973	0.01
Idaho	941	0.06
New Hampshire	673	0.05
New Mexico	673	0.03
Kentucky	567	0.01
South Dakota	511	0.06
Mississippi	285	0.01
Delaware	208	0.02
Maine	172	0.01
Vermont	121	0.02
West Virginia	72	<0.01
District of Columbia	69	0.01
North Dakota	67	0.01
Montana	51	0.01
Wyoming	42	0.01

Place	Population	%
Rhode Island	3,380	0.32
Alaska	2,121	0.30
Minnesota	12,009	0.23
California	69,303	0.19
Iowa	5,744	0.19
Kansas	5,406	0.19
Hawaii	2,620	0.19
Washington	11,568	0.17
Arkansas	4,614	0.16
Oregon	5,792	0.15
Utah	3,189	0.12
Tennessee	7,276	0.11
Connecticut	3,964	0.11
Nevada	2,581	0.10
United States	**232,130**	**0.08**
Wisconsin	4,562	0.08
Georgia	6,638	0.07
North Carolina	6,562	0.07
Massachusetts	4,530	0.07
Texas	15,784	0.06
Illinois	7,102	0.06
Nebraska	1,130	0.06
Idaho	941	0.06
South Dakota	511	0.06
Virginia	3,980	0.05
Colorado	2,576	0.05
New Hampshire	673	0.05
Ohio	4,183	0.04
Arizona	2,388	0.04
Louisiana	1,902	0.04
Oklahoma	1,469	0.04
Florida	6,152	0.03
Michigan	3,380	0.03
Pennsylvania	3,280	0.03
Alabama	1,551	0.03
South Carolina	1,432	0.03
New Mexico	673	0.03
New York	4,471	0.02
Indiana	1,466	0.02
Maryland	1,420	0.02
Missouri	1,180	0.02
Delaware	208	0.02
Vermont	121	0.02
New Jersey	973	0.01
Kentucky	567	0.01
Mississippi	285	0.01
Maine	172	0.01
District of Columbia	69	0.01
North Dakota	67	0.01
Montana	51	0.01
Wyoming	42	0.01
West Virginia	72	<0.01

Please refer to the Explanation of Data in the front of the book for more detailed information.

Race

Asian: Laotian

Top 150 Places Sorted by Population

Based on all places, regardless of total population

Place	Population	%
Fresno, CA (city) Fresno County	6,733	1.36
Sacramento, CA (city) Sacramento County	6,675	1.43
San Diego, CA (city) San Diego County	6,058	0.46
Stockton, CA (city) San Joaquin County	3,581	1.23
Oakland, CA (city) Alameda County	3,071	0.79
Fort Worth, TX (city) Tarrant County	3,009	0.41
Portland, OR (city) Multnomah County	2,603	0.45
Des Moines, IA (city) Polk County	2,269	1.12
Nashville-Davidson, TN (metro govt) Davidson County	2,115	0.35
Seattle, WA (city) King County	2,085	0.34
Anchorage, AK (municipality) Anchorage Municipality	1,922	0.66
Richmond, CA (city) Contra Costa County	1,886	1.82
Lowell, MA (city) Middlesex County	1,765	1.66
Milwaukee, WI (city) Milwaukee County	1,749	0.29
Fort Smith, AR (city) Sebastian County	1,726	2.00
Brooklyn Park, MN (city) Hennepin County	1,597	2.11
Wichita, KS (city) Sedgwick County	1,594	0.42
San Jose, CA (city) Santa Clara County	1,590	0.17
Murfreesboro, TN (city) Rutherford County	1,581	1.45
Merced, CA (city) Merced County	1,482	1.88
Elgin, IL (city) Kane County	1,445	1.34
Woonsocket, RI (city) Providence County	1,430	3.47
Charlotte, NC (city) Mecklenburg County	1,426	0.19
Columbus, OH (city) Franklin County	1,412	0.18
Philadelphia, PA (city) Philadelphia County	1,350	0.09
Modesto, CA (city) Stanislaus County	1,257	0.62
Holland, MI (charter township) Ottawa County	1,250	3.51
St. Petersburg, FL (city) Pinellas County	1,235	0.50
Providence, RI (city) Providence County	1,213	0.68
Amarillo, TX (city) Potter County	1,195	0.63
Visalia, CA (city) Tulare County	1,194	0.96
Minneapolis, MN (city) Hennepin County	1,166	0.30
Urban Honolulu, HI (cdp) Honolulu County	1,152	0.34
Florin, CA (cdp) Sacramento County	1,128	2.37
Redding, CA (city) Shasta County	1,124	1.25
Dallas, TX (city) Dallas County	1,114	0.09
Rockford, IL (city) Winnebago County	1,027	0.67
Haltom City, TX (city) Tarrant County	976	2.30
Elk Grove, CA (city) Sacramento County	937	0.61
Long Beach, CA (city) Los Angeles County	893	0.19
Los Angeles, CA (city) Los Angeles County	871	0.02
Santa Rosa, CA (city) Sonoma County	849	0.51
Oklahoma City, OK (city) Oklahoma County	805	0.14
San Pablo, CA (city) Contra Costa County	798	2.74
Renton, WA (city) King County	798	0.88
West Valley City, UT (city) Salt Lake County	792	0.61
Grand Prairie, TX (city) Dallas County	779	0.44
Phoenix, AZ (city) Maricopa County	777	0.05
Anaheim, CA (city) Orange County	749	0.22
Rochester, MN (city) Olmsted County	735	0.69
Smyrna, TN (town) Rutherford County	707	1.77
Springdale, AR (city) Washington County	696	1.00
Garland, TX (city) Dallas County	691	0.30
Rochester, NY (city) Monroe County	668	0.32
New York, NY (city) Kings County	664	0.01
San Francisco, CA (city) San Francisco County	651	0.08
Olathe, KS (city) Johnson County	633	0.50
La Vergne, TN (city) Rutherford County	612	1.88
Kent, WA (city) King County	604	0.65
High Point, NC (city) Guilford County	579	0.55
Gresham, OR (city) Multnomah County	569	0.54
Storm Lake, IA (city) Buena Vista County	562	5.30
West Sacramento, CA (city) Yolo County	557	1.14
Escondido, CA (city) San Diego County	557	0.39
Worthington, MN (city) Nobles County	529	4.14
Chicago, IL (city) Cook County	529	0.02
Santa Ana, CA (city) Orange County	527	0.16
Sunrise Manor, NV (cdp) Clark County	520	0.27
Bryn Mawr-Skyway, WA (cdp) King County	515	3.29
Westminster, CO (city) Adams County	511	0.48
Albuquerque, NM (city) Bernalillo County	500	0.09
Lemon Hill, CA (cdp) Sacramento County	497	3.62
West Jordan, UT (city) Salt Lake County	496	0.48
Bridgeport, CT (city/town) Fairfield County	474	0.33
Las Vegas, NV (city) Clark County	473	0.08

Place	Population	%
Kansas City, KS (city) Wyandotte County	468	0.32
Moreno Valley, CA (city) Riverside County	454	0.23
Irving, TX (city) Dallas County	453	0.21
New Iberia, LA (city) Iberia Parish	443	1.45
Fairfield, CA (city) Solano County	437	0.41
Tacoma, WA (city) Pierce County	430	0.22
Porterville, CA (city) Tulare County	429	0.79
Shakopee, MN (city) Scott County	420	1.13
East Hill-Meridian, WA (cdp) King County	419	1.40
Sioux Falls, SD (city) Minnehaha County	419	0.27
Clovis, CA (city) Fresno County	417	0.44
Garden Grove, CA (city) Orange County	412	0.24
Union, NY (town) Broome County	406	0.72
St. Cloud, MN (city) Stearns County	405	0.62
South Elgin, IL (village) Kane County	402	1.83
Murrieta, CA (city) Riverside County	402	0.39
Euless, TX (city) Tarrant County	392	0.76
Jacksonville, FL (city) Duval County	391	0.05
Greensboro, NC (city) Guilford County	389	0.14
San Antonio, TX (city) Medina County	389	0.03
Akron, OH (city) Summit County	388	0.19
Van Buren, AR (city) Crawford County	385	1.69
North Highlands, CA (cdp) Sacramento County	382	0.89
St. Paul, MN (city) Ramsey County	379	0.13
Oaklawn-Sunview, KS (cdp) Sedgwick County	377	11.51
Eagan, MN (city) Dakota County	375	0.58
Antelope, CA (cdp) Sacramento County	372	0.81
Fort Wayne, IN (city) Allen County	369	0.15
Riverside, CA (city) Riverside County	369	0.12
Boise City, ID (city) Ada County	366	0.18
North Las Vegas, NV (city) Clark County	365	0.17
Pinellas Park, FL (city) Pinellas County	359	0.73
Thornton, CO (city) Adams County	358	0.30
Winfield, KS (city) Cowley County	356	2.89
Brooklyn Center, MN (city) Hennepin County	355	1.18
Houston, TX (city) Harris County	351	0.02
Madison, WI (city) Dane County	350	0.15
Ceres, CA (city) Stanislaus County	348	0.77
Fitchburg, MA (city) Worcester County	345	0.86
New Britain, CT (city/town) Hartford County	341	0.47
Burnsville, MN (city) Dakota County	340	0.56
East Hartford, CT (cdp/town) Hartford County	336	0.66
Bloomington, MN (city) Hennepin County	336	0.41
Everett, WA (city) Snohomish County	326	0.32
Tucson, AZ (city) Pima County	323	0.06
Temecula, CA (city) Riverside County	322	0.32
Green Bay, WI (city) Brown County	315	0.30
Vancouver, WA (city) Clark County	315	0.19
Suisun City, CA (city) Solano County	311	1.11
Aloha, OR (cdp) Washington County	307	0.62
Memphis, TN (city) Shelby County	299	0.05
Bakersfield, CA (city) Kern County	297	0.09
Fruitridge Pocket, CA (cdp) Sacramento County	291	5.02
St. Louis, MO (city) St. Louis city County	290	0.09
Enterprise, NV (cdp) Clark County	289	0.27
Buffalo, NY (city) Erie County	288	0.11
Spring Valley, NV (cdp) Clark County	287	0.16
St. Cloud, MN (city) Stearns County	284	0.54
Hillsboro, OR (city) Washington County	284	0.31
Johnson City, NY (village) Broome County	278	1.83
Banning, CA (city) Riverside County	276	0.93
Lawrence, KS (city) Douglas County	269	0.31
Sioux City, IA (city) Woodbury County	266	0.32
Montgomery, AL (city) Montgomery County	264	0.13
San Bernardino, CA (city) San Bernardino County	260	0.12
Raleigh, NC (city) Wake County	259	0.06
Paradise, NV (cdp) Clark County	257	0.12
Hercules, CA (city) Contra Costa County	255	1.06
San Marcos, CA (city) San Diego County	248	0.30
Pomona, CA (city) Los Angeles County	244	0.16
Pasco, WA (city) Franklin County	242	0.40
Lynn, MA (city) Essex County	242	0.27
Salina, KS (city) Saline County	239	0.50
Aurora, CO (city) Arapahoe County	239	0.07
Lealman, FL (cdp) Pinellas County	238	1.20

Race

Asian: Laotian

Top 150 Places Sorted by Percent of Total Population

Based on all places, regardless of total population

Place	Population	%
Oaklawn-Sunview, KS (cdp) Sedgwick County	377	11.51
Belleville, AR (city) Yell County	45	10.20
Mountain Lake, MN (city) Cottonwood County	206	9.79
Lake, MN (township) Roseau County	155	7.42
Warroad, MN (city) Roseau County	132	7.41
Mount Airy, GA (town) Habersham County	93	7.24
Delton, MN (township) Cottonwood County	8	6.50
Fields Landing, CA (cdp) Humboldt County	17	6.16
Andrea, MN (township) Wilkin County	4	6.15
Butterfield, MN (city) Watonwan County	36	6.14
Vandalia, MI (village) Cass County	18	5.98
Magnolia, MN (city) Rock County	13	5.86
Deer, MN (township) Roseau County	6	5.71
La Grande, WA (cdp) Pierce County	6	5.50
Storm Lake, IA (city) Buena Vista County	562	5.30
Raymond, WA (city) Pacific County	151	5.24
Lakeside, IA (city) Buena Vista County	31	5.20
Fruitridge Pocket, CA (cdp) Sacramento County	291	5.02
Worthington, MN (city) Nobles County	529	4.14
Gardner, FL (cdp) Hardee County	18	3.89
Teresita, OK (cdp) Cherokee County	6	3.77
Naponee, NE (village) Franklin County	4	3.77
Odin, MN (city) Watonwan County	4	3.77
Weed, CA (city) Siskiyou County	109	3.67
Hersey, MN (township) Nobles County	8	3.65
Lemon Hill, CA (cdp) Sacramento County	497	3.62
Holland, MI (charter township) Ottawa County	1,250	3.51
Woonsocket, RI (city) Providence County	1,430	3.47
Cornelia, GA (city) Habersham County	139	3.34
Bryn Mawr-Skyway, WA (cdp) King County	515	3.29
Midway, MN (township) Cottonwood County	7	3.20
New Milford, IL (village) Winnebago County	22	3.16
Montalvin Manor, CA (cdp) Contra Costa County	86	2.99
Tecumseh, NE (city) Johnson County	50	2.98
Pohlitz, MN (township) Roseau County	1	2.94
Winfield, KS (city) Cowley County	356	2.89
Bayview, CA (cdp) Contra Costa County	49	2.79
Carthage, SD (city) Miner County	4	2.78
Dakota City, NE (city) Dakota County	53	2.76
Algona, WA (city) King County	83	2.75
San Pablo, CA (city) Contra Costa County	798	2.74
Tara Hills, CA (cdp) Contra Costa County	140	2.73
Alto, GA (town) Habersham County	32	2.73
Cottonwood, CA (cdp) Shasta County	90	2.71
Baldwin, GA (city) Habersham County	89	2.71
Clemons, IA (city) Marshall County	4	2.70
Webster City, IA (city) Hamilton County	217	2.69
Lorain, MN (township) Nobles County	8	2.69
Alpha, MN (city) Jackson County	3	2.59
Unionville Center, OH (village) Union County	6	2.58
Danforth, MN (township) Pine County	2	2.56
Kibler, AR (city) Crawford County	24	2.50
Bayou La Batre, AL (city) Mobile County	62	2.42
Highwater, MN (township) Cottonwood County	4	2.41
Florin, CA (cdp) Sacramento County	1,128	2.37
Carl, GA (town) Barrow County	6	2.35
Jackson, MN (city) Jackson County	77	2.33
Haltom City, TX (city) Tarrant County	976	2.30
Westside, MN (township) Nobles County	5	2.29
Patterson Tract, CA (cdp) Tulare County	40	2.28
Jackson, NE (village) Dakota County	5	2.24
Fowlerville, NY (cdp) Livingston County	5	2.20
Rodeo, CA (cdp) Contra Costa County	189	2.18
Danielson, CT (borough) Windham County	87	2.15
Thor, IA (city) Humboldt County	4	2.15
Newmarket, NH (cdp) Rockingham County	113	2.13
Badger, MN (city) Roseau County	8	2.13
Brooklyn Park, MN (city) Hennepin County	1,597	2.11
South Oroville, CA (cdp) Butte County	119	2.07
Danville, AR (city) Yell County	49	2.03
Cade, LA (cdp) St. Martin Parish	35	2.03
Kamrar, IA (city) Hamilton County	4	2.01
Fort Smith, AR (city) Sebastian County	1,726	2.00
Newmarket, NH (town) Rockingham County	178	1.99
Leesburg, IN (town) Kosciusko County	11	1.98
Bloomington, ID (city) Bear Lake County	4	1.94
St. Charles, MN (city) Winona County	72	1.93
Terril, IA (city) Dickinson County	7	1.91
Mayfair, CA (cdp) Fresno County	87	1.90
Connell, WA (city) Franklin County	80	1.90
Skelly, TX (town) Carson County	9	1.90
Merced, CA (city) Merced County	1,482	1.88
La Vergne, TN (city) Rutherford County	612	1.88
Nichols, IA (city) Muscatine County	7	1.87
Bethel Heights, AR (city) Benton County	44	1.85
Central Pacolet, SC (town) Spartanburg County	4	1.85
South Elgin, IL (village) Kane County	402	1.83
Johnson City, NY (village) Broome County	278	1.83
Richmond, CA (city) Contra Costa County	1,886	1.82
West Park, CA (cdp) Fresno County	21	1.82
North Richmond, CA (cdp) Contra Costa County	67	1.80
Cassopolis, MI (village) Cass County	32	1.80
Smyrna, TN (town) Rutherford County	707	1.77
Sergeant Bluff, IA (city) Woodbury County	75	1.77
Glen Alpine, NC (town) Burke County	26	1.71
Van Buren, AR (city) Crawford County	385	1.69
St. Cloud, MN (city) Benton County	108	1.69
Lowell, MA (city) Middlesex County	1,765	1.66
Carver, MN (city) Carver County	61	1.64
Mount Pleasant, IA (city) Henry County	138	1.59
Hanover, VA (cdp) Hanover County	4	1.59
West Liberty, IA (city) Muscatine County	59	1.58
Penn, MI (township) Cass County	28	1.58
Elk, MN (township) Nobles County	4	1.58
Franklin, MN (city) Renville County	8	1.57
Royal, IA (city) Clay County	7	1.57
Clarks Grove, MN (city) Freeborn County	11	1.56
Shasta Lake, CA (city) Shasta County	157	1.54
Orland, CA (city) Glenn County	112	1.54
Minneota, MN (township) Jackson County	4	1.54
Zeeland, MI (charter township) Ottawa County	153	1.53
East Brooklyn, CT (cdp) Windham County	24	1.47
Tooleville, CA (cdp) Tulare County	5	1.47
Manzano Springs, NM (cdp) Torrance County	2	1.46
Murfreesboro, TN (city) Rutherford County	1,581	1.45
New Iberia, LA (city) Iberia Parish	443	1.45
Pacific, WA (city) King County	95	1.44
Burke, MN (township) Pipestone County	3	1.44
Seward, MN (township) Nobles County	3	1.44
Sacramento, CA (city) Sacramento County	6,675	1.43
Franklin, CA (cdp) Merced County	88	1.43
Holy Cross, MN (township) Clay County	2	1.43
Grover, NC (town) Cleveland County	10	1.41
Casey, IA (city) Guthrie County	6	1.41
East Hill-Meridian, WA (cdp) King County	419	1.40
Willows, CA (city) Glenn County	86	1.39
Rollingwood, CA (cdp) Contra Costa County	41	1.38
Wallace, NE (village) Lincoln County	5	1.37
Fresno, CA (city) Fresno County	6,733	1.36
De Pue, IL (village) Bureau County	25	1.36
Drexel, NC (town) Burke County	25	1.35
Elgin, IL (city) Kane County	1,445	1.34
Oxford, WI (village) Marquette County	8	1.32
South Sioux City, NE (city) Dakota County	175	1.31
Parkway, CA (cdp) Sacramento County	190	1.30
Faxon, MN (township) Sibley County	9	1.28
Chester, AR (town) Crawford County	2	1.26
Redding, CA (city) Shasta County	1,124	1.25
Mount Holly, NC (city) Gaston County	170	1.24
Moranville, MN (township) Roseau County	11	1.24
Stockton, CA (city) San Joaquin County	3,581	1.23
Bayfield, WI (city) Bayfield County	6	1.23
Spruce, MN (township) Roseau County	7	1.22
Diablo Grande, CA (cdp) Stanislaus County	10	1.21
Lealman, FL (cdp) Pinellas County	238	1.20
Anderson, CA (city) Shasta County	119	1.20
Maywood Park, OR (city) Multnomah County	9	1.20
Hayward, MN (city) Freeborn County	3	1.20
Brooklyn Center, MN (city) Hennepin County	355	1.18
Dewald, MN (township) Nobles County	3	1.18

Please refer to the Explanation of Data in the front of the book for more detailed information.

Race

Asian: Laotian

Top 150 Places Sorted by Percent of Total Population

Based on places with total population of 7,500 or more

Place	Population	%
Storm Lake, IA (city) Buena Vista County	562	5.30
Worthington, MN (city) Nobles County	529	4.14
Lemon Hill, CA (cdp) Sacramento County	497	3.62
Holland, MI (charter township) Ottawa County	1,250	3.51
Woonsocket, RI (city) Providence County	1,430	3.47
Bryn Mawr-Skyway, WA (cdp) King County	515	3.29
Winfield, KS (city) Cowley County	356	2.89
San Pablo, CA (city) Contra Costa County	798	2.74
Webster City, IA (city) Hamilton County	217	2.69
Florin, CA (cdp) Sacramento County	1,128	2.37
Haltom City, TX (city) Tarrant County	976	2.30
Rodeo, CA (cdp) Contra Costa County	189	2.18
Brooklyn Park, MN (city) Hennepin County	1,597	2.11
Fort Smith, AR (city) Sebastian County	1,726	2.00
Newmarket, NH (town) Rockingham County	178	1.99
Merced, CA (city) Merced County	1,482	1.88
La Vergne, TN (city) Rutherford County	612	1.88
South Elgin, IL (village) Kane County	402	1.83
Johnson City, NY (village) Broome County	278	1.83
Richmond, CA (city) Contra Costa County	1,886	1.82
Smyrna, TN (town) Rutherford County	707	1.77
Van Buren, AR (city) Crawford County	385	1.69
Lowell, MA (city) Middlesex County	1,765	1.66
Mount Pleasant, IA (city) Henry County	138	1.59
Shasta Lake, CA (city) Shasta County	157	1.54
Zeeland, MI (charter township) Ottawa County	153	1.53
Murfreesboro, TN (city) Rutherford County	1,581	1.45
New Iberia, LA (city) Iberia Parish	443	1.45
Sacramento, CA (city) Sacramento County	6,675	1.43
East Hill-Meridian, WA (cdp) King County	419	1.40
Fresno, CA (city) Fresno County	6,733	1.36
Elgin, IL (city) Kane County	1,445	1.34
South Sioux City, NE (city) Dakota County	175	1.31
Parkway, CA (cdp) Sacramento County	190	1.30
Redding, CA (city) Shasta County	1,124	1.25
Mount Holly, NC (city) Gaston County	170	1.24
Stockton, CA (city) San Joaquin County	3,581	1.23
Lealman, FL (cdp) Pinellas County	238	1.20
Anderson, CA (city) Shasta County	119	1.20
Brooklyn Center, MN (city) Hennepin County	355	1.18
West Sacramento, CA (city) Yolo County	557	1.14
Shakopee, MN (city) Scott County	420	1.13
Des Moines, IA (city) Polk County	2,269	1.12
Suisun City, CA (city) Solano County	311	1.11
Kings Mountain, NC (city) Cleveland County	111	1.08
Tukwila, WA (city) King County	205	1.07
Hercules, CA (city) Contra Costa County	255	1.06
Killingly, CT (town) Windham County	183	1.05
Springdale, AR (city) Washington County	696	1.00
Gardner, KS (city) Johnson County	189	0.99
Visalia, CA (city) Tulare County	1,194	0.96
Watauga, TX (city) Tarrant County	220	0.94
Banning, CA (city) Riverside County	276	0.93
Vineyard, CA (cdp) Sacramento County	232	0.93
Oroville, CA (city) Butte County	145	0.93
El Sobrante, CA (cdp) Contra Costa County	117	0.92
Orrville, OH (city) Wayne County	76	0.91
Pinole, CA (city) Contra Costa County	166	0.90
North Highlands, CA (cdp) Sacramento County	382	0.89
Renton, WA (city) King County	798	0.88
Fitchburg, MA (city) Worcester County	345	0.86
Park, MI (township) Ottawa County	150	0.84
Antelope, CA (cdp) Sacramento County	372	0.81
Oakland, CA (city) Alameda County	3,071	0.79
Porterville, CA (city) Tulare County	429	0.79
Savage, MN (city) Scott County	213	0.79
Southbridge Town, MA (city) Worcester County	130	0.78
Troutdale, OR (city) Multnomah County	124	0.78
Ceres, CA (city) Stanislaus County	348	0.77
Oroville East, CA (cdp) Butte County	64	0.77
Euless, TX (city) Tarrant County	392	0.76
Springfield, VA (cdp) Fairfax County	228	0.75
Rogers, MN (city) Hennepin County	64	0.74
Pinellas Park, FL (city) Pinellas County	359	0.73
Union, NY (town) Broome County	406	0.72

Place	Population	%
Pleasant Hill, IA (city) Polk County	63	0.72
St. Michael, MN (city) Wright County	114	0.70
Rochester, MN (city) Olmsted County	735	0.69
Providence, RI (city) Providence County	1,213	0.68
Sterling, VA (cdp) Loudoun County	188	0.68
SeaTac, WA (city) King County	183	0.68
Austin, MN (city) Mower County	169	0.68
Rockford, IL (city) Winnebago County	1,027	0.67
Fairview, OR (city) Multnomah County	60	0.67
Anchorage, AK (municipality) Anchorage Municipality	1,922	0.66
East Hartford, CT (cdp/town) Hartford County	336	0.66
Kingsgate, WA (cdp) King County	86	0.66
Kent, WA (city) King County	604	0.65
Fort Oglethorpe, GA (city) Catoosa County	60	0.65
Eureka, CA (city) Humboldt County	174	0.64
Kapolei, HI (cdp) Honolulu County	97	0.64
Damascus, OR (city) Clackamas County	67	0.64
Amarillo, TX (city) Potter County	1,195	0.63
Modesto, CA (city) Stanislaus County	1,257	0.62
St. Cloud, MN (city) Stearns County	405	0.62
Aloha, OR (cdp) Washington County	307	0.62
Elk Grove, CA (city) Sacramento County	937	0.61
West Valley City, UT (city) Salt Lake County	792	0.61
New Hope, MN (city) Hennepin County	122	0.60
Des Moines, WA (city) King County	176	0.59
Eagan, MN (city) Dakota County	375	0.58
Richfield, MN (city) Hennepin County	203	0.58
Happy Valley, OR (city) Clackamas County	81	0.58
Johnston, RI (town) Providence County	165	0.57
Dumas, TX (city) Moore County	84	0.57
Burnsville, MN (city) Dakota County	340	0.56
White Center, WA (cdp) King County	76	0.56
High Point, NC (city) Guilford County	579	0.55
Henrietta, NY (town) Monroe County	235	0.55
French Valley, CA (cdp) Riverside County	127	0.55
Collingdale, PA (borough) Delaware County	48	0.55
Gresham, OR (city) Multnomah County	569	0.54
St. Cloud, MN (city) Stearns County	284	0.54
Fairwood, WA (cdp) King County	103	0.54
Linda, CA (cdp) Yuba County	96	0.54
North Aurora, IL (village) Kane County	90	0.54
Blacklick Estates, OH (cdp) Franklin County	47	0.54
Crystal, MN (city) Hennepin County	118	0.53
Lathrop, CA (city) San Joaquin County	96	0.53
Chaska, MN (city) Carver County	124	0.52
Riverdale, GA (city) Clayton County	78	0.52
Santa Rosa, CA (city) Sonoma County	849	0.51
Garden Acres, CA (cdp) San Joaquin County	54	0.51
St. Petersburg, FL (city) Pinellas County	1,235	0.50
Olathe, KS (city) Johnson County	633	0.50
Salina, KS (city) Saline County	239	0.50
Kearns, UT (cdp) Salt Lake County	178	0.50
Holland, MI (city) Ottawa County	131	0.50
Lake Park, FL (town) Palm Beach County	41	0.50
Marumsco, VA (cdp) Prince William County	173	0.49
Rio Linda, CA (cdp) Sacramento County	74	0.49
Westminster, CO (city) Adams County	511	0.48
West Jordan, UT (city) Salt Lake County	496	0.48
Grand Island, NE (city) Hall County	232	0.48
Wausau, WI (city) Marathon County	188	0.48
New Britain, CT (city/town) Hartford County	341	0.47
Holland, MI (city) Ottawa County	156	0.47
Foothill Farms, CA (cdp) Sacramento County	155	0.47
Graham, NC (city) Alamance County	67	0.47
San Diego, CA (city) San Diego County	6,058	0.46
Liberal, KS (city) Seward County	95	0.46
Orchards, WA (cdp) Clark County	89	0.46
Portland, OR (city) Multnomah County	2,603	0.45
Binghamton, NY (city) Broome County	211	0.45
Garden City, KS (city) Finney County	119	0.45
Gardner, MA (city) Worcester County	91	0.45
Otsego, MN (city) Wright County	61	0.45
Grand Prairie, TX (city) Dallas County	779	0.44
Clovis, CA (city) Fresno County	417	0.44
Rockingham, NC (city) Richmond County	42	0.44

Please refer to the Explanation of Data in the front of the book for more detailed information.

Race

Asian: Malaysian

U.S. and 50 States Sorted by Population and Percent of Total Population

Place	Population	%
United States	**26,179**	**0.01**
California	5,595	0.02
New York	3,908	0.02
Texas	2,048	0.01
Illinois	939	0.01
Virginia	857	0.01
New Jersey	833	0.01
Washington	798	0.01
Florida	769	<0.01
Pennsylvania	768	0.01
Georgia	679	0.01
Michigan	629	0.01
Massachusetts	593	0.01
Ohio	528	<0.01
Maryland	482	0.01
Indiana	471	0.01
Minnesota	431	0.01
Tennessee	390	0.01
Colorado	378	0.01
Arizona	365	0.01
North Carolina	363	<0.01
Missouri	344	0.01
Wisconsin	338	0.01
Connecticut	324	0.01
Kansas	321	0.01
Iowa	304	0.01
Oklahoma	299	0.01
Hawaii	297	0.02
Oregon	296	0.01
Nevada	237	0.01
Alabama	151	<0.01
Nebraska	132	0.01
Louisiana	129	<0.01
Utah	128	<0.01
South Carolina	122	<0.01
Kentucky	118	<0.01
Arkansas	111	<0.01
New Hampshire	74	0.01
Rhode Island	72	0.01
District of Columbia	66	0.01
Mississippi	65	<0.01
West Virginia	63	<0.01
New Mexico	61	<0.01
Idaho	55	<0.01
Delaware	48	0.01
Alaska	46	0.01
Maine	33	<0.01
Montana	31	<0.01
Vermont	28	<0.01
North Dakota	22	<0.01
Wyoming	22	<0.01
South Dakota	18	<0.01

Place	Population	%
California	5,595	0.02
New York	3,908	0.02
Hawaii	297	0.02
United States	**26,179**	**0.01**
Texas	2,048	0.01
Illinois	939	0.01
Virginia	857	0.01
New Jersey	833	0.01
Washington	798	0.01
Pennsylvania	768	0.01
Georgia	679	0.01
Michigan	629	0.01
Massachusetts	593	0.01
Maryland	482	0.01
Indiana	471	0.01
Minnesota	431	0.01
Tennessee	390	0.01
Colorado	378	0.01
Arizona	365	0.01
Missouri	344	0.01
Wisconsin	338	0.01
Connecticut	324	0.01
Kansas	321	0.01
Iowa	304	0.01
Oklahoma	299	0.01
Oregon	296	0.01
Nevada	237	0.01
Nebraska	132	0.01
New Hampshire	74	0.01
Rhode Island	72	0.01
District of Columbia	66	0.01
Delaware	48	0.01
Alaska	46	0.01
Florida	769	<0.01
Ohio	528	<0.01
North Carolina	363	<0.01
Alabama	151	<0.01
Louisiana	129	<0.01
Utah	128	<0.01
South Carolina	122	<0.01
Kentucky	118	<0.01
Arkansas	111	<0.01
Mississippi	65	<0.01
West Virginia	63	<0.01
New Mexico	61	<0.01
Idaho	55	<0.01
Maine	33	<0.01
Montana	31	<0.01
Vermont	28	<0.01
North Dakota	22	<0.01
Wyoming	22	<0.01
South Dakota	18	<0.01

Please refer to the Explanation of Data in the front of the book for more detailed information.

Race

Asian: Malaysian

Top 150 Places Sorted by Population

Based on all places, regardless of total population

Place	Population	%
New York, NY (city) Kings County	3,220	0.04
Queens, NY (borough) Queens County	1,620	0.07
Manhattan, NY (borough) New York County	766	0.05
Brooklyn, NY (borough) Kings County	708	0.03
San Francisco, CA (city) San Francisco County	358	0.04
Los Angeles, CA (city) Los Angeles County	342	0.01
San Diego, CA (city) San Diego County	315	0.02
San Jose, CA (city) Santa Clara County	304	0.03
Houston, TX (city) Harris County	260	0.01
Nashville-Davidson, TN (metro govt) Davidson County	195	0.03
Seattle, WA (city) King County	178	0.03
Chicago, IL (city) Cook County	165	0.01
Madison, WI (city) Dane County	162	0.07
Fremont, CA (city) Alameda County	158	0.07
Austin, TX (city) Travis County	149	0.02
State College, PA (borough) Centre County	145	0.34
West Lafayette, IN (city) Tippecanoe County	135	0.46
Philadelphia, PA (city) Philadelphia County	130	0.01
Boston, MA (city) Suffolk County	124	0.02
Minneapolis, MN (city) Hennepin County	123	0.03
Columbus, OH (city) Franklin County	121	0.02
Ames, IA (city) Story County	114	0.19
Wichita, KS (city) Sedgwick County	102	0.03
Phoenix, AZ (city) Maricopa County	100	0.01
Urban Honolulu, HI (cdp) Honolulu County	98	0.03
Sunnyvale, CA (city) Santa Clara County	96	0.07
Staten Island, NY (borough) Richmond County	96	0.02
Lincoln, NE (city) Lancaster County	95	0.04
Oklahoma City, OK (city) Oklahoma County	89	0.02
Irvine, CA (city) Orange County	84	0.04
Portland, OR (city) Multnomah County	83	0.01
Plano, TX (city) Collin County	82	0.03
West Haven, CT (city/town) New Haven County	81	0.15
Milpitas, CA (city) Santa Clara County	81	0.12
Ann Arbor, MI (city) Washtenaw County	81	0.07
Dallas, TX (city) Dallas County	81	0.01
Arcadia, CA (city) Los Angeles County	80	0.14
Arlington, VA (cdp) Arlington County	78	0.04
Charlotte, NC (city) Mecklenburg County	78	0.01
Sugar Land, TX (city) Fort Bend County	72	0.09
Santa Clara, CA (city) Santa Clara County	71	0.06
Kansas City, MO (city) Jackson County	71	0.02
Henrietta, NY (town) Monroe County	70	0.16
Pittsburgh, PA (city) Allegheny County	69	0.02
San Antonio, TX (city) Medina County	67	0.01
Washington, DC (city) District of Columbia	66	0.01
East Lansing, MI (city) Ingham County	65	0.14
East Lansing, MI (city) Ingham County	65	0.13
Fort Worth, TX (city) Tarrant County	64	0.01
Cambridge, MA (city) Middlesex County	63	0.06
The Woodlands, TX (cdp) Montgomery County	60	0.06
Long Beach, CA (city) Los Angeles County	60	0.01
Bloomington, IN (city) Monroe County	59	0.07
Rowland Heights, CA (cdp) Los Angeles County	57	0.12
Hoboken, NJ (city) Hudson County	57	0.11
Alhambra, CA (city) Los Angeles County	57	0.07
Tysons Corner, VA (cdp) Fairfax County	56	0.29
Arlington, TX (city) Tarrant County	55	0.02
Oakland, CA (city) Alameda County	55	0.01
Anaheim, CA (city) Orange County	53	0.02
Carbondale, IL (city) Jackson County	52	0.20
Bellevue, WA (city) King County	52	0.04
Chandler, AZ (city) Maricopa County	51	0.02
Overland Park, KS (city) Johnson County	50	0.03
Monterey Park, CA (city) Los Angeles County	49	0.08
Iowa City, IA (city) Johnson County	48	0.07
Des Moines, IA (city) Polk County	48	0.02
Las Vegas, NV (city) Clark County	48	0.01
Daly City, CA (city) San Mateo County	47	0.05
Amherst, NY (town) Erie County	47	0.04
Berkeley, CA (city) Alameda County	47	0.04
Virginia Beach, VA (ind. city) Virginia Beach independent city	47	0.01
Champaign, IL (city) Champaign County	46	0.06
Jacksonville, FL (city) Duval County	46	0.01
Milwaukee, WI (city) Milwaukee County	46	0.01
Tulsa, OK (city) Tulsa County	46	0.01
Stillwater, OK (city) Payne County	45	0.10
Richmond, CA (city) Contra Costa County	45	0.04
Sacramento, CA (city) Sacramento County	45	0.01
San Gabriel, CA (city) Los Angeles County	44	0.11
Indianapolis, IN (city) Marion County	44	0.01
Raleigh, NC (city) Wake County	44	0.01
Kalamazoo, MI (city) Kalamazoo County	43	0.06
Hayward, CA (city) Alameda County	43	0.03
Jersey City, NJ (city) Hudson County	43	0.02
Atlanta, GA (city) Fulton County	43	0.01
Fresno, CA (city) Fresno County	43	0.01
Merrifield, VA (cdp) Fairfax County	42	0.28
Longmont, CO (city) Boulder County	42	0.05
El Monte, CA (city) Los Angeles County	42	0.04
Denver, CO (city) Denver County	42	0.01
Pomona, CA (city) Los Angeles County	41	0.03
Fort Wayne, IN (city) Allen County	41	0.02
West Covina, CA (city) Los Angeles County	40	0.04
Fort Collins, CO (city) Larimer County	40	0.03
Hacienda Heights, CA (cdp) Los Angeles County	39	0.07
Irving, TX (city) Dallas County	39	0.02
Cupertino, CA (city) Santa Clara County	38	0.07
Folsom, CA (city) Sacramento County	38	0.05
Spring Valley, NV (cdp) Clark County	38	0.02
Walnut, CA (city) Los Angeles County	37	0.13
Skokie, IL (village) Cook County	37	0.06
College Station, TX (city) Brazos County	37	0.04
Fullerton, CA (city) Orange County	37	0.03
Vallejo, CA (city) Solano County	37	0.03
Herndon, VA (town) Fairfax County	36	0.15
Orlando, FL (city) Orange County	36	0.02
Urbana, IL (city) Champaign County	35	0.08
Richardson, TX (city) Dallas County	35	0.04
North Hempstead, NY (town) Nassau County	35	0.02
Tucson, AZ (city) Pima County	35	0.01
Chino Hills, CA (city) San Bernardino County	34	0.05
St. Cloud, MN (city) Stearns County	34	0.05
Johns Creek, GA (city) Fulton County	34	0.04
Pasadena, CA (city) Los Angeles County	34	0.02
Fayetteville, AR (city) Washington County	33	0.04
Frisco, TX (city) Collin County	33	0.03
Huntington Beach, CA (city) Orange County	33	0.02
Torrance, CA (city) Los Angeles County	33	0.02
Missouri City, TX (city) Fort Bend County	32	0.05
Chula Vista, CA (city) San Diego County	32	0.01
Golden, CO (city) Jefferson County	31	0.16
Fort Lee, NJ (borough) Bergen County	31	0.09
Diamond Bar, CA (city) Los Angeles County	31	0.06
Rancho Cucamonga, CA (city) San Bernardino County	31	0.02
Salt Lake City, UT (city) Salt Lake County	31	0.02
Paradise, NV (cdp) Clark County	31	0.01
Temple City, CA (city) Los Angeles County	30	0.08
Chino, CA (city) San Bernardino County	30	0.04
Lawrence, KS (city) Douglas County	30	0.03
Olathe, KS (city) Johnson County	30	0.02
Oyster Bay, NY (town) Nassau County	30	0.01
Bronx, NY (borough) Bronx County	30	<0.01
McLean, VA (cdp) Fairfax County	29	0.06
Castro Valley, CA (cdp) Alameda County	29	0.05
Palo Alto, CA (city) Santa Clara County	29	0.05
San Ramon, CA (city) Contra Costa County	29	0.04
Hempstead, NY (town) Nassau County	29	<0.01
Alameda, CA (city) Alameda County	28	0.04
Columbia, MO (city) Boone County	28	0.03
Edison, NJ (township) Middlesex County	28	0.03
Edmond, OK (city) Oklahoma County	28	0.03
Rancho Cordova, CA (city) Sacramento County	27	0.04
Santa Clarita, CA (city) Los Angeles County	27	0.02
Baltimore, MD (city) Baltimore city County	27	<0.01
Elk Grove, CA (city) Sacramento County	26	0.02
Thousand Oaks, CA (city) Ventura County	26	0.02
Lexington-Fayette, KY (cons. govt) Fayette County	26	0.01
St. Louis, MO (city) St. Louis city County	26	0.01
Duluth, GA (city) Gwinnett County	25	0.09

Race

Asian: Malaysian

Top 150 Places Sorted by Percent of Total Population

Based on all places, regardless of total population

Place	Population	%
Woodston, KS (city) Rooks County	4	2.94
Millbourne, PA (borough) Delaware County	21	1.81
Kelly, WI (town) Bayfield County	5	1.08
Congerville, IL (village) Woodford County	5	1.05
Forest Home, NY (cdp) Tompkins County	5	0.87
Graball, TN (cdp) Sumner County	2	0.85
Elmwood Park, WI (village) Racine County	4	0.80
Mahinahina, HI (cdp) Maui County	6	0.68
Kragnes, MN (township) Clay County	2	0.68
Holyrood, KS (city) Ellsworth County	3	0.67
Sunny Slopes, CA (cdp) Mono County	1	0.55
West Sunbury, PA (borough) Butler County	1	0.52
West Lafayette, IN (city) Tippecanoe County	135	0.46
Cave Springs, AR (city) Benton County	8	0.46
South Prairie, WA (town) Pierce County	2	0.46
Kachemak, AK (city) Kenai Peninsula Borough	2	0.42
Arnold Line, MS (cdp) Lamar County	7	0.41
Melville, RI (cdp) Newport County	5	0.38
Plainfield, WI (town) Waushara County	2	0.36
Dallas, WI (town) Barron County	2	0.35
Grand View-on-Hudson, NY (village) Rockland County	1	0.35
State College, PA (borough) Centre County	145	0.34
Portage, NY (town) Livingston County	3	0.34
Kingston, NJ (cdp) Middlesex County	5	0.33
Young Harris, GA (city) Towns County	3	0.33
Columbus Junction, IA (city) Louisa County	6	0.32
Harmony, ME (town) Somerset County	3	0.32
Blairsville, GA (city) Union County	2	0.31
Stockton, KS (city) Rooks County	4	0.30
Elim, AK (city) Nome Census Area	1	0.30
Kampsville, IL (village) Calhoun County	1	0.30
Tysons Corner, VA (cdp) Fairfax County	56	0.29
Boronda, CA (cdp) Monterey County	5	0.29
Inman Mills, SC (cdp) Spartanburg County	3	0.29
Merrifield, VA (cdp) Fairfax County	42	0.28
Milesburg, PA (borough) Centre County	3	0.27
Lake Sherwood, WI (cdp) Adams County	1	0.27
Maunaloa, HI (cdp) Maui County	1	0.27
University at Buffalo, NY (cdp) Erie County	15	0.25
Oronoko, MI (charter township) Berrien County	21	0.23
Poquonock Bridge, CT (cdp) New London County	4	0.23
Kodiak Station, AK (cdp) Kodiak Island Borough	3	0.23
Woodway, WA (city) Snohomish County	3	0.23
Belleville, AR (city) Yell County	1	0.23
Dunn Loring, VA (cdp) Fairfax County	19	0.22
Jordan, PA (township) Clearfield County	1	0.22
Harmar, PA (township) Allegheny County	6	0.21
Ocean View, DE (town) Sussex County	4	0.21
Fern Forest, HI (cdp) Hawaii County	2	0.21
Carbondale, IL (city) Jackson County	52	0.20
Brocton, NY (village) Chautauqua County	3	0.20
Inverness, CO (cdp) Arapahoe County	3	0.20
Versailles, PA (borough) Allegheny County	3	0.20
Ames, IA (city) Story County	114	0.19
Providence, KY (city) Webster County	6	0.19
Grayson, GA (city) Gwinnett County	5	0.19
Troy, NH (town) Cheshire County	4	0.19
Kaanapali, HI (cdp) Maui County	2	0.19
Drakes Branch, VA (town) Charlotte County	1	0.19
San Marino, CA (city) Los Angeles County	24	0.18
St. Cloud, MN (city) Sherburne County	12	0.18
Berrien, MI (township) Berrien County	9	0.18
San Miguel, CA (cdp) Contra Costa County	6	0.18
Camino Tassajara, CA (cdp) Contra Costa County	4	0.18
Brandon, VT (cdp) Rutland County	3	0.18
Colrain, MA (town) Franklin County	3	0.18
Galien, MI (village) Berrien County	1	0.18
Matawan, NJ (borough) Monmouth County	15	0.17
University of California Davis, CA (cdp) Yolo County	10	0.17
Windy Hills, KY (city) Jefferson County	4	0.17
Adamstown, PA (borough) Lancaster County	3	0.17
Adamstown, PA (borough) Lancaster County	3	0.17
Washington Mills, NY (cdp) Oneida County	2	0.17
Bonanza, AR (city) Sebastian County	1	0.17
Henrietta, NY (town) Monroe County	70	0.16
Golden, CO (city) Jefferson County	31	0.16
Purdue University, IN (cdp) Tippecanoe County	19	0.16
East Pasadena, CA (cdp) Los Angeles County	10	0.16
West Loch Estate, HI (cdp) Honolulu County	9	0.16
Loudoun Valley Estates, VA (cdp) Loudoun County	6	0.16
Northfield, OH (village) Summit County	6	0.16
Crossville, AL (town) DeKalb County	3	0.16
Del Rio, CA (cdp) Stanislaus County	2	0.16
Spencerville, NM (cdp) San Juan County	2	0.16
Breesport, NY (cdp) Chemung County	1	0.16
West Haven, CT (city/town) New Haven County	81	0.15
Herndon, VA (town) Fairfax County	36	0.15
East Richmond Heights, CA (cdp) Contra Costa County	5	0.15
New Berlin, NY (town) Chenango County	4	0.15
Black Point-Green Point, CA (cdp) Marin County	2	0.15
Brown City, MI (city) Sanilac County	2	0.15
Brown City, MI (city) Sanilac County	2	0.15
Kenduskeag, ME (town) Penobscot County	2	0.15
Chevy Chase Section Five, MD (village) Montgomery County	1	0.15
Middleburg, VA (town) Loudoun County	1	0.15
Parkway Village, KY (city) Jefferson County	1	0.15
Riverview, SC (cdp) York County	1	0.15
Wainscott, NY (cdp) Suffolk County	1	0.15
Arcadia, CA (city) Los Angeles County	80	0.14
East Lansing, MI (city) Ingham County	65	0.14
La Selva Beach, CA (cdp) Santa Cruz County	4	0.14
Bernardston, MA (town) Franklin County	3	0.14
Oakhurst, OK (cdp) Tulsa County	3	0.14
Baldwin, FL (town) Duval County	2	0.14
Bremen, OH (village) Fairfield County	2	0.14
Hudson, MI (township) Charlevoix County	1	0.14
Kilbuck, PA (township) Allegheny County	1	0.14
Loma Linda, MO (town) Newton County	1	0.14
East Lansing, MI (city) Ingham County	65	0.13
Walnut, CA (city) Los Angeles County	37	0.13
Northfield, IL (village) Cook County	7	0.13
Bryn Mawr, PA (cdp) Montgomery County	5	0.13
Berwyn Heights, MD (town) Prince George's County	4	0.13
North Barrington, IL (village) Lake County	4	0.13
Piney Point Village, TX (city) Harris County	4	0.13
Shadow Lake, WA (cdp) King County	3	0.13
Chadwicks, NY (cdp) Oneida County	2	0.13
Vienna, WI (town) Dane County	2	0.13
Westwood, KS (city) Johnson County	2	0.13
Felch, MI (township) Dickinson County	1	0.13
Moe, MN (township) Douglas County	1	0.13
Milpitas, CA (city) Santa Clara County	81	0.12
Rowland Heights, CA (cdp) Los Angeles County	57	0.12
Lake Barcroft, VA (cdp) Fairfax County	11	0.12
Layhill, MD (cdp) Montgomery County	6	0.12
Hokendauqua, PA (cdp) Lehigh County	4	0.12
Moorefield, WV (town) Hardy County	3	0.12
Biggs, CA (city) Butte County	2	0.12
Montgomery, WV (city) Fayette County	2	0.12
Wheeler AFB, HI (cdp) Honolulu County	2	0.12
Afton, NY (village) Chenango County	1	0.12
Eaton, WI (town) Manitowoc County	1	0.12
Triadelphia, WV (town) Ohio County	1	0.12
West Wood, UT (cdp) Carbon County	1	0.12
Hoboken, NJ (city) Hudson County	57	0.11
San Gabriel, CA (city) Los Angeles County	44	0.11
Cloverly, MD (cdp) Montgomery County	16	0.11
Castle Pines, CO (cdp) Douglas County	4	0.11
Kahaluu-Keauhou, HI (cdp) Hawaii County	4	0.11
North El Monte, CA (cdp) Los Angeles County	4	0.11
South Toms River, NJ (borough) Ocean County	4	0.11
Three Oaks, FL (cdp) Lee County	4	0.11
University Center, VA (cdp) Loudoun County	4	0.11
Brownstown, PA (cdp) Lancaster County	3	0.11
Kemah, TX (city) Galveston County	2	0.11
Reinholds, PA (cdp) Lancaster County	2	0.11
Star City, WV (town) Monongalia County	2	0.11
Berlin, WI (town) Marathon County	1	0.11
Cummington, MA (town) Hampshire County	1	0.11
Russell Gardens, NY (village) Nassau County	1	0.11

Please refer to the Explanation of Data in the front of the book for more detailed information.

Race

Asian: Malaysian

Top 150 Places Sorted by Percent of Total Population

Based on places with total population of 7,500 or more

Place	Population	%
West Lafayette, IN (city) Tippecanoe County	135	0.46
State College, PA (borough) Centre County	145	0.34
Tysons Corner, VA (cdp) Fairfax County	56	0.29
Merrifield, VA (cdp) Fairfax County	42	0.28
Oronoko, MI (charter township) Berrien County	21	0.23
Dunn Loring, VA (cdp) Fairfax County	19	0.22
Carbondale, IL (city) Jackson County	52	0.20
Ames, IA (city) Story County	114	0.19
San Marino, CA (city) Los Angeles County	24	0.18
Matawan, NJ (borough) Monmouth County	15	0.17
Henrietta, NY (town) Monroe County	70	0.16
Golden, CO (city) Jefferson County	31	0.16
Purdue University, IN (cdp) Tippecanoe County	19	0.16
West Haven, CT (city/town) New Haven County	81	0.15
Herndon, VA (town) Fairfax County	36	0.15
Arcadia, CA (city) Los Angeles County	80	0.14
East Lansing, MI (city) Ingham County	65	0.14
East Lansing, MI (city) Ingham County	65	0.13
Walnut, CA (city) Los Angeles County	37	0.13
Milpitas, CA (city) Santa Clara County	81	0.12
Rowland Heights, CA (cdp) Los Angeles County	57	0.12
Lake Barcroft, VA (cdp) Fairfax County	11	0.12
Hoboken, NJ (city) Hudson County	57	0.11
San Gabriel, CA (city) Los Angeles County	44	0.11
Cloverly, MD (cdp) Montgomery County	16	0.11
Stillwater, OK (city) Payne County	45	0.10
Avenel, NJ (cdp) Middlesex County	17	0.10
Avocado Heights, CA (cdp) Los Angeles County	16	0.10
Stanford, CA (cdp) Santa Clara County	14	0.10
Mayfield, KY (city) Graves County	10	0.10
Burtonsville, MD (cdp) Montgomery County	8	0.10
Commerce, TX (city) Hunt County	8	0.10
O'Hara, PA (township) Allegheny County	8	0.10
Sugar Land, TX (city) Fort Bend County	72	0.09
Fort Lee, NJ (borough) Bergen County	31	0.09
Duluth, GA (city) Gwinnett County	25	0.09
Loma Linda, CA (city) San Bernardino County	20	0.09
Oshtemo, MI (charter township) Kalamazoo County	19	0.09
Princeton Meadows, NJ (cdp) Middlesex County	13	0.09
Shorewood, WI (village) Milwaukee County	12	0.09
Sitka, AK (borough) Sitka City and Borough	8	0.09
Monterey Park, CA (city) Los Angeles County	49	0.08
Urbana, IL (city) Champaign County	35	0.08
Temple City, CA (city) Los Angeles County	30	0.08
Hercules, CA (city) Contra Costa County	19	0.08
Duarte, CA (city) Los Angeles County	16	0.08
Cinco Ranch, TX (cdp) Fort Bend County	15	0.08
Rolla, MO (city) Phelps County	15	0.08
Albany, CA (city) Alameda County	14	0.08
Princeton, NJ (borough) Mercer County	10	0.08
Florham Park, NJ (borough) Morris County	9	0.08
Des Peres, MO (city) St. Louis County	7	0.08
Pawling, NY (town) Dutchess County	7	0.08
Rincon, GA (town) Effingham County	7	0.08
Seven Corners, VA (cdp) Fairfax County	7	0.08
Clarkston, GA (city) DeKalb County	6	0.08
Tega Cay, SC (city) York County	6	0.08
Queens, NY (borough) Queens County	1,620	0.07
Madison, WI (city) Dane County	162	0.07
Fremont, CA (city) Alameda County	158	0.07
Sunnyvale, CA (city) Santa Clara County	96	0.07
Ann Arbor, MI (city) Washtenaw County	81	0.07
Bloomington, IN (city) Monroe County	59	0.07
Alhambra, CA (city) Los Angeles County	57	0.07
Iowa City, IA (city) Johnson County	48	0.07
Hacienda Heights, CA (cdp) Los Angeles County	39	0.07
Cupertino, CA (city) Santa Clara County	38	0.07
Issaquah, WA (city) King County	20	0.07
Silver Firs, WA (cdp) Snohomish County	15	0.07
Arbutus, MD (cdp) Baltimore County	14	0.07
Millburn, NJ (township) Essex County	14	0.07
Manchester, MO (city) St. Louis County	13	0.07
Franconia, VA (cdp) Fairfax County	12	0.07
Murphy, TX (city) Collin County	12	0.07
Ewa Beach, HI (cdp) Honolulu County	11	0.07
Bemidji, MN (city) Beltrami County	10	0.07
East San Gabriel, CA (cdp) Los Angeles County	10	0.07
Highland Park, NJ (borough) Middlesex County	10	0.07
Patton, PA (township) Centre County	10	0.07
Lockhart, TX (city) Caldwell County	9	0.07
Somerville, NJ (borough) Somerset County	9	0.07
Greatwood, TX (cdp) Fort Bend County	8	0.07
Oak Hills, OR (cdp) Washington County	8	0.07
Gages Lake, IL (cdp) Lake County	7	0.07
Klahanie, WA (cdp) King County	7	0.07
North Logan, UT (city) Cache County	6	0.07
Waihee-Waiehu, HI (cdp) Maui County	6	0.07
Waimea, HI (cdp) Hawaii County	6	0.07
Westwood, MI (cdp) Kalamazoo County	6	0.07
Santa Clara, CA (city) Santa Clara County	71	0.06
Cambridge, MA (city) Middlesex County	63	0.06
The Woodlands, TX (cdp) Montgomery County	60	0.06
Champaign, IL (city) Champaign County	46	0.06
Kalamazoo, MI (city) Kalamazoo County	43	0.06
Skokie, IL (village) Cook County	37	0.06
Diamond Bar, CA (city) Los Angeles County	31	0.06
McLean, VA (cdp) Fairfax County	29	0.06
Rancho Palos Verdes, CA (city) Los Angeles County	23	0.06
Braintree Town, MA (city) Norfolk County	20	0.06
Ithaca, NY (city) Tompkins County	18	0.06
Leander, TX (city) Williamson County	17	0.06
Mason, OH (city) Warren County	17	0.06
Pullman, WA (city) Whitman County	17	0.06
Los Altos, CA (city) Santa Clara County	16	0.06
West Windsor, NJ (township) Mercer County	15	0.06
El Cerrito, CA (city) Contra Costa County	14	0.06
Plainsboro, NJ (township) Middlesex County	13	0.06
Kihei, HI (cdp) Maui County	12	0.06
King of Prussia, PA (cdp) Montgomery County	12	0.06
Coralville, IA (city) Johnson County	11	0.06
McNair, VA (cdp) Fairfax County	11	0.06
Morrisville, NC (town) Wake County	11	0.06
Calverton, MD (cdp) Montgomery County	10	0.06
Murray, KY (city) Calloway County	10	0.06
Stafford, TX (city) Fort Bend County	10	0.06
Indiana, PA (borough) Indiana County	9	0.06
Glenmont, MD (cdp) Montgomery County	8	0.06
Malibu, CA (city) Los Angeles County	8	0.06
Beachwood, NJ (borough) Ocean County	7	0.06
Dranesville, VA (cdp) Fairfax County	7	0.06
Cheval, FL (cdp) Hillsborough County	6	0.06
Paris, TN (city) Henry County	6	0.06
Cresskill, NJ (borough) Bergen County	5	0.06
Dumbarton, VA (cdp) Henrico County	5	0.06
Manhasset, NY (cdp) Nassau County	5	0.06
Mansfield, NJ (township) Burlington County	5	0.06
Mentone, CA (cdp) San Bernardino County	5	0.06
Plainville, MA (town) Norfolk County	5	0.06
West Earl, PA (township) Lancaster County	5	0.06
Manhattan, NY (borough) New York County	766	0.05
Daly City, CA (city) San Mateo County	47	0.05
Longmont, CO (city) Boulder County	42	0.05
Folsom, CA (city) Sacramento County	38	0.05
Chino Hills, CA (city) San Bernardino County	34	0.05
St. Cloud, MN (city) Stearns County	34	0.05
Missouri City, TX (city) Fort Bend County	32	0.05
Castro Valley, CA (cdp) Alameda County	29	0.05
Palo Alto, CA (city) Santa Clara County	29	0.05
Cerritos, CA (city) Los Angeles County	24	0.05
Sammamish, WA (city) King County	22	0.05
Blacksburg, VA (town) Montgomery County	21	0.05
Bartlett, IL (village) DuPage County	19	0.05
Brighton, NY (cdp/town) Monroe County	18	0.05
Oakton, VA (cdp) Fairfax County	18	0.05
Gurnee, IL (village) Lake County	17	0.05
Kaneohe, HI (cdp) Honolulu County	16	0.05
Dover, NH (city) Strafford County	14	0.05
Morgantown, WV (city) Monongalia County	14	0.05
Belmont, CA (city) San Mateo County	13	0.05
Athens, OH (city) Athens County	12	0.05

Please refer to the Explanation of Data in the front of the book for more detailed information.

Race

Asian: Nepalese

U.S. and 50 States Sorted by Population and Percent of Total Population

Place	Population	%
United States	**59,490**	**0.02**
New York	7,625	0.04
Texas	7,513	0.03
California	6,231	0.02
Virginia	4,770	0.06
Maryland	3,412	0.06
Massachusetts	2,865	0.04
Colorado	2,751	0.05
Georgia	1,959	0.02
Illinois	1,459	0.01
Minnesota	1,438	0.03
Pennsylvania	1,429	0.01
Washington	1,158	0.02
North Carolina	1,039	0.01
Ohio	992	0.01
New Jersey	989	0.01
Florida	945	0.01
Connecticut	944	0.03
Michigan	847	0.01
Arizona	836	0.01
New Hampshire	829	0.06
Nebraska	698	0.04
Kentucky	695	0.02
Utah	693	0.03
Iowa	598	0.02
Missouri	566	0.01
Kansas	545	0.02
Oregon	543	0.01
Wisconsin	500	0.01
Oklahoma	464	0.01
Alabama	430	0.01
Louisiana	396	0.01
Idaho	376	0.02
North Dakota	294	0.04
Indiana	278	<0.01
Nevada	238	0.01
New Mexico	237	0.01
Tennessee	220	<0.01
South Dakota	209	0.03
West Virginia	195	0.01
District of Columbia	161	0.03
Vermont	159	0.03
South Carolina	154	<0.01
Hawaii	146	0.01
Rhode Island	128	0.01
Arkansas	122	<0.01
Alaska	114	0.02
Mississippi	88	<0.01
Wyoming	71	0.01
Delaware	61	0.01
Maine	51	<0.01
Montana	29	<0.01

Place	Population	%
Virginia	4,770	0.06
Maryland	3,412	0.06
New Hampshire	829	0.06
Colorado	2,751	0.05
New York	7,625	0.04
Massachusetts	2,865	0.04
Nebraska	698	0.04
North Dakota	294	0.04
Texas	7,513	0.03
Minnesota	1,438	0.03
Connecticut	944	0.03
Utah	693	0.03
South Dakota	209	0.03
District of Columbia	161	0.03
Vermont	159	0.03
United States	**59,490**	**0.02**
California	6,231	0.02
Georgia	1,959	0.02
Washington	1,158	0.02
Kentucky	695	0.02
Iowa	598	0.02
Kansas	545	0.02
Idaho	376	0.02
Alaska	114	0.02
Illinois	1,459	0.01
Pennsylvania	1,429	0.01
North Carolina	1,039	0.01
Ohio	992	0.01
New Jersey	989	0.01
Florida	945	0.01
Michigan	847	0.01
Arizona	836	0.01
Missouri	566	0.01
Oregon	543	0.01
Wisconsin	500	0.01
Oklahoma	464	0.01
Alabama	430	0.01
Louisiana	396	0.01
Nevada	238	0.01
New Mexico	237	0.01
West Virginia	195	0.01
Hawaii	146	0.01
Rhode Island	128	0.01
Wyoming	71	0.01
Delaware	61	0.01
Indiana	278	<0.01
Tennessee	220	<0.01
South Carolina	154	<0.01
Arkansas	122	<0.01
Mississippi	88	<0.01
Maine	51	<0.01
Montana	29	<0.01

Please refer to the Explanation of Data in the front of the book for more detailed information.

Race

Asian: Nepalese

Top 150 Places Sorted by Population

Based on all places, regardless of total population

Place	Population	%
New York, NY (city) Kings County	6,187	0.08
Queens, NY (borough) Queens County	5,319	0.24
Irving, TX (city) Dallas County	1,590	0.74
Houston, TX (city) Harris County	995	0.05
Somerville, MA (city) Middlesex County	792	1.05
Chicago, IL (city) Cook County	627	0.02
Fort Worth, TX (city) Tarrant County	594	0.08
Arlington, VA (cdp) Arlington County	506	0.24
Denver, CO (city) Denver County	497	0.08
Aurora, CO (city) Arapahoe County	414	0.13
Brooklyn, NY (borough) Kings County	393	0.02
San Francisco, CA (city) San Francisco County	388	0.05
Los Angeles, CA (city) Los Angeles County	387	0.01
Clarkston, GA (city) DeKalb County	381	5.04
Boulder, CO (city) Boulder County	358	0.37
Austin, TX (city) Travis County	353	0.04
Baltimore, MD (city) Baltimore city County	347	0.06
Euless, TX (city) Tarrant County	338	0.66
Dallas, TX (city) Dallas County	335	0.03
Omaha, NE (city) Douglas County	312	0.08
Phoenix, AZ (city) Maricopa County	310	0.02
Manchester, NH (city) Hillsborough County	308	0.28
Sunnyvale, CA (city) Santa Clara County	305	0.22
Louisville-Jefferson County, KY (metro govt) Jefferson County	291	0.05
Manhattan, NY (borough) New York County	281	0.02
Scottdale, GA (cdp) DeKalb County	277	2.61
Arlington, TX (city) Tarrant County	275	0.08
Tucson, AZ (city) Pima County	274	0.05
Towson, MD (cdp) Baltimore County	273	0.49
Lexington-Fayette, KY (cons. govt) Fayette County	266	0.09
Syracuse, NY (city) Onondaga County	262	0.18
West Hartford, CT (cdp/town) Hartford County	245	0.39
Seattle, WA (city) King County	245	0.04
Artesia, CA (city) Los Angeles County	226	1.37
Cambridge, MA (city) Middlesex County	226	0.21
El Cerrito, CA (city) Contra Costa County	222	0.94
Fargo, ND (city) Cass County	221	0.21
Philadelphia, PA (city) Philadelphia County	220	0.01
Boston, MA (city) Suffolk County	215	0.03
Idylwood, VA (cdp) Fairfax County	214	1.24
Des Moines, IA (city) Polk County	213	0.10
San Antonio, TX (city) Medina County	213	0.02
Concord, NH (city) Merrimack County	212	0.50
Berkeley, CA (city) Alameda County	211	0.19
Boise City, ID (city) Ada County	211	0.10
St. Cloud, MN (city) Stearns County	207	0.31
Oakland, CA (city) Alameda County	204	0.05
Salt Lake City, UT (city) Salt Lake County	196	0.11
Cary, NC (town) Wake County	190	0.14
Columbus, OH (city) Franklin County	190	0.02
Denton, TX (city) Denton County	189	0.17
Moorhead, MN (city) Clay County	180	0.47
Arlington, MA (cdp/town) Middlesex County	180	0.42
Portland, OR (city) Multnomah County	180	0.03
Chantilly, VA (cdp) Fairfax County	174	0.76
Wichita, KS (city) Sedgwick County	174	0.05
West Falls Church, VA (cdp) Fairfax County	166	0.57
Rochester, NY (city) Monroe County	165	0.08
Woodland, CA (city) Yolo County	162	0.29
St. Louis, MO (city) St. Louis city County	161	0.05
Washington, DC (city) District of Columbia	161	0.03
Buffalo, NY (city) Erie County	160	0.06
Bronx, NY (borough) Bronx County	159	0.01
Montgomery Village, MD (cdp) Montgomery County	158	0.49
Charlotte, NC (city) Mecklenburg County	157	0.02
Germantown, MD (cdp) Montgomery County	156	0.18
Plano, TX (city) Collin County	156	0.06
Oakton, VA (cdp) Fairfax County	155	0.45
Jersey City, NJ (city) Hudson County	155	0.06
Santa Rosa, CA (city) Sonoma County	153	0.09
Oklahoma City, OK (city) Oklahoma County	153	0.03
Fremont, CA (city) Alameda County	152	0.07
Madison, WI (city) Dane County	151	0.06
Davis, CA (city) Yolo County	150	0.23
Alexandria, VA (ind. city) Alexandria independent city	148	0.11
High Point, NC (city) Guilford County	147	0.14
San Diego, CA (city) San Diego County	146	0.01
Merrifield, VA (cdp) Fairfax County	142	0.93
Raleigh, NC (city) Wake County	140	0.03
San Jose, CA (city) Santa Clara County	139	0.01
Erie, PA (city) Erie County	138	0.14
Longmont, CO (city) Boulder County	136	0.16
Provo, UT (city) Utah County	133	0.12
Minneapolis, MN (city) Hennepin County	133	0.03
Centreville, VA (cdp) Fairfax County	131	0.18
Fairfax, VA (ind. city) Fairfax independent city	127	0.56
Jacksonville, FL (city) Duval County	127	0.02
South Salt Lake, UT (city) Salt Lake County	123	0.52
Thornton, CO (city) Adams County	123	0.10
Baton Rouge, LA (city) East Baton Rouge Parish	123	0.05
Carney, MD (cdp) Baltimore County	122	0.41
St. Cloud, MN (city) Sherburne County	117	1.72
St. Paul, MN (city) Ramsey County	117	0.04
Gaithersburg, MD (city) Montgomery County	113	0.19
Lansing, MI (city) Ingham County	113	0.10
Lansing, MI (city) Ingham County	113	0.10
Colorado Springs, CO (city) El Paso County	113	0.03
Pittsburgh, PA (city) Allegheny County	111	0.04
Abilene, TX (city) Taylor County	110	0.09
Beckley, WV (city) Raleigh County	109	0.62
Sioux Falls, SD (city) Minnehaha County	109	0.07
Worcester, MA (city) Worcester County	109	0.06
Marumsco, VA (cdp) Prince William County	108	0.31
Mountain View, CA (city) Santa Clara County	108	0.15
Cleveland, OH (city) Cuyahoga County	108	0.03
Urban Honolulu, HI (cdp) Honolulu County	106	0.03
Wells Branch, TX (cdp) Travis County	105	0.87
Woodlawn, MD (cdp) Baltimore County	105	0.28
Silver Spring, MD (cdp) Montgomery County	100	0.14
Marshall, MN (city) Lyon County	99	0.72
Alameda, CA (city) Alameda County	99	0.13
Rockville, MD (city) Montgomery County	98	0.16
Grand Prairie, TX (city) Dallas County	97	0.06
Annandale, VA (cdp) Fairfax County	96	0.23
Millcreek, UT (cdp) Salt Lake County	96	0.15
Anchorage, AK (municipality) Anchorage Municipality	96	0.03
Kent, WA (city) King County	93	0.10
Providence, RI (city) Providence County	93	0.05
Herndon, VA (town) Fairfax County	92	0.39
Sacramento, CA (city) Sacramento County	90	0.02
South Riding, VA (cdp) Loudoun County	89	0.37
Edmond, OK (city) Oklahoma County	89	0.11
Lubbock, TX (city) Lubbock County	89	0.04
Cockeysville, MD (cdp) Baltimore County	88	0.42
Brookings, SD (city) Brookings County	88	0.40
North Bethesda, MD (cdp) Montgomery County	88	0.20
Nashua, NH (city) Hillsborough County	88	0.10
Reno, NV (city) Washoe County	88	0.04
Branford, CT (town) New Haven County	87	0.31
Lancaster, PA (city) Lancaster County	87	0.15
Haltom City, TX (city) Tarrant County	85	0.20
Akron, OH (city) Summit County	85	0.04
Nashville-Davidson, TN (metro govt) Davidson County	85	0.01
Wheaton, MD (cdp) Montgomery County	82	0.17
Dunwoody, GA (city) DeKalb County	81	0.18
Greensboro, NC (city) Guilford County	81	0.03
Seven Corners, VA (cdp) Fairfax County	80	0.86
Lorton, VA (cdp) Fairfax County	80	0.43
Scranton, PA (city) Lackawanna County	80	0.11
Santa Clara, CA (city) Santa Clara County	80	0.07
Anaheim, CA (city) Orange County	80	0.02
Burlington, VT (city) Chittenden County	79	0.19
Aspen Hill, MD (cdp) Montgomery County	78	0.16
Albany, CA (city) Alameda County	77	0.42
Manhattan, KS (city) Riley County	77	0.15
Overland Park, KS (city) Johnson County	77	0.04
Cincinnati, OH (city) Hamilton County	77	0.03
Sudley, VA (cdp) Prince William County	76	0.47
Albuquerque, NM (city) Bernalillo County	76	0.01
St. Cloud, MN (city) Stearns County	75	0.14

SECTION THREE

Please refer to the Explanation of Data in the front of the book for more detailed information.

Race

Asian: Nepalese

Top 150 Places Sorted by Percent of Total Population

Based on all places, regardless of total population

Place	Population	%
Blue Sky, CO (cdp) Morgan County	3	12.50
Hillsboro, VA (town) Loudoun County	6	7.50
Clarkston, GA (city) DeKalb County	381	5.04
Crossgate, KY (city) Jefferson County	7	3.11
Scottdale, GA (cdp) DeKalb County	277	2.61
Mockingbird Valley, KY (city) Jefferson County	4	2.40
Nelson Lagoon, AK (cdp) Aleutians East Borough	1	1.92
St. Cloud, MN (city) Sherburne County	117	1.72
Windham, NY (cdp) Greene County	6	1.63
Artesia, CA (city) Los Angeles County	226	1.37
Idylwood, VA (cdp) Fairfax County	214	1.24
New Village, NJ (cdp) Warren County	5	1.19
Westwood, KY (city) Jefferson County	7	1.10
Stone Mountain, GA (city) DeKalb County	63	1.09
Lower Kalskag, AK (city) Bethel Census Area	3	1.06
Somerville, MA (city) Middlesex County	792	1.05
Turkey, NC (town) Sampson County	3	1.03
Derby, OH (cdp) Pickaway County	4	0.98
El Cerrito, CA (city) Contra Costa County	222	0.94
Mackey, IN (town) Gibson County	1	0.94
Merrifield, VA (cdp) Fairfax County	142	0.93
Hiram, OH (village) Portage County	13	0.92
Reece City, AL (town) Etowah County	6	0.92
Searsburg, VT (town) Bennington County	1	0.92
Wells Branch, TX (cdp) Travis County	105	0.87
Seven Corners, VA (cdp) Fairfax County	80	0.86
Calverton, VA (cdp) Fauquier County	2	0.84
Red Mesa, AZ (cdp) Apache County	4	0.83
Boardman, OR (city) Morrow County	25	0.78
Chantilly, VA (cdp) Fairfax County	174	0.76
Irving, TX (city) Dallas County	1,590	0.74
Marshall, MN (city) Lyon County	99	0.72
Kelly, WY (cdp) Teton County	1	0.72
Atlanta, WI (town) Rusk County	4	0.68
Euless, TX (city) Tarrant County	338	0.66
Monroe, SD (town) Turner County	1	0.63
Beckley, WV (city) Raleigh County	109	0.62
West Falls Church, VA (cdp) Fairfax County	166	0.57
Fairfax, VA (ind. city) Fairfax independent city	127	0.56
South Salt Lake, UT (city) Salt Lake County	123	0.52
Sonoma, CA (city) Sonoma County	55	0.52
Millbourne, PA (borough) Delaware County	6	0.52
Forest Home, NY (cdp) Tompkins County	3	0.52
Free Union, VA (cdp) Albemarle County	1	0.52
Winooski, VT (city) Chittenden County	37	0.51
Haymarket, VA (town) Prince William County	9	0.51
Concord, NH (city) Merrimack County	212	0.50
Lauderdale, MN (city) Ramsey County	12	0.50
Towson, MD (cdp) Baltimore County	273	0.49
Montgomery Village, MD (cdp) Montgomery County	158	0.49
Yorkshire, VA (cdp) Prince William County	37	0.49
Merritt Park, NY (cdp) Dutchess County	6	0.48
Moorhead, MN (city) Clay County	180	0.47
Sudley, VA (cdp) Prince William County	76	0.47
Crested Butte, CO (town) Gunnison County	7	0.47
Oakton, VA (cdp) Fairfax County	155	0.45
Jerome, AZ (town) Yavapai County	2	0.45
Lorton, VA (cdp) Fairfax County	80	0.43
Shorewood, WI (village) Milwaukee County	56	0.43
Castle Shannon, PA (borough) Allegheny County	36	0.43
Arlington, MA (cdp/town) Middlesex County	180	0.42
Cockeysville, MD (cdp) Baltimore County	88	0.42
Albany, CA (city) Alameda County	77	0.42
Bull Run, VA (cdp) Prince William County	63	0.42
Carney, MD (cdp) Baltimore County	122	0.41
Fairfield, IA (city) Jefferson County	39	0.41
Brookings, SD (city) Brookings County	88	0.40
Wixom, MI (city) Oakland County	54	0.40
West Hartford, CT (cdp/town) Hartford County	245	0.39
Herndon, VA (town) Fairfax County	92	0.39
Whitehall, PA (borough) Allegheny County	55	0.39
Woodburn, VA (cdp) Fairfax County	33	0.39
Morrisville, NC (town) Wake County	70	0.38
Star City, WV (town) Monongalia County	7	0.38
Boulder, CO (city) Boulder County	358	0.37
South Riding, VA (cdp) Loudoun County	89	0.37
Fair Lakes, VA (cdp) Fairfax County	29	0.37
Fayette, IA (city) Fayette County	5	0.37
Greenbriar, VA (cdp) Fairfax County	29	0.36
Indian Head, MD (town) Charles County	14	0.36
Ravensworth, VA (cdp) Fairfax County	9	0.36
Egan, SD (city) Moody County	1	0.36
Burtonsville, MD (cdp) Montgomery County	29	0.35
Windham, NY (town) Greene County	6	0.35
Vail, CO (town) Eagle County	18	0.34
Annawan, IL (town) Henry County	3	0.34
Blue Ridge Summit, PA (cdp) Franklin County	3	0.34
Nelliston, NY (village) Montgomery County	2	0.34
Westminster, VT (village) Windham County	1	0.34
University Park, NM (cdp) Doña Ana County	14	0.33
Argyle, NY (village) Washington County	1	0.33
St. Cloud, MN (city) Stearns County	207	0.31
Marumsco, VA (cdp) Prince William County	108	0.31
Branford, CT (town) New Haven County	87	0.31
McNair, VA (cdp) Fairfax County	54	0.31
Harrisburg, OH (village) Franklin County	1	0.31
Northeast Ithaca, NY (cdp) Tompkins County	8	0.30
Limestone Creek, FL (cdp) Palm Beach County	3	0.30
Woodland, CA (city) Yolo County	162	0.29
Ruston, LA (city) Lincoln Parish	63	0.29
Branford Center, CT (cdp) New Haven County	17	0.29
Early, TX (city) Brown County	8	0.29
Brewster, NY (village) Putnam County	7	0.29
Savanna, OK (town) Pittsburg County	2	0.29
Manchester, NH (city) Hillsborough County	308	0.28
Woodlawn, MD (cdp) Baltimore County	105	0.28
Caldwell, NJ (borough) Essex County	22	0.28
Nantucket, MA (cdp) Nantucket County	21	0.28
New London, NH (cdp) Merrimack County	4	0.28
Woodbridge, VA (cdp) Prince William County	11	0.27
Todd Creek, CO (cdp) Adams County	10	0.27
Westwood, KS (city) Johnson County	4	0.27
North Kensington, MD (cdp) Montgomery County	25	0.26
Elmsford, NY (village) Westchester County	12	0.26
Sewickley, PA (borough) Allegheny County	10	0.26
Belmont, MA (cdp/town) Middlesex County	61	0.25
Plymouth, MA (cdp) Plymouth County	19	0.25
Madison, WI (town) Dane County	16	0.25
Derwood, MD (cdp) Montgomery County	6	0.25
Morris, MN (township) Stevens County	1	0.25
Wells, VT (cdp) Rutland County	1	0.25
Queens, NY (borough) Queens County	5,319	0.24
Arlington, VA (cdp) Arlington County	506	0.24
County Center, VA (cdp) Prince William County	8	0.24
Eldridge, CA (cdp) Sonoma County	3	0.24
Orange, MI (township) Kalkaska County	3	0.24
Davis, CA (city) Yolo County	150	0.23
Annandale, VA (cdp) Fairfax County	96	0.23
West Springfield Town, MA (city) Hampden County	66	0.23
Addison, TX (town) Dallas County	30	0.23
Superior, CO (town) Boulder County	29	0.23
Mountain House, CA (cdp) San Joaquin County	22	0.23
Maryville, IL (village) Madison County	17	0.23
Laurel Hill, VA (cdp) Fairfax County	16	0.23
St. Cloud, MN (city) Benton County	15	0.23
Potomac Mills, VA (cdp) Prince William County	13	0.23
Fishkill, NY (village) Dutchess County	5	0.23
North Corbin, KY (cdp) Laurel County	4	0.23
Ringle, WI (town) Marathon County	4	0.23
Sunnyvale, CA (city) Santa Clara County	305	0.22
Fair Oaks, VA (cdp) Fairfax County	65	0.22
North Druid Hills, GA (cdp) DeKalb County	41	0.22
La Vista, NE (city) Sarpy County	34	0.22
Hooksett, NH (town) Merrimack County	30	0.22
Lake Barcroft, VA (cdp) Fairfax County	21	0.22
Greenville, NY (cdp) Westchester County	16	0.22
Frankenlust, MI (township) Bay County	8	0.22
Bryn Athyn, PA (borough) Montgomery County	3	0.22
Cambridge, MA (city) Middlesex County	226	0.21
Fargo, ND (city) Cass County	221	0.21

Please refer to the Explanation of Data in the front of the book for more detailed information.

Race

Asian: Nepalese

Top 150 Places Sorted by Percent of Total Population

Based on places with total population of 7,500 or more

Place	Population	%
Clarkston, GA (city) DeKalb County	381	5.04
Scottdale, GA (cdp) DeKalb County	277	2.61
Artesia, CA (city) Los Angeles County	226	1.37
Idylwood, VA (cdp) Fairfax County	214	1.24
Somerville, MA (city) Middlesex County	792	1.05
El Cerrito, CA (city) Contra Costa County	222	0.94
Merrifield, VA (cdp) Fairfax County	142	0.93
Wells Branch, TX (cdp) Travis County	105	0.87
Seven Corners, VA (cdp) Fairfax County	80	0.86
Chantilly, VA (cdp) Fairfax County	174	0.76
Irving, TX (city) Dallas County	1,590	0.74
Marshall, MN (city) Lyon County	99	0.72
Euless, TX (city) Tarrant County	338	0.66
Beckley, WV (city) Raleigh County	109	0.62
West Falls Church, VA (cdp) Fairfax County	166	0.57
Fairfax, VA (ind. city) Fairfax independent city	127	0.56
South Salt Lake, UT (city) Salt Lake County	123	0.52
Sonoma, CA (city) Sonoma County	55	0.52
Concord, NH (city) Merrimack County	212	0.50
Towson, MD (cdp) Baltimore County	273	0.49
Montgomery Village, MD (cdp) Montgomery County	158	0.49
Yorkshire, VA (cdp) Prince William County	37	0.49
Moorhead, MN (city) Clay County	180	0.47
Sudley, VA (cdp) Prince William County	76	0.47
Oakton, VA (cdp) Fairfax County	155	0.45
Lorton, VA (cdp) Fairfax County	80	0.43
Shorewood, WI (village) Milwaukee County	56	0.43
Castle Shannon, PA (borough) Allegheny County	36	0.43
Arlington, MA (cdp/town) Middlesex County	180	0.42
Cockeysville, MD (cdp) Baltimore County	88	0.42
Albany, CA (city) Alameda County	77	0.42
Bull Run, VA (cdp) Prince William County	63	0.42
Carney, MD (cdp) Baltimore County	122	0.41
Fairfield, IA (city) Jefferson County	39	0.41
Brookings, SD (city) Brookings County	88	0.40
Wixom, MI (city) Oakland County	54	0.40
West Hartford, CT (cdp/town) Hartford County	245	0.39
Herndon, VA (town) Fairfax County	92	0.39
Whitehall, PA (borough) Allegheny County	55	0.39
Woodburn, VA (cdp) Fairfax County	33	0.39
Morrisville, NC (town) Wake County	70	0.38
Boulder, CO (city) Boulder County	358	0.37
South Riding, VA (cdp) Loudoun County	89	0.37
Fair Lakes, VA (cdp) Fairfax County	29	0.37
Greenbriar, VA (cdp) Fairfax County	29	0.36
Burtonsville, MD (cdp) Montgomery County	29	0.35
St. Cloud, MN (city) Stearns County	207	0.31
Marumsco, VA (cdp) Prince William County	108	0.31
Branford, CT (town) New Haven County	87	0.31
McNair, VA (cdp) Fairfax County	54	0.31
Woodland, CA (city) Yolo County	162	0.29
Ruston, LA (city) Lincoln Parish	63	0.29
Manchester, NH (city) Hillsborough County	308	0.28
Woodlawn, MD (cdp) Baltimore County	105	0.28
Caldwell, NJ (borough) Essex County	22	0.28
North Kensington, MD (cdp) Montgomery County	25	0.26
Belmont, MA (cdp/town) Middlesex County	61	0.25
Queens, NY (borough) Queens County	5,319	0.24
Arlington, VA (cdp) Arlington County	506	0.24
Davis, CA (city) Yolo County	150	0.23
Annandale, VA (cdp) Fairfax County	96	0.23
West Springfield Town, MA (city) Hampden County	66	0.23
Addison, TX (town) Dallas County	30	0.23
Superior, CO (town) Boulder County	29	0.23
Mountain House, CA (cdp) San Joaquin County	22	0.23
Sunnyvale, CA (city) Santa Clara County	305	0.22
Fair Oaks, VA (cdp) Fairfax County	65	0.22
North Druid Hills, GA (cdp) DeKalb County	41	0.22
La Vista, NE (city) Sarpy County	34	0.22
Hooksett, NH (town) Merrimack County	30	0.22
Lake Barcroft, VA (cdp) Fairfax County	21	0.22
Cambridge, MA (city) Middlesex County	226	0.21
Fargo, ND (city) Cass County	221	0.21
North Decatur, GA (cdp) DeKalb County	35	0.21
Nantucket, MA (town) Nantucket County	21	0.21
White Marsh, MD (cdp) Baltimore County	20	0.21
North Bethesda, MD (cdp) Montgomery County	88	0.20
Haltom City, TX (city) Tarrant County	85	0.20
Springfield, VA (cdp) Fairfax County	62	0.20
Parkville, MD (cdp) Baltimore County	61	0.20
San Pablo, CA (city) Contra Costa County	58	0.20
Moscow, ID (city) Latah County	47	0.20
Berkeley, CA (city) Alameda County	211	0.19
Gaithersburg, MD (city) Montgomery County	113	0.19
Burlington, VT (city) Chittenden County	79	0.19
Perry Hall, MD (cdp) Baltimore County	55	0.19
Hyattsville, MD (city) Prince George's County	34	0.19
Vienna, VA (town) Fairfax County	30	0.19
Newington Forest, VA (cdp) Fairfax County	24	0.19
University of Virginia, VA (cdp) Albemarle County	15	0.19
Syracuse, NY (city) Onondaga County	262	0.18
Germantown, MD (cdp) Montgomery County	156	0.18
Centreville, VA (cdp) Fairfax County	131	0.18
Dunwoody, GA (city) DeKalb County	81	0.18
Kirksville, MO (city) Adair County	32	0.18
Gunbarrel, CO (cdp) Boulder County	17	0.18
Denton, TX (city) Denton County	189	0.17
Wheaton, MD (cdp) Montgomery County	82	0.17
Dickinson, ND (city) Stark County	30	0.17
Redland, MD (cdp) Montgomery County	30	0.17
Hybla Valley, VA (cdp) Fairfax County	27	0.17
Rossville, MD (cdp) Baltimore County	26	0.17
Neabsco, VA (cdp) Prince William County	21	0.17
Bellmawr, NJ (borough) Camden County	20	0.17
Fairfax Station, VA (cdp) Fairfax County	20	0.17
Gainesville, VA (cdp) Prince William County	20	0.17
Federal Heights, CO (city) Adams County	19	0.17
Wyomissing, PA (borough) Berks County	18	0.17
Barrington, NH (town) Strafford County	15	0.17
Longmont, CO (city) Boulder County	136	0.16
Rockville, MD (city) Montgomery County	98	0.16
Aspen Hill, MD (cdp) Montgomery County	78	0.16
Mankato, MN (city) Blue Earth County	64	0.16
Mankato, MN (city) Blue Earth County	64	0.16
Northglenn, CO (city) Adams County	57	0.16
Laramie, WY (city) Albany County	49	0.16
Secaucus, NJ (town) Hudson County	26	0.16
Humble, TX (city) Harris County	24	0.16
Cherry Creek, CO (cdp) Arapahoe County	18	0.16
Mountain View, CA (city) Santa Clara County	108	0.15
Millcreek, UT (cdp) Salt Lake County	96	0.15
Lancaster, PA (city) Lancaster County	87	0.15
Manhattan, KS (city) Riley County	77	0.15
Bellevue, NE (city) Sarpy County	73	0.15
Stillwater, OK (city) Payne County	70	0.15
Blacksburg, VA (town) Montgomery County	64	0.15
Leesburg, VA (town) Loudoun County	63	0.15
Watertown Town, MA (city) Middlesex County	48	0.15
Tukwila, WA (city) King County	28	0.15
Falls Church, VA (ind. city) Falls Church independent city	18	0.15
Countryside, VA (cdp) Loudoun County	15	0.15
Cary, NC (town) Wake County	190	0.14
High Point, NC (city) Guilford County	147	0.14
Erie, PA (city) Erie County	138	0.14
Silver Spring, MD (cdp) Montgomery County	100	0.14
St. Cloud, MN (city) Stearns County	75	0.14
Mansfield, CT (town) Tolland County	37	0.14
Franklin Farm, VA (cdp) Fairfax County	27	0.14
Golden, CO (city) Jefferson County	27	0.14
South Hadley, MA (town) Hampshire County	25	0.14
Menomonie, WI (city) Dunn County	23	0.14
Bull Mountain, OR (cdp) Washington County	13	0.14
Aurora, CO (city) Arapahoe County	414	0.13
Alameda, CA (city) Alameda County	99	0.13
Medford, MA (city) Middlesex County	71	0.13
Bedford, TX (city) Tarrant County	62	0.13
Kent, OH (city) Portage County	39	0.13
Greenbelt, MD (city) Prince George's County	31	0.13
Lincolnia, VA (cdp) Fairfax County	29	0.13
New Brighton, MN (city) Ramsey County	27	0.13

SECTION THREE

Please refer to the Explanation of Data in the front of the book for more detailed information.

Race

Asian: Pakistani

U.S. and 50 States Sorted by Population and Percent of Total Population

Place	Population	%
United States	**409,163**	**0.13**
New York	70,622	0.36
Texas	59,678	0.24
California	53,474	0.14
Illinois	33,000	0.26
New Jersey	28,541	0.32
Virginia	27,100	0.34
Florida	16,035	0.09
Maryland	15,600	0.27
Georgia	11,202	0.12
Michigan	11,056	0.11
Pennsylvania	10,330	0.08
Massachusetts	7,071	0.11
Connecticut	6,640	0.19
North Carolina	6,477	0.07
Ohio	5,330	0.05
Washington	4,594	0.07
Missouri	3,710	0.06
Indiana	3,098	0.05
Arizona	3,008	0.05
Wisconsin	2,984	0.05
Minnesota	2,840	0.05
Tennessee	2,243	0.04
Oklahoma	2,236	0.06
Colorado	2,021	0.04
Louisiana	2,007	0.04
Kansas	1,925	0.07
Nevada	1,793	0.07
Alabama	1,537	0.03
Kentucky	1,402	0.03
Delaware	1,198	0.13
South Carolina	1,127	0.02
Utah	1,086	0.04
Oregon	1,074	0.03
Iowa	967	0.03
Arkansas	815	0.03
Rhode Island	696	0.07
District of Columbia	688	0.11
West Virginia	602	0.03
New Hampshire	579	0.04
Mississippi	546	0.02
New Mexico	498	0.02
Nebraska	413	0.02
Hawaii	303	0.02
Maine	192	0.01
Alaska	184	0.03
Idaho	151	0.01
Vermont	141	0.02
Wyoming	112	0.02
South Dakota	103	0.01
North Dakota	97	0.01
Montana	37	<0.01

Place	Population	%
New York	70,622	0.36
Virginia	27,100	0.34
New Jersey	28,541	0.32
Maryland	15,600	0.27
Illinois	33,000	0.26
Texas	59,678	0.24
Connecticut	6,640	0.19
California	53,474	0.14
United States	**409,163**	**0.13**
Delaware	1,198	0.13
Georgia	11,202	0.12
Michigan	11,056	0.11
Massachusetts	7,071	0.11
District of Columbia	688	0.11
Florida	16,035	0.09
Pennsylvania	10,330	0.08
North Carolina	6,477	0.07
Washington	4,594	0.07
Kansas	1,925	0.07
Nevada	1,793	0.07
Rhode Island	696	0.07
Missouri	3,710	0.06
Oklahoma	2,236	0.06
Ohio	5,330	0.05
Indiana	3,098	0.05
Arizona	3,008	0.05
Wisconsin	2,984	0.05
Minnesota	2,840	0.05
Tennessee	2,243	0.04
Colorado	2,021	0.04
Louisiana	2,007	0.04
Utah	1,086	0.04
New Hampshire	579	0.04
Alabama	1,537	0.03
Kentucky	1,402	0.03
Oregon	1,074	0.03
Iowa	967	0.03
Arkansas	815	0.03
West Virginia	602	0.03
Alaska	184	0.03
South Carolina	1,127	0.02
Mississippi	546	0.02
New Mexico	498	0.02
Nebraska	413	0.02
Hawaii	303	0.02
Vermont	141	0.02
Wyoming	112	0.02
Maine	192	0.01
Idaho	151	0.01
South Dakota	103	0.01
North Dakota	97	0.01
Montana	37	<0.01

Please refer to the Explanation of Data in the front of the book for more detailed information.

Race

Asian: Pakistani

Top 150 Places Sorted by Population

Based on all places, regardless of total population

Place	Population	%
New York, NY (city) Kings County	46,369	0.57
Brooklyn, NY (borough) Kings County	19,840	0.79
Queens, NY (borough) Queens County	18,084	0.81
Houston, TX (city) Harris County	8,258	0.39
Chicago, IL (city) Cook County	7,926	0.29
Hempstead, NY (town) Nassau County	4,976	0.65
Los Angeles, CA (city) Los Angeles County	3,973	0.10
Sugar Land, TX (city) Fort Bend County	3,546	4.50
Jersey City, NJ (city) Hudson County	3,490	1.41
Manhattan, NY (borough) New York County	2,940	0.19
Staten Island, NY (borough) Richmond County	2,777	0.59
Bronx, NY (borough) Bronx County	2,728	0.20
Philadelphia, PA (city) Philadelphia County	2,683	0.18
Carrollton, TX (city) Denton County	2,374	1.99
Plano, TX (city) Collin County	2,314	0.89
Fremont, CA (city) Alameda County	2,242	1.05
San Jose, CA (city) Santa Clara County	2,131	0.23
Skokie, IL (village) Cook County	2,121	3.27
Brookhaven, NY (town) Suffolk County	2,081	0.43
Sacramento, CA (city) Sacramento County	2,061	0.44
Austin, TX (city) Travis County	2,030	0.26
Stockton, CA (city) San Joaquin County	1,904	0.65
Lodi, CA (city) San Joaquin County	1,709	2.75
Irvine, CA (city) Orange County	1,631	0.77
Islip, NY (town) Suffolk County	1,520	0.45
New Territory, TX (cdp) Fort Bend County	1,501	9.88
Woodbridge, NJ (township) Middlesex County	1,481	1.49
Canton, MI (charter township) Wayne County	1,479	1.64
Richardson, TX (city) Dallas County	1,465	1.48
High Point, NC (city) Guilford County	1,399	1.34
Oyster Bay, NY (town) Nassau County	1,330	0.45
Edison, NJ (township) Middlesex County	1,274	1.27
Huntington, NY (town) Suffolk County	1,264	0.62
Irving, TX (city) Dallas County	1,252	0.58
San Antonio, TX (city) Medina County	1,194	0.09
Arlington, TX (city) Tarrant County	1,174	0.32
Dallas, TX (city) Dallas County	1,152	0.10
San Diego, CA (city) San Diego County	1,132	0.09
Arlington, VA (cdp) Arlington County	1,113	0.54
Euless, TX (city) Tarrant County	1,097	2.14
Fort Worth, TX (city) Tarrant County	1,081	0.15
Naperville, IL (city) DuPage County	1,060	0.75
Woodlawn, MD (cdp) Baltimore County	1,055	2.79
Torrance, CA (city) Los Angeles County	1,050	0.72
North Hempstead, NY (town) Nassau County	1,029	0.45
Dale City, VA (cdp) Prince William County	1,013	1.54
San Francisco, CA (city) San Francisco County	1,012	0.13
Santa Clara, CA (city) Santa Clara County	974	0.84
Columbus, OH (city) Franklin County	927	0.12
Springfield, VA (cdp) Fairfax County	926	3.04
Old Bridge, NJ (township) Middlesex County	926	1.42
Piscataway, NJ (township) Middlesex County	920	1.64
Four Corners, TX (cdp) Fort Bend County	912	7.37
Glendale Heights, IL (village) DuPage County	877	2.56
Yonkers, NY (city) Westchester County	874	0.45
Centreville, VA (cdp) Fairfax County	852	1.20
Bolingbrook, IL (village) Will County	835	1.14
Aurora, IL (city) Kane County	829	0.42
Pembroke Pines, FL (city) Broward County	782	0.51
Anaheim, CA (city) Orange County	782	0.23
Oklahoma City, OK (city) Oklahoma County	782	0.13
South Brunswick, NJ (township) Middlesex County	766	1.76
Frisco, TX (city) Collin County	747	0.64
Babylon, NY (town) Suffolk County	739	0.35
Colonie, NY (town) Albany County	736	0.90
Valley Stream, NY (village) Nassau County	733	1.95
Corona, CA (city) Riverside County	731	0.48
Germantown, MD (cdp) Montgomery County	722	0.84
Hoffman Estates, IL (village) Cook County	712	1.37
Lombard, IL (village) DuPage County	710	1.64
Ellicott City, MD (cdp) Howard County	710	1.08
East Meadow, NY (cdp) Nassau County	708	1.86
Allen, TX (city) Collin County	696	0.83
Upper Darby, PA (township) Delaware County	693	0.84
Washington, DC (city) District of Columbia	688	0.11
Woodland, CA (city) Yolo County	677	1.22
Columbia, MD (cdp) Howard County	668	0.67
Troy, MI (city) Oakland County	663	0.82
Boston, MA (city) Suffolk County	659	0.11
Ashburn, VA (cdp) Loudoun County	651	1.50
Elmont, NY (cdp) Nassau County	650	1.96
Alexandria, VA (ind. city) Alexandria independent city	648	0.46
Elk Grove, CA (city) Sacramento County	645	0.42
Bayonne, NJ (city) Hudson County	642	1.02
Hanover Park, IL (village) Cook County	631	1.66
Milwaukee, WI (city) Milwaukee County	629	0.11
Charlotte, NC (city) Mecklenburg County	625	0.09
Indianapolis, IN (city) Marion County	625	0.08
Franklin, NJ (township) Somerset County	609	0.98
Phoenix, AZ (city) Maricopa County	608	0.04
West Bloomfield, MI (charter township) Oakland County	600	0.93
Sayreville, NJ (borough) Middlesex County	595	1.39
Lorton, VA (cdp) Fairfax County	594	3.19
Lincolnia, VA (cdp) Fairfax County	593	2.59
Amherst, NY (town) Erie County	592	0.48
Miramar, FL (city) Broward County	587	0.48
North Brunswick, NJ (township) Middlesex County	586	1.44
Lincolnwood, IL (village) Cook County	580	4.61
Brownstown, MI (charter township) Wayne County	579	1.89
Cary, NC (town) Wake County	579	0.43
Garland, TX (city) Dallas County	572	0.25
Annandale, VA (cdp) Fairfax County	571	1.39
Kansas City, MO (city) Jackson County	553	0.12
Carteret, NJ (borough) Middlesex County	551	2.41
Schaumburg, IL (village) Cook County	550	0.74
Raleigh, NC (city) Wake County	545	0.13
Iselin, NJ (cdp) Middlesex County	538	2.88
Mission Bend, TX (cdp) Fort Bend County	538	1.47
Madison Park, NJ (cdp) Middlesex County	537	7.52
Overland Park, KS (city) Johnson County	535	0.31
Missouri City, TX (city) Fort Bend County	526	0.78
San Ramon, CA (city) Contra Costa County	525	0.73
Ramapo, NY (town) Rockland County	524	0.41
Bellevue, WA (city) King County	523	0.43
Rochester Hills, MI (city) Oakland County	522	0.74
Rancho Cucamonga, CA (city) San Bernardino County	521	0.32
Hicksville, NY (cdp) Nassau County	518	1.25
Coral Springs, FL (city) Broward County	508	0.42
Sterling Heights, MI (city) Macomb County	501	0.39
Farmington Hills, MI (city) Oakland County	500	0.63
Lewisville, TX (city) Denton County	487	0.51
Stafford, TX (city) Fort Bend County	486	2.75
Albany, NY (city) Albany County	483	0.49
Bartlett, IL (village) DuPage County	482	1.17
Baltimore, MD (city) Baltimore city County	476	0.08
Wichita, KS (city) Sedgwick County	473	0.12
Sterling, VA (cdp) Loudoun County	468	1.68
Morton Grove, IL (village) Cook County	466	2.00
Parsippany-Troy Hills, NJ (township) Morris County	462	0.87
Atlanta, GA (city) Fulton County	462	0.11
Herndon, VA (town) Fairfax County	460	1.97
Aurora, CO (city) Arapahoe County	458	0.14
Chandler, AZ (city) Maricopa County	455	0.19
Union City, CA (city) Alameda County	450	0.65
Tulsa, OK (city) Tulsa County	450	0.11
Atlantic City, NJ (city) Atlantic County	436	1.10
Hoover, AL (city) Jefferson County	436	0.53
Reston, VA (cdp) Fairfax County	434	0.74
Tampa, FL (city) Hillsborough County	432	0.13
Boonton, NJ (town) Morris County	428	5.13
Berkeley, CA (city) Alameda County	428	0.38
Seattle, WA (city) King County	427	0.07
North Valley Stream, NY (cdp) Nassau County	425	2.56
Jacksonville, FL (city) Duval County	423	0.05
Palatine, IL (village) Cook County	422	0.62
Nashville-Davidson, TN (metro govt) Davidson County	417	0.07
College Station, TX (city) Brazos County	416	0.44
Garden Grove, CA (city) Orange County	416	0.24
Niles, IL (village) Cook County	413	1.39
Lake Ridge, VA (cdp) Prince William County	409	1.00

SECTION THREE

Please refer to the Explanation of Data in the front of the book for more detailed information.

Race

Asian: Pakistani

Top 150 Places Sorted by Percent of Total Population

Based on all places, regardless of total population

Place	Population	%
New Territory, TX (cdp) Fort Bend County	1,501	9.88
Madison Park, NJ (cdp) Middlesex County	537	7.52
Four Corners, TX (cdp) Fort Bend County	912	7.37
Oak Grove, VA (cdp) Loudoun County	122	6.87
Boonton, NJ (town) Morris County	428	5.13
Hebo, OR (cdp) Tillamook County	11	4.74
Arcola, VA (cdp) Loudoun County	11	4.72
Bellerose Terrace, NY (cdp) Nassau County	103	4.69
Lincolnwood, IL (village) Cook County	580	4.61
Sugar Land, TX (city) Fort Bend County	3,546	4.50
South Valley Stream, NY (cdp) Nassau County	249	4.18
Society Hill, NJ (cdp) Middlesex County	160	4.18
Skokie, IL (village) Cook County	2,121	3.27
Ten Mile Run, NJ (cdp) Somerset County	63	3.22
Lorton, VA (cdp) Fairfax County	594	3.19
Springfield, VA (cdp) Fairfax County	926	3.04
Iselin, NJ (cdp) Middlesex County	538	2.88
Woodlawn, MD (cdp) Baltimore County	1,055	2.79
Lodi, CA (city) San Joaquin County	1,709	2.75
Stafford, TX (city) Fort Bend County	486	2.75
Whitesville, VA (cdp) Accomack County	6	2.74
Oak Brook, IL (village) DuPage County	215	2.73
Lincolnia, VA (cdp) Fairfax County	593	2.59
Heathcote, NJ (cdp) Middlesex County	151	2.59
Glendale Heights, IL (village) DuPage County	877	2.56
North Valley Stream, NY (cdp) Nassau County	425	2.56
Newington, VA (cdp) Fairfax County	327	2.53
Sawpit, CO (town) San Miguel County	1	2.50
Laurel Hill, VA (cdp) Fairfax County	168	2.45
University Center, VA (cdp) Loudoun County	88	2.45
Carteret, NJ (borough) Middlesex County	551	2.41
Pomona, NJ (cdp) Atlantic County	170	2.39
Middlebush, NJ (cdp) Somerset County	55	2.36
Reiner, MN (township) Pennington County	2	2.30
Murphy, TX (city) Collin County	390	2.20
Newington Forest, VA (cdp) Fairfax County	274	2.20
Hybla Valley, VA (cdp) Fairfax County	345	2.18
Monmouth Junction, NJ (cdp) Middlesex County	63	2.18
Euless, TX (city) Tarrant County	1,097	2.14
Ceresco, MN (township) Blue Earth County	5	2.09
Cumberland Gap, TN (town) Claiborne County	10	2.02
Morton Grove, IL (village) Cook County	466	2.00
Carrollton, TX (city) Denton County	2,374	1.99
Herricks, NY (cdp) Nassau County	85	1.98
Herndon, VA (town) Fairfax County	460	1.97
Elmont, NY (cdp) Nassau County	650	1.96
Avenel, NJ (cdp) Middlesex County	333	1.96
Doctor Phillips, FL (cdp) Orange County	215	1.96
Valley Stream, NY (village) Nassau County	733	1.95
Woodlawn, VA (cdp) Fairfax County	401	1.93
Rose Hill, VA (cdp) Fairfax County	389	1.92
Burtonsville, MD (cdp) Montgomery County	160	1.92
Endeavor, WI (village) Marquette County	9	1.92
Randolph, MO (village) Clay County	1	1.92
Dayton, NJ (cdp) Middlesex County	135	1.91
Brownstown, MI (charter township) Wayne County	579	1.89
Groveton, VA (cdp) Fairfax County	276	1.89
Live Oak, CA (city) Sutter County	158	1.88
Franklin Park, NJ (cdp) Somerset County	248	1.87
Camino Tassajara, CA (cdp) Contra Costa County	41	1.87
East Meadow, NY (cdp) Nassau County	708	1.86
Loudoun Valley Estates, VA (cdp) Loudoun County	68	1.86
Archdale, NC (city) Randolph County	211	1.85
Cherry Hill, VA (cdp) Prince William County	289	1.81
County Center, VA (cdp) Prince William County	59	1.80
Blawenburg, NJ (cdp) Somerset County	5	1.79
South Brunswick, NJ (township) Middlesex County	766	1.76
Victor, CA (cdp) San Joaquin County	5	1.71
Bay Hill, FL (cdp) Orange County	83	1.70
Laytonsville, MD (town) Montgomery County	6	1.70
Sterling, VA (cdp) Loudoun County	468	1.68
Neabsco, VA (cdp) Prince William County	203	1.68
Hanover Park, IL (village) Cook County	631	1.66
McNair, VA (cdp) Fairfax County	290	1.66
Six Mile Run, NJ (cdp) Somerset County	53	1.66
Piney Point Village, TX (city) Harris County	52	1.66
Burr Ridge, IL (village) DuPage County	174	1.65
Dulles Town Center, VA (cdp) Loudoun County	76	1.65
Canton, MI (charter township) Wayne County	1,479	1.64
Piscataway, NJ (township) Middlesex County	920	1.64
Lombard, IL (village) DuPage County	710	1.64
Brambleton, VA (cdp) Loudoun County	161	1.64
Potomac Mills, VA (cdp) Prince William County	92	1.64
Lake Barcroft, VA (cdp) Fairfax County	155	1.62
Garden City Park, NY (cdp) Nassau County	124	1.59
Chantilly, VA (cdp) Fairfax County	364	1.58
Morton, PA (borough) Delaware County	42	1.57
Franconia, VA (cdp) Fairfax County	282	1.55
Dale City, VA (cdp) Prince William County	1,013	1.54
Huntington, VA (cdp) Fairfax County	172	1.53
Pleasant Plains, NJ (cdp) Somerset County	14	1.52
South Barrington, IL (village) Cook County	69	1.51
Ashburn, VA (cdp) Loudoun County	651	1.50
Woodbridge, NJ (township) Middlesex County	1,481	1.49
Richardson, TX (city) Dallas County	1,465	1.48
Mount Vernon, VA (cdp) Fairfax County	184	1.48
Mission Bend, TX (cdp) Fort Bend County	538	1.47
Seven Corners, VA (cdp) Fairfax County	136	1.47
Deal, NJ (borough) Monmouth County	11	1.47
North Brunswick, NJ (township) Middlesex County	586	1.44
Bailey's Crossroads, VA (cdp) Fairfax County	339	1.43
Muttontown, NY (village) Nassau County	50	1.43
Old Bridge, NJ (township) Middlesex County	926	1.42
Woodbridge, NJ (cdp) Middlesex County	273	1.42
Sugarland Run, VA (cdp) Loudoun County	168	1.42
Jersey City, NJ (city) Hudson County	3,490	1.41
Town and Country, MO (city) St. Louis County	153	1.41
Hedwig Village, TX (city) Harris County	36	1.41
Forsyth, IL (village) Macon County	49	1.40
Sayreville, NJ (borough) Middlesex County	595	1.39
Annandale, VA (cdp) Fairfax County	571	1.39
Niles, IL (village) Cook County	413	1.39
North Bellmore, NY (cdp) Nassau County	278	1.39
Scarville, IA (city) Winnebago County	1	1.39
South Riding, VA (cdp) Loudoun County	335	1.38
North Bay Shore, NY (cdp) Suffolk County	262	1.38
Kendall Park, NJ (cdp) Middlesex County	129	1.38
Hoffman Estates, IL (village) Cook County	712	1.37
Fair Lakes, VA (cdp) Fairfax County	108	1.36
West Springfield, VA (cdp) Fairfax County	304	1.35
Country Life Acres, MO (village) St. Louis County	1	1.35
High Point, NC (city) Guilford County	1,399	1.34
Elwood, NY (cdp) Suffolk County	149	1.33
Broadlands, VA (cdp) Loudoun County	163	1.32
Searingtown, NY (cdp) Nassau County	65	1.32
North Laurel, MD (cdp) Howard County	59	1.32
North Plainfield, NJ (borough) Somerset County	287	1.31
Laurel, MD (city) Prince George's County	325	1.29
Woodbridge, VA (cdp) Prince William County	52	1.28
Montague, NY (town) Lewis County	1	1.28
Edison, NJ (township) Middlesex County	1,274	1.27
Rockville, CT (cdp) Tolland County	94	1.26
Hicksville, NY (cdp) Nassau County	518	1.25
Lansdowne, VA (cdp) Loudoun County	140	1.24
Little Ferry, NJ (borough) Bergen County	132	1.24
North Springfield, VA (cdp) Fairfax County	90	1.24
Woodland, CA (city) Yolo County	677	1.22
Glen Ellyn, IL (village) DuPage County	334	1.22
Stone Ridge, VA (cdp) Loudoun County	88	1.22
Crompond, NY (cdp) Westchester County	28	1.22
Dix Hills, NY (cdp) Suffolk County	325	1.21
Dranesville, VA (cdp) Fairfax County	144	1.21
Ardsley, NY (village) Westchester County	54	1.21
Millbourne, PA (borough) Delaware County	14	1.21
Louriston, MN (township) Chippewa County	2	1.21
Centreville, VA (cdp) Fairfax County	852	1.20
Scottdale, GA (cdp) DeKalb County	128	1.20
Freedom Plains, NY (cdp) Dutchess County	5	1.19
Gainesville, VA (cdp) Prince William County	136	1.18
Center, MO (city) Ralls County	6	1.18

Please refer to the Explanation of Data in the front of the book for more detailed information.

Race

Asian: Pakistani

Top 150 Places Sorted by Percent of Total Population

Based on places with total population of 7,500 or more

Place	Population	%
New Territory, TX (cdp) Fort Bend County	1,501	9.88
Four Corners, TX (cdp) Fort Bend County	912	7.37
Boonton, NJ (town) Morris County	428	5.13
Lincolnwood, IL (village) Cook County	580	4.61
Sugar Land, TX (city) Fort Bend County	3,546	4.50
Skokie, IL (village) Cook County	2,121	3.27
Lorton, VA (cdp) Fairfax County	594	3.19
Springfield, VA (cdp) Fairfax County	926	3.04
Iselin, NJ (cdp) Middlesex County	538	2.88
Woodlawn, MD (cdp) Baltimore County	1,055	2.79
Lodi, CA (city) San Joaquin County	1,709	2.75
Stafford, TX (city) Fort Bend County	486	2.75
Oak Brook, IL (village) DuPage County	215	2.73
Lincolnia, VA (cdp) Fairfax County	593	2.59
Glendale Heights, IL (village) DuPage County	877	2.56
North Valley Stream, NY (cdp) Nassau County	425	2.56
Newington, VA (cdp) Fairfax County	327	2.53
Carteret, NJ (borough) Middlesex County	551	2.41
Murphy, TX (city) Collin County	390	2.20
Newington Forest, VA (cdp) Fairfax County	274	2.20
Hybla Valley, VA (cdp) Fairfax County	345	2.18
Euless, TX (city) Tarrant County	1,097	2.14
Morton Grove, IL (village) Cook County	466	2.00
Carrollton, TX (city) Denton County	2,374	1.99
Herndon, VA (town) Fairfax County	460	1.97
Elmont, NY (cdp) Nassau County	650	1.96
Avenel, NJ (cdp) Middlesex County	333	1.96
Doctor Phillips, FL (cdp) Orange County	215	1.96
Valley Stream, NY (village) Nassau County	733	1.95
Woodlawn, VA (cdp) Fairfax County	401	1.93
Rose Hill, VA (cdp) Fairfax County	389	1.92
Burtonsville, MD (cdp) Montgomery County	160	1.92
Brownstown, MI (charter township) Wayne County	579	1.89
Groveton, VA (cdp) Fairfax County	276	1.89
Live Oak, CA (city) Sutter County	158	1.88
Franklin Park, NJ (cdp) Somerset County	248	1.87
East Meadow, NY (cdp) Nassau County	708	1.86
Archdale, NC (city) Randolph County	211	1.85
Cherry Hill, VA (cdp) Prince William County	289	1.81
South Brunswick, NJ (township) Middlesex County	766	1.76
Sterling, VA (cdp) Loudoun County	468	1.68
Neabsco, VA (cdp) Prince William County	203	1.68
Hanover Park, IL (village) Cook County	631	1.66
McNair, VA (cdp) Fairfax County	290	1.66
Burr Ridge, IL (village) DuPage County	174	1.65
Canton, MI (charter township) Wayne County	1,479	1.64
Piscataway, NJ (township) Middlesex County	920	1.64
Lombard, IL (village) DuPage County	710	1.64
Brambleton, VA (cdp) Loudoun County	161	1.64
Lake Barcroft, VA (cdp) Fairfax County	155	1.62
Garden City Park, NY (cdp) Nassau County	124	1.59
Chantilly, VA (cdp) Fairfax County	364	1.58
Franconia, VA (cdp) Fairfax County	282	1.55
Dale City, VA (cdp) Prince William County	1,013	1.54
Huntington, VA (cdp) Fairfax County	172	1.53
Ashburn, VA (cdp) Loudoun County	651	1.50
Woodbridge, NJ (township) Middlesex County	1,481	1.49
Richardson, TX (city) Dallas County	1,465	1.48
Mount Vernon, VA (cdp) Fairfax County	184	1.48
Mission Bend, TX (cdp) Fort Bend County	538	1.47
Seven Corners, VA (cdp) Fairfax County	136	1.47
North Brunswick, NJ (township) Middlesex County	586	1.44
Bailey's Crossroads, VA (cdp) Fairfax County	339	1.43
Old Bridge, NJ (township) Middlesex County	926	1.42
Woodbridge, NJ (cdp) Middlesex County	273	1.42
Sugarland Run, VA (cdp) Loudoun County	168	1.42
Jersey City, NJ (city) Hudson County	3,490	1.41
Town and Country, MO (city) St. Louis County	153	1.41
Sayreville, NJ (borough) Middlesex County	595	1.39
Annandale, VA (cdp) Fairfax County	571	1.39
Niles, IL (village) Cook County	413	1.39
North Bellmore, NY (cdp) Nassau County	278	1.39
South Riding, VA (cdp) Loudoun County	335	1.38
North Bay Shore, NY (cdp) Suffolk County	262	1.38
Kendall Park, NJ (cdp) Middlesex County	129	1.38
Hoffman Estates, IL (village) Cook County	712	1.37
Fair Lakes, VA (cdp) Fairfax County	108	1.36
West Springfield, VA (cdp) Fairfax County	304	1.35
High Point, NC (city) Guilford County	1,399	1.34
Elwood, NY (cdp) Suffolk County	149	1.33
Broadlands, VA (cdp) Loudoun County	163	1.32
North Plainfield, NJ (borough) Somerset County	287	1.31
Laurel, MD (city) Prince George's County	325	1.29
Edison, NJ (township) Middlesex County	1,274	1.27
Hicksville, NY (cdp) Nassau County	518	1.25
Lansdowne, VA (cdp) Loudoun County	140	1.24
Little Ferry, NJ (borough) Bergen County	132	1.24
Woodland, CA (city) Yolo County	677	1.22
Glen Ellyn, IL (village) DuPage County	334	1.22
Dix Hills, NY (cdp) Suffolk County	325	1.21
Dranesville, VA (cdp) Fairfax County	144	1.21
Centreville, VA (cdp) Fairfax County	852	1.20
Scottdale, GA (cdp) DeKalb County	128	1.20
Gainesville, VA (cdp) Prince William County	136	1.18
Bartlett, IL (village) DuPage County	482	1.17
South Huntington, NY (cdp) Suffolk County	110	1.17
Franklin Square, NY (cdp) Nassau County	341	1.16
Reisterstown, MD (cdp) Baltimore County	302	1.16
Budd Lake, NJ (cdp) Morris County	104	1.16
Bolingbrook, IL (village) Will County	835	1.14
Kingstowne, VA (cdp) Fairfax County	174	1.12
Scaggsville, MD (cdp) Howard County	269	1.11
Fords, NJ (cdp) Middlesex County	168	1.11
Countryside, VA (cdp) Loudoun County	112	1.11
Atlantic City, NJ (city) Atlantic County	436	1.10
Merrifield, VA (cdp) Fairfax County	168	1.10
Vernon, CT (town) Tolland County	318	1.09
Ellicott City, MD (cdp) Howard County	710	1.08
Fayetteville, GA (city) Fayette County	173	1.08
Deer Park, NY (cdp) Suffolk County	296	1.07
Fremont, CA (city) Alameda County	2,242	1.05
Marumsco, VA (cdp) Prince William County	368	1.05
Floris, VA (cdp) Fairfax County	88	1.05
Southchase, FL (cdp) Orange County	166	1.04
Bayonne, NJ (city) Hudson County	642	1.02
Selden, NY (cdp) Suffolk County	203	1.02
Farmingville, NY (cdp) Suffolk County	158	1.02
Lake Ridge, VA (cdp) Prince William County	409	1.00
Villa Park, IL (village) DuPage County	220	1.00
Lilburn, GA (city) Gwinnett County	115	0.99
Mountain House, CA (cdp) San Joaquin County	96	0.99
Triangle, VA (cdp) Prince William County	81	0.99
Franklin, NJ (township) Somerset County	609	0.98
Clarksburg, MD (cdp) Montgomery County	135	0.98
Bloomingdale, IL (village) DuPage County	213	0.97
Sudley, VA (cdp) Prince William County	155	0.96
Leesburg, VA (town) Loudoun County	403	0.95
Carol Stream, IL (village) DuPage County	376	0.95
Teaneck, NJ (township) Bergen County	376	0.95
Linton Hall, VA (cdp) Prince William County	338	0.95
Greatwood, TX (cdp) Fort Bend County	110	0.95
Streamwood, IL (village) Cook County	373	0.94
Mountain Park, GA (cdp) Gwinnett County	109	0.94
West Bloomfield, MI (charter township) Oakland County	600	0.93
South Windsor, CT (town) Hartford County	239	0.93
Colleyville, TX (city) Tarrant County	212	0.93
Cascades, VA (cdp) Loudoun County	111	0.93
August, CA (cdp) San Joaquin County	78	0.93
Galloway, NJ (township) Atlantic County	345	0.92
Cloverly, MD (cdp) Montgomery County	139	0.92
Burke, VA (cdp) Fairfax County	375	0.91
Bradley Gardens, NJ (cdp) Somerset County	129	0.91
Horizon West, FL (cdp) Orange County	127	0.91
Bellmawr, NJ (borough) Camden County	105	0.91
Colonie, NY (town) Albany County	736	0.90
Niskayuna, NY (town) Schenectady County	195	0.90
Lowes Island, VA (cdp) Loudoun County	97	0.90
New Hyde Park, NY (village) Nassau County	87	0.90
Plano, TX (city) Collin County	2,314	0.89
Pittsfield, MI (charter township) Washtenaw County	308	0.89

Please refer to the Explanation of Data in the front of the book for more detailed information.

Race

Asian: Sri Lankan

U.S. and 50 States Sorted by Population and Percent of Total Population

Place	Population	%
United States	**45,381**	**0.01**
California	11,929	0.03
New York	6,153	0.03
Texas	2,916	0.01
Maryland	2,836	0.05
New Jersey	2,656	0.03
Virginia	1,529	0.02
Florida	1,517	0.01
Illinois	1,320	0.01
Massachusetts	1,254	0.02
Pennsylvania	1,100	0.01
Ohio	1,029	0.01
Minnesota	944	0.02
Michigan	887	0.01
Washington	861	0.01
Georgia	743	0.01
North Carolina	721	0.01
Connecticut	669	0.02
Nevada	610	0.02
Arizona	587	0.01
Oregon	491	0.01
Indiana	372	0.01
Missouri	341	0.01
Kansas	307	0.01
Wisconsin	307	0.01
Colorado	291	0.01
Hawaii	231	0.02
District of Columbia	221	0.04
Tennessee	214	<0.01
South Carolina	212	<0.01
Kentucky	206	<0.01
Louisiana	204	<0.01
Iowa	180	0.01
Oklahoma	164	<0.01
North Dakota	131	0.02
New Mexico	122	0.01
Alabama	122	<0.01
Arkansas	122	<0.01
Nebraska	116	0.01
Mississippi	109	<0.01
Rhode Island	106	0.01
Utah	102	<0.01
New Hampshire	79	0.01
Delaware	69	0.01
West Virginia	69	<0.01
Alaska	49	0.01
Idaho	46	<0.01
Vermont	43	0.01
Maine	40	<0.01
Wyoming	31	0.01
South Dakota	12	<0.01
Montana	11	<0.01

Place	Population	%
Maryland	2,836	0.05
District of Columbia	221	0.04
California	11,929	0.03
New York	6,153	0.03
New Jersey	2,656	0.03
Virginia	1,529	0.02
Massachusetts	1,254	0.02
Minnesota	944	0.02
Connecticut	669	0.02
Nevada	610	0.02
Hawaii	231	0.02
North Dakota	131	0.02
United States	**45,381**	**0.01**
Texas	2,916	0.01
Florida	1,517	0.01
Illinois	1,320	0.01
Pennsylvania	1,100	0.01
Ohio	1,029	0.01
Michigan	887	0.01
Washington	861	0.01
Georgia	743	0.01
North Carolina	721	0.01
Arizona	587	0.01
Oregon	491	0.01
Indiana	372	0.01
Missouri	341	0.01
Kansas	307	0.01
Wisconsin	307	0.01
Colorado	291	0.01
Iowa	180	0.01
New Mexico	122	0.01
Nebraska	116	0.01
Rhode Island	106	0.01
New Hampshire	79	0.01
Delaware	69	0.01
Alaska	49	0.01
Vermont	43	0.01
Wyoming	31	0.01
Tennessee	214	<0.01
South Carolina	212	<0.01
Kentucky	206	<0.01
Louisiana	204	<0.01
Oklahoma	164	<0.01
Alabama	122	<0.01
Arkansas	122	<0.01
Mississippi	109	<0.01
Utah	102	<0.01
West Virginia	69	<0.01
Idaho	46	<0.01
Maine	40	<0.01
South Dakota	12	<0.01
Montana	11	<0.01

Please refer to the Explanation of Data in the front of the book for more detailed information.

Race

Asian: Sri Lankan

Top 150 Places Sorted by Population

Based on all places, regardless of total population

Place	Population	%
New York, NY (city) Kings County	4,369	0.05
Los Angeles, CA (city) Los Angeles County	2,358	0.06
Staten Island, NY (borough) Richmond County	1,766	0.38
Queens, NY (borough) Queens County	1,536	0.07
Manhattan, NY (borough) New York County	563	0.04
Chicago, IL (city) Cook County	376	0.01
San Jose, CA (city) Santa Clara County	358	0.04
Houston, TX (city) Harris County	324	0.02
Brooklyn, NY (borough) Kings County	270	0.01
Torrance, CA (city) Los Angeles County	266	0.18
San Diego, CA (city) San Diego County	248	0.02
Austin, TX (city) Travis County	244	0.03
Anaheim, CA (city) Orange County	237	0.07
Bronx, NY (borough) Bronx County	234	0.02
Washington, DC (city) District of Columbia	221	0.04
Irvine, CA (city) Orange County	217	0.10
Long Beach, CA (city) Los Angeles County	212	0.05
Aspen Hill, MD (cdp) Montgomery County	203	0.42
Columbus, OH (city) Franklin County	202	0.03
Germantown, MD (cdp) Montgomery County	201	0.23
Hempstead, NY (town) Nassau County	201	0.03
San Francisco, CA (city) San Francisco County	191	0.02
Arlington, VA (cdp) Arlington County	185	0.09
Pasadena, CA (city) Los Angeles County	182	0.13
Plano, TX (city) Collin County	178	0.07
Rockville, MD (city) Montgomery County	176	0.29
Fremont, CA (city) Alameda County	172	0.08
Philadelphia, PA (city) Philadelphia County	172	0.01
Cary, NC (town) Wake County	161	0.12
South Brunswick, NJ (township) Middlesex County	157	0.36
Newark, NJ (city) Essex County	152	0.05
Spring Valley, NV (cdp) Clark County	150	0.08
Wheaton, MD (cdp) Montgomery County	147	0.30
Edison, NJ (township) Middlesex County	147	0.15
Santa Clarita, CA (city) Los Angeles County	147	0.08
Bethesda, MD (cdp) Montgomery County	145	0.24
Las Vegas, NV (city) Clark County	141	0.02
Urban Honolulu, HI (cdp) Honolulu County	136	0.04
Seattle, WA (city) King County	133	0.02
Amherst, NY (town) Erie County	130	0.11
Riverside, CA (city) Riverside County	122	0.04
Phoenix, AZ (city) Maricopa County	122	0.01
Woodbridge, NJ (township) Middlesex County	121	0.12
Gaithersburg, MD (city) Montgomery County	117	0.20
Thousand Oaks, CA (city) Ventura County	115	0.09
Wichita, KS (city) Sedgwick County	115	0.03
Tucson, AZ (city) Pima County	114	0.02
Arlington, TX (city) Tarrant County	113	0.03
Sunnyvale, CA (city) Santa Clara County	108	0.08
Lancaster, CA (city) Los Angeles County	107	0.07
Fort Worth, TX (city) Tarrant County	106	0.01
Dallas, TX (city) Dallas County	103	0.01
Montgomery Village, MD (cdp) Montgomery County	100	0.31
North Bethesda, MD (cdp) Montgomery County	100	0.23
Lake Forest, CA (city) Orange County	100	0.13
Fargo, ND (city) Cass County	100	0.09
Brookhaven, NY (town) Suffolk County	100	0.02
Piscataway, NJ (township) Middlesex County	98	0.17
Oakland, CA (city) Alameda County	97	0.02
Cerritos, CA (city) Los Angeles County	95	0.19
Jersey City, NJ (city) Hudson County	95	0.04
Boston, MA (city) Suffolk County	95	0.02
Sacramento, CA (city) Sacramento County	94	0.02
Olney, MD (cdp) Montgomery County	93	0.27
Stanton, CA (city) Orange County	91	0.24
Minneapolis, MN (city) Hennepin County	90	0.02
Portland, OR (city) Multnomah County	89	0.02
Glenmont, MD (cdp) Montgomery County	88	0.65
Corona, CA (city) Riverside County	88	0.06
Palmdale, CA (city) Los Angeles County	88	0.06
Redland, MD (cdp) Montgomery County	87	0.50
San Antonio, TX (city) Medina County	86	0.01
Baltimore, MD (city) Baltimore city County	85	0.01
New Rochelle, NY (city) Westchester County	83	0.11
Burbank, CA (city) Los Angeles County	82	0.08
West Covina, CA (city) Los Angeles County	82	0.08
Simi Valley, CA (city) Ventura County	82	0.07
Cincinnati, OH (city) Hamilton County	82	0.03
Santa Clara, CA (city) Santa Clara County	81	0.07
Potomac, MD (cdp) Montgomery County	80	0.18
St. Paul, MN (city) Ramsey County	80	0.03
Palm Springs, CA (city) Riverside County	78	0.18
Ann Arbor, MI (city) Washtenaw County	77	0.07
East Brunswick, NJ (township) Middlesex County	75	0.16
Raleigh, NC (city) Wake County	75	0.02
Vancouver, WA (city) Clark County	74	0.05
Tustin, CA (city) Orange County	73	0.10
Baton Rouge, LA (city) East Baton Rouge Parish	73	0.03
Aurora, IL (city) Kane County	72	0.04
Lexington-Fayette, KY (cons. govt) Fayette County	72	0.02
Union City, NJ (city) Hudson County	71	0.11
Berkeley, CA (city) Alameda County	71	0.06
Coral Springs, FL (city) Broward County	71	0.06
Orange, CA (city) Orange County	70	0.05
Flower Mound, TX (town) Denton County	69	0.11
Henderson, NV (city) Clark County	69	0.03
Arcadia, CA (city) Los Angeles County	67	0.12
Silver Spring, MD (cdp) Montgomery County	67	0.09
Cambridge, MA (city) Middlesex County	67	0.06
Gardena, CA (city) Los Angeles County	66	0.11
Folsom, CA (city) Sacramento County	66	0.09
Huntington Beach, CA (city) Orange County	66	0.03
Tampa, FL (city) Hillsborough County	66	0.02
Charlotte, NC (city) Mecklenburg County	66	0.01
Mountain View, CA (city) Santa Clara County	65	0.09
Davis, CA (city) Yolo County	64	0.10
Paradise, NV (cdp) Clark County	64	0.03
Naperville, IL (city) DuPage County	62	0.04
Lubbock, TX (city) Lubbock County	61	0.03
Louisville-Jefferson County, KY (metro govt) Jefferson County	61	0.01
Winchester, MA (cdp/town) Middlesex County	60	0.28
Framingham, MA (cdp/town) Middlesex County	60	0.09
Bloomington, MN (city) Hennepin County	60	0.07
Garden Grove, CA (city) Orange County	60	0.04
Madison, WI (city) Dane County	60	0.03
Columbia, MD (cdp) Howard County	59	0.06
North Hempstead, NY (town) Nassau County	59	0.03
Oyster Bay, NY (town) Nassau County	59	0.02
San Ramon, CA (city) Contra Costa County	58	0.08
Irving, TX (city) Dallas County	57	0.03
Beaverton, OR (city) Washington County	56	0.06
West Falls Church, VA (cdp) Fairfax County	55	0.19
Clarkstown, NY (town) Rockland County	55	0.07
San Buenaventura (Ventura), CA (city) Ventura County	55	0.05
Fullerton, CA (city) Orange County	55	0.04
Rancho Palos Verdes, CA (city) Los Angeles County	54	0.13
College Station, TX (city) Brazos County	54	0.06
Enterprise, NV (cdp) Clark County	54	0.05
Buffalo, NY (city) Erie County	54	0.02
North Brunswick, NJ (township) Middlesex County	53	0.13
Ames, IA (city) Story County	53	0.09
Lakewood, CA (city) Los Angeles County	53	0.07
Kendall Park, NJ (cdp) Middlesex County	52	0.56
Skokie, IL (village) Cook County	52	0.08
Pearland, TX (city) Brazoria County	52	0.06
Farmington Hills, MI (city) Oakland County	51	0.06
Costa Mesa, CA (city) Orange County	51	0.05
Bellevue, WA (city) King County	51	0.04
Nashville-Davidson, TN (metro govt) Davidson County	51	0.01
Plainsboro, NJ (township) Middlesex County	50	0.22
Glendale, CA (city) Los Angeles County	49	0.03
Rancho Cucamonga, CA (city) San Bernardino County	49	0.03
Atlanta, GA (city) Fulton County	49	0.01
Cypress, CA (city) Orange County	48	0.10
Richmond, CA (city) Contra Costa County	48	0.05
Chandler, AZ (city) Maricopa County	48	0.02
Fontana, CA (city) San Bernardino County	48	0.02
Norfolk, VA (ind. city) Norfolk independent city	48	0.02
Chino Hills, CA (city) San Bernardino County	47	0.06
Newton, MA (city) Middlesex County	47	0.06

SECTION THREE

Race

Asian: Sri Lankan

Top 150 Places Sorted by Percent of Total Population

Based on all places, regardless of total population

Place	Population	%
Ste. Marie, IL (village) Jasper County	4	1.64
Mud Bay, AK (cdp) Haines Borough	3	1.42
Covenant Life, AK (cdp) Haines Borough	1	1.16
Glenview, KY (city) Jefferson County	4	0.75
Mosier, OR (city) Wasco County	3	0.69
Glenmont, MD (cdp) Montgomery County	88	0.65
Poquott, NY (village) Suffolk County	6	0.63
Moorhead, MN (township) Clay County	1	0.59
Allenhurst, GA (city) Liberty County	4	0.58
Mono City, CA (cdp) Mono County	1	0.58
Kendall Park, NJ (cdp) Middlesex County	52	0.56
Fairfax, OH (village) Hamilton County	9	0.53
Redland, MD (cdp) Montgomery County	87	0.50
Dane, WI (village) Dane County	5	0.50
Highland, MD (cdp) Howard County	5	0.48
Quechee, VT (cdp) Windsor County	3	0.46
Bellerose Terrace, NY (cdp) Nassau County	10	0.45
Independence, CA (cdp) Inyo County	3	0.45
Fern Forest, HI (cdp) Hawaii County	4	0.43
Aspen Hill, MD (cdp) Montgomery County	203	0.42
Derwood, MD (cdp) Montgomery County	10	0.42
Watchtower, NY (cdp) Ulster County	10	0.42
Calverton, VA (cdp) Fauquier County	1	0.42
Fishers Island, NY (cdp) Suffolk County	1	0.42
Heathcote, NJ (cdp) Middlesex County	24	0.41
Stowe, VT (cdp) Lamoille County	2	0.40
Exton, PA (cdp) Chester County	19	0.39
Staten Island, NY (borough) Richmond County	1,766	0.38
Four Bridges, OH (cdp) Butler County	11	0.38
Dellwood, MN (city) Washington County	4	0.38
Forestburgh, NY (town) Sullivan County	3	0.37
South Brunswick, NJ (township) Middlesex County	157	0.36
North Kensington, MD (cdp) Montgomery County	33	0.35
East Pasadena, CA (cdp) Los Angeles County	21	0.34
Le Sauk, MN (township) Stearns County	6	0.34
South Floral Park, NY (village) Nassau County	6	0.34
Wakefield, NE (city) Dixon County	5	0.34
Forest Glen, MD (cdp) Montgomery County	22	0.33
Slippery Rock, PA (borough) Butler County	12	0.33
Allentown, NJ (borough) Monmouth County	6	0.33
Bedford, NY (cdp) Westchester County	6	0.33
North El Monte, CA (cdp) Los Angeles County	12	0.32
Laurel Hill, NC (cdp) Scotland County	4	0.32
Boulevard, CA (cdp) San Diego County	1	0.32
Montgomery Village, MD (cdp) Montgomery County	100	0.31
Travilah, MD (cdp) Montgomery County	38	0.31
Harbor Isle, NY (cdp) Nassau County	4	0.31
Norris Canyon, CA (cdp) Contra Costa County	3	0.31
Wheaton, MD (cdp) Montgomery County	147	0.30
Fords, NJ (cdp) Middlesex County	46	0.30
Kenvil, NJ (cdp) Morris County	9	0.30
Rockville, MD (city) Montgomery County	176	0.29
Charter Oak, CA (cdp) Los Angeles County	27	0.29
Woodburn, VA (cdp) Fairfax County	25	0.29
Perry, PA (township) Berks County	7	0.29
Buckeystown, MD (cdp) Frederick County	3	0.29
Winchester, MA (cdp/town) Middlesex County	60	0.28
Garden City Park, NY (cdp) Nassau County	22	0.28
Bartonsville, MD (cdp) Frederick County	4	0.28
Brooklyn, WI (town) Green County	3	0.28
Fox, PA (township) Sullivan County	1	0.28
Olney, MD (cdp) Montgomery County	93	0.27
Urbana, MD (cdp) Frederick County	25	0.27
Las Flores, CA (cdp) Orange County	16	0.27
Layhill, MD (cdp) Montgomery County	14	0.27
Princess Anne, MD (town) Somerset County	9	0.27
Wilton Center, CT (cdp) Fairfield County	2	0.27
Princeton Meadows, NJ (cdp) Middlesex County	36	0.26
University of California Davis, CA (cdp) Yolo County	15	0.26
Mountain Lakes, NJ (borough) Morris County	11	0.26
Towamensing Trails, PA (cdp) Carbon County	6	0.26
Vance, AL (town) Tuscaloosa County	4	0.26
Diablo, CA (cdp) Contra Costa County	3	0.26
French Lake, MN (township) Wright County	3	0.26
Titusville, NY (cdp) Dutchess County	2	0.25
Bethesda, MD (cdp) Montgomery County	145	0.24
Stanton, CA (city) Orange County	91	0.24
Dayton, NJ (cdp) Middlesex County	17	0.24
Society Hill, NJ (cdp) Middlesex County	9	0.24
Princeton Junction, NJ (cdp) Mercer County	6	0.24
Germantown, MD (cdp) Montgomery County	201	0.23
North Bethesda, MD (cdp) Montgomery County	100	0.23
Haverford College, PA (cdp) Delaware County	3	0.23
Melville, RI (cdp) Newport County	3	0.23
Cedro, NM (cdp) Bernalillo County	1	0.23
Plainsboro, NJ (township) Middlesex County	50	0.22
Clemson, SC (city) Pickens County	31	0.22
Mountain View, AR (city) Stone County	6	0.22
Richmondville, NY (village) Schoharie County	2	0.22
Hillsboro Pines, FL (cdp) Broward County	1	0.22
Innsbrook, VA (cdp) Henrico County	16	0.21
Pompey, NY (town) Onondaga County	15	0.21
East Richmond Heights, CA (cdp) Contra Costa County	7	0.21
Vails Gate, NY (cdp) Orange County	7	0.21
Lynchburg, MS (cdp) DeSoto County	5	0.21
Rancho Viejo, TX (town) Cameron County	5	0.21
Westwood, PA (cdp) Chester County	2	0.21
Big Water, UT (town) Kane County	1	0.21
Gaithersburg, MD (city) Montgomery County	117	0.20
Duarte, CA (city) Los Angeles County	42	0.20
Franklin Park, NJ (cdp) Somerset County	26	0.20
Gold River, CA (cdp) Sacramento County	16	0.20
Ancient Oaks, PA (cdp) Lehigh County	13	0.20
Fair Oaks Ranch, TX (city) Bexar County	12	0.20
Mayflower Village, CA (cdp) Los Angeles County	11	0.20
San Pasqual, CA (cdp) Los Angeles County	4	0.20
Cerritos, CA (city) Los Angeles County	95	0.19
West Falls Church, VA (cdp) Fairfax County	55	0.19
Lomita, CA (city) Los Angeles County	38	0.19
Bradley Gardens, NJ (cdp) Somerset County	27	0.19
Clarksburg, MD (cdp) Montgomery County	26	0.19
Oak Brook, IL (village) DuPage County	15	0.19
Duncan, SC (town) Spartanburg County	6	0.19
Bald Eagle, PA (township) Clinton County	4	0.19
Hines, OR (city) Harney County	3	0.19
Bradbury, CA (city) Los Angeles County	2	0.19
Torrance, CA (city) Los Angeles County	266	0.18
Potomac, MD (cdp) Montgomery County	80	0.18
Palm Springs, CA (city) Riverside County	78	0.18
Reading, MA (cdp/town) Middlesex County	45	0.18
Montgomery, NJ (township) Somerset County	40	0.18
Iselin, NJ (cdp) Middlesex County	34	0.18
Morrisville, NC (town) Wake County	34	0.18
Farmingdale, NY (village) Nassau County	15	0.18
Ann Arbor, MI (charter township) Washtenaw County	8	0.18
Bloomfield Hills, MI (city) Oakland County	7	0.18
East Ithaca, NY (cdp) Tompkins County	4	0.18
Gates Mills, OH (village) Cuyahoga County	4	0.18
Union City, OH (village) Darke County	3	0.18
Castanea, PA (cdp) Clinton County	2	0.18
Linton, ND (city) Emmons County	2	0.18
Piscataway, NJ (township) Middlesex County	98	0.17
Starkville, MS (city) Oktibbeha County	40	0.17
North Plainfield, NJ (borough) Somerset County	37	0.17
East San Gabriel, CA (cdp) Los Angeles County	25	0.17
Dunn Loring, VA (cdp) Fairfax County	15	0.17
Garden City South, NY (cdp) Nassau County	7	0.17
Green, IN (town) Howard County	4	0.17
Altamont, NY (village) Albany County	3	0.17
Castanea, PA (township) Clinton County	2	0.17
Craig, AK (city) Prince of Wales-Hyder Census Area	2	0.17
Ripton, VT (town) Addison County	1	0.17
Southport, ME (town) Lincoln County	1	0.17
East Brunswick, NJ (township) Middlesex County	75	0.16
Greenbriar, VA (cdp) Fairfax County	13	0.16
St. Cloud, MN (city) Sherburne County	11	0.16
Boxborough, MA (town) Middlesex County	8	0.16
Samoset, FL (cdp) Manatee County	6	0.16
King City, OR (city) Washington County	5	0.16
Osceola, WI (village) Polk County	4	0.16

Please refer to the Explanation of Data in the front of the book for more detailed information.

Race

Asian: Sri Lankan

Top 150 Places Sorted by Percent of Total Population

Based on places with total population of 7,500 or more

Place	Population	%
Glenmont, MD (cdp) Montgomery County	88	0.65
Kendall Park, NJ (cdp) Middlesex County	52	0.56
Redland, MD (cdp) Montgomery County	87	0.50
Aspen Hill, MD (cdp) Montgomery County	203	0.42
Staten Island, NY (borough) Richmond County	1,766	0.38
South Brunswick, NJ (township) Middlesex County	157	0.36
North Kensington, MD (cdp) Montgomery County	33	0.35
Montgomery Village, MD (cdp) Montgomery County	100	0.31
Travilah, MD (cdp) Montgomery County	38	0.31
Wheaton, MD (cdp) Montgomery County	147	0.30
Fords, NJ (cdp) Middlesex County	46	0.30
Rockville, MD (city) Montgomery County	176	0.29
Charter Oak, CA (cdp) Los Angeles County	27	0.29
Woodburn, VA (cdp) Fairfax County	25	0.29
Winchester, MA (cdp/town) Middlesex County	60	0.28
Garden City Park, NY (cdp) Nassau County	22	0.28
Olney, MD (cdp) Montgomery County	93	0.27
Urbana, MD (cdp) Frederick County	25	0.27
Princeton Meadows, NJ (cdp) Middlesex County	36	0.26
Bethesda, MD (cdp) Montgomery County	145	0.24
Stanton, CA (city) Orange County	91	0.24
Germantown, MD (cdp) Montgomery County	201	0.23
North Bethesda, MD (cdp) Montgomery County	100	0.23
Plainsboro, NJ (township) Middlesex County	50	0.22
Clemson, SC (city) Pickens County	31	0.22
Innsbrook, VA (cdp) Henrico County	16	0.21
Gaithersburg, MD (city) Montgomery County	117	0.20
Duarte, CA (city) Los Angeles County	42	0.20
Franklin Park, NJ (cdp) Somerset County	26	0.20
Gold River, CA (cdp) Sacramento County	16	0.20
Cerritos, CA (city) Los Angeles County	95	0.19
West Falls Church, VA (cdp) Fairfax County	55	0.19
Lomita, CA (city) Los Angeles County	38	0.19
Bradley Gardens, NJ (cdp) Somerset County	27	0.19
Clarksburg, MD (cdp) Montgomery County	26	0.19
Oak Brook, IL (village) DuPage County	15	0.19
Torrance, CA (city) Los Angeles County	266	0.18
Potomac, MD (cdp) Montgomery County	80	0.18
Palm Springs, CA (city) Riverside County	78	0.18
Reading, MA (cdp/town) Middlesex County	45	0.18
Montgomery, NJ (township) Somerset County	40	0.18
Iselin, NJ (cdp) Middlesex County	34	0.18
Morrisville, NC (town) Wake County	34	0.18
Farmingdale, NY (village) Nassau County	15	0.18
Piscataway, NJ (township) Middlesex County	98	0.17
Starkville, MS (city) Oktibbeha County	40	0.17
North Plainfield, NJ (borough) Somerset County	37	0.17
East San Gabriel, CA (cdp) Los Angeles County	25	0.17
Dunn Loring, VA (cdp) Fairfax County	15	0.17
East Brunswick, NJ (township) Middlesex County	75	0.16
Greenbriar, VA (cdp) Fairfax County	13	0.16
Edison, NJ (township) Middlesex County	147	0.15
West Carson, CA (cdp) Los Angeles County	32	0.15
La Cañada Flintridge, CA (city) Los Angeles County	30	0.15
Castaic, CA (cdp) Los Angeles County	28	0.15
Woodbridge, NJ (cdp) Middlesex County	28	0.15
Albany, CA (city) Alameda County	27	0.15
McNair, VA (cdp) Fairfax County	27	0.15
Jollyville, TX (cdp) Williamson County	24	0.15
Eggertsville, NY (cdp) Erie County	23	0.15
Stanford, CA (cdp) Santa Clara County	21	0.15
Purdue University, IN (cdp) Tippecanoe County	18	0.15
Camp Hill, PA (borough) Cumberland County	12	0.15
Lexington, MA (cdp/town) Middlesex County	44	0.14
West Lafayette, IN (city) Tippecanoe County	40	0.14
West Windsor, NJ (township) Mercer County	38	0.14
Cockeysville, MD (cdp) Baltimore County	30	0.14
Oxford, MS (city) Lafayette County	27	0.14
Creve Coeur, MO (city) St. Louis County	25	0.14
West Whiteland, PA (township) Chester County	25	0.14
Hunters Creek, FL (cdp) Orange County	20	0.14
Lake Barcroft, VA (cdp) Fairfax County	13	0.14
Bernardsville, NJ (borough) Somerset County	11	0.14
Rolling Hills Estates, CA (city) Los Angeles County	11	0.14
Pasadena, CA (city) Los Angeles County	182	0.13
Lake Forest, CA (city) Orange County	100	0.13
Rancho Palos Verdes, CA (city) Los Angeles County	54	0.13
North Brunswick, NJ (township) Middlesex County	53	0.13
Brighton, NY (cdp/town) Monroe County	46	0.13
Claremont, CA (city) Los Angeles County	46	0.13
Burlington, MA (cdp/town) Middlesex County	32	0.13
Okemos, MI (cdp) Ingham County	28	0.13
Stevenson Ranch, CA (cdp) Los Angeles County	23	0.13
Holmdel, NJ (township) Monmouth County	22	0.13
Cloverly, MD (cdp) Montgomery County	19	0.13
Metuchen, NJ (borough) Middlesex County	17	0.13
Emeryville, CA (city) Alameda County	13	0.13
Brookdale, NJ (cdp) Essex County	12	0.13
Potsdam, NY (village) St. Lawrence County	12	0.13
Burtonsville, MD (cdp) Montgomery County	11	0.13
Old Town, ME (city) Penobscot County	10	0.13
Wood-Ridge, NJ (borough) Bergen County	10	0.13
Cary, NC (town) Wake County	161	0.12
Woodbridge, NJ (township) Middlesex County	121	0.12
Arcadia, CA (city) Los Angeles County	67	0.12
South Riding, VA (cdp) Loudoun County	28	0.12
Ballenger Creek, MD (cdp) Frederick County	22	0.12
Nanuet, NY (cdp) Rockland County	21	0.12
El Segundo, CA (city) Los Angeles County	20	0.12
Idylwood, VA (cdp) Fairfax County	20	0.12
Pike Creek Valley, DE (cdp) New Castle County	14	0.12
Congers, NY (cdp) Rockland County	10	0.12
Gateway, FL (cdp) Lee County	10	0.12
Amherst, NY (town) Erie County	130	0.11
New Rochelle, NY (city) Westchester County	83	0.11
Union City, NJ (city) Hudson County	71	0.11
Flower Mound, TX (town) Denton County	69	0.11
Gardena, CA (city) Los Angeles County	66	0.11
Lawrence, NJ (township) Mercer County	38	0.11
Los Altos, CA (city) Santa Clara County	32	0.11
Pullman, WA (city) Whitman County	32	0.11
South Pasadena, CA (city) Los Angeles County	29	0.11
Ridgewood, NJ (village) Bergen County	27	0.11
Ilchester, MD (cdp) Howard County	26	0.11
North Potomac, MD (cdp) Montgomery County	26	0.11
Acton, MA (town) Middlesex County	25	0.11
Fairland, MD (cdp) Montgomery County	25	0.11
East Lyme, CT (town) New London County	21	0.11
Lakeland South, WA (cdp) King County	13	0.11
Leonia, NJ (borough) Bergen County	10	0.11
Bothell East, WA (cdp) Snohomish County	9	0.11
Yorkshire, VA (cdp) Prince William County	8	0.11
Irvine, CA (city) Orange County	217	0.10
Tustin, CA (city) Orange County	73	0.10
Davis, CA (city) Yolo County	64	0.10
Cypress, CA (city) Orange County	48	0.10
Covina, CA (city) Los Angeles County	46	0.10
Middletown, CT (city/town) Middlesex County	46	0.10
Pittsfield, MI (charter township) Washtenaw County	34	0.10
Elmont, NY (cdp) Nassau County	33	0.10
Centereach, NY (cdp) Suffolk County	30	0.10
Walnut, CA (city) Los Angeles County	29	0.10
Savage, MN (city) Scott County	27	0.10
Bergenfield, NJ (borough) Bergen County	26	0.10
Carbondale, IL (city) Jackson County	25	0.10
Tysons Corner, VA (cdp) Fairfax County	20	0.10
Avon, CT (town) Hartford County	19	0.10
Rolla, MO (city) Phelps County	19	0.10
Sharon, MA (town) Norfolk County	18	0.10
Kirksville, MO (city) Adair County	17	0.10
Damascus, MD (cdp) Montgomery County	16	0.10
La Grange, NY (town) Dutchess County	16	0.10
La Palma, CA (city) Orange County	15	0.10
Orange, CT (cdp/town) New Haven County	14	0.10
Paradise Valley, AZ (town) Maricopa County	13	0.10
San Marino, CA (city) Los Angeles County	13	0.10
Grand Terrace, CA (city) San Bernardino County	12	0.10
Home Gardens, CA (cdp) Riverside County	11	0.10
River Forest, IL (village) Cook County	11	0.10
Scottdale, GA (cdp) DeKalb County	11	0.10

Please refer to the Explanation of Data in the front of the book for more detailed information.

Race

Asian: Taiwanese

U.S. and 50 States Sorted by Population and Percent of Total Population

Place	Population	%
United States	**230,382**	**0.07**
California	109,928	0.30
New York	18,868	0.10
Texas	16,555	0.07
New Jersey	10,317	0.12
Washington	8,130	0.12
Illinois	6,705	0.05
Maryland	5,440	0.09
Massachusetts	5,353	0.08
Florida	4,218	0.02
Virginia	4,130	0.05
Pennsylvania	3,830	0.03
Georgia	3,819	0.04
Michigan	3,347	0.03
Ohio	3,172	0.03
North Carolina	2,151	0.02
Arizona	1,920	0.03
Oregon	1,888	0.05
Colorado	1,668	0.03
Indiana	1,646	0.03
Missouri	1,632	0.03
Nevada	1,476	0.05
Minnesota	1,365	0.03
Connecticut	1,215	0.03
Hawaii	1,161	0.09
Wisconsin	1,036	0.02
Tennessee	935	0.01
Utah	814	0.03
Kansas	807	0.03
Louisiana	684	0.02
Iowa	601	0.02
Oklahoma	591	0.02
Alabama	528	0.01
Kentucky	504	0.01
South Carolina	477	0.01
District of Columbia	402	0.07
Arkansas	380	0.01
New Mexico	366	0.02
New Hampshire	339	0.03
Rhode Island	325	0.03
Delaware	283	0.03
Idaho	265	0.02
Nebraska	216	0.01
Mississippi	172	0.01
West Virginia	171	0.01
Vermont	117	0.02
Maine	109	0.01
Alaska	88	0.01
Montana	83	0.01
North Dakota	74	0.01
Wyoming	41	0.01
South Dakota	40	<0.01

Place	Population	%
California	109,928	0.30
New Jersey	10,317	0.12
Washington	8,130	0.12
New York	18,868	0.10
Maryland	5,440	0.09
Hawaii	1,161	0.09
Massachusetts	5,353	0.08
United States	**230,382**	**0.07**
Texas	16,555	0.07
District of Columbia	402	0.07
Illinois	6,705	0.05
Virginia	4,130	0.05
Oregon	1,888	0.05
Nevada	1,476	0.05
Georgia	3,819	0.04
Pennsylvania	3,830	0.03
Michigan	3,347	0.03
Ohio	3,172	0.03
Arizona	1,920	0.03
Colorado	1,668	0.03
Indiana	1,646	0.03
Missouri	1,632	0.03
Minnesota	1,365	0.03
Connecticut	1,215	0.03
Utah	814	0.03
Kansas	807	0.03
New Hampshire	339	0.03
Rhode Island	325	0.03
Delaware	283	0.03
Florida	4,218	0.02
North Carolina	2,151	0.02
Wisconsin	1,036	0.02
Louisiana	684	0.02
Iowa	601	0.02
Oklahoma	591	0.02
New Mexico	366	0.02
Idaho	265	0.02
Vermont	117	0.02
Tennessee	935	0.01
Alabama	528	0.01
Kentucky	504	0.01
South Carolina	477	0.01
Arkansas	380	0.01
Nebraska	216	0.01
Mississippi	172	0.01
West Virginia	171	0.01
Maine	109	0.01
Alaska	88	0.01
Montana	83	0.01
North Dakota	74	0.01
Wyoming	41	0.01
South Dakota	40	<0.01

Please refer to the Explanation of Data in the front of the book for more detailed information.

Race

Asian: Taiwanese

Top 150 Places Sorted by Population

Based on all places, regardless of total population

Place	Population	%
New York, NY (city) Kings County	13,682	0.17
Queens, NY (borough) Queens County	8,962	0.40
San Jose, CA (city) Santa Clara County	6,579	0.70
Irvine, CA (city) Orange County	5,790	2.73
Los Angeles, CA (city) Los Angeles County	5,282	0.14
Arcadia, CA (city) Los Angeles County	4,846	8.60
Fremont, CA (city) Alameda County	4,572	2.14
Rowland Heights, CA (cdp) Los Angeles County	3,476	7.09
San Diego, CA (city) San Diego County	3,400	0.26
Manhattan, NY (borough) New York County	3,318	0.21
Diamond Bar, CA (city) Los Angeles County	3,162	5.69
Hacienda Heights, CA (cdp) Los Angeles County	2,944	5.45
Houston, TX (city) Harris County	2,910	0.14
San Francisco, CA (city) San Francisco County	2,806	0.35
Cupertino, CA (city) Santa Clara County	2,753	4.72
Walnut, CA (city) Los Angeles County	2,064	7.08
Temple City, CA (city) Los Angeles County	1,964	5.52
Cerritos, CA (city) Los Angeles County	1,945	3.97
Seattle, WA (city) King County	1,940	0.32
Alhambra, CA (city) Los Angeles County	1,866	2.25
Sunnyvale, CA (city) Santa Clara County	1,736	1.24
Austin, TX (city) Travis County	1,683	0.21
Plano, TX (city) Collin County	1,604	0.62
San Marino, CA (city) Los Angeles County	1,498	11.39
Torrance, CA (city) Los Angeles County	1,436	0.99
Chino Hills, CA (city) San Bernardino County	1,422	1.90
Sugar Land, TX (city) Fort Bend County	1,394	1.77
Bellevue, WA (city) King County	1,374	1.12
West Covina, CA (city) Los Angeles County	1,347	1.27
Chicago, IL (city) Cook County	1,319	0.05
Saratoga, CA (city) Santa Clara County	1,233	4.12
Monterey Park, CA (city) Los Angeles County	1,233	2.05
Brooklyn, NY (borough) Kings County	1,075	0.04
Berkeley, CA (city) Alameda County	1,066	0.95
Palo Alto, CA (city) Santa Clara County	1,061	1.65
San Gabriel, CA (city) Los Angeles County	1,009	2.54
Boston, MA (city) Suffolk County	976	0.16
Pasadena, CA (city) Los Angeles County	887	0.65
Santa Clara, CA (city) Santa Clara County	862	0.74
Milpitas, CA (city) Santa Clara County	860	1.29
Ann Arbor, MI (city) Washtenaw County	858	0.75
El Monte, CA (city) Los Angeles County	816	0.72
East San Gabriel, CA (cdp) Los Angeles County	809	5.44
North Hempstead, NY (town) Nassau County	809	0.36
Fullerton, CA (city) Orange County	782	0.58
Edison, NJ (township) Middlesex County	759	0.76
Mountain View, CA (city) Santa Clara County	757	1.02
Rancho Palos Verdes, CA (city) Los Angeles County	750	1.80
Tustin, CA (city) Orange County	741	0.98
Anaheim, CA (city) Orange County	740	0.22
Philadelphia, PA (city) Philadelphia County	736	0.05
Cambridge, MA (city) Middlesex County	725	0.69
Urban Honolulu, HI (cdp) Honolulu County	641	0.19
Columbus, OH (city) Franklin County	626	0.08
Eastvale, CA (cdp) Riverside County	622	1.16
Dallas, TX (city) Dallas County	621	0.05
Rancho Cucamonga, CA (city) San Bernardino County	609	0.37
Naperville, IL (city) DuPage County	597	0.42
Yorba Linda, CA (city) Orange County	555	0.86
Huntington Beach, CA (city) Orange County	548	0.29
Riverside, CA (city) Riverside County	547	0.18
Fountain Valley, CA (city) Orange County	529	0.96
Parsippany-Troy Hills, NJ (township) Morris County	526	0.99
North Potomac, MD (cdp) Montgomery County	512	2.10
Rockville, MD (city) Montgomery County	506	0.83
Chino, CA (city) San Bernardino County	503	0.65
San Ramon, CA (city) Contra Costa County	480	0.67
Pleasanton, CA (city) Alameda County	478	0.68
Orange, CA (city) Orange County	477	0.35
Rosemead, CA (city) Los Angeles County	461	0.86
Pittsburgh, PA (city) Allegheny County	461	0.15
Cypress, CA (city) Orange County	453	0.95
Davis, CA (city) Yolo County	446	0.68
Pomona, CA (city) Los Angeles County	445	0.30
Union City, CA (city) Alameda County	441	0.63
Redmond, WA (city) King County	439	0.81
Hempstead, NY (town) Nassau County	438	0.06
San Mateo, CA (city) San Mateo County	433	0.45
Richardson, TX (city) Dallas County	430	0.43
South Pasadena, CA (city) Los Angeles County	428	1.67
Madison, WI (city) Dane County	426	0.18
Urbana, IL (city) Champaign County	422	1.02
Troy, MI (city) Oakland County	415	0.51
Johns Creek, GA (city) Fulton County	412	0.54
Brookline, MA (cdp/town) Norfolk County	411	0.70
Jersey City, NJ (city) Hudson County	406	0.16
Baltimore, MD (city) Baltimore city County	406	0.07
Washington, DC (city) District of Columbia	402	0.07
Oyster Bay, NY (town) Nassau County	401	0.14
Oakland, CA (city) Alameda County	401	0.10
Los Altos, CA (city) Santa Clara County	398	1.37
East Brunswick, NJ (township) Middlesex County	393	0.83
Arlington, TX (city) Tarrant County	389	0.11
College Station, TX (city) Brazos County	386	0.41
San Antonio, TX (city) Medina County	385	0.03
Upland, CA (city) San Bernardino County	382	0.52
Foster City, CA (city) San Mateo County	378	1.24
Santa Monica, CA (city) Los Angeles County	370	0.41
Spring Valley, NV (cdp) Clark County	370	0.21
Newport Beach, CA (city) Orange County	369	0.43
Sacramento, CA (city) Sacramento County	367	0.08
Placentia, CA (city) Orange County	358	0.71
Long Beach, CA (city) Los Angeles County	356	0.08
Potomac, MD (cdp) Montgomery County	354	0.79
Arlington, VA (cdp) Arlington County	352	0.17
Thousand Oaks, CA (city) Ventura County	346	0.27
Cary, NC (town) Wake County	346	0.26
Phoenix, AZ (city) Maricopa County	339	0.02
Newton, MA (city) Middlesex County	338	0.40
Portland, OR (city) Multnomah County	337	0.06
Buena Park, CA (city) Orange County	332	0.41
Atlanta, GA (city) Fulton County	321	0.08
Claremont, CA (city) Los Angeles County	317	0.91
Livingston, NJ (township) Essex County	313	1.07
Chandler, AZ (city) Maricopa County	310	0.13
Millbrae, CA (city) San Mateo County	300	1.39
Lake Forest, CA (city) Orange County	293	0.38
Evanston, IL (city) Cook County	290	0.39
Las Vegas, NV (city) Clark County	288	0.05
El Cerrito, CA (city) Contra Costa County	287	1.22
West Windsor, NJ (township) Mercer County	282	1.04
Brea, CA (city) Orange County	281	0.72
Germantown, MD (cdp) Montgomery County	278	0.32
Holmdel, NJ (township) Monmouth County	274	1.63
Covina, CA (city) Los Angeles County	273	0.57
Champaign, IL (city) Champaign County	272	0.34
Durham, NC (city) Durham County	269	0.12
Raleigh, NC (city) Wake County	269	0.07
McLean, VA (cdp) Fairfax County	263	0.55
Missouri City, TX (city) Fort Bend County	262	0.39
Bloomington, IN (city) Monroe County	260	0.32
La Palma, CA (city) Orange County	259	1.66
Piscataway, NJ (township) Middlesex County	259	0.46
Baldwin Park, CA (city) Los Angeles County	259	0.34
Tempe, AZ (city) Maricopa County	259	0.16
Minneapolis, MN (city) Hennepin County	258	0.07
Walnut Creek, CA (city) Contra Costa County	249	0.39
Gainesville, FL (city) Alachua County	249	0.20
Lexington, MA (cdp/town) Middlesex County	248	0.79
Palos Verdes Estates, CA (city) Los Angeles County	246	1.83
Sammamish, WA (city) King County	245	0.54
Gaithersburg, MD (city) Montgomery County	243	0.41
Vancouver, WA (city) Clark County	239	0.15
Laguna Niguel, CA (city) Orange County	235	0.37
Overland Park, KS (city) Johnson County	234	0.13
Artesia, CA (city) Los Angeles County	233	1.41
Bridgewater, NJ (township) Somerset County	233	0.52
Denver, CO (city) Denver County	232	0.04
Redwood City, CA (city) San Mateo County	227	0.30
Charlotte, NC (city) Mecklenburg County	223	0.03

SECTION THREE

Please refer to the Explanation of Data in the front of the book for more detailed information.

Race

Asian: Taiwanese

Top 150 Places Sorted by Percent of Total Population

Based on all places, regardless of total population

Place	Population	%
San Marino, CA (city) Los Angeles County	1,498	11.39
Arcadia, CA (city) Los Angeles County	4,846	8.60
Point Comfort, TX (city) Calhoun County	54	7.33
Rowland Heights, CA (cdp) Los Angeles County	3,476	7.09
Walnut, CA (city) Los Angeles County	2,064	7.08
Diamond Bar, CA (city) Los Angeles County	3,162	5.69
Temple City, CA (city) Los Angeles County	1,964	5.52
Hacienda Heights, CA (cdp) Los Angeles County	2,944	5.45
East San Gabriel, CA (cdp) Los Angeles County	809	5.44
Cupertino, CA (city) Santa Clara County	2,753	4.72
Bradbury, CA (city) Los Angeles County	47	4.48
Saratoga, CA (city) Santa Clara County	1,233	4.12
Cerritos, CA (city) Los Angeles County	1,945	3.97
Blawenburg, NJ (cdp) Somerset County	9	3.21
East Pasadena, CA (cdp) Los Angeles County	196	3.19
North El Monte, CA (cdp) Los Angeles County	114	3.06
Irvine, CA (city) Orange County	5,790	2.73
Mayflower Village, CA (cdp) Los Angeles County	146	2.65
San Gabriel, CA (city) Los Angeles County	1,009	2.54
Littlejohn Island, ME (cdp) Cumberland County	3	2.54
Russell Gardens, NY (village) Nassau County	23	2.43
University of California Davis, CA (cdp) Yolo County	138	2.39
Forest Home, NY (cdp) Tompkins County	13	2.27
Alhambra, CA (city) Los Angeles County	1,866	2.25
Norris Canyon, CA (cdp) Contra Costa County	21	2.19
Fremont, CA (city) Alameda County	4,572	2.14
North Potomac, MD (cdp) Montgomery County	512	2.10
Dutch John, UT (cdp) Daggett County	3	2.07
Monterey Park, CA (city) Los Angeles County	1,233	2.05
San Pasqual, CA (cdp) Los Angeles County	39	1.91
Chino Hills, CA (city) San Bernardino County	1,422	1.90
Palos Verdes Estates, CA (city) Los Angeles County	246	1.83
Rancho Palos Verdes, CA (city) Los Angeles County	750	1.80
Thomaston, NY (village) Nassau County	47	1.80
Sugar Land, TX (city) Fort Bend County	1,394	1.77
Port Lavaca, TX (city) Calhoun County	206	1.68
South Pasadena, CA (city) Los Angeles County	428	1.67
La Palma, CA (city) Orange County	259	1.66
Palo Alto, CA (city) Santa Clara County	1,061	1.65
Villa Park, CA (city) Orange County	96	1.65
Holmdel, NJ (township) Monmouth County	274	1.63
Hillsborough, CA (town) San Mateo County	170	1.57
Los Altos Hills, CA (town) Santa Clara County	122	1.54
Travilah, MD (cdp) Montgomery County	185	1.52
Ann Arbor, MI (charter township) Washtenaw County	66	1.51
University Gardens, NY (cdp) Nassau County	63	1.49
East Ithaca, NY (cdp) Tompkins County	33	1.48
Artesia, CA (city) Los Angeles County	233	1.41
Millbrae, CA (city) San Mateo County	300	1.39
Haugen, WI (village) Barron County	4	1.39
Rolling Hills Estates, CA (city) Los Angeles County	111	1.38
Los Altos, CA (city) Santa Clara County	398	1.37
Acalanes Ridge, CA (cdp) Contra Costa County	15	1.32
Milpitas, CA (city) Santa Clara County	860	1.29
Stanford, CA (cdp) Santa Clara County	178	1.29
West Covina, CA (city) Los Angeles County	1,347	1.27
Loyola, CA (cdp) Santa Clara County	41	1.26
East Hanover, NJ (township) Morris County	140	1.25
Sunnyvale, CA (city) Santa Clara County	1,736	1.24
Foster City, CA (city) San Mateo County	378	1.24
Society Hill, NJ (cdp) Middlesex County	47	1.23
El Cerrito, CA (city) Contra Costa County	287	1.22
Berkeley Lake, GA (city) Gwinnett County	19	1.21
Emeryville, CA (city) Alameda County	121	1.20
Eastvale, CA (cdp) Riverside County	622	1.16
Albany, CA (city) Alameda County	215	1.16
Hanover, NJ (township) Morris County	159	1.16
Troutville, VA (town) Botetourt County	5	1.16
La Habra Heights, CA (city) Los Angeles County	60	1.13
Rolling Hills, CA (city) Los Angeles County	21	1.13
Bellevue, WA (city) King County	1,374	1.12
North Hills, NY (village) Nassau County	56	1.10
Yarrow Point, WA (town) King County	11	1.10
San Pedro, NM (cdp) Santa Fe County	2	1.09
Bellaire, TX (city) Harris County	182	1.08

Place	Population	%
Indian Creek, IL (village) Lake County	5	1.08
Livingston, NJ (township) Essex County	313	1.07
West Windsor, NJ (township) Mercer County	282	1.04
Mountain View, CA (city) Santa Clara County	757	1.02
Urbana, IL (city) Champaign County	422	1.02
Bethany, OR (cdp) Washington County	211	1.02
Lansing, NY (village) Tompkins County	36	1.02
Oak Brook, IL (village) DuPage County	79	1.00
Torrance, CA (city) Los Angeles County	1,436	0.99
Parsippany-Troy Hills, NJ (township) Morris County	526	0.99
Georgetown, IL (cdp) McDonough County	4	0.99
Tustin, CA (city) Orange County	741	0.98
Englewood Cliffs, NJ (borough) Bergen County	52	0.98
Purdue University, IN (cdp) Tippecanoe County	118	0.97
Fountain Valley, CA (city) Orange County	529	0.96
Piney Point Village, TX (city) Harris County	30	0.96
Berkeley, CA (city) Alameda County	1,066	0.95
Cypress, CA (city) Orange County	453	0.95
Mansfield Center, CT (cdp) Tolland County	9	0.95
O'Brien, TX (city) Haskell County	1	0.94
Lanesboro, MN (city) Fillmore County	7	0.93
Darfur, MN (city) Watonwan County	1	0.93
Hays, TX (city) Hays County	2	0.92
Claremont, CA (city) Los Angeles County	317	0.91
Industry, CA (city) Los Angeles County	2	0.91
Floris, VA (cdp) Fairfax County	75	0.90
Canyonville, OR (city) Douglas County	17	0.90
Crossgate, KY (city) Jefferson County	2	0.89
North Gate, CA (cdp) Contra Costa County	6	0.88
Thornburg, PA (borough) Allegheny County	4	0.88
Newcastle, WA (city) King County	90	0.87
Eastgate, WA (cdp) King County	43	0.87
Harbor Hills, NY (cdp) Nassau County	5	0.87
Yorba Linda, CA (city) Orange County	555	0.86
Rosemead, CA (city) Los Angeles County	461	0.86
New Territory, TX (cdp) Fort Bend County	131	0.86
Klahanie, WA (cdp) King County	91	0.85
Lake Success, NY (village) Nassau County	25	0.85
Boyden, IA (city) Sioux County	6	0.85
Laytonsville, MD (town) Montgomery County	3	0.85
Warren, NJ (township) Somerset County	129	0.84
Derwood, MD (cdp) Montgomery County	20	0.84
Woodway, WA (city) Snohomish County	11	0.84
Saddle Rock, NY (village) Nassau County	7	0.84
Rockville, MD (city) Montgomery County	506	0.83
East Brunswick, NJ (township) Middlesex County	393	0.83
Montville, NJ (township) Morris County	176	0.82
University at Buffalo, NY (cdp) Erie County	50	0.82
Greenvale, NY (cdp) Nassau County	9	0.82
Redmond, WA (city) King County	439	0.81
Medina, WA (city) King County	24	0.81
Flemington, GA (city) Liberty County	6	0.81
Lauderdale, MN (city) Ramsey County	19	0.80
Talmage, CA (cdp) Mendocino County	9	0.80
Golf, IL (village) Cook County	4	0.80
Potomac, MD (cdp) Montgomery County	354	0.79
Lexington, MA (cdp/town) Middlesex County	248	0.79
Mercer Island, WA (city) King County	176	0.78
Montgomery, NJ (township) Somerset County	174	0.78
Princeton, NJ (borough) Mercer County	96	0.78
Annandale, NJ (cdp) Hunterdon County	13	0.77
Edison, NJ (township) Middlesex County	759	0.76
Great Neck Estates, NY (village) Nassau County	21	0.76
Valley Acres, CA (cdp) Kern County	4	0.76
Fisher Island, FL (cdp) Miami-Dade County	1	0.76
Ann Arbor, MI (city) Washtenaw County	858	0.75
Moraga, CA (town) Contra Costa County	120	0.75
Oak Hills, OR (cdp) Washington County	85	0.75
Jupiter Inlet Colony, FL (town) Palm Beach County	3	0.75
Santa Clara, CA (city) Santa Clara County	862	0.74
Green Brook, NJ (township) Somerset County	53	0.74
Lebanon, NJ (borough) Hunterdon County	10	0.74
Isla Vista, CA (cdp) Santa Barbara County	169	0.73
Laguna Woods, CA (city) Orange County	119	0.73
Catheys Valley, CA (cdp) Mariposa County	6	0.73

Please refer to the Explanation of Data in the front of the book for more detailed information.

Race

Asian: Taiwanese

Top 150 Places Sorted by Percent of Total Population

Based on places with total population of 7,500 or more

Place	Population	%
San Marino, CA (city) Los Angeles County	1,498	11.39
Arcadia, CA (city) Los Angeles County	4,846	8.60
Rowland Heights, CA (cdp) Los Angeles County	3,476	7.09
Walnut, CA (city) Los Angeles County	2,064	7.08
Diamond Bar, CA (city) Los Angeles County	3,162	5.69
Temple City, CA (city) Los Angeles County	1,964	5.52
Hacienda Heights, CA (cdp) Los Angeles County	2,944	5.45
East San Gabriel, CA (cdp) Los Angeles County	809	5.44
Cupertino, CA (city) Santa Clara County	2,753	4.72
Saratoga, CA (city) Santa Clara County	1,233	4.12
Cerritos, CA (city) Los Angeles County	1,945	3.97
Irvine, CA (city) Orange County	5,790	2.73
San Gabriel, CA (city) Los Angeles County	1,009	2.54
Alhambra, CA (city) Los Angeles County	1,866	2.25
Fremont, CA (city) Alameda County	4,572	2.14
North Potomac, MD (cdp) Montgomery County	512	2.10
Monterey Park, CA (city) Los Angeles County	1,233	2.05
Chino Hills, CA (city) San Bernardino County	1,422	1.90
Palos Verdes Estates, CA (city) Los Angeles County	246	1.83
Rancho Palos Verdes, CA (city) Los Angeles County	750	1.80
Sugar Land, TX (city) Fort Bend County	1,394	1.77
Port Lavaca, TX (city) Calhoun County	206	1.68
South Pasadena, CA (city) Los Angeles County	428	1.67
La Palma, CA (city) Orange County	259	1.66
Palo Alto, CA (city) Santa Clara County	1,061	1.65
Holmdel, NJ (township) Monmouth County	274	1.63
Hillsborough, CA (town) San Mateo County	170	1.57
Los Altos Hills, CA (town) Santa Clara County	122	1.54
Travilah, MD (cdp) Montgomery County	185	1.52
Artesia, CA (city) Los Angeles County	233	1.41
Millbrae, CA (city) San Mateo County	300	1.39
Rolling Hills Estates, CA (city) Los Angeles County	111	1.38
Los Altos, CA (city) Santa Clara County	398	1.37
Milpitas, CA (city) Santa Clara County	860	1.29
Stanford, CA (cdp) Santa Clara County	178	1.29
West Covina, CA (city) Los Angeles County	1,347	1.27
East Hanover, NJ (township) Morris County	140	1.25
Sunnyvale, CA (city) Santa Clara County	1,736	1.24
Foster City, CA (city) San Mateo County	378	1.24
El Cerrito, CA (city) Contra Costa County	287	1.22
Emeryville, CA (city) Alameda County	121	1.20
Eastvale, CA (cdp) Riverside County	622	1.16
Albany, CA (city) Alameda County	215	1.16
Hanover, NJ (township) Morris County	159	1.16
Bellevue, WA (city) King County	1,374	1.12
Bellaire, TX (city) Harris County	182	1.08
Livingston, NJ (township) Essex County	313	1.07
West Windsor, NJ (township) Mercer County	282	1.04
Mountain View, CA (city) Santa Clara County	757	1.02
Urbana, IL (city) Champaign County	422	1.02
Bethany, OR (cdp) Washington County	211	1.02
Oak Brook, IL (village) DuPage County	79	1.00
Torrance, CA (city) Los Angeles County	1,436	0.99
Parsippany-Troy Hills, NJ (township) Morris County	526	0.99
Tustin, CA (city) Orange County	741	0.98
Purdue University, IN (cdp) Tippecanoe County	118	0.97
Fountain Valley, CA (city) Orange County	529	0.96
Berkeley, CA (city) Alameda County	1,066	0.95
Cypress, CA (city) Orange County	453	0.95
Claremont, CA (city) Los Angeles County	317	0.91
Floris, VA (cdp) Fairfax County	75	0.90
Newcastle, WA (city) King County	90	0.87
Yorba Linda, CA (city) Orange County	555	0.86
Rosemead, CA (city) Los Angeles County	461	0.86
New Territory, TX (cdp) Fort Bend County	131	0.86
Klahanie, WA (cdp) King County	91	0.85
Warren, NJ (township) Somerset County	129	0.84
Rockville, MD (city) Montgomery County	506	0.83
East Brunswick, NJ (township) Middlesex County	393	0.83
Montville, NJ (township) Morris County	176	0.82
Redmond, WA (city) King County	439	0.81
Potomac, MD (cdp) Montgomery County	354	0.79
Lexington, MA (cdp/town) Middlesex County	248	0.79
Mercer Island, WA (city) King County	176	0.78
Montgomery, NJ (township) Somerset County	174	0.78
Princeton, NJ (borough) Mercer County	96	0.78
Edison, NJ (township) Middlesex County	759	0.76
Ann Arbor, MI (city) Washtenaw County	858	0.75
Moraga, CA (town) Contra Costa County	120	0.75
Oak Hills, OR (cdp) Washington County	85	0.75
Santa Clara, CA (city) Santa Clara County	862	0.74
Isla Vista, CA (cdp) Santa Barbara County	169	0.73
Laguna Woods, CA (city) Orange County	119	0.73
El Monte, CA (city) Los Angeles County	816	0.72
Brea, CA (city) Orange County	281	0.72
Placentia, CA (city) Orange County	358	0.71
Ithaca, NY (city) Tompkins County	214	0.71
West Lafayette, IN (city) Tippecanoe County	211	0.71
San Jose, CA (city) Santa Clara County	6,579	0.70
Brookline, MA (cdp/town) Norfolk County	411	0.70
Cambridge, MA (city) Middlesex County	725	0.69
Burlingame, CA (city) San Mateo County	198	0.69
Willowbrook, IL (village) DuPage County	59	0.69
Pleasanton, CA (city) Alameda County	478	0.68
Davis, CA (city) Yolo County	446	0.68
San Ramon, CA (city) Contra Costa County	480	0.67
Martinsville, NJ (cdp) Somerset County	79	0.66
Pasadena, CA (city) Los Angeles County	887	0.65
Chino, CA (city) San Bernardino County	503	0.65
Short Hills, NJ (cdp) Essex County	86	0.65
Blackhawk, CA (cdp) Contra Costa County	60	0.64
Union City, CA (city) Alameda County	441	0.63
Princeton, NJ (township) Mercer County	103	0.63
Plano, TX (city) Collin County	1,604	0.62
Paramus, NJ (borough) Bergen County	160	0.61
Oak Park, CA (cdp) Ventura County	84	0.61
Piedmont, CA (city) Alameda County	65	0.61
Park Forest Village, PA (cdp) Centre County	59	0.61
Plainsboro, NJ (township) Middlesex County	136	0.59
Millburn, NJ (township) Essex County	118	0.59
Syosset, NY (cdp) Nassau County	111	0.59
Cresskill, NJ (borough) Bergen County	51	0.59
Fullerton, CA (city) Orange County	782	0.58
Berkeley Heights, NJ (township) Union County	76	0.58
Covina, CA (city) Los Angeles County	273	0.57
Issaquah, WA (city) King County	174	0.57
Greentree, NJ (cdp) Camden County	65	0.57
Cherry Creek, CO (cdp) Arapahoe County	62	0.56
Rossmoor, CA (cdp) Orange County	57	0.56
McLean, VA (cdp) Fairfax County	263	0.55
University of Virginia, VA (cdp) Albemarle County	42	0.55
Johns Creek, GA (city) Fulton County	412	0.54
Sammamish, WA (city) King County	245	0.54
Monrovia, CA (city) Los Angeles County	199	0.54
Jollyville, TX (cdp) Williamson County	87	0.54
Clayton, MO (city) St. Louis County	85	0.53
Upland, CA (city) San Bernardino County	382	0.52
Bridgewater, NJ (township) Somerset County	233	0.52
Lisle, IL (village) DuPage County	117	0.52
Ferguson, PA (township) Centre County	92	0.52
Troy, MI (city) Oakland County	415	0.51
San Dimas, CA (city) Los Angeles County	169	0.51
Ithaca, NY (town) Tompkins County	102	0.51
Tysons Corner, VA (cdp) Fairfax County	101	0.51
Bradley Gardens, NJ (cdp) Somerset County	73	0.51
Jericho, NY (cdp) Nassau County	68	0.50
Lomita, CA (city) Los Angeles County	100	0.49
Lansing, NY (town) Tompkins County	54	0.49
Gold River, CA (cdp) Sacramento County	39	0.49
Garden City Park, NY (cdp) Nassau County	38	0.49
Belmont, CA (city) San Mateo County	125	0.48
Dublin, CA (city) Alameda County	215	0.47
Laguna Hills, CA (city) Orange County	144	0.47
Kendall Park, NJ (cdp) Middlesex County	44	0.47
South San Gabriel, CA (cdp) Los Angeles County	38	0.47
Piscataway, NJ (township) Middlesex County	259	0.46
Campbell, CA (city) Santa Clara County	180	0.46
Tenafly, NJ (borough) Bergen County	67	0.46
East Foothills, CA (cdp) Santa Clara County	38	0.46
San Mateo, CA (city) San Mateo County	433	0.45

Please refer to the Explanation of Data in the front of the book for more detailed information.

Race

Asian: Thai

U.S. and 50 States Sorted by Population and Percent of Total Population

Place	Population	%
United States	**237,583**	**0.08**
California	67,707	0.18
Texas	16,472	0.07
Florida	15,333	0.08
New York	11,763	0.06
Illinois	9,800	0.08
Washington	9,699	0.14
Virginia	9,170	0.11
Nevada	7,783	0.29
Maryland	5,513	0.10
Georgia	5,168	0.05
Arizona	4,977	0.08
North Carolina	4,782	0.05
Massachusetts	4,712	0.07
Colorado	4,232	0.08
Pennsylvania	4,103	0.03
Ohio	4,024	0.03
New Jersey	3,923	0.04
Hawaii	3,701	0.27
Oregon	3,692	0.10
Michigan	3,212	0.03
Minnesota	2,734	0.05
Missouri	2,471	0.04
Utah	2,276	0.08
Iowa	2,212	0.07
Tennessee	2,183	0.03
Indiana	2,176	0.03
Wisconsin	2,050	0.04
Oklahoma	1,943	0.05
South Carolina	1,797	0.04
Connecticut	1,705	0.05
Kansas	1,576	0.06
Alaska	1,533	0.22
Alabama	1,481	0.03
Louisiana	1,466	0.03
Kentucky	1,235	0.03
Arkansas	1,018	0.03
New Mexico	944	0.05
Nebraska	921	0.05
Idaho	799	0.05
New Hampshire	705	0.05
Mississippi	703	0.02
Rhode Island	591	0.06
Delaware	544	0.06
Maine	516	0.04
District of Columbia	497	0.08
West Virginia	389	0.02
Montana	324	0.03
South Dakota	284	0.03
Vermont	266	0.04
Wyoming	259	0.05
North Dakota	219	0.03

Place	Population	%
Nevada	7,783	0.29
Hawaii	3,701	0.27
Alaska	1,533	0.22
California	67,707	0.18
Washington	9,699	0.14
Virginia	9,170	0.11
Maryland	5,513	0.10
Oregon	3,692	0.10
United States	**237,583**	**0.08**
Florida	15,333	0.08
Illinois	9,800	0.08
Arizona	4,977	0.08
Colorado	4,232	0.08
Utah	2,276	0.08
District of Columbia	497	0.08
Texas	16,472	0.07
Massachusetts	4,712	0.07
Iowa	2,212	0.07
New York	11,763	0.06
Kansas	1,576	0.06
Rhode Island	591	0.06
Delaware	544	0.06
Georgia	5,168	0.05
North Carolina	4,782	0.05
Minnesota	2,734	0.05
Oklahoma	1,943	0.05
Connecticut	1,705	0.05
New Mexico	944	0.05
Nebraska	921	0.05
Idaho	799	0.05
New Hampshire	705	0.05
Wyoming	259	0.05
New Jersey	3,923	0.04
Missouri	2,471	0.04
Wisconsin	2,050	0.04
South Carolina	1,797	0.04
Maine	516	0.04
Vermont	266	0.04
Pennsylvania	4,103	0.03
Ohio	4,024	0.03
Michigan	3,212	0.03
Tennessee	2,183	0.03
Indiana	2,176	0.03
Alabama	1,481	0.03
Louisiana	1,466	0.03
Kentucky	1,235	0.03
Arkansas	1,018	0.03
Montana	324	0.03
South Dakota	284	0.03
North Dakota	219	0.03
Mississippi	703	0.02
West Virginia	389	0.02

Please refer to the Explanation of Data in the front of the book for more detailed information.

Race

Asian: Thai

Top 150 Places Sorted by Population

Based on all places, regardless of total population

Place	Population	%
Los Angeles, CA (city) Los Angeles County	14,122	0.37
New York, NY (city) Kings County	7,244	0.09
Queens, NY (borough) Queens County	4,124	0.18
Chicago, IL (city) Cook County	3,168	0.12
San Francisco, CA (city) San Francisco County	2,879	0.36
San Diego, CA (city) San Diego County	2,061	0.16
Manhattan, NY (borough) New York County	1,657	0.10
Las Vegas, NV (city) Clark County	1,492	0.26
Seattle, WA (city) King County	1,479	0.24
Houston, TX (city) Harris County	1,462	0.07
Long Beach, CA (city) Los Angeles County	1,266	0.27
Spring Valley, NV (cdp) Clark County	1,231	0.69
San Jose, CA (city) Santa Clara County	1,178	0.12
Visalia, CA (city) Tulare County	1,134	0.91
San Antonio, TX (city) Medina County	1,099	0.08
Urban Honolulu, HI (cdp) Honolulu County	1,073	0.32
Anchorage, AK (municipality) Anchorage Municipality	969	0.33
Phoenix, AZ (city) Maricopa County	964	0.07
Portland, OR (city) Multnomah County	960	0.16
Austin, TX (city) Travis County	929	0.12
Brooklyn, NY (borough) Kings County	883	0.04
Dallas, TX (city) Dallas County	868	0.07
Des Moines, IA (city) Polk County	806	0.40
Paradise, NV (cdp) Clark County	795	0.36
Sacramento, CA (city) Sacramento County	784	0.17
Sunrise Manor, NV (cdp) Clark County	776	0.41
Enterprise, NV (cdp) Clark County	767	0.71
Boston, MA (city) Suffolk County	762	0.12
Fort Worth, TX (city) Tarrant County	756	0.10
North Las Vegas, NV (city) Clark County	726	0.33
Henderson, NV (city) Clark County	686	0.27
Arlington, VA (cdp) Arlington County	672	0.32
Cerritos, CA (city) Los Angeles County	651	1.33
Denver, CO (city) Denver County	649	0.11
Anaheim, CA (city) Orange County	632	0.19
Philadelphia, PA (city) Philadelphia County	627	0.04
Tucson, AZ (city) Pima County	611	0.12
Irvine, CA (city) Orange County	598	0.28
Columbus, OH (city) Franklin County	594	0.08
Glendale, CA (city) Los Angeles County	592	0.31
Monterey Park, CA (city) Los Angeles County	569	0.94
Alhambra, CA (city) Los Angeles County	561	0.68
Colorado Springs, CO (city) El Paso County	557	0.13
Jacksonville, FL (city) Duval County	557	0.07
Bellflower, CA (city) Los Angeles County	552	0.72
Burbank, CA (city) Los Angeles County	538	0.52
Oklahoma City, OK (city) Oklahoma County	529	0.09
Torrance, CA (city) Los Angeles County	524	0.36
Fresno, CA (city) Fresno County	515	0.10
Aurora, CO (city) Arapahoe County	513	0.16
Washington, DC (city) District of Columbia	497	0.08
Bellevue, WA (city) King County	480	0.39
Tampa, FL (city) Hillsborough County	474	0.14
Oakland, CA (city) Alameda County	472	0.12
Charlotte, NC (city) Mecklenburg County	461	0.06
Santa Clarita, CA (city) Los Angeles County	456	0.26
Nashville-Davidson, TN (metro govt) Davidson County	450	0.07
West Covina, CA (city) Los Angeles County	449	0.42
Moreno Valley, CA (city) Riverside County	427	0.22
Riverside, CA (city) Riverside County	427	0.14
Arlington, TX (city) Tarrant County	420	0.11
Bronx, NY (borough) Bronx County	414	0.03
Berkeley, CA (city) Alameda County	410	0.36
Rancho Cucamonga, CA (city) San Bernardino County	403	0.24
Huntington Beach, CA (city) Orange County	403	0.21
Fremont, CA (city) Alameda County	400	0.19
Albuquerque, NM (city) Bernalillo County	392	0.07
Tacoma, WA (city) Pierce County	391	0.20
Lakewood, CA (city) Los Angeles County	386	0.48
Reno, NV (city) Washoe County	365	0.16
Fayetteville, NC (city) Cumberland County	364	0.18
Stockton, CA (city) San Joaquin County	357	0.12
Virginia Beach, VA (ind. city) Virginia Beach independent city	353	0.08
Indianapolis, IN (city) Marion County	352	0.04
Pasadena, CA (city) Los Angeles County	347	0.25
Plano, TX (city) Collin County	347	0.13
Rowland Heights, CA (cdp) Los Angeles County	346	0.71
Norwalk, CA (city) Los Angeles County	344	0.33
Raleigh, NC (city) Wake County	343	0.08
Chandler, AZ (city) Maricopa County	334	0.14
Mesa, AZ (city) Maricopa County	328	0.07
Wichita, KS (city) Sedgwick County	325	0.08
Springfield, VA (cdp) Fairfax County	323	1.06
Chino Hills, CA (city) San Bernardino County	323	0.43
Fairfield, CA (city) Solano County	323	0.31
Irving, TX (city) Dallas County	315	0.15
Alexandria, VA (ind. city) Alexandria independent city	312	0.22
Pomona, CA (city) Los Angeles County	312	0.21
St. Petersburg, FL (city) Pinellas County	311	0.13
Minneapolis, MN (city) Hennepin County	311	0.08
Simi Valley, CA (city) Ventura County	308	0.25
Temecula, CA (city) Riverside County	303	0.30
Arcadia, CA (city) Los Angeles County	301	0.53
Wheaton, MD (cdp) Montgomery County	300	0.62
Madison, WI (city) Dane County	298	0.13
Walnut, CA (city) Los Angeles County	294	1.01
Downey, CA (city) Los Angeles County	289	0.26
Buena Park, CA (city) Orange County	288	0.36
Hacienda Heights, CA (cdp) Los Angeles County	287	0.53
San Bernardino, CA (city) San Bernardino County	286	0.14
Fullerton, CA (city) Orange County	284	0.21
Hempstead, NY (town) Nassau County	278	0.04
Yonkers, NY (city) Westchester County	268	0.14
Glendale, AZ (city) Maricopa County	267	0.12
Omaha, NE (city) Douglas County	265	0.06
Bakersfield, CA (city) Kern County	264	0.08
Quincy, MA (city) Norfolk County	262	0.28
Kansas City, MO (city) Jackson County	262	0.06
Daly City, CA (city) San Mateo County	257	0.25
Elk Grove, CA (city) Sacramento County	257	0.17
Garden Grove, CA (city) Orange County	256	0.15
Atlanta, GA (city) Fulton County	256	0.06
Sunnyvale, CA (city) Santa Clara County	252	0.18
Milwaukee, WI (city) Milwaukee County	252	0.04
Newport News, VA (ind. city) Newport News independent city	248	0.14
Pittsburgh, PA (city) Allegheny County	245	0.08
Boise City, ID (city) Ada County	244	0.12
Providence, RI (city) Providence County	241	0.14
Wright, FL (cdp) Okaloosa County	239	1.03
Louisville-Jefferson County, KY (metro govt) Jefferson County	236	0.04
Rosemead, CA (city) Los Angeles County	235	0.44
Skokie, IL (village) Cook County	234	0.36
Gilbert, AZ (town) Maricopa County	233	0.11
Temple City, CA (city) Los Angeles County	232	0.65
Santa Ana, CA (city) Orange County	232	0.07
El Monte, CA (city) Los Angeles County	230	0.20
Renton, WA (city) King County	228	0.25
St. Paul, MN (city) Ramsey County	228	0.08
Aspen Hill, MD (cdp) Montgomery County	227	0.47
Killeen, TX (city) Bell County	227	0.18
Melbourne, FL (city) Brevard County	226	0.30
Victorville, CA (city) San Bernardino County	224	0.19
Centreville, VA (cdp) Fairfax County	221	0.31
Baltimore, MD (city) Baltimore city County	220	0.04
Richmond, CA (city) Contra Costa County	217	0.21
San Gabriel, CA (city) Los Angeles County	212	0.53
Brandon, FL (cdp) Hillsborough County	211	0.20
Brookhaven, NY (town) Suffolk County	211	0.04
Gardena, CA (city) Los Angeles County	210	0.36
Tulare, CA (city) Tulare County	210	0.35
Denton, TX (city) Denton County	209	0.18
Durham, NC (city) Durham County	207	0.09
Santa Clara, CA (city) Santa Clara County	206	0.18
Spokane, WA (city) Spokane County	206	0.10
Beaverton, OR (city) Washington County	205	0.23
Diamond Bar, CA (city) Los Angeles County	203	0.37
Fort Wayne, IN (city) Allen County	202	0.08
Orlando, FL (city) Orange County	201	0.08
Lowell, MA (city) Middlesex County	200	0.19
Fontana, CA (city) San Bernardino County	200	0.10

Race

Asian: Thai

Top 150 Places Sorted by Percent of Total Population

Based on all places, regardless of total population

Place	Population	%
Bryce Canyon City, UT (town) Garfield County	32	16.16
Hollister, OK (town) Tillman County	3	6.00
Sunrise, AK (cdp) Kenai Peninsula Borough	1	5.56
Grand Canyon Village, AZ (cdp) Coconino County	108	5.39
Northway, AK (cdp) Southeast Fairbanks Census Area	3	4.23
Crown Point, AK (cdp) Kenai Peninsula Borough	3	4.05
Smolan, KS (city) Saline County	8	3.72
Lucien, OK (cdp) Noble County	3	3.41
Atlanta, MN (township) Becker County	4	3.36
Aspen Springs, CA (cdp) Mono County	2	3.08
Highwater, MN (township) Cottonwood County	5	3.01
Phillipsville, CA (cdp) Humboldt County	4	2.86
Tonyville, CA (cdp) Tulare County	9	2.85
Meade, MI (township) Mason County	5	2.76
Chautauqua, KS (city) Chautauqua County	3	2.70
Fountain, MI (village) Mason County	5	2.59
Ouzinkie, AK (city) Kodiak Island Borough	4	2.48
Green Mountain, IA (cdp) Marshall County	3	2.38
Balsam, MN (township) Aitkin County	1	2.38
Cinco Bayou, FL (town) Okaloosa County	9	2.35
Hallam, NE (village) Lancaster County	5	2.35
Lakewood, MN (township) Lake of the Woods County	2	2.35
Cactus, TX (city) Moore County	69	2.17
Grand Portage, MN (unorganized territory) Cook County	12	2.12
Little York, IN (town) Washington County	4	2.08
Kasaan, AK (city) Prince of Wales-Hyder Census Area	1	2.04
Tusayan, AZ (cdp) Coconino County	11	1.97
Riverdale, ND (city) McLean County	4	1.95
Bloomington, ID (city) Bear Lake County	4	1.94
Firth, ID (city) Bingham County	9	1.89
Lake Delton, WI (village) Sauk County	53	1.82
Wintergreen, VA (cdp) Nelson County	3	1.82
Pine Flat, CA (cdp) Tulare County	3	1.81
Botines, TX (cdp) Webb County	2	1.71
Animas, NM (cdp) Hidalgo County	4	1.69
Eldorado, MD (town) Dorchester County	1	1.69
New London, NC (town) Stanly County	10	1.67
North Buena Vista, IA (city) Clayton County	2	1.65
Clarks, NE (village) Merrick County	6	1.63
Ukiah, OR (city) Umatilla County	3	1.61
Johnstown, NE (village) Brown County	1	1.56
Willapa, WA (cdp) Pacific County	3	1.43
Hebgen Lake Estates, MT (cdp) Gallatin County	1	1.43
Stowe, VT (cdp) Lamoille County	7	1.41
Acacia Villas, FL (cdp) Palm Beach County	6	1.41
Forest Home, NY (cdp) Tompkins County	8	1.40
Scotts Mills, OR (city) Marion County	5	1.40
Kimbolton, OH (cdp) Guernsey County	2	1.39
Wyeville, WI (village) Monroe County	2	1.36
Taloga, OK (town) Dewey County	4	1.34
Cerritos, CA (city) Los Angeles County	651	1.33
Mary Esther, FL (city) Okaloosa County	49	1.27
Shalimar, FL (town) Okaloosa County	9	1.26
Platte Center, NE (village) Platte County	4	1.19
Viola, AR (town) Fulton County	4	1.19
Pilot Mound, MN (township) Fillmore County	4	1.18
Ocean City, FL (cdp) Okaloosa County	65	1.17
Mono City, CA (cdp) Mono County	2	1.16
Indian Creek, FL (village) Miami-Dade County	1	1.16
Lindsay, CA (city) Tulare County	134	1.14
Elk Mound, WI (village) Dunn County	10	1.14
Tatitlek, AK (cdp) Valdez-Cordova Census Area	1	1.14
Clearview Acres, WY (cdp) Sweetwater County	9	1.13
Wrightstown, NJ (borough) Burlington County	9	1.12
Springfield, VA (cdp) Fairfax County	323	1.06
Bear Creek, TX (village) Hays County	4	1.05
Elmer, OK (town) Jackson County	1	1.04
Wright, FL (cdp) Okaloosa County	239	1.03
Lodoga, CA (cdp) Colusa County	2	1.02
Deering, ND (city) McHenry County	1	1.02
Walnut, CA (city) Los Angeles County	294	1.01
Strand, MN (township) Norman County	1	1.01
Dahlgren Center, VA (cdp) King George County	6	1.00
Orosi, CA (cdp) Tulare County	87	0.99
Kingston Mines, IL (village) Peoria County	3	0.99
Elm Springs, AR (city) Washington County	15	0.98
Fort Walton Beach, FL (city) Okaloosa County	190	0.97
Yosemite Valley, CA (cdp) Mariposa County	10	0.97
Lemon Cove, CA (cdp) Tulare County	3	0.97
Mosquito Lake, AK (cdp) Haines Borough	3	0.97
Windemere, TX (cdp) Travis County	10	0.96
Dahlgren, IL (village) Hamilton County	5	0.95
Monterey Park, CA (city) Los Angeles County	569	0.94
Bark Ranch, CO (cdp) Boulder County	2	0.94
Beaver, UT (city) Beaver County	29	0.93
Belle Mead, NJ (cdp) Somerset County	2	0.93
Visalia, CA (city) Tulare County	1,134	0.91
North El Monte, CA (cdp) Los Angeles County	34	0.91
Hiawassee, GA (city) Towns County	8	0.91
Melbourne Village, FL (town) Brevard County	6	0.91
Swall Meadows, CA (cdp) Mono County	2	0.91
University of California Davis, CA (cdp) Yolo County	52	0.90
Central City, CO (city) Gilpin County	6	0.90
Udolpho, MN (township) Mower County	4	0.89
Colp, IL (village) Williamson County	2	0.89
Medora, ND (city) Billings County	1	0.89
Wabedo, MN (township) Cass County	3	0.88
Addington, OK (town) Jefferson County	1	0.88
Detroit, KS (cdp) Dickinson County	1	0.88
Brooksville, ME (town) Hancock County	8	0.86
Cairo, MN (township) Renville County	2	0.86
Trent, SD (town) Moody County	2	0.86
Laytonsville, MD (town) Montgomery County	3	0.85
Glenmont, MD (cdp) Montgomery County	114	0.84
Watchtower, NY (cdp) Ulster County	20	0.84
Aetna Estates, CO (cdp) Arapahoe County	7	0.84
Bluffton, MN (township) Otter Tail County	4	0.84
Evansville, MN (township) Douglas County	2	0.83
Culver, KS (city) Ottawa County	1	0.83
Noonan, ND (city) Divide County	1	0.83
Greenvale, NY (cdp) Nassau County	9	0.82
Pine Haven, WY (town) Crook County	4	0.82
Rodney Village, DE (cdp) Kent County	12	0.81
Gardiner, OR (cdp) Douglas County	2	0.81
Longville, LA (cdp) Beauregard Parish	5	0.79
Stinson Beach, CA (cdp) Marin County	5	0.79
Ellendale, DE (town) Sussex County	3	0.79
Hawaiian Acres, HI (cdp) Hawaii County	21	0.78
Deerfield, MA (cdp) Franklin County	5	0.78
Wilcox, PA (cdp) Elk County	3	0.78
St. Paul, IA (city) Lee County	1	0.78
Loma Linda, CA (city) San Bernardino County	178	0.77
Carnelian Bay, CA (cdp) Placer County	4	0.76
Fairview, MN (township) Lyon County	3	0.76
Stephenson, MI (township) Menominee County	5	0.75
Milledgeville, TN (town) McNairy County	2	0.75
Pike, CA (cdp) Sierra County	1	0.75
Callaway, FL (city) Bay County	106	0.74
Waipio Acres, HI (cdp) Honolulu County	39	0.74
Patterson Tract, CA (cdp) Tulare County	13	0.74
Laona, MN (township) Roseau County	4	0.74
Faxon, OK (town) Comanche County	1	0.74
Lakewood Village, TX (city) Denton County	4	0.73
Norway, IA (city) Benton County	4	0.73
Duncombe, IA (city) Webster County	3	0.73
San Cristobal, NM (cdp) Taos County	2	0.73
Bellflower, CA (city) Los Angeles County	552	0.72
South San Gabriel, CA (cdp) Los Angeles County	58	0.72
Hudson, MI (township) Charlevoix County	5	0.72
Early, IA (city) Sac County	4	0.72
Westport, MN (township) Pope County	2	0.72
Enterprise, NV (cdp) Clark County	767	0.71
Rowland Heights, CA (cdp) Los Angeles County	346	0.71
Greenleaf, ID (city) Canyon County	6	0.71
Alna, ME (town) Lincoln County	5	0.71
Prairie Farm, WI (town) Barron County	4	0.71
Leadington, MO (city) St. Francois County	3	0.71
Lyon Mountain, NY (cdp) Clinton County	3	0.71
Layhill, MD (cdp) Montgomery County	36	0.70
Tribes Hill, NY (cdp) Montgomery County	7	0.70

Please refer to the Explanation of Data in the front of the book for more detailed information.

Race

Asian: Thai

Top 150 Places Sorted by Percent of Total Population

Based on places with total population of 7,500 or more

Place	Population	%
Cerritos, CA (city) Los Angeles County	651	1.33
Lindsay, CA (city) Tulare County	134	1.14
Springfield, VA (cdp) Fairfax County	323	1.06
Wright, FL (cdp) Okaloosa County	239	1.03
Walnut, CA (city) Los Angeles County	294	1.01
Orosi, CA (cdp) Tulare County	87	0.99
Fort Walton Beach, FL (city) Okaloosa County	190	0.97
Monterey Park, CA (city) Los Angeles County	569	0.94
Visalia, CA (city) Tulare County	1,134	0.91
Glenmont, MD (cdp) Montgomery County	114	0.84
Loma Linda, CA (city) San Bernardino County	178	0.77
Callaway, FL (city) Bay County	106	0.74
Bellflower, CA (city) Los Angeles County	552	0.72
South San Gabriel, CA (cdp) Los Angeles County	58	0.72
Enterprise, NV (cdp) Clark County	767	0.71
Rowland Heights, CA (cdp) Los Angeles County	346	0.71
Spring Valley, NV (cdp) Clark County	1,231	0.69
Alhambra, CA (city) Los Angeles County	561	0.68
Avocado Heights, CA (cdp) Los Angeles County	102	0.66
Temple City, CA (city) Los Angeles County	232	0.65
Kemp Mill, MD (cdp) Montgomery County	82	0.65
Hybla Valley, VA (cdp) Fairfax County	99	0.63
Destin, FL (city) Okaloosa County	78	0.63
Wheaton, MD (cdp) Montgomery County	300	0.62
Franconia, VA (cdp) Fairfax County	111	0.61
Lincolnwood, IL (village) Cook County	77	0.61
Panama City Beach, FL (city) Bay County	71	0.59
Ocean Pointe, HI (cdp) Honolulu County	49	0.59
Rose Hill, VA (cdp) Fairfax County	116	0.57
Navarre, FL (cdp) Santa Rosa County	175	0.56
El Cerrito, CA (city) Contra Costa County	131	0.56
Niceville, FL (city) Okaloosa County	72	0.56
Hershey, PA (cdp) Dauphin County	78	0.55
Waimalu, HI (cdp) Honolulu County	76	0.55
Lake Barcroft, VA (cdp) Fairfax County	53	0.55
Signal Hill, CA (city) Los Angeles County	60	0.54
Holualoa, HI (cdp) Hawaii County	46	0.54
Arcadia, CA (city) Los Angeles County	301	0.53
Hacienda Heights, CA (cdp) Los Angeles County	287	0.53
San Gabriel, CA (city) Los Angeles County	212	0.53
West Springfield, VA (cdp) Fairfax County	120	0.53
Emeryville, CA (city) Alameda County	53	0.53
Burbank, CA (city) Los Angeles County	538	0.52
Stanford, CA (cdp) Santa Clara County	72	0.52
Kingsgate, WA (cdp) King County	66	0.51
Dunn Loring, VA (cdp) Fairfax County	45	0.51
Sterling, VA (cdp) Loudoun County	139	0.50
East San Gabriel, CA (cdp) Los Angeles County	75	0.50
Fife, WA (city) Pierce County	46	0.50
Lincolnia, VA (cdp) Fairfax County	113	0.49
Lakewood, CA (city) Los Angeles County	386	0.48
Worthington, MN (city) Nobles County	61	0.48
Springfield, FL (city) Bay County	43	0.48
Aspen Hill, MD (cdp) Montgomery County	227	0.47
Suisun City, CA (city) Solano County	133	0.47
Artesia, CA (city) Los Angeles County	76	0.46
Whitney, NV (cdp) Clark County	174	0.45
SeaTac, WA (city) King County	120	0.45
Vienna, VA (town) Fairfax County	71	0.45
La Palma, CA (city) Orange County	70	0.45
Rosemead, CA (city) Los Angeles County	235	0.44
Clearfield, UT (city) Davis County	132	0.44
Ewa Gentry, HI (cdp) Honolulu County	100	0.44
Mililani Mauka, HI (cdp) Honolulu County	92	0.44
Stevenson Ranch, CA (cdp) Los Angeles County	78	0.44
Storm Lake, IA (city) Buena Vista County	47	0.44
Chino Hills, CA (city) San Bernardino County	323	0.43
Mililani Town, HI (cdp) Honolulu County	118	0.43
South Pasadena, CA (city) Los Angeles County	111	0.43
Albany, CA (city) Alameda County	79	0.43
Newington, VA (cdp) Fairfax County	56	0.43
Newington Forest, VA (cdp) Fairfax County	54	0.43
Sugarland Run, VA (cdp) Loudoun County	51	0.43
West Covina, CA (city) Los Angeles County	449	0.42
Monrovia, CA (city) Los Angeles County	155	0.42
Spring Lake, NC (town) Cumberland County	50	0.42
George Mason, VA (cdp) Fairfax County	40	0.42
Conover, NC (city) Catawba County	34	0.42
Sunrise Manor, NV (cdp) Clark County	776	0.41
Cypress, CA (city) Orange County	197	0.41
Wilmette, IL (village) Cook County	111	0.41
Lorton, VA (cdp) Fairfax County	77	0.41
Royal Kunia, HI (cdp) Honolulu County	59	0.41
Des Moines, IA (city) Polk County	806	0.40
Watertown Town, MA (city) Middlesex County	127	0.40
Rosamond, CA (cdp) Kern County	73	0.40
College, AK (cdp) Fairbanks North Star Borough	52	0.40
Browns Mills, NJ (cdp) Burlington County	45	0.40
Bellevue, WA (city) King County	480	0.39
Falls Church, VA (ind. city) Falls Church independent city	48	0.39
Claremont, CA (city) Los Angeles County	131	0.38
Morton Grove, IL (village) Cook County	89	0.38
Duarte, CA (city) Los Angeles County	82	0.38
Tysons Corner, VA (cdp) Fairfax County	75	0.38
Makakilo, HI (cdp) Honolulu County	70	0.38
Rutherford, NJ (borough) Bergen County	69	0.38
North Lynnwood, WA (cdp) Snohomish County	63	0.38
Halawa, HI (cdp) Honolulu County	53	0.38
Grand Terrace, CA (city) San Bernardino County	46	0.38
Huntington, VA (cdp) Fairfax County	43	0.38
North Kensington, MD (cdp) Montgomery County	36	0.38
Four Corners, MD (cdp) Montgomery County	30	0.38
Los Angeles, CA (city) Los Angeles County	14,122	0.37
Diamond Bar, CA (city) Los Angeles County	203	0.37
Oakton, VA (cdp) Fairfax County	127	0.37
Millbrae, CA (city) San Mateo County	79	0.37
Kailua, HI (cdp) Hawaii County	44	0.37
San Francisco, CA (city) San Francisco County	2,879	0.36
Paradise, NV (cdp) Clark County	795	0.36
Torrance, CA (city) Los Angeles County	524	0.36
Berkeley, CA (city) Alameda County	410	0.36
Buena Park, CA (city) Orange County	288	0.36
Skokie, IL (village) Cook County	234	0.36
Gardena, CA (city) Los Angeles County	210	0.36
Shoreline, WA (city) King County	190	0.36
Derry, PA (township) Dauphin County	89	0.36
Kings Park West, VA (cdp) Fairfax County	48	0.36
Tulare, CA (city) Tulare County	210	0.35
Chantilly, VA (cdp) Fairfax County	81	0.35
Clinton, UT (city) Davis County	71	0.35
Marina, CA (city) Monterey County	69	0.35
Merrifield, VA (cdp) Fairfax County	54	0.35
San Marino, CA (city) Los Angeles County	46	0.35
Citrus, CA (cdp) Los Angeles County	38	0.35
Pleasant Hill, IA (city) Polk County	31	0.35
Floris, VA (cdp) Fairfax County	29	0.35
San Dimas, CA (city) Los Angeles County	112	0.34
Pemberton, NJ (township) Burlington County	95	0.34
La Crescenta-Montrose, CA (cdp) Los Angeles County	66	0.34
Mango, FL (cdp) Hillsborough County	38	0.34
Klahanie, WA (cdp) King County	36	0.34
Newcastle, WA (city) King County	35	0.34
Del Aire, CA (cdp) Los Angeles County	34	0.34
Anchorage, AK (municipality) Anchorage Municipality	969	0.33
North Las Vegas, NV (city) Clark County	726	0.33
Norwalk, CA (city) Los Angeles County	344	0.33
Beaumont, CA (city) Riverside County	123	0.33
McNair, VA (cdp) Fairfax County	57	0.33
Kingstowne, VA (cdp) Fairfax County	51	0.33
Clarksburg, MD (cdp) Montgomery County	45	0.33
Waipio, HI (cdp) Honolulu County	39	0.33
Box Elder, SD (city) Pennington County	26	0.33
Urban Honolulu, HI (cdp) Honolulu County	1,073	0.32
Arlington, VA (cdp) Arlington County	672	0.32
Rockville, MD (city) Montgomery County	193	0.32
Antelope, CA (cdp) Sacramento County	146	0.32
Burke, VA (cdp) Fairfax County	133	0.32
Summerlin South, NV (cdp) Clark County	78	0.32
Castaic, CA (cdp) Los Angeles County	61	0.32
Frederickson, WA (cdp) Pierce County	60	0.32

Race

Asian: Vietnamese

U.S. and 50 States Sorted by Population and Percent of Total Population

Place	Population	%
United States	**1,737,433**	**0.56**
California	647,589	1.74
Texas	227,968	0.91
Washington	75,843	1.13
Florida	65,772	0.35
Virginia	59,984	0.75
Georgia	49,264	0.51
Massachusetts	47,636	0.73
Pennsylvania	44,605	0.35
New York	34,510	0.18
North Carolina	30,665	0.32
Louisiana	30,202	0.67
Oregon	29,485	0.77
Illinois	29,101	0.23
Arizona	27,872	0.44
Minnesota	27,086	0.51
Maryland	26,605	0.46
Colorado	23,933	0.48
New Jersey	23,535	0.27
Michigan	19,456	0.20
Oklahoma	18,098	0.48
Missouri	16,530	0.28
Kansas	16,074	0.56
Ohio	15,639	0.14
Hawaii	13,266	0.98
Nevada	12,366	0.46
Tennessee	11,351	0.18
Connecticut	10,804	0.30
Iowa	9,543	0.31
Utah	9,338	0.34
Nebraska	8,677	0.48
Alabama	8,488	0.18
Indiana	8,175	0.13
South Carolina	7,840	0.17
Mississippi	7,721	0.26
Arkansas	6,302	0.22
Wisconsin	6,191	0.11
Kentucky	5,813	0.13
New Mexico	5,403	0.26
New Hampshire	2,907	0.22
Maine	2,170	0.16
Idaho	2,154	0.14
District of Columbia	1,856	0.31
Delaware	1,688	0.19
Rhode Island	1,615	0.15
Alaska	1,446	0.20
Vermont	1,206	0.19
West Virginia	1,104	0.06
South Dakota	1,002	0.12
North Dakota	791	0.12
Montana	481	0.05
Wyoming	283	0.05

Place	Population	%
California	647,589	1.74
Washington	75,843	1.13
Hawaii	13,266	0.98
Texas	227,968	0.91
Oregon	29,485	0.77
Virginia	59,984	0.75
Massachusetts	47,636	0.73
Louisiana	30,202	0.67
United States	**1,737,433**	**0.56**
Kansas	16,074	0.56
Georgia	49,264	0.51
Minnesota	27,086	0.51
Colorado	23,933	0.48
Oklahoma	18,098	0.48
Nebraska	8,677	0.48
Maryland	26,605	0.46
Nevada	12,366	0.46
Arizona	27,872	0.44
Florida	65,772	0.35
Pennsylvania	44,605	0.35
Utah	9,338	0.34
North Carolina	30,665	0.32
Iowa	9,543	0.31
District of Columbia	1,856	0.31
Connecticut	10,804	0.30
Missouri	16,530	0.28
New Jersey	23,535	0.27
Mississippi	7,721	0.26
New Mexico	5,403	0.26
Illinois	29,101	0.23
Arkansas	6,302	0.22
New Hampshire	2,907	0.22
Michigan	19,456	0.20
Alaska	1,446	0.20
Delaware	1,688	0.19
Vermont	1,206	0.19
New York	34,510	0.18
Tennessee	11,351	0.18
Alabama	8,488	0.18
South Carolina	7,840	0.17
Maine	2,170	0.16
Rhode Island	1,615	0.15
Ohio	15,639	0.14
Idaho	2,154	0.14
Indiana	8,175	0.13
Kentucky	5,813	0.13
South Dakota	1,002	0.12
North Dakota	791	0.12
Wisconsin	6,191	0.11
West Virginia	1,104	0.06
Montana	481	0.05
Wyoming	283	0.05

Please refer to the Explanation of Data in the front of the book for more detailed information.

Race

Asian: Vietnamese

Top 150 Places Sorted by Population

Based on all places, regardless of total population

Place	Population	%
San Jose, CA (city) Santa Clara County	106,647	11.27
Garden Grove, CA (city) Orange County	48,774	28.54
Houston, TX (city) Harris County	37,178	1.77
Westminster, CA (city) Orange County	37,176	41.44
San Diego, CA (city) San Diego County	36,713	2.81
Santa Ana, CA (city) Orange County	24,260	7.48
Los Angeles, CA (city) Los Angeles County	23,325	0.62
New York, NY (city) Kings County	16,378	0.20
Philadelphia, PA (city) Philadelphia County	16,268	1.07
San Francisco, CA (city) San Francisco County	16,075	2.00
Anaheim, CA (city) Orange County	15,674	4.66
Seattle, WA (city) King County	14,987	2.46
Portland, OR (city) Multnomah County	13,921	2.38
Arlington, TX (city) Tarrant County	13,105	3.59
Fountain Valley, CA (city) Orange County	11,861	21.44
Boston, MA (city) Suffolk County	11,670	1.89
Milpitas, CA (city) Santa Clara County	11,042	16.53
Garland, TX (city) Dallas County	10,877	4.79
Oklahoma City, OK (city) Oklahoma County	10,848	1.87
Chicago, IL (city) Cook County	10,118	0.38
Rosemead, CA (city) Los Angeles County	10,046	18.69
Oakland, CA (city) Alameda County	10,038	2.57
Wichita, KS (city) Sedgwick County	9,902	2.59
El Monte, CA (city) Los Angeles County	9,667	8.52
Irvine, CA (city) Orange County	9,000	4.24
Austin, TX (city) Travis County	8,430	1.07
Urban Honolulu, HI (cdp) Honolulu County	8,307	2.46
Fort Worth, TX (city) Tarrant County	8,223	1.11
Huntington Beach, CA (city) Orange County	8,215	4.32
Elk Grove, CA (city) Sacramento County	7,796	5.09
Sacramento, CA (city) Sacramento County	7,730	1.66
Charlotte, NC (city) Mecklenburg County	7,550	1.03
Phoenix, AZ (city) Maricopa County	7,091	0.49
Stockton, CA (city) San Joaquin County	6,552	2.25
Dallas, TX (city) Dallas County	6,307	0.53
New Orleans, LA (city) Orleans Parish	6,214	1.81
Grand Prairie, TX (city) Dallas County	6,135	3.50
Fremont, CA (city) Alameda County	5,952	2.78
Stanton, CA (city) Orange County	5,762	15.09
Worcester, MA (city) Worcester County	5,759	3.18
Renton, WA (city) King County	5,753	6.33
Denver, CO (city) Denver County	5,528	0.92
Alhambra, CA (city) Los Angeles County	5,348	6.44
Brooklyn, NY (borough) Kings County	5,041	0.20
Lincoln, NE (city) Lancaster County	5,039	1.95
Long Beach, CA (city) Los Angeles County	4,952	1.07
Santa Clara, CA (city) Santa Clara County	4,924	4.23
Orange, CA (city) Orange County	4,664	3.42
Tacoma, WA (city) Pierce County	4,651	2.34
Greensboro, NC (city) Guilford County	4,474	1.66
Queens, NY (borough) Queens County	4,322	0.19
San Antonio, TX (city) Medina County	4,266	0.32
Jacksonville, FL (city) Duval County	4,210	0.51
Kansas City, MO (city) Jackson County	4,128	0.90
Albuquerque, NM (city) Bernalillo County	4,059	0.74
San Gabriel, CA (city) Los Angeles County	3,834	9.65
Sugar Land, TX (city) Fort Bend County	3,796	4.82
Hayward, CA (city) Alameda County	3,712	2.57
Midway City, CA (cdp) Orange County	3,651	43.03
Riverside, CA (city) Riverside County	3,544	1.17
Bronx, NY (borough) Bronx County	3,526	0.25
Annandale, VA (cdp) Fairfax County	3,467	8.45
Florin, CA (cdp) Sacramento County	3,461	7.28
Sunnyvale, CA (city) Santa Clara County	3,433	2.45
Carrollton, TX (city) Denton County	3,430	2.88
Plano, TX (city) Collin County	3,333	1.28
Monterey Park, CA (city) Los Angeles County	3,323	5.51
Quincy, MA (city) Norfolk County	3,297	3.57
Tustin, CA (city) Orange County	3,244	4.29
Pearland, TX (city) Brazoria County	3,244	3.55
West Covina, CA (city) Los Angeles County	3,230	3.04
Raleigh, NC (city) Wake County	3,210	0.79
Aurora, CO (city) Arapahoe County	3,110	0.96
St. Louis, MO (city) St. Louis city County	3,058	0.96
San Leandro, CA (city) Alameda County	3,000	3.53
Nashville-Davidson, TN (metro govt) Davidson County	2,986	0.50
Chandler, AZ (city) Maricopa County	2,943	1.25
West Valley City, UT (city) Salt Lake County	2,927	2.26
Manhattan, NY (borough) New York County	2,919	0.18
Louisville-Jefferson County, KY (metro govt) Jefferson County	2,914	0.49
Baton Rouge, LA (city) East Baton Rouge Parish	2,913	1.27
Richardson, TX (city) Dallas County	2,861	2.88
Union City, CA (city) Alameda County	2,851	4.10
Spring Valley, NV (cdp) Clark County	2,777	1.56
Brooklyn Park, MN (city) Hennepin County	2,774	3.66
Kent, WA (city) King County	2,634	2.85
Des Moines, IA (city) Polk County	2,626	1.29
Tucson, AZ (city) Pima County	2,547	0.49
Corona, CA (city) Riverside County	2,520	1.65
Memphis, TN (city) Shelby County	2,515	0.39
West Falls Church, VA (cdp) Fairfax County	2,499	8.56
Mission Bend, TX (cdp) Fort Bend County	2,493	6.83
Port Arthur, TX (city) Jefferson County	2,479	4.61
Costa Mesa, CA (city) Orange County	2,475	2.25
Springfield, VA (cdp) Fairfax County	2,420	7.94
Fresno, CA (city) Fresno County	2,412	0.49
Vineyard, CA (cdp) Sacramento County	2,380	9.58
Alameda, CA (city) Alameda County	2,379	3.22
Torrance, CA (city) Los Angeles County	2,369	1.63
St. Paul, MN (city) Ramsey County	2,357	0.83
Glendale, AZ (city) Maricopa County	2,326	1.03
Columbus, OH (city) Franklin County	2,319	0.29
Gilbert, AZ (town) Maricopa County	2,307	1.11
Fullerton, CA (city) Orange County	2,277	1.68
Baldwin Park, CA (city) Los Angeles County	2,178	2.89
St. Petersburg, FL (city) Pinellas County	2,159	0.88
Randolph, MA (cdp/town) Norfolk County	2,150	6.70
Everett, WA (city) Snohomish County	2,140	2.08
Fort Smith, AR (city) Sebastian County	2,124	2.46
Irving, TX (city) Dallas County	2,120	0.98
Virginia Beach, VA (ind. city) Virginia Beach independent city	2,097	0.48
Lowell, MA (city) Middlesex County	2,057	1.93
Bellevue, WA (city) King County	2,013	1.65
Springfield, MA (city) Hampden County	1,997	1.30
Centreville, VA (cdp) Fairfax County	1,966	2.76
Pomona, CA (city) Los Angeles County	1,966	1.32
Escondido, CA (city) San Diego County	1,947	1.35
Malden, MA (city) Middlesex County	1,874	3.15
Tampa, FL (city) Hillsborough County	1,863	0.55
Washington, DC (city) District of Columbia	1,856	0.31
Upper Darby, PA (township) Delaware County	1,849	2.23
Las Vegas, NV (city) Clark County	1,841	0.32
Lake Forest, CA (city) Orange County	1,819	2.35
Tulsa, OK (city) Tulsa County	1,806	0.46
Germantown, MD (cdp) Montgomery County	1,803	2.09
Kentwood, MI (city) Kent County	1,786	3.67
Temple City, CA (city) Los Angeles County	1,780	5.01
Arlington, VA (cdp) Arlington County	1,767	0.85
Pinellas Park, FL (city) Pinellas County	1,763	3.59
Minneapolis, MN (city) Hennepin County	1,760	0.46
Eastvale, CA (cdp) Riverside County	1,756	3.27
Jersey City, NJ (city) Hudson County	1,753	0.71
Ontario, CA (city) San Bernardino County	1,752	1.07
Gardena, CA (city) Los Angeles County	1,737	2.95
Orlando, FL (city) Orange County	1,734	0.73
Enterprise, NV (cdp) Clark County	1,732	1.60
Vancouver, WA (city) Clark County	1,719	1.06
Pennsauken, NJ (township) Camden County	1,687	4.70
White Center, WA (cdp) King County	1,679	12.44
Amarillo, TX (city) Potter County	1,654	0.87
Mesa, AZ (city) Maricopa County	1,648	0.38
Lakewood, CO (city) Jefferson County	1,636	1.14
Haltom City, TX (city) Tarrant County	1,623	3.83
Federal Way, WA (city) King County	1,607	1.80
Moreno Valley, CA (city) Riverside County	1,604	0.83
Allen, TX (city) Collin County	1,584	1.88
Pflugerville, TX (city) Travis County	1,580	3.37
Syracuse, NY (city) Onondaga County	1,554	1.07
Westminster, CO (city) Adams County	1,538	1.45
Buena Park, CA (city) Orange County	1,479	1.84

Please refer to the Explanation of Data in the front of the book for more detailed information.

Race

Asian: Vietnamese

Top 150 Places Sorted by Percent of Total Population

Based on all places, regardless of total population

Place	Population	%
Midway City, CA (cdp) Orange County	3,651	43.03
Westminster, CA (city) Orange County	37,176	41.44
Garden Grove, CA (city) Orange County	48,774	28.54
Fountain Valley, CA (city) Orange County	11,861	21.44
Morrow, GA (city) Clayton County	1,332	20.67
Rosemead, CA (city) Los Angeles County	10,046	18.69
Amelia, LA (cdp) St. Mary Parish	450	18.30
Oak Island, TX (cdp) Chambers County	64	17.63
Blue Sky, CO (cdp) Morgan County	4	16.67
Milpitas, CA (city) Santa Clara County	11,042	16.53
Bayou La Batre, AL (city) Mobile County	395	15.44
Stanton, CA (city) Orange County	5,762	15.09
Lake City, GA (city) Clayton County	350	13.40
Unity, OR (city) Baker County	9	12.68
White Center, WA (cdp) King County	1,679	12.44
Ravensworth, VA (cdp) Fairfax County	281	11.39
Avondale, LA (cdp) Jefferson Parish	560	11.30
San Jose, CA (city) Santa Clara County	106,647	11.27
Moorefield Station, VA (cdp) Loudoun County	8	10.39
Buras, LA (cdp) Plaquemines Parish	98	10.37
North Springfield, VA (cdp) Fairfax County	740	10.17
San Gabriel, CA (city) Los Angeles County	3,834	9.65
Vineyard, CA (cdp) Sacramento County	2,380	9.58
Seven Corners, VA (cdp) Fairfax County	877	9.48
Four Corners, TX (cdp) Fort Bend County	1,134	9.16
Henderson, LA (town) St. Martin Parish	152	9.08
South San Gabriel, CA (cdp) Los Angeles County	711	8.81
Palacios, TX (city) Matagorda County	415	8.80
West Falls Church, VA (cdp) Fairfax County	2,499	8.56
El Monte, CA (city) Los Angeles County	9,667	8.52
Annandale, VA (cdp) Fairfax County	3,467	8.45
Bryn Mawr-Skyway, WA (cdp) King County	1,321	8.44
Lynn, CO (cdp) Las Animas County	1	8.33
St. Martin, MS (cdp) Jackson County	628	8.12
Springfield, VA (cdp) Fairfax County	2,420	7.94
Oak Grove, VA (cdp) Loudoun County	141	7.93
Olowalu, HI (cdp) Maui County	6	7.50
Santa Ana, CA (city) Orange County	24,260	7.48
Murphy, TX (city) Collin County	1,319	7.45
Florin, CA (cdp) Sacramento County	3,461	7.28
Larch Way, WA (cdp) Snohomish County	241	7.26
Woodlynne, NJ (borough) Camden County	210	7.05
East Foothills, CA (cdp) Santa Clara County	574	6.94
Mission Bend, TX (cdp) Fort Bend County	2,493	6.83
D'Iberville, MS (city) Harrison County	639	6.74
Randolph, MA (cdp/town) Norfolk County	2,150	6.70
Farley, MN (township) Polk County	3	6.67
Forest Park, GA (city) Clayton County	1,224	6.63
Kings Park, VA (cdp) Fairfax County	284	6.55
Alondra Park, CA (cdp) Los Angeles County	561	6.53
Sachse, TX (city) Dallas County	1,324	6.51
Seadrift, TX (city) Calhoun County	88	6.45
Canyondam, CA (cdp) Plumas County	2	6.45
Alhambra, CA (city) Los Angeles County	5,348	6.44
Alum Rock, CA (cdp) Santa Clara County	998	6.42
Renton, WA (city) King County	5,753	6.33
Tukwila, WA (city) King County	1,152	6.03
Happy Valley, OR (city) Clackamas County	819	5.89
Riverton, WA (cdp) King County	372	5.81
Orogrande, NM (cdp) Otero County	3	5.77
Conception, MO (cdp) Nodaway County	12	5.71
Monterey Park, CA (city) Los Angeles County	3,323	5.51
Empire, LA (cdp) Plaquemines Parish	54	5.44
San Leon, TX (cdp) Galveston County	268	5.39
Fulton, TX (town) Aransas County	73	5.38
Wakefield, VA (cdp) Fairfax County	600	5.32
Harvey, LA (cdp) Jefferson Parish	1,081	5.31
Gulf Hills, MS (cdp) Jackson County	373	5.22
Bayview, CA (cdp) Contra Costa County	91	5.19
Elk Grove, CA (city) Sacramento County	7,796	5.09
Triumph, LA (cdp) Plaquemines Parish	11	5.09
University of California Davis, CA (cdp) Yolo County	294	5.08
Chantilly, VA (cdp) Fairfax County	1,158	5.03
Temple City, CA (city) Los Angeles County	1,780	5.01
Long Branch, VA (cdp) Fairfax County	380	5.00
McKinnon, WY (cdp) Sweetwater County	3	5.00
Woodburn, VA (cdp) Fairfax County	420	4.95
Lake Stickney, WA (cdp) Snohomish County	385	4.95
Clarkston, GA (city) DeKalb County	372	4.92
Mount Calvary, WI (village) Fond du Lac County	37	4.86
Abbeville, LA (city) Vermilion Parish	593	4.84
Sugar Land, TX (city) Fort Bend County	3,796	4.82
Garland, TX (city) Dallas County	10,877	4.79
Talmage, CA (cdp) Mendocino County	54	4.78
Meadows Place, TX (city) Fort Bend County	222	4.76
Pennsauken, NJ (township) Camden County	1,687	4.70
Erath, LA (town) Vermilion Parish	99	4.68
East Hill-Meridian, WA (cdp) King County	1,395	4.67
Anaheim, CA (city) Orange County	15,674	4.66
Fair Lakes, VA (cdp) Fairfax County	369	4.65
Merrifield, VA (cdp) Fairfax County	706	4.64
Port Arthur, TX (city) Jefferson County	2,479	4.61
Laurel Hill, VA (cdp) Fairfax County	313	4.57
Timberlane, LA (cdp) Jefferson Parish	466	4.55
Lawndale, CA (city) Los Angeles County	1,453	4.43
Lilburn, GA (city) Gwinnett County	514	4.43
Epworth, IA (city) Dubuque County	82	4.41
South El Monte, CA (city) Los Angeles County	875	4.35
Stafford, TX (city) Fort Bend County	769	4.35
Loudoun Valley Estates, VA (cdp) Loudoun County	159	4.35
Huntington Beach, CA (city) Orange County	8,215	4.32
Tustin, CA (city) Orange County	3,244	4.29
North El Monte, CA (cdp) Los Angeles County	159	4.27
Byersville, NY (cdp) Livingston County	2	4.26
Irvine, CA (city) Orange County	9,000	4.24
Alderwood Manor, WA (cdp) Snohomish County	358	4.24
Santa Clara, CA (city) Santa Clara County	4,924	4.23
South Riding, VA (cdp) Loudoun County	1,012	4.17
Telford, PA (borough) Montgomery County	111	4.17
Marrero, LA (cdp) Jefferson Parish	1,378	4.16
Union City, CA (city) Alameda County	2,851	4.10
Lealman, FL (cdp) Pinellas County	807	4.06
Colesville, MD (cdp) Montgomery County	595	4.06
Marina, CA (city) Monterey County	799	4.05
Norris Canyon, CA (cdp) Contra Costa County	38	3.97
Stone Ridge, VA (cdp) Loudoun County	284	3.94
North Lynnwood, WA (cdp) Snohomish County	648	3.91
Bridge City, LA (cdp) Jefferson Parish	301	3.91
Hillandale, MD (cdp) Montgomery County	236	3.91
St. Francisville, MO (cdp) Clark County	7	3.91
Calverton, MD (cdp) Montgomery County	689	3.89
Telford, PA (borough) Montgomery County	187	3.84
Haltom City, TX (city) Tarrant County	1,623	3.83
Doraville, GA (city) DeKalb County	317	3.81
Barling, AR (city) Sebastian County	176	3.79
Whitemarsh Island, GA (cdp) Chatham County	257	3.78
Martha Lake, WA (cdp) Snohomish County	578	3.74
Lynnwood, WA (city) Snohomish County	1,337	3.73
Estelle, LA (cdp) Jefferson Parish	602	3.68
Kentwood, MI (city) Kent County	1,786	3.67
Riverdale, GA (city) Clayton County	555	3.67
Brooklyn Park, MN (city) Hennepin County	2,774	3.66
Burien, WA (city) King County	1,220	3.66
Woodmere, LA (cdp) Jefferson Parish	439	3.63
Boothville, LA (cdp) Plaquemines Parish	31	3.63
East San Gabriel, CA (cdp) Los Angeles County	536	3.60
Lake Barcroft, VA (cdp) Fairfax County	344	3.60
Dunn Loring, VA (cdp) Fairfax County	317	3.60
Pass Christian, MS (city) Harrison County	166	3.60
Thunderbolt, GA (town) Chatham County	96	3.60
Arlington, TX (city) Tarrant County	13,105	3.59
Pinellas Park, FL (city) Pinellas County	1,763	3.59
Quincy, MA (city) Norfolk County	3,297	3.57
Clarksburg, MD (cdp) Montgomery County	491	3.57
Pearland, TX (city) Brazoria County	3,244	3.55
Dulles Town Center, VA (cdp) Loudoun County	163	3.54
San Leandro, CA (city) Alameda County	3,000	3.53
Atlantic City, NJ (city) Atlantic County	1,394	3.52
Padre Ranchitos, AZ (cdp) Yuma County	6	3.51
Grand Prairie, TX (city) Dallas County	6,135	3.50

Please refer to the Explanation of Data in the front of the book for more detailed information.

Race

Asian: Vietnamese

Top 150 Places Sorted by Percent of Total Population

Based on places with total population of 7,500 or more

Place	Population	%
Midway City, CA (cdp) Orange County	3,651	43.03
Westminster, CA (city) Orange County	37,176	41.44
Garden Grove, CA (city) Orange County	48,774	28.54
Fountain Valley, CA (city) Orange County	11,861	21.44
Rosemead, CA (city) Los Angeles County	10,046	18.69
Milpitas, CA (city) Santa Clara County	11,042	16.53
Stanton, CA (city) Orange County	5,762	15.09
White Center, WA (cdp) King County	1,679	12.44
San Jose, CA (city) Santa Clara County	106,647	11.27
San Gabriel, CA (city) Los Angeles County	3,834	9.65
Vineyard, CA (cdp) Sacramento County	2,380	9.58
Seven Corners, VA (cdp) Fairfax County	877	9.48
Four Corners, TX (cdp) Fort Bend County	1,134	9.16
South San Gabriel, CA (cdp) Los Angeles County	711	8.81
West Falls Church, VA (cdp) Fairfax County	2,499	8.56
El Monte, CA (city) Los Angeles County	9,667	8.52
Annandale, VA (cdp) Fairfax County	3,467	8.45
Bryn Mawr-Skyway, WA (cdp) King County	1,321	8.44
St. Martin, MS (cdp) Jackson County	628	8.12
Springfield, VA (cdp) Fairfax County	2,420	7.94
Santa Ana, CA (city) Orange County	24,260	7.48
Murphy, TX (city) Collin County	1,319	7.45
Florin, CA (cdp) Sacramento County	3,461	7.28
East Foothills, CA (cdp) Santa Clara County	574	6.94
Mission Bend, TX (cdp) Fort Bend County	2,493	6.83
D'Iberville, MS (city) Harrison County	639	6.74
Randolph, MA (cdp/town) Norfolk County	2,150	6.70
Forest Park, GA (city) Clayton County	1,224	6.63
Alondra Park, CA (cdp) Los Angeles County	561	6.53
Sachse, TX (city) Dallas County	1,324	6.51
Alhambra, CA (city) Los Angeles County	5,348	6.44
Alum Rock, CA (cdp) Santa Clara County	998	6.42
Renton, WA (city) King County	5,753	6.33
Tukwila, WA (city) King County	1,152	6.03
Happy Valley, OR (city) Clackamas County	819	5.89
Monterey Park, CA (city) Los Angeles County	3,323	5.51
Wakefield, VA (cdp) Fairfax County	600	5.32
Harvey, LA (cdp) Jefferson Parish	1,081	5.31
Elk Grove, CA (city) Sacramento County	7,796	5.09
Chantilly, VA (cdp) Fairfax County	1,158	5.03
Temple City, CA (city) Los Angeles County	1,780	5.01
Long Branch, VA (cdp) Fairfax County	380	5.00
Woodburn, VA (cdp) Fairfax County	420	4.95
Lake Stickney, WA (cdp) Snohomish County	385	4.95
Clarkston, GA (city) DeKalb County	372	4.92
Abbeville, LA (city) Vermilion Parish	593	4.84
Sugar Land, TX (city) Fort Bend County	3,796	4.82
Garland, TX (city) Dallas County	10,877	4.79
Pennsauken, NJ (township) Camden County	1,687	4.70
East Hill-Meridian, WA (cdp) King County	1,395	4.67
Anaheim, CA (city) Orange County	15,674	4.66
Fair Lakes, VA (cdp) Fairfax County	369	4.65
Merrifield, VA (cdp) Fairfax County	706	4.64
Port Arthur, TX (city) Jefferson County	2,479	4.61
Timberlane, LA (cdp) Jefferson Parish	466	4.55
Lawndale, CA (city) Los Angeles County	1,453	4.43
Lilburn, GA (city) Gwinnett County	514	4.43
South El Monte, CA (city) Los Angeles County	875	4.35
Stafford, TX (city) Fort Bend County	769	4.35
Huntington Beach, CA (city) Orange County	8,215	4.32
Tustin, CA (city) Orange County	3,244	4.29
Irvine, CA (city) Orange County	9,000	4.24
Alderwood Manor, WA (cdp) Snohomish County	358	4.24
Santa Clara, CA (city) Santa Clara County	4,924	4.23
South Riding, VA (cdp) Loudoun County	1,012	4.17
Marrero, LA (cdp) Jefferson Parish	1,378	4.16
Union City, CA (city) Alameda County	2,851	4.10
Lealman, FL (cdp) Pinellas County	807	4.06
Colesville, MD (cdp) Montgomery County	595	4.06
Marina, CA (city) Monterey County	799	4.05
North Lynnwood, WA (cdp) Snohomish County	648	3.91
Bridge City, LA (cdp) Jefferson Parish	301	3.91
Calverton, MD (cdp) Montgomery County	689	3.89
Haltom City, TX (city) Tarrant County	1,623	3.83
Doraville, GA (city) DeKalb County	317	3.81

Place	Population	%
Martha Lake, WA (cdp) Snohomish County	578	3.74
Lynnwood, WA (city) Snohomish County	1,337	3.73
Estelle, LA (cdp) Jefferson Parish	602	3.68
Kentwood, MI (city) Kent County	1,786	3.67
Riverdale, GA (city) Clayton County	555	3.67
Brooklyn Park, MN (city) Hennepin County	2,774	3.66
Burien, WA (city) King County	1,220	3.66
Woodmere, LA (cdp) Jefferson Parish	439	3.63
East San Gabriel, CA (cdp) Los Angeles County	536	3.60
Lake Barcroft, VA (cdp) Fairfax County	344	3.60
Dunn Loring, VA (cdp) Fairfax County	317	3.60
Arlington, TX (city) Tarrant County	13,105	3.59
Pinellas Park, FL (city) Pinellas County	1,763	3.59
Quincy, MA (city) Norfolk County	3,297	3.57
Clarksburg, MD (cdp) Montgomery County	491	3.57
Pearland, TX (city) Brazoria County	3,244	3.55
San Leandro, CA (city) Alameda County	3,000	3.53
Atlantic City, NJ (city) Atlantic County	1,394	3.52
Grand Prairie, TX (city) Dallas County	6,135	3.50
Kings Park West, VA (cdp) Fairfax County	468	3.50
SeaTac, WA (city) King County	932	3.46
Lincolnia, VA (cdp) Fairfax County	786	3.44
Orange, CA (city) Orange County	4,664	3.42
Montclair, CA (city) San Bernardino County	1,241	3.38
Norcross, GA (city) Gwinnett County	308	3.38
Pflugerville, TX (city) Travis County	1,580	3.37
Eastvale, CA (cdp) Riverside County	1,756	3.27
Newcastle, WA (city) King County	336	3.24
Alameda, CA (city) Alameda County	2,379	3.22
Worcester, MA (city) Worcester County	5,759	3.18
Malden, MA (city) Middlesex County	1,874	3.15
Glendale Heights, IL (village) DuPage County	1,077	3.15
Burke, VA (cdp) Fairfax County	1,284	3.13
Sterling, VA (cdp) Loudoun County	863	3.10
Gaines, MI (charter township) Kent County	773	3.07
West Covina, CA (city) Los Angeles County	3,230	3.04
Lorton, VA (cdp) Fairfax County	562	3.02
Bothell East, WA (cdp) Snohomish County	237	2.96
Gardena, CA (city) Los Angeles County	1,737	2.95
Sugarland Run, VA (cdp) Loudoun County	343	2.91
Placentia, CA (city) Orange County	1,467	2.90
Baldwin Park, CA (city) Los Angeles County	2,178	2.89
Carrollton, TX (city) Denton County	3,430	2.88
Richardson, TX (city) Dallas County	2,861	2.88
Terrytown, LA (cdp) Jefferson Parish	669	2.87
El Sobrante, CA (cdp) Riverside County	364	2.86
Jersey Village, TX (city) Harris County	218	2.86
Kent, WA (city) King County	2,634	2.85
Idylwood, VA (cdp) Fairfax County	493	2.85
Newington Forest, VA (cdp) Fairfax County	353	2.84
San Diego, CA (city) San Diego County	36,713	2.81
Fremont, CA (city) Alameda County	5,952	2.78
Centreville, VA (cdp) Fairfax County	1,966	2.76
Campbell, CA (city) Santa Clara County	1,074	2.73
Bethany, OR (cdp) Washington County	562	2.72
Aloha, OR (cdp) Washington County	1,337	2.71
Greenbriar, VA (cdp) Fairfax County	218	2.67
Fairfax, VA (ind. city) Fairfax independent city	596	2.64
Fair Oaks, VA (cdp) Fairfax County	785	2.60
Wichita, KS (city) Sedgwick County	9,902	2.59
West Springfield, VA (cdp) Fairfax County	580	2.58
White Oak, MD (cdp) Montgomery County	449	2.58
Oakland, CA (city) Alameda County	10,038	2.57
Hayward, CA (city) Alameda County	3,712	2.57
Egg Harbor, NJ (township) Atlantic County	1,109	2.56
Savage, MN (city) Scott County	685	2.55
Oak Ridge, FL (cdp) Orange County	578	2.55
Rowlett, TX (city) Dallas County	1,424	2.53
Wheaton, MD (cdp) Montgomery County	1,215	2.52
Everett, MA (city) Middlesex County	1,051	2.52
Newark, CA (city) Alameda County	1,068	2.51
Biloxi, MS (city) Harrison County	1,096	2.49
Highland, CA (city) San Bernardino County	1,312	2.47
Seattle, WA (city) King County	14,987	2.46
Urban Honolulu, HI (cdp) Honolulu County	8,307	2.46

Please refer to the Explanation of Data in the front of the book for more detailed information.

Race

Hawaii Native/Pacific Islander

U.S. and 50 States Sorted by Population and Percent of Total Population

Place	Population	%
United States	**1,225,195**	**0.40**
Hawaii	355,816	26.16
California	286,145	0.77
Washington	70,322	1.05
Texas	47,646	0.19
Florida	39,914	0.21
Utah	36,777	1.33
New York	36,423	0.19
Nevada	32,848	1.22
Oregon	25,785	0.67
Arizona	25,106	0.39
Georgia	15,577	0.16
Virginia	15,422	0.19
Colorado	15,200	0.30
North Carolina	14,774	0.15
Illinois	13,546	0.11
New Jersey	12,999	0.15
Pennsylvania	12,424	0.10
Missouri	11,296	0.19
Alaska	11,154	1.57
Ohio	10,525	0.09
Massachusetts	10,257	0.16
Maryland	9,826	0.17
Michigan	9,348	0.09
Oklahoma	8,206	0.22
Arkansas	7,849	0.27
Tennessee	7,785	0.12
Indiana	6,385	0.10
Minnesota	6,206	0.12
Alabama	5,914	0.12
South Carolina	5,880	0.13
Connecticut	5,397	0.15
Wisconsin	5,117	0.09
Kentucky	5,111	0.12
Idaho	5,094	0.32
Kansas	4,938	0.17
Louisiana	4,879	0.11
New Mexico	4,698	0.23
Iowa	3,847	0.13
Nebraska	2,823	0.15
Mississippi	2,776	0.09
Rhode Island	2,260	0.21
Montana	1,732	0.18
District of Columbia	1,320	0.22
West Virginia	1,254	0.07
Delaware	1,216	0.14
New Hampshire	1,160	0.09
Wyoming	1,063	0.19
Maine	988	0.07
South Dakota	920	0.11
North Dakota	782	0.12
Vermont	465	0.07

Place	Population	%
Hawaii	355,816	26.16
Alaska	11,154	1.57
Utah	36,777	1.33
Nevada	32,848	1.22
Washington	70,322	1.05
California	286,145	0.77
Oregon	25,785	0.67
United States	**1,225,195**	**0.40**
Arizona	25,106	0.39
Idaho	5,094	0.32
Colorado	15,200	0.30
Arkansas	7,849	0.27
New Mexico	4,698	0.23
Oklahoma	8,206	0.22
District of Columbia	1,320	0.22
Florida	39,914	0.21
Rhode Island	2,260	0.21
Texas	47,646	0.19
New York	36,423	0.19
Virginia	15,422	0.19
Missouri	11,296	0.19
Wyoming	1,063	0.19
Montana	1,732	0.18
Maryland	9,826	0.17
Kansas	4,938	0.17
Georgia	15,577	0.16
Massachusetts	10,257	0.16
North Carolina	14,774	0.15
New Jersey	12,999	0.15
Connecticut	5,397	0.15
Nebraska	2,823	0.15
Delaware	1,216	0.14
South Carolina	5,880	0.13
Iowa	3,847	0.13
Tennessee	7,785	0.12
Minnesota	6,206	0.12
Alabama	5,914	0.12
Kentucky	5,111	0.12
North Dakota	782	0.12
Illinois	13,546	0.11
Louisiana	4,879	0.11
South Dakota	920	0.11
Pennsylvania	12,424	0.10
Indiana	6,385	0.10
Ohio	10,525	0.09
Michigan	9,348	0.09
Wisconsin	5,117	0.09
Mississippi	2,776	0.09
New Hampshire	1,160	0.09
West Virginia	1,254	0.07
Maine	988	0.07
Vermont	465	0.07

Please refer to the Explanation of Data in the front of the book for more detailed information.

Race

Hawaii Native/Pacific Islander

Top 150 Places Sorted by Population

Based on all places, regardless of total population

Place	Population	%
Urban Honolulu, HI (cdp) Honolulu County	61,970	18.37
New York, NY (city) Kings County	24,098	0.29
Hilo, HI (cdp) Hawaii County	16,587	38.34
Los Angeles, CA (city) Los Angeles County	15,031	0.40
San Diego, CA (city) San Diego County	11,945	0.91
Kaneohe, HI (cdp) Honolulu County	11,509	33.27
Sacramento, CA (city) Sacramento County	10,699	2.29
Nanakuli, HI (cdp) Honolulu County	10,276	81.13
Kailua, HI (cdp) Honolulu County	9,732	25.19
Waianae, HI (cdp) Honolulu County	9,141	69.37
Pearl City, HI (cdp) Honolulu County	9,078	19.03
Waipahu, HI (cdp) Honolulu County	9,072	23.74
San Jose, CA (city) Santa Clara County	8,116	0.86
Anchorage, AK (municipality) Anchorage Municipality	8,053	2.76
Queens, NY (borough) Queens County	7,691	0.34
Kahului, HI (cdp) Maui County	7,672	29.13
Long Beach, CA (city) Los Angeles County	7,498	1.62
Las Vegas, NV (city) Clark County	6,856	1.17
Hayward, CA (city) Alameda County	6,708	4.65
East Honolulu, HI (cdp) Honolulu County	6,635	13.29
Kapolei, HI (cdp) Honolulu County	6,396	42.12
Wahiawa, HI (cdp) Honolulu County	6,296	35.33
Bronx, NY (borough) Bronx County	6,213	0.45
Mililani Town, HI (cdp) Honolulu County	6,209	22.47
San Francisco, CA (city) San Francisco County	6,173	0.77
Brooklyn, NY (borough) Kings County	5,784	0.23
Makakilo, HI (cdp) Honolulu County	5,581	30.58
Ewa Gentry, HI (cdp) Honolulu County	5,572	24.56
West Valley City, UT (city) Salt Lake County	5,557	4.29
Maili, HI (cdp) Honolulu County	5,441	57.35
Portland, OR (city) Multnomah County	5,229	0.90
Phoenix, AZ (city) Maricopa County	5,180	0.36
Makaha, HI (cdp) Honolulu County	4,982	60.18
Wailuku, HI (cdp) Maui County	4,912	32.08
Ewa Beach, HI (cdp) Honolulu County	4,890	32.70
Seattle, WA (city) King County	4,754	0.78
Salt Lake City, UT (city) Salt Lake County	4,660	2.50
Paradise, NV (cdp) Clark County	4,287	1.92
Springdale, AR (city) Washington County	4,172	5.98
Kailua, HI (cdp) Hawaii County	4,099	34.23
Hawaiian Paradise Park, HI (cdp) Hawaii County	4,081	35.79
Tacoma, WA (city) Pierce County	4,002	2.02
Waimea, HI (cdp) Hawaii County	3,926	42.62
Halawa, HI (cdp) Honolulu County	3,782	26.99
Chicago, IL (city) Cook County	3,770	0.14
Waihee-Waiehu, HI (cdp) Maui County	3,737	42.27
Waimanalo Beach, HI (cdp) Honolulu County	3,727	83.17
Manhattan, NY (borough) New York County	3,727	0.24
Mililani Mauka, HI (cdp) Honolulu County	3,587	17.05
North Las Vegas, NV (city) Clark County	3,577	1.65
Oakland, CA (city) Alameda County	3,574	0.91
Stockton, CA (city) San Joaquin County	3,566	1.22
Modesto, CA (city) Stanislaus County	3,467	1.72
San Antonio, TX (city) Medina County	3,453	0.26
Oceanside, CA (city) San Diego County	3,428	2.05
Kihei, HI (cdp) Maui County	3,343	16.01
Houston, TX (city) Harris County	3,341	0.16
Elk Grove, CA (city) Sacramento County	3,319	2.17
Henderson, NV (city) Clark County	3,287	1.28
Federal Way, WA (city) King County	3,204	3.59
Ahuimanu, HI (cdp) Honolulu County	3,197	36.29
Laie, HI (cdp) Honolulu County	3,139	51.14
Philadelphia, PA (city) Philadelphia County	3,125	0.20
Waimanalo, HI (cdp) Honolulu County	3,116	57.16
Kapaa, HI (cdp) Kauai County	3,112	29.09
Kalaoa, HI (cdp) Hawaii County	3,098	32.12
Carson, CA (city) Los Angeles County	3,088	3.37
Hauula, HI (cdp) Honolulu County	2,888	69.62
Waimalu, HI (cdp) Honolulu County	2,877	20.95
Royal Kunia, HI (cdp) Honolulu County	2,851	19.63
San Mateo, CA (city) San Mateo County	2,803	2.88
Anaheim, CA (city) Orange County	2,778	0.83
Mesa, AZ (city) Maricopa County	2,777	0.63
Spring Valley, NV (cdp) Clark County	2,774	1.55
Chula Vista, CA (city) San Diego County	2,746	1.13
Colorado Springs, CO (city) El Paso County	2,701	0.65
Lahaina, HI (cdp) Maui County	2,611	22.31
Reno, NV (city) Washoe County	2,564	1.14
Killeen, TX (city) Bell County	2,549	1.99
Kent, WA (city) King County	2,536	2.74
Fremont, CA (city) Alameda County	2,514	1.17
Fairfield, CA (city) Solano County	2,503	2.38
Vallejo, CA (city) Solano County	2,436	2.10
Makawao, HI (cdp) Maui County	2,432	33.85
Vancouver, WA (city) Clark County	2,411	1.49
Pukalani, HI (cdp) Maui County	2,392	31.58
East Palo Alto, CA (city) San Mateo County	2,386	8.47
Waipio, HI (cdp) Honolulu County	2,335	20.00
Riverside, CA (city) Riverside County	2,283	0.75
West Jordan, UT (city) Salt Lake County	2,268	2.19
Provo, UT (city) Utah County	2,258	2.01
Sunrise Manor, NV (cdp) Clark County	2,214	1.17
Kahaluu, HI (cdp) Honolulu County	2,197	46.37
Lakewood, WA (city) Pierce County	2,155	3.71
Jacksonville, FL (city) Duval County	2,152	0.26
Fresno, CA (city) Fresno County	2,133	0.43
Tucson, AZ (city) Pima County	2,080	0.40
Salem, OR (city) Marion County	2,018	1.30
Enterprise, NV (cdp) Clark County	2,004	1.85
Kaunakakai, HI (cdp) Maui County	1,942	56.70
San Bruno, CA (city) San Mateo County	1,934	4.70
Spokane, WA (city) Spokane County	1,907	0.91
Hawaiian Beaches, HI (cdp) Hawaii County	1,875	43.81
Haiku-Pauwela, HI (cdp) Maui County	1,853	22.83
Aurora, CO (city) Arapahoe County	1,852	0.57
South San Francisco, CA (city) San Mateo County	1,797	2.82
Mountain View, HI (cdp) Hawaii County	1,778	45.31
Parkland, WA (cdp) Pierce County	1,774	4.95
Boston, MA (city) Suffolk County	1,767	0.29
Moreno Valley, CA (city) Riverside County	1,760	0.91
Ewa Villages, HI (cdp) Honolulu County	1,755	28.73
Aiea, HI (cdp) Honolulu County	1,732	18.55
Garden Grove, CA (city) Orange County	1,673	0.98
Orem, UT (city) Utah County	1,666	1.89
Fort Worth, TX (city) Tarrant County	1,651	0.22
El Paso, TX (city) El Paso County	1,647	0.25
Fayetteville, NC (city) Cumberland County	1,631	0.81
Waikoloa Village, HI (cdp) Hawaii County	1,624	25.53
Auburn, WA (city) King County	1,620	2.31
Hawaiian Ocean View, HI (cdp) Hawaii County	1,609	36.26
Anahola, HI (cdp) Kauai County	1,599	71.93
Denver, CO (city) Denver County	1,598	0.27
Holualoa, HI (cdp) Hawaii County	1,592	18.65
Kahuku, HI (cdp) Honolulu County	1,589	60.79
Virginia Beach, VA (ind. city) Virginia Beach independent city	1,579	0.36
Albuquerque, NM (city) Bernalillo County	1,579	0.29
Huntington Beach, CA (city) Orange County	1,578	0.83
Santa Ana, CA (city) Orange County	1,576	0.49
Taylorsville, UT (city) Salt Lake County	1,567	2.67
Union City, CA (city) Alameda County	1,563	2.25
Dallas, TX (city) Dallas County	1,549	0.13
Antioch, CA (city) Contra Costa County	1,529	1.49
Lihue, HI (cdp) Kauai County	1,511	23.41
Waipio Acres, HI (cdp) Honolulu County	1,507	28.78
Austin, TX (city) Travis County	1,506	0.19
San Bernardino, CA (city) San Bernardino County	1,497	0.71
Kualapuu, HI (cdp) Maui County	1,487	73.36
Kansas City, MO (city) Jackson County	1,467	0.32
Tracy, CA (city) San Joaquin County	1,466	1.77
Concord, CA (city) Contra Costa County	1,445	1.18
Kekaha, HI (cdp) Kauai County	1,436	40.60
Santa Rosa, CA (city) Sonoma County	1,420	0.85
Spanaway, WA (cdp) Pierce County	1,418	5.21
Daly City, CA (city) San Mateo County	1,396	1.38
Florin, CA (cdp) Sacramento County	1,388	2.92
Torrance, CA (city) Los Angeles County	1,363	0.94
Columbus, OH (city) Franklin County	1,346	0.17
Hawthorne, CA (city) Los Angeles County	1,337	1.59
Heeia, HI (cdp) Honolulu County	1,326	26.72
Oklahoma City, OK (city) Oklahoma County	1,322	0.23

Race

Hawaii Native/Pacific Islander

Top 150 Places Sorted by Percent of Total Population

Based on all places, regardless of total population

Place	Population	%
Waimanalo Beach, HI (cdp) Honolulu County	3,727	83.17
Nanakuli, HI (cdp) Honolulu County	10,276	81.13
Kualapuu, HI (cdp) Maui County	1,487	73.36
Anahola, HI (cdp) Kauai County	1,599	71.93
Ualapu'e, HI (cdp) Maui County	302	71.06
Maunaloa, HI (cdp) Maui County	263	69.95
Hauula, HI (cdp) Honolulu County	2,888	69.62
Waianae, HI (cdp) Honolulu County	9,141	69.37
Hana, HI (cdp) Maui County	844	68.34
Kahuku, HI (cdp) Honolulu County	1,589	60.79
Makaha, HI (cdp) Honolulu County	4,982	60.18
Waikane, HI (cdp) Honolulu County	454	58.35
Maili, HI (cdp) Honolulu County	5,441	57.35
Waiohinu, HI (cdp) Hawaii County	122	57.28
Waimanalo, HI (cdp) Honolulu County	3,116	57.16
Kaunakakai, HI (cdp) Maui County	1,942	56.70
Keokea, HI (cdp) Maui County	903	56.02
Kalaeloa, HI (cdp) Honolulu County	25	52.08
Laie, HI (cdp) Honolulu County	3,139	51.14
Kaaawa, HI (cdp) Honolulu County	703	50.98
Hawi, HI (cdp) Hawaii County	540	49.95
Punaluu, HI (cdp) Honolulu County	554	47.59
Makaha Valley, HI (cdp) Honolulu County	634	47.28
Kahaluu, HI (cdp) Honolulu County	2,197	46.37
Pakala Village, HI (cdp) Kauai County	134	45.58
Mountain View, HI (cdp) Hawaii County	1,778	45.31
Kukuihaele, HI (cdp) Hawaii County	148	44.05
Hawaiian Beaches, HI (cdp) Hawaii County	1,875	43.81
Naalehu, HI (cdp) Hawaii County	378	43.65
Fern Acres, HI (cdp) Hawaii County	656	43.62
Ainaloa, HI (cdp) Hawaii County	1,284	43.31
Waimea, HI (cdp) Hawaii County	3,926	42.62
Waihee-Waiehu, HI (cdp) Maui County	3,737	42.27
Kapolei, HI (cdp) Honolulu County	6,396	42.12
Pahala, HI (cdp) Hawaii County	558	41.15
Halaula, HI (cdp) Hawaii County	191	40.72
Kekaha, HI (cdp) Kauai County	1,436	40.60
Waimea, HI (cdp) Kauai County	731	39.41
Eden Roc, HI (cdp) Hawaii County	362	38.43
Hilo, HI (cdp) Hawaii County	16,587	38.34
Paauilo, HI (cdp) Hawaii County	220	36.97
Ahuimanu, HI (cdp) Honolulu County	3,197	36.29
Kapaau, HI (cdp) Hawaii County	629	36.27
Hawaiian Ocean View, HI (cdp) Hawaii County	1,609	36.26
Hawaiian Paradise Park, HI (cdp) Hawaii County	4,081	35.79
Wahiawa, HI (cdp) Honolulu County	6,296	35.33
Kailua, HI (cdp) Hawaii County	4,099	34.23
Orchidlands Estates, HI (cdp) Hawaii County	957	34.00
Makawao, HI (cdp) Maui County	2,432	33.85
Haliimaile, HI (cdp) Maui County	325	33.71
Nanawale Estates, HI (cdp) Hawaii County	475	33.31
Kaneohe, HI (cdp) Honolulu County	11,509	33.27
Honaunau-Napoopoo, HI (cdp) Hawaii County	854	33.27
Pahoa, HI (cdp) Hawaii County	314	33.23
Honalo, HI (cdp) Hawaii County	801	33.06
Ewa Beach, HI (cdp) Honolulu County	4,890	32.70
Kurtistown, HI (cdp) Hawaii County	422	32.51
Olowalu, HI (cdp) Maui County	26	32.50
Kalaoa, HI (cdp) Hawaii County	3,098	32.12
Wailuku, HI (cdp) Maui County	4,912	32.08
Haleiwa, HI (cdp) Honolulu County	1,268	31.94
Hawaiian Acres, HI (cdp) Hawaii County	854	31.63
Kealakekua, HI (cdp) Hawaii County	638	31.60
Pukalani, HI (cdp) Maui County	2,392	31.58
Pepeekeo, HI (cdp) Hawaii County	561	31.36
Hanapepe, HI (cdp) Kauai County	815	30.89
Waikapu, HI (cdp) Maui County	915	30.86
Captain Cook, HI (cdp) Hawaii County	1,049	30.59
Makakilo, HI (cdp) Honolulu County	5,581	30.58
Fern Forest, HI (cdp) Hawaii County	278	29.86
Papaikou, HI (cdp) Hawaii County	391	29.76
Kahului, HI (cdp) Maui County	7,672	29.13
Kapaa, HI (cdp) Kauai County	3,112	29.09
Waipio Acres, HI (cdp) Honolulu County	1,507	28.78
Ewa Villages, HI (cdp) Honolulu County	1,755	28.73
Honokaa, HI (cdp) Hawaii County	648	28.70
Iroquois Point, HI (cdp) Honolulu County	946	28.04
Keaau, HI (cdp) Hawaii County	631	28.01
Volcano, HI (cdp) Hawaii County	721	28.00
Honomu, HI (cdp) Hawaii County	141	27.70
Koloa, HI (cdp) Kauai County	589	27.47
Halawa, HI (cdp) Honolulu County	3,782	26.99
Heeia, HI (cdp) Honolulu County	1,326	26.72
Laupahoehoe, HI (cdp) Hawaii County	154	26.51
Wainiha, HI (cdp) Kauai County	84	26.42
Waikoloa Village, HI (cdp) Hawaii County	1,624	25.53
Kailua, HI (cdp) Honolulu County	9,732	25.19
Hanamaulu, HI (cdp) Kauai County	962	25.08
Ewa Gentry, HI (cdp) Honolulu County	5,572	24.56
Wainaku, HI (cdp) Hawaii County	300	24.51
Paia, HI (cdp) Maui County	650	24.36
Discovery Harbour, HI (cdp) Hawaii County	230	24.24
Waipahu, HI (cdp) Honolulu County	9,072	23.74
Wailua, HI (cdp) Kauai County	534	23.69
Lihue, HI (cdp) Kauai County	1,511	23.41
Lawai, HI (cdp) Kauai County	543	22.98
Haiku-Pauwela, HI (cdp) Maui County	1,853	22.83
Haena, HI (cdp) Kauai County	98	22.74
Lanai City, HI (cdp) Maui County	705	22.73
Mililani Town, HI (cdp) Honolulu County	6,209	22.47
Waialua, HI (cdp) Honolulu County	867	22.46
Lahaina, HI (cdp) Maui County	2,611	22.31
Whitmore Village, HI (cdp) Honolulu County	995	22.12
Wailua Homesteads, HI (cdp) Kauai County	1,143	22.03
Kalihiwai, HI (cdp) Kauai County	93	21.73
Omao, HI (cdp) Kauai County	278	21.37
Eleele, HI (cdp) Kauai County	510	21.34
Waimalu, HI (cdp) Honolulu County	2,877	20.95
Maunawili, HI (cdp) Honolulu County	424	20.78
Milan, MN (city) Chippewa County	76	20.60
Kaumakani, HI (cdp) Kauai County	153	20.43
West Loch Estate, HI (cdp) Honolulu County	1,109	20.22
Waipio, HI (cdp) Honolulu County	2,335	20.00
Royal Kunia, HI (cdp) Honolulu County	2,851	19.63
Kalaheo, HI (cdp) Kauai County	897	19.52
Pearl City, HI (cdp) Honolulu County	9,078	19.03
Holualoa, HI (cdp) Hawaii County	1,592	18.65
Aiea, HI (cdp) Honolulu County	1,732	18.55
Urban Honolulu, HI (cdp) Honolulu County	61,970	18.37
Paukaa, HI (cdp) Hawaii County	78	18.35
Hanalei, HI (cdp) Kauai County	80	17.78
Kahaluu-Keauhou, HI (cdp) Hawaii County	630	17.75
Puhi, HI (cdp) Kauai County	515	17.72
Kula, HI (cdp) Maui County	1,129	17.50
Leilani Estates, HI (cdp) Hawaii County	272	17.44
Mililani Mauka, HI (cdp) Honolulu County	3,587	17.05
Waikele, HI (cdp) Honolulu County	1,261	16.86
Kihei, HI (cdp) Maui County	3,343	16.01
Kapalua, HI (cdp) Maui County	55	15.58
Ocean Pointe, HI (cdp) Honolulu County	1,251	14.96
Pupukea, HI (cdp) Honolulu County	669	14.70
Kilauea, HI (cdp) Kauai County	394	14.06
Napili-Honokowai, HI (cdp) Maui County	1,003	13.81
Mokuleia, HI (cdp) Honolulu County	242	13.36
Point Baker, AK (cdp) Prince of Wales-Hyder Census Area	2	13.33
East Honolulu, HI (cdp) Honolulu County	6,635	13.29
Makena, HI (cdp) Maui County	13	13.13
Qui-nai-elt Village, WA (cdp) Grays Harbor County	7	12.96
Olinda, HI (cdp) Maui County	138	12.73
Launiupoko, HI (cdp) Maui County	67	11.39
Poipu, HI (cdp) Kauai County	102	10.42
Kawela Bay, HI (cdp) Honolulu County	34	10.30
Urbancrest, OH (village) Franklin County	97	10.10
Whale Pass, AK (cdp) Prince of Wales-Hyder Census Area	3	9.68
Bethel Heights, AR (city) Benton County	214	9.02
East Palo Alto, CA (city) San Mateo County	2,386	8.47
Furnace Creek, CA (cdp) Inyo County	2	8.33
Maalaea, HI (cdp) Maui County	27	7.67
Mahinahina, HI (cdp) Maui County	65	7.39
Naomi, PA (cdp) Fayette County	5	7.25

Please refer to the Explanation of Data in the front of the book for more detailed information.

Race

Hawaii Native/Pacific Islander

Top 150 Places Sorted by Percent of Total Population

Based on places with total population of 7,500 or more

Place	Population	%
Nanakuli, HI (cdp) Honolulu County	10,276	81.13
Waianae, HI (cdp) Honolulu County	9,141	69.37
Makaha, HI (cdp) Honolulu County	4,982	60.18
Maili, HI (cdp) Honolulu County	5,441	57.35
Waimea, HI (cdp) Hawaii County	3,926	42.62
Waihee-Waiehu, HI (cdp) Maui County	3,737	42.27
Kapolei, HI (cdp) Honolulu County	6,396	42.12
Hilo, HI (cdp) Hawaii County	16,587	38.34
Ahuimanu, HI (cdp) Honolulu County	3,197	36.29
Hawaiian Paradise Park, HI (cdp) Hawaii County	4,081	35.79
Wahiawa, HI (cdp) Honolulu County	6,296	35.33
Kailua, HI (cdp) Hawaii County	4,099	34.23
Kaneohe, HI (cdp) Honolulu County	11,509	33.27
Ewa Beach, HI (cdp) Honolulu County	4,890	32.70
Kalaoa, HI (cdp) Hawaii County	3,098	32.12
Wailuku, HI (cdp) Maui County	4,912	32.08
Pukalani, HI (cdp) Maui County	2,392	31.58
Makakilo, HI (cdp) Honolulu County	5,581	30.58
Kahului, HI (cdp) Maui County	7,672	29.13
Kapaa, HI (cdp) Kauai County	3,112	29.09
Halawa, HI (cdp) Honolulu County	3,782	26.99
Kailua, HI (cdp) Honolulu County	9,732	25.19
Ewa Gentry, HI (cdp) Honolulu County	5,572	24.56
Waipahu, HI (cdp) Honolulu County	9,072	23.74
Haiku-Pauwela, HI (cdp) Maui County	1,853	22.83
Mililani Town, HI (cdp) Honolulu County	6,209	22.47
Lahaina, HI (cdp) Maui County	2,611	22.31
Waimalu, HI (cdp) Honolulu County	2,877	20.95
Waipio, HI (cdp) Honolulu County	2,335	20.00
Royal Kunia, HI (cdp) Honolulu County	2,851	19.63
Pearl City, HI (cdp) Honolulu County	9,078	19.03
Holualoa, HI (cdp) Hawaii County	1,592	18.65
Aiea, HI (cdp) Honolulu County	1,732	18.55
Urban Honolulu, HI (cdp) Honolulu County	61,970	18.37
Mililani Mauka, HI (cdp) Honolulu County	3,587	17.05
Kihei, HI (cdp) Maui County	3,343	16.01
Ocean Pointe, HI (cdp) Honolulu County	1,251	14.96
East Honolulu, HI (cdp) Honolulu County	6,635	13.29
East Palo Alto, CA (city) San Mateo County	2,386	8.47
Springdale, AR (city) Washington County	4,172	5.98
Eloy, AZ (city) Pinal County	981	5.90
Schofield Barracks, HI (cdp) Honolulu County	872	5.33
Spanaway, WA (cdp) Pierce County	1,418	5.21
Parkland, WA (cdp) Pierce County	1,774	4.95
San Bruno, CA (city) San Mateo County	1,934	4.70
Hayward, CA (city) Alameda County	6,708	4.65
Marina, CA (city) Monterey County	903	4.58
SeaTac, WA (city) King County	1,157	4.30
West Valley City, UT (city) Salt Lake County	5,557	4.29
Fife, WA (city) Pierce County	377	4.11
Midland, WA (cdp) Pierce County	344	3.84
Lakewood, WA (city) Pierce County	2,155	3.71
Elk Plain, WA (cdp) Pierce County	527	3.71
Federal Way, WA (city) King County	3,204	3.59
Tukwila, WA (city) King County	674	3.53
Frederickson, WA (cdp) Pierce County	650	3.47
Carson, CA (city) Los Angeles County	3,088	3.37
Fort Lewis, WA (cdp) Pierce County	359	3.25
Des Moines, WA (city) King County	925	3.12
Kearns, UT (cdp) Salt Lake County	1,111	3.11
Cherryland, CA (cdp) Alameda County	440	2.99
Florin, CA (cdp) Sacramento County	1,388	2.92
San Mateo, CA (city) San Mateo County	2,803	2.88
South San Francisco, CA (city) San Mateo County	1,797	2.82
Suisun City, CA (city) Solano County	780	2.77
Anchorage, AK (municipality) Anchorage Municipality	8,053	2.76
Kent, WA (city) King County	2,536	2.74
Parkway, CA (cdp) Sacramento County	400	2.73
Magna, UT (cdp) Salt Lake County	712	2.69
Neosho, MO (city) Newton County	318	2.69
Newark, CA (city) Alameda County	1,141	2.68
Taylorsville, UT (city) Salt Lake County	1,567	2.67
Lacey, WA (city) Thurston County	1,133	2.67
White Center, WA (cdp) King County	346	2.56
Burien, WA (city) King County	836	2.51
Seaside, CA (city) Monterey County	829	2.51
Salt Lake City, UT (city) Salt Lake County	4,660	2.50
Euless, TX (city) Tarrant County	1,247	2.43
Fort Hood, TX (cdp) Bell County	716	2.42
Fairfield, CA (city) Solano County	2,503	2.38
Enid, OK (city) Garfield County	1,156	2.34
Fairview, CA (cdp) Alameda County	233	2.33
Auburn, WA (city) King County	1,620	2.31
Sacramento, CA (city) Sacramento County	10,699	2.29
Port Orchard, WA (city) Kitsap County	255	2.29
Union City, CA (city) Alameda County	1,563	2.25
Miami, OK (city) Ottawa County	306	2.25
Twentynine Palms, CA (city) San Bernardino County	556	2.22
North Salt Lake, UT (city) Davis County	359	2.20
West Jordan, UT (city) Salt Lake County	2,268	2.19
Bremerton, WA (city) Kitsap County	825	2.19
West Sacramento, CA (city) Yolo County	1,064	2.18
Lakeland North, WA (cdp) King County	282	2.18
Elk Grove, CA (city) Sacramento County	3,319	2.17
Fort Irwin, CA (cdp) San Bernardino County	191	2.16
Four Corners, OR (cdp) Marion County	336	2.11
Vallejo, CA (city) Solano County	2,436	2.10
East Hill-Meridian, WA (cdp) King County	619	2.07
Oceanside, CA (city) San Diego County	3,428	2.05
West Carson, CA (cdp) Los Angeles County	444	2.05
Patterson, CA (city) Stanislaus County	419	2.05
Signal Hill, CA (city) Los Angeles County	226	2.05
Tacoma, WA (city) Pierce County	4,002	2.02
DuPont, WA (city) Pierce County	166	2.02
Provo, UT (city) Utah County	2,258	2.01
Fort Campbell North, KY (cdp) Christian County	275	2.01
Kaneohe Station, HI (cdp) Honolulu County	191	2.01
Killeen, TX (city) Bell County	2,549	1.99
Graham, WA (cdp) Pierce County	464	1.98
Silverdale, WA (cdp) Kitsap County	378	1.97
La Presa, CA (cdp) San Diego County	668	1.95
North Fair Oaks, CA (cdp) San Mateo County	286	1.95
Ashland, CA (cdp) Alameda County	425	1.94
Paradise, NV (cdp) Clark County	4,287	1.92
Oak Harbor, WA (city) Island County	421	1.91
Hayesville, OR (cdp) Marion County	381	1.91
Lemon Grove, CA (city) San Diego County	481	1.90
Orem, UT (city) Utah County	1,666	1.89
Lemon Hill, CA (cdp) Sacramento County	260	1.89
Barstow, CA (city) San Bernardino County	421	1.86
Enterprise, NV (cdp) Clark County	2,004	1.85
South Hill, WA (cdp) Pierce County	956	1.82
La Grande, OR (city) Union County	237	1.81
Lake Stickney, WA (cdp) Snohomish County	140	1.80
Del Aire, CA (cdp) Los Angeles County	179	1.79
Pittsburg, CA (city) Contra Costa County	1,126	1.78
Vineyard, CA (cdp) Sacramento County	443	1.78
Tracy, CA (city) San Joaquin County	1,466	1.77
Menlo Park, CA (city) San Mateo County	566	1.77
Woods Cross, UT (city) Davis County	173	1.77
Antelope, CA (cdp) Sacramento County	798	1.74
Fort Drum, NY (cdp) Jefferson County	226	1.74
Lakeland South, WA (cdp) King County	200	1.73
Modesto, CA (city) Stanislaus County	3,467	1.72
El Sobrante, CA (cdp) Contra Costa County	218	1.72
Copperas Cove, TX (city) Coryell County	547	1.71
American Canyon, CA (city) Napa County	331	1.70
Pacifica, CA (city) San Mateo County	631	1.69
Bryn Mawr-Skyway, WA (cdp) King County	263	1.68
University Place, WA (city) Pierce County	520	1.67
Saratoga Springs, UT (city) Utah County	296	1.66
North Las Vegas, NV (city) Clark County	3,577	1.65
St. George, UT (city) Washington County	1,189	1.63
Fairview, OR (city) Multnomah County	145	1.63
Long Beach, CA (city) Los Angeles County	7,498	1.62
Redwood City, CA (city) San Mateo County	1,242	1.62
Rancho Cordova, CA (city) Sacramento County	1,044	1.61
Morganton, NC (city) Burke County	272	1.61
Lackland AFB, TX (cdp) Bexar County	160	1.61
Spring Valley, CA (cdp) San Diego County	450	1.60

SECTION THREE

Race

Hawaii Native/Pacific Islander: Not Hispanic

U.S. and 50 States Sorted by Population and Percent of Total Population

Place	Population	%
United States	**1,014,888**	**0.33**
Hawaii	311,205	22.88
California	233,405	0.63
Washington	64,689	0.96
Utah	34,819	1.26
Texas	34,506	0.14
Florida	31,138	0.17
Nevada	28,415	1.05
Oregon	23,486	0.61
New York	21,768	0.11
Arizona	20,167	0.32
Virginia	12,670	0.16
Colorado	12,023	0.24
Georgia	11,896	0.12
North Carolina	11,417	0.12
Alaska	10,515	1.48
Missouri	10,075	0.17
Illinois	9,816	0.08
Pennsylvania	8,756	0.07
Ohio	8,702	0.08
New Jersey	8,299	0.09
Michigan	7,917	0.08
Maryland	7,746	0.13
Arkansas	7,116	0.24
Oklahoma	7,062	0.19
Massachusetts	7,034	0.11
Tennessee	6,070	0.10
Minnesota	5,232	0.10
Indiana	5,116	0.08
South Carolina	4,709	0.10
Idaho	4,414	0.28
Kentucky	4,235	0.10
Wisconsin	4,187	0.07
Alabama	4,112	0.09
Kansas	4,104	0.14
Louisiana	3,859	0.09
Connecticut	3,528	0.10
Iowa	3,290	0.11
New Mexico	2,841	0.14
Mississippi	2,155	0.07
Nebraska	2,128	0.12
Montana	1,528	0.15
Rhode Island	1,437	0.14
West Virginia	1,102	0.06
New Hampshire	945	0.07
Wyoming	875	0.16
Maine	856	0.06
Delaware	842	0.09
District of Columbia	821	0.14
South Dakota	745	0.09
North Dakota	696	0.10
Vermont	419	0.07

Place	Population	%
Hawaii	311,205	22.88
Alaska	10,515	1.48
Utah	34,819	1.26
Nevada	28,415	1.05
Washington	64,689	0.96
California	233,405	0.63
Oregon	23,486	0.61
United States	**1,014,888**	**0.33**
Arizona	20,167	0.32
Idaho	4,414	0.28
Colorado	12,023	0.24
Arkansas	7,116	0.24
Oklahoma	7,062	0.19
Florida	31,138	0.17
Missouri	10,075	0.17
Virginia	12,670	0.16
Wyoming	875	0.16
Montana	1,528	0.15
Texas	34,506	0.14
Kansas	4,104	0.14
New Mexico	2,841	0.14
Rhode Island	1,437	0.14
District of Columbia	821	0.14
Maryland	7,746	0.13
Georgia	11,896	0.12
North Carolina	11,417	0.12
Nebraska	2,128	0.12
New York	21,768	0.11
Massachusetts	7,034	0.11
Iowa	3,290	0.11
Tennessee	6,070	0.10
Minnesota	5,232	0.10
South Carolina	4,709	0.10
Kentucky	4,235	0.10
Connecticut	3,528	0.10
North Dakota	696	0.10
New Jersey	8,299	0.09
Alabama	4,112	0.09
Louisiana	3,859	0.09
Delaware	842	0.09
South Dakota	745	0.09
Illinois	9,816	0.08
Ohio	8,702	0.08
Michigan	7,917	0.08
Indiana	5,116	0.08
Pennsylvania	8,756	0.07
Wisconsin	4,187	0.07
Mississippi	2,155	0.07
New Hampshire	945	0.07
Vermont	419	0.07
West Virginia	1,102	0.06
Maine	856	0.06

Please refer to the Explanation of Data in the front of the book for more detailed information.

Race

Hawaii Native/Pacific Islander: Not Hispanic

Top 150 Places Sorted by Population

Based on all places, regardless of total population

Place	Population	%
Urban Honolulu, HI (cdp) Honolulu County	56,359	16.71
Hilo, HI (cdp) Hawaii County	14,293	33.04
New York, NY (city) Kings County	13,217	0.16
Los Angeles, CA (city) Los Angeles County	10,779	0.28
Kaneohe, HI (cdp) Honolulu County	10,022	28.97
San Diego, CA (city) San Diego County	9,844	0.75
Sacramento, CA (city) Sacramento County	9,762	2.09
Nanakuli, HI (cdp) Honolulu County	9,142	72.18
Kailua, HI (cdp) Honolulu County	8,804	22.79
Waipahu, HI (cdp) Honolulu County	8,211	21.49
Pearl City, HI (cdp) Honolulu County	7,804	16.36
Waianae, HI (cdp) Honolulu County	7,743	58.76
Anchorage, AK (municipality) Anchorage Municipality	7,652	2.62
Kahului, HI (cdp) Maui County	6,692	25.41
Long Beach, CA (city) Los Angeles County	6,549	1.42
San Jose, CA (city) Santa Clara County	6,460	0.68
Hayward, CA (city) Alameda County	6,093	4.23
East Honolulu, HI (cdp) Honolulu County	6,083	12.19
Las Vegas, NV (city) Clark County	5,849	1.00
Queens, NY (borough) Queens County	5,685	0.25
Kapolei, HI (cdp) Honolulu County	5,476	36.06
San Francisco, CA (city) San Francisco County	5,432	0.67
West Valley City, UT (city) Salt Lake County	5,385	4.16
Wahiawa, HI (cdp) Honolulu County	5,273	29.59
Mililani Town, HI (cdp) Honolulu County	5,239	18.96
Portland, OR (city) Multnomah County	4,848	0.83
Ewa Gentry, HI (cdp) Honolulu County	4,583	20.20
Makakilo, HI (cdp) Honolulu County	4,551	24.94
Maili, HI (cdp) Honolulu County	4,483	47.25
Salt Lake City, UT (city) Salt Lake County	4,437	2.38
Seattle, WA (city) King County	4,368	0.72
Wailuku, HI (cdp) Maui County	4,291	28.02
Springdale, AR (city) Washington County	4,152	5.95
Ewa Beach, HI (cdp) Honolulu County	4,075	27.25
Makaha, HI (cdp) Honolulu County	3,993	48.24
Phoenix, AZ (city) Maricopa County	3,828	0.26
Paradise, NV (cdp) Clark County	3,771	1.69
Tacoma, WA (city) Pierce County	3,665	1.85
Kailua, HI (cdp) Hawaii County	3,616	30.20
Waimea, HI (cdp) Hawaii County	3,542	38.45
Brooklyn, NY (borough) Kings County	3,463	0.14
Waimanalo Beach, HI (cdp) Honolulu County	3,455	77.10
Halawa, HI (cdp) Honolulu County	3,347	23.88
Waihee-Waiehu, HI (cdp) Maui County	3,320	37.55
Hawaiian Paradise Park, HI (cdp) Hawaii County	3,213	28.17
Mililani Mauka, HI (cdp) Honolulu County	3,151	14.98
North Las Vegas, NV (city) Clark County	3,074	1.42
Oakland, CA (city) Alameda County	3,073	0.79
Elk Grove, CA (city) Sacramento County	3,048	1.99
Federal Way, WA (city) King County	3,035	3.40
Laie, HI (cdp) Honolulu County	3,005	48.96
Modesto, CA (city) Stanislaus County	2,976	1.48
Kihei, HI (cdp) Maui County	2,968	14.21
Oceanside, CA (city) San Diego County	2,962	1.77
Henderson, NV (city) Clark County	2,913	1.13
Stockton, CA (city) San Joaquin County	2,869	0.98
Carson, CA (city) Los Angeles County	2,773	3.02
Waimanalo, HI (cdp) Honolulu County	2,740	50.27
Ahuimanu, HI (cdp) Honolulu County	2,731	31.00
Kalaoa, HI (cdp) Hawaii County	2,710	28.10
Hauula, HI (cdp) Honolulu County	2,687	64.78
Kapaa, HI (cdp) Kauai County	2,598	24.28
San Mateo, CA (city) San Mateo County	2,588	2.66
Royal Kunia, HI (cdp) Honolulu County	2,494	17.17
Waimalu, HI (cdp) Honolulu County	2,490	18.14
Spring Valley, NV (cdp) Clark County	2,474	1.39
Kent, WA (city) King County	2,408	2.61
Lahaina, HI (cdp) Maui County	2,401	20.51
Mesa, AZ (city) Maricopa County	2,391	0.54
East Palo Alto, CA (city) San Mateo County	2,310	8.20
Reno, NV (city) Washoe County	2,266	1.01
Anaheim, CA (city) Orange County	2,238	0.67
Vancouver, WA (city) Clark County	2,237	1.38
Killeen, TX (city) Bell County	2,209	1.73
Chicago, IL (city) Cook County	2,186	0.08
Colorado Springs, CO (city) El Paso County	2,185	0.52
Fremont, CA (city) Alameda County	2,174	1.02
West Jordan, UT (city) Salt Lake County	2,145	2.07
Fairfield, CA (city) Solano County	2,140	2.03
Provo, UT (city) Utah County	2,120	1.88
Vallejo, CA (city) Solano County	2,103	1.81
San Antonio, TX (city) Medina County	2,094	0.16
Pukalani, HI (cdp) Maui County	2,054	27.12
Waipio, HI (cdp) Honolulu County	2,021	17.31
Lakewood, WA (city) Pierce County	2,006	3.45
Chula Vista, CA (city) San Diego County	1,993	0.82
Makawao, HI (cdp) Maui County	1,990	27.70
Philadelphia, PA (city) Philadelphia County	1,938	0.13
Salem, OR (city) Marion County	1,934	1.25
Kahaluu, HI (cdp) Honolulu County	1,912	40.35
Houston, TX (city) Harris County	1,887	0.09
Bronx, NY (borough) Bronx County	1,854	0.13
Kaunakakai, HI (cdp) Maui County	1,830	53.43
San Bruno, CA (city) San Mateo County	1,792	4.36
Jacksonville, FL (city) Duval County	1,791	0.22
Enterprise, NV (cdp) Clark County	1,779	1.64
Manhattan, NY (borough) New York County	1,776	0.11
Riverside, CA (city) Riverside County	1,762	0.58
Sunrise Manor, NV (cdp) Clark County	1,747	0.92
Spokane, WA (city) Spokane County	1,744	0.83
Parkland, WA (cdp) Pierce County	1,671	4.67
Tucson, AZ (city) Pima County	1,596	0.31
South San Francisco, CA (city) San Mateo County	1,595	2.51
Orem, UT (city) Utah County	1,576	1.78
Auburn, WA (city) King County	1,564	2.23
Haiku-Pauwela, HI (cdp) Maui County	1,534	18.90
Kahuku, HI (cdp) Honolulu County	1,514	57.92
Taylorsville, UT (city) Salt Lake County	1,512	2.58
Aurora, CO (city) Arapahoe County	1,510	0.46
Aiea, HI (cdp) Honolulu County	1,498	16.04
Garden Grove, CA (city) Orange County	1,460	0.85
Waikoloa Village, HI (cdp) Hawaii County	1,455	22.87
Hawaiian Beaches, HI (cdp) Hawaii County	1,449	33.86
Anahola, HI (cdp) Kauai County	1,442	64.87
Fresno, CA (city) Fresno County	1,431	0.29
Holualoa, HI (cdp) Hawaii County	1,424	16.68
Ewa Villages, HI (cdp) Honolulu County	1,415	23.17
Hawaiian Ocean View, HI (cdp) Hawaii County	1,410	31.78
Moreno Valley, CA (city) Riverside County	1,409	0.73
Kualapuu, HI (cdp) Maui County	1,382	68.18
Fayetteville, NC (city) Cumberland County	1,376	0.69
Virginia Beach, VA (ind. city) Virginia Beach independent city	1,375	0.31
Union City, CA (city) Alameda County	1,374	1.98
Huntington Beach, CA (city) Orange County	1,374	0.72
Mountain View, HI (cdp) Hawaii County	1,341	34.17
Spanaway, WA (cdp) Pierce County	1,331	4.89
Lihue, HI (cdp) Kauai County	1,327	20.56
Florin, CA (cdp) Sacramento County	1,271	2.68
Antioch, CA (city) Contra Costa County	1,271	1.24
Kekaha, HI (cdp) Kauai County	1,259	35.60
Kansas City, MO (city) Jackson County	1,258	0.27
Waipio Acres, HI (cdp) Honolulu County	1,247	23.82
Fort Worth, TX (city) Tarrant County	1,237	0.17
Santa Rosa, CA (city) Sonoma County	1,221	0.73
Daly City, CA (city) San Mateo County	1,203	1.19
Boston, MA (city) Suffolk County	1,202	0.19
Denver, CO (city) Denver County	1,198	0.20
Euless, TX (city) Tarrant County	1,196	2.33
Heeia, HI (cdp) Honolulu County	1,180	23.78
Hawthorne, CA (city) Los Angeles County	1,176	1.40
Concord, CA (city) Contra Costa County	1,172	0.96
Tracy, CA (city) San Joaquin County	1,155	1.39
Columbus, OH (city) Franklin County	1,149	0.15
Enid, OK (city) Garfield County	1,139	2.31
St. George, UT (city) Washington County	1,123	1.54
Everett, WA (city) Snohomish County	1,122	1.09
San Bernardino, CA (city) San Bernardino County	1,120	0.53
El Paso, TX (city) El Paso County	1,119	0.17
Torrance, CA (city) Los Angeles County	1,118	0.77
SeaTac, WA (city) King County	1,115	4.14

SECTION THREE

Please refer to the Explanation of Data in the front of the book for more detailed information.

Race

Hawaii Native/Pacific Islander: Not Hispanic

Top 150 Places Sorted by Percent of Total Population

Based on all places, regardless of total population

Place	Population	%
Waimanalo Beach, HI (cdp) Honolulu County	3,455	77.10
Nanakuli, HI (cdp) Honolulu County	9,142	72.18
Kualapuu, HI (cdp) Maui County	1,382	68.18
Anahola, HI (cdp) Kauai County	1,442	64.87
Hauula, HI (cdp) Honolulu County	2,687	64.78
Ualapu'e, HI (cdp) Maui County	274	64.47
Hana, HI (cdp) Maui County	757	61.30
Maunaloa, HI (cdp) Maui County	223	59.31
Waianae, HI (cdp) Honolulu County	7,743	58.76
Kahuku, HI (cdp) Honolulu County	1,514	57.92
Waikane, HI (cdp) Honolulu County	429	55.14
Kaunakakai, HI (cdp) Maui County	1,830	53.43
Waiohinu, HI (cdp) Hawaii County	111	52.11
Kalaeloa, HI (cdp) Honolulu County	25	52.08
Keokea, HI (cdp) Maui County	817	50.68
Waimanalo, HI (cdp) Honolulu County	2,740	50.27
Laie, HI (cdp) Honolulu County	3,005	48.96
Makaha, HI (cdp) Honolulu County	3,993	48.24
Maili, HI (cdp) Honolulu County	4,483	47.25
Kaaawa, HI (cdp) Honolulu County	625	45.32
Punaluu, HI (cdp) Honolulu County	527	45.27
Pakala Village, HI (cdp) Kauai County	126	42.86
Kukuihaele, HI (cdp) Hawaii County	137	40.77
Kahaluu, HI (cdp) Honolulu County	1,912	40.35
Hawi, HI (cdp) Hawaii County	425	39.32
Naalehu, HI (cdp) Hawaii County	334	38.57
Waimea, HI (cdp) Hawaii County	3,542	38.45
Waihee-Waiehu, HI (cdp) Maui County	3,320	37.55
Kapolei, HI (cdp) Honolulu County	5,476	36.06
Kekaha, HI (cdp) Kauai County	1,259	35.60
Makaha Valley, HI (cdp) Honolulu County	477	35.57
Fern Acres, HI (cdp) Hawaii County	531	35.31
Pahala, HI (cdp) Hawaii County	471	34.73
Waimea, HI (cdp) Kauai County	644	34.72
Mountain View, HI (cdp) Hawaii County	1,341	34.17
Ainaloa, HI (cdp) Hawaii County	1,010	34.06
Hawaiian Beaches, HI (cdp) Hawaii County	1,449	33.86
Hilo, HI (cdp) Hawaii County	14,293	33.04
Olowalu, HI (cdp) Maui County	26	32.50
Hawaiian Ocean View, HI (cdp) Hawaii County	1,410	31.78
Ahuimanu, HI (cdp) Honolulu County	2,731	31.00
Paauilo, HI (cdp) Hawaii County	183	30.76
Pahoa, HI (cdp) Hawaii County	290	30.69
Honaunau-Napoopoo, HI (cdp) Hawaii County	779	30.35
Kailua, HI (cdp) Hawaii County	3,616	30.20
Honalo, HI (cdp) Hawaii County	729	30.09
Halaula, HI (cdp) Hawaii County	140	29.85
Wahiawa, HI (cdp) Honolulu County	5,273	29.59
Haliimaile, HI (cdp) Maui County	281	29.15
Kaneohe, HI (cdp) Honolulu County	10,022	28.97
Eden Roc, HI (cdp) Hawaii County	271	28.77
Kealakekua, HI (cdp) Hawaii County	577	28.58
Hawaiian Paradise Park, HI (cdp) Hawaii County	3,213	28.17
Kalaoa, HI (cdp) Hawaii County	2,710	28.10
Wailuku, HI (cdp) Maui County	4,291	28.02
Kurtistown, HI (cdp) Hawaii County	363	27.97
Captain Cook, HI (cdp) Hawaii County	958	27.94
Kapaau, HI (cdp) Hawaii County	484	27.91
Makawao, HI (cdp) Maui County	1,990	27.70
Ewa Beach, HI (cdp) Honolulu County	4,075	27.25
Orchidlands Estates, HI (cdp) Hawaii County	767	27.25
Pukalani, HI (cdp) Maui County	2,054	27.12
Haleiwa, HI (cdp) Honolulu County	1,072	27.00
Nanawale Estates, HI (cdp) Hawaii County	385	27.00
Waikapu, HI (cdp) Maui County	800	26.98
Hanapepe, HI (cdp) Kauai County	703	26.65
Pepeekeo, HI (cdp) Hawaii County	476	26.61
Wainiha, HI (cdp) Kauai County	84	26.42
Kahului, HI (cdp) Maui County	6,692	25.41
Makakilo, HI (cdp) Honolulu County	4,551	24.94
Honokaa, HI (cdp) Hawaii County	556	24.62
Papaikou, HI (cdp) Hawaii County	323	24.58
Hawaiian Acres, HI (cdp) Hawaii County	661	24.48
Kapaa, HI (cdp) Kauai County	2,598	24.28
Fern Forest, HI (cdp) Hawaii County	225	24.17
Keaau, HI (cdp) Hawaii County	542	24.06
Iroquois Point, HI (cdp) Honolulu County	810	24.01
Volcano, HI (cdp) Hawaii County	618	24.00
Halawa, HI (cdp) Honolulu County	3,347	23.88
Waipio Acres, HI (cdp) Honolulu County	1,247	23.82
Heeia, HI (cdp) Honolulu County	1,180	23.78
Ewa Villages, HI (cdp) Honolulu County	1,415	23.17
Koloa, HI (cdp) Kauai County	493	22.99
Waikoloa Village, HI (cdp) Hawaii County	1,455	22.87
Kailua, HI (cdp) Honolulu County	8,804	22.79
Hanamaulu, HI (cdp) Kauai County	846	22.06
Haena, HI (cdp) Kauai County	93	21.58
Waipahu, HI (cdp) Honolulu County	8,211	21.49
Discovery Harbour, HI (cdp) Hawaii County	202	21.29
Paia, HI (cdp) Maui County	551	20.65
Milan, MN (city) Chippewa County	76	20.60
Lihue, HI (cdp) Kauai County	1,327	20.56
Lahaina, HI (cdp) Maui County	2,401	20.51
Honomu, HI (cdp) Hawaii County	103	20.24
Wailua, HI (cdp) Kauai County	456	20.23
Ewa Gentry, HI (cdp) Honolulu County	4,583	20.20
Wainaku, HI (cdp) Hawaii County	246	20.10
Kalihiwai, HI (cdp) Kauai County	86	20.09
Lanai City, HI (cdp) Maui County	623	20.08
Maunawili, HI (cdp) Honolulu County	403	19.75
Waialua, HI (cdp) Honolulu County	762	19.74
Lawai, HI (cdp) Kauai County	460	19.47
Laupahoehoe, HI (cdp) Hawaii County	112	19.28
Wailua Homesteads, HI (cdp) Kauai County	996	19.20
Whitmore Village, HI (cdp) Honolulu County	860	19.12
Mililani Town, HI (cdp) Honolulu County	5,239	18.96
Haiku-Pauwela, HI (cdp) Maui County	1,534	18.90
Kaumakani, HI (cdp) Kauai County	138	18.42
Omao, HI (cdp) Kauai County	239	18.37
Waimalu, HI (cdp) Honolulu County	2,490	18.14
Eleele, HI (cdp) Kauai County	427	17.87
West Loch Estate, HI (cdp) Honolulu County	959	17.48
Waipio, HI (cdp) Honolulu County	2,021	17.31
Royal Kunia, HI (cdp) Honolulu County	2,494	17.17
Urban Honolulu, HI (cdp) Honolulu County	56,359	16.71
Holualoa, HI (cdp) Hawaii County	1,424	16.68
Hanalei, HI (cdp) Kauai County	74	16.44
Kalaheo, HI (cdp) Kauai County	752	16.37
Pearl City, HI (cdp) Honolulu County	7,804	16.36
Paukaa, HI (cdp) Hawaii County	69	16.24
Aiea, HI (cdp) Honolulu County	1,498	16.04
Kahaluu-Keauhou, HI (cdp) Hawaii County	565	15.92
Puhi, HI (cdp) Kauai County	456	15.69
Kapalua, HI (cdp) Maui County	54	15.30
Mililani Mauka, HI (cdp) Honolulu County	3,151	14.98
Kula, HI (cdp) Maui County	944	14.63
Kihei, HI (cdp) Maui County	2,968	14.21
Waikele, HI (cdp) Honolulu County	1,062	14.20
Leilani Estates, HI (cdp) Hawaii County	220	14.10
Pupukea, HI (cdp) Honolulu County	613	13.47
Kilauea, HI (cdp) Kauai County	364	12.99
Qui-nai-elt Village, WA (cdp) Grays Harbor County	7	12.96
Napili-Honokowai, HI (cdp) Maui County	928	12.78
Ocean Pointe, HI (cdp) Honolulu County	1,059	12.67
East Honolulu, HI (cdp) Honolulu County	6,083	12.19
Olinda, HI (cdp) Maui County	117	10.79
Mokuleia, HI (cdp) Honolulu County	193	10.66
Urbancrest, OH (village) Franklin County	97	10.10
Makena, HI (cdp) Maui County	10	10.10
Whale Pass, AK (cdp) Prince of Wales-Hyder Census Area	3	9.68
Launiupoko, HI (cdp) Maui County	54	9.18
Kawela Bay, HI (cdp) Honolulu County	30	9.09
Bethel Heights, AR (city) Benton County	214	9.02
Poipu, HI (cdp) Kauai County	83	8.48
Furnace Creek, CA (cdp) Inyo County	2	8.33
East Palo Alto, CA (city) San Mateo County	2,310	8.20
Maalaea, HI (cdp) Maui County	26	7.39
Naomi, PA (cdp) Fayette County	5	7.25
Mahinahina, HI (cdp) Maui County	63	7.16
Puako, HI (cdp) Hawaii County	52	6.74

Please refer to the Explanation of Data in the front of the book for more detailed information.

Race

Hawaii Native/Pacific Islander: Not Hispanic

Top 150 Places Sorted by Percent of Total Population

Based on places with total population of 7,500 or more

Place	Population	%
Nanakuli, HI (cdp) Honolulu County	9,142	72.18
Waianae, HI (cdp) Honolulu County	7,743	58.76
Makaha, HI (cdp) Honolulu County	3,993	48.24
Maili, HI (cdp) Honolulu County	4,483	47.25
Waimea, HI (cdp) Hawaii County	3,542	38.45
Waihee-Waiehu, HI (cdp) Maui County	3,320	37.55
Kapolei, HI (cdp) Honolulu County	5,476	36.06
Hilo, HI (cdp) Hawaii County	14,293	33.04
Ahuimanu, HI (cdp) Honolulu County	2,731	31.00
Kailua, HI (cdp) Hawaii County	3,616	30.20
Wahiawa, HI (cdp) Honolulu County	5,273	29.59
Kaneohe, HI (cdp) Honolulu County	10,022	28.97
Hawaiian Paradise Park, HI (cdp) Hawaii County	3,213	28.17
Kalaoa, HI (cdp) Hawaii County	2,710	28.10
Wailuku, HI (cdp) Maui County	4,291	28.02
Ewa Beach, HI (cdp) Honolulu County	4,075	27.25
Pukalani, HI (cdp) Maui County	2,054	27.12
Kahului, HI (cdp) Maui County	6,692	25.41
Makakilo, HI (cdp) Honolulu County	4,551	24.94
Kapaa, HI (cdp) Kauai County	2,598	24.28
Halawa, HI (cdp) Honolulu County	3,347	23.88
Kailua, HI (cdp) Honolulu County	8,804	22.79
Waipahu, HI (cdp) Honolulu County	8,211	21.49
Lahaina, HI (cdp) Maui County	2,401	20.51
Ewa Gentry, HI (cdp) Honolulu County	4,583	20.20
Mililani Town, HI (cdp) Honolulu County	5,239	18.96
Haiku-Pauwela, HI (cdp) Maui County	1,534	18.90
Waimalu, HI (cdp) Honolulu County	2,490	18.14
Waipio, HI (cdp) Honolulu County	2,021	17.31
Royal Kunia, HI (cdp) Honolulu County	2,494	17.17
Urban Honolulu, HI (cdp) Honolulu County	56,359	16.71
Holualoa, HI (cdp) Hawaii County	1,424	16.68
Pearl City, HI (cdp) Honolulu County	7,804	16.36
Aiea, HI (cdp) Honolulu County	1,498	16.04
Mililani Mauka, HI (cdp) Honolulu County	3,151	14.98
Kihei, HI (cdp) Maui County	2,968	14.21
Ocean Pointe, HI (cdp) Honolulu County	1,059	12.67
East Honolulu, HI (cdp) Honolulu County	6,083	12.19
East Palo Alto, CA (city) San Mateo County	2,310	8.20
Springdale, AR (city) Washington County	4,152	5.95
Eloy, AZ (city) Pinal County	958	5.76
Spanaway, WA (cdp) Pierce County	1,331	4.89
Schofield Barracks, HI (cdp) Honolulu County	777	4.75
Parkland, WA (cdp) Pierce County	1,671	4.67
San Bruno, CA (city) San Mateo County	1,792	4.36
Hayward, CA (city) Alameda County	6,093	4.23
West Valley City, UT (city) Salt Lake County	5,385	4.16
SeaTac, WA (city) King County	1,115	4.14
Marina, CA (city) Monterey County	805	4.08
Fife, WA (city) Pierce County	366	3.99
Lakewood, WA (city) Pierce County	2,006	3.45
Elk Plain, WA (cdp) Pierce County	490	3.45
Midland, WA (cdp) Pierce County	308	3.44
Tukwila, WA (city) King County	653	3.42
Federal Way, WA (city) King County	3,035	3.40
Frederickson, WA (cdp) Pierce County	602	3.22
Carson, CA (city) Los Angeles County	2,773	3.02
Kearns, UT (cdp) Salt Lake County	1,063	2.98
Des Moines, WA (city) King County	874	2.95
Fort Lewis, WA (cdp) Pierce County	322	2.92
Florin, CA (cdp) Sacramento County	1,271	2.68
San Mateo, CA (city) San Mateo County	2,588	2.66
Anchorage, AK (municipality) Anchorage Municipality	7,652	2.62
Kent, WA (city) King County	2,408	2.61
Magna, UT (cdp) Salt Lake County	689	2.60
Taylorsville, UT (city) Salt Lake County	1,512	2.58
Neosho, MO (city) Newton County	303	2.56
Parkway, CA (cdp) Sacramento County	371	2.53
South San Francisco, CA (city) San Mateo County	1,595	2.51
Lacey, WA (city) Thurston County	1,054	2.49
White Center, WA (cdp) King County	335	2.48
Suisun City, CA (city) Solano County	694	2.47
Cherryland, CA (cdp) Alameda County	363	2.46
Newark, CA (city) Alameda County	1,030	2.42
Salt Lake City, UT (city) Salt Lake County	4,437	2.38
Euless, TX (city) Tarrant County	1,196	2.33
Burien, WA (city) King County	776	2.33
Seaside, CA (city) Monterey County	770	2.33
Enid, OK (city) Garfield County	1,139	2.31
Auburn, WA (city) King County	1,564	2.23
Miami, OK (city) Ottawa County	297	2.19
Fort Hood, TX (cdp) Bell County	636	2.15
North Salt Lake, UT (city) Davis County	342	2.10
Sacramento, CA (city) Sacramento County	9,762	2.09
West Jordan, UT (city) Salt Lake County	2,145	2.07
Four Corners, OR (cdp) Marion County	330	2.07
Lakeland North, WA (cdp) King County	265	2.05
Fairfield, CA (city) Solano County	2,140	2.03
Port Orchard, WA (city) Kitsap County	226	2.03
East Hill-Meridian, WA (cdp) King County	604	2.02
Fairview, CA (cdp) Alameda County	202	2.02
Bremerton, WA (city) Kitsap County	753	2.00
Elk Grove, CA (city) Sacramento County	3,048	1.99
Union City, CA (city) Alameda County	1,374	1.98
Twentynine Palms, CA (city) San Bernardino County	489	1.95
Graham, WA (cdp) Pierce County	447	1.90
Provo, UT (city) Utah County	2,120	1.88
West Carson, CA (cdp) Los Angeles County	405	1.87
West Sacramento, CA (city) Yolo County	907	1.86
Tacoma, WA (city) Pierce County	3,665	1.85
DuPont, WA (city) Pierce County	152	1.85
Vallejo, CA (city) Solano County	2,103	1.81
Fort Irwin, CA (cdp) San Bernardino County	160	1.81
Orem, UT (city) Utah County	1,576	1.78
La Grande, OR (city) Union County	233	1.78
Oceanside, CA (city) San Diego County	2,962	1.77
Hayesville, OR (cdp) Marion County	352	1.77
Fort Campbell North, KY (cdp) Christian County	242	1.77
Woods Cross, UT (city) Davis County	172	1.76
Killeen, TX (city) Bell County	2,209	1.73
Menlo Park, CA (city) San Mateo County	551	1.72
Oak Harbor, WA (city) Island County	380	1.72
Silverdale, WA (cdp) Kitsap County	330	1.72
Paradise, NV (cdp) Clark County	3,771	1.69
Del Aire, CA (cdp) Los Angeles County	169	1.69
South Hill, WA (cdp) Pierce County	883	1.68
Vineyard, CA (cdp) Sacramento County	418	1.68
Lake Stickney, WA (cdp) Snohomish County	131	1.68
Ashland, CA (cdp) Alameda County	367	1.67
Enterprise, NV (cdp) Clark County	1,779	1.64
Lemon Hill, CA (cdp) Sacramento County	225	1.64
North Fair Oaks, CA (cdp) San Mateo County	240	1.63
Signal Hill, CA (city) Los Angeles County	180	1.63
Saratoga Springs, UT (city) Utah County	288	1.62
Lackland AFB, TX (cdp) Bexar County	159	1.60
La Presa, CA (cdp) San Diego County	543	1.59
Lakeland South, WA (cdp) King County	184	1.59
Patterson, CA (city) Stanislaus County	323	1.58
Kaneohe Station, HI (cdp) Honolulu County	150	1.58
St. George, UT (city) Washington County	1,123	1.54
Pittsburg, CA (city) Contra Costa County	976	1.54
University Place, WA (city) Pierce County	480	1.54
Fairview, OR (city) Multnomah County	137	1.54
Copperas Cove, TX (city) Coryell County	490	1.53
Lemon Grove, CA (city) San Diego County	387	1.53
Barstow, CA (city) San Bernardino County	344	1.52
Bryn Mawr-Skyway, WA (cdp) King County	237	1.51
Fort Drum, NY (cdp) Jefferson County	196	1.51
Antelope, CA (cdp) Sacramento County	688	1.50
American Canyon, CA (city) Napa County	289	1.49
Modesto, CA (city) Stanislaus County	2,976	1.48
North Lynnwood, WA (cdp) Snohomish County	244	1.47
El Sobrante, CA (cdp) Contra Costa County	186	1.47
Mountlake Terrace, WA (city) Snohomish County	289	1.45
Orchards, WA (cdp) Clark County	280	1.43
Long Beach, CA (city) Los Angeles County	6,549	1.42
North Las Vegas, NV (city) Clark County	3,074	1.42
Redwood City, CA (city) San Mateo County	1,092	1.42
Hawthorne, CA (city) Los Angeles County	1,176	1.40
Rancho Cordova, CA (city) Sacramento County	910	1.40

Race

Hawaii Native/Pacific Islander: Hispanic

U.S. and 50 States Sorted by Population and Percent of Total Population

Place	Population	%
United States	**210,307**	**0.07**
California	52,740	0.14
Hawaii	44,611	3.28
New York	14,655	0.08
Texas	13,140	0.05
Florida	8,776	0.05
Washington	5,633	0.08
Arizona	4,939	0.08
New Jersey	4,700	0.05
Nevada	4,433	0.16
Illinois	3,730	0.03
Georgia	3,681	0.04
Pennsylvania	3,668	0.03
North Carolina	3,357	0.04
Massachusetts	3,223	0.05
Colorado	3,177	0.06
Virginia	2,752	0.03
Oregon	2,299	0.06
Maryland	2,080	0.04
Utah	1,958	0.07
Connecticut	1,869	0.05
New Mexico	1,857	0.09
Ohio	1,823	0.02
Alabama	1,802	0.04
Tennessee	1,715	0.03
Michigan	1,431	0.01
Indiana	1,269	0.02
Missouri	1,221	0.02
South Carolina	1,171	0.03
Oklahoma	1,144	0.03
Louisiana	1,020	0.02
Minnesota	974	0.02
Wisconsin	930	0.02
Kentucky	876	0.02
Kansas	834	0.03
Rhode Island	823	0.08
Arkansas	733	0.03
Nebraska	695	0.04
Idaho	680	0.04
Alaska	639	0.09
Mississippi	621	0.02
Iowa	557	0.02
District of Columbia	499	0.08
Delaware	374	0.04
New Hampshire	215	0.02
Montana	204	0.02
Wyoming	188	0.03
South Dakota	175	0.02
West Virginia	152	0.01
Maine	132	0.01
North Dakota	86	0.01
Vermont	46	0.01

Place	Population	%
Hawaii	44,611	3.28
Nevada	4,433	0.16
California	52,740	0.14
New Mexico	1,857	0.09
Alaska	639	0.09
New York	14,655	0.08
Washington	5,633	0.08
Arizona	4,939	0.08
Rhode Island	823	0.08
District of Columbia	499	0.08
United States	**210,307**	**0.07**
Utah	1,958	0.07
Colorado	3,177	0.06
Oregon	2,299	0.06
Texas	13,140	0.05
Florida	8,776	0.05
New Jersey	4,700	0.05
Massachusetts	3,223	0.05
Connecticut	1,869	0.05
Georgia	3,681	0.04
North Carolina	3,357	0.04
Maryland	2,080	0.04
Alabama	1,802	0.04
Nebraska	695	0.04
Idaho	680	0.04
Delaware	374	0.04
Illinois	3,730	0.03
Pennsylvania	3,668	0.03
Virginia	2,752	0.03
Tennessee	1,715	0.03
South Carolina	1,171	0.03
Oklahoma	1,144	0.03
Kansas	834	0.03
Arkansas	733	0.03
Wyoming	188	0.03
Ohio	1,823	0.02
Indiana	1,269	0.02
Missouri	1,221	0.02
Louisiana	1,020	0.02
Minnesota	974	0.02
Wisconsin	930	0.02
Kentucky	876	0.02
Mississippi	621	0.02
Iowa	557	0.02
New Hampshire	215	0.02
Montana	204	0.02
South Dakota	175	0.02
Michigan	1,431	0.01
West Virginia	152	0.01
Maine	132	0.01
North Dakota	86	0.01
Vermont	46	0.01

Please refer to the Explanation of Data in the front of the book for more detailed information.

Race

Hawaii Native/Pacific Islander: Hispanic

Top 150 Places Sorted by Population

Based on all places, regardless of total population

Place	Population	%
New York, NY (city) Kings County	10,881	0.13
Urban Honolulu, HI (cdp) Honolulu County	5,611	1.66
Bronx, NY (borough) Bronx County	4,359	0.31
Los Angeles, CA (city) Los Angeles County	4,252	0.11
Brooklyn, NY (borough) Kings County	2,321	0.09
Hilo, HI (cdp) Hawaii County	2,294	5.30
San Diego, CA (city) San Diego County	2,101	0.16
Queens, NY (borough) Queens County	2,006	0.09
Manhattan, NY (borough) New York County	1,951	0.12
San Jose, CA (city) Santa Clara County	1,656	0.18
Chicago, IL (city) Cook County	1,584	0.06
Kaneohe, HI (cdp) Honolulu County	1,487	4.30
Houston, TX (city) Harris County	1,454	0.07
Waianae, HI (cdp) Honolulu County	1,398	10.61
San Antonio, TX (city) Medina County	1,359	0.10
Phoenix, AZ (city) Maricopa County	1,352	0.09
Pearl City, HI (cdp) Honolulu County	1,274	2.67
Philadelphia, PA (city) Philadelphia County	1,187	0.08
Nanakuli, HI (cdp) Honolulu County	1,134	8.95
Makakilo, HI (cdp) Honolulu County	1,030	5.64
Wahiawa, HI (cdp) Honolulu County	1,023	5.74
Las Vegas, NV (city) Clark County	1,007	0.17
Makaha, HI (cdp) Honolulu County	989	11.95
Ewa Gentry, HI (cdp) Honolulu County	989	4.36
Kahului, HI (cdp) Maui County	980	3.72
Mililani Town, HI (cdp) Honolulu County	970	3.51
Maili, HI (cdp) Honolulu County	958	10.10
Long Beach, CA (city) Los Angeles County	949	0.21
Sacramento, CA (city) Sacramento County	937	0.20
Kailua, HI (cdp) Honolulu County	928	2.40
Kapolei, HI (cdp) Honolulu County	920	6.06
Hawaiian Paradise Park, HI (cdp) Hawaii County	868	7.61
Waipahu, HI (cdp) Honolulu County	861	2.25
Ewa Beach, HI (cdp) Honolulu County	815	5.45
Chula Vista, CA (city) San Diego County	753	0.31
San Francisco, CA (city) San Francisco County	741	0.09
Fresno, CA (city) Fresno County	702	0.14
Stockton, CA (city) San Joaquin County	697	0.24
Dallas, TX (city) Dallas County	694	0.06
Wailuku, HI (cdp) Maui County	621	4.06
Hayward, CA (city) Alameda County	615	0.43
Albuquerque, NM (city) Bernalillo County	608	0.11
Boston, MA (city) Suffolk County	565	0.09
East Honolulu, HI (cdp) Honolulu County	552	1.11
Anaheim, CA (city) Orange County	540	0.16
El Paso, TX (city) El Paso County	528	0.08
Riverside, CA (city) Riverside County	521	0.17
Paradise, NV (cdp) Clark County	516	0.23
Colorado Springs, CO (city) El Paso County	516	0.12
Kapaa, HI (cdp) Kauai County	514	4.80
North Las Vegas, NV (city) Clark County	503	0.23
Oakland, CA (city) Alameda County	501	0.13
Washington, DC (city) District of Columbia	499	0.08
Modesto, CA (city) Stanislaus County	491	0.24
Tucson, AZ (city) Pima County	484	0.09
Kailua, HI (cdp) Hawaii County	483	4.03
Sunrise Manor, NV (cdp) Clark County	467	0.25
Santa Ana, CA (city) Orange County	467	0.14
Ahuimanu, HI (cdp) Honolulu County	466	5.29
Oceanside, CA (city) San Diego County	466	0.28
Makawao, HI (cdp) Maui County	442	6.15
Mountain View, HI (cdp) Hawaii County	437	11.14
Mililani Mauka, HI (cdp) Honolulu County	436	2.07
Halawa, HI (cdp) Honolulu County	435	3.10
Austin, TX (city) Travis County	431	0.05
Hawaiian Beaches, HI (cdp) Hawaii County	426	9.95
Providence, RI (city) Providence County	419	0.24
Waihee-Waiehu, HI (cdp) Maui County	417	4.72
Fort Worth, TX (city) Tarrant County	414	0.06
Bakersfield, CA (city) Kern County	410	0.12
Hempstead, NY (town) Nassau County	402	0.05
Anchorage, AK (municipality) Anchorage Municipality	401	0.14
Denver, CO (city) Denver County	400	0.07
Kalaoa, HI (cdp) Hawaii County	388	4.02
Waimalu, HI (cdp) Honolulu County	387	2.82
Mesa, AZ (city) Maricopa County	386	0.09
Seattle, WA (city) King County	386	0.06
Waimea, HI (cdp) Hawaii County	384	4.17
Portland, OR (city) Multnomah County	381	0.07
San Bernardino, CA (city) San Bernardino County	377	0.18
Waimanalo, HI (cdp) Honolulu County	376	6.90
Kihei, HI (cdp) Maui County	375	1.80
Oxnard, CA (city) Ventura County	374	0.19
Henderson, NV (city) Clark County	374	0.15
Fairfield, CA (city) Solano County	363	0.34
Jacksonville, FL (city) Duval County	361	0.04
Royal Kunia, HI (cdp) Honolulu County	357	2.46
Moreno Valley, CA (city) Riverside County	351	0.18
Oklahoma City, OK (city) Oklahoma County	347	0.06
Aurora, CO (city) Arapahoe County	342	0.11
Ewa Villages, HI (cdp) Honolulu County	340	5.57
Killeen, TX (city) Bell County	340	0.27
Fremont, CA (city) Alameda County	340	0.16
Pukalani, HI (cdp) Maui County	338	4.46
Lawrence, MA (city) Essex County	337	0.44
Tacoma, WA (city) Pierce County	337	0.17
Vallejo, CA (city) Solano County	333	0.29
Paterson, NJ (city) Passaic County	333	0.23
Charlotte, NC (city) Mecklenburg County	329	0.04
Newark, NJ (city) Essex County	324	0.12
Haiku-Pauwela, HI (cdp) Maui County	319	3.93
Carson, CA (city) Los Angeles County	315	0.34
Waipio, HI (cdp) Honolulu County	314	2.69
Tracy, CA (city) San Joaquin County	311	0.38
Springfield, MA (city) Hampden County	311	0.20
Indianapolis, IN (city) Marion County	309	0.04
Spring Valley, NV (cdp) Clark County	300	0.17
Salinas, CA (city) Monterey County	299	0.20
Victorville, CA (city) San Bernardino County	298	0.26
Reno, NV (city) Washoe County	298	0.13
Reading, PA (city) Berks County	292	0.33
Palmdale, CA (city) Los Angeles County	291	0.19
Kahaluu, HI (cdp) Honolulu County	285	6.02
Jersey City, NJ (city) Hudson County	281	0.11
Vacaville, CA (city) Solano County	278	0.30
Ontario, CA (city) San Bernardino County	276	0.17
Ainaloa, HI (cdp) Hawaii County	274	9.24
Concord, CA (city) Contra Costa County	273	0.22
Waimanalo Beach, HI (cdp) Honolulu County	272	6.07
Yonkers, NY (city) Westchester County	272	0.14
Elk Grove, CA (city) Sacramento County	271	0.18
Memphis, TN (city) Shelby County	270	0.04
Fontana, CA (city) San Bernardino County	268	0.14
Bridgeport, CT (city/town) Fairfield County	267	0.19
Manteca, CA (city) San Joaquin County	266	0.40
Waipio Acres, HI (cdp) Honolulu County	260	4.97
Antioch, CA (city) Contra Costa County	258	0.25
Fayetteville, NC (city) Cumberland County	255	0.13
Torrance, CA (city) Los Angeles County	245	0.17
Lancaster, CA (city) Los Angeles County	245	0.16
Miami, FL (city) Miami-Dade County	245	0.06
Staten Island, NY (borough) Richmond County	244	0.05
Nashville-Davidson, TN (metro govt) Davidson County	240	0.04
Vista, CA (city) San Diego County	239	0.25
Cleveland, OH (city) Cuyahoga County	235	0.06
Aiea, HI (cdp) Honolulu County	234	2.51
El Cajon, CA (city) San Diego County	232	0.23
Islip, NY (town) Suffolk County	227	0.07
Enterprise, NV (cdp) Clark County	225	0.21
Allentown, PA (city) Lehigh County	224	0.19
Rancho Cucamonga, CA (city) San Bernardino County	223	0.13
Salt Lake City, UT (city) Salt Lake County	223	0.12
Milwaukee, WI (city) Milwaukee County	221	0.04
Hartford, CT (city/town) Hartford County	218	0.17
San Mateo, CA (city) San Mateo County	215	0.22
Tampa, FL (city) Hillsborough County	215	0.06
Langley Park, MD (cdp) Prince George's County	213	1.14
Garden Grove, CA (city) Orange County	213	0.12
Corona, CA (city) Riverside County	211	0.14
Lahaina, HI (cdp) Maui County	210	1.79

Race

Hawaii Native/Pacific Islander: Hispanic

Top 150 Places Sorted by Percent of Total Population

Based on all places, regardless of total population

Place	Population	%
Makaha, HI (cdp) Honolulu County	989	11.95
Makaha Valley, HI (cdp) Honolulu County	157	11.71
Mountain View, HI (cdp) Hawaii County	437	11.14
Halaula, HI (cdp) Hawaii County	51	10.87
Hawi, HI (cdp) Hawaii County	115	10.64
Maunaloa, HI (cdp) Maui County	40	10.64
Waianae, HI (cdp) Honolulu County	1,398	10.61
Maili, HI (cdp) Honolulu County	958	10.10
Hawaiian Beaches, HI (cdp) Hawaii County	426	9.95
Eden Roc, HI (cdp) Hawaii County	91	9.66
Ainaloa, HI (cdp) Hawaii County	274	9.24
Nanakuli, HI (cdp) Honolulu County	1,134	8.95
Kapaau, HI (cdp) Hawaii County	145	8.36
Fern Acres, HI (cdp) Hawaii County	125	8.31
Hawaiian Paradise Park, HI (cdp) Hawaii County	868	7.61
Honomu, HI (cdp) Hawaii County	38	7.47
Laupahoehoe, HI (cdp) Hawaii County	42	7.23
Hawaiian Acres, HI (cdp) Hawaii County	193	7.15
Anahola, HI (cdp) Kauai County	157	7.06
Hana, HI (cdp) Maui County	87	7.04
Waimanalo, HI (cdp) Honolulu County	376	6.90
Orchidlands Estates, HI (cdp) Hawaii County	190	6.75
Point Baker, AK (cdp) Prince of Wales-Hyder Census Area	1	6.67
Ualapu'e, HI (cdp) Maui County	28	6.59
Pahala, HI (cdp) Hawaii County	87	6.42
Nanawale Estates, HI (cdp) Hawaii County	90	6.31
Paauilo, HI (cdp) Hawaii County	37	6.22
Makawao, HI (cdp) Maui County	442	6.15
Waimanalo Beach, HI (cdp) Honolulu County	272	6.07
Kapolei, HI (cdp) Honolulu County	920	6.06
Kahaluu, HI (cdp) Honolulu County	285	6.02
Wahiawa, HI (cdp) Honolulu County	1,023	5.74
Fern Forest, HI (cdp) Hawaii County	53	5.69
Kaaawa, HI (cdp) Honolulu County	78	5.66
Makakilo, HI (cdp) Honolulu County	1,030	5.64
Ewa Villages, HI (cdp) Honolulu County	340	5.57
Ewa Beach, HI (cdp) Honolulu County	815	5.45
Keokea, HI (cdp) Maui County	86	5.33
Hilo, HI (cdp) Hawaii County	2,294	5.30
Ahuimanu, HI (cdp) Honolulu County	466	5.29
Kualapuu, HI (cdp) Maui County	105	5.18
Papaikou, HI (cdp) Hawaii County	68	5.18
Waiohinu, HI (cdp) Hawaii County	11	5.16
Naalehu, HI (cdp) Hawaii County	44	5.08
Kekaha, HI (cdp) Kauai County	177	5.00
Waipio Acres, HI (cdp) Honolulu County	260	4.97
Haleiwa, HI (cdp) Honolulu County	196	4.94
Tibbie, AL (cdp) Washington County	2	4.88
Hauula, HI (cdp) Honolulu County	201	4.85
Kapaa, HI (cdp) Kauai County	514	4.80
Pepeekeo, HI (cdp) Hawaii County	85	4.75
Waihee-Waiehu, HI (cdp) Maui County	417	4.72
Waimea, HI (cdp) Kauai County	87	4.69
Haliimaile, HI (cdp) Maui County	44	4.56
Kurtistown, HI (cdp) Hawaii County	59	4.55
Hawaiian Ocean View, HI (cdp) Hawaii County	199	4.49
Koloa, HI (cdp) Kauai County	96	4.48
Pukalani, HI (cdp) Maui County	338	4.46
Wainaku, HI (cdp) Hawaii County	54	4.41
Ewa Gentry, HI (cdp) Honolulu County	989	4.36
Kaneohe, HI (cdp) Honolulu County	1,487	4.30
Hanapepe, HI (cdp) Kauai County	112	4.25
Waimea, HI (cdp) Hawaii County	384	4.17
Honokaa, HI (cdp) Hawaii County	92	4.07
Wailuku, HI (cdp) Maui County	621	4.06
Kailua, HI (cdp) Hawaii County	483	4.03
Iroquois Point, HI (cdp) Honolulu County	136	4.03
Kalaoa, HI (cdp) Hawaii County	388	4.02
Volcano, HI (cdp) Hawaii County	103	4.00
Keaau, HI (cdp) Hawaii County	89	3.95
Haiku-Pauwela, HI (cdp) Maui County	319	3.93
Waikapu, HI (cdp) Maui County	115	3.88
Kahului, HI (cdp) Maui County	980	3.72
Paia, HI (cdp) Maui County	99	3.71
Seven Springs, NC (town) Wayne County	4	3.64
Mililani Town, HI (cdp) Honolulu County	970	3.51
Lawai, HI (cdp) Kauai County	83	3.51
Eleele, HI (cdp) Kauai County	83	3.47
Wailua, HI (cdp) Kauai County	78	3.46
Maryhill, WA (cdp) Klickitat County	2	3.45
Leilani Estates, HI (cdp) Hawaii County	52	3.33
Kaunakakai, HI (cdp) Maui County	112	3.27
Kukuihaele, HI (cdp) Hawaii County	11	3.27
Waikane, HI (cdp) Honolulu County	25	3.21
Port Royal, VA (town) Caroline County	4	3.17
Kalaheo, HI (cdp) Kauai County	145	3.16
Halawa, HI (cdp) Honolulu County	435	3.10
Makena, HI (cdp) Maui County	3	3.03
Hanamaulu, HI (cdp) Kauai County	116	3.02
Kealakekua, HI (cdp) Hawaii County	61	3.02
Whitmore Village, HI (cdp) Honolulu County	135	3.00
Omao, HI (cdp) Kauai County	39	3.00
Honalo, HI (cdp) Hawaii County	72	2.97
Discovery Harbour, HI (cdp) Hawaii County	28	2.95
Heeia, HI (cdp) Honolulu County	146	2.94
Carrollton, AL (town) Pickens County	30	2.94
Honaunau-Napoopoo, HI (cdp) Hawaii County	75	2.92
Tyonek, AK (cdp) Kenai Peninsula Borough	5	2.92
Havelock, IA (city) Pocahontas County	4	2.90
Kula, HI (cdp) Maui County	185	2.87
Kahuku, HI (cdp) Honolulu County	75	2.87
Nickelsville, VA (town) Scott County	11	2.87
Lihue, HI (cdp) Kauai County	184	2.85
Wailua Homesteads, HI (cdp) Kauai County	147	2.83
Waimalu, HI (cdp) Honolulu County	387	2.82
West Loch Estate, HI (cdp) Honolulu County	150	2.73
Merigold, MS (town) Bolivar County	12	2.73
Waialua, HI (cdp) Honolulu County	105	2.72
Pakala Village, HI (cdp) Kauai County	8	2.72
Mokuleia, HI (cdp) Honolulu County	49	2.71
Ray, AL (cdp) Coosa County	12	2.71
Waipio, HI (cdp) Honolulu County	314	2.69
Pearl City, HI (cdp) Honolulu County	1,274	2.67
Waikele, HI (cdp) Honolulu County	199	2.66
Waikoloa Village, HI (cdp) Hawaii County	169	2.66
Captain Cook, HI (cdp) Hawaii County	91	2.65
Lanai City, HI (cdp) Maui County	82	2.64
Reed Point, MT (cdp) Stillwater County	5	2.59
Pahoa, HI (cdp) Hawaii County	24	2.54
Aiea, HI (cdp) Honolulu County	234	2.51
Shumway, IL (village) Effingham County	5	2.48
Royal Kunia, HI (cdp) Honolulu County	357	2.46
Kailua, HI (cdp) Honolulu County	928	2.40
Clutier, IA (city) Tama County	5	2.35
Punaluu, HI (cdp) Honolulu County	27	2.32
Ocean Pointe, HI (cdp) Honolulu County	192	2.30
Brazos, NM (cdp) Rio Arriba County	1	2.27
Waipahu, HI (cdp) Honolulu County	861	2.25
Launiupoko, HI (cdp) Maui County	13	2.21
Laie, HI (cdp) Honolulu County	134	2.18
Lake Alice, MN (township) Hubbard County	2	2.15
Paukaa, HI (cdp) Hawaii County	9	2.12
Fort Garland, CO (cdp) Costilla County	9	2.08
Shoal Creek Estates, MO (village) Newton County	2	2.08
Mililani Mauka, HI (cdp) Honolulu County	436	2.07
Edwards, MN (township) Kandiyohi County	5	2.07
Puhi, HI (cdp) Kauai County	59	2.03
Kaumakani, HI (cdp) Kauai County	15	2.00
Tasley, VA (cdp) Accomack County	6	2.00
Yoder, WY (town) Goshen County	3	1.99
Blyn, WA (cdp) Clallam County	2	1.98
Holualoa, HI (cdp) Hawaii County	168	1.97
Monmouth, CA (cdp) Fresno County	3	1.97
Olinda, HI (cdp) Maui County	21	1.94
Poipu, HI (cdp) Kauai County	19	1.94
Collinsville, AL (town) DeKalb County	38	1.92
Northland, MN (township) Polk County	3	1.88
Staples, TX (city) Guadalupe County	5	1.87
Kahaluu-Keauhou, HI (cdp) Hawaii County	65	1.83
Houlton, WI (cdp) St. Croix County	7	1.81

Please refer to the Explanation of Data in the front of the book for more detailed information.

Race

Hawaii Native/Pacific Islander: Hispanic

Top 150 Places Sorted by Percent of Total Population

Based on places with total population of 7,500 or more

Place	Population	%
Makaha, HI (cdp) Honolulu County	989	11.95
Waianae, HI (cdp) Honolulu County	1,398	10.61
Maili, HI (cdp) Honolulu County	958	10.10
Nanakuli, HI (cdp) Honolulu County	1,134	8.95
Hawaiian Paradise Park, HI (cdp) Hawaii County	868	7.61
Kapolei, HI (cdp) Honolulu County	920	6.06
Wahiawa, HI (cdp) Honolulu County	1,023	5.74
Makakilo, HI (cdp) Honolulu County	1,030	5.64
Ewa Beach, HI (cdp) Honolulu County	815	5.45
Hilo, HI (cdp) Hawaii County	2,294	5.30
Ahuimanu, HI (cdp) Honolulu County	466	5.29
Kapaa, HI (cdp) Kauai County	514	4.80
Waihee-Waiehu, HI (cdp) Maui County	417	4.72
Pukalani, HI (cdp) Maui County	338	4.46
Ewa Gentry, HI (cdp) Honolulu County	989	4.36
Kaneohe, HI (cdp) Honolulu County	1,487	4.30
Waimea, HI (cdp) Hawaii County	384	4.17
Wailuku, HI (cdp) Maui County	621	4.06
Kailua, HI (cdp) Hawaii County	483	4.03
Kalaoa, HI (cdp) Hawaii County	388	4.02
Haiku-Pauwela, HI (cdp) Maui County	319	3.93
Kahului, HI (cdp) Maui County	980	3.72
Mililani Town, HI (cdp) Honolulu County	970	3.51
Halawa, HI (cdp) Honolulu County	435	3.10
Waimalu, HI (cdp) Honolulu County	387	2.82
Waipio, HI (cdp) Honolulu County	314	2.69
Pearl City, HI (cdp) Honolulu County	1,274	2.67
Aiea, HI (cdp) Honolulu County	234	2.51
Royal Kunia, HI (cdp) Honolulu County	357	2.46
Kailua, HI (cdp) Honolulu County	928	2.40
Ocean Pointe, HI (cdp) Honolulu County	192	2.30
Waipahu, HI (cdp) Honolulu County	861	2.25
Mililani Mauka, HI (cdp) Honolulu County	436	2.07
Holualoa, HI (cdp) Hawaii County	168	1.97
Kihei, HI (cdp) Maui County	375	1.80
Lahaina, HI (cdp) Maui County	210	1.79
Urban Honolulu, HI (cdp) Honolulu County	5,611	1.66
Langley Park, MD (cdp) Prince George's County	213	1.14
East Honolulu, HI (cdp) Honolulu County	552	1.11
Morganton, NC (city) Burke County	133	0.79
Schofield Barracks, HI (cdp) Honolulu County	95	0.58
Haverstraw, NY (village) Rockland County	66	0.55
Cherryland, CA (cdp) Alameda County	77	0.52
Immokalee, FL (cdp) Collier County	121	0.50
Marina, CA (city) Monterey County	98	0.50
Patterson, CA (city) Stanislaus County	96	0.47
Dover, OH (city) Tuscarawas County	59	0.46
Country Club, CA (cdp) San Joaquin County	43	0.46
Lawrence, MA (city) Essex County	337	0.44
Hayward, CA (city) Alameda County	615	0.43
Kaneohe Station, HI (cdp) Honolulu County	41	0.43
Spring Lake, NC (town) Cumberland County	50	0.42
Signal Hill, CA (city) Los Angeles County	46	0.42
Manteca, CA (city) San Joaquin County	266	0.40
Imperial Beach, CA (city) San Diego County	104	0.40
Midland, WA (cdp) Pierce County	36	0.40
Tracy, CA (city) San Joaquin County	311	0.38
La Presa, CA (cdp) San Diego County	125	0.37
Lemon Grove, CA (city) San Diego County	94	0.37
Carthage, MO (city) Jasper County	53	0.37
Gadsden, AL (city) Etowah County	132	0.36
Burlington, WA (city) Skagit County	30	0.36
San Bruno, CA (city) San Mateo County	142	0.35
Fort Irwin, CA (cdp) San Bernardino County	31	0.35
August, CA (cdp) San Joaquin County	29	0.35
Fairfield, CA (city) Solano County	363	0.34
Carson, CA (city) Los Angeles County	315	0.34
Barstow, CA (city) San Bernardino County	77	0.34
Reading, PA (city) Berks County	292	0.33
Ceres, CA (city) Stanislaus County	148	0.33
Piney Green, NC (cdp) Onslow County	44	0.33
Fort Lewis, WA (cdp) Pierce County	37	0.33
South San Francisco, CA (city) San Mateo County	202	0.32
West Sacramento, CA (city) Yolo County	157	0.32
Spanaway, WA (cdp) Pierce County	87	0.32
San Lorenzo, CA (cdp) Alameda County	74	0.32
Bronx, NY (borough) Bronx County	4,359	0.31
Chula Vista, CA (city) San Diego County	753	0.31
Suisun City, CA (city) Solano County	86	0.31
Bostonia, CA (cdp) San Diego County	47	0.31
North Fair Oaks, CA (cdp) San Mateo County	46	0.31
Fairview, CA (cdp) Alameda County	31	0.31
Sleepy Hollow, NY (village) Westchester County	31	0.31
Vacaville, CA (city) Solano County	278	0.30
National City, CA (city) San Diego County	173	0.30
Pacifica, CA (city) San Mateo County	110	0.30
Oakley, CA (city) Contra Costa County	107	0.30
Santa Fe Springs, CA (city) Los Angeles County	48	0.30
Lamont, CA (cdp) Kern County	46	0.30
Guymon, OK (city) Texas County	34	0.30
Newman, CA (city) Stanislaus County	31	0.30
Fort Polk South, LA (cdp) Vernon Parish	27	0.30
Vallejo, CA (city) Solano County	333	0.29
Perth Amboy, NJ (city) Middlesex County	147	0.29
Parkland, WA (cdp) Pierce County	103	0.29
Spring Valley, CA (cdp) San Diego County	81	0.29
French Valley, CA (cdp) Riverside County	67	0.29
Port Hueneme, CA (city) Ventura County	64	0.29
New Philadelphia, OH (city) Tuscarawas County	50	0.29
Inwood, NY (cdp) Nassau County	28	0.29
Oceanside, CA (city) San Diego County	466	0.28
Galt, CA (city) Sacramento County	67	0.28
Lomita, CA (city) Los Angeles County	56	0.28
Sun Valley, NV (cdp) Washoe County	54	0.28
Lathrop, CA (city) San Joaquin County	51	0.28
Discovery Bay, CA (cdp) Contra Costa County	37	0.28
East La Mirada, CA (cdp) Los Angeles County	27	0.28
Toppenish, WA (city) Yakima County	25	0.28
Killeen, TX (city) Bell County	340	0.27
Union City, CA (city) Alameda County	189	0.27
Fort Hood, TX (cdp) Bell County	80	0.27
East Palo Alto, CA (city) San Mateo County	76	0.27
Twentynine Palms, CA (city) San Bernardino County	67	0.27
Bay Point, CA (cdp) Contra Costa County	57	0.27
Grand Terrace, CA (city) San Bernardino County	32	0.27
Healdsburg, CA (city) Sonoma County	30	0.27
River Rouge, MI (city) Wayne County	21	0.27
Victorville, CA (city) San Bernardino County	298	0.26
Lakewood, WA (city) Pierce County	149	0.26
Lompoc, CA (city) Santa Barbara County	112	0.26
Newark, CA (city) Alameda County	111	0.26
Holyoke, MA (city) Hampden County	105	0.26
Chelsea, MA (city) Suffolk County	93	0.26
Ashland, CA (cdp) Alameda County	58	0.26
Frederickson, WA (cdp) Pierce County	48	0.26
Alum Rock, CA (cdp) Santa Clara County	40	0.26
Elk Plain, WA (cdp) Pierce County	37	0.26
Ripon, CA (city) San Joaquin County	37	0.26
Bonita, CA (cdp) San Diego County	32	0.26
Port Orchard, WA (city) Kitsap County	29	0.26
Woodbury, NJ (city) Gloucester County	26	0.26
Gonzales, CA (city) Monterey County	21	0.26
Sunrise Manor, NV (cdp) Clark County	467	0.25
Antioch, CA (city) Contra Costa County	258	0.25
Vista, CA (city) San Diego County	239	0.25
Florin, CA (cdp) Sacramento County	117	0.25
Maywood, CA (city) Los Angeles County	69	0.25
Desert Hot Springs, CA (city) Riverside County	64	0.25
Central Falls, RI (city) Providence County	49	0.25
Silverdale, WA (cdp) Kitsap County	48	0.25
Rosamond, CA (cdp) Kern County	45	0.25
Cocoa, FL (city) Brevard County	43	0.25
Lemon Hill, CA (cdp) Sacramento County	35	0.25
El Sobrante, CA (cdp) Contra Costa County	32	0.25
Batesville, AR (city) Independence County	26	0.25
Stockton, CA (city) San Joaquin County	697	0.24
Modesto, CA (city) Stanislaus County	491	0.24
Providence, RI (city) Providence County	419	0.24
Union City, NJ (city) Hudson County	162	0.24
Pittsburg, CA (city) Contra Costa County	150	0.24

SECTION THREE

Please refer to the Explanation of Data in the front of the book for more detailed information.

Race

Hawaii Native/Pacific Islander: Fijian

U.S. and 50 States Sorted by Population and Percent of Total Population

Place	Population	%
United States	**32,304**	**0.01**
California	24,059	0.06
Washington	2,639	0.04
Oregon	888	0.02
Hawaii	711	0.05
Texas	454	<0.01
Nevada	369	0.01
Utah	366	0.01
New York	321	<0.01
Florida	255	<0.01
Arizona	237	<0.01
Georgia	189	<0.01
Virginia	136	<0.01
Illinois	133	<0.01
Colorado	123	<0.01
Missouri	93	<0.01
Pennsylvania	92	<0.01
Ohio	90	<0.01
Maryland	89	<0.01
Michigan	77	<0.01
North Carolina	76	<0.01
New Jersey	74	<0.01
Massachusetts	65	<0.01
Minnesota	61	<0.01
Idaho	56	<0.01
Kansas	44	<0.01
Wisconsin	43	<0.01
Alaska	42	0.01
Oklahoma	40	<0.01
South Carolina	40	<0.01
Tennessee	39	<0.01
Rhode Island	37	<0.01
Indiana	35	<0.01
Kentucky	35	<0.01
New Mexico	31	<0.01
Connecticut	30	<0.01
Arkansas	27	<0.01
Alabama	24	<0.01
District of Columbia	23	<0.01
Montana	23	<0.01
Louisiana	22	<0.01
Iowa	21	<0.01
Nebraska	19	<0.01
South Dakota	16	<0.01
Mississippi	12	<0.01
Delaware	10	<0.01
North Dakota	10	<0.01
Vermont	8	<0.01
Wyoming	8	<0.01
New Hampshire	6	<0.01
Maine	4	<0.01
West Virginia	2	<0.01

Place	Population	%
California	24,059	0.06
Hawaii	711	0.05
Washington	2,639	0.04
Oregon	888	0.02
United States	**32,304**	**0.01**
Nevada	369	0.01
Utah	366	0.01
Alaska	42	0.01
Texas	454	<0.01
New York	321	<0.01
Florida	255	<0.01
Arizona	237	<0.01
Georgia	189	<0.01
Virginia	136	<0.01
Illinois	133	<0.01
Colorado	123	<0.01
Missouri	93	<0.01
Pennsylvania	92	<0.01
Ohio	90	<0.01
Maryland	89	<0.01
Michigan	77	<0.01
North Carolina	76	<0.01
New Jersey	74	<0.01
Massachusetts	65	<0.01
Minnesota	61	<0.01
Idaho	56	<0.01
Kansas	44	<0.01
Wisconsin	43	<0.01
Oklahoma	40	<0.01
South Carolina	40	<0.01
Tennessee	39	<0.01
Rhode Island	37	<0.01
Indiana	35	<0.01
Kentucky	35	<0.01
New Mexico	31	<0.01
Connecticut	30	<0.01
Arkansas	27	<0.01
Alabama	24	<0.01
District of Columbia	23	<0.01
Montana	23	<0.01
Louisiana	22	<0.01
Iowa	21	<0.01
Nebraska	19	<0.01
South Dakota	16	<0.01
Mississippi	12	<0.01
Delaware	10	<0.01
North Dakota	10	<0.01
Vermont	8	<0.01
Wyoming	8	<0.01
New Hampshire	6	<0.01
Maine	4	<0.01
West Virginia	2	<0.01

Please refer to the Explanation of Data in the front of the book for more detailed information.

Race

Hawaii Native/Pacific Islander: Fijian

Top 150 Places Sorted by Population

Based on all places, regardless of total population

Place	Population	%
Sacramento, CA (city) Sacramento County	3,244	0.70
Hayward, CA (city) Alameda County	2,535	1.76
Modesto, CA (city) Stanislaus County	1,355	0.67
Elk Grove, CA (city) Sacramento County	1,279	0.84
Stockton, CA (city) San Joaquin County	665	0.23
Florin, CA (cdp) Sacramento County	500	1.05
San Jose, CA (city) Santa Clara County	490	0.05
San Bruno, CA (city) San Mateo County	441	1.07
Los Angeles, CA (city) Los Angeles County	420	0.01
Santa Rosa, CA (city) Sonoma County	419	0.25
South San Francisco, CA (city) San Mateo County	414	0.65
Union City, CA (city) Alameda County	403	0.58
San Mateo, CA (city) San Mateo County	390	0.40
West Sacramento, CA (city) Yolo County	387	0.79
Portland, OR (city) Multnomah County	366	0.06
Fremont, CA (city) Alameda County	348	0.16
Arden-Arcade, CA (cdp) Sacramento County	262	0.28
San Francisco, CA (city) San Francisco County	250	0.03
Newark, CA (city) Alameda County	247	0.58
Pittsburg, CA (city) Contra Costa County	234	0.37
Rancho Cordova, CA (city) Sacramento County	233	0.36
Tracy, CA (city) San Joaquin County	222	0.27
Seattle, WA (city) King County	219	0.04
New York, NY (city) Kings County	213	<0.01
East Palo Alto, CA (city) San Mateo County	208	0.74
Kent, WA (city) King County	201	0.22
Vallejo, CA (city) Solano County	190	0.16
Seaside, CA (city) Monterey County	183	0.55
Fairfield, CA (city) Solano County	183	0.17
Daly City, CA (city) San Mateo County	178	0.18
Oakland, CA (city) Alameda County	174	0.04
Vineyard, CA (cdp) Sacramento County	173	0.70
Urban Honolulu, HI (cdp) Honolulu County	165	0.05
Antelope, CA (cdp) Sacramento County	164	0.36
Turlock, CA (city) Stanislaus County	156	0.23
Redwood City, CA (city) San Mateo County	156	0.20
Antioch, CA (city) Contra Costa County	139	0.14
Ceres, CA (city) Stanislaus County	133	0.29
Renton, WA (city) King County	133	0.15
Richmond, CA (city) Contra Costa County	132	0.13
Federal Way, WA (city) King County	127	0.14
Hawthorne, CA (city) Los Angeles County	126	0.15
Santa Clara, CA (city) Santa Clara County	123	0.11
Everett, WA (city) Snohomish County	119	0.12
Vancouver, WA (city) Clark County	115	0.07
Fresno, CA (city) Fresno County	114	0.02
Castro Valley, CA (cdp) Alameda County	110	0.18
Manteca, CA (city) San Joaquin County	106	0.16
Woodland, CA (city) Yolo County	105	0.19
San Leandro, CA (city) Alameda County	104	0.12
Marina, CA (city) Monterey County	102	0.52
Laie, HI (cdp) Honolulu County	100	1.63
East Hill-Meridian, WA (cdp) King County	96	0.32
Parkway, CA (cdp) Sacramento County	94	0.64
Cherryland, CA (cdp) Alameda County	93	0.63
North Highlands, CA (cdp) Sacramento County	90	0.21
Sunnyvale, CA (city) Santa Clara County	86	0.06
Bellingham, WA (city) Whatcom County	82	0.10
Suisun City, CA (city) Solano County	80	0.28
Ashland, CA (cdp) Alameda County	79	0.36
Folsom, CA (city) Sacramento County	79	0.11
San Diego, CA (city) San Diego County	79	0.01
Mountlake Terrace, WA (city) Snohomish County	77	0.39
Foster City, CA (city) San Mateo County	77	0.25
Auburn, WA (city) King County	76	0.11
Queens, NY (borough) Queens County	76	<0.01
Inglewood, CA (city) Los Angeles County	75	0.07
Manhattan, NY (borough) New York County	73	<0.01
Lathrop, CA (city) San Joaquin County	69	0.38
Henderson, NV (city) Clark County	69	0.03
Rosemont, CA (cdp) Sacramento County	66	0.29
Anaheim, CA (city) Orange County	65	0.02
San Pablo, CA (city) Contra Costa County	64	0.22
Pacifica, CA (city) San Mateo County	64	0.17
Mountain View, CA (city) Santa Clara County	64	0.09
Shoreline, WA (city) King County	63	0.12
Carmichael, CA (cdp) Sacramento County	61	0.10
Foothill Farms, CA (cdp) Sacramento County	58	0.18
Citrus Heights, CA (city) Sacramento County	58	0.07
Milpitas, CA (city) Santa Clara County	57	0.09
Riverbank, CA (city) Stanislaus County	56	0.25
Livermore, CA (city) Alameda County	56	0.07
Houston, TX (city) Harris County	56	<0.01
Roseville, CA (city) Placer County	55	0.05
Riverside, CA (city) Riverside County	54	0.02
Fairview, CA (cdp) Alameda County	52	0.52
Menlo Park, CA (city) San Mateo County	52	0.16
Bellflower, CA (city) Los Angeles County	52	0.07
Millbrae, CA (city) San Mateo County	51	0.24
Lynnwood, WA (city) Snohomish County	51	0.14
San Bernardino, CA (city) San Bernardino County	51	0.02
Rohnert Park, CA (city) Sonoma County	50	0.12
Dublin, CA (city) Alameda County	50	0.11
Buena Park, CA (city) Orange County	50	0.06
Paradise, NV (cdp) Clark County	50	0.02
Long Beach, CA (city) Los Angeles County	50	0.01
Beaverton, OR (city) Washington County	49	0.05
Blaine, WA (city) Whatcom County	48	1.02
SeaTac, WA (city) King County	48	0.18
San Rafael, CA (city) Marin County	48	0.08
Corona, CA (city) Riverside County	47	0.03
Spring Valley, NV (cdp) Clark County	47	0.03
El Sobrante, CA (cdp) Contra Costa County	46	0.36
Rio Linda, CA (cdp) Sacramento County	46	0.30
Petaluma, CA (city) Sonoma County	46	0.08
Hillsboro, OR (city) Washington County	46	0.05
Patterson, CA (city) Stanislaus County	45	0.22
Brooklyn, NY (borough) Kings County	45	<0.01
Phoenix, AZ (city) Maricopa County	45	<0.01
Tacoma, WA (city) Pierce County	44	0.02
Mather, CA (cdp) Sacramento County	43	0.97
Campbell, CA (city) Santa Clara County	43	0.11
Carson, CA (city) Los Angeles County	43	0.05
Springfield, OR (city) Lane County	42	0.07
Davis, CA (city) Yolo County	42	0.06
Gresham, OR (city) Multnomah County	42	0.04
San Ramon, CA (city) Contra Costa County	41	0.06
Las Vegas, NV (city) Clark County	41	0.01
North Lynnwood, WA (cdp) Snohomish County	40	0.24
Brentwood, CA (city) Contra Costa County	40	0.08
Marysville, WA (city) Snohomish County	40	0.07
Hercules, CA (city) Contra Costa County	39	0.16
Burien, WA (city) King County	39	0.12
North Las Vegas, NV (city) Clark County	39	0.02
Salida, CA (cdp) Stanislaus County	38	0.28
Novato, CA (city) Marin County	38	0.07
Orem, UT (city) Utah County	38	0.04
Santa Monica, CA (city) Los Angeles County	38	0.04
Tukwila, WA (city) King County	37	0.19
Lodi, CA (city) San Joaquin County	37	0.06
Clovis, CA (city) Fresno County	36	0.04
Berkeley, CA (city) Alameda County	36	0.03
Concord, CA (city) Contra Costa County	36	0.03
Lemon Hill, CA (cdp) Sacramento County	35	0.25
Eugene, OR (city) Lane County	35	0.02
Tucson, AZ (city) Pima County	35	0.01
Culver City, CA (city) Los Angeles County	34	0.09
Bellevue, WA (city) King County	34	0.03
Del Aire, CA (cdp) Los Angeles County	33	0.33
Perris, CA (city) Riverside County	33	0.05
Yuba City, CA (city) Sutter County	33	0.05
Galt, CA (city) Sacramento County	32	0.14
Fruitridge Pocket, CA (cdp) Sacramento County	31	0.53
Alderwood Manor, WA (cdp) Snohomish County	31	0.37
Edmonds, WA (city) Snohomish County	31	0.08
Colusa, CA (city) Colusa County	30	0.50
San Lorenzo, CA (cdp) Alameda County	30	0.13
Norwalk, CA (city) Los Angeles County	30	0.03
Moreno Valley, CA (city) Riverside County	30	0.02
Taylorsville, UT (city) Salt Lake County	29	0.05

SECTION THREE

Race

Hawaii Native/Pacific Islander: Fijian

Top 150 Places Sorted by Percent of Total Population

Based on all places, regardless of total population

Place	Population	%
Camp Sherman, OR (cdp) Jefferson County	5	2.15
Hayward, CA (city) Alameda County	2,535	1.76
Laie, HI (cdp) Honolulu County	100	1.63
Jacksonville, VT (village) Windham County	3	1.35
San Bruno, CA (city) San Mateo County	441	1.07
Cleveland, IL (village) Henry County	2	1.06
Florin, CA (cdp) Sacramento County	500	1.05
Blaine, WA (city) Whatcom County	48	1.02
Mather, CA (cdp) Sacramento County	43	0.97
Hot Springs Landing, NM (cdp) Sierra County	1	0.91
Elk Grove, CA (city) Sacramento County	1,279	0.84
West Sacramento, CA (city) Yolo County	387	0.79
East Palo Alto, CA (city) San Mateo County	208	0.74
Sacramento, CA (city) Sacramento County	3,244	0.70
Vineyard, CA (cdp) Sacramento County	173	0.70
Bayview, CA (cdp) Contra Costa County	12	0.68
Modesto, CA (city) Stanislaus County	1,355	0.67
South San Francisco, CA (city) San Mateo County	414	0.65
Parkway, CA (cdp) Sacramento County	94	0.64
Cherryland, CA (cdp) Alameda County	93	0.63
Montgomery Creek, CA (cdp) Shasta County	1	0.61
Union City, CA (city) Alameda County	403	0.58
Newark, CA (city) Alameda County	247	0.58
Cashel, MN (township) Swift County	1	0.57
Keokea, HI (cdp) Maui County	9	0.56
Seaside, CA (city) Monterey County	183	0.55
Rollingwood, CA (cdp) Contra Costa County	16	0.54
Fruitridge Pocket, CA (cdp) Sacramento County	31	0.53
Hoodsport, WA (cdp) Mason County	2	0.53
Marina, CA (city) Monterey County	102	0.52
Fairview, CA (cdp) Alameda County	52	0.52
Larch Way, WA (cdp) Snohomish County	17	0.51
Kaaawa, HI (cdp) Honolulu County	7	0.51
Colusa, CA (city) Colusa County	30	0.50
Myrtle Springs, TX (cdp) Van Zandt County	4	0.48
Rollins, MT (cdp) Lake County	1	0.48
Whittier, AK (city) Valdez-Cordova Census Area	1	0.45
Morada, CA (cdp) San Joaquin County	16	0.42
Kahuku, HI (cdp) Honolulu County	11	0.42
San Mateo, CA (city) San Mateo County	390	0.40
Dayton, WY (town) Sheridan County	3	0.40
Mountlake Terrace, WA (city) Snohomish County	77	0.39
Waikane, HI (cdp) Honolulu County	3	0.39
Center, MO (city) Ralls County	2	0.39
Wye, MT (cdp) Missoula County	2	0.39
Guinda, CA (cdp) Yolo County	1	0.39
Lathrop, CA (city) San Joaquin County	69	0.38
Pittsburg, CA (city) Contra Costa County	234	0.37
Alderwood Manor, WA (cdp) Snohomish County	31	0.37
Rancho Cordova, CA (city) Sacramento County	233	0.36
Antelope, CA (cdp) Sacramento County	164	0.36
Ashland, CA (cdp) Alameda County	79	0.36
El Sobrante, CA (cdp) Contra Costa County	46	0.36
Hauula, HI (cdp) Honolulu County	15	0.36
Lake Stickney, WA (cdp) Snohomish County	27	0.35
Dade City North, FL (cdp) Pasco County	11	0.35
Keyes, CA (cdp) Stanislaus County	19	0.34
Del Aire, CA (cdp) Los Angeles County	33	0.33
East Hill-Meridian, WA (cdp) King County	96	0.32
Meadowdale, WA (cdp) Snohomish County	9	0.32
Byron, CA (cdp) Contra Costa County	4	0.31
Rio Linda, CA (cdp) Sacramento County	46	0.30
Sand City, CA (city) Monterey County	1	0.30
Ceres, CA (city) Stanislaus County	133	0.29
Rosemont, CA (cdp) Sacramento County	66	0.29
Belvedere, CA (city) Marin County	6	0.29
Arden-Arcade, CA (cdp) Sacramento County	262	0.28
Suisun City, CA (city) Solano County	80	0.28
Salida, CA (cdp) Stanislaus County	38	0.28
Meadow Glade, WA (cdp) Clark County	7	0.28
Tracy, CA (city) San Joaquin County	222	0.27
Mayfield, MI (township) Grand Traverse County	4	0.26
Glen Ellen, CA (cdp) Sonoma County	2	0.26
Santa Rosa, CA (city) Sonoma County	419	0.25
Foster City, CA (city) San Mateo County	77	0.25

Place	Population	%
Riverbank, CA (city) Stanislaus County	56	0.25
Lemon Hill, CA (cdp) Sacramento County	35	0.25
Chatsworth, IL (town) Livingston County	3	0.25
Millbrae, CA (city) San Mateo County	51	0.24
North Lynnwood, WA (cdp) Snohomish County	40	0.24
Tenino, WA (city) Thurston County	4	0.24
Stockton, CA (city) San Joaquin County	665	0.23
Turlock, CA (city) Stanislaus County	156	0.23
Algona, WA (city) King County	7	0.23
Marin City, CA (cdp) Marin County	6	0.23
Crowder, OK (town) Pittsburg County	1	0.23
Kent, WA (city) King County	201	0.22
San Pablo, CA (city) Contra Costa County	64	0.22
Patterson, CA (city) Stanislaus County	45	0.22
Elverta, CA (cdp) Sacramento County	12	0.22
Coalville, UT (city) Summit County	3	0.22
Nooksack, WA (city) Whatcom County	3	0.22
Whitingham, VT (town) Windham County	3	0.22
Alhambra Valley, CA (cdp) Contra Costa County	2	0.22
Goshen, KY (city) Oldham County	2	0.22
Hull, IL (village) Pike County	1	0.22
North Highlands, CA (cdp) Sacramento County	90	0.21
La Riviera, CA (cdp) Sacramento County	23	0.21
Mountain House, CA (cdp) San Joaquin County	20	0.21
Bear Creek, FL (cdp) Pinellas County	4	0.21
North Plains, OR (city) Washington County	4	0.21
Redwood City, CA (city) San Mateo County	156	0.20
Atherton, CA (town) San Mateo County	14	0.20
Mayfair, CA (cdp) Fresno County	9	0.20
Woodland, CA (city) Yolo County	105	0.19
Tukwila, WA (city) King County	37	0.19
Walnut Grove, WA (cdp) Clark County	19	0.19
Corte Madera, CA (town) Marin County	18	0.19
Wilton, CA (cdp) Sacramento County	10	0.19
Oracle, AZ (cdp) Pinal County	7	0.19
Monument Hills, CA (cdp) Yolo County	3	0.19
South Dos Palos, CA (cdp) Merced County	3	0.19
Clinton, MT (cdp) Missoula County	2	0.19
Daly City, CA (city) San Mateo County	178	0.18
Castro Valley, CA (cdp) Alameda County	110	0.18
Foothill Farms, CA (cdp) Sacramento County	58	0.18
SeaTac, WA (city) King County	48	0.18
Clearview, WA (cdp) Snohomish County	6	0.18
Ashton, ID (city) Fremont County	2	0.18
Greenville, CA (cdp) Plumas County	2	0.18
Maxwell, CA (cdp) Colusa County	2	0.18
Meridian Station, MS (cdp) Lauderdale County	2	0.18
Fairfield, CA (city) Solano County	183	0.17
Pacifica, CA (city) San Mateo County	64	0.17
Lakeland North, WA (cdp) King County	22	0.17
Vernal, UT (city) Uintah County	15	0.17
Birch Bay, WA (cdp) Whatcom County	14	0.17
Pukalani, HI (cdp) Maui County	13	0.17
Scappoose, OR (city) Columbia County	11	0.17
Strawberry, CA (cdp) Marin County	9	0.17
El Verano, CA (cdp) Sonoma County	7	0.17
Fetters Hot Springs-Agua Caliente, CA (cdp) Sonoma County	7	0.17
Sleepy Hollow, CA (cdp) Marin County	4	0.17
Belford, NJ (cdp) Monmouth County	3	0.17
Berrien Springs, MI (village) Berrien County	3	0.17
Haymarket, VA (town) Prince William County	3	0.17
Fremont, CA (city) Alameda County	348	0.16
Vallejo, CA (city) Solano County	190	0.16
Manteca, CA (city) San Joaquin County	106	0.16
Menlo Park, CA (city) San Mateo County	52	0.16
Hercules, CA (city) Contra Costa County	39	0.16
Bothell East, WA (cdp) Snohomish County	13	0.16
Riverton, WA (cdp) King County	10	0.16
Vine Hill, CA (cdp) Contra Costa County	6	0.16
Dundee, OR (city) Yamhill County	5	0.16
Lochsloy, WA (cdp) Snohomish County	4	0.16
Hana, HI (cdp) Maui County	2	0.16
Renton, WA (city) King County	133	0.15
Hawthorne, CA (city) Los Angeles County	126	0.15
Coos Bay, OR (city) Coos County	24	0.15

Please refer to the Explanation of Data in the front of the book for more detailed information.

Race

Hawaii Native/Pacific Islander: Fijian

Top 150 Places Sorted by Percent of Total Population

Based on places with total population of 7,500 or more

Place	Population	%
Hayward, CA (city) Alameda County	2,535	1.76
San Bruno, CA (city) San Mateo County	441	1.07
Florin, CA (cdp) Sacramento County	500	1.05
Elk Grove, CA (city) Sacramento County	1,279	0.84
West Sacramento, CA (city) Yolo County	387	0.79
East Palo Alto, CA (city) San Mateo County	208	0.74
Sacramento, CA (city) Sacramento County	3,244	0.70
Vineyard, CA (cdp) Sacramento County	173	0.70
Modesto, CA (city) Stanislaus County	1,355	0.67
South San Francisco, CA (city) San Mateo County	414	0.65
Parkway, CA (cdp) Sacramento County	94	0.64
Cherryland, CA (cdp) Alameda County	93	0.63
Union City, CA (city) Alameda County	403	0.58
Newark, CA (city) Alameda County	247	0.58
Seaside, CA (city) Monterey County	183	0.55
Marina, CA (city) Monterey County	102	0.52
Fairview, CA (cdp) Alameda County	52	0.52
San Mateo, CA (city) San Mateo County	390	0.40
Mountlake Terrace, WA (city) Snohomish County	77	0.39
Lathrop, CA (city) San Joaquin County	69	0.38
Pittsburg, CA (city) Contra Costa County	234	0.37
Alderwood Manor, WA (cdp) Snohomish County	31	0.37
Rancho Cordova, CA (city) Sacramento County	233	0.36
Antelope, CA (cdp) Sacramento County	164	0.36
Ashland, CA (cdp) Alameda County	79	0.36
El Sobrante, CA (cdp) Contra Costa County	46	0.36
Lake Stickney, WA (cdp) Snohomish County	27	0.35
Del Aire, CA (cdp) Los Angeles County	33	0.33
East Hill-Meridian, WA (cdp) King County	96	0.32
Rio Linda, CA (cdp) Sacramento County	46	0.30
Ceres, CA (city) Stanislaus County	133	0.29
Rosemont, CA (cdp) Sacramento County	66	0.29
Arden-Arcade, CA (cdp) Sacramento County	262	0.28
Suisun City, CA (city) Solano County	80	0.28
Salida, CA (cdp) Stanislaus County	38	0.28
Tracy, CA (city) San Joaquin County	222	0.27
Santa Rosa, CA (city) Sonoma County	419	0.25
Foster City, CA (city) San Mateo County	77	0.25
Riverbank, CA (city) Stanislaus County	56	0.25
Lemon Hill, CA (cdp) Sacramento County	35	0.25
Millbrae, CA (city) San Mateo County	51	0.24
North Lynnwood, WA (cdp) Snohomish County	40	0.24
Stockton, CA (city) San Joaquin County	665	0.23
Turlock, CA (city) Stanislaus County	156	0.23
Kent, WA (city) King County	201	0.22
San Pablo, CA (city) Contra Costa County	64	0.22
Patterson, CA (city) Stanislaus County	45	0.22
North Highlands, CA (cdp) Sacramento County	90	0.21
La Riviera, CA (cdp) Sacramento County	23	0.21
Mountain House, CA (cdp) San Joaquin County	20	0.21
Redwood City, CA (city) San Mateo County	156	0.20
Woodland, CA (city) Yolo County	105	0.19
Tukwila, WA (city) King County	37	0.19
Walnut Grove, WA (cdp) Clark County	19	0.19
Corte Madera, CA (town) Marin County	18	0.19
Daly City, CA (city) San Mateo County	178	0.18
Castro Valley, CA (cdp) Alameda County	110	0.18
Foothill Farms, CA (cdp) Sacramento County	58	0.18
SeaTac, WA (city) King County	48	0.18
Fairfield, CA (city) Solano County	183	0.17
Pacifica, CA (city) San Mateo County	64	0.17
Lakeland North, WA (cdp) King County	22	0.17
Vernal, UT (city) Uintah County	15	0.17
Birch Bay, WA (cdp) Whatcom County	14	0.17
Pukalani, HI (cdp) Maui County	13	0.17
Fremont, CA (city) Alameda County	348	0.16
Vallejo, CA (city) Solano County	190	0.16
Manteca, CA (city) San Joaquin County	106	0.16
Menlo Park, CA (city) San Mateo County	52	0.16
Hercules, CA (city) Contra Costa County	39	0.16
Bothell East, WA (cdp) Snohomish County	13	0.16
Renton, WA (city) King County	133	0.15
Hawthorne, CA (city) Los Angeles County	126	0.15
Coos Bay, OR (city) Coos County	24	0.15
San Anselmo, CA (town) Marin County	18	0.15

Place	Population	%
Antioch, CA (city) Contra Costa County	139	0.14
Federal Way, WA (city) King County	127	0.14
Lynnwood, WA (city) Snohomish County	51	0.14
Galt, CA (city) Sacramento County	32	0.14
North Fair Oaks, CA (cdp) San Mateo County	21	0.14
Richmond, CA (city) Contra Costa County	132	0.13
San Lorenzo, CA (cdp) Alameda County	30	0.13
Discovery Bay, CA (cdp) Contra Costa County	17	0.13
Ferndale, WA (city) Whatcom County	15	0.13
Sonoma, CA (city) Sonoma County	14	0.13
Everett, WA (city) Snohomish County	119	0.12
San Leandro, CA (city) Alameda County	104	0.12
Shoreline, WA (city) King County	63	0.12
Rohnert Park, CA (city) Sonoma County	50	0.12
Burien, WA (city) King County	39	0.12
Bryn Mawr-Skyway, WA (cdp) King County	19	0.12
Ewa Beach, HI (cdp) Honolulu County	18	0.12
Lakeland South, WA (cdp) King County	14	0.12
Fairview, OR (city) Multnomah County	11	0.12
Santa Clara, CA (city) Santa Clara County	123	0.11
Folsom, CA (city) Sacramento County	79	0.11
Auburn, WA (city) King County	76	0.11
Dublin, CA (city) Alameda County	50	0.11
Campbell, CA (city) Santa Clara County	43	0.11
El Cerrito, CA (city) Contra Costa County	26	0.11
Halawa, HI (cdp) Honolulu County	15	0.11
White Center, WA (cdp) King County	15	0.11
Tamalpais-Homestead Valley, CA (cdp) Marin County	12	0.11
Ahuimanu, HI (cdp) Honolulu County	10	0.11
Fife, WA (city) Pierce County	10	0.11
Bellingham, WA (city) Whatcom County	82	0.10
Carmichael, CA (cdp) Sacramento County	61	0.10
Belmont, CA (city) San Mateo County	25	0.10
Highland, UT (city) Utah County	15	0.10
Nanakuli, HI (cdp) Honolulu County	13	0.10
Williamsburg, FL (cdp) Orange County	8	0.10
Mountain View, CA (city) Santa Clara County	64	0.09
Milpitas, CA (city) Santa Clara County	57	0.09
Culver City, CA (city) Los Angeles County	34	0.09
Burlingame, CA (city) San Mateo County	27	0.09
Des Moines, WA (city) King County	26	0.09
Five Corners, WA (cdp) Clark County	17	0.09
Pinole, CA (city) Contra Costa County	17	0.09
Makakilo, HI (cdp) Honolulu County	16	0.09
Kapolei, HI (cdp) Honolulu County	13	0.09
Pacific Grove, CA (city) Monterey County	13	0.09
Mill Valley, CA (city) Marin County	12	0.09
Delhi, CA (cdp) Merced County	10	0.09
Fort Knox, KY (cdp) Hardin County	9	0.09
Larkfield-Wikiup, CA (cdp) Sonoma County	8	0.09
San Rafael, CA (city) Marin County	48	0.08
Petaluma, CA (city) Sonoma County	46	0.08
Brentwood, CA (city) Contra Costa County	40	0.08
Edmonds, WA (city) Snohomish County	31	0.08
Orangevale, CA (cdp) Sacramento County	27	0.08
Fairwood, WA (cdp) King County	15	0.08
Artesia, CA (city) Los Angeles County	14	0.08
Wahiawa, HI (cdp) Honolulu County	14	0.08
Wailuku, HI (cdp) Maui County	12	0.08
Garden Acres, CA (cdp) San Joaquin County	9	0.08
Maili, HI (cdp) Honolulu County	8	0.08
North Bend, OR (city) Coos County	8	0.08
East Foothills, CA (cdp) Santa Clara County	7	0.08
Oak Hills, CA (cdp) San Bernardino County	7	0.08
Rodeo, CA (cdp) Contra Costa County	7	0.08
Sound Beach, NY (cdp) Suffolk County	6	0.08
Vancouver, WA (city) Clark County	115	0.07
Inglewood, CA (city) Los Angeles County	75	0.07
Citrus Heights, CA (city) Sacramento County	58	0.07
Livermore, CA (city) Alameda County	56	0.07
Bellflower, CA (city) Los Angeles County	52	0.07
Springfield, OR (city) Lane County	42	0.07
Marysville, WA (city) Snohomish County	40	0.07
Novato, CA (city) Marin County	38	0.07
Valinda, CA (cdp) Los Angeles County	17	0.07

Race

Hawaii Native/Pacific Islander: Guamanian or Chamorro

U.S. and 50 States Sorted by Population and Percent of Total Population

Place	Population	%
United States	**147,798**	**0.05**
California	44,425	0.12
Washington	14,829	0.22
Texas	10,167	0.04
Hawaii	6,647	0.49
Florida	5,904	0.03
Nevada	5,512	0.20
Arizona	4,276	0.07
Georgia	3,856	0.04
North Carolina	3,682	0.04
Virginia	3,592	0.04
New York	3,407	0.02
Colorado	3,056	0.06
Oregon	3,014	0.08
Alabama	2,325	0.05
Tennessee	2,124	0.03
Maryland	2,100	0.04
Ohio	1,977	0.02
Illinois	1,928	0.02
Pennsylvania	1,605	0.01
South Carolina	1,568	0.03
Missouri	1,551	0.03
Oklahoma	1,470	0.04
New Jersey	1,447	0.02
Kentucky	1,287	0.03
Louisiana	1,189	0.03
Massachusetts	1,179	0.02
Indiana	1,113	0.02
Michigan	1,072	0.01
Kansas	1,002	0.04
Utah	880	0.03
Idaho	860	0.05
Mississippi	817	0.03
New Mexico	805	0.04
Connecticut	770	0.02
Nebraska	729	0.04
Minnesota	727	0.01
Arkansas	719	0.02
Wisconsin	716	0.01
Alaska	667	0.09
Iowa	572	0.02
Rhode Island	360	0.03
Delaware	319	0.04
Montana	228	0.02
South Dakota	216	0.03
New Hampshire	195	0.01
West Virginia	194	0.01
District of Columbia	187	0.03
Wyoming	174	0.03
Maine	152	0.01
North Dakota	126	0.02
Vermont	81	0.01

Place	Population	%
Hawaii	6,647	0.49
Washington	14,829	0.22
Nevada	5,512	0.20
California	44,425	0.12
Alaska	667	0.09
Oregon	3,014	0.08
Arizona	4,276	0.07
Colorado	3,056	0.06
United States	**147,798**	**0.05**
Alabama	2,325	0.05
Idaho	860	0.05
Texas	10,167	0.04
Georgia	3,856	0.04
North Carolina	3,682	0.04
Virginia	3,592	0.04
Maryland	2,100	0.04
Oklahoma	1,470	0.04
Kansas	1,002	0.04
New Mexico	805	0.04
Nebraska	729	0.04
Delaware	319	0.04
Florida	5,904	0.03
Tennessee	2,124	0.03
South Carolina	1,568	0.03
Missouri	1,551	0.03
Kentucky	1,287	0.03
Louisiana	1,189	0.03
Utah	880	0.03
Mississippi	817	0.03
Rhode Island	360	0.03
South Dakota	216	0.03
District of Columbia	187	0.03
Wyoming	174	0.03
New York	3,407	0.02
Ohio	1,977	0.02
Illinois	1,928	0.02
New Jersey	1,447	0.02
Massachusetts	1,179	0.02
Indiana	1,113	0.02
Connecticut	770	0.02
Arkansas	719	0.02
Iowa	572	0.02
Montana	228	0.02
North Dakota	126	0.02
Pennsylvania	1,605	0.01
Michigan	1,072	0.01
Minnesota	727	0.01
Wisconsin	716	0.01
New Hampshire	195	0.01
West Virginia	194	0.01
Maine	152	0.01
Vermont	81	0.01

Please refer to the Explanation of Data in the front of the book for more detailed information.

Race

Hawaii Native/Pacific Islander: Guamanian or Chamorro

Top 150 Places Sorted by Population

Based on all places, regardless of total population

Place	Population	%
San Diego, CA (city) San Diego County	3,999	0.31
Los Angeles, CA (city) Los Angeles County	1,840	0.05
New York, NY (city) Kings County	1,784	0.02
Urban Honolulu, HI (cdp) Honolulu County	1,596	0.47
San Jose, CA (city) Santa Clara County	1,396	0.15
Chula Vista, CA (city) San Diego County	1,389	0.57
Killeen, TX (city) Bell County	1,077	0.84
Las Vegas, NV (city) Clark County	1,045	0.18
Fairfield, CA (city) Solano County	1,013	0.96
North Las Vegas, NV (city) Clark County	978	0.45
San Antonio, TX (city) Medina County	968	0.07
Long Beach, CA (city) Los Angeles County	937	0.20
Phoenix, AZ (city) Maricopa County	917	0.06
Vallejo, CA (city) Solano County	866	0.75
Colorado Springs, CO (city) El Paso County	779	0.19
Spanaway, WA (cdp) Pierce County	730	2.68
Tacoma, WA (city) Pierce County	726	0.37
Parkland, WA (cdp) Pierce County	708	1.98
Sacramento, CA (city) Sacramento County	707	0.15
Paradise, NV (cdp) Clark County	703	0.32
Houston, TX (city) Harris County	693	0.03
Vancouver, WA (city) Clark County	685	0.42
Seattle, WA (city) King County	612	0.10
Chicago, IL (city) Cook County	592	0.02
Brooklyn, NY (borough) Kings County	568	0.02
San Francisco, CA (city) San Francisco County	566	0.07
Lakewood, WA (city) Pierce County	559	0.96
Sunrise Manor, NV (cdp) Clark County	547	0.29
El Paso, TX (city) El Paso County	530	0.08
Fayetteville, NC (city) Cumberland County	528	0.26
Oceanside, CA (city) San Diego County	525	0.31
Jacksonville, FL (city) Duval County	522	0.06
Lacey, WA (city) Thurston County	515	1.21
Spring Valley, NV (cdp) Clark County	499	0.28
Queens, NY (borough) Queens County	483	0.02
Hayward, CA (city) Alameda County	470	0.33
Portland, OR (city) Multnomah County	470	0.08
Fremont, CA (city) Alameda County	458	0.21
Tucson, AZ (city) Pima County	457	0.09
Virginia Beach, VA (ind. city) Virginia Beach independent city	453	0.10
Federal Way, WA (city) King County	419	0.47
Bremerton, WA (city) Kitsap County	417	1.11
Stockton, CA (city) San Joaquin County	414	0.14
El Cajon, CA (city) San Diego County	404	0.41
Riverside, CA (city) Riverside County	384	0.13
Oklahoma City, OK (city) Oklahoma County	384	0.07
Bronx, NY (borough) Bronx County	376	0.03
Vacaville, CA (city) Solano County	372	0.40
Henderson, NV (city) Clark County	363	0.14
Elk Grove, CA (city) Sacramento County	350	0.23
Enterprise, NV (cdp) Clark County	349	0.32
Moreno Valley, CA (city) Riverside County	344	0.18
Clarksville, TN (city) Montgomery County	333	0.25
Anaheim, CA (city) Orange County	328	0.10
Modesto, CA (city) Stanislaus County	324	0.16
Suisun City, CA (city) Solano County	321	1.14
La Presa, CA (cdp) San Diego County	312	0.91
Anchorage, AK (municipality) Anchorage Municipality	312	0.11
Aurora, CO (city) Arapahoe County	308	0.09
Oakland, CA (city) Alameda County	305	0.08
National City, CA (city) San Diego County	303	0.52
Temecula, CA (city) Riverside County	303	0.30
Lawton, OK (city) Comanche County	297	0.31
Murrieta, CA (city) Riverside County	296	0.29
Albuquerque, NM (city) Bernalillo County	294	0.05
South Hill, WA (cdp) Pierce County	293	0.56
Mesa, AZ (city) Maricopa County	293	0.07
Spokane, WA (city) Spokane County	287	0.14
Fort Worth, TX (city) Tarrant County	283	0.04
Salinas, CA (city) Monterey County	281	0.19
Santee, CA (city) San Diego County	276	0.52
Lakewood, CA (city) Los Angeles County	275	0.34
Oxnard, CA (city) Ventura County	275	0.14
Austin, TX (city) Travis County	274	0.03
Ewa Gentry, HI (cdp) Honolulu County	272	1.20
Antioch, CA (city) Contra Costa County	272	0.27
Reno, NV (city) Washoe County	272	0.12
Philadelphia, PA (city) Philadelphia County	272	0.02
Elk Plain, WA (cdp) Pierce County	270	1.90
Denver, CO (city) Denver County	270	0.04
Charlotte, NC (city) Mecklenburg County	268	0.04
Kent, WA (city) King County	264	0.29
Fresno, CA (city) Fresno County	264	0.05
Dallas, TX (city) Dallas County	262	0.02
Carson, CA (city) Los Angeles County	261	0.28
Boise City, ID (city) Ada County	260	0.13
Tracy, CA (city) San Joaquin County	254	0.31
Frederickson, WA (cdp) Pierce County	253	1.35
San Leandro, CA (city) Alameda County	252	0.30
Columbus, GA (city) Muscogee County	247	0.13
Morganton, NC (city) Burke County	246	1.45
Memphis, TN (city) Shelby County	243	0.04
Manhattan, NY (borough) New York County	242	0.02
La Mesa, CA (city) San Diego County	241	0.42
Mililani Town, HI (cdp) Honolulu County	239	0.87
Salem, OR (city) Marion County	238	0.15
Victorville, CA (city) San Bernardino County	237	0.20
Marina, CA (city) Monterey County	231	1.17
Lemon Grove, CA (city) San Diego County	229	0.90
Fort Hood, TX (cdp) Bell County	226	0.76
Alameda, CA (city) Alameda County	223	0.30
Corona, CA (city) Riverside County	222	0.15
Bakersfield, CA (city) Kern County	221	0.06
Garden Grove, CA (city) Orange County	218	0.13
Indianapolis, IN (city) Marion County	216	0.03
Escondido, CA (city) San Diego County	209	0.15
Huntington Beach, CA (city) Orange County	209	0.11
Makakilo, HI (cdp) Honolulu County	208	1.14
Pearl City, HI (cdp) Honolulu County	207	0.43
Roseville, CA (city) Placer County	205	0.17
Spring Valley, CA (cdp) San Diego County	204	0.72
Schofield Barracks, HI (cdp) Honolulu County	202	1.23
Security-Widefield, CO (cdp) El Paso County	202	0.61
Hillsboro, OR (city) Washington County	202	0.22
Cincinnati, OH (city) Hamilton County	202	0.07
Nashville-Davidson, TN (metro govt) Davidson County	198	0.03
Sierra Vista, AZ (city) Cochise County	197	0.45
Barstow, CA (city) San Bernardino County	195	0.86
Yuba City, CA (city) Sutter County	189	0.29
Vista, CA (city) San Diego County	188	0.20
Union City, CA (city) Alameda County	187	0.27
Norfolk, VA (ind. city) Norfolk independent city	187	0.08
Washington, DC (city) District of Columbia	187	0.03
San Bernardino, CA (city) San Bernardino County	186	0.09
Fountain, CO (city) El Paso County	185	0.72
Kapolei, HI (cdp) Honolulu County	182	1.20
Manteca, CA (city) San Joaquin County	182	0.27
Chandler, AZ (city) Maricopa County	182	0.08
Columbus, OH (city) Franklin County	181	0.02
Copperas Cove, TX (city) Coryell County	180	0.56
Milpitas, CA (city) Santa Clara County	177	0.27
Beaverton, OR (city) Washington County	177	0.20
Renton, WA (city) King County	174	0.19
Antelope, CA (cdp) Sacramento County	168	0.37
Gadsden, AL (city) Etowah County	165	0.45
Citrus Heights, CA (city) Sacramento County	164	0.20
Santa Clara, CA (city) Santa Clara County	164	0.14
Baltimore, MD (city) Baltimore city County	164	0.03
Irvine, CA (city) Orange County	163	0.08
Graham, WA (cdp) Pierce County	161	0.69
Concord, CA (city) Contra Costa County	161	0.13
Tempe, AZ (city) Maricopa County	161	0.10
Chattanooga, TN (city) Hamilton County	160	0.10
Lancaster, CA (city) Los Angeles County	160	0.10
Parkwood, WA (cdp) Kitsap County	158	2.22
Marysville, WA (city) Snohomish County	158	0.26
Kansas City, MO (city) Jackson County	157	0.03
Port Orchard, WA (city) Kitsap County	155	1.39
Kaneohe, HI (cdp) Honolulu County	155	0.45
Everett, WA (city) Snohomish County	155	0.15

Please refer to the Explanation of Data in the front of the book for more detailed information.

Race

Hawaii Native/Pacific Islander: Guamanian or Chamorro

Top 150 Places Sorted by Percent of Total Population

Based on all places, regardless of total population

Place	Population	%
Point Baker, AK (cdp) Prince of Wales-Hyder Census Area	2	13.33
Thompson Springs, UT (cdp) Grand County	2	5.13
Tibbie, AL (cdp) Washington County	2	4.88
Port Royal, VA (town) Caroline County	4	3.17
Nickelsville, VA (town) Scott County	11	2.87
Ray, AL (cdp) Coosa County	12	2.71
Spanaway, WA (cdp) Pierce County	730	2.68
Bladen, NE (village) Webster County	6	2.53
East Ellijay, GA (city) Gilmer County	13	2.38
Avalon, GA (town) Stephens County	5	2.35
Navy Yard City, WA (cdp) Kitsap County	57	2.30
Parkwood, WA (cdp) Kitsap County	158	2.22
Daphnedale Park, CA (cdp) Modoc County	4	2.17
Dugway, UT (cdp) Tooele County	17	2.14
Collinsville, AL (town) DeKalb County	42	2.12
Sebree, KY (city) Webster County	33	2.06
Whitewater, MN (township) Winona County	4	2.02
Tasley, VA (cdp) Accomack County	6	2.00
Parkland, WA (cdp) Pierce County	708	1.98
Wellington, ME (town) Piscataquis County	5	1.92
Elk Plain, WA (cdp) Pierce County	270	1.90
Wheatland, MO (city) Hickory County	7	1.89
Tracyton, WA (cdp) Kitsap County	97	1.85
Whitesville, VA (cdp) Accomack County	4	1.83
Houlton, WI (cdp) St. Croix County	7	1.81
Ridgeville, AL (town) Etowah County	2	1.79
Acampo, CA (cdp) San Joaquin County	6	1.76
Bell, FL (town) Gilchrist County	8	1.75
East Port Orchard, WA (cdp) Kitsap County	100	1.69
McChord AFB, WA (cdp) Pierce County	42	1.68
Paauilo, HI (cdp) Hawaii County	10	1.68
Volta, CA (cdp) Merced County	4	1.63
Quiogue, NY (cdp) Suffolk County	13	1.59
Holly, MN (township) Murray County	2	1.57
Kirkman, IA (city) Shelby County	1	1.56
Robbins, NC (town) Moore County	17	1.55
Wheeler AFB, HI (cdp) Honolulu County	25	1.53
Deerfield, VA (cdp) Augusta County	2	1.52
Capulin, NM (cdp) Union County	1	1.52
Iroquois Point, HI (cdp) Honolulu County	50	1.48
Ellijay, GA (city) Gilmer County	24	1.48
Morganton, NC (city) Burke County	246	1.45
Greensboro, MD (town) Caroline County	28	1.45
Transit, MN (township) Sibley County	4	1.45
Fordyce, NE (village) Cedar County	2	1.44
Bethel, WA (cdp) Kitsap County	53	1.43
Paukaa, HI (cdp) Hawaii County	6	1.41
Port Orchard, WA (city) Kitsap County	155	1.39
Yakutat, AK (cdp) Yakutat City and Borough	9	1.36
Frederickson, WA (cdp) Pierce County	253	1.35
McClellan Park, CA (cdp) Sacramento County	10	1.35
Providence, AL (town) Marengo County	3	1.35
Hartly, DE (town) Kent County	1	1.35
Hanley Falls, MN (city) Yellow Medicine County	4	1.32
Union Springs, AL (city) Bullock County	52	1.31
Highland Park, FL (village) Polk County	3	1.30
Waikane, HI (cdp) Honolulu County	10	1.29
Preston, NV (cdp) White Pine County	1	1.28
Ocean Pointe, HI (cdp) Honolulu County	105	1.26
Robinson Mill, CA (cdp) Butte County	1	1.25
Tanglewilde, WA (cdp) Thurston County	73	1.24
Schofield Barracks, HI (cdp) Honolulu County	202	1.23
Keener, NC (cdp) Sampson County	7	1.23
Kekaha, HI (cdp) Kauai County	43	1.22
Lacey, WA (city) Thurston County	515	1.21
Ewa Gentry, HI (cdp) Honolulu County	272	1.20
Kapolei, HI (cdp) Honolulu County	182	1.20
West Loch Estate, HI (cdp) Honolulu County	66	1.20
Baring, ME (plantation) Washington County	3	1.20
Fort Lee, VA (cdp) Prince George County	40	1.18
Marina, CA (city) Monterey County	231	1.17
Waipio Acres, HI (cdp) Honolulu County	60	1.15
Suisun City, CA (city) Solano County	321	1.14
Makakilo, HI (cdp) Honolulu County	208	1.14
New Llano, LA (town) Vernon Parish	28	1.12
Burley, WA (cdp) Kitsap County	23	1.12
Purple Sage, WY (cdp) Sweetwater County	6	1.12
Bremerton, WA (city) Kitsap County	417	1.11
Donald, WA (cdp) Yakima County	1	1.10
Lewiston Woodville, NC (town) Bertie County	6	1.09
Grand Forks AFB, ND (cdp) Grand Forks County	25	1.06
Ellendale, DE (town) Sussex County	4	1.05
Gargatha, VA (cdp) Accomack County	4	1.05
Hope, AK (cdp) Kenai Peninsula Borough	2	1.04
Cocoa West, FL (cdp) Brevard County	61	1.03
De Soto, GA (city) Sumter County	2	1.03
Hickam Housing, HI (cdp) Honolulu County	70	1.01
Colebrook, PA (township) Clinton County	2	1.01
Clover Creek, WA (cdp) Pierce County	65	1.00
Sunol, CA (cdp) Alameda County	9	0.99
Concow, CA (cdp) Butte County	7	0.99
Shalimar, FL (town) Okaloosa County	7	0.98
McGuire AFB, NJ (cdp) Burlington County	36	0.97
Santa Clara, TX (city) Guadalupe County	7	0.97
Quitaque, TX (city) Briscoe County	4	0.97
Fairfield, CA (city) Solano County	1,013	0.96
Lakewood, WA (city) Pierce County	559	0.96
Durham, OR (city) Washington County	13	0.96
Lawtey, FL (city) Bradford County	7	0.96
Hilltop, WV (cdp) Fayette County	6	0.96
Henryville, MN (township) Renville County	2	0.96
Erlands Point-Kitsap Lake, WA (cdp) Kitsap County	28	0.95
Burke, NY (village) Franklin County	2	0.95
McGrew, NE (village) Scotts Bluff County	1	0.95
Washburn, WI (town) Bayfield County	5	0.94
Fife, WA (city) Pierce County	85	0.93
Fern Acres, HI (cdp) Hawaii County	14	0.93
Kaumakani, HI (cdp) Kauai County	7	0.93
Doyle, TN (town) White County	5	0.93
Fort Greely, AK (cdp) Southeast Fairbanks Census Area	5	0.93
Lazy Y U, AZ (cdp) Mohave County	4	0.93
Brewster, NY (village) Putnam County	22	0.92
New Solum, MN (township) Marshall County	3	0.92
Grand Lake Stream, ME (plantation) Washington County	1	0.92
La Presa, CA (cdp) San Diego County	312	0.91
Dunbar, WI (town) Marinette County	10	0.91
Mappsville, VA (cdp) Accomack County	4	0.91
Copper Center, AK (cdp) Valdez-Cordova Census Area	3	0.91
Lemon Grove, CA (city) San Diego County	229	0.90
Saluda, SC (town) Saluda County	32	0.90
Arapahoe, NC (town) Pamlico County	5	0.90
Rolla, KS (city) Morton County	4	0.90
Blountsville, AL (town) Blount County	15	0.89
Cape Charles, VA (town) Northampton County	9	0.89
Momeyer, NC (town) Nash County	2	0.89
Hollis, AK (cdp) Prince of Wales-Hyder Census Area	1	0.89
Roy, WA (city) Pierce County	7	0.88
Bluejacket, OK (town) Craig County	3	0.88
Brice, OH (village) Franklin County	1	0.88
Swan Lake, MT (cdp) Lake County	1	0.88
Mililani Town, HI (cdp) Honolulu County	239	0.87
Mullan, ID (city) Shoshone County	6	0.87
Ashton, IA (city) Osceola County	4	0.87
Barstow, CA (city) San Bernardino County	195	0.86
Laupahoehoe, HI (cdp) Hawaii County	5	0.86
Pearson, GA (city) Atkinson County	18	0.85
Diablo Grande, CA (cdp) Stanislaus County	7	0.85
Killeen, TX (city) Bell County	1,077	0.84
Royal Kunia, HI (cdp) Honolulu County	122	0.84
Forest, MS (city) Scott County	48	0.84
Kahaluu, HI (cdp) Honolulu County	40	0.84
Whitewater, KS (city) Butler County	6	0.84
Enetai, WA (cdp) Kitsap County	19	0.83
Spruce Creek, PA (township) Huntingdon County	2	0.83
Steilacoom, WA (town) Pierce County	49	0.82
Nellis AFB, NV (cdp) Clark County	26	0.82
Holloman AFB, NM (cdp) Otero County	25	0.82
Harrison, PA (township) Bedford County	8	0.82
Efland, NC (cdp) Orange County	6	0.82
Idaho City, ID (city) Boise County	4	0.82

Please refer to the Explanation of Data in the front of the book for more detailed information.

Race

Hawaii Native/Pacific Islander: Guamanian or Chamorro

Top 150 Places Sorted by Percent of Total Population

Based on places with total population of 7,500 or more

Place	Population	%
Spanaway, WA (cdp) Pierce County	730	2.68
Parkland, WA (cdp) Pierce County	708	1.98
Elk Plain, WA (cdp) Pierce County	270	1.90
Morganton, NC (city) Burke County	246	1.45
Port Orchard, WA (city) Kitsap County	155	1.39
Frederickson, WA (cdp) Pierce County	253	1.35
Ocean Pointe, HI (cdp) Honolulu County	105	1.26
Schofield Barracks, HI (cdp) Honolulu County	202	1.23
Lacey, WA (city) Thurston County	515	1.21
Ewa Gentry, HI (cdp) Honolulu County	272	1.20
Kapolei, HI (cdp) Honolulu County	182	1.20
Marina, CA (city) Monterey County	231	1.17
Suisun City, CA (city) Solano County	321	1.14
Makakilo, HI (cdp) Honolulu County	208	1.14
Bremerton, WA (city) Kitsap County	417	1.11
Fairfield, CA (city) Solano County	1,013	0.96
Lakewood, WA (city) Pierce County	559	0.96
Fife, WA (city) Pierce County	85	0.93
La Presa, CA (cdp) San Diego County	312	0.91
Lemon Grove, CA (city) San Diego County	229	0.90
Mililani Town, HI (cdp) Honolulu County	239	0.87
Barstow, CA (city) San Bernardino County	195	0.86
Killeen, TX (city) Bell County	1,077	0.84
Royal Kunia, HI (cdp) Honolulu County	122	0.84
Waianae, HI (cdp) Honolulu County	107	0.81
Maili, HI (cdp) Honolulu County	75	0.79
American Canyon, CA (city) Napa County	150	0.77
Fort Hood, TX (cdp) Bell County	226	0.76
Vallejo, CA (city) Solano County	866	0.75
Silverdale, WA (cdp) Kitsap County	140	0.73
Wahiawa, HI (cdp) Honolulu County	130	0.73
Spring Valley, CA (cdp) San Diego County	204	0.72
Fountain, CO (city) El Paso County	185	0.72
Graham, WA (cdp) Pierce County	161	0.69
Dover, OH (city) Tuscarawas County	89	0.69
Kapaa, HI (cdp) Kauai County	72	0.67
Oak Harbor, WA (city) Island County	145	0.66
Mililani Mauka, HI (cdp) Honolulu County	136	0.65
Makaha, HI (cdp) Honolulu County	54	0.65
Radcliff, KY (city) Hardin County	139	0.64
Waimalu, HI (cdp) Honolulu County	86	0.63
Bonita, CA (cdp) San Diego County	79	0.63
Fort Lewis, WA (cdp) Pierce County	70	0.63
Fort Irwin, CA (cdp) San Bernardino County	56	0.63
Security-Widefield, CO (cdp) El Paso County	202	0.61
Ewa Beach, HI (cdp) Honolulu County	91	0.61
Fort Campbell North, KY (cdp) Christian County	84	0.61
Hawaiian Paradise Park, HI (cdp) Hawaii County	70	0.61
DuPont, WA (city) Pierce County	49	0.60
Nanakuli, HI (cdp) Honolulu County	75	0.59
Langley Park, MD (cdp) Prince George's County	108	0.58
Chula Vista, CA (city) San Diego County	1,389	0.57
South Hill, WA (cdp) Pierce County	293	0.56
Copperas Cove, TX (city) Coryell County	180	0.56
Midland, WA (cdp) Pierce County	50	0.56
Halawa, HI (cdp) Honolulu County	77	0.55
Fort Carson, CO (cdp) El Paso County	75	0.54
Fort Drum, NY (cdp) Jefferson County	70	0.54
National City, CA (city) San Diego County	303	0.52
Santee, CA (city) San Diego County	276	0.52
Harker Heights, TX (city) Bell County	134	0.50
Imperial Beach, CA (city) San Diego County	128	0.49
Carthage, MO (city) Jasper County	69	0.48
Urban Honolulu, HI (cdp) Honolulu County	1,596	0.47
Federal Way, WA (city) King County	419	0.47
Casa de Oro-Mount Helix, CA (cdp) San Diego County	88	0.47
North Hanover, NJ (township) Burlington County	36	0.47
Waipio, HI (cdp) Honolulu County	54	0.46
North Las Vegas, NV (city) Clark County	978	0.45
Sierra Vista, AZ (city) Cochise County	197	0.45
Gadsden, AL (city) Etowah County	165	0.45
Kaneohe, HI (cdp) Honolulu County	155	0.45
Kihei, HI (cdp) Maui County	94	0.45
Orchards, WA (cdp) Clark County	86	0.44
Pearl City, HI (cdp) Honolulu County	207	0.43
Tukwila, WA (city) King County	83	0.43
Vancouver, WA (city) Clark County	685	0.42
La Mesa, CA (city) San Diego County	241	0.42
Twentynine Palms, CA (city) San Bernardino County	104	0.42
Signal Hill, CA (city) Los Angeles County	46	0.42
El Cajon, CA (city) San Diego County	404	0.41
Tumwater, WA (city) Thurston County	71	0.41
Mountain Home, ID (city) Elmore County	58	0.41
Ahuimanu, HI (cdp) Honolulu County	36	0.41
Vacaville, CA (city) Solano County	372	0.40
Le Ray, NY (town) Jefferson County	88	0.40
University Place, WA (city) Pierce County	120	0.39
Benicia, CA (city) Solano County	104	0.39
French Valley, CA (cdp) Riverside County	89	0.39
Five Corners, WA (cdp) Clark County	69	0.38
Rosamond, CA (cdp) Kern County	69	0.38
New Philadelphia, OH (city) Tuscarawas County	65	0.38
Tacoma, WA (city) Pierce County	726	0.37
Antelope, CA (cdp) Sacramento County	168	0.37
Puyallup, WA (city) Pierce County	136	0.37
Fairbanks, AK (city) Fairbanks North Star Borough	116	0.37
Ridgecrest, CA (city) Kern County	102	0.37
Cusseta-Chattahoochee County, GA (unified govt) Chattahoochee County	42	0.37
Waipahu, HI (cdp) Honolulu County	136	0.36
Seaside, CA (city) Monterey County	118	0.36
Northport, AL (city) Tuscaloosa County	85	0.36
Bostonia, CA (cdp) San Diego County	55	0.36
Lakewood, CA (city) Los Angeles County	275	0.34
Hayward, CA (city) Alameda County	470	0.33
Lakeside, CA (cdp) San Diego County	69	0.33
Hayesville, OR (cdp) Marion County	66	0.33
Lakeland North, WA (cdp) King County	43	0.33
Kailua, HI (cdp) Hawaii County	39	0.33
Country Club, CA (cdp) San Joaquin County	31	0.33
Fort Polk South, LA (cdp) Vernon Parish	30	0.33
Holualoa, HI (cdp) Hawaii County	28	0.33
Cedar Hills, OR (cdp) Washington County	27	0.33
Box Elder, SD (city) Pennington County	26	0.33
Paradise, NV (cdp) Clark County	703	0.32
Enterprise, NV (cdp) Clark County	349	0.32
Hilo, HI (cdp) Hawaii County	138	0.32
Kailua, HI (cdp) Honolulu County	122	0.32
Ashland, CA (cdp) Alameda County	70	0.32
Havelock, NC (city) Craven County	67	0.32
Linda, CA (cdp) Yuba County	56	0.32
Walnut Grove, WA (cdp) Clark County	31	0.32
Kaneohe Station, HI (cdp) Honolulu County	30	0.32
San Diego, CA (city) San Diego County	3,999	0.31
Oceanside, CA (city) San Diego County	525	0.31
Lawton, OK (city) Comanche County	297	0.31
Tracy, CA (city) San Joaquin County	254	0.31
Lompoc, CA (city) Santa Barbara County	131	0.31
Cherryland, CA (cdp) Alameda County	45	0.31
Artondale, WA (cdp) Pierce County	39	0.31
Kalaoa, HI (cdp) Hawaii County	30	0.31
Temecula, CA (city) Riverside County	303	0.30
San Leandro, CA (city) Alameda County	252	0.30
Alameda, CA (city) Alameda County	223	0.30
Junction City, KS (city) Geary County	70	0.30
San Diego Country Estates, CA (cdp) San Diego County	30	0.30
Cedartown, GA (city) Polk County	29	0.30
Sunrise Manor, NV (cdp) Clark County	547	0.29
Murrieta, CA (city) Riverside County	296	0.29
Kent, WA (city) King County	264	0.29
Yuba City, CA (city) Sutter County	189	0.29
Cypress, CA (city) Orange County	137	0.29
Belle Chasse, LA (cdp) Plaquemines Parish	37	0.29
Spring Valley Lake, CA (cdp) San Bernardino County	24	0.29
Spring Valley, NV (cdp) Clark County	499	0.28
Carson, CA (city) Los Angeles County	261	0.28
East Honolulu, HI (cdp) Honolulu County	139	0.28
Newark, CA (city) Alameda County	119	0.28
Fremont, NE (city) Dodge County	74	0.28
Winter Gardens, CA (cdp) San Diego County	57	0.28
Fort Leonard Wood, MO (cdp) Pulaski County	42	0.28

Please refer to the Explanation of Data in the front of the book for more detailed information.

Race

Hawaii Native/Pacific Islander: Marshallese

U.S. and 50 States Sorted by Population and Percent of Total Population

Place	Population	%
United States	**22,434**	**0.01**
Hawaii	7,412	0.54
Arkansas	4,324	0.15
Washington	2,207	0.03
California	1,761	<0.01
Oklahoma	1,028	0.03
Oregon	970	0.03
Utah	793	0.03
Arizona	666	0.01
Texas	550	<0.01
Iowa	406	0.01
Florida	290	<0.01
North Carolina	182	<0.01
Missouri	174	<0.01
Colorado	167	<0.01
Ohio	124	<0.01
Georgia	120	<0.01
Alabama	117	<0.01
Nevada	108	<0.01
Indiana	82	<0.01
Kansas	80	<0.01
Idaho	75	<0.01
Nebraska	64	<0.01
Virginia	64	<0.01
North Dakota	53	0.01
Minnesota	50	<0.01
Alaska	49	0.01
Michigan	47	<0.01
Tennessee	42	<0.01
Illinois	41	<0.01
Kentucky	37	<0.01
New York	37	<0.01
Maryland	34	<0.01
Massachusetts	30	<0.01
New Jersey	30	<0.01
Louisiana	28	<0.01
Wisconsin	25	<0.01
Pennsylvania	22	<0.01
Mississippi	18	<0.01
South Carolina	18	<0.01
New Mexico	17	<0.01
New Hampshire	16	<0.01
Connecticut	15	<0.01
Vermont	12	<0.01
Wyoming	12	<0.01
Rhode Island	11	<0.01
Maine	9	<0.01
Montana	6	<0.01
District of Columbia	5	<0.01
Delaware	3	<0.01
South Dakota	2	<0.01
West Virginia	1	<0.01

Place	Population	%
Hawaii	7,412	0.54
Arkansas	4,324	0.15
Washington	2,207	0.03
Oklahoma	1,028	0.03
Oregon	970	0.03
Utah	793	0.03
United States	**22,434**	**0.01**
Arizona	666	0.01
Iowa	406	0.01
North Dakota	53	0.01
Alaska	49	0.01
California	1,761	<0.01
Texas	550	<0.01
Florida	290	<0.01
North Carolina	182	<0.01
Missouri	174	<0.01
Colorado	167	<0.01
Ohio	124	<0.01
Georgia	120	<0.01
Alabama	117	<0.01
Nevada	108	<0.01
Indiana	82	<0.01
Kansas	80	<0.01
Idaho	75	<0.01
Nebraska	64	<0.01
Virginia	64	<0.01
Minnesota	50	<0.01
Michigan	47	<0.01
Tennessee	42	<0.01
Illinois	41	<0.01
Kentucky	37	<0.01
New York	37	<0.01
Maryland	34	<0.01
Massachusetts	30	<0.01
New Jersey	30	<0.01
Louisiana	28	<0.01
Wisconsin	25	<0.01
Pennsylvania	22	<0.01
Mississippi	18	<0.01
South Carolina	18	<0.01
New Mexico	17	<0.01
New Hampshire	16	<0.01
Connecticut	15	<0.01
Vermont	12	<0.01
Wyoming	12	<0.01
Rhode Island	11	<0.01
Maine	9	<0.01
Montana	6	<0.01
District of Columbia	5	<0.01
Delaware	3	<0.01
South Dakota	2	<0.01
West Virginia	1	<0.01

Please refer to the Explanation of Data in the front of the book for more detailed information.

Race

Hawaii Native/Pacific Islander: Marshallese

Top 150 Places Sorted by Population

Based on all places, regardless of total population

Place	Population	%
Springdale, AR (city) Washington County	3,740	5.36
Urban Honolulu, HI (cdp) Honolulu County	1,921	0.57
Waipahu, HI (cdp) Honolulu County	984	2.57
Enid, OK (city) Garfield County	934	1.89
Spokane, WA (city) Spokane County	606	0.29
Hawaiian Ocean View, HI (cdp) Hawaii County	540	12.17
Kahului, HI (cdp) Maui County	521	1.98
Sacramento, CA (city) Sacramento County	400	0.09
Auburn, WA (city) King County	399	0.57
Salem, OR (city) Marion County	334	0.22
Hilo, HI (cdp) Hawaii County	289	0.67
Keene, TX (city) Johnson County	274	4.49
Everett, WA (city) Snohomish County	246	0.24
West Valley City, UT (city) Salt Lake County	237	0.18
Dubuque, IA (city) Dubuque County	231	0.40
Kailua, HI (cdp) Hawaii County	212	1.77
Bethel Heights, AR (city) Benton County	194	8.18
Federal Way, WA (city) King County	188	0.21
Costa Mesa, CA (city) Orange County	177	0.16
Tucson, AZ (city) Pima County	177	0.03
Waimea, HI (cdp) Hawaii County	168	1.82
San Diego, CA (city) San Diego County	164	0.01
Parkway, CA (cdp) Sacramento County	161	1.10
Kahaluu-Keauhou, HI (cdp) Hawaii County	132	3.72
Tempe, AZ (city) Maricopa County	131	0.08
Halawa, HI (cdp) Honolulu County	128	0.91
Phoenix, AZ (city) Maricopa County	127	0.01
Waikoloa Village, HI (cdp) Hawaii County	121	1.90
Pepeekeo, HI (cdp) Hawaii County	113	6.32
Wahiawa, HI (cdp) Honolulu County	109	0.61
Garden Grove, CA (city) Orange County	109	0.06
Wailuku, HI (cdp) Maui County	108	0.71
Waterloo, IA (city) Black Hawk County	106	0.15
Mesa, AZ (city) Maricopa County	106	0.02
Fayetteville, AR (city) Washington County	103	0.14
Waianae, HI (cdp) Honolulu County	100	0.76
Waimalu, HI (cdp) Honolulu County	100	0.73
Tigard, OR (city) Washington County	98	0.20
Rogers, AR (city) Benton County	98	0.18
Honalo, HI (cdp) Hawaii County	93	3.84
Ewa Gentry, HI (cdp) Honolulu County	93	0.41
Lemon Hill, CA (cdp) Sacramento County	84	0.61
Santa Ana, CA (city) Orange County	82	0.03
Four Corners, OR (cdp) Marion County	80	0.50
Keizer, OR (city) Marion County	78	0.21
Tustin, CA (city) Orange County	77	0.10
Hanamaulu, HI (cdp) Kauai County	75	1.96
Pearl City, HI (cdp) Honolulu County	70	0.15
Royal Kunia, HI (cdp) Honolulu County	67	0.46
Aurora, CO (city) Arapahoe County	67	0.02
Town and Country, WA (cdp) Spokane County	59	1.21
Huntsville, AL (city) Madison County	57	0.03
Cleburne, TX (city) Johnson County	56	0.19
Kalaoa, HI (cdp) Hawaii County	55	0.57
Makaha, HI (cdp) Honolulu County	54	0.65
La Grande, OR (city) Union County	51	0.39
Ewa Beach, HI (cdp) Honolulu County	51	0.34
Evansville, IN (city) Vanderburgh County	49	0.04
Waihee-Waiehu, HI (cdp) Maui County	46	0.52
Kihei, HI (cdp) Maui County	45	0.22
Mililani Town, HI (cdp) Honolulu County	45	0.16
Springfield, MO (city) Christian County	45	0.03
Kealakekua, HI (cdp) Hawaii County	44	2.18
Winston-Salem, NC (city) Forsyth County	44	0.02
Reno, NV (city) Washoe County	42	0.02
Honokaa, HI (cdp) Hawaii County	41	1.82
Whitmore Village, HI (cdp) Honolulu County	40	0.89
Magna, UT (cdp) Salt Lake County	39	0.15
Springfield, OR (city) Lane County	39	0.07
Marysville, WA (city) Snohomish County	39	0.06
Kent, WA (city) King County	39	0.04
Kansas City, MO (city) Jackson County	38	0.01
North Lynnwood, WA (cdp) Snohomish County	37	0.22
Florin, CA (cdp) Sacramento County	37	0.08
Tualatin, OR (city) Washington County	36	0.14
Ogden, UT (city) Weber County	35	0.04
Holualoa, HI (cdp) Hawaii County	34	0.40
Pittsburg, KS (city) Crawford County	34	0.17
Kaneohe, HI (cdp) Honolulu County	34	0.10
Logan, UT (city) Cache County	34	0.07
Lakewood, WA (city) Pierce County	34	0.06
Makakilo, HI (cdp) Honolulu County	32	0.18
Spokane Valley, WA (city) Spokane County	32	0.04
Koloa, HI (cdp) Kauai County	30	1.40
Pacific, WA (city) King County	30	0.45
Kailua, HI (cdp) Honolulu County	30	0.08
Eugene, OR (city) Lane County	30	0.02
North Logan, UT (city) Cache County	29	0.35
Bentonville, AR (city) Benton County	29	0.08
Taylorsville, UT (city) Salt Lake County	28	0.05
Lihue, HI (cdp) Kauai County	27	0.42
Fife, WA (city) Pierce County	27	0.29
Hayesville, OR (cdp) Marion County	27	0.14
Leesburg, FL (city) Lake County	26	0.13
Fort Hood, TX (cdp) Bell County	26	0.09
Asheville, NC (city) Buncombe County	26	0.03
West Jordan, UT (city) Salt Lake County	26	0.03
Elk Grove, CA (city) Sacramento County	26	0.02
Des Moines, WA (city) King County	25	0.08
Pinellas Park, FL (city) Pinellas County	25	0.05
Cedar Rapids, IA (city) Linn County	25	0.02
Celina, OH (city) Mercer County	24	0.23
Lithia Springs, GA (cdp) Douglas County	24	0.15
North Salt Lake, UT (city) Davis County	24	0.15
Huntington Beach, CA (city) Orange County	24	0.01
East Porterville, CA (cdp) Tulare County	23	0.34
Layton, UT (city) Davis County	23	0.03
Chadron, NE (city) Dawes County	22	0.38
Kapaa, HI (cdp) Kauai County	22	0.21
Nanakuli, HI (cdp) Honolulu County	22	0.17
Fayetteville, NC (city) Cumberland County	22	0.01
Hawaiian Beaches, HI (cdp) Hawaii County	21	0.49
Hawaiian Paradise Park, HI (cdp) Hawaii County	21	0.18
Pleasant Grove, UT (city) Utah County	21	0.06
Boise City, ID (city) Ada County	21	0.01
Lowell, AR (city) Benton County	20	0.27
Lynnwood, WA (city) Snohomish County	20	0.06
Bountiful, UT (city) Davis County	20	0.05
San Jose, CA (city) Santa Clara County	20	<0.01
Discovery Harbour, HI (cdp) Hawaii County	19	2.00
Eleele, HI (cdp) Kauai County	19	0.79
Merritt Island, FL (cdp) Brevard County	19	0.05
Lacey, WA (city) Thurston County	19	0.04
Sparks, NV (city) Washoe County	19	0.02
Portland, OR (city) Multnomah County	19	<0.01
Corvallis, OR (city) Benton County	18	0.03
Avondale, AZ (city) Maricopa County	18	0.02
Ahuimanu, HI (cdp) Honolulu County	17	0.19
Ottumwa, IA (city) Wapello County	17	0.07
University Place, WA (city) Pierce County	17	0.05
Fremont, CA (city) Alameda County	17	0.01
Tacoma, WA (city) Pierce County	17	0.01
Colorado Springs, CO (city) El Paso County	17	<0.01
Kalaheo, HI (cdp) Kauai County	16	0.35
Waipio Acres, HI (cdp) Honolulu County	16	0.31
South Ogden, UT (city) Weber County	16	0.10
Mount Vernon, WA (city) Skagit County	16	0.05
Clarksville, TN (city) Montgomery County	16	0.01
Newport News, VA (ind. city) Newport News independent city	16	0.01
San Bernardino, CA (city) San Bernardino County	16	0.01
Bakersfield, CA (city) Kern County	16	<0.01
Papaikou, HI (cdp) Hawaii County	15	1.14
Waimanalo, HI (cdp) Honolulu County	15	0.28
Lake Stickney, WA (cdp) Snohomish County	15	0.19
Newport, AR (city) Jackson County	15	0.19
Haiku-Pauwela, HI (cdp) Maui County	15	0.18
Maili, HI (cdp) Honolulu County	15	0.16
Lahaina, HI (cdp) Maui County	15	0.13
Meridian, ID (city) Ada County	15	0.02
Anchorage, AK (municipality) Anchorage Municipality	15	0.01

Please refer to the Explanation of Data in the front of the book for more detailed information.

Race

Hawaii Native/Pacific Islander: Marshallese

Top 150 Places Sorted by Percent of Total Population

Based on all places, regardless of total population

Place	Population	%
Hawaiian Ocean View, HI (cdp) Hawaii County	540	12.17
Bethel Heights, AR (city) Benton County	194	8.18
Pepeekeo, HI (cdp) Hawaii County	113	6.32
Springdale, AR (city) Washington County	3,740	5.36
Waiohinu, HI (cdp) Hawaii County	11	5.16
Keene, TX (city) Johnson County	274	4.49
Honalo, HI (cdp) Hawaii County	93	3.84
Kahaluu-Keauhou, HI (cdp) Hawaii County	132	3.72
Jackson, NE (village) Dakota County	7	3.14
Waipahu, HI (cdp) Honolulu County	984	2.57
Kealakekua, HI (cdp) Hawaii County	44	2.18
Elkton, MN (city) Mower County	3	2.13
Discovery Harbour, HI (cdp) Hawaii County	19	2.00
Garfield, AR (town) Benton County	10	1.99
Kahului, HI (cdp) Maui County	521	1.98
Hanamaulu, HI (cdp) Kauai County	75	1.96
Oak Hall, VA (cdp) Accomack County	5	1.96
Waikoloa Village, HI (cdp) Hawaii County	121	1.90
Enid, OK (city) Garfield County	934	1.89
Waimea, HI (cdp) Hawaii County	168	1.82
Honokaa, HI (cdp) Hawaii County	41	1.82
Kailua, HI (cdp) Hawaii County	212	1.77
Edmore, ND (city) Ramsey County	3	1.65
Clio, CA (cdp) Plumas County	1	1.52
North Enid, OK (town) Garfield County	13	1.51
Charleston, UT (town) Wasatch County	6	1.45
Koloa, HI (cdp) Kauai County	30	1.40
Town and Country, WA (cdp) Spokane County	59	1.21
Eschbach, WA (cdp) Yakima County	5	1.20
Papaikou, HI (cdp) Hawaii County	15	1.14
Parkway, CA (cdp) Sacramento County	161	1.10
Zanesfield, OH (village) Logan County	2	1.02
Halawa, HI (cdp) Honolulu County	128	0.91
Whitmore Village, HI (cdp) Honolulu County	40	0.89
Bridge Creek, OK (town) Grady County	3	0.89
West Scio, OR (cdp) Linn County	1	0.83
Eleele, HI (cdp) Kauai County	19	0.79
Waianae, HI (cdp) Honolulu County	100	0.76
Waimalu, HI (cdp) Honolulu County	100	0.73
Hines, MN (township) Beltrami County	5	0.73
Wailuku, HI (cdp) Maui County	108	0.71
Hilo, HI (cdp) Hawaii County	289	0.67
Makaha, HI (cdp) Honolulu County	54	0.65
Mill City, OR (city) Linn County	12	0.65
Gustine, TX (town) Comanche County	3	0.63
Sun Valley, AZ (cdp) Navajo County	2	0.63
Wahiawa, HI (cdp) Honolulu County	109	0.61
Lemon Hill, CA (cdp) Sacramento County	84	0.61
Watterson Park, KY (city) Jefferson County	6	0.61
Urban Honolulu, HI (cdp) Honolulu County	1,921	0.57
Auburn, WA (city) King County	399	0.57
Kalaoa, HI (cdp) Hawaii County	55	0.57
Mulford, CO (cdp) Garfield County	1	0.57
Honeyville, UT (city) Box Elder County	8	0.56
Index, WA (town) Snohomish County	1	0.56
Paradise, UT (town) Cache County	5	0.55
Martin's Additions, MD (village) Montgomery County	5	0.54
Waihee-Waiehu, HI (cdp) Maui County	46	0.52
Queenland, MD (cdp) Prince George's County	10	0.52
Pahala, HI (cdp) Hawaii County	7	0.52
Milton, KY (city) Trimble County	3	0.52
Teasdale, UT (cdp) Wayne County	1	0.52
Four Corners, OR (cdp) Marion County	80	0.50
Hawaiian Beaches, HI (cdp) Hawaii County	21	0.49
Warm Beach, WA (cdp) Snohomish County	12	0.49
Sutton, NH (town) Merrimack County	9	0.49
Garber, OK (city) Garfield County	4	0.49
Mount Pleasant, AR (town) Izard County	2	0.48
Ross, MN (township) Roseau County	2	0.47
Royal Kunia, HI (cdp) Honolulu County	67	0.46
Sturgeon Lake, MN (city) Pine County	2	0.46
Pacific, WA (city) King County	30	0.45
Quinhagak, AK (city) Bethel Census Area	3	0.45
Lihue, HI (cdp) Kauai County	27	0.42
Eden Roc, HI (cdp) Hawaii County	4	0.42
Ewa Gentry, HI (cdp) Honolulu County	93	0.41
Dubuque, IA (city) Dubuque County	231	0.40
Holualoa, HI (cdp) Hawaii County	34	0.40
La Grande, OR (city) Union County	51	0.39
Riverside, UT (cdp) Box Elder County	3	0.39
Chadron, NE (city) Dawes County	22	0.38
Makaha Valley, HI (cdp) Honolulu County	5	0.37
Mountain Village, AK (city) Wade Hampton Census Area	3	0.37
West Wood, UT (cdp) Carbon County	3	0.36
North Logan, UT (city) Cache County	29	0.35
Kalaheo, HI (cdp) Kauai County	16	0.35
Kapaau, HI (cdp) Hawaii County	6	0.35
Ewa Beach, HI (cdp) Honolulu County	51	0.34
East Porterville, CA (cdp) Tulare County	23	0.34
Iroquois Point, HI (cdp) Honolulu County	11	0.33
Eden, UT (cdp) Weber County	2	0.33
Philadelphia, NY (village) Jefferson County	4	0.32
Ithaca, WI (town) Richland County	2	0.32
Waipio Acres, HI (cdp) Honolulu County	16	0.31
Anahola, HI (cdp) Kauai County	7	0.31
Donald, OR (city) Marion County	3	0.31
Johnson, AR (city) Washington County	10	0.30
Deweyville, UT (town) Box Elder County	1	0.30
Spokane, WA (city) Spokane County	606	0.29
Fife, WA (city) Pierce County	27	0.29
Lanai City, HI (cdp) Maui County	9	0.29
Kaaawa, HI (cdp) Honolulu County	4	0.29
Ricardo, TX (cdp) Kleberg County	3	0.29
Waimanalo, HI (cdp) Honolulu County	15	0.28
Kingsley, IA (city) Plymouth County	4	0.28
Lowell, AR (city) Benton County	20	0.27
Ainaloa, HI (cdp) Hawaii County	8	0.27
Keaau, HI (cdp) Hawaii County	6	0.27
Molena, GA (city) Pike County	1	0.27
Kenneth City, FL (town) Pinellas County	13	0.26
Eldon, MO (city) Miller County	12	0.26
Canaan, ME (town) Somerset County	6	0.26
Middletown, PA (township) Susquehanna County	1	0.26
Stafford, OR (cdp) Clackamas County	4	0.25
Georgetown, IL (cdp) McDonough County	1	0.25
Everett, WA (city) Snohomish County	246	0.24
Fort Lee, VA (cdp) Prince George County	8	0.24
Van Horn, TX (town) Culberson County	5	0.24
Labish Village, OR (cdp) Marion County	1	0.24
Marshall, AK (city) Wade Hampton Census Area	1	0.24
Celina, OH (city) Mercer County	24	0.23
Waialua, HI (cdp) Honolulu County	9	0.23
Honaunau-Napoopoo, HI (cdp) Hawaii County	6	0.23
Banks, OR (city) Washington County	4	0.23
Salem, OR (city) Marion County	334	0.22
Kihei, HI (cdp) Maui County	45	0.22
North Lynnwood, WA (cdp) Snohomish County	37	0.22
Beulah, ND (city) Mercer County	7	0.22
West Fork, AR (city) Washington County	5	0.22
Federal Way, WA (city) King County	188	0.21
Keizer, OR (city) Marion County	78	0.21
Kapaa, HI (cdp) Kauai County	22	0.21
Philadelphia, NY (town) Jefferson County	4	0.21
Firth, ID (city) Bingham County	1	0.21
New Melle, MO (city) St. Charles County	1	0.21
Tigard, OR (city) Washington County	98	0.20
Coldwater, OH (village) Mercer County	9	0.20
Cleburne, TX (city) Johnson County	56	0.19
Ahuimanu, HI (cdp) Honolulu County	17	0.19
Lake Stickney, WA (cdp) Snohomish County	15	0.19
Newport, AR (city) Jackson County	15	0.19
West Valley City, UT (city) Salt Lake County	237	0.18
Rogers, AR (city) Benton County	98	0.18
Makakilo, HI (cdp) Honolulu County	32	0.18
Hawaiian Paradise Park, HI (cdp) Hawaii County	21	0.18
Haiku-Pauwela, HI (cdp) Maui County	15	0.18
Lowry Crossing, TX (city) Collin County	3	0.18
Pittsburg, KS (city) Crawford County	34	0.17
Nanakuli, HI (cdp) Honolulu County	22	0.17
Vinita, OK (city) Craig County	10	0.17

Please refer to the Explanation of Data in the front of the book for more detailed information.

Race

Hawaii Native/Pacific Islander: Marshallese

Top 150 Places Sorted by Percent of Total Population

Based on places with total population of 7,500 or more

Place	Population	%
Springdale, AR (city) Washington County	3,740	5.36
Waipahu, HI (cdp) Honolulu County	984	2.57
Kahului, HI (cdp) Maui County	521	1.98
Enid, OK (city) Garfield County	934	1.89
Waimea, HI (cdp) Hawaii County	168	1.82
Kailua, HI (cdp) Hawaii County	212	1.77
Parkway, CA (cdp) Sacramento County	161	1.10
Halawa, HI (cdp) Honolulu County	128	0.91
Waianae, HI (cdp) Honolulu County	100	0.76
Waimalu, HI (cdp) Honolulu County	100	0.73
Wailuku, HI (cdp) Maui County	108	0.71
Hilo, HI (cdp) Hawaii County	289	0.67
Makaha, HI (cdp) Honolulu County	54	0.65
Wahiawa, HI (cdp) Honolulu County	109	0.61
Lemon Hill, CA (cdp) Sacramento County	84	0.61
Urban Honolulu, HI (cdp) Honolulu County	1,921	0.57
Auburn, WA (city) King County	399	0.57
Kalaoa, HI (cdp) Hawaii County	55	0.57
Waihee-Waiehu, HI (cdp) Maui County	46	0.52
Four Corners, OR (cdp) Marion County	80	0.50
Royal Kunia, HI (cdp) Honolulu County	67	0.46
Ewa Gentry, HI (cdp) Honolulu County	93	0.41
Dubuque, IA (city) Dubuque County	231	0.40
Holualoa, HI (cdp) Hawaii County	34	0.40
La Grande, OR (city) Union County	51	0.39
North Logan, UT (city) Cache County	29	0.35
Ewa Beach, HI (cdp) Honolulu County	51	0.34
Spokane, WA (city) Spokane County	606	0.29
Fife, WA (city) Pierce County	27	0.29
Everett, WA (city) Snohomish County	246	0.24
Celina, OH (city) Mercer County	24	0.23
Salem, OR (city) Marion County	334	0.22
Kihei, HI (cdp) Maui County	45	0.22
North Lynnwood, WA (cdp) Snohomish County	37	0.22
Federal Way, WA (city) King County	188	0.21
Keizer, OR (city) Marion County	78	0.21
Kapaa, HI (cdp) Kauai County	22	0.21
Tigard, OR (city) Washington County	98	0.20
Cleburne, TX (city) Johnson County	56	0.19
Ahuimanu, HI (cdp) Honolulu County	17	0.19
Lake Stickney, WA (cdp) Snohomish County	15	0.19
Newport, AR (city) Jackson County	15	0.19
West Valley City, UT (city) Salt Lake County	237	0.18
Rogers, AR (city) Benton County	98	0.18
Makakilo, HI (cdp) Honolulu County	32	0.18
Hawaiian Paradise Park, HI (cdp) Hawaii County	21	0.18
Haiku-Pauwela, HI (cdp) Maui County	15	0.18
Pittsburg, KS (city) Crawford County	34	0.17
Nanakuli, HI (cdp) Honolulu County	22	0.17
Costa Mesa, CA (city) Orange County	177	0.16
Mililani Town, HI (cdp) Honolulu County	45	0.16
Maili, HI (cdp) Honolulu County	15	0.16
Waterloo, IA (city) Black Hawk County	106	0.15
Pearl City, HI (cdp) Honolulu County	70	0.15
Magna, UT (cdp) Salt Lake County	39	0.15
Lithia Springs, GA (cdp) Douglas County	24	0.15
North Salt Lake, UT (city) Davis County	24	0.15
Fayetteville, AR (city) Washington County	103	0.14
Tualatin, OR (city) Washington County	36	0.14
Hayesville, OR (cdp) Marion County	27	0.14
Leesburg, FL (city) Lake County	26	0.13
Lahaina, HI (cdp) Maui County	15	0.13
Pleasant View, UT (city) Weber County	9	0.11
Tustin, CA (city) Orange County	77	0.10
Kaneohe, HI (cdp) Honolulu County	34	0.10
South Ogden, UT (city) Weber County	16	0.10
Fort Lewis, WA (cdp) Pierce County	11	0.10
Sacramento, CA (city) Sacramento County	400	0.09
Fort Hood, TX (cdp) Bell County	26	0.09
Schofield Barracks, HI (cdp) Honolulu County	14	0.09
West Lealman, FL (cdp) Pinellas County	14	0.09
Newport East, RI (cdp) Newport County	11	0.09
La Riviera, CA (cdp) Sacramento County	10	0.09
Tempe, AZ (city) Maricopa County	131	0.08
Florin, CA (cdp) Sacramento County	37	0.08
Kailua, HI (cdp) Honolulu County	30	0.08
Bentonville, AR (city) Benton County	29	0.08
Des Moines, WA (city) King County	25	0.08
Elk Plain, WA (cdp) Pierce County	11	0.08
Fort Carson, CO (cdp) El Paso County	11	0.08
Evanston, WY (city) Uinta County	10	0.08
Monmouth, OR (city) Polk County	8	0.08
Clarksville, AR (city) Johnson County	7	0.08
Sitka, AK (borough) Sitka City and Borough	7	0.08
Washington Terrace, UT (city) Weber County	7	0.08
Springfield, OR (city) Lane County	39	0.07
Logan, UT (city) Cache County	34	0.07
Ottumwa, IA (city) Wapello County	17	0.07
North Ogden, UT (city) Weber County	13	0.07
Middletown, RI (town) Newport County	11	0.07
Edgewood, WA (city) Pierce County	7	0.07
St. Marys, OH (city) Auglaize County	6	0.07
Hyrum, UT (city) Cache County	5	0.07
Garden Grove, CA (city) Orange County	109	0.06
Marysville, WA (city) Snohomish County	39	0.06
Lakewood, WA (city) Pierce County	34	0.06
Pleasant Grove, UT (city) Utah County	21	0.06
Lynnwood, WA (city) Snohomish County	20	0.06
Lady Lake, FL (town) Lake County	9	0.06
Martha Lake, WA (cdp) Snohomish County	9	0.06
Arkansas City, KS (city) Cowley County	7	0.06
Red Bank, NJ (borough) Monmouth County	7	0.06
Waipio, HI (cdp) Honolulu County	7	0.06
Aiea, HI (cdp) Honolulu County	6	0.06
Collegedale, TN (city) Hamilton County	5	0.06
Picnic Point, WA (cdp) Snohomish County	5	0.06
Taylorsville, UT (city) Salt Lake County	28	0.05
Pinellas Park, FL (city) Pinellas County	25	0.05
Bountiful, UT (city) Davis County	20	0.05
Merritt Island, FL (cdp) Brevard County	19	0.05
University Place, WA (city) Pierce County	17	0.05
Mount Vernon, WA (city) Skagit County	16	0.05
Rockledge, FL (city) Brevard County	12	0.05
Kapolei, HI (cdp) Honolulu County	8	0.05
Troutdale, OR (city) Multnomah County	8	0.05
Fort Campbell North, KY (cdp) Christian County	7	0.05
Tavares, FL (city) Lake County	7	0.05
Lexington, NE (city) Dawson County	5	0.05
Sandy, OR (city) Clackamas County	5	0.05
Walnut Grove, WA (cdp) Clark County	5	0.05
Alderwood Manor, WA (cdp) Snohomish County	4	0.05
Arab, AL (city) Marshall County	4	0.05
Birch Bay, WA (cdp) Whatcom County	4	0.05
Pukalani, HI (cdp) Maui County	4	0.05
Evansville, IN (city) Vanderburgh County	49	0.04
Kent, WA (city) King County	39	0.04
Ogden, UT (city) Weber County	35	0.04
Spokane Valley, WA (city) Spokane County	32	0.04
Lacey, WA (city) Thurston County	19	0.04
Kearns, UT (cdp) Salt Lake County	14	0.04
Hinesville, GA (city) Liberty County	13	0.04
Tarpon Springs, FL (city) Pinellas County	9	0.04
Frederickson, WA (cdp) Pierce County	8	0.04
Cusseta-Chattahoochee County, GA (unified govt) Chattahoochee County	5	0.04
Fort Drum, NY (cdp) Jefferson County	5	0.04
Piney Green, NC (cdp) Onslow County	5	0.04
Country Club, CA (cdp) San Joaquin County	4	0.04
Woods Cross, UT (city) Davis County	4	0.04
Ocean Pointe, HI (cdp) Honolulu County	3	0.04
South San Gabriel, CA (cdp) Los Angeles County	3	0.04
Yreka, CA (city) Siskiyou County	3	0.04
Tucson, AZ (city) Pima County	177	0.03
Santa Ana, CA (city) Orange County	82	0.03
Huntsville, AL (city) Madison County	57	0.03
Springfield, MO (city) Christian County	45	0.03
Asheville, NC (city) Buncombe County	26	0.03
West Jordan, UT (city) Salt Lake County	26	0.03
Layton, UT (city) Davis County	23	0.03
Corvallis, OR (city) Benton County	18	0.03
Parkland, WA (cdp) Pierce County	12	0.03

Please refer to the Explanation of Data in the front of the book for more detailed information.

Race

Hawaii Native/Pacific Islander: Native Hawaiian

U.S. and 50 States Sorted by Population and Percent of Total Population

Place	Population	%
United States	**527,077**	**0.17**
Hawaii	289,970	21.32
California	74,932	0.20
Washington	19,863	0.30
Nevada	16,339	0.61
Texas	13,192	0.05
Oregon	9,719	0.25
Arizona	9,549	0.15
Florida	8,023	0.04
Utah	6,525	0.24
Colorado	5,670	0.11
New York	5,108	0.03
Virginia	4,699	0.06
North Carolina	4,182	0.04
Georgia	3,976	0.04
Illinois	3,636	0.03
Pennsylvania	3,043	0.02
Ohio	3,037	0.03
Alaska	3,006	0.42
Oklahoma	2,766	0.07
Michigan	2,708	0.03
Missouri	2,673	0.04
Maryland	2,346	0.04
Tennessee	2,224	0.04
Indiana	2,223	0.03
New Jersey	2,066	0.02
Idaho	1,921	0.12
New Mexico	1,854	0.09
Minnesota	1,847	0.03
Massachusetts	1,780	0.03
South Carolina	1,654	0.04
Wisconsin	1,638	0.03
Kansas	1,554	0.05
Alabama	1,529	0.03
Kentucky	1,505	0.03
Arkansas	1,251	0.04
Louisiana	1,245	0.03
Iowa	1,109	0.04
Connecticut	1,017	0.03
Montana	868	0.09
Nebraska	794	0.04
Mississippi	699	0.02
Wyoming	457	0.08
West Virginia	442	0.02
Rhode Island	397	0.04
New Hampshire	385	0.03
Maine	350	0.03
South Dakota	336	0.04
North Dakota	282	0.04
Delaware	266	0.03
District of Columbia	264	0.04
Vermont	158	0.03

Place	Population	%
Hawaii	289,970	21.32
Nevada	16,339	0.61
Alaska	3,006	0.42
Washington	19,863	0.30
Oregon	9,719	0.25
Utah	6,525	0.24
California	74,932	0.20
United States	**527,077**	**0.17**
Arizona	9,549	0.15
Idaho	1,921	0.12
Colorado	5,670	0.11
New Mexico	1,854	0.09
Montana	868	0.09
Wyoming	457	0.08
Oklahoma	2,766	0.07
Virginia	4,699	0.06
Texas	13,192	0.05
Kansas	1,554	0.05
Florida	8,023	0.04
North Carolina	4,182	0.04
Georgia	3,976	0.04
Missouri	2,673	0.04
Maryland	2,346	0.04
Tennessee	2,224	0.04
South Carolina	1,654	0.04
Arkansas	1,251	0.04
Iowa	1,109	0.04
Nebraska	794	0.04
Rhode Island	397	0.04
South Dakota	336	0.04
North Dakota	282	0.04
District of Columbia	264	0.04
New York	5,108	0.03
Illinois	3,636	0.03
Ohio	3,037	0.03
Michigan	2,708	0.03
Indiana	2,223	0.03
Minnesota	1,847	0.03
Massachusetts	1,780	0.03
Wisconsin	1,638	0.03
Alabama	1,529	0.03
Kentucky	1,505	0.03
Louisiana	1,245	0.03
Connecticut	1,017	0.03
New Hampshire	385	0.03
Maine	350	0.03
Delaware	266	0.03
Vermont	158	0.03
Pennsylvania	3,043	0.02
New Jersey	2,066	0.02
Mississippi	699	0.02
West Virginia	442	0.02

Please refer to the Explanation of Data in the front of the book for more detailed information.

Race

Hawaii Native/Pacific Islander: Native Hawaiian

Top 150 Places Sorted by Population

Based on all places, regardless of total population

Place	Population	%
Urban Honolulu, HI (cdp) Honolulu County	41,781	12.39
Hilo, HI (cdp) Hawaii County	14,694	33.96
Kaneohe, HI (cdp) Honolulu County	10,685	30.88
Nanakuli, HI (cdp) Honolulu County	9,051	71.46
Kailua, HI (cdp) Honolulu County	9,028	23.37
Waianae, HI (cdp) Honolulu County	8,018	60.85
Pearl City, HI (cdp) Honolulu County	7,464	15.65
East Honolulu, HI (cdp) Honolulu County	6,117	12.26
Kapolei, HI (cdp) Honolulu County	5,673	37.36
Kahului, HI (cdp) Maui County	5,634	21.39
Mililani Town, HI (cdp) Honolulu County	5,400	19.54
Wahiawa, HI (cdp) Honolulu County	4,771	26.77
Maili, HI (cdp) Honolulu County	4,616	48.65
Makakilo, HI (cdp) Honolulu County	4,616	25.30
Wailuku, HI (cdp) Maui County	4,465	29.16
Makaha, HI (cdp) Honolulu County	4,393	53.07
Ewa Gentry, HI (cdp) Honolulu County	4,239	18.68
Waipahu, HI (cdp) Honolulu County	4,175	10.92
Los Angeles, CA (city) Los Angeles County	4,062	0.11
Las Vegas, NV (city) Clark County	3,778	0.65
Ewa Beach, HI (cdp) Honolulu County	3,722	24.89
Hawaiian Paradise Park, HI (cdp) Hawaii County	3,683	32.30
Waimanalo Beach, HI (cdp) Honolulu County	3,644	81.32
Waimea, HI (cdp) Hawaii County	3,577	38.83
Waihee-Waiehu, HI (cdp) Maui County	3,506	39.66
Mililani Mauka, HI (cdp) Honolulu County	3,256	15.48
San Diego, CA (city) San Diego County	3,194	0.24
Kailua, HI (cdp) Hawaii County	3,181	26.56
Ahuimanu, HI (cdp) Honolulu County	2,944	33.42
Kapaa, HI (cdp) Kauai County	2,817	26.33
Waimanalo, HI (cdp) Honolulu County	2,791	51.20
Kalaoa, HI (cdp) Hawaii County	2,675	27.74
Kihei, HI (cdp) Maui County	2,485	11.90
Halawa, HI (cdp) Honolulu County	2,453	17.50
New York, NY (city) Kings County	2,448	0.03
Paradise, NV (cdp) Clark County	2,336	1.05
Makawao, HI (cdp) Maui County	2,327	32.39
Pukalani, HI (cdp) Maui County	2,209	29.17
Hauula, HI (cdp) Honolulu County	2,188	52.75
San Jose, CA (city) Santa Clara County	2,161	0.23
Lahaina, HI (cdp) Maui County	2,146	18.34
Waimalu, HI (cdp) Honolulu County	2,118	15.43
Kahaluu, HI (cdp) Honolulu County	2,066	43.60
Royal Kunia, HI (cdp) Honolulu County	2,055	14.15
Waipio, HI (cdp) Honolulu County	2,005	17.17
Kaunakakai, HI (cdp) Maui County	1,887	55.09
Henderson, NV (city) Clark County	1,846	0.72
Hawaiian Beaches, HI (cdp) Hawaii County	1,755	41.00
Haiku-Pauwela, HI (cdp) Maui County	1,698	20.92
Mountain View, HI (cdp) Hawaii County	1,690	43.07
Anchorage, AK (municipality) Anchorage Municipality	1,679	0.58
Phoenix, AZ (city) Maricopa County	1,675	0.12
North Las Vegas, NV (city) Clark County	1,567	0.72
Anahola, HI (cdp) Kauai County	1,558	70.09
San Francisco, CA (city) San Francisco County	1,489	0.18
Aiea, HI (cdp) Honolulu County	1,474	15.78
Ewa Villages, HI (cdp) Honolulu County	1,459	23.89
Kualapuu, HI (cdp) Maui County	1,458	71.93
Spring Valley, NV (cdp) Clark County	1,439	0.81
Seattle, WA (city) King County	1,414	0.23
Laie, HI (cdp) Honolulu County	1,412	23.00
Holualoa, HI (cdp) Hawaii County	1,379	16.15
Lihue, HI (cdp) Kauai County	1,372	21.25
Kekaha, HI (cdp) Kauai County	1,359	38.42
Portland, OR (city) Multnomah County	1,314	0.23
Heeia, HI (cdp) Honolulu County	1,251	25.21
Sacramento, CA (city) Sacramento County	1,236	0.26
Waikoloa Village, HI (cdp) Hawaii County	1,208	18.99
Waipio Acres, HI (cdp) Honolulu County	1,180	22.54
Ainaloa, HI (cdp) Hawaii County	1,168	39.39
Haleiwa, HI (cdp) Honolulu County	1,151	28.99
Kula, HI (cdp) Maui County	1,085	16.82
San Antonio, TX (city) Medina County	1,076	0.08
Wailua Homesteads, HI (cdp) Kauai County	1,073	20.68
Waikele, HI (cdp) Honolulu County	1,070	14.31
Enterprise, NV (cdp) Clark County	1,064	0.98
Hawaiian Ocean View, HI (cdp) Hawaii County	1,035	23.33
Long Beach, CA (city) Los Angeles County	1,018	0.22
Tacoma, WA (city) Pierce County	990	0.50
Captain Cook, HI (cdp) Hawaii County	987	28.78
Ocean Pointe, HI (cdp) Honolulu County	969	11.59
Sunrise Manor, NV (cdp) Clark County	957	0.51
Reno, NV (city) Washoe County	922	0.41
Kahuku, HI (cdp) Honolulu County	912	34.89
Keokea, HI (cdp) Maui County	890	55.21
Colorado Springs, CO (city) El Paso County	884	0.21
West Loch Estate, HI (cdp) Honolulu County	881	16.06
Oceanside, CA (city) San Diego County	877	0.52
Orchidlands Estates, HI (cdp) Hawaii County	855	30.37
Waikapu, HI (cdp) Maui County	852	28.74
Kalaheo, HI (cdp) Kauai County	843	18.35
Honaunau-Napoopoo, HI (cdp) Hawaii County	835	32.53
Hanamaulu, HI (cdp) Kauai County	829	21.62
Hana, HI (cdp) Maui County	814	65.91
Stockton, CA (city) San Joaquin County	800	0.27
Hanapepe, HI (cdp) Kauai County	795	30.14
Waialua, HI (cdp) Honolulu County	790	20.47
Hawaiian Acres, HI (cdp) Hawaii County	788	29.19
Hayward, CA (city) Alameda County	784	0.54
Whitmore Village, HI (cdp) Honolulu County	782	17.38
Eloy, AZ (city) Pinal County	776	4.67
Mesa, AZ (city) Maricopa County	775	0.18
Fremont, CA (city) Alameda County	735	0.34
Chicago, IL (city) Cook County	731	0.03
Houston, TX (city) Harris County	713	0.03
Napili-Honokowai, HI (cdp) Maui County	708	9.75
Tucson, AZ (city) Pima County	704	0.14
Waimea, HI (cdp) Kauai County	699	37.68
Volcano, HI (cdp) Hawaii County	693	26.91
Albuquerque, NM (city) Bernalillo County	688	0.13
Provo, UT (city) Utah County	685	0.61
Bronx, NY (borough) Bronx County	669	0.05
Fairfield, CA (city) Solano County	668	0.63
Huntington Beach, CA (city) Orange County	668	0.35
Oakland, CA (city) Alameda County	664	0.17
Anaheim, CA (city) Orange County	653	0.19
Honalo, HI (cdp) Hawaii County	638	26.33
Torrance, CA (city) Los Angeles County	634	0.44
Kaaawa, HI (cdp) Honolulu County	629	45.61
Pupukea, HI (cdp) Honolulu County	628	13.80
Fern Acres, HI (cdp) Hawaii County	614	40.82
Kapaau, HI (cdp) Hawaii County	612	35.29
Lanai City, HI (cdp) Maui County	611	19.70
Paia, HI (cdp) Maui County	608	22.79
Fresno, CA (city) Fresno County	608	0.12
Manhattan, NY (borough) New York County	608	0.04
Honokaa, HI (cdp) Hawaii County	593	26.26
Keaau, HI (cdp) Hawaii County	590	26.19
Riverside, CA (city) Riverside County	586	0.19
Vancouver, WA (city) Clark County	584	0.36
Makaha Valley, HI (cdp) Honolulu County	582	43.40
Iroquois Point, HI (cdp) Honolulu County	581	17.22
Chula Vista, CA (city) San Diego County	577	0.24
Modesto, CA (city) Stanislaus County	567	0.28
Brooklyn, NY (borough) Kings County	564	0.02
Vacaville, CA (city) Solano County	556	0.60
Jacksonville, FL (city) Duval County	548	0.07
Kealakekua, HI (cdp) Hawaii County	546	27.04
Pahala, HI (cdp) Hawaii County	540	39.82
Philadelphia, PA (city) Philadelphia County	538	0.04
Koloa, HI (cdp) Kauai County	536	25.00
Hawi, HI (cdp) Hawaii County	535	49.49
Austin, TX (city) Travis County	535	0.07
Spokane, WA (city) Spokane County	524	0.25
Vallejo, CA (city) Solano County	523	0.45
Orem, UT (city) Utah County	521	0.59
Federal Way, WA (city) King County	520	0.58
Wailua, HI (cdp) Kauai County	514	22.80
Lawai, HI (cdp) Kauai County	509	21.54
Denver, CO (city) Denver County	494	0.08

SECTION THREE

Race

Hawaii Native/Pacific Islander: Native Hawaiian

Top 150 Places Sorted by Percent of Total Population

Based on all places, regardless of total population

Place	Population	%
Waimanalo Beach, HI (cdp) Honolulu County	3,644	81.32
Kualapuu, HI (cdp) Maui County	1,458	71.93
Nanakuli, HI (cdp) Honolulu County	9,051	71.46
Ualapu'e, HI (cdp) Maui County	300	70.59
Anahola, HI (cdp) Kauai County	1,558	70.09
Maunaloa, HI (cdp) Maui County	253	67.29
Hana, HI (cdp) Maui County	814	65.91
Waianae, HI (cdp) Honolulu County	8,018	60.85
Keokea, HI (cdp) Maui County	890	55.21
Kaunakakai, HI (cdp) Maui County	1,887	55.09
Waikane, HI (cdp) Honolulu County	417	53.60
Makaha, HI (cdp) Honolulu County	4,393	53.07
Hauula, HI (cdp) Honolulu County	2,188	52.75
Waiohinu, HI (cdp) Hawaii County	110	51.64
Waimanalo, HI (cdp) Honolulu County	2,791	51.20
Hawi, HI (cdp) Hawaii County	535	49.49
Maili, HI (cdp) Honolulu County	4,616	48.65
Kaaawa, HI (cdp) Honolulu County	629	45.61
Pakala Village, HI (cdp) Kauai County	130	44.22
Kahaluu, HI (cdp) Honolulu County	2,066	43.60
Makaha Valley, HI (cdp) Honolulu County	582	43.40
Kukuihaele, HI (cdp) Hawaii County	145	43.15
Mountain View, HI (cdp) Hawaii County	1,690	43.07
Naalehu, HI (cdp) Hawaii County	364	42.03
Punaluu, HI (cdp) Honolulu County	483	41.49
Hawaiian Beaches, HI (cdp) Hawaii County	1,755	41.00
Fern Acres, HI (cdp) Hawaii County	614	40.82
Halaula, HI (cdp) Hawaii County	187	39.87
Pahala, HI (cdp) Hawaii County	540	39.82
Waihee-Waiehu, HI (cdp) Maui County	3,506	39.66
Ainaloa, HI (cdp) Hawaii County	1,168	39.39
Waimea, HI (cdp) Hawaii County	3,577	38.83
Kekaha, HI (cdp) Kauai County	1,359	38.42
Waimea, HI (cdp) Kauai County	699	37.68
Kapolei, HI (cdp) Honolulu County	5,673	37.36
Kapaau, HI (cdp) Hawaii County	612	35.29
Kahuku, HI (cdp) Honolulu County	912	34.89
Hilo, HI (cdp) Hawaii County	14,694	33.96
Paauilo, HI (cdp) Hawaii County	201	33.78
Eden Roc, HI (cdp) Hawaii County	317	33.65
Ahuimanu, HI (cdp) Honolulu County	2,944	33.42
Honaunau-Napoopoo, HI (cdp) Hawaii County	835	32.53
Olowalu, HI (cdp) Maui County	26	32.50
Makawao, HI (cdp) Maui County	2,327	32.39
Hawaiian Paradise Park, HI (cdp) Hawaii County	3,683	32.30
Nanawale Estates, HI (cdp) Hawaii County	446	31.28
Kaneohe, HI (cdp) Honolulu County	10,685	30.88
Kurtistown, HI (cdp) Hawaii County	398	30.66
Orchidlands Estates, HI (cdp) Hawaii County	855	30.37
Pahoa, HI (cdp) Hawaii County	285	30.16
Hanapepe, HI (cdp) Kauai County	795	30.14
Hawaiian Acres, HI (cdp) Hawaii County	788	29.19
Pukalani, HI (cdp) Maui County	2,209	29.17
Wailuku, HI (cdp) Maui County	4,465	29.16
Haleiwa, HI (cdp) Honolulu County	1,151	28.99
Captain Cook, HI (cdp) Hawaii County	987	28.78
Waikapu, HI (cdp) Maui County	852	28.74
Kalaoa, HI (cdp) Hawaii County	2,675	27.74
Kealakekua, HI (cdp) Hawaii County	546	27.04
Volcano, HI (cdp) Hawaii County	693	26.91
Fern Forest, HI (cdp) Hawaii County	250	26.85
Wahiawa, HI (cdp) Honolulu County	4,771	26.77
Kailua, HI (cdp) Hawaii County	3,181	26.56
Kapaa, HI (cdp) Kauai County	2,817	26.33
Honalo, HI (cdp) Hawaii County	638	26.33
Honokaa, HI (cdp) Hawaii County	593	26.26
Papaikou, HI (cdp) Hawaii County	345	26.26
Keaau, HI (cdp) Hawaii County	590	26.19
Haliimaile, HI (cdp) Maui County	251	26.04
Honomu, HI (cdp) Hawaii County	131	25.74
Makakilo, HI (cdp) Honolulu County	4,616	25.30
Heeia, HI (cdp) Honolulu County	1,251	25.21
Wainiha, HI (cdp) Kauai County	80	25.16
Laupahoehoe, HI (cdp) Hawaii County	146	25.13
Koloa, HI (cdp) Kauai County	536	25.00
Ewa Beach, HI (cdp) Honolulu County	3,722	24.89
Ewa Villages, HI (cdp) Honolulu County	1,459	23.89
Kailua, HI (cdp) Honolulu County	9,028	23.37
Hawaiian Ocean View, HI (cdp) Hawaii County	1,035	23.33
Laie, HI (cdp) Honolulu County	1,412	23.00
Pepeekeo, HI (cdp) Hawaii County	409	22.86
Wailua, HI (cdp) Kauai County	514	22.80
Paia, HI (cdp) Maui County	608	22.79
Wainaku, HI (cdp) Hawaii County	277	22.63
Waipio Acres, HI (cdp) Honolulu County	1,180	22.54
Discovery Harbour, HI (cdp) Hawaii County	208	21.92
Hanamaulu, HI (cdp) Kauai County	829	21.62
Haena, HI (cdp) Kauai County	93	21.58
Lawai, HI (cdp) Kauai County	509	21.54
Kahului, HI (cdp) Maui County	5,634	21.39
Lihue, HI (cdp) Kauai County	1,372	21.25
Haiku-Pauwela, HI (cdp) Maui County	1,698	20.92
Kalaeloa, HI (cdp) Honolulu County	10	20.83
Wailua Homesteads, HI (cdp) Kauai County	1,073	20.68
Omao, HI (cdp) Kauai County	269	20.68
Waialua, HI (cdp) Honolulu County	790	20.47
Maunawili, HI (cdp) Honolulu County	410	20.10
Eleele, HI (cdp) Kauai County	474	19.83
Lanai City, HI (cdp) Maui County	611	19.70
Kalihiwai, HI (cdp) Kauai County	84	19.63
Mililani Town, HI (cdp) Honolulu County	5,400	19.54
Waikoloa Village, HI (cdp) Hawaii County	1,208	18.99
Ewa Gentry, HI (cdp) Honolulu County	4,239	18.68
Kaumakani, HI (cdp) Kauai County	138	18.42
Kalaheo, HI (cdp) Kauai County	843	18.35
Lahaina, HI (cdp) Maui County	2,146	18.34
Halawa, HI (cdp) Honolulu County	2,453	17.50
Whitmore Village, HI (cdp) Honolulu County	782	17.38
Iroquois Point, HI (cdp) Honolulu County	581	17.22
Waipio, HI (cdp) Honolulu County	2,005	17.17
Hanalei, HI (cdp) Kauai County	77	17.11
Kula, HI (cdp) Maui County	1,085	16.82
Leilani Estates, HI (cdp) Hawaii County	257	16.47
Paukaa, HI (cdp) Hawaii County	69	16.24
Holualoa, HI (cdp) Hawaii County	1,379	16.15
West Loch Estate, HI (cdp) Honolulu County	881	16.06
Aiea, HI (cdp) Honolulu County	1,474	15.78
Puhi, HI (cdp) Kauai County	455	15.66
Pearl City, HI (cdp) Honolulu County	7,464	15.65
Mililani Mauka, HI (cdp) Honolulu County	3,256	15.48
Waimalu, HI (cdp) Honolulu County	2,118	15.43
Waikele, HI (cdp) Honolulu County	1,070	14.31
Royal Kunia, HI (cdp) Honolulu County	2,055	14.15
Pupukea, HI (cdp) Honolulu County	628	13.80
Makena, HI (cdp) Maui County	13	13.13
Qui-nai-elt Village, WA (cdp) Grays Harbor County	7	12.96
Mokuleia, HI (cdp) Honolulu County	229	12.64
Kilauea, HI (cdp) Kauai County	350	12.49
Urban Honolulu, HI (cdp) Honolulu County	41,781	12.39
Olinda, HI (cdp) Maui County	134	12.36
East Honolulu, HI (cdp) Honolulu County	6,117	12.26
Kahaluu-Keauhou, HI (cdp) Hawaii County	435	12.26
Kihei, HI (cdp) Maui County	2,485	11.90
Ocean Pointe, HI (cdp) Honolulu County	969	11.59
Kapalua, HI (cdp) Maui County	39	11.05
Waipahu, HI (cdp) Honolulu County	4,175	10.92
Poipu, HI (cdp) Kauai County	99	10.11
Napili-Honokowai, HI (cdp) Maui County	708	9.75
Whale Pass, AK (cdp) Prince of Wales-Hyder Census Area	3	9.68
Launiupoko, HI (cdp) Maui County	52	8.84
Furnace Creek, CA (cdp) Inyo County	2	8.33
Maalaea, HI (cdp) Maui County	27	7.67
Puako, HI (cdp) Hawaii County	50	6.48
Kawela Bay, HI (cdp) Honolulu County	21	6.36
Princeville, HI (cdp) Kauai County	111	5.14
Wailea, HI (cdp) Maui County	290	4.88
Attu Station, AK (cdp) Aleutians West Census Area	1	4.76
Eloy, AZ (city) Pinal County	776	4.67
Mahinahina, HI (cdp) Maui County	41	4.66
Elderon, WI (village) Marathon County	8	4.47

Please refer to the Explanation of Data in the front of the book for more detailed information.

Race

Hawaii Native/Pacific Islander: Native Hawaiian

Top 150 Places Sorted by Percent of Total Population

Based on places with total population of 7,500 or more

Place	Population	%
Nanakuli, HI (cdp) Honolulu County	9,051	71.46
Waianae, HI (cdp) Honolulu County	8,018	60.85
Makaha, HI (cdp) Honolulu County	4,393	53.07
Maili, HI (cdp) Honolulu County	4,616	48.65
Waihee-Waiehu, HI (cdp) Maui County	3,506	39.66
Waimea, HI (cdp) Hawaii County	3,577	38.83
Kapolei, HI (cdp) Honolulu County	5,673	37.36
Hilo, HI (cdp) Hawaii County	14,694	33.96
Ahuimanu, HI (cdp) Honolulu County	2,944	33.42
Hawaiian Paradise Park, HI (cdp) Hawaii County	3,683	32.30
Kaneohe, HI (cdp) Honolulu County	10,685	30.88
Pukalani, HI (cdp) Maui County	2,209	29.17
Wailuku, HI (cdp) Maui County	4,465	29.16
Kalaoa, HI (cdp) Hawaii County	2,675	27.74
Wahiawa, HI (cdp) Honolulu County	4,771	26.77
Kailua, HI (cdp) Hawaii County	3,181	26.56
Kapaa, HI (cdp) Kauai County	2,817	26.33
Makakilo, HI (cdp) Honolulu County	4,616	25.30
Ewa Beach, HI (cdp) Honolulu County	3,722	24.89
Kailua, HI (cdp) Honolulu County	9,028	23.37
Kahului, HI (cdp) Maui County	5,634	21.39
Haiku-Pauwela, HI (cdp) Maui County	1,698	20.92
Mililani Town, HI (cdp) Honolulu County	5,400	19.54
Ewa Gentry, HI (cdp) Honolulu County	4,239	18.68
Lahaina, HI (cdp) Maui County	2,146	18.34
Halawa, HI (cdp) Honolulu County	2,453	17.50
Waipio, HI (cdp) Honolulu County	2,005	17.17
Holualoa, HI (cdp) Hawaii County	1,379	16.15
Aiea, HI (cdp) Honolulu County	1,474	15.78
Pearl City, HI (cdp) Honolulu County	7,464	15.65
Mililani Mauka, HI (cdp) Honolulu County	3,256	15.48
Waimalu, HI (cdp) Honolulu County	2,118	15.43
Royal Kunia, HI (cdp) Honolulu County	2,055	14.15
Urban Honolulu, HI (cdp) Honolulu County	41,781	12.39
East Honolulu, HI (cdp) Honolulu County	6,117	12.26
Kihei, HI (cdp) Maui County	2,485	11.90
Ocean Pointe, HI (cdp) Honolulu County	969	11.59
Waipahu, HI (cdp) Honolulu County	4,175	10.92
Eloy, AZ (city) Pinal County	776	4.67
Schofield Barracks, HI (cdp) Honolulu County	364	2.22
Lackland AFB, TX (cdp) Bexar County	128	1.29
Kaneohe Station, HI (cdp) Honolulu County	117	1.23
Paradise, NV (cdp) Clark County	2,336	1.05
Enterprise, NV (cdp) Clark County	1,064	0.98
Marina, CA (city) Monterey County	183	0.93
Elk Plain, WA (cdp) Pierce County	122	0.86
Spanaway, WA (cdp) Pierce County	230	0.84
Spring Valley, NV (cdp) Clark County	1,439	0.81
Lakewood, WA (city) Pierce County	473	0.81
Suisun City, CA (city) Solano County	221	0.79
Frederickson, WA (cdp) Pierce County	148	0.79
Fort Lewis, WA (cdp) Pierce County	86	0.78
Whitney, NV (cdp) Clark County	289	0.75
Silverdale, WA (cdp) Kitsap County	141	0.73
Henderson, NV (city) Clark County	1,846	0.72
North Las Vegas, NV (city) Clark County	1,567	0.72
Forest Grove, OR (city) Washington County	149	0.71
Pahrump, NV (cdp) Nye County	249	0.68
Parkland, WA (cdp) Pierce County	241	0.67
DuPont, WA (city) Pierce County	55	0.67
Lacey, WA (city) Thurston County	279	0.66
Las Vegas, NV (city) Clark County	3,778	0.65
Discovery Bay, CA (cdp) Contra Costa County	87	0.65
Midland, WA (cdp) Pierce County	58	0.65
Oak Harbor, WA (city) Island County	141	0.64
Cherryland, CA (cdp) Alameda County	94	0.64
Fairfield, CA (city) Solano County	668	0.63
Oak Hills, OR (cdp) Washington County	71	0.63
Fife, WA (city) Pierce County	58	0.63
Clearlake, CA (city) Lake County	94	0.62
Camp Pendleton South, CA (cdp) San Diego County	66	0.62
Provo, UT (city) Utah County	685	0.61
Vacaville, CA (city) Solano County	556	0.60
University Place, WA (city) Pierce County	186	0.60
Monmouth, OR (city) Polk County	57	0.60

Place	Population	%
Picnic Point, WA (cdp) Snohomish County	53	0.60
Orem, UT (city) Utah County	521	0.59
Anchorage, AK (municipality) Anchorage Municipality	1,679	0.58
Federal Way, WA (city) King County	520	0.58
Graham, WA (cdp) Pierce County	136	0.58
Rockcreek, OR (cdp) Washington County	53	0.57
Lake Stickney, WA (cdp) Snohomish County	44	0.57
Cedar Hills, UT (city) Utah County	55	0.56
Gardena, CA (city) Los Angeles County	324	0.55
Pacifica, CA (city) San Mateo County	203	0.55
Summerlin South, NV (cdp) Clark County	133	0.55
Rodeo, CA (cdp) Contra Costa County	48	0.55
Hayward, CA (city) Alameda County	784	0.54
Winchester, NV (cdp) Clark County	151	0.54
Aloha, OR (cdp) Washington County	260	0.53
Lake Stevens, WA (city) Snohomish County	149	0.53
Fairwood, WA (cdp) King County	102	0.53
Newman, CA (city) Stanislaus County	54	0.53
Oceanside, CA (city) San Diego County	877	0.52
Hillsboro, OR (city) Washington County	477	0.52
College, AK (cdp) Fairbanks North Star Borough	68	0.52
Sunrise Manor, NV (cdp) Clark County	957	0.51
Manteca, CA (city) San Joaquin County	340	0.51
Junction City, KS (city) Geary County	118	0.51
French Valley, CA (cdp) Riverside County	117	0.51
Mountlake Terrace, WA (city) Snohomish County	101	0.51
Mountain House, CA (cdp) San Joaquin County	49	0.51
Tacoma, WA (city) Pierce County	990	0.50
South Hill, WA (cdp) Pierce County	261	0.50
Puyallup, WA (city) Pierce County	186	0.50
Security-Widefield, CO (cdp) El Paso County	163	0.50
Clearfield, UT (city) Davis County	151	0.50
Soquel, CA (cdp) Santa Cruz County	48	0.50
Stanford, CA (cdp) Santa Clara County	67	0.49
Union City, CA (city) Alameda County	332	0.48
Juneau, AK (borough) Juneau City and Borough	149	0.48
Imperial Beach, CA (city) San Diego County	126	0.48
San Lorenzo, CA (cdp) Alameda County	112	0.48
Maple Valley, WA (city) King County	109	0.48
Knik-Fairview, AK (cdp) Matanuska-Susitna Borough	71	0.48
Port Orchard, WA (city) Kitsap County	53	0.48
Kalifornsky, AK (cdp) Kenai Peninsula Borough	38	0.48
Tracy, CA (city) San Joaquin County	393	0.47
American Fork, UT (city) Utah County	124	0.47
Washington, UT (city) Washington County	88	0.47
Corvallis, OR (city) Benton County	249	0.46
Brentwood, CA (city) Contra Costa County	238	0.46
East Hill-Meridian, WA (cdp) King County	137	0.46
Patterson, CA (city) Stanislaus County	93	0.46
Summit, WA (cdp) Pierce County	37	0.46
Vallejo, CA (city) Solano County	523	0.45
Kent, WA (city) King County	417	0.45
St. George, UT (city) Washington County	327	0.45
Dublin, CA (city) Alameda County	208	0.45
Newark, CA (city) Alameda County	192	0.45
San Bruno, CA (city) San Mateo County	184	0.45
Belmont, CA (city) San Mateo County	116	0.45
West Carson, CA (cdp) Los Angeles County	98	0.45
Salmon Creek, WA (cdp) Clark County	89	0.45
Cheney, WA (city) Spokane County	48	0.45
Walnut Grove, WA (cdp) Clark County	44	0.45
Country Club, CA (cdp) San Joaquin County	42	0.45
Torrance, CA (city) Los Angeles County	634	0.44
Lynnwood, WA (city) Snohomish County	158	0.44
Foothill Farms, CA (cdp) Sacramento County	146	0.44
Benicia, CA (city) Solano County	118	0.44
Ashland, OR (city) Jackson County	89	0.44
Orchards, WA (cdp) Clark County	87	0.44
Tukwila, WA (city) King County	84	0.44
North Lynnwood, WA (cdp) Snohomish County	73	0.44
Fairview, CA (cdp) Alameda County	44	0.44
Half Moon, NC (cdp) Onslow County	37	0.44
Auburn, WA (city) King County	301	0.43
Bremerton, WA (city) Kitsap County	164	0.43
Twentynine Palms, CA (city) San Bernardino County	108	0.43

Please refer to the Explanation of Data in the front of the book for more detailed information.

Race

Hawaii Native/Pacific Islander: Samoan

U.S. and 50 States Sorted by Population and Percent of Total Population

Place	Population	%	Place	Population	%
United States	**184,440**	**0.06**	Hawaii	37,463	2.75
California	60,876	0.16	Alaska	5,953	0.84
Hawaii	37,463	2.75	Utah	13,086	0.47
Washington	18,351	0.27	Washington	18,351	0.27
Utah	13,086	0.47	Nevada	5,257	0.19
Alaska	5,953	0.84	California	60,876	0.16
Texas	5,490	0.02	Oregon	2,892	0.08
Nevada	5,257	0.19	**United States**	**184,440**	**0.06**
Arizona	3,547	0.06	Arizona	3,547	0.06
Oregon	2,892	0.08	Idaho	895	0.06
Missouri	2,740	0.05	Missouri	2,740	0.05
Florida	2,493	0.01	Colorado	2,050	0.04
Colorado	2,050	0.04	New Mexico	624	0.03
Georgia	1,828	0.02	Montana	267	0.03
New York	1,654	0.01	Wyoming	151	0.03
North Carolina	1,600	0.02	Texas	5,490	0.02
Virginia	1,569	0.02	Georgia	1,828	0.02
Ohio	1,278	0.01	North Carolina	1,600	0.02
Illinois	1,191	0.01	Virginia	1,569	0.02
Pennsylvania	1,118	0.01	Tennessee	1,022	0.02
Tennessee	1,022	0.02	Oklahoma	855	0.02
Idaho	895	0.06	Kentucky	704	0.02
Oklahoma	855	0.02	Kansas	657	0.02
Michigan	848	0.01	Nebraska	345	0.02
Indiana	830	0.01	North Dakota	117	0.02
Maryland	731	0.01	Florida	2,493	0.01
Kentucky	704	0.02	New York	1,654	0.01
Kansas	657	0.02	Ohio	1,278	0.01
New Jersey	642	0.01	Illinois	1,191	0.01
Minnesota	640	0.01	Pennsylvania	1,118	0.01
New Mexico	624	0.03	Michigan	848	0.01
Louisiana	572	0.01	Indiana	830	0.01
South Carolina	555	0.01	Maryland	731	0.01
Massachusetts	511	0.01	New Jersey	642	0.01
Alabama	488	0.01	Minnesota	640	0.01
Wisconsin	458	0.01	Louisiana	572	0.01
Arkansas	371	0.01	South Carolina	555	0.01
Connecticut	357	0.01	Massachusetts	511	0.01
Nebraska	345	0.02	Alabama	488	0.01
Mississippi	329	0.01	Wisconsin	458	0.01
Iowa	300	0.01	Arkansas	371	0.01
Montana	267	0.03	Connecticut	357	0.01
Wyoming	151	0.03	Mississippi	329	0.01
West Virginia	142	0.01	Iowa	300	0.01
Maine	126	0.01	West Virginia	142	0.01
North Dakota	117	0.02	Maine	126	0.01
Rhode Island	93	0.01	Rhode Island	93	0.01
South Dakota	91	0.01	South Dakota	91	0.01
Delaware	82	0.01	Delaware	82	0.01
District of Columbia	82	0.01	District of Columbia	82	0.01
New Hampshire	69	0.01	New Hampshire	69	0.01
Vermont	50	0.01	Vermont	50	0.01

Please refer to the Explanation of Data in the front of the book for more detailed information.

Race

Hawaii Native/Pacific Islander: Samoan

Top 150 Places Sorted by Population

Based on all places, regardless of total population

Place	Population	%
Urban Honolulu, HI (cdp) Honolulu County	8,520	2.53
Anchorage, AK (municipality) Anchorage Municipality	5,202	1.78
Long Beach, CA (city) Los Angeles County	4,513	0.98
Waipahu, HI (cdp) Honolulu County	2,831	7.41
San Francisco, CA (city) San Francisco County	2,542	0.32
San Diego, CA (city) San Diego County	2,490	0.19
Los Angeles, CA (city) Los Angeles County	2,480	0.07
West Valley City, UT (city) Salt Lake County	2,413	1.86
Carson, CA (city) Los Angeles County	2,352	2.56
San Jose, CA (city) Santa Clara County	1,954	0.21
Tacoma, WA (city) Pierce County	1,784	0.90
Oceanside, CA (city) San Diego County	1,781	1.07
Nanakuli, HI (cdp) Honolulu County	1,602	12.65
Federal Way, WA (city) King County	1,459	1.63
Laie, HI (cdp) Honolulu County	1,397	22.76
Seattle, WA (city) King County	1,352	0.22
Sacramento, CA (city) Sacramento County	1,233	0.26
Pearl City, HI (cdp) Honolulu County	1,187	2.49
Las Vegas, NV (city) Clark County	1,123	0.19
Salt Lake City, UT (city) Salt Lake County	1,100	0.59
Kent, WA (city) King County	1,079	1.17
West Jordan, UT (city) Salt Lake County	1,079	1.04
Ewa Beach, HI (cdp) Honolulu County	1,058	7.07
Ewa Gentry, HI (cdp) Honolulu County	1,030	4.54
Anaheim, CA (city) Orange County	1,023	0.30
Makakilo, HI (cdp) Honolulu County	976	5.35
Waianae, HI (cdp) Honolulu County	963	7.31
Halawa, HI (cdp) Honolulu County	952	6.79
Independence, MO (city) Jackson County	940	0.80
Wahiawa, HI (cdp) Honolulu County	935	5.25
Maili, HI (cdp) Honolulu County	917	9.66
Kaneohe, HI (cdp) Honolulu County	872	2.52
Hayward, CA (city) Alameda County	859	0.60
Lakewood, WA (city) Pierce County	826	1.42
Paradise, NV (cdp) Clark County	791	0.35
Taylorsville, UT (city) Salt Lake County	782	1.33
Phoenix, AZ (city) Maricopa County	768	0.05
New York, NY (city) Kings County	764	0.01
Garden Grove, CA (city) Orange County	760	0.44
Kapolei, HI (cdp) Honolulu County	755	4.97
Compton, CA (city) Los Angeles County	735	0.76
Parkland, WA (cdp) Pierce County	708	1.98
Provo, UT (city) Utah County	705	0.63
Santa Ana, CA (city) Orange County	695	0.21
SeaTac, WA (city) King County	693	2.58
St. George, UT (city) Washington County	658	0.90
Hauula, HI (cdp) Honolulu County	655	15.79
North Las Vegas, NV (city) Clark County	642	0.30
Stockton, CA (city) San Joaquin County	637	0.22
Makaha, HI (cdp) Honolulu County	630	7.61
Moreno Valley, CA (city) Riverside County	628	0.32
Royal Kunia, HI (cdp) Honolulu County	619	4.26
Riverside, CA (city) Riverside County	618	0.20
Mililani Town, HI (cdp) Honolulu County	609	2.20
Daly City, CA (city) San Mateo County	603	0.60
Orem, UT (city) Utah County	595	0.67
San Bernardino, CA (city) San Bernardino County	594	0.28
Vista, CA (city) San Diego County	572	0.61
Kailua, HI (cdp) Honolulu County	569	1.47
Killeen, TX (city) Bell County	565	0.44
Colorado Springs, CO (city) El Paso County	551	0.13
Kearns, UT (cdp) Salt Lake County	549	1.54
Henderson, NV (city) Clark County	543	0.21
Lakewood, CA (city) Los Angeles County	534	0.67
Bellflower, CA (city) Los Angeles County	507	0.66
Waimalu, HI (cdp) Honolulu County	504	3.67
Portland, OR (city) Multnomah County	497	0.09
Des Moines, WA (city) King County	496	1.67
Hilo, HI (cdp) Hawaii County	486	1.12
Kahuku, HI (cdp) Honolulu County	480	18.36
Oxnard, CA (city) Ventura County	474	0.24
South San Francisco, CA (city) San Mateo County	473	0.74
Auburn, WA (city) King County	471	0.67
Vallejo, CA (city) Solano County	463	0.40
Oakland, CA (city) Alameda County	460	0.12
East Palo Alto, CA (city) San Mateo County	430	1.53
Spring Valley, NV (cdp) Clark County	426	0.24
Mesa, AZ (city) Maricopa County	412	0.09
San Bruno, CA (city) San Mateo County	403	0.98
Columbus, OH (city) Franklin County	399	0.05
Sunrise Manor, NV (cdp) Clark County	396	0.21
Chula Vista, CA (city) San Diego County	396	0.16
Renton, WA (city) King County	389	0.43
Fresno, CA (city) Fresno County	388	0.08
Burien, WA (city) King County	384	1.15
Spanaway, WA (cdp) Pierce County	382	1.40
Torrance, CA (city) Los Angeles County	380	0.26
East Honolulu, HI (cdp) Honolulu County	367	0.74
San Antonio, TX (city) Medina County	365	0.03
Vancouver, WA (city) Clark County	361	0.22
Paramount, CA (city) Los Angeles County	360	0.67
Fairfield, CA (city) Solano County	348	0.33
Modesto, CA (city) Stanislaus County	334	0.17
Tukwila, WA (city) King County	333	1.74
Kansas City, MO (city) Jackson County	333	0.07
Enterprise, NV (cdp) Clark County	331	0.31
Huntington Beach, CA (city) Orange County	327	0.17
Ewa Villages, HI (cdp) Honolulu County	326	5.34
Antioch, CA (city) Contra Costa County	325	0.32
South Hill, WA (cdp) Pierce County	322	0.61
Iroquois Point, HI (cdp) Honolulu County	316	9.37
Kahului, HI (cdp) Maui County	306	1.16
Sandy, UT (city) Salt Lake County	301	0.34
Twentynine Palms, CA (city) San Bernardino County	299	1.19
West Carson, CA (cdp) Los Angeles County	293	1.35
Fontana, CA (city) San Bernardino County	290	0.15
El Paso, TX (city) El Paso County	290	0.04
Waipio, HI (cdp) Honolulu County	287	2.46
Westminster, CA (city) Orange County	285	0.32
Lehi, UT (city) Utah County	281	0.59
Chicago, IL (city) Cook County	281	0.01
Tracy, CA (city) San Joaquin County	280	0.34
Aurora, CO (city) Arapahoe County	276	0.08
Waimanalo, HI (cdp) Honolulu County	275	5.04
Magna, UT (cdp) Salt Lake County	274	1.03
Reno, NV (city) Washoe County	274	0.12
Gardena, CA (city) Los Angeles County	269	0.46
Santa Rosa, CA (city) Sonoma County	264	0.16
San Mateo, CA (city) San Mateo County	261	0.27
Houston, TX (city) Harris County	261	0.01
Corona, CA (city) Riverside County	260	0.17
Marina, CA (city) Monterey County	256	1.30
Fremont, CA (city) Alameda County	255	0.12
Norwalk, CA (city) Los Angeles County	252	0.24
Union City, CA (city) Alameda County	251	0.36
Lawton, OK (city) Comanche County	248	0.26
Victorville, CA (city) San Bernardino County	243	0.21
Buena Park, CA (city) Orange County	241	0.30
Sunnyvale, CA (city) Santa Clara County	241	0.17
Santa Clara, CA (city) Santa Clara County	240	0.21
National City, CA (city) San Diego County	238	0.41
Concord, CA (city) Contra Costa County	232	0.19
Clarksville, TN (city) Montgomery County	232	0.17
Kailua, HI (cdp) Hawaii County	230	1.92
Richmond, CA (city) Contra Costa County	230	0.22
Lacey, WA (city) Thurston County	229	0.54
El Cajon, CA (city) San Diego County	227	0.23
Fayetteville, NC (city) Cumberland County	226	0.11
Pomona, CA (city) Los Angeles County	224	0.15
Bakersfield, CA (city) Kern County	224	0.06
Mililani Mauka, HI (cdp) Honolulu County	223	1.06
Kihei, HI (cdp) Maui County	222	1.06
San Leandro, CA (city) Alameda County	222	0.26
Midland, WA (cdp) Pierce County	220	2.45
Frederickson, WA (cdp) Pierce County	220	1.18
Fort Worth, TX (city) Tarrant County	216	0.03
Brooklyn, NY (borough) Kings County	216	0.01
East Hill-Meridian, WA (cdp) King County	215	0.72
Medford, OR (city) Jackson County	214	0.29
Hawthorne, CA (city) Los Angeles County	214	0.25

SECTION THREE

Please refer to the Explanation of Data in the front of the book for more detailed information.

Race

Hawaii Native/Pacific Islander: Samoan

Top 150 Places Sorted by Percent of Total Population

Based on all places, regardless of total population

Place	Population	%
Laie, HI (cdp) Honolulu County	1,397	22.76
Kalaeloa, HI (cdp) Honolulu County	10	20.83
Kahuku, HI (cdp) Honolulu County	480	18.36
Hauula, HI (cdp) Honolulu County	655	15.79
Nanakuli, HI (cdp) Honolulu County	1,602	12.65
Urbancrest, OH (village) Franklin County	93	9.69
Maili, HI (cdp) Honolulu County	917	9.66
Iroquois Point, HI (cdp) Honolulu County	316	9.37
Makaha, HI (cdp) Honolulu County	630	7.61
Punaluu, HI (cdp) Honolulu County	87	7.47
Waipahu, HI (cdp) Honolulu County	2,831	7.41
Waianae, HI (cdp) Honolulu County	963	7.31
Ewa Beach, HI (cdp) Honolulu County	1,058	7.07
Halawa, HI (cdp) Honolulu County	952	6.79
Makakilo, HI (cdp) Honolulu County	976	5.35
Ewa Villages, HI (cdp) Honolulu County	326	5.34
Wahiawa, HI (cdp) Honolulu County	935	5.25
Waimanalo, HI (cdp) Honolulu County	275	5.04
Kapolei, HI (cdp) Honolulu County	755	4.97
Makaha Valley, HI (cdp) Honolulu County	65	4.85
Darwin, CA (cdp) Inyo County	2	4.65
Kaaawa, HI (cdp) Honolulu County	64	4.64
Egegik, AK (city) Lake and Peninsula Borough	5	4.59
Ewa Gentry, HI (cdp) Honolulu County	1,030	4.54
Royal Kunia, HI (cdp) Honolulu County	619	4.26
Waimanalo Beach, HI (cdp) Honolulu County	189	4.22
Maxfield, ME (town) Penobscot County	4	4.12
Waipio Acres, HI (cdp) Honolulu County	204	3.90
Eden Roc, HI (cdp) Hawaii County	36	3.82
Waimalu, HI (cdp) Honolulu County	504	3.67
Whittier, AK (city) Valdez-Cordova Census Area	8	3.64
Whitmore Village, HI (cdp) Honolulu County	158	3.51
Farnam, NE (village) Dawson County	6	3.51
Nikep, MD (cdp) Allegany County	4	3.45
Waikane, HI (cdp) Honolulu County	26	3.34
West Loch Estate, HI (cdp) Honolulu County	163	2.97
Kualapuu, HI (cdp) Maui County	57	2.81
Kawela Bay, HI (cdp) Honolulu County	9	2.73
Playas, NM (cdp) Hidalgo County	2	2.70
Ualapu'e, HI (cdp) Maui County	11	2.59
Reed Point, MT (cdp) Stillwater County	5	2.59
SeaTac, WA (city) King County	693	2.58
Fern Forest, HI (cdp) Hawaii County	24	2.58
Carson, CA (city) Los Angeles County	2,352	2.56
Urban Honolulu, HI (cdp) Honolulu County	8,520	2.53
Kaneohe, HI (cdp) Honolulu County	872	2.52
Northland, MN (township) Polk County	4	2.50
Pearl City, HI (cdp) Honolulu County	1,187	2.49
Bethany, IN (town) Morgan County	2	2.47
Waipio, HI (cdp) Honolulu County	287	2.46
Midland, WA (cdp) Pierce County	220	2.45
Haleiwa, HI (cdp) Honolulu County	97	2.44
Quitaque, TX (city) Briscoe County	10	2.43
Aiea, HI (cdp) Honolulu County	212	2.27
Waimea, HI (cdp) Kauai County	42	2.26
Waikele, HI (cdp) Honolulu County	165	2.21
Wintersburg, AZ (cdp) Maricopa County	3	2.21
Mililani Town, HI (cdp) Honolulu County	609	2.20
Adak, AK (city) Aleutians West Census Area	7	2.15
Hawaiian Beaches, HI (cdp) Hawaii County	91	2.13
Ahuimanu, HI (cdp) Honolulu County	187	2.12
Waialua, HI (cdp) Honolulu County	82	2.12
Nisqually Indian Community, WA (cdp) Thurston County	12	2.09
Shoal Creek Estates, MO (village) Newton County	2	2.08
Vernon, UT (town) Tooele County	5	2.06
Kahaluu, HI (cdp) Honolulu County	97	2.05
Nanawale Estates, HI (cdp) Hawaii County	29	2.03
Fort Bridger, WY (cdp) Uinta County	7	2.03
Ocean Pointe, HI (cdp) Honolulu County	169	2.02
Pahoa, HI (cdp) Hawaii County	19	2.01
Mountain View, HI (cdp) Hawaii County	78	1.99
Parkland, WA (cdp) Pierce County	708	1.98
Honomu, HI (cdp) Hawaii County	10	1.96
Kailua, HI (cdp) Hawaii County	230	1.92
Barrow, AK (city) North Slope Borough	81	1.92
Bobtown, VA (cdp) Accomack County	4	1.90
Fife, WA (city) Pierce County	173	1.89
West Valley City, UT (city) Salt Lake County	2,413	1.86
Stony River, AK (cdp) Bethel Census Area	1	1.85
Kalaoa, HI (cdp) Hawaii County	175	1.81
Rockville, MO (city) Bates County	3	1.81
Anchorage, AK (municipality) Anchorage Municipality	5,202	1.78
Riverton, WA (cdp) King County	114	1.78
Baker, CA (cdp) San Bernardino County	13	1.77
Tukwila, WA (city) King County	333	1.74
Hickam Housing, HI (cdp) Honolulu County	119	1.72
Kekaha, HI (cdp) Kauai County	61	1.72
Algona, WA (city) King County	51	1.69
Copperton, UT (cdp) Salt Lake County	14	1.69
Arimo, ID (city) Bannock County	6	1.69
Des Moines, WA (city) King County	496	1.67
Unalaska, AK (city) Aleutians West Census Area	73	1.67
Folden, MN (township) Otter Tail County	5	1.67
Kaunakakai, HI (cdp) Maui County	57	1.66
Federal Way, WA (city) King County	1,459	1.63
Boulevard Park, WA (cdp) King County	86	1.63
Naalehu, HI (cdp) Hawaii County	14	1.62
Princeton, SC (cdp) Laurens County	1	1.61
Sereno del Mar, CA (cdp) Sonoma County	2	1.59
White Center, WA (cdp) King County	212	1.57
Olean, MO (town) Miller County	2	1.56
Volcano, HI (cdp) Hawaii County	40	1.55
Sharpsburg, KY (city) Bath County	5	1.55
Kearns, UT (cdp) Salt Lake County	549	1.54
Arlington, OR (city) Gilliam County	9	1.54
East Palo Alto, CA (city) San Mateo County	430	1.53
Kailua, HI (cdp) Honolulu County	569	1.47
Hawaiian Paradise Park, HI (cdp) Hawaii County	164	1.44
Delhi, MN (city) Redwood County	1	1.43
Lakewood, WA (city) Pierce County	826	1.42
Waikoloa Village, HI (cdp) Hawaii County	90	1.41
Kanarraville, UT (town) Iron County	5	1.41
Spanaway, WA (cdp) Pierce County	382	1.40
Fort Garland, CO (cdp) Costilla County	6	1.39
Gentry, MO (village) Gentry County	1	1.39
Ainaloa, HI (cdp) Hawaii County	41	1.38
West Carson, CA (cdp) Los Angeles County	293	1.35
Herlong, CA (cdp) Lassen County	4	1.34
Taylorsville, UT (city) Salt Lake County	782	1.33
Keaau, HI (cdp) Hawaii County	30	1.33
Maunaloa, HI (cdp) Maui County	5	1.33
Waihee-Waiehu, HI (cdp) Maui County	116	1.31
Wainaku, HI (cdp) Hawaii County	16	1.31
Marina, CA (city) Monterey County	256	1.30
Keokea, HI (cdp) Maui County	21	1.30
Alborn, MN (township) St. Louis County	6	1.30
Heeia, HI (cdp) Honolulu County	64	1.29
Chignik Lagoon, AK (cdp) Lake and Peninsula Borough	1	1.28
Fern Acres, HI (cdp) Hawaii County	19	1.26
Pacific, WA (city) King County	82	1.24
Hawaiian Ocean View, HI (cdp) Hawaii County	54	1.22
Rawls Springs, MS (cdp) Forrest County	15	1.20
Graham, MN (township) Benton County	7	1.20
Twentynine Palms, CA (city) San Bernardino County	299	1.19
Launiupoko, HI (cdp) Maui County	7	1.19
Frederickson, WA (cdp) Pierce County	220	1.18
Kent, WA (city) King County	1,079	1.17
Anahola, HI (cdp) Kauai County	26	1.17
Kahului, HI (cdp) Maui County	306	1.16
Arrow Point, MO (village) Barry County	1	1.16
Burien, WA (city) King County	384	1.15
Hawaiian Acres, HI (cdp) Hawaii County	31	1.15
Allenhurst, GA (city) Liberty County	8	1.15
Mahinahina, HI (cdp) Maui County	10	1.14
Signal Hill, CA (city) Los Angeles County	125	1.13
Waimea, HI (cdp) Hawaii County	104	1.13
Hilo, HI (cdp) Hawaii County	486	1.12
Lahaina, HI (cdp) Maui County	130	1.11
Rader Creek, MT (cdp) Jefferson County	4	1.10
Redwood Falls, MN (township) Redwood County	2	1.10

Race

Hawaii Native/Pacific Islander: Samoan

Top 150 Places Sorted by Percent of Total Population

Based on places with total population of 7,500 or more

Place	Population	%
Nanakuli, HI (cdp) Honolulu County	1,602	12.65
Maili, HI (cdp) Honolulu County	917	9.66
Makaha, HI (cdp) Honolulu County	630	7.61
Waipahu, HI (cdp) Honolulu County	2,831	7.41
Waianae, HI (cdp) Honolulu County	963	7.31
Ewa Beach, HI (cdp) Honolulu County	1,058	7.07
Halawa, HI (cdp) Honolulu County	952	6.79
Makakilo, HI (cdp) Honolulu County	976	5.35
Wahiawa, HI (cdp) Honolulu County	935	5.25
Kapolei, HI (cdp) Honolulu County	755	4.97
Ewa Gentry, HI (cdp) Honolulu County	1,030	4.54
Royal Kunia, HI (cdp) Honolulu County	619	4.26
Waimalu, HI (cdp) Honolulu County	504	3.67
SeaTac, WA (city) King County	693	2.58
Carson, CA (city) Los Angeles County	2,352	2.56
Urban Honolulu, HI (cdp) Honolulu County	8,520	2.53
Kaneohe, HI (cdp) Honolulu County	872	2.52
Pearl City, HI (cdp) Honolulu County	1,187	2.49
Waipio, HI (cdp) Honolulu County	287	2.46
Midland, WA (cdp) Pierce County	220	2.45
Aiea, HI (cdp) Honolulu County	212	2.27
Mililani Town, HI (cdp) Honolulu County	609	2.20
Ahuimanu, HI (cdp) Honolulu County	187	2.12
Ocean Pointe, HI (cdp) Honolulu County	169	2.02
Parkland, WA (cdp) Pierce County	708	1.98
Kailua, HI (cdp) Hawaii County	230	1.92
Fife, WA (city) Pierce County	173	1.89
West Valley City, UT (city) Salt Lake County	2,413	1.86
Kalaoa, HI (cdp) Hawaii County	175	1.81
Anchorage, AK (municipality) Anchorage Municipality	5,202	1.78
Tukwila, WA (city) King County	333	1.74
Des Moines, WA (city) King County	496	1.67
Federal Way, WA (city) King County	1,459	1.63
White Center, WA (cdp) King County	212	1.57
Kearns, UT (cdp) Salt Lake County	549	1.54
East Palo Alto, CA (city) San Mateo County	430	1.53
Kailua, HI (cdp) Honolulu County	569	1.47
Hawaiian Paradise Park, HI (cdp) Hawaii County	164	1.44
Lakewood, WA (city) Pierce County	826	1.42
Spanaway, WA (cdp) Pierce County	382	1.40
West Carson, CA (cdp) Los Angeles County	293	1.35
Taylorsville, UT (city) Salt Lake County	782	1.33
Waihee-Waiehu, HI (cdp) Maui County	116	1.31
Marina, CA (city) Monterey County	256	1.30
Twentynine Palms, CA (city) San Bernardino County	299	1.19
Frederickson, WA (cdp) Pierce County	220	1.18
Kent, WA (city) King County	1,079	1.17
Kahului, HI (cdp) Maui County	306	1.16
Burien, WA (city) King County	384	1.15
Signal Hill, CA (city) Los Angeles County	125	1.13
Waimea, HI (cdp) Hawaii County	104	1.13
Hilo, HI (cdp) Hawaii County	486	1.12
Lahaina, HI (cdp) Maui County	130	1.11
Oceanside, CA (city) San Diego County	1,781	1.07
Mililani Mauka, HI (cdp) Honolulu County	223	1.06
Kihei, HI (cdp) Maui County	222	1.06
Wailuku, HI (cdp) Maui County	163	1.06
Lakeland North, WA (cdp) King County	136	1.05
West Jordan, UT (city) Salt Lake County	1,079	1.04
Magna, UT (cdp) Salt Lake County	274	1.03
Schofield Barracks, HI (cdp) Honolulu County	162	0.99
North Salt Lake, UT (city) Davis County	161	0.99
Long Beach, CA (city) Los Angeles County	4,513	0.98
San Bruno, CA (city) San Mateo County	403	0.98
Pukalani, HI (cdp) Maui County	70	0.92
Tacoma, WA (city) Pierce County	1,784	0.90
St. George, UT (city) Washington County	658	0.90
Lakeland South, WA (cdp) King County	97	0.84
Fort Lewis, WA (cdp) Pierce County	93	0.84
Independence, MO (city) Jackson County	940	0.80
The Dalles, OR (city) Wasco County	107	0.79
Kapaa, HI (cdp) Kauai County	84	0.79
Compton, CA (city) Los Angeles County	735	0.76
Eloy, AZ (city) Pinal County	124	0.75
Elk Plain, WA (cdp) Pierce County	106	0.75
South San Francisco, CA (city) San Mateo County	473	0.74
East Honolulu, HI (cdp) Honolulu County	367	0.74
Bryn Mawr-Skyway, WA (cdp) King County	115	0.74
Oronoko, MI (charter township) Berrien County	68	0.74
Shelton, WA (city) Mason County	72	0.73
East Hill-Meridian, WA (cdp) King County	215	0.72
East Rancho Dominguez, CA (cdp) Los Angeles County	106	0.70
Woods Cross, UT (city) Davis County	68	0.70
Hurricane, UT (city) Washington County	95	0.69
Barstow, CA (city) San Bernardino County	155	0.68
Patterson, CA (city) Stanislaus County	139	0.68
Holualoa, HI (cdp) Hawaii County	58	0.68
Orem, UT (city) Utah County	595	0.67
Lakewood, CA (city) Los Angeles County	534	0.67
Auburn, WA (city) King County	471	0.67
Paramount, CA (city) Los Angeles County	360	0.67
Bellflower, CA (city) Los Angeles County	507	0.66
Graham, WA (cdp) Pierce County	154	0.66
Provo, UT (city) Utah County	705	0.63
Fort Irwin, CA (cdp) San Bernardino County	55	0.62
Vista, CA (city) San Diego County	572	0.61
South Hill, WA (cdp) Pierce County	322	0.61
Hayward, CA (city) Alameda County	859	0.60
Daly City, CA (city) San Mateo County	603	0.60
La Presa, CA (cdp) San Diego County	205	0.60
Salt Lake City, UT (city) Salt Lake County	1,100	0.59
Lehi, UT (city) Utah County	281	0.59
Lawndale, CA (city) Los Angeles County	187	0.57
Ashland, CA (cdp) Alameda County	126	0.57
Taft, CA (city) Kern County	53	0.57
Washington, UT (city) Washington County	105	0.56
Highland, UT (city) Utah County	87	0.56
Cherryland, CA (cdp) Alameda County	83	0.56
Lacey, WA (city) Thurston County	229	0.54
Fort Hood, TX (cdp) Bell County	156	0.53
Saratoga Springs, UT (city) Utah County	95	0.53
Lemon Grove, CA (city) San Diego County	132	0.52
Hinesville, GA (city) Liberty County	171	0.51
Del Aire, CA (cdp) Los Angeles County	51	0.51
Eagle Mountain, UT (city) Utah County	107	0.50
Lindon, UT (city) Utah County	50	0.50
Lomita, CA (city) Los Angeles County	100	0.49
Bountiful, UT (city) Davis County	206	0.48
Newark, CA (city) Alameda County	198	0.47
Sumner, WA (city) Pierce County	44	0.47
Gardena, CA (city) Los Angeles County	269	0.46
Harker Heights, TX (city) Bell County	124	0.46
Loma Linda, CA (city) San Bernardino County	107	0.46
Garden Grove, CA (city) Orange County	760	0.44
Killeen, TX (city) Bell County	565	0.44
DuPont, WA (city) Pierce County	36	0.44
Renton, WA (city) King County	389	0.43
Cedar Hills, UT (city) Utah County	42	0.43
Pacifica, CA (city) San Mateo County	156	0.42
Pleasant Grove, UT (city) Utah County	142	0.42
Seaside, CA (city) Monterey County	138	0.42
Haiku-Pauwela, HI (cdp) Maui County	34	0.42
National City, CA (city) San Diego County	238	0.41
Bremerton, WA (city) Kitsap County	156	0.41
Vallejo, CA (city) Solano County	463	0.40
Spanish Fork, UT (city) Utah County	140	0.40
Midvale, UT (city) Salt Lake County	111	0.40
South Jordan, UT (city) Salt Lake County	195	0.39
Herriman, UT (city) Salt Lake County	84	0.39
Fairview, CA (cdp) Alameda County	39	0.39
Alum Rock, CA (cdp) Santa Clara County	59	0.38
Fort Drum, NY (cdp) Jefferson County	49	0.38
Stanton, CA (city) Orange County	141	0.37
Copperas Cove, TX (city) Coryell County	117	0.37
Fort Leonard Wood, MO (cdp) Pulaski County	56	0.37
Union City, CA (city) Alameda County	251	0.36
American Fork, UT (city) Utah County	95	0.36
Golden Valley, AZ (cdp) Mohave County	30	0.36
Paradise, NV (cdp) Clark County	791	0.35
Sandy, UT (city) Salt Lake County	301	0.34

Race

Hawaii Native/Pacific Islander: Tongan

U.S. and 50 States Sorted by Population and Percent of Total Population

Place	Population	%
United States	**57,183**	**0.02**
California	22,893	0.06
Utah	13,235	0.48
Hawaii	8,085	0.59
Texas	2,287	0.01
Washington	1,934	0.03
Arizona	1,792	0.03
Nevada	1,590	0.06
Oregon	1,006	0.03
Alaska	762	0.11
Florida	683	<0.01
Colorado	397	0.01
Idaho	311	0.02
Missouri	156	<0.01
New York	138	<0.01
Virginia	138	<0.01
Pennsylvania	137	<0.01
North Carolina	123	<0.01
Indiana	114	<0.01
Michigan	108	<0.01
Minnesota	100	<0.01
Georgia	93	<0.01
Illinois	82	<0.01
Ohio	81	<0.01
Maryland	74	<0.01
Massachusetts	64	<0.01
South Carolina	61	<0.01
Tennessee	59	<0.01
Kansas	58	<0.01
Oklahoma	58	<0.01
Wisconsin	55	<0.01
Iowa	50	<0.01
New Mexico	50	<0.01
South Dakota	46	0.01
Louisiana	46	<0.01
Kentucky	42	<0.01
Montana	37	<0.01
Arkansas	34	<0.01
Wyoming	32	0.01
New Jersey	27	<0.01
Nebraska	25	<0.01
Alabama	18	<0.01
West Virginia	17	<0.01
Mississippi	16	<0.01
North Dakota	15	<0.01
Connecticut	12	<0.01
Delaware	12	<0.01
Rhode Island	10	<0.01
New Hampshire	8	<0.01
Maine	6	<0.01
District of Columbia	5	<0.01
Vermont	1	<0.01

Place	Population	%
Hawaii	8,085	0.59
Utah	13,235	0.48
Alaska	762	0.11
California	22,893	0.06
Nevada	1,590	0.06
Washington	1,934	0.03
Arizona	1,792	0.03
Oregon	1,006	0.03
United States	**57,183**	**0.02**
Idaho	311	0.02
Texas	2,287	0.01
Colorado	397	0.01
South Dakota	46	0.01
Wyoming	32	0.01
Florida	683	<0.01
Missouri	156	<0.01
New York	138	<0.01
Virginia	138	<0.01
Pennsylvania	137	<0.01
North Carolina	123	<0.01
Indiana	114	<0.01
Michigan	108	<0.01
Minnesota	100	<0.01
Georgia	93	<0.01
Illinois	82	<0.01
Ohio	81	<0.01
Maryland	74	<0.01
Massachusetts	64	<0.01
South Carolina	61	<0.01
Tennessee	59	<0.01
Kansas	58	<0.01
Oklahoma	58	<0.01
Wisconsin	55	<0.01
Iowa	50	<0.01
New Mexico	50	<0.01
Louisiana	46	<0.01
Kentucky	42	<0.01
Montana	37	<0.01
Arkansas	34	<0.01
New Jersey	27	<0.01
Nebraska	25	<0.01
Alabama	18	<0.01
West Virginia	17	<0.01
Mississippi	16	<0.01
North Dakota	15	<0.01
Connecticut	12	<0.01
Delaware	12	<0.01
Rhode Island	10	<0.01
New Hampshire	8	<0.01
Maine	6	<0.01
District of Columbia	5	<0.01
Vermont	1	<0.01

Please refer to the Explanation of Data in the front of the book for more detailed information.

Race

Hawaii Native/Pacific Islander: Tongan

Top 150 Places Sorted by Population

Based on all places, regardless of total population

Place	Population	%
Salt Lake City, UT (city) Salt Lake County	2,940	1.58
West Valley City, UT (city) Salt Lake County	2,362	1.82
Urban Honolulu, HI (cdp) Honolulu County	1,723	0.51
East Palo Alto, CA (city) San Mateo County	1,526	5.42
Oakland, CA (city) Alameda County	1,463	0.37
Sacramento, CA (city) Sacramento County	1,382	0.30
San Mateo, CA (city) San Mateo County	1,324	1.36
Euless, TX (city) Tarrant County	885	1.73
West Jordan, UT (city) Salt Lake County	818	0.79
Hayward, CA (city) Alameda County	719	0.50
Mesa, AZ (city) Maricopa County	705	0.16
Provo, UT (city) Utah County	680	0.60
Hawthorne, CA (city) Los Angeles County	656	0.78
Los Angeles, CA (city) Los Angeles County	649	0.02
San Bruno, CA (city) San Mateo County	612	1.49
Taylorsville, UT (city) Salt Lake County	539	0.92
Redwood City, CA (city) San Mateo County	539	0.70
Anchorage, AK (municipality) Anchorage Municipality	527	0.18
San Jose, CA (city) Santa Clara County	526	0.06
Orem, UT (city) Utah County	509	0.58
Portland, OR (city) Multnomah County	497	0.09
Reno, NV (city) Washoe County	494	0.22
Laie, HI (cdp) Honolulu County	484	7.89
Kihei, HI (cdp) Maui County	437	2.09
Kearns, UT (cdp) Salt Lake County	434	1.21
Sandy, UT (city) Salt Lake County	404	0.46
Kahuku, HI (cdp) Honolulu County	398	15.23
Phoenix, AZ (city) Maricopa County	385	0.03
Concord, CA (city) Contra Costa County	380	0.31
Long Beach, CA (city) Los Angeles County	371	0.08
Lahaina, HI (cdp) Maui County	328	2.80
Waipahu, HI (cdp) Honolulu County	327	0.86
Menlo Park, CA (city) San Mateo County	326	1.02
South Jordan, UT (city) Salt Lake County	324	0.64
Kahului, HI (cdp) Maui County	316	1.20
Riverside, CA (city) Riverside County	281	0.09
Magna, UT (cdp) Salt Lake County	274	1.03
Hauula, HI (cdp) Honolulu County	270	6.51
Anaheim, CA (city) Orange County	259	0.08
South San Francisco, CA (city) San Mateo County	250	0.39
Fort Worth, TX (city) Tarrant County	250	0.03
Millcreek, UT (cdp) Salt Lake County	241	0.39
Ontario, CA (city) San Bernardino County	237	0.14
Pittsburg, CA (city) Contra Costa County	235	0.37
Antioch, CA (city) Contra Costa County	226	0.22
Inglewood, CA (city) Los Angeles County	221	0.20
San Francisco, CA (city) San Francisco County	220	0.03
Seattle, WA (city) King County	215	0.04
Bountiful, UT (city) Davis County	211	0.50
Mountain View, CA (city) Santa Clara County	202	0.27
Rancho Cucamonga, CA (city) San Bernardino County	195	0.12
Napili-Honokowai, HI (cdp) Maui County	192	2.64
Fremont, CA (city) Alameda County	192	0.09
Lehi, UT (city) Utah County	189	0.40
Stockton, CA (city) San Joaquin County	188	0.06
Moreno Valley, CA (city) Riverside County	187	0.10
Sunnyvale, CA (city) Santa Clara County	186	0.13
Sparks, NV (city) Washoe County	184	0.20
San Diego, CA (city) San Diego County	180	0.01
Riverton, UT (city) Salt Lake County	177	0.46
Fontana, CA (city) San Bernardino County	176	0.09
Kaneohe, HI (cdp) Honolulu County	175	0.51
Hilo, HI (cdp) Hawaii County	172	0.40
Newark, CA (city) Alameda County	172	0.40
Lawndale, CA (city) Los Angeles County	170	0.52
Union City, CA (city) Alameda County	168	0.24
Spanish Fork, UT (city) Utah County	165	0.48
St. George, UT (city) Washington County	165	0.23
Aurora, CO (city) Arapahoe County	162	0.05
North Fair Oaks, CA (cdp) San Mateo County	157	1.07
Federal Way, WA (city) King County	155	0.17
Lennox, CA (cdp) Los Angeles County	154	0.68
San Bernardino, CA (city) San Bernardino County	151	0.07
Henderson, NV (city) Clark County	144	0.06
Santa Clara, CA (city) Santa Clara County	140	0.12
Kailua, HI (cdp) Honolulu County	133	0.34
Vallejo, CA (city) Solano County	133	0.11
Elk Grove, CA (city) Sacramento County	133	0.09
Las Vegas, NV (city) Clark County	133	0.02
South Salt Lake, UT (city) Salt Lake County	132	0.56
Seaside, CA (city) Monterey County	130	0.39
Bedford, TX (city) Tarrant County	130	0.28
Richmond, CA (city) Contra Costa County	130	0.13
Castro Valley, CA (cdp) Alameda County	129	0.21
Belmont, CA (city) San Mateo County	128	0.50
Kailua, HI (cdp) Hawaii County	122	1.02
Kent, WA (city) King County	122	0.13
Ewa Beach, HI (cdp) Honolulu County	121	0.81
North Salt Lake, UT (city) Davis County	120	0.74
Florin, CA (cdp) Sacramento County	119	0.25
Pearl City, HI (cdp) Honolulu County	119	0.25
Midvale, UT (city) Salt Lake County	114	0.41
Kalaoa, HI (cdp) Hawaii County	113	1.17
Paradise, NV (cdp) Clark County	112	0.05
Wailuku, HI (cdp) Maui County	111	0.72
Gilbert, AZ (town) Maricopa County	111	0.05
Kapaa, HI (cdp) Kauai County	110	1.03
Wahiawa, HI (cdp) Honolulu County	109	0.61
San Leandro, CA (city) Alameda County	109	0.13
Millbrae, CA (city) San Mateo County	107	0.50
Springville, UT (city) Utah County	105	0.36
Tooele, UT (city) Tooele County	104	0.33
Santa Ana, CA (city) Orange County	104	0.03
Logan, UT (city) Cache County	103	0.21
Ogden, UT (city) Weber County	103	0.12
Saratoga Springs, UT (city) Utah County	101	0.57
Layton, UT (city) Davis County	101	0.15
Murray, UT (city) Salt Lake County	100	0.21
Juneau, AK (borough) Juneau City and Borough	99	0.32
Nanakuli, HI (cdp) Honolulu County	98	0.77
Tracy, CA (city) San Joaquin County	97	0.12
Cherryland, CA (cdp) Alameda County	95	0.65
SeaTac, WA (city) King County	95	0.35
Draper, UT (city) Salt Lake County	94	0.22
Tacoma, WA (city) Pierce County	94	0.05
Pleasant Grove, UT (city) Utah County	93	0.28
Ewa Gentry, HI (cdp) Honolulu County	91	0.40
San Tan Valley, AZ (cdp) Pinal County	90	0.11
Holladay, UT (city) Salt Lake County	89	0.34
Eagle Mountain, UT (city) Utah County	88	0.41
Makakilo, HI (cdp) Honolulu County	87	0.48
Nampa, ID (city) Canyon County	87	0.11
Palo Alto, CA (city) Santa Clara County	85	0.13
Adelanto, CA (city) San Bernardino County	83	0.26
Waianae, HI (cdp) Honolulu County	82	0.62
Bellflower, CA (city) Los Angeles County	81	0.11
Waihee-Waiehu, HI (cdp) Maui County	80	0.90
Victorville, CA (city) San Bernardino County	80	0.07
Sunrise Manor, NV (cdp) Clark County	78	0.04
Makaha, HI (cdp) Honolulu County	76	0.92
American Fork, UT (city) Utah County	76	0.29
Arden-Arcade, CA (cdp) Sacramento County	74	0.08
Norwalk, CA (city) Los Angeles County	74	0.07
Hurst, TX (city) Tarrant County	72	0.19
Chula Vista, CA (city) San Diego County	72	0.03
Patterson, CA (city) Stanislaus County	71	0.35
Burien, WA (city) King County	71	0.21
East Honolulu, HI (cdp) Honolulu County	70	0.14
Tempe, AZ (city) Maricopa County	70	0.04
Eastvale, CA (cdp) Riverside County	69	0.13
Pacifica, CA (city) San Mateo County	68	0.18
Arlington, TX (city) Tarrant County	67	0.02
Sun Valley, NV (cdp) Washoe County	66	0.34
San Lorenzo, CA (cdp) Alameda County	66	0.28
Rialto, CA (city) San Bernardino County	66	0.07
New York, NY (city) Kings County	66	<0.01
Bay Point, CA (cdp) Contra Costa County	65	0.30
Salinas, CA (city) Monterey County	65	0.04
Waimanalo, HI (cdp) Honolulu County	64	1.17
Antelope, CA (cdp) Sacramento County	63	0.14

SECTION THREE

Please refer to the Explanation of Data in the front of the book for more detailed information.

Race

Hawaii Native/Pacific Islander: Tongan

Top 150 Places Sorted by Percent of Total Population

Based on all places, regardless of total population

Place	Population	%
Kahuku, HI (cdp) Honolulu County	398	15.23
Kalaeloa, HI (cdp) Honolulu County	6	12.50
Laie, HI (cdp) Honolulu County	484	7.89
Hauula, HI (cdp) Honolulu County	270	6.51
East Palo Alto, CA (city) San Mateo County	1,526	5.42
Kapalua, HI (cdp) Maui County	15	4.25
Bluebell, UT (cdp) Duchesne County	12	4.10
Lahaina, HI (cdp) Maui County	328	2.80
Napili-Honokowai, HI (cdp) Maui County	192	2.64
Glennallen, AK (cdp) Valdez-Cordova Census Area	11	2.28
Kihei, HI (cdp) Maui County	437	2.09
Mahinahina, HI (cdp) Maui County	18	2.05
Koosharem, UT (town) Sevier County	6	1.83
West Valley City, UT (city) Salt Lake County	2,362	1.82
Kaaawa, HI (cdp) Honolulu County	25	1.81
Tabiona, UT (town) Duchesne County	3	1.75
Euless, TX (city) Tarrant County	885	1.73
Palmyra, UT (cdp) Utah County	8	1.63
Salt Lake City, UT (city) Salt Lake County	2,940	1.58
San Bruno, CA (city) San Mateo County	612	1.49
Halaula, HI (cdp) Hawaii County	7	1.49
Hana, HI (cdp) Maui County	17	1.38
San Mateo, CA (city) San Mateo County	1,324	1.36
Anahola, HI (cdp) Kauai County	30	1.35
Kearns, UT (cdp) Salt Lake County	434	1.21
Waikapu, HI (cdp) Maui County	36	1.21
Kahului, HI (cdp) Maui County	316	1.20
Alamo, NV (cdp) Lincoln County	13	1.20
Kalaoa, HI (cdp) Hawaii County	113	1.17
Waimanalo, HI (cdp) Honolulu County	64	1.17
Kaanapali, HI (cdp) Maui County	12	1.15
North Fair Oaks, CA (cdp) San Mateo County	157	1.07
Haliimaile, HI (cdp) Maui County	10	1.04
Highland Beach, MD (town) Anne Arundel County	1	1.04
Magna, UT (cdp) Salt Lake County	274	1.03
Kapaa, HI (cdp) Kauai County	110	1.03
Punaluu, HI (cdp) Honolulu County	12	1.03
Menlo Park, CA (city) San Mateo County	326	1.02
Kailua, HI (cdp) Hawaii County	122	1.02
Orchidlands Estates, HI (cdp) Hawaii County	27	0.96
Taylorsville, UT (city) Salt Lake County	539	0.92
Makaha, HI (cdp) Honolulu County	76	0.92
Waihee-Waiehu, HI (cdp) Maui County	80	0.90
Barrow, AK (city) North Slope Borough	38	0.90
Waikane, HI (cdp) Honolulu County	7	0.90
Briarcliffe Acres, SC (town) Horry County	4	0.88
Waipahu, HI (cdp) Honolulu County	327	0.86
Puhi, HI (cdp) Kauai County	25	0.86
Verdi, NV (cdp) Washoe County	12	0.85
Kurtistown, HI (cdp) Hawaii County	11	0.85
Launiupoko, HI (cdp) Maui County	5	0.85
Bunkerville, NV (cdp) Clark County	11	0.84
Elk Ridge, UT (city) Utah County	20	0.82
Ewa Beach, HI (cdp) Honolulu County	121	0.81
West Jordan, UT (city) Salt Lake County	818	0.79
Loomis, NE (village) Phelps County	3	0.79
Hawthorne, CA (city) Los Angeles County	656	0.78
Kahaluu, HI (cdp) Honolulu County	37	0.78
Nanakuli, HI (cdp) Honolulu County	98	0.77
North Salt Lake, UT (city) Davis County	120	0.74
Woodland Hills, UT (city) Utah County	10	0.74
Wailuku, HI (cdp) Maui County	111	0.72
Chateaugay, NY (village) Franklin County	6	0.72
Haleiwa, HI (cdp) Honolulu County	28	0.71
Redwood City, CA (city) San Mateo County	539	0.70
Honaunau-Napoopoo, HI (cdp) Hawaii County	18	0.70
Fremont, UT (cdp) Wayne County	1	0.69
Lennox, CA (cdp) Los Angeles County	154	0.68
Gorst, WA (cdp) Kitsap County	4	0.68
Wailua Homesteads, HI (cdp) Kauai County	35	0.67
Quail Ridge, FL (cdp) Pasco County	7	0.67
Metzger, OR (cdp) Washington County	25	0.66
Cherryland, CA (cdp) Alameda County	95	0.65
Ephraim, UT (city) Sanpete County	40	0.65
Hanamaulu, HI (cdp) Kauai County	25	0.65

Place	Population	%
Alborn, MN (township) St. Louis County	3	0.65
South Jordan, UT (city) Salt Lake County	324	0.64
Eden Roc, HI (cdp) Hawaii County	6	0.64
Pahoa, HI (cdp) Hawaii County	6	0.63
Waianae, HI (cdp) Honolulu County	82	0.62
Wahiawa, HI (cdp) Honolulu County	109	0.61
Provo, UT (city) Utah County	680	0.60
Woods Cross, UT (city) Davis County	59	0.60
Kukuihaele, HI (cdp) Hawaii County	2	0.60
Maili, HI (cdp) Honolulu County	56	0.59
Lihue, HI (cdp) Kauai County	38	0.59
Orem, UT (city) Utah County	509	0.58
Makawao, HI (cdp) Maui County	42	0.58
Saratoga Springs, UT (city) Utah County	101	0.57
Granite, UT (cdp) Salt Lake County	11	0.57
South Salt Lake, UT (city) Salt Lake County	132	0.56
Hawaiian Acres, HI (cdp) Hawaii County	15	0.56
Kualapuu, HI (cdp) Maui County	11	0.54
Iroquois Point, HI (cdp) Honolulu County	18	0.53
Staatsburg, NY (cdp) Dutchess County	2	0.53
Lawndale, CA (city) Los Angeles County	170	0.52
Del Aire, CA (cdp) Los Angeles County	52	0.52
Rough and Ready, CA (cdp) Nevada County	5	0.52
Lyons, MN (township) Wadena County	1	0.52
Urban Honolulu, HI (cdp) Honolulu County	1,723	0.51
Kaneohe, HI (cdp) Honolulu County	175	0.51
Boulevard Park, WA (cdp) King County	27	0.51
Hayward, CA (city) Alameda County	719	0.50
Bountiful, UT (city) Davis County	211	0.50
Belmont, CA (city) San Mateo County	128	0.50
Millbrae, CA (city) San Mateo County	107	0.50
Ahuimanu, HI (cdp) Honolulu County	43	0.49
Hawaiian Beaches, HI (cdp) Hawaii County	21	0.49
Spanish Fork, UT (city) Utah County	165	0.48
Makakilo, HI (cdp) Honolulu County	87	0.48
Riverton, WA (cdp) King County	31	0.48
Heeia, HI (cdp) Honolulu County	24	0.48
Kekaha, HI (cdp) Kauai County	17	0.48
Waiohinu, HI (cdp) Hawaii County	1	0.47
Sandy, UT (city) Salt Lake County	404	0.46
Riverton, UT (city) Salt Lake County	177	0.46
Hawaiian Paradise Park, HI (cdp) Hawaii County	52	0.46
White City, UT (cdp) Salt Lake County	25	0.46
West Bountiful, UT (city) Davis County	24	0.46
Mountain View, CA (cdp) Contra Costa County	11	0.46
Hawi, HI (cdp) Hawaii County	5	0.46
Warm Springs, CA (cdp) Riverside County	12	0.45
Makaha Valley, HI (cdp) Honolulu County	6	0.45
Whittier, AK (city) Valdez-Cordova Census Area	1	0.45
Cove, UT (cdp) Cache County	2	0.43
Holualoa, HI (cdp) Hawaii County	36	0.42
Bluffdale, UT (city) Salt Lake County	32	0.42
Waipio Acres, HI (cdp) Honolulu County	22	0.42
Thorne Bay, AK (city) Prince of Wales-Hyder Census Area	2	0.42
Midvale, UT (city) Salt Lake County	114	0.41
Eagle Mountain, UT (city) Utah County	88	0.41
Royal Kunia, HI (cdp) Honolulu County	59	0.41
Osceola, IN (town) St. Joseph County	10	0.41
Lehi, UT (city) Utah County	189	0.40
Hilo, HI (cdp) Hawaii County	172	0.40
Newark, CA (city) Alameda County	172	0.40
Ewa Gentry, HI (cdp) Honolulu County	91	0.40
Elizabethtown, NY (cdp) Essex County	3	0.40
Kaumakani, HI (cdp) Kauai County	3	0.40
Merrill, IA (city) Plymouth County	3	0.40
Elmwood Park, WI (village) Racine County	2	0.40
Harrison, WI (town) Grant County	2	0.40
South San Francisco, CA (city) San Mateo County	250	0.39
Millcreek, UT (cdp) Salt Lake County	241	0.39
Seaside, CA (city) Monterey County	130	0.39
Mapleton, UT (city) Utah County	31	0.39
Samoset, FL (cdp) Manatee County	15	0.39
Golden Valley, NV (cdp) Washoe County	6	0.39
Lyman, UT (town) Wayne County	1	0.39
Mountain View, HI (cdp) Hawaii County	15	0.38

Please refer to the Explanation of Data in the front of the book for more detailed information.

Race

Hawaii Native/Pacific Islander: Tongan

Top 150 Places Sorted by Percent of Total Population

Based on places with total population of 7,500 or more

Place	Population	%
East Palo Alto, CA (city) San Mateo County	1,526	5.42
Lahaina, HI (cdp) Maui County	328	2.80
Kihei, HI (cdp) Maui County	437	2.09
West Valley City, UT (city) Salt Lake County	2,362	1.82
Euless, TX (city) Tarrant County	885	1.73
Salt Lake City, UT (city) Salt Lake County	2,940	1.58
San Bruno, CA (city) San Mateo County	612	1.49
San Mateo, CA (city) San Mateo County	1,324	1.36
Kearns, UT (cdp) Salt Lake County	434	1.21
Kahului, HI (cdp) Maui County	316	1.20
Kalaoa, HI (cdp) Hawaii County	113	1.17
North Fair Oaks, CA (cdp) San Mateo County	157	1.07
Magna, UT (cdp) Salt Lake County	274	1.03
Kapaa, HI (cdp) Kauai County	110	1.03
Menlo Park, CA (city) San Mateo County	326	1.02
Kailua, HI (cdp) Hawaii County	122	1.02
Taylorsville, UT (city) Salt Lake County	539	0.92
Makaha, HI (cdp) Honolulu County	76	0.92
Waihee-Waiehu, HI (cdp) Maui County	80	0.90
Waipahu, HI (cdp) Honolulu County	327	0.86
Ewa Beach, HI (cdp) Honolulu County	121	0.81
West Jordan, UT (city) Salt Lake County	818	0.79
Hawthorne, CA (city) Los Angeles County	656	0.78
Nanakuli, HI (cdp) Honolulu County	98	0.77
North Salt Lake, UT (city) Davis County	120	0.74
Wailuku, HI (cdp) Maui County	111	0.72
Redwood City, CA (city) San Mateo County	539	0.70
Lennox, CA (cdp) Los Angeles County	154	0.68
Cherryland, CA (cdp) Alameda County	95	0.65
South Jordan, UT (city) Salt Lake County	324	0.64
Waianae, HI (cdp) Honolulu County	82	0.62
Wahiawa, HI (cdp) Honolulu County	109	0.61
Provo, UT (city) Utah County	680	0.60
Woods Cross, UT (city) Davis County	59	0.60
Maili, HI (cdp) Honolulu County	56	0.59
Orem, UT (city) Utah County	509	0.58
Saratoga Springs, UT (city) Utah County	101	0.57
South Salt Lake, UT (city) Salt Lake County	132	0.56
Lawndale, CA (city) Los Angeles County	170	0.52
Del Aire, CA (cdp) Los Angeles County	52	0.52
Urban Honolulu, HI (cdp) Honolulu County	1,723	0.51
Kaneohe, HI (cdp) Honolulu County	175	0.51
Hayward, CA (city) Alameda County	719	0.50
Bountiful, UT (city) Davis County	211	0.50
Belmont, CA (city) San Mateo County	128	0.50
Millbrae, CA (city) San Mateo County	107	0.50
Ahuimanu, HI (cdp) Honolulu County	43	0.49
Spanish Fork, UT (city) Utah County	165	0.48
Makakilo, HI (cdp) Honolulu County	87	0.48
Sandy, UT (city) Salt Lake County	404	0.46
Riverton, UT (city) Salt Lake County	177	0.46
Hawaiian Paradise Park, HI (cdp) Hawaii County	52	0.46
Holualoa, HI (cdp) Hawaii County	36	0.42
Bluffdale, UT (city) Salt Lake County	32	0.42
Midvale, UT (city) Salt Lake County	114	0.41
Eagle Mountain, UT (city) Utah County	88	0.41
Royal Kunia, HI (cdp) Honolulu County	59	0.41
Lehi, UT (city) Utah County	189	0.40
Hilo, HI (cdp) Hawaii County	172	0.40
Newark, CA (city) Alameda County	172	0.40
Ewa Gentry, HI (cdp) Honolulu County	91	0.40
South San Francisco, CA (city) San Mateo County	250	0.39
Millcreek, UT (cdp) Salt Lake County	241	0.39
Seaside, CA (city) Monterey County	130	0.39
Mapleton, UT (city) Utah County	31	0.39
Oakland, CA (city) Alameda County	1,463	0.37
Pittsburg, CA (city) Contra Costa County	235	0.37
Highland, UT (city) Utah County	58	0.37
Springville, UT (city) Utah County	105	0.36
Lindon, UT (city) Utah County	36	0.36
SeaTac, WA (city) King County	95	0.35
Patterson, CA (city) Stanislaus County	71	0.35
Hyrum, UT (city) Cache County	27	0.35
Kailua, HI (cdp) Honolulu County	133	0.34
Holladay, UT (city) Salt Lake County	89	0.34
Sun Valley, NV (cdp) Washoe County	66	0.34
Tooele, UT (city) Tooele County	104	0.33
Pukalani, HI (cdp) Maui County	25	0.33
Juneau, AK (borough) Juneau City and Borough	99	0.32
Fairview, CA (cdp) Alameda County	32	0.32
Haiku-Pauwela, HI (cdp) Maui County	26	0.32
Concord, CA (city) Contra Costa County	380	0.31
Halawa, HI (cdp) Honolulu County	44	0.31
Sacramento, CA (city) Sacramento County	1,382	0.30
Bay Point, CA (cdp) Contra Costa County	65	0.30
American Fork, UT (city) Utah County	76	0.29
Marina, CA (city) Monterey County	58	0.29
Bedford, TX (city) Tarrant County	130	0.28
Pleasant Grove, UT (city) Utah County	93	0.28
San Lorenzo, CA (cdp) Alameda County	66	0.28
Mountain View, CA (city) Santa Clara County	202	0.27
Hurricane, UT (city) Washington County	37	0.27
Waipio, HI (cdp) Honolulu County	32	0.27
Alondra Park, CA (cdp) Los Angeles County	23	0.27
North Logan, UT (city) Cache County	22	0.27
Adelanto, CA (city) San Bernardino County	83	0.26
Tukwila, WA (city) King County	49	0.26
Lemon Hill, CA (cdp) Sacramento County	36	0.26
Florin, CA (cdp) Sacramento County	119	0.25
Pearl City, HI (cdp) Honolulu County	119	0.25
Herriman, UT (city) Salt Lake County	54	0.25
Aiea, HI (cdp) Honolulu County	23	0.25
Union City, CA (city) Alameda County	168	0.24
St. George, UT (city) Washington County	165	0.23
El Sobrante, CA (cdp) Contra Costa County	29	0.23
Reno, NV (city) Washoe County	494	0.22
Antioch, CA (city) Contra Costa County	226	0.22
Draper, UT (city) Salt Lake County	94	0.22
Watauga, TX (city) Tarrant County	51	0.22
Ashland, CA (cdp) Alameda County	48	0.22
Kapolei, HI (cdp) Honolulu County	34	0.22
White Center, WA (cdp) King County	30	0.22
Smithfield, UT (city) Cache County	21	0.22
Castro Valley, CA (cdp) Alameda County	129	0.21
Logan, UT (city) Cache County	103	0.21
Murray, UT (city) Salt Lake County	100	0.21
Burien, WA (city) King County	71	0.21
Inglewood, CA (city) Los Angeles County	221	0.20
Sparks, NV (city) Washoe County	184	0.20
Cedar City, UT (city) Iron County	59	0.20
Ocean Pointe, HI (cdp) Honolulu County	17	0.20
Hurst, TX (city) Tarrant County	72	0.19
Bryn Mawr-Skyway, WA (cdp) King County	29	0.19
Anchorage, AK (municipality) Anchorage Municipality	527	0.18
Pacifica, CA (city) San Mateo County	68	0.18
Federal Way, WA (city) King County	155	0.17
Rubidoux, CA (cdp) Riverside County	57	0.17
Des Moines, WA (city) King County	51	0.17
Burlingame, CA (city) San Mateo County	50	0.17
Payson, UT (city) Utah County	32	0.17
Waimalu, HI (cdp) Honolulu County	23	0.17
Hillsborough, CA (town) San Mateo County	18	0.17
Meadow Lakes, AK (cdp) Matanuska-Susitna Borough	13	0.17
Richland Hills, TX (city) Tarrant County	13	0.17
Mesa, AZ (city) Maricopa County	705	0.16
Cottonwood Heights, UT (city) Salt Lake County	55	0.16
East Hill-Meridian, WA (cdp) King County	48	0.16
Foster City, CA (city) San Mateo County	48	0.16
Parkway, CA (cdp) Sacramento County	23	0.16
Oak Hills, CA (cdp) San Bernardino County	14	0.16
Layton, UT (city) Davis County	101	0.15
San Carlos, CA (city) San Mateo County	42	0.15
Sitka, AK (borough) Sitka City and Borough	13	0.15
Ontario, CA (city) San Bernardino County	237	0.14
East Honolulu, HI (cdp) Honolulu County	70	0.14
Antelope, CA (cdp) Sacramento County	63	0.14
Vineyard, CA (cdp) Sacramento County	36	0.14
Farmington, UT (city) Davis County	26	0.14
Pinole, CA (city) Contra Costa County	25	0.14
Waimea, HI (cdp) Hawaii County	13	0.14

SECTION THREE

Please refer to the Explanation of Data in the front of the book for more detailed information.

Race

White

U.S. and 50 States Sorted by Population and Percent of Total Population

Place	Population	%
United States	**231,040,398**	**74.83**
California	22,953,374	61.61
Texas	18,276,506	72.68
Florida	14,488,435	77.06
New York	13,155,274	67.89
Pennsylvania	10,604,187	83.48
Ohio	9,751,547	84.53
Illinois	9,423,048	73.44
Michigan	8,006,969	81.01
North Carolina	6,697,465	70.24
New Jersey	6,210,995	70.64
Georgia	5,951,521	61.43
Virginia	5,681,937	71.02
Indiana	5,583,367	86.11
Washington	5,471,864	81.37
Massachusetts	5,400,458	82.48
Missouri	5,070,826	84.67
Tennessee	5,019,639	79.10
Wisconsin	4,995,836	87.85
Arizona	4,852,961	75.92
Minnesota	4,634,915	87.39
Colorado	4,240,231	84.31
Kentucky	3,878,336	89.38
Maryland	3,488,887	60.43
Oregon	3,337,309	87.11
Alabama	3,337,077	69.82
South Carolina	3,127,075	67.61
Oklahoma	2,906,285	77.47
Louisiana	2,895,868	63.88
Connecticut	2,846,192	79.63
Iowa	2,830,454	92.91
Kansas	2,468,364	86.51
Utah	2,447,583	88.56
Arkansas	2,296,665	78.76
Nevada	1,890,043	69.99
Mississippi	1,782,807	60.08
West Virginia	1,765,642	95.29
Nebraska	1,607,717	88.03
New Mexico	1,473,005	71.53
Idaho	1,432,824	91.40
Maine	1,284,877	96.73
New Hampshire	1,255,950	95.40
Montana	908,645	91.84
Rhode Island	882,280	83.82
South Dakota	715,167	87.84
Delaware	637,392	70.98
North Dakota	616,350	91.64
Vermont	606,588	96.94
Hawaii	564,323	41.49
Wyoming	522,739	92.75
Alaska	518,949	73.07
District of Columbia	243,650	40.49

Place	Population	%
Vermont	606,588	96.94
Maine	1,284,877	96.73
New Hampshire	1,255,950	95.40
West Virginia	1,765,642	95.29
Iowa	2,830,454	92.91
Wyoming	522,739	92.75
Montana	908,645	91.84
North Dakota	616,350	91.64
Idaho	1,432,824	91.40
Kentucky	3,878,336	89.38
Utah	2,447,583	88.56
Nebraska	1,607,717	88.03
Wisconsin	4,995,836	87.85
South Dakota	715,167	87.84
Minnesota	4,634,915	87.39
Oregon	3,337,309	87.11
Kansas	2,468,364	86.51
Indiana	5,583,367	86.11
Missouri	5,070,826	84.67
Ohio	9,751,547	84.53
Colorado	4,240,231	84.31
Rhode Island	882,280	83.82
Pennsylvania	10,604,187	83.48
Massachusetts	5,400,458	82.48
Washington	5,471,864	81.37
Michigan	8,006,969	81.01
Connecticut	2,846,192	79.63
Tennessee	5,019,639	79.10
Arkansas	2,296,665	78.76
Oklahoma	2,906,285	77.47
Florida	14,488,435	77.06
Arizona	4,852,961	75.92
United States	**231,040,398**	**74.83**
Illinois	9,423,048	73.44
Alaska	518,949	73.07
Texas	18,276,506	72.68
New Mexico	1,473,005	71.53
Virginia	5,681,937	71.02
Delaware	637,392	70.98
New Jersey	6,210,995	70.64
North Carolina	6,697,465	70.24
Nevada	1,890,043	69.99
Alabama	3,337,077	69.82
New York	13,155,274	67.89
South Carolina	3,127,075	67.61
Louisiana	2,895,868	63.88
California	22,953,374	61.61
Georgia	5,951,521	61.43
Maryland	3,488,887	60.43
Mississippi	1,782,807	60.08
Hawaii	564,323	41.49
District of Columbia	243,650	40.49

Please refer to the Explanation of Data in the front of the book for more detailed information.

Race

White

Top 150 Places Sorted by Population

Based on all places, regardless of total population

Place	Population	%
New York, NY (city) Kings County	3,797,402	46.45
Los Angeles, CA (city) Los Angeles County	2,031,586	53.57
Chicago, IL (city) Cook County	1,270,097	47.12
Brooklyn, NY (borough) Kings County	1,120,592	44.74
Houston, TX (city) Harris County	1,116,036	53.16
San Antonio, TX (city) Medina County	1,001,202	75.43
Phoenix, AZ (city) Maricopa County	995,467	68.86
Manhattan, NY (borough) New York County	956,864	60.34
Queens, NY (borough) Queens County	941,608	42.21
San Diego, CA (city) San Diego County	824,542	63.07
Philadelphia, PA (city) Philadelphia County	655,021	42.92
Dallas, TX (city) Dallas County	633,355	52.88
Austin, TX (city) Travis County	562,451	71.16
El Paso, TX (city) El Paso County	539,737	83.15
Hempstead, NY (town) Nassau County	532,650	70.11
Indianapolis, IN (city) Marion County	526,672	64.19
Jacksonville, FL (city) Duval County	507,456	61.75
Columbus, OH (city) Franklin County	505,454	64.22
Fort Worth, TX (city) Tarrant County	472,242	63.71
Portland, OR (city) Multnomah County	468,194	80.20
Seattle, WA (city) King County	449,536	73.86
San Jose, CA (city) Santa Clara County	442,231	46.75
Denver, CO (city) Denver County	433,792	72.28
Louisville-Jefferson County, KY (metro govt) Jefferson County	433,271	72.53
Bronx, NY (borough) Bronx County	427,659	30.88
San Francisco, CA (city) San Francisco County	420,823	52.26
Brookhaven, NY (town) Suffolk County	419,725	86.36
Albuquerque, NM (city) Bernalillo County	401,578	73.57
Oklahoma City, OK (city) Oklahoma County	388,546	66.99
Las Vegas, NV (city) Clark County	385,348	66.01
Tucson, AZ (city) Pima County	380,875	73.23
Charlotte, NC (city) Mecklenburg County	379,739	51.92
Nashville-Davidson, TN (metro govt) Davidson County	376,470	62.62
Mesa, AZ (city) Maricopa County	351,626	80.09
Staten Island, NY (borough) Richmond County	350,679	74.81
Boston, MA (city) Suffolk County	348,258	56.39
Colorado Springs, CO (city) El Paso County	346,511	83.21
Virginia Beach, VA (ind. city) Virginia Beach independent city	311,177	71.05
Omaha, NE (city) Douglas County	309,021	75.56
Miami, FL (city) Miami-Dade County	298,092	74.62
Wichita, KS (city) Sedgwick County	289,470	75.70
Kansas City, MO (city) Jackson County	284,126	61.80
Milwaukee, WI (city) Milwaukee County	282,615	47.51
Tulsa, OK (city) Tulsa County	264,373	67.46
Fresno, CA (city) Fresno County	263,929	53.36
Minneapolis, MN (city) Hennepin County	257,575	67.33
Islip, NY (town) Suffolk County	254,235	75.77
Corpus Christi, TX (city) Nueces County	253,562	83.08
Oyster Bay, NY (town) Nassau County	252,713	86.19
Washington, DC (city) District of Columbia	243,650	40.49
Raleigh, NC (city) Wake County	240,430	59.53
Sacramento, CA (city) Sacramento County	233,865	50.13
Long Beach, CA (city) Los Angeles County	231,897	50.17
Lexington-Fayette, KY (cons. govt) Fayette County	230,553	77.94
Lincoln, NE (city) Lancaster County	229,200	88.71
Arlington, TX (city) Tarrant County	225,760	61.78
Tampa, FL (city) Hillsborough County	219,680	65.44
Anchorage, AK (municipality) Anchorage Municipality	212,398	72.78
Aurora, CO (city) Arapahoe County	212,302	65.31
Bakersfield, CA (city) Kern County	211,351	60.82
Hialeah, FL (city) Miami-Dade County	211,188	94.00
Laredo, TX (city) Webb County	210,309	89.08
Henderson, NV (city) Clark County	208,655	80.96
Pittsburgh, PA (city) Allegheny County	208,065	68.06
Scottsdale, AZ (city) Maricopa County	198,503	91.31
Memphis, TN (city) Shelby County	196,701	30.41
Toledo, OH (city) Lucas County	195,953	68.23
Fort Wayne, IN (city) Allen County	194,759	76.77
Baltimore, MD (city) Baltimore city County	192,897	31.06
Madison, WI (city) Dane County	190,519	81.69
Anaheim, CA (city) Orange County	189,689	56.41
Spokane, WA (city) Spokane County	189,684	90.79
Boise City, ID (city) Ada County	188,702	91.75
Riverside, CA (city) Riverside County	184,386	60.68
St. Paul, MN (city) Ramsey County	181,147	63.55
Chandler, AZ (city) Maricopa County	180,690	76.52
Plano, TX (city) Collin County	180,479	69.46
Lubbock, TX (city) Lubbock County	178,875	77.92
Gilbert, AZ (town) Maricopa County	177,075	84.95
Reno, NV (city) Washoe County	175,322	77.84
Huntington, NY (town) Suffolk County	174,612	85.90
St. Petersburg, FL (city) Pinellas County	172,891	70.63
Atlanta, GA (city) Fulton County	166,869	39.73
North Hempstead, NY (town) Nassau County	166,538	73.58
Des Moines, IA (city) Polk County	161,365	79.32
Glendale, AZ (city) Maricopa County	161,331	71.16
Santa Ana, CA (city) Orange County	158,778	48.93
Babylon, NY (town) Suffolk County	157,336	73.66
Brownsville, TX (city) Cameron County	156,312	89.31
Cleveland, OH (city) Cuyahoga County	156,136	39.35
Arlington, VA (cdp) Arlington County	155,517	74.90
Huntington Beach, CA (city) Orange County	153,515	80.80
Cincinnati, OH (city) Hamilton County	152,515	51.36
Amarillo, TX (city) Potter County	151,640	79.52
Oakland, CA (city) Alameda County	151,162	38.69
Overland Park, KS (city) Johnson County	150,038	86.54
Springfield, MO (city) Christian County	146,257	91.70
St. Louis, MO (city) St. Louis city County	146,158	45.78
Salt Lake City, UT (city) Salt Lake County	145,969	78.29
Chesapeake, VA (ind. city) Chesapeake independent city	144,601	65.07
Glendale, CA (city) Los Angeles County	144,049	75.14
Orlando, FL (city) Orange County	143,262	60.12
Paradise, NV (cdp) Clark County	143,067	64.11
Chula Vista, CA (city) San Diego County	142,343	58.36
Tacoma, WA (city) Pierce County	142,044	71.60
Modesto, CA (city) Stanislaus County	140,979	70.08
Eugene, OR (city) Lane County	140,868	90.19
Knoxville, TN (city) Knox County	140,108	78.33
Cape Coral, FL (city) Lee County	139,231	90.23
Buffalo, NY (city) Erie County	138,013	52.82
Vancouver, WA (city) Clark County	137,927	85.25
Sioux Falls, SD (city) Minnehaha County	137,010	89.03
Garland, TX (city) Dallas County	136,442	60.14
Greensboro, NC (city) Guilford County	135,483	50.24
Fort Collins, CO (city) Larimer County	132,255	91.85
Santa Clarita, CA (city) Los Angeles County	132,184	74.97
Worcester, MA (city) Worcester County	131,504	72.64
Peoria, AZ (city) Yavapai County	130,783	84.89
Akron, OH (city) Summit County	129,298	64.94
Salem, OR (city) Marion County	128,226	82.92
Grand Rapids, MI (city) Kent County	128,050	68.10
Santa Rosa, CA (city) Sonoma County	126,600	75.44
Port St. Lucie, FL (city) St. Lucie County	126,189	76.66
Aurora, IL (city) Kane County	123,599	62.46
Tempe, AZ (city) Maricopa County	122,818	75.95
Lakewood, CO (city) Jefferson County	122,636	85.77
Stockton, CA (city) San Joaquin County	122,069	41.85
Winston-Salem, NC (city) Forsyth County	121,879	53.08
Norfolk, VA (ind. city) Norfolk independent city	121,016	49.84
Irving, TX (city) Dallas County	120,665	55.79
Irvine, CA (city) Orange County	117,576	55.36
New Orleans, LA (city) Orleans Parish	117,460	34.16
Oceanside, CA (city) San Diego County	117,020	70.04
Pasadena, TX (city) Harris County	116,045	77.86
Yonkers, NY (city) Westchester County	114,948	58.65
Cedar Rapids, IA (city) Linn County	114,533	90.66
Metairie, LA (cdp) Jefferson Parish	113,195	81.74
Sterling Heights, MI (city) Macomb County	112,990	87.12
North Las Vegas, NV (city) Clark County	112,539	51.87
Huntsville, AL (city) Madison County	112,214	62.30
Naperville, IL (city) DuPage County	111,144	78.35
McAllen, TX (city) Hidalgo County	111,011	85.47
Smithtown, NY (town) Suffolk County	111,000	94.23
Spring Valley, NV (cdp) Clark County	110,236	61.79
Rancho Cucamonga, CA (city) San Bernardino County	109,730	66.39
Warren, MI (city) Macomb County	108,186	80.70
Olathe, KS (city) Johnson County	107,898	85.72
Pembroke Pines, FL (city) Broward County	107,718	69.61
Tallahassee, FL (city) Leon County	107,544	59.29
Fort Lauderdale, FL (city) Broward County	106,175	64.15

Please refer to the Explanation of Data in the front of the book for more detailed information.

Race

White

Top 150 Places Sorted by Percent of Total Population

Based on all places, regardless of total population

Place	Population	%
Lilly, PA (borough) Cambria County	968	100.00
Dugger, IN (town) Sullivan County	920	100.00
Chapman, PA (township) Clinton County	848	100.00
Cottonwood, MN (township) Brown County	840	100.00
Middlebourne, WV (town) Tyler County	815	100.00
Washington, PA (township) Lawrence County	799	100.00
Houtzdale, PA (borough) Clearfield County	797	100.00
Scio, OH (village) Harrison County	763	100.00
Stratford, IA (city) Hamilton County	743	100.00
Morrill, MN (township) Morrison County	696	100.00
Stanton, IA (city) Montgomery County	689	100.00
Verdunville, WV (cdp) Logan County	687	100.00
Coffeen, IL (city) Montgomery County	685	100.00
Warner, WI (town) Clark County	669	100.00
Greenville, PA (township) Somerset County	668	100.00
Worden, WI (town) Clark County	666	100.00
Montgomery, MN (township) Le Sueur County	665	100.00
Eldred, PA (township) Warren County	650	100.00
Russia, OH (village) Shelby County	640	100.00
Allardt, TN (city) Fentress County	634	100.00
Noxen, PA (cdp) Wyoming County	633	100.00
Southampton, PA (township) Somerset County	630	100.00
Chester, MA (cdp) Hampden County	627	100.00
Putnam, NY (town) Washington County	609	100.00
Sutersville, PA (borough) Westmoreland County	605	100.00
Franklin, PA (township) Columbia County	595	100.00
Odessa, NY (village) Schuyler County	591	100.00
Gillford, MN (township) Wabasha County	572	100.00
Austin, PA (borough) Potter County	562	100.00
Stoutsville, OH (village) Fairfield County	560	100.00
Barclay, MN (township) Cass County	559	100.00
Bruno, WV (cdp) Logan County	544	100.00
Watson, PA (township) Lycoming County	537	100.00
Chatfield, MN (township) Fillmore County	531	100.00
Cairnbrook, PA (cdp) Somerset County	520	100.00
DeKalb Junction, NY (cdp) St. Lawrence County	519	100.00
Farina, IL (village) Fayette County	518	100.00
Canadohta Lake, PA (cdp) Crawford County	516	100.00
Newport, IN (town) Vermillion County	515	100.00
Goodrich, WI (town) Taylor County	510	100.00
Mesquite, TX (cdp) Starr County	505	100.00
Plymouth, IL (village) Hancock County	505	100.00
West Shenango, PA (township) Crawford County	504	100.00
Minnewaska, MN (township) Pope County	500	100.00
Hawthorn, PA (borough) Clarion County	494	100.00
Verona, OH (village) Preble County	494	100.00
Highland, PA (township) Elk County	492	100.00
Summerhill, PA (borough) Cambria County	490	100.00
North Bend, WI (town) Jackson County	488	100.00
Granite, MN (township) Morrison County	481	100.00
Crestview, KY (city) Campbell County	475	100.00
Barree, PA (township) Huntingdon County	469	100.00
Greeley Center, NE (village) Greeley County	466	100.00
Martensdale, IA (city) Warren County	465	100.00
Drummond, WI (town) Bayfield County	463	100.00
Scott, WI (town) Crawford County	462	100.00
Delhi, IA (city) Delaware County	460	100.00
Garrett, PA (borough) Somerset County	456	100.00
Broad Top City, PA (borough) Huntingdon County	452	100.00
Ramey, PA (borough) Clearfield County	451	100.00
Coloma, WI (village) Waushara County	450	100.00
Hillsboro, TN (cdp) Coffee County	450	100.00
Pinesburg, MD (cdp) Washington County	449	100.00
Wilkinson, IN (town) Hancock County	449	100.00
Clover, PA (township) Jefferson County	448	100.00
Lake, MN (township) Wabasha County	442	100.00
Spruce Hill, MN (township) Douglas County	441	100.00
Ewing, VA (cdp) Lee County	439	100.00
Delta, MO (city) Cape Girardeau County	438	100.00
Emerson, IA (city) Mills County	438	100.00
Portia, AR (town) Lawrence County	437	100.00
Herrick, IL (village) Shelby County	436	100.00
Goshen, PA (township) Clearfield County	435	100.00
McDermott, OH (cdp) Scioto County	434	100.00
Waynesville, IL (village) De Witt County	434	100.00

Place	Population	%
New Haven, IL (village) Gallatin County	433	100.00
Stony Run, MN (township) Yellow Medicine County	432	100.00
White Bear Lake, MN (township) Pope County	431	100.00
Hornbeak, TN (town) Obion County	424	100.00
Garceno, TX (cdp) Starr County	420	100.00
Harrod, OH (village) Allen County	417	100.00
Richland, MN (township) Rice County	416	100.00
Barrett, MN (city) Grant County	415	100.00
Bloom, PA (township) Clearfield County	414	100.00
Justice, WV (cdp) Mingo County	412	100.00
Morris, PA (township) Huntingdon County	410	100.00
Beallsville, OH (village) Monroe County	409	100.00
Strasburg, ND (city) Emmons County	409	100.00
Dowell, IL (village) Jackson County	408	100.00
Hanoverton, OH (village) Columbiana County	408	100.00
St. Michael, PA (cdp) Cambria County	408	100.00
Axtell, KS (city) Marshall County	406	100.00
Sparland, IL (village) Marshall County	406	100.00
Atlasburg, PA (cdp) Washington County	401	100.00
Freeburn, KY (cdp) Pike County	399	100.00
Aquadale, NC (cdp) Stanly County	397	100.00
Jackson, PA (township) Lycoming County	396	100.00
Vanleer, TN (town) Dickson County	395	100.00
London Mills, IL (village) Fulton County	392	100.00
Skanawan, WI (town) Lincoln County	391	100.00
Bascom, OH (cdp) Seneca County	390	100.00
Cedar Creek, NE (village) Cass County	390	100.00
Camargito, TX (cdp) Starr County	388	100.00
Ewing, NE (village) Holt County	387	100.00
James, MO (town) Moniteau County	386	100.00
Clifton, WI (town) Grant County	385	100.00
Troy, IN (town) Perry County	385	100.00
Gilman City, MO (city) Harrison County	383	100.00
Lynnville, IA (city) Jasper County	379	100.00
Pathfork, KY (cdp) Harlan County	379	100.00
Amherst Junction, WI (village) Portage County	377	100.00
Fayette, WI (town) Lafayette County	376	100.00
Carbon, PA (township) Huntingdon County	375	100.00
Jump River, WI (town) Taylor County	375	100.00
Mooreland, IN (town) Henry County	375	100.00
Chippewa, WI (town) Ashland County	374	100.00
Green Camp, OH (village) Marion County	374	100.00
Holy Cross, IA (city) Dubuque County	374	100.00
Neche, ND (city) Pembina County	371	100.00
Port Jefferson, OH (village) Shelby County	371	100.00
Arona, PA (borough) Westmoreland County	370	100.00
Freeport, OH (village) Harrison County	369	100.00
Berrysburg, PA (borough) Dauphin County	368	100.00
New Deal, TN (cdp) Sumner County	368	100.00
York, MN (township) Fillmore County	368	100.00
Lewisville, IN (town) Henry County	366	100.00
Wilton, MN (township) Waseca County	365	100.00
Medo, MN (township) Blue Earth County	364	100.00
Ellenboro, WV (town) Ritchie County	363	100.00
Lacona, IA (city) Warren County	361	100.00
Ryan, IA (city) Delaware County	361	100.00
Fairhaven, MN (cdp) Stearns County	358	100.00
Orient, IL (city) Franklin County	358	100.00
Wharton, OH (village) Wyandot County	358	100.00
Noyes, PA (township) Clinton County	357	100.00
Stoystown, PA (borough) Somerset County	355	100.00
Bloss, PA (township) Tioga County	353	100.00
Waltham, ME (town) Hancock County	353	100.00
Winesburg, OH (cdp) Holmes County	352	100.00
Pleasant View, KY (cdp) Whitley County	350	100.00
Roma Creek, TX (cdp) Starr County	350	100.00
Springhill, PA (township) Greene County	349	100.00
Conesville, OH (village) Coshocton County	347	100.00
Canton, MN (city) Fillmore County	346	100.00
Burleene, MN (township) Todd County	345	100.00
Sigel, MN (township) Brown County	344	100.00
Star City, IN (cdp) Pulaski County	344	100.00
Montgomery, IN (town) Daviess County	343	100.00
Blanford, IN (cdp) Vermillion County	342	100.00
Fisk, MO (city) Butler County	342	100.00

Please refer to the Explanation of Data in the front of the book for more detailed information.

Race

White

Top 150 Places Sorted by Percent of Total Population

Based on places with total population of 7,500 or more

Place	Population	%
Kiryas Joel, NY (village) Orange County	20,092	99.59
Elma, NY (town) Erie County	11,232	99.25
Mount Pleasant, PA (township) Westmoreland County	10,827	99.23
Louisville, OH (city) Stark County	9,112	99.19
Eidson Road, TX (cdp) Maverick County	8,887	99.19
Shelby, OH (city) Richland County	9,239	99.16
La Homa, TX (cdp) Hidalgo County	11,882	99.14
Boston, NY (town) Erie County	7,946	99.04
Roma, TX (city) Starr County	9,669	99.02
St. Marys, PA (city) Elk County	12,940	99.01
Barre, VT (town) Washington County	7,844	98.99
Putnam, MI (township) Livingston County	8,161	98.95
Clay, MI (township) St. Clair County	8,968	98.92
Jerseyville, IL (city) Jersey County	8,368	98.85
Mack, OH (cdp) Hamilton County	11,450	98.83
Waterloo, IL (city) Monroe County	9,695	98.82
Hamburg, NY (village) Erie County	9,297	98.81
West Deer, PA (township) Allegheny County	11,626	98.77
Barton, NY (town) Tioga County	8,748	98.76
Economy, PA (borough) Beaver County	8,858	98.75
Sand Lake, NY (town) Rensselaer County	8,423	98.75
Aurora, NY (town) Erie County	13,609	98.74
Galion, OH (city) Crawford County	10,380	98.74
Penn, PA (township) Westmoreland County	19,751	98.73
Weare, NH (town) Hillsborough County	8,673	98.73
Mooresville, IN (town) Morgan County	9,207	98.72
Allegheny, PA (township) Westmoreland County	8,059	98.71
New Franklin, OH (city) Summit County	14,036	98.66
Paris, IL (city) Edgar County	8,719	98.66
Lawrence, PA (township) Clearfield County	7,578	98.66
Vermilion, OH (city) Lorain County	10,450	98.64
Lehigh, PA (township) Northampton County	10,381	98.62
Hampstead, NH (town) Rockingham County	8,405	98.62
Hastings, NY (town) Oswego County	9,315	98.57
Livonia, NY (town) Livingston County	7,697	98.57
Farmington, ME (town) Franklin County	7,649	98.57
Alpena, MI (township) Alpena County	8,929	98.55
Stillwater, NY (town) Saratoga County	8,167	98.55
Dallas, PA (township) Luzerne County	8,863	98.54
Waterboro, ME (town) York County	7,581	98.54
Greenfield, NY (town) Saratoga County	7,659	98.51
Glocester, RI (town) Providence County	9,600	98.50
Dexter, MO (city) Stoddard County	7,746	98.50
New Ulm, MN (city) Brown County	13,318	98.49
Eden, NY (town) Erie County	7,572	98.49
Lancaster, NY (village) Erie County	10,194	98.47
Standish, ME (town) Cumberland County	9,723	98.47
Wells, ME (town) York County	9,442	98.47
The Villages, FL (cdp) Sumter County	50,651	98.46
North Huntingdon, PA (township) Westmoreland County	30,138	98.46
Highland, MI (charter township) Oakland County	18,907	98.46
Scituate, RI (town) Providence County	10,170	98.46
Warren, PA (city) Warren County	9,560	98.46
Micco, FL (cdp) Brevard County	8,913	98.46
Frankfort, NY (town) Herkimer County	7,518	98.45
Signal Mountain, TN (town) Hamilton County	7,437	98.45
Hamburg, MI (township) Livingston County	20,834	98.44
Westport, MA (town) Bristol County	15,289	98.44
Mayfield, MI (township) Lapeer County	7,831	98.44
Martinsville, IN (city) Morgan County	11,642	98.43
Monitor, MI (charter township) Bay County	10,566	98.43
Sandy, PA (township) Clearfield County	10,458	98.43
Marion, MI (township) Livingston County	9,839	98.43
Sullivan, NY (town) Madison County	15,096	98.42
Lisbon, WI (town) Waukesha County	9,995	98.41
North Madison, OH (cdp) Lake County	8,411	98.41
York, ME (town) York County	12,328	98.40
Alexandria, KY (city) Campbell County	8,341	98.40
Jackson, PA (township) Lebanon County	8,032	98.40
Harrison, OH (city) Hamilton County	9,738	98.39
Oconomowoc, WI (town) Waukesha County	8,273	98.39
Skowhegan, ME (town) Somerset County	8,450	98.38
Ash, MI (township) Monroe County	7,657	98.38
Milton, VT (town) Chittenden County	10,183	98.37
Moundsville, WV (city) Marshall County	9,166	98.37
Cohasset, MA (town) Norfolk County	7,419	98.37
Burrillville, RI (town) Providence County	15,694	98.36
Glenshaw, PA (cdp) Allegheny County	8,834	98.36
Somerset, MA (cdp/town) Bristol County	17,865	98.35
East Huntingdon, PA (township) Westmoreland County	7,832	98.35
Mukwonago, WI (town) Waukesha County	7,827	98.34
Raymond, NH (town) Rockingham County	9,969	98.33
Marysville, MI (city) St. Clair County	9,792	98.32
Gray, ME (town) Cumberland County	7,631	98.32
Halifax, MA (town) Plymouth County	7,392	98.32
Adams, MA (town) Berkshire County	8,342	98.31
Latrobe, PA (city) Westmoreland County	8,196	98.30
Handy, MI (township) Livingston County	7,869	98.29
Lower Burrell, PA (city) Westmoreland County	11,559	98.28
Berlin, NH (city) Coos County	9,878	98.28
Mount Washington, KY (city) Bullitt County	8,960	98.28
Bellevue, OH (city) Sandusky County	8,059	98.26
Columbia, IL (city) Monroe County	9,537	98.25
Swansea, MA (town) Bristol County	15,586	98.24
West Donegal, PA (township) Lancaster County	8,115	98.24
Winslow, ME (cdp/town) Kennebec County	7,657	98.24
Wapakoneta, OH (city) Auglaize County	9,692	98.23
Templeton, MA (town) Worcester County	7,871	98.23
Highland, IL (city) Madison County	9,742	98.22
Merton, WI (town) Waukesha County	8,190	98.22
Butler, PA (township) Butler County	16,940	98.21
Seymour, TN (cdp) Sevier County	10,724	98.21
Acushnet, MA (town) Bristol County	10,119	98.21
Center, PA (township) Butler County	7,757	98.21
Sun City West, AZ (cdp) Maricopa County	24,093	98.20
Holiday City-Berkeley, NJ (cdp) Ocean County	12,600	98.20
West Frankfort, IL (city) Franklin County	8,035	98.20
Fairview, PA (township) Erie County	9,919	98.19
Concord, NY (town) Erie County	8,340	98.19
Plaistow, NH (town) Rockingham County	7,471	98.19
Muskego, WI (city) Waukesha County	23,695	98.18
Norwalk, IA (city) Warren County	8,782	98.18
Ellicott, NY (town) Chautauqua County	8,555	98.18
Alpena, MI (city) Alpena County	10,291	98.17
Elwood, IN (city) Madison County	8,456	98.17
Buxton, ME (town) York County	7,887	98.17
St. Marys, OH (city) Auglaize County	8,179	98.16
Norway, WI (town) Racine County	7,802	98.16
Ellwood City, PA (borough) Lawrence County	7,775	98.16
Derry, PA (township) Westmoreland County	14,234	98.15
Sutton, MA (town) Worcester County	8,797	98.15
Woodstock, CT (town) Windham County	7,817	98.15
Shaler, PA (township) Allegheny County	28,219	98.13
Bloomingdale, TN (cdp) Sullivan County	9,703	98.13
Brazil, IN (city) Clay County	7,764	98.13
Englewood, FL (cdp) Sarasota County	14,582	98.11
Indianola, IA (city) Warren County	14,503	98.11
Oceola, MI (township) Livingston County	11,710	98.11
Columbia City, IN (city) Whitley County	8,585	98.11
Chippewa, PA (township) Beaver County	7,476	98.11
Kingsbury, NY (town) Washington County	12,430	98.10
Suamico, WI (village) Brown County	11,130	98.10
Bow, NH (town) Merrimack County	7,376	98.10
Marinette, WI (city) Marinette County	10,759	98.09
Moore, PA (township) Northampton County	9,022	98.09
Barrington, NH (town) Strafford County	8,412	98.09
Vernon, WI (town) Waukesha County	7,456	98.09
Trenton, OH (city) Butler County	11,640	98.07
Monson, MA (town) Hampden County	8,395	98.07
Lisbon, ME (town) Androscoggin County	8,833	98.05
Bay Village, OH (city) Cuyahoga County	15,344	98.04
Danville, IN (town) Hendricks County	8,824	98.03
Georgetown, MA (town) Essex County	8,022	98.03
Algoma, MI (township) Kent County	9,735	98.02
Douglas, MA (town) Worcester County	8,303	98.02
Unity, PA (township) Westmoreland County	22,157	98.01
Wadsworth, OH (city) Medina County	21,138	98.01
Mountain Home, AR (city) Baxter County	12,199	98.00
Kennebunk, ME (town) York County	10,582	98.00
Duxbury, MA (town) Plymouth County	14,757	97.99

SECTION THREE

Please refer to the Explanation of Data in the front of the book for more detailed information.

Race

White: Not Hispanic

U.S. and 50 States Sorted by Population and Percent of Total Population

Place	Population	%
United States	**201,856,108**	**65.38**
California	15,763,625	42.31
Texas	11,669,272	46.41
New York	11,534,988	59.53
Florida	11,115,250	59.12
Pennsylvania	10,248,965	80.69
Ohio	9,543,218	82.72
Illinois	8,324,628	64.88
Michigan	7,740,156	78.31
North Carolina	6,354,005	66.64
Georgia	5,535,598	57.14
Indiana	5,377,916	82.94
Virginia	5,341,329	66.76
New Jersey	5,315,821	60.46
Washington	5,097,076	75.80
Massachusetts	5,082,983	77.63
Missouri	4,947,306	82.61
Tennessee	4,882,031	76.93
Wisconsin	4,811,054	84.60
Minnesota	4,497,934	84.80
Kentucky	3,805,193	87.69
Arizona	3,795,629	59.38
Colorado	3,611,570	71.81
Maryland	3,257,918	56.43
Alabama	3,257,662	68.16
Oregon	3,107,886	81.12
South Carolina	3,017,747	65.24
Louisiana	2,782,654	61.38
Oklahoma	2,750,713	73.33
Iowa	2,739,834	89.94
Connecticut	2,595,143	72.61
Kansas	2,289,938	80.26
Utah	2,266,547	82.01
Arkansas	2,215,467	75.98
West Virginia	1,750,043	94.44
Mississippi	1,745,642	58.83
Nevada	1,527,298	56.56
Nebraska	1,525,184	83.51
Idaho	1,341,827	85.60
Maine	1,272,487	95.79
New Hampshire	1,232,088	93.59
Montana	889,028	89.85
New Mexico	859,633	41.75
Rhode Island	820,838	77.98
South Dakota	703,177	86.37
North Dakota	607,632	90.34
Delaware	601,625	67.00
Vermont	599,675	95.83
Hawaii	497,162	36.55
Alaska	495,498	69.77
Wyoming	491,793	87.26
District of Columbia	218,422	36.30

Place	Population	%
Vermont	599,675	95.83
Maine	1,272,487	95.79
West Virginia	1,750,043	94.44
New Hampshire	1,232,088	93.59
North Dakota	607,632	90.34
Iowa	2,739,834	89.94
Montana	889,028	89.85
Kentucky	3,805,193	87.69
Wyoming	491,793	87.26
South Dakota	703,177	86.37
Idaho	1,341,827	85.60
Minnesota	4,497,934	84.80
Wisconsin	4,811,054	84.60
Nebraska	1,525,184	83.51
Indiana	5,377,916	82.94
Ohio	9,543,218	82.72
Missouri	4,947,306	82.61
Utah	2,266,547	82.01
Oregon	3,107,886	81.12
Pennsylvania	10,248,965	80.69
Kansas	2,289,938	80.26
Michigan	7,740,156	78.31
Rhode Island	820,838	77.98
Massachusetts	5,082,983	77.63
Tennessee	4,882,031	76.93
Arkansas	2,215,467	75.98
Washington	5,097,076	75.80
Oklahoma	2,750,713	73.33
Connecticut	2,595,143	72.61
Colorado	3,611,570	71.81
Alaska	495,498	69.77
Alabama	3,257,662	68.16
Delaware	601,625	67.00
Virginia	5,341,329	66.76
North Carolina	6,354,005	66.64
United States	**201,856,108**	**65.38**
South Carolina	3,017,747	65.24
Illinois	8,324,628	64.88
Louisiana	2,782,654	61.38
New Jersey	5,315,821	60.46
New York	11,534,988	59.53
Arizona	3,795,629	59.38
Florida	11,115,250	59.12
Mississippi	1,745,642	58.83
Georgia	5,535,598	57.14
Nevada	1,527,298	56.56
Maryland	3,257,918	56.43
Texas	11,669,272	46.41
California	15,763,625	42.31
New Mexico	859,633	41.75
Hawaii	497,162	36.55
District of Columbia	218,422	36.30

Please refer to the Explanation of Data in the front of the book for more detailed information.

Race

White: Not Hispanic

Top 150 Places Sorted by Population

Based on all places, regardless of total population

Place	Population	%
New York, NY (city) Kings County	2,804,430	34.30
Los Angeles, CA (city) Los Angeles County	1,148,305	30.28
Brooklyn, NY (borough) Kings County	917,717	36.64
Chicago, IL (city) Cook County	881,920	32.72
Manhattan, NY (borough) New York County	785,299	49.52
Phoenix, AZ (city) Maricopa County	693,617	47.98
Queens, NY (borough) Queens County	638,051	28.60
San Diego, CA (city) San Diego County	625,399	47.84
Philadelphia, PA (city) Philadelphia County	581,693	38.12
Houston, TX (city) Harris County	555,181	26.44
Indianapolis, IN (city) Marion County	496,520	60.52
Columbus, OH (city) Franklin County	485,567	61.70
Jacksonville, FL (city) Duval County	467,544	56.89
Hempstead, NY (town) Nassau County	460,994	60.68
Portland, OR (city) Multnomah County	441,039	75.55
Seattle, WA (city) King County	426,420	70.06
Louisville-Jefferson County, KY (metro govt) Jefferson County	418,417	70.05
Austin, TX (city) Travis County	397,176	50.25
Brookhaven, NY (town) Suffolk County	379,158	78.01
San Antonio, TX (city) Medina County	365,813	27.56
San Francisco, CA (city) San Francisco County	358,844	44.56
Dallas, TX (city) Dallas County	354,625	29.61
Nashville-Davidson, TN (metro govt) Davidson County	348,544	57.97
Oklahoma City, OK (city) Oklahoma County	348,078	60.01
Charlotte, NC (city) Mecklenburg County	339,512	46.42
Denver, CO (city) Denver County	323,478	53.90
Fort Worth, TX (city) Tarrant County	318,763	43.01
Colorado Springs, CO (city) El Paso County	307,046	73.73
Staten Island, NY (borough) Richmond County	305,118	65.09
Boston, MA (city) Suffolk County	299,393	48.48
Virginia Beach, VA (ind. city) Virginia Beach independent city	294,477	67.23
Las Vegas, NV (city) Clark County	293,301	50.24
San Jose, CA (city) Santa Clara County	292,431	30.91
Mesa, AZ (city) Maricopa County	289,620	65.97
Omaha, NE (city) Douglas County	285,554	69.82
Kansas City, MO (city) Jackson County	261,254	56.82
Wichita, KS (city) Sedgwick County	257,465	67.33
Tucson, AZ (city) Pima County	254,236	48.88
Tulsa, OK (city) Tulsa County	243,101	62.03
Minneapolis, MN (city) Hennepin County	241,570	63.14
Albuquerque, NM (city) Bernalillo County	238,484	43.69
Oyster Bay, NY (town) Nassau County	236,944	80.81
Milwaukee, WI (city) Milwaukee County	231,019	38.84
Lexington-Fayette, KY (cons. govt) Fayette County	221,623	74.92
Raleigh, NC (city) Wake County	221,203	54.77
Lincoln, NE (city) Lancaster County	220,308	85.27
Washington, DC (city) District of Columbia	218,422	36.30
Pittsburgh, PA (city) Allegheny County	203,879	66.69
Anchorage, AK (municipality) Anchorage Municipality	199,952	68.52
Islip, NY (town) Suffolk County	198,326	59.11
Scottsdale, AZ (city) Maricopa County	185,299	85.24
Fort Wayne, IN (city) Allen County	184,757	72.83
Henderson, NV (city) Clark County	184,438	71.56
Toledo, OH (city) Lucas County	183,797	63.99
Memphis, TN (city) Shelby County	182,870	28.27
Spokane, WA (city) Spokane County	182,799	87.50
Madison, WI (city) Dane County	181,869	77.99
Baltimore, MD (city) Baltimore city County	181,450	29.22
Boise City, ID (city) Ada County	179,647	87.35
Sacramento, CA (city) Sacramento County	175,948	37.72
Arlington, TX (city) Tarrant County	170,093	46.54
St. Paul, MN (city) Ramsey County	167,111	58.62
Aurora, CO (city) Arapahoe County	162,069	49.86
St. Petersburg, FL (city) Pinellas County	161,333	65.91
Huntington, NY (town) Suffolk County	160,914	79.17
Tampa, FL (city) Hillsborough County	160,715	47.87
Bronx, NY (borough) Bronx County	158,245	11.42
Atlanta, GA (city) Fulton County	157,119	37.41
Fresno, CA (city) Fresno County	156,548	31.65
Plano, TX (city) Collin County	156,421	60.20
Gilbert, AZ (town) Maricopa County	156,360	75.01
Chandler, AZ (city) Maricopa County	150,495	63.74
North Hempstead, NY (town) Nassau County	149,607	66.10
Cincinnati, OH (city) Hamilton County	148,354	49.96
Des Moines, IA (city) Polk County	147,960	72.73
Reno, NV (city) Washoe County	145,975	64.81
Long Beach, CA (city) Los Angeles County	145,170	31.40
Overland Park, KS (city) Johnson County	143,091	82.53
Springfield, MO (city) Christian County	142,587	89.40
St. Louis, MO (city) St. Louis city County	139,920	43.82
Chesapeake, VA (ind. city) Chesapeake independent city	138,994	62.55
Cleveland, OH (city) Cuyahoga County	138,590	34.93
Bakersfield, CA (city) Kern County	137,595	39.60
Arlington, VA (cdp) Arlington County	137,530	66.24
Babylon, NY (town) Suffolk County	136,259	63.79
Knoxville, TN (city) Knox County	136,185	76.13
Eugene, OR (city) Lane County	133,599	85.54
Sioux Falls, SD (city) Minnehaha County	133,542	86.78
Huntington Beach, CA (city) Orange County	133,155	70.08
Tacoma, WA (city) Pierce County	131,049	66.05
Lubbock, TX (city) Lubbock County	130,123	56.68
Vancouver, WA (city) Clark County	128,851	79.64
Greensboro, NC (city) Guilford County	126,944	47.07
Akron, OH (city) Summit County	126,928	63.75
Salt Lake City, UT (city) Salt Lake County	125,726	67.44
Buffalo, NY (city) Erie County	124,612	47.69
Glendale, CA (city) Los Angeles County	123,773	64.56
Fort Collins, CO (city) Larimer County	122,560	85.12
Glendale, AZ (city) Maricopa County	120,817	53.29
Amarillo, TX (city) Potter County	116,456	61.07
Grand Rapids, MI (city) Kent County	115,639	61.50
Cape Coral, FL (city) Lee County	115,414	74.80
Peoria, AZ (city) Yavapai County	113,903	73.93
Salem, OR (city) Marion County	113,323	73.28
Norfolk, VA (ind. city) Norfolk independent city	113,086	46.58
Oakland, CA (city) Alameda County	111,751	28.60
Cedar Rapids, IA (city) Linn County	111,714	88.43
Worcester, MA (city) Worcester County	111,403	61.53
Winston-Salem, NC (city) Forsyth County	111,232	48.44
Sterling Heights, MI (city) Macomb County	111,121	85.68
Paradise, NV (cdp) Clark County	109,049	48.86
Riverside, CA (city) Riverside County	109,018	35.88
New Orleans, LA (city) Orleans Parish	107,823	31.36
Huntsville, AL (city) Madison County	107,686	59.79
Warren, MI (city) Macomb County	106,146	79.18
Smithtown, NY (town) Suffolk County	105,870	89.87
Naperville, IL (city) DuPage County	105,833	74.61
Modesto, CA (city) Stanislaus County	104,608	52.00
Santa Rosa, CA (city) Sonoma County	104,546	62.30
Irvine, CA (city) Orange County	104,511	49.21
Tempe, AZ (city) Maricopa County	104,218	64.44
Corpus Christi, TX (city) Nueces County	104,028	34.08
Lakewood, CO (city) Jefferson County	103,725	72.55
Port St. Lucie, FL (city) St. Lucie County	103,666	62.98
Santa Clarita, CA (city) Los Angeles County	102,899	58.36
Amherst, NY (town) Erie County	102,429	83.71
Orlando, FL (city) Orange County	102,017	42.81
Metairie, LA (cdp) Jefferson Parish	101,649	73.40
Olathe, KS (city) Johnson County	100,468	79.82
Tallahassee, FL (city) Leon County	99,500	54.86
Independence, MO (city) Jackson County	98,789	84.56
Evansville, IN (city) Vanderburgh County	97,793	83.28
Anaheim, CA (city) Orange County	97,490	28.99
El Paso, TX (city) El Paso County	96,505	14.87
Chattanooga, TN (city) Hamilton County	95,846	57.16
Fargo, ND (city) Cass County	95,614	90.59
Cary, NC (town) Wake County	95,613	70.70
Topeka, KS (city) Shawnee County	92,945	72.91
Rockford, IL (city) Winnebago County	92,788	60.70
Billings, MT (city) Yellowstone County	92,745	89.03
Little Rock, AR (city) Pulaski County	92,351	47.72
Thousand Oaks, CA (city) Ventura County	91,960	72.59
Manchester, NH (city) Hillsborough County	91,901	83.88
Spring Valley, NV (cdp) Clark County	90,750	50.87
Durham, NC (city) Durham County	89,618	39.25
Provo, UT (city) Utah County	89,596	79.65
Norman, OK (city) Cleveland County	89,381	80.58
Springfield, IL (city) Sangamon County	89,342	76.85
Urban Honolulu, HI (cdp) Honolulu County	89,225	26.46
Dearborn, MI (city) Wayne County	88,708	90.38

SECTION THREE

Please refer to the Explanation of Data in the front of the book for more detailed information.

Race

White: Not Hispanic

Top 150 Places Sorted by Percent of Total Population

Based on all places, regardless of total population

Place	Population	%
Worden, WI (town) Clark County	666	100.00
Eldred, PA (township) Warren County	650	100.00
Sutersville, PA (borough) Westmoreland County	605	100.00
Austin, PA (borough) Potter County	562	100.00
Bruno, WV (cdp) Logan County	544	100.00
Farina, IL (village) Fayette County	518	100.00
Newport, IN (town) Vermillion County	515	100.00
Hawthorn, PA (borough) Clarion County	494	100.00
Verona, OH (village) Preble County	494	100.00
Highland, PA (township) Elk County	492	100.00
Scott, WI (town) Crawford County	462	100.00
Spruce Hill, MN (township) Douglas County	441	100.00
Ewing, VA (cdp) Lee County	439	100.00
Herrick, IL (village) Shelby County	436	100.00
Waynesville, IL (village) De Witt County	434	100.00
Hornbeak, TN (town) Obion County	424	100.00
Richland, MN (township) Rice County	416	100.00
Beallsville, OH (village) Monroe County	409	100.00
Hanoverton, OH (village) Columbiana County	408	100.00
Axtell, KS (city) Marshall County	406	100.00
Ewing, NE (village) Holt County	387	100.00
Clifton, WI (town) Grant County	385	100.00
Pathfork, KY (cdp) Harlan County	379	100.00
Fayette, WI (town) Lafayette County	376	100.00
Carbon, PA (township) Huntingdon County	375	100.00
Port Jefferson, OH (village) Shelby County	371	100.00
Arona, PA (borough) Westmoreland County	370	100.00
Freeport, OH (village) Harrison County	369	100.00
Berrysburg, PA (borough) Dauphin County	368	100.00
York, MN (township) Fillmore County	368	100.00
Ellenboro, WV (town) Ritchie County	363	100.00
Ryan, IA (city) Delaware County	361	100.00
Noyes, PA (township) Clinton County	357	100.00
Stoystown, PA (borough) Somerset County	355	100.00
Bloss, PA (township) Tioga County	353	100.00
Winesburg, OH (cdp) Holmes County	352	100.00
Pleasant View, KY (cdp) Whitley County	350	100.00
Springhill, PA (township) Greene County	349	100.00
Conesville, OH (village) Coshocton County	347	100.00
Burleene, MN (township) Todd County	345	100.00
Sigel, MN (township) Brown County	344	100.00
Blanford, IN (cdp) Vermillion County	342	100.00
Washington, WI (town) Rusk County	339	100.00
Fahlun, MN (township) Kandiyohi County	335	100.00
Arnot, PA (cdp) Tioga County	332	100.00
Payne Gap, KY (cdp) Letcher County	329	100.00
Saxon, WI (town) Iron County	324	100.00
Dakota, MN (city) Winona County	323	100.00
New Munich, MN (city) Stearns County	320	100.00
Dunmor, KY (cdp) Muhlenberg County	317	100.00
Ridgeway, IA (city) Winneshiek County	315	100.00
Aristes, PA (cdp) Columbia County	311	100.00
Benson, VT (cdp) Rutland County	308	100.00
Spartansburg, PA (borough) Crawford County	305	100.00
Bowman, TN (cdp) Cumberland County	302	100.00
Wyoming, WI (town) Iowa County	302	100.00
Mickinock, MN (township) Roseau County	301	100.00
Milton Mills, NH (cdp) Strafford County	299	100.00
Mount Olivet, KY (city) Robertson County	299	100.00
Blakesburg, IA (city) Wapello County	296	100.00
Hewett, WI (town) Clark County	293	100.00
Itmann, WV (cdp) Wyoming County	293	100.00
Loud, MI (township) Montmorency County	293	100.00
Dixie, WV (cdp) Nicholas County	291	100.00
Le Raysville, PA (borough) Bradford County	290	100.00
Sherman, WI (town) Iron County	290	100.00
Oma, WI (town) Iron County	289	100.00
West Union, IL (cdp) Clark County	288	100.00
De Soto, WI (village) Vernon County	287	100.00
James City, PA (cdp) Elk County	287	100.00
Leavenworth, MN (township) Brown County	287	100.00
Chauncey, WV (cdp) Logan County	283	100.00
Hartleton, PA (borough) Union County	283	100.00
Larwill, IN (town) Whitley County	283	100.00
Ottawa, MN (township) Le Sueur County	283	100.00

Place	Population	%
Holland, IA (city) Grundy County	282	100.00
Cairo, WV (town) Ritchie County	281	100.00
Somerville, OH (village) Butler County	281	100.00
Deep River, IA (city) Poweshiek County	279	100.00
Mount Clare, IL (village) Macoupin County	278	100.00
Grainfield, KS (city) Gove County	277	100.00
Murry, WI (town) Rusk County	277	100.00
Northeast Piscataquis, ME (unorganized territory) Piscataquis County	273	100.00
Hendricks, WV (town) Tucker County	272	100.00
Lodi, MN (township) Mower County	270	100.00
Ford, WI (town) Taylor County	268	100.00
Casstown, OH (village) Miami County	267	100.00
Valley Head, WV (cdp) Randolph County	267	100.00
Polk, PA (township) Jefferson County	265	100.00
Plainville, IL (village) Adams County	264	100.00
Blain, PA (borough) Perry County	263	100.00
Wingate, IN (town) Montgomery County	263	100.00
Burlington, MI (village) Calhoun County	261	100.00
Chester, SD (cdp) Lake County	261	100.00
Hunter, ND (city) Cass County	261	100.00
La Motte, IA (city) Jackson County	260	100.00
Tenhassen, MN (township) Martin County	260	100.00
Hope, ND (city) Steele County	258	100.00
Greeley, IA (city) Delaware County	256	100.00
Racine, WV (cdp) Boone County	256	100.00
Eden, MN (township) Brown County	254	100.00
Addieville, IL (village) Washington County	252	100.00
Foster, PA (township) Schuylkill County	251	100.00
West Abington, PA (township) Lackawanna County	250	100.00
Woodville, ME (town) Penobscot County	248	100.00
Glasgow, MN (township) Wabasha County	247	100.00
Granby, MN (township) Nicollet County	246	100.00
Halbur, IA (city) Carroll County	246	100.00
Tunnelhill, PA (borough) Cambria County	245	100.00
Eitzen, MN (city) Houston County	243	100.00
Donnelly, MN (city) Stevens County	241	100.00
Goose Lake, IA (city) Clinton County	240	100.00
Moscow, MD (cdp) Allegany County	240	100.00
Winnebago, MN (township) Houston County	240	100.00
Briarcliff, AR (city) Baxter County	236	100.00
North Star, OH (village) Darke County	236	100.00
Ezel, KY (cdp) Morgan County	235	100.00
Roseland, NE (village) Adams County	235	100.00
Skagen, MN (township) Roseau County	235	100.00
Solem, MN (township) Douglas County	233	100.00
Wells, MI (township) Marquette County	231	100.00
Byron, MN (township) Waseca County	230	100.00
Moose Creek, MN (township) Clearwater County	230	100.00
New Folden, MN (township) Marshall County	230	100.00
Lake Bronson, MN (city) Kittson County	229	100.00
Osceola, NY (town) Lewis County	229	100.00
Hereim, MN (township) Roseau County	228	100.00
West Glacier, MT (cdp) Flathead County	227	100.00
Wyaconda, MO (city) Clark County	227	100.00
Gervais, MN (township) Red Lake County	226	100.00
Kansas, AL (town) Walker County	226	100.00
Wilmore, PA (borough) Cambria County	225	100.00
Brookville, MN (township) Redwood County	224	100.00
Gilman, MN (city) Benton County	224	100.00
Jackson Center, PA (borough) Mercer County	224	100.00
Coldiron, KY (cdp) Harlan County	223	100.00
Harvel, IL (village) Montgomery County	223	100.00
Lewistown, OH (cdp) Logan County	222	100.00
Mackville, KY (city) Washington County	222	100.00
Uniopolis, OH (village) Auglaize County	222	100.00
Birdsall, NY (town) Allegany County	221	100.00
Frankclay, MO (cdp) St. Francois County	221	100.00
Heckscherville, PA (cdp) Schuylkill County	220	100.00
Cross Timbers, MO (city) Hickory County	216	100.00
Blairsburg, IA (city) Hamilton County	215	100.00
Longfellow, PA (cdp) Mifflin County	215	100.00
New Minden, IL (village) Washington County	215	100.00
Wind Ridge, PA (cdp) Greene County	215	100.00
Woodland Hills, NE (cdp) Otoe County	215	100.00
Langor, MN (township) Beltrami County	213	100.00

Please refer to the Explanation of Data in the front of the book for more detailed information.

Race

White: Not Hispanic

Top 150 Places Sorted by Percent of Total Population

Based on places with total population of 7,500 or more

Place	Population	%
Mount Pleasant, PA (township) Westmoreland County	10,781	98.81
Elma, NY (town) Erie County	11,179	98.78
St. Marys, PA (city) Elk County	12,903	98.72
Kiryas Joel, NY (village) Orange County	19,869	98.48
Mack, OH (cdp) Hamilton County	11,401	98.41
Allegheny, PA (township) Westmoreland County	8,032	98.38
Lawrence, PA (township) Clearfield County	7,551	98.31
Boston, NY (town) Erie County	7,881	98.23
Penn, PA (township) Westmoreland County	19,638	98.17
Shelby, OH (city) Richland County	9,146	98.16
Economy, PA (borough) Beaver County	8,798	98.08
Louisville, OH (city) Stark County	9,008	98.06
West Deer, PA (township) Allegheny County	11,541	98.05
Clay, MI (township) St. Clair County	8,884	97.99
Jerseyville, IL (city) Jersey County	8,294	97.98
New Franklin, OH (city) Summit County	13,938	97.97
North Huntingdon, PA (township) Westmoreland County	29,984	97.96
Mooresville, IN (town) Morgan County	9,136	97.96
Skowhegan, ME (town) Somerset County	8,412	97.94
Aurora, NY (town) Erie County	13,495	97.92
Standish, ME (town) Cumberland County	9,665	97.88
Hastings, NY (town) Oswego County	9,249	97.87
Glenshaw, PA (cdp) Allegheny County	8,790	97.87
Lower Burrell, PA (city) Westmoreland County	11,507	97.84
Waterboro, ME (town) York County	7,526	97.83
Paris, IL (city) Edgar County	8,644	97.82
Hampstead, NH (town) Rockingham County	8,336	97.81
Sandy, PA (township) Clearfield County	10,391	97.80
Milton, VT (town) Chittenden County	10,123	97.79
East Huntingdon, PA (township) Westmoreland County	7,785	97.76
Derry, PA (township) Westmoreland County	14,175	97.75
Dallas, PA (township) Luzerne County	8,792	97.75
Weare, NH (town) Hillsborough County	8,587	97.75
Livonia, NY (town) Livingston County	7,633	97.75
Putnam, MI (township) Livingston County	8,062	97.74
Latrobe, PA (city) Westmoreland County	8,148	97.72
Martinsville, IN (city) Morgan County	11,554	97.68
Harrison, OH (city) Hamilton County	9,666	97.67
Warren, PA (city) Warren County	9,484	97.67
Buxton, ME (town) York County	7,847	97.67
Westport, MA (town) Bristol County	15,168	97.66
Galion, OH (city) Crawford County	10,266	97.66
York, ME (town) York County	12,234	97.65
Waterloo, IL (city) Monroe County	9,579	97.64
Alpena, MI (township) Alpena County	8,845	97.63
Barre, VT (town) Washington County	7,736	97.63
Hamburg, NY (village) Erie County	9,185	97.62
Gray, ME (town) Cumberland County	7,575	97.60
Chippewa, PA (township) Beaver County	7,437	97.60
Alexandria, KY (city) Campbell County	8,273	97.59
Center, PA (township) Butler County	7,706	97.57
Wells, ME (town) York County	9,354	97.55
Barton, NY (town) Tioga County	8,641	97.55
Suamico, WI (village) Brown County	11,064	97.51
Farmington, ME (town) Franklin County	7,567	97.51
Adams, MA (town) Berkshire County	8,273	97.50
Somerset, MA (cdp/town) Bristol County	17,705	97.47
Scituate, RI (town) Providence County	10,068	97.47
Sand Lake, NY (town) Rensselaer County	8,314	97.47
Moundsville, WV (city) Marshall County	9,081	97.46
Frankfort, NY (town) Herkimer County	7,442	97.46
Shaler, PA (township) Allegheny County	28,024	97.45
Raymond, NH (town) Rockingham County	9,877	97.43
Glocester, RI (town) Providence County	9,496	97.43
Lehigh, PA (township) Northampton County	10,254	97.42
Butler, PA (township) Butler County	16,801	97.41
Bloomingdale, TN (cdp) Sullivan County	9,632	97.41
Halifax, MA (town) Plymouth County	7,322	97.39
Sullivan, NY (town) Madison County	14,937	97.38
Winslow, ME (cdp/town) Kennebec County	7,590	97.38
Hamburg, MI (township) Livingston County	20,601	97.34
Bridgetown, OH (cdp) Hamilton County	14,024	97.34
Burrillville, RI (town) Providence County	15,529	97.33
Alpena, MI (city) Alpena County	10,203	97.33
Elizabeth, PA (township) Allegheny County	12,915	97.32
St. Marys, OH (city) Auglaize County	8,108	97.31
Fairview, PA (township) Erie County	9,827	97.28
Unity, PA (township) Westmoreland County	21,990	97.27
Lancaster, NY (village) Erie County	10,069	97.27
Lisbon, ME (town) Androscoggin County	8,763	97.27
Stillwater, NY (town) Saratoga County	8,061	97.27
Swansea, MA (town) Bristol County	15,431	97.26
Highland, IL (city) Madison County	9,645	97.24
Jackson, PA (township) Lebanon County	7,938	97.24
Cohasset, MA (town) Norfolk County	7,333	97.23
Acushnet, MA (town) Bristol County	10,017	97.22
Kennedy, PA (township) Allegheny County	7,459	97.22
Kennebunk, ME (town) York County	10,496	97.20
Eaton, OH (city) Preble County	8,172	97.20
Micco, FL (cdp) Brevard County	8,798	97.19
Eden, NY (town) Erie County	7,472	97.19
Lisbon, WI (town) Waukesha County	9,871	97.18
DuBois, PA (city) Clearfield County	7,574	97.18
Sun City West, AZ (cdp) Maricopa County	23,840	97.17
Windham, ME (town) Cumberland County	16,520	97.17
Conway, NH (town) Carroll County	9,829	97.17
Wapakoneta, OH (city) Auglaize County	9,588	97.17
Schroeppel, NY (town) Oswego County	8,260	97.17
New Ulm, MN (city) Brown County	13,138	97.16
Marinette, WI (city) Marinette County	10,657	97.16
Merton, WI (town) Waukesha County	8,101	97.16
Brazil, IN (city) Clay County	7,687	97.16
Oconomowoc, WI (town) Waukesha County	8,168	97.15
Mount Washington, KY (city) Bullitt County	8,855	97.13
Sutton, MA (town) Worcester County	8,706	97.13
Ellwood City, PA (borough) Lawrence County	7,694	97.13
The Villages, FL (cdp) Sumter County	49,955	97.11
Brandon, SD (city) Minnehaha County	8,531	97.11
Marion, MI (township) Livingston County	9,706	97.10
Signal Mountain, TN (town) Hamilton County	7,335	97.10
Baxter, MN (city) Crow Wing County	7,388	97.08
Newstead, NY (town) Erie County	8,340	97.04
Gorham, ME (town) Cumberland County	15,894	97.03
Hanson, MA (town) Plymouth County	9,906	97.03
Marysville, MI (city) St. Clair County	9,663	97.03
West Donegal, PA (township) Lancaster County	8,015	97.03
Wrentham, MA (town) Norfolk County	10,627	97.01
Wadsworth, OH (city) Medina County	20,921	97.00
Berlin, NH (city) Coos County	9,749	97.00
Barrington, NH (town) Strafford County	8,319	97.00
North Madison, OH (cdp) Lake County	8,291	97.00
Woodstock, CT (town) Windham County	7,725	97.00
Lakeville, MA (town) Plymouth County	10,282	96.98
Greenfield, NY (town) Saratoga County	7,540	96.98
Royalton, NY (town) Niagara County	7,429	96.98
Soddy-Daisy, TN (city) Hamilton County	12,329	96.97
Edgewood, KY (city) Kenton County	8,315	96.97
Dexter, MO (city) Stoddard County	7,626	96.97
Mountain Brook, AL (city) Jefferson County	19,792	96.96
Duxbury, MA (town) Plymouth County	14,599	96.95
Brighton, PA (township) Beaver County	7,976	96.95
Hibbing, MN (city) St. Louis County	15,861	96.94
Pembroke, MA (town) Plymouth County	17,287	96.92
Bow, NH (town) Merrimack County	7,287	96.91
Columbia, IL (city) Monroe County	9,406	96.90
Grand Rapids, WI (town) Wood County	7,409	96.90
Highland, MI (charter township) Oakland County	18,605	96.89
Marshfield, MA (town) Plymouth County	24,345	96.87
Ellicott, NY (town) Chautauqua County	8,441	96.87
West Frankfort, IL (city) Franklin County	7,926	96.87
Menominee, MI (city) Menominee County	8,329	96.86
Indianola, IA (city) Warren County	14,317	96.85
Seymour, TN (cdp) Sevier County	10,573	96.83
Little Falls, MN (city) Morrison County	8,078	96.82
Arab, AL (city) Marshall County	7,792	96.80
Palmyra, NY (town) Wayne County	7,720	96.80
Tiverton, RI (town) Newport County	15,273	96.79
Concord, NY (town) Erie County	8,221	96.79
Hot Springs Village, AR (cdp) Garland County	12,393	96.77
Templeton, MA (town) Worcester County	7,754	96.77

Race

White: Hispanic

U.S. and 50 States Sorted by Population and Percent of Total Population

Place	Population	%
United States	**29,184,290**	**9.45**
California	7,189,749	19.30
Texas	6,607,234	26.28
Florida	3,373,185	17.94
New York	1,620,286	8.36
Illinois	1,098,420	8.56
Arizona	1,057,332	16.54
New Jersey	895,174	10.18
Colorado	628,661	12.50
New Mexico	613,372	29.79
Georgia	415,923	4.29
Washington	374,788	5.57
Nevada	362,745	13.43
Pennsylvania	355,222	2.80
North Carolina	343,460	3.60
Virginia	340,608	4.26
Massachusetts	317,475	4.85
Michigan	266,813	2.70
Connecticut	251,049	7.02
Maryland	230,969	4.00
Oregon	229,423	5.99
Ohio	208,329	1.81
Indiana	205,451	3.17
Wisconsin	184,782	3.25
Utah	181,036	6.55
Kansas	178,426	6.25
Oklahoma	155,572	4.15
Tennessee	137,608	2.17
Minnesota	136,981	2.58
Missouri	123,520	2.06
Louisiana	113,214	2.50
South Carolina	109,328	2.36
Idaho	90,997	5.80
Iowa	90,620	2.97
Nebraska	82,533	4.52
Arkansas	81,198	2.78
Alabama	79,415	1.66
Kentucky	73,143	1.69
Hawaii	67,161	4.94
Rhode Island	61,442	5.84
Mississippi	37,165	1.25
Delaware	35,767	3.98
Wyoming	30,946	5.49
District of Columbia	25,228	4.19
New Hampshire	23,862	1.81
Alaska	23,451	3.30
Montana	19,617	1.98
West Virginia	15,599	0.84
Maine	12,390	0.93
South Dakota	11,990	1.47
North Dakota	8,718	1.30
Vermont	6,913	1.10

Place	Population	%
New Mexico	613,372	29.79
Texas	6,607,234	26.28
California	7,189,749	19.30
Florida	3,373,185	17.94
Arizona	1,057,332	16.54
Nevada	362,745	13.43
Colorado	628,661	12.50
New Jersey	895,174	10.18
United States	**29,184,290**	**9.45**
Illinois	1,098,420	8.56
New York	1,620,286	8.36
Connecticut	251,049	7.02
Utah	181,036	6.55
Kansas	178,426	6.25
Oregon	229,423	5.99
Rhode Island	61,442	5.84
Idaho	90,997	5.80
Washington	374,788	5.57
Wyoming	30,946	5.49
Hawaii	67,161	4.94
Massachusetts	317,475	4.85
Nebraska	82,533	4.52
Georgia	415,923	4.29
Virginia	340,608	4.26
District of Columbia	25,228	4.19
Oklahoma	155,572	4.15
Maryland	230,969	4.00
Delaware	35,767	3.98
North Carolina	343,460	3.60
Alaska	23,451	3.30
Wisconsin	184,782	3.25
Indiana	205,451	3.17
Iowa	90,620	2.97
Pennsylvania	355,222	2.80
Arkansas	81,198	2.78
Michigan	266,813	2.70
Minnesota	136,981	2.58
Louisiana	113,214	2.50
South Carolina	109,328	2.36
Tennessee	137,608	2.17
Missouri	123,520	2.06
Montana	19,617	1.98
Ohio	208,329	1.81
New Hampshire	23,862	1.81
Kentucky	73,143	1.69
Alabama	79,415	1.66
South Dakota	11,990	1.47
North Dakota	8,718	1.30
Mississippi	37,165	1.25
Vermont	6,913	1.10
Maine	12,390	0.93
West Virginia	15,599	0.84

Please refer to the Explanation of Data in the front of the book for more detailed information.

Race

White: Hispanic

Top 150 Places Sorted by Population

Based on all places, regardless of total population

Place	Population	%
New York, NY (city) Kings County	992,972	12.15
Los Angeles, CA (city) Los Angeles County	883,281	23.29
San Antonio, TX (city) Medina County	635,389	47.87
Houston, TX (city) Harris County	560,855	26.71
El Paso, TX (city) El Paso County	443,232	68.28
Chicago, IL (city) Cook County	388,177	14.40
Queens, NY (borough) Queens County	303,557	13.61
Phoenix, AZ (city) Maricopa County	301,850	20.88
Dallas, TX (city) Dallas County	278,730	23.27
Bronx, NY (borough) Bronx County	269,414	19.45
Miami, FL (city) Miami-Dade County	248,931	62.32
Brooklyn, NY (borough) Kings County	202,875	8.10
Laredo, TX (city) Webb County	202,024	85.57
Hialeah, FL (city) Miami-Dade County	201,485	89.68
San Diego, CA (city) San Diego County	199,143	15.23
Manhattan, NY (borough) New York County	171,565	10.82
Austin, TX (city) Travis County	165,275	20.91
Albuquerque, NM (city) Bernalillo County	163,094	29.88
Fort Worth, TX (city) Tarrant County	153,479	20.71
San Jose, CA (city) Santa Clara County	149,800	15.84
Corpus Christi, TX (city) Nueces County	149,534	48.99
Brownsville, TX (city) Cameron County	146,067	83.46
Santa Ana, CA (city) Orange County	127,132	39.17
Tucson, AZ (city) Pima County	126,639	24.35
Denver, CO (city) Denver County	110,314	18.38
Fresno, CA (city) Fresno County	107,381	21.71
McAllen, TX (city) Hidalgo County	95,480	73.52
Anaheim, CA (city) Orange County	92,199	27.42
Las Vegas, NV (city) Clark County	92,047	15.77
Chula Vista, CA (city) San Diego County	87,377	35.82
Long Beach, CA (city) Los Angeles County	86,727	18.76
Riverside, CA (city) Riverside County	75,368	24.80
Bakersfield, CA (city) Kern County	73,756	21.23
Philadelphia, PA (city) Philadelphia County	73,328	4.81
Hempstead, NY (town) Nassau County	71,656	9.43
Oxnard, CA (city) Ventura County	70,993	35.87
Fontana, CA (city) San Bernardino County	68,142	34.75
Pasadena, TX (city) Harris County	66,432	44.57
East Los Angeles, CA (cdp) Los Angeles County	65,446	51.74
Mesa, AZ (city) Maricopa County	62,006	14.12
San Francisco, CA (city) San Francisco County	61,979	7.70
San Bernardino, CA (city) San Bernardino County	60,877	29.00
Edinburg, TX (city) Hidalgo County	60,399	78.34
Mission, TX (city) Hidalgo County	59,631	77.38
Tampa, FL (city) Hillsborough County	58,965	17.56
Ontario, CA (city) San Bernardino County	58,397	35.62
Sacramento, CA (city) Sacramento County	57,917	12.42
Pomona, CA (city) Los Angeles County	56,755	38.08
Pharr, TX (city) Hidalgo County	56,610	80.41
Islip, NY (town) Suffolk County	55,909	16.66
Arlington, TX (city) Tarrant County	55,667	15.23
Pembroke Pines, FL (city) Broward County	55,129	35.62
Fountainebleau, FL (cdp) Miami-Dade County	51,906	86.85
Milwaukee, WI (city) Milwaukee County	51,596	8.67
Irving, TX (city) Dallas County	51,534	23.83
Garland, TX (city) Dallas County	50,587	22.30
Aurora, CO (city) Arapahoe County	50,233	15.45
Salinas, CA (city) Monterey County	49,890	33.16
Tamiami, FL (cdp) Miami-Dade County	49,390	89.36
Elizabeth, NJ (city) Union County	49,173	39.35
Moreno Valley, CA (city) Riverside County	49,008	25.34
Boston, MA (city) Suffolk County	48,865	7.91
Lubbock, TX (city) Lubbock County	48,752	21.24
Stockton, CA (city) San Joaquin County	48,126	16.50
South Gate, CA (city) Los Angeles County	47,308	50.12
Kendale Lakes, FL (cdp) Miami-Dade County	46,496	82.81
Downey, CA (city) Los Angeles County	46,331	41.45
Harlingen, TX (city) Cameron County	45,801	70.63
Kendall, FL (cdp) Miami-Dade County	45,677	60.60
Newark, NJ (city) Essex County	45,565	16.44
Staten Island, NY (borough) Richmond County	45,561	9.72
Grand Prairie, TX (city) Dallas County	43,694	24.91
Miami Beach, FL (city) Miami-Dade County	42,371	48.27
Aurora, IL (city) Kane County	42,062	21.25
Norwalk, CA (city) Los Angeles County	41,912	39.71
Paterson, NJ (city) Passaic County	41,726	28.54
Palmdale, CA (city) Los Angeles County	41,369	27.08
Orlando, FL (city) Orange County	41,245	17.31
El Monte, CA (city) Los Angeles County	41,121	36.24
Brookhaven, NY (town) Suffolk County	40,567	8.35
Glendale, AZ (city) Maricopa County	40,514	17.87
Oklahoma City, OK (city) Oklahoma County	40,468	6.98
Charlotte, NC (city) Mecklenburg County	40,227	5.50
Jacksonville, FL (city) Duval County	39,912	4.86
Colorado Springs, CO (city) El Paso County	39,465	9.48
Oakland, CA (city) Alameda County	39,411	10.09
North Las Vegas, NV (city) Clark County	39,211	18.07
Sunrise Manor, NV (cdp) Clark County	39,201	20.70
Las Cruces, NM (city) Doña Ana County	38,857	39.81
Cicero, IL (town) Cook County	38,225	45.57
Santa Maria, CA (city) Santa Barbara County	37,420	37.59
Hollywood, FL (city) Broward County	37,371	26.55
Miramar, FL (city) Broward County	37,347	30.60
The Hammocks, FL (cdp) Miami-Dade County	37,099	72.74
Modesto, CA (city) Stanislaus County	36,371	18.08
Corona, CA (city) Riverside County	36,341	23.85
Pico Rivera, CA (city) Los Angeles County	35,921	57.07
Rancho Cucamonga, CA (city) San Bernardino County	35,404	21.42
Odessa, TX (city) Ector County	35,271	35.29
Amarillo, TX (city) Potter County	35,184	18.45
Doral, FL (city) Miami-Dade County	34,526	75.54
Pueblo, CO (city) Pueblo County	34,453	32.32
Union City, NJ (city) Hudson County	34,214	51.48
Paradise, NV (cdp) Clark County	34,018	15.24
Rialto, CA (city) San Bernardino County	33,700	33.98
Whittier, CA (city) Los Angeles County	33,447	39.20
Country Club, FL (cdp) Miami-Dade County	33,339	70.78
Garden Grove, CA (city) Orange County	32,408	18.97
Homestead, FL (city) Miami-Dade County	32,207	53.22
Wichita, KS (city) Sedgwick County	32,005	8.37
Baldwin Park, CA (city) Los Angeles County	31,924	42.35
Yonkers, NY (city) Westchester County	31,778	16.22
Escondido, CA (city) San Diego County	31,753	22.06
Oceanside, CA (city) San Diego County	31,484	18.84
West Covina, CA (city) Los Angeles County	31,456	29.65
Yuma, AZ (city) Yuma County	31,151	33.47
Jersey City, NJ (city) Hudson County	31,108	12.56
Huntington Park, CA (city) Los Angeles County	30,678	52.79
Chandler, AZ (city) Maricopa County	30,195	12.79
Indianapolis, IN (city) Marion County	30,152	3.68
Orange, CA (city) Orange County	30,090	22.06
Kendall West, FL (cdp) Miami-Dade County	30,038	83.08
Montebello, CA (city) Los Angeles County	29,942	47.91
Socorro, TX (city) El Paso County	29,720	92.84
San Juan, TX (city) Hidalgo County	29,484	87.09
Reno, NV (city) Washoe County	29,347	13.03
Santa Clarita, CA (city) Los Angeles County	29,285	16.61
North Bergen, NJ (township) Hudson County	29,220	48.08
Town 'n' Country, FL (cdp) Hillsborough County	27,932	35.61
Nashville-Davidson, TN (metro govt) Davidson County	27,926	4.64
Visalia, CA (city) Tulare County	27,811	22.35
Indio, CA (city) Riverside County	27,810	36.57
Midland, TX (city) Midland County	27,728	24.95
Lynwood, CA (city) Los Angeles County	27,711	39.72
Weston, FL (city) Broward County	27,385	41.92
Elgin, IL (city) Kane County	27,155	25.10
Portland, OR (city) Multnomah County	27,155	4.65
Lancaster, CA (city) Los Angeles County	27,060	17.28
Bridgeport, CT (city/town) Fairfield County	26,580	18.43
Victorville, CA (city) San Bernardino County	26,546	22.90
Westchester, FL (cdp) Miami-Dade County	26,451	88.58
Weslaco, TX (city) Hidalgo County	26,290	73.70
West New York, NJ (town) Hudson County	26,232	52.77
Compton, CA (city) Los Angeles County	26,083	27.04
Mesquite, TX (city) Dallas County	25,949	18.56
Springfield, MA (city) Hampden County	25,848	16.89
Providence, RI (city) Providence County	25,783	14.48
Del Rio, TX (city) Val Verde County	25,780	72.43
South Whittier, CA (cdp) Los Angeles County	25,691	44.95
Pasadena, CA (city) Los Angeles County	25,636	18.70

Race

White: Hispanic

Top 150 Places Sorted by Percent of Total Population

Based on all places, regardless of total population

Place	Population	%
Los Alvarez, TX (cdp) Starr County	303	100.00
Los Ebanos, TX (cdp) Starr County	280	100.00
Olmito and Olmito, TX (cdp) Starr County	271	100.00
El Cenizo, TX (cdp) Starr County	249	100.00
La Paloma Ranchettes, TX (cdp) Starr County	239	100.00
Ranchitos East, TX (cdp) Webb County	212	100.00
El Quiote, TX (cdp) Starr County	208	100.00
Fronton, TX (cdp) Starr County	180	100.00
East Lopez, TX (cdp) Starr County	166	100.00
Loma Vista, TX (cdp) Starr County	160	100.00
Eugenio Saenz, TX (cdp) Starr County	159	100.00
La Escondida, TX (cdp) Starr County	153	100.00
Los Altos, TX (cdp) Webb County	140	100.00
Campo Verde, TX (cdp) Starr County	132	100.00
Villarreal, TX (cdp) Starr County	131	100.00
El Socio, TX (cdp) Starr County	130	100.00
La Casita, TX (cdp) Starr County	128	100.00
Miguel Barrera, TX (cdp) Starr County	128	100.00
Flor del Rio, TX (cdp) Starr County	122	100.00
North Escobares, TX (cdp) Starr County	118	100.00
Loma Linda West, TX (cdp) Starr County	114	100.00
Sammy Martinez, TX (cdp) Starr County	110	100.00
Buena Vista, TX (cdp) Starr County	102	100.00
Old Escobares, TX (cdp) Starr County	97	100.00
Northridge, TX (cdp) Starr County	78	100.00
Hilltop, TX (cdp) Starr County	77	100.00
La Carla, TX (cdp) Starr County	70	100.00
Martinez, TX (cdp) Starr County	69	100.00
San Fernando, TX (cdp) Starr County	68	100.00
Pablo Pena, TX (cdp) Starr County	63	100.00
Zarate, TX (cdp) Starr County	59	100.00
Santa Cruz, TX (cdp) Starr County	54	100.00
Tanquecitos South Acres II, TX (cdp) Webb County	50	100.00
La Chuparosa, TX (cdp) Starr County	49	100.00
El Brazil, TX (cdp) Starr County	47	100.00
Sunset, TX (cdp) Starr County	47	100.00
Garciasville, TX (cdp) Starr County	46	100.00
Cuevitas, TX (cdp) Hidalgo County	40	100.00
El Mesquite, TX (cdp) Starr County	38	100.00
Guadalupe-Guerra, TX (cdp) Starr County	37	100.00
Benjamin Perez, TX (cdp) Starr County	34	100.00
Sandoval, TX (cdp) Starr County	32	100.00
Netos, TX (cdp) Starr County	31	100.00
Elias-Fela Solis, TX (cdp) Starr County	30	100.00
Hillside Acres, TX (cdp) Webb County	30	100.00
Quesada, TX (cdp) Starr County	25	100.00
Los Veteranos I, TX (cdp) Webb County	24	100.00
Jardin de San Julian, TX (cdp) Starr County	22	100.00
Laredo Ranchettes, TX (cdp) Webb County	22	100.00
Rafael Pena, TX (cdp) Starr County	17	100.00
Anacua, TX (cdp) Starr County	12	100.00
Las Haciendas, TX (cdp) Webb County	7	100.00
Roma Creek, TX (cdp) Starr County	349	99.71
San Carlos I, TX (cdp) Webb County	315	99.68
Camargito, TX (cdp) Starr County	386	99.48
Garza-Salinas II, TX (cdp) Starr County	715	99.44
Airport Heights, TX (cdp) Starr County	160	99.38
La Presa, TX (cdp) Webb County	317	99.37
Nina, TX (cdp) Starr County	140	99.29
Falconaire, TX (cdp) Starr County	131	99.24
Rancho Viejo, TX (cdp) Starr County	226	99.12
Barrera, TX (cdp) Starr County	107	99.07
Olivia Lopez de Gutierrez, TX (cdp) Starr County	92	98.92
El Rancho Vela, TX (cdp) Starr County	271	98.91
Mikes, TX (cdp) Starr County	900	98.90
La Rosita, TX (cdp) Starr County	84	98.82
El Chaparral, TX (cdp) Starr County	458	98.71
Eidson Road, TX (cdp) Maverick County	8,843	98.69
Abram, TX (cdp) Hidalgo County	2,040	98.69
San Carlos II, TX (cdp) Webb County	257	98.47
Sullivan City, TX (city) Hidalgo County	3,938	98.40
Rivereno, TX (cdp) Starr County	60	98.36
Tanquecitos South Acres, TX (cdp) Webb County	229	98.28
Los Barreras, TX (cdp) Starr County	283	98.26
East Alto Bonito, TX (cdp) Starr County	809	98.18
JF Villarreal, TX (cdp) Starr County	102	98.08
Indio, TX (cdp) Starr County	49	98.00
La Coma, TX (cdp) Webb County	47	97.92
Los Ebanos, TX (cdp) Hidalgo County	328	97.91
Chapeno, TX (cdp) Starr County	46	97.87
Penitas, TX (city) Hidalgo County	4,303	97.73
Palo Blanco, TX (cdp) Starr County	199	97.55
Salineño North, TX (cdp) Starr County	112	97.39
Doolittle, TX (cdp) Hidalgo County	2,696	97.36
Bonanza Hills, TX (cdp) Webb County	36	97.30
Granjeno, TX (city) Hidalgo County	285	97.27
West Sharyland, TX (cdp) Hidalgo County	2,244	97.18
La Puerta, TX (cdp) Starr County	614	97.15
La Victoria, TX (cdp) Starr County	166	97.08
La Joya, TX (city) Hidalgo County	3,858	96.81
Amaya, TX (cdp) Zavala County	90	96.77
Pueblo Nuevo, TX (cdp) Webb County	504	96.74
Chula Vista, TX (cdp) Cameron County	278	96.53
Palmview, TX (city) Hidalgo County	5,270	96.52
Chaparrito, TX (cdp) Starr County	110	96.49
Tierra Dorada, TX (cdp) Starr County	27	96.43
San Carlos, TX (cdp) Hidalgo County	3,015	96.33
La Homa, TX (cdp) Hidalgo County	11,538	96.27
Santa Rosa, TX (cdp) Starr County	232	96.27
Los Veteranos II, TX (cdp) Webb County	23	95.83
Chula Vista, TX (cdp) Maverick County	3,658	95.81
La Loma de Falcon, TX (cdp) Starr County	91	95.79
Mi Ranchito Estate, TX (cdp) Starr County	269	95.73
Mesquite, TX (cdp) Starr County	483	95.64
Westway, TX (cdp) El Paso County	4,002	95.56
Doffing, TX (cdp) Hidalgo County	4,864	95.54
Siesta Acres, TX (cdp) Maverick County	1,801	95.54
Ranchitos Del Norte, TX (cdp) Starr County	107	95.54
Santel, TX (cdp) Starr County	42	95.45
Regino Ramirez, TX (cdp) Starr County	81	95.29
South Alamo, TX (cdp) Hidalgo County	3,201	95.24
La Grulla, TX (city) Starr County	1,544	95.19
Lago, TX (cdp) Cameron County	194	95.10
El Cenizo, TX (city) Webb County	3,106	94.90
Las Quintas Fronterizas, TX (cdp) Maverick County	3,117	94.74
Faysville, TX (cdp) Hidalgo County	415	94.53
Four Points, TX (cdp) Webb County	17	94.44
Rio Bravo, TX (city) Webb County	4,526	94.41
Moraida, TX (cdp) Starr County	200	94.34
El Refugio, TX (cdp) Starr County	312	94.26
Roma, TX (city) Starr County	9,170	93.91
Lago Vista, TX (cdp) Starr County	108	93.91
Grand Acres, TX (cdp) Cameron County	46	93.88
Medina, TX (cdp) Zapata County	3,693	93.85
Elm Creek, TX (cdp) Maverick County	2,316	93.80
Los Arcos, TX (cdp) Webb County	119	93.70
La Minita, TX (cdp) Starr County	160	93.57
Loma Grande, TX (cdp) Zavala County	100	93.46
San Ygnacio, TX (cdp) Zapata County	623	93.40
Narciso Pena, TX (cdp) Starr County	28	93.33
Fernando Salinas, TX (cdp) Starr County	14	93.33
San Pedro, TX (cdp) Cameron County	494	93.21
Hidalgo, TX (city) Hidalgo County	10,432	93.16
Lopezville, TX (cdp) Hidalgo County	4,033	93.08
Quemado, TX (cdp) Maverick County	214	93.04
West Alto Bonito, TX (cdp) Starr County	647	92.96
Las Pilas, TX (cdp) Webb County	26	92.86
Socorro, TX (city) El Paso County	29,720	92.84
Salineño, TX (cdp) Starr County	186	92.54
Lopeño, TX (cdp) Zapata County	161	92.53
Fabrica, TX (cdp) Maverick County	854	92.52
Loma Linda East, TX (cdp) Jim Wells County	235	92.52
Amada Acres, TX (cdp) Starr County	85	92.39
Ramirez-Perez, TX (cdp) Starr County	72	92.31
Casas, TX (cdp) Starr County	36	92.31
Santa Anna, TX (cdp) Starr County	12	92.31
North Alamo, TX (cdp) Hidalgo County	2,985	92.27
Manuel Garcia II, TX (cdp) Starr County	71	92.21
B and E, TX (cdp) Starr County	477	92.08
Concepcion, TX (cdp) Duval County	57	91.94

Please refer to the Explanation of Data in the front of the book for more detailed information.

Race

White: Hispanic

Top 150 Places Sorted by Percent of Total Population

Based on places with total population of 7,500 or more

Place	Population	%
Eidson Road, TX (cdp) Maverick County	8,843	98.69
La Homa, TX (cdp) Hidalgo County	11,538	96.27
Roma, TX (city) Starr County	9,170	93.91
Hidalgo, TX (city) Hidalgo County	10,432	93.16
Socorro, TX (city) El Paso County	29,720	92.84
Alton, TX (city) Hidalgo County	11,310	91.65
Sweetwater, FL (city) Miami-Dade County	12,243	90.70
Hialeah Gardens, FL (city) Miami-Dade County	19,552	89.92
Hialeah, FL (city) Miami-Dade County	201,485	89.68
Tamiami, FL (cdp) Miami-Dade County	49,390	89.36
Westchester, FL (cdp) Miami-Dade County	26,451	88.58
Rio Grande City, TX (city) Starr County	12,211	88.27
San Elizario, TX (cdp) El Paso County	11,900	87.48
San Juan, TX (city) Hidalgo County	29,484	87.09
Fountainebleau, FL (cdp) Miami-Dade County	51,906	86.85
Eagle Pass, TX (city) Maverick County	22,469	85.60
Laredo, TX (city) Webb County	202,024	85.57
Coral Terrace, FL (cdp) Miami-Dade County	20,858	85.57
Fabens, TX (cdp) El Paso County	6,956	84.24
Brownsville, TX (city) Cameron County	146,067	83.46
Kendall West, FL (cdp) Miami-Dade County	30,038	83.08
Westwood Lakes, FL (cdp) Miami-Dade County	9,826	83.00
Olympia Heights, FL (cdp) Miami-Dade County	11,173	82.84
Kendale Lakes, FL (cdp) Miami-Dade County	46,496	82.81
University Park, FL (cdp) Miami-Dade County	22,099	81.86
Robstown, TX (city) Nueces County	9,327	81.20
Pharr, TX (city) Hidalgo County	56,610	80.41
Donna, TX (city) Hidalgo County	12,701	80.40
Mercedes, TX (city) Hidalgo County	12,317	79.11
San Benito, TX (city) Cameron County	19,103	78.78
Raymondville, TX (city) Willacy County	8,869	78.60
Miami Lakes, FL (town) Miami-Dade County	23,009	78.37
Edinburg, TX (city) Hidalgo County	60,399	78.34
Sunset, FL (cdp) Miami-Dade County	12,763	77.88
Mission, TX (city) Hidalgo County	59,631	77.38
Doral, FL (city) Miami-Dade County	34,526	75.54
Alice, TX (city) Jim Wells County	14,262	74.65
Weslaco, TX (city) Hidalgo County	26,290	73.70
McAllen, TX (city) Hidalgo County	95,480	73.52
Alamo, TX (city) Hidalgo County	13,391	72.96
The Hammocks, FL (cdp) Miami-Dade County	37,099	72.74
Del Rio, TX (city) Val Verde County	25,780	72.43
Richmond West, FL (cdp) Miami-Dade County	23,085	72.20
Horizon City, TX (city) El Paso County	12,037	71.93
Sunland Park, NM (city) Doña Ana County	10,126	71.79
Country Club, FL (cdp) Miami-Dade County	33,339	70.78
Harlingen, TX (city) Cameron County	45,801	70.63
Pearsall, TX (city) Frio County	6,416	70.15
Nogales, AZ (city) Santa Cruz County	14,557	69.86
El Paso, TX (city) El Paso County	443,232	68.28
Miami Springs, FL (city) Miami-Dade County	9,421	68.22
Leisure City, FL (cdp) Miami-Dade County	15,130	66.78
The Crossings, FL (cdp) Miami-Dade County	15,169	66.65
Country Walk, FL (cdp) Miami-Dade County	10,646	66.55
Pecos, TX (city) Reeves County	5,728	65.24
San Luis, AZ (city) Yuma County	16,541	64.85
Somerton, AZ (city) Yuma County	9,077	63.53
Glenvar Heights, FL (cdp) Miami-Dade County	10,639	62.96
Miami, FL (city) Miami-Dade County	248,931	62.32
Calexico, CA (city) Imperial County	23,931	62.04
South Miami Heights, FL (cdp) Miami-Dade County	22,008	61.65
Anthony, NM (cdp) Doña Ana County	5,738	61.30
Three Lakes, FL (cdp) Miami-Dade County	9,155	60.84
Espanola, NM (city) Rio Arriba County	6,204	60.68
Kendall, FL (cdp) Miami-Dade County	45,677	60.60
Key Biscayne, FL (village) Miami-Dade County	7,455	60.39
Uvalde, TX (city) Uvalde County	9,478	60.17
Kingsville, TX (city) Kleberg County	15,458	58.97
Rio Rico, AZ (cdp) Santa Cruz County	11,175	58.93
South Houston, TX (city) Harris County	10,005	58.91
Fort Stockton, TX (city) Pecos County	4,810	58.07
Beeville, TX (city) Bee County	7,419	57.68
Walnut Park, CA (cdp) Los Angeles County	9,196	57.60
Firebaugh, CA (city) Fresno County	4,340	57.49
Pico Rivera, CA (city) Los Angeles County	35,921	57.07
Douglas, AZ (city) Cochise County	9,838	56.61
Galena Park, TX (city) Harris County	6,006	55.17
Hondo, TX (city) Medina County	4,855	55.15
Jacinto City, TX (city) Harris County	5,798	54.94
Commerce, CA (city) Los Angeles County	7,015	54.71
Maywood, CA (city) Los Angeles County	14,767	53.90
Princeton, FL (cdp) Miami-Dade County	11,821	53.64
Mendota, CA (city) Fresno County	5,876	53.35
Homestead, FL (city) Miami-Dade County	32,207	53.22
Huntington Park, CA (city) Los Angeles County	30,678	52.79
West New York, NJ (town) Hudson County	26,232	52.77
West Whittier-Los Nietos, CA (cdp) Los Angeles County	13,469	52.74
Hereford, TX (city) Deaf Smith County	8,085	52.60
Las Vegas, NM (city) San Miguel County	7,231	52.58
Bell, CA (city) Los Angeles County	18,614	52.47
East Los Angeles, CA (cdp) Los Angeles County	65,446	51.74
Coral Gables, FL (city) Miami-Dade County	24,169	51.67
Union City, NJ (city) Hudson County	34,214	51.48
Parlier, CA (city) Fresno County	7,419	51.19
Arvin, CA (city) Kern County	9,826	50.90
Cudahy, CA (city) Los Angeles County	12,057	50.65
Egypt Lake-Leto, FL (cdp) Hillsborough County	17,803	50.46
Cutler Bay, FL (town) Miami-Dade County	20,216	50.18
Avocado Heights, CA (cdp) Los Angeles County	7,729	50.15
South Gate, CA (city) Los Angeles County	47,308	50.12
El Centro, CA (city) Imperial County	21,334	50.08
Deming, NM (city) Luna County	7,374	49.64
Santa Fe Springs, CA (city) Los Angeles County	8,045	49.59
South El Monte, CA (city) Los Angeles County	9,967	49.55
Bell Gardens, CA (city) Los Angeles County	20,794	49.42
Aldine, TX (cdp) Harris County	7,801	49.16
Corpus Christi, TX (city) Nueces County	149,534	48.99
Meadow Woods, FL (cdp) Orange County	12,515	48.97
Buenaventura Lakes, FL (cdp) Osceola County	12,714	48.75
San Fernando, CA (city) Los Angeles County	11,488	48.59
West Puente Valley, CA (cdp) Los Angeles County	10,959	48.41
Miami Beach, FL (city) Miami-Dade County	42,371	48.27
Pleasanton, TX (city) Atascosa County	4,307	48.21
North Bergen, NJ (township) Hudson County	29,220	48.08
Montebello, CA (city) Los Angeles County	29,942	47.91
San Antonio, TX (city) Medina County	635,389	47.87
Coachella, CA (city) Riverside County	19,434	47.74
Guttenberg, NJ (town) Hudson County	5,333	47.72
La Puente, CA (city) Los Angeles County	18,847	47.34
Santa Paula, CA (city) Ventura County	13,841	47.21
Sanger, CA (city) Fresno County	11,431	47.10
Leon Valley, TX (city) Bexar County	4,774	47.03
Dover, NJ (town) Morris County	8,530	46.98
Chaparral, NM (cdp) Otero County	6,853	46.84
Imperial, CA (city) Imperial County	6,903	46.77
Lindsay, CA (city) Tulare County	5,498	46.72
Lamesa, TX (city) Dawson County	4,372	46.40
South Valley, NM (cdp) Bernalillo County	18,751	45.76
Cicero, IL (town) Cook County	38,225	45.57
Port Lavaca, TX (city) Calhoun County	5,520	45.07
South Whittier, CA (cdp) Los Angeles County	25,691	44.95
Pasadena, TX (city) Harris County	66,432	44.57
Socorro, NM (city) Socorro County	4,021	44.43
Golden Gate, FL (cdp) Collier County	10,601	44.24
Cloverleaf, TX (cdp) Harris County	10,119	44.11
West Odessa, TX (cdp) Ector County	10,003	44.05
Valinda, CA (cdp) Los Angeles County	10,019	43.90
Orosi, CA (cdp) Tulare County	3,804	43.38
South San Jose Hills, CA (cdp) Los Angeles County	8,908	43.35
Naranja, FL (cdp) Miami-Dade County	3,582	43.14
Lamont, CA (cdp) Kern County	6,513	43.08
Bloomington, CA (cdp) San Bernardino County	10,240	42.93
Vincent, CA (cdp) Los Angeles County	6,795	42.68
Kissimmee, FL (city) Osceola County	25,359	42.49
Baldwin Park, CA (city) Los Angeles County	31,924	42.35
Dinuba, CA (city) Tulare County	9,069	42.27
Reedley, CA (city) Fresno County	10,211	42.20
Selma, CA (city) Fresno County	9,763	42.05
Seguin, TX (city) Guadalupe County	10,578	42.02
Perth Amboy, NJ (city) Middlesex County	21,333	41.98

Please refer to the Explanation of Data in the front of the book for more detailed information.

Master Place Name Index

Grey House Publishing
2012 Title List

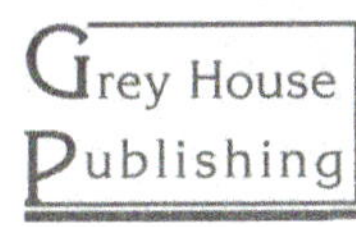

Visit **www.greyhouse.com** for Product Information, Table of Contents and Sample Pages

General Reference
America's College Museums
American Environmental Leaders: From Colonial Times to the Present
An African Biographical Dictionary
An Encyclopedia of Human Rights in the United States
Encyclopedia of African-American Writing
Encyclopedia of Gun Control & Gun Rights
Encyclopedia of Invasions & Conquests
Encyclopedia of Prisoners of War & Internment
Encyclopedia of Religion & Law in America
Encyclopedia of Rural America
Encyclopedia of the United States Cabinet, 1789-2010
Encyclopedia of War Journalism
Encyclopedia of Warrior Peoples & Fighting Groups
From Suffrage to the Senate: America's Political Women
Nations of the World
Political Corruption in America
Speakers of the House of Representatives, 1789-2009
The Environmental Debate: A Documentary History
The Evolution Wars: A Guide to the Debates
The Religious Right: A Reference Handbook
The Value of a Dollar: 1860-2009
The Value of a Dollar: Colonial Era
US Land & Natural Resource Policy
Weather America
Working Americans 1770-1869 Vol. IX: Revol. War to the Civil War
Working Americans 1880-1999 Vol. I: The Working Class
Working Americans 1880-1999 Vol. II: The Middle Class
Working Americans 1880-1999 Vol. III: The Upper Class
Working Americans 1880-1999 Vol. IV: Their Children
Working Americans 1880-2003 Vol. V: At War
Working Americans 1880-2005 Vol. VI: Women at Work
Working Americans 1880-2006 Vol. VII: Social Movements
Working Americans 1880-2007 Vol. VIII: Immigrants
Working Americans 1880-2009 Vol. X: Sports & Recreation
Working Americans 1880-2010 Vol. XI: Inventors & Entrepreneurs
Working Americans 1880-2011 Vol. XII: Our History through Music
World Cultural Leaders of the 20th & 21st Centuries

Business Information
Directory of Business Information Resources
Directory of Mail Order Catalogs
Directory of Venture Capital & Private Equity Firms
Environmental Resource Handbook
Food & Beverage Market Place
Grey House Homeland Security Directory
Grey House Performing Arts Directory
Hudson's Washington News Media Contacts Directory
New York State Directory
Sports Market Place Directory
The Rauch Guides – Industry Market Research Reports
Sweets Directory by McGraw Hill Construction

Statistics & Demographics
America's Top-Rated Cities
America's Top-Rated Small Towns & Cities
America's Top-Rated Smaller Cities
Comparative Guide to American Hospitals
Comparative Guide to American Suburbs
Profiles of... Series – State Handbooks

Health Information
Comparative Guide to American Hospitals
Complete Directory for Pediatric Disorders
Complete Directory for People with Chronic Illness
Complete Directory for People with Disabilities
Complete Mental Health Directory
Directory of Health Care Group Purchasing Organizations
Directory of Hospital Personnel
HMO/PPO Directory
Medical Device Register
Older Americans Information Directory

Education Information
Charter School Movement
Comparative Guide to American Elementary & Secondary Schools
Complete Learning Disabilities Directory
Educators Resource Directory
Special Education

Financial Ratings Series
TheStreet.com Ratings Guide to Bond & Money Market Mutual Funds
TheStreet.com Ratings Guide to Common Stocks
TheStreet.com Ratings Guide to Exchange-Traded Funds
TheStreet.com Ratings Guide to Stock Mutual Funds
TheStreet.com Ratings Ultimate Guided Tour of Stock Investing
Weiss Ratings Consumer Box Set
Weiss Ratings Guide to Banks & Thrifts
Weiss Ratings Guide to Credit Unions
Weiss Ratings Guide to Health Insurers
Weiss Ratings Guide to Life & Annuity Insurers
Weiss Ratings Guide to Property & Casualty Insurers

Bowker's Books In Print® Titles
Books In Print®
Books In Print® Supplement
American Book Publishing Record® Annual
American Book Publishing Record® Monthly
Books Out Loud™
Bowker's Complete Video Directory™
Children's Books In Print®
Complete Directory of Large Print Books & Serials™
El-Hi Textbooks & Serials In Print®
Forthcoming Books®
Law Books & Serials In Print™
Medical & Health Care Books In Print™
Publishers, Distributors & Wholesalers of the US™
Subject Guide to Books In Print®
Subject Guide to Children's Books In Print®

Canadian General Reference
Associations Canada
Canadian Almanac & Directory
Canadian Environmental Resource Guide
Canadian Parliamentary Guide
Financial Services Canada
Governments Canada
Libraries Canada
The History of Canada

Grey House Publishing
4919 Route 22, PO Box 56, Amenia NY 12501-0056 | (800) 562-2139 | www.greyhouse.com | books@greyhouse.com